sky SPORTS

FOOTBALL
YEARBOOK
2015-2016

**Compiled by
John Anderson**

headline

Front cover photographs:
(left and background) Harry Kane (Tottenham Hotspur) – *Alex Livesey/Getty Images*;
(centre) Diego Costa (Chelsea) – *Alex Livesey/Getty Images*;
(right) Wayne Rooney (Manchester United) – *Martin Rickett/PA Archive/Press
Association Images*

Spine photograph:
Chelsea manager Jose Mourinho with the Premier League trophy,
May 2015 – *Mike Hewitt/Getty Images*

Back cover photographs:
(above) Paul Paton (Dundee United) and Stefan Scepovic (Celtic) – *Action
Images/Graham Stuart Livepic*;
(below) Lionel Messi (Barcelona) and Arturo Vidal (Juventus),
UEFA Champions League Final, June 2015 – *Dylan Martinez/Reuters/Action Images*

Cataloguing in Publication Data is available from the British Library

ISBN 978 1 4722 2415 6 (Hardback)
ISBN 978 1 4722 2416 3 (Trade paperback)

Typeset by Wearset Ltd, Boldon, Tyne and Wear

Printed and bound in the UK by
CPI Mackays, Chatham ME5 8TD

HEADLINE PUBLISHING GROUP
An Hachette UK Company
Carmelite House
50 Victoria Embankment
London EC4Y 0DC

www.headline.co.uk
www.hachette.co.uk

CONTENTS

Contents

INTERNATIONAL FOOTBALL

NON-LEAGUE FOOTBALL

INFORMATION AND RECORDS

WELCOME

Welcome to the 2015–16 edition of the *Sky Sports Football Yearbook*.

Last season was another fantastic year for football on Sky Sports. Jose Mourinho delivered the title back to West London for the first time in his second stint at Chelsea, Leicester made a miraculous escape to stay in the Barclays Premier League, and in the SkyBet Championship we saw one of the most thrilling races for promotion in recent memory.

We stand on the verge of our 24th season covering the Premier League and we are proud of what we have done in the past and how we continue to push ourselves to achieve more in the future.

Sky Sports will offer at least four more seasons of the Premier League and because of the drama of the past, we know how much excitement is waiting in the future. Bournemouth will become the 47th team to play in the Premier League, one of the tremendous stories of last season's Championship climax.

Last season we added Thierry Henry to our roster of experts who provide their views and analysis across our live Premier League coverage. Thierry, someone who truly deserves the 'legend' tag, retired from the game and joined the likes of Gary Neville, Jamie Carragher, Jamie Redknapp and Graeme Souness, who continue to engage and entertain viewers every week.

That we are constantly able to raise the bar each season was proven again when the Royal Television Society recognised Gary Neville's analysis, awarding him 'Best Sports Presenter, Commentator or Pundit' for a second successive year.

The Football League forms a big part of our schedule, and that will be increasing this season to a schedule of more games than ever before; 112 matches across the SkyBet Football League, as well as the Capital One Cup, Johnstone's Paint Trophy and the dramatic end-of-season play-off finals. Across the 72 clubs who make up the Football League there is a huge amount of passion and tradition, and to showcase that in the best way possible for our viewers is what motivates us every day.

On the international front we will have the exciting conclusion to the UEFA Euro 2016 qualifying campaign. With many of the Home Nations in contention for a place in France next summer, there is sure to be drama as those groups go down to the wire, and perhaps even a play-off in November.

Sky Sports News HQ provides a huge outlet for the volume of content and rolling news that fans crave every day, and is the perfect companion to our live games.

Our expert analysis, on-air touchscreen, interactive coverage, online and digital platforms, as well as on-demand and social media content, all contribute to giving the viewer what they want, through the medium they choose. That ability to provide our content in new and flexible ways is an important one, because the viewer is always changing their habits and we have to provide for what they want tomorrow as well as today.

I can't wait for another exciting year of live football on Sky Sports. For all the teams, players and managers involved I wish you good luck; and for all the fans at home, we look forward to bringing you more live coverage of the game that we all love.

Gary Hughes
Head of Football, Sky Sports

Gary Hughes

FOREWORD

Last season posed a lot of questions and that is one of the main reasons I'm excited about the coming year, and why I'll be fascinated to see the development of a number of clubs.

Chelsea ran away with it: a first title for Jose Mourinho with what I would term the 'new Chelsea', in his second spell at the club as manager.

Mourinho has won the league three times in his five seasons at Stamford Bridge and he is the man to beat. Chelsea are the team to beat and the others have got to chase them down.

They were criticised towards the end of last season, but I thought that was massively unfair. You don't see a title-winning team that plays well the whole way through. You have to be pragmatic at times and recognise the strengths of other teams. Mourinho does that – he adapts.

It is for Manchester City, Arsenal, Manchester United, Liverpool and others to respond to the challenge that has been laid down by Chelsea.

Can they narrow the gap and mount a greater challenge? How will Chelsea react if they have a constant competitor at the top? You never know how much it can inspire other teams when one side dominates, and that was what Chelsea did last year.

I think this season will see a response from those teams who were little more than a distant chasing pack; they have no other option.

I'm also intrigued to see the impact that the promoted teams can make, and particularly two young managers in Eddie Howe and Alex Neil. Howe appeared on *Monday Night Football* with Ed, Jamie and me at the end of last season, and he showed himself to be intelligent with an astute tactical understanding. His achievement in bringing a club like Bournemouth from the brink of relegation from the Football League to the Premier League, is little short of incredible. He will need every ounce of the enthusiasm and energy he has shown so far to enjoy this season, as the step up can be huge.

Similarly for Neil, the turnaround from him joining Norwich City earlier this year put them on course for a strong end to the season that saw them win the play-off final. Fans of Norwich, Watford and Bournemouth will need patience in the early part of the season: stay with your team, your manager and hope they can live up to the standards that the Premier League sets every week. Leicester City showed that a team can never be written off, and if you can hit a run of form at the right time anything can happen.

I'm looking forward to the first *Monday Night Football* of the season, getting amongst the matches and seeing how the new signings bed in. As much as you need a break at the end of every season, you can't wait to get back to football. With no World Cup or European Championship this summer, that's even more the case!

The questions of last season will be answered, and Sky Sports will be the place to see those big moments from the start right to the finish.

Gary Neville

Gary Neville

INTRODUCTION

The 46th edition of the Yearbook is our thirteenth with sponsors Sky Sports and includes every game of the 2016 European Championship qualifying campaign up-to-date. Full match line-ups and league tables are included for all of the qualifying matches. Other international football at various levels is also well catered for in this edition, including the Women's World Cup Finals in Canada.

The concise feature entitled Cups and Ups and Downs is again included with dates of those events affecting cup finals, plus promotion and relegation issues. In a season where a record number of managerial changes were made, the Managers In and Out section is once again included, with a diary of managerial changes throughout the year. Some old favourites make an appearance with the FA Cup Final line-ups from 1872, updated to include this year's final, together with the League Cup Final line-ups from 1961, also updated to the current season. A significant addition is the full results of the English Women's International team from 1972 to the current season.

At European level, both the Champions League and Europa League have their usual comprehensive details included, with results, goalscorers, attendances, full line-ups and formations from the qualifying rounds onwards and also including all the league tables from the respective group stages.

The 2014–15 season ended with Chelsea worthy Premier League winners with a handsome 8-point gap to second-placed Manchester City. They were top of the league for a record 274 days, surpassing Sir Alex Ferguson's Manchester United's total of 257 days in the 1993–94 season. An incredible season in the Championship, which had witnessed multiple changes at the top of the league, ended with final-day drama when Watford conceded an injury-time equaliser to Sheffield Wednesday and Bournemouth won to become champions and reach the Premier League for the first time in their history.

All of these statistics are reproduced in the pages devoted not only to the Premier League, but the three Football League competitions too, as well as all major allied cup competitions.

While transfer fees are invariably those reported at the time and rarely given as official figures, the edition reflects those listed at the time.

In the club-by-club pages that contain the line-ups of all league matches, appearances are split into starting and substitute appearances. In the Players Directory the totals show figures combined.

The Players Directory and its accompanying A to Z index enables the reader to quickly find the club of any specific player.

Throughout the book players sent off are designated with ■, substitutes in the club pages are 12, 13 and 14. Included again in main competitions are the formations for each team.

In addition to competitions already mentioned there is full coverage of Scottish Premier League and Scottish League and cup competitions. There are also sections devoted to Welsh, Irish, Women's football, the Under-21s and various other UEFA youth levels, schools, reserve team, academies, referees and the leading non-league competitions as well as the work of the chaplains at clubs. The chief tournaments outside the UK at club and national level are not forgotten. The International Directory itself features Europe in some depth as well as every FIFA-affiliated country's international results for the period 14 July 2014 to 30 June 2015.

Naturally there are international appearances and goals scored by players for England, Scotland, Northern Ireland, Wales and the Republic. For easy reference, those players making appearances and scoring goals in the season covered are picked out in bold type.

The Yearbook would like to extend its appreciation to the publishers Headline for excellent support in the preparation of this edition, particularly Jonathan Taylor for photographic selection throughout the book and to Graham Green for his continued support.

ACKNOWLEDGEMENTS

In addition the Yearbook is also keen to thank the following individuals and organisations for their co-operation.

Special thanks to Gary Hughes, Gary Neville and Ed Chamberlin from Sky Sports for their pieces, and to Jamie Carragher for his Sky Sports team of the season.

Thanks are also due to Ian Nannestad for the Obituaries, Did You Know and Fact File features in the club section. Many thanks also to John English for his conscientious proof reading and compilation of the International Directory.

The Yearbook is grateful to the Football Association, the Scottish Professional Football League, the Football League, Rev. Nigel Sands for his contribution to the Chaplain's page and Bob Bannister, Kenny Holmes and Martin Cooper for their help.

Sincere thanks to George Schley and Simon Dunnington for their excellent work on the database, and to Andy Cordiner, Geoff Turner, Brian Tait, Mick Carruthers, Robin Middlemiss and the staff at Wearset for their much appreciated efforts in the production of the book throughout the year.

EDITORIAL

Could this be the start of a dynasty for Chelsea and Jose Mourinho? They are going to be tough to catch again this year. Last season's dominance started when Andre Schurrle scored that brilliant goal against Burnley on the first *Monday Night Football* of the season. That set the tone for Chelsea for the rest of the year. Solid at the back with enough flare going forward, inspired by the Player of the Year Eden Hazard. Having gone close the season before last, the missing pieces of the jigsaw were filled by Diego Costa and Cesc Fabregas, and Mourinho's men found the right formula to win the League with ease.

Will the Chelsea faithful be celebrating the same feat come May? As with Liverpool in the 1980s and Manchester United in the '90s, are we witnessing the beginning of a dominant period for Chelsea?

Mr Abramovich has his sights set on just that and this time around Mourinho seems to be moulding a team with the intention of succeeding over a long period of time. Mourinho is a master at identifying the gaps in his squad and is able to get the very best from his men. John Terry looks better than ever, the spine is evident, and they have a wealth of young talent.

As we move from one season to the next, looking back at some of the great Premier League moments, there are two players who spring to mind straight away who have provided us with some of the best: Steven Gerrard and Frank Lampard. We must pay tribute to these two legends. In typical fashion they both scored in their final Premier League appearances. As they embark upon a new challenge in the MLS, we must not forget what they have done for the game in this country. They are two Premier League greats and will be sorely missed.

Whether it's watching great players, Premier League title triumphs, escape from relegation or simply winning three points – the passion and the dedication of the fans in this country never ceases to amaze. One of the perks of my job is getting to travel up and down the country watching football in different stadiums each and every week. When Jermain Defoe scored the sensational winner in the North East derby, I had never seen anything like it. The stadium was rocking; it was one of those moments that will stay with me for a long time. An iconic moment from last season.

I am already itching to get to the first *Super Sunday* of the season and especially excited to see the battle at the top. Chelsea are definitely the favourites but as Graeme Souness and Gary Neville will tell you, retaining the League title is incredibly difficult.

It all starts again on 8 August. Bring it on.

Ed Chamberlin

SKY SPORTS TEAM OF THE SEASON

JAMIE CARRAGHER'S
PREMIER LEAGUE TEAM OF THE SEASON 2014–15

David De Gea
(Manchester U)

Branislav Ivanovic	Laurent Koscielny	John Terry	Cesar Azpilicueta
(Chelsea)	*(Arsenal)*	*(Chelsea)*	*(Chelsea)*

Alexis Sanchez	Cesc Fabregas	Nemanja Matic	Eden Hazard
(Arsenal)	*(Chelsea)*	*(Chelsea)*	*(Chelsea)*

Harry Kane   Sergio Aguero
(Tottenham H)   *(Manchester C)*

EUROPEAN GOLDEN SHOE

The European Golden Shoe award is presented to the leading goalscorer in European League football. However, the determination of the winner comes from a points system which depends on the status of the country involved. The goals total is multiplied by a factor of either two, one and a half, or just by one.

The top 30 places were as follows:

	Scorer	Team	Country	Goals	Factor	Points
1	Cristiano Ronaldo	Real Madrid	Spain	48	2.0	96.0
2	Lionel Messi	Barcelona	Spain	43	2.0	86.0
3	Sergio Aguero	Manchester C	England	26	2.0	52.0
4	Jonathon Soriano	Red Bull Salzburg	Austria	31	1.5	46.5
5	Mauro Icardi	Internazionale	Italy	22	2.0	44.0
6	Luca Toni	Verona	Italy	22	2.0	44.0
7	Neymar	Barcelona	Spain	22	2.0	44.0
8	Antoine Griezmann	Atletico Madrid	Spain	22	2.0	44.0
9	Jackson Martinez	Porto	Portugal	21	2.0	42.0
10	Harry Kane	Tottenham H	England	21	2.0	42.0
11	Eran Zahavi	Maccabi Tel Aviv	Israel	27	1.5	40.5
12	Robert Beric	Rapid Vienna	Austria	27	1.5	40.5
13	Alexandre Lacazette	Olympique Lyonnais	France	27	1.5	40.5
14	Diego Costa	Chelsea	England	20	2.0	40.0
15	Jonas	Benfica	Portugal	20	2.0	40.0
16	Carlos Tevez	Juventus	Italy	20	2.0	40.0
17	Carlos Bacca	Sevilla	Spain	20	2.0	40.0
18	Rodrigo Lima	Benfica	Portugal	19	2.0	38.0
19	Alexander Meier	Eintracht Frankfurt	Germany	19	2.0	38.0
20	Gonzalo Higuain	Napoli	Italy	18	2.0	36.0
21	Charlie Austin	QPR	England	18	2.0	36.0
22	Artiz Aduriz	Athletic Bilbao	Spain	18	2.0	36.0
23	Robert Lewandowski	Bayern Munich	Germany	17	2.0	34.0
24	Alberto Bueno	Rayo Vallecano	Spain	17	2.0	34.0
25	Arjen Robben	Bayern Munich	Germany	17	2.0	34.0
26	Marco	Nacional	Portugal	17	2.0	34.0
27	Shkelzen Gashi	FC Basel	Switzerland	22	1.5	33.0
28	Fernandao	Bursaspor	Turkey	22	1.5	33.0
29	Memphis Depay	PSV Eindhoven	Netherlands	22	1.5	33.0
30	Luis Suarez	Barcelona	Spain	16	2.0	32.0

FOOTBALL AWARDS 2014–15

FOOTBALLER OF THE YEAR

The Football Writers' Association Sir Stanley Matthews Trophy for the Footballer of the Year was awarded to Eden Hazard of Chelsea and Belgium. Harry Kane (Tottenham H and England) was runner-up and John Terry (Chelsea) came third.

Past Winners
1947–48 Stanley Matthews (Blackpool), 1948–49 Johnny Carey (Manchester U), 1949–50 Joe Mercer (Arsenal), 1950–51 Harry Johnston (Blackpool), 1951–52 Billy Wright (Wolverhampton W), 1952–53 Nat Lofthouse (Bolton W), 1953–54 Tom Finney (Preston NE), 1954–55 Don Revie (Manchester C), 1955–56 Bert Trautmann (Manchester C), 1956–57 Tom Finney (Preston NE), 1957–58 Danny Blanchflower (Tottenham H), 1958–59 Syd Owen (Luton T), 1959–60 Bill Slater (Wolverhampton W), 1960–61 Danny Blanchflower (Tottenham H), 1961–62 Jimmy Adamson (Burnley), 1962–63 Stanley Matthews (Stoke C), 1963–64 Bobby Moore (West Ham U), 1964–65 Bobby Collins (Leeds U), 1965–66 Bobby Charlton (Manchester U), 1966–67 Jackie Charlton (Leeds U), 1967–68 George Best (Manchester U), 1968–69 Dave Mackay (Derby Co) shared with Tony Book (Manchester C), 1969–70 Billy Bremner (Leeds U), 1970–71 Frank McLintock (Arsenal), 1971–72 Gordon Banks (Stoke C), 1972–73 Pat Jennings (Tottenham H), 1973–74 Ian Callaghan (Liverpool), 1974–75 Alan Mullery (Fulham), 1975–76 Kevin Keegan (Liverpool), 1976–77 Emlyn Hughes (Liverpool), 1977–78 Kenny Burns (Nottingham F), 1978–79 Kenny Dalglish (Liverpool), 1979–80 Terry McDermott (Liverpool), 1980–81 Frans Thijssen (Ipswich T), 1981–82 Steve Perryman (Tottenham H), 1982–83 Kenny Dalglish (Liverpool), 1983–84 Ian Rush (Liverpool), 1984–85 Neville Southall (Everton), 1985–86 Gary Lineker (Everton), 1986–87 Clive Allen (Tottenham H), 1987–88 John Barnes (Liverpool), 1988–89 Steve Nicol (Liverpool), 1989–90 John Barnes (Liverpool), 1990–91 Gordon Strachan (Leeds U), 1991–92 Gary Lineker (Tottenham H), 1992–93 Chris Waddle (Sheffield W), 1993–94 Alan Shearer (Blackburn R), 1994–95 Jurgen Klinsmann (Tottenham H), 1995–96 Eric Cantona (Manchester U), 1996–97 Gianfranco Zola (Chelsea), 1997–98 Dennis Bergkamp (Arsenal), 1998–99 David Ginola (Tottenham H), 1999–2000 Roy Keane (Manchester U), 2000–01 Teddy Sheringham (Manchester U), 2001–02 Robert Pires (Arsenal), 2002–03 Thierry Henry (Arsenal), 2003–04 Thierry Henry (Arsenal), 2004–05 Frank Lampard (Chelsea), 2005–06 Thierry Henry (Arsenal), 2006–07 Cristiano Ronaldo (Manchester U), 2007–08 Cristiano Ronaldo (Manchester U), 2008–09 Ryan Giggs (Manchester U), 2009–10 Wayne Rooney (Manchester U), 2010–11 Scott Parker (West Ham U), 2011–12 Robin van Persie (Arsenal), 2012–13 Gareth Bale (Tottenham H), 2013–14 Luis Suarez (Liverpool), 2014–15 Eden Hazard (Chelsea).

THE PFA AWARDS 2015

Player of the Year: Eden Hazard, Chelsea and Belgium
Young Player of the Year: Harry Kane, Tottenham H and England
Women's Player of the Year: Ji So-Yun, Chelsea and South Korea
Women's Young Player of the Year: Leah Williamson, Arsenal and England

SCOTTISH AWARDS 2014–15

SCOTTISH PFA PLAYER OF THE YEAR AWARDS 2015

Player of the Year: Stefan Johansen, Celtic and Norway
Young Player of the Year: Jason Denayer, Celtic (on loan from Manchester C) and Belgium
Manager of the Year: John Hughes, Inverness CT
Championship Player of the Year: Scott Allan, Hibernian and Scotland U21
League One Player of the Year: Declan McManus, Morton and Scotland U21
League Two Player of the Year: Bobby Linn, Arbroath
Goal of the Season: Stephen Mallan, St Mirren
Special Merit Award: Jordan Moore, Dundee U

SCOTTISH FOOTBALL WRITERS' ASSOCIATION 2015

Player of the Year: Craig Gordon, Celtic and Scotland
Young Player of the Year: Ryan Christie, Inverness CT
Manager of the Year: John Hughes, Inverness CT
International Player of the Year: Ikechi Anya, Watford

OTHER AWARDS

EUROPEAN FOOTBALLER OF THE YEAR 2014

Cristiano Ronaldo, Real Madrid and Portugal

EUROPEAN WOMEN'S PLAYER OF THE YEAR 2014

Nadine Kessler, Wolfsburg and Germany

FIFA BALLON D'OR PLAYER OF THE YEAR 2014

Cristiano Ronaldo, Real Madrid and Portugal

FIFA BALLON D'OR WOMEN'S PLAYER OF THE YEAR 2014

Nadine Kessler, Wolfsburg and Germany

FIFA PUSKAS AWARD GOAL OF THE YEAR

James Rodriguez, Real Madrid and Colombia – Colombia v Uruguay, FIFA World Cup Round of 16, 28 June 2014

PREMIER LEAGUE AWARDS 2014–15

PLAYER OF THE MONTH AWARDS 2014–15

August	Diego Costa (Chelsea)
September	Graziano Pelle (Southampton)
October	Diafra Sakho (West Ham U)
November	Sergio Aguero (Manchester C)
December	Charlie Austin (QPR)
January	Harry Kane (Tottenham H)
February	Harry Kane (Tottenham H)
March	Olivier Giroud (Arsenal)
April	Christian Benteke (Aston Villa)

MANAGER OF THE MONTH AWARDS 2014–15

August	Garry Monk (Swansea C)
September	Ronald Koeman (Southampton)
October	Sam Allardyce (West Ham U)
November	Alan Pardew (Newcastle U)
December	Manuel Pellegrini (Manchester C)
January	Ronald Koeman (Southampton)
February	Tony Pulis (WBA)
March	Arsene Wenger (Arsenal)
April	Nigel Pearson (Leicester C)

SKY BET LEAGUE AWARDS 2014–15

SKY BET FOOTBALL LEAGUE PLAYER OF THE MONTH AWARDS 2014–15

	Sky Bet Championship	*Sky Bet League 1*	*Sky Bet League 2*
August	Igor Vetokele (Charlton Ath)	Conor Hourihane (Barnsley)	Matt Tubbs (AFC Wimbledon)
September	Tyrone Mings (Ipswich T)	Eoin Doyle (Chesterfield)	Luke Wilkinson (Luton T)
October	Callum Wilson (Bournemouth)	Jonathan Forte (Oldham Ath)	Mark Cullen (Luton T)
November	Andre Gray (Brentford)	Carl Baker (Milton Keynes D)	David Worrall (Southend U)
December	Daryl Murphy (Ipswich T)	Rory McArdle (Bradford C)	Paris Cowan-Hall (Wycombe W)
January	Lee Tomlin (Middlesbrough)	Dele Alli (Milton Keynes D)	Rory Donnelly (Tranmere R)
February	Henri Lansbury (Nottingham F)	Izale McLeod (Crawley T)	Jed Wallace (Portsmouth)
March	Troy Denney (Watford)	Andrew Flint (Bristol C)	Bobby Grant (Shrewsbury T)
April	Tom Ince (Derby Co)	Jermaine Beckford (Preston NE)	Adam Barrett (Southend U)

SKY BET FOOTBALL LEAGUE MANAGER OF THE MONTH AWARDS 2014–15

	Sky Bet Championship	*Sky Bet League 1*	*Sky Bet League 2*
August	Kenny Jackett (Wolves)	Darren Ferguson (Peterborough U)	Jim Bentley (Morecambe)
September	Mick McCarthy (Ipswich T)	Steve Cotterill (Bristol C)	Phil Brown (Southend U)
October	Eddie Howe (Bournemouth)	Simon Grayson (Preston NE)	John Still (Luton T)
November	Mark Warburton (Brentford)	Mark Cooper (Swindon T)	Phil Brown (Southend U)
December	Eddie Howe (Bournemouth)	Phil Parkinson (Bradford C)	Neal Ardley (AFC Wimbledon)
January	Aitor Karanka (Middlesbrough)	Karl Robinson (Milton Keynes D)	Chris Wilder (Northampton T)
February	Alex Neil (Norwich C)	Simon Grayson (Preston NE)	Andy Awford (Portsmouth)
March	Eddie Howe (Bournemouth)	Steve Cotterill (Bristol C)	Gareth Ainsworth (Wycombe W)
April	Slavisa Jokanovic (Watford)	Karl Robinson (Milton Keynes D)	Phil Brown (Southend U)

LEAGUE MANAGERS ASSOCIATION AWARDS 2014–15

LMA MANAGER OF THE YEAR SPONSORED BY BARCLAYS
Eddie Howe, Bournemouth

BARCLAYS PREMIER LEAGUE MANAGER OF THE YEAR
Jose Mourinho, Chelsea

SKY BET FOOTBALL LEAGUE CHAMPIONSHIP MANAGER OF THE YEAR
Eddie Howe, Bournemouth

SKY BET FOOTBALL LEAGUE 1 MANAGER OF THE YEAR
Steve Cotterill, Bristol C

SKY BET FOOTBALL LEAGUE 2 MANAGER OF THE YEAR
Gareth Ainsworth, Wycombe W

FA CUP MANAGER OF THE YEAR
Phil Parkinson, Bradford C

LMA SPECIAL ACHIEVEMENT AWARDS
Steve Cotterill, Bristol C
Dean Smith, Walsall

LMA SERVICE TO FOOTBALL AWARD
Gordon Guthrie MBE, Derby Co

LMA HALL OF FAME – 1000 CLUB INDUCTEE
Danny Wilson

BARCLAYS PREMIER LEAGUE 2014–15

(P) Promoted into division at end of 2013–14 season.

			Total					Home					Away						
		P	W	D	L	F	A	W	D	L	F	A	W	D	L	F	A	GD	Pts
1	Chelsea	38	26	9	3	73	32	15	4	0	36	9	11	5	3	37	23	41	87
2	Manchester C	38	24	7	7	83	38	14	3	2	44	14	10	4	5	39	24	45	79
3	Arsenal	38	22	9	7	71	36	12	5	2	41	14	10	4	5	30	22	35	75
4	Manchester U	38	20	10	8	62	37	14	2	3	41	15	6	8	5	21	22	25	70
5	Tottenham H	38	19	7	12	58	53	10	3	6	31	24	9	4	6	27	29	5	64
6	Liverpool	38	18	8	12	52	48	10	5	4	30	20	8	3	8	22	28	4	62
7	Southampton	38	18	6	14	54	33	11	4	4	37	13	7	2	10	17	20	21	60
8	Swansea C	38	16	8	14	46	49	9	5	5	27	22	7	3	9	19	27	−3	56
9	Stoke C	38	15	9	14	48	45	10	3	6	32	22	5	6	8	16	23	3	54
10	Crystal Palace	38	13	9	16	47	51	6	3	10	21	27	7	6	6	26	24	−4	48
11	Everton	38	12	11	15	48	50	7	7	5	27	21	5	4	10	21	29	−2	47
12	West Ham U	38	12	11	15	44	47	9	4	6	25	18	3	7	9	19	29	−3	47
13	WBA	38	11	11	16	38	51	7	4	8	24	26	4	7	8	14	25	−13	44
14	Leicester C (P)	38	11	8	19	46	55	7	5	7	28	22	4	3	12	18	33	−9	41
15	Newcastle U	38	10	9	19	40	63	7	5	7	26	27	3	4	12	14	36	−23	39
16	Sunderland	38	7	17	14	31	53	4	8	7	16	27	3	9	7	15	26	−22	38
17	Aston Villa	38	10	8	20	31	57	5	6	8	18	25	5	2	12	13	32	−26	38
18	Hull C	38	8	11	19	33	51	5	5	9	19	24	3	6	10	14	27	−18	35
19	Burnley (P)	38	7	12	19	28	53	4	7	8	14	21	3	5	11	14	32	−25	33
20	QPR (P)	38	8	6	24	42	73	6	5	8	23	24	2	1	16	19	49	−31	30

BARCLAYS PREMIER LEAGUE LEADING GOALSCORERS 2014–15

	League	FA Cup	Capital One Cup	Other	Total
Sergio Aguero *(Manchester C)*	26	0	0	6	32
Harry Kane *(Tottenham H)*	21	0	3	7	31
Alexis Sanchez *(Arsenal)*	16	3	1	4	24
Diego Costa *(Chelsea)*	20	0	0	0	20
Saido Berahino *(WBA)*	14	5	1	0	20
Eden Hazard *(Chelsea)*	14	0	2	3	19
Charlie Austin *(QPR)*	18	0	0	0	18
Olivier Giroud *(Arsenal)*	14	2	0	2	18
Graziano Pelle *(Southampton)*	12	1	3	0	16
Christian Benteke *(Aston Villa)*	13	2	0	0	15
Wayne Rooney *(Manchester U)*	12	2	0	0	14
Mame Biram Diouf *(Stoke C)*	12	0	1	0	13
Nacer Chadli *(Tottenham H)*	11	1	1	0	13
Leonardo Ulloa *(Leicester C)*	11	2	0	0	13
David Silva *(Manchester C)*	12	0	0	0	12
Papiss Cisse *(Newcastle U)*	11	0	0	0	11
Wilfried Bony *(Manchester C)*	11	0	0	0	11
(Includes 9 League goals scored for Swansea C.)					
Danny Ings *(Burnley)*	11	0	0	0	11
Sadio Mane *(Southampton)*	11	0	0	0	11

Other matches consist of European games, Community Shield.

BARCLAYS PREMIER LEAGUE – RESULTS 2014–15

Home \ Away	Arsenal	Aston Villa	Burnley	Chelsea	Crystal Palace	Everton	Hull C	Leicester C	Liverpool	Manchester C	Manchester U	Newcastle U	QPR	Southampton	Stoke C	Sunderland	Swansea C	Tottenham H	WBA	West Ham U
Arsenal	—	5-0	3-0	0-0	2-1	2-0	2-2	2-1	4-1	2-2	1-2	4-1	2-1	1-0	3-0	0-0	0-1	1-1	4-1	3-0
Aston Villa	0-3	—	0-1	1-2	0-0	3-2	2-1	2-1	0-2	0-2	1-1	0-0	3-3	1-1	1-2	0-0	0-1	1-2	2-1	1-0
Burnley	0-1	1-1	—	1-3	2-3	1-3	1-0	0-1	0-1	1-1	0-0	1-1	2-1	1-0	0-0	0-0	0-1	0-0	2-2	1-3
Chelsea	2-0	3-0	1-1	—	1-0	1-0	2-0	2-0	1-1	1-1	1-0	2-0	2-1	1-1	2-1	3-1	4-2	3-0	2-0	2-0
Crystal Palace	1-2	0-1	0-0	1-2	—	0-1	0-2	2-0	3-1	0-0	1-2	1-1	3-1	1-3	1-1	1-3	1-0	2-1	0-2	1-3
Everton	2-2	3-0	1-0	3-6	2-3	—	1-1	2-2	0-0	1-1	3-0	3-0	3-1	1-0	0-1	0-2	0-0	1-2	0-0	2-1
Hull C	1-3	2-0	1-0	2-3	2-0	1-1	—	0-1	1-0	2-4	0-0	0-3	2-1	0-1	0-1	1-1	0-1	1-2	0-0	2-2
Leicester C	1-1	1-0	2-2	1-3	0-1	2-2	0-0	—	1-3	0-1	5-3	3-0	5-1	2-0	1-0	0-0	2-0	4-3	0-1	2-1
Liverpool	2-2	2-0	2-0	1-2	1-3	0-0	0-0	2-2	—	2-1	1-2	2-0	2-1	2-1	1-0	0-0	4-1	4-0	2-1	2-0
Manchester C	0-2	3-2	2-2	1-1	3-0	1-0	1-1	2-0	3-1	—	1-0	5-0	6-0	2-0	0-1	3-2	2-1	3-0	3-0	2-0
Manchester U	1-1	3-1	3-1	1-1	2-0	2-1	3-0	3-1	3-0	4-2	—	3-1	4-0	1-2	2-1	2-0	1-2	1-2	0-1	1-2
Newcastle U	1-2	1-0	3-3	2-1	0-0	0-0	2-2	1-0	1-0	0-2	4-0	—	1-0	1-2	1-1	0-1	2-3	3-0	1-1	2-0
QPR	2-0	2-0	0-0	0-1	3-1	0-0	0-1	3-2	2-3	2-2	2-1	2-1	—	0-1	2-2	1-0	1-1	1-2	3-2	0-0
Southampton	0-1	1-1	1-1	1-2	2-0	2-0	0-1	0-1	0-2	0-3	1-1	4-0	2-1	—	0-1	8-0	0-1	2-2	0-0	0-0
Stoke C	3-2	1-0	0-0	0-2	3-1	2-0	1-0	0-0	6-1	1-4	1-1	1-0	3-1	2-1	—	3-1	2-1	3-0	2-0	2-2
Sunderland	0-2	0-0	2-0	0-0	1-1	1-1	1-3	0-0	0-1	1-4	2-1	1-0	0-2	2-1	3-1	—	0-0	2-2	0-0	1-1
Swansea C	2-1	1-0	1-0	0-5	1-1	1-1	3-1	2-0	0-1	2-4	0-0	2-2	2-0	0-1	2-0	1-1	—	1-2	3-0	1-1
Tottenham H	1-2	2-1	2-1	5-3	0-0	2-1	2-0	4-3	0-3	0-1	1-1	1-2	4-0	1-0	1-2	2-1	3-2	—	0-1	2-2
WBA	0-1	1-0	2-2	3-0	2-0	2-0	1-0	2-3	0-0	1-3	2-2	0-2	1-4	1-0	1-0	2-2	2-0	0-3	—	1-2
West Ham U	1-2	1-0	1-3	0-1	1-3	2-1	3-0	2-0	3-1	2-1	1-1	1-0	2-0	1-3	1-1	1-0	3-1	0-1	1-1	—

SKY BET CHAMPIONSHIP 2014–15

(P) Promoted into division at end of 2013–14 season.   (R) Relegated into division at end of 2013–14 season.

			Total				Home					Away						
		P	W	D	L	F	A	W	D	L	F	A	W	D	L	F	A	GD	Pts
1	Bournemouth	46	26	12	8	98	45	13	7	3	48	25	13	5	5	50	20	53	90
2	Watford	46	27	8	11	91	50	14	4	5	48	22	13	4	6	43	28	41	89
3	Norwich C (R)¶	46	25	11	10	88	48	12	6	5	50	24	13	5	5	38	24	40	86
4	Middlesbrough	46	25	10	11	68	37	15	5	3	42	12	10	5	8	26	25	31	85
5	Brentford (P)	46	23	9	14	78	59	12	6	5	46	28	11	3	9	32	31	19	78
6	Ipswich T	46	22	12	12	72	54	15	5	3	40	18	7	7	9	32	36	18	78
7	Wolverhampton W (P)	46	22	12	12	70	56	13	6	4	42	23	9	6	8	28	33	14	78
8	Derby Co	46	21	14	11	85	56	12	7	4	48	24	9	7	7	37	32	29	77
9	Blackburn R	46	17	16	13	66	59	11	6	6	37	28	6	10	7	29	31	7	67
10	Birmingham C	46	16	15	15	54	64	10	7	6	29	31	6	8	9	25	33	−10	63
11	Cardiff C (R)	46	16	14	16	57	61	10	5	8	31	30	6	9	8	26	31	−4	62
12	Charlton Ath	46	14	18	14	54	60	9	9	5	32	27	5	9	9	22	33	−6	60
13	Sheffield W	46	14	18	14	43	49	5	11	7	16	20	9	7	7	27	29	−6	60
14	Nottingham F	46	15	14	17	71	69	9	5	9	37	32	6	9	8	34	37	2	59
15	Leeds U	46	15	11	20	50	61	8	6	9	22	24	7	5	11	28	37	−11	56
16	Huddersfield T	46	13	16	17	58	75	8	8	7	34	34	5	8	10	24	41	−17	55
17	Fulham (R)	46	14	10	22	62	83	9	5	9	36	38	5	5	13	26	45	−21	52
18	Bolton W	46	13	12	21	54	67	9	8	6	35	27	4	4	15	19	40	−13	51
19	Reading	46	13	11	22	48	69	8	5	10	24	25	5	6	12	24	44	−21	50
20	Brighton & HA	46	10	17	19	44	54	6	8	9	26	29	4	9	10	18	25	−10	47
21	Rotherham U* (P)	46	11	16	19	46	67	8	7	8	31	34	3	9	11	15	33	−21	46
22	Millwall	46	9	14	23	42	76	5	7	11	25	40	4	7	12	17	36	−34	41
23	Wigan Ath	46	9	12	25	39	64	3	8	12	18	29	6	4	13	21	35	−25	39
24	Blackpool	46	4	14	28	36	91	4	7	12	18	35	0	7	16	18	56	−55	26

*Rotherham U deducted 3 points for fielding an ineligible player. ¶Norwich C promoted via play-offs.

SKY BET CHAMPIONSHIP LEADING GOALSCORERS 2014–15

	League	FA Cup	Capital One Cup	Play-Offs	Total
Daryl Murphy *(Ipswich T)*	27	0	0	0	27
Callum Wilson *(Bournemouth)*	20	1	2	0	23
Rudy Gestede *(Blackburn R)*	20	2	0	0	22
Troy Deeney *(Watford)*	21	0	0	0	21
Jordan Rhodes *(Blackburn R)*	21	0	0	0	21
Chris Martin *(Derby Co)*	18	1	2	0	21
Cameron Jerome *(Norwich C)*	18	0	1	2	21
Odion Ighalo *(Watford)*	20	0	0	0	20
Patrick Bamford *(Middlesbrough)*	17	1	1	0	19
Ross McCormack *(Fulham)*	17	1	1	0	19
Andre Gray *(Brentford)*	16	0	1	1	18
Yann Kermorgant *(Bournemouth)*	15	2	0	0	17
Matej Vydra *(Watford)*	16	0	0	0	16
Clayton Donaldson *(Birmingham C)*	15	0	1	0	16
Britt Assombalonga *(Nottingham F)*	15	0	0	0	15
Bradley Johnson *(Norwich C)*	15	0	0	0	15
Matt Ritchie *(Bournemouth)*	15	0	0	0	15
Bakary Sako *(Wolverhampton W)*	15	0	0	0	15
Michail Antonio *(Nottingham F)*	14	0	1	0	15
Nouha Dicko *(Wolverhampton W)*	14	0	1	0	15

SKY BET CHAMPIONSHIP – RESULTS 2014–15

Home \ Away	Birmingham C	Blackburn R	Blackpool	Bolton W	Bournemouth	Brentford	Brighton & HA	Cardiff C	Charlton Ath	Derby Co	Fulham	Huddersfield T	Ipswich T	Leeds U	Middlesbrough	Millwall	Norwich C	Nottingham F	Reading	Rotherham U	Sheffield W	Watford	Wigan Ath	Wolverhampton W
Birmingham C	—	2-2	1-0	0-1	0-8	1-0	1-0	0-0	1-0	0-4	1-2	1-1	2-2	1-1	1-1	0-1	0-0	2-1	6-1	2-1	0-2	2-1	3-1	2-1
Blackburn R	1-0	—	1-1	1-0	3-2	2-3	0-1	1-1	2-0	2-3	2-1	0-0	3-2	2-1	0-0	2-0	1-2	3-3	3-1	2-1	1-2	2-2	3-1	0-1
Blackpool	1-0	1-2	—	1-1	1-6	1-2	1-0	1-0	0-3	0-1	0-1	0-0*	0-2	3-1	1-2	1-0	1-3	4-4	1-1	1-1	0-1	0-1	1-3	0-0
Bolton W	0-1	2-1	1-1	—	1-2	3-1	1-0	3-0	1-1	0-2	3-1	1-0	0-0	1-1	1-2	2-0	1-2	2-2	1-1	3-2	0-0	3-4	3-1	2-2
Bournemouth	4-2	0-0	4-0	3-0	—	1-0	3-2	5-3	1-0	2-2	2-0	1-1	2-2	1-3	3-0	2-2	1-2	1-2	3-0	1-1	2-2	2-0	2-0	2-1
Brentford	1-1	1-1	4-0	1-0	1-0	—	3-2	1-2	1-1	2-1	2-1	4-1	2-4	2-0	0-1	0-1	0-3	2-2	3-1	1-0	0-0	1-2	3-0	4-0
Brighton & HA	4-3	1-1	0-0	2-1	3-1	3-2	—	1-1	3-2	2-1	1-2	0-0	1-2	2-0	0-1	0-0	2-4	2-3	2-2	0-0	2-1	0-2	1-0	1-1
Cardiff C	2-0	1-1	3-2	1-2	1-1	1-2	1-1	—	1-2	0-2	1-0	3-1	3-1	3-1	0-0	2-4	2-3	2-1	2-1	1-1	1-1	2-4	1-1	0-1
Charlton Ath	1-1	1-3	2-2	2-1	0-3	1-1	0-1	1-1	—	3-2	1-1	3-0	0-1	2-1	0-1	0-0	2-2	2-1	3-2	1-0	3-2	1-0	2-1	1-1
Derby Co	2-2	2-0	4-0	0-3	2-0	3-0	3-0	2-2	3-2	—	3-2	3-2	1-1	2-0	1-2	0-0	1-0	1-2	0-3	1-1	4-0	2-2	1-2	5-0
Fulham	1-1	0-1	2-2	2-1	1-5	1-4	0-2	1-1	2-0	2-0	—	3-1	1-2	0-3	0-1	0-0	2-2	3-2	2-1	2-0	0-0	0-5	0-0	0-1
Huddersfield T	0-1	1-1	4-2	4-0	0-4	2-1	1-1	0-0	3-0	4-4	3-1	—	2-1	1-2	4-3	0-1	1-0	3-0	2-2	0-0	1-1	3-1	2-1	1-4
Ipswich T	4-2	1-1	3-1	3-2	1-1	3-2	2-0	3-1	3-0	0-1	2-1	2-2	—	4-1	1-2	2-1	2-2	2-1	3-0	2-0	2-3	1-0	0-0	2-1
Leeds U	1-1	0-3	3-1	1-0	1-0	0-1	0-2	1-2	2-2	2-0	2-0	3-0	4-1	—	1-0	1-0	0-2	0-0	0-1	2-0	1-3	2-3	0-1	1-2
Middlesbrough	2-0	2-2	1-1	1-0	0-0	4-0	0-0	2-1	3-1	2-0	2-0	1-0	1-0	0-1	—	3-0	4-0	3-0	0-0	0-1	2-0	1-1	1-0	2-1
Millwall	1-3	3-1	2-1	0-1	0-2	2-3	0-0	1-0	2-1	3-3	0-0	1-3	2-1	2-0	3-0	—	1-4	0-0	0-1	1-1	0-2	0-2	2-0	3-3
Norwich C	2-2	1-3	4-0	2-1	1-1	1-2	3-3	3-2	0-1	1-1	4-2	5-0	2-2	1-1	4-0	1-4	—	3-1	0-0	2-0	1-3	3-0	0-1	2-0
Nottingham F	1-3	2-0	2-0	4-1	2-1	1-3	0-0	1-1	0-1	1-1	5-3	0-1	2-0	0-2	0-1	6-1	3-1	—	1-2	0-0	2-0	1-3	3-0	1-2
Reading	0-1	0-0	3-0	0-0	0-1	0-2	2-1	1-1	0-1	0-3	3-0	1-2	1-0	2-1	0-0	0-1	1-2	4-0	—	3-0	0-2	0-1	1-2	3-3
Rotherham U	0-1	1-2	1-1	4-2	0-2	0-2	1-0	1-3	1-1	3-3	3-3	2-2	2-0	2-1	0-3	3-2	4-0	0-3	4-0	—	2-3	0-2	3-0	1-0
Sheffield W	0-0	1-0	1-0	1-2	0-2	1-0	0-0	0-1	1-1	0-0	1-0	1-1	2-3	1-2	2-0	3-1	1-1	0-0	2-1	0-0	—	0-3	0-2	0-1
Watford	1-0	1-0	7-2	3-0	1-1	2-1	1-1	0-1	5-0	1-2	3-3	4-2	0-1	4-1	2-0	3-1	0-0	2-2	4-1	3-0	1-1	—	2-1	0-1
Wigan Ath	4-0	3-1	1-0	1-1	1-3	0-0	2-1	1-0	0-3	0-2	3-0	0-1	0-0	0-1	1-1	0-0	0-3	0-0	2-2	1-2	0-1	0-2	—	0-1
Wolverhampton W	0-0	3-1	1-1	1-0	1-0	1-0	1-1	1-0	0-0	0-4	3-0	1-3	2-1	4-3	2-0	4-2	0-1	0-3	1-2	5-0	3-0	2-2	2-2	—

*Blackpool v Huddersfield, Saturday 2 May 2015, match abandoned after 48 minutes because of pitch invasion. Result stands.

SKY BET LEAGUE 1 2014–15

(P) Promoted into division at end of 2013–14 season.   (R) Relegated into division at end of 2013–14 season.

		P	W	D	L	F	A	W	D	L	F	A	W	D	L	F	A	GD	Pts
				Total						*Home*					*Away*				
1	Bristol C	46	29	12	5	96	38	16	5	2	48	17	13	7	3	48	21	58	99
2	Milton Keynes D	46	27	10	9	101	44	16	3	4	60	19	11	7	5	41	25	57	91
3	Preston NE¶	46	25	14	7	79	40	13	9	1	43	21	12	5	6	36	19	39	89
4	Swindon T	46	23	10	13	76	57	12	5	6	38	28	11	5	7	38	29	19	79
5	Sheffield U	46	19	14	13	66	53	10	7	6	35	24	9	7	7	31	29	13	71
6	Chesterfield (P)	46	19	12	15	68	55	12	4	7	42	26	7	8	8	26	29	13	69
7	Bradford C	46	17	14	15	55	55	8	6	9	26	33	9	8	6	29	22	0	65
8	Rochdale (P)	46	19	6	21	72	66	11	3	9	36	29	8	3	12	36	37	6	63
9	Peterborough U	46	18	9	19	53	56	10	5	8	27	26	8	4	11	26	30	–3	63
10	Fleetwood T (P)	46	17	12	17	49	52	8	9	6	28	27	9	3	11	21	25	–3	63
11	Barnsley (R)	46	17	11	18	62	61	11	5	7	41	29	6	6	11	21	32	1	62
12	Gillingham	46	16	14	16	65	66	11	6	6	37	29	5	8	10	28	37	–1	62
13	Doncaster R (R)	46	16	13	17	58	62	7	6	10	24	29	9	7	7	34	33	–4	61
14	Walsall	46	14	17	15	50	54	8	8	7	28	24	6	9	8	22	30	–4	59
15	Oldham Ath	46	14	15	17	54	67	8	8	7	32	34	6	7	10	22	33	–13	57
16	Scunthorpe U (P)	46	14	14	18	62	75	9	6	8	27	28	5	8	10	35	47	–13	56
17	Coventry C	46	13	16	17	49	60	6	9	8	25	33	7	7	9	24	27	–11	55
18	Port Vale	46	15	9	22	55	65	8	5	10	31	31	7	4	12	24	34	–10	54
19	Colchester U	46	14	10	22	58	77	7	4	12	30	36	7	6	10	28	41	–19	52
20	Crewe Alex	46	14	10	22	43	75	8	7	8	21	28	6	3	14	22	47	–32	52
21	Notts Co	46	12	14	20	45	63	5	6	12	24	33	7	8	8	21	30	–18	50
22	Crawley T	46	13	11	22	53	79	9	6	8	30	33	4	5	14	23	46	–26	50
23	Leyton Orient	46	12	13	21	59	69	5	6	12	30	34	7	7	9	29	35	–10	49
24	Yeovil T (R)	46	10	10	26	36	75	5	7	11	17	33	5	3	15	19	42	–39	40

¶*Preston NE promoted via play-offs.*

SKY BET LEAGUE 1 LEADING GOALSCORERS 2014–15

	League	FA Cup	Capital One Cup	J Paint Trophy	Play-Offs	Total
Eoin Doyle *(Chesterfield)*	26	3	1	0	0	30
(Includes 5 League goals for Cardiff C in Championship.)						
Joe Garner *(Preston NE)*	25	0	0	1	1	27
Ian Henderson *(Rochdale)*	22	0	0	0	0	22
Andy Williams *(Swindon T)*	21	0	0	1	0	22
Will Grigg *(Milton Keynes D)*	20	0	2	0	0	22
Matt Done *(Sheffield U)*	17	3	0	1	1	22
(Includes 10 League goals and 3 FA Cup goals for Rochdale.)						
Izale McLeod *(Crawley T)*	19	0	1	1	0	21
Aaron Wilbraham *(Bristol C)*	18	0	0	3	0	21
Tom Bradshaw *(Walsall)*	17	2	0	1	0	20
Jermaine Beckford *(Preston NE)*	12	0	2	0	6	20
Cody McDonald *(Gillingham)*	16	0	0	2	0	18
Michael Smith *(Swindon T)*	13	0	2	1	2	18
Paddy Madden *(Scunthorpe U)*	14	2	0	1	0	17
Dele Alli *(Milton Keynes D)*	16	0	0	0	0	16
Peter Vincenti *(Rochdale)*	13	2	0	1	0	16
Aden Flint *(Bristol C)*	14	0	0	1	0	15
Jonathan Forte *(Oldham Ath)*	14	0	0	0	0	14
Kieran Agard *(Bristol C)*	13	1	0	0	0	14
Billy Clarke *(Bradford C)*	13	1	0	0	0	14

SKY BET LEAGUE 1 – RESULTS 2014-15

	Barnsley	Bradford C	Bristol C	Chesterfield	Colchester U	Coventry C	Crawley T	Crewe Alex	Doncaster R	Fleetwood T	Gillingham	Leyton Orient	Milton Keynes D	Notts Co	Oldham Ath	Peterborough U	Port Vale	Preston NE	Rochdale	Scunthorpe U	Sheffield U	Swindon T	Walsall	Yeovil T
Barnsley	—	3-1	2-2	1-1	3-2	1-0	0-1	2-0	1-1	1-2	4-1	2-0	3-5	2-3	1-0	1-1	2-1	1-1	5-0	1-2	0-2	0-3	3-0	2-0
Bradford C	1-0	—	0-6	0-1	1-1	3-2	1-0	2-0	1-2	1-1	1-1	3-1	2-1	4-0	2-0	0-1	3-1	0-3	1-2	2-0	0-2	1-2	1-1	1-3
Bristol C	2-2	2-2	—	3-2	2-1	0-0	1-0	3-0	3-0	2-0	0-0	0-0	3-2	4-0	1-0	2-0	3-1	0-1	1-0	2-0	1-3	3-0	8-2	2-1
Chesterfield	2-1	0-1	0-2	—	6-0	2-3	3-0	1-0	2-2	3-0	3-0	2-3	0-1	1-1	1-1	3-2	3-0	0-2	2-1	4-1	3-2	0-3	1-0	0-0
Colchester U	3-1	0-0	3-2	2-1	—	0-1	2-3	2-3	0-1	2-1	1-2	2-0	0-1	1-1	2-2	1-3	1-2	1-0	1-4	2-2	2-3	1-1	0-2	2-0
Coventry C	2-2	1-1	1-3	0-0	1-0	—	2-2	1-3	1-3	1-1	1-0	0-1	2-2	0-1	1-1	1-4	2-3	0-2	2-2	1-1	1-0	1-0	0-0	2-1
Crawley T	5-1	1-3	1-2	1-1	1-0	1-2	—	1-1	0-5	1-0	1-2	1-0	2-2	2-0	2-0	1-4	1-2	2-1	0-4	2-2	1-0	1-0	0-0	2-0
Crewe Alex	1-2	0-1	1-2	0-0	0-3	1-2	0-0	—	1-1	0-0	3-1	1-1	0-5	2-0	0-1	1-1	1-2	1-1	2-5	2-2	1-1	0-0	1-1	1-0
Doncaster R	1-0	0-3	1-3	3-2	2-0	2-0	0-0	2-1	—	0-0	1-2	0-2	0-0	0-0	0-1	0-2	1-3	1-1	2-5	5-2	0-1	1-2	0-2	1-0
Fleetwood T	0-0	0-2	3-3	0-0	2-3	1-0	1-0	2-1	3-1	—	1-0	1-1	0-3	2-1	0-2	1-1	1-0	1-1	1-0	2-2	1-1	2-2	0-1	4-0
Gillingham	0-1	1-0	1-3	2-3	2-2	3-1	1-1	2-0	1-1	0-1	—	3-2	4-2	3-1	3-2	2-1	2-2	0-1	1-0	0-3	2-0	2-2	0-0	2-0
Leyton Orient	0-0	0-2	1-3	1-2	0-2	2-2	4-1	4-1	1-1	0-1	3-3	—	0-0	0-1	3-0	0-1	3-1	0-2	2-3	1-4	1-1	1-2	0-3	3-0
Milton Keynes D	2-0	1-2	0-1	1-2	6-0	0-0	2-0	6-1	3-0	2-1	4-2	6-1	—	4-1	7-0	3-0	1-0	0-2	2-2	2-2	1-0	2-1	0-3	5-1
Notts Co	1-1	1-1	1-2	0-1	2-1	0-0	5-3	2-1	2-1	0-1	1-0	1-1	0-1	—	0-0	1-1	0-1	1-3	1-2	2-2	1-0	0-3	1-2	0-0
Oldham Ath	1-3	2-1	1-1	0-0	0-1	4-1	1-1	1-2	2-2	1-1	0-0	1-3	1-3	3-0	—	1-1	0-1	0-4	3-0	3-2	2-2	2-1	2-1	0-4
Peterborough U	2-1	2-0	0-3	1-0	0-2	0-1	4-3	1-1	0-0	1-0	1-2	1-0	3-2	3-0	2-2	—	3-1	0-1	2-1	1-2	2-2	2-1	0-0	1-0
Port Vale	2-1	2-2	0-3	1-2	1-2	0-2	2-3	0-1	3-0	1-0	2-1	3-0	0-0	0-2	0-1	2-1	—	2-2	1-0	2-2	2-1	0-1	1-1	4-1
Preston NE	1-0	1-2	1-1	3-3	4-2	1-0	2-0	5-1	2-2	1-1	2-1	2-2	1-1	1-1	1-0	2-0	2-0	—	1-0	2-0	1-1	3-0	1-0	1-1
Rochdale	0-1	0-2	1-1	1-0	2-1	1-3	4-1	4-0	1-3	2-0	2-1	1-2	2-3	2-2	0-3	2-0	1-0	3-0	—	3-1	1-2	2-4	4-0	2-1
Scunthorpe U	0-1	0-2	1-1	2-0	1-1	2-1	2-1	2-1	0-1	2-1	2-1	1-2	0-1	1-1	0-1	2-0	1-0	3-0	2-1	—	1-1	3-1	2-1	2-1
Sheffield U	0-1	1-1	1-2	2-0	4-1	1-2	1-0	1-2	3-2	1-0	2-1	2-2	0-1	1-1	1-1	1-2	1-0	1-0	1-0	4-0	—	2-0	1-1	2-0
Swindon T	2-0	2-1	1-0	3-1	2-2	1-1	1-2	2-0	0-1	1-0	0-3	2-2	0-3	3-0	2-2	1-0	0-1	3-1	2-3	3-1	5-2	—	3-3	0-1
Walsall	3-1	0-0	1-1	1-0	0-0	0-2	5-0	0-1	3-0	1-0	1-1	1-1	1-1	0-0	2-0	0-0	0-1	0-2	3-2	1-4	1-1	1-4	—	1-2
Yeovil T	1-1	1-0	0-3	2-3	0-1	0-0	2-1	1-1	0-3	0-1	0-1	0-3	0-2	1-1	2-1	1-0	1-2	0-2	0-3	1-1	1-0	1-1	0-1	—

SKY BET LEAGUE 2 2014–15

(P) *Promoted into division at end of 2013–14 season.*   (R) *Relegated into division at end of 2013–14 season.*

				Total				Home					Away					
		P	W	D	L	F	A	W	D	L	F	A	W	D	L	F	A	GD	Pts
1	Burton Alb	46	28	10	8	69	39	16	4	3	34	13	12	6	5	35	26	30	94
2	Shrewsbury T (R)	46	27	8	11	67	31	17	4	2	43	11	10	4	9	24	20	36	89
3	Bury	46	26	7	13	60	40	14	3	6	33	20	12	4	7	27	20	20	85
4	Wycombe W	46	23	15	8	67	45	10	7	6	30	25	13	8	2	37	20	22	84
5	Southend U¶	46	24	12	10	54	38	12	8	3	25	9	12	4	7	29	29	16	84
6	Stevenage (R)	46	20	12	14	62	54	15	3	5	37	23	5	9	9	25	31	8	72
7	Plymouth Arg	46	20	11	15	55	37	13	6	4	34	14	7	5	11	21	23	18	71
8	Luton T (P)	46	19	11	16	54	44	13	4	6	37	19	6	7	10	17	25	10	68
9	Newport Co	46	18	11	17	51	54	9	7	7	30	25	9	4	10	21	29	–3	65
10	Exeter C	46	17	13	16	61	65	8	8	7	30	29	9	5	9	31	36	–4	64
11	Morecambe	46	17	12	17	53	52	8	6	9	26	28	9	6	8	27	24	1	63
12	Northampton T	46	18	7	21	67	62	13	2	8	39	27	5	5	13	28	35	5	61
13	Oxford U	46	15	16	15	50	49	7	9	7	27	24	8	7	8	23	25	1	61
14	Dagenham & R	46	17	8	21	58	59	9	3	11	30	26	8	5	10	28	33	–1	59
15	AFC Wimbledon	46	14	16	16	54	60	10	8	5	34	25	4	8	11	20	35	–6	58
16	Portsmouth	46	14	15	17	52	54	11	6	6	34	23	3	9	11	18	31	–2	57
17	Accrington S	46	15	11	20	58	77	10	6	7	33	32	5	5	13	25	45	–19	56
18	York C	46	11	19	16	46	51	5	10	8	16	21	6	9	8	30	30	–5	52
19	Cambridge U (P)	46	13	12	21	61	66	7	5	11	34	33	6	7	10	27	33	–5	51
20	Carlisle U (R)	46	14	8	24	56	74	9	5	9	35	37	5	3	15	21	37	–18	50
21	Mansfield T	46	13	9	24	38	62	10	5	8	24	24	3	4	16	14	38	–24	48
22	Hartlepool U	46	12	9	25	39	70	8	5	10	22	30	4	4	15	17	40	–31	45
23	Cheltenham T	46	9	14	23	40	67	5	8	10	22	30	4	6	13	18	37	–27	41
24	Tranmere R (R)	46	9	12	25	45	67	5	7	11	26	34	4	5	14	19	33	–22	39

¶*Southend U promoted via play-offs.*

SKY BET LEAGUE 2 LEADING GOALSCORERS 2014–15

	League	FA Cup	Capital One Cup	J Paint Trophy	Play-Offs	Total
Matt Tubbs *(Portsmouth)*	21	2	1	0	0	24
Jamie Cureton *(Dagenham & R)*	19	0	1	0	0	20
Reuben Reid *(Plymouth Arg)*	18	0	2	0	0	20
Marc Richards *(Northampton T)*	18	0	0	0	0	18
James Collins *(Shrewsbury T)*	15	1	1	0	0	17
Jed Wallace *(Portsmouth)*	14	1	0	2	0	17
Barry Corr *(Southend U)*	14	1	0	0	1	16
Danny Hylton *(Oxford U)*	14	0	2	0	0	16
Tom Nichols *(Exeter C)*	15	0	0	0	0	15
Adebayo Akinfenwa *(AFC Wimbledon)*	13	1	0	1	0	15
Paul Hayes *(Wycombe W)*	12	1	0	0	2	15
Mark Cullen *(Luton T)*	13	1	0	0	0	14
Daniel Nardiello *(Bury)*	10	2	0	2	0	14
Lewis Alessandra *(Plymouth Arg)*	11	0	0	2	0	13
Aaron O'Connor *(Newport Co)*	11	1	0	0	0	12
Jack Redshaw *(Morecambe)*	11	0	0	1	0	12
Kevin Ellison *(Morecambe)*	11	0	0	0	0	11
Joe Pigott *(Southend U)*	9	0	0	0	1	10

   (Includes 3 League goals for Newport Co.)

SKY BET LEAGUE 2 – RESULTS 2014-15

Home \ Away	AFC Wimbledon	Accrington S	Burton Alb	Bury	Cambridge U	Carlisle U	Cheltenham T	Dagenham & R	Exeter C	Hartlepool U	Luton T	Mansfield T	Morecambe	Newport Co	Northampton T	Oxford U	Plymouth Arg	Portsmouth	Shrewsbury T	Southend U	Stevenage	Tranmere R	Wycombe W	York C
AFC Wimbledon	—	2-1	3-0	3-2	1-2	1-3	1-1	1-0	4-1	1-2	3-2	0-1	1-0	2-0	2-2	0-0	0-0	1-0	2-2	0-0	2-3	2-2	0-0	2-1
Accrington S	1-0	—	1-0	0-1	2-1	3-1	2-1	1-1	2-3	3-1	2-2	2-1	2-1	0-2	1-5	1-0	1-0	0-2	2-2	1-2	2-2	3-2	1-1	2-2
Burton Alb	0-0	3-1	—	1-0	1-3	1-1	1-0	2-1	1-0	4-0	1-0	2-1	0-2	0-2	3-1	2-0	1-1	2-0	1-0	2-1	1-1	2-0	1-0	2-0
Bury	2-0	0-2	0-1	—	2-0	2-1	1-2	0-2	0-2	1-0	1-0	2-0	1-2	1-2	2-1	0-1	2-0	3-0	1-0	2-0	2-1	2-0	1-1	2-2
Cambridge U	4-4	2-2	2-3	0-2	—	5-0	1-2	1-1	1-2	2-1	0-1	3-1	1-2	4-0	2-1	5-1	2-0	2-2	0-0	0-1	1-1	1-2	0-1	0-3
Carlisle U	0-0	2-2	3-4	0-3	5-0	—	1-0	1-0	1-3	3-3	0-1	2-1	1-2	2-3	3-2	2-1	0-3	1-1	1-1	1-1	3-0	1-0	2-3	0-3
Cheltenham T	1-1	2-1	1-3	1-0	1-0	0-0	—	1-0	1-3	1-0	0-1	1-1	1-1	1-1	0-2	2-1	0-1	0-1	1-1	1-1	0-2	2-0	1-4	0-1
Dagenham & R	4-0	4-0	1-3	1-0	2-3	4-2	3-1	—	1-2	2-0	0-0	2-0	0-3	0-1	3-2	0-0	0-3	2-2	3-0	2-0	0-0	0-1	0-1	2-0
Exeter C	1-1	2-2	3-1	1-3	1-3	0-0	1-0	1-0	—	5-1	0-1	3-1	2-1	3-2	0-1	2-1	2-3	3-1	3-1	5-1	0-0	1-2	2-1	1-1
Hartlepool U	1-1	4-0	1-3	2-1	2-1	3-3	2-0	1-0	1-2	—	3-0	1-0	1-1	2-1	1-1	1-3	0-0	1-0	1-1	3-1	1-3	0-0	1-3	1-3
Luton T	3-2	2-2	2-1	1-1	0-1	1-0	1-0	3-1	1-0	1-2	—	3-0	0-2	2-0	1-0	1-1	2-0	0-0	2-0	2-0	2-0	1-0	2-3	2-2
Mansfield T	0-1	2-1	2-1	2-1	3-1	2-1	1-0	3-1	0-1	1-2	1-2	—	1-0	2-3	1-0	2-1	1-0	1-2	3-0	3-0	1-0	1-0	0-2	1-4
Morecambe	1-0	2-1	0-1	1-2	1-1	1-0	2-0	1-1	1-0	1-1	1-0	1-1	—	1-0	2-0	1-1	0-1	1-0	2-2	2-0	1-0	0-0	1-3	1-1
Newport Co	2-0	0-2	1-3	2-3	4-0	1-0	2-0	3-0	3-0	2-1	1-0	1-0	0-1	—	2-0	0-1	2-0	1-1	0-1	2-0	0-0	1-1	0-2	3-1
Northampton T	2-2	1-5	3-1	2-1	2-1	2-1	0-2	3-2	0-1	1-1	2-1	3-2	2-1	3-0	—	1-3	2-3	0-1	2-1	1-1	1-1	1-0	1-2	3-0
Oxford U	0-0	0-1	1-3	1-0	1-1	2-1	2-0	0-1	2-1	4-1	2-1	0-1	1-0	3-2	2-1	—	0-0	0-1	0-0	2-3	3-2	2-0	2-3	0-0
Plymouth Arg	1-0	1-0	1-1	2-0	1-0	4-0	2-0	1-0	2-0	1-0	2-0	1-0	1-0	2-0	2-0	1-3	—	0-1	2-1	1-2	3-2	2-0	1-2	1-1
Portsmouth	0-2	1-0	1-0	0-0	2-0	3-0	1-0	1-0	1-0	1-0	2-0	2-0	1-0	0-0	2-0	2-1	3-0	—	0-2	1-0	2-0	3-2	0-1	1-1
Shrewsbury T	2-0	4-0	5-0	3-0	3-1	3-0	3-1	2-0	4-0	2-0	2-0	1-1	3-0	0-1	1-2	0-0	0-2	2-1	—	1-1	3-2	3-2	1-1	1-1
Southend U	0-1	1-2	1-1	1-0	2-0	3-1	2-0	0-0	1-0	1-0	1-0	2-0	2-0	2-0	2-0	2-0	0-2	3-0	1-1	—	2-0	1-0	2-2	1-0
Stevenage	1-1	3-1	0-1	0-2	1-1	1-2	2-0	3-3	1-0	0-2	1-1	3-0	2-1	1-0	0-0	2-3	0-0	2-0	3-2	4-2	—	2-2	1-3	2-3
Tranmere R	2-2	3-2	2-0	2-0	1-2	1-0	2-0	0-1	1-2	0-0	1-0	1-0	0-0	1-1	1-0	2-0	0-0	3-2	3-2	1-0	2-2	—	1-2	1-1
Wycombe W	2-0	2-2	1-3	1-0	1-3	1-3	0-1	0-1	2-0	0-1	1-1	0-1	2-1	1-2	0-1	2-3	0-1	2-2	3-2	4-1	1-2	0-2	—	1-0
York C	2-3	1-0	2-0	2-0	2-2	0-3	1-0	0-2	0-0	1-0	0-0	1-1	1-0	0-2	1-1	0-1	0-0	0-0	0-1	2-3	2-3	2-0	0-0	—

FOOTBALL LEAGUE PLAY-OFFS 2014–15

■ *Denotes player sent off.*

SKY BET CHAMPIONSHIP SEMI-FINALS FIRST LEG
Friday, 8 May 2015
Brentford (0) 1 *(Gray 54)*
Middlesbrough (1) 2 *(Vossen 26, Amorebieta 90)*   11,691
Brentford: (4231) Button; Odubajo, Dean, Tarkowski, Bidwell; Diagouraga, Douglas, Jota (Dallas 77), Judge (Smith 88), Pritchard; Gray.
Middlesbrough: (4231) Konstantopoulos; Whitehead, Ayala, Gibson, Friend; Clayton, Leadbitter; Adomah, Vossen (Forshaw 83), Tomlin (Amorebieta 73); Bamford (Garcia 90).

Saturday, 9 May 2015
Ipswich T (1) 1 *(Anderson 45)*
Norwich C (1) 1 *(Howson 41)*   29,166
Ipswich T: (4231) Bialkowski; Chambers, Smith, Berra, Mings; Bru (Tabb 71), Skuse; Varney (Anderson 31), Bishop (Parr 77), Sears; Murphy.
Norwich C: (4231) Ruddy; Whittaker, Martin, Bassong, Olsson; Tettey, Dorrans (Hoolahan 69); Redmond, Howson, Johnson; Jerome (Hooper 86).

SKY BET CHAMPIONSHIP SEMI-FINALS SECOND LEG
Friday, 15 May 2015
Middlesbrough (1) 3 *(Tomlin 23, Garcia 55, Adomah 78)*
Brentford (0) 0   33,266
Middlesbrough: (442) Konstantopoulos; Whitehead, Ayala, Gibson, Friend; Adomah, Leadbitter (Woodgate 90), Clayton, Tomlin (Forshaw 82); Vossen, Garcia (Reach 68).
Brentford: (4231) Button; Odubajo, Dean, Tarkowski, Bidwell; Diagouraga (Long 71), Douglas; Jota (Toral 60), Pritchard, Judge; Gray.
Middlesbrough won 5-1 on aggregate.

Saturday, 16 May 2015
Norwich C (0) 3 *(Hoolahan 50 (pen), Redmond 64, Jerome 76)*
Ipswich T (0) 1 *(Smith 60)*   26,994
Norwich C: (4411) Ruddy; Whittaker, Martin, Bassong, Olsson; Redmond, Howson, Tettey, Johnson (Bennett E 87); Hoolahan (Dorrans 74); Jerome (Hooper 83).
Ipswich T: (4231) Bialkowski; Chambers, Smith, Berra■, Mings; Bru (Tabb 71), Skuse; Anderson (Hunt N 83), Bishop (McGoldrick 71), Sears; Murphy.
Norwich C won 4-2 on aggregate.

SKY BET CHAMPIONSHIP FINAL (at Wembley)
Monday, 25 May 2015
Middlesbrough (0) 0
Norwich C (2) 2 *(Jerome 12, Redmond 15)*   85,656
Middlesbrough: (4231) Konstantopoulos; Whitehead (Nsue 46), Ayala, Gibson, Friend; Clayton, Leadbitter; Adomah, Vossen (Garcia 68), Tomlin; Bamford.
Norwich C: (4411) Ruddy; Whittaker, Martin, Bassong, Olsson; Redmond (O'Neil 87), Howson, Tettey, Johnson; Hoolahan (Dorrans 75); Jerome (Grabban 74).

SKY BET LEAGUE ONE SEMI-FINALS FIRST LEG
Thursday, 7 May 2015
Chesterfield (0) 0
Preston NE (1) 1 *(Beckford 6)*   8409
Chesterfield: (4231) Lee; Darikwa, Evatt, Hird, Jones; Morsy, Ryan; O'Shea (Gnanduillet 88), Roberts, Gardner (Banks 77); Clucas.
Preston NE: (3142) Johnstone; Clarke, Huntington, Wright; Welsh; Humphrey, Johnson, Gallagher (Kilkenny 79), Laird (Woods 79); Garner, Beckford (Robinson 87).

Sheffield U (1) 1 *(Freeman 19)*
Swindon T (0) 2 *(Ricketts 51, Byrne 90)*   20,890
Sheffield U: (4411) Howard; Freeman, Brayford (Scougall 46 (Doyle 88)), McEveley, Harris; Flynn, Basham, Coutts, Murphy; Holt (Done 74); Davies S.
Swindon T: (352) Foderingham; Thompson N, Stephens, Turnbull; Byrne, Luongo, Kasim, Gladwin (Swift 68), Ricketts; Hylton (Williams 76), Smith M (Obika 90).

SKY BET LEAGUE ONE SEMI-FINALS SECOND LEG
Sunday, 10 May 2015
Preston NE (1) 3 *(Beckford 38, 87, Garner 62 (pen))*
Chesterfield (0) 0   15,641
Preston NE: (433) Johnstone; Clarke, Wright, Huntington, Woods (Humphrey 76); Kilkenny, Welsh, Johnson (Laird 71); Beckford, Garner, Gallagher (Browne 53).
Chesterfield: (4231) Murphy; Darikwa, Hird, Evatt, Jones (Ariyibi 67); Ryan, Morsy; O'Shea, Roberts (Gardner 82), Clucas; Banks (Gnanduillet 64).
Preston NE won 4-0 on aggregate.

Norwich City's Cameron Jerome scores his side's opening goal in their 2-0 victory over Middlesbrough at Wembley on 25 May. (David Klein/LANDOV/Press Association Images)

Man of the Match Jermaine Beckford curls in Preston North End's third goal as they cruise past Swindon Town 4-0 at Wembley on 24 May to clinch their place in the Championship.
(Andrew Matthews/PA Wire/Press Association Images)

Monday, 11 May 2015

Swindon T (3) 5 *(Gladwin 4, 10, Smith M 18, 59 (pen), Obika 84)*

Sheffield U (2) 5 *(Thompson N 19 (og), Basham 38, Davies S 65, Done 88, Adams 90)*   13,065

Swindon T: (352) Foderingham; Thompson N (Obika 57), Stephens, Turnbull; Byrne, Luongo, Kasim, Gladwin (Branco 90), Ricketts; Hylton (Rodgers 62), Smith M.
Sheffield U: (442) Howard; Freeman, Alcock, McEveley, Harris; Flynn (Adams 85), Coutts, Basham, Murphy; Done, McNulty (Davies S 60).
Swindon T won 7-6 on aggregate.

SKY BET LEAGUE ONE FINAL (at Wembley)
Sunday, 24 May 2015

Preston NE (3) 4 *(Beckford 3, 44, 57, Huntington 13)*

Swindon T (0) 0   48,236

Preston NE: (433) Johnstone; Clarke, Wright, Huntington, Welsh; Kilkenny, Welsh, Johnson (Laird 82); Beckford (Davies K 68), Garner, Gallagher (Browne 37).
Swindon T: (352) Foderingham; Stephens, Thompson N (Ricketts 5), Turnbull; Byrne, Luongo, Kasim, Gladwin (Thompson L 58), Toffolo (Williams 66); Obika, Smith M.

SKY BET LEAGUE TWO SEMI-FINALS FIRST LEG
Saturday, 9 May 2015

Plymouth Arg (0) 2 *(Ansah 86, Banton 89)*

Wycombe W (2) 3 *(Hayes 10, Amadi-Holloway 22, Craig 52)*   14,175

Plymouth Arg: (352) McCormick; Nelson, McHugh (Ansah 53), Hartley; Mellor, Jones (Banton 53), Reid B, O'Connor, Holmes-Dennis; Reid R (Brunt 65), Alessandra.
Wycombe W: (4231) Lynch; Bean, Mawson, Pierre, Jacobson; Yennaris, Wood; Amadi-Holloway (Murphy 77), Saunders, Craig (Onyedinma 71); Hayes (Bloomfield 46).

Sunday, 10 May 2015

Stevenage (0) 1 *(Parrett 51)*

Southend U (0) 1 *(Corr 60)*   5183

Stevenage: (4231) Day; Whelpdale, Wells, Dembele (Ashton 46), Okimo; Bond, Parrett; Pett (Conlon 78), Lee, Deacon (Kennedy 46); Beardsley.

Southend U: (433) Bentley; White, Bolger, Barrett, Coker; Leonard, Timlin (Deegan 35), Atkinson; McLaughlin (Weston 78), Corr (Pigott 82), Worrall.

SKY BET LEAGUE TWO SEMI-FINALS SECOND LEG
Thursday, 14 May 2015

Southend U (0) 3 *(Leonard 67, McLaughlin 108, Timlin 120)*

Stevenage (0) 1 *(Pett 55)*   8998

Southend U: (442) Bentley; White, Bolger, Barrett, Coker; Yennaris, Wood; Hayes (McClure 85), Worrall (Deegan 113); Corr, Pigott (Weston 106).
Stevenage: (442) Day; Bond, Wells, Lee (Deacon 82), Okimo; Whelpdale (Pett 41), Walton, Parrett, Martin (Henry 69); Kennedy, Beardsley.
aet; Southend U won 4-2 on aggregate.

Wycombe W (2) 2 *(Hayes 8, Mawson 35)*

Plymouth Arg (0) 1 *(Brunt 71)*   7750

Wycombe W: (4231) Lynch; Bean, Mawson, Pierre, Jacobson; Yennaris, Wood; Hayes (McClure 85), Saunders, Ephraim (Onyedinma 86); Amadi-Holloway.
Plymouth Arg: (352) McCormick; Nelson, McHugh (Ansah 46), Hartley; Mellor, Reid B, O'Connor, Blizzard (Banton 46), Holmes-Dennis; Alessandra, Reid R (Brunt 46).
Wycombe W won 5-3 on aggregate.

SKY BET LEAGUE TWO FINAL (at Wembley)
Saturday, 23 May 2015

Southend U (0) 1 *(Pigott 120)*

Wycombe W (0) 1 *(Bentley 95 (og))*   38,252

Southend U: (433) Bentley; White, Bolger, Barrett, Coker; Atkinson (Weston 80), Leonard, Timlin; Worrall (Payne 97), Corr, McLaughlin (Pigott 60).
Wycombe W: (4231) Lynch; Bean, Mawson, Pierre, Jacobson; Yennaris (Murphy 111), Wood; Hayes, Saunders (Bloomfield 4), Ephraim (Craig 85); Amadi-Holloway.
aet; Southend U won 7-6 on penalties.
Referee: Simon Hooper.

REVIEW OF THE SEASON 2014–15

Chelsea led the top flight from the opening round of fixtures to the last to win their first Premier League crown in five years.

The Blues combined wonderful fluid football in the first-half of the season – as new signing Diego Costa racked up an incredible nine goals in six games – with gritty resolve after lifting the Capital One Cup at the start of March.

For boss Jose Mourinho, it was his third league title with the club; the latest was founded on John Terry's stubborn defensive work and the creative flair of summer arrival Cesc Fabregas and PFA Player of the Year Eden Hazard. Chelsea were a formidable proposition at both ends of the pitch.

Dethroned Manchester City looked set to take the title race to the wire when they pulled level with Chelsea with an identical record on New Year's Day but, with Yaya Toure away winning the Africa Cup of Nations with Ivory Coast, Manuel Pellegrini's side went four league games without a win before taking just three points from a possible 18 from the start of March.

Third place and a second FA Cup in two seasons went to Arsene Wenger's Arsenal who, despite gathering more points than any other team in 2015, paid the price for a slow start to the season which saw them win just two of their first eight.

Alexis Sanchez – 25 goals in all competitions – did at least give Arsenal fans plenty to cheer through the campaign and the Chilean rounded off a fine debut

Manager Jose Mourinho and captain John Terry lift the Capital One Cup. (Matt Childs/Action Images via Reuters)

year in England with a stunning strike against Aston Villa to help retain the FA Cup.

Meanwhile, at Old Trafford, British transfer fee record-breaker Angel di Maria soon went off the boil after an exciting start and on-loan Monaco ace Radamel Falcao never fired, but Louis van Gaal, nonetheless, returned Manchester United to the top four and the Champions League.

A remarkable breakthrough season from 31-goal man Harry Kane – who also netted on his international debut as Roy Hodgson's men continued their breeze through Euro 2016 qualifying – helped Mauricio Pochettino's Tottenham Hotspur to a fifth-place finish and the Capital One Cup Final.

However, for Liverpool the loss of Luis Suarez and absence of injury-hit Daniel Sturridge proved too much for Brendan Rodgers' men.

Liverpool's return to the Champions League was over quickly – and featured controversial team selections – while tributes for departing skipper Steven Gerrard – set for a new chapter in the MLS with LA Galaxy – were tinged with disappointment as the Reds were unable to match their title-challenging feats of 2013–14. A protracted Raheem Sterling contract saga did little to lift the mood at Anfield.

However, there were smiles on the south coast, where Southampton shrugged off pre-season predictions of relegation to finish seventh, while Swansea and Stoke enjoyed a campaign of progress under Garry Monk and Mark Hughes, respectively.

Despite this strike from Eden Hazard, Tottenham Hotspur beat Chelsea 5-3 at White Hart Lane on New Year's Day.
(Adam Davy/PA Wire/Press Association Images)

Alan Pardew had ended Chelsea's unbeaten start to the season while in charge of Newcastle United but seemed happy to bring his four-year stay at St James' Park to a close and return to Crystal Palace, where the former Eagles player lifted the south London club from the relegation zone to their best-ever Premier League finish of 10th.

Everton struggled with their Europa League commitments and failed to reproduce the form which had seen them finish fifth the previous season, while Sam Allardyce was unable to please the West Ham United faithful, despite raising the club to the giddy heights of third in December, before slipping to a 12th-place finish, one ahead of the Tony Pulis-rescued West Bromwich Albion.

With Chelsea cantering to the crown, attention in the final weeks of the season was focused on the dramatic battle to avoid the drop, with the at times controversial Nigel Pearson inspiring his Leicester team to an incredible run of seven wins in their last nine to become just the third team to be bottom at Christmas but stay up.

Pardew-less Newcastle slumped to a club-record eight-game losing streak from the start of March and only a final-day win over West Ham spared John Carver the embarrassment of taking the team from 10th to the Championship.

Harry Kane, the PFA's Young Player of the Year, scores past Leicester City keeper Kasper Schmeichel in Spurs' thrilling 4-3 victory at White Hart Lane in March. (Matt Childs/Action Images via Reuters)

There was a narrow escape for North East rivals Sunderland, too. The Black Cats celebrated a record fifth successive Tyne-Wear derby win – thanks to a wonder-goal from Jermain Defoe – but needed a tearful Dick Advocaat to lead them on a five-game unbeaten run to secure survival. Previous incumbent, Gus Poyet had earlier in the season presided over a humiliating 8-0 thrashing by Southampton.

Fellow mid-season appointment, Tim Sherwood, just did enough to maintain Aston Villa's top-flight status after the club's woeful goal-scoring record under Paul Lambert left them facing relegation – but an FA Cup Final hammering by Arsenal suggests the former Tottenham coach has plenty to do this summer.

That left Hull – who won just twice before Christmas and twice in their final 12 – Sean Dyche's hard-working Burnley – the league's lowest scorers – and Queens Park Rangers – who had to wait until February for their first away win of the season – relegated.

Taking their place in the top flight will be Eddie Howe's Bournemouth, whose fairytale season culminated in them winning a thrilling Championship title race, runners-up Watford, who missed out on the crown after a last-minute, final-day equaliser from Sheffield Wednesday, and Norwich, who saw off East Anglia neighbours Ipswich in the play-offs before clinching an immediate Premier League return with a Wembley win over Middlesbrough.

Millwall, Wigan and Blackpool seemed destined for the drop for much of the season and will play in League One in 2015–16, while comfortable third-tier champions Bristol City, runners-up Milton Keynes Dons – who notched an impressive 101 goals and shocked Manchester United 4-0 in the Capital One Cup second round – and play-off winners Preston North End make the step up.

Elsewhere in League One, Capital One Cup semi-finalists Sheffield United suffered an eighth play-off failure, while fellow cup heroes Bradford City – who stunned Chelsea 4-2 at Stamford Bridge in the FA Cup before knocking out Sunderland – missed out on the post-season drama altogether.

At the bottom of the division, Colchester United and Crewe Alexandra escaped relegation to League Two by just two points, with Notts County, Crawley Town, last season's play-off final losers Leyton Orient – who were only playing in this division after a penalty shootout failure – and Yeovil Town falling through the trap door.

Jimmy Floyd Hasselbaink's Burton Albion won the fourth tier, ahead of Shrewsbury Town and Bury, while Southend United also earned promotion in dramatic fashion through the play-offs. Wycombe Wanderers, who just avoided relegation to non-league the previous season, were on course to go up but conceded a 122nd-minute extra-time equaliser and lost out on penalties.

Meanwhile, Cheltenham Town and Tranmere Rovers saw their Football League statuses taken by Conference winners Barnet and play-off champs Bristol Rovers, after Ronnie Moore somehow inspired bottom-at-Christmas Hartlepool United to escape the drop.

Peter Smith

CUPS AND UPS AND DOWNS DIARY

JULY 2014
13   FIFA World Cup Final: Germany 1 Argentina 0 *(aet).*

JANUARY 2015
25   Welsh Premier League Word Cup Final: The New Saints 3 Bala T 0.

MARCH 2015
1   Capital One Cup Final: Chelsea 2 Tottenham H 0.
10   The New Saints champions of Welsh Premier League.
15   Scottish League Cup Presented by QTS Final: Celtic 2 Dundee U 0.
22   Hearts champions of Scottish Championship and promoted to Scottish Premiership.
      Johnstone's Paint Trophy Final: Bristol C 2 Walsall 0.
29   FA Trophy Final: North Ferriby 3 Wrexham 3.
      (aet; North Ferriby won 5-4 on penalties)

APRIL 2015
4   AFC Telford U relegated from Vanarama Conference Premier.
      Montrose finish bottom of Scottish League 2 and will face a play-off against Brora Rangers to maintain their league status.
5   Scottish Petrofac Training Cup Final: Livingston 4 Alloa Ath 0.
6   Blackpool relegated from Football League Championship.
11   Yeovil T relegated from Football League 1 to Football League 2.
      Stirling Alb relegated from Scottish League 1 to Scottish League 2.
14   Dartford and Nuneaton T relegated from Vanarama Conference Premier.
18   Bristol C champions of Football League 1 and promoted to Football League Championship.
      Albion R champions of Scottish League 2 and promoted to Scottish League 1.
      Burton Alb promoted from Football League 2 to Football League 1.
25   Watford promoted from Football League Championship to Premier League.
      Shrewsbury T promoted from Football League 2 to Football League 1.
      Tranmere R and Cheltenham T relegated from Football League 2 to Vanarama Conference Premier.
      Barnet champions of Vanarama Conference Premier and promoted to Football League 2.
      Alfreton T relegated from Vanarama Conference Premier.
      Bristol R, Grimsby T, Eastleigh and Forest Green R confirmed as Vanarama Conference Premier Play-Off contenders.
27   Bournemouth secure promotion from Football League Championship to Premier League (barring a 19-goal turnaround in goal difference in last game).
28   Millwall and Wigan Ath relegated from Football League Championship to Football League 1.

MAY 2015
2   Celtic champions of Scottish Premiership.
      Bournemouth champions of Football League Championship.
      Burton Alb champions of Football League 2.
      Bury promoted from Football League 2 to Football League 1.
      Morton champions of Scottish League 1 and promoted to Scottish Championship.
      Cowdenbeath relegated from Scottish League 1 to Scottish League 2.
      Welsh FA Cup Final: The New Saints 2 Newtown 0.
3   Chelsea champions of Premier League.
      Milton Keynes D runners-up of Football League 1 and promoted to Football League Championship.
      Leyton O, Crawley T and Notts Co all relegated from Football League 1 to Football League 2.
8   St Mirren relegated from Scottish Premiership to Scottish Championship.
9   Burnley relegated from Premier League to Football League Championship.
      FA Vase Final: North Shields 2 Glossop North End 1 *(aet).*
      Scottish Championship Play-Off Final 1st leg: Forfar Ath 3 Alloa Ath 1.
      Scottish League 2 Relegation Play-Off Final 1st leg: Brora Rangers 1 Montrose 0.
13   Scottish League 1 Play-Off Final 1st leg: Queen's Park 0 Stenhousemuir 1.
10   QPR relegated from Premier League to Football League Championship.
16   Scottish League 2 Relegation Play-Off Final 2nd leg: Montrose 3 Brora Rangers 1.
      (Montrose won 3-2 on aggregate and remain in Scottish League 2)
      Scottish League 1 Play-Off Final 2nd leg: Stenhousemuir 1 Queen's Park 1.
      (Stenhousemuir won 2-1 on aggregate and remain in Scottish League 1)
17   Scottish Championship Play-Off Final 2nd leg: Alloa Ath 3 Forfar Ath 0.
      (Alloa Ath won 4-3 on aggregate and remain in Scottish Championship)
23   Football League 2 Play-Off Final: Southend U 1 Wycombe W 1.
      (aet; Southend U won 7-6 on penalties and promoted to Football League 1)
24   Hull C relegated from Premier League to Football League Championship.
      Football League 1 Play-Off Final: Preston NE 4 Swindon 0.
      (Preston NE promoted to Football League Championship)
25   Football League Championship Play-Off Final: Norwich C 2 Middlesbrough 0.
      (Norwich C promoted to Premier League)
27   Europa League Final: Sevilla 3 Dnipro Dnipropetrovsk 2.
28   Scottish Premier League Play-Off Final 1st leg: Rangers 1 Motherwell 3.
30   FA Cup Final: Arsenal 4 Aston Villa 0.
      Scottish FA Cup Final: Inverness CT 2 Falkirk 1.
31   Scottish Premier League Play-Off Final 2nd leg: Motherwell 3 Rangers 0.
      (Motherwell won 6-1 on aggregate and remain in Scottish Premiership)

JUNE 2015
6   Champions League Final: Barcelona 3 Juventus 1.

THE FA COMMUNITY SHIELD WINNERS 1908–2014

CHARITY SHIELD 1908–2001

1908	Manchester U v QPR	1-1
Replay	Manchester U v QPR	4-0
1909	Newcastle U v Northampton T	2-0
1910	Brighton v Aston Villa	1-0
1911	Manchester U v Swindon T	8-4
1912	Blackburn R v QPR	2-1
1913	Professionals v Amateurs	7-2
1920	WBA v Tottenham H	2-0
1921	Tottenham H v Burnley	2-0
1922	Huddersfield T v Liverpool	1-0
1923	Professionals v Amateurs	2-0
1924	Professionals v Amateurs	3-1
1925	Amateurs v Professionals	6-1
1926	Amateurs v Professionals	6-3
1927	Cardiff C v Corinthians	2-1
1928	Everton v Blackburn R	2-1
1929	Professionals v Amateurs	3-0
1930	Arsenal v Sheffield W	2-1
1931	Arsenal v WBA	1-0
1932	Everton v Newcastle U	5-3
1933	Arsenal v Everton	3-0
1934	Arsenal v Manchester C	4-0
1935	Sheffield W v Arsenal	1-0
1936	Sunderland v Arsenal	2-1
1937	Manchester C v Sunderland	2-0
1938	Arsenal v Preston NE	2-1
1948	Arsenal v Manchester U	4-3
1949	Portsmouth v Wolverhampton W	1-1*
1950	English World Cup XI v FA Canadian Touring Team	4-2
1951	Tottenham H v Newcastle U	2-1
1952	Manchester U v Newcastle U	4-2
1953	Arsenal v Blackpool	3-1
1954	Wolverhampton W v WBA	4-4*
1955	Chelsea v Newcastle U	3-0
1956	Manchester U v Manchester C	1-0
1957	Manchester U v Aston Villa	4-0
1958	Bolton W v Wolverhampton W	4-1
1959	Wolverhampton W v Nottingham F	3-1
1960	Burnley v Wolverhampton W	2-2*
1961	Tottenham H v FA XI	3-2
1962	Tottenham H v Ipswich T	5-1
1963	Everton v Manchester U	4-0
1964	Liverpool v West Ham U	2-2*
1965	Manchester U v Liverpool	2-2*
1966	Liverpool v Everton	1-0
1967	Manchester U v Tottenham H	3-3*
1968	Manchester C v WBA	6-1
1969	Leeds U v Manchester C	2-1
1970	Everton v Chelsea	2-1
1971	Leicester C v Liverpool	1-0

1972	Manchester C v Aston Villa	1-0
1973	Burnley v Manchester C	1-0
1974	Liverpool v Leeds U	1-1
	Liverpool won 6-5 on penalties.	
1975	Derby Co v West Ham U	2-0
1976	Liverpool v Southampton	1-0
1977	Liverpool v Manchester U	0-0*
1978	Nottingham F v Ipswich T	5-0
1979	Liverpool v Arsenal	3-1
1980	Liverpool v West Ham U	1-0
1981	Aston Villa v Tottenham H	2-2*
1982	Liverpool v Tottenham H	1-0
1983	Manchester U v Liverpool	2-0
1984	Everton v Liverpool	1-0
1985	Everton v Manchester U	2-0
1986	Everton v Liverpool	1-1*
1987	Everton v Coventry C	1-0
1988	Liverpool v Wimbledon	2-1
1989	Liverpool v Arsenal	1-0
1990	Liverpool v Manchester U	1-1*
1991	Arsenal v Tottenham H	0-0*
1992	Leeds U v Liverpool	4-3
1993	Manchester U v Arsenal	1-1
	Manchester U won 5-4 on penalties.	
1994	Manchester U v Blackburn R	2-0
1995	Everton v Blackburn R	1-0
1996	Manchester U v Newcastle U	4-0
1997	Manchester U v Chelsea	1-1
	Manchester U won 4-2 on penalties.	
1998	Arsenal v Manchester U	3-0
1999	Arsenal v Manchester U	2-1
2000	Chelsea v Manchester U	2-0
2001	Liverpool v Manchester U	2-1

COMMUNITY SHIELD 2002–14

2002	Arsenal v Liverpool	1-0
2003	Manchester U v Arsenal	1-1
	Manchester U won 4-3 on penalties.	
2004	Arsenal v Manchester U	3-1
2005	Chelsea v Arsenal	2-1
2006	Liverpool v Chelsea	2-1
2007	Manchester U v Chelsea	1-1
	Manchester U won 3-0 on penalties.	
2008	Manchester U v Portsmouth	0-0
	Manchester U won 3-1 on penalties.	
2009	Chelsea v Manchester U	2-2
	Chelsea won 4-1 on penalties.	
2010	Manchester U v Chelsea	3-1
2011	Manchester U v Manchester C	3-2
2012	Manchester C v Chelsea	3-2
2013	Manchester U v Wigan Ath	2-0
2014	Arsenal v Manchester C	3-0

* *Each club retained shield for six months.*

THE FA COMMUNITY SHIELD 2014

Arsenal (2) 3, Manchester C (0) 0

at Wembley, Sunday 10 August 2014, attendance 71,523

Arsenal: (4-1-4-1) Szczesny; Debuchy, Koscielny (Monreal 45), Chambers, Gibbs; Arteta; Sanchez (Oxlade-Chamberlain 45), Wilshere (Flamini 68), Ramsey (Campbell 86), Cazorla (Rosicky 70); Sanogo (Giroud 45).
Scorers: Cazorla 21, Ramsey 42, Giroud 61.

Manchester C: (4-2-3-1) Caballero; Clichy, Boyata, Nastasic, Kolarov (Richards 76); Fernando, Toure (Zuculini 60); Navas (Sinclair 85), Jovetic, Nasri (Silva 45); Dzeko (Milner 60).

Referee: Michael Oliver.

ACCRINGTON STANLEY

FOUNDATION

Accrington Football Club, founder members of the Football League in 1888, were not connected with Accrington Stanley. In fact both clubs ran concurrently between 1891 when Stanley were formed and 1895 when Accrington FC folded. Actually Stanley Villa was the original name, those responsible for forming the club living in Stanley Street and using the Stanley Arms as their meeting place. They became Accrington Stanley in 1893. In 1894–95 they joined the Accrington & District League, playing at Moorhead Park. Subsequently they played in the North-East Lancashire Combination and the Lancashire Combination before becoming founder members of the Third Division (North) in 1921, two years after moving to Peel Park. In 1962 they resigned from the Football League, were wound up, re-formed in 1963, disbanded in 1966 only to restart as Accrington Stanley (1968), returning to the Lancashire Combination in 1970.

Store First Stadium, Livingstone Road, Accrington, Lancashire BB5 5BX.

Telephone: (0871) 434 1968. *Fax:* (01254) 356 951.

Ticket Office: (0871) 434 1968.

Website: www.accringtonstanley.co.uk

Email: info@accringtonstanley.co.uk

Ground Capacity: 5,070.

Record Attendance: 13,181 v Hull C, Division 3 (N), 28 September 1948 (at Peel Park); 4,368 v Colchester U, FA Cup 1st rd, 3 January 2004 (at Fraser Eagle Stadium – Crown Inn).

Pitch Measurements: 101.5m × 65m (111yd × 71yd)

Chairman: Peter Marsden.

Chief Executive: Alan Pickup.

Manager: John Coleman.

Assistant Manager: Jimmy Bell.

Physio: Paul Morgan.

Colours: Red shirts with white trim, red shorts, red socks with white trim.

Year Formed: 1891, reformed 1968.

Turned Professional: 1919.

Club Nickname: 'The Reds', 'Stanley'.

Previous Names: 1891, Stanley Villa; 1893, Accrington Stanley.

Grounds: 1891, Moorhead Park; 1897, Bell's Ground; 1919, Peel Park; 1970, Crown Ground (renamed Interlink Express Stadium, Fraser Eagle Stadium, Store First Stadium 2013).

First Football League Game: 27 August 1921, Division 3 (N), v Rochdale (a) L 3-6 – Tattersall; Newton, Baines, Crawshaw, Popplewell, Burkinshaw, Oxley, Makin, Green (1), Hosker (2), Hartles.

HONOURS

Football League – Division 3 (N): *Runners-up* 1954–55, 1957–58.

Conference: *Champions* 2005–06.

FA Cup: Best season: 4th rd, 1927, 1937, 1959, 2010.

Football League Cup: Best season: never past 2nd rd.

Northern Premier League: *Champions* 2002–03.

Northern League – Division 1: *Champions* 1999–2000.

North-West Counties: *Runners-up* 1986–87.

Cheshire County League – Division 2: *Champions* 1980–81; *Runners-up* 1979–80.

Lancashire Combination: *Champions* 1973–74, 1977–78; *Runners-up* 1971–72, 1975–76.

Lancashire Combination Cup: *Winners* 1971–72, 1972–73, 1973–74, 1976–77.

sky SPORTS FACT FILE

In September 1955 Accrington Stanley hammered Bradford Park Avenue 7-0 at Peel Park to inflict what was then the heaviest Football League defeat ever for the West Yorkshire club. The tally included four goals in a spell of just eight minutes during the first half. The result left Stanley top of the Division Three North table.

Record League Victory: 8–0 v New Brighton, Division 3 (N), 17 March 1934 – Maidment; Armstrong (pen), Price, Dodds, Crawshaw, McCulloch, Wyper, Lennox (2), Cheetham (4), Leedham (1), Watson.

Record Cup Victory: 7–0 v Spennymoor U, FA Cup 2nd rd, 8 December 1938 – Tootill; Armstrong, Whittaker, Latham, Curran, Lee, Parry (2), Chadwick, Jepson (3), McLoughlin (2), Barclay.

Record Defeat: 1–9 v Lincoln C, Division 3 (N), 3 March 1951.

Most League Points (2 for a win): 61, Division 3 (N), 1954–55.

Most League Points (3 for a win): 73, FL 2, 2010–11.

Most League Goals: 96, Division 3 (N), 1954–55.

Highest League Scorer in Season: George Stewart, 35, Division 3 (N), 1955–56; George Hudson, 35, Division 4, 1960–61.

Most League Goals in Total Aggregate: George Stewart, 136, 1954–58.

Most League Goals in One Match: 5, Billy Harker v Gateshead, Division 3 (N), 16 November 1935; George Stewart v Gateshead, Division 3 (N), 27 November 1954.

Most Capped Player: Romuald Boco, 19 (48), Benin.

Most League Appearances: Andy Procter, 264, 2006–12, 2014–15.

Youngest League Player: Ian Gibson, 15 years 358 days, v Norwich C, 23 March 1959.

Record Transfer Fee Received: £50,000 (rising to £250,000) from Blackpool for Brett Ormerod, March 1997.

Record Transfer Fee Paid: £85,000 (rising to £150,000) to Swansea C for Ian Craney, January 2008.

Football League Record: 1921 Original Member of Division 3 (N); 1958–60 Division 3; 1960–62 Division 4; 2006– FL 2.

MANAGERS

William Cronshaw *c.*1894
John Haworth 1897–1910
Johnson Haworth *c.*1916
Sam Pilkingson 1919–24
  (*Tommy Booth p-m 1923–24*)
Ernie Blackburn 1924–32
Amos Wade 1932–35
John Hacking 1935–49
Jimmy Porter 1949–51
Walter Crook 1951–53
Walter Galbraith 1953–58
George Eastham snr 1958–59
Harold Bodle 1959–60
James Harrower 1960–61
Harold Mather 1962–63
Jimmy Hinksman 1963–64
Terry Neville 1964–65
Ian Bryson 1965
Danny Parker 1965–66
Gerry Keenan
Gary Pierce
Dave Thornley
Phil Staley
Eric Whalley
Stan Allen 1995–96
Tony Greenwood 1996–98
Billy Rodaway 1998
Wayne Harrison 1998–99
John Coleman 1999–2012
Paul Cook 2012
Leam Richardson 2012–13
James Beattie 2013–15
John Coleman September 2014–

LATEST SEQUENCES

Longest Sequence of League Wins: 7, 27.12.1954 – 5.2.1955.

Longest Sequence of League Defeats: 9, 8.3.1930 – 21.4.1930.

Longest Sequence of League Draws: 4, 10.9.1927 – 27.9.1927.

Longest Sequence of Unbeaten League Matches: 14, 15.3.2011 – 6.8.2011.

Longest Sequence Without a League Win: 18, 17.9.1938 – 31.12.1938.

Successive Scoring Runs: 22 from 14.11.1936.

Successive Non-scoring Runs: 5 from 15.3.1930.

TEN YEAR LEAGUE RECORD

		P	W	D	L	F	A	Pts	Pos
2005-06	Conf	42	28	7	7	76	45	91	1
2006-07	FL 2	46	13	11	22	70	81	50	20
2007-08	FL 2	46	16	3	27	49	83	51	17
2008-09	FL 2	46	13	11	22	42	59	50	16
2009-10	FL 2	46	18	7	21	62	74	61	15
2010-11	FL 2	46	18	19	9	73	55	73	5
2011-12	FL 2	46	14	15	17	54	66	57	14
2012-13	FL 2	46	14	12	20	51	68	54	18
2013-14	FL 2	46	14	15	17	54	56	57	15
2014-15	FL 2	46	15	11	20	58	77	56	17

DID YOU KNOW

Accrington Stanley reached the fourth round of the FA Cup in 1926–27 for the first time in their history as a result of victories over Rochdale, Chilton Colliery and Exeter City. They then faced Chelsea at Stamford Bridge in what proved a humbling experience as they were well beaten 7-2.

ACCRINGTON STANLEY – FOOTBALL LEAGUE TWO 2014–15 LEAGUE RECORD

Match No.	Date	Venue	Opponents	Result	H/T Score	Lg Pos.	Goalscorers	Attendance
1	Aug 9	H	Southend U	L	0-1	0-0	16		1505
2	16	A	Cheltenham T	L	1-2	0-1	19	Naismith [77]	2340
3	19	A	Shrewsbury T	L	0-4	0-3	24		4298
4	23	H	Luton T	D	2-2	2-2	23	Gray [9], Joyce [16]	1562
5	30	A	Bury	L	1-2	1-1	24	Naismith [19]	3381
6	Sept 6	H	Tranmere R	W	3-2	1-0	21	Gray 2 (1 pen) [8 (p), 78], Naismith [82]	2151
7	13	H	AFC Wimbledon	W	1-0	0-0	21	Gray [83]	1238
8	16	A	Oxford U	L	1-3	1-2	20	Carver [17]	4111
9	20	A	Northampton T	W	5-4	3-1	17	Atkinson [22], O'Sullivan 2 [28, 75], Archer (og) [37], Maguire [84]	4731
10	27	H	Plymouth Arg	W	1-0	1-0	16	Naismith [13]	1511
11	Oct 4	A	Mansfield T	W	1-0	1-0	11	Joyce (pen) [10]	2699
12	11	H	Dagenham & R	L	1-2	1-0	16	Maguire [39]	1412
13	18	A	Stevenage	L	1-2	1-1	18	Molyneux [19]	2398
14	21	H	Hartlepool U	W	3-1	2-1	14	McCartan 2 [19, 78], Atkinson [45]	947
15	25	A	Newport Co	D	1-1	0-0	15	Maguire [62]	3254
16	31	H	Morecambe	W	2-1	2-0	9	Joyce (pen) [5], McCartan [11]	1710
17	Nov 15	A	Carlisle U	L	0-1	0-1	15		4069
18	22	H	Cambridge U	W	2-1	1-0	12	Mingoia 2 [34, 72]	1364
19	28	H	Exeter C	L	2-3	0-1	12	O'Sullivan [65], McCartan [73]	1443
20	Dec 13	A	Portsmouth	W	3-2	2-2	11	Atkinson [11], O'Sullivan [15], Mingoia [78]	14,300
21	20	H	Wycombe W	D	1-1	0-1	11	Maguire [49]	1325
22	26	A	York C	L	0-1	0-1	13		3873
23	Jan 3	A	Exeter C	W	2-1	0-1	13	McCartan [67], Aldred [90]	3626
24	17	A	Tranmere R	L	0-3	0-2	14		4872
25	24	A	AFC Wimbledon	L	1-2	0-1	15	Buxton [88]	3859
26	27	H	Bury	L	0-1	0-0	15		2067
27	31	H	Northampton T	L	1-5	1-2	16	Mingoia [40]	1328
28	Feb 7	A	Plymouth Arg	L	0-1	0-1	19		6005
29	10	H	Oxford U	W	1-0	0-0	15	Gornell [90]	1065
30	14	A	Southend U	W	2-1	0-0	14	Mingoia [53], Gornell [71]	5241
31	20	H	Cheltenham T	D	1-1	0-1	14	McCartan [59]	1216
32	24	H	Burton Alb	W	1-0	1-0	15	Windass [23]	919
33	28	A	Luton T	L	0-2	0-1	15		8700
34	Mar 3	H	Shrewsbury T	L	1-2	1-1	15	Windass (pen) [38]	1137
35	7	H	Portsmouth	D	1-1	1-1	15	Windass [16]	1994
36	14	A	Burton Alb	L	0-3	0-1	15		3293
37	17	A	Wycombe W	D	2-2	1-1	17	Gornell [45], Mingoia [61]	2621
38	21	H	York C	D	2-2	0-0	16	Maguire [69], Windass [90]	1454
39	27	H	Newport Co	L	0-2	0-0	16		1111
40	Apr 3	A	Morecambe	D	1-1	1-1	17	Jones [28]	1982
41	6	H	Carlisle U	W	3-1	0-0	17	Mingoia [25], Windass [62], Conneely [65]	2274
42	11	A	Cambridge U	D	2-2	1-1	17	Mingoia [39], Conneely [90]	5569
43	14	A	Hartlepool U	D	1-1	1-0	17	Windass [38]	4159
44	18	H	Stevenage	D	2-2	2-1	17	Maguire 2 [15, 40]	1351
45	25	A	Dagenham & R	L	0-4	0-1	17		2038
46	May 2	H	Mansfield T	W	2-1	0-1	17	Conneely [47], Gornell [71]	1921

Final League Position: 17

GOALSCORERS

League (58): Mingoia 8, Maguire 7, McCartan 6, Windass 6 (1 pen), Gornell 4, Gray 4 (1 pen), Naismith 4, O'Sullivan 4, Atkinson 3, Conneely 3, Joyce 3 (2 pens), Aldred 1, Buxton 1, Carver 1, Jones 1, Molyneux 1, own goal 1.
FA Cup (3): Aldred 1, Carver 1, Joyce 1.
Capital One Cup (1): Gray 1.
Johnstone's Paint Trophy (1): Carver 1.

Simpson L 6 + 2	Buxton A 15 + 2	Aldred T 25	Winnard D 35 + 2	Liddle M 7 + 8	Mingoia P 34 + 2	Joyce L 45	Hunt N 28 + 1	Naismith K 25 + 10	Windass J 23 + 12	Gray J 10 + 7	Alabi J 1 + 1	McCartan S 11 + 20	Atkinson R 44	Mustoe J 4	Bowerman G 2 + 1	Hatfield W 2 + 5	Lynch J 1 + 1	Carver M 6 + 11	Lumley J 5	Procter A 29	O'Sullivan J 13	Maguire S 29 + 4	Chapman A 3	Molyneux L 7 + 3	Joronen J 4	Barry A 9 + 4	Rose J 4	Crooks M 11 + 5	Macey M 4	Conneely S 12 + 4	Davies S 19	Gornell T 14 + 1	Bruna G 6	Jones L 11	Gilchrist J 1 + 4	Whitehead D 1 + 1	Hazeldine M — + 1	Match No.
1	2	3	4	5	6	7¹	8	9²	10	11	12	13																										1
1	5²	2	3		12		8	7	6	10	11¹				4	9	13																					2
1*		3	4		6	7	2	14	8	11¹			5	10²	9¹	12	13																					3
	2	3			9	7	8¹	6	12	11		4	5	10²		1	13																					4
	2	3			9³	7	8¹	6	12	11		13	4	5		10²		14	1																			5
	5	3			6¹	8	2	9	12	10		4				13		11	1	7²																		6
	5	4			6²	7	2	9	12	11¹		3				13		10	1	8																		7
	5²	4	12		9¹	7	2	6	13	11*		14	3					10³	1	8																		8
	3	5			7	2	10	12		14	4				13			11²	1	6	8³	9¹																9
	3	5	14	6	2	10	9³				4				13			12		7	8²	11¹	1															10
	3	5			6	2	10¹	13			4							9²		8	6	11	1	1	12													11
13		3	5		7	2	11²		12		4									6	8	9	1¹	10														12
	3	8			9	5			11³			12	2					13		7	6	10²		4¹	1	14												13
	2	4			6				11²			9¹	3		14			13		7	5	10¹		8	1	12												14
	3	5			7	2				12		14	4					13		8	6	11		10¹	1	9²												15
12		3	5		9	2			14			11¹	4					13		7	8²	6		10	1³													16
	3	5	13		6	2³	11²		12			10¹	4							7	8	9	14			1												17
	4	2	5	8	7				13			3						12		6	10³	9¹	14			1	11²											18
	4	2	5	8¹	6				13			12	3							7	10	9				1	11²											19
	4	2	5	10	6	12						13	3¹					14			8²	9		7³	1	11												20
1		3	5		6	2	11					10	4							7	8	9¹					12											21
1		4	5		6	8	2		14	13		12	3							7²		11³	9			10¹												22
1		3		5	8	6	2	12				11¹	4							7		9	10²			13												23
	3	5		10¹	6			11¹	12	14		8	4							7²		9				13			1	2								24
14	3	4	5		8		9	13	12			10	2							7³		11				6²			1									25
5³		3	13	8	7		10¹	12				9	4					14		6		11¹							1	2								26
5		2	8	6			10¹	14	13			4						11¹		7³		9				12			1	3								27
	5	12	8³	6	2	13	9					10¹	4									14				7				3²	1	11						28
5³		4	12	10	7	2	13	9¹				14	3							6										1	11	8²						29
		3			8	6	2	12	9				4							7								5		1	11	10¹						30
		5			8	6	2¹	12	9			13	4							7		14						3¹		1	11	10²						31
		4			2	6			10	9²		12	3							7						8		13		5	1	11¹						32
		3²	5		6				9¹	10		13	4							7		14				8³		12		2	1	11						33
		3	4²	6	5				13	7		12	2							9						8¹		10			1	11						34
		4			5	6			9	10			2							7						8*		3			1	11						35
					9	6			5	8³		14	2							7¹		10²						3		12	1	11			4	13		36
		4			6	8			9	7			3									11²						5		13	1	10			2¹		12	37
		3			9	8			5	11		12	4									6						7			1	10²			2¹	13		38
		4			5	6			9	11		12	3									8¹						7²			1	10			2	13		39
13					5	6			9³	8		10¹	4									12						7²		4	14	11*			2			40
	5¹		13	6	8	2	14	7				10¹	4									11						12	1			9²	3	10³				41
	5²		12	6	8	2	14	10¹				13	4									11						7	1			9¹	3					42
	5³	14	13	6	8	2			10²			12	4									11						7	1			9¹	3					43
	9²		5	13	6	8	2*		10				4									11¹						7	1			12	4					44
	2		5		9³	3			7			6²	8									10¹				14			1				4	12	11	13	45
			5		6	7	2		9				3									11						8	1	10				4				46

FA Cup

First Round	Notts Co	(a)	0-0
Replay	Notts Co	(h)	2-1
Second Round	Yeovil T	(h)	1-1
Replay	Yeovil T	(a)	0-2

Capital One Cup

First Round	Leeds U	(a)	1-2

Johnstone's Paint Trophy

First Round	Carlisle U	(h)	1-3

AFC WIMBLEDON

FOUNDATION

While the history of AFC Wimbledon is straightforward since it was a new club formed in 2002, there were in effect two clubs operating for two years with Wimbledon connections. The other club was MK Dons, of course. In August 2001, the Football League had rejected the existing Wimbledon's application to move to Milton Keynes. In May 2002, they rejected local sites and were given permission to move by an independent commission set up by the Football League. AFC Wimbledon was founded in the summer of 2002 and held its first trials on Wimbledon Common. In subsequent years, there was considerable debate over the rightful home of the trophies obtained by the former Wimbledon football club. In October 2006, an agreement was reached between Milton Keynes Dons FC, its Supporters Association, the Wimbledon Independent Supporters Association and the Football Supporters Federation to transfer such trophies and honours to the London Borough of Merton.

The Cherry Red Records Stadium, Kingsmeadow, Jack Goodchild Way, 422a Kingston Road, Kingston-upon-Thames, Surrey KT1 3PB.

Telephone: (0208) 547 3528.

Fax: (0808) 2800 816.

Website: www.afcwimbledon.co.uk

Email: info@afcwimbledon.co.uk

Ground Capacity: 5,027.

Record Attendance: 4,784 v Liverpool, FA Cup 3rd rd, 5 January 2015.

Pitch Measurements: 104m × 66m (113.5yd × 72yd)

President: Dickie Guy.

Chief Executive: Erik Samuelson.

Manager: Neal Ardley.

Assistant Manager: Neil Cox.

First Team Coach: Simon Bassey.

Physio: Stuart Douglas.

Club Nickname: 'The Dons'.

Colours: All blue with yellow trim.

Year Formed: 2002.

Turned Professional: 2002.

HONOURS

Blue Square Conference: *Runners-up* 2010–11; promoted via play-offs.

Blue Square South: *Champions* 2008–09.

FA Cup: Best season: 3rd rd, 2015.

Football League Cup: Best season: never past 1st rd.

Isthmian League – Premier Division: *Play-off Winners* 2007–08. **Division 1:** *Champions* 2004–05.

Combined Counties League: *Champions* 2003–04.

Combined Counties League: *Challenge Cup Winners* 2004.

Surrey Senior Cup: *Winners* 2005; *Runners-up* 2006.

Supporters Direct Cup: *Winners* 2003, 2006, 2010; *Runners-up* 2005, 2007.

Phil Ledger Memorial Cup: *Winners* 2011.

sky SPORTS FACT FILE

Keeper Seb Brown was the hero for AFC Wimbledon when they achieved promotion to the Football League in 2010–11. Brown saved two spot-kicks in the play-off final penalty shoot-out to give the Dons victory over Luton Town after the teams finished goalless at the end of extra time.

Grounds: 2002, Kingsmeadow (renamed The Cherry Red Stadium).

First Football League Game: 6 August 2011, FL 2 v Bristol R (h) L 2–3 – Brown; Hatton, Gwillim (Bush), Porter (Minshull), Stuart (1), Johnson B, Moore L, Wellard, Jolley (Ademeno (1)), Midson, Yussuff.

Record League Victory: 4–0 v Burton Alb, FL 2, 24 March 2012 – Brown; Hatton, Gwillim, Moncur (1), Mitchel-King, Balkestein, Moore S (1), Knott (Wellard), Jolley, Midson, Moore L (1) (Harrison (1)); 4-0 v Portsmouth, FL 2, 16 November 2012 – Worner; Bennett, Fuller, Frampton (2), Kennedy, Sweeney (Moore L), Moore S (1), Porter, Pell, Smith (1), Mohamed (Francomb).

Record Cup Victory: 4–3 v York City, FA Cup 1st rd replay, 12 November 2012 – Brown; Fenlon (Osano), Mambo, Mitchel-King, Cummings, Jolley, Gregory, Johnson (Harrison (1)), Yussuff (Long), Midson (1), Strutton (2).

Record Defeat: 2–6 v Burton Alb, FL 2, 25 August 2012.

Most League Points (3 for a win): 58, FL 2, 2014–15.

Most League Goals: 62, FL 2, 2011–12.

Highest League Scorer in Season: Jack Midson, 18, 2011–12.

Most League Goals in Total Aggregate: Kevin Cooper, 107, 2002–04.

Most Capped Player: Shane Smeltz, 5 (51), New Zealand.

Most League Appearances: Sammy Moore, 139, 2011–15.

Youngest League Player: Ben Harrison, 17 years 195 days v Accrington S, 13 September 2014.

Record Transfer Fee Received: £120,000 from Coventry C for Chris Hussey, January 2010.

Record Transfer Fee Paid: £25,000 (in excess of) to Stevenage for Byron Harrison, January 2012.

Football League Record: 2011 Promoted from Conference Premier; 2011– FL 2.

LATEST SEQUENCES

Longest Sequence of League Wins: 4, 17.9.2011 – 8.10.2011.

Longest Sequence of League Defeats: 6, 26.11.2011 – 2.1.2012.

Longest Sequence of League Draws: 3, 12.1.2013 – 2.2.2013.

Longest Sequence of Unbeaten League Matches: 5, 1.1.2013 – 2.2.2013.

Longest Sequence Without a League Win: 12, 15.10.2011 – 2.1.2012.

Successive Scoring Runs: 8 from 16.2.2013.

Successive Non-scoring Runs: 3 from 24.2.2015.

MANAGERS

Terry Eames 2002–04
Nicky English *(Caretaker)* 2004
Dave Anderson 2004–07
Terry Brown 2007–12
Neal Ardley October 2012–

TEN YEAR LEAGUE RECORD

		P	W	D	L	F	A	Pts	Pos
2005-06	Isth PR	42	22	11	9	67	36	77	4
2006-07	Isth PR	42	21	15	6	76	37	75	5
2007-08	Isth PR	42	22	9	11	81	47	75	3
2008-09	Conf S	42	26	10	6	86	36	88	1
2009-10	Conf P	44	18	10	16	61	47	64	8
2010-11	Conf P	46	27	9	10	83	47	90	2
2011-12	FL 2	46	15	9	22	62	78	54	16
2012-13	FL 2	46	14	11	21	54	76	53	20
2013-14	FL 2	46	14	14	18	49	57	53*	20
2014-15	FL 2	46	14	16	16	54	60	58	15

* 3 pts deducted.

DID YOU KNOW

AFC Wimbledon's defeated Sandhurst Town 2-1 in their first competitive match in August 2002. Striker Kevin Cooper scored the club's opening goal and went on to become leading scorer in each of the Dons' first two seasons netting a total of 107.

AFC WIMBLEDON – FOOTBALL LEAGUE TWO 2014–15 LEAGUE RECORD

Match No.	Date		Venue	Opponents	Result	H/T Score	Lg Pos.	Goalscorers	Attendance
1	Aug	9	H	Shrewsbury T	D 2-2	1-1	10	Tubbs [26], Rigg [74]	4162
2		16	A	Luton T	W 1-0	1-0	7	Tubbs [42]	9101
3		19	A	Southend U	W 1-0	0-0	5	Francomb [60]	5364
4		23	H	Hartlepool U	L 1-2	1-0	9	Tubbs [11]	3576
5		30	H	Stevenage	L 2-3	1-1	13	Tubbs [34], Azeez [90]	3791
6	Sept	6	A	Carlisle U	D 4-4	2-2	12	Rigg [4], Tubbs 2 (1 pen) [22, 81 (p)], Azeez [90]	3955
7		13	A	Accrington S	L 0-1	0-0	15		1238
8		16	H	Burton Alb	W 3-0	2-0	12	Tubbs [21], Akinfenwa 2 [37, 67]	3195
9		20	H	Morecambe	W 1-0	1-0	10	Akinfenwa [27]	3822
10		27	A	Newport Co	L 1-4	0-1	12	Akinfenwa [70]	2804
11	Oct	4	A	Cheltenham T	D 1-1	1-1	13	Barrett [41]	2795
12		11	H	Bury	W 3-2	2-0	10	Akinfenwa 2 [26, 37], Tubbs [53]	4268
13		18	A	Wycombe W	L 0-2	0-0	12		4329
14		21	H	Plymouth Arg	D 0-0	0-0	12		4318
15		25	H	Tranmere R	D 2-2	2-1	12	Smith [16], Akinfenwa [44]	4195
16	Nov	1	A	Northampton T	L 0-2	0-1	17		4548
17		15	H	Dagenham & R	W 1-0	1-0	14	Fuller [19]	3887
18		22	A	Oxford U	D 0-0	0-0	16		5443
19		29	H	Cambridge U	L 1-2	1-1	16	Tubbs [2]	4306
20	Dec	13	A	York C	W 3-2	1-0	13	Goodman [24], Rigg [62], Tubbs [64]	3245
21		20	H	Mansfield T	L 0-1	0-0	15		3790
22		26	A	Portsmouth	W 2-0	2-0	12	Sutherland [9], Tubbs [17]	17,558
23		28	H	Exeter C	W 4-1	1-0	11	Tubbs [9], Ribeiro (og) [48], Azeez [71], Akinfenwa [86]	4417
24	Jan	10	A	Stevenage	L 1-2	1-1	12	Francomb [35]	3306
25		17	H	Carlisle U	L 1-3	1-1	13	Akinfenwa [1]	4186
26		24	H	Accrington S	W 2-1	1-0	12	Rigg [37], Azeez [78]	3859
27		31	A	Morecambe	D 1-1	1-1	13	Reeves [12]	1841
28	Feb	7	H	Newport Co	W 2-0	1-0	12	Akinfenwa 2 [11, 72]	3817
29		10	A	Burton Alb	D 0-0	0-0	11		2399
30		14	A	Shrewsbury T	L 0-2	0-1	13		4992
31		21	H	Luton T	W 3-2	2-1	12	Potter [28], Bulman [42], Connolly [90]	4050
32		24	A	Cambridge U	D 0-0	0-0	10		4259
33		28	A	Hartlepool U	L 0-1	0-0	11		3345
34	Mar	3	H	Southend U	D 0-0	0-0	11		3658
35		7	H	York C	W 2-1	1-1	11	Oshilaja [19], Smith [90]	4086
36		14	A	Exeter C	L 2-3	1-0	12	Akinfenwa [4], Hamon (og) [89]	3713
37		17	A	Mansfield T	L 1-2	0-0	13	Francomb (pen) [69]	3151
38		21	H	Portsmouth	W 1-0	1-0	12	Chorley (og) [6]	4485
39		28	A	Tranmere R	D 1-1	1-0	12	Akinfenwa [29]	5592
40	Apr	3	H	Northampton T	D 2-2	0-0	12	Rigg [58], Reeves [60]	4667
41		6	A	Dagenham & R	L 0-4	0-1	13		2346
42		11	H	Oxford U	D 0-0	0-0	13		4234
43		14	A	Plymouth Arg	D 1-1	0-0	13	Azeez [62]	6900
44		18	H	Wycombe W	D 0-0	0-0	13		4535
45		25	A	Bury	L 0-2	0-0	15		4099
46	May	2	H	Cheltenham T	D 1-1	1-1	15	Smith [44]	4374

Final League Position: 15

GOALSCORERS

League (54): Akinfenwa 13, Tubbs 12 (1 pen), Azeez 5, Rigg 5, Francomb 3 (1 pen), Smith 3, Reeves 2, Barrett 1, Bulman 1, Connolly 1, Fuller 1, Goodman 1, Oshilaja 1, Potter 1, Sutherland 1, own goals 3.
FA Cup (6): Tubbs 2, Akinfenwa 1, Frampton 1, Rigg 1, Smith 1.
Capital One Cup (1): Tubbs 1 (1 pen).
Johnstone's Paint Trophy (6): Akinfenwa 1, Azeez 1, Barrett 1, Francomb 1, Rigg 1, Sainte-Luce 1.

Shea J 38	Fuller B 45	Moore S 25+5	Barrett A 23	Smith J 21	Bennett A 16	Rigg S 39+5	Bulman D 40+1	Akinfenwa A 43+2	Tubbs M 22	Francomb G 31+6	Sainte-Luce K 1+8	Phillips M 2+3	Kennedy C 20+6	Azeez A 12+31	Pell H 1+8	Nicholson J 2	Beere T 6+12	Harrison B 5+2	Frampton A 3+1	Sutherland F 4+3	Oakley G —+6	Goodman J 13+1	Fitzpatrick D —+3	Oshilaja A 23	Reeves J 23	Connolly D 2+6	Potter A 10+5	Nightingale W 3+1	Tanner C 16+3	Winfield D 7	McDonnell J 3+1	Worner R 5	Sweeney R 2+1	Gallagher D —+1	Match No.
1	2	3	4	5	6[2]	7	8	9	10	11[1]	12	13																							1
1	2	7	4		3	9[1]	8	10	11[3]	6[2]	14		5	12	13																				2
1	2	7	4		3	9	8	11	10[1]	6[2]	13		5	14	12																				3
1	2	8[1]	4		3	9	7	11	10	6[3]	13		5[1]	14	12																				4
1	2	8	4		3	9[2]	7	10	11	6[1]		12	5	13																					5
1	2	8[1]	4		3	9[1]	7	11	10		12		5	13			6[1]	14																	6
1	2	7	4		3	9[3]	8	10[2]	11		12	14		13			6[1]	5																	7
1	2	8	3	4		9[2]	7	11[1]	10[1]	6[3]	14			13			12	5																	8
1	2	8	3	4		9[2]	7	11		6			13	10[1]			12	5																	9
1	2	8	3	4		9[1]	7	10	11	6[2]	14		12	13				5[3]																	10
1	2	8	4	5	3	9	7	11	10[1]	6[2]			13				12																		11
1	2	7[1]	4	5	3	9	8	10	11[2]	6[3]			13				12	14																	12
1	2	8	4	5	3	9[3]		11	10	6[1]	12		14	13			7[2]																		13
1	2	7	3	5		9	8	10	11	6				11[1]					4																14
1	2	7	3	5		9[1]	8	11	10[3]	6[4]			13	12	14				4																15
1	2[3]	7	3	5		9	8	11	10	6[2]			12						4	13	14														16
1	2	12	3	5	4	9	8	11	10[2]	6			13							7															17
1	2	8	3	5	4		7	10	9	12			11[1]								6[2]	13													18
1	2	8	4	5[1]	3	9[1]	7	11	10	13			12	14							6[2]														19
1	2	7	3			9	8[1]	11	10	6[2]			5	13	12		14					4													20
1	2	7[1]	3			9	8	10[2]	11	6			5	12[2]	14			13				4													21
1	2		3			9[1]	8	11[2]	6				5	10	12		7	13				4													22
1	2[9]		4			9[2]	7	12	11	6			5	10[1]	8		14	3	13																23
1	2					9	7	11		6			5	10								12		4	3	8									24
1	2					7[1]	8	10		11			3	9[1]									6	5	4[2]	12	13	14							25
	2	14				9[2]	7	10[1]		8			5	13										6	3	12		4	11[2]						26
	2					9[2]	7	10[2]		8			3	14			13							5	4	12		6	11[1]						27
	2					9[2]	8	11		6		12	5	14										3	7	10[1]	13	4[1]							28
	2	9				13	8	10[1]		12			3[1]	14										4	7		6[2]		11[3]						29
1[1]	2					14	7	13		6			5	9[1]										4	8	10[2]			11	3	12				30
1	2					9[3]	7	11					5	13			12							4	8	14	6[1]		10[2]	3					31
1	2	7		5		12	13	10						4[1]			9[2]							11	8	14	6[3]			3					32
1	2	12				9[1]	7	10					5	13										4	8	14	6[3]		11[2]	3					33
	2					13	7	11					5	12			6							3	8		9[1]		10[2]	4	1				34
	2					12	8	10		6		4		11[1]										3	7		9[2]		13		1				35
	2	14		5		8[1]	11[1]		6				12	13										3	7		9[1]		10[2]	4	1				36
	2	7		5		9[2]	11			12			6[1]	13										4	8	14	10[3]	3		1					37
	2	8		5		9[2]	11						13			12						4		3	7		6[1]	10		1					38
	2	6		5[2]		9[3]	10						13				7	12				3		4	8	14	11[1]			1					39
	2					9[3]	7	11		12			13				6[2]	5				4		3	8		10			1					40
	2					5[3]	7	10		6[1]			13				14					3		4	8	9	11			1		12		41
1	2			5		11	7	10		6[4]			13				14					12		4[2]	8		9[1]						3		42
1	2			5[1]		9	7	11		6[2]			10[3]				13					3		4	8		12							14	43
1	2					9[3]	8	10		5[1]			11				12	13				3	14	4	6		7[2]								44
1	2			5[1]		9	8	11		6			10[2]					4				3	7	13	12								7		45
1	2	13		5[2]		9		11[1]					4				14				12	3	8	6	10[2]						7			46

FA Cup

First Round	York C	(a)	1-1
Replay	York C	(h)	3-1
Second Round	Wycombe W	(a)	1-0
Third Round	Liverpool	(h)	1-2

Capital One Cup

First Round	Milton Keynes D	(a)	1-3

Johnstone's Paint Trophy

First Round	Southend U	(h)	2-2
(AFC Wimbledon won 4-2 on penalties)			
Second Round	Milton Keynes D	(a)	3-2
Southern Quarter-Finals	Bristol C	(a)	1-2

ARSENAL

FOUNDATION

Formed by workers at the Royal Arsenal, Woolwich in 1886, they began as Dial Square (name of one of the workshops), and included two former Nottingham Forest players, Fred Beardsley and Morris Bates. Beardsley wrote to his old club seeking help and they provided the new club with a full set of red jerseys and a ball. The club became known as the 'Woolwich Reds' although their official title soon after formation was Woolwich Arsenal.

Emirates Stadium, Highbury House, 75 Drayton Park, Islington, London N5 1BU.

Telephone: (020) 7619 5003.

Fax: (020) 7704 4001.

Ticket Office: (020) 7619 5000.

Website: www.arsenal.com

Email: info@arsenal.com

Ground Capacity: 60,272.

Record Attendance: 73,295 v Sunderland, Div 1, 9 March 1935 (at Highbury); 73,707 v RC Lens, UEFA Champions League, 25 November 1998 (at Wembley); 60,162 v Manchester U, FA Premier League, 3 November 2007 (at Emirates).

Pitch Measurements: 105m × 68m (114yd × 74yd)

Chairman: Sir John 'Chips' Keswick.

Chief Executive: Ivan Gazidis.

Manager: Arsène Wenger.

Assistant Manager: Steve Bould.

Physio: Colin Lewin.

Colours: Red shirts with white sleeves, white shorts, white socks with red hoops.

Year Formed: 1886.

Turned Professional: 1891.

Previous Names: 1886, Dial Square; 1886, Royal Arsenal; 1891, Woolwich Arsenal; 1914, Arsenal.

Club Nickname: 'The Gunners'.

Grounds: 1886, Plumstead Common; 1887, Sportsman Ground; 1888, Manor Ground; 1890, Invicta Ground; 1893, Manor Ground; 1913, Highbury; 2006, Emirates Stadium.

HONOURS

FA Premier League:
Champions 1997–98, 2001–02, 2003–04. *Runners-up* 1998–99, 1999–2000, 2000–01, 2002–03, 2004–05.

Football League – Division 1:
Champions 1930–31, 1932–33, 1933–34, 1934–35, 1937–38, 1947–48, 1952–53, 1970–71, 1988–89, 1990–91; *Runners-up* 1925–26, 1931–32, 1972–73; Division 2: *Runners-up* 1903–04.

FA Cup: *Winners* 1930, 1936, 1950, 1971, 1979, 1993, 1998, 2002, 2003, 2005, 2014, 2015; *Runners-up* 1927, 1932, 1952, 1972, 1978, 1980, 2001.

Double performed: 1970–71, 1997–98, 2001–02.

Football League Cup: *Winners* 1987, 1993; *Runners-up* 1968, 1969, 1988, 2007, 2011.

European Competitions
European Cup: 1971–72, 1991–92.
UEFA Champions League: 1998–99, 1999–2000, 2000–01, 2001–02, 2002–03, 2003–04, 2004–05, 2005–06 (*runners-up*), 2006–07, 2007–08 (*q-f*), 2008–09 (*s-f*), 2009–10, 2010–11, 2011–12, 2012–13, 2013–14, 2014–15.
Fairs Cup: 1963–64, 1969–70 (*winners*), 1970–71. **UEFA Cup:** 1978–79, 1981–82, 1982–83, 1996–97, 1997–98, 1999–2000 (*runners-up*).
European Cup-Winners' Cup: 1979–80 (*runners-up*), 1993–94 (*winners*), 1994–95 (*runners-up*). **Super Cup:** 1994 (*runners-up*).

sky SPORTS FACT FILE

Arsenal were elected to the old First Division in March 1919, when membership was increased from 20 clubs to 22. They have remained in the top flight ever since, the only club to retain continuous membership over this period.

First Football League Game: 2 September 1893, Division 2, v Newcastle U (h) D 2–2 – Williams; Powell, Jeffrey; Devine, Buist, Howat; Gemmell, Henderson, Shaw (1), Elliott (1), Booth.

Record League Victory: 12–0 v Loughborough T, Division 2, 12 March 1900 – Orr; McNichol, Jackson; Moir, Dick (2), Anderson (1); Hunt, Cottrell (2), Main (2), Gaudie (3), Tennant (2).

Record Cup Victory: 11–1 v Darwen, FA Cup 3rd rd, 9 January 1932 – Moss; Parker, Hapgood; Jones, Roberts, John; Hulme (2), Jack (3), Lambert (2), James, Bastin (4).

Record Defeat: 0–8 v Loughborough T, Division 2, 12 December 1896.

Most League Points (2 for a win): 66, Division 1, 1930–31.

Most League Points (3 for a win): 90, FA Premier League, 2003–04.

Most League Goals: 127, Division 1, 1930–31.

Highest League Scorer in Season: Ted Drake, 42, 1934–35.

Most League Goals in Total Aggregate: Thierry Henry, 175, 1999–2007; 2011–12.

Most League Goals in One Match: 7, Ted Drake v Aston Villa, Division 1, 14 December 1935.

Most Capped Player: Thierry Henry, 81 (123), France.

Most League Appearances: David O'Leary, 558, 1975–93.

Youngest League Player: Jack Wilshere, 16 years 256 days v Blackburn R, 13 September 2008.

Record Transfer Fee Received: £25,400,000 (rising to £29,800,000) from Barcelona for Cesc Fabregas, August 2011.

Record Transfer Fee Paid: £42,400,000 to Real Madrid for Mesut Ozil, September 2013.

Football League Record: 1893 Elected to Division 2; 1904–13 Division 1; 1913–19 Division 2; 1919–92 Division 1; 1992– FA Premier League.

MANAGERS
Sam Hollis 1894–97
Tom Mitchell 1897–98
George Elcoat 1898–99
Harry Bradshaw 1899–1904
Phil Kelso 1904–08
George Morrell 1908–15
Leslie Knighton 1919–25
Herbert Chapman 1925–34
George Allison 1934–47
Tom Whittaker 1947–56
Jack Crayston 1956–58
George Swindin 1958–62
Billy Wright 1962–66
Bertie Mee 1966–76
Terry Neill 1976–83
Don Howe 1984–86
George Graham 1986–95
Bruce Rioch 1995–96
Arsène Wenger September 1996–

LATEST SEQUENCES

Longest Sequence of League Wins: 14, 10.2.2002 – 18.8.2002.

Longest Sequence of League Defeats: 7, 12.2.1977 – 12.3.1977.

Longest Sequence of League Draws: 6, 4.3.1961 – 1.4.1961.

Longest Sequence of Unbeaten League Matches: 49, 7.5.2003 – 24.10.2004.

Longest Sequence Without a League Win: 23, 28.9.1912 – 1.3.1913.

Successive Scoring Runs: 55 from 19.5.2001.

Successive Non-scoring Runs: 6 from 25.2.1987.

TEN YEAR LEAGUE RECORD

		P	W	D	L	F	A	Pts	Pos
2005-06	PR Lge	38	20	7	11	68	31	67	4
2006-07	PR Lge	38	19	11	8	63	35	68	4
2007-08	PR Lge	38	24	11	3	74	31	83	3
2008-09	PR Lge	38	20	12	6	68	37	72	4
2009-10	PR Lge	38	23	6	9	83	41	75	3
2010-11	PR Lge	38	19	11	8	72	43	68	4
2011-12	PR Lge	38	21	7	10	74	49	70	3
2012-13	PR Lge	38	21	10	7	72	37	73	4
2013-14	PR Lge	38	24	7	7	68	41	79	4
2014-15	PR Lge	38	22	9	7	71	36	75	3

DID YOU KNOW ?

Fans of Woolwich Arsenal are believed to be the first to develop a terrace chant. In the early 1890s they adapted a popular music hall song to chant 'Ta ra ra boom de ay, the Arsenal's won today' at matches.

ARSENAL – FA PREMIERSHIP 2014–15 LEAGUE RECORD

Match No.	Date	Venue	Opponents	Result	H/T Score	Lg Pos.	Goalscorers	Attendance
1	Aug 16	H	Crystal Palace	W 2-1	1-1	1	Koscielny [45], Ramsey [90]	59,962
2	23	A	Everton	D 2-2	0-2	3	Ramsey [83], Giroud [90]	39,490
3	31	A	Leicester C	D 1-1	1-1	7	Sanchez [20]	31,535
4	Sept 13	H	Manchester C	D 2-2	0-1	7	Wilshere [63], Sanchez [74]	60,003
5	20	A	Aston Villa	W 3-0	3-0	4	Ozil [32], Welbeck [34], Cissokho (og) [36]	40,013
6	27	H	Tottenham H	D 1-1	0-0	4	Oxlade-Chamberlain [74]	59,900
7	Oct 5	A	Chelsea	L 0-2	0-1	8		41,607
8	18	H	Hull C	D 2-2	1-1	6	Sanchez [13], Welbeck [90]	60,004
9	25	A	Sunderland	W 2-0	1-0	5	Sanchez 2 [30, 90]	44,449
10	Nov 1	H	Burnley	W 3-0	0-0	4	Sanchez 2 [70, 90], Chambers [72]	60,012
11	9	A	Swansea C	L 1-2	0-0	6	Sanchez [63]	20,812
12	22	H	Manchester U	L 1-2	0-0	8	Giroud [90]	60,074
13	29	A	WBA	W 1-0	0-0	6	Welbeck [60]	24,228
14	Dec 3	H	Southampton	W 1-0	0-0	6	Sanchez [89]	60,025
15	6	A	Stoke C	L 2-3	0-3	6	Cazorla [68], Ramsey [70]	27,367
16	13	H	Newcastle U	W 4-1	1-0	6	Giroud 2 [15, 58], Cazorla 2 (1 pen) [54, 88 (p)]	59,949
17	21	A	Liverpool	D 2-2	1-1	6	Debuchy [45], Giroud [64]	44,703
18	26	H	QPR	W 2-1	1-0	6	Sanchez [37], Rosicky [65]	59,947
19	28	A	West Ham U	W 2-1	2-0	5	Cazorla (pen) [41], Welbeck [44]	34,977
20	Jan 1	A	Southampton	L 0-2	0-1	6		31,492
21	11	H	Stoke C	W 3-0	2-0	5	Koscielny [6], Sanchez 2 [33, 49]	59,956
22	18	A	Manchester C	W 2-0	1-0	5	Cazorla (pen) [24], Giroud [67]	45,596
23	Feb 1	H	Aston Villa	W 5-0	1-0	5	Giroud [8], Ozil [56], Walcott [63], Cazorla (pen) [75], Bellerin [90]	59,958
24	7	A	Tottenham H	L 1-2	1-0	6	Ozil [11]	35,659
25	10	H	Leicester C	W 2-1	2-0	4	Koscielny [27], Walcott [41]	60,032
26	21	A	Crystal Palace	W 2-1	2-0	3	Cazorla (pen) [8], Giroud [45]	24,721
27	Mar 1	H	Everton	W 2-0	1-0	3	Giroud [39], Rosicky [89]	59,925
28	4	A	QPR	W 2-1	0-0	3	Giroud [64], Sanchez [69]	17,977
29	14	H	West Ham U	W 3-0	1-0	3	Giroud [45], Ramsey [81], Flamini [84]	60,002
30	21	A	Newcastle U	W 2-1	2-0	3	Giroud 2 [24, 28]	50,544
31	Apr 4	H	Liverpool	W 4-1	3-0	2	Bellerin [37], Ozil [40], Sanchez [45], Giroud [90]	60,081
32	11	A	Burnley	W 1-0	1-0	2	Ramsey [12]	20,615
33	26	H	Chelsea	D 0-0	0-0	3		60,066
34	May 4	A	Hull C	W 3-1	3-0	3	Sanchez 2 [28, 45], Ramsey [33]	23,628
35	11	H	Swansea C	L 0-1	0-0	3		59,989
36	17	A	Manchester U	D 1-1	0-1	3	Blackett (og) [82]	75,323
37	20	A	Sunderland	D 0-0	0-0	3		59,987
38	24	H	WBA	W 4-1	4-0	3	Walcott 3 [4, 14, 37], Wilshere [17]	59,971

Final League Position: 3

GOALSCORERS

League (71): Sanchez 16, Giroud 14, Cazorla 7 (5 pens), Ramsey 6, Walcott 5, Ozil 4, Welbeck 4, Koscielny 3, Bellerin 2, Rosicky 2, Wilshere 1, Chambers 1, Debuchy 1, Flamini 1, Oxlade-Chamberlain 1, own goals 2.
FA Cup (15): Sanchez 4, Giroud 3, Mertesacker 2, Walcott 2, Monreal 1, Ozil 1, Rosicky 1, Welbeck 1.
Capital One Cup (1): Sanchez 1.
UEFA Champions League (19): Sanchez 4, Podolski 3, Ramsey 3, Welbeck 3, Oxlade-Chamberlain 2, Arteta 1 (1 pen), Gibbs 1, Giroud 1, Sanogo 1.

Szczesny W 17	Debuchy M 10	Chambers C 17+6	Koscielny L 26+1	Gibbs K 18+4	Arteta M 6+1	Sanchez A 34+1	Ramsey A 23+6	Wilshere J 9+5	Cazorla S 33+4	Sanogo Y 2+1	Monreal N 26+2	Giroud O 21+6	Oxlade-Chamberlain A 17+6	Mertesacker P 35	Flamini M 15+8	Ozil M 21+1	Campbell J —+4	Podolski L —+7	Welbeck D 18+7	Rosicky T 5+10	Bellerin H 17+3	Walcott T 4+10	Martinez D 3+1	Coquelin F 19+3	Maitland-Niles A —+1	Akpom C —+3	Ospina D 18	Gabriel A 4+2	Match No.
1	2	3	4	5[1]	6	7	8	9[3]	10	11[1]	12	13	14																1
1	2	3				11[2]	8	9[3]	13		5	12	7[1]	4	6	10	14												2
1	2	12	4[2]			7	8	9[1]	11[3]		5	13		3	6[2]	10	14												3
1	2[1]	12		14		7	8	9			5	13	3	6		10	11[2]												4
1			4	5	6		8[3]	12	9			7[1]		3		10	14	11[2]	13										5
1	2		4	5	6[3]		8[2]	9[1]	13		14	7		3	12	10	11												6
1	2		4	5			8[2]	9[1]	10[3]		12			3	6	7	13	11	14										7
1			5			7	12	9[2]	8		4	10		3	6[1]				13	11	2								8
1	2		5[1]		6[2]		9	13	10		4			8[1]	3	7	11	14	12										9
1	2		5		6[2]		9	12	10		4			8[1]	3	7	14	11[3]	13										10
1	2		5		9	6[3]	13	10	14		4			8	3	7[2]	11	12											11
1[3]	2		5	7	10		6[1]	9[2]	12		4			14	8	3	11	13											12
	2		4	12			8	6	9		5[1]	11[2]	13		3	7			10				1						13
	2		4				10	6	9		5	12		8[2]	3	7	13	11[1]					1						14
			3		5		10	7	9			11[2]	8	4	6		14	13	12			2[1]	1						15
1		3			5		8[3]		9			11[4]	7[1]	4	6	12	10				2	13	14						16
1		3			5		9[2]		8		13	10[2]		6[1]	4	7	14	11			2			12					17
1	2	12			5		8	9			4	10[4]		3	7	11[1]	6[2]		13										18
1	2	13	4	12			11		9		5			8[2]	3	7	10[1]		6										19
1	2[6]		4	5			11		9					8	3	10				12		7	13					6	20
	2[1]		4				10		9		5	11[3]	14	8[2]	3					6	12	13		7			1		21
			4	13			10[2]	8[3]	9		5	11	14	7[1]	3					12	2			6			1		22
			4			6[1]		9			5	11[3]	14	3	10				8[2]	12	2		13	7			1		23
			4			6	8[2]		5		10			3	11				9[3]	12	2		13	7[1]		14	1		24
			4			10[2]	13[3]	8	5		12			3	11		14		9[1]	6	2			7			1		25
	2		4	13			10[1]	7	5		11			3					9[1]	8[2]	12			6			1	14	26
	14		4	5			10[3]	6	11					8[1]					9	13	12	2		7[2]			1	3	27
	12		5				11	13	8			10		3					9	14	6[1]	2		7			1	4	28
	2		4				10[1]	6	13		5	11		3			14		9[3]	12		7		6[2]			1		29
	2		4				8[1]	6	9[3]		5	11		13	10[2]		12			14		7					1	3	30
			4[1]				10	8[3]	7		5	11		3	13				9[2]	14	2			6			1	12	31
	13		4				10[2]	8	7		5	11[1]		3					9	12	2			6			1		32
			4				10	8	6		5	11[2]		3					9	12	2		13	7[1]			1		33
			4				10	8[1]	12	7	5	11[2]		3					9		2		13	6			1		34
			4				10	8	12	6	5	11[1]		3					9		2		13	7[2]			1		35
			4				10[2]	8	13	7[1]	5	11		3			14		9	12	2[3]			6			1		36
			4	5			10	7	8[2]	6	11			3					9[1]	12	2	13					1		37
			5				10	13	8[1]	6	12	11[3]	14	3					9		2	7[1]					1	4	38

FA Cup

Third Round	Hull C	(h)		2-0
Fourth Round	Brighton & HA	(a)		3-2
Fifth Round	Middlesbrough	(h)		2-0
Sixth Round	Manchester U	(a)		2-1
Semi-Finals	Reading	Wembley		2-1
(aet)				
Final	Aston Villa	Wembley		4-0

Capital One Cup

Third Round	Southampton	(h)		1-2

UEFA Champions League

Play-Off 1st leg	Besiktas	(a)	0-0
Play-Off 2nd leg	Besiktas	(h)	1-0
Group D	Borussia Dortmund	(a)	0-2
Group D	Galatasaray	(h)	4-1
Group D	Anderlecht	(a)	2-1
Group D	Anderlecht	(h)	3-3
Group D	Borussia Dortmund	(h)	2-0
Group D	Galatasaray	(a)	4-1
Round of 16 1st leg	Monaco	(h)	1-3
Round of 16 2nd leg	Monaco	(a)	2-0

ASTON VILLA

FOUNDATION

Cricketing enthusiasts of Villa Cross Wesleyan Chapel, Aston, Birmingham decided to form a football club during the winter of 1874–75. Football clubs were few and far between in the Birmingham area and in their first game against Aston Brook St Mary's rugby team they played one half rugby and the other soccer. In 1876 they were joined by Scottish soccer enthusiast George Ramsay who was immediately appointed captain and went on to lead Aston Villa from obscurity to one of the country's top clubs in a period of less than ten years.

Villa Park, Birmingham B6 6HE.
Telephone: (0121) 327 2299.
Fax: (0121) 322 2107.
Ticket Office/Consumer Sales: (0800) 612 0970.
Website: www.avfc.co.uk
Email: postmaster@avfc.co.uk
Ground Capacity: 42,682.
Record Attendance: 76,588 v Derby Co, FA Cup 6th rd, 2 March 1946.
Pitch Measurements: 105m × 68m (114yd × 74yd)
Chairman: Randolph Lerner.
Chief Executive: Paul Faulkner.
Manager: Tim Sherwood.
Assistant Manager: Kevin MacDonald.
Physio: Alan Smith.
Colours: Claret shirts, sky blue sleeves with claret trim, white shorts with sky blue trim, sky blue socks with claret hoops.
Year Formed: 1874.
Turned Professional: 1885.
Club Nickname: 'The Villans'.
Grounds: 1874, Wilson Road and Aston Park (also used Aston Lower Grounds for some matches); 1876, Wellington Road, Perry Barr; 1897, Villa Park.
First Football League Game: 8 September 1888, Football League, v Wolverhampton W (a) D 1–1 – Warner; Cox, Coulton; Yates, Harry Devey, Dawson; Albert Brown, Green (1), Allen, Garvey, Hodgetts.
Record League Victory: 12–2 v Accrington S, Division 1, 12 March 1892 – Warner; Evans, Cox; Harry Devey, Jimmy Cowan, Baird; Athersmith (1), Dickson (2), John Devey (4), Lewis Campbell (4), Hodgetts (1).

HONOURS

FA Premier League:
Runners-up 1992–93.
Football League – Division 1:
Champions 1893–94, 1895–96, 1896–97, 1898–99, 1899–1900, 1909–10, 1980–81;
Runners-up 1888–89, 1902–03, 1907–08, 1910–11, 1912–13, 1913–14, 1930–31, 1932–33, 1989–90;
Division 2: *Champions* 1937–38, 1959–60; *Runners-up* 1974–75, 1987–88;
Division 3: *Champions* 1971–72.
FA Cup: *Winners* 1887, 1895, 1897, 1905, 1913, 1920, 1957;
Runners-up 1892, 1924, 2000, 2015.
Double Performed: 1896–97.
Football League Cup: *Winners* 1961, 1975, 1977, 1994, 1996;
Runners-up 1963, 1971, 2010.
European Competitions
European Cup: 1981–82 (*winners*), 1982–83. **UEFA Cup:** 1975–76, 1977–78, 1983–84, 1990–91, 1993–94, 1994–95, 1996–97, 1997–98, 1998–99, 2001–02, 2008–09.
Europa League: 2009–10, 2010–11.
World Club Championship: 1982.
Super Cup: 1982 (*winners*). **Intertoto Cup:** 2000, 2001 (*winners*), 2002, 2008 (*winners*).

sky SPORTS FACT FILE

Herbert Kingaby was an Aston Villa player for only a few months and made just a handful of appearances in 1906, but his name remains in the history books due to the fact that, with the support of the Players' Union, he unsuccessfully challenged the retain and transfer system in the courts.

Record Cup Victory: 13–0 v Wednesbury Old Ath, FA Cup 1st rd, 30 October 1886 – Warner; Coulton, Simmonds; Yates, Robertson, Burton (2); Richard Davis (1), Albert Brown (3), Hunter (3), Loach (2), Hodgetts (2).

Record Defeat: 0–8 v Chelsea, FA Premier League, 23 December 2012.

Most League Points (2 for a win): 70, Division 3, 1971–72.

Most League Points (3 for a win): 78, Division 2, 1987–88.

Most League Goals: 128, Division 1, 1930–31.

Highest League Scorer in Season: 'Pongo' Waring, 49, Division 1, 1930–31.

Most League Goals in Total Aggregate: Harry Hampton, 215, 1904–15.

Most League Goals in One Match: 5, Harry Hampton v Sheffield W, Division 1, 5 October 1912; 5, Harold Halse v Derby Co, Division 1, 19 October 1912; 5, Len Capewell v Burnley, Division 1, 29 August 1925; 5, George Brown v Leicester C, Division 1, 2 January 1932; 5, Gerry Hitchens v Charlton Ath, Division 2, 18 November 1959.

Most Capped Player: Steve Staunton 64 (102), Republic of Ireland.

Most League Appearances: Charlie Aitken, 561, 1961–76.

Youngest League Player: Jimmy Brown, 15 years 349 days v Bolton W, 17 September 1969.

Record Transfer Fee Received: £26,000,000 from Manchester C for James Milner, August 2010.

Record Transfer Fee Paid: £18,000,000 (rising to £24,000,000) to Sunderland for Darren Bent, January 2011.

Football League Record: 1888 Founder Member of the League; 1936–38 Division 2; 1938–59 Division 1; 1959–60 Division 2; 1960–67 Division 1; 1967–70 Division 2; 1970–72 Division 3; 1972–75 Division 2; 1975–87 Division 1; 1987–88 Division 2; 1988–92 Division 1; 1992– FA Premier League.

MANAGERS
George Ramsay 1884–1926 (*Secretary-Manager*)
W. J. Smith 1926–34 (*Secretary-Manager*)
Jimmy McMullan 1934–35
Jimmy Hogan 1936–44
Alex Massie 1945–50
George Martin 1950–53
Eric Houghton 1953–58
Joe Mercer 1958–64
Dick Taylor 1964–67
Tommy Cummings 1967–68
Tommy Docherty 1968–70
Vic Crowe 1970–74
Ron Saunders 1974–82
Tony Barton 1982–84
Graham Turner 1984–86
Billy McNeill 1986–87
Graham Taylor 1987–90
Dr Jozef Venglos 1990–91
Ron Atkinson 1991–94
Brian Little 1994–98
John Gregory 1998–2002
Graham Taylor OBE 2002–03
David O'Leary 2003–06
Martin O'Neill 2006–10
Gerard Houllier 2010–11
Alex McLeish 2011–12
Paul Lambert 2012–15
Tim Sherwood February 2015–

LATEST SEQUENCES

Longest Sequence of League Wins: 9, 15.10.1910 – 10.12.1910.

Longest Sequence of League Defeats: 11, 23.3.1963 – 4.5.1963.

Longest Sequence of League Draws: 6, 12.9.1981 – 10.10.1981.

Longest Sequence of Unbeaten League Matches: 15, 12.3.1949 – 27.8.1949.

Longest Sequence Without a League Win: 13, 24.3.2012 – 15.9.2012.

Successive Scoring Runs: 35 from 10.11.1895.

Successive Non-scoring Runs: 6 from 26.12.14.

TEN YEAR LEAGUE RECORD								
		P	W	D	L	F	A	Pts	Pos
2005-06	PR Lge	38	10	12	16	42	55	42	16
2006-07	PR Lge	38	11	17	10	43	41	50	11
2007-08	PR Lge	38	16	12	10	71	51	60	6
2008-09	PR Lge	38	17	11	10	54	48	62	6
2009-10	PR Lge	38	17	13	8	52	39	64	6
2010-11	PR Lge	38	12	12	14	48	59	48	9
2011-12	PR Lge	38	7	17	14	37	53	38	16
2012-13	PR Lge	38	10	11	17	47	69	41	15
2013-14	PR Lge	38	10	8	20	39	61	38	15
2014-15	PR Lge	38	10	8	20	31	57	38	17

DID YOU KNOW ?

Aston Villa are one of only seven clubs to have achieved a double of winning the League Championship and FA Cup in the same season. Villa achieved the feat in 1896–97 and it was to be another 64 years before the double was won again.

ASTON VILLA – FA PREMIERSHIP 2014–15 LEAGUE RECORD

Match No.	Date	Venue	Opponents	Result		H/T Score	Lg Pos.	Goalscorers	Attendance
1	Aug 16	A	Stoke C	W	1-0	0-0	3	Weimann [50]	27,478
2	23	H	Newcastle U	D	0-0	0-0	4		30,267
3	31	H	Hull C	W	2-1	2-0	3	Agbonlahor [14], Weimann [36]	28,336
4	Sept 13	A	Liverpool	W	1-0	1-0	2	Agbonlahor [9]	44,689
5	20	H	Arsenal	L	0-3	0-3	3		40,013
6	27	A	Chelsea	L	0-3	0-1	6		41,616
7	Oct 4	H	Manchester C	L	0-2	0-0	7		32,964
8	18	A	Everton	L	0-3	0-1	11		39,505
9	27	A	QPR	L	0-2	0-1	15		18,022
10	Nov 2	H	Tottenham H	L	1-2	1-0	15	Weimann [16]	32,049
11	8	A	West Ham U	D	0-0	0-0	16		34,857
12	24	H	Southampton	D	1-1	1-0	16	Agbonlahor [29]	25,311
13	29	A	Burnley	D	1-1	1-0	16	Cole [38]	19,910
14	Dec 2	A	Crystal Palace	W	1-0	1-0	12	Benteke [32]	23,935
15	7	H	Leicester C	W	2-1	1-1	11	Clark [17], Hutton [71]	27,692
16	13	A	WBA	L	0-1	0-0	12		24,684
17	20	H	Manchester U	D	1-1	1-0	12	Benteke [18]	41,273
18	26	A	Swansea C	L	0-1	0-1	13		20,683
19	28	H	Sunderland	D	0-0	0-0	13		35,436
20	Jan 1	H	Crystal Palace	D	0-0	0-0	12		29,047
21	10	A	Leicester C	L	0-1	0-1	13		31,728
22	17	H	Liverpool	L	0-2	0-1	14		39,758
23	Feb 1	A	Arsenal	L	0-5	0-1	16		59,958
24	7	H	Chelsea	L	1-2	0-1	16	Okore [48]	35,969
25	10	A	Hull C	L	0-2	0-1	18		21,467
26	21	H	Stoke C	L	1-2	1-1	19	Sinclair [20]	31,880
27	28	A	Newcastle U	L	0-1	0-1	29		51,573
28	Mar 3	A	WBA	W	2-1	1-0	17	Agbonlahor [22], Benteke (pen) [90]	31,272
29	14	A	Sunderland	W	4-0	4-0	16	Benteke 2 [16, 44], Agbonlahor 2 [18, 37]	45,746
30	21	H	Swansea C	L	0-1	0-0	16		35,598
31	Apr 4	A	Manchester U	L	1-3	0-1	16	Benteke [80]	75,397
32	7	H	QPR	D	3-3	2-1	16	Benteke 3 [10, 33, 83]	33,708
33	11	A	Tottenham H	W	1-0	1-0	15	Benteke [35]	35,687
34	25	A	Manchester C	L	2-3	0-1	15	Cleverley [68], Sanchez [85]	45,036
35	May 2	H	Everton	W	3-2	2-0	14	Benteke 2 [10, 45], Cleverley [64]	37,859
36	9	H	West Ham U	W	1-0	1-0	14	Cleverley [31]	39,294
37	16	A	Southampton	L	1-6	1-5	15	Benteke [45]	31,636
38	24	H	Burnley	L	0-1	0-1	17		40,792

Final League Position: 17

GOALSCORERS

League (31): Benteke 13 (1 pen), Agbonlahor 6, Cleverley 3, Weimann 3, Clark 1, Cole 1, Hutton 1, Okore 1, Sanchez 1, Sinclair 1.
FA Cup (9): Benteke 2, Delph 2, Sinclair 2, Bacuna 1, Gil 1, Weimann 1.
Capital One Cup (0).

Guzan B 34	Hutton A 27+3	Vlaar R 19+1	Senderos P 7+1	Cissokho A 24+1	Westwood A 25+2	Delph F 27+1	N'Zogbia C 19+8	Richardson K 16+6	Weimann A 20+11	Agbonlahor G 30+4	Grealish J 7+10	Bacuna L 10+9	Sanchez C 20+8	Bent D —+7	Baker N 8+3	Cleverley T 31	Clark C 22+3	Benteke C 26+3	Cole J 3+9	Lowton M 8+4	Okore J 22+1	Gil C 4+1	Sinclair S 5+4	Hepburn-Murphy R —+1	Given S 3	Steer J 1	Match No.
1	2	3	4	5	6	7	8¹	9	10²	11	12	13															1
1	2	4	3	5¹	7	8	9¹	6³	11	10			12	13	14												2
1	2	4	3	5	7	8	9¹	6³	10	11¹²	13		12	14													3
1	2	3		5	7	8	12	11	10¹	9²			13	14	4	6¹											4
1	2	4		5				9	13	10²	6¹	11	12	14	8³	7	3										5
1	2	3		5	7	8	13	11¹	9¹	10			12		4	6											6
1	2	3		5	7	8	9¹	11³	10¹				13	14	4	6	12										7
1	2	3		5	7			9²	8	13	11				4³	6	12	10¹	14								8
1		3		5	7²			11¹	9				8	12	12	6	4	10	13	2							9
1		3		5¹	6			9²	13	11¹	12		7	14	4	8		10⁴		2							10
1		3	12	5	7			9¹		11	10		8			4²	6	13		2							11
1	2			5	7			9¹	12	11	10		8²			6	4	13		3							12
1	2			5	7			13	11²	10	12		8		6	4¹		9³	14	3							13
1	2			5	7			13	11	9	12		6²	4	10	8¹				3							14
1	2			5	7³			9²	12	11	13	14	8	6¹	4	10				3							15
1	2	13		5²	12		9¹	8⁴	14	11	7³				6	4	10			3							16
1	4	6¹		8	13		7²	11⁴	12	9				5	10	2	3										17
1	2	4		6¹	7		12	10	13	8		9²	5	11		3											18
1	2	3		5	6⁴	10³	9	14	12	7	8¹	4²	11	13													19
1	2	4¹		5			9	11	13	6	7	8²	12	10	14	3											20
1	2			5²	7		14	13	12	9		8²	6	4⁴	10	11¹	3										21
1	2			5	7²	8		13	11		6	4	9¹	10		3	12										22
1	2		14	7		5	11²	12		8¹	6³	4	10		3	9	13										23
1	2			5	8	9		10³	11¹		7²	4	12	14		3	6	13									24
1	2			5	7	8		11¹	10			4	12	13		3	6	9²									25
1	2	3⁴		12		8		5²	13	11		7		4	10				6¹	9							26
1	2			7	8	12		13	9²		14	6	4	10		5³	3	11¹									27
1	2			6	8	9¹		14	10³	12	13	8	4	11	5	3											28
1				7	6³		13	10		2	12		8	4¹	11²	5	3	9	14								29
1	5			13	8	6³		14	11		2	12	7²	4	10¹	3	9										30
1	2²			8	6³		9¹	11		12	7	13	4	10	14	5	3										31
1	3			8	14	5	9	11³	2¹	7	6²	4	10	12	13												32
1	3			8	5	13	9¹	11²	2	7⁴	12	6	4³	10	14												33
1	3			7²	10	12	5	8	2¹	9	6	11	13	4													34
	13	4		7²	8	9³	5	11	2¹	12	6	10	14	3										1			35
	13	4		7	8	9²	5	12	11¹	2³	14	6	10	3										1			36
	5	4		7	8	9²	12	11³	2¹	6	10	13	3	14										1			37
	13	3		7	8	5	9	11	2²	4	6¹	10	12												1		38

FA Cup

Third Round	Blackpool	(h)	1-0
Fourth Round	Bournemouth	(h)	2-1
Fifth Round	Leicester C	(h)	2-1
Sixth Round	WBA	(h)	2-0
Semi-Finals	Liverpool	Wembley	2-1
Final	Arsenal	Wembley	0-4

Capital One Cup

Second Round	Leyton Orient	(h)	0-1

BARNET

FOUNDATION

Barnet Football Club was formed in 1888 as an amateur organisation and they played at a ground in Queen's Road until they disbanded in 1901. A club known as Alston Works FC was then formed and they played at Totteridge Lane until changing to Barnet Alston FC in 1906. They moved to their present ground a year later, combining with The Avenue to form Barnet and Alston in 1912. The club progressed to senior amateur football by way of the Athenian and Isthmian Leagues, turning professional in 1965. It was as a Southern League and Conference club that they made their name.

The Hive Stadium, Camrose Avenue, Edgware HA8 6AG.

Telephone: (020) 831 3800.

Ticket Office: (020) 831 3800 (ext. 1028)

Website: www.barnetfc.com

Email: tellus@barnetfc.com

Ground Capacity: 5,176.

Record Attendance: 11,026 v Wycombe Wanderers, FA Amateur Cup 4th rd, 1951–52.

Pitch Measurements: 105m × 68m (115yd × 75yd)

Chairman: Anthony Kleanthous.

Group Finance Director: Andrew Adie.

Head Coach: Martin Allen.

Physio: Jayde Cook.

Colours: Black and amber striped shirts, black shorts, black socks.

Year Formed: 1888.

Turned Professional: 1965.

Previous Name: 1906, Barnet Alston FC; 1919, Barnet.

Club Nickname: 'The Bees'.

Grounds: 1888, Queen's Road; 1901, Totteridge Lane; 1907, Barnet Lane; 2013, The Hive.

First Football League Game: 17 August 1991, Division 4, v Crewe Alex (h) L 4–7 – Phillips; Blackford, Cooper (Murphy), Horton, Bodley (Stein), Johnson, Showler, Carter (2), Bull (2), Lowe, Evans.

Record League Victory: 7–0 v Blackpool, Division 3, 11 November 2000 – Naisbitt; Stockley, Sawyers, Niven (Brown), Heald, Arber (1), Currie (3), Doolan, Richards (2) (McGleish), Cottee (1) (Riza), Toms.

Record Cup Victory: 6–1 v Newport Co, FA Cup 1st rd, 21 November 1970 – McClelland; Lye, Jenkins, Ward, Embery, King, Powell (1), Ferry, Adams (1), Gray, George (3), (1 og).

HONOURS

Football League – FL 2: Best season: 12th, 2007–08.

Conference: *Champions* 2014–15.

FA Amateur Cup: *Winners* 1946.

FA Trophy: *Runners-up* 1972.

GM Vauxhall Conference: *Winners* 1990–91.

Conference: *Winners* 2004–05.

FA Cup: 4th rd, 2007, 2008.

League Cup: Best season: 3rd rd, 2006.

sky SPORTS FACT FILE

Barnet featured in one of the first live football games to be televised by the BBC. The channel showed the opening 20 minutes of the Bees' Athenian League game against Wealdstone in October 1946. After a break the plan was to show the entire second half but the broadcast was cut short 80 minutes into the game because of poor light.

Record Defeat: 1–9 v Peterborough U, Division 3, 5 September 1998.

Most League Points (3 for a win): 79, Division 3, 1992–93.

Most League Goals: 81, Division 4, 1991–92.

Highest League Scorer in Season: Dougie Freedman, 24, Division 3, 1994–95.

Most League Goals in Total Aggregate: Sean Devine, 47, 1995–99.

Most League Goals in One Match: 4, Dougie Freedman v Rochdale, Division 3, 13 September 1994; 4, Lee Hodges v Rochdale, Division 3, 8 April 1996.

Most Capped Player: Ken Charlery, 4, St Lucia.

Most League Appearances: Lee Harrison, 270, 1996–2002, 2006–09.

Youngest League Player: Kieran Adams, 17 years 71 days v Mansfield T, 31 December 1994.

Record Transfer Fee Received: £800,000 from Crystal Palace for Dougie Freedman, September 1995.

Record Transfer Fee Paid: £130,000 to Peterborough U for Greg Heald, August 1997.

Football League Record: 1991 Promoted to Division 4 from GMVC; 1991–92 Division 4; 1992–93 Division 3; 1993–94 Division 2; 1994–2001 Division 3; 2001–05 Conference; 2005–13 FL 2; 2013–15 Conference Premier; 2015– FL 2.

LATEST SEQUENCES

Longest Sequence of League Wins: 6, 28.8.1993 – 25.9.1999.

Longest Sequence of League Defeats: 11, 8.5.1993 – 2.10.1993.

Longest Sequence of League Draws: 4, 22.1.1994 – 12.2.1994.

Longest Sequence of Unbeaten League Matches: 12, 5.12.1992 – 2.3.1993.

Longest Sequence Without a League Win: 14, 24.4.1993 – 10.10.1993.

Successive Scoring Runs: 12 from 19.3.1995.

Successive Non-scoring Runs: 5 from 12.2.2000.

MANAGERS

Lester Finch
George Wheeler
Dexter Adams
Tommy Coleman
Gerry Ward
Gordon Ferry
Brian Kelly
Bill Meadows 1976–79
Barry Fry 1979–85
Roger Thompson 1985
Don McAllister 1985–86
Barry Fry 1986–93
Edwin Stein 1993
Gary Phillips (*Player-Manager*) 1993–94
Ray Clemence 1994–96
Alan Mullery (*Director of Football*) 1996–97
Terry Bullivant 1997
John Still 1997–2000
Tony Cottee 2000–01
John Still 2001–02
Peter Shreeves 2002–03
Martin Allen 2003–04
Paul Fairclough 2004–08
Ian Hendon 2008–10
Mark Stimson 2010–11
Martin Allen 2011
Lawrie Sanchez 2011–12
Mark Robson 2012
Edgar Davids 2012–14
Ulrich Landvreugd and Dick Schreuder 2014
Martin Allen March 2014–

TEN YEAR LEAGUE RECORD

		P	W	D	L	F	A	Pts	Pos
2005-06	FL 2	46	12	18	16	44	57	54	18
2006-07	FL 2	46	16	11	19	55	70	59	14
2007-08	FL 2	46	16	12	18	56	63	60	12
2008-09	FL 2	46	11	15	20	56	74	48	17
2009-10	FL 2	46	12	12	22	47	63	48	21
2010-11	FL 2	46	12	12	22	58	77	48	22
2011-12	FL 2	46	12	10	24	52	79	46	22
2012-13	FL 2	46	13	12	21	47	59	51	23
2013-14	Conf P	46	19	13	14	58	53	70	8
2014-15	Conf P	46	28	8	10	94	46	92	1

DID YOU KNOW ?

Barnet turned professional in the summer of 1965 when they joined the first division of the Southern League. They won 10 out of their first 11 league games including a 10-1 opening day victory over Hinckley Athletic.

BARNSLEY

FOUNDATION

Many clubs owe their inception to the Church and Barnsley are among them, for they were formed in 1887 by the Rev. T. T. Preedy, curate of Barnsley St Peter's, and went under that name until it was dropped in 1897 a year before being admitted to the Second Division of the Football League.

Oakwell Stadium, Grove Street, Barnsley, South Yorkshire S71 1ET.

Telephone: (01226) 211 211.

Fax: (01226) 211 444.

Ticket Office: (0871) 22 66 777.

Website: www.barnsleyfc.co.uk

Email: thereds@barnsleyfc.co.uk

Ground Capacity: 23,287.

Record Attendance: 40,255 v Stoke C, FA Cup 5th rd, 15 February 1936.

Pitch Measurements: 100.5m × 67m (110yd × 73yd)

Chairman: Maurice Watkins.

Chief Executive: Ben Mansford.

Head Coach: Lee Johnson.

Assistant Head Coach: Tommy Wright.

Head Physio: Craig Sedgwick.

Colours: Red shirts with white trim, white shorts, red socks.

Year Formed: 1887.

Turned Professional: 1888.

Previous Name: 1887, Barnsley St Peter's; 1897, Barnsley.

Club Nickname: 'The Tykes', 'The Reds', 'The Colliers'.

Ground: 1887, Oakwell.

HONOURS

Football League – Division 1: *Runners-up* 1996–97;
Division 3 (N): *Champions* 1933–34, 1938–39, 1954–55; *Runners-up* 1953–54;
Division 3: *Runners-up* 1980–81;
Division 4: *Runners-up* 1967–68.
FA Cup: *Winners* 1912; *Runners-up* 1910.
Football League Cup: Best season: quarter-final, 1982.

First Football League Game: 1 September 1898, Division 2, v Lincoln C (a) L 0–1 – Fawcett; McArtney, Nixon; King, Burleigh, Porteous; Davis, Lees, Murray, McCullough, McGee.

Record League Victory: 9–0 v Loughborough T, Division 2, 28 January 1899 – Greaves; McArtney, Nixon; Porteous, Burleigh, Howard; Davis (4), Hepworth (1), Lees (1), McCullough (1), Jones (2). 9–0 v Accrington S, Division 3 (N), 3 February 1934 – Ellis; Cookson, Shotton; Harper, Henderson, Whitworth; Spence (2), Smith (1), Blight (4), Andrews (1), Ashton (1).

Record Cup Victory: 6–0 v Blackpool, FA Cup 1st rd replay, 20 January 1910 – Mearns; Downs, Ness; Glendinning, Boyle (1), Utley; Bartrop, Gadsby (1), Lillycrop (2), Tufnell (2), Forman. 6–0 v Peterborough U, League Cup 1st rd 2nd leg, 15 September 1981 – Horn; Joyce, Chambers, Glavin (2), Banks, McCarthy, Evans, Parker (2), Aylott (1), McHale, Barrowclough (1).

Record Defeat: 0–9 v Notts Co, Division 2, 19 November 1927.

Most League Points (2 for a win): 67, Division 3 (N), 1938–39.

sky SPORTS FACT FILE

John Fair Broley signed for Barnsley in 1899 and featured regularly as a goalkeeper in the reserves, making 3 first-team appearances in 1900–01. He became a significant figure in local politics and in 1913 was the first Labour Councillor to be elected in Barnsley. He later became an Alderman and served as Mayor on two occasions.

Most League Points (3 for a win): 82, Division 1, 1999–2000.

Most League Goals: 118, Division 3 (N), 1933–34.

Highest League Scorer in Season: Cecil McCormack, 33, Division 2, 1950–51.

Most League Goals in Total Aggregate: Ernest Hine, 123, 1921–26 and 1934–38.

Most League Goals in One Match: 5, Frank Eaton v South Shields, Division 3 (N), 9 April 1927; 5, Peter Cunningham v Darlington, Division 3 (N), 4 February 1933; 5, Beau Asquith v Darlington, Division 3 (N), 12 November 1938; 5, Cecil McCormack v Luton T, Division 2, 9 September 1950.

Most Capped Player: Gerry Taggart, 35 (51), Northern Ireland.

Most League Appearances: Barry Murphy, 514, 1962–78.

Youngest League Player: Reuben Noble-Lazarus, 15 years 45 days v Ipswich T, 30 September 2008.

Record Transfer Fee Received: £4,500,000 from Blackburn R for Ashley Ward, December 1998.

Record Transfer Fee Paid: £1,500,000 to Partizan Belgrade for Georgi Hristov, July 1997.

Football League Record: 1898 Elected to Division 2; 1932–34 Division 3 (N); 1934–38 Division 2; 1938–39 Division 3 (N); 1946–53 Division 2; 1953–55 Division 3 (N); 1955–59 Division 2; 1959–65 Division 3; 1965–68 Division 4; 1968–72 Division 3; 1972–79 Division 4; 1979–81 Division 3; 1981–92 Division 2; 1992–97 Division 1; 1997–98 FA Premier League; 1998–2002 Division 1; 2002–04 Division 2; 2004–06 FL 1; 2006–14 FL C; 2014– FL 1.

LATEST SEQUENCES

Longest Sequence of League Wins: 10, 5.3.1955 – 23.4.1955.

Longest Sequence of League Defeats: 9, 14.3.1953 – 25.4.1953.

Longest Sequence of League Draws: 7, 28.3.1911 – 22.4.1911.

Longest Sequence of Unbeaten League Matches: 21, 1.1.1934 – 5.5.1934.

Longest Sequence Without a League Win: 26, 13.12.1952 – 26.8.1953.

Successive Scoring Runs: 44 from 2.10.1926.

Successive Non-scoring Runs: 6 from 27.11.1971.

MANAGERS

Arthur Fairclough 1898–1901
  (*Secretary-Manager*)
John McCartney 1901–04
  (*Secretary-Manager*)
Arthur Fairclough 1904–12
John Hastie 1912–14
Percy Lewis 1914–19
Peter Sant 1919–26
John Commins 1926–29
Arthur Fairclough 1929–30
Brough Fletcher 1930–37
Angus Seed 1937–53
Tim Ward 1953–60
Johnny Steele 1960–71
  (*continued as General Manager*)
John McSeveney 1971–72
Johnny Steele (*General Manager*) 1972–73
Jim Iley 1973–78
Allan Clarke 1978–80
Norman Hunter 1980–84
Bobby Collins 1984–85
Allan Clarke 1985–89
Mel Machin 1989–93
Viv Anderson 1993–94
Danny Wilson 1994–98
John Hendrie 1998–99
Dave Bassett 1999–2000
Nigel Spackman 2001
Steve Parkin 2001–02
Glyn Hodges 2002–03
Gudjon Thordarson 2003–04
Paul Hart 2004–05
Andy Ritchie 2005–06
Simon Davey 2007–09
  (*caretaker from November 2006*)
Mark Robins 2009–11
Keith Hill 2011–12
David Flitcroft 2012–13
Danny Wilson 2013–15
Lee Johnson February 2015–

TEN YEAR LEAGUE RECORD

		P	W	D	L	F	A	Pts	Pos
2005-06	FL 1	46	18	18	10	62	44	72	5
2006-07	FL C	46	15	5	26	53	85	50	20
2007-08	FL C	46	14	13	19	52	65	55	18
2008-09	FL C	46	13	13	20	45	58	52	20
2009-10	FL C	46	14	12	20	53	69	54	18
2010-11	FL C	46	14	14	18	55	66	56	17
2011-12	FL C	46	13	9	24	49	74	48	21
2012-13	FL C	46	14	13	19	56	70	55	21
2013-14	FL C	46	9	12	25	44	77	39	23
2014-15	FL 1	46	17	11	18	62	61	62	11

DID YOU KNOW ?

Sam Kennedy, who scored 5 goals in 9 appearances for Barnsley in 1926–27 including a hat-trick against Notts County, was a multi-talented sportsman. At one time he was the heavyweight boxing champion of Lincolnshire, while in 1947 he reached the last 8 of the English Amateur Golf Championship.

BARNSLEY – FOOTBALL LEAGUE ONE 2014–15 LEAGUE RECORD

Match No.	Date	Venue	Opponents	Result	H/T Score	Lg Pos.	Goalscorers	Attendance
1	Aug 9	H	Crawley T	L 0-1	0-0	20		10,105
2	16	A	Crewe Alex	W 2-1	0-1	15	Lita [57], Cranie [75]	4502
3	19	A	Coventry C	D 2-2	2-2	15	Hourihane [31], Lita [45]	2376
4	23	H	Gillingham	W 4-1	2-0	5	Hourihane [22], Winnall [30], Cole [68], Jennings [76]	9163
5	30	A	Yeovil T	D 1-1	1-0	7	Hourihane [27]	3991
6	Sept 13	H	Milton Keynes D	L 3-5	0-2	13	Hourihane 2 [82, 87], Cole [90]	9192
7	17	A	Fleetwood T	D 0-0	0-0	15		3535
8	20	A	Port Vale	L 1-2	0-1	19	Hourihane (pen) [59]	5415
9	27	H	Swindon T	L 0-3	0-0	21		8879
10	Oct 4	A	Rochdale	W 1-0	1-0	17	Ramage [10]	4380
11	12	H	Bradford C	W 3-1	0-1	13	McArdle (og) [48], Winnall [65], Hemmings [90]	10,499
12	18	A	Peterborough U	L 1-2	1-1	13	Cole [15]	7217
13	21	H	Notts Co	L 2-3	2-1	16	Cole [8], Hourihane [12]	8596
14	25	H	Bristol C	D 2-2	0-1	15	Winnall [59], Hourihane (pen) [68]	9000
15	Nov 1	A	Sheffield U	W 1-0	0-0	12	Winnall [56]	24,495
16	14	H	Colchester U	W 3-2	1-1	11	Winnall [4], Hourihane (pen) [55], Ramage [70]	9191
17	22	A	Chesterfield	L 1-2	0-1	13	Treacy [85]	8544
18	29	H	Scunthorpe U	L 1-2	1-2	15	Trotta [29]	9340
19	Dec 2	H	Doncaster R	D 1-1	1-0	14	Nyatanga [5]	10,058
20	13	A	Walsall	L 1-3	1-2	15	Nyatanga [29]	4433
21	20	H	Leyton Orient	W 2-0	2-0	14	Hourihane [13], Cole [38]	8742
22	26	A	Preston NE	L 0-1	0-1	16		13,793
23	Jan 10	H	Yeovil T	W 2-0	0-0	16	Waring [50], Hourihane (pen) [75]	8518
24	17	A	Doncaster R	L 0-1	0-0	16		9005
25	24	A	Milton Keynes D	L 0-2	0-0	18		8310
26	31	H	Port Vale	W 2-1	1-0	17	Neal (og) [45], Pearson [46]	8660
27	Feb 3	H	Oldham Ath	W 1-0	1-0	13	Hemmings [12]	9135
28	7	A	Swindon T	L 0-2	0-0	15		8380
29	10	H	Fleetwood T	L 1-2	1-2	17	Ramage [5]	8328
30	14	A	Crawley T	L 1-5	0-1	19	Hemmings [65]	2296
31	21	H	Crewe Alex	W 2-0	0-0	18	Nyatanga [66], Rachubka (og) [79]	8635
32	24	A	Scunthorpe U	W 1-0	0-0	16	Scowen [51]	3508
33	28	A	Gillingham	W 1-0	0-0	12	Waring [56]	5905
34	Mar 3	H	Coventry C	W 1-0	0-0	10	Waring [57]	9567
35	7	H	Walsall	W 3-0	1-0	7	Waring 2 [15, 71], Winnall [89]	9275
36	14	A	Oldham Ath	W 3-1	2-1	6	Nyatanga 2 [33, 70], Hourihane [39]	6344
37	17	A	Leyton Orient	D 0-0	0-0	6		4107
38	21	H	Preston NE	D 1-1	0-1	7	Ibehre [79]	12,471
39	28	A	Bristol C	D 2-2	1-1	7	Ibehre [44], Scowen [53]	11,937
40	Apr 4	H	Sheffield U	L 0-2	0-1	9		17,532
41	6	A	Colchester U	L 1-3	1-0	11	Waring [40]	5157
42	11	H	Chesterfield	D 1-1	0-1	10	Winnall [62]	11,268
43	14	A	Notts Co	D 1-1	1-0	9	Winnall [9]	4287
44	18	H	Peterborough U	D 1-1	0-1	10	Berry [90]	8924
45	25	A	Bradford C	L 0-1	0-1	13		15,560
46	May 3	H	Rochdale	W 5-0	0-0	11	Scowen 2 [67, 76], Holgate [84], Hourihane [90], Winnall [90]	9593

Final League Position: 11

GOALSCORERS

League (62): Hourihane 13 (4 pens), Winnall 9, Waring 6, Cole 5, Nyatanga 5, Scowen 4, Hemmings 3, Ramage 3, Ibehre 2, Lita 2, Berry 1, Cranie 1, Holgate 1, Jennings 1, Pearson 1, Treacy 1, Trotta 1, own goals 3.
FA Cup (8): Winnall 3, Jennings 2, Cole 1, Hemmings 1, Hourihane 1.
Capital One Cup (0).
Johnstone's Paint Trophy (4): Berry 1, Cole 1, Hemmings 1, Winnall 1.

Davies A 22+1	Brown R 10+3	Cranie M 39	Nyatanga L 45	Dudgeon J 14	Bailey J 19+6	Hourihane C 45+1	Berry L 25+6	Jennings D 9+11	Winnall S 23+9	Rose D 1 / John D 8+1	Treacy K 6+6	Boakye-Yiadom N —+1	Lita L 11+8	Bree J 6+5	Digby P 5+6	Oates R —+9	Cole D 15+4	Hemmings K 11+12	Abbott B 4+1	Mvoto J 13+2	Noble-Lazarus R —+1	Turnbull R 22 / Stewart C 3+1	Ramage P 19	Williams R 5 / Wildsmith J 2	Trotta M 3+2	Holgate M 18+2	Cowgill J 1+1	Smith G 16+2	Williams G 1+3	Pearson B 21+1	Kiwomya A 3+2	Waring G 17+2	Lalkovic M 13+4	Phenix M —+2 / Maris G 1+1	Scowen J 19+2	O'Sullivan J 7+1	Ibehre J 4+5	*Match No.*
1	2	3	4	5	6	7	8^{1}	9▮	10	11^{2}	12	13																										1
1	2	4	3	5	7	8	6		10^{3}		9^{2}		11^{1}	12	13	14																						2
1	2	4	3	5	7	8	6		10^{3}		9^{2}		11^{1}		12		13	14																				3
1	2	3	4	5		9	7	12	10^{3}		6^{1}		11^{2}				13	14	8																			4
1	2	3	4	5		9	7	12	10^{1}		6^{2}		11^{3}				14	13	8																			5
1	2	3	4	5		8	6	9	14				11^{2}		12		13	10^{1}	7^{3}																			6
1	2	6	3	5		9	8^{2}	10^{3}	14				12				11	7^{1}		4	13																	7
	2^{3}	7	3	5	14	8		6	13		9^{1}		10^{2}	12			11			4		1																8
		7^{2}	4	5	6	8		12	10^{1}		13			2			11	9		3		1																9
	12	3	5		6	9	7		10^{2}		8^{1}			2			11	13				1	4															10
	12	4	5		7	8	9		10^{1}				13	2			11^{2}	14				1	3	6^{3}														11
		3	5		8▮	7	6^{1}		10^{3}				14	2	13		11	12				1	4	9^{2}														12
	12	3	5			8	6		10		13			2^{2}	7^{1}		11					1	4	9														13
		2	3	5	8	6	7	12	9								11					1	4	10^{1}														14
		2	4	5	8	7	6		10^{1}					13			11^{2}	12				1	3	9														15
		2	4	5	7	8	6	12	10^{1}					13			9	11^{2}				1	3															16
		2	4	5^{3}	7^{1}	8	6		11		13		14				10	9^{2}				1	3		12													17
		2	4	5	7^{3}	8	6		10^{1}		14						11	12		13		1	3^{2}		9													18
	2		4		7	8	6^{2}				12		9				11		13			1	3		10^{1}	5												19
	5	6	4^{3}			8	3	9					12				11	13	7^{1}			1			10^{2}	2	14											20
13		4	5		7	8	6	9					12				10^{2}	11^{1}				1▮	3			2												21
1			3		5^{3}	8	7	10					11^{1}			13		9^{2}					4		14	6		2	12									22
						8		14					10^{1}		6					3		1	4^{3}			2		5	12	7	9^{2}	11	13					23
			4			8	7	9^{2}					13							3		1				2▮		5			11	10^{1}	6	12				24
			3			9	7^{2}									12				4		1						5	2	8	6^{1}	11	10^{3}	14	13			25
		2	5			7		8^{1}	13						14			11^{3}		4		1	3							6		10	9^{2}		12			26
		2	5			8		14	12				13					11^{3}		3		1	4							7		10^{2}	6^{1}		9			27
		2^{2}	5			13		12							7^{1}					4		1	3					9		8	14	11	10^{3}		6			28
		2	5			9^{2}		14										11		3^{1}		1	4					12		7	13	10	6^{3}		8			29
		4	3			7							10^{2}			12		13		14		1				9		2^{3}		8		11^{1}	5		6			30
1		2	4		8	9^{1}							10^{3}			14		11^{2}		3								5		7		13			6	12		31
1		2	4		9	10^{2}	14									13				3▮						12		5		8		11^{1}			7	6^{3}		32
1		2	3		12	9										13										4		5		8		11^{2}	10		7	6^{1}		33
1		3	4		12	9	13		14																	2		5		7		11^{1}	10^{2}		8	6^{3}		34
1		3	4		12	9			13																	2		5		6^{3}		11^{2}	10^{1}		8	7	14	35
1		3	4		13	9			12	5																2				6^{1}		11^{2}	10^{3}		8	7	14	36
1		3	4			7	13		10^{1}	5																2				8		11^{2}	12▮		6	9^{3}	14	37
1		3	4		7	8		13	11	5								14				9^{1}				2						10^{3}				6^{2}	12	38
		2	4		12	7			10^{2}											3		6^{1}		1				5		8		13			9		11	39
		3	4			8^{2}		13	10	5								14				9^{3}		1		2		12		7					6		11^{1}	40
1		3	4		7^{1}	6^{2}	14		13	5												12				2				8		11	10^{3}		9			41
1		2	4			8^{2}	13		10	9^{1}													3					5		6		11^{3}	14		7		12	42
1		2	3			7^{3}	12		10	9						14							4			13		5^{2}		8					6		11^{1}	43
1			4			9	6		11	12				14	8^{3}											2	3^{1}	5^{2}		13			10		7			44
1		3	4			9	7^{2}			5					8^{1}											2				6			12	13	10		11	45
1			4			10	7^{2}		11					2^{3}	14	12										3		5	13	6				9^{1}	8			46

FA Cup

First Round	Burton Alb	(h)	5-0
Second Round	Chester FC	(h)	0-0
Replay	Chester FC	(a)	3-0
Third Round	Middlesbrough	(h)	0-2

Capital One Cup

First Round	Crewe Alex	(h)	0-2

Johnstone's Paint Trophy

First Round	York C	(h)	2-0
Second Round	Oldham Ath	(a)	2-2

(*Oldham won 4-2 on penalties*)

BIRMINGHAM CITY

FOUNDATION

In 1875, cricketing enthusiasts who were largely members of Trinity Church, Bordesley, determined to continue their sporting relationships throughout the year by forming a football club which they called Small Heath Alliance. For their earliest games played on waste land in Arthur Street, the team included three Edden brothers and two James brothers.

St Andrew's Stadium, Birmingham B9 4RL.
Telephone: (0844) 557 1875.
Fax: (0844) 557 1975.
Ticket Office: (0844) 557 1875 (then option 2).
Website: www.bcfc.com
Email: reception@bcfc.com
Ground Capacity: 29,409.
Record Attendance: 66,844 v Everton, FA Cup 5th rd, 11 February 1939.
Pitch Measurements: 100m × 66m (109.5yd × 72yd)
Directors: Pano Pavlakis, Ryan Yeung, Shui Cheong Ma.
Manager: Gary Rowett.
Assistant Manager: Kevin Summerfield.
Physio: Dave Hunt.
Colours: Blue shirts, white shorts, blue socks.
Year Formed: 1875.
Turned Professional: 1885.

HONOURS

Football League – FL C:
Runners-up 2006–07, 2008–09;
Division 2: *Champions* 1892–93, 1920–21, 1947–48, 1954–55, 1994–95;
Runners-up 1893–94, 1900–01, 1902–03, 1971–72, 1984–85;
Division 3: *Runners-up* 1991–92.
FA Cup: *Runners-up* 1931, 1956.
Football League Cup: *Winners* 1963, 2011; *Runners-up* 2001.
Leyland DAF Cup: *Winners* 1991.
Auto Windscreens Shield:
Winners 1995.
European Competitions
European Fairs Cup: 1955–58, 1958–60 (*runners-up*), 1960–61 (*runners-up*), 1961–62.
Europa League: 2011–12.

Previous Names: 1875, Small Heath Alliance; 1888, dropped 'Alliance'; 1905, Birmingham; 1945, Birmingham City.

Club Nickname: 'Blues'.

Grounds: 1875, waste ground near Arthur St; 1877, Muntz St, Small Heath; 1906, St Andrew's.

First Football League Game: 3 September 1892, Division 2, v Burslem Port Vale (h) W 5–1 – Charsley; Bayley, Speller; Ollis, Jenkyns, Devey; Hallam (1), Edwards (1), Short (1), Wheldon (2), Hands.

Record League Victory: 12–0 v Walsall T Swifts, Division 2, 17 December 1892 – Charsley; Bayley, Jones; Ollis, Jenkyns, Devey; Hallam (2), Walton (3), Mobley (3), Wheldon (2), Hands (2). 12–0 v Doncaster R, Division 2, 11 April 1903 – Dorrington; Goldie, Wassell; Beer, Dougherty (1), Howard; Athersmith, Leonard (4), McRoberts (1), Wilcox (4), Field (1), (1 og).

Record Cup Victory: 9–2 v Burton W, FA Cup 1st rd, 31 October 1885 – Hedges; Jones, Evetts (1); Fred James, Felton, Arthur James (1); Davenport (2), Stanley (4), Simms, Figures, Morris (1).

Record Defeat: 1–9 v Sheffield W, Division 1, 13 December 1930. 1–9 v Blackburn R, Division 1, 5 January 1895.

sky SPORTS FACT FILE

Birmingham City fans adopted their 'Keep Right On' anthem in the 1955–56 season when they reached the FA Cup final. The song was originally part of the players' pre-match routine but the fans got to know about it and they sang it for the first time during the Cup semi-final match with Sunderland at Hillsborough.

Most League Points (2 for a win): 59, Division 2, 1947–48.

Most League Points (3 for a win): 89, Division 2, 1994–95.

Most League Goals: 103, Division 2, 1893–94 (only 28 games).

Highest League Scorer in Season: Joe Bradford, 29, Division 1, 1927–28.

Most League Goals in Total Aggregate: Joe Bradford, 249, 1920–35.

Most League Goals in One Match: 5, Walter Abbott v Darwen, Division 2, 26 November, 1898; 5, John McMillan v Blackpool, Division 2, 2 March 1901; 5, James Windridge v Glossop, Division 2, 23 January 1915.

Most Capped Player: Maik Taylor, 58 (including 8 on loan at Fulham) (88), Northern Ireland.

Most League Appearances: Frank Womack, 491, 1908–28.

Youngest League Player: Trevor Francis, 16 years 139 days v Cardiff C, 5 September 1970.

Record Transfer Fee Received: £6,700,000 (rising to £8,000,000) from Liverpool for Jermaine Pennant, July 2006.

Record Transfer Fee Paid: £6,000,000 to Valencia for Nikola Zigic, May 2010; £6,000,000 to Manchester U for Ben Foster, June 2010.

Football League Record: 1892 Elected to Division 2; 1894–96 Division 1; 1896–1901 Division 2; 1901–02 Division 1; 1902–03 Division 2; 1903–08 Division 1; 1908–21 Division 2; 1921–39 Division 1; 1946–48 Division 2; 1948–50 Division 1; 1950–55 Division 2; 1955–65 Division 1; 1965–72 Division 2; 1972–79 Division 1; 1979–80 Division 2; 1980–84 Division 1; 1984–85 Division 2; 1985–86 Division 1; 1986–89 Division 2; 1989–92 Division 1; 1992–94 Division 3; 1994–95 Division 2; 1995–2002 Division 1; 2002–06 FA Premier League; 2006–07 FL C; 2007–08 FA Premier League; 2008–09 FL C; 2009–11 FA Premier League; 2011– FL C.

LATEST SEQUENCES

Longest Sequence of League Wins: 13, 17.12.1892 – 16.9.1893.

Longest Sequence of League Defeats: 8, 28.9.1985 – 23.11.1985.

Longest Sequence of League Draws: 8, 18.9.1990 – 23.10.1990.

Longest Sequence of Unbeaten League Matches: 20, 3.9.1994 – 2.1.1995.

Longest Sequence Without a League Win: 17, 28.9.1985 – 18.1.1986.

Successive Scoring Runs: 24 from 24.9.1892.

Successive Non-scoring Runs: 6 from 11.2.1989.

MANAGERS

Alfred Jones 1892–1908 (*Secretary-Manager*)
Alec Watson 1908–10
Bob McRoberts 1910–15
Frank Richards 1915–23
Billy Beer 1923–27
William Harvey 1927–28
Leslie Knighton 1928–33
George Liddell 1933–39
William Camkin and Ted Goodier 1939–45
Harry Storer 1945–48
Bob Brocklebank 1949–54
Arthur Turner 1954–58
Pat Beasley 1959–60
Gil Merrick 1960–64
Joe Mallett 1964–65
Stan Cullis 1965–70
Fred Goodwin 1970–75
Willie Bell 1975–77
Sir Alf Ramsay 1977–78
Jim Smith 1978–82
Ron Saunders 1982–86
John Bond 1986–87
Garry Pendrey 1987–89
Dave Mackay 1989–91
Lou Macari 1991
Terry Cooper 1991–93
Barry Fry 1993–96
Trevor Francis 1996–2001
Steve Bruce 2001–07
Alex McLeish 2007–11
Chris Hughton 2011–12
Lee Clark 2012–14
Gary Rowett October 2014–

TEN YEAR LEAGUE RECORD

		P	W	D	L	F	A	Pts	Pos
2005-06	PR Lge	38	8	10	20	28	50	34	18
2006-07	FL C	46	26	8	12	67	42	86	2
2007-08	PR Lge	38	8	11	19	46	62	35	19
2008-09	FL C	46	23	14	9	54	37	83	2
2009-10	PR Lge	38	13	11	14	38	47	50	9
2010-11	PR Lge	38	8	15	15	37	58	39	18
2011-12	FL C	46	20	16	10	78	51	76	4
2012-13	FL C	46	15	16	15	63	69	61	12
2013-14	FL C	46	11	11	24	58	74	44	21
2014-15	FL C	46	16	15	15	54	64	63	10

DID YOU KNOW ?

Full back Eli Ashurst joined Birmingham in January 1922 and went on to make 70 first-team appearances. He became ill with TB and played his last game for the club in February 1926. He never recovered and passed away in December 1927.

BIRMINGHAM CITY – FL CHAMPIONSHIP 2014–15 LEAGUE RECORD

Match No.	Date	Venue	Opponents	Result	H/T Score	Lg Pos.	Goalscorers	Attendance
1	Aug 9	A	Middlesbrough	L	0-2	0-1	20		18,371
2	16	H	Brighton & HA	W	1-0	0-0	16	Thomas [49]	14,955
3	19	H	Ipswich T	D	2-2	1-0	15	Edgar [30], Donaldson [63]	14,022
4	23	A	Brentford	D	1-1	1-0	16	Caddis (pen) [17]	9076
5	30	A	Wigan Ath	L	0-4	0-3	20		11,708
6	Sept 13	H	Leeds U	D	1-1	1-0	20	Thomas [37]	15,266
7	16	H	Sheffield W	L	0-2	0-0	20		14,085
8	20	A	Norwich C	D	2-2	2-0	20	Reilly [8], Gray [41]	26,351
9	27	H	Fulham	L	1-2	1-0	21	Cotterill [38]	14,132
10	30	A	Millwall	W	3-1	2-0	19	Donaldson [32], Cotterill [40], Thomas [84]	9086
11	Oct 4	A	Charlton Ath	D	1-1	0-1	20	Davis [53]	16,369
12	18	H	Bolton W	L	0-1	0-1	21		15,149
13	21	A	Blackburn R	L	0-1	0-0	21		12,852
14	25	H	Bournemouth	L	0-8	0-3	23		13,837
15	Nov 1	A	Wolverhampton W	D	0-0	0-0	22		25,135
16	4	H	Watford	W	2-1	1-1	22	Donaldson 2 [2, 85]	18,309
17	8	H	Cardiff C	D	0-0	0-0	23		15,950
18	22	A	Rotherham U	W	1-0	0-0	19	Donaldson [62]	10,937
19	29	H	Nottingham F	W	2-1	1-0	17	Cotterill [10], Caddis (pen) [89]	18,595
20	Dec 6	A	Blackpool	L	0-1	0-0	19		11,672
21	13	H	Reading	W	6-1	4-1	15	Caddis [4], Gray 3 [11, 24, 45], Shinnie [46], Cotterill [60]	15,240
22	20	A	Huddersfield T	W	1-0	0-0	15	Cotterill [70]	13,203
23	26	H	Derby Co	L	0-4	0-2	16		23,851
24	28	A	Nottingham F	W	3-1	3-0	14	Cotterill [35], Donaldson 2 [38, 45]	26,212
25	Jan 10	H	Wigan Ath	W	3-1	2-1	12	Donaldson 3 [2, 14, 64]	16,117
26	17	A	Leeds U	D	1-1	1-0	11	Caddis (pen) [8]	23,534
27	27	A	Sheffield W	D	0-0	0-0	11		18,385
28	31	H	Norwich C	D	0-0	0-0	11		17,835
29	Feb 7	A	Fulham	D	1-1	1-1	11	Cotterill [14]	19,086
30	10	H	Millwall	L	0-1	0-0	11		14,186
31	18	H	Middlesbrough	D	1-1	1-0	12	Caddis (pen) [45]	15,101
32	21	A	Brighton & HA	L	3-4	1-1	15	Donaldson [13], Thomas [76], Novak [90]	25,768
33	24	A	Ipswich T	L	2-4	0-1	17	Davis 2 [57, 79]	17,161
34	28	H	Brentford	W	1-0	1-0	13	Tarkowski (og) [40]	15,333
35	Mar 4	H	Blackpool	W	1-0	1-0	13	Shinnie [36]	15,111
36	7	A	Derby Co	D	2-2	0-1	14	Caddis (pen) [90], Donaldson [90]	31,522
37	14	H	Huddersfield T	D	1-1	1-1	15	Cotterill [10]	14,747
38	21	A	Cardiff C	L	0-2	0-0	15		20,602
39	Apr 3	H	Rotherham U	W	2-1	2-0	15	Tesche [27], Donaldson [43]	16,569
40	6	A	Bournemouth	L	2-4	2-2	15	Donaldson [18], Cotterill [21]	11,084
41	11	H	Wolverhampton W	W	2-1	1-1	14	Kiernan [25], Gray [61]	19,330
42	14	H	Blackburn R	D	2-2	0-1	14	Grounds [64], Gray [78]	15,066
43	18	A	Watford	L	0-1	0-0	14		19,156
44	22	H	Reading	W	1-0	0-0	13	Donaldson [83]	14,604
45	25	H	Charlton Ath	W	1-0	0-0	11	Dyer [82]	17,775
46	May 2	A	Bolton W	W	1-0	1-0	10	Tesche [42]	18,614

Final League Position: 10

GOALSCORERS

League (54): Donaldson 15, Cotterill 9, Caddis 6 (5 pens), Gray 6, Thomas 4, Davis 3, Shinnie 2, Tesche 2, Dyer 1, Edgar 1, Grounds 1, Kiernan 1, Novak 1, Reilly 1, own goal 1.
FA Cup (4): Thomas 2, Grounds 1, Novak 1.
Capital One Cup (3): Caddis 1, Donaldson 1, Duffy 1.

Randolph D 45	Eardley N 4	Hall G 7	Grounds J 45	Robinson P 30+4	Shinnie A 24+3	Edgar D 14+2	Gleeson S 34+5	Thomas W 9+24	Novak L 9+12	Gray D 28+13	Duffy M 1+3	Donaldson C 44+2	Spector J 20+4	Cotterill D 42	Davis D 36+6	Caddis P 44+1	Brown R —+1	Johnstone D —+2	Shea B 2+4	Reilly C 4+13	Arthur K 7+2	Packwood W —+1	Doyle C 1	Morrison M 21	Moussi G —+2	Zigic N —+9	Dyer L 7+11	Kiernan R 11+1	Tesche R 12	Fabbrini D 5	Match No.
1	2	3	4	5	6^2	7	8	9^1	10	11	12	13																			1
1			4	5	13		3	12	11^1	9^3		10	2	6	7^2	8	14														2
1			4	5	14		3	12	11^3	9		10	2	6^1	8^2	7		13													3
1			4	5			3	13	11^3	9	12	10	2	6	7^2	8		14													4
1			4		5		3	7^3	12	11^2	14	13	10	2	9^1	8	6														5
1	2		5	4^3	12		3	11		13		10	14	6	8^2	7			9^1												6
1	2^3		5	4			3	14	11	13		10	12	9	8^2	7			6^1												7
1			5	4^1			3	13		11^2		10	2	9	6	7		12		8											8
1			5	4			3		13	9^1		8^3	11	2^2	10	7	14			12	6										9
1			5	4			3	9	13			11		6	7	2				8^1	10^2	12									10
1			5	4			3	9	13			12		11	8	6	2			7^2	10^1										11
1^1			5	4			3	7^2	14	13	9	11		10^1	6^3	2				12	8										12
	2^4		5	4	14		3	7	12			9^3		11	10^1	6				13	8^2		1								13
1		2	5	4			3^4	8^1	11^2	9^3		10		6	12	7				13	14										14
1			5	4	9^3		6	14				11^2		8	7	2		12	13	10^1				3							15
1			5	4	9^1		6	13				12		8	7	2				10^2				3							16
1			5	4	9^2		6	12^4				13		8	7	2				10^1				3							17
1			5	4	9^1		6		12	8^2		11		10	7	2				13				3							18
1			5	4	9^2		6		12	10^1		11		8	7	2				13				3							19
1			5	4			7		9^3	10^1	14	11		8^2	6	2		13	12					3							20
1			5	4	8^2		7	14		9^1		11^3		10	6	2								3	12	13					21
1			5	4	9^1	14	7		12	10^2		11		8	6	2				13				3							22
1			5	4	10^1		7	12	14	9		11^3		6^2	8	2				3						13					23
1			5	4	9^3		7			10^1		11		8^2	6	2				12				3		14	13				24
1			5	4	9^2		7	13	12	10^1		11		8	6	2				3						14					25
1			5	4	9^1	12	7		13	10^3		11		8^2	6	2				3						14					26
1			5	4	9^1		7	14	10			11^3	12	8	6	2				3^2						13					27
1			5	4	12		7			10		11^1	3	8	6	2										9^2	13				28
1			5	4	9^2		7			12		11	3	8	6	2				14						13	10^1				29
1			5	4	9^3		7		12	13		11	3	8	6	2				14						10^2					30
1			5	4	9^2		7	14		10^3		11	3	8	6^1	2				12						13					31
1			5	4	9^1		6	13	12	8		11	3			2				14						13	10^2	7^3			32
1			5	4			7	11	9	12		10^2	3	6^2	8	2				14						13					33
1			5		9^1		7^4			13	10^5	11	3	8^2	6	2										12	4				34
1			5		9^2				12	14	10^3	11	3	8	6	2				13								4	7^1		35
1			5		9^1			12	11^2	14	13		3	8	7	2										10^3	4	6			36
1			5		9^2			12		10^1		11^3	3	8	7	2										13	14	4	6		37
1			5	14			7	13		10^1		11	3^2	6	8^3	2										12	4	9			38
1			5		9^1		7			10^2		11		8	13	2								3		12	4	6			39
1			5	4^4	9^1			13		12		11^2		8	6	2								3		10^3	14	7			40
1			5						10^3			11	12	8	13	2								3		14	4^2	7	9^1		41
1			5					7	13			10	11		9^3	14	2							4		12	3	6^1	9^4		42
1			5		9^3			6	13	14		10^2	11		8	12	2							3			4	7	7^1		43
1			9		12			7	11^3		14		10	2			5^5							3		13	4	6	8^2		44
1			5						13			10	11	3	8^2	6	2							4		12		7	9^1		45
1			5					6	13			8	11^2	4		12	2							3		10		7	9^1		46

FA Cup

Third Round	Blyth Spartans	(a)	3-2
Fourth Round	WBA	(h)	1-2

Capital One Cup

First Round	Cambridge U	(h)	3-1
(aet)			
Second Round	Sunderland	(h)	0-3

BLACKBURN ROVERS

FOUNDATION

It was in 1875 that some public school old boys called a meeting at which the Blackburn Rovers club was formed and the colours blue and white adopted. The leading light was John Lewis, later to become a founder of the Lancashire FA, a famous referee who was in charge of two FA Cup finals, and a vice-president of both the FA and the Football League.

Ewood Park, Blackburn, Lancashire BB2 4JF.

Telephone: (01254) 372 001.

Fax: (01254) 671 042.

Ticket Office: (01254) 372 000.

Website: www.rovers.co.uk

Email: (via website)

Ground Capacity: 31,154.

Record Attendance: 62,522 v Bolton W, FA Cup 6th rd, 2 March 1929.

Pitch Measurements: 105m × 65.84m (115yd × 72yd)

Managing Director: Derek Shaw.

Directors: Robert Coar, Gandhi Babu.

Manager: Gary Bowyer.

Assistant Manager: Terry McPhillips.

Physio: Neil Fitzhenry.

Colours: Blue and white halved shirts, white shorts with blue trim, blue socks.

Year Formed: 1875.

Turned Professional: 1880.

Club Nickname: 'Rovers'.

HONOURS

FA Premier League:
Champions 1994–95;
Runners-up 1993–94.

Football League – Division 1:
Champions 1911–12, 1913–14;
Runners-up 2000–01;
Division 2: *Champions* 1938–39;
Runners-up 1957–58;
Division 3: *Champions* 1974–75;
Runners-up 1979–80.

FA Cup: *Winners* 1884, 1885, 1886, 1890, 1891, 1928; *Runners-up* 1882, 1960.

Football League Cup: *Winners* 2002.

Full Members' Cup: *Winners* 1987.

European Competitions
European Cup: 1995–96.
UEFA Cup: 1994–95, 1998–99, 2002–03, 2003–04, 2006–07, 2007–08.
Intertoto Cup: 2007.

Grounds: 1875, all matches played away; 1876, Oozehead Ground; 1877, Pleasington Cricket Ground; 1878, Alexandra Meadows; 1881, Leamington Road; 1890, Ewood Park.

First Football League Game: 15 September 1888, Football League, v Accrington (h) D 5–5 – Arthur; Beverley, James Southworth; Douglas, Almond, Forrest; Beresford (1), Walton, John Southworth (1), Fecitt (1), Townley (2).

Record League Victory: 9–0 v Middlesbrough, Division 2, 6 November 1954 – Elvy; Suart, Eckersley; Clayton, Kelly, Bell; Mooney (3), Crossan (2), Briggs, Quigley (3), Langton (1).

Record Cup Victory: 11–0 v Rossendale, FA Cup 1st rd, 13 October 1884 – Arthur; Hopwood, McIntyre; Forrest, Blenkhorn, Lofthouse; Sowerbutts (2), Jimmy Brown (1), Fecitt (4), Barton (3), Birtwistle (1).

sky SPORTS FACT FILE

Blackburn Rovers played their first competitive European games in the short-lived Friendship Cup in 1961–62. They beat Nancy at home 3-1 and lost the away leg 1-0, providing the Football League with 2 points against the French League in the competition between clubs of the two competitions.

Record Defeat: 0–8 v Arsenal, Division 1, 25 February 1933; 0-8 v Lincoln C, Division 2, 29 August 1953.

Most League Points (2 for a win): 60, Division 3, 1974–75.

Most League Points (3 for a win): 91, Division 1, 2000–01.

Most League Goals: 114, Division 2, 1954–55.

Highest League Scorer in Season: Ted Harper, 43, Division 1, 1925–26.

Most League Goals in Total Aggregate: Simon Garner, 168, 1978–92.

Most League Goals in One Match: 7, Tommy Briggs v Bristol R, Division 2, 5 February 1955.

Most Capped Player: Morten Gamst Pedersen, 70 (82), Norway.

Most League Appearances: Derek Fazackerley, 596, 1970–86.

Youngest League Player: Harry Dennison, 16 years 155 days v Bristol C, 8 April 1911.

Record Transfer Fee Received: £18,000,000 from Manchester C for Roque Santa Cruz, June 2009.

Record Transfer Fee Paid: £8,000,000 to Huddersfield T for Jordan Rhodes, August 2012; £8,000,000 to Manchester U for Andy Cole, December 2001.

Football League Record: 1888 Founder Member of the League; 1936–39 Division 2; 1946–48 Division 1; 1948–58 Division 2; 1958–66 Division 1; 1966–71 Division 2; 1971–75 Division 3; 1975–79 Division 2; 1979–80 Division 3; 1980–92 Division 2; 1992–99 FA Premier League; 1999–2001 Division 1; 2001–12 FA Premier League; 2012– FL C.

LATEST SEQUENCES

Longest Sequence of League Wins: 8, 1.3.1980 – 7.4.1980.

Longest Sequence of League Defeats: 7, 12.3.1966 – 16.4.1966.

Longest Sequence of League Draws: 5, 11.10.1975 – 1.11.1975.

Longest Sequence of Unbeaten League Matches: 23, 30.9.1987 – 27.3.1988.

Longest Sequence Without a League Win: 16, 11.11.1978 – 24.3.1979.

Successive Scoring Runs: 32 from 24.4.1954.

Successive Non-scoring Runs: 4 from 25.11.2009.

MANAGERS

Thomas Mitchell 1884–96
 (*Secretary-Manager*)
J. Walmsley 1896–1903
 ((*Secretary-Manager*)
R. B. Middleton 1903–25
Jack Carr 1922–26
 (*Team Manager under Middleton to 1925*)
Bob Crompton 1926–31
 (*Hon. Team Manager*)
Arthur Barritt 1931–36
 (*had been Secretary from 1927*)
Reg Taylor 1936–38
Bob Crompton 1938–41
Eddie Hapgood 1944–47
Will Scott 1947
Jack Bruton 1947–49
Jackie Bestall 1949–53
Johnny Carey 1953–58
Dally Duncan 1958–60
Jack Marshall 1960–67
Eddie Quigley 1967–70
Johnny Carey 1970–71
Ken Furphy 1971–73
Gordon Lee 1974–75
Jim Smith 1975–78
Jim Iley 1978
John Pickering 1978–79
Howard Kendall 1979–81
Bobby Saxton 1981–86
Don Mackay 1987–91
Kenny Dalglish 1991–95
Ray Harford 1995–96
Roy Hodgson 1997–98
Brian Kidd 1998–99
Graeme Souness 2000–04
Mark Hughes 2004–08
Paul Ince 2008
Sam Allardyce 2008–10
Steve Kean 2010–12
Henning Berg 2012
Michael Appleton 2013
Gary Bowyer March 2013–

TEN YEAR LEAGUE RECORD

		P	W	D	L	F	A	Pts	Pos
2005-06	PR Lge	38	19	6	13	51	42	63	6
2006-07	PR Lge	38	15	7	16	52	54	52	10
2007-08	PR Lge	38	15	13	10	50	48	58	7
2008-09	PR Lge	38	10	11	17	40	60	41	15
2009-10	PR Lge	38	13	11	14	41	55	50	10
2010-11	PR Lge	38	11	10	17	46	59	43	15
2011-12	PR Lge	38	8	7	23	48	78	31	19
2012-13	FL C	46	14	16	16	55	62	58	17
2013-14	FL C	46	18	16	12	70	62	70	8
2014-15	FL C	46	17	16	13	66	59	67	9

DID YOU KNOW

Blackburn Rovers have traditionally played in blue-and-white halved shirts for almost all their long history, although the change colours have altered. A colour clash for the 1957–58 FA Cup semi-final with Bolton saw them switch to black-and-white stripes. Rovers lost 2-1 and have not worn the colours since.

BLACKBURN ROVERS – FL CHAMPIONSHIP 2014–15 LEAGUE RECORD

Match No.	Date	Venue	Opponents	Result	H/T Score	Lg Pos.	Goalscorers	Attendance
1	Aug 8	H	Cardiff C	D	1-1	1-1	1	Cairney [40]	15,625
2	16	A	Blackpool	W	2-1	1-0	5	Gestede 2 [26, 47]	12,130
3	19	A	Norwich C	L	1-3	1-1	14	Cairney [1]	25,835
4	23	H	Bournemouth	W	3-2	3-0	10	Rhodes [13], Hanley [21], Gestede [24]	13,900
5	30	A	Wolverhampton W	L	1-3	0-2	14	Rhodes (pen) [59]	21,260
6	Sept 13	H	Wigan Ath	W	3-1	0-0	8	Marshall 2 [53, 82], Rhodes [56]	15,782
7	17	H	Derby Co	L	2-3	1-2	13	Keogh (og) [1], Gestede [78]	13,566
8	20	A	Fulham	W	1-0	0-0	9	Rhodes [58]	16,456
9	27	H	Watford	D	2-2	0-2	10	Gestede [46], Tunnicliffe [77]	14,084
10	30	A	Rotherham U	L	0-2	0-2	11		9525
11	Oct 4	H	Huddersfield T	D	0-0	0-0	12		14,662
12	18	A	Ipswich T	D	1-1	0-0	13	Marshall [90]	16,972
13	21	H	Birmingham C	W	1-0	0-0	11	Marshall [51]	12,852
14	25	A	Nottingham F	W	3-1	0-1	8	Baptiste [68], Gestede [75], Rhodes [77]	27,345
15	Nov 1	H	Reading	W	3-1	1-1	7	Gestede 2 [17, 68], Marshall [55]	14,237
16	4	A	Millwall	D	2-2	1-0	8	Duffy [37], Gestede [65]	8250
17	8	A	Brighton & HA	D	1-1	0-1	7	Gestede [51]	24,840
18	22	H	Leeds U	W	2-1	0-1	6	Rhodes 2 (1 pen) [71, 88 (p)]	21,432
19	29	A	Middlesbrough	D	1-1	0-0	6	Gestede [90]	18,152
20	Dec 6	H	Sheffield W	L	1-2	1-1	7	Baptiste [16]	14,920
21	13	A	Brentford	L	1-3	1-1	8	Gestede [45]	11,848
22	20	H	Charlton Ath	W	2-0	2-0	8	Rhodes 2 [6, 19]	13,231
23	26	A	Bolton W	L	1-2	1-0	8	King [41]	23,203
24	28	H	Middlesbrough	D	0-0	0-0	9		22,340
25	Jan 11	H	Wolverhampton W	L	0-1	0-0	10		15,335
26	17	A	Wigan Ath	D	1-1	1-0	10	Evans [15]	14,652
27	27	A	Derby Co	L	0-2	0-0	10		26,373
28	31	H	Fulham	W	2-1	1-0	9	Marshall [12], Rhodes [61]	13,603
29	Feb 7	A	Watford	L	0-1	0-0	9		15,011
30	10	H	Rotherham U	W	2-1	1-0	9	Conway [41], Rhodes [86]	13,403
31	17	A	Cardiff C	D	1-1	0-0	9	Gestede [90]	19,057
32	21	H	Blackpool	D	1-1	1-1	10	Rhodes [14]	14,906
33	24	H	Norwich C	L	1-2	1-0	10	Baptiste [22]	13,530
34	28	A	Bournemouth	D	0-0	0-0	11		10,196
35	Mar 4	A	Sheffield W	W	2-1	2-0	10	Rhodes [17], Henley [26]	19,593
36	11	H	Bolton W	W	1-0	0-0	10	Rhodes [90]	15,362
37	14	H	Charlton Ath	W	3-1	2-0	10	Rhodes 2 [15, 78], Conway [18]	14,888
38	17	H	Brentford	L	2-3	2-1	10	Gestede [5], Taylor, C [45]	13,382
39	21	H	Brighton & HA	L	0-1	0-1	10		13,605
40	Apr 4	A	Leeds U	W	3-0	0-0	10	Cairney [62], Rhodes [69], Spearing [80]	25,293
41	11	A	Reading	D	0-0	0-0	10		17,564
42	14	A	Birmingham C	D	2-2	1-0	9	Kilgallon [8], Rhodes [68]	15,066
43	18	H	Nottingham F	D	3-3	2-2	9	Gestede 3 [3, 35, 82]	13,876
44	21	H	Millwall	W	2-0	0-0	9	Gestede [78], Rhodes [90]	12,884
45	25	A	Huddersfield T	D	2-2	2-1	9	Gestede [28], Rhodes [31]	17,056
46	May 2	H	Ipswich T	W	3-2	2-1	9	Rhodes [36], Conway [42], Gestede [58]	16,869

Final League Position: 9

GOALSCORERS

League (66): Rhodes 21 (2 pens), Gestede 20, Marshall 6, Baptiste 3, Cairney 3, Conway 3, Duffy 1, Evans 1, Hanley 1, Henley 1, Kilgallon 1, King 1, Spearing 1, Taylor, C 1, Tunnicliffe 1, own goal 1.
FA Cup (9): King 3, Taylor, C 3, Gestede 2 (1 pen), Conway 1.
Capital One Cup (0).

Robinson P 7	Baptiste A 29+3	Hanley G 31	Kilgallon M 22	Olsson M 41	Cairney T 32+7	Lowe J 11+1	Evans C 37+1	Conway C 29+9	Rhodes J 40+5	Gestede R 31+8	Williamson L 23+5	King J 5+11	Marshall B 37+5	Varney L —+11	Dunn D 1+8	Henley A 15+3	Taylor C 7+9	Tunnicliffe R 10+7	Duffy S 18+1	Steele J 31	Eastwood S 6	Brown C 11+9	Spearing J 12+3	Spurr T 10+2	Henry D 3	Raya D 2	Taylor P 2+3	O'Sullivan J 1+1	Lenihan D 2+1	Match No.
1	2	3	4¹	5	6	7	8	9	10	11	12																			1
1	2	4		5	7	3	8	9	10²	11	12	6¹	13																	2
1	3	4		5	6	2	7	9¹	10²	11	8¹	12	13	14																3
1	4	3		5	7	2	8	9	10²	11	12		6¹		13															4
1	3	4			6	2	7	8¹	11		9²		10¹	14	12	5	13													5
1	2	3	4	5	7		8	9²	10	11¹	6³	12				13	14													6
1	2	3	4³	5	7		8²	9¹	11	10		6	13			12	14													7
	2	3		5	6¹		8	12	11³	10	7²		9	14		13			4	1										8
	2¹	3		5	6		8	12	11	10	7²		9			13			4	1										9
		3		5			8	9	10	11²	13	2	12	14		6³	7		4	1										10
		3		5	7		6		11		9	8	2			12	10¹		4	1										11
12			4⁴	5	6³		7	9¹	10²	11	8		2			13	14	3		1										12
		3		5	6		8		10²	11¹	7		9		13	12	2		4	1										13
	2	3		5	10		8²	13	11¹	12	7		9³	14		6			4	1										14
	2	3		5	6		7	14	10	11²	8¹		9³		13	12			4	1										15
	2	3		5	6		8	12	10²	11	9¹		13			7			4	1										16
	2	3		5	8¹		7	12	13	11²	9		10			6			4	1										17
	2	3		5	6⁴		7¹	10	11³	8²	9				13	14	12		4	1										18
	2	3³		5			7¹	13	11²	10	8		9		12	6			4	1		14								19
	2	3		5	7		6²	10	11¹	8³	9			14		12			4	1		13								20
	2²	3		5	14		8	6³	12	11	7¹		9		13		10		4	1										21
	2	3		5	8³		7		11	10²	12	13	9¹	14		6			4	1										22
		3		5	10²		8	13	11	12	9⁵		6³		14	2	7		4	1										23
	2		4	5¹	12			6	10	11	7²		9		13		8	3		1										24
	2²	3		5	7			12	10	11¹	8³	14	9			6			4	1		13								25
14		3	4	5¹	7³	2	8	6	10	12	9				13					1		11²								26
	2	3¹	4	5	10²	7	8	9	14	12³	11					6				1		13								27
		3	4	5	13	2	7	9	10	6¹	12									1		11	8²							28
		3	4	5	13	2	7	6	11	12	14		9²							1		10³	8¹							29
12		3	4	5	6¹	2³	8	9	10	14					13					1		11²	7							30
		3	4	5	7		8¹	9	11	10					2		6²			1		13	12							31
	2	3	4		6		8²	9	10	11¹					13		12³			1		14	7	5						32
	2	3	4		6		8	9	10²	11	12³				13					1		14	7¹							33
	3	4		5	14		8	9	12	11	13		10³		2		6¹			1			7²							34
	4						10				9		7		2	6				1		11	8	5	3					35
	4			5¹	7		8²	9	11	14	12		6		2					1		10³	13		3					36
	4			8	13		9²	10	7³	6					2		12			1		11	14	5	3¹					37
	3	4		8	7			11	10³		9¹				2		6			1		13	12	5						38
	3	4		5	8			11	12		9				2		6¹				1	10²	7	13						39
	3	4		5	6			10	11¹		8		9		2²		13³	7			1						12		14	40
	3			5	6¹			10	7		9				2						1	11	8	4			12			41
	3			5	13		8	9	11	12					2						1	10²	7	4			6¹			42
		4		5	7		6	10	11		8		9¹		2						1		3				12			43
		4³		5	14		8	9	13	11					2						1	10²	7		3		6¹		12	44
				5	12		8	9	11	10	7²		13		2								4			1	6¹		3	45
				5			9	8	11	10³	6	12	13		7¹	2							4			1			3	46

FA Cup

Third Round	Charlton Ath	(a)	2-1
Fourth Round	Swansea C	(h)	3-1
Fifth Round	Stoke C	(h)	4-1
Sixth Round	Liverpool	(a)	0-0
Replay	Liverpool	(h)	0-1

Capital One Cup

First Round	Scunthorpe U	(h)	0-1

BLACKPOOL

FOUNDATION

Old boys of St John's School, who had formed themselves into a football club, decided to establish a club bearing the name of their town and Blackpool FC came into being at a meeting at the Stanley Arms Hotel in the summer of 1887. In their first season playing at Raikes Hall Gardens, the club won both the Lancashire Junior Cup and the Fylde Cup.

Bloomfield Road, Seasiders Way, Blackpool, Lancashire FY1 6JJ.

Telephone: (01253) 685 000.

Fax: (01253) 405 011.

Ticket Office: (0844) 847 1953.

Website: www.blackpoolfc.co.uk

Email: secretary@blackpoolfc.co.uk

Ground Capacity: 16,063.

Record Attendance: 38,098 v Wolverhampton W, Division 1, 17 September 1955.

Pitch Measurements: 100m × 64m (109.5yd × 70yd)

Chairman: Karl Oyston.

Manager: Neil McDonald.

First-Team Coach: Richie Kyle.

Physio: Phil Horner.

Colours: Tangerine shirts, white shorts, tangerine socks.

Year Formed: 1887.

Turned Professional: 1887.

HONOURS

Football League – Division 1:
Runners-up 1955–56;
Division 2: *Champions* 1929–30;
Runners-up 1936–37, 1969–70;
Division 4: *Runners-up* 1984–85.
FA Cup: *Winners* 1953;
Runners-up 1948, 1951.
Football League Cup: Best season: semi-final, 1962.
Anglo-Italian Cup: *Winners* 1971;
Runners-up 1972.
LDV Vans Trophy: *Winners* 2002, 2004.

Previous Name: 'South Shore' combined with Blackpool in 1899, twelve years after the latter had been formed on the breaking up of the old 'Blackpool St John's' club.

Club Nickname: 'The Seasiders'.

Grounds: 1887, Raikes Hall Gardens; 1897, Athletic Grounds; 1899, Raikes Hall Gardens; 1899, Bloomfield Road.

First Football League Game: 5 September 1896, Division 2, v Lincoln C (a) L 1–3 – Douglas; Parr, Bowman; Stuart, Stirzaker, Norris; Clarkin, Donnelly, Robert Parkinson, Mount (1), Jack Parkinson.

Record League Victory: 7–0 v Reading, Division 2, 10 November 1928 – Mercer; Gibson, Hamilton, Watson, Wilson, Grant, Ritchie, Oxberry (2), Hampson (5), Tufnell, Neal. 7–0 v Preston NE (away), Division 1, 1 May 1948 – Robinson; Shimwell, Crosland; Buchan, Hayward, Kelly; Hobson, Munro (1), McIntosh (5), McCall, Rickett (1). 7–0 v Sunderland, Division 1, 5 October 1957 – Farm; Armfield, Garrett, Kelly J, Gratrix, Kelly H, Matthews, Taylor (2), Charnley (2), Durie (2), Perry (1).

Record Cup Victory: 7–1 v Charlton Ath, League Cup 2nd rd, 25 September 1963 – Harvey; Armfield, Martin; Crawford, Gratrix, Cranston; Lea, Ball (1), Charnley (4), Durie (1), Oates (1).

sky SPORTS FACT FILE

Between 1949–50 and 1958–59 Blackpool finished in the top 10 of the First Division in all but one season, achieving their best-ever position as runners-up in 1955–56. This success was not always reflected in attendances and in 1953–54 they were the worst supported of all 22 First Division clubs, despite having won the FA Cup the previous season.

Record Defeat: 1–10 v Small Heath, Division 2, 2 March 1901 and v Huddersfield T, Division 1, 13 December 1930.

Most League Points (2 for a win): 58, Division 2, 1929–30 and Division 2, 1967–68.

Most League Points (3 for a win): 86, Division 4, 1984–85.

Most League Goals: 98, Division 2, 1929–30.

Highest League Scorer in Season: Jimmy Hampson, 45, Division 2, 1929–30.

Most League Goals in Total Aggregate: Jimmy Hampson, 248, 1927–38.

Most League Goals in One Match: 5, Jimmy Hampson v Reading, Division 2, 10 November 1928; 5, Jimmy McIntosh v Preston NE, Division 1, 1 May 1948.

Most Capped Player: Jimmy Armfield, 43, England.

Most League Appearances: Jimmy Armfield, 568, 1952–71.

Youngest League Player: Matty Kay, 16 years 32 days v Scunthorpe U, 13 November 2005.

Record Transfer Fee Received: £6,750,000 from Liverpool for Charlie Adam, July 2011.

Record Transfer Fee Paid: £1,250,000 to Leicester C for D.J. Campbell, August 2010.

Football League Record: 1896 Elected to Division 2; 1899 Failed re-election; 1900 Re-elected; 1900–30 Division 2; 1930–33 Division 1; 1933–37 Division 2; 1937–67 Division 1; 1967–70 Division 2; 1970–71 Division 1; 1971–78 Division 2; 1978–81 Division 3; 1981–85 Division 4; 1985–90 Division 3; 1990–92 Division 4; 1992–2000 Division 2; 2000–01 Division 3; 2001–04 Division 2; 2004–07 FL 1; 2007–10 FL C; 2010–11 FA Premier League; 2011–15 FL C; 2015– FL 1.

LATEST SEQUENCES

Longest Sequence of League Wins: 9, 21.11.1936 – 1.1.1937.

Longest Sequence of League Defeats: 8, 26.11.1898 – 7.1.1899.

Longest Sequence of League Draws: 5, 4.12.1976 – 1.1.1977.

Longest Sequence of Unbeaten League Matches: 17, 6.4.1968 – 21.9.1968.

Longest Sequence Without a League Win: 19, 19.12.1970 – 24.4.1971.

Successive Scoring Runs: 33 from 23.2.1929.

Successive Non-scoring Runs: 5 from 25.11.1989.

MANAGERS

Tom Barcroft 1903–33
(*Secretary-Manager*)
John Cox 1909–11
Bill Norman 1919–23
Maj. Frank Buckley 1923–27
Sid Beaumont 1927–28
Harry Evans 1928–33
(*Hon. Team Manager*)
Alex 'Sandy' Macfarlane 1933–35
Joe Smith 1935–58
Ronnie Suart 1958–67
Stan Mortensen 1967–69
Les Shannon 1969–70
Bob Stokoe 1970–72
Harry Potts 1972–76
Allan Brown 1976–78
Bob Stokoe 1978–79
Stan Ternent 1979–80
Alan Ball 1980–81
Allan Brown 1981–82
Sam Ellis 1982–89
Jimmy Mullen 1989–90
Graham Carr 1990
Bill Ayre 1990–94
Sam Allardyce 1994–96
Gary Megson 1996–97
Nigel Worthington 1997–99
Steve McMahon 2000–04
Colin Hendry 2004–05
Simon Grayson 2005–08
Ian Holloway 2009–12
Michael Appleton 2012–13
Paul Ince 2013–14
José Riga 2014
Lee Clark 2014–15
Neil McDonald June 2015–

TEN YEAR LEAGUE RECORD

		P	W	D	L	F	A	Pts	Pos
2005-06	FL 1	46	12	17	17	56	64	53	19
2006-07	FL 1	46	24	11	11	76	49	83	3
2007-08	FL C	46	12	18	16	59	64	54	19
2008-09	FL C	46	13	17	16	47	58	56	16
2009-10	FL C	46	19	13	14	74	58	70	6
2010-11	PR Lge	38	10	9	19	55	78	39	19
2011-12	FL C	46	20	15	11	79	59	75	5
2012-13	FL C	46	14	17	15	62	63	59	15
2013-14	FL C	46	11	13	22	38	66	46	20
2014-15	FL C	46	4	14	28	36	91	26	24

DID YOU KNOW

Benny Green who played for Blackpool between 1913 and 1915 joined the King's Own Royal Lancaster Regiment in July 1916. He went with his regiment to France towards the end of the year and was killed in action on 26 April 1917.

BLACKPOOL – FL CHAMPIONSHIP 2014–15 LEAGUE RECORD

Match No.	Date	Venue	Opponents	Result		H/T Score	Lg Pos.	Goalscorers	Attendance
1	Aug 9	A	Nottingham F	L	0-2	0-2	20		28,028
2	16	H	Blackburn R	L	1-2	0-1	23	Cywka [53]	12,130
3	19	H	Brentford	L	1-2	1-1	24	Delfouneso [17]	9939
4	23	A	Wigan Ath	L	0-1	0-1	23		12,113
5	30	A	Millwall	L	1-2	0-1	24	Ranger [71]	9877
6	Sept 13	H	Wolverhampton W	D	0-0	0-0	23		12,233
7	16	H	Watford	L	0-1	0-0	23		9695
8	20	A	Brighton & HA	D	0-0	0-0	23		24,569
9	27	H	Norwich C	L	1-3	0-0	24	Delfouneso [46]	11,232
10	30	A	Middlesbrough	D	1-1	1-1	24	Miller [25]	15,213
11	Oct 3	H	Cardiff C	W	1-0	0-0	23	Zoko [64]	10,502
12	18	A	Huddersfield T	L,	2-4	2-3	24	McMahon [45], Daniels [45]	14,238
13	21	H	Derby Co	L	0-1	0-0	24		11,036
14	25	A	Reading	L	0-3	0-1	24		15,625
15	Nov 1	H	Ipswich T	L	0-2	0-1	24		10,918
16	5	A	Fulham	D	2-2	2-1	24	Miller [2], Murphy [26]	14,325
17	8	A	Leeds U	L	1-3	0-3	24	Ranger [75]	18,698
18	22	H	Bolton W	D	1-1	0-0	24	Murphy [75]	12,181
19	29	A	Rotherham U	D	1-1	0-0	24	Davies [85]	9381
20	Dec 6	A	Birmingham C	W	1-0	0-0	24	Davies [56]	11,672
21	13	A	Charlton Ath	D	2-2	1-1	24	Eagles [25], Davies [89]	15,411
22	20	H	Bournemouth	L	1-6	0-2	24	Delfouneso [65]	10,014
23	26	A	Sheffield W	L	0-1	0-1	24		26,609
24	28	H	Rotherham U	D	1-1	0-0	24	Telford [84]	11,623
25	Jan 10	H	Millwall	W	1-0	1-0	24	Clarke [33]	9994
26	17	A	Wolverhampton W	L	0-2	0-0	24		28,132
27	24	A	Watford	L	2-7	2-0	24	Orlandi [8], Davies [42]	17,015
28	31	H	Brighton & HA	W	1-0	0-0	24	O'Hara [75]	10,575
29	Feb 7	A	Norwich C	L	0-4	0-2	24		26,017
30	10	H	Middlesbrough	L	1-2	0-0	24	Gibson (og) [85]	10,806
31	14	H	Nottingham F	D	4-4	1-0	24	Madine [45], Orlandi [66], Davies [73], Ferguson [90]	11,712
32	21	A	Blackburn R	D	1-1	1-1	24	Hall [42]	14,906
33	24	A	Brentford	L	0-4	0-2	24		8765
34	28	H	Wigan Ath	L	1-3	0-1	24	Madine [85]	11,679
35	Mar 4	A	Birmingham C	L	0-1	0-1	24		15,111
36	7	H	Sheffield W	L	0-1	0-0	24		11,887
37	14	A	Bournemouth	L	0-4	0-3	24		10,013
38	17	H	Charlton Ath	L	0-3	0-1	24		9168
39	21	H	Leeds U	D	1-1	1-0	24	Madine [44]	11,688
40	Apr 4	A	Bolton W	D	1-1	1-0	24	Jacobs [9]	17,076
41	7	A	Reading	D	1-1	1-0	24	O'Hara (pen) [6]	9614
42	11	H	Ipswich T	L	2-3	1-2	24	Orlandi [4], Cameron [63]	19,290
43	14	A	Derby Co	L	0-4	0-3	24		27,227
44	18	H	Fulham	L	0-1	0-1	24		10,122
45	25	A	Cardiff C	L	2-3	0-2	24	Orlandi [48], Clarke [90]	26,357
46	May 2	H	Huddersfield T	D	0-0	0-0	24		

Final League Position: 24

GOALSCORERS

League (36): Davies 5, Orlandi 4, Delfouneso 3, Madine 3, Clarke 2, Miller 2, Murphy 2, O'Hara 2 (1 pen), Ranger 2, Cameron 1, Cywka 1, Daniels 1, Eagles 1, Ferguson 1, Hall 1, Jacobs 1, McMahon 1, Telford 1, Zoko 1, own goal 1.
FA Cup (0).
Capital One Cup (0).

Lewis J 34	McMahon T 28+4	Daniels D 19	Sene S —+1	Clarke P 37+2	Perkins D 45	Lundstram J 16+1	Feruz I —+2	Mellis J 4+9	Cywka T 5+1	Zenjov S 2+6	Ferguson D 6+4	Orlandi A 23+5	Delfouneso N 21+17	Telford D 9+5	Maher N 6+4	Joan Oriol G 11	Miller H 16+6	Cameron H 10+1	Zoko F 7+7	Davies S 11+6	Oriol E 8+2	Rothwell J 1+2	Ranger N 5+9	Madine G 14+1	Rentmeister J 7+1	Cubero J 10+2	Parish E 12+1	Diehna J 1+1	Mendy F 1+2	Aldred T 6	Dunne C 21+1	Blackman A 2+1	Addison M 6	Murphy J 8+1	Barkhuizen T 4+3	Lenihan B 2	O'Hara J 26+1	Kennedy T 5	Samuel B 1+5	Eagles C 7	Jacobs M 5	Foley K 4	Nosworthy N 5	O'Keefe S 3+1	O'Dea D 16+3	Waddington M 1+2	Oliver C 4+2	Hall G 11+1	Henshall A —+2	Match No.
1	2	3	4	5	6	7	8	9¹	10	11	12																																							1
1	2	4	3	7³	8	6¹	11²	13		9				5	10	12	14																																	2
1	2	3	4	7	6		8¹	14		10				5	11²	9³		12	13																															3
1	2	3	4	8	6		14	11³		9				5	12	10⁴		13	7¹																															4
1	2	3	4	7	6³		8	9¹		5	11²	10	13	14	12																																		5
1	2	4	3	6	7		14	9²	10³		5	12	13		8¹	11																																	6
1	2	3	4	6	7		8³	14		12				5	11	10¹		9²	13																															7
1	2	3		8	7²		6¹	12		5	11	14		9³	13	4																																	8
1	4	3	2	7	12		13	14	9		5	10	6²		11¹		8²																																9
1	2	3		7	12	13		8¹	11		5	10	14		9³		4	6²																															10
	2	4		8	7	14		6		5²	11	10³		9³	13	3	1	12																															11
1	2	3	4	7	8	14		10		11	13		9³	12		5²	6¹																																12
1	5	2	4	7	6³	13		9¹	8		11	12	10²		3		14																																13
1		2	3	6	7	14		5²	9		11	10¹	8³	12	4	13																																	14
1	6	2	3	7		13	11³	8¹	10	12		9	4		5²	14																																	15
1	2¹	3	4	7	6	12		9³	14		11¹		13		5	10	8²																																16
1		3	4	9	7³	14		8¹		11		13		5	10²	6	2	12																															17
1		3	4	6		8³		12		13		14		11¹		10	2	9	5	7²																													18
1		4	9			13		14		12	11³		10²		8	5	6	2	3	7¹																													19
1	13	4	9			12		14	11²		10		6	5	8³	2	3	7¹																															20
1	6	3	7			13		12	11²		8³		9	5	10¹	2	4	14																															21
1	6	4	10			13		11		12		9	5	8³	2	3²	7¹	14																															22
1	2	3	4	7	13		12	11⁸	10²		14	9³	8	6	5¹																																		23
1	2	3	7²	9¹		12	11	13		5	8	6	10³	4	14																																		24
1	2	14	3	6	8	10	11¹		5		7		4²	9³	12	13																																	25
1	2	3	8	14		9	10	11³		5		7		13	6²	4¹	12																																26
5	3¹	7²	14		9	6	13	12	10	11³	1		8		2	4																																	27
2	3	6	10²	12	9		8¹	11	1		5		7		4	13																																	28
2	3	6²	10	13	14		9³	11	12	1		5		7		4	8¹																																29
1	2	3	6	8	14	9	12	10³	11²		13	5¹		7		4																																	30
1	2¹	14	6	13	8	9³	10⁴	12	11		4⁸	5		7		3																																	31
1	12	3	6	10	13	9²	2¹	8³	14	11		5		7		4																																	32
1	2	4	7	14	12	10¹	8	11	3²	6⁸	9⁸		13	5																																			33
1	2	8	6³	12	10	9¹	13	11	3	7²	4	14	5																																				34
13		7	6	10	8¹	2²	11	1	5	4	12	9		3																																			35
13	8	5	11	10	3	1		6	2¹	9	12		7²	4																																			36
13		8	14	6	10	11	12	1	3	5	2¹	9⁸	7²	4																																			37
1		4	8¹	5	6³	13	10	11	12	7	2	14	9²	3																																			38
1		3	8	9	10	6	5	7	11	4	2																																						39
1		3	8	9¹	10	6	5	12	7	11	4	2																																					40
1²		3	8	9³	10	6	13	5	7	14	11	4	2¹																																				41
3	7	12	11	14	2	9²	10	6³	1	5	8	13	4¹																																				42
3	7	9	2¹	11²	10	6	1	5	12	8	13	4																																					43
3	7¹	8²	14	13	12	10	11	6	1	5	2¹	9	4																																				44
3	7	13	12	2	11	10¹	6³	1	5	4	8	9⁴	14																																				45
2	6	11	10	5¹	12	7	1	9	4	8	3																																						46

FA Cup
Third Round   Aston Villa   (a)   0-1

Capital One Cup
First Round   Shrewsbury T   (a)   0-1

BOLTON WANDERERS

FOUNDATION

In 1874 boys of Christ Church Sunday School, Blackburn Street, led by their master Thomas Ogden, established a football club which went under the name of the school and whose president was vicar of Christ Church. Membership was 6d (two and a half pence). When their president began to lay down too many rules about the use of church premises, the club broke away and formed Bolton Wanderers in 1877, holding their earliest meetings at the Gladstone Hotel.

Macron Stadium, Burnden Way, Lostock, Bolton BL6 6JW.

Telephone: (0844) 871 2932. *Fax:* (01204) 673 773.

Ticket Office: (0844) 871 2932.

Website: www.bwfc.co.uk

Email: reception@bwfc.co.uk

Ground Capacity: 28,063.

Record Attendance: 69,912 v Manchester C, FA Cup 5th rd, 18 February 1933 (at Burnden Park); 28,353 v Leicester C, FA Premier League, 23 December 2003 (at The Reebok Stadium).

Pitch Measurements: 105m × 68m (115yd × 74.5yd)

Chairman: Phil A. Gartside.

Chief Operating Officer: Bradley Cooper.

Manager: Neil Lennon.

Assistant Manager: Johan Mjallby.

Head of Sports Science: Mark Leather.

Colours: White shirts with blue body trim, blue shorts, blue socks with white hoops.

Year Formed: 1874.

Turned Professional: 1880.

Previous Name: 1874, Christ Church FC; 1877, Bolton Wanderers.

Club Nickname: 'The Trotters'.

Grounds: Park Recreation Ground and Cockle's Field before moving to Pike's Lane ground 1881; 1895, Burnden Park; 1997, Reebok Stadium (renamed Macron Stadium 2014).

First Football League Game: 8 September 1888, Football League, v Derby Co (h) L 3–6 – Harrison; Robinson, Mitchell; Roberts, Weir, Bullough, Davenport (2), Milne, Coupar, Barbour, Brogan (1).

Record League Victory: 8–0 v Barnsley, Division 2, 6 October 1934 – Jones; Smith, Finney; Goslin, Atkinson, George Taylor; George T. Taylor (2), Eastham, Milsom (1), Westwood (4), Cook, (1 og).

Record Cup Victory: 13–0 v Sheffield U, FA Cup 2nd rd, 1 February 1890 – Parkinson; Robinson (1), Jones; Bullough, Davenport, Roberts; Rushton, Brogan (3), Cassidy (5), McNee, Weir (4).

HONOURS

Football League – Division 1: *Champions* 1996–97;
Division 2: *Champions* 1908–09, 1977–78; *Runners-up* 1899–1900, 1904–05, 1910–11, 1934–35, 1992–93;
Division 3: *Champions* 1972–73.
FA Cup: *Winners* 1923, 1926, 1929, 1958; *Runners-up* 1894, 1904, 1953.
Football League Cup: *Runners-up* 1995, 2004.
Freight Rover Trophy: *Runners-up* 1986.
Sherpa Van Trophy: *Winners* 1989.
European Competitions
UEFA Cup: 2005–06, 2007–08.

sky SPORTS FACT FILE

Bolton Wanderers won just one of their first 4 home games in 1924–25, but then won every single home game to the end of the season, a run of 17 consecutive wins. It was still not quite enough to achieve success as they finished in third place in the First Division.

Record Defeat: 1–9 v Preston NE, FA Cup 2nd rd, 5 November 1887.

Most League Points (2 for a win): 61, Division 3, 1972–73.

Most League Points (3 for a win): 98, Division 1, 1996–97.

Most League Goals: 100, Division 1, 1996–97.

Highest League Scorer in Season: Joe Smith, 38, Division 1, 1920–21.

Most League Goals in Total Aggregate: Nat Lofthouse, 255, 1946–61.

Most League Goals in One Match: 5, Tony Caldwell v Walsall, Division 3, 10 September 1983.

Most Capped Player: Ricardo Gardner, 72 (112), Jamaica.

Most League Appearances: Eddie Hopkinson, 519, 1956–70.

Youngest League Player: Ray Parry, 15 years 267 days v Wolverhampton W, 13 October 1951.

Record Transfer Fee Received: £15,000,000 from Chelsea for Nicolas Anelka, January 2008.

Record Transfer Fee Paid: £8,200,000 to Toulouse for Johan Elmander, July 2008.

Football League Record: 1888 Founder Member of the League; 1899–1900 Division 2; 1900–03 Division 1; 1903–05 Division 2; 1905–08 Division 1; 1908–09 Division 2; 1909–10 Division 1; 1910–11 Division 2; 1911–33 Division 1; 1933–35 Division 2; 1935–64 Division 1; 1964–71 Division 2; 1971–73 Division 3; 1973–78 Division 2; 1978–80 Division 1; 1980–83 Division 2; 1983–87 Division 3; 1987–88 Division 4; 1988–92 Division 3; 1992–93 Division 2; 1993–95 Division 1; 1995–96 FA Premier League; 1996–97 Division 1; 1997–98 FA Premier League; 1998–2001 Division 1; 2001–12 FA Premier League; 2012– FL C.

LATEST SEQUENCES

Longest Sequence of League Wins: 11, 5.11.1904 – 2.1.1905.

Longest Sequence of League Defeats: 11, 7.4.1902 – 18.10.1902.

Longest Sequence of League Draws: 6, 25.1.1913 – 8.3.1913.

Longest Sequence of Unbeaten League Matches: 23, 13.10.1990 – 9.3.1991.

Longest Sequence Without a League Win: 26, 7.4.1902 – 10.1.1903.

Successive Scoring Runs: 24 from 22.11.1996.

Successive Non-scoring Runs: 5 from 30.1.2010.

MANAGERS

Tom Rawthorne 1874–85
  (*Secretary*)
J. J. Bentley 1885–86
  (*Secretary*)
W. G. Struthers 1886–87
  (*Secretary*)
Fitzroy Norris 1887
  (*Secretary*)
J. J. Bentley 1887–95
  (*Secretary*)
Harry Downs 1895–96
  (*Secretary*)
Frank Brettell 1896–98
  (*Secretary*)
John Somerville 1898–1910
Will Settle 1910–15
Tom Mather 1915–19
Charles Foweraker 1919–44
Walter Rowley 1944–50
Bill Ridding 1951–68
Nat Lofthouse 1968–70
Jimmy McIlroy 1970
Jimmy Meadows 1971
Nat Lofthouse 1971
  (*then Admin. Manager to 1972*)
Jimmy Armfield 1971–74
Ian Greaves 1974–80
Stan Anderson 1980–81
George Mulhall 1981–82
John McGovern 1982–85
Charlie Wright 1985
Phil Neal 1985–92
Bruce Rioch 1992–95
Roy McFarland 1995–96
Colin Todd 1996–99
Roy McFarland and Colin Todd
  joint managers 1995–96
Sam Allardyce 1999–2007
Sammy Lee 2007
Gary Megson 2007–09
Owen Coyle 2010–12
Dougie Freedman 2012–14
Neil Lennon October 2014–

TEN YEAR LEAGUE RECORD

		P	W	D	L	F	A	Pts	Pos
2005-06	PR Lge	38	15	11	12	49	41	56	8
2006-07	PR Lge	38	16	8	14	47	52	56	7
2007-08	PR Lge	38	9	10	19	36	54	37	16
2008-09	PR Lge	38	11	8	19	41	53	41	13
2009-10	PR Lge	38	10	9	19	42	67	39	14
2010-11	PR Lge	38	12	10	16	52	56	46	14
2011-12	PR Lge	38	10	6	22	46	77	36	18
2012-13	FL C	46	18	14	14	69	61	68	7
2013-14	FL C	46	14	17	15	59	60	59	14
2014-15	FL C	46	13	12	21	54	67	51	18

DID YOU KNOW ?

Bolton Wanderers were a power to be reckoned with in the 1950s, finishing in top 10 positions on all but three occasions between 1950–51 and 1959–60. During this period 9 players won England caps while 13 won representative honours for the Football League XI.

BOLTON WANDERERS – FL CHAMPIONSHIP 2014–15 LEAGUE RECORD

Match No.	Date	Venue	Opponents	Result	H/T Score	Lg Pos.	Goalscorers	Attendance
1	Aug 9	A	Watford	L	0-3	0-2	23		15,546
2	16	H	Nottingham F	D	2-2	2-2	20	Mason [4], Wheater [29]	15,753
3	19	H	Middlesbrough	L	1-2	1-1	22	Davies, C (pen) [27]	13,847
4	23	A	Brighton & HA	L	1-2	1-1	22	Mills [25]	24,435
5	30	A	Leeds U	L	0-1	0-1	22		21,901
6	Sept 13	H	Sheffield W	D	0-0	0-0	22		15,799
7	16	H	Rotherham U	W	3-2	0-1	21	Mason 3 [60, 80, 84]	13,630
8	20	A	Wolverhampton W	L	0-1	0-1	21		22,695
9	27	H	Derby Co	L	0-2	0-1	22		15,006
10	Oct 1	A	Fulham	L	0-4	0-2	23		14,496
11	4	H	Bournemouth	L	0-0	0-0	24	Spearing [52]	13,033
12	18	A	Birmingham C	W	1-0	1-0	23	Mills [20]	15,149
13	21	A	Charlton Ath	L	1-2	0-1	23	Moxey [54]	13,433
14	25	H	Brentford	W	3-1	0-0	22	Danns [61], Davies, M [76], Davies, C [90]	14,811
15	31	A	Norwich C	L	1-2	0-1	22	Lee [86]	26,070
16	Nov 4	H	Cardiff C	W	3-0	0-2	23	Feeney 2 [9, 36], Mills [76]	12,961
17	7	H	Wigan Ath	W	3-1	0-0	18	Clayton [50], Davies, C [55], Lee (pen) [61]	17,282
18	22	A	Blackpool	D	1-1	0-0	21	Lee [82]	12,181
19	29	H	Huddersfield T	W	1-0	0-0	18	Davies, C [67]	15,924
20	Dec 6	A	Reading	D	0-0	0-0	17		15,421
21	13	H	Ipswich T	D	0-0	0-0	18		15,186
22	19	A	Millwall	W	1-0	0-0	14	Pratley [68]	8635
23	26	H	Blackburn R	W	2-1	0-1	14	Heskey [59], Pratley [62]	23,203
24	28	A	Huddersfield T	L	1-2	1-1	15	Pratley [1]	15,773
25	Jan 10	H	Leeds U	D	1-1	0-1	16	Gudjohnsen (pen) [48]	18,844
26	17	A	Sheffield W	W	2-1	2-1	14	Feeney [2], Pratley [25]	22,617
27	27	A	Rotherham U	L	2-4	0-3	16	Trotter [77], Mills [79]	8760
28	31	H	Wolverhampton W	D	2-2	2-1	14	Clough 2 [23, 25]	15,869
29	Feb 7	A	Derby Co	L	1-4	0-2	17	Twardzik [51]	30,310
30	10	H	Fulham	W	3-1	1-1	13	Gudjohnsen [44], Janko [80], Le Fondre [89]	12,790
31	14	H	Watford	L	3-4	2-1	15	Clough 2 [37, 85], Le Fondre [41]	14,230
32	21	A	Nottingham F	L	1-4	1-2	18	Le Fondre (pen) [45]	22,441
33	24	A	Middlesbrough	L	0-1	0-1	19		16,569
34	28	H	Brighton & HA	W	1-0	0-0	17	Clough [64]	14,115
35	Mar 3	H	Reading	D	1-1	0-0	17	Gudjohnsen [60]	12,795
36	11	A	Blackburn R	L	0-1	0-0	18		15,362
37	14	H	Millwall	W	2-0	0-0	16	Le Fondre 2 [10, 45]	14,719
38	17	A	Ipswich T	L	0-1	0-0	16		16,923
39	21	A	Wigan Ath	D	1-1	0-0	17	Walker [70]	15,861
40	Apr 4	H	Blackpool	D	1-1	0-1	16	Gudjohnsen [90]	17,076
41	6	A	Cardiff C	W	3-0	0-0	16	Gudjohnsen [55], Davies, C 2 [59, 73]	20,219
42	11	H	Norwich C	L	1-2	1-1	17	Le Fondre [18]	16,027
43	14	H	Charlton Ath	D	1-1	0-1	17	Le Fondre [79]	12,994
44	18	A	Brentford	D	2-2	1-2	17	Le Fondre [39], Davies, M [71]	11,874
45	27	A	Bournemouth	L	0-3	0-2	18		10,070
46	May 2	H	Birmingham C	L	0-1	0-1	18		18,614

Final League Position: 18

GOALSCORERS

League (54): Le Fondre 8 (1 pen), Davies, C 6 (1 pen), Clough 5, Gudjohnsen 5 (1 pen), Mason 4, Mills 4, Pratley 4, Feeney 3, Lee 3 (1 pen), Davies, M 2, Clayton 1, Danns 1, Heskey 1, Janko 1, Moxey 1, Spearing 1, Trotter 1, Twardzik 1, Walker 1, Wheater 1.
FA Cup (2): Clough 1, Gudjohnsen 1 (1 pen).
Capital One Cup (7): Beckford 2, Danns 2, Davies, C 1 (1 pen), Mills 1, Pratley 1.

Lonergan A 28 +1	McNaughton K 8 +1	Mills M 37	Ream T 42 +2	Moxey D 14 +6	Spearing J 15 +6	Amos B 8 +1	Lee C 22 +1	McCarthy P 5	Pratley D 19 +3	Danns R 36 +5	Davies C 17 +10	Feeney L 35 +6	Dervite D 34 +3	Beckford J 5 +8	Bogdan A 10	Wheater D 13 +4	Mason J 9 +3	Coke G 3 +1	Trotter L 7 +7	White H 2 +1	Rochinha D 4	Garvan O 3	Davies M 9 +6	Herd C 2	Clayton M 5 +4	Woolery K — +1	Vela J 25 +4	Threlkeld O 3 +1	Hall R 2 +7	Wilkinson C 2 +2	Gudjohnsen E 12 +9	Heskey E 11 +5	Walker T 9 +2	Taylor Q 1	Kellett A 1	Le Fondre A 16 +1	Clough Z 6 +2	Bannan B 15 +1	Slavchev S — +1	Twardzik F 1 +2	Janko S 6 +4	Eaves T — +1	Match No.
1	2	3	4	5¹	6		7	8		9²	10³	11	12	13	14																												1
	2	3	5		7	8³	6	12		9²	11¹			14		1	4	10	13																								2
	2³	3	5		7		9		13	11²	6		12		1	4	10		8¹	14																							3
12		3	5		6	8³	7		9¹	10	14				1²	4	11	13	2																								4
		3	5		6	7¹	8		9	11³	14	12	13		1	4³	10		2																							5
1		3	4	5	7		9	12		14	6	2	13			11¹						8³	10²																				6
1		3	2	5	6	14	12	7³	8²	11	13	4				10						9¹																					7
1		3	2	5	6		10		14	11²	8	4	12			9³			7¹	13																							8
1	2	3		5	7		10¹			13	12	6	4			11			9²	8																							9
1		3²	7	5	6			9¹	10	11³	8	4	13			14			12	2																							10
1		3	5		7		6	12	9³	11²		4	10			13			8¹	2	14																						11
1	2	3	12	5²	7		10	9¹	8	13	6	4	11																														12
1	2	3	13	5¹	7		10	9	8		6²	4	11			12		14																									13
1	2	3	5		6		9	7³	8	13		4	10²			11¹			12								14																14
1		3	5		9¹		10	8³	7	14		4	11²				12		6	13	2																						15
1		3	5		12		9	10	7	11³	2²	4	14						8¹	13	6																						16
1		3	5		12		9		7	11	8¹	4				6			10	2																							17
1		3	5		12		9	7²	6	11	8¹	4				13			10³	2		14																					18
1		3	5				9	7	6	11	8¹	4							10	2	12																						19
1		3	5		14		9	7	6¹	11³	8²	4							10	2	13	12																					20
1		3	5		12		9	6¹	7		8	2		4²					10¹	14		11	13																				21
1		3	5				9	7	6		8	4		12					2		10¹	13	11²																				22
1		3	5				9	7	6	10¹	4		14	13					2		8³	11²	12																				23
1		3	5				9	10¹	7	8	4		14	6¹					2		13	11³	12																				24
1		3	5				10	7	13	8	4⁴	12	6¹						2			9²	11	14																			25
1		3	5				9	6	11¹	7	2	4							8			12	10																				26
1		3	4	14			8	7		5	2	13	12						6			11²	10³		9¹																		27
1		5	12				9¹	8		6	4	3	7						2	13									10	11²													28
1		5	6				2	4		3²	7³								2	13									11	10	9	12	13										29
1		5					8	9	4	3									6			13	10²								11	12	7³		14	2¹							30
1		5					6	10	4	3									2			12									11	9	7²						8¹	13			31
1²	3⁸	4³	12		4		7		5	2									6										13		11	10	8		9¹								32
		5					1			7		9	4		3				2									10¹	11		13	12	8					6²				33
12	4	5	14				1			7¹	6²				3				2									13	10³		11	9	8					6				34
2³	3	5					1			7		9	13			4²			12									14			11	10¹	8					6				35
	3	5	12				1		4	7	13	9					8		2												11¹	10						6²				36
	3	5					1		4	7³	13	9				12	14		2									10¹		6	11		8²									37
	2	4					1		11			3				7	6	8⁴	5									13	10¹	9	12											38
	2	4	14				1		3	13	5					6	8³		12									11	9¹	10²	7											39
	3	5					1		4	6	13	8¹				9²			2									14	12	10³	11	7										40
	3	5	12					14	10	13	4		1			7						8³	11	6¹								9						2²				41
	4	5						12		7	3		1					9²	10	8¹		11		6								13						14				42
	3	5								7	8	4	1					9¹	13		2³			12	10²		11					14										43
	6	5³						4		7	3	1				9²			12						2¹		13	10	8	11										14		44
	3	4						7	5³	2⁴	1					6¹	14		13					12		11	9	10²	8												45
	4	5						7¹	13		1					8²			2								9³	11	12	3	10		6					14				46

FA Cup

Third Round	Wigan Ath	(h)	1-0
Fourth Round	Liverpool	(a)	0-0
Replay	Liverpool	(h)	1-2

Capital One Cup

First Round	Bury	(h)	3-2
(aet)			
Second Round	Crewe Alex	(a)	3-2
(aet)			
Third Round	Chelsea	(a)	1-2

AFC BOURNEMOUTH

FOUNDATION

There was a Bournemouth FC as early as 1875, but the present club arose out of the remnants of the Boscombe St John's club (formed 1890). The meeting at which Boscombe FC came into being was held at a house in Gladstone Road in 1899. They began by playing in the Boscombe and District Junior League.

Goldsands Stadium, Dean Court, Kings Park, Bournemouth, Dorset BH7 7AF.

Telephone: (0844) 576 1910.

Fax: (01202) 726 373.

Ticket Office: (0844) 576 1910.

Website: www.afcb.co.uk

Email: enquiries@afcb.co.uk

Ground Capacity: 12,081.

Record Attendance: 28,799 v Manchester U, FA Cup 6th rd, 2 March 1957.

Pitch Measurements: 105m × 67.5m (115yd × 74yd)

Chairman: Jeff Mostyn.

Chief Executive: Neill Blake.

Manager: Eddie Howe.

Assistant Manager: Jason Tindall.

Physio: Steve Hard.

Colours: Red and black striped shirts, black shorts, red socks with black trim.

Year Formed: 1899.

Turned Professional: 1910.

Previous Names: 1890, Boscombe St John's; 1899, Boscombe FC; 1923, Bournemouth & Boscombe Ath FC; 1972, AFC Bournemouth.

Club Nickname: 'Cherries'.

Grounds: 1899, Castlemain Road, Pokesdown; 1910, Dean Court (renamed Fitness First Stadium 2001, Seward Stadium 2011, Goldsands Stadium 2012).

First Football League Game: 25 August 1923, Division 3 (S), v Swindon T (a) L 1–3 – Heron; Wingham, Lamb; Butt, Charles Smith, Voisey; Miller, Lister (1), Davey, Simpson, Robinson.

Record League Victory: 8–0 v Birmingham C, FL C, 25 October 2014 – Boruc; Francis, Elphick, Cook, Daniels; Ritchie (1), Arter (Gosling), Surman, Pugh (3); Pitman (1) (Rantie 2 (1 pen)), Wilson (1) (Fraser). 10–0 win v Northampton T at start of 1939–40 expunged from the records on outbreak of war.

Record Cup Victory: 11–0 v Margate, FA Cup 1st rd, 20 November 1971 – Davies; Machin (1), Kitchener, Benson, Jones, Powell, Cave (1), Boyer, MacDougall (9 incl. 1p), Miller, Scott (De Garis).

HONOURS

Football League – FL C: *Champions* 2014–15;

FL 1: *Runners-up* 2012–13;

FL 2: *Runners-up* 2009–10.

Division 3: *Champions* 1986–87;

Division 3 (S): *Runners-up* 1947–48;

Division 4: *Runners-up* 1970–71.

FA Cup: Best season: 6th rd, 1957.

Football League Cup: Best season: quarter-final, 2015.

Associate Members' Cup: *Winners* 1984.

Auto Windscreens Shield: *Runners-up* 1998.

sky SPORTS FACT FILE

Goalkeeper Len Brooks played in the first 7 games of the 1938–39 season for Bournemouth before vanishing. In a letter to the club he claimed he was ill, but 12 months later he signed for Southern League club Colchester United. He was subsequently ordered to repay wages to the Cherries and incurred a one-month suspension.

Record Defeat: 0–9 v Lincoln C, Division 3, 18 December 1982.

Most League Points (2 for a win): 62, Division 3, 1971–72.

Most League Points (3 for a win): 97, Division 3, 1986–87.

Most League Goals: 98, FL C, 2014–15.

Highest League Scorer in Season: Ted MacDougall, 42, 1970–71.

Most League Goals in Total Aggregate: Ron Eyre, 202, 1924–33.

Most League Goals in One Match: 4, Jack Russell v Clapton Orient, Division 3 (S), 7 January 1933; 4, Jack Russell v Bristol C, Division 3 (S), 28 January 1933; 4, Harry Mardon v Southend C, Division 3 (S), 1 January 1938; 4, Jack McDonald v Torquay U, Division 3 (S), 8 November 1947; 4, Ted MacDougall v Colchester U, 18 September 1970; 4, Brian Clark v Rotherham U, 10 October 1972; 4, Luther Blissett v Hull C, 29 November 1988; 4, James Hayter v Bury, Division 2, 21 October 2000.

Most Capped Player: Tokelo Rantie, 17 (29), South Africa.

Most League Appearances: Steve Fletcher, 628, 1992–2007; 2008–13.

Youngest League Player: Jimmy White, 15 years 321 days v Brentford, 30 April 1958.

Record Transfer Fee Received: £1,000,000 from Burnley for Danny Ings, August 2011.

Record Transfer Fee Paid: £8,000,000 to Ipswich T for Tyrone Mings, June 2015.

Football League Record: 1923 Elected to Division 3 (S) and remained a Third Division club for record number of years until 1970; 1970–71 Division 4; 1971–75 Division 3; 1975–82 Division 4; 1982–87 Division 3; 1987–90 Division 2; 1990–92 Division 3; 1992–2002 Division 2; 2002–03 Division 3; 2003–04 Division 2; 2004–08 FL 1; 2008–10 FL 2; 2010–13 FL 1; 2013–15 FL C; 2015– FA Premier League.

MANAGERS
Vincent Kitcher 1914–23
(*Secretary-Manager*)
Harry Kinghorn 1923–25
Leslie Knighton 1925–28
Frank Richards 1928–30
Billy Birrell 1930–35
Bob Crompton 1935–36
Charlie Bell 1936–39
Harry Kinghorn 1939–47
Harry Lowe 1947–50
Jack Bruton 1950–56
Fred Cox 1956–58
Don Welsh 1958–61
Bill McGarry 1961–63
Reg Flewin 1963–65
Fred Cox 1965–70
John Bond 1970–73
Trevor Hartley 1974–75
John Benson 1975–78
Alec Stock 1979–80
David Webb 1980–82
Don Megson 1983
Harry Redknapp 1983–92
Tony Pulis 1992–94
Mel Machin 1994–2000
Sean O'Driscoll 2000–06
Kevin Bond 2006–08
Jimmy Quinn 2008
Eddie Howe 2008–11
Lee Bradbury 2011–12
Paul Groves 2012
Eddie Howe October 2012–

LATEST SEQUENCES

Longest Sequence of League Wins: 8, 12.3.2013 – 20.4.2013.

Longest Sequence of League Defeats: 7, 13.8.1994 – 13.9.1994.

Longest Sequence of League Draws: 5, 25.4.2000 – 12.8.2000.

Longest Sequence of Unbeaten League Matches: 18, 6.3.1982 – 28.8.1982.

Longest Sequence Without a League Win: 14, 6.3.1974 – 27.4.1974.

Successive Scoring Runs: 31 from 28.10.2000.

Successive Non-scoring Runs: 6 from 1.2.1975.

TEN YEAR LEAGUE RECORD

		P	W	D	L	F	A	Pts	Pos
2005-06	FL 1	46	12	19	15	49	53	55	17
2006-07	FL 1	46	13	13	20	50	64	52	19
2007-08	FL 1	46	17	7	22	62	72	48*	21
2008-09	FL 2	46	17	12	17	59	51	46†	21
2009-10	FL 2	46	25	8	13	61	44	83	2
2010-11	FL 1	46	19	14	13	75	54	71	6
2011-12	FL 1	46	15	13	18	48	52	58	11
2012-13	FL 1	46	24	11	11	76	53	83	2
2013-14	FL C	46	18	12	16	67	66	66	10
2014-15	FL C	46	26	12	8	98	45	90	1

*10 pts deducted; †17 pts deducted.

DID YOU KNOW ?

In 2015–16 Bournemouth and Southampton will meet in league action for the first time since 1957–58. On that occasion the Cherries lost 7-0 at The Dell, but ran out 5-2 winners at Dean Court. Goalscorers that day were Brian Bedford (2), Reg Cutler (2) and Ray Hampson.

AFC BOURNEMOUTH – FL CHAMPIONSHIP 2014–15 LEAGUE RECORD

Match No.	Date	Venue	Opponents	Result	Score	H/T Pos.	Lg Goalscorers	Atten- dance
1	Aug 9	A	Huddersfield T	W	4-0	2-0	1	Pugh [1], Wilson 2 [32, 64], Kermorgant [50]	12,371
2	16	H	Brentford	W	1-0	0-0	1	Stanislas [72]	10,114
3	19	H	Nottingham F	L	1-2	0-0	5	Wilson [58]	10,768
4	23	A	Blackburn R	L	2-3	0-3	11	Pitman (pen) [81], Cook [90]	13,900
5	30	A	Norwich C	D	1-1	1-1	11	Wilson [45]	25,814
6	Sept 13	H	Rotherham U	D	1-1	0-0	13	Cook [60]	8480
7	16	H	Leeds U	L	1-3	1-0	15	Surman [6]	9307
8	20	A	Watford	D	1-1	0-0	15	Arter [63]	14,320
9	27	H	Wigan Ath	W	2-0	1-0	14	Kermorgant [36], Francis [70]	8754
10	30	A	Derby Co	L	0-2	0-0	15		26,725
11	Oct 4	A	Bolton W	W	2-1	0-0	11	Wilson 2 [46, 68]	13,033
12	18	H	Charlton Ath	W	1-0	1-0	9	Wilson [3]	10,360
13	21	H	Reading	W	3-0	0-0	8	Wilson [50], Pitman 2 [55, 64]	8899
14	25	A	Birmingham C	W	8-0	3-0	4	Pitman [3], Wilson [35], Ritchie [40], Pugh 3 [63, 69, 84], Rantie 2 (1 pen) [82 (p), 86]	13,837
15	Nov 1	H	Brighton & HA	W	3-2	2-1	2	Greer (og) [25], Pugh [38], Kermorgant (pen) [76]	10,166
16	4	A	Sheffield W	W	2-0	0-0	1	Surman [65], Fraser [69]	16,881
17	8	A	Middlesbrough	D	0-0	0-0	2		22,930
18	22	H	Ipswich T	D	2-2	1-0	2	Kermorgant [2], Ritchie [54]	11,115
19	29	H	Millwall	D	2-2	2-0	4	Cook [22], Pitman [25]	10,016
20	Dec 6	A	Wolverhampton W	W	2-1	0-1	3	Arter [73], Ritchie [85]	20,196
21	13	H	Cardiff C	W	5-3	3-1	1	Ritchie [1], Arter [43], Pugh [45], Kermorgant [67], Wilson [89]	10,440
22	20	A	Blackpool	W	6-1	2-0	1	Ritchie 2 [18, 59], Wilson [42], Pitman (pen) [67], Pugh [73], Arter [76]	10,014
23	26	H	Fulham	W	2-0	1-0	1	Pitman [9], Arter [90]	10,926
24	28	A	Millwall	W	2-0	2-0	1	Kermorgant (pen) [32], Arter [42]	10,407
25	Jan 10	A	Norwich C	L	1-2	1-1	1	Ritchie [18]	11,318
26	17	A	Rotherham U	W	2-0	1-0	1	Elphick [45], Wilson [62]	9157
27	20	A	Leeds U	L	0-1	0-1	1		17,634
28	30	H	Watford	W	2-0	1-0	1	Kermorgant (pen) [35], Ritchie [57]	10,904
29	Feb 7	A	Wigan Ath	W	3-1	2-0	1	Wilson 2 [37, 57], Kermorgant [41]	10,621
30	10	A	Derby Co	D	2-2	2-1	2	Ritchie [12], Wilson [44]	11,031
31	14	H	Huddersfield T	D	1-1	1-0	1	Kermorgant [16]	10,007
32	21	A	Brentford	L	1-3	1-2	3	Pugh [30]	11,459
33	25	A	Nottingham F	L	1-2	1-2	4	Surman [3]	20,637
34	28	H	Blackburn R	D	0-0	0-0	4		10,196
35	Mar 3	H	Wolverhampton W	W	2-1	1-1	4	Kermorgant 2 (1 pen) [10, 49 (p)]	9851
36	6	A	Fulham	W	5-1	2-0	2	Pitman 2 [29, 61], Ritchie 2 [37, 71], Cook [84]	16,317
37	14	H	Blackpool	W	4-0	0-0	1	Pitman 3 [10, 36, 39], Wilson (pen) [49]	10,013
38	17	A	Cardiff C	D	1-1	1-0	3	Arter [16]	19,819
39	21	H	Middlesbrough	W	3-0	1-0	1	Kermorgant (pen) [12], Arter [48], Pitman (pen) [74]	10,998
40	Apr 3	A	Ipswich T	D	1-1	0-1	2	Jones [82]	22,672
41	6	H	Birmingham C	W	4-2	2-2	1	Cook [39], Wilson [45], Kermorgant (pen) [48], Daniels [74]	11,084
42	10	A	Brighton & HA	W	2-0	0-0	1	Kermorgant [70], Wilson [81]	25,919
43	14	A	Reading	W	1-0	1-0	1	Wilson [4]	18,917
44	18	H	Sheffield W	D	2-2	0-1	2	Kermorgant [69], Ritchie [84]	11,280
45	27	H	Bolton W	W	3-0	2-0	2	Pugh [39], Ritchie [44], Wilson [78]	10,070
46	May 2	A	Charlton Ath	W	3-0	2-0	1	Ritchie 2 [10, 85], Arter [12]	21,280

Final League Position: 1

GOALSCORERS

League (98): Wilson 20 (1 pen), Kermorgant 15 (6 pens), Ritchie 15, Pitman 13 (3 pens), Arter 9, Pugh 9, Cook 5, Surman 3, Rantie 2 (1 pen), Daniels 1, Elphick 1, Francis 1, Fraser 1, Jones 1, Stanislas 1, own goal 1.
FA Cup (6): Kermorgant 2, Fraser 1, MacDonald 1, Stanislas 1, Wilson 1.
Capital One Cup (11): Gosling 5, Wilson 2, Daniels 1, O'Kane 1, Pitman 1, own goal 1.

Camp L 9	Francis S 42	Elphick T 46	Cook S 46	Daniels C 41 + 1	O'Kane E 8 + 3	Ritchie M 44 + 2	Pugh M 35 + 7	Arter H 43	Wilson C 45	Kermorgant Y 26 + 12	Rantie T — + 12	Gosling D 1 + 17	Stanislas J 6 + 7	Fraser R 6 + 15	Smith A 6 + 23	Pitman B 18 + 16	Surman A 40 + 1	Harte I 4	Boruc A 37	Flahavan D — +1	MacDonald S 3 + 2	Ward E — +2	Jones K — + 6	Match No.
1	2	3	4	5	6	7	8²	9	10¹	11³	12	13	14											1
1	2	3	4	5	6	7¹	8¹	9¹	11	10			14	12	13									2
1		3	4	5	7	6²	13	8	10	11	14		9³	12	2									3
1		3	4	5	6	7³		9	11	10²	13		8¹	12	2	14								4
1	2	3	4	5	7	12	13	6	11				9	10²	8¹									5
1	2	3	4	5	6	7²	8³	9	11	10¹		13		12	14									6
1	2	3	4		7		9	11	10	12	8²	13	14	6	5¹									7
	2	3	4		6	8¹	12	9	11	10²	13			7	5		1							8
	2	3	4	12	6	13	8¹	11	10³	14	9²			7	5		1							9
1¹	2	3	4		6	8	12	9²	11¹	14	10³			7	5	13								10
	2	3	4	5		6¹	9	7	11²	10⁴						12	13	8		1				11
	2	3	4	5		6	9	8	10							11	7		1					12
	2	3	4	5		6¹	9²	7	11³		13	14		12		10	8		1					13
	2	3	4	5		6	9	7¹	11³		13	12		14		10¹	8		1					14
	2	3	4	5		8¹	10	6	11¹	13		14		12		9³	7		1					15
	2	3	4	5		6¹	9	7	11²	12	14			13		10¹	8		1					16
	2	3	4	5		6²	9	7	11	10¹				12		13	8		1					17
	2	3	4	5		6	9	7	11¹	10	12²					13	8		1					18
	2	3	4	5	13	6	9³	7²		10¹				12	14	11	8		1					19
	2	3	4	5²		6	9¹	7	11³	13		14		12		10	8		1					20
	2	3	4	5		6¹	9	8	11³	12	14			13		10²	7		1					21
	2	3	4	5		6	9¹	7	11²	12		13		14		10³	8		1					22
	2	3	4	5		6²	9	7	11³	12				14		10³	8		1					23
	2	3	4	5		6¹	13	8	11	10²	12	14	9¹				7		1					24
	2	3	4	5		6	9²	7	11	12		14		13		10³	8¹		1					25
1	2	3	4	5		6¹	9²	8	11³	13		12				14	10	7						26
	2	3	4	5		6²	9	8³	10	12		13	14				11¹	7	1					27
	2	3	4	5	12	6³	9	8	10²	11¹						13	14	7	1					28
	2	3	4	5		8³	10²	6	11	9¹						13	14	7	1		12			29
	2	3	4	5		6¹	9³	7	10	11²						13	14	8	1		12			30
		3	4	5		6	9²	8	11	10¹				12	2	13	7		1					31
	2	3	4	5³		6	9		11	10²				12	14	13	7		1		8			32
	2	3	4	12		6	13		11		14			9¹	5³	10	7		1		8²			33
	2	3	4	5		12	9²	8	11¹	10	13			6			7		1					34
	2	3	4	5		6³	9¹	8	11	10²						12	14	7	1		13			35
	2	3	4	5		6²	9³	8	11¹	12		14		13		10	7		1					36
	2	3¹	4	5		6	9²		11³	14		13				12	10	8	1		7			37
	2	3	4	5		6²	9	7	11	12						13	10¹	8	1					38
	2	3	4	5		6¹	9	7	11²	10¹	14					13	12	8	1					39
	2	3	4¹	5		6		8	11	12				9³	13	10³	7		1				14	40
	2	3	4	5		6		7	10¹	11³				9¹	12	13	8		1				14	41
	2	3	4	5		6	9¹	7	11³	10²	13					12	8		1				14	42
	2	3	4	5		6	9¹	7	11²	10³						12	13	8	1				14	43
2²	3	4¹	5			6	9³	7	11	10²						12		8	1			14	13	44
		3	4	5		6¹	9³	8	11	10¹	14		13	2	12		7		1					45
	2	3	4	5		6	9³	7	11	10²				12			8		1				14	46

FA Cup

Third Round	Rotherham U	(a)	5-1
Fourth Round	Aston Villa	(a)	1-2

Capital One Cup

First Round	Exeter C	(a)	2-0
Second Round	Northampton T	(h)	3-0
Third Round	Cardiff C	(a)	3-0
Fourth Round	WBA	(h)	2-1
Quarter-Finals	Liverpool	(h)	1-3

BRADFORD CITY

FOUNDATION

Bradford was a rugby stronghold around the turn of the 20th century but after Manningham RFC held an archery contest to help them out of financial difficulties in 1903, they were persuaded to give up the handling code and turn to soccer. So they formed Bradford City and continued at Valley Parade. Recognising this as an opportunity to spread the dribbling code in this part of Yorkshire, the Football League immediately accepted the new club's first application for membership of the Second Division.

Coral Windows Stadium, Valley Parade, Bradford, West Yorkshire BD8 7DY.

Telephone: (0871) 978 1911.

Fax: (01274) 773 356.

Ticket Office: (0871) 978 8000.

Website: www.bradfordcityfc.co.uk

Email: bradfordcityfc@compuserve.com

Ground Capacity: 24,965.

Record Attendance: 39,146 v Burnley, FA Cup 4th rd, 11 March 1911.

Pitch Measurements: 103.5m × 64m (113yd × 70yd)

Joint Chairmen: Julian Rhodes and Mark Lawn.

Chief Operating Officer: James Mason.

Manager: Phil Parkinson.

Assistant Manager: Steve Parkin.

Head Physio: Matt Barrass.

Colours: Claret and amber striped shirts, black shorts, amber socks.

Year Formed: 1903.

Turned Professional: 1903.

Club Nickname: 'The Bantams'.

Ground: 1903, Valley Parade (renamed Bradford & Bingley Stadium 1999, Intersonic Stadium 2007, Coral Windows Stadium 2007).

First Football League Game: 1 September 1903, Division 2, v Grimsby T (a) L 0–2 – Seymour; Wilson, Halliday; Robinson, Millar, Farnall; Guy, Beckram, Forrest, McMillan, Graham.

Record League Victory: 11–1 v Rotherham U, Division 3 (N), 25 August 1928 – Sherlaw; Russell, Watson; Burkinshaw (1), Summers, Bauld; Harvey (2), Edmunds (3), White (3), Cairns, Scriven (2).

Record Cup Victory: 11–3 v Walker Celtic, FA Cup 1st rd (replay), 1 December 1937 – Parker; Rookes, McDermott; Murphy, Mackie, Moore; Bagley (1), Whittingham (1), Deakin (4 incl. 1p), Cooke (1), Bartholomew (4).

HONOURS

Football League –
Division 1: *Runners-up* 1998–99;
Division 2: *Champions* 1907–08;
Division 3: *Champions* 1984–85;
Division 3 (N): *Champions* 1928–29;
Division 4: *Runners-up* 1981–82.

FA Cup: *Winners* 1911.

Football League Cup: *Runners-up* 2012–13.

European Competitions:
Intertoto Cup: 2000.

sky SPORTS FACT FILE

Bradford City's Valley Parade ground was closed for 18 months following the tragic stadium fire in May 1985. During this period they played their home games at Leeds Road, Elland Road and Bradford Northern's Odsal Stadium. The highest attendance during this period was 16,009 for the League Cup tie with Nottingham Forest at Odsal in November 1986.

Record Defeat: 1–9 v Colchester U, Division 4,
30 December 1961.

Most League Points (2 for a win): 63, Division 3 (N),
1928–29.

Most League Points (3 for a win): 94, Division 3, 1984–85.

Most League Goals: 128, Division 3 (N), 1928–29.

Highest League Scorer in Season: David Layne, 34,
Division 4, 1961–62.

Most League Goals in Total Aggregate: Bobby Campbell,
121, 1981–84, 1984–86.

Most League Goals in One Match: 7, Albert Whitehurst v
Tranmere R, Division 3 (N), 6 March 1929.

Most Capped Player: Jamie Lawrence, 19 (24), Jamaica.

Most League Appearances: Cec Podd, 502, 1970–84.

Youngest League Player: Robert Cullingford, 16 years
141 days v Mansfield T, 22 April 1970.

Record Transfer Fee Received: £2,000,000 from
Newcastle U for Des Hamilton, March 1997; £2,000,000
from Newcastle U for Andrew O'Brien, March 2001.

Record Transfer Fee Paid: £2,500,000 to Leeds U for
David Hopkin, July 2000.

Football League Record: 1903 Elected to Division 2;
1908–22 Division 1; 1922–27 Division 2; 1927–29
Division 3 (N); 1929–37 Division 2; 1937–61 Division 3;
1961–69 Division 4; 1969–72 Division 3; 1972–77 Division 4;
1977–78 Division 3; 1978–82 Division 4; 1982–85 Division 3;
1985–90 Division 2; 1990–92 Division 3; 1992–96 Division 2;
1996–99 Division 1; 1999–2001 FA Premier League;
2001–04 Division 1; 2004–07 FL 1; 2007–13 FL 2; 2013– FL 1.

LATEST SEQUENCES

Longest Sequence of League Wins: 10, 26.11.1983 – 3.2.1984.

Longest Sequence of League Defeats: 8, 21.1.1933 –
11.3.1933.

Longest Sequence of League Draws: 6, 30.1.1976 –
13.3.1976.

Longest Sequence of Unbeaten League Matches: 21,
11.1.1969 – 2.5.1969.

Longest Sequence Without a League Win: 16, 28.8.1948 –
20.11.1948.

Successive Scoring Runs: 30 from 26.12.1961.

Successive Non-scoring Runs: 7 from 18.4.1925.

MANAGERS

Robert Campbell 1903–05
Peter O'Rourke 1905–21
David Menzies 1921–26
Colin Veitch 1926–28
Peter O'Rourke 1928–30
Jack Peart 1930–35
Dick Ray 1935–37
Fred Westgarth 1938–43
Bob Sharp 1943–46
Jack Barker 1946–47
John Milburn 1947–48
David Steele 1948–52
Albert Harris 1952
Ivor Powell 1952–55
Peter Jackson 1955–61
Bob Brocklebank 1961–64
Bill Harris 1965–66
Willie Watson 1966–69
Grenville Hair 1967–68
Jimmy Wheeler 1968–71
Bryan Edwards 1971–75
Bobby Kennedy 1975–78
John Napier 1978
George Mulhall 1978–81
Roy McFarland 1981–82
Trevor Cherry 1982–87
Terry Dolan 1987–89
Terry Yorath 1989–90
John Docherty 1990–91
Frank Stapleton 1991–94
Lennie Lawrence 1994–95
Chris Kamara 1995–98
Paul Jewell 1998–2000
Chris Hutchings 2000
Jim Jefferies 2000–01
Nicky Law 2001–03
Bryan Robson 2003–04
Colin Todd 2004–07
Stuart McCall 2007–10
Peter Taylor 2010–11
Peter Jackson 2011
Phil Parkinson August 2011–

TEN YEAR LEAGUE RECORD		P	W	D	L	F	A	Pts	Pos
2005-06	FL 1	46	14	19	13	51	49	61	11
2006-07	FL 1	46	11	14	21	47	65	47	22
2007-08	FL 2	46	17	11	18	63	61	62	10
2008-09	FL 2	46	18	13	15	66	55	67	9
2009-10	FL 2	46	16	14	16	59	62	62	14
2010-11	FL 2	46	15	7	24	43	68	52	18
2011-12	FL 2	46	12	14	20	54	59	50	18
2012-13	FL 2	46	18	15	13	63	52	69	7
2013-14	FL 1	46	14	17	15	57	54	59	11
2014-15	FL 1	46	17	14	15	55	55	65	7

DID YOU KNOW

Half back Joe Hargreaves made
over 200 appearances for
Bradford City between 1911 and
1924. In June 1924, just two
months after playing his final
match, he was tragically killed in
a motorcycle accident when he
overturned when negotiating a
bend near Mirfield in West
Yorkshire.

BRADFORD CITY – FOOTBALL LEAGUE ONE 2014–15 LEAGUE RECORD

Match No.	Date		Venue	Opponents	Result	H/T Score	Lg Pos.	Goalscorers	Attendance
1	Aug	9	H	Coventry C	W 3-2	1-1	4	Hanson 2 [27, 90], Sheehan (pen) [49]	14,621
2		16	A	Walsall	D 0-0	0-0	8		4520
3		19	A	Crawley T	W 3-1	0-0	2	Hanson [49], Knott [62], Bennett [77]	2225
4		23	H	Peterborough U	L 0-1	0-0	8		13,546
5		30	A	Rochdale	W 2-0	0-0	4	Kennedy [60], Hanson [66]	4758
6	Sept	6	H	Yeovil T	L 1-3	1-2	5	McArdle [26]	12,601
7		13	H	Swindon T	L 1-2	1-2	8	Thompson (og) [10]	12,486
8		16	A	Milton Keynes D	W 2-1	2-1	5	McLean [24], Clarke [26]	7139
9		20	A	Colchester U	D 0-0	0-0	6		3524
10		27	H	Port Vale	D 1-1	1-1	9	Yeates [45]	12,703
11	Oct	4	H	Crewe Alex	W 2-0	0-0	7	McLean [72], Liddle [74]	12,386
12		12	A	Barnsley	L 1-3	1-0	7	Kennedy [1]	10,499
13		18	H	Sheffield U	L 0-2	0-0	11		14,784
14		21	A	Bristol C	D 2-2	1-1	12	Clarke [20], Routis [85]	12,548
15		25	A	Oldham Ath	L 1-2	1-2	12	Halliday [45]	5832
16	Nov	1	H	Doncaster R	L 1-2	1-0	14	Stead [45]	13,348
17		15	A	Preston NE	W 2-1	1-0	13	McArdle [26], Yeates [86]	10,302
18		22	H	Gillingham	D 1-1	0-0	12	Legge (og) [56]	12,434
19		29	H	Leyton Orient	W 3-1	1-0	10	Knott [42], Clarke [79], Stead [81]	12,489
20	Dec	13	A	Chesterfield	W 1-0	0-0	10	Clarke [57]	6809
21		20	H	Scunthorpe U	D 1-1	1-0	8	McArdle [32]	12,831
22		26	A	Fleetwood T	W 2-0	1-0	5	Hanson [42], Morais [78]	4278
23		28	H	Notts Co	W 1-0	1-0	5	Knott [41]	14,518
24	Jan	10	H	Rochdale	L 1-2	1-1	5	Stead [32]	13,571
25		17	A	Yeovil T	L 0-1	0-1	6		4009
26		31	H	Colchester U	D 1-1	0-1	8	Morais [77]	13,917
27	Feb	7	A	Port Vale	D 2-2	1-0	9	Hanson [41], Morais [65]	5205
28		9	H	Milton Keynes D	W 2-1	0-0	6	Clarke [56], Hanson [70]	11,948
29		18	A	Leyton Orient	W 2-0	2-0	7	Hanson 2 [21, 32]	4760
30		21	H	Walsall	D 1-1	0-0	6	Clarke [51]	13,534
31		24	A	Swindon T	L 1-2	0-2	6	Clarke [54]	6812
32		28	A	Peterborough U	L 0-2	0-0	8		6494
33	Mar	3	H	Crawley T	W 1-0	1-0	8	Zoko [9]	11,683
34		10	A	Coventry C	D 1-1	0-1	9	Yeates [69]	8566
35		14	A	Notts Co	D 1-1	1-0	9	Stead [45]	5166
36		21	H	Fleetwood T	D 2-2	1-0	12	Stead [10], Routis [50]	12,963
37		28	H	Oldham Ath	W 2-0	0-0	10	Clarke 2 [71, 90]	14,010
38		31	H	Chesterfield	L 0-1	0-1	10		12,551
39	Apr	3	A	Doncaster R	W 3-0	0-0	7	MacKenzie [55], Clarke [64], McMahon [90]	8592
40		6	H	Preston NE	L 0-3	0-0	9		16,032
41		11	A	Gillingham	L 0-1	0-0	9		5221
42		14	H	Bristol C	L 0-6	0-2	11		12,609
43		18	A	Sheffield U	D 1-1	0-0	12	Clarke [83]	21,879
44		21	A	Scunthorpe U	D 1-1	0-1	10	Clarke [63]	3176
45		25	H	Barnsley	W 1-0	1-0	8	Stead [17]	15,560
46	May	3	A	Crewe Alex	W 1-0	1-0	7	Clarke [23]	7608

Final League Position: 7

GOALSCORERS

League (55): Clarke 13, Hanson 9, Stead 6, Knott 3, McArdle 3, Morais 3, Yeates 3, Kennedy 2, McLean 2, Routis 2, Bennett 1, Halliday 1, Liddle 1, MacKenzie 1, McMahon 1, Sheehan 1 (1 pen), Zoko 1, own goals 2.
FA Cup (19): Stead 5, Knott 3, Morais 3, Halliday 2, Yeates 2, Clarke 1, Hanson 1, own goals 2.
Capital One Cup (3): Hanson 1, Knott 1, Mclean 1.
Johnstone's Paint Trophy (0).

Pickford J 33	Darby S 45	Davies A 28	McArdle R 43	Sheehan A 13 + 10	Liddle G 39 + 2	Kennedy J 17 + 3	Knott B 31 + 9	Yeates M 26 + 15	Hanson J 31 + 7	Clarke B 32 + 4	Dolan M 3 + 10	McLean A 7 + 6	Meredith J 38 + 2	Bennett M 4 + 7	Shariff M — + 1	Morais F 22 + 8	Routis C 16 + 2	McBurnie O — + 7	Stead J 27 + 5	Halliday B 12 + 2	Zoko F 3 + 13	Williams B 12 + 2	MacKenzie G 9 + 3	Burke D 2	Alnwick J 1	McMahon T 4 + 4	Mottley-Henry D — + 1	Webb-Foster R — + 1	Match No.
1	2	3	4	5	6	7	8¹	9	10	11²	12	13																	1
1	2	3	4		6	7	8¹	9¹	11			13	12	5	10²	14													2
1	2	3	4	5	7	8	6²	13	11		14	10²	12	9¹															3
1	2	4¹	3	5	7	6	8	14	10		13	12	11³	9²															4
1	2		3	4	6	7	8¹		10	12	14	13	5	11³	9²														5
1	2		4	3	6²	7	8	13	11	9		12	5	10¹															6
1	2		4	3*	6	7¹	8	9	10	11		13	5²	14	12														7
1	2		3		8	7	9³	6		10¹		11³	5	14	13	4	12												8
1	2		3		6	7	8²	9		11³		10¹	5	13	12	4	14												9
1	2		4		7	6	9¹	8		11³		10¹	5	14	12	3	13												10
1	2	4	3	5	6	7¹	12	8		11		10¹	14	9³	13														11
1	2¹	4	3	5	6	7	8²	9		10³		11	14	12	13														12
1	2*	4	3	5		7	13	8	10²	9³		11¹		12	6	14													13
1		4¹	3	12	7	6		10	13	9²		5		14	2	11	8¹												14
1	2		4¹	5	7	8³	13	9	10	14		12		3¹		11	6³												15
1	2	3		4		7³	8	10	12	13		5		9	14	11¹	6²												16
1	2	3	4	14	12	8		9	13	10²		5		6³		11	7¹												17
1	2	3	4		8		12	9	13	11¹		5		6²	14	10²	7												18
1	2	4	3		7		8	9	13	10		5				11²	6¹	12											19
1	2	4	3		7		12	9	13	11³		5		6		10¹	8¹	14											20
1	2	3	4		7		8³	9	13	10²		5		6		11¹	12	14											21
1	2	4	3		6	13	12	9¹	11			5		7		10³	8¹	14											22
1	2	3¹	4	12	8	14	7¹		11			5		6		10³	9	13											23
1*	2		3	4	6	14	9³	13	10			5		7²		11	8¹	12											24
1	2	3²	4	14	9		7	12	10			5		6		11³	8¹	13											25
1	2	4	3		7		8	12	11			5		6		10	9¹												26
1*	2	4	3		8		7¹	12²	10			5		9		11	6	13											27
1	2	3	4		7		6²	12	10	8¹		5		9		11	13												28
1	2	4³	3	14	7			9	11²	10¹		5		6			8	12	13										29
1	2		4	13	7		8	6¹		10²		5				11	9	12	3										30
1	2		3	12	7		8	13		10		5²				11³	9	14	4	6¹									31
1	2	3	4	5		8¹	7	13		10				14	11	9³	12			6²									32
1	2		3	12		14	8	11		7³		5		6²		13	9	10¹	4										33
	2	4¹	3	12	6		14	13	10	9		5		7³			11	8²	1										34
	2		3		7			9	12	14	8	5		13	6²	11¹		10³		4		1							35
	2		3		6			9²	11	8	13	5				7³		10¹	12	14	1	4							36
	2	3¹	4		6		13	8¹	10	9		5				7¹		11			1	12		14					37
	2²		3		7		8	12	10	9		5				6³		11	14	1	4¹		13						38
	2		4		7		8¹	9¹	11	10²	14	5				6		13			1	3		12					39
	2		4	6²	8		12	10	9	13		5				7¹	3*	11³			1					14			40
	2		4	6¹	8		12	10	9			5				7³		11	13	1	3²						14		41
	2	3		7			8³	9²	10	11		5				6¹	13	12			1	4		14					42
	2	4	3*				8¹	12³	10	11		5				6		13	9²	1	14		7						43
	2	4		3			8¹		10	9	13	5				6		11²	12	1			7						44
	2	3		7			9¹		10	8	12	5				4		11		1			6						45
	2	3	4	13	12				10	9³	7²	5				6¹		11	14	1			8						46

FA Cup

First Round	FC Halifax T	(a)	2-1
Second Round	Dartford	(h)	4-1
Third Round	Millwall	(a)	3-3
Replay	Millwall	(h)	4-0
Fourth Round	Chelsea	(a)	4-2
Fifth Round	Sunderland	(h)	2-0
Sixth Round	Reading	(h)	0-0
Replay	Reading	(a)	0-3

Capital One Cup

First Round	Morecambe	(a)	1-0
Second Round	Leeds U	(h)	2-1
Third Round	Milton Keynes D	(a)	0-2

Johnstone's Paint Trophy

First Round	Oldham Ath	(a)	0-1

BRENTFORD

FOUNDATION

Formed as a small amateur concern in 1889 they were very successful in local circles. They won the championship of the West London Alliance in 1893 and a year later the West Middlesex Junior Cup before carrying off the Senior Cup in 1895. After winning both the London Senior Amateur Cup and the Middlesex Senior Cup in 1898 they were admitted to the Second Division of the Southern League.

Griffin Park, Braemar Road, Brentford, Middlesex TW8 0NT.

Telephone: (0845) 3456 442.

Ticket Office: (0845) 3456 442 (option 1).

Website: www.brentfordfc.co.uk

Email: enquiries@brentfordfc.co.uk

Ground Capacity: 12,802.

Record Attendance: 38,678 v Leicester C, FA Cup 6th rd, 26 February 1949.

Pitch Measurements: 101.5m × 68.5m (111yd × 75yd)

Chairman: Cliff Crown.

Chief Executive: Mark Devlin.

Manager: Marinus Dijkhuizen.

Assistant Manager: Roy Hendriksen.

Physio: Daryl Martin.

Colours: Red and white striped shirts, black shorts, black socks with white hoops.

Year Formed: 1889.

Turned Professional: 1899.

Club Nickname: 'The Bees'.

HONOURS

Football League – Division 1: Best season: 5th, 1935–36; **FL C:** Best season: 5th, 2014–15;

Division 2: *Champions* 1934–35, 1994–95; **Division 3:** *Champions* 1991–92, 1998–99;

Division 3 (S): *Champions* 1932–33, *Runners-up* 1929–30, 1957–58;

Division 4: *Champions* 1962–63;

FL 1: *Runners-up* 2013–14.

FL 2: *Champions* 2008–09.

FA Cup: Best season: 6th rd, 1938, 1946, 1949, 1989.

Football League Cup: Best season: 4th rd, 1983, 2011.

Freight Rover Trophy: *Runners-up* 1985.

LDV Vans Trophy: *Runners-up* 2001.

Johnstone's Paint Trophy: *Runners-up* 2011.

Grounds: 1889, Clifden Road; 1891, Benns Fields, Little Ealing; 1895, Shotters Field; 1898, Cross Road, S. Ealing; 1900, Boston Park; 1904, Griffin Park.

First Football League Game: 28 August 1920, Division 3, v Exeter C (a) L 0–3 – Young; Hodson, Rosier, Jimmy Elliott, Levitt, Amos, Smith, Thompson, Spreadbury, Morley, Henery.

Record League Victory: 9–0 v Wrexham, Division 3, 15 October 1963 – Cakebread; Coote, Jones; Slater, Scott, Higginson; Summers (1), Brooks (2), McAdams (2), Ward (2), Hales (1), (1 og).

Record Cup Victory: 7–0 v Windsor & Eton (away), FA Cup 1st rd, 20 November 1982 – Roche; Rowe, Harris (Booker), McNichol (1), Whitehead, Hurlock (2), Kamara, Joseph (1), Mahoney (3), Bowles, Roberts. *N.B.* 8–0 v Uxbridge: Frail, Jock Watson, Caie, Bellingham, Parsonage (1), Jay, Atherton, Leigh (1), Bell (2), Buchanan (2), Underwood (2), FA Cup, 3rd Qual rd, 31 October 1903.

Record Defeat: 0–7 v Swansea T, Division 3 (S), 8 November 1924; v Walsall, Division 3 (S), 19 January 1957; v Peterborough U, 24 November 2007.

sky SPORTS FACT FILE

Only two Brentford players have gained full international honours and both gained a single cap. Billy Scott played against Wales in October 1936 while Leslie Smith played against Romania in May 1939. Smith also appeared 13 times in unofficial international matches during the war.

Most League Points (2 for a win): 62, Division 3 (S), 1932–33 and Division 4, 1962–63.

Most League Points (3 for a win): 94, FL 1, 2013–14.

Most League Goals: 98, Division 4, 1962–63.

Highest League Scorer in Season: Jack Holliday, 38, Division 3 (S), 1932–33.

Most League Goals in Total Aggregate: Jim Towers, 153, 1954–61.

Most League Goals in One Match: 5, Jack Holliday v Luton T, Division 3 (S), 28 January 1933; 5, Billy Scott v Barnsley, Division 2, 15 December 1934; 5, Peter McKennan v Bury, Division 2, 18 February 1949.

Most Capped Player: John Buttigieg, 22 (98), Malta.

Most League Appearances: Ken Coote, 514, 1949–64.

Youngest League Player: Danis Salman, 15 years 248 days v Watford, 15 November 1975.

Record Transfer Fee Received: £3,000,000 from Wigan Ath for Adam Forshaw, September 2014.

Record Transfer Fee Paid: £2,100,000 to FC Twente for Andreas Bjelland, July 2015.

Football League Record: 1920 Original Member of Division 3; 1921–33 Division 3 (S); 1933–35 Division 2; 1935–47 Division 1; 1947–54 Division 2; 1954–62 Division 3 (S); 1962–63 Division 4; 1963–66 Division 3; 1966–72 Division 4; 1972–73 Division 3; 1973–78 Division 4; 1978–92 Division 3; 1992–93 Division 1; 1993–98 Division 2; 1998–99 Division 3; 1999–2004 Division 2; 2004–07 FL 1; 2007–09 FL 2; 2009–14 FL 1; 2014– FL C.

LATEST SEQUENCES

Longest Sequence of League Wins: 9, 30.4.1932 – 24.9.1932.

Longest Sequence of League Defeats: 9, 20.10.1928 – 25.12.1928.

Longest Sequence of League Draws: 5, 16.3.1957 – 6.4.1957.

Longest Sequence of Unbeaten League Matches: 26, 20.2.1999 – 16.10.1999.

Longest Sequence Without a League Win: 18, 9.9.2006 – 26.12.2006.

Successive Scoring Runs: 26 from 4.3.1963.

Successive Non-scoring Runs: 7 from 7.3.2000.

MANAGERS

Will Lewis 1900–03
(Secretary-Manager)
Dick Molyneux 1902–06
W. G. Brown 1906–08
Fred Halliday 1908–12, 1915–21, 1924–26
(only Secretary to 1922)
Ephraim Rhodes 1912–15
Archie Mitchell 1921–24
Harry Curtis 1926–49
Jackie Gibbons 1949–52
Jimmy Bain 1952–53
Tommy Lawton 1953
Bill Dodgin Snr 1953–57
Malcolm Macdonald 1957–65
Tommy Cavanagh 1965–66
Billy Gray 1966–67
Jimmy Sirrel 1967–69
Frank Blunstone 1969–73
Mike Everitt 1973–75
John Docherty 1975–76
Bill Dodgin Jnr 1976–80
Fred Callaghan 1980–84
Frank McLintock 1984–87
Steve Perryman 1987–90
Phil Holder 1990–93
David Webb 1993–97
Eddie May 1997
Micky Adams 1997–98
Ron Noades 1998–2000
Ray Lewington 2000–01
Steve Coppell 2001–02
Wally Downes 2002–04
Martin Allen 2004–06
Leroy Rosenior 2006
Scott Fitzgerald 2006–07
Terry Butcher 2007
Andy Scott 2007–11
Nicky Forster 2011
Uwe Rosler 2011–13
Mark Warburton 2013–15
Marinus Dijkhuizen June 2015–

TEN YEAR LEAGUE RECORD

		P	W	D	L	F	A	Pts	Pos
2005-06	FL 1	46	20	16	10	72	52	76	3
2006-07	FL 1	46	8	13	25	40	79	37	24
2007-08	FL 2	46	17	8	21	52	70	59	14
2008-09	FL 2	46	23	16	7	65	36	85	1
2009-10	FL 1	46	14	20	12	55	52	62	9
2010-11	FL 1	46	17	10	19	55	62	61	11
2011-12	FL 1	46	18	13	15	63	52	67	9
2012-13	FL 1	46	21	16	9	62	47	79	3
2013-14	FL 1	46	28	10	8	72	43	94	2
2014-15	FL C	46	23	9	14	78	59	78	5

DID YOU KNOW

Brentford's 6-6 draw with Dagenham & Redbridge in a League Cup tie in August 2014 equalled the record number of goals scored in a game in the competition. The teams were level 4-4 after 90 minutes, both scoring twice in extra time. The Bees eventually went through 4-2 on penalties.

BRENTFORD – FL CHAMPIONSHIP 2014–15 LEAGUE RECORD

Match No.	Date	Venue	Opponents	Result	H/T Score	Lg Pos.	Goalscorers	Attendance
1	Aug 9	H	Charlton Ath	D	1-1	0-0	11	Smith [85]	9690
2	16	A	Bournemouth	L	0-1	0-0	19		10,114
3	19	A	Blackpool	W	2-1	1-1	12	Pritchard [37], Dallas [52]	9939
4	23	H	Birmingham C	D	1-1	0-1	15	Odubajo [79]	9076
5	30	A	Rotherham U	W	2-0	1-0	8	Gray [45], Proschwitz [90]	9016
6	Sept 13	H	Brighton & HA	W	3-2	2-1	6	Odubajo [18], Gray [32], Douglas [55]	10,089
7	16	H	Norwich C	L	0-3	0-0	10		10,074
8	20	A	Middlesbrough	L	0-4	0-1	14		15,485
9	27	H	Leeds U	W	2-0	1-0	11	Jota [45], McCormack [77]	10,886
10	30	A	Watford	L	1-2	0-1	12	Douglas [57]	15,502
11	Oct 4	H	Reading	W	3-1	2-0	10	Jota [11], Pritchard [32], Douglas [81]	10,776
12	18	A	Wigan Ath	D	0-0	0-0	10		12,061
13	21	H	Sheffield W	D	0-0	0-0	12		10,826
14	25	A	Bolton W	L	1-3	0-0	13	Toral [83]	14,811
15	Nov 1	H	Derby Co	W	2-1	0-1	12	Gray [49], Dallas [90]	10,608
16	5	A	Nottingham F	W	3-1	2-0	9	Toral [17], Gray [35], Pritchard (pen) [48]	21,072
17	8	A	Millwall	W	3-2	1-0	6	Gray 2 [42, 56], Shittu (og) [64]	13,048
18	21	H	Fulham	W	2-1	0-0	4	Dean [81], Jota [90]	12,255
19	29	H	Wolverhampton W	W	4-0	1-0	3	Judge [29], Dallas [74], Gray [82], Jota [90]	10,923
20	Dec 6	A	Huddersfield T	L	1-2	0-1	5	Douglas [70]	13,038
21	13	H	Blackburn R	W	3-1	1-1	5	Douglas [16], Gray [55], Jota [61]	11,848
22	20	A	Cardiff C	W	3-2	3-0	3	Pritchard [11], Gray [22], Jota [33]	21,784
23	26	H	Ipswich T	L	2-4	0-3	5	Saunders 2 [80, 90]	12,165
24	28	A	Wolverhampton W	L	1-2	0-1	6	Batth (og) [87]	23,598
25	Jan 10	A	Rotherham U	W	1-0	0-0	5	Dallas [57]	10,851
26	17	A	Brighton & HA	W	1-0	1-0	5	Gray [29]	27,186
27	24	A	Norwich C	W	2-1	1-1	4	Jota [21], Pritchard (pen) [71]	26,148
28	31	H	Middlesbrough	L	0-1	0-1	5		11,853
29	Feb 7	A	Leeds U	W	1-0	0-0	4	Pritchard [65]	23,164
30	10	H	Watford	L	1-2	0-0	6	Gray [53]	10,524
31	14	A	Charlton Ath	L	0-3	0-1	7		14,875
32	21	H	Bournemouth	W	3-1	2-1	7	Douglas [9], Pritchard [45], Long [90]	11,459
33	24	H	Blackpool	W	4-0	2-0	7	Toral 3 [16, 18, 89], Gray [52]	8765
34	28	A	Birmingham C	L	0-1	0-1	7		15,333
35	Mar 3	H	Huddersfield T	W	4-1	1-1	6	Long 2 [4, 51], Pritchard [70], Toral [90]	9625
36	7	A	Ipswich T	D	1-1	1-1	6	Douglas [25]	20,132
37	14	H	Cardiff C	L	1-2	1-0	6	Gray [28]	11,217
38	17	A	Blackburn R	W	3-2	1-2	6	Long [44], Jota [52], Gray [84]	13,382
39	21	H	Millwall	D	2-2	0-1	7	Pritchard (pen) [85], Odubajo [90]	10,179
40	Apr 3	A	Fulham	W	4-1	1-0	5	Dallas 2 [24, 58], Jota [90], Judge [90]	23,271
41	6	H	Nottingham F	D	2-2	1-0	7	Gray [80], Jota [90]	11,499
42	11	A	Derby Co	D	1-1	1-0	7	Pritchard [28]	30,043
43	14	A	Sheffield W	L	0-1	0-0	7		17,416
44	18	H	Bolton W	D	2-2	2-1	7	Pritchard [35], Douglas [42]	11,874
45	25	A	Reading	W	2-0	1-0	7	Judge [7], Tarkowski [65]	20,048
46	May 2	H	Wigan Ath	W	3-0	1-0	5	Pritchard [26], Jota [46], Gray [80]	11,842

Final League Position: 5

GOALSCORERS

League (78): Gray 16, Pritchard 12 (3 pens), Jota 11, Douglas 8, Dallas 6, Toral 6, Long 4, Judge 3, Odubajo 3, Saunders 2, Dean 1, McCormack 1, Proschwitz 1, Smith 1, Tarkowski 1, own goals 2.
FA Cup (0).
Capital One Cup (6): Dallas 2, Dean 1, Gray 1, Moore 1, Proschwitz 1.
Championship Play-Offs (1): Gray 1.

Button D 46	McCormack A 14+4	Tarkowski J 34	Craig T 22+1	Bidwell J 42+1	Douglas J 44	Odubajo M 44+1	Pritchard A 43+2	Judge A 33+4	Dallas S 23+15	Gray A 43+2	Tebar M 1+3	Proschwitz N 1+17	Smith T 1+27	Jota R 37+5	Dean H 33+2	Hogan S —+1	Toral J 8+26	Betinho A —+1	Diagouraga T 31+7	Saunders S —+5	Long C 2+8	Yennaris N 1	Moore L 3	Match No.
1	2	3	4	5	6	7^1	8^3	9	10	11^2	12	13	14											1
1	2	3	4	5	6	7^1	8	10	12	11^3	9^2	14	13											2
1	2	3	4	5	6	7^1	8	10	9	11^2		13	12											3
1	2^2	3	4^4	5	6	14	8	10	13	11	9^1	7^3	12											4
1	2		4	5	6		9	8	7	11^1			14	10^2	3		12		13					5
1	2		4	5	6	7	9^2	10	12	11^1		13		8^1	3		14							6
1	2		4	5	6	7	9	8	10^1	11^2			12		3		13							7
1	2	3		5	6	7^4	9^3	8		11		13	12	10^1	4		14							8
1	2	3	4	5	6	7	8^3	9		11^2	12	13		10^1			14							9
1	2	3	4	5	7	8	12	9		11		13		10^1					6^2					10
1	2	3	4	5	6	7	9^1	8		11^2	12			10^3			14		13					11
1	2	3	4	5	6	7^2	9	8		11^1		13		10			12							12
1	2	3		5	6	7	8	9^2		11^2		12		10^1	4		14		13					13
1	2^2		4	5	6	7	8^1	9		11		13		10^3	3		14		12					14
1				4	5	6	2	12	8	13	11^2		14	10^3	3		7^1		9					15
1				4	5	6	2	10	9	13	11^2		14	12	3		7^3		8					16
1				4	5	2		9^1	8	12	11		14	7^2	3		10^3		6	13				17
1				4	5	6	2	8	9	12	11^1		14	13	3		10^1		7^2					18
1				4	5	6	2	8	10	12	11^1		13	14	3		7^3		9					19
1				4	5	6	2	8	10	12	11^3		13	14	3		9^1		7^2					20
1				4	5	6	2	9^3	10	12	11^1	13	14	7^2	3				8					21
1		3		5	6^1	2		8	10	13	11^3		14	7^2	4		12		9					22
1				4	5	6^2	2	8	10^1		11^3	13		7	3		12		9	14				23
1		3	4	5	6	2		8^3	9	10^1	11			7^4			12		13	14				24
1				4	5	6	2	9	10	11^1		13		8^2	3		12		7					25
1				4	5	6	2	8^2	10	11		13		7^3	3		12		9	14				26
1				4	5	7	2	9	10^1	11^2		12		8^3	3		14		6		13			27
1		3		5	7	2	9	10	11^1				14	8	4^3		12		6^2		13			28
1				4	5	6	2	9^2	10	12	11		14	8^1	3		13		7					29
1	4^3		12	5^4	6	2		9^2	10	11			14	8^1	3		13		7					30
1				4		7	2	9	10^1	11			14	8^2	3		12		6^3		13		5	31
1	14	3	4			7	2	9	10^2	5	11^1			8	3		12		6^3		13			32
1			4		6^3	2	9		5	11^1			14	8^2	3		10		7	12	13			33
1	14		4	13	6	2^1		9	12	5	11			8^2	10		7^3		3		3			34
1		3		5	6	2		9	10^2			13	14	8			12		7^1	11^3	4			35
1		3	4	5	7	2		9	10^2	8	11^3	12					13		6	14		4^1		36
1				4	5^2	6	2	9	12	10^2	11		14	8	3		13		7^1					37
1				4	5	6	2	9^2	8	10		13		7	3		14		12	11^3				38
1				4	5	6	2	8	12	10^1	11		14	7	3^1		13		9^2					39
1				4	5	6	2	9^3	12	10^1	11^2		14	8	3		7		13					40
1				4	5	2		8	9	10^2	11	13		7	3^1		12		6					41
1				4	5	6	2	9^2	10	12	11^3		13	8	3		14		7					42
1	14			4	5^1	6	2	9	10^3	11		13		8	3		12		7^2					43
1				4	5	6	2	10^1	9	12	11^3		14	8	3		13		7					44
1				4	5	7	2	9^3	10	13	11^3		14	8^2	3		12		6					45
1	14			4	5	7	2	10^1	9	12	11^3		13	8	3				6^2					46

FA Cup
Third Round   Brighton & HA   (h)   0-2

Capital One Cup
First Round   Dagenham & R   (a)   6-6
(aet; Brentford won 4-2 on penalties)
Second Round   Fulham   (h)   0-1

Championship Play-Offs
Semi-Finals 1st leg   Middlesbrough   (h)   1-2
Semi-Finals 2nd leg   Middlesbrough   (a)   0-3

BRIGHTON & HOVE ALBION

FOUNDATION

A professional club Brighton United was formed in November 1897 at the Imperial Hotel, Queen's Road, but folded in March 1900 after less than two seasons in the Southern League at the County Ground. An amateur team Brighton & Hove Rangers was then formed by some prominent United supporters and after one season at Withdean, decided to turn semi-professional and play at the County Ground. Rangers were accepted into the Southern League but folded in June 1901. John Jackson, the former United manager, organised a meeting at the Seven Stars public house, Ship Street on 24 June 1901 at which a new third club Brighton & Hove United was formed. They took over Rangers' place in the Southern League and pitch at County Ground. The name was changed to Brighton & Hove Albion before a match was played because of objections by Hove FC.

American Express Community Stadium, Village Way, Falmer, Brighton BN1 9BL.
Telephone: (0344) 324 6282.
Fax: (01273) 878 238.
Ticket Office: (0844) 327 1901.
Website: www.seagulls.co.uk
Email: supporter.services@bhafc.co.uk
Ground Capacity: 30,303.
Record Attendance: 36,747 v Fulham, Division 2, 27 December 1958 (at Goldstone Ground); 8,691 v Leeds U, FL 1, 20 October 2007 (at Withdean); 30,278 v Arsenal, FA Cup 4th rd, 25 January 2015 (at Amex).
Pitch Measurements: 105m × 68m (115yd × 74.5yd)
Chairman: Tony Bloom.
Chief Executive: Paul Barber.
Manager: Chris Hughton.
First Team Coach: Colin Calderwood.
Physios: Fraser Young and Paul Watson.
Colours: Blue and white striped shirts with blue sleeves, blue shorts, blue socks with white trim.
Year Formed: 1901.
Turned Professional: 1901.
Club Nickname: 'The Seagulls'.
Grounds: 1901, County Ground; 1902, Goldstone Ground; 1997, groundshare at Gillingham FC; 1999, Withdean Stadium; 2011, American Express Community Stadium.
First Football League Game: 28 August 1920, Division 3, v Southend U (a) L 0–2 – Hayes; Woodhouse, Little; Hall, Comber, Bentley; Longstaff, Ritchie, Doran, Rodgerson, March.
Record League Victory: 9–1 v Newport Co, Division 3 (S), 18 April 1951 – Ball; Tennant (1p), Mansell (1p); Willard, McCoy, Wilson; Reed, McNichol (4), Garbutt, Bennett (2), Keene (1). 9–1 v Southend U, Division 3, 27 November 1965 – Powney; Magill, Baxter; Leck, Gall, Turner; Gould (1), Collins (1), Livesey (2), Smith (3), Goodchild (2).

HONOURS

Football League – Division 1: Best season: 13th, 1981–82;
Division 2: *Champions* 2001–02;
Runners-up 1978–79;
FL 1: *Champions* 2010–11.
Division 3 (S): *Champions* 1957–58;
Runners-up 1953–54, 1955–56;
Division 3: *Champions* 2000–01;
Runners-up 1971–72, 1976–77, 1987–88;
Division 4: *Champions* 1964–65.
FA Cup: *Runners-up* 1983.
Football League Cup: Best season: 5th rd, 1979.
Charity Shield: *Winners* 1910.

sky SPORTS FACT FILE

Brighton & Hove Albion were in prime position to win the Division Three South title in 1953–54, but won just 5 of their last 14 games and finished as runners-up to Ipswich Town. However, Albion were the best supported team in the division that season, attracting an average gate of 18,880 to the Goldstone Ground.

Record Cup Victory: 10–1 v Wisbech, FA Cup 1st rd, 13 November 1965 – Powney; Magill, Baxter; Collins (1), Gall, Turner; Gould, Smith (2), Livesey (3), Cassidy (2), Goodchild (1), (1 og).

Record Defeat: 0–9 v Middlesbrough, Division 2, 23 August 1958.

Most League Points (2 for a win): 65, Division 3 (S), 1955–56 and Division 3, 1971–72.

Most League Points (3 for a win): 95, FL 1, 2010–11.

Most League Goals: 112, Division 3 (S), 1955–56.

Highest League Scorer in Season: Peter Ward, 32, Division 3, 1976–77.

Most League Goals in Total Aggregate: Tommy Cook, 114, 1922–29.

Most League Goals in One Match: 5, Jack Doran v Northampton T, Division 3 (S), 5 November 1921; 5, Adrian Thorne v Watford, Division 3 (S), 30 April 1958.

Most Capped Player: Steve Penney, 17, Northern Ireland.

Most League Appearances: Ernie 'Tug' Wilson, 509, 1922–36.

Youngest League Player: Ian Chapman, 16 years 259 days v Birmingham C, 14 February 1987.

Record Transfer Fee Received: £8,000,000 from Leicester C for Leonardo Ulloa, July 2014.

Record Transfer Fee Paid: £2,500,000 to Peterborough U for Craig Mackail-Smith, July 2011.

Football League Record: 1920 Original Member of Division 3; 1921–58 Division 3 (S); 1958–62 Division 2; 1962–63 Division 3; 1963–65 Division 4; 1965–72 Division 3; 1972–73 Division 2; 1973–77 Division 3; 1977–79 Division 2; 1979–83 Division 1; 1983–87 Division 2; 1987–88 Division 3; 1988–96 Division 2; 1996–2001 Division 3; 2001–02 Division 2; 2002–03 Division 1; 2003–04 Division 2; 2004–06 FL C; 2006–11 FL 1; 2011– FL C.

LATEST SEQUENCES

Longest Sequence of League Wins: 9, 2.10.1926 – 20.11.1926.

Longest Sequence of League Defeats: 12, 17.8.2002 – 26.10.2002.

Longest Sequence of League Draws: 6, 16.2.1980 – 15.3.1980.

Longest Sequence of Unbeaten League Matches: 16, 8.10.1930 – 28.1.1931.

Longest Sequence Without a League Win: 15, 21.10.1972 – 27.1.1973.

Successive Scoring Runs: 31 from 4.2.1956.

Successive Non-scoring Runs: 6 from 23.9.1970.

MANAGERS

John Jackson 1901–05
Frank Scott-Walford 1905–08
John Robson 1908–14
Charles Webb 1919–47
Tommy Cook 1947
Don Welsh 1947–51
Billy Lane 1951–61
George Curtis 1961–63
Archie Macaulay 1963–68
Fred Goodwin 1968–70
Pat Saward 1970–73
Brian Clough 1973–74
Peter Taylor 1974–76
Alan Mullery 1976–81
Mike Bailey 1981–82
Jimmy Melia 1982–83
Chris Cattlin 1983–86
Alan Mullery 1986–87
Barry Lloyd 1987–93
Liam Brady 1993–95
Jimmy Case 1995–96
Steve Gritt 1996–98
Brian Horton 1998–99
Jeff Wood 1999
Micky Adams 1999–2001
Peter Taylor 2001–02
Martin Hinshelwood 2002
Steve Coppell 2002–03
Mark McGhee 2003–06
Dean Wilkins 2006–08
Micky Adams 2008–09
Russell Slade 2009
Gus Poyet 2009–13
Óscar Garcia 2013–14
Sammi Hyypia 2014
Chris Hughton December 2014–

TEN YEAR LEAGUE RECORD

		P	W	D	L	F	A	Pts	Pos
2005-06	FL C	46	7	17	22	39	71	38	24
2006-07	FL 1	46	14	11	21	49	58	53	18
2007-08	FL 1	46	19	12	15	58	50	69	7
2008-09	FL 1	46	13	13	20	55	70	52	16
2009-10	FL 1	46	15	14	17	56	60	59	13
2010-11	FL 1	46	28	11	7	85	40	95	1
2011-12	FL C	46	17	15	14	52	52	66	10
2012-13	FL C	46	19	18	9	69	43	75	4
2013-14	FL C	46	19	15	12	55	40	72	6
2014-15	FL C	46	10	17	19	44	54	47	20

DID YOU KNOW ?

Tommy Cook, who remains Brighton & Hove Albion's leading all-time scorer, was also the club's first-ever England international when he lined up against Wales in February 1925. It was not until 1982 that Steve Foster became the second Albion player to be capped by England, a gap of almost 60 years.

BRIGHTON & HOVE ALBION – FL CHAMPIONSHIP 2014–15 LEAGUE RECORD

Match No.	Date	Venue	Opponents	Result	H/T Score	Lg Pos.	Goalscorers	Attendance
1	Aug 9	H	Sheffield W	L	0-1	0-1	18		26,993
2	16	A	Birmingham C	L	0-1	0-0	22		14,955
3	19	A	Leeds U	W	2-0	1-0	16	Teixeira [5], LuaLua [84]	21,429
4	23	H	Bolton W	W	2-1	1-1	13	Mackail-Smith [37], Teixeira [64]	24,435
5	30	H	Charlton Ath	D	2-2	0-1	13	Dunk 2 [67, 90]	26,189
6	Sept 13	A	Brentford	L	2-3	1-2	17	Greer [39], Holla [61]	10,089
7	16	A	Ipswich T	L	0-2	0-0	18		15,726
8	20	H	Blackpool	D	0-0	0-0	18		24,569
9	27	A	Nottingham F	D	0-0	0-0	17		23,811
10	30	H	Cardiff C	D	1-1	1-1	18	Saltor [20]	23,712
11	Oct 4	A	Watford	D	1-1	0-0	19	Dunk [77]	16,531
12	18	H	Middlesbrough	L	1-2	0-1	20	Greer [88]	26,642
13	21	A	Huddersfield T	D	1-1	1-1	20	Dunk [39]	10,817
14	25	H	Rotherham U	D	1-1	1-0	21	Bennett, J [45]	24,370
15	Nov 1	A	Bournemouth	L	2-3	1-2	21	Adrian Colunga [28], Baldock [60]	10,166
16	4	H	Wigan Ath	W	1-0	1-0	20	Gardner [1]	23,044
17	8	H	Blackburn R	D	1-1	1-0	20	Gardner [42]	24,840
18	22	A	Norwich C	D	3-3	1-1	20	Saltor [33], LuaLua [66], Adrian Colunga (pen) [77]	26,379
19	29	H	Fulham	L	1-2	0-0	22	Bent [52]	28,802
20	Dec 6	A	Derby Co	L	0-3	0-3	22		28,637
21	12	H	Millwall	L	0-1	0-1	22		24,085
22	20	A	Wolverhampton W	D	1-1	1-0	22	Bent [10]	22,882
23	26	H	Reading	D	2-2	1-2	23	Forster-Caskey [40], Calderon [90]	26,173
24	29	A	Fulham	W	2-0	0-0	21	Adrian Colunga (pen) [60], March [87]	20,619
25	Jan 10	A	Charlton Ath	W	1-0	0-0	19	Ince [62]	17,865
26	17	H	Brentford	L	0-1	0-1	19		27,186
27	21	H	Ipswich T	W	3-2	3-1	19	Baldock [18], Teixeira 2 [38, 45]	23,880
28	31	A	Blackpool	L	0-1	0-0	21		10,575
29	Feb 7	H	Nottingham F	L	2-3	1-1	21	Dunk [42], Kayal [90]	26,267
30	10	A	Cardiff C	D	0-0	0-0	21		19,206
31	14	A	Sheffield W	D	0-0	0-0	21		19,274
32	21	H	Birmingham C	W	4-3	1-1	20	Teixeira 2 [8, 58], Calderon 2 [50, 85]	25,768
33	24	H	Leeds U	W	2-0	1-0	18	Baldock [26], Calderon [63]	25,274
34	28	A	Bolton W	L	0-1	0-0	20		14,115
35	Mar 3	H	Derby Co	W	2-0	0-0	19	Stephens [69], LuaLua [77]	24,002
36	10	A	Reading	L	1-2	0-1	19	O'Grady (pen) [53]	14,748
37	14	H	Wolverhampton W	D	1-1	0-0	19	Saltor [70]	27,019
38	17	A	Millwall	D	0-0	0-0	19		9105
39	21	A	Blackburn R	W	1-0	1-0	16	Kilgallon (og) [26]	13,605
40	Apr 3	H	Norwich C	L	0-1	0-0	16		28,890
41	6	A	Rotherham U	L	0-1	0-1	18		9872
42	10	H	Bournemouth	L	0-2	0-0	19		25,919
43	14	H	Huddersfield T	D	0-0	0-0	19		23,270
44	18	A	Wigan Ath	L	1-2	0-1	20	Stephens [55]	11,100
45	25	H	Watford	L	0-2	0-1	20		28,841
46	May 2	A	Middlesbrough	D	0-0	0-0	20		33,381

Final League Position: 20

GOALSCORERS

League (44): Teixeira 6, Dunk 5, Calderon 4, Adrian Colunga 3 (2 pens), Baldock 3, LuaLua 3, Saltor 3, Bent 2, Gardner 2, Greer 2, Stephens 2, Bennett, J 1, Forster-Caskey 1, Holla 1, Ince 1, Kayal 1, Mackail-Smith 1, March 1, O'Grady 1 (1 pen), own goal 1.
FA Cup (4): O'Grady 2, Baldock 1, Dunk 1.
Capital One Cup (9): Forster-Caskey 2 (2 pens), Ince 2, Mackail-Smith 2, Adrian Colunga 1, Dunk 1, LuaLua 1.

Stockdale D 42	Saltor B 33+2	Greer G 37	Hughes A 7+3	Calderon I 30+5	Crofts A 7	Ince R 23+9	Forster-Caskey J 28+1	Fenelon S 1+1	O'Grady C 15+13	LuaLua K 15+19	Agustien K 1+1	Buckley W —+1	Mackail-Smith C 15+15	Chicksen A 4+1	Teixeira J 27+5	Dunk L 38	Holla D 23+1	Bennett J 41	Adrian Colunga P 11+6	Gardner G 14+3	Baldock S 19+1	McCourt P —+10	Al Habsi A 1	Walton C 3	Bennett E 7	Halford G 14+5	Bent D 5	March S 6+5	Best L 6+7	Kayal B 17+1	Stephens D 10+6	Ledesma E 2+2	Carayol M 4+1	Tilley J —+1	Match No.
1	2	3	4	5³	6⁸	7	8¹	9²	10	11	12	13	14																						1
1	6	3	4	2		7	8	13	10	11¹					9¹	5	12																		2
1	6	3	14	2		13	8		12		7²				11	5	10¹	4	9³																3
1	6	3		2⁸	7	14	9		12						11	13	10¹	4	8	5⁸															4
1	2	3			6²		8¹			13					9³	11	4	7	5	10	12	14													5
1		3	12	2	8					13					14	11²	4¹	7	5	9³	6	10													6
1	2	3			6	8				11					9²	13	4	7¹	5	12		10													7
1	2	3			6	8				12					13	11¹	4	7¹	5	9³		10²	14												8
1	2	3			6	12	8²			11					10		4	7¹	5	9³	14		13												9
1	2	3				8			12	11					10¹		9²	4	7	5		6	13												10
1	2	3		6²	7³				10	12						9	4	13	5	11¹	8		14												11
1		3		2			8³		13	11					9²	4	7¹	5	14	6	10	12													12
1		3		2		13	8		10²	11▪				5		4	7¹		12	6	9														13
1		3		2		7	8¹		10						13	4		5	11	6²	9	12													14
	3	2³	12		8				13				14		9	4	7	5	11¹	6	10²		1												15
	3	2		12	7	10				13					9¹	4		5		6	11³			1	8²	14									16
	3	2		7	8¹	13	11							4			5	6	10²	12			1	9											17
1	2¹	3	4	12	7	8				11							5	9²	6	10					13										18
1	2		3			12	7		10²				14				4	5	9⁸	6					8¹	11	13								19
1	2		3			12	7								9¹		4	5		6	13				10	11	8²								20
1	2						6						5	10	4			12	7		13				8²	3	11	9¹							21
1	6⁸		2		13	8				11³				4	7	5	14	12							3	10¹	9²								22
1		2				8						12		4	7²	5	11	6		14				9¹	3	10³	13								23
1	14	2		7					13				11²	9³	4	6	5	8							10¹	3	12								24
1	13	3	2		6²	9¹			12				11¹	4	7	5		10							14	8									25
1		3		2	7	9³			14				11	4⁸	6	5	12	10²							13	8¹									26
1	8	3	4	2	7				11²					9¹	6	5		10							13	12									27
1	2	3	8¹	6	9				11³				14		4	7	5	10²							13	12									28
1	2	3	8²	7					11	12				9	4	6³	5								10	13	14								29
1	8	3	2		6	9			12	13			10²	4	5										11¹	7³	14								30
1	6	3	2		9				14				9	4	5		11²							13	10¹	8³	12								31
1	2	3	8	6					14				12	9²	4	5		10							11¹	7³	13								32
1	2	3	8	6		14	13						11¹	9	4	5		10³								7²	12								33
1	2³	3	8	6		14	13						11¹	9	4	5										7²	12								34
1	2	3	8						11	12			13	9³	4	6	5	10¹								7²	13	14							35
1	13	3		6²	9				11	10				4	5										2	12	7		8¹						36
1	2	3	8						12	13			11²	10¹	4	7³	5								9	6	14								37
1	2	4	8						14	12			10¹	13		6	5								3	11²	7³	9							38
1	2	4	12		6	13			11				10¹			5									3		7	9	8²						39
1	2	3	8³			7			11²	12			14	9		5		4							13	6¹	10								40
1	2				7				10³	11¹			13	14	4	5		3							12	8	6	9²							41
1	2		8	12						13			14	9²	4	5		3							11	7¹	6		10³						42
1	2		8						14	12			13	9¹	4	5		3							11²	6	7		10³						43
1	2	3	8³						12	10			11²		6¹	5		4							13	7	9		14						44
1	5¹	3	14			8²			11	13			12		4	9		2								6	7		10³						45
	3	13			7¹	9²			10³	11			12		4	5		1		2							8	6					14		46

FA Cup

Third Round	Brentford	(a)	2-0
Fourth Round	Arsenal	(h)	2-3

Capital One Cup

First Round	Cheltenham T	(h)	2-0
Second Round (aet)	Swindon T	(a)	4-2
Third Round	Burton Alb	(a)	3-0
Fourth Round	Tottenham H	(a)	0-2

BRISTOL CITY

FOUNDATION

The name Bristol City came into being in 1897 when the Bristol South End club, formed three years earlier, decided to adopt professionalism and apply for admission to the Southern League after competing in the Western League. The historic meeting was held at the Albert Hall, Bedminster. Bristol City employed Sam Hollis from Woolwich Arsenal as manager and gave him £40 to buy players. In 1900 they merged with Bedminster, another leading Bristol club.

Ashton Gate Stadium, Bristol BS3 2EJ.
Telephone: (0117) 963 0600.
Fax: (0117) 9630 700.
Ticket Office: (0117) 963 0600.
Website: www.bcfc.co.uk
Email: enquiries@bcfc.co.uk
Ground Capacity: 13.649.
Record Attendance: 43,335 v Preston NE, FA Cup 5th rd, 16 February 1935.
Pitch Measurements: 105m × 68.5m (115yd × 75yd)
Chairman: Keith Dawe.
Chief Executive: John Pelling.
Manager: Steve Cotterill.
Assistant Manager: John Pemberton.
Physio: Steve Allen.
Colours: Red shirts with white trim, white shorts, red socks with white trim.
Year Formed: 1894.
Turned Professional: 1897.
Previous Name: 1894, Bristol South End; 1897, Bristol City.
Club Nickname: 'Robins'.

HONOURS

Football League –
Division 1: *Runners-up* 1906–07;
Division 2: *Champions* 1905–06;
Runners-up 1975–76, 1997–98;
FL 1: *Champions* 2014–15;
Runners-up 2006–07;
Division 3 (S): *Champions* 1922–23, 1926–27, 1954–55;
Runners-up 1937–38;
Division 3: *Runners-up* 1964–65, 1989–90.
FA Cup: *Runners-up* 1909.
Football League Cup: Best season: semi-final, 1971, 1989.
Welsh Cup: *Winners* 1934.
Anglo-Scottish Cup: *Winners* 1978.
Freight Rover Trophy: *Winners* 1986; *Runners-up* 1987.
Auto Windscreens Shield: *Runners-up* 2000.
LDV Vans Trophy: *Winners* 2003.
Johnstone's Paint Trophy: *Winners* 2015.

Grounds: 1894, St John's Lane; 1904, Ashton Gate.
First Football League Game: 7 September 1901, Division 2, v Blackpool (a) W 2–0 – Moles; Tuft, Davies; Jones, McLean, Chambers; Bradbury, Connor, Boucher, O'Brien (2), Flynn.
Record League Victory: 9–0 v Aldershot, Division 3 (S), 28 December 1946 – Eddols; Morgan, Fox; Peacock, Roberts, Jones (1); Chilcott, Thomas, Clark (4 incl. 1p), Cyril Williams (1), Hargreaves (3).
Record Cup Victory: 11–0 v Chichester C, FA Cup 1st rd, 5 November 1960 – Cook; Collinson, Thresher; Connor, Alan Williams, Etheridge; Tait (1), Bobby Williams (1), Atyeo (5), Adrian Williams (3), Derrick, (1 og).

sky SPORTS FACT FILE

Inside forward John Donaldson played the final four games of the 1931–32 season for Bristol City and later moved to play for Coleraine in Ireland. In February 1939 he was tragically knifed to death in a Glasgow billiards hall. His attacker James Gray received a sentence of 3 years in prison for culpable homicide.

Record Defeat: 0–9 v Coventry C, Division 3 (S), 28 April 1934.

Most League Points (2 for a win): 70, Division 3 (S), 1954–55.

Most League Points (3 for a win): 99, FL 1, 2014–15.

Most League Goals: 104, Division 3 (S), 1926–27.

Highest League Scorer in Season: Don Clark, 36, Division 3 (S), 1946–47.

Most League Goals in Total Aggregate: John Atyeo, 314, 1951–66.

Most League Goals in One Match: 6, Tommy 'Tot' Walsh v Gillingham, Division 3 (S), 15 January 1927.

Most Capped Player: Billy Wedlock, 26, England.

Most League Appearances: John Atyeo, 596, 1951–66.

Youngest League Player: Marvin Brown, 16 years 105 days v Bristol R, 17 October 1999.

Record Transfer Fee Received: £3,500,000 from Wolverhampton W for Ade Akinbiyi, September 1999.

Record Transfer Fee Paid: £2,250,000 to Crewe Alex for Nicky Maynard, August 2008.

Football League Record: 1901 Elected to Division 2; 1906–11 Division 1; 1911–22 Division 2; 1922–23 Division 3 (S); 1923–24 Division 2; 1924–27 Division 3 (S); 1927–32 Division 2; 1932–55 Division 3 (S); 1955–60 Division 2; 1960–65 Division 3; 1965–76 Division 2; 1976–80 Division 1; 1980–81 Division 2; 1981–82 Division 3; 1982–84 Division 4; 1984–90 Division 3; 1990–92 Division 2; 1992–95 Division 1; 1995–98 Division 2; 1998–99 Division 1; 1999–2004 Division 2; 2004–07 FL 1; 2007–13 FL C; 2013–15 FL 1; 2015– FL C.

LATEST SEQUENCES

Longest Sequence of League Wins: 14, 9.9.1905 – 2.12.1905.

Longest Sequence of League Defeats: 7, 6.10.2012 – 11.11.2012.

Longest Sequence of League Draws: 4, 6.11.1999 – 27.11.1999.

Longest Sequence of Unbeaten League Matches: 24, 9.9.1905 – 10.2.1906.

Longest Sequence Without a League Win: 21, 16.3.2013 – 22.10.2013.

Successive Scoring Runs: 25 from 26.12.1905.

Successive Non-scoring Runs: 6 from 20.12.1980.

MANAGERS

Sam Hollis 1897–99
Bob Campbell 1899–1901
Sam Hollis 1901–05
Harry Thickett 1905–10
Frank Bacon 1910–11
Sam Hollis 1911–13
George Hedley 1913–17
Jack Hamilton 1917–19
Joe Palmer 1919–21
Alex Raisbeck 1921–29
Joe Bradshaw 1929–32
Bob Hewison 1932–49
  (*under suspension 1938–39*)
Bob Wright 1949–50
Pat Beasley 1950–58
Peter Doherty 1958–60
Fred Ford 1960–67
Alan Dicks 1967–80
Bobby Houghton 1980–82
Roy Hodgson 1982
Terry Cooper 1982–88
  (*Director from 1983*)
Joe Jordan 1988–90
Jimmy Lumsden 1990–92
Denis Smith 1992–93
Russell Osman 1993–94
Joe Jordan 1994–97
John Ward 1997–98
Benny Lennartsson 1998–99
Tony Pulis 1999–2000
Tony Fawthrop 2000
Danny Wilson 2000–04
Brian Tinnion 2004–05
Gary Johnson 2005–10
Steve Coppell 2010
Keith Millen 2010–11
Derek McInnes 2011–13
Sean O'Driscoll 2013
Steve Cotterill December 2013–

TEN YEAR LEAGUE RECORD

		P	W	D	L	F	A	Pts	Pos
2005-06	FL 1	46	18	11	17	66	62	65	9
2006-07	FL 1	46	25	10	11	63	39	85	2
2007-08	FL C	46	20	14	12	54	53	74	4
2008-09	FL C	46	15	16	15	54	54	61	10
2009-10	FL C	46	15	18	13	56	65	63	10
2010-11	FL C	46	17	9	20	62	65	60	15
2011-12	FL C	46	12	13	21	44	68	49	20
2012-13	FL C	46	11	8	27	59	84	41	24
2013-14	FL 1	46	13	19	14	70	67	58	12
2014-15	FL 1	46	29	12	5	96	38	99	1

DID YOU KNOW ?

Bristol City attracted a club record average attendance of 26,575 in 1955–56 following their promotion from Division Three South the previous season. The derby game with Bristol Rovers attracted 39,583 fans to Ashton Gate, a record for a League game at the ground.

BRISTOL CITY – FOOTBALL LEAGUE ONE 2014–15 LEAGUE RECORD

Match No.	Date	Venue	Opponents	Result	H/T Score	Lg Pos.	Goalscorers	Attendance
1	Aug 9	A	Sheffield U	W 2-1	1-1	5	Wilbraham [20], Elliott, W [72]	19,889
2	16	H	Colchester U	W 2-1	0-1	1	Wilbraham 2 [46, 68]	11,626
3	19	H	Leyton Orient	D 0-0	0-0	3		11,692
4	23	A	Rochdale	D 1-1	1-0	4	Freeman [16]	3115
5	31	A	Notts Co	W 2-1	0-1	3	Wilbraham [60], Emmanuel-Thomas (pen) [90]	5678
6	Sept 6	H	Scunthorpe U	W 2-0	0-0	2	Flint [52], Cunningham [83]	12,007
7	13	H	Doncaster R	W 3-0	2-0	1	Wilbraham [13], Little [30], Agard [82]	11,733
8	16	A	Port Vale	W 3-0	1-0	1	Wilbraham 2 [13, 61], Flint [48]	4050
9	20	A	Fleetwood T	D 3-3	1-1	1	Agard 2 [31, 47], Wilbraham [51]	3700
10	27	H	Milton Keynes D	W 3-2	2-0	1	Agard 2 (1 pen) [4, 35 (p)], Elliott, W [74]	13,119
11	Oct 4	A	Walsall	D 1-1	1-0	1	Bryan [11]	5574
12	11	H	Chesterfield	W 3-2	1-1	1	Evatt (og) [9], Williams [46], Burns [90]	12,558
13	18	A	Coventry C	W 3-1	2-0	1	Pack [11], Agard [45], Wagstaff [90]	11,888
14	21	H	Bradford C	D 2-2	1-1	1	Flint 2 [8, 82]	12,548
15	25	A	Barnsley	D 2-2	1-0	1	Ayling [36], Wilbraham [79]	9000
16	Nov 1	A	Oldham Ath	W 1-0	0-0	1	Agard [57]	12,696
17	15	A	Swindon T	L 0-1	0-0	1		12,565
18	22	H	Preston NE	L 0-1	0-1	1		13,245
19	28	A	Peterborough U	W 3-0	2-0	1	Freeman 2 [11, 64], Wilbraham [16]	6804
20	Dec 13	H	Crawley T	W 1-0	0-0	1	Ayling [87]	11,660
21	20	A	Crewe Alex	L 0-1	0-0	1		4927
22	26	H	Yeovil T	W 2-1	1-0	1	Smith, M [31], Emmanuel-Thomas (pen) [64]	13,731
23	28	A	Gillingham	W 3-1	2-0	1	Smith, M 2 [34, 44], Wagstaff [55]	6216
24	Jan 10	H	Notts Co	W 4-0	2-0	1	Bryan [8], Smith, M [43], Emmanuel-Thomas [62], Williams [84]	12,817
25	17	A	Scunthorpe U	W 2-0	1-0	2	Emmanuel-Thomas (pen) [35], Freeman [85]	3611
26	Feb 1	H	Fleetwood T	W 2-0	0-0	1	Smith, M [52], Emmanuel-Thomas [90]	11,654
27	7	A	Milton Keynes D	D 0-0	0-0	1		15,642
28	10	H	Port Vale	W 3-1	1-0	1	Emmanuel-Thomas [34], Bryan [59], Smith, M [67]	10,890
29	14	H	Sheffield U	L 1-3	1-0	1	Smith, M [41]	11,767
30	17	H	Peterborough U	W 2-0	1-0	1	Flint [9], Agard [48]	11,101
31	21	A	Colchester U	L 2-3	0-3	1	Tavernier [50], Flint [61]	4300
32	24	A	Doncaster R	W 3-1	2-0	1	Freeman [10], Cunningham (pen) [33], Wilbraham [69]	5495
33	28	H	Rochdale	W 1-0	1-0	1	Wilbraham [14]	11,841
34	Mar 3	A	Leyton Orient	W 3-1	2-1	1	Freeman [12], Flint [21], Wilbraham [60]	4511
35	7	A	Crawley T	W 2-1	0-0	1	Flint [48], Ayling [84]	3333
36	10	A	Yeovil T	W 3-0	0-0	1	Agard [47], Freeman [49], Saville [86]	6591
37	14	H	Gillingham	D 0-0	0-0	1		11,601
38	17	H	Crewe Alex	W 3-0	2-0	1	Wilbraham [32], Flint [42], Emmanuel-Thomas [84]	10,719
39	28	H	Barnsley	D 2-2	1-1	1	Pack (pen) [13], Bryan [84]	11,937
40	Apr 3	A	Oldham Ath	D 1-1	0-0	1	Wilbraham [71]	4577
41	7	A	Swindon T	W 3-0	1-0	1	Agard [36], Bryan [80], Wilbraham [87]	12,302
42	11	A	Preston NE	D 1-1	0-0	1	Wilbraham [63]	16,441
43	14	A	Bradford C	W 6-0	2-0	1	Tavernier 2 [17, 73], Bryan [35], Ayling [54], Flint [66], Wilbraham [79]	12,609
44	18	H	Coventry C	D 0-0	0-0	1		12,093
45	25	A	Chesterfield	W 2-0	1-0	1	Agard [31], Flint [59]	9615
46	May 3	H	Walsall	W 8-2	2-2	1	Flint 3 [16, 67, 88], Emmanuel-Thomas 2 (1 pen) [22 (p), 63], Agard 2 [57, 90], Pack [62]	11,960

Final League Position: 1

GOALSCORERS

League (96): Wilbraham 18, Flint 14, Agard 13 (1 pen), Emmanuel-Thomas 9 (4 pens), Freeman 7, Smith, M 7, Bryan 6, Ayling 4, Pack 3 (1 pen), Tavernier 3, Cunningham 2 (1 pen), Elliott, W 2, Wagstaff 2, Williams 2, Burns 1, Little 1, Saville 1, own goal 1.
FA Cup (6): Emmanuel-Thomas 3, Agard 1, Cunningham 1, Smith, M 1.
Capital One Cup (1): Bryan 1.
Johnstone's Paint Trophy (14): Smith, M 5, Wilbraham 3, Smith, K 2, Burns 1, Flint 1, Little 1, Williams 1.

Fielding F 46	Ayling L 46	Flint A 46	Williams D 44	Little M 35+2	Elliott W 26+10	Smith K 44	Freeman L 44+2	Cunningham G 9+15	Baldock S 4	Wilbraham A 33+4	Pack M 22+12	Wagstaff S 2+24	Emmanuel-Thomas J 10+26	El-Abd A —+2	Bryan J 39+2	Agard K 34+5	Burns W —+3	Kane T 1+4	Reid B —+2	Smith M 11+3	Osborne K —+1	Tavernier J 9+3	Saville G 1+6	Match No.
1	2	3	4	5	6^3	7	8^2	9	10^1	11	12	13	14											1
1	2	3	4	5	6^1	7	8^2	9^1	11	10	13	14			12									2
1	4	3	2	5	6	7	13			10	11^1	8^2	14	12	9^0									3
1	2	4	3	7	5	8	9^1	6	10	11			12											4
1	2	3	4	5	6	8	7	13		10			12		9^1	11^2								5
1	4	3	2	9	8	7	6	12		10^1	13	14			5^3	11^2								6
1	4	3	2	5^2	8	7	6^3			10^1	12	13	14		9	11								7
1	4	3	5	2	7	8	6^1	12		10^2	13	14			9^2	11								8
1	4	3	2	5	8	6	7^1	14		10	13	12			9^2	11^3								9
1	2	3	4	5	6	7	8^1			10		13	12		9	11^2								10
1	2	3	4	6	9	5	7^1			11		12												11
1	2	3	4	5	6	7^1	8^2			11	13		14		9	10^3	12							12
1	2	3	4	5	6		7^2			10^1	8	14	12		9	11^3	13							13
1	4	3	2	5	6		8	12		10	7		13		9^2	11^1								14
1	4	3	5	2	7	6	9^1	14		10	13	12			8^0	11^2								15
1	2	3	4	5	6	8	7^1			11	13	12			9	10^2								16
1	2	3	4		6^4	7	8	12		11	14	5^3			9^2	10^1		13						17
1	2	3	4	5^1		6	8^2			11	7^3		12		9	10		13	14					18
1	3	2	4	5^1		6	7^3			10	8	13			9	11^2		14		12				19
1	4	3	2	9^0	8^1	7	6			12	13	14			5	11				10^2				20
1	3	4	5^4	2	7^2	8	9^1	6		10	12		14			11^3				13				21
1	6	2		5		8	7	4		13	14	12			9	11^2	3^0	10^1						22
1	2	3	4		14	7	8^1	9^2		6	5^1	11			13		12	10						23
1	4	3	2	9	8^3	7	6^1			12	11				5		14	10^3	13					24
1	2	3	4	12	6^3	7	8	14		10					9^1			11				5^2	13	25
1	2	3	4	5	6		7^2	12				14	13		9	10^3				11		8^1		26
1	2	3	4	5	6	7	8			12			11^1		9	13				10^2				27
1	2	3	4^3					6^2		7	8	12	13		10	9	14			11^1	5			28
1	2	3	4	5^1	6^1	7	8	13				14	11		9^2	12				10				29
1	2	3	4	5	14	8	6^3			12	7		13		9	11^1				10^2				30
1	2^2	3	4	12	6	7	8					14	10^3		9	13				11^1	5			31
1	2	3	4	5			7	8^3	9	10^4	6	14	13			12								32
1	2	3	4	5	13	7	8^2	9^3		10	6				12	11^1						14		33
1	2	3	4	5		6	8^3			10^1	7	14	13		9	11^2						12		34
1	6	4	3	2		5	9^3	13		11	7		12		8^1	10^2						14		35
1	6	4	3	2		5^3	9^2	12		11	7		14		8	10						13		36
1	2	3	4^1	5		6	7	12		10	8		13		9^2	11^3				14				37
1	2	3		5^1		6	8^3	4		11^1	7	14	10		9	13				12				38
1	3	4	2	5^1	13	6	7			10	8		12		9	11^2								39
1	2	3	4	5^3	13	7	9			10	6^2		12		8	11^1						14		40
1	2	3	4		13	6	8^3			11^2	7	14	12		9	10^1					5			41
1	2	3	4		13	6	8^1			11	7		12		9	10^2					5			42
1	2	3	4		6	7^1	12			11^1	8		14		9^3	10					5	13		43
1	2	3	4	12		6	8^2			10	7		13		9	11					5^1			44
1	2	3	4		14	7	8^1	12		6	13	10^2			9^3	11					5			45
1	2	3	4		14	6	8^1				7	13	11^2		9	10	12				5^2			46

FA Cup

First Round	Gillingham	(a)	2-1
Second Round	AFC Telford U	(h)	1-0
Third Round	Doncaster R	(a)	1-1
Replay	Doncaster R	(h)	2-0
Fourth Round	West Ham U	(h)	0-1

Capital One Cup

First Round	Oxford U	(h)	1-2

Johnstone's Paint Trophy

Second Round	Cheltenham T	(a)	3-1
Southern Quarter-Finals	AFC Wimbledon	(h)	2-1
Southern Semi-Finals	Coventry C	(h)	2-0
Southern Final 1st leg	Gillingham	(a)	4-2
Southern Final 2nd leg	Gillingham	(h)	1-1
Final	Walsall Wembley		2-0

BRISTOL ROVERS

FOUNDATION

Bristol Rovers were formed at a meeting in Stapleton Road, Eastville, in 1883. However, they first went under the name of the Black Arabs (wearing black shirts). Changing their name to Eastville Rovers in their second season in 1888–89, they won the Gloucestershire Senior Cup. Original members of the Bristol & District League in 1892, this eventually became the Western League and Eastville Rovers adopted professionalism in 1897.

The Memorial Stadium, Filton Avenue, Horfield, Bristol BS7 0BF.
Telephone: (0117) 909 6648.
Fax: (0117) 907 4312.
Ticket Office: (0117) 952 4001 (option 1).
Website: www.bristolrovers.co.uk
Email: dave@bristolrovers.co.uk
Ground Capacity: 11,626.
Record Attendance: 38,472 v Preston NE, FA Cup 4th rd, 30 January 1960 (at Eastville); 9,464 v Liverpool, FA Cup 4th rd, 8 February 1992 (at Twerton Park); 12,011 v WBA, FA Cup 6th rd, 9 March 2008 (at Memorial Stadium).
Pitch Measurements: 100.5m × 67m (110yd × 73yd)
Chairman: Nick Higgs.
Manager: Darrell Clarke.
Assistant Manager: Marcus Stewart.
Physio: Phil Kite.
Colours: Blue and white quarters, blue shorts with white trim, white socks.
Year Formed: 1883.
Turned Professional: 1897.
Previous Names: 1883, Black Arabs; 1884, Eastville Rovers; 1897, Bristol Eastville Rovers; 1898, Bristol Rovers. *Club Nicknames:* 'The Pirates', 'The Gas'.
Grounds: 1883, Purdown; Three Acres, Ashley Hill; Rudgeway, Fishponds; 1897, Eastville; 1986, Twerton Park; 1996, The Memorial Stadium.
First Football League Game: 28 August 1920, Division 3, v Millwall (a) L 0–2 – Stansfield; Bethune, Panes; Boxley, Kenny, Steele; Chance, Bird, Sims, Bell, Palmer.
Record League Victory: 7–0 v Brighton & HA, Division 3 (S), 29 November 1952 – Hoyle; Bamford, Fox; Pitt, Warren, Sampson; McIlvenny, Roost (2), Lambden (1), Bradford (1), Petherbridge (2), (1 og). 7–0 v Swansea T, Division 2, 2 October 1954 – Radford; Bamford, Watkins; Pitt, Muir, Anderson; Petherbridge, Bradford (2), Meyer, Roost (1), Hooper (2), (2 og). 7–0 v Shrewsbury T, Division 3, 21 March 1964 – Hall; Hillard, Gwyn Jones; Oldfield, Stone (1), Mabbutt; Jarman (2), Brown (1), Biggs (1p), Hamilton, Bobby Jones (2).
Record Cup Victory: 7–1 v Dorchester, FA Cup 4th qualifying rd, 25 October 2014 – Midenhall; Locyer, Trotman (McChrystal), Parkes, Monkhouse (2), Clarke, Mansell (1) (Thomas), Brown, Gosling, Harrison (3), Taylor (1) (White).
Record Defeat: 0–12 v Luton T, Division 3 (S), 13 April 1936.

HONOURS

Football League – Division 2: Best season: 4th, 1994–95; **Division 3 (S):** *Champions* 1952–53; **Division 3:** *Champions* 1989–90; *Runners-up* 1973–74.

Conference: *Runners-up* 2014–15.

FA Cup: Best season: 6th rd, 1951, 1958, 2008.

Football League Cup: Best season: 5th rd, 1971, 1972.

Leyland DAF: *Runners-up* 1990.

Johnstone's Paint Trophy: *Runners-up* 2007.

sky SPORTS FACT FILE

Les Berry, who appeared for Bristol Rovers as a goalkeeper in the 1930s, was better known for his achievements as a cricketer. He played for Leicestershire between 1924 and 1952 and is the only player to have scored more than 30,000 first class runs for the county. His record of 45 centuries also still stands as a county record.

Most League Points (2 for a win): 64, Division 3 (S), 1952–53.

Most League Points (3 for a win): 93, Division 3, 1989–90.

Most League Goals: 92, Division 3 (S), 1952–53.

Highest League Scorer in Season: Geoff Bradford, 33, Division 3 (S), 1952–53.

Most League Goals in Total Aggregate: Geoff Bradford, 242, 1949–64.

Most League Goals in One Match: 4, Sidney Leigh v Exeter C, Division 3 (S), 2 May 1921; 4, Jonah Wilcox v Bournemouth, Division 3 (S), 12 December 1925; 4, Bill Culley v QPR, Division 3 (S), 5 March 1927; 4, Frank Curran v Swindon T, Division 3 (S), 25 March 1939; 4, Vic Lambden v Aldershot, Division 3 (S), 29 March 1947; 4, George Petherbridge v Torquay U, Division 3 (S), 1 December 1951; 4, Vic Lambden v Colchester U, Division 3 (S), 14 May 1952; 4, Geoff Bradford v Rotherham U, Division 2, 14 March 1959; 4, Robin Stubbs v Gillingham, Division 2, 10 October 1970; 4, Alan Warboys v Brighton & HA, Division 3, 1 December 1973; 4, Jamie Cureton v Reading, Division 2, 16 January 1999.

Most Capped Player: Vitalijs Astafjevs, 31 (167), Latvia.

Most League Appearances: Stuart Taylor, 546, 1966–80.

Youngest League Player: Ronnie Dix, 15 years 173 days v Charlton Ath, 25 February 1928.

Record Transfer Fee Received: £2,100,000 from Fulham for Barry Hayles, November 1998; £2,100,000 from WBA for Jason Roberts, July 2000.

Record Transfer Fee Paid: £375,000 to QPR for Andy Tillson, November 1992.

Football League Record: 1920 Original Member of Division 3; 1921–53 Division 3 (S); 1953–62 Division 2; 1962–74 Division 3; 1974–81 Division 2; 1981–90 Division 3; 1990–92 Division 2. 1992–93 Division 1; 1993–2001 Division 2; 2001–04 Division 3; 2004–07 FL 2; 2007–11 FL 1; 2011–14 FL 2; 2014–15 Conference Premier; 2015– FL 2.

LATEST SEQUENCES

Longest Sequence of League Wins: 12, 18.10.1952 – 17.1.1953.

Longest Sequence of League Defeats: 8, 26.10.2002 – 21.12.2002.

Longest Sequence of League Draws: 5, 1.11.1975 – 22.11.1975.

Longest Sequence of Unbeaten League Matches: 32, 7.4.1973 – 27.1.1974.

Longest Sequence Without a League Win: 20, 5.4.1980 – 1.11.1980.

Successive Scoring Runs: 26 from 26.3.1927.

Successive Non-scoring Runs: 6 from 14.10.1922.

MANAGERS

Alfred Homer 1899–1920
   (*continued as Secretary to 1928*)
Ben Hall 1920–21
Andy Wilson 1921–26
Joe Palmer 1926–29
Dave McLean 1929–30
Albert Prince-Cox 1930–36
Percy Smith 1936–37
Brough Fletcher 1938–49
Bert Tann 1950–68 (*continued as General Manager to 1972*)
Fred Ford 1968–69
Bill Dodgin Snr 1969–72
Don Megson 1972–77
Bobby Campbell 1978–79
Harold Jarman 1979–80
Terry Cooper 1980–81
Bobby Gould 1981–83
David Williams 1983–85
Bobby Gould 1985–87
Gerry Francis 1987–91
Martin Dobson 1991
Dennis Rofe 1992
Malcolm Allison 1992–93
John Ward 1993–96
Ian Holloway 1996–2001
Garry Thompson 2001
Gerry Francis 2001
Garry Thompson 2001–02
Ray Graydon 2002–04
Ian Atkins 2004–05
Paul Trollope 2005–10
Dave Penney 2011
Paul Buckle 2011–12
Mark McGhee 2012
John Ward 2012–14
Darrell Clarke March 2014–

TEN YEAR LEAGUE RECORD

		P	W	D	L	F	A	Pts	Pos
2005-06	FL 2	46	17	9	20	59	67	60	12
2006-07	FL 2	46	20	12	14	49	42	72	6
2007-08	FL 1	46	12	17	17	45	53	53	16
2008-09	FL 1	46	17	12	17	79	61	63	11
2009-10	FL 1	46	19	5	22	59	70	62	11
2010-11	FL 1	46	11	12	23	48	82	45	22
2011-12	FL 2	46	15	12	19	60	70	57	13
2012-13	FL 2	46	16	12	18	60	69	60	14
2013-14	FL 2	46	12	14	20	43	54	50	23
2014-15	Conf P	46	25	16	5	73	34	91	2

DID YOU KNOW ?

Bristol Rovers' biggest FA Cup victory was in November 1900 when they defeated Weymouth, then an amateur team, by the margin of 15-1 in a fourth qualifying round tie. Rovers were 5-1 up at half-time and added 10 more in a one-sided second half.

BURNLEY

FOUNDATION

On 18 May 1882 Burnley (Association) Football Club was still known as Burnley Rovers as members of that rugby club had decided on that date to play Association Football in the future. It was only a matter of days later that the members met again and decided to drop Rovers from the club's name.

Turf Moor, Harry Potts Way, Burnley, Lancashire BB10 4BX.

Telephone: (0871) 221 1882.

Fax: (01282) 700 014.

Ticket Office: (0871) 221 1914.

Website: www.burnleyfootballclub.com

Email: info@burnleyfc.com

Ground Capacity: 21,401.

Record Attendance: 54,775 v Huddersfield T, FA Cup 3rd rd, 23 February 1924.

Pitch Measurements: 103.5m × 65m (113yd × 71yd)

Chairmen: Mike Garlick and John Banaszkiewicz.

Chief Executive: Lee Hoos.

Manager: Sean Dyche.

Assistant Manager: Ian Woan.

Head Physio: Ally Beattie.

Colours: Claret shirts with blue sleeves, white shorts with blue trim, claret socks.

Year Formed: 1882.

Turned Professional: 1883.

Previous Name: 1882, Burnley Rovers; 1882, Burnley.

Club Nickname: 'The Clarets'.

Grounds: 1882, Calder Vale; 1883, Turf Moor.

HONOURS

Football League – Division 1: *Champions* 1920–21, 1959–60; *Runners-up* 1919–20, 1961–62; **Division 2:** *Champions* 1897–98, 1972–73; *Runners-up* 1912–13, 1946–47, 1999–2000; **Division 3:** *Champions* 1981–82; **Division 4:** *Champions* 1991–92. Record 30 consecutive Division 1 games without defeat 1920–21.

FL C: *Runners-up* 2013–14.

FA Cup: *Winners* 1914; *Runners-up* 1947, 1962.

Football League Cup: Best season: semi-final, 1961, 1969, 1983, 2009.

Anglo–Scottish Cup: *Winners* 1979.

Sherpa Van Trophy: *Runners-up* 1988.

European Competitions **European Cup:** 1960–61. **European Fairs Cup:** 1966–67.

First Football League Game: 8 September 1888, Football League, v Preston NE (a) L 2–5 – Smith; Lang, Bury, Abrahams, Friel, Keenan, Brady, Tait, Poland (1), Gallocher (1), Yates.

Record League Victory: 9–0 v Darwen, Division 1, 9 January 1892 – Hillman; Walker, McFettridge, Lang, Matthews, Keenan, Nicol (3), Bowes, Espie (1), McLardie (3), Hill (2).

Record Cup Victory: 9–0 v Crystal Palace, FA Cup 2nd rd (replay), 10 February 1909 – Dawson; Barron, McLean; Cretney (2), Leake, Moffat; Morley, Ogden, Smith (3), Abbott (2), Smethams (1). 9–0 v New Brighton, FA Cup 4th rd, 26 January 1957 – Blacklaw; Angus, Winton; Seith, Adamson, Miller; Newlands (1), McIlroy (3), Lawson (3), Cheesebrough (1), Pilkington (1). 9–0 v Penrith, FA Cup 1st rd, 17 November 1984 – Hansbury; Miller, Hampton, Phelan, Overson (Kennedy), Hird (3 incl. 1p), Grewcock (1), Powell (2), Taylor (3), Biggins, Hutchison.

Record Defeat: 0–11 v Darwen, FA Cup 1st rd, 17 October 1885.

sky SPORTS FACT FILE

After beating Midland League club Gainsborough Trinity 4-1 in an FA Cup tie in February 1913, Burnley signed up the goalkeeper and two full backs from their opponents. Best known was 'keeper Ronnie Sewell who later played for England, but his colleagues Sam Gunton and Cliff Jones did not progress to similar honours.

Most League Points (2 for a win): 62, Division 2, 1972–73.

Most League Points (3 for a win): 93, FL C, 2013–14.

Most League Goals: 102, Division 1, 1960–61.

Highest League Scorer in Season: George Beel, 35, Division 1, 1927–28.

Most League Goals in Total Aggregate: George Beel, 179, 1923–32.

Most League Goals in One Match: 6, Louis Page v Birmingham C, Division 1, 10 April 1926.

Most Capped Player: Jimmy McIlroy, 51 (55), Northern Ireland.

Most League Appearances: Jerry Dawson, 522, 1907–28.

Youngest League Player: Tommy Lawton, 16 years 174 days v Doncaster R, 28 March 1936.

Record Transfer Fee Received: £7,000,000 from Southampton for Jay Rodriguez, June 2012.

Record Transfer Fee Paid: £3,000,000 to Hibernian for Steven Fletcher, June 2009; £3,000,000 to Hull C for George Boyd, September 2014.

Football League Record: 1888 Original Member of the Football League; 1897–98 Division 2; 1898–1900 Division 1; 1900–13 Division 2; 1913–30 Division 1; 1930–47 Division 2; 1947–71 Division 1; 1971–73 Division 2; 1973–76 Division 1; 1976–80 Division 2; 1980–82 Division 3; 1982–83 Division 2; 1983–85 Division 3; 1985–92 Division 4; 1992–94 Division 2; 1994–95 Division 1; 1995–2000 Division 2; 2000–04 Division 1; 2004–09 FL C; 2009–10 FA Premier League; 2010–14 FL C; 2014–15 FA Premier League; 2015– FL C.

LATEST SEQUENCES

Longest Sequence of League Wins: 10, 16.11.1912 – 18.1.1913.

Longest Sequence of League Defeats: 8, 2.1.1995 – 25.2.1995.

Longest Sequence of League Draws: 6, 21.2.1931 – 28.3.1931.

Longest Sequence of Unbeaten League Matches: 30, 6.9.1920 – 25.3.1921.

Longest Sequence Without a League Win: 24, 16.4.1979 – 17.11.1979.

Successive Scoring Runs: 27 from 13.2.1926.

Successive Non-scoring Runs: 6 from 21.3.2015.

MANAGERS

Harry Bradshaw 1894–99
  (*Secretary-Manager from 1897*)
Club Directors 1899–1900
J. Ernest Mangnall 1900–03
  (*Secretary-Manager*)
Spen Whittaker 1903–10
  (*Secretary-Manager*)
John Haworth 1910–24
  (*Secretary-Manager*)
Albert Pickles 1925–31
  (*Secretary-Manager*)
Tom Bromilow 1932–35
Selection Committee 1935–45
Cliff Britton 1945–48
Frank Hill 1948–54
Alan Brown 1954–57
Billy Dougall 1957–58
Harry Potts 1958–70
  (*General Manager to 1972*)
Jimmy Adamson 1970–76
Joe Brown 1976–77
Harry Potts 1977–79
Brian Miller 1979–83
John Bond 1983–84
John Benson 1984–85
Martin Buchan 1985
Tommy Cavanagh 1985–86
Brian Miller 1986–89
Frank Casper 1989–91
Jimmy Mullen 1991–96
Adrian Heath 1996–97
Chris Waddle 1997–98
Stan Ternent 1998–2004
Steve Cotterill 2004–07
Owen Coyle 2007–10
Brian Laws 2010
Eddie Howe 2011–12
Sean Dyche October 2012–

TEN YEAR LEAGUE RECORD

		P	W	D	L	F	A	Pts	Pos
2005-06	FL C	46	14	12	20	46	54	54	17
2006-07	FL C	46	15	12	19	52	49	57	15
2007-08	FL C	46	16	14	16	60	67	62	13
2008-09	FL C	46	21	13	12	72	60	76	5
2009-10	PR Lge	38	8	6	24	42	82	30	18
2010-11	FL C	46	18	14	14	65	61	68	8
2011-12	FL C	46	17	11	18	61	58	62	13
2012-13	FL C	46	16	13	17	62	60	61	11
2013-14	FL C	46	26	15	5	72	37	93	2
2014-15	PR Lge	38	7	12	19	28	53	33	19

DID YOU KNOW

Burnley is widely recognised as the club that attracts the highest attendances compared to population in English football. In 1947–48 the Clarets recorded an average attendance of 33,621, the highest in the club's history. This represented around 40% of the total population of the town.

BURNLEY – FA PREMIERSHIP 2014–15 LEAGUE RECORD

Match No.	Date	Venue	Opponents	Result	H/T Score	Lg Pos.	Goalscorers	Attendance
1	Aug 18	H	Chelsea	L	1-3	1-3	19	Arfield [14]	20,699
2	23	A	Swansea C	L	0-1	0-1	20		20,565
3	30	H	Manchester U	D	0-0	0-0	20		21,099
4	Sept 13	A	Crystal Palace	D	0-0	0-0	18		23,829
5	20	H	Sunderland	D	0-0	0-0	17		20,026
6	28	A	WBA	L	0-4	0-2	20		24,286
7	Oct 4	A	Leicester C	D	2-2	1-2	19	Kightly [39], Wallace [90]	31,448
8	18	H	West Ham U	L	1-3	0-0	19	Boyd [60]	18,936
9	26	H	Everton	L	1-3	1-2	19	Ings [20]	19,927
10	Nov 1	A	Arsenal	L	0-3	0-0	20		60,012
11	8	H	Hull C	W	1-0	0-0	20	Barnes [50]	16,998
12	22	A	Stoke C	W	2-1	2-1	18	Ings 2 [12, 13]	27,018
13	29	H	Aston Villa	D	1-1	0-1	19	Ings (pen) [87]	19,910
14	Dec 2	H	Newcastle U	D	1-1	1-0	17	Boyd [34]	18,791
15	6	A	QPR	L	0-2	0-0	19		17,785
16	13	H	Southampton	W	1-0	0-0	17	Barnes [73]	17,287
17	20	A	Tottenham H	L	1-2	1-2	18	Barnes [27]	35,681
18	26	H	Liverpool	L	0-1	0-0	19		21,335
19	28	A	Manchester C	D	2-2	0-2	19	Boyd [47], Barnes [81]	45,608
20	Jan 1	A	Newcastle U	D	3-3	1-2	19	Dummett (og) [19], Ings [66], Boyd [86]	51,761
21	10	H	QPR	W	2-1	2-1	17	Arfield [12], Ings [37]	17,523
22	17	H	Crystal Palace	L	2-3	2-1	17	Mee [12], Ings [16]	17,782
23	31	A	Sunderland	L	0-2	0-2	17		44,022
24	Feb 8	H	WBA	D	2-2	2-1	17	Barnes [11], Ings [32]	16,904
25	11	A	Manchester U	L	1-3	1-2	19	Ings [12]	75,356
26	21	A	Chelsea	D	1-1	0-1	18	Mee [81]	41,629
27	28	H	Swansea C	L	0-1	0-0	18		17,388
28	Mar 4	A	Liverpool	L	0-2	0-1	19		44,717
29	14	H	Manchester C	W	1-0	0-0	18	Boyd [61]	21,216
30	21	A	Southampton	L	0-2	0-1	18		30,864
31	Apr 5	H	Tottenham H	D	0-0	0-0	18		18,829
32	11	H	Arsenal	L	0-1	0-1	19		20,615
33	18	A	Everton	L	0-1	0-1	20		39,496
34	25	H	Leicester C	L	0-1	0-0	20		19,582
35	May 2	A	West Ham U	L	0-1	0-1	20		34,946
36	9	A	Hull C	W	1-0	0-0	19	Ings [62]	24,877
37	16	H	Stoke C	D	0-0	0-0	19		18,636
38	24	A	Aston Villa	W	1-0	1-0	19	Ings [6]	40,792

Final League Position: 19

GOALSCORERS

League (28): Ings 11 (1 pen), Barnes 5, Boyd 5, Arfield 2, Mee 2, Kightly 1, Wallace 1, own goal 1.
FA Cup (3): Sordell 1, Vokes 1, Wallace 1.
Capital One Cup (0).

Heaton T 38	Trippier K 38	Duff M 21	Shackell J 38	Mee B 32 + 1	Arfield S 36 + 1	Marney D 20	Jones D 36	Taylor M 7 + 3	Ings D 35	Jutkiewicz L 10 + 15	Kightly M 10 + 7	Barnes A 28 + 7	Sordell M 2 + 12	Wallace R 1 + 14	Reid S 1 + 6	Boyd G 35	Chalobah N — + 4	Ward S 7 + 2	Keane M 17 + 4	Lafferty D — + 1	Vokes S 5 + 10	Long K — + 1	Ulvestad F 1 + 1	Match No.
1	2	3	4	5	6	7	8	9²	10¹	11³	12	13	14											1
1	2	3	4	5	6	7	8¹	9¹	10	11²		13	14	12										2
1	2	3	4	5	6	7	8	9¹	11²	10	12				13									3
1	2	3	4	5	6	8	7		11¹	10	12					9								4
1	2	3	4	5	6	8	7¹		10		12	11³	13	14		9²								5
1	2	3	4	5	7			11¹	10	12		14				6¹	8²	9	13					6
1	2³	3	4	5	7			11	10	12		13	9²		8	6¹	14							7
1	2	3	4	5	7		8		10²	11¹		9³	12	13		6	14							8
1	2	3	4		7		8		10²	11	12	9¹	13			6¹	14	5						9
1	2	3	4	9	7²	8			10	12		11¹				6	13	5						10
1	2	3	4	6¹	7	8			11	13	12	10²				9		5						11
1	2	3²	4		7	8		11³	12	9¹	10		14			6		5	13					12
1	2		4	13	7	8¹		11	12	9³	10²	14				6		5	3					13
1	2		4	12	9	7	8		10	13		11²				6		5¹	3					14
1	2		4	5	9²	7	8¹		11	13		10³	14	12		6			3					15
1	2		4	5¹	9	7	8		11			10				6		3			12			16
1	2		4	5	9¹	7	8		10	14	12	11³			13	6²		3						17
1	2		4	5¹	9	7	8²		11	14		10¹			13	6		3	12					18
1	2		4	5	9	7	8		10			11				6		3						19
1	2		4¹	5	9	8²	7		10	13		11		14		6		3				12²		20
1	2		4	5	9	7	8		11			10¹				6		3			12			21
1	2		4	5	9	7	8³		11			10¹	14	13		6²		3			12			22
1	2		4	5	9	7	8		11³	12		10¹		13		6²		3			14			23
1	2		4	5	9	7¹	8		11		12	10				6		3						24
1	2		4	5		7	8		11	13		9²	10¹			6		3	12					25
1	2		4	5		7	8		11			9¹	10			6		3	12					26
1	2		4	5		8	7		11	13		9¹	10²			6		3	12					27
1	2		4	5		8	7		11³	14		9¹	10²	12		6		3	13					28
1	2	3	4	5		7	8		11²			9		13		6		12			10¹			29
1	2	3	4	5		7	8		11¹	12		9¹	14	13		6					10²			30
1	2	3	4	5		7	8		10	12		9				6					11¹			31
1	2	3	4	5		7	8¹	12	10			9				6					11			32
1	2	3	4	5		7	8³	14	10	12		9⁴		13		6¹					11²			33
1	2	3	4	5		8	7	9¹	10	11²	14		13	12		6⁴								34
1	2	3⁴	4	5		7	8	9²	11	10²	13	14				6¹		12						35
1	2	3	4	5		7	8	9¹	10²	11						6		12	13					36
1	2	3	4	5		7	8²	9¹	10		12	11¹				6					13	14		37
1	2		4	5	9		8	13	11²			10¹		14		6		3			12	7³		38

FA Cup
Third Round   Tottenham H   (h)   1-1
Replay   Tottenham H   (a)   2-4

Capital One Cup
Second Round   Sheffield W   (h)   0-1

BURTON ALBION

FOUNDATION

Once upon a time there were three Football League clubs bearing the name Burton. Then there was none. In reality it had been two. Originally Burton Swifts and Burton Wanderers competed in it until 1901 when they amalgamated to form Burton United. This club disbanded in 1910. There was no senior club representing the town until 1924 when Burton Town, formerly known as Burton All Saints, played in the Birmingham & District League, subsequently joining the Midland League in 1935–36. When the Second World War broke out the club fielded a team in a truncated version of the Birmingham & District League taking over from the club's reserves. But it was not revived in peacetime. So it was not until a further decade that a club bearing the name of Burton reappeared. Founded in 1950 Burton Albion made progress from the Birmingham & District League, too, then into the Southern League and because of its geographical situation later had spells in the Northern Premier League. In April 2009 Burton Albion restored the name of the town to the Football League competition as champions of the Blue Square Premier League.

Pirelli Stadium, Princess Way, Burton-on-Trent, Staffordshire DE13 0AR.

Telephone: (01283) 565 938.

Fax: (01283) 523 199.

Ticket Office: (01283) 565 938.

Website: www.burtonalbionfc.co.uk

Email: bafc@burtonalbionfc.co.uk

Ground Capactiy: 6,972.

HONOURS

Football League – FL 2 *Champions* 2014–15.
Conference: *Champions* 2008–09.
FA Cup: Best season: 4th rd, 2011.
Football League Cup: Best season: 3rd rd, 2013, 2015.
FA Trophy: *Runners-up* 1986–87.

Record Attendance: 5,806 v Weymouth, Southern League Cup final 2nd leg 1964 (at Eton Park); 6,192 v Oxford U, Blue Square Premier, 17 April 2009 (at Pirelli Stadium).

Pitch Measurements: 100m × 68.5m (109.5yd × 75yd)

Chairman: Ben Robinson.

Manager: Jimmy Floyd Hasselbaink.

Assistant Manager: David Oldfield.

Physio: Nick Fenton.

Colours: Yellow shirts with black trim, black shorts, black socks with yellow trim.

Year Formed: 1950.

Turned Professional: 1950.

Club Nickname: 'The Brewers'.

sky SPORTS FACT FILE

Burton Albion, then members of the Birmingham League, applied to join the Football League Division Three North in 1955 but did not receive a single vote when the decision was made at the annual meeting. The bottom two clubs in the division, Grimsby Town and Chester, were both re-elected.

Grounds: 1950, Eton Park; 2005, Pirelli Stadium.

First Football League Game: 8 August 2009, FL 2, v Shrewsbury T (a) L 1–3 – Redmond; Edworthy, Boertien, Austin, Branston, McGrath, Maghoma, Penn, Phillips (Stride), Walker, Shroot (Pearson) (1).

Record League Victory: 6-1 v Aldershot T, FL 2, 12 December 2009 – Krysiak; James, Boertien, Stride, Webster, McGrath, Jackson, Penn, Kabba (2), Pearson (3) (Harrad) (1), Gilroy (Maghoma).

Record Cup Victory: 12–1 v Coalville T, Birmingham Senior Cup, 6 September 1954.

Record Defeat: 0–10 v Barnet, Southern League, 7 February 1970.

Most League Points (3 for a win): 94, FL 2, 2014–15.

Most League Goals: 71, FL 2, 2009–10; 2012–13.

Highest League Scorer in Season: Shaun Harrad, 21, 2009–10.

Most League Goals in Total Aggregate: Billy Kee, 39, 2011–15.

Most League Goals in One Match: 3, Greg Pearson v Aldershot T, FL 2, 12 December 2009; 3, Shaun Harrad v Rotherham U, FL 2, 11 September 2010.

Most Capped Player: Jacques Maghoma, 2, DR Congo.

Most League Appearances: Jacques Maghoma, 155, 2009–13.

Youngest League Player: Sam Austin, 17 years 310 days v Stevenage, 25 October 2014.

Record Transfer Fee Received: £200,000 from Derby Co for Adam Legzdins, June 2011.

Record Transfer Fee Paid: £25,000 to Kidderminster H for Russell Penn, July 2009.

Football League Record: 2009 Promoted from Blue Square Premier; 2009–15 FL 2; 2015– FL 1.

MANAGERS
Reg Weston
Sammy Crooks 1957
Eddie Shimwell 1958
Bill Townsend 1959–62
Peter Taylor 1962–65
Richie Norman
Reg Gutteridge
Harold Bodle 1974–76
Ian Storey-Moore 1978–81
Neil Warnock 1981–86
Brian Fidler 1986–88
Vic Halom 1988
Bobby Hope 1988
Chris Wright 1988–89
Ken Blair 1989–90
Steve Powell 1990–91
Brian Fidler 1991–92
Brian Kenning 1992–94
John Barton 1994–98
Nigel Clough 1998–2009
Roy McFarland 2009
Paul Peschisolido 2009–12
Gary Rowett 2012–14
Jimmy Floyd Hasselbaink November 2014–

LATEST SEQUENCES

Longest Sequence of League Wins: 4, 7.3.2015 – 21.3.2015.

Longest Sequence of League Defeats: 8, 25.2.2012 – 24.3.2012.

Longest Sequence of League Draws: 6, 25.4.2011 – 16.8.2011.

Longest Sequence of Unbeaten League Matches: 13, 6.12.2014 – 21.2.2015.

Longest Sequence Without a League Win: 16, 31.12.2011 – 24.3.2012.

Successive Scoring Runs: 18 from 16.4.2011 – 8.10.2011.

Successive Non-scoring Runs: 5 from 25.2.2012 – 10.3.2012.

TEN YEAR LEAGUE RECORD

		P	W	D	L	F	A	Pts	Pos
2005-06	Conf	42	16	12	14	50	52	60	9
2006-07	Conf	46	22	9	15	52	47	75	6
2007-08	Conf P	46	23	12	11	79	56	81	5
2008-09	Conf P	46	27	7	12	81	52	88	1
2009-10	FL 2	46	17	11	18	71	71	62	13
2010-11	FL 2	46	12	15	19	56	70	51	19
2011-12	FL 2	46	14	12	20	54	81	54	17
2012-13	FL 2	46	22	10	14	71	65	76	4
2013-14	FL 2	46	19	15	12	47	42	72	6
2014-15	FL 2	46	28	10	8	69	39	94	1

DID YOU KNOW ?

Burton Albion's first competitive match saw them play Gloucester City Reserves in a Birmingham League fixture on 19 August 1950. A crowd of 5,000 at the Brewers' then home ground in Wellington Street saw them go down to a 2-0 defeat.

BURTON ALBION – FOOTBALL LEAGUE TWO 2014–15 LEAGUE RECORD

Match No.	Date	Venue	Opponents	Result	H/T Score	Lg Pos.	Goalscorers	Attendance
1	Aug 9	A	Oxford U	W 1-0	1-0	3	Akins [42]	5370
2	16	H	Dagenham & R	W 2-1	0-1	4	Kee 2 (1 pen) [84 (p), 88]	2150
3	19	H	Exeter C	W 1-0	0-1	2	Beavon [41]	2099
4	23	A	Newport Co	D 1-1	0-1	4	Mousinho [51]	2872
5	30	H	Mansfield T	W 2-1	1-0	1	Sutton (og) [42], McFadzean [71]	2966
6	Sept 7	H	Portsmouth	W 2-0	1-0	1	McGurk [2], Akins [55]	2980
7	13	H	York C	W 2-0	0-0	1	Akins [55], Mousinho [79]	2890
8	16	A	AFC Wimbledon	L 0-3	0-2	1		3195
9	20	A	Bury	L 1-3	0-0	2	Blyth [88]	4536
10	27	H	Cheltenham T	W 1-0	1-0	1	Beavon [34]	2225
11	Oct 3	H	Cambridge U	L 1-3	0-1	1	Akins [81]	2683
12	11	A	Northampton T	W 2-1	1-0	2	Blyth [45], MacDonald [85]	4935
13	18	H	Morecambe	L 0-2	0-0	3		2560
14	21	A	Carlisle U	W 4-3	4-2	2	McCrory [5], Bell [27], Blyth [40], MacDonald [45]	4266
15	25	A	Stevenage	L 0-1	0-0	3		3051
16	Nov 1	H	Plymouth Arg	D 1-1	1-1	5	MacDonald [32]	3083
17	17	A	Wycombe W	W 3-1	1-0	4	Edwards [38], MacDonald [49], Blyth [68]	3981
18	22	H	Luton T	W 1-0	0-0	2	Edwards [47]	4772
19	29	A	Shrewsbury T	L 0-1	0-0	4		5170
20	Dec 6	A	Exeter C	D 1-1	0-0	4	Blyth [60]	3381
21	13	H	Hartlepool U	W 4-0	1-0	2	MacDonald 2 [45, 46], Cansdell-Sherriff [65], Beavon [69]	2474
22	19	A	Southend U	D 0-0	0-0	2		5266
23	26	H	Tranmere R	W 2-0	2-0	3	McCrory (pen) [23], Cansdell-Sherriff [38]	4206
24	Jan 3	H	Shrewsbury T	W 1-0	0-0	2	Taft [60]	4555
25	10	H	Mansfield T	W 2-1	2-0	2	Palmer [8], Maynard [24]	3506
26	17	A	Portsmouth	D 1-1	0-1	2	Lenihan [82]	14,323
27	24	A	York C	D 1-1	0-0	3	McGurk [87]	3398
28	31	H	Bury	W 1-0	0-0	2	Edwards [62]	3049
29	Feb 7	A	Cheltenham T	W 3-1	2-0	1	Beavon [21], McGurk [36], Edwards [49]	2389
30	10	A	AFC Wimbledon	D 0-0	0-0	2		2399
31	14	H	Oxford U	W 2-0	1-0	2	McGurk [13], Akins [89]	2954
32	21	A	Dagenham & R	W 3-1	0-0	1	McGurk [71], El Khayati [75], McCrory [90]	1718
33	24	A	Accrington S	L 0-1	0-1	1		919
34	28	A	Newport Co	L 0-1	0-0	1		2974
35	Mar 7	A	Hartlepool U	W 1-0	0-0	1	Cuvelier [90]	3289
36	14	H	Accrington S	W 3-0	1-0	1	McCrory (pen) [27], Beavon [74], Palmer [85]	3293
37	18	H	Southend U	W 2-1	0-1	1	Palmer [56], El Khayati [89]	2669
38	21	H	Tranmere R	W 4-1	2-1	1	McCrory [18], Akins [22], El Khayati [72], Dugdale (og) [89]	5390
39	30	H	Stevenage	D 1-1	1-1	1	Dembele (og) [45]	3024
40	Apr 3	A	Plymouth Arg	D 1-1	1-0	1	Stewart [33]	8649
41	6	H	Wycombe W	W 1-0	0-0	1	McGurk [55]	4284
42	11	A	Luton T	W 1-0	0-0	1	Palmer [79]	8680
43	15	H	Carlisle U	D 1-1	0-1	1	Johnstone [90]	3892
44	18	A	Morecambe	W 2-1	1-0	1	Akins 2 (1 pen) [30, 60 (p)]	2139
45	25	H	Northampton T	W 3-1	3-0	1	Diamond (og) [4], Edwards [31], Akins (pen) [41]	5720
46	May 2	A	Cambridge U	W 3-2	1-1	1	Beavon [11], Edwards [77], Stewart [88]	7109

Final League Position: 1

GOALSCORERS

League (69): Akins 9 (2 pens), Beavon 6, Edwards 6, MacDonald 6, McGurk 6, Blyth 5, McCrory 5 (2 pens), Palmer 4, El Khayati 3, Cansdell-Sherriff 2, Kee 2 (1 pen), Mousinho 2, Stewart 2, Bell 1, Cuvelier 1, Johnstone 1, Lenihan 1, Maynard 1, McFadzean 1, Taft 1, own goals 4.
FA Cup (0).
Capital One Cup (3): Beavon 1, Knowles 1, McGurk 1.
Johnstone's Paint Trophy (0).

McLaughlin J 45	Edwards P 45	Sharps I 16+3	Taft G 22+8	McFadzean C 7+2	Akins L 32+3	Mousinho J 42	Weir R 39+2	MacDonald A 20+1	Beavon S 41+3	Knowles D 4+7	Palmer M 21+12	McGurk A 27+10	Kee B —+2	Cansdell-Sherriff S 37	Harness M 1+17	Bell L 3+2	Blyth J 15+7	Slade L —+6	McCrory D 32+2	Austin S —+1	Lenihan D 15+2	Lyness D 1	Morris B 3+2	Maynard K 5+5	Phillips J —+1	Naylor T 13+4	El Khayati A 9+9	Calero I 3+3	Antoine-Curier M 1+4	Cuvelier F —+1	Reilly C 1+1	Stewart K 4+3	Johnstone D 2+3	Dunn J —+1	Shearer S —+1	Match No.
1	2	3	4	5	6	7	8	9^1	10^2	11^1	12	13	14																							1
1	2	3	5		6	8^1	7	9^1	10	11^3	13			12		4	14																			2
1	2	3		5	6	7	8	9	10	11^1				4		12																				3
1	2	4	5	9^1	6	8	7	12	10		11^1			3		13																				4
1	2	3	5	6^2		8	7^1	9	10^1		11			4	12	13																				5
1	2	3	5	13	9	8	7	6^2	11		14	10^1		4^3			12																			6
1	2	3	5		9	8	7	6^1	10^2		14	11^3		4	13		12																			7
1	2^2	3	5	13	6^3	7	8	9	10		12			4^1	14		11																			8
1	2^1	3	5	10^2		9	7		11	13	8			4	6^3		12	14																		9
1	2	4		5	6^3	7	8	9	10^2		13	11^1		3	14		12																			10
1	2	3	12	5^2	6	8	7	9^3	11			10^1		4	14		13																			11
1	2	3	5^2		7	4	8^1	9		6	10^1			13	11	14	12																			12
1	2	3	5		7^3		8^2	9	12	14	6	10^1		4	13		11																			13
1	2	3	5^1	6		9	10^4		8	13		4		7	11^2		12																			14
1	2	3		6			10^3	8	5		4	12	7^2	11^1		9	13	14																		15
	2	3		7		9	10^2	11		6^1	12		4	14	8^1			5				13	1													16
1	3		14	11^3	7	13	6	10^1		9	8^2		5		12		4	2																		17
1	2	3			8	6	9^2	11		7^1	10^3		4	14		13	5				12															18
1	2	5			4	7	6^1	10		8^2	11^1		3		14	9					12	13														19
1					3	8	6	10	12	14			4		11^1	13	5		7		9^2	2^3														20
1	2				3	7^2	9^1	10^3	12	14			4	13	11		5		8		6															21
1	2				4	7	9^2	10		12	13		3		11		5		8		6^1															22
1	2	13			3	7	9^2	10		6^2			4^1		11		5		8				12	14												23
1	2	14	4		3	8		10^1	12	9^2	13				11		5		7		6^3															24
1	2	14	4		13	3	8	11^1		9^3	12				10		5		7		6^2															25
1	2		4		12	3	8	11^1		9^2	14		13		10		5		7		6^3															26
1	2		4		12	3	8	10^1	14	9^3	13				11		5		7		6^2															27
1	2	13	4		6	3	8	10		9^1					11^2		5		7							12										28
1	2		4		6	3	7	10^2		9^1					11^3		5		8							14	12	13								29
1	2		4		10	3	8	11		9			13				5									7^1	12	6^2								30
1	2	14			6	3	8	11^2			10^3	4					5		7							12	13	9^1								31
1	2				6	3	7	11^3			10^1	4					5		8							14	12	9^2	13							32
1	2				6^3	3	7	10^3		9	11	11^1	4				5		8							9^2	12	14								33
1	2^1				6	3	7	11^3			10	4					5		8							12	9^2	14	13							34
1	2	14			6	3	7	10	9^2		4						5									8	12	11^1	13^3							35
1	2				6^2	3	7	11	9	10^1	4						5									8	14	12^3	13							36
1	2	14			6	4	7^4	11^1	12	10^3	3						5		8							13			9^2							37
1	2	5			6^2	3		10^1	14	7	4	13					12	9								8	11^3									38
1	2				6	3		11	12	7	10^1	4					5									8	9									39
1	2	13			6	4		12		7^3	11^1	3					5									8	14						9	10^2		40
1	2	5				3	13	10^3	12	11		4			14		9^1									7	6^2					8				41
1	2				6^2	3	7	10^3	9	11^1	4						5									8	13					14	12			42
1	2				3	8	12		6^2	10^3	4						5							14		7^1	9					13	11			43
1	2				9	4	6	10^1			3						5							14		7	11^3					8^2	13	12		44
1	2				8	3	6^1	11	13	12	4						5							7		10^3						9^2	14			45
1^4	2	12			6	3	7^3	10		11^1	4^2						5									8	9					13			14	46

FA Cup
First Round   Barnsley   (a)   0-5

Capital One Cup
First Round   Wigan Ath   (h)   2-1
Second Round   QPR   (h)   1-0
Third Round   Brighton & HA   (h)   0-3

Johnstone's Paint Trophy
Second Round   Doncaster R   (h)   0-3

BURY

JD Stadium, Gigg Lane, Bury, Lancashire BL9 9HR.

Telephone: (0871) 222 1885.

Fax: (0161) 764 5521.

Ticket Office: (0871) 221 1885.

Website: www.buryfc.co.uk

Email: info@buryfc.co.uk

Ground Capacity: 11,376.

Record Attendance: 35,000 v Bolton W, FA Cup 3rd rd, 9 January 1960.

Pitch Measurements: 102.5m × 65.8m (112yd × 72yd)

Chairman: Stewart Day.

Chief Executive: Glenn Thomas.

Manager: David Flitcroft.

Assistant Manager: Chris Brass.

Physio: Tom Walsh.

Colours: White shirts with blue trim, blue shorts, blue socks with white hoops.

Year Formed: 1885.

Turned Professional: 1885.

Club Nickname: 'The Shakers'.

Ground: 1885, Gigg Lane (renamed JD Stadium 2013).

First Football League Game: 1 September 1894, Division 2, v Manchester C (h) W 4–2 – Lowe; Gillespie, Davies; White, Clegg, Ross; Wylie, Barbour (2), Millar (1), Ostler (1), Plant.

Record League Victory: 8–0 v Tranmere R, Division 3, 10 January 1970 – Forrest; Tinney, Saile; Anderson, Turner, McDermott; Hince (1), Arrowsmith (1), Jones (4), Kerr (1), Grundy, (1 og).

Record Cup Victory: 12–1 v Stockton, FA Cup 1st rd (replay), 2 February 1897 – Montgomery; Darroch, Barbour; Hendry (1), Clegg, Ross (1); Wylie (3), Pangbourn, Millar (4), Henderson (2), Plant, (1 og).

Record Defeat: 0–10 v Blackburn R, FA Cup pr rd, 1 October 1887. 0–10 v West Ham U, Milk Cup 2nd rd 2nd leg, 25 October 1983.

Most League Points (2 for a win): 68, Division 3, 1960–61.

Most League Points (3 for a win): 85, FL 2, 2014–15.

Most League Goals: 108, Division 3, 1960–61.

Highest League Scorer in Season: Craig Madden, 35, Division 4, 1981–82.

Most League Goals in Total Aggregate: Craig Madden, 129, 1978–86.

Most League Goals in One Match: 5, Eddie Quigley v Millwall, Division 2, 15 February 1947; 5, Ray Pointer v Rotherham U, Division 2, 2 October 1965.

Most Capped Player: Bill Gorman, 11 (13), Republic of Ireland and (4), Northern Ireland.

Most League Appearances: Norman Bullock, 505, 1920–35.

Youngest League Player: Brian Williams, 16 years 133 days v Stockport Co, 18 March 1972.

Record Transfer Fee Received: £1,100,000 from Ipswich T for David Johnson, November 1997.

Record Transfer Fee Paid: £200,000 to Ipswich T for Chris Swailes, November 1997; £200,000 to Swindon T for Darren Bullock, February 1999.

Football League Record: 1894 Elected to Division 2; 1895–1912 Division 1; 1912–24 Division 2; 1924–29 Division 1; 1929–57 Division 2; 1957–61 Division 3; 1961–67 Division 2; 1967–68 Division 3; 1968–69 Division 2; 1969–71 Division 3; 1971–74 Division 4; 1974–80 Division 3; 1980–85 Division 4; 1985–96 Division 3; 1996–97 Division 2; 1997–99 Division 1; 1999–2002 Division 2; 2002–04 Division 3; 2004–11 FL 2; 2011–13 FL 1; 2013–15 FL 2; 2015– FL 1.

LATEST SEQUENCES

Longest Sequence of League Wins: 9, 26.9.1960 – 19.11.1960.

Longest Sequence of League Defeats: 8, 18.8.2001 – 25.9.2001.

Longest Sequence of League Draws: 6, 6.3.1999 – 3.4.1999.

Longest Sequence of Unbeaten League Matches: 18, 4.2.1961 – 29.4.1961.

Longest Sequence Without a League Win: 19, 1.4.1911 – 2.12.1911.

Successive Scoring Runs: 24 from 1.9.1894.

Successive Non-scoring Runs: 6 from 11.1.1969.

MANAGERS

T. Hargreaves 1887
  (*Secretary-Manager*)
H. S. Hamer 1887–1907
  (*Secretary-Manager*)
Archie Montgomery 1907–15
William Cameron 1919–23
James Hunter Thompson 1923–27
Percy Smith 1927–30
Arthur Paine 1930–34
Norman Bullock 1934–38
Charlie Dean 1938–44
Jim Porter 1944–45
Norman Bullock 1945–49
John McNeil 1950–53
Dave Russell 1953–61
Bob Stokoe 1961–65
Bert Head 1965–66
Les Shannon 1966–69
Jack Marshall 1969
Colin McDonald 1970
Les Hart 1970
Tommy McAnearney 1970–72
Alan Brown 1972–73
Bobby Smith 1973–77
Bob Stokoe 1977–78
David Hatton 1978–79
Dave Connor 1979–80
Jim Iley 1980–84
Martin Dobson 1984–89
Sam Ellis 1989–90
Mike Walsh 1990–95
Stan Ternent 1995–98
Neil Warnock 1998–99
Andy Preece 1999–2003
Graham Barrow 2003–05
Chris Casper 2005–08
Alan Knill 2008–11
Richie Barker 2011–12
Kevin Blackwell 2012–13
David Flitcroft December 2013–

TEN YEAR LEAGUE RECORD

		P	W	D	L	F	A	Pts	Pos
2005-06	FL 2	46	12	17	17	45	57	52*	19
2006-07	FL 2	46	13	11	22	46	61	50	21
2007-08	FL 2	46	16	11	19	58	61	59	13
2008-09	FL 2	46	21	15	10	63	43	78	4
2009-10	FL 2	46	19	12	15	54	59	69	9
2010-11	FL 2	46	23	12	11	82	50	81	2
2011-12	FL 1	46	15	11	20	60	79	56	14
2012-13	FL 1	46	9	14	23	45	73	41	22
2013-14	FL 2	46	13	20	13	59	51	59	12
2014-15	FL 2	46	26	7	13	60	40	85	3

*1 pt deducted.

DID YOU KNOW

Striker Ryan Lowe set a Bury club record when he scored in nine consecutive League Two games between January and March 2011. The Shakers won six of the nine games and at the end of the season won promotion to League One.

BURY – FOOTBALL LEAGUE TWO 2014–15 LEAGUE RECORD

Match No.	Date		Venue	Opponents		Result	H/T Score	Lg Pos.	Goalscorers	Attendance
1	Aug	9	H	Cheltenham T	L	0-1	0-1	16		3376
2		16	A	Hartlepool U	W	2-0	1-0	11	Nardiello [18], Rose [73]	3246
3		19	A	Luton T	D	1-1	0-0	12	Rose [62]	7890
4		23	H	Plymouth Arg	W	2-1	2-0	7	Soares [5], Rose [15]	3156
5		30	H	Accrington S	W	2-1	1-1	6	Rose [35], Mayor [62]	3381
6	Sept	6	A	Wycombe W	D	0-0	0-0	6		3483
7		13	A	Carlisle U	W	3-0	0-0	3	Rose [48], Jones [59], Lowe [80]	3975
8		16	H	Stevenage	W	2-1	1-1	2	Lowe [13], Jones [47]	2638
9		20	H	Burton Alb	W	3-1	0-0	1	Nardiello 2 [48, 66], Lowe [57]	4536
10		27	A	Exeter C	L	1-2	0-1	3	Soares [59]	3215
11	Oct	4	H	Tranmere R	W	2-0	0-0	1	Etuhu [55], Nardiello [87]	4481
12		11	A	AFC Wimbledon	L	2-3	0-2	3	Mayor [49], Lowe (pen) [73]	4268
13		18	H	Portsmouth	W	3-0	2-0	2	Mayor [9], Lowe [44], Rose [61]	4259
14		21	A	Shrewsbury T	L	0-5	0-3	4		4233
15		25	A	Southend U	D	1-1	0-1	5	Jones [71]	5174
16	Nov	1	H	Cambridge U	W	2-0	2-0	4	Adams [13], Rose [28]	3704
17		15	A	Morecambe	L	0-1	0-0	5		2665
18		22	H	Newport Co	L	1-3	0-2	7	Rose [61]	3166
19		29	H	Dagenham & R	L	0-2	0-0	8		3042
20	Dec	13	A	Oxford U	L	1-2	0-0	9	Mayor [63]	6912
21		20	H	York C	D	2-2	0-0	9	Tutte [57], Nardiello [62]	3313
22		26	A	Northampton T	W	3-2	2-1	9	Tutte [30], Soares [45], Mayor [57]	4563
23		28	H	Mansfield T	W	2-0	1-0	8	Lowe [40], Mayor [77]	3196
24	Jan	3	A	Dagenham & R	L	0-1	0-0	8		1877
25		17	H	Wycombe W	D	1-1	1-0	10	Mayor [32]	2932
26		24	H	Carlisle U	W	2-1	1-1	7	Nardiello 2 (1 pen) [16 ipl, 62]	3589
27		27	A	Accrington S	W	1-0	0-0	7	Cameron [81]	2067
28		31	A	Burton Alb	L	0-1	0-0	7		3049
29	Feb	7	H	Exeter C	D	1-1	1-1	7	Nardiello [45]	3513
30		10	A	Stevenage	D	0-0	0-0	8		2165
31		14	A	Cheltenham T	W	2-1	2-1	8	Mayor [4], Rose [17]	2375
32		21	H	Hartlepool U	W	1-0	0-0	7	Tutte [75]	3172
33		28	A	Plymouth Arg	W	2-0	0-0	6	Nardiello [62], Rose [90]	7374
34	Mar	3	H	Luton T	W	1-0	1-0	5	Soares [9]	2915
35		7	H	Oxford U	L	0-1	0-0	6		3645
36		14	A	Mansfield T	W	1-0	1-0	5	Tafazolli (og) [21]	2868
37		17	A	York C	W	1-0	1-0	4	Soares [9]	3194
38		21	H	Northampton T	W	2-1	0-1	4	Etuhu [66], El-Abd [90]	3969
39	Apr	3	A	Cambridge U	W	2-0	1-0	4	Cameron [23], Soares [53]	5427
40		6	H	Morecambe	L	1-2	1-0	4	Eaves [17]	4045
41		11	A	Newport Co	W	2-0	1-0	4	Lowe [21], Nardiello [88]	3123
42		14	H	Shrewsbury T	W	1-0	0-0	4	Riley [57]	4277
43		18	A	Portsmouth	W	1-0	1-0	4	Lowe [45]	14,569
44		21	H	Southend U	L	0-1	0-0	5		8396
45		25	H	AFC Wimbledon	W	2-0	1-0	4	Soares [33], Lowe [77]	4099
46	May	2	A	Tranmere R	W	1-0	0-0	3	Soares [61]	7518

Final League Position: 3

GOALSCORERS

League (60): Nardiello 10 (1 pen), Rose 10, Lowe 9 (1 pen), Mayor 8, Soares 8, Jones 3, Tutte 3, Cameron 2, Etuhu 2, Adams 1, Eaves 1, El-Abd 1, Riley 1, own goal 1.
FA Cup (4): Nardiello 2, Cameron 1, Tutte 1.
Capital One Cup (2): Lowe 1, McNulty 1.
Johnstone's Paint Trophy (4): Nardiello 2 (1 pen), Cameron 1, Lowe 1.

Jalal S 5	Jones C 25 + 15	McNulty J 22 + 3	Mills P 18	Hussey C 30 + 8	Adams N 29 + 9	Soares T 43	Nardiello D 19 + 13	Mayor D 43 + 1	Lowe R 23 + 11	Tutte A 37 + 5	Poole J — + 4	Cameron N 45 + 1	Lainton R 17	Etuhu K 43	Rose D 19 + 16	Sedgwick C 1 + 19	Widdowson J — + 1	Holmes D — + 6	Platt C — + 2	Kennedy T 1 + 1	Duffus C 1 + 2	Loach S 2	White H 2	Thompson J — + 1	El-Abd A 24	Milsom R 2	Hope H 10 + 9	Dudley A — + 1	Pope N 22	Riley J 16 + 1	Eaves T 7 + 2	Holding R — + 1	Match No.
1	2	3	4	5	6²	7	8¹	9	10	11	12	13																					1
		4	3	5	6²	9	11	12	10¹	8		2	1	7³	13	14																	2
		4	3		7²	5		9¹	11	6	12	2	1	6		10⁹																	3
		3	4	13	8	9	12	7	11²	5¹	14	2	1	6		10³																	4
13	4⁸	3	12	8³	5²	9	11¹	6		2	1	7	10		14																		5
2		4	5	12	8⁸	6	11¹	9	14	3	1	7	10⁹	13																			6
	5	4	3	10²	9	13	8	12	7¹		2	1	6	11³	14																		7
	5	4	3	13	7	6	14	9²	11¹		2	1	8	10⁹	12																		8
2	5	4		7	9	12	6	10⁹	14		3	1	8¹	11²	13																		9
2	5	4¹		9³	8	11²	6	10			3	1	7	13		12	14																10
1	2	5	3	13	6	9	12		11¹	7²		4		8	10⁹	14																	11
1	5	4	3³	13	9¹	7	11²	6	10		2		8	12		14																	12
	5	4	3	9	6	13	8²	11¹	12		2	1	7	10³	14																		13
	5	4	3	13	9³	7		8¹	11	12		2	1	6	10¹	14																	14
12	4⁸	3		6		8	13	7		2	1	9	14	10²							5	11¹											15
2	5	4		6	8	9²	10²	12		3	1	7	11¹									13	14										16
	4	3	5	11¹	6	12	8		9⁸		2		7	10									13	1									17
	4		5	6	7	12	9	11¹		3		8	10									1	2²	13									18
5			6	8	10	9	13	12		2	1	7²	11¹											3	4								19
1	2	5		14	13	8		6	12	7		4		11³										3		9¹	10²						20
1	5		3²	12	9		11	8¹	10⁹	6		2		7	14									4		13							21
13			5		6	11²	9¹	12	8		4	1	7		14							2⁸		3		10³						22
	13		5	9	2		6	11³	7		3⁸		1	8	12	14								4		10¹						23
13			5	9²	2		6	11	7		3	1	8¹	12										4		10¹	14						24
2			5	14	6	13	9	10¹	7		4		8	12										3		11³		1				25
2			5	12	8	10¹	9		6⁹		4		7	13	14									3		11²		1				26
6¹			5	13	2	10	9		8		4		7³	14										3		11²		1	12			27
13			2	12	9	11	6		8		4		7²	14										4		10¹		1	5⁵			28
2¹	13		9	6²	8	10	11		7		4		3³	14										3³		14		1	5			29
6²	4		5	14	10	12	9		8⁹		3		7	11¹										13				1	2			30
13	4		5	6		10¹	9³		7²		3		8	11	12									14				1	2			31
12			5	9¹		11³	10		7		4		8	6²	14									3		13		1	2			32
13			5	6²	10	11¹	9		7		3		8	12										4				1	2			33
13			5	7¹	9	11²	10	12	8⁹		3		6		14									4				1	2			34
14	13		5	6²	9		10	12	7		4		8³	11¹										3⁸				1	2			35
12	4		5	6¹	10		9⁸		7		3		8	13										14				1	2	11³		36
12	3		5	7²	9		10⁸		8¹		4		6	14										13				1	2	11		37
12			5	6¹	10		9	13	7³		3		8											4		14		1	2⁴	11²		38
2³			5		6	12	9	10¹	8		4		7	13										3				1	11²	14		39
2²			5	13	9	10¹	8	12	6		4		7											3		14		1	11³			40
2			5	6¹	12	9	11³	7			4		8	14	13									3				1	10²			41
6			5	10	11¹	9	7²				4		8	14										3				1	2	12		42
6			5	10		9¹	12	7			4		8²	14	13									3				1	2	11³		43
13			5	9	11²	8	10	7			4		6³	12										3				1	2¹	14		44
2			5	14	8	11		13	10		4		6⁴	12										3		9³		1	7¹			45
12			5	6	13	9	11³	7²			3		8	14										4		10¹		1	2			46

FA Cup

First Round	Hemel Hempstead	(h)	3-1
Second Round	Luton T	(h)	1-1
Replay	Luton T	(a)	0-1

Capital One Cup

First Round	Bolton W	(a)	2-3
(aet)			

Johnstone's Paint Trophy

Second Round	Morecambe	(h)	3-1
Northern Quarter-Finals	Tranmere R	(h)	1-2

CAMBRIDGE UNITED

FOUNDATION

The football revival in Cambridge began soon after World War II when the Abbey United club (formed 1912) decided to turn professional in 1949. In 1951 they changed their name to Cambridge United. They were competing in the United Counties League before graduating to the Eastern Counties League in 1951 and the Southern League in 1958.

The R Costings Abbey Stadium, Newmarket Road, Cambridge CB5 8LN.

Telephone: (01223) 566 500.

Ticket Office: (01223) 566 500.

Website: www.cambridgeunited.com

Email: info@cambridge-united.co.uk

Ground Capacity: 8,696.

Record Attendance: 14,000 v Chelsea, Friendly, 1 May 1970.

Pitch Measurements: 100.5m × 67.5m (110yd × 74yd).

Chairman: Dave Doggett.

Vice-chairman: Eddie Clarke.

Head Coach: Richard Money.

Assistant Coach: Alan Neilson.

Physio: Greg Reid.

HONOURS

Football League – Division 2: Best season: 5th, 1991–92; **Division 3:** *Champions* 1990–91; *Runners-up* 1977–78, 1998–99; **Division 4:** *Champions* 1976–77; *Promoted from Division 4* 1989–90 (play-offs).

Skrill Conference: *Promoted to FL 2* 2013–14 (play-offs).

FA Cup: Best season: 6th rd, 1990 (shared record for Fourth Division club), 1991.

Football League Cup: Best season: quarter-final, 1993.

LDV Vans Trophy: *Runners-up* 2002.

Colours: Amber and black striped shirts, black shorts, amber stockings.

Year Formed: 1912.

Turned Professional: 1949.

Ltd Co.: 1948.

Previous Name: 1919, Abbey United; 1951, Cambridge United.

Club Nickname: The 'U's'.

Grounds: 1932, Abbey Stadium (renamed R Costings Abbey Stadium 2009).

First Football League Game: 15 August 1970, Division 4, v Lincoln C (h) D 1–1 – Roberts; Thompson, Meldrum (1), Slack, Eades, Hardy, Leggett, Cassidy, Lindsey, McKinven, Harris.

Record League Victory: 6–0 v Darlington, Division 4, 18 September 1971 – Roberts; Thompson, Akers, Guild, Eades, Foote, Collins (1p), Horrey, Hollett, Greenhalgh (4), Phillips, (1 og). 6–0 v Hartlepool U, Division 4, 11 February 1989 – Vaughan; Beck, Kimble, Turner, Chapple (1), Daish, Clayton, Holmes, Taylor (3 incl. 1p), Bull (1), Leadbitter (1).

Record Cup Victory: 5–1 v Bristol C, FA Cup 5th rd second replay, 27 February 1990 – Vaughan; Fensome, Kimble, Bailie (O'Shea), Chapple, Daish, Cheetham (Robinson), Leadbitter (1), Dublin (2), Taylor (1), Philpott (1).

Record Defeat: 0–7 v Sunderland, League Cup 2nd rd, 1 October 2002.

sky SPORTS FACT FILE

Cambridge United had the distinction of being the first club to gain promotion via a Wembley play-off final when they defeated Chesterfield 1-0 on 26 May 1990 to go up to the Third Division. Dion Dublin scored the second half winner in front of a crowd of 26,404. Previously play-off finals were played on a home and away basis over two legs.

Most League Points (2 for a win): 65, Division 4, 1976–77.

Most League Points (3 for a win): 86, Division 3, 1990–91.

Most League Goals: 87, Division 4, 1976–77.

Highest League Scorer in Season: David Crown, 24, Division 4, 1985–86.

Most League Goals in Total Aggregate: John Taylor, 86, 1988–92; 1996–2001.

Most League Goals in One Match: 5, Steve Butler v Exeter C, Division 2, 4 April 1994.

Most Capped Player: Tom Finney, 7 (15), Northern Ireland.

Most League Appearances: Steve Spriggs, 416, 1975–87.

Youngest League Player: Andy Sinton, 16 years 228 days v Wolverhampton W, 2 November 1982.

Record Transfer Fee Received: £1,000,000 from Manchester U for Dion Dublin, August 1992; £1,000,000 from Leicester C for Trevor Benjamin, July 2000.

Record Transfer Fee Paid: £192,000 to Luton T for Steve Claridge, November 1992.

Football League Record: 1970 Elected to Division 4; 1973–74 Division 3; 1974–77 Division 4; 1977–78 Division 3; 1978–84 Division 2; 1984–85 Division 3; 1985–90 Division 4; 1990–91 Division 3; 1991–92 Division 2; 1992–93 Division 1; 1993–95 Division 2; 1995–99 Division 3; 1999–2002 Division 2; 2002–04 Division 3; 2004–05 FL2; 2005–14 Conference; 2014– FL 2.

MANAGERS
Bill Whittaker 1949–55
Gerald Williams 1955
Bert Johnson 1955–59
Bill Craig 1959–60
Alan Moore 1960–63
Roy Kirk 1964–66
Bill Leivers 1967–74
Ron Atkinson 1974–78
John Docherty 1978–83
John Ryan 1984–85
Ken Shellito 1985
Chris Turner 1985–90
John Beck 1990–92
Ian Atkins 1992–93
Gary Johnson 1993–95
Tommy Taylor 1995–96
Roy McFarland 1996–2001
John Beck 2001
John Taylor 2001–04
Claude Le Roy 2004
Herve Renard 2004
Steve Thompson 2004–05
Rob Newman 2005–06
Jimmy Quinn 2006–08
Gary Brabin 2008–09
Martin Ling 2009–11
Jez George 2011–12
Richard Money October 2012–

LATEST SEQUENCES

Longest Sequence of League Wins: 7, 19.2.1977 – 1.4.1977.

Longest Sequence of League Defeats: 7, 8.4.1985 – 30.4.1985.

Longest Sequence of League Draws: 6, 6.9.1986 – 30.9.1986.

Longest Sequence of Unbeaten League Matches: 14, 9.9.1972 – 10.11.1972.

Longest Sequence Without a League Win: 31, 8.10.1983 – 23.4.1984.

Successive Scoring Runs: 26 from 9.4.2002.

Successive Non-scoring Runs: 5 from 29.9.1973.

TEN YEAR LEAGUE RECORD

		P	W	D	L	F	A	Pts	Pos
2005-06	Conf	42	15	10	17	51	57	55	12
2006-07	Conf	46	15	10	21	57	66	55	17
2007-08	Conf P	46	25	11	10	68	41	86	2
2008-09	Conf P	46	24	14	8	65	39	86	2
2009-10	Conf P	44	15	14	15	65	53	59	10
2010-11	Conf P	46	11	17	18	53	61	50	17
2011-12	Conf P	46	19	14	13	57	41	71	9
2012-13	Conf P	46	15	14	17	68	69	59	14
2013-14	Conf P	46	23	13	10	72	35	82	2
2014-15	FL 2	46	13	12	21	61	66	51	19

DID YOU KNOW ?

Brothers Tony and Jose Gallego both went on to play for Cambridge United after fleeing from Bilbao as refugees of the Spanish Civil War. Tony, a goalkeeper, appeared in the Football League for Norwich City while Jose also played for Brentford, Southampton and Colchester United.

CAMBRIDGE UNITED – FOOTBALL LEAGUE TWO 2014–15 LEAGUE RECORD

Match No.	Date	Venue	Opponents	Result	H/T Score	Lg Pos.	Goalscorers	Attendance
1	Aug 9	H	Plymouth Arg	W 1-0	0-0	3	Coulson [61]	6009
2	16	A	Portsmouth	L 1-2	0-1	12	Appiah [69]	16,671
3	19	A	York C	D 2-2	2-1	13	Elliott [27], Appiah (pen) [38]	3176
4	23	H	Morecambe	L 1-2	0-1	17	Elliott [55]	3152
5	30	H	Carlisle U	W 5-0	3-0	9	Diallo [25], Simpson 2 [33, 45], Stockley 2 [83, 87]	3512
6	Sept 8	A	Newport Co	D 1-1	0-0	11	Chadwick [48]	2594
7	13	A	Dagenham & R	W 3-2	0-1	6	Donaldson [54], Nelson [61], Bird [77]	2049
8	16	H	Exeter C	L 1-2	1-1	11	Bird [8]	3266
9	20	H	Luton T	L 0-1	0-0	14		6533
10	27	A	Wycombe W	L 0-1	0-0	18		3610
11	Oct 3	A	Burton Alb	W 3-1	0-0	13	Elliott 2 [35, 76], Donaldson [64]	2683
12	11	H	Oxford U	W 5-1	2-1	11	Appiah 2 [41, 45], Donaldson [54], Elliott [59], Simpson [89]	4435
13	18	A	Mansfield T	D 0-0	0-0	11		2925
14	21	H	Cheltenham T	L 1-2	1-1	15	Appiah [25]	3252
15	25	H	Hartlepool U	W 2-1	1-0	11	Donaldson [26], Dunk [87]	4933
16	Nov 1	H	Bury	L 0-2	0-2	14		3704
17	14	H	Northampton T	W 2-1	0-0	8	Cunnington [51], Bird [79]	5644
18	22	A	Accrington S	L 1-2	0-1	13	Nelson [90]	1364
19	29	A	AFC Wimbledon	D 2-2	1-1	10	Appiah [12], Hughes [58]	4306
20	Dec 13	A	Shrewsbury T	D 0-0	0-0	12		5346
21	19	A	Tranmere R	D 1-1	0-0	11	Nelson [89]	4578
22	26	H	Southend U	L 0-1	0-0	14		7053
23	28	A	Stevenage	L 2-3	1-3	14	Bird [22], Cunnington [86]	4579
24	Jan 10	A	Carlisle U	W 1-0	0-0	14	Hughes [48]	3406
25	17	H	Newport Co	W 4-0	2-0	12	McGeehan 2 [12, 64], KaiKai [43], Hughes [79]	6076
26	27	A	Dagenham & R	D 1-1	1-0	12	McGeehan [23]	4068
27	31	A	Luton T	L 2-3	0-3	14	Hunt [67], Simpson [86]	10,054
28	Feb 7	H	Wycombe W	L 0-1	0-0	14		6894
29	10	H	Exeter C	D 2-2	1-0	14	Simpson [37], Woodman (og) [50]	3012
30	14	A	Plymouth Arg	L 0-2	0-0	15		6413
31	21	H	Portsmouth	L 2-6	1-4	16	Mendez-Laing [22], Simpson [54]	6528
32	24	H	AFC Wimbledon	D 0-0	0-0	16		4259
33	28	A	Morecambe	W 2-0	1-0	16	Donaldson [45], Slew [59]	1593
34	Mar 3	H	York C	L 0-3	0-1	16		4037
35	7	A	Shrewsbury T	D 1-1	0-1	17	KaiKai [90]	5075
36	14	A	Stevenage	D 1-1	0-1	16	Simpson [90]	5503
37	17	H	Tranmere R	L 1-2	0-1	18	KaiKai [63]	4202
38	21	A	Southend U	D 0-0	0-0	18		7224
39	28	A	Hartlepool U	L 1-2	1-1	19	Harrold [32]	5009
40	Apr 3	H	Bury	L 0-2	0-1	19		5427
41	6	A	Northampton T	W 1-0	1-0	18	Dunk [1]	5520
42	11	H	Accrington S	D 2-2	1-1	18	Elliott [8], Bird [79]	5569
43	14	A	Cheltenham T	L 1-3	1-1	19	Bird [33]	2415
44	18	H	Mansfield T	W 3-1	2-0	18	KaiKai 2 [3, 43], Elliott [88]	4667
45	25	A	Oxford U	L 0-2	0-2	18		5954
46	May 2	A	Burton Alb	L 2-3	1-1	19	Elliott [25], Simpson (pen) [69]	7109

Final League Position: 19

GOALSCORERS

League (61): Elliott 8, Simpson 8 (1 pen), Appiah 6 (1 pen), Bird 6, Donaldson 5, KaiKai 5, Hughes 3, McGeehan 3, Nelson 3, Cunnington 2, Dunk 2, Stockley 2, Chadwick 1, Coulson 1, Diallo 1, Harrold 1, Hunt 1, Mendez-Laing 1, Slew 1, own goal 1.
FA Cup (6): Appiah 2, Chadwick 1, Donaldson 1, KaiKai 1, Simpson 1.
Capital One Cup (1): Donaldson 1.
Johnstone's Paint Trophy (0).

Dunn C 43	Tait R 34+3	Coulson J 46	Bonner T 4	Taylor G 41+2	Donaldson R 38	Champion T 38	Diallo I 7+1	Dunk H 21+11	Cunnington A 4+3	Appiah K 19	Simpson R 23+12	Sam-Yorke D —+2	Chadwick L 8+14	Hughes L 26+4	Elliott T 30	Whittall S —+2	Lanzoni M 3	Nelson M 33	Stockley J 1+2	Taylor B 1+6	Bird R 10+14	Harrold M 6+1	Lennon H —+2	Austin M 1	Margetts J —+1	Hurst L —+4	Naylor T 5+3	Norris W 3	Blair M 1+1	KaiKai S 11+14	Chiedozie J 2+4	Miller I 8	Atkinson W —+2	McGeehan C 4	Ball D 9+2	Hunt J 4+5	Morrissey G 3+5	Slew J 9+4	Akintunde J —+1	Mendez-Laing N 10+1	Match No.
1	2	3	4	5	6	7	8³	9	10¹	11³	12	13	14																												1
1	2¹	3	4²	5	6	7		9	13	11	12		14	8³				10																							2
1	12	4	3	5	9	8				11	7¹	14	6³	2				10²	13																						3
1	2	3	4	5	6	7	8¹	9¹		11²			14	12	13			10																							4
1		3		5	9¹	7	8³				11²			12	6	10	2	4	13	14																					5
1		3		4	10	7		9²			12³			6	11		2	5	13				8¹	14																	6
1	2	3		5	8	7		6¹			10			4	11³	14	12					9²	13																		7
1	6²	3		5	7		8	9			10²			2¹	4	14	13	11			12																				8
1	2	3		5	6		12	8²		11	10¹			9				4				13	7⁴																		9
1	2	3		5	7¹		6²	8		11³	9			10				4			14	12	13																		10
1	2		4	5	6		8			11	7				9	10		3																							11
1	2		4	5⁹				12			10	7		6¹	8	11²		3			13	14																			12
1	2	3		5⁹	9	7		12			10	8¹		13	6	11		4																							13
1	2¹		4	5⁹	9	7		12			11			14	6	10		3			13						8²														14
1	2		4	5	9	7¹		13			12			11²	14	8³		3					12																		15
1	2	3		5	9	7		12			11	8²		6¹	13	10³		4					14																		16
1	2		4	5	6³	7		10²	11		9			12	3		14	13					8¹																		17
1	2	3		5			8			14	10	11¹		9²	7			4					13		12	6³															18
1	2		4	5		7					6	14		12	8			3					11²						13	9⁵	10¹										19
1	2	3		5		7					10	9²		13	8			4					11³				6¹		12		4	14									20
1		3	2			7		11¹	10	8⁴		14	5					4			9²				6		12		13³												21
1	2	3		5		7		13	10²		6	8		9¹	6						12								11³	9¹	4	14									22
1	2	3		5	9	7		13			11¹	6²		8	10			4					14						12³												23
1	2	4		5	9¹	7		12						6	10³			3					13						11²	14			8							24
1	2	4		5	6¹		8	9²						13	11			3					12						14			10	7³							25
1	2	4		5	6³	7					12				11			3					10¹									8	9² 13							26
1	2	4		5	9	7					11¹				10³			3					13									8⁸	14	6² 12						27
1	2	4		5	7	8					10	12			3								6¹										9	11						28
1		3		5	6	7		8						11¹				4					9² 13										2	12	10³ 14					30
1	12	4		5	6	7						8		2³				3			11²						13							14	10¹	9				31
1	2	4		5	6	7					12				10²		8¹								11					13		3			14		10	9		32
1	2	4		5	6²	7					13				12		8³						11¹						3					14	10	9				33
1	2	4		5⁴	6	7					12				13		8³						11¹						3					14	10	9				34
1	2	4		5	6	7²					12				8¹	13							11³										14		10	9				35
1	2	13		6	7			5			12				8²			3					11³			14								10²	9¹	9				36
1	2²	4			6	7					5		14	10			3³													12			8¹		13		9			37
1		3		5	6	7							8	10				11¹							4		12		8¹	9									38
1	2³	4			6	7					5			12									11¹						13		3				9²	14				39
		4		2	6	7					5				8²			10¹					3							11					12	14		9³	13		40
1		3		5	7	8		9¹					13		10			4			11³									12								2 14		6²	41
		4		5	8²	7		9³							10			3					11						1	13							2 14 12		6¹	42
1		3		5	7	8		9²							10¹			4					11							12							2 14 13		6²	43
1		4		12	6¹	7					5							11					3							13						2	8 10²			44
13		4		9							5				12			3			11²		6⁵						1	14					7		2¹ 8 10			45
	2	3		5	7¹			9					11		8	10²		4					12						1	6											46

FA Cup

First Round	Fleetwood T	(h)	1-0
Second Round	Mansfield T	(h)	2-2
Replay	Mansfield T	(a)	1-0
Third Round	Luton T	(h)	2-1
Fourth Round	Manchester U	(h)	0-0
Replay	Manchester U	(a)	0-3

Capital One Cup

| First Round | Birmingham C | (a) | 1-3 |
| *(aet)* | | | |

Johnstone's Paint Trophy

| First Round | Crawley T | (a) | 0-2 |

CARDIFF CITY

FOUNDATION

Credit for the establishment of a first class professional football club in such a rugby stronghold as Cardiff is due to members of the Riverside club formed in 1899 out of a cricket club of that name. Cardiff became a city in 1905 and in 1908 the South Wales and Monmouthshire FA granted Riverside permission to call themselves Cardiff City. The club turned professional under that name in 1910.

Cardiff City Stadium, Leckwith Road, Cardiff CF11 8AZ.

Telephone: (0845) 365 1115. *Fax:* (0845) 365 1116.

Ticket Office: (0845) 345 1400.

Website: www.cardiffcityfc.co.uk

Email: club@cardiffcityfc.co.uk

Ground Capacity: 33,280.

Record Attendance: 57,893 v Arsenal, Division 1, 22 April 1953 (at Ninian Park); 28,018 v Liverpool, FA Premier League, 22 March 2014 (at Cardiff City Stadium).

Ground Record Attendance: 62,634, Wales v England, 17 October 1959 (at Ninian Park).

Pitch Measurements: 105m × 68m (114yd × 75yd)

Chairman: Mehmet Dalman.

Chief Executive: Ken Choo.

Manager: Russell Slade.

Assistant Manager: Scott Young.

Physio: Adam Rattenberry.

Colours: Blue shirts with white trim, blue shorts, blue socks with white trim.

Year Formed: 1899.

Turned Professional: 1910.

Previous Names: 1899, Riverside; 1902, Riverside Albion; 1908, Cardiff City.

Club Nickname: 'The Bluebirds'.

HONOURS

Football League Division 1: *Runners-up* 1923–24;
Division 2: *Runners-up* 1920–21, 1951–52, 1959–60;
FL C: *Champions* 2012–13;
Division 3 (S): *Champions* 1946–47;
Division 3: *Champions* 1992–93. *Runners-up* 1975–76, 1982–83, 2000–01;
Division 4: *Runners-up* 1987–88.

FA Cup: *Winners* 1927 (only occasion the Cup has been won by a club outside England); *Runners-up* 1925, 2008.

Football League Cup: *Runners-up* 2012.

Welsh Cup: *Winners* 22 times (joint record).

Charity Shield: *Winners* 1927.

European Competitions
European Cup-Winners' Cup: 1964–65, 1965–66, 1967–68 (*s-f*), 1968–69, 1969–70, 1970–71, 1971–72, 1973–74, 1974–75, 1976–77, 1977–78, 1988–89, 1992–93, 1993–94.

Grounds: Riverside, Sophia Gardens, Old Park and Fir Gardens; 1910, Ninian Park; 2009, Cardiff City Stadium.

First Football League Game: 28 August 1920, Division 2, v Stockport Co (a) W 5–2 – Kneeshaw; Brittan, Layton; Keenor (1), Smith, Hardy; Grimshaw (1), Gill (2), Cashmore, West, Evans (1).

Record League Victory: 9–2 v Thames, Division 3 (S), 6 February 1932 – Farquharson; Eric Morris, Roberts; Galbraith, Harris, Ronan; Emmerson (1), Keating (1), Jones (1), McCambridge (1), Robbins (5).

sky SPORTS FACT FILE

When official competitions resumed after the break for the Second World War, Cardiff City won their first 5 home games and in fact went undefeated at Ninian Park in the 1946–47 season. The Bluebirds' first post-war home defeat was against Tottenham Hotspur in September 1947.

Record Cup Victory: 8–0 v Enfield, FA Cup 1st rd, 28 November 1931 – Farquharson; Smith, Roberts; Harris (1), Galbraith, Ronan; Emmerson (2), Keating (3); O'Neill (2), Robbins, McCambridge.

Record Defeat: 2–11 v Sheffield U, Division 1, 1 January 1926.

Most League Points (2 for a win): 66, Division 3 (S), 1946–47.

Most League Points (3 for a win): 87, FL C, 2012–13.

Most League Goals: 95, Division 3, 2000–01.

Highest League Scorer in Season: Robert Earnshaw, 31, Division 2, 2002–03.

Most League Goals in Total Aggregate: Len Davies, 128, 1920–31.

Most League Goals in One Match: 5, Hugh Ferguson v Burnley, Division 1, 1 September 1928; 5, Walter Robbins v Thames, Division 3 (S), 6 February 1932; 5, William Henderson v Northampton T, Division 3 (S), 22 April 1933.

Most Capped Player: Alf Sherwood, 39 (41), Wales.

Most League Appearances: Phil Dwyer, 471, 1972–85.

Youngest League Player: Bob Adams, 15 years 355 days v Southend U, 18 February 1933.

Record Transfer Fee Received: £8,000,000 from QPR for Steven Caulker, July 2014.

Record Transfer Fee Paid: £11,000,000 to Sevilla for Gary Medel, August 2013.

Football League Record: 1920 Elected to Division 2; 1921–29 Division 1; 1929–31 Division 2; 1931–47 Division 3 (S); 1947–52 Division 2; 1952–57 Division 1; 1957–60 Division 2; 1960–62 Division 1; 1962–75 Division 2; 1975–76 Division 3; 1976–82 Division 2; 1982–83 Division 3; 1983–85 Division 2; 1985–86 Division 3; 1986–88 Division 4; 1988–90 Division 3; 1990–92 Division 4; 1992–93 Division 3; 1993–95 Division 2; 1995–99 Division 3; 1999–2000 Division 2; 2000–01 Division 3; 2001–03 Division 2; 2003–04 Division 1; 2004–13 FL C; 2013–14 FA Premier League; 2014– FL C.

LATEST SEQUENCES

Longest Sequence of League Wins: 9, 26.10.1946 – 28.12.1946.

Longest Sequence of League Defeats: 7, 4.11.1933 – 25.12.1933.

Longest Sequence of League Draws: 6, 29.11.1980 – 17.1.1981.

Longest Sequence of Unbeaten League Matches: 21, 21.9.1946 – 1.3.1947.

Longest Sequence Without a League Win: 15, 21.11.1936 – 6.3.1937.

Successive Scoring Runs: 24 from 25.8.2012.

Successive Non-scoring Runs: 8 from 20.12.1952.

MANAGERS

Davy McDougall 1910–11
Fred Stewart 1911–33
Bartley Wilson 1933–34
B. Watts-Jones 1934–37
Bill Jennings 1937–39
Cyril Spiers 1939–46
Billy McCandless 1946–48
Cyril Spiers 1948–54
Trevor Morris 1954–58
Bill Jones 1958–62
George Swindin 1962–64
Jimmy Scoular 1964–73
Frank O'Farrell 1973–74
Jimmy Andrews 1974–78
Richie Morgan 1978–81
Graham Williams 1981–82
Len Ashurst 1982–84
Jimmy Goodfellow 1984
Alan Durban 1984–86
Frank Burrows 1986–89
Len Ashurst 1989–91
Eddie May 1991–94
Terry Yorath 1994–95
Eddie May 1995
Kenny Hibbitt (*Chief Coach*) 1995–96
Phil Neal 1996
Russell Osman 1996–97
Kenny Hibbitt 1997–98
Frank Burrows 1998–2000
Billy Ayre 2000
Bobby Gould 2000
Alan Cork 2000–02
Lennie Lawrence 2002–05
Dave Jones 2005–11
Malky Mackay 2011–13
Ole Gunnar Solskjaer 2014
Russell Slade October 2014–

TEN YEAR LEAGUE RECORD

		P	W	D	L	F	A	Pts	Pos
2005-06	FL C	46	16	12	18	58	59	60	11
2006-07	FL C	46	17	13	16	57	53	64	13
2007-08	FL C	46	16	16	14	59	55	64	12
2008-09	FL C	46	19	17	10	65	53	74	7
2009-10	FL C	46	22	10	14	73	54	76	4
2010-11	FL C	46	23	11	12	76	54	80	4
2011-12	FL C	46	19	18	9	66	53	75	6
2012-13	FL C	46	25	12	9	72	45	87	1
2013-14	PR Lge	38	7	9	22	32	74	30	20
2014-15	FL C	46	16	14	16	57	61	62	11

DID YOU KNOW ?

Cardiff City centre half Stan Montgomery also played cricket for Glamorgan. He still holds the county's record fifth wicket partnership after hitting 264 along with Maurice Robinson in the game with Hampshire at Bournemouth in 1949.

CARDIFF CITY – FL CHAMPIONSHIP 2014–15 LEAGUE RECORD

Match No.	Date	Venue	Opponents	Result		H/T Score	Lg Pos.	Goalscorers	Attendance
1	Aug 8	A	Blackburn R	D	1-1	1-1	1	Jones [18]	15,625
2	16	H	Huddersfield T	W	3-1	2-1	3	Whittingham [28], Jones 2 [35, 56]	20,749
3	19	A	Wigan Ath	W	1-0	0-0	2	Maynard [53]	20,662
4	23	A	Wolverhampton W	L	0-1	0-0	8		21,221
5	30	A	Fulham	D	1-1	0-1	8	Jones [55]	17,508
6	Sept 13	H	Norwich C	L	2-4	2-0	15	Ralls [4], Gunnarsson [22]	21,746
7	16	H	Middlesbrough	L	0-1	0-1	17		19,711
8	20	A	Derby Co	D	2-2	0-0	16	Gunnarsson [51], Whittingham [55]	27,251
9	27	H	Sheffield W	W	2-1	1-0	15	Morrison, S [39], Pilkington [61]	20,901
10	30	A	Brighton & HA	D	1-1	1-1	13	Jones [21]	23,712
11	Oct 3	A	Blackpool	L	0-1	0-0	14		10,502
12	18	H	Nottingham F	W	2-1	2-0	12	Macheda [22], Whittingham [27]	21,263
13	21	H	Ipswich T	W	3-1	1-1	10	Whittingham [37], Macheda [47], Le Fondre [69]	20,191
14	25	A	Millwall	L	0-1	0-0	11		10,135
15	Nov 1	H	Leeds U	W	3-1	0-0	11	Ecuele Manga [61], Macheda [67], Jones [83]	24,220
16	4	A	Bolton W	L	0-3	0-2	11		12,961
17	8	A	Birmingham C	D	0-0	0-0	12		15,950
18	21	H	Reading	W	2-1	2-0	11	Pearce (og) [20], Whittingham (pen) [45]	20,643
19	29	A	Watford	W	1-0	1-0	8	Le Fondre [12]	15,668
20	Dec 6	H	Rotherham U	D	0-0	0-0	9		20,419
21	13	A	Bournemouth	L	3-5	1-3	11	Jones [45], Morrison, S 2 [48, 78]	10,440
22	20	H	Brentford	L	2-3	0-3	11	Noone [48], Jones [75]	21,784
23	26	A	Charlton Ath	D	1-1	1-0	11	Adeyemi [12]	17,543
24	28	A	Watford	L	2-4	1-2	12	Le Fondre [20], Jones [90]	22,208
25	Jan 10	H	Fulham	W	1-0	1-0	11	Morrison, S [14]	22,515
26	17	A	Norwich C	L	2-3	0-3	13	Revell [61], Harris [64]	25,995
27	20	A	Middlesbrough	L	1-2	0-0	13	Jones [86]	16,035
28	31	H	Derby Co	L	0-2	0-2	13		22,287
29	Feb 7	A	Sheffield W	D	1-1	1-0	15	Jones [7]	22,344
30	10	H	Brighton & HA	D	0-0	0-0	16		19,206
31	17	H	Blackburn R	D	1-1	0-0	15	Morrison, S [84]	19,057
32	21	H	Huddersfield T	D	0-0	0-0	17		12,798
33	24	A	Wigan Ath	W	1-0	1-0	13	Gunnarsson [20]	10,016
34	28	H	Wolverhampton W	L	0-1	0-1	15		21,165
35	Mar 3	A	Rotherham U	W	3-1	3-0	13	Ecuele Manga [24], Macheda [26], McAleny [35]	8534
36	7	H	Charlton Ath	L	1-2	0-0	15	Macheda [56]	20,488
37	14	A	Brentford	W	2-1	0-1	14	Macheda [53], Revell [68]	11,217
38	17	H	Bournemouth	D	1-1	0-1	13	Ecuele Manga [62]	19,819
39	21	H	Birmingham C	W	2-0	0-0	14	Doyle [50], Whittingham (pen) [76]	20,602
40	Apr 4	A	Reading	D	1-1	0-1	13	McAleny [90]	17,953
41	6	H	Bolton W	L	0-3	0-0	13		20,219
42	11	A	Leeds U	W	2-1	1-1	12	Morrison, S [14], Gunnarsson [62]	22,401
43	14	A	Ipswich T	L	1-3	1-2	13	Doyle [13]	17,722
44	18	H	Millwall	D	0-0	0-0	13		19,639
45	25	H	Blackpool	W	3-2	2-0	13	Mason [19], Doyle 2 (2 pens) [31, 76]	26,357
46	May 2	A	Nottingham F	W	2-1	2-0	11	Ralls [14], Doyle [24]	21,988

Final League Position: 11

GOALSCORERS

League (57): Jones 11, Macheda 6, Morrison, S 6, Whittingham 6 (2 pens), Doyle 5 (2 pens), Gunnarsson 4, Ecuele Manga 3, Le Fondre 3, McAleny 2, Ralls 2, Revell 2, Adeyemi 1, Harris 1, Mason 1, Maynard 1, Noone 1, Pilkington 1, own goal 1.
FA Cup (4): Jones 2, Harris 1, Ralls 1.
Capital One Cup (5): Macheda 2, Burgstaller 1, Ralls 1, own goal 1.

Marshall D 38	Brayford J 26	Hudson M 3	Connolly M 20+3	Da Silva F 22+6	Whittingham P 43	Gunnarsson A 43+2	Daehli M 7+2	Le Fondre A 19+4	Jones K 25+9	Maynard N 3+7	Adeyemi T 11+9	Burgstaller G 1+2	Eikrem M —+3	Guerra J —+3	Morrison S 41	Pilkington A 15+5	Dikgacoi K 1+1	Ralls J 15+13	Macheda F 13+8	John D 2+4	Ecuele Manga B 29	Cala J 1	Noone C 33+4	Morrison R 1+6	Turner B 11	Gabbidon D —+1	Kim B 2	Harris K 3+11	Moore S 8+2	Malone S 12+1	Revell A 8+8	Peltier L 15	O'Keefe S 4+2	Doyle E 11+5	McAleny C 6+2	Kennedy M 9+5	Mason J 5+2	Match No.
1	2	3	4	5	6	7	8¹	9²	10²	11	12	13	14																									1
1	2	3	4	5	8	12	9³	10	11²			7	6¹	14	13																							2
1	2		4	5	9	8	6³	13	11¹	10²				14	3	12																						3
1	3	2		5	9	7³		10	12	11¹	8	13			4	6²	14																					4
1	2		4	5	8		9²	11³	10		14				3	6	7¹	12	13																			5
1	2	3	5²		8	7		10²		14	13				4	9¹					6	11	12															6
1	2		4		8	12	7³	13	10	9				14	6²						11¹		3	5														7
1	2		4		7	8²		12	11	13	9				6						5		11¹	3	5													8
1	2		5²	9	7	8		11¹							4	6	14	13			3		10³	12														9
1	2		5	9	8	10²		11³			7¹				4	6		14			3		12	13														10
1	2		5	8	7		14	11³							3	6		9²	12	4			13	10¹														11
1	2			8	7¹	14	10	12			13³				4	6		5	11²	4	3		9															12
1	2		5	8	7		11¹		12						4	6		13	10²	3			9															13
1	2		5	8	7¹		11²		14						4	6		12	10³	3			9	13														14
1	2		5	8	7		11³		13						4	6²		12	10¹	3			9	14														15
1	2		5	8	7		11¹		13						4	6²		9²	10	3			6	12														16
1	5		2	13	8	7		10		12					4³	9		11¹			6²		3	14														17
1	5		2¹	13	8	7		12	10	14					3	6		11²			9³		4															18
1	5		2²	12	8	7³		10	11		14				3	6¹	13				9		4															19
1	5		2³	13	8	7		11¹	10²						3			12			9	14	4	6														20
1	5		2		8	7³		11	10³		14				3			13			9	4	6¹	12														21
1	2		5¹	8	7			10	12							11²	13	3			9		4	6														22
1	2			8	6		10¹	11		7²					3	13	5				9		4	12														23
1	2			7	8³		10¹	11		6¹					4	12	14	5	3		9		13															24
	2			8	7	11¹	10²	6							3	13					9		4		14	1	5¹	12										25
	2			8	7	10²	6³								3	14					13		9	4	12	1	5¹	11										26
	2	5		8	7		12		6³						3	13	14				9²		4	10	1		11¹											27
			4	13	10	8²		12	14						3						6		9³	1	5	11	2	7¹										28
		13		8	7			10							3			4			14			1	5	12	2⁴	6	9²	11¹								29
1				9	8			11							4			3	6		13		5		2	7¹	12	10²										30
1	14			8	7²			11	13						4			3	6				5⁴	12	2	10¹	9											31
1	12			8	7			11							4			3	9				5⁴	14	2	10³	13	6²										32
1		2		8	7			11²							4		5		3		9		13	12	2	10²	11	6¹										33
1		5		8⁰	7			11							4				3		9		13	2	10²	12	6¹											34
1¹		5			7			14							3		8	9³	4				12	10²	2	13	11	6										35
	2			8	7¹			11							4		12	10³	3		9		1	14	5		6²	13										36
		5	8	7				14							4		12	10⁸	3		9		13⁹	1	11¹	2³		6²										37
	5	2		8	7¹			11²	14						4		12		3		9		1	10		13	6⁴											38
	2			8	7²		10	14							4			9	3		6³		5	11¹	1	12	13											39
1	5			7	8			4							9³	3	6						14		2¹	10¹	11	12	13									40
1	2			7	8³			4							9	3	6¹						14		5	10¹	11²	13	12									41
1				7	8			4							9	3	6²		13		5		2	14	12	10¹	11³											42
1	6¹			8	7			4					13		9³	3	12				14		5	2	11²	10												43
1	12			8	7			4					13		9³	3	6²				5¹		2	10	14	11												44
1		5			7			14					4		13	8¹	3	9³					2	12	10	6	11²											45
1⁸		5			7			3	12				9		4	14	13				2	8		11⁴			6³	10¹										46

FA Cup

| Third Round | Colchester U | (h) | 3-1 |
| Fourth Round | Reading | (h) | 1-2 |

Capital One Cup

First Round	Coventry C	(a)	2-1
Second Round	Port Vale	(a)	3-2
Third Round	Bournemouth	(h)	0-3

CARLISLE UNITED

FOUNDATION

Carlisle United came into being when members of Shaddongate United voted to change its name on 17 May 1904. The new club was admitted to the Second Division of the Lancashire Combination in 1905–06, winning promotion the following season. Devonshire Park was officially opened on 2 September 1905, when St Helens Town were the visitors. Despite defeat in a disappointing 3–2 start, a respectable mid-table position was achieved.

Brunton Park, Warwick Road, Carlisle, Cumbria CA1 1LL.

Telephone: (01228) 526 237.

Fax: (01228) 554 141.

Ticket Office: (0844) 371 1921.

Website: www.carlisleunited.co.uk

Email: enquiries@carlisleunited.co.uk

Ground Capacity: 17,949.

Record Attendance: 27,500 v Birmingham C, FA Cup 3rd rd, 5 January 1957 and v Middlesbrough, FA Cup 5th rd, 7 February 1970.

Pitch Measurements: 102.5m × 67.5m (112yd × 74yd)

Chairman: Andrew Jenkins.

Managing Director: John Nixon.

Manager: Keith Curle.

Assistant Manager: Colin West.

Physio: Neil Dalton.

Colours: Blue shirts with white and red trim, white shorts with blue and red trim, red socks.

Year Formed: 1904. *Turned Professional:* 1921.

Previous Name: 1904, Shaddongate United; 1904, Carlisle United.

Club Nicknames: 'The Cumbrians', 'The Blues'.

Grounds: 1904, Milholme Bank; 1905, Devonshire Park; 1909, Brunton Park.

First Football League Game: 25 August 1928, Division 3 (N), v Accrington S (a) W 3–2 – Prout; Coulthard, Cook; Harrison, Ross, Pigg; Agar (1), Hutchison, McConnell (1), Ward (1), Watson.

Record League Victory: 8–0 v Hartlepool U, Division 3 (N), 1 September 1928 – Prout; Smiles, Cook; Robinson (1) Ross, Pigg; Agar (1), Hutchison (1), McConnell (4), Ward (1), Watson. 8–0 v Scunthorpe U, Division 3 (N), 25 December 1952 – MacLaren; Hill, Scott; Stokoe, Twentyman, Waters; Harrison (1), Whitehouse (5), Ashman (2), Duffett, Bond.

Record Cup Victory: 6–0 v Shepshed Dynamo, FA Cup 1st rd, 16 November 1996 – Caig; Hopper, Archdeacon (pen), Walling, Robinson, Pounewatchy, Peacock (1), Conway (1) (Jansen), Smart (McAlindon (1)), Hayward, Aspinall (Thorpe), (2 og). 6–0 v Tipton T, FA Cup 1st rd, 6 November 2010 – Collin; Simek, Murphy, Chester, Cruise, Robson (McKenna), Berrett, Taiwo (Hurst), Marshall, Zoko (Curran) (2), Madine (4).

HONOURS

Football League – Division 1: 22nd, 1974–75;

Division 3: *Champions* 1964–65, 1994–95; *Runners-up* 1981–82;

Division 4: *Runners-up* 1963–64; **FL 2:** *Champions* 2005–06.

FA Cup: 6th rd, 1975.

Football League Cup: Best season: semi-final, 1970.

Auto Windscreens Shield: *Winners* 1997; *Runners-up* 1995.

LDV Vans Trophy: *Runners-up* 2003, 2006.

Johnstone's Paint Trophy: *Winners* 2011; *Runners-up* 2010.

sky SPORTS FACT FILE

In the early hours of 11 March 1953 the 1,000-seater main stand at Carlisle United's Brunton Park ground was gutted by a fire. The club lost their entire stock of playing kit but, undeterred, they managed to fulfil their Division Three North home fixture against Tranmere Rovers the following day with United winning 4-0.

Record Defeat: 1–11 v Hull C, Division 3 (N), 14 January 1939.

Most League Points (2 for a win): 62, Division 3 (N), 1950–51.

Most League Points (3 for a win): 91, Division 3, 1994–95.

Most League Goals: 113, Division 4, 1963–64.

Highest League Scorer in Season: Jimmy McConnell, 42, Division 3 (N), 1928–29.

Most League Goals in Total Aggregate: Jimmy McConnell, 124, 1928–32.

Most League Goals in One Match: 5, Hugh Mills v Halifax T, Division 3 (N), 11 September 1937; 5, Jim Whitehouse v Scunthorpe U, Division 3 (N), 25 December 1952.

Most Capped Player: Eric Welsh, 4, Northern Ireland.

Most League Appearances: Allan Ross, 466, 1963–79.

Youngest League Player: John Slaven, 16 years 162 days v Scunthorpe U, 16 March 2002.

Record Transfer Fee Received: £1,000,000 from Crystal Palace for Matt Jansen, February 1998.

Record Transfer Fee Paid: £140,000 to Blackburn R for Joe Garner, August 2007.

Football League Record: 1928 Elected to Division 3 (N); 1958–62 Division 4; 1962–63 Division 3; 1963–64 Division 4; 1964–65 Division 3; 1965–74 Division 2; 1974–75 Division 1; 1975–77 Division 2; 1977–82 Division 3; 1982–86 Division 2; 1986–87 Division 3; 1987–92 Division 4; 1992–95 Division 3; 1995–96 Division 2; 1996–97 Division 3; 1997–98 Division 2; 1998–2004 Division 3; 2004–05 Conference; 2005–06 FL 2; 2006–14 FL 1; 2014– FL 2.

LATEST SEQUENCES

Longest Sequence of League Wins: 7, 18.2.2006 – 8.4.2006.

Longest Sequence of League Defeats: 12, 27.9.2003 – 13.12.2003.

Longest Sequence of League Draws: 6, 11.2.1978 – 11.3.1978.

Longest Sequence of Unbeaten League Matches: 19, 1.10.1994 – 11.2.1995.

Longest Sequence Without a League Win: 15, 12.4.2014 – 20.9.2014.

Successive Scoring Runs: 26 from 23.8.1947.

Successive Non-scoring Runs: 5 from 16.8.2003.

MANAGERS

Harry Kirkbride 1904–05
  (Secretary-Manager)
McCumiskey 1905–06
  (Secretary-Manager)
Jack Houston 1906–08
  (Secretary-Manager)
Bert Stansfield 1908–10
Jack Houston 1910–12
Davie Graham 1912–13
George Bristow 1913–30
Billy Hampson 1930–33
Bill Clarke 1933–35
Robert Kelly 1935–36
Fred Westgarth 1936–38
David Taylor 1938–40
Howard Harkness 1940–45
Bill Clark 1945–46
  (Secretary-Manager)
Ivor Broadis 1946–49
Bill Shankly 1949–51
Fred Emery 1951–58
Andy Beattie 1958–60
Ivor Powell 1960–63
Alan Ashman 1963–67
Tim Ward 1967–68
Bob Stokoe 1968–70
Ian MacFarlane 1970–72
Alan Ashman 1972–75
Dick Young 1975–76
Bobby Moncur 1976–80
Martin Harvey 1980
Bob Stokoe 1980–85
Bryan 'Pop' Robson 1985
Bob Stokoe 1985–86
Harry Gregg 1986–87
Cliff Middlemass 1987–91
Aidan McCaffery 1991–92
David McCreery 1992–93
Mick Wadsworth (*Director of Coaching*) 1993–96
Mervyn Day 1996–97
David Wilkes and John Halpin
  (*Directors of Coaching*), and
  Michael Knighton 1997–99
Nigel Pearson 1998–99
Keith Mincher 1999
Martin Wilkinson 1999–2000
Ian Atkins 2000–01
Roddy Collins 2001–02; 2002–03
Paul Simpson 2003–06
Neil McDonald 2006–07
John Ward 2007–08
Greg Abbott 2008–13
Graham Kavanagh 2013–14
Keith Curle September 2014–

TEN YEAR LEAGUE RECORD

		P	W	D	L	F	A	Pts	Pos
2005-06	FL 2	46	25	11	10	84	42	86	1
2006-07	FL 1	46	19	11	16	54	55	68	8
2007-08	FL 1	46	23	11	12	64	46	80	4
2008-09	FL 1	46	12	14	20	56	69	50	20
2009-10	FL 1	46	15	13	18	63	66	58	14
2010-11	FL 1	46	16	11	19	60	62	59	12
2011-12	FL 1	46	18	15	13	65	66	69	8
2012-13	FL 1	46	14	13	19	56	77	55	17
2013-14	FL 1	46	11	12	23	43	76	45	22
2014-15	FL 2	46	14	8	24	56	74	50	20

DID YOU KNOW ?

When Carlisle United lost 3-2 at home to Wycombe Wanderers on 21 February 2015 they set a new club record of 26 consecutive Football League games without a draw. United extended the run by a further three games before being held to a 0-0 draw at York City.

CARLISLE UNITED – FOOTBALL LEAGUE TWO 2014–15 LEAGUE RECORD

Match No.	Date	Venue	Opponents	Result		H/T Score	Lg Pos.	Goalscorers	Atten- dance
1	Aug 9	H	Luton T	L	0-1	0-1	16		6766
2	16	A	Wycombe W	L	1-3	0-0	22	Potts [57]	3121
3	19	A	Cheltenham T	D	0-0	0-0	19		2341
4	23	H	Southend U	D	1-1	1-1	20	Sweeney [43]	3847
5	30	A	Cambridge U	L	0-5	0-3	22		3512
6	Sept 6	H	AFC Wimbledon	D	4-4	2-2	22	Dempsey 2 [13, 45], Gillies [52], Potts [70]	3955
7	13	H	Bury	L	0-3	0-0	24		3975
8	16	A	Shrewsbury T	L	0-1	0-1	24		3833
9	20	A	Mansfield T	L	2-3	0-3	24	Amoo [61], Dempsey [71]	3117
10	27	H	Tranmere R	W	1-0	0-0	24	Amoo [72]	3873
11	Oct 4	A	Hartlepool U	W	3-0	0-0	23	Rigg [54], Elliott [82], Beck [89]	3927
12	11	H	Stevenage	W	3-0	2-0	20	Potts [17], Rigg [28], Beck [87]	4011
13	18	A	Plymouth Arg	L	0-1	0-1	21		6529
14	21	H	Burton Alb	L	3-4	2-4	21	Dempsey [12], Potts [45], Asamoah [65]	4266
15	25	H	Oxford U	W	2-1	0-1	20	Beck [73], Asamoah [89]	4392
16	Nov 1	A	Portsmouth	L	0-3	0-2	22		15,533
17	15	H	Accrington S	W	1-0	1-0	20	Asamoah [21]	4069
18	22	A	Dagenham & R	L	2-4	1-3	22	Asamoah [16], Grainger [53]	2097
19	29	H	Newport Co	L	2-3	0-1	22	Potts [52], Amoo [90]	3642
20	Dec 13	A	Exeter C	L	0-2	0-0	23		3402
21	20	H	Northampton T	W	2-1	1-1	21	Archibald-Henville [17], Potts [61]	4421
22	26	A	Morecambe	W	1-0	0-0	20	Amoo [51]	4165
23	28	H	York C	L	0-3	0-1	21		5716
24	Jan 3	A	Newport Co	L	1-2	1-1	22	Meppen-Walter [11]	3273
25	10	H	Cambridge U	D	0-0	0-0	22		3406
26	17	A	AFC Wimbledon	W	3-1	1-1	21	O'Hanlon [16], Rigg [56], Amoo [90]	4186
27	24	A	Bury	L	1-2	1-1	22	Rigg [22]	3589
28	31	H	Mansfield T	W	2-1	0-1	20	Wyke [72], Dempsey [79]	3827
29	Feb 7	A	Tranmere R	W	2-0	0-0	18	Wyke 2 [65, 69]	5358
30	10	H	Shrewsbury T	L	1-2	0-0	19	Wyke [66]	3624
31	14	A	Luton T	L	0-1	0-1	19		8502
32	21	H	Wycombe W	L	2-3	0-1	21	Dempsey [67], Grainger (pen) [82]	4021
33	28	A	Southend U	L	0-2	0-0	23		5576
34	Mar 3	A	Cheltenham T	W	1-0	1-0	21	Wyke [31]	3116
35	7	H	Exeter C	L	1-3	1-1	21	Rigg [39]	3724
36	14	A	York C	D	0-0	0-0	21		4274
37	17	A	Northampton T	W	2-0	0-0	20	Kennedy [69], Dempsey [71]	3682
38	21	H	Morecambe	D	1-1	0-0	20	Potts [53]	4343
39	28	A	Oxford U	L	1-2	1-1	21	Corry [9]	5515
40	Apr 3	H	Portsmouth	D	2-2	1-2	21	Dempsey [2], Wyke [90]	5230
41	6	A	Accrington S	L	1-3	0-1	21	Dempsey [90]	2274
42	11	H	Dagenham & R	W	1-0	0-0	20	Kennedy [55]	3660
43	15	A	Burton Alb	D	1-1	1-0	21	Grainger [2]	3892
44	18	H	Plymouth Arg	W	2-0	1-0	20	Dicker [29], Paynter [50]	4651
45	25	A	Stevenage	L	0-1	0-0	20		3632
46	May 2	H	Hartlepool U	D	3-3	3-0	20	Dempsey [25], Rigg [31], Kennedy [33]	8105

Final League Position: 20

GOALSCORERS

League (56): Dempsey 10, Potts 7, Rigg 6, Wyke 6, Amoo 5, Asamoah 4, Beck 3, Grainger 3 (1 pen), Kennedy 3, Archibald-Henville 1, Corry 1, Dicker 1, Elliott 1, Gillies 1, Meppen-Walter 1, O'Hanlon 1, Paynter 1, Sweeney 1.
FA Cup (1): Asamoah 1.
Capital One Cup (0).
Johnstone's Paint Trophy (4): Dempsey 1, Paynter 1, Potts 1, Sweeney 1.

Gillespie M 19	Symington D 9+3	Grainger D 41	O'Hanlon S 28+1	Meppen-Walter C 17+2	Robson M 5+6	Marrow A 4	Potts B 34+5	Dicker G 16+4	Paynter B 9+9	Amoo D 12+15	Elliott S 4+11	Kearns D 3+7	Sweeney A 26+3	Dempsey K 4+2	Brough P 27+2	Thirlwell P 14+4	Marriott J 3+1	Gillies J 3+3	Beck M 11+16	Archibald-Henville T 24	White H 8	Hanford D 25	Rigg S 19+9	Iliev G 4	Asamoah D 13+14	Anderson T 8	Taylor C —+1	Brown C 8	Hammell C —+3	Young M 20	Griffith A 10+1	Wyke C 16+1	Spiegel R 2	Kennedy J 11	Corry P 4+2	Moiakana J 1	Buddle N 1+2	Atkinson D 6+1	Match No.
1	2	3[2]	4	5	6	7	8	9	10	11[1]	12	13																											1
1	2		4	3	9[1]	7[4]	5	10[3]	11[2]			13	14		6	8	12																						2
1	2	5	3			8	7	10		12		6			9	4	11[1]																						3
1	5	4	2			6	7[3]	10			13		8	12	9	3	11[1]																						4
1	2	5	3		8[3]		10[2]	6	12			7	14	9	4	11[1]	13																						5
1	2	3	4		8[3]	6[4]		14	11[2]			7	10[1]	5	13			9	12																				6
1	6	4	2		8			13	11[2]			7	9	5	14	10	12	3[3]																					7
1	2	3			8	7[3]	10[2]	13	12			6	11	5	4[4]			9[1]	14																				8
1		4		6[1]	7	9	12	11[2]	14	8[3]	10	5			13	3	2																						9
	4			6	8[3]	12	9	13	14	11	5[2]	7			10	3	2	1																					10
	5			7	12	14	6[3]	13		11	9[1]	3			10	4	2	1	8[2]																				11
14	5		12		8[2]	7		13			6	9[3]	4		10	3	2	1	11[1]																				12
6[1]		13	12	9	8		14		7[3]	5	3[2]				11	4	2	1	10																				13
	5	3	9[1]	6	8[2]		14		7	11		4			13		2	1	10[3]	12																			14
	3		4	8	7		12	9[2]		6	2				10		5	1	11[1]	13																			15
	5	3[3]	12	8	6		14		7	9[2]		11			2[4]	1	10[1]	13	4																				16
	5	3	9		8	11[3]	12		6[2]	13	7					1	14	10[1]	4	2																			17
	5	4	9[3]		7	11[1]		6[2]	12	8					13		1	14	10	3	2																		18
	5	3	14	6			13		9	8	7[1]	4			12		1	11	10[2]		2[2]																		19
	5		12	13	14	11		6	8	7[1]		10[3]	3		1		9	4	2[2]																				20
	5	13	9		6[2]			7	8			10	4		1		11[1]	3	2	12																			21
13	5	7	11[2]		9[1]		6	8	14			10[1]	4		1		12	3	2																				22
14	5	3	9[2]		6[3]		8[1]	7				11			1	12	10	4	2	13																			23
	5	9[1]	13	10			7	6	8[2]		12		3	1	14	11[2]	4	2																					24
1	5	4	6[2]		7		12		9	8			13	3		11[1]	10		2																				25
1	2	10	5		8[3]		13		4[1]	6			14	3		7[2]	12		9	11																			26
1	5[3]	3	6		9[2]		12		8	10			14	4		11			2	7[1]	13																		27
1	2	4	8		9[1]		12		14	6				3		11[3]	13		5	7	10[2]																		28
1	5	3	7					14	10[2]	9[1]	13			4		8[3]	12		2	6	11[1]																		29
	4	3	8		6		12		13	9[2]		5			1	11[3]	14		2	7	10[1]																		30
	5	4	7[1]		13		12		9	6			14	3		1	10[3]		2	8[1]	11																		31
	3	4	6[3]		8		12		9[1]	7	5		14[4]			13	10[2]		2	11	1																		32
	3						6[3]		7	9	5	8[2]	12	4		10	13		2	11	1																		33
	4						6		8	7	5		3			10[1]	12		2	9	11																		34
	5	3[3]	13				6		8[1]	9		12	4		1	10	14		2	7[1]	11																		35
	5	4		6[1]	13		9			14	3		1	11			2	8[1]	10[3]	7	12																		36
	4	3		9	13	6[1]		10	5	14			1	12		11[2]			2			7	8[1]																37
	4			6[3]	12		13		9	5		3			1	10[2]	14		2	11		7	8																38
	2								10[1]	8			3[4]	1	9	12			4	11[2]		7	5	6[3]	13	14													39
	4	3		6	14	12			8[2]	5			1	11[3]	13				10	7	9[1]							2											40
	5	4		6[2]	14	13			9	8[3]		1			13	10[2]			2	14	11	7							2										41
1	5	3		12	7[1]				8	6			4[4]			13	10[2]		2	14	11[3]	9																	42
1	2	3[2]		14	5[1]				7	6		11[3]				13	10		9			8			12	4													43
1	2	3		12	8[2]	13			6	5			12			11[3]	10[1]		9			7	14			4													44
1	2	5		3	14				9	8			12			13			11[1]	6[2]	10[3]	7																	45
1				6[3]					8[2]	9	5	14				11[1]				13		12	2		10	7						3	4						46

FA Cup
First Round   Peterborough U   (a)   1-2

Capital One Cup
First Round   Derby Co   (h)   0-2

Johnstone's Paint Trophy
First Round   Accrington S   (a)   3-1
Second Round   Tranmere R   (a)   1-1
(Tranmere R won 5-4 on penalties)

CHARLTON ATHLETIC

FOUNDATION

The club was formed on 9 June 1905, by a group of 14- and 15-year-old youths living in streets by the Thames in the area which now borders the Thames Barrier. The club's progress through local leagues was so rapid that after the First World War they joined the Kent League where they spent a season before turning professional and joining the Southern League in 1920. A year later they were elected to the Football League's Division 3 (South).

The Valley, Floyd Road, Charlton, London SE7 8BL.

Telephone: (020) 8333 4000.

Fax: (020) 8333 4001.

Ticket Office: (03330) 144 444.

Website: www.cafc.co.uk

Email: customerservices@cafc.co.uk

Ground Capacity: 27,111.

Record Attendance: 75,031 v Aston Villa, FA Cup 5th rd, 12 February 1938 (at The Valley).

Pitch Measurements: 101.5m × 65.8m (111yd × 72yd)

Non-Executive Chairman: Richard Murray.

Head Coach: Guy Luzon.

First-Team Coach: Damian Matthew.

Head Physio: Erol Umut.

Colours: Red shirts with white trim, red shorts, red socks with white hoops.

Year Formed: 1905.

Turned Professional: 1920.

Club Nickname: 'The Addicks'.

Grounds: 1906, Siemen's Meadow; 1907, Woolwich Common; 1909, Pound Park; 1913, Horn Lane; 1920, The Valley; 1923, Catford (The Mount); 1924, The Valley; 1985, Selhurst Park; 1991, Upton Park; 1992, The Valley.

First Football League Game: 27 August 1921, Division 3 (S), v Exeter C (h) W 1–0 – Hughes; Johnny Mitchell, Goodman; Dowling (1), Hampson, Dunn; Castle, Bailey, Halse, Green, Wilson.

Record League Victory: 8–1 v Middlesbrough, Division 1, 12 September 1953 – Bartram; Campbell, Ellis; Fenton, Ufton, Hammond; Hurst (2), O'Linn (2), Leary (1), Firmani (3), Kiernan.

Record Cup Victory: 7–0 v Burton A, FA Cup 3rd rd, 7 January 1956 – Bartram; Campbell, Townsend; Hewie, Ufton, Hammond; Hurst (1), Gauld (1), Leary (3), White, Kiernan (2).

Record Defeat: 1–11 v Aston Villa, Division 2, 14 November 1959.

Most League Points (2 for a win): 61, Division 3 (S), 1934–35.

HONOURS

Football League – FL 1 *Champions* 2011–12; **Division 1:** *Champions* 1999–2000; *Runners-up* 1936–37; **Division 2:** *Runners-up* 1935–36, 1985–86;
Division 3 (S): *Champions* 1928–29, 1934–35.

FA Cup: *Winners* 1947; *Runners-up* 1946.

Football League Cup: Best season: quarter-final, 2007.

Full Members' Cup: *Runners-up* 1987.

sky SPORTS FACT FILE

Charlton Athletic did particularly well during the emergency competitions in World War Two, playing in the League South Cup final at Wembley on two occasions. In 1942–43 they lost 7-1 to Arsenal while the following season they defeated Chelsea 3-1. The Addicks also reached the FA Cup final in 1945–46, losing to Derby County in extra time.

Most League Points (3 for a win): 101, FL 1, 2011–12.

Most League Goals: 107, Division 2, 1957–58.

Highest League Scorer in Season: Ralph Allen, 32, Division 3 (S), 1934–35.

Most League Goals in Total Aggregate: Stuart Leary, 153, 1953–62.

Most League Goals in One Match: 5, Wilson Lennox v Exeter C, Division 3 (S), 2 February 1929; 5, Eddie Firmani v Aston Villa, Division 1, 5 February 1955; 5, John Summers v Huddersfield T, Division 2, 21 December 1957; 5, John Summers v Portsmouth, Division 2, 1 October 1960.

Most Capped Player: Jonatan Johansson, 42 (106), Finland.

Most League Appearances: Sam Bartram, 579, 1934–56.

Youngest League Player: Jonjo Shelvey, 16 years 59 days v Burnley, 26 April 2008.

Record Transfer Fee Received: £16,500,000 from Tottenham H for Darren Bent, May 2007.

Record Transfer Fee Paid: £4,750,000 to Wimbledon for Jason Euell, January 2001.

Football League Record: 1921 Elected to Division 3 (S); 1929–33 Division 2; 1933–35 Division 3 (S); 1935–36 Division 2; 1936–57 Division 1; 1957–72 Division 2; 1972–75 Division 3; 1975–80 Division 2; 1980–81 Division 3; 1981–86 Division 2; 1986–90 Division 1; 1990–92 Division 2; 1992–98 Division 1; 1998–99 FA Premier League; 1999–2000 Division 1; 2000–07 FA Premier League; 2007–09 FL C; 2009–12 FL 1; 2012– FL C.

MANAGERS

Walter Rayner 1920–25
Alex Macfarlane 1925–27
Albert Lindon 1928
Alex Macfarlane 1928–32
Albert Lindon 1932–33
Jimmy Seed 1933–56
Jimmy Trotter 1956–61
Frank Hill 1961–65
Bob Stokoe 1965–67
Eddie Firmani 1967–70
Theo Foley 1970–74
Andy Nelson 1974–79
Mike Bailey 1979–81
Alan Mullery 1981–82
Ken Craggs 1982
Lennie Lawrence 1982–91
Steve Gritt/Alan Curbishley 1991–95
Alan Curbishley 1995–2006
Iain Dowie 2006
Les Reed 2006
Alan Pardew 2006–08
Phil Parkinson 2008–11
Chris Powell 2011–14
José Riga 2014
Bob Peeters 2014–15
Guy Luzon January 2015–

LATEST SEQUENCES

Longest Sequence of League Wins: 12, 26.12.1999 – 7.3.2000.

Longest Sequence of League Defeats: 10, 11.4.1990 – 15.9.1990.

Longest Sequence of League Draws: 6, 13.12.1992 – 16.1.1993.

Longest Sequence of Unbeaten League Matches: 15, 4.10.1980 – 20.12.1980.

Longest Sequence Without a League Win: 18, 18.10.2008 – 17.1.2009.

Successive Scoring Runs: 25 from 26.12.1935.

Successive Non-scoring Runs: 5 from 6.9.1922.

TEN YEAR LEAGUE RECORD

		P	W	D	L	F	A	Pts	Pos
2005-06	PR Lge	38	13	8	17	41	55	47	13
2006-07	PR Lge	38	8	10	20	34	60	34	19
2007-08	FL C	46	17	13	16	63	58	64	11
2008-09	FL C	46	8	15	23	52	74	39	24
2009-10	FL 1	46	23	15	8	71	48	84	4
2010-11	FL 1	46	15	14	17	62	66	59	13
2011-12	FL 1	46	30	11	5	82	36	101	1
2012-13	FL C	46	17	14	15	65	59	65	9
2013-14	FL C	46	13	12	21	41	61	51	18
2014-15	FL C	46	14	18	14	54	60	60	12

DID YOU KNOW ?

In December 1923 Charlton Athletic moved from The Valley to a new ground, The Mount in Catford. The directors had hoped this would produce an increase in attendances but the move was disastrous and the club quickly returned to their former home.

CHARLTON ATHLETIC – FL CHAMPIONSHIP 2014–15 LEAGUE RECORD

Match No.	Date	Venue	Opponents	Result	H/T Score	Lg Pos.	Goalscorers	Attendance
1	Aug 9	A	Brentford	D	1-1	0-0	11	Vetokele [64]	9690
2	16	H	Wigan Ath	W	2-1	1-1	5	Cousins [8], Moussa [90]	15,334
3	19	H	Derby Co	W	3-2	2-1	4	Tucudean [11], Buyens (pen) [45], Vetokele [78]	15,317
4	23	A	Huddersfield T	D	1-1	0-0	5	Vetokele [90]	11,333
5	30	H	Brighton & HA	D	2-2	1-0	6	Vetokele 2 [4, 75]	26,189
6	Sept 13	H	Watford	W	1-0	1-0	5	Buyens (pen) [3]	17,628
7	16	H	Wolverhampton W	D	1-1	1-0	5	Bikey [25]	15,973
8	20	A	Rotherham U	D	1-1	1-0	7	Gudmundsson [27]	9620
9	27	H	Middlesbrough	D	0-0	0-0	8		16,110
10	30	A	Norwich C	W	1-0	0-0	7	Jackson [86]	25,983
11	Oct 4	H	Birmingham C	D	1-1	1-0	6	Vetokele [11]	16,369
12	18	A	Bournemouth	L	0-1	0-1	8		10,360
13	21	H	Bolton W	W	2-1	1-0	7	Tucudean [28], Jackson [51]	13,433
14	24	A	Fulham	L	0-3	0-2	7		17,923
15	Nov 1	H	Sheffield W	D	1-1	0-1	9	Vetokele [70]	16,850
16	4	A	Leeds U	D	2-2	0-0	9	Gudmundsson 2 (1 pen) [62, 81 (p)]	18,698
17	8	A	Reading	W	1-0	1-0	8	Vetokele [39]	16,989
18	22	H	Millwall	D	0-0	0-0	9		19,189
19	29	H	Ipswich T	L	0-1	0-0	10		16,613
20	Dec 6	A	Nottingham F	D	1-1	1-0	11	Harriott [9]	22,297
21	13	H	Blackpool	D	2-2	1-1	10	Buyens (pen) [38], Cousins [55]	15,411
22	20	A	Blackburn R	L	0-2	0-2	12		13,231
23	26	H	Cardiff C	D	1-1	0-1	12	Gudmundsson [88]	17,543
24	30	A	Ipswich T	L	0-3	0-1	13		26,157
25	Jan 10	H	Brighton & HA	L	0-1	0-0	14		17,865
26	17	A	Watford	L	0-5	0-3	16		17,703
27	24	A	Wolverhampton W	D	0-0	0-0	17		23,487
28	31	H	Rotherham U	D	1-1	0-0	18	Cousins [83]	14,447
29	Feb 7	A	Middlesbrough	L	1-3	1-1	19	Gudmundsson [37]	18,903
30	10	A	Norwich C	L	2-3	0-2	20	Watt [61], Vetokele [68]	15,094
31	14	H	Brentford	W	3-1	1-0	18	Gudmundsson [27], Vetokele [55], Bulot [90]	14,875
32	20	A	Wigan Ath	W	3-0	2-0	12	Bulot [17], Vetokele [45], Eagles [88]	11,344
33	24	A	Derby Co	L	0-2	0-2	16		28,277
34	28	H	Huddersfield T	W	3-0	1-0	12	Gudmundsson [34], Watt 2 [48, 71]	25,545
35	Mar 3	H	Nottingham F	W	2-1	2-1	12	Bulot 2 [7, 38]	14,937
36	7	A	Cardiff C	W	2-1	0-0	12	Watt [74], Buyens (pen) [87]	20,488
37	14	H	Blackburn R	L	1-3	0-2	12	Buyens (pen) [57]	14,888
38	17	A	Blackpool	W	3-0	1-0	11	Eagles [31], Church [61], Gudmundsson [88]	9168
39	21	H	Reading	W	3-2	0-1	11	Buyens 2 (1 pen) [58 (p), 70], Church [80]	15,007
40	Apr 3	A	Millwall	L	1-2	0-0	11	Diarra [67]	14,722
41	7	H	Fulham	D	1-1	1-1	11	Gudmundsson [16]	16,521
42	11	A	Sheffield W	D	1-1	0-1	11	Gudmundsson [75]	23,257
43	14	A	Bolton W	D	1-1	1-0	12	Bulot [9]	12,994
44	18	H	Leeds U	W	2-1	0-1	10	Watt [75], Buyens (pen) [80]	18,053
45	25	A	Birmingham C	L	0-1	0-0	10		17,775
46	May 2	H	Bournemouth	L	0-3	0-2	12		21,280

Final League Position: 12

GOALSCORERS

League (54): Vetokele 11, Gudmundsson 10 (1 pen), Buyens 8 (7 pens), Bulot 5, Watt 5, Cousins 3, Church 2, Eagles 2, Jackson 2, Tucudean 2, Bikey 1, Diarra 1, Harriott 1, Moussa 1.
FA Cup (1): Gudmundsson 1.
Capital One Cup (4): Wilson 2, Buyens 1 (1 pen), Church 1.

Henderson S 31	Solly C 38	Ben Haim T 37	Bikey A 29 + 2	Wiggins R 21	Gudmundsson J 38 + 3	Buyens Y 38 + 2	Jackson J 25 + 1	Cousins J 43 + 1	Tucudean G 14 + 6	Vetokele I 37 + 4	Harriott C 11 + 10	Fox M 23 + 8	Moussa F 4 + 10	Pope N 7 + 1	Wilson L 10 + 14	Gomez J 16 + 5	Church S 3 + 14	Bulot F 19 + 9	Ahearne-Grant K 2 + 3	Morrison M 1 + 1	Coquelin F 3 + 2	Onyewu O 1 + 2	Pigot J — + 1	Etheridge N 4	Watt T 16 + 6	Dmitrovic M 4 + 1	Veljkovic M 3	Lepoint C 1 + 5	Johnson R 14	Eagles C 5 + 10	Diarra A 8 + 4	Match No.
1	2	3	4	5	6³	7	8	9¹	10²	11	12	13	14																			1
1¹	2	4	3	5	6	7	8³	9	11²	10			12	13	14																	2
		3	4	5	6²	7	8	9	10³	11		14	12	1	13	2																3
	2	3	4	5²	6	7	8	9³	11¹	10	14		12	1			13															4
1	2	3	4	5	6¹	7	8	9³	11²	10		14			13		12															5
1	2	3	4	5	6¹	7	8²	9	11³	10	14		13		12																	6
1		3	4	5		7	8	9	10¹	11			12		6²	2		13														7
1	2	3	4	5	6¹	7	8	9³		11	13	14	10²				12															8
1	2	3	4	5	6¹	7		9³	10	13	11			12	14		8²															9
1		3	4	5		8	7	9		11²		14	12		6	2¹	10³	13														10
1	2		4	5		7	8³	9¹	13	11		14	12		6²		10	3														11
1	2	3	4	5	6¹	7	8²	9		11³	13		12		14			10														12
1		3	4	5		7	8	9	11¹		14	12	10³		2		6²	13														13
1	2	3	4		12		8	7	11			5³	10²		6			9¹	13	14												14
1	2	3	4	5	12	7	8²	6	11	13			10¹		14			9³														15
1		3	4	5	10	7²	8	6	11³	12	9¹				2					13	14											16
1	2	3	4		10¹	7	8	6	13	11²	9³	5				14				12												17
	2	3	4		8³	6²	7¹	10	13	11	12	5		1	14					9												18
	2	3	4		6¹		8³	9	13	11	10²	5		1	12					14		7										19
	2	3	4		6¹		8²	9		11	10	5		1	12					13		7										20
	7	3	4		9	6		8	12	11	10¹	5		1	2																	21
	7	3	4		9	6		8²		10	11³	5¹		1	12	2		14				13										22
	2	3	4		6	7	8²	10	11	12	9¹				5¹						13	1										23
	2	4	3		6	7	8¹	9	10	11					5	12						1										24
	2	3	4	5	9		8¹	7	11²	10					6³	12	14			1	13											25
	2	3	4	5	9³	7		8	10²	11					6¹	14	13			1	12											26
	2	3	4		6	7		9	10²	11³	5				14	13					12		8¹									27
	2	3	4	5	6	7		9	10³	11³					14						12	1	8²	13								28
	2	3			6	7³	12	9	13		5				10¹					4		11	1	8²	14							29
	2	3	4	5	6	7	8²	9		11	13						10¹					12	1									30
1	2	4		5³	6	13	8¹	7		10²		12			14		9					11				3						31
1	2	3			6	7		8²		10¹	14	5			13		9					11³				4	12					32
1	2	3			6	8			10	14	5				7²		9¹					11³				4	13	12				33
1	2				6¹	7		8	10		5				12	3	9²					11³				4	14	13				34
1		12				7		8	10²	6¹	5				2²	3	9					11			14		13	4				35
1²	2				6	7		9			5				3	14	10³					11	12		8¹	4	13					36
1	2	3			6	7²		8	10		5					13	9¹					11				4	12					37
1	2				6	12		8			5				3	10	14					11³			13	4	9²	7¹				38
1					6	8		7			5				2	12	9					11¹			13	4	10²	3				39
1	2¹		12		6			8	10²		5				3	14	13					11²				4	9¹	7				40
1		3			6			7	10²		5				2	13	9¹					11				4	12	8				41
1	2				6	7		8	10		5				3	11²						12				4	9¹	13				42
1	2			5	6	7		8	10¹						13	9						11²				4	12	3				43
1	2	4			13	8		12	10¹		5				3	14	9					11					6¹	7²				44
1	2	3			6	8		7¹	10³		5					13	9²					11				4	12	14				45
1	2	3			6	8			10²		5				14	12	9²					11				4	13	7¹				46

FA Cup

Third Round   Blackburn R   (h)   1-2

Capital One Cup

First Round   Colchester U   (h)   4-0
Second Round   Derby Co   (a)   0-1

CHELSEA

FOUNDATION

Chelsea may never have existed but for the fact that Fulham rejected an offer to rent the Stamford Bridge ground from Mr H. A. Mears who had owned it since 1904. Fortunately he was determined to develop it as a football stadium rather than sell it to the Great Western Railway and got together with Frederick Parker, who persuaded Mears of the financial advantages of developing a major sporting venue. Chelsea FC was formed in 1905 and applications made to join both the Southern League and Football League. The latter competition was decided upon because of its comparatively meagre representation in the south of England.

Stamford Bridge, Fulham Road, London SW6 1HS.
Telephone: (0871) 984 1955. *Fax:* (020) 7381 4831.
Ticket Office: (0871) 984 1905.
Website: www.chelseafc.com
Email: enquiries@chelseafc.com
Ground Capacity: 41,798.
Record Attendance: 82,905 v Arsenal, Division 1, 12 October 1935.
Pitch Measurements: 103m × 67.5m (112yd × 74yd)
Chairman: Bruce Buck.
Chief Executive: Marina Granovskaia.
Manager: Jose Mourinho.
Technical Director: Michael Emenalo.
Assistant First Team Coach: Steve Holland.
Medical Director: Paco Biosca.
Colours: Chelse blue shirt with core blue trim, Chelsea blue shorts with white trim, white socks with Chelsea blue trim.
Year Formed: 1905. *Turned Professional:* 1905.
Club Nickname: 'The Blues'.
Ground: 1905, Stamford Bridge.
First Football League Game: 2 September 1905, Division 2, v Stockport Co (a) L 0–1 – Foulke; Mackie, McEwan; Key, Harris, Miller; Moran, Jack Robertson, Copeland, Windridge, Kirwan.
Record League Victory: 8–0 v Wigan Ath, FA Premier League, 9 May 2010 – Cech; Ivanovic (Belletti), Ashley Cole (1), Ballack (Matic), Terry, Alex, Kalou (1) (Joe Cole), Lampard (pen), Anelka (2), Drogba (3, 1 pen), Malouda; 8–0 v Aston Villa, FA Premier League, 23 December 2012 – Cech; Azpilicueta, Ivanovic (1), Cahill, Cole, Luiz (1), Lampard (1) (Ramirez (2)), Moses, Mata (Piazon), Hazard (1), Torres (1) (Oscar (1)).

HONOURS

FA Premier League:
Champions 2004–05, 2005–06, 2009–10, 2104–15. *Runners-up* 2003–04, 2006–07, 2007–08, 2010–11.

Football League – Division 1:
Champions 1954–55; **Division 2:**
Champions 1983–84, 1988–89;
Runners-up 1906–07, 1911–12, 1929–30, 1962–63, 1976–77.

FA Cup: *Winners* 1970, 1997, 2000, 2007, 2009, 2010, 2012. *Runners-up* 1915, 1967, 1994, 2002.

Football League Cup: *Winners* 1965, 1998, 2005, 2007, 2015; *Runners-up* 1972, 2008.

Full Members' Cup: *Winners* 1986.

Zenith Data Systems Cup:
Winners 1990.

European Competitions
Champions League: 1999–2000, 2003–04 (s-f), 2004–05 (s-f), 2005–06, 2006–07 (s-f), 2007–08 (runners-up), 2008–09 (s-f), 2009–10, 2010–11, 2011–12 (winners), 2012–13, 2013–14 (s-f), 2014–15. **European Fairs Cup:** 1958–60, 1965–66, 1968–69.
European Cup-Winners' Cup: 1970–71 (winners), 1971–72, 1994–95, 1997–98 (winners), 1998–99 (s-f). **UEFA Cup:** 2000–01, 2001–02, 2002–03, 2012. **Super Cup:** 1998–99 (winners), **Europa League:** 2012–13 (winners). **Club World Cup:** 2012 (runners-up).

sky SPORTS FACT FILE

The first Swiss player to appear in England's top flight was Willi Steffen, a full back who played as an amateur for Chelsea in 1946–47. Fluent in French, German and Italian he came to London to learn English and joined Chelsea as his tutor was the wife of the club's manager, Billy Birrell.

Record Cup Victory: 13–0 v Jeunesse Hautcharage, ECWC, 1st rd 2nd leg, 29 September 1971 – Bonetti; Boyle, Harris (1), Hollins (1p), Webb (1), Hinton, Cooke, Baldwin (3), Osgood (5), Hudson (1), Houseman (1).

Record Defeat: 1–8 v Wolverhampton W, Division 1, 26 September 1953.

Most League Points (2 for a win): 57, Division 2, 1906–07.

Most League Points (3 for a win): 99, Division 2, 1988–89.

Most League Goals: 103, FA Premier League, 2009–10.

Highest League Scorer in Season: Jimmy Greaves, 41, 1960–61.

Most League Goals in Total Aggregate: Bobby Tambling, 164, 1958–70.

Most League Goals in One Match: 5, George Hilsdon v Glossop, Division 2, 1 September 1906; 5, Jimmy Greaves v Wolverhampton W, Division 1, 30 August 1958; 5, Jimmy Greaves v Preston NE, Division 1, 19 December 1959; 5, Jimmy Greaves v WBA, Division 1, 3 December 1960; 5, Bobby Tambling v Aston Villa, Division 1, 17 September 1966; 5, Gordon Durie v Walsall, Division 2, 4 February 1989.

Most Capped Player: Frank Lampard, 104 (106), England.

Most League Appearances: Ron Harris, 655, 1962–80.

Youngest League Player: Ian Hamilton, 16 years 138 days v Tottenham H, 18 March 1967.

Record Transfer Fee Received: £50,000,000 from Paris Saint-Germain for David Luiz, July 2014.

Record Transfer Fee Paid: £50,000,000 to Liverpool for Fernando Torres, January 2011.

Football League Record: 1905 Elected to Division 2; 1907–10 Division 1; 1910–12 Division 2; 1912–24 Division 1; 1924–30 Division 2; 1930–62 Division 1; 1962–63 Division 2; 1963–75 Division 1; 1975–77 Division 2; 1977–79 Division 1; 1979–84 Division 2; 1984–88 Division 1; 1988–89 Division 2; 1989–92 Division 1; 1992– FA Premier League.

MANAGERS

John Tait Robertson 1905–07
David Calderhead 1907–33
Leslie Knighton 1933–39
Billy Birrell 1939–52
Ted Drake 1952–61
Tommy Docherty 1961–67
Dave Sexton 1967–74
Ron Suart 1974–75
Eddie McCreadie 1975–77
Ken Shellito 1977–78
Danny Blanchflower 1978–79
Geoff Hurst 1979–81
John Neal 1981–85 (*Director to 1986*)
John Hollins 1985–88
Bobby Campbell 1988–91
Ian Porterfield 1991–93
David Webb 1993
Glenn Hoddle 1993–96
Ruud Gullit 1996–98
Gianluca Vialli 1998–2000
Claudio Ranieri 2000–04
Jose Mourinho 2004–07
Avram Grant 2007–08
Luiz Felipe Scolari 2008–09
Guus Hiddink 2009
Carlo Ancelotti 2009–11
Andre Villas-Boas 2011–12
Roberto Di Matteo 2012
Rafael Benitez 2012–13
Jose Mourinho June 2013–

LATEST SEQUENCES

Longest Sequence of League Wins: 11, 25.4.2009 – 20.9.2009.
Longest Sequence of League Defeats: 7, 1.11.1952 – 20.12.1952.
Longest Sequence of League Draws: 6, 20.8.1969 – 13.9.1969.
Longest Sequence of Unbeaten League Matches: 40, 23.10.2004 – 29.10.2005.
Longest Sequence Without a League Win: 21, 3.11.1987 – 2.4.1988.
Successive Scoring Runs: 27 from 29.10.1988.
Successive Non-scoring Runs: 9 from 14.3.1981.

TEN YEAR LEAGUE RECORD

		P	W	D	L	F	A	Pts	Pos
2005-06	PR Lge	38	29	4	5	72	22	91	1
2006-07	PR Lge	38	24	11	3	64	24	83	2
2007-08	PR Lge	38	25	10	3	65	26	85	2
2008-09	PR Lge	38	25	8	5	68	24	83	3
2009-10	PR Lge	38	27	5	6	103	32	86	1
2010-11	PR Lge	38	21	8	9	69	33	71	2
2011-12	PR Lge	38	18	10	10	65	46	64	6
2012-13	PR Lge	38	22	9	7	75	39	75	3
2013-14	PR Lge	38	25	7	6	71	27	82	3
2014-15	PR Lge	38	26	9	3	73	32	87	1

DID YOU KNOW ?

England international Jack Cock, who scored over 50 goals for Chelsea between 1919 and 1923, was one of the first footballers to enter the world of show business. He was a music hall singer and also appeared in a film, *The Winning Goal*, during his time at Stamford Bridge.

CHELSEA – FA PREMIERSHIP 2014–15 LEAGUE RECORD

Match No.	Date	Venue	Opponents	Result	H/T Score	Lg Pos.	Goalscorers	Attendance
1	Aug 18	A	Burnley	W 3-1	3-1	1	Costa [17], Schurrle [21], Ivanovic [34]	20,699
2	23	H	Leicester C	W 2-0	0-0	1	Costa [62], Hazard, E [77]	41,604
3	30	A	Everton	W 6-3	2-1	1	Costa 2 [1, 90], Ivanovic [3], Coleman (og) [67], Matic [74], Ramires [77]	39,402
4	Sept 13	H	Swansea C	W 4-2	1-1	1	Costa 3 [45, 56, 67], Remy [81]	41,400
5	21	A	Manchester C	D 1-1	0-0	1	Schurrle [71]	45,602
6	27	H	Aston Villa	W 3-0	1-0	1	Oscar [7], Costa [59], Willian [79]	41,616
7	Oct 5	H	Arsenal	W 2-0	1-0	1	Hazard, E (pen) [27], Costa [78]	41,607
8	18	A	Crystal Palace	W 2-1	1-0	1	Oscar [6], Fabregas [51]	24,451
9	26	A	Manchester U	D 1-1	0-0	1	Drogba [53]	75,327
10	Nov 1	H	QPR	W 2-1	1-0	1	Oscar [32], Hazard, E (pen) [75]	41,486
11	8	A	Liverpool	W 2-1	1-1	1	Cahill [14], Costa [67]	44,698
12	22	H	WBA	W 2-0	2-0	1	Costa [11], Hazard, E [25]	41,600
13	29	A	Sunderland	D 0-0	0-0	1		45,232
14	Dec 3	H	Tottenham H	W 3-0	2-0	1	Hazard, E [19], Drogba [22], Remy [73]	41,518
15	6	A	Newcastle U	L 1-2	0-0	1	Drogba [83]	52,019
16	13	H	Hull C	W 2-0	1-0	1	Hazard, E [7], Costa [68]	41,626
17	22	A	Stoke C	W 2-0	1-0	1	Terry [2], Fabregas [78]	27,550
18	26	H	West Ham U	W 2-0	1-0	1	Terry [31], Costa [62]	41,589
19	28	A	Southampton	D 1-1	1-1	1	Hazard, E [45]	31,641
20	Jan 1	A	Tottenham H	L 3-5	1-3	1	Costa [18], Hazard, E [61], Terry [87]	35,903
21	10	H	Newcastle U	W 2-0	1-0	1	Oscar [43], Costa [59]	41,612
22	17	A	Swansea C	W 5-0	4-0	1	Oscar 2 [1, 36], Costa 2 [20, 34], Schurrle [79]	20,785
23	31	H	Manchester C	D 1-1	1-1	1	Remy [41]	41,620
24	Feb 7	A	Aston Villa	W 2-1	1-0	1	Hazard, E [8], Ivanovic [66]	35,969
25	11	H	Everton	W 1-0	0-0	1	Willian [89]	41,592
26	21	H	Burnley	D 1-1	1-0	1	Ivanovic [14]	41,629
27	Mar 4	A	West Ham U	W 1-0	1-0	1	Hazard, E [22]	34,927
28	15	H	Southampton	D 1-1	1-1	1	Costa [11]	41,624
29	22	A	Hull C	W 3-2	2-2	1	Hazard, E [2], Costa [9], Remy [77]	24,598
30	Apr 4	H	Stoke C	W 2-1	1-1	1	Hazard, E (pen) [39], Remy [62]	41,098
31	12	A	QPR	W 1-0	0-0	1	Fabregas [88]	17,939
32	18	H	Manchester U	W 1-0	1-0	1	Hazard, E [38]	41,422
33	26	A	Arsenal	D 0-0	0-0	1		60,066
34	29	A	Leicester C	W 3-1	0-1	1	Drogba [48], Terry [79], Ramires [83]	32,021
35	May 3	H	Crystal Palace	W 1-0	1-0	1	Hazard, E [45]	41,566
36	10	H	Liverpool	D 1-1	1-1	1	Terry [5]	41,547
37	18	A	WBA	L 0-3	0-1	1		24,750
38	24	H	Sunderland	W 3-1	1-1	1	Costa (pen) [37], Remy 2 [70, 88]	41,620

Final League Position: 1

GOALSCORERS

League (73): Costa 20 (1 pen), Hazard, E 14 (3 pens), Remy 7, Oscar 6, Terry 5, Drogba 4, Ivanovic 4, Fabregas 3, Schurrle 3, Ramires 2, Willian 2, Cahill 1, Matic 1, own goal 1.
FA Cup (5): Cahill 1, Ramires 1, Remy 1, Willian 1, Zouma 1.
Capital One Cup (11): Hazard, E 2 (1 pen), Drogba 1, Ivanovic 1, Luis 1, Oscar 1, Schurrle 1, Terry 1, Zouma 1, own goals 2.
UEFA Champions League (20): Hazard, E 3 (2 pens), Drogba 2 (1 pen), Fabregas 2 (1 pen), Matic 2, Terry 2, Cahill 1, Ivanovic 1, Mikel 1, Ramires 1, Remy 1, Schurrle 1, Willian 1, own goals 2.

Courtois T 32	Ivanovic B 38	Cahill G 33 + 3	Terry J 38	Azpilicueta C 29	Fabregas F 33 + 1	Matic N 35 + 1	Schurrle A 5 + 9	Oscar E 26 + 2	Hazard E 38	Costa D 24 + 2	Willian d 28 + 8	Mikel J 6 + 12	Drogba D 8 + 20	Ramires 11 + 12	Luis F 9 + 6	Remy L 6 + 13	Salah M — + 3	Cech P 6 + 1	Zouma K 7 + 8	Loftus-Cheek R 2 + 1	Cuadrado J 4 + 8	Ake N — + 1	Brown I — + 1	Christensen A — + 1	Match No.
1	2	3	4	5	6	7	8³	9¹	10²	11	12	13	14												1
1	2	3	4	5	7	6	8²	9³	10	11¹	13		14	12											2
1	2	3	4	5	9¹	7		10²	11	8³	12	14	6	13											3
1	2	3	4	5	6³	7	8¹	9	10	11²			12			13	14								4
1	2	3	4	5	6	7	12	9²	10	11³		13	14	8¹											5
1	2	3	4	5	6	7	12	9⁴	10¹	11²	8	13	14												6
1³	2	3	4	5	7	6	8¹	9²	10	11	14	13			12										7
1	2	3	4	5*	7	6		9	10¹	8³	14		12	11²	13										8
1	2*	3	4		6	7	13	9¹	10²	8³	12	11		5							14				9
1	2	3	4		6	7	13	9	10	11²	8³		12	14	5										10
1	2	3	4	5	7	6		9	10²	11³		14	8¹	13	12										11
1	2	3	4	5	7	6		9⁴	10	11¹	8²		13	14	12										12
1	2	3	4	5	6	7	14	9²	10	11³	8¹		13		12										13
1	2	3¹	4	5	6³	7		9	10	8	14	11¹			13				12						14
1	2	3	4	5²	6		12	9	10	11	8³	7	14	13											15
	2	3	4			7	13	9	10	11	8³	6²	12	14	5			1							16
1	2	3	4	5	9	7	12	10²	11¹	8³	6	13		14											17
1	2	3	4	5	6	7		9³	10	11²	8¹	13	12	14											18
1	2	3	4		9	7	8²	10	11¹²	12	6¹	13			5	14									19
1	2	3	4	5	6	7		9¹	10	11	8²		12					13							20
	2		4	5¹	6	7		9⁴	10	11²	8	13	12	14				1	3						21
	2	3	4		6³	7	14	9	10	11	8²	12			5			1	13						22
1	2	13	4	5		7		9²	10	8¹		12	6	11³					3	14					23
1	2	3	4	5		7		9²	10	8¹	13	11³	6						12						24
	2	14	4	5	12	7		10	9³	13	6	11¹²						1	3		8¹				25
1	2		4		6	7*		9³	10	11	12	14	13		5¹				3		8²				26
1	2	3	4	5	6			9⁴	10¹	11²	12	14	8	13					7						27
1	2	3	4	5	6	7⁴		9¹	10	11	8³	12							13	14					28
1	2	3	4		9	7		12	10	11¹	8²		6³		5	13					14				29
1	2	3	4	5	6	7		9²	10	12³	8		13			11¹					14				30
1	2	3	4	5	9¹	7		12	10	8²		11	6³						14	13					31
1	2	3	4	5	9³	7		8¹	10²	13	14	11	12						6						32
1	2	3	4	5	6³	7		11¹	10	9²	12	8							13		14				33
	2	3	4	5	6²	7		10¹	9³	14	11	8						1	12		13				34
1	2	3	4	5	6	7		10²	9³	12	11		14						13		8¹				35
1	2	12	4		9	13		10	8	7		5	11²						3¹	6³	14				36
1	2	3	4		9¹	7		10	11¹		5		8⁹						6²	12	13	14			37
	2	3	4	5		7		10	12	9	6¹	11¹²			13			1			8³		14		38

FA Cup

Third Round	Watford	(h)	3-0
Fourth Round	Bradford C	(h)	2-4

Capital One Cup

Third Round	Bolton W	(h)	2-1
Fourth Round	Shrewsbury T	(a)	2-1
Quarter-Finals	Derby Co	(a)	3-1
Semi-Finals 1st leg	Liverpool	(a)	1-1
Semi-Finals 2nd leg	Liverpool	(h)	1-0
(aet; Chelsea won 2-1 on aggregate)			
Final	Tottenham H	Wembley	2-0

UEFA Champions League

Group G	Schalke 04	(h)	1-1
Group G	Sporting Lisbon	(a)	1-0
Group G	Maribor	(h)	6-0
Group G	Maribor	(a)	1-1
Group G	Schalke 04	(a)	5-0
Group G	Sporting Lisbon	(h)	3-1
Round of 16 1st leg	Paris Saint-Germain	(a)	1-1
Round of 16 2nd leg	Paris Saint-Germain	(h)	2-2
(aet; Paris Saint-Germain won on away goals)			

CHELTENHAM TOWN

FOUNDATION

Although a scratch team representing Cheltenham played a match against Gloucester in 1884, the earliest recorded match for Cheltenham Town FC was a friendly against Dean Close School on 12 March 1892. The School won 4–3 and the match was played at Prestbury (half a mile from Whaddon Road). Cheltenham Town played Wednesday afternoon friendlies at a local cricket ground until entering the Mid Gloucester League. In those days the club played in deep red coloured shirts and were nicknamed 'the Rubies'. The club moved to Whaddon Lane for season 1901–02 and changed to red and white colours two years later.

The Abbey Business Stadium, Whaddon Road, Cheltenham, Gloucestershire GL52 5NA.

Telephone: (01242) 573 558.

Fax: (01242) 224 675.

Ticket Office: (01242) 588 117.

Website: www.ctfc.com

Email: info@ctfc.com

Ground Capacity: 7,036.

Record Attendance: 10,389 v Blackpool, FA Cup 3rd rd, 13 January 1934 (at Cheltenham Athletic Ground); 8,326 v Reading, FA Cup 1st rd, 17 November 1956 (at Whaddon Road).

Pitch Measurements: 102.5m × 66m (112yd × 72yd)

Chairman: Paul Baker.

Vice-chairman: Colin Farmer.

Manager: Gary Johnson.

Assistant Manager: Russell Milton.

Physio: Ian Weston.

Colours: Red and white striped shirts, white shorts, white socks.

Year Formed: 1892.

Turned Professional: 1932.

Club Nickname: 'The Robins'.

Grounds: Pre-1932, Agg-Gardner's Recreation Ground; Whaddon Lane; Carter's Lane; 1932, Whaddon Road (renamed The Abbey Business Stadium 2009).

First Football League Game: 7 August 1999, Division 3, v Rochdale (h) L 0–2 – Book; Griffin, Victory, Banks, Freeman, Brough (Howarth), Howells, Bloomer (Devaney), Grayson, Watkins (McAuley), Yates.

Record League Victory: 5–0 v Mansfield T, FL 2, 6 May 2006 – Higgs; Gallinagh, Bell, McCann (1) (Connolly), Caines, Duff, Wilson, Bird (1p), Gillespie (1) (Spencer), Guinan (Odejayi (1)), Vincent (1).

HONOURS

Football League – Division 3: Best season: 4th, 2001–02.

FA Cup: Best season: 5th rd, 2002.

Football League Cup: Best season: never past 2nd rd.

Football Conference:
Champions 1998–99,
Runners-up 1997–98.

FA Trophy: *Winners* 1997–98.

sky SPORTS FACT FILE

In 1933–34 Cheltenham Town reached the third round of the FA Cup despite losing a qualifying round replay. The were reinstated after protesting that opponents Llanelly had fielded ineligible players and Cheltenham went on to defeat Calne & Harris United, Barnet and Carlisle United before going out to Blackpool in a game switched to Cheltenham RFC's home ground.

Record Cup Victory: 12–0 v Chippenham R, FA Cup 3rd qual. rd, 2 November 1935 – Bowles; Whitehouse, Williams; Lang, Devonport (1), Partridge (2); Perkins, Hackett, Jones (4), Black (4), Griffiths (1).

Record Defeat: 1–8 v Crewe Alex, FL 2, 2 April 2011.
N.B. 1–10 v Merthyr T, Southern League, 8 March 1952.

Most League Points (2 for a win): 60, Southern League Division 1, 1963–64.

Most League Points (3 for a win): 78, Division 3, 2001–02.

Most League Goals: 66, Division 3, 2001–02; 66, FL 2, 2011–12.

Highest League Scorer in Season: Julian Alsop, 20, Division 3, 2001–02.

Most League Goals in Total Aggregate: Julian Alsop, 39, 2000–03; 2009–10.

Most League Goals in One Match: 3, Martin Devaney v Plymouth Arg, Division 3, 23 September 2000; 3, Neil Grayson v Cardiff C, Division 3, 1 April 2001; 3, Damien Spencer v Hull C, Division 3, 23 August 2003; 3, Damien Spencer v Milton Keynes D, FL 1, 31 January 2009; 3, Michael Pook v Burton Alb, FL 2, 13 March 2010.

Most Capped Player: Grant McCann, 7 (39), Northern Ireland.

Most League Appearances: David Bird, 288, 2001–11.

Youngest League Player: Kyle Haynes, 17 years 85 days v Oldham Ath, 24 March 2009.

Record Transfer Fee Received: £400,000 from Colchester U for Steve Gillespie, July 2008.

Record Transfer Fee Paid: £60,000 to Aldershot T for Jermaine McGlashan, January 2012.

Football League Record: 1999 Promoted to Division 3; 2002 Division 2; 2003–04 Division 3; 2004–06 FL 2; 2006–09 FL 1; 2009–15 FL 2; 2015– Conference Premier.

LATEST SEQUENCES

Longest Sequence of League Wins: 5, 29.10.2011 – 10.12.2011.
Longest Sequence of League Defeats: 7, 27.1.2009 – 28.2.2009.
Longest Sequence of League Draws: 5, 5.4.2003 – 21.4.2003.
Longest Sequence of Unbeaten League Matches: 16, 1.12.2001 – 12.3.2002.
Longest Sequence Without a League Win: 14, 20.12.2008 – 7.3.2009.
Successive Scoring Runs: 17 from 16.2.2008.
Successive Non-scoring Runs: 5 from 10.3.2012 – 30.3.2012.

MANAGERS

George Blackburn 1932–34
George Carr 1934–37
Jimmy Brain 1937–48
Cyril Dean 1948–50
George Summerbee 1950–52
William Raeside 1952–53
Arch Anderson 1953–58
Ron Lewin 1958–60
Peter Donnelly 1960–61
Tommy Cavanagh 1961
Arch Anderson 1961–65
Harold Fletcher 1965–66
Bob Etheridge 1966–73
Willie Penman 1973–74
Dennis Allen 1974–79
Terry Paine 1979
Alan Grundy 1979–82
Alan Wood 1982–83
John Murphy 1983–88
Jim Barron 1988–90
John Murphy 1990
Dave Lewis 1990–91
Ally Robertson 1991–92
Lindsay Parsons 1992–95
Chris Robinson 1995–97
Steve Cotterill 1997–2002
Graham Allner 2002–03
Bobby Gould 2003
John Ward 2003–07
Keith Downing 2007–08
Martin Allen 2008–09
Mark Yates 2009–14
Paul Buckle 2014–15
Gary Johnson March 2015–

TEN YEAR LEAGUE RECORD

		P	W	D	L	F	A	Pts	Pos
2005-06	FL 2	46	19	15	12	65	53	72	5
2006-07	FL 1	46	15	9	22	49	61	54	17
2007-08	FL 1	46	13	12	21	42	64	51	19
2008-09	FL 1	46	9	12	25	51	91	39	23
2009-10	FL 2	46	10	18	18	54	71	48	22
2010-11	FL 2	46	13	13	20	56	77	52	17
2011-12	FL 2	46	23	8	15	66	50	77	6
2012-13	FL 2	46	20	15	11	58	51	75	5
2013-14	FL 2	46	13	16	17	53	63	55	17
2014-15	FL 2	46	9	14	23	40	67	41	23

DID YOU KNOW ?

Cheltenham Town won the 1998–99 Conference title and promotion to the Football League although they managed just one victory in their final five games of the season. The Robins still finished clear of their nearest rivals Kettering Town by a four-point margin.

CHELTENHAM TOWN – FOOTBALL LEAGUE TWO 2014–15 LEAGUE RECORD

Match No.	Date		Venue	Opponents	Result		H/T Score	Lg Pos.	Goalscorers	Atten- dance
1	Aug	9	A	Bury	W	1-0	1-0	3	Hanks [42]	3376
2		16	H	Accrington S	W	2-1	1-0	4	Harrison [34], Arthur [84]	2340
3		19	H	Carlisle U	D	0-0	0-0	6		2341
4		23	A	Tranmere R	W	3-2	0-2	3	Richards, M [67], Arthur [69], Wynter [73]	4607
5		30	H	Hartlepool U	W	1-0	0-0	1	Arthur [90]	2735
6	Sept	6	A	Morecambe	D	0-0	0-0	1		2273
7		13	A	Luton T	L	0-1	0-1	5		7793
8		16	H	Southend U	L	0-1	0-0	8		2303
9		20	H	Dagenham & R	D	1-1	0-0	7	Hanks [87]	2597
10		27	A	Burton Alb	L	0-1	0-1	9		2225
11	Oct	4	H	AFC Wimbledon	D	1-1	1-1	10	Taylor, M [8]	2795
12		11	A	Shrewsbury T	L	1-3	0-0	14	Harrison [48]	4817
13		18	A	Northampton T	W	3-2	1-0	10	Gornell 2 [45, 78], Marquis [84]	2447
14		21	A	Cambridge U	W	2-1	1-1	9	Richards, M [10], Gornell [55]	3252
15		25	A	Plymouth Arg	L	0-3	0-2	10		6837
16	Nov	1	H	York C	L	0-1	0-1	13		2469
17		15	A	Stevenage	L	1-5	0-3	16	Harrison [76]	2668
18		22	H	Wycombe W	L	1-4	1-2	18	Elliott [3]	2833
19		29	H	Oxford U	D	1-1	0-0	17	Harrison [52]	3002
20	Dec	13	A	Mansfield T	D	1-1	0-0	18	Kotwica [87]	3324
21		20	H	Portsmouth	D	1-1	1-0	18	Sterling-James [42]	3331
22		26	A	Exeter C	L	0-1	0-0	18		4591
23		28	H	Newport Co	L	0-1	0-1	19		3417
24	Jan	3	A	Oxford U	W	2-1	2-1	17	Dunn [40], Stewart [45]	5360
25		10	A	Hartlepool U	L	0-2	0-1	18		3155
26		16	H	Morecambe	D	1-1	1-0	16	Dunn (pen) [18]	2122
27		24	H	Luton T	D	1-1	1-1	17	Kotwica [20]	3611
28		31	A	Dagenham & R	L	1-3	0-0	21	Dunn (pen) [62]	2696
29	Feb	7	H	Burton Alb	L	1-3	0-2	22	Burns [55]	2389
30		10	A	Southend U	L	0-2	0-2	22		5013
31		14	H	Bury	L	1-2	1-2	23	Johnstone [24]	2375
32		20	A	Accrington S	D	1-1	1-0	23	Burns [31]	1216
33		28	H	Tranmere R	W	2-0	1-0	21	Holmes (og) [9], Brown, T [61]	3070
34	Mar	3	A	Carlisle U	L	0-1	0-1	23		3116
35		7	H	Mansfield T	D	1-1	0-0	22	Burns [47]	2597
36		13	A	Newport Co	D	1-1	1-1	22	Burns [13]	2951
37		17	A	Portsmouth	D	2-2	2-2	23	Richards, E [18], Packwood [22]	13,558
38		21	H	Exeter C	L	1-2	0-1	23	Moore-Taylor (og) [89]	2880
39		28	H	Plymouth Arg	L	0-3	0-1	24		3831
40	Apr	3	A	York C	L	0-1	0-0	24		4151
41		6	H	Stevenage	L	0-1	0-0	24		2858
42		11	A	Wycombe W	L	1-2	0-1	24	Berry [54]	3907
43		14	H	Cambridge U	W	3-1	1-1	23	Harrad [2], Haynes [57], Sparrow [75]	2415
44		18	A	Northampton T	L	0-2	0-0	23		4579
45		25	H	Shrewsbury T	L	0-1	0-1	23		5117
46	May	2	A	AFC Wimbledon	D	1-1	1-1	23	Berry [25]	4374

Final League Position: 23

GOALSCORERS

League (40): Burns 4, Harrison 4, Arthur 3, Dunn 3 (2 pens), Gornell 3, Berry 2, Hanks 2, Kotwica 2, Richards, M 2, Brown, T 1, Elliott 1, Harrad 1, Haynes 1, Johnstone 1, Marquis 1, Packwood 1, Richards, E 1, Sparrow 1, Sterling-James 1, Stewart 1, Taylor, M 1, Wynter 1, own goals 2.
FA Cup (5): Harrison 3, Gornell 1, Richards, M 1.
Capital One Cup (0).
Johnstone's Paint Trophy (3): Arthur 1, Gornell 1, Marquis 1.

Carson T 46	Taylor M 31+2	Brown T 42+1	Elliott S 17	Vaughan L 31+1	Richards M 44+1	Taylor J 16	Hall A 1	Braham-Barrett C 45	Harrison B 17+6	Haynes D 5+3	Gornell T 18+7	Hanks J 16+17	Packwood W 5	Arthur K 1+6	Wynter J 12+4	Sterling-James O 9+13	Marquis J 8+5	McDonald S 3+1	Black P 3	Kotwica Z 8+9	Lawrence J —+1	De Vita R 7+3	Deaman J 13+5	Haworth A —+5	Bancessi E 2+2	Bowen J 1+2	Ferdinand K 15+1	Williams H 3+5	Dale B 1+1	Jones L 5+1	Stewart K 4	Dunn J 5	Gray J 3+1	Berry D 8+4	Burns W 14	Johnstone D 4+1	Manset M 8+4	Richards E 6+3	Sparrow M 11	Mills P 8	Harrad S 10+2	Match No.
1	2	3	4	5	6	7	8^2	9	10^1	11	12	13																														1
1	3	2	4	5	8	7		9	10^1	11	6	12																														2
1	3	2	4	5	8	7		9	10	11	6^1	12																														3
1	5	4	3^1	2	8	9		6	11	10^2	14	13	7	12^3																												4
1	3	2	4	5^4	8	7		9	10^1	11^2					14	6	13	12																								5
1	2	3	4		6	8		9	10^2	14		7^3	12		5	13	11^1																									6
1	3	2	4^3		8	7		9	12	14	6^1	11			5^2	13	10																								7
1	3	2	4		8	7^4		9	10	13	12				5^1	6^2	11																								8
1	3	4		2	8			5	10^1	14	13		6	7^2	11	9^3	12																								9
1	2	3	4	5	8			9	10	12	6					11^1	7^2		13																						10
1	3		4	5	7			9	10^1	13	6					11^2	12		8^3	2	14																				11
1	2	12	3^2	5	8	7		9	11							13				6^1	4^3	14	10																		12
1	4^1	3	5	2	9	8		6	10^2	11	14					13					12		7^3																		13
1		2	3	5	6	7		9	13	10^2	8^1					12	11				4																				14
1		2	4	5	6	7^4		9	10^3	11	14					8^1					3	13	12																		15
1		2	4	5	8	7		9	14	11	6^2						10^3				12	3^1	13																		16
1	3	4^2	2	7	8				10		9^1	14				13	5	12	11^3			6																			17
1		3	5^2	9	8^2			6	10	11^1						12	13			14	4				7^3																18
1	4	3			8	7		5	10	11^2	13					12			9^1	2			6																		19
1	4	3			8^1			5	10^2	11	7					12			14	9^3	2	13				6															20
1	3	4		2	8			5	12	11^2	7					10				9^1		13				6															21
1	3^1	4		2	7			5		11	8^2					10				12	9^3	13				6	14														22
1		4	2	8				5		11^1						6				9		3				7	10	12													23
1	3		2	9				5		10^2	12					6^2					14					8^1		4	7	11											24
1	3		2	8				5	12	11^2						6^1										9	13		4	7	10										25
1	3	4		5				8^1		14	12					9^3									13	6	11^2		2	7	10										26
1	3	4			7			5	12										11							6			2	8	10^1	9									27
1	3	4			7^2			5									12		11							6	13		2		10^1	9									28
1	3	4^2			9^1			5				8							13							7			14		12	2	6	10	11^3	13						29
1	4	3		14				5^2		12		8^1				13									7				9^3	2	6	10		11							30
1	3	4		2	8			5		13							12			9^2						7^3							6	11^1	14	10					31
1	3	4		2	8			5		7^1		9					12									13						14	6^2	11^3		10					32
1	3	4		2	8			5		14																				13	9^3	12		11		6^2	7	10^1		33
1	4	3		2	8			5				13																		6			12	10^1	9	7^3	11			34
1	3	4		2	8			5	11			14																		9^2			10^1	13	6^3	7	12			35
1		4			6			7	10		3	13								12										2	9		12		8^2	5	11^1		36
1	13	4			6			7	10^3		3^2	14					12													2				9^1	8	5	11	10	37
1	4		14	8				5	11^2	12	3		13																	2^4	9					6^1	7	10	38
1	2		5	8				9^3		7		14		13			4															11	12	6^1	3	10^2	39
1		4	2	8				5	13^2	12	3	9			6^2																11		14			7^2	10^1	40
1		4	2	8				5	13	7	3^1	6			9^3		12														11		10^2			14	41
1	14	3		2	8			5	12			9^3			6			4^1											13	11^2	10		7			11	42
1	3	4		2^1	8			5	6					9														12		10		7			11	43
1	3^1	4			7			5		12			9^3		13			6^2	14									2		11		8			10	44
1		4			8			5		13			12		9	3											2	6		11^2	7				10^1	45
1		4			7			5		8			13		9	14	3			12		10^3	11^2				2	6^1									46

FA Cup
| First Round | Swindon T | (h) | 5-0 |
| Second Round | Dover Ath | (h) | 0-1 |

Capital One Cup
| First Round | Brighton & HA | (a) | 0-2 |

Johnstone's Paint Trophy
| First Round | Oxford U | (h) | 2-0 |
| Second Round | Bristol C | (h) | 1-3 |

CHESTERFIELD

The Proact Stadium, 1866 Sheffield Road, Whittington Moor, Chesterfield, Derbyshire S41 8NZ.

Telephone: (01246) 209 765.

Fax: (01246) 556 799.

Ticket Office: (01246) 488 232.

Website: www.chesterfield-fc.co.uk

Email: reception@chesterfield-fc.co.uk

Ground Capacity: 10,379.

Record Attendance: 30,968 v Newcastle U, Division 2, 7 April 1939 (at Saltergate); 10,089 v Rotherham U, FL 2, 18 March 2011 (at b2net Stadium (now called the Proact Stadium)).

Pitch Measurements: 103m × 67m (112.5yd × 73.5yd)

Chairman: Dave Allen.

Chief Executive: Chris Turner.

Manager: Dean Saunders.

Assistant Manager: Leam Richardson.

Sports Therapist: Jamie Hewitt.

Colours: Blue shirts with white trim, white shorts with blue trim, blue socks with white trim.

Year Formed: 1866.

Turned Professional: 1891.

Previous Name: 1867, Chesterfield Town; 1919, Chesterfield.

Club Nicknames: 'The Blues', 'The Spireites'.

Grounds: 1867, Drill Field; 1871, Recreation Ground, Saltergate; 2010, b2net Stadium (renamed The Proact Stadium 2012).

First Football League Game: 2 September 1899, Division 2, v Sheffield W (a) L 1–5 – Hancock; Pilgrim, Fletcher, Ballantyne, Bell, Downie; Morley, Thacker, Gooing, Munday (1), Geary.

Record League Victory: 10–0 v Glossop NE, Division 2, 17 January 1903 – Clutterbuck; Thorpe, Lerper; Haig, Banner, Thacker; Tomlinson (2), Newton (1), Milward (3), Munday (2), Steel (2).

Record Cup Victory: 6–1 v Hartlepool U (h), FA Cup 1st rd, 3 November 2012 – O'Donnell; Talbot, Forbes (1), Cooper (Westcarr (1)), Smith, Whitaker, Clay (1), Togwell, Randall (1) (Broadhead), Darika, Boden (1) (Lester (1)).

HONOURS

Football League – Division 2: Best season: 4th, 1946–47;
Division 3 (N): *Champions* 1930–31, 1935–36; *Runners-up* 1933–34;
FL 2: *Champions* 2010–11, 2013–14;
Division 4: *Champions* 1969–70, 1984–85.
FA Cup: Best season: semi-final, 1997.
Football League Cup: Best season: 4th rd, 1965, 2007.
Johnstone's Paint Trophy: *Winners* 2012; *Runners-up* 2014.
Anglo-Scottish Cup: *Winners* 1981.

sky SPORTS FACT FILE

Chesterfield were reformed by the local Borough Council in April 1919 and the club was, perhaps uniquely, run by the Council's Sports Committee for a time, despite opposition from the FA. Tom Callaghan is the only manager of a senior club to have been appointed by a local authority selection panel.

Record Defeat: 0–10 v Gillingham, Division 3, 5 September 1987.

Most League Points (2 for a win): 64, Division 4, 1969–70.

Most League Points (3 for a win): 91, Division 4, 1984–85.

Most League Goals: 102, Division 3 (N), 1930–31.

Highest League Scorer in Season: Jimmy Cookson, 44, Division 3 (N), 1925–26.

Most League Goals in Total Aggregate: Ernie Moss, 162, 1969–76, 1979–81 and 1984–86.

Most League Goals in One Match: 4, Jimmy Cookson v Accrington S, Division 3 (N), 16 January 1926; 4, Jimmy Cookson v Ashington, Division 3 (N), 1 May 1926; 4, Jimmy Cookson v Wigan Borough, Division 3 (N), 4 September 1926; 4, Tommy Lyon v Southampton, Division 2, 3 December 1938.

Most Capped Player: Walter McMillen, 4 (7), Northern Ireland; Mark Williams, 4 (36), Northern Ireland.

Most League Appearances: Dave Blakey, 617, 1948–67.

Youngest League Player: Dennis Thompson, 16 years 160 days v Notts Co, 26 December 1950.

Record Transfer Fee Received: £750,000 from Southampton for Kevin Davies, May 1997.

Record Transfer Fee Paid: £250,000 to Watford for Jason Lee, August 1998.

Football League Record: 1899 Elected to Division 2; 1909 failed re-election; 1921–31 Division 3 (N); 1931–33 Division 2; 1933–36 Division 3 (N); 1936–51 Division 2; 1951–58 Division 3 (N); 1958–61 Division 3; 1961–70 Division 4; 1970–83 Division 3; 1983–85 Division 4; 1985–89 Division 3; 1989–92 Division 4; 1992–95 Division 3; 1995–2000 Division 2; 2000–01 Division 3; 2001–04 Division 2; 2004–07 FL 1; 2007–11 FL 2; 2011–12 FL 1; 2012–14 FL 2; 2014– FL 1.

LATEST SEQUENCES

Longest Sequence of League Wins: 10, 6.9.1933 – 4.11.1933.

Longest Sequence of League Defeats: 9, 22.10.1960 – 27.12.1960.

Longest Sequence of League Draws: 8, 26.11.2005 – 2.1.2006.

Longest Sequence of Unbeaten League Matches: 21, 26.12.1994 – 29.4.1995.

Longest Sequence Without a League Win: 18, 11.9.1999 – 3.1.2000.

Successive Scoring Runs: 46 from 25.12.1929.

Successive Non-scoring Runs: 7 from 23.9.1977.

MANAGERS

E. Russell Timmeus 1891–95 (*Secretary-Manager*)
Gilbert Gillies 1895–1901
E. F. Hind 1901–02
Jack Hoskin 1902–06
W. Furness 1906–07
George Swift 1907–10
G. H. Jones 1911–13
R. L. Weston 1913–17
T. Callaghan 1919
J. J. Caffrey 1920–22
Harry Hadley 1922
Harry Parkes 1922–27
Alec Campbell 1927
Ted Davison 1927–32
Bill Harvey 1932–38
Norman Bullock 1938–45
Bob Brocklebank 1945–48
Bobby Marshall 1948–52
Ted Davison 1952–58
Duggie Livingstone 1958–62
Tony McShane 1962–67
Jimmy McGuigan 1967–73
Joe Shaw 1973–76
Arthur Cox 1976–80
Frank Barlow 1980–83
John Duncan 1983–87
Kevin Randall 1987–88
Paul Hart 1988–91
Chris McMenemy 1991–93
John Duncan 1993–2000
Nicky Law 2000–01
Dave Rushbury 2002–03
Roy McFarland 2003–07
Lee Richardson 2007–09
John Sheridan 2009–12
Paul Cook 2012–15
Dean Saunders May 2015–

TEN YEAR LEAGUE RECORD

		P	W	D	L	F	A	Pts	Pos
2005-06	FL 1	46	14	14	18	63	73	56	16
2006-07	FL 1	46	12	11	23	45	53	47	21
2007-08	FL 2	46	19	12	15	76	56	69	8
2008-09	FL 2	46	16	15	15	62	57	63	10
2009-10	FL 2	46	21	7	18	61	62	70	8
2010-11	FL 2	46	24	14	8	85	51	86	1
2011-12	FL 1	46	10	12	24	56	81	42	22
2012-13	FL 2	46	18	13	15	60	45	67	8
2013-14	FL 2	46	23	15	8	71	40	84	1
2014-15	FL 1	46	19	12	15	68	55	69	6

DID YOU KNOW ?

Centre half Allan Sliman joined Chesterfield for a then club record fee of £1,700 in June 1932 and went on to play over 250 games for the Spireites. He later enlisted in the RAF but was killed in action when his plane was shot down in August 1945.

CHESTERFIELD – FOOTBALL LEAGUE ONE 2014–15 LEAGUE RECORD

Match No.	Date	Venue	Opponents	Result	H/T Score	Lg Pos.	Goalscorers	Attendance
1	Aug 9	A	Leyton Orient	W	2-1	1-0	5	Boco 7, Doyle 79	5619
2	16	H	Rochdale	W	2-1	1-0	1	Doyle 2 (2 pens) 39, 76	5682
3	19	H	Milton Keynes D	L	0-1	0-0	6		5811
4	23	A	Fleetwood T	D	0-0	0-0	11		3512
5	30	A	Port Vale	W	2-1	1-1	5	Doyle 9, Roberts 46	5593
6	Sept 13	H	Scunthorpe U	W	4-1	0-0	4	Doyle 3 (1 pen) 55, 64, 72 (p), Morsy 88	6227
7	16	A	Preston NE	D	3-3	1-3	3	Doyle 3 (1 pen) 31, 79, 90 (p)	8399
8	20	A	Doncaster R	L	2-3	1-2	5	Clucas 42, Doyle 61	7954
9	27	H	Notts Co	D	1-1	0-1	8	Margreitter 62	7422
10	Oct 4	H	Sheffield U	W	3-2	2-0	6	Ryan 26, Roberts 45, Doyle 73	9723
11	11	A	Bristol C	L	2-3	1-1	6	Doyle 2 (1 pen) 25 (p), 59	12,558
12	18	H	Oldham Ath	D	1-1	0-0	8	Clucas 57	7130
13	21	A	Colchester U	L	1-2	1-0	10	Clucas 1	2718
14	25	A	Walsall	L	0-1	0-0	10		4230
15	28	H	Swindon T	L	0-3	0-2	11		6144
16	Nov 1	H	Yeovil T	D	0-0	0-0	11		6462
17	15	A	Crewe Alex	D	0-0	0-0	14		4557
18	22	H	Barnsley	W	2-1	1-0	11	Doyle 2 42, 58	8544
19	29	A	Crawley T	D	1-1	0-0	12	Roberts 59	2459
20	Dec 13	H	Bradford C	L	0-1	0-0	13		6809
21	20	A	Gillingham	W	3-2	1-1	11	Clucas 22, Legge (og) 54, Ryan 69	6841
22	26	H	Peterborough U	W	3-2	2-0	9	Zakuani (og) 10, Gnanduillet 34, Doyle 54	8353
23	28	H	Coventry C	D	0-0	0-0	7		10,166
24	Jan 10	H	Port Vale	W	3-0	1-0	7	Gnanduillet 13, Doyle (pen) 60, Raglan 70	7034
25	17	A	Swindon T	L	1-3	1-2	8	Clucas 22	7981
26	27	H	Crawley T	W	3-0	1-0	5	Doyle 2 34, 53, O'Shea 51	5329
27	31	H	Doncaster R	D	2-2	1-2	5	Doyle 43, Ryan 87	7839
28	Feb 7	A	Notts Co	W	1-0	0-0	5	Lavery 67	6649
29	10	H	Preston NE	L	0-2	0-1	7		6309
30	14	H	Leyton Orient	L	2-3	1-1	7	O'Shea (pen) 19, Omozusi (og) 54	6524
31	17	A	Scunthorpe U	L	0-2	0-0	8		3601
32	21	A	Rochdale	L	0-1	0-0	10		2967
33	28	H	Fleetwood T	W	3-0	2-0	7	Lavery 31, Hird 42, Morsy 63	6497
34	Mar 3	A	Milton Keynes D	W	2-1	0-1	7	Roberts 66, Lavery 90	7335
35	14	H	Coventry C	L	2-3	1-1	11	O'Shea 42, Ariyibi 85	7205
36	17	H	Gillingham	W	3-0	2-0	9	Clucas 2 3, 88, O'Shea 12	4804
37	21	A	Peterborough U	L	0-1	0-1	6		6612
38	28	H	Walsall	W	1-0	0-0	6	Hird 86	6358
39	31	H	Bradford C	W	1-0	1-0	6	Harrison 45	12,551
40	Apr 3	A	Yeovil T	W	3-2	0-1	6	Hird 59, O'Shea 2 66, 69	4520
41	6	H	Crewe Alex	W	1-0	1-0	6	Darikwa 26	6942
42	11	A	Barnsley	D	1-1	1-0	6	O'Shea 26	11,268
43	14	H	Colchester U	W	6-0	3-0	6	Roberts 2 (1 pen) 6, 84 (p), Clucas 2 16, 17, Gardner 58, Ryan 60	6508
44	18	A	Oldham Ath	D	0-0	0-0	6		4557
45	25	H	Bristol C	L	0-2	0-1	6		9615
46	May 3	A	Sheffield U	D	1-1	0-1	6	Evatt 51	26,078

Final League Position: 6

GOALSCORERS

League (68): Doyle 21 (6 pens), Clucas 9, O'Shea 7 (1 pen), Roberts 6 (1 pen), Ryan 4, Hird 3, Lavery 3, Gnanduillet 2, Morsy 2, Ariyibi 1, Boco 1, Darikwa 1, Evatt 1, Gardner 1, Harrison 1, Margreitter 1, Raglan 1, own goals 3.
FA Cup (11): Clucas 3, Doyle 3 (1 pen), O'Shea 2, Roberts 2, own goal 1.
Capital One Cup (3): Banks 1, Doyle 1, Humphreys 1.
Johnstone's Paint Trophy (0).
League One Play-Offs (0).

Lee T 46	Darikwa T 46	Cooper L 1	Evatt J 38+1	Jones D 27+6	Ryan J 42+2	Morsy S 39	Roberts G 33+1	Boco R 11+2	Humphreys R 9+10	Doyle E 26	O'Shea J 27+14	Hird S 28	Gnanduillet A 12+14	Banks O 11+13	Onowvigun M —+2	Gardner D 8+9	Johnson D 7+4	Raglan C 15+3	Broadhead J —+1	Margreitter G 11+2	Clucas S 40+1	Ariyibi G 5+12	Wright M —+1	Gobern O 3	Dieseruvwe E —+9	Talbot D 8+1	Harrison B 4+8	Lavery C 6+2	Duffy M 1+2	Carter A 2	Match No.
1	2	3	4	5	6	7	8	9	10	11																					1
1	3		2	6	5^3	4	10	11^2		9	7^1	8	12	13	14																2
1	2	3	5	7^3	6	10	8^2			11	9^1	4	13	12		14															3
1	2		4	5	7	6	9^1	11		8	10^2	3	12	13																	4
1	2		3^1	5	6	9	10^3			8			4^2	11	14		7^1	12	13												5
1	2	3		5	6	7	9^2	8		11^3			13							12	4	10^1	14								6
1	2	3	5^1	7	6	8^2	11				12	13	14			10				9	4^2										7
1	2	3	7	6^2	8^1	5^3	11						13	14	12	9					4	10									8
1	2	3	7							11	9^1	10	6	12		8				4	5										9
1*	2	3		5	7	6	9^2			11^1	10^3		14			8					4	13	12								10
1	2	3		5	6^3	7	10^1	12		11			14	13		9^2					4	8									11
1	2	3		5^3	8	7	9^1	10					13	12	14	6^2					4	11									12
1	2	3		5	6	7	11	8^1		9^2			13	12							4	10									13
1	2	3		5	6^1	7				11	13		12	14		8^2					4	10	9^3								14
1	2	3		6	7^1	5	11				14			12		8^2				9	4	13	10^3								15
1	2			5	6					11	12	9^1	14	13		8^1					4	10	7^2								16
1	2		4	5	6	7	10			11	12					8^1		3			9										17
1	2	3		5	8	10				11	12	9^1		13		6^2					4	14	7^3								18
1	2	3*	4^2	9	7	10				11		6^1	14	13		5					12	8^2									19
1	2^3		7	8*	9^1	12	11	6^2		10			13			3				5	4	14									20
1	6		2	7	9	11	8			10						4		10			3										21
1	2	3	12	9^3	6^1	8	11	14		7		10^2	13							5	4										22
1	2	3	12	9	6^3	8	11	13		7^2		10^1	14							5	4										23
1	2		12	7	9	6^2	8^1	11				13	14			3		10^3		5	4										24
1	2			5	7	9	8	10^1			12	3	11	13		6^2					4	14									25
1	2^2			5	8	7^3	11	6^1		3	12	10	14							9	4	13									26
1	2		12	5^2	7	6	11			9^1			14			8^3		3		10	4	13									27
1	2		3	5	7	8	9	4		10^1						6				13	12	11^2									28
1	2	3		5^1	7	8	6	4*			12					9				13	11^1	10^2	14								29
1	2	3	12	8^2	7		6				13	10^3								5	4	14				11		9^1			30
1	2		13	7	6	9^1	8									3				5	12				10^2	11^3	14		4		31
1	2		3	7	8^1		4	10		9	12					6^2					11^3	13					14		5		32
1	2		5^3	7	8		4	6		10	14										12					13	11^1				33
1	2		4		6	7	8^1			10	3	9^3									5	12				13	14	11^2			34
1	2		3^3	5^2	6		9				12	8	4			7^1					10	13				14		11			35
1	2	3		7	9^2		8			12		4	6^1			14					11	10^3				13				5	36
1	2^2	4	13	7	6		10^1			9		3	8^3								11	12				14		5			37
1	2	3		9	7	10^2	8^1					4	6^2								11	12				14		5	13		38
1	2		4		8	6	10^1		7			13	3								11	12				5		9^2			39
1	2	3			6	7	10	8^3				13	4			14				9^1		12				5		11^2			40
1	2	3			7	6	9^2			13		8	4							12	11	10^1				5					41
1	2		3^1		7	6	9^2			14		8	4							12	11	10^3				5		13			42
1	2		4	12	6	7	10			9		3	14					8^2			11^1					13		5^3			43
1	2	3		5	6	7	9			10			12					8^1			4	11									44
1	2	3		5	7^1	6	9			8^2			4	12				10^3			11					14					45
1	2	3		5	6	7	9			8^2			4	13				10^1			11					12					46

FA Cup

First Round	Braintree T	(a)	6-0
Second Round	Milton Keynes D	(a)	1-0
Third Round	Scunthorpe U	(a)	2-2
Replay	Scunthorpe U	(h)	2-0
(aet)			
Fourth Round	Derby Co	(a)	0-2

Johnstone's Paint Trophy

First Round	Scunthorpe U	(a)	0-2

Capital One Cup

First Round	Huddersfield T	(h)	3-5
(aet)			

League One Play-Offs

Semi-Finals 1st leg	Preston NE	(h)	0-1
Semi-Finals 2nd leg	Preston NE	(a)	0-3

COLCHESTER UNITED

FOUNDATION

Colchester United was formed in 1937 when a number of enthusiasts of the much older Colchester Town club decided to establish a professional concern as a limited liability company. The new club continued at Layer Road which had been the amateur club's home since 1909.

Weston Homes Community Stadium, United Way, Colchester, Essex CO4 5UP.

Telephone: (01206) 755 100.

Fax: (01206) 715 327.

Ticket Office: (0845) 437 9089.

Website: www.cu-fc.com

Email: media@colchesterunited.net

Ground Capacity: 10,105.

Record Attendance: 19,072 v Reading, FA Cup 1st rd, 27 November 1948 (at Layer Road); 10,064 v Norwich C, FL 1, 16 January 2010 (at Community Stadium).

Pitch Measurements: 100.5m × 65m (110yd × 71yd)

Executive Chairman: Robbie Cowling.

Vice-chairman: Richard Cowling.

Manager: Tony Humes.

Assistant Manager: Richard Hall.

Physio: Tony Flynn.

Colours: Royal blue and white striped shirts, royal blue shorts with white trim, white socks with blue hoops.

Year Formed: 1937.

Turned Professional: 1937.

Club Nickname: 'The U's'.

Grounds: 1937, Layer Road; 2008, Weston Homes Community Stadium.

First Football League Game: 19 August 1950, Division 3 (S), v Gillingham (a) D 0–0 – Wright; Kettle, Allen; Bearryman, Stewart, Elder; Jones, Curry, Turner, McKim, Church.

Record League Victory: 9–1 v Bradford C, Division 4, 30 December 1961 – Ames; Millar, Fowler; Harris, Abrey, Ron Hunt; Foster, Bobby Hunt (4), King (4), Hill (1), Wright.

Record Cup Victory: 9-1 v Leamington, FA Cup 1st rd, 5 November 2005 – Davison; Stockley (Garcia), Duguid, Brown (1), Chilvers, Watson (1), Halford (1), Izzet (Danns) (2), Iwelumo (1) (Williams), Cureton (2), Yeates (1).

HONOURS

Football League – FL 1: *Runners-up* 2005–06;
Division 4: *Runners-up* 1961–62.
FA Cup: Best season: 6th rd, 1971.
Football League Cup: Best season: 5th rd, 1975.
Auto Windscreens Shield: *Runners-up* 1997.
GM Vauxhall Conference: *Winners* 1991–92.
FA Trophy: *Winners* 1992.

sky SPORTS FACT FILE

The BBC televised a small number of games as an experiment in the late 1940s. Although mostly involving amateur teams, one of the matches shown was the FA Cup 4th qualifying round tie between Colchester United and Wealdstone on 12 November 1949. This was the U's first-ever televised match, but the occasion ended in a 1-0 defeat.

Record Defeat: 0–8 v Leyton Orient, Division 4, 15 October 1988.

Most League Points (2 for a win): 60, Division 4, 1973–74.

Most League Points (3 for a win): 81, Division 4, 1982–83.

Most League Goals: 104, Division 4, 1961–62.

Highest League Scorer in Season: Bobby Hunt, 38, Division 4, 1961–62.

Most League Goals in Total Aggregate: Martyn King, 130, 1956–64.

Most League Goals in One Match: 4, Bobby Hunt v Bradford C, Division 4, 30 December 1961; 4, Martyn King v Bradford C, Division 4, 30 December 1961; 4, Bobby Hunt v Doncaster R, Division 4, 30 April 1962.

Most Capped Player: Bela Balogh, 2 (9), Hungary.

Most League Appearances: Micky Cook, 613, 1969–84.

Youngest League Player: Lindsay Smith, 16 years 218 days v Grimsby T, 24 April 1971.

Record Transfer Fee Received: £2,500,000 from Reading for Greg Halford, January 2007.

Record Transfer Fee Paid: £400,000 to Cheltenham T for Steve Gillespie, July 2008.

Football League Record: 1950 Elected to Division 3 (S); 1958–61 Division 3; 1961–62 Division 4; 1962–65 Division 3; 1965–66 Division 4; 1966–68 Division 3; 1968–74 Division 4; 1974–76 Division 3, 1976–77 Division 4; 1977–81 Division 3; 1981–90 Division 4; 1990–92 Conference; 1992–98 Division 3; 1998–2004 Division 2; 2004–06 FL 1; 2006–08 FL C; 2008– FL 1.

MANAGERS

Ted Fenton 1946–48
Jimmy Allen 1948–53
Jack Butler 1953–55
Benny Fenton 1955–63
Neil Franklin 1963–68
Dick Graham 1968–72
Jim Smith 1972–75
Bobby Roberts 1975–82
Allan Hunter 1982–83
Cyril Lea 1983–86
Mike Walker 1986–87
Roger Brown 1987–88
Jock Wallace 1989
Mick Mills 1990
Ian Atkins 1990–91
Roy McDonough 1991–94
George Burley 1994
Steve Wignall 1995–99
Mick Wadsworth 1999
Steve Whitton 1999–2003
Phil Parkinson 2003–06
Geraint Williams 2006–08
Paul Lambert 2008–09
Aidy Boothroyd 2009–10
John Ward 2010–12
Joe Dunne 2012–14
Tony Humes September 2014–

LATEST SEQUENCES

Longest Sequence of League Wins: 7, 31.12.2005 – 7.2.2006.

Longest Sequence of League Defeats: 9, 20.11.2012 – 12.1.2013.

Longest Sequence of League Draws: 6, 21.3.1977 – 11.4.1977.

Longest Sequence of Unbeaten League Matches: 20, 22.12.1956 – 19.4.1957.

Longest Sequence Without a League Win: 20, 2.3.1968 – 31.8.1968.

Successive Scoring Runs: 24 from 15.9.1962.

Successive Non-scoring Runs: 5 from 11.2.2006.

TEN YEAR LEAGUE RECORD

		P	W	D	L	F	A	Pts	Pos
2005-06	FL 1	46	22	13	11	58	40	79	2
2006-07	FL C	46	20	9	17	70	56	69	10
2007-08	FL C	46	7	17	22	62	86	38	24
2008-09	FL 1	46	18	9	19	58	58	63	12
2009-10	FL 1	46	20	12	14	64	52	72	8
2010-11	FL 1	46	16	14	16	57	63	62	10
2011-12	FL 1	46	13	20	13	61	66	59	10
2012-13	FL 1	46	14	9	23	47	68	51	20
2013-14	FL 1	46	13	14	19	53	61	53	16
2014-15	FL 1	46	14	10	22	58	77	52	19

DID YOU KNOW ?

Colchester United's Player of the Year award dates from 1964–65, with the first-ever recipient being goalkeeper Percy Ames. Although several players have won the award twice, the only three-times winner was another goalkeeper, Mike Walker, who was successful in 1979–80, 1980–81 and 1982–83.

COLCHESTER UNITED – FOOTBALL LEAGUE ONE 2014–15 LEAGUE RECORD

Match No.	Date	Venue	Opponents	Result	H/T Score	Lg Pos.	Goalscorers	Attendance
1	Aug 9	H	Oldham Ath	D	2-2	1-2	10	Okuonghae [7], Moncur [58]	4023
2	16	A	Bristol C	L	1-2	1-0	17	Moncur [9]	11,626
3	19	A	Notts Co	L	1-2	0-1	22	Sears [69]	3792
4	23	H	Doncaster R	L	0-1	0-0	22		3162
5	30	H	Peterborough U	L	1-3	0-2	23	Sears [64]	4014
6	Sept 6	A	Walsall	D	0-0	0-0	23		4009
7	13	A	Leyton Orient	W	2-0	0-0	21	Watt [62], Sears [73]	5313
8	16	H	Sheffield U	L	2-3	1-0	22	Moncur [31], Sears [77]	3084
9	20	H	Bradford C	D	0-0	0-0	23		3524
10	27	A	Crewe Alex	W	3-0	0-0	20	Sears [57], Healey [63], Watt [67]	3909
11	Oct 4	A	Preston NE	L	2-4	2-2	21	Healey [16], Gilbey [37]	8478
12	11	H	Fleetwood T	W	2-1	1-1	16	Massey 2 [40, 76]	3383
13	18	A	Scunthorpe U	D	1-1	1-1	16	Sears [33]	3303
14	21	A	Chesterfield	W	2-1	0-1	14	Healey [50], Sears [87]	2718
15	25	H	Swindon T	D	2-2	0-1	14	Healey [47], Massey [52]	7871
16	Nov 1	H	Port Vale	L	1-2	0-0	18	Sears [79]	3571
17	14	A	Barnsley	L	2-3	1-1	18	Watt [15], Sears [75]	9191
18	22	H	Coventry C	L	0-1	0-0	21		4433
19	29	A	Milton Keynes D	L	0-6	0-3	22		7646
20	Dec 13	H	Rochdale	L	1-4	0-3	23	Massey [50]	2920
21	20	A	Yeovil T	W	1-0	0-0	21	Eastmond [72]	6837
22	26	H	Gillingham	L	1-2	0-2	23	Szmidics [51]	4544
23	28	A	Crawley T	D	0-0	0-0	23		2046
24	Jan 10	A	Peterborough U	W	2-0	0-0	22	Sears [54], Hewitt [84]	5524
25	17	H	Walsall	L	0-2	0-1	22		2980
26	24	H	Leyton Orient	W	2-0	1-0	21	Massey [14], Gorkss [47]	5668
27	31	A	Bradford C	D	1-1	1-0	21	Porter [5]	13,917
28	Feb 7	A	Crewe Alex	L	2-3	1-0	21	Porter [45], Marriott [84]	3134
29	10	A	Sheffield U	L	1-4	0-2	21	Szmidics [70]	17,162
30	14	A	Oldham Ath	W	1-0	1-0	21	Szmidics [2]	5668
31	17	H	Milton Keynes D	L	0-1	0-1	21		2974
32	21	H	Bristol C	W	3-2	3-0	20	Lapslie [3], Bonne [14], Porter [26]	4300
33	28	A	Doncaster R	L	0-2	0-1	22		6330
34	Mar 3	H	Notts Co	L	0-1	0-0	22		2505
35	7	A	Rochdale	L	1-2	0-1	22	Porter (pen) [63]	2625
36	14	H	Crawley T	L	2-3	1-2	23	Szmidics [11], Fox [49]	3592
37	17	H	Yeovil T	W	2-0	0-0	23	Fox (pen) [54], Murphy [58]	2336
38	21	A	Gillingham	D	2-2	0-0	23	Moncur [62], Porter [87]	5319
39	Apr 3	A	Port Vale	W	2-1	0-0	23	Moncur [57], Murphy [77]	4471
40	6	H	Barnsley	W	3-1	0-1	23	Massey [62], Murphy [80], Moncur [86]	5157
41	11	A	Coventry C	L	0-1	0-1	23		8933
42	14	A	Chesterfield	L	0-6	0-3	23		6508
43	18	H	Scunthorpe U	D	2-2	0-1	23	Eastman [81], Porter [85]	4551
44	25	A	Fleetwood T	W	3-2	0-0	23	Moncur [47], Massey [84], Porter (pen) [87]	3129
45	28	H	Swindon T	D	1-1	1-0	22	Murphy [1]	4395
46	May 3	H	Preston NE	W	1-0	0-0	19	Moncur [82]	8413

Final League Position: 19

GOALSCORERS

League (58): Sears 10, Moncur 8, Massey 7, Porter 7 (2 pens), Healey 4, Murphy 4, Szmidics 4, Watt 3, Fox 2 (1 pen), Bonne 1, Eastman 1, Eastmond 1, Gilbey 1, Gorkss 1, Hewitt 1, Lapslie 1, Marriott 1, Okuonghae 1.
FA Cup (8): Sears 3 (1 pen), Gilbey 1, Massey 1, Moncur 1, Szmodics 1, Watt 1.
Capital One Cup (0).
Johnstone's Paint Trophy (3): Drey Wright 1, Sears 1, Watt 1 (1 pen).

This appearance grid lists, for each of the 46 league matches, the shirt number worn by each player (a superscript indicates goals scored). Column headings give each player's name followed by their appearances (+ substitute appearances).

Player	1	2	3	4	5	6	7	8	9	10	11	12	13	14	15	16	17	18	19	20	21	22	23	24	25	26	27	28	29	30	31	32	33	34	35	36	37	38	39	40	41	42	43	44	45	46
Walker S 45	1	1	1	1	1	1	1	1	1	1	1	1	1	1	1	1	1	1	1	1	1	1	1	1	1	1	1	1	1	1	1	1	1	1	1	1	1	1	1	1	1		1	1	1	1
Clohessy S 31 +1	2	2	2	2	2	2	2	2	2	2	2					5					2	2²	2	2	2	2	2	2	2	2	2	2	2¹													
Okuonghae M 8 +1	3		3	3	3	3	3¹									12			3			3		3									3													
Eastman T 46	4	4	4	4	4	4	4		4	4	4	4	4	4	4	4	4	4	4	4						4	4	4	4			4	4	4	4	4	4	4	4	4	4	4	4	4	4	4
Gordon B 16 +2	5	5	5	5	5	5¹	5	5	5	5	5	5	5	5	5	5			4		6	5	5¹							3	3		3	8	8	7²	8	8	7	3	8	8	6¹	6²	7¹	7³
Gilbey A 32 +2	6	6	6¹	7	7	7	6	7	8	6	6	4	6	12	3	4	8	8	6³	8		6³	11	13	13	11²	9	10	10¹	10	12	7	12	9	9	11	12	12	10	9	6	6	11	9	9	8²
Eastmond C 6 +4	7¹		14	12			13	9	7	7²	7								12	13	5	10	10	10²	6	12	6	6	8²	9¹	10	9	7	6³	9	12	8²	6	6	8	7	7	8	8	8	9
Massey G 39 +7	8²	8²	12	13	11³	11²	9	10	11¹	9	9	8	9	8	9	9	10³	11²	14	13	3	8	6	13	9²	9⁴	10¹	9	9	8²	8²	6²	9	6	6	6	6	13	12	8	7	8	8	8	8	9
Sears F 24	9	9	9	11	9		10	6	10	11²	12	9	10	10	12	10	11	10	9	11	9	11	9	7	10³	8³	8	7				10	14	9	9			11	11		7					
Wright Drey 1 +4	10³		10	10			7¹	12		13	10¹	12	13	8	11	6¹	7	8		9²	10				11									6³		3³				12						
Ibehre J 5	11	11¹	8	8³	8	8	14	12				7²	8¹	6¹	8	11²	14				7		7²	12	11	14										8¹							9²	11¹	13	12
Moncur G 34 +7	12	10³	11¹	9¹	10²	9	12	11¹									12		11¹	10¹	11		8	11	7	6	11	11	12	13	6³	10	8	7²	10	8¹	9	7¹	13	7¹	10	11¹	12	7	6	10¹
Vose D 2 +5	13	13	7³	14	6¹	13	8²	13		10						7¹									12	3	12	8	7	7																
Holman D —+4	14	14	13		13		11³																			14																				
Osborne K 4		3		6¹																																										
Kent F 9 +1		7																																												
Bean M 3		12							3	3	3	3	2	2	2	2	2	12	2	2																										
Szmidics S 17 +14					6¹	6						13	13	13	13	13	14	14			11 8	12 14	8	8	8	8³	10¹	6	9¹	9¹	9	9²	14	7²	10	8¹	13	13	7¹	12	13	9²	11¹	9	13	12
Watt S 17 +4			13	6¹	13	10 12 13			9	11¹	10¹	11¹ 11²	11²	12	11	11²	6¹	9¹	10²	9²			9¹ 7	9²	9	6 14		7	6 13	6³	8 11¹	10	12 11¹	7	7	8	7¹	11	12	7¹	13	9²	11¹	7 13	11¹	10¹
Murphy J 11											14																									9										
Smith D —+1									13		10¹													10³ 11¹					14							14 2 6				14						
Wright David —+2																								7 12	7 12	6 14			7 12	6 13	7	3	2													
Lawrence B —+1																																				3							3			
Healey R 7 +14												2	2	2		2	5	13 5	5	5	4	4		4 5 14	3 5 14	3	3	3	3	4	4 4	3 2	5	2	2¹ 13 5	13 5	11² 5	2 9² 5¹	5	5	1 2³ 5 9¹	13 5	12 5	12 5	12 5	14 13 5
Hewitt E 21												6	7	7	7	7² 12	3 9²	6³	5 3⁴ 13	3	4	4	13	3 5 14	5 7 10¹	5 7 11 12	5 8 11 12	5 7 11	5 7 11	5 7 11 12	5 7¹11	8¹11 13	5 10	2 5 10 14	11²	13 5 10	8² 9¹ 10	8² 9¹	6 10	2² 13 9¹ 11³	2³ 5 9¹ 11	13 5 10	12 5 10	12 5 10	14 13 5 11
Fox D 29 +1																																														

(Note: the rightmost columns — O'Donoghue M 1, Khumalo B 10, Roofe K —+2, Kpekawa C 3+1, Brindley R 7+1, Packwood W 1, Harney J —+1, Lewington C 1, Gorkss K 7, Wynter A 16+2, Sembie-Ferris D 2+8, Briggs M 17+1, Lapslie T 11, Porter C 20+1, Marriott J —+5, McEvoy K —+1 — contain the remaining scattered appearance entries for matches 17–46.)

FA Cup

First Round	Gosport Bor	(a)	6-3
Second Round	Peterborough U	(h)	1-0
Third Round	Cardiff C	(a)	1-3

Capital One Cup

First Round	Charlton Ath	(a)	0-4

Johnstone's Paint Trophy

Second Round	Gillingham	(h)	3-3
(Gillingham won 4-2 penalties)			

COVENTRY CITY

FOUNDATION

Workers at Singers' cycle factory formed a club in 1883. The first success of Singers' FC was to win the Birmingham Junior Cup in 1891 and this led in 1894 to their election to the Birmingham & District League. Four years later they changed their name to Coventry City and joined the Southern League in 1908 at which time they were playing in blue and white quarters.

Ricoh Arena, Phoenix Way, Coventry CV6 6GE.

Telephone: (02476) 992 326 or (02476) 992 327.

Ticket Office: (02476) 992 326.

Website: www.ccfc.co.uk

Email: info@ccfc.co.uk

Ground Capacity: 32,604.

Record Attendance: 51,455 v Wolverhampton W, Division 2, 29 April 1967 (at Highfield Road); 31,407 v Chelsea, FA Cup 6th rd, 7 March 2009 (at Ricoh Arena).

Pitch Measurements: 100m × 68m (109yd × 74.5yd)

Chairman: Tim Fisher.

Chief Executive: Steve Waggott.

Manager: Tony Mowbray.

Assistant Manager: Neil MacFarlane.

Physio: David Hart.

Colours: Sky blue shirts with grey horizontal stripes, sky blue shorts, sky blue socks.

Year Formed: 1883.

Turned Professional: 1893.

Previous Name: 1883, Singers' FC; 1898, Coventry City.

Club Nickname: 'Sky Blues'.

Grounds: 1883, Binley Road; 1887, Stoke Road; 1899, Highfield Road; 2005, Ricoh Arena; 2013, Sixfields Stadium (groundshare with Northampton T); 2014, Ricoh Arena.

First Football League Game: 30 August 1919, Division 2, v Tottenham H (h) L 0–5 – Lindon; Roberts, Chaplin, Allan, Hawley, Clarke, Sheldon, Mercer, Sambrooke, Lowes, Gibson.

Record League Victory: 9–0 v Bristol C, Division 3 (S), 28 April 1934 – Pearson; Brown, Bisby; Perry, Davidson, Frith; White (2), Lauderdale, Bourton (5), Jones (2), Lake.

Record Cup Victory: 8–0 v Rushden & D, League Cup 2nd rd, 2 October 2002 – Debec; Caldwell, Quinn, Betts (1p), Konjic (Shaw), Davenport, Pipe, Safri (Stanford), Mills (2) (Bothroyd (2)), McSheffery (3), Partridge.

Record Defeat: 2–10 v Norwich C, Division 3 (S), 15 March 1930.

Most League Points (2 for a win): 60, Division 4, 1958–59 and Division 3, 1963–64.

HONOURS

Football League – Division 1:
Best season: 6th, 1969–70;
Division 2: *Champions* 1966–67;
Division 3: *Champions* 1963–64;
Division 3 (S): *Champions* 1935–36;
Runners-up 1933–34;
Division 4: *Runners-up* 1958–59.

FA Cup: *Winners* 1987.

Football League Cup: Best season: semi-final, 1981, 1990.

European Competitions
European Fairs Cup: 1970–71.

sky SPORTS FACT FILE

Coventry City were one of the pioneers of the commercialisation of the game under Jimmy Hill in the 1960s. The Bantams became the Sky Blues and fans were courted with a new social club, pre-match entertainment and much-improved facilities providing a blueprint for the modern game which has since become standard at all clubs.

Most League Points (3 for a win): 66, Division 1, 2001–02.

Most League Goals: 108, Division 3 (S), 1931–32.

Highest League Scorer in Season: Clarrie Bourton, 49, Division 3 (S), 1931–32.

Most League Goals in Total Aggregate: Clarrie Bourton, 173, 1931–37.

Most League Goals in One Match: 5, Clarrie Bourton v Bournemouth, Division 3 (S), 17 October 1931; 5, Arthur Bacon v Gillingham, Division 3 (S), 30 December 1933.

Most Capped Player: Magnus Hedman, 44 (58), Sweden.

Most League Appearances: Steve Ogrizovic, 507, 1984–2000.

Youngest League Player: Ben Mackey, 16 years 167 days v Ipswich T, 12 April 2003.

Record Transfer Fee Received: £13,000,000 from Internazionale for Robbie Keane, July 2000.

Record Transfer Fee Paid: £6,500,000 to Norwich C for Craig Bellamy, August 2000.

Football League Record: 1919 Elected to Division 2; 1925–26 Division 3 (N); 1926–36 Division 3 (S); 1936–52 Division 2; 1952–58 Division 3 (S); 1958–59 Division 4; 1959–64 Division 3; 1964–67 Division 2; 1967–92 Division 1; 1992–2001 FA Premier League; 2001–04 Division 1; 2004–12 FL C; 2012– FL 1.

LATEST SEQUENCES

Longest Sequence of League Wins: 6, 25.4.1964 – 5.9.1964.

Longest Sequence of League Defeats: 9, 30.8.1919 – 11.10.1919.

Longest Sequence of League Draws: 6, 1.11.2003 – 29.11.2003.

Longest Sequence of Unbeaten League Matches: 25, 26.11.1966 – 13.5.1967.

Longest Sequence Without a League Win: 19, 30.8.1919 – 20.12.1919.

Successive Scoring Runs: 25 from 10.9.1966.

Successive Non-scoring Runs: 11 from 11.10.1919.

MANAGERS

H. R. Buckle 1909–10
Robert Wallace 1910–13
 (*Secretary-Manager*)
Frank Scott-Walford 1913–15
William Clayton 1917–19
H. Pollitt 1919–20
Albert Evans 1920–24
Jimmy Kerr 1924–28
James McIntyre 1928–31
Harry Storer 1931–45
Dick Bayliss 1945–47
Billy Frith 1947–48
Harry Storer 1948–53
Jack Fairbrother 1953–54
Charlie Elliott 1954–55
Jesse Carver 1955–56
George Raynor 1956
Harry Warren 1956–57
Billy Frith 1957–61
Jimmy Hill 1961–67
Noel Cantwell 1967–72
Bob Dennison 1972
Joe Mercer 1972–75
Gordon Milne 1972–81
Dave Sexton 1981–83
Bobby Gould 1983–84
Don Mackay 1985–86
George Curtis 1986–87
 (*became Managing Director*)
John Sillett 1987–90
Terry Butcher 1990–92
Don Howe 1992
Bobby Gould 1992–93
 (*with Don Howe, June 1992*)
Phil Neal 1993–95
Ron Atkinson 1995–96
 (*became Director of Football*)
Gordon Strachan 1996–2001
Roland Nilsson 2001–02
Gary McAllister 2002–04
Eric Black 2004
Peter Reid 2004–05
Micky Adams 2005–07
Iain Dowie 2007–08
Chris Coleman 2008–10
Aidy Boothroyd 2010–11
Andy Thorn 2011–12
Mark Robins 2012–13
Steven Pressley 2013–15
Tony Mowbray March 2015–

TEN YEAR LEAGUE RECORD

		P	W	D	L	F	A	Pts	Pos
2005-06	FL C	46	16	15	15	62	65	63	8
2006-07	FL C	46	16	8	22	47	62	56	17
2007-08	FL C	46	14	11	21	52	64	53	21
2008-09	FL C	46	13	15	18	47	58	54	17
2009-10	FL C	46	13	15	18	47	64	54	19
2010-11	FL C	46	14	13	19	54	58	55	18
2011-12	FL C	46	9	13	24	41	65	40	23
2012-13	FL 1	46	18	11	17	66	59	55*	15
2013-14	FL 1	46	16	13	17	74	77	51*	18
2014-15	FL 1	46	13	16	17	49	60	55	17

* 10 pts deducted.

DID YOU KNOW ?

Coventry City were in such a serious financial position towards the end of the 1914–15 season that the club received a summons for non-payment of rates and the reserve team sometimes played with less than a full team in their Birmingham League fixtures. By July there was just one board member remaining.

COVENTRY CITY – FOOTBALL LEAGUE ONE 2014–15 LEAGUE RECORD

Match No.	Date	Venue	Opponents	Result	H/T Score	Lg Pos.	Goalscorers	Attendance
1	Aug 9	A	Bradford C	L	2-3	1-1	16	Johnson 2 [41,89]	14,621
2	16	H	Sheffield U	W	1-0	0-0	14	Harris (og) [78]	2279
3	19	H	Barnsley	D	2-2	2-2	14	McQuoid [4], Clarke [44]	2376
4	23	A	Milton Keynes D	D	0-0	0-0	15		10,600
5	30	A	Swindon T	D	1-1	1-0	15	McQuoid [41]	7299
6	Sept 5	H	Gillingham	W	1-0	1-0	8	Nouble [10]	27,306
7	13	H	Yeovil T	W	2-1	1-0	5	Johnson [7], Jackson [68]	11,085
8	16	A	Scunthorpe U	L	1-2	1-1	8	Nouble [17]	2866
9	20	A	Rochdale	L	0-1	0-1	11		3583
10	27	H	Preston NE	L	0-2	0-0	14		10,006
11	Oct 4	H	Crawley T	D	2-2	2-2	15	McQuoid [14], Jackson [27]	7708
12	11	A	Crewe Alex	L	1-2	0-2	15	Grant (og) [48]	5058
13	18	A	Bristol C	L	1-3	0-2	17	Miller [76]	11,888
14	21	A	Oldham Ath	L	1-4	1-3	20	Maddison [35]	3224
15	25	H	Peterborough U	W	3-2	0-2	17	Haynes [49], O'Brien [62], Nouble [64]	8957
16	Nov 1	A	Leyton Orient	D	2-2	1-0	19	O'Brien 2 [35,90]	5464
17	15	H	Notts Co	L	0-1	0-0	20		8116
18	22	A	Colchester U	W	1-0	0-0	18	Madine [74]	4433
19	29	H	Walsall	D	0-0	0-0	18		8076
20	Dec 13	A	Port Vale	W	2-0	0-0	14	Johnson [57], Madine [90]	5321
21	20	A	Fleetwood T	D	1-1	0-1	17	Jackson [80]	10,254
22	26	A	Doncaster R	L	0-2	0-2	19		6916
23	28	H	Chesterfield	D	0-0	0-0	17		10,166
24	Jan 3	A	Walsall	W	2-0	1-0	16	O'Brien [6], Tudgay [87]	5930
25	12	H	Swindon T	L	0-3	0-2	18		7098
26	17	A	Gillingham	L	1-3	1-0	18	Madine (pen) [35]	5141
27	24	A	Yeovil T	D	0-0	0-0	17		4422
28	31	H	Rochdale	D	2-2	2-1	19	Samuel [24], Odelusi [38]	7606
29	Feb 7	H	Preston NE	L	0-1	0-1	20		13,363
30	10	H	Scunthorpe U	D	1-1	0-1	20	Tudgay [90]	6885
31	21	A	Sheffield U	D	2-2	1-0	21	Samuel 2 [33,47]	20,314
32	28	H	Milton Keynes D	W	2-1	2-0	20	Stokes [9], Samuel [12]	9934
33	Mar 3	A	Barnsley	L	0-1	0-0	20		9567
34	7	H	Port Vale	L	2-3	1-2	20	O'Brien [4], Odelusi [70]	9446
35	10	H	Bradford C	D	1-1	1-0	20	Nouble [45]	8566
36	14	A	Chesterfield	W	3-2	1-1	20	Tudgay [9], Odelusi [65], Nouble [75]	7205
37	17	H	Fleetwood T	W	2-0	0-0	18	Samuel [88], Nouble [90]	3017
38	21	H	Doncaster R	L	1-3	1-0	18	Samuel [5]	8699
39	28	A	Peterborough U	W	1-0	0-0	17	Turgott [70]	7325
40	Apr 1	H	Leyton Orient	L	0-1	0-0	17		8010
41	6	A	Notts Co	D	0-0	0-0	18		6706
42	11	H	Colchester U	W	1-0	1-0	16	O'Brien [36]	8933
43	14	A	Oldham Ath	D	1-1	0-1	16	Johnson [90]	7256
44	18	A	Bristol C	D	0-0	0-0	16		12,093
45	25	H	Crewe Alex	L	1-3	0-2	18	Proschwitz [85]	13,983
46	May 3	A	Crawley T	W	2-1	0-0	17	Tudgay [73], Maddison [90]	5744

Final League Position: 17

GOALSCORERS

League (49): Nouble 6, O'Brien 6, Samuel 6, Johnson 5, Tudgay 4, Jackson 3, Madine 3 (1 pen), McQuoid 3, Odelusi 3, Maddison 2, Clarke 1, Haynes 1, Miller 1, Proschwitz 1, Stokes 1, Turgott 1, own goals 2.
FA Cup (1): Johnson 1.
Capital One Cup (1): Miller 1.
Johnstone's Paint Trophy (6): McQuoid 2, Phillips 2, Madine 1, Nouble 1.

Allsop R 24	Clarke J 10+1	Willis J 33+1	Webster A 25+5	Johnson R 20	Pugh D 5	Thomas C 13+3	Swanson D 8+7	O'Brien J 43+1	Tudgay M 18+4	McQuoid J 12+2	Fleck J 43+1	Miller S 1+11	Haynes R 20+6	Daniels B —+2	Jackson S 12+16	Phillips A 14+5	Nouble F 28+3	Hines S 6+3	Finch J 8+8	Coulibaly M 1+3	Maddison J 2+10	Barton A 24+3	Burge L 18	Martin A 26+1	Madine G 11	Pennington M 24	Thomas G —+6	Jones J 4	Odelusi S 4+10	Samuel D 12+1	Williams L 4+1	Stokes C 16	Proschwitz N 6+3	Turgott B —+3	Ward G 11	Match No.
1	2²	3	4	5	6	7¹	8	9	10	11	12	13																								1
1	5	2	3	4		14	7³	8	11	10²	6¹	12	9	13																						2
1	5	2	3	4			7¹	8	11³	10²	6	12	9	14	13																					3
1	4	5	2	3		12	6²	8	10³	11¹	7	13	9		14																					4
1		2	3	4		6	14	7	10²	11¹	8	12²	9		13	5																				5
1	5	2	3	4		8²		7	10³	12	6		9						11¹	13	14															6
1	5	2²	3	4		6		7		10³	8		9			12	14	11¹	13																	7
1	5	2	3²	4⁴		6¹	13	7		8			14	9		11³	10	12																		8
1	5	4	3¹		9	6²	12	7	14		8³				11		10	2	13																	9
1	5	2	3³			6²	7	11	13	8	14	9			10¹			4		12																10
1	12	2	3		9	6¹		8		10³	7	14			11	5²		4	13																	11
1		2			5	7¹		9³		10	8	13			11	6		3²	4⁴	12	14															12
1	2	3	4		9¹			7		10⁴		14	12		11	5		6³	13	8																13
1		4	3²		14			8²	13		7	10¹	9		12	5	2		11	6																14
	2		3		6			8²		10¹	9		5		12		11	4	13		7	1														15
	2	12³	3²					6		8		5	13		11		9¹		14	7	1	4	10													16
1	2¹	3				13	6			9		5			12¹	11	8		7		4	10														17
1		4	5			12	6²			8		9			2	10¹	7			13		3	11													18
1		3	5			12	6			8		9²			13	11¹	7					4	10	2												19
1	14	3	5			10¹	6		8²	7³		12								13		9	4	11	2											20
1		4				6¹	7		10²	9		5	13						12	8		3	11	2												21
1		3				6²				9		5			12		13		8¹		10⁴	7⁴		3	11	2										22
1		4				7		6		8		5			9		11						3	10	2											23
1	4					7		6	11	9		5			8¹	2²	10		12			13			3											24
1		4				7	12	6¹		8		5			9²		10						3	11	2	13										25
1		2	4			7²	10³			9	13	5			6¹		8		14			12		3	11											26
		2	4	5				7	12	8					10¹		6		9					3	11			1								27
		2	4	5²				6		8		12			13		11		7					3			1	1	9¹	10						28
		2	4²					6	12	7							11¹					8	1	3		5	13		10	9						29
		5²						6¹	9	8		12			14	2						7		4		3	13	1	10	11³						30
								6	10	8		14			2							7²		4		3	13	1	11	9¹	5³					31
								6¹	11²	8					2							7	1	4		3	12		10	9³	5	13				32
								9	10²	8					5	13						7¹	1	4		2			6³		3	12	14		33
								6¹	10¹	8					14	2	9					7²	1	4		3			12	11	13	5			34
		12						6²	11	8					2¹	10						7	1	4		3			9²	13		5	14		35
	2							9		7					13	10¹						8	1	4		3			12	11²	5			6	36
	2	14						12	9¹	7					10							8²	1	4		3			13	11	5³			6	37
	2							9¹		10					14	13	11³					6²	1	4		3			12	8	5			7	38
	2	14						7¹	6²	8					9³							1	4	3					12	11	5	13	10		39
	2							9²		7		13			10							1	4	3	12		8¹	11³		5		14	6		40
	2							7							11²	6					12	9	1	3	4		13			5	10¹		8		41
	2		4					9¹		8					13	10					12	6²	1		3		14			5	11³		7		42
	2¹		4					9²		7					13	10					12	8³	1		3		14			5	11		6		43
	2²		4					9⁴		8					12	11¹					13	6	1		3		14			5	10		7		44
			4					10		7					2¹	9					13	8³	1	12	3²		14			5	11		6		45
	2	14	3					9²	11	7					13						12	6¹	1	5			4				10³		8		46

FA Cup
First Round Worcester (h) 1-2

Capital One Cup
First Round Cardiff C (h) 1-2

Johnstone's Paint Trophy
First Round Wycombe W (a) 1-0
Second Round Exeter C (h) 3-1
Southern Quarter-Finals Plymouth Arg (h) 2-0
Southern Semi-Finals Bristol C (a) 0-2

CRAWLEY TOWN

FOUNDATION

Formed in 1896, Crawley Town initially entered the West Sussex League before switching to the mid-Sussex League in 1901, winning the Second Division in its second season. The club remained at such level until 1951 when it became members of the Sussex County League and five years later moved to the Metropolitan League while remaining as an amateur club. It was not until 1962 that the club turned semi-professional and a year later, joined the Southern League. Many honours came the club's way, but the most successful run was achieved in 2010–11 when they reached the fifith round of the FA Cup and played before a crowd of 74,778 spectators at Old Trafford against Manchester United. Crawley Town spent 48 years at the Town Mead ground before a new site was occupied at Broadfield in 1997, ideally suited to access from the neighbouring motorway. History was also made on 9 April when the team won promotion to the Football League after beating Tamworth 3-0 to stretch their unbeaten League record to 26 games. They finished the season with a Conference record points total of 105 and at the same time, established another milestone for the longest unbeaten run, having extended it to 30 matches by the end of the season.

Checkatrade.com Stadium, Winfield Way, Crawley, West Sussex RH11 9RX.

Telephone: (01293) 410 000.

Fax: (01293) 410 002.

Ticket Office: (01293) 410 005.

Website: www.crawleytownfc.com

Email: feedback@crawleytownfc.com

Ground Capacity: 5,748.

Record Attendance: 5,880 v Reading, FA Cup 3rd rd, 5 January 2013.

Pitch Measurements: 103.5m × 66m (113yd × 72yd)

Chairman: Dave Pottinger.

Chief Executive: Michael Dunford.

Manager: Mark Yates.

Assistant Manager: Jimmy Dack.

Head of Medical: Niall Clarke.

Colours: Red shirts with white trim, red shorts with white trim, red socks with white trim.

Year Formed: 1896. *Turned Professional:* 1962.

Club Nickname: 'The Red Devils'.

Grounds: Up to 1997, Town Mead; 1997 Broadfield Stadium (renamed Checkatrade.com Stadium 2013).

First Football League Game: 6 August 2011, FL 2 v Port Vale (a) D 2-2 – Shearer; Hunt, Howell, Bulman, McFadzean (1), Dempster (Thomas), Simpson, Torres, Tubbs (Neilson), Barnett (1) (Wassmer), Smith.

MANAGERS

John Maggs 1978–90
Brian Sparrow 1990–92
Steve Wicks 1992–93
Ted Shepherd 1993–95
Colin Pates 1995–96
Billy Smith 1997–99
Cliff Cant 1999–2000
Billy Smith 2000–03
Francis Vines 2003–05
John Collins 2005–06
David Woozley, Ben Judge, John Yems 2006–07
Steve Evans 2007–12
Sean O'Driscoll 2012
Richie Barker 2012–13
John Gregory 2013–14
Dean Saunders 2014–15
Mark Yates May 2015–

sky SPORTS FACT FILE

In the days before they embraced professionalism Crawley Town regularly entered the FA Amateur Cup, although with little success. Their final season in the competition was 1961–62 when they defeated Sidley United and Camberley before going down 5-2 at home to Dorking in the 2nd qualifying round.

Record League Victory: 5–1 v Barnsley, FL 1, 14 February 2015 – Price; Dickson, Bradley (1), Ward, Fowler (Smith); Young, Elliott (1), Edwards, Wordsworth (Morgan), Pogba (Tomlin); McLeod (3).

Record League Defeat: 6-0 v Morecambe, FL 2, 10 September 2011.

Most League Points (3 for a win): 84, FL 2, 2011–12.

Most League Goals: 76, FL 2, 2011–12.

Highest League Scorer in Season: Tyrone Barnett, 14, 2011–12.

Most League Goals in Total Aggregate: Billy Clarke, 20, 2011–14; Matt Tubbs, 20, 2011–12, 2013–14.

Most League Goals in One Match: 3, Izale McLeod v Barnsley, FL 1, 14 February 2015.

Most Capped Player: Dean Morgan, 1 (3), Montserrat.

Most League Appearances: Dannie Bulman, 135, 2011–14.

Youngest League Player: Hiram Boateng, 18 years 55 days v Stevenage, 4 March 2014.

Record Transfer Fee Received: £1,100,000 from Peterborough U for Tyrone Barnett, July 2012.

Record Transfer Fee Paid: £100,000 to Peterborough U for Sergio Raul Torres, July 2010; £100,000 to Peterborough U for Emile Sinclair, August 2013.

Football League Record: 2011 Promoted from Conference Premier; 2011–12 FL 2; 2012–15 FL 1; 2015– FL 2.

LATEST SEQUENCES

Longest Sequence of League Wins: 7, 17.9.2011 – 25.10.2011.

Longest Sequence of League Defeats: 6, 22.3.2014 – 8.4.2014.

Longest Sequence of League Draws: 5, 25.10.2014 – 29.11.2014.

Longest Sequence of Unbeaten League Matches: 13, 17.9.2011 – 17.12.2011.

Longest Sequence Without a League Win: 13, 25.10.2014 – 27.1.2015.

Successive Scoring Runs: 16 from 17.9.2011 – 2.1.2012.

Successive Non-scoring Runs: 4 from 22.10.2013.

HONOURS

Football League – FL 2: Best season: 3rd (promoted), 2011–12.

FA Cup: Best season: 5th rd, 2011, 2012.

Football League Cup: Best season: 3rd rd, 2013.

Blue Square Premier: *Champions* 2010–11.

Southern League: *Champions* 2003–04.

Southern League Cup: *Winners* 2003, 2004.

Southern League Championship Trophy: *Winners* 2004, 2005.

Southern League Merit Cup: *Winners* 1971.

Sussex Professional Cup: *Winners* 1970.

Sussex Senior Cup: *Winners* 1990, 1991, 2003, 2005.

Sussex Intermediate Cup: *Winners* 1928.

Sussex Floodlit Cup: *Winners* 1991, 1992, 1993, 1999.

Southern Counties Floodlit League: *Champions* 1985–86.

Mid-Sussex Senior League: *Champions* 1902–03.

Montgomery Cup: *Winners* 1926.

Gilbert Rice Floodlit Cup: *Winners* 1980, 1984.

Roy Hayden Trophy: *Winners* 1991, 1992.

William Hill Senior Cup: *Winners* 1993.

Metropolitan League Challenge Cup: *Winners* 1959.

Highest Placed Amateur Award: 1961–62.

FA Ronnie Radford Award: 2011.

TEN YEAR LEAGUE RECORD

		P	W	D	L	F	A	Pts	Pos
2005-06	Conf	42	12	11	19	48	55	44	17
2006-07	Conf	46	17	12	17	52	52	53	18
2007-08	Conf P	46	19	9	18	73	67	60	15
2008-09	Conf P	46	19	14	13	77	55	70	9
2009-10	Conf P	44	19	9	16	50	57	66	7
2010-11	Conf P	46	31	12	3	93	50	105	1
2011-12	FL 2	46	23	15	8	76	54	84	3
2012-13	FL 1	46	18	14	14	59	58	68	10
2013-14	FL 1	46	14	15	17	48	54	57	14
2014-15	FL 1	46	13	11	22	53	79	50	22

DID YOU KNOW ?

Goalkeeper John Maggs joined Crawley Town in August 1963 and went on to make 440 Southern League appearances before retiring through injury. He later served the club as manager, chairman, director, chief executive and stadium manager before leaving after over 35 years' service.

CRAWLEY TOWN – FOOTBALL LEAGUE ONE 2014–15 LEAGUE RECORD

Match No.	Date		Venue	Opponents	Result		H/T Score	Lg Pos.	Goalscorers	Atten- dance
1	Aug	9	A	Barnsley	W	1-0	0-0	8	McLeod [82]	10,105
2		16	H	Swindon T	W	1-0	0-0	5	McLeod (pen) [51]	2710
3		19	H	Bradford C	L	1-3	0-0	7	Walsh [54]	2225
4		23	A	Sheffield U	L	0-1	0-0	13		18,178
5		30	A	Milton Keynes D	L	0-2	0-1	16		7148
6	Sept	6	H	Rochdale	L	0-4	0-1	19		2534
7		13	H	Fleetwood T	W	1-0	0-0	12	McLeod [78]	1905
8		16	A	Doncaster R	D	0-0	0-0	14		5197
9		20	A	Preston NE	L	0-2	0-1	18		10,388
10		27	H	Yeovil T	W	2-0	0-0	12	Elliott 2 [57, 59]	2351
11	Oct	4	A	Coventry C	D	2-2	2-2	14	Edwards [33], McLeod [37]	7708
12		11	H	Peterborough U	L	1-4	1-2	14	McLeod [2]	2832
13		18	A	Notts Co	L	3-5	0-3	15	Edwards [50], Harrold [55], Elliott [84]	6086
14		21	H	Walsall	W	1-0	0-0	13	Henderson [89]	2204
15		25	A	Gillingham	D	1-1	1-1	13	Edwards [29]	4850
16	Nov	1	H	Crewe Alex	D	1-1	0-1	15	McLeod [68]	2329
17		15	A	Oldham Ath	D	1-1	1-1	15	Edwards [42]	3924
18		22	H	Scunthorpe U	D	2-2	0-1	17	Leacock [76], McLeod (pen) [80]	2178
19		29	H	Chesterfield	D	1-1	0-0	17	Tomlin [70]	2459
20	Dec	13	A	Bristol C	L	0-1	0-0	20		11,660
21		20	H	Port Vale	L	1-2	0-2	20	Henderson [88]	2320
22		26	A	Leyton Orient	L	1-4	1-2	21	Smith [10]	4108
23		28	H	Colchester U	D	0-0	0-0	20		2046
24	Jan	10	H	Milton Keynes D	D	2-2	1-0	23	McLeod 2 (1 pen) [14 (p), 48]	2468
25		17	A	Rochdale	L	1-4	0-2	23	Elliott [76]	2255
26		24	A	Fleetwood T	L	0-1	0-1	24		2601
27		27	A	Chesterfield	L	0-3	0-1	24		5329
28		31	H	Preston NE	W	2-1	1-0	22	Wordsworth [18], Fowler [87]	2550
29	Feb	7	A	Yeovil T	L	1-2	1-0	23	McLeod [27]	3807
30		10	H	Doncaster R	L	0-5	0-1	23		2581
31		14	H	Barnsley	W	5-1	1-0	22	McLeod 3 [45, 73, 83], Bradley [48], Elliott [59]	2296
32		21	A	Swindon T	W	2-1	1-0	22	Wordsworth [5], Tomlin [88]	7692
33		28	H	Sheffield U	D	1-1	0-0	23	Wood [63]	3320
34	Mar	3	A	Bradford C	L	0-1	0-1	23		11,683
35		7	H	Bristol C	L	1-2	0-0	23	Wordsworth [60]	3333
36		14	A	Colchester U	W	3-2	2-1	22	Dickson [15], Tomlin [41], McLeod (pen) [75]	3592
37		17	A	Port Vale	W	3-2	1-2	21	Wordsworth [43], McLeod [56], Wood [69]	3852
38		21	H	Leyton Orient	W	1-0	1-0	19	McLeod (pen) [33]	3255
39		28	H	Gillingham	L	1-2	0-1	21	McLeod [63]	3570
40	Apr	3	A	Crewe Alex	D	0-0	0-0	22		5353
41		6	H	Oldham Ath	W	2-0	2-0	19	McLeod [15], Wood [33]	2520
42		11	A	Scunthorpe U	L	1-2	0-1	20	McLeod [77]	3009
43		14	A	Walsall	L	0-5	0-1	22		3296
44		18	H	Notts Co	W	2-0	2-0	19	Youga [14], Ward [16]	2580
45		25	A	Peterborough U	L	3-4	1-1	21	Elliott [29], Pogba [57], Simpson [66]	6270
46	May	3	H	Coventry C	L	1-2	0-0	22	Pogba [49]	5744

Final League Position: 22

GOALSCORERS

League (53): McLeod 19 (5 pens), Elliott 6, Edwards 4, Wordsworth 4, Tomlin 3, Wood 3, Henderson 2, Pogba 2, Bradley 1, Dickson 1, Fowler 1, Harrold 1, Leacock 1, Simpson 1, Smith 1, Walsh 1, Ward 1, Youga 1.
FA Cup (0).
Capital One Cup (2): McLeod 1, own goal 1.
Johnstone's Paint Trophy (4): Banya 1, Edwards 1, McLeod 1 (1 pen), own goal 1.

Jensen B 19 + 1	Oyebanjo L 26 + 5	Leacock D 23	Dickson R 30 + 2	Walsh J 28	Young L 29 + 9	Henderson C 13 + 4	Smith J 28 + 8	Edwards G 29 + 8	Simpson J 8	McLeod I 41 + 1	Bawling B 13 + 15	Banya C — + 9	Bradley S 25 + 1	Tomlin G 29 + 6	O'Connor E 1 + 3	Harrold M 4 + 16	Rose M — + 1	Sadler M 10	Keane K 12	Wright J 2 + 2	Ashdown J 9	Elliot M 22 + 5	Price L 18	Miller S 4 + 1	Ward D 17 + 1	Anderson B — + 1	Wordsworth A 18	Morgan D 3 + 10	Fowler L 16 + 3	Pogba M 14 + 3	Wood R 10	Cofie J — + 1	Youga K 5	Match No.
1	2	3	4	5	6^1	7	8	9	10^2	11	12	13																						1
1	2	3	5	4		8^1	7	6^2		10	13	12	9	11^1	14																			2
1	2	4	3	8		12	7	6^1		10	9	13		5^2	11																			3
1	2^1	3	5	4	10^2	8	9	6		11	7	13		12																				4
1	2	4	5	3		9	7	6^2		11	8^1		10	12	13																			5
1	2	3	5		6^2	8	7		10		14	4	13	9^3	11^1	12																		6
1		3	9	4	13	8^1	2			11	12			6^2				5	7	10														7
		3	9	4			12	8		11	2	13		10^3		14		5	7	6^2	1													8
		3		4	14	9^1	2	8		11	7^2			10^3		13		5		12	1	6												9
	2	3		4		6	8	7^2	10^1					13				5	11	12	1	9												10
	2	4		5	12		9	6			10^2	7^1			13			3	11		1	8												11
	2	4			8		9			10^1		13	3	11^2		12		5	7^1		1	6												12
1	2	3		4	10		8	7		11^2		13				12		5	6^1			9												13
	2	3		4	8	12	7^3	6	10^1	11^2	13					14		5			1	9												14
	2	3		4	6^1	7^2	13	9	10	14	12					11^3		5	8		1													15
	2	3		4	8	9^1		6	10	11						12		5	7^1		1													16
	3	5	4	12	8^1	7	10			9			2	11				6		1														17
	3	6	5	12		7	8			10	2^2		4^1	11				9				13	1											18
	2	4	3	5	12		8	9		11^4	6^1			10^2				7				1		13										19
	3	4		6	8		7			2			5	11^2		12		9				13	1	10^1										20
	2	8	3	9^1	13	7				5			4^2	10		12		6	1			11												21
1	4^3	2	5	13	7	8	9			6^1				12	14	11		3				10^2												22
1		5	8	6	2	4^2		11	3	13			12		9^1			7				10												23
1^1	2		4	12	7^3	8	6^2		10			5	11		13			9					3	14										24
	2	5	3	13		6^3	9^1		10	12			11^2		14			8^1	1		4	7												25
	2	5^1	3	6		8^2	11		10	12			14					7^3	1		4		9^1	13										26
	2		5	4	8		6^2	10		11	13				14			7^3	1		3		9^1	12										27
	2		3	5	8^2		10^1	7		11	12							6	1		4	9		13										28
	2	5	3				7^2	9^1		11	12							8	1		4	10	14	13	6^1									29
	2^2		5	3^4			9^3	10		11	12		14					8	1		4	7		13	6^1									30
			2		6			14	8		11			3	12			7	1		4		9^1	13	5^3	10^2								31
		5		2			14	8		11^2	12			4	7^3		13				1		6		9	10^1	3							32
		3		2			12	6^3		10	13		5	9							1		14	7		8^1	11^2	4						33
			13			2^1				6		11		5	9						1		3	8	12	7	10^2	4						34
		5			9^2				13		11			2	6						1		3	7	12	8	10^1	4						35
		9^2		2				13		11	14			5	6^1					12	1		4	7		8	10^3	3						36
	9	5		14							11^2			2	6^3					13	1		4	8	12	7	10^3	3						37
12	14		10		2					11			5	8^6						13	1^3		3	7		6	9^1	4						38
1	12		9^1		2^2			13		10			5	11						8^3			4	6		7		3	14					39
1	2	3^2	12					9		11			5	6										8	13	7	10^1	4						40
1	2	5	6		13	12				11^1			4	9^3						8						10^2	7^1	14	3					41
1	2	5^2		9^1			12			11			4	6	14					8^3						10	7	13			3			42
1	2	5^3		9		14	12			11			4	6										8	10^1	7^2	13				3			43
1	14			2				12		9^3	11			4	6^1									3		7	13	8	10^2		5			44
1	12			2		13		7^3	11^3				3	6						9^1			4		14	8	10				5			45
1	12			2^3			14	9^2	10	13			4	6						8			3			7	11				5^1		46

FA Cup
First Round   Yeovil T   (a)   0-1

Capital One Cup
First Round   Ipswich T   (h)   1-0
(aet)
Second Round   Norwich C   (a)   1-3

Johnstone's Paint Trophy
First Round   Cambridge U   (h)   2-0
Second Round   Luton T   (a)   1-0
Southern Quarter-Finals   Gillingham   (h)   1-2

CREWE ALEXANDRA

FOUNDATION

The first match played at Crewe was on 1 December 1877 against Basford, the leading North Staffordshire team of that time. During the club's history they have also played in a number of other leagues including the Football Alliance, Football Combination, Lancashire League, Manchester League, Central League and Lancashire Combination. Two former players, Aaron Scragg in 1899 and Jackie Pearson in 1911, had the distinction of refereeing FA Cup finals. Pearson was also capped for England against Ireland in 1892.

The Alexandra Stadium, Gresty Road, Crewe, Cheshire CW2 6EB.

Telephone: (01270) 213 014.

Fax: (01270) 216 320.

Ticket Office: (01270) 252 610.

Website: www.crewealex.net

Email: info@crewealex.net

Ground Capacity: 10,109.

Record Attendance: 20,000 v Tottenham H, FA Cup 4th rd, 30 January 1960.

Pitch Measurements: 100.5m × 67m (110yd × 73.1yd)

Chairman: John Bowler.

Vice-chairman: David Rowlinson.

Director of Football: Dario Gradi MBE.

Manager: Steve Davis.

Assistant Manager: Neil Baker.

Physio: Rob Sharp.

Colours: Red shirts with white and black trim, white shorts, red socks with white trim.

Year Formed: 1877. *Turned Professional:* 1893. *Club Nickname:* 'The Railwaymen'.

Ground: 1898, Gresty Road.

First Football League Game: 3 September 1892, Division 2, v Burton Swifts (a) L 1–7 – Hickton; Moore, Cope; Linnell, Johnson, Osborne; Bennett, Pearson (1), Bailey, Barnett, Roberts.

Record League Victory: 8–0 v Rotherham U, Division 3 (N), 1 October 1932 – Foster; Pringle, Dawson; Ward, Keenor (1), Turner (1); Gillespie, Swindells (1), McConnell (2), Deacon (2), Weale (1).

Record Cup Victory: 8–0 v Hartlepool U, Auto Windscreens Shield 1st rd, 17 October 1995 – Gayle; Collins (1), Booty, Westwood (Unsworth), Macauley (1), Whalley (1), Garvey (1), Murphy (1), Savage (1) (Rivers (1p)), Lennon, Edwards, (1 og). 8–0 v Doncaster R, LDV Vans Trophy 3rd rd, 10 November 2002 – Bankole; Wright, Walker, Foster, Tierney; Lunt (1), Brammer, Sorvel, Vaughan (1) (Bell); Ashton (3) (Miles), Jack (2) (Jones (1)).

HONOURS

Football League – Division 2: *Runners-up* 2002–03.

FA Cup: Best season: semi-final, 1888.

Football League Cup: Best season: never past 3rd rd.

Welsh Cup: *Winners* 1936, 1937.

Johnstone's Paint Trophy: *Winners* 2013.

sky SPORTS FACT FILE

The only Crewe Alexandra player to win full international honours for England was Jackie Pearson who played at inside right against Ireland in March 1892. Like many of his colleagues, Pearson was employed by the London, Midland & Scottish Railway. He later became a referee, taking charge of the 1911 FA Cup final.

Record Defeat: 2–13 v Tottenham H, FA Cup 4th rd replay, 3 February 1960.

Most League Points (2 for a win): 59, Division 4, 1962–63.

Most League Points (3 for a win): 86, Division 2, 2002–03.

Most League Goals: 95, Division 3 (N), 1931–32.

Highest League Scorer in Season: Terry Harkin, 35, Division 4, 1964–65.

Most League Goals in Total Aggregate: Bert Swindells, 126, 1928–37.

Most League Goals in One Match: 5, Tony Naylor v Colchester U, Division 3, 24 April 1993.

Most Capped Player: Clayton Ince, 38 (79), Trinidad & Tobago.

Most League Appearances: Tommy Lowry, 436, 1966–78.

Youngest League Player: Steve Walters, 16 years 119 days v Peterborough U, 6 May 1988.

Record Transfer Fee Received: £3,000,000 (rising to £6,000,000) from Manchester U for Nick Powell, June 2012.

Record Transfer Fee Paid: £650,000 to Torquay U for Rodney Jack, June 1998.

Football League Record: 1892 Original Member of Division 2; 1896 Failed re-election; 1921 Re-entered Division (N); 1958–63 Division 4; 1963–64 Division 3; 1964–68 Division 4; 1968–69 Division 3; 1969–89 Division 4; 1989–91 Division 3; 1991–92 Division 4; 1992–94 Division 3; 1994–97 Division 2; 1997–2002 Division 1; 2002–03 Division 2; 2003–04 Division 1; 2004–06 FL C; 2006–09 FL 1; 2009–12 FL 2; 2012– FL 1.

LATEST SEQUENCES

Longest Sequence of League Wins: 7, 30.4.1994 – 3.9.1994.

Longest Sequence of League Defeats: 10, 16.4.1979 – 22.8.1979.

Longest Sequence of League Draws: 5, 18.9.2010 – 9.10.2010.

Longest Sequence of Unbeaten League Matches: 17, 25.3.1995 – 16.9.1995.

Longest Sequence Without a League Win: 30, 22.9.1956 – 6.4.1957.

Successive Scoring Runs: 26 from 7.4.1934.

Successive Non-scoring Runs: 9 from 6.11.1974.

MANAGERS

W. C. McNeill 1892–94
  (*Secretary-Manager*)
J. G. Hall 1895–96
  (*Secretary-Manager*)
R. Roberts (*1st team Secretary-Manager*) 1897
J. B. Blomerley 1898–1911
  (*Secretary-Manager, continued as Hon. Secretary to 1925*)
Tom Bailey (*Secretary only*) 1925–38
George Lillycrop (*Trainer*) 1938–44
Frank Hill 1944–48
Arthur Turner 1948–51
Harry Catterick 1951–53
Ralph Ward 1953–55
Maurice Lindley 1956–57
Willie Cook 1957–58
Harry Ware 1958–60
Jimmy McGuigan 1960–64
Ernie Tagg 1964–71
  (*continued as Secretary to 1972*)
Dennis Viollet 1971
Jimmy Melia 1972–74
Ernie Tagg 1974
Harry Gregg 1975–78
Warwick Rimmer 1978–79
Tony Waddington 1979–81
Arfon Griffiths 1981–82
Peter Morris 1982–83
Dario Gradi 1983–2007
Steve Holland 2007–08
Gudjon Thordarson 2008–09
Dario Gradi 2009–11
Steve Davis October 2011–

TEN YEAR LEAGUE RECORD

		P	W	D	L	F	A	Pts	Pos
2005-06	FL C	46	9	15	22	57	86	42	22
2006-07	FL 1	46	17	9	20	66	72	60	13
2007-08	FL 1	46	12	14	20	47	65	50	20
2008-09	FL 1	46	12	10	24	59	82	46	22
2009-10	FL 2	46	15	10	21	68	73	55	18
2010-11	FL 2	46	18	11	17	87	65	65	10
2011-12	FL 2	46	20	12	14	67	59	72	7
2012-13	FL 1	46	18	10	18	54	62	64	13
2013-14	FL 1	46	13	12	21	54	80	51	19
2014-15	FL 1	46	14	10	22	43	75	52	20

DID YOU KNOW ?

Crewe Alexandra won the last 10 home games of 1937–38 and the first 6 of 1938–39, a total of 16 consecutive wins. The run was eventually broken by Oldham Athletic who won 2-1 at Gresty Road on 5 November 1938.

CREWE ALEXANDRA – FOOTBALL LEAGUE ONE 2014–15 LEAGUE RECORD

Match No.	Date	Venue	Opponents	Result	H/T Score	Lg Pos.	Goalscorers	Attendance
1	Aug 9	A	Fleetwood T	L	1-2	0-0	17	Inman (pen) [90]	3774
2	16	H	Barnsley	L	1-2	1-0	20	Waters [22]	4502
3	19	H	Rochdale	L	2-5	1-2	23	Haber 2 [9, 62]	3742
4	23	A	Swindon T	L	0-2	0-1	24		6530
5	30	A	Gillingham	L	0-2	0-2	24		4998
6	Sept 13	H	Port Vale	W	2-1	2-1	24	Ray [6], Oliver [19]	6357
7	16	A	Yeovil T	D	1-1	0-0	24	Waters [62]	3509
8	20	A	Milton Keynes D	L	1-6	1-2	24	McFadzean (og) [7]	7049
9	27	H	Colchester U	L	0-3	0-0	24		3909
10	30	H	Notts Co	L	0-3	0-1	24		3495
11	Oct 4	A	Bradford C	L	0-2	0-0	24		12,386
12	11	H	Coventry C	W	2-1	2-0	24	Brandy [26], Cooper [32]	5058
13	18	A	Walsall	W	1-0	0-0	24	Dugdale [84]	4127
14	21	H	Peterborough U	W	1-0	1-0	22	Haber (pen) [31]	3524
15	25	H	Sheffield U	L	0-1	0-0	23		5699
16	Nov 1	A	Crawley T	D	1-1	1-0	24	Cooper [19]	2329
17	15	H	Chesterfield	D	0-0	0-0	23		4557
18	22	A	Leyton Orient	L	1-4	0-2	24	Grant [70]	5516
19	29	H	Doncaster R	D	1-1	1-0	24	Ikpeazu [30]	4530
20	Dec 13	A	Scunthorpe U	L	1-2	1-1	24	Ajose [30]	3006
21	20	H	Bristol C	W	1-0	0-0	24	Ness [74]	4927
22	26	A	Oldham Ath	W	2-1	0-0	22	Ajose 2 (1 pen) [70 (p), 86]	4782
23	28	H	Preston NE	D	1-1	0-0	21	Cooper [81]	6429
24	Jan 10	H	Gillingham	W	3-1	2-0	19	Ajose (pen) [27], Davis [32], Ikpeazu [84]	4436
25	17	A	Notts Co	L	1-2	0-1	21	Ness [47]	4643
26	24	A	Port Vale	W	1-0	1-0	20	Ajose [39]	8002
27	31	H	Milton Keynes D	L	0-5	0-3	20		4319
28	Feb 7	A	Colchester U	W	3-2	0-1	19	Jones [68], Ajose [73], Grant [81]	3134
29	10	H	Yeovil T	W	1-0	1-0	18	Ajose [38]	3523
30	14	H	Fleetwood T	W	2-0	1-0	17	Ajose [42], Haber [59]	4135
31	17	A	Doncaster R	L	1-2	1-0	18	Ray [8]	6164
32	21	A	Barnsley	L	0-2	0-0	19		8635
33	28	H	Swindon T	D	0-0	0-0	18		4781
34	Mar 3	A	Rochdale	L	0-4	0-1	19		1954
35	7	H	Scunthorpe U	W	2-0	0-0	18	Leigh [54], Haber [55]	4213
36	14	A	Preston NE	L	1-5	1-2	19	Turton [34]	10,203
37	17	A	Bristol C	L	0-3	0-2	20		10,719
38	21	H	Oldham Ath	L	0-1	0-0	21		4669
39	28	A	Sheffield U	W	2-1	1-0	18	Dalla Valle [12], Colclough [90]	19,672
40	Apr 3	H	Crawley T	D	0-0	0-0	19		5353
41	6	A	Chesterfield	L	0-1	0-1	21		6942
42	11	H	Leyton Orient	D	1-1	1-1	21	Dalla Valle [10]	4419
43	14	A	Peterborough U	D	1-1	1-0	19	Dalla Valle [3]	4338
44	18	H	Walsall	D	1-1	1-0	20	Haber [13]	4644
45	25	A	Coventry C	W	3-1	2-0	19	Dalla Valle [23], Colclough [35], Haber [73]	13,983
46	May 3	H	Bradford C	L	0-1	0-1	20		7608

Final League Position: 20

GOALSCORERS

League (43): Ajose 8 (2 pens), Haber 7 (1 pen), Dalla Valle 4, Cooper 3, Colclough 2, Grant 2, Ikpeazu 2, Ness 2, Ray 2, Waters 2, Brandy 1, Davis 1, Dugdale 1, Inman 1 (1 pen), Jones 1, Leigh 1, Oliver 1, Turton 1, own goal 1.
FA Cup (0).
Capital One Cup (4): Haber 1, Inman 1, Tootle 1, Waters 1.
Johnstone's Paint Trophy (0).

Shearer S 2	Tootle M 15	Ray G 35	Dugdale A 16+2	Guthrie J 21+4	Turton O 39+5	Grant A 42+1	Nolan L 6+7	Inman B 12+9	Oliver V 6+3	Waters B 11+5	Saunders C 1+3	Haber M 25+11	Baillie J 12+1	Leigh G 36+2	Ness J 31+3	Molyneux L 2+1	Garratt B 30	Atkinson C 8+11	Audel T 2	Brandy F 6+2	Cooper G 5+17	Tate A 26	Haynes D 2+1	Davis H 31	Jones J 21+3	Ajose N 23+4	Ikpeazu U 11+6	Stewart A 2+8	Dalla Valle L 10+7	Rachubka P 14+1	Colclough R 3+4	Match No.
1	2	3	4	5^3	6	7^1	8	9	10^2	11	12	13	14																			1
1	2	4	3	14	10^1	7		8^1	11	6		13			5^2	9	12															2
	2	4	3		10	6^2		13	7		8			5	9	11^1	1	12														3
	2	3	4	5	6	7		13	14	9		10^2			8^1	11^3	1	12														4
	2	3	4	5	7^3	12	8	9		10^1	14	11		13			1	6^2														5
	2	3	4	5	7	8	6	12	11^1	9^2		10^3		13			1	14														6
	2	3		5	8	7	6		11^1	9		10					1	12	4													7
	2		4		5	13	7	6		11^3	9^1	10			8^2		1			3	12	14										8
	2		4		5^2	10	7			12	13	6		11^1			1				14	3										9
	2	3^2	12	5^1	13	7			10	6		11			9	8^3	1	14				4										10
	5	2	4		13	8	7^1			14		10		9			1	6^3			12	11	3^2									11
	5	2	3		8	6	7					9					1	12			10^1	11	4									12
	5	2	4		6	7		11^1		13		12			8		1	14			10^3	9^2	3									13
	2	3	4		8	7		9^1				10			6	13	1				11^2	12	5									14
	2	3^4		4		8	7		9^2		14	10^1			5	12	1				6^3	11		13								15
		3	5	6								13	14	8	2		1	7			11^3	9^2			10^1	4	12					16
		3	4		6	7		8						5	9		1				10	12		11^1	2							17
		4	5^2		2	7		10		9^1	11^1	14		6	8		1				12			3	13							18
		3	4	13	6	7		14				12		5	9^2		1							2		10^1	11^3					19
		4	5		9^1	8		12						2	6	7	1				13			3^2		10	11					20
		4			8^2	6	13					14		5	9	7	1				12	3		2		11^3	10^1					21
	2^4		4^1	6^2	7									5	9	8	1				12			3	14	11	10^3	13				22
			4		6^2	7				11^1				5	9	8	1				13				10	12	2					23
			5	12	7									2	3	10	1					4			6	11^2	8^1	9		13		24
		12	4^1		6									5	9	7	1				14	3			2	8	11^2	10^3		13		25
	2			12	7^2									5^2	8	9	1					4			3	6	10	11^1	14	13		26
	6^3				7		14							2^1	3	9	1				13	5			4	11	8		12		10^2	27
	2			5	6									12	8	9	1				3				4	7	10		11^1			28
	4			5	8									11	9	7	1				3				2	6	10^1		12			29
	4			5	8^1	13								10^2	9	7	1				14	3			2	6	11^3		12			30
	4			9	6	12								10	5	7	1				14	3			2	8^2	11^1		13^3			31
	4			5	9^1				14			11	7				1^2				12	3^3			2	6	10				13	32
	4			12	5	7		13				10			9^1	8						3^4			2	6^2	11^3	14		1		33
	3			5	8^1	6		10^2		14		12			9			13				4			7^3	11		2		1		34
				4	2	8						11^2			5	9^3					12				6	3	7	10^1	13	14	1	35
	4			5	2	7						11			9			14			12	8^3			3	6^1	10^3	13		1		36
	3			4	9	6^1	14					10			8			13				7^3			2	5	12	11^2		1		37
				4	5	7						10^3			9^1	6					14	2^2			3	8	11	12	13	1		38
				2	6		14								5	7		8^2				3		4		9^1	10^3	13	11	1	12	39
				5	6		13							14	4	8		7				3		2		9^2	10^2	11^1		1	12	40
				5			9^3					14			2^1	6		8				3		4		7^2	13	10^1	11	1	12	41
				2			12	11^3							5	8^2		6^1				4		3		7	14	13	10	1	9	42
	3			12	5	7						10^1			8							14		4^2	2	6	9^2	13	11	1		43
	3			2	7	12						10^2			5							8^1			4	6	9			1	13	44
				4			5	2	9	13					11									3^1	7			12	10	1	8^1	45
				2	4^1	5	6								10^2			8	12						3	7^3	13	14	9	1	11	46

FA Cup
First Round   Sheffield U   (h)   0-0
Replay   Sheffield U   (a)   0-2

Capital One Cup
First Round   Barnsley   (a)   2-0
Second Round   Bolton W   (h)   2-3
(aet)

Johnstone's Paint Trophy
First Round   Rochdale   (h)   0-3

CRYSTAL PALACE

FOUNDATION

There was a Crystal Palace club as early as 1861 but the present organisation was born in 1905 after the formation of a club by the company that controlled the Crystal Palace (building) had been rejected by the FA, who did not like the idea of the Cup Final hosts running their own club. A separate company had to be formed and they had their home on the old Cup Final ground until 1915.

Selhurst Park Stadium, Whitehorse Lane, London SE25 6PU.

Telephone: (020) 8768 6000.

Fax: (020) 8771 5311.

Ticket Office: (0871) 200 0071.

Website: www.cpfc.co.uk

Email: info@cpfc.co.uk

Ground Capacity: 25,747.

Record Attendance: 51,482 v Burnley, Division 2, 11 May 1979 (at Selhurst Park).

Pitch Measurements: 101m × 68m (109yd × 75yd)

Co-Chairmen: Steve Parish and Martin Long.

Chief Executive: Phil Alexander.

Manager: Alan Pardew.

Assistant Manager: Keith Millen.

Physio: Alex Manos.

Colours: Red and blue striped shirts, blue shorts with red trim, blue socks with red trim.

Year Formed: 1905.

Turned Professional: 1905.

Club Nickname: 'The Eagles'.

Grounds: 1905, Crystal Palace; 1915, Herne Hill; 1918, The Nest; 1924, Selhurst Park.

First Football League Game: 28 August 1920, Division 3, v Merthyr T (a) L 1–2 – Alderson; Little, Rhodes; McCracken, Jones, Feebury; Bateman, Conner, Smith, Milligan (1), Whibley.

Record League Victory: 9–0 v Barrow, Division 4, 10 October 1959 – Rouse; Long, Noakes; Truett, Evans, McNichol; Gavin (1), Summersby (4 incl. 1p), Sexton, Byrne (2), Colfar (2).

Record Cup Victory: 8–0 v Southend U, Rumbelows League Cup 2nd rd (1st leg), 25 September 1990 – Martyn; Humphrey (Thompson (1)), Shaw, Pardew, Young, Thorn, McGoldrick, Thomas, Bright (3), Wright (3), Barber (Hodges (1)).

Record Defeat: 0–9 v Burnley, FA Cup 2nd rd replay, 10 February 1909; 0–9 v Liverpool, Division 1, 12 September 1990.

HONOURS

Football League –
Division 1: *Champions* 1993–94;
Division 2: *Champions* 1978–79;
Runners-up 1968–69;
Division 3: *Runners-up* 1963–64;
Division 3 (S): *Champions* 1920–21;
Runners-up 1928–29, 1930–31, 1938–39;
Division 4: *Runners-up* 1960–61.

FA Cup: *Runners-up* 1990.

Football League Cup: Best season: semi-final, 1993, 1995, 2001, 2012.

Zenith Data Systems Cup:
Winners 1991.

European Competition
Intertoto Cup: 1998.

sky SPORTS FACT FILE

Winger Billy Davies became the first Crystal Palace player to win full international honours when he lined up for Wales against Scotland at Dundee in March 1908. He later won further caps whilst at West Bromwich Albion, before returning to Palace for whom he made over 200 first-team appearances.

Most League Points (2 for a win): 64, Division 4, 1960–61.

Most League Points (3 for a win): 90, Division 1, 1993–94.

Most League Goals: 110, Division 4, 1960–61.

Highest League Scorer in Season: Peter Simpson, 46, Division 3 (S), 1930–31.

Most League Goals in Total Aggregate: Peter Simpson, 153, 1930–36.

Most League Goals in One Match: 6, Peter Simpson v Exeter C, Division 3 (S), 4 October 1930.

Most Capped Player: Miles Jedinak, 26 (58), Australia.

Most League Appearances: Jim Cannon, 571, 1973–88.

Youngest League Player: John Bostock, 15 years 287 days v Watford, 29 October 2007.

Record Transfer Fee Received: £15,000,000 from Manchester U for Wilfried Zaha, January 2013.

Record Transfer Fee Paid: £10,000,000 to Paris Saint-Germain for Yohan Cabaye, July 2015.

Football League Record: 1920 Original Members of Division 3; 1921–25 Division 2; 1925–58 Division 3 (S); 1958–61 Division 4; 1961–64 Division 3; 1964–69 Division 2; 1969–73 Division 1; 1973–74 Division 2; 1974–77 Division 3; 1977–79 Division 2; 1979–81 Division 1; 1981–89 Division 2; 1989–92 Division 1; 1992–93 FA Premier League; 1993–94 Division 1; 1994–95 FA Premier League; 1995–97 Division 1; 1997–98 FA Premier League; 1998–2004 Division 1; 2004–05 FA Premier League; 2005–13 FL C; 2013– FA Premier League.

LATEST SEQUENCES

Longest Sequence of League Wins: 8, 9.2.1921 – 26.3.1921.

Longest Sequence of League Defeats: 8, 10.1.1998 – 14.3.1998.

Longest Sequence of League Draws: 5, 21.9.2002 – 19.10.2002.

Longest Sequence of Unbeaten League Matches: 18, 22.2.1969 – 13.8.1969.

Longest Sequence Without a League Win: 20, 3.3.1962 – 8.9.1962.

Successive Scoring Runs: 24 from 27.4.1929.

Successive Non-scoring Runs: 9 from 19.11.1994.

MANAGERS

John T. Robson 1905–07
Edmund Goodman 1907–25
  (*Secretary 1905–33*)
Alex Maley 1925–27
Fred Mavin 1927–30
Jack Tresadern 1930–35
Tom Bromilow 1935–36
R. S. Moyes 1936
Tom Bromilow 1936–39
George Irwin 1939–47
Jack Butler 1947–49
Ronnie Rooke 1949–50
Charlie Slade and Fred Dawes
  (*Joint Managers*) 1950–51
Laurie Scott 1951–54
Cyril Spiers 1954–58
George Smith 1958–60
Arthur Rowe 1960–62
Dick Graham 1962–66
Bert Head 1966–72 (*continued as General Manager to 1973*)
Malcolm Allison 1973–76
Terry Venables 1976–80
Ernie Walley 1980
Malcolm Allison 1980–81
Dario Gradi 1981
Steve Kember 1981–82
Alan Mullery 1982–84
Steve Coppell 1984–93
Alan Smith 1993–95
Steve Coppell (*Technical Director*) 1995–96
Dave Bassett 1996–97
Steve Coppell 1997–98
Attilio Lombardo 1998
Terry Venables (*Head Coach*) 1998–99
Steve Coppell 1999–2000
Alan Smith 2000–01
Steve Bruce 2001
Trevor Francis 2001–03
Steve Kember 2003
Iain Dowie 2003–06
Peter Taylor 2006–07
Neil Warnock 2007–10
Paul Hart 2010
George Burley 2010–11
Dougie Freedman 2011–12
Ian Holloway 2012–13
Tony Pulis 2013–14
Neil Warnock 2014
Alan Pardew January 2015

TEN YEAR LEAGUE RECORD

		P	W	D	L	F	A	Pts	Pos
2005-06	FL C	46	21	12	13	67	48	75	6
2006-07	FL C	46	18	11	17	59	51	65	12
2007-08	FL C	46	18	17	11	58	42	71	5
2008-09	FL C	46	15	12	19	52	55	57	15
2009-10	FL C	46	14	17	15	50	53	49*	21
2010-11	FL C	46	12	12	22	44	69	48	20
2011-12	FL C	46	13	17	16	46	51	56	17
2012-13	FL C	46	19	15	12	73	62	72	5
2013-14	PR Lge	38	13	6	19	33	48	45	11
2014-15	PR Lge	38	13	9	16	47	51	48	10

* 10 pts deducted.

DID YOU KNOW ?

Although Crystal Palace have won two play-off finals at Wembley, their only cup success at the national stadium came in April 1991 when they defeated Everton 4-1 after extra time in the final of the Full Members' Cup (known by its sponsorship name as the Zenith Data Systems Cup).

CRYSTAL PALACE – FA PREMIERSHIP 2014–15 LEAGUE RECORD

Match No.	Date	Venue	Opponents	Result	H/T Score	Lg Pos.	Goalscorers	Attendance
1	Aug 16	A	Arsenal	L	1-2	1-1	16	Hangeland [35]	59,962
2	23	H	West Ham U	L	1-3	0-2	19	Chamakh [48]	24,242
3	30	A	Newcastle U	D	3-3	1-1	19	Gayle [1], Puncheon [48], Zaha [90]	49,226
4	Sept 13	H	Burnley	D	0-0	0-0	17		23,829
5	21	A	Everton	W	3-2	1-1	15	Jedinak (pen) [30], Campbell [54], Bolasie [69]	37,574
6	27	H	Leicester C	W	2-0	0-0	9	Campbell [51], Jedinak [54]	24,311
7	Oct 4	A	Hull C	L	0-2	0-0	14		24,281
8	18	H	Chelsea	L	1-2	0-1	16	Campbell [90]	24,451
9	25	A	WBA	D	2-2	2-0	15	Hangeland [16], Jedinak (pen) [45]	24,738
10	Nov 3	H	Sunderland	L	1-3	0-1	17	Brown (og) [55]	23,212
11	8	A	Manchester U	L	0-1	0-0	17		75,325
12	23	H	Liverpool	W	3-1	1-1	15	Gayle [17], Ledley [78], Jedinak [81]	24,862
13	29	A	Swansea C	D	1-1	1-1	14	Jedinak (pen) [25]	20,240
14	Dec 2	H	Aston Villa	L	0-1	0-1	15		23,935
15	6	A	Tottenham H	D	0-0	0-0	15		35,860
16	13	H	Stoke C	D	1-1	1-1	16	McArthur [11]	23,038
17	20	A	Manchester C	L	0-3	0-0	17		45,302
18	26	H	Southampton	L	1-3	0-1	18	Dann [86]	24,565
19	28	A	QPR	D	0-0	0-0	18		18,011
20	Jan 1	A	Aston Villa	D	0-0	0-0	18		29,047
21	10	H	Tottenham H	W	2-1	0-0	15	Gayle (pen) [69], Puncheon [80]	24,193
22	17	A	Burnley	W	3-2	1-2	12	Gayle 2 [28, 87], Puncheon [48]	17,782
23	31	H	Everton	L	0-1	0-1	13		25,197
24	Feb 7	A	Leicester C	W	1-0	0-0	13	Ledley [55]	31,695
25	11	H	Newcastle U	D	1-1	0-1	13	Campbell [71]	25,118
26	21	H	Arsenal	L	1-2	0-2	13	Murray [90]	24,721
27	28	A	West Ham U	W	3-1	1-0	12	Murray 2 [41, 63], Dann [51]	34,857
28	Mar 3	A	Southampton	L	0-1	0-0	12		28,351
29	14	H	QPR	W	3-1	3-0	12	Zaha [21], McArthur [40], Ward [42]	24,886
30	21	A	Stoke C	W	2-1	2-1	11	Murray (pen) [41], Zaha [45]	27,532
31	Apr 6	H	Manchester C	W	2-1	1-0	11	Murray [34], Puncheon [48]	24,718
32	11	A	Sunderland	W	4-1	0-0	11	Murray [48], Bolasie 3 [51, 53, 62]	42,073
33	18	H	WBA	L	0-2	0-1	11		24,765
34	25	H	Hull C	L	0-2	0-0	11		23,876
35	May 3	A	Chelsea	L	0-1	0-1	12		41,566
36	9	H	Manchester U	L	1-2	0-1	12	Puncheon [57]	25,009
37	16	A	Liverpool	W	3-1	1-1	12	Puncheon [43], Zaha [60], Murray [90]	44,673
38	24	H	Swansea C	W	1-0	0-0	10	Chamakh [57]	25,076

Final League Position: 10

GOALSCORERS

League (47): Murray 7 (1 pen), Puncheon 6, Gayle 5 (1 pen), Jedinak 5 (3 pens), Bolasie 4, Campbell 4, Zaha 4, Chamakh 2, Dann 2, Hangeland 2, Ledley 2, McArthur 2, Ward 1, own goal 1.
FA Cup (8): Chamakh 2, Dann 2, Campbell 1, Doyle 1, Gayle 1, Sanogo 1.
Capital One Cup (5): Gayle 4 (1 pen), KaiKai 1.

Speroni J 36	Kelly M 27 + 4	Dann S 34	Hangeland B 12 + 2	Ward J 37	Puncheon J 31 + 6	Jedinak M 24	Ledley J 30 + 2	Bolasie Y 31 + 3	Chamakh M 15 + 3	Campbell F 13 + 7	Delaney D 28 + 1	Gayle D 11 + 14	O'Keefe S 1 + 1	Bannan B 2 + 5	Williams Jon —+ 2	Murray G 9 + 8	Mariappa A 8 + 4	Zaha W 23 + 8	McArthur J 29 + 3	Doyle K —+ 3	Guedioura A —+ 7	Fryers Z —+ 1	Hennessey W 2 + 1	Thomas J —+ 1	Sanogo Y 3 + 7	Mutch J 4 + 3	Souare P 7 + 2	Ameobi S —+ 4	Lee C 1 + 2	Match No.
1	2	3^1	4	5	6*	7	8	9^2	10	11^3	12	13	14																	1
1	2	3		5	7			9	10	11^3	4	12	8^2	6^1	13	14														2
1	5	3		8	6	7		9^1	10^3	12	4	11^2				14	2	13												3
1		3		5	6	8	13		10^2	4	11^3				14		2	9^1	7	12										4
1	2	3		5	8	7		9	10^3	11^1	4							6^2	13	12	14									5
1	2	3		5	9	7	8	11^1	12	10^2	4							6	13											6
1	2	3^1		5	9	7	8	11	13	10^3	4	14				12		6^2												7
1	2		3	5	9^3	7	8^2	11	10	4*						12	14	6^1	13											8
1^1	2		4	5	13	7	8	9	10^2	11						3		6^3	14	12										9
1	2	3	4^1	5	12	7*	8	9	10^2	11				13				6												10
1		3		5	6		8	9^2	10^3	11^1	4	12		13			2		7	14										11
1	2	3	12	5	6^1	7	8	9^3	10	4^2	11				14			13												12
1	5	3	4	2	6^1	7	8	9	10^2	13	11^3							14	12											13
1	2^2	3	4	5	13	7		9	10	12	11^1							6	8											14
1	2	3	4	5	12	6	9	10	11									7^1	8											15
1	2	3	4	5	12	7	8	11	10^1			13			14			9^2	6^3											16
1	2	3	4	5	7^2	6	9^1	10		11^3					14	12	8					13								17
1	14	3		5	9	7	8^2	11^3		10^1	4	12					2	13	6											18
1		3		5	9	7	8	11		12	4						2	10^1	6											19
1	5	3			6	7		9	10	4	12	13					2	11^1	8^2											20
1	5	3		2	7		6		10^3	4	14				9^2	11^1	13	8	12											21
1	5^1	3		2	6		8			4	11				13	14	9^3	7	12								10^2			22
1	5^2	3		2	6		8	10^1		4	9					14	13	7							11^3	12				23
1	5	3^1	12	2		8	7			4	11^2					10	6	14							13	9^3				24
1	5^2		3	2	6		8	14	10^3	12	4	13					9	7							11^1					25
1		3		2	8			6^2	12	11^3	4	10^1				13	7								9	5		14		26
1	5	3		2	8		6	14	10^1	4					11*		7^2	12								9^3	13			27
1	5	3		2	10		7	9		4	11						6	8^1										12		28
1	5	3		2	6^3	7	11			4	12					10^1	13	9^2	8								14			29
1	12	3		2	9		7	10		4	13					11^1	8^2	6								5^3	14			30
1	5	3		2	8		6	10^3		4	14					11^1	7^3	9							12	13				31
1	12	3		2	8	7	13	11^1		4						10	9	6^3								14	5^2			32
1		3		2	6	7^2	5^1	11		4	12					10	9	8^3								14	13			33
1	2	3			6	7^2		11		4	14					10^3	9^1	8								12	5		13	34
1	12	3		5	6^2		8	11		4						13	2^3	9	7							14	10^1			35
1		3		2	12	6^1	7^2	8	14	4						11	10^3	9									5	13		36
	3	4		2	6		8	11^3	10^1						14		12	7				1			13	5	9^3			37
	3	4		2	6	7		11^2	10^1	14							12	9	8^3			1			13	5				38

FA Cup

Third Round	Dover Ath	(a)	4-0
Fourth Round	Southampton	(a)	3-2
Fifth Round	Liverpool	(h)	1-2

Capital One Cup

Second Round	Walsall	(a)	3-0
Third Round	Newcastle U	(h)	2-3
(aet)			

DAGENHAM & REDBRIDGE

FOUNDATION

The roots of Dagenham & Redbridge lie firmly in the Essex side of the Greater London area. Though formed only in 1992 their complex origins date back to the 19th century involving Ilford (founded 1881) and Leytonstone (1886) who merged in 1979 to form Leytonstone-Ilford. They and Walthamstow Avenue (1900) joined together in 1988 to become Redbridge Forest who in turn merged with Dagenham FC (1949) in 1992. Victoria Road has existed as a football ground since 1917. Initially used by Sterling Works, in the summer of 1955 Briggs Sports vacated the premises and Dagenham FC moved in and the pitch was enclosed.

The London Borough of Barking and Dagenham Stadium, Victoria Road, Dagenham, Essex RM10 7XL.

Telephone: (020) 8592 1549.

Fax: (020) 8593 7227.

Ticket Office: (020) 8592 1549 (extension 21).

Website: www.daggers.co.uk

Email: info@daggers.co.uk

Ground Capacity: 6,077.

Record Attendance: 5,949 v Ipswich T, FA Cup 3rd rd, 5 January 2002.

Pitch Measurements: 100.5m × 64m (110yd × 70yd)

Chairman: David Bennett.

Managing Director: Stephen Thompson MBE.

Manager: Wayne Burnett.

First Team Coaches: Darren Currie and Warren Hackett.

Physio: John Gowens.

Colours: Red shirts with blue and white trim, blue shorts, blue socks.

Year Formed: 1992.

Turned Professional: 1992.

Club Nickname: 'The Daggers'.

Ground: 1992, Victoria Road (renamed The London Borough of Barking and Dagenham Stadium 2009).

First Football League Game: 11 August 2007, FL 2 v Stockport Co (a) L 0–1 – Roberts; Foster, Griffiths, Rainford, Uddin, Boardman, Saunders (Strevens), Southam, Benson (Moore), Nurse, Sloma (Huke).

Record League Victory: 6–0 v Chester C, FL 2, 9 August 2008 – Roberts; Okuonghae, Griffiths, Arber, Uddin, Taiwo, Saunders (2), Green (1) (Southam), Benson (1) (Nurse), Strevens (1p) (Nwokeji (1)), Gain.

MANAGERS

John Still 1992–94
Dave Cusack 1994–95
Graham Carr 1995–96
Ted Hardy 1996–99
Garry Hill 1999–2004
John Still 2004–13
Wayne Burnett February 2013–

sky SPORTS FACT FILE

Dagenham & Redbridge defeated Leyton Orient 14-13 on penalties to win their Football League Trophy first round tie in September 2011. The game ended 1-1 and the first 26 penalties were converted in the shoot-out before Daggers' keeper James Shea ended the deadlock when he saved from the O's Ben Chorley.

Record Cup Victory: 6–1 v Stowmarket T, FA Cup 2nd qual rd, 28 September 1992; 6–1 v Wealdstone (a), FA Cup 3rd qual rd, 12 October 1992.

Record Defeat: 0–9 v Hereford U, Conference, 27 February 2004.

Most League Points (3 for a win): 72, FL 2, 2009–10.

Most League Goals: 77, FL 2, 2008–09.

Highest League Scorer in Season: Paul Benson, 28, Conference, 2006–07.

Most League Goals in Total Aggregate: 40, Paul Benson, 2007–11.

Most League Goals in One Match: 4, Paul Benson v Shrewsbury T, FL 2, 18 August 2009.

Most Capped Player: Andre Boucaud, 10 (24), Trinidad & Tobago.

Most League Appearances: Scott Doe, 243, 2009–15.

Youngest League Player: Jodi Jones, 17 years 111 days v Portsmouth, 10 February 2015.

Record Transfer Fee Received: £700,000 from Peterborough U for Dwight Gayle, January 2013.

Record Transfer Fee Paid: £20,000 to Plymouth Arg for Damien McCrory, February 2010.

Football League Record: 2006–07 Promoted from Conference; 2007–10 FL 2; 2010–11 FL 1; 2011– FL 2.

LATEST SEQUENCES

Longest Sequence of League Wins: 5, 12.2.2008 – 1.3.2008.

Longest Sequence of League Defeats: 9, 8.10.2011 – 10.12.2011.

Longest Sequence of League Draws: 3, 21.9.2010 – 28.9.2010.

Longest Sequence of Unbeaten League Matches: 8, 1.3.2014 – 5.4.2014.

Longest Sequence Without a League Win: 10, 8.10.2011 – 17.12.2011.

Successive Scoring Runs: 16 from 12.4.2008.

Successive Non-scoring Runs: 4 from 13.12.2014.

HONOURS

Football League – FL 1: Best season: 21st, 2010–11.

FA Cup: Best season: 3rd rd, 2008, 2012.

Football League Cup: Best season: never beyond 1st rd.

Conference: *Champions* 2006–07. *Runners-up* 2001–02.

Isthmian League (Premier): *Champions* 1999–2000.

Essex Senior Cup: *Winners* 1997–98, 2000–01; *Runners-up* 2001–02.

AS DAGENHAM FC

FA Trophy: *Winners* 1979–80; *Runners-up* 1976–77. **Amateur Cup:** *Runners-up* 1969–70, 1970–71.

AS ILFORD

FA Amateur Cup: *Winners* 1929, 1930. **Isthmian League:** *Champions* 1906–07, 1920–21, 1921–22.

AS LEYTONSTONE

FA Amateur Cup: *Winners* 1947, 1948, 1968. **Isthmian League:** *Champions* 1918–19, 1937–38, 1938–39, 1946–47, 1947–48, 1949–50, 1950–51, 1951–52, 1965–66.

AS LEYTONSTONE/ILFORD

Isthmian League: *Champions* 1981–82, 1988–89.

AS WALTHAMSTOW AVENUE

FA Amateur Cup: *Winners* 1952, 1961. **Isthmian League:** *Champions* 1945–46, 1948–49, 1952–53, 1954–55. **Athenian League:** *Champions* 1929–30, 1932–33, 1933–34, 1937–38, 1938–39.

AS REDBRIDGE FOREST

Isthmian League: *Winners* 1990–91.

TEN YEAR LEAGUE RECORD

		P	W	D	L	F	A	Pts	Pos
2005-06	Conf	42	16	19	16	63	59	58	10
2006-07	Conf	46	28	11	7	93	48	95	1
2007-08	FL 2	46	13	10	23	49	70	49	20
2008-09	FL 2	46	19	11	16	77	53	68	8
2009-10	FL 2	46	20	12	14	69	58	72	7
2010-11	FL 1	46	12	11	23	52	70	47	21
2011-12	FL 2	46	14	8	24	50	72	50	19
2012-13	FL 2	46	13	12	21	55	62	51	22
2013-14	FL 2	46	15	15	16	53	59	60	9
2014-15	FL 2	46	17	8	21	58	59	59	14

DID YOU KNOW ?

In winning the Isthmian League championship in 1999–2000 Dagenham & Redbridge won 20 out of their 21 home league games. The other game ended in a draw against Chesham United. The Daggers finished the season with 101 points putting them 24 clear of their nearest rivals.

DAGENHAM & REDBRIDGE – FOOTBALL LEAGUE TWO 2014–15 LEAGUE RECORD

Match No.	Date		Venue	Opponents	Result		H/T Score	Lg Pos.	Goalscorers	Attendance
1	Aug	9	H	Morecambe	L	0-3	0-0	24		1529
2		16	A	Burton Alb	L	1-2	1-0	24	Cureton [18]	2150
3		19	A	Hartlepool U	W	2-0	1-0	18	Howell [5], Ogogo [64]	2792
4		23	H	Mansfield T	W	2-0	1-0	10	Howell [45], Ogogo [60]	1558
5		30	A	Oxford U	D	3-3	1-1	12	Hemmings [7], Cureton [46], Ogogo [71]	4391
6	Sept	6	H	Northampton T	L	0-2	0-2	16		2186
7		13	H	Cambridge U	L	2-3	1-0	19	Howell [20], Porter [82]	2049
8		16	A	Portsmouth	L	0-3	0-1	19		13,648
9		20	A	Cheltenham T	D	1-1	0-0	21	Cureton [58]	2597
10		27	H	York C	W	2-0	1-0	19	Labadie 2 [35, 62]	1801
11	Oct	3	H	Exeter C	L	1-2	1-0	19	Cureton [11]	2138
12		11	A	Accrington S	W	2-1	0-1	18	Yusuff 2 [57, 64]	1412
13		18	A	Newport Co	L	0-1	0-0	19		1654
14		21	A	Luton T	L	1-3	0-2	20	Doidge [86]	7746
15		25	A	Wycombe W	D	1-1	0-0	21	Cureton [63]	3316
16	Nov	1	H	Shrewsbury T	L	1-2	1-0	21	Bingham [6]	1698
17		15	A	AFC Wimbledon	L	0-1	0-1	22		3887
18		22	H	Carlisle U	W	4-2	3-1	21	Bingham [23], Chambers 2 [24, 46], Cureton [39]	2097
19		29	A	Bury	W	2-0	0-0	20	Jakubiak [55], Cureton [74]	3042
20	Dec	13	H	Tranmere R	L	0-1	0-0	20		1840
21		20	A	Plymouth Arg	L	0-3	0-1	20		7176
22		26	H	Stevenage	L	0-2	0-0	22		1779
23		28	A	Southend U	D	0-0	0-0	23		6966
24	Jan	3	H	Bury	W	1-0	0-0	21	Murphy [51]	1877
25		10	H	Oxford U	D	0-0	0-0	21		1892
26		17	A	Northampton T	L	0-1	0-0	23		4122
27		27	A	Cambridge U	D	1-1	0-1	22	Hemmings [61]	4068
28		31	H	Cheltenham T	W	3-1	0-0	19	Cureton [55], Hemmings [71], Jakubiak [90]	2696
29	Feb	7	A	York C	W	2-0	1-0	17	Cureton 2 [19, 52]	2958
30		10	H	Portsmouth	D	0-0	0-0	18		2310
31		15	A	Morecambe	W	3-2	1-1	17	Howell [1], Obileye [48], Cureton [52]	1351
32		21	H	Burton Alb	L	1-3	0-0	18	Jakubiak [67]	1718
33		28	A	Mansfield T	L	1-2	0-0	19	Cureton [80]	2546
34	Mar	3	H	Hartlepool U	W	2-0	1-0	18	Harrison (og) [22], Bingham [66]	1799
35		7	A	Tranmere R	W	3-2	1-1	16	Cureton [40], Hemmings [50], Bingham [54]	4762
36		14	H	Southend U	L	1-3	1-2	18	Obileye [23]	3393
37		17	H	Plymouth Arg	W	2-0	1-0	15	Ogogo [30], Cureton [88]	1713
38		21	A	Stevenage	W	1-0	0-0	15	Howell [54]	2795
39		28	H	Wycombe W	L	0-1	0-0	15		2362
40	Apr	3	A	Shrewsbury T	L	0-2	0-2	16		6143
41		6	H	AFC Wimbledon	W	4-0	1-0	15	Cureton 3 [2, 71, 74], Doe [58]	2346
42		11	A	Carlisle U	L	0-1	0-0	15		3660
43		14	H	Luton T	D	0-0	0-0	15		2461
44		18	A	Newport Co	W	3-2	0-0	14	Hemmings [78], Doidge [81], Jakubiak [88]	2737
45		25	H	Accrington S	W	4-0	1-0	13	Partridge [20], Cureton [47], Raymond [67], Jones [90]	2038
46	May	2	A	Exeter C	L	1-2	0-0	14	Cureton [90]	3645

Final League Position: 14

GOALSCORERS

League (58): Cureton 19, Hemmings 5, Howell 5, Bingham 4, Jakubiak 4, Ogogo 4, Chambers 2, Doidge 2, Labadie 2, Obileye 2, Yusuff 2, Doe 1, Jones 1, Murphy 1, Partridge 1, Porter 1, Raymond 1, own goal 1.
FA Cup (0).
Capital One Cup (6): Hemmings 2, Boucaud 1, Chambers 1, Cureton 1, Porter 1.
Johnstone's Paint Trophy (0).

O'Brien L 9 + 1	Batt D 24 + 4	Doe S 39	Saah B 22 + 1	Connors J 14 + 3	Howell L 29 + 2	Ogogo A 28 + 4	Boucaud A 36 + 5	Hemmings A 36 + 5	Cureton J 40 + 5	Porter G 7 + 12	Goldberg B — + 5	Partridge M 20 + 4	Labadie J 16 + 8	Gayle I 6	Green N 6 + 1	Enigbokan-Bloomfield M — + 1	Yusuff A 9 + 9	Cousins M 37	Doidge C 3 + 8	Bingham B 32 + 2	Murphy R 6 + 3	Obileye A 25 + 1	Jakubiak A 6 + 17	Agyemang P 2 + 2	Widdowson J 20 + 1	Carr D — + 6	Jones J 2 + 6	Fenelon S 3 + 1	Raymond F 2	Match No.
1	2	3	4	5	6¹	7	8	9²	10	11	12	13																		1
1		4	3	5	6	7¹	8³	11	10²	9	13	14		2	12															2
1		3	4	5	6	8	7	10¹	9²	11	12	13		2																3
1		3	4	5	6	7	8	11¹	10²	9	12	13		2																4
1	12	4	3	5³	6	7	8	11¹	10	9²	13	14		2																5
1	2	3			6¹	7	8	11	10		9²	13		5³	4	12	14													6
1			4		7	8	6²	9¹	10	11	13			2	3	5	12													7
	2	3	7¹	6	8⁴	13	10³	9²	11	4	14	5		12				1												8
	2	3	13	8	6	12	10³	9³	11¹	4	7	5						1	14											9
	2	3	5	7³	8	6	12	10²	11¹	13	4	9					14	1												10
	2	3	5		7	9²	6¹	11	10	12	4	8						1	13											11
	2	3	4	5	8		9	11³	6	13	7	12						1	10²	14										12
	2	3	4	5	7⁴	14	9³	13	10	6³	8¹	11						1	12											13
	2	3	4		7²	14	10	11³	12		6			5			9¹	1	13	8										14
	2	3	4		7		10	6³	9	14	12			5²			11	1	13	8										15
	2	4	3		6¹		10³	13	11		12	8		5			9²	1		7	14									16
5²		3		7³	2		10	13	9	8		4					11¹	1		6	12	14								17
	2	3	4		13	6	11²	7	12		9						10³	1	14	8¹		5								18
	5	2	3		9	10²	8	7				11¹						1		6		4	12	13						19
	2	3	5		13	6³	10	8¹			9²							1		7		4	14	11	12					20
	5	2	4		6		11³	7¹			10²							1		8	13	3	12	14	9					21
	2	4	5		9			13			8	12						1		7	10²	3¹	14	11³	6					22
		3	14	5	12		8²	11	10	9⁵				2¹	7		13	1		6		4								23
13		3		5			12	9	10	6				2²	8¹		14	1		7	11¹	4								24
13		3		5			12	9	10	6²				2¹	8			1		7³	11	4	14							25
	2	4	5		7		10³	13	14		8						12	1		6	9²	3	11¹							26
	2	3			7²	12	8³	9	11¹		14							1		6	10	4	13		5					27
	2	3			7	13	8	9	11²									1		6	10¹	4	12		5					28
		3			6	2	7	10	11²	13								1		8	4	9¹			5	12				29
		3			6	2	8	9	11¹									1		7	4	10⁵			5	12	13			30
		4	13		6	2	7²	9	10	12								1		8	3	11¹			5					31
		3			6	2	8	9²	11	12								1		7	4	10¹			5	13				32
		4			6¹	2	7	11	9									1		8	3	10²			5	13	12			33
12	2	3			6		8	9	10								1¹		7²	4	13	5	14		11³					34
1	2	3			6		7²	9	10³					14	13				8	4	12	5			11¹					35
1	2¹	3			6³	13	8	9	10									7		4	12	5			14	11²				36
	13	3		9	5	8¹	6	10	11³		14							1		7²	4			2	12					37
		3			7	4	9	10	12		13	6						1	11²	5¹	8		2							38
		3			6¹	2	8	9	11	10²								1		7	4	13	5		12					39
	2¹	3			6	8	9	10	11			13						1		7²	4	12	5							40
		3			6	2	8	9¹	11³									1	10²	7	4	12	5		13	14				41
		3	5³		6	8	10¹	11²				2	7				12	1	14	9	4⁴	13								42
		3			6	8	9¹	10	11²			2	4					1		7	13		5		12					43
		3			6³	8	9	10²	11	14		2	4				11²	1		13	12	5							7¹	44
		3	14		13	8³	12	9				2	4				11²	1		7				5¹	10		6			45
		3			12	7	8¹	9	10	11		2	4					1	14	5			13³			6²				46

FA Cup

First Round	Southport	(h)	0-0
Replay	Southport	(a)	0-2

Capital One Cup

First Round	Brentford	(h)	6-6

(aet; Brentford won 4-2 on penalties)

Johnstone's Paint Trophy

Second Round	Leyton Orient	(h)	0-2

DERBY COUNTY

FOUNDATION

Derby County was formed by members of the Derbyshire County Cricket Club in 1884, when football was booming in the area and the cricketers thought that a football club would help boost finances for the summer game. To begin with, they sported the cricket club's colours of amber, chocolate and pale blue, and went into the game at the top immediately entering the FA Cup.

The iPro Stadium, Pride Park, Derby DE24 8XL.

Telephone: (0871) 472 1884.

Fax: (01332) 667 519.

Ticket Office: (0871) 472 1884 (option 1).

Website: www.dcfc.co.uk

Email: derby.county@dcfc.co.uk

Ground Capacity: 33,010.

Record Attendance: 41,826 v Tottenham H, Division 1, 20 September 1969 (at Baseball Ground); 33,378 v Liverpool, FA Premier League, 18 March 2000 (at Pride Park).

Stadium Record Attendance: 33,597, England v Mexico, 25 May 2001 (at Pride Park).

Pitch Measurements: 100.5m × 66m (110yd × 72yd)

Chairman: Andy Appleby.

Chief Executive: Sam Rush.

Head Coach: Paul Clement.

First Team Coach: Paul Simpson.

Physio: Neil Sullivan.

HONOURS

Football League – Division 1:
Champions 1971–72, 1974–75;
Runners-up 1895–96, 1929–30,
1935–36, 1995–96;
Division 2: *Champions* 1911–12,
1914–15, 1968–69, 1986–87;
Runners-up 1925–26;
Division 3 (N): *Champions* 1956–57;
Runners-up 1955–56.
FA Cup: *Winners* 1946;
Runners-up 1898, 1899, 1903.
Football League Cup: Best season:
semi-final, 1968, 2009.
Texaco Cup: *Winners* 1972.
European Competitions
European Cup: 1972–73, 1975–76.
UEFA Cup: 1974–75, 1976–77.
Anglo-Italian Cup: *Runners-up* 1993.

Colours: White shirts with black trim, black shorts, white socks with black trim.

Year Formed: 1884.

Turned Professional: 1884.

Club Nickname: 'The Rams'.

Grounds: 1884, Racecourse Ground; 1895, Baseball Ground; 1997, Pride Park (renamed The iPro Stadium 2013).

First Football League Game: 8 September 1888, Football League, v Bolton W (a) W 6–3 – Marshall; Latham, Ferguson, Williamson; Monks, Walter Roulstone; Bakewell (2), Cooper (2), Higgins, Harry Plackett, Lol Plackett (2).

Record League Victory: 9–0 v Wolverhampton W, Division 1, 10 January 1891 – Bunyan; Archie Goodall, Roberts; Walker, Chalmers, Walter Roulstone (1); Bakewell, McLachlan, Johnny Goodall (1), Holmes (2), McMillan (5). 9–0 v Sheffield W, Division 1, 21 January 1899 – Fryer; Methven, Staley; Cox, Archie Goodall, May; Oakden (1), Bloomer (6), Boag, McDonald (1), Allen, (1 og).

sky SPORTS FACT FILE

Harry Storer, who played for Derby County between 1921 and 1929 winning 2 England caps, was also an excellent cricketer with Derbyshire between 1920 and 1936. In 1929 he established a record first wicket partnership of 322 with Joseph Bowden playing for Derbyshire against Essex; this had yet to be surpassed at the start of the 2015 season.

Record Cup Victory: 12–0 v Finn Harps, UEFA Cup 1st rd 1st leg, 15 September 1976 – Moseley; Thomas, Nish, Rioch (1), McFarland, Todd (King), Macken, Gemmill, Hector (5), George (3), James (3).

Record Defeat: 2–11 v Everton, FA Cup 1st rd, 1889–90.

Most League Points (2 for a win): 63, Division 2, 1968–69 and Division 3 (N), 1955–56 and 1956–57.

Most League Points (3 for a win): 85, FL C, 2013–14.

Most League Goals: 111, Division 3 (N), 1956–57.

Highest League Scorer in Season: Jack Bowers, 37, Division 1, 1930–31; Ray Straw, 37 Division 3 (N), 1956–57.

Most League Goals in Total Aggregate: Steve Bloomer, 292, 1892–1906 and 1910–14.

Most League Goals in One Match: 6, Steve Bloomer v Sheffield W, Division 1, 2 January 1899.

Most Capped Player: Deon Burton, 42 (59), Jamaica.

Most League Appearances: Kevin Hector, 486, 1966–78 and 1980–82.

Youngest League Player: Mason Bennett, 15 years 99 days v Middlesbrough 22 October 2011.

Record Transfer Fee Received: £7,000,000 from Leeds U for Seth Johnson, October 2001.

Record Transfer Fee Paid: £4,750,000 to Hull C for Tom Ince, July 2015.

Football League Record: 1888 Founder Member of the Football League; 1907–12 Division 2; 1912–14 Division 1; 1914–15 Division 2; 1915–21 Division 1; 1921–26 Division 2; 1926–53 Division 1; 1953–55 Division 2; 1955–57 Division 3 (N); 1957–69 Division 2; 1969–80 Division 1; 1980–84 Division 2; 1984–86 Division 3; 1986–87 Division 2; 1987–91 Division 1; 1991–92 Division 2; 1992–96 Division 1; 1996–2002 FA Premier League; 2002–04 Division 1; 2004–07 FL C; 2007–08 FA Premier League; 2008– FL C.

MANAGERS

W. D. Clark 1896–1900
Harry Newbould 1900–06
Jimmy Methven 1906–22
Cecil Potter 1922–25
George Jobey 1925–41
Ted Magner 1944–46
Stuart McMillan 1946–53
Jack Barker 1953–55
Harry Storer 1955–62
Tim Ward 1962–67
Brian Clough 1967–73
Dave Mackay 1973–76
Colin Murphy 1977
Tommy Docherty 1977–79
Colin Addison 1979–82
Johnny Newman 1982
Peter Taylor 1982–84
Roy McFarland 1984
Arthur Cox 1984–93
Roy McFarland 1993–95
Jim Smith 1995–2001
Colin Todd 2001–02
John Gregory 2002–03
George Burley 2003–05
Phil Brown 2005–06
Billy Davies 2006–07
Paul Jewell 2007–08
Nigel Clough 2009–13
Steve McClaren 2013–15
Paul Clement June 2015–

LATEST SEQUENCES

Longest Sequence of League Wins: 9, 15.3.1969 – 19.4.1969.

Longest Sequence of League Defeats: 8, 12.12.1987 – 10.2.1988.

Longest Sequence of League Draws: 6, 26.3.1927 – 18.4.1927.

Longest Sequence of Unbeaten League Matches: 22, 8.3.1969 – 20.9.1969.

Longest Sequence Without a League Win: 36, 22.9.2007 – 30.8.2008.

Successive Scoring Runs: 29 from 3.12.1960.

Successive Non-scoring Runs: 8 from 30.10.1920.

TEN YEAR LEAGUE RECORD

		P	W	D	L	F	A	Pts	Pos
2005-06	FL C	46	10	20	16	53	67	50	20
2006-07	FL C	46	25	9	12	62	46	84	3
2007-08	PR Lge	38	1	8	29	20	89	11	20
2008-09	FL C	46	14	12	20	55	67	54	18
2009-10	FL C	46	15	11	20	53	63	56	14
2010-11	FL C	46	13	10	23	58	71	49	19
2011-12	FL C	46	18	10	18	50	58	64	12
2012-13	FL C	46	16	13	17	65	62	61	10
2013-14	FL C	46	25	10	11	84	52	85	3
2014-15	FL C	46	21	14	11	85	56	77	8

DID YOU KNOW ?

Archie Goodall made over 400 appearances for Derby County between 1889 and 1902, appearing in two FA Cup finals for the club. After retiring he developed a career in the music hall with a novelty act walking backwards around a metal hoop. It was said he defied gravity, causing 'almost breathless amazement'.

DERBY COUNTY – FL CHAMPIONSHIP 2014–15 LEAGUE RECORD

Match No.	Date	Venue	Opponents	Result	H/T Score	Lg Pos.	Goalscorers	Attendance
1	Aug 9	H	Rotherham U	W 1-0	0-0	7	Hendrick [82]	30,105
2	16	A	Sheffield W	D 0-0	0-0	8		25,186
3	19	A	Charlton Ath	L 2-3	1-2	12	Ward 2 [31, 85]	15,317
4	23	H	Fulham	W 5-1	1-0	7	Ward [23], Bryson [59], Martin 2 [61, 87], Dawkins [88]	26,577
5	30	H	Ipswich T	D 1-1	1-0	7	Martin [13]	26,673
6	Sept 14	A	Nottingham F	D 1-1	0-0	10	Shotton [80]	30,227
7	17	A	Blackburn R	W 3-2	2-1	7	Ward 2 [9, 58], Hughes [37]	13,566
8	20	H	Cardiff C	D 2-2	0-1	8	Ibe [61], Bryson [84]	27,251
9	27	A	Bolton W	W 2-0	1-0	6	Martin 2 [38, 57]	15,006
10	30	H	Bournemouth	W 2-0	0-0	4	Hughes [81], Martin [90]	26,725
11	Oct 4	H	Millwall	D 0-0	0-0	4		27,749
12	18	A	Reading	W 3-0	2-0	2	Martin 2 [18, 79], Ibe [38]	18,141
13	21	A	Blackpool	W 1-0	0-0	1	Martin (pen) [81]	11,036
14	25	H	Wigan Ath	L 1-2	1-0	1	Eustace [45]	28,824
15	Nov 1	A	Brentford	L 1-2	1-0	5	Martin [27]	10,608
16	4	H	Huddersfield T	W 3-2	2-1	4	Ibe [7], Russell [45], Dawkins [77]	27,153
17	8	H	Wolverhampton W	W 5-0	3-0	1	Shotton [16], Hendrick 2 [28, 55], Russell 2 [42, 60]	30,398
18	22	A	Watford	W 2-1	1-0	1	Ibe [39], Bryson [81]	17,421
19	29	A	Leeds U	L 0-2	0-1	1		26,028
20	Dec 6	H	Brighton & HA	W 3-0	3-0	1	Martin 2 [10, 20], Russell [15]	28,637
21	13	A	Middlesbrough	L 0-2	0-1	3		17,434
22	20	H	Norwich C	D 2-2	1-0	5	Russell [43], Martin (pen) [55]	27,974
23	26	A	Birmingham C	W 4-0	2-0	3	Ibe [9], Martin [23], Forsyth [77], Russell [89]	23,851
24	30	H	Leeds U	W 2-0	1-0	3	Mowatt (og) [41], Buxton [47]	31,690
25	Jan 10	A	Ipswich T	W 1-0	0-0	2	Martin [57]	20,861
26	17	H	Nottingham F	L 1-2	1-0	3	Lansbury (og) [16]	32,705
27	27	H	Blackburn R	W 2-0	0-0	2	Bent 2 [68, 90]	26,373
28	31	A	Cardiff C	W 2-0	2-0	2	Malone (og) [22], Martin [45]	22,287
29	Feb 7	H	Bolton W	W 4-1	2-0	2	Ince 2 [39, 47], Hendrick 2 [45, 68]	30,310
30	10	A	Bournemouth	D 2-2	1-2	3	Ince [30], Bent [68]	11,031
31	17	A	Rotherham U	D 3-3	1-1	2	Ince 2 [36, 64], Bent [83]	11,035
32	21	H	Sheffield W	W 3-2	0-1	2	Buxton 2 [47, 68], Bent (pen) [77]	31,628
33	24	H	Charlton Ath	W 2-0	2-0	1	Hendrick [9], Lingard [17]	28,277
34	28	A	Fulham	L 0-2	0-2	1		20,242
35	Mar 3	A	Brighton & HA	L 0-2	0-0	2		24,002
36	7	H	Birmingham C	D 2-2	1-0	2	Ward [20], Ince [48]	31,522
37	14	A	Norwich C	D 1-1	0-1	4	Hanson [66]	26,766
38	17	H	Middlesbrough	L 0-1	0-0	5		31,939
39	20	A	Wolverhampton W	L 0-2	0-0	5		27,480
40	Apr 3	H	Watford	D 2-2	1-1	6	Bent (pen) [45], Ince [57]	31,748
41	6	A	Wigan Ath	W 2-0	0-0	5	Martin [51], Bent [81]	14,697
42	11	A	Brentford	D 1-1	1-1	5	Bent [90]	30,043
43	14	H	Blackpool	W 4-0	3-0	5	Bryson [3], Ince [28], Bent 2 (1 pen) [29, 65 (p)]	27,227
44	18	A	Huddersfield T	D 4-4	1-3	5	Ince 2 [16, 79], Dawkins [52], Lingard [61]	15,889
45	25	A	Millwall	D 3-3	1-2	6	Ince [42], Martin (pen) [70], Hendrick [85]	12,571
46	May 2	H	Reading	L 0-3	0-1	8		30,806

Final League Position: 8

GOALSCORERS

League (85): Martin 18 (3 pens), Ince 11, Bent 10 (3 pens), Hendrick 7, Russell 6, Ward 6, Ibe 5, Bryson 4, Buxton 3, Dawkins 3, Hughes 2, Lingard 2, Shotton 2, Eustace 1, Forsyth 1, Hanson 1, own goals 3.
FA Cup (4): Bent 2, Hughes 1, Martin 1 (1 pen).
Capital One Cup (11): Dawkins 2, Hendrick 2, Martin 2 (1 pen), Russell 2, Bryson 1, Calero 1, own goal 1.

Grant L 40	Christie C 34+4	Keogh R 45	Buxton J 18+1	Forsyth C 44	Bryson C 25+13	Hughes W 37+5	Hendrick J 34+7	Dawkins S 15+19	Martin C 31+4	Russell J 2+12	Mascarell O 18+5	Ward J 21+4	Best L —+15	Eustace J 13	Shotton R 23+2	Ibe J 13+7	Calero I —+2	Whitbread Z 8+1	Butland J 6	Coutts P —+7	Thomas K —+4	Bent D 11+4	Bennett M —+2	Ince T 18	Lingard J 6+8	Thorne G 3	Albentosa R 7+1	Hanson J 2	Warnock S 6+1	Sammon C 1	Match No.
1	2	3	4	5	6	7^3	8	9^2	10	11^1	12	13	14																		1
1	2	4	3	5	6	7^1	8	9^2	10	14	12	11^3	13																		2
1	2	3	4	5	6	7^2	8^1	9^3	10	13	12	11	14																		3
1	2	3	4	5	8^3	13	6	12	10	11^2			9^1	14	7																4
1	2	3	4	5	8	12	6^2	14	10	11^3			9	13	7^1																5
1		3	4^4	5	6^1	8	11	10	9^2		12			7^3	2	13	14														6
1	2	3		5	6	8^2	11^1	10	12	14	9^3				7	13		4													7
1	2	3		5	6	8	11^2	10	14		9^1	13			7^3		12	4													8
1	2	3		5	6	8		10	12	11^2		13	9^1		7		9^1	4													9
1	2	3		5	8	6	14	10	12	11^3		13	9^1		7^2		4	11^1													10
1	2	3		5	6	8	12	10	14	11^2		13	7^3		9^1		4														11
1	2	3^2		5	8	14	10	12	9^1		7	13	11		4																12
	2	3		5	13	8^1	6	10	9	7	12		4	11^2		1															13
	2	3		5	6	8^1	12	13	10	9		14	7^2	11^3	4	1															14
	2	3	4	5	6^2	12	8	11^3	10	9^1	7		13		1	14															15
	2	3		5		8	6	12	10	11^2	7		4	9^1	1	13															16
	2	3		5		8	6	11^2	10	9^2	7^1		4	12	13	1	14														17
	2	3		5	12	8^1	6	13	10	9^2	7		4	11^3		1	14														18
1	2	3		5	14	8	6	12	10	11^1	7^2		4	9^3			13														19
1	2		4	5	8		6	11^1	10^3	9^2	7	12	14	3	13																20
1	2	3		5	8	14	6	11^3	10	9	7^2		13	4^1	12																21
1	2	3		5	8^3	12	6^2	13	10	9	7		4	11^1			14														22
1	2	4		5		8	6^2		10^1	9		13	7	3	11		12														23
1	2	3	4	5	12	8	6^3	13	10	9^2		7		11^1		14															24
1	2	3	4	5	12	8	6^2	13	10	9^3			7^4	14	11^1																25
1	2	3	4	5	6	8^2	12		10	9	7	11^1													13						26
1		3	4	5		8	6	9^3	10		7	11^2		2										12	13						27
1	12	3	4^3	5	14	8	6	11^1	10		7	9^2		2											13						28
1		3	4	5	14	8^2	6	13	10^1		7	9^2		2										12	11						29
1	2	3	4	5		8	6	13	10^1		7	11^2												12	9						30
1	2	3	4	5	14	8	6^1	13			7^3	11^2												10	9	12					31
1	2	3	4	5	12	8	6	11^1																10	9	13	7^2				32
1	2	3		5	14	8^3	6	12		13	7		4											10	9^{11}	7^2					33
1	2^1	3	12	5	14	8	6		13	7			4											10^3	9	11^2					34
1		3	4	5	8		6	13	10^1	7^3	11^2		2									14		9	12						35
1	2	3		5	13	8^2	6	14	10^1	7	11^3													9	12	4					36
1	12	3		5	13	6^2	8	10	11^1	2^3														9	4	7	14				37
1	2^1	3		5	6	8	12	10	11^3				14											9	13	4	7^2				38
1	2	3		5	7	6	12	8^1													11			9	10	4					39
1	2^2	3		5	7^3	9	12	14	10	4											11	8	13	6^1							40
1	13	2	4	6	7	14	12	8	10^1												11	9^3		3	5^2						41
1		2	4	7^3	8	12	11	6^2				14									10	9	13	3	5^{11}						42
1		2		6	7^2	8	12	13	3	4	14	10^1	9^3	11										5							43
1	13	3		8^3	7^1	6	12	14	2	4^2		10	9	11										5							44
1		3	4	8	6	7^1	14	12	2			9^{11}?	11^2	13										5^3	10						45
1		3	5	8	6	13	11^1	14	2			10	9	12	4^2									7^3							46

FA Cup

Third Round	Southport	(h)	1-0
Fourth Round	Chesterfield	(h)	2-0
Fifth Round	Reading	(h)	1-2

Capital One Cup

First Round	Carlisle U	(a)	2-0
Second Round	Charlton Ath	(h)	1-0
Third Round	Reading	(h)	2-0
Fourth Round	Fulham	(a)	5-2
Quarter-Finals	Chelsea	(h)	1-3

DONCASTER ROVERS

FOUNDATION

In 1879, Mr Albert Jenkins assembled a team to play a match against the Yorkshire Institution for the Deaf. The players remained together as Doncaster Rovers, joining the Midland Alliance in 1889 and the Midland Counties League in 1891.

Keepmoat Stadium, Stadium Way, Lakeside, Doncaster, South Yorkshire DN4 5JW.

Telephone: (01302) 764 664.

Fax: (01302) 363 525.

Ticket Office: (01302) 762 576.

Website: www.doncasterroversfc.co.uk

Email: info@doncasterroversfc.co.uk

Ground Capacity: 15,231.

Record Attendance: 37,149 v Hull C, Division 3 (N), 2 October 1948 (at Belle Vue); 15,001 v Leeds U, FL 1, 1 April 2008 (at Keepmoat Stadium).

Pitch Measurements: 100m × 66m (109.5yd × 72yd)

Chairman: David Blunt.

Chief Executive: Gavin Baldwin.

Manager: Paul Dickov.

Assistant Manager: Brian Horton.

Physio: Alex Dalton.

Colours: Red and white hooped shirts, black shorts with white trim, white socks with red trim.

Year Formed: 1879.

Turned Professional: 1885.

Club Nickname: 'Rovers', 'Donny'.

Grounds: 1880–1916, Intake Ground; 1920, Benetthorpe Ground; 1922, Low Pasture, Belle Vue; 2007, Keepmoat Stadium.

HONOURS

Football League Division 3: *Champions* 2003–04; **Division 3 (N):** *Champions* – 1934–35, 1946–47, 1949–50; *Runners-up* 1937–38, 1938–39; **FL 1:** *Champions* 2012–13; **Division 4:** *Champions* 1965–66, 1968–69; *Runners-up* 1983–84.

FA Cup: Best season: 5th rd, 1952, 1954, 1955, 1956.

Football League Cup: Best season: 5th rd, 1976, 2006.

Johnstone's Paint Trophy: *Winners* 2007.

Football Conference: *Champions* 2002–03

Sheffield County Cup: *Winners* 1891, 1912, 1936, 1938, 1956, 1968, 1976, 1986.

Midland Counties League: *Champions* 1897, 1899.

Conference Trophy: *Winners* 1999, 2000.

Sheffield & Hallamshire Senior Cup: *Winners* 2001, 2002.

First Football League Game: 7 September 1901, Division 2, v Burslem Port Vale (h) D 3–3 – Eggett; Simpson, Layton; Longden, Jones, Wright, Langham, Murphy, Price, Goodson (2), Bailey (1).

Record League Victory: 10–0 v Darlington, Division 4, 25 January 1964 – Potter; Raine, Meadows, Windross (1), White, Ripley (2), Robinson, Book (2), Hale (4), Jeffrey, Broadbent (1).

Record Cup Victory: 7–0 v Blyth Spartans, FA Cup 1st rd, 27 November 1937 – Imrie; Shaw, Rodgers, McFarlane, Bycroft, Cyril Smith, Burton (1), Killourhy (4), Morgan (2), Malam, Dutton.

Record Defeat: 0–12 v Small Heath, Division 2, 11 April 1903.

sky SPORTS FACT FILE

Centre forward Les Lievesley scored 21 goals from 66 appearances playing for Doncaster Rovers between 1930 and 1932. He became a well respected coach and after the war was employed by Torino. Les was on board the flight which crashed in April 1949 killing players and officials of the Italian club in what has become known as the Superga Disaster.

Most League Points (2 for a win): 72, Division 3 (N), 1946–47.

Most League Points (3 for a win): 92, Division 3, 2003–04.

Most League Goals: 123, Division 3 (N), 1946–47.

Highest League Scorer in Season: Clarrie Jordan, 42, Division 3 (N), 1946–47.

Most League Goals in Total Aggregate: Tom Keetley, 180, 1923–29.

Most League Goals in One Match: 6, Tom Keetley v Ashington, Division 3 (N), 16 February 1929.

Most Capped Player: Len Graham, 14, Northern Ireland.

Most League Appearances: Fred Emery, 417, 1925–36.

Youngest League Player: Alick Jeffrey, 15 years 229 days v Fulham, 15 September 1954.

Record Transfer Fee Received: £2,000,000 from Reading for Matthew Mills, July 2009.

Record Transfer Fee Paid: £1,150,000 to Sheffield U for Billy Sharp, August 2010.

Football League Record: 1901 Elected to Division 2; 1903 Failed re-election; 1904 Re-elected; 1905 Failed re-election; 1923 Re-elected to Division 3 (N); 1935–37 Division 2; 1937–47 Division 3 (N); 1947–48 Division 2; 1948–50 Division 3 (N); 1950–58 Division 2; 1958–59 Division 3; 1959–66 Division 4; 1966–67 Division 3; 1967–69 Division 4; 1969–71 Division 3; 1971–81 Division 4; 1981–83 Division 3; 1983–84 Division 4; 1984–88 Division 3; 1988–92 Division 4; 1992–98 Division 3; 1998–2003 Conference; 2003–04 Division 3; 2004–08 FL 1; 2008–12 FL C; 2012–13 FL 1; 2013–14 FL C; 2014– FL 1.

LATEST SEQUENCES

Longest Sequence of League Wins: 10, 22.1.1947 – 4.4.1947.

Longest Sequence of League Defeats: 9, 14.1.1905 – 1.4.1905.

Longest Sequence of League Draws: 4, 29.10.1932 – 19.11.1932.

Longest Sequence of Unbeaten League Matches: 20, 26.12.1968 – 12.4.1969.

Longest Sequence Without a League Win: 20, 9.8.1997 – 29.11.1997.

Successive Scoring Runs: 27 from 10.11.1934.

Successive Non-scoring Runs: 7 from 27.9.1947.

MANAGERS

Arthur Porter 1920–21
Harry Tufnell 1921–22
Arthur Porter 1922–23
Dick Ray 1923–27
David Menzies 1928–36
Fred Emery 1936–40
Bill Marsden 1944–46
Jackie Bestall 1946–49
Peter Doherty 1949–58
Jack Hodgson and Sid Bycroft
  (*Joint Managers*) 1958
Jack Crayston 1958–59
  (*continued as Secretary-Manager to 1961*)
Jackie Bestall (*TM*) 1959–60
Norman Curtis 1960–61
Danny Malloy 1961–62
Oscar Hold 1962–64
Bill Leivers 1964–66
Keith Kettleborough 1966–67
George Raynor 1967–68
Lawrie McMenemy 1968–71
Maurice Setters 1971–74
Stan Anderson 1975–78
Billy Bremner 1978–85
Dave Cusack 1985–87
Dave Mackay 1987–89
Billy Bremner 1989–91
Steve Beaglehole 1991–93
Ian Atkins 1994
Sammy Chung 1994–96
Kerry Dixon (*Player-Manager*)
  1996–97
Dave Cowling 1997
Mark Weaver 1997–98
Ian Snodin 1998–99
Steve Wignall 1999–2001
Dave Penney 2002–06
Sean O'Driscoll 2006–11
Dean Saunders 2011–13
Brian Flynn 2013
Paul Dickov May 2013–

TEN YEAR LEAGUE RECORD

		P	W	D	L	F	A	Pts	Pos
2005-06	FL 1	46	20	9	17	55	51	69	8
2006-07	FL 1	46	16	15	15	52	47	63	11
2007-08	FL 1	46	23	11	12	65	41	80	3
2008-09	FL C	46	17	7	22	42	53	58	14
2009-10	FL C	46	15	15	16	59	58	60	12
2010-11	FL C	46	11	15	20	55	81	48	21
2011-12	FL C	46	8	12	26	43	80	36	24
2012-13	FL 1	46	25	9	12	62	44	84	1
2013-14	FL C	46	11	11	24	39	70	44	22
2014-15	FL 1	46	16	13	17	58	62	61	13

DID YOU KNOW ?

Doncaster Rovers' former ground, Belle Vue, was for many years the largest playing surface in the Football League. The pitch measured 119 yards by 79 yards before it was reduced in size in 1981. Unusually the ground had separate tunnels for the home and away teams.

DONCASTER ROVERS – FOOTBALL LEAGUE ONE 2014–15 LEAGUE RECORD

Match No.	Date	Venue	Opponents	Result		H/T Score	Lg Pos.	Goalscorers	Attendance
1	Aug 9	A	Yeovil T	W	3-0	1-0	1	Main [8], Forrester [63], Robinson [90]	5235
2	16	H	Port Vale	L	1-3	0-3	10	Bennett [74]	6437
3	19	H	Preston NE	D	1-1	0-0	10	Tyson [90]	6513
4	23	A	Colchester U	W	1-0	0-0	8	Bennett [65]	3162
5	30	H	Oldham Ath	L	0-2	0-1	11		6313
6	Sept 13	A	Bristol C	L	0-3	0-2	19		11,733
7	16	H	Crawley T	D	0-0	0-0	18		5197
8	20	H	Chesterfield	W	3-2	2-1	15	Tyson [7], Bennett [32], McCombe [50]	7954
9	27	A	Walsall	L	0-3	0-1	18		3741
10	Oct 4	A	Scunthorpe U	W	2-1	1-1	13	Coppinger [29], Tyson [49]	5420
11	18	A	Fleetwood T	L	1-3	1-2	14	Tyson [17]	3785
12	21	H	Leyton Orient	L	0-2	0-1	17		5205
13	25	H	Milton Keynes D	D	0-0	0-0	20		5976
14	Nov 1	A	Bradford C	W	2-1	0-1	17	Wabara [59], Main [69]	13,348
15	15	H	Sheffield U	L	0-1	0-0	17		11,037
16	22	A	Rochdale	W	3-1	1-1	16	Bennett [25], Robinson [86], Main [90]	3229
17	29	A	Crewe Alex	D	1-1	0-1	16	Coppinger [80]	4530
18	Dec 2	A	Barnsley	D	1-1	0-1	16	Robinson [52]	10,058
19	13	H	Gillingham	L	1-2	0-0	17	Main (pen) [90]	5542
20	20	A	Swindon T	W	1-0	1-0	16	Robinson (pen) [26]	7793
21	26	H	Coventry C	W	2-0	2-0	13	Butler [2], Forrester [22]	6916
22	28	A	Peterborough U	D	0-0	0-0	14		6895
23	Jan 10	A	Oldham Ath	D	2-2	0-1	14	Tyson [78], Coppinger [90]	4181
24	17	H	Barnsley	W	1-0	0-0	13	Forrester [84]	9005
25	20	H	Notts Co	D	0-0	0-0	10		5547
26	31	A	Chesterfield	D	2-2	2-1	12	Coppinger [3], Butler [9]	7839
27	Feb 7	H	Walsall	L	0-2	0-1	13		6089
28	10	A	Crawley T	W	5-0	1-0	11	Butler [38], Wellens [56], Tyson [64], Forrester [73], Main [90]	2581
29	14	A	Yeovil T	W	3-0	1-0	8	Tyson [22], Furman [57], Bennett [77]	5950
30	17	H	Crewe Alex	W	2-1	0-1	6	Furman [62], Wellens [90]	6164
31	21	A	Port Vale	L	0-3	0-2	7		5713
32	24	H	Bristol C	L	1-3	0-2	7	Main [57]	5495
33	28	H	Colchester U	W	2-0	1-0	6	Stevens [39], Tyson (pen) [83]	6330
34	Mar 3	A	Preston NE	D	2-2	0-1	6	Forrester [81], Main [84]	8703
35	7	A	Gillingham	D	1-1	1-1	6	Forrester [40]	5909
36	14	H	Peterborough U	L	0-2	0-1	10		11,520
37	17	H	Swindon T	L	1-2	1-0	12	Main [41]	5258
38	21	A	Coventry C	W	3-1	0-1	9	Wellens [50], Clarke-Harris [72], Forrester [84]	8699
39	Apr 3	H	Bradford C	L	0-3	0-0	12		8592
40	7	A	Sheffield U	L	2-3	1-1	12	Bennett 2 [17, 59]	20,487
41	11	H	Rochdale	D	1-1	1-0	13	Bennett [17]	5695
42	14	A	Leyton Orient	W	1-0	0-0	13	Jones [56]	4410
43	18	H	Fleetwood T	D	0-0	0-0	13		6211
44	21	A	Milton Keynes D	L	0-3	0-0	13		8159
45	25	A	Notts Co	L	1-2	0-1	14	Tyson (pen) [90]	5857
46	May 3	H	Scunthorpe U	W	5-2	3-0	13	Canavan (og) [12], Tyson 3 (2 pens) [33, 74 (p), 80 (p)], Jones [45]	9394

Final League Position: 13

GOALSCORERS

League (58): Tyson 12 (4 pens), Bennett 8, Main 8 (1 pen), Forrester 7, Coppinger 4, Robinson 4 (1 pen), Butler 3, Wellens 3, Furman 2, Jones 2, Clarke-Harris 1, McCombe 1, Stevens 1, Wabara 1, own goal 1.
FA Cup (6): Main 2, Coppinger 1, McCullough 1, Wellens 1, own goal 1.
Capital One Cup (4): Coppinger 1, Forrester 1, Tyson 1 (1 pen), Wakefield 1.
Johnstone's Paint Trophy (3): Forrester 1, Tyson 1 (1 pen), Wellens 1.

Steer J 13	Wabara R 42 + 1	McCullough L 33	Jones R 10	Evina C 17 + 2	Coppinger J 33 + 1	Furman D 32 + 2	Keegan P 30 + 2	Forrester H 24 + 16	Main C 23 + 15	Tyson N 31 + 8	Robinson T 13 + 19	De Val Fernandez M 8 + 3	Bennett K 31 + 11	Wakefield L 3 + 2	McCombe J 16 + 2	Wellens R 37 + 2	Marosi M 2 + 1	Peterson A — + 1	Butler A 33	Johnstone S 10	Stevens E 27 + 1	McKay J 1 + 3	Whitehouse B — + 4	Middleton H 1 + 3	Bywater S 21	Ikpeazu U 3 + 4	Razak A 5 + 4	Clarke-Harris J 3 + 6	Mandeville L — + 3	Lund M 4	Match No.
1	2	3	4	5	6	7	8	9³	10²	11¹	12	13	14																		1
1	2	4	3	5	6	7¹	8	9⁴	11¹¹	10²	12	13	14																		2
1	2	4	3²	5	6	9¹	8			13	11	7	10	12																	3
1	2	3		5		8	9	6			12	11¹	7	10	4																4
1	2	4	3	5	8	9²	6	13		11	12	7³	10¹			14															5
1	2	3¹	5	10		6²	9⁴			13	11		6³		8	12	7														6
1	2	3		5	6	7				10	11		9		4	8															7
1	2	4		5	9	8	12			10¹	13	6²	11		3	7															8
1²	2	4		5	9	8	7¹	10			11		6³		3	13	12	14													9
1		5	3			8	10	12	9		11		6¹		2	4	7														10
1	2	4		5	6		7	10¹	12	11	14	8⁵	13		3²	9															11
1	5	4			7	9		10¹	13	11	14	6¹	12	2	3²	8															12
1	2	3		5			8	9	10¹	11	12		6			7			4												13
	2	3		5¹	9			7	13	10		6²	12			8			4	1											14
		4			6			7³	9	10¹	11²	12	13		2	3	8		4	1	5	14									15
	2	3			6²			7¹	12	10	11³	13	9			8			4	1	5	14									16
	5	3			6	14		7²	13	11	10¹	12	9³			8			4	1	2										17
	2	3			6		8	12	11¹	10			9			7			4	1	5										18
	2	3			6	7¹	12	11		10			9			8			4	1	5										19
	2	3			10	6	7	12	13		11²		8¹			9			4	1	5										20
	2	3			11	6	7	9¹³	13	10¹	12		8³						4	1	5	14									21
	2	3			7	8	6	10²	13	11³	9¹								4	1	5	14	12								22
	2	4			7		6	10	13	12	11¹		9²			8			3	1	5										23
	2	3			6		7	13	10¹	12	11³		9²			8			4		5	14	1								24
	2	4	12	6		7	9	13	11	10			8						3		5²		1								25
	2	4		6²	14	7	9	10³	13		12³		8						3		5		1			11¹					26
	2			8²	6¹	9	10³	12	14	13		3	7						4		5		1			11					27
	2	14		8	6	10	13	11³	12		7		3	9²					4		5¹		1								28
	2			7	6	10¹	12	11³	14		9		3	8⁴					4		5		1				13				29
	2			7	6		12	10		8²			3	9					4		5		1			11²	13				30
	2			8		10¹²	12	11¹	14		7		3	6					4		5		1			13	9²				31
	2			7	6³	10⁴	12	11		8¹			3	9					4		5		1			13	14				32
	2	3			8	7	13	11¹	10¹		12		9						4		5		1			14	6²				33
	2	4		13	9⁴	6¹	12	11	10				7						3		5		1			14	8³				34
	2	3		9³	7		12	10	11²	14		13	8						4		5		1				6¹				35
	2	3		7¹		9	10	11²	13	12			8						4		5		1			14	6				36
	2	3		7		13	10	11	12		6¹		8						4		5		1				9²				37
	5	4		9		12	10³	11²	14		7		8						3		2		1			6¹	13				38
	2	3		6¹	7		9¹	10	12		13		8						4		5		1					11²	14		39
	2			6²	8	13	10	11¹		9		3	7			8			4		5		1					12			40
	2			6	7²	13	10³	11¹	9			3	8						4		5		1					12	14		41
	2	4	5³	6	8			11¹	10				7						3		13	7²	1					12			42
		3	5	6¹	8		13	10²	11³		9		7						4				1					12	14	2	43
	6¹	3	5		8		11²	12	10³		9		7						4				14					13		2	44
	3	5	7	6		8¹	12	10		9³					1				4		11²	14	13							2	45
13	3	5	6	11		9	12	10³		8¹			7		1				4			14								2²	46

FA Cup

First Round	Weston Super Mare	(a)	4-1	
Second Round	Oldham Ath	(a)	1-0	
Third Round	Bristol C	(h)	1-1	
Replay	Bristol C	(a)	0-2	

Capital One Cup

First Round	York C	(a)	1-0
Second Round	Watford	(a)	2-1
Third Round	Fulham	(a)	1-2

Johnstone's Paint Trophy

Second Round	Burton Alb	(a)	3-0
Northern Quarter-Finals	Notts Co	(h)	0-1

EVERTON

Goodison Park, Goodison Road, Liverpool L4 4EL.

Telephone: (0871) 663 1878.

Fax: (0151) 286 9112.

Ticket Office: (0871) 663 1878.

Website: www.evertonfc.com

Email: everton@evertonfc.com

Ground Capacity: 39,571.

Record Attendance: 78,299 v Liverpool, Division 1, 18 September 1948.

Pitch Measurements: 100.48m × 68m (109yd × 74yd)

Chairman: Bill Kenwright CBE.

Chief Executive: Robert Elstone.

Manager: Roberto Martinez.

Assistant Manager: Graeme Jones.

Physio: Matt Connery.

Colours: Blue shirts with white trim, white shorts with blue trim, blue socks with white trim.

Year Formed: 1878.

Turned Professional: 1885.

Previous Name: 1878, St Domingo FC; 1879, Everton.

Club Nickname: 'The Toffees'.

Grounds: 1878, Stanley Park; 1882, Priory Road; 1884, Anfield Road; 1892, Goodison Park.

First Football League Game: 8 September 1888, Football League, v Accrington (h) W 2–1 – Smalley; Dick, Ross; Holt, Jones, Dobson; Fleming (2), Waugh, Lewis, Edgar Chadwick, Farmer.

Record League Victory: 9–1 v Manchester C, Division 1, 3 September 1906 – Scott; Balmer, Crelley; Booth, Taylor (1), Abbott (1); Sharp, Bolton (1), Young (4), Settle (2), George Wilson. 9–1 v Plymouth Arg, Division 2, 27 December 1930 – Coggins; Williams, Cresswell; McPherson, Griffiths, Thomson; Critchley, Dunn, Dean (4), Johnson (1), Stein (4).

HONOURS

Football League – Division 1:
Champions 1890–91, 1914–15, 1927–28, 1931–32, 1938–39, 1962–63, 1969–70, 1984–85, 1986–87;
Runners-up 1889–90, 1894–95, 1901–02, 1904–05, 1908–09, 1911–12, 1985–86;
Division 2: *Champions* 1930–31;
Runners-up 1953–54.

FA Cup: *Winners* 1906, 1933, 1966, 1984, 1995; *Runners-up* 1893, 1897, 1907, 1968, 1985, 1986, 1989, 2009.

Football League Cup:
Runners-up 1977, 1984.

League Super Cup: *Runners-up* 1986.

Simod Cup: *Runners-up* 1989.

Zenith Data Systems Cup:
Runners-up 1991.

European Competitions
European Cup: 1963–64, 1970–71.
European Cup-Winners' Cup:
1966–67, 1984–85 (*winners*), 1995–96.
European Fairs Cup: 1962–63, 1964–65, 1965–66.
Champions League: 2005–06.
UEFA Cup: 1975–76, 1978–79, 1979–80, 2005–06, 2007–08, 2008–09.
Europa League: 2009–10, 2014–15.

sky SPORTS FACT FILE

Sandy Young scored the winning goal for Everton in the 1906 FA Cup final and in 1914 he emigrated to Australia. The following year he was found guilty of the manslaughter of his brother John and sentenced to three years in prison.

Record Cup Victory: 11–2 v Derby Co, FA Cup 1st rd, 18 January 1890 – Smalley; Hannah, Doyle (1); Kirkwood, Holt (1), Parry; Latta, Brady (3), Geary (3), Edgar Chadwick, Millward (3).

Record Defeat: 4–10 v Tottenham H, Division 1, 11 October 1958.

Most League Points (2 for a win): 66, Division 1, 1969–70.

Most League Points (3 for a win): 90, Division 1, 1984–85.

Most League Goals: 121, Division 2, 1930–31.

Highest League Scorer in Season: William Ralph 'Dixie' Dean, 60, Division 1, 1927–28 (All-time League record).

Most League Goals in Total Aggregate: William Ralph 'Dixie' Dean, 349, 1925–37.

Most League Goals in One Match: 6, Jack Southworth v WBA, Division 1, 30 December 1893.

Most Capped Player: Neville Southall, 92, Wales.

Most League Appearances: Neville Southall, 578, 1981–98.

Youngest League Player: Jose Baxter, 16 years 191 days v Blackburn R, 16 August 2008.

Record Transfer Fee Received: £25,000,000 (rising to £29,000,000) from Manchester U for Wayne Rooney, August 2004.

Record Transfer Fee Paid: £28,000,000 to Chelsea for Romelu Lukaku, July 2014.

Football League Record: 1888 Founder Member of the Football League; 1930–31 Division 2; 1931–51 Division 1; 1951–54 Division 2; 1954–92 Division 1; 1992– FA Premier League.

MANAGERS

W. E. Barclay 1888–89
(Secretary-Manager)
Dick Molyneux 1889–1901
(Secretary-Manager)
William C. Cuff 1901–18
(Secretary-Manager)
W. J. Sawyer 1918–19
(Secretary-Manager)
Thomas H. McIntosh 1919–35
(Secretary-Manager)
Theo Kelly 1936–48
Cliff Britton 1948–56
Ian Buchan 1956–58
Johnny Carey 1958–61
Harry Catterick 1961–73
Billy Bingham 1973–77
Gordon Lee 1977–81
Howard Kendall 1981–87
Colin Harvey 1987–90
Howard Kendall 1990–93
Mike Walker 1994
Joe Royle 1994–97
Howard Kendall 1997–98
Walter Smith 1998–2002
David Moyes 2002–13
Roberto Martinez July 2013–

LATEST SEQUENCES

Longest Sequence of League Wins: 12, 24.3.1894 – 13.10.1894.

Longest Sequence of League Defeats: 6, 27.8.2005– 15.10.2005.

Longest Sequence of League Draws: 5, 4.5.1977 – 16.5.1977.

Longest Sequence of Unbeaten League Matches: 20, 29.4.1978 – 16.12.1978.

Longest Sequence Without a League Win: 14, 6.3.1937 – 4.9.1937.

Successive Scoring Runs: 40 from 15.3.1930.

Successive Non-scoring Runs: 6 from 27.8.2005.

TEN YEAR LEAGUE RECORD

		P	W	D	L	F	A	Pts	Pos
2005-06	PR Lge	38	14	8	16	34	49	50	11
2006-07	PR Lge	38	15	13	10	52	36	58	6
2007-08	PR Lge	38	19	8	11	55	33	65	5
2008-09	PR Lge	38	17	12	9	55	37	63	5
2009-10	PR Lge	38	16	13	9	60	49	61	8
2010-11	PR Lge	38	13	15	10	51	45	54	7
2011-12	PR Lge	38	15	11	12	50	40	56	7
2012-13	PR Lge	38	16	15	7	55	40	63	6
2013-14	PR Lge	38	21	9	8	61	39	72	5
2014-15	PR Lge	38	12	11	15	48	50	47	11

DID YOU KNOW

Everton were founder members of the Football League and up to the end of the 2014–15 season had spent a record 112 seasons out of 116 in top flight football, well clear of their nearest rivals Aston Villa and Liverpool.

EVERTON – FA PREMIERSHIP 2014–15 LEAGUE RECORD

Match No.	Date	Venue	Opponents	Result	H/T Score	Lg Pos.	Goalscorers	Atten- dance
1	Aug 16	A	Leicester C	D	2-2	2-1	6	McGeady [20], Naismith [45]	31,603
2	23	H	Arsenal	D	2-2	2-0	10	Coleman [19], Naismith [45]	39,490
3	30	H	Chelsea	L	3-6	1-2	16	Mirallas [45], Naismith [69], Eto'o [76]	39,402
4	Sept 13	A	WBA	W	2-0	1-0	9	Lukaku [2], Mirallas [66]	23,567
5	21	H	Crystal Palace	L	2-3	1-1	14	Lukaku [9], Baines (pen) [83]	37,574
6	27	A	Liverpool	D	1-1	0-0	13	Jagielka [90]	44,511
7	Oct 5	A	Manchester U	L	1-2	0-1	17	Naismith [55]	75,294
8	18	H	Aston Villa	W	3-0	1-0	12	Jagielka [18], Lukaku [48], Coleman [76]	39,505
9	26	A	Burnley	W	3-1	2-1	9	Eto'o [2 4, 85], Lukaku [29]	19,927
10	Nov 1	H	Swansea C	D	0-0	0-0	9		39,149
11	9	A	Sunderland	D	1-1	0-0	10	Baines (pen) [76]	43,476
12	22	H	West Ham U	W	2-1	1-0	9	Lukaku [26], Osman [73]	39,182
13	30	A	Tottenham H	L	1-2	1-2	10	Mirallas [15]	35,901
14	Dec 3	H	Hull C	D	1-1	1-0	11	Lukaku [34]	34,645
15	6	A	Manchester C	L	0-1	0-1	11		45,603
16	15	H	QPR	W	3-1	2-0	10	Barkley [33], Mirallas [43], Onuoha (og) [53]	34,035
17	20	A	Southampton	L	0-3	0-1	10		31,475
18	26	H	Stoke C	L	0-1	0-1	12		39,166
19	28	A	Newcastle U	L	2-3	1-1	12	Kone [5], Mirallas [84]	52,313
20	Jan 1	A	Hull C	L	0-2	0-2	13		23,865
21	10	H	Manchester C	D	1-1	0-0	12	Naismith [78]	39,499
22	19	H	WBA	D	0-0	0-0	12		34,739
23	31	A	Crystal Palace	W	1-0	1-0	12	Lukaku [2]	25,197
24	Feb 7	H	Liverpool	D	0-0	0-0	12		39,621
25	11	A	Chelsea	L	0-1	0-0	12		41,592
26	22	H	Leicester C	D	2-2	0-0	12	Naismith [57], Upson (og) [88]	38,904
27	Mar 1	A	Arsenal	L	0-2	0-1	14		59,925
28	4	A	Stoke C	L	0-2	0-1	14		26,431
29	15	H	Newcastle U	W	3-0	1-0	14	McCarthy [20], Lukaku (pen) [56], Barkley [90]	38,806
30	22	A	QPR	W	2-1	1-0	13	Coleman [18], Lennon [77]	17,706
31	Apr 4	H	Southampton	W	1-0	1-0	11	Jagielka [16]	39,390
32	11	A	Swansea C	D	1-1	1-0	12	Lennon [41]	20,468
33	18	H	Burnley	W	1-0	1-0	12	Mirallas [29]	39,496
34	26	H	Manchester U	W	3-0	2-0	10	McCarthy [5], Stones [35], Mirallas [74]	39,497
35	May 2	A	Aston Villa	L	2-3	0-2	11	Lukaku (pen) [59], Jagielka [90]	37,859
36	9	H	Sunderland	L	0-2	0-0	11		38,246
37	16	A	West Ham U	W	2-1	0-0	10	Osman [68], Lukaku [90]	34,977
38	24	H	Tottenham H	L	0-1	0-1	11		39,365

Final League Position: 11

GOALSCORERS

League (48): Lukaku 10 (2 pens), Mirallas 7, Naismith 6, Jagielka 4, Coleman 3, Eto'o 3, Baines 2 (2 pens), Barkley 2, Lennon 2, McCarthy 2, Osman 2, Kone 1, McGeady 1, Stones 1, own goals 2.
FA Cup (3): Lukaku 2, Mirallas 1.
Capital One Cup (0).
UEFA Europa League (21): Lukaku 8 (2 pens), Mirallas 3, Coleman 2, Jagielka 2, Naismith 2, Baines 1 (1 pen), Eto'o 1, Osman 1, own goal 1.

Howard T 32	Stones J 23	Jagielka P 37	Distin S 12 + 1	Baines L 31	McCarthy J 27 + 1	Barry G 33	McGeady A 10 + 6	Naismith S 22 + 9	Pienaar S 3 + 6	Lukaku R 32 + 4	Mirallas K 18 + 11	Coleman S 34 + 1	Osman L 13 + 8	Atsu C 1 + 4	Eto'o S 8 + 6	Besic M 15 + 8	Gibson D 3 + 6	Hibbert T 4	Browning T — + 2	Oviedo B 2 + 4	Alcaraz A 6 + 2	Barkley R 22 + 7	Kone A 7 + 5	Robles J 6 + 1	Garbutt L 3 + 1	Lennon A 12 + 2	Galloway B 2	Match No.
1	2	3	4	5	6	7	8¹	9	10²	11	12	13																1
1		3	4	5	6	7	13	9	10³	11²	8¹	2	12	14														2
1		3	4	5	6	7	10¹	9		11²	8	2			12	13												3
1		3	4	5	6	7	8²	9		11¹	10	2	12		13													4
1	2¹	3	4²	5	6	7	13	10	12	8					9³	11	14											5
1		3	4	5	6	7	12	10	9	11¹		2	14		8²							13						6
1		3	4	5	6	7	8³	9	10¹	11		2²	14		13							12						7
1		4		5	6	7	8¹	12		11²		2	10		13	14						3	9¹					8
1		4		5	6	7	8	13		11¹		2	10²		9							3	12					9
1		4		5	6	7	8²	9	14	13		2			11	12						3³	10					10
1		3	4	5	6	7²	8³	13		11		2		14	9	12						10¹						11
1		3	4		6		9³	11	8¹			2	7		14	12	13	5				10²						12
1		3	4	5		7	13			11	8¹	2	12		9²	6						10						13
1		3	4	5		7	13	12		11	10²	2			8	6¹						9						14
1		3	4	5		7				11	10²		8	13	9	6¹	2					12						15
1		3	4	5		7	8³	9	12	11¹	10²	2			13	7						6	14					16
1		3	4	5		7	8			11		2			9	6						10						17
1¹		3	4²	5	6²	7		9		11	8	2	14								12	10	13					18
	4	10	6	7	8²		14	2		9										3		12	11¹	1	5			19
	3	8	4	9						11²	12	5			6¹				2		13	7	10	1				20
	3	4		5		7	8¹	10		11	12	2				6						9		1				21
	3	4		5		7	8			11	10²	2				6					12	9	13	1				22
	3	4		5		7	8	9		11²	10¹	2				6					12		13	1				23
	3	4			6	7		10¹		11	9³	2			8²					5	14	13		1		12		24
1		3	4		12	7	10	11		13		2			6³	14		5				9¹				8²		25
1		3	4	5		7	10³			11	14	2	12		6¹	13						9²				8		26
1		3	4		6	7²	13	10		9³		2			8¹	14						11			5	12		27
1		3	4		6		8¹	10		11³	14	2			7	13						12			5	9²		28
1		4		5	7³						10²	2			9	13				3	14	8	12			11	6¹	29
1		3	4	5		7	13				10²	2			9	14						12	11¹			6		30
1		3	4	5	6	7	12					2	10			13						9¹	11²			8		31
1		3	4	5	8	6	13	12				2	10³			14						9¹	11²			7		32
1		3	4	5	8²	6	13	12		10¹		2			14							9	11³			7		33
1		3	4	5	9	6		14		11³	12	2	10¹									8²	13			7		34
1		3	4	5	6	7	9³			11	10¹	2				13						12				8		35
1		3	4	5²	6	7		14		11	12	2	10									9		13		8²		36
1		3	4		6	7	13			11	12	2	10									9¹				8²	5	37
1		3	4	14	6	7	13			11	8²	2	10								12	9³					5¹	38

FA Cup

Third Round	West Ham U	(h)	1-1
Replay	West Ham U	(a)	2-2

(aet; West Ham U won 9-8 on penalties)

Capital One Cup

Third Round	Swansea C	(a)	0-3

UEFA Europa League

Group H	Wolfsburg	(h)	4-1
Group H	Krasnodar	(a)	1-1
Group H	Lille	(a)	0-0
Group H	Lille	(h)	3-0
Group H	Wolfsburg	(a)	2-0
Group H	Krasnodar	(h)	0-1
Round of 32 1st leg	Young Boys	(a)	4-1
Round of 32 2nd leg	Young Boys	(h)	3-1
Round of 16 1st leg	Dynamo Kiev	(h)	2-1
Round of 16 2nd leg	Dynamo Kiev	(a)	2-5

EXETER CITY

FOUNDATION

Exeter City was formed in 1904 by the amalgamation of St Sidwell's United and Exeter United. The club first played in the East Devon League and then the Plymouth & District League. After an exhibition match between West Bromwich Albion and Woolwich Arsenal, which was held to test interest as Exeter was then a rugby stronghold, it was decided to form Exeter City. At a meeting at the Red Lion Hotel in 1908, the club turned professional.

St James Park, Stadium Way, Exeter, Devon EX4 6PX.

Telephone: (01392) 411 243.

Fax: (01392) 413 959.

Ticket Office: (01392) 411 243.

Website: www.exetercityfc.co.uk

Email: reception@exetercityfc.co.uk

Ground Capacity: 8,714.

Record Attendance: 20,984 v Sunderland, FA Cup 6th rd (replay), 4 March 1931.

Pitch Measurements: 104m × 64m (113.5yd × 70yd)

Vice Chairman: Julian Tagg.

Manager: Paul Tisdale.

Director of Football: Steve Perryman.

Physio: Graham McAnuff.

Colours: Red and white striped shirts with red sleeves, black shorts, white socks with black trim.

Year Formed: 1904.

Turned Professional: 1908.

Club Nickname: 'The Grecians'.

Ground: 1904, St James Park.

HONOURS

Football League – FL 1: Best season: 8th, 2010–11; **Division 3 (S):** *Runners-up* 1932–33; **Division 4:** *Champions* 1989–90; *Runners-up* 1976–77; **FL 2:** *Runners-up* 2008–09.

FA Cup: Best season: 6th rd replay, 1931; 6th rd, 1981.

Football League Cup: Best season: never beyond 4th rd.

Division 3 (S) Cup: *Winners* 1934.

First Football League Game: 28 August 1920, Division 3, v Brentford (h) W 3–0 – Pym; Coleburne, Feebury (1p); Crawshaw, Carrick, Mitton; Appleton, Makin, Wright (1), Vowles (1), Dockray.

Record League Victory: 8–1 v Coventry C, Division 3 (S), 4 December 1926 – Bailey; Pollard, Charlton; Pullen, Pool, Garrett; Purcell (2), McDevitt, Blackmore (2), Dent (2), Compton (2). 8–1 v Aldershot, Division 3 (S), 4 May 1935 – Chesters; Gray, Miller; Risdon, Webb, Angus; Jack Scott (1), Wrightson (1), Poulter (3), McArthur (1), Dryden (1), (1 og).

Record Cup Victory: 14–0 v Weymouth, FA Cup 1st qual rd, 3 October 1908 – Fletcher; Craig, Bulcock; Ambler, Chadwick, Wake; Parnell (1), Watson (1), McGuigan (4), Bell (6), Copestake (2).

Record Defeat: 0–9 v Notts Co, Division 3 (S), 16 October 1948. 0–9 v Northampton T, Division 3 (S), 12 April 1958.

sky SPORTS FACT FILE

Exeter City's first competitive fixture saw them defeat a team from the 110th Battery of the Royal Artillery in an East Devon League match in September 1904. City initially played in green and white shirts only switching to red and white six years later following the club's elevation to the Southern League.

Most League Points (2 for a win): 62, Division 4, 1976–77.

Most League Points (3 for a win): 89, Division 4, 1989–90.

Most League Goals: 88, Division 3 (S), 1932–33.

Highest League Scorer in Season: Fred Whitlow, 33, Division 3 (S), 1932–33.

Most League Goals in Total Aggregate: Tony Kellow, 129, 1976–78, 1980–83, 1985–88.

Most League Goals in One Match: 4, Harold 'Jazzo' Kirk v Portsmouth, Division 3 (S), 3 March 1923; 4, Fred Dent v Bristol R, Division 3 (S), 5 November 1927; 4, Fred Whitlow v Watford, Division 3 (S), 29 October 1932.

Most Capped Player: Dermot Curtis, 1 (17), Eire.

Most League Appearances: Arnold Mitchell, 495, 1952–66.

Youngest League Player: Cliff Bastin, 16 years 31 days v Coventry C, 14 April 1928.

Record Transfer Fee Received: £500,000 from Manchester C for Martin Phillips, November 1995.

Record Transfer Fee Paid: £65,000 to Blackpool for Tony Kellow, March 1980.

Football League Record: 1920 Elected to Division 3; 1921–58 Division 3 (S); 1958–64 Division 4; 1964–66 Division 3; 1966–77 Division 4; 1977–84 Division 3; 1984–90 Division 4; 1990–92 Division 3; 1992–94 Division 2; 1994–2003 Division 3; 2003–08 Conference; 2008–09 FL 2; 2009–12 FL 1; 2012– FL 2.

LATEST SEQUENCES

Longest Sequence of League Wins: 7, 23.4.1977 – 20.8.1977.

Longest Sequence of League Defeats: 7, 14.1.1984 – 25.2.1984.

Longest Sequence of League Draws: 6, 13.9.1986 – 4.10.1986.

Longest Sequence of Unbeaten League Matches: 13, 23.8.1986 – 25.10.1986.

Longest Sequence Without a League Win: 18, 21.2.1995 – 19.8.1995.

Successive Scoring Runs: 22 from 15.9.1958.

Successive Non-scoring Runs: 6 from 17.1.1986.

MANAGERS

Arthur Chadwick 1910–22
Fred Mavin 1923–27
Dave Wilson 1928–29
Billy McDevitt 1929–35
Jack English 1935–39
George Roughton 1945–52
Norman Kirkman 1952–53
Norman Dodgin 1953–57
Bill Thompson 1957–58
Frank Broome 1958–60
Glen Wilson 1960–62
Cyril Spiers 1962–63
Jack Edwards 1963–65
Ellis Stuttard 1965–66
Jock Basford 1966–67
Frank Broome 1967–69
Johnny Newman 1969–76
Bobby Saxton 1977–79
Brian Godfrey 1979–83
Gerry Francis 1983–84
Jim Iley 1984–85
Colin Appleton 1985–87
Terry Cooper 1988–91
Alan Ball 1991–94
Terry Cooper 1994–95
Peter Fox 1995–2000
Noel Blake 2000–01
John Cornforth 2001–02
Neil McNab 2002–03
Gary Peters 2003
Eamonn Dolan 2003–04
Alex Inglethorpe 2004–06
Paul Tisdale June 2006–

TEN YEAR LEAGUE RECORD

		P	W	D	L	F	A	Pts	Pos
2005-06	Conf	42	18	9	15	65	48	63	7
2006-07	Conf	46	22	12	12	67	48	78	5
2007-08	Conf P	46	22	17	7	83	58	83	4
2008-09	FL 2	46	22	13	11	65	50	79	2
2009-10	FL 1	46	11	18	17	48	60	51	18
2010-11	FL 1	46	20	10	16	66	73	70	8
2011-12	FL 1	46	10	12	24	46	75	42	23
2012-13	FL 2	46	18	10	18	63	62	64	10
2013-14	FL 2	46	14	13	19	54	57	55	16
2014-15	FL 2	46	17	13	16	61	65	64	10

DID YOU KNOW ?

In March 1925 Exeter City took a break from their Division Three South fixtures when they travelled to Amsterdam to take on the Dutch club Ajax. The Grecians won the game 5-1 with Harry Kirk netting a hat-trick.

EXETER CITY – FOOTBALL LEAGUE TWO 2014–15 LEAGUE RECORD

Match No.	Date	Venue	Opponents	Result		H/T Score	Lg Pos.	Goalscorers	Attendance
1	Aug 9	H	Portsmouth	D	1-1	1-0	12	Nichols [27]	5694
2	16	A	Plymouth Arg	L	0-3	0-2	18		11,418
3	19	A	Burton Alb	L	0-1	0-1	20		2099
4	23	H	York C	D	1-1	1-0	21	Wheeler [8]	2741
5	30	A	Northampton T	L	0-1	0-0	21		4053
6	Sept 6	H	Mansfield T	L	1-2	0-2	24	Grimes [67]	2771
7	13	H	Oxford U	D	1-1	1-1	23	Cummins (pen) [4]	3076
8	16	A	Cambridge U	W	2-1	1-1	23	Cummins [17], Nicholls [63]	3266
9	20	A	Tranmere R	W	2-1	1-1	20	Cummins [6], Moore-Taylor [69]	4725
10	27	H	Bury	W	2-1	1-0	17	Grimes [5], Keohane [83]	3215
11	Oct 3	A	Dagenham & R	W	2-1	0-1	11	Keohane (pen) [81], Davies [90]	2138
12	11	H	Hartlepool U	L	1-2	0-0	17	Ribeiro [80]	3547
13	18	A	Southend U	D	1-1	0-1	17	Cummins [77]	5749
14	21	H	Wycombe W	W	2-1	1-1	13	Wheeler [26], Bennett [60]	3129
15	26	A	Morecambe	W	2-0	1-0	10	Beeley (og) [9], Nichols [89]	1787
16	Nov 1	H	Luton T	D	1-1	0-1	11	Nichols (pen) [72]	5400
17	16	A	Newport Co	D	2-2	2-0	12	Nichols (pen) [22], Cummins [40]	4070
18	22	H	Shrewsbury T	W	3-2	0-2	9	Nichols 2 [46, 90], Wheeler [75]	3933
19	28	A	Accrington S	W	3-2	1-0	8	Sercombe [45], Nichols [49], Grimes [69]	1443
20	Dec 6	H	Burton Alb	D	1-1	0-0	8	Ribeiro [87]	3381
21	13	H	Carlisle U	W	2-0	0-0	7	Bennett [58], Grimes [89]	3402
22	20	A	Stevenage	L	0-1	0-0	8		2878
23	26	H	Cheltenham T	W	1-0	0-0	8	Nichols [62]	4591
24	28	A	AFC Wimbledon	L	1-4	0-1	9	Sercombe [90]	4417
25	Jan 3	H	Accrington S	L	1-2	1-0	9	Nichols [35]	3626
26	10	H	Northampton T	L	0-2	0-2	10		3519
27	17	A	Mansfield T	W	3-2	1-0	8	Nichols [37], Bennett [77], Nicholls (pen) [83]	3881
28	24	A	Oxford U	D	2-2	1-1	9	Davies [37], Nicholls [88]	6791
29	31	H	Tranmere R	L	1-2	1-1	9	Nichols [37]	4044
30	Feb 7	A	Bury	D	1-1	1-1	9	Davies [13]	3513
31	10	H	Cambridge U	D	2-2	0-1	9	Nichols [65], Wheeler [88]	3012
32	14	A	Portsmouth	L	0-1	0-0	10		14,097
33	21	H	Plymouth Arg	L	1-3	0-1	13	Davies [45]	7440
34	28	A	York C	D	0-0	0-0	14		3209
35	Mar 7	A	Carlisle U	W	3-1	1-1	13	Harley 2 [30, 56], Sercombe [90]	3724
36	14	H	AFC Wimbledon	W	3-2	0-1	11	Nichols 2 (1 pen) [54, 66 (p)], Wheeler [70]	3713
37	17	H	Stevenage	D	0-0	0-0	11		3149
38	21	H	Cheltenham T	W	2-1	1-0	10	Nichols [26], Cummins [86]	2880
39	28	H	Morecambe	D	1-1	0-1	11	Nicholls [80]	3538
40	Apr 3	A	Luton T	W	3-2	0-2	10	Harley [51], Moore-Taylor [76], Wheeler [90]	8755
41	6	H	Newport Co	W	2-0	0-0	10	Wheeler [77], Harley (pen) [90]	4478
42	11	A	Shrewsbury T	L	0-4	0-1	10		5442
43	14	A	Wycombe W	L	1-2	0-1	10	Sercombe [76]	3245
44	18	H	Southend U	L	0-1	0-0	11		4039
45	25	A	Hartlepool U	L	1-2	1-2	11	Cummins [17]	4994
46	May 2	H	Dagenham & R	W	2-1	0-0	10	Keohane [61], Nichols [70]	3645

Final League Position: 10

GOALSCORERS

League (61): Nichols 15 (3 pens), Cummins 7 (1 pen), Wheeler 7, Nicholls 5 (1 pen), Davies 4, Grimes 4, Harley 4 (1 pen), Sercombe 4, Bennett 3, Keohane 3 (1 pen), Moore-Taylor 2, Ribeiro 2, own goal 1.
FA Cup (0).
Capital One Cup (0).
Johnstone's Paint Trophy (1): Watkins 1.

Pym C 25	Tillson J 3	Baldwin P 6+1	Bennett S 26+2	Woodman C 31+1	Dawson A 2+1	Grimes M 22+1	Sercombe L 39+1	Oakley M 44+1	Keohane J 11+12	Nichols T 24+12	Wheeler D 14+31	Butterfield D 26+4	Cummins G 26+8	Watkins O —+2	Davies A 34+5	Jay M 1+2	Ribeiro C 33+4	Moore-Taylor J 25+1	Nicholls A 27+5	Noble D 8+7	Riley-Lowe C 3	Hamon J 21	Harley R 22+3	Morrison C 13+12	McAllister J 13+1	McCready T 1+2	Holmes L 6+2	Match No.
1	2	3	4	5	6	7	8²	9	10	11¹	12	13																1
1	3²	4	2		6	8	7	10	11³	12	9¹	13	14															2
1	5¹	4	3		6	9	7	8	10²	12	2	11	13															3
1		3	8	5	4	10¹	7	9		12		2			11		6											4
1		3	4	6	13	9	7	5		12		2²			11		8	10¹										5
1	4³	3	6			12	8	9	13	14	7				11		2¹	5²	10									6
1		3	5		8³	6	7	13	9²	11		14			4¹		2	10	12									7
1		3	5		8³	6	7	13	9²	11					14		4¹	2	10	12								8
1		2¹	8		6	7	3		14	9²	13	11³			5		12	4	10									9
1		3			6	7	4	12	13			2¹	11²		10		5	9	8									10
1		4			7	8³	3	13	10¹	12		2			9	14	6	5	11²									11
1		10	3		8			5	9	13	12	7³	11²		2		4		14	6¹								12
1		3	9		8	7²	4	10		12	5	11			6¹		2		13									13
1		3	9		8		6	10	13	7¹	4	11²			5		2		12									14
1		4	8		7		3	9	13	10²	6	11¹			5		2		12									15
1		7	5		8	13	6	10¹	14	2	4	11³			9²		3		12									16
1		7²	5		6	8	4	12	10	13	3	11			2			9¹										17
			5		8	6	4	11¹	10	12	2	9			13		3		7²		1							18
			5		9	6	4	10¹	14	3	11¹	12			2		8³	7			1	13						19
		13	5		8	6	4	10¹	12	3	11³				2		9²	7			1	14						20
		4	5		9		7			6²	3	13			11¹		2	10	8		1	12						21
		3	5		8	6	7			9	4				12		2¹	10			1	11² 13						22
		3	5		9	8	4		10	12	2				14		13	6¹			1	7³	11²					23
		6¹	5		8	3		12	9	4	10²				2		13	11³			1	7	14					24
		13	5		7		4	14	11	12	3				6		2	9¹			1	8³	10³					25
			5		7	3		9²	13	4¹	14				8		2	12	6		1	11	10³					26
		3	9		6	2		10²	12³		14				5		4	13	7		1	8	11¹					27
		2¹	5		6	3		10	13	14	11³				8		12	4	9	7²	1							28
1			5		7	6	14	10	12	3	11¹				2		9	8²										29
1			6		7	10		9²	12	4	14				2		5	8						13	11³	3¹		30
1			5		8	3¹		11	14	7					2		12	4	10					9²	13	6³		31
1			9		7	3		10¹	13	2					5		6	4	11³	14				8²	12			32
1		2¹	5²		6	8		11	13						9		4	3	14				7	10¹	12			33
					7			13	11	12	3				6		2	4	9¹		1		8	10²	5			34
					7	12		11²	14	2¹	13				6		3	4	9		1		8	10³	5			35
					6	7		10	12						2		3	4	9²	5	1		8	11¹		13		36
					6	7		10²	12						2		3	4	9¹	5	1		8	11		13		37
1					6³	7		10	9²		11¹				2		3	4					8	14	5	12	13	38
						7		11¹ 13	14						5		4³	3	12		1		8	10²	2	6¹	9	39
					6	8			12						11¹		5	4	3	10²	1		9	13	2		7	40
			12		6	7			13						10²		2	3	4	9¹	1		8	14	5³		11	41
		2			6	7²			12		9	11³			5		3	14			1		8	13	4		10	42
1					7	4		12	13				11³		6¹		2	3	10²				8	14	5		9	43
1		3			6	7		8¹ 12	10³		13				2	14		4					9	11²	5			44
		3			7	6		9² 14	12			11³			2			4	10¹		1		8	13	5			45
	14					7	12	9	13						2		3	4	10²		1		6	11³	5		8¹	46

FA Cup
First Round   Warrington T   (a)   0-1

Capital One Cup
First Round   Bournemouth   (h)   0-2

Johnstone's Paint Trophy
Second Round   Coventry C   (a)   1-3

FLEETWOOD TOWN

FOUNDATION

Originally formed in 1908 as Fleetwood FC, it was liquidated in 1976. Re-formed as Fleetwood Town in 1977, it folded again in 1996. Once again, it was re-formed a year later as Fleetwood Wanderers, but a sponsorship deal saw the club's name immediately changed to Fleetwood Freeport through the local retail outlet centre. This sponsorship ended in 2002, but since then local energy businessman Andy Pilley took charge and the club has risen through the non-league pyramid until finally achieving Football League status in 2012 as Fleetwood Town.

Highbury Stadium, Park Avenue, Fleetwood, Lancashire FY7 6TX.

Telephone: (01253) 775 080.

Ticket Office: (01253) 775 080

Website: www.fleetwoodtownfc.com

Email: info@fleetwoodtownfc.com

Ground Capacity: 5,311.

Record Attendance: (Before 1997) 6,150 v Rochdale, FA Cup 1st rd, 13 November 1965; (Since 1997) 5,194 v York C, FL 2 Play-Off semi-final 2nd leg, 16 May 2014.

Pitch Measurements: 100.5m × 65m (110yd × 71yd)

Chairman: Andy Pilley.

Chief Executive: Steve Curwood.

Manager: Graham Alexander.

Assistant Manager: Chris Lucketti.

Physio: Luke Bussey.

Colours: Red shirts with white trim, white shorts with red trim, red socks with white trim.

Year Formed: 1908 (re-formed 1997).

Club Nicknames: 'The Trawlermen', 'The Cod Army'.

Grounds: 1908, North Euston Hotel; 1934, Memorial Park (now Highbury Stadium).

First Football League Game: 18 August 2012, FL 2, v Torquay U (h) D 0–0 – Davies; Beeley, Mawene, McNulty, Howell, Nicolson, Johnson, McGuire, Ball, Parkin, Mangan.

Record League Victory: 13–0 v Oldham T, North West Counties Div 2, 5 December 1998.

Record Defeat: 0–7 v Billingham T, FA Cup 1st qual rd, 15 September 2001.

MANAGER

Alan Tinsley 1997
Mark Hughes 1998
Brian Wilson 1998–99
Mick Hoyle 1990–2001
Les Attwood 2001
Mark Hughes 2001
Alan Tinsley 2001–02
Mick Hoyle 2002–03
Tony Greenwood 2003–08
Micky Mellon 2008–12
Graham Alexander December 2012–

sky SPORTS FACT FILE

Fleetwood Town will meet their neighbours Blackpool in League action for the first time ever in 2015–16 following the Seasiders' relegation to League One. The two clubs did however meet in an FA Cup tie in 2011–12 with Blackpool winning 5-1 at Highbury Stadium.

Most League Points (3 for a win): 76, FL 2, 2013–14

Most League Goals: 66, FL 2, 2013–14.

Most League Goals in Total Aggregate: David Ball, 23, 2012–15.

Most League Goals in One Match: 3, Steven Schumacher v Newport Co, FL 2, 2 November 2013.

Most Capped Player: Conor McLaughlin, 9, Northern Ireland.

Most League Appearances: David Ball, 96, 2012–15.

Youngest League Player: Jamie Allen, 17 years 227 days v Northampton T, 5 January 2013.

Record Transfer Fee Received: £1,000,000 from Leicester C for Jamie Vardy, May 2012.

Record Transfer Fee Paid: £300,000 to Kidderminster H for Jamille Matt, January 2013.

Football League Record: 2012 Promoted from Conference Premier; 2012–14 FL 2; 2014–FL 1.

LATEST SEQUENCES

Longest Sequence of League Wins: 4, 1.1.2014 – 27.1.2014.

Longest Sequence of League Defeats: 4, 6.4.2013 – 27.4.2013.

Longest Sequence of League Draws: 3, 27.10.2012 – 10.11.2012.

Longest Sequence of Unbeaten League Matches: 7, 25.3.2014 – 26.4.2014.

Longest Sequence Without a League Win: 7, 23.8.2014 – 27.9.2014.

Successive Scoring Runs: 9 from 25.3.2014.

Successive Non-scoring Runs: 4 from 22.2.2014.

HONOURS

1908 Foundation

Lancashire Combination: Champions 1923–24. *Runners-Up:* 1933–34, 1934–35.

Northern Premier League Challenge Cup: *Winners:* 1971.

Lancashire Combination Cup: *Winners:* 1926, 1932, 1933, 1934. *Runners-up:* 1953, 1967.

1976 Foundation

Northern Premier League First Division: *Champions:* 1987–88.

North West Counties Football League First Division: *Champions:* 1983–84.

Northern Premier League President's Cup: *Winners:* 1990.

FA Vase: *Runners-cup:* 1984–85.

Northern Premier League Challenge Cup: *Runners-up:* 1989.

1997 Foundation

FL 1: Best season: 10th, 2014–15.

FA Cup: Best season: 3rd rd, 2011–12.

Conference: *Champions:* 2011–12.

Conference North: *Runners-up and Play-off winners:* 2009–10.

Northern Premier League Premier Division: *Champions:* 2007–08.

Northern Premier League First Division: *Runners-up* (promoted): 2005–06.

North West Counties Football League Premier Division: *Champions:* 2004–05.

North West Counties Football League First Divison: *Champions:* 1998–99.

Peter Swales Memorial Shield: *Winners:* 2008.

Northern Premier League Challenge Cup: *Winners:* 2007.

North West Counties Football League First Division Trophy: *Winners:* 1999.

Lancashire League West Division Reserve League: *Winners:* 2008–09.

TEN YEAR LEAGUE RECORD

		P	W	D	L	F	A	Pts	Pos
2005-06	Uni 1	42	22	10	10	72	48	76	2
2006-07	Uni Pr	42	19	10	13	71	60	67	8
2007-08	Uni Pr	40	28	7	5	81	39	91	1
2008-09	Conf N	42	17	11	14	70	66	62	8
2009-10	Conf N	42	26	7	7	86	44	85	2
2010-11	Conf P	46	22	12	12	68	42	78	5
2011-12	Conf P	46	31	10	5	102	48	103	1
2012-13	FL 2	46	15	15	16	55	57	60	13
2013-14	FL 2	46	22	10	14	66	52	76	4
2014-15	FL 1	46	17	12	17	49	52	63	10

DID YOU KNOW ?

When winning the Northern Premier League title in 2007–08, Fleetwood Town finished the season with a run of 14 games without defeat. Included in this was a spell of 7 consecutive away games when they did not concede a single goal.

FLEETWOOD TOWN – FOOTBALL LEAGUE ONE 2014–15 LEAGUE RECORD

Match No.	Date		Venue	Opponents	Result		H/T Score	Lg Pos.	Goalscorers	Atten- dance
1	Aug	9	H	Crewe Alex	W	2-1	0-0	5	Ball [47], Proctor [54]	3774
2		16	A	Notts Co	W	1-0	1-0	4	Proctor [45]	5051
3		19	A	Scunthorpe U	W	2-0	0-0	1	Proctor [70], Evans [80]	2773
4		23	H	Chesterfield	D	0-0	0-0	1		3512
5		30	H	Leyton Orient	D	1-1	0-1	2	Dobbie [83]	3222
6	Sept	6	A	Oldham Ath	L	0-1	0-1	3		4425
7		13	A	Crawley T	L	0-1	0-0	7		1905
8		17	H	Barnsley	D	0-0	0-0	8		3535
9		20	H	Bristol C	D	3-3	1-1	9	Morris [22], Proctor [61], Dobbie [89]	3700
10		27	A	Peterborough U	L	0-1	0-1	11		5698
11	Oct	4	H	Port Vale	W	1-0	0-0	10	Dobbie (pen) [80]	4196
12		11	A	Colchester U	L	1-2	1-1	12	McAlinden [18]	3383
13		18	A	Doncaster R	W	3-1	2-1	9	Dobbie [11], McAlinden [37], Ball [73]	3785
14		21	A	Milton Keynes D	L	1-2	0-0	11	Ball [52]	6736
15		25	A	Preston NE	L	2-3	2-0	11	Jordan [1], Laird (og) [7]	13,280
16	Nov	1	H	Gillingham	W	1-0	1-0	10	Hitchcock [3]	2951
17		15	A	Yeovil T	W	1-0	0-0	10	Hughes, J [87]	3577
18		22	H	Walsall	L	0-1	0-1	10		3224
19		29	A	Swindon T	L	0-1	0-0	11		10,506
20	Dec	13	H	Sheffield U	D	1-1	0-1	11	Sarcevic [53]	4269
21		20	A	Coventry C	D	1-1	1-0	12	Webster (og) [19]	10,254
22		26	A	Bradford C	L	0-2	0-1	14		4278
23		28	A	Rochdale	W	2-0	2-0	11	Roberts [17], Morris [38]	3123
24	Jan	3	H	Swindon T	D	2-2	0-0	12	Morris 2 [49, 59]	3346
25		10	A	Leyton Orient	W	1-0	0-0	9	Evans [46]	4947
26		17	H	Oldham Ath	L	0-2	0-0	11		4312
27		24	H	Crawley T	W	1-0	1-0	6	Sarcevic [43]	2601
28	Feb	1	A	Bristol C	L	0-2	0-0	11		11,654
29		7	H	Peterborough U	D	1-1	0-0	11	Roberts [78]	3188
30		10	A	Barnsley	W	2-1	2-1	9	McLaughlin [14], McAlinden [33]	8328
31		14	A	Crewe Alex	L	0-2	0-1	11		4135
32		21	H	Notts Co	W	2-1	1-1	8	McAlinden [25], Ball [62]	3529
33		28	A	Chesterfield	L	0-3	0-2	11		6497
34	Mar	3	H	Scunthorpe U	D	2-2	1-1	14	Proctor [3], Morris [71]	2667
35		7	A	Sheffield U	W	2-1	2-1	12	Morris [25], Haughton [35]	18,668
36		14	H	Rochdale	W	1-0	0-0	8	Morris [59]	3822
37		17	H	Coventry C	L	0-2	0-0	9		3017
38		21	A	Bradford C	D	2-2	0-1	10	Proctor [86], Pond [90]	12,963
39		29	H	Preston NE	D	1-1	0-1	12	Ball [85]	5110
40	Apr	3	A	Gillingham	W	1-0	1-0	11	Evans [18]	7961
41		6	H	Yeovil T	W	4-0	3-0	8	Ball 2 [7, 16], Proctor [32], Hunter [83]	3086
42		11	A	Walsall	L	0-1	0-0	8		3534
43		14	H	Milton Keynes D	L	0-3	0-0	8		2752
44		18	A	Doncaster R	D	0-0	0-0	8		6211
45		25	H	Colchester U	L	2-3	0-0	10	Proctor [65], Ball [74]	3129
46	May	3	A	Port Vale	W	2-1	2-0	10	Morris [17], Roberts [26]	5355

Final League Position: 10

GOALSCORERS

League (49): Ball 8, Morris 8, Proctor 8, Dobbie 4 (1 pen), McAlinden 4, Evans 3, Roberts 3, Sarcevic 2, Haughton 1, Hitchcock 1, Hughes, J 1, Hunter 1, Jordan 1, McLaughlin 1, Pond 1, own goals 2.
FA Cup (0).
Capital One Cup (0).
Johnstone's Paint Trophy (1): Evans 1.

Maxwell C 46	Hogan L 4	Pond N 24 + 3	Jordan S 40 + 2	McLaughlin C 38 + 1	Schumacher S 27 + 5	Sarcevic A 29 + 8	Morris J 43 + 2	Evans G 40 + 3	Ball D 20 + 12	Dobbie S 18 + 9	Proctor J 32 + 9	Blair M 3 + 5	Crainey S 26 + 2	Campbell A — + 2	Murdoch S 5 + 6	Cresswell R — + 1	Hughes Matty 2 + 4	Roberts M 27	Andrew D 6 + 1	Haughton N 11 + 11	McAlinden L 10 + 9	Southern K 1 + 1	Hughes J 20 + 2	Hitchcock T 4 + 2	Hornby-Forbes T 11 + 6	Paterson M 3	Hunter A 3 + 9	Chicksen A 13	Match No.
1	2	3	4	5	6	7	8	9²	10	11¹	12	13																	1
1		3	4	2	7	6¹	9	8	10²		11			5	12	13													2
1	3		4	2	7	6	9	8¹	11¹		10			5	12	13													3
1	4	3		2	7	8²	9	6	11¹		10	12	5	13															4
1		3	4	2	7	8²	9	6	11¹	12	10	13	5																5
1	2	3	4		6	7¹	8	9	12	11²	10	13	5																6
1		3	4	2	6	13	8	9	12	10²	11	7¹	5																7
1		3	4	2	7		8	9	12	11¹	10	6	6	5															8
1		3	4	2	7¹	14	6	8	11²	10	12	9¹	5		13														9
1		3	4	2	6¹	7	8	9	12	10²	11	5¹			13														10
1			4	2	7	8²	9	6	13	11¹	10²			3	5	12	14												11
1			4		6	7¹	8	9²	12	13	10³		2	3	5	14	11												12
1	3		4	2	7²		9	6	11	8¹	13		5			10³	12	14											13
1		3	4	2	6		8	7	11³	9¹	12		5			14	10²	13											14
1	4	3		2	6	11²	10¹	7³		14	9	12	5					13	8										15
1		3	4	2			12	9²	6		11¹		5				13			7	8	10							16
1	14	3			7	13	9¹	6		10³			5				4			8	12	2	11²						17
1			4	2	7³	12	13	6		10			5				3²		14	8	9¹		11						18
1		3		2	6³	9		7		12			5				4		14	8	11¹	13	10²						19
1			4	2		8	10	9¹			11					6	3	5	12		7								20
1			4	2	13	7	8²	9			10					11¹	3	5		6	12								21
1			4	2		9	8³	7¹		11	10		12				3	5¹	13	6	14								22
1			4	2	13		8³	7		9¹	10		5			12	3			6	11²	14							23
1			4	2		8	9¹	6		10²	11		5				3			7	13								24
1			4	2	12	9	8²	7		10¹	11		5				3			6	13								25
1			4	2		8	9²	6	14	11³	10		5¹				3		12	13	7								26
1			4	2	13	8	9²	6	12		11		5				3		10¹	7									27
1			4	2		8	7	12	13	10¹			3				9	11²	6	5									28
1			4	2		8	7³	11²	13	10			5				3	9	14	6			12						29
1			4	2	12	9	7	11²		5	13		3				8¹	10³	6			14							30
1			4	2	7	10	8¹	9²	13		5³		3				12	11	6			14							31
1	14		4	2	7	8	11¹	13	5¹		12		3				9²	10³	6										32
1			4	2	7³	8	14	10²	13				12				3	9¹	11¹	6				5					33
1			4	2	14	8	7¹	10²	13		11		6				3	9¹	12					5					34
1	12	4²	2	8		10³	6		13	11		14	7				3	9¹						5					35
1	4		2	7		10	6²		11			8					3	9¹	12			13		5					36
1	4		2	7	12	9	6³		14	11		8¹					3		10²		8	13	5²						37
1	4		2	7	12	10		13	9¹	11		6¹					3				8	14	5²						38
1	4	3		8	7	10		13		11			5²		9			6			12	2¹							39
1	4	14		6	9	8	7¹	11³		10	12		3							2²		13	5						40
1	4	5		6	7³	8	13	10¹	11		9²		14						2	12	3	5							41
1	3	4		6	9	8	7²	10¹		11			12						2	13	5								42
1	2	4	3		7	8	6¹	11²		12								13			5	10	9						43
1	4	3	6		9	7	8²	10¹		13							12	14			2	11³	5						44
1	4	3	7		6	13	14	12		11			8²					9			5¹	10³	2						45
1	3	13	12	6¹	7	8²	9	11		10							4	5			2								46

FA Cup
First Round   Cambridge U   (a)   0-1

Capital One Cup
First Round   Rotherham U   (a)   0-1
(aet)

Johnstone's Paint Trophy
First Round   Morecambe   (h)   1-3

FULHAM

FOUNDATION

Churchgoers were responsible for the foundation of Fulham, which first saw the light of day as Fulham St Andrew's Church Sunday School FC in 1879. They won the West London Amateur Cup in 1887 and the championship of the West London League in its initial season of 1892–93. The name Fulham had been adopted in 1888.

Craven Cottage, Stevenage Road, London SW6 6HH.
Telephone: (0843) 208 1222.
Fax: (0870) 442 0236 (Motspur Park).
Ticket Line: (0843) 208 1234.
Website: www.fulhamfc.co.uk
Email: enquiries@fulhamfc.com
Ground Capacity: 25,700.
Record Attendance: 49,335 v Millwall, Division 2, 8 October 1938.
Pitch Measurements: 100m × 65m (109yd × 71yd)
Chairman: Shadid Khan.
Chief Executive: Alistair Mackintosh.
Manager: Kit Symons.
First Team Coach: Sam Reed.
Director of Sports Medicine and Exercise Science: Mark Taylor.

HONOURS

Football League –
Division 1: *Champions* 2000–01;
Division 2: *Champions* 1948–49, 1998–99; *Runners-up* 1958–59;
Division 3 (S): *Champions* 1931–32;
Division 3: *Runners-up* 1970–71, 1996–97.
FA Cup: *Runners-up* 1975.
Football League Cup: Best season: quarter-final, 1968, 1971, 2000, 2005.
European Competitions
UEFA Cup: 2002–03.
Intertoto Cup: 2002 (*winners*).
Europa League: 2009–10 (*runners-up*), 2011–12.

Colours: White shirts with grey stripes, black shorts with red trim, white socks with red trim.
Year Formed: 1879.
Turned Professional: 1898.
Reformed: 1987.
Previous Name: 1879, Fulham St Andrew's; 1888, Fulham.
Club Nickname: 'The Cottagers'.
Grounds: 1879, Star Road, Fulham; c.1883, Eel Brook Common, 1884, Lillie Road; 1885, Putney Lower Common; 1886, Ranelagh House, Fulham; 1888, Barn Elms, Castelnau; 1889, Purser's Cross (Roskell's Field), Parsons Green Lane; 1891, Eel Brook Common; 1891, Half Moon, Putney; 1895, Captain James Field, West Brompton; 1896, Craven Cottage.
First Football League Game: 3 September 1907, Division 2, v Hull C (h) L 0–1 – Skene; Ross, Lindsay; Collins, Morrison, Goldie; Dalrymple, Freeman, Bevan, Hubbard, Threlfall.
Record League Victory: 10–1 v Ipswich T, Division 1, 26 December 1963 – Macedo; Cohen, Langley; Mullery (1), Keetch, Robson (1); Key, Cook (1), Leggat (4), Haynes, Howfield (3).
Record Cup Victory: 7–0 v Swansea C, FA Cup 1st rd, 11 November 1995 – Lange; Jupp (1), Herrera, Barkus (Brooker (1)), Moore, Angus, Thomas (1), Morgan, Brazil (Hamill), Conroy (3) (Bolt), Cusack (1).
Record Defeat: 0–10 v Liverpool, League Cup 2nd rd 1st leg, 23 September 1986.

sky SPORTS FACT FILE

Goalkeeper Wilf Nixon, who played for Fulham between 1910 and 1921, is one of the very few footballers to have become a centurion. Born in 1882, he died in April 1985 at the age of 102. He fought with the Footballers' Battalion in the First World War when he was taken as a prisoner of war.

Most League Points (2 for a win): 60, Division 2, 1958–59 and Division 3, 1970–71.

Most League Points (3 for a win): 101, Division 2, 1998–99. 101, Division 1, 2000–01.

Most League Goals: 111, Division 3 (S), 1931–32.

Highest League Scorer in Season: Frank Newton, 43, Division 3 (S), 1931–32.

Most League Goals in Total Aggregate: Gordon Davies, 159, 1978–84, 1986–91.

Most League Goals in One Match: 5, Fred Harrison v Stockport Co, Division 2, 5 September 1908; 5, Bedford Jezzard v Hull C, Division 2, 8 October 1955; 5, Jimmy Hill v Doncaster R, Division 2, 15 March 1958; 5, Steve Earle v Halifax T, Division 3, 16 September 1969.

Most Capped Player: Johnny Haynes, 56, England.

Most League Appearances: Johnny Haynes, 594, 1952–70.

Youngest League Player: Matthew Briggs, 16 years 65 days v Middlesbrough, 13 May 2007.

Record Transfer Fee Received: £15,000,000 from Tottenham H for Moussa Dembele, August 2012.

Record Transfer Fee Paid: £12,400,00 to Olympiacos for Konstantinos Mitroglou, January 2014.

Football League Record: 1907 Elected to Division 2; 1928–32 Division 3 (S); 1932–49 Division 2; 1949–52 Division 1; 1952–59 Division 2; 1959–68 Division 1; 1968–69 Division 2; 1969–71 Division 3; 1971–80 Division 2; 1980–82 Division 3; 1982–86 Division 2; 1986–92 Division 3; 1992–94 Division 2; 1994–97 Division 3; 1997–99 Division 2; 1999–2001 Division 1; 2001–14 FA Premier League; 2014– FL C.

LATEST SEQUENCES

Longest Sequence of League Wins: 12, 7.5.2000 – 18.10.2000.

Longest Sequence of League Defeats: 11, 2.12.1961 – 24.2.1962.

Longest Sequence of League Draws: 6, 23.12.2006 – 20.1.2007.

Longest Sequence of Unbeaten League Matches: 15, 26.1.1999 – 13.4.1999.

Longest Sequence Without a League Win: 15, 25.2.1950 – 23.8.1950.

Successive Scoring Runs: 26 from 28.3.1931.

Successive Non-scoring Runs: 6 from 21.8.1971.

MANAGERS

Harry Bradshaw 1904–09
Phil Kelso 1909–24
Andy Ducat 1924–26
Joe Bradshaw 1926–29
Ned Liddell 1929–31
Jim McIntyre 1931–34
Jimmy Hogan 1934–35
Jack Peart 1935–48
Frank Osborne 1948–64
  (was Secretary-Manager or General Manager for most of this period and Team Manager 1953–56)
Bill Dodgin Snr 1949–53
Duggie Livingstone 1956–58
Bedford Jezzard 1958–64
  (General Manager for last two months)
Vic Buckingham 1965–68
Bobby Robson 1968
Bill Dodgin Jnr 1968–72
Alec Stock 1972–76
Bobby Campbell 1976–80
Malcolm Macdonald 1980–84
Ray Harford 1984–96
Ray Lewington 1986–90
Alan Dicks 1990–91
Don Mackay 1991–94
Ian Branfoot 1994–96
  (continued as General Manager)
Micky Adams 1996–97
Ray Wilkins 1997–98
Kevin Keegan 1998–99
  (Chief Operating Officer)
Paul Bracewell 1999–2000
Jean Tigana 2000–03
Chris Coleman 2003–07
Lawrie Sanchez 2007
Roy Hodgson 2007–10
Mark Hughes 2010–11
Martin Jol 2011–13
Rene Muelenstein 2013–14
Felix Magath 2014
Kit Symons October 2014–

TEN YEAR LEAGUE RECORD

		P	W	D	L	F	A	Pts	Pos
2005-06	PR Lge	38	14	6	18	48	58	48	12
2006-07	PR Lge	38	8	15	15	38	60	39	16
2007-08	PR Lge	38	8	12	18	38	60	36	17
2008-09	PR Lge	38	14	11	13	39	34	53	7
2009-10	PR Lge	38	12	10	16	39	46	46	12
2010-11	PR Lge	38	11	16	11	49	43	49	8
2011-12	PR Lge	38	14	10	14	48	51	52	9
2012-13	PR Lge	38	11	10	17	50	60	43	12
2013-14	PR Lge	38	9	5	24	40	85	32	19
2014-15	FL C	46	14	10	22	62	83	52	17

DID YOU KNOW ?

After playing for Fulham against Coventry City in November 1924 forward Harvey Darvill was taken to hospital with severe abdominal pains. He died four days later from a ruptured blood vessel in the stomach, believed to have been caused by an earlier collision with a goalkeeper.

FULHAM – FL CHAMPIONSHIP 2014–15 LEAGUE RECORD

Match No.	Date	Venue	Opponents	Result		H/T Score	Lg Pos.	Goalscorers	Attendance
1	Aug 9	A	Ipswich T	L	1-2	0-1	17	Hoogland [86]	17,218
2	16	H	Millwall	L	0-1	0-1	21		18,988
3	20	H	Wolverhampton W	L	0-1	0-1	23		18,627
4	23	A	Derby Co	L	1-5	0-1	24	Parker [54]	26,577
5	30	H	Cardiff C	D	1-1	1-0	23	Hoogland [22]	17,508
6	Sept 13	A	Reading	L	0-3	0-1	24		18,790
7	17	A	Nottingham F	L	3-5	1-2	24	McCormack 2 [31, 65], Rodallega [51]	22,572
8	20	H	Blackburn R	L	0-1	0-0	24		16,456
9	27	A	Birmingham C	W	2-1	0-1	23	Hoogland [63], Rodallega [71]	14,132
10	Oct 1	H	Bolton W	W	4-0	2-0	22	Rodallega [9], Amorebieta [45], Christensen [67], Hoogland [79]	14,496
11	4	A	Middlesbrough	L	0-2	0-0	22		16,201
12	18	H	Norwich C	W	1-0	1-0	22	Kavanagh [22]	20,776
13	21	A	Rotherham U	D	3-3	1-1	22	McCormack (pen) [33], Woodrow [58], Burn [90]	8981
14	24	H	Charlton Ath	W	3-0	2-0	19	Parker [6], Rodallega 2 [12, 89]	17,923
15	Nov 1	A	Wigan Ath	D	3-3	2-1	20	Christensen [30], Ruiz 2 (1 pen) [36, 88 (p)]	12,084
16	5	H	Blackpool	D	2-2	1-2	21	Parker [45], Ruiz [73]	14,325
17	8	H	Huddersfield T	W	3-1	1-0	17	Rodallega [18], Christensen [77], McCormack [84]	17,734
18	21	A	Brentford	L	1-2	0-0	17	Rodallega [57]	12,255
19	29	A	Brighton & HA	W	2-1	0-0	16	Rodallega [62], Christensen [77]	28,802
20	Dec 5	H	Watford	L	0-5	0-3	16		16,772
21	13	A	Leeds U	W	1-0	0-0	14	Rodallega [60]	27,264
22	20	H	Sheffield W	W	4-0	2-0	13	McCormack [34], Hutchinson [45], Christensen [67], Woodrow (pen) [90]	21,123
23	26	A	Bournemouth	L	0-2	0-1	15		10,926
24	29	H	Brighton & HA	L	0-2	0-0	17		20,619
25	Jan 10	A	Cardiff C	L	0-1	0-1	18		22,515
26	17	H	Reading	W	2-1	0-0	15	Kacaniklic [55], Ruiz [90]	17,831
27	21	H	Nottingham F	W	3-2	3-1	14	McCormack 3 [7, 18, 35]	15,512
28	31	A	Blackburn R	L	1-2	0-1	15	McCormack [66]	13,603
29	Feb 7	A	Birmingham C	D	1-1	1-1	16	Rodallega [5]	19,086
30	10	A	Bolton W	L	1-3	1-1	18	Hutchinson [21]	12,790
31	14	H	Ipswich T	L	1-2	0-2	19	McCormack [74]	19,816
32	21	A	Millwall	D	0-0	0-0	19		12,707
33	24	A	Wolverhampton W	L	0-3	0-3	20		17,744
34	28	H	Derby Co	W	2-0	2-0	19	Bodurov [31], Woodrow [45]	20,242
35	Mar 3	A	Watford	L	0-1	0-1	20		15,809
36	6	H	Bournemouth	L	1-5	0-2	20	Smith [66]	16,317
37	14	A	Sheffield W	D	1-1	0-0	20	Smith [75]	22,182
38	18	H	Leeds U	L	0-3	0-1	21		19,200
39	21	A	Huddersfield T	W	2-0	1-0	20	Kacaniklic [2], Fofana [90]	11,635
40	Apr 3	H	Brentford	L	1-4	0-1	20	McCormack (pen) [67]	23,271
41	7	A	Charlton Ath	D	1-1	1-1	20	McCormack [8]	16,521
42	10	A	Wigan Ath	D	2-2	2-1	20	McCormack [4], Smith [35]	15,994
43	15	A	Rotherham U	D	1-1	0-1	20	McCormack [67]	15,011
44	18	A	Blackpool	W	1-0	1-0	18	Smith [8]	10,122
45	25	H	Middlesbrough	W	4-3	1-0	17	Turner [45], McCormack 3 (2 pens) [55 (p), 67 (p), 90]	22,731
46	May 2	A	Norwich C	L	2-4	0-2	17	Johnson (og) [90], Smith [83]	26,662

Final League Position: 17

GOALSCORERS

League (62): McCormack 17 (4 pens), Rodallega 10, Christensen 5, Smith 5, Hoogland 4, Ruiz 4 (1 pen), Parker 3, Woodrow 3 (1 pen), Hutchinson 2, Kacaniklic 2, Amorebieta 1, Bodurov 1, Burn 1, Fofana 1, Kavanagh 1, Turner 1, own goal 1.
FA Cup (4): Woodrow 2, McCormack 1 (1 pen), Rodallega 1.
Capital One Cup (5): Dembele 2, Burn 1, McCormack 1, Ruiz 1.

Joronen J 4	Hoogland T 22+3	Bodurov N 36+2	Hutchinson S 25	Stafylidis K 34+4	Burgess C 4	Parker S 35+2	Hyndman E 9	David C 3+2	Dembele M 2+9	McCormack R 43+1	Eisfeld T 2+5	Woodrow C 10+19	Roberts P 2+15	Christensen L 24+1	Williams G 7+7	Rodallega H 30+3	Kavanagh S 14+5	Fotheringham M 2	Williams R 1+1	Kacaniklic A 8+6	Voser K 2+1	Bettinelli M 39	Burn D 20	Chihi A —+1	Kiraly G 3+1	Smith M 8+7	Zverotic E 5+5	Amorebieta F 7	Ruiz B 23+6	Grimmer J 13	Fofana S 13+8	Tunnicliffe R 22	Richards A 14	Turner M 9	Husband J 5	Guthrie D 6	Match No.
1	2	3	4^2	5	6	7	8	9^3	10	11^1	12	13	14																								1
1	2	3		5	4	7	8	14		12	11^3	13		6^1	9^2	10																					2
1	2	3	9	4	7				12	11		10^3	6		13		5^2	8^1	14																		3
1	2^3	3	9^2	4	8					11		14	10	6^1		5			7	12	13																4
	6	3		5			8^3	7	9^1	13	11	14	10^2							2	1	4	12														5
	6	3		5			7	8^1	9^2	11			14	12		5				2^3		4		1	10^4	13											6
	6	2	3^1	9		8		12		11			13			10		7^2				4		1		5											7
	2		3^3	8^1		7				11				13	6	12	10					1	4				5	9^2									8
	2	3		12		6	7^1			11		13		8		10						1	4				5	9^2									9
	2	3		8		6^2				11^1		13	14	7	12	10^3						1	4				5	9									10
	2	3		8^2		6				10			13	7	12	11						1	4			14		5^1	9^3								11
	2^2	3		8		6			13	11				7		10	5					1	4				12	9^1									12
		3		5		13	7^1		12	11	6^3	10^2		8	9							1	4		14	2											13
	2	3		5		6				11^2		12	14	7		10^1	8					1	4			13		9^3									14
		3		5		6			12	11^4				7	8^1	10						1	4			2		9									15
		3		12		6			11^2			14	13	7	8^3	10						1	4			2	5^1	9									16
		3		5		6			12	11	13			7	8^2	10						1	4			2		9^1									17
		3		5		8				11	12			7	9	10						1	4			2		6^1									18
		3	4	5		6	8^3			10		13		7		11						1					14	9^2	2^1	12							19
		3		5		6				11				7	13	10						1^4	4	12				9^1	2	8^2							20
		3	4	5		6				11		12		7		10^1						1				13		9	2	8^2							21
		3	4	5		6				11		13	14	7	12	10^3						1						9^1	2	8^2							22
		3	4	5		6				11		14	13	7^3	12	10^1						1						9^2	2	8							23
		4	3	5^2		6	7^1			9		12	14		10^2	11	13					1							2	8							24
		4	3	5		6			14	9		10^3			11^2	12			13			1							2	7^1	8						25
		4	3	5		6				11		12			10^2			9^1				1							13	2	8	7					26
		4	3	5		6^2				11		13			10^1			9				1							12	2	8	7					27
		4	3	5		7^3			13	11		9^1		8	10^4			12				1								14	6	2					28
		4	3	5						10			12	7^1	11			9				1								8	6	2					29
		4	3	5		12				11		13		7	14	10^3			9^1			1								2	8^2	6					30
		4	3	5		6				11		12	14	7^3		10^2			9^1			1							13		8	2					31
		4	3	5		6				11		7			10^1			9^1				1							12	13	8^2	2					32
		4	3	5						11		13		7	10^1	12			1										9		8^2	6	2				33
13		4	3	5		6^2			14	11		10^1		7^1		12			1										9		8	2					34
		4	3	5						11		10^1			12	8^1	14		1					13		9^2		7	6	2						35
2		4	3	13		6				10					11^2	8^1			1					12		5^4	9^3	14	7								36
2^2		4	9	7						11	12				6^1				1					10					13	8	5	3					37
7		3	5^4	6						10^2								12	1					11		9^1			13	8	2	4					38
7	12	3^4								10^1				14	8^2		9^3		1					11					2	13	6	5	4				39
12	3									11		10^2			14		9^1		1					13			2^1	7	8			4	5	6		40
2				6						11					9²		13	1	3					10		12			7		4	5	8^1			41
6		14		8						11^3	12				9^1				1	4				10^2		13	2		7		3	5					42
12				6						10									1	4				11		9					8^1	2	3	5	7		43
6										11	12				9				1	4				10^1						7	2	3	5	8		44
2	3									11	13				10^3	8			1					14		9^1		12	6	5	4		7^2			45
2^2	12	3								11		14			10^1	8^1			1	4				13		9			7	5		6				46

FA Cup

Third Round	Wolverhampton W	(h)	0-0
Replay	Wolverhampton W	(a)	3-3
(aet; Fulham won 5-3 on penalties)			
Fourth Round	Sunderland	(a)	0-0
Replay	Sunderland	(h)	1-3

Capital One Cup

Second Round	Brentford	(a)	1-0
Third Round	Doncaster R	(h)	2-1
Fourth Round	Derby Co	(h)	2-5

GILLINGHAM

FOUNDATION

The success of the pioneering Royal Engineers of Chatham excited the interest of the residents of the Medway Towns and led to the formation of many clubs including Excelsior. After winning the Kent Junior Cup and the Chatham District League in 1893, Excelsior decided to go for bigger things and it was at a meeting in the Napier Arms, Brompton, in 1893 that New Brompton FC came into being, buying and developing the ground which is now Priestfield Stadium. They changed their name to Gillingham in 1913, when they also changed their strip from black and white stripes to predominantly blue.

MEMS Priestfield Stadium, Redfern Avenue, Gillingham, Kent ME7 4DD.

Telephone: (01634) 300 000.

Fax: (01634) 850 986.

Ticket Office: (01634) 300 000 (option 1).

Website: www.gillinghamfootballclub.com

Email: info@priestfield.com

Ground Capacity: 11,440.

Record Attendance: 23,002 v QPR, FA Cup 3rd rd, 10 January 1948.

Pitch Measurements: 100.5m × 64m (110yd × 70yd)

Chairman: Paul D. P. Scally.

Vice-chairman: Michael Anderson.

Manager: Justin Edinburgh.

Assistant Manager: Andy Hessenthaler.

Physio: Gary Hemens.

Colours: Blue shirts with white stripe, blue shorts with white trim, white socks with blue trim.

Year Formed: 1893.

Turned Professional: 1894.

Previous Name: 1893, New Brompton; 1913, Gillingham.

Club Nickname: 'The Gills'.

Ground: 1893, Priestfield Stadium (renamed KRBS Priestfield Stadium 2009, MEMS Priestfield Stadium 2011).

First Football League Game: 28 August 1920, Division 3, v Southampton (h) D 1–1 – Branfield; Robertson, Sissons; Battiste, Baxter, Wigmore; Holt, Hall, Gilbey (1), Roe, Gore.

Record League Victory: 10–0 v Chesterfield, Division 3, 5 September 1987 – Kite; Haylock, Pearce, Shipley (2) (Lillis), West, Greenall (1), Pritchard (2), Shearer (2), Lovell, Elsey (2), David Smith (1).

HONOURS

Football League – FL C: 22nd, 2007–08; **Division 3:** *Runners-up* 1995–96; **Division 4:** *Champions* 1963–64; *Runners-up* 1973–74; **FL 2:** *Champions* 2012–13.

FA Cup: Best season: 6th rd, 2000.

Football League Cup: Best season: 4th rd, 1964, 1997.

sky SPORTS FACT FILE

Forward Billy Jervis made his only appearance for Gillingham against Barrow in October 1961. The Gills arrived late having missed their rail connection in London and the game was eventually abandoned after 76 minutes with Barrow 7-0 up. The Football League ordered the result to stand and as a result Jervis's appearance counts for official records.

Record Cup Victory: 10–1 v Gorleston, FA Cup 1st rd, 16 November 1957 – Brodie; Parry, Hannaway; Riggs, Boswell, Laing; Payne, Fletcher (2), Saunders (5), Morgan (1), Clark (2).

Record Defeat: 2–9 v Nottingham F, Division 3 (S), 18 November 1950.

Most League Points (2 for a win): 62, Division 4, 1973–74.

Most League Points (3 for a win): 85, Division 2, 1999–2000.

Most League Goals: 90, Division 4, 1973–74.

Highest League Scorer in Season: Ernie Morgan, 31, Division 3 (S), 1954–55; Brian Yeo, 31, Division 4, 1973–74.

Most League Goals in Total Aggregate: Brian Yeo, 135, 1963–75.

Most League Goals in One Match: 6, Fred Cheesmur v Merthyr T, Division 3 (S), 26 April 1930.

Most Capped Player: Andrew Crofts, 12 (27), Wales.

Most League Appearances: John Simpson, 571, 1957–72.

Youngest League Player: Luke Freeman, 15 years 247 days v Hartlepool U, 24 November 2007.

Record Transfer Fee Received: £1,500,000 from Manchester C for Robert Taylor, November 1999.

Record Transfer Fee Paid: £600,000 to Reading for Carl Asaba, August 1998.

Football League Record: 1920 Original Member of Division 3; 1921 Division 3 (S); 1938 Failed re-election; Southern League 1938–44; Kent League 1944–46; Southern League 1946–50; 1950 Re-elected to Division 3 (S); 1958–64 Division 4; 1964–71 Division 3; 1971–74 Division 4; 1974–89 Division 3; 1989–92 Division 4; 1992–96; Division 3; 1996–2000 Division 2; 2000–04 Division 1; 2004–05 FL C; 2005–08 FL 1; 2008–09 FL 2; 2009–10 FL 1; 2010–13 FL 2; 2013– FL 1.

LATEST SEQUENCES

Longest Sequence of League Wins: 7, 18.12.1954 – 29.1.1955.

Longest Sequence of League Defeats: 10, 20.9.1988 – 5.11.1988.

Longest Sequence of League Draws: 5, 28.8.1993 – 18.9.1993.

Longest Sequence of Unbeaten League Matches: 20, 13.10.1973 – 10.2.1974.

Longest Sequence Without a League Win: 15, 1.4.1972 – 2.9.1972.

Successive Scoring Runs: 20 from 31.10.1959.

Successive Non-scoring Runs: 6 from 11.2.1961.

MANAGERS

W. Ironside Groombridge
  1896–1906 *(Secretary-Manager)*
  (previously Financial Secretary)
Steve Smith 1906–08
W. I. Groombridge 1908–19
  (Secretary-Manager)
George Collins 1919–20
John McMillan 1920–23
Harry Curtis 1923–26
Albert Hoskins 1926–29
Dick Hendrie 1929–31
Fred Mavin 1932–37
Alan Ure 1937–38
Bill Harvey 1938–39
Archie Clark 1939–58
Harry Barratt 1958–62
Freddie Cox 1962–65
Basil Hayward 1966–71
Andy Nelson 1971–74
Len Ashurst 1974–75
Gerry Summers 1975–81
Keith Peacock 1981–87
Paul Taylor 1988
Keith Burkinshaw 1988–89
Damien Richardson 1989–92
Glenn Roeder 1992–93
Mike Flanagan 1993–95
Neil Smillie 1995
Tony Pulis 1995–99
Peter Taylor 1999–2000
Andy Hessenthaler 2000–04
Stan Ternent 2004–05
Neale Cooper 2005
Ronnie Jepson 2005–07
Mark Stimson 2007–10
Andy Hessenthaler 2010–12
Martin Allen 2012–13
Peter Taylor 2013–14
Justin Edinburgh February 2015–

TEN YEAR LEAGUE RECORD

		P	W	D	L	F	A	Pts	Pos
2005-06	FL 1	46	16	12	18	50	64	60	14
2006-07	FL 1	46	17	8	21	56	77	59	16
2007-08	FL 1	46	11	13	22	44	73	46	22
2008-09	FL 2	46	21	12	13	58	55	75	5
2009-10	FL 1	46	12	14	20	48	64	50	21
2010-11	FL 2	46	17	17	12	67	57	68	8
2011-12	FL 2	46	20	10	16	79	62	70	8
2012-13	FL 2	46	23	14	9	66	39	83	1
2013-14	FL 1	46	15	8	23	60	79	53	17
2014-15	FL 1	46	16	14	16	65	66	62	12

DID YOU KNOW

When Gillingham won the Division Four title in 1963–64 they were unbeaten in 26 home League and Cup games. The defence provided a secure foundation and only 6 teams managed to score more than a single goal against them in their 46 League games. The Gills were also the best supported team in the division that season.

GILLINGHAM – FOOTBALL LEAGUE ONE 2014–15 LEAGUE RECORD

Match No.	Date	Venue	Opponents	Result	H/T Score	Lg Pos.	Goalscorers	Attendance
1	Aug 9	A	Milton Keynes D	L	2-4	2-1	22	McDonald [7], Kedwell (pen) [29]	7595
2	16	H	Yeovil T	W	2-0	1-0	13	Martin [35], Kedwell [55]	5173
3	19	H	Swindon T	D	2-2	1-1	13	Kedwell [9], Hause [51]	5264
4	23	A	Barnsley	L	1-4	0-2	18	Kedwell [74]	9163
5	30	H	Crewe Alex	W	2-0	2-0	13	Dack [18], McDonald [45]	4998
6	Sept 5	A	Coventry C	L	0-1	0-1	14		27,306
7	13	A	Oldham Ath	D	0-0	0-0	15		3785
8	16	H	Peterborough U	W	2-1	1-1	10	McDonald 2 (1 pen) [26, 86 (p)]	4819
9	20	H	Walsall	D	0-0	0-0	12		5344
10	27	A	Sheffield U	L	1-2	0-0	13	Norris [83]	18,487
11	Oct 4	A	Notts Co	L	0-1	0-1	18		4800
12	11	H	Scunthorpe U	L	0-3	0-1	20		7042
13	18	A	Rochdale	D	1-1	0-1	18	McDonald [83]	2574
14	21	H	Preston NE	L	0-1	0-0	19		4632
15	25	H	Crawley T	D	1-1	1-1	21	Legge [44]	4850
16	Nov 1	A	Fleetwood T	L	0-1	0-1	22		2951
17	15	H	Leyton Orient	W	3-2	0-0	19	Legge 2 [55, 74], McDonald [90]	5891
18	22	A	Bradford C	D	1-1	0-0	20	German [90]	12,434
19	29	H	Port Vale	D	2-2	1-1	20	Egan 2 [29, 55]	4799
20	Dec 13	A	Doncaster R	W	2-1	0-0	18	Norris 2 [51, 77]	5542
21	20	H	Chesterfield	L	2-3	0-1	19	McDonald [59], Egan [61]	6841
22	26	A	Colchester U	W	2-1	2-0	18	Martin [25], Dack [34]	4544
23	28	A	Bristol C	L	1-3	0-2	19	McDonald [47]	6216
24	Jan 3	A	Port Vale	L	1-2	1-1	20	McDonald [31]	4783
25	10	A	Crewe Alex	L	1-3	0-2	21	Dack [55]	4436
26	17	H	Coventry C	W	3-1	0-1	19	Marquis [82], McDonald (pen) [88], McGlashan [90]	5141
27	24	H	Oldham Ath	W	3-2	2-2	16	Marquis 2 [7, 14], Dack [70]	4959
28	Feb 1	A	Walsall	D	1-1	0-0	18	Dack [69]	3951
29	7	H	Sheffield U	W	2-0	0-0	17	McGlashan [86], McDonald [90]	5704
30	10	A	Peterborough U	W	2-1	1-0	15	Dack [30], Marquis [79]	4449
31	14	H	Milton Keynes D	W	4-2	2-1	12	McDonald [9], Dack [38], Garmston [75], Marquis [81]	5107
32	21	A	Yeovil T	D	2-2	0-1	11	Marquis [49], Norris [87]	4293
33	28	H	Barnsley	L	0-1	0-0	14		5905
34	Mar 3	A	Swindon T	W	3-0	1-0	12	McDonald 2 [29, 88], Hessenthaler [46]	7025
35	7	H	Doncaster R	D	1-1	1-1	14	Marquis [44]	5909
36	14	H	Bristol C	D	0-0	0-0	14		11,601
37	17	A	Chesterfield	L	0-3	0-2	14		4804
38	21	H	Colchester U	D	2-2	0-0	14	Ehmer [82], Loft [90]	5319
39	28	A	Crawley T	W	2-1	1-0	14	Dack [40], McGlashan [81]	3570
40	Apr 3	A	Fleetwood T	L	0-1	0-1	14		7961
41	6	A	Leyton Orient	D	3-3	2-1	14	McGlashan [35], McDonald 2 (1 pen) [43, 56 (p)]	6634
42	11	H	Bradford C	W	1-0	0-0	12	Marquis [72]	5221
43	14	A	Preston NE	D	2-2	0-2	13	McGlashan [58], Legge [90]	9417
44	18	H	Rochdale	W	1-0	1-0	9	Dack [14]	5430
45	25	A	Scunthorpe U	L	1-2	1-2	12	Norris [2]	3763
46	May 3	H	Notts Co	W	3-1	0-0	12	Egan [88], Dickenson [90], Norris [90]	8443

Final League Position: 12

GOALSCORERS

League (65): McDonald 16 (3 pens), Dack 9, Marquis 8, Norris 6, McGlashan 5, Egan 4, Kedwell 4 (1 pen), Legge 4, Martin 2, Dickenson 1, Ehmer 1, Garmston 1, German 1, Hause 1, Hessenthaler 1, Loft 1.
FA Cup (1): Kedwell 1 (1 pen).
Capital One Cup (2): Dickenson 1, Morris, A 1.
Johnstone's Paint Trophy (10): McDonald 2, McGlashan 2, Dack 1, Dickenson 1, Egan 1, German 1, Loft 1, Norris 1 (1 pen).

Nelson S 24	Egan J 45	Hause K 14	Legge L 21+1	Martin J 22+3	Morris A 20+3	Loft D 36	Hessenthaler J 35+2	McGlashan J 23+17	Kedwell D 10+4	McDonald C 38+5	Morris G 9+1	German A 1+9	Dickenson B 17+17	Bywater S 13	Hare J 2	Fish M 2+1	Pritchard J 14+11	Davies C 5	Dack B 35+7	Hoyte G 26+4	Norris L 13+24	Linganzi A 3+4	Doughty M 9	Chicksen A 3	Ehmer M 27	Galbraith D 3+4	Lennon H 2	Marquis J 18+3	Garmston B 7+1	Muldoon O 3	Bell A 6+1	Freiter M —+1	Match No.
1¹	2	3	4	5	6	7	8²	9	10	11²	12	13	14																				1
	2	4	3	9¹	7	8	5		10				11³	13	1	6²	12	14															2
	3	4	2				8	13	10		12	1					5²		12	8	2	14											3
	3	5	4		6²		7	11³	10	13		9¹	1				12		8	2	14												4
	3	4		5	8		7	9¹	10²	11¹		12	1				14		6	2	13												5
	3	4		5	9		7	6²		11		14	10²	1			12		2¹	8	13												6
	3	4		5	9		7	6		11²		14	10	1			12		2¹	8²	13												7
	3	4		5	2	7²	8⁹	6		10		14	1				12		9		11¹	13											8
	3	4		5	2	8	7³	6		10		13	12	1					9²		11¹	14											9
	3	4		6		8	13		11¹			10	1				7	5	2	12	9²												10
	3	4		5	2	7	8²	6³		11		14	10¹	1			9		13	12													11
	4			5	2³	8⁴		6		10		14	13	1			7¹	3	9		11²	12											12
	3	5¹	4			8	14		11			6	1			2	9		10¹	13	12	7²											13
1	4		3	5		7	6¹	10³	11		14	9					8²		12	2	13												14
1	3		4	5		7	6⁴	10¹	11			9					13	2	14		8³												15
	3	4	2	9		7²		12	10³	11			1				6	13	5¹	14	8												16
1	3		4		6	7	9²	10		13			11				12	2	8⁴	5													17
1	2	3²	4		6	7	12	14	11³	13	10						8¹	5			9												18
1	3		2		6	7	12		11³	13	10						14	5¹			8²	9	4										19
1	3		2	9		7	5			10							8¹		11		6		4	12									20
1	3		2	9		6	5	12	14	13			11²				8¹		10³		7	4											21
1	4		6	2²				13	10				14				7		9³		11¹	12	8		5	3							22
1	2		5			7	13	10²	11				12				6³				14	9¹	8		4	3							23
1	2		4	5	8¹	9		13	11			10²					14		6	12		3³											24
1		4			6	7	9²	10		13	2						8		5	12				3		11¹							25
1	3			7	8	12	11		13								6²		9	2					4			10	5¹				26
1	3	14		8	7¹	13	10		12								6		9	2				4		11³	5²						27
1	4			2	8²	9	10										6³								3	13	11	12					28
1	3			8	7	13	11										6¹		9	2					4	12		10²	5				29
1	3	13		8	7	12	11¹												9	2	14				4	6²		10	5³				30
1	3			8	7	12	11												9	2	13				4	6²		10¹	5				31
1	3			7	6	12	10³						14				8²		2	13					4	9¹		11	5				32
1	3	12		8	7³	6	11										9		2¹	13					4	14		10	5²				33
1	3		5		9	6	11										7		8	2	12				4			10¹					34
1	3		5	12	7	8	14		11³								6²		9¹	2	13				4			10					35
1	3		5	7	9	12	11										8		2	13					4			10²	6¹				36
1	3		5²	6	8	12	13		11								9		2	14					4			10¹	7¹				37
	3		6²	8	7	12		10	1				14				9		2	11¹					4			13			5³		38
	3		2	7		8		12	1	13							9		6	11¹					4			10²			5		39
	3²	14	6	9		7		12	1	13							8		2	11¹					4			10³			5		40
	2	4²	13	9	7¹	6		11	1								8		12	10					3						5		41
	2	4	12	8	6³	7		10	1	14							9			11²					3			13			5¹		42
	2	4	7¹	9		6		11²	1	12			14				8			13					3			10			5³		43
	2	3	7	8⁹		5²		11¹	1	9			13				6			12					4			10		14			44
	2	4²	6	7	5¹	10		1	8				12	13			11								3			14	9¹				45
	2	3	8¹	6		5		10²	1	9							7			12					4			11				13	46

FA Cup

First Round	Bristol C	(h)	1-2

Capital One Cup

First Round	Yeovil T	(a)	2-1
Second Round	Newcastle U	(h)	0-1

Johnstone's Paint Trophy

First Round	Stevenage	(a)	1-0
Second Round	Colchester U	(a)	3-3

(Gillingham won 4-2 on penalties)

Southern Quarter-Finals	Crawley T	(a)	2-1
Southern Semi-Finals	Leyton Orient	(h)	1-0
Southern Final 1st leg	Bristol C	(h)	2-4
Southern Final 2nd leg	Bristol C	(a)	1-1

HARTLEPOOL UNITED

FOUNDATION

The inspiration for the launching of Hartlepool United was the West Hartlepool club which won the FA Amateur Cup in 1904–05. They had been in existence since 1881 and their cup success led in 1908 to the formation of the new professional concern which first joined the North-Eastern League. In those days they were Hartlepools United and won the Durham Senior Cup in their first two seasons.

Victoria Park, Clarence Road, Hartlepool TS24 8BZ.

Telephone: (01429) 272 584.

Fax: (01429) 863 007.

Ticket Office: (01429) 272 584 (option 2).

Website: www.hartlepoolunited.co.uk

Email: enquires@hartlepoolunited.co.uk

Ground Capacity: 7,856.

Record Attendance: 17,426 v Manchester U, FA Cup 3rd rd, 5 January 1957.

Pitch Measurements: 100.5m × 67.5m (110yd × 74yd)

Chairman: Ken Hodcroft.

Chief Executive: Russ Green.

Manager: Ronnie Moore.

Assistant Manager: Sam Collins.

Physio: Ian Gallagher.

Colours: Blue and white striped shirts, blue shorts, white socks with blue trim.

Year Formed: 1908.

Turned Professional: 1908.

Previous Names: 1908, Hartlepools United; 1968, Hartlepool; 1977, Hartlepool United.

Club Nickname: 'The Pool', 'Monkey Hangers'.

Ground: 1908, Victoria Park.

First Football League Game: 27 August 1921, Division 3 (N), v Wrexham (a) W 2–0 – Gill; Thomas, Crilly; Dougherty, Hopkins, Short; Kessler, Mulholland (1), Lister (1), Robertson, Donald.

Record League Victory: 10–1 v Barrow, Division 4, 4 April 1959 – Oakley; Cameron, Waugh; Johnson, Moore, Anderson; Scott (1), Langland (1), Smith (3), Clark (2), Luke (2), (1 og).

Record Cup Victory: 6–0 v North Shields, FA Cup 1st rd, 30 November 1946 – Heywood; Brown, Gregory; Spelman, Lambert, Jones; Price, Scott (2), Sloan (4), Moses, McMahon; 6–0 v Gainsborough Trinity (a), FA Cup 1st rd, 10 November 2007 – Budtz; McCunnie, Humphreys, Liddle (1) (Antwi), Nelson, Clark, Moore (1), Sweeney, Barker (2) (Monkhouse), Mackay (Porter 1), Brown (1).

Record Defeat: 1–10 v Wrexham, Division 4, 3 March 1962.

HONOURS

Football League –
FL 2: *Runners-up* 2006–07;
Division 3: *Runners-up* 2002–03;
Division 3 (N): *Runners-up* 1956–57.
FA Cup: Best season: 4th rd, 1955, 1978, 1989, 1993, 2005, 2009.
Football League Cup: Best season: 4th rd, 1975.

sky SPORTS FACT FILE

In their 1951–52 FA Cup campaign Hartlepool United defeated Rhyl and Watford before being given an away draw at First Division club Burnley in the third round. United took 5,000 fans to Turf Moor in three special trains and a fleet of 80 buses which formed a mile long convoy. Burnley scraped through into the fourth round with a 1-0 victory in a hard fought game.

Most League Points (2 for a win): 60, Division 4, 1967–68.

Most League Points (3 for a win): 88, FL 2, 2006–07.

Most League Goals: 90, Division 3 (N), 1956–57.

Highest League Scorer in Season: William Robinson, 28, Division 3 (N), 1927–28; Joe Allon, 28, Division 4, 1990–91.

Most League Goals in Total Aggregate: Ken Johnson, 98, 1949–64.

Most League Goals in One Match: 5, Harry Simmons v Wigan Borough, Division 3 (N), 1 January 1931; 5, Bobby Folland v Oldham Ath, Division 3 (N), 15 April 1961.

Most Capped Player: Ambrose Fogarty, 1 (11), Republic of Ireland.

Most League Appearances: Richie Humphreys, 481, 2001–13.

Youngest League Player: David Foley, 16 years 105 days v Port Vale, 25 August 2003.

Record Transfer Fee Received: £750,000 from Ipswich T for Tommy Miller, July 2001.

Record Transfer Fee Paid: £80,000 to Mansfield T for Darrell Clarke, July 2001.

Football League Record: 1921 Original Member of Division 3 (N); 1958–68 Division 4; 1968–69 Division 3; 1969–91 Division 4; 1991–92 Division 3; 1992–94 Division 2; 1994–2003 Division 3; 2003–04 Division 2; 2004–06 FL 1; 2006–07 FL 2; 2007–13 FL 1; 2013– FL 2.

LATEST SEQUENCES

Longest Sequence of League Wins: 9, 18.11.2006 – 1.1.2007.

Longest Sequence of League Defeats: 8, 27.1.1993 – 27.2.1993.

Longest Sequence of League Draws: 6, 30.4.2011 – 20.8.2011.

Longest Sequence of Unbeaten League Matches: 23, 18.11.2006 – 30.3.2007.

Longest Sequence Without a League Win: 20, 8.9.2012 – 26.12.2012.

Successive Scoring Runs: 27 from 18.11.2006.

Successive Non-scoring Runs: 11 from 9.1.1993.

MANAGERS

Alfred Priest 1908–12
Percy Humphreys 1912–13
Jack Manners 1913–20
Cecil Potter 1920–22
David Gordon 1922–24
Jack Manners 1924–27
Bill Norman 1927–31
Jack Carr 1932–35
  (had been Player-Coach from 1931)
Jimmy Hamilton 1935–43
Fred Westgarth 1943–57
Ray Middleton 1957–59
Bill Robinson 1959–62
Allenby Chilton 1962–63
Bob Gurney 1963–64
Alvan Williams 1964–65
Geoff Twentyman 1965
Brian Clough 1965–67
Angus McLean 1967–70
John Simpson 1970–71
Len Ashurst 1971–74
Ken Hale 1974–76
Billy Horner 1976–83
Johnny Duncan 1983
Mike Docherty 1983
Billy Horner 1984–86
John Bird 1986–88
Bobby Moncur 1988–89
Cyril Knowles 1989–91
Alan Murray 1991–93
Viv Busby 1993
John MacPhail 1993–94
David McCreery 1994–95
Keith Houchen 1995–96
Mick Tait 1996–99
Chris Turner 1999–2002
Mike Newell 2002–03
Neale Cooper 2003–05
Martin Scott 2005–06
Danny Wilson 2006–08
Chris Turner 2008–10
Mick Wadsworth 2010–11
Neale Cooper 2011–12
John Hughes 2012–13
Colin Cooper 2013–14
Ronnie Moore December 2014–

TEN YEAR LEAGUE RECORD

		P	W	D	L	F	A	Pts	Pos
2005-06	FL 1	46	11	17	18	44	59	50	21
2006-07	FL 2	46	26	10	10	65	40	88	2
2007-08	FL 1	46	15	9	22	63	66	54	15
2008-09	FL 1	46	13	11	22	66	79	50	19
2009-10	FL 1	46	14	11	21	59	67	50*	20
2010-11	FL 1	46	15	12	19	47	65	57	16
2011-12	FL 1	46	14	14	18	50	55	56	13
2012-13	FL 1	46	9	14	23	39	67	41	23
2013-14	FL 2	46	14	11	21	50	56	53	19
2014-15	FL 2	46	12	9	25	39	70	45	22

*3 pts deducted.

DID YOU KNOW ?

Hartlepools United ended their first season as members of the Football League with a five-match tour of Spain. United defeated Racing Club Santander in the three fixtures between the teams in May 1922; later the same month they faced Oviedo, losing the first game 5-0 but going on to win the second match 1-0.

HARTLEPOOL UNITED – FOOTBALL LEAGUE TWO 2014–15 LEAGUE RECORD

Match No.	Date		Venue	Opponents		Result	H/T Score	Lg Pos.	Goalscorers	Atten- dance
1	Aug	9	A	Stevenage	L	0-1	0-0	16		3023
2		16	H	Bury	L	0-2	0-1	23		3246
3		19	H	Dagenham & R	L	0-2	0-1	23		2792
4		23	A	AFC Wimbledon	W	2-1	0-1	19	Wyke [46], Harewood [68]	3576
5		30	A	Cheltenham T	L	0-1	0-0	20		2735
6	Sept	6	H	Shrewsbury T	W	2-0	1-0	18	Wyke [5], Walker [79]	3368
7		13	H	Tranmere R	D	0-0	0-0	20		3245
8		16	A	Northampton T	L	1-5	1-3	21	Wyke [1]	3653
9		20	A	Plymouth Arg	L	0-2	0-1	23		6146
10		27	H	Portsmouth	D	0-0	0-0	22		3439
11	Oct	4	H	Carlisle U	L	0-3	0-0	24		3927
12		11	A	Exeter C	W	2-1	0-0	21	Woods [49], Wyke [66]	3547
13		18	H	Luton T	L	1-2	0-1	22	Austin (pen) [90]	4225
14		21	A	Accrington S	L	1-3	1-2	23	Bates [42]	947
15		25	A	Cambridge U	L	1-2	0-1	24	Walker [59]	4933
16	Nov	1	H	Newport Co	D	2-2	0-1	24	Walker [80], Duckworth [87]	3172
17		15	A	Southend U	L	0-1	0-0	24		5436
18		22	H	York C	L	1-3	1-0	24	Fenwick [27]	4234
19		29	H	Wycombe W	L	1-3	0-1	24	Harewood [84]	3053
20	Dec	13	A	Burton Alb	L	0-4	0-1	24		2474
21		20	H	Oxford U	D	1-1	0-0	24	Ironside [53]	4070
22		26	A	Mansfield T	D	1-1	0-1	24	Duckworth [51]	3357
23		28	H	Morecambe	L	0-2	0-1	24		4108
24	Jan	3	A	Wycombe W	L	0-1	0-1	24		3607
25		10	H	Cheltenham T	W	2-0	1-0	24	Fenwick [38], Bingham [68]	3155
26		17	A	Shrewsbury T	L	0-3	0-0	24		4601
27		24	A	Tranmere R	D	1-1	1-1	24	Fenwick [14]	5488
28		31	H	Plymouth Arg	W	3-2	1-1	24	Franks 2 [8, 54], Fenwick [76]	3291
29	Feb	7	A	Portsmouth	L	0-1	0-1	24		14,397
30		10	H	Northampton T	W	1-0	0-0	24	Morgan [51]	2856
31		14	H	Stevenage	L	1-3	0-1	24	Fenwick [49]	3388
32		21	A	Bury	L	0-1	0-0	24		3172
33		28	H	AFC Wimbledon	W	1-0	0-0	24	Bird [73]	3345
34	Mar	3	A	Dagenham & R	L	0-2	0-1	24		1799
35		7	H	Burton Alb	L	0-1	0-0	24		3289
36		14	A	Morecambe	W	1-0	1-0	24	Parrish (og) [35]	1673
37		17	A	Oxford U	W	2-0	1-0	24	Bird [33], Austin [51]	4375
38		21	H	Mansfield T	W	1-0	0-0	24	Walker (pen) [47]	4166
39		28	H	Cambridge U	W	2-1	1-1	22	Walker [20], Harrison [67]	5009
40	Apr	3	A	Newport Co	D	2-2	2-1	22	Minshull (og) [15], Hugill [37]	3531
41		6	H	Southend U	L	0-1	0-0	22		5393
42		11	A	York C	L	0-1	0-0	22		5424
43		14	H	Accrington S	D	1-1	0-1	22	Harewood [80]	4159
44		18	A	Luton T	L	0-3	0-2	22		8231
45		25	H	Exeter C	W	2-1	2-1	22	Fenwick [15], Hugill [44]	4994
46	May	2	A	Carlisle U	D	3-3	0-3	22	Hugill 2 [63, 86], Duckworth [64]	8105

Final League Position: 22

GOALSCORERS

League (39): Fenwick 6, Walker 5 (1 pen), Hugill 4, Wyke 4, Duckworth 3, Harewood 3, Austin 2 (1 pen), Bird 2, Franks 2, Bates 1, Bingham 1, Harrison 1, Ironside 1, Morgan 1, Woods 1, own goals 2.
FA Cup (3): Franks 3.
Capital One Cup (2): Austin 1 (1 pen), Franks 1.
Johnstone's Paint Trophy (1): Duckworth 1.

Flinders S 46	Duckworth M 37	Bates M 25	Collins S 7	Austin N 46	Walker B 25+3	Miller T 14+1	Parnaby S 5	Compton J 17+4	James L 3+1	Harewood M 17+17	Brobbel R 13+2	Franks J 38+7	Holden D 7+4	Woods M 16+7	Hawkins L 4+8	Wyke C 13	Richards J 5+4	Harrison S 36	Jones D 23+2	Smith C 3+5	Crooks M 2+1	Featherstone N 22+3	Schmeltz S 2+3	Fenwick S 10+9	Ironside J 3+1	Campbell A 1+1	Lanzoni M 1	Dolan M 2	Green K —+1	Tshibola A 23	Bingham R 5	Mirfin D 15	Morgan M 4+1	Jones J 1+10	Bird R 6	Hugill J 8	Nelson-Addy E 1+1	Match No.
1	2	3	4	5	6^1	7	8^2	9	10	11	12	13																										1
1	2	3		4	8	7	6^1		11	10	12	9	5																									2
1	5	4		3	7^2			6^3	12	11	13	8	10	2	9^1	14																						3
1	10	3	4	2	6	8				7	9	5						11^1	12																			4
1	2	4	3	5	8	7		13	14	10^3	9^1	6^2		12			11																					5
1		4		2	7	8	5^2	6^1		9	10	13			11	12	3																					6
1		4		5	7	8		9^2		12	6^3	10^1	13	14		11	2	3																				7
1		3		5	7	8	2^1			12	6	10^2			14	11^3	13	4																				8
1		3		5	7	8		9		11	6^1	10^2	13	12			2	4																				9
1	5	4		2	7	8		6^2		13	9	11^1	12				10		3																			10
1	2	3		5	8^1	7				10	6		9	12		11		4																				11
1	2	7		3		6				11	12		8	9^1	10			4	5																			12
1	2	8^2		3	13	7				11	14		6^1	9^2	10			4	5	12																		13
1	2	6		3		7				10^2	13		9	8^3	11^1			4	5	14	12																	14
1	2		3	5	6	7				12	11^2	9^1		14			10		4		13	8^3																15
1	2		3	5	7					10		9		8^1		11	4					6	12															16
1	2		3	5	8					14		6					10^2	12	4			11^1	7	9^3	13													17
1	2^3		3	5	7					11^2		9					6^1	4	14			8		10	12	13												18
1		3		2	6^2					11		13					5					7	12	10			9^1	4	8									19
1		4		3	9^3			8^1		11^2		10	5	12			2					7		13						6	14							20
1		3		2				12		10		9	5	7				4				8	6^2	13	11^1													21
1	6	4		2				10^4		9		5	8^2					3				7		12	11^1													22
1	6^2	3		2	7			13		9		5						4				8	12	11^1	10													23
1	7	3		2				9		10^2		12^4					4	5				6^1		13						8	11							24
1	5			2				9		6		7					4	3						11						8	10							25
1	2			5				9^1		10^2		6		7	13			4	3					12						8	11							26
1	2	7		5						12		11		8				3	4					10^1						6	9							27
1	2	6		5						11		8						3	4					10						7	9							28
1	5	6^1		9				13		14		7					2	3		12		10								8^2	4	11^3						29
1	2			5				9^2		10		6^3		7			3	13	14	12										8	4	11^1						30
1	5			2				9		10^2		6		7			3					12								8	4	11^1	13					31
1	2			5	13			9		12		6^1		7			3	10		12										8^3	4	11^2	14					32
1	2			5				9				6^2		7^1			3	10	12											8	4	13	11					33
1	3			2	14			8		12		9^3					5	6^1	7^2											10	4	13	11					34
1		2						9^2		10^1		12					3	5	13	7										8	4	14	6	11^3				35
1	9			5	6^1					10				12			2	4		7										8	3		11					36
1	5			9	8					12		10					2	4		7										6	3	11^1						37
1	9			5	7^1					10				13			4^2	2		6										8	3	12^1	11					38
1	9			5	6					13		10		12			2	4		7										8^1	3						11^2	39
1	9			5	6					13		10					3^1	4		7										8	2	12					11^2	40
1	9			5	6^1					12		10		13			3	4		7										8	2						11^2	41
1	6^1			2^2	8^3					11		12					5	3		9		13								7	4	14	10					42
1	9^2			5						14		10^3			6^1		3	4		7		13								8	2	12	11					43
1	2			5						11		6					4	3		7		9^2								8		12			10^1	13		44
1	4			2	13			9^1		12		6					3	5		8		11								7					10^2			45
1	2	4		5						12		6					3			8		10^1								7					13	11	9^2	46

FA Cup

| First Round | East Thurrock | (h) | 2-0 |
| Second Round | Blyth Spartans | (h) | 1-2 |

Capital One Cup

| First Round | Port Vale | (a) | 2-6 |

Johnstone's Paint Trophy

| Second Round | Sheffield U | (h) | 1-2 |

HUDDERSFIELD TOWN

FOUNDATION

A meeting, attended largely by members of the Huddersfield & District FA, was held at the Imperial Hotel in 1906 to discuss the feasibility of establishing a football club in this rugby stronghold. However, it was not until a man with both the enthusiasm and the money to back the scheme came on the scene that real progress was made. This benefactor was Mr Hilton Crowther and it was at a meeting at the Albert Hotel in 1908 that the club formally came into existence with an investment of £2,000 and joined the North-Eastern League.

John Smith's Stadium, Stadium Way, Leeds Road, Huddersfield, West Yorkshire HD1 6PX.

Telephone: (01484) 484 112.

Fax: (01484) 484 101.

Ticket Office: (01484) 484 123.

Website: www.htafc.com

Email: info@htafc.com

Ground Capacity: 24,590.

Record Attendance: 67,037 v Arsenal, FA Cup 6th rd, 27 February 1932 (at Leeds Road); 23,678 v Liverpool, FA Cup 3rd rd, 12 December 1999 (at Alfred McAlpine Stadium).

Pitch Measurements: 105m × 67.5m (115yd × 74yd)

Chairman: Dean Hoyle.

Chief Executive: Nigel Clibbens.

Manager: Chris Powell.

Assistant Manager: Alex Dyer.

Physio: James Haycock.

Colours: Blue and white striped shirts, white shorts with blue trim, black socks with white trim.

Year Formed: 1908.

Turned Professional: 1908.

Club Nickname: 'The Terriers'.

Grounds: 1908, Leeds Road; 1994, The Alfred McAlpine Stadium (renamed the Galpharm Stadium 2004, John Smith's Stadium 2012).

First Football League Game: 3 September 1910, Division 2, v Bradford PA (a) W 1–0 – Mutch; Taylor, Morris; Beaton, Hall, Bartlett; Blackburn, Wood, Hamilton (1), McCubbin, Jee.

Record League Victory: 10–1 v Blackpool, Division 1, 13 December 1930 – Turner; Goodall, Spencer; Redfern, Wilson, Campbell; Bob Kelly (1), McLean (4), Robson (3), Davies (1), Smailes (1).

Record Cup Victory: 7–0 v Lincoln U, FA Cup 1st rd, 16 November 1991 – Clarke; Trevitt, Charlton, Donovan (2), Mitchell, Doherty, O'Regan (1), Stapleton (1) (Wright), Roberts (2), Onuora (1), Barnett (Ireland). *N.B.* 11–0 v Heckmondwike (a), FA Cup pr rd, 18 September 1909 – Doggart; Roberts, Ewing; Hooton, Stevenson, Randall; Kenworthy (2), McCreadie (1), Foster (4), Stacey (4), Jee.

HONOURS

Football League – Division 1:
Champions 1923–24, 1924–25, 1925–26; *Runners-up* 1926–27, 1927–28, 1933–34;
Division 2: *Champions* 1969–70;
Runners-up 1919–20, 1952–53;
Division 4: *Champions* 1979–80.

FA Cup: *Winners* 1922;
Runners-up 1920, 1928, 1930, 1938.

Football League Cup: Best season: semi-final, 1968.

Autoglass Trophy: *Runners-up* 1994.

sky SPORTS FACT FILE

Huddersfield Town played their first-ever game on 2 September 1908. The Terriers hosted Bradford Park Avenue for a friendly match and after trailing at half time went on to win 2-1 with an own goal from Jimmy Freeborough and a strike from Richard Morris.

Record Defeat: 1–10 v Manchester C, Division 2, 7 November 1987.

Most League Points (2 for a win): 66, Division 4, 1979–80.

Most League Points (3 for a win): 87, FL 1, 2010–11.

Most League Goals: 101, Division 4, 1979–80.

Highest League Scorer in Season: Sam Taylor, 35, Division 2, 1919–20; George Brown, 35, Division 1, 1925–26; Jordan Rhodes, 35, 2011–12.

Most League Goals in Total Aggregate: George Brown, 142, 1921–29; Jimmy Glazzard, 142, 1946–56.

Most League Goals in One Match: 5, Dave Mangnall v Derby Co, Division 1, 21 November 1931; 5, Alf Lythgoe v Blackburn R, Division 1, 13 April 1935; 5, Jordan Rhodes v Wycombe W, FL 1, 6 January 2012.

Most Capped Player: Jimmy Nicholson, 31 (41), Northern Ireland.

Most League Appearances: Billy Smith, 521, 1914–34.

Youngest League Player: Denis Law, 16 years 303 days v Notts Co, 24 December 1956.

Record Transfer Fee Received: £8,000,000 from Blackburn R for Jordan Rhodes, August 2012.

Record Transfer Fee Paid: £1,500,000 to Bradford C for Nahki Wells, January 2014.

Football League Record: 1910 Elected to Division 2; 1920–52 Division 1; 1952–53 Division 2; 1953–56 Division 1; 1956–70 Division 2; 1970–72 Division 1; 1972–73 Division 2; 1973–75 Division 3; 1975–80 Division 4; 1980–83 Division 3; 1983–88 Division 2; 1988–92 Division 3; 1992–95 Division 2; 1995–2001 Division 1; 2001–03 Division 2; 2003–04 Division 3; 2004–12 FL 1; 2012– FL C.

LATEST SEQUENCES

Longest Sequence of League Wins: 11, 5.4.1920 – 4.9.1920.

Longest Sequence of League Defeats: 7, 8.10.1955 – 19.11.1955.

Longest Sequence of League Draws: 6, 3.3.1987 – 3.4.1987.

Longest Sequence of Unbeaten League Matches: 43, 1.1.2011 – 19.11.2011.

Longest Sequence Without a League Win: 22, 4.12.1971 – 29.4.1972.

Successive Scoring Runs: 27 from 12.3.2005.

Successive Non-scoring Runs: 7 from 14.10.2000.

MANAGERS

Fred Walker 1908–10
Richard Pudan 1910–12
Arthur Fairclough 1912–19
Ambrose Langley 1919–21
Herbert Chapman 1921–25
Cecil Potter 1925–26
Jack Chaplin 1926–29
Clem Stephenson 1929–42
Ted Magner 1942–43
David Steele 1943–47
George Stephenson 1947–52
Andy Beattie 1952–56
Bill Shankly 1956–59
Eddie Boot 1960–64
Tom Johnston 1964–68
Ian Greaves 1968–74
Bobby Collins 1974
Tom Johnston 1975–78
    (had been General Manager since 1975)
Mike Buxton 1978–86
Steve Smith 1986–87
Malcolm Macdonald 1987–88
Eoin Hand 1988–92
Ian Ross 1992–93
Neil Warnock 1993–95
Brian Horton 1995–97
Peter Jackson 1997–99
Steve Bruce 1999–2000
Lou Macari 2000–02
Mick Wadsworth 2002–03
Peter Jackson 2003–07
Andy Ritchie 2007–08
Stan Ternent 2008
Lee Clark 2008–12
Simon Grayson 2012–13
Mark Robins 2013–14
Chris Powell September 2014–

TEN YEAR LEAGUE RECORD

		P	W	D	L	F	A	Pts	Pos
2005-06	FL 1	46	19	16	11	72	59	73	4
2006-07	FL 1	46	14	17	15	60	69	59	15
2007-08	FL 1	46	20	6	20	50	62	66	10
2008-09	FL 1	46	18	14	14	62	65	68	9
2009-10	FL 1	46	23	11	12	82	56	80	6
2010-11	FL 1	46	25	12	9	77	48	87	3
2011-12	FL 1	46	21	18	7	79	47	81	4
2012-13	FL C	46	15	13	18	53	73	58	19
2013-14	FL C	46	14	11	21	58	65	53	17
2014-15	FL C	46	13	16	17	58	75	55	16

DID YOU KNOW ?

Huddersfield Town defender Larrett (Larry) Roebuck was the first professional player from the Football League to be killed during the First World War. Although he died on 18 October 1914 his death was not officially confirmed until January 1916.

HUDDERSFIELD TOWN – FL CHAMPIONSHIP 2014–15 LEAGUE RECORD

Match No.	Date	Venue	Opponents	Result		H/T Score	Lg Pos.	Goalscorers	Attendance
1	Aug 9	H	Bournemouth	L	0-4	0-2	24		12,371
2	16	A	Cardiff C	L	1-3	1-2	24	Wallace [45]	20,749
3	19	A	Reading	W	2-1	2-0	20	Butterfield [10], Bunn [38]	15,035
4	23	H	Charlton Ath	D	1-1	0-0	20	Wells [50]	11,333
5	30	A	Watford	L	2-4	0-1	21	Bunn [48], Wallace [63]	14,409
6	Sept 13	H	Middlesbrough	L	1-2	0-1	21	Stead [86]	17,993
7	16	H	Wigan Ath	D	0-0	0-0	22		11,083
8	20	A	Leeds U	L	0-3	0-2	22		29,131
9	27	H	Millwall	W	2-1	1-1	20	Wells 2 (1 pen) [37, 57 (p)]	11,712
10	Oct 1	A	Wolverhampton W	W	3-1	2-0	18	Bunn [21], Scannell [39], Coady [51]	19,059
11	4	A	Blackburn R	D	0-0	0-0	18		14,662
12	18	A	Blackpool	W	4-2	3-2	17	Holt [4], Bunn 2 [11, 16], Butterfield [61]	14,238
13	21	A	Brighton & HA	D	1-1	1-1	16	Butterfield [10]	10,817
14	25	A	Ipswich T	D	2-2	0-1	17	Wells 2 (1 pen) [70 (p), 82]	16,751
15	Nov 1	H	Nottingham F	W	3-0	2-0	14	Lynch [1], Wells [20], Holt [54]	15,317
16	4	A	Derby Co	L	2-3	1-2	15	Bunn [22], Hudson [90]	27,153
17	8	A	Fulham	L	1-3	0-1	16	Lynch [75]	17,734
18	22	H	Sheffield W	D	0-0	0-0	14		14,389
19	29	A	Bolton W	L	0-1	0-0	19		15,924
20	Dec 6	H	Brentford	W	2-1	1-0	15	Scannell [18], Bidwell (og) [48]	13,038
21	13	A	Norwich C	L	0-5	0-0	17		25,595
22	20	A	Birmingham C	L	0-1	0-0	20		13,203
23	26	A	Rotherham U	D	2-2	1-0	19	Vaughan [35], Coady [61]	11,681
24	28	H	Bolton W	W	2-1	1-1	18	Butterfield [43], Wells [85]	15,773
25	Jan 10	A	Watford	W	3-1	0-0	15	Wells [52], Vaughan [77], Lynch [83]	13,843
26	17	A	Middlesbrough	L	0-2	0-0	17		18,576
27	24	A	Wigan Ath	W	1-0	0-0	15	Coady [82]	12,064
28	31	H	Leeds U	L	1-2	1-1	17	Bunn [26]	20,029
29	Feb 7	A	Millwall	W	3-1	1-1	14	Scannell [17], Butterfield [74], Vaughan (pen) [86]	10,281
30	10	H	Wolverhampton W	L	1-4	0-1	15	Vaughan [63]	11,843
31	14	A	Bournemouth	D	1-1	0-1	14	Vaughan [65]	10,007
32	21	H	Cardiff C	D	0-0	0-0	16		12,798
33	24	H	Reading	W	3-0	1-0	12	Bunn [10], Wells [55], Miller [74]	10,282
34	28	A	Charlton Ath	L	0-3	0-1	14		25,545
35	Mar 3	A	Brentford	L	1-4	1-1	15	Bunn [22]	9625
36	7	H	Rotherham U	L	0-2	0-1	16		13,342
37	14	A	Birmingham C	D	1-1	1-1	18	Lolley [27]	14,747
38	17	H	Norwich C	D	2-2	0-0	17	Miller [55], Vaughan [90]	11,879
39	21	H	Fulham	L	0-2	0-1	18		11,635
40	Apr 4	A	Sheffield W	D	1-1	0-0	18	Miller [89]	20,851
41	6	H	Ipswich T	W	2-1	2-0	17	Wells [12], Vaughan [30]	13,231
42	11	A	Nottingham F	W	1-0	1-0	16	Scannell [43]	21,572
43	14	A	Brighton & HA	D	0-0	0-0	16		23,270
44	18	H	Derby Co	D	4-4	3-1	15	Gobern [38], Hudson [41], James [45], Wells [72]	15,889
45	25	H	Blackburn R	D	2-2	1-2	16	Butterfield [39], Lolley [84]	17,056
46	May 2	A	Blackpool	D	0-0	0-0	16		

Final League Position: 16

GOALSCORERS

League (58): Wells 11 (2 pens), Bunn 9, Vaughan 7 (1 pen), Butterfield 6, Scannell 4, Coady 3, Lynch 3, Miller 3, Holt 2, Hudson 2, Lolley 2, Wallace 2, Gobern 1, James 1, Stead 1, own goal 1.
FA Cup (0).
Capital One Cup (5): Wells 3 (1 pen), Lolley 1, Stead 1.

Smithies A 44	Crooks M 1	Peltier L 8+3	Lynch J 34	Hammill A 1+4	Hogg J 23+3	Majewski R 3+5	Norwood O 1	Dixon P 8+3	Wells N 29+6	Ward D 2+10	Scannell S 37+5	Lolley J 3+14	Coady C 42+3	Smith T 40+1	Wallace M 15+11	Butterfield J 45	Stead J 2+5	Bunn H 24+6	Sinnott J —+1	Vaughan J 21+5	Robinson J 30	Hudson M 41	Holt G 14+1	Paterson M —+3	Murphy J 2	Poyet D 2	Gerrard A 1+2	Gobern O 7+5	Edgar D 9+3	Miller I 9+7	Boyle W —+1	Carroll J 1+1	Charles J —+1	James R 6	Wilkinson J 1	Match No.
1	2	3	4	5[1]	6[2]	7[3]	8	9	10	11	12	13	14																							1
1			4	12	7[3]	9[2]		5	11	13			6	2	3	8	10[1]	14																		2
1			4		7	13		5	10[1]			9[2]	6	2	3[4]	8	11[2]	14		13																3
1	7[1]	4	14		12			5	10[3]			9[2]	6	2	3[4]	8		11		13																4
1		4	13		8			2[1]	12		9		7		3	6	14	11[2]	10[3]	5																5
1	7[2]	3						9	14		13	6	2		8	12	11[3]		10[1]	5	4															6
1	6	3[2]						11	9[1]	12		8	2	13	7	10			5	4																7
1	2	4		8[2]				10	12	9[1]		7		6	13	11			5	3																8
1	6[2]	4		7[3]				10[1]		13		9	2	14	8		11		5	3	12															9
1		4		7[2]			14		9[3]		8	2	13	6	12	11			5	3	10[1]															10
1	12	4						11[1]	6		8	2		7	9				5	3	10															11
1		4	6					12	9		7	2		8	11[2]				5	3	10[1]	13														12
1		4	6					12	9[1]		7	2		8	11				5	3	10															13
1	2[2]	4	8[1]		9		11	13			6	5		7	12				3	10																14
1	12	4						10[2]	13	6[1]		7	2	8	9			5	3	11[3]	14															15
1		4			13			10[2]	12	6[1]		7	2	8[3]	9			5	3	11	14															16
1		4	6[1]				5[1]	12	13	9		7	2	8		11			3	10																17
1		4					5	12	13	9		6[2]	2	8	11[1]				3	10	1	7														18
1	4[1]						11	14	9[3]	13	7	2	12	6			5	3	10	8[2]																19
1		8		13	10[2]		6		7	2	4	9		12	5	3	11[1]																			20
1		6		12	11[1]		9		7	2	4[4]	8			5	3	10																			21
1	2	6[3]			12		9	14	7		8		11[1]	13	5	3	10[2]			4																22
1	13	6			12		9		7	2	4	8[1]	9	11[2]	5	3	10[3]				14	12														23
1	13	6			12		9		7	2	4	8[2]	11	10[3]	5	3					14															24
1	4				10		6	12	7	2	8		11[1]	5	3					9																25
1	13	4	6[3]		11		9	14	7	2	8		10[1]	5[2]	3					12																26
1	4				11[2]		9		6	2	12	8		13	10	5	3				7[1]															27
1	4[3]				10[1]		5	14	8	2[2]	13	6		12	11	9	3	1			7															28
1					10[*]			6	7		4	8		9[1]	11[2]	5	3				13	2	12													29
1								6	12	7		4[1]	8	9[2]	11	5	3				13	10														30
1			13					7		9	2	4	8[2]	10	11[1]	5	3				6	12														31
1			6[3]		11[2]		5[1]	13	7	2	4	8		14	10	9	3				7	10[3]	14													32
1			6				9[2]	13		2	4	8		11[1]	12	5	3				7	10[3]	14													33
1			7[3]					6	14	13	12	4	8	9[1]		10	5	3			2[2]	11														34
1			6					5[1]		14	2	4	8	10		11	9[2]	3			7[3]	13	12													35
1	4[2]		7[3]	13				5	10[1]	6		2	14	8		11	9	3			12															36
1	4		6					12	9[1]	7	2	14	8		11[2]	10	5[1]	3			13															37
1	4		6					5	7	2		8		10[8]	3					13	12	11[1]	9[2]													38
1	4		6[2]	13				11	5	12	7	9[3]	8			3					2[1]	10		14												39
1	4							11[1]	5		6	2	8			10	3				7	12									9					40
1	4							11[1]	5[3]	13	6	2	14	8		10[2]	3				7	12									9					41
1	4		12					11[3]	5	6	2	14	8[2]			10[1]	3				7	13									9					42
1	4							11[1]	5	8	2	12	6				3				7	10									9					43
1	4		12					10[2]	5	7[1]	2	8	13				3				6	11									9					44
1	9							11	5	12	6	2	8		13		3				7	10[1]													4[2]	45
1	4								5	6	2	8		10	3						7	11									9					46

FA Cup
Third Round   Reading   (h)   0-1

Capital One Cup
First Round   Chesterfield   (a)   5-3
(aet)
Second Round   Nottingham F   (h)   0-2

HULL CITY

FOUNDATION

The enthusiasts who formed Hull City in 1904 were brave men indeed. More than that, they were audacious for they immediately put the club on the map in this Rugby League fortress by obtaining a three-year agreement with the Hull Rugby League club to rent their ground! They had obtained quite a number of conversions to the dribbling code, before the Rugby League forbade the use of any of their club grounds by Association Football clubs. By that time, Hull City were well away, having entered the FA Cup in their initial season and the Football League, Second Division after only a year.

The KC Stadium, West Park, Hull, East Yorkshire HU3 6HU.

Telephone: (01482) 504 600.

Fax: (01482) 304 882.

Ticket Office: (01482) 505 600.

Website: www.hullcitytigers.com

Email: info@hulltigers.com

Ground Capacity: 25,400.

Record Attendance: 55,019 v Manchester U, FA Cup 6th rd, 26 February 1949 (at Boothferry Park); 25,512 v Sunderland, FL C, 28 October 2007 (at KC Stadium).

Pitch Measurements: 105m × 68m (115yd × 74yd)

Chairman: Dr Assem Allam.

Vice-chairman: Ehab Allam.

Manager: Steve Bruce.

Assistant Manager: Mike Phelan.

Physio: Stuart Leake.

Colours: Amber shirts with black stripes, black shorts, amber socks with black trim.

Year Formed: 1904.

Turned Professional: 1905.

Club Nickname: 'The Tigers'.

Grounds: 1904, Boulevard Ground (Hull RFC); 1905, Anlaby Road (Hull CC); 1944, Boulevard Ground; 1946, Boothferry Park; 2002, Kingston Communications Stadium.

First Football League Game: 2 September 1905, Division 2, v Barnsley (h) W 4–1 – Spendiff; Langley, Jones; Martin, Robinson, Gordon (2); Rushton, Spence (1), Wilson (1), Howe, Raisbeck.

Record League Victory: 11–1 v Carlisle U, Division 3 (N), 14 January 1939 – Ellis; Woodhead, Dowen; Robinson (1), Blyth, Hardy; Hubbard (2), Richardson (2), Dickinson (2), Davies (2), Cunliffe (2).

Record Cup Victory: 8–2 v Stalybridge Celtic (a), FA Cup 1st rd, 26 November 1932 – Maddison; Goldsmith, Woodhead; Gardner, Hill (1), Denby; Forward (1), Duncan, McNaughton (1), Wainscoat (4), Sargeant (1).

HONOURS

FA Premier League: Best season 16th, 2013–14.

Football League – FL C: *Runners-up* 2012–13;

FL 1: *Runners-up* 2004–05;

Division 3 (N): *Champions* 1932–33, 1948–49;

Division 3: *Champions* 1965–66; *Runners-up* 1958–59, 2003–04;

Division 4: *Runners-up* 1982–83.

FA Cup: *Runners-up* 2014.

Football League Cup: Best season: 4th, 1974, 1976, 1978, 2014.

Associate Members' Cup: *Runners-up* 1984.

European Competitions Europa League: 2014–15.

sky SPORTS FACT FILE

George Salvidge, who served as a Lance Corporal in the York & Lancaster Regiment, was killed in action at Tobruk in November 1941. A winger, he was a regular with Hull City's reserve team and made four first-team appearances during his time with the club.

Record Defeat: 0–8 v Wolverhampton W, Division 2, 4 November 1911.

Most League Points (2 for a win): 69, Division 3, 1965–66.

Most League Points (3 for a win): 90, Division 4, 1982–83.

Most League Goals: 109, Division 3, 1965–66.

Highest League Scorer in Season: Bill McNaughton, 39, Division 3 (N), 1932–33.

Most League Goals in Total Aggregate: Chris Chilton, 193, 1960–71.

Most League Goals in One Match: 5, Ken McDonald v Bristol C, Division 2, 17 November 1928; 5, Simon 'Slim' Raleigh v Halifax T, Division 3 (N), 26 December 1930.

Most Capped Player: Theo Whitmore, 28 (105), Jamaica.

Most League Appearances: Andy Davidson, 520, 1952–67.

Youngest League Player: Matthew Edeson, 16 years 63 days v Fulham, 10 October 1992.

Record Transfer Fee Received: £12,000,000 from Southampton for Shane Long, August 2014.

Record Transfer Fee Paid: £10,000,000 to Palermo for Abel Hernandez, September 2014.

Football League Record: 1905 Elected to Division 2; 1930–33 Division 3 (N); 1933–36 Division 2; 1936–49 Division 3 (N); 1949–56 Division 2; 1956–58 Division 3 (N); 1958–59 Division 3; 1959–60 Division 2; 1960–66 Division 3; 1966–78 Division 2; 1978–81 Division 3; 1981–83 Division 4; 1983–85 Division 3; 1985–91 Division 2; 1991–92 Division 3; 1992–96 Division 2; 1996–2004 Division 3; 2004–05 FL 1; 2005–08 FL C; 2008–10 FA Premier League; 2010–13 FL C; 2013–15 FA Premier League; 2015– FL C.

LATEST SEQUENCES

Longest Sequence of League Wins: 10, 23.2.1966 – 20.4.1966.

Longest Sequence of League Defeats: 8, 7.4.1934 – 8.9.1934.

Longest Sequence of League Draws: 5, 14.2.2012 – 10.3.2012.

Longest Sequence of Unbeaten League Matches: 19, 13.3.2001 – 22.9.2001.

Longest Sequence Without a League Win: 27, 27.3.1989 – 4.11.1989.

Successive Scoring Runs: 26 from 10.4.1990.

Successive Non-scoring Runs: 6 from 13.11.1920.

MANAGERS

James Ramster 1904–05
  (Secretary-Manager)
Ambrose Langley 1905–13
Harry Chapman 1913–14
Fred Stringer 1914–16
David Menzies 1916–21
Percy Lewis 1921–23
Bill McCracken 1923–31
Haydn Green 1931–34
John Hill 1934–36
David Menzies 1936
Ernest Blackburn 1936–46
Major Frank Buckley 1946–48
Raich Carter 1948–51
Bob Jackson 1952–55
Bob Brocklebank 1955–61
Cliff Britton 1961–70
  (continued as General Manager to 1971)
Terry Neill 1970–74
John Kaye 1974–77
Bobby Collins 1977–78
Ken Houghton 1978–79
Mike Smith 1979–82
Bobby Brown 1982
Colin Appleton 1982–84
Brian Horton 1984–88
Eddie Gray 1988–89
Colin Appleton 1989
Stan Ternent 1989–91
Terry Dolan 1991–97
Mark Hateley 1997–98
Warren Joyce 1998–2000
Brian Little 2000–02
Jan Molby 2002
Peter Taylor 2002–06
Phil Parkinson 2006
Phil Brown *(after caretaker role December 2006)* 2007–10
Ian Dowie *(consultant)* 2010
Nigel Pearson 2010–11
Nick Barmby 2011–12
Steve Bruce June 2012–

TEN YEAR LEAGUE RECORD

		P	W	D	L	F	A	Pts	Pos
2005-06	FL C	46	12	16	18	49	55	52	18
2006-07	FL C	46	13	10	23	51	67	49	21
2007-08	FL C	46	21	12	13	65	47	75	3
2008-09	PR Lge	38	8	11	19	39	64	35	17
2009-10	PR Lge	38	6	12	20	34	75	30	19
2010-11	FL C	46	16	17	13	52	51	65	11
2011-12	FL C	46	19	11	16	47	44	68	8
2012-13	FL C	46	24	7	15	61	52	79	2
2013-14	PR Lge	38	10	7	21	38	53	37	16
2014-15	PR Lge	38	8	11	19	33	51	35	18

DID YOU KNOW ?

Hull City played their first-ever game on 1 September 1904. Notts County were the visitors to The Boulevard for a friendly fixture. George Rushton scored twice to put the Tigers 2-0 up, before County fought back to draw 2-2.

HULL CITY – FA PREMIERSHIP 2014–15 LEAGUE RECORD

Match No.	Date	Venue	Opponents	Result		H/T Score	Lg Pos.	Goalscorers	Attendance
1	Aug 16	A	QPR	W	1-0	0-0	3	Chester [52]	17,603
2	24	H	Stoke C	D	1-1	1-0	5	Jelavic [42]	24,348
3	31	A	Aston Villa	L	1-2	0-2	9	Jelavic [74]	28,336
4	Sept 15	H	West Ham U	D	2-2	1-0	10	Hernandez [39], Diame [64]	21,275
5	20	A	Newcastle U	D	2-2	0-0	9	Jelavic [48], Diame [68]	49,119
6	27	H	Manchester C	L	2-4	2-2	14	Mangala (og) [21], Hernandez (pen) [32]	22,859
7	Oct 4	H	Crystal Palace	W	2-0	0-0	8	Diame [60], Jelavic [89]	24,281
8	18	A	Arsenal	D	2-2	1-1	9	Diame [17], Hernandez [46]	60,004
9	25	A	Liverpool	D	0-0	0-0	9		44,591
10	Nov 1	H	Southampton	L	0-1	0-1	13		22,828
11	8	A	Burnley	L	0-1	0-0	14		16,998
12	23	H	Tottenham H	L	1-2	1-0	16	Livermore [8]	23,561
13	29	A	Manchester U	L	0-3	0-2	17		75,345
14	Dec 3	A	Everton	D	1-1	0-1	17	Aluko [59]	34,645
15	6	H	WBA	D	0-0	0-0	18		23,279
16	13	A	Chelsea	L	0-2	0-1	19		41,626
17	20	H	Swansea C	L	0-1	0-1	19		21,913
18	26	A	Sunderland	W	3-1	1-1	17	Ramirez [32], Chester [51], Jelavic [90]	44,817
19	28	H	Leicester C	L	0-1	0-1	17		23,809
20	Jan 1	H	Everton	W	2-0	2-0	15	Elmohamady [33], Jelavic [43]	23,865
21	10	A	WBA	L	0-1	0-0	18		24,818
22	18	A	West Ham U	L	0-3	0-0	18		34,914
23	31	H	Newcastle U	L	0-3	0-1	18		23,925
24	Feb 7	A	Manchester C	D	1-1	1-0	17	Meyler [35]	45,233
25	10	A	Aston Villa	W	2-0	1-0	15	Jelavic [22], N'Doye [74]	21,467
26	21	H	QPR	W	2-1	1-1	15	Jelavic [16], N'Doye [89]	24,466
27	28	A	Stoke C	L	0-1	0-0	15		26,473
28	Mar 3	H	Sunderland	D	1-1	1-0	15	N'Doye [15]	23,017
29	14	A	Leicester C	D	0-0	0-0	15		31,456
30	22	H	Chelsea	L	2-3	2-2	15	Elmohamady [26], Hernandez [28]	24,598
31	Apr 4	A	Swansea C	L	1-3	0-2	15	McShane [50]	20,333
32	11	A	Southampton	L	0-2	0-0	17		30,359
33	25	A	Crystal Palace	W	2-0	0-0	16	N'Doye 2 [51, 90]	23,876
34	28	H	Liverpool	W	1-0	1-0	15	Dawson [37]	24,843
35	May 4	H	Arsenal	L	1-3	0-3	17	Quinn [56]	23,628
36	9	H	Burnley	L	0-1	0-0	18		24,877
37	16	A	Tottenham H	L	0-2	0-0	18		35,857
38	24	H	Manchester U	D	0-0	0-0	18		24,745

Final League Position: 18

GOALSCORERS

League (33): Jelavic 8, N'Doye 5, Diame 4, Hernandez 4 (1 pen), Chester 2, Elmohamady 2, Aluko 1, Dawson 1, Livermore 1, McShane 1, Meyler 1, Quinn 1, Ramirez 1, own goal 1.
FA Cup (0).
Capital One Cup (2): Brady 1, Ince 1.
UEFA Europa League (4): Brady 2 (1 pen), Aluko 1, Elmohamady 1.

McGregor A 26	Chester J 23	Bruce A 17+5	Davies C 21	Elmohamady A 38	Huddlestone T 30+1	Livermore J 35	Robertson A 17+7	Ince T 3+4	Snodgrass R 1	Jelavic N 21+5	Quinn S 17+11	McShane P 19+1	Meyler D 19+9	Rosenior L 5+8	Boyd G —+1	Dawson M 28	Brady R 17+10	Aluko S 13+12	Diame M 10+2	Hernandez A 15+10	Ben Arfa H 5+3	Ramirez G 11+11	Harper S 10	Jakupovic E 2+1	Maguire H —+3	Sagbo Y —+4	Figueroa M 2+1	N'Doye D 13+2	Match No.
1	2	3¹	4	5	6	7	8	9²	10³	11	12	13	14																1
1	3*	2	5	7	6	9	10²			11³	8¹	4	13	12	14														2
1		4³	5	7²	6	9	11¹			10	8	2		12		3	13	14											3
1		4	2	7	6	5				10	9²					3	12			8¹	11¹	13	14						4
1		4	2	7	6	5²				10³	9		13	14		3				7	11²	12	13						5
1		4	6	8	9¹	5³				10				2		3	14			7	11²	12	13						6
	2	14	4	5¹	8	7	9²			11				13			6	10¹		12	1								7
	2	14	3	5	6	7	9							4¹			8	11²	10	13	1³	12							8
	2	3	4	5	8	6				14						9	12	7²	11³	10¹	13		1						9
	2		4	5	8	6	13			14	3²					9¹	12	7	11	10¹		1							10
	2³		4	5	6¹	7				12	3		8	11²	9	10	14	13	1										11
1			4	2	6²	7	5			11	14		12	13		3	10³			8¹	9⁴								12
1	2		4	5		7	9			11	14		13			3	8³	12	6²	10¹									13
1	3			5	7	6	14			11	9²		8³	4		2	13	12	10¹										14
1	3			5	7	8	12			14	9¹		6	4²		2	13	10³	11										15
1	3	12	5	2	8⁴	7	6			10¹			9			4³	13	11²		14									16
1	3	4¹	5²	2		8	6			11¹			7				12		10	9				13	14				17
1	2	3	4	6			13			14	8		7	5			9²	11³		10¹		12							18
1		3	4	6		2			13	12	8⁴		7¹	5			9	10³		14		11²							19
1	2	3	4	6		8	5²			11			7	12²			13			10		9¹		14					20
1	2	3	4	6	14	8			13	11²	9¹		7				12			10³								5	21
5¹	3²	4³	9	7	6					10		8				2	11							13	14	12			22
1		4	2	8	7	5²	13			11			6¹			3	14	12		10³		9							23
1	3		5	7	6	12				14	4	8				2	10²	11¹		9³								13	24
1	3		5	7	6¹					10³	14	4	8			2	9			13		12						11²	25
1	3¹		5	7	6²					10		4	8¹			2	9	14		13		12						11	26
1	3		5	7	6					13		4	8¹			2		11²		14		10					9³	12	27
1	3		5	7	6	9				11¹		4	8			2				12								10	28
1	3		5	7¹	6	9³				11¹	12	4	13			2				14		8²						10	29
1	3		5	7						12	4	6²				2	13	14		11		8³						10	30
1	3²		5	7						12	4	8⁴				2	9	14	13	11¹		6³						10	31
	2³	4		6	8²	7				9	5					3		11¹	12	14			1		13			10	32
	2	14		5	7	6				8²	4		13			3	9¹	11³		12		1						10	33
	2	13		5	7	6				8²	4		14			3	9	11³		12		1						10¹	34
	2			5	7	6³	13			14	8²	4	12			3	9	11¹				1						10	35
	2			5	7	6¹				13	8	4³	12			3	9	11¹²	14			1						10	36
	2			5	7¹		13			11²	8	4	6			3	9			12		1						10	37
	2³			5	7		14			11	8	4	6²			3	9	13		12		1						10¹	38

FA Cup
Third Round   Arsenal   (a)   0-2

Capital One Cup
Third Round   WBA   (a)   2-3

UEFA Europa League
Third Qualifying 1st leg   Trencin   (a)   0-0
Third Qualifying 2nd leg   Trencin   (h)   2-1
Play-Offs 1st leg   Lokeren   (a)   0-1
Play-Offs 2nd leg   Lokeren   (h)   2-1

IPSWICH TOWN

FOUNDATION

Considering that Ipswich Town only reached the Football League in 1938, many people outside of East Anglia may be surprised to learn that this club was formed at a meeting held in the Town Hall as far back as 1878 when Mr T. C. Cobbold, MP, was voted president. Originally it was the Ipswich Association FC to distinguish it from the older Ipswich Football Club which played rugby. These two amalgamated in 1888 and the handling game was dropped in 1893.

Portman Road, Ipswich, Suffolk IP1 2DA.

Telephone: (01473) 400 500.

Fax: (01473) 400 040.

Ticket Office: (03330) 050 503

Website: www.itfc.co.uk

Email: customerservices@itfc.co.uk

Ground Capacity: 30,311.

Record Attendance: 38,010 v Leeds U, FA Cup 6th rd, 8 March 1975.

Pitch Measurements: 102m × 66m (111.5yd × 72yd)

Managing Directors: Ian Milne, Jonathan Symonds.

Manager: Mick McCarthy.

Assistant Manager: Terry Connor.

Physios: Matt Byard, Alex Chapman.

Colours: Blue shirts with white trim, white shorts with blue trim, blue socks with white tops.

Year Formed: 1878.

Turned Professional: 1936.

HONOURS

Football League – Division 1:
Champions 1961–62;
Runners-up 1980–81, 1981–82;
Division 2: *Champions* 1960–61, 1967–68, 1991–92;
Division 3 (S): *Champions* 1953–54, 1956–57.

FA Cup: *Winners* 1978.

Football League Cup: Best season: semi-final, 1982, 1985, 2001, 2011.

Texaco Cup: *Winners* 1973.

European Competitions
European Cup: 1962–63.
European Cup-Winners' Cup: 1978–79.
UEFA Cup: 1973–74, 1974–75, 1975–76, 1977–78, 1979–80, 1980–81 (*winners*), 1981–82, 1982–83, 2001–02, 2002–03.

Previous Name: 1878, Ipswich Association FC; 1888, Ipswich Town.

Club Nicknames: 'The Blues', 'Town', 'The Tractor Boys'.

Grounds: 1878, Broom Hill and Brook's Hall; 1884, Portman Road.

First Football League Game: 27 August 1938, Division 3 (S), v Southend U (h) W 4–2 – Burns; Dale, Parry; Perrett, Fillingham, McLuckie; Williams, Davies (1), Jones (2), Alsop (1), Little.

Record League Victory: 7–0 v Portsmouth, Division 2, 7 November 1964 – Thorburn; Smith, McNeil; Baxter, Bolton, Thompson; Broadfoot (1), Hegan (2), Baker (1), Leadbetter, Brogan (3). 7–0 v Southampton, Division 1, 2 February 1974 – Sivell; Burley, Mills (1), Morris, Hunter, Beattie (1), Hamilton (2), Viljoen, Johnson, Whymark (2), Lambert (1) (Woods). 7–0 v WBA, Division 1, 6 November 1976 – Sivell; Burley, Mills, Talbot, Hunter, Beattie (1), Osborne, Wark (1), Mariner (1) (Bertschin), Whymark (4), Woods.

sky SPORTS FACT FILE

Ipswich Town suffered one of their worst ever seasons in 1963–64, just two seasons after winning the Football League title. They suffered both their worst ever home and away defeats to Manchester United and Fulham respectively, while their final total of 25 points was their lowest in the era of two points for a win.

Record Cup Victory: 10–0 v Floriana, European Cup prel. rd, 25 September 1962 – Bailey; Malcolm, Compton; Baxter, Laurel, Elsworthy (1); Stephenson, Moran (2), Crawford (5), Phillips (2), Blackwood.

Record Defeat: 1–10 v Fulham, Division 1, 26 December 1963.

Most League Points (2 for a win): 64, Division 3 (S), 1953–54 and 1955–56.

Most League Points (3 for a win): 87, Division 1, 1999–2000.

Most League Goals: 106, Division 3 (S), 1955–56.

Highest League Scorer in Season: Ted Phillips, 41, Division 3 (S), 1956–57.

Most League Goals in Total Aggregate: Ray Crawford, 204, 1958–63 and 1966–69.

Most League Goals in One Match: 5, Alan Brazil v Southampton, Division 1, 16 February 1981.

Most Capped Player: Allan Hunter, 47 (53), Northern Ireland.

Most League Appearances: Mick Mills, 591, 1966–82.

Youngest League Player: Jason Dozzell, 16 years 56 days v Coventry C, 4 February 1984.

Record Transfer Fee Received: £8,000,000 from Sunderland for Connor Wickham, June 2011; £8,000,000 from AFC Bournemouth for Tyrone Mings, June 2015.

Record Transfer Fee Paid: £5,000,000 to Sampdoria for Matteo Sereni, August 2001.

Football League Record: 1938 Elected to Division 3 (S); 1954–55 Division 2; 1955–57 Division 3 (S); 1957–61 Division 2; 1961–64 Division 1; 1964–68 Division 2; 1968–86 Division 1; 1986–92 Division 2; 1992–95 FA Premier League; 1995–2000 Division 1; 2000–02 FA Premier League; 2002–04 Division 1; 2004– FL C.

MANAGERS
Mick O'Brien 1936–37
Scott Duncan 1937–55
(continued as Secretary)
Alf Ramsey 1955–63
Jackie Milburn 1963–64
Bill McGarry 1964–68
Bobby Robson 1969–82
Bobby Ferguson 1982–87
Johnny Duncan 1987–90
John Lyall 1990–94
George Burley 1994–2002
Joe Royle 2002–06
Jim Magilton 2006–09
Roy Keane 2009–11
Paul Jewell 2011–12
Mick McCarthy November 2012–

LATEST SEQUENCES

Longest Sequence of League Wins: 8, 23.9.1953 – 31.10.1953.

Longest Sequence of League Defeats: 10, 4.9.1954 – 16.10.1954.

Longest Sequence of League Draws: 7, 10.11.1990 – 21.12.1990.

Longest Sequence of Unbeaten League Matches: 23, 8.12.1979 – 26.4.1980.

Longest Sequence Without a League Win: 21, 28.8.1963 – 14.12.1963.

Successive Scoring Runs: 31 from 7.3.2004.

Successive Non-scoring Runs: 7 from 28.2.1995.

TEN YEAR LEAGUE RECORD

		P	W	D	L	F	A	Pts	Pos
2005-06	FL C	46	14	14	18	53	66	56	15
2006-07	FL C	46	18	8	20	64	59	62	14
2007-08	FL C	46	18	15	13	65	56	69	8
2008-09	FL C	46	17	15	14	62	53	66	9
2009-10	FL C	46	12	20	14	50	61	56	15
2010-11	FL C	46	18	8	20	62	68	62	13
2011-12	FL C	46	17	10	19	69	77	61	15
2012-13	FL C	46	16	12	18	48	61	60	14
2013-14	FL C	46	18	14	14	60	54	68	9
2014-15	FL C	46	22	12	12	72	54	78	6

DID YOU KNOW ?

Ipswich Town were elected as members of the Football League in May 1938 after two seasons as a professional club. They topped the poll with 36 votes and Gillingham, who had finished bottom of the Division Three South table, were voted out.

IPSWICH TOWN – FL CHAMPIONSHIP 2014–15 LEAGUE RECORD

Match No.	Date	Venue	Opponents	Result	H/T Score	Lg Pos.	Goalscorers	Atten-dance
1	Aug 9	H	Fulham	W 2-1	1-0	6	Murphy [32], McGoldrick [61]	17,218
2	16	A	Reading	L 0-1	0-1	13		17,198
3	19	A	Birmingham C	D 2-2	0-1	10	Berra 2 [50, 90]	14,022
4	23	H	Norwich C	L 0-1	0-1	17		25,245
5	30	A	Derby Co	D 1-1	0-1	19	Berra [52]	26,673
6	Sept 13	H	Millwall	W 2-0	1-0	14	McGoldrick [45], Murphy [63]	16,190
7	16	A	Brighton & HA	W 2-0	0-0	9	Parr [79], Murphy [88]	15,726
8	22	A	Wigan Ath	W 2-1	1-0	7	Hyam [20], Sammon [63]	12,817
9	27	H	Rotherham U	W 2-0	2-0	4	Murphy [3], McGoldrick [6]	16,447
10	30	A	Sheffield W	D 1-1	0-1	5	Williams [62]	18,093
11	Oct 5	A	Nottingham F	D 2-2	1-0	6	Murphy 2 [19, 71]	24,354
12	18	H	Blackburn R	D 1-1	0-0	6	McGoldrick [65]	16,972
13	21	A	Cardiff C	L 1-3	1-1	9	Murphy [29]	20,191
14	25	H	Huddersfield T	D 2-2	1-0	10	Smith [21], Berra [55]	16,751
15	Nov 1	A	Blackpool	W 2-0	1-0	8	McGoldrick [26], Murphy [61]	10,918
16	4	H	Wolverhampton W	W 2-1	1-0	5	Murphy 2 [35, 59]	17,267
17	8	H	Watford	W 1-0	0-0	4	Smith [83]	22,490
18	22	A	Bournemouth	D 2-2	0-1	4	Bishop [50], Murphy [76]	11,115
19	29	A	Charlton Ath	W 1-0	0-0	2	Hunt, N [90]	16,613
20	Dec 6	H	Leeds U	W 4-1	3-1	2	Murphy 2 [12, 45], McGoldrick (pen) [26], Berra [48]	21,489
21	13	A	Bolton W	D 0-0	0-0	4		15,186
22	20	H	Middlesbrough	W 2-0	2-0	2	Murphy [25], Tabb [45]	21,187
23	26	H	Brentford	W 4-2	3-0	2	Murphy 2 [1, 21], Anderson [30], Smith [82]	12,165
24	30	H	Charlton Ath	W 3-0	1-0	2	Smith [31], Murphy [59], McGoldrick [90]	26,157
25	Jan 10	H	Derby Co	L 0-1	0-0	3		20,861
26	17	A	Millwall	W 3-1	2-1	2	Hunt, N 2 [5, 14], Parr [77]	11,063
27	21	A	Brighton & HA	L 2-3	1-3	3	Murphy [22], Sears [78]	23,880
28	31	H	Wigan Ath	D 0-0	0-0	4		19,155
29	Feb 7	A	Rotherham U	L 0-2	0-1	5		10,336
30	10	H	Sheffield W	W 2-1	0-1	4	Murphy [52], Chambers [67]	17,306
31	14	A	Fulham	W 2-1	2-0	4	Murphy 2 [5, 45]	19,816
32	21	H	Reading	L 0-1	0-1	4		21,298
33	24	H	Birmingham C	W 4-2	1-0	3	Mings [24], Sears 2 [49, 64], Bru [90]	17,161
34	Mar 1	A	Norwich C	L 0-2	0-1	6		27,005
35	4	A	Leeds U	L 1-2	0-0	7	Sears [74]	19,730
36	7	H	Brentford	D 1-1	1-1	7	Murphy [9]	20,132
37	14	A	Middlesbrough	L 1-4	1-2	7	Murphy [11]	18,909
38	17	H	Bolton W	W 1-0	0-0	7	Tabb [79]	16,923
39	21	H	Watford	W 1-0	0-0	6	Chaplow [90]	19,038
40	Apr 3	H	Bournemouth	D 1-1	1-0	7	Sears [6]	22,672
41	6	A	Huddersfield T	L 1-2	0-2	8	Varney [48]	13,231
42	11	H	Blackpool	W 3-2	2-1	6	Sears 2 [24, 28], Berra [83]	19,290
43	14	A	Cardiff C	W 3-1	2-1	6	Sears [8], Skuse [29], Murphy [90]	17,722
44	18	A	Wolverhampton W	D 1-1	1-0	6	Stearman (og) [21]	23,409
45	25	H	Nottingham F	W 2-1	1-0	5	Murphy [22], Sears [83]	25,199
46	May 2	A	Blackburn R	L 2-3	1-2	6	Murphy 2 (1 pen) [2, 82 (p)]	16,869

Final League Position: 6

GOALSCORERS

League (72): Murphy 27 (1 pen), Sears 9, McGoldrick 7 (1 pen), Berra 6, Smith 4, Hunt, N 3, Parr 2, Tabb 2, Anderson 1, Bishop 1, Bru 1, Chambers 1, Chaplow 1, Hyam 1, Mings 1, Sammon 1, Skuse 1, Varney 1, Williams 1, own goal 1.
FA Cup (1): Ambrose 1.
Capital One Cup (0).
Championship Play-Offs (2): Anderson 1, Smith 1.

Gerken D 16	Chambers L 45	Smith T 39+3	Mings T 38+2	Hewitt E 2+1	Hyam L 14+2	Skuse C 40	Tabb J 33+7	Murphy D 43+1	Bajner B 1+4	McGoldrick D 24+2	Wordsworth A —+1	Bru K 16+15	Anderson P 20+15	Sammon C 8+11	Henshall A —+4	Parr J 24+7	Bishop T 23+10	Nouble F —+1	Ambrose D 1+5	Williams J 4+3	Hunt S 10+7	Bialkowski B 30+1	Hunt N 3+8	Sears F 14+7	Clarke M —+4	Varney L 5+5	Chaplow R 3+3	Wood C 3+5	Fryers Z 2+1	Match No.
1	2	3	4	5	6	7[1]	8[1]	9	10	11[3]	12	13	14																	1
1	2	3	4	5	6[3]	8	7	9[1]	10	14	11[1]		12	13																2
1	2	4	3	5		8	7	9[2]	11[3]	13	12		6	10[1]	14															3
1	2	3	4	5		7[1]	8	9[1]	10		11		12	6[1]	14	13														4
1	2[2]	3	4	12		7		9	10			11	6[3]		13	5	8[1]	14												5
1	3	4	12	5[3]		13	7	9	10		11		6[2]	14		2	8[1]													6
1	3	4	14	5		13	7	9	10		11[2]		6[1]	14		2	8[3]													7
1	3	4	14	5		6	7[3]	11		9[2]		12		10		2	8[1]	13												8
1	3	4		5	13	8		12	9	11[3]		7	6[1]	10[2]		2														9
1	3	4		5		7	6	9		10		14	13	11[1]		2	8[2]			12[3]										10
1	3	4	14	5		6[1]	7	12	9	10[3]				11		2	8[2]													11
1		4	3	5		7	12			10		6[2]	13	9		2				14	8[1]	11[3]								12
1	3		4	5		7		9	12	10		6[2]	14	11[1]		2	13				8[3]									13
1	2	4	3			6[3]	7	12	9			10		13	11[2]	5	8[1]			14										14
	2	4	3	5		8	7[3]	13	9		10[2]	12	14			6[1]						1								15
	2	4	3	5		6		8[3]	9		10[2]	7	12	14						13	11[1]	1								16
	2	4	3	5				7	9	10[1]		6		13			12			8[2]	11	1								17
	2	4	3	5[2]		8	7		11	10		6[1]	9	14		13	12[3]					1								18
	3		4	5		6	7	11		10			9[1]	12		2				8[2]	1		13							19
	2	4	3	5		7	8[3]	9		10		13	6[1]	14			12				11[2]	1	1							20
	2	4	3	5		7	8[3]	11		10		12	9[1]				6[2]		14		1	13								21
	2	4	3			8[3]	9	11		10		12	6[1]	14		5	7[2]		13			1								22
	2	4	3			6	8[3]	10		11		13	7[1]			5	9[2]				14	1	12							23
	2	4	3			6	8	10		11[2]		13	7[1]			5	9[2]				12	1	14							24
	2	4	3	5		6		8[2]	11			10	14	7[1]			9[3]				12	1	13							25
	2	4	3	5				7	11			8	6[1]			13				9[2]	1		10[3]	12	14					26
	2	4	3	5		6		8[3]	10			9	7[2]				13				14	1	11[2]	12						27
	2	4	3	5		7		9[2]			10	14	12				11	1	13											28
	2	4	3	5		6		8[3]	11	10[2]		9	7[1]				13				14	1	12							29
	2	4	3	12		8			11			13				5	7[2]	6	9[3]		1	14	10[3]							30
	2	4	3	5		7		9[2]	11			8	14			12	6[2]				1	13	10[1]							31
	2	4	3	5		7		9[2]	11			8	12			13	6[2]				1	10[1]		14						32
	2	4	3	5		8[2]	12	11				7	6[2]	9								1	10[1]	14		13				33
	2	4	3	5		8		9	11[3]			7[2]		13								1	10			12	6[1]	14		34
	2	4	3	5		7		8	13			12	6[2]	9								1	14		10[1]		11[3]			35
1	2	4	3	5		7		8	11			9	12					1					10[2]				6[1]	13		36
1[1]	2	4	3	5		7		9[1]	11			6	8[2]					12				10		14			13			37
	2	4	3	5		8		9	11			13		6[3]	7[2]		1					10[1]	14	12						38
	2	4	3	5		7		8	11			6[3]	12					1				13	10[2]	14	9[1]					39
	2	4	3			7		8	10					6[3]				1				11[2]	14	9[1]	12	13	5			40
	2	4	3			7		8[3]	9					13		14		1				12	10	6[2]	11[1]	5				41
	2	4	3	5[2]		7		9[3]	10			12		14	8		13	1				11		6[1]						42
	2	4	3	5		8	12	11					13			6[3]	7[1]			9[2]	1	10							14	43
	2	4	3	5		6	8	11					12			7[2]	9[1]			13	1	10[3]				14			44
	2	4	3	5		7		10				13	14			6[3]	8[1]			9[2]	1	11	12							45
	2	4	3	5		8	9[2]	11				14	13			6[3]	7[1]			12	1	10								46

FA Cup

Third Round	Southampton	(a)	1-1
Replay	Southampton	(h)	0-1

Capital One Cup

First Round (*aet*)	Crawley T	(a)	0-1

Championship Play-Offs

Semi-Finals 1st leg	Norwich C	(h)	1-1
Semi-Finals 2nd leg	Norwich C	(a)	1-3

LEEDS UNITED

FOUNDATION

Immediately the Leeds City club (founded in 1904) was wound up by the FA in October 1919, following allegations of illegal payments to players, a meeting was called by a Leeds solicitor, Mr Alf Masser, at which Leeds United was formed. They joined the Midland League, playing their first game in that competition in November 1919. It was in this same month that the new club had discussions with the directors of a virtually bankrupt Huddersfield Town who wanted to move to Leeds in an amalgamation. But Huddersfield survived even that crisis.

Elland Road, Leeds, West Yorkshire LS11 0ES.

Telephone: (0871) 334 1919.

Fax: (0113) 367 6050.

Ticket Office: (0871) 334 1992.

Website: www.leedsunited.com

Email: reception@leedsunited.com

Ground Capacity: 37,890.

Record Attendance: 57,892 v Sunderland, FA Cup 5th rd (replay), 15 March 1967.

Pitch Measurements: 105m × 67.5m (115yd × 74yd)

Directors: Massimo Cellino, Edoardo Cellino, Ercole Cellino, Daniel Atty, Andrew Umbers, Salem Patel, Jinesh Patel, Giampaolo Caboni.

Manager: Uwe Rosler.

Assistant Manager: Gunnar Halle.

Physio: Harvey Sharman.

Colours: White shirts with blue trim, white shorts with blue trim, white socks with blue trim.

Year Formed: 1919, as Leeds United after disbandment (by FA order) of Leeds City (formed in 1904).

Turned Professional: 1920.

Club Nickname: 'The Whites'.

Ground: 1919, Elland Road.

HONOURS

Football League – Division 1: Champions 1968–69, 1973–74, 1991–92; *Runners-up* 1964–65, 1965–66, 1969–70, 1970–71, 1971–72; **Division 2: Champions** 1923–24, 1963–64, 1989–90; *Runners-up* 1927–28, 1931–32, 1955–56; **FL 1:** *Runners-up* 2009–10.

FA Cup: *Winners* 1972; *Runners-up* 1965, 1970, 1973.

Football League Cup: *Winners* 1968; *Runners-up* 1996.

European Competitions
European Cup: 1969–70, 1974–75 (*runners-up*).
Champions League: 1992–93, 2000–01 (*s-f*).
European Cup-Winners' Cup: 1972–73 (*runners-up*).
European Fairs Cup: 1965–66, 1966–67 (*runners-up*), 1967–68 (*winners*), 1968–69, 1970–71 (*winners*).
UEFA Cup: 1971–72, 1973–74, 1979–80, 1995–96, 1998–99, 1999–2000 (*s-f*), 2001–02, 2002–03.

First Football League Game: 28 August 1920, Division 2, v Port Vale (a) L 0–2 – Down; Duffield, Tillotson; Musgrove, Baker, Walton; Mason, Goldthorpe, Thompson, Lyon, Best.

Record League Victory: 8–0 v Leicester C, Division 1, 7 April 1934 – Moore; George Milburn, Jack Milburn; Edwards, Hart, Copping; Mahon (2), Firth (2), Duggan (2), Furness (2), Cochrane.

sky **SPORTS** FACT FILE

A total of 31 Leeds United players have won full international caps for England to the end of the 2014–15 season. The first United player to represent England was Willis Edwards who appeared at right half against Wales on 1 March 1926. He went on to win 16 caps, captaining the team on 5 occasions.

Record Cup Victory: 10–0 v Lyn (Oslo), European Cup 1st rd 1st leg, 17 September 1969 – Sprake; Reaney, Cooper, Bremner (2), Charlton, Hunter, Madeley, Clarke (2), Jones (3), Giles (2) (Bates), O'Grady (1).

Record Defeat: 1–8 v Stoke C, Division 1, 27 August 1934.

Most League Points (2 for a win): 67, Division 1, 1968–69.

Most League Points (3 for a win): 86, FL 1, 2009–10.

Most League Goals: 98, Division 2, 1927–28.

Highest League Scorer in Season: John Charles, 42, Division 2, 1953–54.

Most League Goals in Total Aggregate: Peter Lorimer, 168, 1965–79 and 1983–86.

Most League Goals in One Match: 5, Gordon Hodgson v Leicester C, Division 1, 1 October 1938.

Most Capped Player: Lucas Radebe, 58 (70), South Africa.

Most League Appearances: Jack Charlton, 629, 1953–73.

Youngest League Player: Peter Lorimer, 15 years 289 days v Southampton, 29 September 1962.

Record Transfer Fee Received: £30,800,000 from Manchester U for Rio Ferdinand, July 2002.

Record Transfer Fee Paid: £18,000,000 to West Ham U for Rio Ferdinand, November 2000.

Football League Record: 1920 Elected to Division 2; 1924–27 Division 1; 1927–28 Division 2; 1928–31 Division 1; 1931–32 Division 2; 1932–47 Division 1; 1947–56 Division 2; 1956–60 Division 1; 1960–64 Division 2; 1964–82 Division 1; 1982–90 Division 2; 1990–92 Division 1; 1992–2004 FA Premier League; 2004–07 FL C; 2007–10 FL 1; 2010– FL C.

LATEST SEQUENCES

Longest Sequence of League Wins: 9, 18.4.2009 – 5.9.2009.

Longest Sequence of League Defeats: 6, 28.12.2003 – 7.2.2004.

Longest Sequence of League Draws: 5, 19.4.1997 – 9.8.1997.

Longest Sequence of Unbeaten League Matches: 34, 26.10.1968 – 26.8.1969.

Longest Sequence Without a League Win: 17, 1.2.1947 – 26.5.1947.

Successive Scoring Runs: 30 from 27.8.1927.

Successive Non-scoring Runs: 6 from 30.1.1982.

MANAGERS

Dick Ray 1919–20
Arthur Fairclough 1920–27
Dick Ray 1927–35
Bill Hampson 1935–47
Willis Edwards 1947–48
Major Frank Buckley 1948–53
Raich Carter 1953–58
Bill Lambton 1958–59
Jack Taylor 1959–61
Don Revie OBE 1961–74
Brian Clough 1974
Jimmy Armfield 1974–78
Jock Stein CBE 1978
Jimmy Adamson 1978–80
Allan Clarke 1980–82
Eddie Gray MBE 1982–85
Billy Bremner 1985–88
Howard Wilkinson 1988–96
George Graham 1996–98
David O'Leary 1998–2002
Terry Venables 2002–03
Peter Reid 2003
Eddie Gray *(Caretaker)* 2003–04
Kevin Blackwell 2004–06
Dennis Wise 2006–08
Gary McAllister 2008
Simon Grayson 2008–12
Neil Warnock 2012–13
Brian McDermott 2013–14
Dave Hockaday 2014
Darko Milanic 2014
Neil Redfearn 2014–15
Uwe Rosler May 2015–

TEN YEAR LEAGUE RECORD

		P	W	D	L	F	A	Pts	Pos
2005-06	FL C	46	21	15	10	57	38	78	5
2006-07	FL C	46	13	7	26	46	72	36*	24
2007-08	FL 1	46	27	10	9	72	38	76†	5
2008-09	FL 1	46	26	6	14	77	49	84	4
2009-10	FL 1	46	25	11	10	77	44	86	2
2010-11	FL C	46	19	15	12	81	70	72	7
2011-12	FL C	46	17	10	19	65	68	61	14
2012-13	FL C	46	17	10	19	57	66	61	13
2013-14	FL C	46	16	9	21	59	67	57	15
2014-15	FL C	46	15	11	20	50	61	56	15

*10 pts deducted; †15 pts deducted.

DID YOU KNOW ?

Brian Close, who captained Yorkshire and England at cricket, was on Leeds United's books as a youngster. He won England youth international honours, the first United player to do so, and progressed to the reserves before being released at the end of the 1949–50 season.

LEEDS UNITED – FL CHAMPIONSHIP 2014–15 LEAGUE RECORD

Match No.	Date	Venue	Opponents	Result	H/T Score	Lg Pos.	Goalscorers	Attendance
1	Aug 9	A	Millwall	L 0-2	0-1	20		16,205
2	16	H	Middlesbrough	W 1-0	0-0	16	Sharp [88]	24,484
3	19	H	Brighton & HA	L 0-2	0-1	19		21,429
4	23	A	Watford	L 1-4	1-1	21	Tamas (og) [32]	15,674
5	30	H	Bolton W	W 1-0	1-0	18	Warnock [17]	21,901
6	Sept 13	A	Birmingham C	D 1-1	0-1	19	Mowatt [76]	15,266
7	16	A	Bournemouth	W 3-1	0-1	13	Doukara [67], Bellusci [82], Antenucci [89]	9307
8	20	H	Huddersfield T	W 3-0	2-0	11	Austin [19], Antenucci [45], Doukara [69]	29,131
9	27	A	Brentford	L 0-2	0-1	13		10,886
10	Oct 1	H	Reading	D 0-0	0-0	12		20,705
11	4	H	Sheffield W	D 1-1	0-0	14	Bellusci [79]	24,094
12	17	A	Rotherham U	L 1-2	1-0	14	Antenucci [30]	11,350
13	21	A	Norwich C	D 1-1	0-0	15	Doukara [63]	26,565
14	25	H	Wolverhampton W	L 1-2	1-0	18	Antenucci [18]	27,883
15	Nov 1	A	Cardiff C	L 1-3	0-0	19	Mowatt [77]	24,220
16	4	A	Charlton Ath	D 2-2	0-0	17	Mowatt 2 [49, 67]	18,698
17	8	H	Blackpool	W 3-1	3-0	15	Cooper [9], Doukara [31], Antenucci [42]	18,698
18	22	A	Blackburn R	L 1-2	1-0	16	Doukara [33]	21,432
19	29	H	Derby Co	W 2-0	1-0	15	Antenucci 2 [43, 50]	26,028
20	Dec 6	A	Ipswich T	L 1-4	1-3	16	Antenucci [4]	21,489
21	13	H	Fulham	L 0-1	0-0	19		27,264
22	20	A	Nottingham F	D 1-1	0-1	18	Sharp (pen) [54]	22,664
23	26	H	Wigan Ath	L 0-2	0-1	20		28,375
24	30	A	Derby Co	L 0-2	0-1	20		31,690
25	Jan 10	A	Bolton W	D 1-1	1-0	21	Austin (pen) [3]	18,844
26	17	H	Birmingham C	D 1-1	0-1	20	Murphy [86]	23,534
27	20	H	Bournemouth	W 1-0	1-0	19	Murphy [36]	17,634
28	31	A	Huddersfield T	W 2-1	1-1	19	Byram [7], Sharp [90]	20,029
29	Feb 7	A	Brentford	L 0-1	0-0	20		23,164
30	10	A	Reading	W 2-0	0-0	17	Murphy [63], Byram [90]	18,124
31	14	H	Millwall	W 1-0	1-0	12	Mowatt [39]	24,000
32	21	A	Middlesbrough	W 1-0	1-0	11	Mowatt [3]	25,531
33	24	A	Brighton & HA	L 0-2	0-1	14		25,274
34	28	H	Watford	L 2-3	2-1	16	Sharp [7], Austin [19]	24,705
35	Mar 4	H	Ipswich T	W 2-1	0-0	15	Mowatt [71], Sharp [77]	19,730
36	7	A	Wigan Ath	W 1-0	0-0	13	Mowatt [51]	16,163
37	14	H	Nottingham F	D 0-0	0-0	13		30,722
38	18	A	Fulham	W 3-0	1-0	12	Byram [40], Bamba [48], Antenucci [88]	19,200
39	21	A	Blackpool	D 1-1	0-1	13	Antenucci [62]	11,688
40	Apr 4	H	Blackburn R	L 0-3	0-0	14		25,293
41	6	A	Wolverhampton W	L 3-4	1-2	16	Taylor, C [11], Batth (og) [65], Mowatt [74]	25,169
42	11	H	Cardiff C	L 1-2	1-1	15	Philips [17]	22,401
43	14	H	Norwich C	L 0-2	0-0	15		21,471
44	18	A	Charlton Ath	L 1-2	1-0	16	Morison [40]	18,053
45	25	A	Sheffield W	W 2-1	0-1	15	Taylor, C [57], Morison [72]	28,227
46	May 2	H	Rotherham U	D 0-0	0-0	15		31,850

Final League Position: 15

GOALSCORERS

League (50): Antenucci 10, Mowatt 9, Doukara 5, Sharp 5 (1 pen), Austin 3 (1 pen), Byram 3, Murphy 3, Bellusci 2, Morison 2, Taylor, C 2, Bamba 1, Cooper 1, Philips 1, Warnock 1, own goals 2.
FA Cup (0).
Capital One Cup (3): Doukara 2, Smith 1.

Silvestri M 43	Byram S 36 + 3	Pearce J 20 + 1	Wootton S 23	Warnock S 21	Austin R 24 + 6	Murphy L 26 + 4	Tonge M 4 + 6	Hunt N 1	Doukara S 17 + 8	Ajose N 2 + 1	Smith M 1 + 2	Cook L 33 + 4	Poleon D — + 4	Bianchi T 24	Cooper L 25 + 4	Sharp B 17 + 16	Bellusci G 29 + 1	Antenucci M 24 + 12	Mowatt A 37 + 1	Sloth C 7 + 6	Taylor C 22 + 1	Benedicic Z — + 1	Berardi G 19 + 3	Morison S 17 + 9	Adryan T 9 + 3	Montenegro B — + 5	Dawson C — + 3	Bamba S 19	Cani E — + 4	Philips K 2	Ngoyi G 1	Taylor S 3	White A — + 1	Match No.
1	2	3	4	5	6	7	8		9¹	10³	11²	12	13	14																				1
1	2		4		5	6³	7		12		11²	9¹		14	13		8	10																2
1	2	3		5	6	9²	8		12	11¹		14	13	4	7	10¹																		3
1	2◼		4	5	7	10	6²		14			13	12	8	11¹	3◼	9²																	4
1		4	2	5¹					6					7	10	3	11	8	9²	12	13													5
1		4	5	12					13			6		7	10³	3	11	8	9²	2														6
1	12	4	5²	7					9			6		13	8	10¹	3	11	2															7
1	12	4	5	7¹		14	10³		6			8		3	11	9²	2◼	13																8
1	2	4	5	9	14	13	11		6¹			7²		3	10	8³	12																	9
1	2	4	13	12	10	6²	5		8			14		3	11¹	7³	9																	10
1	2	4	7	12	11²	6	13		3			10¹		8	9²	5	14																	11
1		4	5	7	11³	9²			6¹	13		3	10	8	2	14	12																	12
1	2	4		7	10¹	12			6			3		11	8²	13	5	9																13
1		4	5	12	6	7¹			3	10		8³	13	2	11	9²	14																	14
1	14	4	5	9	6	7³			3	11		8	13	2¹	10²	12																		15
1	2		5	11	7				4	6²		3	10	8	12	9¹	13																	16
1	2	3	5	12		13			11	7	4	6²	14	10²	8	9¹																		17
1	2	4	5		10	7¹			3	6²	13	12	11	8	9																			18
1	2		5	12	13	10			7	4	6¹	3	11	8	9²																			19
1	2	4	5	12		13	10¹		7	3	6	11	8	9²																				20
1	2	3	5²		10³				7	4	6	12	11	8	14	9¹	13																	21
1	2	3	5	13		14			6	4	7	10¹	11²	9	12	8¹																		22
1	2		5	13	6				14	9	4	7¹	11³	3	10	8²	12																	23
1	2		5²	9					11¹	6	4	7³	13	3	10	8	12	14																24
1	8				9	6			7			4			3	12	10¹	5	2	11														25
1	8	2			6	7			13			9²	4		12	3	10¹	5	11															26
1	8	13	2		9²	6			7			4		12	3◼	10³	5	14	11¹															27
1	8	2			9	7			6²			4		13	12	10¹	5	11							3									28
1	8	2			9	7¹			6			4		10	12	5	11²							3	13									29
1	8	2			6				9			7¹	4		10	12	5	11							3									30
1	8	2			9¹	6			7			4	12	10	5	11								3										31
1	8	2			9	7			6	12		4¹	10	5	11									3										32
1		2			9	6			14	7	4	13	10²	8³	5	11¹	3	12																33
1	8²	2			9³	6			7	4	11	13	10¹	5	12	3	14																	34
1	8	2			6	7			5	11¹	4	12	9	10²	13	3																		35
1		2			8	7			10²	4	13	6	9	10¹	5	11¹	8²	3	12															36
1		2			7	13			6	11	4	12	9	10¹	5	8²	3																	37
1	8	2			7	6			11¹	4	13	9²	10	5	12	3																		38
1	8	2			6	14			7	11³	4	13	9¹	10²	5	12	3																	39
1	8	2¹			6◼	7			13	14	3	12	9	10	5³	11²	4																	40
1	7	2			6				4	12	11¹	9	10	5	3	8																		41
1	7	2			6	14			12	3	11¹	9	10	5³	13	4	8²																	42
1	8¹	2			7				4	11	12	9	10²	5	13	3									6									43
		6¹	2	7	8				4	11²	9	5	10	12	13	3															1			44
	8	2	6	7					4	12	9¹	10	5	11	3																1			45
	8	2	6	7					4	12	9¹	10	5²	11³	14	3															1	13	46

FA Cup
Third Round   Sunderland   (a)   0-1

Capital One Cup
First Round   Accrington S   (h)   2-1
Second Round   Bradford C   (a)   1-2

LEICESTER CITY

FOUNDATION

In 1884 a number of young footballers, who were mostly old boys of Wyggeston School, held a meeting at a house on the Roman Fosse Way and formed Leicester Fosse FC. They collected 9d (less than 4p) towards the cost of a ball, plus the same amount for membership. Their first professional, Harry Webb from Stafford Rangers, was signed in 1888 for 2s 6d (12p) per week, plus travelling expenses.

King Power Stadium, Filbert Way, Leicester LE2 7FL.
Telephone: (0344) 815 5000.
Fax: (0116) 291 5778.
Ticket Office: (0344) 815 5000.
Website: www.lcfc.co.uk
Email: sales@lcfc.co.uk
Ground Capacity: 32,312.
Record Attendance: 47,298 v Tottenham H, FA Cup 5th rd, 18 February 1928 (at Filbert Street); 32,148 v Newcastle U, FA Premier League, 26 December 2003 (at Walkers Stadium); 32,188 v Real Madrid, Friendly, 30 July 2011 (at King Power Stadium).
Pitch Measurements: 110m × 74m (120.5yd × 81yd)
Chairman: Khun Vichai Srivaddhanaprabha.
Chief Executive: Susan Whelan.
Manager: Claudio Ranieri.
Assistant Managers: Craig Shakespeare, Steve Walsh.
Physio: Dave Rennie.
Colours: Blue shirts with yellow trim, white shorts with blue and yellow trim, blue socks with white trim.
Year Formed: 1884.
Turned Professional: 1888.
Previous Name: 1884, Leicester Fosse; 1919, Leicester City.
Club Nickname: 'The Foxes'.
Grounds: 1884, Victoria Park; 1887, Belgrave Road; 1888, Victoria Park; 1891, Filbert Street; 2002, Walkers Stadium (now known as King Power Stadium from 2011).
First Football League Game: 1 September 1894, Division 2, v Grimsby T (a) L 3–4 – Thraves; Smith, Bailey; Seymour, Brown, Henrys; Hill, Hughes, McArthur (1), Skea (2), Priestman.
Record League Victory: 10–0 v Portsmouth, Division 1, 20 October 1928 – McLaren; Black, Brown; Findlay, Carr, Watson; Adcock, Hine (3), Chandler (6), Lochhead, Barry (1).
Record Cup Victory: 8–1 v Coventry C (a), League Cup 5th rd, 1 December 1964 – Banks; Sjoberg, Norman (2); Roberts, King, McDerment; Hodgson (2), Cross, Goodfellow, Gibson (1), Stringfellow (2), (1 og).

HONOURS

Football League – Division 1:
Runners-up 1928–29, 2002–03;
Division 2: *Champions* 1924–25, 1936–37, 1953–54, 1956–57, 1970–71, 1979–80; *Runners-up* 1907–08;
FL C: *Champions* 2013–14.
FL 1: *Champions* 2008–09.
FA Cup: *Runners-up* 1949, 1961, 1963, 1969.
Football League Cup: *Winners* 1964, 1997, 2000; *Runners-up* 1965, 1999.
European Competitions
European Cup-Winners' Cup: 1961–62.
UEFA Cup: 1997–98, 2000–01.

sky SPORTS FACT FILE

The old Leicester Fosse club was placed in liquidation in July 1919 and a new company, The Leicester City Football Club Company Limited was incorporated on 7 August 1919. They were able to use the title 'City' as the town of Leicester was granted city status in June 1919.

Record Defeat: 0–12 (as Leicester Fosse) v Nottingham F,
Division 1, 21 April 1909.

Most League Points (2 for a win): 61, Division 2, 1956–57.

Most League Points (3 for a win): 102, FL C, 2013–14.

Most League Goals: 109, Division 2, 1956–57.

Highest League Scorer in Season: Arthur Rowley, 44,
Division 2, 1956–57.

Most League Goals in Total Aggregate: Arthur Chandler,
259, 1923–35.

Most League Goals in One Match: 6, John Duncan v
Port Vale, Division 2, 25 December 1924; 6, Arthur
Chandler v Portsmouth, Division 1, 20 October 1928.

Most Capped Player: John O'Neill, 39, Northern Ireland.

Most League Appearances: Adam Black, 528, 1920–35.

Youngest League Player: Dave Buchanan, 16 years 192 days
v Oldham Ath, 1 January 1979.

Record Transfer Fee Received: £11,000,000 from Liverpool
for Emile Heskey, March 2000.

Record Transfer Fee Paid: £9,500,000 to HNK Rijeka for
Andrej Kramaric, January 2015.

Football League Record: 1894 Elected to Division 2;
1908–09 Division 1; 1909–25 Division 2; 1925–35 Division 1;
1935–37 Division 2; 1937–39 Division 1; 1946–54 Division 2;
1954–55 Division 1; 1955–57 Division 2; 1957–69 Division 1;
1969–71 Division 2; 1971–78 Division 1; 1978–80 Division 2;
1980–81 Division 1; 1981–83 Division 2; 1983–87 Division 1;
1987–92 Division 2; 1992–94 Division 1; 1994–95 FA
Premier League; 1995–96 Division 1; 1996–2002 FA Premier
League; 2002–03 Division 1; 2003–04 FA Premier League;
2004–08 FL C; 2008–09 FL 1; 2009–14 FL C; 2014–
FA Premier League.

LATEST SEQUENCES

Longest Sequence of League Wins: 9, 21.12.2013 – 1.2.2014.

Longest Sequence of League Defeats: 8, 17.3.2001 – 28.4.2001.

Longest Sequence of League Draws: 6, 2.10.2004 – 2.11.2004.

Longest Sequence of Unbeaten League Matches: 23,
1.11.2008 – 7.3.2009.

Longest Sequence Without a League Win: 18, 12.4.1975 –
1.11.1975.

Successive Scoring Runs: 32 from 23.11.2013.

Successive Non-scoring Runs: 7 from 21.11.1987.

MANAGERS

Frank Gardner 1884–92
Ernest Marson 1892–94
J. Lee 1894–95
Henry Jackson 1895–97
William Clark 1897–98
George Johnson 1898–1912
Jack Bartlett 1912–14
Louis Ford 1914–15
Harry Linney 1915–19
Peter Hodge 1919–26
Willie Orr 1926–32
Peter Hodge 1932–34
Arthur Lochhead 1934–36
Frank Womack 1936–39
Tom Bromilow 1939–45
Tom Mather 1945–46
John Duncan 1946–49
Norman Bullock 1949–55
David Halliday 1955–58
Matt Gillies 1958–68
Frank O'Farrell 1968–71
Jimmy Bloomfield 1971–77
Frank McLintock 1977–78
Jock Wallace 1978–82
Gordon Milne 1982–86
Bryan Hamilton 1986–87
David Pleat 1987–91
Gordon Lee 1991
Brian Little 1991–94
Mark McGhee 1994–95
Martin O'Neill 1995–2000
Peter Taylor 2000–01
Dave Bassett 2001–02
Micky Adams 2002–04
Craig Levein 2004–06
Robert Kelly 2006–07
Martin Allen 2007
Gary Megson 2007
Ian Holloway 2007–08
Nigel Pearson 2008–10
Paulo Sousa 2010
Sven-Göran Eriksson 2010–11
Nigel Pearson 2011–15
Claudio Ranieri July 2015–

TEN YEAR LEAGUE RECORD

		P	W	D	L	F	A	Pts	Pos
2005-06	FL C	46	13	15	18	51	59	54	16
2006-07	FL C	46	13	14	19	49	64	53	19
2007-08	FL C	46	12	16	18	42	45	52	22
2008-09	FL 1	46	27	15	4	84	39	96	1
2009-10	FL C	46	21	13	12	61	45	76	5
2010-11	FL C	46	19	10	17	76	71	67	10
2011-12	FL C	46	18	12	16	66	55	66	9
2012-13	FL C	46	19	11	16	71	48	68	6
2013-14	FL C	46	31	9	6	83	43	102	1
2014-15	PR Lge	38	11	8	19	46	55	41	14

DID YOU KNOW ?

Left half Reg Halton, who played
for Leicester City between 1950
and 1953, was one of numerous
Foxes' players who were also
talented cricketers. In July 1952
he scored 212 runs in just 226
minutes playing for Staffordshire
against Yorkshire Seconds at
Scarborough.

LEICESTER CITY – FA PREMIERSHIP 2014–15 LEAGUE RECORD

Match No.	Date	Venue	Opponents	Result	H/T Score	Lg Pos.	Goalscorers	Attendance
1	Aug 16	H	Everton	D	2-2	1-2	6	Ulloa [22], Wood [86]	31,603
2	23	A	Chelsea	L	0-2	0-0	14		41,604
3	31	H	Arsenal	D	1-1	1-1	15	Ulloa [22]	31,535
4	Sept 13	A	Stoke C	W	1-0	0-0	10	Ulloa [64]	27,500
5	21	H	Manchester U	W	5-3	1-2	7	Ulloa 2 (1 pen) [17, 83 (p)], Nugent (pen) [62], Cambiasso [64], Vardy [79]	31,784
6	27	A	Crystal Palace	L	0-2	0-0	10		24,311
7	Oct 4	H	Burnley	D	2-2	2-1	9	Schlupp [33], Mahrez [40]	31,448
8	18	A	Newcastle U	L	0-1	0-0	13		51,886
9	25	A	Swansea C	L	0-2	0-1	16		20,259
10	Nov 1	H	WBA	L	0-1	0-0	17		31,819
11	8	A	Southampton	L	0-2	0-0	18		31,297
12	22	H	Sunderland	D	0-0	0-0	17		31,825
13	29	A	QPR	L	2-3	1-2	20	Cambiasso [4], Schlupp [67]	18,054
14	Dec 2	H	Liverpool	L	1-3	1-1	20	Mignolet (og) [21]	32,000
15	7	A	Aston Villa	L	1-2	1-1	20	Ulloa [13]	27,692
16	13	H	Manchester C	L	0-1	0-1	20		31,643
17	20	A	West Ham U	L	0-2	0-1	20		34,977
18	26	H	Tottenham H	L	1-2	0-1	20	Ulloa [48]	31,870
19	28	A	Hull C	W	1-0	1-0	20	Mahrez [32]	23,809
20	Jan 1	A	Liverpool	D	2-2	0-2	20	Nugent [58], Schlupp [60]	44,720
21	10	H	Aston Villa	W	1-0	1-0	20	Konchesky [45]	31,728
22	17	H	Stoke C	L	0-1	0-0	20		31,772
23	31	A	Manchester U	L	1-3	0-3	20	Wasilewski [80]	75,329
24	Feb 7	H	Crystal Palace	L	0-1	0-0	20		31,695
25	10	A	Arsenal	L	1-2	0-2	20	Kramaric [61]	60,032
26	22	H	Everton	D	2-2	0-0	20	Nugent [63], Cambiasso [70]	38,904
27	Mar 4	A	Manchester C	L	0-2	0-1	20		45,000
28	14	H	Hull C	D	0-0	0-0	20		31,456
29	21	A	Tottenham H	L	3-4	1-2	20	Vardy [38], Morgan [50], Nugent [90]	35,950
30	Apr 4	H	West Ham U	W	2-1	1-1	20	Cambiasso [12], King [86]	31,863
31	11	A	WBA	W	3-2	1-2	20	Nugent [20], Huth [80], Vardy [90]	26,768
32	18	H	Swansea C	W	2-0	1-0	18	Ulloa [15], King [89]	31,121
33	25	A	Burnley	W	1-0	0-0	17	Vardy [60]	19,582
34	29	H	Chelsea	L	1-3	1-0	17	Albrighton [45]	32,021
35	May 2	H	Newcastle U	W	3-0	2-0	17	Ulloa 2 (1 pen) [1, 48 (p)], Morgan [17]	31,576
36	9	H	Southampton	W	2-0	2-0	15	Mahrez 2 [7, 19]	31,939
37	16	A	Sunderland	D	0-0	0-0	14		46,705
38	24	H	QPR	W	5-1	2-0	14	Vardy [16], Albrighton [43], Ulloa [51], Cambiasso [52], Kramaric [86]	31,467

Final League Position: 14

GOALSCORERS

League (46): Ulloa 11 (2 pens), Cambiasso 5, Nugent 5 (1 pen), Vardy 5, Mahrez 4, Schlupp 3, Albrighton 2, King 2, Kramaric 2, Morgan 2, Huth 1, Konchesky 1, Wasilewski 1, Wood 1, own goal 1.
FA Cup (4): Ulloa 2, Kramaric 1, Schlupp 1.
Capital One Cup (0).

Schmeichel K 24	De Laet R 20+6	Morgan W 37	Moore L 10+1	Konchesky P 26	Mahrez R 25+5	King A 16+8	Drinkwater D 16+7	Knockaert A 3+6	Ulloa J 29+8	Nugent D 16+13	Hammond D 9+3	Schlupp J 30+2	Wood C —+7	Albrighton M 10+8	Taylor-Fletcher G —+1	Vardy J 26+8	Hamer B 8	Cambiasso E 27+4	James M 20+7	Simpson D 13+1	Wasilewski M 22+3	Powell N —+3	Lawrence T —+3	Kramaric A 6+7	Schwarzer M 6	Huth R 14	Upson M 5	Match No.
1	2	3	4	5	6	7	8^2	9^3	10^1	11	12	13	14															1
1	2	3	4	5	6^1	7			11^{12}	10		8^3	9	14		12		13										2
1	2	3	4	5	6^2	8	14		10^1	11		7	9^1			12		13										3
1	2	3	4	5	6^1	7^2	12		10	11		8	9^1			11^1	1	13										4
1	2	3	4	5		12	7		9	10^2	6		14			11^1		8^2	13									5
1	2^3	3	4	5	13		8		10	11	6^2		9			7	14	12										6
1	2	3	4	5	6^2		7	13	11^1	12	8^3	9				10		14										7
1	2	3	4	5			9	14	11	12		10^3			7^2	13	6^1	8										8
1	2	3	4	5	8	13	7^2		11	9	6^3				10^1	14	12											9
1	2	4		5		9	7^3		12	11^2			14			10^1		6	8	3	13							10
1	2^3	4	12		9^2	8			11^1				5	13		10		6	7	3	14							11
1	2	4		5	6				13	10^1	12		9^2	14		11^3		7	8	3								12
1	2	4		5	6^3	14			11^2	12		9		13		10		8^1	7	3								13
1	2	4^4		5^1	6				10				9			12		11	8	7	3							14
1		4		5^4	6				10^3	12			9^1	13	14	11^2		8	7	2	3							15
	4		5	6	7	9^3	14	12			10^2			11^1	1	8		2	3	13								16
	4		5^1	6	7	9	14	12	13			10			11^2	1	8^1		2	3								17
	4		5^1	6	8^2	7	14	11	10^5			9			13	1		12	2	3								18
13	4		5^4	6^3		14			11^2	10			9	12		1		7^1	8	2	3							19
5	4			6		8^1		14	12	9^2	10			11^3	1	13		7	8	2	3							20
	4		5		14		9	11^2	10	7^3				6^1		13	1		8^4	2	3	12						21
	4		5			8	7	6	14	11^1			9^2			10^3	1			2	3	13	12					22
5	4				8	7			10^1	13		9		14		6^2		12		2	3	11^3	1					23
	4		5	6			11		10^5	9^3		12	14			7	8	2^1	3			13	1					24
	3^2			6	7				13	14		10^1				9	8	12				11	1	4		5^3		25
	3			6	7^2	14				12		10^3				13		9^5	8	2		11	1	4		5		26
	3			6^2	7^3				14	12		10				13		9	8	2		11^1	1	4		5		27
	2^2	3^1			7				12	14		6				10		8	9			13	11^3	1	4		5^3	28
1	2	3			13	14			11	7		6				10		9^5	8	12				4^1		5^3		29
1	2^2	4			8^1	14			11^3	9		5		12		10		7	6				13	3				30
1	2^2	4			14	13			11^1	10		5		6		9		8	7^3	12				3				31
1	12	4			13	6	14		10^3			8		5		11		7				2^2	9^1	3				32
1	13	5			6	9	7^3		11^1			2^4		10		8	14		3				12	4				33
1	13	5			6	14	9^3	7	10			2		11^2		8	12		3					4^1				34
1	12	4			9				11^1	13	8	5		10		7^5	6		2^3				14	3				35
	1	4			9		12		10^3	13	14	8		5		11^1		7	6^2	2				3				36
	1	4			9^1	6	12		10^2			8		5		11		7		2			13	3				37
1	12	4			9	7	14		10			8		5		11^1		6^3		2^2			13	3				38

FA Cup

Third Round	Newcastle U	(h)	1-0
Fourth Round	Tottenham H	(a)	2-1
Fifth Round	Aston Villa	(a)	1-2

Capital One Cup

Second Round	Shrewsbury T	(h)	0-1

LEYTON ORIENT

FOUNDATION

There is some doubt about the foundation of Leyton Orient, and, indeed, some confusion with clubs like Leyton and Clapton over their early history. As regards the foundation, the most favoured version is that Leyton Orient was formed originally by members of Homerton Theological College who established Glyn Cricket Club in 1881 and then carried on through the following winter playing football. Eventually many employees of the Orient Shipping Line became involved and so the name Orient was chosen in 1888.

Matchroom Stadium, Brisbane Road, Leyton, London E10 5NF.

Telephone: (0871) 310 1881.

Fax: (0871) 310 1882.

Ticket Office: (0871) 310 1883.

Website: www.leytonorient.com

Email: info@leytonorient.net

Ground Capacity: 9,255.

Record Attendance: 34,345 v West Ham U, FA Cup 4th rd, 25 January 1964.

Pitch Measurements: 100.5m × 65m (110yd × 71yd)

Chairman: Francesco Becchetti.

Chief Executive: Alessandro Angelieri.

Head Coach: Ian Hendon.

Assistant Coach: Kevin Nugent.

Physio: Mike Preston.

Colours: Red shirts with white trim, red shorts, red socks.

Year Formed: 1881.

Turned Professional: 1903.

Previous Names: 1881, Glyn Cricket and Football Club; 1886, Eagle Football Club; 1888, Orient Football Club; 1898, Clapton Orient; 1946, Leyton Orient; 1966, Orient; 1987, Leyton Orient.

Club Nickname: 'The O's'.

Grounds: 1884, Glyn Road; 1896, Whittles Athletic Ground; 1900, Millfields Road; 1930, Lea Bridge Road; 1937, Brisbane Road (renamed Matchroom Stadium).

First Football League Game: 2 September 1905, Division 2, v Leicester Fosse (a) L 1–2 – Butler; Holmes, Codling; Lamberton, Boden, Boyle; Kingaby (1), Wootten, Leigh, Evenson, Bourne.

Record League Victory: 8–0 v Crystal Palace, Division 3 (S), 12 November 1955 – Welton; Lee, Earl; Blizzard, Aldous, McKnight; White (1), Facey (3), Burgess (2), Heckman, Hartburn (2). 8–0 v Rochdale, Division 4, 20 October 1987 – Wells; Howard, Dickenson (1), Smalley (1), Day, Hull, Hales (2), Castle (Sussex), Shinners (2), Godfrey (Harvey), Comfort (2). 8–0 v Colchester U, Division 4, 15 October 1988 – Wells; Howard, Dickenson, Hales (1p), Day (1), Sitton (1), Baker (1), Ward, Hull (3), Juryeff, Comfort (1). 8–0 v Doncaster R, Division 3, 28 December 1997 – Hyde; Channing, Naylor, Smith (1p), Hicks, Clark, Ling, Roger Joseph, Griffiths (3) (Harris), Richards (2) (Baker (1)), Inglethorpe (1) (Simpson).

HONOURS

Football League – Division 1: 22nd, 1962–63;
Division 2: *Runners-up* 1961–62;
Division 3: *Champions* 1969–70;
Division 3 (S): *Champions* 1955–56;
Runners-up 1954–55.
FA Cup: Best season: semi-final 1978.
Football League Cup: Best season: 5th rd, 1963.

sky SPORTS FACT FILE

Centre half Willy Van Den Eynden joined Clapton Orient in November 1913 and played 12 Football League games for the O's. Van den Eynden was said to have been a Belgian international and worked as an architect, having come to London to improve his English. In July 1914 he was sentenced to 3 months' imprisonment and deportation.

Record Cup Victory: 9–2 v Chester, League Cup 3rd rd, 15 October 1962 – Robertson; Charlton, Taylor; Gibbs, Bishop, Lea; Deeley (1), Waites (3), Dunmore (2), Graham (3), Wedge.

Record Defeat: 0–8 v Aston Villa, FA Cup 4th rd, 30 January 1929.

Most League Points (2 for a win): 66, Division 3 (S), 1955–56.

Most League Points (3 for a win): 86, FL 1, 2013–14.

Most League Goals: 106, Division 3 (S), 1955–56.

Highest League Scorer in Season: Tom Johnston, 35, Division 2, 1957–58.

Most League Goals in Total Aggregate: Tom Johnston, 121, 1956–58, 1959–61.

Most League Goals in One Match: 4, Wally Leigh v Bradford C, Division 2, 13 April 1906; 4, Albert Pape v Oldham Ath, Division 2, 1 September 1924; 4, Peter Kitchen v Millwall, Division 3, 21 April 1984.

Most Capped Players: Jobi McAnuff, 10 (17), Jamaica.

Most League Appearances: Peter Allen, 432, 1965–78.

Youngest League Player: Paul Went, 15 years 327 days v Preston NE, 4 September 1965.

Record Transfer Fee Received: £1,000,000 from Fulham for Gabriel Zakuani, July 2006; £1,000,000 from Brentford for Moses Odubajo, June 2014.

Record Transfer Fee Paid: £175,000 to Wigan Ath for Paul Beesley, October 1989.

Football League Record: 1905 Elected to Division 2; 1929–56 Division 3 (S); 1956–62 Division 2; 1962–63 Division 1; 1963–66 Division 2; 1966–70 Division 3; 1970–82 Division 2; 1982–85 Division 3; 1985–89 Division 4; 1989–92 Division 3; 1992–95 Division 2; 1995–2004 Division 3; 2004–06 FL 2; 2006–15 FL 1; 2015– FL 2.

LATEST SEQUENCES

Longest Sequence of League Wins: 10, 21.1.1956 – 30.3.1956.

Longest Sequence of League Defeats: 9, 1.4.1995 – 6.5.1995.

Longest Sequence of League Draws: 6, 30.11.1974 – 28.12.1974.

Longest Sequence of Unbeaten League Matches: 15, 13.4.2013 – 19.10.2013.

Longest Sequence Without a League Win: 23, 6.10.1962 – 13.4.1963.

Successive Scoring Runs: 22 from 12.3.1927.

Successive Non-scoring Runs: 8 from 19.11.1994.

MANAGERS

Sam Omerod 1905–06
Ike Ivenson 1906
Billy Holmes 1907–22
Peter Proudfoot 1922–29
Arthur Grimsdell 1929–30
Peter Proudfoot 1930–31
Jimmy Seed 1931–33
David Pratt 1933–34
Peter Proudfoot 1935–39
Tom Halsey 1939
Bill Wright 1939–45
Willie Hall 1945
Bill Wright 1945–46
Charlie Hewitt 1946–48
Neil McBain 1948–49
Alec Stock 1949–59
Les Gore 1959–61
Johnny Carey 1961–63
Benny Fenton 1963–64
Dave Sexton 1965
Dick Graham 1966–68
Jimmy Bloomfield 1968–71
George Petchey 1971–77
Jimmy Bloomfield 1977–81
Paul Went 1981
Ken Knighton 1981–83
Frank Clark 1983–91
(Managing Director)
Peter Eustace 1991–94
Chris Turner/John Sitton 1994–95
Pat Holland 1995–96
Tommy Taylor 1996–2001
Paul Brush 2001–03
Martin Ling 2003–09
Geraint Williams 2009–10
Russell Slade 2010–14
Kevin Nugent 2014
Mauro Milanese 2014
Fabio Liverani 2014–15
Ian Hendon May 2015–

TEN YEAR LEAGUE RECORD

		P	W	D	L	F	A	Pts	Pos
2005-06	FL 2	46	22	15	9	67	51	81	3
2006-07	FL 1	46	12	15	19	61	77	51	20
2007-08	FL 1	46	16	12	18	49	63	60	14
2008-09	FL 1	46	15	11	20	45	57	56	14
2009-10	FL 1	46	13	12	21	53	63	51	17
2010-11	FL 1	46	19	13	14	71	62	70	7
2011-12	FL 1	46	13	11	22	48	75	50	20
2012-13	FL 1	46	21	8	17	55	48	71	7
2013-14	FL 1	46	25	11	10	85	45	86	3
2014-15	FL 1	46	12	13	21	59	69	49	23

DID YOU KNOW ?

In 1994–95, for the only time in their history, Leyton Orient failed to win a single League game away from home, drawing 2 and losing 21 of their games. However, they did manage a Cup win on their travels, running out 3–1 winners at non-league Tiverton Town in an FA Cup first round tie.

LEYTON ORIENT – FOOTBALL LEAGUE ONE 2014–15 LEAGUE RECORD

Match No.	Date		Venue	Opponents	Result		H/T Score	Lg Pos.	Goalscorers	Attendance
1	Aug	9	H	Chesterfield	L	1-2	0-1	17	Henderson [83]	5619
2		16	A	Oldham Ath	W	3-1	1-1	10	Henderson [20], Mooney [58], Lisbie [81]	3754
3		19	A	Bristol C	D	0-0	0-0	12		11,692
4		23	H	Walsall	D	0-0	0-0	14		4400
5		30	A	Fleetwood T	D	1-1	1-0	14	Henderson [34]	3222
6	Sept	13	H	Colchester U	L	0-2	0-0	20		5313
7		16	A	Notts Co	D	1-1	0-1	19	Dagnall (pen) [51]	4024
8		20	A	Scunthorpe U	W	2-1	1-0	17	Cuthbert [3], McAnuff [51]	3264
9		27	H	Rochdale	L	2-3	2-1	19	McAnuff [13], Vincelot [42]	4405
10	Oct	4	H	Swindon T	L	1-2	0-1	20	Henderson [90]	5422
11		11	A	Sheffield U	D	2-2	1-0	22	Simpson, J [38], Vincelot [90]	19,179
12		18	A	Milton Keynes D	D	0-0	0-0	20		5014
13		21	A	Doncaster R	W	2-0	1-0	15	Simpson, J [2], Henderson [62]	5205
14		25	A	Port Vale	L	0-3	0-0	18		4773
15		28	H	Preston NE	L	0-2	0-1	19		4650
16	Nov	1	H	Coventry C	D	2-2	0-1	20	Cuthbert [54], Simpson, J [70]	5464
17		15	A	Gillingham	L	2-3	0-0	21	Plasmati (pen) [48], Dagnall [90]	5891
18		22	H	Crewe Alex	W	4-1	2-0	19	Plasmati [23], Dagnall [35], Cox [61], Mooney [86]	5516
19		29	A	Bradford C	L	1-3	0-1	19	Mooney [74]	12,489
20	Dec	13	H	Peterborough U	L	1-2	1-1	22	Batt [39]	5546
21		20	A	Barnsley	L	0-2	0-2	23		8742
22		26	H	Crawley T	W	4-1	2-1	20	Cox [6], Dagnall 2 [19, 90], Mooney [88]	4108
23		29	A	Yeovil T	W	3-0	1-0	19	Dagnall [34], Lisbie [62], Cox [85]	4132
24	Jan	10	A	Fleetwood T	L	0-1	0-0	20		4947
25		16	H	Preston NE	D	2-2	1-1	19	Mooney [5], Dagnall [78]	8555
26		24	A	Colchester U	L	0-2	0-1	22		5668
27		31	H	Scunthorpe U	L	1-4	0-2	23	Henderson (pen) [68]	5184
28	Feb	10	H	Notts Co	L	0-1	0-1	24		3534
29		14	A	Chesterfield	W	3-2	1-1	23	Mooney 2 [35, 70], Cox [90]	6524
30		18	H	Bradford C	L	0-2	0-2	23		4760
31		21	A	Oldham Ath	W	3-0	2-0	23	Dossena [3], Mooney (pen) [25], Simpson, J [90]	4423
32		28	A	Walsall	W	2-0	0-0	21	Hedges [56], Dagnall [59]	5239
33	Mar	3	H	Bristol C	L	1-3	1-2	21	Dagnall [4]	4511
34		7	A	Peterborough U	L	0-1	0-1	21		6525
35		14	H	Yeovil T	W	3-0	2-0	21	Dagnall [2], Hedges [7], McAnuff [59]	5117
36		17	H	Barnsley	D	0-0	0-0	22		4107
37		21	A	Crawley T	L	0-1	0-1	22		3255
38		28	H	Port Vale	W	3-1	0-1	22	Mooney (pen) [56], Collins (og) [61], Cox [84]	5623
39	Apr	1	A	Coventry C	W	1-0	0-0	18	Wright [78]	8010
40		6	H	Gillingham	D	3-3	1-2	20	James (pen) [31], Henderson [67], Wright [85]	6634
41		11	A	Crewe Alex	D	1-1	1-1	19	Henderson [30]	4419
42		14	A	Doncaster R	L	0-1	0-0	20		4410
43		18	A	Milton Keynes D	L	1-6	0-4	21	Simpson, J [69]	10,137
44		21	A	Rochdale	L	0-1	0-0	21		1914
45		25	H	Sheffield U	D	1-1	0-0	22	Baudry [71]	7249
46	May	3	A	Swindon T	D	2-2	1-0	23	Cox [40], Dagnall [47]	8609

Final League Position: 23

GOALSCORERS

League (59): Dagnall 11 (1 pen), Mooney 9 (2 pens), Henderson 8 (1 pen), Cox 6, Simpson, J 5, McAnuff 3, Cuthbert 2, Hedges 2, Lisbie 2, Plasmati 2 (1 pen), Vincelot 2, Wright 2, Batt 1, Baudry 1, Dossena 1, James 1 (1 pen), own goal 1.
FA Cup (0).
Capital One Cup (4): Vincelot 2, Baudry 1, Cox 1.
Johnstone's Paint Trophy (7): Simpson, J 3, Dagnall 2, Bartley 1, Pritchard 1.

Legdins A 11	Omozusi E 24+1	Baudry M 28+3	Clarke N 31+2	Lowry S 31+3	Pritchard B 22+9	Vincelot R 27	James L 10+3	Cox D 27+10	Lisbie K 5+2	Mooney D 20+13	Simpson J 12+16	McAnuff J 25+9	Henderson D 16+7	Cuthbert S 36+2	Dagnall C 34+4	Bartley M 17+5	Woods G 16+1	Petrasso M 2+1	Batt S 5+11	Price J 4+1	Lee H —+2	Plasmati G 7+7	Wright J 26+3	Kashket S —+1	Dossena A 13+2	Sawyer G 12+1	Adeboyejo V —+1	Agyemang M —+1	Lundstram J 3+1	Eardley N 1	Hedges R 11+6	Cisak A 19	O'Neill L 8	Taylor J 3	Match No.
1	2	3	4	5	6²	7	8	9	10¹	11	12	13	14																						1
1		3	4	5	8	7		9	13	6	10²	12	11¹	2																					2
1	2	4	5		13	7	8	6	10³	11¹	14	9²	12	3																					3
1	5	3	4		7	8²	9		10³	12	6	11¹	2	13	14																				4
1	5²	3	4	14	12	8	7	9		10	13	6³	11¹	2																					5
		3	4	5	6		12		9	14	13	10	2³	11	7¹	1	8³																		6
	2		4	5	8	7		13		10¹	14	9	12	3	11³	1	6²																		7
	5		4	3		7	8	9³		13	6¹	11	2	10²		1	12	14																	8
	2	4		5	12	7	8²	9		14		6¹	11³	3	10	1		13																	9
	3	4	5		7		9			11²	6	12	2	10¹	8	1	13																		10
	5		3	4	6¹	8				9²	11⁸	10³	2	12	13	1		14	7																11
	3⁴	4	5	9	7					11		10	2	12	1		6¹	8																	12
	5		3	2						6	9	11	4	10¹	8	1	13	7²	12																13
	2	4	7	5	13					11³	6²	10⁸	3	9¹	8	1	14																		14
	2	4		5	7²					9		10³	6	3		8	1		13				11¹	12	14										15
	5	4	3		13					9		10	6	2		8	1		12				11¹	7²											16
1	14	4	3¹	6	7			9		12	11²			2	13				10³	8		5													17
1	2	4		6	7			9		12				3	10				14				11¹	8³		5²	13								18
1	2	4		6²				9		13		12		3	11⁸				8				10¹	7		5									19
1		3	4	9	7			10			12	6¹		2					11²				8			5	13								20
1	2²	13		3	6	8		14		12		9		4					11				10¹	7³		5									21
1³	2			4	13	8		6¹		12		9		3	10		14		11²				7		5										22
	2		3	6	8³			9	10²	12				4	11		1					13	7¹			5		14							23
	2		4	6	7			9¹	13	10²				3	11		1						14	8³	5				12						24
	13	4	3	6						10²	11¹			2	9		1						12	8	5			7							25
		3	4	13	7			8		10¹					11		1						12		14	2³		6	5	9²					26
	2	3	4	6¹	7			9		14		12		10	1		1						11²		5		8³	13							27
		3		4	6²	7		13	10	11¹				2	9⁸				12				8		5					14	1				28
	2		3	4	6³	7		9		11¹					10	12			14				8²		5					13	1				29
	2		3	4	6³	7		9²		11		14		10	8¹								13		5					12	1				30
		3	4		7			12	10²	14	6¹			11	13								8		2	5				9³	1				31
	4		3²	7				12	11	13	9			14	10¹								8		5					6²	1	2			32
	3		4		8			12	10³	13	9¹			11									14	7	5					6²	1	2			33
	3		6	8¹				13	10²		9³	12	4	11	14								7		5					1	2				34
	4		13					12	14	8	10³	3	9	7²									6	5					11¹	1	2				35
	4		7					12	13	14	9¹	11³	3	10									8	5					6¹	1	2				36
	4							9²	12	13	14	11¹	3	10	7³								8	5					6	1	2				37
	4	12			14	9		10²		3	11	8				13	7		5										1	2¹	6³				38
14	3	4	5		13			9	11	2	10²	8		7														12	1		6³				39
	3	14	4		8	9		11³		13	12	2	10			7	5²											6¹	1						40
	3	4	5²					9	11	2	10	7		13	8	12							7	5³				6¹	1						41
	3	4	12					14	13	9¹	11	2	10	8									7	5³				6²	1						42
	3	4	5	8				10	6⁸	2	11²	7		12		13							14	1			9¹								43
2	3	4	5	12	13	9²		10	14	11	8			7³									6¹	1											44
5	3	4		7¹	9	14	11	12		2	10	8²		6³		13								1											45
5¹	4	3	12	6	9²			11³	13	14	10	8		7										1	2										46

FA Cup

First Round	Oldham Ath	(a)	0-1

Capital One Cup

First Round	Plymouth Arg	(a)	3-3

(aet; Leyton Orient won 6-5 on penalties)

Second Round	Aston Villa	(a)	1-0
Third Round	Sheffield U	(h)	0-1

Johnstone's Paint Trophy

First Round	Peterborough U	(a)	3-2
Second Round	Dagenham & R	(a)	2-0
Southern Quarter-Finals	Northampton T	(h)	2-0
Southern Semi-Finals	Gillingham	(a)	0-1

LIVERPOOL

FOUNDATION

But for a dispute between Everton FC and their landlord at Anfield in 1892, there may never have been a Liverpool club. This dispute persuaded the majority of Evertonians to quit Anfield for Goodison Park, leaving the landlord, Mr John Houlding, to form a new club. He originally tried to retain the name 'Everton' but when this failed, he founded Liverpool Association FC on 15 March 1892.

Anfield Stadium, Anfield Road, Anfield, Liverpool L4 0TH.

Telephone: (0151) 263 2361.

Fax: (0151) 260 8813.

Ticket Office: (0843) 170 5555.

Website: www.liverpoolfc.com

Email: customerservices@liverpoolfc.com

Ground Capacity: 45,276.

Record Attendance: 61,905 v Wolverhampton W, FA Cup 4th rd, 2 February 1952.

Pitch Measurements: 101m × 68m (110yd × 74yd)

Chairman: Tom Werner.

Managing Director: Ian Ayre.

Manager: Brendan Rodgers.

Assistant Manager: Sean O'Driscoll.

Physio: Chris Morgan.

Colours: Red shirts, red shorts, red socks.

Year Formed: 1892.

Turned Professional: 1892.

Club Nicknames: 'The Reds', 'Pool'.

Ground: 1892, Anfield.

First Football League Game: 2 September 1893, Division 2, v Middlesbrough Ironopolis (a) W 2–0 – McOwen; Hannah, McLean; Henderson, McQue (1), McBride; Gordon, McVean (1), Matt McQueen, Stott, Hugh McQueen.

HONOURS

FA Premier League: *Runners-up* 2001–02, 2008–09, 2013–14.
Football League – Division 1:
Champions 1900–01, 1905–06, 1921–22, 1922–23, 1946–47, 1963–64, 1965–66, 1972–73, 1975–76, 1976–77, 1978–79, 1979–80, 1981–82, 1982–83, 1983–84, 1985–86, 1987–88, 1989–90; *Runners-up* 1898–99, 1909–10, 1968–69, 1973–74, 1974–75, 1977–78, 1984–85, 1986–87, 1988–89, 1990–91; **Division 2:** *Champions* 1893–94, 1895–96, 1904–05, 1961–62.
FA Cup: *Winners* 1965, 1974, 1986, 1989, 1992, 2001, 2006; *Runners-up* 1914, 1950, 1971, 1977, 1988, 1996, 2012.
Football League Cup: *Winners* 1981, 1982, 1983, 1984, 1995, 2001, 2003, 2012; *Runners-up* 1978, 1987, 2005.
League Super Cup: *Winners* 1986.
European Competitions: European Cup: 1964–65, 1966–67, 1973–74, 1976–77 (*winners*), 1977–78 (*winners*), 1978–79, 1979–80, 1980–81 (*winners*), 1981–82, 1982–83, 1983–84 (*winners*), 1984–85 (*runners-up*). **Champions League:** 2001–02, 2002–03, 2004–05 (*winners*), 2005–06, 2006–07 (*runners-up*), 2007–08 (*s-f*), 2008–09 (*q-f*), 2009–10, 2014–15. **European Cup-Winners' Cup:** 1965–66 (*runners-up*), 1971–72, 1974–75, 1992–93, 1996–97 (*s-f*). **European Fairs Cup:** 1967–68, 1968–69, 1969–70, 1970–71. **UEFA Cup:** 1972–73 (*winners*), 1975–76 (*winners*), 1991–92, 1995–96, 1997–98, 1998–99, 2000–01 (*winners*), 2002–03, 2003–04. **Europa League:** 2009–10, 2010–11, 2012–13, 2014–15. **Super Cup:** 1977 (*winners*), 1978, 1984, 2001 (*winners*), 2005 (*winners*). **World Club Championship:** 1981, 1984.
FIFA Club World Cup: 2005.

Record League Victory: 10–1 v Rotherham T, Division 2, 18 February 1896 – Storer; Goldie, Wilkie; McCartney, McQue, Holmes; McVean (3), Ross (2), Allan (4), Becton (1), Bradshaw.

sky SPORTS FACT FILE

Jim Harley, a full back on Liverpool's books between 1934 and 1949, was one of the fastest defenders of his time. In 1936, competing under the pseudonym 'JH Mitchell of Letham' he won the famous Powderhall New Year Sprint over 130 yards. His prize was £100 plus a gold medal.

Record Cup Victory: 11–0 v Stromsgodset Drammen, ECWC 1st rd 1st leg, 17 September 1974 – Clemence; Smith (1), Lindsay (1p), Thompson (2), Cormack (1), Hughes (1), Boersma (2), Hall, Heighway (1), Kennedy (1), Callaghan (1).

Record Defeat: 1–9 v Birmingham C, Division 2, 11 December 1954.

Most League Points (2 for a win): 68, Division 1, 1978–79.

Most League Points (3 for a win): 90, Division 1, 1987–88.

Most League Goals: 106, Division 2, 1895–96.

Highest League Scorer in Season: Roger Hunt, 41, Division 2, 1961–62.

Most League Goals in Total Aggregate: Roger Hunt, 245, 1959–69.

Most League Goals in One Match: 5, Andy McGuigan v Stoke C, Division 1, 4 January 1902; 5, John Evans v Bristol R, Division 2, 15 September 1954; 5, Ian Rush v Luton T, Division 1, 29 October 1983.

Most Capped Player: Steven Gerrard, 114, England.

Most League Appearances: Ian Callaghan, 640, 1960–78.

Youngest League Player: Jack Robinson, 16 years 250 days v Hull C, 9 May 2010.

MANAGERS
W. E. Barclay 1892–96
Tom Watson 1896–1915
David Ashworth 1920–23
Matt McQueen 1923–28
George Patterson 1928–36
(continued as Secretary)
George Kay 1936–51
Don Welsh 1951–56
Phil Taylor 1956–59
Bill Shankly 1959–74
Bob Paisley 1974–83
Joe Fagan 1983–85
Kenny Dalglish 1985–91
Graeme Souness 1991–94
Roy Evans 1994–98
(then Joint Manager)
Gerard Houllier 1998–2004
Rafael Benitez 2004–10
Roy Hodgson 2010–11
Kenny Dalglish 2011–12
Brendan Rodgers June 2012–

Record Transfer Fee Received: £75,000,000 from Barcelona for Luis Suarez, July 2014.

Record Transfer Fee Paid: £35,000,000 to Newcastle U for Andy Carroll, January 2011.

Football League Record: 1893 Elected to Division 2; 1894–95 Division 1; 1895–96 Division 2; 1896–1904 Division 1; 1904–05 Division 2; 1905–54 Division 1; 1954–62 Division 2; 1962–92 Division 1; 1992– FA Premier League.

LATEST SEQUENCES

Longest Sequence of League Wins: 12, 21.4.1990 – 6.10.1990.

Longest Sequence of League Defeats: 9, 29.4.1899 – 14.10.1899.

Longest Sequence of League Draws: 6, 19.2.1975 – 19.3.1975.

Longest Sequence of Unbeaten League Matches: 31, 4.5.1987 – 16.3.1988.

Longest Sequence Without a League Win: 14, 12.12.1953 – 20.3.1954.

Successive Scoring Runs: 29 from 27.4.1957.

Successive Non-scoring Runs: 5 from 21.4.2000.

TEN YEAR LEAGUE RECORD

		P	W	D	L	F	A	Pts	Pos
2005-06	PR Lge	38	25	7	6	57	25	82	3
2006-07	PR Lge	38	20	8	10	57	27	68	3
2007-08	PR Lge	38	21	13	4	67	28	76	4
2008-09	PR Lge	38	25	11	2	77	27	86	2
2009-10	PR Lge	38	18	9	11	61	35	63	7
2010-11	PR Lge	38	17	7	14	59	44	58	6
2011-12	PR Lge	38	14	10	14	47	40	52	8
2012-13	PR Lge	38	16	13	9	71	43	61	7
2013-14	PR Lge	38	26	6	6	101	50	84	2
2014-15	PR Lge	38	18	8	12	52	48	62	6

DID YOU KNOW ?

In their early days Liverpool would organise an annual picnic during the close season when players and club members would travel to the countryside and take part in athletic sports before adjourning to a local public house for dinner and refreshments.

LIVERPOOL – FA PREMIERSHIP 2014–15 LEAGUE RECORD

Match No.	Date	Venue	Opponents	Result	H/T Score	Lg Pos.	Goalscorers	Attendance
1	Aug 17	H	Southampton	W 2-1	1-0	2	Sterling [23], Sturridge [79]	44,736
2	25	A	Manchester C	L 1-3	0-1	9	Zabaleta (og) [83]	45,471
3	31	A	Tottenham H	W 3-0	1-0	5	Sterling [8], Gerrard (pen) [49], Moreno [60]	36,130
4	Sept 13	H	Aston Villa	L 0-1	0-1	8		44,689
5	20	A	West Ham U	L 1-3	1-2	10	Sterling [26]	34,977
6	27	H	Everton	D 1-1	0-0	12	Gerrard [65]	44,511
7	Oct 4	H	WBA	W 2-1	1-0	6	Lallana [45], Henderson [61]	44,708
8	19	A	QPR	W 3-2	0-0	5	Dunne (og) [67], Caulker (og) [90], Coutinho [90]	18,069
9	25	H	Hull C	D 0-0	0-0	7		44,591
10	Nov 1	A	Newcastle U	L 0-1	0-0	7		52,166
11	8	H	Chelsea	L 1-2	1-1	8	Can [9]	44,698
12	23	A	Crystal Palace	L 1-3	1-1	12	Lambert [2]	24,862
13	29	H	Stoke C	W 1-0	0-0	11	Johnson [85]	44,735
14	Dec 2	A	Leicester C	W 3-1	1-1	8	Lallana [26], Gerrard [54], Henderson [83]	32,000
15	6	H	Sunderland	D 0-0	0-0	9		44,716
16	14	A	Manchester U	L 0-3	0-2	10		75,331
17	21	H	Arsenal	D 2-2	1-1	10	Coutinho [45], Skrtel [90]	44,703
18	26	A	Burnley	W 1-0	0-0	9	Sterling [62]	21,335
19	29	H	Swansea C	W 4-1	1-0	8	Moreno [33], Lallana 2 [51, 61], Shelvey (og) [69]	44,714
20	Jan 1	H	Leicester C	D 2-2	2-0	8	Gerrard 2 (2 pens) [17, 40]	44,720
21	10	A	Sunderland	W 1-0	1-0	8	Markovic [8]	45,369
22	17	A	Aston Villa	W 2-0	1-0	7	Borini [24], Lambert [79]	39,758
23	31	H	West Ham U	W 2-0	0-0	7	Sterling [51], Sturridge [80]	44,718
24	Feb 7	A	Everton	D 0-0	0-0	7		39,621
25	10	H	Tottenham H	W 3-2	1-1	7	Markovic [15], Gerrard (pen) [53], Balotelli [83]	44,577
26	22	A	Southampton	W 2-0	1-0	6	Coutinho [3], Sterling [73]	31,723
27	Mar 1	H	Manchester C	W 2-1	1-1	5	Henderson [11], Coutinho [75]	44,590
28	4	H	Burnley	W 2-0	1-0	5	Henderson [29], Sturridge [51]	44,717
29	16	A	Swansea C	W 1-0	0-0	5	Henderson [68]	20,828
30	22	H	Manchester U	L 1-2	0-1	5	Sturridge [69]	44,405
31	Apr 4	A	Arsenal	L 1-4	0-3	5	Henderson (pen) [76]	60,081
32	13	H	Newcastle U	W 2-0	1-0	5	Sterling [9], Allen [70]	44,611
33	25	A	WBA	D 0-0	0-0	5		26,663
34	28	A	Hull C	L 0-1	0-1	5		24,843
35	May 2	H	QPR	W 2-1	1-0	5	Coutinho [19], Gerrard [87]	44,707
36	10	A	Chelsea	D 1-1	1-1	5	Gerrard [44]	41,547
37	16	H	Crystal Palace	L 1-3	1-1	5	Lallana [26]	44,673
38	24	A	Stoke C	L 1-6	0-5	6	Gerrard [70]	27,602

Final League Position: 6

GOALSCORERS

League (52): Gerrard 9 (4 pens), Sterling 7, Henderson 6 (1 pen), Coutinho 5, Lallana 5, Sturridge 4, Lambert 2, Markovic 2, Moreno 2, Allen 1, Balotelli 1, Borini 1, Can 1, Johnson 1, Skrtel 1, own goals 4.
FA Cup (8): Coutinho 3, Gerrard 2, Lallana 1, Sterling 1, Sturridge 1.
Capital One Cup (8): Sterling 3, Balotelli 1, Lovren 1, Markovic 1, Rossiter 1, Suso 1.
UEFA Champions League (5): Gerrard 2 (1 pen), Balotelli 1, Henderson 1, Lambert 1.
UEFA Europa League (1): Balotelli 1 (1 pen).

Mignolet S 35 + 1	Manquillo J 10	Skrtel M 33	Lovren D 22 + 4	Johnson G 15 + 4	Gerrard S 25 + 4	Lucas 16 + 4	Henderson J 36 + 1	Coutinho P 32 + 3	Sterling R 34 + 1	Sturridge D 7 + 5	Allen J 16 + 5	Lambert R 7 + 18	Moreno A 26 + 2	Markovic L 11 + 8	Can E 23 + 4	Sakho M 15 + 1	Balotelli M 10 + 6	Jose Enrique 2 + 2	Lallana A 23 + 4	Borini F 3 + 9	Toure K 7 + 5	Jones B 3	Ibe J 7 + 5	Sinclair J — + 2	Match No.
1	2	3	4	5	6	7¹	8	9²	10	11	12	13													1
1		3	4	2	7		6	11¹	9²	10	8³	14	5	12	13										2
1	2		3		6		7	9¹	10	8³			5	13	12	4	11²	14							3
1	2		3		6		7	9	12			13	5	8¹		4	11²		10³	14					4
1	2²	3	4		6	7³	8		9			14	5			12	11		13	10¹					5
1	2	3	4		6		7	12	10			13	5	8¹			11²		9						6
1	2¹	3	4	12	6	14	9	7³	8			11²	5				13		10						7
1		3	4	2	9		6	12	8³		13				7¹		11	5	10²		14				8
1	2	3	4		7		14	12	9		6²	13	5		8¹		10		11³						9
1		3	4	2	6		7	10¹	5			8²	13	9			11		12						10
1		3	4	2	7		6	9²	11			12	14	5		8³			10¹		13				11
1	2	3	4	5	7			11		9		8²	10			13			6¹	12					12
1		3	13	2	12	6¹	8	9²	10		7	11			5				4						13
1	2³	3	14	5	9	7	6		10¹			13	11	12			8²			4					14
1		3		2	12	7	6		9¹	10		11	5	13			8²			4					15
1		3	4	2²	6		5	9	10	7			8¹	14	13		11³		12		1				16
1		3			7	6	5	9	10			13		8²	4		11	12⁴	2¹	1					17
12		3			6	7	5	9²	10			14		8	13	4		11		2¹	1²				18
1	5	3			6	7	11³	10³				8	12	2	4	13		9¹	14						19
1					6	7³	5	9	10			14		8²	13	2	4		11¹	12	3				20
1		3	12		9¹	7	6	11					8	5	2	4	13		10²						21
1		3			7	6	11	9¹				12	8²	5	2	4		13	10³				14		22
1		3			7	6	10²	11	12				8	5¹	2	4			9				13		23
1		3			9	7²	6	11³	10¹	13	12	14	8		2	4							5		24
1		3	12		7¹		6	10		11³			8	9²	2	4	13		14				5		25
1		3	2	14		6	10	11	13	7		12	8³	4					9²				5¹		26
1		3	4			6	11	10	12	7		8¹	5²	2					9		13				27
1		3	4	13		6	11	5	10²	7	14	8³		2					9		12				28
1		3		13	12	6	11	9	10	7		8¹		2	4				5²						29
1		3			12⁴		6	11	5	10	7		8¹		2	4	13		9²						30
1						6	5	10	11	12	7		8	9¹	2¹	4					3				31
1			4	2		7	6	10	11²		8	13	5		3						12		9¹		32
1		3	4	5	7		6	9	10				2				11²		12	13			8¹		33
1		3	4³	5		6	8	11			7	12	14	2			10²		13				9¹		34
1		3	4	5³	7¹	14	6	8	9			10¹		13	2				11²				12		35
1		3	4	5	7³	14	6	8	9			10¹			2				11²				13	12	36
1		3	4		6	13	7	9	10			12	8¹		2				11³				5²	14	37
1		3				10	7	6	9			8³	14	5¹		2²	4		11		13		12		38

FA Cup

Third Round	AFC Wimbledon	(a)	2-1
Fourth Round	Bolton W	(h)	0-0
Replay	Bolton W	(a)	2-1
Fifth Round	Crystal Palace	(a)	2-1
Sixth Round	Blackburn R	(h)	0-0
Replay	Blackburn R	(a)	1-0
Semi-Finals	Aston Villa	Wembley	1-2

Capital One Cup

Third Round	Middlesbrough	(h)	2-2

(aet; Liverpool won 14-13 on penalties)

Fourth Round	Swansea C	(h)	2-1
Quarter-Finals	Bournemouth	(a)	3-1
Semi-Finals 1st leg	Chelsea	(h)	1-1
Semi-Finals 2nd leg	Chelsea	(a)	0-1

(aet; Chelsea won 2-1 on aggregate)

UEFA Champions League

Group B	Ludogorets Razgrad	(h)	2-1
Group B	FC Basel	(a)	0-1
Group B	Real Madrid	(h)	0-3
Group B	Real Madrid	(a)	0-1
Group B	Ludogorets Razgrad	(a)	2-2
Group B	FC Basel	(h)	1-1

UEFA Europa League

Round of 32 1st leg	Besiktas	(h)	1-0
Round of 32 2nd leg	Besiktas	(a)	0-1

(aet; Besiktas won 5-4 on penalties)

LUTON TOWN

FOUNDATION

Formed by an amalgamation of two leading local clubs, Wanderers and Excelsior a works team, at a meeting in Luton Town Hall in April 1885. The Wanderers had three months earlier changed their name to Luton Town Wanderers and did not take too kindly to the formation of another Town club but were talked around at this meeting. Wanderers had already appeared in the FA Cup and the new club entered in its inaugural season.

Kenilworth Road Stadium, 1 Maple Road, Luton, Bedfordshire LU4 8AW.

Telephone: (01582) 411 622.

Fax: (01582) 405 070.

Ticket Office: (01582) 416 976.

Website: www.lutontown.co.uk

Email: info@lutontown.co.uk

Ground Capacity: 9,915.

Record Attendance: 30,069 v Blackpool, FA Cup 6th rd replay, 4 March 1959.

Pitch Measurements: 100.8m × 65.8m (110yd × 72yd).

Chairman: Nick Owen.

Managing Director: Gary Sweet.

Manager: John Still.

Assistant Manager: Terry Harris.

Physio: Simon Parsell.

Colours: Orange shirts, navy blue shorts, white socks with orange trim.

Year Formed: 1885.

Turned Professional: 1890.

Ltd Co.: 1897.

Club Nickname: 'The Hatters'.

Grounds: 1885, Excelsior, Dallow Lane; 1897, Dunstable Road; 1905, Kenilworth Road.

First Football League Game: 4 September 1897, Division 2, v Leicester Fosse (a) D 1–1 – Williams; McCartney, McEwen; Davies, Stewart, Docherty; Gallacher, Coupar, Birch, McInnes, Ekins (1).

Record League Victory: 12–0 v Bristol R, Division 3 (S), 13 April 1936 – Dolman; Mackey, Smith; Finlayson, Nelson, Godfrey; Rich, Martin (1), Payne (10), Roberts (1), Stephenson.

Record Cup Victory: 9–0 v Clapton, FA Cup 1st rd (replay after abandoned game), 30 November 1927 – Abbott; Kingham, Graham; Black, Rennie, Fraser; Pointon, Yardley (4), Reid (2), Woods (1), Dennis (2).

HONOURS

Football League – Division 1: Best season: 7th, 1986–87;
Division 2: *Champions* 1981–82; *Runners-up* 1954–55, 1973–74;
Division 3: *Runners-up* 1969–70, 2001–02; **Division 4:** *Champions* 1967–68; **Division 3 (S):** *Champions* 1936–37; *Runners-up* 1935–36.
FL 1: *Champions* 2004–05.
Skrill Premier: *Champions* 2013–14.
FA Cup: *Runners-up* 1959.
Football League Cup: *Winners* 1988; *Runners-up* 1989.
Simod Cup: *Runners-up* 1988.
Johnstone's Paint Trophy: *Winners* 2009.

sky SPORTS FACT FILE

Luton Town began their 1935–36 campaign by failing to win any of their opening five fixtures leaving them bottom of Division Three South by mid-September. Their fortunes then had a dramatic turn around as they dropped just four points in the next 17 games to top the table by early January.

Record Defeat: 0–9 v Small Heath, Division 2, 12 November 1898.

Most League Points (2 for a win): 66, Division 4, 1967–68.

Most League Points (3 for a win): 98, FL 1 2004–05.

Most League Goals: 103, Division 3 (S), 1936–37.

Highest League Scorer in Season: Joe Payne, 55, Division 3 (S), 1936–37.

Most League Goals in Total Aggregate: Gordon Turner, 243, 1949–64.

Most League Goals in One Match: 10, Joe Payne v Bristol R, Division 3 (S), 13 April 1936.

Most Capped Player: Mal Donaghy, 58 (91), Northern Ireland.

Most League Appearances: Bob Morton, 495, 1948–64.

Youngest League Player: Mike O'Hara, 16 years 32 days v Stoke C, 1 October 1960.

Record Transfer Fee Received: £3,000,000 from WBA for Curtis Davies, August 2005; £3,000,000 from Birmingham C for Rowan Vine, January 2007.

Record Transfer Fee Paid: £850,000 to Odense for Lars Elstrup, August 1989.

Football League Record: 1897 Elected to Division 2; 1900 Failed re-election; 1920 Division 3; 1921–37 Division 3 (S); 1937–55 Division 2; 1955–60 Division 1; 1960–63 Division 2; 1963–65 Division 3; 1965–68 Division 4; 1968–70 Division 3; 1970–74 Division 2; 1974–75 Division 1; 1975–82 Division 2; 1982–96 Division 1; 1996–2001 Division 2; 2001–02 Division 3; 2002–04 Division 2; 2004–05 FL 1; 2005–07 FL C; 2007–08 FL 1; 2008–09 FL 2; 2009–14 Conference Premier; 2014– FL 2.

MANAGERS

Charlie Green 1901–28
(Secretary-Manager)
George Thomson 1925
John McCartney 1927–29
George Kay 1929–31
Harold Wightman 1931–35
Ted Liddell 1936–38
Neil McBain 1938–39
George Martin 1939–47
Dally Duncan 1947–58
Syd Owen 1959–60
Sam Bartram 1960–62
Bill Harvey 1962–64
George Martin 1965–66
Allan Brown 1966–68
Alec Stock 1968–72
Harry Haslam 1972–78
David Pleat 1978–86
John Moore 1986–87
Ray Harford 1987–89
Jim Ryan 1990–91
David Pleat 1991–95
Terry Westley 1995
Lennie Lawrence 1995–2000
Ricky Hill 2000
Lil Fuccillo 2000
Joe Kinnear 2001–03
Mike Newell 2003–07
Kevin Blackwell 2007–08
Mick Harford 2008–09
Richard Money 2009–11
Gary Brabin 2011–12
Paul Buckle 2012–13
John Still February 2013–

LATEST SEQUENCES

Longest Sequence of League Wins: 12, 19.2.2002 – 6.4.2002.

Longest Sequence of League Defeats: 8, 11.11.1899 – 6.1.1900.

Longest Sequence of League Draws: 5, 28.8.1971 – 18.9.1971.

Longest Sequence of Unbeaten League Matches: 19, 8.4.1969 – 7.10.1969.

Longest Sequence Without a League Win: 16, 9.9.1964 – 6.11.1964.

Successive Scoring Runs: 25 from 24.10.1931.

Successive Non-scoring Runs: 5 from 10.4.1973.

TEN YEAR LEAGUE RECORD

		P	W	D	L	F	A	Pts	Pos
2005-06	FL C	46	17	10	19	66	67	61	10
2006-07	FL C	46	10	10	26	53	81	40	23
2007-08	FL 1	46	11	10	25	43	63	33*	24
2008-09	FL 2	46	13	17	16	58	65	26†	24
2009-10	Conf P	44	26	10	8	84	40	88	2
2010-11	Conf P	46	23	15	8	85	37	84	3
2011-12	Conf P	46	22	15	9	78	42	81	5
2012-13	Conf P	46	18	13	15	70	62	67	7
2013-14	Conf P	46	30	11	5	102	35	101	1
2014-15	FL 2	46	19	11	16	54	44	68	8

*10 pts deducted; †30 points deducted.

DID YOU KNOW ?

Luton Town's first home game under floodlights saw them take on the Turkish champions Fenerbahce at Kenilworth Road on 7 October 1953. A crowd of 13,768 saw the Hatters win the game 7-4 with centre-forward Bert Mitchell notching a hat-trick.

LUTON TOWN – FOOTBALL LEAGUE TWO 2014–15 LEAGUE RECORD

Match No.	Date	Venue	Opponents	Result	H/T Score	Lg Pos.	Goalscorers	Attendance
1	Aug 9	A	Carlisle U	W 1-0	1-0	3	Cullen [30]	6766
2	16	H	AFC Wimbledon	L 0-1	0-1	14		9101
3	19	H	Bury	D 1-1	0-0	14	Ruddock [90]	7890
4	23	A	Accrington S	D 2-2	2-2	12	Rooney [32], Howells [42]	1562
5	30	A	Shrewsbury T	L 0-2	0-1	18		5888
6	Sept 6	H	Plymouth Arg	L 0-1	0-0	19		7864
7	13	H	Cheltenham T	W 1-0	1-0	18	Cullen [8]	7793
8	16	A	York C	D 0-0	0-0	18		3649
9	20	A	Cambridge U	W 1-0	0-0	13	Cullen [81]	6533
10	27	H	Oxford U	W 2-0	1-0	8	Wilkinson [2], Howells [67]	9101
11	Oct 4	A	Stevenage	W 2-1	1-1	7	Wilkinson [10], Wall [83]	5236
12	11	H	Southend U	W 2-0	2-0	4	Lawless [17], Cullen [34]	9238
13	18	A	Hartlepool U	W 2-1	1-0	4	Cullen [39], Stevenson [81]	4225
14	21	H	Dagenham & R	W 3-1	2-0	3	Cullen 3 [42, 45, 68]	7746
15	25	H	Northampton T	W 1-0	0-0	1	Guttridge [90]	10,040
16	Nov 1	A	Exeter C	D 1-1	1-0	2	Griffiths [3]	5400
17	15	H	Tranmere R	W 1-0	0-0	1	Miller [70]	9061
18	22	A	Burton Alb	L 0-1	0-0	3		4772
19	29	H	Mansfield T	W 3-0	1-0	2	Benson [19], Whalley 2 [59, 63]	8418
20	Dec 13	A	Morecambe	L 0-3	0-2	4		2263
21	20	H	Newport Co	W 3-0	1-0	3	Wilkinson [5], Rooney [61], Howells [90]	8383
22	26	A	Wycombe W	D 1-1	1-1	4	Smith, J [8]	7539
23	28	H	Portsmouth	D 1-1	1-1	4	Rooney [13]	10,071
24	Jan 8	H	Shrewsbury T	D 0-0	0-0	4		7666
25	17	A	Plymouth Arg	W 1-0	1-0	4	Drury [22]	8420
26	24	A	Cheltenham T	D 1-1	1-1	4	Whalley [21]	3611
27	31	H	Cambridge U	W 3-2	3-0	4	Drury [19], Wilkinson [31], Smith, J [45]	10,054
28	Feb 7	A	Oxford U	D 1-1	1-1	4	Stockley [36]	7541
29	10	H	York C	D 2-2	0-0	5	Cullen 2 [65, 71]	7763
30	14	H	Carlisle U	W 1-0	1-0	4	Cullen [38]	8502
31	17	A	Mansfield T	L 0-1	0-1	4		2998
32	21	A	AFC Wimbledon	L 2-3	1-2	4	Stockley [45], Lee [68]	4050
33	28	H	Accrington S	W 2-0	1-0	4	Stockley [41], Guttridge [60]	8700
34	Mar 3	A	Bury	L 0-1	0-1	4		2915
35	7	H	Morecambe	L 2-3	1-2	5	McGeehan [43], Lawless [76]	8667
36	14	A	Portsmouth	L 0-2	0-1	6		17,149
37	17	A	Newport Co	L 0-1	0-1	6		2536
38	24	H	Wycombe W	L 2-3	2-3	6	Lee 2 [7, 38]	8379
39	28	A	Northampton T	L 1-2	0-0	5	Lawless [46]	5668
40	Apr 3	H	Exeter C	L 2-3	2-0	9	Guttridge [21], Cullen [45]	8755
41	6	A	Tranmere R	W 1-0	0-0	9	McGeehan [81]	6035
42	11	H	Burton Alb	L 0-1	0-0	9		8680
43	14	A	Dagenham & R	D 0-0	0-0	8		2461
44	18	H	Hartlepool U	W 3-0	2-0	8	McGeehan [5], Howells (pen) [15], Griffiths [71]	8231
45	25	A	Southend U	L 0-1	0-0	8		10,730
46	May 2	H	Stevenage	W 2-0	2-0	8	Cullen [5], Harriman [45]	10,054

Final League Position: 8

GOALSCORERS

League (54): Cullen 13, Howells 4 (1 pen), Wilkinson 4, Guttridge 3, Lawless 3, Lee 3, McGeehan 3, Rooney 3, Stockley 3, Whalley 3, Drury 2, Griffiths 2, Smith, J 2, Benson 1, Harriman 1, Miller 1, Ruddock 1, Stevenson 1, Wall 1.
FA Cup (7): Benson 1, Cullen 1, Guttridge 1, Harriman 1, Howells 1, Miller 1, Rooney 1.
Capital One Cup (1): Rooney 1 (1 pen).
Johnstone's Paint Trophy (0).

Tyler M 31	Connolly P 4	McNulty S 41	Lacey A 10 + 8	Griffiths S 35	Wilkinson L 42	Robinson M 7 + 2	Drury A 30 + 5	Howells J 28 + 8	Benson P 16 + 5	Cullen M 33 + 9	Stevenson J 2 + 9	Rooney L 8 + 3	Franks F 10 + 3	Guttridge L 17 + 10	Wall A 1 + 6	Ruddock P 10 + 6	Lafayette R 1 + 10	Lawless A 7 + 8	Williams C 3	Smith J 35	Whalley S 14 + 4	Doyle N 27	Walker C — + 3	Harriman M 35	Miller R 2 + 10	Stockley J 11 + 2	Hall R 4 + 3	Oduwa N 3 + 8	Justham E 15	McGeehan C 13 + 2	Lee E 9 + 2	Kinsella L 2 + 1	Match No.
1	2	3	4	5	6	7	8²	9¹	10	11	12	13																					1
1		3		5	4	8	6³	9	11	10	14			2²	7	12	13																2
1		3		5¹	4	8	9	13	10¹	11			6	2	7²		12	14															3
1	2	3	7²		4	6	8	5	10	11¹		9			12	13																	4
1	2	3	12		4	6¹		5	10	9³	8	11¹			7²		14	13															5
1	2	3	4	5			7²	10¹		11¹	14	6		9		8	13	12															6
1	2	3³	9	4		14	13			11	12			6¹		7	10		5²	8													7
1		4	5	3		6	9¹		11³	13	12			10		7	14		2	8²													8
1		3	7	5	4	14	12			11	8			10¹	9³	6	13		2²														9
1		3	2	5	4		13	10		11	14			9	12					8²	6³	7¹											10
1		3	2	5	4		6		10²	11³	12			14	9					7¹		8	13										11
1	4	12	13	5	3		8			11					6		10			9		7		2¹									12
1		4		5	3		6		12	10¹	13			14		11²				7		8		2	9³								13
1		3		5	4		11		12	10¹						6				7		8	13	2	9²								14
1		3		5	4		8		12	11	13			14		6²		10¹		7		9²		2									15
1		3	13	5²	4		6	9¹	11	10¹				12						8		7		2	14								16
1		3			4		14	9	10	11³			2	6¹	12					8		7²		5	13								17
1		3		5	4¹		14	9	11					10²	12					7	6	8¹		2	13								18
1		3		5			9	12	10³	11¹		14	4							7	6²	8	13	2									19
1		3²	12		2		8²	5		11³			4				13			6	10	7		9¹	14								20
1		3		5	4		8	12		11		10¹				13				9	6²	7		2									21
1		3		5	4		9	12		11¹		10³				13				7	8²	6		2	14								22
1		3		5¹	4		8	14		11¹		10				12				7	6²	9		2	13								23
1		3		5²	4		8	10				6¹								7	12	9		2	13	11							24
1		3		5	4		9	10												6	8	7		2		11							25
1		3		5	4		6²	11¹		12						13				8	10¹	7		2	14	9							26
1		3		5³	4²		8	10		14			12			13				7	6¹	9		2		11							27
1		4			3		10	5		13				14						7	6¹	8		2		11³	9²	12					28
1		3⁴	12		4¹		8³	5		13										7	14	9		2		11	10²	6					29
1		12	5	4⁴	8³	9	14			11³			3			13				7			2	10		6¹							30
1		3	7		8²	2	9¹		10			4	14							5			6		11³	12	13						31
		4	5			8¹					3	9	14			12				7			2		11²		10⁴	1	6	13		32
		5	4				9		13		3	6				12				7			2		11¹			1	8	10²		33
	4		5	3			9³		14			7				12				6			2		10¹		13	1	8	11¹		34
	3		5¹	4			9		11			10				12				7³	6²		2				14	1	8	13		35
	3²			4		9	5	14	11³			12	8			6					10¹		2				13	1	7			36
	3			4		9	5	13	10¹			12	7			6³							2²				14	1	8	11		37
	3			4	12	6	9	10	14			2²	8										5				13	1	7³	11¹		38
	3⁴	12		4		7		10	11²							9³			6		8		2	13				1	14		5	39
	3	14		4			10	11³				9				6			7²		8		2		13			1	12		5¹	40
	4		5	3			14	10³	11							12			7¹		8		2		13	6²		1	9			41
	3		5	4			9	10	12			14				6²							2		13		1	7	11³			42
	4		5	3				10²	14			13				6²			7	12³	8¹		2		9²			1	6	11		43
	3		5	4			9³		11			13							7	6¹			2	14		12		1	8	10²		44
	3		5¹	4			9		11			13	14						7	12	6		2					1	8²	10³		45
	3		5³	4			10¹		6			13							8		9²		2			12		1	7	11	14	46

FA Cup

First Round	Newport Co	(h)	4-2	
Second Round	Bury	(a)	1-1	
Replay	Bury	(h)	1-0	
Third Round	Cambridge U	(a)	1-2	

Capital One Cup

First Round	Swindon T	(h)	1-2

Johnstone's Paint Trophy

Second Round	Crawley T	(h)	0-1

MANCHESTER CITY

Etihad Stadium, Etihad Campus, Manchester M11 3FF.

Telephone: (0161) 444 1894.

Fax: (0161) 438 7999.

Ticket Office: (0161) 444 1894.

Website: www.mcfc.co.uk

Email: mcfc@mcfc.co.uk

Ground Capacity: 46,708.

Record Attendance: 84,569 v Stoke C, FA Cup 6th rd, 3 March 1934 (at Maine Road; British record for any game outside London or Glasgow); 47,435 v QPR, FA Premier League, 13 May 2012 (at Etihad Stadium).

Pitch Measurements: 105m × 68m (114yd × 74yd)

Chairman: Khaldoon Al Mubarak.

Chief Executive: Ferran Soriano.

Manager: Manuel Pellegrini

Assistant Managers: Ruben Cousillas Fuse, Brian Kidd.

Fitness Coach: Jose Cabello.

Colours: Sky blue shirts with navy blue trim, sky blue shorts with navy blue trim, sky blue socks with navy blue trim.

Year Formed: 1887 as Ardwick FC; 1894 as Manchester City.

Turned Professional: 1887 as Ardwick FC.

Previous Names: 1880, St Mark's Church, West Gorton; 1884, Gorton; 1887, Ardwick; 1894, Manchester City.

Club Nicknames: 'The Blues', 'The Citizens'.

Grounds: 1880, Clowes Street; 1881, Kirkmanshulme Cricket Ground; 1882, Queens Road; 1884, Pink Bank Lane; 1887, Hyde Road (1894–1923 as City); 1923, Maine Road; 2003, City of Manchester Stadium (renamed Etihad Stadium 2011).

First Football League Game: 3 September 1892, Division 2, v Bootle (h) W 7–0 – Douglas; McVickers, Robson; Middleton, Russell, Hopkins; Davies (3), Morris (2), Angus (1), Weir (1), Milarvie.

Record League Victory: 10–1 v Huddersfield T, Division 2, 7 November 1987 – Nixon; Gidman, Hinchcliffe, Clements, Lake, Redmond, White (3), Stewart (3), Adcock (3), McNab (1), Simpson.

Record Cup Victory: 10–1 v Swindon T, FA Cup 4th rd, 29 January 1930 – Barber; Felton, McCloy; Barrass, Cowan, Heinemann; Toseland, Marshall (5), Tait (3), Johnson (1), Brook (1).

HONOURS

FA Premier League: *Champions* 2011–12, 2013–14; *Runners-up* 2012–13, 2014–15.
Football League – Division 1: *Champions* 1936–37, 1967–68, 2001–02; *Runners-up* 1903–04, 1920–21, 1976–77, 1999–2000; **Division 2:** *Champions* 1898–99, 1902–03, 1909–10, 1927–28, 1946–47, 1965–66; *Runners-up* 1895–96, 1950–51, 1988–89.

FA Cup: *Winners* 1904, 1934, 1956, 1969, 2011; *Runners-up* 1926, 1933, 1955, 1981, 2013.

Football League Cup: *Winners* 1970, 1976, 2014; *Runners-up* 1974.

Full Members Cup: *Runners-up* 1986.

European Competitions
Champions League: 2011–12, 2012–13, 2013–14, 2014–15. **European Cup:** 1968–69. **European Cup-Winners' Cup:** 1969–70 (*winners*), 1970–71. **UEFA Cup:** 1972–73, 1976–77, 1977–78, 1978–79, 2003–04, 2008–09. **Europa League:** 2010–11, 2011–12.

Record Defeat: 1–9 v Everton, Division 1, 3 September 1906.

Most League Points (2 for a win): 62, Division 2, 1946–47.

Most League Points (3 for a win): 99, Division 1, 2001–02.

Most League Goals: 108, Division 2, 1926–27, 108, Division 1, 2001–02.

Highest League Scorer in Season: Tommy Johnson, 38, Division 1, 1928–29.

Most League Goals in Total Aggregate: Tommy Johnson, 158, 1919–30.

Most League Goals in One Match: 5, Fred Williams v Darwen, Division 2, 18 February 1899; 5, Tom Browell v Burnley, Division 2, 24 October 1925; 5, Tom Johnson v Everton, Division 1, 15 September 1928; 5, George Smith v Newport Co, Division 2, 14 June 1947.

Most Capped Player: Joe Hart, 52, England.

Most League Appearances: Alan Oakes, 564, 1959–76.

Youngest League Player: Glyn Pardoe, 15 years 314 days v Birmingham C, 11 April 1962.

Record Transfer Fee Received: £21,000,000 from Chelsea for Shaun Wright-Phillips, July 2005.

Record Transfer Fee Paid: £44,000,000 (rising to £49,000,000 to Liverpool for Raheem Sterling, July 2015.

Football League Record: 1892 Ardwick elected founder member of Division 2; 1894 Newly-formed Manchester C elected to Division 2; 1899 Division 1 1899–1902, 1903–09, 1910–26, 1928–38, 1947–50, 1951–63, 1966–83, 1985–87, 1989–92; Division 2 1902–03, 1909–10, 1926–28, 1938–47, 1950–51, 1963–66, 1983–85, 1987–89; 1992–96 FA Premier League; 1996–98 Division 1; 1998–99 Division 2; 1999–2000 Division 1; 2000–01 FA Premier League; 2001–02 Division 1; 2002– FA Premier League.

LATEST SEQUENCES

Longest Sequence of League Wins: 9, 8.4.1912 – 28.9.1912.

Longest Sequence of League Defeats: 8, 23.8.1995 – 14.10.1995.

Longest Sequence of League Draws: 7, 5.10.2009 – 28.11.2009.

Longest Sequence of Unbeaten League Matches: 22, 16.11.1946 – 19.4.1947.

Longest Sequence Without a League Win: 17, 26.12.1979 – 7.4.1980.

Successive Scoring Runs: 44 from 3.10.1936.

Successive Non-scoring Runs: 6 from 30.1.1971.

MANAGERS

Joshua Parlby 1893–95
(Secretary-Manager)
Sam Omerod 1895–1902
Tom Maley 1902–06
Harry Newbould 1906–12
Ernest Magnall 1912–24
David Ashworth 1924–25
Peter Hodge 1926–32
Wilf Wild 1932–46
(continued as Secretary to 1950)
Sam Cowan 1946–47
John 'Jock' Thomson 1947–50
Leslie McDowall 1950–63
George Poyser 1963–65
Joe Mercer 1965–71
(continued as General Manager to 1972)
Malcolm Allison 1972–73
Johnny Hart 1973
Ron Saunders 1973–74
Tony Book 1974–79
Malcolm Allison 1979–80
John Bond 1980–83
John Benson 1983
Billy McNeill 1983–86
Jimmy Frizzell 1986–87
(continued as General Manager)
Mel Machin 1987–89
Howard Kendall 1989–90
Peter Reid 1990–93
Brian Horton 1993–95
Alan Ball 1995–96
Steve Coppell 1996
Frank Clark 1996–98
Joe Royle 1998–2001
Kevin Keegan 2001–05
Stuart Pearce 2005–07
Sven-Göran Eriksson 2007–08
Mark Hughes 2008–09
Roberto Mancini 2009–13
Manuel Pellegrini June 2013–

TEN YEAR LEAGUE RECORD

			P	W	D	L	F	A	Pts	Pos
2005-06	PR Lge	38	13	4	21	43	48	43	15
2006-07	PR Lge	38	11	9	18	29	44	42	14
2007-08	PR Lge	38	15	10	13	45	53	55	9
2008-09	PR Lge	38	15	5	18	58	50	50	10
2009-10	PR Lge	38	18	13	7	73	45	67	5
2010-11	PR Lge	38	21	8	9	60	33	71	3
2011-12	PR Lge	38	28	5	5	93	29	89	1
2012-13	PR Lge	38	23	9	6	66	34	78	2
2013-14	PR Lge	38	27	5	6	102	37	86	1
2014-15	PR Lge	38	24	7	7	83	38	79	2

DID YOU KNOW ?

Manchester City director John Allison was a pioneer in the treatment of sports injuries. In the early 1900s injured players were brought to Allison's football hospital in Hyde Road, Manchester, to rehabilitate much in the same way as players are sent to Lilleshall today.

MANCHESTER CITY – FA PREMIERSHIP 2014–15 LEAGUE RECORD

Match No.	Date	Venue	Opponents	Result	H/T Score	Lg Pos.	Goalscorers	Attendance
1	Aug 17	A	Newcastle U	W 2-0	1-0	1	Silva [38], Aguero [90]	50,816
2	25	H	Liverpool	W 3-1	1-0	2	Jovetic 2 [41, 55], Aguero [69]	45,471
3	30	H	Stoke C	L 0-1	0-0	4		45,622
4	Sept 13	A	Arsenal	D 2-2	1-0	5	Aguero [28], Demichelis [83]	60,003
5	21	H	Chelsea	D 1-1	0-0	6	Lampard [85]	45,602
6	27	A	Hull C	W 4-2	2-2	3	Aguero [7], Dzeko 2 [11, 68], Lampard [87]	22,859
7	Oct 4	A	Aston Villa	W 2-0	0-0	2	Toure [82], Aguero [88]	32,964
8	18	H	Tottenham H	W 4-1	2-1	2	Aguero 4 (2 pens) [13, 20 (p), 68 (p), 75]	45,549
9	25	A	West Ham U	L 1-2	0-1	3	Silva [77]	34,977
10	Nov 2	H	Manchester U	W 1-0	0-0	3	Aguero [63]	45,358
11	8	A	QPR	D 2-2	1-1	3	Aguero 2 [32, 83]	18,005
12	22	H	Swansea C	W 2-1	1-1	3	Jovetic [19], Toure [62]	45,448
13	30	A	Southampton	W 3-0	0-0	2	Toure [51], Lampard [80], Clichy [88]	30,919
14	Dec 3	A	Sunderland	W 4-1	2-1	2	Aguero 2 [21, 71], Jovetic [38], Zabaleta [55]	41,152
15	6	H	Everton	W 1-0	1-0	2	Toure (pen) [24]	45,603
16	13	A	Leicester C	W 1-0	1-0	2	Lampard [40]	31,643
17	20	H	Crystal Palace	W 3-0	0-0	2	Silva 2 [49, 61], Toure [81]	45,302
18	26	A	WBA	W 3-1	3-0	2	Fernando [8], Toure (pen) [13], Silva [34]	26,040
19	28	H	Burnley	D 2-2	2-0	2	Silva [23], Fernandinho [33]	45,608
20	Jan 1	H	Sunderland	W 3-2	0-0	1	Toure [57], Jovetic [66], Lampard [73]	45,367
21	10	A	Everton	D 1-1	0-0	2	Fernandinho [74]	39,499
22	18	H	Arsenal	L 0-2	0-1	2		45,596
23	31	A	Chelsea	D 1-1	1-1	2	Silva [45]	41,620
24	Feb 7	H	Hull C	D 1-1	0-1	2	Milner [90]	45,233
25	11	A	Stoke C	W 4-1	1-1	2	Aguero 2 (1 pen) [33, 70 (p)], Milner [55], Nasri [76]	27,011
26	21	A	Newcastle U	W 5-0	3-0	2	Aguero (pen) [2], Nasri [12], Dzeko [21], Silva 2 [51, 53]	45,602
27	Mar 1	A	Liverpool	L 1-2	1-1	2	Dzeko [25]	44,590
28	4	H	Leicester C	W 2-0	1-0	2	Silva [45], Milner [88]	45,000
29	14	A	Burnley	L 0-1	0-0	2		21,216
30	21	H	WBA	W 3-0	2-0	2	Bony [27], Fernando [40], Silva [77]	45,018
31	Apr 6	A	Crystal Palace	L 1-2	0-1	4	Toure [78]	24,718
32	12	H	Manchester U	L 2-4	1-2	4	Aguero 2 [8, 89]	75,313
33	19	H	West Ham U	W 2-0	2-0	4	Collins (og) [18], Aguero [36]	45,041
34	25	H	Aston Villa	W 3-2	1-0	2	Aguero [3], Kolarov [66], Fernandinho [89]	45,036
35	May 3	A	Tottenham H	W 1-0	1-0	2	Aguero [29]	35,784
36	10	H	QPR	W 6-0	2-0	2	Aguero 3 (1 pen) [4, 50, 65 (p)], Kolarov [32], Milner [70], Silva [87]	44,564
37	17	A	Swansea C	W 4-2	2-1	2	Toure 2 [21, 74], Milner [36], Bony [90]	20,669
38	24	H	Southampton	W 2-0	1-0	2	Lampard [31], Aguero [88]	45,919

Final League Position: 2

GOALSCORERS
League (83): Aguero 26 (5 pens), Silva 12, Toure 10 (2 pens), Lampard 6, Jovetic 5, Milner 5, Dzeko 4, Fernandinho 3, Bony 2, Fernando 2, Kolarov 2, Nasri 2, Clichy 1, Demichelis 1, Zabaleta 1, own goal 1.
FA Cup (2): Milner 2.
Capital One Cup (7): Dzeko 2, Lampard 2, Jesus Navas 1, Pozo 1, Toure 1 (1 pen).
UEFA Champions League (10): Aguero 6 (2 pens), Milner 1, Nasri 1, Toure 1, Zabaleta 1.

Hart J 36	Clichy G 23	Kompany V 23+2	Demichelis M 28+3	Kolarov A 16+5	Nasri S 18+6	Fernando F 22+3	Toure Y 27+2	Silva D 32	Dzeko E 11+11	Jovetic S 9+8	Fernandinho L 25+8	Milner J 18+14	Aguero S 30+3	Zabaleta P 29	Jesus Navas G 23+12	Sagna B 8+1	Lampard F 10+22	Mangala E 24+1	Caballero W 2	Boyata D 1+1	Pozo J 1+2	Sinclair S —+2	Bony W 2+8	Match No.
1	2	3	4	5	6^3	7	8	9	10^2	11^1	12	13	14											1
1	5	3	4		6	8	7	9^1	10^2	11^1		14	13	2	12									2
1		3	4	5	6^3	7^1	8	9	14	10^2	12	11	13	2										3
1	5	3	4	14	12			9	13				6^1	10	11^2	2	8	7^3						4
1		3		5^2			8	9	10^3	7^1	6	11	2^4	13	12	14		4						5
	5	3		14			8	9^2	10	7^3	6	11^1	13	2	12			4	1					6
1		3	5		13	8		9^1	10^3	7^2	6	11		2	14		12	4						7
1	5	3	4		6^1	14		9^2	13	12	10	11		8	2			7^3						8
1	5^2	3		13			8^1	7	9	10^3	12	14	11	2	6			4						9
1	5	3	4	12	8	7		13	11^1	14	9^3	10^2	2	6										10
1	5		3	10^2	7	9		12^3		6^1	14	11		8	2	13		4						11
1	5	3	4	9^2	14	8		10^1	7^3	13	11		2	6	12									12
1	5	3	14	9^3		8		10^1	7	12	11		2	6^2		13	4^4							13
1	5		4	10^3		7		9^2	8	12	11^1		2	6	13						3	14		14
1	5	3		10	7	8		13		9	11^1		2	6^2	14		4				12^3			15
1	5	3^2	14	8	7	6	10			12			13	2	9^3	4					11^1			16
1		3	5	10^2	13	6	9^3			7	11^1		2	8		12	4						14	17
1	5		3	12	10^2	6	7^3	9^1		13	11		8	2	14		4							18
1		3	5	10^1	6		9		12	7^3	11^2		2	8		13	4						14	19
	5	3	13	10^3		6	9^1	11^2	7	14			2	8	12		4	1						20
1	5	3	14	10^2	7		9	11^1	6^3		12		8	2	13		4							21
1	5	3	4	7		9	14	12	6^3	10^2	11^1		2	8^1	13									22
1	5	3	4		6^2		9^1	13	14	7	10	11^3	8	2	12									23
1	5	3	4		6	7^3		9^1	11^2	14	8	13	10	2	12									24
1		3	5	6^2	7		9^3	12	8	10	11^1		2	14	13	4								25
1		3	5	6^1	8		9^3	10	7		11^2		2	12		14	4					13		26
1		3	5	6^3	7		9	11^2	8^1	12	10		2		14	4						13		27
1		3	5		8	7	9	14		12		11^1	6	2	13	4							10^2	28
1	5	3	4			7^3	9^2	10^1	13	8		11	2	6	14							12		29
1	5	3			7		9^1	13	12		14	11	2	6	8^2	4						10^3		30
1	5	3	4	13		7		9^1	11^3		8^1	14	10	6^2	2	12								31
1	5	3^2	4	13		7	9			8	10^2	11	2	6^3	14	12								32
1		3	5	12	7	9	10^1	14	13		11^2	2	8				9							33
1		3	5	7	6^1	10		12	13	11^3		2	8	9^2	4							14		34
1		3	5	12^3	6	10	7		8	11^2	2			9^1	4	14						13		35
1		3	5	6	13	10	7^3		8^1	11	2		14	9^2	4							12		36
1	13	3	5	6^3	10	7^2	8		11	2	12		9^1	4								14		37
1	14	3	5	6^1	10	7	8^2		11	2	13		9^3	4								12		38

FA Cup

Third Round	Sheffield W	(h)	2-1
Fourth Round	Middlesbrough	(h)	0-2

Capital One Cup

Third Round	Sheffield W	(h)	7-0
Fourth Round	Newcastle U	(h)	0-2

UEFA Champions League

Group E	Bayern Munich	(a)	0-1
Group E	Roma	(h)	1-1
Group E	CSKA Moscow	(a)	2-2
Group E	CSKA Moscow	(h)	1-2
Group E	Bayern Munich	(h)	3-2
Group E	Roma	(a)	2-0
Round of 16 1st leg	Barcelona	(h)	1-2
Round of 16 2nd leg	Barcelona	(a)	0-1

MANCHESTER UNITED

FOUNDATION

Manchester United was formed as comparatively recently as 1902 after their predecessors, Newton Heath, went bankrupt. However, it is usual to give the date of the club's foundation as 1878 when the dining room committee of the carriage and waggon works of the Lancashire and Yorkshire Railway Company formed Newton Heath L and YR Cricket and Football Club. They won the Manchester Cup in 1886 and as Newton Heath FC were admitted to the Second Division in 1892.

Old Trafford, Sir Matt Busby Way, Manchester M16 0RA.

Telephone: (0161) 868 8000.

Fax: (0161) 868 8804.

Ticket Office: (0161) 868 8000 (option 1).

Website: www.manutd.com

Email: enquiries@manutd.co.uk

Ground Capacity: 75,635.

Record Attendance: 76,098 v Blackburn R, FA Premier League, 31 March 2007.

Ground Record Attendance: 76,962 Wolverhampton W v Grimsby T, FA Cup semi-final, 25 March 1939.

Pitch Measurements: 105m × 68m (114yd × 74yd)

Co-Chairmen: Joel and Avram Glazer.

Chief Executive: Edward Woodward.

Manager: Louis van Gaal.

Assistant Manager: Ryan Giggs.

Physio: Matt Radcliffe.

Colours: Red shirts with white trim, white shorts, black socks with red trim.

Year Formed: 1878 as Newton Heath LYR; 1902, Manchester United.

Turned Professional: 1885.

Previous Name: 1880, Newton Heath; 1902, Manchester United.

Club Nickname: 'Red Devils'.

Grounds: 1880, North Road, Monsall Road; 1893, Bank Street; 1910, Old Trafford (played at Maine Road 1941–49).

HONOURS

FA Premier League: *Champions* 1992–93, 1993–94, 1995–96, 1996–97, 1998–99, 1999–2000, 2000–01, 2002–03, 2006–07, 2007–08, 2008–09, 2010–11, 2012–13; *Runners-up* 1994–95, 1997–98, 2005–06, 2009–10, 2011–12.

Football League – Division 1: *Champions* 1907–08, 1910–11, 1951–52, 1955–56, 1956–57, 1964–65, 1966–67; *Runners-up* 1946–47, 1947–48, 1948–49, 1950–51, 1958–59, 1963–64, 1967–68, 1979–80, 1987–88, 1991–92. **Division 2:** *Champions* 1935–36, 1974–75; *Runners-up* 1896–97, 1905–06, 1924–25, 1937–38.

FA Cup: *Winners* 1909, 1948, 1963, 1977, 1983, 1985, 1990, 1994, 1996, 1999, 2004; *Runners-up* 1957, 1958, 1976, 1979, 1995, 2005, 2007.

Football League Cup: *Winners* 1992, 2006, 2009, 2010; *Runners-up* 1983, 1991, 1994, 2003.

European Competitions
European Cup: 1956–57 (*s-f*), 1957–58 (*s-f*), 1965–66 (*s-f*), 1967–68 (*winners*), 1968–69 (*s-f*). **Champions League:** 1993–94, 1994–95, 1996–97 (*s-f*), 1997–98, 1998–99 (*winners*), 1999–2000, 2000–01, 2001–02 (*s-f*), 2002–03, 2003–04, 2004–05, 2005–06, 2006–07 (*s-f*), 2007–08 (*winners*), 2008–09 (*runners-up*), 2009–10, 2010–11 (*runners-up*), 2011–12, 2012–13, 2013–14. **European Cup-Winners' Cup:** 1963–64, 1977–78, 1983–84, 1990–91 (*winners*). 1991–92. **Inter Cities Fairs Cup:** 1964–65. **UEFA Cup:** 1976–77, 1980–81, 1982–83, 1984–85, 1992–93, 1995–96. **Europa League:** 2011–12. **Super Cup:** 1991 (*winners*), 1999, 2008. **World Club Championship:** 1968, 1999 (*winners*). **FIFA Club World Cup:** 2008 (*winners*). *NB: In 1958–59 FA refused permission to compete in European Cup.*

First Football League Game: 3 September 1892, Division 1, v Blackburn R (a) L 3–4 – Warner; Clements, Brown; Perrins, Stewart, Erentz; Farman (1), Coupar (1), Donaldson (1), Carson, Mathieson.

Record League Victory (as Newton Heath): 10–1 v Wolverhampton W, Division 1, 15 October 1892 – Warner; Mitchell, Clements; Perrins, Stewart (3), Erentz; Farman (1), Hood (1), Donaldson (3), Carson (1), Hendry (1).

Record League Victory (as Manchester U): 9–0 v Ipswich T, FA Premier League, 4 March 1995 – Schmeichel; Keane (1) (Sharpe), Irwin, Bruce (Butt), Kanchelskis, Pallister, Cole (5), Ince (1), McClair, Hughes (2), Giggs.

Record Cup Victory: 10–0 v RSC Anderlecht, European Cup prel. rd 2nd leg, 26 September 1956 – Wood; Foulkes, Byrne; Colman, Jones, Edwards; Berry (1), Whelan (2), Taylor (3), Viollet (4), Pegg.

Record Defeat: 0–7 v Blackburn R, Division 1, 10 April 1926; 0–7 v Aston Villa, Division 1, 27 December 1930; 0–7 v Wolverhampton W, Division 2, 26 December 1931.

Most League Points (2 for a win): 64, Division 1, 1956–57.

Most League Points (3 for a win): 92, FA Premier League, 1993–94.

Most League Goals: 103, Division 1, 1956–57 and 1958–59.

Highest League Scorer in Season: Dennis Viollet, 32, 1959–60.

Most League Goals in Total Aggregate: Bobby Charlton, 199, 1956–73.

Most League Goals in One Match: 5, Andy Cole v Ipswich T, FA Premier League, 3 March 1995; 5, Dimitar Berbatov v Blackburn R, FA Premier League, 27 November 2010.

Most Capped Player: Bobby Charlton, 106, England.

Most League Appearances: Ryan Giggs, 672, 1991–2014.

Youngest League Player: Jeff Whitefoot, 16 years 105 days v Portsmouth, 15 April 1950.

Record Transfer Fee Received: £80,000,000 from Real Madrid for Cristiano Ronaldo, July 2009.

Record Transfer Fee Paid: £59,700,000 to Real Madrid for Angel Di Maria, August 2014.

Football League Record: 1892 Newton Heath elected to Division 1; 1894–1906 Division 2; 1906–22 Division 1; 1922–25 Division 2; 1925–31 Division 1; 1931–36 Division 2; 1936–37 Division 1; 1937–38 Division 2; 1938–74 Division 1; 1974–75 Division 2; 1975–92 Division 1; 1992– FA Premier League.

MANAGERS

J. Ernest Mangnall 1903–12
John Bentley 1912–14
John Robson 1914–21
(Secretary-Manager from 1916)
John Chapman 1921–26
Clarence Hilditch 1926–27
Herbert Bamlett 1927–31
Walter Crickmer 1931–32
Scott Duncan 1932–37
Walter Crickmer 1937–45
(Secretary-Manager)
Matt Busby 1945–69
(continued as General Manager then Director)
Wilf McGuinness 1969–70
Sir Matt Busby 1970–71
Frank O'Farrell 1971–72
Tommy Docherty 1972–77
Dave Sexton 1977–81
Ron Atkinson 1981–86
Sir Alex Ferguson 1986–2013
David Moyes 2013–14
Louis van Gaal May 2014–

LATEST SEQUENCES

Longest Sequence of League Wins: 14, 15.10.1904 – 3.1.1905.

Longest Sequence of League Defeats: 14, 26.4.1930 – 25.10.1930.

Longest Sequence of League Draws: 6, 30.10.1988 – 27.11.1988.

Longest Sequence of Unbeaten League Matches: 29, 11.4.2010 – 1.2.2011.

Longest Sequence Without a League Win: 16, 19.4.1930 – 25.10.1930.

Successive Scoring Runs: 36 from 3.12.2007.

Successive Non-scoring Runs: 5 from 7.2.1981.

TEN YEAR LEAGUE RECORD

		P	W	D	L	F	A	Pts	Pos
2005-06	PR Lge	38	25	8	5	72	34	83	2
2006-07	PR Lge	38	28	5	5	83	27	89	1
2007-08	PR Lge	38	27	6	5	80	22	87	1
2008-09	PR Lge	38	28	6	4	68	24	90	1
2009-10	PR Lge	38	27	4	7	86	28	85	2
2010-11	PR Lge	38	23	11	4	78	37	80	1
2011-12	PR Lge	38	28	5	5	89	33	89	2
2012-13	PR Lge	38	28	5	5	86	43	89	1
2013-14	PR Lge	38	19	7	12	64	43	64	7
2014-15	PR Lge	38	20	10	8	62	37	70	4

DID YOU KNOW ?

It was recently revealed that when George Best was born his name was registered as Ronald Samuel Best. His parents very quickly changed his name to George, apparently because Ronald Samuel was too much of a mouthful.

MANCHESTER UNITED – FA PREMIERSHIP 2014–15 LEAGUE RECORD

Match No.	Date	Venue	Opponents	Result	H/T Score	Lg Pos.	Goalscorers	Atten-dance
1	Aug 16	H	Swansea C	L	1-2	0-1	16	Rooney [53]	75,339
2	24	A	Sunderland	D	1-1	1-1	12	Mata [17]	43,217
3	30	A	Burnley	D	0-0	0-0	14		21,099
4	Sept14	H	QPR	W	4-0	3-0	9	Di Maria [24], Ander Herrera [36], Rooney [44], Mata [58]	75,355
5	21	A	Leicester C	L	3-5	2-1	12	Van Persie [13], Di Maria [16], Ander Herrera [57]	31,784
6	27	H	West Ham U	W	2-1	2-1	7	Rooney [5], Van Persie [22]	75,317
7	Oct 5	A	Everton	W	2-1	1-0	4	Di Maria [27], Falcao [62]	75,294
8	20	A	WBA	D	2-2	0-1	6	Fellaini [48], Blind [87]	25,794
9	26	H	Chelsea	D	1-1	0-0	8	Van Persie [90]	75,327
10	Nov 2	A	Manchester C	L	0-1	0-0	10		45,358
11	8	H	Crystal Palace	W	1-0	0-0	6	Mata [67]	75,325
12	22	A	Arsenal	W	2-1	0-0	4	Gibbs (og) [56], Rooney [85]	60,074
13	29	H	Hull C	W	3-0	2-0	4	Smalling [16], Rooney [42], Van Persie [66]	75,345
14	Dec 2	A	Stoke C	W	2-1	1-1	4	Fellaini [21], Mata [59]	75,388
15	8	A	Southampton	W	2-1	1-1	3	Van Persie 2 [12, 71]	31,420
16	14	H	Liverpool	W	3-0	0-0	3	Rooney [12], Mata [40], Van Persie [71]	75,331
17	20	A	Aston Villa	D	1-1	0-1	3	Falcao [53]	41,273
18	26	H	Newcastle U	W	3-1	2-0	3	Rooney 2 [23, 36], Van Persie [53]	75,318
19	28	A	Tottenham H	D	0-0	0-0	3		35,711
20	Jan 1	A	Stoke C	D	1-1	1-1	3	Falcao [26]	27,203
21	11	H	Southampton	L	0-1	0-0	4		75,395
22	17	A	QPR	W	2-0	0-0	4	Fellaini [58], Wilson [90]	18,098
23	31	H	Leicester C	W	3-1	3-0	3	Van Persie [27], Falcao [32], Morgan (og) [44]	75,329
24	Feb 8	A	West Ham U	D	1-1	0-0	4	Blind [90]	34,499
25	11	H	Burnley	W	3-1	2-1	3	Smalling 2 [6, 45], Van Persie (pen) [82]	75,356
26	21	A	Swansea C	L	1-2	1-1	4	Ander Herrera [28]	20,809
27	28	H	Sunderland	W	2-0	0-0	3	Rooney 2 (1 pen) [66 (p), 84]	75,344
28	Mar 4	A	Newcastle U	W	1-0	0-0	4	Young [89]	49,801
29	15	H	Tottenham H	W	3-0	3-0	4	Fellaini [9], Carrick [19], Rooney [34]	75,112
30	22	A	Liverpool	W	2-1	1-0	4	Mata 2 [14, 59]	44,405
31	Apr 4	H	Aston Villa	W	3-1	1-0	3	Ander Herrera 2 [43, 90], Rooney [79]	75,397
32	12	H	Manchester C	W	4-2	2-1	3	Young [14], Fellaini [27], Mata [67], Smalling [73]	75,313
33	18	A	Chelsea	L	0-1	0-1	3		41,422
34	26	A	Everton	L	0-3	0-2	4		39,497
35	May 2	H	WBA	L	0-1	0-0	4		75,454
36	9	A	Crystal Palace	W	2-1	1-0	4	Mata (pen) [19], Fellaini [78]	25,009
37	17	H	Arsenal	D	1-1	1-0	4	Ander Herrera [30]	75,323
38	24	A	Hull C	D	0-0	0-0	4		24,745

Final League Position: 4

GOALSCORERS

League (62): Rooney 12 (1 pen), Van Persie 10 (1 pen), Mata 9 (1 pen), Ander Herrera 6, Fellaini 6, Falcao 4, Smalling 4, Di Maria 3, Blind 2, Young 2, Carrick 1, Wilson 1, own goals 2.
FA Cup (9): Ander Herrera 2, Rooney 2 (1 pen), Di Maria 1, Fellaini 1, Mata 1, Rojo 1, Wilson 1.
Capital One Cup (0).

De Gea D 37	Jones P 22	Smalling C 21+4	Blackett T 6+5	Lingard J 1	Fletcher D 4+7	Ander Herrera A 19+7	Young A 23+3	Mata J 27+6	Hernandez J 1	Rooney W 33	Januzaj A 7+11	Nani —+1	Fellaini M 19+8	Valencia A 29+3	Cleverley T 1	Van Persie R 25+2	Keane M —+1	Welbeck D —+2	Evans J 12+2	Di Maria A 20+7	Anderson —+1	De Silva R 6+4	Rojo M 20+2	Blind D 25	Falcao R 14+12	McNair P 12+4	Shaw L 15+1	Thorpe T —+1	Wilson J 2+11	Carrick M 16+2	Pereira A —+1	Valdes V 1+1	Match No.
1	2	3	4	5²	6	7¹	8	9	10³	11	12	13	14																				1
1	2	3³	4		6¹		8	9		11	14			5	7	10³	12	13															2
1	3		4		6		8	9¹		11	14			5		10²		13	2	7³	12												3
1			4			7		9¹		10	14			12		11			3	8²		2¹	5	6	13								4
1	12	4⁸				7		14		9	13					10			3¹	8³		2	5	6	11²								5
1		12				7²		9⁸				13				10			8			2	4	6	11³	3	5	14					6
1		12						9					14	7²		10			8			2	4	6	11¹	3	5³		13				7
1	3				9²	14	8³			7		12		11		10¹			2	4		6	13	5									8
1	3					8¹				10			9	7¹		11			8²			2	4	6		5	12						9
1	3							9		7¹			8	2		11²			10			4³	6		13	5		14	12				10
1					14			12		9	7²		8	2		11			10¹				4		3²	5	13	6					11
1	3	4		14		12³		9					6	5		10²			11						2	8¹	13	7					12
1	3			14	12	5	8	11		6	2¹		10³			9²						4	13						7				13
1	3			13	9⁵	5	8²			14			7	2		10			4	12					11¹	6			5				14
1	3³			14	13	9	8²	11		7			6			10		12		4			2¹				5						15
1	2³				12	8	9	7¹		6	5		10	4									13	14			11²	3					16
1	2	12		6²		8	9	7					5³	10¹					4	13			11				14	3					17
1	2			12		9	7	8					6⁵	10					4		14		11²	3			13	5¹					18
1	2	13				9	7	8					6⁵	10					4²	12			11	3¹	14			5					19
1	2	3			12	6²	7	8	13				10						4		14		11³		9¹			5					20
1	2	3	13		12		7	8				14	6	10³						11¹			4		9²			5					21
1	2				14		7²	8				12	6						3¹	10³			4	9	11			13	5				22
1	3					13		7	8				2¹	10²					9				4	6	11³	12	5	14					23
1	3	13						7	8²			12	2						9				4	6	11¹		5⁸						24
1	3¹	12			13			7	9				10						4	8			5	6³	11²	2		14					25
1	3				7	13	14	11		9	12		10						8¹			4	6		2⁴	5³							26
1		3			6	10	14		9²	12	13	2							4	8³			5	7	11¹								27
1		3			6	10	13	11	12		9²	2							4	8³			5¹	7				14					28
1	4	3				8	10	7²		11			9¹	2							14		5	13				6²	12				29
1	4	3				8²	10³	7		11			9	2						12			14	5¹	13			6					30
1	3					8	10²	7		11			9	2						12			4	5	13			6					31
1	4¹	3				8	10	7³		11			9²	2						13			12	5	14			6					32
1		3	14			6	10²	7¹		8	13		9	2						12				11	4	5³							33
1		3				8	10	7¹		11³			9²	2	14					13				6	12	4	5						34
1		3				6	10	7		9			8	2	11					12				5³	13	4¹							35
1	4	3¹				8	10	7		11²			9	2					12				6	13	14	5³							36
1³	4	3	13			8	10	7					9	2	12								5¹	6	11²							14	37
	4	3				8	9²	7²		11	12		13⁸	2						10¹				5	6				14			1	38

FA Cup

Third Round	Yeovil T	(a)	2-0
Fourth Round	Cambridge U	(a)	0-0
Replay	Cambridge U	(h)	3-0
Fifth Round	Preston NE	(a)	3-1
Sixth Round	Arsenal	(h)	1-2

Capital One Cup

Second Round	Milton Keynes D	(a)	0-4

MANSFIELD TOWN

FOUNDATION

The club was formed as Mansfield Wesleyans in 1897, and changed their name to Mansfield Wesley in 1906 and Mansfield Town in 1910. This was after the Mansfield Wesleyan Chapel trustees had requested that the club change its name as 'it has no longer had any connection with either the chapel or school'. The new club participated in the Notts and Derby District League, but in the following season 1911–12 joined the Central Alliance.

One Call Stadium, Quarry Lane, Mansfield, Nottinghamshire NG18 5DA.

Telephone: (01623) 482 482.

Fax: (01623) 482 495.

Ticket Office: (01623) 482 482.

Website: www.mansfieldtown.net

Email: info@mansfieldtown.net

Ground Capacity: 9,186.

Record Attendance: 24,467 v Nottingham F, FA Cup 3rd rd, 10 January 1953.

Pitch Measurements: 103.5m × 64m (113yd × 70yd)

Chairman: John Radford.

Chief Executive: Carolyn Radford.

Manager: Adam Murray.

First-Team Coach: Micky Moore.

Physio: Matt Fenney.

Colours: Yellow shirts with blue trim, blue shorts, yellow socks with blue trim.

Year Formed: 1897.

Turned Professional: 1906.

Ltd Co.: 1922.

Previous Name: 1897, Mansfield Wesleyans; 1906, Mansfield Wesley; 1910, Mansfield Town.

Grounds: 1897–99, Westfield Lane; 1899–1901, Ratcliffe Gate; 1901–12, Newgate Lane; 1912–16, Ratcliffe Gate; 1916, Field Mill (renamed One Call Stadium 2012).

Club Nickname: 'The Stags'.

First Football League Game: 29 August 1931, Division 3 (S), v Swindon T (h) W 3–2 – Wilson; Clifford, England; Wake, Davis, Blackburn; Gilhespy, Readman (1), Johnson, Broom (2), Baxter.

Record League Victory: 9–2 v Rotherham U, Division 3 (N), 27 December 1932 – Wilson; Anthony, England; Davies, S. Robinson, Slack; Prior, Broom, Readman (3), Hoyland (3), Bowater (3).

Record Cup Victory: 8–0 v Scarborough (a), FA Cup 1st rd, 22 November 1952 – Bramley; Chessell, Bradley; Field, Plummer, Lewis; Scott, Fox (3), Marron (2), Sid Watson (1), Adam (2).

Record Defeat: 1–8 v Walsall, Division 3 (N), 19 January 1933.

HONOURS

Football League: Division 2: Best season: 21st, 1977–78; **Division 3:** *Champions* 1976–77; Promoted to **Division 2** (3rd) 2001–02; **Division 4:** *Champions* 1974–75; **Division 3 (N):** *Runners-up* 1950–51.

FA Cup: Best season: 6th rd, 1969.

Football League Cup: Best season: 5th rd, 1976.

Freight Rover Trophy: *Winners* 1987.

Conference: *Winners* 2012–13.

sky SPORTS FACT FILE

An end-of-season fixture congestion forced Mansfield Town to play four League fixtures in five days during March 1937. They scored 16 goals in winning three of the four games with leading scorer Ted Harston netting 11 including five against Port Vale and a hat-trick against Wrexham.

Most League Points (2 for a win): 68, Division 4, 1974–75.

Most League Points (3 for a win): 81, Division 4, 1985–86.

Most League Goals: 108, Division 4, 1962–63.

Highest League Scorer in Season: Ted Harston, 55, Division 3 (N), 1936–37.

Most League Goals in Total Aggregate: Harry Johnson, 104, 1931–36.

Most League Goals in One Match: 7, Ted Harston v Hartlepools U, Division 3N, 23 January 1937.

Most Capped Player: John McClelland, 6 (53), Northern Ireland.

Most League Appearances: Rod Arnold, 440, 1970–83.

Youngest League Player: Cyril Poole, 15 years 351 days v New Brighton, 27 February 1937.

Record Transfer Fee Received: £175,000 from Sunderland for Liam Lawrence, June 2004.

Record Transfer Fee Paid: £150,000 to Carlisle U for Lee Peacock, October 1997.

Football League Record: 1931 Elected to Division 3 (S); 1932–37 Division 3 (N); 1937–47 Division 3 (S); 1947–58 Division 3 (N); 1958–60 Division 3; 1960–63 Division 4; 1963–72 Division 3; 1972–75 Division 4; 1975–77 Division 3; 1977–78 Division 2; 1978–80 Division 3; 1980–86 Division 4; 1986–91 Division 3; 1991–92 Division 4; 1992–93 Division 2; 1993–2002 Division 3; 2002–03 Division 2; 2003–04 Division 3; 2004–08 FL 2; 2008–13 Conference Premier; 2013– FL 2.

LATEST SEQUENCES

Longest Sequence of League Wins: 7, 13.9.1991 – 26.10.1991.

Longest Sequence of League Defeats: 7, 18.1.1947 – 15.3.1947.

Longest Sequence of League Draws: 5, 18.10.1986 – 22.11.1986.

Longest Sequence of Unbeaten League Matches: 20, 14.2.1976 – 21.8.1976.

Longest Sequence Without a League Win: 14, 25.3.2000 – 2.9.2000.

Successive Scoring Runs: 27 from 1.10.1962.

Successive Non-scoring Runs: 8 from 25.3.2000.

MANAGERS

John Baynes 1922–25
Ted Davison 1926–28
Jack Hickling 1928–33
Henry Martin 1933–35
Charlie Bell 1935
Harold Wightman 1936
Harold Parkes 1936–38
Jack Poole 1938–44
Lloyd Barke 1944–45
Roy Goodall 1945–49
Freddie Steele 1949–51
George Jobey 1952–53
Stan Mercer 1953–55
Charlie Mitten 1956–58
Sam Weaver 1958–60
Raich Carter 1960–63
Tommy Cummings 1963–67
Tommy Eggleston 1967–70
Jock Basford 1970–71
Danny Williams 1971–74
Dave Smith 1974–76
Peter Morris 1976–78
Billy Bingham 1978–79
Mick Jones 1979–81
Stuart Boam 1981–83
Ian Greaves 1983–89
George Foster 1989–93
Andy King 1993–96
Steve Parkin 1996–99
Billy Dearden 1999–2002
Stuart Watkiss 2002
Keith Curle 2002–04
Carlton Palmer 2004–05
Peter Shirtliff 2005–06
Billy Dearden 2006–08
Paul Holland 2008
Billy McEwan 2008
David Holdsworth 2008–10
Duncan Russell 2010–11
Paul Cox 2011–14
Adam Murray December 2014–

TEN YEAR LEAGUE RECORD

		P	W	D	L	F	A	Pts	Pos
2005-06	FL 2	46	13	15	18	59	66	54	16
2006-07	FL 2	46	14	12	20	58	63	54	17
2007-08	FL 2	46	11	9	26	48	68	42	23
2008-09	Conf P	46	19	9	18	57	55	62	12
2009-10	Conf P	44	17	11	16	69	60	62	9
2010-11	Conf P	46	17	10	19	73	75	61	13
2011-12	Conf P	46	25	14	7	87	48	89	3
2012-13	Conf P	46	30	5	11	92	52	95	1
2013-14	FL 2	46	15	15	16	49	58	60	11
2014-15	FL 2	46	13	9	24	38	62	48	21

DID YOU KNOW ?

Mansfield Town began the 1949–50 season in great form and topped the table after being undefeated in the opening 10 fixtures of the season. Their run only came to an end when they were defeated at Tranmere Rovers on the first Saturday in October.

MANSFIELD TOWN – FOOTBALL LEAGUE TWO 2014–15 LEAGUE RECORD

Match No.	Date	Venue	Opponents	Result	H/T Score	Lg Pos.	Goalscorers	Attendance
1	Aug 9	A	Northampton T	L 0-1	0-1	16		5202
2	16	H	Oxford U	W 2-1	1-0	12	Tafazolli [39], Murray [88]	3042
3	19	H	Newport Co	W 1-0	1-0	9	Clements [2]	2448
4	23	A	Dagenham & R	L 0-2	0-1	11		1558
5	30	H	Burton Alb	L 1-2	0-1	16	Rhead [75]	2966
6	Sept 6	A	Exeter C	W 2-1	2-0	10	Bingham [14], Bell, F [40]	2771
7	13	A	Wycombe W	L 1-2	1-1	13	Rhead [4]	3106
8	16	H	Morecambe	W 1-0	0-0	10	Fisher [90]	2185
9	20	H	Carlisle U	W 3-2	3-0	8	Beevers [4], Bingham 2 [37, 41]	3117
10	27	A	Stevenage	L 0-3	0-2	11		2820
11	Oct 4	H	Accrington S	L 0-1	0-1	15		2699
12	11	A	Portsmouth	D 1-1	0-0	15	Heslop [46]	15,585
13	18	H	Cambridge U	D 0-0	0-0	16		2925
14	21	A	Tranmere R	D 0-0	0-0	17		4092
15	25	A	York C	D 1-1	0-1	17	Carr [61]	3370
16	Nov 1	H	Southend U	L 1-2	0-1	18	Palmer [78]	2719
17	15	A	Shrewsbury T	L 0-2	0-0	19		5001
18	22	H	Plymouth Arg	W 1-0	1-0	17	Oliver [45]	2926
19	29	A	Luton T	L 0-3	0-1	18		8418
20	Dec 13	H	Cheltenham T	D 1-1	0-0	19	Oliver [55]	3324
21	20	A	AFC Wimbledon	W 1-0	0-0	16	Oliver [47]	3790
22	26	H	Hartlepool U	D 1-1	1-0	16	Brown [10]	3357
23	28	A	Bury	L 0-2	0-1	17		3196
24	Jan 10	A	Burton Alb	L 1-2	0-2	20	Lambe [51]	3506
25	17	H	Exeter C	L 2-3	0-1	20	Kee [57], Oliver [68]	3881
26	24	H	Wycombe W	D 0-0	0-0	20		2759
27	31	A	Carlisle U	L 1-2	1-0	23	Oliver [45]	3827
28	Feb 7	H	Stevenage	W 1-0	0-0	20	Lambe [51]	2436
29	10	A	Morecambe	L 1-2	1-2	21	Heslop [27]	1156
30	14	H	Northampton T	D 1-1	0-0	21	Oliver [48]	4614
31	17	H	Luton T	W 1-0	1-0	18	Bingham [32]	2998
32	21	A	Oxford U	L 0-3	0-1	19		6954
33	28	H	Dagenham & R	W 2-1	0-0	18	Lambe [46], Brown [82]	2546
34	Mar 3	A	Newport Co	W 1-0	0-0	17	Lambe [87]	2481
35	7	A	Cheltenham T	D 1-1	0-0	19	Kee [68]	2597
36	14	H	Bury	L 0-1	0-1	19		2868
37	17	H	AFC Wimbledon	W 2-1	0-0	16	Beevers [56], Bingham [87]	3151
38	21	A	Hartlepool U	L 0-1	0-0	17		4166
39	28	H	York C	L 1-4	0-2	18	Rhead [77]	3133
40	Apr 3	A	Southend U	L 0-2	0-2	18		5925
41	6	H	Shrewsbury T	L 0-1	0-0	20		3108
42	11	A	Plymouth Arg	L 1-2	0-1	21	Oliver [64]	6626
43	14	H	Tranmere R	W 1-0	1-0	20	Lambe [44]	3051
44	18	A	Cambridge U	L 1-3	0-2	21	Bingham [64]	4667
45	25	H	Portsmouth	L 1-2	0-1	21	Thomas [68]	4222
46	May 2	A	Accrington S	L 1-2	1-0	21	McGuire [39]	1921

Final League Position: 21

GOALSCORERS

League (38): Oliver 7, Bingham 6, Lambe 5, Rhead 3, Beevers 2, Brown 2, Heslop 2, Kee 2, Bell, F 1, Carr 1, Clements 1, Fisher 1, McGuire 1, Murray 1, Palmer 1, Tafazolli 1, Thomas 1.
FA Cup (4): Bingham 1, Palmer 1, own goals 2.
Capital One Cup (1): Fisher 1.
Johnstone's Paint Trophy (0).

Studer S 17	Sutton R 34	Dempster J 4	Tafazolli R 35 + 1	Bell F 10 + 6	Beevers L 33 + 2	Heslop S 21 + 4	Murray A 11 + 3	Taylor R 10 + 6	Hawkridge T 4 + 1	Fisher A 6 + 8	Palmer O 2 + 14	Shires C — + 1	Clucas S 2 + 3	Hearn L — + 3	Clements C 30 + 4	McGuire J 25 + 4	Rhead M 16 + 16	Evtimov D 10	Riley M 31 + 2	Marsden L 9 + 1	Bingham R 15 + 13	Lambe R 20 + 10	Freeman K 11	Sendles-White J 7	Carr D 3 + 1	Oliver V 28 + 2	Waterfall L 5	Brown J 21 + 3	Smith A 4	Raynes M 10	Elder C 21	Ravenhill R 12 + 1	Kee B 8 + 5	Fletcher D — + 1	Blair M 2 + 1	Ridgeley L 15	Fitzpatrick J 1 + 2	Thomas J 11 + 1	Monakana J 2 + 4	Match No.
1	2	3	4	5[2]	6	7	8	9[1]	10	11[3]	12		13		14																									1
1	2	3	4	13	5	6	14	9	11[2]	12	10				7[3]	8[1]																								2
1	2	3	4		5	6	13	9	11[2]	12	14				7[3]	8	10[1]																							3
1	2	3	4	14	5	8		9	11[3]	12	13				7[1]	6	10																							4
	2	3	13	4[1]	14	8		6[2]	12	10[3]	9					7	11	1	5																					5
	2[3]		4	7[2]	6	13	8	12			14				5	10		1	3	9	11[1]																			6
	2		4	8[1]	9[2]	6	13				12				7	10		1	3	5	11																			7
	2		4	9[3]	5	14	7				12	13			6	10[3]		1	3	8	11[1]																			8
	2	3		7[2]	9		6				14				8[1]	12	10	1	4	5	11[3]	13																		9
	2[3]		4		3	9	6				14	12				13	10[2]	1	5	8	11	7[1]																		10
1	4		7[1]	8	2		11[4]				13					6	9[2]		3		10	12	5																	11
1	2		7[1]	5	8[2]		13				12				14	6	10[3]		4		11	9	3																	12
1	2		8[1]	5	6		12	10							7				4		11	9	3																	13
1	2		7[2]	5	8		12	10[1]							6				4		11	14	9[3]	3	13															14
1	3			5		7	9			12					8				2	10					4	6	11[1]													15
1				13	5	7	9			14					12	8[2]			3	2	10				4	6[1]	11[3]													16
1		4		9		6					12				8	7[4]	10[2]		2		13		5			11[1]		3												17
1			3	12	5	8		11[1]							6[2]		13		2				9	2	7	10														18
1			3	13	5	9		10[2]							8		14		4				7[1]	2	6[3]		11		12											19
	2		4	10[2]	12	8		13							7				14	6[1]	5[2]	3	9																	20
	2		3					13			9[4]			14	7[2]	8	11[1]	1			12		5			10[2]	4	6												21
	5		2[8]											14	7	4	10[1]	1	12		13	6[2]	8			9	3	11												22
	2					5[3]	7							14		6	13	1	3		10[1]	12	8			11[4]	4	9												23
	2														8	12	3				6[1]					11			9	1	4	5[2]	7	10	13					24
	2[1]														7	13	14		3				6[2]			11			9	1	4	5	8[2]	10		12				25
	2		4										14		7		12					13				10[2]		6	1	3	5	8	11[1]		9[3]					26
	2		3				8										13					10				11		9[1]	1	4	5	7	12		6[2]					27
	2		3		5										6	7	10[1]					12				9		13		4	8	11[2]			1				28
	2		3		5[3]	7										6	11[1]		14			9				10		13		4[2]	8				1		12		29
	2		4		5	9	13										3		12		6[2]					11		10				8			1			7[1]	30
	2		4			6[3]									13		14		3		12	5[1]				10[2]		9			11	7			1			8	31
	2		3		9														5		12	14				11[3]		10[2]			4	8	13		1		7[1]	6	32
	2		4		9														3							11		10			5	6	12		1		7[1]	13	33
1			3		2	8[3]									9	7			5							12		14			10	4	11[1]				13	6[2]		34
			4		2	8[1]									9				3							6		11			10[2]	5	7	12		1		13		35
			3		2										8				4		14	10[1]				11		7[2]			5	6	12		1		9[3]	13	36
			3		2										7	8	12		4		14	6				10[3]		9[1]			5		11[2]		1			13	37
					2[1]	9[2]		7[3]							8	6			4		14	13				12		10[4]	3	5		11			1				38
			4		5						12	14			6	8	13		2[2]		11					7[3]			3	9		10[1]			1				39
	3		14		2[2]	9[1]	7								8		13		4		12	10				11[3]			5	6					1				40
	4				2						11[1]	14			7	8[1]	12		3		13	9				10[3]			5						1			6	41
1			3		2										7	6	12		4		11[2]	9[1]				10[3]			5						1			8	42
1	2		4												7	8[1]	12			14		10[8]				11		6[1]	3	5	13							9[3]	43
1	2		3		5					10[5]					9		12				13					11[1]		7	4		6[2]					14	8		44
	3[8]		4												13	8[2]	14	11			2[1]	7[3]	12					10		5			1	9	6				45
			4[1]		13									14	8	6	12		3[2]	2		9				11		10[3]		5			1		7				46

FA Cup

First Round	Concord R	(h)	1-1	
Replay	Concord R	(a)	1-0	
Second Round	Cambridge U	(a)	2-2	
Replay	Cambridge U	(h)	0-1	

Capital One Cup

First Round	Sheffield U	(a)	1-2

Johnstone's Paint Trophy

First Round	Notts Co	(a)	0-2

MIDDLESBROUGH

FOUNDATION

A previous belief that Middlesbrough Football Club was founded at a tripe supper at the Corporation Hotel has proved to be erroneous. In fact, members of Middlesbrough Cricket Club were responsible for forming it at a meeting in the gymnasium of the Albert Park Hotel in 1875.

Riverside Stadium, Middlesbrough TS3 6RS.

Telephone: (0844) 499 6789.

Fax: (01642) 757 697.

Ticket Office: (0844) 499 1234.

Website: www.mfc.co.uk

Email: enquiries@mfc.co.uk

Ground Capacity: 34,733.

Record Attendance: 53,536 v Newcastle U, Division 1, 27 December 1949 (at Ayresome Park); 34,814 v Newcastle U, FA Premier League, 5 March 2003 (at Riverside Stadium); 35,000, England v Slovakia, Euro 2004 qualifier, 11 June 2003.

Pitch Measurements: 105m × 68m (115yd × 74.5yd)

Chairman: Steve Gibson.

Chief Executive: Neil Bausor.

Head Coach: Aitor Karanka.

Assistant Head Coach: Steve Agnew.

Head of Medical: Chris Moseley.

HONOURS

Football League – Division 1:
Champions 1994–95;
Runners-up 1997–98.
Division 2: *Champions* 1926–27, 1928–29, 1973–74;
Runners-up 1901–02, 1991–92;
Division 3: *Runners-up* 1966–67, 1986–87.
FA Cup: *Runners-up* 1997.
Football League Cup: *Winners* 2004; *Runners-up* 1997, 1998.
Amateur Cup: *Winners* 1895, 1898.
Anglo-Scottish Cup: *Winners* 1976.
Zenith Data Systems Cup: *Runners-up* 1990.
European Competitions
UEFA Cup: 2004–05, 2005–06 (*runners-up*).

Colours: Red shirts with white trim, white shorts with red trim, red socks with white hoops.

Year Formed: 1876; re-formed 1986.

Turned Professional: 1889; became amateur 1892, and professional again, 1899.

Club Nickname: 'Boro'.

Grounds: 1877, Old Archery Ground, Albert Park; 1879, Breckon Hill; 1882, Linthorpe Road Ground; 1903, Ayresome Park; 1995, Riverside Stadium.

First Football League Game: 2 September 1899, Division 2, v Lincoln C (a) L 0–3 – Smith; Shaw, Ramsey; Allport, McNally, McCracken; Wanless, Longstaffe, Gettins, Page, Pugh.

Record League Victory: 9–0 v Brighton & HA, Division 2, 23 August 1958 – Taylor; Bilcliff, Robinson; Harris (2p), Phillips, Walley; Day, McLean, Clough (5), Peacock (2), Holliday.

Record Cup Victory: 7–0 v Hereford U, Coca-Cola Cup 2nd rd, 1st leg, 18 September 1996 – Miller; Fleming (1), Branco (1), Whyte, Vickers, Whelan, Emerson (1), Mustoe, Stamp, Juninho, Ravanelli (4).

sky SPORTS FACT FILE

Centre forward George Elliott scored 214 goals from 266 appearances for Boro before retiring at the end of the 1924–25 season. Shortly afterwards he was involved in an accident when a young boy died after being dragged for 10 miles under a car driven by Elliott. He was later found not guilty of manslaughter at Durham Assizes.

Record Defeat: 0–9 v Blackburn R, Division 2, 6 November 1954.

Most League Points (2 for a win): 65, Division 2, 1973–74.

Most League Points (3 for a win): 94, Division 3, 1986–87.

Most League Goals: 122, Division 2, 1926–27.

Highest League Scorer in Season: George Camsell, 59, Division 2, 1926–27 (Second Division record).

Most League Goals in Total Aggregate: George Camsell, 325, 1925–39.

Most League Goals in One Match: 5, John Wilkie v Gainsborough T, Division 2, 2 March 1901; 5, Andy Wilson v Nottingham F, Division 1, 6 October 1923; 5, George Camsell v Manchester C, Division 2, 25 December 1926; 5, George Camsell v Aston Villa, Division 1, 9 September 1935; 5, Brian Clough v Brighton & HA, Division 2, 22 August 1958.

Most Capped Player: Wilf Mannion, 26, England.

Most League Appearances: Tim Williamson, 563, 1902–23.

Youngest League Player: Luke Williams, 16 years 200 days v Barnsley, 18 December 2009.

Record Transfer Fee Received: £12,000,000 from Atletico Madrid for Juninho, July 1997; £12,000,000 from Aston Villa for Stewart Downing, July 2009.

Record Transfer Fee Paid: £12,000,000 to Heerenveen for Afonso Alves, January 2008.

Football League Record: 1899 Elected to Division 2; 1902–24 Division 1; 1924–27 Division 2; 1927–28 Division 1; 1928–29 Division 2; 1929–54 Division 1; 1954–66 Division 2; 1966–67 Division 3; 1967–74 Division 2; 1974–82 Division 1; 1982–86 Division 2; 1986–87 Division 3; 1987–88 Division 2; 1988–89 Division 1; 1989–92 Division 2; 1992–93 FA Premier League; 1993–95 Division 1; 1995–97 FA Premier League; 1997–98 Division 1; 1998–2009 FA Premier League; 2009– FL C.

MANAGERS

John Robson 1899–1905
Alex Mackie 1905–06
Andy Aitken 1906–09
J. Gunter 1908–10
    (Secretary-Manager)
Andy Walker 1910–11
Tom McIntosh 1911–19
Jimmy Howie 1920–23
Herbert Bamlett 1923–26
Peter McWilliam 1927–34
Wilf Gillow 1934–44
David Jack 1944–52
Walter Rowley 1952–54
Bob Dennison 1954–63
Raich Carter 1963–66
Stan Anderson 1966–73
Jack Charlton 1973–77
John Neal 1977–81
Bobby Murdoch 1981–82
Malcolm Allison 1982–84
Willie Maddren 1984–86
Bruce Rioch 1986–90
Colin Todd 1990–91
Lennie Lawrence 1991–94
Bryan Robson 1994–2001
Steve McClaren 2001–06
Gareth Southgate 2006–09
Gordon Strachan 2009–10
Tony Mowbray 2010–13
Aitor Karanka November 2013–

LATEST SEQUENCES

Longest Sequence of League Wins: 9, 16.2.1974 – 6.4.1974.

Longest Sequence of League Defeats: 8, 26.12.1995 – 17.2.1996.

Longest Sequence of League Draws: 8, 3.4.1971 – 1.5.1971.

Longest Sequence of Unbeaten League Matches: 24, 8.9.1973 – 19.1.1974.

Longest Sequence Without a League Win: 19, 3.10.1981 – 6.3.1982.

Successive Scoring Runs: 26 from 21.9.1946.

Successive Non-scoring Runs: 7, 25.1.2014 – 1.3.2014.

TEN YEAR LEAGUE RECORD

		P	W	D	L	F	A	Pts	Pos
2005-06	PR Lge	38	12	9	17	48	58	45	14
2006-07	PR Lge	38	12	10	16	44	49	46	12
2007-08	PR Lge	38	10	12	16	43	53	42	13
2008-09	PR Lge	38	7	11	20	28	57	32	19
2009-10	FL C	46	16	14	16	58	50	62	11
2010-11	FL C	46	17	11	18	68	68	62	12
2011-12	FL C	46	18	16	12	52	51	70	7
2012-13	FL C	46	18	5	23	61	70	59	16
2013-14	FL C	46	16	16	14	62	50	64	12
2014-15	FL C	46	25	10	11	68	37	85	4

DID YOU KNOW ?

Middlesbrough went the entire 1903–04 season without recording an away League win, yet were unbeaten away from home in 3 FA Cup ties, winning at Millwall and Preston and drawing at Manchester City before going out in a replay at home to City.

MIDDLESBROUGH – FL CHAMPIONSHIP 2014–15 LEAGUE RECORD

Match No.	Date	Venue	Opponents	Result		H/T Score	Lg Pos.	Goalscorers	Attendance
1	Aug 9	H	Birmingham C	W	2-0	1-0	3	Ayala [33], Garcia [66]	18,371
2	16	A	Leeds U	L	0-1	0-0	11		24,484
3	19	A	Bolton W	W	2-1	1-1	8	Leadbitter (pen) [45], Garcia [78]	13,847
4	23	H	Sheffield W	L	2-3	0-2	12	Leadbitter 2 (2 pens) [72, 90]	17,820
5	30	H	Reading	L	0-1	0-1	16		14,970
6	Sept 13	A	Huddersfield T	W	2-1	1-0	10	Leadbitter 2 (1 pen) [36, 90 (p)]	17,993
7	16	A	Cardiff C	W	1-0	1-0	8	Garcia [2]	19,711
8	20	H	Brentford	W	4-0	1-0	5	Leadbitter [35], Adomah [50], Bamford [68], Garcia [89]	15,485
9	27	A	Charlton Ath	D	0-0	0-0	7		16,110
10	30	H	Blackpool	D	1-1	1-1	8	Ayala [19]	15,213
11	Oct 4	H	Fulham	W	2-0	0-0	5	Reach [46], Adomah [82]	16,201
12	18	A	Brighton & HA	W	2-1	1-0	3	Tomlin [8], Adomah [53]	26,642
13	21	A	Wolverhampton W	L	0-2	0-1	3		18,391
14	25	H	Watford	D	1-1	0-0	5	Garcia [49]	17,491
15	Nov 1	A	Rotherham U	W	3-0	2-0	3	Bamford [8], Wildschut [19], Tomlin [87]	11,282
16	4	H	Norwich C	W	4-0	2-0	2	Bamford [6], Leadbitter 2 (1 pen) [33 (p), 69], Wildschut [95]	16,468
17	8	H	Bournemouth	D	0-0	0-0	3		22,930
18	22	A	Wigan Ath	D	1-1	0-1	3	Bamford [58]	16,347
19	29	H	Blackburn R	D	1-1	0-0	5	Bamford [83]	18,152
20	Dec 6	A	Millwall	W	5-1	4-0	4	Vossen 3 [21, 34, 44], Bamford [28], Garcia [79]	10,328
21	13	H	Derby Co	W	2-0	1-0	2	Bamford [6], Leadbitter (pen) [63]	17,434
22	20	A	Ipswich T	L	0-2	0-2	4		21,187
23	26	H	Nottingham F	W	3-0	0-0	4	Friend [53], Vossen [79], Leadbitter (pen) [88]	32,277
24	28	A	Blackburn R	D	0-0	0-0	3		22,340
25	Jan 10	A	Reading	D	0-0	0-0	4		17,131
26	17	H	Huddersfield T	W	2-0	0-0	4	Tomlin 2 [61, 90]	18,576
27	20	H	Cardiff C	W	2-1	0-0	2	Bamford [63], Tomlin [79]	16,035
28	31	A	Brentford	W	1-0	1-0	3	Leadbitter (pen) [44]	11,853
29	Feb 7	A	Charlton Ath	W	3-1	1-1	2	Bamford [6], Vossen [48], Tomlin [88]	18,903
30	10	A	Blackpool	W	2-1	0-0	1	Woodgate [81], Garcia [88]	10,806
31	18	A	Birmingham C	D	1-1	0-1	1	Bamford [74]	15,101
32	21	H	Leeds U	L	0-1	0-1	2		25,531
33	24	H	Bolton W	W	1-0	1-0	2	Adomah [34]	16,569
34	28	A	Sheffield W	L	0-2	0-0	2		23,774
35	Mar 3	H	Millwall	W	3-0	2-0	1	Bamford [26], Garcia [30], Vossen [78]	16,078
36	7	A	Nottingham F	L	1-2	1-1	4	Mancienne (og) [27]	24,200
37	14	H	Ipswich T	W	4-1	2-0	3	Ayala [4], Adomah [30], Bamford 2 [64, 79]	18,909
38	17	A	Derby Co	W	1-0	0-0	2	Bamford [64]	31,939
39	21	A	Bournemouth	L	0-3	0-1	3		10,998
40	Apr 3	H	Wigan Ath	W	1-0	1-0	1	Bamford [20]	23,082
41	6	A	Watford	L	0-2	0-1	4		19,656
42	11	H	Rotherham U	W	2-0	0-0	4	Tomlin [50], Bamford [66]	19,537
43	14	H	Wolverhampton W	W	2-1	2-0	3	Vossen [3], Bamford [11]	20,520
44	17	A	Norwich C	W	1-0	1-0	1	Tettey (og) [8]	26,993
45	25	A	Fulham	L	3-4	0-1	3	Reach [63], Ayala [73], Garcia [88]	22,731
46	May 2	H	Brighton & HA	D	0-0	0-0	4		33,381

Final League Position: 4

GOALSCORERS

League (68): Bamford 17, Leadbitter 11 (8 pens), Garcia 9, Tomlin 7, Vossen 7, Adomah 5, Ayala 4, Reach 2, Wildschut 2, Friend 1, Woodgate 1, own goals 2.
FA Cup (4): Ayala 1, Bamford 1, Garcia 1, Vossen 1.
Capital One Cup (8): Tomlin 2, Bamford 1 (1 pen), Garcia 1, Leadbitter 1, Reach 1, Williams, L 1, own goal 1.
Championship Play-Offs (5): Adomah 1, Amorebieta 1, Garcia 1, Tomlin 1, Vossen 1.

Mejias T 6+1	Hines S 3	Gibson B 33+3	Ayala D 29+1	Friend G 42	Whitehead D 11+7	Leadbitter G 40+3	Adomah A 40+3	Tomlin L 32+10	Reach A 27+12	Garcia E 25+17	Omeruo K 17+2	Nsue E 12+14	Williams L —+4	Damia A 6	Clayton A 37+4	Bamford P 32+6	Konstantopoulos D 40	Vossen J 20+13	Fredericks R 16+1	Wildschut Y 3+8	Husband J 2+1	Ledesma E 1	Veljkovic M 1+2	Williams R —+1	Kalas T 16+1	Forshaw A 6+12	Woodgate J 5+2	Tiendalli D 2	Amorebieta F 2+2	Match No.
1	2	3³	4	5	6	7	8	9²	10	11	12	13	14																	1
1		3		5	8¹	7	6	10³	9²	11	4	13	14		2	12														2
1	4	13	5	14		7	9	10¹	12	11	3	6¹			2	8²														3
1		4	5	6		7	8	9²	10	11	3		13		2¹	12														4
1	3²		5	14		7	8	9²	10	11	4		13		2	6¹	12													5
	3	4	5		8	6³	10¹	9	11²			14		2	7	13	1	12												6
	3	5		8	6	13	9	10²	4	12			2³	7	14	1	11¹													7
	4		5	7⁸	6³	8		14	13	3	10			12	9¹	1	11²	2												8
	12	3	5	13	6⁸	8²	9	11³	4¹		2			7	10	1		14												9
	4	3		8		11	9	12		13			7¹	10	1		2		5	6²										10
	3	5	13	7	8	9³	10¹	11²	4	14			6		1	12	2													11
	4	3	5	13	7	6³	10²	9	11		14			8¹		1	12	2												12
	3	5	8	7	6	13	9³	12	4						11³	1	10¹	2	14											13
	4	3	5	6		8	9²	12	11					7	10¹	1	13	2												14
	4	3	5²		7		12	6	10²			2		8	11¹	1	13		9	14										15
	4	3	5		6	8¹	9	12	11²					7	10³	1	14	2	13											16
	4	3	5		6	13	9¹	10	12					7	11	1	14	2	8²											17
	3	4	5		7	6	10	9¹	11²		2³			8	12	1		13	14											18
	14	3¹	5	7	6	10	9			13	4	12			8	1	11³	2²												19
	4	5		7	6		9³	13	3	2				8²	11	1	10¹		14		12									20
	4	3	5	8	6		9	12		2				11¹	1	10²	13													21
	3	5		7	6³	12	9	14	4²	2				8	10	1	11¹			13										22
	4		5	7	8	9³	13	11³	3	2				6	10¹	1	12					14								23
	4	3	5	2	7		13	9	11					14	12	1	10²		6²		8¹									24
	3	4	5	8	7	6	12	9²	13					11	1	10²						2								25
	3	4	5		6	10	8	12	11¹					7	9²	1	13					2								26
	3	4	5	14	7	12	8³	10	11²					6	9	1	13					2¹								27
	4		5		6	8²	9	13	14	3				7	10³	1	11²	2							12					28
	4		5		7	8¹	9	13	14	3				6	11³	1	10²	2							12					29
	12	3²		2¹	13	8	14	10	11					6		1	9³								5	7	4			30
12	4		5		6	13	8²	14		3	10³				9	1⁸	11³	2								7				31
1	4		5		8³	6	12	9³	11		2¹			7	13		10								3	14				32
	4		5		6	10	9	8¹	13					7	11²	1		2							3	12				33
	4		5		7³	12	8	13		11	2²			6	10	1			14	5					3	9¹				34
	4		5		6²	8	9¹		11					7	10³	1	12	2	14						3	13				35
	4		5		6²	8¹	9		11			12		7	10	1	13	2³							3	14				36
	3	4³	5		7¹	8		10			14			6	9	1	11²								2	13	12			37
	4		5		6	10³	8²	13			14			7	11	1	9¹								2	12	3			38
	4		5	14	6²	10	9	8	13		2¹			7³	11	1									3	12				39
	4		5		7	8	12	10	13					6	9¹	1	11²								2	3				40
		5		7	8	9³	10	12						6¹	11	1									13	14	3	2²	4	41
	3	4¹	5	13		8	9²		11		14			6³	10	1									2	7	12			42
	4		5		8²	9			12	13				6	10	1	11¹								2	7	3³		14	43
	4	3	5		7	8	10³	13						6	11¹	1	9³								2	12			14	44
	4	3	5⁸		7	8	10	13	14					6²	11	1	9¹	2³								12				45
	4	3			6	10	9¹	14	11			13		7		1	12								8³		2²	5		46

FA Cup		
Third Round	Barnsley	(a) 2-0
Fourth Round	Manchester C	(a) 2-0
Fifth Round	Arsenal	(a) 0-2
Capital One Cup		
First Round	Oldham Ath	(a) 3-0
Second Round	Preston NE	(h) 3-1
Third Round	Liverpool	(a) 2-2
(aet; Liverpool won 14-13 on penalties)		
Championship Play-Offs		
Semi-Finals 1st leg	Brentford	(a) 2-1
Semi-Finals 2nd leg	Brentford	(h) 3-0
Final	Norwich C	Wembley 0-2

MILLWALL

FOUNDATION

Formed in 1885 as Millwall Rovers by employees of Morton & Co, a jam and marmalade factory in West Ferry Road. The founders were predominantly Scotsmen. Their first headquarters was The Islanders pub in Tooke Street, Millwall. Their first trophy was the East End Cup in 1887.

The Den, Zampa Road, London SE16 3LN.

Telephone: (020) 7232 1222. *Fax:* (020) 7231 3663.

Ticket Office: (0844) 826 2004.

Website: www.millwallfc.co.uk

Email: questions@millwallplc.com

Ground Capacity: 19,734.

Record Attendance: 48,672 v Derby Co, FA Cup 5th rd, 20 February 1937 (at The Den, Cold Blow Lane); 20,093 v Arsenal, FA Cup 3rd rd, 10 January 1994 (at The Den, Bermondsey).

Pitch Measurements: 101m × 68m (110yd × 74yd)

Chairman: John G. Berylson.

Chief Executive: Andy Ambler.

Manager: Neil Harris.

Coach: Nigel Gibbs.

Physio: Bobby Bacic.

Colours: Blue shirts, white shorts, blue socks.

Year Formed: 1885.

Turned Professional: 1893.

Previous Names: 1885, Millwall Rovers; 1889, Millwall Athletic; 1899, Millwall; 1985, Millwall Football & Athletic Company.

Club Nickname: 'The Lions'.

Grounds: 1885, Glengall Road, Millwall; 1886, Back of 'Lord Nelson'; 1890, East Ferry Road; 1901, North Greenwich; 1910, The Den, Cold Blow Lane; 1993, The Den, Bermondsey.

First Football League Game: 28 August 1920, Division 3, v Bristol R (h) W 2–0 – Lansdale; Fort, Hodge; Voisey (1), Riddell, McAlpine; Waterall, Travers, Broad (1), Sutherland, Dempsey.

Record League Victory: 9–1 v Torquay U, Division 3 (S), 29 August 1927 – Lansdale, Tilling, Hill, Amos, Bryant (3), Graham, Chance, Hawkins (3), Landells (1), Phillips (2), Black. 9–1 v Coventry C, Division 3 (S), 19 November 1927 – Lansdale, Fort, Hill, Amos, Collins (1), Graham, Chance, Landells (4), Cock (2), Phillips (2), Black.

Record Cup Victory: 7–0 v Gateshead, FA Cup 2nd rd, 12 December 1936 – Yuill; Ted Smith, Inns; Brolly, Hancock, Forsyth; Thomas (1), Mangnall (1), Ken Burditt (2), McCartney (2), Thorogood (1).

Record Defeat: 1–9 v Aston Villa, FA Cup 4th rd, 28 January 1946.

HONOURS

Football League – Division 1:
Best season: 3rd, 1993–94;
Division 2: *Champions* 1987–88, 2000–01; **Division 3 (S):**
Champions 1927–28, 1937–38;
Runners-up 1952–53;
Division 3: *Runners–up* 1965–66, 1984–85;
Division 4: *Champions* 1961–62;
Runners-up 1964–65.

FA Cup: *Runners-up* 2004; *Semi-final* 1900, 1903, 1937 (first Division 3 side to reach semi-final), 2013.

Football League Cup: Best season: 5th rd, 1974, 1977, 1995.

Football League Trophy: *Winners* 1983.

Auto Windscreens Shield:
Runners-up 1999.

European Competitions
UEFA Cup: 2004–05.

sky SPORTS FACT FILE

The Den was one of several Football League grounds to suffer damage during the Second World War. In April 1943 a section of terracing was severely damaged by a stray bomber and shortly afterwards a fire destroyed the main stand. The Lions spent much of the 1943–44 season playing their home games elsewhere as a result.

Most League Points (2 for a win): 65, Division 3 (S), 1927–28 and Division 3, 1965–66.

Most League Points (3 for a win): 93, Division 2, 2000–01.

Most League Goals: 127, Division 3 (S), 1927–28.

Highest League Scorer in Season: Richard Parker, 37, Division 3 (S), 1926–27.

Most League Goals in Total Aggregate: Neil Harris, 124, 1995–2004; 2006–11.

Most League Goals in One Match: 5, Richard Parker v Norwich C, Division 3 (S), 28 August 1926.

Most Capped Player: Eamonn Dunphy, 22 (23), Republic of Ireland.

Most League Appearances: Barry Kitchener, 523, 1967–82.

Youngest League Player: Moses Ashikodi, 15 years 240 days v Brighton & HA, 22 February 2003.

Record Transfer Fee Received: £2,800,000 from Norwich C for Steve Morison, June 2011.

Record Transfer Fee Paid: £800,000 to Derby Co for Paul Goddard, December 1989.

Football League Record: 1920 Original Members of Division 3; 1921 Division 3 (S); 1928–34 Division 2; 1934–38 Division 3 (S); 1938–48 Division 2; 1948–58 Division 3 (S); 1958–62 Division 4; 1962–64 Division 3; 1964–65 Division 4; 1965–66 Division 3; 1966–75 Division 2; 1975–76 Division 3; 1976–79 Division 2; 1979–85 Division 3; 1985–88 Division 2; 1988–90 Division 1; 1990–92 Division 2; 1992–96 Division 1; 1996–2001 Division 2; 2001–04 Division 1; 2004–06 FL C; 2006–10 FL 1; 2010–15 FL C; 2015– FL 1.

LATEST SEQUENCES

Longest Sequence of League Wins: 10, 10.3.1928 – 25.4.1928.

Longest Sequence of League Defeats: 11, 10.4.1929 – 16.9.1929.

Longest Sequence of League Draws: 5, 22.12.1973 – 12.1.1974.

Longest Sequence of Unbeaten League Matches: 19, 22.8.1959 – 31.10.1959.

Longest Sequence Without a League Win: 20, 26.12.1989 – 5.5.1990.

Successive Scoring Runs: 22 from 27.11.1954.

Successive Non-scoring Runs: 6 from 27.4.2013.

MANAGERS

F. B. Kidd 1894–99
(Hon. Treasurer/Manager)
E. R. Stopher 1899–1900
(Hon. Treasurer/Manager)
George Saunders 1900–11
(Hon. Treasurer/Manager)
Herbert Lipsham 1911–19
Robert Hunter 1919–33
Bill McCracken 1933–36
Charlie Hewitt 1936–40
Bill Voisey 1940–44
Jack Cock 1944–48
Charlie Hewitt 1948–56
Ron Gray 1956–57
Jimmy Seed 1958–59
Reg Smith 1959–61
Ron Gray 1961–63
Billy Gray 1963–66
Benny Fenton 1966–74
Gordon Jago 1974–77
George Petchey 1978–80
Peter Anderson 1980–82
George Graham 1982–86
John Docherty 1986–90
Bob Pearson 1990
Bruce Rioch 1990–92
Mick McCarthy 1992–96
Jimmy Nicholl 1996–97
John Docherty 1997
Billy Bonds 1997–98
Keith Stevens 1998–2000
(then Joint Manager)
*(plus **Alan McLeary** 1999–2000)*
Mark McGhee 2000–03
Dennis Wise 2003–05
Steve Claridge 2005
Colin Lee 2005
David Tuttle 2005–06
Nigel Spackman 2006
Willie Donachie 2006–07
Kenny Jackett 2007–13
Steve Lomas 2013
Ian Holloway 2014–15
Neil Harris March 2015–

TEN YEAR LEAGUE RECORD

		P	W	D	L	F	A	Pts	Pos
2005-06	FL C	46	8	17	21	35	61	40	23
2006-07	FL 1	46	19	9	18	59	62	66	10
2007-08	FL 1	46	14	10	22	45	60	52	17
2008-09	FL 1	46	25	7	14	63	53	82	5
2009-10	FL 1	46	24	13	9	76	44	85	3
2010-11	FL C	46	18	13	15	62	48	67	9
2011-12	FL C	46	15	12	19	55	57	57	16
2012-13	FL C	46	15	11	20	51	62	56	20
2013-14	FL C	46	11	15	20	46	74	48	19
2014-15	FL C	46	9	14	23	42	76	41	22

DID YOU KNOW ?

Millwall achieved their best-ever average attendance of 27,387 in the 1938–39 season. This made them the fourth best supported club in London, with a lead of more than 7,000 over local rivals West Ham United.

MILLWALL – FL CHAMPIONSHIP 2014–15 LEAGUE RECORD

Match No.	Date	Venue	Opponents	Result	H/T Score	Lg Pos.	Goalscorers	Attendance
1	Aug 9	H	Leeds U	W 2-0	1-0	3	Beevers [8], Williams (pen) [88]	16,205
2	16	A	Fulham	W 1-0	1-0	2	Woolford [12]	18,988
3	19	A	Sheffield W	D 1-1	0-0	3	Gueye [90]	20,636
4	23	H	Rotherham U	L 0-1	0-0	9		10,282
5	30	H	Blackpool	W 2-1	1-0	5	McDonald [33], Malone [51]	9877
6	Sept 13	A	Ipswich T	L 0-2	0-1	7		16,190
7	16	A	Reading	L 2-3	1-2	12	Fuller [39], Beevers [54]	15,091
8	20	H	Nottingham F	D 0-0	0-0	13		12,038
9	27	A	Huddersfield T	L 1-2	1-1	16	Upson [41]	11,712
10	30	H	Birmingham C	L 1-3	0-2	16	Gregory [54]	9086
11	Oct 4	A	Derby Co	D 0-0	0-0	16		27,749
12	18	H	Wolverhampton W	D 3-3	0-1	18	Gregory [67], Fuller 2 [82, 87]	13,428
13	21	A	Wigan Ath	D 0-0	0-0	18		10,201
14	25	H	Cardiff C	W 1-0	0-0	15	Shittu [54]	10,135
15	Nov 1	A	Watford	L 1-3	1-2	16	Woolford [12]	17,000
16	4	H	Blackburn R	D 2-2	0-1	16	Martin [72], Williams [88]	8250
17	8	H	Brentford	L 2-3	0-1	18	Gregory [58], Dunne [59]	13,048
18	22	A	Charlton Ath	D 0-0	0-0	18		19,189
19	29	A	Bournemouth	D 2-2	0-2	20	Upson [75], Gueye [88]	10,016
20	Dec 6	H	Middlesbrough	L 1-5	0-4	20	McDonald [78]	10,328
21	12	A	Brighton & HA	W 1-0	1-0	17	Gregory [15]	24,085
22	19	A	Bolton W	L 0-1	0-0	20		8635
23	26	A	Norwich C	L 1-6	0-2	21	Easter [86]	26,714
24	28	H	Bournemouth	L 0-2	0-2	21		10,407
25	Jan 10	A	Blackpool	L 0-1	0-1	22		9994
26	17	H	Ipswich T	L 1-3	1-2	22	Gueye [43]	11,063
27	27	H	Reading	D 0-0	0-0	22		8317
28	31	A	Nottingham F	W 1-0	0-0	22	Fuller [83]	23,018
29	Feb 7	H	Huddersfield T	L 1-3	1-1	22	Maierhofer [28]	10,281
30	10	A	Birmingham C	W 1-0	0-0	22	Dunne [51]	14,186
31	14	A	Leeds U	L 0-1	0-1	22		24,000
32	21	H	Fulham	D 0-0	0-0	22		12,707
33	24	H	Sheffield W	L 1-3	0-0	22	Fabbrini [90]	8568
34	28	A	Rotherham U	L 1-2	1-0	22	Woolford [20]	10,329
35	Mar 3	A	Middlesbrough	L 0-3	0-2	22		16,078
36	7	H	Norwich C	L 1-4	0-2	23	Gregory (pen) [82]	11,116
37	14	A	Bolton W	L 0-2	0-2	23		14,719
38	17	H	Brighton & HA	D 0-0	0-0	23		9105
39	21	A	Brentford	D 2-2	1-0	23	Gregory [28], O'Brien [64]	10,179
40	Apr 3	H	Charlton Ath	W 2-1	0-0	22	Gueye [79], Hooiveld [87]	14,722
41	11	H	Watford	L 0-2	0-1	23		12,075
42	14	H	Wigan Ath	W 2-0	0-0	22	Abdou [74], Gueye [90]	8494
43	18	A	Cardiff C	D 0-0	0-0	22		19,639
44	21	A	Blackburn R	L 0-2	0-0	22		12,884
45	25	H	Derby Co	D 3-3	2-1	22	Gregory 3 (2 pens) [26, 36 (p), 50 (p)]	12,571
46	May 2	A	Wolverhampton W	L 2-4	0-1	22	O'Brien [58], Philpot [82]	24,480

Final League Position: 22

GOALSCORERS

League (42): Gregory 9 (3 pens), Gueye 5, Fuller 4, Woolford 3, Beevers 2, Dunne 2, McDonald 2, O'Brien 2, Upson 2, Williams 2 (1 pen), Abdou 1, Easter 1, Fabbrini 1, Hooiveld 1, Maierhofer 1, Malone 1, Martin 1, Philpot 1, Shittu 1.
FA Cup (3): Fuller 2, McDonald 1.
Capital One Cup (1): Briggs 1.

Forde D 46	Edwards C 8	Beevers M 24 + 1	Dunne A 35 + 4	Malone S 17 + 3	Martin L 22 + 5	Williams S 38	Abdou N 29 + 4	Woolford M 33 + 5	McDonald S 23 + 1	Fuller R 16 + 22	Gueye M 9 + 23	Easter J 2 + 7	Gregory L 28 + 11	Bailey N 5 + 3	Wright J 1	Powell J 5	Ranegie M 3 + 4	Webster B 9 + 2	Upson E 15 + 11	Onyedinma F 1 + 1	Chaplow R 6 + 1	Hoyte J 1 + 1	O'Brien A 13 + 6	Briggs M 7 + 1	Wilkinson A 9	Philpot J — + 1	Shittu D 7 + 1	Martinez A 4	Pavey A — + 1	Marquis J 1	Nelson S 14	Harding D 20	Maierhofer S 6 + 4	Cummings S 12	Fabbrini D 11 + 1	Hooiveld J 15	Cowan-Hall P — + 5	Tonge M 5 + 1	Taylor-Fletcher G 6 + 4	Match No.
1	2	3	4	5	6²	7	8	9³	10	11¹	12	13	14																											1
1	2	4	3	5	6	7	8²	9¹	10	11	14	13	12																											2
1	2	4	3	5	8¹	7	6³	10	9	13	12	14	11²																											3
1	2	4	3	5	9²	8	6	10	11³	12	13	14			7¹																									4
1	2	4	3	5	8²	6		10	9	11¹	13						7³	12	14																					5
1	2	4	3	5		9		6¹	8	13	12	10⁴					7²	11	14																					6
1	5	4	2	9		6	12	10	11								14	3¹	13		7²	8³																		7
1	2³	4	3	5		7		6	8	9	13	14	10²					11¹	12																					8
1		4	3	5		8	2	11	9	10	13					7³			12		6²		14																	9
1		4	3	5		6	7		9	14		11							10³		8¹		12	2²			13													10
1		2	12		5	7¹	10	9	13		11²						4	14		6		8³	3																	11
1		2	14	12	4⁴	8¹	9	10	13		11						3			7²	6³	5																		12
1		3	5	9²			6¹	8	10		11³					4	12	13	7		14	2																		13
1		4			8	7		13	9	11¹		10					12	6			5²	2	3																	14
1		4	12	8¹	6		10	9	11¹²	13						3	7		14		5³	2																		15
1		4	13	10	7		8	9	11¹	14		12					6¹				5	2*	3																	16
1		4¹	2	10	7			12	11	8³		9		13		14	6²				5	3																		17
1		4	2	5	8	6		10²	9	13	14	12	11¹				3	7³																						18
1		4¹	2	5	8³	6		10²	9	13	14	12	11				3	7																						19
1		2	8		4		14	9	11	12		10				7²	3¹	6³									5	13												20
1		4	14	5		7	12	10	9	13		8¹		11³													2	3	6²											21
1		3	5	13	8	14	9	10³	12	6¹		11															2²	4	7											22
1		4	2		8	7	12		11³	10²	13	14															5	3	6¹	9										23
1		14	5	8³	6*	7	10	9	12	13		11									6						2²	3¹			4									24
1		3		8		7	10	9²	11*	14		13											6				2				4	5³	12							25
1		12		7			13	6	11				8		4													3	5	10	2²	9¹								26
1	13		14	7	8			6¹	10																		4*	5	11²	2	9³	3	12							27
1		4	5	10¹	6	7			14	8³	13							12														11²	2	9	3					28
1		5	3		7		6	14		13	10¹		12										8²									11³	2	9	3					29
1	13		3		8²	7	14	10					12						13												5	11³	2	9¹	4			6	30
1		3		8	6			10		14			12						13							7¹					5	11²	2	9³	4				31
1		3			7	2	8²	13					11					14					10³								5	5³	12	2²	9¹		6¹	12	32
1		3			7	2²	9¹	13	14				11³					12					10³								5			6	4	8		8	10	33
1		3			6	2	8	12					11³					14					13								5			9²	4		7	10¹	34
1		3			7²	2	8	13					11³					12					14								5			9	4		6¹	10	35
1		2			6		8¹	11³					13	7²					14													3	5			9	4	12	10	36
1		3			7	6		12	14	10													8²					9³			5			2	4	13	11¹	37
1					8	7	9²		12									11					6¹								3	5	13	2	14	4		10³	38
1					7	8	10						11										9								3	5	13	2	4			12	39
1					7	8²	9						12							10	14		6³								3	5	13	2	4				40
1	4			13	8	7²	9¹						12							10			6								3	5³	14	2						41
1	4			9¹	8²	7	14						13							11	12		6*								3	5		2					42
1	4	2		6³		7	9			13	12		10²	8									11¹								3	5							14	43
1	4	2			7	6			11²	9³	12		8										10								3	5¹						13	14	44
1		2		6¹	7	9			12	13			10²	8									11³								3	5					4	14		45
1	4	2		6²	8				10					7¹					9				11					13⁴		14	3	5						12		46

FA Cup

Third Round	Bradford C	(h)	3-3
Replay	Bradford C	(a)	0-4

Capital One Cup

First Round	Wycombe W	(h)	1-0
Second Round	Southampton	(h)	0-2

MILTON KEYNES DONS

FOUNDATION

In July 2004 Wimbledon became MK Dons and relocated to Milton Keynes. In 2007 it recognised itself as a new club with no connection to the old Wimbledon FC. In August of that year the replica trophies and other Wimbledon FC memorabilia were returned to the London Borough of Merton.

Stadiummk, Stadium Way West, Milton Keynes, Buckinghamshire MK1 1ST.

Telephone: (01908)) 622 922.

Fax: (01908) 622 933.

Ticket Office: (0333) 200 5343

Website: www.mkdons.com

Email: info@mkdons.com

Ground Capacity: 30,582.

Record Attendance: 26,969 v Manchester U, League Cup 2nd rd, 26 August 2014.

Pitch Measurements: 104m × 67.5m (114yd × 74yd)

Chairman: Pete Winkelman.

Executive Director: Andrew Cullen.

Manager: Karl Robinson.

Head of Coaching: Richie Barker.

Head of Sports Medicine: Simon Crampton.

Colours: White shirts with red and black trim, white shorts with red trim, white socks.

Year Formed: 2004.

Turned Professional: 2004.

Club Nickname: 'The Dons'.

Grounds: 2003, The National Hockey Stadium; 2007, Stadiummk.

First Football League Game: 7 August 2004, FL 1, v Barnsley (h) D 1–1 – Rachubka; Palmer, Lewington, Harding, Williams, Oyedele, Kamara, Smith, Smart (Herve), McLeod (1) (Hornuss), Small.

Record League Victory: 7–0 v Oldham Ath, FL 1, 20 December 2014 – Martin; Spence, McFadzean, Kay (Baldock), Lewington; Potter (1), Alli (1); Baker C (1), Carruthers (Green), Bowditch (1) (Afobe (1)); Grigg (2).

Record Cup Victory: 6–0 v Nantwich T, FA Cup 1st rd, 12 November 2011 – Martin; Chicksen, Baldock G, Doumbe (1), Flanagan, Williams S, Powell (1) (O'Shea (1), Chadwick (Galloway), Bowditch (2), MacDonald (Williams G (1)), Balanta.

HONOURS

Football League – FL 2: *Champions* 2007–08; **FL 1:** *Runners-up* 2014–15.
Johnstone's Paint Trophy: *Winners* 2008.
FA Cup: Best season: 5th rd, 2013.
Football League Cup: Best season: 4th rd, 2015.

sky SPORTS FACT FILE

Milton Keynes Dons achieved the landmark of 750 Football League goals in regular season play when Lewis Baker netted after 74 minutes in their 4-1 win over Notts County on 21 March 2015. Their total of 101 League goals for the season is the best in the club's history.

Record Defeat: 0–5 v Hartlepool U, FL 1, 31 January 2005; 0–5 v Huddersfield T, FL 1, 18 February 2006; 0–5 v Tottenham H, Carling Cup 3rd rd, 24 October 2006; 0–5 v Rochdale, FL 2, 27 January 2007; 0–5 v Carlisle U, FL 1, 13 February 2010.

Most League Points (3 for a win): 97, FL 2, 2007–08.

Most League Goals: 101, FL 1, 2014–15.

Highest League Scorer in Season: Izale McLeod, 21, 2006–07.

Most League Goals in Total Aggregate: Izale McLeod, 62, 2004–07; 2012–14.

Most Capped Player: Ali Gerba (31), Canada.

Most League Goals in One Match: 3, Clive Platt v Barnet, FL 2, 20 January 2007; 3, Mark Wright v Bury, FL 2, 2 February 2008; 3, Aaron Wilbraham v Cheltenham T, FL 1, 31 January 2009; 3, Sam Baldock v Colchester U, FL 1, 12 March 2011; 3, Sam Baldock v Chesterfield, FL 1, 20 August 2012; 3, Dean Bowditch v Bury, FL 1, 22 September 2012; 3, Dele Alli v Notts Co, FL 1, 11 March 2014; 3, Dele Alli v Crewe Alex, FL 1, 20 September 2014; 3, Benik Afobe v Colchester U, FL 1, 29 November 2014; 3, Robert Hall v Leyton Orient, FL 1, 18 April 2015.

Most League Appearances: Dean Lewington, 469, 2004–15.

Youngest League Player: Brendon Galloway, 16 years 42 days v Rochdale, 28 April 2012.

Record Transfer Fee Received: £5,000,000 from Tottenham H for Dele Alli, February 2015.

Record Transfer Fee Paid: £100,000 to Plymouth Arg for Scott Taylor, January 2006.

Football League Record: 2004–06 FL 1; 2006–08 FL 2; 2008–15 FL 1; 2015– FL C.

MANAGERS

Stuart Murdock 2002–04
Danny Wilson 2004–06
Martin Allen 2006–07
Paul Ince 2007–08
Roberto Di Matteo 2008–09
Paul Ince 2009–10
Karl Robinson May 2010–

LATEST SEQUENCES

Longest Sequence of League Wins: 8, 7.9.2007 – 20.10.2007.

Longest Sequence of League Defeats: 4, 14.11.2009 – 1.12.2009.

Longest Sequence of League Draws: 4, 12.2.2013 – 2.3.2013.

Longest Sequence of Unbeaten League Matches: 18, 29.1.2008 – 3.5.2008.

Longest Sequence Without a League Win: 11, 13.3.2010 – 2.5.2010.

Successive Scoring Runs: 18 from 7.4.2007.

Successive Non-scoring Runs: 4, 17.12.2005.

TEN YEAR LEAGUE RECORD

		P	W	D	L	F	A	Pts	Pos
2005-06	FL 1	46	12	14	20	45	66	50	22
2006-07	FL 2	46	25	9	12	76	58	84	4
2007-08	FL 2	46	29	10	7	82	37	97	1
2008-09	FL 1	46	26	9	11	83	47	87	3
2009-10	FL 1	46	17	9	20	60	68	60	12
2010-11	FL 1	46	23	8	15	67	60	77	5
2011-12	FL 1	46	22	14	10	84	47	80	5
2012-13	FL 1	46	19	13	14	62	45	70	8
2013-14	FL 1	46	17	9	20	63	65	60	10
2014-15	FL 1	46	27	10	9	101	44	91	2

DID YOU KNOW ?

When Milton Keynes Dons won the League Two title in 2007–08 they went unbeaten for the final 18 games. They won their last 7 away games as well as 2 Johnstone's Paint Trophy ties, making a run of 9 successive away victories.

MILTON KEYNES DONS – FOOTBALL LEAGUE ONE 2014–15 LEAGUE RECORD

Match No.	Date	Venue	Opponents	Result	H/T Score	Lg Pos.	Goalscorers	Attendance
1	Aug 9	H	Gillingham	W 4-2	1-2	2	Hause (og) [44], Grigg [68], McFadzean [70], Legge (og) [73]	7595
2	16	A	Peterborough U	L 2-3	0-1	9	Alli [48], Powell [87]	7115
3	19	A	Chesterfield	W 1-0	0-0	4	Afobe [49]	5811
4	23	H	Coventry C	D 0-0	0-0	7		10,600
5	30	H	Crawley T	W 2-0	1-0	3	Alli [15], Afobe [90]	7148
6	Sept 13	A	Barnsley	W 5-3	2-0	3	Afobe [33], Carruthers [45], Alli [52], Grigg [71], Reeves [79]	9192
7	16	H	Bradford C	L 1-2	1-2	4	Lewington [41]	7139
8	20	H	Crewe Alex	W 6-1	2-1	2	Alli 3 [3, 48, 84], Grigg [16], Afobe [70], Reeves [90]	7049
9	27	A	Bristol C	L 2-3	0-2	4	Bowditch [51], Afobe [73]	13,119
10	Oct 4	A	Yeovil T	W 2-0	0-0	4	Grigg [69], Powell [84]	4000
11	18	A	Leyton Orient	D 0-0	0-0	5		5014
12	21	H	Fleetwood T	W 2-1	0-0	4	McFadzean [61], Afobe (pen) [84]	6736
13	25	A	Doncaster R	D 0-0	0-0	7		5976
14	Nov 1	H	Swindon T	W 2-1	0-1	3	Alli [51], Kay [59]	9494
15	22	H	Port Vale	W 1-0	1-0	4	Baker, C [3]	12,007
16	25	H	Rochdale	D 2-2	1-1	4	Grigg [19], Green [84]	6720
17	29	H	Colchester U	W 6-0	3-0	4	Alli [11], Afobe 3 [37, 45, 58], Reeves (pen) [67], Hodson [90]	7646
18	Dec 2	A	Sheffield U	W 1-0	0-0	3	Alli [87]	17,030
19	13	A	Preston NE	D 1-1	1-0	3	Baker, C [39]	9856
20	20	H	Oldham Ath	W 7-0	2-0	2	Grigg 2 [17, 49], Bowditch [43], Potter [51], Alli [77], Afobe [84], Baker, C [90]	7998
21	26	A	Notts Co	W 1-0	1-0	2	Powell [31]	5897
22	28	H	Walsall	L 0-3	0-1	4		9311
23	Jan 10	A	Crawley T	D 2-2	0-1	3	Grigg [76], Alli [90]	2468
24	17	H	Sheffield U	W 1-0	0-0	3	Baker, C [67]	9633
25	24	H	Barnsley	W 2-0	0-0	3	Alli [57], Grigg [63]	8310
26	27	A	Scunthorpe U	D 1-1	0-0	3	McFadzean [77]	3005
27	31	A	Crewe Alex	W 5-0	3-0	1	Cole 2 [12, 38], Bowditch [28], Baker, C [72], Powell [90]	4319
28	Feb 7	H	Bristol C	D 0-0	0-0	3		15,642
29	9	A	Bradford C	L 1-2	0-0	3	Alli [54]	11,948
30	14	A	Gillingham	L 2-4	1-2	3	Cole [36], Reeves (pen) [67]	5107
31	17	A	Colchester U	W 1-0	1-0	2	Alli [44]	2974
32	21	H	Peterborough U	W 3-0	3-0	2	Grigg [4], Reeves 2 [30, 45]	11,162
33	28	A	Coventry C	L 1-2	0-2	2	Powell [56]	9934
34	Mar 3	H	Chesterfield	L 1-2	1-0	3	Baker, L [28]	7335
35	7	H	Preston NE	L 0-2	0-0	4		10,618
36	14	A	Walsall	D 1-1	1-1	4	Grigg [32]	3887
37	17	A	Oldham Ath	W 3-1	2-0	4	Bowditch [25], Powell [37], Reeves [65]	2445
38	21	H	Notts Co	W 4-1	0-0	4	Baker, C [63], Baker, L [74], Grigg 2 [84, 90]	11,911
39	Apr 4	A	Swindon T	W 3-0	0-0	3	Powell [60], Grigg 2 [72, 88]	10,087
40	7	H	Scunthorpe U	W 2-0	2-0	3	Grigg 2 (1 pen) [2, 5 (p)]	8087
41	11	A	Port Vale	D 0-0	0-0	3		4379
42	14	H	Fleetwood T	W 3-0	0-0	3	Baker, L [55], Grigg [74], Alli [76]	2752
43	18	H	Leyton Orient	W 6-1	4-0	3	Bowditch [22], Robert Hall 3 [24, 37, 59], Grigg (pen) [29], Alli [81]	10,137
44	21	H	Doncaster R	W 3-0	0-0	3	Bowditch [66], Baker, C 2 [77, 84]	8159
45	25	A	Rochdale	W 3-2	2-0	3	Carruthers [16], Bowditch [29], Powell [76]	3501
46	May 3	H	Yeovil T	W 5-1	4-0	2	Baker, C [7], Lewington 2 [24, 74], Potter [36], Grigg [39]	16,965

Final League Position: 2

GOALSCORERS

League (101): Grigg 20 (2 pens), Alli 16, Afobe 10 (1 pen), Baker, C 9, Powell 8, Bowditch 7, Reeves 7 (2 pens), Baker, L 3, Cole 3, Robert Hall 3, Lewington 3, McFadzean 3, Carruthers 2, Potter 2, Green 1, Hodson 1, Kay 1, own goals 2.
FA Cup (4): Afobe 2 (1 pen), Baker, C 1, Green 1.
Capital One Cup (10): Afobe 6 (1 pen), Grigg 2, McFadzean 1, Powell 1.
Johnstone's Paint Trophy (2): Afobe 1, Powell 1.

Martin D 39	Hodson L 12 + 2	McFadzean K 41	Kay A 45	Lewington D 41	Green D 4 + 10	Potter D 40	Reeves B 25 + 5	Alli B 39	Bowditch D 26 + 9	Grigg W 31 + 13	Afobe B 11 + 11	Powell D 30 + 12	Hitchcock T 1 + 11	Randall M 2 + 7	McLoughlin I 7 + 1	Baldock G 6 + 3	Carruthers S 20 + 12	Spence J 33 + 5	Flanagan T 3 + 3	Baker C 24 + 8	Clarke-Harris J 2 + 3	Cole D 5 + 10	Andrews K 2 + 3	Williams G 2 + 2	Baker L 8 + 4	Walsh J 2	Hall Robert S 5 + 2	Match No.
1	2	3	4	5	6	7	8[1]	9	10[2]	11[3]	12	13	14															1
1	2	3	4	5	8	6	9[2]	7	10[1]	11[3]	12	14		13														2
1[2]	2[3]	3	4	5		6	9	7	10[1]	14	11	8			12	13												3
	3	4	5		7	9[3]	8	10[2]	11[1]	13	6	14			1	2	12											4
1	3[4]	4	5		7[1]		9	10[3]		11	6	8[2]	12			2	13	14										5
1		3	5			14	11[1]	9	12	10[2]	6	13	7			2	8[3]	4										6
1	3	4	5		7	8[1]	9	13	11	12	10	14			2[3]	6[2]												7
1	3	4	5		7	8	9	10[2]	11[3]	12	6	14			2[1]		13											8
1	4	3	2		6	9[1]	7	10[3]	12	11	8				5[2]	14	13											9
1	3		5		6[1]	8	7		9[3]	11	10		12			14	2	4[2]	13									10
1	3	4	5			9[3]	6	8	13	11	10[2]		7[1]			12	2	12										11
1	3[3]	4	5		7	8	9	10[2]	11[1]	13	6					12	2	14										12
1		4	5		6	9[2]	7		11[3]	12	10	14				8[1]	2	3	13									13
1	3	4	5		7	8[2]	9	10[1]	14	11[3]	6					12	2		13									14
1	3	4	5	14	7	8[3]	9	13	12	11	10[2]					2		6[1]										15
1	5[3]		4		14	6	9[2]	7	10[1]	11	13	12				2	3	8										16
1	5	3[3]	4		12	6	9	7[1]		14	11	10				2	13	8[2]										17
1	5	3	4		13[4]	6	7[3]	9		11[1]	12	10[2]				2	14	8										18
1		4	3	5		7	9[3]	6	12	14	11[1]	8[2]				13	2		10									19
1		4[3]	5	14	6		7	10[1]	11	13					12	9[2]	2		8									20
1		4	3	5	13	6		7	9[1]	12	11	10[2]				14	2		8[3]									21
1		3	4	5	13	7		8	10[1]	11	12	14				9[3]	2		6[2]									22
1		4	3[3]	5		7	6	11	12	10		13	14			8[1]	2[4]		9									23
1		4	3	5			8[1]	9	10[3]	11			13		14	7[2]	2		6	12								24
1		3	4	5	14		8	9[1]	11		6[2]						2		10[3]	12	13							25
1		3	4	5	6[2]	7		8	14	11[3]		13					2		9	10[1]	12							26
1		3	4	5		6		7[2]	10[1]			9	14				12	2		8	13	11[2]						27
1		3	4	5		7		8	9[3]	11[2]		10[1]				12	2		6	14	13							28
1	2		4	5	6[2]	8		10		13		12					3		9	11[1]	14	7[3]						29
		3	5		6[3]	12	7		13		8	14		1		10[1]	2		9		11[2]	4						30
	4	3	5			6	12	7[1]		11[3]		8		1		13	2		9		14		10[2]					31
	3	4	5			6	9[1]			11		8[3]		1		7[2]	2		10	14	13	12						32
	3	4	5			6	9[2]			12		8		1		7[1]	2		10	11[3]		13	14					33
	13	3	4	5[4]		6	9			11		8		1			2[2]		12		14	10[3]	7[1]					34
	3	4		14		7	13		9[3]	10		12		1		8	2[2]		6	11[1]				5				35
1	3	4	5			7	11[2]		9[1]	10[3]		12				8	2		6	14		13						36
1	2	3	4	5			9[3]		10[2]	11		6[1]	14			8	13		12			7						37
1	2	3	4	5			9[1]		13	12		10[3]	14			6			8	11[2]		7						38
1	2	3	4	5		7		6	8[2]	11[3]		10				9[1]	13			14		12						39
1	2	3	4			7		6	12	11[2]		13	14			10[1]						9			8[3]			40
1	2	3	4				8		7[1]	6	10	9[2]				11						13	5	12				41
1		4	3	5	14	7		6		11[3]		10[1]	13				2			12		9			8[3]			42
1		3	4	5		6[2]		7	10[3]	11[1]		13					2		14	12		9			8			43
1		3	4	2		9		10	13	11		14				8[1]	5		12						6[2]	7[3]		44
1		4	3	5			7	10[2]	11			13				9[1]	2		8						6	12		45
1	14	3[2]	4	5		6	13	7	12	11[1]						10[3]	2		9							8		46

FA Cup
First Round — Port Vale — (a) 4-3
Second Round — Chesterfield — (h) 0-1

Capital One Cup
First Round — AFC Wimbledon — (h) 3-1
Second Round — Manchester U — (h) 4-0
Third Round — Bradford C — (h) 2-0
Fourth Round — Sheffield U — (h) 1-2

Johnstone's Paint Trophy
Second Round — AFC Wimbledon — (h) 2-3

MORECAMBE

FOUNDATION

Several attempts to start a senior football club in a rugby stronghold finally succeeded on 7 May 1920 at the West View Hotel, Morecambe and a team competed in the Lancashire Combination for 1920–21. The club shared with a local cricket club at Woodhill Lane for the first season and a crowd of 3,000 watched the first game. The club moved to Roseberry Park, the name of which was changed to Christie Park after J.B. Christie who as President had purchased the ground.

Globe Arena, Christie Way, Westgate, Morecambe, Lancashire LA4 4TB.

Telephone: (01524) 411 797.

Fax: (01524) 832 230.

Ticket Office: (01524) 411 797.

Website: www.morecambefc.com

Email: office@morecambefc.com

Ground Capacity: 6,384.

Record Attendance: 9,383 v Weymouth, FA Cup 3rd rd, 6 January 1962 (at Christie Park). 5,375 v Newcastle U, League Cup, 28 August 2013 (at Globe Arena).

Pitch Measurements: 100.5m × 67.5m (110yd × 74yd)

Chairman: Peter McGuigan.

Manager: Jim Bentley.

Assistant Manager: Ken McKenna.

Physio: Simon Farnworth.

Colours: Red panelled shirts with black and white trim, white shorts with red trim, black socks with red trim.

Year Formed: 1920.

Turned Professional: 1920.

Club Nickname: 'The Shrimps'.

HONOURS

Football League – FL 2: Best season: 4th, 2009–10.
FA Cup: Best season: 3rd rd, 1962, 2001, 2003.
Football League Cup: Best season: 3rd rd, 2008.
Northern Premier League: *Runners-up* – 1994–95.
Presidents Cup: *Winners* 1991–92.
FA Trophy: *Winners* 1973–74.
Lancs Senior Cup: *Winners* 1967–68.
Lancs Combination – *Champions* 1924–25, 1961–62, 1962–63, 1967–68.
Runners-up 1925–26.
Lancs Combination Cup: *Winners* 1926–27, 1945–46, 1964–65, 1966–67, 1967–68.
Runners-up 1923–24, 1924–25, 1962–63.
Lancs Junior Cup: *Winners* 1927, 1928, 1962, 1963, 1969, 1986, 1987, 1994, 1996, 1999, 2004.

Grounds: 1920, Woodhill Lane; 1921, Christie Park; 2010, Globe Arena.

First Football League game: 11 August 2007, FL 2, v Barnet (h) D 0–0 – Lewis; Yates, Adams, Artell, Bentley, Stanley, Baker (Burns), Sorvel, Twiss (Newby), Curtis, Hunter (Thompson).

sky SPORTS FACT FILE

Morecambe's final League Two game at their former Christie Park ground was staged in May 2010 when the Shrimps defeated Aldershot Town to end the season in their highest ever position of 4th in the table. The club had one last fixture at the stadium against Dagenham & Redbridge in the play-off semi final when they won 2-1 but lost over the two legs.

Record League Victory: 6–0 v Crawley T, FL 2, 10 September 2011 – Roche; Reid, Wilson (pen), McCready, Haining (Parrish), Fenton (1), Drummond, McDonald, Price (Jevons), Carlton (3) (Alessandra), Ellison (1).

Record Cup Victory: 6–2 v Nelson (a), Lancashire Trophy, 27 January 2004.

Record Defeat: 2–7 v Port Vale, FL 2, 30 April 2011.

Most League Points (3 for a win): 73, FL 2, 2009–10.

Most League Goals: 73, FL 2, 2009–10.

Highest League Scorer in Season: Phil Jevons, 18, 2009–10.

Most League Goals in Total Aggregate: Kevin Ellison, 47, 2011–15.

Most League Goals in One Match: 3, Jon Newby v Rotherham U, FL 2, 29 March 2008.

Most League Appearances: Stuart Drummond, 277, 2007–15.

Youngest League Player: Aaron McGowan, 16 years 263 days, 20 April 2013.

Record Transfer Fee Received: £225,000 from Stockport Co for Carl Baker, July 2008.

Record Transfer Fee Paid: £50,000 to Southport for Carl Baker, July 2007.

Football League Record: 2006–07 Promoted from Conference; 2007– FL 2.

MANAGERS

Jimmy Milne 1947–48
Albert Dainty 1955–56
Ken Horton 1956–61
Joe Dunn 1961–64
Geoff Twentyman 1964–65
Ken Waterhouse 1965–69
Ronnie Clayton 1969–70
Gerry Irving/Ronnie Mitchell 1970
Ken Waterhouse 1970–72
Dave Roberts 1972–75
Alan Spavin 1975–76
Johnny Johnson 1976–77
Tommy Ferber 1977–78
Mick Hogarth 1978–79
Don Curbage 1979–81
Jim Thompson 1981
Les Rigby 1981–84
Sean Gallagher 1984–85
Joe Wojciechowicz 1985–88
Eric Whalley 1988
Billy Wright 1988–89
Lawrie Milligan 1989
Bryan Griffiths 1989–93
Leighton James 1994
Jim Harvey 1994–2006
Sammy McIlroy 2006–11
Jim Bentley May 2011–

LATEST SEQUENCES

Longest Sequence of League Wins: 7, 31.10.2009 – 12.12.2009.

Longest Sequence of League Defeats: 4, 23.2.2008 – 12.3.2008.

Longest Sequence of League Draws: 5, 3.1.2015 – 31.1.2015.

Longest Sequence of Unbeaten League Matches: 12, 31.1.2009 – 21.3.2009.

Longest Sequence Without a League Win: 10, 29.12.2013 – 1.3.2014.

Successive Scoring Runs: 17 from 13.8.2011.

Successive Non-scoring Runs: 3 from 16.9.2014.

TEN YEAR LEAGUE RECORD

		P	W	D	L	F	A	Pts	Pos
2005-06	Conf	42	22	8	12	68	41	74	5
2006-07	Conf	46	23	12	11	64	46	81	3
2007-08	FL 2	46	16	12	18	59	63	60	11
2008-09	FL 2	46	15	18	13	53	56	63	11
2009-10	FL 2	46	20	13	13	73	64	73	4
2010-11	FL 2	46	13	12	21	54	73	51	20
2011-12	FL 2	46	14	14	18	63	57	56	15
2012-13	FL 2	46	15	13	18	55	61	58	16
2013-14	FL 2	46	13	15	18	52	64	54	18
2014-15	FL 2	46	17	12	17	53	52	63	11

DID YOU KNOW ?

John Yzendoorn emigrated to Australia after a brief spell with Morecambe in the late 1970s and went on to enjoy a successful football career on the other side of the world. He made his debut for Australia when he came on as a substitute against Czechoslovakia in February 1980 and went on to win 13 caps.

MORECAMBE – FOOTBALL LEAGUE TWO 2014–15 LEAGUE RECORD

Match No.	Date	Venue	Opponents	Result	H/T Score	Lg Pos.	Goalscorers	Attendance
1	Aug 9	A	Dagenham & R	W 3-0	0-0	1	Ellison [49], Amond (pen) [54], Redshaw [90]	1529
2	16	H	Newport Co	W 3-2	0-2	1	Ellison 2 [58, 63], Mullin [84]	1506
3	19	H	Oxford U	W 1-0	1-0	1	Ellison [39]	1615
4	23	A	Cambridge U	W 2-1	1-0	1	Mullin 2 [16, 61]	3152
5	30	A	Tranmere R	L 1-2	1-0	3	Hughes [39]	4656
6	Sept 6	H	Cheltenham T	D 0-0	0-0	2		2273
7	13	H	Plymouth Arg	W 2-1	1-1	2	Ellison [19], Devitt [83]	1865
8	16	A	Mansfield T	L 0-1	0-0	4		2185
9	20	A	AFC Wimbledon	L 0-1	0-1	5		3822
10	27	H	Northampton T	L 0-1	0-1	6		1725
11	Oct 4	A	Southend U	W 1-0	1-0	5	Redshaw [5]	5284
12	11	H	Wycombe W	L 1-3	1-2	7	Fleming [45]	1710
13	18	A	Burton Alb	W 2-0	0-0	6	Ellison [59], Kenyon [61]	2560
14	21	H	York C	D 1-1	0-0	7	Redshaw [90]	1346
15	26	H	Exeter C	L 0-2	0-1	8		1787
16	31	A	Accrington S	L 1-2	0-2	8	Mullin [51]	1710
17	Nov 15	H	Bury	W 1-0	0-0	8	Ellison [70]	2665
18	22	A	Portsmouth	L 0-3	0-1	11		14,349
19	29	A	Stevenage	D 1-1	1-1	11	Amond [85]	2464
20	Dec 13	H	Luton T	W 3-0	2-0	10	Ellison [17], Hughes [45], Amond [81]	2263
21	20	A	Shrewsbury T	L 0-1	0-0	10		4708
22	26	H	Carlisle U	L 0-1	0-0	11		4165
23	28	A	Hartlepool U	W 2-0	1-0	12	Redshaw 2 [22, 81]	4108
24	Jan 3	H	Stevenage	D 0-0	0-0	11		1530
25	10	H	Tranmere R	D 0-0	0-0	11		2232
26	16	A	Cheltenham T	D 1-1	0-1	11	Amond (pen) [83]	2122
27	24	A	Plymouth Arg	D 1-1	0-1	11	Redshaw [52]	6314
28	31	H	AFC Wimbledon	D 1-1	1-0	11	Amond [42]	1841
29	Feb 7	A	Northampton T	L 1-2	1-1	13	Devitt [41]	4307
30	10	H	Mansfield T	W 2-1	2-1	12	Mullin [17], Ellison [24]	1156
31	15	H	Dagenham & R	L 2-3	1-1	12	Fleming [24], Redshaw [90]	1351
32	21	A	Newport Co	W 1-0	1-0	11	Redshaw [8]	2883
33	28	H	Cambridge U	L 0-2	0-1	13		1593
34	Mar 3	A	Oxford U	D 1-1	1-0	12	Ellison [11]	6924
35	7	A	Luton T	W 3-2	2-1	12	Redshaw [18], Wilson [29], Wilkinson (og) [86]	8667
36	14	H	Hartlepool U	L 0-1	0-0	14		1673
37	17	H	Shrewsbury T	L 1-4	1-2	14	Redshaw [28]	1363
38	21	A	Carlisle U	D 1-1	0-0	14	Amond (pen) [78]	4343
39	28	A	Exeter C	D 1-1	1-0	13	McGowan [17]	3538
40	Apr 3	H	Accrington S	D 1-1	1-1	13	Ellison [25]	1982
41	6	A	Bury	W 2-1	0-1	12	Amond [79], Mullin [85]	4045
42	11	H	Portsmouth	W 3-1	1-0	12	Kenyon 2 [10, 69], Amond [90]	2065
43	14	A	York C	L 1-2	1-1	12	Mullin [10]	2854
44	18	H	Burton Alb	L 1-2	0-1	12	Hughes [90]	2139
45	25	A	Wycombe W	W 1-0	0-0	12	Mullin [86]	5177
46	May 2	H	Southend U	W 3-1	1-1	11	Redshaw [4], Wildig [54], Devitt [66]	4108

Final League Position: 11

GOALSCORERS

League (53): Ellison 11, Redshaw 11, Amond 8 (3 pens), Mullin 8, Devitt 3, Hughes 3, Kenyon 3, Fleming 2, McGowan 1, Wildig 1, Wilson 1, own goal 1.
FA Cup (0).
Capital One Cup (0).
Johnstone's Paint Trophy (4): Amond 2, Beeley 1, Redshaw 1.

Roche B 14	Beeley S 41+1	Hughes M 40	Parrish A 45	Wilson L 34	Fleming A 31+4	Goodall A 22+6	Kenyon A 29+8	Sampson J 3+13	Amond P 17+20	Ellison K 35+8	Redshaw J 28+12	Devitt J 30+6	Wright A 10+7	Williams R 9+3	Mullin P 20+22	Drummond S 11+3	Doyle C 1+1	Widdowson J 8	Edwards R 31	McGowan A 4+4	McCready T 1+6	Barkhuizen T 1+4	Davies S 10	Arestidou A 17	Stewart T —+1	Ward D 5	Wildig A 9	Match No.
1	2	3	4	5	6	7	8^2	9^1	10^3	11	12	13	14															1
1	2	3	4		6	7	5		10^2	11		9^3	13		8^1	12	14											2
1	2	4	3	5		8	6	9^1	13	10	11^2	7^3	14		12													3
1	2	3		5		7^1	13	12		11	14	9	6		10^2	8^3		4										4
1	2	4^4	3		8^1	7			12	10	14	9^2	6		11^3		13	5										5
1	2		4		8^3	7	14		13	11	10	9^2	6^1		12			5	3									6
1			4		8	7^2	13	12	9	10		11^3	2	14	6^1			5	3									7
1		4	3		7		8	11^2	10^1	13		14			12	6		5	3	9^2								8
1	5		3		6^1	7				11	10	12			9	8		4	2									9
1	2		3		6^1	12	7^3	14	9	11	10			8^2	13		5	4										10
1	2	3	4		12	5	7	14	13	9	10	6^3	8^1		11^2													11
1	2	3	4		8	5	7^3	14	12	9^2	10^1	6^4			11						13							12
1	2	3	4		8^3		7	14	10	9		6^2	12		11^1			5				13						13
1	2	3	4		7		6	14	11^3	10	12	8^1			9^2			5				13						14
	2	3	4	5	8		10^2	14		11		7^3	6	13							12	9^1		1				15
	2	4	3	5	7	6^2	8	13	9^1	11		14	10^2									12		1				16
	5	3	2	9	8	6	7^2		10^3	12	14	11^1								4		13		1				17
	4	2	5^1	8	7	9^3	6		10	12	13	11^2								3	14			1				18
	3	2	5		6^1		12		11^3	9^2		7	10	8						4	14	13		1				19
	9	4	5	2		8		12	11		6	10^1	7							3			1					20
	5	3	2	8		12	7^1		13	11	14	9^3	10^2	6						4			1					21
	5	3	2	8		6^1		11		9	12	10^2	13		7					4^3	14		1					22
13	3	2	9^2		7			12	11		8	10^1							4	5	6		1					23
	5	3	2	8		6		14	13	11	10^3	9^1	12		7					4^2			1					24
	5	3	4	9		6^3	14		13	11^3	10	7^2		8						2	12			1				25
8		3	2		7		13	11	10^2	9		12			6				4	5^1			1					26
	5	3	2	8	14	13	7^2		10^3	12	11	9					6^1		4					1				27
	5	3	2	9		7	6^2	12	11	13	10^1	8^3			14				4					1				28
	5	3	2^1	8		7^3	6	14	10^2	12	11	9			13				4					1				29
	5	3	2	9	8^2	6		13	14	11	12	7^1			10^3				4					1				30
	2	4	5	6	7	9		14	13	11	12	8^2			10^3				3^1					1				31
	2	3	5	10		9	6^2		12	8	11^1		14	7^3	13				4					1				32
	5	3^2	2	9		12	8^1	7		11	10	14	6^3		13				4					1				33
	5	2	4	8		6	12			13	11	10^1	9^2	7^3	14				3					1				34
	5^1	3	4	9	8		13		14	10	11^2	6^3	7	12					2^4					1				35
	2^3	3	4	5	8			13		9	11	10	6^1	7^2	12					14				1				36
	5^2	3	4	9	8			13		11	10^1		6^3	14	7				2						1^1	12		37
	5	3	2^3	9		13	6		12	10	11	7^1			14				4							1	8^2	38
		3	4	9	8		6^2		13	11^3	10^1	12			14				2	5						1	7	39
	5	3^1	2	9		7	12		14	11	10	6^3			13				4							1	8^2	40
	2			5		6	7	4^2	8	13	11^3	10^1			12				14	3						1	9	41
	2		3	5		8	6		10	13		9^1	12		11^3				4	14						1	7^2	42
	5	2	4	8		6			10	12	13	9			11^2				3^1							1	7	43
	2	3	4	5	6		7			13	11	10^2	9^1		12										1		8	44
	2	3	4	5	8^2		6			13	11	10^1	9		12										1		7	45
	2	4	3	5	8^3		6			10	11^1	9^2			13	12					14						7	46

FA Cup
First Round   Dover Ath   (a)   0-1

Capital One Cup
First Round   Bradford C   (h)   0-1

Johnstone's Paint Trophy
First Round   Fleetwood T   (a)   3-1
Second Round   Bury   (a)   1-3

NEWCASTLE UNITED

FOUNDATION

In October 1882 a club called Stanley, which had been formed in 1881, changed its name to Newcastle East End to avoid confusion with two other local clubs, Stanley Nops and Stanley Albion. Shortly afterwards another club, Rosewood, merged with them. Newcastle West End had been formed in August 1882 and they played on a pitch which was part of the Town Moor. They moved to Brandling Park in 1885 and St James' Park 1886 (home of Newcastle Rangers). West End went out of existence after a bad run and the remaining committee men invited East End to move to St James' Park. They accepted and, at a meeting in Bath Lane Hall in 1892, changed their name to Newcastle United.

St James' Park, Newcastle-upon-Tyne NE1 4ST.

Telephone: (0844) 372 1892.

Fax: (0191) 201 8600.

Ticket Office: (0844) 372 1892 (option 1).

Website: www.nufc.co.uk

Email: admin@nufc.co.uk

Ground Capacity: 52,405.

Record Attendance: 68,386 v Chelsea, Division 1, 3 September 1930.

Pitch Measurements: 105m × 68m (114yd × 74yd)

Managing Director: Lee Charnley.

Head Coach: Steve McClaren.

Assistant Head Coach: Ian Cathro.

Physio: Derek Wright.

Colours: Black and white striped shirts, black shorts, black socks.

Year Formed: 1881.

Turned Professional: 1889.

Previous Names: 1881, Stanley; 1882, Newcastle East End; 1892, Newcastle United.

Club Nickname: 'The Magpies', 'The Toon'.

Grounds: 1881, South Byker; 1886, Chillingham Road, Heaton; 1892, St James' Park.

First Football League Game: 2 September 1893, Division 2, v Royal Arsenal (a) D 2–2 – Ramsay; Jeffery, Miller; Crielly, Graham, McKane; Bowman, Crate (1), Thompson, Sorley (1), Wallace. Graham not Crate scored according to some reports.

Record League Victory: 13–0 v Newport Co, Division 2, 5 October 1946 – Garbutt; Cowell, Graham; Harvey, Brennan, Wright; Milburn (2), Bentley (1), Wayman (4), Shackleton (6), Pearson.

HONOURS

FA Premier League:
Runners-up 1995–96, 1996–97.

Football League – Division 1:
Champions 1904–05, 1906–07, 1908–09, 1926–27, 1992–93;
Division 2: *Champions* 1964–65;
Runners-up 1897–98, 1947–48;
FL C: *Champions* 2009–10.

FA Cup: *Winners* 1910, 1924, 1932, 1951, 1952, 1955; *Runners-up* 1905, 1906, 1908, 1911, 1974, 1998, 1999.

Football League Cup:
Runners-up 1976.

Texaco Cup: *Winners* 1974, 1975.

European Competitions
Champions League: 1997–98, 2002–03, 2003–04. **European Fairs Cup:** 1968–69 (*winners*), 1969–70, 1970–71.
UEFA Cup: 1977–78, 1994–95, 1996–97, 1999–2000, 2003–04 (*s-f*), 2004–05, 2006–07.
European Cup Winners' Cup: 1998–99.
Europa League: 2012–13.
Anglo-Italian Cup: 1972–73 (*winners*).
Intertoto Cup: 2001 (*runners-up*), 2005, 2006 (*winners*).

sky SPORTS FACT FILE

Bill Mellor, goalkeeper for Newcastle United either side of the First World War, began his professional sporting career with Barrow Northern Union (Rugby League) club. After making his debut as a 16-year-old, he went on to play make over 100 appearances in the handling game before switching codes.

Record Cup Victory: 9–0 v Southport (at Hillsborough), FA Cup 4th rd, 1 February 1932 – McInroy; Nelson, Fairhurst; McKenzie, Davidson, Weaver (1); Boyd (1), Jimmy Richardson (3), Cape (2), McMenemy (1), Lang (1).

Record Defeat: 0–9 v Burton Wanderers, Division 2, 15 April 1895.

Most League Points (2 for a win): 57, Division 2, 1964–65.

Most League Points (3 for a win): 102, FL C, 2009–10.

Most League Goals: 98, Division 1, 1951–52.

Highest League Scorer in Season: Hughie Gallacher, 36, Division 1, 1926–27.

Most League Goals in Total Aggregate: Jackie Milburn, 177, 1946–57.

Most League Goals in One Match: 6, Len Shackleton v Newport Co, Division 2, 5 October 1946.

Most Capped Player: Shay Given, 82 (130), Republic of Ireland.

Most League Appearances: Jim Lawrence, 432, 1904–22.

Youngest League Player: Steve Watson, 16 years 223 days v Wolverhampton W, 10 November 1990.

Record Transfer Fee Received: £35,000,000 from Liverpool for Andy Carroll, January 2011.

Record Transfer Fee Paid: £16,000,000 to Real Madrid for Michael Owen, September 2005.

Football League Record: 1893 Elected to Division 2; 1898–1934 Division 1; 1934–48 Division 2; 1948–61 Division 1; 1961–65 Division 2; 1965–78 Division 1; 1978–84 Division 2; 1984–89 Division 1; 1989–92 Division 2; 1992–93 Division 1; 1993–2009 FA Premier League; 2009–10 FL C; 2010– FA Premier League.

LATEST SEQUENCES

Longest Sequence of League Wins: 13, 25.4.1992 – 18.10.1992.

Longest Sequence of League Defeats: 10, 23.8.1977 – 15.10.1977.

Longest Sequence of League Draws: 4, 15.11.2008 – 6.12.2008.

Longest Sequence of Unbeaten League Matches: 17, 13.2.2010 – 2.5.2010.

Longest Sequence Without a League Win: 21, 14.1.1978 – 23.8.1978.

Successive Scoring Runs: 25 from 15.4.1939.

Successive Non-scoring Runs: 6 from 29.10.1988.

MANAGERS

Frank Watt 1895–32
(Secretary-Manager)
Andy Cunningham 1930–35
Tom Mather 1935–39
Stan Seymour 1939–47
(Hon. Manager)
George Martin 1947–50
Stan Seymour 1950–54
(Hon. Manager)
Duggie Livingstone 1954–56
Stan Seymour 1956–58
(Hon. Manager)
Charlie Mitten 1958–61
Norman Smith 1961–62
Joe Harvey 1962–75
Gordon Lee 1975–77
Richard Dinnis 1977
Bill McGarry 1977–80
Arthur Cox 1980–84
Jack Charlton 1984
Willie McFaul 1985–88
Jim Smith 1988–91
Ossie Ardiles 1991–92
Kevin Keegan 1992–97
Kenny Dalglish 1997–98
Ruud Gullit 1998–99
Sir Bobby Robson 1999–2004
Graeme Souness 2004–06
Glenn Roeder 2006–07
Sam Allardyce 2007–08
Kevin Keegan 2008
Joe Kinnear 2008–09
Alan Shearer 2009
Chris Hughton 2009–10
Alan Pardew 2010–15
John Carver 2015
Steve McClaren June 2015–

TEN YEAR LEAGUE RECORD

		P	W	D	L	F	A	Pts	Pos
2005-06	PR Lge	38	17	7	14	47	42	58	7
2006-07	PR Lge	38	11	10	17	38	47	43	13
2007-08	PR Lge	38	11	10	17	45	65	43	12
2008-09	PR Lge	38	7	13	18	40	59	34	18
2009-10	FL C	46	30	12	4	90	35	102	1
2010-11	PR Lge	38	11	13	14	56	57	46	12
2011-12	PR Lge	38	19	8	11	56	51	65	5
2012-13	PR Lge	38	11	8	19	45	68	41	16
2013-14	PR Lge	38	15	4	19	43	59	49	10
2014-15	PR Lge	38	10	9	19	40	63	39	15

DID YOU KNOW

Winger Tommy Pearson, who made over 200 appearances for Newcastle United between 1933 and 1948, was also a talented golfer. He won several local competitions and in 1939, as a member of the Carrick Knowe club in Edinburgh, he reached the last 32 of the Scottish Amateur Championship.

NEWCASTLE UNITED – FA PREMIERSHIP 2014–15 LEAGUE RECORD

Match No.	Date	Venue	Opponents	Result	H/T Score	Lg Pos.	Goalscorers	Attendance
1	Aug 17	H	Manchester C	L	0-2	0-1	20		50,816
2	23	A	Aston Villa	D	0-0	0-0	15		30,267
3	30	H	Crystal Palace	D	3-3	1-1	15	Janmaat [37], Aarons [73], Williamson [88]	49,226
4	Sept 13	A	Southampton	L	0-4	0-2	20		29,678
5	20	H	Hull C	D	2-2	0-0	18	Cisse 2 [73, 87]	49,119
6	29	A	Stoke C	L	0-1	0-1	19		26,332
7	Oct 4	A	Swansea C	D	2-2	1-1	18	Cisse 2 [43, 75]	20,622
8	18	H	Leicester C	W	1-0	0-0	18	Obertan [71]	51,886
9	26	A	Tottenham H	W	2-1	0-1	14	Sammy Ameobi [46], Perez [58]	35,650
10	Nov 1	H	Liverpool	W	1-0	0-0	11	Perez [73]	52,166
11	9	A	WBA	W	2-0	1-0	8	Perez [45], Coloccini [62]	26,476
12	22	H	QPR	W	1-0	0-0	5	Sissoko [78]	51,915
13	29	A	West Ham U	L	0-1	0-0	8		34,977
14	Dec 2	A	Burnley	D	1-1	0-1	10	Cisse [48]	18,791
15	6	H	Chelsea	W	2-1	0-0	7	Cisse 2 [57, 78]	52,019
16	13	A	Arsenal	L	1-4	0-1	7	Perez [63]	59,949
17	21	H	Sunderland	L	0-1	0-0	9		52,315
18	26	A	Manchester U	L	1-3	0-2	10	Cisse (pen) [87]	75,318
19	28	H	Everton	W	3-2	1-1	9	Cisse [34], Perez [51], Colback [68]	52,313
20	Jan 1	H	Burnley	D	3-3	2-1	10	Taylor, S [15], Colback [26], Sissoko [78]	51,761
21	10	A	Chelsea	L	0-2	0-1	10		41,612
22	17	A	Southampton	L	1-2	1-1	11	Gouffran [29]	49,307
23	31	A	Hull C	W	3-0	1-0	11	Cabella [40], Sammy Ameobi [50], Gouffran [78]	23,925
24	Feb 8	H	Stoke C	D	1-1	0-0	11	Colback [74]	47,763
25	11	A	Crystal Palace	D	1-1	1-0	11	Cisse [42]	25,118
26	21	A	Manchester C	L	0-5	0-3	11		45,602
27	28	H	Aston Villa	W	1-0	1-0	11	Cisse [37]	51,573
28	Mar 4	H	Manchester U	L	0-1	0-0	11		49,801
29	15	A	Everton	L	0-3	0-1	11		38,806
30	21	H	Arsenal	L	1-2	0-2	12	Sissoko [48]	50,544
31	Apr 5	A	Sunderland	L	0-1	0-1	13		47,563
32	13	A	Liverpool	L	0-2	0-1	13		44,611
33	19	H	Tottenham H	L	1-3	0-1	14	Colback [46]	47,427
34	25	H	Swansea C	L	2-3	1-1	14	Perez [20], De Jong, S [87]	46,884
35	May 2	A	Leicester C	L	0-3	0-2	15		31,576
36	9	H	WBA	D	1-1	1-1	17	Perez [41]	47,894
37	16	A	QPR	L	1-2	1-0	17	Riviere [24]	17,608
38	24	H	West Ham U	W	2-0	0-0	15	Sissoko [54], Gutierrez [85]	52,094

Final League Position: 15

GOALSCORERS

League (40): Cisse 11 (1 pen), Perez 7, Colback 4, Sissoko 4, Sammy Ameobi 2, Gouffran 2, Aarons 1, Cabella 1, Coloccini 1, De Jong 1, Gutierrez 1, Janmaat 1, Obertan 1, Riviere 1, Taylor, S 1, Williamson 1.
FA Cup (0).
Capital One Cup (6): Riviere 2 (1 pen), Aarons 1, Dummett 1, Sissoko 1, own goal 1.

Krul T 30	Janmaat D 37	Williamson M 27 + 4	Coloccini P 32	Dummett P 24 + 1	Colback J 35	Anita V 17 + 2	Cabella R 21 + 10	Sissoko M 34	Gouffran Y 24 + 7	Riviere E 15 + 8	Obertan G 8 + 5	Aarons R — + 4	Perez A 25 + 11	De Jong S 1 + 3	Taylor S 7 + 3	Haidara M 12 + 3	Tiote C 10 + 1	Ameobi Sammy 15 + 10	Cisse P 11 + 11	Abeid M 7 + 6	Taylor R 11 + 3	Armstrong A 1 + 10	Elliot R 3	Ainwick J 5 + 1	Vuckic H — + 1	Gutierrez J 6 + 4	Match No.
1	2	3	4	5	6	7³	8	9	10¹	11²	12	13	14														1
1	2	3⁴	4	5	7	6¹	8	9	10	11²				13³	12	14											2
1	2²	3	4		7	14	8	6	10¹	11			12	13	9²		5										3
1	2	3	4		7	6³	8²	9	10	11			13		5	12	14										4
1	2	3	4	5	7		9	8	10²	11¹			14		6³	13	12										5
1	2	3	4	5	7		9²	8	10¹	11³	13				6	14	12										6
1	2	3	4	5	9³		8		10²	13	6		14		7	12	11¹										7
1	2		4	5²	7	6³	14	9	10¹		8		12		3	13			11								8
1	2		4	5	7	6³	13	9	10		8²		11¹		3	14			12								9
1	2		4	5	7		14	9			8³		10⁵	12	3	13			11²	6							10
1	2	12	3³	4	7		8¹	9	13	11			10²		5			6		14							11
1	2	3	4		7		8¹	9	12	11³			10		5			13	6²	14							12
	2¹	3	4		7		13	9⁴	8³	11			14		5			6²	10	12			1				13
	2	3⁴	4				13	8	14				9⁴	12	5	7	10¹	11	6				1				14
	2	14	4	5	7		8³	9		11			10¹		3⁴			6	13		1²	12					15
	2	3	4	5	7		13		10	12			8²		6	9¹	11³						1	14			16
	2		4	5	7		14	9	8³	11					3	6²	10¹	13			12		1				17
	2		4	5²	7	6	13	9	8	11³					3	12	10¹						1	14			18
	2	3	4	5	7		13	8	10¹	12			9		6		11²						1				19
	2	13	4	5	7			9	10²	11¹			8		3³	14	6						1	12			20
1	2	3	4	5	7	6	8	9¹	10²	13							11		12								21
1	2	14	3	4¹	7	6⁴	8	9	10³	13							11		5	12							22
1	2	3	4		7	6	8²	9	12	11¹							5	10³	13	14							23
1	2	3	4		7	6¹	8¹	9	13	11							5	10²	12	14							24
1	2	3	4	13	7		9²	6	10	14							5	8¹	11³	12							25
1	2¹	3	4		6	7³	9	8²					14				5	10	11	12	13						26
1	2	3	4				8		14	11²	6³		13				5¹	9	10	12	7						27
1	2	3	4				8		14	10³	6		12					9¹	11	5²	7					13	28
1	2	3	4⁴		7	6		9	8³	11¹								12	10²	5						14	29
1		3	4	5	6²	7	8	9		11								10¹		12	13					2	30
1		3	4	5		6¹	9	8	12									10	11²	2	13					7	31
1		3	4	5	6		10	9⁴	14									8³	11¹	2	7³	13				12	32
1	2	3	4	5²			8	9³		11			13					10		12	6¹	7				14	33
1	2¹	3	4	5	6			9³		11			10²						14	12	13	7				8	34
1	2⁴	3⁴	4	5	6			9		11³			10²							12	14	7¹				8	35
1		3	4		7			9	10	11¹			8²					13	12	14	5	6				2³	36
1	2	3	4		7			9	10¹	11²			13					8	14	12	5	6³					37
1	2	3	4	5	7	6¹	8	9	12				10						11								38

FA Cup

Third Round	Leicester C	(a)	0-1

Capital One Cup

Second Round	Gillingham	(a)	1-0
Third Round *(aet)*	Crystal Palace	(a)	3-2
Fourth Round	Manchester C	(a)	2-0
Quarter-Finals	Tottenham H	(a)	0-4

NEWPORT COUNTY

FOUNDATION

In 1912 Newport County were formed following a meeting at The Tredegar Arms Hotel. A professional football club had existed in the town called Newport FC, but they ceased to exist in 1907. The first season as Newport County was in the second division of the Southern League. They started life playing at Somerton Park where they remained through their League years. They were elected to the Football League for the beginning of the 1920–21 season as founder members of Division 3. At the end of the 1987–88 season, they were relegated from the Football League and replaced by Lincoln City. On February 27 1989, Newport County went out of business and from the ashes Newport AFC was born. Starting down the pyramid in the Hellenic League, they eventally gained promotion to the Conference in 2011 and were promoted to the Football League after a play-off with Wrexham in 2013.

Rodney Parade, Newport, South Wales NP19 0UU.

Telephone: (01633) 670 690.

Ticket Office: (01633) 674 990.

Website: www.newport-county.co.uk

Email: office@newport-county.co.uk

Ground Capacity: 7,616.

Record Attendance: 24,268 v Cardiff C, Division 3 (S), 16 October 1937 (Somerton Park); 4,660 v Swansea C, FA Cup 1st rd, 11 November 2006 (Newport Stadium); 6,615 v Grimsby T, Conference National Play-off semi-final, 28 April 2013 (Rodney Parade).

Pitch Measurements: 100m × 64m (109.5yd × 70yd)

Chairman: Les Scadding.

Manager: Terry Butcher.

Assistant Manager: Russell Osman.

Physio: Adam Roche.

Colours: Amber shirts with black trim, amber shorts with black trim, amber socks with black hoops.

Year Formed: 1912.

Turned Professional: 1912.

Club Nicknames: 'The Exiles', 'The Ironsides', 'The Port', 'The County'.

Grounds: 1912–89, 1990–92, Somerton Park; 1992–94, Meadow Park Stadium; 1994, Newport Stadium; 2012, Rodney Parade.

First Football League Game: 28 August 1920, Division 3, v Reading (h) L 0–1.

HONOURS

Football League – Division 3 (S): *Champions* 1938–39.

FA Cup: Best season: 5th rd, 1949.

Football League Cup: Best season: never past 3rd rd.

Welsh Cup: *Winners* 1980; *Runners-up* 1963, 1987.

FA Trophy: *Runners-up* 2012.

**European Competitions
European Cup Winners' Cup:** 1980–81 (*quarter-finals*).

sky SPORTS FACT FILE

Newport County's recent move to Rodney Parade is not the first time they have shared with the city's rugby union club. Mid-way through the 1939–40 season County's Somerton Park ground was requisitioned by the Civil Defence for the war effort. The club switched to playing their home fixtures at Newport RFC until the ground was needed for cricket. County's final five home games were staged at the Lovell's Athletic stadium at Rexville.

Record League Victory: 10-0 v Merthyr T, Division 3(S), 10 April 1930 – Martin (5), Gittins (2), Thomas (1), Bagley (1), Lawson (1).

Record Cup Victory: 7-0 v Working, FA Cup 1st rd, 24 November 1928 – Young (3), Pugh (2) Gittins (1), Reid (1).

Record Defeat: 0–13 v Newcastle U, Division 2, 5 October 1946.

Most League Points (2 for a win): 61, Division 4, 1979–80.

Most League Points (3 for a win): 78, Division 3, 1982–83.

Most League Goals: 85, Division 4, 1964–65.

Highest League Scorer in Season: Tudor Martin, 34, Division 3 (S), 1929–30.

Most League Goals in Total Aggregate: Reg Parker, 99, 1948–54.

Most League Goals in One Match: 5, Tudor Martin v Merthyr T, Dvision 3 (S), 10 April 1930.

Most Capped Player: Nigel Vaughan, 3 (10), Wales.

Most League Appearances: Len Weare, 527, 1955–70.

Youngest League Player: Regan Poole, 16 years 94 days v Shrewsbury T, 20 September 2014.

Record Transfer Fee Received: £500,000 from Peterborough U for Conor Washington, January 2014.

Record Transfer Fee Paid: £80,000 to Swansea C for Alan Waddle, January 1981.

Football League Record: 1920 Original member of Division 3; 1921–31 Divsion 3 (S) – dropped out of Football League; 1932 Re-elected to Division 3 (S); 1932–39 Division 3 (S); 1946–47 Division 2; 1947–58 Division 3 (S); 1958–62 Division 3; 1962–80 Division 4; 1980–87 Division 3; 1987–88 Division 4 (relegated from Football League); 2011 Promoted to Conference; 2011–13 Conference Premier; 2013– FL 2.

LATEST SEQUENCES

Longest Sequence of League Wins: 4, 26.12.2014 – 10.1.2015.

Longest Sequence of League Defeats: 4, 6.4.2015 – 18.4.2015.

Longest Sequence of League Draws: 3, 25.10.2014 – 16.11.2014.

Longest Sequence of Unbeaten League Matches: 9, 10.11.2014 – 13.12.2014

Longest Sequence Without a League Win: 8, 22.2.2014 – 19.3.2013.

Successive Scoring Runs: 9 from 11.10.2014.

Successive Non-scoring Runs: 4 from 17.1.2015.

MANAGERS

Davy McDougle 1912–13
(Player-Manager)
Sam Hollis 1913–17
Harry Parkes 1919–22
Jimmy Hindmarsh 1922–35
Louis Page 1935–36
Tom Bromilow 1936–37
Billy McCandless 1937–45
Tom Bromilow 1945–50
Fred Stansfield 1950–53
Billy Lucas 1953–61
Bobby Evans 1961–62
Billy Lucas 1962–67
Leslie Graham 1967–69
Bobby Ferguson 1969–70
(Player-Manager)
Billy Lucas 1970–74
Brian Harris 1974–75
Dave Elliott 1975–76
(Player-Manager)
Jimmy Scoular 1976–77
Colin Addison 1977–78
Len Ashurst 1978–82
Colin Addison 1982–85
Bobby Smith 1985–86
John Relish 1986
Jimmy Mullen 1986–87
John Lewis 1987
Brian Eastick 1987–88
David Williams 1988
Eddie May 1988
John Mahoney 1988–89
John Relish 1989–93
Graham Rogers 1993–96
Chris Price 1997
Tim Harris 1997–2002
Peter Nicholas 2002–04
John Cornforth 2004–05
Peter Beadle 2005–08
Dean Holdsworth 2008–11
Anthony Hudson 2011
Justin Edinburgh 2011–15
Jimmy Dack 2015
Terry Butcher April 2015–

DID YOU KNOW ?

Newport County's achievement in winning promotion to the Football League was recognised in July 2013 when the local Council awarded them the Freedom of the City. Only 16 individuals and organisations had previously been granted the honour since 1909.

TEN YEAR LEAGUE RECORD

		P	W	D	L	F	A	Pts	Pos
2005-06	Conf S	42	12	8	22	50	67	44	18
2006-07	Conf S	42	21	7	14	83	57	70	6
2007-08	Conf S	42	18	12	12	64	49	66	10
2008-09	Conf S	42	16	11	15	50	51	59	10
2009-10	Conf S	42	32	7	3	93	26	103	1
2010-11	Conf P	46	18	15	13	78	60	69	9
2011-12	Conf P	46	11	14	21	53	65	47	19
2012-13	Conf P	46	25	10	11	85	60	85	3
2013-14	FL 2	46	14	16	16	56	59	58	14
2014-15	FL 2	46	18	11	17	51	54	65	9

NEWPORT COUNTY – FOOTBALL LEAGUE TWO 2014–15 LEAGUE RECORD

Match No.	Date	Venue	Opponents	Result		H/T Score	Lg Pos.	Goalscorers	Attendance
1	Aug 9	H	Wycombe W	L	0-2	0-2	23		3634
2	16	A	Morecambe	L	2-3	2-0	21	Chapman [27], O'Connor [29]	1506
3	19	A	Mansfield T	L	0-1	0-1	22		2448
4	23	H	Burton Alb	D	1-1	1-0	22	Zebroski [37]	2872
5	30	A	Portsmouth	W	1-0	0-0	19	Sandell [84]	16,191
6	Sept 8	H	Cambridge U	D	1-1	0-0	19	Willmott [90]	2594
7	13	H	Northampton T	W	3-2	2-0	17	Zebroski [18], Jones, D [33], Minshull [53]	2875
8	16	A	Tranmere R	D	0-0	0-0	17		3948
9	20	A	Shrewsbury T	D	0-0	0-0	16		4904
10	27	H	AFC Wimbledon	W	4-1	1-0	15	Yakubu [18], Pigott 2 [46, 65], O'Connor [90]	2804
11	Oct 4	A	Oxford U	L	0-1	0-1	18		5072
12	11	H	York C	W	3-1	0-1	13	Hughes [51], Zebroski [65], Jones, D [72]	2822
13	18	A	Dagenham & R	W	1-0	0-0	9	Zebroski [90]	1654
14	21	H	Southend U	W	1-0	0-0	8	Byrne [74]	2558
15	25	H	Accrington S	D	1-1	0-0	7	Pigott [72]	3254
16	Nov 1	A	Hartlepool U	D	2-2	1-0	8	Zebroski [38], O'Connor [57]	3172
17	16	A	Exeter C	D	2-2	0-2	9	Klukowski [49], Porter [51]	4070
18	22	A	Bury	W	3-1	2-0	8	O'Connor 3 [3, 43, 90]	3166
19	29	A	Carlisle U	W	3-2	1-0	7	Klukowski [9], Yakubu [47], Jeffers [90]	3642
20	Dec 13	H	Stevenage	W	2-0	2-0	6	O'Connor [26], Jones, D [45]	2976
21	20	A	Luton T	L	0-3	0-1	7		8383
22	26	H	Plymouth Arg	W	2-0	1-0	7	Zebroski [9], Byrne [82]	5020
23	28	A	Cheltenham T	W	1-0	1-0	5	Zebroski [11]	3417
24	Jan 3	H	Carlisle U	W	2-1	1-1	4	Chapman (pen) [45], Minshull [70]	3273
25	10	H	Portsmouth	W	1-0	0-0	3	Byrne [68]	4575
26	17	A	Cambridge U	L	0-4	0-2	5		6076
27	24	A	Northampton T	L	0-3	0-2	6		4226
28	31	H	Shrewsbury T	L	0-1	0-0	6		3706
29	Feb 7	A	AFC Wimbledon	L	0-2	0-1	6		3817
30	10	H	Tranmere R	D	1-1	0-1	6	Byrne [83]	2327
31	14	A	Wycombe W	W	2-1	1-0	6	Klukowski 2 [20, 79]	3196
32	21	H	Morecambe	L	0-1	0-1	8		2883
33	28	A	Burton Alb	W	1-0	0-0	7	Storey [59]	2974
34	Mar 3	H	Mansfield T	L	0-1	0-0	7		2481
35	7	A	Stevenage	L	1-2	0-1	9	Chapman [88]	2941
36	13	H	Cheltenham T	D	1-1	1-1	9	Storey [38]	2951
37	17	H	Luton T	W	1-0	1-0	8	O'Connor [21]	2536
38	21	A	Plymouth Arg	D	0-0	0-0	7		6847
39	27	A	Accrington S	W	2-0	0-0	6	Davies (og) [66], Jeffers [90]	1111
40	Apr 3	H	Hartlepool U	D	2-2	1-2	6	Jones, D [44], O'Connor [48]	3531
41	6	A	Exeter C	L	0-2	0-0	7		4478
42	11	A	Bury	L	0-2	0-1	8		3123
43	14	A	Southend U	L	0-2	0-1	9		5480
44	18	H	Dagenham & R	L	2-3	0-0	9	Tutonda [90], O'Connor [90]	2737
45	25	A	York C	W	2-0	0-0	9	Tutonda [48], Minshull [75]	3459
46	May 2	H	Oxford U	L	0-1	0-1	9		4295

Final League Position: 9

GOALSCORERS

League (51): O'Connor 10, Zebroski 7, Byrne 4, Jones, D 4, Klukowski 4, Chapman 3 (1 pen), Minshull 3, Pigott 3, Jeffers 2, Storey 2, Tutonda 2, Yakubu 2, Hughes 1, Porter 1, Sandell 1, Willmott 1, own goal 1.
FA Cup (2): Klukowski 1, O'Connor 1.
Capital One Cup (1): Jeffers 1.
Johnstone's Paint Trophy (1): Klukowski 1.

Pidgeley L 4	Willmott R 14 + 2	Jones D 43	Feely K 17 + 5	Sandell A 32 + 6	Flynn M 3 + 8	Minshull L 34 + 5	Byrne M 39 + 3	O'Connor A 32 + 7	Howe R 5 + 9	Zebroski C 28 + 8	Klukowski Y 24 + 14	Yakubu I 32 + 1	Chapman A 27 + 9	Hughes A 16	Jeffers S 11 + 10	Jolley C — + 5	Jackson R 31 + 3	Day J 36	Pigott J 6 + 4	Poole R 11	Tancock S 4	Crow D — + 2	Loveridge J 2 + 5	Porter M 21 + 6	Obeng C 4 + 1	Stephens J 6 + 1	Parker J — + 4	Storey M 14 + 4	Tutonda D 10 + 2	Collins A — + 2	Patten K — + 1	Owen-Evans T — + 1	Match No.
1	2	3	4	5	6[2]	7[1]	8	9[3]	10	11	12	13	14																				1
1	2	3		9		7	8	11[3]	10[1]	12			4	6[2]	5	13	14																2
1	5	3	4	9[3]		8[1]	7	11	13	10[2]	14	2	6				12																3
1	9	3	2			8	7	10[1]	11				6	4	12		5																4
	9[1]	3	2	14		8	7	12		11[3]			5	4	10[2]	13	6	1															5
	9	3	4[1]	12		8[3]	7	11[2]		10	14		6	5		13	2	1															6
	9	4	3	13		7	6	11[2]		10	14		8[1]	2			5[3]	1	12														7
	5	3	2[2]	9		7	6	12		11[1]	13		8	4		14		1	10[3]														8
	9	4		5		8	6	14		11[2]			7	2[4]		12	13	1	10[3]	3[1]													9
	8	3	6	9[1]		7	13	10[3]		12			4	5[2]				1		11		2	14										10
	7	3	6			8	11[2]			13	9[3]		4	5[1]				1		10		2	14	12									11
6[2]		3		12		7		14		10	11		4		2		5	1		5[3]		8[1]		9	13								12
		4	12	6	13	8	9	14		11	2		3[3]	5				1				10[1]		7[2]									13
		3	2	6	13	7	8[2]	11		10				5				1	12				4[3]	14	9[1]								14
		3	2	9		6	7	10[1]		11[3]	13		4					1	12					14	8[2]	5							15
		2		5[1]	7	6		10[1]		11	12	3	4					1						13	8[2]	9							16
		3			6[1]		10[2]		11	8	2	12	4			7[1]	9[3]	1	13					14	7	5							17
		4		6		7[1]	12	10		11	9	3		5			13	1						8	2[2]								18
		4		6		8	12	10[2]		11	9[1]	3	14	5	13		2							7[3]			1						19
		3		9		6	13	10[1]		8	2		4[3]	11[1]	5									7	12	1							20
		2		4		7[1]	6		13	10	5	3	12	11	9									8[2]			1						21
		2		8	13	7[3]	9		12	10	14	3	6[2]	11[1]	5						4						1						22
		2		9	14		8		12	10	7	3	6[1]	11[2]	5						4[3]			13			1						23
		2		9		7		8[1]	10[3]	12	11[2]		3	6	14		5	1			4			13									24
		3		9		8[2]	6	10[3]	13		12	4	7[1]	11	5		1		2					14									25
		4		9[2]		7[1]	8	10		11	12	2	6[2]		5		1		3					14				13					26
		3	2[2]	8	12		7	13	11[1]	10		4	6	9[3]	5		1											14					27
		4	3	6		14	8[2]	11		10[1]	13	5	7[3]				2	1						9				12					28
		4	2[4]	9		14	8	10		11[2]	13	3	7[3]				5	1						6[1]				12					29
9		3		4		8[3]	7	10[1]	14		12	2			13		5	1						6				11[2]					30
		3	14				6	11[1]	10[2]		8	4	12		13		2	1						7				9[1]	5				31
12		2				4		7	13	11[3]	3	14		10[2]			5	1						6[1]				8	9				32
		3		12		13	6		14	10[2]	9	4	8[1]				2	1						7				11[3]	5				33
		3		12		7[1]	6		10[5]	9[3]	4	8					2	1						13			14	11	5				34
	7	4	12			14	9		13[4]	11[3]	3[1]	6					2	1						8[2]				10	5				35
		4	3	12	14	7	6	11	13		9		8[2]				2	1										10[1]	5[3]				36
		3	4	9	13	6		11[1]		12	8[3]	2	14		10[2]		5	1						7									37
		3		4		8[1]	7	10[2]		13	9	2	12	14			5	1						6				11[3]					38
		3		4		8	6	10		9	2			14	5[3]	12		1						7		13		11[1]	12				39
		3		4		7	8	10		5[2]	2	13	12					1						6[1]				11	9				40
		4		6		14	9[1]	10		12	2	5[4]	7[2]	11[3]				1	3					8				13					41
	3	13	4			7[2]	6	11		10[5]	9[2]		8	14	5	1	2							12									42
		4	14	5			9	10		13		3[1]	8	11[3]	2	1								7[2]				6	12				43
		4	5			8	10			9[1]		7[3]		2	1	3											12	11[2]	6	13	14		44
		4				3	9	10		7[2]		8[1]		5	1	2											11	6	12			13	45
12		2		7[1]	6	8	10	9				5				3							1				11[1]	4				46

FA Cup
First Round   Luton T   (a)   2-4

Capital One Cup
First Round   Reading   (a)   1-3

Johnstone's Paint Trophy
First Round   Swindon T   (h)   1-2

NORTHAMPTON TOWN

FOUNDATION

Formed in 1897 by schoolteachers connected with the Northampton & District Elementary Schools' Association, they survived a financial crisis at the end of their first year when they were £675 in the red and became members of the Midland League – a fast move indeed for a new club. They achieved Southern League membership in 1901.

Sixfields Stadium, Upton Way, Northampton NN5 5QA.

Telephone: (01604) 683 700.

Fax: (01604) 751 613.

Ticket Office: (01604) 683 777.

Website: www.ntfc.co.uk

Email: gareth.willsher@ntfc.tv

Ground Capacity: 7,500 (rising).

Record Attendance: 24,523 v Fulham, Division 1, 23 April 1966 (at County Ground); 7,557 v Manchester C, Division 2, 26 September 1998 (at Sixfields Stadium).

Pitch Measurements: 106m × 66m (116yd × 72yd)

Chairman: David Cardoza.

Manager: Chris Wilder.

Assistant Manager: Alan Knill.

Physio: Anders Braastad.

Colours: Claret shirts with white trim, claret shorts, claret socks with white hoops.

Year Formed: 1897.

Turned Professional: 1901.

Grounds: 1897, County Ground; 1994, Sixfields Stadium.

Club Nickname: 'The Cobblers'.

First Football League Game: 28 August 1920, Division 3, v Grimsby T (a) L 0–2 – Thorpe; Sproston, Hewison; Jobey, Tomkins, Pease; Whitworth, Lockett, Thomas, Freeman, MacKechnie.

Record League Victory: 10–0 v Walsall, Division 3 (S), 5 November 1927 – Hammond; Watson, Jeffs; Allen, Brett, Odell; Daley, Smith (3), Loasby (3), Hoten (1), Wells (3).

Record Cup Victory: 10–0 v Sutton T, FA Cup prel rd, 7 December 1907 – Cooch; Drennan, Lloyd Davies, Tirrell (1), McCartney, Hickleton, Badenock (3), Platt (3), Lowe (1), Chapman (2), McDiarmid.

Record Defeat: 0–11 v Southampton, Southern League, 28 December 1901.

HONOURS

Football League – Division 1: 21st, 1965–66;
Division 2: *Runners-up* 1964–65;
Division 3: *Champions* 1962–63;
Division 3 (S): *Runners-up* 1927–28, 1949–50;
Division 4: *Champions* 1986–87; *Runners-up* 1975–76;
FL 2: *Runners-up* 2005–06.
FA Cup: Best season: 5th rd, 1934, 1950, 1970.
Football League Cup: Best season: 5th rd, 1965, 1967.

sky SPORTS FACT FILE

When Northampton Town won promotion to the old First Division in 1964–65 they conceded just 50 goals in their 42 games. Goalkeeper Bryan Harvey had the distinction of saving six penalties during the campaign including two from the Southampton and England winger Terry Paine.

Most League Points (2 for a win): 68, Division 4, 1975–76.

Most League Points (3 for a win): 99, Division 4, 1986–87.

Most League Goals: 109, Division 3, 1962–63 and Division 3 (S), 1952–53.

Highest League Scorer in Season: Cliff Holton, 36, Division 3, 1961–62.

Most League Goals in Total Aggregate: Jack English, 135, 1947–60.

Most League Goals in One Match: 5, Ralph Hoten v Crystal Palace, Division 3 (S), 27 October 1928.

Most Capped Player: Edwin Lloyd Davies, 12 (16), Wales.

Most League Appearances: Tommy Fowler, 521, 1946–61.

Youngest League Player: Adrian Mann, 16 years 297 days v Bury, 5 May 1984.

Record Transfer Fee Received: £470,000 from Blackburn R for Mark Bunn, September 2008.

Record Transfer Fee Paid: £165,000 to Oldham Ath for Josh Low, July 2003.

Football League Record: 1920 Original Member of Division 3; 1921 Division 3 (S); 1958–61 Division 4; 1961–63 Division 3; 1963–65 Division 2; 1965–66 Division 1; 1966–67 Division 2; 1967–69 Division 3; 1969–76 Division 4; 1976–77 Division 3; 1977–87 Division 4; 1987–90 Division 3; 1990–92 Division 4; 1992–97 Division 3; 1997–99 Division 2; 1999–2000 Division 3; 2000–03 Division 2; 2003–04 Division 3; 2004–06 FL 2; 2006–09 FL 1; 2009– FL 2.

LATEST SEQUENCES

Longest Sequence of League Wins: 8, 27.8.1960 – 19.9.1960.

Longest Sequence of League Defeats: 8, 26.10.1935 – 21.12.1935.

Longest Sequence of League Draws: 6, 5.2.2011 – 26.2.2011.

Longest Sequence of Unbeaten League Matches: 21, 27.9.1986 – 6.2.1987.

Longest Sequence Without a League Win: 18, 5.2.2011 – 25.4.2011.

Successive Scoring Runs: 27 from 23.8.1986.

Successive Non-scoring Runs: 7 from 7.4.1939.

MANAGERS

Arthur Jones 1897–1907
  (Secretary-Manager)
Herbert Chapman 1907–12
Walter Bull 1912–13
Fred Lessons 1913–19
Bob Hewison 1920–25
Jack Tresadern 1925–30
Jack English 1931–35
Syd Puddefoot 1935–37
Warney Cresswell 1937–39
Tom Smith 1939–49
Bob Dennison 1949–54
Dave Smith 1954–59
David Bowen 1959–67
Tony Marchi 1967–68
Ron Flowers 1968–69
Dave Bowen 1969–72
  *(continued as General Manager
  and Secretary 1972–85 when
  joined the board)*
Billy Baxter 1972–73
Bill Dodgin Jnr 1973–76
Pat Crerand 1976–77
By committee 1977
Bill Dodgin Jnr 1977
John Petts 1977–78
Mike Keen 1978–79
Clive Walker 1979–80
Bill Dodgin Jnr 1980–82
Clive Walker 1982–84
Tony Barton 1984–85
Graham Carr 1985–90
Theo Foley 1990–92
Phil Chard 1992–93
John Barnwell 1993–94
Ian Atkins 1995–99
Kevin Wilson 1999–2001
Kevan Broadhurst 2001–03
Terry Fenwick 2003
Martin Wilkinson 2003
Colin Calderwood 2003–06
John Gorman 2006
Stuart Gray 2007–09
Ian Sampson 2009–11
Gary Johnson 2011
Aidy Boothroyd 2011–13
Chris Wilder January 2014–

TEN YEAR LEAGUE RECORD

		P	W	D	L	F	A	Pts	Pos
2005-06	FL 2	46	22	17	7	63	37	83	2
2006-07	FL 1	46	15	14	17	48	51	59	14
2007-08	FL 1	46	17	15	14	60	55	66	9
2008-09	FL 1	46	12	13	21	61	65	49	21
2009-10	FL 2	46	18	13	15	62	53	67	11
2010-11	FL 2	46	11	19	16	63	71	52	16
2011-12	FL 2	46	12	12	22	56	79	48	20
2012-13	FL 2	46	21	10	15	64	55	73	6
2013-14	FL 2	46	13	14	19	42	57	53	21
2014-15	FL 2	46	18	7	21	67	62	61	12

DID YOU KNOW

Northampton Town won the Southern League in 1908–09 which earned them the right to play Football League champions Newcastle United for the FA Charity Shield. The game was played at Stamford Bridge with the Magpies winning 2-0.

NORTHAMPTON TOWN – FOOTBALL LEAGUE TWO 2014–15 LEAGUE RECORD

Match No.	Date	Venue	Opponents	Result	H/T Score	Lg Pos.	Goalscorers	Attendance
1	Aug 9	H	Mansfield T	W 1-0	1-0	3	Mohamed [26]	5202
2	16	A	York C	D 1-1	0-0	9	Richards [90]	3448
3	19	A	Portsmouth	L 0-2	0-2	15		15,004
4	23	H	Shrewsbury T	D 1-1	0-0	13	Sinclair [90]	4369
5	30	H	Exeter C	W 1-0	0-0	8	Richards [89]	4053
6	Sept 6	A	Dagenham & R	W 2-0	2-0	7	Richards 2 [8, 23]	2186
7	13	A	Newport Co	L 2-3	0-2	9	D'Ath [76], Richards [85]	2875
8	16	H	Hartlepool U	W 5-1	3-1	5	Richards 2 (1 pen) [12 (pl, 76)], Mohamed 2 [20, 35], D'Ath [67]	3653
9	20	H	Accrington S	L 4-5	1-3	9	Richards [26], Toney 2 [78, 89], Carter [90]	4731
10	27	A	Morecambe	W 1-0	1-0	5	Toney [33]	1725
11	Oct 4	A	Wycombe W	D 1-1	1-0	6	Cresswell [31]	3822
12	11	H	Burton Alb	L 1-2	0-1	9	Cresswell [80]	4935
13	18	A	Cheltenham T	L 2-3	0-1	12	Byrom [48], Moyo [86]	2447
14	21	H	Oxford U	L 1-3	1-2	16	Stevens [4]	4577
15	25	A	Luton T	L 0-1	0-0	18		10,040
16	Nov 1	H	AFC Wimbledon	W 2-0	1-0	15	Mohamed [32], Nicholls [90]	4548
17	14	A	Cambridge U	L 1-2	0-0	15	Toney [50]	5644
18	22	H	Stevenage	W 1-0	1-0	14	Richards [20]	4431
19	29	A	Southend U	L 0-2	0-0	15		5500
20	Dec 13	H	Plymouth Arg	L 2-3	0-2	16	Toney [79], Murdoch [89]	4318
21	20	A	Carlisle U	L 1-2	1-1	19	Richards (pen) [45]	4421
22	26	H	Bury	L 2-3	1-2	19	Richards [6], Hackett [77]	4563
23	28	A	Tranmere R	L 1-2	1-1	20	Richards [44]	5394
24	Jan 3	A	Southend U	D 1-1	0-0	20	D'Ath [72]	4587
25	10	A	Exeter C	W 2-0	2-0	16	Richards [20], O'Toole [29]	3519
26	17	A	Dagenham & R	W 1-0	0-0	15	Holmes [60]	4122
27	24	H	Newport Co	W 3-0	2-0	14	Cresswell [13], O'Toole [29], D'Ath [82]	4226
28	31	A	Accrington S	W 5-1	2-1	12	Holmes [5], Richards 2 (1 pen) [32 (pl), 67], D'Ath 2 [65, 80]	1328
29	Feb 7	H	Morecambe	W 2-1	1-1	11	Byrom [1], Richards [54]	4307
30	10	A	Hartlepool U	L 0-1	0-0	13		2856
31	14	H	Mansfield T	D 1-1	0-0	11	Richards (pen) [90]	4614
32	21	H	York C	W 3-0	1-0	10	Hackett [4], Moloney [48], Toney [89]	4694
33	28	A	Shrewsbury T	W 2-1	1-0	10	Hackett [20], Byrom [47]	5310
34	Mar 3	H	Portsmouth	W 1-0	1-0	10	Holmes [25]	4871
35	7	A	Plymouth Arg	L 0-2	0-1	10		6501
36	14	H	Tranmere R	W 1-0	0-0	10	Cresswell [62]	4428
37	17	H	Carlisle U	L 0-2	0-0	10		3682
38	21	A	Bury	L 1-2	1-0	11	Holmes [10]	3969
39	28	H	Luton T	W 2-1	0-0	10	Holmes (pen) [64], Gray [86]	5668
40	Apr 3	A	AFC Wimbledon	D 2-2	0-0	11	Gray 2 [66, 69]	4667
41	6	H	Cambridge U	L 0-1	0-1	11		5520
42	11	A	Stevenage	L 1-2	1-0	11	Diamond [39]	3378
43	14	A	Oxford U	D 1-1	1-0	11	Toney [38]	4836
44	18	H	Cheltenham T	W 2-0	0-0	10	Toney [57], Richards [70]	4579
45	25	A	Burton Alb	L 1-3	0-3	10	D'Ath [53]	5720
46	May 2	H	Wycombe W	L 2-3	0-2	12	Wood (og) [67], Cresswell [85]	5723

Final League Position: 12

GOALSCORERS

League (67): Richards 18 (4 pens), Toney 8, D'Ath 7, Cresswell 5, Holmes 5 (1 pen), Mohamed 4, Byrom 3, Gray 3, Hackett 3, O'Toole 2, Carter 1, Diamond 1, Moloney 1, Moyo 1, Murdoch 1, Nicholls 1, Sinclair 1, Stevens 1, own goal 1.
FA Cup (1): Toney 1.
Capital One Cup (3): D'Ath 2, Toney 1.
Johnstone's Paint Trophy (2): Mohamed 1, Moyo 1.

Duke M 29+1	Alfei D 9+2	Diamond Z 18+3	Collins L 36+1	Robertson G 20+1	Hackett C 20+18	Carter D 12+11	Ravenhill R 8+4	Mohamed K 17+6	Richards M 26+5	O'Toole J 24+11	Toney J 23+17	Morris I —+2	Horwood E 23+2	D'Ath L 31+10	Moyo D —+3	Tozer B 15+7	Byrom J 37+2	Sinclair E 1+9	Cresswell R 31+1	Watson R 5	Archer J 13	Stevens E 4	Nicholls A 4+2	Langmead K 4+3	Newey T 5+4	Murdoch S 8	Banks O 3	Moloney B 22	Taylor J 21	Holmes R 21	Bodin B —+4	Gray J 7+1	De Girolamo D 5+1	Jalal S 4	Match No.
1	2	3	4	5	6²	7¹	8	9	10	11³	12	13	14																						1
1	2	4	3	5	8³	7¹	13	10	6	11	12		9²	14																					2
1	2²	3	4	5	13		8	6¹	11		7	10		9³	12	14																			3
1		3	4	5¹	6²			14	9	11		7	10³		12		2	8	13																4
1		3	4³	5	6			14	9	10		7²	13		12		2	8	11¹																5
1			4		5	6¹		9	10³	12	11²		13	14		2	8		3	7															6
	12	3		5²	6	8			11	13	10		14			2³	7		4	9¹	1														7
	2	3¹	12	5	6³			9	11²	14	13		10			7			4	8	1														8
	2³		3	5²	6	14		9	11		12		10¹	13	7		3	8	1																9
			4	5	6¹	13	14	9²		12	11		10¹			2	7		3	8	1														10
			4	5¹	9	12	8	6²	13	14	11³		10¹			2	7		3		1														11
13			4		6			7	9¹		11		12			2²	8		3		1	5	10³	14											12
2			4		6²		8³	12		14	10			9	13		7		3		1	5	11¹												13
2²			4			7¹		6		8	11		10¹	13	9	14	3				1	5	12												14
			4	13		7³	10	8²	12		6		2	9	14	3					1	5	11¹												15
			4			9³		11¹	10²		6		2	8	12	3		1		13	14	5	7												16
	3	12	9³		6	10	13	11		2	8¹	14	4		1					5²	7														17
	4	5	6²	7	13	9¹	10		12		2	14			1	11¹	3		8																18
14		4	5	12	10	8³	13	11		2	6²		1•			3		7¹	9																19
1		4	5	6³	8		9²	11		13			14	2			12		3									7	10¹						20
1	3			13	8			12	11		10	2	14			5³	6¹							4			7	9²							21
1	2¹	4		5	12	8		14	10	13	11•	9	6²	3													7³								22
1	2	4¹	3	5•	6			9	11	10		13				7	14									12	8								23
1		4		14				13	11		10¹			5		6³	8	12	3									2	7	9²					24
1		4		13				10¹	11²		5		6			7	12	3										2	8	9					25
1		3		12				10	11	13	2	9				7		4										5	8	6²					26
1		4		14				11³	10²	12	5	6	13	8			3											2	7	9¹					27
1	12	4		14				10	6¹		5	9¹		8		3•												2	7	11²	13				28
1	3¹	4		13				11	10³		5	6	12	8			14											2	7	9²					29
1		4		14				11	10²	13	5	6¹	12	8														2	7	9¹					30
1	3²							11	9•	12	5	8		7		4							13					2	6³	10¹	14				31
1	3			10²	13			11		12	5	6		8¹		4												2	7	9					32
1	13	4		6¹	12				11		5	7²		8		3												2	9	10					33
1		4		6³	13		12		11		5	10²		8		3							14					2	7	9¹					34
1		4		12			7		12	10	5	6²		3		•												2	8	9	13	11¹			35
1		4		12	8			10¹	13	5	9		3			14							5					2	7	6¹	11¹				36
1		4³		6	8²			10¹	12	9		14	3			5												2	7	13	11				37
1		3		12				13	11	10	7	4				5												2	6	8¹		9²			38
1	14	3		12				10¹	13	6	8	4		5¹														2	7	9	11³				39
1	4¹	3		13	14			10¹	12	6²	8	5																2	7	9	11³				40
1	4³			6¹	14			12		5²	10	8	3															2	7	9	11	13			41
1	4³	3		14				10	5¹	12	13	7	8•															2	6	9²	11				42
	4	3	12	13		7	11¹		5	6		14	8															2	9²	10³	1			1	43
	3	4		14				12	7	11²		5¹	9	8														2	13	10³	1				44
	3	4¹	14				12	11	5		9	8	13															2²	7	6	10²	1			45
	2			12	13			10	7¹	11	4²	9	8	3														6	5				1		46

FA Cup

First Round	Rochdale		(h)	0-0
Replay	Rochdale		(a)	1-2

Capital One Cup

First Round	Wolverhampton W		(a)	3-2
Second Round	Bournemouth		(a)	0-3

Johnstone's Paint Trophy

Second Round	Portsmouth		(a)	2-1
Southern Quarter-Finals	Leyton Orient		(a)	0-2

NORWICH CITY

FOUNDATION

Formed in 1902, largely through the initiative of two local schoolmasters who called a meeting at the Criterion Cafe, they were shocked by an FA Commission which in 1904 declared the club professional and ejected them from the FA Amateur Cup. However, this only served to strengthen their determination. New officials were appointed and a professional club established at a meeting in the Agricultural Hall in March 1905.

Carrow Road, Norwich, Norfolk NR1 1JE.

Telephone: (01603) 760 760.

Fax: (01603) 613 886.

Ticket Office: (0844) 444 1902.

Website: www.canaries.co.uk

Email: reception@ncfc-canaries.co.uk

Ground Capacity: 27,254.

Record Attendance: 25,037 v Sheffield W, FA Cup 5th rd, 16 February 1935 (at The Nest); 43,984 v Leicester C, FA Cup 6th rd, 30 March 1963 (at Carrow Road).

Pitch Measurements: 105m × 68m (114yd × 74yd)

Chairman: Alan Bowkett.

Joint Majority Shareholders: Delia Smith and Michael Wynn-Jones.

Chief Executive: David McNally.

Manager: Alex Neil.

First Team Coaches: Frank McAvoy and Gary Holt.

Physio: Neal Reynolds.

Colours: Yellow shirts with green trim, green shorts with yellow trim, yellow socks with green trim.

Year Formed: 1902.

Turned Professional: 1905.

Club Nickname: 'The Canaries'.

Grounds: 1902, Newmarket Road; 1908, The Nest, Rosary Road; 1935, Carrow Road.

First Football League Game: 28 August 1920, Division 3, v Plymouth Arg (a) D 1–1 – Skermer; Gray, Gadsden; Wilkinson, Addy, Martin; Laxton, Kidger, Parker, Whitham (1), Dobson.

Record League Victory: 10–2 v Coventry C, Division 3 (S), 15 March 1930 – Jarvie; Hannah, Graham; Brown, O'Brien, Lochhead (1); Porter (1), Anderson, Hunt (5), Scott (2), Slicer (1).

Record Cup Victory: 8–0 v Sutton U, FA Cup 4th rd, 28 January 1989 – Gunn; Culverhouse, Bowen, Butterworth, Linighan, Townsend (Crook), Gordon, Fleck (3), Allen (4), Phelan, Putney (1).

Record Defeat: 2–10 v Swindon T, Southern League, 5 September 1908.

HONOURS

FA Premier League: Best season: 3rd, 1992–93.

Football League – Division 1: *Champions* 2003–04;

FL C: *Runners-up* 2010–11;

Division 2: *Champions* 1971–72, 1985–86;

FL 1: *Champions* 2009–10;

Division 3 (S): *Champions* 1933–34; *Runners-up* 1950–51;

Division 3: *Runners-up* 1959–60.

FA Cup: semi-finals, 1959, 1989, 1992.

Football League Cup: *Winners* 1962, 1985; *Runners-up* 1973, 1975.

European Competitions UEFA Cup: 1993–94.

sky SPORTS FACT FILE

Goalkeeper Michael Theoklitos joined Norwich City in the summer of 2009, and was selected for the opening match of the season against Colchester United. The Canaries suffered a record home defeat, losing 7-1, and Michael never played for the team again. He returned to Australia and a successful career with Brisbane Roar.

Most League Points (2 for a win): 64, Division 3 (S), 1950–51.

Most League Points (3 for a win): 95, FL 1, 2009–10.

Most League Goals: 99, Division 3 (S), 1952–53.

Highest League Scorer in Season: Ralph Hunt, 31, Division 3 (S), 1955–56.

Most League Goals in Total Aggregate: Johnny Gavin, 122, 1945–54, 1955–58.

Most League Goals in One Match: 5, Tommy Hunt v Coventry C, Division 3 (S), 15 March 1930; 5, Roy Hollis v Walsall, Division 3 (S), 29 December 1951.

Most Capped Player: Mark Bowen, 35 (41), Wales.

Most League Appearances: Ron Ashman, 592, 1947–64.

Youngest League Player: Ryan Jarvis, 16 years 282 days v Walsall, 19 April 2003.

Record Transfer Fee Received: £8,000,000 from QPR for Leroy Fer, August 2014.

Record Transfer Fee Paid: £8,500,000 to Sporting Lisbon for Ricky van Wolfswinkel, July 2013.

Football League Record: 1920 Original Member of Division 3; 1921 Division 3 (S): 1934–39 Division 2; 1946–58 Division 3 (S); 1958–60 Division 3; 1960–72 Division 2; 1972–74 Division 1; 1974–75 Division 2; 1975–81 Division 1; 1981–82 Division 2; 1982–85 Division 1; 1985–86 Division 2; 1986–92 Division 1; 1992–95 FA Premier League; 1995–2004 Division 1; 2004–05 FA Premier League; 2005–09 FL C; 2009–10 FL 1; 2010–11 FL C; 2011–14 FA Premier League; 2014–15 FL C; 2015– FA Premier League.

LATEST SEQUENCES

Longest Sequence of League Wins: 10, 23.11.1985 – 25.1.1986.

Longest Sequence of League Defeats: 7, 1.4.1995 – 6.5.1995.

Longest Sequence of League Draws: 7, 15.1.1994 – 26.2.1994.

Longest Sequence of Unbeaten League Matches: 20, 31.8.1950 – 30.12.1950.

Longest Sequence Without a League Win: 25, 22.9.1956 – 23.2.1957.

Successive Scoring Runs: 25 from 14.9.2009.

Successive Non-scoring Runs: 5 from 18.9.2007.

MANAGERS

John Bowman 1905–07
James McEwen 1907–08
Arthur Turner 1909–10
Bert Stansfield 1910–15
Major Frank Buckley 1919–20
Charles O'Hagan 1920–21
Albert Gosnell 1921–26
Bert Stansfield 1926
Cecil Potter 1926–29
James Kerr 1929–33
Tom Parker 1933–37
Bob Young 1937–39
Jimmy Jewell 1939
Bob Young 1939–45
Duggie Lochhead 1945–46
Cyril Spiers 1946–47
Duggie Lochhead 1947–50
Norman Low 1950–55
Tom Parker 1955–57
Archie Macaulay 1957–61
Willie Reid 1961–62
George Swindin 1962
Ron Ashman 1962–66
Lol Morgan 1966–69
Ron Saunders 1969–73
John Bond 1973–80
Ken Brown 1980–87
Dave Stringer 1987–92
Mike Walker 1992–94
John Deehan 1994–95
Martin O'Neill 1995
Gary Megson 1995–96
Mike Walker 1996–98
Bruce Rioch 1998–2000
Bryan Hamilton 2000
Nigel Worthington 2000–06
Peter Grant 2006–07
Glenn Roeder 2007–09
Bryan Gunn 2009
Paul Lambert 2009–12
Chris Hughton 2012–14
Neil Adams 2014–15
Alex Neil January 2015–

TEN YEAR LEAGUE RECORD

		P	W	D	L	F	A	Pts	Pos
2005-06	FL C	46	18	8	20	56	65	62	9
2006-07	FL C	46	16	9	21	56	71	57	16
2007-08	FL C	46	15	10	21	49	59	55	17
2008-09	FL C	46	12	10	24	57	70	46	22
2009-10	FL 1	46	29	8	9	89	47	95	1
2010-11	FL C	46	23	15	8	83	58	84	2
2011-12	PR Lge	38	12	11	15	52	66	47	12
2012-13	PR Lge	38	10	14	14	41	58	44	11
2013-14	PR Lge	38	8	9	21	28	62	33	18
2014-15	FL C	46	25	11	10	88	48	86	3

DID YOU KNOW

Jimmy Jewell refereed the 1938 FA Cup final and the following January he was appointed as secretary-manager of Norwich City. He proved unable to keep the Canaries in Division Two and left to join the RAF when war broke out. He later commentated on games for BBC television.

NORWICH CITY – FL CHAMPIONSHIP 2014–15 LEAGUE RECORD

Match No.	Date	Venue	Opponents	Result	H/T Score	Lg Pos.	Goalscorers	Attendance
1	Aug 10	A	Wolverhampton W	L 0-1	0-0	17		22,053
2	16	H	Watford	W 3-0	1-0	10	Johnson 32, Grabban 59, Tettey 61	26,375
3	19	H	Blackburn R	W 3-1	1-1	5	Grabban 2 23, 90, Johnson 87	25,835
4	23	A	Ipswich T	W 1-0	1-0	3	Grabban 24	25,245
5	30	H	Bournemouth	D 1-1	1-1	4	Grabban 15	25,814
6	Sept13	A	Cardiff C	W 4-2	0-2	2	Olsson 54, Hoolahan 68, Turner 71, Jerome 87	21,746
7	16	H	Brentford	W 3-0	0-0	1	Tettey 68, Jerome 2 75, 83	10,074
8	20	H	Birmingham C	D 2-2	0-2	2	Jerome 2 52, 55	26,351
9	27	A	Blackpool	W 3-1	0-0	1	Daniels (og) 54, Grabban 80, Josh Murphy 81	11,232
10	30	H	Charlton Ath	L 0-1	0-0	1		25,983
11	Oct 4	A	Rotherham U	D 1-1	0-1	1	Jerome 77	26,114
12	18	A	Fulham	L 0-1	0-1	4		20,776
13	21	H	Leeds U	D 1-1	0-0	5	Martin 59	26,565
14	25	A	Sheffield W	D 0-0	0-0	6		20,898
15	31	H	Bolton W	W 2-1	1-0	3	Jerome 2 12, 61	26,070
16	Nov 4	A	Middlesbrough	L 0-4	0-2	7		16,468
17	8	A	Nottingham F	L 1-2	1-0	10	Howson 16	24,783
18	22	H	Brighton & HA	D 3-3	1-1	10	Howson 38, Martin 49, Hooper 85	26,379
19	29	H	Reading	L 1-2	1-2	11	Hooper 10	26,002
20	Dec 6	A	Wigan Ath	W 1-0	1-0	8	Howson 5	11,475
21	13	H	Huddersfield T	W 5-0	0-0	7	Johnson 2 46, 51, Redmond 48, Jerome 69, Grabban 77	25,595
22	20	A	Derby Co	D 2-2	0-1	7	Jerome 51, Whittaker 89	27,974
23	26	H	Millwall	W 6-1	2-0	7	Whittaker 13, Jerome 18, Johnson 2 54, 61, Hooper 2 69, 90	26,714
24	28	A	Reading	L 1-2	0-2	7	Johnson 71	19,430
25	Jan 10	A	Bournemouth	W 2-1	1-1	7	Hooper 36, Jerome 80	11,318
26	17	H	Cardiff C	W 3-2	3-0	7	Hooper 15, Lafferty 25, Jerome 45	25,995
27	24	H	Brentford	L 1-2	1-1	8	Redmond 27	26,148
28	31	A	Birmingham C	D 0-0	0-0	8		17,835
29	Feb 7	H	Blackpool	W 4-0	2-0	7	Hooper 3 (1 pen) 12, 24, 56 (p), Redmond 90	26,017
30	10	A	Charlton Ath	W 3-2	2-0	7	Howson 14, Grabban 43, Jerome 83	15,094
31	14	H	Wolverhampton W	W 2-0	1-0	6	Johnson 28, Grabban 67	26,322
32	21	A	Watford	W 3-0	0-0	5	Grabban 2 (1 pen) 65 (p), 85, Jerome 70	18,602
33	24	A	Blackburn R	W 2-1	0-1	5	Jerome 65, Johnson 84	13,530
34	Mar 1	H	Ipswich T	W 2-0	1-0	3	Johnson 24, Grabban 62	27,005
35	4	H	Wigan Ath	L 0-1	0-1	5		26,208
36	7	A	Millwall	W 4-1	2-0	5	Howson 2 38, 60, Hooper (pen) 45, Hoolahan 57	11,116
37	14	H	Derby Co	D 1-1	1-0	5	Jerome 31	26,766
38	17	H	Huddersfield T	D 2-2	0-0	4	Hoolahan 67, Loza 90	11,879
39	21	H	Nottingham F	W 3-1	1-0	4	Howson 45, Jerome 56, Hoolahan (pen) 59	26,976
40	Apr 3	A	Brighton & HA	W 1-0	0-0	3	Johnson 62	28,890
41	6	H	Sheffield W	W 2-0	0-0	2	Johnson 2 33, 45	26,993
42	11	A	Bolton W	W 2-1	1-1	2	Dorrans 9, Hooper 90	16,027
43	14	A	Leeds U	W 2-0	0-0	2	Howson 57, Dorrans 90	21,471
44	17	H	Middlesbrough	L 0-1	0-1	4		26,993
45	25	A	Rotherham U	D 1-1	0-0	4	Hooper 59	11,498
46	May 2	H	Fulham	W 4-2	2-0	3	Johnson 2 36, 90, Redmond 39, Dorrans 81	26,662

Final League Position: 3

GOALSCORERS

League (88): Jerome 18, Johnson 15, Grabban 12 (1 pen), Hooper 12 (2 pens), Howson 8, Hoolahan 4 (1 pen), Redmond 4, Dorrans 3, Martin 2, Tettey 2, Whittaker 2, Lafferty 1, Loza 1, Josh Murphy 1, Olsson 1, Turner 1, own goal 1.
FA Cup (0).
Capital One Cup (3): Josh Murphy 2, Jerome 1.
Championship Play-Offs (6): Jerome 2, Redmond 2, Hoolahan 1 (1 pen), Howson 1.

Ruddy J 46	Whittaker S 37	Martin R 45	Turner M 22 + 1	Olsson M 42	Johnson B 40 + 1	Bennett E 3 + 6	Surman A 1	Hoolahan W 27 + 9	Grabban L 23 + 12	Redmond N 33 + 10	Garrido J 3 + 4	Tettey A 34 + 2	Lafferty K 11 + 7	O'Neil G 10 + 11	Fer L — + 1	Bennett R 3 + 4	Murphy Josh 1 + 12	Jerome C 32 + 9	Hooiveld J 6	Odjidja-Ofoa V 1 + 4	Howson J 32 + 2	Loza J — + 2	Hooper G 16 + 14	Cuellar C 8	McGrandles C — + 1	Bassong S 18	Andreu T — + 6	Dorrans G 12 + 3	Morris C — + 1	Match No.
1	2³	3	4	5⁵	6	7	8¹	9²	10	11	12	13	14																	1
1	2	3	4		7	13		10¹	11	8	5	6²	9³	12	14															2
1	2	3	4		7	13		9	11	8¹	5²	6	10³					12	14											3
1	5	2	4		7	13		9¹	11	10	12	6	8³	14		3²														4
1	2	3	4		7			9	11	10¹	5	6	8²					12	13											5
1	2	3	5		7			9¹	11	10³	14	6	8³	13				12			4									6
1	2	5	3		7	14		9¹	10³	6²	8	12		11							4	13								7
1	2	3	5	8				9¹	10²	6		7	13					12	11	4										8
1	2	3	5		7			9¹	10³	8²	6²	14						12	11³	4	13									9
1	2	3	4	5	7			9¹	10³	8	6²							13	11	12	14									10
1	2	3	5		7			9¹	10	8		12						13	11	4²	6									11
1	2	3	4	5	7			9²	10¹	8		6						12	11		13									12
1	2	3	4	5				14	8		6	10¹						9³	11²	13	7		12							13
1	2	3	4	5	8²			10	13		6		12					11		9¹	7									14
1	2	3	4	5	13			12	8		7	10	6²					11¹		9										15
1	2	3	4	5				14	8		7²	10¹	6					13	11³		9	12								16
1		2	4	5	8			10			6	12	7					11¹		9		3								17
1	2	3	5	8⁸				10¹	7		6	13	14					11²	4³	9	12									18
1	2	3	4	5¹				13	8		7³	9²	14					12	10		6	11								19
1	2	3	5	8				6	13	7		12	10¹					9	11²	4										20
1	2	3	5	8				13	14	12		6	7²					10¹	9	11³	4									21
1	2	3	5	8				13	14	12		6¹	7³					10	9	11²	4									22
1	2	3	5	8²				13	12	7		6³						10¹	9	11	4	14								23
1	2	3	5	8				12	14	13		6³	7¹	4				10²	9	11										24
1	2²	3	4	5	8			7¹	6	14	13	12³		11				9⁸	10											25
1	2	3	5	8				12	14	7		9¹	6					13	10²	11³	4									26
1	6¹	2	4	5	7	12		13	14	8		10²		11				9³	3											27
1	2	3		5	7	10²		9¹	11³	8		13	12					14			4									28
1	2	3	12	5	7			9¹	10³	8		14						6	11		4²	13								29
1	2	3	5	8				12	10	7²	6							13		9	11¹	4								30
1	2	3	5³	8				10	7²	14	6							13		9	11¹	4	12							31
1	2	3	5	8				9¹	10³	13	6							11²	7	14	4	12								32
1	2	3	5	7				10²	11	8¹	13							12	9		4	14	6²							33
1	2	3	5	7				10²	11	8¹	6							12³	9	14	4	13								34
1	2	3	5	8				12	6³									10	7	11²	4	14	9¹	13						35
1	2	3	5	8				7²	12			13						10	11³	9	4	14	6¹							36
1	2	3	5	9				10	7									11	6	12	4	8¹								37
1	2	3	5	8⁹				12	7			13						10	9² 14	11¹	4	13	6							38
1	2	3	5	10²				9¹	12		7	13						11	8			4	6							39
1	2	3	5	10				9²	12	6								11¹	8	13		4	8²							40
1	2	3	5	9¹				10²	12	7								11	14 6	13		4	8²							41
1	2¹	3	5					10³ 12	8²	6			14					11	9	13		4	7							42
1	2	3	5		12			10²	8¹	6								11	9	13		4	7							43
1	2	3	5	9¹				10² 12	13	7								11	6	14		4	8³							44
1		2	5	10				9²	11⁸	8¹					3			13	7	12		4	6							45
1		3	5	10	2			9²		8			6	14				12	7³	11		4¹	13							46

FA Cup
Third Round — Preston NE (a) 0-2

Capital One Cup
Second Round — Crawley T (h) 3-1
Third Round — Shrewsbury T (a) 0-1

Championship Play-Offs
Semi-Finals 1st leg — Ipswich T (a) 1-1
Semi-Finals 2nd leg — Ipswich T (h) 3-1
Final — Middlesbrough Wembley 2-0

NOTTINGHAM FOREST

FOUNDATION

One of the oldest football clubs in the world, Nottingham Forest was formed at a meeting in the Clinton Arms in 1865. Known originally as the Forest Football Club, the game which first drew the founders together was 'shinney', a form of hockey. When they determined to change to football in 1865, one of their first moves was to buy a set of red caps to wear on the field.

The City Ground, Pavilion Road, Nottingham NG2 5FJ.
Telephone: (0115) 982 4444.
Fax: (0115) 982 4455.
Ticket Office: (0115) 982 4388
Website: www.nottinghamforest.co.uk
Email: info@nottinghamforest.co.uk
Ground Capacity: 30,445.
Record Attendance: 49,946 v Manchester U, Division 1, 28 October 1967.
Pitch Measurements: 102.5m × 67.5m (112yd × 74yd)
Chairman: Fawaz Mubarak Al-Hasawi.
Manager: Dougie Freedman.
Assistant Manager: Lennie Lawrence.
Physio: Andrew Balderston.
Colours: Red shirt with white trim, white shorts with red trim, red socks with white trim.
Year Formed: 1865.
Turned Professional: 1889.
Previous Name: Forest Football Club.
Club Nickname: 'The Reds'.
Grounds: 1865, Forest Racecourse; 1879, The Meadows; 1880, Trent Bridge Cricket Ground; 1882, Parkside, Lenton; 1885, Gregory, Lenton; 1890, Town Ground; 1898, City Ground.

HONOURS

Football League – Division 1:
Champions 1977–78, 1997–98;
Runners-up 1966–67, 1978–79, 1993–94; **FL 1:** *Runners-up* 2007–08;
Division 2: *Champions* 1906–07, 1921–22; *Runners-up* 1956–57;
Division 3 (S): *Champions* 1950–51.
FA Cup: *Winners* 1898, 1959; *Runners-up* 1991.
Football League Cup: *Winners* 1978, 1979, 1989, 1990; *Runners-up* 1980, 1992.
Anglo-Scottish Cup: *Winners* 1977.
Simod Cup: *Winners* 1989.
Zenith Data Systems Cup: *Winners*: 1992.
European Competitions
European Cup: 1978–79 (*winners*), 1979–80 (*winners*), 1980–81.
European Fairs Cup: 1961–62, 1967–68. **UEFA Cup:** 1983–84, 1984–85, 1995–96. **Super Cup:** 1979 (*winners*), 1980.
World Club Championship: 1980.

First Football League Game: 3 September 1892, Division 1, v Everton (a) D 2–2 – Brown; Earp, Scott; Hamilton, Albert Smith, McCracken; McCallum, 'Tich' Smith, Higgins (2), Pike, McInnes.

Record League Victory: 12–0 v Leicester Fosse, Division 1, 12 April 1909 – Iremonger; Dudley, Maltby; Hughes (1), Needham, Armstrong; Hooper (3), Marrison, West (3), Morris (2), Spouncer (3 incl. 1p).

Record Cup Victory: 14–0 v Clapton (away), FA Cup 1st rd, 17 January 1891 – Brown; Earp, Scott; Albert Smith, Russell, Jeacock; McCallum (2), 'Tich' Smith (1), Higgins (5), Lindley (4), Shaw (2).

Record Defeat: 1–9 v Blackburn R, Division 2, 10 April 1937.

Most League Points (2 for a win): 70, Division 3 (S), 1950–51.

Most League Points (3 for a win): 94, Division 1, 1997–98.

sky SPORTS FACT FILE

Goalkeeper Bill Fiske joined Nottingham Forest from Blackpool in June 1914 but was called up as an Army reservist before he could make his debut. He played a handful of first-team games later that season and survived for most of the war, but was killed in action on 27 May 1918.

Most League Goals: 110, Division 3 (S), 1950–51.

Highest League Scorer in Season: Wally Ardron, 36, Division 3 (S), 1950–51.

Most League Goals in Total Aggregate: Grenville Morris, 199, 1898–1913.

Most League Goals in One Match: 4, Enoch West v Sunderland, Division 1, 9 November 1907; 4, Tommy Gibson v Burnley, Division 2, 25 January 1913; 4, Tom Peacock v Port Vale, Division 2, 23 December 1933; 4, Tom Peacock v Barnsley, Division 2, 9 November 1935; 4, Tom Peacock v Port Vale, Division 2, 23 November 1935; 4, Tom Peacock v Doncaster R, Division 2, 26 December 1935; 4, Tommy Capel v Gillingham, Division 3 (S), 18 November 1950; 4, Wally Ardron v Hull C, Division 2, 26 December 1952; 4, Tommy Wilson v Barnsley, Division 2, 9 February 1957; 4, Peter Withe v Ipswich T, Division 1, 4 October 1977; 4, Marlon Harewood v Stoke C, Division 1, 22 February 2003; Gareth McCleary v Leeds U, FL C, 20 March 2012.

Most Capped Player: Stuart Pearce, 76 (78), England.

Most League Appearances: Bob McKinlay, 614, 1951–70.

Youngest League Player: Craig Westcarr, 16 years 257 days v Burnley, 13 October 2001.

Record Transfer Fee Received: £8,500,000 from Liverpool for Stan Collymore, June 1995.

Record Transfer Fee Paid: £5,500,000 to Peterborough U for Britt Assombalonga, August 2014.

Football League Record: 1892 Elected to Division 1; 1906–07 Division 2; 1907–11 Division 1; 1911–22 Division 2; 1922–25 Division 1; 1925–49 Division 2; 1949–51 Division 3 (S); 1951–57 Division 2; 1957–72 Division 1; 1972–77 Division 2; 1977–92 Division 1; 1992–93 FA Premier League; 1993–94 Division 1; 1994–97 FA Premier League; 1997–98 Division 1; 1998–99 FA Premier League; 1999–2004 Division 1; 2004–05 FL C; 2005–08 FL 1; 2008– FL C.

MANAGERS

Harry Radford 1889–97
  (Secretary-Manager)
Harry Haslam 1897–1909
  (Secretary-Manager)
Fred Earp 1909–12
Bob Masters 1912–25
John Baynes 1925–29
Stan Hardy 1930–31
Noel Watson 1931–36
Harold Wightman 1936–39
Billy Walker 1939–60
Andy Beattie 1960–63
Johnny Carey 1963–68
Matt Gillies 1969–72
Dave Mackay 1972
Allan Brown 1973–75
Brian Clough 1975–93
Frank Clark 1993–96
Stuart Pearce 1996–97
Dave Bassett 1997–99
  (previously General Manager)
Ron Atkinson 1999
David Platt 1999–2001
Paul Hart 2001–04
Joe Kinnear 2004
Gary Megson 2005–06
Colin Calderwood 2006–08
Billy Davies 2009–11
Steve McClaren 2011
Steve Cotterill 2011–12
Sean O'Driscoll 2012
Alex McLeish 2012–13
Billy Davies 2013–14
Stuart Pearce 2014–15
Dougie Freedman February 2015–

LATEST SEQUENCES

Longest Sequence of League Wins: 7, 9.5.1979 – 1.9.1979.

Longest Sequence of League Defeats: 14, 21.3.1913 – 27.9.1913.

Longest Sequence of League Draws: 7, 29.4.1978 – 2.9.1978.

Longest Sequence of Unbeaten League Matches: 42, 26.11.1977 – 25.11.1978.

Longest Sequence Without a League Win: 19, 8.9.1998 – 16.1.1999.

Successive Scoring Runs: 22 from 28.3.1931.

Successive Non-scoring Runs: 7 from 26.11.2011.

TEN YEAR LEAGUE RECORD

		P	W	D	L	F	A	Pts	Pos
2005-06	FL 1	46	19	12	15	67	52	69	7
2006-07	FL 1	46	23	13	10	65	41	82	4
2007-08	FL 1	46	22	16	8	64	32	82	2
2008-09	FL C	46	13	14	19	50	65	53	19
2009-10	FL C	46	22	13	11	65	40	79	3
2010-11	FL C	46	20	15	11	69	50	75	6
2011-12	FL C	46	14	8	24	48	63	50	19
2012-13	FL C	46	17	16	13	63	59	67	8
2013-14	FL C	46	16	17	13	67	64	65	11
2014-15	FL C	46	15	14	17	71	69	59	14

DID YOU KNOW ❓

Nottingham Forest were the last Football League club to change from being a members' club run by a committee to becoming a limited company. Nottingham Forest Football Club Limited was incorporated on 20 April 1982.

NOTTINGHAM FOREST – FL CHAMPIONSHIP 2014–15 LEAGUE RECORD

Match No.	Date	Venue	Opponents	Result	H/T Score	Lg Pos.	Goalscorers	Attendance
1	Aug 9	H	Blackpool	W 2-0	2-0	3	Antonio [25], Burke, C [30]	28,028
2	16	A	Bolton W	D 2-2	2-2	3	Assombalonga 2 (1 pen) [27, 35 (p)]	15,753
3	19	A	Bournemouth	W 2-1	0-0	1	Assombalonga [67], Fryatt [72]	10,768
4	23	H	Reading	W 4-0	1-0	1	Antonio 2 [17, 47], Fryatt [53], Assombalonga [64]	22,795
5	30	A	Sheffield W	W 1-0	1-0	1	Lansbury [37]	20,656
6	Sept 14	H	Derby Co	D 1-1	0-0	1	Assombalonga [72]	30,227
7	17	H	Fulham	W 5-3	2-1	1	Assombalonga 3 (1 pen) [9, 21 (p), 79], Antonio [77], Paterson [89]	22,572
8	20	A	Millwall	D 0-0	0-0	1		12,038
9	27	H	Brighton & HA	D 0-0	0-0	2		23,811
10	30	A	Wigan Ath	D 0-0	0-0	2		14,078
11	Oct 5	H	Ipswich T	D 2-2	0-1	2	Tesche [63], Antonio [90]	24,354
12	18	A	Cardiff C	L 1-2	0-2	5	Assombalonga [89]	21,263
13	21	A	Watford	D 2-2	1-1	6	Antonio 2 [31, 67]	16,095
14	25	H	Blackburn R	L 1-3	1-0	7	Fryatt [37]	27,345
15	Nov 1	A	Huddersfield T	L 0-3	0-2	10		15,317
16	5	H	Brentford	L 1-3	0-2	11	Antonio [82]	21,072
17	8	H	Norwich C	W 2-1	0-1	11	Assombalonga [85], Antonio [90]	24,783
18	22	A	Wolverhampton W	W 3-0	0-0	8	Assombalonga [65], Fryatt [68], Lansbury [83]	25,513
19	29	A	Birmingham C	L 1-2	0-1	9	Assombalonga [84]	18,595
20	Dec 6	H	Charlton Ath	D 1-1	0-1	110	Tesche [59]	22,297
21	13	A	Rotherham U	D 0-0	0-0	9		11,228
22	20	H	Leeds U	D 1-1	1-0	9	Fryatt [45]	22,664
23	26	A	Middlesbrough	L 0-3	0-0	10		32,277
24	28	H	Birmingham C	L 1-3	0-3	10	Assombalonga [90]	26,212
25	Jan 10	H	Sheffield W	L 0-2	0-1	13		22,209
26	17	A	Derby Co	W 2-1	0-1	12	Assombalonga [75], Osborn [90]	32,705
27	21	A	Fulham	L 2-3	1-3	12	Lansbury 2 [45, 62]	15,512
28	31	H	Millwall	L 0-1	0-0	12		23,018
29	Feb 7	A	Brighton & HA	W 3-2	1-1	12	Collins [44], Lansbury [63], Osborn [86]	26,267
30	11	H	Wigan Ath	W 3-0	1-0	10	Assombalonga [33], Burke, C [50], Lansbury [61]	19,619
31	14	A	Blackpool	D 4-4	0-1	10	Blackstock [68], Gardner [70], Lansbury (pen) [77], Burke, C [90]	11,712
32	21	H	Bolton W	W 4-1	2-1	9	Burke, C 2 [8, 68], Antonio [17], Lansbury (pen) [65]	22,441
33	25	H	Bournemouth	W 2-1	2-1	9	Lascelles [21], Lansbury [44]	20,637
34	28	A	Reading	W 3-0	0-0	9	Osborn [56], Fryatt [70], Gardner [80]	18,586
35	Mar 3	A	Charlton Ath	L 1-2	1-2	9	Antonio [14]	14,937
36	7	H	Middlesbrough	W 2-1	1-1	9	Gardner [34], Blackstock [65]	24,200
37	14	A	Leeds U	D 0-0	0-0	9		30,722
38	18	H	Rotherham U	W 2-0	0-0	9	Blackstock [43], Antonio [45]	20,569
39	21	A	Norwich C	L 1-3	0-1	9	Burke, C [76]	26,976
40	Apr 3	H	Wolverhampton W	L 1-2	0-0	9	Blackstock [90]	27,185
41	6	A	Brentford	D 2-2	0-0	9	Walker [61], Kane [77]	11,499
42	11	H	Huddersfield T	L 0-1	0-1	9		21,572
43	15	A	Watford	L 1-3	0-2	10	Gardner [72]	20,723
44	18	A	Blackburn R	D 3-3	2-2	11	Antonio 2 [7, 88], Lansbury [45]	13,876
45	25	A	Ipswich T	L 1-2	0-1	12	Berra (og) [53]	25,199
46	May 2	H	Cardiff C	L 1-2	0-2	14	Blackstock [90]	21,988

Final League Position: 14

GOALSCORERS

League (71): Assombalonga 15 (2 pens), Antonio 14, Lansbury 10 (2 pens), Burke, C 6, Fryatt 6, Blackstock 5, Gardner 4, Osborn 3, Tesche 2, Collins 1, Kane 1, Lascelles 1, Paterson 1, Walker 1, own goal 1.
FA Cup (0).
Capital One Cup (4): Antonio 1, Grant 1, Lansbury 1, own goal 1.

Darlow K 42	Hunt J 15 + 2	Mancienne M 34 + 2	Fox D 25 + 2	Harding D 6 + 2	Burke C 34 + 7	Cohen C 6	Reid A 6	Antonio M 46	Fryatt M 17 + 8	Assombalonga B 27 + 2	McLaughlin S 1 + 5	Osborn B 27 + 10	Lichaj E 37 + 5	Hobbs J 17	Veldwijk L — + 11	Paterson J 4 + 17	Lansbury H 36 + 3	Tesche R 18 + 4	Lascelles J 20 + 6	Wilson K 22 + 1	Vaughan D 10 + 3	Grant J — + 1	Ince T 4 + 2	Blackstock D 11 + 8	De Vries D 4	Kane T 7 + 1	Gardner G 16 + 2	Collins D 7 + 1	Burke O — + 2	Barrow M 2 + 2	Walker T — + 1	Akpom C 5 + 2	Match No.
1	2	3	4	5	6³	7¹	8	9¹	10	11	12	13	14																				1
1	2		4	5	6¹	7	8	9¹	10²	11		13	12	3	14																		2
1	12	4	5²		6	7	8³	9¹	10	11	14	13	2	3																			3
1	2	3	4	5¹	6²	7	8	9¹	10	11		13	12		14																		4
1	2	4			6	7	8	9²	14	11			5	3³			10¹	12	13														5
1	2	3			8	6¹	7²	10				13¹	5	4	14		9	12															6
1	2	3	4		8			10		11		7²	5³			13	9	6¹	14	12													7
1	2²	3	12		8			10		11			5			13	9	6¹		4	7												8
1	2	3	5		8			10²		11		7				13	12	9³	6¹		4	14											9
1	2	3			8			10	12	11		7¹	5				9	6	4														10
1	2	3	14	7¹				8	10	11			5²		13		9	6	12	4³													11
1	2²	3	12	7				8	11	10		5³			14		9¹	6		4	13												12
1		3		5	9			11	12	10¹		8	2				7		4	6													13
1	2	3		5	6			9	11¹	10						13	12	7²		4	8												14
1	12	3	5		14			8		11		13	2¹				9	7³	4		6²		10										15
1	2¹	7	5		6³			11		13		9	12			14	8		4²	3		10											16
1	2¹	3	5²					6	10	11		8	13				12	14	7	4		9³											17
1		3	5		6			9³	10²	11¹		7	2				14	8	12	4			13										18
1		3	5³		6²			9	10¹	11ᵇ		7	2				12	8	4			13	14										19
1		3	5					9	11			7	2				10	8¹	12	4			6²	13									20
1		3	5					9		11			2				6	8	7		4		12	10¹									21
1	5³	7¹	4		13			9	10	12			2				14	8	6		3		11²										22
1		3	5		6			9²	10	11¹		8	2		13			7		4ⁿ	12												23
1		3	5¹		12			9	10	11		14	2			13	6³	8²	7	4													24
1				9³				11		10¹		8	5	3	14	13		6	4		7				1	2⁴	12						25
								11¹		10	12	8	5	3		7	9²	13	4						1	2	6						26
								6		11	12	9	5¹	3			8	10	4						1	2	7						27
				6¹				9	12	11	5	8			3		13	7	10²	4						1	2						28
1		5	6		11	12	10²	9	2	3		8¹		13															7	4				29
1		5	6³		10²	12	11¹	9	2	3		13	8						14										7	4				30
1		5	7		10	11³		9¹	2	3⁴		8					12		13										6	4	14			31
1		5	7¹		10⁴	14		9	2			13	12	8			4		11³										6	3				32
1	12	5	7²		10³	13		9	2		14	8		3				11¹											6	4				33
1	6	5	12		7²	11³		9	2			10¹	8				3		14										13	4				34
1		5	7		10	11³		9	2	14		8²					3		12										6¹	4				35
1	6		7		10			12	5			9²					3	4									11¹	2	8	13				36
1	2		6		10			7	5			8					3	4									11		9					37
1	2		7¹		10			9	5			8					3	4									11²		6		12	13		38
1	2		12		10			9¹	5			13	8				3	4									11²		6		7³	14		39
1	2		7³		10²			9¹	5			12	8				3	4									14		6			13	11	40
1	6	5	8²		10			13	2	3		9					4	7									14				12³	11¹	41
1	6	5	7		10¹			13	2	3		8²					4	9³											14		12	11	42
1	6		9		11²			8¹	5	3			13				4ⁿ										2	7			14	12	10³	43
1	12	5³	13		11			2	3			7		4			8		10¹				6						9⁴		14		44
1	5	12	13		11			8⁵	2¹	4		7		3			6		10										14		9³		45
1	5		9³		11¹			14		3		13	6	4			8		10				2	7²							12		46

FA Cup
Third Round — Rochdale — (a) 0-1

Capital One Cup
First Round — Tranmere R — (a) 1-0
Second Round — Huddersfield T — (a) 2-0
Third Round — Tottenham H — (a) 1-3

NOTTS COUNTY

FOUNDATION

According to the official history of Notts County 'the true date of Notts' foundation has to be the meeting at the George Hotel on 7 December 1864'. However, there is documented evidence of continuous play from 1862, when club members played organised matches amongst themselves in The Park in Nottingham. They are the world's oldest professional football club.

Meadow Lane Stadium, Meadow Lane, Nottingham NG2 3HJ.

Telephone: (0115) 952 9000.

Fax: (0115) 955 3994.

Ticket Office: (0115) 955 7210.

Website: www.nottscountyfc.co.uk

Email: office@nottscountyfc.co.uk

Ground Capacity: 20,229.

Record Attendance: 47,310 v York C, FA Cup 6th rd, 12 March 1955.

Pitch Measurements: 103.5m × 64m (113yd × 70yd)

Executive Chairman: Ray Trew.

Chief Executive: Aileen Trew.

Manager: Ricardo Moniz.

Assistant Manager: David Kevan.

Physio: Rebecca Knight.

Colours: Black and white striped shirts, white shorts with black trim, white socks with black trim.

Year Formed: 1862* (*see Foundation*). *Turned Professional:* 1885.

Club Nickname: 'The Magpies'.

Grounds: 1862, The Park; 1864, The Meadows; 1877, Beeston Cricket Ground; 1880, Castle Ground; 1883, Trent Bridge; 1910, Meadow Lane.

First Football League Game: 15 September 1888, Football League, v Everton (a) L 1–2 – Holland; Guttridge, McLean; Brown, Warburton, Shelton; Hodder, Harker, Jardine, Albert Moore (1), Wardle.

Record League Victory: 11–1 v Newport Co, Division 3 (S), 15 January 1949 – Smith; Southwell, Purvis; Gannon, Baxter, Adamson; Houghton (1), Sewell (4), Lawton (4), Pimbley, Johnston (2).

Record Cup Victory: 15–0 v Rotherham T (at Trent Bridge), FA Cup 1st rd, 24 October 1885 – Sherwin; Snook, Henry Thomas Moore; Dobson (1), Emmett (1), Chapman; Gunn (1), Albert Moore (2), Jackson (3), Daft (2), Cursham (4), (1 og).

Record Defeat: 1–9 v Blackburn R, Division 1, 16 November 1889. 1–9 v Aston Villa, Division 1, 29 September 1888. 1–9 v Portsmouth, Division 2, 9 April 1927.

Most League Points (2 for a win): 69, Division 4, 1970–71.

HONOURS

Football League – Division 1: Best season: 3rd, 1890–91, 1900–01; **Division 2:** *Champions* 1896–97, 1913–14, 1922–23; *Runners-up* 1894–95, 1980–81; **Division 3 (S):** *Champions* 1930–31, 1949–50; *Runners-up* 1936–37; **Division 3:** *Champions* 1997–98; *Runners-up* 1972–73; **Division 4:** *Champions* 1970–71; *Runners-up* 1959–60; **FL 2:** *Champions* 2009–10.

FA Cup: *Winners* 1894; *Runners-up* 1891.

Football League Cup: Best season: 5th rd, 1964, 1973, 1976.

Anglo-Italian Cup: *Winners* 1995; *Runners-up* 1994.

sky SPORTS FACT FILE

Although a total of 17 Notts County players have been capped for England only two have been honoured since the end of the First World War. Defender Billy Ashurst won 5 caps between 1923 and 1925 while Tommy Lawton was capped on four occasions during his stay at Meadow Lane between 1947 and 1948.

Most League Points (3 for a win): 99, Division 3, 1997–98.

Most League Goals: 107, Division 4, 1959–60.

Highest League Scorer in Season: Tom Keetley, 39, Division 3 (S), 1930–31.

Most League Goals in Total Aggregate: Les Bradd, 125, 1967–78.

Most League Goals in One Match: 5, Robert Jardine v Burnley, Division 1, 27 October 1888; 5, Daniel Bruce v Port Vale, Division 2, 26 February 1895; 5, Bertie Mills v Barnsley, Division 2, 19 November 1927.

Most Capped Player: Kevin Wilson, 15 (42), Northern Ireland.

Most League Appearances: Albert Iremonger, 564, 1904–26.

Youngest League Player: Tony Bircumshaw, 16 years 54 days v Brentford, 3 April 1961.

Record Transfer Fee Received: £2,500,000 from Derby Co for Craig Short, September 1992.

Record Transfer Fee Paid: £800,000 to Manchester C for Kasper Schmeichel, July 2009.

Football League Record: 1888 Founder Member of the Football League; 1893–97 Division 2; 1897–1913 Division 1; 1913–14 Division 2; 1914–20 Division 1; 1920–23 Division 2; 1923–26 Division 1; 1926–30 Division 2; 1930–31 Division 3 (S); 1931–35 Division 2; 1935–50 Division 3 (S); 1950–58 Division 2; 1958–59 Division 3; 1959–60 Division 4; 1960–64 Division 3; 1964–71 Division 4; 1971–73 Division 3; 1973–81 Division 2; 1981–84 Division 1; 1984–85 Division 2; 1985–90 Division 3; 1990–91 Division 2; 1991–95 Division 1; 1995–97 Division 2; 1997–98 Division 3; 1998–2004 Division 2; 2004–10 FL 2; 2010–15 FL 1; 2015– FL 2.

LATEST SEQUENCES

Longest Sequence of League Wins: 10, 3.12.1997 – 31.1.1998.

Longest Sequence of League Defeats: 9, 15.3.2011 – 16.4.2011.

Longest Sequence of League Draws: 6, 16.8.2008 – 20.9.2008.

Longest Sequence of Unbeaten League Matches: 19, 26.4.1930 – 6.12.1930.

Longest Sequence Without a League Win: 20, 3.12.1996 – 31.3.1997.

Successive Scoring Runs: 35 from 10.10.1959.

Successive Non-scoring Runs: 5 from 15.3.2011.

MANAGERS

Edwin Browne 1883–93, **Tom Featherstone** 1893, **Tom Harris** 1893–1913, **Albert Fisher** 1913–27, **Horace Henshall** 1927–34, **Charlie Jones** 1934, **David Pratt** 1935, **Percy Smith** 1935–36, **Jimmy McMullan** 1936–37, **Harry Parkes** 1938–39, **Tony Towers** 1939–42, **Frank Womack** 1942–43, **Major Frank Buckley** 1944–46, **Arthur Stollery** 1946–49, **Eric Houghton** 1949–53, **George Poyser** 1953–57, **Tommy Lawton** 1957–58, **Frank Hill** 1958–61, **Tim Coleman** 1961–63, **Eddie Lowe** 1963–65, **Tim Coleman** 1965–66, **Jack Burkitt** 1966–67, **Andy Beattie** (*General Manager*) 1967, **Billy Gray** 1967–68, **Jack Wheeler** (*Caretaker Manager*) 1968–69, **Jimmy Sirrel** 1969–75, **Ron Fenton** 1975–77, **Jimmy Sirrel** 1978–82 (*continued as General Manager to 1984*), **Howard Wilkinson** 1982–83, **Larry Lloyd** 1983–84, **Richie Barker** 1984–85, **Jimmy Sirrel** 1985–87, **John Barnwell** 1987–88, **Neil Warnock** 1989–93, **Mick Walker** 1993–94, **Russell Slade** 1994–95, **Howard Kendall** 1995, **Colin Murphy** 1995–96 (*General Manager*), **Steve Thompson** 1995–96, **Sam Allardyce** 1997–99, **Gary Brazil** 1999–2000, **Jocky Scott** 2000–01, **Gary Brazil** 2001–02, **Billy Dearden** 2002–04, **Gary Mills** 2004, **Ian Richardson** 2004–05, **Gudjon Thordarson** 2005–06, **Steve Thompson** 2006–07, **Ian McParland** 2007–09, **Hans Backe** 2009, **Sven-Göran Eriksson** 2009–10 (*Director of Football*), **Steve Cotterill** 2010, **Craig Short** 2010, **Paul Ince** 2010–11, **Martin Allen** 2011–12, **Keith Curle** 2012–13, **Chris Kiwomya** 2013, **Shaun Derry** 2013–15 **Ricardo Moniz** April 2015–

TEN YEAR LEAGUE RECORD

		P	W	D	L	F	A	Pts	Pos
2005-06	FL 2	46	12	16	18	48	63	52	21
2006-07	FL 2	46	16	14	16	55	53	62	13
2007-08	FL 2	46	10	18	18	37	53	48	21
2008-09	FL 2	46	11	14	21	49	69	47	19
2009-10	FL 2	46	27	12	7	96	31	93	1
2010-11	FL 1	46	14	8	24	46	60	50	19
2011-12	FL 1	46	21	10	15	75	63	73	7
2012-13	FL 1	46	16	17	13	61	49	65	12
2013-14	FL 1	46	15	5	26	64	77	50	20
2014-15	FL 1	46	12	14	20	45	63	50	21

DID YOU KNOW ?

Goalkeeper Gordon Bradley, who made over 200 appearances for Notts County between 1950 and 1958, was also a professional lawn tennis player. Competing with the likes of the legendary Fred Perry, he reached the semi-finals of the British Professional Championships on at least two occasions.

NOTTS COUNTY – FOOTBALL LEAGUE ONE 2014–15 LEAGUE RECORD

Match No.	Date	Venue	Opponents	Result	H/T Score	Lg Pos.	Goalscorers	Atten-dance
1	Aug 9	A	Preston NE	D 1-1	0-0	12	Cassidy [52]	12,857
2	16	H	Fleetwood T	L 0-1	0-1	18		5051
3	19	H	Colchester U	W 2-1	1-0	16	Murray [6], Noble [71]	3792
4	23	A	Port Vale	W 2-0	1-0	10	Jones [11], Noble [87]	5090
5	31	H	Bristol C	L 1-2	1-0	10	Ismail [13]	5678
6	Sept13	A	Peterborough U	D 0-0	0-0	14		6567
7	16	H	Leyton Orient	D 1-1	1-0	15	Ismail (pen) [25]	4024
8	20	H	Oldham Ath	D 0-0	0-0	16		5109
9	27	A	Chesterfield	D 1-1	1-0	16	Adams [15]	7422
10	30	A	Crewe Alex	W 3-0	1-0	10	Cassidy 2 [44, 62], Harrad [52]	3495
11	Oct 4	H	Gillingham	W 1-0	1-0	8	Harrad [35]	4800
12	18	H	Crawley T	W 5-3	3-0	6	Thompson, G 3 [9, 37, 63], Ismail [18], Jones [80]	6086
13	21	A	Barnsley	W 3-2	1-2	5	Thompson, G [20], Petrasso 2 [62, 71]	8596
14	25	A	Scunthorpe U	W 1-0	0-0	3	Ismail (pen) [89]	4008
15	Nov 1	H	Walsall	L 1-2	1-1	6	Thompson, G [31]	5884
16	15	A	Coventry C	W 1-0	0-0	4	Thompson, G [72]	8116
17	22	H	Yeovil T	L 1-2	0-0	6	Petrasso [63]	7746
18	28	A	Sheffield U	D 1-1	1-0	6	Edwards [31]	19,385
19	Dec 13	H	Swindon T	L 0-3	0-1	7		4753
20	20	A	Rochdale	D 2-2	1-0	7	Edwards [42], Thompson, G [90]	2814
21	26	H	Milton Keynes D	L 0-1	0-1	8		5897
22	28	A	Bradford C	L 0-1	0-1	9		14,518
23	Jan 10	A	Bristol C	L 0-4	0-2	12		12,817
24	17	H	Crewe Alex	W 2-1	1-0	10	Noble (pen) [45], Daniels [86]	4643
25	20	A	Doncaster R	D 0-0	0-0	9		5547
26	24	H	Peterborough U	L 1-2	1-1	10	Thompson, G [41]	5960
27	31	A	Oldham Ath	L 0-3	0-2	13		3493
28	Feb 7	H	Chesterfield	L 0-1	0-0	16		6649
29	10	A	Leyton Orient	W 1-0	1-0	14	Bajner [20]	3534
30	17	H	Sheffield U	L 1-2	1-1	17	Noble [35]	6893
31	21	A	Fleetwood T	L 1-2	1-1	17	Thompson, G [11]	3529
32	28	H	Port Vale	L 0-1	0-1	19		5179
33	Mar 3	A	Colchester U	W 1-0	0-0	18	McCourt [68]	2505
34	7	A	Swindon T	L 0-3	0-0	19		8013
35	14	H	Bradford C	D 1-1	0-1	18	Edwards [75]	5166
36	17	H	Rochdale	L 1-2	1-1	19	Thompson, G [30]	3159
37	21	A	Milton Keynes D	L 1-4	0-0	20	Whitehouse [79]	11,991
38	28	H	Scunthorpe U	D 2-2	1-1	20	Jones [10], Bajner [73]	4990
39	Apr 3	A	Walsall	D 0-0	0-0	21		4353
40	6	H	Coventry C	D 0-0	0-0	22		6706
41	11	A	Yeovil T	D 1-1	0-1	22	Thompson, G [79]	3947
42	14	A	Barnsley	D 1-1	0-1	21	Bajner [90]	4287
43	18	A	Crawley T	L 0-2	0-2	22		2580
44	21	H	Preston NE	L 1-3	0-2	22	Spencer [72]	4769
45	25	H	Doncaster R	W 2-1	1-0	20	Thompson, G [8], Noble [60]	5857
46	May 3	A	Gillingham	L 1-3	0-0	21	Burke [61]	8443

Final League Position: 21

GOALSCORERS

League (45): Thompson, G 12, Noble 5 (1 pen), Ismail 4 (2 pens), Bajner 3, Cassidy 3, Edwards 3, Jones 3, Petrasso 3, Harrad 2, Adams 1, Burke 1, Daniels 1, McCourt 1, Murray 1, Spencer 1, Whitehouse 1.
FA Cup (1): Murray 1.
Capital One Cup (0).
Johnstone's Paint Trophy (5): Murray 2, Cassidy 1, McLaughlin 1, Noble 1.

Carroll R 45	Dumbuya M 27+2	Mullins H 32	Hollis H 41	Adams B 31+3	Murray R 7+13	Wroe N 6+6	Jones G 39+4	Thompson G 36+5	Cassidy J 15+1	Smith A 20+3	Dawson A 1+1	Noble L 30+3	Thompson C 20+11	Balmy J —+1	Campbell-Ryce J 3+1	Ismail Z 10+4	McCourt P 11+1	Keane C 2	Lita L 3+3	Harrad S 4+8	Brown R 3	Haynes D 1+1	Spencer J 8+1	Laing L 10	Cranston J 9	Traore D 2+2	Pilkington K 1	McLaughlin S 13	Petrasso M 5+3	Williams J 8	Edwards M 17+1	McKenzie T 2+2	Hall R 2+2	Whitehouse E 3+4	Bishop C 2+1	Burke G 6+1	Santos A 1+2	Hayhurst W 8+4	Thomas K 2+3	Daniels B 1+2	White H 2+1	Bajner B 8+11	Woolery K 3+2	Newton S 6+2	Match No.
1	2	3	4	5	6	7	8	9	10	11	12																																		1
1	2	3	4	5¹	10	6	7		11			9³	8¹	12	13	14																													2
1	2	3	4		10	9⁴	7		11			8	12			6¹	5¹																												3
1	2	3	4	5¹	11		8		10	7²		9	12			6		13																											4
1	2	3	4		13		7		11	8²		9	14			10	5¹		6²	12																									5
1		4		12			7		11	8		9¹	2			10		6		13			3	5																					6
1		3		12			7¹	13	11	6³		9	2			10		8²					4	5	14																				7
1	2		4		9²		7	13	10			8				6		12		11¹			3	5																				8
1		3	8²		9¹		13	11	7			10	2			6		12					4	5																				9
1	2		4	12	8		7²	10				9				13		11¹					3	5		6																		10
1	2		4	5		7	6	10¹	13			8				12		11²					3			9																		11
1	2³	3		14		7	6					8	12			10¹		11²					4	5		9	13																	12
1	2	4	12			7	11					6				9							3	5¹		10	8																	13
1	2	4	5	12		7	11					6				13		9¹					3			10	8²																	14
1	2		4	5	13	14	7¹	10²				8				6		12								9³	11	3																15
1			3	5	10¹		7	11				8	6					12								9		2	4																16
1			4	5²	14		7¹	10	11³			8	2					13								9	6	3¹	12															17
1	2		4	12			7	10¹	11			8	13					13						5²		9	6¹	3		14														18
1			4	5			7³	10	11¹			8¹	2²					13					3			6	9	12		14														19
1	2	3	5	12		6	10			7¹																14	11³	13	4		9²	8												20
1		3	4	5	10²		13	6	12	7³																8	9		2		14	11¹												21
1	2	3	4	5	14		7	11³	10	8²																	9				6¹	13	12											22
1	5	4	3	2	13		6	8		7²			10														9³	12			11¹	14												23
1	2	3	4	5			7	10³		8⁴	14					6															12		9²	6	11¹	13								24
1	13	4	3	5			7¹	10	8			6																14	9	11⁴					2²	12								25
1		3	4	5	13		12	6	7³			8																14	9	10²	2	11												26
1	2	3	4				6¹					8	7									5							9	12	13			11²	10									27
1	2	7	3	5			12	13				8¹				9⁴	4												6	14			11²	10										28
1	2	3		5			7	6				9	8																4			10	12		11¹									29
1	2	3		5			7²	11				8	6																4			9¹					10	12	13	10				30
1	2³	3		6			8²	11				10	9				13												5³							12	14	7	4					31
1		2	4	5			13	10				8²	7	6		9												3						11¹	12									32
1		2	3	5			9¹	11²				7	8	6		10³		12										4						13	14									33
1		2	3	5			8³	12		14		7⁴	6⁴	10		9		11¹										4																34
1		2	4	5²		14	8	10				6				9		11³										3		7¹					12		13							35
1		2	4	8		14	6	10				7				9¹		11²										3		5³			12			13								36
1		2	3	10²			8	11	7			6³	9					14										13	4¹	12										5					37
	2¹	3	4	14		13	6	9	7²	8													10²	1	11								12			5								38
1	2	4	3			14	8	7		13						9¹							10³					6					11²			12		5					39
1	5	3	4		6³	8	11¹		7²	12						10	14										2					13			9									40
1	2	3	4¹	12			7	11	6				13			9²							10					8					14					5³						41
1	2	3		5			8²	11	6			12				7							10³					4					9¹	14		13								42
1	2	3		5²			7	10	6			14				9¹							11³					4					8	13		12								43
1		5	3				8	10	9³			12	14					11										6	4²		7	2¹			13									44
1		2	4	5			7	6	12			8²	13					10										3			9			11¹										45
1	13	3³	4	5			7	6				8				12		14					10¹					2			9⁴			11										46

FA Cup

First Round	Accrington S	(h)	0-0
Replay	Accrington S	(a)	1-2

Capital One Cup

First Round	Sheffield W	(a)	0-3

Johnstone's Paint Trophy

First Round	Mansfield T	(h)	2-0
Second Round	Scunthorpe U	(a)	2-1
Northern Quarter-Finals	Doncaster R	(a)	1-0
Northern Semi-Finals	Preston NE	(h)	0-1

OLDHAM ATHLETIC

FOUNDATION

It was in 1895 that John Garland, the landlord of the Featherstall and Junction Hotel, decided to form a football club. As Pine Villa they played in the Oldham Junior League. In 1899 the local professional club, Oldham County, went out of existence and one of the liquidators persuaded Pine Villa to take over their ground at Sheepfoot Lane and change their name to Oldham Athletic.

SportsDirect.com Park, Furtherwood Road, Oldham, Lancs OL1 2PB.

Telephone: (0161) 624 4972.

Fax: (0161) 627 5915.

Ticket Office: (0161) 785 5150.

Website: www.oldhamathletic.co.uk

Email: enquiries@oldhamathletic.co.uk

Ground Capacity: 10,904.

Record Attendance: 46,471 v Sheffield W, FA Cup 4th rd, 25 January 1930.

Pitch Measurements: 100m × 68.5m (109.5yd × 75yd)

Chairman: Simon Corney.

Chief Executive: Neil Joy.

Manager: Darren Kelly.

Assistant Manager: Dean Holden.

Physio: Craig Schofield.

Colours: Blue shirts with white trim, white shorts with blue trim, blue socks with white trim.

Year Formed: 1895.

Turned Professional: 1899.

Previous Name: 1895, Pine Villa; 1899, Oldham Athletic.

Club Nickname: 'The Latics'.

Grounds: 1895, Sheepfoot Lane; 1900, Hudson Field; 1906, Sheepfoot Lane; 1907, Boundary Park (renamed SportsDirect.com Park 2014).

First Football League Game: 9 September 1907, Division 2, v Stoke (a) W 3–1 – Hewitson; Hodson, Hamilton; Fay, Walders, Wilson; Ward, Billy Dodds (1), Newton (1), Hancock, Swarbrick (1).

Record League Victory: 11–0 v Southport, Division 4, 26 December 1962 – Bollands; Branagan, Marshall; McCall, Williams, Scott; Ledger (1), Johnstone, Lister (6), Colquhoun (1), Whitaker (3).

Record Cup Victory: 10–1 v Lytham, FA Cup 1st rd, 28 November 1925 – Gray; Wynne, Grundy; Adlam, Heaton, Naylor (1), Douglas, Pynegar (2), Ormston (2), Barnes (3), Watson (2).

HONOURS

Football League – Division 1:
Runners-up 1914–15;
Division 2: *Champions* 1990–91;
Runners-up 1909–10;
Division 3 (N): *Champions* 1952–53;
Division 2: *Champions* 1973–74;
Division 4: *Runners-up* 1962–63.

FA Cup: Best season: semi-final, 1913, 1990, 1994.

Football League Cup:
Runners-up 1990.

sky SPORTS FACT FILE

Oldham Athletic's biggest two League victories were achieved 10 years apart against Chester (11-2, January 1952) and Southport (11-0, December 1962). On both occasions the matches were played on snow-covered pitches and a Latics player hit a double hat-trick, Eric Gemmell netting 7 against Chester and Bert Lister hitting 6 against Southport.

Record Defeat: 4–13 v Tranmere R, Division 3 (N), 26 December 1935.

Most League Points (2 for a win): 62, Division 3, 1973–74.

Most League Points (3 for a win): 88, Division 2, 1990–91.

Most League Goals: 95, Division 4, 1962–63.

Highest League Scorer in Season: Tom Davis, 33, Division 3 (N), 1936–37.

Most League Goals in Total Aggregate: Roger Palmer, 141, 1980–94.

Most League Goals in One Match: 7, Eric Gemmell v Chester, Division 3 (N), 19 January 1952.

Most Capped Player: Gunnar Halle, 24 (64), Norway.

Most League Appearances: Ian Wood, 525, 1966–80.

Youngest League Player: Wayne Harrison, 16 years 347 days v Notts Co, 27 October 1984.

Record Transfer Fee Received: £1,700,000 from Aston Villa for Earl Barrett, February 1992.

Record Transfer Fee Paid: £750,000 to Aston Villa for Ian Olney, June 1992.

Football League Record: 1907 Elected to Division 2; 1910–23 Division 1; 1923–35 Division 2; 1935–53 Division 3 (N); 1953–54 Division 2; 1954–58 Division 3 (N); 1958–63 Division 4; 1963–69 Division 3; 1969–71 Division 4; 1971–74 Division 3; 1974–91 Division 2; 1991–92 Division 1; 1992–94 FA Premier League; 1994–97 Division 1; 1997–2004 Division 2; 2004– FL 1.

LATEST SEQUENCES

Longest Sequence of League Wins: 10, 12.1.1974 – 12.3.1974.

Longest Sequence of League Defeats: 8, 15.12.1934 – 2.2.1935.

Longest Sequence of League Draws: 5, 26.12.1982 – 15.1.1983.

Longest Sequence of Unbeaten League Matches: 20, 1.5.1990 – 10.11.1990.

Longest Sequence Without a League Win: 17, 4.9.1920 – 18.12.1920.

Successive Scoring Runs: 25 from 25.8.1962.

Successive Non-scoring Runs: 6 from 12.2.2011.

MANAGERS

David Ashworth 1906–14
Herbert Bamlett 1914–21
Charlie Roberts 1921–22
David Ashworth 1923–24
Bob Mellor 1924–27
Andy Wilson 1927–32
Bob Mellor 1932–33
Jimmy McMullan 1933–34
Bob Mellor 1934–45
   (continued as Secretary to 1953)
Frank Womack 1945–47
Billy Wootton 1947–50
George Hardwick 1950–56
Ted Goodier 1956–58
Norman Dodgin 1958–60
Danny McLennan 1960
Jack Rowley 1960–63
Les McDowall 1963–65
Gordon Hurst 1965–66
Jimmy McIlroy 1966–68
Jack Rowley 1968–69
Jimmy Frizzell 1970–82
Joe Royle 1982–94
Graeme Sharp 1994–97
Neil Warnock 1997–98
Andy Ritchie 1998–2001
Mick Wadsworth 2001–02
Iain Dowie 2002–03
Brian Talbot 2004–05
Ronnie Moore 2005–06
John Sheridan 2006–09
Joe Royle 2009
Dave Penney 2009–10
Paul Dickov 2010–13
Lee Johnson 2013–15
Dean Holden 2015
Darren Kelly May 2015–

TEN YEAR LEAGUE RECORD

		P	W	D	L	F	A	Pts	Pos
2005-06	FL 1	46	18	11	17	58	60	65	10
2006-07	FL 1	46	21	12	13	69	47	75	6
2007-08	FL 1	46	18	13	15	58	46	67	8
2008-09	FL 1	46	16	17	13	66	65	65	10
2009-10	FL 1	46	13	13	20	39	57	52	16
2010-11	FL 1	46	13	17	16	53	60	56	17
2011-12	FL 1	46	14	12	20	50	66	54	16
2012-13	FL 1	46	14	9	23	46	59	51	19
2013-14	FL 1	46	14	14	18	50	59	56	15
2014-15	FL 1	46	14	15	17	54	67	57	15

DID YOU KNOW ?

George Joynson made 5 appearances as a forward for Oldham Athletic during the period 1912 to 1914, also playing and scoring regularly for the reserves. In July 1914 he was struck down with sunstroke whilst at Blackpool and he passed away in hospital shortly afterwards.

OLDHAM ATHLETIC – FOOTBALL LEAGUE ONE 2014–15 LEAGUE RECORD

Match No.	Date	Venue	Opponents	Result	H/T Score	Lg Pos.	Goalscorers	Attendance
1	Aug 9	A	Colchester U	D 2-2	2-1	10	Forte 2 [18, 40]	4023
2	16	H	Leyton Orient	L 1-3	1-1	19	Forte [16]	3754
3	19	H	Port Vale	D 1-1	0-1	21	Wilson, J [64]	3592
4	23	A	Preston NE	L 0-1	0-1	21		11,678
5	30	A	Doncaster R	W 2-0	1-0	17	Clarke-Harris [4], Forte (pen) [59]	6313
6	Sept 6	H	Fleetwood T	W 1-0	1-0	11	Forte (pen) [45]	4425
7	13	H	Gillingham	D 0-0	0-0	11		3785
8	16	A	Swindon T	D 2-2	1-1	13	Dayton [23], Morgan-Smith [84]	6332
9	20	A	Notts Co	D 0-0	0-0	14		5109
10	27	H	Scunthorpe U	W 3-2	1-2	10	Forte [29], Philliskirk 2 [66, 83]	3837
11	Oct 4	A	Peterborough U	D 2-2	1-1	12	Forte [6], Kusunga [66]	5508
12	11	H	Walsall	W 2-1	1-1	8	Wilkinson [31], Jones [75]	4178
13	18	A	Chesterfield	D 1-1	0-0	10	Forte (pen) [49]	7130
14	21	H	Coventry C	W 4-1	3-1	8	Philliskirk [9], Forte 2 [29, 41], Ibehre [78]	3224
15	25	H	Bradford C	W 2-1	2-1	6	Forte [7], Jones [24]	5832
16	Nov 1	A	Bristol C	L 0-1	0-0	9		12,696
17	15	H	Crawley T	D 1-1	1-1	9	Johnson [7]	3924
18	22	A	Sheffield U	D 1-1	1-0	8	Forte [16]	19,767
19	29	A	Rochdale	W 3-0	1-0	6	Johnson 2 [24, 80], Forte (pen) [72]	7269
20	Dec 13	H	Yeovil T	L 0-4	0-3	8		3706
21	20	A	Milton Keynes D	L 0-7	0-2	10		7998
22	26	H	Crewe Alex	L 1-2	0-0	11	Elokobi [75]	4782
23	Jan 10	A	Doncaster R	D 2-2	1-0	13	Ibehre [23], Elokobi [54]	4181
24	17	A	Fleetwood T	W 2-0	0-0	12	Winchester [51], Jones [64]	4312
25	24	A	Gillingham	L 2-3	2-2	14	Kelly [20], Poleon [23]	4959
26	31	H	Notts Co	W 3-0	2-0	10	Elokobi [30], Morgan-Smith [32], Forte [73]	3493
27	Feb 3	A	Barnsley	L 0-1	0-1	10		9135
28	7	A	Scunthorpe U	W 1-0	0-0	6	Winchester [84]	4125
29	10	H	Swindon T	W 2-1	2-0	5	Jones [10], Wilkinson [11]	3451
30	14	H	Colchester U	L 0-1	0-1	6		5668
31	21	A	Leyton Orient	L 0-3	0-2	9		4423
32	28	H	Preston NE	L 0-4	0-2	13		5935
33	Mar 3	A	Port Vale	W 1-0	1-0	11	Jones [42]	4423
34	7	A	Yeovil T	L 1-2	1-0	15	Winchester [44]	3917
35	14	H	Barnsley	L 1-3	1-2	15	Jones [42]	6344
36	17	A	Milton Keynes D	L 1-3	0-2	16	Turner [80]	2445
37	21	A	Crewe Alex	W 1-0	0-0	13	Wilkinson [74]	4669
38	24	H	Rochdale	W 3-0	1-0	11	Turner 2 [30, 61], Forte [58]	5322
39	28	A	Bradford C	L 0-2	0-0	13		14,010
40	Apr 3	H	Bristol C	D 1-1	0-0	13	Winchester [75]	4577
41	6	A	Crawley T	L 0-2	0-2	13		2520
42	11	H	Sheffield U	D 2-2	2-0	14	Poleon 2 [22, 43]	5072
43	14	A	Coventry C	D 1-1	1-0	14	Philliskirk [13]	7256
44	18	H	Chesterfield	D 0-0	0-0	14		4557
45	25	A	Walsall	L 0-2	0-2	16		4699
46	May 3	H	Peterborough U	D 1-1	1-0	15	Poleon [9]	3943

Final League Position: 15

GOALSCORERS

League (54): Forte 15 (4 pens), Jones 6, Philliskirk 4, Poleon 4, Winchester 4, Elokobi 3, Johnson 3, Turner 3, Wilkinson 3, Ibehre 2, Morgan-Smith 2, Clarke-Harris 1, Dayton 1, Kelly 1, Kusunga 1, Wilson, J 1.
FA Cup (1): Jones 1.
Capital One Cup (0).
Johnstone's Paint Trophy (5): Philliskirk 2, Poleon 2, Bove 1.

Rachubka P 22	Wilson B 33	Kusungu G 12+6	Wilson J 40+1	Mills J 28+2	Winchester C 36+5	Dayton J 5+12	Jones M 45	Kelly L 37	Forte J 32+2	Clarke-Harris J 5	Elokobi G 20+4	Gros W —+1	Philliskirk D 37+6	Brown C 22+2	Dieng T 15+7	Noble D —+2	Morgan-Smith A 3+10	Poleon D 21+14	Wilkinson C 10+7	Turner R 9+5	Ibehre J 8+3	Tidser M 1+4	Johnson D 5+1	Kenny P 3	Mellor D 1+1	Mellis J 2+5	Kean J 11	Murphy R 3+8	Jacobs D —+2	Lockwood A 11+1	Sadler M 7+1	Woodland L 6	Coleman J 10+1	Gerrard A 6	Bove J —+5	Tuohy J —+1	Match No.
1	2	3	4	5	6³	7²	8	9	10¹	11	12	13	14																								1
1		4	5	8³	13	6	9	10	11²	3		12	2	7¹	14																						2
1		4	5	6¹		8	7	9	11	3		10	2		12																					3
1	2		3	5²	8³	12	7	6	10	11	4		9¹						14	13																4
1	2		3	5	6	12	8	7	9¹	11	3		10																							5
1	2	3	5	6			7	8	9¹		4		10				12	11																		6
1	2	4	5	6	9²	8	7			3		10¹				14	11³	12	13																	7
1	9	4	5	3	6¹	7	8³		2		11²	13				12	10	14																		8
1	2		3	5	6¹	12	8	7	9²		4		14				13	10³	11																	9
1	2	12	4	5	6³		7	8	9		3²		13				14	10¹	11																	10
1	2	4	3		6²		13	8		7	9¹		11	5			12	10																		11
1	2		3	5	6¹	14	7	8	13			10		4			11²	9³	12																	12
1	2²	14	3	5	6¹	13	7	8	9			10		4			11³		12																	13
1		2	4	5	14	6²	8³	7	9¹			10		3			12		11	13																14
1		2	3	5	7²	12	8	6	10¹			9		4			13		11																	15
1	2³	4	3	5	14	8²	7	6	10¹			9	13				12		11																	16
1	2		4	5		13	7	6²	10³			9		3			14		11	12	8¹															17
1		2	4	5			7	8	9			10		3			12		11⁴	6¹																18
2	3	4¹	5			8	7	10²		13		11	6³				12			14	9	1														19
5	3²	2	8	12		6			4			10		7¹			13		11	9	1															20
4	3	2	5¹			6		9	12	11	7²		10³				13	14	8	1																21
1	2		3	5	7¹	14	8		10²		4	9³					12			11	6	13														22
1	2		3	5⁴	7²	14	8	6	10¹		4	9		13			11			12																23
1	2³	12	3		7²	14	8	6		4		9	5	13	11	10¹																				24
1	2		4		7¹	13	8	6		3	9²	5	11	10			12																			25
2		3		7²		8	6	12		4	9	5	14	11¹	10³						13	1														26
2		4	14	6		8	7	9		3	10³	5¹	11²	13						12	1															27
2		4	5	9		8³	6	10	3		7²	14	11¹				12	1	13																	28
2		3	5	7²		8	6	10	4		13	14	11³		9¹	1	12																			29
2		3	5	12		8³	6	10	4		9	13	14	7²	1	11¹																				30
2	12	3	5³	6			7	9	4¹	11	13	10	8²	1	14																					31
2³	4²	3			7	6		8	5	9	10	13	1	11¹	12	14																				32
2		3	6¹		8	7	11	10	5	13	9²	12	1		4																					33
2⁴		4	9		8	7	11¹	10³	5	14	6	12	1	13	3²																					34
	4		6¹	7		9		10²	2	11	13	3⁴	5	8																						35
3	4		6	9		10	12	2³	7	11²	14	1	5	8	13																					36
			7	8		10	2	12	11¹	1	3	5	6	1	4																					37
	13		7	6		10	9	2⁵	14	12	11¹	1	4	5	8²	1	3																			38
			7	8		10	9³	2⁵	12	11	13	3	5	6¹	1	4	14																			39
		13	14	7		9	10	2		6	12	11³	3	5	8¹	1	4²																			40
	3	5²	6¹	8	4		2		12	7	9³		14	11	10	1	13																			41
	4	5¹	8	7	6		9²	2		10	11		13	3	12	1																				42
5	14	4	9³	8	7		6	2		13	10¹	11²		12	3		1																			43
2		4	6	8	7		13	10	5	9				11¹		1	3²	12																		44
	4	12	8	7		6	2	9²		10¹	11³		5	14	3	1	13																			45
2¹	3	7³	9	8		10	5	14		6	11²			1	4	12	13																			46

FA Cup

First Round	Leyton Orient	(h)	1-0
Second Round	Doncaster R	(h)	0-1

Capital One Cup

First Round	Middlesbrough	(h)	0-3

Johnstone's Paint Trophy

First Round	Bradford C	(h)	1-0
Second Round	Barnsley	(h)	2-2

(Oldham Ath won 4-2 on penalties)

Northern Quarter-Finals	Preston NE	(h)	2-2

(Preston NE won 10-9 on penalties)

OXFORD UNITED

FOUNDATION

There had been an Oxford United club around the time of World War I but only in the Oxfordshire Thursday League and there is no connection with the modern club which began as Headington in 1893, adding 'United' a year later. Playing first on Quarry Fields and subsequently Wootten's Fields, they owe much to a Dr Hitchings for their early development.

The Kassam Stadium, Grenoble Road, Oxford OX4 4XP.

Telephone: (01865) 337 500.

Fax: (01865) 337 501.

Ticket Office: (01865) 337 533.

Website: www.oufc.co.uk

Email: admin@oufc.co.uk

Ground Capacity: 12,205.

Record Attendance: 22,730 v Preston NE, FA Cup 6th rd, 29 February 1964 (at Manor Ground); 12,243 v Leyton Orient, FL 2, 6 May 2006 (at The Kassam Stadium).

Pitch Measurements: 105m × 65m (115yd × 71yd)

Chairman: Darryl Eales.

Chief Executive: Mark Ashton.

Head Coach: Michael Appleton.

Assistant Head Coach: Mickey Lewis.

Physio: Andrew Procter.

Colours: Yellow shirts with blue trim, blue shorts with yellow trim, blue socks with yellow trim.

Year Formed: 1893.

Turned Professional: 1949.

Previous Names: 1893, Headington; 1894, Headington United; 1960, Oxford United.

Club Nickname: 'The U's'.

Grounds: 1893, Headington Quarry; 1894, Wootten's Fields; 1898, Sandy Lane Ground; 1902, Britannia Field; 1909, Sandy Lane; 1910, Quarry Recreation Ground; 1914, Sandy Lane; 1922, The Paddock Manor Road; 1925, Manor Ground; 2001, The Kassam Stadium.

First Football League Game: 18 August 1962, Division 4, v Barrow (a) L 2–3 – Medlock; Beavon, Quartermain; Ron Atkinson, Kyle, Jones; Knight, Graham Atkinson (1), Houghton (1), Cornwell, Colfar.

Record League Victory: 7–0 v Barrow, Division 4, 19 December 1964 – Fearnley; Beavon, Quartermain; Ron Atkinson (1), Kyle, Jones; Morris, Booth (3), Willey (1), Graham Atkinson (1), Harrington (1).

Record Cup Victory: 9–1 v Dorchester T, FA Cup 1st rd, 11 November 1995 – Whitehead; Wood (2), Mike Ford (1), Smith, Elliott, Gilchrist, Rush (1), Massey (Murphy), Moody (3), Bobby Ford (1), Angel (Beauchamp (1)).

HONOURS

Football League – Division 1:
Best season: 12th, 1997–98;
Division 2: *Champions* 1984–85;
Runners-up 1995–96;
Division 3: *Champions* 1967–68, 1983–84.

FA Cup: Best season: 6th rd, 1964 (shared record for 4th Division club).

Football League Cup: *Winners* 1986.

sky SPORTS FACT FILE

Oxford United, then known as Headington United, marked their first home game as a professional club by defeating Huntley & Palmer's 9-4 in an FA Cup extra preliminary round tie in September 1949 with centre-forward Fred Tapping scoring four goals. It was the club's only victory in their opening seven competitive games as a professional club.

Record Defeat: 0–7 v Sunderland, Division 1, 19 September 1998.

Most League Points (2 for a win): 61, Division 4, 1964–65.

Most League Points (3 for a win): 95, Division 3, 1983–84.

Most League Goals: 91, Division 3, 1983–84.

Highest League Scorer in Season: John Aldridge, 30, Division 2, 1984–85.

Most League Goals in Total Aggregate: Graham Atkinson, 77, 1962–73.

Most League Goals in One Match: 4, Tony Jones v Newport Co, Division 4, 22 September 1962; 4, Arthur Longbottom v Darlington, Division 4, 26 October 1963; 4, Richard Hill v Walsall, Division 2, 26 December 1988; 4, John Durnin v Luton T, 14 November 1992; 4, Tom Craddock v Accrington S, FL 2, 20 October 2011.

Most Capped Player: Jim Magilton, 18 (52), Northern Ireland.

Most League Appearances: John Shuker, 478, 1962–77.

Youngest League Player: Jason Seacole, 16 years 149 days v Mansfield T, 7 September 1976.

Record Transfer Fee Received: £1,600,000 from Leicester C for Matt Elliott, January 1997.

Record Transfer Fee Paid: £475,000 to Aberdeen for Dean Windass, August 1998.

Football League Record: 1962 Elected to Division 4; 1965–68 Division 3; 1968–76 Division 2; 1976–84 Division 3; 1984–85 Division 2; 1985–88 Division 1; 1988–92 Division 2; 1992–94 Division 1; 1994–96 Division 2; 1996–99 Division 1; 1999–2001 Division 2; 2001–04 Division 3; 2004–06 FL 2; 2006–10 Conference; 2010– FL 2.

MANAGERS

Harry Thompson 1949–58
(Player-Manager) 1949-51
Arthur Turner 1959–69
(continued as General Manager to 1972)
Ron Saunders 1969
Gerry Summers 1969–75
Mick Brown 1975–79
Bill Asprey 1979–80
Ian Greaves 1980–82
Jim Smith 1982–85
Maurice Evans 1985–88
Mark Lawrenson 1988
Brian Horton 1988–93
Denis Smith 1993–97
Malcolm Crosby 1997–98
Malcolm Shotton 1998–99
Micky Lewis 1999–2000
Denis Smith 2000
David Kemp 2000–01
Mark Wright 2001
Ian Atkins 2001–04
Graham Rix 2004
Ramon Diaz 2004–05
Brian Talbot 2005–06
Darren Patterson 2006
Jim Smith 2006–07
Darren Patterson 2007–08
Chris Wilder 2008–14
Gary Waddock 2014
Michael Appleton July 2014–

LATEST SEQUENCES

Longest Sequence of League Wins: 6, 13.4.2013 – 17.8.2013.

Longest Sequence of League Defeats: 8, 18.4.2014 – 23.8.2014.

Longest Sequence of League Draws: 5, 7.10.1978 – 28.10.1978.

Longest Sequence of Unbeaten League Matches: 20, 17.3.1984 – 29.9.1984.

Longest Sequence Without a League Win: 27, 14.11.1987 – 27.8.1988.

Successive Scoring Runs: 17 from 10.9.1983.

Successive Non-scoring Runs: 6 from 26.3.1988.

TEN YEAR LEAGUE RECORD

		P	W	D	L	F	A	Pts	Pos
2005-06	FL 2	46	11	16	19	43	57	49	23
2006-07	Conf	46	22	15	9	66	33	81	2
2007-08	Conf P	46	20	11	15	56	48	71	9
2008-09	Conf P	46	24	10	12	72	51	77*	7
2009-10	Conf P	44	25	11	8	64	31	86	3
2010-11	FL 2	46	17	12	17	58	60	63	12
2011-12	FL 2	46	17	17	12	59	48	68	9
2012-13	FL 2	46	19	8	19	60	61	65	9
2013-14	FL 2	46	16	14	16	53	50	62	8
2014-15	FL 2	46	15	16	15	50	49	61	13

*5 pts deducted.

DID YOU KNOW ?

Oxford United won promotion to top flight football in 1984–85 when they finished champions of the old Division Two. Boss Jim Smith won the divisional manager of the year award and six of the U's players were selected in the PFA Division Two team of the season.

OXFORD UNITED – FOOTBALL LEAGUE TWO 2014–15 LEAGUE RECORD

Match No.	Date	Venue	Opponents	Result	H/T Score	Lg Pos.	Goalscorers	Attendance
1	Aug 9	H	Burton Alb	L	0-1	0-1	16		5370
2	16	A	Mansfield T	L	1-2	0-1	19	Hylton (pen) [79]	3042
3	19	A	Morecambe	L	0-1	0-1	21		1615
4	23	H	Portsmouth	L	0-1	0-0	24		6852
5	30	H	Dagenham & R	D	3-3	1-1	23	Jakubiak [3], Hylton 2 (1 pen) [55, 61 (p)]	4391
6	Sept 6	A	Southend U	D	1-1	0-1	23	Hylton (pen) [67]	5315
7	13	A	Exeter C	D	1-1	1-1	22	O'Dowda [15]	3076
8	16	H	Accrington S	W	3-1	2-1	22	Hylton [15], Collins [36], Barnett [71]	4111
9	20	H	Stevenage	D	0-0	0-0	22		4658
10	27	A	Luton T	L	0-2	0-1	23		9101
11	Oct 4	H	Newport Co	W	1-0	1-0	20	Collins [40]	5072
12	11	A	Cambridge U	L	1-5	1-2	23	Hylton [9]	4435
13	18	H	Tranmere R	W	2-0	1-0	20	Barnett [28], Potter [73]	4748
14	21	A	Northampton T	W	3-1	2-1	19	Hylton 2 (1 pen) [25, 27 (p)], Potter [50]	4577
15	25	A	Carlisle U	L	1-2	1-0	19	Hylton [45]	4392
16	Nov 1	H	Wycombe W	L	1-2	1-0	19	Hylton (pen) [37]	7552
17	15	A	York C	W	1-0	1-0	18	Roberts [35]	3363
18	22	H	AFC Wimbledon	D	0-0	0-0	19		5443
19	29	A	Cheltenham T	D	1-1	0-0	19	Barnett [61]	3002
20	Dec 13	H	Bury	W	2-1	0-0	17	Jones (og) [69], Barnett [90]	6912
21	20	A	Hartlepool U	D	1-1	0-0	17	Hylton [65]	4070
22	26	H	Shrewsbury T	L	0-2	0-2	17		7502
23	28	A	Plymouth Arg	W	2-1	0-1	16	Campbell [69], Roberts [83]	11,020
24	Jan 3	H	Cheltenham T	L	1-2	1-2	16	Burns [20]	5360
25	10	A	Dagenham & R	D	0-0	0-0	15		1892
26	17	H	Southend U	L	2-3	2-1	17	O'Dowda [13], Long, S [45]	7207
27	24	H	Exeter C	D	2-2	1-1	16	Hylton [18], Roberts [90]	6791
28	31	A	Stevenage	W	2-0	0-0	15	Mullins [59], O'Dowda [68]	3146
29	Feb 7	H	Luton T	D	1-1	1-1	15	Mullins [43]	7541
30	10	A	Accrington S	L	0-1	0-0	17		1065
31	14	A	Burton Alb	L	0-2	0-1	17		2954
32	21	H	Mansfield T	W	3-0	1-0	17	MacDonald 2 [31, 54], Hylton (pen) [63]	6954
33	28	A	Portsmouth	D	0-0	0-0	17		16,355
34	Mar 3	H	Morecambe	D	1-1	0-1	19	Baldock [87]	6924
35	7	A	Bury	W	1-0	0-0	18	O'Dowda [85]	3645
36	14	H	Plymouth Arg	D	0-0	0-0	17		8057
37	17	H	Hartlepool U	L	0-2	0-1	19		4375
38	21	A	Shrewsbury T	L	0-2	0-1	19		5265
39	28	H	Carlisle U	W	2-1	1-1	16	Hoban [38], Vassell [80]	5515
40	Apr 3	A	Wycombe W	W	3-2	2-0	15	Roofe 2 [11, 60], Rose [22]	6892
41	6	H	York C	D	0-0	0-0	16		9406
42	11	A	AFC Wimbledon	D	0-0	0-0	16		4234
43	14	H	Northampton T	D	1-1	0-1	16	MacDonald [90]	4836
44	18	A	Tranmere R	W	3-0	0-0	15	Roofe 2 [51, 68], Rose [52]	5777
45	25	H	Cambridge U	W	2-0	2-0	14	Roofe [31], Hylton [45]	5954
46	May 2	A	Newport Co	W	1-0	1-0	13	Roofe [30]	4295

Final League Position: 13

GOALSCORERS

League (50): Hylton 14 (6 pens), Roofe 6, Barnett 4, O'Dowda 4, MacDonald 3, Roberts 3, Collins 2, Mullins 2, Potter 2, Rose 2, Baldock 1, Burns 1, Campbell 1, Hoban 1, Jakubiak 1, Long, S 1, Vassell 1, own goal 1.
FA Cup (6): Barnett 2, Roberts 2, Potter 1, Rose 1.
Capital One Cup (3): Hylton 2, Morris 1.
Johnstone's Paint Trophy (0).

Long G 10	Riley J 22	Raynes M 3+1	Wright J 42	Newey T 12	Potter A 9+6	Ruffels J 29+4	Collins M 38+1	Brown J 6+5	Rose D 25+4	Morris C 5+2	Mullins J 42+2	Hylton D 41+3	O'Dowda C 20+19	Hunt D 2+1	Meades J 5+2	Jakubiak A 2+7	Hoskins W 2+2	Hawtin A —+1	Barnett T 11+1	Howard B 7	Humphreys S —+1	Clarke R 31	Whing A 18+3	Roberts J 5+20	Holmes-Dennis T 14	Burns W 6+3	Campbell J 1+2	Dunkley C 7+2	Long S 8+2	Hoban P 15+5	Ashby J 2	Skarz J 18	Brindley R 3	MacDonald A 14+1	Baldock G 12	Roofe K 12+4	Ghanduillet A —+4	Rasulo G —+1	Vassell K 2+4	Match No.
1	2	3³	4	5	6	7	8	9¹	10³	11	12	13	14																											1
1	8	13	4	5	9²	7	10		11	3	14					2³	6¹		12																					2
1	2		4	5	14	7	6	10³	9³	11³	3	8	13						12																					3
1	2		4	5	14	8¹	7	6	9¹	10²	3	11	12						13																					4
1	2		4	5		8¹	7	6		11²	3	9	13				10	12																						5
1	2¹		4	5	14	7		10²	6		3	9	13	12		8	11³																							6
1	8		4	5		7	6	14	13		3	9	10²	2³		12				11¹																				7
1	2		4	5		7	6	12			14	3	8¹	10		13				11³	9²																			8
1	2		4	5		7	6	12				3	8	10						11	9¹																			9
1	2		4	5		7	6³	13	12		3	8²	11	14		10				10	9¹																			10
	2	4		5		13	6	14	7³	12	3	8	10²						11¹	9¹	1																			11
	2	3		5			6¹	8²	7		4	11	10						13		9²	1	12	14																12
	2	3		12	13	7²		9¹			4	6	8³							11		1	10	14	5															13
	2		4	5		9²	13	8		6	3	11¹								10		1	7	12	5															14
	2		4			9¹		8		6²	3	4	11	12						10		1	7	13	5															15
	2		4			6²		8¹		9	3	10	13							11		1	7	12	5															16
	2		4	6		9				8	3	6	12							11¹		1	7	10	5															17
	2		4	6					6		3	9	10	13						12	8¹	1	7	11²	5									4						18
	2		4			6¹	12			8	3	10	9							11		1	7		5															19
	2		4	12			7¹		10		3	9								11		1	6		5	8														20
6	3			7		4			2²	5				13								1	8		9	10	11¹	12												21
2²	4			12		10	7		3	11				5¹								1	8³	14	9	6		13												22
	4			7	9¹				13	10	12											1	6	11	5	8²	14	3	2³											23
	4			7			12		2	11	14	5										1	6¹	10	8²	9³	13	3												24
	4			6					3	11	12	5		13								1	7	10¹	8	9²		2												25
	3			6					2	11	7	14	10²									1	8		9	13		4¹	5³	12										26
	4			8²		6			3	10	9¹		5									1		12		13		2	11	7										27
	5			7		6			4	10¹	9²											1	8	12		13			11		2	3								28
	4			7	8				3	10	9											1		12				13	11		5	2¹	6²							29
	4			7	6				3	8¹	10											1		13				12	11		5	2²	9							30
	3			8					4	7¹	10											1	6²	13				11	9	5			2	12					31
	4			7	8²				3	10³	9											1	14	13				5	11				6¹	2	12				32
	3			7	8				4	10	9¹											1							11	5			6	2	12				33
	4			8	7				3	11³	9²											1	14						10	5			6¹	2	12	13			34
	4			8	7				3	10²	12											1	13						11	5			6²	2	9				35
	4			8	7				3		9²											1	12						11³	5			6¹	2	10	14	13		36
	4			7	8				3	11	13											1	12						10	5			11¹	2	9	13			37
	4			7	8				3	10	13											1	12						10¹	5²			9	2	6³	14			38
	4			8	7			9¹		3	11²	13										1	14						10³	5			2	6			12	9	39
	4			7	8			9		3	11¹	13										1							10	5			2	6²			12	9	40
	4			7	8			9³		3	13	14										1							12	5			6²	2	10		11¹		41
	4		14		8				3	11	13		1									7³							10²	5			6¹	2	9		12		42
	4			7	8²	12			3	11	9³		1										13						2	5			14	6			10¹		43
	4			8	7			9		11¹			1	14								13	3	2	12				5			6²	10³						44
				7	8			9		3²	11³												12					4	2	14	5			6	10¹			13	45
				7	8³			6		10¹	14											13	3					5	4²	12	2			11	9				46

FA Cup

First Round	Grimsby T	(a)	3-1
Second Round	Tranmere R	(h)	2-2
Replay	Tranmere R	(a)	1-2

Capital One Cup

First Round	Bristol C	(a)	2-1
Second Round	WBA	(a)	1-1

(aet; WBA won 7-6 on penalties)

Johnstone's Paint Trophy

First Round	Cheltenham T	(a)	0-2

PETERBOROUGH UNITED

FOUNDATION

The old Peterborough & Fletton club, founded in 1923, was suspended by the FA during season 1932–33 and disbanded. Local enthusiasts determined to carry on and in 1934 a new professional club, Peterborough United, was formed and entered the Midland League the following year. Peterborough's first success came in 1939–40, but from 1955–56 to 1959–60 they won five successive titles. During the 1958–59 season they were undefeated in the Midland League. They reached the third round of the FA Cup, won the Northamptonshire Senior Cup, the Maunsell Cup and were runners-up in the East Anglian Cup.

ABAX Stadium, London Road, Peterborough PE2 8AL.
Telephone: (01733) 563 947. *Fax:* (01733) 344 140.
Ticket Office: (0844) 847 1934.
Website: www.theposh.com
Email: info@theposh.com
Ground Capacity: 15,314.
Record Attendance: 30,096 v Swansea T, FA Cup 5th rd, 20 February 1965.
Pitch Measurements: 102.5m × 64m (112yd × 70yd)
Chairman: Darragh MacAnthony.
Chief Executive: Bob Symns.
Manager: Dave Robertson.
Coach: Grant McCann.
Physio: Jonathan Chatfield.
Colours: Blue shirts with white trim, blue shorts, blue socks with white trim.
Year Formed: 1934.
Turned Professional: 1934.
Club Nickname: 'The Posh'.
Ground: 1934, London Road Stadium (renamed ABAX Stadium 2014).
First Football League Game: 20 August 1960, Division 4, v Wrexham (h) W 3–0 – Walls; Stafford, Walker; Rayner, Rigby, Norris; Hails, Emery (1), Bly (1), Smith, McNamee (1).
Record League Victory: 9–1 v Barnet (a) Division 3, 5 September 1998 – Griemink; Hooper (1), Drury (Farell), Gill, Bodley, Edwards, Davies, Payne, Grazioli (5), Quinn (2) (Rowe), Houghton (Etherington) (1).
Record Cup Victory: 9–1 v Rushden T, FA Cup 1st qual rd, 6 October 1945 – Hilliard; Bryan, Parrott, Warner, Hobbs, Woods, Polhill (1), Fairchild, Laxton (6), Tasker (1), Rodgers (1); 9–1 v Kingstonian, FA Cup 1st rd, 25 November 1992. Match ordered to be replayed by FA. Peterborough won replay 1–0.
Record Defeat: 1–8 v Northampton T, FA Cup 2nd rd (2nd replay), 18 December 1946.

HONOURS

Football League – Division 1:
Best season: 10th, 1992–93;
Division 2: 1991–92 (play-offs);
FL 1: *Runners-up* 2008–09;
FL 2: *Runners-up* 2007–08;
Division 4: *Champions* 1960–61, 1973–74.

FA Cup: Best season: 6th rd, 1965.

Football League Cup: semi-final, 1966.

Johnstone's Paint Trophy:
Winners 2014.

sky SPORTS FACT FILE

In their first season in the Football League, Peterborough won the Fourth Division title, finishing 2 points clear of closest rivals Crystal Palace. The average attendance for matches at London Road of 14,203 has yet to be beaten.

Most League Points (2 for a win): 66, Division 4, 1960–61.

Most League Points (3 for a win): 92, FL 2, 2007–08.

Most League Goals: 134, Division 4, 1960–61.

Highest League Scorer in Season: Terry Bly, 52, Division 4, 1960–61.

Most League Goals in Total Aggregate: Jim Hall, 122, 1967–75.

Most League Goals in One Match: 5, Guiliano Grazioli v Barnet, Division 3, 5 September 1998.

Most Capped Player: Craig Morgan, 19 (23), Wales.

Most League Appearances: Tommy Robson, 482, 1968–81.

Youngest League Player: Matthew Etherington, 15 years 262 days v Brentford, 3 May 1997.

Record Transfer Fee Received: £5,500,000 from Nottingham F for Britt Assombalonga, August 2014.

Record Transfer Fee Paid: £1,250,000 to Watford for Britt Assombalonga, July 2013.

Football League Record: 1960 Elected to Division 4; 1961–68 Division 3, when they were demoted for financial irregularities; 1968–74 Division 4; 1974–79 Division 3; 1979–91 Division 4; 1991–92 Division 3; 1992–94 Division 1; 1994–97 Division 2; 1997–2000 Division 3; 2000–04 Division 2; 2004–05 FL 1; 2005–08 FL 2; 2008–09 FL 1; 2009–10 FL C; 2010–11 FL 1; 2011–13 FL C; 2013– FL 1.

LATEST SEQUENCES

Longest Sequence of League Wins: 9, 1.2.1992 – 14.3.1992.

Longest Sequence of League Defeats: 8, 16.12.2006 – 27.1.2007.

Longest Sequence of League Draws: 8, 18.12.1971 – 12.2.1972.

Longest Sequence of Unbeaten League Matches: 17, 15.1.2008 – 5.4.2008.

Longest Sequence Without a League Win: 17, 23.9.1978 – 30.12.1978.

Successive Scoring Runs: 33 from 20.9.1960.

Successive Non-scoring Runs: 6 from 13.8.2002.

MANAGERS

Jock Porter 1934–36
Fred Taylor 1936–37
Vic Poulter 1937–38
Sam Haden 1938–48
Jack Blood 1948–50
Bob Gurney 1950–52
Jack Fairbrother 1952–54
George Swindin 1954–58
Jimmy Hagan 1958–62
Jack Fairbrother 1962–64
Gordon Clark 1964–67
Norman Rigby 1967–69
Jim Iley 1969–72
Noel Cantwell 1972–77
John Barnwell 1977–78
Billy Hails 1978–79
Peter Morris 1979–82
Martin Wilkinson 1982–83
John Wile 1983–86
Noel Cantwell 1986–88 *(continued as General Manager)*
Mick Jones 1988–89
Mark Lawrenson 1989–90
Dave Booth 1990–91
Chris Turner 1991–92
Lil Fuccillo 1992–93
Chris Turner 1993–94
John Still 1994–95
Mick Halsall 1995–96
Barry Fry 1996–2005
Mark Wright 2005–06
Steve Bleasdale 2006
Keith Alexander 2006–07
Darren Ferguson 2007–09
Mark Cooper 2009–10
Jim Gannon 2010
Gary Johnson 2010–11
Darren Ferguson 2011–15
Dave Robertson March 2015–

TEN YEAR LEAGUE RECORD

		P	W	D	L	F	A	Pts	Pos
2005-06	FL 2	46	17	11	18	57	49	62	9
2006-07	FL 2	46	18	11	17	70	61	65	10
2007-08	FL 2	46	28	8	10	84	43	92	2
2008-09	FL 1	46	26	11	9	78	54	89	2
2009-10	FL C	46	8	10	28	46	80	34	24
2010-11	FL 1	46	23	10	13	106	75	79	4
2011-12	FL C	46	13	11	22	67	77	50	18
2012-13	FL C	46	15	9	22	66	75	54	22
2013-14	FL 1	46	23	5	18	72	58	74	6
2014-15	FL 1	46	18	9	19	53	56	63	9

DID YOU KNOW ?

Winger Jimmy Rooney spent two seasons on the books of Peterborough United and managed just 7 first-team appearances. He later emigrated to Australia and went on to win 57 caps for his adopted country, featuring in all three games in the 1974 World Cup finals.

PETERBOROUGH UNITED – FOOTBALL LEAGUE ONE 2014–15 LEAGUE RECORD

Match No.	Date	Venue	Opponents	Result	H/T Score	Lg Pos.	Goalscorers	Attendance
1	Aug 9	A	Rochdale	W 1-0	0-0	8	Vassell [61]	3613
2	16	H	Milton Keynes D	W 3-2	1-0	1	McEvoy [45], Vassell 2 [81, 85]	7115
3	19	H	Sheffield U	L 1-2	1-1	5	Brisley [34]	6578
4	23	A	Bradford C	W 1-0	0-0	2	Vassell [57]	13,546
5	30	A	Colchester U	W 3-1	2-0	1	Washington [21], Ntlhe [25], Anderson, J [77]	4014
6	Sept 6	H	Port Vale	W 3-1	1-0	1	Maddison [30], Vassell [72], Payne [79]	6024
7	13	H	Notts Co	D 0-0	0-0	2		6567
8	16	A	Gillingham	L 1-2	1-1	2	Taylor [44]	4819
9	20	A	Yeovil T	L 0-1	0-0	3		3970
10	27	H	Fleetwood T	W 1-0	1-0	2	Washington [45]	5698
11	Oct 4	H	Oldham Ath	D 2-2	1-1	3	Bostwick [18], Maddison [51]	5508
12	11	A	Crawley T	W 4-1	2-1	2	Smith [11], Washington 2 [40, 58], Maddison [55]	2832
13	18	H	Barnsley	W 2-1	1-1	2	Washington [45], Maddison [69]	7217
14	21	A	Crewe Alex	L 0-1	0-1	2		3524
15	25	A	Coventry C	L 2-3	2-0	4	Taylor [17], Maddison [28]	8957
16	Nov 1	H	Scunthorpe U	L 1-2	0-1	7	Washington [57]	6275
17	15	A	Walsall	D 0-0	0-0	7		5495
18	22	H	Swindon T	L 1-2	0-1	7	Newell [90]	7182
19	28	H	Bristol C	L 0-3	0-2	9		6804
20	Dec 13	A	Leyton Orient	W 2-1	1-1	9	McLean [9], Oztumer [47]	5546
21	20	H	Preston NE	L 0-1	0-1	8		6803
22	26	A	Chesterfield	L 2-3	0-2	10	Bostwick [62], Maddison [71]	8353
23	28	H	Doncaster R	D 0-0	0-0	10		6895
24	Jan 10	H	Colchester U	L 0-2	0-0	11		5524
25	17	A	Port Vale	L 1-2	1-1	15	Washington [21]	4446
26	24	H	Notts Co	W 2-1	1-1	13	Maddison [13], Burgess [62]	5960
27	31	H	Yeovil T	W 1-0	1-0	11	Beautyman [28]	5146
28	Feb 7	A	Fleetwood T	D 1-1	0-0	10	Newell [64]	3188
29	10	H	Gillingham	L 1-2	0-1	13	Payne [55]	4449
30	14	H	Rochdale	W 2-1	2-1	10	Beautyman [4], Burgess [7]	5163
31	17	A	Bristol C	L 0-2	0-1	10		11,101
32	21	A	Milton Keynes D	L 0-3	0-3	15		11,162
33	28	H	Bradford C	W 2-0	0-0	10	Zakuani [52], Bostwick (pen) [90]	6494
34	Mar 3	A	Sheffield U	W 2-1	0-0	9	Payne [88], Washington [90]	18,604
35	7	H	Leyton Orient	W 1-0	1-0	8	Taylor [25]	6525
36	14	A	Doncaster R	W 2-0	1-0	7	James [16], Washington [88]	11,520
37	17	A	Preston NE	L 0-2	0-1	7		8856
38	21	H	Chesterfield	W 1-0	1-0	6	Bostwick [27]	6612
39	28	H	Coventry C	L 0-1	0-0	8		7325
40	Apr 3	A	Scunthorpe U	L 0-2	0-1	10		4216
41	6	H	Walsall	D 0-0	0-0	10		6711
42	11	A	Swindon T	L 0-1	0-0	11		7126
43	14	A	Crewe Alex	D 1-1	0-1	10	Washington [86]	4338
44	18	A	Barnsley	D 1-1	1-0	11	Washington [16]	8924
45	25	H	Crawley T	W 4-3	1-1	9	Washington 2 [43, 90], Bostwick 2 [51, 87]	6270
46	May 3	A	Oldham Ath	D 1-1	0-1	9	Bostwick [76]	3943

Final League Position: 9

GOALSCORERS

League (53): Washington 13, Bostwick 7 (1 pen), Maddison 7, Vassell 5, Payne 3, Taylor 3, Beautyman 2, Burgess 2, Newell 2, Anderson, J 1, Brisley 1, James 1, McEvoy 1, McLean 1, Ntlhe 1, Oztumer 1, Smith 1, Zakuani 1.
FA Cup (2): Burgess 2.
Capital One Cup (0):
Johnstone's Paint Trophy (2): James 1, Maddison 1.

Alnwick B 41	Bostwick M 37 + 1	Baldwin J 11	Zakuani G 20 + 2	Nthle K 25 + 3	Mendez-Laing N 6 + 8	Anderson J 19 + 5	Payne J 38 + 3	Taylor J 22 + 2	Vassell K 12 + 5	Washington C 31 + 9	McEvoy K 2 + 5	Barnett T — + 4	Ferdinand K 2 + 10	Smith M 40 + 3	Brisley S 11 + 4	Santos R 22 + 2	Burgess C 28 + 2	Newell J 35 + 4	McCann G 2 + 4	Maddison M 23 + 6	James L 21 + 11	Oztumer E 11 + 9	McLean A 10 + 8	Mackail-Smith C 3	Beautyman H 15 + 3	Loach S 5	Norris D 3 + 5	Anderson H 6 + 4	Williams L 1 + 1	Sheehan A 1 + 1	Edwards J 1 + 2	Da Silva Lopes L 2	Match No.
1	2	3	4	5	6^1	7	8	9^3	10^2	11	12	13	14																				1
1	4			5	6	8^4	7	9^1	13	11	10^3	14	12	2	3																		2
1				5^1	6	8	7	9^2	10	11		13	14	2	3		4^1	12															3
1					7^3	8	6		11^2	10		13		5	12	2	4	3	9^1	14													4
1		12	6^4			7	9		10	11				2^3	14	4^2	3^1	5	8	13													5
1	4					7^2	8	6	12	10			13	5		2	3		14	9^1	11^3												6
1	4					7^1	8	6	10	11^2			14	5		2^1	3	12		9	13												7
1	3					8^1	7	6^2	10	14			13	2		5	4	12		9	11^3												8
1	3	4				8	7^2			11	10^1			5		2		6	13	9	12												9
1	3			5^1		14	7	9^3		11			13	2			4	12	8^2	6	10												10
1	2	3				8	7			9^2	14			12	5		4	6^3		11	10^1	13											11
1	2	3				6^1	8	10^2		11	12			5			4	9	13	7^2		14											12
1	3	2				8^2	6	10^3		11	13		14	5			12	4^1	9	7													13
1	4^1	3^4	12			14	7^3	8	10^1	11			13	2		5^2		6	9														14
1	3		2^3			13	6	7	10^2	11^1				5			4	9	8	12	14												15
1	6	4^2				11	13		9		12	14		5		2	3	8	7^1	10^3													16
1	7			5	12	14	8^1	6^3	10	11^2				2		3	4	9		13													17
1	8			5	6^2	12	7^1		10^3		13			2		3	4	9		14	11												18
1	12		3	5		8^2	7^1							2			4	9		6^3	14	10	11	13									19
1	2		4	5		12	7							3	6^4						13	9	10	11	8^1								20
1	2		3^2	5	12	8^1	7			13									9	10	11	6											21
1	2	3				14	7			6^3				5^2			4	8		12	11	9	10^1				7						22
1	3					14	7			13	12			2^3		4	5	6^2		10	9	11^1			8								23
1	3			5	12		7			13				2			4	9^1	10^2	11	6	14			8^1								24
	4			5^1	12		6			11				2		3	8	9	13	10^1	14	7^2				1							25
	2					8				10^2	11^1			5	3		4	9		7^3	13	12	14		6	1							26
	3		14				9			10^2	11^1			2	4		5	6		8^3	12		13		7	1							27
	2			6^3	12					10^2				5	3		4	9		7	11				8	1							28
	3			6			11^2							5	2^1		4	9		7	10	13	12		8	1							29
1	2			12			6	13						5	3		4	9^3		10	8^2	11^1			7		14						30
1	2			14			6	12						5	3^1		4	9^2		10	13	11^2			8		7						31
1	3			5			7	9		14				2^1	13		4			12	11	8^3			10		6^2						32
1	2		3	8			6	9^2		11^3				5		4		7		10^1				12			14	13					33
1	8		3	5			7	6	11^2	12				2		4		9		10^1	13												34
1	8		3	5			7	6^3	14	11				2		4		9^2		12^4	13	10^1											35
1	3		8	5^2			7	6	13	11				2	14	4		9^1		10^3								12					36
1	7^1		3	5			6	9	12	10^0				2		4		8		11								13					37
1	8		4	5			7	6		11				2^1	12	3^4		9		10							13						38
1	8			5			7	6		11^3				2	4^2		3	9^1		13	10							14	12				39
1	8		4^1	5						11^2				2			3			9			12		7^2		13	6	10	14			40
1	3		4	5			7	6^1		13				2			14			9^1	10	11^2			8		12						41
1	4		3	5			7^2			11				2			8			9^1	10	12			13		6						42
1	7		3	4			6^1			10				2				9		11	13	8^3					12	5^2					43
1	7		3	5^4						11^1				2			4			10^2	12		8					6			9	13	44
1	7		3				14			11				2		4^1	13	5^2		10	8							6			12	9^1	45
1	7		3^2				12			10				2	13	4		9		14	8^1							5			11^8	6^3	46

FA Cup

First Round	Carlisle U	(h)	2-1	
Second Round	Colchester U	(a)	0-1	

Capital One Cup

First Round	Portsmouth	(a)	0-1

Johnstone's Paint Trophy

First Round	Leyton Orient	(h)	2-3

PLYMOUTH ARGYLE

FOUNDATION

The club was formed in September 1886 as the Argyle Athletic Club by former public and private school pupils who wanted to continue playing the game. The meeting was held in a room above the Borough Arms (a coffee house), Bedford Street, Plymouth. It was common then to choose a local street/terrace as a club name and Argyle or Argyll was a fashionable name throughout the land due to Queen Victoria's great interest in Scotland.

Home Park, Plymouth, Devon PL2 3DQ.

Telephone: (01752) 562 561.

Fax: (01752) 606 167.

Ticket Office: (0845) 872 3335.

Website: www.pafc.co.uk

Email: argyle@pafc.co.uk

Ground Capacity: 16,388.

Record Attendance: 43,596 v Aston Villa, Division 2, 10 October 1936.

Pitch Measurements: 105m × 68.5m (115yd × 75yd)

Chairman: James Brent.

Chief Executive: Martyn Starnes.

Manager: Derek Adams.

First Team Coach: Sean McCarthy.

Physio: Paul Atkinson.

HONOURS

Football League – Division 2: *Champions* 2003–04;
Division 3 (S): *Champions* 1929–30, 1951–52; *Runners-up* 1921–22, 1922–23, 1923–24, 1924–25, 1925–26, 1926–27 (record of six consecutive years);
Division 3: *Champions* 1958–59, 2001–02; *Runners-up* 1974–75, 1985–86.
FA Cup: Best season: semi-final, 1984.
Football League Cup: Best season: semi-final, 1965, 1974.

Colours: Dark green shirts with white trim, white shorts with green trim, green socks with white trim.

Year Formed: 1886.

Turned Professional: 1903.

Previous Name: 1886, Argyle Athletic Club; 1903, Plymouth Argyle.

Club Nickname: 'The Pilgrims'.

Ground: 1886, Home Park.

First Football League Game: 28 August 1920, Division 3, v Norwich C (h) D 1–1 – Craig; Russell, Atterbury; Logan, Dickinson, Forbes; Kirkpatrick, Jack, Bowler, Heeps (1), Dixon.

Record League Victory: 8–1 v Millwall, Division 2, 16 January 1932 – Harper; Roberts, Titmuss; Mackay, Pullan, Reed; Grozier, Bowden (2), Vidler (3), Leslie (1), Black (1), (1 og). 8–1 v Hartlepool U (a), Division 2, 7 May 1994 – Nicholls; Patterson (Naylor), Hill, Burrows, Comyn, McCall (1), Barlow, Castle (1), Landon (3), Marshall (1), Dalton (2).

Record Cup Victory: 6–0 v Corby T, FA Cup 3rd rd, 22 January 1966 – Leiper; Book, Baird; Williams, Nelson, Newman; Jones (1), Jackson (1), Bickle (3), Piper (1), Jennings.

sky SPORTS FACT FILE

Plymouth Argyle went on a month-long tour of the United States at the end of the 1953–54 season travelling each way on an ocean liner. The Pilgrims played matches in Los Angeles, Chicago, Denver, Detroit and New York winning 8 of their 10 fixtures including a 16-2 victory over a Colorado All Star XI.

Record Defeat: 0–9 v Stoke C, Division 2, 17 December 1960.

Most League Points (2 for a win): 68, Division 3 (S), 1929–30.

Most League Points (3 for a win): 102, Division 3, 2001–02.

Most League Goals: 107, Division 3 (S), 1925–26 and 1951–52.

Highest League Scorer in Season: Jack Cock, 32, Division 3 (S), 1926–27.

Most League Goals in Total Aggregate: Sammy Black, 174, 1924–38.

Most League Goals in One Match: 5, Wilf Carter v Charlton Ath, Division 2, 27 December 1960.

Most Capped Player: Moses Russell, 20 (23), Wales.

Most League Appearances: Kevin Hodges, 530, 1978–92.

Youngest League Player: Lee Phillips, 16 years 43 days v Gillingham, 29 October 1996.

Record Transfer Fee Received: £2,000,000 from Hull C for Peter Halmosi, July 2008.

Record Transfer Fee Paid: £500,000 to Cardiff C for Steve MacLean, January 2008.

Football League Record: 1920 Original Member of Division 3; 1921–30 Division 3 (S); 1930–50 Division 2; 1950–52 Division 3 (S); 1952–56 Division 2; 1956–58 Division 3 (S); 1958–59 Division 3; 1959–68 Division 2; 1968–75 Division 3; 1975–77 Division 2; 1977–86 Division 3; 1986–95 Division 2; 1995–96 Division 3; 1996–98 Division 2; 1998–2002 Division 3; 2002–04 Division 2; 2004–10 FL C; 2010–11 FL 1; 2011– FL 2.

LATEST SEQUENCES

Longest Sequence of League Wins: 9, 8.3.1986 – 12.4.1986.

Longest Sequence of League Defeats: 9, 12.10.1963 – 7.12.1963.

Longest Sequence of League Draws: 5, 26.2.2000 – 14.3.2000.

Longest Sequence of Unbeaten League Matches: 22, 20.4.1929 – 21.12.1929.

Longest Sequence Without a League Win: 13, 13.4.2009 – 27.9.2009.

Successive Scoring Runs: 39 from 15.4.1939.

Successive Non-scoring Runs: 5 from 21.11.2009.

MANAGERS

Frank Brettell 1903–05
Bob Jack 1905–06
Bill Fullerton 1906–07
Bob Jack 1910–38
Jack Tresadern 1938–47
Jimmy Rae 1948–55
Jack Rowley 1955–60
Neil Dougall 1961
Ellis Stuttard 1961–63
Andy Beattie 1963–64
Malcolm Allison 1964–65
Derek Ufton 1965–68
Billy Bingham 1968–70
Ellis Stuttard 1970–72
Tony Waiters 1972–77
Mike Kelly 1977–78
Malcolm Allison 1978–79
Bobby Saxton 1979–81
Bobby Moncur 1981–83
Johnny Hore 1983–84
Dave Smith 1984–88
Ken Brown 1988–90
David Kemp 1990–92
Peter Shilton 1992–95
Steve McCall 1995
Neil Warnock 1995–97
Mick Jones 1997–98
Kevin Hodges 1998–2000
Paul Sturrock 2000–04
Bobby Williamson 2004–05
Tony Pulis 2005–06
Ian Holloway 2006–07
Paul Sturrock 2007–09
Paul Mariner 2009–10
Peter Reid 2010–11
Carl Fletcher 2011–13
John Sheridan 2013–15
Derek Adams June 2015–

TEN YEAR LEAGUE RECORD

		P	W	D	L	F	A	Pts	Pos
2005-06	FL C	46	13	17	16	39	46	56	14
2006-07	FL C	46	17	16	13	63	62	67	11
2007-08	FL C	46	17	13	16	60	50	64	10
2008-09	FL C	46	13	12	21	44	57	51	21
2009-10	FL C	46	11	8	27	43	68	41	23
2010-11	FL 1	46	15	7	24	51	74	42*	23
2011-12	FL 2	46	10	16	20	47	64	46	21
2012-13	FL 2	46	13	13	20	46	55	52	21
2013-14	FL 2	46	16	12	18	51	58	60	10
2014-15	FL 2	46	20	11	15	55	37	71	7

* 10 pts deducted.

DID YOU KNOW

Plymouth Argyle were unbeaten in their opening 21 League and FA Cup fixtures of the 1929–30 season before losing in a Christmas Day game at Coventry City. They finished the campaign with 11 wins in their final 12 matches and clinched the Division Three South title over the Easter holiday period.

PLYMOUTH ARGYLE – FOOTBALL LEAGUE TWO 2014–15 LEAGUE RECORD

Match No.	Date	Venue	Opponents	Result	H/T Score	Lg Pos.	Goalscorers	Attendance
1	Aug 9	A	Cambridge U	L	0-1	0-0	16		6009
2	16	H	Exeter C	W	3-0	2-0	10	Harvey [14], Reid, R [36], Nelson [83]	11,418
3	19	H	Stevenage	D	1-1	0-0	10	Smalley (pen) [90]	6240
4	23	A	Bury	L	1-2	0-2	14	Reid, R (pen) [66]	3156
5	30	H	Southend U	W	2-0	0-0	10	Alessandra [52], Reid, R [68]	6247
6	Sept 6	A	Luton T	W	1-0	0-0	8	Blizzard [68]	7864
7	13	A	Morecambe	L	1-2	1-1	10	Hartley [25]	1865
8	16	H	Wycombe W	L	0-1	0-1	13		5657
9	20	H	Hartlepool U	W	2-0	1-0	12	Morgan [14], Thomas [77]	6146
10	27	A	Accrington S	L	0-1	0-1	14		1511
11	Oct 4	H	Shrewsbury T	W	1-0	1-0	8	Reid, R [33]	6229
12	11	A	Tranmere R	W	1-0	1-0	6	Reid, R [29]	4952
13	18	A	Carlisle U	W	1-0	1-0	5	Alessandra [15]	6529
14	21	A	AFC Wimbledon	D	0-0	0-0	6		4318
15	25	H	Cheltenham T	W	3-0	2-0	6	Reid, R [23], Hartley [45], Alessandra [76]	6837
16	Nov 1	A	Burton Alb	D	1-1	0-1	6	Reid, R (pen) [70]	3083
17	15	H	Portsmouth	W	3-0	3-0	4	Reid, R 2 (1 pen) [6 (p), 30], Alessandra [21]	10,354
18	22	A	Mansfield T	L	0-1	0-1	6		2926
19	29	H	York C	D	1-1	1-0	6	Reid, B [3]	6808
20	Dec 13	A	Northampton T	W	3-2	2-0	5	Hartley [2], Kellett [40], Alessandra [62]	4318
21	20	H	Dagenham & R	W	3-0	1-0	5	Reid, R 2 (1 pen) [41, 78 (p)], Reid, B [50]	7176
22	26	A	Newport Co	L	0-2	0-1	6		5020
23	28	H	Oxford U	L	1-2	1-0	7	Alessandra [19]	11,020
24	Jan 3	A	York C	D	0-0	0-0	7		3869
25	10	A	Southend U	D	0-0	0-0	7		5767
26	17	H	Luton T	L	0-1	0-1	9		8420
27	24	H	Morecambe	D	1-1	1-0	10	Reid, R [45]	6314
28	31	A	Hartlepool U	L	2-3	1-0	10	Brunt [30], Lee [90]	3291
29	Feb 7	A	Accrington S	W	1-0	1-0	8	Alessandra [42]	6005
30	10	A	Wycombe W	W	2-0	2-0	7	Alessandra [19], Hartley [29]	3078
31	14	H	Cambridge U	W	2-0	0-0	7	Brunt [81], Alessandra [84]	6413
32	21	A	Exeter C	W	3-1	1-1	6	Reid, R 3 (1 pen) [27, 57 (p), 71]	7440
33	28	H	Bury	L	0-2	0-0	8		7374
34	Mar 3	A	Stevenage	L	0-1	0-0	8		3022
35	7	H	Northampton T	W	2-0	1-0	7	O'Connor [28], Alessandra [86]	6501
36	14	A	Oxford U	D	0-0	0-0	7		8057
37	17	A	Dagenham & R	L	0-2	0-1	9		1713
38	21	H	Newport Co	D	0-0	0-0	8		6847
39	28	A	Cheltenham T	W	3-0	1-0	7	Reid, R 2 [34, 60], Ansah [86]	3831
40	Apr 3	H	Burton Alb	D	1-1	0-1	7	McHugh [86]	8649
41	6	A	Portsmouth	L	1-2	0-0	8	Lee [78]	16,581
42	11	H	Mansfield T	W	2-1	1-0	7	O'Connor [2], McHugh [63]	6626
43	14	H	AFC Wimbledon	D	1-1	0-0	7	O'Connor [54]	6900
44	18	A	Carlisle U	L	0-2	0-1	7		4651
45	25	H	Tranmere R	W	3-2	2-1	7	Reid, R (pen) [7], Holmes-Dennis [37], Alessandra [81]	9769
46	May 2	H	Shrewsbury T	W	2-0	2-0	7	Reid, B [3], Mellor [44]	8963

Final League Position: 7

GOALSCORERS
League (55): Reid, R 18 (6 pens), Alessandra 11, Hartley 4, O'Connor 3, Reid, B 3, Brunt 2, Lee 2, McHugh 2, Ansah 1, Blizzard 1, Harvey 1, Holmes-Dennis 1, Kellett 1, Mellor 1, Morgan 1, Nelson 1, Smalley 1 (1 pen), Thomas 1.
FA Cup (2): Hartley 1, Morgan 1.
Capital One Cup (3): Reid, R 2, McHugh 1.
Johnstone's Paint Trophy (3): Alessandra 2, Smalley 1.
League Two Play-Offs (3): Ansah 1, Banton 1, Brunt 1.

McCormick L 46	Mellor K 36 + 1	Nelson C 42	Hartley P 38 + 1	McHugh C 43 + 1	Alessandra L 43 + 1	Cox L 21 + 11	Norburn O 7 + 7	Banton J 11 + 14	Reid R 42	Smalley D 3 + 13	Morgan M 5 + 11	Blizzard D 24 + 7	Thomas N 1 + 8	O'Connor A 40	Harvey T 3 + 10	Allen R — + 3	Purrington B 4 + 4	Bray A — + 1	Reid B 33	Kellett A 12	Bentley A 3	Flanagan T 4	Lee O 9 + 6	Bittner J — + 1	Brunt R 4 + 12	Talbot D 9	Holmes-Dennis T 17	Ansah Z 2 + 6	Jones G 4 + 2	Match No.
1	2	3	4	5	6²	7	8¹	9³	10	11	12	13	14																	1
1	2	3	4	5	7			9	10⁴	11³		12	14	8¹	6		13													2
1	2	3	4	5	6	7²		9		11³	14	13		8	10¹	12														3
1	2	3	4	5¹	10	13	7	9³	11	6²	14			8			12													4
1	2	3	4	5	6	7²	12	9¹	10		11³		14	8	13															5
1	2	3	4	5	6	7		10	11	13		9		8				12²												6
1	2	3	4	5	6	9¹		11	12	10²	7	13		8			12²													7
1	2	3	4	5²		13	7³	9	11	6¹		8	10	14	12															8
1	2	3	4³	13	7	9		11¹		10²	8	12	6	14	5															9
1	2	3		4	9	14		12	10	8	11³	7²	13	5¹	6															10
1	5	4	3	2	10		11	12	7¹	8	6	9							9											11
1	6	3	5	4	10²	8	14	11³	12	13	7¹	2							9											12
1	9	2	4	3	10²	6		11	12	13	8	5							7											13
1	2	3	5	4	11¹			10²	12	13	9			8					7	6										14
1	5	2	4	3¹	10²		13	11³	12		8			7	14				6	9										15
1	6	2	4	3²	11	12		14	10	13	9¹			5³					7	8										16
1	5	2	4	3	10²	6³		11¹	12	14	8			7	13					9										17
1	5	2	4	3¹	10	8	12	14	11	13		8²		7³						9										18
1	5	2	4		10	7		11¹	12			8		3					6	9										19
1	5	2	4		10²	6	12	13	11³			8¹		3	14				7	9										20
1	5			3	10¹	6	8	12	11²	13				2	14				7³	9	4									21
1	2			3	10¹	6	7²	13	11	12				5					8	4	9									22
1	5			3	10	6	8		11					2					7	9	4*									23
1	5	4	3¹	2	10³	7	12	14	11		13			6					8²	9										24
1	6	4		3	11¹	8		7²	10		12	13	5							9		2								25
1	5	2		3	11	6¹		10				8²	13		12		9		4	7										26
1²	5	2		3	11	6¹		10					14	12		9		7			4	8³	12	13						27
1	3	2	12	4	11	7		10						13		8			6³	14			9²	5¹						28
1		3	4	6	10	12	14		11¹					7					6				8²	13	9					29
1		3	4	6	10	12			11²					7					9¹				8³	13	2	5				30
1		2	4	3	10	13			11²					7		14			6				8¹	12	5	9³				31
1		4	5	3	10³	12			11¹				14	9					7²				2*	13	8	6				32
1	13	2	4	3²	11	8¹		12						14		7			6					10³	5	9				33
1		4	3	5	10	13		12						6		8			7²				11¹	2	9					34
1	5	2	4	3¹	10²			14	11³					12		7			6				13	8	9					35
1	5	3	2	4	11²			12	10¹					8					6³			13	14	7	9					36
1	9	4	2	3	10¹			12	11			13		7²					8				6³	14	5					37
1	5	2	4	3	10			12	11			13		7¹					6					9						38
1		3	5	4	11¹			8¹	10²			9		2					7			14	13		6	12				39
1		2	4	3	10²			7³	11³			8		6								12	14		9	13	5			40
1	2*	4	3²	12				6²	11			7		9								13	14		8	10¹	5			41
1	5	4	3¹	10	13			11²				7	2	6								8³			9	14	5			42
1		2	4	3	10			11²				8¹	7	6								13			9	12	5			43
1		2	4	3¹	10	14		11²				8	7	6										13	9	12	5³			44
1	5	2	4	3	10¹			14	11³			8²	7	13	6										9	12				45
1	5	2	4	3		14			6²	7	12	8										10¹			9	11³	13			46

FA Cup

First Round	AFC Fylde	(h)	2-0
Second Round	Sheffield U	(a)	0-3

Capital One Cup

First Round	Leyton Orient	(h)	3-3

(aet; Leyton Orient won 6-5 on penalties)

Johnstone's Paint Trophy

Second Round	Swindon T	(h)	3-2
Southern Quarter-Finals	Coventry C	(a)	0-2

League Two Play-Offs

Semi-Finals 1st leg	Wycombe W	(h)	2-3
Semi-Finals 2nd leg	Wycombe W	(a)	1-2

PORT VALE

FOUNDATION

Port Vale Football Club was formed in 1876 and took its name from the venue of the inaugural meeting at 'Port Vale House' situated in a suburb of Stoke-on-Trent. Upon moving to Burslem in 1884 the club changed its name to 'Burslem Port Vale' and after several seasons in the Midland League became founder members of the Football League Division Two in 1892. The prefix 'Burslem' was dropped from the name as a new ground several miles away was acquired.

Vale Park, Hamil Road, Burslem, Stoke-on-Trent, Staffordshire ST6 1AW.

Telephone: (01782) 655 800.

Ticket Office: (01782) 655 821.

Website: www.port-vale.co.uk

Email: enquiries@port-vale.co.uk

Ground Capacity: 19,148.

Record Attendance: 22,993 v Stoke C, Division 2, 6 March 1920 (at Recreation Ground); 49,768 v Aston Villa, FA Cup 5th rd, 20 February 1960 (at Vale Park).

Pitch Measurements: 104m × 69.5m (114yd × 76yd)

Chairman: Norman Smurthwaite.

Manager: Robert Page.

Assistant Manager: Mark Grew.

Physio: James Rowland.

Colours: White shirts with orange and black trim, black shorts with white trim, white socks with black trim.

Year Formed: 1876.

Turned Professional: 1885.

Previous Names: 1876, Port Vale; 1884, Burslem Port Vale; 1909, Port Vale.

Club Nickname: 'Valiants'.

Grounds: 1876, Limekin Lane, Longport; 1881, Westport; 1884, Moorland Road, Burslem; 1886, Athletic Ground, Cobridge; 1913, Recreation Ground, Hanley; 1950, Vale Park.

First Football League Game: 3 September 1892, Division 2, v Small Heath (a) L 1–5 – Frail; Clutton, Elson; Farrington, McCrindle, Delves; Walker, Scarratt, Bliss (1), Jones. (Only 10 men).

Record League Victory: 9–1 v Chesterfield, Division 2, 24 September 1932 – Leckie; Shenton, Poyser; Sherlock, Round, Jones; McGrath, Mills, Littlewood (6), Kirkham (2), Morton (1).

Record Cup Victory: 7–1 v Irthlingborough, FA Cup 1st rd, 12 January 1907 – Matthews; Dunn, Hamilton; Eardley, Baddeley, Holyhead; Carter, Dodds (2), Beats, Mountford (2), Coxon (3).

HONOURS

Football League – Division 2: *Runners-up* 1993–94; **Division 3 (N):** *Champions* 1929–30, 1953–54; *Runners-up* 1952–53; **Division 4:** *Champions* 1958–59.

FA Cup: Best season: semi-final, 1954, when in Division 3.

Football League Cup: Best season: 4th rd, 2007.

Autoglass Trophy: *Winners* 1993.

Anglo-Italian Cup: *Runners-up* 1996.

LDV Vans Trophy: *Winners* 2001.

sky SPORTS FACT FILE

Norman Hallam, a wing-half who made 63 Football League appearances for Port Vale, gave up full-time football in July 1948 to become a Methodist Minister. He continued as a part-time player and made occasional further appearances for the club when his Church duties allowed.

Record Defeat: 0–10 v Sheffield U, Division 2, 10 December 1892. 0–10 v Notts Co, Division 2, 26 February 1895.

Most League Points (2 for a win): 69, Division 3 (N), 1953–54.

Most League Points (3 for a win): 89, Division 2, 1992–93.

Most League Goals: 110, Division 4, 1958–59.

Highest League Scorer in Season: Wilf Kirkham 38, Division 2, 1926–27.

Most League Goals in Total Aggregate: Wilf Kirkham, 153, 1923–29, 1931–33.

Most League Goals in One Match: 6, Stewart Littlewood v Chesterfield, Division 2, 24 September 1922.

Most Capped Player: Chris Birchall, 24 (43), Trinidad & Tobago.

Most League Appearances: Roy Sproson, 760, 1950–72.

Youngest League Player: Malcolm McKenzie, 15 years 347 days v Newport Co, 12 April 1966.

Record Transfer Fee Received: £2,000,000 from Wimbledon for Gareth Ainsworth, October 1998.

Record Transfer Fee Paid: £500,000 to Lincoln C for Gareth Ainsworth, September 1997.

Football League Record: 1892 Original Member of Division 2. Failed re-election in 1896; Re-elected 1898; Resigned 1907; Returned in Oct, 1919, when they took over the fixtures of Leeds City; 1929–30 Division 3 (N); 1930–36 Division 2; 1936–38 Division 3 (N); 1938–52 Division 3 (S); 1952–54 Division 3 (N); 1954–57 Division 2; 1957–58 Division 3 (S); 1958–59 Division 4; 1959–65 Division 3; 1965–70 Division 4; 1970–78 Division 3; 1978–83 Division 4; 1983–84 Division 3; 1984–86 Division 4; 1986–89 Division 3; 1989–94 Division 2; 1994–2000 Division 1; 2000–04 Division 2; 2004–08 FL 1; 2008–13 FL 2; 2013– FL 1.

LATEST SEQUENCES

Longest Sequence of League Wins: 8, 8.4.1893 – 30.9.1893.

Longest Sequence of League Defeats: 9, 9.3.1957 – 20.4.1957.

Longest Sequence of League Draws: 6, 26.4.1981 – 12.9.1981.

Longest Sequence of Unbeaten League Matches: 19, 5.5.1969 – 8.11.1969.

Longest Sequence Without a League Win: 17, 7.12.1991 – 21.3.1992.

Successive Scoring Runs: 22 from 12.9.1992.

Successive Non-scoring Runs: 4 from 7.4.2009.

MANAGERS

Sam Gleaves 1896–1905
 (Secretary-Manager)
Tom Clare 1905–11
A. S. Walker 1911–12
H. Myatt 1912–14
Tom Holford 1919–24
 (continued as Trainer)
Joe Schofield 1924–30
Tom Morgan 1930–32
Tom Holford 1932–35
Warney Cresswell 1936–37
Tom Morgan 1937–38
Billy Frith 1945–46
Gordon Hodgson 1946–51
Ivor Powell 1951
Freddie Steele 1951–57
Norman Low 1957–62
Freddie Steele 1962–65
Jackie Mudie 1965–67
Sir Stanley Matthews
 (General Manager) 1965–68
Gordon Lee 1968–74
Roy Sproson 1974–77
Colin Harper 1977
Bobby Smith 1977–78
Dennis Butler 1978–79
Alan Bloor 1979
John McGrath 1980–83
John Rudge 1983–99
Brian Horton 1999–2004
Martin Foyle 2004–07
Lee Sinnott 2007–08
Dean Glover 2008–09
Micky Adams 2009–10
Jim Gannon 2011
Micky Adams 2011–14
Robert Page October 2014–

TEN YEAR LEAGUE RECORD

		P	W	D	L	F	A	Pts	Pos
2005-06	FL 1	46	16	12	18	49	54	60	13
2006-07	FL 1	46	18	6	22	64	65	60	12
2007-08	FL 1	46	9	11	26	47	81	38	23
2008-09	FL 2	46	13	9	24	44	66	48	18
2009-10	FL 2	46	17	17	12	61	50	68	10
2010-11	FL 2	46	17	14	15	54	49	65	11
2011-12	FL 2	46	20	9	17	68	60	59*	12
2012-13	FL 2	46	21	15	10	87	52	78	3
2013-14	FL 1	46	18	7	21	59	73	61	9
2014-15	FL 1	46	15	9	22	55	65	54	18

*10 pts deducted.

DID YOU KNOW ?

Port Vale's first visit to Wembley came in 1993 when they reached the final of the Football League Trophy. Vale overcame Stockport County 2-1 with Paul Kerr and Bernie Slaven scoring Vale's goals in front of a crowd of 35,885.

PORT VALE – FOOTBALL LEAGUE ONE 2014–15 LEAGUE RECORD

Match No.	Date	Venue	Opponents	Result	H/T Score	Lg Pos.	Goalscorers	Attendance
1	Aug 9	H	Walsall	D	1-1	1-0	12	Pope [25]	7050
2	16	A	Doncaster R	W	3-1	3-0	7	Williamson [27], Pope [39], Dickinson [41]	6437
3	19	A	Oldham Ath	D	1-1	1-0	9	Pope [8]	3592
4	23	H	Notts Co	L	0-2	0-1	15		5090
5	30	H	Chesterfield	L	1-2	1-1	17	Marshall [41]	5593
6	Sept 6	A	Peterborough U	L	1-3	0-1	20	Slew [83]	6024
7	13	A	Crewe Alex	L	1-2	1-2	22	Slew [32]	6357
8	16	A	Bristol C	L	0-3	0-1	23		4050
9	20	H	Barnsley	W	2-1	1-0	21	O'Connor [24], Marshall [89]	5415
10	27	A	Bradford C	D	1-1	1-1	22	Lines (pen) [12]	12,703
11	Oct 4	A	Fleetwood T	L	0-1	0-0	22		4196
12	11	H	Yeovil T	W	4-1	2-0	19	Pope 2 [18, 29], Lines [46], Daniel [90]	4798
13	18	A	Preston NE	L	0-2	0-1	22		9381
14	21	H	Scunthorpe U	D	2-2	1-1	18	Williamson [7], Birchall [70]	3590
15	25	A	Leyton Orient	W	3-0	0-0	16	Yates [63], Williamson [66], Clarke (og) [81]	4773
16	Nov 1	H	Colchester U	W	2-1	0-0	13	Marshall [56], Daniel [60]	3571
17	15	H	Rochdale	W	1-0	0-0	12	Brown [64]	5043
18	22	A	Milton Keynes D	L	0-1	0-1	15		12,007
19	29	A	Gillingham	D	2-2	1-1	14	N'Guessan [18], Brown [90]	4799
20	Dec 13	H	Coventry C	L	0-2	0-0	16		5321
21	20	A	Crawley T	W	2-1	2-0	15	Brown [30], Dodds [42]	2320
22	26	H	Sheffield U	W	2-1	1-0	12	Williamson [16], N'Guessan (pen) [79]	8524
23	28	A	Swindon T	L	0-1	0-0	15		9248
24	Jan 3	H	Gillingham	W	2-1	1-1	8	Williamson [11], Daniel [90]	4783
25	10	A	Chesterfield	L	0-3	0-1	10		7034
26	17	H	Peterborough U	W	2-1	1-1	9	Birchall [32], Williamson [47]	4446
27	24	H	Crewe Alex	L	0-1	0-1	12		8002
28	31	A	Barnsley	L	1-2	0-1	14	Daniel [66]	8660
29	Feb 7	H	Bradford C	D	2-2	0-1	14	Campion [58], O'Connor (pen) [90]	5205
30	10	A	Bristol C	L	1-3	0-1	16	Marshall [77]	10,890
31	14	A	Walsall	W	1-0	1-0	14	Pope [28]	4504
32	21	A	Doncaster R	W	3-0	2-0	12	Marshall [7], Veseli [38], Moore [87]	5713
33	28	A	Notts Co	W	1-0	1-0	9	Marshall [7]	5179
34	Mar 3	A	Oldham Ath	L	0-1	0-1	13		4423
35	7	A	Coventry C	W	3-2	2-1	11	Pope [40], Marshall [45], O'Connor [76]	9446
36	14	H	Swindon T	L	0-1	0-1	12		5120
37	17	H	Crawley T	L	2-3	2-1	13	Dodds 2 [4, 45]	3852
38	21	A	Sheffield U	L	0-1	0-1	15		18,729
39	28	A	Leyton Orient	L	1-3	1-0	15	Birchall [28]	5623
40	Apr 3	H	Colchester U	L	1-2	0-0	15	Dodds [84]	4471
41	6	A	Rochdale	L	0-1	0-0	16		2948
42	11	H	Milton Keynes D	D	0-0	0-0	18		4379
43	14	A	Scunthorpe U	D	1-1	1-0	18	Duffy [43]	3002
44	17	H	Preston NE	D	2-2	0-1	18	O'Connor 2 (2 pens) [52, 85]	7210
45	25	A	Yeovil T	W	2-1	1-0	17	Pope [13], Brown [82]	4127
46	May 3	H	Fleetwood T	L	1-2	0-2	18	O'Connor [90]	5355

Final League Position: 18

GOALSCORERS

League (55): Pope 8, Marshall 7, O'Connor 6 (3 pens), Williamson 6, Brown 4, Daniel 4, Dodds 4, Birchall 3, Lines 2 (1 pen), N'Guessan 2 (1 pen), Slew 2, Campion 1, Dickinson 1, Duffy 1, Moore 1, Veseli 1, Yates 1, own goal 1.
FA Cup (3): N'Guessan 2, Williamson 1.
Capital One Cup (8): Williamson 3, Brown 2, Pope 2, O'Connor 1.
Johnstone's Paint Trophy (2): Pope 2.

Johnson S 6+1	Veseli F 37	Duffy R 27	McGivern R 18+2	Dickinson C 43	Marshall M 45+1	O'Connor M 44	Lines C 19+8	Dodds L 24+13	Williamson B 33+10	Pope T 28+5	Jennings S 1+3	Robertson C 21+3	Brown M 30+6	Birchall C 12+15	Daniel C 8+20	Moore B 9+6	Slew J 5+4	Neal C 40	Yates A 24+1	Zubar S 2	Streete R 1+1	N'Guessan D 10+1	Campion A 4+8	Nimely A —+1	Luer G —+2	Inniss R 5	O'Sullivan T 1+4	Collins N 7	Junior F 1	Coulibaly M 1+3	Match No.
1	2[2]	3	4	5	6	7	8[1]	9[3]	10	11	12	13	14																		1
1	2	3	4	5	9	7[1]	8	13	10[3]	11	12		14	6[2]																	2
1	2	3	4	5	9[2]	8[1]	7		10	11		13	14	6[3]	12																3
1	2[1]	3	4	5	9	8	7	14	10[2]	11				6[3]	12	13															4
1	2	3	4	5	6	8	7[1]		11[2]	10			14		9[3]	12	13														5
	2		4	5	6	8[3]		14	13	10[3]	9	3	7		11[2]	12		1													6
		3	4	5	9	8	7	12	13	10				6[2]	11[1]			1	2												7
	2	3	4	5	14	6	7			10			8[2]	11[1]	9[3]	12	13	1													8
		3	4	5	9	7[3]	8	6[1]	14	10			12		13	11[1]		1	2												9
		4	3	5	9	8	7	6[1]	13	10			12		11[2]			1	2												10
		3	4	5	9[2]	8	7	6	12	10			13		11[2]			1	2												11
		3		5	9	7[1]	8	6	11[2]	10			13			12		1	2	4											12
		3[1]	12	5	9	7	8	6[3]	10[3]	11					14	13		1	2	4[*]											13
		3	4	5	9	8	7	6	11[2]	10			12			13		1	2												14
	5	4	3[3]		9[2]	8	7	14		10			6		11[1]			1	2			12	13								15
	3			5	9[2]	8	7	13		11			6			12		1	2			4	10[1]								16
	4			5	8	7		10		12		3	9	13	6[2]			1	2			11[1]									17
	4			5	10	8[2]	9[3]	13		12		3	6	14	7[3]			1	2			11[1]									18
	4			5	7[1]	8		11	9[3]			3	6	13				1	2			10[2]	14								19
	4	5[2]		7	8			13		10		3	6[1]	14	9[3]			1	2			11		12							20
	4	3		5	9	7[2]		6		10[1]	12	8	13		11			1	2												21
	4	3		5	6	8		12	10[2]	11		7		13	9[1]			1	2												22
	3	4		5	6	8[3]	13	9[1]		11		7			10[3]	14		1	2												23
	3	4		5	6	7	12	10		11[2]		8[1]		13	9[3]	14		1	2												24
	4	3		5	6	8	13	10[1]		11		7[3]			12	9[2]	14	1	2												25
	4			5	9	8			10	11		3	7	6[1]	12			1	2												26
	4			5	9	7	14		10[1]	11	12	3	8[2]	6[1]	13			1	2												27
	4			5	6	8	7		10	11[1]		3	12		9			1	2												28
	2	3[2]		5	9	8	6[3]			10		4	7	12	11[1]			1				13	14								29
	2	4		5	9	8	12			11		3	7[3]	6[1]		14		1				10[2]	13								30
	2			5	9[2]	7	12		10[3]	11		4	8[1]	14		6		1									3	13			31
	5				2	9[1]	8		12	11[2]		4	7	13		6		1									3				32
	2			5	9	7			12	10[1]		3	8			6		1									4				33
	2			5	9[3]	8	13	14	10	11		4[1]	7[2]		12	6		1									3				34
	2		12	5	9	8			13	10[3]		4	7		14	6[1]		1									3[2]				35
	2	4		5	6	8	12		11	10[2]		3	7	13	9[1]			1	2												36
	3			5		6	7		10	12	11[2]	4	8[3]		9[1]			1	2			14						13			37
	4			5		9	8		10	11[2]	12	3	7[*]		13	6[3]		1	2			14									38
12	2			5	9	7			10	14	11[2]	3		6[3]	13			1[*]									4	8[1]			39
1	3			5	9	8			10	11[2]	12	14	7	6[1]					2									4[3]		13	40
	2	4		5	9				10	12	11[2]	3	8	6[1]	13			1										7			41
	2	4		5	9	8			10[1]	6[2]	13		7									11						3		12	42
	2	4		5	9[1]	8			11	6			7	13	12							10[2]						3			43
	2	3[*]		5	9	7			6[2]	10[2]	12		8					1	13			11[1]						4		14	44
	2			5	9	7[1]			6[2]	10[3]	11	4	8	13	12			1									14	3			45
	2	3		5	9	8			10[3]	11		7[2]	14					1				13						12	4	6[1]	46

FA Cup
First Round — Milton Keynes D (h) 3-4

Capital One Cup
First Round — Hartlepool U (h) 6-2
Second Round — Cardiff C (h) 2-3

Johnstone's Paint Trophy
Second Round — Preston NE (a) 2-3

PORTSMOUTH

Fratton Park, Frogmore Road, Portsmouth, Hampshire PO4 8RA.

Telephone: (02392) 731 204.

Fax: (02392) 734 129.

Ticket Office: (02392) 778 559.

Website: www.portsmouthfc.co.uk

Email: info@pompeyfc.co.uk

Ground Capacity: 18,204.

Record Attendance: 51,385 v Derby Co, FA Cup 6th rd, 26 February 1949.

Pitch Measurements: 100m × 66m (109.5yd × 72yd)

Chairman: Iain McInnes.

Chief Executive: Mark Catlin.

Manager: Paul Cook.

Assistant Manager: Leam Richardson.

Colours: Blue shirts with red and white trim, white shorts with blue trim, red socks.

Year Formed: 1898.

Turned Professional: 1898.

Club Nickname: 'Pompey'.

Ground: 1898, Fratton Park.

First Football League Game: 28 August 1920, Division 3, v Swansea T (h) W 3–0 – Robson; Probert, Potts; Abbott, Harwood, Turner; Thompson, Stringfellow (1), Reid (1), James (1), Beedie.

Record League Victory: 9–1 v Notts Co, Division 2, 9 April 1927 – McPhail; Clifford, Ted Smith; Reg Davies (1), Foxall, Moffat; Forward (1), Mackie (2), Haines (3), Watson, Cook (2).

Record Cup Victory: 7–0 v Stockport Co, FA Cup 3rd rd, 8 January 1949 – Butler; Rookes, Ferrier; Scoular, Flewin, Dickinson; Harris (3), Barlow, Clarke (2), Phillips (2), Froggatt.

Record Defeat: 0–10 v Leicester C, Division 1, 20 October 1928.

Most League Points (2 for a win): 65, Division 3, 1961–62.

HONOURS

Football League – Division 1:
Champions 1948–49, 1949–50, 2002–03;
Division 2: *Runners-up* 1926–27, 1986–87;
Division 3 (S): *Champions* 1923–24;
Division 3: *Champions* 1961–62, 1982–83.
FA Cup: *Winners* 1939, 2008;
Runners-up 1929, 1934, 2010.
Football League Cup: Best season: 5th rd, 1961, 1986, 1994, 2010.
European Competitions
UEFA Cup: 2008–09.

sky SPORTS FACT FILE

Mike Barnard, an inside forward who played for Portsmouth in the 1950s, was also a first class cricketer with Hampshire. He made over 100 first-team appearances for Pompey and 276 first class appearances for Hampshire with whom he scored six centuries.

Most League Points (3 for a win): 98, Division 1, 2002–03.

Most League Goals: 97, Division 1, 2002–03.

Highest League Scorer in Season: Guy Whittingham, 42, Division 1, 1992–93.

Most League Goals in Total Aggregate: Peter Harris, 194, 1946–60.

Most League Goals in One Match: 5, Alf Strange v Gillingham, Division 3, 27 January 1923; 5, Peter Harris v Aston Villa, Division 1, 3 September 1958.

Most Capped Player: Jimmy Dickinson, 48, England.

Most League Appearances: Jimmy Dickinson, 764, 1946–65.

Youngest League Player: Clive Green, 16 years 259 days v Wrexham, 21 August 1976.

Record Transfer Fee Received: £20,000,000 from Real Madrid for Lassana Diarra, January 2009.

Record Transfer Fee Paid: £9,000,000 (rising to £11,000,000) to Liverpool for Peter Crouch, July 2008.

Football League Record: 1920 Original Member of Division 3; 1921 Division 3 (S); 1924–27 Division 2; 1927–59 Division 1; 1959–61 Division 2; 1961–62 Division 3; 1962–76 Division 2; 1976–78 Division 3; 1978–80 Division 4; 1980–83 Division 3; 1983–87 Division 2; 1987–88 Division 1; 1988–92 Division 2; 1992–2003 Division 1; 2003–10 FA Premier League; 2010–12 FL C; 2012–13 FL 1; 2013– FL 2.

LATEST SEQUENCES

Longest Sequence of League Wins: 7, 17.8.2002 – 17.9.2002.

Longest Sequence of League Defeats: 9, 26.12.2012 – 9.2.2013.

Longest Sequence of League Draws: 5, 16.12.2000 – 13.1.2001.

Longest Sequence of Unbeaten League Matches: 15, 18.4.1924 – 18.10.1924.

Longest Sequence Without a League Win: 25, 29.11.1958 – 22.8.1959.

Successive Scoring Runs: 23 from 30.8.1930.

Successive Non-scoring Runs: 6 from 27.12.1993.

MANAGERS

Frank Brettell 1898–1901
Bob Blyth 1901–04
Richard Bonney 1905–08
Bob Brown 1911–20
John McCartney 1920–27
Jack Tinn 1927–47
Bob Jackson 1947–52
Eddie Lever 1952–58
Freddie Cox 1958–61
George Smith 1961–70
Ron Tindall 1970–73
  (General Manager to 1974)
John Mortimore 1973–74
Ian St John 1974–77
Jimmy Dickinson 1977–79
Frank Burrows 1979–82
Bobby Campbell 1982–84
Alan Ball 1984–89
John Gregory 1989–90
Frank Burrows 1990–91
Jim Smith 1991–95
Terry Fenwick 1995–98
Alan Ball 1998–99
Tony Pulis 2000
Steve Claridge 2000–01
Graham Rix 2001–02
Harry Redknapp 2002–04
Velimir Zajec 2004–05
Alain Perrin 2005
Harry Redknapp 2005–08
Tony Adams 2008–09
Paul Hart 2009
Avram Grant 2009–10
Steve Cotterill 2010–11
Michael Appleton 2011–12
Guy Whittingham 2012–13
Richie Barker 2013–14
Andy Awford 2014–15
Paul Cook May 2015–

TEN YEAR LEAGUE RECORD

		P	W	D	L	F	A	Pts	Pos
2005-06	PR Lge	38	10	8	20	37	62	38	17
2006-07	PR Lge	38	14	12	12	45	42	54	9
2007-08	PR Lge	38	16	9	13	48	40	57	8
2008-09	PR Lge	38	10	11	17	38	57	41	14
2009-10	PR Lge	38	7	7	24	34	66	19*	20
2010-11	FL C	46	15	13	18	53	60	58	16
2011-12	FL C	46	13	11	22	50	59	40†	22
2012-13	FL 1	46	10	12	24	51	69	32‡	24
2013-14	FL 2	46	14	17	15	56	66	59	13
2014-15	FL 2	46	14	15	17	52	54	57	16

*9 pts deducted; †10 pts deducted; ‡10 pts deducted.

DID YOU KNOW ?

After joining the Southern League in 1899–1900 Portsmouth remained unbeaten at Fratton Park for the first three seasons of their history. The record finally ended when they went down to a 1-0 defeat at the hands of Northampton Town on 18 October 1902.

PORTSMOUTH – FOOTBALL LEAGUE TWO 2014–15 LEAGUE RECORD

Match No.	Date	Venue	Opponents	Result	H/T Score	Lg Pos.	Goalscorers	Attendance
1	Aug 9	A	Exeter C	D	1-1	0-1	12	Wallace [74]	5694
2	16	H	Cambridge U	W	2-1	1-0	7	Taylor [34], Dunn (og) [66]	16,671
3	19	H	Northampton T	W	2-0	2-0	4	Wallace [26], Westcarr [39]	15,004
4	23	A	Oxford U	W	1-0	0-0	2	Westcarr [80]	6852
5	30	H	Newport Co	L	0-1	0-0	7		16,191
6	Sept 7	A	Burton Alb	L	0-2	0-1	8		2980
7	13	A	Southend U	L	0-2	0-0	11		7023
8	16	H	Dagenham & R	W	3-0	1-0	9	Dunne [40], Wallace (pen) [69], Barcham [90]	13,648
9	20	H	Wycombe W	D	1-1	0-0	11	Ertl [70]	16,171
10	27	A	Hartlepool U	D	0-0	0-0	8		3439
11	Oct 4	A	York C	D	0-0	0-0	9		3856
12	11	H	Mansfield T	D	1-1	0-0	12	Robinson [70]	15,585
13	18	A	Bury	L	0-3	0-2	14		4259
14	21	H	Stevenage	W	3-2	1-1	11	Wallace [34], Storey [57], Devera [79]	13,281
15	25	A	Shrewsbury T	L	1-2	0-1	13	Wallace (pen) [3]	5515
16	Nov 1	H	Carlisle U	W	3-0	2-0	9	Westcarr [2], Storey [26], Hollands [74]	15,533
17	15	A	Plymouth Arg	L	0-3	0-3	13		10,354
18	22	H	Morecambe	W	3-0	1-0	10	Westcarr [11], Wallace 2 [54, 88]	14,349
19	29	A	Tranmere R	L	1-3	0-1	12	Wallace [57]	5163
20	Dec 13	A	Accrington S	L	2-3	2-2	13	Bean [17], Westcarr [31]	14,300
21	20	A	Cheltenham T	D	1-1	0-1	13	Atangana [56]	3331
22	26	H	AFC Wimbledon	L	0-2	0-2	14		17,558
23	28	A	Luton T	D	1-1	1-1	14	Taylor [36]	10,071
24	Jan 10	A	Newport Co	L	0-1	0-0	17		4575
25	17	H	Burton Alb	D	1-1	1-0	16	Wallace [36]	14,323
26	24	H	Southend U	L	1-2	1-1	18	Webster [24]	15,573
27	31	A	Wycombe W	D	0-0	0-0	18		5829
28	Feb 7	H	Hartlepool U	W	1-0	0-0	16	Tubbs [60]	14,397
29	10	A	Dagenham & R	D	0-0	0-0	16		2310
30	14	H	Exeter C	W	1-0	0-0	16	Wallace [90]	14,097
31	21	A	Cambridge U	W	6-2	4-1	14	Wallace [2], Tubbs 3 [24, 45, 81], Robinson [33], Taylor [74]	6528
32	24	H	Tranmere R	W	3-2	0-1	13	Westcarr [76], Taylor 2 [82, 85]	13,660
33	28	H	Oxford U	D	0-0	0-0	12		16,355
34	Mar 3	A	Northampton T	L	0-1	0-1	13		4871
35	7	A	Accrington S	D	1-1	1-1	14	Taylor [20]	1994
36	14	H	Luton T	W	2-0	1-0	13	Tubbs [3], Taylor [62]	17,149
37	17	H	Cheltenham T	D	2-2	2-2	12	Tubbs [17], Taylor [43]	13,558
38	21	A	AFC Wimbledon	L	0-1	0-1	13		4485
39	28	H	Shrewsbury T	L	0-2	0-1	14		14,749
40	Apr 3	A	Carlisle U	D	2-2	2-1	14	Wallace [38], Tubbs [45]	5230
41	6	H	Plymouth Arg	W	2-1	0-0	14	Wallace [46], Taylor [76]	16,581
42	11	A	Morecambe	L	1-3	0-1	14	Chaplin [85]	2065
43	14	A	Stevenage	L	0-1	0-1	14		3615
44	18	H	Bury	L	0-1	0-1	16		14,569
45	25	A	Mansfield T	W	2-1	1-0	16	Tubbs (pen) [2], Wallace [55]	4222
46	May 2	H	York C	D	1-1	0-0	16	Tubbs [82]	17,254

Final League Position: 16

GOALSCORERS

League (52): Wallace 14 (2 pens), Taylor 9, Tubbs 9 (1 pen), Westcarr 6, Robinson 2, Storey 2, Atangana 1, Barcham 1, Bean 1, Chaplin 1, Devera 1, Dunne 1, Ertl 1, Hollands 1, Webster 1, own goal 1.
FA Cup (2): Hollands 1, Wallace 1 (1 pen).
Capital One Cup (1): Storey 1.
Johnstone's Paint Trophy (4): Wallace 2, Taylor 1, Westcarr 1.

Jones P 46	Webster A 12+3	Whatmough J 21+1	Chorley B 15+1	Shorey N 19+1	Wallace J 43+1	Dunne J 34+2	Hollands D 39+5	Barcham A 6+13	Westcarr C 21+12	Taylor R 31+6	Atangana N 16+14	Storey M 10+7	Bird R —+2	Robinson P 33	Devera J 37+2	Holmes R 9+4	Butler D 26+4	Wynter A 10	Ertl J 7+7	Agyemang P 3+5	Close B 3+3	Drennan M 3+1	Tarbuck B —+2	Awford N 1	Fish M 3	Bean M 6	Holmes L 3+2	Chaplin C 1+8	Tubbs M 23	McCallum P —+7	Passley J 12	Fogden W 3+6	East D 2+2	Nosworthy N 6+1	Kpekawa C 2	May A —+1	Match No.
1	2	3	4	5	6	7	8	9^1	10^3	11^2	12	13	14																								1
1	2*	3		5	8	7	6			11^2	9^3	10^1	14	4	12	13																					2
1			4	5	9	6	12		10^3	11^1	7	13		3	2	8^2	14																				3
1	14		4	8	12	7	6		10^2	13	9	11^1		3	2	5^1																					4
1		3	9^2	7	5	8^3	14	11	10	13	12			4	2	6^1																					5
1			5^2	6	8	7			10	11		12		4		9^3	14		2^1	3	13																6
1			4	5^2	8^2	6	7	12	10			9^1		3		11	13		2	14																	7
1	2			6	7^1	8	14		10^3			12		3	4	9	5			11^1	13																8
1			3^1	8	5	7	14		10^2			13		9	2	4	6		12	11^3																	9
1			4	7	6^2	8	14		10^3			12		3	2	9	5			11^1	13																10
1			3^3	9	8	7	6		10^2			13	14	4	2		5		12	11^1																	11
1			9	6	7	8				11^3		13	14	3	2		5		4^2	12	10^1																12
1			4	7		8			10			6^2		3	12	9	5^1		2		14	13	11^1														13
1			3	5	6^1	8	7		10^2			12		11	4		2		9		13																14
1			3	5	6	7	8		10^1	11^2	12	13		4	2				9^3		14																15
1				5	6^3	7	8		10^2	11^1	12			4	3	9	2		14		13																16
1	6^1		4	5^1	7		8					13	14	11	3	10	12	2							9^2												17
1	3			6			7					11	10	12	9	4	5									2	8^1										18
1	3^1	12		6			8			11		10^2		9	4			14	5							2	7^2	13									19
1	3						8^1			11	10	13	6^2	4			12	5								7	2	9^3	14								20
1	4			8			7			12				11	9^1	3		2	5								6	10									21
1	2		4	6			8^1					13		10	11	12	3		5*								7	9^2									22
1	2			5	6			12	10^2	13	11^3	8^1		3	4				7										9	14							23
1	2			5	6		14	7^2	12	13	10^3	9		3	4				8^1											11							24
1	2			5	6		7^1	14	8^2	10^3	9			3	4														12	11	13						25
1	2			5	6		7	13	9^1	11^1	14	8^2		4	3															10	12*						26
1	4	2^1		7	8	6			10					3	12	9												13		11^2	5						27
1	2			8	6	7			11					3	4	9													12	10^1	5						28
1	4		9^2	6	7				13	10		12		3	2	8														11^1	5						29
1	4		9^1	6	7				12	10		13		3	2	8														11	5^2						30
1	4			7	6^2		8^1		10^3			14		3	2	9	12												13	11	5						31
1	4		9	6	7^2		12		13	10				3	2^3	8													14	11	5^1						32
1		3	9	6			12		13	10	7			4	2	8														11^2	5^1						33
1		3*	9	7			13		12	10	6^3			4	2	8^2														11	5^1	14					34
1	4			6	7		8^1	13	14	11^3				3	2	9														10	5^2	12					35
1	12		4	7	6	8		5^1	14	11				3^2	2	9														10				13			36
1	4^2		3	7	6^3	8		5^1	10						2	9														11	14		13	12			37
1	4		9	7^1	8^3				13	10				3																11	12	14		2	5^2	6	38
1	4			7	6		8^1			11^2					2														13	10	14	12	5^3	3	9		39
1	13		4^2	6	7		14			10		8		3	5															11^1	2	9	12^3				40
1			8^1	6			13		12	11	7			3	5															9^2	2	10	4				41
1	14			8	6		13			11^3	7			4	5														12	9	2^1	10^2	3			42
1	2		5		8	9			12	11^1	7^1			3	6															10^2	13	14	4			43
1		3	5	9	7		11				6				2				12									8^2		13	10^3			4^1	14		44
1	2		13	9	6	7				11^1				3	5	4			8^3											12	10^2			14			45
1	4		6^1	7	9									2	5	3	8		12											11	10						46

FA Cup

First Round	Aldershot T	(h)	2-2
Replay	Aldershot T	(a)	0-1

Capital One Cup

First Round	Peterborough U	(h)	1-0
Second Round	Stoke C	(a)	0-3

Johnstone's Paint Trophy

First Round	Yeovil T	(a)	3-1
Second Round	Northampton T	(h)	1-2

PRESTON NORTH END

FOUNDATION

North End Cricket and Rugby Club, which was formed in 1863, indulged in most sports before taking up soccer in about 1879. In 1881 they decided to stick to football to the exclusion of other sports and even a 16–0 drubbing by Blackburn Rovers in an invitation game at Deepdale, a few weeks after taking this decision, did not deter them for they immediately became affiliated to the Lancashire FA.

Deepdale Stadium, Sir Tom Finney Way, Deepdale, Preston, Lancashire PR1 6RU.
Telephone: (0844) 856 1964.
Fax: (01772) 693 366.
Ticket Office: (0844) 856 1966.
Website: www.pne.co.uk
Email: enquiries@pne.co.uk
Ground Capacity: 21,945.
Record Attendance: 42,684 v Arsenal, Division 1, 23 April 1938.
Pitch Measurements: 100.5m × 67.5m (110yd × 74yd)
Chief Executive: John Kay.
Manager: Simon Grayson.
Assistant Manager: Glynn Snodin.
Head Physio: Matthew Jackson.
Colours: White shirts, blue shorts, white socks.
Year Formed: 1880.
Turned Professional: 1885.
Club Nicknames: 'The Lilywhites', 'North End'.
Ground: 1881, Deepdale.

HONOURS

Football League – Division 1:
Champions 1888–89 (first champions) 1889–90; *Runners-up* 1890–91, 1891–92, 1892–93, 1905–06, 1952–53, 1957–58;
Division 2: *Champions* 1903–04, 1912–13, 1950–51, 1999–2000; *Runners-up* 1914–15, 1933–34;
Division 3: *Champions* 1970–71, 1995–96;
Division 4: *Runners-up* 1986–87.
FA Cup: *Winners* 1889, 1938; *Runners-up* 1888, 1922, 1937, 1954, 1964.
Football League Cup: Best season: 4th rd, 2003.
Double Performed: 1888–89.
Football League Cup: Best season: 4th rd, 1963, 1966, 1972, 1981.

First Football League Game: 8 September 1888, Football League, v Burnley (h) W 5–2 – Trainer; Howarth, Holmes; Robertson, William Graham, Johnny Graham; Gordon (1), Jimmy Ross (2), Goodall, Dewhurst (2), Drummond.
Record League Victory: 10–0 v Stoke, Division 1, 14 September 1889 – Trainer; Howarth, Holmes; Kelso, Russell (1), Johnny Graham; Gordon, Jimmy Ross (2), Nick Ross (3), Thomson (2), Drummond (2).
Record Cup Victory: 26–0 v Hyde, FA Cup 1st rd, 15 October 1887 – Addison; Howarth, Nick Ross; Russell (1), Thomson (5), Johnny Graham (1); Gordon (5), Jimmy Ross (8), John Goodall (1), Dewhurst (3), Drummond (2).
Record Defeat: 0–7 v Nottingham F, Division 2, 9 April 1927; 0–7 v Blackpool, Division 1, 1 May 1948.
Most League Points (2 for a win): 61, Division 3, 1970–71.
Most League Points (3 for a win): 95, Division 2, 1999–2000.
Most League Goals: 100, Division 2, 1927–28 and Division 1, 1957–58.

sky SPORTS FACT FILE

Jim Mitchell, Preston North End's goalkeeper in the 1922 FA Cup final, is one of the last keepers to play at senior level wearing spectacles. Mitchell, who played as an amateur, had previously represented the Great Britain team in the 1920 Olympic Games.

Highest League Scorer in Season: Ted Harper, 37, Division 2, 1932–33.

Most League Goals in Total Aggregate: Tom Finney, 187, 1946–60.

Most League Goals in One Match: 4, Jimmy Ross v Stoke, Division 1, 6 October 1888; 4, Nick Ross v Derby Co, Division 1, 11 January 1890; 4, George Drummond v Notts Co, Division 1, 12 December 1891; 4, Frank Becton v Notts Co, Division 1, 31 March 1893; 4, George Harrison v Grimsby T, Division 2, 3 November 1928; 4, Alex Reid v Port Vale, Division 2, 23 February 1929; 4, James McClelland v Reading, Division 2, 6 September 1930; 4, Dick Rowley v Notts Co, Division 2, 16 April 1932; 4, Ted Harper v Burnley, Division 2, 29 August 1932; 4, Ted Harper v Lincoln C, Division 2, 11 March 1933; 4, Charlie Wayman v QPR, Division 2, 25 December 1950; 4, Alex Bruce v Colchester U, Division 3, 28 February 1978; 4, Joe Garner v Crewe Alex, FL 1, 14 March 2015.

Most Capped Player: Tom Finney, 76, England.

Most League Appearances: Alan Kelly, 447, 1961–75.

Youngest League Player: Steve Doyle, 16 years 166 days v Tranmere R, 15 November 1974.

Record Transfer Fee Received: £6,000,000 from Portsmouth for David Nugent, August 2007.

Record Transfer Fee Paid: £1,500,000 to Manchester U for David Healy, December 2000.

Football League Record: 1888 Founder Member of League; 1901–04 Division 2; 1904–12 Division 1; 1912–13 Division 2; 1913–14 Division 1; 1914–15 Division 1; 1919–25 Division 1; 1925–34 Division 2; 1934–49 Division 1; 1949–51 Division 2; 1951–61 Division 1; 1961–70 Division 2; 1970–71 Division 3; 1971–74 Division 2; 1974–78 Division 3; 1978–81 Division 2; 1981–85 Division 3; 1985–87 Division 4; 1987–92 Division 3; 1992–93 Division 2; 1993–96 Division 3; 1996–2000 Division 2; 2000–04 Division 1; 2004–11 FL C; 2011–15 FL 1; 2015– FL C.

LATEST SEQUENCES

Longest Sequence of League Wins: 14, 25.12.1950 – 27.3.1951.

Longest Sequence of League Defeats: 8, 22.9.1984 – 27.10.1984.

Longest Sequence of League Draws: 6, 24.2.1979 – 20.3.1979.

Longest Sequence of Unbeaten League Matches: 23, 8.9.1888 – 14.9.1889.

Longest Sequence Without a League Win: 15, 14.4.1923 – 20.10.1923.

Successive Scoring Runs: 30 from 15.11.1952.

Successive Non-scoring Runs: 6 from 19.11.1960.

MANAGERS

Charlie Parker 1906–15
Vincent Hayes 1919–23
Jim Lawrence 1923–25
Frank Richards 1925–27
Alex Gibson 1927–31
Lincoln Hayes 1931–32
Run by committee 1932–36
Tommy Muirhead 1936–37
Run by committee 1937–49
Will Scott 1949–53
Scot Symon 1953–54
Frank Hill 1954–56
Cliff Britton 1956–61
Jimmy Milne 1961–68
Bobby Seith 1968–70
Alan Ball Snr 1970–73
Bobby Charlton 1973–75
Harry Catterick 1975–77
Nobby Stiles 1977–81
Tommy Docherty 1981
Gordon Lee 1981–83
Alan Kelly 1983–85
Tommy Booth 1985–86
Brian Kidd 1986
John McGrath 1986–90
Les Chapman 1990–92
Sam Allardyce 1992 (*Caretaker*)
John Beck 1992–94
Gary Peters 1994–98
David Moyes 1998–2002
Kelham O'Hanlon 2002 (*Caretaker*)
Craig Brown 2002–04
Billy Davies 2004–06
Paul Simpson 2006–07
Alan Irvine 2007–09
Darren Ferguson 2010
Phil Brown 2011
Graham Westley 2012–13
Simon Grayson February 2013–

TEN YEAR LEAGUE RECORD

		P	W	D	L	F	A	Pts	Pos
2005-06	FL C	46	20	20	6	59	30	80	4
2006-07	FL C	46	22	8	16	64	53	74	7
2007-08	FL C	46	15	11	20	50	56	56	15
2008-09	FL C	46	21	11	14	66	54	74	6
2009-10	FL C	46	13	15	18	58	73	54	17
2010-11	FL C	46	10	12	24	54	79	42	22
2011-12	FL 1	46	13	15	18	54	68	54	15
2012-13	FL 1	46	14	17	15	54	49	59	14
2013-14	FL 1	46	23	16	7	72	46	85	5
2014-15	FL 1	46	25	14	7	79	40	89	3

DID YOU KNOW ?

Preston North End's play-off victory over Swindon Town in May 2015 was the first time they had played at Wembley since 1994. They reached two play-off finals in the interim years but both were staged at the Millennium Stadium in Cardiff.

PRESTON NORTH END – FOOTBALL LEAGUE ONE 2014–15 LEAGUE RECORD

Match No.	Date	Venue	Opponents	Result	H/T Score	Lg Pos.	Goalscorers	Attendance
1	Aug 9	H	Notts Co	D	1-1	0-0	12	Garner [89]	12,857
2	16	A	Scunthorpe U	W	4-0	2-0	6	Garner 2 [17, 82], Llera (og) [39], Humphrey [48]	4013
3	19	A	Doncaster R	D	1-1	0-0	8	Humphrey [66]	6513
4	23	H	Oldham Ath	W	1-0	1-0	3	King [4]	11,678
5	30	H	Sheffield U	D	1-1	1-1	6	Little [11]	11,058
6	Sept 13	A	Walsall	L	1-3	1-1	10	Garner [36]	4776
7	16	H	Chesterfield	D	3-3	3-1	12	Browne [7], Garner [15], Brownhill [28]	8399
8	20	H	Crawley T	W	2-0	1-0	8	Wright [23], Garner (pen) [65]	10,388
9	27	A	Coventry C	W	2-0	0-0	6	Clarke [62], Garner (pen) [67]	10,006
10	Oct 4	H	Colchester U	W	4-2	2-2	5	Wiseman [21], Browne [25], Gallagher [47], Humphrey [57]	8478
11	18	H	Port Vale	W	2-0	1-0	4	Gallagher [42], Browne [81]	9381
12	21	A	Gillingham	W	1-0	0-0	3	Huntington [59]	4632
13	25	H	Fleetwood T	W	3-2	0-2	2	Garner 3 [60, 63, 79]	13,280
14	28	A	Leyton Orient	W	2-0	1-0	2	Robinson [19], Huntington [75]	4650
15	Nov 1	A	Rochdale	L	0-3	0-2	2		6102
16	4	A	Swindon T	L	0-1	0-0	2		6646
17	15	H	Bradford C	L	1-2	0-1	3	Garner [85]	10,302
18	22	A	Bristol C	W	1-0	1-0	3	Robinson [28]	13,245
19	29	A	Yeovil T	W	2-0	1-0	3	Huntington [5], Gallagher [90]	4343
20	Dec 13	H	Milton Keynes D	D	1-1	0-1	4	Wiseman [68]	9856
21	20	A	Peterborough U	W	1-0	1-0	4	Beckford [45]	6803
22	26	H	Barnsley	W	1-0	1-0	4	Gallagher (pen) [16]	13,793
23	28	A	Crewe Alex	D	1-1	0-0	3	Beckford [83]	6429
24	Jan 10	A	Sheffield U	L	1-2	0-0	4	Brownhill [90]	19,902
25	16	H	Leyton Orient	D	2-2	1-1	3	Beckford [23], Gallagher (pen) [68]	8555
26	20	H	Yeovil T	D	1-1	0-1	4	Ebanks-Blake [76]	7491
27	31	A	Crawley T	L	1-2	0-1	4	Huntington [56]	2550
28	Feb 7	H	Coventry C	W	1-0	1-0	4	Davies, K [21]	13,363
29	10	A	Chesterfield	W	2-0	1-0	4	Garner 2 [30, 79]	6309
30	21	A	Scunthorpe U	W	2-0	0-0	4	Johnson [57], Gallagher [71]	9415
31	24	H	Walsall	W	1-0	1-0	4	Johnson [18]	7779
32	28	A	Oldham Ath	W	4-0	2-0	3	Huntington [2], Johnson [32], Garner [52], Beckford [82]	5935
33	Mar 3	H	Doncaster R	D	2-2	1-0	2	Johnson [13], Beckford [90]	8703
34	7	A	Milton Keynes D	W	2-0	0-0	2	Robinson [66], Garner [70]	10,618
35	14	H	Crewe Alex	W	5-1	2-1	2	Garner 4 [11, 24, 72, 79], Beckford [82]	10,203
36	17	H	Peterborough U	W	2-0	1-0	2	Johnson [37], Beckford [81]	8856
37	21	A	Barnsley	D	1-1	1-0	2	Garner [37]	12,471
38	29	H	Fleetwood T	D	1-1	1-0	2	Johnson [9]	5110
39	Apr 3	H	Rochdale	W	1-0	1-0	2	Beckford [36]	12,288
40	6	A	Bradford C	W	3-0	0-0	2	Gallagher [47], Johnson [53], Humphrey [80]	16,032
41	11	H	Bristol C	D	1-1	0-0	2	Beckford [59]	16,441
42	14	A	Gillingham	D	2-2	2-0	2	Beckford [36], Robinson [45]	9417
43	17	A	Port Vale	D	2-2	1-0	2	Johnson [12], Garner (pen) [59]	7210
44	21	A	Notts Co	W	3-1	2-0	2	Beckford 2 [23, 86], Garner [31]	4769
45	25	H	Swindon T	W	3-0	2-0	2	Garner 3 [2, 45, 51]	17,621
46	May 3	A	Colchester U	L	0-1	0-0	3		8413

Final League Position: 3

GOALSCORERS

League (79): Garner 25 (3 pens), Beckford 12, Johnson 8, Gallagher 7 (2 pens), Huntington 5, Humphrey 4, Robinson 4, Browne 3, Brownhill 2, Wiseman 2, Clarke 1, Davies, K 1, Ebanks-Blake 1, King 1, Little 1, Wright 1, own goal 1.
FA Cup (11): Gallagher 5 (1 pen), Robinson 3 (1 pen), Huntington 2, Laird 1.
Capital One Cup (3): Hugill 1, Kilkenny 1, Little 1.
Johnstone's Paint Trophy (7): Clarke 1, Gallagher 1, Garner 1, Hugill 1, Humphrey 1, Huntington 1, Laird 1.
League One Play-Offs (8): Beckford 6, Garner 1 (1 pen), Huntington 1.

Jones J 17	Woods C 12+6	Clarke T 42+1	Wright B 27	Davies B 4	Browne A 14+6	Kilkenny N 24+11	Little A 5+7	Brownhill J 13+5	Garner J 36+1	Gallagher P 45+1	Humphrey C 32+12	Davies K 8+24	Hayhurst W 2+5	King J 10+8	Laird S 27+4	Hugill J —+3	Wiseman S 17+5	Buchanan D 17	Robinson C 18+7	Reid K 5+9	Ryan J —+1	Huntington P 32	Welsh J 30+2	Stuckmann T 7	Beckford J 19+4	Ebanks-Blake S 1+8	Johnstone S 22	Johnson D 20	Match No.
1	2	3	4	5	6	7¹	8²	9	10	11¹	12	13	14																1
1	2	3	4²	5	8	7		6	10	11¹	9³		13	12	14														2
1	2	3	4	5	9	6²	13	8	11	10³	7¹		14	12															3
1	2	3	4¹		12		7	9²	11	10³	8		6	5	13	14													4
1	12	4		5²	9	7	10¹	8³	11	14	6		3		13	2													5
1	2	3	4		14	8	10²		11	7³	9¹	13		6	12		5												6
1	2	3	4		8	7¹		6	10	9²		11³	12		5	13	14												7
1	2	3	4		6	7		9	11	8	13	10²		12		5¹													8
1	14	3	4		6	7		9	11	10¹	8³		2²	5	13	12													9
1		3	4		6	7		9²	11²	10	8¹		2	5	13	12	14												10
1		4			6	7		11¹	9	8³	13	14	3	2	5	12	10⁶												11
1					7	8		10	9	6²	13		3	2	5	11¹¹		4											12
1					7¹	6		11	9	14	12		3	2³	5	10	8²	4	13										13
1	13				14	6¹		11	9²	8	12		3		2	5	10¹	4	7										14
1	3				13	7¹		11	9	8	12		14		2	5	10²	4	6³										15
1	3				10	8³		12	11	9²	6¹	14		2	5		13	4	7										16
1	2				6	7		11	9³	8²	12		3	13		5¹	10	14											17
	3				6			10¹	8	9²	12	13		2	5	11		4	7	1									18
	3				6¹	13		9	8	14		12		2	5		10	4	7²	1	11³								19
	3				8	13		9	6¹	10		5		2		12		4	7	1	11²								20
	3				12	8	13	9²	6³	10		14	5	2				4	7	1	11¹								21
2	3				7	12		9²	6	10	13		5					4	8	1	11¹								22
	3				6	14	11²	8	9³	12	10		5		2			4	7¹	1	13								23
	3				7	12		9	6²	11		2	5	13	14			4	8³	1	10¹	14							24
	3				14	8		7²	10	6¹	13		12	2	5³	9		4		11		1							25
	2	4³			6¹			7	5	10		9		12			13	3	8	11²	14	1							26
4	3				6¹			11	12	13		2²		7				5	9	10		1	8						27
2²	4				7¹	12	13	8³	11	10		9	5					3	14		1	6							28
	3	4			14			10¹	6	12	11		9	5²		11		2	7	13	1	8¹							29
	2	4			12			10²	7²	5	13		9			11		3	8¹	14	1	6							30
	2²	4			13			10¹	9	6	14		5	12		11²		3	8	1	7								31
	3				13			11³	7¹	6²		5	2		10			4	8	12	14	1	9						32
	2	3			12			11¹	10³	6	13		5		9²			4	8	14	1	7							33
14	2	3			11²	10		6¹	12			5		9³			4	8	13	1	7								34
	2	3			13			10	6	12		5		11³			4	7¹	9²	14	1	8							35
14	2	3			10³	6	13	12				5		11¹			4	7	9²	1	8								36
	3	2			13			10	6	12		5		9¹			4	8	11²	1	7								37
13	3				14	10	7³	5	12	4	9			2¹	6			11²	1	8									38
2	4	3			13			10	6	12		5		11²				7	9¹	1	8								39
	3	2			13	14		11	6	5¹		12	9			4²	8³	10	1	7									40
	2	3			10¹	8	5³	14	4	9		13	12			7	11²	1	6										41
2	3	4			14			9	6	12		5¹	13		11		7	10³	1	8²									42
	2	4			10	6	12	14	5			9³			3	8¹	11²	13	1	7									43
12	5	4			13			10³	9²	14		2		6¹			3	8	11	1	7								44
	2	3			14			11³	9	7	12		5		13			4	8¹	10²	1	6							45
	2	4			11	9		6³	13			5¹			12			3	8	10²	14	1	7						46

FA Cup

First Round	Havant and W	(a)	3-0
Second Round	Shrewsbury T	(h)	1-0
Third Round	Norwich C	(h)	2-0
Fourth Round	Sheffield U	(h)	1-1
Replay	Sheffield U	(a)	3-1
Fifth Round	Manchester U	(h)	1-3

Capital One Cup

First Round	Rochdale	(a)	2-0
Second Round	Middlesbrough	(a)	1-3

Johnstone's Paint Trophy

First Round	Shrewsbury T		(h)	1-0
Second Round	Port Vale		(h)	3-2
Northern Quarter-Finals	Oldham Ath		(a)	2-2
(Preston NE won 10-9 on penalties)				
Northern Semi-Finals	Notts Co		(a)	1-0
Northern Final 1st leg	Walsall		(h)	0-2
Northern Final 2nd leg	Walsall		(a)	0-0

League One Play-Offs

Semi-Finals 1st leg	Chesterfield		(a)	1-0
Semi-Finals 2nd leg	Chesterfield		(h)	3-0
Final	Swindon T	Wembley		4-0

QUEENS PARK RANGERS

FOUNDATION

There is an element of doubt about the date of the foundation of this club, but it is believed that in either 1885 or 1886 it was formed through the amalgamation of Christchurch Rangers and St Jude's Institute FC. The leading light was George Wodehouse, whose family maintained a connection with the club until comparatively recent times. Most of the players came from the Queen's Park district so this name was adopted after a year as St Jude's Institute.

Loftus Road Stadium, South Africa Road, Shepherds Bush, London W12 7PJ.

Telephone: (020) 8743 0262.

Fax: (020) 8749 0994.

Ticket Office: (08444) 777 007.

Website: www.qpr.co.uk

Email: customerservices@qpr.co.uk

Ground Capacity: 18,439.

Record Attendance: 41,097 v Leeds U, FA Cup 3rd rd, 9 January 1932 (at White City); 35,353 v Leeds U, Division 1, 27 April 1974 (at Loftus Road).

Pitch Measurements: 100m × 65.85m (109yd × 72yd)

Chairman: Tony Fernandes.

Chief Executive: Mark Donnelly.

Manager: Chris Ramsey.

Assistant Manager: Kevin Bond.

Physio: Nigel Cox.

Colours: Blue and white hooped shirts, white shorts with blue trim, white socks with blue trim.

Year Formed: 1885* (*see Foundation*).

Turned Professional: 1898.

HONOURS

Football League – Division 1:
Runners-up 1975–76;
FL C: *Champions* 2010–11;
Division 2: *Champions* 1982–83;
Runners-up 1967–68, 1972–73, 2003–04;
Division 3 (S): *Champions* 1947–48;
Runners-up 1946–47;
Division 3: *Champions* 1966–67.
FA Cup: *Runners-up* 1982.
Football League Cup: *Winners* 1967;
Runners-up 1986.
European Competitions
UEFA Cup: 1976–77, 1984–85.

Previous Name: 1885, St Jude's; 1887, Queens Park Rangers. *Club Nicknames:* 'Rangers', 'The Hoops', 'R's'.

Grounds: 1885* (*see Foundation*), Welford's Fields; 1888–99, London Scottish Ground, Brondesbury, Home Farm, Kensal Rise Green, Gun Club Wormwood Scrubs, Kilburn Cricket Ground; 1899, Kensal Rise Athletic Ground; 1901, Latimer Road, Notting Hill; 1904, Agricultural Society, Park Royal; 1907, Park Royal Ground; 1917, Loftus Road; 1931, White City; 1933, Loftus Road; 1962, White City; 1963, Loftus Road.

First Football League Game: 28 August 1920, Division 3, v Watford (h) L 1–2 – Price; Blackman, Wingrove; McGovern, Grant, O'Brien; Faulkner, Birch (1), Smith, Gregory, Middlemiss.

Record League Victory: 9–2 v Tranmere R, Division 3, 3 December 1960 – Drinkwater; Woods, Ingham; Keen, Rutter, Angell; Lazarus (2), Bedford (2), Evans (2), Andrews (1), Clark (2).

Record Cup Victory: 8–1 v Bristol R (a), FA Cup 1st rd, 27 November 1937 – Gilfillan; Smith, Jefferson; Lowe, James, March; Cape, Mallett, Cheetham (3), Fitzgerald (3) Bott (2). 8–1 v Crewe Alex, Milk Cup 1st rd, 3 October 1983 – Hucker; Neill, Dawes, Waddock (1), McDonald (1), Fenwick, Micklewhite (1), Stewart (1), Allen (1), Stainrod (3), Gregory.

sky SPORTS FACT FILE

Evelyn Lintott was the first Queens Park Rangers player to be capped for England when he appeared against Ireland in February 1908. He also worked as a schoolteacher in Willesden at the time. He was killed in action on the first day of the Battle of the Somme, 1 July 1916.

Record Defeat: 1–8 v Mansfield T, Division 3, 15 March 1965. 1–8 v Manchester U, Division 1, 19 March 1969.

Most League Points (2 for a win): 67, Division 3, 1966–67.

Most League Points (3 for a win): 88, FL C, 2010–11.

Most League Goals: 111, Division 3, 1961–62.

Highest League Scorer in Season: George Goddard, 37, Division 3 (S), 1929–30.

Most League Goals in Total Aggregate: George Goddard, 174, 1926–34.

Most League Goals in One Match: 4, George Goddard v Merthyr T, Division 3 (S), 9 March 1929; 4, George Goddard v Swindon T, Division 3 (S), 12 April 1930; 4, George Goddard v Exeter C, Division 3 (S), 20 December 1930; 4, George Goddard v Watford, Division 3 (S), 19 September 1931; 4, Tom Cheetham v Aldershot, Division 3 (S), 14 September 1935; 4, Tom Cheetham v Aldershot, Division 3 (S), 12 November 1938.

Most Capped Player: Alan McDonald, 52, Northern Ireland.

Most League Appearances: Tony Ingham, 514, 1950–63.

Youngest League Player: Frank Sibley, 16 years 97 days v Bristol C, 10 March 1964.

Record Transfer Fee Received: £12,000,000 from Anzhi Makhachkala for Chris Samba, July 2013.

Record Transfer Fee Paid: £12,500,000 to Anzhi Makhachkala for Chris Samba, January 2013.

Football League Record: 1920 Original Members of Division 3; 1921–48 Division 3 (S); 1948–52 Division 2; 1952–58 Division 3 (S); 1958–67 Division 3; 1967–68 Division 2; 1968–69 Division 1; 1969–73 Division 2; 1973–79 Division 1; 1979–83 Division 2; 1983–92 Division 1; 1992–96 FA Premier League; 1996–2001 Division 1; 2001–04 Division 2; 2004–11 FL C; 2011–13 FA Premier League; 2013–14 FL C; 2014–15 FA Premier League; 2015– FL C.

LATEST SEQUENCES

Longest Sequence of League Wins: 8, 7.11.1931 – 28.12.1931.

Longest Sequence of League Defeats: 9, 25.2.1969 – 5.4.1969.

Longest Sequence of League Draws: 6, 29.1.2000 – 5.3.2000.

Longest Sequence of Unbeaten League Matches: 20, 11.3.1972 – 23.9.1972.

Longest Sequence Without a League Win: 20, 7.12.1968 – 7.4.1969.

Successive Scoring Runs: 33 from 9.12.1961.

Successive Non-scoring Runs: 6 from 18.3.1939.

MANAGERS

James Cowan 1906–13
Jimmy Howie 1913–20
Ned Liddell 1920–24
Will Wood 1924–25
  (had been Secretary since 1903)
Bob Hewison 1925–31
John Bowman 1931
Archie Mitchell 1931–33
Mick O'Brien 1933–35
Billy Birrell 1935–39
Ted Vizard 1939–44
Dave Mangnall 1944–52
Jack Taylor 1952–59
Alec Stock 1959–65
  (General Manager to 1968)
Bill Dodgin Jnr 1968
Tommy Docherty 1968
Les Allen 1968–71
Gordon Jago 1971–74
Dave Sexton 1974–77
Frank Sibley 1977–78
Steve Burtenshaw 1978–79
Tommy Docherty 1979–80
Terry Venables 1980–84
Gordon Jago 1984
Alan Mullery 1984
Frank Sibley 1984–85
Jim Smith 1985–88
Trevor Francis 1988–89
Don Howe 1989–91
Gerry Francis 1991–94
Ray Wilkins 1994–96
Stewart Houston 1996–97
Ray Harford 1997–98
Gerry Francis 1998–2001
Ian Holloway 2001–06
Gary Waddock 2006
John Gregory 2006–07
Luigi Di Canio 2007–08
Iain Dowie 2008
Paulo Sousa 2008–09
Jim Magilton 2009
Paul Hart 2009–10
Neil Warnock 2010–12
Mark Hughes 2012
Harry Redknapp 2012–15
Chris Ramsey February 2015–

TEN YEAR LEAGUE RECORD

		P	W	D	L	F	A	Pts	Pos
2005-06	FL C	46	12	14	20	50	65	50	21
2006-07	FL C	46	14	11	21	54	68	53	18
2007-08	FL C	46	14	16	16	60	66	58	14
2008-09	FL C	46	15	16	15	42	44	61	11
2009-10	FL C	46	14	15	17	58	65	57	13
2010-11	FL C	46	24	16	6	71	32	88	1
2011-12	PR Lge	38	10	7	21	43	66	37	17
2012-13	PR Lge	38	4	13	21	30	60	25	20
2013-14	FL C	46	23	11	12	60	44	80	4
2014-15	PR Lge	38	8	6	24	42	73	30	20

DID YOU KNOW ?

Gordon Reed, who made 9 appearances as a centre forward for Queens Park Rangers in the 1934–35 season, was a singer and guitarist who performed with dance bands during the close season. He eventually left football and led his own dance band in the late 1930s.

QUEENS PARK RANGERS – FA PREMIERSHIP 2014–15 LEAGUE RECORD

Match No.	Date	Venue	Opponents	Result	H/T Score	Lg Pos.	Goalscorers	Attendance
1	Aug 16	H	Hull C	L	0-1	0-0	18		17,603
2	24	A	Tottenham H	L	0-4	0-3	20		36,109
3	30	H	Sunderland	W	1-0	1-0	12	Austin [45]	17,930
4	Sept 14	A	Manchester U	L	0-4	0-3	16		75,355
5	20	H	Stoke C	D	2-2	1-1	16	Caulker [42], Kranjcar [88]	16,163
6	27	A	Southampton	L	1-2	0-0	18	Austin [66]	30,504
7	Oct 5	A	West Ham U	L	0-2	0-1	20		34,907
8	19	H	Liverpool	L	2-3	0-0	20	Vargas [87], Gerrard (og) [90]	18,069
9	27	H	Aston Villa	W	2-0	1-0	19	Austin 2 [17, 69]	18,022
10	Nov 1	A	Chelsea	L	1-2	0-1	19	Austin [62]	41,486
11	8	H	Manchester C	D	2-2	1-1	19	Austin [21], Demichelis (og) [76]	18,005
12	22	A	Newcastle U	L	0-1	0-0	20		51,915
13	29	H	Leicester C	W	3-2	2-1	18	Morgan (og) [37], Fer [45], Austin [73]	18,054
14	Dec 2	A	Swansea C	L	0-2	0-0	19		20,145
15	6	H	Burnley	W	2-0	0-0	17	Fer [51], Austin [74]	17,785
16	15	A	Everton	L	1-3	0-2	18	Zamora [80]	34,035
17	20	H	WBA	W	3-2	1-2	15	Austin 3 (1 pen) [24 (p), 48, 86]	17,560
18	26	A	Arsenal	L	1-2	0-1	16	Austin (pen) [79]	59,947
19	28	H	Crystal Palace	D	0-0	0-0	15		18,011
20	Jan 1	H	Swansea C	D	1-1	1-0	16	Fer [20]	17,729
21	10	A	Burnley	L	1-2	1-2	19	Austin (pen) [33]	17,523
22	17	H	Manchester U	L	0-2	0-0	19		18,098
23	31	A	Stoke C	L	1-3	1-2	19	Kranjcar [36]	27,512
24	Feb 7	H	Southampton	L	0-1	0-0	19		18,082
25	10	A	Sunderland	W	2-0	2-0	17	Fer [17], Zamora [45]	39,077
26	21	A	Hull C	L	1-2	1-1	17	Austin [39]	24,466
27	Mar 4	H	Arsenal	L	1-2	0-0	18	Austin [82]	17,977
28	7	H	Tottenham H	L	1-2	0-1	18	Sandro [75]	17,992
29	14	A	Crystal Palace	L	1-3	0-3	19	Phillips [83]	24,886
30	22	H	Everton	L	1-2	0-1	19	Vargas [65]	17,706
31	Apr 4	A	WBA	W	4-1	3-0	18	Vargas [15], Austin [37], Zamora [43], Barton [90]	25,735
32	7	A	Aston Villa	D	3-3	1-2	18	Phillips [7], Hill [55], Austin [78]	33,708
33	12	A	Chelsea	L	0-1	0-0	18		17,939
34	25	H	West Ham U	D	0-0	0-0	19		18,036
35	May 2	A	Liverpool	L	1-2	0-1	19	Fer [73]	44,707
36	10	A	Manchester C	L	0-6	0-2	20		44,564
37	16	H	Newcastle U	W	2-1	0-1	20	Phillips [54], Fer [61]	17,608
38	24	A	Leicester C	L	1-5	0-2	20	Austin [57]	31,467

Final League Position: 20

GOALSCORERS

League (42): Austin 18 (3 pens), Fer 6, Phillips 3, Vargas 3, Zamora 3, Kranjcar 2, Barton 1, Caulker 1, Hill 1, Sandro 1, own goals 3.
FA Cup (0).
Capital One Cup (0).

Green R 36	Caulker S 34 + 1	Ferdinand R 11	Dunne R 22 + 1	Simpson D 1	Faurlin A 1 + 1	Mutch J 6 + 3	Barton J 27 + 1	Traore A 7 + 9	Remy L 2	Austin C 35	Phillips M 20 + 5	Hoilett J 9 + 13	Zamora B 19 + 12	Isla M 24 + 2	Fer L 27 + 2	Onuoha N 22 + 1	Hill C 15 + 4	Taarabt A 3 + 4	Sandro 17	Kranjcar N 11 + 11	Vargas E 16 + 5	Henry K 27 + 6	McCarthy A 2 + 1	Yun S 19 + 4	Zarate M — + 4	Wright-Phillips S 1 + 3	Doughty M — + 3	Furlong D 3	Grego-Cox R 1 + 3	Comley B — + 1	Kpekawa C — + 1	Match No.
1	2	3	4^3	5^1	6^2	7	8	9	10	11	12	13	14																			1
1	2	3	4^2		13	7	6	9	11		10^3		14	5	8^1	12																2
1		3	4			7	8	13		11^2	6	9^3	12	2	10^1					5	14											3
1	4	3				12				11^3	10	6		2	7		5^2			8^1	9	13	14									4
1		3	4			7^3	6^2	5		10	12		14	2	8	9				11^1	13											5
1		3	4					5		11	6^3	13	14	2	8	7^2			10	9^1	12											6
1		3	4				14	5		11	6^3	12		2	8	13			9^1	10^2	7											7
	4	3					13	11		12	10^1	6	9	2^3	8^2	14			7				1	5								8
1	4	3					13	11		12	10^3	2	9^2	8	14	6			7			5										9
1	4	3					13	11		9^2	12	2	10^1	8	6	7						5										10
1	4	3					12	11		10	2	9	8^1	6	7	5																11
1	4	3				6	11	13		10	9	2	7^1	12	8^2	5																12
1	4		13			7	12	11	14	2	9	3	6^2	10^1	8	5^3																13
1	4	3				7^1	11	12		10	2	9	8	6	5																	14
1	4	3	13			7	11^4	14		10^3	2	9^2	12	6^1	8	5																15
1		3				7	8	6^2	10	12	2	9^1	4	13	11	5																16
1	4	3				7	10	13		11^2	9	2	12	14	6^3	8	5^1															17
1	4	3				6^2	9			11	12	14	5	13	2	8	10	7^3														18
1	4	3				7	10	13		6	11^2	2	9^1	5	12	8																19
1	4	3				8	11	12		10^1	2	9	5	6	7																	20
1	4	3				8	13	11		12	2	9	5^3	10	6^1	7^2							14									21
1	12	3^2				7		10		11^3	2	9^1	4	5	13				14	6	8											22
1		3				8		11		13	12	2	9	4	5^2				10^1	7	6^1	14										23
1	4	3^1				8	9^2	11	6		13	7	2	5	10^3		14				12											24
1	4	3				7		8^2	11	2^3	9^1			10		6			5	13	12	14										25
1	4	3				8^1	14	10^2	6	11^3				9				7	5	13		12	2									26
1	4							10	6	9^2	11	14		3^1	12	8^2	13		7	5					2							27
1	4	3						11	9	12	10	6^2		2		8^1			7^3	5	14			13								28
1	4							11	9			3	12	10	8^1	13		7	5	6^3		2^1	14									29
1	4					7		11	6	9^2	10^3	2		3	14	8^1	12	13	9^2	13	5^3											30
1	4					7		10	6	11^1		2		3	14	8	12	9^2	13	5^3												31
1	4					8	13	10	6			11		2^1		3	5		7^2	9^3	12					14						32
1	4	14				7		10	6	13	11^2	2^1		3	5		8^3	12	9													33
1	4	3				7		11	6		10^2			13	2	5^1	8		9	12												34
1	4^1	3				7		11	6		13			10	2^4	5	8		9^2	12												35
1	2	3				7		10	5	12	11^3			9^2		4		13	6		8^1	14										36
1^3	4^1	3				7		11	6	9^2				10	2	5				8	12	14				13						37
	3					8		10	6					9	2	4				7^1	1	5^2							11	12	13	38

FA Cup
Third Round   Sheffield U   (h)   0-3

Capital One Cup
Second Round   Burton Alb   (a)   0-1

READING

Madejski Stadium, Junction 11, M4, Reading, Berkshire RG2 0FL.

Telephone: (0118) 968 1100.

Fax: (0870) 999 1001.

Ticket Office: (0118) 968 1313.

Website: www.readingfc.co.uk

Email: customerservice@readingfc.co.uk

Ground Capacity: 24,182.

Record Attendance: 33,042 v Brentford, FA Cup 5th rd, 19 February 1927 (at Elm Park); 24,184 v Everton, FA Premier League, 17 November 2012 (at Madejski Stadium).

Pitch Measurements: 105m × 68m (115yd × 74.5yd)

Co-Chairman: Sir John Madejski.

Co-Chairwoman: Khunying Sasima Srivikorn.

Chief Executive: Nigel Howe.

Manager: Steve Clarke.

Assistant Manager: Kevin Keen.

Head of Sports Science: Nick Harvey.

Colours: Blue and white hooped shirts, blue shorts with red and white trim, white socks with blue trim.

Year Formed: 1871.

Turned Professional: 1895.

Club Nickname: 'The Royals'.

Grounds: 1871, Reading Recreation; Reading Cricket Ground; 1882, Coley Park; 1889, Caversham Cricket Ground; 1896, Elm Park; 1998, Madejski Stadium.

First Football League Game: 28 August 1920, Division 3, v Newport Co (a) W 1–0 – Crawford; Smith, Horler; Christie, Mavin, Getgood; Spence, Weston, Yarnell, Bailey (1), Andrews.

Record League Victory: 10–2 v Crystal Palace, Division 3 (S), 4 September 1946 – Groves; Glidden, Gulliver; McKenna, Ratcliffe, Young; Chitty, Maurice Edelston (3), McPhee (4), Barney (1), Deverell (2).

Record Cup Victory: 6–0 v Leyton, FA Cup 2nd rd, 12 December 1925 – Duckworth; Eggo, McConnell; Wilson, Messer, Evans; Smith (2), Braithwaite (1), Davey (1), Tinsley, Robson (2).

HONOURS

FA Premier League: Best season: 8th, 2006–07.

Football League – FL C:
Champions 2005–06, 2011–12;
Division 1: *Runners-up* 1994–95;
Division 2: *Champions* 1993–94;
Runners-up 2001–02;
Division 3: *Champions* 1985–86;
Division 3 (S): *Champions* 1925–26;
Runners-up 1931–32, 1934–35, 1948–49, 1951–52;
Division 4: *Champions* 1978–79.

FA Cup: Best season: semi-final, 1927.

Football League Cup: Best season: 5th rd, 1996, 1998.

Simod Cup: *Winners* 1988.

sky SPORTS FACT FILE

Centre half Ben Butler, who played for Reading between 1908 and 1912, later enlisted in the Footballers' Battalion in the First World War. He was severely wounded, having a leg blown off, and died shortly afterwards on 13 May 1916. He was the first professional footballer in the battalion to be killed during the war.

Record Defeat: 0–18 v Preston NE, FA Cup 1st rd, 1893–94.

Most League Points (2 for a win): 65, Division 4, 1978–79.

Most League Points (3 for a win): 106, Championship, 2005–06 (Football League Record).

Most League Goals: 112, Division 3 (S), 1951–52.

Highest League Scorer in Season: Ronnie Blackman, 39, Division 3 (S), 1951–52.

Most League Goals in Total Aggregate: Ronnie Blackman, 158, 1947–54.

Most League Goals in One Match: 6, Arthur Bacon v Stoke C, Division 2, 3 April 1931.

Most Capped Player: Kevin Doyle, 26 (61), Republic of Ireland.

Most League Appearances: Martin Hicks, 500, 1978–91.

Youngest League Player: Peter Castle, 16 years 49 days v Watford, 30 April 2003.

Record Transfer Fee Received: £7,000,000 from TSG 1899 Hoffenheim for Gylfi Sigurdsson, August 2010.

Record Transfer Fee Paid: £2,500,000 to Nantes for Emerse Fae, August 2007.

Football League Record: 1920 Original Member of Division 3; 1921–26 Division 3 (S); 1926–31 Division 2; 1931–58 Division 3 (S); 1958–71 Division 3; 1971–76 Division 4; 1976–77 Division 3; 1977–79 Division 4; 1979–83 Division 3; 1983–84 Division 4; 1984–86 Division 3; 1986–88 Division 2; 1988–92 Division 3; 1992–94 Division 2; 1994–98 Division 1; 1998–2002 Division 2; 2002–04 Division 1; 2004–06 FL C; 2006–08 FA Premier League; 2008–12 FL C; 2012–13 FA Premier League; 2013– FL C.

LATEST SEQUENCES

Longest Sequence of League Wins: 13, 17.8.1985 – 19.10.1985.

Longest Sequence of League Defeats: 8, 29.12.2007 – 24.2.2008.

Longest Sequence of League Draws: 6, 23.3.2002 – 20.4.2002.

Longest Sequence of Unbeaten League Matches: 33, 9.8.2005 – 14.2.2006.

Longest Sequence Without a League Win: 14, 30.4.1927 – 29.10.1927.

Successive Scoring Runs: 32 from 1.10.1932.

Successive Non-scoring Runs: 6 from 29.3.2008.

MANAGERS

Thomas Sefton 1897–1901
  (Secretary-Manager)
James Sharp 1901–02
Harry Matthews 1902–20
Harry Marshall 1920–22
Arthur Chadwick 1923–25
H. S. Bray 1925–26
  (Secretary only since 1922 and 1926–35)
Andrew Wylie 1926–31
Joe Smith 1931–35
Billy Butler 1935–39
John Cochrane 1939
Joe Edelston 1939–47
Ted Drake 1947–52
Jack Smith 1952–55
Harry Johnston 1955–63
Roy Bentley 1963–69
Jack Mansell 1969–71
Charlie Hurley 1972–77
Maurice Evans 1977–84
Ian Branfoot 1984–89
Ian Porterfield 1989–91
Mark McGhee 1991–94
Jimmy Quinn/Mick Gooding 1994–97
Terry Bullivant 1997–98
Tommy Burns 1998–99
Alan Pardew 1999–2003
Steve Coppell 2003–09
Brendan Rodgers 2009
Brian McDermott 2009–13
Nigel Adkins 2013–14
Steve Clarke December 2014–

TEN YEAR LEAGUE RECORD

		P	W	D	L	F	A	Pts	Pos
2005-06	FL C	46	31	13	2	99	32	106	1
2006-07	PR Lge	38	16	7	15	52	47	55	8
2007-08	PR Lge	38	10	6	22	41	66	36	18
2008-09	FL C	46	21	14	11	72	40	77	4
2009-10	FL C	46	17	12	17	68	63	63	9
2010-11	FL C	46	20	17	9	77	51	77	5
2011-12	FL C	46	27	8	11	69	41	89	1
2012-13	PR Lge	38	6	10	22	43	73	28	19
2013-14	FL C	46	19	14	13	70	56	71	7
2014-15	FL C	46	13	11	22	48	69	50	19

DID YOU KNOW ?

Reading's Elm Park ground was the first Football League ground to host a women's international match. On 9 November 1973 England defeated Netherlands 1-0 in only their fifth-ever international fixture.

READING – FL CHAMPIONSHIP 2014–15 LEAGUE RECORD

Match No.	Date	Venue	Opponents	Result	H/T Score	Lg Pos.	Goalscorers	Attendance
1	Aug 9	A	Wigan Ath	D 2-2	0-1	9	Cummings [71], Morrison [77]	12,174
2	16	H	Ipswich T	W 1-0	1-0	5	Taylor, J [26]	17,198
3	19	H	Huddersfield T	L 1-2	0-2	10	Cox [79]	15,035
4	23	A	Nottingham F	L 0-4	0-1	19		22,795
5	30	A	Middlesbrough	W 1-0	1-0	15	Cox [7]	14,970
6	Sept 13	H	Fulham	W 3-0	1-0	9	Murray 2 [15, 54], Blackman [85]	18,790
7	16	H	Millwall	W 3-2	2-1	6	Cox 2 [6, 84], Blackman (pen) [15]	15,091
8	20	A	Sheffield W	L 0-1	0-0	10		29,848
9	28	H	Wolverhampton W	D 3-3	1-0	11	Hector [19], Taylor, J [55], Murray [89]	17,454
10	Oct 1	A	Leeds U	D 0-0	0-0	10		20,705
11	4	A	Brentford	L 1-3	0-2	13	Cox [49]	10,776
12	18	H	Derby Co	L 0-3	0-2	16		18,141
13	21	A	Bournemouth	L 0-3	0-0	17		8899
14	25	H	Blackpool	W 3-0	1-0	14	Murray [23], Clarke (og) [69], Blackman (pen) [90]	15,625
15	Nov 1	A	Blackburn R	L 1-3	1-1	15	Murray [44]	14,237
16	4	H	Rotherham U	W 3-0	1-0	13	Mackie [29], Cox 2 [55, 64]	13,775
17	8	H	Charlton Ath	L 0-1	0-1	14		16,989
18	21	A	Cardiff C	L 1-2	0-2	14	Hector [81]	20,643
19	29	A	Norwich C	W 2-1	2-1	14	Cooper 2 [14, 45]	26,002
20	Dec 6	H	Bolton W	D 0-0	0-0	14		15,421
21	13	A	Birmingham C	L 1-6	1-4	16	Murray [19]	15,240
22	20	H	Watford	L 0-1	0-0	17		18,522
23	26	A	Brighton & HA	D 2-2	2-1	17	Murray 2 [1, 26]	26,173
24	28	H	Norwich C	W 2-1	2-0	16	Robson-Kanu (pen) [25], Cox [34]	19,430
25	Jan 10	H	Middlesbrough	D 0-0	0-0	17		17,131
26	17	A	Fulham	L 1-2	0-0	18	Pogrebnyak [63]	17,831
27	27	A	Millwall	D 0-0	0-0	18		8317
28	31	H	Sheffield W	W 2-0	2-0	16	Pogrebnyak [29], Chalobah [40]	17,755
29	Feb 7	A	Wolverhampton W	W 2-1	1-1	13	Pogrebnyak [1], Williams [70]	20,274
30	10	H	Leeds U	L 0-2	0-0	14		18,124
31	17	H	Wigan Ath	L 0-1	0-1	17		14,601
32	21	A	Ipswich T	W 1-0	1-0	14	Mackie [14]	21,298
33	24	A	Huddersfield T	L 0-3	0-1	15		10,282
34	28	H	Nottingham F	L 0-3	0-0	18		18,586
35	Mar 3	A	Bolton W	D 1-1	0-0	18	Mackie [90]	12,795
36	10	H	Brighton & HA	W 2-1	1-0	16	Mackie 2 [24, 56]	14,748
37	14	A	Watford	L 1-4	0-2	17	Karacan [70]	16,660
38	21	A	Charlton Ath	L 2-3	1-0	19	Pogrebnyak 2 [40, 90]	15,007
39	Apr 4	H	Cardiff C	D 1-1	1-0	19	Pogrebnyak [4]	17,953
40	7	A	Blackpool	D 1-1	0-1	18	Hall (og) [46]	9614
41	11	H	Blackburn R	D 0-0	0-0	18		17,564
42	14	H	Bournemouth	L 0-1	0-1	18		18,917
43	22	H	Birmingham C	L 0-1	0-0	19		14,604
44	25	H	Brentford	L 0-2	0-1	19		20,048
45	28	A	Rotherham U	L 1-2	0-0	20	Norwood [87]	11,123
46	May 2	A	Derby Co	W 3-0	1-0	19	Appiah [2], Hector [72], McCleary (pen) [85]	30,806

Final League Position: 19

GOALSCORERS

League (48): Cox 8, Murray 8, Pogrebnyak 6, Mackie 5, Blackman 3 (2 pens), Hector 3, Cooper 2, Taylor, J 2, Appiah 1, Chalobah 1, Cummings 1, Karacan 1, McCleary 1 (1 pen), Morrison 1, Norwood 1, Robson-Kanu 1 (1 pen), Williams 1, own goals 2.
FA Cup (9): Robson-Kanu 3, McCleary 2, Blackman 1, Mackie 1, Norwood 1, Yakubu 1.
Capital One Cup (4): Blackman 1, Pogrebnyak 1, Tanner 1, Taylor, J 1.

Federici A 43	Gunter C 38	Morrison S 1	Pearce A 39 + 1	Cummings S 4 + 1	Blackman N 16 + 21	Hector M 40 + 1	Obita J 43	Taylor J 14 + 8	Edwards R 4 + 3	Pogrebnyak P 17 + 9	Guthrie D 2 + 7	Cox S 28 + 9	Akpan H 14 + 6	Cooper J 9 + 6	Stacey J 2 + 4	Kuhl A 3 + 3	Mackie J 18 + 14	Tanner C — + 3	Norwood O 32 + 6	Tshibola A — + 1	Murray G 18	Andersen M 3	Robson-Kanu H 26 + 3	Williams D 21 + 4	Ferdinand A 1 + 1	Kelly S 14 + 1	McCleary G 22 + 4	Karacan J 5 + 3	Chalobah N 15	Yakubu A 3 + 4	Keown N 1 + 1	Travner J 1	Knight Z 2	Novakovich A — + 2	Ake N 5	Appiah K 2 + 4	Fosu T — + 1	Match No.
1	2	3	4	5	6	7	8	9^2	10^1	11	12	13																										1
1	2		4	5	6^2	3	9	7^3	12	11		10^1	8	13	14																							2
1	2		4	5^2	6^3	3	8	9^1		11		10	7				12	13	14																			3
1	2		4	5	6	3	11^3	9^2	7^1			10					8		13	12	14																	4
1	2		4			3	5	9	6			10^3	12	14		7^2	11	13	8^1																			5
1	2		4		13	3	5	9	14	12		10	8^3			6^1		7	11^2																			6
1	2		4		9^2	3	5	12	13			10	7^1	14		6^3		8	11																			7
	2		4		6		5	9			12	14	10^3	8^2	3		13		7	11^1	1																	8
1	2		4		6	3	5	9^2			12	10^1	7^3			14	13	8	11																			9
1	2	3		6	4	5	9^2			12	10^1	7^3					14	8	11	13																		10
1	2		4		6	3	5		10^2	14		12				7^1	13	8	11		9^3																	11
1	2		4		14	3	5	8		13		10				12	6^3		7^2	11	9^1																	12
1	2		4		9	3	5	12				13					10^1	7		6	8			11^2														13
1	2		4		14	3	5	12				13					10^1	7		6^3	8		11^2	9														14
1	2	3			6		5	9^1				12	7^3	4			13	8	11		10^2	14																15
1	2		4			12	9	14				10^1	13				6	7	11			8^3	3^2	5														16
1	5		4		13	3	9		14			10^2					6^1	8	11		12	7	2^3															17
1	5	$4^•$		14		3	9	13				11^2					7	10		6^3	8^1	2	12															18
1	5			13		3	9	12						4			7	10^2	11		8^1	14	2	6^3														19
1	5			13		3	9	14						4			7	10	11^1		8^2	2	6^3															20
1	5	12		13		3^1	9^1	14				10		4			7	11			8^2	2	6^3															21
1	2		4		9	3	5					10	12				7	11			8^1	6																22
1	2		4	12	13	3	5	6^1				10					7	11^3	9^2	8	14																	23
1	2		4		14	3	5		13	10^3							12	8	11^1		9	7	6^2															24
1	2		4		12	3	5			10^1	13	11					6^3	7^2			9	8	14															25
1	2	3		12		4	5			11^2		10^1					13	8			9	7	6															26
1			4	11^3		3	5			10		12					14	7				9^1	6	2	13	8^2												27
1			4	13		3	5			11		10^1					14	12				9^2	7	2	6	8												28
1			4	13		3	5			11		10^2	14					12				9^3	7	2	6	8^1												29
1			4	11^1		3	5			10^3		13					12	7^2				6	2	9	8	14												30
1			4	13			5			10		11^1	14				8				9^2	7^3	2	6	3	12												31
1			4			3	5			11		10^3	12	14			6^2	6				9^1	7	2	13	8												32
1			4	13		3	5	11^2			8^3	7					12	6			14	2^3	9		10													33
1	2		4			3	5			10	13	11^1					9^2	7				6	8	12														34
1	2		4	12		3	5			11		13					6	7			9^1	14	10^3	8^2														35
1	2			9		3				12				7	4		10^2	13			11^3	6^1	5	8	14													36
				13				9^3				8	10	7	5	6	1						12	11	3	2	4^1	14										37
1	2	3		13		4	5		11								10	8^1				9^2	$7^•$			6	12											38
1	2	3		14		4	5		11				8				10^1	13				9^3				6^2					7	12					39
1	2	3					5			12	14		13				8				9			6^1		11^3	4			7	10^2						40
1	2		4		5			11^3		13		10	12				9					6^1	8^2	7							3	14					41
1	2	3		4	5			10									11^{12}	9			7^3	6^2	14				8	13									42
1	2		11^1	4	9						3	13					10^2					6^3	7	8						14	5	12					43
1	2	3		14	4	5				12							13	10	7			11^1	8				9^3	6^2									44
		5						3	11^3		10^2		9		4	14	13	7		1				2	12	6	8^1									11	12	45
1	2		4				3	5					14	10^3				6^2					13			8	9^1	7									46

ROCHDALE

FOUNDATION

Considering the love of rugby in their area, it is not surprising that Rochdale had difficulty in establishing an Association Football club. The earlier Rochdale Town club formed in 1900 went out of existence in 1907 when the present club was immediately established and joined the Manchester League, before graduating to the Lancashire Combination in 1908.

Spotland Stadium, Willbutts Lane, Rochdale, Lancs OL11 5DS.

Telephone: (0844) 826 1907.

Fax: (01706) 648 466.

Ticket Office: (0844) 826 1907 (option 8).

Website: www.rochdaleafc.co.uk

Email: admin@rochdaleafc.co.uk

Ground Capacity: 10,037.

Record Attendance: 24,231 v Notts Co, FA Cup 2nd rd, 10 December 1949.

Pitch Measurements: 104m × 69.5m (114yd × 76yd)

Chairman: Chris Dunphy.

Chief Executive: Colin Garlick.

Manager: Keith Hill.

Assistant Manager: Chris Beech.

Physio: Andy Thorpe.

Colours: Blue shirts with white trim, blue shorts, blue socks.

Year Formed: 1907.

Turned Professional: 1907.

Club Nickname: 'The Dale'.

Ground: 1907, St Clements Playing Fields (original name Spotland).

First Football League Game: 27 August 1921, Division 3 (N), v Accrington Stanley (h) W 6–3 – Crabtree; Nuttall, Sheehan; Hill, Farrer, Yarwood; Hoad, Sandiford, Dennison (2), Owens (3), Carney (1).

Record League Victory: 8–1 v Chesterfield, Division 3 (N), 18 December 1926 – Hill; Brown, Ward; Hillhouse, Parkes, Braidwood; Hughes, Bertram, Whitehurst (5), Schofield (2), Martin (1).

Record Cup Victory: 8–2 v Crook T, FA Cup 1st rd, 26 November 1927 – Moody; Hopkins, Ward; Braidwood, Parkes, Barker; Tompkinson, Clennell (3) Whitehurst (4), Hall, Martin (1).

Record Defeat: 1–9 v Tranmere R, Division 3 (N), 25 December 1931.

HONOURS

Football League – FL 1: Best season: 8th, 2014–15; **Division 3 (N):** *Runners-up* 1923–24, 1926–27.

FA Cup: Best season: 5th rd, 1990, 2003.

Football League Cup: *Runners-up* 1962.

sky SPORTS FACT FILE

During the First World War Rochdale were one of a handful of non-league clubs invited to join in the Football League's emergency competitions. Dale took part in the Lancashire Section tournaments between 1915–16 and 1918–19 whilst members of the Central League. It was not until 1921–22 that the club was elected to membership of the Football League.

Most League Points (2 for a win): 62, Division 3 (N), 1923–24.

Most League Points (3 for a win): 82, FL 2, 2009–10.

Most League Goals: 105, Division 3 (N), 1926–27.

Highest League Scorer in Season: Albert Whitehurst, 44, Division 3 (N), 1926–27.

Most League Goals in Total Aggregate: Reg Jenkins, 119, 1964–73.

Most League Goals in One Match: 6, Tommy Tippett v Hartlepools U, Division 3 (N), 21 April 1930.

Most Capped Player: Leo Bertos, 6 (56), New Zealand.

Most League Appearances: Gary Jones, 470, 1998–2001; 2003–12.

Youngest League Player: Zac Hughes, 16 years 105 days v Exeter C, 19 September 1987.

Record Transfer Fee Received: £750,000 from Brentford for Scott Hogan, July 2014.

Record Transfer Fee Paid: £150,000 to Stoke C for Paul Connor, March 2001.

Football League Record: 1921 Elected to Division 3 (N); 1958–59 Division 3; 1959–69 Division 4; 1969–74 Division 3; 1974–92 Division 4; 1992–2004 Division 3; 2004–10 FL 2; 2010–12 FL 1; 2012–14 FL 2; 2014– FL 1.

LATEST SEQUENCES

Longest Sequence of League Wins: 8, 29.9.1969 – 3.11.1969.

Longest Sequence of League Defeats: 17, 14.11.1931 – 12.3.1932.

Longest Sequence of League Draws: 6, 17.8.1968 – 14.9.1968.

Longest Sequence of Unbeaten League Matches: 20, 15.9.1923 – 19.1.1924.

Longest Sequence Without a League Win: 28, 14.11.1931 – 29.8.1932.

Successive Scoring Runs: 29 from 10.10.2008.

Successive Non-scoring Runs: 9 from 14.3.1980.

MANAGERS

Billy Bradshaw 1920
Run by committee 1920–22
Tom Wilson 1922–23
Jack Peart 1923–30
Will Cameron 1930–31
Herbert Hopkinson 1932–34
Billy Smith 1934–35
Ernest Nixon 1935–37
Sam Jennings 1937–38
Ted Goodier 1938–52
Jack Warner 1952–53
Harry Catterick 1953–58
Jack Marshall 1958–60
Tony Collins 1960–68
Bob Stokoe 1967–68
Len Richley 1968–70
Dick Conner 1970–73
Walter Joyce 1973–76
Brian Green 1976–77
Mike Ferguson 1977–78
Doug Collins 1979
Bob Stokoe 1979–80
Peter Madden 1980–83
Jimmy Greenhoff 1983–84
Vic Halom 1984–86
Eddie Gray 1986–88
Danny Bergara 1988–89
Terry Dolan 1989–91
Dave Sutton 1991–94
Mick Docherty 1994–96
Graham Barrow 1996–99
Steve Parkin 1999–2001
John Hollins 2001–02
Paul Simpson 2002–03
Alan Buckley 2003
Steve Parkin 2003–06
Keith Hill 2007–11
  (caretaker from December 2006)
Steve Eyre 2011
John Coleman 2012–13
Keith Hill January 2013–

TEN YEAR LEAGUE RECORD

		P	W	D	L	F	A	Pts	Pos
2005-06	FL 2	46	14	14	18	66	69	56	14
2006-07	FL 2	46	18	12	16	70	50	66	9
2007-08	FL 2	46	23	11	12	77	54	80	5
2008-09	FL 2	46	19	13	14	70	59	70	6
2009-10	FL 2	46	25	7	14	82	48	82	3
2010-11	FL 1	46	18	14	14	63	55	68	9
2011-12	FL 1	46	8	14	24	47	81	38	24
2012-13	FL 2	46	16	13	17	68	70	61	12
2013-14	FL 2	46	24	9	13	69	48	81	3
2014-15	FL 1	46	19	6	21	72	66	63	8

DID YOU KNOW ?

Rochdale applied for re-election to the Football League on 10 occasions prior to 1987 when automatic promotion and relegation was introduced. They came close to losing their place in 1980 when they polled only 26 votes, just enough to put them ahead of challengers Altrincham who had 25 votes.

ROCHDALE – FOOTBALL LEAGUE ONE 2014–15 LEAGUE RECORD

Match No.	Date	Venue	Opponents	Result		H/T Score	Lg Pos.	Goalscorers	Attendance
1	Aug 9	H	Peterborough U	L	0-1	0-0	20		3613
2	16	A	Chesterfield	L	1-2	0-1	21	Henderson (pen) [90]	5682
3	19	A	Crewe Alex	W	5-2	2-1	17	Henderson [31], Done 3 [42, 55, 72], Vincenti [66]	3742
4	23	H	Bristol C	D	1-1	0-1	17	Henderson [56]	3115
5	30	H	Bradford C	L	0-2	0-0	20		4758
6	Sept 6	A	Crawley T	W	4-0	1-0	13	Done [10], Vincenti 2 [54, 66], Andrew [75]	2534
7	13	A	Sheffield U	L	0-0	0-0	17		19,122
8	16	H	Walsall	W	4-0	3-0	11	Done [5], Eastham [30], Henderson [37], Butler (og) [71]	2082
9	20	H	Coventry C	W	1-0	1-0	7	Henderson (pen) [29]	3583
10	27	A	Leyton Orient	W	3-2	1-2	5	Done 2 [4, 66], Vincenti [48]	4405
11	Oct 4	H	Barnsley	L	0-1	0-1	9		4380
12	18	H	Gillingham	D	1-1	1-0	12	Vincenti [25]	2574
13	21	A	Swindon T	W	3-2	0-1	9	Lund [49], Vincenti [60], Hery [90]	6718
14	25	A	Yeovil T	W	3-0	2-0	8	O'Connell [6], Henderson 2 [16, 53]	3601
15	Nov 1	H	Preston NE	W	3-0	2-0	4	O'Connell [28], Henderson [32], Done [61]	6102
16	15	H	Port Vale	L	0-1	0-0	8		5043
17	22	H	Doncaster R	L	1-3	1-1	9	Done [8]	3229
18	25	A	Milton Keynes D	D	2-2	1-1	7	Flanagan (og) [20], Noble-Lazarus [76]	6720
19	29	H	Oldham Ath	L	0-3	0-1	9		7269
20	Dec 13	A	Colchester U	W	4-1	3-0	6	Lund [26], Vincenti [29], Henderson (pen) [41], O'Connell [56]	2920
21	20	H	Notts Co	D	2-2	0-1	6	Henderson [46], Vincenti [64]	2814
22	26	A	Scunthorpe U	L	1-2	0-0	7	Done [69]	4004
23	28	H	Fleetwood T	L	0-2	0-2	8		3123
24	Jan 10	A	Bradford C	W	2-1	1-1	8	Vincenti [13], Andrew [90]	13,571
25	17	H	Crawley T	W	4-1	2-0	5	Tanser [33], Henderson 2 [38, 88], Andrew [90]	2255
26	31	A	Coventry C	D	2-2	1-2	7	Camps [33], Andrew [66]	7606
27	Feb 10	A	Walsall	L	2-3	0-3	12	Vincenti [55], Eastham [63]	3567
28	14	A	Peterborough U	L	1-2	1-2	15	Rafferty [24]	5163
29	21	H	Chesterfield	W	1-0	0-0	13	Henderson [65]	2967
30	24	H	Sheffield U	L	1-2	0-1	13	O'Connell [74]	3574
31	28	A	Bristol C	L	0-1	0-1	15		11,841
32	Mar 3	H	Crewe Alex	W	4-0	1-0	15	Henderson 2 (2 pens) [38, 73], Bunney 2 [57, 80]	1954
33	7	A	Colchester U	W	2-1	1-0	13	Bennett [6], Henderson [55]	2625
34	14	H	Fleetwood T	L	0-1	0-0	13		3822
35	17	A	Notts Co	W	2-1	1-1	10	Henderson [35], Vincenti [54]	3159
36	21	H	Scunthorpe U	W	3-1	1-0	8	Rose [22], Henderson [61], Vincenti [84]	2738
37	24	A	Oldham Ath	L	0-3	0-1	8		5322
38	28	H	Yeovil T	W	2-1	0-0	6	Bennett [51], O'Connell [53]	2650
39	Apr 3	A	Preston NE	L	0-1	0-1	8		12,288
40	6	H	Port Vale	W	1-0	0-0	7	Andrew [90]	2948
41	11	A	Doncaster R	D	1-1	0-1	7	Henderson [59]	5695
42	14	H	Swindon T	L	2-4	1-4	7	Henderson (pen) [45], Thompson (og) [90]	2344
43	18	A	Gillingham	L	0-1	0-1	7		5430
44	21	H	Leyton Orient	W	1-0	0-0	7	Henderson [66]	1914
45	25	H	Milton Keynes D	L	2-3	0-2	7	Vincenti [66], Henderson [86]	3501
46	May 3	A	Barnsley	L	0-5	0-0	8		9593

Final League Position: 8

GOALSCORERS

League (72): Henderson 22 (6 pens), Vincenti 13, Done 10, Andrew 5, O'Connell 5, Bennett 2, Bunney 2, Eastham 2, Lund 2, Camps 1, Hery 1, Noble-Lazarus 1, Rafferty 1, Rose 1, Tanser 1, own goals 3.
FA Cup (8): Done 3, Vincenti 2 (1 pen), Bennett 1, Lancashire 1, Noble-Lazarus 1.
Capital One Cup (0).
Johnstone's Paint Trophy (3): Andrew 1, Done 1, Vincenti 1.

Lillis J 14+2	Rafferty J 28+3	Lancashire O 16+5	Tanser S 27+3	Rose M 26+6	Bennett R 33+6	Allen J 33+2	Lund M 12+2	Done M 23	Henderson I 44	Donnelly G 1+2	Andrew C 5+27	Vincenti P 36+1	Bunney J 10+9	Kennedy T 22+1	Dawson S 27+3	Hery B 12+9	Diba Musangu J —+1	Logan C 19	Eastham A 40+1	Camps C 6+6	Fenelon S —+4	O'Connell J 28+1	Bell N —+3	Cannon A 16+2	Muldoon J 2+1	Noble-Lazarus R 7+12	Cywka T 1+2	Logan J 4+4	Brandy F 1+3	Jones J 13	Match No.
	2¹	3	4	5	6	7²	8	9	10	11³	12	13	14																		1
1⁴	2		4³		6		7¹	9	10	14	11			3	5	8	12	13													2
	2		4		6	11		9²	10		12	8³		5	14	7¹		1	3	13											3
	2		4	14	6	7			10	11¹		9²	12	5	13	8¹		1	3												4
	2¹		4		6	7			10			9²	13	14	11¹	5	8	1	3	12											5
	2		5		13	9		11²	10	12		6¹				8	7³	1	3	14	4										6
	2²		5		6³		8¹	10	11	14	9			12	7			1	3	13	4										7
	2		5		14	7		11¹	10	13	9³					8	6²	1	3	12	4										8
	2²		5		13	7		11¹	10		8	12				9	6³	1	3		4		14								9
		12	5		2	6²		11¹	8		10	14				9	7²	1	3■	4	13										10
		2³	3	5				7	6²		10	11	12	9¹	13			1	8	14	4										11
					5	7	2	8	13	10²	11	12		9		6¹		1	3			4									12
					5²	12	2	6	8	10	11	13		9³	7¹	14		1	3			4									13
					6	5	2	8¹	7		10²	11	12	13				1	3			4									14
		13	12³		5	8	2¹	6	11		9		14	10		7²		1	3			4									15
			2³		5	7²	9	6	12	11		10¹				8		1	3			4				13	14				16
		13	3		12	5¹	2	7	6	10■	11²			9				1	4							8					17
		13			5		2	6	11		14	7²	12					1	3			4	8		10³		9¹				18
					5		2	7³	6		14	8		9²				1	3			4				11¹	10	13			19
	2	7			5			6²	10		8	12	11¹	9	13			1	3			4									20
12	5	3			6	13		7	9		10¹	14	11²	8			1³		2			4									21
1	2				5			6¹	8²		10	9	13	7					4				3	12		14	11³				22
1	5	3			8			6	9	11	12	10¹				7²			2³	13		4			14						23
1	2	4	5²		12	6			10	11³	14	7		8					3	9¹						13					24
1	2	4			5	7			13		10¹	11	12	9³					3	8¹				14							25
1	2³	4			5	14		6¹	9			11	12	7					3	10²				13							26
1	4				5²			7³	10			11	8	13					3	9¹		12	2		14						27
1	2				6			9²	11		12		14	10		5			3³	13		4				7¹					28
1	2	3¹			8				10		9		11	5		7²	13		12			4		6							29
1	2				7	14			10			9²	5	6					3			4	13	12		8¹	11¹				30
	2¹				6	7	8		11			9	10²	5					3			4		2³		10¹	13			1	31
	2¹				12	7	6	8	10			9	11	5					3			4				13				1	32
					6	7	9		10			8	11²	5		12						4	3	2¹		13				1	33
		14	12		7	6	9		11			10³	8¹	5					3			4		2⁴		13				1	34
					10	6	9		11			7	5	8								4	3	2						1	35
					7	6	8		11¹			10	13	5		9²			3			4		2		12				1	36
		14			7	6	9¹		11			8²	5	10³		13			3			4		2		12				1	37
12		4	11²		7	8			10			9	5							6¹		3	2		13				1	38
1		4			7	6			10			13	9²	11¹		5			8³				3	2		12	14				39
	5				7	6			11			12	8	4		9²			3				14	2³		10¹		13		1	40
	5²				7	6	9		11			13	8	4					3				12	2					10¹	1	41
	5				7²	6²	9		11			13	10¹	8		4			14				3	2		12				1	42
14	2				12	7	6■		10			11³	9¹	4									5			8²		13		1■	43
1	2	9	8		7	6¹			11			12	10	4									5							1	44
		3	5		7²	6	10¹		11			12	8	14		4						9³	2			13				1	45
1	2■	4	6		12	13			11			7	5						3				14	8¹		10²		9³			46

FA Cup

First Round	Northampton T	(a)	0-0
Replay	Northampton T	(h)	2-1
Second Round	Aldershot T	(a)	0-0
Replay	Aldershot T	(h)	4-1
Third Round	Nottingham F	(h)	1-0
Fourth Round	Stoke C	(h)	1-4

Capital One Cup

First Round	Preston NE	(h)	0-2

Johnstone's Paint Trophy

First Round	Crewe Alex	(a)	3-0
Second Round	Walsall	(h)	0-1

ROTHERHAM UNITED

FOUNDATION

Rotherham were formed in 1870 before becoming Town in the late 1880s. Thornhill United were founded in 1877 and changed their name to Rotherham County in 1905. The Town amalgamated with Rotherham County to form Rotherham United in 1925.

The AESSEAL New York Stadium, New York Way, Rotherham, South Yorkshire S60 1AH.

Telephone: (0844) 4140 733.

Fax: (0844) 4140 744.

Ticket Office: (0844) 4140 754.

Website: www.themillers.co.uk

Email: office@rotherhamunited.net

Ground Capacity: 12,009.

Record Attendance: 25,170 v Sheffield U, Division 2, 13 December 1952 (at Millmoor); 7,082 v Aldershot T, FL 2 Play-offs semi-final 2nd leg, 19 May 2010 (at Don Valley); 11,758 v Sheffield U, FL 1, 7 September 2013 (at New York Stadium).

Pitch Measurements: 102m × 66m (111.5yd × 72yd)

Chairman: Tony Stewart.

Chief Operating Officer: Paul Douglas.

Manager: Steve Evans.

Assistant Manager: Paul Raynor.

Head of Medical: Denis Circuit.

HONOURS

Football League – Division 2:
Runners-up 2000–01;
Division 3: *Champions* 1980–81;
Runners-up 1999–2000;
Division 3 (N): *Champions* 1950–51;
Runners-up 1946–47, 1947–48, 1948–49;
Division 4: *Champions* 1988–89;
Runners-up 1991–92.

FL 2: *Runners-up* 2012–13.

FA Cup: Best season: 5th rd, 1953, 1968.

Football League Cup:
Runners-up 1961.

Auto Windscreens Shield:
Winners 1996.

Colours: Red shirts with white trim, white shorts with red trim, red socks with white trim.

Year Formed: 1870. *Turned Professional:* 1905. *Club Nickname:* 'The Millers'.

Previous Names: 1877, Thornhill United; 1905, Rotherham County; 1925, amalgamated with Rotherham Town under Rotherham United.

Grounds: 1870, Red House Ground; 1907, Millmoor; 2008, Don Valley Stadium; 2012, New York Stadium (renamed The AESSEAL New York Stadium 2014).

First Football League Game: 2 September 1893, Division 2, Rotherham T v Lincoln C (a) D 1–1 – McKay; Thickett, Watson; Barr, Brown, Broadhead; Longden, Cutts, Leatherbarrow, McCormick, Pickering, (1 og). 30 August 1919, Division 2, Rotherham Co v Nottingham F (h) W 2–0 – Branston; Alton, Baines; Bailey, Coe, Stanton; Lee (1), Cawley (1), Glennon, Lees, Lamb.

Record League Victory: 8–0 v Oldham Ath, Division 3 (N), 26 May 1947 – Warnes; Selkirk, Ibbotson; Edwards, Horace Williams, Danny Williams; Wilson (2), Shaw (1), Ardron (3), Guest (1), Hainsworth (1).

Record Cup Victory: 6–0 v Spennymoor U, FA Cup 2nd rd, 17 December 1977 – McAlister; Forrest, Breckin, Womble, Stancliffe, Green, Finney, Phillips (3), Gwyther (2) (Smith), Goodfellow, Crawford (1). 6–0 v Wolverhampton W, FA Cup 1st rd, 16 November 1985 – O'Hanlon; Forrest, Dungworth, Gooding (1), Smith (1), Pickering, Birch (2), Emerson, Tynan (1), Simmons (1), Pugh. 6–0 v Kings Lynn, FA Cup 2nd rd, 6 December 1997 – Mimms; Clark, Hurst (Goodwin), Garner (1) (Hudson) (1), Warner (Bass), Richardson (1), Berry (1), Thompson, Druce (1), Glover (1), Roscoe.

Record Defeat: 1–11 v Bradford C, Division 3 (N), 25 August 1928.

sky SPORTS FACT FILE

Rotherham United had to wait until the 21st game of 2004–05 before recording their first League win of the season. The 1-0 win over Yorkshire rivals Leeds United was most welcome, but the Millers remained rooted to the foot of the Championship table and were relegated at the end of the season.

Most League Points (2 for a win): 71, Division 3 (N), 1950–51.
Most League Points (3 for a win): 91, Division 2, 2000–01.
Most League Goals: 114, Division 3 (N), 1946–47.
Highest League Scorer in Season: Wally Ardron, 38, Division 3 (N), 1946–47.
Most League Goals in Total Aggregate: Gladstone Guest, 130, 1946–56.
Most League Goals in One Match: 4, Roland Bastow v York C, Division 3 (N), 9 November 1935; 4, Roland Bastow v Rochdale, Division 3 (N), 7 March 1936; 4, Wally Ardron v Crewe Alex, Division 3 (N), 5 October 1946; 4, Wally Ardron v Carlisle U, Division 3 (N), 13 September 1947; 4, Wally Ardron v Hartlepools U, Division 3 (N), 13 October 1948; 4, Ian Wilson v Liverpool, Division 2, 2 May 1955; 4, Carl Gilbert v Swansea C, Division 3, 28 September 1971; 4, Carl Airey v Chester, Division 3, 31 August 1987; 4, Shaun Goater v Hartlepool U, Division 3, 9 April 1994; 4, Lee Glover v Hull C, Division 3, 28 December 1997; 4, Darren Byfield v Millwall, Division 1, 10 August 2002; 4, Adam Le Fondre v Cheltenham T, FL 2, 21 August 2010.
Most Capped Player: Kari Arnason, 20 (39), Iceland.
Most League Appearances: Danny Williams, 461, 1946–62.
Youngest League Player: Kevin Eley, 16 years 72 days v Scunthorpe U, 15 May 1984.
Record Transfer Fee Received: £900,000 from Bristol C for Kieran Agard, August 2014.
Record Transfer Fee Paid: £400,000 to Oldham Ath for Jonson Clarke-Harris, September 2014.
Football League Record: 1893 Rotherham Town elected to Division 2; 1896 Failed re-election; 1919 Rotherham County elected to Division 2; 1923–51 Division 3 (N); 1951–68 Division 2; 1968–73 Division 3; 1973–75 Division 4; 1975–81 Division 3; 1981–83 Division 2; 1983–88 Division 3; 1988–89 Division 4; 1989–91 Division 3; 1991–92 Division 4; 1992–97 Division 3; 1997–2000 Division 3; 2000–01 Division 2; 2001–04 Division 1; 2004–05 FL C; 2005–07 FL 1; 2007–13 FL 2; 2013–14 FL 1; 2014– FL C.

MANAGERS

Billy Heald 1925–29 *(Secretary only for several years)*
Stanley Davies 1929–30
Billy Heald 1930–33
Reg Freeman 1934–52
Andy Smailes 1952–58
Tom Johnston 1958–62
Danny Williams 1962–65
Jack Mansell 1965–67
Tommy Docherty 1967–68
Jimmy McAnearney 1968–73
Jimmy McGuigan 1973–79
Ian Porterfield 1979–81
Emlyn Hughes 1981–83
George Kerr 1983–85
Norman Hunter 1985–87
Dave Cusack 1987–88
Billy McEwan 1988–91
Phil Henson 1991–94
Archie Gemmill/John McGovern 1994–96
Danny Bergara 1996–97
Ronnie Moore 1997–2005
Mick Harford 2005
Alan Knill 2005–07
Mark Robins 2007–09
Ronnie Moore 2009–11
Andy Scott 2011–12
Steve Evans April 2012–

LATEST SEQUENCES

Longest Sequence of League Wins: 9, 2.2.1982 – 6.3.1982.
Longest Sequence of League Defeats: 8, 7.4.1956 – 18.8.1956.
Longest Sequence of League Draws: 6, 13.10.1969 – 22.11.1969.
Longest Sequence of Unbeaten League Matches: 18, 13.10.1969 – 7.2.1970.
Longest Sequence Without a League Win: 21, 9.5.2004 – 20.11.2004.
Successive Scoring Runs: 30 from 3.4.1954.
Successive Non-scoring Runs: 6 from 21.8.2004.

TEN YEAR LEAGUE RECORD

		P	W	D	L	F	A	Pts	Pos
2005-06	FL 1	46	12	16	18	52	62	52	20
2006-07	FL 1	46	13	9	24	58	75	38	23
2007-08	FL 2	46	21	11	14	62	58	64*	9
2008-09	FL 2	46	21	12	13	60	46	58†	14
2009-10	FL 2	46	21	10	15	55	52	73	5
2010-11	FL 2	46	17	15	14	75	60	66	9
2011-12	FL 2	46	18	13	15	67	63	67	10
2012-13	FL 2	46	24	7	15	74	59	79	2
2013-14	FL 1	46	24	14	8	86	58	86	4
2014-15	FL C	46	11	16	19	46	67	46‡	21

*10 pts deducted; †17 pts deducted; ‡3 pts deducted.

DID YOU KNOW ?

Rotherham United played for their first three seasons in amber shirts with a black 'V' and black shorts. They only switched to their now traditional red and white strip for the 1928–29 season.

ROTHERHAM UNITED – FL CHAMPIONSHIP 2014–15 LEAGUE RECORD

Match No.	Date	Venue	Opponents	Result	H/T Score	Lg Pos.	Goalscorers	Attendance
1	Aug 9	A	Derby Co	L	0-1	0-0	18		30,105
2	16	H	Wolverhampton W	W	1-0	0-0	14	Hall [76]	10,752
3	19	H	Watford	L	0-2	0-0	18		9361
4	23	A	Millwall	W	1-0	0-0	14	Pringle [49]	10,282
5	30	H	Brentford	L	0-2	0-1	17		9016
6	Sept 13	A	Bournemouth	D	1-1	0-0	18	Bowery [90]	8480
7	16	A	Bolton W	L	2-3	1-0	19	Wordsworth [33], Bowery [82]	13,630
8	20	H	Charlton Ath	D	1-1	0-1	19	Becchio [70]	9620
9	27	A	Ipswich T	L	0-2	0-2	19		16,447
10	30	H	Blackburn R	W	2-0	2-0	17	Arnason [5], Becchio [32]	9525
11	Oct 4	A	Norwich C	D	1-1	1-0	17	Green (pen) [44]	26,114
12	17	H	Leeds U	W	2-1	0-1	15	Revell [58], Clarke-Harris [65]	11,350
13	21	H	Fulham	D	3-3	1-1	14	Revell [28], Clarke-Harris [55], Bodurov (og) [86]	8981
14	25	A	Brighton & HA	D	1-1	0-1	16	Revell [48]	24,370
15	Nov 1	H	Middlesbrough	L	0-3	0-2	17		11,282
16	4	A	Reading	L	0-3	0-1	18		13,775
17	8	A	Sheffield W	D	0-0	0-0	19		26,986
18	22	H	Birmingham C	L	0-1	0-0	22		10,937
19	29	H	Blackpool	D	1-1	0-0	21	Bowery [78]	9381
20	Dec 6	A	Cardiff C	D	0-0	0-0	21		20,419
21	13	H	Nottingham F	D	0-0	0-0	21		11,228
22	20	A	Wigan Ath	W	2-1	1-0	19	Lawrence [40], Revell [65]	12,641
23	26	H	Huddersfield T	D	2-2	0-1	18	Clarke-Harris [88], Frecklington [90]	11,681
24	28	A	Blackpool	D	1-1	0-0	19	Ledesma [57]	11,623
25	Jan 10	A	Brentford	L	0-1	0-0	20		10,851
26	17	H	Bournemouth	L	0-2	0-1	21		9157
27	27	H	Bolton W	W	4-2	3-0	21	Pringle [2], Sammon [23], Green [44], Derbyshire [57]	8760
28	31	A	Charlton Ath	D	1-1	0-0	20	Ward [90]	14,447
29	Feb 7	A	Ipswich T	W	2-0	1-0	18	Derbyshire [38], Sammon [64]	10,336
30	10	A	Blackburn R	L	1-2	0-1	19	Derbyshire [72]	13,403
31	17	A	Derby Co	D	3-3	1-1	20	Green [35], Smallwood [49], Derbyshire [54]	11,035
32	21	A	Wolverhampton W	L	0-5	0-2	21		20,336
33	24	A	Watford	L	0-3	0-1	21		13,468
34	28	H	Millwall	W	2-1	0-0	21	Ward [47], Arnason [85]	10,329
35	Mar 3	H	Cardiff C	L	1-3	0-3	21	Ward [80]	8534
36	7	A	Huddersfield T	W	2-0	1-0	20	Arnason [44], Sammon [60]	13,342
37	14	H	Wigan Ath	L	1-2	1-2	21	Derbyshire [45]	10,062
38	18	H	Nottingham F	L	0-2	0-2	20		20,569
39	21	H	Sheffield W	L	2-3	0-0	21	Pringle [57], Bowery [87]	11,707
40	Apr 3	A	Birmingham C	L	1-2	0-2	21	Derbyshire [48]	16,569
41	6	H	Brighton & HA	W	1-0	1-0	20	Derbyshire [8]	9872
42	11	A	Middlesbrough	L	0-2	0-0	21		19,537
43	15	A	Fulham	D	1-1	1-1	21	Derbyshire [4]	15,011
44	25	H	Norwich C	D	1-1	0-0	21	Bowery [86]	11,498
45	28	H	Reading	W	2-1	0-0	19	Derbyshire [52], Frecklington [58]	11,123
46	May 2	A	Leeds U	D	0-0	0-0	21		31,850

Final League Position: 21

GOALSCORERS

League (46): Derbyshire 9, Bowery 5, Revell 4, Arnason 3, Clarke-Harris 3, Green 3 (1 pen), Pringle 3, Sammon 3, Ward 3, Becchio 2, Frecklington 2, Hall 1, Lawrence 1, Ledesma 1, Smallwood 1, Wordsworth 1, own goal 1.
FA Cup (1): Brindley 1.
Capital One Cup (1): Derbyshire 1 (1 pen).

Collin A 36	Broadfoot K 24+1	Morgan C 34+1	Arnason K 42+1	Skarz J 17	Agard K 1+1	Frecklington L 24+5	Green P 34+3	Pringle B 39+1	Revell A 20+4	Derbyshire M 28+6	Bowery J 6+27	Swift J 1+2	Taylor P 13+4	Hall R 2+1	Smallwood R 37+4	Tidser M —+1	Wordsworth A 3+3	Wood R 3+3	Brindley R 1+1	Lafferty D 11	Brandy F —+1	Richardson F 19+4	Clarke-Harris J 5+10	Becchio L 3+2	Martinez D 8	Leach S 2	Milsom R 3+5	Wilson L 3	Ledesme E 6+1	Wootton S 7	Yates J —+1	James R 7	Lawrence T 6	Newton C 6+7	Hammill A 4+10	Barmby J 2	Ward D 10+6	Fryers Z 10	Sammon C 11+4	Hunt J 14+2	Rawson F 4	Match No.
1	2	3	4	5	6	7	8	9	10[2]	11[1]	12	13																														1
1	2	3	4	5	14	7	8	9	11	13					6[1]	10[2]	12[3]																									2
1	2	3	4	5		8[3]	6[1]	9[1]	10	13					14	11		7	12																							3
1	2	3	4	5[3]		8		9[2]	11[1]	13					6			7		10	12	14																				4
1	2		4	5		7[2]		6	10[1]	11[3]	13				9			8		12	3	14																				5
1		3	4	5			7	6[2]	12	10[1]	14				9			8				2	10[3]	11[2]																		6
1		3	4	5			7	8	12	10[1]	14				6[2]	7		9				2	13	11[3]																		7
1		3	4	5		13	8	14	11[3]	9					10[2]			7[1]				2	12		1																	8
	4	3		5[1]		8	7	6	10	12	11[2]				9[3]							2	13	14	1																	9
1	3[3]	12	4	5		8	7	9	11[2]		14				6[1]							2	10																			10
1		3	4	5		7	8	9	11	10[1]	13				14	6[2]						2	12																			11
1		3	4	5		7	8	9	11	10[2]						12	6[3]	14				2	13																			12
1		3	4	5		7	8	9	10						12		6[2]	13				2	11[1]																			13
1		3	4	5		8	7	9	11		6[1]				10[2]		13					2	12																			14
1	5	3	4			8	7	9[2]	10[1]	13	12[4]				6[3]		14					2	11																			15
1	12	3	4[1]	5[2]		8[3]	7	6	10	11	13				9							2									14											16
1	4	3		5		7	8	9	11						10		6					2																				17
1		3	4	5		7[1]	13	9	10		14				6[2]			8				2	11[3]				12															18
1	4[1]	3	12			7		9	14	10	13				8												6[3]		2	5			11[2]									19
1	4	3				7		9[1]	11		12	13			8							14					6[1]		2	5									10[2]			20
1		3	4			7		9[2]	11		13		12		8												6[1]		2	5									10			21
1		3	4		14	7		9	11[1]		12	13			8												6[2]		2	5									10[3]			22
1		3	4			13	7	9[1]	11[2]		12				8							14					6[1]		2	5									10			23
1		3	4			7					12		6		8								11[2]				9[1]		2	5		13							10			24
1		3	4			7		11[2]							8							14					9[1]		2	5[2]			12	6	9[1]				10[3]	13		25
1		3	4			7									8							2					13						12	6	9[2]		10[1]	5[3]	11			26
1		3	4			7		9[3]							8		13					2												6	14				5	10[2]		27
1		3	4			7		9[1]							8							2												6[1]	14		13	5	10[3]			28
1		3	4			7		9			13				8							2												6[1]	14		12	5	10[3]			29
1		3	4			7		9[1]							8							2											13	6[2]			14	5	10[3]	12		30
1	3		4			7	6[2]								8							12							9[3]					13	14		10	5		2[1]		31
1	3		4			7			10[3]						8								13						8[1]						14	9[2]	11	5	10[3]	12		32
1		3	4				6	9		11[3]					7								14						8[2]								13	5	10[1]	2		33
1	3		4				7	9		11[2]					8																			6[1]			12	10[1]	5	13	2	34
1	3		4				7	9		11[2]					8																			6[1]			12	10	5	13	2	35
1		3			6	9[*]		8[2]		11	13				7					5	14													12					10[3]	2	4	36
1		4			7			9[3]	10	11	13				6[1]					5													14	12				8[2]	2	3	37
1		4			7			9	10	11[3]	14				6[2]					5	12						13							13	5	10[3]		8	2[1]	3	38
	3	4					7	9		10[3]	12				8					5						1	13	6									11[2]	2			39
	4	3					7	9		11	12				8[2]					5						1		6[3]	14			13						10[1]	2		40
	4						7	9	10	11					8[1]					5						1							6						12	2	3	41
	3	7[1]				13		9[3]		11[2]	8				6				4	5						1							10				12	14	2		42
	4	3	7				9		10	11					6					5						1							8						2		43
	4	3	8			6		9[2]		11	13				7					5						1							12						10[1]	2		44
	4[3]	3	8			6	14	9		11[1]	13				7	12				5						1													10[1]	2		45
		3	8			6[3]	14	9		11[1]	12				7		4			5		13				1				2									10[2]			46

FA Cup
Third Round — Bournemouth — (h) — 1-5

Capital One Cup
First Round — Fleetwood T — (h) — 1-0
(aet)
Second Round — Swansea C — (a) — 0-1

SCUNTHORPE UNITED

FOUNDATION

The year of foundation for Scunthorpe United has often been quoted as 1910, but the club can trace its history back to 1899 when Brumby Hall FC, who played on the Old Showground, consolidated their position by amalgamating with some other clubs and changing their name to Scunthorpe United. The year 1910 was when that club amalgamated with North Lindsey United as Scunthorpe and Lindsey United. The link is Mr W. T. Lockwood whose chairmanship covers both years.

Glanford Park, Jack Brownsword Way, Scunthorpe, North Lincolnshire DN15 8TD.

Telephone: (0871) 221 1899.

Fax: (01724) 857 986.

Ticket Office: (0871) 221 1899 (option 1).

Website: www.scunthorpe-united.co.uk

Email: admin@scunthorpe-united.co.uk

Ground Capacity: 9,144.

Record Attendance: 23,935 v Portsmouth, FA Cup 4th rd, 30 January 1954 (at Old Showground); 9,077 v Manchester U, League Cup 3rd rd, 22 September 2010 (at Glanford Park).

Pitch Measurements: 102.5m × 66m (112yd × 72yd)

Chairman: Peter Swann.

Chief Executive: James Rodwell.

Manager: Mark Robins.

Assistant Manager: David Kelly.

Physio: Joe Sharp.

Colours: Claret and light blue striped shirts, claret shorts, claret socks.

Year Formed: 1899.

Turned Professional: 1912.

Previous Names: Amalgamated first with Brumby Hall then North Lindsey United to become Scunthorpe and Lindsey United, 1910; 1958, Scunthorpe United.

Club Nickname: 'The Iron'.

Grounds: 1899, Old Showground; 1988, Glanford Park.

First Football League Game: 19 August 1950, Division 3 (N), v Shrewsbury T (h) D 0–0 – Thompson; Barker, Brownsword; Allen, Taylor, McCormick; Mosby, Payne, Gorin, Rees, Boyes.

Record League Victory: 8–1 v Luton T, Division 3, 24 April 1965 – Sidebottom; Horstead, Hemstead; Smith, Neale, Lindsey; Bramley (1), Scott, Thomas (5), Mahy (1), Wilson (1). 8–1 v Torquay U (a), Division 3, 28 October 1995 – Samways; Housham, Wilson, Ford (1), Knill (1), Hope (Nicholson), Thornber, Bullimore (Walsh), McFarlane (4) (Young), Eyre (2), Paterson.

HONOURS

Football League – FL 1: *Champions* 2006–07;
FL 2: *Runners-up* 2004–05, 2013–14;
Division 3 (N): *Champions* 1957–58.

FA Cup: Best season: 5th rd, 1958, 1970.

Football League Cup: Best season: 4th rd, 2010.

Johnstone's Paint Trophy: *Runners-up* 2008–09.

sky SPORTS FACT FILE

Scunthorpe United, then a Midland League club, faced Rotherham United in the second round of the FA Cup in 1929–30. They drew 3-3 at the Old Showground before losing 5-4 in the replay. Centre-forward Arthur Smalley, who scored in both games, was sold to Blackpool immediately after the replay.

Record Cup Victory: 9–0 v Boston U, FA Cup 1st rd, 21 November 1953 – Malan; Hubbard, Brownsword; Sharpe, White, Bushby; Mosby (1), Haigh (3), Whitfield (2), Gregory (1), Mervyn Jones (2).

Record Defeat: 0–8 v Carlisle U, Division 3 (N), 25 December 1952.

Most League Points (2 for a win): 66, Division 3 (N), 1956–57, 1957–58.

Most League Points (3 for a win): 91, FL 1, 2006–07.

Most League Goals: 88, Division 3 (N), 1957–58.

Highest League Scorer in Season: Barrie Thomas, 31, Division 2, 1961–62.

Most League Goals in Total Aggregate: Steve Cammack, 110, 1979–81, 1981–86.

Most League Goals in One Match: 5, Barrie Thomas v Luton T, Division 3, 24 April 1965.

Most Capped Player: Grant McCann, 11 (39), Northern Ireland.

Most League Appearances: Jack Brownsword, 597, 1950–65.

Youngest League Player: Hakeeb Adelakun, 16 years 201 days Tranmere R, 29 December 2012.

Record Transfer Fee Received: £2,500,000 from Celtic for Gary Hooper, August 2010.

Record Transfer Fee Paid: £700,000 to Hibernian for Rob Jones, July 2009.

Football League Record: 1950 Elected to Division 3 (N); 1958–64 Division 2; 1964–68 Division 3; 1968–72 Division 4; 1972–73 Division 3; 1973–83 Division 4; 1983–84 Division 3; 1984–92 Division 4; 1992–99 Division 3; 1999–2000 Division 2; 2000–04 Division 3; 2004–05 FL 2; 2005–07 FL 1; 2007–08 FL C; 2008–09 FL 1; 2009–11 FL C; 2011–13 FL 1; 2013–14 FL 2; 2014– FL 1.

MANAGERS

Harry Allcock 1915–53
(Secretary-Manager)
Tom Crilly 1936–37
Bernard Harper 1946–48
Leslie Jones 1950–51
Bill Corkhill 1952–56
Ron Suart 1956–58
Tony McShane 1959
Bill Lambton 1959
Frank Soo 1959–60
Dick Duckworth 1960–64
Fred Goodwin 1964–66
Ron Ashman 1967–73
Ron Bradley 1973–74
Dick Rooks 1974–76
Ron Ashman 1976–81
John Duncan 1981–83
Allan Clarke 1983–84
Frank Barlow 1984–87
Mick Buxton 1987–91
Bill Green 1991–93
Richard Money 1993–94
David Moore 1994–96
Mick Buxton 1996–97
Brian Laws 1997–2004; 2004–06
Nigel Adkins 2006–10
Ian Baraclough 2010–11
Alan Knill 2011–12
Brian Laws 2012–13
Russ Wilcox 2013–14
Mark Robins October 2014–

LATEST SEQUENCES

Longest Sequence of League Wins: 7, 27.1.2007 – 3.3.2007.

Longest Sequence of League Defeats: 8, 29.11.1997 – 20.1.1998.

Longest Sequence of League Draws: 6, 2.1.1984 – 25.2.1984.

Longest Sequence of Unbeaten League Matches: 28, 23.11.2013 – 21.4.2014.

Longest Sequence Without a League Win: 14, 22.3.1975 – 6.9.1975.

Successive Scoring Runs: 24 from 13.1.2007.

Successive Non-scoring Runs: 7 from 19.4.1975.

TEN YEAR LEAGUE RECORD

		P	W	D	L	F	A	Pts	Pos
2005-06	FL 1	46	15	15	16	68	73	60	12
2006-07	FL 1	46	26	13	7	73	35	91	1
2007-08	FL C	46	11	13	22	46	69	46	23
2008-09	FL 1	46	22	10	14	82	63	76	6
2009-10	FL C	46	14	10	22	62	84	52	20
2010-11	FL C	46	12	6	28	43	87	42	24
2011-12	FL 1	46	10	22	14	55	59	52	18
2012-13	FL 1	46	13	9	24	49	73	48	21
2013-14	FL 2	46	20	21	5	68	44	81	2
2014-15	FL 1	46	14	14	18	62	75	56	16

DID YOU KNOW ?

In 1950 the Football League was increased by four clubs. Scunthorpe United finished fourth in the opening ballot for two extra Division Three North places but tied with Wigan Athletic in the second round of voting. It took a third ballot to separate the clubs with United elected by 30 votes to 18.

SCUNTHORPE UNITED – FOOTBALL LEAGUE ONE 2014–15 LEAGUE RECORD

Match No.	Date		Venue	Opponents	Result		H/T Score	Lg Pos.	Goalscorers	Atten- dance
1	Aug	9	A	Swindon T	L	1-3	1-3	23	Madden [20]	7060
2		16	H	Preston NE	L	0-4	0-2	24		4013
3		19	H	Fleetwood T	L	0-2	0-0	24		2773
4		23	A	Yeovil T	D	1-1	0-0	23	Madden [82]	3943
5		30	H	Walsall	W	2-1	0-0	21	Adelakun [51], McSheffrey [54]	3098
6	Sept	6	A	Bristol C	L	0-2	0-0	22		12,007
7		13	H	Chesterfield	L	1-4	0-0	23	Madden [46]	6227
8		16	H	Coventry C	W	2-1	1-1	21	Madden [38], Taylor [62]	2866
9		20	H	Leyton Orient	L	1-2	0-1	22	Sparrow [49]	3264
10		27	A	Oldham Ath	L	2-3	2-1	23	Boyce [26], Fallon [34]	3837
11	Oct	4	H	Doncaster R	L	1-2	1-1	23	Fallon [24]	5420
12		11	A	Gillingham	W	3-0	1-0	23	Madden [41], Bishop [72], McSheffrey [90]	7042
13		18	A	Colchester U	D	1-1	1-1	23	Fallon [20]	3303
14		21	A	Port Vale	D	2-2	1-1	24	Bishop [4], Taylor [79]	3590
15		25	H	Notts Co	L	0-1	0-0	24		4008
16	Nov	1	A	Peterborough U	W	2-1	1-0	21	Williams, L [14], Santos (og) [64]	6275
17		22	A	Crawley T	D	2-2	1-0	23	Madden [26], Taylor [55]	2178
18		29	A	Barnsley	W	2-1	2-1	21	Madden 2 [30, 45]	9340
19	Dec	13	H	Crewe Alex	W	2-1	1-1	19	Williams, L [10], Llera [77]	3006
20		20	A	Bradford C	D	1-1	0-1	18	Adelakun [90]	12,831
21		26	H	Rochdale	W	2-1	0-0	17	O'Neil [58], Madden [77]	4004
22	Jan	10	A	Walsall	W	4-1	2-0	17	Chambers (og) [24], Hopper [39], Madden (pen) [63], Bishop [65]	3738
23		17	H	Bristol C	L	0-2	0-1	17		3611
24		27	A	Milton Keynes D	D	1-1	0-0	17	Hopper [57]	3005
25		31	A	Leyton Orient	W	4-1	2-0	16	O'Neil [13], McSheffrey [28], Hopper 2 [49, 80]	5184
26	Feb	7	H	Oldham Ath	L	0-1	0-0	18		4125
27		10	A	Coventry C	D	1-1	1-0	19	McSheffrey [21]	6885
28		14	H	Swindon T	W	3-1	0-1	18	Madden [62], Canavan [76], van Veen [79]	3763
29		17	H	Chesterfield	W	2-0	0-0	14	Canavan [58], Madden [87]	3601
30		21	A	Preston NE	L	0-2	0-0	16		9415
31		24	H	Barnsley	L	0-1	0-0	17		3508
32		28	H	Yeovil T	D	1-1	0-1	17	Adelakun [61]	3783
33	Mar	3	A	Fleetwood T	D	2-2	1-1	17	McSheffrey [45], Evans [74]	2667
34		7	A	Crewe Alex	L	0-2	0-0	17		4213
35		14	H	Sheffield U	D	1-1	1-1	17	Bishop [37]	5550
36		21	A	Rochdale	L	1-3	0-1	17	van Veen [60]	2738
37		24	A	Sheffield U	L	0-4	0-2	18		19,442
38		28	A	Notts Co	D	2-2	1-1	19	Robinson [1], Canavan [86]	4990
39	Apr	3	H	Peterborough U	W	2-0	1-0	17	Madden [40], Robinson [73]	4216
40		7	A	Milton Keynes D	L	0-2	0-2	18		8087
41		11	H	Crawley T	W	2-1	1-0	17	Dickson (og) [19], Madden [62]	3009
42		14	A	Port Vale	D	1-1	0-1	17	Wootton, K [90]	3002
43		18	A	Colchester U	D	2-2	1-0	17	Robinson [30], Adelakun [90]	4551
44		21	H	Bradford C	D	1-1	1-0	16	McSheffrey [26]	3176
45		25	H	Gillingham	W	2-1	2-1	15	Adelakun [11], McSheffrey [19]	3763
46	May	3	A	Doncaster R	L	2-5	0-3	16	Butler (og) [53], Adelakun [90]	9394

Final League Position: 16

GOALSCORERS

League (62): Madden 14 (1 pen), McSheffrey 7, Adelakun 6, Bishop 4, Hopper 4, Canavan 3, Fallon 3, Robinson 3, Taylor 3, O'Neil 2, van Veen 2, Williams, L 2, Boyce 1, Evans 1, Llera 1, Sparrow 1, Wootton, K 1, own goals 4.
FA Cup (6): Madden 2, McSheffrey 2, Davey 1, Taylor 1.
Capital One Cup (1): Bishop 1.
Johnstone's Paint Trophy (3): Madden 1, McAllister 1, McSheffrey 1.

Slocombe S 9	Nolan E 4+2	Canavan N 31+1	Llera M 15	Williams M 40	Myrie-Williams J 7+8	McAllister S 13+10	Bishop N 34+1	Syers D 1+5	McSheffrey G 35+6	Madden P 46	Burton D 1+4	Taylor L 11+7	Lundstram J 5+2	Sparrow M 6+3	Robinson T 8	Severn J 1+1	Dawson A 3	Adelakun H 7+25	Hawkridge T 10+1	Olejnik R 13	O'Neill L 13	Addison M 3	Kee B —+12	Brisley S 6+1	Boyce A 25+4	Fallon R 4	Osbourne I 24+4	Williams L 6	O'Neil L 21+1	Davey A 13	Brindley R 3	Murphy J 3	Hopper T 12	Clarke L 23	Daniels L 23	Evans G 9+7	van Veen K 11+9	Wootton K 1+11	Townsend C 5+1	Match No.
1	2	3	4	5¹	6²	7	8	9¹	10	11	12³	13	14																											1
	2	3	4		6²	7	8		9¹	11	12	10³				1		5	13	14																				2
		5	4		12	7	8¹		10²	11				6					9	1	2	3	13																	3
			4	5	6¹		8		13	10		11³					7	14	9²	1	2	3	12																	4
			4	5	13	7	8		11¹	10²							14	9	6¹	1	2	3	12																	5
	5	3	4	6	13	8¹	7		11	10²		12					2	9³		1		14																		6
	3	4		9	13	8			10	11		12	7²				5¹	6²		1	2	14																		7
	4	3	5	13	7				9³	10		11¹	8				12	6²		1	2	14																		8
	4	3	5	13	7²				9	10		11³	8				12	6¹		1	2	14																		9
			5	6	8	7¹			9³	11				13				12		1	2	14		3	4	10²														10
			5	12		7			9¹	11				10				8		13	6²	1	2		3	4	10													11
			5	6²	8	7			9	10	13							12		1	2			4	3	11¹														12
			5	6	7¹	8			9³	11		12						14		1	2	12	3	10²	13															13
			5	9⁴	13	8			11	14	10²							7³		1	2	12	3	4		6¹														14
			5		7				9¹	11²		10						12		1	2	13	3	4		6	8													15
1		4	5		13	7			9	6		11¹									2	12		3		8	10²													16
1		4²	5	13	14	8			9³	11		10						2				12	3			7¹														17
1		3	5		12	8			9¹	10		11²						2				13				7	6	4												18
1		4	5		6				8			11¹						13	10²							12	9	7	3	2										19
1		3	5		8				6²	10		13						12							4	11¹	9	7		2										20
1		4	5		12	9			10	8		11²						13							3	7	6¹		2											21
1	14	3	5		12	7			9	10²		13													4		6	2			8³	11								22
1²	13	4	5		6				14	8								12³							3		7	9¹			10	11	2							23
		4	5		14	7			12	6		13													3		8	2¹			10²	11³	9	1						24
		4	5		8				10	6³		13						12							3		7	9²			11¹	2	1	14						25
		4	5		6				10	8								14							3		7²	9³			11¹	2	1	12	13					26
		3	5		6				10²	9								14									7³	8	4			11¹	2	1	12	13				27
		3	5		12	6¹				9								14										8	4			11	2	1	10²	7³	13			28
		3	5		6					9												13		12			7	4³			10²	2	1	8	11¹				29
		4	5		6¹				12	8								13							3		13	9			10	2	1	7³	11²	14			30
12		4	5³		6				13	8								3									7¹	9²			10	2	1	14	11				31
		4				14				10²	8							12									6	9	3			11³	2	1	7¹	13		5	32
		3				13				10	8																7	9²	4			11¹	2	1	6	12		5	33
		3				13				11²	9																8¹	7	4			2	1	6	10³	14	5	34
		4	5			8³				10¹	11							12							3		7	9			2	1	6²	13	14		35
		4	5			5⁴				13	10							12							3		7	14			2	1	6¹	11	9³	8	36
		4	3⁴							9²	10	7						11¹							14		8³	6			2	1	12	13		5	37
		4	5							9	10⁵				11			13									8	7	3			2	1	6¹	12			38
		4¹	5				13		9²	6		7			11³										12		8		3			2	1	10	14			39
			5				13		8²	9		7			10										4		6³		3			2	1	14	11¹	12		40
		4	5		6				10³	8		14			9²			13							12		7		3¹			2	1	11				41
		4	5¹		6				9	8					10³			12							3		7					2	1	11²	13	14		42
		4	5		6³				10	8		9²			11¹			14							3		7					2	1	13	12			43
		4	5		6	14			9³	8		12			11¹			10							3		7²					2	1	13				44
		4	5		6	13			9²	8		7			11¹			10							3							2	1	12				45
		4	5	7	6³	13			10²	9					8										3							2	1	12	11¹	14		46

FA Cup

First Round	Forest Green R	(a)	2-0
Second Round	Worcester	(h)	1-1
Replay	Worcester	(a)	1-1

(aet; Scunthorpe U won 14-13 on penalties)

Third Round	Chesterfield	(h)	2-2
Replay	Chesterfield	(a)	0-2

(aet)

Capital One Cup

First Round	Blackburn R	(a)	1-0
Second Round	Reading	(h)	0-1

Johnstone's Paint Trophy

First Round	Chesterfield	(h)	2-0
Second Round	Notts Co	(h)	1-2

SHEFFIELD UNITED

FOUNDATION

In March 1889, Yorkshire County Cricket Club formed Sheffield United six days after an FA Cup semi-final between Preston North End and West Bromwich Albion had finally convinced Charles Stokes, a member of the cricket club, that the formation of a professional football club would prove successful at Bramall Lane. The United's first secretary, Mr J. B. Wostinholm, was also secretary of the cricket club.

Bramall Lane Ground, Cherry Street, Bramall Lane, Sheffield, South Yorkshire S2 4SU.

Telephone: (0871) 995 1899.

Fax: (0871) 663 2430.

Ticket Office: (0871) 995 1889.

Website: www.sufc.co.uk

Email: info@sufc.co.uk

Ground Capacity: 32,609.

Record Attendance: 68,287 v Leeds U, FA Cup 5th rd, 15 February 1936.

Pitch Measurements: 100.5m × 67m (110yd × 73yd)

Co-Chairmen: Kevin McCabe, James Phipps.

Manager: Nigel Adkins.

Assistant Manager: Andy Crosby.

Physio: Ed Owen.

Colours: Red and white striped shirts, red shorts with white trim, red socks with white trim.

Year Formed: 1889.

Turned Professional: 1889.

Club Nickname: 'The Blades'.

Ground: 1889, Bramall Lane.

HONOURS

Football League
Division 1: *Champions* 1897–98;
Runners-up 1896–97, 1899–1900;
Division 2: *Champions* 1952–53;
Runners-up 1892–93, 1938–39,
1960–61, 1970–71, 1989–90;
FL C: *Runners-up* 2005–06;
Division 3: *Runners-up* 1988–89;
Division 4: *Champions* 1981–82.
FA Cup: *Winners* 1899, 1902, 1915,
1925; *Runners-up* 1901, 1936.

Football League Cup: Best season: semi-final, 2003, 2015.

First Football League Game: 3 September 1892, Division 2, v Lincoln C (h) W 4–2 – Lilley; Witham, Cain; Howell, Hendry, Needham (1); Wallace, Dobson, Hammond (3), Davies, Drummond.

Record League Victory: 10–0 v Burslem Port Vale (a), Division 2, 10 December 1892 – Howlett; Witham, Lilley; Howell, Hendry, Needham; Drummond (1), Wallace (1), Hammond (4), Davies (2), Watson (2). 10-0 v Burnley, Division 1 (h), 19 January 1929.

Record Cup Victory: 6–1 v Scarborough (a), FA Cup 1st qualifying rd, 5 October 1889 – Howlett; Stringer, Gilmartin, Mack, Hobson, Hudson, Galbraith (2), Robertson (1), Fraser (2), Duncan, Mosforth (1). 6–1 v Loughborough, FA Cup 4th qualifying rd, 6 December 1890. 6–1 v Lincoln C, League Cup, 22 August 2000 – Tracey; Uhlenbeek, Weber, Woodhouse (Ford), Murphy, Sandford, Devlin (pen), Ribeiro (Santos), Bent (3), Kelly (1) (Thompson), Jagielka, og (1).

sky SPORTS FACT FILE

Joe Carr, who was a regular in Sheffield United's first team in 1938–39 when they won promotion to the First Division, was called up to the Army shortly after the outbreak of the Second World War. He had only served for a short time before he lost his life, aged just 21, at Dunkirk in May 1940.

Record Defeat: 0–13 v Bolton W, FA Cup 2nd rd, 1 February 1890.

Most League Points (2 for a win): 60, Division 2, 1952–53.

Most League Points (3 for a win): 96, Division 4, 1981–82.

Most League Goals: 102, Division 1, 1925–26.

Highest League Scorer in Season: Jimmy Dunne, 41, Division 1, 1930–31.

Most League Goals in Total Aggregate: Harry Johnson, 201, 1919–30.

Most League Goals in One Match: 5, Harry Hammond v Bootle, Division 2, 26 November 1892; 5, Harry Johnson v West Ham U, Division 1, 26 December 1927.

Most Capped Player: Billy Gillespie, 25, Northern Ireland.

Most League Appearances: Joe Shaw, 632, 1948–66.

Youngest League Player: Louis Reed, 16 years 257 days v Rotherham U, 8 April 2014.

Record Transfer Fee Received: £4,000,000 from Everton for Phil Jagielka, July 2007; £4,000,000 from Tottenham H for Kyle Naughton, July 2009; £4,000,000 from Tottenham H for Kyle Walker, July 2009.

Record Transfer Fee Paid: £4,000,000 to Everton for James Beattie, August 2007.

Football League Record: 1892 Elected to Division 2; 1893–1934 Division 1; 1934–39 Division 2; 1946–49 Division 1; 1949–53 Division 2; 1953–56 Division 1; 1956–61 Division 2; 1961–68 Division 1; 1968–71 Division 1; 1971–76 Division 1; 1976–79 Division 2; 1979–81 Division 3; 1981–82 Division 4; 1982–84 Division 3; 1984–88 Division 2; 1988–89 Division 3; 1989–90 Division 2; 1990–92 Division 1; 1992–94 FA Premier League; 1994–2004 Division 1; 2004–06 FL C; 2006–07 FA Premier League; 2007–11 FL C; 2011– FL 1.

MANAGERS

J. B. Wostinholm 1889–99
(Secretary-Manager)
John Nicholson 1899–1932
Ted Davison 1932–52
Reg Freeman 1952–55
Joe Mercer 1955–58
Johnny Harris 1959–68
(continued as General Manager to 1970)
Arthur Rowley 1968–69
Johnny Harris *(General Manager resumed Team Manager duties)* 1969–73
Ken Furphy 1973–75
Jimmy Sirrel 1975–77
Harry Haslam 1978–81
Martin Peters 1981
Ian Porterfield 1981–86
Billy McEwan 1986–88
Dave Bassett 1988–95
Howard Kendall 1995–97
Nigel Spackman 1997–98
Steve Bruce 1998–99
Adrian Heath 1999
Neil Warnock 1999–2007
Bryan Robson 2007–08
Kevin Blackwell 2008–10
Gary Speed 2010
Micky Adams 2010–11
Danny Wilson 2011–13
David Weir 2013
Nigel Clough 2013–15
Nigel Adkins June 2015–

LATEST SEQUENCES

Longest Sequence of League Wins: 8, 20.8.2005 – 27.9.2005.

Longest Sequence of League Defeats: 7, 19.8.1975 – 20.9.1975.

Longest Sequence of League Draws: 6, 6.5.2001 – 8.9.2001.

Longest Sequence of Unbeaten League Matches: 22, 2.9.1899 – 13.1.1900.

Longest Sequence Without a League Win: 19, 27.9.1975 – 7.2.1976.

Successive Scoring Runs: 34 from 30.3.1956.

Successive Non-scoring Runs: 6 from 4.12.1993.

TEN YEAR LEAGUE RECORD

		P	W	D	L	F	A	Pts	Pos
2005-06	FL C	46	26	12	8	76	46	90	2
2006-07	PR Lge	38	10	8	20	32	55	38	18
2007-08	FL C	46	17	15	14	56	51	66	9
2008-09	FL C	46	22	14	10	64	39	80	3
2009-10	FL C	46	17	14	15	62	55	65	8
2010-11	FL C	46	11	9	26	44	79	42	23
2011-12	FL 1	46	27	9	10	92	51	90	3
2012-13	FL 1	46	19	18	9	56	42	75	5
2013-14	FL 1	46	18	13	15	48	46	67	7
2014-15	FL 1	46	19	14	13	66	53	71	5

DID YOU KNOW

Billy Bromage, a winger who played for Sheffield United in the early 1900s, was one of six brothers to play football professionally. Billy spent six years with the Blades while one of his brothers, George, also played for United between 1921 and 1924.

SHEFFIELD UNITED – FOOTBALL LEAGUE ONE 2014–15 LEAGUE RECORD

Match No.	Date	Venue	Opponents	Result	H/T Score	Lg Pos.	Goalscorers	Attendance
1	Aug 9	H	Bristol C	L	1-2	1-1	17	Higdon [32]	19,889
2	16	A	Coventry C	L	0-1	0-0	21		2279
3	19	A	Peterborough U	W	2-1	1-1	18	Baxter [25], Davies, B [84]	6578
4	23	H	Crawley T	W	1-0	0-0	12	Baxter [48]	18,178
5	30	A	Preston NE	D	1-1	1-1	12	Baxter [41]	11,058
6	Sept 13	H	Rochdale	W	1-0	0-0	9	Campbell-Ryce [84]	19,122
7	16	A	Colchester U	W	3-2	0-1	6	Davies, B 2 (1 pen) [83, 88 (p)], Flynn [85]	3084
8	20	A	Swindon T	L	2-5	0-1	10	McNulty [66], Davies, B [72]	7536
9	27	H	Gillingham	W	2-1	0-0	7	Higdon [87], Murphy [90]	18,487
10	Oct 4	A	Chesterfield	L	2-3	0-2	11	McNulty [81], Collins [90]	9723
11	11	H	Leyton Orient	D	2-2	0-1	10	McCarthy [90], McNulty [90]	19,179
12	18	A	Bradford C	W	2-0	0-0	7	Harris [66], McNulty [83]	14,784
13	21	H	Yeovil T	W	2-0	1-0	6	McNulty [14], Murphy [67]	19,353
14	25	A	Crewe Alex	W	1-0	0-0	5	Scougall [69]	5699
15	Nov 1	H	Barnsley	L	0-1	0-0	8		24,495
16	15	A	Doncaster R	W	1-0	0-0	5	Murphy [64]	11,037
17	22	H	Oldham Ath	D	1-1	0-1	5	Campbell-Ryce [63]	19,767
18	25	H	Notts Co	D	1-1	0-1	5	Murphy [76]	19,385
19	Dec 2	H	Milton Keynes D	L	0-1	0-0	5		17,030
20	13	A	Fleetwood T	D	1-1	1-0	5	Harris [8]	4269
21	20	A	Walsall	D	1-1	0-0	5	O'Grady [56]	20,209
22	26	A	Port Vale	L	1-2	0-1	6	Campbell-Ryce [55]	8524
23	Jan 10	A	Preston NE	W	2-1	0-0	6	McNulty [52], Campbell-Ryce [70]	19,902
24	17	A	Milton Keynes D	L	0-1	0-0	7		9633
25	31	H	Swindon T	W	2-0	0-0	5	Murphy 2 [73, 90]	19,490
26	Feb 7	A	Gillingham	L	0-2	0-0	7		5704
27	10	A	Colchester U	W	4-1	2-0	6	Baxter 2 (1 pen) [8, 80 (p)], Done [37], McEveley [59]	17,162
28	14	A	Bristol C	W	3-1	0-1	5	Done 2 [54, 77], Murphy [82]	11,767
29	17	A	Notts Co	W	2-1	1-1	5	Murphy [16], Done [75]	6893
30	21	H	Coventry C	D	2-2	0-1	5	Doyle [78], Murphy [80]	20,314
31	24	A	Rochdale	W	2-1	1-0	5	McNulty [21], Brayford [61]	3574
32	28	A	Crawley T	D	1-1	0-0	5	McNulty (pen) [81]	3320
33	Mar 3	H	Peterborough U	L	1-2	0-0	5	Done [65]	18,604
34	7	H	Fleetwood T	L	1-2	1-2	5	Done [39]	18,668
35	14	A	Scunthorpe U	D	1-1	1-1	5	Freeman [45]	5550
36	17	A	Walsall	D	1-1	1-0	5	Baxter [8]	3950
37	21	H	Port Vale	W	1-0	1-0	5	Baxter (pen) [29]	18,729
38	24	H	Scunthorpe U	W	4-0	2-0	5	Holt [14], Baxter 2 (2 pens) [40, 86], Murphy [81]	19,442
39	28	H	Crewe Alex	L	1-2	0-1	5	Holt [55]	19,672
40	Apr 4	A	Barnsley	W	2-0	1-0	5	Davies, S [42], Holt [71]	17,532
41	7	H	Doncaster R	W	3-2	1-1	5	Baxter (pen) [29], Done [52], Davies, S [71]	20,487
42	11	A	Oldham Ath	D	2-2	0-2	5	Holt [56], Murphy [73]	5072
43	14	A	Yeovil T	L	0-1	0-0	5		3841
44	18	H	Bradford C	D	1-1	0-0	5	Holt [57]	21,879
45	25	A	Leyton Orient	D	1-1	0-0	5	Harris [77]	7249
46	May 3	H	Chesterfield	D	1-1	1-0	5	McNulty [34]	26,078

Final League Position: 5

GOALSCORERS

League (66): Murphy 11, Baxter 10 (5 pens), McNulty 9 (1 pen), Done 7, Holt 5, Campbell-Ryce 4, Davies, B 4 (1 pen), Harris 3, Davies, S 2, Higdon 2, Brayford 1, Collins 1, Doyle 1, Flynn 1, Freeman 1, McCarthy 1, McEveley 1, O'Grady 1, Scougall 1.
FA Cup (10): Baxter 2 (2 pens), Campbell-Ryce 2, Flynn 2, McNulty 2, De Girolamo 1, Murphy 1.
Capital One Cup (9): Higdon 3, Adams 2, McNulty 2, Butler 1, own goal 1.
Johnstone's Paint Trophy (2): Baxter 1, Campbell-Ryce 1.
League One Play-Offs (6): Adams 1, Basham 1, Davies, S 1, Done 1, Freeman 1, own goal 1.

Howard M 35	Davies B 11+3	Alcock C 17+7	McGahey H 11+4	Harris R 35+5	Scougall S 20+5	Basham C 35+2	Reed L 10+9	Flynn R 18+14	Higdon M 9+4	Murphy J 41+2	Campbell-Ryce J 14+5	McNulty M 11+20	Baxter J 28+6	McEveley J 31+3	Doyle M 35+8	Collins N 8	Wallace J 7+3	McCarthy P 10+1	Porter C —+1	O'Grady C 4	Wallace K 2+2	Cuvelier F 1+2	Adams C 5+5	Kennedy T 10+1	Turner I 11	Brayford J 22	Freeman K 13+6	Coutts P 19+1	Holt J 11+5	Done M 12+3	Davies S 10+3	Calvert-Lewin D —+2	Match No.
1	2	3	4	5	6¹	7³	8	9²	10	11	12	13	14																				1
1	2	3	4	5	6²	7	8³	9¹	11	10				12	13	14																	2
1	6	2	4			8		13	12	9		11²	10¹	5	7	3																	3
1	6	2	3	14		7	13	12	11³	9			10²	5¹	8	4																4
1	2		4	14		7		11¹	9	6	12	10²	5	8³	3	13																	5
1	2¹	5	3		7²		13		9²	6	12	10	11	8	4	14																	6
1	6	2	4	9	14		12	13	11²		10		5³	7	3	8¹																7
1	9	2	3	14	10¹	7³	12	13		11		6		5	8	4²																	8
1	6³	2	4	12	10		13	14	9		11¹		5²	8	3	7																9
1	2			14	9		8¹	11⁵	10	13	12		5¹	6	3	7²	4																10
1		4		2	10¹	14		6		9	13	12	11²	5	8	7³	3																11
1		2	12	5	10²	8		14		6	9¹	13	11	4³	7		3																12
1	2	4	5	10¹	3	7	13	12	9	6³	11²	14		8																			13
1		5	9¹	4²	13		6	10	14	11³	12	8		7	3																		14
1	2	5	10		13		9	6³	12	11¹	4	8	7²	3	14																		15
1	2	14	5	8	9		13		11	6³		10¹	4	12	7²	3³																	16
1	2		5	10	7		6		9	12		11¹	4	8		3																	17
1		5	10	2	14	13	11³	9	6	12	7²	4	8¹			3																	18
1	2	14	5	10¹	2³	7		9	6	12	13	3	8		4		11²																19
1		5		12		2	11²	6		13	8¹	4	7		3		10	9³	14														20
1	12	5	7	3		2³		6		13	10²	4	8				11		14	9¹													21
1	2³	5	9¹	4⁴	13		8	10	14		3	6		12			11		7²														22
1	12	5	7¹		2		9	6²	11	10³	4	8	13			14			3														23
1	2²	5	8²	12		13	10	6	11¹	9	4	7				14	3																24
6			13	3	7	10²	12			14				8¹		11	4	1	2	5	9³												25
1	6¹		2	3	7		10	12	14	9²	8				11³			4			5	13											26
		5	3				9¹	6²	13	10	4	8			14			1	2		7	12	11³										27
		5	6				9		10²	4	8				13	3	1	2	14		7	12³	11¹										28
1	13	5	3	6²			10	12			8							4	1	2	14	7	9¹	11³									29
		5	3				9	6³	14	10⁴	4	8					12	1	2	13	7¹		11²										30
		5	6	14	8³		10	11²		4	7						3	1	2	13	9¹		12										31
		2	9	10²		11	13		4	8							5¹	1	3	12	7		6										32
		5	3	13	6		9	10¹		4	8							1	2	14	7³	12	11²										33
		5¹	3				9		13	7¹	4	8				14	12		1	2		6		10	11²								34
	13	5		6			11			4	8							1	3	2²	7¹	12	9	10									35
1	14	5		8²	13	9		10	4	7							3	2		6³	11¹	12											36
1	14	5	4	12		9		10¹	13							3	2	7	8³	6²	11												37
	14	5	3	9¹	11		12	8	13					1	4	2	6²	7		10²													38
1	12	5	3	9¹	11		8²	13							4	2	6	7	14	10³													39
1		5	13	7	11	10		14				3	4	2	6	8²	12	9³															40
1	14	5²	3	6¹		10³	12	13		8					4	2	8	7	9	11													41
1		12	3	7³	6	10	11²		8					4¹	2	5	13	9	14														42
1	13	9³	4	2²	12		14	7						3	5	8	10	6	11¹														43
1	12		3		9		10¹	8					13	4²	2	5	7	6	11														44
1		5	12	3		10		6	14					9³	4	2	7	8	11¹	13													45
1		5	6¹		7²	13		11	10	4	8³				9	3	2				14	12											46

FA Cup

First Round	Crewe Alex	(a)	0-0
Replay	Crewe Alex	(h)	2-0
Second Round	Plymouth Arg	(h)	3-0
Third Round	QPR	(a)	3-0
Fourth Round	Preston NE	(a)	1-1
Replay	Preston NE	(h)	1-3
Fourth Round	Milton Keynes D	(a)	2-1
Quarter-Finals	Southampton	(h)	1-0
Semi-Finals 1st leg	Tottenham H	(a)	0-1
Semi-Finals 2nd leg	Tottenham H	(h)	2-2

Capital One Cup

First Round	Mansfield T	(h)	2-1
Second Round	West Ham U	(a)	1-1

(aet; Sheffield U won 5-4 on penalties)

Third Round	Leyton Orient	(a)	1-0

Johnstone's Paint Trophy

Second Round	Hartlepool U	(a)	2-1
Northern Quarter-Finals	Walsall	(a)	0-1

League One Play-Offs

Semi-Finals 1st leg	Swindon T	(h)	1-2
Semi-Finals 2nd leg	Swindon T	(a)	5-5

SHEFFIELD WEDNESDAY

FOUNDATION

Sheffield being one of the principal centres of early Association Football, this club was formed as long ago as 1867 by the Sheffield Wednesday Cricket Club (formed 1825) and their colours from the start were blue and white. The inaugural meeting was held at the Adelphi Hotel and the original committee included Charles Stokes who was subsequently a founder member of Sheffield United.

Hillsborough Stadium, Sheffield, South Yorkshire S6 1SW.

Telephone: (0871) 995 1867.

Fax: (0114) 221 2122.

Ticket Office: (0871) 900 1867.

Website: www.swfc.co.uk

Email: footballenquiries@swfc.co.uk

Ground Capacity: 38,702.

Record Attendance: 72,841 v Manchester C, FA Cup 5th rd, 17 February 1934.

Pitch Measurements: 106m × 64m (116yd × 70yd)

Chairman: Dejphon Chansiri.

Vice-Chairman: Paul Aldridge.

Head Coach: Carlos Carvalhal.

Coach: Lee Bullen.

Head Physio: Paul Smith.

HONOURS

Football League – Division 1: *Champions* 1902–03, 1903–04, 1928–29, 1929–30; *Runners-up* 1960–61; **Division 2:** *Champions* 1899–1900, 1925–26, 1951–52, 1955–56, 1958–59; *Runners-up* 1949–50, 1983–84. **FL 1:** *Runners-up* 2011–12. **FA Cup:** *Winners* 1896, 1907, 1935; *Runners-up* 1890, 1966, 1993.

Football League Cup: *Winners* 1991; *Runners-up* 1993.

European Competitions European Fairs Cup: 1961–62, 1963–64. **UEFA Cup:** 1992–93. **Intertoto Cup:** 1995.

Colours: Blue and white striped shirts, blue shorts with white trim, blue socks with white trim.

Year Formed: 1867 (fifth oldest League club).

Turned Professional: 1887.

Previous Name: The Wednesday until 1929.

Club Nickname: 'The Owls'.

Grounds: 1867, Highfield; 1869, Myrtle Road; 1877, Sheaf House; 1887, Olive Grove; 1899, Owlerton (since 1912 known as Hillsborough). Some games were played at Endcliffe in the 1880s. Until 1895 Bramall Lane was used for some games.

First Football League Game: 3 September 1892, Division 1, v Notts Co (a) W 1–0 – Allan; Tom Brandon (1), Mumford; Hall, Betts, Harry Brandon; Spiksley, Brady, Davis, Bob Brown, Dunlop.

Record League Victory: 9–1 v Birmingham, Division 1, 13 December 1930 – Brown; Walker, Blenkinsop; Strange, Leach, Wilson; Hooper (3), Seed (2), Ball (2), Burgess (1), Rimmer (1).

Record Cup Victory: 12–0 v Halliwell, FA Cup 1st rd, 17 January 1891 – Smith; Thompson, Brayshaw; Harry Brandon (1), Betts, Cawley (2); Winterbottom, Mumford (2), Bob Brandon (1), Woolhouse (5), Ingram (1).

sky SPORTS FACT FILE

Sheffield Wednesday adopted a live monkey as a mascot for the 1908–09 season. Unfortunately the monkey failed to bring any luck and the team suffered a disastrous FA Cup defeat at home to Glossop. It appears the monkey was subsequently 'transferred' to a local theatre as a novelty act.

Record Defeat: 0–10 v Aston Villa, Division 1, 5 October 1912.

Most League Points (2 for a win): 62, Division 2, 1958–59.

Most League Points (3 for a win): 93, FL 1, 2011–12.

Most League Goals: 106, Division 2, 1958–59.

Highest League Scorer in Season: Derek Dooley, 46, Division 2, 1951–52.

Most League Goals in Total Aggregate: Andrew Wilson, 199, 1900–20.

Most League Goals in One Match: 6, Doug Hunt v Norwich C, Division 2, 19 November 1938.

Most Capped Player: Nigel Worthington, 50 (66), Northern Ireland.

Most League Appearances: Andrew Wilson, 501, 1900–20.

Youngest League Player: Peter Fox, 15 years 269 days v Orient, 31 March 1973.

Record Transfer Fee Received: £3,000,000 from WBA for Chris Brunt, August 2007.

Record Transfer Fee Paid: £4,500,000 to Celtic for Paolo Di Canio, August 1997.

Football League Record: 1892 Elected to Division 1; 1899–1900 Division 2; 1900–20 Division 1; 1920–26 Division 2; 1926–37 Division 1; 1937–50 Division 2; 1950–51 Division 1; 1951–52 Division 2; 1952–55 Division 1; 1955–56 Division 2; 1956–58 Division 1; 1958–59 Division 2; 1959–70 Division 1; 1970–75 Division 2; 1975–80 Division 3; 1980–84 Division 2; 1984–90 Division 1; 1990–91 Division 2; 1991–92 Division 1; 1992–2000 FA Premier League; 2000–03 Division 1; 2003–04 Division 2; 2004–05 FL 1; 2005–10 FL C; 2010–12 FL 1; 2012– FL C.

LATEST SEQUENCES

Longest Sequence of League Wins: 9, 23.4.1904 – 15.10.1904.

Longest Sequence of League Defeats: 8, 9.9.2000 – 17.10.2000.

Longest Sequence of League Draws: 7, 15.3.2008 – 14.4.2008.

Longest Sequence of Unbeaten League Matches: 19, 10.12.1960 – 8.4.1961.

Longest Sequence Without a League Win: 20, 11.1.1975 – 30.8.1975.

Successive Scoring Runs: 40 from 14.11.1959.

Successive Non-scoring Runs: 8 from 8.3.1975.

MANAGERS

Arthur Dickinson 1891–1920
  (Secretary-Manager)
Robert Brown 1920–33
Billy Walker 1933–37
Jimmy McMullan 1937–42
Eric Taylor 1942–58
  (continued as General Manager to 1974)
Harry Catterick 1958–61
Vic Buckingham 1961–64
Alan Brown 1964–68
Jack Marshall 1968–69
Danny Williams 1969–71
Derek Dooley 1971–73
Steve Burtenshaw 1974–75
Len Ashurst 1975–77
Jackie Charlton 1977–83
Howard Wilkinson 1983–88
Peter Eustace 1988–89
Ron Atkinson 1989–91
Trevor Francis 1991–95
David Pleat 1995–97
Ron Atkinson 1997–98
Danny Wilson 1998–2000
Peter Shreeves *(Acting)* 2000
Paul Jewell 2000–01
Peter Shreeves 2001
Terry Yorath 2001–02
Chris Turner 2002–04
Paul Sturrock 2004–06
Brian Laws 2006–09
Alan Irvine 2010–11
Gary Megson 2011–12
Dave Jones 2012–13
Stuart Gray 2014–15
Carlos Carvalhal July 2015–

TEN YEAR LEAGUE RECORD

		P	W	D	L	F	A	Pts	Pos
2005-06	FL C	46	13	13	20	39	52	52	19
2006-07	FL C	46	20	11	15	70	66	71	9
2007-08	FL C	46	14	13	19	54	55	55	16
2008-09	FL C	46	16	13	17	51	58	61	12
2009-10	FL C	46	11	14	21	49	69	47	22
2010-11	FL 1	46	16	10	20	67	67	58	15
2011-12	FL 1	46	28	9	9	81	48	93	2
2012-13	FL C	46	16	10	20	53	61	58	18
2013-14	FL C	46	13	14	19	63	65	53	16
2014-15	FL C	46	14	18	14	43	49	60	13

DID YOU KNOW ?

Goalkeeper Teddy Davison made 424 appearances for Sheffield Wednesday between 1908 and 1925. He won a single cap for England, appearing against Wales in March 1922. Standing at just 5 feet 7 inches he is believed to have been England's shortest-ever goalkeeper.

SHEFFIELD WEDNESDAY – FL CHAMPIONSHIP 2014–15 LEAGUE RECORD

Match No.	Date	Venue	Opponents	Result	H/T Score	Lg Pos.	Goalscorers	Attendance
1	Aug 9	A	Brighton & HA	W	1-0	1-0	7	Coke [40]	26,993
2	16	H	Derby Co	D	0-0	0-0	8		25,186
3	19	H	Millwall	D	1-1	0-0	9	Maguire [57]	20,636
4	23	A	Middlesbrough	W	3-2	2-0	6	Nuhiu 2 [6, 57], May [42]	17,820
5	30	H	Nottingham F	L	0-1	0-1	10		20,656
6	Sept 13	H	Bolton W	D	0-0	0-0	11		15,799
7	16	A	Birmingham C	W	2-0	0-0	7	May [67], Helan [89]	14,085
8	20	H	Reading	W	1-0	0-0	6	May [83]	29,848
9	27	A	Cardiff C	L	1-2	0-1	9	Morrison, S (og) [50]	20,901
10	30	H	Ipswich T	D	1-1	1-0	9	Nuhiu [5]	18,093
11	Oct 4	A	Leeds U	D	1-1	0-0	9	Maguire [52]	24,094
12	18	H	Watford	L	0-3	0-2	11		20,909
13	21	A	Brentford	D	0-0	0-0	13		10,826
14	25	H	Norwich C	D	0-0	0-0	12		20,898
15	Nov 1	A	Charlton Ath	D	1-1	1-0	13	Drenthe [27]	16,850
16	4	H	Bournemouth	L	0-2	0-0	14		16,881
17	8	H	Rotherham U	D	0-0	0-0	13		26,986
18	22	A	Huddersfield T	D	0-0	0-0	13		14,389
19	29	H	Wigan Ath	W	2-1	1-1	13	May 2 [27, 71]	20,609
20	Dec 6	A	Blackburn R	W	2-1	1-1	12	Lee [3], Dielna [90]	14,920
21	13	A	Wolverhampton W	L	0-1	0-0	13		20,598
22	20	A	Fulham	L	0-4	0-2	14		21,123
23	26	H	Blackpool	W	1-0	0-0	13	Maguire (pen) [39]	26,609
24	30	A	Wigan Ath	W	1-0	0-0	10	Nuhiu [77]	14,571
25	Jan 10	A	Nottingham F	W	2-0	1-0	8	Lee [45], Maguire [50]	22,209
26	17	H	Bolton W	L	1-2	1-2	9	Maguire (pen) [28]	22,617
27	27	H	Birmingham C	D	0-0	0-0	9		18,385
28	31	A	Reading	L	0-2	0-2	10		17,755
29	Feb 7	H	Cardiff C	D	1-1	0-1	10	Keane (pen) [75]	22,344
30	10	A	Ipswich T	L	1-2	1-0	10	Lee [20]	17,306
31	14	H	Brighton & HA	D	0-0	0-0	11		19,274
32	21	A	Derby Co	L	2-3	1-0	12	McGugan [20], Keane [55]	31,628
33	24	A	Millwall	W	3-1	0-0	11	McGugan [52], Nuhiu [72], May [83]	8568
34	28	A	Middlesbrough	W	2-0	0-0	10	Nuhiu (pen) [52], Keane [54]	23,774
35	Mar 4	H	Blackburn R	L	1-2	0-2	11	Maguire [61]	19,593
36	7	A	Blackpool	W	1-0	0-0	10	McGugan [54]	11,887
37	14	H	Fulham	D	1-1	0-0	11	May [54]	22,182
38	17	A	Wolverhampton W	L	0-3	0-1	12		18,687
39	21	A	Rotherham U	W	3-2	0-0	12	Lavery [86], Lee [90], Nuhiu [90]	11,707
40	Apr 4	H	Huddersfield T	D	1-1	0-0	12	Bus [86]	20,851
41	6	A	Norwich C	L	0-2	0-2	12		26,993
42	11	H	Charlton Ath	D	1-1	1-0	13	Lavery [41]	23,257
43	14	H	Brentford	W	1-0	0-0	11	Lee [75]	17,416
44	18	A	Bournemouth	D	2-2	0-0	12	Lee [36], Maguire (pen) [90]	11,280
45	25	H	Leeds U	L	1-2	1-0	14	Maguire (pen) [36]	28,227
46	May 2	A	Watford	D	1-1	0-1	13	Nuhiu [90]	20,250

Final League Position: 13

GOALSCORERS

League (43): Maguire 8 (4 pens), Nuhiu 8 (1 pen), May 7, Lee 6, Keane 3 (1 pen), McGugan 3, Lavery 2, Bus 1, Coke 1, Dielna 1, Drenthe 1, Helan 1, own goal 1.
FA Cup (1): Nuhiu 1.
Capital One Cup (4): Nuhiu 2 (1 pen), Madine 1, Maghoma 1.

Westwood K 43	Palmer L 35	Lees T 44	Loovens G 26	Mattock J 24 + 3	Maguire C 35 + 7	Coke G 9 + 4	Lee K 28 + 5	Hutchinson S 16 + 4	Maghoma J 28 + 4	Nuhiu A 31 + 12	Semedo J 27 + 3	Madine G 1 + 9	May S 26 + 13	Helan J 25 + 13	McCabe R — + 1	Hope H 1 + 3	Zayatte K 11	Drenthe R 7 + 8	Dielna C 14 + 9	Buxton L 7 + 2	Taylor-Fletcher G 2 + 2	McGugan L 21 + 1	Lavery C 7 + 6	Baker L 2 + 2	Keane W 12 + 1	Vermijl M 8 + 3	Bus S 2 + 5	Filipe Melo S 4 + 2	Kirkland C 3 + 1	Isgrove L 7 + 1	Match No.
1	2	3	4	5	6	7	8	9	10[1]	11[2]	12	13																			1
1	2	3	4	5	6	12	8[1]	7	9	11[2]			13	10																	2
1	2	3	4	5	6	12		8[1]	9[2]	11[3]	7		13	10	14																3
1	2	3	4	5	6	7			9[1]	10[3]	8	12	11[2]	13	14																4
1	2	3	4	5[1]	6[3]	8			9	11	7[1]	12	10	13		14															5
1	2	3		5	6[1]		8		9	11	7		10				4	12													6
1	2	3	4	5	6		8[2]		9	10[1]	7	13	11[2]	14			12														7
1	2	3	4	5	6[3]		8[1]		9[2]	10	7		11	13			12		14												8
1	2		4	5	6[3]		8[1]		9	10	7[2]		14	11			12	13	3												9
1	7		4	5	6[1]				9[2]	10	8		11	13			3[3]	14	12	2											10
1	2	3	4	5	6[1]	14	8		9	10[3]	7[2]	12	11	13																	11
1	2	3	4	5				7[3]	8	9	14	12	10	11			6[1]		13												12
1	2	3	4	5	6		8[2]			10	7	12	11[1]	9			13														13
1	2	3	4		6[2]			7	14	10[2]	8		11	9			12	5[1]	13												14
1	2	3	4	5[1]	6		13		9[3]	11	7		8				10[2]	12	14												15
1	2	3	4		8[1]	9		7[2]		10	11		12	5			6[3]	13													16
1	2	3	4		6[1]	8	13		9	12	7		10	5								11[2]									17
1	2	3	4		13		14		9[3]	12	7		11	5			6					10[2]	8[1]								18
1	2	3	4		9				10	8			11	5			6[1]					7	12								19
1	2	3	4	12	9		7		10[3]				11	5			6[1]	14				8[2]	13								20
1	2	3	4		6		7[2]		10[1]				11	5			9	13				8	12								21
1	2	3	4[2]	5[1]	6		7[1]		12	8			11	10			13	14				9									22
1	2	3		5	6		12		13	8			11[2]	9			10	4				7[1]									23
1	2	3	4	5[1]	11[2]		13		6	10	7		14	9			12					8[2]									24
1	2	3	4		9[3]		8		6[2]	11	7		10[1]	12			5						14	13							25
1	4	3			6		8[2]	12[4]	9[1]	11	7[3]		10	13			5						14								26
1	2	3	4	5	6[2]			9	10	8			13	12									7	11[1]							27
1	2	3	4	5[1]	10		8		6[1]	9			12	13			14						7[2]	11							28
1		3	5[1]	6[2]		7[1]	8			12			10	9			4					14			11	2	13				29
1		3	5			7	8[1]		13				10	9			4	14				6[3]			11	2[2]		12			30
1	2	3				7	12	9	13	6[2]			14	5			4					8	10[1]		11[3]						31
1[*]	2	3		13	12	6	8[1]	9[2]	11				5				4					7	10[3]						14		32
	2	3			6	12	9[3]	11	7				13	14			4		5			8[1]	10[2]					1			33
1	2	3			13		6[3]	12	9	10	7		14				4		5			8[1]	11[2]								34
1	2	3			12			7	9[1]	11	8[2]		14	13			4[3]		5			6	10								35
1	2	3		13	9		6	7[2]		11				5			4					8			10[1]	12					36
1	2[3]	3			6			9[1]	8	14	10			13	5		4					7			11[2]	12					37
1		3			6			8[1]	9	10			11[2]	5			4					7	12			2		13			38
1		3	5	14		7	8[2]		9	11[3]			13				4					10	12			2	13			6[1]	39
1		3	5	14		8[2]	9		11[3]				12				4					7	10[1]			2	13			6	40
1		3	5	6		7			12								4	13				10	11[1]			2[3]	14	8	9[1]		41
1		3		6	13	7		12					14	5			4			2		8[3]	11[2]		10[1]			9			42
1		3		13	6		14						11[3]	5			4			2		8[2]	10		12	7		9[1]			43
		3		8	9	6[1]	12	14						5			4[3]			2			11			13	7	1	1	10[2]	44
1	4		10		8		9[2]		7				12	5[2]			3						11		13	2	14			6[1]	45
	3		9		6[3]			12	7				13	5			4						11[2]		10	2		8	1	14	46

FA Cup

Third Round	Manchester C	(a)	1-2

Capital One Cup

First Round	Notts Co	(h)	3-0
Second Round	Burnley	(a)	1-0
Third Round	Manchester C	(a)	0-7

SHREWSBURY TOWN

FOUNDATION

Shrewsbury School having provided a number of the early England and Wales international players it is not surprising that there was a Town club as early as 1876 which won the Birmingham Senior Cup in 1879. However, the present Shrewsbury Town club was formed in 1886 and won the Welsh FA Cup as early as 1891.

Greenhous Meadow, Oteley Road, Shrewsbury, Shropshire SY2 6ST.

Telephone: (01743) 289 177.

Fax: (01743) 246 942.

Ticket Office: (01743) 273 943.

Website: www.shrewsburytown.com

Email: info@shrewsburytown.co.uk

Ground Capacity: 9,875.

Record Attendance: 18,917 v Walsall, Division 3, 26 April 1961 (at Gay Meadow); 10,210 v Chelsea, League Cup 4th rd, 28 October 2014 (at Greenhous Meadow).

Pitch Measurements: 105m × 68.5m (115yd × 75yd)

Chairman: Roland Wycherley.

Manager: Micky Mellon.

Assistant Manager: Mike Jackson.

Physio: Chris Skitt.

HONOURS

Football League – Division 2: Best season: 8th, 1983–84, 1984–85; **Division 3:** *Champions* 1978–79, 1993–94; **Division 4:** *Runners-up* 1974–75. **FL 2:** *Runners-up* 2011–12, 2014–15. **FA Cup:** Best season: 6th rd, 1979, 1982. **Football League Cup:** Best season: semi-final, 1961. **Welsh Cup:** *Winners* 1891, 1938, 1977, 1979, 1984, 1985; *Runners-up* 1931, 1948, 1980. **Auto Windscreens Shield:** *Runners-up* 1996.

Colours: Blue and yellow striped shirts with blue sleeves, blue shorts, blue socks.

Year Formed: 1886.

Turned Professional: 1896.

Club Nicknames: 'Town', 'Blues', 'Salop'. The name 'Salop' is a colloquialism for the county of Shropshire. Since Shrewsbury is the only club in Shropshire, cries of 'Come on Salop' are frequently used!

Grounds: 1886, Old Racecourse Ground; 1889, Ambler's Field; 1893, Sutton Lane; 1895, Barracks Ground; 1910, Gay Meadow; 2007, New Meadow (re-named ProStar Stadium 2008; Greenhous Meadow 2010).

First Football League Game: 19 August 1950, Division 3 (N), v Scunthorpe U (a) D 0–0 – Egglestone; Fisher, Lewis; Wheatley, Depear, Robinson; Griffin, Hope, Jackson, Brown, Barker.

Record League Victory: 7–0 v Swindon T, Division 3 (S), 6 May 1955 – McBride; Bannister, Skeech; Wallace, Maloney, Candlin; Price, O'Donnell (1), Weigh (4), Russell, McCue (2); 7-0 v Gillingham, FL 2, 13 September 2008 – Daniels; Herd, Tierney, Davies (2), Jackson (1) (Langmead), Coughlan (1), Cansdell-Sherriff (1), Thornton, Hibbert (1) (Hindmarch), Holt (pen), McIntyre (Ashton).

Record Cup Victory: 11–2 v Marine, FA Cup 1st rd, 11 November 1995 – Edwards; Seabury (Dempsey (1)), Withe (1), Evans (1), Whiston (2), Scott (1), Woods, Stevens (1), Spink (3) (Anthrobus), Walton, Berkley, (1 og).

sky SPORTS FACT FILE

Shrewsbury Town's most successful season was in 1978–79 when they won the Division Three championship and reached the quarter-finals of the FA Cup. Town were unbeaten at home in their League campaign and secured the title with a 4-1 victory over Exeter City in their final game.

Record Defeat: 1–8 v Norwich C, Division 3 (S), 13 September 1952; 1–8 v Coventry C, Division 3, 22 October 1963.

Most League Points (2 for a win): 62, Division 4, 1974–75.

Most League Points (3 for a win): 89, FL 2, 2014–15.

Most League Goals: 101, Division 4, 1958–59.

Highest League Scorer in Season: Arthur Rowley, 38, Division 4, 1958–59.

Most League Goals in Total Aggregate: Arthur Rowley, 152, 1958–65 (thus completing his League record of 434 goals).

Most League Goals in One Match: 5, Alf Wood v Blackburn R, Division 3, 2 October 1971.

Most Capped Player: Jimmy McLaughlin, 5 (12), Northern Ireland; Bernard McNally, 5, Northern Ireland.

Most League Appearances: Mickey Brown, 418, 1986–91; 1992–94; 1996–2001.

Youngest League Player: Graham French, 16 years 177 days v Reading, 30 September 1961.

Record Transfer Fee Received: £600,000 (rising to £1,500,000) from Manchester C for Joe Hart, May 2006.

Record Transfer Fee Paid: £170,000 to Nottingham F for Grant Holt, June 2008.

Football League Record: 1950 Elected to Division 3 (N); 1951–58 Division 3 (S); 1958–59 Division 4; 1959–74 Division 3; 1974–75 Division 4; 1975–79 Division 3; 1979–89 Division 2; 1989–94 Division 3; 1994–97 Division 2; 1997–2003 Division 3; 2003–04 Conference; 2004–12 FL 2; 2012–14 FL 1; 2014–15 FL 2; 2015– FL 1.

LATEST SEQUENCES

Longest Sequence of League Wins: 7, 28.10.1995 – 16.12.1995.

Longest Sequence of League Defeats: 11, 9.4.2003 – 14.8.2004.

Longest Sequence of League Draws: 6, 30.10.1963 – 14.12.1963.

Longest Sequence of Unbeaten League Matches: 16, 30.10.1993 – 26.2.1994.

Longest Sequence Without a League Win: 18, 8.3.2003 – 14.8.2004.

Successive Scoring Runs: 28 from 7.9.1960.

Successive Non-scoring Runs: 6 from 1.1.1991.

MANAGERS

W. Adams 1905–12
(Secretary-Manager)
A. Weston 1912–34
(Secretary-Manager)
Jack Roscamp 1934–35
Sam Ramsey 1935–36
Ted Bousted 1936–40
Leslie Knighton 1945–49
Harry Chapman 1949–50
Sammy Crooks 1950–54
Walter Rowley 1955–57
Harry Potts 1957–58
Johnny Spuhler 1958
Arthur Rowley 1958–68
Harry Gregg 1968–72
Maurice Evans 1972–73
Alan Durban 1974–78
Richie Barker 1978
Graham Turner 1978–84
Chic Bates 1984–87
Ian McNeill 1987–90
Asa Hartford 1990–91
John Bond 1991–93
Fred Davies 1994–97
(previously Caretaker-Manager 1993–94)
Jake King 1997–99
Kevin Ratcliffe 1999–2003
Jimmy Quinn 2003–04
Gary Peters 2004–08
Paul Simpson 2008–10
Graham Turner 2010–14
Mike Jackson 2014
Micky Mellon May 2014–

TEN YEAR LEAGUE RECORD

		P	W	D	L	F	A	Pts	Pos
2005-06	FL 2	46	16	13	17	55	55	61	10
2006-07	FL 2	46	18	17	11	68	46	71	7
2007-08	FL 2	46	12	14	20	56	65	50	18
2008-09	FL 2	46	17	18	11	61	44	69	7
2009-10	FL 2	46	17	12	17	55	54	63	12
2010-11	FL 2	46	22	13	11	72	49	79	4
2011-12	FL 2	46	26	10	10	66	41	88	2
2012-13	FL 1	46	13	16	17	54	60	55	16
2013-14	FL 1	46	9	15	22	44	65	42	23
2014-15	FL 2	46	27	8	11	67	31	89	2

DID YOU KNOW ❓

Shrewsbury Town won the 1937–38 Welsh Cup by defeating Swansea Town in a replay which was held over until early the following season. The clubs drew 2-2 in the first game but Town, who were Midland League champions, won the replay at Gay Meadow 2-1 in September 1938.

SHREWSBURY TOWN – FOOTBALL LEAGUE TWO 2014–15 LEAGUE RECORD

Match No.	Date	Venue	Opponents	Result		H/T Score	Lg Pos.	Goalscorers	Attendance
1	Aug 9	A	AFC Wimbledon	D	2-2	1-1	10	Collins 2 [9, 84]	4162
2	16	H	Tranmere R	W	2-1	0-1	6	Demetriou [90], Mangan [90]	5249
3	19	H	Accrington S	W	4-0	3-0	3	Mangan 2 [7, 65], Akpa Akpro (pen) [44], Goldson [45]	4298
4	23	A	Northampton T	D	1-1	0-0	6	Collins [63]	4369
5	30	H	Luton T	W	2-0	1-0	4	Clark 2 [3, 70]	5888
6	Sept 6	A	Hartlepool U	L	0-2	0-1	4		3368
7	13	A	Stevenage	L	0-1	0-1	7		2840
8	16	H	Carlisle U	W	1-0	1-0	6	Grandison [42]	3833
9	20	H	Newport Co	D	0-0	0-0	6		4904
10	27	A	Southend U	L	0-1	0-1	7		6951
11	Oct 4	A	Plymouth Arg	L	0-1	0-1	12		6229
12	11	H	Cheltenham T	W	3-1	0-0	8	Collins [50], Mangan [55], Knight-Percival [69]	4817
13	18	A	York C	W	1-0	0-0	7	Collins [87]	3651
14	21	H	Bury	W	5-0	3-0	5	Akpa Akpro 3 [3, 35, 51], Goldson [19], Clark [73]	4233
15	25	H	Portsmouth	W	2-1	1-1	4	Wesolowski [13], Goldson [72]	5515
16	Nov 1	A	Dagenham & R	W	2-1	0-1	3	Mangan [70], Lawrence (pen) [90]	1698
17	15	H	Mansfield T	W	2-0	0-0	2	Grant [59], Collins [75]	5001
18	22	A	Exeter C	L	2-3	2-0	4	Collins 2 [13, 34]	3933
19	29	H	Burton Alb	W	1-0	0-0	3	Akpa Akpro [82]	5170
20	Dec 13	A	Cambridge U	D	0-0	0-0	3		5346
21	20	H	Morecambe	W	1-0	0-0	2	Mangan [86]	4708
22	26	A	Oxford U	W	2-0	2-0	1	Collins [13], Ellis [18]	7502
23	28	H	Wycombe W	D	0-0	0-0	1		7239
24	Jan 3	A	Burton Alb	L	0-1	0-0	3		4555
25	8	A	Luton T	D	0-0	0-0	3		7666
26	17	H	Hartlepool U	W	3-0	0-0	3	Mangan 2 [50, 68], Collins [59]	4601
27	24	H	Stevenage	W	3-2	2-2	2	Collins 2 [22, 88], Lawrence (pen) [24]	4565
28	31	A	Newport Co	W	1-0	0-0	1	Akpa Akpro [77]	3706
29	Feb 7	H	Southend U	D	1-1	0-0	3	Barnett [85]	5276
30	10	A	Carlisle U	W	2-1	0-0	1	Demetriou [90], Collins [90]	3624
31	14	H	AFC Wimbledon	W	2-0	1-0	1	Lawrence [45], Vernon [49]	4992
32	21	A	Tranmere R	L	1-2	0-2	2	Goldson [82]	5987
33	28	H	Northampton T	L	1-2	0-1	2	Demetriou [84]	5310
34	Mar 3	A	Accrington S	W	2-1	1-1	1	Grant 2 [11, 87]	1137
35	7	H	Cambridge U	D	1-1	1-0	2	Grant [16]	5075
36	14	A	Wycombe W	L	0-1	0-1	3		4697
37	17	A	Morecambe	W	4-1	2-1	2	Goldson [33], Collins [35], Grandison [84], Barnett [90]	1363
38	21	H	Oxford U	W	2-0	1-0	2	Lawrence 2 (1 pen) [2 (p), 82]	5265
39	28	A	Portsmouth	W	2-0	1-0	2	Grant 2 [25, 66]	14,749
40	Apr 3	H	Dagenham & R	W	2-0	2-0	2	Goldson 2 [17, 22]	6143
41	6	A	Mansfield T	W	1-0	0-0	2	Barnett [50]	3108
42	11	H	Exeter C	W	4-0	1-0	2	Akpa Akpro 2 [18, 73], Collins [62], Barnett [90]	5442
43	14	A	Bury	L	0-1	0-0	2		4277
44	18	H	York C	W	1-0	1-0	2	Ellis [12]	6400
45	25	A	Cheltenham T	W	1-0	1-0	2	Akpa Akpro [20]	5117
46	May 2	H	Plymouth Arg	L	0-2	0-2	2		8963

Final League Position: 2

GOALSCORERS

League (67): Collins 15, Akpa Akpro 9 (1 pen), Mangan 8, Goldson 7, Grant 6, Lawrence 5 (3 pens), Barnett 4, Clark 3, Demetriou 3, Ellis 2, Grandison 2, Knight-Percival 1, Vernon 1, Wesolowski 1.
FA Cup (3): Collins 1, Ellis 1, Lawrence 1.
Capital One Cup (4): Mangan 2, Collins 1, Vernon 1.
Johnstone's Paint Trophy (0).

Leutwiler J 46	Woods R 41 + 2	Clark J 18 + 9	Knight-Percival N 28	Ellis M 32	Akpa Akpro J 26 + 19	Lawrence L 30 + 3	Gayle C 27 + 1	Collins J 42 + 3	Goldson C 44	Vernon S 12 + 10	Vincent A 4 + 4	Wesolowski J 18 + 3	Mangan A 10 + 20	Demetriou M 40 + 2	Caton J — + 2	Robinson A — + 2	Grandison J 32 + 4	Ginnelly J — + 3	Griffith A 1 + 4	Grimmer J 6	Grant R 28 + 5	Passley J 6	Halstead M — + 1	Southern K 3 + 3	Mandron M 2 + 1	Barnett T 8 + 10	Randall C — + 1	Wildig A — + 1	Sharpe R 2 + 1	Match No.
1	2	3³	4	5	6²	7¹	8	9	10	11	12	13	14																	1
1	8	6	5		14		2	10⁴	4	11¹		9¹	7	13	3	12														2
1	14	9¹	4		10	8	2		3			6⁹	7¹¹	11	5	13	12													3
1	12	9	3		11²	8⁶	2	13	4	14		6³	7	10¹	5															4
1	6	7³	3		12		5	10¹	4	11²		8		9	13	2	14													5
1	7	6	4	3	14		9³	11	2	10²		8	13	5¹			12													6
1	8	7¹	5	3	10			11	4	12		6	9				2													7
1	6	9	5	4	10			11¹	3		12	7	8				2													8
1	8	11¹	2	3	9¹			14	4	10²	13	7	6				5	12												9
1	6	13	3		10	7²	5³	11¹	4		14	8	12⁸	9			2													10
1	8	13	3		6			10	4	11¹	9²	7		2			5	12												11
1	6	8¹	4		13	12	5	10	3			7	11²	9			2													12
1	6	13	4		12			10	3	14			11²	9			2				8³	5	7¹							13
1	6²	12	4		11¹			10	3	13		7		9			2	14	5	8³										14
1	6	14	4		11	13		10³	3			7¹	12	9			2		5	8²										15
1	7		5		11¹	8³		10	4			13	12	6			3⁴		14	2	9²									16
1		12	4		10²	8		11	2	13		7		9			3			5	6¹									17
1	7	12	5		11	8¹		10	4			9		6			3			2										18
1	8		3		10			11	5			9	12	6			4				7¹	2								19
1¹	7		4	2	11²	6		10	3			13		9							8	5	12							20
1	8		4	3	11²	6		10	2			12		9				13			7¹	5								21
1	6		4	3	13	8		10²	2	11¹		12		9							7	5								22
1	6		4	3	12	7		10	2	11²		13		9							8¹	5								23
1	6		4	2³		7¹		11	3	10		12	13	9							8	5								24
1	6	4⁴	2	10¹	5	8		11	3			7		9							12									25
1	7		3	14	6	5		11¹	4	13		8⁴	10³	9			2				12									26
1	7²		4	3	12	8	5³	10	2			11¹		9			13				6			14						27
1	7		3	4	12	8	2³	10	5					6			13				9¹			14⁴	11²					28
1	7		4²	3	14	8	5³	10	2					9			12				6				11¹	13				29
1	6	14		2	13	7	5¹	11	3	12				9			4				8³					10²				30
1	6	7		4	12	8¹		11	3	9				5			2³				14					10²	13			31
1	6	8¹		3	13	7²	14	10	4	9				5³			2				12					11				32
1	7	6²		3	13			10	4	8¹				5			2				12			9³		11	14			33
1	7	6		4	12		5	11	3					9			2				8					10¹				34
1	7	6		3	12		5	10	4					9			2				8²		13			11¹				35
1	7	6²		3	14	12	5	10	4	13				9			2				8					11¹				36
1	6			3	10²	7	5	11³	4		13	14					2				8					12		9¹		37
1	6			3³	10	8	5	11¹	4			12					2				7					13		9⁸		38
1	8			3	11²	6	5	10¹	2			13	9				4				7					12				39
1	7			3¹	11	8	5	10²	2			13	9				4	14			6³					12				40
1	7			4	10²	8	5	11¹	3			13	9				2				6³					12			14	41
1	8¹			4	10¹	7	2	11²		14		13	5				3				9			6		12				42
1	9			4	11	7	2²	10³				13	5				3				6			8¹	14	12				43
1	6	14		3	12	7	5	13	4			11¹	9				2				8²					10³				44
1	7			3	11²	6	5	10¹	4			13	9				2				8					12				45
1	7			3³	11	8	5¹	10²	4	12		14	9				2				6					13				46

FA Cup

First Round	Walsall	(a)	2-2	
Replay	Walsall	(h)	1-0	
Second Round	Preston NE	(a)	0-1	

Johnstone's Paint Trophy

First Round	Preston NE	(a)	0-1	

Capital One Cup

First Round	Blackpool	(h)	1-0	
Second Round	Leicester C	(a)	1-0	
Third Round	Norwich C	(h)	1-0	
Fourth Round	Chelsea	(h)	1-2	

SOUTHAMPTON

FOUNDATION

The club was formed by members of the St Mary's Church of England Young Men's Association at a meeting of the Y.M.A. in November 1885 and it was named as such. For the sake of brevity this was usually shortened to St Mary's Y.M.A. The rector Canon Albert Basil Orme Wilberforce was elected president. The name was changed to plain St Mary's during 1887–88 and did not become Southampton St Mary's until 1894, the inaugural season in the Southern League.

St Mary's Stadium, Britannia Road, Southampton, Hampshire SO14 5FP.

Telephone: (0845) 688 9448.

Fax: (02380) 727 727.

Ticket Office: (0845) 688 9288.

Website: www.saintsfc.co.uk

Email: sfc@saintsfc.co.uk

Ground Capacity: 32,505.

Record Attendance: 31,044 v Manchester U, Division 1, 8 October 1969 (at The Dell); 32,363 v Coventry C, FL C, 28 April 2012 (at St Mary's).

Pitch Measurements: 105m × 68m (114yd × 74yd)

Executive Chairman: Katharina Liebherr.

Manager: Ronald Koeman.

Assistant Manager: Erwin Koeman.

Physios: Tom Sturdy and Steve Wright.

Colours: Red and white striped shirts, black shorts, red socks with white hoops.

Year Formed: 1885.

Turned Professional: 1894.

Previous Names: 1885, St Mary's Young Men's Association; 1887–88, St Mary's; 1894–95 Southampton St Mary's; 1897, Southampton.

Club Nickname: 'Saints'.

Grounds: 1885, 'The Common' (from 1887 also used the County Cricket Ground and Antelope Cricket Ground); 1889, Antelope Cricket Ground; 1896 The County Cricket Ground; 1898, The Dell; 2001, St Mary's.

First Football League Game: 28 August 1920, Division 3, v Gillingham (a) D 1–1 – Allen; Parker, Titmuss; Shelley, Campbell, Turner; Barratt, Dominy (1), Rawlings, Moore, Foxall.

Record League Victory: 8–0 v Sunderland, FA Premier League, 18 October 2014 – Forster; Clyne, Fonte, Alderweireld, Bertrand; Davis S (Mane), Schneiderlin, Cork (1); Long (Wanyama (1)), Pelle (2) (Mayuka), Tadic (1) (plus 3 Sunderland own goals).

HONOURS

Football League – FL C: *Runners-up* 2011–12; **FL 1:** *Runners-up* 2010–11; **Division 1:** *Runners-up* 1983–84; **Division 2:** *Runners-up* 1965–66, 1977–78; **Division 3:** *Champions* 1959–60; *Runners-up* 1920–21; **Division 3 (S):** *Champions* 1921–22.

FA Cup: *Winners* 1976; *Runners-up* 1900, 1902, 2003.

Football League Cup: *Runners-up* 1979.

Zenith Data Systems Cup: *Runners-up* 1992.

Johnstone's Paint Trophy: *Winners* 2009–10.

**European Competitions
European Fairs Cup:** 1969–70.
UEFA Cup: 1971–72, 1981–82, 1982–83, 1984–85, 2003–04.
European Cup-Winners' Cup: 1976–77.

sky SPORTS FACT FILE

Future England star Ted Drake who began his career with Southampton was also a promising cricketer attached to Hampshire. He made his debut in First Class cricket for Hampshire against Glamorgan in July 1931, four months before he appeared for Saints' first team.

Record Cup Victory: 7–1 v Ipswich T, FA Cup 3rd rd, 7 January 1961 – Reynolds; Davies, Traynor, Conner, Page, Huxford, Paine (1), O'Brien (3 incl. 1p), Reeves, Mulgrew (2), Penk (1).

Record Defeat: 0–8 v Tottenham H, Division 2, 28 March 1936; 0–8 v Everton, Division 1, 20 November 1971.

Most League Points (2 for a win): 61, Division 3 (S), 1921–22 and Division 3, 1959–60.

Most League Points (3 for a win): 92, FL 1, 2010–11.

Most League Goals: 112, Division 3 (S), 1957–58.

Highest League Scorer in Season: Derek Reeves, 39, Division 3, 1959–60.

Most League Goals in Total Aggregate: Mike Channon, 185, 1966–77, 1979–82.

Most League Goals in One Match: 5, Charlie Wayman v Leicester C, Division 2, 23 October 1948.

Most Capped Player: Peter Shilton, 49 (125), England.

Most League Appearances: Terry Paine, 713, 1956–74.

Youngest League Player: Theo Walcott, 16 years 143 days v Wolverhampton W, 6 August 2005.

Record Transfer Fee Received: £27,000,000 (rising to £32,000,000) from Manchester U for Luke Shaw, July 2014.

Record Transfer Fee Paid: £12,800,000 (rising to £18,000,000) to AS Roma for Pablo Daniel Osvaldo, August 2013.

Football League Record: 1920 Original Member of Division 3; 1921–22 Division 3 (S); 1922–53 Division 2; 1953–58 Division 3 (S); 1958–60 Division 3; 1960–66 Division 2; 1966–74 Division 1; 1974–78 Division 2; 1978–92 Division 1; 1992–2005 FA Premier League; 2005–09 FL C; 2009–11 FL 1; 2011–12 FL C; 2012– FA Premier League.

LATEST SEQUENCES

Longest Sequence of League Wins: 10, 16.4.2011 – 20.8.2011.

Longest Sequence of League Defeats: 5, 16.8.1998 – 12.9.1998.

Longest Sequence of League Draws: 8, 29.8.2005 – 15.10.2005.

Longest Sequence of Unbeaten League Matches: 19, 5.9.1921 – 31.12.1921.

Longest Sequence Without a League Win: 20, 30.8.1969 – 27.12.1969.

Successive Scoring Runs: 28 from 10.2.2008.

Successive Non-scoring Runs: 5 from 2.4.2001.

MANAGERS

Cecil Knight 1894–95
(Secretary-Manager)
Charles Robson 1895–97
Er Arnfield 1897–1911
(Secretary-Manager)
(continued as Secretary)
George Swift 1911–12
Er Arnfield 1912–19
Jimmy McIntyre 1919–24
Arthur Chadwick 1925–31
George Kay 1931–36
George Gross 1936–37
Tom Parker 1937–43
J. R. Sarjantson stepped down
from the board to act as
Secretary-Manager 1943–47 with
the next two listed being Team
Managers during this period
Arthur Dominy 1943–46
Bill Dodgin Snr 1946–49
Sid Cann 1949–51
George Roughton 1952–55
Ted Bates 1955–73
Lawrie McMenemy 1973–85
Chris Nicholl 1985–91
Ian Branfoot 1991–94
Alan Ball 1994–95
Dave Merrington 1995–96
Graeme Souness 1996–97
Dave Jones 1997–2000
Glenn Hoddle 2000–01
Stuart Gray 2001
Gordon Strachan 2001–04
Paul Sturrock 2004
Steve Wigley 2004
Harry Redknapp 2004–05
George Burley 2005–08
Nigel Pearson 2008
Jan Poortvliet 2008–09
Mark Wotte 2009
Alan Pardew 2009–10
Nigel Adkins 2010–13
Mauricio Pochettino 2013–14
Ronald Koeman June 2014–

TEN YEAR LEAGUE RECORD

		P	W	D	L	F	A	Pts	Pos
2005-06	FL C	46	13	19	14	49	50	58	12
2006-07	FL C	46	21	12	13	77	53	75	6
2007-08	FL C	46	13	15	18	56	72	54	20
2008-09	FL C	46	10	15	21	46	69	45	23
2009-10	FL 1	46	23	14	9	85	47	73*	7
2010-11	FL 1	46	28	8	10	86	38	92	2
2011-12	FL C	46	26	10	10	85	46	88	2
2012-13	PR Lge	38	9	14	15	49	60	41	14
2013-14	PR Lge	38	15	11	12	54	46	56	8
2014-15	PR Lge	38	18	6	14	54	33	60	7

*10 pts deducted.

DID YOU KNOW

Southampton's former ground The Dell was damaged twice during the Second World War. Firstly, in November 1940 a German bomb landed in one of the penalty areas, and secondly, in March 1941 explosives stored by the RAF damaged the West Stand.

SOUTHAMPTON – FA PREMIERSHIP 2014–15 LEAGUE RECORD

Match No.	Date	Venue	Opponents	Result	H/T Score	Lg Pos.	Goalscorers	Attendance
1	Aug 17	A	Liverpool	L	1-2	0-1	14	Clyne [56]	44,736
2	23	H	WBA	D	0-0	0-0	13		27,598
3	30	A	West Ham U	W	3-1	1-1	4	Schneiderlin 2 [45, 68], Pelle [83]	34,907
4	Sept 13	H	Newcastle U	W	4-0	2-0	2	Pelle 2 [6, 19], Cork [54], Schneiderlin [90]	29,678
5	20	A	Swansea C	W	1-0	0-0	2	Wanyama [80]	20,596
6	27	H	QPR	W	2-1	0-0	3	Bertrand [54], Pelle [68]	30,504
7	Oct 5	A	Tottenham H	L	0-1	0-1	3		35,564
8	18	H	Sunderland	W	8-0	3-0	2	Vergini (og) [12], Pelle 2 [18, 69], Cork [37], Bridcutt (og) [63], Tadic [78], Wanyama [79], Van Aanholt (og) [86]	29,615
9	25	H	Stoke C	W	1-0	1-0	2	Mane [33]	30,017
10	Nov 1	A	Hull C	W	1-0	1-0	2	Wanyama [3]	22,828
11	8	H	Leicester C	W	2-0	0-0	2	Long 2 [75, 80]	31,297
12	24	A	Aston Villa	D	1-1	0-1	3	Clyne [81]	25,311
13	30	H	Manchester C	L	0-3	0-0	3		30,919
14	Dec 3	A	Arsenal	L	0-1	0-0	5		60,025
15	8	H	Manchester U	L	1-2	1-1	5	Pelle [31]	31,420
16	13	A	Burnley	L	0-1	0-0	5		17,287
17	20	H	Everton	W	3-0	1-0	4	Lukaku (og) [38], Pelle [65], Yoshida [82]	31,475
18	26	A	Crystal Palace	W	3-1	1-0	4	Mane [17], Bertrand [48], Alderweireld [53]	24,565
19	28	H	Chelsea	D	1-1	1-1	4	Mane [17]	31,641
20	Jan 1	H	Arsenal	W	2-0	1-0	2	Mane [34], Tadic [56]	31,492
21	11	A	Manchester U	W	1-0	0-0	3	Tadic [69]	75,395
22	17	A	Newcastle U	W	2-1	1-1	3	Elia 2 [14, 62]	49,307
23	Feb 1	H	Swansea C	L	0-1	0-0	4		30,943
24	7	A	QPR	W	1-0	0-0	3	Mane [90]	18,082
25	11	H	West Ham U	D	0-0	0-0	4		31,241
26	22	H	Liverpool	L	0-2	0-1	5		31,723
27	28	A	WBA	L	0-1	0-1	5		25,303
28	Mar 3	H	Crystal Palace	W	1-0	0-0	5	Mane [83]	28,351
29	15	A	Chelsea	D	1-1	1-1	6	Tadic (pen) [19]	41,624
30	21	H	Burnley	W	2-0	1-0	6	Long [37], Shackell (og) [58]	30,864
31	Apr 4	A	Everton	L	0-1	0-1	6		39,390
32	11	H	Hull C	W	2-0	0-0	5	Ward-Prowse (pen) [56], Pelle [81]	30,359
33	18	A	Stoke C	L	1-2	1-0	6	Schneiderlin [22]	26,467
34	25	H	Tottenham H	D	2-2	1-1	7	Pelle 2 [29, 65]	31,622
35	May 2	A	Sunderland	L	1-2	1-1	7	Mane [22]	39,613
36	9	A	Leicester C	L	0-2	0-2	7		31,939
37	16	H	Aston Villa	W	6-1	5-1	7	Mane 3 [13, 14, 16], Long 2 [26, 38], Pelle [81]	31,636
38	24	A	Manchester C	L	0-2	0-1	7		45,919

Final League Position: 7

GOALSCORERS

League (54): Pelle 12, Mane 10, Long 5, Schneiderlin 4, Tadic 4 (1 pen), Wanyama 3, Bertrand 2, Clyne 2, Cork 2, Elia 2, Alderweireld 1, Ward-Prowse 1 (1 pen), Yoshida 1, own goals 5.
FA Cup (4): Long 1, Pelle 1, Schneiderlin 1, own goal 1.
Capital One Cup (7): Pelle 3, Clyne 1, Cork 1, Long 1, Tadic 1 (1 pen).

Forster F 30	Clyne N 35	Fonte J 37	Yoshida M 18+4	Bertrand R 34	Davis S 32+3	Schneiderlin M 24+2	Wanyama V 26+6	Ward-Prowse J 16+9	Pelle G 37+1	Tadic D 24+7	Long S 16+16	Isgrove L —+1	Cork J 5+7	Ramirez G —+1	Alderweireld T 26	Gardos F 5+6	Mane S 24+6	Targett M 3+3	Mayuka E —+5	Reed H 5+4	Hesketh J 1+1	Gape D —+1	McCarthy J —+1	Elia E 9+7	Seager R —+1	Djuricic F 3+6	Davis K 6+1	Gazzaniga P 2	Match No.
1	2	3	4	5	6²	7	8	9	10	11¹	12	13																	1
1	2	3	4	5	8²	6	7	9	11	10	12		13																2
1	2	3	4	5	8	7		6²	10	11	9¹		13	12															3
1	2	3		5	6	7	12	13	10	11²	9³		8¹		4	14													4
1	2	3	4¹	5	13	8	14	6³	10	11	9		7²		12														5
1	2	3		5	6	8	7¹		10		9¹²		13		4		11²	14											6
1	2	3		5	6	8	7¹		10		9		12		4		11												7
1	2	3		5	6²	7	12		10¹	11	9³		8		4		13	14											8
1	2	3		5	6¹	7	12		10		9		8²		4	13	11												9
1	2	3		5	6	8	7		10	11¹	9²		13		4		12												10
1	2	3		5	6³	8¹	7		10		9		13	12	4		11²	14											11
1	2	3		5		7	6		11		8		9²	13	4		10¹	12											12
1	2	3	12	5	6²	8¹	7		10		9		13		4		11³	14											13
1	2	3	12	5	6		7		10	11²	9³		8¹		4		13	14											14
1	2	3	4	5	6		7		11		9²		8¹				10	13	12										15
1	2	3		5		7		6	12	11	9		13		4		10¹			8²									16
1	2	3	4	5	8				9¹	10			11²		6			12		7	13								17
1	2³		5	6	8¹	9	12	7	11²		13				4	3	10							14					18
1		3	2²		6¹	8⁴	7	12	10		9³	14			4	13	11	5											19
1	3	13	5		6		7	8	11		10¹	14			2	4³	9²												20
1	2	3		5	6²	8	7	9	10		13				4³	12				14				11¹					21
1	2	3		5	6			8¹¹		9¹	12		13			4		14		7				10²					22
1	2	3	4	5⁴	6			9	11	8						12				7¹				10²	13				23
1	2	3	4		7	13	6³	8	11	14					12	9	5²							10¹					24
1	2	3	5		8			7	13	10	12				4	9³			6²					11¹	14				25
1	2	3	4		8³	12	7	6	10	14						13	5							11	9²				26
1	5	3	4	8	13	7	6³		10		9¹	14			2²	11								12					27
1	2	3		5		7	6	14	11¹²	12	13					10								8²	9³				28
1	2	3		5	9³	7	6	13	14	10²	11¹				4	8								12					29
1¹	2	3		5	6	7	13		11	10²	8				4	9										12			30
	2	3		5		7	6	9²	11	13	8				4¹	12								10³		14	1		31
	3	4	5	9	7	6³	12	11	13	8¹					2	10²								14			1		32
	2	3	4	5¹	8²	7		12	11	10³	13				6	9								14			1		33
	2	3	4	5	10³	7⁴		8¹	11		12				6	9		14						13			1		34
	2	3	4	5	13		6¹	9⁴	11		8²				7	10³								14		12	1		35
	2	3		5	8¹		7		11		13				4	9		6						10²		12	1	1	36
	2	3	12	5	7¹		6	9³	11¹²		8				4	10								14		13	1	1	37
	2	3		5	7²		6	12	11		8				4	10								13		9¹	1		38

FA Cup

Third Round	Ipswich T	(h)	1-1
Replay	Ipswich T	(a)	1-0
Fourth Round	Crystal Palace	(h)	2-3

Capital One Cup

Second Round	Millwall	(a)	2-0
Third Round	Arsenal	(a)	2-1
Fourth Round	Stoke C	(a)	3-2
Quarter-Finals	Sheffield U	(a)	0-1

SOUTHEND UNITED

Roots Hall Stadium, Victoria Avenue, Southend-on-Sea, Essex SS2 6NQ.

Telephone: (01702) 304 050.

Fax: (01702) 304 124.

Ticket Office: (08444) 770 077.

Website: www.southendunited.co.uk

Email: info@southend-united.co.uk

Ground Capacity: 12,149.

Record Attendance: 22,862 v Tottenham H, FA Cup 3rd rd replay, 11 January 1936 (at Southend Stadium); 31,090 v Liverpool, FA Cup 3rd rd, 10 January 1979 (at Roots Hall).

Pitch Measurements: 100.5m × 67.5m (110yd × 74yd)

Chairman: Ronald Martin.

Chief Executive: Steve Kavanagh.

Manager: Phil Brown.

Assistant Manager: Dave Penney.

Physio: Ben Clarkson.

Colours: White shirts with navy blue trim, navy blue shorts, navy blue socks.

Year Formed: 1906.

Turned Professional: 1906.

Club Nicknames: 'The Blues', 'The Shrimpers'.

Grounds: 1906, Roots Hall, Prittlewell; 1920, Kursaal; 1934, Southend Stadium; 1955, Roots Hall Football Ground.

First Football League Game: 28 August 1920, Division 3, v Brighton & HA (a) W 2–0 – Capper; Reid, Newton; Wileman, Henderson, Martin; Nicholls, Nuttall, Fairclough (2), Myers, Dorsett.

Record League Victory: 9–2 v Newport Co, Division 3 (S), 5 September 1936 – McKenzie; Nelson, Everest (1); Deacon, Turner, Carr; Bolan, Lane (1), Goddard (4), Dickinson (2), Oswald (1).

Record Cup Victory: 10–1 v Golders Green, FA Cup 1st rd, 24 November 1934 – Moore; Morfitt, Kelly; Mackay, Joe Wilson, Carr (1); Lane (1), Johnson (5), Cheesmuir (2), Deacon (1), Oswald. 10–1 v Brentwood, FA Cup 2nd rd, 7 December 1968 – Roberts; Bentley, Birks; McMillan (1) Beesley, Kurila; Clayton, Chisnall, Moore (4), Best (5), Hamilton. 10–1 v Aldershot, Leyland DAF Cup Prel rd, 6 November 1990 – Sansome; Austin, Powell, Cornwell, Prior (1), Tilson (3), Cawley, Butler, Ansah (1), Benjamin (1), Angell (4).

Record Defeat: 1–9 v Brighton & HA, Division 3, 27 November 1965.

Most League Points (2 for a win): 67, Division 4, 1980–81.

Most League Points (3 for a win): 85, Division 3, 1990–91.

Most League Goals: 92, Division 3 (S), 1950–51.

Highest League Scorer in Season: Jim Shankly, 31, 1928–29; Sammy McCrory, 1957–58, both in Division 3 (S).

Most League Goals in Total Aggregate: Roy Hollis, 122, 1953–60.

Most League Goals in One Match: 5, Jim Shankly v Merthyr T, Division 3 (S), 1 March 1930.

Most Capped Player: George Mackenzie, 9, Eire.

Most League Appearances: Sandy Anderson, 452, 1950–63.

Youngest League Player: Phil O'Connor, 16 years 76 days v Lincoln C, 26 December 1969.

Record Transfer Fee Received: £2,000,000 (rising to £2,750,000) from Nottingham F for Stan Collymore, June 1993.

Record Transfer Fee Paid: £80,000 to Crystal Palace for Stan Collymore, November 1992.

Football League Record: 1920 Original Member of Division 3; 1921–58 Division 3 (S); 1958–66 Division 3; 1966–72 Division 4; 1972–76 Division 3; 1976–78 Division 4; 1978–80 Division 3; 1980–81 Division 4; 1981–84 Division 3; 1984–87 Division 4; 1987–89 Division 3; 1989–90 Division 4; 1990–91 Division 3; 1991–92 Division 2; 1992–97 Division 1; 1997–98 Division 2; 1998–2004 Division 3; 2004–05 FL 2; 2005–06 FL 1; 2006–07 FL C; 2007–10 FL 1; 2010–15 FL 2; 2015– FL 1.

LATEST SEQUENCES

Longest Sequence of League Wins: 8, 29.8.2005 – 9.10.2005.

Longest Sequence of League Defeats: 6, 14.4.2007 – 18.8.2007.

Longest Sequence of League Draws: 6, 30.1.1982 – 19.2.1982.

Longest Sequence of Unbeaten League Matches: 16, 20.2.1932 – 29.8.1932.

Longest Sequence Without a League Win: 17, 26.8.2006 – 2.12.2006.

Successive Scoring Runs: 24 from 23.3.1929.

Successive Non-scoring Runs: 6 from 6.6.1979.

MANAGERS

Bob Jack 1906–10
George Molyneux 1910–11
O. M. Howard 1911–12
Joe Bradshaw 1912–19
Ned Liddell 1919–20
Tom Mather 1920–21
Ted Birnie 1921–34
David Jack 1934–40
Harry Warren 1946–56
Eddie Perry 1956–60
Frank Broome 1960
Ted Fenton 1961–65
Alvan Williams 1965–67
Ernie Shepherd 1967–69
Geoff Hudson 1969–70
Arthur Rowley 1970–76
Dave Smith 1976–83
Peter Morris 1983–84
Bobby Moore 1984–86
Dave Webb 1986–87
Dick Bate 1987
Paul Clark 1987–88
Dave Webb *(General Manager)* 1988–92
Colin Murphy 1992–93
Barry Fry 1993
Peter Taylor 1993–95
Steve Thompson 1995
Ronnie Whelan 1995–97
Alvin Martin 1997–99
Alan Little 1999–2000
David Webb 2000–01
Rob Newman 2001–03
Steve Wignall 2003
Steve Tilson 2003–10
Paul Sturrock 2010–13
Phil Brown March 2013–

TEN YEAR LEAGUE RECORD

		P	W	D	L	F	A	Pts	Pos
2005-06	FL 1	46	23	13	10	72	43	82	1
2006-07	FL C	46	10	12	24	47	80	42	22
2007-08	FL 1	46	22	10	14	70	55	76	6
2008-09	FL 1	46	21	8	17	58	61	71	8
2009-10	FL 1	46	10	13	23	51	72	43	23
2010-11	FL 2	46	16	13	17	62	56	61	13
2011-12	FL 2	46	25	8	13	77	48	83	4
2012-13	FL 2	46	16	13	17	61	55	61	11
2013-14	FL 2	46	19	15	12	56	39	72	5
2014-15	FL 2	46	24	12	10	54	38	84	5

DID YOU KNOW ?

Southend United were unable to use their own ground during the Second World War as it was in a restricted area. From the start of the 1940–41 season United played their home games at Chelmsford City's stadium with the Chelmsford boss Harry Warren being appointed manager of Southend.

SOUTHEND UNITED – FOOTBALL LEAGUE TWO 2014–15 LEAGUE RECORD

Match No.	Date	Venue	Opponents	Result	H/T Score	Lg Pos.	Goalscorers	Attendance
1	Aug 9	A	Accrington S	W 1-0	0-0	3	Barnard (pen) [85]	1505
2	16	H	Stevenage	W 2-0	2-0	3	Weston [9], Coker [20]	5397
3	19	H	AFC Wimbledon	L 0-1	0-0	8		5364
4	23	A	Carlisle U	D 1-1	1-1	8	Clifford [45]	3847
5	30	A	Plymouth Arg	L 0-2	0-0	14		6247
6	Sept 6	H	Oxford U	D 1-1	1-0	13	Payne [36]	5315
7	13	H	Portsmouth	W 2-0	0-0	8	Corr [56], Coulthirst [90]	7023
8	16	A	Cheltenham T	W 1-0	0-0	7	Clifford [52]	2303
9	20	A	York C	W 3-2	1-1	4	Weston (pen) [9], Hurst [52], Payne [78]	3307
10	27	H	Shrewsbury T	W 1-0	1-0	4	Coulthirst [2]	6951
11	Oct 4	H	Morecambe	L 0-1	0-1	4		5284
12	11	A	Luton T	L 0-2	0-2	5		9238
13	18	H	Exeter C	D 1-1	1-0	8	Worrall [33]	5749
14	21	A	Newport Co	L 0-1	0-0	10		2558
15	25	H	Bury	D 1-1	1-0	9	Corr [37]	5174
16	Nov 1	A	Mansfield T	W 2-1	1-0	7	Leonard [17], Worrall [69]	2719
17	15	H	Hartlepool U	W 1-0	0-0	7	Worrall [65]	5436
18	22	A	Tranmere R	W 2-1	2-0	5	Payne [16], Aimson (og) [23]	4621
19	29	H	Northampton T	W 2-0	0-0	5	Corr (pen) [69], Worrall [79]	5500
20	Dec 13	A	Wycombe W	L 1-4	1-2	8	Payne [2]	4123
21	19	H	Burton Alb	D 0-0	0-0	5		5266
22	26	A	Cambridge U	W 1-0	0-0	5	Corr [57]	7053
23	28	H	Dagenham & R	D 0-0	0-0	6		6966
24	Jan 3	A	Northampton T	D 1-1	0-0	6	Coulthirst [47]	4587
25	10	H	Plymouth Arg	D 0-0	0-0	6		5767
26	17	A	Oxford U	W 3-2	1-2	6	Worrall [25], Pigott [48], Corr [82]	7207
27	24	A	Portsmouth	W 2-1	1-1	5	Leonard [29], Pigott [70]	15,573
28	31	H	York C	W 1-0	0-0	5	Coulthirst (pen) [88]	6126
29	Feb 7	A	Shrewsbury T	D 1-1	0-0	5	Payne [54]	5276
30	10	H	Cheltenham T	W 2-0	2-0	4	Pigott 2 [9, 34]	5013
31	14	H	Accrington S	L 1-2	0-0	5	Corr [72]	5241
32	21	A	Stevenage	L 2-4	0-1	5	Pigott [49], Corr (pen) [56]	3918
33	28	H	Carlisle U	W 2-0	0-0	5	Timlin [50], Corr [72]	5576
34	Mar 3	A	AFC Wimbledon	D 0-0	0-0	6		3658
35	7	H	Wycombe W	D 2-2	1-1	4	Corr 2 [14, 60]	6204
36	14	A	Dagenham & R	W 3-1	2-1	4	Pigott [16], Leonard [45], Corr (pen) [52]	3393
37	18	A	Burton Alb	L 1-2	1-0	5	Corr [45]	2669
38	21	H	Cambridge U	D 0-0	0-0	5		7224
39	Apr 3	H	Mansfield T	W 2-0	2-0	5	Corr [21], Atkinson [28]	5925
40	6	A	Hartlepool U	W 1-0	0-0	5	Atkinson [53]	5393
41	11	H	Tranmere R	W 1-0	1-0	5	Corr [38]	5846
42	14	H	Newport Co	W 2-0	1-0	5	Bolger [45], McLaughlin [51]	5480
43	18	A	Exeter C	W 1-0	0-0	5	Timlin [90]	4039
44	21	A	Bury	W 1-0	0-0	4	Worrall [74]	8396
45	25	H	Luton T	W 1-0	0-0	3	Timlin [81]	10,730
46	May 2	A	Morecambe	L 1-3	1-1	5	Payne [10]	4108

Final League Position: 5

GOALSCORERS

League (54): Corr 14 (3 pens), Payne 6, Pigott 6, Worrall 6, Coulthirst 4 (1 pen), Leonard 3, Timlin 3, Atkinson 2, Clifford 2, Weston 2 (1 pen), Barnard 1 (1 pen), Bolger 1, Coker 1, Hurst 1, McLaughlin 1, own goal 1.
FA Cup (1): Corr 1 (1 pen).
Capital One Cup (1): Leonard 1.
Johnstone's Paint Trophy (2): Payne 2.
League Two Play-Offs (5): Corr 1, Leonard 1, McLaughlin 1, Pigott 1, Timlin 1.

Bentley D 42	White J 40 + 2	Bolger C 21 + 2	Prosser L 29 + 1	Coker B 32	Hurst K 19 + 9	Leonard R 39 + 2	Clifford C 10 + 2	Weston M 17 + 17	Corr B 30 + 9	Coulthirst S 12 + 10	Worrall D 23 + 15	Barnard L 2 + 7	Atkinson W 26 + 10	Payne J 20 + 14	Thompson A 27 + 1	Williams Jerome 18 + 3	Deegan G 19 + 3	Ibehre M — + 1	Timlin M 29 + 3	Sokolik J 1	O'Toole J 2	Williams Jason — + 2	Pigott J 17 + 3	Cassidy J 12 + 5	Barrett A 9 + 1	Smith T 4	McLaughlin S 6	Match No.
1	2	3	4	5	6²	7	8	9	10³	11¹	12	13	14															1
1	2	3	4	5	6²	7	8	10	9	11¹	12	13																2
1	2¹	3	4	5	6	7	8	11	10³	9¹	13	12			14													3
1	2	4	3	5	6²	8	7	11	10¹	9³	13	14	12															4
1	2	3⁴	4	5	6¹	8	7	11³	10²	13	14		9		12													5
1	2		4	5	14	7²	8	10	13	11¹	12		6		9¹	3												6
1	2		4				11³	7		10¹	9	14	12		13	8²	3	5	6									7
1	2		4			9	7²	12	10	11³			13	14	8¹	3	5	6										8
1	2		4			9		6³	11	10¹	12		13	7²	3	5	8	14										9
1	2	14	4		10¹			8	9²	13	11		12	7³	3	5	6											10
1	2		4		9			6¹	10⁵	11	14	12	13	8²	3	5	7											11
1	2	4³			9	12	8	10	13	11²		6¹	14	3	5	7												12
1			4		14	2		12	13		6	11¹	7	10³	3	5	8		9²									13
1	2		4			6		10	11²	14		12	7	13	3	5	9		8³									14
1	3		4			2		12	10		6	11¹	9²	13	5	7			8									15
1	2		4			6		11¹	10	12	9		5	7			8	3										16
1	5	3	4		9	7			10		6		11	2			8											17
1	5	3	4		9¹	7²	12		11		6		10	2	13		8											18
1	5	3	4					10¹	11	13	7		12	9²	2	14			6		8³							19
1	14	5	4		13	2		9¹	11		6			10		3⁴	12		7²		8³							20
1	2	3	4	5	9	6			12	10¹		11		8	7													21
1	2	3	4	5	9²	7		12	11	14	6³		8¹	10					13									22
1	2	3⁴	4	5		7		10	11³	12	8²		6	9¹					13		14							23
1	2	4⁴	5		7			10	11¹	12		6	9	3					8²		13							24
1	2		5		7		12		11¹	9		13	8²	3	4	6			10									25
1	2		5		7			12		6²		9	14	3	4	8⁴			13				11¹	10³				26
1	2		5		8			13	12⁴		6		9³	14	3	4			7				11²	10¹				27
1	2		5	13	7			12		14	6³		9²	3	4				8				10	11				28
1	2		5		6			14	13	12			7	9²	3	4			8				11³	10¹				29
	2		5¹	14	7			13					6	9²	3	4			8				11	10³	12			30
	2		5¹	14	7				13		12		6³	9	3	4			8				10	11²		1		31
1	2	4	5	12	8			11¹	14	6							9²		7³				10	13	3			32
	2	4	5	13	7			11		6¹			9	12	3				8				10²		1			33
	2	4	5		7			11²		6			8¹	12	3				9				10	13	1			34
1	2	4	5	9¹	7			12	10	6			13	3					8				11²					35
1	2	4	5	9²	7			12	10	6			3	13					8¹				11³	14				36
1	2	4	5	9	7			13	10	6¹			12	3³					8				11²	14				37
1	2	4¹	5	9²	7			11		6			12	13	3	14			8				10³					38
1	2	12	5		7			14	10				6		3³				8				11¹	13	4		9²	39
1	2	3	5		7			14	10³	13			6						8				12	11¹	4		9²	40
1	2	3	5						10²	13			6				7		8				12	11	4		9¹	41
1	2³	3	5	12						13			6¹			14	7		8				10	11	4		9²	42
1		3	5	2				14	12				6	13			7		8				10²	11³	4		9¹	43
1		3	5	2				14	11	13			6³	12			7		8					10¹	4		9²	44
1		3	13	5⁴	2			14	10				9	6¹	12³		7		8					11²	4			45
1	13	3		5⁴	12	2			11				9	6¹	10		8²		7				14		4			46

FA Cup
First Round   Chester FC   (h)   1-2

Capital One Cup
First Round   Walsall   (h)   1-2

Johnstone's Paint Trophy
First Round   AFC Wimbledon   (a)   2-2
(*AFC Wimbledon won 4-2 on penalties*)

League Two Play-Offs
Semi-Finals 1st leg   Stevenage   (a)   1-1
Semi-Finals 2nd leg   Stevenage   (h)   3-1
(*aet*)
Final   Wycombe W   Wembley   1-1
(*aet; Southend U won 7-6 on penalties*)

STEVENAGE

FOUNDATION

There have been several clubs associated with the town of Stevenage. Stevenage Town was formed in 1884. They absorbed Stevenage Rangers in 1955 and later played at Broadhall Way. The club went into liquidation in 1968 and Stevenage Athletic was formed, but they, too, followed a similar path in 1976. Then Stevenage Borough was founded. The Broadhall Way pitch was dug up and remained unused for three years. Thus the new club started its life in the modest surrounds of the King George V playing fields with a roped-off ground in the Chiltern League. A change of competition followed to the Wallspan Southern Combination and by 1980 the club returned to the council-owned Broadhall Way when "Borough" was added to the name. Entry into the United Counties League was so successful the league and cup were won in the first season. On to the Isthmian League Division Two and the climb up the pyramid continued. In 1995–96 Stevenage Borough won the Conference but was denied a place in the Football League as the ground did not measure up to the competition's standards. Subsequent improvements changed this and the 7,100 capacity venue became one of the best appointed grounds in non-league football. After winning elevation to the Football League the club dropped Borough from its title.

Lamex Stadium, Broadhall Way, Stevenage, Hertfordshire SG2 8RH.

Telephone: (01438) 223223.

Fax: (01438) 743666.

Ticket Office: (01438) 223 223.

Website: stevenagefc.com

Email: info@stevenagefc.com

Ground Capacity: 6,772.

Record Attendance: 8,040 v Newcastle U, FA Cup 4th rd, 25 January 1998.

Pitch Measurements: 104.5m × 64.5m (114yd × 70.5yd)

Chairman: Phil Wallace.

Chief Executive: Barry Webber.

Manager: Teddy Sheringham.

Assistant Manager: Dino Maamria.

Physio: Paul Dando.

Colours: White shirts with red stripes, red shorts with white trim, red socks with white trim.

HONOURS

Football League – FL 1: Best season: 6th, 2011–12.
FA Cup: Best season: 5th rd, 2012.
Football League Cup: Best season: 2nd rd, 2012.
Blue Square Premier League: *Champions* 2009–10.
Conference: *Champions* 1995–96.
FA Trophy: *Winners* 2007, 2009; *Runners-up* 2002, 2010.
Herts Senior Cup: *Winners* 2009.
Isthmian League Premier Division: *Champions* 1993–94.
Isthmian League Division 1: *Champions* 1991–92.
Isthmian League Division 2 (N): *Champions* 1985–86, 1990–91.
United Counties League Division 1: *Champions* 1980–81.
United Counties League Cup: *Winners* 1981.

sky SPORTS FACT FILE

Winger George Boyd was capped by the England C team during his time at Stevenage before switching his allegiance and appearing for the Scotland national team. George made his senior debut for Stevenage as a 17-year-old and was later sold to Peterborough United in January 2007.

Nickname: 'The Boro'.

Previous Name: 1976, Stevenage Borough; 2010, Stevenage.

Grounds: 1976, King George V playing fields; 1980, Broadhall Way (renamed Lamex Stadium 2009).

First Football League Game: 7 August 2010, FL 2, v Macclesfield T (h) D 2–2 – Day; Henry, Laird, Bostwick, Roberts, Foster, Wilson (Sinclair), Byrom, Griffin (1), Winn (Odubade), Vincenti (1) (Beardsley).

Year Formed: 1976.

Turned Professional: 1976.

Record League Victory: 6–0 v Yeovil T, FL 2, 14 April 2012 – Day; Lascelles (1), Laird, Roberts (1), Ashton (1), Shroot (Mousinho), Wilson (Myrie-Williams), Long, Agyemang (1), Reid (Slew), Freeman (2).

Record Victory: 11–1 v British Timken Ath 1980–81.

Record Defeat: 0–7 v Southwick 1987–88.

Most League Points (3 for a win): 73, FL 1, 2011–12.

Most League Goals: 69, FL 1, 2011–12.

Highest League Scorer in Season: Francois Zoko, 14, 2013–14.

Most Goals in Total Aggregate: Luke Freeman, 15, 2011–14.

Most League Goals in One Match: 3, Chris Holroyd v Hereford U, FL 2, 28 September 2010; 3, Dani Lopez v Sheffield U, FL 1, 16 March 2013.

Most Capped Player: Marcus Haber, 5 (including 3 on loan at Notts Co) (17), Canada.

Most League Appearances: Chris Day, 189, 2010–15.

Youngest League Player: Ryan Johnson, 17 years 213 days v Brentford, 3 May 2014.

Record Transfer Fee Received: £260,000 from Peterborough U for George Boyd, January 2007.

Record Transfer Fee Paid: £75,000 (rising to £150,000) to Exeter C for James Dunne, May 2012.

Football League Record: 2011 Promoted from Conference Premier; 2010–11 FL 2; 2011–14 FL 1; 2014– FL 2.

MANAGERS

Derek Montgomery 1976–83
Frank Cornwell 1983–87
John Bailey 1987–88
Brian Wilcox 1988–90
Paul Fairclough 1990–98
Richard Hill 1998–2000
Steve Wignall 2000
Paul Fairclough 2000–02
Wayne Turner 2002–03
Graham Westley 2003–06
Mark Stimson 2006–07
Peter Taylor 2007–08
Graham Westley 2008–12
Gary Smith 2012–13
Graham Westley 2013–15
Teddy Sheringham May 2015–

LATEST SEQUENCES

Longest Sequence of League Wins: 6, 12.3.2011 – 2.4.2011.

Longest Sequence of League Defeats: 6, 13.4.2013 – 17.8.2013.

Longest Sequence of League Draws: 5, 17.3.2012 – 31.3.2012.

Longest Sequence of Unbeaten League Matches: 17, 9.4.2012 – 6.10.2012.

Longest Sequence Without a League Win: 10, 11.3.2014 – 21.4.2014.

Successive Scoring Runs: 17 from 9.4.2012.

Successive Non-scoring Runs: 4 from 6.4.2013.

TEN YEAR LEAGUE RECORD

		P	W	D	L	F	A	Pts	Pos
2005-06	Conf	42	19	12	11	62	47	69	6
2006-07	Conf	46	20	10	16	76	66	70	8
2007-08	Conf P	46	24	7	15	82	55	79	6
2008-09	Conf P	46	23	12	11	73	54	81	5
2009-10	Conf P	44	30	9	5	79	24	99	1
2010-11	FL 2	46	18	15	13	62	45	69	6
2011-12	FL 1	46	18	19	9	69	44	73	6
2012-13	FL 1	46	15	9	22	47	64	54	18
2013-14	FL 1	46	11	9	26	46	72	42	24
2014-15	FL 2	46	20	12	14	62	54	72	6

DID YOU KNOW ?

Stevenage did the double over Runcorn on their way to the Conference championship in 1995–96 winning 4-1 at home and 8-0 at Canal Street with striker Barry Hayles scoring a hat-trick on both occasions.

STEVENAGE – FOOTBALL LEAGUE TWO 2014–15 LEAGUE RECORD

Match No.	Date	Venue	Opponents	Result	H/T Score	Lg Pos.	Goalscorers	Attendance
1	Aug 9	H	Hartlepool U	W	1-0	0-0	3	Whelpdale [60]	3023
2	16	A	Southend U	L	0-2	0-2	15		5397
3	19	A	Plymouth Arg	D	1-1	0-0	15	Calcutt [54]	6240
4	23	H	Wycombe W	L	1-3	1-2	18	Charles [31]	2832
5	30	A	AFC Wimbledon	W	3-2	1-1	15	Wells [42], Lancaster [59], Lee [74]	3791
6	Sept 6	H	York C	L	2-3	0-2	17	Whelpdale [58], Pett [64]	3090
7	13	H	Shrewsbury T	W	1-0	1-0	12	Charles [36]	2840
8	16	A	Bury	L	1-2	1-1	14	Marriott [10]	2638
9	20	A	Oxford U	D	0-0	0-0	15		4658
10	27	H	Mansfield T	W	3-0	2-0	13	Whelpdale 2 [3, 83], Lee [5]	2820
11	Oct 4	A	Luton T	L	1-2	1-1	17	Pett [33]	5236
12	11	A	Carlisle U	L	0-3	0-2	19		4011
13	18	H	Accrington S	W	2-1	1-1	15	Whelpdale [1], Lee [48]	2398
14	21	A	Portsmouth	L	2-3	1-1	18	Wells [23], Beardsley [74]	13,281
15	25	H	Burton Alb	W	1-0	0-0	14	Sharps (og) [84]	3051
16	Nov 1	A	Tranmere R	D	2-2	1-0	16	Ihiekwe (og) [14], Barnard [64]	5456
17	15	H	Cheltenham T	W	5-1	3-0	11	Beardsley 2 [5, 34], Lee [8], Barnard 2 [74, 81]	2668
18	22	A	Northampton T	L	0-1	0-1	15		4431
19	29	H	Morecambe	D	1-1	0-0	14	Walton (pen) [62]	2464
20	Dec 13	A	Newport Co	L	0-2	0-2	15		2976
21	20	H	Exeter C	W	1-0	0-0	13	Lee [84]	2878
22	26	A	Dagenham & R	W	2-0	0-0	10	Lee [50], Whelpdale [73]	1779
23	28	H	Cambridge U	W	3-2	3-1	10	Lee [14], Pett [32], Parrett [38]	4579
24	Jan 3	A	Morecambe	D	0-0	0-0	10		1530
25	10	H	AFC Wimbledon	W	2-1	1-1	8	Pett [32], Walton (pen) [69]	3306
26	17	A	York C	W	2-0	1-0	7	Marriott [39], Pett [64]	3107
27	24	A	Shrewsbury T	L	2-3	2-2	8	Marriott [10], Wells [42]	4565
28	31	H	Oxford U	L	0-2	0-0	8		3146
29	Feb 7	A	Mansfield T	L	0-1	0-0	10		2436
30	10	H	Bury	D	0-0	0-0	10		2165
31	14	A	Hartlepool U	W	3-1	1-0	9	Martin [38], Kennedy 2 [52, 65]	3388
32	21	A	Southend U	W	4-2	1-0	9	Deacon [30], Walton (pen) [74], Kennedy [86], Parrett [90]	3918
33	28	H	Wycombe W	D	2-2	2-1	9	Pett [30], Parrett [45]	3664
34	Mar 3	H	Plymouth Arg	W	1-0	0-0	9	Andrade [89]	3022
35	7	H	Newport Co	W	2-1	1-0	8	Lee [31], Dembele [67]	2941
36	14	A	Cambridge U	D	1-1	1-0	8	Wells [17]	5503
37	17	A	Exeter C	D	0-0	0-0	7		3149
38	21	H	Dagenham & R	L	0-1	0-0	9		2795
39	30	A	Burton Alb	D	1-1	1-1	9	Naylor (og) [12]	3024
40	Apr 3	H	Tranmere R	D	2-2	1-2	8	Dembele [4], Lee [78]	3344
41	6	A	Cheltenham T	W	1-0	0-0	6	Kennedy (pen) [78]	2858
42	11	H	Northampton T	W	2-1	0-1	6	Whelpdale [65], Walton [90]	3378
43	14	H	Portsmouth	W	1-0	1-0	6	Pett [3]	3615
44	18	A	Accrington S	D	2-2	1-2	6	Walton (pen) [19], Beardsley [89]	1351
45	25	H	Carlisle U	W	1-0	0-0	6	Parrett [47]	3632
46	May 2	A	Luton T	L	0-2	0-2	6		10,054

Final League Position: 6

GOALSCORERS

League (62): Lee 9, Pett 7, Whelpdale 7, Walton 5 (4 pens), Beardsley 4, Kennedy 4 (1 pen), Parrett 4, Wells 4, Barnard 3, Marriott 3, Charles 2, Dembele 2, Andrade 1, Calcutt 1, Deacon 1, Lancaster 1, Martin 1, own goals 3.
FA Cup (1): Charles 1.
Capital One Cup (0).
Johnstone's Paint Trophy (0).
League Two Play-Offs (2): Parrett 1, Pett 1.

Beasant S 8	Ashton J 15 + 2	Wells D 43	Worley H 3	Dembele B 25 + 2	Pett T 28 + 6	Lee C 38 + 6	Bond A 16 + 4	Whelpdale C 35 + 4	Marriott A 8 + 5	Charles D 29	Calcutt C — + 8	Okimo J 26 + 3	Deacon R 11 + 13	Walton S 25 + 4	Johnson R — + 4	Henry R 34	Lancaster C 4 + 1	Zola C 1 + 6	Conlon T 6 + 7	Richens M 2	Beardsley C 23 + 6	Day C 38	Parrott D 28 + 2	McAllister D 13 + 3	Adams C 5 + 4	Jebb J 4 + 5	Clarke J — + 1	Barnard L 6	Brunt R 3 + 2	N'Guessan J — + 3	Kennedy B 6 + 9	Andrade B 5 + 11	Johnson D 1 + 3	Martin D 9 + 1	Keane K 5 + 2	Lisbie K 3	Match No.
1	2	3	4	5	6³	7	8	9	10	11²	12	13	14																								1
1	2	4	3¹	5¹	9²	8	12	6	11	10		13		14	13	7																					2
1		3	4	5	13	7¹	9	6²		10²	12	2	11	8	14																						3
1	2		4	3³	12	11	8²	6	13	10¹		5	9	7	14																						4
1			4		9³	8²	3	6	14	10	12	5	13	7		2	11¹																				5
1	4¹				12	6	7	3⁴	9	13	10		5²		8	2	11²	14																			6
1		3			5	10²	8	6	13	4	12	14	7³		2	11¹		9																			7
1	12	3			5	13	9		7	11	4			14⁴	6			8¹	2³	10²																	8
		3			5	13	7		9¹	10³	4	12			8	11²			2	6	1	14															9
	3	4			9¹	11	8	6		5	14		13		2				12		10³	1	7²														10
	3	4			11³	6	8	9		5	14		13		2				12		10¹	1	7²														11
	13	4			9	10	7¹	6²		3	14		5		12	2					11³	1	8														12
	3	4			9¹	11		6		5					2	14					10²	1	8³	7	12	13											13
	3	4				7	12	9		5					2						10	1	8²	6	11¹		13										14
	3	4			12³	11		6		5			14		2						13	1	9²	7	8	10¹											15
	3²	4			6		7		5	13	14	12			2						11¹	1	8	10³			9										16
	3				9		13	4		5	10¹	8³			2		14				11²	1	7	12		6											17
	3	4	5		6³	14		10²			13				2					1	12	7	9	8¹	11												18
	4²				6¹	12		3		5	9	8			2						11¹	1	7	13		10	14										19
	3		2		9		6¹			4	7²				5						11³	1	8	14	12	10	13										20
	3				9	12		13		4	5				2						14	1	7	8	11²		10³	6¹									21
	3				9	10²		6		4	5	12			2						13	1	8¹	7			11										22
	3				6	11		9¹		4	5	13			2						12	1	7	8			10²										23
		4			6	10²		9³	11¹	3	5	13			2	14	12				1	7	8														24
		4			9	13		6	10²	3	5		7		2	12					11¹	1	8														25
		3			6	10		9	11	4	5		8		2						1	7															26
		3¹			6²	8		10	11	4	5		9		2	13					14	1	7	12³													27
		3			7			4		5	6²	9			2	11³					10	1	8¹	14							12	13					28
		3	5³		8			9		4			13		2						14	1		7¹							12	10	6	11²			29
	3	4	13		9	7	6		5¹				8		2						10	1									12		11¹				30
		4			3	13	7	6			5	2									11	1	8¹							9¹	12	14	10²				31
		3			5	13	11²	4³	6		2	7				14					10¹	1	8								12			9			32
		3			5	10¹	12		6		2	7³		4		14					11⁴	1	8								13			9²			33
		3			4	9	10		6¹		5²	7		2							1	8									11	13	14	12³			34
		3			4	6	9	14			5			8		2					11²	1	7¹								10³	13			12		35
		3			4	6	10	13			5					2						1	7								11¹	12	9	8			36
		3			4	6¹	10²				5					2						1	7								12	14	13	9³	8	11	37
		3			4²	6¹	9		12		5					2						1	7								13	14	10³	8	11	38
		4			3	7					5			6		2						1	8¹			13					12	10²		9	11	39
		3			4	6	13		10			5³	14	7²				12			1					2¹					11	9		8			40
		4			3		11	8	2			5	14	7³							10¹	1	9								12	13		6²			41
		3			4	6²	10³	7	2			5		13					9		11	1	8									12					42
		3			4	9	13	2	11			5		8³					6¹		10²	1	7									14			12		43
		3			4	9	10	2³	6¹			5		7²					13		11	1	8				14					12					44
		3			4	9		2	6			5		8³					10		1	7²				14					13	12		11¹			45
3		4³				11						5²	8	2¹		14	7		1		12	10									13	6		9			46

FA Cup

First Round	Maidstone U	(h)	0-0
Replay	Maidstone U	(a)	1-2

Capital One Cup

First Round	Watford	(h)	0-1

Johnstone's Paint Trophy

First Round	Gillingham	(h)	0-1

League Two Play-Offs

Semi-Finals 1st leg	Southend U	(h)	1-1
Semi-Finals 2nd leg	Southend U	(a)	1-3
(aet)			

STOKE CITY

Britannia Stadium, Stanley Matthews Way, Stoke-on-Trent, Staffordshire ST4 4EG.

Telephone: (01782) 367 598.

Fax: (01782) 592 221.

Ticket Office: (01782) 367 599.

Website: www.stokecityfc.com

Email: info@stokecityfc.com

Ground Capacity: 27,740.

Record Attendance: 51,380 v Arsenal, Division 1, 29 March 1937 (at Victoria Ground); 28,218 v Everton, FA Cup 3rd rd, 5 January 2002 (at Britannia Stadium).

Pitch Measurements: 100m × 66m (109yd × 72yd)

Chairman: Peter Coates.

Chief Executive: Tony Scholes.

Manager: Mark Hughes.

Assistant Manager: Mark Bowen.

Physio: Chris Banks.

Colours: Red and white striped shirts with red sleeves and white trim, white shorts with red trim, red socks with white trim.

Year Formed: 1863* *(see Foundation).*

Turned Professional: 1885.

Previous Names: 1868, Stoke Ramblers; 1870, Stoke; 1925, Stoke City.

Club Nickname: 'The Potters'.

Grounds: 1875, Sweeting's Field; 1878, Victoria Ground (previously known as the Athletic Club Ground); 1997, Britannia Stadium.

First Football League Game: 8 September 1888, Football League, v WBA (h) L 0–2 – Rowley; Clare, Underwood; Ramsey, Shutt, Smith; Sayer, McSkimming, Staton, Edge, Tunnicliffe.

Record League Victory: 8–0 v Sunderland, FA Premier League, 18 October 2014 – Forster; Clyne, Fonte, Alderweireld, Bertrand; Davis S (Mane), Schneiderlin, Cork (1); Long (Wanyama (1)), Pelle (2) (Mayuka), Tadic (1) (plus 3 Sunderland own goals).

Record Cup Victory: 7–1 v Burnley, FA Cup 2nd rd (replay), 20 February 1896 – Clawley; Clare, Eccles; Turner, Grewe, Robertson; Willie Maxwell, Dickson, Alan Maxwell (3), Hyslop (4), Schofield.

HONOURS

Football League – Division 1: Best season: 4th, 1935–36, 1946–47; **FL C:** *Runners-up* 2007–08; **Division 2:** *Champions* 1932–33, 1962–63, 1992–93; *Runners-up* 1921–22; **Division 3 (N):** *Champions* 1926–27.

FA Cup: *Runners-up* 2011.

Football League Cup: *Winners* 1972; *Runners-up* 1964.

Autoglass Trophy: *Winners:* 1992.

Auto Windscreens Shield: *Winners:* 2000.

European Competitions UEFA Cup: 1972–73, 1974–75. **Europa League:** 2011–12.

Record Defeat: 0–10 v Preston NE, Division 1, 14 September 1889.

Most League Points (2 for a win): 63, Division 3 (N), 1926–27.

Most League Points (3 for a win): 93, Division 2, 1992–93.

Most League Goals: 92, Division 3 (N), 1926–27.

Highest League Scorer in Season: Freddie Steele, 33, Division 1, 1936–37.

Most League Goals in Total Aggregate: Freddie Steele, 142, 1934–49.

Most League Goals in One Match: 7, Neville Coleman v Lincoln C, Division 2, 23 February 1957.

Most Capped Player: Glenn Whelan, 64, Republic of Ireland.

Most League Appearances: Eric Skeels, 507, 1958–76.

Youngest League Player: Peter Bullock, 16 years 163 days v Swansea C, 19 April 1958.

Record Transfer Fee Received: £8,000,000 from Chelsea for Asmir Begovic, July 2015.

Record Transfer Fee Paid: £10,000,000 (rising to £12,000,000) to Tottenham H for Peter Crouch, August 2011.

Football League Record: 1888 Founder Member of Football League; 1890 Not re-elected; 1891 Re-elected; relegated in 1907, and after one year in Division 2, resigned for financial reasons; 1919 re-elected to Division 2; 1922–23 Division 1; 1923–26 Division 2; 1926–27 Division 3 (N); 1927–33 Division 2; 1933–53 Division 1; 1953–63 Division 2; 1963–77 Division 1; 1977–79 Division 2; 1979–85 Division 1; 1985–90 Division 2; 1990–92 Division 3; 1992–93 Division 2; 1993–98 Division 2; 1998–2002 Division 2; 2002–04 Division 1; 2004–08 FL C; 2008– FA Premier League.

LATEST SEQUENCES

Longest Sequence of League Wins: 8, 30.3.1895 – 21.9.1895.

Longest Sequence of League Defeats: 11, 6.4.1985 – 17.8.1985.

Longest Sequence of League Draws: 5, 13.5.2012 – 15.9.2012.

Longest Sequence of Unbeaten League Matches: 25, 5.9.1992 – 20.2.1993.

Longest Sequence Without a League Win: 17, 22.4.1989 – 14.10.1989.

Successive Scoring Runs: 21 from 24.12.1921.

Successive Non-scoring Runs: 8 from 29.12.1984.

MANAGERS

Tom Slaney 1874–83
(Secretary-Manager)
Walter Cox 1883–84
(Secretary-Manager)
Harry Lockett 1884–90
Joseph Bradshaw 1890–92
Arthur Reeves 1892–95
William Rowley 1895–97
H. D. Austerberry 1897–1908
A. J. Barker 1908–14
Peter Hodge 1914–15
Joe Schofield 1915–19
Arthur Shallcross 1919–23
John 'Jock' Rutherford 1923
Tom Mather 1923–35
Bob McGrory 1935–52
Frank Taylor 1952–60
Tony Waddington 1960–77
George Eastham 1977–78
Alan A'Court 1978
Alan Durban 1978–81
Richie Barker 1981–83
Bill Asprey 1984–85
Mick Mills 1985–89
Alan Ball 1989–91
Lou Macari 1991–93
Joe Jordan 1993–94
Lou Macari 1994–97
Chic Bates 1997–98
Chris Kamara 1998
Brian Little 1998–99
Gary Megson 1999
Gudjon Thordarson 1999–2002
Steve Cotterill 2002
Tony Pulis 2002–05
Johan Boskamp 2005–06
Tony Pulis 2006–13
Mark Hughes May 2013–

TEN YEAR LEAGUE RECORD

		P	W	D	L	F	A	Pts	Pos
2005-06	FL C	46	17	7	22	54	63	58	13
2006-07	FL C	46	19	16	11	62	41	73	8
2007-08	FL C	46	21	16	9	69	55	79	2
2008-09	PR Lge	38	12	9	17	38	55	45	12
2009-10	PR Lge	38	11	14	13	34	48	47	11
2010-11	PR Lge	38	13	7	18	46	48	46	13
2011-12	PR Lge	38	11	12	15	36	53	45	14
2012-13	PR Lge	38	9	15	14	34	45	42	13
2013-14	PR Lge	38	13	11	14	45	52	50	9
2014-15	PR Lge	38	15	9	14	48	45	54	9

DID YOU KNOW

In May 1969 Stoke City played a friendly against Barcelona at the Nou Camp as warm-up for the Spanish club who were to play in the European Cup Winners' Cup final the following week. The Potters surprised their hosts and were 3-0 up at one stage, finishing as 3-2 winners.

STOKE CITY – FA PREMIERSHIP 2014–15 LEAGUE RECORD

Match No.	Date	Venue	Opponents	Result	H/T Score	Lg Pos.	Goalscorers	Atten- dance
1	Aug 16	H	Aston Villa	L	0-1	0-0	18		27,478
2	24	A	Hull C	D	1-1	0-1	14	Shawcross [83]	24,348
3	30	A	Manchester C	W	1-0	0-0	9	Diouf [58]	45,622
4	Sept13	H	Leicester C	L	0-1	0-0	12		27,500
5	20	A	QPR	D	2-2	1-1	13	Diouf [11], Crouch [51]	16,163
6	29	H	Newcastle U	W	1-0	1-0	11	Crouch [15]	26,332
7	Oct 4	A	Sunderland	L	1-3	1-2	15	Adam [15]	42,713
8	19	H	Swansea C	W	2-1	1-0	10	Adam (pen) [43], Walters [76]	27,017
9	25	A	Southampton	L	0-1	0-1	11		30,017
10	Nov 1	H	West Ham U	D	2-2	1-0	12	Moses [33], Diouf [56]	27,174
11	9	A	Tottenham H	W	2-1	2-0	9	Bojan [6], Walters [33]	35,699
12	22	H	Burnley	L	1-2	1-2	10	Walters [32]	27,018
13	29	A	Liverpool	L	0-1	0-0	12		44,735
14	Dec 2	A	Manchester U	L	1-2	1-1	13	Nzonzi [39]	75,388
15	6	H	Arsenal	W	3-2	3-0	12	Crouch [1], Bojan [35], Walters [45]	27,367
16	13	A	Crystal Palace	D	1-1	1-1	11	Crouch [13]	23,038
17	22	H	Chelsea	L	0-2	0-1	13		27,550
18	26	A	Everton	W	1-0	1-0	11	Bojan (pen) [38]	39,166
19	28	H	WBA	W	2-0	0-0	11	Diouf 2 [51, 66]	27,070
20	Jan 1	H	Manchester U	D	1-1	1-1	11	Shawcross [2]	27,203
21	11	A	Arsenal	L	0-3	0-2	11		59,956
22	17	A	Leicester C	W	1-0	0-0	10	Bojan [63]	31,772
23	31	H	QPR	W	3-1	2-1	9	Walters 3 [21, 34, 90]	27,512
24	Feb 8	A	Newcastle U	D	1-1	0-0	10	Crouch [90]	47,763
25	11	H	Manchester C	L	1-4	1-1	10	Crouch [38]	27,011
26	21	A	Aston Villa	W	2-1	1-1	10	Diouf [45], Moses (pen) [90]	31,880
27	28	H	Hull C	W	1-0	0-0	10	Crouch [71]	26,473
28	Mar 4	A	Everton	W	2-0	1-0	8	Moses [32], Diouf [84]	26,431
29	14	A	WBA	L	0-1	0-1	8		24,323
30	21	H	Crystal Palace	L	1-2	1-2	10	Diouf [14]	27,532
31	Apr 4	A	Chelsea	L	1-2	1-1	10	Adam [44]	41,098
32	11	A	West Ham U	D	1-1	0-1	10	Arnautovic [90]	34,946
33	18	H	Southampton	W	2-1	0-0	9	Diouf [47], Adam [84]	26,467
34	25	H	Sunderland	D	1-1	1-1	9	Adam [27]	26,706
35	May 2	A	Swansea C	L	0-2	0-0	10		20,661
36	9	H	Tottenham H	W	3-0	2-0	9	Adam [21], Nzonzi [32], Vertonghen (og) [86]	27,104
37	16	A	Burnley	D	0-0	0-0	9		18,636
38	24	H	Liverpool	W	6-1	5-0	9	Diouf 2 [22, 26], Walters [30], Adam [41], Nzonzi [45], Crouch [86]	27,602

Final League Position: 9

GOALSCORERS

League (48): Diouf 11, Crouch 8, Walters 8, Adam 7 (1 pen), Bojan 4 (1 pen), Moses 3 (1 pen), Nzonzi 3, Shawcross 2, Arnautovic 1, own goal 1.
FA Cup (8): Ireland 3, Arnautovic 1, Crouch 1, Krkic 1, Moses 1, Walters 1.
Capital One Cup (7): Muniesa 2, Walters 2, Crouch 1, Diouf 1, Nzonzi 1.

Begovic A 35	Bardsley P 24 + 1	Shawcross R 32	Wilson M 25 + 2	Pieters E 29 + 2	Nzonzi S 38	Whelan G 26 + 2	Bojan K 14 + 2	Ireland S 11 + 6	Arnautovic M 20 + 9	Diouf M 28 + 6	Crouch P 17 + 16	Adam C 15 + 14	Sidwell S 5 + 7	Odemwingie P 1 + 6	Walters J 28 + 4	Moses V 19	Muniesa M 14 + 5	Assaidi O 1 + 8	Cameron G 21 + 6	Huth R — + 1	Wollscheid P 12	Shenton O — + 1	Dionatan T — + 1	Butland J 3	Match No.
1	2	3	4	5	6	7^1	8	9	10	11^2	12	13													1
1	2	3	4	5	9	7^3	12		10^2	11	13	14	6^1	8											2
1	2	3	4	5	8	7					10	11	13		12^3	6^2	9^1	14							3
1	2	3	4	5^1	7	6	9^3				12	11			8^2	10	14	13							4
1	2	3	4	5	7	6			13	8	11	9^2	12		10^1										5
1	2	3	4		7	6		13	12	8^1	11	9^2			10^1		5	14							6
1	2	3	4		6	7^2	13	8			11^3	9		14	10^1		5	12							7
1	2	3	4	5	6			9^3		8^1	11	7			13	10^2	14	12							8
1	2	3	4	5	6				13		12	11	7^2		8^1	10^3	14	9							9
1		3	4	5	6		9^1				11	12	7		8	10			2						10
1	2^3	3	4^2	5	6		9^1	14			11		7		8	10	13	12							11
1	2	3			7				12	11^2	13	14	6^3		8	10^1	5		4						12
1		3	4	5	7		12^3	9	10^2	11	14	13			6^1	8			2						13
1	2	3	4	5	6			9		8^2	13	11				10^1	12		7						14
1	2	3		5	6	12		9^3		10^1	11	13			8		4^2	14	7						15
1	2	3	4	5	7			9^1	12		10	11			8		6								16
1	2	3		5	6			9	10^3		12	11^1	13		8		4		7^2	14					17
1		3		5	7	6		9^2	10^3		11^1	14	12		8		4	13	2						18
1		3	14	5	6	7^1		9^2		8	10	11^3	13		12		4		2						19
1		3		5	7	8			9^1		11	10			6		4	12	2						20
1		3		5^2	6^2	7			9^1	14	10	11	12		8			13	2		4				17
1	2			5	7	6			9	8^1	12				11	10^2	4	13	3						22
1	2	3^3		5	6	7			9^1	8^2	13	14			11	10	12		4						23
1	2			5^2	6	7			9^1	8	13				11	10	12		4		3				24
1				5	6^1	7^3			8	9	11	13	12		10^2		4		2	14	3				25
1	2		4	5^2	7	8		6^1	9		13				10	11	12		3						26
1	2		4	5	6	7		9^2			11	13	12		8	10			3						27
1	2		4	5	6	7			14	13	11^1	9^2			8	10	12		3^3						28
1	2	3	4	5^3	6	7			13	14	11	9			8^2	10^1	12								29
1		3	4	5	7				9	10	8	11^1			6		12		2						30
1		3		5	7	8			12	10^1	13	9^2			6^2	11	14		2		4				31
1		3	13	5^2	7	6^2			14	8	12	9			11	10^1			2		4				32
1		3		5	7	6^1			9^2	10	11^3	13	12	14	8				2		4				33
1	14	3		5	6				9	10	11^2	12	7		13	8^2			2^3		4				34
	2	3	4^1	5	7	6			12	10	11^2	13			9^2		14		8^1					1	35
	2	3		5	6	7^1			12	10	11	9^3	14	13	8^1				4					1	36
	2	3		5	6	7			10^2	11	13	9^3	14	12	8^1				4					1	37
1	2	3	13	5	6	7			10^1	11	14	9	12		8^3				4^2						38

FA Cup

Third Round	Wrexham	(h)	3-1
Fourth Round	Rochdale	(a)	4-1
Fifth Round	Blackburn R	(a)	1-4

Capital One Cup

Second Round	Portsmouth	(h)	3-0
Third Round	Sunderland	(a)	2-1
Fourth Round	Southampton	(h)	2-3

SUNDERLAND

FOUNDATION

A Scottish schoolmaster named James Allan, working at Hendon Board School, took the initiative in the foundation of Sunderland in 1879 when they were formed as The Sunderland and District Teachers' Association FC at a meeting in the Adults School, Norfolk Street. Due to financial difficulties, they quickly allowed members from outside the teaching profession and so became Sunderland AFC in October 1880.

Stadium of Light, Sunderland, Tyne and Wear SR5 1SU.

Telephone: (0871) 911 1200.

Fax: (0191) 551 5123.

Ticket Office: (0871) 911 1973.

Website: www.safc.com

Email: enquiries@safc.com

Ground Capacity: 48,707.

Record Attendance: 75,118 v Derby Co, FA Cup 6th rd replay, 8 March 1933 (at Roker Park); 48,353 v Liverpool, FA Premier League, 13 April 2002 (at Stadium of Light) (FA Premier League figure 46,062).

Pitch Measurements: 105m × 68m (114yd × 74yd)

Chairman: Ellis Short.

Chief Executive: Margaret Byrne.

Head Coach: Dick Advocaat.

Assistant Head Coach: Zeljko Petrovic.

Physio: Peter Brand.

Colours: Red and white striped shirts, black shorts with red trim, black socks with red trim.

Year Formed: 1879.

Turned Professional: 1886.

Previous Names: 1879, Sunderland and District Teachers AFC; 1880, Sunderland.

Club Nickname: 'The Black Cats'.

Grounds: 1879, Blue House Field, Hendon; 1882, Groves Field, Ashbrooke; 1883, Horatio Street; 1884, Abbs Field, Fulwell; 1886, Newcastle Road; 1898, Roker Park; 1997, Stadium of Light.

First Football League Game: 13 September 1890, Football League, v Burnley (h) L 2–3 – Kirtley; Porteous, Oliver; Wilson, Auld, Gibson; Spence (1), Miller, Campbell (1), Scott, Davy Hannah.

Record League Victory: 9–1 v Newcastle U (a), Division 1, 5 December 1908 – Roose; Forster, Melton; Daykin, Thomson, Low; Mordue (1), Hogg (3), Brown, Holley (3), Bridgett (2).

Record Cup Victory: 11–1 v Fairfield, FA Cup 1st rd, 2 February 1895 – Doig; McNeill, Johnston; Dunlop, McCreadie (1), Wilson; Gillespie (1), Millar (5), Campbell, Jimmy Hannah (3), Scott (1).

HONOURS

Football League: Division 1: *Champions* 1891–92, 1892–93, 1894–95, 1901–02, 1912–13, 1935–36, 1995–96, 1998–99; *Runners-up* 1893–94, 1897–98, 1900–01, 1922–23, 1934–35; **Division 2:** *Champions* 1975–76; *Runners-up* 1963–64, 1979–80. **FL C:** *Champions* 2004–05, 2006–07; **Division 3:** *Champions* 1987–88.

FA Cup: *Winners* 1937, 1973; *Runners-up* 1913, 1992.

Football League Cup: *Runners-up* 1985, 2014.

European Competitions
European Cup-Winners' Cup: 1973–74.

sky SPORTS FACT FILE

What is believed to be the earliest artwork featuring professional football shows a goalmouth scene during the match between Sunderland and Aston Villa at the Black Cats' Newcastle Road ground in January 1895. The painting, by Thomas Hemy, was once offered as a raffle prize by the directors but the winning ticket was unclaimed.

Record Defeat: 0–8 v Sheff Wed, Division 1, 26 December 1911; 0–8 v West Ham U, Division 1, 19 October 1968; 0–8 v Watford, Division 1, 25 September 1982; 0–8 v Southampton, FA Premier League, 18 October 2014.

Most League Points (2 for a win): 61, Division 2, 1963–64.

Most League Points (3 for a win): 105, Division 1, 1998–99.

Most League Goals: 109, Division 1, 1935–36.

Highest League Scorer in Season: Dave Halliday, 43, Division 1, 1928–29.

Most League Goals in Total Aggregate: Charlie Buchan, 209, 1911–25.

Most League Goals in One Match: 5, Charlie Buchan v Liverpool, Division 1, 7 December 1919; 5, Bobby Gurney v Bolton W, Division 1, 7 December 1935; 5, Dominic Sharkey v Norwich C, Division 2, 20 February 1962.

Most Capped Player: Seb Larsson, 41 (74), Sweden.

Most League Appearances: Jim Montgomery, 537, 1962–77.

Youngest League Player: Derek Forster, 15 years 184 days v Leicester C, 22 August 1964.

Record Transfer Fee Received: £18,000,000 (rising to £24,000,000) from Aston Villa for Darren Bent, January 2011.

Record Transfer Fee Paid: £12,000,000 (rising to £14,000,000) to Wolverhampton W for Steven Fletcher, August 2012.

Football League Record: 1890 Elected to Division 1; 1958–64 Division 2; 1964–70 Division 1; 1970–76 Division 2; 1976–77 Division 1; 1977–80 Division 2; 1980–85 Division 1; 1985–87 Division 2; 1987–88 Division 3; 1988–90 Division 2; 1990–91 Division 1; 1991–92 Division 2; 1992–96 Division 1; 1996–97 FA Premier League; 1997–99 Division 1; 1999–2003 FA Premier League; 2003–04 Division 1; 2004–05 FL C; 2005–06 FA Premier League; 2006–07 FL C; 2007– FA Premier League.

MANAGERS

Tom Watson 1888–96
Bob Campbell 1896–99
Alex Mackie 1899–1905
Bob Kyle 1905–28
Johnny Cochrane 1928–39
Bill Murray 1939–57
Alan Brown 1957–64
George Hardwick 1964–65
Ian McColl 1965–68
Alan Brown 1968–72
Bob Stokoe 1972–76
Jimmy Adamson 1976–78
Ken Knighton 1979–81
Alan Durban 1981–84
Len Ashurst 1984–85
Lawrie McMenemy 1985–87
Denis Smith 1987–91
Malcolm Crosby 1991–93
Terry Butcher 1993
Mick Buxton 1993–95
Peter Reid 1995–2002
Howard Wilkinson 2002–03
Mick McCarthy 2003–06
Niall Quinn 2006
Roy Keane 2006–08
Ricky Sbragia 2008–09
Steve Bruce 2009–11
Martin O'Neill 2011–13
Paolo Di Canio 2013
Gus Poyet 2013–15
Dick Advocaat March 2015–

LATEST SEQUENCES

Longest Sequence of League Wins: 13, 14.11.1891 – 2.4.1892.

Longest Sequence of League Defeats: 17, 18.1.2003 – 16.8.2003.

Longest Sequence of League Draws: 6, 26.3.1949 – 19.4.1949.

Longest Sequence of Unbeaten League Matches: 19, 3.5.1998 – 14.11.1998.

Longest Sequence Without a League Win: 22, 21.12.2002 – 16.8.2003.

Successive Scoring Runs: 29 from 8.11.1997.

Successive Non-scoring Runs: 10 from 27.11.1976.

TEN YEAR LEAGUE RECORD

		P	W	D	L	F	A	Pts	Pos
2005-06	PR Lge	38	3	6	29	26	69	15	20
2006-07	FL C	46	27	7	12	76	47	88	1
2007-08	PR Lge	38	11	6	21	36	59	39	15
2008-09	PR Lge	38	9	9	20	34	54	36	16
2009-10	PR Lge	38	11	11	16	48	56	44	13
2010-11	PR Lge	38	12	11	15	45	56	47	10
2011-12	PR Lge	38	11	12	15	45	46	45	13
2012-13	PR Lge	38	9	12	17	41	54	39	17
2013-14	PR Lge	38	10	8	20	41	60	38	14
2014-15	PR Lge	38	7	17	14	31	53	38	16

DID YOU KNOW ?

On 12 November 1955 Sunderland went to the top of the First Division table following a 4-4 draw with Burnley. The following Saturday they travelled to play mid-table Luton Town only to lose 8-2, a score that equalled the highest number of goals conceded by the club in a Football League match.

SUNDERLAND – FA PREMIERSHIP 2014–15 LEAGUE RECORD

Match No.	Date		Venue	Opponents	Result	H/T Score	Lg Pos.	Goalscorers	Attendance
1	Aug	16	A	WBA	D	2-2	1-1	6	Cattermole [5], Larsson [85]	25,468
2		24	H	Manchester U	D	1-1	1-1	11	Rodwell [30]	43,217
3		30	A	QPR	L	0-1	0-1	13		17,930
4	Sept	13	H	Tottenham H	D	2-2	1-1	13	Johnson [4], Kane (og) [82]	40,799
5		20	A	Burnley	D	0-0	0-0	15		20,026
6		27	H	Swansea C	D	0-0	0-0	15		41,325
7	Oct	4	H	Stoke C	W	3-1	2-1	11	Wickham [4], Fletcher 2 [23, 79]	42,713
8		18	A	Southampton	L	0-8	0-3	17		29,615
9		25	H	Arsenal	L	0-2	0-1	17		44,449
10	Nov	3	A	Crystal Palace	W	3-1	1-0	15	Fletcher 2 [31, 90], Gomez [79]	23,212
11		9	H	Everton	D	1-1	0-0	14	Larsson [67]	43,476
12		22	A	Leicester C	D	0-0	0-0	14		31,825
13		29	H	Chelsea	D	0-0	0-0	13		45,232
14	Dec	3	H	Manchester C	L	1-4	1-2	14	Wickham [19]	41,152
15		6	A	Liverpool	D	0-0	0-0	14		44,716
16		13	H	West Ham U	D	1-1	1-1	15	Gomez (pen) [22]	41,694
17		21	A	Newcastle U	W	1-0	0-0	14	Johnson [90]	52,315
18		26	H	Hull C	L	1-3	1-1	14	Johnson [1]	44,817
19		28	A	Aston Villa	D	0-0	0-0	14		35,436
20	Jan	1	A	Manchester C	L	2-3	0-0	14	Rodwell [68], Johnson (pen) [71]	45,367
21		10	H	Liverpool	L	0-1	0-1	16		45,369
22		17	A	Tottenham H	L	1-2	1-1	16	Larsson [31]	35,973
23		31	H	Burnley	W	2-0	2-0	14	Wickham [20], Defoe [34]	44,022
24	Feb	7	A	Swansea C	D	1-1	1-0	14	Defoe [42]	20,355
25		10	H	QPR	L	0-2	0-2	14		39,077
26		21	H	WBA	D	0-0	0-0	16		40,943
27		28	A	Manchester U	L	0-2	0-0	16		75,344
28	Mar	3	A	Hull C	D	1-1	0-1	16	Rodwell [77]	23,017
29		14	H	Aston Villa	L	0-4	0-4	17		45,746
30		21	A	West Ham U	L	0-1	0-0	17		34,914
31	Apr	5	H	Newcastle U	W	1-0	1-0	15	Defoe [45]	47,563
32		11	H	Crystal Palace	L	1-4	0-0	16	Wickham [90]	42,073
33		25	A	Stoke C	D	1-1	1-1	18	Wickham [1]	26,706
34	May	2	H	Southampton	W	2-1	1-1	18	Gomez 2 (2 pens) [21, 55]	39,613
35		9	A	Everton	W	2-0	0-0	16	Graham [53], Defoe [85]	38,246
36		16	H	Leicester C	D	0-0	0-0	16		46,705
37		20	A	Arsenal	D	0-0	0-0	15		59,987
38		24	A	Chelsea	L	1-3	1-1	16	Fletcher [26]	41,620

Final League Position: 16

GOALSCORERS

League (31): Fletcher 5, Wickham 5, Defoe 4, Gomez 4 (3 pens), Johnson 4 (1 pen), Larsson 3, Rodwell 3, Cattermole 1, Graham 1, own goal 1.
FA Cup (4): Alvarez 1, Gomez 1 (1 pen), Van Aanholt 1, own goal 1.
Capital One Cup (4): Altidore 1, Gomez 1, Johnson 1, Wickham 1.

Mannone V 10	Brown W 23 + 2	O'Shea J 37	Roberge V 1	Van Aanholt P 26 + 2	Cattermole L 26 + 2	Johnson A 23 + 9	Larsson S 36	Rodwell J 17 + 6	Wickham C 31 + 5	Fletcher S 20 + 10	Gomez J 22 + 7	Buckley W 9 + 13	Altidore J 2 + 9	Vergini S 28 + 3	Bridcutt L 10 + 8	Giaccherini E 2 + 6	Alvarez R 5 + 8	Jones B 14	Pantilimon C 28	Reveillere A 15 + 1	Coates S 9 + 1	Graham D 7 + 7	Mandron M — + 1	Defoe J 17	Match No.
1	2¹	3	4	5	6	7²	8	9¹	10	11	12	13	14												1
1	4	3		5	7		6	8¹	11	10³	12	9²	13	2	14										2
1	4	3		5	7	9	6	8¹	11	10²		13	14	2¹	12										3
1	4	3		5	6	10	8³	9¹	11	14	13			2		12	7²								4
1	4	3		5	6	10¹	7³	8	11	12	14	13		2			9²								5
1		4		5	6	10¹	8	9³	11¹²	12	7			3	13	2									6
1		4		5	6	12	8²	14	10	11	9¹	7³		3	13	2									7
1	4³	3		5	6	14	8¹	13	10	11	9²	7		2	12										8
1	4	3		5	6	7²	8	9¹	12	11¹³	13	10	14	2											9
12	4			5²	6		8	10³	11	9	7¹	13	3	14					1	2					10
	4	3				7³	8	13	10	11	9¹	12		2	6				1	5					11
	4	3			7	9	6²	11	10	8¹	13			2	12				1	5					12
	4	3			6	7	8	9¹	10	11¹²	12			13	2				1	5					13
		3			6		8	9	7¹	11²		10	12	2	13			1	5	4					14
	4	3			13	7²	8¹	10		9	14	11³		2	6		12		1	5					15
	4	3			6	7¹	8	10	12	9	11²			13	2				1	5					16
	4	5		6³	7	8²	14	10¹	11	9		13		2	12				1		3				17
		4		6	10	8		11	9³	14	13	2¹		12		7¹	5		1		3				18
	4	3		12	7	8³		10	11	9	14			2¹	6²	13			5	1					19
	4	3			10	8	6	11		9²	7³			2¹	12	13			5	1		14			20
	4	3	5		7²	8	11³	9	12					2	6⁴	10¹			1			13	14		21
	4	3	8		9	6	7	12	10¹		14			2		5²			1	2		13		11³	22
		4	5		10³	8		7²	12	9		3	6		14				1	2		13		11¹	23
		4	5		12	7		13	9	3	8			6²					1	2		10¹		11	24
13	4		5		9	6	11³	14	8²	3	7			12					1	2¹				10	25
	4	3	14	7	9	8		13	12			2¹			6²				1	5		10³		11	26
	4⁴	3	5	6	7²	8		10³	14	9		12							1	2		13		11¹	27
	4	3	13	6³		7	9	14				2¹	8		12				1	5		11²		10	28
	4	3	5			8	9	12	10²		6			7¹					1	2		13		11	29
	4³	3	5	13	7	8	11	9²	6			12							1	2		14		10¹	30
		4	5	7	12	6		11	10	8			3		2	1								9¹	31
		4	5	7¹	12		6	11	10	8²		3	13		2	1								9	32
		4	5	7			8	11		9	6¹			2		1		3			12			10	33
	4³	5	7	14	6²	13	11	8			12			2		1		3		10				9¹	34
	4	5	7	12	6¹		11³	13	8				14			2		1		3		10²		9	35
	4	5	7	12	8		11	13		6²				2¹		1		14		3		10³		9	36
	4	5	7	8²	6	13		9¹	12		14			2		1		3			11³			10	37
1	4	5		8¹	7	6	9	11			12			2			3							10	38

FA Cup

Third Round	Leeds U	(h)	1-0	
Fourth Round	Fulham	(h)	0-0	
Replay	Fulham	(a)	3-1	
Fifth Round	Bradford C	(a)	0-2	

Capital One Cup

Second Round	Birmingham C	(a)	3-0
Third Round	Stoke C	(h)	1-2

SWANSEA CITY

Liberty Stadium, Morfa, Landore, Swansea SA1 2FA.
Telephone: (01792) 616 600.
Fax: (01792) 616 606.
Ticket Office: (0844) 815 6665.
Website: www.swanseacity.net
Email: info@swanseacityfc.co.uk
Ground Capacity: 20,827.
Record Attendance: 32,796 v Arsenal, FA Cup 4th rd, 17 February 1968 (at Vetch Field); 20,828 v Liverpool, FA Premier League, 16 March 2015 (at Liberty Stadium).
Pitch Measurements: 105m × 68m (114yd × 74yd)
Chairman: Huw Jenkins.
Vice-chairman: Leigh Dineen.
Manager: Garry Monk.
Assistant Manager: Josep Clotet.
Head Physio: Kate Rees.
Colours: White shirts with black trim, white shorts with black trim, white socks with black trim.
Year Formed: 1912.
Turned Professional: 1912.
Previous Name: 1912, Swansea Town; 1970, Swansea City.
Club Nicknames: 'The Swans', 'The Jacks'.
Grounds: 1912, Vetch Field; 2005, Liberty Stadium.

HONOURS

Football League – Division 1:
Best season: 6th, 1981–82;
FL 1: *Champions* 2007–08;
Division 3(S): *Champions* 1924–25, 1948–49;
Division 3: *Champions* 1999–2000.
FA Cup: Best season: semi-final, 1926, 1964.
Football League Cup: *Winners* 2013.
Welsh Cup: *Winners* 11 times; *Runners-up* 8 times.
Autoglass Trophy: *Winners* 1994, 2006.
Football League Trophy: *Winners* 2006.
European Competitions
Europa League: 2013–14.
European Cup-Winners' Cup:
1961–62, 1966–67, 1981–82, 1982–83, 1983–84, 1989–90, 1991–92.

First Football League Game: 28 August 1920, Division 3, v Portsmouth (a) L 0–3 – Crumley; Robson, Evans; Smith, Holdsworth, Williams; Hole, Ivor Jones, Edmundson, Rigsby, Spottiswood.
Record League Victory: 8–0 v Hartlepool U, Division 4, 1 April 1978 – Barber; Evans, Bartley, Lally (1) (Morris), May, Bruton, Kevin Moore, Robbie James (3 incl. 1p), Curtis (3), Toshack (1), Chappell.
Record Cup Victory: 12–0 v Sliema W (Malta), ECWC 1st rd 1st leg, 15 September 1982 – Davies; Marustik, Hadziabdic (1), Irwin (1), Kennedy, Rajkovic (1), Loveridge (2) (Leighton James), Robbie James, Charles (2), Stevenson (1), Latchford (1) (Walsh (3)).
Record Defeat: 0–8 v Liverpool, FA Cup 3rd rd, 9 January 1990; 0–8 v Monaco, ECWC, 1st rd 2nd leg, 1 October 1991.

sky SPORTS FACT FILE

Goalkeeper Roger Freestone kept 8 consecutive clean sheets for Swansea City between 19 November 1999 and 3 January 2000, going 753 minutes without conceding a goal. In total he kept 22 clean sheets that season as the Swans went on to win the Third Division title.

Most League Points (2 for a win): 62, Division 3 (S), 1948–49.

Most League Points (3 for a win): 92, FL 1, 2007–08.

Most League Goals: 90, Division 2, 1956–57.

Highest League Scorer in Season: Cyril Pearce, 35, Division 2, 1931–32.

Most League Goals in Total Aggregate: Ivor Allchurch, 166, 1949–58, 1965–68.

Most League Goals in One Match: 5, Jack Fowler v Charlton Ath, Division 3S, 27 December 1924.

Most Capped Player: Ashley Williams, 50 (51), Wales.

Most League Appearances: Wilfred Milne, 587, 1919–37.

Youngest League Player: Nigel Dalling, 15 years 289 days v Southport, 6 December 1974.

Record Transfer Fee Received: £25,000,000 (rising to £28,000,000) from Manchester C for Wilfried Bony, January 2015.

Record Transfer Fee Paid: £12,000,000 to Vitesse Arnhem for Wilfried Bony, July 2013.

Football League Record: 1920 Original Member of Division 3; 1921–25 Division 3 (S); 1925–47 Division 2; 1947–49 Division 3 (S); 1949–65 Division 2; 1965–67 Division 3; 1967–70 Division 4; 1970–73 Division 3; 1973–78 Division 4; 1978–79 Division 3; 1979–81 Division 2; 1981–83 Division 1; 1983–84 Division 2; 1984–86 Division 3; 1986–88 Division 4; 1988–92 Division 3; 1992–96 Division 2; 1996–2000 Division 3; 2000–01 Division 2; 2001–04 Division 3; 2004–05 FL 2; 2005–08 FL 1; 2008–11 FL C; 2011– FA Premier League.

LATEST SEQUENCES

Longest Sequence of League Wins: 9, 27.11.1999 – 22.01.2000.

Longest Sequence of League Defeats: 9, 26.1.1991 – 19.3.1991.

Longest Sequence of League Draws: 8, 25.11.2008 – 28.12.2008.

Longest Sequence of Unbeaten League Matches: 19, 19.10.1970 – 9.3.1971.

Longest Sequence Without a League Win: 15, 25.3.1989 – 2.9.1989.

Successive Scoring Runs: 27 from 28.8.1947.

Successive Non-scoring Runs: 6 from 6.2.1996.

MANAGERS

Walter Whittaker 1912–14
William Bartlett 1914–15
Joe Bradshaw 1919–26
Jimmy Thomson 1927–31
Neil Harris 1934–39
Haydn Green 1939–47
Bill McCandless 1947–55
Ron Burgess 1955–58
Trevor Morris 1958–65
Glyn Davies 1965–66
Billy Lucas 1967–69
Roy Bentley 1969–72
Harry Gregg 1972–75
Harry Griffiths 1975–77
John Toshack 1978–83
  (resigned October re-appointed in December) 1983–84
Colin Appleton 1984
John Bond 1984–85
Tommy Hutchison 1985–86
Terry Yorath 1986–89
Ian Evans 1989–90
Terry Yorath 1990–91
Frank Burrows 1991–95
Bobby Smith 1995
Kevin Cullis 1996
Jan Molby 1996–97
Micky Adams 1997
Alan Cork 1997–98
John Hollins 1998–2001
Colin Addison 2001–02
Nick Cusack 2002
Brian Flynn 2002–04
Kenny Jackett 2004–07
Roberto Martinez 2007–09
Paulo Sousa 2009–10
Brendan Rodgers 2010–12
Michael Laudrup 2012–14
Garry Monk February 2014–

TEN YEAR LEAGUE RECORD

		P	W	D	L	F	A	Pts	Pos
2005-06	FL 1	46	18	17	11	78	55	71	6
2006-07	FL 1	46	20	12	14	69	53	72	7
2007-08	FL 1	46	27	11	8	82	42	92	1
2008-09	FL C	46	16	20	10	63	50	68	8
2009-10	FL C	46	17	18	11	40	37	69	7
2010-11	FL C	46	24	8	14	69	42	80	3
2011-12	PR Lge	38	12	11	15	44	51	47	11
2012-13	PR Lge	38	11	13	14	47	51	46	9
2013-14	PR Lge	38	11	9	18	54	54	42	12
2014-15	PR Lge	38	16	8	14	46	49	56	8

DID YOU KNOW ?

Swansea Town won their first major trophy in their first season of football, winning the Welsh Cup in April 1913. In the final they defeated Pontypridd 1-0 at Mid Rhondda's ground in Tonypandy, the teams having previously drawn 0-0 at Ninian Park.

SWANSEA CITY – FA PREMIERSHIP 2014–15 LEAGUE RECORD

Match No.	Date	Venue	Opponents	Result		H/T Score	Lg Pos.	Goalscorers	Atten- dance
1	Aug 16	A	Manchester U	W	2-1	1-0	1	Ki [28], Sigurdsson [72]	75,339
2	23	H	Burnley	W	1-0	1-0	2	Dyer [23]	20,565
3	30	H	WBA	W	3-0	2-0	2	Dyer 2 [2, 71], Routledge [24]	20,318
4	Sept 13	A	Chelsea	L	2-4	1-1	3	Terry (og) [11], Shelvey [86]	41,400
5	20	H	Southampton	L	0-1	0-0	5		20,596
6	27	A	Sunderland	D	0-0	0-0	5		41,325
7	Oct 4	H	Newcastle U	D	2-2	1-1	4	Bony [17], Routledge [50]	20,622
8	19	A	Stoke C	L	1-2	1-1	8	Bony (pen) [34]	27,017
9	25	H	Leicester C	W	2-0	1-0	6	Bony 2 [34, 57]	20,259
10	Nov 1	A	Everton	D	0-0	0-0	6		39,149
11	9	H	Arsenal	W	2-1	0-0	5	Sigurdsson [75], Gomis [78]	20,812
12	22	A	Manchester C	L	1-2	1-1	7	Bony [9]	45,448
13	29	H	Crystal Palace	D	1-1	1-1	7	Bony [15]	20,240
14	Dec 2	H	QPR	W	2-0	0-0	6	Ki [78], Routledge [83]	20,145
15	7	A	West Ham U	L	1-3	1-1	8	Bony [19]	34,125
16	14	H	Tottenham H	L	1-2	0-1	9	Bony [48]	20,650
17	20	A	Hull C	W	1-0	1-0	8	Ki [15]	21,913
18	26	H	Aston Villa	W	1-0	1-0	8	Sigurdsson [13]	20,683
19	29	A	Liverpool	L	1-4	0-1	9	Sigurdsson [52]	44,714
20	Jan 1	A	QPR	D	1-1	0-1	9	Bony [90]	17,729
21	10	H	West Ham U	D	1-1	0-1	9	Noble (og) [74]	20,745
22	17	H	Chelsea	L	0-5	0-4	9		20,785
23	Feb 1	A	Southampton	W	1-0	0-0	9	Shelvey [83]	30,943
24	7	H	Sunderland	D	1-1	0-1	9	Ki [66]	20,355
25	11	A	WBA	L	0-2	0-0	9		23,516
26	21	H	Manchester U	W	2-1	1-1	9	Ki [30], Gomis [73]	20,809
27	28	A	Burnley	W	1-0	0-0	8	Heaton (og) [64]	17,388
28	Mar 4	A	Tottenham H	L	2-3	1-1	9	Ki [19], Sigurdsson [89]	34,008
29	16	H	Liverpool	L	0-1	0-0	9		20,828
30	21	A	Aston Villa	W	1-0	0-0	8	Gomis [87]	35,598
31	Apr 4	H	Hull C	W	3-1	2-0	8	Ki [18], Gomis 2 [37, 90]	20,333
32	11	H	Everton	D	1-1	0-1	8	Shelvey (pen) [69]	20,468
33	18	A	Leicester C	L	0-2	0-1	8		31,121
34	25	A	Newcastle U	W	3-2	1-1	8	Nelson Oliveira [45], Sigurdsson [49], Cork [71]	46,884
35	May 2	H	Stoke C	W	2-0	0-0	8	Montero [76], Ki [90]	20,661
36	11	A	Arsenal	W	1-0	0-0	8	Gomis [85]	59,989
37	17	H	Manchester C	L	2-4	1-2	8	Sigurdsson [45], Gomis [64]	20,669
38	24	A	Crystal Palace	L	0-1	0-0	8		25,076

Final League Position: 8

GOALSCORERS

League (46): Bony 9 (1 pen), Ki 8, Gomis 7, Sigurdsson 7, Dyer 3, Routledge 3, Shelvey 3 (1 pen), Cork 1, Montero 1, Nelson Oliveira 1, own goals 3.
FA Cup (7): Gomis 2, Barrow 1, Carroll 1, Dyer 1, Routledge 1, Sigurdsson 1.
Capital One Cup (5): Emnes 2, Dyer 1, Gomis 1, Sigurdsson 1.

Fabianski L 37	Rangel A 22 + 5	Amat J 7 + 3	Williams A 37	Taylor N 34	Ki S 30 + 3	Shelvey J 28 + 3	Dyer N 23 + 9	Sigurdsson G 32	Routledge W 27 + 2	Bony W 16 + 4	Tiendalli D 1 + 2	Montero J 15 + 15	Gomis B 18 + 13	Carroll T 8 + 5	Fernandez F 27 + 1	Emnes M 3 + 14	Richards A 7 + 3	Bartley K 7	Barrow M 1 + 10	Briton L 7 + 2	Tremmel G 1 + 1	Nelson Oliveira M 4 + 6	Fulton J 1 + 1	Naughton K 10	Cork J 15	Grimes M — + 3	Gorre K — + 1	Match No.
1	2	3	4	5^2	6	7	8^1	9	10	11^3	12	13	14															1
1	2	3	4	5	7	6	8^2	9	10^1	11^3	14	13	12															2
1	2	3	4	5	6	7^1	8	9	10^2	11^3		12	13	14														3
1	2	3^2	4	5	7	6	8	9	10^1	14		13	11^2		12													4
1	2		4	5	7^2	6	8^1	9	10	11^4		12			3	13												5
1	2		4	5	7	6	8^1	9	10	13		12	11^2		3		14											6
1			4	5	6	7	8^2	9^1	10	11		13			3	12	2											7
1	2		4	5	6		8^3	9^1	10	11		13	12	7^2	3	14												8
1	2		4	5	6	7	14	9^2	8^3	11^1		10	13	12	3													9
1	2		4	5	7	6^4	14	9^3	8	11^1		10^2	12	13	3													10
1	2		4	5	6			9		11^3		10	13	7^2	3		8^1	12	14									11
1	2		4	5	6	12	8^2	9^1		11		10	14	7^3	3			13										12
1	2		4	5	6	7		9	8^1	11^2		10	13		3			12										13
1			4	5	7	13	12	9^3	8	11		10^1		14			2	3				6^2						14
1	2^1		4		7		14	9	8	11		10^3	13				5	3				6^2	12					15
	2^2		4	5	7	12		9	8	11^3		10	14				13	3				6^1	1					16
1	14		4	5	6	9	8		10			13	11^1	7^3	3	12	2^2											17
1	2		4	5	7	6^1	8	9^3	12	11		10^2	13		3	14												18
1	12		4	5	14	7	8	9	10	11^1		13			3		2^2					6^2						19
1	2		4	5	7		8^1	9^2	10	13		11			3	12		6										20
1	2		4	5			8^1	9^2	10^3	11				7	3	13			12	6		14						21
1			4	5			8^2	6	10^1		2	11		7	3	12			14			9^3		13				22
1	13	14	4	5				9	8			11		7	3	10^1		12^3		6				2^2				23
1	13		4	5^3	6	9^2	10					12	11		3				8^1			14		2	7			24
1			4	5	7			9^2	8^1			13	10	11	3							12		2	6			25
1	13		4	5	6		8^2	9^1				10	12	11	3									2	7			26
1	14		4	5	6	8				11^2		12	10^1	9^3	3		13							2	7			27
1			4	5	6		8^2	9	11			13	10^1		3							12		2	7			28
1		3	4	5	6^2	8	13		10^1	11^2		12	9			14								2	7			29
1			4	5	7		8^2	13	9	11		12	10^1		3							14		2	6			30
1	12		4	5	6	8^1	13	11	9			10			3									2^2	7^3	14		31
1	2		4	5	7		8^2	13	9	11		10^1			3	12									6			32
1	2	5	4		7^2		8	13	9	11^3		12			3	14								10^1	6			33
1	2	5	4		13	7	8	9^2				10^1			3	14								11^3	6	12		34
1	2		4	5	13		8^3	9				10^2			3	12			14					11^1	6			35
1	2^3		4	5	6^1		8	9^2	10			11	13		3	12	14								7			36
1			4	5		7^2	8^1	9^3				10	11		3	14	2			12	13				6			37
1							8^3					10^1	11		3	9	5	4	12	7^2				2	6	13	14	38

FA Cup

Third Round	Tranmere R	(a)	6-2
Fourth Round	Blackburn R	(a)	1-3

Capital One Cup

Second Round	Rotherham U	(h)	1-0
Third Round	Everton	(h)	3-0
Fourth Round	Liverpool	(a)	1-2

SWINDON TOWN

FOUNDATION

It is generally accepted that Swindon Town came into being in 1881, although there is no firm evidence that the club's founder, Rev. William Pitt, captain of the Spartans (an offshoot of a cricket club), changed his club's name to Swindon Town before 1883, when the Spartans amalgamated with St Mark's Young Men's Friendly Society.

The County Ground, County Road, Swindon, Wiltshire SN1 2ED.

Telephone: (0871) 876 1879.

Fax: (0844) 880 1112.

Ticket Office: (0871) 876 1993.

Website: www.swindontownfc.co.uk

Email: enquiries@swindontownfc.co.uk

Ground Capacity: 15,547.

Record Attendance: 32,000 v Arsenal, FA Cup 3rd rd, 15 January 1972.

Pitch Measurements: 100.5m × 67m (110yd × 73.5yd)

Chairman: Lee Power.

General Manager: Steve Anderson.

Manager: Mark Cooper.

First Team Coach: Luke Williams.

Physio: Paul Godfrey.

Colours: Red shirts with white trim, white shorts with red trim, red socks with white trim.

Year Formed: 1881* (*see Foundation*).

Turned Professional: 1894.

Club Nickname: 'The Robins'.

Grounds: 1881, The Croft; 1896, County Ground.

First Football League Game: 28 August 1920, Division 3, v Luton T (h) W 9–1 – Nash; Kay, Macconachie; Langford, Hawley, Wareing; Jefferson (1), Fleming (4), Rogers, Batty (2), Davies (1), (1 og).

Record League Victory: 9–1 v Luton T, Division 3 (S), 28 August 1920 – Nash; Kay, Macconachie; Langford, Hawley, Wareing; Jefferson (1), Fleming (4), Rogers, Batty (2), Davies (1), (1 og).

Record Cup Victory: 10–1 v Farnham U Breweries (away), FA Cup 1st rd (replay), 28 November 1925 – Nash; Dickenson, Weston, Archer, Bew, Adey; Denyer (2), Wall (1), Richardson (4), Johnson (3), Davies.

HONOURS

Football League: FL 2: *Champions* 2011–12;
Division 2: *Champions* 1995–96;
Division 3: *Runners-up* 1962–63, 1968–69;
Division 4: *Champions* 1985–86.

FA Cup: Best season: semi-final, 1910, 1912.

Football League Cup: *Winners* 1969.

Johnstone's Paint Trophy: *Runners-up* 2012.

Anglo-Italian Cup: *Winners* 1970.

sky SPORTS FACT FILE

Rev Edward Reid, who was Curate of the nearby village of Kempsford, made a number of appearances for Swindon Town in the Southern League. Reid, a forward, scored on his debut against Brentford in April 1903 and appeared throughout the following season. His team mates presented him with a gold watch when he moved on to a new post in Exeter.

Record Defeat: 1–10 v Manchester C, FA Cup 4th rd (replay), 25 January 1930.

Most League Points (2 for a win): 64, Division 3, 1968–69.

Most League Points (3 for a win): 102, Division 4, 1985–86.

Most League Goals: 100, Division 3 (S), 1926–27.

Highest League Scorer in Season: Harry Morris, 47, Division 3 (S), 1926–27.

Most League Goals in Total Aggregate: Harry Morris, 216, 1926–33.

Most League Goals in One Match: 5, Harry Morris v QPR, Division 3 (S), 18 December 1926; 5, Harry Morris v Norwich C, Division 3 (S), 26 April 1930; 5, Keith East v Mansfield T, Division 3, 20 November 1965.

Most Capped Player: Rod Thomas, 30 (50), Wales.

Most League Appearances: John Trollope, 770, 1960–80.

Youngest League Player: Paul Rideout, 16 years 107 days v Hull C, 29 November 1980.

Record Transfer Fee Received: £1,500,000 (rising to £1,900,000) from WBA for Simon Cox, July 2009.

Record Transfer Fee Paid: £800,000 to West Ham U for Joey Beauchamp, August 1994.

Football League Record: 1920 Original Member of Division 3; 1921–58 Division 3 (S); 1958–63 Division 3; 1963–65 Division 2; 1965–69 Division 3; 1969–74 Division 2; 1974–82 Division 3; 1982–86 Division 4; 1986–87 Division 3; 1987–92 Division 2; 1992–93 Division 1; 1993–94 FA Premier League; 1994–95 Division 1; 1995–96 Division 2; 1996–2000 Division 1; 2000–04 Division 2; 2004–06 FL 1; 2006–07 FL 2; 2007–11 FL 1; 2011–12 FL 2; 2012– FL 1.

MANAGERS

Sam Allen 1902–33
Ted Vizard 1933–39
Neil Harris 1939–41
Louis Page 1945–53
Maurice Lindley 1953–55
Bert Head 1956–65
Danny Williams 1965–69
Fred Ford 1969–71
Dave Mackay 1971–72
Les Allen 1972–74
Danny Williams 1974–78
Bobby Smith 1978–80
John Trollope 1980–83
Ken Beamish 1983–84
Lou Macari 1984–89
Ossie Ardiles 1989–91
Glenn Hoddle 1991–93
John Gorman 1993–94
Steve McMahon 1994–98
Jimmy Quinn 1998–2000
Colin Todd 2000
Andy King 2000–01
Roy Evans 2001
Andy King 2001–05
Iffy Onuora 2005–06
Dennis Wise 2006
Paul Sturrock 2006–07
Maurice Malpas 2008
Danny Wilson 2008–11
Paul Hart 2011
Paolo Di Canio 2011–13
Kevin MacDonald 2013
Mark Cooper August 2013–

LATEST SEQUENCES

Longest Sequence of League Wins: 10, 31.12.2011 – 28.2.2012

Longest Sequence of League Defeats: 8, 29.8.2005 – 8.10.2005.

Longest Sequence of League Draws: 6, 22.11.1991 – 28.12.1991.

Longest Sequence of Unbeaten League Matches: 22, 12.1.1986 – 23.8.86.

Longest Sequence Without a League Win: 19, 30.10.1999 – 4.3.2000.

Successive Scoring Runs: 31 from 17.4.1926.

Successive Non-scoring Runs: 5 from 5.4.1997.

TEN YEAR LEAGUE RECORD

		P	W	D	L	F	A	Pts	Pos
2005-06	FL 1	46	11	15	20	46	65	48	23
2006-07	FL 2	46	25	10	11	58	38	85	3
2007-08	FL 1	46	16	13	17	63	56	61	13
2008-09	FL 1	46	12	17	17	68	71	53	15
2009-10	FL 1	46	22	16	8	73	57	82	5
2010-11	FL 1	46	9	14	23	50	72	41	24
2011-12	FL 2	46	29	6	11	75	32	93	1
2012-13	FL 1	46	20	14	12	72	39	74	6
2013-14	FL 1	46	19	9	18	63	59	66	8
2014-15	FL 1	46	23	10	13	76	57	79	4

DID YOU KNOW ?

After winning the League Cup in 1969 Swindon Town were denied entry to the Inter Cities Fairs Cup because they were not a First Division team. As compensation it was agreed they should meet the Coppa Italia winners for the Anglo Italian League Cup. Town went on to defeat AS Roma 5-2 on aggregate in the two-legged match.

SWINDON TOWN – FOOTBALL LEAGUE ONE 2014–15 LEAGUE RECORD

Match No.	Date	Venue	Opponents	Result	H/T Score	Lg Pos.	Goalscorers	Attendance
1	Aug 9	H	Scunthorpe U	W 3-1	3-1	3	Luongo [3], Smith, M 2 [12, 45]	7060
2	16	A	Crawley T	L 0-1	0-0	12		2710
3	19	A	Gillingham	D 2-2	1-1	10	Williams [43], Bywater (og) [90]	5264
4	23	H	Crewe Alex	W 2-0	1-0	6	Kasim [34], Williams [77]	6530
5	30	H	Coventry C	D 1-1	0-1	8	Branco [72]	7299
6	Sept 13	A	Bradford C	W 2-1	2-1	6	Obika 2 [23, 43]	12,486
7	16	H	Oldham Ath	D 2-2	1-1	7	Obika [27], Williams [80]	6332
8	20	H	Sheffield U	W 5-2	1-0	4	Smith, M 2 (1 pen) [13, 55 (p)], Obika [58], Williams [76], Thompson, L [86]	7536
9	27	A	Barnsley	W 3-0	0-0	3	Byrne [58], Reeves [82], Williams [83]	8879
10	Oct 4	A	Leyton Orient	W 2-1	1-0	2	Smith, M [29], Byrne [47]	5422
11	18	A	Yeovil T	D 1-1	0-1	3	Williams [71]	5679
12	21	H	Rochdale	L 2-3	1-0	7	Rodgers [35], Smith, M [77]	6718
13	25	H	Colchester U	D 2-2	1-0	9	Smith, M 2 [27, 48]	7871
14	28	A	Chesterfield	W 3-0	2-0	3	Kasim [30], Byrne [34], Williams [70]	6144
15	Nov 1	A	Milton Keynes D	L 1-2	1-0	5	Obika [6]	9494
16	4	H	Preston NE	W 1-0	0-0	3	Williams [84]	6646
17	15	H	Bristol C	W 1-0	0-0	2	Smith, M [78]	12,565
18	22	A	Peterborough U	W 2-1	1-0	2	Williams [33], Obika [47]	7182
19	29	H	Fleetwood T	W 1-0	0-0	2	Gladwin [86]	10,506
20	Dec 13	A	Notts Co	W 3-0	1-0	2	Williams 2 [6, 54], Luongo [59]	4753
21	20	H	Doncaster R	L 0-1	0-1	3		7793
22	26	A	Walsall	W 4-1	1-1	3	Smith, M [3], Luongo [46], Williams 2 [51, 57]	5696
23	28	H	Port Vale	W 1-0	0-0	2	Williams [56]	9248
24	Jan 3	A	Fleetwood T	D 2-2	0-0	2	Williams [71], Thompson, L [88]	3346
25	12	A	Coventry C	W 3-0	2-0	1	Williams 2 (1 pen) [8, 18 (p)], Obika [81]	7098
26	17	H	Chesterfield	W 3-1	2-1	1	Stephens [17], Swift [25], Williams [47]	7981
27	31	H	Sheffield U	L 0-2	0-0	3		19,490
28	Feb 7	H	Barnsley	W 2-0	1-0	2	Branco [14], Gladwin [84]	8380
29	10	A	Oldham Ath	L 1-2	0-2	2	Luongo [63]	3451
30	14	A	Scunthorpe U	L 1-3	1-0	2	Smith, M [44]	3763
31	21	H	Crawley T	L 1-2	0-1	3	Williams [58]	7692
32	24	H	Bradford C	W 2-1	2-0	3	Luongo 2 [15, 34]	6812
33	28	A	Crewe Alex	D 0-0	0-0	4		4781
34	Mar 3	H	Gillingham	L 0-3	0-1	4		7025
35	7	H	Notts Co	W 3-0	0-0	3	Swift [58], Williams (pen) [64], Toffolo [89]	8013
36	14	A	Port Vale	W 1-0	1-0	3	Branco [8]	5120
37	17	H	Doncaster R	W 2-1	0-1	3	Smith, M (pen) [54], Obika [90]	5258
38	Apr 4	H	Milton Keynes D	L 0-3	0-0	4		10,087
39	7	A	Bristol C	L 0-3	0-1	4		12,302
40	11	H	Peterborough U	W 1-0	0-0	4	Hylton [71]	7126
41	14	A	Rochdale	W 4-2	4-1	4	Gladwin 3 (1 pen) [20, 33, 40 (p)], Smith, M [23]	2344
42	18	H	Yeovil T	L 0-1	0-0	4		8490
43	21	H	Walsall	D 3-3	0-1	4	Gladwin 2 (2 pens) [59, 67], Turnbull [81]	6305
44	25	A	Preston NE	L 0-3	0-2	4		17,621
45	28	A	Colchester U	D 1-1	0-1	4	Gladwin [53]	4395
46	May 3	H	Leyton Orient	D 2-2	0-1	4	Rodgers [61], Williams (pen) [86]	8609

Final League Position: 4

GOALSCORERS

League (76): Williams 21 (3 pens), Smith, M 13 (2 pens), Gladwin 8 (3 pens), Obika 8, Luongo 6, Branco 3, Byrne 3, Kasim 2, Rodgers 2, Swift 2, Thompson, L 2, Hylton 1, Reeves 1, Stephens 1, Toffolo 1, Turnbull 1, own goal 1.
FA Cup (0).
Capital One Cup (4): Smith, M 2 (1 pen), Kasim 1, Thompson, L 1.
Johnstone's Paint Trophy (4): Gladwin 1, Obika 1, Smith, M 1 (1 pen), Williams 1.
League One Play-Offs (7): Gladwin 2, Smith, M 2 (1 pen), Byrne 1, Obika 1, Ricketts 1.

Foderingham W 44	Thompson N 35	Turnbull J 44	Lelan J 2+3	Byrne N 42	Luongo M 33+1	Thompson L 30+2	Kasim Y 28+7	Smith B 7	Gladwin B 28+6	Smith M 32+8	Williams A 28+18	Branco R 26+3	Barthram J 3+2	Randall W 2+2	Barker G 1+4	Waldon C 1	Obika J 21+11	Reeves J 1+9	Stephens J 36+1	Ball A 7+3	Rodgers A 7+3	Toffolo H 22+6	Swift J 12+6	Hylton J 1+10	Ricketts S 8+1	Belford T 2	Marshall L 1+1	Smith T —+1	Cooke J 1+1	Agombar H 1	Belford C —+1	Match No.
1	2	3	4²	5	6	7	8	9	10	11¹	12	13																				1
1	3	4		2	7	9⁴	8		11¹	10	12	5	6²	13																		2
1	3	4	13	5		7²	6	9	8¹	10	11	2				12																3
1	2	3		5		8	7	9¹	6²	10	11		4	12		13																4
1		2	3	5	6	7	8	9		10	4				12	11¹																5
1	3	5	14	2	8	9	7	6²	11¹	12	4						10³	13														6
1	3	4		6	8	7¹	5	9⁴	10³	12	2		14	11	13																	7
1	4	3	14	5	6¹	8	7	9		10	12	2³					11²	13														8
1	2	4		5	6	7¹	8		10	12							11²	13	3	9												9
1	4	5		2	7	9	8		10	11¹							12		3	6												10
1	2⁴	4		5	6	8	7	13	10	12							11¹		3	9²												11
1		4		5	6	12	3		7²	10	11						14	13	2	9²	8¹											12
1		4		5	6	2	8			10	11¹						13	7	3	9²	12											13
1	3	4		5	6	8³	7			10	12						11²	13	2	9¹	14											14
1	2	3		5	8	6²	7¹	14	10	13							11		4	9²	12											15
1	3	4			6	8	7		5	11	12						10¹		2		9											16
1	3	4		5		8			7	11	12	2					10¹	6			9											17
1	3	4		5	12	8³	13		6¹	10	2						11		7	14	9²											18
1	3¹	4		5	7	6	8¹		14	13	10						11²		2	12	9											19
1	3	4		5	8	7²	6²		9	13	10						11¹	12	2		14											20
1	3	4		5	7	6	8²		9	12	11						10¹		2	13												21
1	3²	4		5	8³	6	13		9¹	11	10	7						14	2		12											22
1		4		5	6	8			7	12	10	3					11¹		2		9											23
1		4		5		8			6	10²	11	2					12	3		13	9	7¹										24
1	3	4		5		6			7	10²	11³	12					13		2		8	9²	14									25
1	3	4		5		7			11¹	10	2	14					12		8		13	9²	6³									26
1	3	4		5		7			12	10¹	2						11²		8		9	6	13									27
1		4		5	6	8	7		13	12	11¹	2					3				9	10²										28
1		4			8	7	6³		5	10¹	12	3					11²		2		9	13	14									29
1	5	4		8		7	6²		12	10	9	3¹					2				11	13										30
1	3	4		5		12	7		8	11²	10								2		9¹	6	13									31
1	3	4		5	6	8			9¹	11	10	2							7		12											32
1	3	4		5	6	8³	13		9²	10¹	11	2					14		7⁴		12											33
1	3	4		5	8	7			14	11²	10³	2¹					12				9	6	13									34
1	3	4		5	6		12		8²	11¹	2								7		9	10	13									35
1	3	4		5	7³	12			6	14	11¹	2					13		8		9	10²										36
1	4	5		2			9		10¹	11	12	3					13		7		6	8²										37
1	3	4		5	8	13			9³	11	12	2					14		7			10²		6¹								38
1		4		5	8	6			9¹	10	11²	2					12		7			13	3									39
1		4		5	8		14		10³	11¹	3						7²		9		12		13	2								40
1	3			5	8				6¹	10²	13						11³		2		7	9	12	14	4							41
1	2			5	7	12			8	11²	13						10		3		6¹	9²	14	4								42
1	3	2		5		8	10			14					12		11²		7		6³	9¹		13	4							43
			4						11¹	12				9	5	8³		2	7²			10		3	1		6	13	14			44
1	3³	2		5	6		7		8	10²	12			11			4		9¹			13	14									45
		4³							10	2	5	9					13		7			8	3	1⁴	14			11¹	6²	12		46

FA Cup
First Round	Cheltenham T	(a)	0-5

Capital One Cup
First Round	Luton T	(a)	2-1
Second Round	Brighton & HA	(h)	2-4
(aet)			

Johnstone's Paint Trophy
First Round	Newport Co	(a)	2-1
Second Round	Plymouth Arg	(a)	2-3

League One Play-Offs
Semi-Finals 1st leg	Sheffield U	(a)	2-1
Semi-Finals 2nd leg	Sheffield U	(h)	5-5
Final	Preston NE	Wembley	0-4

TOTTENHAM HOTSPUR

FOUNDATION

The Hotspur Football Club was formed from an older cricket club in 1882. Most of the founders were old boys of St John's Presbyterian School and Tottenham Grammar School. The Casey brothers were well to the fore as the family provided the club's first goalposts (painted blue and white) and their first ball. They soon adopted the local YMCA as their meeting place, but after a couple of moves settled at the Red House, which is still their headquarters, although now known simply as 748 High Road.

White Hart Lane, Bill Nicholson Way, 748 High Road, Tottenham, London N17 0AP.

Telephone: (0844) 499 5000.

Fax: (020) 3544 8563.

Ticket Office: (0844) 499 5000.

Website: www.tottenhamhotspur.com

Email: email@tottenhamhotspur.com

Ground Capacity: 36,284.

Record Attendance: 75,038 v Sunderland, FA Cup 6th rd, 5 March 1938.

Pitch Measurements: 100m × 67m (109yd × 73yd)

Chairman: Daniel Levy.

Head Coach: Mauricio Pochettino.

Assistant Head Coach: Jesus Perez.

Head Physio: Geoff Scott.

Colours: White shirts, navy blue shorts, white socks with navy blue trim.

Year Formed: 1882. *Turned Professional:* 1895.

Previous Name: 1882, Hotspur Football Club; 1884, Tottenham Hotspur.

Club Nickname: 'Spurs'.

Grounds: 1882, Tottenham Marshes; 1888, Northumberland Park; 1899, White Hart Lane.

HONOURS

Football League – Division 1: *Champions* 1950–51, 1960–61; *Runners-up* 1921–22, 1951–52, 1956–57, 1962–63; **Division 2:** *Champions* 1919–20, 1949–50; *Runners-up* 1908–09, 1932–33.

FA Cup: *Winners* 1901 (as non-League club), 1921, 1961, 1962, 1967, 1981, 1982, 1991; *Runners-up* 1987.

Football League Cup: *Winners* 1971, 1973, 1999, 2008; *Runners-up* 1982, 2002, 2009, 2015.

European Competitions European Cup: 1961–62. **Champions League:** 2010–11. **European Cup-Winners' Cup:** 1962–63 (*winners*), 1963–64, 1967–68, 1981–82, 1982–83, 1991–92. **UEFA Cup:** 1971–72 (*winners*), 1972–73, 1973–74 (*runners-up*), 1983–84 (*winners*), 1984–85, 1999–2000, 2006–07, 2007–08, 2008–09. **Europa League:** 2011–12, 2012–13, 2013–14, 2014–15. **Intertoto Cup:** 1995.

First Football League Game: 1 September 1908, Division 2, v Wolverhampton W (h) W 3–0 – Hewitson; Coquet, Burton; Morris (1), Danny Steel, Darnell; Walton, Woodward (2), Macfarlane, Bobby Steel, Middlemiss.

Record League Victory: 9–0 v Bristol R, Division 2, 22 October 1977 – Daines; Naylor, Holmes, Hoddle (1), McAllister, Perryman, Pratt, McNab, Moores (3), Lee (4), Taylor (1).

Record Cup Victory: 13–2 v Crewe Alex, FA Cup 4th rd (replay), 3 February 1960 – Brown; Hills, Henry; Blanchflower, Norman, Mackay; White, Harmer (1), Smith (4), Allen (5), Jones (3 incl. 1p).

sky SPORTS FACT FILE

Tottenham Hotspur were elected to the Football League in 1908 only after three ballots were held. On the first two occasions they tied with Lincoln City in the vote of member clubs. The matter was then decided by the Management Committee members who voted to accept Spurs by 5 votes to 3.

Record Defeat: 0–8 v Cologne, UEFA Intertoto Cup, 22 July 1995.

Most League Points (2 for a win): 70, Division 2, 1919–20.

Most League Points (3 for a win): 77, Division 1, 1984–85.

Most League Goals: 115, Division 1, 1960–61.

Highest League Scorer in Season: Jimmy Greaves, 37, Division 1, 1962–63.

Most League Goals in Total Aggregate: Jimmy Greaves, 220, 1961–70.

Most League Goals in One Match: 5, Ted Harper v Reading, Division 2, 30 August 1930; 5, Alf Stokes v Birmingham C, Division 1, 18 September 1957; 5, Bobby Smith v Aston Villa, Division 1, 29 March 1958; 5, Jermain Defoe v Wigan Ath, FA Premier League, 22 November 2009.

Most Capped Player: Pat Jennings, 74 (119), Northern Ireland.

Most League Appearances: Steve Perryman, 655, 1969–86.

Youngest League Player: Ally Dick, 16 years 301 days v Manchester C, 20 February 1982.

Record Transfer Fee Received: £85,300,000 from Real Madrid for Gareth Bale, September 2013.

Record Transfer Fee Paid: £30,000,000 to AS Roma for Erik Lamela, August 2013.

Football League Record: 1908 Elected to Division 2; 1909–15 Division 1; 1919–20 Division 2; 1920–28 Division 1; 1928–33 Division 2; 1933–35 Division 1; 1935–50 Division 2; 1950–77 Division 1; 1977–78 Division 2; 1978–92 Division 1; 1992– FA Premier League.

LATEST SEQUENCES

Longest Sequence of League Wins: 13, 23.4.1960 – 1.10.1960.

Longest Sequence of League Defeats: 7, 1.1.1994 – 27.2.1994.

Longest Sequence of League Draws: 6, 9.1.1999 – 27.2.1999.

Longest Sequence of Unbeaten League Matches: 22, 31.8.1949 – 31.12.1949.

Longest Sequence Without a League Win: 16, 29.12.1934 – 13.4.1935.

Successive Scoring Runs: 32 from 24.2.1962.

Successive Non-scoring Runs: 6 from 28.12.1985.

MANAGERS

Frank Brettell 1898–99
John Cameron 1899–1906
Fred Kirkham 1907–08
Peter McWilliam 1912–27
Billy Minter 1927–29
Percy Smith 1930–35
Jack Tresadern 1935–38
Peter McWilliam 1938–42
Arthur Turner 1942–46
Joe Hulme 1946–49
Arthur Rowe 1949–55
Jimmy Anderson 1955–58
Bill Nicholson 1958–74
Terry Neill 1974–76
Keith Burkinshaw 1976–84
Peter Shreeves 1984–86
David Pleat 1986–87
Terry Venables 1987–91
Peter Shreeves 1991–92
Doug Livermore 1992–93
Ossie Ardiles 1993–94
Gerry Francis 1994–97
Christian Gross *(Head Coach)* 1997–98
George Graham 1998–2001
Glenn Hoddle 2001–03
David Pleat *(Caretaker)* 2003–04
Jacques Santini 2004
Martin Jol 2004–07
Juande Ramos 2007–08
Harry Redknapp 2008–12
Andre Villas-Boas 2012–13
Tim Sherwood 2013–14
Mauricio Pochettino May 2014–

TEN YEAR LEAGUE RECORD

		P	W	D	L	F	A	Pts	Pos
2005-06	PR Lge	38	18	11	9	53	38	65	5
2006-07	PR Lge	38	17	9	12	57	54	60	5
2007-08	PR Lge	38	11	13	14	66	61	46	11
2008-09	PR Lge	38	14	9	15	45	45	51	8
2009-10	PR Lge	38	21	7	10	67	41	70	4
2010-11	PR Lge	38	16	14	8	55	46	62	5
2011-12	PR Lge	38	20	9	9	66	41	69	4
2012-13	PR Lge	38	21	9	8	66	46	72	5
2013-14	PR Lge	38	21	6	11	55	51	69	6
2014-15	PR Lge	38	19	7	12	58	53	64	5

DID YOU KNOW ?

Tottenham Hotspur drew 3-3 with Manchester United in the FA Charity Shield match at Old Trafford in August 1967. Goalkeeper Pat Jennings achieved the unusual feat of scoring in the match when his long kick downfield bounced over the United keeper and into the net.

TOTTENHAM HOTSPUR – FA PREMIERSHIP 2014–15 LEAGUE RECORD

Match No.	Date	Venue	Opponents	Result	H/T Score	Lg Pos.	Goalscorers	Attendance
1	Aug 16	A	West Ham U	W 1-0	0-0	3	Dier [90]	34,977
2	24	H	QPR	W 4-0	3-0	1	Chadli 2 [12, 37], Dier [30], Adebayor [65]	36,109
3	31	H	Liverpool	L 0-3	0-1	6		36,130
4	Sept 13	A	Sunderland	D 2-2	1-1	6	Chadli [2], Eriksen [48]	40,799
5	21	H	WBA	L 0-1	0-0	9	.	35,861
6	27	A	Arsenal	D 1-1	0-0	8	Chadli [56]	59,900
7	Oct 5	H	Southampton	W 1-0	1-0	6	Eriksen [40]	35,564
8	18	A	Manchester C	L 1-4	1-2	8	Eriksen [15]	45,549
9	26	H	Newcastle U	L 1-2	1-0	11	Adebayor [18]	35,650
10	Nov 2	A	Aston Villa	W 2-1	0-1	8	Chadli [84], Kane [90]	32,049
11	9	H	Stoke C	L 1-2	0-2	12	Chadli [77]	35,699
12	23	A	Hull C	W 2-1	0-1	10	Kane [61], Eriksen [90]	23,561
13	30	H	Everton	W 2-1	2-1	7	Eriksen [21], Soldado [45]	35,901
14	Dec 3	A	Chelsea	L 0-3	0-2	10		41,518
15	6	H	Crystal Palace	D 0-0	0-0	10		35,860
16	14	A	Swansea C	W 2-1	1-0	7	Kane [4], Eriksen [89]	20,650
17	20	H	Burnley	W 2-1	2-1	6	Kane [21], Lamela [35]	35,681
18	26	A	Leicester C	W 2-1	1-0	7	Kane [1], Eriksen [71]	31,870
19	28	H	Manchester U	D 0-0	0-0	7		35,711
20	Jan 1	H	Chelsea	W 5-3	3-1	5	Kane 2 [30, 52], Rose [44], Townsend (pen) [45], Chadli [78]	35,903
21	10	A	Crystal Palace	L 1-2	0-0	5	Kane [49]	24,193
22	17	H	Sunderland	W 2-1	1-1	5	O'Shea (og) [3], Eriksen [88]	35,973
23	31	A	WBA	W 3-0	2-0	5	Eriksen [6], Kane 2 (1 pen) [15, 64 (p)]	25,079
24	Feb 7	H	Arsenal	W 2-1	0-1	5	Kane 2 [56, 86]	35,659
25	10	A	Liverpool	L 2-3	1-1	6	Kane [26], Dembele [61]	44,577
26	22	H	West Ham U	D 2-2	0-1	7	Rose [81], Kane [90]	35,837
27	Mar 4	H	Swansea C	W 3-2	1-1	7	Chadli [7], Mason [51], Townsend [60]	34,008
28	7	A	QPR	W 2-1	1-0	6	Kane 2 [34, 68]	17,992
29	15	A	Manchester U	L 0-3	0-3	7		75,112
30	21	H	Leicester C	W 4-3	2-1	7	Kane 3 (1 pen) [6, 13, 64 (p)], Schlupp (og) [85]	35,950
31	Apr 5	A	Burnley	D 0-0	0-0	6		18,829
32	11	H	Aston Villa	L 0-1	0-1	7		35,687
33	19	A	Newcastle U	W 3-1	1-0	6	Chadli [30], Eriksen [53], Kane [90]	47,427
34	25	A	Southampton	D 2-2	1-1	6	Lamela [43], Chadli [70]	31,622
35	May 3	H	Manchester C	L 0-1	0-1	6		35,784
36	9	A	Stoke C	L 0-3	0-2	6		27,104
37	16	H	Hull C	W 2-0	0-0	6	Chadli [54], Rose [61]	35,857
38	24	A	Everton	W 1-0	1-0	5	Kane [24]	39,365

Final League Position: 5

GOALSCORERS

League (58): Kane 21 (2 pens), Chadli 11, Eriksen 10, Rose 3, Adebayor 2, Dier 2, Lamela 2, Townsend 2 (1 pen), Dembele 1, Mason 1, Soldado 1, own goals 2.
FA Cup (6): Capoue 1, Chadli 1, Chiriches 1, Paulinho 1, Rose 1, Townsend 1 (1 pen).
Capital One Cup (12): Kane 3, Eriksen 2, Soldado 2, Bentaleb 1, Chadli 1, Lamela 1, Mason 1, Townsend 1 (1 pen).
UEFA Europa League (15): Kane 7, Lamela 2, Soldado 2, Townsend 2 (2 pens), Paulinho 1, Stambouli 1.

Lloris H 35	Naughton K 5	Kaboul Y 11	Dier E 25+3	Rose D 27+1	Bentaleb N 25+1	Capoue E 11+1	Eriksen C 37+1	Lamela E 25+8	Lennon A 3+6	Adebayor E 9+4	Holtby L —+1	Townsend A 10+7	Kane H 28+6	Vertonghen J 31+1	Chadli N 28+7	Dembele M 10+16	Soldado R 7+17	Davies B 9+5	Chiriches V 8+2	Stambouli B 4+8	Paulinho 3+12	Mason R 29+2	Fazio F 20	Walker K 15	Vorm M 3+1	Yedlin D —+1	Match No.
1	2*	3	4	5	6	7	8	9¹	10³	11¹	12	13	14														1
1		3	2	5	7³	6	9	8		11¹		13		4	10²	12	14										2
1		3	2	5¹	6³	7	9²	8		11		12		4	10¹	6			4	12							3
1		3	2	5		7	9³	8	14	11²		13			10¹	6			4	12							4
1		3	2	5			6³	9	8	14	11			10¹	7²	12		4		13							5
1	2	3	14	5²	13	7	9¹	8	12	11				4	10³					6							6
1	2¹	3	12	5		6	9³	8²		11				14	4	10	13			7¹	4⁸						7
1		3	2	5			6³	9	8¹			12		14	10	13	11		7¹								8
1		3	2	5		6²	9	8³	13	11¹	12			4	10	14			7								9
1	2	3		5		7²	6³	12		10¹		14	13	4	9	11			8								10
1	2*	3				6¹	9³	13			14			8²	11		10	12		7	4						11
1	2²						10	8	13				9	4		6²	11¹	5	12		14	7	3				12
1		13		7			10	12	8⁹				9	4			11²	5	2¹		14	6	3				13
1				7			10	9¹	8²				11	4	12		14	5	2		13	6³	3				14
1		2		7			10	8²	14				9	4	12		11¹	5			13	6³	3				15
1				7			10	8²					9	4	14	12	11¹	5	13		6²	3	2				16
1			14	6			9³	8					11²	4	10		13	5	12		7¹	3	2				17
1			5	7			9	8					11²	4	10¹		13		6³	14	12	3	2				18
1							9	13					8¹	11	4	10²	12		5	2	6	7	3				19
1			5²	6			9						8¹	11	4	10	12		14		13	7³	3	2			20
1			5	12			9						8²	11	4	10	7	13			6¹		3	2			21
1		3	5				8					12	13	9	4	10²	7¹	11³			6	14		2			22
1			5				10	8					11¹	4	12	9³	14				13	6	7³	3	2		23
1		3	5	7			10	8³					11	4	12	9²					13	14	6¹		2		24
1		3	5	6			10¹	8					11	4	13	9²	14				12	7³			2		25
1		3	5	7			12	10					8²	11	4	14	9¹	13				6³			2		26
1		3	5²	6			9						8³	11¹	4	10	12	13	14			7			2		27
1		3		7			9²	13					8²	11	4	10¹	12		5		14	6			2		28
1		3	5	6			9	13		14			8¹	11	4	10²	12					7¹			2		29
1³		3	5	7			9						8²	11	4	10	14				13	6¹		2	12		30
		3	5	7			8	13				14	11		10²			12	4		9	6³		2¹	1		31
		4	5	7			10	13				8³	11		9¹		12		2²			6	3	1	1	14	32
		2	5³	7			9	8					11	4	10¹	12	13				6²	14	3	1			33
1		2		7¹			9	8					11	4	10³	13	14	5³	12			6	3				34
1		2	5	6			9¹	8		14			11	4	10²		12				13	7³	3				35
1		2		7			9	8¹					11	5	10²	13	12		4⁸			6	3				36
1		2	5	7			9¹	8					11²	4	10	12	14				13	6³	3				37
1		2		5			9	8				13	11¹	4	10²	6³	14				12	7	3				38

FA Cup

Third Round	Burnley	(a)	1-1
Replay	Burnley	(h)	4-2
Fourth Round	Leicester C	(h)	1-2

Capital One Cup

Third Round	Nottingham F	(h)	3-1
Fourth Round	Brighton & HA	(h)	2-0
Quarter-Finals	Newcastle U	(h)	4-0
Semi-Finals 1st leg	Sheffield U	(h)	1-0
Semi-Finals 2nd leg	Sheffield U	(a)	2-2
Final	Chelsea	Wembley	0-2

UEFA Europa League

Play-Offs 1st leg	AEL Limassol	(a)	2-1
Play-Offs 2nd leg	AEL Limassol	(h)	3-0
Group C	Partizan Belgrade	(a)	0-0
Group C	Besiktas	(h)	1-1
Group C	Asteras Tripolis	(h)	5-1
Group C	Asteras Tripolis	(a)	2-1
Group C	Partizan Belgrade	(h)	1-0
Group C	Besiktas	(a)	0-1
Round of 32 1st leg	Fiorentina	(h)	1-1
Round of 32 2nd leg	Fiorentina	(a)	0-2

TRANMERE ROVERS

FOUNDATION

Formed in 1884 as Belmont they adopted their present title the following year and eventually joined their first league, the West Lancashire League, in 1889–90, the same year as their first success in the Wirral Challenge Cup. The club almost folded in 1899–1900 when all the players left en bloc to join a rival club, but they survived the crisis and went from strength to strength, winning the 'Combination' title in 1907–08 and the Lancashire Combination in 1913–14. They joined the Football League in 1921 from the Central League.

Prenton Park, Prenton Road West, Birkenhead, Merseyside CH42 9PY.

Telephone: (0333) 014 4452.

Fax: (0151) 609 0606.

Ticket Office: (0333) 014 4452.

Website: www.tranmererovers.co.uk

Email: customerservice@tranmererovers.co.uk

Ground Capacity: 16,587.

Record Attendance: 24,424 v Stoke C, FA Cup 4th rd, 5 February 1972.

Pitch Measurements: 100.5m × 64m (110yd × 70yd)

Chairman: Mark Palios.

Vice Chairman: Nicola Palios.

Manager: Gary Brabin.

Assistant Manager: Alan Rogers.

Physio: Gregg Blundell.

Colours: White shirts with blue and green trim, white shorts with green trim, white socks with blue and green trim.

Year Formed: 1884.

Turned Professional: 1912.

Previous Name: 1884, Belmont AFC; 1885, Tranmere Rovers.

Club Nickname: 'Rovers'.

Grounds: 1884, Steeles Field; 1887, Ravenshaws Field/Old Prenton Park; 1912, Prenton Park.

First Football League Game: 27 August 1921, Division 3 (N), v Crewe Alex (h) W 4–1 – Bradshaw; Grainger, Stuart (1); Campbell, Milnes (1), Heslop; Moreton, Groves (1), Hyam, Ford (1), Hughes.

Record League Victory: 13–4 v Oldham Ath, Division 3 (N), 26 December 1935 – Gray; Platt, Fairhurst; McLaren, Newton, Spencer; Eden, MacDonald (1), Bell (9), Woodward (2), Urmson (1).

Record Cup Victory: 13–0 v Oswestry U, FA Cup 2nd prel rd, 10 October 1914 – Ashcroft; Stevenson, Bullough, Hancock, Taylor, Holden (1), Moreton (1), Cunningham (2), Smith (5), Leck (3), Gould (1).

HONOURS

Football League – Division 1:
Best season: 4th, 1992–93;
Division 3 (N): *Champions* 1937–38;
Division 4: *Runners-up* 1988–89.

FA Cup: Best season: 6th rd, 2000, 2001, 2004.

Football League Cup:
Runners-up 2000.

Welsh Cup: *Winners* 1935;
Runners-up 1934.

Leyland DAF Cup: *Winners* 1990;
Runners-up 1991.

sky SPORTS FACT FILE

Tranmere Rovers attracted an attendance of 17,430 for their Fourth Division home fixture with Bradford Park Avenue on Good Friday 16 April 1965 when both teams were challenging for promotion. The game ended goalless and Rovers went on to miss out on promotion by goal average to Colchester United by the margin of 0.08 goals.

Record Defeat: 1–9 v Tottenham H, FA Cup 3rd rd (replay), 14 January 1953.

Most League Points (2 for a win): 60, Division 4, 1964–65.

Most League Points (3 for a win): 80, Division 4, 1988–89; Division 3, 1989–90; Division 2, 2002–03.

Most League Goals: 111, Division 3 (N), 1930–31.

Highest League Scorer in Season: Bunny Bell, 35, Division 3 (N), 1933–34.

Most League Goals in Total Aggregate: Ian Muir, 142, 1985–95.

Most League Goals in One Match: 9, Bunny Bell v Oldham Ath, Division 3 (N), 26 December 1935.

Most Capped Player: John Aldridge, 30 (69), Republic of Ireland.

Most League Appearances: Harold Bell, 595, 1946–64 (incl. League record 401 consecutive appearances).

Youngest League Player: Iain Hume, 16 years 167 days v Swindon T, 15 April 2000.

Record Transfer Fee Received: £2,250,000 from WBA for Jason Koumas, August 2002.

Record Transfer Fee Paid: £450,000 to Aston Villa for Shaun Teale, August 1995.

Football League Record: 1921 Original Member of Division 3 (N): 1938–39 Division 2; 1946–58 Division 3 (N); 1958–61 Division 3; 1961–67 Division 4; 1967–75 Division 3; 1975–76 Division 4; 1976–79 Division 3; 1979–89 Division 4; 1989–91 Division 3; 1991–92 Division 2; 1992–2001 Division 1; 2001–04 Division 2; 2004–14 FL 1; 2014–15 FL 2; 2015– Conference Premier.

MANAGERS

Bert Cooke 1912–35
Jackie Carr 1935–36
Jim Knowles 1936–39
Bill Ridding 1939–45
Ernie Blackburn 1946–55
Noel Kelly 1955–57
Peter Farrell 1957–60
Walter Galbraith 1961
Dave Russell 1961–69
Jackie Wright 1969–72
Ron Yeats 1972–75
John King 1975–80
Bryan Hamilton 1980–85
Frank Worthington 1985–87
Ronnie Moore 1987
John King 1987–96
John Aldridge 1996–2001
Dave Watson 2001–02
Ray Mathias 2002–03
Brian Little 2003–06
Ronnie Moore 2006–09
John Barnes 2009
Les Parry 2009–12
Ronnie Moore 2012–14
Robert Edwards 2014
Micky Adams 2014–15
Gary Brabin May 2015–

LATEST SEQUENCES

Longest Sequence of League Wins: 9, 9.2.1990 – 19.3.1990.

Longest Sequence of League Defeats: 8, 29.10.1938 – 17.12.1938.

Longest Sequence of League Draws: 5, 26.12.1997 – 31.1.1998.

Longest Sequence of Unbeaten League Matches: 18, 16.3.1970 – 4.9.1970.

Longest Sequence Without a League Win: 16, 8.11.1969 – 14.3.1970.

Successive Scoring Runs: 32 from 24.2.1934.

Successive Non-scoring Runs: 7 from 20.12.1997.

TEN YEAR LEAGUE RECORD

		P	W	D	L	F	A	Pts	Pos
2005-06	FL 1	46	13	15	18	50	52	54	18
2006-07	FL 1	46	18	13	15	58	53	67	9
2007-08	FL 1	46	18	11	17	52	47	65	11
2008-09	FL 1	46	21	11	14	62	49	74	7
2009-10	FL 1	46	14	9	23	45	72	51	19
2010-11	FL 1	46	15	11	20	53	60	56	17
2011-12	FL 1	46	14	14	18	49	53	56	12
2012-13	FL 1	46	19	10	17	58	48	67	11
2013-14	FL 1	46	12	11	23	52	79	47	21
2014-15	FL 2	46	9	12	25	45	67	39	24

DID YOU KNOW ?

Tranmere Rovers featured in an astonishing 6-6 draw with Newcastle United in a Zenith Data Systems Cup clash at Prenton Park in October 1991. John Aldridge scored a hat-trick for Rovers who eventually went through 3-2 on penalties to earn a second round home tie with Grimsby Town.

TRANMERE ROVERS – FOOTBALL LEAGUE TWO 2014–15 LEAGUE RECORD

Match No.	Date	Venue	Opponents	Result	H/T Score	Lg Pos.	Goalscorers	Attendance
1	Aug 9	H	York C	D	1-1	0-0	12	Rowe [90]	6287
2	16	A	Shrewsbury T	L	1-2	1-0	17	Bell-Baggie [42]	5249
3	19	A	Wycombe W	W	2-0	1-0	11	Stockton [19], Power [54]	3005
4	23	H	Cheltenham T	L	2-3	2-0	15	Richards [12], Laird [45]	4607
5	30	H	Morecambe	W	2-1	0-1	11	Stockton 2 [58, 90]	4656
6	Sept 6	A	Accrington S	L	2-3	0-1	15	Bell-Baggie 2 [46, 70]	2151
7	13	A	Hartlepool U	D	0-0	0-0	14		3245
8	16	H	Newport Co	D	0-0	0-0	15		3948
9	20	H	Exeter C	L	1-2	1-1	18	Holmes [25]	4725
10	27	A	Carlisle U	L	0-1	0-0	20		3873
11	Oct 4	A	Bury	L	0-2	0-0	22		4481
12	11	H	Plymouth Arg	L	0-1	0-1	24		4952
13	18	A	Oxford U	L	0-2	0-1	24		4748
14	21	H	Mansfield T	D	0-0	0-0	24		4092
15	25	A	AFC Wimbledon	D	2-2	1-2	23	Gnanduillet 2 [20, 65]	4195
16	Nov 1	H	Stevenage	D	2-2	0-1	23	Ihiekwe [90], Jennings [66]	5456
17	15	A	Luton T	L	0-1	0-0	23		9061
18	22	H	Southend U	L	1-2	0-2	23	Power (pen) [53]	4621
19	29	H	Portsmouth	W	3-1	1-0	23	Fenelon [2], Rowe [68], Power [78]	5163
20	Dec 13	A	Dagenham & R	W	1-0	0-0	22	Power [74]	1840
21	19	H	Cambridge U	D	1-1	0-0	21	Stockton [74]	4578
22	26	A	Burton Alb	L	0-2	0-2	23		4206
23	28	H	Northampton T	W	2-1	1-1	22	Odejayi [32], Kirby [63]	5394
24	Jan 10	A	Morecambe	D	0-0	0-0	23		2232
25	17	A	Accrington S	W	3-0	2-0	22	Donnelly, R 2 [12, 57], Fenelon [23]	4872
26	24	H	Hartlepool U	D	1-1	1-1	21	Odejayi [12]	5488
27	31	A	Exeter C	W	2-1	1-1	17	Myrie-Williams [29], Donnelly, R [50]	4044
28	Feb 7	A	Carlisle U	L	0-2	0-0	21		5358
29	10	A	Newport Co	D	1-1	1-0	20	Donnelly, R [45]	2327
30	14	A	York C	L	0-2	0-1	22		3714
31	21	H	Shrewsbury T	W	2-1	2-0	20	Donnelly, R [29], Holmes [32]	5987
32	24	A	Portsmouth	L	2-3	1-0	20	Myrie-Williams [28], Jones (og) [50]	13,660
33	28	A	Cheltenham T	L	0-2	0-1	20		3070
34	Mar 3	H	Wycombe W	L	1-2	1-2	22	Hugill [32]	4161
35	7	H	Dagenham & R	L	2-3	1-1	23	Gardner [43], Power [87]	4762
36	14	A	Northampton T	L	0-1	0-0	23		4428
37	17	A	Cambridge U	W	2-1	1-0	22	Power [45], Gardner [68]	4202
38	21	H	Burton Alb	L	1-4	1-2	22	Odejayi [35]	5390
39	28	H	AFC Wimbledon	D	1-1	0-1	23	Green [90]	5592
40	Apr 3	A	Stevenage	D	2-2	2-1	23	Myrie-Williams [37], Odejayi [45]	3344
41	6	H	Luton T	L	0-1	0-0	23		6035
42	11	A	Southend U	L	0-1	0-1	23		5846
43	14	A	Mansfield T	L	0-1	0-1	24		3051
44	18	H	Oxford U	L	0-3	0-0	24		5777
45	25	A	Plymouth Arg	L	2-3	1-2	24	Power [34], Odejayi [89]	9769
46	May 2	H	Bury	L	0-1	0-0	24		7518

Final League Position: 24

GOALSCORERS

League (45): Power 7 (1 pen), Donnelly, R 5, Odejayi 5, Stockton 4, Bell-Baggie 3, Myrie-Williams 3, Fenelon 2, Gardner 2, Gnanduillet 2, Holmes 2, Rowe 2, Green 1, Hugill 1, Ihiekwe 1, Jennings 1, Kirby 1, Laird 1, Richards 1, own goal 1.
FA Cup (7): Power 3 (1 pen), Stockton 2, Koumas 1, Odejayi 1.
Capital One Cup (0).
Johnstone's Paint Trophy (5): Power 3, Johnson 1, Odejayi 1.

Fon Williams O 38	Holmes D 33+3	Ihiekwe M 37+1	Holness M 15+2	Myrie-Williams J 16+2	Woodards D 4+1	Kirby J 7+10	Power M 45	Laird M 27+7	Dugdale A 15+1	Richards E 9+4	Kounas J 8+12	Stockton C 15+7	Rowe J 3+4	Bell-Baggie A 8+4	Hume J 3+9	Odejayi K 27+13	Hill M 9+2	Gill M 8	McGahey H 2+2	McDonald C —+1	Donacien J 31	Brezovan P 8	Donnelly G 4+7	Davies B 3	Hugill J 4+2	Fanino M —+1	Barker G 4	Gardner D 2+2	Gnanduillet A 4	Johnson D 4	Jago B —+2	Ridehalgh L 13+5	Jennings S 30	Thompson Josh 15	Gumbs E —+1	Green G 5+1	Aimson W 2	Fenelon S 9+1	Jahraldo-Martin C 1+1	Madjo G —+2	Omotola T —+1	Shuker C 1+2	Donnelly R 15+5	Taylor R 15	Molyneux L 7+4	Duggan M —+1	Match No.
1	2	3	4	5	6	7¹	8		9	10²	11	12	13	14																																	1
1	2²	3		4	10	8	7				11¹			6¹	14		5	9	12																												2
1		3	4	2	10	8	6		9	7	11						5																													3
1	12	4	3	9¹	6³	2	8	10²	7	11	13			14			5																													4
1	2	3				7	8	10¹		11	6	9	12	5					4																											5
	2	3			13	8	7	10²	12	11	9¹	6		5			4	1																												6
1	2	3		9	10	6		11		8¹				5	7		4		12																											7
1	2	4	12	6²	8	11	13	10¹		8¹	7	3	14				5																													8
1	2	4		6	7	10²	14	11³		8	12	9¹		3	13	5																														9
1	2	3		8¹	7		11	13	12	9		6²		4	10³	5	14																													10
1	2	3		13	7	8	14	12		9²	11	6³		4	10¹	5																														11
	5	3	4	7¹	12	13	9	14	11	6³	2	1	8¹		10																															12
	5	4	3	6	12	14	8	13	10³	7²	2	1	9	11¹																																13
1	5	3	4	6²	7	8	13	14		2	12	9¹	10	11³																																14
1	5	3	4	6³	8	7	12			2	14	9¹	10	11¹²	13																															15
1	5¹	3	4	8	6	14	10³			2	13	9	11¹²	12	7																															16
12	2	3	8	7²	13	5¹	1	10	11	9	6	4³	14																																	17
	3	4	8	13	11	12	2	1	6¹	5	7	10²																																		18
1	3	4	12	8	13	11³	7¹	14	2	6	9	5²	10																																	19
1	2	4	5	9	7²	13	12	11	3	6	8	10¹																																		20
1	2	4³	5	12	8	7	13	10¹	3	6	9	11²	14																																	21
1	5		6	8	10	13	2	9¹	7²	4³	11¹	12	14																																	22
1	5	3	13	6	9	12	2	7	4	11	14	8²																																		23
1	2	3	4¹	8	9³	14	10	13	6	7	5	11²	12																																	24
1	2	3	13	8²	12	10	7	4	11¹	6¹	5	9	14																																	25
1	2	3	12	8	13	14	11³	6	4	10¹	7	5	9²																																	26
1	2³	6²	8	3	14	11¹	12	7	4	13	10	5	9																																	27
1	2	6	7	3	14	13	12	10³	8	4¹	11	5	9²																																	28
1	2³	6³	8	13	14	12	10	7	3	11	5	9¹																																		29
1	2	6¹	12	8	3	13	11²	10³	4	7	9	5	14																																	30
1	2	9¹	8	6	4	10	12	7	3	11	5																																			31
1	2	14	7	8	9	4	10	13	12	6	3¹	11²	5³																																	32
1	2	4	6	14	8	13	3	12	11¹	10	7	9²	5³																																	33
1	5	2	14	6	7	3	12	10	4³	11²	13	8¹																																		34
1	13	9	7	3	8²	14	2	10¹	12	6	4³	11	5																																	35
1	3	6	7	11	2	13	10	5	8¹	4³	14	12	9¹																																	36
1	4	9¹	8	6	12	10	3	14	11¹	5	7¹	2²	13																																	37
1	3	6	14	7	8³	4	10	2	11¹	13	5²	9	12																																	38
	3	6	7	4	12	10	2	1	5¹	8	9	11²	13																																	39
	3	9²	7	2	13	11	4	1	5	6	10	8¹	12																																	40
	2	6²	7³	12	4	13	11	3	5	8	10	14	9¹																																	41
1	5	2	12	14	6²	8	4	7	3³	13	9																																			42
1	2	3	6²	7	11³	13	12	14	4	8	9	10¹	5²																																	43
1	2	3	6²	7	12	13	11	10	14	4	8	9¹	5³																																	44
1	2	6	5²	3	7	13	11	9¹	4	8	12	10																																		45
1	2	14	7	4	8¹	9³	11	5	3	13	6	12	10¹																																	46

FA Cup

First Round	Bristol R	(h)	1-0
Second Round	Oxford U	(a)	2-2
Replay	Oxford U	(h)	2-1
Third Round	Swansea C	(h)	2-6

Capital One Cup

First Round	Nottingham F	(h)	0-1

Johnstone's Paint Trophy

Second Round	Carlisle U	(h)	1-1
(Tranmere R won 5-4 on penalties)			
Northern Quarter-Finals	Bury	(a)	2-1
Northern Semi-Finals	Walsall	(h)	2-2
(Walsall won 5-4 on penalties)			

WALSALL

FOUNDATION

Two of the leading clubs around Walsall in the 1880s were Walsall Swifts (formed 1877) and Walsall Town (formed 1879). The Swifts were winners of the Birmingham Senior Cup in 1881, while the Town reached the 4th round (5th round modern equivalent) of the FA Cup in 1883. These clubs amalgamated as Walsall Town Swifts in 1888, becoming simply Walsall in 1895.

Banks's Stadium, Bescot Crescent, Walsall WS1 4SA.
Telephone: (01922) 622 791. *Fax:* (01922) 613 202.
Ticket Office: (01922) 651 414/416.
Website: www.saddlers.co.uk
Email: info@walsallfc.co.uk
Ground Capacity: 10,989.
Record Attendance: 25,453 v Newcastle U, Division 2, 29 August 1961 (at Fellows Park); 11,049 v Rotherham U, Division 1, 9 May 2004 (at Bescot Stadium).
Pitch Measurements: 100.5m × 67m (110yd × 73yd)
Chairman: Jeff Bonser.
Chief Executive: Stefan Gamble.
Manager: Dean Smith.
First Team Coach: Richard O'Kelly.
Physio: Jon Whitney.
Colours: Red shirts with black and white trim, white shorts with red trim, red socks with white trim.
Year Formed: 1888.
Turned Professional: 1888.
Previous Names: Walsall Swifts (founded 1877) and Walsall Town (founded 1879) amalgamated in 1888 as Walsall Town Swifts; 1895, Walsall.
Club Nickname: 'The Saddlers'.
Grounds: 1888, Fellows Park; 1990, Bescot Stadium (renamed Banks's Stadium 2007).
First Football League Game: 3 September 1892, Division 2, v Darwen (h) L 1–2 – Hawkins; Withington, Pinches; Robinson, Whitrick, Forsyth; Marshall, Holmes, Turner, Gray (1), Pangbourn.
Record League Victory: 10–0 v Darwen, Division 2, 4 March 1899 – Tennent; Ted Peers (1), Davies; Hickinbotham, Jenkyns, Taggart; Dean (3), Vail (2), Aston (4), Martin, Griffin.
Record Cup Victory: 7–0 v Macclesfield T (a), FA Cup 2nd rd, 6 December 1997 – Walker; Evans, Marsh, Viveash (1), Ryder, Peron, Boli (2 incl. 1p) (Ricketts), Porter (2), Keates, Watson (Platt), Hodge (2 incl. 1p).
Record Defeat: 0–12 v Small Heath, 17 December 1892; 0–12 v Darwen, 26 December 1896, both Division 2.
Most League Points (2 for a win): 65, Division 4, 1959–60.
Most League Points (3 for a win): 89, FL 2, 2006–07.
Most League Goals: 102, Division 4, 1959–60.

HONOURS

Football League –
Division 2: *Runners-up,* 1998–99;
FL 2: *Champions* 2006–07;
Division 3: *Runners-up* 1960–61, 1994–95;
Division 4: *Champions* 1959–60; *Runners-up* 1979–80.
FA Cup: Best season: 5th rd, 1939, 1975, 1978, 1987, 2002, 2003 and last 16 1889.
Football League Cup: Best season: semi-final, 1984.
Johnstone's Paint Trophy: *Runners-up* 2014–15.

sky SPORTS FACT FILE

Jack Flavell made 22 Football League appearances for Walsall in the 1950s but was better known as a cricketer for Worcestershire. He played in four tests for England and was Wisden Cricketer of the Year in 1965.

Highest League Scorer in Season: Gilbert Alsop, 40, Division 3 (N), 1933–34 and 1934–35.

Most League Goals in Total Aggregate: Tony Richards, 184, 1954–63; Colin Taylor, 184, 1958–63, 1964–68, 1969–73.

Most League Goals in One Match: 5, Gilbert Alsop v Carlisle U, Division 3 (N), 2 February 1935; 5, Bill Evans v Mansfield T, Division 3 (N), 5 October 1935; 5, Johnny Devlin v Torquay U, Division 3 (S), 1 September 1949.

Most Capped Player: Mick Kearns, 15 (18), Republic of Ireland.

Most League Appearances: Colin Harrison, 473, 1964–82.

Youngest League Player: Geoff Morris, 16 years 218 days v Scunthorpe U, 14 September 1965.

Record Transfer Fee Received: £1,000,000 from Coventry C for Scott Dann, January 2008.

Record Transfer Fee Paid: £175,000 to Birmingham C for Alan Buckley, June 1979.

Football League Record: 1892 Elected to Division 2; 1895 Failed re-election; 1896–1901 Division 2; 1901 Failed re-election; 1921 Original Member of Division 3 (N); 1927–31 Division 3 (S); 1931–36 Division 3 (N); 1936–58 Division 3 (S); 1958–60 Division 4; 1960–61 Division 3; 1961–63 Division 2; 1963–79 Division 3; 1979–80 Division 4; 1980–88 Division 3; 1988–89 Division 2; 1989–90 Division 3; 1990–92 Division 4; 1992–95 Division 3; 1995–99 Division 2; 1999–2000 Division 1; 2000–01 Division 2; 2001–04 Division 1; 2004–06 FL 1; 2006–07 FL 2; 2007– FL 1.

LATEST SEQUENCES

Longest Sequence of League Wins: 7, 9.4.2005 – 9.8.2005.

Longest Sequence of League Defeats: 15, 29.10.1988 – 4.2.1989.

Longest Sequence of League Draws: 5, 7.5.1988 – 17.9.1988.

Longest Sequence of Unbeaten League Matches: 21, 6.11.1979 – 22.3.1980.

Longest Sequence Without a League Win: 18, 15.10.1988 – 4.2.1989.

Successive Scoring Runs: 27 from 6.11.1979.

Successive Non-scoring Runs: 5 from 10.4.2004.

MANAGERS

H. Smallwood 1888–91 *(Secretary-Manager)*
A. G. Burton 1891–93
J. H. Robinson 1893–95
C. H. Ailso 1895–96 *(Secretary-Manager)*
A. E. Parsloe 1896–97 *(Secretary-Manager)*
L. Ford 1897–98 *(Secretary-Manager)*
G. Hughes 1898–99 *(Secretary-Manager)*
L. Ford 1899–1901 *(Secretary-Manager)*
J. E. Shutt 1908–13 *(Secretary-Manager)*
Haydn Price 1914–20
Joe Burchell 1920–26
David Ashworth 1926–27
Jack Torrance 1927–28
James Kerr 1928–29
Sid Scholey 1929–30
Peter O'Rourke 1930–32
Bill Slade 1932–34
Andy Wilson 1934–37
Tommy Lowes 1937–44
Harry Hibbs 1944–51
Tony McPhee 1951
Brough Fletcher 1952–53
Major Frank Buckley 1953–55
John Love 1955–57
Billy Moore 1957–64
Alf Wood 1964
Reg Shaw 1964–68
Dick Graham 1968
Ron Lewin 1968–69
Billy Moore 1969–72
John Smith 1972–73
Ronnie Allen 1973
Doug Fraser 1973–77
Dave Mackay 1977–78
Alan Ashman 1978
Frank Sibley 1979
Alan Buckley 1979–86
Neil Martin *(Joint Manager with Buckley)* 1981–82
Tommy Coakley 1986–88
John Barnwell 1989–90
Kenny Hibbitt 1990–94
Chris Nicholl 1994–97
Jan Sorensen 1997–98
Ray Graydon 1998–2002
Colin Lee 2002–04
Paul Merson 2004–06
Kevin Broadhurst 2006
Richard Money 2006–08
Jimmy Mullen 2008–09
Chris Hutchings 2009–11
Dean Smith January 2011–

TEN YEAR LEAGUE RECORD

		P	W	D	L	F	A	Pts	Pos
2005-06	FL 1	46	11	14	21	47	70	47	24
2006-07	FL 2	46	25	14	7	66	34	89	1
2007-08	FL 1	46	16	16	14	52	46	64	12
2008-09	FL 1	46	17	10	19	61	66	61	13
2009-10	FL 1	46	16	14	16	60	63	62	10
2010-11	FL 1	46	12	12	22	56	75	48	20
2011-12	FL 1	46	10	20	16	51	57	50	19
2012-13	FL 1	46	17	17	12	65	58	68	9
2013-14	FL 1	46	14	16	16	49	49	58	13
2014-15	FL 1	46	14	17	15	50	54	59	14

DID YOU KNOW ?

Walsall player Walter Kimberley was taken prisoner of war in the first few months of the 1914–18 conflict. Kimberley, who served in the Coldstream Guards, was held in Germany before being released in an exchange of prisoners. He contracted consumption while captive and passed away in 1917.

WALSALL – FOOTBALL LEAGUE ONE 2014–15 LEAGUE RECORD

Match No.	Date		Venue	Opponents	Result	H/T Score	Lg Pos.	Goalscorers	Atten-dance
1	Aug	9	A	Port Vale	D	1-1	0-1	12	Bradshaw [59]	7050
2		16	H	Bradford C	D	0-0	0-0	16		4520
3		19	H	Yeovil T	L	1-2	0-0	20	Bradshaw [72]	3758
4		23	A	Leyton Orient	D	0-0	0-0	20		4400
5		30	A	Scunthorpe U	L	1-2	0-0	22	Bradshaw [70]	3098
6	Sept	6	H	Colchester U	D	0-0	0-0	21		4009
7		13	H	Preston NE	W	3-1	1-1	18	Sawyers [7], Bradshaw [49], Downing [76]	4776
8		16	H	Rochdale	L	0-4	0-3	20		2082
9		20	A	Gillingham	D	0-0	0-0	20		5344
10		27	H	Doncaster R	W	3-0	1-0	17	Baxendale [45], Bradshaw [57], Forde [64]	3741
11	Oct	4	H	Bristol C	D	1-1	0-1	16	Sawyers [85]	5574
12		11	A	Oldham Ath	L	1-2	1-1	18	Cook [10]	4178
13		18	H	Crewe Alex	L	0-1	0-0	21		4127
14		21	A	Crawley T	L	0-1	0-0	23		2204
15		25	H	Chesterfield	W	1-0	0-0	19	Bradshaw [61]	4230
16	Nov	1	A	Notts Co	W	2-1	1-1	16	Jones (og) [16], Bradshaw (pen) [64]	5884
17		15	H	Peterborough U	D	0-0	0-0	16		5495
18		22	A	Fleetwood T	W	1-0	1-0	14	Sawyers [35]	3224
19		29	A	Coventry C	D	0-0	0-0	13		8076
20	Dec	13	H	Barnsley	W	3-1	2-1	12	Cook 2 [31, 90], Bradshaw [34]	4433
21		20	A	Sheffield U	D	1-1	0-0	13	Bradshaw [59]	20,209
22		26	H	Swindon T	L	1-4	1-1	15	Bradshaw [18]	5696
23		28	A	Milton Keynes D	W	3-0	1-0	11	Potter (og) [4], Bradshaw 2 [62, 77]	9311
24	Jan	3	A	Coventry C	L	0-2	0-1	13		5930
25		10	H	Scunthorpe U	L	1-4	0-2	15	Cain [51]	3738
26		17	A	Colchester U	W	2-0	1-0	14	Forde [33], Cain [75]	2980
27	Feb	1	H	Gillingham	D	1-1	0-0	15	Grimes [74]	3951
28		7	A	Doncaster R	W	2-0	1-0	12	Cook [3], Hiwula [70]	6089
29		10	A	Rochdale	W	3-2	3-0	10	O'Connor [13], Forde [19], Hiwula [22]	3567
30		14	H	Port Vale	L	0-1	0-1	13		4504
31		21	A	Bradford C	D	1-1	0-0	14	Hiwula [74]	13,534
32		24	A	Preston NE	L	0-1	0-1	14		7779
33		28	H	Leyton Orient	L	0-2	0-0	16		5239
34	Mar	3	A	Yeovil T	W	1-0	1-0	16	Hiwula [32]	3668
35		7	A	Barnsley	L	0-3	0-1	16		9275
36		14	H	Milton Keynes D	D	1-1	1-1	16	Bradshaw [8]	3887
37		17	H	Sheffield U	D	1-1	0-1	15	Grimes [71]	3950
38		28	A	Chesterfield	L	0-1	0-0	16		6358
39	Apr	3	H	Notts Co	D	0-0	0-0	16		4353
40		6	A	Peterborough U	D	0-0	0-0	15		6711
41		11	H	Fleetwood T	W	1-0	0-0	15	Bradshaw [86]	3534
42		14	H	Crawley T	W	5-0	1-0	15	Hiwula 2 [16, 66], Morris [67], Taylor [81], Cook [90]	3296
43		18	A	Crewe Alex	D	1-1	0-1	15	Bradshaw [81]	4644
44		21	A	Swindon T	D	3-3	1-0	14	Morris [18], Hiwula [53], Sawyers [74]	6305
45		25	H	Oldham Ath	W	2-0	2-0	11	Bradshaw 2 (1 pen) [18, 24 (p)]	4699
46	May	3	A	Bristol C	L	2-8	2-2	14	Hiwula 2 [13, 36]	11,960

Final League Position: 14

GOALSCORERS

League (50): Bradshaw 17 (2 pens), Hiwula 9, Cook 5, Sawyers 4, Forde 3, Cain 2, Grimes 2, Morris 2, Baxendale 1, Downing 1, O'Connor 1, Taylor 1, own goals 2.
FA Cup (2): Bradshaw 2.
Capital One Cup (2): Benning 1, Morris 1.
Johnstone's Paint Trophy (6): Forde 2, Bradshaw 1, Cain 1, Manset 1, Sawyers 1.

O'Donnell R 44	O'Connor J 30+2	Chambers J 31	Downing P 33+2	Taylor A 37+2	Benning M 11+9	Sawyers R 37+5	Chambers A 45	Baxendale J 17+11	Grimes A 11+16	Bradshaw T 29	Clifford B 7+6	Bakayoko A —+7	Kinsella L 4	Holden D 2+2	Forde A 24+13	Morris K 9+5	Flanagan R 9+7	Manset M 4+15	Butler A 7	Cook J 27+5	Purkiss B 31+1	Cain M 28+4	Mantom S 6+6	Henry R 4+5	Hiwula J 17+2	Preston M —+1	Murphy J —+2	MacGillivray C 2	Match No.
1	2	3	4	5	6	7	8	9²	10	11¹	12	13																	1
1	4²	3		5	10¹	9	6			8	11	7		2	12	13													2
1		3		5	10¹	9¹	7			8	11	6²	14	2	4	12	13												3
1			4	5		12	7	6²	11¹	10	8³			2	3	9	14	13											4
1	2	3¹	4	5			7	13	6²	10	8				12	9¹	14		11										5
1	3	4	5	14		6	12		10	8²		2		13	9³	7¹	11												6
1	2	3		5	10	9¹	7²	14		11¹	12				8	6	13			4									7
1	2	3		5	9	10			13	14		7³			6¹	12	8	11²		4									8
1	2	3		5¹	12	10¹	7		9	11³			14		6		8	13		4									9
1	2	3		5		10²	7	9	14	11¹	12				6		8³	13		4									10
1	2	3		5		10	7	9¹		11³	13				6		8²	14	4	12									11
1	2	3		5		7	9	10³		8¹					6²	13	14	12	4	11									12
1		4		5	9³	10	8	14			13				6¹		7²	12	3	11	2								13
1		4	3	5		7	6	8²	12						10³		13			11¹	2	9	14						14
1		4	3	5	14	7	6	8¹		11					12			13		10²	2	9³	13						15
1		4	3	5	12	10¹	7			14	11²				9		13			6³	2	8							16
1		3	4	5	13	10	7			12					9²		11¹			6	2	8							17
1		4	3	5		10	7	6³	9²		13				12		14			11¹	2	8							18
1		4	3	5		10	7	6¹	9²						12		13			11	2	8							19
1		4	3			10	8	6²		11¹					12		13			9	2	7	5						20
1		4	3		13	10³	8	6²	14	11					12					9¹	2	7	5						21
1		3	4			10	7		12	11²					6		13			9	2	8	5						22
1	2	4	3	5	12	10	8	13		11⁴					6¹		14			9³	7								23
1	2	4³	3	5	12	10	8	9¹		11					6²		14			13	7								24
1	2	4	3	5		10⁸	8			13	11				6³		12	14		9²	7								25
1	4²	3	12	5¹		10	7	13			11				6					9¹	2	8	14						26
1	12	4¹	3	5		10	7			13	11²				6					9	2	8							27
1	3		4	5		9³	7	13	11²						10	14				8	2	6¹		12					28
1	4		3	5		9	7	12							8³					10²	2	6¹		13	11	14			29
1	4		3	5		8	9	6²	12						10					2	7¹		13	11¹³	14				30
1	3		4	5¹		8²	7	14	13						10					6¹	2	9		12	11				31
1	3	4		12		13	6	14	8¹						10²					9	2	7		5²	11				32
1	3	4		5		10	7	13	11²		14						12			9¹	2	8³		6					33
1		4	3	5		9	6	8¹	12	11					7²					2	13			10					34
1	12	2	4	5		7	6	9¹	13	10					8³					3²	14			11					35
1	3		4	5		9	7			11					12					8²	2	6		10¹	13				36
1	3		4	5	10	8		12				13			6					9²	2	14	7³	11¹					37
1	3	4		5	12		9¹	8²							7³	14				11	2	13	6	10					38
1	3	4		5		9	6		13			14			12	10³				11²	2	7		8¹					39
1	3	4		5		10²	7					14			12	6				11¹	2	8	13	9³					40
1	4	3		5		9	6			11³					10²					8¹	2	7	14	13	12				41
1	4	3		5		7²	6			10³					14		13			2	8¹	12		11					42
1	4		3	5		8²	7			11					6¹					12	2	9	13	10					43
1	4	3		5	13	7			11					12	10¹					14	2	6	8²	9³					44
	3	4		5	13	7³			11¹	6					12		14			2	9²	8	10					1	45
	3	4	12	13	5³	14	6			10					9					2¹	7²	8	11					1	46

FA Cup

First Round	Shrewsbury T	(h)	2-2
Replay	Shrewsbury T	(a)	0-1

Capital One Cup

First Round	Southend U	(a)	2-1
Second Round	Crystal Palace	(h)	0-3

Johnstone's Paint Trophy

Second Round	Rochdale	(a)	1-0
Northern Quarter-Finals	Sheffield U	(h)	1-0
Northern Semi-Finals	Tranmere R	(a)	2-2
(*Walsall won 5-4 on penalties*)			
Northern Final 1st leg	Preston NE	(a)	2-0
Northern Final 2nd leg	Preston NE	(h)	0-0
Final	Bristol C	Wembley	0-2

WATFORD

FOUNDATION

The club was formed as Watford Rovers in 1881. The name was changed to West Herts in 1893 and then the name Watford was adopted after rival club Watford St Mary's was absorbed in 1898.

Vicarage Road Stadium, Vicarage Road, Watford, Hertfordshire WD18 0ER.

Telephone: (01923) 496 000.

Fax: (01923) 496 001.

Ticket Office: (01923) 496 001.

Website: www.watfordfc.com

Email: yourvoice@watfordfc.com

Ground Capacity: 17,477.

Record Attendance: 34,099 v Manchester U, FA Cup 4th rd (replay), 3 February 1969.

Pitch Measurements: 100.5m × 67.5m (110yd × 74yd)

Executive Chairman: Raffaele Riva.

Chief Executive: Scott Duxbury.

Head Coach: Quique Flores.

Assistant Coach: Dean Austin.

Physio: Kevin Powell.

Colours: Yellow shirts with black trim, black shorts with yellow trim, yellow socks with black trim.

Year Formed: 1881.

Turned Professional: 1897.

Previous Names: 1881, Watford Rovers; 1893, West Herts; 1898, Watford.

Club Nickname: 'The Hornets'.

Grounds: 1883, Vicarage Meadow, Rose and Crown Meadow; 1889, Colney Butts; 1890, Cassio Road; 1922, Vicarage Road.

First Football League Game: 28 August 1920, Division 3, v QPR (a) W 2–1 – Williams; Horseman, Fred Gregory; Bacon, Toone, Wilkinson; Bassett, Ronald (1), Hoddinott, White (1), Waterall.

Record League Victory: 8–0 v Sunderland, Division 1, 25 September 1982 – Sherwood; Rice, Rostron, Taylor, Terry, Bolton, Callaghan (2), Blissett (4), Jenkins (2), Jackett, Barnes.

Record Cup Victory: 10–1 v Lowestoft T, FA Cup 1st rd, 27 November 1926 – Yates; Prior, Fletcher (1); Frank Smith, Bert Smith, Strain; Stephenson, Warner (3), Edmonds (3), Swan (1), Daniels (1), (1 og).

Record Defeat: 0–10 v Wolverhampton W, FA Cup 1st rd (replay), 24 January 1912.

HONOURS

Football League – FL C: *Runners-up* 2014–15;
Division 1: *Runners-up* 1982–83;
Division 2: *Champions* 1997–98;
Runners-up 1981–82;
Division 3: *Champions* 1968–69;
Runners-up 1978–79;
Division 4: *Champions* 1977–78.
FA Cup: *Runners-up* 1984; semi-final, 1970, 1984, 1987, 2003, 2007.
Football League Cup: Best season: semi-final, 1979, 2005.
European Competitions
UEFA Cup: 1983–84.

sky SPORTS FACT FILE

Watford were involved in a marathon FA Cup encounter with Nottingham Forest in January 1946 which lasted 328 minutes. The teams were level after two 90-minute legs, with the second game being abandoned in extra time due to poor light. The replay at White Hart Lane was decided in the Hornets' favour 15 minutes into extra time.

Most League Points (2 for a win): 71, Division 4, 1977–78.

Most League Points (3 for a win): 89, FL C, 2014–15

Most League Goals: 92, Division 4, 1959–60.

Highest League Scorer in Season: Cliff Holton, 42, Division 4, 1959–60.

Most League Goals in Total Aggregate: Luther Blissett, 148, 1976–83, 1984–88, 1991–92.

Most League Goals in One Match: 5, Eddie Mummery v Newport Co, Division 3 (S), 5 January 1924.

Most Capped Players: John Barnes, 31 (79), England; Kenny Jackett, 31, Wales.

Most League Appearances: Luther Blissett, 415, 1976–83, 1984–88, 1991–92.

Youngest League Player: Keith Mercer, 16 years 125 days v Tranmere R, 16 February 1973.

Record Transfer Fee Received: £9,600,000 from Aston Villa for Ashley Young, January 2007.

Record Transfer Fee Paid: £6,300,000 to Tottenham H for Etienne Capoue, July 2015.

Football League Record: 1920 Original Member of Division 3; 1921–58 Division 3 (S); 1958–60 Division 4; 1960–69 Division 3; 1969–72 Division 2; 1972–75 Division 3; 1975–78 Division 2; 1978–79 Division 3; 1979–82 Division 2; 1982–88 Division 1; 1988–92 Division 2; 1992–96 Division 1; 1996–98 Division 2; 1998–99 Division 1; 1999–2000 FA Premier League; 2000–04 Division 1; 2004–06 FL C; 2006–07 FA Premier League; 2007–15 FL C; 2015– FA Premier League.

LATEST SEQUENCES

Longest Sequence of League Wins: 7, 28.8.2000 – 14.10.2000.

Longest Sequence of League Defeats: 9, 26.12.1972 – 27.2.1973.

Longest Sequence of League Draws: 7, 16.2.2008 – 22.3.2008.

Longest Sequence of Unbeaten League Matches: 22, 1.10.1996 – 1.3.1997.

Longest Sequence Without a League Win: 19, 27.11.1971 – 8.4.1972.

Successive Scoring Runs: 22 from 20.8.1985.

Successive Non-scoring Runs: 7 from 18.12.1971.

MANAGERS

John Goodall 1903–10
Harry Kent 1910–26
Fred Pagnam 1926–29
Neil McBain 1929–37
Bill Findlay 1938–47
Jack Bray 1947–48
Eddie Hapgood 1948–50
Ron Gray 1950–51
Haydn Green 1951–52
Len Goulden 1952–55
  (General Manager to 1956)
Johnny Paton 1955–56
Neil McBain 1956–59
Ron Burgess 1959–63
Bill McGarry 1963–64
Ken Furphy 1964–71
George Kirby 1971–73
Mike Keen 1973–77
Graham Taylor 1977–87
Dave Bassett 1987–88
Steve Harrison 1988–90
Colin Lee 1990
Steve Perryman 1990–93
Glenn Roeder 1993–96
Graham Taylor 1996
Kenny Jackett 1996–97
Graham Taylor 1997–2001
Gianluca Vialli 2001–02
Ray Lewington 2002–05
Adrian Boothroyd 2005–08
Brendan Rodgers 2008–09
Malky Mackay 2009–11
Sean Dyche 2011–12
Gianfranco Zola 2012–13
Beppe Sannino 2013–14
Oscar Garcia 2014
Billy McKinlay 2014
Slavisa Jokanovic 2014–15
Quique Flores June 2015–

TEN YEAR LEAGUE RECORD

		P	W	D	L	F	A	Pts	Pos
2005-06	FL C	46	22	15	9	77	53	81	3
2006-07	PR Lge	38	5	13	20	29	59	28	20
2007-08	FL C	46	18	16	12	62	56	70	6
2008-09	FL C	46	16	10	20	68	72	58	13
2009-10	FL C	46	14	12	20	61	68	54	16
2010-11	FL C	46	16	13	17	77	71	61	14
2011-12	FL C	46	16	16	14	56	64	64	11
2012-13	FL C	46	23	8	15	85	58	77	3
2013-14	FL C	46	15	15	16	74	64	60	13
2014-15	FL C	46	27	8	11	91	50	89	2

DID YOU KNOW ?

Fred Titmus, who won 53 caps for the England cricket team and was a mainstay of the national side for many years as a spin bowler, was on the books of Watford as a youngster before his cricket career took off. He played for the reserves but never made the first team.

WATFORD – FL CHAMPIONSHIP 2014–15 LEAGUE RECORD

Match No.	Date	Venue	Opponents	Result	H/T Score	Lg Pos.	Goalscorers	Attendance
1	Aug 9	H	Bolton W	W 3-0	2-0	2	Deeney [17], Vydra [23], Forestieri [80]	15,546
2	16	A	Norwich C	L 0-3	0-1	12		26,375
3	19	A	Rotherham U	W 2-0	0-0	7	Dyer [74], Munari [87]	9361
4	23	H	Leeds U	W 4-1	1-1	2	Forestieri 2 [20, 67], Deeney (pen) [58], Tozser [90]	15,674
5	30	H	Huddersfield T	W 4-2	1-0	2	Deeney [15], Abdi 2 [54, 90], Andrews [68]	14,409
6	Sept 13	A	Charlton Ath	L 0-1	0-1	4		17,628
7	16	A	Blackpool	W 1-0	0-0	3	Vydra (pen) [68]	9695
8	20	H	Bournemouth	D 1-1	0-0	4	Cathcart [83]	14,320
9	27	A	Blackburn R	D 2-2	2-0	3	Vydra [30], Tozser [41]	14,084
10	30	H	Brentford	W 2-1	1-0	3	Ighalo [42], Vydra [70]	15,502
11	Oct 4	H	Brighton & HA	D 1-1	0-0	2	Tozser [53]	16,531
12	18	A	Sheffield W	W 3-0	2-0	1	Ighalo [21], Abdi [38], Vydra [69]	20,909
13	21	H	Nottingham F	D 2-2	1-1	2	Ighalo [29], Vydra (pen) [52]	16,095
14	25	A	Middlesbrough	D 1-1	0-0	2	Deeney [61]	17,491
15	Nov 1	H	Millwall	W 3-1	2-1	1	Vydra [36], Tozser [45], Munari [64]	17,000
16	4	A	Birmingham C	L 1-2	1-1	3	Forestieri [7]	18,309
17	8	A	Ipswich T	L 0-1	0-0	5		22,490
18	22	H	Derby Co	L 1-2	0-1	7	Munari [67]	17,421
19	29	H	Cardiff C	L 0-1	0-1	7		15,668
20	Dec 5	A	Fulham	W 5-0	3-0	6	Abdi 2 [15, 51], Deeney 3 (1 pen) [20 (p), 37, 90]	16,772
21	13	A	Wigan Ath	W 2-1	1-1	6	Deeney 2 [20, 82]	15,297
22	20	H	Reading	W 1-0	0-0	6	Abdi [70]	18,522
23	26	H	Wolverhampton W	L 0-1	0-0	6		17,443
24	28	A	Cardiff C	W 4-2	2-1	5	Guedioura 2 [42, 63], Ighalo [45], Angella [83]	22,208
25	Jan 10	A	Huddersfield T	L 1-3	0-0	6	Ighalo [65]	13,843
26	17	A	Charlton Ath	W 5-0	3-0	6	Cathcart [15], Deeney [25], Ighalo 2 [44, 58], Tozser [90]	17,703
27	24	H	Blackpool	W 7-2	0-2	6	Ighalo 4 [47, 54, 73, 81], Deeney [53], Vydra [59], Angella [66]	17,015
28	30	A	Bournemouth	L 0-2	0-1	6		10,904
29	Feb 7	H	Blackburn R	W 1-0	0-0	6	Ighalo [83]	15,011
30	10	A	Brentford	W 2-1	0-0	5	Ighalo 2 [68, 90]	10,524
31	14	A	Bolton W	W 4-3	1-2	5	Ighalo [25], Abdi [69], Ekstrand [74], Deeney [90]	14,230
32	21	H	Norwich C	L 0-3	0-0	6		18,602
33	24	H	Rotherham U	W 3-0	1-0	6	Ighalo 2 [18, 56], Deeney [54]	13,468
34	28	A	Leeds U	W 3-2	1-2	3	Deeney [39], Vydra 2 [56, 81]	24,705
35	Mar 3	H	Fulham	W 1-0	1-0	3	Deeney [9]	15,809
36	7	A	Wolverhampton W	D 2-2	1-1	3	Vydra [30], Deeney [65]	23,146
37	14	H	Reading	W 4-1	2-0	2	Abdi [1], Vydra [39], Deeney [48], Forestieri [85]	16,660
38	17	A	Wigan Ath	W 2-0	0-0	1	Deeney 2 (1 pen) [54, 90 (p)]	10,684
39	21	H	Ipswich T	L 0-1	0-0	2		19,038
40	Apr 3	A	Derby Co	D 2-2	1-1	4	Vydra [23], Ighalo [75]	31,748
41	6	H	Middlesbrough	W 2-0	1-0	3	Deeney [37], Ighalo [65]	19,656
42	11	A	Millwall	W 2-0	1-0	3	Vydra [26], Guedioura [56]	12,075
43	15	H	Nottingham F	W 3-1	2-0	3	Ighalo [4], Connolly [41], Abdi [87]	20,723
44	18	H	Birmingham C	W 1-0	0-0	1	Cathcart [56]	19,156
45	25	A	Brighton & HA	W 2-0	1-0	1	Deeney [29], Vydra [90]	28,841
46	May 2	H	Sheffield W	D 1-1	1-0	2	Vydra [25]	20,250

Final League Position: 2

GOALSCORERS

League (91): Deeney 21 (3 pens), Ighalo 20, Vydra 16 (2 pens), Abdi 9, Forestieri 5, Tozser 5, Cathcart 3, Guedioura 3, Munari 3, Angella 2, Andrews 1, Connolly 1, Dyer 1, Ekstrand 1.
FA Cup (0).
Capital One Cup (2): Dyer 2.

Gomes H 44	Tamas G 6+1	Ekstrand J 23+1	Angella G 32+3	Paredes J 32+7	Abdi A 28+4	McGugan L 5+1	Tozser D 34+11	Pudil D 19+4	Deeney T 37+5	Vydra M 31+11	Munari G 21+7	Forestieri F 10+14	Dyer L 4+10	Andrews K 4+5	Hoban T 20+7	Fabbrini D 2	Anya I 27+8	Ighalo O 22+13	Murray S 2+4	Cathcart C 28+1	Doyley L 5+1	Bassong S 11	Bond J 2+1	Guedioura A 13+4	Layun M 14+3	Byers G —+1	Watson B 19+1	Mensah B —+1	Motta M 7+2	Connolly M 4+2	Match No.
1	2	3	4	5	6	7[2]	8	9[1]	10	11[2]	12	13	14																		1
1	2	3[4]	4	5	6[3]	7[1]	8	9	10	11[1]		13	12	14																	2
1	2	3		5			14		10	11[2]	6	13	8	4			7[3]	9[1] 12													3
1		3	4	5[3]	8[2]		6	9	10		7	11[1]		14	2		12	13													4
1	2[4]	3	4	14	6		8	9	10	7[3]	11[2]		12	13			5[1]														5
1		3	4	12	6	8[2]	7	9	10	11[1]		13		2[3]			5	14													6
1	14	3	4	2	7[3]	9[1]	8	5	10	11[2]		12			6		13														7
1	4[2]	3		2	8[1]		7	5	10		13	11[3]		9	14	6	12														8
1	14	3	2		6	5		10	9	13	12		7[3]	11[2]	8[1]	4															9
1		3		2	13		6	5[1]	10[1]	9		8		14	7[2]	12	11[3]	4													10
1		4		2	9[1]	12	7		11	6		10[2]		5		8		13	3												11
1		3		12	6[2]		7	5	14	9	8	10[3]	13			11[1]			2	4											12
1		3		2	6[1]		7	5	13	9	8	10		14			11[3] 12			4[2]											13
1		3		2			7	5	12	9	6	10[2]		13			8	11[1]		4	1										14
1		4		2			7	5[2]	11	10[3]	6		13	8	12			9		14	3[1]										15
1		3		2		6	7		11	13			9[1]		12	4		8	10[2]		5										16
1		3		2			7	5	10	9	6	11[2]		8[1]			12	13			4										17
1		3		2			7		11	12	13	9	10[1]	6[3]			14	8[2]		5	4	1									18
1		3	4	5[2]	6[1]		7		10	11	8	12			9					2		13									19
1		3	5	8			7[2] 14		10	11[3]	6	12			9[1]					2		4	13								20
1		2	5[2]	6[1]			7		10	11[2]	8		12				9	13		4		3	14								21
1		2[4]	12	8			7		9	10[3] 11[2]			13				5[1]	14		3		4	6								22
1			5	8			7[2]		10	11[1]	6[3]	13					9	12		3	2	4	14								23
1		4	5[1]	6[3]			13	9	14			8	11[2]				12	10		3			7								24
1[2]		4		8			7	9[1]	10	11[3]	6						2	14	13	3				12		5					25
1		3	5				7	12	10	13	8[3]						4	9[1] 11[2]		2					6	14					26
1		3	5				7[3] 14	11		9	13						4[1]	8[2] 10		2					6		12				27
1		3[4]					7	12	10[2] 13	6[1]							4	9 11[3]		2					5		8 14				28
1		3	5	13			14		10	12	8						4[2]	9 11		2					6[1]	7[3]					29
1		4	2	12			7		11[3] 13		10						14	5[1] 9		3					8	6[2]					30
1		3	4[1]	5	8		14		12	10[2]		13						9 11		2					6	7[3]					31
1		3[4]	4	5	6		14		10	13 12								9 11		2					8[2]	7[3]					32
1		3	4		9		8		10[2] 13	12 14				5				11[3]		2					6[1]	7					33
1	4[2]	12	2[1]	9			8		10 11	13				14			5			3					6[3]	7					34
1		3		6[2]				9[1] 10 11[1]			14						4		13	2					8 12	7	5				35
1		4	2[1]	9[3]	8			10 11 12 13							5[·]					3					6	7[1]	14				36
1		3 14		9[1]	8	5		10 11[2]		12							4								6[·] 13	7	2				37
1		3	4 13				14		11	10[2] 6 12		5						2[3]		9					8	7[1]					38
1	4[2]	12					8[1]		11 14		5						13 10		3					9 6[3]	7	2				39
1		4					12		11 10[1]								13 9[2]		3					7 8[·]	6	2[·] 14				40
1		3	5				7		10 13								4	9 11[3]		2[1]					6[·] 14	8	12				41
1		3	5[·] 12				7		10 11[1]		4						9[·] 13							6	8	14 2				42
1		3	13	8			14		10		12						9[·] 11		2					6	7	5[1] 4[2]				43
1		4	2	9[3]			14		11	10[1]	5						12 13		3					6 8[2]	7					44
1	2	5	8[1]	12			11 13			14							9[2] 10[1]		3					6	7			4		45
1		3	12	8			13		10 11[3]								9[1] 14		2					6	7	5[2] 4				46

FA Cup
Third Round   Chelsea   (a)   0-3

Capital One Cup
First Round   Stevenage   (a)   1-0
Second Round   Doncaster R   (h)   1-2

WEST BROMWICH ALBION

FOUNDATION

There is a well known story that when employees of Salter's Spring Works in West Bromwich decided to form a football club, they had to send someone to the nearby Association Football stronghold of Wednesbury to purchase a football. A weekly subscription of 2d (less than 1p) was imposed and the name of the new club was West Bromwich Strollers.

The Hawthorns, West Bromwich, West Midlands B71 4LF.

Telephone: (0871) 271 1100.

Fax: (0871) 271 9851.

Ticket Office: (0121) 227 2227.

Website: www.wba.co.uk

Email: enquiries@wbafc.co.uk

Ground Capacity: 26,445.

Record Attendance: 64,815 v Arsenal, FA Cup 6th rd, 6 March 1937.

Pitch Measurements: 105m × 68m (114yd × 74yd)

Chairman: Jeremy Peace.

Chief Executive: Mark Jenkins.

Head Coach: Tony Pulis.

Assistant Head Coaches: David Kemp and Mark O'Connor.

Physio: Richie Rawlins.

Colours: White shirts with navy blue stripes, navy blue shorts with white trim, navy blue socks with white hoops.

Year Formed: 1878.

Turned Professional: 1885.

Previous Name: 1878, West Bromwich Strollers; 1881, West Bromwich Albion.

Club Nicknames: 'The Throstles', 'The Baggies', 'Albion'.

Grounds: 1878, Coopers Hill; 1879, Dartmouth Park; 1881, Bunns Field, Walsall Street; 1882, Four Acres (Dartmouth Cricket Club); 1885, Stoney Lane; 1900, The Hawthorns.

First Football League Game: 8 September 1888, Football League, v Stoke (a) W 2–0 – Roberts; Jack Horton, Green; Ezra Horton, Perry, Bayliss; Bassett, Woodhall (1), Hendry, Pearson, Wilson (1).

Record League Victory: 12–0 v Darwen, Division 1, 4 April 1892 – Reader; Jack Horton, McCulloch; Reynolds (2), Perry, Groves; Bassett (3), McLeod, Nicholls (1), Pearson (4), Geddes (1), (1 og).

Record Cup Victory: 10–1 v Chatham (away), FA Cup 3rd rd, 2 March 1889 – Roberts; Jack Horton, Green; Timmins (1), Charles Perry, Ezra Horton; Bassett (2), Walter Perry (1), Bayliss (2), Pearson, Wilson (3), (1 og).

HONOURS

Football League – Division 1:
Champions 1919–20;
Runners-up 1924–25, 1953–54, 2001–02, 2003–04.
FL C: *Champions* 2007–08;
Runners-up 2009–10.
Division 2: *Champions* 1901–02, 1910–11; *Runners-up* 1930–31, 1948–49.
FA Cup: *Winners* 1888, 1892, 1931, 1954, 1968; *Runners-up* 1886, 1887, 1895, 1912, 1935.
Football League Cup: *Winners* 1966; *Runners-up* 1967, 1970.
European Competitions
European Cup-Winners' Cup: 1968–69.
European Fairs Cup: 1966–67.
UEFA Cup: 1978–79, 1979–80, 1981–82.

sky SPORTS FACT FILE

Harold Bache was capped for the England AFA team, which was then separated from the Football Association, scoring 7 goals in a 20-0 victory over France in March 1910. He later signed for West Bromwich Albion and won representative honours for the Football League but was killed in action at Ypres on 16 February 1916.

Record Defeat: 3–10 v Stoke C, Division 1, 4 February 1937.

Most League Points (2 for a win): 60, Division 1, 1919–20.

Most League Points (3 for a win): 91, FL C, 2009–10.

Most League Goals: 105, Division 2, 1929–30.

Highest League Scorer in Season: William 'Ginger' Richardson, 39, Division 1, 1935–36.

Most League Goals in Total Aggregate: Tony Brown, 218, 1963–79.

Most League Goals in One Match: 6, Jimmy Cookson v Blackpool, Division 2, 17 September 1927.

Most Capped Player: James Morrison, 39, Scotland.

Most League Appearances: Tony Brown, 574, 1963–80.

Youngest League Player: Charlie Wilson, 16 years 73 days v Oldham Ath, 1 October 1921.

Record Transfer Fee Received: £8,000,000 from Aston Villa for Curtis Davies, July 2008.

Record Transfer Fee Paid: £10,000,000 to Dynamo Kyiv for Brown Ideye, July 2014.

Football League Record: 1888 Founder Member of Football League; 1901–02 Division 2; 1902–04 Division 1; 1904–11 Division 2; 1911–27 Division 1; 1927–31 Division 2; 1931–38 Division 1; 1938–49 Division 2; 1949–73 Division 1; 1973–76 Division 2; 1976–86 Division 1; 1986–91 Division 2; 1991–92 Division 3; 1992–93 Division 2; 1993–2002 Division 1; 2002–03 FA Premier League; 2003–04 Division 1; 2004–06 FA Premier League; 2006–08 FL C; 2008–09 FA Premier League; 2009–10 FL C; 2010– FA Premier League.

LATEST SEQUENCES

Longest Sequence of League Wins: 11, 5.4.1930 – 8.9.1930.

Longest Sequence of League Defeats: 11, 28.10.1995 – 26.12.1995.

Longest Sequence of League Draws: 5, 30.8.1999 – 3.10.1999.

Longest Sequence of Unbeaten League Matches: 17, 7.9.1957 – 7.12.1957.

Longest Sequence Without a League Win: 15, 16.10.2004 – 16.1.2005.

Successive Scoring Runs: 36 from 26.4.1958.

Successive Non-scoring Runs: 4 from 1.3.2003.

MANAGERS

Louis Ford 1890–92
(Secretary-Manager)
Henry Jackson 1892–94
(Secretary-Manager)
Edward Stephenson 1894–95
(Secretary-Manager)
Clement Keys 1895–96
(Secretary-Manager)
Frank Heaven 1896–1902
(Secretary-Manager)
Fred Everiss 1902–48
Jack Smith 1948–52
Jesse Carver 1952
Vic Buckingham 1953–59
Gordon Clark 1959–61
Archie Macaulay 1961–63
Jimmy Hagan 1963–67
Alan Ashman 1967–71
Don Howe 1971–75
Johnny Giles 1975–77
Ronnie Allen 1977
Ron Atkinson 1978–81
Ronnie Allen 1981–82
Ron Wylie 1982–84
Johnny Giles 1984–85
Nobby Stiles 1985–86
Ron Saunders 1986–87
Ron Atkinson 1987–88
Brian Talbot 1988–91
Bobby Gould 1991–92
Ossie Ardiles 1992–93
Keith Burkinshaw 1993–94
Alan Buckley 1994–97
Ray Harford 1997
Denis Smith 1997–1999
Brian Little 1999–2000
Gary Megson 2000–04
Bryan Robson 2004–06
Tony Mowbray 2006–09
Roberto Di Matteo 2009–11
Roy Hodgson 2011–12
Steve Clarke 2012–13
Pepe Mel 2014
Alan Irvine 2014
Tony Pulis January 2015–

TEN YEAR LEAGUE RECORD

		P	W	D	L	F	A	Pts	Pos
2005-06	PR Lge	38	7	9	22	31	58	30	19
2006-07	FL C	46	22	10	14	81	55	76	4
2007-08	FL C	46	23	12	11	88	55	81	1
2008-09	PR Lge	38	8	8	22	36	67	32	20
2009-10	FL C	46	26	13	7	89	48	91	2
2010-11	PR Lge	38	12	11	15	56	71	47	11
2011-12	PR Lge	38	13	8	17	45	52	47	10
2012-13	PR Lge	38	14	7	17	53	57	49	8
2013-14	PR Lge	38	7	15	16	43	59	36	17
2014-15	PR Lge	38	11	11	16	38	51	44	13

DID YOU KNOW ?

West Bromwich Albion were the subject of a short documentary film, *The Saturday Men*, made in 1962. The film was part of the Ford Motor Company's Look at Britain series and took a behind the scenes look at the club and the lives of the players.

WEST BROMWICH ALBION – FA PREMIERSHIP 2014–15 LEAGUE RECORD

Match No.	Date	Venue	Opponents	Result	H/T Score	Lg Pos.	Goalscorers	Attendance
1	Aug 16	H	Sunderland	D	2-2	1-1	6	Berahino 2 (1 pen) [42 (p), 74]	25,468
2	23	A	Southampton	D	0-0	0-0	11		27,598
3	30	A	Swansea C	L	0-3	0-2	17		20,318
4	Sept 13	A	Everton	L	0-2	0-1	19		23,567
5	21	A	Tottenham H	W	1-0	0-0	16	Morrison [74]	35,861
6	28	H	Burnley	W	4-0	2-0	10	Dawson [30], Berahino 2 [45, 56], Dorrans [90]	24,286
7	Oct 4	A	Liverpool	L	1-2	0-1	13	Berahino (pen) [56]	44,708
8	20	H	Manchester U	D	2-2	1-0	14	Sessegnon [8], Berahino [66]	25,794
9	25	H	Crystal Palace	D	2-2	0-2	12	Anichebe [51], Berahino (pen) [90]	24,738
10	Nov 1	A	Leicester C	W	1-0	0-0	10	Cambiasso (og) [47]	31,819
11	9	H	Newcastle U	L	0-2	0-1	13		26,476
12	22	A	Chelsea	L	0-2	0-2	13		41,600
13	29	H	Arsenal	L	0-1	0-0	15		24,228
14	Dec 2	H	West Ham U	L	1-2	1-2	16	Dawson [10]	23,975
15	6	A	Hull C	D	0-0	0-0	16		23,279
16	13	H	Aston Villa	W	1-0	0-0	14	Gardner [72]	24,684
17	20	A	QPR	L	2-3	2-1	14	Lescott [10], Varela [20]	17,560
18	26	H	Manchester C	L	1-3	0-3	15	Ideye [87]	26,040
19	28	A	Stoke C	L	0-2	0-0	16		27,070
20	Jan 1	A	West Ham U	D	1-1	1-1	17	Berahino [42]	34,914
21	10	H	Hull C	W	1-0	0-0	14	Berahino [78]	24,818
22	19	A	Everton	D	0-0	0-0	14		34,739
23	31	H	Tottenham H	L	0-3	0-2	15		25,079
24	Feb 8	A	Burnley	D	2-2	1-2	15	Brunt [45], Ideye [67]	16,904
25	11	A	Swansea C	W	2-0	0-0	14	Ideye [60], Berahino [74]	23,516
26	21	A	Sunderland	D	0-0	0-0	14		40,943
27	28	H	Southampton	W	1-0	1-0	13	Berahino [2]	25,303
28	Mar 3	A	Aston Villa	L	1-2	0-1	13	Berahino [66]	31,272
29	14	H	Stoke C	W	1-0	1-0	13	Ideye [19]	24,323
30	21	A	Manchester C	L	0-3	0-2	13		45,018
31	Apr 4	H	QPR	L	1-4	0-3	14	Anichebe [58]	25,735
32	11	H	Leicester C	L	2-3	2-1	14	Fletcher [8], Gardner [26]	26,768
33	18	A	Crystal Palace	W	2-0	1-0	13	Morrison [2], Gardner [53]	24,765
34	25	H	Liverpool	D	0-0	0-0	13		26,663
35	May 2	A	Manchester U	L	1-0	0-0	13	Olsson [63]	75,454
36	9	A	Newcastle U	D	1-1	1-1	13	Anichebe [32]	47,894
37	18	H	Chelsea	W	3-0	1-0	13	Berahino 2 (1 pen) [9, 47 (p)], Brunt [60]	24,750
38	24	A	Arsenal	L	1-4	0-4	13	McAuley [57]	59,971

Final League Position: 13

GOALSCORERS

League (38): Berahino 14 (4 pens), Ideye 4, Anichebe 3, Gardner 3, Brunt 2, Dawson 2, Morrison 2, Dorrans 1, Fletcher 1, Lescott 1, McAuley 1, Olsson 1, Sessegnon 1, Varela 1, own goal 1.
FA Cup (13): Berahino 5, Anichebe 3, Ideye 2, Morrison 2, Brunt 1.
Capital One Cup (5): Berahino 1, Ideye 1, McAuley 1, own goals 2.

Foster B 28	Wisdom A 22+2	Dawson C 29	Olsson J 9+4	Pocognoli S 15	Dorrans G 19+2	Gardner C 30+5	Mulumbu Y 10+7	Brunt C 33+1	Berahino S 32+6	Anichebe V 11+10	Baird C 9+10	Sessegnon S 20+8	Yacob C 16+4	Ideye B 13+11	Davidson J 1+1	Morrison J 29+4	Gamboa C 1+9	Samaras G —+5	Blanco S —+3	Lescott J 34	Myhill B 10+1	Varela S 3+4	McAuley G 24	McManaman C 5+3	Fletcher D 15	Match No.
1	2	3	4	5	6^1	7^2	8	9^2	10	11	12	13	14													1
1	2	3	4	5^1	10	7	8	9	6^1	11^2				14		12	13									2
1	2	3	4		10^1	7	8	9^2	6		12					5^3	13	14								3
1	2	3	4	5^1	6	8		9^1	10					11^2		7	14	12	13							4
1	2	3		5	8	7		10	11	12				9^1		6				4						5
1	2	3		5^2	8	7^1		10	11					9^3	14	6	13	12		4						6
1		3		5	8^3	6	12	10^2	11					9		7^1	2	14	13	4						7
	2	3		5	8	6	12	10	11					9^1		7				4	1					8
1	2	3		5	8^2	7		10	11	12				9^1		6			13	4						9
1	2	3		5^3	8	7		10	11^1	13				9^3	12	6	14			4						10
1	2	3		5^3	6^1		7^2	9	11	10				13		8	12	14		4						11
1	2	3			8^2	7		10	11^1	13		5^3	9	$6^•$		14	12			4						12
1	2	3		5^1	8	7		6^2	10	11	12			9^1			13	14		4						13
1	2	3			8	7^1	12	6^2	10	11		5^3	9		14					4		13				14
1	2			5	8	7^1	6		13	11^2			10^2	14		9				4		12	3			15
1	2			5	8^1	10			12				6			11	7			4		9	3			16
1	2			5^1	7	9			12				8			11^2	6	13		4		10	3			17
1	2			5^2	9^3	7	12	11					8			14	6	13		4		10^1	3			18
1	2				8^1	9	14	6	13			5	10^2	11		7^3				4		12	3			19
1	2				8^3		7^2	10	11^1			5	9	12	13	6				4		14	3			20
1	2				13			6	10	12	5	9^2	7	11^1		8				4		3				21
1	2				13	9		6	10^3	11^2	5	12	7	14		8^1				4		3				22
1	2^1	4				14	13	9	11	10			7	12		8^3				5		3		6^2		23
1	2					8	12	10^2	5^1	11	7	13		14		4				3		9^3	7			24
1	2				13		5	9			12	6	11	8^1		4				3		10^2	7			25
1	2				9^1		5	10		12		8	11	6^1		4				3		13	7			26
1	2				9	12	5	11^2		14	13	7	10^1	6^2		4				3			8			27
1	2				10		5	9		12		7	11	8^1		4				3			6			28
1^3	2	14			8		5	10^1	13	6		11^2	9			4	12			3		7				29
	2	4			8	13		11^2	12	9	6^1		10			5	1	$3^•$				7				30
		13			6^1	$14^•$	5	11	12	2^3	9^2		10			8	4	1		3		7				31
	2	13			6^3		5	10	12		14	8	11^2			9^1	4	1		3		7				32
12	2^3	13			9^1		5	10^2	11	14		8				6	4	1		3		7				33
	2				6		5	11^3	10^2	14		7	13			9^1	4	1		3		12	8			34
14	2	4			6^1	7^2	10	11^3		12		8	13			9				5	1	3				35
	2	4			6^3	9^1	10	13	11^2			12	8			5	1					3	14	7		36
	2	4			12			11^3	10		14		7	13		8^1	5	1		3		9^2	6			37
	2	4^1			13			11	10	12	14		7^2			8	5	1		3		9^2	6			38

FA Cup

Third Round	Gateshead	(h)	7-0	
Fourth Round	Birmingham C	(a)	2-1	
Fifth Round	West Ham U	(h)	4-0	
Sixth Round	Aston Villa	(a)	0-2	

Capital One Cup

Second Round	Oxford U	(h)	1-1
(aet; WBA won 7-6 on penalties)			
Third Round	Hull C	(h)	3-2
Fourth Round	Bournemouth	(a)	1-2

WEST HAM UNITED

FOUNDATION

Thames Ironworks FC was formed by employees of this famous shipbuilding company in 1895 and entered the FA Cup in their initial season at Chatham and the London League in their second. The committee wanted to introduce professional players, so Thames Ironworks was wound up in June 1900 and relaunched a month later as West Ham United.

The Boleyn Ground, Upton Park, Green Street, London E13 9AZ.

Telephone: (020) 8548 2748.

Fax: (020) 8548 2758.

Ticket Office: (0871) 529 1966.

Website: www.whufc.com

Email: customerservices@westhamunited.co.uk

Ground Capacity: 35,345.

Record Attendance: 42,322 v Tottenham H, Division 1, 17 October 1970.

Pitch Measurements: 100.58m × 66m (109yd × 72yd)

Joint Chairmen: David Sullivan and David Gold.

Vice-chairman: Karren Brady.

Manager: Slaven Bilic.

Assistant Coach: Julian Dicks.

Physio: Dominic Rogan.

Colours: Claret shirts with sky blue trim, sky blue shorts with claret trim, claret socks with sky blue trim.

Year Formed: 1895.

Turned Professional: 1900.

Previous Name: 1895, Thames Ironworks FC; 1900, West Ham United.

Club Nicknames: 'The Hammers', 'The Irons'.

Grounds: 1895, Memorial Recreation Ground, Canning Town; 1904, Boleyn Ground.

First Football League Game: 30 August 1919, Division 2, v Lincoln C (h) D 1–1 – Hufton; Cope, Lee; Lane, Fenwick, McCrae; David Smith, Moyes (1), Puddefoot, Morris, Bradshaw.

Record League Victory: 8–0 v Rotherham U, Division 2, 8 March 1958 – Gregory; Bond, Wright; Malcolm, Brown, Lansdowne; Grice, Smith (2), Keeble (2), Dick (4), Musgrove. 8–0 v Sunderland, Division 1, 19 October 1968 – Ferguson; Bonds, Charles; Peters, Stephenson, Moore (1); Redknapp, Boyce, Brooking (1), Hurst (6), Sissons.

HONOURS

Football League – Division 1:
Runners-up 1992–93
Division 2: *Champions* 1957–58, 1980–81; *Runners-up* 1922–23, 1990–91.
FA Cup: *Winners* 1964, 1975, 1980; *Runners-up* 1923, 2006.
Football League Cup:
Runners-up 1966, 1981.
European Competitions
European Cup-Winners' Cup:
1964–65 (*winners*), 1965–66, 1975–76 (*runners-up*), 1980–81.
UEFA Cup: 1999–2000; 2006–07.
Intertoto Cup: 1999 (*winners*).

sky SPORTS FACT FILE

Charlie Paynter joined West Ham United as a player in 1900. He never made a first-team appearance and his career was ended by injury, but he subsequently joined the club's backroom staff and stayed for almost half a century, serving as manager from November 1932 until August 1950.

Record Cup Victory: 10–0 v Bury, League Cup 2nd rd (2nd leg), 25 October 1983 – Parkes; Stewart (1), Walford, Bonds (Orr), Martin (1), Devonshire (2), Allen, Cottee (4), Swindlehurst, Brooking (2), Pike.

Record Defeat: 2–8 v Blackburn R, Division 1, 26 December 1963.

Most League Points (2 for a win): 66, Division 2, 1980–81.

Most League Points (3 for a win): 88, Division 1, 1992–93.

Most League Goals: 101, Division 2, 1957–58.

Highest League Scorer in Season: Vic Watson, 42, Division 1, 1929–30.

Most League Goals in Total Aggregate: Vic Watson, 298, 1920–35.

Most League Goals in One Match: 6, Vic Watson v Leeds U, Division 1, 9 February 1929; 6, Geoff Hurst v Sunderland, Division 1, 19 October 1968.

Most Capped Player: Bobby Moore, 108, England.

Most League Appearances: Billy Bonds, 663, 1967–88.

MANAGERS
Syd King 1902–32
Charlie Paynter 1932–50
Ted Fenton 1950–61
Ron Greenwood 1961–74
(continued as General Manager to 1977)
John Lyall 1974–89
Lou Macari 1989–90
Billy Bonds 1990–94
Harry Redknapp 1994–2001
Glenn Roeder 2001–03
Alan Pardew 2003–06
Alan Curbishley 2006–08
Gianfranco Zola 2008–10
Avram Grant 2010–11
Sam Allardyce 2011–15
Slaven Bilic June 2015–

Youngest League Player: Billy Williams, 16 years 221 days v Blackpool, 6 May 1922.

Record Transfer Fee Received: £18,000,000 from Leeds U for Rio Ferdinand, November 2000.

Record Transfer Fee Paid: £15,000,000 to Liverpool for Andy Carroll, July 2013.

Football League Record: 1919 Elected to Division 2; 1923–32 Division 1; 1932–58 Division 2; 1958–78 Division 1; 1978–81 Division 2; 1981–89 Division 1; 1989–91 Division 2; 1991–93 Division 1; 1993–2003 FA Premier League; 2003–04 Division 1; 2004–05 FL C; 2005–11 FA Premier League; 2011–12 FL C; 2012– FA Premier League.

LATEST SEQUENCES

Longest Sequence of League Wins: 9, 19.10.1985 – 14.12.1985.

Longest Sequence of League Defeats: 9, 28.3.1932 – 29.8.1932.

Longest Sequence of League Draws: 5, 7.3.2012 – 24.3.2012.

Longest Sequence of Unbeaten League Matches: 27, 27.12.80 – 10.10.81.

Longest Sequence Without a League Win: 17, 31.1.1976 – 21.8.1976.

Successive Scoring Runs: 27 from 5.10.1957.

Successive Non-scoring Runs: 5 from 17.9.2006.

TEN YEAR LEAGUE RECORD

		P	W	D	L	F	A	Pts	Pos
2005-06	PR Lge	38	16	7	15	52	55	55	9
2006-07	PR Lge	38	12	5	21	35	59	41	15
2007-08	PR Lge	38	13	10	15	42	50	49	10
2008-09	PR Lge	38	14	9	15	42	45	51	9
2009-10	PR Lge	38	8	11	19	47	66	35	17
2010-11	PR Lge	38	7	12	19	43	70	33	20
2011-12	FL C	46	24	14	8	81	48	86	3
2012-13	PR Lge	38	12	10	16	45	53	46	10
2013-14	PR Lge	38	11	7	20	40	51	40	13
2014-15	PR Lge	38	12	11	15	44	47	47	12

DID YOU KNOW ?

Thames Ironworks, forerunners of West Ham United, were pioneers of floodlit football, playing several matches under electric light in the 1895–96 season at their Canning Town ground. Opponents included Woolwich Arsenal and West Bromwich Albion.

WEST HAM UNITED – FA PREMIERSHIP 2014–15 LEAGUE RECORD

Match No.	Date	Venue	Opponents	Result	H/T Score	Lg Pos.	Goalscorers	Attendance
1	Aug 16	H	Tottenham H	L	0-1	0-0	18		34,977
2	23	A	Crystal Palace	W	3-1	2-0	6	Zarate [34], Downing [37], Cole, C [62]	24,242
3	30	H	Southampton	L	1-3	1-1	10	Noble [27]	34,907
4	Sept 15	A	Hull C	D	2-2	0-1	13	Valencia [50], Sakho [67]	21,275
5	20	H	Liverpool	W	3-1	2-1	8	Reid [2], Sakho [7], Amalfitano [88]	34,977
6	27	A	Manchester U	L	1-2	1-2	11	Sakho [37]	75,317
7	Oct 5	H	QPR	W	2-0	1-0	7	Onuoha (og) [5], Sakho [59]	34,907
8	18	A	Burnley	W	3-1	0-0	4	Sakho [49], Valencia [54], Cole, C [70]	18,936
9	25	H	Manchester C	W	2-1	1-0	4	Amalfitano [21], Sakho [75]	34,977
10	Nov 1	A	Stoke C	D	2-2	0-1	5	Valencia [60], Downing [73]	27,174
11	8	H	Aston Villa	D	0-0	0-0	4		34,857
12	22	A	Everton	L	1-2	0-1	6	Zarate [56]	39,182
13	29	H	Newcastle U	W	1-0	0-0	5	Cresswell [56]	34,977
14	Dec 2	A	WBA	W	2-1	2-1	5	Nolan [35], Tomkins [45]	23,975
15	7	H	Swansea C	W	3-1	1-1	3	Carroll 2 [41, 66], Sakho [87]	34,125
16	13	A	Sunderland	D	1-1	1-1	4	Downing [29]	41,694
17	20	H	Leicester C	W	2-0	1-0	4	Carroll [24], Downing [56]	34,977
18	26	A	Chelsea	L	0-2	0-1	5		41,589
19	28	H	Arsenal	L	1-2	0-2	6	Kouyate [54]	34,977
20	Jan 1	A	WBA	D	1-1	1-1	7	Sakho [10]	34,914
21	10	A	Swansea C	D	1-1	1-0	7	Carroll [43]	20,745
22	18	H	Hull C	W	3-0	0-0	7	Carroll [49], Amalfitano [69], Downing [72]	34,914
23	31	A	Liverpool	L	0-2	0-0	8		44,718
24	Feb 8	H	Manchester U	D	1-1	0-0	8	Kouyate [49]	34,499
25	11	A	Southampton	D	0-0	0-0	8		31,241
26	22	A	Tottenham H	D	2-2	1-0	8	Kouyate [22], Sakho [62]	35,837
27	28	H	Crystal Palace	L	1-3	0-1	9	Valencia [76]	34,857
28	Mar 4	A	Chelsea	L	0-1	0-1	10		34,927
29	14	A	Arsenal	L	0-3	0-1	10		60,002
30	21	H	Sunderland	W	1-0	0-0	9	Sakho [88]	34,914
31	Apr 4	A	Leicester C	L	1-2	1-1	9	Kouyate [32]	31,863
32	11	A	Stoke C	D	1-1	1-0	9	Cresswell [7]	34,946
33	19	A	Manchester C	L	0-2	0-2	10		45,041
34	25	A	QPR	D	0-0	0-0	10		18,036
35	May 2	H	Burnley	W	1-0	1-0	9	Noble (pen) [24]	34,946
36	9	A	Aston Villa	L	0-1	0-1	10		39,294
37	16	H	Everton	L	1-2	0-0	11	Downing [62]	34,977
38	24	A	Newcastle U	L	0-2	0-0	12		52,094

Final League Position: 12

GOALSCORERS

League (44): Sakho 10, Downing 6, Carroll 5, Kouyate 4, Valencia 4, Amalfitano 3, Cole, C 2, Cresswell 2, Noble 2 (1 pen), Zarate 2, Nolan 1, Reid 1, Tomkins 1, own goal 1.
FA Cup (4): Cole, C 1, Collins 1, Sakho 1, Valencia 1.
Capital One Cup (1): Sakho 1.

Adrian 38	O'Brien J 6 + 3	Collins J 21 + 6	Reid W 29 + 1	Cresswell A 38	Noble M 27 + 1	Kouyate C 30 + 1	Downing S 37	Nolan K 19 + 10	Vaz Te R 3 + 1	Cole C 8 + 15	Demel G 3 + 3	Diame M — + 3	Valencia E 25 + 7	Tomkins J 20 + 2	Zarate M 5 + 2	Sakho D 20 + 3	Poyet D 1 + 2	Morrison R — + 1	Song A 25 + 3	Jenkinson C 29 + 3	Amalfitano M 14 + 10	Jarvis M 4 + 7	Carroll A 12 + 2	Jaaskelainen J — + 1	Nene A — + 8	Burke R 4 + 1	Lee E — + 1	Match No
1	2¹	3⁴	4	5	6	7	8	9	10²	11³	12	13	14															1
1	2		4	5	7	6	8²	10	11³				14	3	9¹	12	13											2
1	2		4	5	6	7	8	10²	11¹	13			14	3	9³		12											3
1			4	5	6	7	8			2²			11	3	9³	10¹			6	13	14							4
1	14		4	5	6	7	9			2³			11¹	3		10			8²	12	13							5
1			4	5		9	14		12	2³			11	3		8	7¹		6	13	10²							6
1			4	5			8	12					11¹	3	9²	10			6	2	7	13						7
1	3	4	5	7		9	13	12					11¹			10			6²	2	8							8
1	3	4	5	7	12	9	14	13					11³			10²			6	2	8¹							9
1	3	4¹	5	6³	8	9	14						10	12					7	2	11²							10
1	3	4	5	7²	8³	9	12						11¹			10			6	2		14						11
1		4	5	6	9²			8	14	11¹				3	12					2	7³	13	10					12
1	3		5	6	7¹	9	13							4	12					2	8	10²	11					13
1	12	4	5		6	10	7		14				13	3	9³					2	8¹		11²					14
1	13	14	4	5		7²	8	9					10²	3		12			6	2¹			11					15
1			4	5		8	9	7¹					12	3		10			6	2			11					16
1	12		4	5		8	9	6²					13	3¹		10³			7	2	14		11					17
1	3		4	5	7¹	8	9³	6					11			12			13	2	14		10²					18
1	2¹		4	5		8²	9	14				13	12	3		10³			6		7		11					19
1	3	4	5		8	9		14					13			11³			6	2	7¹	12	10²					20
1		4	5	6	7		9	8¹					10²	3				13		2	12		11					21
1	14	3³	12	5	6³		8	9					10	4¹					7	2	13		11					22
1	2	3¹	4	5	12		8	9	13	14			11						6		7³		10²					23
1			5	7	3	9	8						11¹	4		10			6	2	12							24
1*			5		3	8		10³					11²	4		10			7	2	6	12	13	14				25
1	14		4	5	6²	8	9			12³			11¹	3		10			7	2	13							26
1			4	5	8	7	9						10	3		11			6¹	2					12			27
1	12	4²	5	7	6¹	9	8						11	3		10				2					13			28
1	2	3		5	6²	4	8	9								11			7		12	10¹			13			29
1	14	3		5	7	4	8	9¹		12						11³			6	2	10²				13			30
1	3	4	5	6	8	9	10²			13						11³			7¹	2	12				14			31
1	3	4	5	7	8	9	13		12				11²			10¹			6³	2	14							32
1	3	4	5	6	8	9	13		10¹				11						7²	2		12						33
1	3		5	8	7	6	10		12				11						2		9¹					4		34
1	3		5	6	7	8	9²		13				11¹						2	10					12	4		35
1	3		5	6³	7	8	9¹		14				11			13			2	10¹					12	4		36
1	3²	4	5	6	7	9			10¹				11						8	2					13	12		37
1		4	5	6²	8	9		11					10³	13					7	2	12					3¹	14	38

FA Cup

Third Round	Everton	(a)	1-1
Replay	Everton	(h)	2-2
(aet; West Ham U won 9-8 on penalties)			
Fourth Round	Bristol C	(a)	1-0
Fifth Round	WBA	(a)	0-4

Capital One Cup

Second Round	Sheffield U	(h)	1-1
(aet; Sheffield U won 5-4 on penalties)			

WIGAN ATHLETIC

FOUNDATION

Following the demise of Wigan Borough and their resignation from the Football League in 1931, a public meeting was called in Wigan at the Queen's Hall in May 1932 at which a new club, Wigan Athletic, was founded in the hope of carrying on in the Football League. With this in mind, they bought Springfield Park for £2,250, but failed to gain admission to the Football League until 46 years later.

The DW Stadium, Loire Drive, Wigan, Lancashire WN5 0UZ.

Telephone: (01942) 774 000.

Fax: (01942) 770 477.

Ticket Office: (0871) 663 3552.

Website: www.wiganlatics.co.uk

Email: feedback@wiganathletic.com

Ground Capacity: 25,133.

Record Attendance: 27,526 v Hereford U, 12 December 1953 (at Springfield Park); 25,133 v Manchester U, FA Premier League, 11 May 2008 (at DW Stadium).

Pitch Measurements: 105m × 68m (114yd × 74.5yd)

Chairman: David Sharpe.

Chief Executive: Jonathan Jackson.

Manager: Gary Caldwell.

Assistant Manager: Graham Barrow.

Physios: Russell Hitchin and Alex Cribley.

Colours: Blue and white striped shirts with blue sleeves, black shorts, blue socks with white trim.

Year Formed: 1932.

Turned Professional: 1932.

Club Nickname: 'The Latics'.

Grounds: 1932, Springfield Park; 1999, JJB Stadium (renamed the DW Stadium in 2009).

First Football League Game: 19 August 1978, Division 4, v Hereford U (a) D 0–0 – Brown; Hinnigan, Gore, Gillibrand, Ward, Davids, Corrigan, Purdie, Houghton, Wilkie, Wright.

Record League Victory: 7–1 v Scarborough, Division 3, 11 March 1997 – Lee Butler; John Butler, Sharp (Morgan), Greenall, McGibbon (Biggins (1)), Martinez (1), Diaz (2), Jones (Lancashire (1)), Lowe (2), Rogers, Kilford.

Record Cup Victory: 6–0 v Carlisle U (a), FA Cup 1st rd, 24 November 1934 – Caunce; Robinson, Talbot; Paterson, Watson, Tufnell; Armes (2), Robson (1), Roberts (2), Felton, Scott (1).

Record Defeat: 1–9 v Tottenham H, FA Premier League, 22 November 2009.

HONOURS

Football League – FL C:
Runners-up 2004–05;
Division 2: *Champions* 2002–03;
Division 3: *Champions* 1996–97.
FA Cup: *Winners* 2013.
Football League Cup:
Runners-up 2006.
Freight Rover Trophy: *Winners* 1985.
Auto Windscreens Shield:
Winners 1999.
European Competitions
Europa League: 2013–14.

sky|SPORTS FACT FILE

Goalkeeper Roy Carroll was the first Wigan Athletic player to win a full international cap when he came on as a substitute for Northern Ireland against Thailand in May 1997, shortly after signing from Hull City. At the time he had yet to make an appearance for the Latics.

Most League Points (2 for a win): 55, Division 4, 1978–79 and 1979–80.

Most League Points (3 for a win): 100, Division 2, 2002–03.

Most League Goals: 84, Division 3, 1996–97.

Highest League Scorer in Season: Graeme Jones, 31, Division 3, 1996–97.

Most League Goals in Total Aggregate: Andy Liddell, 70, 1998–2004.

Most League Goals in One Match: Not more than three goals by one player.

Most Capped Players: Kevin Kilbane, 22 (110), Republic of Ireland; Henri Camara, 22 (99), Senegal.

Most League Appearances: Kevin Langley, 317, 1981–86, 1990–94.

Youngest League Player: Steve Nugent, 16 years 132 days v Leyton Orient, 16 September 1989.

Record Transfer Fee Received: £15,250,000 from Manchester U for Antonio Valencia, June 2009.

Record Transfer Fee Paid: £6,500,000 to Estudiantes for Mauro Boselli, August 2010.

Football League Record: 1978 Elected to Division 4; 1982–92 Division 3; 1992–93 Division 2; 1993–97 Division 3; 1997–2003 Division 2; 2003–04 Division 1; 2004–05 FL C; 2005–13 FA Premier League; 2013–15 FL C; 2015– FL 1.

LATEST SEQUENCES

Longest Sequence of League Wins: 11, 2.11.2002 – 18.1.2003.

Longest Sequence of League Defeats: 8, 10.9.2011 – 6.11.2011.

Longest Sequence of League Draws: 6, 11.12.2001 – 5.1.2002.

Longest Sequence of Unbeaten League Matches: 25, 8.5.1999 – 3.1.2000.

Longest Sequence Without a League Win: 14, 9.5.1989 – 17.10.1989.

Successive Scoring Runs: 24 from 27.4.1996.

Successive Non-scoring Runs: 4 from 17.2.2001.

MANAGERS

Charlie Spencer 1932–37
Jimmy Milne 1946–47
Bob Pryde 1949–52
Ted Goodier 1952–54
Walter Crook 1954–55
Ron Suart 1955–56
Billy Cooke 1956
Sam Barkas 1957
Trevor Hitchen 1957–58
Malcolm Barrass 1958–59
Jimmy Shirley 1959
Pat Murphy 1959–60
Allenby Chilton 1960
Johnny Ball 1961–63
Allan Brown 1963–66
Alf Craig 1966–67
Harry Leyland 1967–68
Alan Saunders 1968
Ian McNeill 1968–70
Gordon Milne 1970–72
Les Rigby 1972–74
Brian Tiler 1974–76
Ian McNeill 1976–81
Larry Lloyd 1981–83
Harry McNally 1983–85
Bryan Hamilton 1985–86
Ray Mathias 1986–89
Bryan Hamilton 1989–93
Dave Philpotts 1993
Kenny Swain 1993–94
Graham Barrow 1994–95
John Deehan 1995–98
Ray Mathias 1998–99
John Benson 1999–2000
Bruce Rioch 2000–01
Steve Bruce 2001
Paul Jewell 2001–07
Chris Hutchings 2007
Steve Bruce 2007–09
Roberto Martinez 2009–13
Owen Coyle 2013
Uwe Rosler 2013–14
Malky Mackay 2014–15
Gary Caldwell April 2015–

TEN YEAR LEAGUE RECORD

		P	W	D	L	F	A	Pts	Pos
2005-06	PR Lge	38	15	6	17	45	52	51	10
2006-07	PR Lge	38	10	8	20	37	59	38	17
2007-08	PR Lge	38	10	10	18	34	51	40	14
2008-09	PR Lge	38	12	9	17	34	45	45	11
2009-10	PR Lge	38	9	9	20	37	79	36	16
2010-11	PR Lge	38	9	15	14	40	61	42	16
2011-12	PR Lge	38	11	10	17	42	62	43	15
2012-13	PR Lge	38	9	9	20	47	73	36	18
2013-14	FL C	46	21	10	15	61	48	73	5
2014-15	FL C	46	9	12	25	39	64	39	23

DID YOU KNOW

Wigan Athletic had a difficult first season in the Football League after they were elected for the 1978–79 season. They failed to score in their first 3 games and after 5 games were bottom of the table. The Latics recovered and finished the season in a respectable 6th place.

WIGAN ATHLETIC – FL CHAMPIONSHIP 2014–15 LEAGUE RECORD

Match No.	Date	Venue	Opponents	Result	H/T Score	Lg Pos.	Goalscorers	Atten- dance
1	Aug 9	H	Reading	D	2-2	1-0	9	McManaman [27], McArthur [90]	12,174
2	16	A	Charlton Ath	L	1-2	1-1	18	McManaman [22]	15,334
3	19	A	Cardiff C	L	0-1	0-0	21		20,662
4	23	H	Blackpool	W	1-0	1-0	17	Riera [35]	12,113
5	30	H	Birmingham C	W	4-0	3-0	12	McManaman 2 [9, 45], Taylor [39], Waghorn [78]	11,708
6	Sept 13	A	Blackburn R	L	1-3	0-0	16	Perch [51]	15,782
7	16	A	Huddersfield T	D	0-0	0-0	16		11,083
8	22	H	Ipswich T	L	1-2	0-1	17	Waghorn [82]	12,817
9	27	A	Bournemouth	L	0-2	0-1	18		8754
10	30	H	Nottingham F	D	0-0	0-0	20		14,078
11	Oct 4	A	Wolverhampton W	D	2-2	2-1	21	Perch [32], Fortune [45]	21,288
12	18	A	Brentford	D	0-0	0-0	19		12,061
13	21	H	Millwall	D	0-0	0-0	19		10,201
14	25	A	Derby Co	W	2-1	0-1	19	McClean 2 [69, 83]	28,824
15	Nov 1	H	Fulham	D	3-3	1-2	18	Forshaw (pen) [9], Espinoza [54], Maloney [82]	12,084
16	4	A	Brighton & HA	L	0-1	0-1	19		23,044
17	7	A	Bolton W	L	1-3	0-0	21	McManaman [79]	17,282
18	22	H	Middlesbrough	D	1-1	1-0	23	Maloney [24]	16,347
19	29	A	Sheffield W	L	1-2	1-1	23	McCann [26]	20,609
20	Dec 6	H	Norwich C	L	0-1	0-1	23		11,475
21	13	A	Watford	L	1-2	1-1	23	McCann [45]	15,297
22	20	H	Rotherham U	L	1-2	0-1	23	Watson [64]	12,641
23	26	A	Leeds U	W	2-0	1-0	22	Cooper (og) [11], McClean [83]	28,375
24	30	H	Sheffield W	L	0-1	0-0	23		14,571
25	Jan 10	A	Birmingham C	L	1-3	1-2	23	McClean [36]	16,117
26	17	H	Blackburn R	D	1-1	0-1	23	McClean [63]	14,652
27	24	H	Huddersfield T	L	0-1	0-0	23		12,064
28	31	A	Ipswich T	D	0-0	0-0	23		19,155
29	Feb 7	H	Bournemouth	L	1-3	0-2	23	Clarke [60]	10,621
30	11	A	Nottingham F	L	0-3	0-1	23		19,619
31	17	A	Reading	W	1-0	1-0	23	Pearce [17]	14,601
32	20	H	Charlton Ath	L	0-3	0-2	23		11,344
33	24	H	Cardiff C	L	0-1	0-1	23		10,016
34	28	A	Blackpool	W	3-1	1-0	23	Kim [45], Maguire [67], McClean [79]	11,679
35	Mar 4	A	Norwich C	W	1-0	1-0	22	Kim [8]	26,208
36	7	H	Leeds U	L	0-1	0-0	22		16,163
37	14	A	Rotherham U	W	2-1	2-1	22	Pennant 2 [31, 36]	10,062
38	17	H	Watford	L	0-2	0-0	22		10,684
39	21	H	Bolton W	D	1-1	0-0	22	Waghorn [90]	15,861
40	Apr 3	A	Middlesbrough	L	0-1	0-1	23		23,082
41	6	H	Derby Co	L	0-2	0-0	23		14,697
42	10	A	Fulham	D	2-2	1-2	22	Pennant [22], Pearce [69]	15,994
43	14	A	Millwall	L	0-2	0-0	23		8494
44	18	H	Brighton & HA	W	2-1	1-0	23	Chow [26], Perch [81]	11,100
45	25	H	Wolverhampton W	L	0-1	0-1	23		16,810
46	May 2	A	Brentford	L	0-3	0-1	23		11,842

Final League Position: 23

GOALSCORERS

League (39): McClean 6, McManaman 5, Pennant 3, Perch 3, Waghorn 3, Kim 2, Maloney 2, McCann 2, Pearce 2, Chow 1, Clarke 1, Espinoza 1, Forshaw 1 (1 pen), Fortune 1, Maguire 1, McArthur 1, Riera 1, Taylor 1, Watson 1, own goal 1.
FA Cup (0).
Capital One Cup (1): Fortune 1.

Carson S 34	Perch J 39 + 2	Boyce E 26 + 1	Kiernan R 16 + 1	Nicholls L 1	Taylor A 26	Huws E 15 + 1	Cowie D 24 + 8	McArthur J 5	McManaman C 19 + 4	Riera O 6 + 7	Waghorn M 6 + 17	Maloney S 10 + 10	Tavernier J 7 + 4	Fortune M 27 + 8	Ramis I 17 + 1	Espinoza R 6 + 6	Barnett L 16 + 4	Kvist Jorgensen W 18 + 8	Delort A 4 + 7	Forshaw A 13 + 3	McClean J 30 + 6	Figueroa M 6	McCann C 11 + 6	Flores J — + 1	Watson B 7 + 2	Ridgewell L 6	Robles L — + 1	Al Habsi A 11	McKay B 1 + 8	Herd C 3	Kim B 17 + 1	Clarke L 9 + 1	Ojo S 7 + 4	Pearce J 16	Maguire H 16	Bong G 14	Pennant J 12 + 1	Murphy J 2 + 3	Sinclair J — + 1	Chow T 3 + 1	Match No.
1	2	3	4		5^1	6	7^2	8	9	10	11^3	12	13	14																											1
1	2		4		5	6	8^1	7	11	10^2	13	12			9^3	3	14																								2
1	2	3			5	6^3	9	7	8	10^1	12	13		14	11^2	4																								3
1	2	3			5	6	10^1	9	8	7^3	11^2	12		14	13	4																								4
1	5	2	4		9	6	7	8	10^3	11^1	13	14					3^2	12																						5
1	2	3			5	6	9^3	8	11^1			14		12			4			7^2	10	13																		6
1	2	3			5	6^3	9	7	10^1	14		13					4			8	11^2	12																		7
1	5	2	4			6			9^1	13	14	11^2				3				7	10^3	8	12																	8
1	5	2	4^2		9	8	7			13	11^1			10	3^3	12				14	6																			9
1	2	3^2			5	8	6^1		9^1	14		13			4	12	7	10		11																				10
1	2				5	7	6		14		10			11^1	3		4	8^3	13	12	9^2																			11
1					5	7^1			8^2	11^3	9	2	13	3		4	14	12	6	10																				12
1		12							13	10^2	6	2	11	3^1	14	4	7		8	9^5	5																			13
1		4^1			6^2	8	9^4		13	2	10		11	3	14		7	12	5																					14
1		4			8^3	7	10^1		13	2	11	14	9^2	3^4		6	12	5																						15
1	5	3			6^1		12	13	11	9	2		10			7^2	8	4	14																					16
1	2	4			6^1		10		8^3		11		9	3	14	7^2	13	5	12																					17
1	14	2^2			5		9			11	10	3	8^3	4	7^1	12		6	13																					18
1	12	2			5		9			10	3^1	13	4	7^2	11		6	8																						19
1	2				5	12	8		9^1	11^3	13	3	14	10	4	6^4	7																							20
1	2	3			5	9	8^1		12		11^2	4	13	10	6	7																								21
1	2	3			5	8^1	10	13	9^3	12		4	14	11	7^2	6																								22
1	2		4		9	6			5	11^1	3	12		10	7	8																								23
1	2	4^2	8		12^4		14	5	11^1	3	13		7	9	10	6^3																								24
1	2	5	6		10^1		13	7		4^3		14		9	11	8	12	3^2																						25
1	2		5	13			11^2	12		3	6	14	9^1	10		8	7^3	4																						26
1	2		5	8	13		9^1	10^3		12		3	7	14		11	6^2	4																						27
	2		5	8	7		9^5	10		3	6			11		4	1	12																						28
		5	6		3	7			11	8		3	7	11	8	4	1	12	2^1	9^2	10	13																		29
	2		5	9	13			3	8	10		4	1	14	7^2	6^3	11^1	12																						30
	2		5	13			10^2	7		9	1	14	8^3	12	11	6^1	3	4																						31
	2		5	14			11^3	8^1	9	12	1	13	7	10^2	6	4	3																							32
7	2	13	12		11^2	10		1	8	9	4	3	5	6^1																										33
1	6	2	13		11	9		7	12	10^8	4	3	5	8^1																										34
1	7	2	12		14	10^3	9	13	8	11^1	4	3	5	6^2																										35
1	7	2^3	12		11^2	13	10	14	8	9	4	3	5	6^1																										36
	6	2	13		11	12	9	1	7	10^2	4	3	5	8^1																										37
	7	2	10^2	13		1	8	11	9^1	4	3	5	6^3	12	14																									38
	7	2^1	14	10^3	13	1	8	11	12	4	3	5	6^2	9																										39
	7	2	13	12	14	11	1	8	10^2	4	3	5	6^3	9^1																										40
	7	2^2	14	10^1	6	9	12	1	8	11^3	4	3	5	13																										41
1	7	2^1	12	11^3	6	9	13	10	4	3	5	8^2	14																											42
1	7	2	12^4	11^1	6^2	9	10	14	4^1	3	5	9^2	13																											43
1	2	13	7^2	12	6^1	11	14	10	4	3	5	8^1	9																											44
1	6	2	14	12	7^2	11$^■$	13	10	4	3	5	8^3	9^1																											45
2	5	1	7	11^3	13	14	10	8^1	4	3	9	12	6^2																											46

FA Cup
Third Round   Bolton W   (a)   0-1

Capital One Cup
First Round   Burton Alb   (a)   1-2

WOLVERHAMPTON WANDERERS

FOUNDATION

Enthusiasts of the game at St Luke's School, Blakenhall formed a club in 1877. In the same neighbourhood a cricket club called Blakenhall Wanderers had a football section. Several St Luke's footballers played cricket for them and shortly before the start of the 1879–80 season the two amalgamated and Wolverhampton Wanderers FC was brought into being.

Molineux Stadium, Waterloo Road, Wolverhampton WV1 4QR.

Telephone: (0871) 222 2220.

Fax: (01902) 687 006.

Ticket Office: (0871) 222 1877.

Website: wolves.co.uk

Email: info@wolves.co.uk

Ground Capacity: 31,700.

Record Attendance: 61,315 v Liverpool, FA Cup 5th rd, 11 February 1939.

Pitch Measurements: 105m × 68m (113yd × 74.5yd)

Chairman: Steve Morgan OBE.

Chief Executive: Jez Moxey.

Head Coach: Kenny Jackett.

Assistant Head Coach: Joe Gallen.

Physio: Carl Howarth.

Colours: Gold shirts with black trim, black shorts with gold trim, gold socks with black trim.

Year Formed: 1877* (*see Foundation*).

Turned Professional: 1888.

Previous Names: 1879, St Luke's combined with Wanderers Cricket Club to become Wolverhampton Wanderers (1923) Ltd. New limited companies followed in 1982 and 1986 (current).

Club Nickname: 'Wolves'.

HONOURS

Football League – Division 1:
Champions 1953–54, 1957–58, 1958–59; *Runners-up* 1937–38, 1938–39, 1949–50, 1954–55, 1959–60;
Division 2: *Champions* 1931–32, 1976–77; *Runners-up* 1966–67, 1982–83; **FL C:** *Champions* 2008–09;
Division 3 (N): *Champions* 1923–24;
Division 3: *Champions* 1988–89;
Division 4: *Champions* 1987–88;
FL 1: *Champions* 2013–14.

FA Cup: *Winners* 1893, 1908, 1949, 1960; *Runners-up* 1889, 1896, 1921, 1939.

Football League Cup: *Winners* 1974, 1980.

Texaco Cup: *Winners* 1971.

Sherpa Van Trophy: *Winners* 1988.

European Competitions
European Cup: 1958–59, 1959–60.
European Cup-Winners' Cup: 1960–61. **UEFA Cup:** 1971–72 (*runners-up*), 1973–74, 1974–75, 1980–81.

Grounds: 1877, Windmill Field; 1879, John Harper's Field; 1881, Dudley Road; 1889, Molineux.

First Football League Game: 8 September 1888, Football League, v Aston Villa (h) D 1–1 – Baynton; Baugh, Mason; Fletcher, Allen, Lowder; Hunter, Cooper, Anderson, White, Cannon, (1 og).

Record League Victory: 10–1 v Leicester C, Division 1, 15 April 1938 – Sidlow; Morris, Dowen; Galley, Cullis, Gardiner; Maguire (1), Horace Wright, Westcott (4), Jones (1), Dorsett (4).

Record Cup Victory: 14–0 v Crosswell's Brewery, FA Cup 2nd rd, 13 November 1886 – Ike Griffiths; Baugh, Mason; Pearson, Allen (1), Lowder; Hunter (4), Knight (2), Brodie (4), Bernie Griffiths (2), Wood. Plus one goal 'scrambled through'.

sky SPORTS FACT FILE

Wolverhampton Wanderers had a difficult time in the first half of 1987–88, spending most of the season in the lower reaches of the old Fourth Division table. The improvement in the New Year was dramatic: only 3 games were lost out of the final 23, and 11 of the last 12 games were won. Wanderers then lost out to Aldershot in the play-offs.

Record Defeat: 1–10 v Newton Heath, Division 1, 15 October 1892.

Most League Points (2 for a win): 64, Division 1, 1957–58.

Most League Points (3 for a win): 103, FL 1, 2013–14.

Most League Goals: 115, Division 2, 1931–32.

Highest League Scorer in Season: Dennis Westcott, 38, Division 1, 1946–47.

Most League Goals in Total Aggregate: Steve Bull, 250, 1986–99.

Most League Goals in One Match: 5, Joe Butcher v Accrington, Division 1, 19 November 1892; 5, Tom Phillipson v Barnsley, Division 2, 26 April 1926; 5, Tom Phillipson v Bradford C, Division 2, 25 December 1926; 5, Billy Hartill v Notts Co, Division 2, 12 October 1929; 5, Billy Hartill v Aston Villa, Division 1, 3 September 1934.

Most Capped Player: Billy Wright, 105, England (70 consecutive).

Most League Appearances: Derek Parkin, 501, 1967–82.

Youngest League Player: Jimmy Mullen, 16 years 43 days v Leeds U, 18 February 1939.

Record Transfer Fee Received: £12,000,000 (rising to £14,000,000) from Sunderland for Steven Fletcher, August 2012.

Record Transfer Fee Paid: £6,500,000 to Reading for Kevin Doyle, June 2009; £6,500,000 to Burnley for Steven Fletcher, June 2010.

Football League Record: 1888 Founder Member of Football League: 1906–23 Division 2; 1923–24 Division 3 (N); 1924–32 Division 2; 1932–65 Division 1; 1965–67 Division 2; 1967–76 Division 1; 1976–77 Division 2; 1977–82 Division 1; 1982–83 Division 2; 1983–84 Division 1; 1984–85 Division 2; 1985–86 Division 3; 1986–88 Division 4; 1988–89 Division 3; 1989–92 Division 2; 1992–2003 Division 1; 2003–04 FA Premier League; 2004–09 FL C; 2009–12 FA Premier League; 2012–13 FL C; 2013–14 FL 1; 2014– FL C.

MANAGERS

George Worrall 1877–85
(Secretary-Manager)
John Addenbrooke 1885–1922
George Jobey 1922–24
Albert Hoskins 1924–26
(had been Secretary since 1922)
Fred Scotchbrook 1926–27
Major Frank Buckley 1927–44
Ted Vizard 1944–48
Stan Cullis 1948–64
Andy Beattie 1964–65
Ronnie Allen 1966–68
Bill McGarry 1968–76
Sammy Chung 1976–78
John Barnwell 1978–81
Ian Greaves 1982
Graham Hawkins 1982–84
Tommy Docherty 1984–85
Bill McGarry 1985
Sammy Chapman 1985–86
Brian Little 1986
Graham Turner 1986–94
Graham Taylor 1994–95
Mark McGhee 1995–98
Colin Lee 1998–2000
Dave Jones 2001–04
Glenn Hoddle 2004–06
Mick McCarthy 2006–12
Stale Solbakken 2012–13
Dean Saunders 2013
Kenny Jackett May 2013–

LATEST SEQUENCES

Longest Sequence of League Wins: 9, 11.1.2014 – 11.3.2014.

Longest Sequence of League Defeats: 8, 5.12.1981 – 13.2.1982.

Longest Sequence of League Draws: 6, 22.4.1995 – 20.8.1995.

Longest Sequence of Unbeaten League Matches: 21, 15.1.2005 – 13.8.2005.

Longest Sequence Without a League Win: 19, 1.12.1984 – 6.4.1985.

Successive Scoring Runs: 41 from 20.12.1958.

Successive Non-scoring Runs: 7 from 2.2.1985.

TEN YEAR LEAGUE RECORD

		P	W	D	L	F	A	Pts	Pos
2005-06	FL C	46	16	19	11	50	42	67	7
2006-07	FL C	46	22	10	14	59	56	76	5
2007-08	FL C	46	18	16	12	53	48	70	7
2008-09	FL C	46	27	9	10	80	52	90	1
2009-10	PR Lge	38	9	11	18	32	56	38	15
2010-11	PR Lge	38	11	7	20	46	66	40	17
2011-12	PR Lge	38	5	10	23	40	82	25	20
2012-13	FL C	46	14	9	23	55	69	51	23
2013-14	FL 1	46	31	10	5	89	31	103	1
2014-15	FL C	46	22	12	12	70	56	78	7

DID YOU KNOW

In their early days as a Football League club Wolverhampton Wanderers played in red and white striped shirts. They switched to gold and black for the 1892–93 season and these have remained as the club colours ever since, although the traditional kit of gold shirts and black shorts dates from the 1930s.

WOLVERHAMPTON WANDERERS – FL CHAMPIONSHIP 2014–15 LEAGUE RECORD

Match No.	Date	Venue	Opponents	Result	H/T Score	Lg Pos.	Goalscorers	Atten- dance
1	Aug 10	H	Norwich C	W 1-0	0-0	7	Edwards [64]	22,053
2	16	A	Rotherham U	L 0-1	0-0	14		10,752
3	20	A	Fulham	W 1-0	1-0	9	Sako [15]	18,627
4	23	H	Cardiff C	W 1-0	0-0	4	Hudson (og) [90]	21,221
5	30	H	Blackburn R	W 3-1	2-0	3	Dicko [13], Sako 2 [33, 68]	21,260
6	Sept 13	A	Blackpool	D 0-0	0-0	3		12,233
7	16	A	Charlton Ath	D 1-1	0-1	4	Batth [65]	15,973
8	20	H	Bolton W	W 1-0	1-0	3	Dicko [42]	22,695
9	28	A	Reading	D 3-3	0-1	3	Henry [51], Evans [54], Blackman (og) [84]	17,454
10	Oct 1	H	Huddersfield T	L 1-3	0-2	7	Sako [71]	19,059
11	4	H	Wigan Ath	D 2-2	1-2	7	Edwards [30], Sako [64]	21,288
12	18	A	Millwall	D 3-3	1-0	7	Batth [23], Ebanks-Landell [61], Sako [64]	13,428
13	21	H	Middlesbrough	W 2-0	1-0	4	Sako (pen) [33], Dicko [73]	18,391
14	25	A	Leeds U	W 2-1	0-1	3	Henry [66], Clarke [85]	27,883
15	Nov 1	H	Birmingham C	D 0-0	0-0	4		25,135
16	4	A	Ipswich T	L 1-2	0-1	6	Henry [53]	17,267
17	8	A	Derby Co	L 0-5	0-3	9		30,398
18	22	H	Nottingham F	L 0-3	0-0	11		25,513
19	29	A	Brentford	L 0-4	0-1	12		10,923
20	Dec 6	H	Bournemouth	L 1-2	1-0	13	Graham, D [41]	20,196
21	13	A	Sheffield W	W 1-0	0-0	12	Clarke [84]	20,598
22	20	H	Brighton & HA	D 1-1	0-1	10	Batth [88]	22,882
23	26	A	Watford	W 1-0	0-0	9	Dicko [57]	17,443
24	28	H	Brentford	W 2-1	1-0	8	Dicko [7], Tarkowski (og) [72]	23,598
25	Jan 11	A	Blackburn R	W 1-0	0-0	8	Edwards [48]	15,335
26	17	H	Blackpool	W 2-0	0-0	8	Edwards [86], Afobe [90]	28,132
27	24	H	Charlton Ath	D 0-0	0-0	7		23,487
28	31	A	Bolton W	D 2-2	1-2	7	Dicko [3], Henry [90]	15,869
29	Feb 7	H	Reading	L 1-2	1-1	8	Afobe [26]	20,274
30	10	A	Huddersfield T	W 4-1	1-0	8	Dicko 2 [12, 90], Coady (og) [47], Afobe [61]	11,843
31	14	A	Norwich C	L 0-2	0-1	8		26,322
32	21	H	Rotherham U	W 5-0	2-0	8	Afobe 2 [21, 63], Dicko [28], Edwards [74], Sako [80]	20,336
33	24	H	Fulham	W 3-0	3-0	8	Batth [10], Sako 2 [40, 45]	17,744
34	28	A	Cardiff C	W 1-0	1-0	8	Sako [26]	21,165
35	Mar 3	A	Bournemouth	L 1-2	1-1	8	Afobe [39]	9851
36	7	H	Watford	D 2-2	1-1	8	Afobe [14], Price [50]	23,146
37	14	A	Brighton & HA	D 1-1	0-0	8	van La Parra [74]	27,019
38	17	H	Sheffield W	W 3-0	1-0	8	Sako (pen) [18], Afobe [55], Henry [67]	18,687
39	20	H	Derby Co	W 2-0	0-0	7	Dicko [48], Grant (og) [69]	27,480
40	Apr 3	A	Nottingham F	W 2-1	0-0	8	Afobe [46], Sako (pen) [72]	27,185
41	6	H	Leeds U	W 4-3	2-1	6	Dicko 2 [19, 45], Afobe [48], Edwards [88]	25,169
42	11	A	Birmingham C	L 1-2	1-1	8	Afobe [21]	19,330
43	14	A	Middlesbrough	L 1-2	0-2	8	Sako [53]	20,520
44	18	H	Ipswich T	D 1-1	0-1	8	Afobe [50]	23,409
45	25	A	Wigan Ath	W 1-0	1-0	8	Afobe [25]	16,810
46	May 2	H	Millwall	W 4-2	1-0	7	Dicko 2 [20, 56], Ebanks-Landell [70], Sako [90]	24,480

Final League Position: 7

GOALSCORERS

League (70): Sako 15 (3 pens), Dicko 14, Afobe 13, Edwards 6, Henry 5, Batth 4, Clarke 2, Ebanks-Landell 2, Evans 1, Graham, D 1, Price 1, van La Parra 1, own goals 5.
FA Cup (3): Edwards 2, van La Parra 1.
Capital One Cup (2): Dicko 1, Ricketts 1.

Ikeme C 33	Doherty M 26 + 7	Batth D 44	Stearman R 38 + 4	Golbourne S 23 + 4	McDonald K 45 + 1	Evans L 17 + 1	van La Parra R 29 + 11	Edwards D 32 + 9	Sako B 39 + 2	Dicko N 30 + 7	Jacobs M 3 + 9	Henry J 23 + 14	Clarke L 5 + 11	Saville G 5 + 2	Rowe T 7 + 7	McAlinden L 1 + 5	Ricketts S 4	Sagbo Y 1 + 3	Ebanks-Landell E 9 + 5	Graham D 5	Iorfa D 20	Hause K 15 + 2	Price J 19 + 4	Afobe B 20 + 1	Kuszczak T 13	Doyle K — + 6	Match No.
1	2	3	4	5	6	7	8^3	9	10^2	11^1	12	13	14														1
1	2	3	4	5	7	6	8^2	9	10^1	11	13	12															2
1	2	3	4	5	6	7	8^1	9	10	11	12																3
1	2	3	4	5	7	6	8^2	9^1	10	11	12	13															4
1	2	3	4	5	6	7^1	8^2	9^2	10	11		12		13	14												5
1	2	3	4	5	7		8^1	9	12	11^2	10^2	13	14	6													6
1	2	3	4	5	6	7		13	10	12	14	8	11^3	9^2													7
1	2	3	4	5	7	8	10^1	9	11^3	6^2	12	13	14														8
1	2	3	4	5	6	7	13	12	10			8^1	11^1	9^3				14									9
1		3	4	5	6	7^1	13		10	11		8^1	14		12				2	9^1							10
1	2	3	4	5	7	6^1	8	10	11^2		12		9		13												11
1	2	3	14	8	7	6^2	10	9	11^1		12		5		13				4^3								12
1	2	3		7	6		9	10^2	11^1	12	8	13		5					4								13
1	2	3	14	6	7	13	9^1		11^1	10^2	8	12		5					4								14
1	2	3		6	7		12	13	9^3	8	11^2		5	10^1	14				4								15
1	2	3		7	6	14	9	10	12^3	8	11		5	13					4								16
1	2	3	12		7		9^3	10	8	11^2	6	14	13	5					4^1								17
1	2	3	12		6	14	9^2	10		8^1	7	13	5						4^3	11							18
1	2	3	5^3	13	7^1	8	9	10		14	6	12							4	11^2							19
1	5^1	3	4	6		8^1	7	10^2	12	9^1	14	13							11^3		2						20
1		3	4		7	11	8	9^2	6^1	12	14								10^3		2	5	13				21
1		3	4		7	11	8^1	9	13	6^1	14								10^2		2	5	12				22
1		3	4		7		8	9^1	10	11^2	13		12^3						14		2	5	6				23
1	14	3	4		7^*		8^2	9	10^3	11^1	12	13									2	5	6				24
1	12	3	4		7		10	9		11^2	8								13		2	5	6^1				25
1	13	3	4		6		10	9		11^3		8^1							14		2	5^2	7	12			26
1	14	3	4	12	7		10	9		13		8^1									2^2	5^3	6	11			27
1	14	3	4	5	7	12	6	9^1		11		13									2^1		8^2	10			28
	2	3	4		7	6^2	8^3	9^1	10	12	14								5	13			11		1		29
	2	3	4	12	6		8^1	13	10^2	11					5							7	9		1		30
		3	4	13	6		8	12	10	11^1					2				5^2			7	9		1		31
		3	4	5^1	7	12	8	9	11^3	6					2				14				10^2	1		13	32
		3	4	5	6	12	9	10^1	11^2	13					2				7				8	1		14	33
13		3	4		6		8^2	9	10	12		14			2^2				5			7	11^1			1	34
	2	3	4		8		6	7	9	11^1					5				10				1			12	35
	2	3	4		6		8	10^*		9^1					5				7				11		1	12	36
	2	3	4		6		8	10	12	9^1					5				7				11		1		37
	2	3	4^3	5	8^2		6^1	14	9	10	12							13				7	11		1		38
	2	3	4	5	7		13	12	9	11^1	6^1				8								10^2	1		14	39
1	14	3	4	5	7		13	12	9	10^1	6^3				2								8			11^2	40
1		3	4	5	7		13	12	9	11^2	6^1				2								8	10			41
1		3	4	5	7		12		9	11	6^1				2								8	10			42
1		3	4	12	6		8^1	9	10	13	14				2				5^2				7^2	11			43
1		3	4	5	8		6^1	7	9	10	12				2									11			44
		4	5	7		6	9^1	11^4							3				2		13	8	10		1	12	45
		4	5	7		6^1	8	9	11						3				2			12	10		1		46

FA Cup

Third Round	Fulham	(a)	0-0	
Replay	Fulham	(h)	3-3	

(aet; Fulham won 5-3 on penalties)

Capital One Cup

First Round	Northampton T	(h)	2-3

WYCOMBE WANDERERS

FOUNDATION

In 1887 a group of young furniture trade workers called a meeting at the Steam Engine public house with the aim of forming a football club and entering junior football. It is thought that they were named after the famous FA Cup winners, The Wanderers, who had visited the town in 1877 for a tie with the original High Wycombe club. It is also possible that they played informally before their formation, although there is no proof of this.

Adams Park, Hillbottom Road, High Wycombe, Buckinghamshire HP12 4HJ.

Telephone: (01494) 472 100. *Fax:* (01494) 441 589.

Ticket Office: (01494) 441 118.

Website: www.wwfc.com

Email: wwfc@wwfc.com

Ground Capacity: 10,284.

Record Attendance: 15,850 v St Albans C, FA Amateur Cup 4th rd, 25 February 1950 (at Loakes Park); 9,921 v Fulham, FA Cup 3rd rd, 9 January 2002 (at Adams Park).

Pitch Measurements: 106.5m × 64m (110yd × 70yd)

Chairman: Don Woodward.

Manager: Gareth Ainsworth.

Assistant Manager: Richard Dobson.

Physio: Cian O'Doherty.

HONOURS

Football League – Division 2: Best season: 6th, 1994–95; **FL 2:** Best season: 3rd, 2008–09 (promoted to FL 1), 2010–11 (promoted to FL 1).

FA Amateur Cup: *Winners* 1931.

FA Trophy: *Winners* 1991, 1993.

GM Vauxhall Conference: *Winners* 1992–93.

FA Cup: Best season: semi-final, 2001.

Football League Cup: Best season: semi-final, 2007.

Colours: Light blue and dark blue quartered shirts, dark blue shorts with light blue trim, dark blue socks.

Year Formed: 1887. *Turned Professional:* 1974.

Club Nicknames: 'The Chairboys' (after High Wycombe's tradition of furniture making), 'The Blues'.

Grounds: 1887, The Rye; 1893, Spring Meadow; 1895, Loakes Park; 1899, Daws Hill Park; 1901, Loakes Park; 1990, Adams Park.

First Football League Game: 14 August 1993, Division 3 v Carlisle U (a) D 2–2: Hyde; Cousins, Horton (Langford), Kerr, Crossley, Ryan, Carroll, Stapleton, Thompson, Scott, Guppy (1) (Hutchinson), (1 og).

Record League Victory: 5–0 v Burnley, Division 2, 15 April 1997 – Parkin; Cousins, Bell, Kavanagh, McCarthy, Forsyth, Carroll (2p) (Simpson), Scott (Farrell), Stallard (1), McGavin (1) (Read (1)), Brown. 5–0 v Northampton T, Division 2, 4 January 2003 – Talia; Senda, Ryan, Thomson, McCarthy, Johnson, Bulman, Simpson (1), Faulconbridge (Harris), Dixon (1) (Roberts 3), Brown (Currie).

Record Cup Victory: 5–0 v Hitchin T (a), FA Cup 2nd rd, 3 December 1994 – Hyde; Cousins, Brown, Crossley, Evans, Ryan (1), Carroll, Bell (1), Thompson, Garner (3) (Hemmings), Stapleton (Langford); 5–0 v Hartlepool U, FL 1, 25 February 2012 – Bull; McCoy, Basey, Eastmond (Bloomfield), Laing, Doherty (1), Hackett, Lewis, Bevon (2) (Strevons), Hayes (2) (McClure), McNamee.

sky SPORTS FACT FILE

Wycombe Wanderers attracted an average home crowd of 4,602 when they won the Conference championship in 1993 to earn promotion to the Football League. The Chairboys' biggest attendance during the campaign was the 7,230 crowd for their clash with Slough Town.

Record Defeat: 0–7 v Shrewsbury T, Johnstone's Paint Trophy, 7 October 2008.

Most League Points (3 for a win): 84, FL 2, 2014–15.

Most League Goals: 72, FL 2, 2005–06.

Highest League Goalscorer in Season: Scott McGleish, 25, 2007–08.

Most League Goals in Total Aggregate: Nathan Tyson, 42, 2004–06.

Most League Goals in One Match: 3, Miquel Desouza v Bradford C, Division 2, 2 September 1995; 3, John Williams v Stockport Co, Division 2, 24 February 1996; 3, Mark Stallard v Walsall, Division 2, 21 October 1997; 3, Sean Devine v Reading, Division 2, 2 October 1999; 3, Sean Divine v Bury, Division 2, 26 February 2000; 3, Stuart Roberts v Northampton T, Division 2, 4 January 2003; 3, Nathan Tyson v Lincoln C, FL 2, 5 March 2005; 3, Nathan Tyson v Kidderminster H, FL 2, 2 April 2005; 3, Nathan Tyson v Stockport Co, FL 2, 10 September 2005; 3, Kevin Betsy v Mansfield T, FL 2, 24 September 2005; 3, Scott McGleish v Mansfield T, FL 2, 8 January 2008; 3, Stuart Beavon v Bury, FL 1, 17 March 2012.

Most Capped Player: Mark Rogers, 7, Canada; Marvin McCoy, 7, Antigua and Barbuda.

Most League Appearances: Steve Brown, 371, 1994–2004.

Youngest League Player: Jordon Ibe, 15 years 311 days v Hartlepool U, 15 October 2011.

Record Transfer Fee Received: £675,000 from Nottingham F for Nathan Tyson, January 2006.

Record Transfer Fee Paid: £200,000 to Barnet for Sean Devine, 15 April 1999.

Football League Record: 1993 Promoted to Division 3 from Conference; 1993–94 Division 3; 1994–2004 Division 2; 2004–09 FL 2; 2009–10 FL 1; 2010–11 FL 2; 2011–12 FL 1; 2012– FL 2.

MANAGERS

First coach appointed 1951.
Prior to Brian Lee's appointment in 1969 the team was selected by a Match Committee which met every Monday evening.
James McCormack 1951–52
Sid Cann 1952–61
Graham Adams 1961–62
Don Welsh 1962–64
Barry Darvill 1964–68
Brian Lee 1969–76
Ted Powell 1976–77
John Reardon 1977–78
Andy Williams 1978–80
Mike Keen 1980–84
Paul Bence 1984–86
Alan Gane 1986–87
Peter Suddaby 1987–88
Jim Kelman 1988–90
Martin O'Neill 1990–95
Alan Smith 1995–96
John Gregory 1996–98
Neil Smillie 1998–99
Lawrie Sanchez 1999–2003
Tony Adams 2003–04
John Gorman 2004–06
Paul Lambert 2006–08
Peter Taylor 2008–09
Gary Waddock 2009–12
Gareth Ainsworth November 2012–

LATEST SEQUENCES

Longest Sequence of League Wins: 6, 19.8.2006 – 16.9.2006.

Longest Sequence of League Defeats: 6, 18.3.2006 – 17.4.2006.

Longest Sequence of League Draws: 5, 24.1.2004 – 21.2.2004.

Longest Sequence of Unbeaten League Matches: 21, 6.8.2005 – 10.12.2005.

Longest Sequence Without a League Win: 13, 16.8.2003 – 18.10.2003 and 10.1.2004 – 20.3.2004.

Successive Scoring Runs: 16 from 13.9.2014.

Successive Non-scoring Runs: 5 from 15.10.1996.

TEN YEAR LEAGUE RECORD

		P	W	D	L	F	A	Pts	Pos
2005-06	FL 2	46	18	17	11	72	56	71	6
2006-07	FL 2	46	16	14	16	52	47	62	12
2007-08	FL 2	46	22	12	12	56	42	78	7
2008-09	FL 2	46	20	18	8	54	33	78	3
2009-10	FL 1	46	10	15	21	56	76	45	22
2010-11	FL 2	46	22	14	10	69	50	80	3
2011-12	FL 1	46	11	10	25	65	88	43	21
2012-13	FL 2	46	17	9	20	50	60	60	15
2013-14	FL 2	46	12	14	20	46	54	50	22
2014-15	FL 2	46	23	15	8	67	45	84	4

DID YOU KNOW ?

Wycombe Wanderers entered the Isthmian League in 1921 after winning the Spartan League championship in the two previous seasons. Their first game in their new league saw them go down to a 4-3 defeat at the hands of Leytonstone.

WYCOMBE WANDERERS – FOOTBALL LEAGUE TWO 2014–15 LEAGUE RECORD

Match No.	Date	Venue	Opponents	Result	H/T Score	Lg Pos.	Goalscorers	Atten- dance
1	Aug 9	A	Newport Co	W 2-0	2-0	2	Murphy [40], Cowan-Hall [44]	3634
2	16	H	Carlisle U	W 3-1	0-0	2	Pierre [55], Hayes (pen) [77], Murphy [80]	3121
3	19	H	Tranmere R	L 0-2	0-1	7		3005
4	23	A	Stevenage	W 3-1	2-1	5	Hayes [40], Murphy [44], McClure [90]	2832
5	30	A	York C	D 0-0	0-0	5		3209
6	Sept 6	H	Bury	D 0-0	0-0	5		3483
7	13	H	Mansfield T	W 2-1	1-1	4	Hayes (pen) [30], Murphy [77]	3106
8	16	H	Plymouth Arg	W 1-0	1-0	3	Hayes [36]	5657
9	20	A	Portsmouth	D 1-1	0-0	3	Wood [50]	16,171
10	27	H	Cambridge U	W 1-0	0-0	2	Hayes [63]	3610
11	Oct 4	H	Northampton T	D 1-1	0-1	2	Amadi-Holloway [90]	3822
12	11	A	Morecambe	W 3-1	2-1	1	Wood [10], Hayes [15], Jacobson [72]	1710
13	18	H	AFC Wimbledon	W 2-0	0-0	1	Scowen [51], Wood [70]	4329
14	21	A	Exeter C	L 1-2	1-1	1	Murphy [7]	3129
15	25	H	Dagenham & R	D 1-1	0-0	2	Murphy [83]	3316
16	Nov 1	A	Oxford U	W 2-1	0-1	1	Hayes [53], Murphy [62]	7552
17	17	H	Burton Alb	L 1-3	0-1	3	Hayes (pen) [65]	3981
18	22	A	Cheltenham T	W 4-1	2-1	1	Cowan-Hall [4], Craig [37], Jacobson [70], McClure [90]	2833
19	29	A	Hartlepool U	W 3-1	1-0	1	Cowan-Hall [33], Bloomfield [76], Mawson [79]	3053
20	Dec 13	H	Southend U	W 4-1	2-1	1	Cowan-Hall [32], McClure 2 [45, 72], Jacobson [67]	4123
21	20	A	Accrington S	D 1-1	1-0	1	Cowan-Hall [9]	1325
22	26	H	Luton T	D 1-1	1-1	2	Cowan-Hall [3]	7539
23	28	A	Shrewsbury T	D 0-0	0-0	2		7239
24	Jan 3	H	Hartlepool U	W 1-0	1-0	1	Onyedinma [37]	3607
25	10	H	York C	W 1-0	0-0	1	Onyedinma [47]	3669
26	17	A	Bury	D 1-1	0-1	1	Onyedinma [68]	2932
27	24	A	Mansfield T	D 0-0	0-0	1		2759
28	31	H	Portsmouth	D 0-0	0-0	3		5829
29	Feb 7	A	Cambridge U	W 1-0	0-0	2	Ephraim [53]	6894
30	10	H	Plymouth Arg	L 0-2	0-2	3		3078
31	14	H	Newport Co	L 1-2	0-1	3	Onyedinma [55]	3196
32	21	A	Carlisle U	W 3-2	1-0	3	Pierre [28], Onyedinma [62], McClure [65]	4021
33	28	H	Stevenage	D 2-2	1-2	3	Onyedinma 2 [10, 71]	3664
34	Mar 3	A	Tranmere R	W 2-1	2-1	3	Hayes (pen) [26], Onyedinma [40]	4161
35	7	A	Southend U	D 2-2	1-1	3	Craig [28], Mawson [85]	6204
36	14	H	Shrewsbury T	W 1-0	1-0	2	Wood [1]	4697
37	17	H	Accrington S	D 2-2	1-1	3	Wood [30], Mawson [70]	2621
38	24	A	Luton T	W 3-2	3-2	3	Saunders [3], Hayes (pen) [22], Mawson [31]	8379
39	28	A	Dagenham & R	W 1-0	0-0	3	Pierre [64]	2362
40	Apr 3	H	Oxford U	L 2-3	0-2	3	Hayes [48], Amadi-Holloway [89]	6892
41	6	A	Burton Alb	L 0-1	0-0	3		4284
42	11	A	Cheltenham T	W 2-1	1-0	3	Pierre [45], Mawson [56]	3907
43	14	H	Exeter C	W 2-1	1-0	3	Saunders [7], Hayes (pen) [90]	3245
44	18	A	AFC Wimbledon	D 0-0	0-0	3		4535
45	25	H	Morecambe	L 0-1	1-0	5		5177
46	May 2	A	Northampton T	W 3-2	2-0	4	Amadi-Holloway [36], Yennaris [39], Mawson [90]	5723

Final League Position: 4

GOALSCORERS

League (67): Hayes 12 (6 pens), Onyedinma 8, Murphy 7, Cowan-Hall 6, Mawson 6, McClure 5, Wood 5, Pierre 4, Amadi-Holloway 3, Jacobson 3, Craig 2, Saunders 2, Bloomfield 1, Ephraim 1, Scowen 1, Yennaris 1.
FA Cup (3): Hayes 1 (1 pen), Pierre 1, Wood 1.
Capital One Cup (0).
Johnstone's Paint Trophy (0).
League Two Play-Offs (6): Hayes 2, Amadi-Holloway 1, Craig 1, Mawson 1, own goal 1.

Ingram M 46	Jombati S 35	Mawson A 45	Pierre A 42	Jacobson J 42	Cowan-Hall P 18+2	Murphy P 32+10	Kretzschmar M 8+8	Wood S 43+1	McClure M 13+14	Hayes P 38+1	Bloomfield M 23+10	Craig S 14+17	Amadi-Holloway A 12+17	Rowe D 10+6	Lewis S 1+5	Scowen J 18	Ephraim H 5+9	Onyedinna F 20+5	Bean M 16+1	Senior C —+1	Saunders S 11	Yennaris N 14	Lynch A —+1	Match No.
1	2	3	4	5	6^1	7	8^2	9	10	11	12	13												1
1	2	4	3	5	6^3	7	8	9	11^1	10^2	12	13	14											2
1	2	4	3	5	6^1	7	8^2	9	11^3	10		14	12	13			7	12						3
1	2	4	3	5	6^1	8		9	14	10^3	13	11^2				7	12							4
1	2	3	4	5	6^1	7	13	9	14	10^2		11^2	12			8								5
1	2	4	3	5	6^3	7	14	9	12	10	13	11^2		8^1										6
1	2	4	3	5		7^1		9	12	10	14	11^3	8	13	6^2									7
1	2	3	4	5		7	6^2	9	10^3	11^1		13	12	14	8									8
1	2	3	4	5	12	7	13	9	11^1	10^2			6		8									9
1	2	4	3	5	6^3	8		9	11^2	10^1	14	13	12			7								10
1	2	4	3	5	6	7		9	11^1	10		12			8									11
1	2	4	3^1	5	6^2	8	10	9		11^2	12	13	14			7								12
1	2	4	3	5	6^1	7	13	9	12	10^1	14	11^2				8								13
1	2	4	3	5	6^3	10	7^1	9	14	11^2	13	12				8								14
1	2	4	3	5	6^2	7	12	9	13	10		11^1				8								15
1	2	4	3	5		8	13	9		10^2	6^3	11^1	14			7	12							16
1	2	4		5	12	7	8^1	9^4		11	6^2	14	3	13	10									17
1	2		3	5	6	9			13	11^1	7	10	4^2	12	8									18
1	5	3	4	2	11^1	6	14		12	10^3	7	9^3				8	13							19
1	2	4	3	5	6^3	7		9^1	11	10^1	13	14				8	12							20
1	2	4	3	5	6	7^2		9	11	10^1	12	13				8								21
1	2	3	4	5	6	7		10		11	12			9^1		8								22
1	2	4	3	5	6	14		12		7^1	13	11^2		9	8		10^3							23
1	2	4	3	5		7		9		11		12	10^1		8		6							24
1	2	3	4	5		7		9	13		12	11^1			8		10^2	6						25
1	2	4	3	5		8		10			9		6				11	7						26
1	2	4	3	5		8^1		9^2	12		6	11				13	10^1	7						27
1	2	4	3	5		8		10	11^2			13	12			7^1	9	6						28
1	2	4	3	5		12		8			7	13	10^1			11^2	9	6						29
1	2	4	3	5		14		8	13		7		10^1			11	9^2	6^3	12					30
1	2	4	3	5		7		8	11^1	12		10^2	13			12	9	6						31
1	2	4	3	5		13		8	9	10^3	7	14				12	11^1	6^2						32
1	2	4		5				9		10	7			3			11				6	8		33
1	2	4		5		13		8	12^8	11	9^3	14		3			10^2				7^1	6		34
1	2	3	4	5		12		9		10	8^1	11^3	14			13					6^2	7		35
1		4	3	5		8		9		6		12					10^1	7			11	2		36
1		4	3	5	12	8		9		8^2		13					11^1	7			6	2		37
1		3	4	5		8			10^1	6	13	12					9^2	7			11	2		38
1		3	4	5				8	11^1	10	6						12	7			9	2		39
1		3	4	5	12			9^3		10	8^1	13				14	11	7			6^2	2		40
1		3	4	5	14			8		10	6^2	12	11^3			13	9	7^1				2		41
1		3	4	5^1	12			8		10	7	13	9^2				11				6	2		42
1		4	3					8		5	12^3	10	7	11^2	9^1		14	13			6	2		43
1		4	3^8		6	13	5		10	7^1	9			14		11	12		8^3	2^2				44
1		4	2		6^2	5		10		7		9^1	13			12	11	8				3		45
1^3		4	3			7		5		10	12	9	11^1			6^2	13	2				8	14	46

FA Cup

First Round	Barnet		(a)	3-1
Second Round	AFC Wimbledon		(h)	0-1

Capital One Cup

First Round	Millwall		(a)	0-1

Johnstone's Paint Trophy

First Round	Coventry C		(h)	0-1

League Two Play-Offs

Semi-Finals 1st leg	Plymouth Arg		(a)	3-2
Semi-Finals 2nd leg	Plymouth Arg		(h)	2-1
Final	Southend U	Wembley		1-1

(aet; Southend U won 7-6 on penalties)

YEOVIL TOWN

FOUNDATION

One of the prime movers of Yeovil football was Ernest J. Sercombe. His association with the club began in 1895 as a playing member of Yeovil Casuals, of which team he became vice-captain and in his last season 1899–1900, he was chosen to play for Somerset against Devon. Upon the reorganisation of the club, he became secretary of the old Yeovil Town FC and with the amalgamation with Petters United in 1914, he continued to serve until his resignation in 1930.

Huish Park, Lufton Way, Yeovil, Somerset BA22 8YF.

Telephone: (01935) 423 662.

Fax: (01935) 847 886.

Ticket Office: (01935) 847 888.

Website: www.ytfc.net

Email: info@ytfc.net

Ground Capacity: 9,565.

Record Attendance: 16,318 v Sunderland, FA Cup 4th rd, 29 January 1949 (at Huish); 9,527 v Leeds U, FL 1, 25 April 2008 (at Huish Park).

Pitch Measurements: 108m × 67m (118yd × 73.5yd)

Chairman: John R. Fry.

Manager: Paul Sturrock.

Assistant Manager: Terry Skiverton.

Physios: Simon Baker, Mike Micciche.

Colours: Green and white hooped shirts, white shorts with green trim, green and white hooped socks.

Year Formed: 1895.

Turned Professional: 1921.

Previous Names: 1895, Yeovil Casuals; 1907, Yeovil Town; 1915, Yeovil & Petters United; 1946, Yeovil Town.

Club Nickname: 'The Glovers'.

HONOURS

Football League – FL 2: *Winners* 2004–05.

Conference: *Champions* 2002–03.

FA Cup: Best season: 5th rd, 1949.

League Cup: Best season: never past 2nd rd.

Southern League: *Champions* 1954–55, 1963–64, 1970–71; *Runners-up*: 1923–24, 1931–32, 1934–35, 1969–70, 1972–73.

Southern League Cup: *Winners* 1948–49, 1954–55, 1960–61, 1965–66; *Runners-up*: 1946–47, 1955–56.

Isthmian League: *Winners* 1987–88; *Runners-up*: 1985–86, 1986–87, 1996–97.

AC Delco Cup: *Winners* 1987–88.

Bob Lord Trophy: *Winners* 1989–90.

FA Trophy: *Winners* 2002.

London Combination: *Runners-up* 1930–31, 1932–33.

Grounds: 1895, Pen Mill Ground; 1921, Huish; 1990, Huish Park.

First Football League Game: 9 August 2003, Division 3 v Rochdale (a) W 3-1: Weale; Williams (Lindegaard), Crittenden, Lockwood, O'Brien, Pluck (Rodrigues), Gosling (El Kholti), Way, Jackson, Gall (2), Johnson (1).

Record League Victory: 6–1 v Oxford U, FL 2, 18 September 2004 – Weale; Rose, O'Brien, Way, Skiverton, Fontaine, Caceres (Tarachulski), Johnson, Jevons (3), Stoicers (2) (Mirza), Terry (Gall 1).

Record Cup Victory: 12–1 v Westbury United, FA Cup 1st qual rd, 1923–24.

sky SPORTS FACT FILE

Yeovil Town won their first Southern League title in 1954–55 when a draw against Hastings United in their final game of the season earned them the championship on goal difference ahead of Weymouth. Town also won the Southern League Cup and the Somerset Professional Cup that season, while their reserve team won the Second Division of the Western League.

Record Defeat: 0–8 v Manchester United, FA Cup 5th rd, 12 February 1949.

Most League Points (3 for a win): 83, FL 2, 2004–05.

Most League Goals: 90, FL 2, 2004–05.

Highest League Goalscorer in Season: Phil Jevons, 27, 2004–05.

Most League Goals in Total Aggregate: Phil Jevons, 42, 2004–06.

Most League Goals in One Match: 3, Phil Jevons v Oxford U, FL 2, 18 September 2004; 3, Phil Jevons v Chester C, FL 2, 30 October 2004; 3, Phil Jevons v Bristol R, FL 2, 12 February 2005; 3, Arron Davies v Chesterfield, FL 1, 4 March 2006.

Most Capped Players: Joel Grant, 6, Jamaica.

Most League Appearances: Terry Skiverton, 195, 2003–09.

Youngest League Player: Steven Caulker, 17 years 222 days v Tranmere R, 8 August 2009.

Record Transfer Fee Received: £1,000,000 from Nottingham F for Arron Davies and Chris Cohen, July 2007.

Record Transfer Fee Paid: £250,000 to Quilmes for Pablo Bastianini, August 2005.

Football League Record: 2003 Promoted to Division 3 from Conference; 2003–04 Division 3; 2004–05 FL 2; 2005–13 FL 1; 2013–14 FL C; 2014–15 FL 1; 2015– FL 2.

LATEST SEQUENCES

Longest Sequence of League Wins: 8, 29.12.2012 – 16.2.2013.

Longest Sequence of League Defeats: 6, 10.3.2015 – 6.4.2015.

Longest Sequence of League Draws: 3, 18.3.2014 – 25.3.2014.

Longest Sequence of Unbeaten League Matches: 9, 29.12.2012 – 23.2.2013.

Longest Sequence Without a League Win: 11, 10.8.2013 – 19.10.2013.

Successive Scoring Runs: 22 from 30.10.2004.

Successive Non-scoring Runs: 4 from 21.10.2014.

MANAGERS

Jack Gregory 1922–28
Tommy Lawes 1928–29
Dave Pratt 1929–33
Louis Page 1933–35
Dave Halliday 1935–38
Billy Kingdon 1938–46
Alec Stock 1946–49
George Patterson 1949–51
Harry Lowe 1951–53
Ike Clarke 1953–57
Norman Dodgin 1957
Jimmy Baldwin 1957–60
Basil Hayward 1960–64
Glyn Davies 1964–65
Joe McDonald 1965–67
Ron Saunders 1967–69
Mike Hughes 1969–72
Cecil Irwin 1972–75
Stan Harland 1975–81
Barry Lloyd 1978–81
Malcolm Allison 1981
Jimmy Giles 1981–83
Trevor Finnigan/Mike Hughes 1983
Steve Coles 1983–84
Ian McFarlane 1984
Gerry Gow 1984–87
Brian Hall 1987–90
Clive Whitehead 1990–91
Steve Rutter 1991–93
Brian Hall 1994–95
Graham Roberts 1995–98
Colin Lippiatt 1998–99
Steve Thompson 1999–2000
Dave Webb 2000
Gary Johnson 2001–05
Steve Thompson 2005–06
Russell Slade 2006–09
Terry Skiverton 2009–12
Gary Johnson 2012–15
Terry Skiverton 2015
Paul Sturrock April 2015–

TEN YEAR LEAGUE RECORD

		P	W	D	L	F	A	Pts	Pos
2005-06	FL 1	46	15	11	20	54	62	56	15
2006-07	FL 1	46	23	10	13	55	39	79	5
2007-08	FL 1	46	14	10	22	38	59	52	18
2008-09	FL 1	46	12	15	19	41	66	51	17
2009-10	FL 1	46	13	14	19	55	59	53	15
2010-11	FL 1	46	16	11	19	56	66	59	14
2011-12	FL 1	46	14	12	20	59	80	54	17
2012-13	FL 1	46	23	8	15	71	56	77	4
2013-14	FL C	46	8	13	25	44	75	37	24
2014-15	FL 1	46	10	10	26	36	75	40	24

DID YOU KNOW

Yeovil played in front of a crowd of 81,565 when they faced Manchester United in an FA Cup fifth round tie in February 1949. United won 8-0 ending Yeovil's run which began in the fourth qualifying round.

YEOVIL TOWN – FOOTBALL LEAGUE ONE 2014–15 LEAGUE RECORD

Match No.	Date	Venue	Opponents	Result	H/T Score	Lg Pos.	Goalscorers	Attendance
1	Aug 9	H	Doncaster R	L	0-3	0-1	24	5235
2	16	A	Gillingham	L	0-2	0-1	23	5173
3	19	A	Walsall	W	2-1	0-0	19	Hayter 56, Dawson 73	3758
4	23	H	Scunthorpe U	D	1-1	0-0	19	Moore 65	3943
5	30	H	Barnsley	D	1-1	0-1	19	Cranie (og) 76	3991
6	Sept 6	A	Bradford C	W	3-1	2-1	12	Martin 2 8, 23, Leitch-Smith 72	12,601
7	13	A	Coventry C	L	1-2	0-1	16	Foley 51	11,085
8	16	H	Crewe Alex	D	1-1	0-0	16	Moore 72	3509
9	20	H	Peterborough U	W	1-0	0-0	13	Grant 88	3970
10	27	A	Crawley T	L	0-2	0-0	15		2351
11	Oct 4	H	Milton Keynes D	L	0-2	0-0	19		4000
12	11	A	Port Vale	L	1-4	0-2	21	Martin 86	4798
13	18	H	Swindon T	D	1-1	1-0	19	Hayter 34	5679
14	21	A	Sheffield U	L	0-2	0-1	21		19,353
15	25	H	Rochdale	L	0-3	0-2	22		3601
16	Nov 1	A	Chesterfield	D	0-0	0-0	23		6462
17	15	H	Fleetwood T	L	0-1	0-0	24		3577
18	22	A	Notts Co	W	2-1	0-0	22	Clarke 2 84, 88	7746
19	29	H	Preston NE	L	0-2	0-1	23		4343
20	Dec 13	A	Oldham Ath	W	4-0	3-0	21	Arthurworrey 21, Gillett 28, Hoskins 40, Moore 90	3706
21	20	H	Colchester U	L	0-1	0-0	22		6837
22	26	A	Bristol C	L	1-2	0-1	24	Nugent 88	13,731
23	29	H	Leyton Orient	L	0-3	0-1	24		4132
24	Jan 10	A	Barnsley	L	0-2	0-0	24		8518
25	17	H	Bradford C	W	1-0	1-0	24	Ugwu 26	4009
26	20	A	Preston NE	D	1-1	1-0	24	Ugwu 45	7491
27	24	H	Coventry C	D	0-0	0-0	23		4422
28	31	A	Peterborough U	L	0-1	0-1	24		5146
29	Feb 7	H	Crawley T	W	2-1	0-1	22	Ugwu 66, Leitch-Smith 72	3807
30	10	A	Crewe Alex	L	0-1	0-1	22		3523
31	14	A	Doncaster R	L	0-3	0-1	24		5950
32	21	H	Gillingham	D	2-2	1-0	24	Ugwu 21, Morgan (pen) 90	4293
33	28	A	Scunthorpe U	D	1-1	1-0	24	Grant 28	3783
34	Mar 3	H	Walsall	L	0-1	0-1	24		3668
35	7	H	Oldham Ath	W	2-1	0-1	24	Grant 55, Hayter 90	3917
36	10	H	Bristol C	L	0-3	0-0	24		6591
37	14	A	Leyton Orient	L	0-3	0-2	24		5117
38	17	A	Colchester U	L	0-2	0-0	24		2336
39	28	A	Rochdale	L	1-2	0-0	24	Hayter 56	2650
40	Apr 3	H	Chesterfield	L	2-3	1-0	24	Hayter 18, Foley 57	4520
41	6	A	Fleetwood T	L	0-4	0-3	24		3086
42	11	H	Notts Co	D	1-1	1-0	24	Hollis (og) 10	3947
43	14	H	Sheffield U	W	1-0	0-0	24	Arthurworrey 67	3841
44	18	A	Swindon T	W	1-0	0-0	24	Berrett 58	8490
45	25	H	Port Vale	L	1-2	0-1	24	Ugwu 80	4127
46	May 3	A	Milton Keynes D	L	1-5	0-4	24	Spence (og) 56	16,965

Final League Position: 24

GOALSCORERS

League (36): Hayter 5, Ugwu 5, Grant 3, Martin 3, Moore 3, Arthurworrey 2, Clarke 2, Foley 2, Leitch-Smith 2, Berrett 1, Dawson 1, Gillett 1, Hoskins 1, Morgan 1 (1 pen), Nugent 1, own goals 3.
FA Cup (4): Clarke 1, Gillett 1, Hiwula 1, Moore 1.
Capital One Cup (1): Gillett 1.
Johnstone's Paint Trophy (1): Ralph 1.

Weale C 8	Moloney B 4 + 1	Martin A 12	Sokolik J 11	Davis L 8	Berrett J 18 + 10	Edwards J 33 + 1	Gillett S 14 + 3	Foley S 37 + 3	Leitch-Smith A 21 + 12	Moore K 20 + 10	Ralph N 9 + 12	Hayter J 23 + 15	Hoskins S 2 + 10	Nugent B 23	Dawson K 12 + 5	Smith N 36 + 5	Price J 5 + 1	Nana Ofori-Twumasi S 18 + 7	Grant J 15 + 6	Kean J 5	Hiwula J 7 + 1	Krysiak A 15	Inniss R 4 + 2	Eastmond C — + 1	Steer J 12	Clarke J 5	Arthurworrey S 29	Eaves T 4 + 1	Bell F 1 + 1	Smith A 3 + 3	Loza J 4 + 1	Ugwu C 21 + 1	Shephard L 20	Webster B 14	Kingsley S 12	Sheehan J 12 + 1	Morgan A 3 + 3	Stewart G — + 1	Loach S 6	Match No.
1	2	3	4	5	6³	7	8	9	10	11²	12	13	14																											1
1	14	3	2		8	7	13	10	11³	5²	12			4	6	9¹																								2
1		3	2		6	8	5²	10		13	11	12		4	7¹	9																							3
1		3	2		7	8	9¹	10	12	14	11¹	13		4	6³	5																							4
1		3	2		7	8³	9	11	12	13	10¹	14		4	6²	5																							5
1		4	2		3		9²	11¹	13	12	10²		8	6	5	7	14																						6
1		4	2		7¹		9²	11	13	14	10⁴		3	6	5	8		12																					7
		4	2³		8		9¹	10	12	14			3	6²	5	7	13	11	1																				8
		3			8			10	11	6			4	12	5	9	2	7¹	1																				9
		4	3		14	8		7²	10¹	11	13			12³	2	9	5	6	1																				10
		4			6³	8	7²		12		9	10¹		3⁴		5	14	2	13	1	11																		11
	2²	3	4		7	6	9	8¹	11	12		14		13	5			1	10¹																				12
				5		8	7			2	10¹			3	12			9	6		11	1	4																13
				9		7	8	13			5³	11¹		4	12	14		2	6²		10	1	3																14
		2¹	5		7	8	12	13		9³	10²			4	6	14					11	1	3																15
				5	10	7		8		11²		13		3	9			6¹			12		1		2	4													16
				5³	8¹	7	14	9	10³			13		3	6	12					11		1		2	4													17
				8¹	7	14	9	10²			12			4	6	5		13			11³		1		2	3													18
				10³	7²	8	14	9			12	13			6¹	5					1		3⁴		2	4	11												19
					8	9²	7	13	14		11¹	10³	4		5		6								1	2	3	12											20
	2²				6	9	7	12		13	10¹	4		5		8³						14	1		3	11													21
	2²				6¹	7	8	9		10		3		5		12							1		4	11	13												22
				14	7	8	6¹	9²		12	10³	4		5		2					13	1			3	11													23
					8²	7		11	6¹	10	9		13	3⁴		5		2					1		4		12												24
					12	8		7	6	4	9					5		2					1		3			10¹	11										25
					14	7		9		3		12	13			2		5					1		4		6¹	11³	10⁵	8										26
						8		7	12	4	13	14			5		6²						1		3		9³	10¹	11	2									27
						7		8	12	3²	14		13			5							1		4		9³	10¹	11	2									28
						6		8	7	2		10		3		5						1			4			11	9										29
				12	7¹			9	11	8²		10³	13	2		5							1		4			14	6	3									30
				8			7	6²	3		11	12	4¹		9							1			2	13		10	5										31
				6¹		7				10²					9			12		1					2			11	5	3	4	8	13						32
				13		7		4³		14					9			10²		1¹					2			11	5	3	8	6		12					33
			9	7			6		2	12³	10¹				14										4			11	5	4	3²	8	13		1				34
						8	13	10³		12					5	14	9¹								4			11	2	3		7	6²	1				35
				13			8¹		10²		12				5		9								3			11	2	4		7	6	1				36
				13	7		10	14			12				3		9³								3			11	2	4	5	8²	6¹	1				37
					7¹		8	12			10				5		6³					14			3			11	2	4	9²		13	1				38
				7			8	6¹	12		10	13			5	2									3			11²		4	9			1				39
				13			8	9¹			10					2	12		1						3			11	6	4	5	7²						40
				12			8	13			10				14	2	7		1						3			11	6²	5	3²	9¹						41
				8			7		12		10¹				5	14	6²		1						3			11³	2	4	9	13						42
				6			7		10						5	12			1						3			11¹	2	4	9	8						43
				8					12	10²					5	6	11¹		1						3			13	2	4	9	7						44
1						7	14	8³		10					12	13									3		6¹	11	2	4²	5	9						45
						7	8			13	12		10²		5		4	9³		1					3		14	11¹	2			6						46

FA Cup

First Round	Crawley T	(h)	1-0
Second Round	Accrington S	(a)	1-1
Replay	Accrington S	(h)	2-0
Third Round	Manchester U	(h)	0-2

Capital One Cup

First Round	Gillingham	(h)	1-2

Johnstone's Paint Trophy

First Round	Portsmouth	(h)	1-3

YORK CITY

FOUNDATION

Although there was a York City club formed in 1903 by a soccer enthusiast from Darlington, this has no connection with the modern club because it went out of existence during World War I. Unlike many others of that period who restarted in 1919, York City did not re-form until 1922 and the tendency now is to ignore the modern club's pre-1922 existence.

Bootham Crescent, York YO30 7AQ.

Telephone: (01904) 624 447.

Fax: (01904) 631 457.

Ticket Office: (01904) 624 447 (ext 1).

Website: www.yorkcityfootballclub.co.uk

Email: enquiries@yorkcityfootballclub.co.uk

Ground Capacity: 7,192.

Record Attendance: 28,123 v Huddersfield T, FA Cup 6th rd, 5 March 1938.

Pitch Measurements: 104m × 64m (113.5yd × 70yd)

Chairman: Jason McGill.

Manager: Russ Wilcox.

Assistant Manager: Steve Torpey.

Physio: Jeff Miller.

Colours: Red shirts with white trim, white shorts, red socks.

Year Formed: 1922.

Turned Professional: 1922.

Ltd Co.: 1922.

Club Nickname: 'Minstermen'.

Previous Grounds: 1922, Fulfordgate; 1932, Bootham Crescent.

First Football League Game: 31 August 1929, Division 3 (N), v Wigan Borough (a) W 2–0 – Farmery; Archibald, Johnson; Beck, Davis, Thompson; Evans, Gardner, Cowie (1), Smailes, Stockill (1).

Record League Victory: 9–1 v Southport, Division 3 (N), 2 February 1957 – Forgan; Phillips, Howe; Brown (1), Cairney, Mollatt; Hill, Bottom (4 incl. 1p), Wilkinson (2), Wragg (1), Fenton (1).

Record Cup Victory: 6–0 v South Shields (a), FA Cup 1st rd, 16 November 1968 – Widdowson; Baker (1p), Richardson; Carr, Jackson, Burrows; Taylor, Ross (3), MacDougall (2), Hodgson, Boyer.

Record Defeat: 0–12 v Chester, Division 3 (N), 1 February 1936.

Most League Points (2 for a win): 62, Division 4, 1964–65.

HONOURS

Football League – Division 3: *Promoted* 1973–74 (3rd); **Division 4:** *Champions* 1983–84. 1992–93 *(play-offs).*

FA Cup: *Semi-finals* 1955, *when in Division 3.*

Football League Cup: Best season: 5th rd, 1962.

FA Trophy: *Winners* 2012; *Runners-up* 2009.

sky SPORTS FACT FILE

York City became the first Football League team to earn over 100 points in a season when they won the Fourth Division title in 1983–84. They defeated Bury 3-0 at Bootham Crescent in the final home game of the season to take them to 101 points. They lost their last away game but ended the season 16 points clear of second-placed Doncaster Rovers.

Most League Points (3 for a win): 101, Division 4, 1983–84.

Most League Goals: 96, Division 4, 1983–84.

Highest League Scorer in Season: Bill Fenton, 31, Division 3 (N), 1951–52; Arthur Bottom, 31, Division 3 (N), 1954–55 and 1955–56.

Most League Goals in Total Aggregate: Norman Wilkinson, 127, 1954–66.

Most League Goals in One Match: 5, Alf Patrick v Rotherham U, Division 3N, 20 November 1948.

Most Capped Player: Peter Scott, 7 (10), Northern Ireland.

Most League Appearances: Barry Jackson, 482, 1958–70.

Youngest League Player: Reg Stockill, 15 years 281 days v Wigan Borough, 31 August 1929.

Record Transfer Fee Received: £950,000 from Sheffield W for Richard Cresswell, March 1999.

Record Transfer Fee Paid: £140,000 to Burnley for Adrian Randall, December 1995.

Football League Record: 1929 Elected to Division 3 (N); 1958–59 Division 4; 1959–60 Division 3; 1960–65 Division 3; 1965–66 Division 3; 1966–71 Division 4; 1971–74 Division 3; 1974–76 Division 2; 1976–77 Division 3; 1977–84 Division 4; 1984–88 Division 3; 1988–92 Division 4; 1992–93 Division 3; 1993–99 Division 2; 1999–04 Division 3; 2004–07 Conference; 2007–12 Conference Premier; 2012– FL 2.

LATEST SEQUENCES

Longest Sequence of League Wins: 7, 31.10.1964 – 26.12.1964.

Longest Sequence of League Defeats: 8, 14.11.1966 – 31.12.1966.

Longest Sequence of League Draws: 6, 3.5.2014 – 30.8.2014.

Longest Sequence of Unbeaten League Matches: 21, 10.9.1973 – 12.1.1974.

Longest Sequence Without a League Win: 23, 1.2.2014 – 6.9.2014.

Successive Scoring Runs: 24 from 3.3.1984.

Successive Non-scoring Runs: 7 from 28.8.1972.

MANAGERS

Bill Sherrington 1924–60
(was Secretary for most of this time but virtually Secretary-Manager for a long pre-war spell)
John Collier 1929–36
Tom Mitchell 1936–50
Dick Duckworth 1950–52
Charlie Spencer 1952–53
Jimmy McCormick 1953–54
Sam Bartram 1956–60
Tom Lockie 1960–67
Joe Shaw 1967–68
Tom Johnston 1968–75
Wilf McGuinness 1975–77
Charlie Wright 1977–80
Barry Lyons 1980–81
Denis Smith 1982–87
Bobby Saxton 1987–88
John Bird 1988–91
John Ward 1991–93
Alan Little 1993–99
Neil Thompson 1999–2000
Terry Dolan 2000–03
Chris Brass 2003–04
Billy McEwan 2005–07
Colin Walker 2007–08
Martin Foyle 2008–10
Gary Mills 2010–13
Nigel Worthington 2013–14
Russ Wilcox October 2014–

TEN YEAR LEAGUE RECORD

		P	W	D	L	F	A	Pts	Pos
2005-06	Conf	42	17	12	13	63	48	63	8
2006-07	Conf	46	23	11	12	65	45	80	4
2007-08	Conf P	46	17	11	18	71	74	62	14
2008-09	Conf P	46	11	19	16	47	51	52	17
2009-10	Conf P	44	22	12	10	62	35	78	5
2010-11	Conf P	46	19	14	13	55	50	71	8
2011-12	Conf P	46	23	14	9	81	45	83	4
2012-13	FL 2	46	12	19	15	50	60	55	17
2013-14	FL 2	46	18	17	11	52	41	71	7
2014-15	FL 2	46	11	19	16	46	51	52	18

DID YOU KNOW

In September 1995 York City travelled to Old Trafford for a Football League Cup second round tie after winning just one of their opening 8 League fixtures. The Minstermen achieved an astonishing 3-0 victory and although they lost the second leg they went through 4-3 on aggregate.

YORK CITY – FOOTBALL LEAGUE TWO 2014–15 LEAGUE RECORD

Match No.	Date		Venue	Opponents	Result	H/T Score	Lg Pos.	Goalscorers	Attendance
1	Aug	9	A	Tranmere R	D 1-1	0-0	12	Lowe [67]	6287
2		16	H	Northampton T	D 1-1	0-0	16	Hyde [67]	3448
3		19	H	Cambridge U	D 2-2	1-2	17	Hyde [43], Fletcher (pen) [82]	3176
4		23	A	Exeter C	D 1-1	0-1	16	Lowe [82]	2741
5		30	H	Wycombe W	D 0-0	0-0	17		3209
6	Sept	6	A	Stevenage	W 3-2	2-0	11	Coulson [3], Fletcher 2 (1 pen) [15, 75 (p)]	3090
7		13	A	Burton Alb	L 0-2	0-0	16		2890
8		16	H	Luton T	D 0-0	0-0	16		3649
9		20	H	Southend U	L 2-3	1-1	19	Penn [45], Winfield [85]	3307
10		27	A	Dagenham & R	L 0-2	0-1	21		1801
11	Oct	4	H	Portsmouth	D 0-0	0-0	21		3856
12		11	A	Newport Co	L 1-3	1-0	22	De Girolamo [7]	2822
13		18	H	Shrewsbury T	L 0-1	0-0	23		3651
14		21	A	Morecambe	D 1-1	0-0	22	Coulson [77]	1346
15		25	H	Mansfield T	D 1-1	1-0	22	De Girolamo [20]	3370
16	Nov	1	H	Cheltenham T	W 1-0	1-0	20	De Girolamo [43]	2469
17		15	H	Oxford U	L 0-1	0-1	21		3363
18		22	A	Hartlepool U	W 3-1	0-1	20	Lowe 2 [53, 55], Hyde [63]	4234
19		29	A	Plymouth Arg	D 1-1	0-1	21	Hyde [90]	6808
20	Dec	13	H	AFC Wimbledon	L 2-3	0-1	21	De Girolamo [55], Zubar [75]	3245
21		20	A	Bury	D 2-2	0-0	22	Hyde [66], Summerfield [78]	3313
22		26	H	Accrington S	W 1-0	1-0	21	Lowe [35]	3873
23		28	A	Carlisle U	W 3-0	1-0	18	Carson [44], Summerfield [68], Coulson [81]	5716
24	Jan	3	H	Plymouth Arg	D 0-0	0-0	18		3869
25		10	A	Wycombe W	L 0-1	0-0	19		3669
26		17	H	Stevenage	L 0-2	0-1	19		3107
27		24	H	Burton Alb	D 1-1	0-0	19	Sinclair [70]	3398
28		31	A	Southend U	L 0-1	0-0	22		6126
29	Feb	7	H	Dagenham & R	L 0-2	0-1	23		2958
30		10	A	Luton T	D 2-2	0-0	23	Carson [55], Sinclair [59]	7763
31		14	H	Tranmere R	W 2-0	1-0	20	Fletcher 2 [20, 58]	3714
32		21	A	Northampton T	L 0-3	0-1	22		4694
33		28	H	Exeter C	D 0-0	0-0	22		3209
34	Mar	3	A	Cambridge U	W 3-0	1-0	20	Fletcher [43], Coulson [49], Hyde [55]	4037
35		7	A	AFC Wimbledon	L 1-2	1-1	20	Hyde [43]	4086
36		14	H	Carlisle U	D 0-0	0-0	20		4274
37		17	H	Bury	L 0-1	0-1	21		3194
38		21	A	Accrington S	D 2-2	0-0	21	Summerfield [63], Hyde [76]	1454
39		28	A	Mansfield T	W 4-1	2-0	20	Lowe [9], Coulthirst 2 [17, 89], Hyde [52]	3133
40	Apr	3	H	Cheltenham T	W 1-0	0-0	20	Winfield [73]	4151
41		6	A	Oxford U	D 0-0	0-0	19		9406
42		11	H	Hartlepool U	W 1-0	0-0	19	Summerfield [67]	5424
43		14	H	Morecambe	W 2-1	1-1	18	Zubar [34], Penn [51]	2854
44		18	A	Shrewsbury T	L 0-1	0-1	19		6400
45		25	H	Newport Co	L 0-2	0-0	19		3459
46	May	2	A	Portsmouth	D 1-1	0-0	18	Halliday [85]	17,254

Final League Position: 18

GOALSCORERS

League (46): Hyde 9, Fletcher 6 (2 pens), Lowe 6, Coulson 4, De Girolamo 4, Summerfield 4, Carson 2, Coulthirst 2, Penn 2, Sinclair 2, Winfield 2, Zubar 2, Halliday 1.
FA Cup (2): Fletcher 1, Hyde 1.
Capital One Cup (0).
Johnstone's Paint Trophy (0).

Mooney J 3+1	McCoy M 30+1	McCombe J 27+4	Lowe K 46	Ilesanmi F 29+4	Meikle L 13+15	Penn R 45	Platt T 7+13	Straker A 7+5	Coulson M 43	Jarvis R 5+3	Hirst B —+3	Summerfield L 26+5	Montrose L 10+4	Hyde J 32+7	Fletcher W 22+7	Winfield D 9+1	Ingham M 17+2	Brunt R 5+1	De Girolamo D 9+3	Cisak A 10	Burton D 1	Zohar S 22+1	Carson J 18+4	Morris C —+8	Halliday B 24	Olejnik R 16	Benning M 9	Sinclair E 9+3	Coulthirst S 10+1	O'Hanlon J —+3	Miller S 2+4	Match No.
1	2	3	4	5	6	7	8	9²	10¹	11³	12	13	14																			1
1	2	3	4	5	6	7	8	9	10					11¹	12																	2
1³	2	3¹	4		5	9	7	6	11			8		10²	14	12	13															3
	2	3	5	12	7	6¹	9²	11				14	8	10³	13	4	1															4
	2	4	3	5	6	7		9²	10			13	8	11¹	12		1															5
	2	3	9	4	5²	10		8¹	6	13		7		12	11		1															6
	2	3	4	5	6²	7	13	9¹	10			8		12	11		1															7
	2	3	4	5	9³	7	6¹	12	10	14		8		13	11²		1															8
	2		3	5	9³	8	12	13	6	14		7¹		10²	11	4	1															9
	2		3	5	12	8	13		6	9		7¹		11²	10	4	1															10
	2	3	4	5	12	9	14		8¹	7²		6	13	11²			1	10														11
12	2	4	3	5	9	7¹	13		10⁵			14	6				1³	11	8¹													12
	2	3	4	5	12		8		6	9⁴		7					1	11	10¹													13
	2	3	4	5	6	7	12		9			8¹		11			1	10														14
	2	3	4	5	9²	8	12	13	6			7¹		11	10		1															15
	2	3	4	5	6	7³		9				13	8	12	14	10¹	1		11²													16
	2		4	5	6¹	7		12	9			13	8²	11	10³					1		3	14									17
	2		3	5	13	8			6			12	7²	11	10¹					1		4	9									18
	2	13	3²	5		7		9				8		10	11¹				12	1		4	6³	14								19
		3	5		7			9				8		10	11¹				6²	1		4	13	12	2							20
		3	5		6			8				7		10	11				9	1		4			2							21
12		3	5		8			6				7		9²	10³				11¹	1		4	14	13	2⁴							22
	2		4	5	13	7³		8				6	14	10	11¹					1		3	9²	12								23
	2	12	3	5	13	7		6²				8		11	10¹					1		4⁴	9									24
	2	3	4	5	12	8¹		6				7		11	10					1		9²	13									25
		3	4	5³	13	8		12	6			7		10	11²					1		9¹	14		2							26
		3	4		8			6				7		10¹	12				9			2				1	5	11				27
		3	4		8²			9				7	13	11³	12							6	14		2	1	5	10⁵				28
		3	4		7			6				8²	12	11¹								9	13		2	1	5	11				29
	2	3		12	7			6				10⁴	13									4	9²	8	5	1		11¹				30
	2	3		12	7			6				10										4	9¹	8	5	1		11				31
	2¹	3		13	6			9				11							12			4	10²	7	5	1		8				32
	2	3		13	7			6				11							10²			4	9¹	8	5	1		12				33
	2	13	4	·	14	6		8²		9¹		11³										3	10	7	5	1		12				34
	2	3		13	7			6				11	10¹									4	9²	8	5	1		12				35
	2	4	5		8			6				11²							13			3	9¹	7		1			10	12		36
	2	14	3	5²	7			9¹				13							10			4³	12	8		1			6	11		37
	2	4			7	12		6	11			3										5		8		1		9				38
	2	3			7³	9		6	11²	4		12										8			5	1⁸			10¹	13	14	39
	4¹	2			6	9²	8	7	11	3		1										12			5				10³	14	13	40
	4	2			6	12	9	7¹	10	3		1										8			5				11			41
	2	3	12		6	13	11¹	7	10	4⁴		1										8			5				9²			42
	3	2	12		6	13	8³	7¹	14	11		1										4			5				10		9²	43
	3	2			9¹	8		6	7	11		1										4			5				10		12	44
	2	3	12		7¹	14	9²	8	11	1		4										5			6				13	10³		45
	4	2	12		8	13	7¹	6	10	3³		9										5			1				11²	14		46

FA Cup

First Round	AFC Wimbledon	(h)	1-1
Replay	AFC Wimbledon	(a)	1-3

Capital One Cup

First Round	Doncaster R	(h)	0-1

Johnstone's Paint Trophy

First Round	Barnsley	(a)	0-2

ENGLISH LEAGUE PLAYERS DIRECTORY

Players listed represent those with their clubs during the 2014–15 season.

Players are listed alphabetically on pages 537–542.
The number alongside each player corresponds to the team number heading. (Aarons, Rolando 54 = team 54 (Newcastle U)). Club names in *italics* indicate loans.

ACCRINGTON S (1)

ALDRED, Tom (D)   102   3
H: 6 2   W: 13 02   b.Bolton 11-9-90
Internationals: Scotland U19.
2008–09	Carlisle U	0	0		
2009–10	Carlisle U	5	0	5	0
2010–11	Watford	0	0		
2010–11	*Stockport Co*	7	0	7	0
2011–12	Watford	0	0		
2011–12	Colchester U	0	0		
2011–12	*Torquay U*	0	0		
2012–13	Colchester U	0	0		
2012–13	Accrington S	13	0		
2013–14	Accrington S	46	2		
2014–15	Accrington S	25	1	84	3
2014–15	*Blackpool*	6	0	6	0

ATKINSON, Rob (D)   191   8
H: 6 1   W: 12 03   b.Beverley 29-4-87
Internationals: England C.
2003–04	Barnsley	1	0		
2004–05	Barnsley	1	0		
2005–06	Barnsley	0	0		
2006–07	Barnsley	6	0		
2007–08	Barnsley	0	0	8	0
2007–08	*Rochdale*	2	0	2	0
2007–08	*Grimsby T*	24	1		
2008–09	Grimsby T	31	2		
2009–10	Grimsby T	37	2	92	5
2012–13	Fleetwood T	18	0	18	0
2012–13	*Accrington S*	12	0		
2013–14	Accrington S	15	0		
2014–15	Accrington S	44	3	71	3

BARRY, Anthony (M)   132   1
H: 5 7   W: 10 00   b.Liverpool 29-5-86
2004–05	Coventry C	0	0		
From Accrington S					
2005–06	Yeovil T	4	0		
2006–07	Yeovil T	24	0		
2007–08	Yeovil T	36	0	64	0
2008–09	Chester C	43	1	43	1
2012–13	Fleetwood T	12	0	12	0
on loan from Forest Green R					
2014–15	Accrington S	13	0	13	0

BOWERMAN, George (F)   67   12
H: 5 10   W: 10 07   b.Sedgley 6-11-91
2010–11	Walsall	0	0		
2011–12	Walsall	22	3		
2012–13	Walsall	28	6		
2013–14	Walsall	0	0	50	9
2013–14	Accrington S	14	3		
2014–15	Accrington S	3	0	17	3

BRUNA, Gerardo (M)   8   0
H: 5 8   W: 10 02   b.Mendoza 29-1-91
Internationals: Spain U17.
2007–08	Liverpool	0	0		
2008–09	Liverpool	0	0		
2009–10	Liverpool	0	0		
2010–11	Liverpool	0	0		
2011–12	Blackpool	1	0		
2012–13	Blackpool	1	0		
2013–14	Blackpool	0	0	2	0
2014–15	Tranmere R	0	0		
2014–15	Accrington S	6	0	6	0

BUXTON, Adam (D)   28   1
H: 6 1   W: 12 10   b.Liverpool 12-5-92
2010–11	Wigan Ath	0	0		
2011–12	Wigan Ath	0	0		
2012–13	Wigan Ath	0	0		
2013–14	Wigan Ath	0	0		
2013–14	*Burton Alb*	0	0		
2014–15	Accrington S	17	1	28	1

CARVER, Marcus (F)   36   1
H: 5 11   W: 11 11   b.Blackburn 22-10-93
2011–12	Accrington S	2	0		
2012–13	Accrington S	11	0		
2013–14	Accrington S	6	0		
2014–15	Accrington S	17	1	36	1

CONNEELY, Seamus (D)   102   5
H: 5 9   W: 10 10   b.Galway 9-7-88
Internationals: Republic of Ireland U21, U23.
2008	Galway U	20	0		
2009	Galway U	34	2		
2010	Galway U	32	0	86	2
2010–11	Sheffield U	0	0		
2011–12	Sheffield U	0	0		
2014–15	Accrington S	16	3	16	3

CROOKS, Matt (M)   20   0
H: 6 0   W: 11 05   b.Leeds 20-1-94
2011–12	Huddersfield T	0	0		
2012–13	Huddersfield T	0	0		
2013–14	Huddersfield T	0	0		
2014–15	Huddersfield T	1	0	1	0
2014–15	*Hartlepool U*	3	0	3	0
2014–15	Accrington S	16	0	16	0

GORNELL, Terry (F)   237   44
H: 5 11   W: 12 04   b.Liverpool 16-12-89
2008–09	Tranmere R	10	1		
2008–09	*Accrington S*	11	4		
2009–10	Tranmere R	27	2		
2010–11	Tranmere R	3	0	40	3
2010–11	Accrington S	40	13		
2011–12	Shrewsbury T	41	9		
2012–13	Shrewsbury T	12	0	53	9
2012–13	Rochdale	19	5	19	5
2013–14	Cheltenham T	34	3		
2014–15	Cheltenham T	25	3	59	6
2014–15	Accrington S	15	4	66	21

GOULDING, Liam (D)   0   0
H: 6 1   W: 12 08   b. 28-4-96
2014–15	Accrington S	0	0		

GRAY, James (F)   76   16
H: 5 11   b.Stockton on Tees 17-10-92
Internationals: Northern Ireland U16, U17, U19, U21.
2012–13	Accrington S	16	2		
2013–14	Accrington S	35	7		
2014–15	Accrington S	17	4	68	13
2014–15	*Northampton T*	8	3	8	3

HATFIELD, Will (M)   87   5
H: 5 8   W: 10 00   b.Liversedge 10-10-91
2009–10	Leeds U	0	0		
2010–11	Leeds U	0	0		
2011–12	Leeds U	0	0		
2011–12	Accrington S	17	3		
2012–13	Accrington S	32	2		
2013–14	Accrington S	31	0		
2014–15	Accrington S	7	0	87	5

HAZELDINE, Max (M)   1   0
H: 5 10   W: 11 11   b. 13-2-97
2014–15	Accrington S	0	0		
2014–15	Accrington S	1	0	1	0

HUNT, Nicky (D)   270   2
H: 6 1   W: 13 07   b.Westhoughton 3-9-83
Internationals: England U21.
2000–01	Bolton W	1	0		
2001–02	Bolton W	0	0		
2002–03	Bolton W	0	0		
2003–04	Bolton W	31	1		
2004–05	Bolton W	29	0		
2005–06	Bolton W	20	0		
2006–07	Bolton W	33	0		
2007–08	Bolton W	14	0		
2008–09	Bolton W	0	0		
2008–09	*Birmingham C*	11	0	11	0
2009–10	Bolton W	0	0	128	1
2009–10	*Derby Co*	21	0	21	0
2010–11	Bristol C	7	0		
2011–12	Bristol C	0	0	7	0
2011–12	Preston NE	17	1	17	1
2012–13	Rotherham U	9	0	9	0
2012–13	Accrington S	11	0		
2013–14	Accrington S	37	0		
2014–15	Accrington S	29	0	77	0

JENKINS, James (M)   0   0
b.Liverpool 18-1-96
2013–14	Accrington S	0	0		
2014–15	Accrington S	0	0		

JOYCE, Luke (M)   272   10
H: 5 11   W: 12 03   b.Bolton 9-7-87
2005–06	Wigan Ath	0	0		
2006–07	Carlisle U	16	1		
2007–08	Carlisle U	3	1		
2008–09	Carlisle U	7	0	26	2
2009–10	Accrington S	41	1		
2010–11	Accrington S	27	1		
2011–12	Accrington S	43	2		
2012–13	Accrington S	44	0		
2013–14	Accrington S	46	1		
2014–15	Accrington S	45	3	246	8

LIDDLE, Michael (D)   101   0
H: 5 6   W: 11 00   b.Hounslow 25-12-89
Internationals: Republic of Ireland U21.
2007–08	Sunderland	0	0		
2008–09	Sunderland	0	0		
2008–09	*Carlisle U*	22	0	22	0
2009–10	Sunderland	0	0		
2010–11	Sunderland	0	0		
2010–11	*Leyton Orient*	1	0	1	0
2011–12	Sunderland	0	0		
2011–12	*Accrington S*	12	0		
2012–13	Accrington S	32	0		
2013–14	Accrington S	19	0		
2014–15	Accrington S	15	0	78	0

LYNCH, Jay (G)   2   0
H: 6 2   W: 13 04   b.Salford 31-3-93
2012–13	Bolton W	0	0		
2013–14	Bolton W	0	0		
2014–15	Accrington S	2	0	2	0

McCARTAN, Shay (M)   50   7
H: 5 10   W: 11 09   b.Newry 18-5-94
Internationals: Northern Ireland U17, U19, U21.
2011–12	Burnley	1	0		
2012–13	Burnley	0	0	1	0
2013–14	Accrington S	18	1		
2014–15	Accrington S	31	6	49	7

MINGOIA, Piero (M)   85   10
H: 5 6   W: 10 12   b.Enfield 20-10-91
2010–11	Watford	5	0		
2011–12	Watford	0	0		
2011–12	*Brentford*	0	0		
2012–13	Watford	0	0		
2012–13	*Accrington S*	7	1		
2013–14	Watford	0	0	5	0
2013–14	Accrington S	37	1		
2014–15	Accrington S	36	8	80	10

MUSTOE, Jordan (M)   61   1
H: 5 11   W: 11 11   b.Birkenhead 28-1-91
2009–10	Wigan Ath	0	0		
2010–11	Wigan Ath	0	0		
2011–12	Wigan Ath	0	0		
2011–12	Barnet	18	0	18	0
2012–13	Wigan Ath	0	0		
2012–13	Morecambe	11	0		
2012–13	*Carlisle U*	14	1	14	1
2013–14	Wigan Ath	0	0		
2013–14	*Bury*	6	0	6	0
2013–14	*Wycombe W*	3	0	3	0
2013–14	*Morecambe*	5	0	16	0
2014–15	Accrington S	4	0	4	0
Transferred to Westerlo January 2015.					

NAISMITH, Kal (F)   73   14
H: 5 7   W: 13 02   b.Glasgow 18-2-92
Internationals: Scotland U16, U17.
2013–14	Accrington S	38	10		
2014–15	Accrington S	35	4	73	14

PROCTER, Andy (M)   330   31
H: 6 0   W: 12 04   b.Blackburn 13-3-83
Internationals: England C.
2006–07	Accrington S	43	3		
2007–08	Accrington S	43	10		
2008–09	Accrington S	37	3		
2009–10	Accrington S	44	5		
2010–11	Accrington S	43	6		
2011–12	Accrington S	25	2		
2011–12	Preston NE	19	0		

Season	Club				
2012–13	Preston NE	15	0	34	0
2013–14	Bury	32	2	32	2
2014–15	Accrington S	29	0	264	29

RODDAN, Craig (M) 1 0
b.Kirkby 22-4-93

Season	Club				
2011–12	Liverpool	0	0		
2012–13	Liverpool	0	0		
2013–14	Liverpool	0	0		
2013–14	Carlisle U	1	0	1	0
2014–15	Accrington S	0	0		

SIMPSON, Luke (G) 8 0
H: 5 10 W: 12 03 b.Bury 23-9-94

Season	Club				
2012–13	Oldham Ath	0	0		
2013–14	Oldham Ath	0	0		
2014–15	Accrington S	8	0	8	0

STEENSON, Kealan (M) 0 0
b. 6-11-96

Season	Club				
2014–15	Accrington S	0	0		

WHITEHEAD, Danny (M) 2 0
H: 5 10 W: 10 11 b.Trafford 23-10-93

Season	Club				
2013–14	West Ham U	0	0		
2014–15	West Ham U	0	0		
2014–15	Accrington S	2	0	2	0

WINDASS, Josh (M) 45 6
H: 5 9 W: 10 10 b.Hull 9-1-93

Season	Club				
2013–14	Accrington S	10	0		
2014–15	Accrington S	35	6	45	6

WINNARD, Dean (D) 235 5
H: 5 9 W: 10 04 b.Wigan 20-8-89

Season	Club				
2006–07	Blackburn R	0	0		
2007–08	Blackburn R	0	0		
2008–09	Blackburn R	0	0		
2009–10	Accrington S	44	0		
2010–11	Accrington S	45	1		
2011–12	Accrington S	30	1		
2012–13	Accrington S	40	1		
2013–14	Accrington S	39	2		
2014–15	Accrington S	37	0	235	5

Scholars
Dass, Reuben; Downey, Dieter; Evans, Christian Paul; Gunner, Callum Richard Peter; Hartley, Jack Kennedy; Hazeldine, Max Cameron; Hickey, Roman Wes; Quansah, Keenan Elliott; Roberts, John Joseph; Scarth, Tyler Brian; Smith, Dylan Liam; Steenson, Kealan Joseph; Walsh, Callum Joseph; Webb, Nathan James; Wolfenden, James Harry.

AFC WIMBLEDON (2)

AGYEI, Daniel (F) 0 0

Season	Club				
2014–15	AFC Wimbledon	0	0		

AKINFENWA, Adebayo (F) 430 142
H: 5 11 W: 13 07 b.Nigeria 10-5-82

Season	Club				
2001	Atlantas	19	4		
2002	Atlantas	4	1	23	5
From Barry T					
2003–04	Boston U	3	0	3	0
2003–04	Leyton Orient	1	0	1	0
2003–04	Rushden & D	0	0		
2003–04	Doncaster R	9	4	9	4
2004–05	Torquay U	37	14	37	14
2005–06	Swansea C	34	9		
2006–07	Swansea C	25	5		
2007–08	Swansea C	0	0	59	14
2007–08	Millwall	7	0	7	0
2007–08	Northampton T	15	7		
2008–09	Northampton T	33	13		
2009–10	Northampton T	40	17		
2010–11	Gillingham	44	11		
2011–12	Northampton T	39	18		
2012–13	Northampton T	41	16	168	71
2013–14	Gillingham	34	10	78	21
2014–15	AFC Wimbledon	45	13	45	13

ARTHUR, Chris (M) 33 1
H: 5 10 W: 12 02 b.Enfield 25-1-90

Season	Club				
2011–12	Northampton T	7	0	7	0
2013–14	AFC Wimbledon	26	1		
2014–15	AFC Wimbledon	0	0	26	1

AZEAZE, Adebayo (F) 72 10
H: 6 0 W: 12 07 b.Orpington 8-1-94
Internationals: England U19.

Season	Club				
2012–13	Charlton Ath	0	0		
2012–13	Wycombe W	4	0	4	0
2012–13	Leyton Orient	1	0	1	0
2013–14	Charlton Ath	0	0		
2013–14	Torquay U	9	2	9	2

Season	Club				
2013–14	Dagenham & R	15	3	15	3
2014–15	AFC Wimbledon	43	5	43	5

BAYES, Ashley (G) 307 0
H: 6 1 W: 13 04 b.Lincoln 19-4-72
Internationals: England U18.

Season	Club				
1989–90	Brentford	1	0		
1990–91	Brentford	0	0		
1991–92	Brentford	1	0		
1992–93	Brentford	2	0	4	0
1993–94	Torquay U	32	0		
1994–95	Torquay U	37	0		
1995–96	Torquay U	28	0	97	0
1996–97	Exeter C	41	0		
1997–98	Exeter C	45	0		
1998–99	Exeter C	41	0	127	0
2000–01	Leyton Orient	39	0		
2001–02	Leyton Orient	13	0	52	0
2002–03	Bohemians	27	0	27	0
From Woking, Hornchurch, Grays Ath, Crawley T, Stevenage, Basingstoke					
2013–14	AFC Wimbledon	0	0		
2014–15	AFC Wimbledon	0	0		

BEERE, Tom (F) 18 0
H: 5 11 W: 11 09 b.Southwark 27-1-95

Season	Club				
2012–13	AFC Wimbledon	0	0		
2013–14	AFC Wimbledon	0	0		
2014–15	AFC Wimbledon	18	0	18	0

BENNETT, Alan (D) 228 7
H: 6 2 W: 12 08 b.Cork 4-10-81
Internationals: Republic of Ireland U21, B. Full caps.

Season	Club				
2006–07	Reading	0	0		
2007–08	Reading	0	0		
2007–08	Southampton	10	0	10	0
2007–08	Brentford	11	1		
2008–09	Reading	0	0		
2008–09	Brentford	44	1		
2009–10	Brentford	13	0	68	2
2009–10	Wycombe W	6	1		
2010–11	Wycombe W	17	0	23	1
2011–12	Cheltenham T	44	2		
2012–13	Cheltenham T	17	0	61	2
2012–13	AFC Wimbledon	18	1		
2013–14	AFC Wimbledon	32	1		
2014–15	AFC Wimbledon	16	0	66	2
Transferred to Cork C February 2015.					

BULMAN, Dannie (M) 364 19
H: 5 9 W: 11 12 b.Ashford 24-1-79

Season	Club				
1998–99	Wycombe W	11	1		
1999–2000	Wycombe W	29	1		
2000–01	Wycombe W	36	4		
2001–02	Wycombe W	46	5		
2002–03	Wycombe W	42	3		
2003–04	Wycombe W	38	0	202	14
From Stevenage, Crawley T.					
2010–11	Oxford U	5	0	5	0
2011–12	Crawley T	41	3		
2012–13	Crawley T	36	1		
2013–14	Crawley T	39	0	116	4
2014–15	AFC Wimbledon	41	1	41	1

CONNOLLY, David (F) 444 165
H: 5 9 W: 11 00 b.Willesden 6-6-77
Internationals: Republic of Ireland U21, Full caps.

Season	Club				
1994–95	Watford	2	0		
1995–96	Watford	11	8		
1996–97	Watford	13	2	26	10
1997–98	Feyenoord	10	2		
1998–99	Wolverhampton W	32	6	32	6
1999–2000	Excelsior	32	29	32	29
2000–01	Feyenoord	15	5	25	7
2001–02	Wimbledon	35	18		
2002–03	Wimbledon	28	24	63	42
2003–04	West Ham U	39	10	39	10
2004–05	Leicester C	44	13		
2005–06	Leicester C	5	4	49	17
2005–06	Wigan Ath	17	1		
2006–07	Wigan Ath	2	0	19	1
2006–07	Sunderland	36	13		
2007–08	Sunderland	3	0		
2008–09	Sunderland	0	0	39	13
2009–10	Southampton	20	5		
2010–11	Southampton	15	3		
2011–12	Southampton	26	6	61	14
2012–13	Portsmouth	17	7		
2013–14	Oxford U	16	4	16	4
2014–15	Portsmouth	0	0	35	11
2014–15	AFC Wimbledon	8	1	8	1

FITZPATRICK, David (M) 3 0
b.Surbiton 10-2-95

Season	Club				
2011–12	QPR	0	0		
2012–13	QPR	0	0		

Season	Club				
2013–14	QPR	0	0		
2014–15	AFC Wimbledon	3	0	3	0

FRAMPTON, Andrew (D) 367 12
H: 5 11 W: 10 10 b.Wimbledon 3-9-79

Season	Club				
1998–99	Crystal Palace	6	0		
1999–2000	Crystal Palace	9	0		
2000–01	Crystal Palace	10	0		
2001–02	Crystal Palace	2	0		
2002–03	Crystal Palace	1	0	28	0
2002–03	Brentford	15	0		
2003–04	Brentford	16	0		
2004–05	Brentford	35	0		
2005–06	Brentford	36	3		
2006–07	Brentford	32	1	134	4
2007–08	Millwall	30	1		
2008–09	Millwall	37	1		
2009–10	Millwall	21	2		
2010–11	Millwall	0	0	88	4
2010–11	Leyton Orient	1	0	1	0
2010–11	Swindon T	23	0	23	0
2011–12	Gillingham	28	0		
2012–13	Gillingham	30	0		
2013–14	Gillingham	0	0	58	0
2013–14	AFC Wimbledon	31	4		
2014–15	AFC Wimbledon	4	0	35	4

FRANCOMB, George (D) 114 6
H: 5 11 W: 11 07 b.Hackney 8-9-91

Season	Club				
2009–10	Norwich C	2	0		
2010–11	Norwich C	0	0		
2010–11	Barnet	13	0	13	0
2011–12	Norwich C	0	0		
2011–12	Hibernian	14	0	14	0
2012–13	Norwich C	0	0	2	0
2012–13	AFC Wimbledon	15	0		
2013–14	AFC Wimbledon	33	3		
2014–15	AFC Wimbledon	37	3	85	6

FULLER, Barry (D) 278 2
H: 5 10 W: 11 10 b.Ashford 25-9-84
Internationals: England C.

Season	Club				
2004–05	Charlton Ath	0	0		
2005–06	Charlton Ath	0	0		
2005–06	Barnet	15	1		
From Stevenage B.					
2007–08	Gillingham	10	0		
2008–09	Gillingham	37	0		
2009–10	Gillingham	36	0		
2010–11	Gillingham	42	0		
2011–12	Gillingham	9	0		
2012–13	Gillingham	0	0	134	0
2012–13	Barnet	39	0	54	1
2013–14	AFC Wimbledon	45	0		
2014–15	AFC Wimbledon	45	1	90	1

GALLAGHER, Dan (M) 1 0
b. 20-6-97

Season	Club				
2014–15	AFC Wimbledon	1	0	1	0

HARRISON, Ben (M) 7 0
b. 2-3-97

Season	Club				
2014–15	AFC Wimbledon	7	0	7	0

JACQUART, Chace (M) 0 0
H: 5 4 W: 9 06 b.Sutton 16-7-95

Season	Club				
2013–14	AFC Wimbledon	0	0		
2014–15	AFC Wimbledon	0	0		

KENNEDY, Callum (D) 106 1
H: 5 11 W: 12 10 b.Chertsey 9-11-89

Season	Club				
2007–08	Swindon T	0	0		
2008–09	Swindon T	4	0		
2009–10	Swindon T	8	0		
2010–11	Swindon T	3	0		
2010–11	Gillingham	3	0	3	0
2010–11	Rotherham U	5	0	5	0
2011–12	Swindon T	18	1	33	1
2012–13	Scunthorpe U	17	0	17	0
2013–14	AFC Wimbledon	22	0		
2014–15	AFC Wimbledon	26	0	48	0

McDONNELL, Joe (G) 4 0
H: 5 10 W: 9 13 b.Basingstoke 19-5-94

Season	Club				
2014–15	AFC Wimbledon	4	0	4	0

MOORE, Sammy (M) 160 14
H: 5 8 W: 9 00 b.Dover 7-9-87

Season	Club				
2006–07	Ipswich T	0	0		
2007–08	Ipswich T	0	0		
2007–08	Brentford	20	2	20	2
2008–09	Brentford	0	0	1	0
2011–12	AFC Wimbledon	41	6		
2012–13	AFC Wimbledon	28	2		
2013–14	AFC Wimbledon	40	4		
2014–15	AFC Wimbledon	30	0	139	12

NICHOLSON, Jake (M) 8 1
H: 6 0 W: 11 07 b.Harrow 19-7-92
Internationals: England U19.

Season	Club				
2010–11	Tottenham H	0	0		

2010–11	*MyPa*	2	0	2 0
2011–12	Tottenham H	0	0	
2012–13	Tottenham H	0	0	
2013–14	AFC Wimbledon	4	1	
2014–15	AFC Wimbledon	2	0	6 1

NIGHTINGALE, Will (M) 4 0
H: 6 1 W: 13 03 b.Wandsworth 2-7-95

2013–14	AFC Wimbledon	0	0	
2014–15	AFC Wimbledon	4	0	4 0

OAKLEY, George (F) 6 0
H: 6 2 W: 13 08 b.Wandsworth 18-11-95

2013–14	AFC Wimbledon	0	0	
2014–15	AFC Wimbledon	6	0	6 0

PELL, Harry (M) 106 9
H: 6 4 W: 13 05 b.Tilbury 21-10-91

2010–11	Bristol R	10	0	10 0
2010–11	*Hereford U*	7	0	
2011–12	Hereford U	30	3	37 3
2012–13	AFC Wimbledon	17	2	
2013–14	AFC Wimbledon	33	4	
2014–15	AFC Wimbledon	9	0	59 6

PHILLIPS, Mark (D) 227 14
H: 6 2 W: 11 00 b.Lambeth 27-1-82

1999–2000	Millwall	0	0	
2000–01	Millwall	0	0	
2001–02	Millwall	1	0	
2002–03	Millwall	7	0	
2003–04	Millwall	0	0	
2004–05	Millwall	25	1	
2005–06	Millwall	22	0	
2006–07	Millwall	12	0	
2006–07	*Darlington*	8	0	8 0
2007–08	Millwall	0	0	67 1
2008–09	Brentford	33	1	
2009–10	Brentford	22	0	55 1
2010–11	Southend U	5	0	
2011–12	Southend U	39	7	
2012–13	Southend U	21	3	
2013–14	Southend U	27	2	92 12
2014–15	AFC Wimbledon	5	0	5 0

PILBEAM, George (D) 0 0
b. 27-9-95

2014–15	AFC Wimbledon	0	0	

REEVES, Jake (M) 73 3
H: 5 8 W: 11 11 b.Lewisham 30-6-93

2010–11	Brentford	1	0	
2011–12	Brentford	8	0	
2012–13	Brentford	6	0	
2012–13	*AFC Wimbledon*	5	0	
2013–14	Brentford	20	0	35 0
2014–15	Swindon T	10	1	10 1
2014–15	AFC Wimbledon	23	2	28 2

RIGG, Sean (F) 266 30
H: 5 9 W: 12 01 b.Bristol 1-10-88

2006–07	Bristol R	18	1	
2007–08	Bristol R	31	1	
2008–09	Bristol R	8	0	
2009–10	Bristol R	0	0	57 2
2009–10	*Port Vale*	26	3	
2010–11	Port Vale	25	3	
2011–12	Port Vale	42	10	93 16
2012–13	Oxford U	44	5	
2013–14	Oxford U	28	2	72 7
2014–15	AFC Wimbledon	44	.5	44 5

SAINTE-LUCE, Kevin (M) 46 3
H: 5 10 W: 11 11 b.Paris 28-4-93
Internationals: Guadeloupe U20.

2012–13	Cardiff C	0	0	
2012–13	AFC Wimbledon	14	2	
2013–14	AFC Wimbledon	23	1	
2014–15	AFC Wimbledon	9	0	46 3

SHEA, James (G) 39 0
H: 5 11 W: 12 00 b.Islington 16-6-91

2009–10	Arsenal	0	0	
2010–11	Arsenal	0	0	
2011–12	Arsenal	0	0	
2011–12	*Dagenham & R*	1	0	1 0
2012–13	Arsenal	0	0	
2013–14	Arsenal	0	0	
2014–15	AFC Wimbledon	38	0	38 0

SMITH, Jack (D) 280 15
H: 5 11 W: 11 05 b.Hemel Hempstead 14-10-83

2001–02	Watford	0	0	
2002–03	Watford	1	0	
2003–04	Watford	17	2	
2004–05	Watford	7	0	25 2
2005–06	Swindon T	38	0	
2006–07	Swindon T	41	3	
2007–08	Swindon T	21	1	
2008–09	Swindon T	38	5	138 9

2009–10	Millwall	31	0	
2010–11	Millwall	9	1	
2011–12	Millwall	33	0	
2012–13	Millwall	17	0	
2013–14	Millwall	6	0	96 1
2014–15	AFC Wimbledon	21	3	21 3

SWEENEY, Ryan (D) 3 0
b.Kingston upon Thames 15-4-97
Internationals: Republic of Ireland U18.

2014–15	AFC Wimbledon	3	0	3 0

WORNER, Ross (G) 81 0
H: 6 1 W: 12 05 b.Hindhead 3-10-89

2010–11	Charlton Ath	8	0	8 0
2011–12	Aldershot T	22	0	
2012–13	Aldershot T	1	0	23 0
2013–14	AFC Wimbledon	45	0	
2014–15	AFC Wimbledon	5	0	50 0

Players retained or with offer of contract
Kaja, Egli; Wilson, Callum Anthony.

Scholars
Agyei, Daniel Ebenezer Kwasi; Ano, Joshua Daniel Kwadjo; Batchelor, Reece Oluwatosin; Bellikli, Neset Can; Bishop, Billy; Bongo, Dominique Munansi; Egan, Alfie Patrick; Frost, Billy James; Haines, Oliver George; Mannion, William John; McKillop, Seanan Bernard James; Overton, Callum Peter William; Roles, Taylor Lewis; Stanton-Cockle, Louie Joe; Stripp, Jason Oliver.

ARSENAL (3)

AJAYI, Semi (D) 0 0
H: 6 4 W: 13 00 b.Croydon 9-11-93
Internationals: Nigeria U21.

2012–13	Charlton Ath	0	0	
2013–14	Charlton Ath	0	0	
2014–15	Arsenal	0	0	
2014–15	*Cardiff C*	0	0	

AKPOM, Chuba (F) 21 0
H: 6 0 W: 12 02 b.London 9-10-95
Internationals: England U16, U17, U19, U20.

2012–13	Arsenal	0	0	
2013–14	Arsenal	1	0	
2013–14	*Brentford*	4	0	4 0
2013–14	*Coventry C*	6	0	6 0
2014–15	Arsenal	3	0	4 0
2014–15	*Nottingham F*	7	0	7 0

ARTETA, Mikel (M) 412 59
H: 5 9 W: 10 08 b.San Sebastian 26-3-82
Internationals: Spain U16, U17, U18, U21.

1999–2000	Barcelona B	26	1	
2000–01	Barcelona B	16	2	42 3
2000–01	Paris St Germain	6	1	
2001–02	Paris St Germain	25	1	31 2
2002–03	Rangers	27	4	
2003–04	Rangers	23	8	50 12
2004–05	Real Sociedad	14	1	14 1
2004–05	Everton	29	1	
2005–06	Everton	29	1	
2006–07	Everton	35	9	
2007–08	Everton	28	1	
2008–09	Everton	26	5	
2009–10	Everton	13	6	
2010–11	Everton	29	3	
2011–12	Everton	2	1	174 27
2011–12	Arsenal	29	6	
2012–13	Arsenal	34	6	
2013–14	Arsenal	31	2	
2014–15	Arsenal	7	0	101 14

BELLERIN, Hector (D) 28 2
H: 5 10 W: 11 09 b.Barcelona 19-3-95
Internationals: Spain U16, U17, U19.

2012–13	Arsenal	0	0	
2013–14	Arsenal	0	0	
2013–14	*Watford*	8	0	8 0
2014–15	Arsenal	20	2	20 2

BIELIK, Krystian (M) 5 0
H: 5 10 W: 11 00 b.Vrinnevi 4-1-98

2014–15	Legia Warsaw	5	0	5 0

CAMPBELL, Joel (F) 113 14
H: 5 10 W: 12 00 b.Costa Rica 26-6-92
Internationals: Costa Rica U17, U20, Full caps.

2009–10	Saprissa	1	0	
2010–11	Saprissa	2	0	3 0
2010–11	Puntarenas	5	0	5 0

2011–12	Arsenal	0	0	
2011–12	*Lorient*	25	3	25 3
2012–13	Arsenal	0	0	
2012–13	*Real Betis*	28	2	28 2
2013–14	Arsenal	0	0	
2013–14	*Olympiacos*	32	8	32 8
2014–15	Arsenal	4	0	4 0
2014–15	*Villarreal*	16	1	16 1

CAZORLA, Santi (M) 358 62
H: 5 5 W: 10 07 b.Lugo De Llanera 13-12-84
Internationals: Spain U21, Full caps.

2003–04	Villarreal	2	0	
2004–05	Villarreal	28	2	
2005–06	Villarreal	23	0	
2006–07	Recreativo Huelva	34	5	34 5
2007–08	Villarreal	36	5	
2008–09	Villarreal	30	8	
2009–10	Villarreal	24	5	
2010–11	Villarreal	37	5	180 25
2011–12	Malaga	38	9	
2012–13	Malaga	0	0	38 9
2012–13	Arsenal	38	12	
2013–14	Arsenal	31	4	
2014–15	Arsenal	37	7	106 23

CHAMBERS, Calum (M) 45 1
H: 6 0 W: 10 05 b.Petersfield 20-1-95
Internationals: England U17, U19, U21, Full caps.

2011–12	Southampton	0	0	
2012–13	Southampton	0	0	
2013–14	Southampton	22	0	22 0
2014–15	Arsenal	23	1	23 1

COQUELIN, Francis (M) 88 1
H: 5 10 W: 11 08 b.Laval 13-5-91
Internationals: France U17, U18, U19, U20, U21.

2008–09	Arsenal	0	0	
2009–10	Arsenal	0	0	
2010–11	Arsenal	0	0	
2010–11	*Lorient*	24	1	24 1
2011–12	Arsenal	10	0	
2012–13	Arsenal	11	0	
2013–14	Arsenal	0	0	
2013–14	*SC Freiburg*	16	0	16 0
2014–15	Arsenal	22	0	43 0
2014–15	*Charlton Ath*	5	0	5 0

DEBUCHY, Mathieu (D) 282 18
H: 5 10 W: 12 02 b.Fretin 28-7-85
Internationals: France U21, Full caps.

2003–04	Lille	16	0	
2004–05	Lille	16	3	
2005–06	Lille	26	4	
2006–07	Lille	22	1	
2007–08	Lille	16	0	
2008–09	Lille	30	0	
2009–10	Lille	31	1	
2010–11	Lille	35	2	
2011–12	Lille	32	5	
2012–13	Lille	15	0	229 16
2012–13	Newcastle U	14	0	
2013–14	Newcastle U	29	1	43 1
2014–15	Arsenal	10	1	10 1

DIABY, Abou (M) 134 15
H: 6 2 W: 12 04 b.Paris 11-5-86
Internationals: France U19, U21, Full caps.

2004–05	Auxerre	5	0	
2005–06	Auxerre	5	1	10 1
2005–06	Arsenal	12	1	
2006–07	Arsenal	15	1	
2007–08	Arsenal	24	3	
2008–09	Arsenal	29	6	
2010–11	Arsenal	16	2	
2011–12	Arsenal	4	0	
2012–13	Arsenal	11	0	
2013–14	Arsenal	1	0	
2014–15	Arsenal	0	0	124 14

FLAMINI, Mathieu (M) 258 17
H: 5 10 W: 10 07 b.Marseille 7-3-84
Internationals: France U21, Full caps.

2003–04	Marseille	14	0	14 0
2004–05	Arsenal	21	1	
2005–06	Arsenal	31	0	
2006–07	Arsenal	30	3	
2007–08	Arsenal	30	3	
2008–09	AC Milan	28	0	
2009–10	AC Milan	23	0	
2010–11	AC Milan	22	2	
2011–12	AC Milan	2	1	
2012–13	AC Milan	17	4	92 7
2013–14	Arsenal	27	2	
2014–15	Arsenal	23	1	152 10

GABRIEL, Armando (D) 120 1
H: 6 2 W: 13 05 b.Sao Paulo 26-11-90

Season	Club				
2010	Vitoria	11	0		
2011	Vitoria	17	0		
2012	Vitoria	35	0		
2013	Vitoria	14	1	77	1
2013–14	Villareal	18	0	18	0
2014–15	Villarreal	19	0	19	0
2014–15	Arsenal	6	0	6	0

GIBBS, Kieran (M) 118 1
H: 5 10 W: 10 02 b.Lambeth 26-9-89
Internationals: England U19, U20, U21, Full caps

Season	Club				
2007–08	Arsenal	0	0		
2007–08	Norwich C	7	0	7	0
2008–09	Arsenal	8	0		
2009–10	Arsenal	3	0		
2010–11	Arsenal	7	0		
2011–12	Arsenal	16	1		
2012–13	Arsenal	27	0		
2013–14	Arsenal	28	0		
2014–15	Arsenal	22	0	111	1

GIROUD, Olivier (F) 249 105
H: 6 3 W: 13 11 b.Chambery 30-9-86
Internationals: France Full caps.

Season	Club				
2005–06	Grenoble	3	0		
2006–07	Grenoble	15	2	18	2
2008–09	Tours	23	8		
2009–10	Tours	38	21	61	29
2010–11	Montpellier	37	12		
2011–12	Montpellier	36	21	73	33
2012–13	Arsenal	34	11		
2013–14	Arsenal	36	16		
2014–15	Arsenal	27	14	97	41

GNABRY, Serge (M) 10 1
H: 5 9 W: 11 06 b.Stuttgart 14-7-95
Internationals: Germany U16, U17, U18, U19, U21.

Season	Club				
2012–13	Arsenal	1	0		
2013–14	Arsenal	9	1		
2014–15	Arsenal	0	0	10	1

HAYDEN, Isaac (D) 0 0
H: 6 2 W: 12 06 b.Chelmsford 22-3-95
Internationals: England U16, U17, U18, U19, U20.

Season	Club		
2011–12	Arsenal	0	0
2012–13	Arsenal	0	0
2013–14	Arsenal	0	0
2014–15	Arsenal	0	0

HUDDART, Ryan (G) 0 0
H: 6 5 b.Margate 6-3-97

Season	Club		
2013–14	Arsenal	0	0
2014–15	Arsenal	0	0

ILIEV, Dejan (G) 0 0
H: 6 5 b.Strumica 25-2-95
Internationals: Macedonia U17, U19, U21.

Season	Club		
2012–13	Arsenal	0	0
2013–14	Arsenal	0	0
2014–15	Arsenal	0	0

IWOBI, Alex (M) 0 0
H: 5 11 W: 11 11 b.Lagos 3-5-96
Internationals: England U16, U17, U18.

Season	Club		
2012–13	Arsenal	0	0
2013–14	Arsenal	0	0
2014–15	Arsenal	0	0

JEBB, Jack (M) 9 0
H: 6 0 W: 11 09 b.London 11-9-95
Internationals: England U16, U17.

Season	Club				
2012–13	Arsenal	0	0		
2013–14	Arsenal	0	0		
2014–15	Arsenal	0	0		
2014–15	Stevenage	9	0	9	0

JENKINSON, Carl (D) 77 1
H: 6 1 W: 12 02 b.Harlow 8-2-92
Internationals: Finland U19, U21. England U17, U21, Full caps.

Season	Club				
2010–11	Charlton Ath	8	0	8	0
2010–11	Arsenal	0	0		
2011–12	Arsenal	9	0		
2012–13	Arsenal	14	0		
2013–14	Arsenal	14	1		
2014–15	Arsenal	0	0	37	1
2014–15	West Ham U	32	0	32	0

KAMARA, Glen (F) 0 0
H: 5 10 W: 11 05 b. 28-10-95
Internationals: Finland U19, U20, U21.

Season	Club		
2012–13	Arsenal	0	0
2013–14	Arsenal	0	0

KOSCIELNY, Laurent (D) 290 20
H: 6 1 W: 11 11 b.Tulle 10-9-85
Internationals: France Full caps.

Season	Club				
2004–05	Guingamp	11	0		
2005–06	Guingamp	9	0		
2006–07	Guingamp	21	0	41	0
2007–08	Tours	33	1		
2008–09	Tours	34	5	67	6
2009–10	Lorient	35	3	35	3
2010–11	Arsenal	30	2		
2011–12	Arsenal	33	2		
2012–13	Arsenal	25	2		
2013–14	Arsenal	32	2		
2014–15	Arsenal	27	3	147	11

LIPMAN, Austin (M) 0 0
b.Leytonstone 20-9-95
Internationals: England U16, U17.

Season	Club		
2012–13	Arsenal	0	0
2013–14	Arsenal	0	0
2014–15	Arsenal	0	0

MACEY, Matt (G) 4 0
H: 6 6 b.Bristol 9-9-94

Season	Club				
2011–12	Bristol R	0	0		
2012–13	Bristol R	0	0		
2013–14	Arsenal	0	0		
2014–15	Arsenal	0	0		
2014–15	Accrington S	4	0	4	0

MAITLAND-NILES, Ainsley (F) 1 0
b.Goodmayes 29-8-97
Internationals: England U17, U18.

Season	Club				
2014–15	Arsenal	1	0	1	0

MARTINEZ, Damian (G) 24 0
H: 6 3 W: 13 05 b.Mar del Plata 2-9-92
Internationals: Argentina U17, U20.

Season	Club				
2010–11	Arsenal	0	0		
2011–12	Arsenal	0	0		
2011–12	Oxford U	1	0	1	0
2012–13	Arsenal	0	0		
2013–14	Arsenal	0	0		
2013–14	Sheffield W	11	0	11	0
2014–15	Arsenal	4	0	4	0
2014–15	Rotherham U	8	0	8	0

MERTESACKER, Per (D) 345 24
H: 6 6 W: 14 -02 b.Hannover 29-9-84
Internationals: Germany U20, U21, Full caps.

Season	Club				
2003–04	Hannover	13	0		
2004–05	Hannover	31	2		
2005–06	Hannover	30	5	74	7
2006–07	Werder Bremen	25	2		
2007–08	Werder Bremen	32	1		
2008–09	Werder Bremen	23	2		
2009–10	Werder Bremen	33	5		
2010–11	Werder Bremen	29	2		
2011–12	Werder Bremen	4	0	146	12
2011–12	Arsenal	21	0		
2012–13	Arsenal	34	3		
2013–14	Arsenal	35	2		
2014–15	Arsenal	35	0	125	5

MIYAICHI, Ryo (F) 27 0
H: 6 0 W: 11 02 b.Okazaki 14-12-92
Internationals: Japan U15, U16, U17, U19, Full caps.

Season	Club				
2010–11	Arsenal	0	0		
2011–12	Arsenal	0	0		
2011–12	Bolton W	12	0	12	0
2012–13	Arsenal	0	0		
2012–13	Wigan Ath	4	0	4	0
2013–14	Arsenal	1	0		
2014–15	Arsenal	0	0	1	0
2014–15	FC Twente	10	0	10	0

MONREAL, Nacho (D) 234 4
H: 5 10 W: 11 04 b.Pamplona 26-2-86
Internationals: Spain U19, U21, Full caps.

Season	Club				
2006–07	Osasuna	11	0		
2007–08	Osasuna	27	0		
2008–09	Osasuna	28	0		
2009–10	Osasuna	31	1		
2010–11	Osasuna	31	1	128	2
2011–12	Malaga	31	0		
2012–13	Malaga	14	1	45	1
2012–13	Arsenal	10	1		
2013–14	Arsenal	23	0		
2014–15	Arsenal	28	0	61	1

O'CONNOR, Stefan (D) 0 0
b.Croydon 23-1-97
Internationals: England U17.

Season	Club		
2014–15	Arsenal	0	0

OLSSON, Kristoffer (M) 10 0
b.Vrinnevi 30-6-95
Internationals: Sweden U17, U19, U21.

Season	Club				
2012–13	Arsenal	0	0		
2013–14	Arsenal	0	0		
2014–15	Arsenal	0	0		
2014–15	FC Midtjylland	10	0	10	0

ORMONDE-OTTEWILL, Brandon (D)0 0
b.London 21-12-95
Internationals: England U16, U19.

Season	Club		
2012–13	Arsenal	0	0
2013–14	Arsenal	0	0
2014–15	Arsenal	0	0

OSPINA, David (G) 304 0
H: 6 0 W: 12 00 b.Medellin 31-8-88
Internationals: Colombia U20, Full caps.

Season	Club				
2006	Atletico Nacional	34	0		
2007	Atletico Nacional	47	0		
2008	Atletico Nacional	16	0	97	0
2008–09	Nice	25	0		
2009–10	Nice	37	0		
2010–11	NIce	35	0		
2011–12	Nice	37	0		
2012–13	Nice	26	0		
2013–14	NIce	29	0	189	0
2014–15	Arsenal	18	0	18	0

OXLADE-CHAMBERLAIN, Alex (M)114 15
H: 5 11 W: 11 00 b.Portsmouth 15-8-93
Internationals: England U18, U19, U21, Full caps.

Season	Club				
2009–10	Southampton	2	0		
2010–11	Southampton	34	9	36	9
2011–12	Arsenal	16	2		
2012–13	Arsenal	25	1		
2013–14	Arsenal	14	2		
2014–15	Arsenal	23	1	78	6

OZIL, Mesut (M) 253 41
H: 5 11 W: 11 06 b.Gelsenkirchen 15-10-88
Internationals: Germany U19, U21, Full caps.

Season	Club				
2005–06	Schalke 04	0	0		
2006–07	Schalke 04	19	0		
2007–08	Schalke 04	11	0	30	0
2007–08	Werder Bremen	12	1		
2008–09	Werder Bremen	27	3		
2009–10	Werder Bremen	31	9		
2010–11	Werder Bremen	0	0	70	13
2010–11	Real Madrid	36	6		
2011–12	Real Madrid	35	4		
2012–13	Real Madrid	32	9		
2013–14	Real Madrid	2	0	105	19
2013–14	Arsenal	26	5		
2014–15	Arsenal	22	4	48	9

PODOLSKI, Lukas (F) 299 111
H: 6 0 W: 13 00 b.Gleiwitz, Poland 4-6-85
Internationals: Germany U17, U18, U19, U21, Full caps.

Season	Club				
2003–04	Cologne	19	10		
2004–05	Cologne	12	21		
2005–06	Cologne	32	12		
2006–07	Bayern Munich	22	4		
2007–08	Bayern Munich	25	5		
2008–09	Bayern Munich	24	6	71	15
2009–10	Cologne	27	2		
2010–11	Cologne	32	13		
2011–12	Cologne	29	18	151	76
2012–13	Arsenal	33	11		
2013–14	Arsenal	20	8		
2014–15	Arsenal	7	0	60	19
2014–15	Inter Milan	17	1	17	1

RAMSEY, Aaron (M) 183 25
H: 5 9 W: 10 07 b.Caerphilly 26-12-90
Internationals: Wales U17, U21, Full caps. Great Britain.

Season	Club				
2006–07	Cardiff C	1	0		
2007–08	Cardiff C	15	1		
2008–09	Arsenal	9	0		
2009–10	Arsenal	18	3		
2010–11	Arsenal	7	1		
2010–11	Nottingham F	5	0	5	0
2010–11	Cardiff C	6	1	22	2
2011–12	Arsenal	34	2		
2012–13	Arsenal	36	1		
2013–14	Arsenal	23	10		
2014–15	Arsenal	29	6	156	23

ROSICKY, Tomas (M) 360 46
H: 5 10 W: 10 10 b.Prague 4-10-80
Internationals: Czech Republic U15, U16, U17, U18, U21, Full caps.

Season	Club				
1998–99	Sparta Prague	3	0		
1999–2000	Sparta Prague	24	5		
2000–01	Sparta Prague	14	3	41	8
2000–01	Borussia Dortmund	15	0		
2001–02	Borussia Dortmund	30	5		
2002–03	Borussia Dortmund	30	3		
2003–04	Borussia Dortmund	19	2		
2004–05	Borussia Dortmund	27	4		

2005–06	Borussia Dortmund	28	5	**149**	**19**
2006–07	Arsenal	26	3		
2007–08	Arsenal	18	6		
2008–09	Arsenal	0	0		
2009–10	Arsenal	25	3		
2010–11	Arsenal	21	0		
2011–12	Arsenal	28	1		
2012–13	Arsenal	10	2		
2013–14	Arsenal	27	2		
2014–15	Arsenal	15	2	**170**	**19**

SANCHEZ, Alexis (F)   **320 92**
H: 5 6   W: 11 09   b.Tocopilla 19-12-88
Internationals: Chile U20, Full caps.

2005	Cobreloa	35	3		
2006	Cobreloa	12	6	**47**	**9**
2006–07	Udinese	0	0		
2006–07	*Colo Colo*	32	5	**32**	**5**
2007–08	*River Plate*	23	4	**23**	**4**
2008–09	Udinese	32	3		
2009–10	Udinese	32	5		
2010–11	Udinese	31	12	**95**	**20**
2011–12	Barcelona	25	11		
2012–13	Barcelona	29	8		
2013–14	Barcelona	34	19	**88**	**38**
2014–15	Arsenal	35	16	**35**	**16**

SANOGO, Yaya (F)   **41 10**
H: 6 3   W: 11 08   b.Massy 27-1-93
Internationals: France U16, U17, U19, U20, U21.

2009–10	Auxerre	0	0		
2010–11	Auxerre	0	0		
2011–12	Auxerre	7	1		
2012–13	Auxerre	13	9	**20**	**10**
2013–14	Arsenal	8	0		
2014–15	Arsenal	3	0	**11**	**0**
2014–15	*Crystal Palace*	10	0	**10**	**0**

SILVA, Wellington (M)   **87 6**
H: 5 6   W: 10 00   b.Rio de Janeiro 6-1-93
Internationals: Brazil U17, U21.

2010–11	Arsenal	0	0		
2010–11	*Levante*	2	0	**2**	**0**
2011–12	Arsenal	0	0		
2011–12	*Alcoyano*	16	3	**16**	**3**
2012–13	Arsenal	0	0		
2013–14	Arsenal	0	0		
2013–14	*Murcia*	38	3	**38**	**3**
2014–15	Arsenal	0	0		
2014–15	*Almeria*	31	0	**31**	**0**

SZCZESNY, Wojciech (G)   **160 0**
H: 5 10   W: 11 11   b.Warsaw 18-4-90
Internationals: Poland U20, U21, Full caps.

2007–08	Arsenal	0	0		
2008–09	Arsenal	0	0		
2009–10	Arsenal	0	0		
2009–10	*Brentford*	28	0	**28**	**0**
2010–11	Arsenal	15	0		
2011–12	Arsenal	38	0		
2012–13	Arsenal	25	0		
2013–14	Arsenal	37	0		
2014–15	Arsenal	17	0	**132**	**0**

TORAL, Jon (M)   **34 6**
H: 6 0   W: 12 07   b.Reus 5-2-95

2013–14	Arsenal	0	0		
2014–15	Arsenal	0	0		
2014–15	*Brentford*	34	6	**34**	**6**

WALCOTT, Theo (F)   **229 54**
H: 5 9   W: 11 01   b.Stanmore 16-3-89
Internationals: England U16, U17, U19, U21, Full caps.

2005–06	Southampton	21	4	**21**	**4**
2005–06	Arsenal	0	0		
2006–07	Arsenal	16	0		
2007–08	Arsenal	25	4		
2008–09	Arsenal	22	2		
2009–10	Arsenal	23	3		
2010–11	Arsenal	28	9		
2011–12	Arsenal	35	8		
2012–13	Arsenal	32	14		
2013–14	Arsenal	13	5		
2014–15	Arsenal	14	5	**208**	**50**

WELBECK, Danny (F)   **151 32**
H: 6 1   W: 11 07   b.Manchester 26-11-90
Internationals: England U17, U18, U19, U21, Full caps.

2007–08	Manchester U	0	0		
2008–09	Manchester U	3	1		
2009–10	Manchester U	5	0		
2009–10	*Preston NE*	8	2	**8**	**2**
2010–11	Manchester U	0	0		
2010–11	*Sunderland*	26	6	**26**	**6**
2011–12	Manchester U	30	9		
2012–13	Manchester U	27	1		
2013–14	Manchester U	25	9		
2014–15	Manchester U	2	0	**92**	**20**
2014–15	Arsenal	25	4	**25**	**4**

WILSHERE, Jack (M)   **114 7**
H: 5 7   W: 11 03   b.Stevenage 1-1-92
Internationals: England U16, U17, U19, U21, Full caps.

2008–09	Arsenal	1	0		
2009–10	Arsenal	1	0		
2009–10	*Bolton W*	14	1	**14**	**1**
2010–11	Arsenal	35	1		
2011–12	Arsenal	0	0		
2012–13	Arsenal	25	0		
2013–14	Arsenal	24	3		
2014–15	Arsenal	14	2	**100**	**6**

ZELALEM, Gedion (M)   **0 0**
H: 5 10   b.Berlin 26-1-97
Internationals: Germany U16, U17. USA U20.

2013–14	Arsenal	0	0	
2014–15	Arsenal	0	0	

Players retained or with offer of contract
Crowley, Daniel; Da Graca, Kristopher
Santos; Dobson, George David; Hinds,
Kaylen Miles; Johnson, Chiori; Moore, Tafari
Lalibela; Pleguezuelo, Julio Jose; Robinson,
Tyrell; Toral, Jon-Miquel.

Scholars
Bola, Marc Joel; Chatzitheodoridis, Ilias;
Donovan, Harry; Eyoma, Aaron Jordan;
Keto, Hugo Oliver; Mavididi, Stephy Alvaro;
Mourgos, Savvas.

ASTON VILLA (4)

AGBONLAHOR, Gabriel (F)   **317 72**
H: 5 11   W: 12 05   b.Birmingham 13-10-86
Internationals: England U21, Full caps.

2005–06	Aston Villa	9	1		
2005–06	*Watford*	2	0	**2**	**0**
2005–06	*Sheffield W*	8	0	**8**	**0**
2006–07	Aston Villa	38	9		
2007–08	Aston Villa	37	11		
2008–09	Aston Villa	36	11		
2009–10	Aston Villa	36	13		
2010–11	Aston Villa	26	3		
2011–12	Aston Villa	33	5		
2012–13	Aston Villa	28	9		
2013–14	Aston Villa	34	3		
2014–15	Aston Villa	34	6	**307**	**72**

BACUNA, Leandro (M)   **107 12**
H: 6 2   W: 12 00   b.Groningen 21-8-91
Internationals: Netherlands U19, U21.

2009–10	FC Groningen	20	2		
2012–13	FC Groningen	33	5	**53**	**7**
2013–14	Aston Villa	35	5		
2014–15	Aston Villa	19	0	**54**	**5**

BAKER, Nathan (D)   **103 0**
H: 6 2   W: 11 11   b.Worcester 23-4-91
Internationals: England U19, U20, U21.

2008–09	Aston Villa	0	0		
2009–10	Aston Villa	0	0		
2009–10	*Lincoln C*	18	0	**18**	**0**
2010–11	Aston Villa	4	0		
2010–11	Aston Villa	8	0		
2011–12	*Millwall*	6	0	**6**	**0**
2012–13	Aston Villa	26	0		
2013–14	Aston Villa	30	0		
2014–15	Aston Villa	11	0	**79**	**0**

BENT, Darren (F)   **413 166**
H: 5 11   W: 12 07   b.Wandsworth 6-2-84
Internationals: England U15, U16, U17, U19, U21, Full caps.

2001–02	Ipswich T	5	1		
2002–03	Ipswich T	35	12		
2003–04	Ipswich T	37	16		
2004–05	Ipswich T	45	20	**122**	**49**
2005–06	Charlton Ath	36	18		
2006–07	Charlton Ath	32	13	**68**	**31**
2007–08	Tottenham H	27	6		
2008–09	Tottenham H	33	12		
2009–10	Tottenham H	0	0	**60**	**18**
2009–10	Sunderland	38	24		
2010–11	Sunderland	20	8	**58**	**32**
2010–11	Aston Villa	16	9		
2011–12	Aston Villa	22	9		
2012–13	Aston Villa	16	3		
2013–14	Aston Villa	0	0		
2013–14	*Fulham*	24	3	**24**	**3**
2014–15	Aston Villa	7	0	**61**	**21**
2014–15	*Brighton & HA*	5	2	**5**	**2**
2014–15	*Derby Co*	15	10	**15**	**10**

BENTEKE, Christian (F)   **193 78**
H: 6 3   W: 13 00   b.Kinshasa 3-12-90
Internationals: Belgium U17, U18, U19, U21, Full caps.

2007–08	Genk	7	0		
2008–09	Genk	3	0		
2008–09	Standard Liege	9	3		
2009–10	*KV Kortrijk*	24	9	**24**	**9**
2010–11	Standard Liege	5	0		
2010–11	*KV Mechelen*	15	5	**15**	**5**
2011–12	Standard Liege	4	0	**18**	**3**
2011–12	Genk	32	16		
2012–13	Genk	5	3	**47**	**19**
2012–13	Aston Villa	34	19		
2013–14	Aston Villa	26	10		
2014–15	Aston Villa	29	13	**89**	**42**

BURKE, Graham (F)   **10 1**
H: 5 11   W: 11 11   b.Dublin 21-9-93
Internationals: Republic of Ireland U19, U21.

2010–11	Aston Villa	0	0		
2011–12	Aston Villa	0	0		
2012–13	Aston Villa	0	0		
2013–14	Aston Villa	0	0		
2013–14	*Shrewsbury T*	3	0	**3**	**0**
2014–15	Aston Villa	0	0		
2014–15	*Notts Co*	7	1	**7**	**1**

CALDER, Ricardo (M)   **0 0**
b.Birmingham 26-1-96
Internationals: England U17.

2013–14	Aston Villa	0	0	
2014–15	Aston Villa	0	0	

CISSOKHO, Aly (D)   **207 3**
H: 5 11   W: 11 10   b.Blois 15-9-87
Internationals: France Full caps.

2006–07	Gueugnon	1	0		
2007–08	Gueugnon	21	0	**22**	**0**
2008–09	Vitoria Setubal	13	0	**13**	**0**
2008–09	Porto	15	0	**15**	**0**
2009–10	Lyon	30	0		
2010–11	Lyon	29	1		
2011–12	Lyon	31	0		
2012–13	Lyon	2	0	**92**	**1**
2012–13	Valencia	25	2		
2013–14	Valencia	0	0	**25**	**2**
2013–14	*Liverpool*	15	0	**15**	**0**
2014–15	Aston Villa	25	0	**25**	**0**

CLARK, Ciaran (D)   **116 6**
H: 6 2   W: 12 00   b.Harrow 26-9-89
Internationals: England U17, U18, U19, U20.
Republic of Ireland Full caps.

2008–09	Aston Villa	0	0		
2009–10	Aston Villa	0	0		
2010–11	Aston Villa	19	3		
2011–12	Aston Villa	15	1		
2012–13	Aston Villa	29	1		
2013–14	Aston Villa	27	0		
2014–15	Aston Villa	25	1	**116**	**6**

COLE, Joe (M)   **409 50**
H: 5 9   W: 11 09   b.Camden 8-11-81
Internationals: England U16, U18, U21, B, Full caps.

1998–99	West Ham U	8	0		
1999–2000	West Ham U	22	1		
2000–01	West Ham U	30	5		
2001–02	West Ham U	30	5		
2002–03	West Ham U	36	4		
2003–04	Chelsea	35	1		
2004–05	Chelsea	28	8		
2005–06	Chelsea	34	7		
2006–07	Chelsea	13	0		
2007–08	Chelsea	33	7		
2008–09	Chelsea	14	2		
2009–10	Chelsea	26	2	**183**	**27**
2010–11	Liverpool	20	2		
2011–12	Liverpool	0	0		
2011–12	*Lille*	31	4	**31**	**4**
2012–13	Liverpool	6	1	**26**	**3**
2012–13	West Ham U	11	2		
2013–14	West Ham U	20	3	**157**	**15**
2014–15	Aston Villa	12	1	**12**	**1**

DELPH, Fabian (D)   **161 9**
H: 5 8   W: 11 00   b.Bradford 21-11-89
Internationals: England U19, U21, Full caps.

2006–07	Leeds U	1	0		
2007–08	Leeds U	1	0		
2008–09	Leeds U	42	6		
2009–10	Aston Villa	8	0		
2010–11	Aston Villa	7	0		
2011–12	Aston Villa	11	0		
2012–13	*Leeds U*	5	0	**49**	**6**
2012–13	Aston Villa	24	0		
2013–14	Aston Villa	34	3		
2014–15	Aston Villa	28	0	**112**	**3**

DONACIEN, Janoi (D) — 31 0
H: 6 0 W: 11 11 b.St Lucia 3-11-93

Season	Club				
2011–12	Aston Villa	0	0		
2012–13	Aston Villa	0	0		
2013–14	Aston Villa	0	0		
2014–15	Aston Villa	0	0		
2014–15	*Tranmere R*	31	0	**31**	**0**

DRENNAN, Michael (F) — 20 3
b.Kilkenny 2-2-94
Internationals: Republic of Ireland U17, U19, U21.

2010–11	Aston Villa	0	0		
2011–12	Aston Villa	0	0		
2012–13	Aston Villa	0	0		
2013–14	Aston Villa	0	0		
2013–14	*Carlisle U*	6	0	**6**	**0**
2013–14	*Portsmouth*	10	3		
2014–15	Aston Villa	0	0		
2014–15	*Portsmouth*	4	0	**14**	**3**

Transferred to Shamrock R January 2015.

GIL, Carles (M) — 77 6
H: 5 7 W: 10 03 b.Valencia 2-11-92
Internationals: Spain U21.

2012–13	Elche	31	4		
2013–14	Elche	33	1	**64**	**5**
2014–15	Valencia	8	1	**8**	**1**
2014–15	Aston Villa	5	0	**5**	**0**

GIVEN, Shay (G) — 481 0
H: 6 0 W: 13 03 b.Lifford 20-4-76
Internationals: Republic of Ireland U21, Full caps.

1994–95	Blackburn R	0	0		
1994–95	*Swindon T*	0	0		
1995–96	Blackburn R	0	0		
1995–96	*Swindon T*	5	0	**5**	**0**
1995–96	*Sunderland*	17	0	**17**	**0**
1996–97	Blackburn R	2	0	**2**	**0**
1997–98	Newcastle U	24	0		
1998–99	Newcastle U	31	0		
1999–2000	Newcastle U	14	0		
2000–01	Newcastle U	34	0		
2001–02	Newcastle U	38	0		
2002–03	Newcastle U	38	0		
2003–04	Newcastle U	38	0		
2004–05	Newcastle U	36	0		
2005–06	Newcastle U	38	0		
2006–07	Newcastle U	22	0		
2007–08	Newcastle U	19	0		
2008–09	Newcastle U	22	0	**354**	**0**
2008–09	Manchester C	15	0		
2009–10	Manchester C	35	0		
2010–11	Manchester C	0	0	**50**	**0**
2011–12	Aston Villa	32	0		
2012–13	Aston Villa	2	0		
2013–14	Aston Villa	0	0		
2013–14	*Middlesbrough*	16	0	**16**	**0**
2014–15	Aston Villa	3	0	**37**	**0**

GREALISH, Jack (M) — 55 5
H: 5 9 W: 10 10 b.Birmingham 10-9-95
Internationals: Republic of Ireland U17, U18, U21.

2012–13	Aston Villa	0	0		
2013–14	Aston Villa	1	0		
2013–14	*Notts Co*	37	5	**37**	**5**
2014–15	Aston Villa	17	0	**18**	**0**

GREEN, Andre (F) — 0 0
b. 2-5-98
Internationals: England U17.

2014–15	Aston Villa	0	0		

GUZAN, Brad (G) — 211 0
H: 6 4 W: 14 11 b.Chicago 9-9-84
Internationals: USA U21, Full caps.

2005	Chivas USA	24	0		
2006	Chivas USA	13	0		
2007	Chivas USA	27	0		
2008	Chivas USA	15	0	**79**	**0**
2008–09	Aston Villa	1	0		
2009–10	Aston Villa	0	0		
2010–11	Aston Villa	0	0		
2010–11	*Hull C*	16	0	**16**	**0**
2011–12	Aston Villa	7	0		
2012–13	Aston Villa	36	0		
2013–14	Aston Villa	38	0		
2014–15	Aston Villa	34	0	**116**	**0**

HEPBURN-MURPHY, Rushian (F) — 1 0
b. 19-9-98
Internationals: England U16, U17.

2014–15	Aston Villa	1	0	**1**	**0**

HERD, Chris (M) — 76 7
H: 5 9 W: 11 04 b.Perth 4-4-89
Internationals: Australia U20, Full caps.

2007–08	Aston Villa	0	0		
2007–08	*Port Vale*	11	2	**11**	**2**
2007–08	*Wycombe W*	4	0	**4**	**0**
2008–09	Aston Villa	0	0		
2009–10	Aston Villa	0	0		
2009–10	*Lincoln C*	20	4	**20**	**4**
2010–11	Aston Villa	6	0		
2011–12	Aston Villa	19	1		
2012–13	Aston Villa	9	0		
2013–14	Aston Villa	2	0		
2014–15	Aston Villa	0	0	**36**	**1**
2014–15	*Bolton W*	2	0	**2**	**0**
2014–15	*Wigan Ath*	3	0	**3**	**0**

HUTTON, Alan (D) — 238 4
H: 6 1 W: 11 05 b.Glasgow 30-11-84
Internationals: Scotland U21, Full caps.

2004–05	Rangers	10	0		
2005–06	Rangers	19	0		
2006–07	Rangers	33	1		
2007–08	Rangers	20	0	**82**	**1**
2007–08	Tottenham H	14	0		
2008–09	Tottenham H	8	0		
2009–10	*Sunderland*	11	0	**11**	**0**
2010–11	Tottenham H	21	2		
2011–12	Tottenham H	0	0	**51**	**2**
2011–12	Aston Villa	31	0		
2012–13	Aston Villa	0	0		
2012–13	*Nottingham F*	7	0	**7**	**0**
2012–13	*Mallorca*	17	0	**17**	**0**
2013–14	Aston Villa	0	0		
2013–14	*Bolton W*	9	0	**9**	**0**
2014–15	Aston Villa	30	1	**61**	**1**

KINSELLA, Lewis (D) — 3 0
b.Watford 2-9-94

2013–14	Aston Villa	0	0		
2014–15	Aston Villa	0	0		
2014–15	*Luton T*	3	0	**3**	**0**

KOZAK, Libor (F) — 96 18
H: 6 4 W: 12 11 b.Brumov-Bylnice 30-5-89
Internationals: Czech Republic U19, U21, Full caps.

2008–09	Lazio	3	0		
2009–10	*Brescia*	25	4	**25**	**4**
2010–11	Lazio	19	6		
2011–12	Lazio	16	4		
2012–13	Lazio	19	0	**57**	**10**
2013–14	Aston Villa	14	4		
2014–15	Aston Villa	0	0	**14**	**4**

LOWTON, Matt (M) — 155 12
H: 5 11 W: 12 04 b.Chesterfield 9-6-89

2008–09	Sheffield U	0	0		
2009–10	Sheffield U	2	0		
2009–10	*Ferencvaros*	5	0	**5**	**0**
2010–11	Sheffield U	32	4		
2011–12	Sheffield U	44	6	**78**	**10**
2012–13	Aston Villa	37	2		
2013–14	Aston Villa	23	0		
2014–15	Aston Villa	12	0	**72**	**2**

N'ZOGBIA, Charles (M) — 278 28
H: 5 9 W: 11 00 b.Le Havre 28-5-86
Internationals: France U21, Full caps.

2004–05	Newcastle U	14	0		
2005–06	Newcastle U	32	5		
2006–07	Newcastle U	22	0		
2007–08	Newcastle U	31	3		
2008–09	Newcastle U	18	1	**117**	**9**
2008–09	Wigan Ath	13	1		
2009–10	Wigan Ath	36	5		
2010–11	Wigan Ath	34	9	**83**	**15**
2011–12	Aston Villa	30	2		
2012–13	Aston Villa	21	2		
2013–14	Aston Villa	0	0		
2014–15	Aston Villa	27	0	**78**	**4**

OKORE, Jores (D) — 91 6
H: 6 0 W: 12 07 b.Abidjan 11-8-92
Internationals: Denmark U21, Full caps.

2010–11	Nordsjaelland	11	0		
2011–12	Nordsjaelland	25	1		
2012–13	Nordsjaelland	29	4	**65**	**5**
2013–14	Aston Villa	3	0		
2014–15	Aston Villa	23	1	**26**	**1**

RICHARDSON, Kieran (M) — 254 24
H: 5 9 W: 11 13 b.Greenwich 21-10-84
Internationals: England U18, U20, U21, Full caps.

2002–03	Manchester U	2	0		
2003–04	Manchester U	0	0		
2004–05	Manchester U	2	0		
2004–05	*WBA*	12	3	**12**	**3**
2005–06	Manchester U	22	1		
2006–07	Manchester U	15	1	**41**	**2**
2007–08	Sunderland	17	3		
2008–09	Sunderland	32	4		
2009–10	Sunderland	29	1		
2010–11	Sunderland	26	4		
2011–12	Sunderland	29	2		
2012–13	Sunderland	1	0	**134**	**14**
2012–13	Fulham	14	1		
2013–14	Fulham	31	4	**45**	**5**
2014–15	Aston Villa	22	0	**22**	**0**

ROBINSON, Callum (F) — 29 4
H: 5 10 W: 11 11 b.Birmingham 2-2-95
Internationals: England U16, U17, U19, U20.

2013–14	Aston Villa	4	0		
2014–15	Aston Villa	0	0	**4**	**0**
2014–15	*Preston NE*	25	4	**25**	**4**

SANCHEZ, Carlos (M) — 273 13
H: 6 0 W: 12 08 b.Quibdo 6-2-86
Internationals: Colombia Full caps.

2005–06	River Plate	14	0		
2006–07	River Plate	26	1	**40**	**1**
2007–08	Valenciennes	34	0		
2008–09	Valenciennes	37	1		
2009–10	Valenciennes	28	5		
2010–11	Valenciennes	28	2		
2011–12	Valenciennes	21	1		
2012–13	Valenciennes	27	2	**175**	**11**
2013–14	Elche	30	0	**30**	**0**
2014–15	Aston Villa	28	1	**28**	**1**

SENDEROS, Philippe (D) — 179 9
H: 6 1 W: 13 10 b.Geneva 14-2-85
Internationals: Switzerland U20, U21, Full caps.

2001–02	Servette	3	0		
2002–03	Servette	23	3	**26**	**3**
2003–04	Arsenal	0	0		
2004–05	Arsenal	13	0		
2005–06	Arsenal	20	2		
2006–07	Arsenal	14	0		
2007–08	Arsenal	17	2		
2008–09	Arsenal	0	0		
2008–09	*AC Milan*	14	0	**14**	**0**
2009–10	Arsenal	0	0	**64**	**4**
2009–10	*Everton*	2	0	**2**	**0**
2010–11	Fulham	3	0		
2011–12	Fulham	21	1		
2012–13	Fulham	21	0		
2013–14	Fulham	12	1	**57**	**2**
2013–14	*Valencia*	8	0	**8**	**0**
2014–15	Aston Villa	8	0	**8**	**0**

SIEGRIST, Benjamin (G) — 0 0
H: 6 4 W: 13 05 b.Basle 31-1-92
Internationals: Switzerland U17, U18, U19, U21.

2008–09	Aston Villa	0	0		
2009–10	Aston Villa	0	0		
2010–11	Aston Villa	0	0		
2011–12	Aston Villa	0	0		
2012–13	Aston Villa	0	0		
2013–14	Aston Villa	0	0		
2013–14	*Burton Alb*	0	0		
2014–15	*Cambridge U*	0	0		

STEER, Jed (G) — 38 0
H: 6 2 W: 14 00 b.Norwich 23-9-92
Internationals: England U16, U17, U19.

2009–10	Norwich C	0	0		
2010–11	Norwich C	0	0		
2011–12	Norwich C	0	0		
2011–12	*Yeovil T*	12	0		
2012–13	*Cambridge U*	0	0		
2012–13	Norwich C	0	0		
2013–14	Aston Villa	0	0		
2014–15	Aston Villa	1	0	**1**	**0**
2014–15	*Doncaster R*	13	0	**13**	**0**
2014–15	*Yeovil T*	12	0	**24**	**0**

STEVENS, Enda (D) — 131 2
H: 6 0 W: 12 04 b.Dublin 9-7-90
Internationals: Republic of Ireland U21.

2008	UCD	2	0	**2**	**0**
2009	St Patrick's Ath	30	1	**30**	**0**
2010	Shamrock R	18	0		
2011	Shamrock R	27	0	**45**	**0**
2011–12	Aston Villa	3	0		
2012–13	Aston Villa	7	0		
2013–14	Aston Villa	0	0		
2013–14	*Notts Co*	2	0	**2**	**0**
2013–14	*Doncaster R*	13	0		
2014–15	Aston Villa	0	0	**7**	**0**
2014–15	*Northampton T*	4	1	**4**	**1**
2014–15	*Doncaster R*	28	1	**41**	**1**

SYLLA, Yacouba (M) — 113 1
H: 6 0 W: 12 07 b.Etampes 29-11-90
Internationals: France U21. Mali Full caps.

2010–11	Clermont Foot	20	0		
2011–12	Clermont Foot	23	0		
2012–13	Clermont Foot	21	0	**64**	**0**

2012–13	Aston Villa	11	0	
2013–14	Aston Villa	11	0	
2014–15	Aston Villa	0	0	22 0
2014–15	*Kayseri Erciyesspor*	27	1	27 1

VLAAR, Ron (D) 221 10
H: 5 11 W: 12 05 b.Hensbraek 16-2-85
Internationals: Netherlands U19, U21, Full caps.

2004–05	AZ	3	0	
2005–06	AZ	7	0	10 0
2005–06	Feyenoord	16	0	
2006–07	Feyenoord	20	1	
2007–08	Feyenoord	4	1	
2009–10	Feyenoord	32	4	
2010–11	Feyenoord	26	2	
2011–12	Feyenoord	34	0	
2012–13	Feyenoord	0	0	132 8
2012–13	Aston Villa	27	2	
2013–14	Aston Villa	32	0	
2014–15	Aston Villa	20	0	79 2

WEIMANN, Andreas (F) 134 21
H: 5 9 W: 11 09 b.Vienna 5-8-91
Internationals: Austria U17, U19, U20, U21, Full caps.

2008–09	Aston Villa	0	0	
2009–10	Aston Villa	0	0	
2010–11	Aston Villa	1	0	
2010–11	*Watford*	18	4	
2011–12	Aston Villa	14	2	
2011–12	*Watford*	3	0	21 4
2012–13	Aston Villa	30	7	
2013–14	Aston Villa	37	5	
2014–15	Aston Villa	31	3	113 17

WESTWOOD, Ashley (M) 220 17
H: 5 10 W: 11 00 b.Nantwich 1-4-90

2008–09	Crewe Alex	2	0	
2009–10	Crewe Alex	36	6	
2010–11	Crewe Alex	46	5	
2011–12	Crewe Alex	41	3	
2012–13	Crewe Alex	3	0	128 14
2012–13	Aston Villa	30	0	
2013–14	Aston Villa	35	3	
2014–15	Aston Villa	27	0	92 3

Players retained or with offer of contract
Abdo, Khalid; Bateman, Liam Vere; Bennett, Joseph; Cowans, Henry Gordon Mander; Gardner, Gary; Jensen, Nicklaus Helenius; Luna Rodriguez, Antonio Manuel; Lyden, Jordan; Lyons-Foster, Kodi; Suliman, Easah; Tonev, Aleksandar Antonov.

Scholars
Bannister, Charlie Brendan Alec; Blackett-Taylor, Corey; Green, Andre; Hailey, Liam; Hale, Rory Danny; Hepburn-Murphy, Rushian; Linley, Joseph; McKirdy, Harry; O'Hare, Callum; Omerovic, Anes; Sundman, Joonas Sebastian; Zeidan, Moustafa.

BARNSLEY (5)

ABBOTT, Brad (M) 5 0
b. 24-12-94

2013–14	Barnsley	0	0	
2014–15	Barnsley	5	0	5 0

BAILEY, James (M) 160 3
H: 6 0 W: 12 05 b.Bollington 18-9-88

2006–07	Crewe Alex	0	0	
2007–08	Crewe Alex	1	0	
2008–09	Crewe Alex	24	0	
2009–10	Crewe Alex	21	0	46 0
2010–11	Derby Co	36	1	
2011–12	Derby Co	22	0	
2012–13	Derby Co	0	0	
2012–13	*Coventry C*	30	2	30 2
2013–14	Derby Co	1	0	59 1
2014–15	Barnsley	25	0	25 0

BERRY, Luke (D) 31 1
H: 5 10 W: 11 05 b.Bassingbourn 12-7-92

2014–15	Barnsley	31	1	31 1

BOAKYE-YIADOM, Nana (F) 1 0
b. 31-5-96

2013–14	Barnsley	0	0	
2014–15	Barnsley	1	0	1 0

BREE, James (D) 12 0
H: 5 10 W: 11 09 b.Wakefield 11-10-97

2013–14	Barnsley	1	0	
2014–15	Barnsley	11	0	12 0

BROWN, Reece (D) 54 0
H: 6 2 W: 13 02 b.Manchester 1-11-91
Internationals: England U19, U20.

2010–11	Manchester U	0	0	
2010–11	*Bradford C*	3	0	3 0
2011–12	Manchester U	0	0	
2011–12	*Doncaster R*	3	0	3 0
2011–12	*Oldham Ath*	15	0	15 0
2012–13	Manchester U	0	0	
2012–13	*Coventry C*	6	0	6 0
2012–13	*Ipswich T*	1	0	1 0
2013–14	*Watford*	1	0	1 0
2013–14	*Carlisle U*	12	0	12 0
2014–15	Barnsley	13	0	13 0

COWGILL, Jack (D) 2 0
H: 6 1 W: 13 05 b.Wakefield 8-1-97

2013–14	Barnsley	0	0	
2014–15	Barnsley	2	0	2 0

CRANIE, Martin (D) 282 2
H: 6 1 W: 12 09 b.Yeovil 23-9-86
Internationals: England U17, U18, U19, U20, U21.

2003–04	Southampton	1	0	
2004–05	Southampton	3	0	
2004–05	*Bournemouth*	3	0	3 0
2005–06	Southampton	11	0	
2006–07	Southampton	1	0	16 0
2006–07	*Yeovil T*	12	0	12 0
2007–08	Portsmouth	2	0	
2007–08	*QPR*	6	0	6 0
2008–09	Portsmouth	0	0	
2008–09	*Charlton Ath*	19	0	19 0
2009–10	Portsmouth	0	0	2 0
2009–10	Coventry C	40	1	
2010–11	Coventry C	30	0	
2011–12	Coventry C	38	0	114 1
2012–13	Barnsley	36	0	
2013–14	Barnsley	35	0	
2014–15	Barnsley	39	1	110 1

DAVIES, Adam (G) 23 0
H: 6 1 W: 11 11 b.Rinteln 17-7-92

2009–10	Everton	0	0	
2010–11	Everton	0	0	
2011–12	Everton	0	0	
2013–14	Sheffield W	0	0	
2014–15	Barnsley	23	0	23 0

DIBBLE, Christian (G) 0 0
H: 6 4 W: 13 11 b.Wilmslow 11-5-94
Internationals: Wales U17, U19, U21.

2012–13	Bury	0	0	
2013–14	Barnsley	0	0	
2014–15	Barnsley	0	0	

DIGBY, Paul (M) 20 0
H: 5 9 W: 10 00 b.Sheffield 2-2-95
Internationals: England U19, U20.

2011–12	Barnsley	4	0	
2012–13	Barnsley	0	0	
2013–14	Barnsley	5	0	
2014–15	Barnsley	11	0	20 0

HEMMINGS, Kane (F) 27 3
b.Burton 8-4-92

2011–12	Rangers	4	0	4 0

From Cowdenbeath.

2014–15	Barnsley	23	3	23 3

HOLGATE, Mason (D) 20 1
b.Doncaster 22-10-96

2014–15	Barnsley	20	1	20 1

HOURIHANE, Conor (M) 171 28
H: 5 11 W: 9 11 b.Cork 2-2-91
Internationals: Republic of Ireland U19, U21.

2008–09	Sunderland	0	0	
2009–10	Sunderland	0	0	
2010–11	Ipswich T	0	0	
2011–12	Plymouth Arg	38	2	
2012–13	Plymouth Arg	42	5	
2013–14	Plymouth Arg	45	8	125 15
2014–15	Barnsley	46	13	46 13

JENNINGS, Dale (F) 82 10
H: 5 7 W: 11 00 b.Liverpool 21-12-92

2010–11	Tranmere R	29	6	29 6
2013–14	Barnsley	27	3	
2013–14	*Milton Keynes D*	6	0	6 0
2014–15	Barnsley	20	1	47 4

LALKOVIC, Milan (F) 77 6
H: 5 9 W: 10 01 b.Kosice 9-12-92
Internationals: Slovakia U17, U19, U21.

2010–11	Chelsea	0	0	
2011–12	Chelsea	0	0	
2011–12	*Doncaster R*	6	0	6 0
2011–12	*Den Haag*	2	0	2 0
2012–13	Chelsea	0	0	

2012–13	*Vitoria Guimaraes*	8	0	8 0
2013–14	Chelsea	0	0	
2013–14	*Walsall*	38	6	38 6
2014–15	*Mlada Boleslav*	6	0	6 0
2014–15	Barnsley	17	0	17 0

LITA, Leroy (F) 345 95
H: 5 7 W: 11 12 b.DR Congo 28-12-84
Internationals: England U21.

2002–03	Bristol C	15	2	
2003–04	Bristol C	26	5	
2004–05	Bristol C	44	24	85 31
2005–06	Reading	26	11	
2006–07	Reading	33	7	
2007–08	Reading	14	1	
2007–08	*Charlton Ath*	8	3	8 3
2008–09	Reading	10	1	83 20
2008–09	*Norwich C*	16	7	16 7
2009–10	Middlesbrough	40	8	
2010–11	Middlesbrough	38	12	78 20
2011–12	Swansea C	16	2	
2012–13	Swansea C	0	0	
2012–13	*Birmingham C*	10	3	10 3
2012–13	*Sheffield W*	17	6	17 6
2013–14	Swansea C	2	0	18 2
2013–14	*Brighton & HA*	5	1	5 1
2014–15	Barnsley	19	2	19 2
2014–15	*Notts Co*	6	0	6 0

MARIS, George (F) 2 0
b.Sheffield 6-3-96

2014–15	Barnsley	2	0	2 0

McHALE, Dominic (M) 0 0
H: 5 11 W: 11 07 b. 1-1-95

2013–14	Barnsley	0	0	
2014–15	Barnsley	0	0	

MVOTO, Jean Yves (D) 43 2
H: 6 4 W: 14 07 b.Paris 6-9-88

2009–10	*Southend U*	0	0	
2010–11	Oldham Ath	0	0	
2012–13	Oldham Ath	0	0	
2013–14	Barnsley	28	2	
2014–15	Barnsley	15	0	43 2

NYATANGA, Lewin (D) 290 15
H: 6 2 W: 12 08 b.Burton 18-8-88
Internationals: Wales U17, U21, Full caps.

2005–06	Derby Co	24	1	
2006–07	Derby Co	7	1	
2006–07	*Sunderland*	11	0	11 0
2006–07	Derby Co	2	1	
2007–08	*Barnsley*	41	1	
2008–09	Derby Co	30	1	63 4
2009–10	Bristol C	20	1	
2010–11	Bristol C	30	1	
2010–11	*Peterborough U*	3	0	3 0
2011–12	Bristol C	29	0	
2012–13	Bristol C	19	2	105 4
2013–14	Barnsley	12	0	
2014–15	Barnsley	45	5	108 7

OATES, Rhys (D) 9 0
H: 6 0 W: 11 09 b.Pontefract 4-12-94

2012–13	Barnsley	0	0	
2013–14	Barnsley	0	0	
2014–15	Barnsley	9	0	9 0

PHENIX, Mike (M) 2 0
H: 5 10 W: 11 00 b.Manchester 15-3-89

2014–15	Barnsley	2	0	2 0

ROSE, Danny (F) 58 14
H: 5 8 W: 9 00 b.Barnsley 10-12-93

2010–11	Barnsley	1	0	
2011–12	Barnsley	4	0	
2012–13	Barnsley	8	1	
2013–14	Barnsley	3	0	
2013–14	*Bury*	6	3	
2014–15	Barnsley	1	0	17 1
2014–15	*Bury*	35	10	41 13

SCOWEN, Josh (M) 112 7
H: 5 10 W: 11 09 b.Cheshunt 28-3-93

2010–11	Wycombe W	2	0	
2011–12	Wycombe W	0	0	
2012–13	Wycombe W	34	1	
2013–14	Wycombe W	37	1	
2014–15	Wycombe W	18	1	91 3
2014–15	Barnsley	21	4	21 4

SMITH, George (D) 18 0
H: 6 0 W: 12 02 b.Barnsley 14-8-96

2014–15	Barnsley	18	0	18 0

TREACY, Keith (M)   172 17
H: 6 0   W: 13 02   b.Dublin 13-9-88
Internationals: Republic of Ireland U21, Full caps.

2005–06	Blackburn R	0	0	
2006–07	Blackburn R	0	0	
2006–07	Stockport Co	4	0	4 0
2007–08	Blackburn R	0	0	
2008–09	Blackburn R	12	0	
2009–10	Blackburn R	0	0	12 0
2009–10	Sheffield U	16	1	16 1
2009–10	Preston NE	17	2	
2010–11	Preston NE	38	7	55 9
2011–12	Burnley	24	2	
2011–12	Sheffield W	7	1	7 1
2012–13	Burnley	15	1	
2013–14	Burnley	27	2	66 5
2014–15	Barnsley	12	1	12 1

TURNBULL, Ross (G)   148 0
H: 6 4   W: 15 00   b.Bishop Auckland 4-1-85
Internationals: England U16, U17, U18, U19.

2002–03	Middlesbrough	0	0	
2003–04	Middlesbrough	0	0	
2003–04	Darlington	1	0	1 0
2003–04	Barnsley	3	0	
2004–05	Middlesbrough	0	0	
2004–05	Bradford C	2	0	2 0
2004–05	Barnsley	23	0	
2005–06	Middlesbrough	2	0	
2005–06	Crewe Alex	29	0	29 0
2006–07	Middlesbrough	0	0	
2007–08	Middlesbrough	3	0	
2007–08	Cardiff C	6	0	6 0
2008–09	Middlesbrough	22	0	
2009–10	Middlesbrough	0	0	27 0
2009–10	Chelsea	2	0	
2010–11	Chelsea	0	0	
2011–12	Chelsea	2	0	
2012–13	Chelsea	3	0	7 0
2013–14	Doncaster R	28	0	28 0
2014–15	Barnsley	22	0	48 0

WILLIAMS, George (D)   6 0
H: 5 9   W: 11 00   b.Hillingdon 14-4-93

2011–12	Milton Keynes D	2	0	2 0
From Worcester C.				
2014–15	Barnsley	4	0	4 0

WINNALL, Sam (F)   110 41
H: 5 9   W: 11 04   b.Wolverhampton 19-1-91

2009–10	Wolverhampton W	0	0	
2010–11	Wolverhampton W	0	0	
2010–11	Burton Alb	19	7	19 7
2011–12	Wolverhampton W	0	0	
2011–12	Hereford U	8	2	8 2
2011–12	Inverness CT	2	0	2 0
2012–13	Wolverhampton W	0	0	
2012–13	Shrewsbury T	4	0	4 0
2013–14	Scunthorpe U	45	23	45 23
2014–15	Barnsley	32	9	32 9

Players retained or with offer of contract
Zezere, Neves Carnerio Pedro.

Scholars
Alton, Jack James; Gooda, Bailey Roy;
Goodwin, Sean; Hanna, Sam James; Jeffs,
Logan Liam; Ndlovu, Talent; Proctor, George
Miles; Reilly, Liam Joseph; Rogerson,
Edward James; Rusling, Danny William;
Templeton, Matthew; Walton, Jack James.

Non-Contract
Crossley, Mark Geoffrey.

BIRMINGHAM C (6)

ADAMS, Charlee (M)   0 0
H: 5 11   W: 12 01   b.Redbridge 16-2-95

2013–14	Birmingham C	0	0
2014–15	Birmingham C	0	0

ARTHUR, Koby (M)   19 3
H: 5 6   W: 10 09   b.Kumasi 3-1-96

2012–13	Birmingham C	2	0	
2013–14	Birmingham C	1	0	
2014–15	Birmingham C	9	0	12 0
2014–15	Cheltenham T	7	3	7 3

BELL, Amari (D)   18 0
H: 5 11   W: 12 00   b.Burton-upon-Trent 5-5-94

2012–13	Birmingham C	0	0	
2013–14	Birmingham C	1	0	
2014–15	Birmingham C	0	0	1 0
2014–15	Swindon T	10	0	10 0
2014–15	Gillingham	7	0	7 0

BROWN, Reece (M)   10 0
H: 5 9   W: 12 04   b.Dudley 3-3-96
Internationals: England U16, U17, U18.

2013–14	Birmingham C	6	0	
2014–15	Birmingham C	1	0	7 0
2014–15	Notts Co	3	0	3 0

CADDIS, Paul (D)   215 16
H: 5 7   W: 10 07   b.Irvine 19-4-88
Internationals: Scotland U19, U21.

2007–08	Celtic	2	0	
2008–09	Celtic	5	0	
2008–09	Dundee U	11	0	11 0
2009–10	Celtic	10	0	17 0
2010–11	Swindon T	38	1	
2011–12	Swindon T	39	4	
2012–13	Swindon T	0	0	
2012–13	Birmingham C	27	0	
2013–14	Swindon T	0	0	77 5
2013–14	Birmingham C	38	5	
2014–15	Birmingham C	45	6	110 11

COTTERILL, David (F)   321 44
H: 5 9   W: 11 02   b.Cardiff 4-12-87
Internationals: Wales U19, U21, Full caps.

2004–05	Bristol C	12	0	
2005–06	Bristol C	45	7	
2006–07	Bristol C	5	1	62 8
2006–07	Wigan Ath	16	1	
2007–08	Wigan Ath	2	0	18 1
2007–08	Sheffield U	16	0	
2008–09	Sheffield U	24	4	
2009–10	Sheffield U	14	2	54 6
2009–10	Swansea C	21	3	
2010–11	Swansea C	14	1	
2010–11	Portsmouth	15	1	15 1
2011–12	Swansea C	0	0	35 4
2011–12	Barnsley	11	1	11 1
2012–13	Doncaster R	44	10	
2013–14	Doncaster R	40	4	84 14
2014–15	Birmingham C	42	9	42 9

DAVIS, David (M)   135 5
H: 5 8   W: 12 03   b.Smethwick 20-2-91

2009–10	Wolverhampton W	0	0	
2009–10	Darlington	5	0	5 0
2010–11	Wolverhampton W	0	0	
2010–11	Walsall	7	0	7 0
2010–11	Shrewsbury T	19	2	19 2
2011–12	Wolverhampton W	7	0	
2011–12	Chesterfield	9	0	9 0
2012–13	Wolverhampton W	28	0	
2013–14	Wolverhampton W	18	0	53 0
2014–15	Birmingham C	42	3	42 3

DONALDSON, Clayton (F)   318 113
H: 6 1   W: 11 07   b.Bradford 7-2-84
Internationals: England C.

2002–03	Hull C	2	0	
2003–04	Hull C	1	0	
2004–05	Hull C	0	0	2 0
From York C				
2007–08	Hibernian	17	5	17 5
2008–09	Crewe Alex	37	6	
2009–10	Crewe Alex	37	13	
2010–11	Crewe Alex	43	28	117 47
2011–12	Brentford	46	11	
2012–13	Brentford	44	18	
2013–14	Brentford	46	17	136 46
2014–15	Birmingham C	46	15	46 15

DOYLE, Colin (G)   48 0
H: 6 5   W: 14 05   b.Cork 12-8-85
Internationals: Republic of Ireland U21, B, Full caps.

2004–05	Birmingham C	0	0	
2004–05	Chester C	0	0	
2004–05	Nottingham F	3	0	3 0
2005–06	Birmingham C	0	0	
2005–06	Millwall	14	0	14 0
2006–07	Birmingham C	19	0	
2007–08	Birmingham C	3	0	
2008–09	Birmingham C	2	0	
2009–10	Birmingham C	0	0	
2010–11	Birmingham C	1	0	
2011–12	Birmingham C	5	0	
2012–13	Birmingham C	0	0	
2013–14	Birmingham C	0	0	
2014–15	Birmingham C	1	0	31 0

DUFFY, Mark (M)   211 15
H: 5 9   W: 11 05   b.Liverpool 7-10-85

2008–09	Morecambe	9	1	
2009–10	Morecambe	35	4	
2010–11	Morecambe	22	0	66 5
2010–11	Scunthorpe U	22	1	
2011–12	Scunthorpe U	37	2	
2012–13	Scunthorpe U	43	5	102 8

EARDLEY, Neal (M)   227 12
H: 5 11   W: 11 10   b.Llandudno 6-11-88
Internationals: Wales U17, U19, U21, Full caps.

2005–06	Oldham Ath	1	0	
2006–07	Oldham Ath	36	2	
2007–08	Oldham Ath	42	6	
2008–09	Oldham Ath	34	2	
2009–10	Oldham Ath	0	0	113 10
2009–10	Blackpool	24	0	
2010–11	Blackpool	31	1	
2011–12	Blackpool	26	1	
2012–13	Blackpool	23	0	104 2
2013–14	Birmingham C	5	0	
2014–15	Birmingham C	4	0	9 0
2014–15	Leyton Orient	1	0	1 0

EDGAR, David (D)   151 8
H: 6 2   W: 12 13   b.Ontario 19-5-87
Internationals: Canada U17, U20, Full caps.

2005–06	Newcastle U	0	0	
2006–07	Newcastle U	3	1	
2007–08	Newcastle U	5	0	
2008–09	Newcastle U	11	1	
2009–10	Newcastle U	0	0	19 2
2009–10	Burnley	0	0	
2009–10	Swansea C	5	1	5 1
2010–11	Burnley	7	0	
2011–12	Burnley	44	2	
2012–13	Burnley	27	2	
2013–14	Burnley	17	0	99 4
2014–15	Birmingham C	16	1	16 1
2014–15	Huddersfield T	12	0	12 0

FRY, James (D)   0 0
H: 5 11   W: 12 03   b.Solihull 3-2-95

2012–13	Birmingham C	0	0
2013–14	Birmingham C	0	0
2014–15	Birmingham C	0	0

GLEESON, Stephen (M)   261 20
H: 6 2   W: 11 00   b.Dublin 3-8-88
Internationals: Republic of Ireland U21, Full caps.

2006–07	Wolverhampton W	3	0	
2006–07	Stockport Co	14	2	
2007–08	Wolverhampton W	0	0	
2007–08	Hereford U	4	0	4 0
2008–09	Stockport Co	6	0	
2008–09	Wolverhampton W	0	0	3 0
2008–09	Stockport Co	21	2	41 4
2008–09	Milton Keynes D	5	0	
2009–10	Milton Keynes D	29	0	
2010–11	Milton Keynes D	36	2	
2011–12	Milton Keynes D	39	5	
2012–13	Milton Keynes D	30	6	
2013–14	Milton Keynes D	35	3	174 16
2014–15	Birmingham C	39	0	39 0

GRAY, Demarai (M)   48 7
H: 5 10   W: 10 04   b.Birmingham 28-6-96
Internationals: England U18, U19, U20.

2013–14	Birmingham C	7	1	
2014–15	Birmingham C	41	6	48 7

GREEN, Matt (F)   56 1
H: 6 0   W: 12 09   b.Bath 2-1-87

2006–07	Cardiff C	6	0	
2007–08	Cardiff C	0	0	6 0
2007–08	Darlington	4	0	4 0
From Torquay U				
2010–11	Oxford U	17	0	17 0
2010–11	Cheltenham T	19	0	19 0
From Mansfield T				
2013–14	Birmingham C	10	1	
2014–15	Birmingham C	0	0	10 1

GROUNDS, Jonathan (D)   210 8
H: 6 1   W: 13 10   b.Thornaby 2-2-88

2007–08	Middlesbrough	5	0	
2008–09	Middlesbrough	2	0	
2008–09	Norwich C	16	3	16 3
2009–10	Middlesbrough	20	0	
2010–11	Middlesbrough	6	1	
2011–12	Middlesbrough	0	0	33 1
2011–12	Chesterfield	13	0	13 0
2011–12	Yeovil T	14	0	14 0
2012–13	Oldham Ath	44	1	
2013–14	Oldham Ath	45	2	89 3
2014–15	Birmingham C	45	1	45 1

GUNNING, Gavin (D)   126 8
H: 5 11   W: 13 08   b.Dublin 26-1-91
Internationals: Republic of Ireland U21.

2007–08	Blackburn R	0	0
2008–09	Blackburn R	0	0

2009–10	Blackburn R	0	0		
2009–10	Tranmere R	6	0	6	0
2009–10	Rotherham U	21	0	21	0
2010–11	Blackburn R	0	0		
2010–11	Bury	2	0	2	0
2010–11	Motherwell	14	0	14	0
2011–12	Dundee U	31	2		
2012–13	Dundee U	25	3		
2013–14	Dundee U	27	3	83	8
2014–15	Birmingham C	0	0		

HANCOX, Mitch (D) 33 0
H: 5 10 W: 11 03 b.Solihull 9-11-93

2011–12	Birmingham C	0	0		
2012–13	Birmingham C	19	0		
2013–14	Birmingham C	14	0		
2014–15	Birmingham C	0	0	33	0

JOHNSTONE, Denny (F) 12 2
H: 6 2 W: 13 01 b. 9-1-95
Internationals: Scotland U16, U17, U18, U19.

2013–14	Celtic	0	0		
2014–15	Birmingham C	0	0		
2014–15	Cheltenham T	5	1	5	1
2014–15	Burton Alb	5	1	5	1

LEE, Oliver (M) 71 6
H: 5 11 W: 12 07 b.Hornchurch 11-7-91

2009–10	West Ham U	0	0		
2010–11	West Ham U	0	0		
2010–11	Dagenham & R	5	0		
2011–12	West Ham U	0	0		
2011–12	Dagenham & R	16	3	21	3
2011–12	Gillingham	8	0	8	0
2012–13	Barnet	11	0	11	0
2012–13	Birmingham C	0	0		
2013–14	Birmingham C	16	1		
2014–15	Birmingham C	0	0	16	1
2014–15	Plymouth Arg	15	2	15	2

MARTIN, Josh (D) 0 0
b.Birmingham 21-10-98

2014–15	Birmingham C	0	0

MORRISON, Michael (D) 246 11
H: 6 0 W: 12 00 b.Bury St Edmunds 3-3-88
Internationals: England C.

2008–09	Leicester C	35	3		
2009–10	Leicester C	31	2		
2010–11	Leicester C	11	0	77	5
2010–11	Sheffield W	12	0	12	0
2011–12	Charlton Ath	45	4		
2012–13	Charlton Ath	44	1		
2013–14	Charlton Ath	45	1		
2014–15	Charlton Ath	2	0	136	6
2014–15	Birmingham C	21	0	21	0

MOUSSI, Guy (M) 232 5
H: 6 1 W: 12 11 b.Paris 23-1-85

2004–05	Angers	15	1		
2005–06	Angers	9	0		
2006–07	Angers	32	0		
2007–08	Angers	35	1	91	2
2008–09	Nottingham F	15	0		
2009–10	Nottingham F	27	3		
2010–11	Nottingham F	31	0		
2011–12	Nottingham F	34	0		
2012–13	Nottingham F	18	0		
2013–14	Nottingham F	11	0	136	3
2013–14	Millwall	3	0	3	0
2014–15	Birmingham C	2	0	2	0

NOVAK, Lee (F) 203 44
H: 6 0 W: 12 04 b.Newcastle 28-9-88

2008–09	Huddersfield T	0	0		
2009–10	Huddersfield T	37	12		
2010–11	Huddersfield T	31	5		
2011–12	Huddersfield T	41	13		
2012–13	Huddersfield T	35	4	144	34
2013–14	Birmingham C	38	9		
2014–15	Birmingham C	21	1	59	10

PACKWOOD, Will (M) 32 1
H: 6 3 W: 12 08 b.Concord 21-5-93
Internationals: USA U17, U18, U20, U23.

2011–12	Birmingham C	0	0		
2012–13	Birmingham C	5	0		
2013–14	Birmingham C	12	0		
2013–14	Bristol R	8	0	8	0
2014–15	Birmingham C	1	0	18	0
2014–15	Colchester U	1	0	1	0
2014–15	Cheltenham T	5	1	5	1

PRESTON, Callum (G) 0 0
b.Stafford 7-1-95

2014–15	Birmingham C	0	0

RANDOLPH, Darren (G) 246 0
H: 6 1 W: 12 02 b.Dublin 12-5-87
Internationals: Republic of Ireland U21, B, Full caps.

2004–05	Charlton Ath	0	0		
2005–06	Charlton Ath	0	0		
2006–07	Charlton Ath	1	0		
2006–07	Gillingham	3	0	3	0
2007–08	Charlton Ath	1	0		
2007–08	Bury	14	0	14	0
2008–09	Charlton Ath	1	0		
2008–09	Hereford U	13	0	13	0
2009–10	Charlton Ath	11	0	14	0
2010–11	Motherwell	37	0		
2011–12	Motherwell	38	0		
2012–13	Motherwell	36	0	111	0
2013–14	Birmingham C	46	0		
2014–15	Birmingham C	45	0	91	0

REILLY, Callum (M) 62 2
H: 6 1 W: 12 03 b.Warrington 3-10-93
Internationals: Republic of Ireland U21.

2012–13	Birmingham C	18	1		
2013–14	Birmingham C	25	0		
2014–15	Birmingham C	17	1	60	2
2014–15	Burton Alb	2	0	2	0

ROBINSON, Paul (D) 629 12
H: 5 9 W: 11 12 b.Watford 14-12-78
Internationals: England U21.

1996–97	Watford	12	0		
1997–98	Watford	22	0		
1998–99	Watford	29	0		
1999–2000	Watford	32	0		
2000–01	Watford	39	0		
2001–02	Watford	38	3		
2002–03	Watford	37	3		
2003–04	Watford	10	0	219	8
2003–04	WBA	31	0		
2004–05	WBA	30	1		
2005–06	WBA	33	0		
2006–07	WBA	42	2		
2007–08	WBA	43	1		
2008–09	WBA	35	0		
2009–10	WBA	0	0	214	4
2009–10	Bolton W	25	0		
2010–11	Bolton W	35	0		
2011–12	Bolton W	17	0	77	0
2011–12	Leeds U	10	0	10	0
2012–13	Birmingham C	35	0		
2013–14	Birmingham C	40	0		
2014–15	Birmingham C	34	0	109	0

SHINNIE, Andrew (M) 112 23
H: 5 11 W: 10 13 b.Aberdeen 17-7-89
Internationals: Scotland U19, U21, Full caps.

2005–06	Rangers	0	0		
2006–07	Rangers	2	0		
2007–08	Rangers	0	0		
2008–09	Rangers	0	0		
2009–10	Rangers	0	0		
2010–11	Rangers	0	0	2	0
2011–12	Inverness CT	19	7		
2012–13	Inverness CT	38	12	57	19
2013–14	Birmingham C	26	2		
2014–15	Birmingham C	27	2	53	4

SPECTOR, Jonathan (D) 230 1
H: 6 0 W: 12 08 b.Chicago 1-3-86
Internationals: USA U17, U20, Full caps.

2003–04	Manchester U	0	0		
2004–05	Manchester U	3	0		
2005–06	Manchester U	0	0		
2005–06	Charlton Ath	20	0	20	0
2006–07	West Ham U	25	0		
2007–08	West Ham U	26	0		
2008–09	West Ham U	9	0		
2009–10	West Ham U	27	0		
2010–11	West Ham U	14	1	101	1
2011–12	Birmingham C	31	0		
2012–13	Birmingham C	29	0		
2013–14	Birmingham C	22	0		
2014–15	Birmingham C	24	0	106	0

THOMAS, Wesley (F) 199 51
H: 5 10 W: 11 00 b.Barking 23-1-87

2008–09	Dagenham & R	5	0		
2009–10	Dagenham & R	23	3	28	3
2010–11	Cheltenham T	41	18	41	18
2011–12	Crawley T	6	1	6	1
2011–12	Bournemouth	36	11		
2012–13	Bournemouth	6	0		
2012–13	Portsmouth	6	3	6	3
2012–13	Blackpool	9	3	9	3
2012–13	Birmingham C	11	3		
2013–14	Bournemouth	10	0	52	11
2013–14	Rotherham U	13	5	13	5
2014–15	Birmingham C	33	4	44	7

TOWNSEND, Nick (G) 0 0
H: 5 11 W: 13 11 b.Solihull 1-11-94

2012–13	Birmingham C	0	0
2013–14	Birmingham C	0	0
2014–15	Birmingham C	0	0

TRUEMAN, Connal (G) 0 0
H: 6 1 W: 11 10 b.Birmingham 26-3-96

2014–15	Birmingham C	0	0
2014–15	Oldham Ath	0	0

TRUSLOVE, Liam (M) 0 0
H: 5 11 W: 10 11 b. 5-9-95

2013–14	Birmingham C	0	0
2014–15	Birmingham C	0	0

ZIGIC, Nikola (F) 413 208
H: 6 8 W: 14 02 b.Backa Topola 25-9-80
Internationals: Serbia Full caps.

1998–99	Backa Topola	14	8		
1999–2000	Backa Topola	28	28		
2000–01	Backa Topola	30	30		
2001–02	Backa Topola	4	2	76	68
2001–02	Mornar Bar	23	15	23	15
2002–03	Kolubara	8	3	8	3
2002–03	Spartak Subotica	11	14	11	14
2003–04	Red Star Belgrade	28	19		
2004–05	Red Star Belgrade	25	15		
2005–06	Red Star Belgrade	23	11		
2006–07	Red Star Belgrade	3	2	79	47
2006–07	Santander	32	11		
2007–08	Valencia	15	1		
2008–09	Santander	19	13	51	24
2009–10	Valencia	13	4	28	5
2010–11	Birmingham C	25	5		
2011–12	Birmingham C	35	11		
2012–13	Birmingham C	35	9		
2013–14	Birmingham C	33	7		
2014–15	Birmingham C	9	0	137	32

Scholars
Bailey-Nicholls, Khaellem-Bryce Khiyah; Bernard, Dominic Archie; Challis, Jack; Cooper, Charlie Terrence; Cotton, Perry Kevin; Dacres-Cogley, Joshua Jacob; Deadfield, Samuel Jack; Dunbar, Kieron Paul; Harding, Wesley Nathan Hylton; Lang, Thomas Antoni Robert; Lubala, Beryly Logos; Mbunga, Edjidja; McDonald, Wesley Nurettin; McFarlane, Raewkon Kyle; McGee, George David; Moseley, Bobby James; O'Keeffe, Corey James John; O'Neill, George Connor; Popa, David; Potter, Jordan William; Seddon, Steven Jeffrey; Smith, Leighton Robert Allen; Tibbetts, Joshua Joseph; Weaver, Jacob William Robert; Webb, Reece.

BLACKBURN R (7)

BAURESS, Bradley (D) 0 0
b. 4-4-98

2014–15	Blackburn R	0	0

BEST, Leon (F) 254 54
H: 6 1 W: 13 03 b.Nottingham 19-9-86
Internationals: Republic of Ireland U21, Full caps.

2004–05	Southampton	3	0		
2004–05	QPR	5	0	5	0
2005–06	Southampton	3	0		
2005–06	Sheffield W	13	2		
2006–07	Southampton	9	4	15	4
2006–07	Bournemouth	15	3	15	3
2006–07	Yeovil T	15	10	15	10
2007–08	Coventry C	34	8		
2008–09	Coventry C	31	2		
2009–10	Coventry C	27	9	92	19
2009–10	Newcastle U	13	0		
2010–11	Newcastle U	11	6		
2011–12	Newcastle U	18	4	42	10
2012–13	Blackburn R	6	0		
2013–14	Blackburn R	8	2		
2013–14	Sheffield W	15	4	28	6
2014–15	Blackburn R	0	0	14	2
2014–15	Derby Co	15	0	15	0
2014–15	Brighton & HA	13	0	13	0

BROWN, Chris (F) 332 58
H: 6 1 W: 13 01 b.Doncaster 11-12-84

2002–03	Sunderland	0	0		
2003–04	Sunderland	2	0		
2003–04	Doncaster R	22	10		
2004–05	Sunderland	37	5		
2005–06	Sunderland	13	1		
2005–06	Hull C	13	1	13	1
2006–07	Sunderland	16	3	66	9

2006–07	Norwich C	4	0	
2007–08	Norwich C	14	1	**18 1**
2007–08	Preston NE	17	5	
2008–09	Preston NE	30	6	
2009–10	Preston NE	43	6	
2010–11	Preston NE	16	1	**106 18**
2011–12	Doncaster R	11	2	
2012–13	Doncaster R	36	8	
2013–14	Doncaster R	40	9	**109 29**
2014–15	Blackburn R	20	0	**20 0**

CAIRNEY, Tom (M)   **146 10**
H: 6 0   W: 11 05   b.Nottingham 20-1-91
Internationals: Scotland U19, U21.

2009–10	Hull C	11	1	
2010–11	Hull C	22	1	
2011–12	Hull C	27	0	
2012–13	Hull C	10	0	
2013–14	Hull C	0	0	**70 2**
2013–14	Blackburn R	37	5	
2014–15	Blackburn R	39	3	**76 8**

CONWAY, Craig (M)   **324 33**
H: 5 7   W: 10 07   b.Irvine 2-5-85
Internationals: Scotland Full caps.

2002–03	Ayr U	1	0	
2003–04	Ayr U	6	0	
2004–05	Ayr U	23	3	
2005–06	Ayr U	31	4	**61 7**
2006–07	Dundee U	30	0	
2007–08	Dundee U	15	1	
2008–09	Dundee U	36	5	
2009–10	Dundee U	33	4	
2010–11	Dundee U	22	3	**136 13**
2011–12	Cardiff C	31	3	
2012–13	Cardiff C	27	2	
2013–14	Cardiff C	0	0	**58 5**
2013–14	Brighton & HA	13	1	**13 1**
2013–14	Blackburn R	18	4	
2014–15	Blackburn R	38	3	**56 7**

DALY, Kellen (D)   **0 0**
b. 17-1-95

2012–13	Blackburn R	0	0
2013–14	Blackburn R	0	0
2014–15	Blackburn R	0	0

DUFFY, Shane (D)   **80 4**
H: 6 4   W: 12 00   b.Derry 1-1-92
Internationals: Northern Ireland U16, U17, U19, U21, B. Republic of Ireland U19, U21, Full caps.

2008–09	Everton	0	0	
2009–10	Everton	0	0	
2010–11	Everton	0	0	
2010–11	Burnley	1	0	**1 0**
2011–12	Everton	4	0	
2011–12	Scunthorpe U	18	2	**18 2**
2012–13	Everton	1	0	
2013–14	Everton	0	0	
2013–14	Yeovil T	37	1	**37 1**
2014–15	Everton	0	0	**5 0**
2014–15	Blackburn R	19	1	**19 1**

DUNN, David (M)   **374 57**
H: 5 9   W: 12 03   b.Gt Harwood 27-12-79
Internationals: England U18, U21, Full caps.

1997–98	Blackburn R	0	0	
1998–99	Blackburn R	15	1	
1999–2000	Blackburn R	22	2	
2000–01	Blackburn R	42	12	
2001–02	Blackburn R	29	7	
2002–03	Blackburn R	28	8	
2003–04	Birmingham C	21	2	
2004–05	Birmingham C	11	2	
2005–06	Birmingham C	15	2	
2006–07	Birmingham C	11	1	**58 7**
2006–07	Blackburn R	11	0	
2007–08	Blackburn R	31	1	
2008–09	Blackburn R	15	1	
2009–10	Blackburn R	23	9	
2010–11	Blackburn R	27	2	
2011–12	Blackburn R	26	2	
2012–13	Blackburn R	15	1	
2013–14	Blackburn R	23	4	
2014–15	Blackburn R	9	0	**316 50**

EASTWOOD, Simon (G)   **63 0**
H: 6 2   W: 10 13   b.Huddersfield 26-6-89
Internationals: England U18, U19.

2005–06	Huddersfield T	0	0	
2006–07	Huddersfield T	0	0	
2007–08	Huddersfield T	0	0	
2008–09	Huddersfield T	0	0	
2009–10	Huddersfield T	0	0	**1 0**
2009–10	Bradford C	22	0	**22 0**
2012–13	Portsmouth	27	0	**27 0**
2013–14	Blackburn R	7	0	
2014–15	Blackburn R	6	0	**13 0**

EVANS, Corry (M)   **153 8**
H: 5 8   W: 10 12   b.Belfast 30-7-90
Internationals: Northern Ireland U16, U17, U19, U21, B, Full caps.

2007–08	Manchester U	0	0	
2008–09	Manchester U	0	0	
2009–10	Manchester U	0	0	
2010–11	Manchester U	0	0	
2010–11	Carlisle U	1	0	**1 0**
2010–11	Hull C	18	3	
2011–12	Hull C	43	2	
2012–13	Hull C	32	1	
2013–14	Hull C	0	0	**93 6**
2013–14	Blackburn R	21	1	
2014–15	Blackburn R	38	1	**59 2**

FORRESTER, Anton (F)   **28 6**
H: 6 0   W: 12 00   b.Liverpool 11-2-94

2010–11	Everton	0	0	
2011–12	Everton	0	0	
2012–13	Blackburn R	0	0	
2013–14	Blackburn R	0	0	
2013–14	Bury	28	6	**28 6**
2014–15	Blackburn R	0	0	

GESTEDE, Rudy (F)   **162 48**
H: 6 4   W: 13 07   b.Nancy 10-10-88
Internationals: France U19. Benin Full caps.

2008–09	Metz	5	0	
2009–10	Cannes	22	4	**22 4**
2010–11	Metz	11	3	**16 3**
2010–11	Metz B	3	1	**3 1**
2011–12	Cardiff C	25	2	
2012–13	Cardiff C	27	5	
2013–14	Cardiff C	3	0	**55 7**
2013–14	Blackburn R	27	13	
2014–15	Blackburn R	39	20	**66 33**

GREEN, Devarn (F)   **0 0**
b. 26-8-96

2014–15	Blackburn R	0	0

HANLEY, Grant (D)   **139 5**
H: 6 2   W: 12 00   b.Dumfries 20-11-91
Internationals: Scotland U19, U21, Full caps.

2008–09	Blackburn R	0	0	
2009–10	Blackburn R	1	0	
2010–11	Blackburn R	7	0	
2011–12	Blackburn R	23	1	
2012–13	Blackburn R	39	2	
2013–14	Blackburn R	38	1	
2014–15	Blackburn R	31	1	**139 5**

HENLEY, Adam (D)   **54 1**
H: 5 10   W: 12 02   b.Knoxville 14-6-94
Internationals: Wales U19, U21.

2011–12	Blackburn R	7	0	
2012–13	Blackburn R	15	0	
2013–14	Blackburn R	14	0	
2014–15	Blackburn R	18	1	**54 1**

KEAN, Jake (G)   **86 0**
H: 6 4   W: 11 13   b.Derby 4-2-91
Internationals: England U20.

2010–11	Blackburn R	0	0	
2010–11	Hartlepool U	19	0	**19 0**
2011–12	Blackburn R	1	0	
2011–12	Rochdale	14	0	**14 0**
2012–13	Blackburn R	18	0	
2013–14	Blackburn R	18	0	
2014–15	Blackburn R	0	0	**37 0**
2014–15	Yeovil T	5	0	**5 0**
2014–15	Oldham Ath	11	0	**11 0**

KILGALLON, Matthew (D)   **274 9**
H: 6 1   W: 12 10   b.York 8-1-84
Internationals: England U20, U21.

2000–01	Leeds U	0	0	
2001–02	Leeds U	0	0	
2002–03	Leeds U	2	0	
2003–04	Leeds U	8	2	
2003–04	West Ham U	3	0	**3 0**
2004–05	Leeds U	26	0	
2005–06	Leeds U	25	1	
2006–07	Leeds U	19	0	**80 3**
2006–07	Sheffield U	6	0	
2007–08	Sheffield U	40	2	
2008–09	Sheffield U	40	1	
2009–10	Sheffield U	21	1	**107 4**
2009–10	Sunderland	7	0	
2010–11	Sunderland	0	0	
2010–11	Middlesbrough	2	0	**2 0**
2010–11	Doncaster R	12	0	**12 0**
2011–12	Sunderland	10	0	
2012–13	Sunderland	6	0	**23 0**
2013–14	Blackburn R	25	1	
2014–15	Blackburn R	22	1	**47 2**

KING, Josh (F)   **92 6**
H: 5 11   W: 11 09   b.Oslo 15-1-92
Internationals: Norway U15, U16, U18, U19, U21, Full caps.

2008–09	Manchester U	0	0	
2009–10	Manchester U	0	0	
2010–11	Manchester U	0	0	
2010–11	Preston NE	8	0	**8 0**
2011–12	Manchester U	0	0	
2011–12	Moenchengladbach	2	0	**2 0**
2011–12	Hull C	18	1	**18 1**
2012–13	Manchester U	0	0	
2012–13	Blackburn R	16	2	
2013–14	Blackburn R	32	2	
2014–15	Blackburn R	16	1	**64 5**

LENIHAN, Darragh (M)   **20 1**
H: 5 10   W: 12 00   b.Dublin 16-3-94
Internationals: Republic of Ireland U17, U19, U21.

2011–12	Blackburn R	0	0	
2012–13	Blackburn R	0	0	
2013–14	Blackburn R	0	0	
2014–15	Blackburn R	3	0	**3 0**
2014–15	Burton Alb	17	1	**17 1**

LOWE, Jason (M)   **127 3**
H: 6 0   W: 12 08   b.Wigan 2-9-91
Internationals: England U20, U21.

2009–10	Blackburn R	0	0	
2010–11	Blackburn R	1	0	
2010–11	Oldham Ath	7	2	**7 2**
2011–12	Blackburn R	32	0	
2012–13	Blackburn R	36	0	
2013–14	Blackburn R	39	1	
2014–15	Blackburn R	12	0	**120 1**

MAHONEY, Connor (M)   **4 0**
H: 5 9   W: 10 08   b.Blackburn 12-2-97
Internationals: England U17, U18.

2013–14	Accrington S	4	0	**4 0**
2013–14	Blackburn R	0	0	
2014–15	Blackburn R	0	0	

MARSHALL, Ben (F)   **212 30**
H: 5 11   W: 11 13   b.Salford 29-3-91
Internationals: England U21.

2009–10	Stoke C	0	0	
2009–10	Northampton T	15	2	**15 2**
2009–10	Cheltenham T	6	2	**6 2**
2010–11	Stoke C	0	0	
2010–11	Carlisle U	33	3	**53 6**
2011–12	Stoke C	0	0	
2011–12	Sheffield W	22	5	**22 5**
2011–12	Leicester C	16	3	
2012–13	Leicester C	40	4	
2013–14	Leicester C	0	0	**56 7**
2013–14	Blackburn R	18	2	
2014–15	Blackburn R	42	6	**60 8**

MORRIS, Josh (M)   **95 10**
H: 5 9   W: 10 00   b.Preston 30-9-91
Internationals: England U20.

2010–11	Blackburn R	4	0	
2011–12	Blackburn R	2	0	
2011–12	Yeovil T	5	0	**5 0**
2012–13	Blackburn R	10	0	
2012–13	Rotherham U	5	0	**5 0**
2013–14	Blackburn R	4	0	
2013–14	Carlisle U	6	0	**6 0**
2013–14	Fleetwood T	14	2	
2014–15	Blackburn R	0	0	**20 0**
2014–15	Fleetwood T	45	8	**59 10**

NYAMBE, Ryan (D)   **0 0**
b. 4-12-97

2014–15	Blackburn R	0	0

O'SULLIVAN, John (M)   **24 4**
H: 5 11   W: 13 01   b.Birmingham 18-9-93
Internationals: Republic of Ireland U19, U21.

2011–12	Blackburn R	0	0	
2012–13	Blackburn R	1	0	
2013–14	Blackburn R	0	0	
2014–15	Blackburn R	2	0	**3 0**
2014–15	Accrington S	13	4	**13 4**
2014–15	Barnsley	8	0	**8 0**

OLSSON, Marcus (M)   **184 13**
H: 5 11   W: 10 10   b.Gavle 17-5-88
Internationals: Sweden U21, Full caps.

2008	Halmstad	21	2	
2009	Halmstad	20	4	
2010	Halmstad	30	4	
2011	Halmstad	29	2	**100 12**
2011–12	Blackburn R	12	0	
2012–13	Blackburn R	23	1	
2013–14	Blackburn R	0	0	
2014–15	Blackburn R	41	0	**84 1**

PRESTON, Jordan (F) 0 0
b. 26-11-95

Season	Club				
2014–15	Blackburn R	0	0		

RAYA, David (G) 2 0
H: 6 0 W: 12 08 b.Barcelona 15-9-95

2013–14	Blackburn R	0	0		
2014–15	Blackburn R	2	0	2	0

RHODES, Jordan (F) 287 155
H: 6 1 W: 11 03 b.Oldham 5-2-90
Internationals: Scotland U21, Full caps.

2007–08	Ipswich T	8	1		
2008–09	Ipswich T	2	0	10	1
2008–09	Rochdale	5	2	5	2
2008–09	Brentford	14	7	14	7
2009–10	Huddersfield T	45	19		
2010–11	Huddersfield T	37	16		
2011–12	Huddersfield T	40	35		
2012–13	Huddersfield T	2	2	124	72
2012–13	Blackburn R	43	27		
2013–14	Blackburn R	46	25		
2014–15	Blackburn R	45	21	134	73

RITTENBERG, Dean (F) 0 0
b. 13-5-96
Internationals: England U18.

2013–14	Blackburn R	0	0		
2014–15	Blackburn R	0	0		

ROBINSON, Paul (G) 421 0
H: 6 1 W: 14 07 b.Beverley 15-10-79
Internationals: England U21, Full caps

1996–97	Leeds U	0	0		
1997–98	Leeds U	0	0		
1998–99	Leeds U	5	0		
1999–2000	Leeds U	0	0		
2000–01	Leeds U	16	0		
2001–02	Leeds U	0	0		
2002–03	Leeds U	38	0		
2003–04	Leeds U	36	0	95	0
2003–04	Tottenham H	0	0		
2004–05	Tottenham H	36	0		
2005–06	Tottenham H	38	0		
2006–07	Tottenham H	38	1		
2007–08	Tottenham H	25	0	137	1
2008–09	Blackburn R	35	0		
2009–10	Blackburn R	35	0		
2010–11	Blackburn R	36	0		
2011–12	Blackburn R	34	0		
2012–13	Blackburn R	21	0		
2013–14	Blackburn R	21	0		
2014–15	Blackburn R	7	0	189	0

SONGO'O, Yann (D) 35 4
H: 6 0 W: 12 00 b.Yaounde 17-11-91
Internationals: France U16. Cameroon U20.

2011–12	Sabadell	6	0	6	0
2013	Sporting Kansas C	0	0		
2013	*Orlando C*	12	1	12	1
2013–14	Ross Co	0	0		
2013–14	*Ross Co*	17	3	17	3
2014–15	Blackburn R	0	0		

SPURR, Tommy (D) 312 9
H: 6 1 W: 11 05 b.Leeds 13-9-87

2005–06	Sheffield W	2	0		
2006–07	Sheffield W	36	0		
2007–08	Sheffield W	41	2		
2008–09	Sheffield W	41	2		
2009–10	Sheffield W	46	1		
2010–11	Sheffield W	26	0	192	5
2011–12	Doncaster R	19	0		
2012–13	Doncaster R	46	1		
2013–14	Doncaster R	0	0	65	1
2013–14	Blackburn R	43	3		
2014–15	Blackburn R	12	0	55	3

TAYLOR, Chris (M) 326 37
H: 5 11 W: 11 00 b.Oldham 20-12-86

2005–06	Oldham Ath	14	0		
2006–07	Oldham Ath	44	4		
2007–08	Oldham Ath	42	5		
2008–09	Oldham Ath	42	10		
2009–10	Oldham Ath	32	1		
2010–11	Oldham Ath	42	11		
2011–12	Oldham Ath	38	2	254	33
2012–13	Millwall	22	3	22	3
2013–14	Blackburn R	34	0		
2014–15	Blackburn R	16	1	50	1

THOMSON, Connor (D) 0 0
H: 6 3 b. 14-2-96

2013–14	Carlisle U	0	0		
2014–15	Carlisle U	0	0		
2014–15	Blackburn R	0	0		

VARNEY, Luke (F) 345 67
H: 5 11 W: 11 00 b.Leicester 28-9-82

2002–03	Crewe Alex				
2003–04	Crewe Alex	8	1		
2004–05	Crewe Alex	26	4		
2005–06	Crewe Alex	27	5		
2006–07	Crewe Alex	34	17	95	27
2007–08	Charlton Ath	39	8		
2008–09	Charlton Ath	18	2	57	10
2008–09	Sheffield W	4	2		
2008–09	Derby Co	10	1		
2009–10	Derby Co	1	0		
2009–10	Sheffield W	39	9	43	11
2010–11	Derby Co	1	0	12	1
2010–11	*Blackpool*	30	5	30	5
2011–12	Portsmouth	30	6	30	6
2012–13	Leeds U	34	4		
2013–14	Leeds U	11	2	45	6
2013–14	*Blackburn R*	12	0		
2014–15	Blackburn R	11	0	23	0
2014–15	*Ipswich T*	10	1	10	1

WILLIAMSON, Lee (M) 480 36
H: 5 10 W: 10 04 b.Derby 7-6-82

1999–2000	Mansfield T	4	0		
2000–01	Mansfield T	15	0		
2001–02	Mansfield T	46	3		
2002–03	Mansfield T	40	0		
2003–04	Mansfield T	35	0		
2004–05	Mansfield T	4	0	144	3
2004–05	Northampton T	37	0	37	0
2005–06	Rotherham U	37	4		
2006–07	Rotherham U	19	5	56	9
2006–07	Watford	5	0		
2007–08	Watford	32	2		
2008–09	Watford	34	2	71	4
2008–09	*Preston NE*	5	1	5	1
2009–10	Sheffield U	20	3		
2010–11	Sheffield U	16	3		
2011–12	Sheffield U	40	13		
2012–13	Sheffield U	0	0	76	19
2012–13	Portsmouth	22	0	22	0
2012–13	Blackburn R	9	0		
2013–14	Blackburn R	32	0		
2014–15	Blackburn R	28	0	69	0

Players retained or with offer of contract
Crump, Ryan; Steele, Jason.

Scholars
Askew, Joshua George Michael Peter;
Callaway, Stuart Peter; Doyle, Jack Marc;
Edgar, Mark David Arthur; Edo, Martin
Adrian; Fisher, Andrew Lee; Hardcastle,
Lewis James; Howarth, Ramirez; Joel,
Samuel Robert Edward; Lavelle, Samuel
Mark; Mansell, Lewis David; Mehew, Oliver
David William; Nyambe, Ryan; Pierce,
George Ramon; Pirretas, Glasmacher Jan;
Platt, Matthew James; Scott, Cameron Henry;
Tanner, Hyuga; Thomson, Connor Kegan;
Tomlinson, Willem David Daniel; Wall, Luke
Sky; Wharton, Scott Bradley; Williams,
Callum James.

BLACKPOOL (8)

BARKHUIZEN, Tom (F) 77 13
H: 5 9 W: 11 00 b.Blackpool 4-7-93

2011–12	Blackpool	0	0		
2011–12	*Hereford U*	38	11	38	11
2012–13	Blackpool	0	0		
2012–13	*Fleetwood T*	13	1	13	1
2013–14	Blackpool	14	1		
2014–15	Blackpool	7	0	21	1
2014–15	*Morecambe*	5	0	5	0

BLACKMAN, Andre (D) 14 0
H: 5 11 W: 11 05 b.Lambeth 10-11-90

2009–10	Bristol C	0	0		
2011–12	Celtic	3	0		
2012–13	Celtic	0	0	3	0
2012–13	*Inverness CT*	2	0	2	0
2013–14	Plymouth Arg	6	0	6	0
2014–15	Blackpool	3	0	3	0

BONEY, Miles (G) 0 0
H: 5 11 W: 11 09 b.Blackpool 1-2-98

2014–15	Blackpool	0	0		

CAMERON, Henry (M) 11 1
H: 5 10 W: 11 00 b. 28-6-97

2013–14	Blackpool	0	0		
2014–15	Blackpool	11	1	11	1

CLARKE, Peter (D) 484 36
H: 6 0 W: 12 00 b.Southport 3-1-82
Internationals: England U20, U21.

1998–99	Everton	0	0		
1999–2000	Everton	0	0		
2000–01	Everton	1	0		
2001–02	Everton	7	0		
2002–03	Everton	0	0		
2002–03	*Blackpool*	16	3		
2002–03	*Port Vale*	13	1	13	1
2003–04	Everton	1	0		
2003–04	*Coventry C*	5	0	5	0
2004–05	Everton	0	0	9	0
2004–05	Blackpool	38	5		
2005–06	Blackpool	46	6		
2006–07	Southend U	38	2		
2007–08	Southend U	45	4		
2008–09	Southend U	43	4	126	10
2009–10	Huddersfield T	46	5		
2010–11	Huddersfield T	46	4		
2011–12	Huddersfield T	31	0		
2012–13	Huddersfield T	43	0		
2013–14	Huddersfield T	26	0	192	9
2014–15	Blackpool	39	2	139	16

CUBERO, Jose (M) 178 16
H: 5 10 W: 11 00 b.San Jose 14-2-87
Internationals: Costa Rica Full caps.

2009–10	Herediano	14	2		
2009–10	*Puntarenas*	17	0	17	0
2010–11	Herediano	34	3		
2011–12	Herediano	40	4		
2012–13	Herediano	19	4		
2013–14	Herediano	42	3	149	16
2014–15	Blackpool	12	0	12	0

CYWKA, Thomasz (M) 120 15
H: 5 10 W: 11 09 b.Gliwice 27-6-88
Internationals: Poland U18, U19, U20, U21.

2006–07	Wigan Ath	0	0		
2006–07	*Oldham Ath*	4	0	4	0
2007–08	Wigan Ath	0	0		
2008–09	Wigan Ath	0	0		
2009–10	Wigan Ath	0	0		
2009–10	Derby Co	5	0		
2010–11	Derby Co	31	4		
2011–12	Derby Co	8	1	44	5
2011–12	*Reading*	4	0	4	0
2012–13	Barnsley	29	5		
2013–14	Barnsley	30	4	59	9
2014–15	Blackpool	6	1	6	1
2014–15	*Rochdale*	3	0	3	0

DAVIES, Steve (F) 238 48
H: 6 0 W: 12 00 b.Liverpool 29-12-87

2005–06	Tranmere R	22	2		
2006–07	Tranmere R	28	1		
2007–08	Tranmere R	10	2	60	5
2008–09	Derby Co	19	3		
2009–10	Derby Co	18	1		
2010–11	Derby Co	20	5		
2011–12	Derby Co	26	11		
2012–13	Derby Co	0	0	83	20
2012–13	*Bristol C*	37	13	37	13
2013–14	Blackpool	28	3		
2014–15	Blackpool	17	5	45	8
2014–15	*Sheffield U*	13	2	13	2

DELFOUNESO, Nathan (F) 72 6
H: 6 1 W: 12 04 b.Birmingham 2-2-91
Internationals: England U16, U17, U19, U21.

2007–08	Aston Villa	0	0		
2008–09	Aston Villa	4	0		
2009–10	Aston Villa	9	1		
2010–11	Aston Villa	11	1		
2010–11	*Burnley*	11	1	11	1
2011–12	Aston Villa	6	0		
2011–12	*Leicester C*	4	0	4	0
2012–13	Aston Villa	1	0		
2012–13	*Blackpool*	40	6		
2013–14	Aston Villa	0	0	31	2
2013–14	*Blackpool*	11	0		
2013–14	*Coventry C*	14	3	14	3
2014–15	Blackpool	38	3	89	9

DIELNA, Joel (D) 19 0
H: 6 2 W: 12 08 b. 27-12-90

2012–13	Vannes	5	0		
2013–14	Vannes	12	0	17	0
2014–15	Blackpool	2	0	2	0

DUNNE, Charles (F) 72 0
H: 5 9 W: 11 09 b.Lambeth 13-2-93
Internationals: Republic of Ireland U21.

2011–12	Wycombe W	3	0		
2012–13	Wycombe W	38	0		
2013–14	Blackpool	0	0		
2013–14	*Wycombe W*	9	0	50	0
2014–15	Blackpool	22	0	22	0

FERGUSON, David (D) 10 1
b.Sunderland 7-6-94

2012–13	Sunderland	0	0		
2013–14	Sunderland	0	0		

2014–15 Sunderland 0 0
2014–15 Blackpool 10 1 **10 1**

GRANT, Robert (M) 214 48
H: 5 11 W: 12 00 b.Liverpool 1-7-90
2006–07 Accrington S 1 0
2007–08 Accrington S 7 0
2008–09 Accrington S 15 1
2009–10 Accrington S 42 14
2010–11 Scunthorpe U 27 0
2010–11 *Rochdale* 6 2
2011–12 Scunthorpe U 29 7
2011–12 *Accrington S* 8 3 **73 18**
2012–13 Scunthorpe U 3 0 **59 7**
2012–13 Rochdale 36 15 **42 17**
2013–14 Blackpool 6 0
2013–14 *Fleetwood T* 1 0 **1 0**
2014–15 Blackpool 0 0 **6 0**
2014–15 *Shrewsbury T* 33 6 **33 6**

HIGHAM, Luke (M) 0 0
2014–15 Blackpool 0 0

MACKENZIE, Gary (D) 222 9
H: 6 3 W: 13 01 b.Lanark 15-10-85
2003–04 Rangers 2 0
2004–05 Rangers 1 0
2005–06 Rangers 0 0 **2 0**
2006–07 Dundee 21 0
2007–08 Dundee 33 1
2008–09 Dundee 19 0
2009–10 Dundee 25 1 **98 2**
2010–11 Milton Keynes D 26 2
2011–12 Milton Keynes D 26 1
2012–13 Milton Keynes D 11 0 **63 3**
2012–13 *Blackpool* 12 2
2013–14 Blackpool 35 1
2014–15 Blackpool 0 0 **47 3**
2014–15 *Bradford C* 12 1 **12 1**

McMAHON, Tony (D) 255 8
H: 5 10 W: 11 04 b.Bishop Auckland 24-3-86
Internationals: England U16, U17, U19.
2003–04 Middlesbrough 0 0
2004–05 Middlesbrough 13 0
2005–06 Middlesbrough 3 0
2006–07 Middlesbrough 0 0
2007–08 Middlesbrough 1 0
2007–08 *Blackpool* 2 0
2008–09 Middlesbrough 13 0
2008–09 *Sheffield W* 15 1 **15 1**
2009–10 Middlesbrough 21 0
2010–11 Middlesbrough 34 2
2011–12 Middlesbrough 34 1 **119 3**
2012–13 Sheffield U 38 2
2013–14 Sheffield U 23 0 **61 2**
2013–14 Blackpool 18 0
2014–15 Blackpool 32 1 **52 1**
2014–15 *Bradford C* 8 1 **8 1**

MELLIS, Jacob (M) 113 10
H: 5 11 W: 10 11 b.Nottingham 8-1-91
Internationals: England U16, U17, U19.
2009–10 Chelsea 0 0
2009–10 *Southampton* 12 0 **12 0**
2010–11 Chelsea 0 0
2010–11 *Barnsley* 15 2
2012–13 Barnsley 36 6
2013–14 Barnsley 30 2 **81 10**
2014–15 Blackpool 13 0 **13 0**
2014–15 *Oldham Ath* 7 0 **7 0**

MENDY, Formose (M) 52 0
H: 6 0 W: 12 00 b.Guediawaye 23-3-89
Internationals: Guineau-Bissau Full caps.
2009–10 Peurtollano 14 0 **14 0**
2011–12 Sporting Gijon 10 0
2012–13 Sporting Gijon 13 0
2013–14 Sporting Gijon 12 0 **35 0**
2014–15 Blackpool 3 0 **3 0**
Transferred to HJK Helsinki April 2015.

MILTON, Daniel (G) 0 0
H: 6 0 W: 12 04 b. 26-11-96
Internationals: Canada U17.
2014–15 Blackpool 0 0

NOSWORTHY, Nyron (D) 417 8
H: 6 0 W: 12 08 b.Brixton 11-10-80
Internationals: Jamaica Full caps.
1998–99 Gillingham 3 0
1999–2000 Gillingham 29 1
2000–01 Gillingham 10 0
2001–02 Gillingham 29 0
2002–03 Gillingham 39 2
2003–04 Gillingham 27 2
2004–05 Gillingham 37 0 **174 5**
2005–06 Sunderland 30 0
2006–07 Sunderland 29 0

2007–08 Sunderland 29 0
2008–09 Sunderland 16 0
2009–10 Sunderland 10 0
2009–10 Sheffield U 19 0
2010–11 Sunderland 0 0 **114 0**
2010–11 *Sheffield U* 32 0 **51 0**
2011–12 Watford 32 2
2012–13 Watford 19 0
2013–14 Watford 5 0 **56 2**
2013–14 *Bristol C* 10 1 **10 1**
2014–15 Blackpool 5 0 **5 0**
2014–15 *Portsmouth* 7 0 **7 0**

O'DEA, Darren (D) 173· 9
H: 6 1 W: 13 01 b.Dublin 4-2-87
Internationals: Eire U21, Full caps.
2006–07 Celtic 14 2
2007–08 Celtic 6 0
2008–09 Celtic 10 1
2009–10 Celtic 19 1 **49 4**
2009–10 *Reading* 8 0 **8 0**
2010–11 Ipswich T 20 0
2011–12 Ipswich T 0 0 **20 0**
2011–12 *Leeds U* 35 2 **35 2**
2012 Toronto 9 0
2013 Toronto 17 1 **26 1**
2013–14 Metallurg Donetsk 16 2
2014–15 Metallurg Donetsk 0 0 **16 2**
2014–15 *Blackpool* 19 0 **19 0**

O'HARA, Jamie (M) 175 18
H: 5 11 W: 12 04 b.Dartford 25-9-86
Internationals: England U21.
2004–05 Tottenham H 0 0
2005–06 Tottenham H 0 0
2005–06 *Chesterfield* 19 5 **19 5**
2006–07 Tottenham H 0 0
2007–08 Tottenham H 17 1
2007–08 *Millwall* 14 2 **14 2**
2008–09 Tottenham H 15 1
2009–10 Tottenham H 2 0
2009–10 *Portsmouth* 26 2 **26 2**
2010–11 Tottenham H 0 0 **34 2**
2010–11 *Wolverhampton W* 14 3
2011–12 Wolverhampton W 19 2
2012–13 Wolverhampton W 20 0
2013–14 Wolverhampton W 2 0
2014–15 Wolverhampton W 0 0 **55 5**
2014–15 *Blackpool* 27 2 **27 2**

OLIVER, Connor (D) 9 0
b. 17-1-94
2013–14 Sunderland 0 0
2013–14 *Hartlepool U* 3 0 **3 0**
2014–15 Blackpool 6 0 **6 0**

ORIOL, Eduardo (D) 74 7
H: 5 9 W: 11 00 b.Cambrils 5-11-86
2011–12 Real Zaragoza 20 2
2012–13 Real Zaragoza 19 0 **39 2**
2013–14 Khazar Lankaran 7 0 **7 0**
2013–14 *AEL Limassol* 18 5 **18 5**
2014–15 Blackpool 10 0 **10 0**
Transferred to Rapid Bucharest January 2015.

ORIOL, Joan (D) 72 0
H: 5 9 W: 10 12 b.Cambrils 5-11-86
2010–11 Villareal 6 0
2011–12 Villareal 21 0
2012–13 Villareal 23 0 **50 0**
2013–14 Osasuna 11 0 **11 0**
2014–15 Blackpool 11 0 **11 0**
Transferred to Rapid Bucharest January 2015.

ORLANDI, Andrea (M) 217 18
H: 6 0 W: 12 01 b.Barcelona 3-8-84
2005–06 Alaves 0 0
2005–06 *Barcelona B* 1 0 **1 0**
2005–06 Barcelona B 32 4
2006–07 Barcelona B 35 1 **67 5**
2007–08 Swansea C 8 0
2008–09 Swansea C 11 1
2009–10 Swansea C 30 1
2010–11 Swansea C 20 0
2011–12 Swansea C 3 1
2012–13 Swansea C 0 0 **72 3**
2012–13 Brighton & HA 35 6
2013–14 Brighton & HA 14 0 **49 6**
2014–15 Blackpool 28 4 **28 4**

PARISH, Elliot (G) 50 0
H: 6 2 W: 13 00 b.Towcester 20-5-90
Internationals: England U20.
2008–09 Aston Villa 0 0
2009–10 Aston Villa 0 0
2010–11 Aston Villa 0 0
2010–11 *Lincoln C* 9 0 **9 0**
2011–12 Aston Villa 0 0

2011–12 Cardiff C 0 0
2012–13 Wycombe W 2 0 **2 0**
2012–13 Cardiff C 0 0
2013–14 Bristol C 19 0 **19 0**
2013–14 *Newport Co* 7 0 **7 0**
2014–15 Blackpool 13 0 **13 0**

PERKINS, David (D) 328 14
H: 5 6 W: 11 06 b.Heysham 21-6-82
Internationals: England C.
2006–07 Rochdale 18 0
2007–08 Rochdale 40 4 **58 4**
2008–09 Colchester U 38 5
2009–10 Colchester U 5 0
2009–10 *Chesterfield* 13 1 **13 1**
2009–10 *Stockport Co* 22 0 **22 0**
2010–11 Colchester U 36 1 **79 7**
2011–12 Barnsley 33 1
2012–13 Barnsley 35 1
2013–14 Barnsley 23 0 **91 2**
2013–14 Blackpool 20 0
2014–15 Blackpool 45 0 **65 0**

RANGER, Nile (F) 101 14
H: 6 2 W: 13 03 b.Wood Green 11-4-91
Internationals: England U19.
2008–09 Newcastle U 0 0
2009–10 Newcastle U 25 2
2010–11 Newcastle U 24 0
2011–12 Newcastle U 0 0
2011–12 *Barnsley* 5 0 **5 0**
2011–12 *Sheffield W* 8 2 **8 2**
2012–13 Newcastle U 0 0 **51 2**
2013–14 Swindon T 23 8 **23 8**
2014–15 Blackpool 14 2 **14 2**

RENTMEISTER, Jeffrey (D) 122 16
b.Oupeye 11-7-84
2008–09 Beveren 15 8
2009–10 Beveren 24 4 **39 12**
2010–11 F91 Dudelange 10 2
2011–12 F91 Dudelange 10 0 **20 2**
2011–12 Vise 15 0
2012–13 Vise 8 1 **23 1**
2012–13 Westerlo 3 0
2013–14 Westerlo 27 1
2014–15 Westerlo 2 0 **32 1**
2014–15 Blackpool 8 0 **8 0**

SAMUEL, Bright (F) 6 0
b. 1-2-97
2014–15 Blackpool 6 0 **6 0**

SENE, Saer (F) 65 17
H: 6 3 W: 11 00 b.Paris 4-11-86
2012 N. E. Revolution 25 11
2013 N. E. Revolution 24 5
2014 N. E. Revolution 10 1 **59 17**
2014 New York Red Bulls 5 0 **5 0**
2014–15 Blackpool 1 0 **1 0**

TELFORD, Dominic (F) 14 1
H: 5 9 W: 11 05 b.Burnley 5-12-96
2014–15 Blackpool 14 1 **14 1**

WADDINGTON, Mark (M) 3 0
H: 6 0 W: 10 06 b.Wigan 11-10-96
2013–14 Blackpool 0 0
2014–15 Blackpool 3 0 **3 0**

ZENJOV, Sergei (F) 196 46
H: 6 0 b.Parnu 20-4-89
Internationals: Estonia U21, Full caps.
2006 Parnu 18 7 **17 8**
2006 TVMK Tallinn 12 3
2007 TVMK Tallinn 22 14 **34 17**
2007–08 Karpaty Lviv 11 0
2008–09 Karpaty Lviv 21 1
2009–10 Karpaty Lviv 25 3
2010–11 Karpaty Lviv 18 4 **18 4**
2011–12 Karpaty Lviv 17 1
2012–13 Karpaty Lviv 10 3
2013–14 Karpaty Lviv 28 9 **119 17**
2014–15 Blackpool 8 0 **8 0**
Transferred to Torpedo Moscow January 2015.

ZOKO, Francois (F) 415 72
H: 6 0 W: 11 05 b.Daloa 13-9-83
Internationals: Ivory Coast U20, U23.
2001–02 Nancy 24 3
2002–03 Nancy 28 2
2003–04 Nancy 19 3 **71 8**
2004–05 Laval 27 7
2005–06 Laval 33 2 **60 9**
2006–07 Mons 23 4
2007–08 Mons 32 8 **55 12**
2008–09 Hacetepe 27 1 **27 1**
2009–10 Ostend 11 4 **11 4**
2010–11 Carlisle U 44 6
2011–12 Carlisle U 45 13

Season	Club	App	Gls	Tot App	Tot Gls
2012–13	Carlisle U	0	0	89	19
2012–13	Notts Co	38	7		
2013–14	Notts Co	1	0	39	7
2013–14	Stevenage	33	10	33	10
2014–15	Blackpool	14	1	14	1
2014–15	*Bradford C*	16	1	16	1

Scholars
Boney, Myles Laurence; Cato, Anthony Robert; Doyle, James Andrew; Gregory, Kit William; Milton, Daniel Brian; Moulden, Joseph Luke; Njie, Alieu; Osayi, Samuel Bright; Pond, Elliot Daniel Lloyd; Richardson, Rowan Francis; Roscoe, Byrne Samuel Alexander; Telford, Dominic; Waddington, Mark Thomas; Wilson, Macauley David James.

BOLTON W (9)

ANDREWS, Keith (M)   375 43
H: 6 0 W: 12 04 b.Dublin 13-9-80
Internationals: Republic of Ireland U17, Full caps.

Season	Club	App	Gls	Tot App	Tot Gls
1997–98	Wolverhampton W	0	0		
1998–99	Wolverhampton W	0	0		
1999–2000	Wolverhampton W	2	0		
2000–01	Wolverhampton W	22	0		
2000–01	Oxford U	4	1	4	1
2001–02	Wolverhampton W	11	0		
2002–03	Wolverhampton W	9	0		
2003–04	Wolverhampton W	1	0		
2003–04	Stoke C	16	0	16	0
2003–04	Walsall	10	2	10	2
2004–05	Wolverhampton W	20	0	65	0
2005–06	Hull C	26	0		
2006–07	Hull C	3	0	29	0
2006–07	Milton Keynes D	34	6		
2007–08	Milton Keynes D	41	12		
2008–09	Milton Keynes D	1	0		
2008–09	Blackburn R	33	4		
2009–10	Blackburn R	32	1		
2010–11	Blackburn R	5	0		
2011–12	Blackburn R	0	0	70	5
2011–12	*Ipswich T*	20	9	20	9
2011–12	*WBA*	14	2	14	2
2012–13	Bolton W	25	4		
2013–14	Bolton W	1	0		
2013–14	*Brighton & HA*	31	1	31	1
2014–15	Bolton W	0	0	26	4
2014–15	*Watford*	9	1	9	1
2014–15	*Milton Keynes D*	5	0	81	18

BAPTISTE, Alex (D)   415 20
H: 6 0 W: 11 11 b.Sutton-in-Ashfield 31-1-86

Season	Club	App	Gls	Tot App	Tot Gls
2002–03	Mansfield T	4	0		
2003–04	Mansfield T	17	0		
2004–05	Mansfield T	41	1		
2005–06	Mansfield T	41	1		
2006–07	Mansfield T	46	3		
2007–08	Mansfield T	25	0	174	5
2008–09	Blackpool	21	1		
2009–10	Blackpool	42	3		
2010–11	Blackpool	21	2		
2011–12	Blackpool	43	1		
2012–13	Blackpool	43	1	170	8
2013–14	Bolton W	39	4		
2014–15	Bolton W	0	0	39	4
2014–15	*Blackburn R*	32	3	32	3

BECKFORD, Jermaine (F)   315 124
H: 6 2 W: 13 02 b.Ealing 9-12-83
Internationals: Jamaica Full caps.

Season	Club	App	Gls	Tot App	Tot Gls
2005–06	Leeds U	5	0		
2006–07	Leeds U	5	0		
2006–07	Carlisle U	4	1	4	1
2006–07	Scunthorpe U	18	8	18	8
2007–08	Leeds U	40	20		
2008–09	Leeds U	34	26		
2009–10	Leeds U	42	25	126	71
2010–11	Everton	32	8		
2011–12	Everton	2	0	34	8
2011–12	Leicester C	39	9		
2012–13	Leicester C	4	0	43	9
2012–13	*Huddersfield T*	21	8	21	8
2013–14	Bolton W	33	7		
2014–15	Bolton W	13	0	46	7
2014–15	*Preston NE*	23	12	23	12

BOGDAN, Adam (G)   105 0
H: 6 4 W: 14 02 b.Budapest 27-9-87
Internationals: Hungary U21, Full caps.

Season	Club	App	Gls	Tot App	Tot Gls
2007–08	Bolton W	0	0		
2008–09	Bolton W	0	0		
2009–10	Bolton W	0	0		
2009–10	*Crewe Alex*	1	0	1	0
2010–11	Bolton W	4	0		
2011–12	Bolton W	20	0		
2012–13	Bolton W	41	0		
2013–14	Bolton W	29	0		
2014–15	Bolton W	10	0	104	0

CLAYTON, Max (F)   83 10
H: 5 9 W: 11 00 b.Crewe 9-8-94
Internationals: England U16, U17, U18, U19.

Season	Club	App	Gls	Tot App	Tot Gls
2010–11	Crewe Alex	2	0		
2011–12	Crewe Alex	24	3		
2012–13	Crewe Alex	35	4		
2013–14	Crewe Alex	13	2	74	9
2014–15	Bolton W	9	1	9	1

CLOUGH, Zach (F)   8 5
b.Manchester 8-3-95

Season	Club	App	Gls	Tot App	Tot Gls
2013–14	Bolton W	0	0		
2014–15	Bolton W	8	5	8	5

DANNS, Neil (M)   361 59
H: 5 10 W: 10 12 b.Liverpool 23-11-82
Internationals: Guyana Full caps.

Season	Club	App	Gls	Tot App	Tot Gls
2000–01	Blackburn R	0	0		
2001–02	Blackburn R	0	0		
2002–03	Blackburn R	2	0		
2003–04	Blackpool	12	2	12	2
2003–04	Blackburn R	1	0		
2003–04	Hartlepool U	9	1	9	1
2004–05	Blackburn R	0	0	3	0
2004–05	Colchester U	32	11		
2005–06	Colchester U	41	8	73	19
2006–07	Birmingham C	29	3		
2007–08	Birmingham C	2	0	31	3
2007–08	Crystal Palace	4	0		
2008–09	Crystal Palace	20	2		
2009–10	Crystal Palace	42	8		
2010–11	Crystal Palace	37	8	103	18
2011–12	Leicester C	29	5		
2012–13	Leicester C	1	0		
2012–13	*Bristol C*	9	2	9	2
2012–13	*Huddersfield T*	17	2	17	2
2013–14	Leicester C	0	0	30	5
2013–14	Bolton W	33	6		
2014–15	Bolton W	41	1	74	7

DAVIES, Craig (F)   342 88
H: 6 2 W: 13 05 b.Burton-on-Trent 9-1-86
Internationals: Wales U17, U19, U21, Full caps.

Season	Club	App	Gls	Tot App	Tot Gls
2004–05	Oxford U	28	6		
2005–06	Oxford U	20	2	48	8
2005–06	Verona	0	0		
2006–07	Wolverhampton W	23	0	23	0
2007–08	Oldham Ath	32	10		
2008–09	Oldham Ath	12	0	44	10
2008–09	*Stockport Co*	9	5	9	5
2008–09	Brighton & HA	16	1		
2009–10	Brighton & HA	5	0	21	1
2009–10	*Yeovil T*	4	0	4	0
2009–10	*Port Vale*	24	7	24	7
2010–11	Chesterfield	41	23	41	23
2011–12	Barnsley	40	11		
2012–13	Barnsley	20	8	60	19
2012–13	Bolton W	18	4		
2013–14	Bolton W	8	0		
2013–14	*Preston NE*	15	5	15	5
2014–15	Bolton W	27	6	53	10

DAVIES, Mark (M)   177 16
H: 5 11 W: 11 08 b.Willenhall 18-2-88
Internationals: England U17, U19.

Season	Club	App	Gls	Tot App	Tot Gls
2004–05	Wolverhampton W	0	0		
2005–06	Wolverhampton W	20	1		
2006–07	Wolverhampton W	7	0		
2007–08	Wolverhampton W	0	0		
2008–09	Wolverhampton W	0	0	27	1
2008–09	*Leicester C*	7	1	7	1
2008–09	Bolton W	10	0		
2009–10	Bolton W	17	0		
2010–11	Bolton W	24	1		
2011–12	Bolton W	35	4		
2012–13	Bolton W	24	6		
2013–14	Bolton W	18	1		
2014–15	Bolton W	15	2	143	14

DERVITE, Dorian (D)   136 5
H: 6 3 W: 13 06 b.Lille 25-7-88
Internationals: France U16, U17, U18, U19, U21.

Season	Club	App	Gls	Tot App	Tot Gls
2008–09	Southend U	18	0	18	0
2010–11	Villarreal B	9	0		
2011–12	Villarreal B	2	0	11	0
2012–13	Villarreal	0	0		
2012–13	Charlton Ath	30	3		
2013–14	Charlton Ath	40	2	70	5
2014–15	Bolton W	37	0	37	0

EAVES, Tom (M)   92 16
H: 6 3 W: 13 07 b.Liverpool 14-1-92

Season	Club	App	Gls	Tot App	Tot Gls
2009–10	Oldham Ath	15	0		
2010–11	Bolton W	0	0		
2010–11	*Oldham Ath*	0	0	15	0
2011–12	Bolton W	0	0		
2012–13	Bolton W	3	0		
2012–13	*Bristol R*	16	7	16	7
2012–13	*Shrewsbury T*	10	6		
2013–14	Bolton W	0	0		
2013–14	*Rotherham U*	8	0	8	0
2013–14	*Shrewsbury T*	25	2	35	8
2014–15	Bolton W	1	0	4	0
2014–15	*Yeovil T*	5	0	5	0
2014–15	*Bury*	9	1	9	1

FEENEY, Liam (M)   234 20
H: 5 10 W: 12 02 b.Hammersmith 21-1-87

Season	Club	App	Gls	Tot App	Tot Gls
2008–09	Southend U	1	0	1	0
2008–09	Bournemouth	14	3		
2009–10	Bournemouth	44	5		
2010–11	Bournemouth	46	4		
2011–12	Bournemouth	5	0	109	12
2011–12	Millwall	34	4		
2012–13	Millwall	22	1		
2013–14	Millwall	17	0	73	5
2013–14	Bolton W	4	0		
2013–14	*Blackburn R*	6	0	6	0
2014–15	Bolton W	41	3	45	3

FITZSIMONS, Ross (G)   0 0
H: 6 1 W: 11 10 b.Hammersmith 28-5-94

Season	Club	App	Gls	Tot App	Tot Gls
2012–13	Crystal Palace	0	0		
2013–14	Crystal Palace	0	0		
2014–15	Crystal Palace	0	0		

GUDJOHNSEN, Eidur (F)   473 112
H: 6 1 W: 14 00 b.Reykjavik 15-9-78
Internationals: Iceland U17, U18, U19, Full caps.

Season	Club	App	Gls	Tot App	Tot Gls
1994–95	Valur	17	7	17	7
1995–96	PSV Eindhoven	13	3	13	3
1996–97	PSV Eindhoven	0	0		
1998	KR	6	0	6	0
1998–99	Bolton W	14	5		
1999–2000	Bolton W	41	13		
2000–01	Chelsea	30	10		
2001–02	Chelsea	32	14		
2002–03	Chelsea	35	10		
2003–04	Chelsea	26	6		
2004–05	Chelsea	37	12		
2005–06	Chelsea	26	2	186	54
2006–07	Barcelona	25	5		
2007–08	Barcelona	23	2		
2008–09	Barcelona	24	3	72	10
2009–10	Monaco	9	0	9	0
2009–10	Tottenham H	11	1	11	1
2010–11	Stoke C	4	0	4	0
2010–11	Fulham	10	0	10	0
2011–12	AEK Athens	10	1	10	1
2012–13	Cercle Brugge	13	6	13	6
2012–13	Club Brugge	18	3		
2013–14	Club Brugge	28	4	46	7
2014–15	Bolton W	21	5	76	23

HALL, Robert (F)   71 9
H: 6 2 W: 10 05 b.Aylesbury 20-10-93
Internationals: England U16, U17, U18, U19.

Season	Club	App	Gls	Tot App	Tot Gls
2010–11	West Ham U	0	0		
2011–12	West Ham U	3	0		
2011–12	*Oxford U*	13	5	13	5
2011–12	*Milton Keynes D*	2	0		
2012–13	West Ham U	1	0	4	0
2012–13	*Birmingham C*	13	0	13	0
2012–13	*Bolton W*	1	0		
2013–14	Bolton W	22	1		
2014–15	Bolton W	9	0	32	1
2014–15	*Milton Keynes D*	7	3	9	3

HESKEY, Emile (F)   604 128
H: 6 2 W: 13 12 b.Leicester 11-1-78
Internationals: England Youth, U21, B, Full caps.

Season	Club	App	Gls	Tot App	Tot Gls
1994–95	Leicester C	1	0		
1995–96	Leicester C	30	7		
1996–97	Leicester C	35	10		
1997–98	Leicester C	35	10		
1998–99	Leicester C	30	6		
1999–2000	Leicester C	23	7	154	40
1999–2000	Liverpool	12	3		
2000–01	Liverpool	36	14		
2001–02	Liverpool	35	9		
2002–03	Liverpool	32	6		
2003–04	Liverpool	35	7	150	39
2004–05	Birmingham C	34	10		
2005–06	Birmingham C	34	4	68	14
2006–07	Wigan Ath	34	8		
2007–08	Wigan Ath	28	4		
2008–09	Wigan Ath	20	3	82	15

2008–09	Aston Villa	14	2		
2009–10	Aston Villa	31	3		
2010–11	Aston Villa	19	3		
2011–12	Aston Villa	28	1	92	9
2012–13	Newcastle Jets	23	9		
2013–14	Newcastle Jets	19	1	42	10
2014–15	Bolton W	16	1	16	1

HOLDING, Rob (D)   1 0
b.Tameside 20-9-95

2014–15	Bolton W	0	0		
2014–15	Bury	1	0	1	0

HUGHES, Andy (M)   544 39
H: 5 11 W: 12 01 b.Stockport 2-1-78

1995–96	Oldham Ath	15	1		
1996–97	Oldham Ath	8	0		
1997–98	Oldham Ath	10	0	33	1
1997–98	Notts Co	15	2		
1998–99	Notts Co	30	3		
1999–2000	Notts Co	35	7		
2000–01	Notts Co	30	5	110	17
2001–02	Reading	39	6		
2002–03	Reading	43	9		
2003–04	Reading	43	3		
2004–05	Reading	41	0	166	16
2005–06	Norwich C	36	2		
2006–07	Norwich C	36	0	72	2
2007–08	Leeds U	40	1		
2008–09	Leeds U	27	0		
2009–10	Leeds U	39	0		
2010–11	Leeds U	10	0	116	1
2010–11	Scunthorpe U	19	0	19	0
2011–12	Charlton Ath	15	0		
2012–13	Charlton Ath	6	0		
2013–14	Charlton Ath	7	0	28	0
2014–15	Bolton W	0	0		

ILIEV, Georg (M)   4 0
b.Sofia 23-10-94
Internationals: Bulgaria U17, U19, U21.

2013–14	Bolton W	0	0		
2014–15	Bolton W	0	0		
2014–15	Carlisle U	4	0	4	0

KELLETT, Andy (D)   16 1
H: 5 8 b.Bolton 10-11-93

2012–13	Bolton W	0	0		
2013–14	Bolton W	3	0		
2014–15	Bolton W	1	0	4	0
2014–15	Plymouth Arg	12	1	12	1
2014–15	Manchester U	0	0		

LESTER, Chris (M)   1 0
b.Salford 27-10-94
Internationals: Northern Ireland U21.

2012–13	Bolton W	0	0		
2013–14	Bolton W	1	0		
2014–15	Bolton W	0	0	1	0

LONERGAN, Andrew (G)   299 1
H: 6 4 W: 13 02 b.Preston 19-10-83
Internationals: Republic of Ireland U16. England U20.

2000–01	Preston NE	1	0		
2001–02	Preston NE	0	0		
2002–03	Preston NE	0	0		
2002–03	Darlington	2	0	2	0
2003–04	Preston NE	8	0		
2004–05	Preston NE	23	1		
2005–06	Preston NE	0	0		
2005–06	Wycombe W	2	0	2	0
2006–07	Preston NE	13	0		
2006–07	Swindon T	1	0	1	0
2007–08	Preston NE	43	0		
2008–09	Preston NE	46	0		
2009–10	Preston NE	45	0		
2010–11	Preston NE	29	0	208	1
2011–12	Leeds U	35	0	35	0
2012–13	Bolton W	5	0		
2013–14	Bolton W	17	0		
2014–15	Bolton W	29	0	51	0

MAHER, Niall (D)   10 0
b.Manchester 31-7-95

2014–15	Bolton W	0	0		
2014–15	Blackpool	10	0	10	0

MEDO, Mohamed (M)   81 17
H: 5 9 W: 10 12 b.Serabu 27-12-81
Internationals: Sierra Leone U17, Full caps.

2007–08	HJK Helsinki	4	4		
2008–09	HJK Helsinki	4	4		
2009–10	HJK Helsinki	3.	3		
2010–11	HJK Helsinki	2	2	13	13
2012–13	Partizan Belgrade	0	0		
2012–13	Bolton W	12	1		
2013–14	Bolton W	35	2		
2014–15	Bolton W	5	0	52	3
2014–15	Maccabi Haifa	16	1	16	1

MILLS, Matthew (D)   279 17
H: 6 3 W: 12 12 b.Swindon 14-7-86
Internationals: England U18, U19.

2004–05	Southampton	0	0		
2004–05	Coventry C	4	0	4	0
2004–05	Bournemouth	12	3	12	3
2005–06	Southampton	4	0	4	0
2005–06	Manchester C	1	0		
2006–07	Manchester C	1	0		
2006–07	Colchester U	9	0	9	0
2007–08	Manchester C	0	0	2	0
2007–08	Doncaster R	34	3		
2008–09	Doncaster R	41	0		
2009–10	Doncaster R	0	0	75	3
2009–10	Reading	23	2		
2010–11	Reading	38	2	61	4
2011–12	Leicester C	25	1	25	1
2012–13	Bolton W	18	1		
2013–14	Bolton W	32	1		
2014–15	Bolton W	37	4	87	6

MOXEY, Dean (D)   206 8
H: 6 2 W: 11 00 b.Exeter 14-1-86
Internationals: England C.

2008–09	Exeter C	43	4	43	4
2009–10	Derby Co	30	0		
2010–11	Derby Co	22	2	52	2
2010–11	Crystal Palace	17	1		
2011–12	Crystal Palace	24	0		
2012–13	Crystal Palace	30	0		
2013–14	Crystal Palace	20	0	91	1
2014–15	Bolton W	20	1	20	1

ODELUSI, Sanmi (F)   30 3
H: 6 0 W: 11 11 b.London 11-6-93

2012–13	Bolton W	1	0		
2013–14	Bolton W	5	0		
2013–14	Milton Keynes D	10	0	10	0
2014–15	Bolton W	0	0	6	0
2014–15	Coventry C	14	3	14	3

PRATLEY, Darren (M)   322 40
H: 6 1 W: 10 12 b.Barking 22-4-85

2001–02	Fulham	0	0		
2002–03	Fulham	0	0		
2003–04	Fulham	1	0		
2004–05	Fulham	0	0		
2004–05	Brentford	14	1		
2005–06	Fulham	0	0	1	0
2005–06	Brentford	32	4	46	5
2006–07	Swansea C	28	1		
2007–08	Swansea C	42	5		
2008–09	Swansea C	37	4		
2009–10	Swansea C	36	7		
2010–11	Swansea C	34	9	177	26
2011–12	Bolton W	25	1		
2012–13	Bolton W	31	2		
2013–14	Bolton W	20	2		
2014–15	Bolton W	22	4	98	9

REAM, Tim (D)   273 7
H: 6 1 W: 11 05 b.St Louis 5-10-87
Internationals: USA Full caps.

2006	St Louis Billikens	19	0		
2007	St Louis Billikens	19	0		
2008	St Louis Billikens	22	0		
2008	Chicago Fire	12	0		
2009	Chicago Fire	7	0	19	0
2009	St Louis Billikens	22	6	82	6
2010	New York RB	30	1		
2011	New York RB	28	0	58	1
2011–12	Bolton W	13	0		
2012–13	Bolton W	15	0		
2013–14	Bolton W	42	0		
2014–15	Bolton W	44	0	114	0

ROCHINHA, Diogo (M)   4 0
b. 3-5-95
Internationals: Portugal U17, U19.
On loan from Benfica.

2014–15	Bolton W	4	0	4	0

SELLERS, Ryan (D)   0 0
b.London 13-10-95

2014–15	Bolton W	0	0		

SLAVCHEV, Simeon (M)   67 15
H: 6 1 W: 12 02 b.Sofia 25-9-93
Internationals: Bulgaria U19, U21, Full caps.

2010–11	Litex Lovech	1	0		
2011–12	Chavdor Etropole	14	0	14	0
2012–13	Litex Lovech	17	1		
2013–14	Litex Lovech	34	14	52	15
2014–15	Sporting Lisbon	1	0		

On loan from Sporting Lisbon.

2014–15	Bolton W	1	0	1	0

SPEARING, Jay (M)   155 7
H: 5 6 W: 11 01 b.Wallasey 25-11-88

2006–07	Liverpool	1	0		
2007–08	Liverpool	0	0		
2008–09	Liverpool	0	0		
2009–10	Liverpool	3	0		
2009–10	Leicester C	7	1	7	1
2010–11	Liverpool	11	0		
2011–12	Liverpool	16	0		
2012–13	Liverpool	0	0		
2012–13	Bolton W	37	2		
2013–14	Liverpool	0	0	30	0
2013–14	Bolton W	45	2		
2014–15	Bolton W	21	1	103	5
2014–15	Blackburn R	15	1	15	1

TAYLOR, Quade (M)   1 0
H: 6 3 W: 11 00 b.Tooting 11-12-93

2010–11	Crystal Palace	0	0		
2011–12	Crystal Palace	0	0		
2012–13	Crystal Palace	0	0		
2013–14	Crystal Palace	0	0		
2014–15	Bolton W	1	0	1	0

THRELKELD, Oscar (D)   6 0
b.Bolton 15-12-94

2013–14	Bolton W	2	0		
2014–15	Bolton W	4	0	6	0

TROTTER, Liam (M)   227 31
H: 6 2 W: 12 02 b.Ipswich 24-8-88

2005–06	Ipswich T	1	0		
2006–07	Ipswich T	0	0		
2006–07	Millwall	2	0		
2007–08	Ipswich T	7	1		
2008–09	Ipswich T	3	1		
2008–09	Grimsby T	15	2	15	2
2008–09	Scunthorpe U	12	1	12	1
2009–10	Ipswich T	12	0	23	2
2009–10	Millwall	20	1		
2010–11	Millwall	35	7		
2011–12	Millwall	35	7		
2012–13	Millwall	36	6		
2013–14	Millwall	19	3	147	24
2013–14	Bolton W	16	1		
2014–15	Bolton W	14	1	30	2

TWARDZIK, Filip (M)   8 1
H: 5 11 W: 10 01 b.Trinec 10-2-93
Internationals: Czech Republic U17, U19.

2011–12	Celtic	1	0		
2012–13	Celtic	2	0		
2013–14	Celtic	1	0		
2014–15	Celtic	1	0	5	0
2014–15	Bolton W	3	1	3	1

VELA, Joshua (M)   43 0
H: 5 11 W: 11 07 b.Salford 14-12-93

2010–11	Bolton W	0	0		
2011–12	Bolton W	3	0		
2012–13	Bolton W	4	0		
2013–14	Bolton W	0	0		
2013–14	Notts Co	7	0	7	0
2014–15	Bolton W	29	0	36	0

WALKER, Tom (M)   11 1
b.Salford 12-12-95

2014–15	Bolton W	11	1	11	1

WHEATER, David (D)   238 16
H: 6 5 W: 12 12 b.Redcar 14-2-87
Internationals: England U16, U17, U18, U19, U21.

2004–05	Middlesbrough	0	0		
2005–06	Middlesbrough	6	0		
2005–06	Doncaster R	7	1	7	1
2006–07	Middlesbrough	2	1		
2006–07	Wolverhampton W	1	0	1	0
2006–07	Darlington	15	2	15	2
2007–08	Middlesbrough	34	3		
2008–09	Middlesbrough	32	1		
2009–10	Middlesbrough	42	1		
2010–11	Middlesbrough	24	3	140	9
2010–11	Bolton W	14	0		
2011–12	Bolton W	24	2		
2012–13	Bolton W	4	0		
2013–14	Bolton W	23	1		
2014–15	Bolton W	17	1	75	4

WHITE, Hayden (D)   18 0
H: 6 1 W: 10 10 b.Greenwich 15-4-95

2013–14	Bolton W	2	0		
2014–15	Bolton W	3	0	5	0
2014–15	Carlisle U	8	0	8	0
2014–15	Bury	2	0	2	0
2014–15	Notts Co	3	0	3	0

WILKINSON, Conor (F)   24 3
H: 6 1 W: 12 02 b.Croydon 23-1-95
Internationals: Republic of Ireland U17, U19, U21.

2012–13	Millwall	0	0		
2013–14	Bolton W	0	0		
2013–14	Torquay U	3	0	3	0

2014–15	Bolton W	4	0	4	0
2014–15	Oldham Ath	17	3	17	3

WOODLAND, Luke (M) 6 0
b. 21-7-97
Internationals: England U16, U17, U18. Philippines Full caps.

2013–14	Bolton W	0	0		
2014–15	Bolton W	0	0		
2014–15	Oldham Ath	6	0	6	0

WOOLERY, Kaiyne (F) 6 0
H: 5 10 W: 11 07 b.Hackney 11-1-95

2014–15	Bolton W	1	0	1	0
2014–15	Notts Co	5	0	5	0

Players retained or with offer of contract
Finney, Alex; John-Baptiste, Alex.

Scholars
Allen, Max Patrick; Ball, James Cameron; Campbell, Harry Joseph Gordon; Campbell-Young, Channing Shelby; Cvetko, Christopher Brian; Garratt, Tyler John; Griffiths, Luke Duncan; Holding, Robert Samuel; Honeyball, Alexander Robert; Jaaskelainen, William Albert; Kennedy, Carl Harvey; Kenyi, Francis; Likoy, Elumba Enock; McKenna, Daniel Joseph; Nolan, Kieran Nathan; Palmer, Tyrell Robert; Perry, Alexander Anthony; Spooner, Callum Michael; Thomas, Jamie Carl; Walker, Thomas James; Wassi, Yvan; Wassi.

Non-Contract
Hughes, Andrew John.

BOURNEMOUTH (10)

ADDISON, Miles (D) 125 4
H: 6 2 W: 13 03 b.Newham 7-1-89
Internationals: England U21.

2005–06	Derby Co	2	0		
2006–07	Derby Co	0	0		
2007–08	Derby Co	1	0		
2008–09	Derby Co	28	1		
2009–10	Derby Co	13	2		
2010–11	Derby Co	21	0		
2011–12	Derby Co	0	0		
2011–12	Barnsley	11	0	11	0
2011–12	Bournemouth	14	1		
2012–13	Derby Co	0	0	65	3
2012–13	Bournemouth	20	0		
2013–14	Bournemouth	0	0		
2013–14	Rotherham U	6	0	6	0
2014–15	Bournemouth	0	0	34	1
2014–15	Scunthorpe U	3	0	3	0
2014–15	Blackpool	6	0	6	0

ALLSOP, Ryan (G) 66 0
H: 6 2 W: 12 06 b.Birmingham 17-6-92
Internationals: England U17.

2012–13	Leyton Orient	20	0	20	0
2012–13	Bournemouth	10	0		
2013–14	Bournemouth	12	0		
2014–15	Bournemouth	0	0	22	0
2014–15	Coventry C	24	0	24	0

ARTER, Harry (M) 168 26
H: 5 9 W: 11 07 b.Sidcup 28-12-89
Internationals: Republic of Ireland U17, U19, Full caps.

2007–08	Charlton Ath	0	0		
2008–09	Charlton Ath	0	0		

From Woking.

2010–11	Bournemouth	18	0		
2010–11	Carlisle U	5	1	5	1
2011–12	Bournemouth	34	5		
2012–13	Bournemouth	37	8		
2013–14	Bournemouth	31	3		
2014–15	Bournemouth	43	9	163	25

BASSELE, Aristide (M) 0 0
H: 5 10 W: 11 09 b.London 15-6-94

2012–13	Bournemouth	0	0		
2013–14	Bournemouth	0	0		
2014–15	Bournemouth	0	0		

BUCHEL, Benjamin (G) 0 0
H: 6 2 W: 11 08 b.Ruggel 4-7-89
Internationals: Liechtenstein Youth, U21, Full caps.

2012–13	Bournemouth	0	0		
2013–14	Bournemouth	0	0		
2014–15	Bournemouth	0	0		

BUCKLEY, Callum (D) 0 0
b. 12-1-96

2014–15	Bournemouth	0	0		

CAMP, Lee (G) 388 0
H: 5 11 W: 11 11 b.Derby 22-8-84
Internationals: England U21. Northern Ireland Full caps.

2002–03	Derby Co	1	0		
2003–04	Derby Co	0	0		
2003–04	QPR	12	0		
2004–05	Derby Co	45	0		
2005–06	Derby Co	40	0		
2006–07	Derby Co	3	0	89	0
2006–07	Norwich C	3	0		
2006–07	QPR	11	0		
2007–08	QPR	46	0		
2008–09	QPR	4	0	73	0
2008–09	Nottingham F	15	0		
2009–10	Nottingham F	45	0		
2010–11	Nottingham F	46	0		
2011–12	Nottingham F	46	0		
2012–13	Nottingham F	26	0	178	0
2012–13	Norwich C	3	0	6	0
2013–14	WBA	0	0		
2013–14	Bournemouth	33	0		
2014–15	Bournemouth	9	0	42	0

CARGILL, Baily (D) 5 0
b. 13-10-95
Internationals: England U20.

2012–13	Bournemouth	0	0		
2013–14	Bournemouth	0	0		
2013–14	Torquay U	5	0	5	0
2014–15	Bournemouth	0	0		

CARMICHAEL, Josh (M) 4 0
H: 6 0 W: 12 06 b.Poole 27-9-94
Internationals: Scotland U16.

2011–12	Bournemouth	1	0		
2012–13	Bournemouth	3	0		
2013–14	Bournemouth	0	0		
2014–15	Bournemouth	0	0	4	0

COLLINS, Chad (G) 0 0
H: 5 11 W: 10 13 b.Southampton 8-10-94

2012–13	Bournemouth	0	0		
2013–14	Bournemouth	0	0		
2014–15	Bournemouth	0	0		

COOK, Steve (D) 146 9
H: 6 1 W: 12 13 b.Hastings 19-4-91

2008–09	Brighton & HA	2	0		
2009–10	Brighton & HA	0	0		
2010–11	Brighton & HA	0	0		
2011–12	Brighton & HA	1	0	3	0
2011–12	Bournemouth	26	0		
2012–13	Bournemouth	33	1		
2013–14	Bournemouth	38	3		
2014–15	Bournemouth	46	5	143	9

COULIBALY, Mohamed (M) 25 0
H: 5 10 W: 11 00 b.Bakel 7-8-88

2011–12	Grasshoppers	5	0		
2012–13	Grasshoppers	5	0	10	0
2013–14	Bournemouth	7	0		
2014–15	Bournemouth	0	0	7	0
2014–15	Coventry C	4	0	4	0
2014–15	Port Vale	4	0	4	0

DANIELS, Charlie (M) 275 12
H: 6 1 W: 12 12 b.Harlow 7-9-86

2005–06	Tottenham H	0	0		
2006–07	Tottenham H	0	0		
2006–07	Chesterfield	2	0	2	0
2007–08	Tottenham H	0	0		
2007–08	Leyton Orient	31	2		
2008–09	Tottenham H	0	0		
2008–09	Gillingham	5	1	5	1
2008–09	Leyton Orient	21	2		
2009–10	Leyton Orient	41	0		
2010–11	Leyton Orient	42	0		
2011–12	Leyton Orient	13	0	148	4
2011–12	Bournemouth	21	2		
2012–13	Bournemouth	34	4		
2013–14	Bournemouth	23	0		
2014–15	Bournemouth	42	1	120	7

ELPHICK, Tommy (M) 271 11
H: 5 11 W: 11 07 b.Brighton 7-9-87

2005–06	Brighton & HA	1	0		
2006–07	Brighton & HA	3	0		
2007–08	Brighton & HA	39	2		
2008–09	Brighton & HA	39	1		
2009–10	Brighton & HA	44	3		
2010–11	Brighton & HA	27	1		
2011–12	Brighton & HA	0	0		
2012–13	Brighton & HA	0	0	153	7
2012–13	Bournemouth	34	2		
2013–14	Bournemouth	38	1		
2014–15	Bournemouth	46	1	118	4

FLAHAVAN, Darryl (G) 357 0
H: 5 11 W: 12 05 b.Southampton 9-9-77
From Woking.

2000–01	Southend U	29	0		
2001–02	Southend U	41	0		
2002–03	Southend U	41	0		
2003–04	Southend U	37	0		
2004–05	Southend U	28	0		
2005–06	Southend U	43	0		
2006–07	Southend U	46	0		
2007–08	Southend U	26	0	291	0
2008–09	Crystal Palace	1	0		
2008–09	Leeds U	0	0		
2009–10	Crystal Palace	1	0		
2009–10	Oldham Ath	18	0	18	0
2010–11	Crystal Palace	0	0	2	0
2011–12	Bournemouth	44	0		
2012–13	Bournemouth	0	0		
2013–14	Bournemouth	1	0		
2014–15	Bournemouth	1	0	46	0

FOUNTAIN, Brad (M) 0 0
b. 29-6-96

2014–15	Bournemouth	0	0		

FRANCIS, Simon (D) 439 9
H: 6 0 W: 12 06 b.Nottingham 16-2-85
Internationals: England U20.

2002–03	Bradford C	25	1		
2003–04	Bradford C	30	0	55	1
2003–04	Sheffield U	5	0		
2004–05	Sheffield U	6	0		
2005–06	Sheffield U	1	0	12	0
2005–06	Grimsby T	5	0	5	0
2005–06	Tranmere R	17	1	17	1
2006–07	Southend U	40	1		
2007–08	Southend U	27	2		
2008–09	Southend U	45	0		
2009–10	Southend U	45	1	157	4
2010–11	Charlton Ath	34	0		
2011–12	Charlton Ath	0	0	34	0
2011–12	Bournemouth	29	0		
2012–13	Bournemouth	42	1		
2013–14	Bournemouth	46	1		
2014–15	Bournemouth	42	1	159	3

FRASER, Ryan (M) 84 4
H: 5 4 W: 10 13 b.Aberdeen 24-2-94
Internationals: Scotland U19, U21.

2010–11	Aberdeen	2	0		
2011–12	Aberdeen	3	0		
2012–13	Aberdeen	16	0	21	0
2012–13	Bournemouth	5	0		
2013–14	Bournemouth	37	3		
2014–15	Bournemouth	21	1	63	4

GILKES, Harrison (M) 0 0

2012–13	Bournemouth	0	0		
2013–14	Bournemouth	0	0		
2014–15	Bournemouth	0	0		

GOODSHIP, Brandon (F) 0 0
b. 1-1-86

2013–14	Bournemouth	0	0		
2014–15	Bournemouth	0	0		

GOSLING, Dan (M) 100 9
H: 6 0 W: 11 00 b.Brixham 2-2-90
Internationals: England U17, U18, U19, U21.

2006–07	Plymouth Arg	12	2		
2007–08	Plymouth Arg	10	0	22	2
2007–08	Everton	11	2		
2008–09	Everton	11	2		
2009–10	Everton	11	2	22	4
2010–11	Newcastle U	1	0		
2011–12	Newcastle U	12	1		
2012–13	Newcastle U	0	0		
2013–14	Newcastle U	8	0	24	1
2013–14	Blackpool	14	2	14	2
2014–15	Bournemouth	18	0	18	0

HARTE, Ian (D) 423 64
H: 5 11 W: 12 06 b.Drogheda 31-8-77
Internationals: Republic of Ireland Full caps.

1995–96	Leeds U	4	0		
1996–97	Leeds U	14	2		
1997–98	Leeds U	12	0		
1998–99	Leeds U	35	4		
1999–2000	Leeds U	33	6		
2000–01	Leeds U	29	7		
2001–02	Leeds U	36	5		
2002–03	Leeds U	27	3		
2003–04	Leeds U	23	1	213	28
2004–05	Levante	24	1		
2005–06	Levante	0	0		
2006–07	Levante	6	0	30	1
2007–08	Sunderland	8	0	8	0
2008–09	Blackpool	4	0	4	0
2008–09	Carlisle U	3	1		

2009–10	Carlisle U	45	16		
2010–11	Carlisle U	4	2	52	19
2010–11	Reading	40	11		
2011–12	Reading	32	4		
2012–13	Reading	16	0	88	15
2013–14	Bournemouth	24	1		
2014–15	Bournemouth	4	0	28	1

HUGHES, Richard (M) 300 16
H: 6 0 W: 12 13 b.Glasgow 25-6-79
Internationals: Scotland Full caps.

1998–99	Bournemouth	44	2		
1999–2000	Bournemouth	21	2		
2000–01	Bournemouth	44	8		
2001–02	Portsmouth	22	2		
2002–03	Portsmouth	6	0		
2002–03	*Grimsby T*	12	1	12	1
2003–04	Portsmouth	11	0		
2004–05	Portsmouth	16	0		
2005–06	Portsmouth	26	0		
2006–07	Portsmouth	18	0		
2007–08	Portsmouth	13	0		
2008–09	Portsmouth	20	0		
2009–10	Portsmouth	10	0		
2010–11	Portsmouth	11	0	131	0
2012–13	Bournemouth	21	1		
2013–14	Bournemouth	5	0		
2014–15	Bournemouth	0	0	157	15

KERMORGANT, Yann (F) 343 100
H: 6 0 W: 13 03 b.Vannes 8-11-81
Internationals: Brittany Full caps.

2004–05	Chatellerault	29	14	29	14
2005–06	Grenoble	26	6		
2006–07	Grenoble	32	10	58	16
2007–08	Reims	33	4		
2008–09	Reims	34	9	67	13
2009–10	Leicester C	20	1		
2010–11	Leicester C	0	0	20	1
2010–11	*Arles-Avignon*	26	3	26	3
2011–12	Charlton Ath	36	12		
2012–13	Charlton Ath	32	12		
2013–14	Charlton Ath	21	5	89	29
2013–14	Bournemouth	16	9		
2014–15	Bournemouth	38	15	54	24

MACDONALD, Shaun (M) 166 10
H: 6 1 W: 11 04 b.Swansea 17-6-88
Internationals: Wales U19, U21, Full caps.

2005–06	Swansea C	7	0		
2006–07	Swansea C	8	0		
2007–08	Swansea C	5	0		
2008–09	*Yeovil T*	4	2		
2009–10	Swansea C	3	0		
2009–10	*Yeovil T*	31	3		
2010–11	Swansea C	0	0		
2010–11	*Yeovil T*	26	4	61	9
2011–12	Swansea C	0	0	24	0
2011–12	Bournemouth	25	1		
2012–13	Bournemouth	28	0		
2013–14	Bournemouth	23	0		
2014–15	Bournemouth	5	0	81	1

MATTHEWS, Sam (M) 0 0
b. 1-3-97

2013–14	Bournemouth	0	0
2014–15	Bournemouth	0	0

McCARTHY, Jake (D) 0 0
H: 5 8 W: 11 00 b. 2-4-96

2013–14	Bournemouth	0	0
2014–15	Bournemouth	0	0

McQUOID, Josh (F) 165 19
H: 5 9 W: 10 10 b.Southampton 15-12-89
Internationals: Northern Ireland U19, U21, B, Full caps.

2006–07	Bournemouth	2	0		
2007–08	Bournemouth	5	0		
2008–09	Bournemouth	16	0		
2009–10	Bournemouth	29	1		
2010–11	Bournemouth	17	9		
2010–11	Millwall	11	1		
2011–12	*Millwall*	5	0	16	1
2011–12	*Burnley*	17	1	17	1
2012–13	Bournemouth	34	3		
2013–14	Bournemouth	1	0		
2013–14	*Peterborough U*	14	1	14	1
2014–15	Bournemouth	0	0	104	13
2014–15	*Coventry C*	14	3	14	3

MULEBA, Jonathan (D) 0 0
b.London 4-9-95

2013–14	Bournemouth	0	0
2014–15	Bournemouth	0	0

O'HANLON, Josh (F) 25 7
H: 6 0 W: 12 00 b. 25-9-95

2013	Longford T	22	7	22	7
2013–14	Bournemouth	0	0		
2014–15	Bournemouth	0	0		
2014–15	*York C*	3	0	3	0

O'KANE, Eunan (M) 204 18
H: 5 8 W: 13 04 b.Derry 10-7-90
Internationals: Northern Ireland U16, U17, U19, U20, U21. Republic of Ireland U21.

2007–08	Everton	0	0		
2008–09	Everton	0	0		
2009–10	Coleraine	13	4	13	4
2009–10	Torquay U	16	1		
2010–11	Torquay U	45	6		
2011–12	Torquay U	45	5		
2012–13	Torquay U	0	0	106	12
2012–13	Bournemouth	37	1		
2013–14	Bournemouth	37	1		
2014–15	Bournemouth	11	0	85	2

PITMAN, Brett (F) 345 115
H: 6 0 W: 11 00 b.Jersey 31-1-88

2005–06	Bournemouth	19	1		
2006–07	Bournemouth	29	5		
2007–08	Bournemouth	39	6		
2008–09	Bournemouth	39	17		
2009–10	Bournemouth	46	26		
2010–11	Bristol C	39	13		
2011–12	Bristol C	35	7		
2012–13	Bristol C	3	0	77	20
2012–13	Bournemouth	26	19		
2013–14	Bournemouth	34	5		
2014–15	Bournemouth	34	13	268	95

PUGH, Marc (M) 345 62
H: 5 11 W: 11 04 b.Bacup 2-4-87

2005–06	Burnley	0	0		
2005–06	Bury	6	1		
2006–07	Bury	35	3	41	4
2007–08	Shrewsbury T	37	4		
2008–09	Shrewsbury T	7	0	44	4
2008–09	*Luton T*	4	0	4	0
2008–09	*Hereford U*	9	1		
2009–10	Hereford U	40	13	49	14
2010–11	Bournemouth	41	12		
2011–12	Bournemouth	42	8		
2012–13	Bournemouth	40	6		
2013–14	Bournemouth	42	5		
2014–15	Bournemouth	42	9	207	40

RANTIE, Tokelo (F) 93 22
b.Parys 8-9-90
Internationals: South Africa Full caps.

2011–12	Orlando Pirates	20	7	20	7
2012	Malmo FF	11	3		
2013	Malmo FF	21	7	32	10
2013–14	Bournemouth	29	3		
2014–15	Bournemouth	12	2	41	5

RITCHIE, Matt (M) 260 67
H: 5 8 W: 11 00 b.Gosport 10-9-89

2008–09	Portsmouth	0	0		
2008–09	*Dagenham & R*	37	11	37	11
2009–10	Portsmouth	2	0		
2009–10	*Notts Co*	16	3	16	3
2009–10	*Swindon T*	4	0		
2010–11	Portsmouth	5	0	7	0
2010–11	Swindon T	36	7		
2011–12	Swindon T	40	10		
2012–13	Swindon T	27	9	107	26
2012–13	Bournemouth	17	3		
2013–14	Bournemouth	30	9		
2014–15	Bournemouth	46	15	93	27

SMITH, Adam (D) 145 4
H: 5 8 W: 10 07 b.Leytonstone 29-4-91
Internationals: England U16, U17, U19, U20, U21.

2007–08	Tottenham H	0	0		
2008–09	Tottenham H	0	0		
2009–10	Tottenham H	0	0		
2009–10	*Wycombe W*	3	0	3	0
2009–10	*Torquay U*	16	0	16	0
2010–11	Tottenham H	0	0		
2010–11	*Bournemouth*	38	1		
2011–12	Tottenham H	1	0		
2011–12	*Milton Keynes D*	17	2	17	2
2011–12	*Leeds U*	3	0	3	0
2012–13	Tottenham H	0	0		
2012–13	*Millwall*	25	1	25	1
2013–14	Tottenham H	0	0	1	0
2013–14	*Derby Co*	8	0	8	0
2013–14	Bournemouth	5	0		
2014–15	Bournemouth	29	0	72	1

STANISLAS, Junior (M) 154 15
H: 6 0 W: 12 00 b.Kidbrooke 26-11-89
Internationals: England U20, U21.

2007–08	West Ham U	0	0		
2008–09	West Ham U	9	2		
2008–09	*Southend U*	6	1	6	1
2009–10	West Ham U	26	3		
2010–11	West Ham U	6	1		
2011–12	West Ham U	1	0	42	6
2011–12	Burnley	31	0		
2012–13	Burnley	35	5		
2013–14	Burnley	27	2	93	7
2014–15	Bournemouth	13	1	13	1

STOCKLEY, Jayden (F) 68 10
H: 6 2 W: 12 07 b.Poole 10-10-93

2009–10	Bournemouth	2	0		
2010–11	Bournemouth	4	0		
2011–12	Bournemouth	10	0		
2011–12	*Accrington S*	9	3	9	3
2012–13	Bournemouth	0	0		
2013–14	Bournemouth	0	0		
2013–14	*Leyton Orient*	8	1	8	1
2013–14	*Torquay U*	19	1	19	1
2014–15	Bournemouth	0	0	16	0
2014–15	*Cambridge U*	3	2	3	2
2014–15	*Luton T*	13	3	13	3

SURMAN, Andrew (M) 306 33
H: 5 10 W: 11 06 b.Johannesburg 20-8-86
Internationals: England U21.

2003–04	Southampton	0	0		
2004–05	Southampton	0	0		
2004–05	*Walsall*	14	2	14	2
2005–06	Southampton	12	2		
2006–07	*Bournemouth*	24	6		
2006–07	Southampton	37	4		
2007–08	Southampton	40	2		
2008–09	Southampton	44	7		
2009–10	Southampton	0	0	133	15
2009–10	*Wolverhampton W*	7	0	7	0
2010–11	Norwich C	22	3		
2011–12	Norwich C	25	4		
2012–13	Norwich C	4	0		
2013–14	Norwich C	0	0		
2013–14	*Bournemouth*	35	0		
2014–15	Norwich C	1	0	52	7
2014–15	Bournemouth	41	3	100	9

WAKEFIELD, Josh (M) 3 0
H: 5 11 W: 11 05 b.Frimley 6-11-93

2011–12	Bournemouth	2	0		
2012–13	Bournemouth	1	0		
2012–13	*Dagenham & R*	0	0		
2013–14	Bournemouth	0	0		
2014–15	Bournemouth	0	0	3	0

WALSH, Mason (M) 0 0
b. 22-11-95

2014–15	Bournemouth	0	0

WARD, Elliot (D) 268 20
H: 6 2 W: 13 00 b.Harrow 19-1-85

2001–02	West Ham U	0	0		
2002–03	West Ham U	0	0		
2003–04	West Ham U	0	0		
2004–05	West Ham U	11	0		
2004–05	*Bristol R*	3	0	3	0
2005–06	West Ham U	4	0	15	0
2005–06	*Plymouth Arg*	16	1	16	1
2006–07	Coventry C	39	3		
2007–08	Coventry C	37	6		
2008–09	Coventry C	33	5		
2009–10	Coventry C	8	0	117	14
2009–10	*Doncaster R*	6	1	6	1
2009–10	*Preston NE*	4	0	4	0
2010–11	Norwich C	39	1		
2011–12	Norwich C	12	0		
2012–13	Norwich C	0	0	51	1
2012–13	*Nottingham F*	31	3	31	3
2013–14	Bournemouth	23	0		
2014–15	Bournemouth	2	0	25	0

WHITFIELD, Ben (M) 0 0
H: 5 5 W: 9 11 b. 28-2-96

2013–14	Bournemouth	0	0
2014–15	Bournemouth	0	0

WILSON, Callum (M) 94 42
H: 5 11 W: 10 06 b.Coventry 27-2-92
Internationals: England U21.

2009–10	Coventry C	0	0		
2010–11	Coventry C	1	0		
2011–12	Coventry C	0	0		
2011–12	Coventry C	11	1		
2013–14	Coventry C	37	21	49	22
2014–15	Bournemouth	45	20	45	20

ZUBAR, Stephane (D) 145 5
H: 6 1 W: 12 11 b.Guadeloupe 9-10-86
Internationals: Guadeloupe Full caps.

2006–07	Caen	0	0		
2006–07	Pau	10	0	10	0
2007–08	Caen	0	0		
2007–08	FC Brussels	11	0	11	0

2008–09	Vaslui	10	0		
2009–10	Vaslui	26	1	36	1
2010–11	Plymouth Arg	29	2		
2011–12	Plymouth Arg	4	0	33	2
2011–12	Bournemouth	22	0		
2012–13	Bournemouth	2	0		
2012–13	Bury	6	0	6	0
2013–14	Bournemouth	0	0		
2014–15	Bournemouth	0	0	24	0
2014–15	Port Vale	2	0	2	0
2014–15	York C	23	2	23	2

Players retained or with offer of contract
Cornick, Harry Charles Frederick; Daniels, Charlie; Holmes, Jordan Thomas; O'Flaherty, Patrick.

Scholars
Butcher, Matthew David; Harfield, Oliver John; Holmes, Luke Harold; Lander, Henry Miles; Lee, Jordan Michael; Millar, Ethan Charles; Neale, Matthew Alexander; O'Sullivan, Daniel Liam; Quigley, Joseph Richard; Randall, Declan Samuel; Simpson, Jack Benjamin; Stanton, Callum James Frank; Surridge, Samuel William; Walker, Benjamin Courtenay; Worthington, Matthew Luke.

BRADFORD C (11)

CLARKE, Billy (F) 246 56
H: 5 7 W: 10 01 b.Cork 13-12-87
Internationals: Republic of Ireland U17, U19, U21.

2004–05	Ipswich T	0	0		
2005–06	Ipswich T	2	0		
2005–06	Colchester U	6	0	6	0
2006–07	Ipswich T	27	3		
2007–08	Ipswich T	20	0		
2007–08	Falkirk	8	1	8	1
2008–09	Ipswich T	0	0	49	3
2008–09	Darlington	20	8	20	8
2008–09	Northampton T	5	3	5	3
2008–09	Brentford	8	6	8	6
2009–10	Blackpool	18	1		
2010–11	Blackpool	0	0		
2011–12	Blackpool	9	0	27	1
2011–12	Sheffield U	5	1	5	1
2011–12	Crawley T	17	3		
2012–13	Crawley T	36	10		
2013–14	Crawley T	29	7	82	20
2014–15	Bradford C	36	13	36	13

DARBY, Stephen (D) 197 0
H: 5 9 W: 10 00 b.Liverpool 6-10-88
Internationals: England U19.

2006–07	Liverpool	0	0		
2007–08	Liverpool	0	0		
2008–09	Liverpool	0	0		
2009–10	Liverpool	1	0		
2009–10	Swindon T	12	0	12	0
2010–11	Liverpool	0	0		
2010–11	Notts Co	23	0	23	0
2011–12	Liverpool	0	0	1	0
2011–12	Rochdale	35	0	35	0
2012–13	Bradford C	35	0		
2013–14	Bradford C	46	0		
2014–15	Bradford C	45	0	126	0

DAVIES, Andrew (D) 243 10
H: 6 3 W: 14 08 b.Stockton 17-12-84
Internationals: England U21.

2002–03	Middlesbrough	1	0		
2003–04	Middlesbrough	10	0		
2004–05	Middlesbrough	3	0		
2004–05	QPR	9	0	9	0
2005–06	Middlesbrough	12	0		
2005–06	Derby Co	23	3	23	3
2006–07	Middlesbrough	23	0		
2007–08	Middlesbrough	4	0		
2007–08	Southampton	23	0		
2008–09	Southampton	0	0	23	0
2008–09	Stoke C	2	0		
2008–09	Preston NE	5	0	5	0
2009–10	Stoke C	0	0		
2009–10	Sheffield U	8	0	8	0
2010–11	Stoke C	0	0		
2010–11	Walsall	3	0	3	0
2010–11	Middlesbrough	6	0	59	0
2011–12	Stoke C	0	0	2	0
2011–12	Crystal Palace	1	0	1	0
2011–12	Bradford C	26	2		
2012–13	Bradford C	28	4		
2013–14	Bradford C	28	1		
2014–15	Bradford C	28	0	110	7

DOLAN, Matthew (M) 54 3
b.Hartlepool 11-2-93

2010–11	Middlesbrough	0	0		
2011–12	Middlesbrough	0	0		
2012–13	Middlesbrough	0	0		
2012–13	Yeovil T	8	1	8	1
2013–14	Middlesbrough	0	0		
2013–14	Hartlepool U	20	2		
2013–14	Bradford C	11	0		
2014–15	Bradford C	13	0	24	0
2014–15	Hartlepool U	2	0	22	2

HALLIDAY, Andrew (M) 130 18
H: 5 8 W: 10 07 b.Glasgow 11-10-91

2008–09	Livingston	12	1		
2009–10	Livingston	32	14	44	15
2010–11	Middlesbrough	12	1		
2011–12	Middlesbrough	1	0		
2011–12	Walsall	7	0	7	0
2012–13	Middlesbrough	19	0		
2013–14	Middlesbrough	4	0		
2013–14	Blackpool	18	1	18	1
2014–15	Middlesbrough	0	0	36	1
2014–15	Bradford C	25	1	25	1

HANSON, James (F) 225 62
H: 6 4 W: 12 04 b.Bradford 9-11-87

2009–10	Bradford C	34	12		
2010–11	Bradford C	36	6		
2011–12	Bradford C	39	13		
2012–13	Bradford C	43	10		
2013–14	Bradford C	35	12		
2014–15	Bradford C	38	9	225	62

KENNEDY, Jason (M) 329 28
H: 6 1 W: 13 02 b.Stockton 11-9-86

2004–05	Middlesbrough	1	0		
2005–06	Middlesbrough	3	0		
2006–07	Middlesbrough	0	0		
2006–07	Boston U	13	1	13	1
2006–07	Bury	12	0	12	0
2007–08	Middlesbrough	0	0	4	0
2007–08	Livingston	18	2	18	2
2007–08	Darlington	13	2		
2008–09	Darlington	46	5	59	7
2009–10	Rochdale	42	0		
2010–11	Rochdale	45	4		
2011–12	Rochdale	44	4		
2012–13	Rochdale	46	4		
2013–14	Bradford C	8	1		
2013–14	Rochdale	7	0	184	12
2014–15	Bradford C	20	2	20	3
2014–15	Carlisle U	11	3	11	3

KNOTT, Billy (M) 96 9
H: 5 8 W: 11 02 b.Canvey Island 28-11-92
Internationals: England U16, U17, U20.

2010–11	Sunderland	0	0		
2011–12	Sunderland	0	0		
2011–12	AFC Wimbledon	20	3	20	3
2012–13	Sunderland	1	0		
2013–14	Sunderland	0	0		
2013–14	Wycombe W	17	1	17	1
2013–14	Port Vale	18	2	18	2
2014–15	Bradford C	40	3	40	3

LIDDLE, Gary (D) 366 23
H: 6 1 W: 12 06 b.Middlesbrough 15-6-86

2003–04	Middlesbrough	0	0		
2004–05	Middlesbrough	0	0		
2005–06	Middlesbrough	0	0		
2006–07	Hartlepool U	42	3		
2007–08	Hartlepool U	41	2		
2008–09	Hartlepool U	43	0		
2009–10	Hartlepool U	40	3		
2010–11	Hartlepool U	42	0		
2011–12	Hartlepool U	39	4	247	18
2012–13	Notts Co	46	0		
2013–14	Notts Co	32	4	78	4
2014–15	Bradford C	41	1	41	1

McARDLE, Rory (D) 326 16
H: 6 1 W: 11 04 b.Doncaster 1-5-87
Internationals: Northern Ireland U21, Full caps.

2005–06	Sheffield W	0	0		
2005–06	Rochdale	19	1		
2006–07	Sheffield W	1	0	1	0
2006–07	Rochdale	25	0		
2007–08	Rochdale	43	3		
2008–09	Rochdale	41	2		
2009–10	Rochdale	20	0	148	6
2010–11	Aberdeen	28	2		
2011–12	Aberdeen	25	0	53	2
2012–13	Bradford C	40	2		
2013–14	Bradford C	41	3		
2014–15	Bradford C	43	3	124	8

McBURNIE, Oliver (F) 15 0
H: 6 2 W: 10 04 b.Bradford 6-4-96
Internationals: Scotland U19.

2013–14	Bradford C	8	0		
2014–15	Bradford C	7	0	15	0

McLEAN, Aaron (F) 339 90
H: 5 9 W: 10 10 b.Hammersmith 25-5-83
Internationals: England C.

1999–2000	Leyton Orient	3	0		
2000–01	Leyton Orient	2	1		
2001–02	Leyton Orient	27	1		
2002–03	Leyton Orient	8	0	40	2
From Aldershot T, Grays Ath.					
2006–07	Peterborough U	16	7		
2007–08	Peterborough U	45	29		
2008–09	Peterborough U	42	18		
2009–10	Peterborough U	35	7		
2010–11	Peterborough U	19	10		
2010–11	Hull C	23	3		
2011–12	Hull C	39	5		
2012–13	Hull C	14	1		
2012–13	Ipswich T	7	1	7	1
2013–14	Hull C	1	0	77	9
2013–14	Birmingham C	7	0	7	0
2013–14	Bradford C	20	4		
2014–15	Bradford C	13	2	33	6
2014–15	Peterborough U	18	1	175	72

MEREDITH, James (D) 102 7
H: 6 1 W: 11 06 b.Albury, Australia 4-4-88

2006–07	Derby Co	0	0		
2006–07	Chesterfield	1	0	1	0
2007–08	Shrewsbury T	3	0	3	0
From York C					
2012–13	Bradford C	32	1		
2013–14	Bradford C	26	0		
2014–15	Bradford C	40	0	98	1

MORAIS, Filipe (M) 254 26
H: 5 9 W: 11 10 b.Lisbon 21-11-85
Internationals: Portugal U21.

2003–04	Chelsea	0	0		
2004–05	Chelsea	0	0		
2005–06	Chelsea	0	0		
2005–06	Milton Keynes D	13	0	13	0
2006–07	Millwall	12	1	12	1
2006–07	St Johnstone	13	1		
2007–08	Hibernian	28	1		
2008–09	Hibernian	2	0	30	1
2008–09	Inverness CT	12	3	12	3
2009–10	St Johnstone	30	2	43	3
2010–11	Oldham Ath	23	3		
2011–12	Oldham Ath	36	5		
2012–13	Oldham Ath	0	0	59	8
2012–13	Stevenage	28	3		
2013–14	Stevenage	27	4	55	7
2014–15	Bradford C	30	3	30	3

MOTTLEY-HENRY, Dylan (F) 1 0
b. 2-8-97

2014–15	Bradford C	1	0	1	0

ROUTIS, Christopher (D) 105 7
H: 6 1 W: 13 03 b.Genf 3-3-90

2010–11	Servette	12	1		
2011–12	Servette	31	3		
2012–13	Servette	22	0		
2013–14	Servette	22	1	87	5
2014–15	Bradford C	18	2	18	2

SHARIFF, Mo (F) 5 0
H: 5 10 b.Newham 5-3-93

2011–12	QPR	0	0		
2011–12	QPR	0	0		
2012–13	QPR	0	0		
2012–13	Dagenham & R	4	0	4	0
2013–14	QPR	0	0		
2014–15	Bradford C	1	0	1	0

SHEEHAN, Alan (D) 247 16
H: 5 11 W: 11 02 b.Athlone 14-9-86
Internationals: Republic of Ireland U21.

2004–05	Leicester C	1	0		
2005–06	Leicester C	2	0		
2006–07	Leicester C	0	0		
2006–07	Mansfield T	10	0	10	0
2007–08	Leicester C	20	1	23	1
2007–08	Leeds U	10	1		
2008–09	Leeds U	11	1		
2008–09	Crewe Alex	3	0	3	0
2009–10	Leeds U	0	0	21	2
2009–10	Oldham Ath	8	1	8	1
2009–10	Swindon T	22	1		
2010–11	Swindon T	21	1	43	2
2011–12	Notts Co	39	2		
2012–13	Notts Co	33	0		
2013–14	Notts Co	42	7	114	9

2014–15 Bradford C 23 1 **23 1**
2014–15 *Peterborough U* 2 0 **2 0**

URWIN, Matthew (G) 0 0
H: 6 1 W: 12 00 b. 28-11-93
2012–13 Blackburn R 0 0
2013–14 Blackburn R 0 0
2014–15 Bradford C 0 0

WEBB-FOSTER, Reece (F) 1 0
b. 7-3-97
2014–15 Bradford C 1 0 **1 0**

WILLIAMS, Ben (G) 309 0
H: 6 0 W: 13 01 b.Manchester 27-8-82
Internationals: England Schools.
2001–02 Manchester U 0 0
2002–03 Manchester U 0 0
2002–03 *Coventry C* 0 0
2002–03 *Chesterfield* 14 0 **14 0**
2003–04 Manchester U 0 0
2003–04 *Crewe Alex* 10 0
2004–05 Crewe Alex 23 0
2005–06 Crewe Alex 17 0
2006–07 Crewe Alex 39 0
2007–08 Crewe Alex 46 0 **135 0**
2008–09 Carlisle U 31 0 **31 0**
2009–10 Colchester U 46 0
2010–11 Colchester U 33 0
2011–12 Colchester U 36 0 **115 0**
2014–15 Bradford C 14 0 **14 0**

YEATES, Mark (F) 352 46
H: 5 8 W: 13 03 b.Dublin 11-1-85
Internationals: Republic of Ireland U21, B.
2002–03 Tottenham H 0 0
2003–04 Tottenham H 1 0
2003–04 *Brighton & HA* 9 0 **9 0**
2004–05 Tottenham H 2 0
2004–05 *Swindon T* 4 0 **4 0**
2005–06 Tottenham H 0 0
2005–06 *Colchester U* 44 5
2006–07 Tottenham H 0 0 **3 0**
2006–07 *Hull C* 5 0 **5 0**
2006–07 *Leicester C* 9 1 **9 1**
2007–08 Colchester U 29 8
2008–09 Colchester U 43 12 **116 25**
2009–10 Middlesbrough 19 1 **19 1**
2009–10 Sheffield U 20 2
2010–11 Sheffield U 35 5 **55 7**
2011–12 Watford 33 3
2012–13 Watford 29 4 **62 7**
2013–14 Bradford C 29 2
2014–15 Bradford C 41 3 **70 5**

Scholars
Barker, Elliott Austin; Brennan, Joseph James; Chippendale, Callum Ross; Cissa, Sumaili; Devine, Daniel Steven; Hallwood, Chandler Benjamin Taylor; Jenkinson, Rhys Brandon; Kershaw, Ross David Thomas; King, James Taylor; Landu, Giovanni; McBurnie, Alexander Cameron; Mellor, Luca Daniel; Mottley-Henry, Dylan; Omolokun, Kesi Olufemi Adrian; Pollard, James Harry; Waters, Jack Donald; Webb-Foster, Reece Patrick; Wright, Samuel Lee.

BRENTFORD (12)

ADAMS, Charlie (M) 13 0
H: 5 6 W: 9 10 b.London 16-5-94
2012–13 Brentford 1 0
2013–14 Brentford 3 0
2014–15 Brentford 0 0 **4 0**
2014–15 *Stevenage* 9 0 **9 0**
Transferred to Louisville C February 2015.

BETINHO, Alberto (F) 12 0
H: 5 10 W: 11 09 b.Santa Maria de Lamas 21-7-93
Internationals: Portugal U16, U17, U18, U19, U20.
2012–13 Sporting Lisbon 3 0
2013–14 Sporting Lisbon 0 0 **3 0**
2013–14 *Setubal* 8 0 **8 0**
On loan from Sporting Lisbon.
2014–15 Brentford 1 0 **1 0**

BIDWELL, Jake (D) 145 0
H: 6 0 W: 11 00 b.Southport 21-3-93
Internationals: England U16, U17, U18, U19.
2009–10 Everton 0 0
2010–11 Everton 0 0
2011–12 Everton 0 0
2011–12 *Brentford* 24 0
2012–13 Everton 0 0
2012–13 *Brentford* 40 0
2013–14 Brentford 38 0
2014–15 Brentford 43 0 **145 0**

BONHAM, Jack (G) 2 0
H: 6 4 W: 14 13 b.Stevenage 14-9-93
Internationals: Republic of Ireland U17.
2010–11 Watford 0 0
2011–12 Watford 0 0
2012–13 Watford 1 0 **1 0**
2013–14 Brentford 1 0
2014–15 Brentford 0 0 **1 0**

BUTTON, David (G) 183 0
H: 6 3 W: 13 00 b.Stevenage 27-2-89
Internationals: England U16, U17, U19, U20.
2005–06 Tottenham H 0 0
2006–07 Tottenham H 0 0
2007–08 *Rochdale* 0 0
2007–08 Tottenham H 0 0
2008–09 Tottenham H 0 0
2008–09 *Bournemouth* 4 0 **4 0**
2008–09 *Luton T* 0 0
2008–09 *Dagenham & R* 3 0 **3 0**
2009–10 Tottenham H 0 0
2009–10 *Crewe Alex* 10 0 **10 0**
2009–10 *Shrewsbury T* 26 0 **26 0**
2010–11 Tottenham H 0 0
2010–11 *Plymouth Arg* 30 0 **30 0**
2011–12 Tottenham H 0 0
2011–12 *Leyton Orient* 1 0 **1 0**
2011–12 *Doncaster R* 7 0 **7 0**
2011–12 *Barnsley* 9 0 **9 0**
2012–13 Tottenham H 0 0
2012–13 Charlton Ath 5 0 **5 0**
2013–14 Brentford 42 0
2014–15 Brentford 46 0 **88 0**

CALVET, Raphael (D) 1 0
H: 6 0 W: 10 13 b.Paris 7-2-94
Internationals: France U16, U17, U18, U20.
2012–13 Auxerre 1 0 **1 0**
2013–14 Brentford 0 0
2014–15 Brentford 0 0

CLARKE, Josh (M) 2 0
H: 5 8 W: 11 00 b.Waltham Forest 5-7-95
2012–13 Brentford 0 0
2013–14 Brentford 1 0
2014–15 Brentford 0 0 **1 0**
2014–15 *Dagenham & R* 0 0
2014–15 *Stevenage* 1 0 **1 0**

CRAIG, Tony (D) 347 7
H: 6 0 W: 10 03 b.Greenwich 20-4-85
2002–03 Millwall 2 1
2003–04 Millwall 9 0
2004–05 Millwall 10 0
2004–05 *Wycombe W* 14 0 **14 0**
2005–06 Millwall 28 0
2006–07 Millwall 30 1
2007–08 Crystal Palace 13 0 **13 0**
2007–08 *Millwall* 5 1
2008–09 Millwall 44 2
2009–10 Millwall 30 2
2010–11 Millwall 24 0
2011–12 Millwall 23 0 **205 7**
2011–12 *Leyton Orient* 4 0 **4 0**
2012–13 Brentford 44 0
2013–14 Brentford 44 0
2014–15 Brentford 23 0 **111 0**

DALLAS, Stuart (M) 96 35
H: 6 0 W: 12 09 b.Cookstown 19-4-91
Internationals: Northern Ireland U21, U23, Full caps.
2010–11 Crusaders 13 16
2011–12 Crusaders 8 8 **21 24**
2012–13 Brentford 7 0
2013–14 Brentford 18 2
2013–14 *Northampton T* 12 3 **12 3**
2014–15 Brentford 38 6 **63 8**

DEAN, Harlee (M) 138 5
H: 6 0 W: 11 10 b.Basingstoke 26-7-91
2008–09 Dagenham & R 0 0
2009–10 Dagenham & R 1 0 **1 0**
2010–11 Southampton 0 0
2011–12 Southampton 0 0
2011–12 *Brentford* 26 1
2012–13 Brentford 44 3
2013–14 Brentford 32 0
2014–15 Brentford 35 1 **137 5**

DIAGOURAGA, Toumani (M) 312 10
H: 6 2 W: 11 05 b.Paris 10-6-87
2004–05 Watford 0 0
2005–06 Watford 1 0
2005–06 *Swindon T* 8 0 **8 0**
2006–07 Watford 0 0
2006–07 *Rotherham U* 7 0 **7 0**
2007–08 Watford 0 0 **1 0**
2007–08 *Hereford U* 41 2
2008–09 Hereford U 45 2 **86 4**
2009–10 Peterborough U 19 0 **19 0**
2009–10 *Brentford* 20 0
2010–11 Brentford 32 1
2011–12 Brentford 35 4
2012–13 Brentford 39 1
2013–14 Brentford 19 0
2013–14 *Portsmouth* 8 0 **8 0**
2014–15 Brentford 38 0 **183 6**

DOUGLAS, Jonathan (M) 442 33
H: 5 11 W: 11 11 b.Monaghan 22-11-81
Internationals: Republic of Ireland Full caps.
1999–2000 Blackburn R 0 0
2000–01 Blackburn R 0 0
2001–02 Blackburn R 0 0
2002–03 Blackburn R 1 0
2002–03 *Chesterfield* 7 1 **7 1**
2003–04 Blackpool 16 3 **16 3**
2003–04 Blackburn R 14 1
2004–05 Blackburn R 1 0
2004–05 *Gillingham* 10 0 **10 0**
2005–06 Blackburn R 0 0
2005–06 *Leeds U* 40 5
2006–07 Blackburn R 0 0 **16 1**
2006–07 Leeds U 35 1
2007–08 Leeds U 24 3
2008–09 Leeds U 43 1 **142 10**
2009–10 Swindon T 43 0
2010–11 Swindon T 39 1 **82 1**
2011–12 Brentford 46 2
2012–13 Brentford 44 4
2013–14 Brentford 35 3
2014–15 Brentford 44 8 **169 17**

FIELD, Tom (D) 0 0
H: 5 10 W: 10 13 b.Kingston upon Thames 2-8-85
2013–14 Brentford 0 0
2014–15 Brentford 0 0

GRAY, Andre (F) 49 16
H: 5 10 W: 12 06 b.Shrewsbury 26-6-91
Internationals: England C.
2009–10 Shrewsbury T 4 0 **4 0**
From Hinckley U, Luton T.
2014–15 Brentford 45 16 **45 16**

GREENE, Aaron (M) 0 0
b.Dublin 2-1-90
2014–15 Brentford 0 0

GRIGG, Will (M) 177 52
H: 5 11 W: 11 00 b.Solihull 3-7-91
Internationals: Northern Ireland U19, U21, Full caps.
2008–09 Walsall 1 0
2009–10 Walsall 0 0
2010–11 Walsall 28 4
2011–12 Walsall 29 4
2012–13 Walsall 41 19 **99 27**
2013–14 Brentford 34 5
2014–15 Brentford 0 0 **34 5**
2014–15 *Milton Keynes D* 44 20 **44 20**

HOGAN, Scott (F) 34 17
H: 5 11 W: 10 01 b. 13-4-92
2009–10 Rochdale 0 0
2013–14 Rochdale 33 17 **33 17**
2014–15 Brentford 1 0 **1 0**

HUTTON, Louis (M) 0 0
H: 5 9 b.Bradford 9-9-94
Internationals: England U16, U17.
2013–14 Manchester C 0 0
2013–14 Brentford 0 0
2014–15 Brentford 0 0

JOTA, Ramallo (M) 81 22
H: 5 11 W: 10 08 b.A Coruna 16-6-91
2010–11 Celta Vigo 4 0
2011–12 Celta Vigo 0 0
2012–13 Celta Vigo 0 0
2013–14 Celta Vigo 0 0 **4 0**
2013–14 *Eibar* 35 11 **35 11**
2014–15 Brentford 42 11 **42 11**

JUDGE, Alan (F) 225 33
H: 5 6 W: 11 03 b.Dublin 11-11-88
Internationals: Republic of Ireland U18, U19, U21, U23.
2006–07 Blackburn R 0 0
2007–08 Blackburn R 0 0
2008–09 Blackburn R 0 0
2008–09 *Plymouth Arg* 17 2
2009–10 Blackburn R 0 0
2009–10 *Plymouth Arg* 37 5 **54 7**
2010–11 Blackburn R 0 0

2010–11	Notts Co	19	1	
2011–12	Notts Co	43	7	
2012–13	Notts Co	39	8	101 16
2013–14	Blackburn R	11	0	11 0
2013–14	Brentford	22	7	
2014–15	Brentford	37	3	59 10

LEE, Richard (G)   158 0
H: 6 0   W: 12 06   b.Oxford 5-10-82
Internationals: England U20.

2000–01	Watford	0	0	
2001–02	Watford	0	0	
2002–03	Watford	4	0	
2003–04	Watford	0	0	
2004–05	Watford	33	0	
2005–06	Watford	0	0	
2005–06	*Blackburn R*	0	0	
2006–07	Watford	10	0	
2007–08	Watford	35	0	
2008–09	Watford	10	0	
2009–10	Watford	0	0	92 0
2010–11	Brentford	22	0	
2011–12	Brentford	37	0	
2012–13	Brentford	3	0	
2013–14	Brentford	4	0	
2014–15	Brentford	0	0	66 0
2014–15	*Fulham*	0	0	

MACLEOD, Lewis (M)   52 11
b.Law 16-6-94
Internationals: Scotland U16, U17, U18, U19, U20.

2012–13	Rangers	21	3	
2013–14	Rangers	18	5	
2014–15	Rangers	13	3	52 11
2014–15	Brentford	0	0	

MALONEY, Joe (M)   0 0
H: 5 6   W: 11 01   b.Brentford 21-3-95

2013–14	Brentford	0	0	
2014–15	Brentford	0	0	

MAWSON, Alfie (D)   45 6
H: 5 8   W: 12 11   b.Hillingdon 19-1-94

2012–13	Brentford	0	0	
2013–14	Brentford	0	0	
2014–15	Brentford	0	0	
2014–15	*Wycombe W*	45	6	45 6

McCORMACK, Alan (M)   356 25
H: 5 8   W: 11 00   b.Dublin 10-1-84

2002–03	Preston NE	0	0	
2003–04	Preston NE	5	0	
2003–04	*Leyton Orient*	10	0	10 0
2004–05	Preston NE	3	0	
2004–05	*Southend U*	7	2	
2005–06	Preston NE	0	0	
2005–06	*Motherwell*	24	2	24 2
2006–07	Preston NE	3	0	11 0
2006–07	*Southend U*	22	3	
2007–08	Southend U	42	8	
2008–09	Southend U	34	2	
2009–10	Southend U	41	3	146 18
2010–11	Charlton Ath	24	1	24 1
2011–12	Swindon T	40	2	
2012–13	Swindon T	40	0	80 2
2013–14	Brentford	43	1	
2014–15	Brentford	18	1	61 2

MILLER-RODNEY, Tyrell (M)   0 0
H: 5 9   W: 10 04   b.Stonebridge 23-4-94

2013–14	Brentford	0	0	
2014–15	Brentford	0	0	

MOORE, Montell (F)   0 0
b. 23-12-95

2014–15	Brentford	0	0	

O'CONNELL, Jack (D)   88 5
H: 6 3   W: 13 05   b.Liverpool 29-3-94
Internationals: England U18, U19.

2012–13	Blackburn R	0	0	
2012–13	*Rotherham U*	3	0	3 0
2013–14	*York C*	18	0	18 0
2013–14	Blackburn R	0	0	
2013–14	*Rochdale*	38	0	
2014–15	Blackburn R	0	0	
2014–15	*Rochdale*	29	5	67 5
2014–15	Brentford	0	0	

O'CONNOR, Kevin (F)   420 32
H: 5 11   W: 12 00   b.Blackburn 24-2-82
Internationals: Republic of Ireland U21.

1999–2000	Brentford	6	0	
2000–01	Brentford	11	1	
2001–02	Brentford	25	0	
2002–03	Brentford	45	5	
2003–04	Brentford	43	1	
2004–05	Brentford	37	2	
2005–06	Brentford	30	7	
2006–07	Brentford	39	6	

2007–08	Brentford	37	3	
2008–09	Brentford	28	0	
2009–10	Brentford	43	4	
2010–11	Brentford	41	2	
2011–12	Brentford	14	1	
2012–13	Brentford	12	0	
2013–14	Brentford	9	0	
2014–15	Brentford	0	0	420 32

O'SHAUGHNESSY, Daniel (D)   0 0
b. 14-9-94
Internationals: Finland U17, U20, U21.

2014–15	Brentford	0	0	

ODUBAJO, Moses (M)   138 16
H: 5 9   W: 11 05   b.Greenwich 28-7-93
Internationals: England U20.

2011–12	Leyton Orient	3	1	
2012–13	Leyton Orient	44	2	
2013–14	Leyton Orient	46	10	93 13
2014–15	Brentford	45	3	45 3

PROSCHWITZ, Nick (F)   133 34
H: 6 3   W: 12 11   b.Weibenfels 28-11-86

2010–11	FC Thun	31	8	31 8
2011–12	Paderborn	32	17	32 17
2012–13	Hull C	27	3	
2013–14	Hull C	2	0	29 3
2013–14	*Barnsley*	14	4	14 4
2014–15	Brentford	18	1	18 1
2014–15	*Coventry C*	9	1	9 1

SMITH, Tommy (F)   519 95
H: 5 8   W: 11 04   b.Hemel Hempstead 22-5-80
Internationals: England Youth, U21.

1997–98	Watford	1	0	
1998–99	Watford	8	2	
1999–2000	Watford	22	2	
2000–01	Watford	43	11	
2001–02	Watford	40	11	
2002–03	Watford	35	7	
2003–04	Watford	0	0	
2003–04	*Sunderland*	35	4	35 4
2004–05	Derby Co	42	11	
2005–06	Derby Co	43	8	
2006–07	Derby Co	5	1	90 20
2006–07	*Watford*	32	1	
2007–08	Watford	44	7	
2008–09	Watford	44	17	
2009–10	Watford	4	2	273 60
2009–10	*Portsmouth*	16	1	
2010–11	Portsmouth	3	0	19 1
2010–11	QPR	33	6	
2011–12	QPR	17	2	
2012–13	QPR	0	0	50 8
2012–13	*Cardiff C*	24	1	
2013–14	*Cardiff C*	0	0	24 1
2014–15	Brentford	28	1	28 1

TARKOWSKI, James (D)   119 8
H: 6 1   W: 12 10   b.Manchester 19-11-92

2010–11	Oldham Ath	9	0	
2011–12	Oldham Ath	16	1	
2012–13	Oldham Ath	21	2	
2013–14	Oldham Ath	26	2	72 5
2013–14	Brentford	13	2	
2014–15	Brentford	34	1	47 3

TEBAR, Marcos (M)   147 4
H: 6 1   W: 12 02   b.Madrid 7-2-86
Internationals: Spain U16, U17.

2008–09	Real Madrid	1	0	1 0
2009–10	Girona	8	0	
2010–11	Girona	35	0	
2011–12	Girona	35	0	
2012–13	Girona	39	4	117 4
2013–14	Almeria	25	0	25 0
2014–15	Brentford	4	0	4 0

UDUMAGA, Jermaine (M)   0 0
b.Wandsworth Hill 22-6-95

2013–14	Crystal Palace	0	0	
2014–15	Crystal Palace	0	0	
2014–15	Brentford	0	0	

Players retained or with offer of contract
Ramallo, Jose Ignacio Peleteiro; Rodrigues
Alves, Herson Domingos; Saunders, Sam
Daniel; Smith, Mark David; Yennaris,
Nicholas.

Scholars
Austin, Courtney Cephas; Carey, Jordan Joe;
Cole, Reece George; Ferry, James Patrick;
Field, Thomas; Guppy, Anthony Adam
William; Jatta, Seika; Kamanzi, Jerry
Rawlings, Khanye, Makhosini Ryan; Laucys,
Audrius; Marsh-Brown, Kyjuon Jaeger;
Massala, Joao Augusto; Mepham,

Christopher James; Milenge, Gradi; Owens,
Seth; Pennant, Romayn James; Roberts,
Thomas George Maurice; Senior, Courtney
Fitzroy; Westbrooke, Zain Sam.

BRIGHTON & HA (13)

ADRIAN COLUNGA, Perez (F)   215 56
H: 5 8   W: 11 00   b.Oviedo 17-11-84

2007–08	Las Palmas	33	13	33 13
2008–09	Recreativo Huelva	33	9	
2009–10	Recreativo Huelva	13	3	46 12
2009–10	Real Zaragoza	16	7	16 7
2010–11	Getafe	29	8	
2011–12	Getafe	4	0	
2011–12	Sportin Gijon	17	3	17 3
2012–13	Getafe	22	6	
2013–14	Getafe	27	4	82 18
2013–14	Brighton & HA	17	3	17 3
2014–15	*Granada*	4	0	4 0

AGUSTIEN, Kemy (M)   208 8
H: 5 10   W: 11 05   b.Tilburg 20-8-86
Internationals: Netherlands U19, U20, U21.
Curacao Full caps.

2004–05	Willem II	21	1	
2005–06	Willem II	34	2	55 3
2006–07	Roda JC	31	2	31 2
2007–08	AZ	25	2	25 2
2008–09	Birmingham C	18	0	18 0
2009–10	*RKC Waalwijk*	19	1	19 1
2010–11	Swansea C	8	0	
2010–11	*Crystal Palace*	8	0	8 0
2011–12	Swansea C	13	0	
2012–13	Swansea C	18	0	39 0
2013–14	Brighton & HA	11	0	
2014–15	Brighton & HA	2	0	13 0

ANKERGREN, Casper (G)   273 0
H: 6 3   W: 14 07   b.Koge 9-11-79
Internationals: Denmark U17, U21.

2001–02	Brondby	1	0	
2002–03	Brondby	16	0	
2003–04	Brondby	1	0	
2004–05	Brondby	32	0	
2005–06	Brondby	18	0	
2006–07	Brondby	18	0	86 0
2006–07	Leeds U	14	0	
2007–08	Leeds U	43	0	
2008–09	Leeds U	33	0	
2009–10	Leeds U	29	0	119 0
2010–11	Brighton & HA	45	0	
2011–12	Brighton & HA	19	0	
2012–13	Brighton & HA	3	0	
2013–14	Brighton & HA	1	0	
2014–15	Brighton & HA	0	0	68 0

ASMUNDSSON, Emil (M)   6 1
b. 8-1-95
Internationals: Iceland U17, U19.

2012	Fylkir	6	1	6 1
2012–13	Brighton & HA	0	0	
2013–14	Brighton & HA	0	0	
2014–15	Brighton & HA	0	0	

BALDOCK, Sam (F)   226 75
H: 5 7   W: 10 07   b.Buckingham 15-3-89
Internationals: England U20.

2005–06	Milton Keynes D	0	0	
2006–07	Milton Keynes D	1	0	
2007–08	Milton Keynes D	5	0	
2008–09	Milton Keynes D	40	12	
2009–10	Milton Keynes D	20	5	
2010–11	Milton Keynes D	30	12	
2011–12	Milton Keynes D	4	4	100 33
2011–12	West Ham U	23	5	
2012–13	West Ham U	0	0	23 5
2012–13	Bristol C	34	10	
2013–14	Bristol C	45	24	
2014–15	Bristol C	4	0	83 34
2014–15	Brighton & HA	20	3	20 3

BARRY, Bradley (D)   0 0

2013–14	Brighton & HA	0	0	
2014–15	Brighton & HA	0	0	

BENNETT, Joe (D)   156 2
H: 5 10   W: 10 04   b.Rochdale 28-3-90
Internationals: England U19, U20, U21.

2008–09	Middlesbrough	1	0	
2009–10	Middlesbrough	12	0	
2010–11	Middlesbrough	31	0	
2011–12	Middlesbrough	41	1	
2012–13	Middlesbrough	0	0	85 1
2012–13	Aston Villa	25	0	
2013–14	Aston Villa	5	0	30 0
2014–15	Brighton & HA	41	1	41 1

CALDERON, Inigo (D)   386 26
H: 5 10   W: 12 02   b.Vitoria 4-1-82

2002–03	Alaves B	35	1	
2003–04	Alaves B	33	0	68 1
2004–05	Alicante	25	0	
2005–06	Alicante	31	4	
2006–07	Alicante	28	1	84 5
2007–08	Alaves	20	0	
2008–09	Alaves	33	2	53 2
2009–10	Brighton & HA	19	1	
2010–11	Brighton & HA	44	7	
2011–12	Brighton & HA	32	4	
2012–13	Brighton & HA	28	0	
2013–14	Brighton & HA	23	2	
2014–15	Brighton & HA	35	4	181 18

CHICKSEN, Adam (D)   98 2
H: 5 8   W: 11 09   b.Milton Keynes 27-9-91

2008–09	Milton Keynes D	1	0	
2009–10	Milton Keynes D	6	0	
2010–11	Milton Keynes D	14	0	
2011–12	Milton Keynes D	20	0	
2011–12	*Leyton Orient*	3	0	3 0
2012–13	Milton Keynes D	32	2	
2013–14	Milton Keynes D	0	0	73 2
2013–14	Brighton & HA	1	0	
2014–15	Brighton & HA	5	0	6 0
2014–15	*Gillingham*	3	0	3 0
2014–15	*Fleetwood T*	13	0	13 0

COLE, George (M)   0 0
b. 22-12-95

2014–15	Brighton & HA	0	0

CROFTS, Andrew (D)   349 35
H: 5 10   W: 12 09   b.Chatham 29-5-84
Internationals: Wales U19, U21, Full caps.

2000–01	Gillingham	1	0	
2001–02	Gillingham	0	0	
2002–03	Gillingham	0	0	
2003–04	Gillingham	8	0	
2004–05	Gillingham	27	2	
2005–06	Gillingham	45	2	
2006–07	Gillingham	43	8	
2007–08	Gillingham	41	5	
2008–09	Gillingham	9	0	174 17
2008–09	*Peterborough U*	9	0	9 0
2009–10	Brighton & HA	44	5	
2010–11	Norwich C	44	8	
2011–12	Norwich C	24	0	
2012–13	Norwich C	0	0	68 8
2013–14	Brighton & HA	24	0	
2013–14	Brighton & HA	23	5	
2014–15	Brighton & HA	7	0	98 10

DALLISON, Tom (M)   0 0
H: 5 10   W: 14 01   b. 2-2-96

2012–13	Arsenal	0	0
2013–14	Brighton & HA	0	0
2014–15	Brighton & HA	0	0

DUNK, Lewis (D)   91 5
H: 6 3   W: 12 02   b.Brighton 1-12-91

2009–10	Brighton & HA	1	0	
2010–11	Brighton & HA	5	0	
2011–12	Brighton & HA	31	0	
2012–13	Brighton & HA	8	0	
2013–14	Brighton & HA	6	0	
2013–14	*Bristol C*	2	0	2 0
2014–15	Brighton & HA	38	5	89 5

FENELON, Shamir (M)   32 3
H: 6 1   W: 12 08   b.Brighton 3-8-94
Internationals: Republic of Ireland U21.

2011–12	Brighton & HA	0	0	
2013–14	Brighton & HA	0	0	
2013–14	*Torquay U*	12	1	12 1
2014–15	Brighton & HA	2	0	2 0
2014–15	*Rochdale*	4	0	4 0
2014–15	*Tranmere R*	10	2	10 2
2014–15	*Dagenham & R*	4	0	4 0

FORSTER-CASKEY, Jake (M)   81 8
H: 5 10   W: 10 00   b.Southend 25-4-94
Internationals: England U16, U17, U18, U20, U21.

2009–10	Brighton & HA	1	0	
2010–11	Brighton & HA	0	0	
2011–12	Brighton & HA	4	1	
2012–13	Brighton & HA	3	0	
2012–13	*Oxford U*	16	3	16 3
2013–14	Brighton & HA	28	3	
2014–15	Brighton & HA	29	1	65 5

GREER, Gordon (D)   406 12
H: 6 2   W: 12 05   b.Glasgow 14-12-80
Internationals: Scotland B, Full caps.

2000–01	Clyde	30	0	30 0
2000–01	Blackburn R	0	0	
2001–02	Blackburn R	0	0	
2002–03	Blackburn R	0	0	
2002–03	*Stockport Co*	5	1	5 1
2003–04	Kilmarnock	25	0	
2004–05	Kilmarnock	22	1	
2005–06	Kilmarnock	27	2	
2006–07	Kilmarnock	33	0	107 3
2007–08	Doncaster R	11	1	
2008–09	Doncaster R	1	0	12 1
2008–09	Swindon T	19	1	
2009–10	Swindon T	44	1	63 2
2010–11	Brighton & HA	32	0	
2011–12	Brighton & HA	42	1	
2012–13	Brighton & HA	38	1	
2013–14	Brighton & HA	40	1	
2014–15	Brighton & HA	37	2	189 5

HARRIS, Charlie (M)   0 0

2014–15	Brighton & HA	0	0

HOLLA, Danny (M)   220 35
H: 5 10   W: 11 09   b.Almere 31-12-87

2006–07	Groningen	6	0	
2007–08	*Zwolle*	23	8	23 8
2007–08	Groningen	6	0	
2008–09	Groningen	34	6	
2009–10	Groningen	22	2	
2010–11	Groningen	22	2	
2011–12	Groningen	13	0	103 10
2011–12	*VVV*	16	2	16 2
2012–13	Den Haag	28	11	
2013–14	Den Haag	26	3	54 14
2014–15	Brighton & HA	24	1	24 1

HUGHES, Aaron (D)   476 5
H: 6 0   W: 11 02   b.Cookstown 8-11-79
Internationals: Northern Ireland Youth, B, Full caps.

1996–97	Newcastle U	0	0	
1997–98	Newcastle U	4	0	
1998–99	Newcastle U	14	0	
1999–2000	Newcastle U	27	2	
2000–01	Newcastle U	35	0	
2001–02	Newcastle U	34	0	
2002–03	Newcastle U	35	1	
2003–04	Newcastle U	34	0	
2004–05	Newcastle U	22	1	205 4
2005–06	Aston Villa	35	0	
2006–07	Aston Villa	19	0	54 0
2007–08	Fulham	30	0	
2008–09	Fulham	38	0	
2009–10	Fulham	34	0	
2010–11	Fulham	38	1	
2011–12	Fulham	19	0	
2012–13	Fulham	24	0	
2013–14	Fulham	13	0	196 1
2013–14	*QPR*	11	0	11 0
2014–15	Brighton & HA	10	0	10 0

HUNT, Robert (M)   0 0
b. 7-7-95

2013–14	Brighton & HA	0	0
2014–15	Brighton & HA	0	0

INCE, Rohan (D)   62 1
H: 6 3   W: 12 08   b.Whitechapel 8-11-92

2010–11	Chelsea	0	0	
2011–12	Chelsea	0	0	
2012–13	Chelsea	0	0	
2012–13	*Yeovil T*	2	0	2 0
2013–14	Brighton & HA	28	0	
2014–15	Brighton & HA	32	1	60 1

KAYAL, Beram (M)   161 5
H: 5 10   W: 11 09   b.Jadeidi 2-5-88
Internationals: Israel U17, U18, U19, U21, Full caps.

2008–09	Maccabi Haifa	30	1	
2009–10	Maccabi Haifa	27	1	57 2
2010–11	Celtic	21	2	
2011–12	Celtic	19	0	
2012–13	Celtic	27	0	
2013–14	Celtic	13	0	
2014–15	Celtic	6	0	86 2
2014–15	Brighton & HA	18	1	18 1

LOPEZ, David (M)   258 34
H: 5 11   W: 11 06   b.Logrono 10-9-82

2004–05	Osasuna	12	1	
2005–06	Osasuna	34	6	
2006–07	Osasuna	31	4	77 11
2007–08	Athletic Bilbao	30	1	
2008–09	Athletic Bilbao	29	3	
2009–10	Athletic Bilbao	17	0	
2010–11	Athletic Bilbao	28	6	
2011–12	Athletic Bilbao	12	1	116 11
2012–13	Athletic Bilbao	31	9	
2013–14	Brighton & HA	34	3	
2014–15	Brighton & HA	0	0	65 12

LUALUA, Kazenga (F)   149 14
H: 5 11   W: 12 00   b.Kinshasa 10-12-90

2007–08	Newcastle U	2	0	
2008–09	Newcastle U	3	0	
2008–09	*Doncaster R*	4	0	4 0
2009–10	Newcastle U	1	0	
2009–10	*Brighton & HA*	11	0	
2010–11	Newcastle U	2	0	
2010–11	*Brighton & HA*	11	4	
2011–12	Newcastle U	0	0	8 0
2011–12	Brighton & HA	27	1	
2012–13	Brighton & HA	22	5	
2013–14	Brighton & HA	32	1	
2014–15	Brighton & HA	34	3	137 14

MACKAIL-SMITH, Craig (F)   297 101
H: 6 3   W: 12 04   b.Watford 25-2-84
Internationals: England C. Scotland Full caps.

2006–07	Peterborough U	15	8	
2007–08	Peterborough U	36	12	
2008–09	Peterborough U	46	23	
2009–10	Peterborough U	43	10	
2010–11	Peterborough U	45	27	
2011–12	Brighton & HA	45	9	
2012–13	Brighton & HA	29	11	
2013–14	Brighton & HA	5	0	
2014–15	Brighton & HA	30	1	109 21
2014–15	*Peterborough U*	3	0	188 80

MAKSIMENKO, Vitalijs (D)   108 3
H: 6 1   W: 11 11   b.Riga 8-12-90
Internationals: Latvia U17, U19, U21, Full caps.

2010	Skonto FC	24	0	
2011	Skonto FC	19	0	
2012	Skonto FC	32	2	75 2
2012–13	Brighton & HA	0	0	
2012–13	*Yeovil T*	3	0	3 0
2013–14	Brighton & HA	1	0	
2013–14	*Kilmarnock*	8	1	8 1
2014–15	Brighton & HA	0	0	1 0
2014–15	*VVV*	21	0	21 0

MARCH, Solly (M)   34 1
b.Lewes 26-7-94
Internationals: England U20.

2012–13	Brighton & HA	0	0	
2013–14	Brighton & HA	23	0	
2014–15	Brighton & HA	11	1	34 1

McCOURT, Paddy (M)   269 33
H: 5 10   W: 10 13   b.Londonderry 16-12-83
Internationals: Northern Ireland U21, B, Full caps.

2001–02	Rochdale	23	4	
2002–03	Rochdale	26	3	
2003–04	Rochdale	24	2	
2004–05	Rochdale	6	0	79 9
2005	Shamrock R	17	7	17 7
2005	Derry C	15	1	
2006	Derry C	22	2	
2007	Derry C	17	2	
2008	Derry C	8	0	62 5
2008–09	Celtic	4	0	
2009–10	Celtic	9	2	
2010–11	Celtic	25	7	
2011–12	Celtic	13	0	
2012–13	Celtic	15	0	66 9
2013–14	Barnsley	23	2	23 2
2014–15	Brighton & HA	10	0	10 0
2014–15	*Notts Co*	12	1	12 1

MONAKANA, Jeffrey (M)   70 5
H: 5 10   W: 10 08   b.Enfield 5-11-93

2012–13	Preston NE	38	4	
2013–14	Preston NE	2	0	40 4
2013–14	*Colchester U*	9	1	9 1
2013–14	Brighton & HA	0	0	
2013–14	*Crawley T*	4	0	4 0
2014–15	Brighton & HA	0	0	
2014–15	*Aberdeen*	10	0	10 0
2014–15	*Mansfield T*	6	0	6 0
2014–15	*Carlisle U*	1	0	1 0

O'GRADY, Chris (F)   376 82
H: 6 3   W: 12 04   b.Nottingham 25-1-86
Internationals: England Youth.

2002–03	Leicester C	1	0	
2003–04	Leicester C	0	0	
2004–05	Leicester C	0	0	
2004–05	*Notts Co*	9	0	9 0
2005–06	Leicester C	3	1	
2005–06	*Rushden & D*	22	4	22 4
2006–07	Leicester C	10	0	24 1
2007–08	Rotherham U	13	4	
2007–08	Rotherham U	38	9	51 13
2008–09	Oldham Ath	13	0	13 0
2008–09	*Bury*	6	0	6 0
2008–09	*Bradford C*	0	0	2 0

2008–09	*Stockport Co*	18	2	**18 2**
2009–10	Rochdale	43	22	
2010–11	Rochdale	46	9	
2011–12	Rochdale	1	0	**90 31**
2011–12	Sheffield W	32	5	
2012–13	Sheffield W	21	4	**53 9**
2012–13	Barnsley	16	5	
2013–14	Barnsley	40	15	**56 20**
2014–15	Brighton & HA	28	1	**28 1**
2014–15	*Sheffield U*	4	1	**4 1**

REA, Glen (D)   **0 0**
b. 3-9-94
Internationals: Republic of Ireland U21.
| 2013–14 | Brighton & HA | 0 | 0 | |
| 2014–15 | Brighton & HA | 0 | 0 | |

SALTOR, Bruno (D)   **300 6**
H: 5 10   W: 11 10   b.Masnou (Barca)
1-10-80
2001–02	Espanyol	1	0	**1 0**
2001–02	*Gimnastic*	12	0	**12 0**
2004–05	Lleida	1	1	
2005–06	Lleida	38	0	**39 1**
2006–07	Almeria	23	0	
2007–08	Almeria	34	0	
2008–09	Almeria	34	0	**91 0**
2009–10	Valencia	26	0	
2010–11	Valencia	19	0	
2011–12	Valencia	14	0	**59 0**
2012–13	Brighton & HA	30	1	
2013–14	Brighton & HA	33	1	
2014–15	Brighton & HA	35	3	**98 5**

SMITH, Josh (G)   **0 0**
| 2013–14 | Brighton & HA | 0 | 0 | |
| 2014–15 | Brighton & HA | 0 | 0 | |

STEPHENS, Dale (M)   **195 27**
H: 5 7   W: 11 04   b.Bolton 12-6-89
2006–07	Bury	3	0	
2007–08	Bury	6	1	**9 1**
2008–09	Oldham Ath	9	0	
2009–10	Oldham Ath	26	2	
2009–10	*Rochdale*	6	1	**6 1**
2010–11	Oldham Ath	34	9	**60 11**
2010–11	*Southampton*	6	0	**6 0**
2011–12	Charlton Ath	30	5	
2012–13	Charlton Ath	28	2	
2013–14	Charlton Ath	26	3	**84 10**
2013–14	Brighton & HA	14	2	
2014–15	Brighton & HA	16	2	**30 4**

STOCKDALE, David (G)   **208 0**
H: 6 3   W: 13 04   b.Leeds 20-9-85
Internationals: England C.
2002–03	York C	1	0	
2003–04	York C	1	0	**1 0**
2006–07	Darlington	6	0	
2007–08	Darlington	41	0	**47 0**
2008–09	Fulham	0	0	
2008–09	*Rotherham U*	8	0	**8 0**
2008–09	*Leicester C*	8	0	**8 0**
2009–10	Fulham	1	0	
2009–10	*Plymouth Arg*	21	0	**21 0**
2010–11	Fulham	7	0	
2011–12	Fulham	8	0	
2011–12	*Ipswich T*	18	0	**18 0**
2012–13	Fulham	2	0	
2012–13	*Hull C*	24	0	**24 0**
2013–14	Fulham	21	0	**39 0**
2014–15	Brighton & HA	42	0	**42 0**

TILLEY, James (F)   **1 0**
b. 13-6-98
| 2014–15 | Brighton & HA | 1 | 0 | **1 0** |

WALTON, Christian (G)   **3 0**
b. 9-11-95
Internationals: England U19, U20.
2011–12	Plymouth Arg	0	0	
2012–13	Plymouth Arg	0	0	
2013–14	Brighton & HA	0	0	
2014–15	Brighton & HA	3	0	**3 0**

Players retained or with offer of contract
Davis, Jason Mytton; Deen, Robin; Doherty,
Harry Daniel; Kandi, Luke Chike; Larusson,
Ragnar Mar; Starkey, Jesse Aaron.

Scholars
Barclay, Benjamin Philip; Barnett, Dylan
Mark; Cadman, Thomas Patrick; Collar,
William Guy; Courtney, Josh; Cox, George
Frederick; Hutchinson, Desmond John;
Maguire-Drew, Jordan Luke; Meyers, Remi
Christopher; Pring, Connor Mark; Rowe-
Hurst, Jack Michael; Tighe, Connor Jay;
Tilley, James Alexander David; Vose, Bailey
Jack; White, Benjamin William;

BRISTOL C (14)

AGARD, Kieran (F)   **155 47**
H: 5 10   W: 10 10   b.Newham 10-10-89
2006–07	Everton	0	0	
2007–08	Everton	0	0	
2008–09	Everton	0	0	
2009–10	Everton	1	0	
2010–11	Everton	0	0	**1 0**
2010–11	*Kilmarnock*	8	1	**8 1**
2010–11	*Peterborough U*	0	0	
2011–12	Yeovil T	29	6	**29 6**
2012–13	Rotherham U	30	6	
2013–14	Rotherham U	46	21	
2014–15	Rotherham U	2	0	**78 27**
2014–15	Bristol C	39	13	**39 13**

AYLING, Luke (D)   **212 6**
H: 5 11   W: 10 08   b.Lambeth 25-8-91
2009–10	Arsenal	0	0	
2009–10	*Yeovil T*	4	0	
2010–11	Yeovil T	37	0	
2011–12	Yeovil T	44	0	
2012–13	Yeovil T	39	0	
2013–14	Yeovil T	42	2	**166 2**
2014–15	Bristol C	46	4	**46 4**

BATTEN, Jack (M)   **0 0**
H: 6 3   W: 13 05   b.Bristol 22-12-95
2012–13	Bristol C	0	0	
2013–14	Bristol C	0	0	
2014–15	Bristol C	0	0	

BRYAN, Joe (D)   **86 9**
H: 5 7   W: 11 05   b.Bristol 17-9-93
2011–12	Bristol C	1	0	
2012–13	Bristol C	13	0	
2012–13	*Plymouth Arg*	10	1	**10 1**
2013–14	Bristol C	21	2	
2014–15	Bristol C	41	6	**76 8**

BURNS, Wes (F)   **52 7**
H: 5 8   W: 10 10   b.Cardiff 28-12-95
Internationals: Wales U21.
2012–13	Bristol C	6	0	
2013–14	Bristol C	20	1	
2014–15	Bristol C	3	1	**29 2**
2014–15	*Oxford U*	9	1	**9 1**
2014–15	*Cheltenham T*	14	4	**14 4**

CUNNINGHAM, Greg (D)   **133 4**
H: 6 0   W: 11 00   b.Galway 31-1-91
Internationals: Republic of Ireland U17, U21,
Full caps.
2008–09	Manchester C	0	0	
2009–10	Manchester C	2	0	
2010–11	Manchester C	0	0	
2010–11	*Leicester C*	13	0	**13 0**
2011–12	Manchester C	0	0	
2011–12	*Nottingham F*	27	0	**27 0**
2012–13	Manchester C	0	0	**2 0**
2012–13	Bristol C	30	1	
2013–14	Bristol C	37	1	
2014–15	Bristol C	24	2	**91 4**

EL-ABD, Adam (D)   **340 6**
H: 5 10   W: 13 05   b.Brighton 11-9-84
Internationals: Egypt Full caps.
2003–04	Brighton & HA	11	0	
2004–05	Brighton & HA	16	0	
2005–06	Brighton & HA	29	0	
2006–07	Brighton & HA	42	1	
2007–08	Brighton & HA	35	1	
2008–09	Brighton & HA	31	0	
2009–10	Brighton & HA	35	1	
2010–11	Brighton & HA	37	1	
2011–12	Brighton & HA	23	0	
2012–13	Brighton & HA	32	1	
2013–14	Brighton & HA	9	0	**300 5**
2013–14	Bristol C	14	0	
2014–15	Bristol C	2	0	**16 0**
2014–15	*Bury*	24	1	**24 1**

ELLIOTT, Wade (M)   **615 63**
H: 5 10   W: 10 03   b.Eastleigh 14-12-78
1999–2000	Bournemouth	12	3	
2000–01	Bournemouth	36	9	
2001–02	Bournemouth	46	8	
2002–03	Bournemouth	44	4	
2003–04	Bournemouth	39	3	
2004–05	Bournemouth	43	4	**220 31**
2005–06	Burnley	36	3	
2006–07	Burnley	42	4	
2007–08	Burnley	46	2	
2008–09	Burnley	42	4	
2009–10	Burnley	38	4	
2010–11	Burnley	44	2	
2011–12	Burnley	4	0	**252 19**

2011–12	Birmingham C	29	2	
2012–13	Birmingham C	44	6	
2013–14	Birmingham C	15	0	**88 8**
2013–14	*Bristol C*	19	3	
2014–15	Bristol C	36	2	**55 5**

EMMANUEL-THOMAS, Jay (M)   **193 40**
H: 5 9   W: 11 05   b.Forest Gate 27-12-90
Internationals: England U17, U19.
2008–09	Arsenal	0	0	
2009–10	Arsenal	0	0	
2009–10	*Blackpool*	11	1	**11 1**
2009–10	*Doncaster R*	14	5	**14 5**
2010–11	Arsenal	1	0	**1 0**
2010–11	*Cardiff C*	14	2	**14 2**
2011–12	Ipswich T	42	6	
2012–13	Ipswich T	29	2	**71 8**
2013–14	Bristol C	46	15	
2014–15	Bristol C	36	9	**82 24**

FIELDING, Frank (G)   **227 0**
H: 5 11   W: 12 00   b.Blackburn 4-4-88
Internationals: England U19, U21.
2006–07	Blackburn R	0	0	
2007–08	Blackburn R	0	.0	
2007–08	*Wycombe W*	36	0	**36 0**
2008–09	Blackburn R	0	0	
2008–09	*Northampton T*	12	0	**12 0**
2008–09	*Rochdale*	23	0	
2009–10	Blackburn R	0	0	
2009–10	*Rochdale*	18	0	**41 0**
2010–11	Blackburn R	0	0	
2010–11	Derby Co	16	0	
2011–12	Derby Co	44	0	
2012–13	Derby Co	16	0	**76 0**
2013–14	Bristol C	16	0	
2014–15	Bristol C	46	0	**62 0**

FLINT, Aiden (D)   **144 21**
H: 6 2   W: 12 00   b.Pinxton 11-7-89
Internationals: England C.
2010–11	Swindon T	3	0	
2011–12	Swindon T	32	2	
2012–13	Swindon T	29	2	**64 4**
2013–14	Bristol C	34	3	
2014–15	Bristol C	46	14	**80 17**

FREEMAN, Luke (F)   **170 24**
H: 6 0   W: 10 00   b.Dartford 22-3-92
Internationals: England U16, 17.
2007–08	Gillingham	1	0	**1 0**
2008–09	Arsenal	0	0	
2009–10	Arsenal	0	0	
2010–11	Arsenal	0	0	
2010–11	*Yeovil T*	13	2	**13 2**
2011–12	Arsenal	0	0	
2011–12	*Stevenage*	26	7	
2012–13	Stevenage	39	2	
2013–14	Stevenage	45	6	**110 15**
2014–15	Bristol C	46	7	**46 7**

GILABERT, Luis (M)   **0 0**
b. 23-10-95
| 2014–15 | Bristol C | 0 | 0 | |

HALL, Lewis (M)   **0 0**
b.Southall 27-6-95
2012–13	Bristol C	0	0	
2013–14	Bristol C	0	0	
2014–15	Bristol C	0	0	

LEMONHEIGH-EVANS, Connor (F) 0 0
b. 24-1-97
Internationals: Wales U17.
| 2013–14 | Bristol C | 0 | 0 | |
| 2014–15 | Bristol C | 0 | 0 | |

LITTLE, Mark (D)   **259 4**
H: 6 1   W: 12 10   b.Worcester 20-8-88
Internationals: England U19.
2005–06	Wolverhampton W	0	0	
2006–07	Wolverhampton W	26	0	
2007–08	Wolverhampton W	1	0	
2007–08	*Northampton T*	17	0	
2008–09	Wolverhampton W	0	0	
2008–09	*Northampton T*	9	0	**26 0**
2009–10	Wolverhampton W	0	0	**27 0**
2009–10	*Chesterfield*	12	0	**12 0**
2009–10	Peterborough U	9	0	
2010–11	Peterborough U	35	0	
2011–12	Peterborough U	35	1	
2012–13	Peterborough U	40	1	
2013–14	Peterborough U	38	1	**157 3**
2014–15	Bristol C	37	1	**37 1**

MAFUTA, Gus (M)
H: 5 10   W: 11 01   b.Clevedon 28-8-94
| 2013–14 | Bristol C | 0 | 0 | |
| 2014–15 | Bristol C | 0 | 0 | |

MORRELL, Joe (M)   0   0
H: 5 3   W: 11 04   b.Ipswich 3-1-97
Internationals: Wales U17, U19.
2013–14   Bristol C   0   0
2014–15   Bristol C   0   0

MURPHY, Billy (M)   0   0
b. 22-12-95
Internationals: Republic of Ireland U19.
2014–15   Bristol C   0   0

OSBORNE, Karleigh (D)   207   8
H: 6 2   W: 12 04   b.Southall 19-3-88
2004–05   Brentford   1   0
2005–06   Brentford   1   0
2006–07   Brentford   21   0
2007–08   Brentford   29   1
2008–09   Brentford   23   4
2009–10   Brentford   19   0
2010–11   Brentford   42   1
2011–12   Brentford   25   0   161   6
2012–13   Millwall   13   1
2013–14   Millwall   1   0   14   1
2013–14   Bristol C   27   1
2014–15   Bristol C   1   0   28   1
2014–15   Colchester U   4   0   4   0

PACK, Marlon (M)   227   18
H: 6 2   W: 11 09   b.Portsmouth 25-3-91
2008–09   Portsmouth   0   0
2009–10   Portsmouth   0   0
2009–10   Wycombe W   8   0   8   0
2009–10   Dagenham & R   17   1   17   1
2010–11   Portsmouth   1   0   1   0
2010–11   Cheltenham T   38   2
2011–12   Cheltenham T   43   5
2012–13   Cheltenham T   43   7
2013–14   Cheltenham T   0   0   124   14
2013–14   Bristol C   43   0
2014–15   Bristol C   34   3   77   3

REID, Bobby (M)   72   5
H: 5 7   W: 10 10   b.Bristol 1-3-93
2010–11   Bristol C   1   0
2011–12   Bristol C   0   0
2011–12   Cheltenham T   1   0   1   0
2012–13   Bristol C   4   1
2012–13   Oldham Ath   7   0   7   0
2013–14   Bristol C   24   1
2014–15   Bristol C   2   0   31   2
2014–15   Plymouth Arg   33   3   33   3

RICHARDS, Dave (G)   0   0
b.Abergavenny 31-12-93
2013–14   Cardiff C   0   0
2014–15   Bristol C   0   0
2014–15   Bristol C   0   0

SMITH, Korey (M)   192   5
H: 5 9   W: 11 01   b.Hatfield 31-1-91
2008–09   Norwich C   2   0
2009–10   Norwich C   37   4
2010–11   Norwich C   28   0
2011–12   Norwich C   0   0
2011–12   Barnsley   12   0   12   0
2012–13   Norwich C   0   0   67   4
2012–13   Yeovil T   17   0   17   0
2012–13   Oldham Ath   10   0
2013–14   Oldham Ath   42   1   52   1
2014–15   Bristol C   44   0   44   0

WAGSTAFF, Scott (M)   192   24
H: 5 10   W: 10 03   b.Maidstone 31-3-90
2007–08   Charlton Ath   2   0
2008–09   Charlton Ath   7   0
2008–09   Bournemouth   5   0   5   0
2009–10   Charlton Ath   30   4
2010–11   Charlton Ath   40   8
2011–12   Charlton Ath   34   4
2012–13   Charlton Ath   9   1   117   17
2012–13   Leyton Orient   0   0   7   0
2013–14   Bristol C   37   5
2014–15   Bristol C   26   2   63   7

WILBRAHAM, Aaron (F)   461   109
H: 6 3   W: 12 04   b.Knutsford 21-10-79
1997–98   Stockport Co   7   1
1998–99   Stockport Co   26   0
1999–2000   Stockport Co   26   4
2000–01   Stockport Co   36   12
2001–02   Stockport Co   21   3
2002–03   Stockport Co   15   7
2003–04   Stockport Co   41   8   172   35
2004–05   Hull C   19   2   19   2
2004–05   Oldham Ath   4   2   4   2
2005–06   Milton Keynes D   31   4
2005–06   Bradford C   5   1   5   1
2006–07   Milton Keynes D   32   7
2007–08   Milton Keynes D   35   10
2008–09   Milton Keynes D   33   16

2009–10   Milton Keynes D   35   10
2010–11   Milton Keynes D   10   2   176   49
2010–11   Norwich C   12   1
2011–12   Norwich C   11   1   23   2
2012–13   Crystal Palace   21   0
2013–14   Crystal Palace   4   0   25   0
2014–15   Bristol C   37   18   37   18

WILLIAMS, Derrick (D)   88   3
H: 5 11   W: 11 11   b.Waterford 17-1-93
Internationals: Republic of Ireland U19, U21.
2009–10   Aston Villa   0   0
2010–11   Aston Villa   0   0
2011–12   Aston Villa   0   0
2012–13   Aston Villa   1   0   1   0
2013–14   Bristol C   43   1
2014–15   Bristol C   44   2   87   3

WYNTER, Jordan (M)   19   1
H: 6 1   W: 11 11   b.Redbridge 24-11-93
2012–13   Arsenal   0   0
2013–14   Bristol C   3   0
2014–15   Bristol C   0   0   3   0
2014–15   Cheltenham T   16   1   16   1

Players retained or with offer of contract
Bishop-Wisdom, Marley Lyndon; Fry, Thomas Owain; Last, Benjamin Frederick; Vyner, Zachary George Onyeao.

Scholars
Alexander, Jack Curtis; Andrews, Jake; Chilekwa, Elijah; Difford, James Mark; Harper, Ashley Stephen; Harris, Charlie; Kellow, George Rogan; Long, Matthew Terence; Mattis, Matthew David; McNulty, Joseph Michael; Moss, Harvey; Selman, Joseph Andrew; Spalding, Henry Lee; Withey, Ben Stephen; Wollacott, Joseph Luke.

BURNLEY (15)

ANDERSON, Thomas (M)   8   0
H: 6 4   W: 13 01   b.Burnley 2-9-93
2012–13   Burnley   0   0
2013–14   Burnley   0   0
2014–15   Burnley   0   0
2014–15   Carlisle U   8   0   8   0

ARFIELD, Scott (M)   286   30
H: 5 10   W: 10 01   b.Livingston 1-11-88
Internationals: Scotland U19, U21, B.
2007–08   Falkirk   35   3
2008–09   Falkirk   37   7
2009–10   Falkirk   36   3   108   13
2010–11   Huddersfield T   40   4
2011–12   Huddersfield T   35   2
2012–13   Huddersfield T   21   1   96   7
2013–14   Burnley   45   8
2014–15   Burnley   37   2   82   10

BARNES, Ashley (F)   233   56
H: 6 0   W: 12 00   b.Bath 30-10-89
Internationals: Austria U20.
2006–07   Plymouth Arg   0   0
2007–08   Plymouth Arg   0   0
2008–09   Plymouth Arg   15   1
2009–10   Torquay U   6   0   6   0
2009–10   Brighton & HA   7   1   22   2
2009–10   Brighton & HA   6   0
2010–11   Brighton & HA   42   18
2011–12   Brighton & HA   43   11
2012–13   Brighton & HA   34   8
2013–14   Brighton & HA   22   5   149   46
2013–14   Burnley   21   3
2014–15   Burnley   35   5   56   8

BOYD, George (M)   347   76
H: 5 10   W: 11 07   b.Chatham 2-10-85
Internationals: Scotland B, Full caps.
2006–07   Peterborough U   20   6
2007–08   Peterborough U   46   12
2008–09   Peterborough U   46   9
2009–10   Peterborough U   32   9
2009–10   Nottingham F   6   1   6   1
2010–11   Peterborough U   43   15
2011–12   Peterborough U   45   7
2012–13   Peterborough U   31   6   263   64
2012–13   Hull C   13   4
2013–14   Hull C   29   2
2014–15   Hull C   1   0   43   6
2014–15   Burnley   35   5   35   5

CISAK, Aleksander (G)   100   0
H: 6 3   W: 14 11   b.Krakow 19-5-89
Internationals: Australia U20.
2006–07   Leicester C   0   0

2007–08   Leicester C   0   0
2008–09   Leicester C   0   0
2009–10   Leicester C   0   0
2010–11   Accrington S   21   0   21   0
2011–12   Oldham Ath   38   0
2012–13   Oldham Ath   10   0   48   0
2012–13   Portsmouth   1   0   1   0
2013–14   Burnley   1   0
2014–15   Burnley   0   0   1   0
2014–15   York C   10   0   10   0
2014–15   Leyton Orient   19   0   19   0

CONLAN, Luke (D)   0   0
H: 5 11   W: 11 05   b.Portaferry 31-10-94
Internationals: Northern Ireland U21.
2011–12   Burnley   0   0
2012–13   Burnley   0   0
2013–14   Burnley   0   0
2014–15   Burnley   0   0

DUFF, Michael (D)   519   19
H: 6 1   W: 11 08   b.Belfast 11-1-78
Internationals: Northern Ireland B, Full caps.
1999–2000   Cheltenham T   31   2
2000–01   Cheltenham T   39   5
2001–02   Cheltenham T   45   3
2002–03   Cheltenham T   44   2
2003–04   Cheltenham T   42   0   201   12
2004–05   Burnley   42   0
2005–06   Burnley   41   0
2006–07   Burnley   44   2
2007–08   Burnley   8   1
2008–09   Burnley   27   1
2009–10   Burnley   11   0
2010–11   Burnley   28   1
2011–12   Burnley   31   0
2012–13   Burnley   24   1
2013–14   Burnley   41   1
2014–15   Burnley   21   0   318   7

DUMMIGAN, Cameron (D)   0   0
H: 5 11   W: 11 00   b. 2-6-96
Internationals: Northern Ireland U17, U19, U21.
2013–14   Burnley   0   0
2014–15   Burnley   0   0

GILCHRIST, Jason (F)   5   0
H: 5 10   W: 10 06   b.St Helens 17-12-94
2013–14   Burnley   0   0
2014–15   Burnley   0   0
2014–15   Accrington S   5   0   5   0

GILKS, Matthew (G)   362   0
H: 6 3   W: 13 12   b.Rochdale 4-6-82
Internationals: Scotland Full caps.
2000–01   Rochdale   3   0
2001–02   Rochdale   19   0
2002–03   Rochdale   20   0
2003–04   Rochdale   12   0
2004–05   Rochdale   30   0
2005–06   Rochdale   46   0
2006–07   Rochdale   46   0   176   0
2007–08   Norwich C   5   0
2008–09   Blackpool   5   0
2008–09   Shrewsbury T   4   0   4   0
2009–10   Blackpool   26   0
2010–11   Blackpool   18   0
2011–12   Blackpool   42   0
2012–13   Blackpool   45   0
2013–14   Blackpool   46   0   182   0
2014–15   Burnley   0   0

HEATON, Tom (G)   219   0
H: 6 1   W: 13 12   b.Chester 15-4-86
Internationals: England 16, U17, U18, U19, U21.
2003–04   Manchester U   0   0
2004–05   Manchester U   0   0
2005–06   Manchester U   0   0
2005–06   Swindon T   14   0   14   0
2006–07   Manchester U   0   0
2007–08   Manchester U   0   0
2008–09   Cardiff C   21   0
2009–10   Manchester U   0   0
2009–10   Rochdale   12   0   12   0
2009–10   Wycombe W   16   0   16   0
2010–11   Cardiff C   27   0
2011–12   Cardiff C   2   0   50   0
2012–13   Bristol C   43   0   43   0
2013–14   Burnley   46   0
2014–15   Burnley   38   0   84   0

HOWIESON, Cameron (M)   2   0
H: 5 9   W: 11 00   b.Dunedin 22-12-94
Internationals: New Zealand U17, U20, U23, Full caps.
2011–12   Doncaster R   2   0
2012–13   Doncaster R   0   0

Season	Club				
2012–13	Burnley	0	0		
2013–14	Burnley	0	0		
2014–15	Burnley	0	0	2	0

INGS, Danny (F)   **149 45**
H: 5 10 W: 11 07 b.Winchester 16-3-92
Internationals: England U21.

Season	Club				
2009–10	Bournemouth	0	0		
2010–11	Bournemouth	26	7		
2011–12	Bournemouth	1	0	27	7
2011–12	Burnley	15	3		
2012–13	Burnley	32	3		
2013–14	Burnley	40	21		
2014–15	Burnley	35	11	122	38

JONES, David (M)   **272 25**
H: 5 11 W: 10 10 b.Southport 4-11-84
Internationals: England U21.

Season	Club				
2003–04	Manchester U	0	0		
2004–05	Manchester U	0	0		
2005–06	Manchester U	0	0		
2005–06	Preston NE	24	3	24	3
2005–06	NEC Nijmegen	17	6	17	6
2006–07	Manchester U	0	0		
2006–07	Derby Co	28	6		
2007–08	Derby Co	14	1	42	7
2008–09	Wolverhampton W	34	4		
2009–10	Wolverhampton W	20	1		
2010–11	Wolverhampton W	12	1	66	6
2011–12	Wigan Ath	16	0		
2012–13	Wigan Ath	13	0	29	0
2012–13	*Blackburn R*	12	2	12	2
2013–14	Burnley	46	1		
2014–15	Burnley	36	0	82	1

JUTKIEWICZ, Lucas (F)   **259 53**
H: 6 1 W: 12 11 b.Southampton 20-3-89

Season	Club				
2005–06	Swindon T	5	0		
2006–07	Swindon T	33	5	38	5
2006–07	Everton	0	0		
2007–08	Everton	0	0		
2007–08	Plymouth Arg	3	0	3	0
2008–09	Everton	1	0		
2008–09	*Huddersfield T*	7	0	7	0
2009–10	Everton	0	0	1	0
2009–10	*Motherwell*	33	12	33	12
2010–11	Coventry C	42	9		
2011–12	Coventry C	25	9	67	18
2011–12	Middlesbrough	19	2		
2012–13	Middlesbrough	24	8		
2013–14	Middlesbrough	22	1	65	11
2013–14	*Bolton W*	20	7	20	7
2014–15	Burnley	25	0	25	0

KEANE, Michael (D)   **64 5**
H: 5 7 W: 12 11 b.Stockport 11-1-93
Internationals: Republic of Ireland U17.
England U19, U20, U21.

Season	Club				
2011–12	Manchester U	0	0		
2012–13	Manchester U	0	0		
2012–13	*Leicester C*	22	2	22	2
2013–14	Manchester U	0	0		
2013–14	*Derby Co*	7	0	7	0
2013–14	*Blackburn R*	13	3	13	3
2014–15	Manchester U	1	0	1	0
2014–15	Burnley	21	0	21	0

KIGHTLY, Michael (M)   **214 35**
H: 5 10 W: 10 10 b.Basildon 24-1-86
Internationals: England U21.

Season	Club				
2002–03	Southend U	1	0		
2003–04	Southend U	11	0		
2004–05	Southend U	1	0	13	0
From Grays Ath.					
2006–07	Wolverhampton W	24	8		
2007–08	Wolverhampton W	21	4		
2008–09	Wolverhampton W	38	8		
2009–10	Wolverhampton W	9	0		
2010–11	Wolverhampton W	4	0		
2011–12	Wolverhampton W	18	3		
2011–12	*Watford*	12	3	12	3
2012–13	Wolverhampton W	0	0	114	23
2012–13	Stoke C	22	3		
2013–14	Stoke C	0	0	22	3
2013–14	*Burnley*	36	5		
2014–15	Burnley	17	1	53	6

LAFFERTY, Danny (D)   **111 8**
H: 6 0 W: 12 08 b.Derry 1-4-89
Internationals: Northern Ireland U17, U19,
U21, B, Full caps.

Season	Club				
2009–10	Celtic	0	0		
2009–10	*Ayr U*	14	1	14	1
2010	Derry C	12	0		
2011	Derry C	34	7	46	7
2011–12	Burnley	5	0		
2012–13	Burnley	24	0		
2013–14	Burnley	10	0		

Season	Club				
2014–15	Burnley	1	0	40	0
2014–15	*Rotherham U*	11	0	11	0

LONG, Kevin (D)   **98 4**
H: 6 3 W: 13 01 b.Cork 18-8-90

Season	Club				
2009	Cork C	16	0	16	0
2009–10	Burnley	0	0		
2010–11	Burnley	0	0		
2010–11	*Accrington S*	15	0		
2011–12	Burnley	0	0		
2011–12	*Accrington S*	24	4	39	4
2011–12	*Rochdale*	16	0	16	0
2012–13	Burnley	14	0		
2012–13	*Portsmouth*	5	0	5	0
2013–14	Burnley	7	0		
2014–15	Burnley	1	0	22	0

MARNEY, Dean (M)   **329 19**
H: 5 10 W: 11 09 b.Barking 31-1-84
Internationals: England U21.

Season	Club				
2002–03	Tottenham H	0	0		
2002–03	*Swindon T*	9	0	9	0
2003–04	Tottenham H	3	0		
2003–04	*QPR*	2	0	2	0
2004–05	Tottenham H	5	2		
2004–05	*Gillingham*	3	0	3	0
2005–06	Tottenham H	0	0	8	2
2005–06	*Norwich C*	13	0	13	0
2006–07	Hull C	37	2		
2007–08	Hull C	41	6		
2008–09	Hull C	31	0		
2009–10	Hull C	16	1	125	9
2009–10	Burnley	0	0		
2010–11	Burnley	36	3		
2011–12	Burnley	37	0		
2012–13	Burnley	38	2		
2013–14	Burnley	38	3		
2014–15	Burnley	20	0	169	8

MEE, Ben (D)   **136 3**
H: 5 11 W: 11 09 b.Sale 21-9-89
Internationals: England U19, U20, U21.

Season	Club				
2007–08	Manchester C	0	0		
2008–09	Manchester C	0	0		
2009–10	Manchester C	0	0		
2010–11	Manchester C	0	0		
2010–11	*Leicester C*	15	0	15	0
2011–12	Manchester C	0	0		
2011–12	*Burnley*	31	0		
2012–13	Burnley	19	1		
2013–14	Burnley	38	0		
2014–15	Burnley	33	2	121	3

O'NEILL, Luke (D)   **43 1**
H: 6 0 W: 11 04 b.Slough 20-8-91
Internationals: England U17.

Season	Club				
2009–10	Leicester C	1	0	1	0
2009–10	*Tranmere R*	4	0	4	0
From Kettering T (loan), Mansfield T					
2012–13	Burnley	1	0		
2013–14	Burnley	0	0		
2013–14	*York C*	15	1	15	1
2013–14	*Southend U*	1	0	1	0
2014–15	Burnley	0	0	1	0
2014–15	*Scunthorpe U*	13	0	13	0
2014–15	*Leyton Orient*	8	0	8	0

REID, Steven (M)   **343 27**
H: 6 0 W: 12 07 b.Kingston 10-3-81
Internationals: England U16. Republic of
Ireland U21, Full caps.

Season	Club				
1997–98	Millwall	1	0		
1998–99	Millwall	25	0		
1999–2000	Millwall	21	0		
2000–01	Millwall	37	7		
2001–02	Millwall	35	5		
2002–03	Millwall	20	6	139	18
2003–04	Blackburn R	16	0		
2004–05	Blackburn R	28	2		
2005–06	Blackburn R	34	4		
2006–07	Blackburn R	3	0		
2007–08	Blackburn R	24	0		
2008–09	Blackburn R	4	0		
2009–10	Blackburn R	4	0	113	6
2009–10	*QPR*	2	0	2	0
2009–10	*WBA*	10	1		
2010–11	WBA	23	1		
2011–12	WBA	22	1		
2012–13	WBA	11	0		
2013–14	WBA	16	0	82	3
2014–15	Burnley	7	0	7	0

SHACKELL, Jason (D)   **384 12**
H: 6 4 W: 13 06 b.Stevenage 27-9-83

Season	Club				
2002–03	Norwich C	2	0		
2003–04	Norwich C	6	0		
2004–05	Norwich C	11	0		
2005–06	Norwich C	17	0		
2006–07	Norwich C	43	3		
2007–08	Norwich C	39	0		
2008–09	Norwich C	15	0	133	3
2008–09	Wolverhampton W	12	0		
2009–10	Wolverhampton W	0	0	12	0
2009–10	*Doncaster R*	21	1	21	1
2010–11	Barnsley	44	3		
2011–12	Barnsley	0	0	44	3
2011–12	*Derby Co*	46	1	46	1
2012–13	Burnley	44	2		
2013–14	Burnley	46	2		
2014–15	Burnley	38	0	128	4

SORDELL, Marvin (F)   **153 33**
H: 5 9 W: 12 06 b.Pinner 17-2-91
Internationals: England U20, U21. Great
Britain.

Season	Club				
2009–10	Watford	6	1		
2009–10	*Tranmere R*	8	1	8	1
2010–11	Watford	43	12		
2011–12	Watford	26	8	75	21
2011–12	Bolton W	3	0		
2012–13	Bolton W	22	4		
2013–14	Bolton W	0	0	25	4
2013–14	*Charlton Ath*	31	7	31	7
2014–15	Burnley	14	0	14	0

TAYLOR, Matthew (D)   **517 64**
H: 5 11 W: 12 03 b.Oxford 27-11-81
Internationals: England U21, B.

Season	Club				
1998–99	Luton T	0	0		
1999–2000	Luton T	41	4		
2000–01	Luton T	45	1		
2001–02	Luton T	43	11	129	16
2002–03	Portsmouth	35	7		
2003–04	Portsmouth	30	0		
2004–05	Portsmouth	32	1		
2005–06	Portsmouth	34	6		
2006–07	Portsmouth	35	8		
2007–08	Portsmouth	13	1	179	23
2007–08	Bolton W	16	3		
2008–09	Bolton W	34	10		
2009–10	Bolton W	37	8		
2010–11	Bolton W	36	2	123	23
2011–12	West Ham U	28	1		
2012–13	West Ham U	28	1		
2013–14	West Ham U	20	0	76	2
2014–15	Burnley	10	0	10	0

TRIPPIER, Keiran (D)   **212 6**
H: 5 10 W: 11 00 b.Bury 19-9-90
Internationals: England U18, U19, U20, U21.

Season	Club				
2007–08	Manchester C	0	0		
2008–09	Manchester C	0	0		
2009–10	Manchester C	0	0		
2009–10	*Barnsley*	3	0		
2010–11	Manchester C	0	0		
2010–11	*Barnsley*	39	2	42	2
2011–12	Manchester C	0	0		
2011–12	*Burnley*	46	3		
2012–13	Burnley	45	0		
2013–14	Burnley	41	1		
2014–15	Burnley	38	0	170	4

ULVESTAD, Fredrik (M)   **108 14**
H: 6 0 W: 12 06 b.Alesund 19-5-92

Season	Club				
2010	Aalesund	0	0		
2011	Aalesund	24	2		
2012	Aalesund	25	2		
2013	Aalesund	27	7		
2014	Aalesund	29	3	106	14
2014–15	Burnley	2	0	2	0

VOKES, Sam (F)   **243 54**
H: 6 1 W: 13 10 b.Lymington 21-10-89
Internationals: Wales U21, Full caps.

Season	Club				
2006–07	Bournemouth	8	1		
2007–08	Bournemouth	41	12	54	16
2008–09	Wolverhampton W	36	6		
2009–10	*Leeds U*	8	1	8	1
2009–10	Wolverhampton W	5	0		
2010–11	Wolverhampton W	2	0		
2010–11	*Bristol C*	1	0	1	0
2010–11	*Sheffield U*	6	1	6	1
2010–11	*Norwich C*	4	1	4	1
2011–12	Wolverhampton W	4	0		
2011–12	*Burnley*	9	2		
2011–12	*Brighton & HA*	14	3	14	3
2012–13	Wolverhampton W	0	0	47	6
2012–13	Burnley	46	4		
2013–14	Burnley	39	20		
2014–15	Burnley	15	0	109	26

WALLACE, Ross (M)   **319 33**
H: 5 6 W: 9 12 b.Dundee 23-5-85
Internationals: Scotland U18, U19, U21, B,
Full caps.

Season	Club				
2001–02	Celtic	0	0		
2002–03	Celtic	0	0		
2003–04	Celtic	8	1		

2004–05	Celtic	16	0		
2005–06	Celtic	11	0		
2006–07	Celtic	2	0	37	1
2006–07	Sunderland	32	6		
2007–08	Sunderland	21	2		
2008–09	Sunderland	0	0	53	8
2008–09	Preston NE	39	5		
2009–10	Preston NE	41	7	80	12
2010–11	Burnley	40	3		
2011–12	Burnley	44	5		
2012–13	Burnley	36	3		
2013–14	Burnley	14	0		
2014–15	Burnley	15	1	149	12

WARD, Stephen (D) 347 24
H: 5 11 W: 12 02 b.Dublin 20-8-85
Internationals: Republic of Ireland U20, U21, B, Full caps.

2003	Bohemians	6	0		
2004	Bohemians	16	2		
2005	Bohemians	29	7		
2006	Bohemians	21	2	72	11
2006–07	Wolverhampton W	18	3		
2007–08	Wolverhampton W	29	0		
2008–09	Wolverhampton W	42	0		
2009–10	Wolverhampton W	22	0		
2010–11	Wolverhampton W	34	1		
2011–12	Wolverhampton W	38	3		
2012–13	Wolverhampton W	39	2		
2013–14	Wolverhampton W	0	0	222	9
2013–14	Brighton & HA	44	4	44	4
2014–15	Burnley	9	0	9	0

Players retained or with offer of contract
Frost, Jamie Peter; Hewitt, Steven Daniel; Nizic, Danijel.

Scholars
Aghayere, Nosakhare Tony; Bianga, Andreas Ntuntumuna; Crawford, Jamal; Dixon, Vashiko Tanaka; Dolling, Joshua Jordan; El-Fitouri, Hamam Abdel Hakim; Hill, Christian Stephen; Hobson, Shaun Jermaine; Jackson, Bradley Allen; Lowe, Nathan Patrick; Massanka, Ntumba; Metz, Khius; Mitchell, Conor; Norvock, Lewis; Nugent, Andrew; Whitmore, Alexander James; Wilson, Brandon James.

BURTON ALB (16)

AKINS, Lucas (F) 214 30
H: 5 10 W: 11 07 b.Huddersfield 25-2-89

2006–07	Huddersfield T	2	0		
2007–08	Huddersfield T	3	0	5	0
2008–09	Hamilton A	1	0		
2008–09	Partick Thistle	9	1	9	1
2009–10	Hamilton A	0	0	11	0
2010–11	Tranmere R	33	2		
2011–12	Tranmere R	44	5	77	7
2012–13	Stevenage	46	10		
2013–14	Stevenage	31	3	77	13
2014–15	Burton Alb	35	9	35	9

ANTOINE-CURIER, Mickael (F) 233 90
H: 6 0 W: 12 00 b.Orsay 5-3-83
Internationals: Guadeloupe Full caps.

2000–01	Preston NE	0	0		
2001–02	Nottingham F	0	0		
2002–03	Nottingham F	0	0		
2002–03	Brentford	11	3	11	3
2003–04	Oldham Ath	8	2	8	2
2003–04	Kidderminster H	1	0	1	0
2003–04	Rochdale	8	1	8	1
2003–04	Sheffield W	1	0	1	0
2003–04	Notts Co	1	4	1	4
2003–04	Grimsby T	5	0	5	0
2004	Vard Haugesund	9	5		
2005	Vard Haugesund	28	28	37	33
2006	FK Haugesund	34	6		
2007	FK Haugesund	15	7	39	15
2007–08	Hibernian	13	3	13	3
2009–10	Hamilton A	26	7		
2010–11	Hamilton A	13	4		
2011–12	Ethnikos Achnas	8	0	8	0
2012	Felda U	20	13	20	13
2013	Atyrau	12	0	12	0
2014–15	Hamilton A	22	8	61	19
2014–15	Burton Alb	5	0	5	0

AUSTIN, Sam (F) 1 0
b. 19-12-96

| 2014–15 | Burton Alb | 1 | 0 | 1 | 0 |

BEAVON, Stuart (F) 217 43
H: 5 7 W: 10 10 b.Reading 5-5-84

2008–09	Wycombe W	8	0		
2009–10	Wycombe W	25	3		
2010–11	Wycombe W	37	3		
2011–12	Wycombe W	43	21		
2012–13	Wycombe W	2	1	115	28
2012–13	Preston NE	31	6		
2013–14	Preston NE	27	3	58	9
2014–15	Burton Alb	44	6	44	6

BELL, Lee (M) 317 14
H: 5 11 W: 12 04 b.Alsager 26-1-83

2000–01	Crewe Alex	0	0		
2001–02	Crewe Alex	0	0		
2002–03	Crewe Alex	17	1		
2003–04	Crewe Alex	3	0		
2004–05	Crewe Alex	17	0		
2005–06	Crewe Alex	17	2		
2006–07	Crewe Alex	0	0		
2007–08	Mansfield T	23	1	23	1
2008–09	Macclesfield T	41	1		
2009–10	Macclesfield T	42	2	83	3
2010–11	Crewe Alex	45	1		
2011–12	Crewe Alex	30	0	129	4
2012–13	Burton Alb	43	4		
2013–14	Burton Alb	34	1		
2014–15	Burton Alb	5	1	82	6

CANSDELL-SHERRIFF, Shane (D) 423 25
H: 5 11 W: 11 08 b.Sydney 10-11-82
Internationals: Australia U17, U23.

1999–2000	Leeds U	0	0		
2000–01	Leeds U	0	0		
2001–02	Leeds U	0	0		
2002–03	Leeds U	0	0		
2002–03	Rochdale	3	0		
2003–04	Aarhus	29	4		
2004–05	Aarhus	26	2		
2005–06	Aarhus	27	1	82	7
2006–07	Tranmere R	43	3		
2007–08	Tranmere R	44	3	87	6
2008–09	Shrewsbury T	31	2		
2009–10	Shrewsbury T	41	1		
2010–11	Shrewsbury T	41	2		
2011–12	Shrewsbury T	37	4	150	9
2012–13	Preston NE	15	1		
2012–13	Rochdale	17	0	20	0
2013–14	Preston NE	0	0	15	1
2013–14	Burton Alb	32	0		
2014–15	Burton Alb	37	2	69	2

DOYLE, Joe (M) 0 0
b. 14-10-95

| 2013–14 | Burton Alb | 0 | 0 | | |
| 2014–15 | Burton Alb | 0 | 0 | | |

EDWARDS, Phil (D) 355 31
H: 5 8 W: 11 03 b.Bootle 8-11-85

2005–06	Wigan Ath	0	0		
2006–07	Accrington S	33	1		
2007–08	Accrington S	31	1		
2008–09	Accrington S	46	0		
2009–10	Accrington S	46	8		
2010–11	Accrington S	44	13	200	23
2011–12	Stevenage	22	0	22	0
2011–12	Rochdale	3	0		
2012–13	Rochdale	44	0	47	0
2013–14	Rochdale	41	2		
2014–15	Burton Alb	45	6	86	8

EL KHAYATI, Abdenasser (F) 45 15
H: 6 1 W: 11 11 b.7-2-89

2008–09	Den Bosh	8	0	8	0
2009–10	Dan Bosh	2	0	2	0
2010–11	Breda	0	0		
2012–13	Olympiacos	0	0		
2013–14	Kozakken Boys	17	12	17	12
2014–15	Burton Alb	18	3	18	3

HARNESS, Marcus (M) 21 0
H: 6 0 W: 11 00 b.1-8-94

| 2013–14 | Burton Alb | 3 | 0 | | |
| 2014–15 | Burton Alb | 18 | 0 | 21 | 0 |

KNOWLES, Dominic (F) 39 3
H: 5 9 W: 11 05 b.Accrington 13-2-92

2010–11	Burnley	0	0		
2011–12	Burnley	0	0		
2013–14	Burton Alb	28	3		
2014–15	Burton Alb	11	0	39	3

LYNESS, Dean (G) 37 0
H: 6 3 W: 11 12 b.Birmingham 20-7-91
Internationals: England U17.

2012–13	Burton Alb	15	0		
2013–14	Burton Alb	21	0		
2014–15	Burton Alb	1	0	37	0

MALETIC, Stefan (D) 55 4
H: 6 5 W: 12 00 b.Belgrade 9-4-87

2009–10	Frem	5	1	5	1
2010–11	FC Oss	9	0		
2011–12	Kozara Gradiska	12	0	12	0
2012–13	Celik Zenica	19	1	19	1
2013–14	Stuttgart K	2	0	2	0
2014–15	Achilles '29	8	2	8	2
2014–15	Burton Alb	0	0		

MAYNARD, Kelvin (D) 156 6
H: 5 11 W: 13 01 b.Paramaribo 29-5-87

2006–07	Volendam	4	0		
2007–08	Volendam	35	0		
2008–09	Volendam	18	0		
2009–10	Volendam	25	0	82	0
2010–11	Olhanense	0	0		
2011–12	Kecskemeti	8	0	8	0
2012–13	Emmen	29	4	29	4
2013–14	Antwerp	27	1	27	1
2014–15	Burton Alb	10	1	10	1

McCRORY, Damien (M) 219 8
H: 6 2 W: 12 10 b.Limerick 22-2-90
Internationals: Republic of Ireland U18, U19.

2008–09	Plymouth Arg	0	0		
2008–09	Port Vale	12	0		
2009–10	Plymouth Arg	0	0		
2009–10	Port Vale	5	0	17	0
2009–10	Grimsby T	10	0	10	0
2009–10	Dagenham & R	20	0		
2010–11	Dagenham & R	23	0		
2011–12	Dagenham & R	33	1	76	1
2012–13	Burton Alb	42	1		
2013–14	Burton Alb	40	1		
2014–15	Burton Alb	34	5	116	7

McGURK, Adam (F) 150 25
H: 5 9 W: 12 13 b.Larne 24-1-89
Internationals: Northern Ireland U21.

2005–06	Aston Villa	0	0		
2006–07	Aston Villa	0	0		
2007–08	Aston Villa	0	0		
2008–09	Aston Villa	0	0		
2009–10	Aston Villa	0	0		

From Hednesford T.

2010–11	Tranmere R	21	3		
2011–12	Tranmere R	31	4		
2012–13	Tranmere R	27	3	79	10
2013–14	Burton Alb	34	9		
2014–15	Burton Alb	37	6	71	15

McLAUGHLIN, Jon (G) 170 0
H: 6 2 W: 13 00 b.Edinburgh 9-9-87

2008–09	Bradford C	0	0		
2009–10	Bradford C	7	0		
2010–11	Bradford C	25	0		
2011–12	Bradford C	23	0		
2012–13	Bradford C	23	0		
2013–14	Bradford C	46	0	125	0
2014–15	Burton Alb	45	0	45	0

MOUSINHO, John (M) 282 20
H: 6 1 W: 12 07 b.Hounslow 30-4-86

2005–06	Brentford	7	0		
2006–07	Brentford	34	0		
2007–08	Brentford	23	2	64	2
2008–09	Wycombe W	34	2		
2009–10	Wycombe W	39	1	73	3
2010–11	Stevenage	38	7		
2011–12	Stevenage	19	3		
2012–13	Preston NE	24	1		
2013–14	Preston NE	2	0	26	1
2013–14	Gillingham	4	1	4	1
2013–14	Stevenage	16	1	73	11
2014–15	Burton Alb	42	2	42	2

PALMER, Matthew (M) 75 4
H: 5 10 W: 12 06 b.Derby 1-8-93

2012–13	Burton Alb	2	0		
2013–14	Burton Alb	40	0		
2014–15	Burton Alb	33	4	75	4

PHILLIPS, Jimmy (M) 121 3
H: 5 7 W: 10 00 b.Stoke 20-9-89

2008–09	Stoke C	0	0		
2009–10	Burton Alb	24	1		
2010–11	Burton Alb	23	0		
2011–12	Burton Alb	33	0		
2012–13	Burton Alb	33	2		
2014–15	Burton Alb	1	0	121	3

SHARPS, Ian (D) 513 18
H: 6 3 W: 14 07 b.Warrington 23-10-80

1998–99	Tranmere R	0	0		
1999–2000	Tranmere R	0	0		
2000–01	Tranmere R	29	0		
2001–02	Tranmere R	30	3		
2002–03	Tranmere R	27	1		
2003–04	Tranmere R	44	1		
2004–05	Tranmere R	39	1	170	6
2005–06	Rotherham U	38	2		
2007–08	Rotherham U	33	2		

2008–09	Rotherham U	45	4		
2009–10	Rotherham U	44	0		
2010–11	Shrewsbury T	43	1		
2011–12	Shrewsbury T	43	1	86	2
2012–13	Rotherham U	23	1	183	9
2012–13	Burton Alb	16	0		
2013–14	Burton Alb	39	1		
2014–15	Burton Alb	19	0	74	1

SLADE, Liam (D) 6 0
H: 6 3 W: 12 08 b. 14-5-95

2013–14	Burton Alb	0	0		
2014–15	Burton Alb	6	0	6	0

TAFT, George (D) 33 1
H: 5 9 W: 11 09 b.Leicester 29-7-93
Internationals: England U18, U19.

2010–11	Leicester C	0	0		
2011–12	Leicester C	0	0		
2012–13	Leicester C	0	0		
2013–14	Leicester C	0	0		
2013–14	York C	3	0	3	0
2014–15	Burton Alb	30	1	30	1

WEIR, Robbie (M) 181 10
H: 5 9 W: 11 07 b.Belfast 9-12-88
Internationals: Northern Ireland U18, U19, U21, B.

2007–08	Sunderland	0	0		
2008–09	Sunderland	0	0		
2009–10	Sunderland	0	0		
2010–11	Sunderland	0	0		
2010–11	Tranmere R	18	0		
2011–12	Tranmere R	39	3	57	3
2012–13	Burton Alb	42	5		
2013–14	Burton Alb	41	2		
2014–15	Burton Alb	40	0	124	7

Players retained or with offer of contract
Fenton, Nicholas Leonard; Myers-Harness, Marcus Anthony.

Scholars
Allen, Shay Courtney; Austin, Samuel Joseph; Coggins, Brad Michael William; Dinanga, Nyambu Marcus; Fox, Benjamin Jake; Gatter, Charlie Anthony; Hornby, Charles Benjamin; Murfin, Matthew Adam; O'Brien, Jack Christopher; Pearson, Michael Thomas; Richards, Christopher Crushi; Sejdic, Mirza; Shelton, Mark John; Smith, Brad; Thorpe, Ashley Nicholas; Troke, Lewis Andrew Harry.

BURY (17)

ADAMS, Nicky (F) 328 30
H: 5 10 W: 11 00 b.Bolton 16-10-86
Internationals: Wales U21.

2005–06	Bury	15	1		
2006–07	Bury	19	1		
2007–08	Bury	43	12		
2008–09	Leicester C	12	0		
2008–09	Rochdale	14	1		
2009–10	Leicester C	18	0	30	0
2009–10	Leyton Orient	6	0	6	0
2010–11	Brentford	7	0	7	0
2010–11	Rochdale	30	0		
2011–12	Rochdale	41	4	85	5
2012–13	Crawley T	46	8		
2013–14	Crawley T	24	1	70	9
2013–14	Rotherham U	15	1	15	1
2013–14	Bury	0	0		
2014–15	Bury	38	1	115	15

BURGESS, Scott (M) 1 0
H: 5 10 W: 11 00 b. 27-6-96

2013–14	Bury	1	0		
2014–15	Bury	0	0	1	0

CAMERON, Nathan (D) 124 6
H: 6 2 W: 12 04 b.Birmingham 21-11-91
Internationals: England U20.

2009–10	Coventry C	0	0		
2010–11	Coventry C	25	0		
2011–12	Coventry C	14	0		
2012–13	Coventry C	9	0	48	0
2012–13	Northampton T	3	0	3	0
2013–14	Bury	27	4		
2014–15	Bury	46	2	73	6

DUDLEY, Anthony (F) 3 0
H: 5 10 W: 11 00 b.Manchester 3-1-96

2013–14	Bury	2	0		
2014–15	Bury	1	0	3	0

ETUHU, Kelvin (F) 136 6
H: 5 11 W: 11 02 b.Kano 30-5-88

2005–06	Manchester C	0	0		
2006–07	Manchester C	0	0		
2006–07	Rochdale	4	2	4	2
2007–08	Manchester C	6	1		
2007–08	Leicester C	4	0	4	0
2008–09	Manchester C	4	0		
2009–10	Manchester C	0	0		
2009–10	Cardiff C	16	0	16	0
2010–11	Manchester C	0	0	10	1
2011–12	Kavala	0	0		
2011–12	Portsmouth	13	1		
2012–13	Portsmouth	0	0	13	1
2012–13	Barnsley	26	0		
2013–14	Barnsley	20	0	46	0
2014–15	Bury	43	2	43	2

HOPE, Hallam (F) 34 6
H: 5 10 W: 12 00 b.Manchester 17-3-94
Internationals: England U16, U17, U18, U19.

2010–11	Everton	0	0		
2011–12	Everton	0	0		
2012–13	Everton	0	0		
2013–14	Northampton T	3	1	3	1
2013–14	Bury	8	5		
2014–15	Everton	0	0		
2014–15	Sheffield W	4	0	4	0
2014–15	Bury	19	0	27	5

HUSSEY, Chris (D) 153 3
H: 5 10 W: 10 03 b.Hammersmith 2-1-89

2009–10	Coventry C	8	0		
2010–11	Coventry C	11	0		
2010–11	Crewe Alex	0	0		
2011–12	Coventry C	29	0		
2012–13	Coventry C	10	0	58	0
2012–13	AFC Wimbledon	19	0		
2013–14	AFC Wimbledon	0	0	19	0
2013–14	Burton Alb	27	1	27	1
2013–14	Bury	11	2		
2014–15	Bury	38	0	49	2

JONES, Craig (M) 211 31
H: 5 7 W: 10 13 b.Chester 20-3-87

2004–05	Airbus UK	2	2		
2005–06	Airbus UK	7	6	9	8
2007–08	Rhyl	27	8		
2008–09	Rhyl	14	2	41	10
2008–09	Connah's Quay	12	0	12	0
2009–10	New Saints FC	26	7	26	7
2010–11	Port Talbot	14	1		
2011–12	Port Talbot	7	0	21	1
2012–13	Bury	25	1		
2013–14	Bury	37	1		
2014–15	Bury	40	3	102	5

LAINTON, Robert (G) 35 0
H: 6 2 W: 12 06 b.Ashton-under-Lyne 12-10-89

2009–10	Bolton W	0	0		
2010–11	Bolton W	0	0		
2011–12	Bolton W	0	0		
2012–13	Bolton W	0	0		
2013–14	Bury	4	0		
2013–14	Burton Alb	14	0	14	0
2014–15	Bury	17	0	21	0

LOWE, Ryan (F) 527 161
H: 5 10 W: 12 08 b.Liverpool 18-9-78

2000–01	Shrewsbury T	30	4		
2001–02	Shrewsbury T	38	7		
2002–03	Shrewsbury T	39	9		
2003–04	Shrewsbury T	0	0		
2004–05	Shrewsbury T	30	3	137	23
2004–05	Chester C	8	4		
2005–06	Chester C	32	10		
2005–06	Crewe Alex	0	0		
2006–07	Crewe Alex	37	8		
2007–08	Crewe Alex	27	4	64	12
2007–08	Stockport Co	4	0	4	0
2008–09	Chester C	45	16	85	30
2009–10	Bury	39	18		
2010–11	Bury	46	27		
2011–12	Bury	5	4		
2011–12	Sheffield W	26	8		
2012–13	Sheffield W	0	0	26	8
2012–13	Milton Keynes D	42	11	42	11
2013–14	Tranmere R	45	19	45	19
2013–14	Bury	0	0		
2014–15	Bury	34	9	124	58

MAYOR, Danny (M) 163 15
H: 6 0 W: 11 12 b.Leyland 18-10-90

2008–09	Preston NE	0	0		
2008–09	Tranmere R	3	0	3	0
2009–10	Preston NE	7	0		
2010–11	Preston NE	21	0		
2011–12	Preston NE	36	2		
2012–13	Preston NE	0	0	64	2
2012–13	Sheffield W	8	0		
2012–13	Southend U	5	0	5	0
2013–14	Sheffield W	0	0	8	0
2013–14	Bury	39	5		
2014–15	Bury	44	8	83	13

McNULTY, Jim (D) 207 5
H: 6 1 W: 12 00 b.Runcorn 13-2-85
Internationals: Scotland U17, U19.

2006–07	Macclesfield T	15	0		
2007–08	Macclesfield T	19	1	34	1
2007–08	Stockport Co	11	0		
2008–09	Stockport Co	26	1	37	1
2008–09	Brighton & HA	5	1		
2009–10	Brighton & HA	8	0		
2009–10	Scunthorpe U	3	0		
2010–11	Brighton & HA	0	0	13	1
2010–11	Scunthorpe U	6	0	9	0
2011–12	Barnsley	44	2		
2012–13	Barnsley	12	0		
2013–14	Barnsley	0	0	56	2
2013–14	Tranmere R	12	0	12	0
2013–14	Bury	21	0		
2014–15	Bury	25	0	46	0

MILLS, Pablo (D) 302 6
H: 5 9 W: 11 04 b.Birmingham 27-5-84
Internationals: England U16, U18, U19.

2002–03	Derby Co	16	0		
2003–04	Derby Co	19	0		
2004–05	Derby Co	22	0		
2005–06	Derby Co	1	0	58	0
2005–06	Milton Keynes D	16	1	16	1
2005–06	Walsall	14	0	14	0
2006–07	Rotherham U	31	1		
2007–08	Rotherham U	33	1		
2008–09	Rotherham U	35	1		
2009–10	Rotherham U	37	0		
2011–12	Crawley T	21	2	21	2
2013–14	Rotherham U	10	0	146	3
2013–14	Bury	21	0		
2014–15	Bury	18	0	39	0
2014–15	Cheltenham T	8	0	8	0

NARDIELLO, Daniel (F) 328 101
H: 5 11 W: 11 04 b.Coventry 22-10-82
Internationals: Wales Full caps.

1999–2000	Manchester U	0	0		
2000–01	Manchester U	0	0		
2001–02	Manchester U	0	0		
2002–03	Manchester U	0	0		
2003–04	Manchester U	0	0		
2003–04	Swansea C	4	0	4	0
2003–04	Barnsley	16	7		
2004–05	Manchester U	0	0		
2004–05	Barnsley	28	7		
2005–06	Barnsley	34	5		
2006–07	Barnsley	30	9		
2007–08	QPR	8	0	8	0
2007–08	Barnsley	11	2	119	30
2008–09	Blackpool	2	0		
2008–09	Hartlepool U	12	3	12	3
2009–10	Blackpool	5	0	7	0
2009–10	Bury	6	4		
2009–10	Oldham Ath	0	2	2	0
2010–11	Exeter C	30	10		
2011–12	Exeter C	36	9	66	19
2012–13	Rotherham U	36	19		
2013–14	Rotherham U	9	5	45	24
2013–14	Bury	27	11		
2014–15	Bury	32	10	65	25

O'BRIEN, Keil (D) 0 0
H: 6 4 W: 13 03 b. 29-6-92

2014–15	Bury	0	0	

PLATT, Clive (F) 617 110
H: 6 4 W: 12 07 b.Wolverhampton 27-10-77

1995–96	Walsall	4	2		
1996–97	Walsall	1	0		
1997–98	Walsall	20	1		
1998–99	Walsall	7	1		
1999–2000	Walsall	0	0	32	4
1999–2000	Rochdale	41	9		
2000–01	Rochdale	43	8		
2001–02	Rochdale	43	7		
2002–03	Rochdale	42	6	169	30
2003–04	Notts Co	19	3	19	3
2003–04	Peterborough U	18	2		
2004–05	Peterborough U	19	4	37	6
2004–05	Milton Keynes D	20	3		
2005–06	Milton Keynes D	40	6		
2006–07	Milton Keynes D	42	18	102	27
2007–08	Colchester U	41	8		
2008–09	Colchester U	43	10		
2009–10	Colchester U	41	7	125	25
2010–11	Coventry C	34	3		

2011–12	Coventry C	33	4	67	7
2012–13	Northampton T	36	5		
2013–14	Northampton T	11	1	47	6
2013–14	Bury	17	2		
2014–15	Bury	2	0	19	2

POOLE, James (F)   112 15
H: 5 11 W: 12 05 b.Stockport 20-3-90

2008–09	Manchester C	0	0		
2009–10	Manchester C	0	0		
2009–10	Bury	9	0		
2010–11	Manchester C	0	0		
2010–11	Hartlepool U	3	1		
2011–12	Hartlepool U	27	7		
2012–13	Hartlepool U	36	4		
2013–14	Hartlepool U	33	3	99	15
2014–15	Bury	4	0	13	0

RILEY, Joe (D)   42 1
H: 6 0 W: 12 05 b.Salford 13-10-91

2011–12	Bolton W	3	0		
2012–13	Bolton W	0	0		
2013–14	Bolton W	0	0		
2014–15	Bolton W	0	0	3	0
2014–15	Oxford U	22	0	22	0
2014–15	Bury	17	1	17	1

RUDDY, Jack (G)   0 0
b. 18-5-97

2014–15	Bury	0	0

SEDGWICK, Chris (M)   576 36
H: 5 11 W: 11 10 b.Sheffield 24-8-80

1997–98	Rotherham U	4	0		
1998–99	Rotherham U	33	4		
1999–2000	Rotherham U	38	5		
2000–01	Rotherham U	21	2		
2001–02	Rotherham U	44	1		
2002–03	Rotherham U	43	1		
2003–04	Rotherham U	40	2		
2004–05	Rotherham U	20	2	243	17
2004–05	Preston NE	24	3		
2005–06	Preston NE	46	4		
2006–07	Preston NE	43	1		
2007–08	Preston NE	42	2		
2008–09	Preston NE	40	1		
2009–10	Preston NE	34	1	229	12
2010–11	Sheffield W	33	4		
2011–12	Sheffield W	10	1	43	5
2012–13	Scunthorpe U	4	0	4	0
2013–14	Bury	37	2		
2014–15	Bury	20	0	57	2

SHAW, Brayden (F)   0 0

2014–15	Bury	0	0

SOARES, Tom (M)   298 32
H: 6 0 W: 11 04 b.Reading 10-7-86
Internationals: England U20, U21.

2003–04	Crystal Palace	3	0		
2004–05	Crystal Palace	22	0		
2005–06	Crystal Palace	44	1		
2006–07	Crystal Palace	37	3		
2007–08	Crystal Palace	39	6		
2008–09	Crystal Palace	4	1	149	11
2008–09	Stoke C	7	0		
2008–09	Charlton Ath	11	1	11	1
2009–10	Stoke C	0	0		
2009–10	Sheffield W	25	2	25	2
2010–11	Stoke C	0	0		
2011–12	Stoke C	0	0	7	0
2011–12	Hibernian	10	2	10	2
2012–13	Bury	23	2		
2013–14	Bury	30	6		
2014–15	Bury	43	8	96	16

THOMPSON, Joe (M)   173 18
H: 6 0 W: 9 07 b.Rochdale 5-3-89

2005–06	Rochdale	1	0		
2006–07	Rochdale	13	0		
2007–08	Rochdale	11	1		
2008–09	Rochdale	30	5		
2009–10	Rochdale	36	6		
2010–11	Rochdale	32	2		
2011–12	Rochdale	16	1		
2012–13	Tranmere R	19	1		
2012–13	Rochdale	7	0	147	15
2013–14	Tranmere R	6	2	25	3
2014–15	Bury	1	0	1	0

TUTTE, Andrew (M)   173 16
H: 5 9 W: 10 10 b.Huyton 21-9-90
Internationals: England U19, U20.

2007–08	Manchester C	0	0		
2008–09	Manchester C	0	0		
2009–10	Manchester C	0	0		
2010–11	Manchester C	0	0		
2010–11	Rochdale	7	0		
2010–11	Shrewsbury T	2	0	2	0
2010–11	Yeovil T	15	2	15	2
2011–12	Rochdale	40	1		
2012–13	Rochdale	37	7		
2013–14	Rochdale	11	2	95	10
2013–14	Bury	19	1		
2014–15	Bury	42	3	61	4

Players retained or with offer of contract
Rose, Daniel Antony.

Scholars
Bourne, Robert; Burgess, Scott Andrew; Crosdale, Raquarn Malique; Durham, Jake Robert; Foulds, Matthew Colin; Gibson, Samuel James; Kimmins, Rowan Michael David; McCarthy, Jamie Paul; Miller, George; Mohamed, Khalid Abdi; Poscha, Marcus Anthony; Potter, Benjamin Oliver; Ruddy, John Robert; Shaw, Brayden Lewis; Williams, Rhys Frederick; Wordingham, Henry Robert.

CAMBRIDGE U (18)

AKINTUNDE, James (M)   1 0
b. 29-3-96

2014–15	Cambridge U	1	0	1	0

ARNOLD, Nathan (M)   62 8
H: 5 7 W: 10 03 b.Mansfield 26-7-87
Internationals: England C.

2005–06	Mansfield T	8	1		
2006–07	Mansfield T	22	3		
2007–08	Mansfield T	32	4	62	8
2014–15	Cambridge U	0	0		

AUSTIN, Mitch (M)   1 0
H: 6 2 W: 12 06 b.Sydney 3-4-91

2014–15	Cambridge U	1	0	1	0

BIRD, Ryan (F)   50 11
H: 6 4 W: 12 06 b.Slough 15-11-87

2013–14	Portsmouth	18	3		
2014–15	Portsmouth	2	0	20	3
2014–15	Cambridge U	24	6	24	6
2014–15	Hartlepool U	6	2	6	2

BONNER, Tom (D)   4 0
H: 6 0 W: 11 07 b.London 6-2-88
Internationals: Scotland U19.

2005–06	Northampton T	0	0		
2014–15	Cambridge U	4	0	4	0

CHADWICK, Luke (M)   406 34
H: 5 11 W: 11 08 b.Cambridge 18-11-80
Internationals: England U18, U21.

1998–99	Manchester U	0	0		
1999–2000	Manchester U	0	0		
2000–01	Manchester U	16	2		
2001–02	Manchester U	8	0		
2002–03	Manchester U	1	0		
2002–03	Reading	15	1	15	1
2003–04	Manchester U	0	0	25	2
2003–04	Burnley	36	5	36	5
2004–05	West Ham U	32	1		
2005–06	West Ham U	0	0	32	1
2005–06	Stoke C	36	2		
2006–07	Stoke C	15	3	51	5
2006–07	Norwich C	4	1		
2007–08	Norwich C	13	1		
2008–09	Norwich C	0	0	17	2
2008–09	Milton Keynes D	24	6		
2009–10	Milton Keynes D	40	2		
2010–11	Milton Keynes D	44	0		
2011–12	Milton Keynes D	42	2		
2012–13	Milton Keynes D	36	6		
2013–14	Milton Keynes D	22	1	208	17
2014–15	Cambridge U	22	1	22	1

CHAMPION, Tom (M)   38 0
b.London 15-5-86

2014–15	Cambridge U	38	0	38	0

CHIEDOZIE, Jordan (M)   6 0
H: 5 11 W: 11 06 b.Owerri 5-5-90

2013–14	Bournemouth	0	0		
2013–14	Bournemouth	0	0		
2014–15	Cambridge U	6	0	6	0

COULSON, Josh (D)   46 1
H: 6 3 W: 11 11 b.Cambridge 28-1-89

2014–15	Cambridge U	46	1	46	1

CUNNINGTON, Adam (F)   16 2
H: 6 3 W: 12 11 b.Leighton Buzzard 7-10-87

2011–12	Dagenham & R	9	0	9	0

From Alfreton T, Tamworth.

2014–15	Cambridge U	7	2	7	2

DIALLO, Issaga (D)   110 1
b. 26-1-87

2009–10	Locarno	27	0		
2010–11	Locarno	29	0	56	0
2011–12	Servette	18	0		
2012–13	Servette	16	0	34	0
2013–14	Kaposvar	12	0	12	0
2014–15	Cambridge U	8	1	8	1

DONALDSON, Ryan (F)   53 5
H: 5 9 W: 11 00 b.Newcastle 1-5-91
Internationals: England U17, U19.

2008–09	Newcastle U	0	0		
2009–10	Newcastle U	2	0		
2010–11	Newcastle U	0	0		
2010–11	Hartlepool U	12	0	12	0
2011–12	Newcastle U	0	0	2	0
2011–12	Tranmere R	1	0	1	0
2014–15	Cambridge U	38	5	38	5

DUNK, Harrison (M)   32 2
b. 25-10-90

2014–15	Cambridge U	32	2	32	2

DUNN, Chris (G)   152 0
H: 6 5 W: 13 11 b.Brentwood 23-10-87

2006–07	Northampton T	0	0		
2007–08	Northampton T	1	0		
2008–09	Northampton T	29	0		
2009–10	Northampton T	29	0		
2010–11	Northampton T	39	0	98	0
2011–12	Coventry C	2	0		
2012–13	Coventry C	1	0		
2013–14	Coventry C	0	0	3	0
2013–14	Yeovil T	8	0	8	0
2014–15	Cambridge U	43	0	43	0

ELLIOTT, Tom (F)   110 16
H: 6 3 W: 12 00 b.Hunslet 9-11-90
Internationals: England U16, U18.

2006–07	Leeds U	3	0		
2007–08	Leeds U	0	0		
2008–09	Leeds U	0	0		
2008–09	Macclesfield T	6	0	6	0
2009–10	Leeds U	0	0		
2009–10	Bury	16	1	16	1
2010–11	Leeds U	0	0	3	0
2010–11	Rotherham U	6	0	6	0
2011–12	Hamilton A	7	0	7	0
2011–12	Stockport Co	42	7	42	7
2014–15	Cambridge U	30	8	30	8

FOY, Matt (F)   0 0

2014–15	Cambridge U	0	0

GAFFNEY, Rory (M)   0 0
H: 6 0 W: 12 04 b. 23-10-89

2014–15	Cambridge U	0	0

HANCOCK, Mitch (D)   0 0
b. 23-10-94

2014–15	Cambridge U	0	0

HORNE, Ryan (M)   0 0

2014–15	Cambridge U	0	0

HUGHES, Liam (F)   30 3
H: 6 4 W: 13 08 b.Rotherham 10-8-92

2014–15	Cambridge U	30	3	30	3

HUNT, Johnny (M)   9 1
H: 5 11 W: 10 03 b.Liverpool 23-8-90
Internationals: England C.

2014–15	Cambridge U	9	1	9	1

HURST, Liam (M)   4 0
H: 5 10 W: 11 09 b. 2-10-94

2014–15	Cambridge U	4	0	4	0

LANZONI, Matteo (D)   103 2
H: 6 0 W: 12 05 b.Como 18-7-88
Internationals: Italy U19.

2007–08	Sampdoria	0	0		
2008–09	Sampdoria	0	0		
2008–09	Bari	0	0		
2009–10	Sampdoria	0	0		
2009–10	Mantova	20	1	20	1
2010–11	Sampdoria	0	0		
2010–11	Portogruaro	18	0	18	0
2011–12	Sampdoria	0	0		
2011–12	Foggia	24	0	24	0
2012–13	Sampdoria	0	0		
2012–13	Carrarese	21	0	21	0
2013–14	Oldham Ath	10	1	10	1
2013–14	Yeovil T	6	0	6	0
2014–15	Cambridge U	3	0	3	0
2014–15	Hartlepool U	1	0	1	0

LOWE, Matt (M)   0 0
b. 11-3-96

2014–15	Cambridge U	0	0

MILLER, Ian (D)   8   0
H: 6 2   W: 12 02   b.Colchester 23-11-83

2014–15	Cambridge U	8	0	8	0

MORRISSEY, Gearoid (M)   8   0
H: 5 11   W: 12 11   b.Cork 17-11-91

2014–15	Cambridge U	8	0	8	0

NELSON, Michael (D)   518   35
H: 6 2   W: 13 03   b.Gateshead 15-3-82

2000–01	Bury	2	1		
2001–02	Bury	31	2		
2002–03	Bury	39	5	72	8
2003–04	Hartlepool U	40	3		
2004–05	Hartlepool U	43	1		
2005–06	Hartlepool U	43	2		
2006–07	Hartlepool U	42	1		
2007–08	Hartlepool U	45	2		
2008–09	Hartlepool U	46	5	259	14
2009–10	Norwich C	31	3		
2010–11	Norwich C	8	2	39	5
2010–11	Scunthorpe U	20	0		
2011–12	Scunthorpe U	10	1	30	1
2011–12	Kilmarnock	15	1		
2012–13	Kilmarnock	21	1	36	2
2012–13	Bradford C	13	0	13	0
2013–14	Hibernian	34	2		
2014–15	Hibernian	2	0	36	2
2014–15	Cambridge U	33	3	33	3

NORRIS, Will (G)   3   0
H: 6 5   W: 11 09   b.Royston 12-7-93

2014–15	Cambridge U	3	0	3	0

SAM-YORKE, Delano (F)   2   0
H: 6 1   W: 13 05   b. 20-1-89

2014–15	Cambridge U	2	0	2	0

SIMPSON, Robbie (F)   216   24
H: 6 1   W: 11 11   b.Poole 15-3-85

2007–08	Coventry C	28	1		
2008–09	Coventry C	33	3	61	4
2009–10	Huddersfield T	13	0		
2010–11	Huddersfield T	0	0		
2010–11	Brentford	27	4	27	4
2011–12	Huddersfield T	0	0	13	0
2011–12	Oldham Ath	29	6		
2012–13	Oldham Ath	37	2		
2013–14	Oldham Ath	0	0	66	8
2013–14	Leyton Orient	14	0	14	0
2014–15	Cambridge U	35	8	35	8

SLEW, Jordan (F)   73   7
H: 6 3   W: 12 11   b.Sheffield 7-9-92
Internationals: England U19.

2010–11	Sheffield U	7	2		
2011–12	Sheffield U	4	1	11	3
2011–12	Blackburn R	1	0		
2011–12	Stevenage	9	0	9	0
2012–13	Blackburn R	0	0		
2012–13	Oldham Ath	3	0	3	0
2012–13	Rotherham U	7	0	7	0
2013–14	Blackburn R	0	0		
2013–14	Ross Co	20	1	20	1
2014–15	Blackburn R	0	0	1	0
2014–15	Port Vale	9	2	9	2
2014–15	Cambridge U	13	1	13	1

TAIT, Richard (D)   37   0
H: 5 11   b.Gala Shields 2-12-89

2007–08	Nottingham F	0	0		
2008–09	Nottingham F	0	0		
2014–15	Cambridge U	37	0	37	0

TAYLOR, Bobby Joe (M)   7   0
b.Ashford 4-2-95

2014–15	Cambridge U	7	0	7	0

TAYLOR, Greg (D)   43   0
b.Bedford 15-1-90
Internationals: England C.

2008–09	Northampton T	0	0		
2014–15	Cambridge U	43	0	43	0

WHITTALL, Sam (M)   2   0
b. 5-10-93

2012–13	Wolverhampton W	0	0		
2013–14	Wolverhampton W	0	0		
2014–15	Cambridge U	2	0	2	0

Players retained or with offer of contract
Burns, Daniel Dene.

Scholars
Boddey, Owen; Brown, Jordan; Burniston,
Joshua Joseph; Chambers-Shaw, Jake; Jonas,
Romario Darnell; Jones, Francis Douglas;
Leavers, Justin; Mason, Dominic; Williams,
Dylan; Williams, Jordan.

CARDIFF C (19)

ADEYEMI, Tom (M)   166   11
H: 6 1   W: 12 04   b.Milton Keynes 24-10-91

2008–09	Norwich C	0	0		
2009–10	Norwich C	11	0		
2010–11	Norwich C	0	0		
2010–11	Bradford C	34	5	34	5
2011–12	Norwich C	0	0		
2011–12	Oldham Ath	36	2	36	2
2012–13	Norwich C	0	0	11	0
2012–13	Brentford	30	2	30	2
2013–14	Birmingham C	35	1	35	1
2014–15	Cardiff C	20	1	20	1

AMONDARAIN, Maximiliano (D)   0   0
H: 6 1   W: 12 05   b.Salto 22-1-93
Internationals: Uruguay U20.

2013–14	Cardiff C	0	0		
2014–15	Cardiff C	0	0		

BARNUM-BOBB, Jazzi (D)   0   0
b.Enfield 9-5-95

2014–15	Cardiff C	0	0		

BELL, Anthony (M)   0   0
b. 10-4-95

2014–15	Cardiff C	0	0		

BOWEN, Jaye (M)   0   0
b. 10-4-95

2014–15	Cardiff C	0	0		

BURGSTALLER, Guido (M)   202   38
H: 6 2   W: 12 00   b.Villach 29-4-89
Internationals: Austria Full caps.

2006–07	FC Karnten	4	1		
2007–08	FC Karnten	29	1	33	2
2008–09	Wiener Neustadt	26	7		
2009–10	Wiener Neustadt	30	0		
2010–11	Wiener Neustadt	25	5	81	12
2011–12	Rapid Vienna	23	7		
2012–13	Rapid Vienna	32	6		
2013–14	Rapid Vienna	30	11	85	24
2014–15	Cardiff C	3	0	3	0

Transferred to Nurnburg January 2015.

CALA, Juan (D)   78   11
H: 6 1   W: 12 03   b.Lebrija 26-11-89
Internationals: Spain U19.

2008–09	Sevilla	0	0		
2009–10	Sevilla	5	3		
2010–11	Sevilla	3	0		
2010–11	Cartagena	25	3	25	3
2011–12	Sevilla	8	1		
2011–12	AEK Athens	13	1	13	1
2012–13	Sevilla	10	0		
2013–14	Sevilla	9	1	32	5
2013–14	Cardiff C	7	2		
2014–15	Cardiff C	1	0	8	2

Transferred to Granada January 2015.

CONNOLLY, Matthew (D)   211   11
H: 6 1   W: 11 03   b.Barnet 24-9-87

2005–06	Arsenal	0	0		
2006–07	Arsenal	0	0		
2006–07	Bournemouth	5	1	5	1
2007–08	Arsenal	0	0		
2007–08	Colchester U	16	2	16	2
2007–08	QPR	20	0		
2008–09	QPR	35	0		
2009–10	QPR	19	2		
2010–11	QPR	36	0		
2011–12	QPR	6	0		
2011–12	Reading	6	0	6	0
2012–13	QPR	0	0	116	2
2012–13	Cardiff C	36	5		
2013–14	Cardiff C	3	0		
2014–15	Cardiff C	23	0	62	5
2014–15	Watford	6	1	6	1

DA SILVA, Fabio (D)   84   1
H: 5 8   W: 10 03   b.Rio de Janeiro 9-7-90
Internationals: Brazil U17, Full caps.

2008–09	Manchester U	0	0		
2009–10	Manchester U	5	0		
2010–11	Manchester U	11	1		
2011–12	Manchester U	5	0		
2012–13	Manchester U	5	0		
2012–13	QPR	21	0	21	0
2013–14	Manchester U	1	0	22	1
2013–14	Cardiff C	13	0		
2014–15	Cardiff C	28	0	41	0

DIKGACOI, Kagisho (M)   210   15
H: 5 11   W: 12 10   b.Brandfort 24-11-84
Internationals: South Africa Full caps.

2004–05	Bloemfontein YT	10	0	10	0
2005–06	Lamontville GA	9	0		

2006–07	Lamontville GA	25	0		
2007–08	Lamontville GA	23	4		
2008–09	Lamontville GA	23	4	80	8
2009–10	Fulham	12	0		
2010–11	Fulham	1	0	13	0
2010–11	Crystal Palace	13	1		
2011–12	Crystal Palace	27	2		
2012–13	Crystal Palace	39	4		
2013–14	Crystal Palace	26	0	105	7
2014–15	Cardiff C	2	0	2	0

DOYLE, Eoin (F)   218   77
H: 6 0   b. 12-3-88

2009	Sligo	15	3		
2010	Sligo	35	6		
2011	Sligo	34	20	84	29
2011–12	Hibernian	13	1		
2012–13	Hibernian	36	10	49	11
2013–14	Chesterfield	43	11		
2014–15	Chesterfield	26	21	69	32
2014–15	Cardiff C	16	5	16	5

ECUELE MANGA, Bruno (D)   204   11
H: 6 2   W: 11 11   b.Libreville 16-7-88
Internationals: Gabon Full caps.

2008–09	Angers	29	1		
2009–10	Angers	28	3	57	4
2010–11	Lorient	31	1		
2011–12	Lorient	32	2		
2012–13	Lorient	17	0		
2013–14	Lorient	35	1		
2014–15	Lorient	3	0	118	4
2014–15	Cardiff C	29	3	29	3

EIKREM, Magnus Wolff (M)   90   8
H: 5 8   W: 10 11   b.Molde 8-8-90
Internationals: Norway U17, U19, U21, Full caps.

2009–10	Manchester U	0	0		
2010–11	Manchester U	0	0		
2011	Molde	28	4		
2012	Molde	27	0		
2013	Molde	13	2	68	6
2013–14	Heerenveen	13	2	13	2
2013–14	Cardiff C	6	0		
2014–15	Cardiff C	3	0	9	0

Transferred to Malmo January 2015.

GABBIDON, Daniel (D)   364   12
H: 6 0   W: 13 05   b.Cwmbran 8-8-79
Internationals: Wales Youth, U21, Full caps.

1998–99	WBA	2	0		
1999–2000	WBA	18	0		
2000–01	WBA	0	0	20	0
2000–01	Cardiff C	43	3		
2001–02	Cardiff C	44	3		
2002–03	Cardiff C	24	0		
2003–04	Cardiff C	41	3		
2004–05	Cardiff C	45	1		
2005–06	West Ham U	32	0		
2006–07	West Ham U	18	0		
2007–08	West Ham U	10	0		
2008–09	West Ham U	0	0		
2009–10	West Ham U	10	0		
2010–11	West Ham U	26	0	96	0
2011–12	QPR	17	0	17	0
2012–13	Crystal Palace	0	0		
2013–14	Crystal Palace	23	1	33	2
2014–15	Cardiff C	1	0	198	10

GUERRA, Javi (F)   278   103
H: 5 11   W: 12 04   b.Velez-Malaga 15-3-82

2006–07	Valencia	2	0	2	0
2007–08	Granada	39	8	39	8
2008–09	Mallorca	0	0		
2008–09	Alaves	40	9	40	9
2009–10	Mallorca	0	0		
2009–10	Levante	37	12	37	12
2010–11	Valladolid	41	28	41	28
2011–12	Valladolid	36	17		
2012–13	Valladolid	30	8		
2013–14	Valladolid	37	16	103	41
2014–15	Cardiff C	3	0	3	0
2014–15	Malaga	13	5	13	5

GUNNARSSON, Aron (M)   278   24
H: 5 9   W: 11 00   b.Akureyri 22-9-89
Internationals: Iceland U17, U19, U21, Full caps.

2007–08	AZ	1	0	1	0
2008–09	Coventry C	40	1		
2009–10	Coventry C	40	1		
2010–11	Coventry C	42	4	122	6
2011–12	Cardiff C	42	5		
2012–13	Cardiff C	45	8		
2013–14	Cardiff C	23	1		
2014–15	Cardiff C	45	4	155	18

HARRIS, Kedeem (M)   43 2
H: 5 9   W: 10 08   b.Westminster 8-6-93

Season	Club				
2009–10	Wycombe W	0	0		
2010–11	Wycombe W	2	0		
2011–12	Wycombe W	17	0	19	0
2011–12	Cardiff C	0	0		
2012–13	Cardiff C	0	0		
2013–14	Cardiff C	0	0		
2013–14	*Brentford*	10	1	10	1
2014–15	Cardiff C	14	1	14	1

HEALEY, Rhys (M)   22 4
H: 5 8   W: 10 10   b.Manchester 6-12-94

2012–13	Cardiff C	0	0		
2013–14	Cardiff C	1	0		
2014–15	Cardiff C	0	0	1	0
2014–15	*Colchester U*	21	4	21	4

JAMES, Tom (D)   1 0
b.Leamington Spa 19-11-88
Internationals: Wales U19.

2013–14	Cardiff C	1	0		
2014–15	Cardiff C	0	0	1	0

JOHN, Declan (M)   41 0
H: 5 10   W: 11 10   b.Merthyr Tydfil 30-6-95
Internationals: Wales U17, U19, Full caps.

2010–11	Llanelli	1	0	1	0
2011–12	Afan Lido	5	0	5	0
2012–13	Cardiff C	0	0		
2013–14	Cardiff C	20	0		
2014–15	Cardiff C	6	0	26	0
2014–15	*Barnsley*	9	0	9	0

JOHNSON, Danny (F)   8 0
b. 28-2-93

2014–15	Cardiff C	0	0		
2014–15	*Tranmere R*	4	0	4	0
2014–15	*Stevenage*	4	0	4	0

JONES, Kenwyne (F)   324 81
H: 6 2   W: 13 06   b.Trinidad & Tobago 5-10-84
Internationals: Trinidad & Tobago Youth, U23, Full caps.

2004–05	Southampton	2	0		
2004–05	*Sheffield W*	7	7	7	7
2004–05	*Stoke C*	13	3		
2005–06	Southampton	34	4		
2006–07	Southampton	34	14		
2007–08	Southampton	1	1	71	19
2007–08	Sunderland	33	7		
2008–09	Sunderland	29	10		
2009–10	Sunderland	32	9	94	26
2010–11	Stoke C	34	9		
2011–12	Stoke C	21	1		
2012–13	Stoke C	26	3		
2013–14	Stoke C	7	0	101	16
2013–14	Cardiff C	11	1		
2014–15	Cardiff C	34	11	45	12
2014–15	*Bournemouth*	6	1	6	1

KENNEDY, Matthew (M)   56 1
H: 5 9   W: 10 02   b.Irvine 1-11-94
Internationals: Scotland U16, U17, U18, U19, U21.

2011–12	Kilmarnock	11	0		
2012–13	Kilmarnock	3	0	14	0
2012–13	Everton	0	0		
2013–14	Everton	0	0		
2013–14	*Tranmere R*	8	0	8	0
2013–14	*Milton Keynes D*	7	1	7	1
2014–15	Everton	0	0		
2014–15	*Hibernian*	13	0	13	0
2014–15	Cardiff C	14	0	14	0

KISS, Filip (M)   131 17
H: 6 1   W: 11 11   b.Dunajska 13-10-90
Internationals: Slovakia U19, U21, Full caps.

2009–10	Petrzalka	25	4	25	4
2010–11	Slovan Bratislava	29	6		
2011–12	Slovan Bratislava	1	0	30	6
2011–12	*Cardiff C*	26	1		
2012–13	Cardiff C	2	0		
2013–14	Cardiff C	0	0		
2013–14	*Ross Co*	17	6		
2014–15	Cardiff C	0	0	28	1
2014–15	*Ross Co*	31	0	48	6

LE FONDRE, Adam (F)   398 157
H: 5 9   W: 11 04   b.Stockport 2-12-86

2004–05	Stockport Co	20	4		
2005–06	Stockport Co	22	6		
2006–07	Stockport Co	21	7	63	17
2006–07	*Rochdale*	7	4		
2007–08	Rochdale	46	16		
2008–09	Rochdale	44	18		
2009–10	Rochdale	1	0	98	38
2009–10	Rotherham U	44	25		
2010–11	Rotherham U	45	23		
2011–12	Rotherham U	4	4	93	52
2011–12	Reading	32	12		
2012–13	Reading	34	12		
2013–14	Reading	38	15	104	39
2014–15	*Cardiff C*	23	3	23	3
2014–15	*Bolton W*	17	8	17	8

LEWIS, Joe (G)   226 0
H: 6 5   W: 12 10   b.Bungay 6-10-87
Internationals: England U16, U17, U19, U21.

2004–05	Norwich C	0	0		
2005–06	Norwich C	0	0		
2006–07	Norwich C	0	0		
2006–07	*Stockport Co*	5	0	5	0
2007–08	Norwich C	0	0		
2007–08	*Morecambe*	19	0	19	0
2008–09	Peterborough U	46	0		
2009–10	Peterborough U	43	0		
2010–11	Peterborough U	45	0		
2011–12	Peterborough U	11	0	167	0
2012–13	Cardiff C	0	0		
2013–14	Cardiff C	1	0		
2014–15	Cardiff C	0	0	1	0
2014–15	*Blackpool*	34	0	34	0

MACHEDA, Federico (F)   104 23
H: 6 0   W: 11 13   b.Rome 22-8-91
Internationals: Italy U16, U17, U19, U21.

2008–09	Manchester U	4	2		
2009–10	Manchester U	5	1		
2010–11	Manchester U	7	1		
2010–11	*Sampdoria*	14	0	14	0
2011–12	Manchester U	3	0		
2011–12	*QPR*	3	0	3	0
2012–13	Manchester U	0	0		
2012–13	*Stuttgart*	14	0	14	0
2013–14	Manchester U	0	0	19	4
2013–14	*Doncaster R*	15	3	15	3
2013–14	*Birmingham C*	18	10	18	10
2014–15	Cardiff C	21	6	21	6

MALONE, Scott (D)   159 12
H: 6 2   W: 11 11   b.Rowley Regis 25-3-91
Internationals: England U19.

2008–09	Wolverhampton W	0	0		
2008–09	*Ujpest*	7	1	7	1
2009–10	Wolverhampton W	0	0		
2009–10	*Southend U*	17	0	17	0
2010–11	Wolverhampton W	0	0		
2010–11	*Burton Alb*	22	1	22	1
2011–12	Wolverhampton W	0	0		
2011–12	*Bournemouth*	32	5	32	5
2012–13	Millwall	15	1		
2013–14	Millwall	33	3		
2014–15	Millwall	20	1	68	5
2014–15	Cardiff C	13	0	13	0

MARSHALL, David (G)   349 0
H: 6 3   W: 13 04   b.Glasgow 5-3-85
Internationals: Scotland Youth, U21, B, Full caps.

2003–04	Celtic	11	0		
2004–05	Celtic	18	0		
2005–06	Celtic	4	0		
2006–07	Celtic	2	0	35	0
2006–07	Norwich C	2	0		
2007–08	Norwich C	46	0		
2008–09	Norwich C	46	0	94	0
2008–09	Cardiff C	0	0		
2009–10	Cardiff C	43	0		
2010–11	Cardiff C	11	0		
2011–12	Cardiff C	45	0		
2012–13	Cardiff C	46	0		
2013–14	Cardiff C	37	0		
2014–15	Cardiff C	38	0	220	0

MASON, Joe (F)   155 36
H: 5 9   W: 11 11   b.Plymouth 13-5-91
Internationals: Republic of Ireland U19, U21.

2009–10	Plymouth Arg	19	3		
2010–11	Plymouth Arg	34	7	53	10
2011–12	Cardiff C	39	9		
2012–13	Cardiff C	28	6		
2013–14	Cardiff C	0	0		
2013–14	*Bolton W*	16	6		
2014–15	Cardiff C	7	1	74	16
2014–15	*Bolton W*	12	4	28	10

MAYNARD, Nicky (F)   236 84
H: 5 11   W: 11 00   b.Winsford 11-12-86

2005–06	Crewe Alex	1	1		
2006–07	Crewe Alex	31	16		
2007–08	Crewe Alex	27	14	59	31
2008–09	Bristol C	43	11		
2009–10	Bristol C	42	20		
2010–11	Bristol C	13	6		
2011–12	Bristol C	27	8	125	45
2011–12	West Ham U	14	2		
2012–13	West Ham U	0	0	14	2
2012–13	Cardiff C	4	1		
2013–14	Cardiff C	8	0		
2013–14	*Wigan Ath*	16	4	16	4
2014–15	Cardiff C	10	1	22	2

McNAUGHTON, Kevin (D)   452 5
H: 5 10   W: 10 06   b.Dundee 28-8-82
Internationals: Scotland B, Full caps.

1999–2000	Aberdeen	0	0		
2000–01	Aberdeen	33	0		
2001–02	Aberdeen	34	0		
2002–03	Aberdeen	22	1		
2003–04	Aberdeen	17	0		
2004–05	Aberdeen	35	2		
2005–06	Aberdeen	34	0	175	3
2006–07	Cardiff C	42	0		
2007–08	Cardiff C	35	1		
2008–09	Cardiff C	39	0		
2009–10	Cardiff C	21	0		
2010–11	Cardiff C	44	0		
2011–12	Cardiff C	42	0		
2012–13	Cardiff C	27	0		
2013–14	Cardiff C	5	0		
2013–14	*Bolton W*	13	1		
2014–15	Cardiff C	0	0	255	1
2014–15	*Bolton W*	9	0	22	1

MOORE, Simon (G)   85 0
H: 6 3   W: 12 02   b.Sandown 19-5-90
Internationals: Isle of Wight Full caps.

2009–10	Brentford	1	0		
2010–11	Brentford	10	0		
2011–12	Brentford	10	0		
2012–13	Brentford	43	0	64	0
2013–14	Cardiff C	0	0		
2013–14	*Bristol C*	11	0	11	0
2014–15	Cardiff C	10	0	10	0

MORRISON, Sean (D)   156 17
H: 6 4   W: 14 00   b.Plymouth 8-1-91

2007–08	Swindon T	2	0		
2008–09	Swindon T	20	1		
2009–10	Swindon T	9	1		
2009–10	*Southend U*	8	0	8	0
2010–11	Swindon T	19	4	50	6
2010–11	Reading	0	0		
2010–11	*Huddersfield T*	0	0		
2011–12	Reading	0	0		
2011–12	*Huddersfield T*	19	1	19	1
2012–13	Reading	16	2		
2013–14	Reading	21	1		
2014–15	Reading	1	1	38	4
2014–15	Cardiff C	41	6	41	6

NOONE, Craig (M)   207 20
H: 6 3   W: 12 07   b.Kirkby 17-11-87

2008–09	Plymouth Arg	21	1		
2009–10	Plymouth Arg	17	1		
2009–10	*Exeter C*	7	2	7	2
2010–11	Plymouth Arg	17	3	55	5
2010–11	Brighton & HA	23	2		
2011–12	Brighton & HA	33	2		
2012–13	Brighton & HA	3	0	59	4
2012–13	Cardiff C	32	7		
2013–14	Cardiff C	17	1		
2014–15	Cardiff C	37	1	86	9

NUGENT, Ben (D)   46 2
H: 6 1   W: 13 00   b.Street 28-11-93

2012–13	Cardiff C	12	1		
2013–14	Cardiff C	0	0		
2013–14	*Brentford*	0	0		
2013–14	*Peterborough U*	11	0	11	0
2014–15	Cardiff C	0	0	12	1
2014–15	*Yeovil T*	23	1	23	1

O'KEEFE, Stuart (M)   56 1
H: 5 8   W: 10 00   b.Eye 4-3-91

2008–09	Southend U	3	0		
2009–10	Southend U	7	0		
2010–11	Southend U	0	0	10	0
2010–11	Crystal Palace	4	0		
2011–12	Crystal Palace	13	0		
2012–13	Crystal Palace	5	0		
2013–14	Crystal Palace	12	1		
2014–15	Crystal Palace	2	0	36	1
2014–15	*Blackpool*	4	0	4	0
2014–15	Cardiff C	6	0	6	0

O'SULLIVAN, Tommy (M)   5 0
H: 5 9   W: 11 04   b.Mountain Ash 18-1-95
Internationals: Wales U17, U19, U21.

2012–13	Cardiff C	0	0		
2013–14	Cardiff C	0	0		
2014–15	Cardiff C	0	0		
2014–15	*Port Vale*	5	0	5	0

OSHILAJA, Adedeji (D) 33 1
H: 5 11 W: 11 10 b.Bermondsey 16-7-93

Season	Club				
2012–13	Cardiff C	0	0		
2013–14	Cardiff C	0	0		
2013–14	Newport Co	8	0	8	0
2013–14	Sheffield W	2	0	2	0
2014–15	Cardiff C	0	0		
2014–15	AFC Wimbledon	23	1	23	1

OWEN, Kane (D) 0 0
H: 5 11 W: 11 05 b.Cardiff 22-10-94

2014–15	Cardiff C	0	0		

PELTIER, Lee (D) 295 5
H: 5 10 W: 12 00 b.Liverpool 11-12-86
Internationals: England U18.

2004–05	Liverpool	0	0		
2005–06	Liverpool	0	0		
2006–07	Liverpool	0	0		
2006–07	Hull C	7	0	7	0
2007–08	Liverpool	0	0		
2007–08	Yeovil T	34	0		
2008–09	Yeovil T	35	1	69	1
2009–10	Huddersfield T	42	0		
2010–11	Huddersfield T	38	1		
2011–12	Leicester C	40	2		
2012–13	Leicester C	0	0	40	2
2012–13	Leeds U	41	0		
2013–14	Leeds U	25	1	66	1
2013–14	Nottingham F	7	0	7	0
2014–15	Huddersfield T	11	0	91	1
2014–15	Cardiff C	15	0	15	0

PILKINGTON, Anthony (M) 262 50
H: 5 11 W: 12 00 b.Blackburn 3-11-87
Internationals: Republic of Ireland U21, Full caps.

2006–07	Stockport Co	24	5		
2007–08	Stockport Co	29	6		
2008–09	Stockport Co	24	5	77	16
2008–09	Huddersfield T	16	2		
2009–10	Huddersfield T	43	7		
2010–11	Huddersfield T	31	10	90	19
2011–12	Norwich C	30	8		
2012–13	Norwich C	30	5		
2013–14	Norwich C	15	1	75	14
2014–15	Cardiff C	20	1	20	1

RALLS, Joe (M) 79 6
H: 5 10 W: 11 00 b.Farnborough 13-10-93
Internationals: England U19.

2011–12	Cardiff C	10	1		
2012–13	Cardiff C	4	0		
2013–14	Cardiff C	0	0		
2013–14	Yeovil T	37	3	37	3
2014–15	Cardiff C	28	2	42	3

REVELL, Alex (F) 385 73
H: 6 3 W: 13 00 b.Cambridge 7-7-83

2000–01	Cambridge U	4	0		
2001–02	Cambridge U	24	2		
2002–03	Cambridge U	9	0		
2003–04	Cambridge U	20	3	57	5

From Braintree T.

2006–07	Brighton & HA	38	7		
2007–08	Brighton & HA	21	6	59	13
2007–08	Southend U	8	0		
2008–09	Southend U	23	4		
2009–10	Southend U	3	0	34	4
2009–10	Swindon T	10	2	10	2
2009–10	Wycombe W	15	6	15	6
2010–11	Leyton Orient	39	13		
2011–12	Leyton Orient	5	0	44	13
2011–12	Rotherham U	40	10		
2012–13	Rotherham U	41	6		
2013–14	Rotherham U	45	8		
2014–15	Rotherham U	24	4	150	28
2014–15	Cardiff C	16	2	16	2

ROCHE, Tyler (M) 0 0
b. 15-9-95

2014–15	Cardiff C	0	0		

SOUTHAM, Macauley (M) 0 0
b. 2-2-96

2014–15	Cardiff C	0	0		

TURNER, Ben (D) 191 7
H: 6 4 W: 14 04 b.Birmingham 21-1-88
Internationals: England U19.

2005–06	Coventry C	1	0		
2006–07	Coventry C	1	0		
2006–07	Peterborough U	8	0	8	0
2006–07	Oldham Ath	1	0	1	0
2007–08	Coventry C	19	0		
2008–09	Coventry C	24	0		
2009–10	Coventry C	13	0		
2010–11	Coventry C	14	4	72	4
2011–12	Cardiff C	37	2		
2012–13	Cardiff C	31	1		
2013–14	Cardiff C	31	0		
2014–15	Cardiff C	11	0	110	3

TUTONDA, David (D) 12 2
b. 11-10-95

2014–15	Cardiff C	0	0		
2014–15	Newport Co	12	2	12	2

WATKINS, Curtis (D) 0 0
b. 11-9-95

2014–15	Cardiff C	0	0		

WHARTON, Theo (M) 0 0
b.Cwmbran 15-11-94
Internationals: Wales U17, U19, U21.

2011–12	Cardiff C	0	0		
2012–13	Cardiff C	0	0		
2013–14	Cardiff C	0	0		
2014–15	Cardiff C	0	0		

WHITTINGHAM, Peter (M) 414 73
H: 5 10 W: 9 13 b.Nuneaton 8-9-84
Internationals: England U20, U21.

2002–03	Aston Villa	4	0		
2003–04	Aston Villa	32	0		
2004–05	Aston Villa	13	1		
2004–05	Burnley	7	0	7	0
2005–06	Aston Villa	4	0		
2005–06	Derby Co	11	0	11	0
2006–07	Aston Villa	3	0	56	1
2006–07	Cardiff C	19	4		
2007–08	Cardiff C	41	5		
2008–09	Cardiff C	33	3		
2009–10	Cardiff C	41	20		
2010–11	Cardiff C	45	11		
2011–12	Cardiff C	46	12		
2012–13	Cardiff C	40	8		
2013–14	Cardiff C	32	3		
2014–15	Cardiff C	43	6	340	72

WICKHAM, Bradley (M) 0 0
b. 31-10-95
Internationals: Wales U19.

2014–15	Cardiff C	0	0		

WILSON, Ben (G) 0 0
H: 6 1 W: 11 09 b.Stanley 9-8-92

2010–11	Sunderland	0	0		
2011–12	Sunderland	0	0		
2013–14	Accrington S	0	0		
2013–14	Cardiff C	0	0		
2014–15	Cardiff C	0	0		

YORWERTH, Josh (D) 0 0
b. 1-1-95
Internationals: Wales U16, U19, U21.

2014–15	Cardiff C	0	0		

Players retained or with offer of contract
Evitt-Healey, Rhys; Mathurin-Harris, Kadeem Raymond; Rodriguez, Javier Guerra; Theopile-Catherine, Kevin; Velikonja, Etien.

Scholars
Abbruzzese, Rhys; Baker, Ashley Thomas; Bellamy, Ellis; Bird, Jamie Eric Jason; Burridge, Thomas Sean; Chappell-Smith, Aidan Paul; Humphries, Lloyd; Menayese, Elvis; Menayese, Rollin; Noor, Abdifatah Mohamed; Parry, Shane Thomas; Patten, Robbie; Pearson, Thomas James; Phipps, Elijah; Rees, Dylan Patrick James; Taylor, William Margam Raymond; Veale, Jamie Lawrence; Wakeman, Luke Oliver; Watkins, Jake Kristian; Williams, Samuel Jack Piotr.

CARLISLE U (20)

AMOO, David (F) 135 19
H: 5 10 W: 12 03 b.Southwark 23-4-91

2007–08	Liverpool	0	0		
2008–09	Liverpool	0	0		
2009–10	Liverpool	0	0		
2010–11	Liverpool	0	0		
2010–11	Milton Keynes D	3	0	3	0
2010–11	Hull C	7	1	7	1
2011–12	Liverpool	0	0		
2011–12	Bury	27	4	27	4
2012–13	Preston NE	17	0	17	0
2012–13	Tranmere R	11	1		
2013–14	Tranmere R	0	0	11	1
2013–14	Carlisle U	43	8		
2014–15	Carlisle U	27	5	70	13

ARCHIBALD-HENVILLE, Troy (D) 162 4
H: 6 2 W: 13 03 b.Newham 4-11-88

2007–08	Tottenham H	0	0		
2008–09	Tottenham H	0	0		
2008–09	Norwich C	0	0		
2008–09	Exeter C	19	0		
2009–10	Tottenham H	0	0		
2009–10	Exeter C	15	0		
2010–11	Exeter C	36	1		
2011–12	Exeter C	45	2	115	3
2012–13	Swindon T	5	0		
2013–14	Carlisle U	4	0		
2013–14	Swindon T	14	0	19	0
2014–15	Carlisle U	24	1	28	1

ASAMOAH, Derek (F) 390 69
H: 5 6 W: 10 04 b.Ghana 1-5-81
Internationals: Ghana Full caps.

2001–02	Northampton T	40	3		
2002–03	Northampton T	42	4		
2003–04	Northampton T	31	3	113	10
2004–05	Mansfield T	30	5	30	5
2004–05	Lincoln C	10	0		
2005–06	Lincoln C	25	2	35	2
2005–06	Chester C	17	8	17	8
2006–07	Shrewsbury T	39	10	39	10
2007–08	Nice	0	0		
2008–09	Hamilton A	3	0	3	0
2009–10	Lokomotiv Sofia	22	6		
2010–11	Lokomotiv Sofia	14	7	36	13
2011	Pohang Steelers	27	7		
2012	Pohang Steelers	30	6		
2013	Pohang Steelers	0	0	57	13
2013	Daegu	33	4	33	4
2014–15	Carlisle U	27	4	27	4

BECK, Mark (F) 66 7
H: 6 5 W: 12 08 b.Sunderland 2-2-94
Internationals: Scotland U19, U21.

2011–12	Carlisle U	2	0		
2012–13	Carlisle U	27	4		
2013–14	Carlisle U	10	0		
2014–15	Carlisle U	27	3	66	7

BROUGH, Patrick (M) 32 0
H: 5 8 b.Carlisle 20-2-96

2013–14	Carlisle U	3	0		
2014–15	Carlisle U	29	0	32	0

BUDDLE, Nathan (D) 3 0
H: 6 3 W: 13 11 b.Ashington 29-9-93

2012–13	Hartlepool U	0	0		
2014–15	Carlisle U	3	0	3	0

CAIG, Tony (G) 310 0
H: 6 0 W: 13 02 b.Whitehaven 11-4-74

1992–93	Carlisle U	1	0		
1993–94	Carlisle U	20	0		
1994–95	Carlisle U	40	0		
1995–96	Carlisle U	33	0		
1996–97	Carlisle U	46	0		
1997–98	Carlisle U	46	0		
1998–99	Carlisle U	37	0		
1998–99	Blackpool	10	0		
1999–2000	Blackpool	33	0		
2000–01	Blackpool	6	0	49	0
2000–01	Charlton Ath	1	0	1	0
2001–02	Hibernian	8	0		
2002–03	Hibernian	5	0	13	0
2003–04	Newcastle U	0	0		
2003–04	Barnsley	3	0	3	0
2007–08	Gretna	7	0	7	0
2008–09	Houston D	6	0		
2008–09	Houston D	8	0	14	0
2012–13	Carlisle U	0	0		
2013–14	Carlisle U	0	0		
2014–15	Carlisle U	0	0	223	0

DEMPSEY, Kyle (M) 47 10
b.Whitehaven 17-9-95

2013–14	Carlisle U	4	0		
2014–15	Carlisle U	43	10	47	10

DICKER, Gary (M) 304 13
H: 6 0 W: 12 00 b.Dublin 31-7-86
Internationals: Republic of Ireland U19, U21.

2004	UCD	9	1		
2005	UCD	31	2		
2006	UCD	28	2	68	5
2006–07	Birmingham C	0	0		
2007–08	Stockport Co	30	0		
2008–09	Stockport Co	25	0	55	0
2009–10	Brighton & HA	9	1		
2010–11	Brighton & HA	46	3		
2011–12	Brighton & HA	18	0		
2012–13	Brighton & HA	23	0		
2013–14	Brighton & HA	0	0	138	6
2013–14	Rochdale	12	1	12	1
2013–14	Crawley T	11	0	11	0
2014–15	Carlisle U	20	1	20	1

ELLIOTT, Stephen (F) 257 51
H: 5 9 W: 11 08 b.Dublin 6-1-84
Internationals: Eire Youth, U21, Full caps.

2003–04	Manchester C	2	0	2	0
2004–05	Sunderland	42	15		
2005–06	Sunderland	15	2		
2006–07	Sunderland	24	5	81	22
2007–08	Wolverhampton W	29	4	29	4
2008–09	Preston NE	37	6		
2009–10	Preston NE	9	1	46	7
2009–10	Norwich C	10	2	10	2
2010–11	Hearts	30	8		
2011–12	Hearts	26	3	56	11
2012–13	Coventry C	18	4		
2013–14	Coventry C	0	0	18	4
2014–15	Carlisle U	15	1	15	1

GILLESPIE, Mark (G) 70 0
H: 6 3 W: 13 07 b.Newcastle 27-3-92

2009–10	Carlisle U	1	0		
2010–11	Carlisle U	0	0		
2011–12	Carlisle U	0	0		
2012–13	Carlisle U	35	0		
2013–14	Carlisle U	15	0		
2014–15	Carlisle U	19	0	70	0

GILLIES, Josh (M) 12 1
H: 5 10 W: 11 07 b.Sunderland 12-6-96
Internationals: England C.

2013–14	Carlisle U	6	0		
2014–15	Carlisle U	6	1	12	1

GRAINGER, Danny (D) 183 10
H: 5 10 W: 10 10 b.Kettering 28-7-86

2008–09	Dundee U	9	0	9	0
2009–10	St Johnstone	36	1		
2010–11	St Johnstone	33	2	69	3
2011–12	Hearts	27	0		
2012–13	Hearts	13	2	40	2
2013–14	St Mirren	13	0	13	0
2013–14	Dunfermline Ath	11	2	11	2
2014–15	Carlisle U	41	3	41	3

GRIFFITH, Anthony (M) 256 2
H: 6 0 W: 12 00 b.Huddersfield 28-10-86
Internationals: Montserrat Full caps.

2005–06	Doncaster R	4	0		
2005–06	Oxford U	5	0		
2006–07	Doncaster R	2	0		
2006–07	Darlington	4	0	4	0
2007–08	Doncaster R	0	0	6	0
2007–08	Port Vale	0	0		
2008–09	Port Vale	38	0		
2009–10	Port Vale	40	0		
2010–11	Port Vale	40	1		
2011–12	Port Vale	43	1		
2012–13	Port Vale	10	0		
2012–13	Leyton Orient	21	0	21	0
2013–14	Port Vale	38	0	209	2
2014–15	Shrewsbury T	5	0	5	0
2014–15	Carlisle U	11	0	11	0

GWINNUT, Brandon (M) 0 0
b. 16-6-95

2013–14	Carlisle U	0	0		
2014–15	Carlisle U	0	0		

HAMMELL, Connor (F) 3 0
b. 14-2-96

2014–15	Carlisle U	3	0	3	0

HANFORD, Dan (G) 53 0
H: 6 2 W: 12 04 b. 6-3-91

2013–14	Floriana	28	0	28	0
2014–15	Carlisle U	25	0	25	0

KEARNS, Daniel (M) 120 9
H: 5 10 W: 12 00 b.Belfast 26-8-91
Internationals: Northern Ireland U19. Republic of Ireland U19, U21, U23.

2010	Dundalk				
2011	Dundalk	37	9	49	9
2011–12	Peterborough U	20	0		
2012–13	Peterborough U	1	0		
2012–13	York C	9	0	9	0
2012–13	Rotherham U	10	0	10	0
2013–14	Peterborough U	11	0	32	0
2013–14	Chesterfield	10	0	10	0
2014–15	Carlisle U	10	0	10	0

MARROW, Alex (M) 96 2
H: 6 1 W: 13 00 b.Tyldesley 21-1-90

2007–08	Blackburn R	0	0		
2008–09	Blackburn R	0	0		
2009–10	Blackburn R	0	0		
2009–10	Oldham Ath	32	1	32	1
2010–11	Blackburn R	0	0		
2010–11	Crystal Palace	21	0		
2011–12	Crystal Palace	1	0		
2011–12	Preston NE	4	0	4	0
2012–13	Crystal Palace	4	0	26	0
2012–13	Fleetwood T	20	0		
2013–14	Blackburn R	3	0	3	0
2013–14	Fleetwood T	7	1	27	1
2014–15	Carlisle U	4	0	4	0

MEPPEN-WALTER, Courtney (D) 39 2
H: 6 0 W: 12 00 b.Bury 2-8-94
Internationals: England U17, U18.

2012–13	Manchester C	0	0		
2013–14	Carlisle U	20	1		
2014–15	Carlisle U	19	1	39	2

O'HANLON, Sean (D) 366 31
H: 6 1 W: 12 04 b.Liverpool 2-1-83
Internationals: England U20.

2003–04	Swindon T	21	1		
2004–05	Swindon T	40	3		
2005–06	Swindon T	40	4	101	8
2006–07	Milton Keynes D	38	4		
2007–08	Milton Keynes D	43	4		
2008–09	Milton Keynes D	40	3		
2009–10	Milton Keynes D	6	0		
2010–11	Milton Keynes D	34	4	161	15
2011–12	Hibernian	22	2		
2012–13	Hibernian	1	0	23	2
2012–13	Carlisle U	19	1		
2013–14	Carlisle U	33	4		
2014–15	Carlisle U	29	1	81	6

PAYNTER, Billy (F) 424 99
H: 6 1 W: 14 01 b.Liverpool 13-7-84

2000–01	Port Vale	1	0		
2001–02	Port Vale	7	0		
2002–03	Port Vale	31	5		
2003–04	Port Vale	44	13		
2004–05	Port Vale	45	10		
2005–06	Port Vale	16	2	144	30
2005–06	Hull C	22	3	22	3
2006–07	Southend U	9	0		
2006–07	Bradford C	15	4	15	4
2007–08	Southend U	0	0	9	0
2007–08	Swindon T	36	8		
2008–09	Swindon T	42	11		
2009–10	Swindon T	42	26	120	45
2010–11	Leeds U	22	1		
2011–12	Leeds U	5	2		
2011–12	Brighton & HA	10	0	10	0
2012–13	Leeds U	3	0	27	3
2012–13	Doncaster R	37	13		
2013–14	Doncaster R	9	0	46	13
2013–14	Sheffield U	13	0	13	0
2014–15	Carlisle U	18	1	18	1

POTTS, Brad (M) 103 9
H: 6 2 W: 12 09 b.Carlisle 3-7-94
Internationals: England U19.

2012–13	Carlisle U	27	0		
2013–14	Carlisle U	37	2		
2014–15	Carlisle U	39	7	103	9

RIGG, Steven (M) 28 6
b.Keswick 30-6-92

2014–15	Carlisle U	28	6	28	6

ROBSON, Matty (D) 322 29
H: 5 10 W: 11 02 b.Spennymoor 23-1-85

2002–03	Hartlepool U	0	0		
2003–04	Hartlepool U	23	1		
2004–05	Hartlepool U	27	2		
2005–06	Hartlepool U	19	1		
2006–07	Hartlepool U	20	2		
2007–08	Hartlepool U	17	1		
2008–09	Hartlepool U	29	2	135	9
2009–10	Carlisle U	39	4		
2010–11	Carlisle U	42	2		
2011–12	Carlisle U	27	2		
2012–13	Carlisle U	36	7		
2013–14	Carlisle U	32	5		
2014–15	Carlisle U	11	0	187	20

SIMEK, Frankie (D) 241 2
H: 6 0 W: 11 06 b.St Louis 13-10-84
Internationals: USA U20, Full caps.

2002–03	Arsenal	0	0		
2003–04	Arsenal	0	0		
2004–05	Arsenal	0	0		
2004–05	QPR	5	0	5	0
2004–05	Bournemouth	8	0	8	0
2005–06	Sheffield W	43	1		
2006–07	Sheffield W	41	1		
2007–08	Sheffield W	17	0		
2008–09	Sheffield W	6	0		
2009–10	Sheffield W	12	0	119	2
2010–11	Carlisle U	46	0		
2011–12	Carlisle U	25	0		
2012–13	Carlisle U	38	0		
2013–14	Carlisle U	0	0		
2014–15	Carlisle U	0	0	109	0

SWEENEY, Anthony (M) 414 53
H: 6 0 W: 11 07 b.Stockton 5-9-83

2001–02	Hartlepool U	2	0		
2002–03	Hartlepool U	4	0		
2003–04	Hartlepool U	11	1		
2004–05	Hartlepool U	44	13		
2005–06	Hartlepool U	35	5		
2006–07	Hartlepool U	35	4		
2007–08	Hartlepool U	36	4		
2008–09	Hartlepool U	44	5		
2009–10	Hartlepool U	42	2		
2010–11	Hartlepool U	40	9		
2011–12	Hartlepool U	39	8		
2012–13	Hartlepool U	34	1		
2013–14	Hartlepool U	19	0	385	52
2014–15	Carlisle U	29	1	29	1

SYMINGTON, David (M) 74 3
H: 5 8 W: 12 03 b.Carlisle 28-1-94

2012–13	Carlisle U	31	3		
2013–14	Carlisle U	31	0		
2014–15	Carlisle U	12	0	74	3

TAYLOR, Carl (M) 1 0

2014–15	Carlisle U	1	0	1	0

THIRLWELL, Paul (M) 371 8
H: 5 11 W: 12 08 b.Washington 13-2-79
Internationals: England U21.

1996–97	Sunderland	0	0		
1997–98	Sunderland	0	0		
1998–99	Sunderland	2	0		
1999–2000	Sunderland	8	0		
1999–2000	Swindon T	12	0	12	0
2000–01	Sunderland	5	0		
2001–02	Sunderland	14	0		
2002–03	Sunderland	19	0		
2003–04	Sunderland	29	0	77	0
2004–05	Sheffield U	30	1	30	1
2005–06	Derby Co	21	0		
2006–07	Derby Co	0	0	21	0
2006–07	Carlisle U	30	0		
2007–08	Carlisle U	13	0		
2008–09	Carlisle U	34	4		
2009–10	Carlisle U	28	1		
2010–11	Carlisle U	23	1		
2011–12	Carlisle U	26	1		
2012–13	Carlisle U	32	0		
2013–14	Carlisle U	27	0		
2014–15	Carlisle U	18	0	231	7

WYKE, Charlie (F) 72 14
b.Middlesbrough 6-12-92

2011–12	Middlesbrough	0	0		
2012–13	Middlesbrough	0	0		
2012–13	Hartlepool U	25	2		
2013–14	Middlesbrough	0	0		
2013–14	AFC Wimbledon	17	2	17	2
2014–15	Middlesbrough	0	0		
2014–15	Hartlepool U	13	4	38	6
2014–15	Carlisle U	17	6	17	6

Scholars
Blackburn, Jason James; Bradbury, Arron Andrew; Douglas, Matthew; Eccles, Daniel John; Elliott, Jack; Fowler, Thomas; Hammell, Connor Rhys; Hurley, Cuan francis; Marshall, Jordan Aaron; Pearson, Ellis James; Quigley, Michael Thomas; Robson, Joe Leigh; Rudd, Karlton Thomas; Taylor, Carl; Wallace, Frankie; White, Thomas Alan.

CHARLTON ATH (21)

AHEARNE-GRANT, Karlan (F) 5 0
b. 19-12-97
Internationals: England U17, U18.

2014–15	Charlton Ath	5	0	5	0

ANSAH, Zak (F) 8 1
H: 5 10 W: 11 00 b.Sidcup 4-5-94
Internationals: England U16, U17.

2010–11	Arsenal	0	0		
2011–12	Arsenal	0	0		
2012–13	Arsenal	0	0		
2013–14	Arsenal	0	0		
2014–15	Charlton Ath	0	0		
2014–15	Plymouth Arg	8	1	8	1

BEENEY, Jordan (G) 0 0
b. 12-5-98

2014–15	Charlton Ath	0	0		

BEN HAIM, Tal (D) 314 3
H: 5 11 W: 11 09 b.Rishon Le Zion 31-3-82
Internationals: Israel U21, Full caps.

2000–01	Maccabi Tel Aviv	1	0		

2001–02	Maccabi Tel Aviv	29	1	
2002–03	Maccabi Tel Aviv	30	0	
2003–04	Maccabi Tel Aviv	26	1	86 2
2004–05	Bolton W	21	1	
2005–06	Bolton W	35	0	
2006–07	Bolton W	32	0	88 1
2007–08	Chelsea	13	0	13 0
2008–09	Manchester C	9	0	
2008–09	Sunderland	5	0	5 0
2009–10	Manchester C	0	0	9 0
2009–10	Portsmouth	22	0	
2010–11	Portsmouth	0	0	
2010–11	*West Ham U*	8	0	8 0
2011–12	Portsmouth	33	0	
2012–13	Portsmouth	0	0	55 0
2012–13	Hapoel Tel-Aviv	0	0	
2012–13	QPR	3	0	3 0
2013–14	Standard Liege	10	0	10 0
2014–15	Charlton Ath	37	0	37 0

BIKEY, Andre (D)   253 14
H: 6 0   W: 12 08   b.Douala 8-1-85
Internationals: Cameroon Full caps.

2003–04	Pacos de Ferreira	2	0	2 0
2004–05	Dep Aves	0	0	
2005	Shinnik	11	1	11 1
2005	Loko Moscow	9	0	
2006	Loko Moscow	5	0	14 0
2006–07	Reading	15	0	
2007–08	Reading	22	3	
2008–09	Reading	25	3	
2009–10	Reading	0	0	62 6
2009–10	Burnley	28	1	
2010–11	Burnley	28	2	
2011–12	Burnley	14	0	70 3
2011–12	*Bristol C*	7	0	7 0
2012–13	Middlesbrough	33	1	33 1
2013–14	Panetolikos	23	2	23 2
2014–15	Charlton Ath	31	1	31 1

BULOT, Frederic (M)   138 14
H: 5 10   W: 10 10   b.Libreville 27-9-90
Internationals: France U16, U17, U18, U19, U21. Gabon Full caps.

2010–11	Monaco	8	0	8 0
2011–12	Caen	38	4	38 4
2012–13	Standard Liege	36	4	
2013–14	Standard Liege	28	1	
2014–15	Standard Liege	0	0	64 5

On loan from Standard Liege

2014–15	Charlton Ath	28	5	28 5

BUYENS, Yoni (M)   294 26
H: 6 0   b.Duffel 10-3-88
Internationals: Belgium, U19, U20, U21.

2006–07	Lierse	20	0	
2007–08	Lierse	33	2	
2008–09	Lierse	34	2	87 4
2009–10	Mechelen	31	1	
2010–11	Mechelen	33	1	64 2
2011–12	Standard Liege	38	4	
2012–13	Standard Liege	41	8	
2013–14	Standard Liege	24	0	
2014–15	Standard Liege	0	0	103 12

On loan from Standard Liege.

2014–15	Charlton Ath	40	8	40 8

CHURCH, Simon (F)   206 34
H: 6 0   W: 13 04   b.Amersham 10-12-88
Internationals: Wales U21, Full caps.

2007–08	Reading	0	0	
2007–08	*Crewe Alex*	12	1	12 1
2007–08	*Yeovil T*	6	0	6 0
2008–09	Reading	0	0	
2008–09	*Wycombe W*	9	0	9 0
2008–09	*Leyton Orient*	13	5	13 5
2009–10	Reading	36	10	
2010–11	Reading	37	5	
2011–12	Reading	31	7	
2012–13	Reading	0	0	104 22
2012–13	*Huddersfield T*	7	1	7 1
2013–14	Charlton Ath	38	3	
2014–15	Charlton Ath	17	2	55 5

COUSINS, Jordan (D)   86 5
H: 5 10   W: 11 05   b.Greenwich 6-3-94
Internationals: England U16, U17, U18, U21.

2011–12	Charlton Ath	0	0	
2012–13	Charlton Ath	0	0	
2013–14	Charlton Ath	42	0	
2014–15	Charlton Ath	44	3	86 5

DANIEL, Kadell (D)   0 0
H: 5 10   W: 9 05   b.London 3-6-94

2012–13	Crystal Palace	0	0	
2013–14	Charlton Ath	0	0	

DIARRA, Alou (M)   335 23
H: 6 3   W: 12 05   b.Villepinte 15-7-81
Internationals: France U20, U21, Full caps.

2002–03	Liverpool	0	0	
2002–03	Le Havre	25	0	25 0
2003–04	Liverpool	0	0	
2003–04	Bastia	35	4	35 4
2004–05	Liverpool	0	0	
2004–05	Lens	34	2	
2005–06	Lens	30	2	64 4
2006–07	Lyon	15	1	15 1
2007–08	Bordeaux	36	4	
2008–09	Bordeaux	35	2	
2009–10	Bordeaux	30	1	
2010–11	Bordeaux	32	4	133 11
2011–12	Marseille	33	2	
2012–13	Marseille	0	0	33 2
2012–13	West Ham U	3	0	
2012–13	*Rennes*	12	0	12 0
2013–14	West Ham U	3	0	6 0
2014–15	Charlton Ath	12	1	12 1

DMITROVIC, Marko (G)   17 0
b. 24-1-92
Internationals: Serbia U19, U21.

2010–11	Red Star Belgrade	0	0	
2011–12	Red Star Belgrade	0	0	
2012–13	Red Star Belgrade	0	0	
2013–14	Ujpest	12	0	
2014–15	Ujpest	0	0	12 0
2014–15	Charlton Ath	5	0	5 0

EAGLES, Chris (M)   311 50
H: 5 10   W: 11 07   b.Hemel Hempstead 19-11-85
Internationals: England Youth.

2003–04	Manchester U	0	0	
2004–05	Manchester U	0	0	
2004–05	*Watford*	13	1	
2005–06	Manchester U	0	0	
2005–06	*Sheffield W*	25	3	25 3
2005–06	*Watford*	17	3	30 4
2006–07	Manchester U	2	1	
2006–07	*NEC Nijmegen*	15	1	15 1
2007–08	Manchester U	4	0	6 1
2008–09	Burnley	43	8	
2009–10	Burnley	34	2	
2010–11	Burnley	43	11	120 21
2011–12	Bolton W	34	4	
2012–13	Bolton W	43	12	
2013–14	Bolton W	16	1	93 17
2014–15	Blackpool	7	1	7 1
2014–15	Charlton Ath	15	2	15 2

EDWARDS, Archie (D)   0 0
b. 10-7-97
Internationals: England U16, U17.

2014–15	Charlton Ath	0	0	

ETHERIDGE, Neil (G)   20 0
H: 6 3   W: 14 00   b.Enfield 7-2-90
Internationals: England U16. Philippines Full caps.

2008–09	Fulham	0	0	
2009–10	Fulham	0	0	
2010–11	Fulham	0	0	
2011–12	Fulham	0	0	
2012–13	Fulham	0	0	
2012–13	*Bristol R*	12	0	12 0
2013–14	Fulham	0	0	
2013–14	*Crewe Alex*	4	0	4 0
2014–15	Oldham Ath	0	0	
2014–15	Charlton Ath	4	0	4 0

FOX, Morgan (D)   44 1
H: 6 1   W: 12 03   b.Chelmsford 21-9-93
Internationals: Wales U21.

2012–13	Charlton Ath	0	0	
2013–14	Charlton Ath	6	0	
2013–14	*Notts Co*	7	1	7 1
2014–15	Charlton Ath	31	0	37 0

GOMEZ, Joseph (D)   21 0
b. 23-5-97
Internationals: England U16, U17, U19.

2014–15	Charlton Ath	21	0	21 0

GUDMUNDSSON, Johann Berg (M) 160 19
H: 6 1   W: 12 06   b.Reykjavik 27-10-90
Internationals: Iceland U19, U21, Full caps.

2009–10	AZ	0	0	
2010–11	AZ	23	1	
2011–12	AZ	30	3	
2012–13	AZ	31	2	
2013–14	AZ	35	3	119 9
2014–15	Charlton Ath	41	10	41 10

HARRIOTT, Callum (M)   66 8
H: 5 5   W: 10 05   b.Norbury 4-3-94
Internationals: England U19.

2010–11	Charlton Ath	3	0	
2011–12	Charlton Ath	0	0	
2012–13	Charlton Ath	14	2	
2013–14	Charlton Ath	28	5	
2014–15	Charlton Ath	21	1	66 8

HENDERSON, Stephen (G)   128 0
H: 6 3   W: 11 00   b.Dublin 2-5-88
Internationals: Republic of Ireland U16, U17, U19, U21.

2005–06	Aston Villa	0	0	
2006–07	Aston Villa	0	0	
2007–08	Bristol C	1	0	
2008–09	Bristol C	1	0	
2009–10	Bristol C	3	0	
2009–10	*Aldershot T*	8	0	8 0
2010–11	Bristol C	0	0	5 0
2010–11	*Yeovil T*	33	0	33 0
2011–12	Portsmouth	25	0	25 0
2011–12	West Ham U	0	0	
2012–13	West Ham U	0	0	
2012–13	*Ipswich T*	24	0	24 0
2013–14	West Ham U	0	0	
2013–14	*Bournemouth*	2	0	2 0
2014–15	Charlton Ath	31	0	31 0

HOLMES-DENNIS, Tareiq (M)   31 1
H: 5 9   W: 11 11   b.Farnborough 31-10-95
Internationals: England U18.

2012–13	Charlton Ath	0	0	
2013–14	Charlton Ath	0	0	
2014–15	Charlton Ath	0	0	
2014–15	*Oxford U*	14	0	14 0
2014–15	*Plymouth Arg*	17	1	17 1

JACKSON, Johnnie (M)   375 63
H: 6 1   W: 12 00   b.Camden 15-8-82
Internationals: England U17, U18, U20.

1999–2000	Tottenham H	0	0	
2000–01	Tottenham H	0	0	
2001–02	Tottenham H	0	0	
2002–03	Tottenham H	0	0	
2002–03	*Swindon T*	13	1	13 1
2002–03	*Colchester U*	8	0	
2003–04	Tottenham H	11	1	
2003–04	*Coventry C*	5	2	5 2
2004–05	Tottenham H	8	0	
2004–05	*Watford*	15	0	15 0
2005–06	Tottenham H	1	0	20 1
2005–06	*Derby Co*	6	0	6 0
2006–07	Colchester U	32	2	
2007–08	Colchester U	46	7	
2008–09	Colchester U	29	4	
2009–10	Colchester U	0	0	115 13
2009–10	*Notts Co*	24	2	24 2
2009–10	*Charlton Ath*	4	0	
2010–11	Charlton Ath	30	13	
2011–12	Charlton Ath	36	12	
2012–13	Charlton Ath	43	12	
2013–14	Charlton Ath	38	5	
2014–15	Charlton Ath	26	2	177 44

JOHNSON, Roger (D)   456 35
H: 6 3   W: 11 00   b.Ashford (Middlesex) 28-4-83

1999–2000	Wycombe W	1	0	
2000–01	Wycombe W	1	0	
2001–02	Wycombe W	7	1	
2002–03	Wycombe W	33	3	
2003–04	Wycombe W	28	2	
2004–05	Wycombe W	42	6	
2005–06	Wycombe W	45	7	157 19
2006–07	Cardiff C	32	2	
2007–08	Cardiff C	42	5	
2008–09	Cardiff C	45	5	119 12
2009–10	Birmingham C	38	0	
2010–11	Birmingham C	38	2	76 2
2011–12	Wolverhampton W	27	0	
2012–13	Wolverhampton W	42	2	
2013–14	Wolverhampton W	0	0	
2013–14	*Sheffield W*	17	0	17 0
2013–14	*West Ham U*	4	0	4 0
2014–15	Wolverhampton W	0	0	69 2
2014–15	Charlton Ath	14	0	14 0

LENNON, Harry (M)   6 0
H: 6 3   W: 11 11   b.Barking 16-12-94

2012–13	Charlton Ath	0	0	
2013–14	Charlton Ath	2	0	
2014–15	Charlton Ath	0	0	2 0
2014–15	*Cambridge U*	2	0	2 0
2014–15	*Gillingham*	2	0	2 0

LEPOINT, Christophe (F)   232 27
H: 6 2   W: 12 06   b. 24-10-84
Internationals: Belgium U19, U20, U21, Full caps.

2002–03	Anderlecht	0	0	
2003–04	1860 Munich	1	0	
2004–05	1860 Munich	8	0	9 0
2005–06	Willem II	10	0	10 0
2005–06	Genclerbirligi Ankara	4	0	4 0
2006–07	Tubize	23	3	
2007–08	Tubize	33	3	56 6
2008–09	Excelsior Mouscron	29	5	29 5
2009–10	Gent	34	6	
2010–11	Gent	10	2	
2011–12	Gent	0	0	
2012–13	Gent	12	1	
2012–13	Wassland-Beveren	16	5	16 5
2013–14	Gent	29	2	
2014–15	Gent	17	0	102 11
2014–15	Charlton Ath	6	0	6 0

MITOV, Dimitar (G)   0 0
b. 22-1-97
Internationals: Bulgaria U19.

2014–15	Charlton Ath	0	0

MOUSSA, Franck (M)   222 33
H: 5 8   W: 10 08   b.Brussels 24-7-89

2005–06	Southend U	1	0	
2006–07	Southend U	4	0	
2007–08	Southend U	16	0	
2008–09	Southend U	26	2	
2008–09	Wycombe W	9	0	9 0
2009–10	Southend U	43	5	90 7
2010–11	Leicester C	8	1	
2010–11	Doncaster R	14	2	14 2
2011–12	Leicester C	0	0	8 1
2011–12	Chesterfield	10	4	10 4
2012–13	Nottingham F	0	0	
2012–13	Coventry C	38	6	
2013–14	Coventry C	39	12	77 18
2014–15	Charlton Ath	14	1	14 1

MULDOON, Oliver (M)   3 0
b. 3-9-94

2014–15	Charlton Ath	0	0	
2014–15	Gillingham	3	0	3 0

MUNNS, Jack (M)   0 0
H: 5 5   W: 10 01   b.Dagenham 18-11-93

2012–13	Aldershot T	0	0
2013–14	Charlton Ath	0	0
2014–15	Charlton Ath	0	0

OBILEYE, Ayo (D)   26 2
b.Hackney 2-9-94

2011–12	Sheffield W	0	0	
2012–13	Sheffield W	0	0	
2013–14	Sheffield W	0	0	
2014–15	Charlton Ath	0	0	
2014–15	Dagenham & R	26	2	26 2

ONYEWU, Oguchi (D)   227 16
H: 6 5   W: 15 04   b.Washington DC 13-5-82
Internationals: USA U17, U20, Full caps

2002–03	Metz	3	0	
2003–04	Metz	2	0	5 0
2003–04	La Louviere	24	1	24 1
2004–05	Standard Liege	30	3	
2005–06	Standard Liege	29	2	
2006–07	Standard Liege	15	1	
2006–07	Newcastle U	11	0	11 0
2007–08	Standard Liege	33	2	
2008–09	Standard Liege	32	3	139 11
2009–10	AC Milan	0	0	
2010–11	AC Milan	0	0	
2010–11	FC Twente	8	0	8 0
2011–12	Sporting Lisbon	17	4	
2012–13	Sporting Lisbon	0	0	17 4
2012–13	Malaga	2	0	2 0
2013–14	QPR	0	0	
2013–14	Sheffield W	18	0	18 0
2014–15	Charlton Ath	3	0	3 0

OSBORNE, Harry (D)
H: 6 0   W: 12 03   b.Greenwich 3-3-94

2011–12	Charlton Ath	0	0
2012–13	Charlton Ath	0	0
2013–14	Charlton Ath	0	0
2014–15	Charlton Ath	0	0

PARZYSZEK, Piotr (F)   47 25
H: 6 2   W: 11 08   b.Torun 8-6-93
Internationals: Poland U18, U20, U21.

2012–13	De Graafschap	26	10	
2013–14	De Graafschap	20	15	46 25
2013–14	Charlton Ath	1	0	
2014–15	Charlton Ath	0	0	1 0

PHILLIPS, Dillon (M)   0 0
H: 6 2   W: 11 11   b. 11-6-95

2012–13	Charlton Ath	0	0
2013–14	Charlton Ath	0	0
2014–15	Charlton Ath	0	0

PIGOTT, Joe (F)   49 10
H: 6 0   W: 9 05   b.London 24-11-93

2012–13	Charlton Ath	0	0	
2013–14	Charlton Ath	11	0	
2013–14	Gillingham	7	1	7 1
2014–15	Charlton Ath	1	0	12 0
2014–15	Newport Co	10	3	10 3
2014–15	Southend U	20	6	20 6

POPE, Nick (G)   53 0
H: 6 3   W: 11 13   b.Cambridge 19-4-92

2011–12	Charlton Ath	0	0	
2012–13	Charlton Ath	1	0	
2013–14	Charlton Ath	0	0	
2013–14	York C	22	0	22 0
2014–15	Charlton Ath	8	0	9 0
2014–15	Bury	22	0	22 0

SHO-SILVA, Oluwatobi (M)   0 0
b. 27-3-95
Internationals: England U18.

2012–13	Charlton Ath	0	0
2013–14	Charlton Ath	0	0
2014–15	Charlton Ath	0	0

SOLLY, Chris (D)   163 2
H: 5 8   W: 10 07   b.Rochester 20-1-91
Internationals: England U16, U17.

2008–09	Charlton Ath	1	0	
2009–10	Charlton Ath	9	0	
2010–11	Charlton Ath	14	1	
2011–12	Charlton Ath	44	0	
2012–13	Charlton Ath	45	1	
2013–14	Charlton Ath	12	0	
2014–15	Charlton Ath	38	0	163 2

THOMAS, Terell (D)   0 0
b. 13-10-97

2014–15	Charlton Ath	0	0

TUCUDEAN, George (F)   123 24
H: 6 2   W: 12 08   b. 30-4-91
Internationals: Romania U17, U21.

2010–11	Dinamo Bucharest	12	4	
2011–12	Dinamo Bucharest	23	2	
2012–13	Dinamo Bucharest	18	6	
2012–13	Standard Liege	11	0	11 0
2013–14	Dinamo Bucharest	22	7	75 19
2014–15	Charlton Ath	20	2	20 2
2014–15	Steaua Bucharest	17	3	17 3

VETOKELE, Igor (F)   123 36
H: 5 8   W: 11 00   b.Ostend 23-3-92
Internationals: Belgium U17, U18, U19, U20, U21. Angola Full caps.

2010–11	Gent	0	0	
2011–12	Cercle Brugge	34	8	
2012–13	Cercle Brugge	4	1	38 9
2012–13	Copenhagen	15	3	
2013–14	Copenhagen	29	13	44 16
2014–15	Charlton Ath	41	11	41 11

WATT, Tony (F)   93 25
H: 5 8   W: 12 00   b.Bellshill 29-3-93
Internationals: Scotland U19, U20, U21.

2009–10	Airdrieonians	1	0	
2010–11	Airdrieonians	15	3	16 3
2011–12	Celtic	3	2	
2012–13	Celtic	20	5	
2013–14	Celtic	2	0	25 7
2013–14	Lierse	17	8	17 8
2014–15	Standard Liege	13	2	13 2
2014–15	Charlton Ath	22	5	22 5

WIGGINS, Rhoys (D)   192 3
H: 5 8   W: 11 05   b.Uxbridge 4-11-87
Internationals: Wales U17, U19, U21.

2006–07	Crystal Palace	0	0	
2007–08	Crystal Palace	0	0	
2008–09	Crystal Palace	1	0	1 0
2008–09	Bournemouth	13	0	
2009–10	Norwich C	0	0	
2009–10	Bournemouth	19	0	
2010–11	Bournemouth	35	2	67 2
2011–12	Charlton Ath	45	1	
2012–13	Charlton Ath	20	0	
2013–14	Charlton Ath	38	0	
2014–15	Charlton Ath	21	0	124 1

WILSON, Lawrie (D)   187 14
H: 5 11   W: 11 06   b.London 11-9-87

2006–07	Colchester U	0	0	
2010–11	Stevenage	42	5	
2011–12	Stevenage	46	5	88 10
2012–13	Charlton Ath	30	2	
2013–14	Charlton Ath	42	2	
2014–15	Charlton Ath	24	0	96 4
2014–15	Rotherham U	3	0	3 0

Players retained or with offer of contract
Assiana, Elan Lumir; Ghoochannejhad, Reza; Kennedy, Mikhail Caolan Patrick; Konsa, Ngoyo Ezri; Lapslie, George Robert; Monlouis, Keiran Dion; Nego, Loic; Wozencroft, Pigott Joseph David.

Scholars
Afolabi, Emmanuel Mayowa; Barnes, Aaron Christopher; Bokciu, Sevdar; Bone, Samuel George; Charles-Cook, Regan Evans; Hanlan, Brandon Alex Graham; Kelly, Alexander Lawrence; Leon, Connor Stephen Williams; Lookman, Ademola Lookman Olajade; Millar, Christopher James; Thomas, Callum; Umerah, Joshua Chukwudinma.

CHELSEA (22)

AKE, Nathan (M)   10 0
H: 5 11   W: 11 01   b.Den Haag 18-2-95
Internationals: Netherlands U15, U16, U17, U19, U21.

2012–13	Chelsea	3	0	
2013–14	Chelsea	1	0	
2014–15	Chelsea	1	0	5 0
2014–15	Reading	5	0	5 0

ATSU, Christian (F)   75 12
H: 5 8   W: 10 09   b.Ada Foah 10-1-92
Internationals: Ghana Full caps.

2010–11	Porto	0	0	
2011–12	Porto	0	0	
2011–12	Rio Ave	27	6	27 6
2012–13	Porto	17	1	17 1
2013–14	Chelsea	0	0	
2013–14	Vitesse	26	5	26 5
2014–15	Chelsea	0	0	
2014–15	Everton	5	0	5 0

AZPILICUETA, Cesar (D)   231 1
H: 5 10   W: 10 13   b.Pamplona 28-8-89
Internationals: Spain U16, U17, U19, U20, U21, U23, Full caps.

2006–07	Osasuna	1	0	
2007–08	Osasuna	29	0	
2008–09	Osasuna	36	0	
2009–10	Osasuna	33	0	99 0
2010–11	Marseille	15	0	
2011–12	Marseille	30	1	
2012–13	Marseille	2	0	47 1
2012–13	Chelsea	27	0	
2013–14	Chelsea	29	0	
2014–15	Chelsea	29	0	85 0

BAKER, Lewis (M)   16 3
b.Luton 25-4-95
Internationals: England U17, U19, U20.

2012–13	Chelsea	0	0	
2013–14	Chelsea	0	0	
2014–15	Chelsea	0	0	
2014–15	Sheffield W	4	0	4 0
2014–15	Milton Keynes D	12	3	12 3

BAMFORD, Patrick (F)   98 43
H: 6 1   W: 11 02   b.Newark 5-9-93
Internationals: Republic of Ireland U18. England U18, U19, U21.

2010–11	Nottingham F	0	0	
2011–12	Nottingham F	2	0	2 0
2012–13	Chelsea	0	0	
2012–13	Milton Keynes D	14	4	
2013–14	Chelsea	0	0	
2013–14	Milton Keynes D	23	14	37 18
2013–14	Derby Co	21	8	21 8
2014–15	Chelsea	0	0	
2014–15	Middlesbrough	38	17	38 17

BEENEY, Mitchell (G)   0 0
H: 6 0   W: 12 04   b.Leeds 3-10-95
Internationals: England U17.

2014–15	Chelsea	0	0

BLACKMAN, Jamal (G)   0 0
H: 6 6   W: 14 09   b.Croydon 27-10-93
Internationals: England U16, U17, U18, U19.

2011–12	Chelsea	0	0
2012–13	Chelsea	0	0
2013–14	Chelsea	0	0
2014–15	Middlesbrough	0	0

BOGA, Jeremie (F)   0   0
H: 5 8   W: 10 10   b.Marseille 3-1-97
Internationals: France U19.

| 2014–15 | Chelsea | 0 | 0 | | |

BROWN, Isaiah (M)   2   0
H: 6 0   W: 10 13   b.Peterborough 7-1-97
Internationals: England U16, U17, U19.

2012–13	WBA	1	0	1	0
2013–14	Chelsea	0	0		
2014–15	Chelsea	1	0	1	0

CAHILL, Gary (D)   303   22
H: 6 2   W: 12 06   b.Dronfield 19-12-85
Internationals: England U20, U21, Full caps.

2003–04	Aston Villa	0	0		
2004–05	Aston Villa	0	0		
2004–05	Burnley	27	1	27	1
2005–06	Aston Villa	7	1		
2006–07	Aston Villa	20	0		
2007–08	Aston Villa	1	0	28	1
2007–08	Sheffield U	16	2	16	2
2007–08	Bolton W	13	0		
2008–09	Bolton W	33	3		
2009–10	Bolton W	29	5		
2010–11	Bolton W	36	3		
2011–12	Bolton W	19	2	130	13
2011–12	Chelsea	10	1		
2012–13	Chelsea	26	2		
2013–14	Chelsea	30	1		
2014–15	Chelsea	36	1	102	5

CECH, Petr (G)   461   0
H: 6 5   W: 14 07   b.Plzen 20-5-82
Internationals: Czech Republic U15, U16, U17, U18, U20, U21, Full caps.

1998–99	Viktoria Plzen	0	0		
1999–2000	Chmel	1	0		
2000–01	Chmel	26	0	27	0
2001–02	Sparta Prague	26	0	26	0
2002–03	Rennes	37	0		
2003–04	Rennes	38	0	75	0
2004–05	Chelsea	35	0		
2005–06	Chelsea	34	0		
2006–07	Chelsea	20	0		
2007–08	Chelsea	26	0		
2008–09	Chelsea	35	0		
2009–10	Chelsea	34	0		
2010–11	Chelsea	38	0		
2011–12	Chelsea	34	0		
2012–13	Chelsea	36	0		
2013–14	Chelsea	34	0		
2014–15	Chelsea	7	0	333	0

CHALOBAH, Nathaniel (D)   88   9
H: 6 1   W: 11 11   b.Sierra Leone 12-12-94
Internationals: England U16, U17, U19, U21.

2010–11	Chelsea	0	0		
2011–12	Chelsea	0	0		
2012–13	Chelsea	0	0		
2012–13	Watford	38	5	38	5
2013–14	Chelsea	0	0		
2013–14	Nottingham F	12	2	12	2
2013–14	Middlesbrough	19	1	19	1
2014–15	Chelsea	0	0		
2014–15	Burnley	4	0	4	0
2014–15	Reading	15	1	15	1

CHRISTENSEN, Andreas (D)   1   0
H: 6 2   W: 11 09   b.Allerod 4-96
Internationals: Denmark U16, U17, U19, U21, Full caps.

2012–13	Chelsea	0	0		
2013–14	Chelsea	0	0		
2014–15	Chelsea	1	0	1	0

COSTA, Diego (F)   255   101
H: 6 1   W: 12 04   b.Lagarto 7-10-88
Internationals: Brazil Full caps. Spain Full caps.

2006–07	Penafiel	13	5	13	5
2006–07	Sporting Braga	7	0	7	0
2007–08	Celta Vigo	30	6	30	6
2008–09	Albacete	35	9	35	9
2009–10	Valladolid	34	8	34	8
2010–11	Atletico Madrid	28	6		
2011–12	Atletico Madrid	0	0		
2011–12	Rayo Vallecano	16	10	16	10
2012–13	Atletico Madrid	31	10		
2013–14	Atletico Madrid	35	27	94	43
2014–15	Chelsea	26	20	26	20

COURTOIS, Thibaut (G)   184   0
H: 6 6   W: 14 02   b.Bree 11-5-92
Internationals: Belgium U18, Full caps.

2008–09	Genk	1	0		
2009–10	Genk	0	0		
2010–11	Genk	40	0	41	0
2011–12	Chelsea	0	0		
2011–12	Atletico Madrid	37	0		
2012–13	Chelsea	0	0		
2012–13	Atletico Madrid	37	0		
2013–14	Chelsea	0	0		
2013–14	Atletico Madrid	37	0	111	0
2014–15	Chelsea	32	0	32	0

CUADRADO, Juan Guillermo (M)   180   25
H: 5 10   W: 10 06   b.Necodi 26-5-88
Internationals: Colombia Full caps.

2008	Medellin	21	2		
2009	Medellin	9	0	30	2
2009–10	Udinese	11	0		
2010–11	Udinese	9	0		
2011–12	Udinese	0	0	20	0
2011–12	Lecce	33	3	33	3
2012–13	Fiorentina	36	5		
2013–14	Fiorentina	32	11		
2014–15	Fiorentina	17	4	85	20
2014–15	Chelsea	12	0	12	0

DAVEY, Alex (D)   13   0
b.Luton 24-11-94
Internationals: Scotland U19.

2012–13	Chelsea	0	0		
2013–14	Chelsea	0	0		
2014–15	Chelsea	0	0		
2014–15	Scunthorpe U	13	0	13	0

DROGBA, Didier (F)   446   176
H: 6 2   W: 14 05   b.Abidjan 11-3-78
Internationals: Ivory Coast Full caps.

1998–99	Le Mans	2	0		
1999–2000	Le Mans	30	6		
2000–01	Le Mans	11	0		
2001–02	Le Mans	21	5	64	11
2001–02	Guingamp	11	3		
2002–03	Guingamp	34	17	45	20
2003–04	Marseille	35	18	35	18
2004–05	Chelsea	26	10		
2005–06	Chelsea	29	12		
2006–07	Chelsea	36	20		
2007–08	Chelsea	19	8		
2008–09	Chelsea	24	5		
2009–10	Chelsea	32	29		
2010–11	Chelsea	24	5		
2011–12	Chelsea	24	5		
2012	Shanghai Shenhua	11	8	11	8
2012–13	Galatasaray	13	5		
2013–14	Galatasaray	24	4	37	15
2014–15	Chelsea	28	4	254	104

FABREGAS, Francesc (M)   342   66
H: 5 11   W: 11 01   b.Arenys de Mar 4-5-87
Internationals: Spain Youth, U21, Full caps.

2003–04	Arsenal	0	0		
2004–05	Arsenal	33	2		
2005–06	Arsenal	34	3		
2006–07	Arsenal	38	2		
2007–08	Arsenal	32	7		
2008–09	Arsenal	22	3		
2009–10	Arsenal	27	15		
2010–11	Arsenal	25	3	212	35
2011–12	Barcelona	28	9		
2012–13	Barcelona	32	11		
2013–14	Barcelona	36	8	96	28
2014–15	Chelsea	34	3	34	3

FERUZ, Islam (F)   3   0
H: 5 4   W: 8 07   b.Somalia 10-9-95
Internationals: Scotland U16, U17, U19, U20, U21.

2011–12	Chelsea	0	0		
2013–14	Chelsea	0	0		
2014–15	Chelsea	0	0		
2014–15	OFI Crete	1	0	1	0
2014–15	Blackpool	2	0	2	0

HAZARD, Eden (M)   253   73
H: 5 7   W: 8 11   b.La Louviere 7-1-91
Internationals: Belgium U15, U16, U17, U19, Full caps.

2007–08	Lille	3	0		
2008–09	Lille	30	4		
2009–10	Lille	37	5		
2010–11	Lille	38	7		
2011–12	Lille	38	20	146	36
2012–13	Chelsea	34	9		
2013–14	Chelsea	35	14		
2014–15	Chelsea	38	14	107	37

HILARIO (G)   253   2
H: 6 2   W: 13 05   b.San Pedro da Cova 21-10-75
Internationals: Portugal U21, B, Full caps.

1994–95	Naval	27	0	27	0
1995–96	Academica	33	2		
1996–97	Porto	18	0		
1997–98	Porto	30	0		
1998–99	Amadora	27	0	27	0
1999–2000	Porto	19	0		
2000–01	Porto	0	0		
2001–02	Varzim	24	0	24	0
2002–03	Porto	0	0	40	0
2002–03	Academica	10	0	43	2
2003–04	Nacional	29	0		
2004–05	Nacional	32	0		
2005–06	Nacional	11	0	72	0
2006–07	Chelsea	11	0		
2007–08	Chelsea	3	0		
2008–09	Chelsea	1	0		
2009–10	Chelsea	3	0		
2010–11	Chelsea	0	0		
2011–12	Chelsea	2	0		
2012–13	Chelsea	0	0		
2013–14	Chelsea	0	0		
2014–15	Chelsea	0	0	20	0

IVANOVIC, Branislav (M)   343   32
H: 6 0   W: 12 04   b.Sremska Mitreovica 22-2-84
Internationals: Serbia U21, Full caps.

2002–03	Sremska	19	2	19	2
2003–04	OFK Belgrade	13	0		
2004–05	OFK Belgrade	27	2		
2005–06	OFK Belgrade	15	3	55	5
2006	Loko Moscow	28	2		
2007	Loko Moscow	26	3	54	5
2007–08	Chelsea	0	0		
2008–09	Chelsea	16	0		
2009–10	Chelsea	28	1		
2010–11	Chelsea	34	4		
2011–12	Chelsea	29	3		
2012–13	Chelsea	34	5		
2013–14	Chelsea	36	3		
2014–15	Chelsea	38	4	215	20

KAKUTA, Gael (F)   102   12
H: 5 8   W: 10 03   b.Lille 21-6-91
Internationals: France U16, U17, U18, U19, U20, U21.

2008–09	Chelsea	0	0		
2009–10	Chelsea	1	0		
2010–11	Chelsea	5	0		
2010–11	Fulham	7	1	7	1
2011–12	Chelsea	0	0		
2011–12	Bolton W	4	0	4	0
2011–12	Dijon	14	4	14	4
2012–13	Chelsea	0	0		
2012–13	Vitesse	22	1		
2013–14	Chelsea	0	0		
2013–14	Vitesse	13	1	35	2
2013–14	Lazio	1	0	1	0
2014–15	Chelsea	0	0	6	0
2014–15	Rayo Vallecano	35	5	35	5

KALAS, Tomas (D)   58   1
H: 6 0   W: 12 00   b.Olomouc 15-5-93
Internationals: Czech Republic U17, U18, U19, U21, Full caps.

2009–10	Sigma Olomouc	1	0		
2010–11	Chelsea	0	0		
2010–11	Sigma Olomouc	4	0	5	0
2011–12	Chelsea	0	0		
2012–13	Chelsea	0	0		
2012–13	Vitesse	34	1	34	1
2013–14	Chelsea	2	0		
2014–15	Chelsea	0	0	2	0
2014–15	Cologne	0	0		
2014–15	Middlesbrough	17	0	17	0

KANE, Todd (D)   57   3
H: 5 11   W: 11 00   b.Huntingdon 17-9-93
Internationals: England U19.

2011–12	Chelsea	0	0		
2012–13	Chelsea	0	0		
2012–13	Preston NE	3	0	3	0
2012–13	Blackburn R	14	0		
2013–14	Chelsea	0	0		
2013–14	Blackburn R	27	2	41	2
2014–15	Chelsea	0	0		
2014–15	Bristol C	5	0	5	0
2014–15	Nottingham F	8	1	8	1

KIWOMYA, Alex (M)   5   0
H: 5 10   W: 10 08   b.Sheffield 20-5-96
Internationals: England U16, U17, U18, U19.

| 2014–15 | Chelsea | 0 | 0 | | |
| 2014–15 | Barnsley | 5 | 0 | 5 | 0 |

LOFTUS-CHEEK, Ruben (M)   3   0
H: 6 4   W: 11 03   b.Lewisham 23-1-96
Internationals: England U16, 17, U19, U21.

2012–13	Chelsea	0	0		
2013–14	Chelsea	0	0		
2014–15	Chelsea	3	0	3	0

LUIS, Filipe (D) — 314 9
H: 6 0 W: 10 06 b.Jaragua do Sul 9-8-85
Internationals: Brazil U20, Full caps.

Season	Club				
2003	Figueirense	7	1		
2004	Figueirense	17	0	24	1
2005–06	Real Madrid	37	0	37	0
2006–07	La Coruna	19	0		
2007–08	La Coruna	33	1		
2008–09	La Coruna	38	2		
2009–10	La Coruna	21	3	111	6
2010–11	Atletico Madrid	27	1		
2011–12	Atletico Madrid	36	0		
2012–13	Atletico Madrid	32	1		
2013–14	Atletico Madrid	32	0	127	2
2014–15	Chelsea	15	0	15	0

MATIC, Nemanja (M) — 221 13
H: 6 4 W: 13 02 b.Sabac 1-8-88
Internationals: Serbia U21, Full caps.

Season	Club				
2005–06	Jedinstvo	7	0		
2006–07	Jedinstvo	9	0	16	0
2006–07	Kosice	13	1		
2007–08	Kosice	25	1		
2008–09	Kosice	29	2	67	4
2009–10	Chelsea	2	0		
2010–11	Chelsea	0	0		
2010–11	Vitesse	27	2	27	2
2011–12	Benfica	16	1		
2012–13	Benfica	26	3		
2013–14	Benfica	14	2	56	6
2013–14	Chelsea	17	0		
2014–15	Chelsea	36	1	55	1

McEACHRAN, Josh (D) — 87 0
H: 5 10 W: 10 03 b.Oxford 1-3-93
Internationals: England U16, U17, U19, U21.

Season	Club				
2010–11	Chelsea	9	0		
2011–12	Chelsea	5	0		
2011–12	Swansea C	4	0	4	0
2012–13	Chelsea	0	0		
2012–13	Middlesbrough	38	0	38	0
2013–14	Chelsea	0	0		
2013–14	Watford	7	0	7	0
2013–14	Wigan Ath	8	0	8	0
2014–15	Chelsea	0	0	11	0
2014–15	Vitesse	19	0	19	0

MIKEL, John Obi (M) — 230 2
H: 6 0 W: 13 05 b.Plateau State 22-4-87
Internationals: Nigeria Youth, Full caps.

Season	Club				
2005	Lyn	6	1	6	1
2006–07	Chelsea	22	0		
2007–08	Chelsea	29	0		
2008–09	Chelsea	34	0		
2009–10	Chelsea	25	0		
2010–11	Chelsea	28	0		
2011–12	Chelsea	22	0		
2012–13	Chelsea	22	0		
2013–14	Chelsea	24	1		
2014–15	Chelsea	18	0	224	1

MOSES, Victor (M) — 193 24
H: 5 10 W: 11 07 b.Lagos 12-12-90
Internationals: England U16, U17, U19, U21. Nigeria Full caps.

Season	Club				
2007–08	Crystal Palace	13	3		
2008–09	Crystal Palace	27	2		
2009–10	Crystal Palace	18	6	58	11
2009–10	Wigan Ath	14	1		
2010–11	Wigan Ath	21	1		
2011–12	Wigan Ath	38	6		
2012–13	Wigan Ath	1	0	74	8
2012–13	Chelsea	23	1		
2013–14	Chelsea	0	0		
2013–14	Liverpool	19	1	19	1
2014–15	Chelsea	0	0	23	1
2014–15	Stoke C	19	3	19	3

OMERUO, Kenneth (D) — 60 0
H: 6 1 W: 12 00 b.Nigeria 10-17-93
Internationals: Nigeria U17, U20, Full caps

Season	Club				
2011–12	Chelsea	0	0		
2012–13	Chelsea	0	0		
2012–13	Den Haag	27	0	27	0
2013–14	Chelsea	0	0		
2013–14	Middlesbrough	14	0		
2014–15	Chelsea	0	0		
2014–15	Middlesbrough	19	0	33	0

OSCAR, Emboaba (M) — 133 28
H: 5 11 W: 10 04 b.Americana 9-9-91
Internationals: Brazil U20, Full caps.

Season	Club				
2008–09	Sao Paulo	1	0		
2009–10	Sao Paulo	3	0	4	0
2010–11	Internacional	7	2		
2011–12	Internacional	27	8	34	10
2012–13	Chelsea	34	4		
2013–14	Chelsea	33	8		
2014–15	Chelsea	28	6	95	18

PASALIC, Mario (M) — 63 14
H: 6 1 W: 12 04 b.Mainz 9-2-95
Internationals: Croatia U16, U17, U19, U21, Full caps.

Season	Club				
2012–13	Hajduk Split	2	0		
2013–14	Hajduk Split	30	11	32	11
2014–15	Chelsea	0	0		
2014–15	Elche	31	3	31	3

RAMIRES (M) — 248 32
H: 5 11 W: 10 03 b.Rio de Janeiro 24-3-87
Internationals: Brazil U23, Full caps.

Season	Club				
2006	Joinville	14	3	14	3
2007	Cruzeiro	32	3		
2008	Cruzeiro	25	6		
2009	Cruzeiro	4	1	61	10
2009–10	Benfica	26	4	26	4
2010–11	Chelsea	29	2		
2011–12	Chelsea	30	5		
2012–13	Chelsea	35	5		
2013–14	Chelsea	30	1		
2014–15	Chelsea	23	2	147	15

REMY, Loic (F) — 225 82
H: 6 0 W: 10 04 b.Lyon 2-1-87
Internationals: France U20, U21, Full caps.

Season	Club				
2006–07	Lyon	6	0		
2007–08	Lyon	6	0	12	0
2007–08	Lens	10	3	10	3
2008–09	Nice	32	10		
2009–10	Nice	34	14		
2010–11	Nice	2	1	68	25
2010–11	Marseille	31	15		
2011–12	Marseille	29	11		
2012–13	Marseille	14	1	74	27
2012–13	QPR	14	6		
2013–14	QPR	7	0		
2013–14	Newcastle U	26	14	26	14
2014–15	QPR	2	0	16	6
2014–15	Chelsea	19	7	19	7

ROMEU, Oriol (M) — 112 1
H: 6 0 W: 12 06 b.Ulldecona 24-9-91
Internationals: Spain U17, U19, U20, U21, U23.

Season	Club				
2008–09	Barcelona B	5	0		
2009–10	Barcelona B	26	0		
2010–11	Barcelona B	18	1	49	1
2010–11	Barcelona	1	0	1	0
2011–12	Chelsea	16	0		
2012–13	Chelsea	0	0		
2013–14	Chelsea	0	0		
2013–14	Valencia	13	0	13	0
2014–15	Chelsea	0	0	22	0
2014–15	Stuttgart	27	0	27	0

SALAH, Mohamed (M) — 112 28
H: 5 9 W: 11 04 b.Basion 15-6-92
Internationals: Egypt U20, U23, Full caps

Season	Club				
2010–11	Al-Mokawloon	21	4		
2011–12	Al-Mokawloon	15	7	36	11
2012–13	Basle	29	5		
2013–14	Basle	18	4	47	9
2013–14	Chelsea	10	2		
2014–15	Chelsea	3	0	13	2
2014–15	Fiorentina	16	6	16	6

SCHURRLE, Andre (F) — 175 49
H: 6 0 W: 11 06 b.Ludwigschafen 6-11-90
Internationals: Germany U19, U20, U21, Full caps.

Season	Club				
2009–10	Mainz	33	5		
2010–11	Mainz	33	15	66	20
2011–12	Bayer Leverkusen	31	7		
2012–13	Bayer Leverkusen	34	11	65	18
2013–14	Chelsea	30	8		
2014–15	Chelsea	14	3	44	11

Transferred to Wolfsburg February 2015.

SOLANKE, Dominic (F) — 0 0
H: 6 1 W: 11 11 b.Reading 14-9-97
Internationals: England U16, U17, U18.

Season	Club				
2014–15	Chelsea	0	0		

SWIFT, John (M) — 22 2
H: 6 0 W: 11 07 b.Portsmouth 23-6-95
Internationals: England U16, U17, U18, U19, U20.

Season	Club				
2013–14	Chelsea	1	0		
2014–15	Chelsea	0	0	1	0
2014–15	Rotherham U	3	0	3	0
2014–15	Swindon T	18	2	18	2

TERRY, John (D) — 465 39
H: 6 1 W: 14 02 b.Barking 7-12-80
Internationals: England U21, Full caps.

Season	Club				
1997–98	Chelsea	0	0		
1998–99	Chelsea	2	0		
1999–2000	Chelsea	4	0		
1999–2000	Nottingham F	6	0	6	0
2000–01	Chelsea	22	1		
2001–02	Chelsea	33	1		
2002–03	Chelsea	20	3		
2003–04	Chelsea	33	2		
2004–05	Chelsea	36	3		
2005–06	Chelsea	36	4		
2006–07	Chelsea	28	1		
2007–08	Chelsea	23	1		
2008–09	Chelsea	35	1		
2009–10	Chelsea	37	2		
2010–11	Chelsea	33	3		
2011–12	Chelsea	31	6		
2012–13	Chelsea	14	4		
2013–14	Chelsea	34	2		
2014–15	Chelsea	38	5	459	39

TRAORE, Bertrand (M) — 48 17
H: 5 10 b.Bob-Dioulasso 6-9-95
Internationals: Burkina Faso U17, Full caps

Season	Club				
2013–14	Vitesse	0	0		
2013–14	Vitesse	15	3		
2014–15	Vitesse	0	0		
2014–15	Vitesse	33	14	48	17

VAN GINKEL, Marco (M) — 115 19
H: 6 1 W: 12 11 b.Amersfoort 1-12-92
Internationals: Netherlands U15, U19, U21, Full caps

Season	Club				
2009–10	Vitesse	3	0		
2010–11	Vitesse	26	5		
2011–12	Vitesse	34	5		
2012–13	Vitesse	33	8	96	18
2013–14	Chelsea	2	0		
2014–15	Chelsea	0	0	2	0
2014–15	AC Milan	17	1	17	1

WALLACE, Oliveira (D) — 46 2
H: 5 9 W: 10 09 b.Rio de Jainero 1-5-94
Internationals: Brazil U17, U20.

Season	Club				
2011	Fluminense	3	0		
2012	Fluminense	18	1	21	1
2013–14	Chelsea	0	0		
2013–14	Inter Milan	3	0	3	0
2014–15	Chelsea	0	0		
2014–15	Vitesse	22	1	22	1

WILLIAN, da Silva (M) — 197 27
H: 5 9 W: 11 10 b.Ribeirao 9-8-88
Internationals: Brazil U20, Full caps.

Season	Club				
2006	Corinthians	5	0		
2007	Corinthians	0	0	5	0
2008–09	Shakhtar Donetsk	29	5		
2009–10	Shakhtar Donetsk	22	5		
2010–11	Shakhtar Donetsk	28	3		
2011–12	Shakhtar Donetsk	27	5		
2012–13	Shakhtar Donetsk	14	2	120	20
2012–13	Anzhi Makhachkala	7	1		
2013–14	Anzhi Makhachkala	4	0	11	1
2013–14	Chelsea	25	4		
2014–15	Chelsea	36	2	61	6

ZOUMA, Kurt (D) — 76 3
H: 6 2 W: 13 04 b.Lyon 27-10-94
Internationals: France U16, U17, U19, U20, U21, Full caps.

Season	Club				
2011–12	St Etienne	20	1		
2012–13	St Etienne	18	2		
2013–14	St Etienne	0	0		
2013–14	St Etienne	23	0	61	3
2014–15	Chelsea	15	0	15	0

Players retained or with offer of contract
Abraham, Tammy; Aina, Temitayo Olufisayo; Ali, Mukhtar Abdullahi; Angban, Bekanty Victorien; Christie-Davies, Isaac David; Clarke-Salter, Jake-Liam; Colkett, Charlie; Cuevas, Bradley Ray; Conroy, Dion John; Cuevas Jara, Cristian Alejandro; Dabo, Sheik Mohamed Fankaty; Davey, Alex James; Davila Plascencia, Ulises Alejandro; Delac, Matej; Houghton, Jordan; Kasmirski, Filipe Luis; Marin, Marko; Mitchell, Reece Steven; Musonda, Charles; Musonda, Tika Kafusha; Palmer, Kasey Remel; Perica, Stipe; Piazon, Lucas Domingues; Sammut, Ruben; Scott, Kyle; Suljic, Ali; Wright, Kevin.

Scholars
Adamczyk, Hubert; Bolkiah, Faiq Jefri; Dasilva, Jay Rhys; Muheim, Miro Max Maria; Tomori, Fikayo; Wakefield, Charlie Mark.

CHELTENHAM T (23)

BERRY, Durrell (D) 107 3
H: 5 11 W: 11 11 b.Derby 27-5-92

2010–11	Aston Villa	0	0		
2011–12	Plymouth Arg	35	0		
2012–13	Plymouth Arg	28	0		
2013–14	Plymouth Arg	32	1		
2014–15	Plymouth Arg	0	0	**95**	**1**
2014–15	Cheltenham T	12	2	**12**	**2**

BLACK, Paul (D) 77 1
H: 6 0 W: 12 10 b.Middleton 18-5-90

2007–08	Oldham Ath	2	0		
2008–09	Oldham Ath	3	0		
2009–10	Oldham Ath	13	1		
2010–11	Oldham Ath	29	0		
2011–12	Oldham Ath	13	0	**60**	**1**
2012–13	Tranmere R	10	0		
2013–14	Tranmere R	0	0	**10**	**0**
2013–14	Mansfield T	0	0		
2013–14	*Carlisle U*	4	0	**4**	**0**
2014–15	Cheltenham T	3	0	**3**	**0**

BOWEN, James (M) 3 0
b. 4-2-96

2013–14	Cheltenham T	0	0		
2014–15	Cheltenham T	3	0	**3**	**0**

BRAHAM-BARRETT, Craig (D) 74 0
H: 5 9 b.England 1-9-88

2013–14	Cheltenham T	29	0		
2014–15	Cheltenham T	45	0	**74**	**0**

BROWN, Troy (D) 152 11
H: 6 1 W: 12 01 b.Croydon 17-9-90
Internationals: Wales U17, U19, U21.

2009–10	Ipswich T	1	0		
2010–11	Ipswich T	12	0	**13**	**0**
2011–12	Rotherham U	6	1	**6**	**1**
2011–12	*Aldershot T*	17	2		
2012–13	Aldershot T	34	3	**51**	**5**
2013–14	Cheltenham T	39	4		
2014–15	Cheltenham T	43	1	**82**	**5**

CARSON, Trevor (G) 178 0
H: 6 0 W: 14 11 b.Downpatrick 5-3-88
Internationals: Northern Ireland U17, U18, U19, U20, U21, B.

2004–05	Sunderland	0	0		
2005–06	Sunderland	0	0		
2006–07	Sunderland	0	0		
2007–08	Sunderland	0	0		
2008–09	Sunderland	0	0		
2008–09	*Chesterfield*	18	0	**18**	**0**
2009–10	Sunderland	0	0		
2010–11	Sunderland	0	0		
2010–11	*Lincoln C*	16	0	**16**	**0**
2010–11	*Brentford*	1	0	**1**	**0**
2011–12	Sunderland	0	0		
2011–12	*Hull C*	0	0		
2011–12	Bury	17	0		
2012–13	Bury	39	0		
2013–14	Bury	5	0	**61**	**0**
2013–14	*Portsmouth*	36	0	**36**	**0**
2014–15	Cheltenham T	46	0	**46**	**0**

DALE, Bobbie (F) 3 0
b. 25-11-95

2013–14	Cheltenham T	1	0		
2014–15	Cheltenham T	2	0	**3**	**0**

DE VITA, Raffaele (F) 171 35
H: 6 0 W: 11 09 b.Rome 23-9-87

2005–06	Blackburn R	0	0		
2006–07	Blackburn R	0	0		
2007–08	Blackburn R	0	0		
2008–09	Livingston	7	1		
2009–10	Livingston	29	9		
2010–11	Livingston	31	12	**67**	**22**
2011–12	Swindon T	38	4		
2012–13	Swindon T	36	8	**74**	**12**
2013–14	Bradford C	20	1	**20**	**1**
2014–15	Cheltenham T	10	0	**10**	**0**

Transferred to Ross Co January 2015.

DEAMAN, Jack (D) 18 0
H: 6 3 W: 11 11 b.Camden 18-5-93

2011–12	Birmingham C	0	0		
2012–13	Birmingham C	0	0		
2012–13	*Cheltenham T*	0	0		
2013–14	Birmingham C	0	0		
2014–15	Cheltenham T	18	0	**18**	**0**

ELLIOTT, Steve (D) 493 26
H: 6 1 W: 14 00 b.Derby 29-10-78
Internationals: England U21.

1996–97	Derby Co	0	0		
1997–98	Derby Co	3	0		
1998–99	Derby Co	11	0		
1999–2000	Derby Co	20	0		
2000–01	Derby Co	6	0		
2001–02	Derby Co	6	0		
2002–03	Derby Co	23	1		
2003–04	Derby Co	4	0	**73**	**1**
2003–04	Blackpool	28	0	**28**	**0**
2004–05	Bristol R	41	2		
2005–06	Bristol R	45	2		
2006–07	Bristol R	39	5		
2007–08	Bristol R	33	3		
2008–09	Bristol R	39	3		
2009–10	Bristol R	21	1	**218**	**16**
2010–11	Cheltenham T	41	1		
2011–12	Cheltenham T	38	2		
2012–13	Cheltenham T	46	4		
2013–14	Cheltenham T	32	1		
2014–15	Cheltenham T	17	1	**174**	**9**

GOULD, Matthew (G) 0 0
b. 7-1-94

2014–15	Cheltenham T	0	0		

HALL, Asa (M) 212 29
H: 6 2 W: 11 09 b.Sandwell 29-11-86
Internationals: England U19, U20.

2004–05	Birmingham C	0	0		
2005–06	Birmingham C	0	0		
2005–06	*Boston U*	12	0	**12**	**0**
2006–07	Birmingham C	0	0		
2007–08	Birmingham C	0	0		
2007–08	*Shrewsbury T*	15	3		
2008–09	Luton T	42	10		
2009–10	Luton T	0	0	**42**	**10**
2010–11	Oxford U	41	4		
2011–12	Oxford U	34	7		
2012–13	Shrewsbury T	15	2		
2012–13	*Aldershot T*	16	0	**16**	**0**
2013–14	Shrewsbury T	17	0	**47**	**5**
2013–14	*Oxford U*	19	3	**94**	**14**
2014–15	Cheltenham T	1	0	**1**	**0**

HANKS, Joe (M) 36 2
b.Gloucester 2-3-95

2012–13	Cheltenham T	1	0		
2013–14	Cheltenham T	2	0		
2014–15	Cheltenham T	33	2	**36**	**2**

HAWORTH, Andrew (M) 86 3
H: 5 11 W: 11 10 b.Lancaster 28-11-88

2007–08	Blackburn R	0	0		
2008–09	Blackburn R	0	0		
2009–10	Blackburn R	0	0		
2009–10	*Rochdale*	7	0		
2010–11	Bury	40	3		
2011–12	Bury	6	0	**46**	**3**
2011–12	*Oxford U*	4	0	**4**	**0**
2011–12	*Bradford C*	3	0	**3**	**0**
2012–13	Falkirk	12	0	**12**	**0**
2012–13	Rochdale	7	0	**14**	**0**
2013–14	Notts Co	2	0	**2**	**0**
2014–15	Cheltenham T	5	0	**5**	**0**

HAYNES, Danny (F) 279 47
H: 5 11 W: 12 04 b.Peckham 19-1-88
Internationals: England U19.

2005–06	Ipswich T	19	3		
2006–07	Ipswich T	31	7		
2006–07	*Millwall*	5	2	**5**	**2**
2007–08	Ipswich T	40	7		
2008–09	Ipswich T	24	0	**114**	**17**
2009–10	Bristol C	38	7		
2010–11	Bristol C	13	1	**51**	**8**
2010–11	Barnsley	20	6		
2011–12	Barnsley	12	0	**32**	**6**
2011–12	Charlton Ath	14	2		
2012–13	Charlton Ath	20	7	**34**	**9**
2013–14	Notts Co	21	3		
2013–14	*Hibernian*	9	1	**9**	**1**
2014–15	Notts Co	2	0	**23**	**3**
2014–15	*Crewe Alex*	3	0	**3**	**0**
2014–15	Cheltenham T	8	1	**8**	**1**

KOTWICA, Zack (M) 35 2
b. 18-1-95

2013–14	Cheltenham T	18	0		
2014–15	Cheltenham T	17	2	**35**	**2**

LAWRENCE, Jamal (F) 1 0
b. 28-10-96

2014–15	Cheltenham T	1	0	**1**	**0**

MANSET, Mathieu (F) 150 21
H: 6 1 W: 13 08 b.Metz 5-8-89

2009–10	Hereford U	29	3		
2010–11	Hereford U	21	7	**50**	**10**
2010–11	Reading	13	2		
2011–12	Reading	15	3	**28**	**5**
2011–12	*Shanghai S*	9	1	**9**	**1**
2012–13	FC Sion	5	1	**5**	**1**
2012–13	Carlisle U	7	0	**7**	**0**
2013–14	Coventry C	9	1	**9**	**1**
2013–14	Antwerp	11	3	**11**	**3**
2014–15	Walsall	19	0	**19**	**0**
2014–15	Cheltenham T	12	0	**12**	**0**

REYNOLDS, Danny (D) 0 0

2014–15	Cheltenham T	0	0		

REYNOLDS, Harry (G) 0 0
b. 3-6-96

2014–15	Cheltenham T	0	0		

RICHARDS, Eliot (M) 151 23
H: 5 9 W: 11 09 b.New Tredegar 1-9-91
Internationals: Wales U19, U21.

2009–10	Bristol R	5	0		
2010–11	Bristol R	13	1		
2011–12	Bristol R	32	7		
2012–13	Bristol R	40	6		
2013–14	Bristol R	22	2	**112**	**16**
2013–14	*Exeter C*	17	5	**17**	**5**
2014–15	Tranmere R	13	1	**13**	**1**
2014–15	Cheltenham T	9	1	**9**	**1**

RICHARDS, Matt (D) 462 41
H: 5 8 W: 11 00 b.Harlow 26-12-84
Internationals: England U16, U17, U18, U21.

2001–02	Ipswich T	0	0		
2002–03	Ipswich T	13	0		
2003–04	Ipswich T	44	1		
2004–05	Ipswich T	24	1		
2005–06	Ipswich T	38	4		
2006–07	Ipswich T	28	2		
2007–08	Ipswich T	0	0		
2007–08	*Brighton & HA*	28	0		
2008–09	*Brighton & HA*	23	1	**51**	**1**
2008–09	Wycombe W	0	0		
2008–09	*Notts Co*	1	0	**1**	**0**
2008–09	Ipswich T	1	0	**148**	**8**
2009–10	Walsall	40	4		
2010–11	Walsall	46	8	**86**	**12**
2011–12	Shrewsbury T	42	5		
2012–13	Shrewsbury T	43	7	**85**	**12**
2013–14	Cheltenham T	46	6		
2014–15	Cheltenham T	45	2	**91**	**8**

STERLING-JAMES, Omari (M) 22 1
b.Birmingham 15-9-93

2014–15	Cheltenham T	22	1	**22**	**1**

TAYLOR, Matthew (D) 198 11
H: 6 0 W: 12 04 b.Chorley 30-1-82

2008–09	Exeter C	31	2		
2009–10	Exeter C	46	5		
2010–11	Exeter C	28	2	**105**	**9**
2011–12	Charlton Ath	41	0		
2012–13	Charlton Ath	12	0	**53**	**0**
2013–14	Bradford C	2	0	**2**	**0**
2013–14	*Colchester U*	5	1	**5**	**1**
2014–15	Cheltenham T	33	1	**33**	**1**

VAUGHAN, Lee (D) 32 0
H: 5 7 W: 10 08 b.Castle Bromwich 17-7-86
Internationals: England C.

2005–06	Walsall	0	0		
2014–15	Cheltenham T	32	0	**32**	**0**

WILLIAMS, Harry (M) 13 0
b.Cheltenham 17-1-96

2013–14	Cheltenham T	5	0		
2014–15	Cheltenham T	8	0	**13**	**0**

Players retained or with offer of contract
Wynter, Jordan James Cecil.

Scholars
Chambers, Karnell Patrick Michael; Craddock, Callum David; Daly, Reece John; Dinsmore, Alexander; Goodwin, Jamie Liam; Lymn, Jordan Kenneth; McCarthy, James Patrick; McFarlane, Callum Robert; Mendes, Samuel; Reynolds, Danny James; Reynolds, Harry; Rowe, Niall Alan; Sheppard, Liam Paul; Tetek, Bojan; Thompson, Lewis James.

CHESTERFIELD (24)

ARIYIBI, Gboly (M) 21 1
b. 18-1-95
Internationals: USA U20.

2013–14	Leeds U	2	0	**2**	**0**
2013–14	*Tranmere R*	2	0	**2**	**0**
2014–15	Chesterfield	17	1	**17**	**1**

BANKS, Oliver (D) 53 8
H: 6 3 W: 11 11 b.Rotherham 21-9-92

2010–11	Rotherham U	1	1		
2011–12	Rotherham U	0	0	**1**	**1**

2013–14	Chesterfield	25	7		
2014–15	Chesterfield	24	0	**49**	**7**
2014–15	*Northampton T*	3	0	**3**	**0**

BEESLEY, Jake (F) 0 0

2013–14	Chesterfield	0	0		
2014–15	Chesterfield	0	0		

BOCO, Romuald (F) 133 15

H: 5 10 W: 10 13 b.Bernay 8-7-85

Internationals: Benin Full caps.

2006–07	Accrington S	32	3		
2007–08	Accrington S	11	0		
2008–09	Accrington S	0	0		
2009–10	Burton Alb	8	0	**8**	**0**
From Sligo					
2012–13	Accrington S	42	10	**85**	**13**
2013–14	Plymouth Arg	27	1	**27**	**1**
2014–15	Chesterfield	13	1	**13**	**1**

Transferred to Bharat January 2015.

BROADHEAD, Jack (D) 1 0

b. 2-10-94

2012–13	Chesterfield	0	0		
2013–14	Chesterfield	0	0		
2014–15	Chesterfield	1	0	**1**	**0**

CHAPMAN, Aaron (G) 3 0

b. 29-5-90

2013–14	Chesterfield	0	0		
2014–15	Chesterfield	0	0		
2014–15	*Accrington S*	3	0	**3**	**0**

CLUCAS, Sam (M) 101 17

H: 5 10 W: 11 08 b.Lincoln 25-9-90

2009–10	Lincoln C	0	0		
2011–12	Hereford U	17	0	**17**	**0**
2013–14	Mansfield T	38	8		
2014–15	Mansfield T	5	0	**43**	**8**
2014–15	Chesterfield	41	9	**41**	**9**

DARIKWA, Tendayi (M) 125 9

H: 6 2 W: 12 02 b.Nottingham 13-12-91

2010–11	Chesterfield	0	0		
2011–12	Chesterfield	2	0		
2012–13	Chesterfield	36	5		
2013–14	Chesterfield	41	3		
2014–15	Chesterfield	46	1	**125**	**9**

DAWES, Charlie (M) 0 0

b. 13-9-95

2014–15	Chesterfield	0	0		

EVATT, Ian (D) 460 20

H: 6 3 W: 13 12 b.Coventry 19-11-81

1998–99	Derby Co	0	0		
1999–2000	Derby Co	0	0		
2000–01	Derby Co	1	0		
2001–02	*Northampton T*	11	0	**11**	**0**
2001–02	Derby Co	3	0		
2002–03	Derby Co	30	0	**34**	**0**
2003–04	Chesterfield	43	5		
2004–05	Chesterfield	41	4		
2005–06	QPR	27	0		
2006–07	QPR	0	0	**27**	**0**
2006–07	Blackpool	44	0		
2007–08	Blackpool	29	0		
2008–09	Blackpool	33	1		
2009–10	Blackpool	36	4		
2010–11	Blackpool	38	1		
2011–12	Blackpool	39	3		
2012–13	Blackpool	11	0	**230**	**9**
2013–14	Chesterfield	35	1		
2014–15	Chesterfield	39	1	**158**	**11**

GARDNER, Dan (M) 39 6

H: 6 1 W: 12 05 b.Manchester 5-4-90

2009–10	Crewe Alex	2	0	**2**	**0**
From Droylsden, FC Halifax T					
2013–14	Chesterfield	16	3		
2014–15	Chesterfield	17	1	**33**	**4**
2014–15	*Tranmere R*	4	2	**4**	**2**

GNANDUILLET, Armand (F) 81 12

H: 6 4 W: 13 12 b.Angers 13-2-92

Internationals: Ivory Coast U20.

2012–13	Chesterfield	13	3		
2013–14	Chesterfield	34	5		
2014–15	Chesterfield	26	2	**73**	**10**
2014–15	*Tranmere R*	4	2	**4**	**2**
2014–15	*Oxford U*	4	0	**4**	**0**

HARRISON, Byron (F) 176 39

H: 6 3 W: 13 02 b.Wandsworth 15-6-87

2010–11	Stevenage	20	8		
2011–12	Stevenage	18	2	**38**	**10**
2011–12	AFC Wimbledon	19	2		
2012–13	AFC Wimbledon	21	8	**40**	**10**
2012–13	Cheltenham T	17	1		
2013–14	Cheltenham T	46	13		
2014–15	Cheltenham T	23	4	**86**	**18**

2014–15	Chesterfield	12	1	**12**	**1**

HIRD, Samuel (D) 266 8

H: 5 7 W: 10 12 b.Askern 7-9-87

2005–06	Leeds U	0	0		
2006–07	Leeds U	0	0		
2006–07	*Doncaster R*	5	0		
2007–08	Doncaster R	4	0		
2007–08	*Grimsby T*	17	0	**17**	**0**
2008–09	Doncaster R	37	1		
2009–10	Doncaster R	36	0		
2010–11	Doncaster R	32	0		
2011–12	Doncaster R	31	0	**145**	**1**
2012–13	Chesterfield	41	2		
2013–14	Chesterfield	35	2		
2014–15	Chesterfield	28	3	**104**	**7**

HUMPHREYS, Richie (M) 638 47

H: 5 11 W: 12 07 b.Sheffield 30-11-77

Internationals: England U20, U21.

1995–96	Sheffield W	5	0		
1996–97	Sheffield W	29	3		
1997–98	Sheffield W	7	0		
1998–99	Sheffield W	19	1		
1999–2000	Sheffield W	0	0		
1999–2000	*Scunthorpe U*	6	2	**6**	**2**
1999–2000	*Cardiff C*	9	2	**9**	**2**
2000–01	Sheffield W	7	0	**67**	**4**
2000–01	Cambridge U	7	3	**7**	**3**
2001–02	Hartlepool U	46	5		
2002–03	Hartlepool U	46	11		
2003–04	Hartlepool U	46	3		
2004–05	Hartlepool U	46	3		
2005–06	Hartlepool U	46	2		
2006–07	Hartlepool U	38	3		
2006–07	*Port Vale*	7	0	**7**	**0**
2007–08	Hartlepool U	45	3		
2008–09	Hartlepool U	45	0		
2009–10	Hartlepool U	38	0		
2010–11	Hartlepool U	25	2		
2011–12	Hartlepool U	29	1		
2012–13	Hartlepool U	31	1	**481**	**34**
2013–14	Chesterfield	42	2		
2014–15	Chesterfield	19	0	**61**	**2**

JONES, Daniel (D) 196 5

H: 6 2 W: 13 00 b.Rowley Regis 14-7-86

2005–06	Wolverhampton W	1	0		
2006–07	Wolverhampton W	8	0		
2007–08	Wolverhampton W	1	0		
2007–08	*Northampton T*	33	3	**33**	**3**
2008–09	Wolverhampton W	0	0		
2008–09	*Oldham Ath*	23	1	**23**	**1**
2009–10	Wolverhampton W	0	0	**10**	**0**
2009–10	*Notts Co*	7	0	**7**	**0**
2009–10	*Bristol R*	17	0	**17**	**0**
2010–11	Sheffield W	25	0		
2011–12	Sheffield W	3	0		
2012–13	Sheffield W	9	0	**37**	**0**
2012–13	Port Vale	16	1		
2013–14	Port Vale	20	0	**36**	**1**
2014–15	Chesterfield	33	0	**33**	**0**

LEE, Tommy (G) 349 0

H: 6 2 W: 12 00 b.Keighley 3-1-86

2005–06	Manchester U	0	0		
2005–06	*Macclesfield T*	11	0		
2006–07	Macclesfield T	34	0		
2007–08	Macclesfield T	18	0	**63**	**0**
2007–08	*Rochdale*	11	0	**11**	**0**
2008–09	Chesterfield	28	0		
2009–10	Chesterfield	42	0		
2010–11	Chesterfield	46	0		
2011–12	Chesterfield	35	0		
2012–13	Chesterfield	32	0		
2013–14	Chesterfield	46	0		
2014–15	Chesterfield	46	0	**275**	**0**

MAGUIRE, Laurence (D) 0 0

b. 8-2-97

2013–14	Chesterfield	0	0		
2014–15	Chesterfield	0	0		

MASSEY, Joe (D) 0 0

2014–15	Chesterfield	0	0		

MORSY, Sam (M) 144 7

H: 5 9 W: 12 06 b.Wolverhampton 10-9-91

2009–10	Port Vale	1	0		
2010–11	Port Vale	16	1		
2011–12	Port Vale	26	1		
2012–13	Port Vale	28	2	**71**	**4**
2013–14	Chesterfield	34	1		
2014–15	Chesterfield	39	2	**73**	**3**

O'SHEA, Jay (M) 234 45

H: 5 9 W: 12 00 b.Dun Laoghaire 10-8-88

Internationals: Republic of Ireland U19, U21, U23.

2007	Bray Wanderers	27	4	**27**	**4**
2008	Galway U	29	8		
2009	Galway U	19	3	**48**	**11**
2009–10	Birmingham C	1	0		
2009–10	*Middlesbrough*	2	0	**2**	**0**
2010–11	Birmingham C	0	0	**1**	**0**
2010–11	*Stevenage*	5	0	**5**	**0**
2010–11	*Port Vale*	5	1	**5**	**1**
2011–12	Milton Keynes D	28	5		
2012–13	Milton Keynes D	11	1	**39**	**6**
2012–13	*Chesterfield*	26	7		
2013–14	Chesterfield	40	9		
2014–15	Chesterfield	41	7	**107**	**23**

ONOVWIGUN, Michael (M) 2 0

b. 9-4-96

2014–15	Chesterfield	2	0	**2**	**0**

RAGLAN, Charlie (D) 18 1

H: 6 0 W: 11 13 b.Wythenshawe 28-4-93

2011–12	Port Vale	0	0		
2012–13	Port Vale	0	0		
2013–14	Port Vale	0	0		
2014–15	Chesterfield	18	1	**18**	**1**

ROBERTS, Gary (F) 347 63

H: 5 10 W: 11 09 b.Chester 18-3-84

Internationals: England C.

2006–07	Accrington S	14	8	**14**	**8**
2006–07	Ipswich T	33	2		
2007–08	Ipswich T	21	1	**54**	**3**
2007–08	*Crewe Alex*	4	0	**4**	**0**
2008–09	Huddersfield T	43	9		
2009–10	Huddersfield T	43	7		
2010–11	Huddersfield T	37	9		
2011–12	Huddersfield T	39	6	**162**	**31**
2012–13	Swindon T	39	4	**39**	**4**
2013–14	Chesterfield	40	11		
2014–15	Chesterfield	34	6	**74**	**17**

RYAN, James (M) 285 32

H: 5 8 W: 11 08 b.Maghull 6-9-88

Internationals: Republic of Ireland U21. Northern Ireland Full caps.

2006–07	Liverpool	0	0		
2007–08	Liverpool	0	0		
2007–08	*Shrewsbury T*	4	0	**4**	**0**
2008–09	Accrington S	44	10		
2009–10	Accrington S	39	3		
2010–11	Accrington S	46	9	**129**	**22**
2011–12	Scunthorpe U	24	2		
2012–13	Scunthorpe U	45	2	**69**	**4**
2013–14	Chesterfield	39	2		
2014–15	Chesterfield	44	4	**83**	**6**

SCULLY, Josh (M) 0 0

b. 6-3-95

2012–13	Chesterfield	0	0		
2013–14	Chesterfield	0	0		
2014–15	Chesterfield	0	0		

TALBOT, Drew (F) 300 23

H: 5 10 W: 11 00 b.Barnsley 19-7-86

2003–04	Sheffield W	0	0		
2004–05	Sheffield W	21	4		
2005–06	Sheffield W	0	0		
2006–07	Sheffield W	8	0	**29**	**4**
2006–07	*Scunthorpe U*	3	1	**3**	**1**
2006–07	Luton T	15	3		
2007–08	Luton T	27	0		
2008–09	Luton T	7	0	**49**	**3**
2008–09	*Chesterfield*	17	2		
2009–10	Chesterfield	30	6		
2010–11	Chesterfield	44	3		
2011–12	Chesterfield	43	2		
2012–13	Chesterfield	42	2		
2013–14	Chesterfield	25	0		
2014–15	Chesterfield	9	0	**210**	**15**
2014–15	*Plymouth Arg*	9	0	**9**	**0**

WRIGHT, Myles (G) 1 0

b. 14-9-96

2014–15	Chesterfield	1	0	**1**	**0**

Players retained or with offer of contract

Dieseruvwe, Emmanuel Aghohho.

Scholars

Bayne, Joseph John; Beesley, Jake Elliott; Coy, Mason Taylor; Dakwa, Edward Junior Munashe; Daly, Derek Kevin; Daswell, Martell Jordan; Fowodu, Temitope Olamide Joseph; Holmes, Brad Geoff; Hudson, Jake Bevan; Jarrald, Thomas Lewis; Maguire, Laurence Henry; Marshall, Thomas Francis; Massey, Joseph Paul; Milner, George Edward; Morrison, Curtis Lloyd; Randle, Luke; Sugden, Lewis Jack; Walshaw, Jordan Thomas.

Non-Contract

Wright, Myles Harvey.

COLCHESTER U (25)

BONNE, Macauley (F)   24 3
H: 5 11 W: 12 00 b.Ipswich 26-10-95
Internationals: Zimbabwe U23.
| 2013–14 | Colchester U | 14 | 2 | | |
| 2014–15 | Colchester U | 10 | 1 | 24 | 3 |

BRANSGROVE, James (G) 0 0
H: 6 4 W: 12 04 b. 12-5-95
| 2013–14 | Colchester U | 0 | 0 |
| 2014–15 | Colchester U | 0 | 0 |

CLOHESSY, Sean (D) 236 7
H: 5 11 W: 12 07 b.Croydon 12-12-86
2005–06	Gillingham	20	1		
2006–07	Gillingham	6	0		
2007–08	Gillingham	17	0	43	1
From Salisbury C.
2010–11	Southend U	46	1		
2011–12	Southend U	45	0		
2012–13	Southend U	46	3	137	4
2013–14	Kilmarnock	24	2	24	2
2014–15	Colchester U	32	0	32	0

CURTIS, Jack (M) 0 0
H: 5 7 W: 11 00 b. 11-9-95
| 2013–14 | Colchester U | 0 | 0 |
| 2014–15 | Colchester U | 0 | 0 |

EASTMAN, Tom (D) 152 6
H: 6 3 W: 13 12 b.Clacton 21-10-91
2009–10	Ipswich T	1	0		
2010–11	Ipswich T	9	0	10	0
2011–12	Colchester U	25	3		
2011–12	Crawley T	6	0	6	0
2012–13	Colchester U	29	2		
2013–14	Colchester U	36	0		
2014–15	Colchester U	46	1	136	6

FOX, David (M) 215 13
H: 5 9 W: 11 08 b.Leek 13-12-83
Internationals: England U16, U17, U19, U20.
2000–01	Manchester U	0	0		
2001–02	Manchester U	0	0		
2002–03	Manchester U	0	0		
2003–04	Manchester U	0	0		
2004–05	Manchester U	0	0		
2004–05	Shrewsbury T	4	1	4	1
2005–06	Manchester U	0	0		
2005–06	Blackpool	7	1		
2006–07	Blackpool	37	4		
2007–08	Blackpool	28	1		
2008–09	Blackpool	22	0	94	6
2009–10	Colchester U	18	3		
2010–11	Norwich C	32	1		
2011–12	Norwich C	28	0		
2012–13	Norwich C	2	0		
2013–14	Colchester U	0	0	62	1
2013–14	Barnsley	7	0	7	0
2014–15	Colchester U	30	2	48	5

GILBEY, Alex (M) 73 2
H: 6 0 W: 11 07 b.Dagenham 9-12-94
2011–12	Colchester U	0	0		
2012–13	Colchester U	3	0		
2013–14	Colchester U	36	1		
2014–15	Colchester U	34	1	73	2

GORDON, Ben (D) 86 1
H: 5 11 W: 12 06 b.Bradford 2-3-91
Internationals: England U16, U17, U20.
2008–09	Chelsea	0	0		
2009–10	Chelsea	0	0		
2009–10	Tranmere R	4	0	4	0
2010–11	Chelsea	0	0		
2010–11	Scunthorpe U	14	0	14	0
2011–12	Chelsea	0	0		
2011–12	Peterborough U	1	0	1	0
2011–12	Kilmarnock	17	0	17	0
2012–13	Chelsea	0	0		
2012–13	Birmingham C	1	0	1	0
2012–13	Yeovil T	3	0	3	0
2013–14	Ross Co	28	1	28	1
2014–15	Colchester U	18	0	18	0

GORKSS, Kaspars (D) 378 25
H: 6 3 W: 13 05 b.Riga 6-11-81
Internationals: Latvia U21, Full caps.
2002	Auda Riga	28	0	28	0
2003	Oster	8	0		
2004	Oster	24	1	32	1
2005	Assyriska	23	0	23	0
2006	Ventspils	28	5	28	5
2006–07	Blackpool	10	0		
2007–08	Blackpool	40	5	50	5
2008–09	QPR	31	0		
2009–10	QPR	41	3		
2010–11	QPR	42	3		
2011–12	QPR	0	0	114	6
2011–12	Reading	42	3		
2012–13	Reading	14	1		
2012–13	Wolverhampton W	15	0	15	0
2013–14	Reading	25	3	81	7
2014–15	Colchester U	7	1	7	1
Transferred to Ergotelis January 2015.

HARNEY, Jamie (D) 1 0
b. 4-3-96
Internationals: Northern Ireland U17, U19, U21.
| 2014–15 | Colchester U | 1 | 0 | 1 | 0 |

HOLMAN, Dan (F) 4 0
H: 5 11 W: 11 03 b.Northampton 5-6-90
| 2014–15 | Colchester U | 4 | 0 | 4 | 0 |

IBEHRE, Jabo (F) 458 83
H: 6 2 W: 13 13 b.Islington 28-1-83
1999–2000	Leyton Orient	3	0		
2000–01	Leyton Orient	5	2		
2001–02	Leyton Orient	28	4		
2002–03	Leyton Orient	25	5		
2003–04	Leyton Orient	35	4		
2004–05	Leyton Orient	19	2		
2005–06	Leyton Orient	33	8		
2006–07	Leyton Orient	30	4		
2007–08	Leyton Orient	31	7	209	36
2008–09	Walsall	39	10	39	10
2009–10	Milton Keynes D	10	1		
2009–10	Southend U	4	0	4	0
2009–10	Stockport Co	20	5	20	5
2010–11	Milton Keynes D	42	3		
2011–12	Milton Keynes D	39	8		
2012–13	Milton Keynes D	3	0	94	12
2012–13	Colchester U	30	8		
2013–14	Colchester U	37	8		
2014–15	Colchester U	5	0	72	16
2014–15	Oldham Ath	11	2	11	2
2014–15	Barnsley	9	2	9	2

KENT, Frankie (D) 11 0
H: 6 2 W: 12 00 b.Romford 21-11-95
| 2013–14 | Colchester U | 1 | 0 | | |
| 2014–15 | Colchester U | 10 | 0 | 11 | 0 |

LAPSLIE, Tom (M) 11 1
H: 5 6 W: 10 12 b. 5-5-95
| 2013–14 | Colchester U | 0 | 0 | | |
| 2014–15 | Colchester U | 11 | 1 | 11 | 1 |

LAWRENCE, Byron (M) 2 0
H: 5 7 W: 10 03 b.Cambridge 12-3-96
2011–12	Ipswich T	0	0		
2012–13	Ipswich T	0	0		
2013–14	Colchester U	1	0	1	0
2014–15	Colchester U	1	0	1	0

LEWINGTON, Chris (G) 128 0
H: 6 1 W: 12 00 b.Sidcup 23-8-88
2009–10	Dagenham & R	0	0		
2010–11	Dagenham & R	3	0		
2011–12	Dagenham & R	41	0		
2012–13	Dagenham & R	41	0		
2013–14	Dagenham & R	42	0	127	0
2014–15	Colchester U	1	0	1	0

LOKKO, Kevin (D) 0 0
b.Whitechapel 3-11-95
| 2014–15 | Colchester U | 0 | 0 |

MASSEY, Gavin (F) 147 19
H: 5 11 W: 11 06 b.Watford 14-10-92
2009–10	Watford	1	0		
2010–11	Watford	3	0		
2011–12	Watford	3	0		
2011–12	Yeovil T	16	3	16	3
2011–12	Colchester U	8	0		
2012–13	Watford	0	0	7	0
2012–13	Colchester U	40	6		
2013–14	Colchester U	30	3		
2014–15	Colchester U	46	7	124	16

MONCUR, George (M) 63 11
H: 5 9 W: 10 00 b.Swindon 18-8-93
Internationals: England U18.
2010–11	West Ham U	0	0		
2011–12	West Ham U	0	0		
2011–12	AFC Wimbledon	20	2	20	2
2012–13	West Ham U	0	0		
2013–14	West Ham U	0	0		
2013–14	Partick Thistle	2	1	2	1
2014–15	Colchester U	41	8	41	8

O'DONOGHUE, Michael (D) 1 0
H: 5 11 W: 11 00 b. 18-1-95
| 2013–14 | Colchester U | 0 | 0 | | |
| 2014–15 | Colchester U | 1 | 0 | 1 | 0 |

OKUONGHAE, Magnus (D) 273 11
H: 6 3 W: 13 04 b.Nigeria 16-2-86
Internationals: England C.
2003–04	Rushden & D	1	0		
2004–05	Rushden & D	3	0		
2005–06	Rushden & D	21	1		
2006–07	Rushden & D	0	0	22	1
2007–08	Dagenham & R	10	0		
2008–09	Dagenham & R	45	2	55	2
2009–10	Colchester U	44	0		
2010–11	Colchester U	14	2		
2011–12	Colchester U	42	0		
2012–13	Colchester U	43	3		
2013–14	Colchester U	44	2		
2014–15	Colchester U	9	1	196	8

OLUFEMI, Tosin (M) 14 0
H: 5 8 W: 10 13 b.Hackney 13-5-94
2012–13	Colchester U	1	0		
2013–14	Colchester U	13	0		
2014–15	Colchester U	0	0	14	0

PORTER, Chris (F) 357 102
H: 6 1 W: 12 09 b.Wigan 12-12-83
2002–03	Bury	2	0		
2003–04	Bury	37	9		
2004–05	Bury	32	9	71	18
2005–06	Oldham Ath	31	7		
2006–07	Oldham Ath	35	21	66	28
2007–08	Motherwell	37	14		
2008–09	Motherwell	22	9	59	23
2008–09	Derby Co	5	3		
2009–10	Derby Co	21	4		
2010–11	Derby Co	18	2	44	9
2011–12	Sheffield U	34	5		
2012–13	Sheffield U	24	4		
2012–13	Shrewsbury T	5	1	5	1
2013–14	Sheffield U	32	7		
2013–14	Chesterfield	3	0	3	0
2014–15	Sheffield U	1	0	88	16
2014–15	Colchester U	21	7	21	7

SEMBI-FERRIS, Dion (F) 10 0
H: 5 8 W: 11 00 b. 23-5-96
| 2013–14 | Colchester U | 0 | 0 | | |
| 2014–15 | Colchester U | 10 | 0 | 10 | 0 |

SMITH, Dominic (F) 1 0
b. 22-9-95
| 2014–15 | Colchester U | 1 | 0 | 1 | 0 |

SZMIDICS, Sammie (M) 38 4
b.Colchester 24-9-95
| 2013–14 | Colchester U | 7 | 0 | | |
| 2014–15 | Colchester U | 31 | 4 | 38 | 4 |

VINCENT-YOUNG, Kane (D) 0 0
H: 5 11 W: 11 00 b. 15-3-96
| 2014–15 | Colchester U | 0 | 0 |

VOSE, Dominic (M) 36 0
H: 5 8 W: 11 03 b.Lambeth 23-11-93
2010–11	West Ham U	0	0		
2011–12	West Ham U	0	0		
2012–13	Barnet	2	0	2	0
2013–14	Colchester U	27	0		
2014–15	Colchester U	7	0	34	0

WALKER, Sam (G) 169 0
H: 6 5 W: 14 00 b.Gravesend 2-10-91
2009–10	Chelsea	0	0		
2010–11	Chelsea	0	0		
2010–11	Barnet	7	0	7	0
2011–12	Chelsea	0	0		
2011–12	Northampton T	21	0	21	0
2011–12	Yeovil T	20	0	20	0
2012–13	Chelsea	0	0		
2012–13	Bristol R	11	0	11	0
2012–13	Colchester U	19	0		
2013–14	Colchester U	46	0		
2014–15	Colchester U	45	0	110	0

WATT, Sanchez (M) 99 11
H: 5 11 W: 12 00 b.Hackney 14-2-91
Internationals: England U16, U17, U19.
2008–09	Arsenal	0	0		
2009–10	Arsenal	0	0		
2009–10	Southend U	4	0	4	0
2009–10	Leeds U	6	0		
2010–11	Arsenal	0	0		
2010–11	Leeds U	22	1	28	1
2011–12	Arsenal	0	0		
2011–12	Sheffield W	4	0	4	0
2011–12	Crawley T	14	2	14	2
2012–13	Arsenal	0	0		
2012–13	Colchester U	6	2		
2013–14	Colchester U	22	3		
2014–15	Colchester U	21	3	49	8

WRIGHT, David (D) 488 9
H: 5 11 W: 11 01 b.Warrington 1-5-80
Internationals: England Youth.

1997–98	Crewe Alex	3	0		
1998–99	Crewe Alex	20	1		
1999–2000	Crewe Alex	45	0		
2000–01	Crewe Alex	42	0		
2001–02	Crewe Alex	30	0		
2002–03	Crewe Alex	31	1		
2003–04	Crewe Alex	40	1	211	3
2004–05	Wigan Ath	31	0		
2005–06	Wigan Ath	2	0		
2005–06	Norwich C	5	0	5	0
2006–07	Wigan Ath	12	0	45	0
2006–07	Ipswich T	19	1		
2007–08	Ipswich T	41	2		
2008–09	Ipswich T	34	1		
2009–10	Ipswich T	26	1	120	5
2010–11	Crystal Palace	28	0		
2011–12	Crystal Palace	22	0		
2012–13	Crystal Palace	1	0	51	0
2012–13	Gillingham	7	0	7	0
2012–13	Colchester U	12	0		
2013–14	Colchester U	35	1		
2014–15	Colchester U	2	0	49	1

WRIGHT, Drey (M) 37 3
H: 5 9 W: 10 11 b.Greenwich 30-4-94

2012–13	Colchester U	21	3		
2013–14	Colchester U	11	0		
2014–15	Colchester U	5	0	37	3

Players retained or with offer of contract
Andrews, Marley Patrick; Brampton, Tyler
Victor; Harrison, Callum John; Segura
Garcia, David; Wynter, Alex James.

Scholars
Atkin, Joel; Brown, George Alan; Carroll,
Ronnie James Alfred; Downey, Milo;
Heenan, Diaz Ray; Issa, Tariq Ahmed;
James, Cameron Lewis; Monk, Thomas
Edward; Ogbodu-Wilson, Osase Junior John;
Robinson, Callum; Sheriff, De-Carrey
Deavon; Stephens, Jamie Jack; Tennent, Joe
Stephen.

COVENTRY C (26)

BANGURA, Alhassan (M) 87 1
H: 5 11 W: 10 07 b.Freetown 24-1-88
Internationals: Sierra Leone Full caps.

2004–05	Watford	2	0		
2005–06	Watford	35	1		
2006–07	Watford	16	0		
2007–08	Watford	7	0		
2008–09	Watford	2	0	62	1
2008–09	Brighton & HA	6	0	6	0
2009–10	Blackpool	9	0	9	0
2010–11	Mersin	5	0	5	0
2010–11	Qabala	5	0	5	0

From Forest Green R.

2014–15	Coventry C	0	0

BARTON, Adam (M) 113 4
H: 5 11 W: 12 01 b.Clitheroe 7-1-91
Internationals: Republic of Ireland U21.
Northern Ireland Full caps.

2008–09	Preston NE	0	0		
2009–10	Preston NE	1	0		
2010–11	Preston NE	33	1		
2011–12	Preston NE	16	0		
2012–13	Preston NE	0	0	50	1
2012–13	Coventry C	22	3		
2013–14	Coventry C	14	0		
2013–14	Fleetwood T	0	0		
2014–15	Coventry C	27	0	63	3

BURGE, Lee (G) 18 0
H: 5 11 W: 11 00 b.Hereford 9-1-93

2011–12	Coventry C	0	0		
2012–13	Coventry C	0	0		
2013–14	Coventry C	0	0		
2014–15	Coventry C	18	0	18	0

CHARLES-COOK, Reice (G) 2 0
H: 6 1 W: 12 08 b.London 8-4-94

2013–14	Bury	2	0	2	0
2014–15	Coventry C	0	0		

FINCH, Jack (M) 16 0
H: 6 1 W: 12 02 b.Southam 6-8-96

2013–14	Coventry C	0	0		
2014–15	Coventry C	16	0	16	0

FLECK, John (M) 170 6
H: 5 9 W: 11 05 b.Glasgow 24-8-91
Internationals: Scotland U17, U19, U21.

2007–08	Rangers	1	0		
2008–09	Rangers	8	1		
2009–10	Rangers	15	1		
2010–11	Rangers	13	0		
2011–12	Rangers	4	0	41	2
2011–12	Blackpool	7	0	7	0
2012–13	Coventry C	35	3		
2013–14	Coventry C	43	1		
2014–15	Coventry C	44	0	122	4

HAYNES, Ryan (D) 29 1
H: 5 7 W: 10 10 b.Northampton 27-9-95

2012–13	Coventry C	1	0		
2013–14	Coventry C	2	0		
2014–15	Coventry C	26	1	29	1

JACKSON, Simeon (M) 242 62
H: 5 10 W: 10 12 b.Kingston, Jamaica
28-3-87
Internationals: Canada U20, Full caps.

2004–05	Rushden & D	3	0		
2005–06	Rushden & D	14	5		
2006–07	Rushden & D	0	0		
2007–08	Rushden & D	0	0	17	5
2007–08	Gillingham	18	4		
2008–09	Gillingham	41	17		
2009–10	Gillingham	42	14	101	35
2010–11	Norwich C	38	13		
2011–12	Norwich C	22	3		
2012–13	Norwich C	13	1	73	17
2013–14	E Braunschweig	9	0	9	0
2013–14	Millwall	14	2	14	2
2014–15	Coventry C	28	3	28	3

JOHNSON, Reda (D) 152 25
H: 6 2 W: 13 10 b.Marseille 21-3-88
Internationals: Benin Full caps.

2005–06	Gueugnon	0	0		
2006–07	Gueugnon	0	0		
2007–08	Amiens	8	0		
2008–09	Amiens	7	0	15	0
2009–10	Plymouth Arg	25	0		
2010–11	Plymouth Arg	17	2	42	2
2010–11	Sheffield W	16	3		
2011–12	Sheffield W	24	7		
2012–13	Sheffield W	16	6		
2013–14	Sheffield W	19	2	75	18
2014–15	Coventry C	20	5	20	5

KELLY-EVANS, Dion (D) 0 0
H: 5 10 W: 12 06 b.Coventry 21-9-96

2014–15	Coventry C	0	0

LAWTON, Ivor (M) 0 0
b.Coventry 5-9-95

2013–14	Coventry C	0	0
2014–15	Coventry C	0	0

MADDISON, James (M) 12 2
H: 5 10 W: 11 07 b.Coventry 23-11-96

2013–14	Coventry C	0	0		
2014–15	Coventry C	12	2	12	2

MARTIN, Aaron (D) 83 4
H: 6 3 W: 11 13 b.Newport (IW) 29-9-89

2009–10	Southampton	2	0		
2010–11	Southampton	8	0		
2011–12	Southampton	10	1		
2012–13	Southampton	0	0		
2012–13	Crystal Palace	4	0	4	0
2012–13	Coventry C	12	0		
2013–14	Southampton	0	0	20	1
2013–14	Birmingham C	8	0	8	0
2014–15	Yeovil T	12	3	12	3
2014–15	Coventry C	27	0	39	0

MILLER, Shaun (F) 222 46
H: 5 10 W: 11 08 b.Alsager 25-9-87

2006–07	Crewe Alex	7	3		
2007–08	Crewe Alex	15	1		
2008–09	Crewe Alex	33	4		
2009–10	Crewe Alex	33	7		
2010–11	Crewe Alex	42	18		
2011–12	Crewe Alex	33	5	163	38
2012–13	Sheffield U	15	4		
2013–14	Sheffield U	13	0	28	4
2013–14	Shrewsbury T	8	3	8	3
2014–15	Coventry C	12	1	12	1
2014–15	Crawley T	5	0	5	0
2014–15	York C	6	0	6	0

NOUBLE, Frank (F) 151 18
H: 6 3 W: 12 08 b.Lewisham 24-9-91
Internationals: England U17, U19.

2009–10	West Ham U	5	0		
2009–10	WBA	3	0	3	0
2009–10	Swindon T	8	0	8	0
2010–11	West Ham U	2	0		
2010–11	Swansea C	6	1	6	1
2010–11	Barnsley	4	0		
2010–11	Charlton Ath	9	1	9	1
2011–12	West Ham U	3	1	13	1
2011–12	Gillingham	13	5	13	5
2011–12	Barnsley	6	0	10	0
2012–13	Wolverhampton W	2	0	2	0
2012–13	Ipswich T	17	2		
2013–14	Ipswich T	38	2		
2014–15	Ipswich T	1	0	56	4
2014–15	Coventry C	31	6	31	6

O'BRIEN, Jim (F) 255 18
H: 6 0 W: 11 11 b.Alexandria 28-9-87
Internationals: Republic of Ireland U19, U21.

2006–07	Celtic	0	0		
2006–07	Dunfermline Ath	13	1	13	1
2007–08	Celtic	1	0	1	0
2007–08	Dundee U	10	0	10	0
2008–09	Motherwell	29	1		
2009–10	Motherwell	35	3	64	4
2010–11	Barnsley	33	1		
2011–12	Barnsley	31	2		
2012–13	Barnsley	30	2		
2013–14	Barnsley	29	2	123	7
2014–15	Coventry C	44	6	44	6

PHILLIPS, Aaron (D) 30 1
H: 5 7 W: 11 00 b.Warwick 20-11-93

2012–13	Coventry C	0	0		
2013–14	Coventry C	11	1		
2014–15	Coventry C	19	0	30	1

PUGH, Danny (M) 254 15
H: 6 0 W: 12 10 b.Cheadle Hulme 19-10-82

2000–01	Manchester U	0	0		
2001–02	Manchester U	0	0		
2002–03	Manchester U	1	0		
2003–04	Manchester U	0	0	1	0
2004–05	Leeds U	38	5		
2005–06	Leeds U	12	0		
2006–07	Preston NE	45	4		
2007–08	Preston NE	7	0		
2007–08	Stoke C	30	0		
2008–09	Stoke C	17	0		
2009–10	Stoke C	7	1		
2010–11	Stoke C	10	0		
2010–11	Preston NE	5	0	57	4
2011–12	Stoke C	3	0	67	1
2011–12	Leeds U	34	2		
2012–13	Leeds U	4	0		
2012–13	Sheffield W	16	1	16	1
2013–14	Leeds U	20	2	108	9
2014–15	Coventry C	5	0	5	0

RICHARDS, Jake (G) 0 0
H: 6 1 W: 11 05 b. 30-12-96

2014–15	Coventry C	0	0

SPENCE, Kyle (F) 0 0
H: 5 5 W: 11 03 b.Croydon 14-1-97
Internationals: Scotland U16.

2014–15	Coventry C	0	0

STOKES, Chris (M) 18 1
H: 5 7 W: 10 04 b.Trowbridge 8-3-91
Internationals: England C, U17.

2009–10	Crewe Alex	2	0	2	0

From Forest Green R.

2014–15	Coventry C	16	1	16	1

SWANSON, Danny (M) 240 22
H: 5 6 W: 9 03 b.Edinburgh 28-12-86

2005–06	Berwick R	27	1		
2006–07	Berwick R	3	0		
2007–08	Berwick R	14	3	44	4
2007–08	Dundee U	12	2		
2008–09	Dundee U	30	0		
2009–10	Dundee U	31	5		
2010–11	Dundee U	21	2		
2011–12	Dundee U	14	3	108	12
2012–13	Peterborough U	27	2		
2013–14	Peterborough U	35	2	62	4
2014–15	Coventry C	15	0	15	0
2014–15	St Johnstone	11	2	11	2

THOMAS, Conor (M) 97 1
H: 6 1 W: 11 05 b.Coventry 29-10-93
Internationals: England U17, U18.

2010–11	Liverpool	0	0		
2010–11	Coventry C	0	0		
2011–12	Coventry C	27	1		
2012–13	Coventry C	11	0		
2013–14	Coventry C	43	0		
2014–15	Coventry C	16	0	97	1

THOMAS, George (M)   7   0
H: 5 8   W: 12 00   b.Leicester 24-3-97
Internationals: Wales U17, U19.

2013–14	Coventry C	1	0		
2014–15	Coventry C	6	0	7	0

TUDGAY, Marcus (F)   386   87
H: 5 10   W: 12 04   b.Shoreham 3-2-83

2002–03	Derby Co	8	0		
2003–04	Derby Co	29	6		
2004–05	Derby Co	34	9		
2005–06	Derby Co	21	2	92	17
2005–06	Sheffield W	18	5		
2006–07	Sheffield W	40	11		
2007–08	Sheffield W	35	7		
2008–09	Sheffield W	42	14		
2009–10	Sheffield W	43	10		
2010–11	Sheffield W	17	2	195	49
2010–11	Nottingham F	22	7		
2011–12	Nottingham F	34	5		
2012–13	Nottingham F	3	0		
2012–13	Barnsley	9	3		
2013–14	Nottingham F	2	1	61	13
2013–14	Barnsley	5	1	14	4
2013–14	*Charlton Ath*	2	0	2	0
2014–15	Coventry C	22	4	22	4

TURGOTT, Blair (M)   17   2
H: 6 0   W: 10 03   b.Bromley 22-5-94
Internationals: England U16, U17, U18, U19.

2011–12	West Ham U	0	0		
2012–13	*Bradford C*	4	0	4	0
2013–14	West Ham U	0	0		
2013–14	*Colchester U*	4	1	4	1
2013–14	*Rotherham U*	1	0	1	0
2013–14	*Dagenham & R*	5	0	5	0
2014–15	West Ham U	0	0		
2014–15	Coventry C	3	1	3	1

WEBSTER, Andy (D)   329   17
H: 6 0   W: 9 13   b.Dundee 23-4-82
Internationals: Scotland U21, B, Full caps.

2000–01	Hearts	4	0		
2001–02	Hearts	26	1		
2002–03	Hearts	21	1		
2003–04	Hearts	32	2		
2004–05	Hearts	35	1		
2005–06	Hearts	30	1		
2006–07	Wigan Ath	4	0		
2007–08	Wigan Ath	0	0	4	0
2007–08	*Rangers*	1	0		
2008–09	*Rangers*	0	0		
2008–09	*Bristol C*	5	0	5	0
2009–10	*Rangers*	0	0		
2009–10	*Dundee U*	26	3	26	3
2010–11	*Rangers*	1	0	2	0
2010–11	Hearts	9	0		
2011–12	Hearts	31	4		
2012–13	Hearts	33	1	221	11
2013–14	Coventry C	41	3		
2014–15	Coventry C	30	0	71	3

WILLIS, Jordan (D)   66   0
H: 5 11   W: 11 00   b.Coventry 24-8-94
Internationals: England U18, U19.

2011–12	Coventry C	3	0		
2012–13	Coventry C	1	0		
2013–14	Coventry C	28	0		
2014–15	Coventry C	34	0	66	0

Scholars
Addai, Corey Kofi Cheremeh; Albini, Jason Antonio; Barnett, Kyle James; Bromley, Luke William; Harries, Cian William Thomas; Kelly-Evans, Devon Jerome; Kelly-Evans, Dion Jermaine; Leahy, Darragh John; Maycock, Callum; Richards, Jake James; Sambou, Bassala; Shipley, Jordan Mark Edward james; Spence, Kyle Cameron Walter; Stevenson, Ben Edward; Thomas, George Stanley; Whitmore, Jacob James.

CRAWLEY T (27)

ANDERSON, Blair (M)   1   0
b. 1-7-92

2014–15	Crawley T	1	0	1	0

BANYA, Charlie (M)   9   0
H: 5 7   W: 9 08   b.Tulse Hill 18-9-93

2011–12	Fulham	0	0		
2012–13	Fulham	0	0		
2013–14	Fulham	0	0		
2014–15	Crawley T	9	0	9	0

BAWLING, Bobson (M)   28   0
b.London 21-9-95

2013–14	Watford	0	0		
2014–15	Crawley T	28	0	28	0

BRADLEY, Sonny (D)   117   4
H: 6 0   W: 11 05   b.Hedon 14-6-92

2011–12	Hull C	2	0		
2011–12	*Aldershot T*	14	0		
2012–13	Hull C	0	0	2	0
2012–13	*Aldershot T*	42	1	56	1
2013–14	Portsmouth	33	2	33	2
2014–15	Crawley T	26	1	26	1

COFIE, John (F)   24   3
H: 6 0   W: 12 11   b.Aboso 21-1-93
Internationals: England U17.

2010–11	Manchester U	0	0		
2011–12	Manchester U	0	0		
2012–13	Manchester U	0	0		
2012–13	*Sheffield U*	16	2	16	2
2012–13	*Notts Co*	7	1	7	1
2013–14	Barnsley	0	0		
2014–15	Molde	0	0		
2014–15	Crawley T	1	0	1	0

DICKSON, Ryan (M)   217   8
H: 5 10   W: 11 05   b.Saltash 14-12-86

2004–05	Plymouth Arg	3	0		
2005–06	Plymouth Arg	0	0		
2006–07	Plymouth Arg	2	0		
2006–07	*Torquay U*	9	1	9	1
2007–08	Plymouth Arg	0	0	5	0
2007–08	Brentford	31	0		
2008–09	Brentford	39	1		
2009–10	Brentford	27	2	97	3
2010–11	Southampton	23	1		
2011–12	Southampton	0	0		
2011–12	*Yeovil T*	5	1	5	1
2011–12	*Leyton Orient*	9	0	9	0
2012–13	Southampton	0	0	23	1
2012–13	*Bradford C*	5	1	5	1
2013–14	Colchester U	32	0	32	0
2014–15	Crawley T	32	1	32	1

EDWARDS, Gwion (M)   62   6
H: 5 9   W: 12 00   b.Carmarthen 1-3-93
Internationals: Wales U19, U21

2011–12	Swansea C	0	0		
2012–13	Swansea C	0	0		
2012–13	*St Johnstone*	6	0		
2013–14	Swansea C	0	0		
2013–14	*St Johnstone*	13	0	19	0
2013–14	*Crawley T*	6	2		
2014–15	Crawley T	37	4	43	6

ELLIOTT, Marvin (M)   413   34
H: 6 0   W: 12 02   b.Wandsworth 15-9-84
Internationals: Jamaica Full caps.

2001–02	Millwall	1	0		
2002–03	Millwall	1	0		
2003–04	Millwall	21	0		
2004–05	Millwall	41	1		
2005–06	Millwall	39	2		
2006–07	Millwall	42	0	144	3
2007–08	Bristol C	45	5		
2008–09	Bristol C	28	3		
2009–10	Bristol C	39	1		
2010–11	Bristol C	46	8		
2011–12	Bristol C	28	2		
2012–13	Bristol C	32	2		
2013–14	Bristol C	24	4		
2014–15	Bristol C	0	0	242	25
2014–15	Crawley T	27	6	27	6

FOWLER, Lee (M)   103   1
H: 5 7   W: 9 13   b.Cardiff 10-6-83
Internationals: Wales Youth, U21.

2001–02	Coventry C	13	0		
2002–03	Coventry C	1	0	14	0
2003–04	Huddersfield T	29	0		
2004–05	Huddersfield T	20	0	49	0

From Scarborough, Burton Alb, Forest Green R, Wrexham

2012–13	Fleetwood T	10	0	10	0
2012–13	Doncaster R	4	0	4	0
2012–13	*Burton Alb*	3	0	3	0
2013–14	The New Saints FC	4	0	4	0
2014–15	Crawley T	19	1	19	1

HARROLD, Matt (F)   354   67
H: 6 1   W: 11 10   b.Leyton 25-7-84

2003–04	Brentford	13	2		
2004–05	Brentford	19	0	32	2
2004–05	*Grimsby T*	6	2	6	2
2005–06	Yeovil T	42	9		
2006–07	Yeovil T	5	0	47	9
2006–07	Southend U	36	3		
2007–08	Southend U	16	0		
2008–09	Southend U	0	0	52	3
2008–09	Wycombe W	37	9		
2009–10	Wycombe W	36	8	73	17
2010–11	Shrewsbury T	41	8	41	8
2011–12	Bristol R	40	16		
2012–13	Bristol R	6	2		
2013–14	Bristol R	30	6	76	24
2014–15	Crawley T	20	1	20	1
2014–15	*Cambridge U*	7	1	7	1

HENDERSON, Conor (M)   22   2
H: 6 1   W: 11 13   b.Sidcup 8-9-91
Internationals: England U17. Republic of Ireland U19, U21.

2008–09	Arsenal	0	0		
2009–10	Arsenal	0	0		
2010–11	Arsenal	0	0		
2011–12	Arsenal	0	0		
2012–13	Arsenal	0	0		
2012–13	*Coventry C*	2	0	2	0
2013–14	Hull C	0	0		
2013–14	*Stevenage*	3	0	3	0
2014–15	Crawley T	17	2	17	2

ISAACS, Bradley (M)   0   0
H: 5 6   W: 9 08   b.Crawley 2-12-95

2013–14	Crawley T	0	0	
2014–15	Crawley T	0	0	

JENSEN, Brian (G)   374   0
H: 6 1   W: 12 04   b.Copenhagen 8-6-75

1997–98	AZ	0	0		
1998–99	AZ	1	0	1	0
1999–2000	WBA	12	0		
2000–01	WBA	33	0		
2001–02	WBA	1	0		
2002–03	WBA	0	0	46	0
2003–04	Burnley	46	0		
2004–05	Burnley	27	0		
2005–06	Burnley	39	0		
2006–07	Burnley	31	0		
2007–08	Burnley	19	0		
2008–09	Burnley	45	0		
2009–10	Burnley	38	0		
2010–11	Burnley	21	0		
2011–12	Burnley	4	0		
2012–13	Burnley	1	0	271	0
2013–14	Bury	36	0	36	0
2014–15	Crawley T	20	0	20	0

LEACOCK, Dean (D)   245   4
H: 6 2   W: 12 04   b.Croydon 10-6-84
Internationals: England U18, U19, U20.

2002–03	Fulham	0	0		
2003–04	Fulham	4	0		
2004–05	Fulham	0	0		
2004–05	*Coventry C*	13	0	13	0
2005–06	Fulham	5	0		
2006–07	Fulham	0	0	9	0
2006–07	Derby Co	38	0		
2007–08	Derby Co	26	0		
2008–09	Derby Co	11	0		
2009–10	Derby Co	17	0		
2010–11	Derby Co	25	1		
2011–12	Derby Co	0	0	117	1
2011–12	*Leyton Orient*	15	0	15	0
2012–13	Notts Co	42	1		
2013–14	Notts Co	26	1	68	2
2014–15	Crawley T	23	1	23	1

MADDISON, Johnny (G)   0   0
H: 6 0   W: 11 12   b.Chester Le Street 4-9-94

2012–13	Crawley T	0	0	
2013–14	Crawley T	0	0	
2014–15	Crawley T	0	0	

McLEOD, Izale (F)   398   133
H: 6 1   W: 11 02   b.Birmingham 15-10-84
Internationals: England U21.

2002–03	Derby Co	29	3		
2003–04	Derby Co	10	1	39	4
2003–04	*Sheffield U*	7	0	7	0
2004–05	Milton Keynes D	43	16		
2005–06	Milton Keynes D	39	17		
2006–07	Milton Keynes D	34	21		
2007–08	Charlton Ath	18	1		
2007–08	*Colchester U*	2	0	2	0
2008–09	Charlton Ath	2	0		
2008–09	*Millwall*	7	2	7	2
2009–10	Charlton Ath	1	0		
2009–10	*Peterborough U*	4	0	4	0
2010–11	Charlton Ath	0	0	31	3
2010–11	Barnet	29	14		
2011–12	Barnet	44	18	73	32
2012–13	Portsmouth	24	10	24	10
2012–13	Milton Keynes D	1	0		
2013–14	Milton Keynes D	36	7	165	62
2013–14	*Northampton T*	4	1	4	1
2014–15	Crawley T	42	19	42	19

MORGAN, Dean (M) 380 51
H: 5 11 W: 13 00 b.Enfield 3-10-83
Internationals: Montserrat Full caps.

Season	Club	App	Gls	Tot	TGls
2000–01	Colchester U	4	0		
2001–02	Colchester U	30	0		
2002–03	Colchester U	37	6		
2003–04	Colchester U	0	0	71	6
2003–04	Reading	13	1		
2004–05	Reading	18	2	31	3
2005–06	Luton T	36	6		
2006–07	Luton T	36	4		
2007–08	Luton T	16	1		
2007–08	Southend U	8	0	8	0
2007–08	Crewe Alex	9	1	9	1
2008–09	Luton T	0	0		
2008–09	Leyton Orient	32	5	32	5
2009–10	Luton T	0	0	88	11
2009–10	Milton Keynes D	9	1	9	1
2009–10	Aldershot T	9	4	9	4
2010–11	Chesterfield	21	1		
2011–12	Chesterfield	17	3	38	4
2011–12	Oxford U	10	1	10	1
2012–13	Wycombe W	33	7		
2013–14	Wycombe W	29	8	62	15
2014–15	Crawley T	13	0	13	0

O'CONNOR, Emmett (M) 0 0
H: 5 9 W: 11 03 b.Ajax, Ontario 13-9-92

Season	Club	App	Gls	Tot	TGls
2014–15	Crawley T	4	0	4	0

OYEBANJO, Lanre (D) 102 0
H: 6 1 W: 11 04 b.Hackney 24-4-90
Internationals: Republic of Ireland U19, U21.

Season	Club	App	Gls	Tot	TGls
2012–13	York C	30	0		
2013–14	York C	41	0	71	0
2014–15	Crawley T	31	0	31	0

POGBA, Mathias (F) 77 0
H: 6 3 W: 12 13 b.Conakry 19-8-90
Internationals: Guinea Full caps.

Season	Club	App	Gls	Tot	TGls
2010–11	Wrexham	0	0		
2012–13	Crewe Alex	34	12		
2013–14	Crewe Alex	22	5	56	17
2014–15	Pescara	4	0	4	0
2014–15	Crawley T	17	2	17	2

RICHEFOND, Ryan (M) 0 0
H: 5 7 W: 9 04 b.Tower Hamlets 16-6-96

Season	Club	App	Gls	Tot	TGls
2013–14	Crawley T	0	0		
2014–15	Crawley T	0	0		

SIMPSON, Josh (M) 160 12
H: 5 10 W: 12 02 b.Cambridge 6-3-87
Internationals: England C.

Season	Club	App	Gls	Tot	TGls
2009–10	Peterborough U	21	2		
2010–11	Peterborough U	0	0	21	2
2010–11	Southend U	17	1	17	1
2011–12	Crawley T	40	2		
2012–13	Crawley T	36	4		
2013–14	Crawley T	38	2		
2014–15	Crawley T	8	1	122	9

SMITH, Jimmy (M) 289 28
H: 6 0 W: 10 03 b.Newham 7-1-87
Internationals: England U16, U17, U19.

Season	Club	App	Gls	Tot	TGls
2004–05	Chelsea	0	0		
2005–06	Chelsea	1	0		
2006–07	Chelsea	0	0		
2006–07	QPR	29	6	29	6
2007–08	Chelsea	0	0		
2007–08	Norwich C	9	0	9	0
2008–09	Chelsea	0	0	1	0
2008–09	Sheffield W	12	0	12	0
2008–09	Leyton Orient	16	0		
2009–10	Leyton Orient	40	2		
2010–11	Leyton Orient	31	7		
2011–12	Leyton Orient	38	6		
2012–13	Leyton Orient	35	3		
2013–14	Leyton Orient	0		160	18
2013–14	Stevenage	42	3	42	3
2014–15	Crawley T	36	1	36	1

TOMLIN, Gavin (F) 239 47
H: 6 0 W: 12 02 b.Gillingham 13-1-83

Season	Club	App	Gls	Tot	TGls
2006–07	Brentford	12	0		
2007–08	Brentford	0	0	12	0

From Fisher Ath.

Season	Club	App	Gls	Tot	TGls
2008–09	Yeovil T	42	7		
2009–10	Yeovil T	35	7	77	14
2010–11	Dagenham & R	19	2		
2010–11	Torquay U	12	4	12	4
2011–12	Dagenham & R	17	0	36	2
2011–12	Gillingham	10	6	10	6
2012–13	Southend U	33	13		
2013–14	Southend U	0	0	33	13
2013–14	Port Vale	24	5	24	5
2014–15	Crawley T	35	3	35	3

WALSH, Joe (D) 99 8
H: 5 11 W: 11 00 b.Cardiff 15-5-92
Internationals: Wales U17, U19, U21.

Season	Club	App	Gls	Tot	TGls
2010–11	Swansea C	0	0		
2011–12	Swansea C	0	0		
2012–13	Crawley T	30	2		
2013–14	Crawley T	39	5		
2014–15	Crawley T	28	1	97	8
2014–15	Milton Keynes D	2	0	2	0

YOUGA, Kelly (D) 105 3
H: 6 1 W: 12 00 b.Bangui 22-9-85
Internationals: Central African Republic Full caps.

Season	Club	App	Gls	Tot	TGls
2005–06	Charlton Ath	0	0		
2005–06	Bristol C	4	0	4	0
2006–07	Charlton Ath	0	0		
2006–07	Bradford C	11	0	11	0
2007–08	Charlton Ath	11	0		
2007–08	Scunthorpe U	19	1	19	1
2008–09	Charlton Ath	33	1		
2009–10	Charlton Ath	18	0		
2010–11	Charlton Ath	0	0		
2011–12	Charlton Ath	0	0	62	1
2011–12	Yeovil T	1	0	1	0
2012–13	AFC Wimbledon	3	0		
2013–14	AFC Wimbledon	0	0	3	0
2014–15	Crawley T	5	1	5	1

YOUNG, Lewis (M) 113 0
H: 5 10 W: 11 02 b.Stevenage 27-9-89

Season	Club	App	Gls	Tot	TGls
2008–09	Watford	1	0		
2009–10	Watford	0	0	1	0
2009–10	Hereford U	6	0	6	0
2010–11	Burton Alb	19	0	19	0
2011–12	Northampton T	30	0	30	0
2012–13	Yeovil T	15	0		
2013–14	Yeovil T	0	0	15	0
2013–14	Bury	4	0	4	0
2014–15	Crawley T	38	0	38	0

Scholars
Low, Sonnie Frank; Read, Alexander Nicholas; Smith, Vincent Cudal Nelson.

CREWE ALEX (28)

ATKINSON, Chris (M) 70 8
H: 6 1 W: 11 13 b.Huddersfield 13-2-92

Season	Club	App	Gls	Tot	TGls
2010–11	Huddersfield T	2	0		
2011–12	Huddersfield T	1	0		
2012–13	Huddersfield T	7	1		
2012–13	Chesterfield	15	5	15	5
2013–14	Huddersfield T	0	0	10	1
2013–14	Tranmere R	22	2	22	2
2013–14	Bradford C	4	0	4	0
2014–15	Crewe Alex	19	0	19	0

AUDEL, Thierry (D) 13 1
H: 6 2 W: 12 08 b. 15-1-87
Internationals: France U19.

Season	Club	App	Gls	Tot	TGls
2007–08	Triestina	2	0		
2008–09	Triestina	0	0		
2009–10	Triestina	7	1	9	1

From Macclesfield T.

Season	Club	App	Gls	Tot	TGls
2013–14	Crewe Alex	2	0		
2014–15	Crewe Alex	2	0	4	0

BAILLIE, James (D) 13 0
b.Warrington 27-3-96

Season	Club	App	Gls	Tot	TGls
2014–15	Crewe Alex	13	0	13	0

COLCLOUGH, Ryan (F) 33 5
H: 6 3 W: 13 01 b.Budapest 27-12-94

Season	Club	App	Gls	Tot	TGls
2012–13	Crewe Alex	18	1		
2013–14	Crewe Alex	8	2		
2014–15	Crewe Alex	7	2	33	5

COOPER, George (M) 22 3
b.Warrington 2-11-96

Season	Club	App	Gls	Tot	TGls
2014–15	Crewe Alex	22	3	22	3

DALLA VALLE, Lauri (F) 60 14
H: 5 9 W: 11 03 b.Joensuu 14-9-91
Internationals: Finland U16, U17, U19, U21.

Season	Club	App	Gls	Tot	TGls
2007	JIPPO	8	0	8	0
2008–09	Liverpool	0	0		
2009–10	Liverpool	0	0		
2010–11	Fulham	0	0		
2010–11	Bournemouth	8	2	8	2
2011–12	Fulham	0	0		
2011–12	Dundee U	12	3	12	3
2011–12	Exeter C	5	0	5	0
2012–13	Fulham	0	0		
2012–13	Crewe Alex	10	5		
2014–15	Crewe Alex	17	4	27	9

DAVIS, Harry (D) 148 10
H: 6 2 W: 12 04 b.Burnley 24-9-91

Season	Club	App	Gls	Tot	TGls
2009–10	Crewe Alex	1	0		
2010–11	Crewe Alex	1	0		
2011–12	Crewe Alex	41	5		
2012–13	Crewe Alex	42	1		
2013–14	Crewe Alex	32	3		
2014–15	Crewe Alex	31	1	148	10

GARRATT, Ben (G) 57 0
H: 6 1 W: 10 06 b.Market Drayton 25-4-94
Internationals: England U17, U18, U19.

Season	Club	App	Gls	Tot	TGls
2011–12	Crewe Alex	0	0		
2012–13	Crewe Alex	1	0		
2013–14	Crewe Alex	26	0		
2014–15	Crewe Alex	30	0	57	0

GRANT, Anthony (M) 328 14
H: 5 10 W: 11 01 b.Lambeth 4-6-87
Internationals: England U16, U17, U19.

Season	Club	App	Gls	Tot	TGls
2004–05	Chelsea	1	0		
2005–06	Chelsea	0	0		
2005–06	Oldham Ath	2	0	2	0
2006–07	Chelsea	0	0		
2006–07	Wycombe W	40	0	40	0
2007–08	Chelsea	0	0	1	0
2007–08	Luton T	4	0	4	0
2007–08	Southend U	10	0		
2008–09	Southend U	35	1		
2009–10	Southend U	38	0		
2010–11	Southend U	43	8		
2011–12	Southend U	33	1	159	10
2012–13	Stevenage	41	0	41	0
2013–14	Crewe Alex	38	2		
2014–15	Crewe Alex	43	2	81	4

GUTHRIE, Jon (D) 50 0
H: 5 10 W: 11 00 b.Devizes 1-2-93

Season	Club	App	Gls	Tot	TGls
2011–12	Crewe Alex	0	0		
2012–13	Crewe Alex	2	0		
2013–14	Crewe Alex	23	0		
2014–15	Crewe Alex	25	0	50	0

HABER, Marcus (F) 139 19
H: 6 3 W: 13 04 b.Vancouver 11-1-89
Internationals: Canada U16, U17, U20, U23 U23, Full caps.

Season	Club	App	Gls	Tot	TGls
2009–10	WBA	0	0		
2009–10	Exeter C	5	0	5	0
2010–11	WBA	0	0		
2010–11	St Johnstone	11	1		
2011–12	St Johnstone	31	2	42	3
2012–13	Stevenage	42	7		
2013–14	Stevenage	3	0	45	7
2013–14	Notts Co	11	2	11	2
2014–15	Crewe Alex	36	7	36	7

INMAN, Bradden (M) 78 10
H: 5 9 W: 11 03 b.Adelaide 10-12-91
Internationals: Scotland U19, U21.

Season	Club	App	Gls	Tot	TGls
2009–10	Newcastle U	0	0		
2010–11	Newcastle U	0	0		
2011–12	Newcastle U	0	0		
2012–13	Newcastle U	0	0		
2012–13	Crewe Alex	21	5		
2013–14	Newcastle U	0	0		
2013–14	Crewe Alex	36	4		
2014–15	Crewe Alex	21	1	78	10

JONES, James (M) 24 1
b. 1-2-96
Internationals: Scotland U19.

Season	Club	App	Gls	Tot	TGls
2014–15	Crewe Alex	24	1	24	1

MURDOCH, Fraser (F) 0 0
b.Manchester 30-9-95
Internationals: Scotland U19.

Season	Club	App	Gls	Tot	TGls
2014–15	Crewe Alex	0	0		

NG, Perry (D) 0 0
H: 5 11 W: 12 02 b.Liverpool 24-6-96

Season	Club	App	Gls	Tot	TGls
2014–15	Crewe Alex	0	0		

NOLAN, Liam (D) 26 0
H: 5 9 W: 10 12 b.Liverpool 20-9-94
Internationals: Northern Ireland U21.

Season	Club	App	Gls	Tot	TGls
2012–13	Crewe Alex	0	0		
2013–14	Crewe Alex	13	0		
2014–15	Crewe Alex	13	0	26	0

OLIVER, Vadaine (F) 64 10
H: 6 2 W: 12 04 b.Sheffield 21-10-91

Season	Club	App	Gls	Tot	TGls
2010–11	Sheffield W	0	0		
2011–12	Sheffield W	0	0		
2013–14	Crewe Alex	25	2		
2014–15	Crewe Alex	9	1	34	3
2014–15	Mansfield T	30	7	30	7

RACHUBKA, Paul (G)   321
H: 6 1 W: 13 05 b.San Luis Opispo 21-5-81
Internationals: England U16, U18, U20.

Season	Club				
1999–2000	Manchester U	0	0		
2000–01	Manchester U	1	0		
2001–02	Manchester U	0	0	1	0
2001–02	Oldham Ath	16	0		
2001–02	Charlton Ath	0	0		
2002–03	Charlton Ath	0	0		
2003–04	Charlton Ath	0	0		
2003–04	Huddersfield T	13	0		
2004–05	Charlton Ath	0	0		
2004–05	Milton Keynes D	4	0	4	0
2004–05	Northampton T	10	0	10	0
2004–05	Huddersfield T	29	0		
2005–06	Huddersfield T	34	0		
2006–07	Huddersfield T	0	0	76	0
2006–07	Peterborough U	4	0	4	0
2006–07	Blackpool	8	0		
2007–08	Blackpool	46	0		
2008–09	Blackpool	42	0		
2009–10	Blackpool	20	0		
2010–11	Blackpool	2	0	118	0
2011–12	Leeds U	6	0		
2011–12	Tranmere R	10	0	10	0
2011–12	Leyton Orient	8	0	8	0
2012–13	Leeds U	0	0	6	0
2012–13	Accrington S	21	0	21	0
2013–14	Oldham Ath	10	0		
2014–15	Oldham Ath	22	0	48	0
2014–15	Crewe Alex	15	0	15	0

RAY, George (D)   48 2
H: 5 10 W: 11 03 b.Warrington 13-10-93
Internationals: Wales U21.

Season	Club				
2011–12	Crewe Alex	0	0		
2012–13	Crewe Alex	4	0		
2013–14	Crewe Alex	9	0		
2014–15	Crewe Alex	35	2	48	2

SAUNDERS, Callum (F)   4 0
H: 5 10 W: 11 11 b.Istanbul 26-9-95
Internationals: Wales U19.

Season	Club				
2014–15	Crewe Alex	4	0	4	0

SHEARER, Scott (G)   289
H: 6 3 W: 12 00 b.Glasgow 15-2-81
Internationals: Scotland B.

Season	Club				
2000–01	Albion R	3	0		
2001–02	Albion R	10	0		
2002–03	Albion R	36	0	49	0
2003–04	Coventry C	30	0		
2004–05	Coventry C	8	0	38	0
2004–05	Rushden & D	13	0	13	0
2005–06	Bristol R	45	0		
2006–07	Bristol R	2	0	47	0
2006–07	Shrewsbury T	20	0	20	0
2007–08	Wycombe W	5	0		
2008–09	Wycombe W	29	0		
2009–10	Wycombe W	29	0		
2010–11	Wycombe W	0	0	63	0
2011–12	Crawley T	25	0	25	0
2012–13	Rotherham U	19	0		
2013–14	Rotherham U	12	0	31	0
2014–15	Crewe Alex	2	0	2	0
2014–15	Burton Alb	1	0	1	0

STEWART, Anthony (D)   66 4
H: 5 10 W: 12 03 b.Brixton 18-9-92

Season	Club				
2011–12	Wycombe W	4	0		
2012–13	Wycombe W	19	1		
2013–14	Wycombe W	33	3	56	4
2014–15	Crewe Alex	10	0	10	0

TOOTLE, Matt (D)   199 2
H: 5 9 W: 11 00 b.Widnes 11-10-90

Season	Club				
2009–10	Crewe Alex	28	1		
2010–11	Crewe Alex	39	0		
2011–12	Crewe Alex	37	0		
2012–13	Crewe Alex	37	1		
2013–14	Crewe Alex	43	0		
2014–15	Crewe Alex	15	0	199	2

TURTON, Oliver (D)   79 2
H: 5 11 W: 11 11 b.Manchester 6-12-92

Season	Club				
2010–11	Crewe Alex	1	0		
2011–12	Crewe Alex	2	0		
2012–13	Crewe Alex	20	0		
2013–14	Crewe Alex	12	1		
2014–15	Crewe Alex	44	1	79	2

WATERS, Billy (M)   25 2
H: 5 9 W: 11 07 b.Epsom 15-10-94

Season	Club				
2012–13	Crewe Alex	0	0		
2013–14	Crewe Alex	9	0		
2014–15	Crewe Alex	16	2	25	2

Players retained or with offer of contract
Ainley, Callum Thomas; Finney, Oliver Vincent; Wintle, Ryan Frank.

Scholars
Brown, Andre Dave; Dowsett, Aaron Joseph Llewellyn; Harrison, Kieran James; Higham, Jonathan Mark; Howell, Joseph Edward James; Kearns, Joseph Glen; Lowery, Thomas Richard; Matthews, Liam Elliott; Moran, Jonathan Lewis Daniel; Morgan, Jamie Lee; Mullarkey, Tobias; Neal, Matthew Saul Andrew; O'Neill, Liam Kieron; Pino, Michael Roberto; Quinn, Thomas Evander; Speed, Christopher David.

CRYSTAL PALACE (29)

ALLASSANI, Reise (M)   0 0
b.Wandsworth 3-1-96
Internationals: England U16, U17.

Season	Club				
2013–14	Crystal Palace	0	0		
2014–15	Crystal Palace	0	0		

AMEOBI, Shola (F)   322 53
H: 6 3 W: 11 13 b.Zaria 12-10-81
Internationals: England U21. Nigeria Full caps.

Season	Club				
1998–99	Newcastle U	0	0		
1999–2000	Newcastle U	0	0		
2000–01	Newcastle U	20	2		
2001–02	Newcastle U	15	0		
2002–03	Newcastle U	28	5		
2003–04	Newcastle U	26	7		
2004–05	Newcastle U	31	2		
2005–06	Newcastle U	30	9		
2006–07	Newcastle U	12	3		
2007–08	Newcastle U	6	0		
2007–08	Stoke C	6	0	6	0
2008–09	Newcastle U	22	4		
2009–10	Newcastle U	18	10		
2010–11	Newcastle U	28	6		
2011–12	Newcastle U	27	2		
2012–13	Newcastle U	23	1		
2013–14	Newcastle U	26	2	312	53
2014–15	Crystal Palace	4	0	4	0

ANDERSON, Keshi (F)   0 0
b. 15-11-95

Season	Club				
2014–15	Crystal Palace	0	0		

APPIAH, Kwesi (F)   52 10
H: 5 11 W: 12 08 b.Thamesmead 12-8-90
Internationals: Ghana Full caps.

Season	Club				
2008–09	Peterborough U	0	0		
From Brackley T, Thurrock, Margate.					
2011–12	Crystal Palace	4	0		
2012–13	Crystal Palace	2	0		
2012–13	Aldershot T	2	0	2	0
2012–13	Yeovil T	5	0	5	0
2013–14	Crystal Palace	0	0		
2013–14	Notts Co	7	0	7	0
2013–14	AFC Wimbledon	7	3	7	3
2014–15	Crystal Palace	0	0	6	0
2014–15	Cambridge U	19	6	19	6
2014–15	Reading	6	1	6	1

BANNAN, Barry (D)   139 4
H: 5 10 W: 10 08 b.Glasgow 1-12-89
Internationals: Scotland U21, Full caps.

Season	Club				
2008–09	Aston Villa	0	0		
2008–09	Derby Co	10	1	10	1
2009–10	Aston Villa	0	0		
2009–10	Blackpool	20	1	20	1
2010–11	Aston Villa	12	0		
2010–11	Leeds U	7	0	7	0
2011–12	Aston Villa	28	1		
2012–13	Aston Villa	24	0		
2013–14	Aston Villa	0	0	64	1
2013–14	Crystal Palace	15	1		
2014–15	Crystal Palace	7	0	22	1
2014–15	Bolton W	16	0	16	0

BLACK, Sonny (M)   0 0
b. 20-6-96

Season	Club				
2014–15	Crystal Palace	0	0		

BOATENG, Hiram (M)   1 0
H: 5 7 W: 11 00 b.Wandsworth 8-1-96

Season	Club				
2012–13	Crystal Palace	0	0		
2013–14	Crystal Palace	0	0		
2013–14	Crawley T	1	0	1	0
2014–15	Crystal Palace	0	0		

BOLASIE, Yannick (M)   222 21
H: 6 3 W: 13 02 b.DR Congo 24-5-89
Internationals: DR Congo Full caps.

Season	Club				
2008–09	Plymouth Arg	0	0		
2008–09	Barnet	20	3		
2009–10	Plymouth Arg	16	1		
2009–10	Barnet	22	2	42	5
2010–11	Plymouth Arg	35	7	51	8
2011–12	Bristol C	23	1		
2012–13	Bristol C	0	0	23	1
2012–13	Crystal Palace	43	3		
2013–14	Crystal Palace	29	0		
2014–15	Crystal Palace	34	4	106	7

CAMPBELL, Frazier (F)   173 39
H: 5 11 W: 12 04 b.Huddersfield 13-9-87
Internationals: England U16, U17, U18, U21, Full caps.

Season	Club				
2005–06	Manchester U	0	0		
2006–07	Manchester U	0	0		
2007–08	Manchester U	1	0		
2007–08	Hull C	34	15	34	15
2008–09	Manchester U	1	0		
2008–09	Tottenham H	10	1	10	1
2009–10	Manchester U	0	0	2	0
2009–10	Sunderland	31	4		
2010–11	Sunderland	3	0		
2011–12	Sunderland	12	1		
2012–13	Sunderland	12	1	58	6
2012–13	Cardiff C	12	7		
2013–14	Cardiff C	37	6	49	13
2014–15	Crystal Palace	20	4	20	4

CHAMAKH, Marouane (F)   323 71
H: 6 1 W: 11 00 b.Tonnens 10-1-84
Internationals: France U19. Morocco Full caps.

Season	Club				
2002–03	Bordeaux	10	1		
2003–04	Bordeaux	25	6		
2004–05	Bordeaux	33	10		
2005–06	Bordeaux	29	7		
2006–07	Bordeaux	29	5		
2007–08	Bordeaux	32	4		
2008–09	Bordeaux	34	13		
2009–10	Bordeaux	38	10	230	56
2010–11	Arsenal	29	7		
2011–12	Arsenal	11	1		
2012–13	Arsenal	0	0		
2012–13	West Ham U	3	0	3	0
2013–14	Arsenal	0	0	40	8
2013–14	Crystal Palace	32	5		
2014–15	Crystal Palace	18	2	50	7

DANN, Scott (D)   302 20
H: 6 2 W: 12 00 b.Liverpool 14-2-87
Internationals: England U21.

Season	Club				
2004–05	Walsall	1	0		
2005–06	Walsall	0	0		
2006–07	Walsall	30	4		
2007–08	Walsall	28	3	59	7
2007–08	Coventry C	16	0		
2008–09	Coventry C	31	3	47	3
2009–10	Birmingham C	30	0		
2010–11	Birmingham C	20	2		
2011–12	Birmingham C	0	0	50	2
2011–12	Blackburn R	27	1		
2012–13	Blackburn R	46	4		
2013–14	Blackburn R	25	0	98	5
2013–14	Crystal Palace	14	1		
2014–15	Crystal Palace	34	2	48	3

DE SILVA, Kyle (F)   10 0
H: 5 10 W: 11 05 b.Croydon 29-11-93

Season	Club				
2010–11	Crystal Palace	0	0		
2011–12	Crystal Palace	6	0		
2012–13	Crystal Palace	1	0		
2012–13	Barnet	3	0	3	0
2013–14	Crystal Palace	0	0		
2014–15	Crystal Palace	0	0	7	0

DELANEY, Damien (D)   511 14
H: 6 3 W: 14 00 b.Cork 20-7-81
Internationals: Republic of Ireland Full caps.

Season	Club				
2000–01	Leicester C	5	0		
2001–02	Leicester C	3	0		
2001–02	Stockport Co	12	1	12	1
2001–02	Huddersfield T	2	0	2	0
2002–03	Leicester C	0	0	8	0
2002–03	Mansfield T	7	0	7	0
2002–03	Hull C	30	1		
2003–04	Hull C	46	2		
2004–05	Hull C	43	1		
2005–06	Hull C	46	0		
2006–07	Hull C	37	1		
2007–08	Hull C	22	0	224	5
2007–08	QPR	17	1		
2008–09	QPR	37	1		
2009–10	QPR	0	0	54	2
2009–10	Ipswich T	36	0		
2010–11	Ipswich T	32	2		
2011–12	Ipswich T	29	0		
2012–13	Ipswich T	1	0	98	2
2012–13	Crystal Palace	40	3		
2013–14	Crystal Palace	37	1		
2014–15	Crystal Palace	29	0	106	4

DOBBIE, Stephen (F) 329 98
H: 5 10 W: 11 00 b.Glasgow 5-12-82

Season	Club				
2002–03	Rangers	0	0		
2002–03	*Northern Spirit*	3	3	3	3
2003–04	Hibernian	28	2		
2004–05	Hibernian	7	0	35	2
2004–05	*St Johnstone*	8	2		
2005–06	St Johnstone	20	1	28	3
2006–07	*Dumbarton*	17	10	17	10
2006–07	Queen of the South	15	10		
2007–08	Queen of the South	36	16		
2008–09	Queen of the South	32	23	83	49
2009–10	Swansea C	6	0		
2009–10	Blackpool	16	4		
2010–11	Swansea C	41	9		
2011–12	Swansea C	8	0	55	9
2011–12	*Blackpool*	7	5		
2012–13	Brighton & HA	15	2	15	2
2012–13	*Crystal Palace*	15	3		
2013–14	Crystal Palace	1	0		
2013–14	*Blackpool*	27	4	50	13
2014–15	Crystal Palace	0	0	16	3
2014–15	*Fleetwood T*	27	4	27	4

FRYERS, Zeki (D) 30 0
H: 6 0 W: 12 00 b.Manchester 9-9-92
Internationals: England U16, U17, U19.

Season	Club				
2011–12	Manchester U	2	0	2	0
2012–13	Standard Liege	7	0	7	0
2012–13	Tottenham H	0	0		
2013–14	Tottenham H	7	0	7	0
2014–15	Crystal Palace	1	0	1	0
2014–15	*Rotherham U*	10	0	10	0
2014–15	*Ipswich T*	3	0	3	0

GARVAN, Owen (M) 257 23
H: 6 0 W: 10 07 b.Dublin 29-1-88
Internationals: Republic of Ireland U21.

Season	Club				
2005–06	Ipswich T	32	3		
2006–07	Ipswich T	27	1		
2007–08	Ipswich T	43	2		
2008–09	Ipswich T	37	7		
2009–10	Ipswich T	25	0	164	13
2010–11	Crystal Palace	26	3		
2011–12	Crystal Palace	22	3		
2012–13	Crystal Palace	27	4		
2013–14	Crystal Palace	2	0		
2013–14	*Millwall*	13	0	13	0
2014–15	Crystal Palace	0	0	77	10
2014–15	*Bolton W*	3	0	3	0

GAYLE, Dwight (F) 95 32
H: 5 10 W: 11 07 b.Walthamstow 20-10-89

Season	Club				
2011–12	Dagenham & R	0	0		
2012–13	Dagenham & R	18	7	18	7
2012–13	Peterborough U	29	13	29	13
2013–14	Crystal Palace	23	7		
2014–15	Crystal Palace	25	5	48	12

GRAY, Jake (F) 4 0
H: 5 11 W: 11 00 b.Aylesbury 25-12-95

Season	Club				
2014–15	Crystal Palace	0	0		
2014–15	*Cheltenham T*	4	0	4	0

GUEDIOURA, Adlene (M) 220 20
H: 6 1 W: 12 08 b.La Roche-sur-Yon 12-11-85
Internationals: Algeria Full caps.

Season	Club				
2004–05	Sedan	0	0		
2005–06	Noisy-Le-Sec	15	1	15	1
2006–07	L'Entente	21	3	21	3
2007–08	Creteil	24	6	24	6
2008–09	Kortrijk	10	0	10	0
2008–09	Charleroi	12	0		
2009–10	Charleroi	13	1	25	1
2009–10	Wolverhampton W	14	1		
2010–11	Wolverhampton W	10	1		
2011–12	Wolverhampton W	10	0	34	2
2011–12	*Nottingham F*	19	1		
2012–13	Nottingham F	33	3		
2013–14	Nottingham F	5	0	59	4
2013–14	Crystal Palace	8	0		
2014–15	Crystal Palace	7	0	15	0
2014–15	*Watford*	17	3	17	3

HANGELAND, Brede (D) 408 19
H: 6 4 W: 13 05 b.Houston 20-6-81
Internationals: Norway U21, Full caps.

Season	Club				
2000	Vidar	0	0		
2001	Viking	22	0		
2002	Viking	26	2		
2003	Viking	26	1		
2004	Viking	14	3		
2005	Viking	26	0	114	6
2005–06	FC Copenhagen	13	1		
2006–07	FC Copenhagen	32	0		
2007–08	FC Copenhagen	18	2	63	3
2007–08	Fulham	15	0		
2008–09	Fulham	37	1		
2009–10	Fulham	32	1		
2010–11	Fulham	37	6		
2011–12	Fulham	38	0		
2012–13	Fulham	35	0		
2013–14	Fulham	23	0	217	8
2014–15	Crystal Palace	14	2	14	2

HENNESSEY, Wayne (G) 183 0
H: 6 0 W: 11 06 b.Anglesey 24-1-87
Internationals: Wales U17, U19, U21, Full caps.

Season	Club				
2004–05	Wolverhampton W	0	0		
2005–06	Wolverhampton W	0	0		
2006–07	Wolverhampton W	0	0		
2006–07	*Bristol C*	0	0		
2006–07	*Stockport Co*	15	0	15	0
2007–08	Wolverhampton W	46	0		
2008–09	Wolverhampton W	35	0		
2009–10	Wolverhampton W	13	0		
2010–11	Wolverhampton W	24	0		
2011–12	Wolverhampton W	34	0		
2012–13	Wolverhampton W	0	0		
2013–14	Wolverhampton W	0	0	152	0
2013–14	*Yeovil T*	12	0	12	0
2013–14	Crystal Palace	1	0		
2014–15	Crystal Palace	3	0	4	0

HUNT, Jack (D) 168 2
H: 5 9 W: 11 02 b.Rothwell 6-12-90

Season	Club				
2009–10	Huddersfield T	0	0		
2010–11	Huddersfield T	19	1		
2010–11	*Chesterfield*	20	0	20	0
2011–12	Huddersfield T	43	1		
2012–13	Huddersfield T	40	0		
2013–14	Huddersfield T	2	0	104	2
2013–14	Crystal Palace	0	0		
2013–14	*Barnsley*	11	0	11	0
2014–15	Crystal Palace	0	0		
2014–15	*Nottingham F*	17	0	17	0
2014–15	*Rotherham U*	16	0	16	0

INNISS, Ryan (D) 16 0
H: 6 5 W: 13 02 b.Kent 5-6-95
Internationals: England U16, U17.

Season	Club				
2012–13	Crystal Palace	0	0		
2013–14	Crystal Palace	0	0		
2013–14	*Cheltenham T*	2	0	2	0
2013–14	*Gillingham*	3	0	3	0
2014–15	Crystal Palace	0	0		
2014–15	*Yeovil T*	6	0	6	0
2014–15	*Port Vale*	5	0	5	0

JEDINAK, Mile (M) 327 39
H: 6 2 W: 13 12 b.Sydney 3-8-84
Internationals: Australia U20, Full caps.

Season	Club				
2000–01	Sydney U	3	0		
2001–02	Sydney U	7	1		
2002–03	Sydney U	18	2		
2003–04	Varteks	0	0		
2004–05	Sydney U	24	3		
2005–06	Sydney U	30	6	82	12
2006–07	Central Coast M	8	0		
2007–08	Central Coast M	22	2		
2008–09	Central Coast M	15	6	45	8
2008–09	Genclerbirligi	15	1		
2009–10	Genclerbirligi	2	0		
2009–10	Antalya	28	5	28	5
2010–11	Genclerbirligi	21	3	38	4
2011–12	Crystal Palace	31	1		
2012–13	Crystal Palace	41	3		
2013–14	Crystal Palace	38	1		
2014–15	Crystal Palace	24	5	134	10

JOHNSON, Andy (F) 390 114
H: 5 7 W: 10 09 b.Bedford 10-2-81
Internationals: England U20, Full caps.

Season	Club				
1997–98	Birmingham C	0	0		
1998–99	Birmingham C	4	0		
1999–2000	Birmingham C	22	1		
2000–01	Birmingham C	34	4		
2001–02	Birmingham C	23	3	83	8
2002–03	Crystal Palace	28	11		
2003–04	Crystal Palace	42	27		
2004–05	Crystal Palace	37	21		
2005–06	Crystal Palace	33	15		
2006–07	Everton	32	11		
2007–08	Everton	29	6	61	17
2008–09	Fulham	31	7		
2009–10	Fulham	8	0		
2010–11	Fulham	27	3		
2011–12	Fulham	20	3	86	13
2012–13	QPR	39	0		
2013–14	QPR	17	2	20	2
2014–15	Crystal Palace	0	0	140	74

KAIKAI, Sullay (F) 30 5
H: 6 0 W: 11 07 b.London 26-8-95

Season	Club				
2013–14	Crystal Palace	0	0		
2013–14	*Crawley T*	5	0	5	0
2014–15	Crystal Palace	0	0		
2014–15	*Cambridge U*	25	5	25	5

KEBE, Jimmy (M) 224 37
H: 6 2 W: 11 07 b.Paris 19-1-84
Internationals: Mali U23, Full caps.

Season	Club				
2005–06	Lens	18	2		
2006–07	*Chateauroux*	18	2	18	2
2007–08	Lens	0	0		
2007–08	*Boulogne*	16	5	16	5
2007–08	Reading	5	0		
2008–09	Reading	41	2		
2009–10	Reading	42	10		
2010–11	Reading	36	9		
2011–12	Reading	33	3		
2012–13	Reading	18	5		
2013–14	Reading	0	0	175	29
2013–14	Crystal Palace	6	0		
2013–14	*Leeds U*	9	1	9	1
2014–15	Crystal Palace	0	0	6	0

KELLY, Martin (D) 71 1
H: 6 3 W: 12 02 b.Bolton 27-4-90
Internationals: England U19, U20, U21, Full caps.

Season	Club				
2007–08	Liverpool	0	0		
2008–09	Liverpool	0	0		
2008–09	*Huddersfield T*	7	1	7	1
2009–10	Liverpool	1	0		
2010–11	Liverpool	11	0		
2011–12	Liverpool	12	0		
2012–13	Liverpool	4	0		
2013–14	Liverpool	5	0	33	0
2014–15	Crystal Palace	31	0	31	0

KETTINGS, Chris (G) 2 0
H: 6 2 W: 12 04 b.Bolton 25-10-92
Internationals: Scotland U19, U21.

Season	Club				
2011–12	Blackpool	0	0		
2011–12	*Birmingham C*	0	0		
2011–12	*Morecambe*	2	0	2	0
2012–13	Blackpool	0	0		
2013–14	Blackpool	0	0		
2013–14	*York C*	0	0		
2014–15	Crystal Palace	0	0		

LEDLEY, Joe (M) 378 49
H: 6 0 W: 11 06 b.Cardiff 23-1-87
Internationals: Wales U17, U19, U21, Full caps.

Season	Club				
2004–05	Cardiff C	28	3		
2005–06	Cardiff C	42	3		
2006–07	Cardiff C	46	2		
2007–08	Cardiff C	41	10		
2008–09	Cardiff C	40	4		
2009–10	Cardiff C	29	3	226	25
2010–11	Celtic	29	2		
2011–12	Celtic	32	7		
2012–13	Celtic	25	7		
2013–14	Celtic	20	4	106	20
2013–14	Crystal Palace	14	2		
2014–15	Crystal Palace	32	2	46	4

LEE, Chung Yong (M) 230 27
H: 5 11 W: 10 09 b.Seoul 2-7-88
Internationals: South Korea U19, U20, Full caps.

Season	Club				
2006	FC Seoul	2	0		
2007	FC Seoul	15	3		
2008	FC Seoul	20	5		
2009	FC Seoul	14	2	51	10
2009–10	Bolton W	34	4		
2010–11	Bolton W	31	3		
2011–12	Bolton W	2	0		
2012–13	Bolton W	41	4		
2013–14	Bolton W	45	3		
2014–15	Bolton W	23	3	176	17
2014–15	Crystal Palace	3	0	3	0

MARIAPPA, Adrian (D) 281 6
H: 5 10 W: 11 12 b.Harrow 3-10-86
Internationals: Jamaica Full caps.

Season	Club				
2005–06	Watford	3	0		
2006–07	Watford	19	0		
2007–08	Watford	25	0		
2008–09	Watford	39	1		
2009–10	Watford	46	1		
2010–11	Watford	45	1		
2011–12	Watford	39	1	216	4
2012–13	Reading	29	1		
2013–14	Reading	0	0	29	1
2013–14	Crystal Palace	24	1		
2014–15	Crystal Palace	12	0	36	1

McARTHUR, James (M) 329 22
H: 5 6 W: 9 13 b.Glasgow 7-10-87
Internationals: Scotland U21, Full caps.

Season	Club				
2004–05	Hamilton A	6	0		
2005–06	Hamilton A	20	1		
2006–07	Hamilton A	36	1		

2007–08	Hamilton A	34	4		
2008–09	Hamilton A	37	2		
2009–10	Hamilton A	35	1	168	9
2010–11	Wigan Ath	18	0		
2011–12	Wigan Ath	31	3		
2012–13	Wigan Ath	34	3		
2013–14	Wigan Ath	41	4		
2014–15	Wigan Ath	5	1	129	11
2014–15	Crystal Palace	32	2	32	2

McCARTHY, Patrick (D)   269 12
H: 6 2   W: 13 07   b.Dublin 31-5-83
Internationals: Republic of Ireland U17, U21, B.

2000–01	Manchester C	0	0		
2001–02	Manchester C	0	0		
2002–03	Manchester C	0	0		
2002–03	Boston U	12	0	12	0
2002–03	Notts Co	6	0	6	0
2003–04	Manchester C	0	0		
2004–05	Manchester C	0	0		
2004–05	Leicester C	12	0		
2005–06	Leicester C	38	2		
2006–07	Leicester C	22	1	72	3
2007–08	Charlton Ath	29	2	29	2
2008–09	Crystal Palace	27	3		
2009–10	Crystal Palace	20	0		
2010–11	Crystal Palace	43	1		
2011–12	Crystal Palace	43	2		
2012–13	Crystal Palace	0	0		
2013–14	Crystal Palace	1	0		
2014–15	Crystal Palace	0	0	134	6
2014–15	Sheffield U	11	1	11	1
2014–15	Bolton W	5	0	5	0

MURRAY, Glenn (F)   339 137
H: 6 1   W: 12 12   b.Maryport 25-9-83

2005–06	Carlisle U	26	3		
2006–07	Carlisle U	1	0	27	3
2006–07	Stockport Co	11	3	11	3
2006–07	Rochdale	31	16		
2007–08	Rochdale	23	9	54	25
2007–08	Brighton & HA	21	9		
2008–09	Brighton & HA	23	11		
2009–10	Brighton & HA	32	12		
2010–11	Brighton & HA	42	22	118	54
2011–12	Crystal Palace	38	6		
2012–13	Crystal Palace	42	30		
2013–14	Crystal Palace	14	1		
2014–15	Crystal Palace	17	7	111	44
2014–15	Reading	18	8	18	8

MUTCH, Jordon (M)   140 16
H: 5 9   W: 10 03   b.Derby 2-12-91
Internationals: England U17, U19, U20, U21.

2007–08	Birmingham C	0	0		
2008–09	Birmingham C	0	0		
2009–10	Birmingham C	0	0		
2009–10	Hereford U	3	0	3	0
2009–10	Doncaster R	17	2	17	2
2010–11	Birmingham C	3	0		
2010–11	Watford	23	5	23	5
2011–12	Birmingham C	21	2	24	2
2012–13	Cardiff C	22	0		
2013–14	Cardiff C	35	7	57	7
2014–15	QPR	9	0	9	0
2014–15	Crystal Palace	7	0	7	0

PRICE, Lewis (G)   125 0
H: 6 3   W: 13 05   b.Bournemouth 19-7-84
Internationals: Wales U19, U21, Full caps.

2002–03	Ipswich T	0	0		
2003–04	Ipswich T	1	0		
2004–05	Ipswich T	8	0		
2004–05	Cambridge U	6	0	6	0
2005–06	Ipswich T	25	0		
2006–07	Ipswich T	34	0	68	0
2007–08	Derby Co	6	0		
2008–09	Derby Co	0	0		
2008–09	Milton Keynes D	2	0	2	0
2008–09	Luton T	1	0	1	0
2009–10	Derby Co	0	0	6	0
2009–10	Brentford	13	0	13	0
2010–11	Crystal Palace	1	0		
2011–12	Crystal Palace	5	0		
2012–13	Crystal Palace	0	0		
2013–14	Crystal Palace	0	0		
2013–14	Mansfield T	5	0	5	0
2014–15	Crystal Palace	0	0	6	0
2014–15	Crawley T	18	0	18	0

PUNCHEON, Jason (M)   334 57
H: 5 9   W: 12 05   b.Croydon 26-6-86

2003–04	Wimbledon	8	0	8	0
2004–05	Milton Keynes D	25	1		
2005–06	Milton Keynes D	1	0		
2006–07	Barnet	37	5		
2007–08	Barnet	41	10	78	15
2008–09	Plymouth Arg	6	0		
2008–09	Milton Keynes D	27	4		
2009–10	Plymouth Arg	0	0	6	0
2009–10	Milton Keynes D	24	7	77	12
2009–10	Southampton	19	3		
2010–11	Southampton	15	0		
2010–11	Millwall	7	5	7	5
2010–11	Blackpool	11	3	11	3
2011–12	Southampton	8	0		
2011–12	QPR	2	0	2	0
2012–13	Southampton	32	6		
2013–14	Southampton	0	0	74	9
2013–14	Crystal Palace	34	7		
2014–15	Crystal Palace	37	6	71	13

RAMAGE, Peter (D)   233 9
H: 6 3   W: 11 02   b.Whitley Bay 22-11-83

2003–04	Newcastle U	4	0		
2004–05	Newcastle U	4	0		
2005–06	Newcastle U	23	0		
2006–07	Newcastle U	21	0		
2007–08	Newcastle U	3	0	51	0
2008–09	QPR	31	0		
2009–10	QPR	33	2		
2010–11	QPR	4	0		
2011–12	QPR	0	0	68	2
2011–12	Crystal Palace	17	0		
2011–12	Birmingham C	14	0	14	0
2012–13	Crystal Palace	40	4		
2013–14	Crystal Palace	0	0		
2013–14	Barnsley	24	0		
2014–15	Crystal Palace	0	0	57	4
2014–15	Barnsley	19	3	43	3

SOUARE, Pape (D)   88 3
H: 5 10   W: 10 10   b.Mbao 6-6-90
Internationals: Senegal U23, Full caps.

2010–11	Lille	4	0		
2011–12	Lille	7	0		
2012–13	Lille	0	0		
2012–13	Reims	23	0	23	0
2013–14	Lille	33	3		
2014–15	Lille	12	0	56	3
2014–15	Crystal Palace	9	0	9	0

SPERONI, Julian (G)   451 0
H: 6 0   W: 11 00   b.Buenos Aires 18-5-79
Internationals: Argentina U20, U21.

1999–2000	Platense	2	0		
2000–01	Platense	0	0	2	0
2001–02	Dundee	17	0		
2002–03	Dundee	38	0		
2003–04	Dundee	37	0	92	0
2004–05	Crystal Palace	6	0		
2005–06	Crystal Palace	4	0		
2006–07	Crystal Palace	5	0		
2007–08	Crystal Palace	46	0		
2008–09	Crystal Palace	45	0		
2009–10	Crystal Palace	45	0		
2010–11	Crystal Palace	45	0		
2011–12	Crystal Palace	42	0		
2012–13	Crystal Palace	46	0		
2013–14	Crystal Palace	37	0		
2014–15	Crystal Palace	36	0	357	0

THOMAS, Jerome (M)   231 22
H: 5 9   W: 11 09   b.Wembley 23-3-83
Internationals: England U19, U20, U21.

2001–02	Arsenal	0	0		
2001–02	QPR	4	1		
2002–03	Arsenal	0	0		
2002–03	QPR	6	2	10	3
2003–04	Arsenal	0	0		
2003–04	Charlton Ath	1	0		
2004–05	Charlton Ath	24	3		
2005–06	Charlton Ath	25	1		
2006–07	Charlton Ath	20	3		
2007–08	Charlton Ath	32	0		
2008–09	Charlton Ath	1	0	103	7
2008–09	Portsmouth	3	0		
2009–10	Portsmouth	0	0	3	0
2009–10	WBA	27	7		
2010–11	WBA	33	3		
2011–12	WBA	29	1		
2012–13	WBA	10	0	99	11
2012–13	Leeds U	6	1	6	1
2013–14	Crystal Palace	9	0		
2014–15	Crystal Palace	1	0	10	0

WARD, Joel (D)   208 8
H: 6 2   W: 11 13   b.Emsworth 29-10-89

2008–09	Portsmouth	0	0		
2008–09	Bournemouth	21	1	21	1
2009–10	Portsmouth	3	0		
2010–11	Portsmouth	42	3		
2011–12	Portsmouth	44	3	89	6
2012–13	Crystal Palace	25	0		
2013–14	Crystal Palace	36	0		
2014–15	Crystal Palace	37	1	98	1

WILLIAMS, Jerome (D)   21 0
H: 5 11   W: 12 02   b.Croydon 7-3-95
Internationals: England U18, U19.

2013–14	Crystal Palace	0	0		
2014–15	Crystal Palace	0	0		
2014–15	Southend U	21	0	21	0

WILLIAMS, Jon (M)   74 2
H: 5 6   W: 10 00   b.Tunbridge Wells 9-10-93
Internationals: Wales U17, U19, U21, Full caps.

2010–11	Crystal Palace	0	0		
2011–12	Crystal Palace	14	0		
2012–13	Crystal Palace	29	0		
2013–14	Crystal Palace	9	0		
2013–14	Ipswich T	13	1		
2014–15	Crystal Palace	2	0	54	0
2014–15	Ipswich T	7	1	20	2

WYNTER, Alex (M)   34 1
H: 6 0   W: 13 04   b.Camberwell 15-9-93

2009–10	Crystal Palace	0	0		
2010–11	Crystal Palace	0	0		
2011–12	Crystal Palace	0	0		
2012–13	Crystal Palace	0	0		
2013–14	Crystal Palace	0	0		
2013–14	Colchester U	6	1		
2014–15	Crystal Palace	0	0		
2014–15	Portsmouth	10	0	10	0
2014–15	Colchester U	18	0	24	1

ZAHA, Wilfried (F)   171 17
H: 5 11   W: 10 05   b.Ivory Coast 10-11-92
Internationals: England U19, U21, Full caps.

2009–10	Crystal Palace	1	0		
2010–11	Crystal Palace	41	1		
2011–12	Crystal Palace	41	6		
2012–13	Crystal Palace	43	6		
2012–13	Manchester U	0	0		
2013–14	Manchester U	2	0	2	0
2013–14	Cardiff C	12	0	12	0
2014–15	Crystal Palace	31	4	157	17

Players retained or with offer of contract
Adarabioyo, Mubarak Olufisayo Olatayo Monthly; Andrews, Corie Anthony; Berkeley-Agyepong, Jacob Kwame; Binnom-Williams, Jerome Craig; Breimyr, Andreas Malde; Croll, Luke Alan; Dymond, Connor William; Ferrier, Morgan James Monthly; Gregory, David Michael; Magri, Samuel John Monthly; Pain, Oliver David.

Scholars
Akiotu, Jason; Bennett, Oliver George; Coker, Andre Jordan Coleridge; Day, Thomas; Egbo, Mandela; Forte, Spencer Ellis Henderson; George, Matthew; Hoare, William James; Hogan, Daniel Peter; King-Elliott, Ryan; Mohammed, Hussein Ali; O'Dwyer, Oliver; Phillips, Michael; Scales, Christian Stephen; Wan-Bissaka, Aaron; Wynter, Ben Douglas.

DAGENHAM & R (30)

BATT, Damian (D)   155 2
H: 5 10   W: 11 06   b.Hoddesdon 16-9-84

2005–06	Barnet	22	0	22	0

From St Albans C, Stevenage, Woking, Fisher Ath, Grays Ath.

2010–11	Oxford U	28	0		
2011–12	Oxford U	40	1		
2012–13	Oxford U	37	1		
2013–14	Oxford U	0	0	105	2
2014–15	Dagenham & R	28	0	28	0

BINGHAM, Billy (D)   117 8
H: 5 11   W: 11 02   b.Welling 15-7-90

2008–09	Dagenham & R	0	0		
2009–10	Dagenham & R	2	0		
2010–11	Dagenham & R	6	0		
2011–12	Dagenham & R	27	2		
2012–13	Dagenham & R	18	2		
2013–14	Dagenham & R	30	0		
2014–15	Dagenham & R	34	4	117	8

BOUCAUD, Andre (M)   158 3
H: 5 8   W: 11 01   b.Enfield 10-10-84
Internationals: Trinidad & Tobago Full caps.

2002–03	Reading	0	0		
2002–03	Peterborough U	6	0		
2003–04	Reading	0	0		
2003–04	Peterborough U	8	1		
2004–05	Peterborough U	22	1		
2005–06	Peterborough U	3	0	39	2

From Kettering T

2007–08	Wycombe W	10	0	10	0

From Kettering T, York C, Luton T

2012–13	Notts Co	39	1		
2013–14	Notts Co	29	0	68	1
2014–15	Dagenham & R	41	0	41	0

CHAMBERS, Ashley (F)   97 12
H: 5 10 W: 11 06 b.Leicester 1-3-90
Internationals: England C, U16, U17, U18, U19.

2005–06	Leicester C	0	0		
2006–07	Leicester C	0	0		
2007–08	Leicester C	5	0		
2008–09	Leicester C	1	0		
2009–10	Leicester C	0	0	6	0
2009–10	Wycombe W	0	0		
2009–10	Grimsby T	0	0		
2012–13	York C	38	10		
2013–14	York C	15	0	53	10
2013–14	*Dagenham & R*	6	0		
2014–15	Dagenham & R	32	2	38	2

CONNORS, Jack (D)   40 0
H: 5 8 W: 9 06 b.Brent 24-10-94
Internationals: Republic of Ireland U21.

2013–14	Dagenham & R	23	0		
2014–15	Dagenham & R	17	0	40	0

COUSINS, Mark (G)   95 0
H: 6 2 W: 12 02 b.Chelmsford 9-1-87

2005–06	Colchester U	0	0		
2006–07	Colchester U	0	0		
2007–08	Colchester U	2	0		
2008–09	Colchester U	9	0		
2009–10	Colchester U	0	0		
2010–11	Colchester U	14	0		
2011–12	Colchester U	10	0		
2012–13	Colchester U	23	0		
2013–14	Colchester U	0	0	58	0
2014–15	Dagenham & R	37	0	37	0

CURETON, Jamie (F)   717 256
H: 5 8 W: 10 07 b.Bristol 28-8-75
Internationals: England U18.

1992–93	Norwich C	0	0		
1993–94	Norwich C	0	0		
1994–95	Norwich C	17	4		
1995–96	Norwich C	12	2		
1995–96	*Bournemouth*	5	0	5	0
1996–97	Bristol R	38	11		
1997–98	Bristol R	43	13		
1998–99	Bristol R	46	25		
1999–2000	Bristol R	46	22		
2000–01	Bristol R	1	1	174	72
2000–01	Reading	43	26		
2001–02	Reading	38	15		
2002–03	Reading	27	9	108	50

From Busan Icons.

2003–04	QPR	13	2		
2004–05	QPR	30	4	43	6
2005–06	Swindon T	30	7	30	7
2005–06	*Colchester U*	8	4		
2006–07	Colchester U	44	23	52	27
2007–08	Norwich C	41	12		
2008–09	Norwich C	22	2		
2008–09	*Barnsley*	8	2	8	2
2009–10	Norwich C	6	2	98	22
2009–10	*Shrewsbury T*	12	0	12	0
2010–11	Exeter C	41	17		
2011–12	*Leyton Orient*	19	1	19	1
2011–12	*Exeter C*	7	1		
2012–13	Exeter C	40	21	88	39
2013–14	Cheltenham T	35	11	35	11
2014–15	Dagenham & R	45	19	45	19

DOE, Scott (D)   243 11
H: 6 0 W: 11 06 b.Reading 6-11-88
Internationals: England C.

2009–10	Dagenham & R	42	0		
2010–11	Dagenham & R	38	0		
2011–12	Dagenham & R	41	6		
2012–13	Dagenham & R	46	3		
2013–14	Dagenham & R	37	1		
2014–15	Dagenham & R	39	1	243	11

DOIDGE, Christian (F)   11 2
H: 6 1 W: 12 02 b.Newport 25-8-92

2014–15	Dagenham & R	11	2	11	2

ENIGBOKAN-BLOOMFIELD,   1 0
Mason (F)
b.Westminster 6-11-96

2014–15	Dagenham & R	1	0	1	0

GAYLE, Ian (D)   10 0
b.Welling 23-10-92

2011–12	Dagenham & R	0	0		
2012–13	Dagenham & R	0	0		
2013–14	Dagenham & R	4	0		
2014–15	Dagenham & R	6	0	10	0

GOLDBERG, Bradley (F)   5 0
H: 5 7 W: 11 03 b.Bromley 20-10-93

2013–14	Dagenham & R	0	0		
2014–15	Dagenham & R	5	0	5	0

GREEN, Nathan (D)   7 0
b. 8-6-92

2014–15	Dagenham & R	7	0	7	0

HEMMINGS, Ashley (M)   136 10
H: 5 8 W: 11 06 b.Lewisham 3-3-91
Internationals: England U17.

2008–09	Wolverhampton W	2	0		
2008–09	*Cheltenham T*	1	0	1	0
2009–10	Wolverhampton W	0	0		
2010–11	Wolverhampton W	0	0		
2010–11	*Torquay U*	9	0	9	0
2011–12	Wolverhampton W	0	0	2	0
2011–12	*Plymouth Arg*	23	2	23	2
2012–13	Walsall	28	1		
2013–14	Walsall	27	2	55	3
2013–14	*Burton Alb*	5	0	5	0
2014–15	Dagenham & R	41	5	41	5

HINES, Zavon (F)   109 11
H: 5 10 W: 10 07 b.Jamaica 27-12-88
Internationals: England U21.

2007–08	West Ham U	0	0		
2007–08	*Coventry C*	7	1	7	1
2008–09	West Ham U	0	0		
2009–10	West Ham U	13	1		
2010–11	West Ham U	9	0	22	1
2011–12	Burnley	13	0	13	0
2011–12	*Bournemouth*	8	1	8	1
2012–13	Bradford C	32	2		
2013–14	Bradford C	0	0	32	2
2013–14	*Dagenham & R*	27	6		
2014–15	Dagenham & R	27	6		

HOWELL, Luke (D)   206 20
H: 5 10 W: 10 05 b.Heathfield 5-1-87

2006–07	Gillingham	1	0	1	0
2007–08	Milton Keynes D	8	0		
2008–09	Milton Keynes D	15	1		
2009–10	Milton Keynes D	29	0		
2010–11	Milton Keynes D	1	0	53	1
2010–11	Lincoln C	25	1	25	1
2011–12	Dagenham & R	10	0		
2012–13	Dagenham & R	46	9		
2013–14	Dagenham & R	40	4		
2014–15	Dagenham & R	31	5	127	18

JONES, Jodi (F)   8 1
b. 22-10-97

2014–15	Dagenham & R	8	1	8	1

LABADIE, Joss (M)   175 25
H: 5 7 W: 11 02 b.Croydon 31-8-90

2008–09	WBA	0	0		
2008–09	*Shrewsbury T*	1	0		
2009–10	WBA	0	0		
2009–10	*Shrewsbury T*	13	5	14	5
2009–10	*Cheltenham T*	11	0	11	0
2009–10	*Tranmere R*	9	3		
2010–11	Tranmere R	34	2		
2011–12	Tranmere R	27	5	70	10
2012–13	Notts Co	24	2		
2012–13	*Torquay U*	7	4		
2013–14	Notts Co	15	1	39	3
2013–14	*Torquay U*	10	1	17	5
2014–15	Dagenham & R	24	2	24	2

NOUBLE, Jon (F)   1 0
H: 6 4 W: 12 04 b.Deptford 19-1-96

2013–14	Dagenham & R	1	0		
2014–15	Dagenham & R	0	0	1	0

O'BRIEN, Liam (G)   31 0
H: 6 1 W: 12 06 b.Ruislip 30-11-91
Internationals: England U19.

2008–09	Portsmouth	0	0		
2009–10	Portsmouth	0	0		
2010–11	Barnet	8	0		
2011–12	Barnet	10	0		
2012–13	Barnet	3	0	21	0
2013–14	Brentford	0	0		
2014–15	Dagenham & R	10	0	10	0

OGOGO, Abu (D)   234 18
H: 5 8 W: 10 02 b.Epsom 3-11-89

2007–08	Arsenal	0	0		
2008–09	Arsenal	0	0		
2008–09	*Barnet*	9	1	9	1
2009–10	Dagenham & R	30	2		
2010–11	Dagenham & R	33	1		
2011–12	Dagenham & R	40	1		
2012–13	Dagenham & R	46	1		
2013–14	Dagenham & R	44	8		
2014–15	Dagenham & R	32	4	225	17

PARTRIDGE, Matt (D)   24 1
H: 6 3 W: 13 02 b.Reading 24-10-84

2012–13	Reading	0	0		
2013–14	Reading	0	0		
2014–15	Dagenham & R	24	1	24	1

PORTER, George (F)   96 3
H: 5 10 W: 12 06 b.Sidcup 27-6-92

2010–11	Leyton Orient	1	0		
2011–12	Leyton Orient	34	1	35	1
2012–13	Burnley	0	0		
2012–13	*Colchester U*	19	1	19	1
2013–14	Burnley	0	0		
2013–14	*AFC Wimbledon*	21	0	21	0
2013–14	*Rochdale*	2	0	2	0
2014–15	Dagenham & R	19	1	19	1

RAYMOND, Frankie (M)   2 1
H: 5 10 W: 11 09 b.Chislehurst 18-11-92

2010–11	Reading	0	0		
2011–12	Reading	0	0		

From Eastleigh, Eastbourne Bor.

2014–15	Dagenham & R	2	1	2	1

SAAH, Brian (M)   237 3
H: 6 3 W: 12 03 b.Rush Green 16-12-86
Internationals: England C.

2003–04	Leyton Orient	6	0		
2004–05	Leyton Orient	12	0		
2005–06	Leyton Orient	3	0		
2006–07	Leyton Orient	32	0		
2007–08	Leyton Orient	25	1		
2008–09	Leyton Orient	15	0	93	1

From Cambridge U.

2011–12	Torquay U	35	1		
2012–13	Torquay U	43	1	78	2
2013–14	Dagenham & R	43	0		
2014–15	Dagenham & R	23	0	66	0

WIDDOWSON, Joe (D)   221 1
H: 6 0 W: 12 00 b.Forest Gate 28-3-89

2007–08	West Ham U	0	0		
2007–08	*Rotherham U*	3	0	3	0
2008–09	West Ham U	0	0		
2008–09	*Grimsby T*	20	1		
2009–10	Grimsby T	38	0	58	1
2010–11	Rochdale	34	0		
2011–12	Rochdale	32	0	66	0
2012–13	Northampton T	39	0		
2013–14	Northampton T	25	0	64	0
2014–15	*Bury*	1	0	1	0
2014–15	*Morecambe*	8	0	8	0
2014–15	Dagenham & R	21	0	21	0

YUSUFF, Ade (F)   18 2
H: 5 7 W: 10 06 b.Lewisham 25-5-94

2014–15	Dagenham & R	18	2	18	2

Scholars
Bolton, Tyler Jon; Burnett, Henry; Clark, Lewis James; Crickmay, Benjamin Michael; Enigbokan-Bloomfield, Mason Ozail; Fitchett, James David; Foxley, Darren Stepan Stanley; Grimme-Yexley, Charles John; Hackett-Fairchild, Reeco Lee; Heather, Kai Joseph; Hursit, Lee; Moulder, Alfie Glen; Nicol-Wilson, David Ronald Adrian; Nottage, James Lloyd Thomas; Olukoga, Ayodeji Sulaimon; Shepherd, James Frederick Alan.

DERBY CO (31)

ALBENTOSA, Raul (D)   122 10
H: 6 4 W: 14 00 b.Alzira 7-9-88

2011–12	San Rocque	31	3	31	3
2012–13	Cadiz	33	3	33	3
2013–14	Eibar	33	2		
2014–15	Eibar	17	2	50	4
2014–15	Derby Co	8	0	8	0

ATKINS, Ross (G)   50 0
H: 6 0 W: 13 00 b.Derby 3-11-89
Internationals: England U18, U19.

2008–09	Derby Co	0	0		
2009–10	Derby Co	0	0		
2010–11	Derby Co	1	0		
2011–12	Derby Co	0	0		
2011–12	*Burton Alb*	45	0		
2012–13	Derby Co	0	0		
2012–13	*Burton Alb*	4	0	49	0
2013–14	Derby Co	0	0		
2013–14	*Crawley T*	0	0		
2014–15	Derby Co	1	0		

BARKER, Shaun (D)   355 18
H: 6 2 W: 12 08 b.Nottingham 19-9-82

2002–03	Rotherham U	11	0		
2003–04	Rotherham U	36	2		

2004–05	Rotherham U	33	2		
2005–06	Rotherham U	43	3	123	7
2006–07	Blackpool	45	3		
2007–08	Blackpool	46	2		
2008–09	Blackpool	43	0	134	5
2009–10	Derby Co	35	5		
2010–11	Derby Co	43	1		
2011–12	Derby Co	20	0		
2012–13	Derby Co	0	0		
2013–14	Derby Co	0	0		
2014–15	Derby Co	0	0	98	6

BENNETT, Mason (F)   46   2
H: 5 10   W: 10 02   b.Shirebrook 15-7-96
Internationals: England U16, U17, U19.

2011–12	Derby Co	9	0		
2012–13	Derby Co	6	0		
2013–14	Derby Co	13	1		
2013–14	*Chesterfield*	5	0	5	0
2014–15	Derby Co	2	0	30	1
2014–15	*Bradford C*	11	1	11	1

BRYSON, Craig (M)   377   51
H: 5 7   W: 10 00   b.Rutherglen 6-11-86
Internationals: Scotland U21, Full caps.

2003–04	Clyde	0	0		
2004–05	Clyde	28	3		
2005–06	Clyde	33	2		
2006–07	Clyde	34	3	95	8
2007–08	Kilmarnock	19	4		
2008–09	Kilmarnock	33	2		
2009–10	Kilmarnock	33	4		
2010–11	Kilmarnock	33	2	118	12
2011–12	Derby Co	44	6		
2012–13	Derby Co	37	5		
2013–14	Derby Co	45	16		
2014–15	Derby Co	38	4	164	31

BUNJAKU, Alban (M)   0   0
H: 6 0   W: 12 04   b.Romford 20-5-94
Internationals: Kosovo Full caps.

2014–15	Derby Co	0	0

BUXTON, Jake (D)   287   16
H: 6 1   W: 13 05   b.Sutton-in-Ashfield 4-3-85

2002–03	Mansfield T	3	0		
2003–04	Mansfield T	9	1		
2004–05	Mansfield T	30	1		
2005–06	Mansfield T	39	0		
2006–07	Mansfield T	30	1		
2007–08	Mansfield T	40	2		
2008–09	Mansfield T	0	0	151	5

From Burton Alb.

2008–09	Derby Co	0	0		
2009–10	Derby Co	19	1		
2010–11	Derby Co	1	0		
2011–12	Derby Co	21	2		
2012–13	Derby Co	31	3		
2013–14	Derby Co	45	2		
2014–15	Derby Co	19	3	136	11

CALERO, Ivan (M)   8   0
H: 5 8   W: 10 01   b.Parla 30-11-94
Internationals: Spain U16, U17, U18, U19.

2014–15	Derby Co	2	0	2	0
2014–15	*Burton Alb*	6	0	6	0

CHRISTIE, Cyrus (D)   140   2
H: 6 2   W: 12 03   b.Coventry 30-9-92
Internationals: Republic of Ireland Full caps.

2011–12	Coventry C	37	0		
2012–13	Coventry C	31	2		
2013–14	Coventry C	34	0	102	2
2014–15	Derby Co	38	0	38	0

DAWKINS, Simon (F)   130   21
H: 5 10   W: 11 01   b.Edgware 1-12-87
Internationals: Jamaica Full caps.

2005–06	Tottenham H	0	0		
2006–07	Tottenham H	0	0		
2007–08	Tottenham H	0	0		
2008–09	Tottenham H	0	0		
2008–09	*Leyton Orient*	11	0	11	0
2009–10	Tottenham H	0	0		
2010–11	Tottenham H	0	0		
2011	*San Jose E*	26	6		
2011–12	Tottenham H	0	0		
2012	*San Jose E*	29	8	55	14
2012–13	Tottenham H	0	0		
2012–13	*Aston Villa*	4	0	4	0
2013–14	Tottenham H	0	0		
2013–14	Derby Co	26	4		
2014–15	Derby Co	34	3	60	7

ETHERIDGE, Ross (G)   0   0

2013–14	Derby Co	0	0
2014–15	Derby Co	0	0
2014–15	*Crewe Alex*	0	0

EUSTACE, John (M)   394   32
H: 5 11   W: 11 12   b.Solihull 3-11-79

1996–97	Coventry C	0	0		
1997–98	Coventry C	0	0		
1998–99	Coventry C	0	0		
1998–99	Dundee U	11	1	11	1
1999–2000	Coventry C	16	1		
2000–01	Coventry C	32	2		
2001–02	Coventry C	6	0		
2002–03	Coventry C	32	4	86	7
2002–03	*Middlesbrough*	1	0	1	0
2003–04	Stoke C	26	5		
2004–05	Stoke C	7	0		
2005–06	Stoke C	0	0		
2006–07	Stoke C	15	0		
2006–07	*Hereford U*	8	0	8	0
2007–08	Stoke C	26	0	74	5
2007–08	Watford	13	0		
2008–09	Watford	17	2		
2008–09	*Derby Co*	9	1		
2009–10	Watford	42	4		
2010–11	Watford	41	6		
2011–12	Watford	39	4		
2012–13	Watford	5	0	157	16
2013–14	Derby Co	35	1		
2014–15	Derby Co	13	1	57	3

FORSYTH, Craig (M)   223   18
H: 6 0   W: 12 00   b.Carnoustie 24-2-89
Internationals: Scotland Full caps.

2006–07	Dundee	1	0		
2007–08	Dundee	0	0		
2007–08	*Montrose*	9	0	9	0
2008–09	Dundee	1	0		
2008–09	*Arbroath*	26	2	26	2
2009–10	Dundee	24	2		
2010–11	Dundee	33	8	59	10
2011–12	Watford	20	3		
2012–13	Watford	2	0	22	3
2012–13	*Bradford C*	7	0	7	0
2012–13	*Derby Co*	10	0		
2013–14	Derby Co	46	2		
2014–15	Derby Co	44	1	100	3

GRANT, Lee (G)   427   0
H: 6 3   W: 13 01   b.Hemel Hempstead 27-1-83
Internationals: England U16, U17, U18, U19, U21.

2000–01	Derby Co	0	0		
2001–02	Derby Co	0	0		
2002–03	Derby Co	29	0		
2003–04	Derby Co	36	0		
2004–05	Derby Co	2	0		
2005–06	Derby Co	0	0		
2005–06	*Burnley*	1	0		
2005–06	*Oldham Ath*	16	0	16	0
2006–07	Derby Co	7	0		
2007–08	Sheffield W	44	0		
2008–09	Sheffield W	46	0		
2009–10	Sheffield W	46	0	136	0
2010–11	Burnley	25	0		
2011–12	Burnley	43	0		
2012–13	Burnley	46	0	115	0
2013–14	Burnley	46	0		
2014–15	Derby Co	40	0	160	0

HANSON, Jamie (F)   2   1
H: 6 3   W: 12 06   b.Burton-upon-Trent 10-11-95
Internationals: England U20.

2012–13	Derby Co	0	0		
2013–14	Derby Co	0	0		
2014–15	Derby Co	2	1	2	1

HENDRICK, Jeff (M)   162   20
H: 6 1   W: 11 11   b.Dublin 31-1-92
Internationals: Republic of Ireland U17, U21, Full caps.

2010–11	Derby Co	4	0		
2011–12	Derby Co	42	3		
2012–13	Derby Co	45	6		
2013–14	Derby Co	30	4		
2014–15	Derby Co	41	7	162	20

HENDRIE, Luke (M)   0   0
b. 27-8-94
Internationals: England U17.

2013–14	Derby Co	0	0
2014–15	Derby Co	0	0

HUGHES, Will (M)   121   7
H: 6 1   W: 11 08   b.Weybridge 7-4-95
Internationals: England U17, U21.

2011–12	Derby Co	3	0		
2012–13	Derby Co	35	2		
2013–14	Derby Co	41	3		
2014–15	Derby Co	42	2	121	7

KEOGH, Richard (D)   365   14
H: 6 0   W: 11 02   b.Harlow 11-8-86
Internationals: Republic of Ireland U21, Full caps.

2004–05	Stoke C	0	0		
2005–06	Bristol C	9	1		
2005–06	*Wycombe W*	3	0	3	0
2006–07	Bristol C	31	2		
2007–08	Bristol C	0	0	40	3
2007–08	*Huddersfield T*	9	1	9	1
2007–08	Carlisle U	7	0		
2007–08	*Cheltenham T*	10	0	10	0
2008–09	Carlisle U	32	1		
2009–10	Carlisle U	41	3	80	4
2010–11	Coventry C	46	1		
2011–12	Coventry C	45	0	91	1
2012–13	Derby Co	46	4		
2013–14	Derby Co	41	1		
2014–15	Derby Co	45	0	132	5

KOBLENZ, Tom (M)   0   0
b.Homburg 21-5-95

2014–15	Derby Co	0	0

LELAN, Josh (D)   5   0
H: 6 1   W: 11 00   b.Derby 21-12-94

2012–13	Derby Co	0	0		
2013–14	Derby Co	0	0		
2014–15	Derby Co	0	0		
2014–15	*Swindon T*	5	0	5	0

LOWE, Max (D)   0   0
b. 11-5-97
Internationals: England U16, U17, U18.

2013–14	Derby Co	0	0
2014–15	Derby Co	0	0

MARTIN, Chris (F)   272   84
H: 6 2   W: 12 06   b.Beccles 4-11-88
Internationals: England U19. Scotland Full caps.

2006–07	Norwich C	18	4		
2007–08	Norwich C	7	0		
2008–09	Norwich C	0	0		
2008–09	*Luton T*	40	11	40	11
2009–10	Norwich C	42	17		
2010–11	Norwich C	30	4		
2011–12	Norwich C	4	0		
2011–12	*Crystal Palace*	26	7	26	7
2012–13	Norwich C	1	0	102	25
2012–13	*Swindon T*	12	1	12	1
2013–14	Derby Co	13	2		
2014–15	Derby Co	35	18	92	40

MASCARELL, Omar (M)   24   0
H: 5 11   W: 11 11   b.Tenerife 2-2-93
Internationals: Spain U17, U18, U19.

2012–13	Real Madrid	1	0		
2013–14	Real Madrid	0	0		
2014–15	Real Madrid	0	0	1	0

On loan from Real Madrid.

2014–15	Derby Co	23	0	23	0

McDONALD, Shaquille (F)   4   0
b. 19-7-95

2012–13	Peterborough U	0	0		
2013–14	Peterborough U	0	0		
2013–14	*York C*	0	0		
2014–15	Derby Co	0	0		
2014–15	*Cheltenham T*	4	0	4	0

MITCHELL, Jonathan (G)   0   0
H: 5 11   W: 13 08   b. 24-11-94

2014–15	Derby Co	0	0

MORCH, Mats (G)   0   0
b.Mandal 8-9-93

2010–11	Derby Co	0	0
2011–12	Derby Co	0	0
2012–13	Derby Co	0	0
2013–14	Derby Co	0	0
2013–14	*Burton Alb*	0	0
2014–15	Derby Co	0	0

NAYLOR, Lee (D)   439   12
H: 5 9   W: 11 03   b.Walsall 19-3-80
Internationals: England U21.

1997–98	Wolverhampton W	16	0		
1998–99	Wolverhampton W	23	1		
1999–2000	Wolverhampton W	30	2		
2000–01	Wolverhampton W	46	1		
2001–02	Wolverhampton W	27	0		
2002–03	Wolverhampton W	32	1		
2003–04	Wolverhampton W	38	0		
2004–05	Wolverhampton W	38	1		
2005–06	Wolverhampton W	40	1		
2006–07	Wolverhampton W	3	0	293	7
2006–07	Celtic	32	0		
2007–08	Celtic	33	1		
2008–09	Celtic	23	1		

2009–10	Celtic	12	1	**100** **3**
2010–11	Cardiff C	27	2	
2011–12	Cardiff C	2	0	**29** **2**
2013–14	Accrington S	13	0	**13** **0**
2013–14	Derby Co	4	0	
2014–15	Derby Co	0	0	**4** **0**

NAYLOR, Tom (D)   **71** **1**
H: 5 11 W: 11 05   b.Sutton-in-Ashfield 28-6-91

2011–12	Derby Co	8	0	
2012–13	Derby Co	0	0	
2012–13	Bradford C	5	0	**5** **0**
2013–14	Derby Co	0	0	
2013–14	Newport Co	33	1	**33** **1**
2014–15	Derby Co	0	0	**8** **0**
2014–15	Cambridge U	8	0	**8** **0**
2014–15	Burton Alb	17	0	**17** **0**

RAWSON, Farrend (D)   **4** **0**
b. 11-7-96

2014–15	Derby Co	0	0	
2014–15	Rotherham U	4	0	**4** **0**

ROOS, Kelle (G)   **0** **0**
H: 6 4 W: 14 02   b. 31-5-92

2013–14	Derby Co	0	0
2014–15	Derby Co	0	0

RUSSELL, Johnny (F)   **180** **46**
H: 5 10 W: 12 03   b.Glasgow 8-4-90
Internationals: Scotland U19, U21, Full caps.

2006–07	Dundee U	1	0	
2007–08	Dundee U	2	0	
2008–09	Dundee U	0	0	
2009–10	Dundee U	0	0	
2010–11	Dundee U	30	9	
2011–12	Dundee U	37	9	
2012–13	Dundee U	32	13	**102** **31**
2013–14	Derby Co	39	9	
2014–15	Derby Co	39	6	**78** **15**

SAMMON, Conor (F)   **299** **48**
H: 5 10 W: 11 11   b.Dublin 13-4-87
Internationals: Republic of Ireland U21, U23, Full caps.

2005	UCD	7	0	
2006	UCD	31	7	
2007	UCD	31	6	**69** **13**
2008	Derry C	16	3	**16** **3**
2008–09	Kilmarnock	17	1	
2009–10	Kilmarnock	25	1	
2010–11	Kilmarnock	23	15	**65** **17**
2010–11	Wigan Ath	7	1	
2011–12	Wigan Ath	25	0	**32** **1**
2012–13	Derby Co	45	8	
2013–14	Derby Co	37	2	
2014–15	Derby Co	1	0	**83** **10**
2014–15	Ipswich T	19	1	**19** **1**
2014–15	Rotherham U	15	3	**15** **3**

SANTOS, Alefe (M)   **27** **1**
H: 5 10 W: 10 06   b.Sao Paulo 28-1-95

2012–13	Bristol R	1	0	
2013	Ponte Preta	0	0	
2013–14	Bristol R	23	1	**24** **1**
2014–15	Derby Co	0	0	
2014–15	Notts Co	3	0	**3** **0**

SHARPE, Rhys (D)   **3** **0**
b. 17-10-94
Internationals: Republic of Ireland U21.

2013–14	Derby Co	0	0	
2014–15	Derby Co	0	0	
2014–15	Shrewsbury T	3	0	**3** **0**

SHOTTON, Ryan (D)   **145** **9**
H: 6 3 W: 13 05   b.Stoke 30-9-88

2006–07	Stoke C	0	0	
2007–08	Stoke C	0	0	
2008–09	Stoke C	0	0	
2008–09	Tranmere R	33	5	**33** **5**
2009–10	Stoke C	0	0	
2009–10	Barnsley	30	0	**30** **0**
2010–11	Stoke C	2	0	
2011–12	Stoke C	23	1	
2012–13	Stoke C	23	0	
2013–14	Stoke C	0	0	**48** **1**
2013–14	Wigan Ath	9	1	**9** **1**
2014–15	Derby Co	25	2	**25** **2**

SSEWANKAMBO, Isak (D)   **13** **0**
H: 5 10 W: 12 02   b.Angered 27-2-96
Internationals: Sweden U19, U21.

2014–15	NAC Breda	13	0	**13** **0**
2014–15	Derby Co	0	0	

THOMAS, Kwame (F)   **9** **0**
H: 5 10 W: 12 00   b.Nottingham 28-9-95
Internationals: England U16, U17, U20.

2011–12	Derby Co	0	0

2012–13	Derby Co	0	0	
2013–14	Derby Co	0	0	
2014–15	Derby Co	4	0	**4** **0**
2014–15	Notts Co	5	0	**5** **0**

THORNE, George (M)   **51** **2**
H: 6 2 W: 13 01   b.Chatham 4-1-93
Internationals: England U16, U17, U18, U19.

2009–10	WBA	1	0	
2010–11	WBA	1	0	
2011–12	WBA	3	0	
2011–12	Portsmouth	14	0	**14** **0**
2012–13	WBA	5	0	
2012–13	Peterborough U	7	1	**7** **1**
2013–14	WBA	0	0	**10** **0**
2013–14	Watford	8	0	**8** **0**
2013–14	Derby Co	9	1	
2014–15	Derby Co	3	0	**12** **1**

VERNAM, Charles (F)   **0** **0**
b. 8-10-96

2013–14	Derby Co	0	0
2014–15	Derby Co	0	0

WARD, Jamie (M)   **302** **82**
H: 5 5 W: 9 04   b.Birmingham 12-5-86
Internationals: Northern Ireland U18, U21, Full caps.

2003–04	Aston Villa	0	0	
2004–05	Aston Villa	0	0	
2005–06	Aston Villa	0	0	
2005–06	Stockport Co	9	1	**9** **1**
2006–07	Torquay U	25	9	**25** **9**
2006–07	Chesterfield	9	3	
2007–08	Chesterfield	35	12	
2008–09	Chesterfield	23	14	**67** **29**
2008–09	Sheffield U	16	2	
2009–10	Sheffield U	28	7	
2010–11	Sheffield U	19	0	**63** **9**
2010–11	Derby Co	13	5	
2011–12	Derby Co	37	4	
2012–13	Derby Co	25	12	
2013–14	Derby Co	38	7	
2014–15	Derby Co	25	6	**138** **34**

WARNOCK, Stephen (D)   **354** **15**
H: 5 7 W: 11 09   b.Ormskirk 12-12-81
Internationals: England Full caps.

1998–99	Liverpool	0	0	
1999–2000	Liverpool	0	0	
2000–01	Liverpool	0	0	
2001–02	Liverpool	0	0	
2002–03	Liverpool	0	0	
2002–03	Bradford C	12	1	**12** **1**
2003–04	Liverpool	0	0	
2003–04	Coventry C	44	3	**44** **3**
2004–05	Liverpool	19	0	
2005–06	Liverpool	20	1	
2006–07	Liverpool	1	0	**40** **1**
2006–07	Blackburn R	13	1	
2007–08	Blackburn R	37	1	
2008–09	Blackburn R	37	3	
2009–10	Blackburn R	1	0	**88** **5**
2009–10	Aston Villa	30	0	
2010–11	Aston Villa	19	0	
2011–12	Aston Villa	35	2	
2012–13	Aston Villa	0	0	**84** **2**
2012–13	Bolton W	15	0	**15** **0**
2012–13	Leeds U	16	1	
2013–14	Leeds U	27	1	
2014–15	Leeds U	21	1	**64** **3**
2014–15	Derby Co	7	0	**7** **0**

WHITBREAD, Zak (D)   **176** **6**
H: 6 2 W: 12 07   b.Houston 4-3-84
Internationals: USA U20.

2002–03	Liverpool	0	0	
2003–04	Liverpool	0	0	
2004–05	Liverpool	0	0	
2005–06	Liverpool	0	0	
2005–06	Millwall	25	0	
2006–07	Millwall	14	0	
2007–08	Millwall	23	3	
2008–09	Millwall	38	0	
2009–10	Millwall	0	0	**100** **3**
2009–10	Norwich C	4	0	
2010–11	Norwich C	22	1	
2011–12	Norwich C	18	0	**44** **1**
2012–13	Leicester C	16	1	
2013–14	Leicester C	3	0	**19** **1**
2013–14	Derby Co	4	1	
2014–15	Derby Co	9	0	**13** **1**

Players retained or with offer of contract
Guy, Callum; Tuite, Jack Patrick; Zanzala, Offrande.

Scholars
Adams, Mohammed; Babos, Alexander Jon; Barnes, Joshua Edwin; Bennett, Thomas Paul; Bird, Jared; Carvell, James Shaun; Clennett, Guy James; Cover, Alexander Robert; Dryden, Samuel; Gordon, Kellan Sheene; Macdonald, Calum Ross; Mellors, Thomas James; Moulton, Jorna Anthony Junior; Rigby, Thomas James; Stabana, Kyron Thomas; Vernam, Charles Terence Priestley; Wassall, Ethan Luca.

DONCASTER R (32)

ASKINS, Ben (M)   **0** **0**
b. 2-1-96

2014–15	Doncaster R	0	0

BENNETT, Kyle (F)   **170** **18**
H: 5 5 W: 9 08   b.Telford 9-9-90
Internationals: England U18.

2007–08	Wolverhampton W	0	0	
2008–09	Wolverhampton W	0	0	
2009–10	Wolverhampton W	0	0	
2010–11	Bury	32	2	**32** **2**
2011–12	Doncaster R	36	4	
2012–13	Doncaster R	35	3	
2013–14	Doncaster R	3	0	
2013–14	Crawley T	4	0	**4** **0**
2013–14	Bradford C	18	1	**18** **1**
2014–15	Doncaster R	42	8	**116** **15**

BUTLER, Andy (D)   **398** **37**
H: 6 0 W: 13 00   b.Doncaster 4-11-83

2003–04	Scunthorpe U	35	2	
2004–05	Scunthorpe U	37	10	
2005–06	Scunthorpe U	16	1	
2006–07	Scunthorpe U	11	1	
2006–07	Grimsby T	4	0	**4** **0**
2007–08	Scunthorpe U	36	2	**135** **16**
2008–09	Huddersfield T	42	4	
2009–10	Huddersfield T	11	0	**53** **4**
2009–10	Blackpool	7	0	**7** **0**
2010–11	Walsall	31	4	
2011–12	Walsall	42	5	
2012–13	Walsall	41	3	
2013–14	Walsall	45	2	
2014–15	Sheffield U	0	0	
2014–15	Walsall	7	0	**166** **14**
2014–15	Doncaster R	33	3	**33** **3**

BYWATER, Steve (G)   **327** **0**
H: 6 2 W: 12 10   b.Manchester 7-6-81
Internationals: England U20, U21.

1997–98	Rochdale	0	0	
1998–99	West Ham U	0	0	
1999–2000	Wycombe W	2	0	**2** **0**
1999–2000	Hull C	4	0	**4** **0**
2000–01	West Ham U	1	0	
2001–02	West Ham U	0	0	
2001–02	Wolverhampton W	0	0	
2001–02	Cardiff C	0	0	
2002–03	West Ham U	0	0	
2003–04	West Ham U	17	0	
2004–05	West Ham U	36	0	
2005–06	West Ham U	1	0	**59** **0**
2005–06	Coventry C	14	0	**14** **0**
2006–07	Derby Co	37	0	
2007–08	Derby Co	18	0	
2007–08	Ipswich T	17	0	**17** **0**
2008–09	Derby Co	31	0	
2009–10	Derby Co	42	0	
2010–11	Derby Co	22	0	**150** **0**
2010–11	Cardiff C	8	0	**8** **0**
2011–12	Sheffield W	32	0	
2012–13	Sheffield W	0	0	**32** **0**
2013–14	Millwall	7	0	
2014–15	Millwall	0	0	**7** **0**
2014–15	Gillingham	13	0	**13** **0**
2014–15	Doncaster R	21	0	**21** **0**

COPPINGER, James (F)   **468** **50**
H: 5 7 W: 10 03   b.Middlesbrough 10-1-81
Internationals: England U16.

1997–98	Newcastle U	0	0	
1998–99	Newcastle U	0	0	
1999–2000	Newcastle U	0	0	
1999–2000	Hartlepool U	10	3	
2000–01	Newcastle U	1	0	
2001–02	Newcastle U	0	0	**1** **0**
2001–02	Hartlepool U	14	2	**24** **5**
2002–03	Exeter C	43	5	**43** **5**
2004–05	Doncaster R	31	0	
2005–06	Doncaster R	36	5	
2006–07	Doncaster R	39	4	
2007–08	Doncaster R	39	5	
2008–09	Doncaster R	32	5	
2009–10	Doncaster R	39	4	

2010–11	Doncaster R	40	7	
2011–12	Doncaster R	38	2	
2012–13	Doncaster R	25	2	
2012–13	*Nottingham F*	6	0	**6 0**
2013–14	Doncaster R	41	4	
2014–15	Doncaster R	34	4	**394 40**

DE VAL FERNANDEZ, Marc (M)   **16 0**
H: 5 11   W: 11 00   b.Blanes 15-2-90

2013–14	Doncaster R	5	0
2014–15	Doncaster R	11	0	**16 0**

EVINA, Cedric (D)   **69 2**
H: 5 11   W: 12 08   b.Cameroon 16-11-91

2009–10	Arsenal	0	0	
2010–11	Arsenal	0	0	
2010–11	Oldham Ath	27	2	**27 2**
2011–12	Charlton Ath	3	0	
2012–13	Charlton Ath	12	0	
2013–14	Charlton Ath	8	0	**23 0**
2014–15	Doncaster R	19	0	**19 0**

FERGUSON, Lewis (M)   **0 0**

2013–14	Doncaster R	0	0
2014–15	Doncaster R	0	0

FORRESTER, Harry (F)   **109 15**
H: 5 9   W: 11 03   b.Milton Keynes 2-1-91
Internationals: England U16, U17.

2007–08	Aston Villa	0	0	
2008–09	Aston Villa	0	0	
2009–10	Aston Villa	0	0	
2010–11	Aston Villa	0	0	
2010–11	Kilmarnock	7	0	**7 0**
2011–12	Brentford	19	0	
2012–13	Brentford	36	8	**55 8**
2013–14	Doncaster R	7	0	
2014–15	Doncaster R	40	7	**47 7**

FURMAN, Dean (M)   **238 15**
H: 6 0   W: 11 08   b.Cape Town 22-6-88
Internationals: South Africa Full caps.

2007–08	Rangers	1	0	
2008–09	*Bradford C*	32	4	**32 4**
2009–10	Oldham Ath	38	0	
2010–11	Oldham Ath	42	5	
2011–12	Oldham Ath	23	1	
2012–13	Oldham Ath	28	2	**131 8**
2012–13	*Doncaster R*	8	0	
2013–14	Doncaster R	32	1	
2014–15	Doncaster R	34	2	**74 3**

JONES, Rob (D)   **322 32**
H: 6 7   W: 12 02   b.Stockton 30-11-79

2002–03	Stockport Co	0	0	
2003–04	Stockport Co	16	2	**16 2**
2003–04	*Macclesfield T*	1	0	**1 0**
2004–05	Grimsby T	20	1	
2005–06	Grimsby T	40	4	**60 5**
2006–07	Hibernian	34	4	
2007–08	Hibernian	30	0	
2008–09	Hibernian	32	4	**96 8**
2009–10	Scunthorpe U	28	1	
2010–11	Scunthorpe U	14	1	**42 2**
2010–11	*Sheffield W*	8	1	
2011–12	Sheffield W	33	4	**41 5**
2012–13	Doncaster R	44	7	
2013–14	Doncaster R	12	1	
2014–15	Doncaster R	10	2	**66 10**

KEEGAN, Paul (M)   **264 13**
H: 5 11   W: 11 05   b.Dublin 5-7-84
Internationals: Republic of Ireland U16, U21, U23.

2000–01	Leeds U	0	0	
2001–02	Leeds U	0	0	
2002–03	Leeds U	0	0	
2003–04	Leeds U	0	0	
2003–04	*Scunthorpe U*	2	0	**2 0**
2004–05	Leeds U	0	0	
2005	Drogheda	11	0	
2006	Drogheda	25	4	
2007	Drogheda	30	1	
2008	Drogheda	27	1	**93 6**
2009	Bohemians	34	2	
2010	Bohemians	32	4	**66 6**
2010–11	Doncaster R	10	0	
2011–12	Doncaster R	2	0	
2012–13	Doncaster R	25	1	
2013–14	Doncaster R	34	0	
2014–15	Doncaster R	32	0	**103 1**

LUND, Mitchell (D)   **4 0**
H: 6 1   W: 11 11   b.Leeds 27-8-96

2014–15	Doncaster R	4	0	**4 0**

MAIN, Curtis (F)   **136 19**
H: 5 9   W: 12 02   b.South Shields 20-6-92

2007–08	Darlington	1	0
2008–09	Darlington	18	2
2009–10	Darlington	26	3

2010–11	Darlington	0	0	**45 5**
2011–12	Middlesbrough	12	2	
2012–13	Middlesbrough	13	3	
2013–14	Middlesbrough	23	1	**48 6**
2013–14	*Shrewsbury T*	5	0	**5 0**
2014–15	Doncaster R	38	8	**38 8**

MANDEVILLE, Liam (F)   **3 0**
b. 17-2-97

2014–15	Doncaster R	3	0	**3 0**

MAROSI, Marko (G)   **3 0**
H: 6 3   W: 12 08   b. 23-10-93
Internationals: Slovakia U21.

2013–14	Wigan Ath	0	0
2014–15	Doncaster R	3	0	**3 0**

McCOMBE, Jamie (D)   **382 27**
H: 6 5   W: 12 05   b.Scunthorpe 1-1-83

2001–02	Scunthorpe U	17	0	
2002–03	Scunthorpe U	31	1	
2003–04	Scunthorpe U	15	0	**63 1**
2003–04	Lincoln C	8	0	
2004–05	Lincoln C	41	3	
2005–06	Lincoln C	38	4	**87 7**
2006–07	Bristol C	41	4	
2007–08	Bristol C	34	3	
2008–09	Bristol C	28	1	
2009–10	Bristol C	16	1	**119 9**
2010–11	Huddersfield T	34	5	
2011–12	Huddersfield T	20	3	
2011–12	*Preston NE*	6	0	**6 0**
2012–13	Huddersfield T	0	0	**54 8**
2012–13	Doncaster R	33	1	
2013–14	Doncaster R	2	0	
2014–15	Doncaster R	18	1	**53 2**

McCULLOUGH, Luke (D)   **48 0**
b.Portadown 15-2-94
Internationals: Northern Ireland U16, U17, U19, U20, U21, Full caps.

2012–13	Manchester U	0	0	
2012–13	*Cheltenham T*	1	0	**1 0**
2013–14	Doncaster R	14	0	
2014–15	Doncaster R	33	0	**47 0**

McKAY, Jack (F)   **4 0**
b.Glasgow 19-11-96

2014–15	Doncaster R	4	0	**4 0**

McKAY, Paul (M)   **0 0**
H: 6 3   W: 12 13   b.Glasgow 19-11-96

2014–15	Doncaster R	0	0

McLAREN, Jack (G)   **0 0**

2014–15	Doncaster R	0	0

MIDDLETON, Harry (M)   **4 0**
H: 5 11   W: 11 00   b.Doncaster 12-4-95

2012–13	Doncaster R	0	0
2013–14	Doncaster R	0	0
2014–15	Doncaster R	4	0	**4 0**

PETERSON, Alex (F)   **6 0**
H: 5 11   W: 11 00   b.Doncaster 17-10-94

2013–14	Doncaster R	5	0
2014–15	Doncaster R	1	0	**6 0**

RAZAK, Abdul (M)   **32 0**
H: 5 10   W: 11 02   b.Abidjan 11-11-92
Internationals: Ivory Coast Full caps.

2010–11	Manchester C	1	0	
2011–12	Manchester C	1	0	
2011–12	*Portsmouth*	3	0	**3 0**
2011–12	*Brighton & HA*	6	0	**6 0**
2012–13	Manchester C	3	0	
2012–13	*Charlton Ath*	2	0	**2 0**
2013–14	Manchester C	0	0	**5 0**
2013–14	*Anzhi Makhachkala*	7	0	**7 0**
2013–14	West Ham U	0	0	
2014–15	West Ham U	0	0	
2014–15	Doncaster R	9	0	**9 0**

ROBINSON, Theo (F)   **275 68**
H: 5 9   W: 10 03   b.Birmingham 22-1-89
Internationals: Jamaica Full caps.

2005–06	Watford	1	0	
2006–07	Watford	1	0	
2007–08	Watford	0	0	
2007–08	*Hereford U*	43	13	**43 13**
2008–09	Watford	3	0	**5 0**
2008–09	*Southend U*	21	7	**21 7**
2009–10	Huddersfield T	37	13	
2010–11	Huddersfield T	1	0	
2010–11	Millwall	11	3	
2010–11	*Derby Co*	13	2	
2011–12	Derby Co	39	10	
2012–13	Derby Co	28	8	
2012–13	*Huddersfield T*	6	0	**44 13**
2013–14	Millwall	0	0	**11 3**
2013–14	Derby Co	0	0	**80 20**

2013–14	Doncaster R	31	5	
2014–15	Doncaster R	32	4	**63 9**
2014–15	*Scunthorpe U*	8	3	**8 3**

TYSON, Nathan (F)   **420 96**
H: 5 10   W: 10 02   b.Reading 4-5-82
Internationals: England U20.

1999–2000	Reading	1	0	
2000–01	Reading	0	0	
2001–02	Reading	1	0	
2001–02	*Swansea C*	11	1	**11 1**
2001–02	*Cheltenham T*	8	1	**8 1**
2002–03	Reading	23	1	
2003–04	Reading	8	0	**33 1**
2003–04	Wycombe W	21	9	
2004–05	Wycombe W	42	22	
2005–06	Wycombe W	15	11	**78 42**
2005–06	Nottingham F	28	10	
2006–07	Nottingham F	24	7	
2007–08	Nottingham F	34	9	
2008–09	Nottingham F	35	5	
2009–10	Nottingham F	33	2	
2010–11	Nottingham F	30	2	**184 35**
2011–12	Derby Co	23	0	
2012–13	Derby Co	16	4	
2012–13	*Millwall*	4	0	**4 0**
2013–14	Derby Co	0	0	**39 4**
2013–14	*Blackpool*	10	0	**10 0**
2013–14	*Fleetwood T*	4	0	**4 0**
2013–14	*Notts Co*	10	0	**10 0**
2014–15	Doncaster R	39	12	**39 12**

WABARA, Reece (D)   **89 1**
H: 6 0   W: 12 06   b.Birmingham 28-12-91
Internationals: England U19, U20.

2008–09	Manchester C	0	0	
2009–10	Manchester C	0	0	
2010–11	Manchester C	1	0	
2011–12	*Ipswich T*	6	0	**6 0**
2012–13	Manchester C	0	0	
2012–13	*Oldham Ath*	25	0	**25 0**
2012–13	*Blackpool*	1	0	**1 0**
2013–14	Manchester C	0	0	**1 0**
2013–14	*Doncaster R*	13	0	
2014–15	Doncaster R	43	1	**56 1**

WAKEFIELD, Liam (D)   **9 0**
H: 6 0   W: 11 00   b.Doncaster 9-4-94

2012–13	Doncaster R	0	0	
2013–14	Doncaster R	4	0	
2014–15	Doncaster R	5	0	**9 0**

WELLENS, Richard (M)   **571 40**
H: 5 9   W: 11 06   b.Manchester 26-3-80

1996–97	Manchester U	0	0	
1997–98	Manchester U	0	0	
1998–99	Manchester U	0	0	
1999–2000	Manchester U	0	0	
1999–2000	Blackpool	8	0	
2000–01	Blackpool	36	8	
2001–02	Blackpool	36	1	
2002–03	Blackpool	39	1	
2003–04	Blackpool	41	3	
2004–05	Blackpool	28	3	**188 16**
2005–06	Oldham Ath	45	4	
2006–07	Oldham Ath	42	4	**87 8**
2007–08	Doncaster R	45	6	
2008–09	Doncaster R	39	3	
2009–10	Leicester C	41	1	
2010–11	Leicester C	45	2	
2011–12	Leicester C	41	1	
2012–13	Leicester C	2	0	
2012–13	*Ipswich T*	7	0	**7 0**
2013–14	Leicester C	0	0	**129 4**
2013–14	Doncaster R	37	0	
2014–15	Doncaster R	39	3	**160 12**

WHITEHOUSE, Billy (M)   **4 0**
H: 5 11   W: 11 05   b.Rotherham 13-6-96

2014–15	Doncaster R	4	0	**4 0**

Scholars

Carberry, Michael George; Davies, Matthew Allen; Gordon, Aron Josiah; Greasley, Benjamin John McHale; Head, Alexander; Iveson, Jonathan; Linley, Jordan Alex; Mbuti, Sala Kevin; McCormick, Joseph David; McLaren, Jack Maurice Peter; Parkin, Matthew David; Pugh, Joseph James; Wanless, Ryan Norman; Williamson, Conner Reece.

EVERTON (33)

ALCARAZ, Antolin (D) 263 0
H: 6 0 W: 12 08 b.Roque Gonzalez 30-7-82
Internationals: Paraguay Full caps.

2002-03	Beira-Mar	7	0		
2003-04	Beira-Mar	24	1		
2004-05	Beira-Mar	24	1		
2005-06	Beira-Mar	31	0		
2006-07	Beira-Mar	26	3	112	5
2007-08	Club Brugge	10	1		
2008-09	Club Brugge	29	3		
2009-10	Club Brugge	29	1	68	5
2010-11	Wigan Ath	34	1		
2011-12	Wigan Ath	25	2		
2012-13	Wigan Ath	10	0	69	3
2013-14	Everton	6	0		
2014-15	Everton	8	0	14	0

BAINES, Leighton (D) 407 27
H: 5 8 W: 11 00 b.Liverpool 11-12-84
Internationals: England U21, Full caps.

2002-03	Wigan Ath	6	0		
2003-04	Wigan Ath	26	0		
2004-05	Wigan Ath	41	1		
2005-06	Wigan Ath	37	0		
2006-07	Wigan Ath	35	3		
2007-08	Wigan Ath	0	0	145	4
2007-08	Everton	22	0		
2008-09	Everton	31	1		
2009-10	Everton	37	1		
2010-11	Everton	38	5		
2011-12	Everton	33	4		
2012-13	Everton	38	5		
2013-14	Everton	32	5		
2014-15	Everton	31	2	262	23

BARKLEY, Ross (M) 93 12
H: 6 2 W: 12 00 b.Liverpool 5-12-93
Internationals: England U16, U17, U19, U20, U21, Full caps.

2010-11	Everton	0	0		
2011-12	Everton	6	0		
2012-13	Everton	7	0		
2012-13	*Sheffield W*	13	4	13	4
2012-13	*Leeds U*	4	0	4	0
2013-14	Everton	34	6		
2014-15	Everton	29	2	76	8

BARRY, Gareth (M) 562 50
H: 5 11 W: 12 06 b.Hastings 23-2-81
Internationals: England B, U21, Full caps.

1997-98	Aston Villa	2	0		
1998-99	Aston Villa	32	2		
1999-2000	Aston Villa	30	1		
2000-01	Aston Villa	30	0		
2001-02	Aston Villa	20	0		
2002-03	Aston Villa	35	3		
2003-04	Aston Villa	36	3		
2004-05	Aston Villa	34	7		
2005-06	Aston Villa	36	3		
2006-07	Aston Villa	35	8		
2007-08	Aston Villa	37	9		
2008-09	Aston Villa	38	5	365	41
2009-10	Manchester C	34	2		
2010-11	Manchester C	33	2		
2011-12	Manchester C	34	1		
2012-13	Manchester C	31	1		
2013-14	Manchester C	0	0	132	6
2013-14	*Everton*	32	3		
2014-15	Everton	33	0	65	3

BESIC, Muhamed (M) 73 1
H: 5 10 W: 11 11 b.Berlin 10-9-92
Internationals: Bosnia-Herzegovina U21, Full caps.

2010-11	Hamburg	3	0		
2011-12	Hamburg	3	0		
2012-13	Hamburg	0	0	3	0
2012-13	Ferencvaros	22	1		
2013-14	Ferencvaros	25	0	47	1
2014-15	Everton	23	0	23	0

BROWNING, Tyias (D) 4 0
H: 5 11 W: 12 00 b.Liverpool 27-5-94
Internationals: England U17, U19, U21.

2011-12	Everton	0	0		
2012-13	Everton	0	0		
2013-14	Everton	0	0		
2013-14	*Wigan Ath*	2	0	2	0
2014-15	Everton	2	0	2	0

COLEMAN, Seamus (D) 161 14
H: 6 4 W: 10 07 b.Donegal 11-10-88
Internationals: Republic of Ireland U21, U23, Full caps.

2008-09	Everton	0	0		
2009-10	Everton	3	0		
2009-10	*Blackpool*	9	1	9	1
2010-11	Everton	34	4		
2011-12	Everton	18	0		
2012-13	Everton	26	0		
2013-14	Everton	36	6		
2014-15	Everton	35	3	152	13

DISTIN, Sylvain (D) 544 11
H: 6 3 W: 14 06 b.Bagnolet 16-12-77

1998-99	Tours	26	3	26	3
1999-2000	Gueugnon	33	1	33	1
2000-01	Paris St Germain	28	0	28	0
2001-02	Newcastle U	28	0	28	0
2002-03	Manchester C	34	0		
2003-04	Manchester C	38	2		
2004-05	Manchester C	38	1		
2005-06	Manchester C	31	0		
2006-07	Manchester C	37	2	178	5
2007-08	Portsmouth	36	0		
2008-09	Portsmouth	38	0		
2009-10	Portsmouth	3	0	77	0
2009-10	Everton	29	0		
2010-11	Everton	38	2		
2011-12	Everton	27	0		
2012-13	Everton	34	0		
2013-14	Everton	33	0		
2014-15	Everton	13	0	174	2

DOWELL, Kieran (F) 0 0
b. 10-10-97
Internationals: England U16, U17, U18.

| 2014-15 | Everton | 0 | 0 | | |

DUFFUS, Courtney (F) 3 0
b.Cheltenham 24-10-95

2013-14	Everton	0	0		
2014-15	Everton	0	0		
2014-15	*Bury*	3	0	3	0

ETO'O, Samuel (F) 416 224
H: 5 11 W: 11 10 b.Nkon 10-3-81
Internationals: Cameroon U23, Full caps.

2000-01	Mallorca	28	11		
2001-02	Mallorca	30	6		
2002-03	Mallorca	30	14		
2003-04	Mallorca	32	17	120	48
2004-05	Barcelona	37	24		
2005-06	Barcelona	34	26		
2006-07	Barcelona	19	11		
2007-08	Barcelona	18	16		
2008-09	Barcelona	36	30	144	107
2009-10	Inter Milan	30	11		
2010-11	Inter Milan	34	21	64	32
2011-12	Anzhi Makhachkala	22	13		
2012-13	Anzhi Makhachkala	25	10		
2013-14	Anzhi Makhachkala	6	2	53	25
2013-14	Chelsea	21	9	21	9
2014-15	Everton	14	3	14	3

Transferred to Sampdoria January 2015.

GALLOWAY, Brendon (M) 12 0
H: 6 2 W: 13 10 b.Zimbabwe 17-3-96
Internationals: England U17, U18, U19.

2011-12	Milton Keynes D	1	0		
2012-13	Milton Keynes D	1	0		
2013-14	Milton Keynes D	8	0	10	0
2014-15	Everton	2	0	2	0

GARBUTT, Luke (D) 58 4
H: 5 10 W: 11 07 b.Harrogate 21-5-93
Internationals: England U16, U17, U18, U19, U20, U21.

2010-11	Everton	0	0		
2011-12	Everton	0	0		
2011-12	*Cheltenham T*	34	2	34	2
2012-13	Everton	0	0		
2013-14	Everton	1	0		
2013-14	*Colchester U*	19	2	19	2
2014-15	Everton	4	0	5	0

GIBSON, Darron (M) 96 5
H: 6 0 W: 12 04 b.Derry 25-10-87
Internationals: Republic of Ireland U21, B, Full caps.

2005-06	Manchester U	0	0		
2006-07	Manchester U	0	0		
2007-08	Manchester U	0	0		
2007-08	*Wolverhampton W*	21	1	21	1
2008-09	Manchester U	3	1		
2009-10	Manchester U	15	2		
2010-11	Manchester U	12	0		
2011-12	Manchester U	1	0	31	3
2011-12	Everton	11	1		
2012-13	Everton	23	1		
2013-14	Everton	1	0		
2014-15	Everton	9	0	44	2

GRANT, Conor (M) 11 1
H: 5 9 W: 12 08 b.Fazakerley 18-4-95

2013-14	Everton	0	0		
2014-15	Everton	0	0		
2014-15	*Motherwell*	11	1	11	1

GREEN, George (M) 6 1
b.Dewsbury 2-1-96
Internationals: England U16, U17, U18.

2013-14	Everton	0	0		
2014-15	Everton	0	0		
2014-15	*Tranmere R*	6	1	6	1

GRIFFITHS, Russell (G) 0 0
b.Gravesend 13-4-96
Internationals: England U19.

| 2014-15 | Everton | 0 | 0 | | |

HIBBERT, Tony (D) 264 0
H: 5 9 W: 11 05 b.Liverpool 20-2-81

1998-99	Everton	0	0		
1999-2000	Everton	0	0		
2000-01	Everton	3	0		
2001-02	Everton	10	0		
2002-03	Everton	24	0		
2003-04	Everton	25	0		
2004-05	Everton	36	0		
2005-06	Everton	29	0		
2006-07	Everton	13	0		
2007-08	Everton	24	0		
2008-09	Everton	17	0		
2009-10	Everton	20	0		
2010-11	Everton	20	0		
2011-12	Everton	32	0		
2012-13	Everton	6	0		
2013-14	Everton	1	0		
2014-15	Everton	4	0	264	0

HOWARD, Tim (G) 459 1
H: 6 3 W: 14 12 b.North Brunswick 6-3-79
Internationals: USA U21, U23, Full caps.

1998	NY/NJ MetroStars	1	0		
1999	NY/NJ MetroStars	9	0		
2000	NY/NJ MetroStars	9	0		
2001	NY/NJ MetroStars	26	0		
2002	NY/NJ MetroStars	27	0		
2003	NY/NJ MetroStars	13	0	85	0
2003-04	Manchester U	32	0		
2004-05	Manchester U	12	0		
2005-06	Manchester U	1	0		
2006-07	Manchester U	0	0	45	0
2006-07	Everton	36	0		
2007-08	Everton	36	0		
2008-09	Everton	38	0		
2009-10	Everton	38	0		
2010-11	Everton	38	0		
2011-12	Everton	38	1		
2012-13	Everton	36	0		
2013-14	Everton	37	0		
2014-15	Everton	32	0	329	1

JAGIELKA, Phil (D) 496 28
H: 6 0 W: 13 01 b.Manchester 17-8-82
Internationals: England U20, U21, B, Full caps.

1999-2000	Sheffield U	1	0		
2000-01	Sheffield U	15	0		
2001-02	Sheffield U	23	3		
2002-03	Sheffield U	42	0		
2003-04	Sheffield U	43	3		
2004-05	Sheffield U	46	0		
2005-06	Sheffield U	46	8		
2006-07	Sheffield U	38	4	254	18
2007-08	Everton	34	1		
2008-09	Everton	34	0		
2009-10	Everton	12	0		
2010-11	Everton	33	1		
2011-12	Everton	30	2		
2012-13	Everton	36	2		
2013-14	Everton	26	0		
2014-15	Everton	37	4	242	10

JONES, Gethin (D) 6 0
b.Perth 13-10-95
Internationals: Wales U17, U19, U21.

| 2014-15 | Everton | 0 | 0 | | |
| 2014-15 | *Plymouth Arg* | 6 | 0 | 6 | 0 |

JUNIOR, Francisco (M) 15 1
H: 5 4 W: 10 02 b.Bissau 18-1-92
Internationals: Portugal U19, U21.

2012-13	Everton	0	0		
2013-14	Everton	0	0		
2013-14	*Vitesse*	2	0	2	0
2014	*Stromsgodset*	12	1	12	1
2014-15	Everton	0	0		
2014-15	*Port Vale*	1	0	1	0

KENNY, Jonjoe (D)   0   0
H: 5 9 W: 10 08 b.Kirkdale 15-3-97
Internationals: England U16, U17, U18.

2014–15	Everton	0	0		

KONE, Arouna (F)   268   88
H: 6 0 W: 11 08 b.Anyama 11-11-83
Internationals: Ivory Coast full caps.

2002–03	Lierse	21	11	21	11
2003–04	Roda JC	28	11		
2004–05	Roda JC	32	14		
2005–06	Roda JC	1	1	61	26
2005–06	PSV Eindhoven	21	11		
2006–07	PSV Eindhoven	31	10		
2007–08	PSV Eindhoven	1	0	53	21
2007–08	Sevilla	21	1		
2008–09	Sevilla	6	0		
2009–10	Sevilla	12	0		
2009–10	Hannover 96	8	2	8	2
2010–11	Sevilla	1	0	40	1
2011–12	Levante	34	15	34	15
2012–13	Wigan Ath	34	11	34	11
2013–14	Everton	5	0		
2014–15	Everton	12	1	17	1

LEDSON, Ryan (M)   0   0
H: 5 9 W: 10 12 b.Liverpool 19-8-97
Internationals: England U16, U17, U18.

2013–14	Everton	0	0		
2014–15	Everton	0	0		

LONG, Chris (F)   14   5
H: 5 7 W: 12 02 b.Huyton 25-2-95
Internationals: England U16, U17, U18, U19, U20.

2013–14	Everton	0	0		
2013–14	Milton Keynes D	4	1	4	1
2014–15	Everton	0	0		
2014–15	Brentford	10	4	10	4

LUKAKU, Romelu (F)   185   75
H: 6 3 W: 13 00 b.Antwerp 13-5-93
Internationals: Belgium U15, U18, U21, Full caps.

2008–09	Anderlecht	1	0		
2009–10	Anderlecht	33	15		
2010–11	Anderlecht	37	16		
2011–12	Anderlecht	2	2	73	33
2011–12	Chelsea	8	0		
2012–13	Chelsea	0	0		
2012–13	WBA	35	17	35	17
2013–14	Chelsea	2	0	10	0
2013–14	Everton	31	15		
2014–15	Everton	36	10	67	25

LUNDSTRAM, John (M)   63   2
H: 5 11 W: 11 09 b.Liverpool 18-2-94
Internationals: England U17, U18, U19, U20.

2011–12	Everton	0	0		
2012–13	Everton	0	0		
2012–13	Doncaster R	14	0	14	0
2013–14	Everton	0	0		
2013–14	Yeovil T	14	2	14	2
2013–14	Leyton Orient	7	0		
2014–15	Everton	0	0		
2014–15	Blackpool	17	0	17	0
2014–15	Leyton Orient	4	0	11	0
2014–15	Scunthorpe U	7	0	7	0

McALENY, Conor (F)   17   2
H: 5 10 W: 12 05 b.Liverpool 12-8-92

2009–10	Everton	0	0		
2010–11	Everton	0	0		
2011–12	Everton	2	0		
2011–12	Scunthorpe U	3	0	3	0
2012–13	Everton	0	0		
2013–14	Everton	0	0		
2013–14	Brentford	4	0	4	0
2014–15	Everton	0	0	2	0
2014–15	Cardiff C	8	2	8	2

McCARTHY, James (M)   277   24
H: 5 11 W: 11 05 b.Glasgow 12-11-90
Internationals: Republic of Ireland U17, U18, U19, U21, Full caps.

2006–07	Hamilton A	23	1		
2007–08	Hamilton A	35	7		
2008–09	Hamilton A	37	6	95	14
2009–10	Wigan Ath	20	1		
2010–11	Wigan Ath	24	3		
2011–12	Wigan Ath	33	0		
2012–13	Wigan Ath	38	3		
2013–14	Wigan Ath	5	0	120	7
2013–14	Everton	34	1		
2014–15	Everton	28	2	62	3

McGEADY, Aiden (M)   289   43
H: 5 10 W: 11 03 b.Glasgow 4-4-86
Internationals: Republic of Ireland Full caps.

2003–04	Celtic	4	1		
2004–05	Celtic	27	4		
2005–06	Celtic	20	4		
2006–07	Celtic	34	5		
2007–08	Celtic	36	7		
2008–09	Celtic	29	3		
2009–10	Celtic	35	7	185	31
2010–11	Spartak Moscow	11	2		
2011–12	Spartak Moscow	31	3		
2012–13	Spartak Moscow	17	5		
2013–14	Spartak Moscow	13	1	72	11
2013–14	Everton	16	0		
2014–15	Everton	16	1	32	1

MIRALLAS, Kevin (F)   265   68
H: 6 0 W: 11 10 b.Leige 5-10-87
Internationals: Belgium U16, U17, U18, U19, U21, Full caps.

2004–05	Lille	1	1		
2005–06	Lille	15	1		
2006–07	Lille	23	2		
2007–08	Lille	35	6	74	10
2008–09	St Etienne	30	3		
2009–10	St Etienne	23	0	53	3
2010–11	Olympiacos	26	14		
2011–12	Olympiacos	24	20		
2012–13	Olympiacos	0	0	50	34
2012–13	Everton	27	6		
2013–14	Everton	32	8		
2014–15	Everton	29	7	88	21

NAISMITH, Steven (F)   293   72
H: 5 10 W: 11 04 b.Irvine 14-9-86
Internationals: Scotland U21, B, Full caps.

2003–04	Kilmarnock	1	0		
2004–05	Kilmarnock	24	1		
2005–06	Kilmarnock	36	13		
2006–07	Kilmarnock	37	15		
2007–08	Kilmarnock	4	0	102	29
2007–08	Rangers	21	5		
2008–09	Rangers	7	0		
2009–10	Rangers	28	3		
2010–11	Rangers	31	11		
2011–12	Rangers	11	9	98	28
2012–13	Everton	31	4		
2013–14	Everton	31	5		
2014–15	Everton	31	6	93	15

OSMAN, Leon (F)   372   48
H: 5 8 W: 10 09 b.Billinge 17-5-81
Internationals: England U16, Full caps.

1998–99	Everton	0	0		
1999–2000	Everton	0	0		
2000–01	Everton	0	0		
2001–02	Everton	0	0		
2002–03	Everton	2	0		
2002–03	Carlisle U	12	1	12	1
2003–04	Everton	4	1		
2003–04	Derby Co	17	3	17	3
2004–05	Everton	29	6		
2005–06	Everton	35	3		
2006–07	Everton	34	3		
2007–08	Everton	28	4		
2008–09	Everton	34	6		
2009–10	Everton	26	2		
2010–11	Everton	26	4		
2011–12	Everton	30	5		
2012–13	Everton	36	5		
2013–14	Everton	38	3		
2014–15	Everton	31	2	343	44

OVIEDO, Bryan (M)   74   4
H: 5 8 W: 10 13 b.Alajuela 18-2-90
Internationals: Costa Rica U20, Full caps.

2009–10	FC Copenhagen	3	0		
2010–11	FC Copenhagen	1	0		
2010–11	Nordsjaelland	14	0	14	0
2011–12	FC Copenhagen	22	2		
2012–13	FC Copenhagen	4	0	30	2
2012–13	Everton	15	0		
2013–14	Everton	9	2		
2014–15	Everton	6	0	30	2

PENNINGTON, Matthew (D)   41   2
H: 6 1 b.Warrington 6-10-94
Internationals: England U19.

2013–14	Everton	0	0		
2013–14	Tranmere R	17	2	17	2
2014–15	Everton	0	0		
2014–15	Coventry C	24	0	24	0

PIENAAR, Steven (M)   314   35
H: 5 10 W: 10 06 b.Westbury 17-3-82
Internationals: South Africa U17, Full caps.

2001–02	Ajax	8	1		
2002–03	Ajax	31	5		
2003–04	Ajax	16	3		
2004–05	Ajax	24	4		
2005–06	Ajax	15	2	94	15
2006–07	Bor Dortmund	25	0	25	0
2007–08	Everton	28	2		
2008–09	Everton	28	2		
2009–10	Everton	30	4		
2010–11	Everton	18	1		
2010–11	Tottenham H	8	0		
2011–12	Tottenham H	2	0		
2011–12	Everton	14	4		
2012–13	Tottenham H	0	0	10	0
2012–13	Everton	35	6		
2013–14	Everton	23	1		
2014–15	Everton	9	0	185	20

ROBLES, Joel (G)   33   0
H: 6 5 W: 13 04 b.Leganes 17-6-90
Internationals: Spain U16, U17, U21, U23.

2009–10	Atletico Madrid	2	0		
2011–12	Rayo Vallecano	13	0	13	0
2012–13	Atletico Madrid	0	0	2	0
2012–13	Wigan Ath	9	0	9	0
2013–14	Everton	2	0		
2014–15	Everton	7	0	9	0

STANEK, Jindrich (G)   0   0
H: 6 4 W: 13 03 b.Strakonice 27-4-96
Internationals: Czech Republic U16, U17, U18, U19.

2013–14	Everton	0	0		
2014–15	Everton	0	0		

STONES, John (D)   68   1
H: 6 2 W: 11 00 b.Barnsley 28-5-94
Internationals: England U19, U20, U21, Full caps

2011–12	Barnsley	2	0		
2012–13	Barnsley	22	0	24	0
2012–13	Everton	0	0		
2013–14	Everton	21	0		
2014–15	Everton	23	1	44	1

WILLIAMS, Joe (M)   0   0
b. 8-12-96

2014–15	Everton	0	0		

Players retained or with offer of contract
Byrne, Sam John; Charsley, Henry William James; Duffus, Tyrone Errol; Dyson, Calum William; Hunt, Connor Charles; Walsh, Liam.

Scholars
Bainbridge, Jack; Brewster, Delial Edmund; Broadhead, Nathan Paul; Connolly, Callum Alexander; Davies, Thomas; Donohue, Michael John; Graham, Aidan James; Hewelt, Mateusz Tomasz; Holland, Nathan Elliot; Kinsella, Steven; Mellen, Jamie David; Myers, Spencer Richard; O'loughlin, Ciaran Patrick; Robinson, Antonee; Thorniley, Jordan; Yarney, Josef Charles; Yates, James John.

EXETER C (34)

BALDWIN, Pat (D)   316   3
H: 6 3 W: 12 07 b.City of London 12-11-82

2002–03	Colchester U	19	0		
2003–04	Colchester U	4	0		
2004–05	Colchester U	38	0		
2005–06	Colchester U	25	0		
2006–07	Colchester U	38	1		
2007–08	Colchester U	26	0		
2008–09	Colchester U	35	0		
2009–10	Colchester U	7	0		
2009–10	Bristol R	6	0	6	0
2009–10	Southend U	18	1		
2010–11	Colchester U	11	0		
2011–12	Colchester U	5	0	208	1
2011–12	Southend U	3	0	20	1
2011–12	Exeter C	9	0		
2012–13	Exeter C	41	1		
2013–14	Exeter C	25	0		
2014–15	Exeter C	7	0	82	1

BENNETT, Scott (D)   132   18
H: 5 10 W: 12 10 b.Newquay 30-11-90

2008–09	Exeter C	0	0		
2009–10	Exeter C	2	0		
2010–11	Exeter C	1	0		
2011–12	Exeter C	15	3		
2012–13	Exeter C	43	6		
2013–14	Exeter C	45	6		
2014–15	Exeter C	28	3	132	18

BUTTERFIELD, Danny (D)   478   9
H: 5 10 W: 11 06 b.Boston 21-11-79

1997–98	Grimsby T	7	0		
1998–99	Grimsby T	12	0		
1999–2000	Grimsby T	29	0		

2000–01	Grimsby T	30	1		
2001–02	Grimsby T	46	2	**124**	**3**
2002–03	Crystal Palace	46	1		
2003–04	Crystal Palace	45	4		
2004–05	Crystal Palace	7	0		
2005–06	Crystal Palace	13	0		
2006–07	Crystal Palace	28	0		
2007–08	Crystal Palace	30	0		
2008–09	Crystal Palace	26	1		
2008–09	*Charlton Ath*	12	0	**12**	**0**
2009–10	Crystal Palace	37	0	**232**	**6**
2010–11	Southampton	34	0		
2011–12	Southampton	10	0		
2012–13	Southampton	0	0		
2012–13	*Bolton W*	6	0	**6**	**0**
2013–14	Southampton	0	0	**44**	**0**
2013–14	Carlisle U	1	0	**1**	**0**
2013–14	Exeter C	29	0		
2014–15	Exeter C	30	0	**59**	**0**

CUMMINS, Graham (F) 262 91
H: 6 2 W: 11 11 b.Cork 29-12-87
Internationals: Republic of Ireland U23.

2006	Cobh Ramblers	14	5		
2007	Cobh Ramblers	35	11		
2008	Cobh Ramblers	28	1	**77**	**17**
2009	Waterford U	28	17	**28**	**17**
2010	Cork C	32	18		
2011	Cork C	30	24	**62**	**42**
2011–12	Preston NE	15	2		
2012–13	Preston NE	19	2		
2013–14	Preston NE	0	0	**34**	**4**
2013–14	*Rochdale*	27	4	**27**	**4**
2014–15	Exeter C	34	7	**34**	**7**

DAVIES, Arron (M) 299 37
H: 5 9 W: 11 00 b.Cardiff 22-6-84
Internationals: Wales U19, 21, Full caps.

2002–03	Southampton	0	0		
2003–04	Southampton	0	0		
2003–04	*Barnsley*	4	0	**4**	**0**
2004–05	Southampton	0	0		
2004–05	Yeovil T	23	8		
2005–06	Yeovil T	39	8		
2006–07	Yeovil T	39	6		
2007–08	Nottingham F	19	1		
2008–09	Nottingham F	13	0		
2009–10	Nottingham F	0	0	**32**	**1**
2009–10	*Brighton & HA*	7	0	**7**	**0**
2009–10	Yeovil T	10	0	**111**	**22**
2010–11	Peterborough U	22	1	**22**	**1**
2011–12	Northampton T	15	4	**15**	**4**
2012–13	Exeter C	37	3		
2013–14	Exeter C	32	2		
2014–15	Exeter C	39	4	**108**	**9**

DAWSON, Aaron (M) 17 0
H: 5 10 W: 10 10 b.Exmouth 24-3-92

2010–11	Exeter C	0	0		
2011–12	Exeter C	2	0		
2012–13	Exeter C	7	0		
2013–14	Exeter C	5	0		
2014–15	Exeter C	3	0	**17**	**0**

GOW, Alan (M) 320 64
H: 6 0 W: 11 00 b.Clydebank 9-10-82
Internationals: Scotland B.

2000–01	Clydebank	3	0		
2001–02	Clydebank	5	0	**8**	**0**
2002–03	Airdrie U	27	5		
2003–04	Airdrie U	32	12		
2004–05	Airdrie U	26	9	**85**	**26**
2005–06	Falkirk	34	6		
2006–07	Falkirk	36	7	**70**	**13**
2007–08	Rangers	0	0		
2008–09	*Blackpool*	17	5	**17**	**5**
2008–09	Norwich C	13	0	**13**	**0**
2009–10	Plymouth Arg	14	2	**14**	**2**
2009–10	*Hibernian*	7	0	**7**	**0**
2010–11	Motherwell	15	1	**15**	**1**
2010–11	Notts Co	16	1	**16**	**1**
2010–11	East Bengal	5	2	**5**	**2**
2011–12	Exeter C	7	3		
2012–13	Exeter C	26	4		
2013–14	Exeter C	25	7		
2013–14	*Bristol R*	4	0	**4**	**0**
2014–15	Exeter C	0	0	**58**	**14**
2014–15	*St Mirren*	8	0	**8**	**0**

HAMON, James (G) 21 0
H: 6 1 W: 11 00 b. 1-7-95

2013–14	Exeter C	0	0		
2014–15	Exeter C	21	0	**21**	**0**

HARLEY, Ryan (M) 191 31
H: 5 11 W: 11 00 b.Bristol 22-1-85

2004–05	Bristol C	2	0		
2005–06	Bristol C	0	0	**2**	**0**
2008–09	Exeter C	31	4		
2009–10	Exeter C	44	10		
2010–11	Exeter C	21	6		
2010–11	Swansea C	0	0		
2010–11	*Exeter C*	21	4		
2011–12	Swansea C	0	0		
2011–12	Brighton & HA	16	2		
2012–13	Brighton & HA	2	0	**18**	**2**
2012–13	*Milton Keynes D*	8	0	**8**	**0**
2013–14	Swindon T	21	1		
2014–15	Swindon T	0	0	**21**	**1**
2014–15	Exeter C	25	4	**142**	**28**

JAY, Matt (D) 5 0
H: 5 10 W: 10 12 b.Torbay 27-2-96

2013–14	Exeter C	2	0		
2014–15	Exeter C	3	0	**5**	**0**

KEADELL, Kavanagh (G) 0 0
b. 6-5-98

2014–15	Exeter C	0	0		

KEOHANE, Jimmy (M) 80 9
H: 5 11 W: 11 05 b.Wexford 22-1-91
Internationals: Republic of Ireland U19.

2010–11	Bristol C	0	0		
2011–12	Bristol C	0	0		
2011–12	Exeter C	4	0		
2012–13	Exeter C	33	3		
2013–14	Exeter C	20	3		
2014–15	Exeter C	23	3	**80**	**9**

McALLISTER, Jamie (D) 530 4
H: 5 10 W: 11 00 b.Glasgow 26-4-78
Internationals: Scotland Full caps.

1995–96	Queen of the South	2	0		
1996–97	Queen of the South	6	0		
1997–98	Queen of the South	15	0		
1998–99	Queen of the South	27	0	**50**	**0**
1999–2000	Aberdeen	34	0		
2000–01	Aberdeen	25	0		
2001–02	Aberdeen	29	0		
2002–03	Aberdeen	29	0	**117**	**0**
2003–04	Livingston	34	1	**34**	**1**
2004–05	Hearts	30	0		
2005–06	Hearts	17	0	**47**	**0**
2006–07	Bristol C	31	1		
2007–08	Bristol C	41	0		
2008–09	Bristol C	35	1		
2009–10	Bristol C	33	0		
2010–11	Bristol C	34	1		
2011–12	Bristol C	12	0	**186**	**3**
2011–12	*Preston NE*	4	0	**4**	**0**
2012–13	Yeovil T	34	0		
2013–14	Yeovil T	38	0	**72**	**0**
2014–15	Kerala Blasters	6	0	**6**	**0**
2014–15	Exeter C	14	0	**14**	**0**

McCREADY, Tom (M) 10 0
H: 6 0 W: 11 11 b.Chester 7-6-91

2014–15	Morecambe	7	0	**7**	**0**
2014–15	Exeter C	3	0	**3**	**0**

MOORE-TAYLOR, Jordan (D) 62 3
H: 5 10 W: 13 01 b.Exeter 21-1-94

2012–13	Exeter C	7	0		
2013–14	Exeter C	29	1		
2014–15	Exeter C	26	2	**62**	**3**

MORRISON, Clinton (F) 617 152
H: 6 0 W: 12 00 b.Tooting 14-5-79
Internationals: Republic of Ireland U21, Full caps.

1996–97	Crystal Palace	0	0		
1997–98	Crystal Palace	1	1		
1998–99	Crystal Palace	37	12		
1999–2000	Crystal Palace	29	13		
2000–01	Crystal Palace	45	14		
2001–02	Crystal Palace	45	22		
2002–03	Birmingham C	28	6		
2003–04	Birmingham C	32	4		
2004–05	Birmingham C	26	4		
2005–06	Birmingham C	1	0	**87**	**14**
2005–06	Crystal Palace	40	13		
2006–07	Crystal Palace	41	12		
2007–08	Crystal Palace	43	16	**281**	**103**
2008–09	Coventry C	45	10		
2009–10	Coventry C	46	11	**91**	**21**
2010–11	Sheffield W	35	6		
2011–12	Sheffield W	19	1	**54**	**7**
2011–12	*Milton Keynes D*	6	3	**6**	**3**
2011–12	*Brentford*	8	0	**8**	**0**
2012–13	Colchester U	32	2		
2013–14	Colchester U	33	2	**65**	**4**
2014–15	Exeter C	25	0	**25**	**0**

NICHOLS, Tom (F) 75 22
H: 5 10 W: 10 10 b.Wellington 1-9-93

2010–11	Exeter C	1	0		
2011–12	Exeter C	7	1		
2012–13	Exeter C	3	0		
2013–14	Exeter C	28	6		
2014–15	Exeter C	36	15	**75**	**22**

NOBLE, David (M) 308 18
H: 6 0 W: 12 04 b.Hitchin 2-2-82
Internationals: England U20. Scotland U21, B.

2000–01	Arsenal	0	0		
2001–02	Arsenal	0	0		
2001–02	*Watford*	15	1	**15**	**1**
2002–03	Arsenal	0	0		
2002–03	West Ham U	0	0		
2003–04	West Ham U	3	0	**3**	**0**
2003–04	Boston U	14	2		
2004–05	Boston U	32	3		
2005–06	Boston U	11	0	**57**	**5**
2005–06	Bristol C	24	1		
2006–07	Bristol C	26	3		
2007–08	Bristol C	26	2		
2008–09	Bristol C	9	1	**85**	**7**
2008–09	*Yeovil T*	2	0	**2**	**0**
2009–10	Exeter C	0	0		
2010–11	Exeter C	36	0		
2011–12	Exeter C	42	2		
2012–13	Rotherham U	22	3		
2013–14	Rotherham U	0	0	**22**	**3**
2013–14	*Cheltenham T*	29	0	**29**	**0**
2014–15	Oldham Ath	2	0	**2**	**0**
2014–15	Exeter C	15	0	**93**	**2**

OAKLEY, Matthew (M) 566 33
H: 5 10 W: 12 06 b.Peterborough 17-8-77
Internationals: England U21.

1994–95	Southampton	1	0		
1995–96	Southampton	10	0		
1996–97	Southampton	28	3		
1997–98	Southampton	33	1		
1998–99	Southampton	22	2		
1999–2000	Southampton	31	3		
2000–01	Southampton	35	1		
2001–02	Southampton	27	1		
2002–03	Southampton	31	0		
2003–04	Southampton	7	0		
2004–05	Southampton	7	1		
2005–06	Southampton	29	2	**261**	**14**
2006–07	Derby Co	37	6		
2007–08	Derby Co	19	3	**56**	**9**
2007–08	Leicester C	20	0		
2008–09	Leicester C	45	8		
2009–10	Leicester C	38	0		
2010–11	Leicester C	34	2		
2011–12	Leicester C	0	0	**137**	**10**
2011–12	*Exeter C*	7	0		
2012–13	Exeter C	36	0		
2013–14	Exeter C	24	0		
2014–15	Exeter C	45	0	**112**	**0**

POPE, Jason (M) 0 0
H: 5 8 W: 10 01 b. 20-9-95

2014–15	Exeter C	0	0		

PYM, Christy (G) 34 0
H: 6 0 W: 11 09 b.Exeter 24-4-95
Internationals: England U20.

2012–13	Exeter C	0	0		
2013–14	Exeter C	9	0		
2014–15	Exeter C	25	0	**34**	**0**

REID, Jamie (F) 10 2
H: 5 11 W: 11 09 b.Torquay 15-7-94
Internationals: Northern Ireland U21.

2012–13	Exeter C	4	2		
2013–14	Exeter C	6	0		
2014–15	Exeter C	0	0	**10**	**2**

RIBEIRO, Christian (D) 124 4
H: 5 11 W: 12 02 b.Neath 14-12-89
Internationals: Wales U17, U19, U21, Full caps.

2006–07	Bristol C	0	0		
2007–08	Bristol C	0	0		
2008–09	Bristol C	0	0		
2009–10	Bristol C	5	0		
2009–10	*Stockport Co*	7	0	**7**	**0**
2009–10	*Colchester U*	2	0	**2**	**0**
2010–11	Bristol C	9	0		
2011–12	Bristol C	0	0	**14**	**0**
2011–12	*Carlisle U*	5	0	**5**	**0**
2011–12	*Scunthorpe U*	10	0		
2012–13	Scunthorpe U	28	2		
2013–14	Scunthorpe U	21	0	**59**	**2**
2014–15	Exeter C	37	2	**37**	**2**

RILEY-LOWE, Conor (D) 3 0
b. 10-1-96

2014–15	Exeter C	3	0	**3**	**0**

ROPER, Luke (M) 0 0

Season	Club				
2012–13	Exeter C	0	0		
2013–14	Exeter C	0	0		
2014–15	Exeter C	0	0		

SERCOMBE, Liam (M) 236 23
H: 5 10 W: 10 10 b.Exeter 25-4-90

Season	Club				
2008–09	Exeter C	29	2		
2009–10	Exeter C	28	1		
2010–11	Exeter C	42	3		
2011–12	Exeter C	33	7		
2012–13	Exeter C	20	1		
2013–14	Exeter C	44	5		
2014–15	Exeter C	40	4	236	23

TILLSON, Jordan (D) 4 0
b.Bath 5-3-93

Season	Club				
2012–13	Exeter C	0	0		
2013–14	Exeter C	1	0		
2014–15	Exeter C	3	0	4	0

WATKINS, Ollie (F) 3 0
b.Torbay 30-12-95

Season	Club				
2013–14	Exeter C	1	0		
2014–15	Exeter C	2	0	3	0

WHEELER, David (M) 80 10
b.Brighton 4-10-90
Internationals: England U18.

Season	Club				
2013–14	Exeter C	35	3		
2014–15	Exeter C	45	7	80	10

WOODMAN, Craig (D) 417 7
H: 5 9 W: 10 11 b.Tiverton 22-12-82

Season	Club				
1999–2000	Bristol C	0	0		
2000–01	Bristol C	2	0		
2001–02	Bristol C	6	0		
2002–03	Bristol C	10	0		
2003–04	Bristol C	21	0		
2004–05	Bristol C	3	0		
2004–05	*Mansfield T*	8	1	8	1
2004–05	*Torquay U*	22	1		
2005–06	Bristol C	37	1		
2005–06	*Torquay U*	2	0	24	1
2006–07	Bristol C	11	0	90	1
2007–08	Wycombe W	29	0		
2008–09	Wycombe W	46	1		
2009–10	Wycombe W	44	1	119	2
2010–11	Brentford	41	1		
2011–12	Brentford	18	0	59	1
2012–13	Exeter C	44	0		
2013–14	Exeter C	41	1		
2014–15	Exeter C	32	0	117	1

Players retained or with offer of contract
Nicholls, Alex.

Scholars
Billingsley, Dean Albert Joseph; Byrne, Alex John; Charles, Joseph Paul; Down, Toby Alan; Egan, Kyle Daren; Gill, Cameron Louis; Green, Brandon Joseph Paul; Harkness, Jamie Scott; Keadell, Kavanagh Billie; Madden, Charlie Thomas; Merritt, Scott Michael; Read, Joshua John Peter; Rehemi, Mustafa; Richards, William Lee.

Non-Contract
Tisdale, Paul Robert.

FLEETWOOD T (35)

ANDREW, Danny (D) 73 0
H: 5 11 W: 11 06 b.Holbeach 23-12-90

Season	Club				
2009–10	Peterborough U	2	0	2	0
2009–10	Cheltenham T	10	0		
2010–11	Cheltenham T	43	4		
2011–12	Cheltenham T	10	0		
2012–13	Cheltenham T	1	0	64	4

From Gloucester C, Macclesfield T.

Season	Club				
2014–15	Fleetwood T	7	0	7	0

BALL, David (F) 169 37
H: 6 0 W: 11 08 b.Whitefield 14-12-89

Season	Club				
2007–08	Manchester C	0	0		
2008–09	Manchester C	0	0		
2009–10	Manchester C	0	0		
2010–11	Manchester C	0	0		
2010–11	*Swindon T*	18	2	18	2
2010–11	*Peterborough U*	19	5		
2011–12	Peterborough U	22	4		
2011–12	*Rochdale*	14	3	14	3
2012–13	Peterborough U	0	0	41	9
2012–13	Fleetwood T	34	7		
2013–14	Fleetwood T	30	8		
2014–15	Fleetwood T	32	8	96	23

BLEEKER, Liam (G) 0 0
b. 28-1-97

Season	Club				
2014–15	Fleetwood T	0	0		

CARTRIGHT, Max (D) 0 0
H: 6 0 W: 10 12 b. 18-11-95

Season	Club				
2013–14	Fleetwood T	0	0		
2014–15	Fleetwood T	0	0		

CRAINEY, Stephen (D) 360 4
H: 5 9 W: 9 11 b.Glasgow 22-6-81
Internationals: Scotland B, U21, Full caps.

Season	Club				
1999–2000	Celtic	9	0		
2000–01	Celtic	2	0		
2001–02	Celtic	15	0		
2002–03	Celtic	13	0		
2003–04	Celtic	2	0	41	0
2003–04	Southampton	5	0	5	0
2004–05	Leeds U	9	0		
2005–06	Leeds U	24	0		
2006–07	Leeds U	19	0	52	0
2007–08	Blackpool	40	1		
2008–09	Blackpool	17	0		
2009–10	Blackpool	41	0		
2010–11	Blackpool	31	0		
2011–12	Blackpool	42	3		
2012–13	Blackpool	43	0	214	4
2013–14	Wigan Ath	20	0	20	0
2014–15	Fleetwood T	28	0	28	0

DAVIES, Scott (G) 113 0
H: 6 0 W: 10 13 b.Blackpool 27-2-87

Season	Club				
2007–08	Morecambe	10	0		
2008–09	Morecambe	0	0		
2009–10	Morecambe	1	0		
2012–13	Fleetwood T	45	0		
2013–14	Fleetwood T	28	0		
2014–15	Fleetwood T	0	0	73	0
2014–15	*Morecambe*	10	0	21	0
2014–15	*Accrington S*	19	0	19	0

DAVIES, Tom (D) 0 0
H: 5 11 W: 11 00 b.Warrington 18-4-92

Season	Club				
2014–15	Fleetwood T	0	0		

DEACON, Keano (M) 0 0
b. 4-4-96

Season	Club				
2013–14	Fleetwood T	0	0		
2014–15	Fleetwood T	0	0		

EVANS, Gary (F) 299 52
H: 6 0 W: 12 08 b.Stockport 26-4-88

Season	Club				
2007–08	Macclesfield T	42	7		
2008–09	Macclesfield T	40	12	82	19
2009–10	Bradford C	43	11		
2010–11	Bradford C	36	3	79	14
2011–12	Rotherham U	32	7		
2012–13	Rotherham U	13	2	45	9
2012–13	Fleetwood T	16	1		
2013–14	Fleetwood T	34	6		
2014–15	Fleetwood T	43	3	93	10

GREEN, Josh (M) 0 0
b. 11-1-95

Season	Club				
2014–15	Fleetwood T	0	0		

HAUGHTON, Nick (M) 22 1
b. 20-9-94

Season	Club				
2013–14	Fleetwood T	0	0		
2014–15	Fleetwood T	22	1	22	1

HOGAN, Liam (D) 20 0
H: 6 0 W: 12 02 b. 8-2-89

Season	Club				
2012–13	Fleetwood T	0	0		
2013–14	Fleetwood T	16	0		
2014–15	Fleetwood T	4	0	20	0

HORNBY-FORBES, Tyler (M) 17 0
b. 8-3-96

Season	Club				
2014–15	Fleetwood T	17	0	17	0

HUGHES, Jeff (D) 395 62
H: 6 1 W: 11 00 b.Larne 29-5-85
Internationals: Northern Ireland U21, Full caps.

Season	Club				
2003–04	Larne	21	1		
2004–05	Larne	29	0	50	1
2005–06	Lincoln C	22	2		
2006–07	Lincoln C	41	6	63	8
2007–08	Crystal Palace	10	0	10	0
2007–08	*Peterborough U*	7	1	7	1
2008–09	Bristol R	43	6		
2009–10	Bristol R	44	12		
2010–11	Bristol R	42	10	129	28
2011–12	Notts Co	45	13		
2012–13	Notts Co	44	7	89	20
2013–14	Fleetwood T	25	3		
2014–15	Fleetwood T	22	1	47	4

HUGHES, Matty (M) 11 0
b. 1-4-92

Season	Club				
2013–14	Fleetwood T	5	0		
2014–15	Fleetwood T	6	0	11	0

HUNTER, Ashley (F) 12 1
H: 5 10 W: 10 08 b.Derby 29-9-93

Season	Club				
2014–15	Fleetwood T	12	1	12	1

JORDAN, Stephen (D) 229 1
H: 6 1 W: 13 00 b.Warrington 6-3-82

Season	Club				
1998–99	Manchester C	0	0		
1999–2000	Manchester C	0	0		
2000–01	Manchester C	0	0		
2001–02	Manchester C	0	0		
2002–03	Manchester C	1	0		
2002–03	*Cambridge U*	11	0	11	0
2003–04	Manchester C	2	0		
2004–05	Manchester C	19	0		
2005–06	Manchester C	18	0		
2006–07	Manchester C	13	0	53	0
2007–08	Burnley	21	0		
2008–09	Burnley	27	0		
2009–10	Burnley	25	0		
2010–11	Burnley	0	0	73	0
2010–11	*Sheffield U*	15	0	15	0
2010–11	*Huddersfield T*	6	0	6	0
2011–12	Rochdale	19	0	19	0
2013–14	Fleetwood T	10	0		
2014–15	Fleetwood T	42	1	52	1

MATT, Jamille (F) 39 11
H: 6 1 W: 11 11 b.Walsall 20-10-89

Season	Club				
2012–13	Fleetwood T	14	3		
2013–14	Fleetwood T	25	8		
2014–15	Fleetwood T	0	0	39	11

MAXWELL, Chris (G) 64 0
H: 6 0 W: 11 07 b.Wrexham 30-7-90
Internationals: Wales U17, U19, U21, U23.

Season	Club				
2012–13	Fleetwood T	0	0		
2013–14	Fleetwood T	18	0		
2014–15	Fleetwood T	46	0	64	0

McLAUGHLIN, Conor (D) 121 1
H: 6 0 W: 11 02 b.Belfast 26-7-91
Internationals: Northern Ireland U21, Full caps.

Season	Club				
2009–10	Preston NE	0	0		
2010–11	Preston NE	7	0		
2011–12	Preston NE	17	0	24	0
2011–12	*Shrewsbury T*	4	0	4	0
2012–13	Preston NE	19	0		
2013–14	Preston NE	35	0		
2014–15	Fleetwood T	39	1	93	1

MOORE, Brendan (G) 0 0

Season	Club				
2014–15	Fleetwood T	0	0		

MURDOCH, Stewart (M) 60 1
H: 6 0 W: 12 00 b.Aberdeen 9-5-90

Season	Club				
2007–08	Falkirk	0	0		
2008–09	Falkirk	0	0		
2009–10	Falkirk	3	0	3	0
2013–14	Fleetwood T	38	0		
2014–15	Fleetwood T	11	0	49	0
2014–15	*Northampton T*	8	1	8	1

POND, Nathan (M) 80 2
H: 6 3 W: 11 00 b.Preston 5-1-85

Season	Club				
2012–13	Fleetwood T	12	0		
2013–14	Fleetwood T	41	1		
2014–15	Fleetwood T	27	1	80	2

PROCTOR, Jamie (F) 149 25
H: 6 2 W: 12 03 b.Preston 25-3-92

Season	Club				
2009–10	Preston NE	1	0		
2010–11	Preston NE	5	1		
2010–11	*Stockport Co*	7	0	7	0
2011–12	Preston NE	31	3	37	4
2012–13	Swansea C	0	0		
2012–13	*Shrewsbury T*	2	0	2	0
2012–13	*Crawley T*	18	7		
2013–14	Crawley T	44	6	62	13
2014–15	Fleetwood T	41	8	41	8

ROBERTS, Mark (D) 233 20
H: 6 1 W: 12 00 b.Northwich 16-10-83

Season	Club				
2002–03	Crewe Alex	1	0		
2003–04	Crewe Alex	0	0		
2004–05	Crewe Alex	6	0		
2005–06	Crewe Alex	0	0		
2005–06	*Chester C*	1	0	1	0
2006–07	Crewe Alex	0	0	6	0
2007–08	Accrington S	34	0	34	0

From Northwich Vic.

Season	Club				
2010–11	Stevenage	42	6		
2011–12	Stevenage	46	6		
2012–13	Stevenage	44	2	132	14
2013–14	Fleetwood T	33	3		
2014–15	Fleetwood T	27	3	60	6

SARCEVIC, Antoni (M)   91 16
H: 5 10   W: 11 00   b.Manchester 13-3-92
Internationals: England C.

Season	Club				
2009–10	Crewe Alex	0	0		
2010–11	Crewe Alex	6	1		
2011–12	Crewe Alex	6	0	12	1
2013–14	Fleetwood T	42	13		
2014–15	Fleetwood T	37	2	79	15

SCHUMACHER, Steven (M)   372 48
H: 5 10   W: 11 00   b.Liverpool 30-4-84

Season	Club				
2000–01	Everton	0	0		
2001–02	Everton	0	0		
2002–03	Everton	0	0		
2003–04	Everton	0	0		
2003–04	*Carlisle U*	4	0	4	0
2004–05	Bradford C	43	6		
2005–06	Bradford C	30	1		
2006–07	Bradford C	44	6	117	13
2007–08	Crewe Alex	26	1		
2008–09	Crewe Alex	15	2		
2009–10	Crewe Alex	32	4	73	7
2010–11	Bury	43	9		
2011–12	Bury	32	6		
2012–13	Bury	39	8	114	23
2013–14	Fleetwood T	32	5		
2014–15	Fleetwood T	32	0	64	5

SOUTHERN, Keith (M)   377 27
H: 5 10   W: 12 06   b.Gateshead 24-4-81

Season	Club				
1998–99	Everton	0	0		
1999–2000	Everton	0	0		
2000–01	Everton	0	0		
2001–02	Everton	0	0		
2002–03	Everton	0	0		
2002–03	Blackpool	38	1		
2003–04	Blackpool	28	2		
2004–05	Blackpool	27	6		
2005–06	Blackpool	42	2		
2006–07	Blackpool	39	5		
2007–08	Blackpool	30	3		
2008–09	Blackpool	35	3		
2009–10	Blackpool	45	2		
2010–11	Blackpool	21	0		
2011–12	Blackpool	25	1	330	25
2012–13	Huddersfield T	29	1		
2013–14	Huddersfield T	10	1	39	2
2014–15	Fleetwood T	2	0	2	0
2014–15	*Shrewsbury T*	6	0	6	0

SOWERBY, Jack (F)   0 0
b. 23-3-95

Season	Club		
2014–15	Fleetwood T	0	0

TAYLOR, Joe (M)   0 0

Season	Club		
2014–15	Fleetwood T	0	0

WRIGHT, Akil (M)   0 0

Season	Club		
2014–15	Fleetwood T	0	0

WRIGHT, Richard (M)   0 0

Season	Club		
2013–14	Fleetwood T	0	0
2014–15	Fleetwood T	0	0

Scholars
Bleeker, Liam James Jan; Coulson, Thomas Matthew; Djabi, Mamadou; Folksman, Jonathan; Glean, Shane Eric Dalglish; Hancox, Jordan Peter; Johnstone, Max Oliver; Myers, Louis Christopher; Nelson, Wesley James; Smith, Andrew James; Smith, Conor James; Stinton, Jake Andrew; Tetteh, Michael Djangmatey; Vaughan-Muscat, Michael; Vile, Daniel Oscar; Williams, Matthew Thomas; Wood, Liam Wayne; Wynne, Elliot.

Non-Contract
Moore, Brendan Albert.

FULHAM (36)

AMOREBIETA, Fernando (D)   229 5
H: 6 3   W: 12 00   b.Iurreta 29-3-85
Internationals: Spain U19. Venezuela Full caps.

Season	Club				
2004–05	Athletic Bilbao	1	0		
2005–06	Athletic Bilbao	15	0		
2006–07	Athletic Bilbao	27	0		
2007–08	Athletic Bilbao	34	0		
2008–09	Athletic Bilbao	29	0		
2009–10	Athletic Bilbao	34	0		
2010–11	Athletic Bilbao	17	0		
2011–12	Athletic Bilbao	28	3		
2012–13	Athletic Bilbao	11	0	195	3
2013–14	Fulham	23	1		
2014–15	Fulham	7	1	30	2
2014–15	*Middlesbrough*	4	0	4	0

ARTHURWORREY, Stephen (D)   46 2
H: 6 4   W: 13 12   b.Hackney 15-10-94

Season	Club				
2011–12	Fulham	0	0		
2012–13	Fulham	0	0		
2013–14	Fulham	0	0		
2013–14	*Tranmere R*	17	0	17	0
2014–15	Fulham	0	0		
2014–15	*Yeovil T*	29	2	29	2

BETTINELLI, Marcus (G)   78 0
H: 6 4   W: 12 13   b.Camberwell 24-5-92
Internationals: England U21.

Season	Club				
2010–11	Fulham	0	0		
2011–12	Fulham	0	0		
2012–13	Fulham	0	0		
2013–14	Fulham	0	0		
2013–14	*Accrington S*	39	0	39	0
2014–15	Fulham	39	0	39	0

BODUROV, Nikolay (D)   228 8
H: 5 11   W: 12 04   b. 30-5-86
Internationals: Bulgaria Full caps.

Season	Club				
2005–06	Pirin Blagoevgrad	13	0		
2006–07	Pirin Blagoevgrad	19	0		
2007–08	Pirin Blagoevgrad	27	1		
2008–09	Pirin Blagoevgrad	22	0	81	1
2009–10	Litex Lovech	18	0		
2010–11	Litex Lovech	25	2		
2011–12	Litex Lovech	19	3		
2012–13	Litex Lovech	18	0		
2013–14	Litex Lovech	27	1		
2014–15	Litex Lovech	2	0	109	6
2014–15	Fulham	38	1	38	1

BURGESS, Cameron (D)   4 0
H: 6 4   W: 12 11   b.Aberdeen 21-10-95
Internationals: Scotland U19. Australia U20, U23.

Season	Club				
2014–15	Fulham	4	0	4	0
2014–15	*Ross Co*	0	0		

Transferred to Ross Co Janury 2015

BURN, Dan (D)   91 3
H: 6 6   W: 13 00   b.Blyth 1-5-92

Season	Club				
2009–10	Darlington	4	0	4	0
2010–11	Fulham	0	0		
2011–12	Fulham	0	0		
2012–13	Fulham	0	0		
2012–13	*Yeovil T*	34	2	34	2
2013–14	Fulham	9	0		
2013–14	*Birmingham C*	24	0	24	0
2014–15	Fulham	20	1	29	1

CASASOLA, Tiago (D)   0 0
H: 6 3   W: 13 05   b.Buenos Aires 11-8-95
Internationals: Argentina U17, U20.

Season	Club		
2014–15	Fulham	0	0

CHIHI, Adil (M)   132 20
H: 6 0   W: 12 04   b.Dusseldorf 21-2-88
Internationals: Morocco Full caps.

Season	Club				
2006–07	Cologne	33	4		
2007–08	Cologne	21	4		
2008–09	Cologne	19	1		
2009–10	Cologne	15	3		
2010–11	Cologne	11	1		
2011–12	Cologne	10	2		
2012–13	Cologne	21	5		
2013–14	Cologne	1	0	131	20
2014–15	Fulham	1	0	1	0

CHRISTENSEN, Lasse Vigen (M)   25 5
H: 5 10   W: 10 04   b.Esbjerg 15-8-94
Internationals: Denmark U16, U17, U18, U19, U21.

Season	Club				
2012–13	Fulham	0	0		
2013–14	Fulham	0	0		
2014–15	Fulham	25	5	25	5

COLE, Larnell (M)   4 0
H: 5 4   W: 12 04   b.Manchester 9-3-93
Internationals: England U19, U20.

Season	Club				
2011–12	Manchester U	0	0		
2012–13	Manchester U	0	0		
2013–14	Manchester U	0	0		
2013–14	Fulham	0	0		
2013–14	*Milton Keynes D*	3	0	3	0
2014–15	Fulham	1	0	1	0

DAVID, Chris (F)   8 1
H: 5 7   W: 11 01   b.Amsterdam 6-3-93
Internationals: Netherlands U17, U18, U19.

Season	Club				
2013–14	Fulham	1	1		
2014–15	Fulham	5	0	6	1
2014–15	*FC Twente*	2	0	2	0

DELLA VERDE, Lyle (M)   0 0
H: 5 9   W: 11 07   b.Leeds 9-1-95

Season	Club		
2014–15	Fulham	0	0

DEMBELE, Moussa (F)   13 0
H: 6 0   W: 11 08   b.Pontoise 12-7-96
Internationals: France U16, U17, U18, U19.

Season	Club				
2013–14	Fulham	2	0		
2014–15	Fulham	11	0	13	0

DONNELLY, Liam (D)   0 0
b.Dungannon 7-3-96
Internationals: Northern Ireland U16, U17, U21, Full caps.

Season	Club		
2013–14	Fulham	0	0
2014–15	Fulham	0	0

EISFELD, Thomas (M)   19 1
H: 5 10   W: 10 03   b.Finsterwalde 18-1-93
Internationals: Germany U20.

Season	Club				
2011–12	Arsenal	0	0		
2012–13	Arsenal	0	0		
2013–14	Arsenal	0	0		
2014–15	Fulham	7	0	7	0
2014–15	*VfL Bochum*	12	1	12	1

FOTHERINGHAM, Mark (M)   214 10
H: 5 9   W: 11 12   b.Dundee 22-10-83
Internationals: Scotland U21

Season	Club				
1999–2000	Celtic	2	0		
2000–01	Celtic	1	0		
2001–02	Celtic	0	0		
2002–03	Celtic	0	0	3	0
2003–04	Dundee	24	4		
2004–05	Dundee	27	0	51	4
2005–06	Freiburg	9	0	9	0
2006–07	Aarau	13	0	13	0
2006–07	Norwich C	14	0		
2007–08	Norwich C	28	2		
2008–09	Norwich C	27	1	69	3
2009–10	Dundee U	3	0	3	0
2009–10	Anorthosis	7	1		
2010–11	Anorthosis	15	1	22	2

From Livingston, Dundee

Season	Club				
2012–13	Ross Co	14	0	14	0
2013–14	Notts Co	28	1	28	1
2014–15	Fulham	2	0	2	0

GRIMMER, Jack (M)   36 1
H: 6 0   W: 12 06   b.Aberdeen 25-1-94
Internationals: Scotland U15, U16, U17, U18, U19, U21.

Season	Club				
2009–10	Aberdeen	2	0		
2010–11	Aberdeen	2	0		
2011–12	Aberdeen	0	0	4	0
2011–12	Fulham	0	0		
2012–13	Fulham	0	0		
2013–14	Fulham	0	0		
2013–14	*Port Vale*	13	1	13	1
2014–15	Fulham	13	0	13	0
2014–15	*Shrewsbury T*	6	0	6	0

HOOGLAND, Tim (D)   148 18
H: 6 0   W: 12 04   b.Marl 11-6-85
Internationals: Germany U18, U19, U20.

Season	Club				
2004–05	Shalke 04	0	0		
2005–06	Shalke 04	0	0		
2006–07	Shalke 04	9	0		
2007–08	Mainz 05	30	5		
2008–09	Mainz 05	33	3		
2009–10	Mainz 05	21	6	84	14
2010–11	Shalke 04	3	0		
2011–12	Shalke 04	3	0		
2012–13	Shalke 04	4	0		
2012–13	VB Stuttgart	4	0	4	0
2013–14	Shalke 04	19	0	35	0
2014–15	Fulham	25	4	25	4

HUTCHINSON, Shaun (D)   146 9
H: 6 1   W: 12 04   b.Newcastle-Upon-Tyne 23-11-90

Season	Club				
2008–09	Motherwell	1	0		
2009–10	Motherwell	5	3		
2010–11	Motherwell	19	1		
2011–12	Motherwell	30	1		
2012–13	Motherwell	31	1		
2013–14	Motherwell	35	1	121	7
2014–15	Fulham	25	2	25	2

HYNDMAN, Emerson (M)   9 0
H: 5 7   W: 9 08   b.Dallas 9-4-96
Internationals: USA U17, U20, U23, Full caps.

Season	Club				
2013–14	Fulham	0	0		
2014–15	Fulham	9	0	9	0

JORONEN, Jesse (G)   0 0
H: 6 6   W: 14 00   b.Rautjarvi 21-3-93
Internationals: Finland U17, U19, U21, Full caps.

Season	Club				
2013–14	Fulham	0	0		
2013–14	*FC Lahti*	18	0	18	0
2014–15	Fulham	4	0	4	0
2014–15	*Accrington S*	4	0	4	0

KACANIKLIC, Alex (M) 86 10
H: 5 11 W: 10 05 b.Helsingborg 13-8-91
Internationals: Sweden U17, U19, Full caps.

2008–09	Liverpool	0	0		
2009–10	Liverpool	0	0		
2010–11	Fulham	0	0		
2011–12	Fulham	4	0		
2011–12	Watford	12	1	12	1
2012–13	Fulham	20	4		
2012–13	Burnley	6	0	6	0
2013–14	Fulham	23	1		
2014–15	Fulham	14	2	61	7
2014–15	FC Copenhagen	7	2	7	2

KAVANAGH, Sean (D) 19 1
H: 5 8 W: 9 11 b. 24-1-94

| 2014–15 | Fulham | 19 | 1 | 19 | 1 |

KIRALY, Gabor (G) 573 0
H: 6 3 W: 13 05 b.Szombathely 1-4-76
Internationals: Hungary U21, Full caps.

1993–94	Haladas	15	0		
1994–95	Haladas	0	0		
1995–96	Haladas	19	0		
1996–97	Haladas	33	0	67	0
1997–98	Hertha Berlin	27	0		
1998–99	Hertha Berlin	34	0		
1999–2000	Hertha Berlin	27	0		
2000–01	Hertha Berlin	34	0		
2001–02	Hertha Berlin	25	0		
2002–03	Hertha Berlin	33	0		
2003–04	Hertha Berlin	18	0	198	0
2004–05	Crystal Palace	32	0		
2005–06	Crystal Palace	43	0		
2006–07	Crystal Palace	29	0	104	0
2006–07	West Ham U	0	0		
2006–07	Aston Villa	5	0	5	0
2007–08	Burnley	27	0	27	0
2008–09	Bayer Leverkusen	0	0		
2009–10	1860 Munich	33	0		
2010–11	1860 Munich	33	0		
2011–12	1860 Munich	32	0		
2012–13	1860 Munich	34	0		
2013–14	1860 Munich	34	0		
2014–15	1860 Munich	2	0	168	0
2014–15	Fulham	4	0	4	0

McCORMACK, Ross (F) 340 112
H: 5 9 W: 11 00 b.Glasgow 18-8-86
Internationals: Scotland U21, B, Full caps.

2003–04	Rangers	2	1		
2004–05	Rangers	1	0		
2005–06	Rangers	8	1	11	2
2005–06	Doncaster R	19	4	19	4
2006–07	Motherwell	12	2		
2007–08	Motherwell	36	9	48	11
2008–09	Cardiff C	38	21		
2009–10	Cardiff C	34	4		
2010–11	Cardiff C	2	0	74	25
2010–11	Leeds U	21	2		
2011–12	Leeds U	45	18		
2012–13	Leeds U	32	5		
2013–14	Leeds U	46	28	144	53
2014–15	Fulham	44	17	44	17

MITROGLOU, Konstantinos (F) 164 82
H: 6 2 W: 12 09 b.Kavala 12-3-88
Internationals: Greece U19, U21, Full caps.

2007–08	Olympiacos	11	4		
2008–09	Olympiacos	7	2		
2009–10	Olympiacos	32	9		
2010–11	Olympiacos	5	1		
2010–11	Panionios	11	8	11	8
2011–12	Olympiacos	0	0		
2011–12	Atromitos	34	17	34	17
2012–13	Olympiacos	25	11		
2013–14	Olympiacos	12	14		
2013–14	Fulham	3	0		
2014–15	Fulham	0	0	3	0
2014–15	Olympiacos	24	16	116	57

NA BANGNA, Buomesca (M) 7 1
H: 5 9 W: 10 03 b.Guinea-Bissau 6-5-93
Internationals: Portugal U17, U18, U19.

2011–12	Fulham	0	0		
2012–13	Fulham	0	0		
2013–14	Fulham	1	0		
2013–14	Crewe Alex	6	1	6	1
2014–15	Fulham	0	0	1	0

PARKER, Scott (M) 433 30
H: 5 9 W: 11 10 b.Lambeth 13-10-80
Internationals: England U16, U18, U21, Full caps.

1997–98	Charlton Ath	3	0		
1998–99	Charlton Ath	4	0		
1999–2000	Charlton Ath	15	1		
2000–01	Charlton Ath	20	1		
2000–01	Norwich C	6	1	6	1
2001–02	Charlton Ath	38	1		
2002–03	Charlton Ath	28	4		
2003–04	Charlton Ath	20	2	128	9
2003–04	Chelsea	11	1		
2004–05	Chelsea	4	0	15	1
2005–06	Newcastle U	26	1		
2006–07	Newcastle U	29	3	55	4
2007–08	West Ham U	18	1		
2008–09	West Ham U	28	1		
2009–10	West Ham U	31	2		
2010–11	West Ham U	32	5		
2011–12	West Ham U	4	1	113	10
2011–12	Tottenham H	29	0		
2012–13	Tottenham H	21	0		
2013–14	Tottenham H	0	0	50	0
2013–14	Fulham	29	2		
2014–15	Fulham	37	3	66	5

PASSLEY, Josh (D) 18 0
H: 6 0 W: 12 06 b.Chelsea 21-9-93

2013–14	Fulham	0	0		
2014–15	Fulham	0	0		
2014–15	Shrewsbury T	6	0	6	0
2014–15	Portsmouth	12	0	12	0

PLUMAIN, Ange (F) 20 1
b.Paris 2-3-95
Internationals: France U16, U18.

2012–13	Lens	20	1	20	1
2013–14	Fulham	0	0		
2014–15	Fulham	0	0		

ROBERTS, Patrick (M) 19 0
b. 5-2-97
Internationals: England U16, U17, U18, U19.

| 2013–14 | Fulham | 2 | 0 | | |
| 2014–15 | Fulham | 17 | 0 | 19 | 0 |

RODAK, Marek (G) 0 0
H: 6 2 W: 10 12 b. 13-12-96
Internationals: Slovakia U16.

| 2014–15 | Fulham | 0 | 0 | | |

RODALLEGA, Hugo (F) 344 116
H: 5 11 W: 11 05 b.Valle del Cauca 25-7-85
Internationals: Colombia U20, Full caps.

2004	Quindio	32	31	32	31
2005	Dep Cali	26	12	26	12
2005–06	Monterrey	14	3		
2006–07	Atlas	17	5	17	5
2006–07	Monterrey	15	1	29	4
2007–08	Necaxa	36	16		
2008–09	Necaxa	17	9	53	25
2008–09	Wigan Ath	15	3		
2009–10	Wigan Ath	38	10		
2010–11	Wigan Ath	36	9		
2011–12	Wigan Ath	23	2	112	24
2012–13	Fulham	29	3		
2013–14	Fulham	13	2		
2014–15	Fulham	33	10	75	15

RUIZ, Bryan (M) 320 99
H: 6 2 W: 12 04 b.Alajuela 18-8-85
Internationals: Costa Rica Full caps.

2004–05	Alajuelense	31	13		
2005–06	Alajuelense	35	8	66	21
2006–07	Gent	15	3		
2007–08	Gent	31	11		
2008–09	Gent	32	12	78	26
2009–10	Twente	34	24		
2010–11	Twente	27	9		
2011–12	Twente	4	2	65	35
2011–12	Fulham	27	2		
2012–13	Fulham	29	5		
2013–14	Fulham	12	1		
2013–14	PSV Eindhoven	14	5	14	5
2014–15	Fulham	29	4	97	12

SMITH, Matt (F) 141 34
H: 6 6 W: 14 00 b.Birmingham 7-6-89

2011–12	Oldham Ath	11	0		
2011–12	Macclesfield T	8	1	8	1
2012–13	Oldham Ath	34	6	62	9
2013–14	Leeds U	39	12		
2014–15	Leeds U	3	0	42	12
2014–15	Fulham	15	5	15	5
2014–15	Bristol C	14	7	14	7

STAFYLIDIS, Konstantinos (D) 68 1
H: 5 9 W: 11 09 b.Koufalia 2-12-93
Internationals: Greece U17, U19, U20, U21, Full caps.

2011–12	PAOK Salonika	11	0		
2012–13	PAOK Salonika	18	1	29	1
2013–14	Bayer Leverkusen	1	0		
2014–15	Bayer Leverkusen	0	0	1	0

On loan from Bayer Leverkusen.

| 2014–15 | Fulham | 38 | 0 | 38 | 0 |

TAGGART, Adam (F) 54 19
H: 5 8 W: 10 12 b.Perth 2-6-93
Internationals: Australia U20, U23, Full caps.

2010–11	Perth Glory	6	1		
2011–12	Perth Glory	4	0	10	1
2012–13	Newcastle Jets	19	2		
2013–14	Newcastle Jets	25	16	44	18
2014–15	Fulham	0	0		

TROTTA, Marcello (F) 74 27
H: 6 1 W: 12 12 b.Caserta 29-9-92
Internationals: Italy U16, U18, U19, U20, U21.

2009–10	Fulham	0	0		
2010–11	Fulham	0	0		
2011–12	Fulham	1	0		
2011–12	Wycombe W	8	8	8	8
2011–12	Watford	1	0	1	0
2012–13	Fulham	0	0		
2012–13	Brentford	22	6		
2013–14	Fulham	0	0		
2013–14	Brentford	37	12	59	18
2014–15	Fulham	0	0	1	0
2014–15	Barnsley	5	1	5	1

Transferred to Avellino January 2015.

TUNNICLIFFE, Ryan (M) 103 1
H: 6 0 W: 14 02 b.Bury 30-12-92
Internationals: England U16, U17.

2009–10	Manchester U	0	0		
2010–11	Manchester U	0	0		
2011–12	Manchester U	0	0		
2011–12	Peterborough U	27	0	27	0
2012–13	Manchester U	0	0		
2012–13	Barnsley	2	0	2	0
2013–14	Manchester U	0	0		
2013–14	Ipswich T	27	0	27	0
2013–14	Fulham	3	0		
2013–14	Wigan Ath	5	0	5	0
2014–15	Fulham	22	0	25	0
2014–15	Blackburn R	17	1	17	1

VOSER, Kay (D) 125 1
H: 5 8 W: 10 12 b. 4-1-87
Internationals: Switzerland U16, U17, U20, U21.

2008–09	Grasshopper	31	0		
2009–10	Grasshopper	30	0		
2010–11	Grasshopper	13	0	74	0
2011–12	Basle	6	0		
2012–13	Basle	13	0		
2013–14	Basle	29	1	48	1
2014–15	Fulham	3	0	3	0

WILLIAMS, George (F) 18 0
H: 5 10 W: 12 04 b.Milton Keynes 7-9-95
Internationals: Wales U17, U19, U21, Full caps.

2012–13	Fulham	0	0		
2013–14	Fulham	0	0		
2014–15	Fulham	14	0	14	0
2014–15	Milton Keynes D	4	0	4	0

WILLIAMS, Ryan (F) 47 7
H: 5 11 W: 12 00 b.Perth 28-10-93
Internationals: Australia U20, U23.

2011–12	Portsmouth	4	0	4	0
2011–12	Fulham	0	0		
2012–13	Fulham	0	0		
2013–14	Fulham	0	0		
2013–14	Oxford U	36	7	36	7
2014–15	Fulham	2	0	2	0
2014–15	Barnsley	5	0	5	0

WOODROW, Cauley (F) 54 6
H: 6 0 W: 12 04 b.Hemel Hempstead 2-12-94
Internationals: England U17, U21.

2011–12	Fulham	0	0		
2012–13	Fulham	0	0		
2013–14	Fulham	6	1		
2013–14	Southend U	19	2	19	2
2014–15	Fulham	29	3	35	4

ZVEROTIC, Elsad (D) 159 3
H: 5 10 W: 11 10 b.Berane 31-10-86
Internationals: Switzerland U18. Montenegro U21, Full caps.

2008–09	Lucerne	27	1		
2009–10	Lucerne	31	0		
2010–11	Lucerne	27	1	85	2
2011–12	Young Boys	23	0		
2012–13	Young Boys	28	1		
2013–14	Young Boys	7	0	58	1
2013–14	Fulham	6	0		
2014–15	Fulham	10	0	16	0

Transferred to Sion February 2015.

Players retained or with offer of contract
Barnes, Dillon; Elworthy, Shane; Evans, Jordan Anthony John; Humphrys, Stephen Peter; Norman, Magnus; Sheckleford, Ryheem Cole; Smile, Joshua Clifford; Stekelenburg, Maarten.

Scholars
Adebayo, Elijah Anuoluwapo; Davies, Aron Paul; De, La Torre Lucas Daniel; Dolan, Anthony; Edun, Adetayo Oluwatosin; Kait, Mattias; Nabay, Foday; Paton, Harrison Theodore; Redford, Aaron; Sambou, Solomon; Shamsi, Ravin; Soutter, Jake Keith; Walker, Joshua James.

GILLINGHAM (37)

DACK, Bradley (M)   86 13
b.Greenwich 31-12-93
2012–13	Gillingham	16	1		
2013–14	Gillingham	28	3		
2014–15	Gillingham	42	9	86	13

DAVIES, Callum (D)   29 0
H: 6 1   W: 11 11   b.Sittingbourne 8-2-93
2010–11	Gillingham	1	0		
2011–12	Gillingham	2	0		
2012–13	Gillingham	14	0		
2013–14	Gillingham	7	0		
2014–15	Gillingham	5	0	29	0

DICKENSON, Brennan (F)   65 5
H: 6 0   W: 12 07   b.Ferndown 26-2-93
2012–13	Brighton & HA	0	0		
2012–13	*Chesterfield*	11	1	11	1
2012–13	*AFC Wimbledon*	7	2	7	2
2013–14	Brighton & HA	0	0		
2013–14	*Northampton T*	13	1	13	1
2014–15	Gillingham	34	1	34	1

EGAN, John (D)   64 5
H: 6 1   W: 11 11   b.Cork 20-10-92
Internationals: Republic of Ireland U17, U19, U21.
2009–10	Sunderland	0	0		
2010–11	Sunderland	0	0		
2011–12	Sunderland	0	0		
2011–12	*Crystal Palace*	1	0	1	0
2011–12	*Sheffield U*	1	0	1	0
2012–13	Sunderland	0	0		
2012–13	*Bradford C*	4	0	4	0
2013–14	Sunderland	0	0		
2013–14	*Southend U*	13	1	13	1
2014–15	Gillingham	45	4	45	4

FISH, Matt (D)   75 3
H: 6 1   W: 10 12   b.Croydon 5-1-89
2011–12	Gillingham	23	1		
2012–13	Gillingham	44	2		
2013–14	Gillingham	2	0		
2014–15	Gillingham	3	0	72	3
2014–15	*Portsmouth*	3	0	3	0

FREITER, Michael (M)   1 0
b. 15-1-96
2012–13	Gillingham	0	0		
2013–14	Gillingham	0	0		
2014–15	Gillingham	1	0	1	0

GALBRAITH, Danny (M)   94 3
b. 19-8-90
2009–10	Hibernian	14	1		
2010–11	Hibernian	22	0		
2011–12	Hibernian	16	0	52	1
2013	Limerick	27	0		
2014	Limerick	8	2	35	2
2014–15	Gillingham	7	0	7	0

GERMAN, Antonio (F)   66 5
H: 5 10   W: 12 03   b.Wembley 26-12-91
2008–09	QPR	3	0		
2009–10	QPR	13	2		
2009–10	*Aldershot T*	3	0	3	0
2010–11	QPR	2	0		
2010–11	*Southend U*	4	0	4	0
2010–11	*Yeovil T*	4	0	4	0
2011–12	QPR	0	0	18	2
From Stockport Co, Bromley.
2011–12	Brentford	2	0		
2012–13	Brentford	2	1	4	1
2012–13	*Gillingham*	7	1		
2013–14	Gillingham	9	0		
2013–14	*Northampton T*	7	0	7	0
2014–15	Gillingham	10	1	26	2

HADDLER, Tom (G)   0 0
b. 30-7-96
| 2014–15 | Gillingham | 0 | 0 | | |

HARE, Josh (D)   2 0
H: 6 0   W: 12 04   b.Cantebury 12-8-94
2012–13	Gillingham	0	0		
2013–14	Gillingham	0	0		
2014–15	Gillingham	2	0	2	0

HESSENTHALER, Jake (M)   56 2
b.Gravesend 20-4-94
2012–13	Gillingham	0	0		
2013–14	Gillingham	19	1		
2014–15	Gillingham	37	1	56	2

HOYTE, Gavin (D)   139 0
H: 5 11   W: 11 00   b.Waltham Forest 6-6-90
Internationals: England U17, U18, U19, U20. Trinidad & Tobago Full caps.
2007–08	Arsenal	0	0		
2008–09	Arsenal	1	0		
2008–09	*Watford*	7	0	7	0
2009–10	Arsenal	0	0		
2009–10	*Brighton & HA*	18	0	18	0
2010–11	Arsenal	0	0		
2010–11	*Lincoln C*	12	0	12	0
2011–12	Arsenal	0	0	1	0
2011–12	*AFC Wimbledon*	3	0	3	0
2012–13	Dagenham & R	26	0		
2013–14	Dagenham & R	42	0	68	0
2014–15	Gillingham	30	0	30	0

KEDWELL, Danny (F)   119 40
H: 5 11   W: 12 13   b.Gillingham 3-8-83
2011–12	Gillingham	40	12		
2012–13	Gillingham	38	14		
2013–14	Gillingham	27	10		
2014–15	Gillingham	14	4	119	40

LEGGE, Leon (D)   175 17
H: 6 1   W: 11 02   b.Bexhill 1-7-85
2009–10	Brentford	29	2		
2010–11	Brentford	30	3		
2011–12	Brentford	28	4		
2012–13	Brentford	7	0	94	9
2012–13	Gillingham	22	2		
2013–14	Gillingham	37	2		
2014–15	Gillingham	22	4	81	8

LINGANZI, Amine (M)   46 1
H: 6 1   W: 10 00   b.Algiers 16-11-89
Internationals: DR Congo Full caps.
2008–09	St Etienne	3	0		
2009–10	St Etienne	0	0	3	0
2009–10	Blackburn R	1	0		
2010–11	Blackburn R	1	0		
2010–11	*Preston NE*	1	0	1	0
2011–12	Blackburn R	0	0		
2012–13	Blackburn R	0	0	2	0
2012–13	*Accrington S*	13	0	13	0
2013–14	Gillingham	20	1		
2014–15	Gillingham	7	0	27	1

LOFT, Doug (M)   260 21
H: 6 0   W: 12 01   b.Maidstone 25-12-86
2005–06	Brighton & HA	3	1		
2006–07	Brighton & HA	11	1		
2007–08	Brighton & HA	13	0		
2008–09	Brighton & HA	12	0	39	2
2008–09	*Dagenham & R*	11	0	11	0
2009–10	Port Vale	32	3		
2010–11	Port Vale	29	1		
2011–12	Port Vale	44	4		
2012–13	Port Vale	32	1		
2013–14	Port Vale	37	9	174	18
2014–15	Gillingham	36	1	36	1

MARTIN, Joe (M)   183 8
H: 6 0   W: 12 13   b.Dagenham 29-11-88
Internationals: England U16, U17.
2005–06	Tottenham H	0	0		
2006–07	Tottenham H	0	0		
2007–08	Tottenham H	0	0		
2007–08	*Blackpool*	1	0		
2008–09	Blackpool	15	0		
2009–10	Blackpool	6	0	22	0
2010–11	Gillingham	17	1		
2011–12	Gillingham	35	1		
2012–13	Gillingham	38	2		
2013–14	Gillingham	46	2		
2014–15	Gillingham	25	2	161	8

McDONALD, Cody (F)   202 73
H: 5 10   W: 11 03   b.Witham 30-5-86
2008–09	Norwich C	7	1		
2009–10	Norwich C	17	3		
2010–11	Norwich C	0	0		
2010–11	*Gillingham*	41	25		
2011–12	Norwich C	0	0	24	4

2011–12	Coventry C	23	4		
2012–13	Coventry C	20	3	43	7
2012–13	*Gillingham*	7	4		
2013–14	Gillingham	44	17		
2014–15	Gillingham	43	16	135	62

McGLASHAN, Jermaine (M)   205 22
H: 5 7   W: 10 00   b.Croydon 14-4-88
2010–11	Aldershot T	38	1		
2011–12	Aldershot T	23	4	61	5
2011–12	*Cheltenham T*	16	2		
2012–13	Cheltenham T	45	4		
2013–14	Cheltenham T	43	6	104	12
2014–15	Gillingham	40	5	40	5

MILLBANK, Aaron (F)   1 0
H: 6 0   W: 11 09   b.Ramsgate 4-2-95
| 2013–14 | Gillingham | 1 | 0 | | |
| 2014–15 | Gillingham | 0 | 0 | 1 | 0 |

MORRIS, Aaron (D)   139 2
H: 6 1   W: 12 05   b.Cardiff 30-12-89
Internationals: Wales Youth, U21.
2008–09	Cardiff C	0	0		
2009–10	Cardiff C	1	0	1	0
2010–11	Aldershot T	22	0		
2011–12	Aldershot T	39	2		
2012–13	Aldershot T	37	0	98	2
2013–14	AFC Wimbledon	17	0	17	0
2014–15	Gillingham	23	0	23	0

MORRIS, Glenn (G)   193 0
H: 6 0   W: 12 03   b.Woolwich 20-12-83
2001–02	Leyton Orient	2	0		
2002–03	Leyton Orient	23	0		
2003–04	Leyton Orient	27	0		
2004–05	Leyton Orient	12	0		
2005–06	Leyton Orient	4	0		
2006–07	Leyton Orient	3	0		
2007–08	Leyton Orient	16	0		
2008–09	Leyton Orient	26	0		
2009–10	Leyton Orient	11	0	124	0
2010–11	Southend U	33	0		
2011–12	Southend U	24	0		
2012–13	Southend U	0	0	57	0
2012–13	*Aldershot T*	2	0	2	0
2014–15	Gillingham	10	0	10	0

NELSON, Stuart (G)   340 0
H: 6 1   W: 12 12   b.Stroud 17-9-81
2003–04	Brentford	9	0		
2004–05	Brentford	43	0		
2005–06	Brentford	45	0		
2006–07	Brentford	19	0	116	0
2007–08	*Leyton Orient*	30	0	30	0
2008–09	Norwich C	0	0		
2010–11	Notts Co	33	0		
2011–12	Notts Co	46	0	79	0
2012–13	Gillingham	45	0		
2013–14	Gillingham	46	0		
2014–15	Gillingham	24	0	115	0

NORRIS, Luke (F)   68 14
H: 6 1   W: 13 05   b.Stevenage 3-6-93
2011–12	Brentford	1	0		
2012–13	Brentford	0	0		
2013–14	Brentford	0	0	2	0
2013–14	*Northampton T*	10	4	10	4
2013–14	*Dagenham & R*	19	4	19	4
2014–15	*Gillingham*	37	6	37	6

PRITCHARD, Josh (M)   25 0
H: 5 9   W: 11 02   b.Stockport 23-9-92
Internationals: Wales U21.
2011–12	Fulham	0	0		
2012–13	Fulham	0	0		
2013–14	Fulham	0	0		
2014–15	Gillingham	25	0	25	0

WEBSTER, Charlie (M)   0 0
2012–13	Gillingham	0	0		
2013–14	Gillingham	0	0		
2014–15	Gillingham	0	0		

Scholars
Adams, Daniel Raymond; Bent, Daniel David; Bowyer-O'Brien, Jake; Crandley, Ryan; Cundle, Gregory Vincent; Dickenson, Mitchell Jack; Emptage, Callum James; Haigh, Christopher David; Hendricks, Connor Ian; Ibbertson, Ross Adam; Leonard, Danny Claydon; Newcombe, Henry John; Nougbele, Joseph; Stannard, Harry; Stewart, Sam Ryan; Thompson, Ricardo Dante Nathaniel; Welch, Mitchell Krane.

HARTLEPOOL U (38)

AUSTIN, Neil (D)   433 15
H: 5 10   W: 11 09   b.Barnsley 26-4-83
Internationals: England U16, U17.
1999–2000	Barnsley	0	0		
2000–01	Barnsley	0	0		
2001–02	Barnsley	0	0		
2002–03	Barnsley	34	0		
2003–04	Barnsley	37	0		
2004–05	Barnsley	15	0		
2005–06	Barnsley	38	0		
2006–07	Barnsley	24	0	148	0
2007–08	Darlington	29	2		
2008–09	Darlington	33	3	62	5
2009–10	Hartlepool U	39	3		
2010–11	Hartlepool U	24	2		
2011–12	Hartlepool U	46	1		
2012–13	Hartlepool U	39	2		
2013–14	Hartlepool U	29	0		
2014–15	Hartlepool U	46	2	223	10

BARBER, Jonathan (G)   0   0
b. 1-10-96
2014–15	Hartlepool U	0	0		

BATES, Matthew (D)   173   7
H: 5 10   W: 12 03   b.Stockton 10-12-86
Internationals: England U18, U19.
2003–04	Middlesbrough	0	0		
2004–05	Middlesbrough	2	0		
2004–05	*Darlington*	4	0	4	0
2005–06	Middlesbrough	16	0		
2006–07	Middlesbrough	1	0		
2006–07	*Ipswich T*	2	0	2	0
2007–08	Middlesbrough	0	0		
2007–08	*Norwich C*	3	0	3	0
2008–09	Middlesbrough	17	1		
2009–10	Middlesbrough	0	0		
2010–11	Middlesbrough	31	3		
2011–12	Middlesbrough	37	2	104	6
2012–13	Bristol C	13	0		
2013–14	Bristol C	0	0	13	0
2013–14	Bradford C	22	0	22	0
2014–15	Hartlepool U	25	1	25	1

COLLINS, Sam (D)   525 19
H: 6 2   W: 14 03   b.Pontefract 5-6-77
1994–95	Huddersfield T	0	0		
1995–96	Huddersfield T	0	0		
1996–97	Huddersfield T	4	0		
1997–98	Huddersfield T	10	0		
1998–99	Huddersfield T	23	0	37	0
1999–2000	Bury	19	0		
2000–01	Bury	34	2		
2001–02	Bury	29	0	82	2
2002–03	Port Vale	44	5		
2003–04	Port Vale	43	4		
2004–05	Port Vale	33	2		
2005–06	Port Vale	15	0	135	11
2005–06	Hull C	17	0		
2006–07	Hull C	6	0		
2007–08	Hull C	0	0	23	0
2007–08	*Swindon T*	4	0	4	0
2007–08	Hartlepool U	10	2		
2008–09	Hartlepool U	40	1		
2009–10	Hartlepool U	44	0		
2010–11	Hartlepool U	42	2		
2011–12	Hartlepool U	36	1		
2012–13	Hartlepool U	41	0		
2013–14	Hartlepool U	24	0		
2014–15	Hartlepool U	7	0	244	6

COMPTON, Jack (M)   125   7
H: 5 8   W: 10 07   b.Torquay 2-9-88
2008–09	Brighton & HA	0	0		
From Havant & Waterlooville,
Weston-Super-Mare.
2010–11	Falkirk	24	3		
2011–12	Falkirk	13	0	37	3
2011–12	*Bradford C*	14	0	14	0
2011–12	*St Johnstone*	0	0		
2012–13	Portsmouth	12	0	12	0
2012–13	*Colchester U*	7	0	7	0
2013–14	Hartlepool U	34	4		
2014–15	Hartlepool U	21	0	55	4

DUCKWORTH, Michael (M)   67   3
b. 28-6-92
2013–14	Hartlepool U	30	0		
2014–15	Hartlepool U	37	3	67	3

FEATHERSTONE, Nicky (M)   162   1
H: 5 7   W: 11 02   b.Ferriby 22-9-88
2006–07	Hull C	2	0		
2007–08	Hull C	6	0		
2008–09	Hull C	0	0		
2009–10	Hull C	0	0	8	0

2009–10	Grimsby T	8	0	8	0
2010–11	Hereford U	27	1		
2011–12	Hereford U	38	0	65	1
2012–13	Walsall	31	0		
2013–14	Walsall	25	0	56	0
2014–15	Scunthorpe U	0	0		
2014–15	Hartlepool U	25	0	25	0

FENWICK, Scott (F)   19   6
b. 9-4-90
2014–15	Hartlepool U	19	6	19	6

FLINDERS, Scott (G)   304   1
H: 6 4   W: 13 00   b.Rotherham 12-6-86
Internationals: England U20.
2004–05	Barnsley	11	0		
2005–06	Barnsley	3	0	14	0
2006–07	Crystal Palace	8	0		
2006–07	Gillingham	9	0	9	0
2006–07	*Brighton & HA*	12	0	12	0
2007–08	Crystal Palace	0	0		
2007–08	*Yeovil T*	9	0	9	0
2008–09	Crystal Palace	0	0	8	0
2009–10	Hartlepool U	46	0		
2010–11	Hartlepool U	26	1		
2011–12	Hartlepool U	45	0		
2012–13	Hartlepool U	46	0		
2013–14	Hartlepool U	43	0		
2014–15	Hartlepool U	46	0	252	1

FRANKS, Jonathan (F)   172 17
H: 5 9   W: 11 03   b.Stockton 8-4-90
*Internationals: England U16, U17, U18, U19,
U20.*
2007–08	Middlesbrough	0	0		
2008–09	Middlesbrough	1	0		
2009–10	Middlesbrough	23	3		
2010–11	Middlesbrough	4	0		
2011–12	Middlesbrough	0	0	28	3
2011–12	*Oxford U*	1	0	1	0
2011–12	*Yeovil T*	14	3	14	3
2012–13	Hartlepool U	45	4		
2013–14	Hartlepool U	39	5		
2014–15	Hartlepool U	45	2	129	11

GREEN, Kieran (M)   1   0
b. 30-6-97
2014–15	Hartlepool U	1	0	1	0

HAREWOOD, Marlon (F)   516 131
H: 6 1   W: 13 07   b.Hampstead 25-8-79
1996–97	Nottingham F	0	0		
1997–98	Nottingham F	1	0		
1998–99	Nottingham F	23	1		
1998–99	*Ipswich T*	6	1	6	1
1999–2000	Nottingham F	34	4		
2000–01	Nottingham F	33	3		
2001–02	Nottingham F	28	11		
2002–03	Nottingham F	44	20		
2003–04	Nottingham F	19	12		
2003–04	West Ham U	28	13		
2004–05	West Ham U	45	17		
2005–06	West Ham U	37	14		
2006–07	West Ham U	32	3	142	47
2007–08	Aston Villa	23	5		
2008–09	Aston Villa	6	0		
2008–09	*Wolverhampton W*	5	0	5	0
2009–10	Aston Villa	0	0	29	5
2009–10	*Newcastle U*	15	5	15	5
2010–11	Blackpool	16	5	16	5
2010–11	*Barnsley*	10	4		
2011	Guangzhou	10	4	10	4
2011–12	Nottingham F	40	0	186	51
2012–13	Barnsley	32	2		
2013–14	Barnsley	0	0	42	6
2013–14	Bristol C	12	1	12	1
2014–15	Hartlepool U	19	3		
2014–15	Hartlepool U	34	3	53	6

HAWKINS, Lewis (M)   19   0
H: 5 10   W: 12 04   b.Middlesbrough 15-6-93
2011–12	Hartlepool U	1	0		
2012–13	Hartlepool U	1	0		
2013–14	Hartlepool U	5	0		
2014–15	Hartlepool U	12	0	19	0

HOLDEN, Darren (D)   58   0
H: 5 11   W: 11 00   b.Krugersdorp 27-8-93
2010–11	Hartlepool U	1	0		
2011–12	Hartlepool U	3	0		
2012–13	Hartlepool U	17	0		
2013–14	Hartlepool U	26	0		
2014–15	Hartlepool U	11	0	58	0

JONES, Dan (D)   26   0
H: 6 0   W: 12 05   b. 14-12-94
2013–14	Hartlepool U	1	0		
2014–15	Hartlepool U	25	0	26	0

MAXTED, Jonathan (G)   0   0
H: 6 0   W: 11 03   b. 26-10-93
2012–13	Doncaster R	0	0		
2013–14	Doncaster R	0	0		
2014–15	Hartlepool U	0	0		

MILLER, Tommy (M)   520 90
H: 6 0   W: 11 07   b.Shotton 8-1-79
1997–98	Hartlepool U	13	1		
1998–99	Hartlepool U	34	4		
1999–2000	Hartlepool U	44	14		
2000–01	Hartlepool U	46	16		
2001–02	Hartlepool U	0	0		
2001–02	Ipswich T	8	0		
2002–03	Ipswich T	30	6		
2003–04	Ipswich T	34	11		
2004–05	Ipswich T	45	13		
2005–06	Sunderland	29	3		
2006–07	Sunderland	4	0	33	3
2006–07	*Preston NE*	7	0	7	0
2007–08	Ipswich T	37	5		
2008–09	Ipswich T	32	5	186	40
2009–10	Sheffield W	20	1		
2010–11	Sheffield W	34	9	54	10
2011–12	Huddersfield T	26	1	26	1
2012–13	Swindon T	34	1		
2013–14	Swindon T	0	0	34	1
2013–14	Bury	28	0	28	0
2014–15	Hartlepool U	15	0	152	35

NEARNEY, Josh (D)   0   0
b. 7-9-95
2014–15	Hartlepool U	0	0		

NELSON-ADDY, Ebby (M)   2   0
b. 13.9.92
From Brackley T, Worcester C
2014–15	Hartlepool U	2	0	2	0

PARNABY, Stuart (D)   166   2
H: 5 11   W: 12 00   b.Durham 19-7-82
Internationals: England U20, U21.
2000–01	Middlesbrough	0	0		
2000–01	*Halifax T*	6	0	6	0
2001–02	Middlesbrough	21	0		
2002–03	Middlesbrough	13	0		
2003–04	Middlesbrough	19	0		
2004–05	Middlesbrough	20	2		
2005–06	Middlesbrough	18	0		
2006–07	Birmingham C	13	0		
2007–08	Birmingham C	13	0		
2008–09	Birmingham C	21	0		
2009–10	Birmingham C	8	0		
2010–11	Birmingham C	5	0	47	0
2012–13	Middlesbrough	14	0		
2013–14	Middlesbrough	3	0	108	2
2014–15	Hartlepool U	5	0	5	0

RICHARDS, Jordan (M)   41   0
H: 5 9   W: 11 05   b.Sunderland 25-4-93
2011–12	Hartlepool U	2	0		
2012–13	Hartlepool U	11	0		
2013–14	Hartlepool U	19	0		
2014–15	Hartlepool U	9	0	41	0

SCHMELTZ, Sidney (M)   108   8
H: 5 10   W: 11 04   b.Nieuwegein 8-6-89
2008–09	Willem II	4	0		
2009–10	Willem II	2	0	6	0
2010–11	Almere C	33	4	33	4
2011–12	S Rotterdam	17	2	17	2
2012–13	Veendam	26	2	26	2
2013–14	Oldham Ath	17	0	17	0
2013–14	*Shrewsbury T*	4	0	4	0
2014–15	Hartlepool U	5	0	5	0

SMITH, Connor (M)   9   0
b. 14-10-96
2013–14	Hartlepool U	1	0		
2014–15	Hartlepool U	8	0	9	0

WALKER, Brad (M)   64   8
H: 6 1   W: 12 08   b. 25-4-95
2012–13	Hartlepool U	0	0		
2013–14	Hartlepool U	36	3		
2014–15	Hartlepool U	28	5	64	8

WOODS, Michael (M)   28   2
H: 6 0   W: 12 07   b.Pocklington 6-4-90
Internationals: England U16, U17, U19, U20.
2006–07	Chelsea	0	0		
2007–08	Chelsea	0	0		
2008–09	Chelsea	0	0		
2009–10	Chelsea	0	0		
2010–11	Chelsea	0	0		
2010–11	Notts Co	0	0		
2011–12	Chelsea	0	0		
2011–12	Yeovil T	5	1	5	1
2012–13	Doncaster R	0	0		
2014–15	Hartlepool U	23	1	23	1

Players retained or with offer of contract
Harrison, Scott Nathan.

Scholars
Armstrong, Dylan Michael; Barber, Jonathan Frederick; Blackford, Jack; Briggs, Frazer Wilkinson; Carr, Jonathon Wesley; Cunningham, Aaron Ross; Dawson, James Edward; Elliott, Dylan Michael; Green, Kieran Thomas; Howes, Scott Anthony; Jewson, Jordan Lewis; Male, Adam; Skidmore, Nathaniel; Smith, Connor Charles; Turnbull, Jack Thomas; Varga, Bradley Brian Miklos; Wood, Callum Peter.

HUDDERSFIELD T (39)

ALLINSON, Lloyd (G)   0   0
H: 6 2   W: 13 00   b.Rothwell 7-9-93
2010–11	Huddersfield T	0	0		
2011–12	Huddersfield T	0	0		
2012–13	Huddersfield T	0	0		
2013–14	Huddersfield T	0	0		
2014–15	Huddersfield T	0	0		

ATKINSON, Ben (M)   0   0
b. 4-9-95
2014–15	Huddersfield T	0	0

BILLING, Phillip (M)   1   0
H: 6 4   W: 12 08   b. 11-6-96
2013–14	Huddersfield T	1	0		
2014–15	Huddersfield T	0	0	1	0

BOJAJ, Florent (F)   0   0
b. 13-4-96
Internationals: Albania U17.
2014–15	Huddersfield T	0	0

BOYLE, William (D)   1   0
H: 6 2   W: 11 00   b.Garforth 1-9-95
2014–15	Huddersfield T	1	0	1	0

BUTTERFIELD, Jacob (D)   183   17
H: 5 10   W: 11 00   b.Bradford 10-6-90
Internationals: England U21.
2007–08	Barnsley	3	0		
2008–09	Barnsley	3	0		
2009–10	Barnsley	20	1		
2010–11	Barnsley	40	2		
2011–12	Barnsley	24	5	90	8
2012–13	Norwich C	0	0		
2012–13	Bolton W	8	0	8	0
2012–13	Crystal Palace	9	0	9	0
2013–14	Norwich C	0	0		
2013–14	Middlesbrough	31	3	31	3
2014–15	Huddersfield T	45	6	45	6

CARR, Daniel (F)   16   2
H: 5 11   W: 11 13   b. 30-11-93
2013–14	Huddersfield T	2	0		
2013–14	Fleetwood T	4	1	4	1
2014–15	Huddersfield T	0	0	2	0
2014–15	Mansfield T	4	1	4	1
2014–15	Dagenham & R	6	0	6	0

CARROLL, Jake (D)   55   2
H: 6 0   W: 12 03   b.Dublin 11-1-91
Internationals: Republic of Ireland U18.
2011	St Patricks	7	0		
2012	St Patricks	19	1		
2013	St Patricks	7	0	33	1
2013–14	Huddersfield T	4	0		
2013–14	Bury	6	1	6	1
2014–15	Huddersfield T	2	0	6	0
2014–15	Partick Thistle	10	0	10	0

CHARLES, Jake (M)   1   0
H: 6 0   W: 10 10   b.Leeds 28-2-96
Internationals: Wales U16, U17, U19.
2013–14	Huddersfield T	0	0		
2014–15	Huddersfield T	1	0	1	0

COADY, Conor (D)   85   8
H: 6 1   W: 11 05   b.Liverpool 25-2-93
Internationals: England U16, U17, U18, U19, U20.
2010–11	Liverpool	0	0		
2011–12	Liverpool	0	0		
2012–13	Liverpool	1	0		
2013–14	Liverpool	0	0	1	0
2013–14	Sheffield U	39	5	39	5
2014–15	Huddersfield T	45	3	45	3

COOGANS, Liam (F)   0   0
H: 5 9   W: 11 00   b.Glasgow 31-10-96

DIXON, Paul (D)   298   6
H: 5 9   W: 11 01   b.Aberdeen 11-10-86
Internationals: Scotland U21, Full caps.
2005–06	Dundee	29	2		
2006–07	Dundee	33	0		
2007–08	Dundee	30	0	92	2
2008–09	Dundee U	29	1		
2009–10	Dundee U	25	0		
2010–11	Dundee U	30	0		
2011–12	Dundee U	37	3	121	4
2012–13	Huddersfield T	37	0		
2013–14	Huddersfield T	37	0		
2014–15	Huddersfield T	11	0	85	0
Transferred to Dundee U February 2015.

GERRARD, Anthony (D)   350   17
H: 6 2   W: 13 07   b.Huyton 6-2-86
Internationals: Republic of Ireland U18.
2004–05	Everton	0	0		
2004–05	Walsall	8	0		
2005–06	Walsall	34	0		
2006–07	Walsall	35	1		
2007–08	Walsall	44	3		
2008–09	Walsall	42	3	163	7
2009–10	Cardiff C	39	2		
2010–11	Cardiff C	0	0		
2010–11	Hull C	41	5	41	5
2011–12	Cardiff C	20	1		
2012–13	Cardiff C	0	0	59	3
2012–13	Huddersfield T	38	1		
2013–14	Huddersfield T	40	1		
2014–15	Huddersfield T	3	0	81	2
2014–15	Oldham Ath	6	0	6	0

GOBERN, Oscar (M)   97   4
H: 5 11   W: 10 10   b.Birmingham 26-1-91
Internationals: England U19.
2008–09	Southampton	6	0		
2009–10	Southampton	4	0		
2009–10	Milton Keynes D	2	0	2	0
2010–11	Southampton	11	1	21	1
2011–12	Huddersfield T	21	2		
2012–13	Huddersfield T	15	0		
2013–14	Huddersfield T	23	0		
2014–15	Huddersfield T	12	1	71	3
2014–15	Chesterfield	3	0	3	0

GUTHRIE, Sam (G)   0   0
b. 25-4-96
2014–15	Huddersfield T	0	0

HAMMILL, Adam (M)   250   21
H: 5 11   W: 11 07   b.Liverpool 25-1-88
Internationals: England U19, U21.
2005–06	Liverpool	0	0		
2006–07	Liverpool	0	0		
2006–07	Dunfermline Ath	13	1	13	1
2007–08	Liverpool	0	0		
2007–08	Southampton	25	0	25	0
2008–09	Liverpool	0	0		
2008–09	Blackpool	22	1	22	1
2008–09	Barnsley	14	1		
2009–10	Barnsley	39	4		
2010–11	Barnsley	25	8	78	13
2011–12	Wolverhampton W	10	0		
2011–12	Wolverhampton W	9	0		
2011–12	Middlesbrough	10	0	10	0
2012–13	Wolverhampton W	4	0	23	0
2012–13	Huddersfield T	16	2		
2013–14	Huddersfield T	44	4		
2014–15	Huddersfield T	5	0	65	6
2014–15	Rotherham U	14	0	14	0

HOGG, Jonathan (M)   167   1
H: 5 7   W: 10 05   b.Middlesbrough 6-12-88
2007–08	Aston Villa	0	0		
2008–09	Aston Villa	0	0		
2009–10	Aston Villa	0	0		
2009–10	Darlington	5	1	5	1
2010–11	Aston Villa	5	0		
2010–11	Portsmouth	19	0	19	0
2011–12	Aston Villa	0	0	5	0
2011–12	Watford	40	0		
2012–13	Watford	38	0	78	0
2013–14	Huddersfield T	34	0		
2014–15	Huddersfield T	26	0	60	0

HOLMES, Ben (M)   0   0
b.Oldham 7-8-96
2014–15	Huddersfield T	0	0

HOLMES, Duane (M)   27   0
H: 5 8   W: 10 03   b.Wakefield 6-11-94
2012–13	Huddersfield T	0	0		
2013–14	Huddersfield T	16	0		
2013–14	Yeovil T	5	0	5	0
2014–15	Huddersfield T	0	0	16	0
2014–15	Bury	6	0	6	0

HUDSON, Mark (D)   363   23
H: 6 1   W: 12 01   b.Guildford 30-3-82
1998–99	Fulham	0	0		
1999–2000	Fulham	0	0		
2000–01	Fulham	0	0		
2001–02	Fulham	0	0		
2002–03	Fulham	0	0		
2003–04	Fulham	0	0		
2003–04	Oldham Ath	15	0	15	0
2003–04	Crystal Palace	14	0		
2004–05	Crystal Palace	7	1		
2005–06	Crystal Palace	15	0		
2006–07	Crystal Palace	39	4		
2007–08	Crystal Palace	45	2	120	7
2008–09	Charlton Ath	43	3	43	3
2009–10	Cardiff C	27	2		
2010–11	Cardiff C	40	0		
2011–12	Cardiff C	39	5		
2012–13	Cardiff C	33	4		
2013–14	Cardiff C	2	0		
2014–15	Cardiff C	3	0	144	11
2014–15	Huddersfield T	41	2	41	2

LOLLEY, Joe (F)   23   3
H: 5 10   W: 11 05   b. 25-8-92
Internationals: England C.
2013–14	Huddersfield T	6	1		
2014–15	Huddersfield T	17	2	23	3

LYNCH, Joel (D)   244   11
H: 6 1   W: 12 10   b.Eastbourne 3-10-87
Internationals: England Youth. Wales Full caps.
2005–06	Brighton & HA	16	1		
2006–07	Brighton & HA	39	0		
2007–08	Brighton & HA	22	1		
2008–09	Brighton & HA	2	0	79	2
2008–09	Nottingham F	23	0		
2009–10	Nottingham F	10	0		
2010–11	Nottingham F	12	0		
2011–12	Nottingham F	35	3	80	3
2012–13	Nottingham F	22	1		
2013–14	Huddersfield T	29	2		
2014–15	Huddersfield T	34	3	85	6

MILLER, Ishmael (F)   206   38
H: 6 3   W: 14 00   b.Manchester 5-3-87
2005–06	Manchester C	1	0		
2006–07	Manchester C	16	0		
2007–08	Manchester C	0	0	17	0
2007–08	WBA	34	9		
2008–09	WBA	15	3		
2009–10	WBA	15	2		
2010–11	WBA	6	0	70	14
2010–11	QPR	12	1	12	1
2011–12	Nottingham F	21	3		
2012–13	Nottingham F	0	0		
2012–13	Middlesbrough	25	5	25	5
2013–14	Nottingham F	4	0	25	3
2013–14	Yeovil T	19	10	19	10
2014–15	Blackpool	22	2	22	2
2014–15	Huddersfield T	16	3	16	3

MURPHY, Joe (G)   447   0
H: 6 2   W: 13 06   b.Dublin 21-8-81
Internationals: Republic of Ireland Youth, U21, Full caps.
1999–2000	Tranmere R	21	0		
2000–01	Tranmere R	20	0		
2001–02	Tranmere R	22	0	63	0
2002–03	WBA	2	0		
2003–04	WBA	3	0		
2004–05	WBA	0	0	5	0
2004–05	Walsall	25	0		
2005–06	Sunderland	0	0		
2005–06	Walsall	14	0	39	0
2006–07	Scunthorpe U	45	0		
2007–08	Scunthorpe U	45	0		
2008–09	Scunthorpe U	42	0		
2009–10	Scunthorpe U	40	0		
2010–11	Scunthorpe U	29	0	201	0
2011–12	Coventry C	46	0		
2012–13	Coventry C	45	0		
2013–14	Coventry C	46	0	137	0
2014–15	Huddersfield T	2	0	2	0
2014–15	Chesterfield	0	0-		

PATERSON, Martin (F)   239   55
H: 5 9   W: 10 11   b.Tunstall 13-5-87
Internationals: Northern Ireland U21, Full caps.
2004–05	Stoke C	3	0		
2005–06	Stoke C	3	0		
2006–07	Stoke C	1	0	15	1
2006–07	Grimsby T	15	6	15	6
2007–08	Scunthorpe U	40	13	40	13
2008–09	Burnley	43	12		
2009–10	Burnley	23	4		
2010–11	Burnley	11	2		

2011–12	Burnley	14	3		
2012–13	Burnley	39	8	130	29
2013–14	Huddersfield T	22	5		
2013–14	*Bristol C*	8	1	8	1
2014–15	Huddersfield T	3	0	25	5
2014–15	*Fleetwood T*	3	0	3	0
2015	*Orlando C*	3	0	3	0

SCANNELL, Sean (F) 244 19
H: 5 9 W: 11 07 b.Croydon 19-9-90
Internationals: Republic of Ireland U17, U18, U19, U21, B.

2007–08	Crystal Palace	23	2		
2008–09	Crystal Palace	25	2		
2009–10	Crystal Palace	26	2		
2010–11	Crystal Palace	19	2		
2011–12	Crystal Palace	37	4	130	12
2012–13	Huddersfield T	34	2		
2013–14	Huddersfield T	38	1		
2014–15	Huddersfield T	42	4	114	7

SINNOTT, Jordan (M) 11 1
H: 5 11 W: 11 12 b. 14-2-94

2012–13	Huddersfield T	1	0		
2013–14	Huddersfield T	0	0		
2013–14	*Bury*	9	1	9	1
2014–15	Huddersfield T	1	0	2	0

SMITH, Tommy (D) 65 0
b.Warrington 14-4-92

2012–13	Huddersfield T	0	0		
2013–14	Huddersfield T	24	0		
2014–15	Huddersfield T	41	0	65	0

SMITHIES, Alex (G) 246 0
H: 6 1 W: 10 01 b.Huddersfield 25-3-90
Internationals: England U16, U17, U18, U19.

2006–07	Huddersfield T	0	0		
2007–08	Huddersfield T	2	0		
2008–09	Huddersfield T	27	0		
2009–10	Huddersfield T	46	0		
2010–11	Huddersfield T	22	0		
2011–12	Huddersfield T	13	0		
2012–13	Huddersfield T	46	0		
2013–14	Huddersfield T	46	0		
2014–15	Huddersfield T	44	0	246	0

STEAD, Jon (F) 418 93
H: 6 3 W: 13 03 b.Huddersfield 7-4-83
Internationals: England U21.

2001–02	Huddersfield T	0	0		
2002–03	Huddersfield T	42	6		
2003–04	Huddersfield T	26	16		
2003–04	Blackburn R	13	6		
2004–05	Blackburn R	29	2	42	8
2005–06	Sunderland	30	1		
2006–07	Sunderland	5	1	35	2
2006–07	Derby Co	17	3	17	3
2006–07	Sheffield U	14	5		
2007–08	Sheffield U	24	3		
2008–09	Sheffield U	1	0	39	8
2008–09	Ipswich T	39	12		
2009–10	Ipswich T	22	6		
2009–10	Coventry C	10	2	10	2
2010–11	Ipswich T	3	1	64	19
2010–11	Bristol C	27	9		
2011–12	Bristol C	24	6		
2012–13	Bristol C	28	5	79	20
2013–14	Huddersfield T	12	1		
2013–14	*Oldham Ath*	5	0	5	0
2013–14	*Bradford C*	8	1		
2014–15	Huddersfield T	7	1	87	24
2014–15	*Bradford C*	32	6	40	7

TRONSTAD, Sondre (M) 9 1
H: 5 8 W: 10 13 b. 26-8-95
Internationals: Norway U16, U17, U18.

2013	IK Start	9	1	9	1
2013–14	Huddersfield T	0	0		
2014–15	Huddersfield T	0	0		

VAUGHAN, James (F) 166 47
H: 5 11 W: 13 00 b.Birmingham 14-7-88
Internationals: England U17, U19, U21.

2004–05	Everton	2	1		
2005–06	Everton	1	0		
2006–07	Everton	14	4		
2007–08	Everton	8	1		
2008–09	Everton	13	0		
2009–10	Everton	8	1		
2009–10	*Derby Co*	2	0	2	0
2010–11	Everton	1	0	47	7
2010–11	*Crystal Palace*	30	9	30	9
2011–12	Norwich C	5	0		
2012–13	Norwich C	0	0	5	0
2012–13	*Huddersfield T*	33	14		
2013–14	Huddersfield T	23	10		
2014–15	Huddersfield T	26	7	82	31

WALLACE, Murray (D) 68 5
H: 6 2 W: 11 07 b.Glasgow 10-1-93
Internationals: Scotland U20, U21.

2011–12	Falkirk	19	2	19	2
2011–12	Huddersfield T	0	0		
2012–13	Huddersfield T	6	1		
2013–14	Huddersfield T	17	0		
2014–15	Huddersfield T	26	2	49	3

WARD, Danny (M) 175 29
H: 5 11 W: 12 05 b.Bradford 11-12-91

2008–09	Bolton W	0	0		
2009–10	Bolton W	2	0		
2009–10	*Swindon T*	28	7	28	7
2010–11	Bolton W	0	0	2	0
2010–11	*Coventry C*	5	0	5	0
2010–11	*Huddersfield T*	7	3		
2011–12	Huddersfield T	39	4		
2012–13	Huddersfield T	28	2		
2013–14	Huddersfield T	38	10		
2014–15	Huddersfield T	12	0	124	19
2014–15	*Rotherham U*	16	3	16	3

WELLS, Nahki (F) 151 60
H: 5 7 W: 11 00 b.Bermuda 1-6-90
Internationals: Bermuda Full caps.

2010–11	Carlisle U	3	0	3	0
2011–12	Bradford C	33	10		
2012–13	Bradford C	39	18		
2013–14	Bradford C	19	14	91	42
2013–14	Huddersfield T	22	7		
2014–15	Huddersfield T	35	11	57	18

WILCZYNSKI, Ed (G) 0 0
H: 6 2 W: 12 08 b. 6-11-94

2013–14	Huddersfield T	0	0		
2014–15	Huddersfield T	0	0		

WILKINSON, Joe (D) 1 0
b. 2-11-95

2014–15	Huddersfield T	1	0	1	0

WRIGHT, Joe (D) 0 0
H: 6 4 W: 12 06 b. 26-2-95
Internationals: Wales U21.

2013–14	Huddersfield T	0	0		
2014–15	Huddersfield T	0	0		

Players retained or with offer of contract
Booty, Regan Jak; Bunn, Harry; Hanson, Jacob Luke; Kane, Danny; Pyke, Rekiel Leshaun; Ryan, Tadhg Ryan.

Scholars
Atkinson, Benjamin Louis; Boyle, Jack; Carroll, Bradley John; Cogill, Dylan Joseph; Horsfall, Fraser Matthew; Pells, Nathaniel William; Porritt, Adam Thomas; Rodgers, Sheiden Lee Tosh; Senior, Jack Christopher Senior; Spencer, Jamie William; Warde, Sam.

HULL C (40)

AIMSON, Will (D) 2 0
H: 5 10 W: 11 00 b.Christchurch 1-1-94

2013–14	Hull C	0	0		
2014–15	Hull C	0	0		
2014–15	*Tranmere R*	2	0	2	0

ALUKO, Sone (M) 189 32
H: 5 8 W: 9 10 b.Birmingham 19-2-89
Internationals: England U16, U17, U18, U19. Nigeria U20, Full caps.

2005–06	Birmingham C	0	0		
2006–07	Birmingham C	0	0		
2007–08	Birmingham C	0	0		
2007–08	*Aberdeen*	20	3		
2008–09	Birmingham C	0	0		
2008–09	*Blackpool*	1	0	1	0
2008–09	*Aberdeen*	14	0		
2009–10	Aberdeen	22	3		
2010–11	Aberdeen	28	2	102	10
2011–12	Rangers	21	12	21	12
2012–13	Hull C	23	8		
2013–14	Hull C	17	1		
2014–15	Hull C	25	1	65	10

BEN ARFA, Hatem (M) 243 38
H: 5 8 W: 10 08 b.Clamart 7-3-87
Internationals: France U16, U17, U18, U19, U21, Full caps.

2003–04	Lyon B	3	0		
2004–05	Lyon B	10	3		
2004–05	Lyon	1	0		
2005–06	Lyon B	12	0		
2005–06	Lyon	9	3		
2006–07	Lyon B	9	3	32	9
2006–07	Lyon	13	1		
2007–08	Lyon	30	6	64	7
2008–09	Marseille	33	6		
2009–10	Marseille	29	3		
2010–11	Marseille	1	0	63	9
2010–11	Newcastle U	4	1		
2011–12	Newcastle U	26	5		
2012–13	Newcastle U	19	4		
2013–14	Newcastle U	27	3	76	13
2014–15	Hull C	8	0	8	0

Transferred to Nice January 2015.

BOWEN, Jarrod (F) 0 0
b.Leominster 1-1-96

2014–15	Hull C	0	0		

BRADY, Robert (F) 114 10
H: 5 9 W: 10 12 b.Belfast 14-1-92
Internationals: Republic of Ireland Youth, U21, Full caps.

2008–09	Manchester U	0	0		
2009–10	Manchester U	0	0		
2010–11	Manchester U	0	0		
2011–12	Manchester U	0	0		
2011–12	*Hull C*	39	3		
2012–13	Manchester U	0	0		
2012–13	Hull C	32	4		
2013–14	Hull C	16	3		
2014–15	Hull C	27	0	114	10

BRUCE, Alex (D) 259 3
H: 6 0 W: 11 06 b.Norwich 28-9-84
Internationals: Republic of Ireland B, U21, Full caps. Northern Ireland Full caps.

2002–03	Blackburn R	0	0		
2003–04	Blackburn R	0	0		
2004–05	Blackburn R	0	0		
2004–05	*Oldham Ath*	12	0	12	0
2004–05	Birmingham C	0	0		
2004–05	*Sheffield W*	6	0	6	0
2005–06	Birmingham C	6	0	6	0
2005–06	*Tranmere R*	11	0	11	0
2006–07	Ipswich T	41	0		
2007–08	Ipswich T	36	0		
2008–09	Ipswich T	25	1		
2009–10	*Leicester C*	3	0	3	0
2010–11	Ipswich T	0	0	115	2
2011–12	Leeds U	21	1		
2011–12	Leeds U	8	0	29	1
2011–12	*Huddersfield T*	3	0	3	0
2012–13	Hull C	32	0		
2013–14	Hull C	20	0		
2014–15	Hull C	22	0	74	0

CHESTER, James (D) 182 9
H: 5 11 W: 11 04 b.Warrington 23-1-89
Internationals: Wales Full caps.

2007–08	Manchester U	0	0		
2008–09	Manchester U	0	0		
2008–09	*Peterborough U*	5	0	5	0
2009–10	Manchester U	0	0		
2009–10	*Plymouth Arg*	3	0	3	0
2010–11	Manchester U	0	0		
2010–11	*Carlisle U*	18	2	18	2
2010–11	Hull C	21	1		
2011–12	Hull C	44	2		
2012–13	Hull C	44	1		
2013–14	Hull C	24	1		
2014–15	Hull C	23	2	156	7

DAVIES, Curtis (D) 329 20
H: 6 2 W: 11 13 b.Waltham Forest 15-3-85
Internationals: England U21.

2003–04	Luton T	6	0		
2004–05	Luton T	44	1		
2005–06	Luton T	6	1	56	2
2005–06	WBA	33	2		
2006–07	WBA	32	0		
2007–08	WBA	0	0	65	2
2007–08	Aston Villa	12	1		
2008–09	Aston Villa	35	1		
2009–10	Aston Villa	2	1		
2010–11	Aston Villa	0	0	49	3
2010–11	*Leicester C*	12	0	12	0
2010–11	Birmingham C	6	0		
2011–12	Birmingham C	42	5		
2012–13	Birmingham C	41	6	89	11
2013–14	Hull C	37	2		
2014–15	Hull C	21	0	58	2

DAWSON, Michael (D) 347 15
H: 6 2 W: 12 02 b.Leyburn 18-11-83
Internationals: England U21, B, Full caps.

2000–01	Nottingham F	0	0		
2001–02	Nottingham F	1	0		
2002–03	Nottingham F	38	5		
2003–04	Nottingham F	30	1		
2004–05	Nottingham F	14	1	83	7
2004–05	Tottenham H	5	0		

2005–06	Tottenham H	32	0		
2006–07	Tottenham H	37	1		
2007–08	Tottenham H	27	1		
2008–09	Tottenham H	16	1		
2009–10	Tottenham H	29	2		
2010–11	Tottenham H	24	1		
2011–12	Tottenham H	7	0		
2012–13	Tottenham H	27	1		
2013–14	Tottenham H	32	0	236	3
2014–15	Hull C	28	1	28	1

DIAME, Mohamed (M)   245 19
H: 6 1 W: 11 02 b.Creteil 14-6-87
Internationals: Senegal U23, Full caps.

2006–07	Lens	0	0		
2007–08	Linares	31	1	31	1
2008–09	Rayo Vallecano	35	2	35	2
2009–10	Wigan Ath	34	1		
2010–11	Wigan Ath	36	1		
2011–12	Wigan Ath	26	3	96	5
2012–13	West Ham U	33	3		
2013–14	West Ham U	35	4		
2014–15	West Ham U	3	0	71	7
2014–15	Hull C	12	4	12	4

DUDGEON, Joe (D)   49 0
H: 5 9 W: 11 02 b.Leeds 26-11-90
Internationals: Northern Ireland U21.

2009–10	Manchester U	0	0		
2010–11	Manchester U	0	0		
2010–11	Carlisle U	2	0	2	0
2011–12	Hull C	24	0		
2012–13	Hull C	9	0		
2013–14	Hull C	0	0		
2014–15	Hull C	0	0	33	0
2014–15	Barnsley	14	0	14	0

ELMOHAMADY, Ahmed (M)   248 22
H: 5 11 W: 12 10 b.El Mahalla El-Kubra
9-9-87
Internationals: Egypt Full caps.

2003–04	Ghazi Al-Mehalla	0	0		
2004–05	Ghazi Al-Mehalla	14	4		
2005–06	Ghazi Al-Mehalla	3	0	17	4
2006–07	ENPPI	12	2		
2007–08	ENPPI	6	1		
2008–09	ENPPI	28	6		
2009–10	ENPPI	12	1	58	10
2010–11	Sunderland	36	0		
2011–12	Sunderland	18	1		
2012–13	Sunderland	2	0	56	1
2012–13	*Hull C*	41	3		
2013–14	*Hull C*	38	2		
2014–15	*Hull C*	38	2	117	7

FIGUEROA, Maynor (D)   244 6
H: 5 11 W: 12 02 b.Jutiapa 2-5-83
Internationals: Honduras U20, U23, Full caps.

2000–01	Victoria La Ceiba	2	0		
2001–02	Victoria La Ceiba	22	2	24	2
2007–08	Wigan Ath	2	0		
2008–09	Wigan Ath	38	1		
2009–10	Wigan Ath	35	1		
2010–11	Wigan Ath	33	1		
2011–12	Wigan Ath	38	0		
2012–13	Wigan Ath	33	1		
2013–14	Wigan Ath	0	0		
2013–14	Hull C	32	0		
2014–15	Hull C	3	0	35	0
2014–15	*Wigan Ath*	6	0	185	4

HARPER, Steve (G)   225 0
H: 6 2 W: 13 10 b.Easington 14-3-75

1993–94	Newcastle U	0	0		
1994–95	Newcastle U	0	0		
1995–96	Newcastle U	0	0		
1995–96	*Bradford C*	1	0	1	0
1996–97	Newcastle U	0	0		
1996–97	*Stockport Co*	0	0		
1997–98	Newcastle U	0	0		
1997–98	*Hartlepool U*	15	0	15	0
1997–98	*Huddersfield T*	24	0	24	0
1998–99	Newcastle U	8	0		
1999–2000	Newcastle U	18	0		
2000–01	Newcastle U	5	0		
2001–02	Newcastle U	0	0		
2002–03	Newcastle U	0	0		
2003–04	Newcastle U	0	0		
2004–05	Newcastle U	2	0		
2005–06	Newcastle U	0	0		
2006–07	Newcastle U	18	0		
2007–08	Newcastle U	21	0		
2008–09	Newcastle U	16	0		
2009–10	Newcastle U	45	0		
2010–11	Newcastle U	0	0		
2011–12	*Brighton & HA*	5	0	5	0
2012–13	Newcastle U	6	0	157	0

2013–14	Hull C	13	0		
2014–15	Hull C	10	0	23	0

HERNANDEZ, Abel (F)   174 47
H: 6 1 W: 11 00 b.Pando Canelones 8-8-90
Internationals: Uruguay U20, U23, Full caps.

2006–07	Central Espanol	6	0		
2007–08	Central Espanol	24	9	30	9
2008–09	Penarol	8	3	8	3
2008–09	Palermo	6	0		
2009–10	Palermo	21	7		
2010–11	Palermo	22	3		
2011–12	Palermo	20	6		
2012–13	Palermo	14	1		
2013–14	Palermo	28	14	111	31
2014–15	Hull C	25	4	25	4

HUDDLESTONE, Tom (M)   312 12
H: 6 2 W: 11 02 b.Nottingham 28-12-86
Internationals: England U16, U17, U19, U20,
U21, Full caps.

2003–04	Derby Co	43	0		
2004–05	Derby Co	45	0	88	0
2005–06	Tottenham H	4	0		
2005–06	*Wolverhampton W*	13	1	13	1
2006–07	Tottenham H	21	1		
2007–08	Tottenham H	28	3		
2008–09	Tottenham H	22	0		
2009–10	Tottenham H	33	2		
2010–11	Tottenham H	14	2		
2011–12	Tottenham H	2	0		
2012–13	Tottenham H	20	0		
2013–14	Tottenham H	0	0	144	8
2013–14	Hull C	36	3		
2014–15	Hull C	31	0	67	3

INCE, Tom (M)   106 37
H: 5 10 W: 10 06 b.Stockport 30-1-92
Internationals: England U17, U19, U21.

2011–12	Blackpool	0	0		
2012–13	Blackpool	44	18		
2013–14	Blackpool	23	7	67	25
2013–14	*Crystal Palace*	8	1	8	1
2014–15	Hull C	7	0	7	0
2014–15	*Nottingham F*	6	0	6	0
2014–15	*Derby Co*	18	11	18	11

JAHRALDO-MARTIN, Calaum (F)   2 0
H: b.St Johns 27-4-93
Internationals: Antigua and Barbuda U20,
Full caps.

2013–14	Hull C	0	0		
2014–15	Hull C	0	0		
2014–15	*Tranmere R*	2	0	2	0

JAKUPOVIC, Eldin (G)   135 1
H: 6 3 W: 13 00 b.Kozarac 2-10-84
Internationals: Bosnia & Herzegovina U21,
Switzerland U21, Full caps.

2004–05	Grasshoppers	8	0		
2005–06	FC Thun	23	0	23	0
2007–08	Grasshoppers	23	1		
2008–09	Grasshoppers	32	0	63	1
2010–11	Olympiacos Volou	26	0	26	0
2011–12	Aris Salonika	1	0	1	0
2012–13	Hull C	5	0		
2013–14	Hull C	1	0		
2013–14	*Leyton Orient*	13	0	13	0
2014–15	Hull C	3	0	9	0

JELAVIC, Nikica (F)   274 91
H: 6 2 W: 13 12 b.Capljina 27-8-85
Internationals: Croatia U17, U18, Full caps.

2002–03	Hajduk Split	2	0		
2003–04	Hajduk Split	2	0		
2004–05	Hajduk Split	0	0		
2005–06	Hajduk Split	9	0		
2006–07	Hajduk Split	22	5	35	5
2007–08	Waregem	23	3	23	3
2008–09	Rapid Vienna	34	7		
2009–10	Rapid Vienna	33	17		
2010–11	Rapid Vienna	3	1	70	25
2010–11	Rangers	23	16		
2011–12	Rangers	22	14	45	30
2011–12	Everton	13	9		
2012–13	Everton	37	7		
2013–14	Everton	9	0	59	16
2013–14	Hull C	16	4		
2014–15	Hull C	26	8	42	12

LENIHAN, Brian (D)   29 0
H: 5 10 W: 12 00 b.Cork 8-6-94
Internationals: Republic of Ireland U21.

2012	Cork C	3	0		
2013	Cork C	3	0		
2014	Cork C	21	0	27	0
2014–15	Hull C	0	0		
2014–15	*Blackpool*	2	0	2	0

LIVERMORE, Jake (M)   154 6
H: 5 9 W: 12 08 b.Enfield 14-11-89
Internationals: England Full caps.

2006–07	Tottenham H	0	0		
2007–08	Tottenham H	0	0		
2007–08	*Milton Keynes D*	5	0	5	0
2008–09	Tottenham H	0	0		
2008–09	*Crewe Alex*	0	0		
2009–10	Tottenham H	1	0		
2009–10	*Derby Co*	16	1	16	1
2009–10	*Peterborough U*	9	1	9	1
2010–11	Tottenham H	0	0		
2010–11	*Ipswich T*	12	0	12	0
2010–11	*Leeds U*	5	0	5	0
2011–12	Tottenham H	24	0		
2012–13	Tottenham H	11	0		
2013–14	Tottenham H	0	0	36	0
2013–14	*Hull C*	36	3		
2014–15	Hull C	35	1	71	4

LUER, Greg (F)   2 0
H: 5 11 W: 11 07 b.Brighton 6-12-94

2014–15	Hull C	0	0		
2014–15	*Port Vale*	2	0	2	0

MAGUIRE, Harry (D)   153 10
H: 6 2 W: 12 06 b.Mosborough 5-3-93
Internationals: England U21.

2010–11	Sheffield U	5	0		
2011–12	Sheffield U	44	1		
2012–13	Sheffield U	44	3		
2013–14	Sheffield U	41	5	134	9
2014–15	Hull C	0	0	3	0
2014–15	*Wigan Ath*	16	1	16	1

MARGETTS, Jonathon (F)   1 0
b.Edenthorpe 28-9-93

2014–15	Hull C	0	0		
2014–15	*Cambridge U*	1	0	1	0

McGREGOR, Allan (G)   310 0
H: 6 0 W: 11 08 b.Edinburgh 31-1-82
Internationals: Scotland U21, B, Full caps.

1998–99	Rangers	0	0		
1999–2000	Rangers	0	0		
2000–01	Rangers	0	0		
2001–02	Rangers	2	0		
2002–03	Rangers	0	0		
2003–04	Rangers	4	0		
2004–05	Rangers	2	0		
2005–06	Rangers	0	0		
2005–06	*Dunfermline Ath*	26	0	26	0
2006–07	Rangers	31	0		
2007–08	Rangers	31	0		
2008–09	Rangers	27	0		
2009–10	Rangers	34	0		
2010–11	Rangers	37	0		
2011–12	Rangers	37	0	205	0
2012–13	Besiktas	27	0	27	0
2013–14	Hull C	26	0		
2014–15	Hull C	26	0	52	0

McSHANE, Paul (D)   238 11
H: 6 0 W: 11 05 b.Wicklow 6-1-86
Internationals: Republic of Ireland U21, Full
caps.

2002–03	Manchester U	0	0		
2003–04	Manchester U	0	0		
2004–05	Manchester U	0	0		
2004–05	*Walsall*	4	1	4	1
2005–06	Manchester U	0	0		
2005–06	*Brighton & HA*	38	3	38	3
2006–07	WBA	32	2	32	2
2007–08	Sunderland	21	0		
2008–09	Sunderland	3	0		
2008–09	*Hull C*	17	1		
2009–10	Sunderland	0	0	24	0
2009–10	Hull C	27	0		
2010–11	Hull C	19	0		
2010–11	*Barnsley*	10	1	10	1
2011–12	Hull C	0	0		
2011–12	*Crystal Palace*	10	0	11	0
2012–13	Hull C	25	2		
2013–14	Hull C	10	0		
2014–15	Hull C	20	1	119	4

MEYLER, David (M)   113 8
H: 6 3 W: 11 09 b.Cork 29-5-89
Internationals: Republic of Ireland U21, Full
caps.

2008	Cork C	2	0	2	0
2008–09	Sunderland	0	0		
2009–10	Sunderland	10	0		
2010–11	Sunderland	5	0		
2011–12	Sunderland	7	0		
2012–13	Sunderland	3	0	25	0
2012–13	*Hull C*	28	5		
2013–14	*Hull C*	30	2		
2014–15	*Hull C*	28	1	86	8

N'DOYE, Dame (F)   271 116
H: 6 1   b.Thies 21-2-85
Internationals: Senegal Full caps.

2005–06	Al-Sadd	27	12	**27 12**
2006–07	Academica Coimbra	25	4	**25 4**
2007–08	Panathaniakos	19	2	**19 2**
2008–09	Irakliou	15	7	**15 7**
2008–09	Copenhagen	11	2	
2009–10	Copenhagen	32	14	
2010–11	Copenhagen	31	25	
2011–12	Copenhagen	30	18	**104 59**
2012–13	Lokomotiv Moscow	25	10	
2013–14	Lokomotiv Moscow	27	13	
2014–15	Lokomotiv Moscow	14	4	**66 27**
2014–15	Hull C	15	5	**15 5**

OXLEY, Mark (G)   78 1
H: 5 11   W: 12 05   b.Aston 2-6-90
Internationals: England U18, U20.

2008–09	Hull C	0	0	
2009–10	Hull C	0	0	
2009–10	*Grimsby T*	3	0	**3 0**
2010–11	Hull C	0	0	
2011–12	Hull C	0	0	
2012–13	Hull C	1	0	
2012–13	*Burton Alb*	3	0	**3 0**
2013–14	Hull C	0	0	
2013–14	*Oldham Ath*	36	0	**36 0**
2014–15	Hull C	0	0	**1 0**
2014–15	*Hibernian*	35	1	**35 1**

QUINN, Stephen (M)   322 24
H: 5 6   W: 9 08   b.Dublin 4-4-86
Internationals: Republic of Ireland U21, Full caps.

2005–06	Sheffield U	0	0	
2005–06	*Milton Keynes D*	15	0	**15 0**
2005–06	*Rotherham U*	16	0	**16 0**
2006–07	Sheffield U	15	2	
2007–08	Sheffield U	19	2	
2008–09	Sheffield U	43	7	
2009–10	Sheffield U	44	4	
2010–11	Sheffield U	37	1	
2011–12	Sheffield U	45	4	
2012–13	Sheffield U	3	0	**206 20**
2012–13	Hull C	42	3	
2013–14	Hull C	15	0	
2014–15	Hull C	28	1	**85 4**

ROBERTSON, Andrew (D)   94 5
H: 5 10   W: 10 00   b.Glasgow 11-3-94
Internationals: Scotland U21, Full caps.

2012–13	Queen's Park	34	2	**34 2**
2013–14	Dundee U	36	3	**36 3**
2014–15	Hull C	24	0	**24 0**

ROSENIOR, Liam (D)   348 15
H: 5 10   W: 11 05   b.Wandsworth 9-7-84
Internationals: England U20, U21.

2001–02	Bristol C	1	0	
2002–03	Bristol C	21	2	
2003–04	Bristol C	0	0	**22 2**
2003–04	Fulham	0	0	
2003–04	*Torquay U*	10	0	**10 0**
2004–05	Fulham	17	0	
2005–06	Fulham	24	0	
2006–07	Fulham	38	0	
2007–08	Fulham	0	0	**79 0**
2007–08	Reading	17	0	
2008–09	Reading	42	0	
2009–10	Reading	5	0	
2009–10	*Ipswich T*	29	1	**29 1**
2010–11	Reading	0	0	**64 0**
2010–11	Hull C	26	0	
2011–12	Hull C	44	0	
2012–13	Hull C	32	0	
2013–14	Hull C	29	1	
2014–15	Hull C	13	0	**144 1**

SAGBO, Yannick (F)   154 27
H: 6 0   W: 12 03   b.Marseille 12-7-88
Internationals: Ivory Coast U23, Full caps.

2008–09	Monaco	5	0	
2009–10	Monaco	14	0	
2010–11	Monaco	1	0	**20 0**
2010–11	Evian TG	30	9	
2011–12	Evian TG	33	10	
2012–13	Evian TG	35	6	**98 25**
2013–14	Hull C	28	2	
2014–15	Hull C	4	0	**32 2**
2014–15	*Wolverhampton W*	4	0	**4 0**

SNODGRASS, Robert (M)   327 67
H: 6 0 `   W: 12 02   b.Glasgow 7-9-87
Internationals: Scotland U20, U21, Full caps.

2003–04	Livingston	3	0	
2004–05	Livingston	17	2	
2005–06	Livingston	27	4	
2006–07	Livingston	6	0	
2006–07	*Stirling Alb*	12	5	**12 5**
2007–08	Livingston	31	9	**81 15**
2008–09	Leeds U	42	9	
2009–10	Leeds U	44	7	
2010–11	Leeds U	37	6	
2011–12	Leeds U	43	13	**166 35**
2012–13	Norwich C	37	6	
2013–14	Norwich C	30	6	**67 12**
2014–15	Hull C	1	0	**1 0**

TOWNSEND, Conor (D)   55 1
H: 5 4   W: 9 11   b.Hessle 4-3-93

2011–12	Hull C	0	0	
2012–13	Hull C	0	0	
2012–13	*Chesterfield*	20	1	**20 1**
2013–14	Hull C	0	0	
2013–14	*Carlisle U*	12	0	**12 0**
2014–15	Hull C	0	0	
2014–15	*Dundee U*	17	0	**17 0**
2014–15	*Scunthorpe U*	6	0	**6 0**

WATSON, Rory (G)   0 0
b. 5-2-96

2014–15	Hull C	0	0	

Players retained or with offer of contract
Bukran, Erik; Clappison, Benjamin Lewis; Clark, Max Oliver; Dixon, Matthew; Ter Horst, Johan.

Scholars
Annan, William John; Barkworth, Ellis; Batty, Daniel Thomas; Clackstone, Joshua Philip; Hinchliffe, Benjamin Jack; Hinchliffe, Matthew James; Langton, Mitchell Jay; Lofts, Luke; Rodgers, Harvey.

IPSWICH T (41)

AMBROSE, Darren (M)   322 61
H: 6 0   W: 11 00   b.Harlow 29-2-84
Internationals: England U21.

2001–02	Ipswich T	1	0	
2002–03	Ipswich T	29	8	
2002–03	Newcastle U	1	0	
2003–04	Newcastle U	24	2	
2004–05	Newcastle U	12	3	**37 5**
2005–06	Charlton Ath	28	3	
2006–07	Charlton Ath	26	3	
2007–08	Charlton Ath	37	7	
2008–09	Charlton Ath	21	0	**112 13**
2008–09	*Ipswich T*	9	0	
2009–10	Crystal Palace	46	15	
2010–11	Crystal Palace	28	7	
2011–12	Crystal Palace	36	7	**110 29**
2012–13	Birmingham C	6	0	
2013–14	Birmingham C	1	0	**7 0**
2013–14	*Apollon Smyrni*	11	6	**11 6**
2014–15	Ipswich T	6	0	**45 8**

ANDERSON, Paul (M)   242 25
H: 5 9   W: 10 04   b.Leicester 23-7-88
Internationals: England U19.

2005–06	Hull C	0	0	
2005–06	Liverpool	0	0	
2006–07	Liverpool	0	0	
2007–08	Liverpool	0	0	
2007–08	*Swansea C*	31	7	**31 7**
2008–09	Liverpool	0	0	
2008–09	*Nottingham F*	26	2	
2009–10	Nottingham F	37	4	
2010–11	Nottingham F	36	3	
2011–12	Nottingham F	17	0	
2012–13	Nottingham F	0	0	**116 9**
2012–13	Bristol C	29	3	**29 3**
2013–14	Ipswich T	31	5	
2014–15	Ipswich T	35	1	**66 6**

BENYU, Kundai (M)   0 0
b. 12-12-97

2014–15	Ipswich T	0	0	

BERRA, Christophe (D)   351 15
H: 6 1   W: 12 10   b.Edinburgh 31-1-85
Internationals: Scotland U21, B, Full caps.

2003–04	Hearts	6	0	
2004–05	Hearts	12	0	
2005–06	Hearts	12	1	
2006–07	Hearts	35	1	
2007–08	Hearts	35	2	
2008–09	Hearts	23	0	**123 4**
2008–09	Wolverhampton W	15	0	
2009–10	Wolverhampton W	32	0	
2010–11	Wolverhampton W	32	0	
2011–12	Wolverhampton W	32	0	
2012–13	Wolverhampton W	30	0	**141 0**
2013–14	Ipswich T	42	5	
2014–15	Ipswich T	46	5	**87 11**

BIALKOWSKI, Bartosz (G)   146 0
H: 6 3   W: 12 10   b.Braniewo 6-7-87
Internationals: Poland U20, U21.

2004–05	Gornik Zabrze	7	0	**7 0**
2005–06	Southampton	5	0	
2006–07	Southampton	8	0	
2007–08	Southampton	1	0	
2008–09	Southampton	0	0	
2009–10	Southampton	7	0	
2009–10	*Barnsley*	2	0	**2 0**
2010–11	Southampton	0	0	
2011–12	Southampton	1	0	**22 0**
2012–13	Notts Co	40	0	
2013–14	Notts Co	44	0	**84 0**
2014–15	Ipswich T	31	0	**31 0**

BISHOP, Teddy (M)   33 1
H: 5 11   W: 10 03   b. 15-7-96

2013–14	Ipswich T	0	0	
2014–15	Ipswich T	33	1	**33 1**

BRU, Kevin (M)   172 10
H: 6 0   W: 11 05   b. 12-12-88
Internationals: France U19. Mauritius Full caps.

2006–07	Rennes	2	0	**2 0**
2007–08	Chatearoux	10	0	**10 0**
2008–09	Clermont Foot Avergne	25	2	**25 2**
2009–10	Dijon	14	2	
2010–11	Dijon	11	0	**25 2**
2010–11	Bologne	9	0	
2011–12	Bologne	19	2	**28 2**
2012–13	Istres	31	2	**31 2**
2013–14	Levski Sofia	20	1	**20 1**
2014–15	Ipswich T	31	1	**31 1**

CHAMBERS, Luke (D)   464 25
H: 6 1   W: 11 13   b.Kettering 29-8-85

2002–03	Northampton T	1	0	
2003–04	Northampton T	24	0	
2004–05	Northampton T	27	0	
2005–06	Northampton T	43	0	
2006–07	Northampton T	29	1	**124 1**
2006–07	Nottingham F	14	0	
2007–08	Nottingham F	42	6	
2008–09	Nottingham F	39	2	
2009–10	Nottingham F	23	3	
2010–11	Nottingham F	44	6	
2011–12	Nottingham F	43	0	**205 17**
2012–13	Ipswich T	44	3	
2013–14	Ipswich T	46	3	
2014–15	Ipswich T	45	1	**135 7**

CLARKE, Matthew (M)   4 0
H: 5 11   W: 11 00   b.Ipswich 22-9-96

2013–14	Ipswich T	0	0	
2014–15	Ipswich T	4	0	**4 0**

CONNOLLY, Dylan (F)   0 0
H: 5 9   W: 10 12   b.Dublin 2-5-95
Internationals: Republic of Ireland U21.

2014–15	Ipswich T	0	0	

GERKEN, Dean (G)   226 0
H: 6 3   W: 12 08   b.Southend 22-5-85

2003–04	Colchester U	1	0	
2004–05	Colchester U	13	0	
2005–06	Colchester U	7	0	
2006–07	Colchester U	27	0	
2007–08	Colchester U	40	0	
2008–09	Colchester U	21	0	**109 0**
2008–09	*Darlington*	7	0	**7 0**
2009–10	Bristol C	39	0	
2010–11	Bristol C	1	0	
2011–12	Bristol C	10	0	
2012–13	Bristol C	3	0	**53 0**
2013–14	Ipswich T	41	0	
2014–15	Ipswich T	16	0	**57 0**

HAMMOND, Kyle (D)   0 0
b. 29-9-95

2013–14	Ipswich T	0	0	
2014–15	Ipswich T	0	0	

HENSHALL, Alex (M)   15 1
H: 5 10   b.Swindon 15-2-94
Internationals: England U16, U17.

2010–11	Manchester C	0	0	
2011–12	Manchester C	0	0	
2012–13	Manchester C	0	0	
2012–13	*Chesterfield*	7	0	**7 0**
2013–14	Manchester C	0	0	
2013–14	*Bristol R*	2	1	**2 1**
2013–14	Ipswich T	0	0	
2014–15	Ipswich T	4	0	**4 0**
2014–15	*Blackpool*	2	0	**2 0**

HEWITT, Elliott (D) 77 1
H: 5 11 W: 11 10 b.Rhyl 30-5-94
Internationals: Wales U17, U21.

Season	Club				
2010–11	Macclesfield T	1	0		
2011–12	Macclesfield T	21	0	22	0
2012–13	Ipswich T	7	0		
2013–14	Ipswich T	4	0		
2013–14	Gillingham	20	0	20	0
2014–15	Ipswich T	3	0	14	0
2014–15	Colchester U	21	1	21	1

HUNT, Steve (M) 418 55
H: 5 9 W: 10 10 b.Port Laoise 1-8-80
Internationals: Republic of Ireland U21, B, Full caps.

Season	Club				
1999–2000	Crystal Palace	3	0		
2000–01	Crystal Palace	0	0	3	0
2001–02	Brentford	35	4		
2002–03	Brentford	42	7		
2003–04	Brentford	40	11		
2004–05	Brentford	19	3	136	25
2005–06	Reading	38	2		
2006–07	Reading	35	4		
2007–08	Reading	37	5		
2008–09	Reading	46	6		
2009–10	Reading	0	0	156	17
2009–10	Hull C	27	6	27	6
2010–11	Wolverhampton W	20	3		
2011–12	Wolverhampton W	24	3		
2012–13	Wolverhampton W	12	1	56	7
2013–14	Ipswich T	23	0		
2014–15	Ipswich T	17	0	40	0

HYAM, Luke (M) 99 3
H: 5 10 W: 11 05 b.Ipswich 24-10-91

Season	Club				
2010–11	Ipswich T	10	0		
2011–12	Ipswich T	8	0		
2012–13	Ipswich T	30	1		
2013–14	Ipswich T	35	1		
2014–15	Ipswich T	16	1	99	3

KENNY, Paddy (G) 567 0
H: 6 1 W: 14 01 b.Halifax 17-5-78
Internationals: Republic of Ireland Full caps.

Season	Club				
1998–99	Bury	0	0		
1999–2000	Bury	46	0		
2000–01	Bury	46	0		
2001–02	Bury	41	0		
2002–03	Bury	0	0	133	0
2002–03	Sheffield U	45	0		
2003–04	Sheffield U	27	0		
2004–05	Sheffield U	40	0		
2005–06	Sheffield U	46	0		
2006–07	Sheffield U	34	0		
2007–08	Sheffield U	40	0		
2008–09	Sheffield U	46	0		
2009–10	Sheffield U	2	0	278	0
2010–11	QPR	44	0		
2011–12	QPR	33	0	77	0
2012–13	Leeds U	46	0		
2013–14	Leeds U	30	0	76	0
2014–15	Bolton W	0	0		
2014–15	Oldham Ath	3	0	3	0
2014–15	Ipswich T	0	0		

MARRIOTT, Jack (F) 12 1
H: 5 8 W: 11 03 b.Beverley 9-9-94

Season	Club				
2012–13	Ipswich T	1	0		
2013–14	Ipswich T	1	0		
2013–14	Gillingham	1	0	1	0
2014–15	Ipswich T	0	0	2	0
2014–15	Carlisle U	4	0	4	0
2014–15	Colchester U	5	1	5	1

McGOLDRICK, David (F) 262 70
H: 6 1 W: 11 10 b.Nottingham 29-11-87
Internationals: Republic of Ireland Full caps.

Season	Club				
2003–04	Notts Co	4	0		
2004–05	Notts Co	0	0		
2005–06	Southampton	0	0		
2005–06	Notts Co	6	0	10	0
2006–07	Southampton	0	0		
2006–07	Bournemouth	12	6	12	6
2007–08	Southampton	8	0		
2007–08	Port Vale	17	2	17	2
2008–09	Southampton	46	12	64	12
2009–10	Nottingham F	33	3		
2010–11	Nottingham F	21	5		
2011–12	Nottingham F	9	0		
2011–12	Sheffield W	4	1	4	1
2012–13	Nottingham F	0	0	63	8
2012–13	Coventry C	22	16	22	16
2012–13	Ipswich T	13	4		
2013–14	Ipswich T	31	14		
2014–15	Ipswich T	26	7	70	25

McQUEEN, Darren (F) 0 0
H: 5 9 W: 11 00 b.Leytonstone 8-5-95

Season	Club		
2014–15	Ipswich T	0	0

MINGS, Tyrone (D) 57 1
H: 6 3 W: 12 00 b.Bath 19-3-93

Season	Club				
2012–13	Ipswich T	1	0		
2013–14	Ipswich T	16	0		
2014–15	Ipswich T	40	1	57	1

MURPHY, Daryl (F) 312 74
H: 6 2 W: 13 12 b.Waterford 15-3-83
Internationals: Republic of Ireland U21, Full caps.

Season	Club				
2000–01	Luton T	0	0		
2001–02	Luton T	0	0		
2005–06	Sunderland	18	1		
2005–06	Sheffield W	4	0	4	0
2006–07	Sunderland	38	10		
2007–08	Sunderland	28	3		
2008–09	Sunderland	23	0		
2009–10	Sunderland	3	0	110	14
2009–10	Ipswich T	18	6		
2010–11	Celtic	18	3		
2011–12	Ipswich T	33	4		
2012–13	Celtic	1	0	19	3
On loan from Celtic					
2012–13	Ipswich T	39	7		
2013–14	Ipswich T	45	13		
2014–15	Ipswich T	44	27	179	57

PARR, Jonathan (M) 244 12
H: 6 0 W: 11 11 b.Oslo 21-10-88
Internationals: Norway U17, U19, U21, Full caps.

Season	Club				
2006	Lyn	11	0	11	0
2007	Aalesund	19	1		
2008	Aalesund	24	4		
2009	Aalesund	27	2		
2010	Aalesund	25	0		
2011	Aalesund	15	1	110	8
2011–12	Crystal Palace	39	2		
2012–13	Crystal Palace	38	0		
2013–14	Crystal Palace	15	0	92	2
2014–15	Ipswich T	31	2	31	2

SEARS, Freddie (F) 206 42
H: 5 8 W: 10 01 b.Hornchurch 27-11-89
Internationals: England U19, U20, U21.

Season	Club				
2007–08	West Ham U	7	1		
2008–09	West Ham U	17	0		
2009–10	West Ham U	1	0		
2009–10	Crystal Palace	18	0	18	0
2009–10	Coventry C	10	0	10	0
2010–11	West Ham U	11	1		
2010–11	Scunthorpe U	9	0	9	0
2011–12	West Ham U	10	0	46	2
2011–12	Colchester U	11	2		
2012–13	Colchester U	35	7		
2013–14	Colchester U	32	12		
2014–15	Colchester U	24	10	102	31
2014–15	Ipswich T	21	9	21	9

SKUSE, Cole (M) 362 10
H: 6 1 W: 11 05 b.Bristol 29-3-86

Season	Club				
2004–05	Bristol C	7	0		
2005–06	Bristol C	38	2		
2006–07	Bristol C	42	0		
2007–08	Bristol C	25	0		
2008–09	Bristol C	33	2		
2009–10	Bristol C	43	2		
2010–11	Bristol C	30	1		
2011–12	Bristol C	36	2		
2012–13	Bristol C	25	0	279	9
2013–14	Ipswich T	43	0		
2014–15	Ipswich T	40	1	83	1

SMITH, Tommy (D) 203 19
H: 6 2 W: 12 02 b.Macclesfield 31-3-90
Internationals: England U17, U18. New Zealand Full caps.

Season	Club				
2007–08	Ipswich T	0	0		
2008–09	Ipswich T	2	0		
2009–10	Ipswich T	14	0		
2009–10	Brentford	8	0	8	0
2010–11	Ipswich T	22	3		
2010–11	Colchester U	6	0	6	0
2011–12	Ipswich T	26	3		
2012–13	Ipswich T	38	3		
2013–14	Ipswich T	45	6		
2014–15	Ipswich T	42	4	189	19

STEWART, Cameron (M) 101 4
H: 5 8 W: 11 05 b.Manchester 8-4-91
Internationals: England U17, U19, U20.

Season	Club				
2009–10	Manchester U	0	0		
2010–11	Manchester U	0	0		
2010–11	Yeovil T	5	0	5	0
2010–11	Hull C	14	0		
2011–12	Hull C	31	1		
2012–13	Hull C	2	0		
2012–13	Burnley	9	0	9	0
2012–13	Blackburn R	7	0	7	0
2013–14	Hull C	0	0	47	1
2013–14	Charlton Ath	18	3	18	3
2013–14	Leeds U	11	0	11	0
2014–15	Ipswich T	0	0		
2014–15	Barnsley	4	0	4	0

TABB, Jay (M) 388 35
H: 5 7 W: 10 00 b.Tooting 21-2-84
Internationals: Republic of Ireland U21.

Season	Club				
2000–01	Brentford	2	0		
2001–02	Brentford	3	0		
2002–03	Brentford	5	0		
2003–04	Brentford	36	9		
2004–05	Brentford	40	5		
2005–06	Brentford	42	6	128	20
2006–07	Coventry C	31	3		
2007–08	Coventry C	42	5		
2008–09	Coventry C	22	3	95	11
2008–09	Reading	9	0		
2009–10	Reading	28	0		
2010–11	Reading	21	0		
2011–12	Reading	19	0		
2012–13	Reading	12	0	89	0
2012–13	Ipswich T	9	1		
2013–14	Ipswich T	27	1		
2014–15	Ipswich T	40	2	76	4

TAYLOR, Paul (F) 110 13
H: 5 11 W: 11 02 b.Liverpool 4-11-87

Season	Club				
2008–09	Chester C	9	0	9	0
2009–10	Montegnee	1	0	1	0
2009–10	Charleoi	3	0	3	0
2010–11	Anderlecht	0	0		
2010–11	Peterborough U	1	0		
2011–12	Peterborough U	44	12		
2012–13	Peterborough U	3	0		
2012–13	Ipswich T	3	0		
2013–14	Ipswich T	18	1		
2013–14	Peterborough U	6	0	54	12
2014–15	Ipswich T	0	0	21	1
2014–15	Rotherham U	17	0	17	0
2014–15	Blackburn R	5	0	5	0

WORDSWORTH, Anthony (M) 219 42
H: 6 1 W: 12 00 b.Camden 3-1-89

Season	Club				
2007–08	Colchester U	3	0		
2008–09	Colchester U	30	3		
2009–10	Colchester U	41	11		
2010–11	Colchester U	35	5		
2011–12	Colchester U	44	13		
2012–13	Colchester U	24	3	177	35
2012–13	Ipswich T	7	1		
2013–14	Ipswich T	10	1		
2014–15	Ipswich T	1	0	18	2
2014–15	Rotherham U	6	1	6	1
2014–15	Crawley T	18	4	18	4

WYATT, Ben (D) 0 0
H: 5 8 W: 10 01 b.Norwich 4-2-96

Season	Club		
2014–15	Ipswich T	0	0

Players retained or with offer of contract
Crowe, Michael Thomas Tallaksen; Guldbrandsen, Neils Victor.

Scholars
Blanchfield, James Elliott; Cole, Travis Sol; Daly, Harry David; Ellis, Edward William Colin; Emmanuel, Joshua Oluwadurotimi; Ford, Samuel George; Fowler, George Ryan; George-Kenlock, Myles Lewis; Ingram, Nicholas Ever Terry; Jones, Ronaldo Patrick; Marsden, Jacob Anthony; McDermid, Samuel David; McLoughlin, Shane Daniel; Patterson, Monty Mark; Ramadan, Cemal; Robinson, Joe Alan; Smith, Chris; Walton-Owen, Amon Jesse Enos; Willbye, Jack Thomas.

LEEDS U (42)

ADRYAN, Tavares (M) 54 2
H: 5 8 W: 10 01 b.Rio de Janeiro 8-10-94
Internationals: Brazil U17, U20.

Season	Club				
2012	Flamengo	23	2		
2013	Flamengo	14	0		
2013–14	Cagliari	5	0	5	0
2014	Flamengo	0	0	37	2
On loan from Flamengo					
2014–15	Leeds U	12	0	12	0

AJOSE, Nicholas (F) 155 41
H: 5 8 W: 11 00 b.Bury 7-10-91
Internationals: England U16, U17. Nigeria U20.

Season	Club		
2009–10	Manchester U	0	0
2010–11	Manchester U	0	0
2010–11	Bury	28	13

2011–12	Peterborough U	2	0		
2011–12	*Scunthorpe U*	7	0	**7**	**0**
2011–12	*Chesterfield*	12	1	**12**	**1**
2012–13	*Crawley T*	19	2	**19**	**2**
2012–13	Peterborough U	0	0		
2012–13	*Bury*	19	4	**47**	**17**
2013–14	Peterborough U	22	7	**24**	**7**
2013–14	*Swindon T*	16	6	**16**	**6**
2014–15	Leeds U	3	0	**3**	**0**
2014–15	*Crewe Alex*	27	8	**27**	**8**

ANTENUCCI, Mirco (F) **247** **77**
H: 5 5 W: 9 06 b.Termoli 8-9-84

2008–09	Catania	4	0		
2008–09	*Pisa*	20	1	**20**	**1**
2009–10	Ascoli	40	24	**40**	**24**
2010–11	Catania	13	1		
2010–11	*Torino*	19	6		
2011–12	Torino	41	10	**60**	**16**
2012–13	Catania	1	0	**18**	**1**
2012–13	*Spezia*	33	6	**33**	**6**
2013–14	Ternana	40	19	**40**	**19**
2014–15	Leeds U	36	10	**36**	**10**

AUSTIN, Rodolph (M) **191** **23**
H: 6 0 W: 12 03 b.Clarendon 1-6-85
Internationals: Jamaica Full caps.

2008–09	SK Brann	19	2		
2009–10	SK Brann	20	2		
2010–11	SK Brann	22	1		
2011–12	SK Brann	29	10	**90**	**15**
2012–13	Leeds U	31	2		
2013–14	Leeds U	40	3		
2014–15	Leeds U	30	3	**101**	**8**

BAMBA, Souleymane (D) **214** **8**
H: 6 3 W: 14 02 b.Ivry-sur-Seine 13-1-85
Internationals: Ivory Coast Full caps.

2004–05	Paris St Germain	1	0		
2005–06	Paris St Germain	0	0	**1**	**0**
2006–07	Dunfermline Ath	23	0		
2007–08	Dunfermline Ath	15	0		
2008–09	Dunfermline Ath	1	0	**39**	**0**
2008–09	Hibernian	29	0		
2009–10	Hibernian	30	2		
2010–11	Hibernian	16	2	**75**	**4**
2010–11	Leicester C	16	2		
2011–12	Leicester C	36	1	**52**	**3**
2012–13	Trabzonspor	18	0		
2013–14	Trabzonspor	9	0	**27**	**0**
2014–15	Palermo	1	0	**1**	**0**

On loan from Palermo.

2014–15	Leeds U	19	1	**19**	**1**

BELLUSCI, Giuseppe (D) **164** **3**
H: 6 1 W: 11 07 b.Trebisacce 21-8-89
Internationals: Italy U21.

2006–07	Ascoli	3	0		
2007–08	Ascoli	2	0		
2008–09	Ascoli	30	1	**35**	**1**
2009–10	Catania	12	0		
2010–11	Catania	9	0		
2011–12	Catania	32	0		
2012–13	Catania	26	0		
2013–14	Catania	20	0	**99**	**0**
2014–15	Leeds U	30	2	**30**	**2**

BENEDICIC, Zan (M) **1** **0**
H: 5 10 W: 11 00 b.Krani 3-10-95
Internationals: Slovenia U17, U18, U21.

2014–15	AC Milan	0	0		

On loan from AC Milan.

2014–15	Leeds U	1	0	**1**	**0**

BERARDI, Gaetano (D) **162** **0**
H: 5 10 W: 11 00 b.Sorengo 21-8-88
Internationals: Switzerland U20, U21, Full caps.

2006–07	Brescia	1	0		
2007–08	Brescia	9	0		
2008–09	Brescia	26	0		
2009–10	Brescia	29	0		
2010–11	Brescia	27	0		
2011–12	Brescia	13	0	**105**	**0**
2011–12	Sampdoria	9	0		
2012–13	Sampdoria	21	0		
2013–14	Sampdoria	5	0	**35**	**0**
2014–15	Leeds U	22	0	**22**	**0**

BIANCHI, Tommaso (M) **202** **15**
H: 6 0 W: 10 10 b.Piombino 1-11-88
Internationals: Italy U19, U20, U21.

2008–09	Piacenza	21	2		
2009–10	Piacenza	18	2		
2010–11	Piacenza	39	4	**78**	**8**
2011–12	Sassuolo	29	0		
2012–13	Sassuolo	30	4		
2013–14	Sassuolo	0	0	**59**	**4**
2013–14	*Modena*	41	3	**41**	**3**
2014–15	Leeds U	24	0	**24**	**0**

BYRAM, Samuel (M) **108** **6**
H: 5 11 W: 11 04 b.Thurrock 16-9-93

2012–13	Leeds U	44	3		
2013–14	Leeds U	25	0		
2014–15	Leeds U	39	3	**108**	**6**

CAIRNS, Alex (G) **1** **0**
H: 6 0 W: 11 05 b.Doncaster 4-1-93

2011–12	Leeds U	1	0		
2012–13	Leeds U	0	0		
2013–14	Leeds U	0	0		
2014–15	Leeds U	0	0	**1**	**0**

CANI, Edgar (F) **188** **37**
H: 6 2 W: 12 08 b. 22-7-89
Internationals: Albania Full caps.

2007–08	Pescara	11	3	**11**	**3**
2007–08	Palermo	1	0		
2008–09	Palermo	0	0		
2008–09	*Ascoli*	24	4	**24**	**4**
2009–10	Palermo	0	0		
2009–10	*Padova*	19	2	**19**	**2**
2009–10	*Piacenza*	14	4	**14**	**4**
2010–11	Palermo	0	0	**1**	**0**
2010–11	*Modena*	34	5	**34**	**5**
2011–12	Polonia Warsaw	26	11		
2012–13	Polonia Warsaw	5	0	**31**	**11**
2012–13	Catania	4	0		
2013–14	Cartania	0	0		
2013–14	*Carpi*	14	1	**14**	**1**
2013–14	*Bari*	17	4	**17**	**4**
2014–15	Catania	15	3	**19**	**3**

On loan from Catania.

2014–15	Leeds U	4	0	**4**	**0**

COKER, Afolabi (D) **0** **0**
b. 3-9-95

2013–14	Leeds U	0	0		
2014–15	Leeds U	0	0		

COOK, Lewis (M) **37** **0**
b. 3-2-97
Internationals: England U16, U17, U18, U19.

2014–15	Leeds U	37	0	**37**	**0**

COOPER, Liam (D) **121** **7**
H: 6 2 W: 13 07 b.Hull 30-8-91
Internationals: Scotland U17, U19.

2008–09	Hull C	0	0		
2009–10	Hull C	2	0		
2010–11	Hull C	2	0		
2010–11	*Carlisle U*	6	1	**6**	**1**
2011–12	Hull C	7	0		
2011–12	*Huddersfield T*	4	0	**4**	**0**
2012–13	Hull C	0	0	**11**	**0**
2012–13	Chesterfield	29	2		
2013–14	Chesterfield	41	3		
2014–15	Chesterfield	1	0	**71**	**5**
2014–15	Leeds U	29	1	**29**	**1**

DAWSON, Chris (M) **4** **0**
b.Dewsbury 2-9-94
Internationals: Wales U21.

2012–13	Leeds U	1	0		
2013–14	Leeds U	0	0		
2014–15	Leeds U	3	0	**4**	**0**

DOUKARA, Souleymane (F) **59** **11**
H: 6 4 W: 13 08 b.Meudon 29-9-91

2012–13	Catania	12	0		
2013–14	Catania	1	0	**13**	**0**
2013–14	*Juve Stabia*	21	6	**21**	**6**
2014–15	Leeds U	25	5	**25**	**5**

GRIMES, Eric (G) **0** **0**
b. 4-2-94
Internationals: Republic of Ireland U17, U19, U21.

2013–14	Leeds U	0	0		
2014–15	Leeds U	0	0		

HUNT, Noel (F) **320** **67**
H: 5 8 W: 11 05 b.Waterford 26-12-82
Internationals: Republic of Ireland U21, B, Full caps.

2002–03	Dunfermline Ath	12	1		
2003–04	Dunfermline Ath	13	2		
2004–05	Dunfermline Ath	23	1		
2005–06	Dunfermline Ath	32	4	**80**	**8**
2006–07	Dundee U	28	10		
2007–08	Dundee U	36	13	**64**	**23**
2008–09	Reading	37	11		
2009–10	Reading	10	2		
2010–11	Reading	33	10		
2011–12	Reading	41	8		
2012–13	Reading	24	2	**145**	**33**
2013–14	Leeds U	19	0		
2014–15	Leeds U	1	0	**20**	**0**
2014–15	*Ipswich T*	11	3	**11**	**3**

KILLOCK, Ross (D) **0** **0**
b. 12-7-94

2012–13	Leeds U	0	0		
2013–14	Leeds U	0	0		
2014–15	Leeds U	0	0		

MONTENEGRO, Brian (F) **125** **22**
H: 5 10 W: 12 00 b.Asuncion 18-6-93
Internationals: Paraguay U20.

2010	Tacuary	31	2		
2011	Tacuary	20	5		
2011–12	*West Ham U*	0	0		
2012	Tacuary	17	2	**68**	**9**
2013	Rubio Nu	14	3	**14**	**3**
2013	Libertad	17	8		
2014	Libertad	19	1	**36**	**9**
2014	Nacional	2	1	**2**	**1**

On loan from Nacional.

2014–15	Leeds U	5	0	**5**	**0**

MORISON, Steven (F) **241** **61**
H: 6 2 W: 13 07 b.Enfield 29-8-83
Internationals: England C. Wales Full caps.

2001–02	Northampton T	1	0		
2002–03	Northampton T	13	1		
2003–04	Northampton T	5	1		
2004–05	Northampton T	4	1	**23**	**3**

From Stevenage B.

2008–09	Millwall	0	0		
2009–10	Millwall	43	20		
2010–11	Millwall	40	15		
2011–12	Norwich C	34	9		
2012–13	Norwich C	19	1	**53**	**10**
2012–13	Leeds U	15	3		
2013–14	Leeds U	0	0		
2013–14	*Millwall*	41	8	**124**	**43**
2014–15	Leeds U	26	2	**41**	**5**

MOWATT, Alex (D) **67** **10**
b. 13-2-95
Internationals: England U19, U20.

2013–14	Leeds U	29	1		
2014–15	Leeds U	38	9	**67**	**10**

MURPHY, Luke (M) **228** **27**
H: 6 1 W: 11 05 b.Alsager 21-10-89

2008–09	Crewe Alex	9	1		
2009–10	Crewe Alex	32	3		
2010–11	Crewe Alex	39	3		
2011–12	Crewe Alex	42	8		
2012–13	Crewe Alex	39	6	**161**	**21**
2013–14	Leeds U	37	3		
2014–15	Leeds U	30	3	**67**	**6**

NGOYI, Granddi (M) **144** **3**
H: 6 1 W: 12 02 b.Melun 17-5-88
Internationals: France U19, U21.

2007–08	Paris St Germain	7	0		
2008–09	Paris St Germain	0	0		
2008–09	*Clermont*	19	1	**19**	**1**
2009–10	Paris St Germain	16	0		
2010–11	Paris St Germain	0	0		
2010–11	*Brest*	25	0	**25**	**0**
2011–12	Paris St Germain	0	0	**23**	**0**
2011–12	*Nantes*	20	1	**20**	**1**
2012–13	Troyes	31	1	**31**	**1**
2013–14	Palermo	20	0		
2014–15	Palermo	5	0	**25**	**0**

On loan from Palermo.

2014–15	Leeds U	1	0	**1**	**0**

PARKIN, Luke (F) **0** **0**
b. 15-8-95

2013–14	Leeds U	0	0		
2014–15	Leeds U	0	0		

PHILIPS, Kalvin (M) **2** **1**
b. 2-12-95

2014–15	Leeds U	2	1	**2**	**1**

SHARP, Billy (F) **348** **140**
H: 5 9 W: 11 00 b.Sheffield 5-2-86

2004–05	Sheffield U	2	0		
2004–05	*Rushden & D*	16	9	**16**	**9**
2005–06	Scunthorpe U	37	23		
2006–07	Scunthorpe U	45	30	**82**	**53**
2007–08	Sheffield U	29	4		
2008–09	Sheffield U	22	4		
2009–10	Sheffield U	0	0	**53**	**8**
2009–10	*Doncaster R*	33	15		
2010–11	Doncaster R	29	15		
2011–12	Doncaster R	20	10		
2011–12	Southampton	15	9		
2012–13	Southampton	2	0		
2012–13	*Nottingham F*	39	10	**39**	**10**
2013–14	Southampton	0	0	**17**	**9**
2013–14	*Reading*	10	2	**10**	**2**
2013–14	*Doncaster R*	16	4	**98**	**44**
2014–15	Leeds U	33	5	**33**	**5**

SILVESTRI, Marco (G) 98 0
H: 6 3 W: 12 08 b.Castelnuovo ne Monti 2-3-91
Internationals: Italy U20, U21.

2011–12	Chievo	0	0		
2011–12	*Reggiana*	27	0	27	0
2012–13	Chievo	0	0		
2012–13	*Padova*	25	0	25	0
2013–14	Chievo	0	0		
2013–14	*Cagliari*	3	0	3	0
2014–15	Leeds U	43	0	43	0

SLOTH, Casper (M) 137 9
H: 5 11 b.Aarhus 26-3-92
Internationals: Denmark U17, U18, U19, U20, U21, Full caps.

2009–10	Aarhus	14	2		
2010–11	Aarhus	19	0		
2011–12	Aarhus	26	1		
2012–13	Aarhus	29	1		
2013–14	Aarhus	32	5		
2014–15	Aarhus	4	0	124	9
2014–15	Leeds U	13	0	13	0

TAYLOR, Charlie (D) 71 2
H: 5 9 W: 11 00 b.York 18-9-93
Internationals: England U19.

2011–12	Leeds U	2	0		
2011–12	*Bradford C*	3	0	3	0
2012–13	Leeds U	0	0		
2012–13	*York C*	4	0	4	0
2012–13	*Inverness CT*	7	0	7	0
2013–14	Leeds U	0	0		
2013–14	*Fleetwood T*	32	0	32	0
2014–15	Leeds U	23	2	25	2

TAYLOR, Stuart (G) 75 0
H: 6 5 W: 13 07 b.Romford 28-11-80
Internationals: FA Schools, England U16, U18, U20, U21.

1998–99	Arsenal	0	0		
1999–2000	Arsenal	0	0		
1999–2000	*Bristol R*	4	0	4	0
2000–01	Arsenal	0	0		
2000–01	*Crystal Palace*	10	0	10	0
2000–01	*Peterborough U*	6	0	6	0
2001–02	Arsenal	10	0		
2002–03	Arsenal	8	0		
2003–04	Arsenal	0	0		
2004–05	Arsenal	0	0	18	0
2004–05	Leicester C	10	0	10	0
2005–06	Aston Villa	2	0		
2006–07	Aston Villa	6	0		
2007–08	Aston Villa	4	0		
2008–09	Aston Villa	0	0	12	0
2008–09	*Cardiff C*	8	0	8	0
2009–10	Manchester C	0	0		
2010–11	Manchester C	0	0		
2011–12	Manchester C	0	0		
2012–13	Manchester C	0	0		
2012–13	Reading	4	0		
2013–14	Reading	0	0	4	0
2014–15	Leeds U	3	0	3	0

TONGE, Michael (M) 388 28
H: 6 0 W: 11 10 b.Manchester 7-4-83
Internationals: England U20, U21.

2000–01	Sheffield U	2	0		
2001–02	Sheffield U	30	3		
2002–03	Sheffield U	44	6		
2003–04	Sheffield U	46	4		
2004–05	Sheffield U	34	2		
2005–06	Sheffield U	30	3		
2006–07	Sheffield U	27	2		
2007–08	Sheffield U	45	1		
2008–09	Sheffield U	4	0	262	21
2008–09	Stoke C	10	0		
2009–10	Stoke C	0	0		
2009–10	*Preston NE*	7	0		
2009–10	*Derby Co*	18	2	18	2
2010–11	Stoke C	2	0		
2010–11	*Preston NE*	5	1	12	1
2011–12	Stoke C	0	0		
2011–12	*Barnsley*	10	0	10	0
2012–13	Stoke C	0	0	12	0
2012–13	Leeds U	35	4		
2013–14	Leeds U	23	0		
2014–15	Leeds U	10	0	68	4
2014–15	*Millwall*	6	0	6	0

WALTERS, Lewis (F) 0 0
b. 28-3-95

| 2013–14 | Leeds U | 0 | 0 | | |
| 2014–15 | Leeds U | 0 | 0 | | |

WHITE, Aidan (D) 117 5
H: 5 7 W: 10 00 b.Otley 10-10-91
Internationals: England U19. Republic of Ireland U21.

2008–09	Leeds U	5	0		
2009–10	Leeds U	8	0		
2010–11	Leeds U	2	0		
2010–11	*Oldham Ath*	24	4	24	4
2011–12	Leeds U	36	0		
2012–13	Leeds U	24	1		
2013–14	Leeds U	9	0		
2013–14	*Sheffield U*	8	0	8	0
2014–15	Leeds U	1	0	85	1

WOOTTON, Scott (D) 83 2
H: 6 2 W: 13 00 b.Birkenhead 12-9-91
Internationals: England U17.

2009–10	Manchester U	0	0		
2010–11	Manchester U	0	0		
2010–11	*Tranmere R*	7	1	7	1
2011–12	Manchester U	0	0		
2011–12	*Peterborough U*	11	0		
2011–12	*Nottingham F*	13	0	13	0
2012–13	Manchester U	0	0		
2012–13	*Peterborough U*	2	1	13	1
2013–14	Manchester U	0	0		
2013–14	Leeds U	20	0		
2014–15	Leeds U	23	0	43	0
2014–15	*Rotherham U*	7	0	7	0

Players retained or with offer of contract
Coyle, Lewie Jacob; Denton, Tyler Jake; McDaid, Robbie John Thomas; Skelton, Jake Daniel; Stokes, Eoghan.

Scholars
Assenso, Isaac Kofi Boateng; Bell, Tyla George Moses; Bennett, Liam Christopher; Berry, Adam Stephen; Crouz, Chydrick Piteu Kamgang; Lyman, Thomas Ian; Mbanje, Munyaradzi; Molloy, Ian Patrick; Mulhern, Euan Francis Peter; Peacock-Farrell, Bailey; Pearce, Tom Mark; Taylor, Michael James; Turnbull, Jack Matthew William; Vann, Jack.

LEICESTER C (43)

ALBRIGHTON, Marc (M) 108 9
H: 6 2 W: 12 06 b.Tamworth 18-11-89
Internationals: England U20, U21.

2008–09	Aston Villa	0	0		
2009–10	Aston Villa	3	0		
2010–11	Aston Villa	29	5		
2011–12	Aston Villa	26	2		
2012–13	Aston Villa	9	0		
2013–14	Aston Villa	19	0	86	7
2013–14	*Wigan Ath*	4	0	4	0
2014–15	Leicester C	18	2	18	2

BARMBY, Jack (M) 19 5
H: 5 10 W: 11 09 b. 14-11-94
Internationals: England U16, U18, U19, U20.

2013–14	Manchester U	0	0		
2013–14	*Hartlepool U*	17	5	17	5
2014–15	Leicester C	0	0		
2014–15	*Rotherham U*	2	0	2	0

BLYTH, Jacob (F) 39 8
b.Nuneaton 14-8-92

2012–13	Leicester C	0	0		
2012–13	*Burton Alb*	2	0		
2012–13	*Notts Co*	4	0	4	0
2013–14	Leicester C	0	0		
2013–14	*Northampton T*	11	3	11	3
2014–15	Leicester C	0	0		
2014–15	*Burton Alb*	22	5	24	5

CAIN, Michael (M) 34 2
H: 6 0 W: 10 08 b.Luton 18-2-94

2011–12	Leicester C	0	0		
2012–13	Leicester C	0	0		
2013–14	Leicester C	0	0		
2013–14	*Mansfield T*	2	0	2	0
2014–15	Leicester C	0	0		
2014–15	*Walsall*	32	2	32	2

CAMBIASSO, Esteban (M) 522 72
H: 5 10 W: 11 07 b.Buenos Aires 18-8-80
Internationals: Argentina U17, U20, Full caps.

1998–99	Independiente	27	3		
1999–2000	Independiente	36	6		
2000–01	Independiente	35	5	98	14
2001–02	River Plate	37	12	37	12
2002–03	Real Madrid	24	0		
2003–04	Real Madrid	17	0	41	0
2004–05	Inter Milan	30	2		
2005–06	Inter Milan	34	5		

2006–07	Inter Milan	21	3		
2007–08	Inter Milan	33	6		
2008–09	Inter Milan	35	4		
2009–10	Inter Milan	30	3		
2010–11	Inter Milan	30	7		
2011–12	Inter Milan	37	4		
2012–13	Inter Milan	33	3		
2013–14	Inter Milan	32	4	315	41
2014–15	Leicester C	31	5	31	5

DAVIS, Joe (D) 27 0
H: 6 0 W: 11 07 b.Burnley 10-11-93

2010–11	Port Vale	1	0		
2011–12	Port Vale	8	0		
2012–13	Port Vale	7	0		
2013–14	Port Vale	11	0	27	0
2014–15	Leicester C	0	0		

DAWSON, Adam (M) 2 0
H: 5 9 W: 12 02 b.Bury 5-10-92

2011–12	Wigan Ath	0	0		
2012–13	Wigan Ath	0	0		
2012–13	*Accrington S*	0	0		
2013–14	Leicester C	0	0		
2014–15	Leicester C	0	0		
2014–15	*Notts Co*	2	0	2	0

DE LAET, Ritchie (D) 145 4
H: 6 1 W: 12 02 b.Antwerp 28-11-88
Internationals: Belgium U21, Full caps.

2007–08	Stoke C	0	0		
2008–09	Stoke C	0	0		
2008–09	Manchester U	1	0		
2009–10	Manchester U	2	0		
2010–11	Manchester U	0	0		
2010–11	*Sheffield U*	6	0	6	0
2010–11	*Preston NE*	5	0	5	0
2010–11	*Portsmouth*	22	0	22	0
2011–12	Manchester U	0	0	3	0
2011–12	*Norwich C*	6	1	6	1
2012–13	Leicester C	41	1		
2013–14	Leicester C	36	2		
2014–15	Leicester C	26	0	103	3

DODOO, Joseph (F) 0 0
b.Nottingham 6-1-95
Internationals: England U18.

| 2013–14 | Leicester C | 0 | 0 | | |
| 2014–15 | Leicester C | 0 | 0 | | |

DRINKWATER, Daniel (M) 200 13
H: 5 10 W: 11 00 b.Manchester 5-3-90
Internationals: England U18, U19.

2008–09	Manchester U	0	0		
2009–10	Manchester U	0	0		
2009–10	*Huddersfield T*	33	2	33	2
2010–11	Manchester U	0	0		
2010–11	*Cardiff C*	9	0	9	0
2010–11	*Watford*	12	0	12	0
2011–12	Manchester U	0	0		
2011–12	*Barnsley*	17	1	17	1
2011–12	Leicester C	19	2		
2012–13	Leicester C	42	1		
2013–14	Leicester C	45	7		
2014–15	Leicester C	23	0	129	10

ELDER, Callum (D) 21 0
H: 5 11 W: 10 08 b.Sydney 27-1-95
Internationals: Australia U20.

2013–14	Leicester C	0	0		
2014–15	Leicester C	0	0		
2014–15	*Mansfield T*	21	0	21	0

GALLAGHER, Paul (F) 362 70
H: 6 1 W: 11 00 b.Bury 9-8-84
Internationals: Scotland U21, B, Full caps.

2002–03	Blackburn R	1	0		
2003–04	Blackburn R	26	3		
2004–05	Blackburn R	16	2		
2005–06	Blackburn R	1	0		
2005–06	*Stoke C*	37	11		
2006–07	Blackburn R	16	1		
2007–08	Blackburn R	0	0		
2007–08	*Preston NE*	19	1		
2007–08	*Stoke C*	7	0	44	11
2008–09	Blackburn R	0	0		
2008–09	*Plymouth Arg*	40	13	40	13
2009–10	Blackburn R	1	0	61	6
2009–10	Leicester C	41	7		
2010–11	Leicester C	41	10		
2011–12	Leicester C	28	8		
2012–13	Leicester C	8	0		
2012–13	*Sheffield U*	6	1	6	1
2013–14	Leicester C	0	0		
2013–14	*Preston NE*	28	6		
2014–15	Leicester C	0	0	118	25
2014–15	*Preston NE*	46	7	93	14

HAMER, Ben (G) · 215 0
H: 5 11 W: 12 04 b.Chard 20-11-87
2006–07	Reading	0	0		
2007–08	Reading	0	0		
2007–08	Brentford	20	0		
2008–09	Reading	0	0		
2008–09	Brentford	45	0		
2009–10	Reading	0	0		
2010–11	Reading	0	0		
2010–11	Brentford	10	0	75	0
2010–11	Exeter C	18	0	18	0
2011–12	Charlton Ath	41	0		
2012–13	Charlton Ath	41	0		
2013–14	Charlton Ath	32	0	114	0
2014–15	Leicester C	8	0	8	0

HAMMOND, Dean (M) 402 39
H: 6 0 W: 11 09 b.Hastings 7-3-83
2002–03	Brighton & HA	4	0		
2003–04	Brighton & HA	0	0		
2003–04	Leyton Orient	8	0	8	0
2004–05	Brighton & HA	30	4		
2005–06	Brighton & HA	41	4		
2006–07	Brighton & HA	37	8		
2007–08	Brighton & HA	24	5		
2007–08	Colchester U	13	0		
2008–09	Colchester U	41	5		
2009–10	Colchester U	2	0	56	5
2009–10	Southampton	40	5		
2010–11	Southampton	41	4		
2011–12	Southampton	43	1		
2012–13	Southampton	0	0	124	10
2012–13	Brighton & HA	37	2	173	23
2013–14	Leicester C	29	1		
2014–15	Leicester C	12	0	41	1

HOPPER, Tom (F) 34 7
H: 6 1 W: 12 00 b.Boston 14-12-93
Internationals: England U18.
2011–12	Leicester C	0	0		
2012–13	Leicester C	0	0		
2012–13	Bury	22	3	22	3
2013–14	Leicester C	0	0		
2014–15	Leicester C	0	0		
2014–15	Scunthorpe U	12	4	12	4

HUTH, Robert (D) 258 16
H: 6 3 W: 14 07 b.Berlin 18-8-84
Internationals: Germany U21, Full caps.
2001–02	Chelsea	1	0		
2002–03	Chelsea	2	0		
2003–04	Chelsea	16	0		
2004–05	Chelsea	10	0		
2005–06	Chelsea	13	0	42	0
2006–07	Middlesbrough	12	1		
2007–08	Middlesbrough	13	1		
2008–09	Middlesbrough	24	0		
2009–10	Middlesbrough	4	0	53	2
2009–10	Stoke C	32	3		
2010–11	Stoke C	35	6		
2011–12	Stoke C	34	3		
2012–13	Stoke C	35	1		
2013–14	Stoke C	12	0		
2014–15	Stoke C	1	0	149	13
2014–15	Leicester C	14	1	14	1

JAMES, Matthew (M) 114 6
H: 6 0 W: 11 12 b.Bacup 22-7-91
Internationals: England U16, U17, U19, U20.
2007–08	Manchester U	0	0		
2008–09	Manchester U	0	0		
2009–10	Manchester U	0	0		
2009–10	Preston NE	18	2		
2010–11	Manchester U	0	0		
2010–11	Preston NE	10	0	28	2
2011–12	Manchester U	0	0		
2012–13	Leicester C	24	3		
2013–14	Leicester C	35	1		
2014–15	Leicester C	27	0	86	4

KING, Andy (M) 270 51
H: 6 0 W: 11 10 b.Barnstaple 29-10-88
Internationals: Wales U19, U21, Full caps.
2007–08	Leicester C	11	1		
2008–09	Leicester C	45	9		
2009–10	Leicester C	43	9		
2010–11	Leicester C	45	15		
2011–12	Leicester C	30	4		
2012–13	Leicester C	42	7		
2013–14	Leicester C	30	4		
2014–15	Leicester C	24	2	270	51

KNOCKAERT, Anthony (M) 127 23
H: 5 8 W: 10 11 b.Lille 20-11-91
Internationals: France U20, U21.
2011–12	Guingamp	34	10	34	10
2012–13	Leicester C	42	8		
2013–14	Leicester C	42	5		
2014–15	Leicester C	9	0	93	13

KONCHESKY, Paul (D) 485 14
H: 5 10 W: 11 07 b.Barking 15-5-81
Internationals: England U18, U20, U21, Full caps.
1997–98	Charlton Ath	3	0		
1998–99	Charlton Ath	2	0		
1999–2000	Charlton Ath	8	0		
2000–01	Charlton Ath	23	0		
2001–02	Charlton Ath	34	1		
2002–03	Charlton Ath	30	3		
2003–04	Charlton Ath	21	0		
2003–04	Tottenham H	12	0	12	0
2004–05	Charlton Ath	28	1	149	5
2005–06	West Ham U	37	1		
2006–07	West Ham U	22	0	59	1
2007–08	Fulham	33	0		
2008–09	Fulham	36	1		
2009–10	Fulham	27	1		
2010–11	Fulham	1	0	97	2
2010–11	Liverpool	15	0	15	0
2010–11	Nottingham F	15	1	15	1
2011–12	Leicester C	42	2		
2012–13	Leicester C	39	1		
2013–14	Leicester C	31	1		
2014–15	Leicester C	26	1	138	5

KRAMARIC, Andrej (F) 142 69
H: 5 10 W: 11 00 b.Zagreb 19-6-91
Internationals: Croatia U16, U17, U18, U19, U20, U21, Full caps.
2008–09	Dinamo Zagreb	1	0		
2009–10	Dinamo Zagreb	24	7		
2010–11	Dinamo Zagreb	12	1		
2011–12	Dinamo Zagreb	1	0		
2011–12	Lokomotiv Zagreb	13	5		
2012–13	Dinamo Zagreb	5	0		
2012–13	Lokomotiv Zagreb	32	15	45	20
2013–14	Dinamo Zagreb	4	2	42	10
2013–14	Rijeka	24	16		
2014–15	Rijeka	18	21	42	37
2014–15	Leicester C	13	2	13	2

LAWRENCE, Tom (F) 38 6
H: 5 9 W: 11 11 b.Wrexham 13-1-94
Internationals: Wales U17, U19, U21.
2012–13	Manchester U	0	0		
2013–14	Manchester U	1	0		
2013–14	Carlisle U	9	3	9	3
2013–14	Yeovil T	19	2	19	2
2014–15	Leicester C	3	0	3	0
2014–15	Rotherham U	6	1	6	1

LOGAN, Conrad (G) 153 0
H: 6 2 W: 14 00 b.Letterkenny 18-4-86
2003–04	Leicester C	0	0		
2004–05	Leicester C	0	0		
2005–06	Leicester C	0	0		
2005–06	Boston U	13	0	13	0
2006–07	Leicester C	18	0		
2007–08	Leicester C	0	0		
2007–08	Stockport Co	34	0		
2008–09	Leicester C	0	0		
2008–09	Luton T	22	0	22	0
2008–09	Stockport Co	7	0	41	0
2009–10	Leicester C	2	0		
2010–11	Leicester C	3	0		
2010–11	Bristol R	16	0	16	0
2011–12	Leicester C	0	0		
2011–12	Rotherham U	19	0	19	0
2012–13	Leicester C	0	0		
2013–14	Leicester C	0	0		
2014–15	Leicester C	0	0	23	0
2014–15	Rochdale	19	0	19	0

MAHREZ, Riyad (M) 107 13
H: 5 10 W: 9 10 b.Sarcelles 21-2-91
Internationals: Algeria Full caps.
2011–12	Le Havre	9	0		
2012–13	Le Havre	32	4		
2013–14	Le Havre	17	2	58	6
2013–14	Leicester C	19	3		
2014–15	Leicester C	30	4	49	7

McCOURT, Jak (M) 11 0
2013–14	Leicester C	0	0		
2013–14	Torquay U	11	0	11	0
2014–15	Leicester C	0	0		

MOORE, Liam (D) 86 1
H: 6 1 W: 13 08 b.Loughborough 31-1-93
Internationals: England U17, U21.
2011–12	Leicester C	2	0		
2011–12	Bradford C	17	0	17	0
2012–13	Leicester C	16	0		
2012–13	Brentford	7	0		
2013–14	Leicester C	30	1		
2014–15	Leicester C	11	0	59	1
2014–15	Brentford	3	0	10	0

MORGAN, Wes (D) 501 18
H: 6 2 W: 14 00 b.Nottingham 21-1-84
Internationals: Jamaica Full caps.
2002–03	Nottingham F	0	0		
2002–03	Kidderminster H	5	1	5	1
2003–04	Nottingham F	32	2		
2004–05	Nottingham F	43	1		
2005–06	Nottingham F	43	2		
2006–07	Nottingham F	38	0		
2007–08	Nottingham F	42	1		
2008–09	Nottingham F	42	1		
2009–10	Nottingham F	44	3		
2010–11	Nottingham F	46	1		
2011–12	Nottingham F	22	1	352	12
2011–12	Leicester C	17	0		
2012–13	Leicester C	45	1		
2013–14	Leicester C	45	2		
2014–15	Leicester C	37	2	144	5

NUGENT, Dave (F) 449 127
H: 5 11 W: 12 13 b.Liverpool 2-5-85
Internationals: England U20, U21, Full caps.
2001–02	Bury	5	0		
2002–03	Bury	31	4		
2003–04	Bury	26	3		
2004–05	Bury	26	11	88	18
2004–05	Preston NE	18	8		
2005–06	Preston NE	32	10		
2006–07	Preston NE	44	15	94	33
2007–08	Portsmouth	15	0		
2008–09	Portsmouth	16	3		
2009–10	Portsmouth	3	0		
2009–10	Burnley	30	6	30	6
2010–11	Portsmouth	44	13	78	16
2011–12	Leicester C	42	15		
2012–13	Leicester C	42	14		
2013–14	Leicester C	46	20		
2014–15	Leicester C	29	5	159	54

PANAYIOTOU, Harry (F) 1 1
H: 5 10 W: 11 05 b.Leicester 28-10-94
Internationals: St Kitts and Nevis Full caps.
2011–12	Leicester C	1	1		
2012–13	Leicester C	0	0		
2013–14	Leicester C	0	0		
2014–15	Leicester C	0	0	1	1
2014–15	Port Vale	0	0		

PEARSON, James (D) 3 0
H: 6 1 W: 11 11 b.Sheffield 19-1-93
2013–14	Leicester C	0	0		
2013–14	Carlisle U	3	0	3	0
2014–15	Leicester C	0	0		
2014–15	Peterborough U	0	0		

SCHLUPP, Jeffrey (M) 107 15
H: 5 8 W: 11 00 b.Hamburg 23-12-92
Internationals: Ghana Full caps.
2010–11	Leicester C	0	0		
2010–11	Brentford	9	6	9	6
2011–12	Leicester C	21	2		
2012–13	Leicester C	19	3		
2013–14	Leicester C	26	1		
2014–15	Leicester C	32	3	98	9

SCHMEICHEL, Kasper (G) 321 0
H: 6 1 W: 13 00 b.Copenhagen 5-11-86
Internationals: Denmark U19, U20, U21, Full caps.
2003–04	Manchester C	0	0		
2004–05	Manchester C	0	0		
2005–06	Manchester C	0	0		
2005–06	Darlington	4	0	4	0
2005–06	Bury	15	0		
2006–07	Manchester C	0	0		
2006–07	Falkirk	15	0	15	0
2006–07	Bury	14	0	29	0
2007–08	Manchester C	7	0		
2007–08	Cardiff C	14	0	14	0
2007–08	Coventry C	9	0	9	0
2008–09	Manchester C	1	0		
2009–10	Manchester C	0	0	8	0
2009–10	Notts Co	43	0	43	0
2010–11	Leeds U	37	0	37	0
2011–12	Leicester C	46	0		
2012–13	Leicester C	46	0		
2013–14	Leicester C	46	0		
2014–15	Leicester C	24	0	162	0

SCHWARZER, Mark (G) 626 0
H: 6 4 W: 14 07 b.Sydney 6-10-72
Internationals: Australia U17, U20, U23, Full caps.
1990–91	Marconi Stallions	1	0		
1991–92	Marconi Stallions	9	0		
1992–93	Marconi Stallions	23	0		
1993–94	Marconi Stallions	25	0	58	0
1994–95	Dynamo Dresden	2	0	2	0
1995–96	Kaiserslautern	4	0		

1996–97	Kaiserslautern	0	0	**4**	**0**
1996–97	Bradford C	13	0	**13**	**0**
1996–97	Middlesbrough	7	0		
1997–98	Middlesbrough	35	0		
1998–99	Middlesbrough	34	0		
1999–2000	Middlesbrough	37	0		
2000–01	Middlesbrough	31	0		
2001–02	Middlesbrough	21	0		
2002–03	Middlesbrough	38	0		
2003–04	Middlesbrough	36	0		
2004–05	Middlesbrough	31	0		
2005–06	Middlesbrough	27	0		
2006–07	Middlesbrough	36	0		
2007–08	Middlesbrough	34	0	**367**	**0**
2008–09	Fulham	38	0		
2009–10	Fulham	37	0		
2010–11	Fulham	31	0		
2011–12	Fulham	30	0		
2012–13	Fulham	36	0	**172**	**0**
2013–14	Chelsea	4	0		
2014–15	Chelsea	0	0	**4**	**0**
2014–15	Leicester C	6	0	**6**	**0**

SCOTT, Kris (M) **0** **0**
H: 5 10 W: 12 02 b.Brsitol 23-5-95
Internationals: USA U20.

2013–14	Swansea C	0	0		
2014–15	Leicester C	0	0		

SIMPSON, Danny (D) **208** **1**
H: 5 9 W: 11 05 b.Eccles 4-1-87

2005–06	Manchester U	0	0		
2006–07	Manchester U	0	0		
2006–07	*Sunderland*	14	0	**14**	**0**
2007–08	Manchester U	3	0		
2007–08	*Ipswich T*	8	0	**8**	**0**
2008–09	Manchester U	0	0		
2008–09	*Blackburn R*	12	0	**12**	**0**
2009–10	Manchester U	0	0	**3**	**0**
2009–10	Newcastle U	39	1		
2010–11	Newcastle U	30	0		
2011–12	Newcastle U	35	0		
2012–13	Newcastle U	19	0	**123**	**1**
2013–14	QPR	33	0		
2014–15	QPR	1	0	**34**	**0**
2014–15	Leicester C	14	0	**14**	**0**

SMITH, Adam (G) **4** **0**
H: 5 11 W: 11 00 b.Sunderland 23-11-92

2010–11	Leicester C	0	0		
2011–12	Leicester C	0	0		
2011–12	*Chesterfield*	0	0		
2011–12	*Bristol R*	0	0		
2012–13	Leicester C	0	0		
2013–14	Leicester C	0	0		
2013–14	*Stevenage*	0	0		
2014–15	Leicester C	0	0		
2014–15	*Mansfield T*	4	0	**4**	**0**

TAYLOR-FLETCHER, Gary (F) **439** **88**
H: 6 0 W: 11 00 b.Widnes 4-6-81

2000–01	Hull C	5	0	**5**	**0**
2001–02	Leyton Orient	9	0		
2002–03	Leyton Orient	12	1	**21**	**1**
2003–04	Lincoln C	42	16		
2004–05	Lincoln C	38	11	**80**	**27**
2005–06	Huddersfield T	43	10		
2006–07	Huddersfield T	39	11	**82**	**21**
2007–08	Blackpool	42	6		
2008–09	Blackpool	38	5		
2009–10	Blackpool	32	6		
2010–11	Blackpool	31	6		
2011–12	Blackpool	37	8		
2012–13	Blackpool	35	5	**215**	**36**
2013–14	Leicester C	21	3		
2014–15	Leicester C	1	0	**22**	**3**
2014–15	*Sheffield W*	4	0	**4**	**0**
2014–15	*Millwall*	10	0	**10**	**0**

ULLOA, Jose (F) **264** **109**
H: 6 1 W: 11 10 b.General Roca 26-7-86

2004–05	San Lorenzo	0	0		
2005–06	San Lorenzo	22	3		
2006–07	San Lorenzo	6	0	**25**	**3**
2007–08	Arsenal Sarandi	6	1	**6**	**1**
2007–08	Olimpo	8	1	**8**	**1**
2008–09	Castellon	33	17		
2009–10	Castellon	32	14		
2010–11	Castellon	1	0	**66**	**31**
2010–11	Almeria	34	7		
2011–12	Almeria	28	29		
2012–13	Almeria	10	3	**72**	**39**
2012–13	Brighton & HA	17	9		
2013–14	Brighton & HA	33	14	**50**	**23**
2014–15	Leicester C	37	11	**37**	**11**

UPSON, Matthew (D) **382** **14**
H: 6 1 W: 11 04 b.Eye 18-4-79
Internationals: England U21, Full caps.

1995–96	Luton T	0	0		
1996–97	Luton T	1	0	**1**	**0**
1996–97	Arsenal	0	0		
1997–98	Arsenal	5	0		
1998–99	Arsenal	5	0		
1999–2000	Arsenal	8	0		
2000–01	Arsenal	2	0		
2000–01	*Nottingham F*	1	0	**1**	**0**
2000–01	*Crystal Palace*	7	0	**7**	**0**
2001–02	Arsenal	14	0		
2002–03	Arsenal	0	0	**34**	**0**
2002–03	*Reading*	14	0	**14**	**0**
2002–03	Birmingham C	14	0		
2003–04	Birmingham C	30	0		
2004–05	Birmingham C	36	2		
2005–06	Birmingham C	24	1		
2006–07	Birmingham C	9	2	**113**	**5**
2006–07	West Ham U	2	0		
2007–08	West Ham U	29	1		
2008–09	West Ham U	37	0		
2009–10	West Ham U	33	3		
2010–11	West Ham U	30	0	**131**	**4**
2011–12	Stoke C	14	1		
2012–13	Stoke C	1	1	**15**	**2**
2012–13	*Brighton & HA*	18	1		
2013–14	Brighton & HA	43	2	**61**	**3**
2014–15	Leicester C	5	0	**5**	**0**

VARDY, Jamie (F) **97** **25**
H: 5 10 W: 11 12 b.Sheffield 11-1-87
Internationals: England Full caps.

2012–13	Leicester C	26	4		
2013–14	Leicester C	37	16		
2014–15	Leicester C	34	5	**97**	**25**

WASILEWSKI, Marcin (D) **297** **33**
H: 6 1 W: 13 11 b.Krakow 9-6-80
Internationals: Poland Full caps.

2002–03	Wisla Plock	24	1		
2003–04	Wisla Plock	21	1		
2004–05	Wisla Plock	15	1	**60**	**3**
2005–06	Amica Wronki	24	4	**24**	**4**
2006–07	Lech Poznan	14	5	**14**	**5**
2006–07	Anderlecht	14	2		
2007–08	Anderlecht	26	3		
2008–09	Anderlecht	30	8		
2009–10	Anderlecht	6	1		
2010–11	Anderlecht	17	3		
2011–12	Anderlecht	30	3		
2012–13	Anderlecht	20	0	**143**	**20**
2013–14	Leicester C	31	0		
2014–15	Leicester C	25	1	**56**	**1**

WATSON, Ryan (M) **5** **0**
H: 6 1 W: 11 07 b.Crewe 7-7-93

2011–12	Wigan Ath	0	0		
2012–13	Wigan Ath	0	0		
2012–13	*Accrington S*	0	0		
2013–14	Leicester C	0	0		
2014–15	Leicester C	0	0		
2014–15	*Northampton T*	5	0	**5**	**0**

WOOD, Chris (F) **179** **46**
H: 6 3 W: 12 10 b.Auckland 7-12-91
Internationals: New Zealand U17, U23, Full caps.

2008–09	WBA	2	0		
2009–10	WBA	18	1		
2010–11	WBA	1	0		
2010–11	*Barnsley*	7	0	**7**	**0**
2010–11	*Brighton & HA*	29	8	**29**	**8**
2011–12	WBA	0	0		
2011–12	*Birmingham C*	23	9	**23**	**9**
2011–12	*Bristol C*	19	3	**19**	**3**
2012–13	WBA	0	0	**21**	**1**
2012–13	*Millwall*	19	11	**19**	**11**
2012–13	Leicester C	20	9		
2013–14	Leicester C	26	4		
2014–15	Leicester C	7	1	**53**	**14**
2014–15	*Ipswich T*	8	0	**8**	**0**

Players retained or with offer of contract
Bailey, Kyle Stuart; Barnes, Harvey Lewis; Chilwell, Benjamin James; Choudhury, Hamza; Fox, Brandon Levi; Hassall, Aaron; Kelly, Michael Eamon James; King, Keenan Rakwarne; Kipre, Cedric; Maddison, Jonathan; Miles, Matthew Richard; Moore, Elliott Jordan; Sesay, Alie; Stankevicius, Simonas.

Scholars
Anderson, Conor Rhys; Bramley, Max; Fura, Toby Carl; Knight, Joshua Michael; Mitchell, Kairo Ellis; Muskwe, Admiral Dalindlela; Olukanmi, Andre Cameron; Percival, Elliot James.

LEYTON ORIENT (44)

ADEBOYEJO, Victor (F) **1** **0**
b. 12-1-98

2014–15	Leyton Orient	1	0	**1**	**0**

AGYEMANG, Montel (M) **1** **0**
H: 5 9 W: 10 08 b. 11-1-97

2014–15	Leyton Orient	1	0	**1**	**0**

BARTLEY, Marvyn (M) **225** **8**
H: 6 1 W: 12 04 b.Reading 4-7-86

2007–08	Bournemouth	20	1		
2008–09	Bournemouth	33	1		
2009–10	Bournemouth	34	0		
2010–11	Bournemouth	26	1	**113**	**3**
2010–11	Burnley	5	0		
2011–12	Burnley	39	3		
2012–13	Burnley	21	0		
2013–14	Burnley	0	0	**65**	**3**
2013–14	*Leyton Orient*	25	2		
2014–15	Leyton Orient	22	0	**47**	**2**

BATT, Shaun (M) **153** **15**
H: 6 3 W: 12 08 b.Harlow 22-2-87

2008–09	Peterborough U	30	2		
2009–10	Peterborough U	20	2	**50**	**4**
2009–10	*Millwall*	16	3		
2010–11	Millwall	0	0		
2011–12	Millwall	4	0		
2011–12	*Crawley T*	5	0	**5**	**0**
2012–13	Millwall	16	1		
2012–13	*Leyton Orient*	11	2		
2013–14	Millwall	0	0	**36**	**4**
2013–14	Leyton Orient	35	4		
2014–15	Leyton Orient	16	1	**62**	**7**

BAUDRY, Mathieu (D) **141** **8**
H: 6 2 W: 12 08 b.Le Havre 24-2-88

2007–08	Troyes	2	1		
2008–09	Troyes	17	0		
2009–10	Troyes	7	0	**26**	**1**
2010–11	Bournemouth	3	1		
2011–12	Bournemouth	7	0	**10**	**1**
2011–12	*Dagenham & R*	11	0	**11**	**0**
2012–13	Leyton Orient	24	3		
2013–14	Leyton Orient	39	2		
2014–15	Leyton Orient	31	1	**94**	**6**

CLARKE, Nathan (D) **422** **11**
H: 6 2 W: 12 00 b.Halifax 30-11-83

2001–02	Huddersfield T	36	1		
2002–03	Huddersfield T	3	0		
2003–04	Huddersfield T	26	1		
2004–05	Huddersfield T	37	0		
2005–06	Huddersfield T	46	0		
2006–07	Huddersfield T	16	0		
2007–08	Huddersfield T	44	2		
2008–09	Huddersfield T	38	3		
2009–10	Huddersfield T	17	1		
2010–11	Huddersfield T	1	0		
2010–11	*Colchester U*	18	0	**18**	**0**
2011–12	Huddersfield T	0	0	**264**	**8**
2011–12	*Oldham Ath*	16	1	**16**	**1**
2011–12	*Bury*	11	0	**11**	**0**
2012–13	Leyton Orient	34	0		
2013–14	Leyton Orient	46	2		
2014–15	Leyton Orient	33	0	**113**	**2**

COX, Dean (M) **355** **56**
H: 5 4 W: 9 08 b.Cuckfield 12-8-87

2005–06	Brighton & HA	1	0		
2006–07	Brighton & HA	42	6		
2007–08	Brighton & HA	42	6		
2008–09	Brighton & HA	40	4		
2009–10	Brighton & HA	21	0	**146**	**16**
2010–11	Leyton Orient	45	11		
2011–12	Leyton Orient	38	7		
2012–13	Leyton Orient	44	4		
2013–14	Leyton Orient	45	12		
2014–15	Leyton Orient	37	6	**209**	**40**

CUTHBERT, Scott (D) **246** **13**
H: 6 2 W: 14 00 b.Alexandria 15-6-87
Internationals: Scotland U19, U20, U21, B.

2004–05	Celtic	0	0		
2005–06	Celtic	0	0		
2006–07	Celtic	0	0		
2006–07	*Livingston*	4	1	**4**	**1**
2007–08	Celtic	0	0		
2008–09	Celtic	0	0		
2008–09	*St Mirren*	29	0	**29**	**0**
2009–10	Swindon T	39	3		
2010–11	Swindon T	41	2	**80**	**5**
2011–12	Leyton Orient	33	1		
2012–13	Leyton Orient	18	0		
2013–14	Leyton Orient	44	4		
2014–15	Leyton Orient	38	2	**133**	**7**

DAGNALL, Chris (F) 380 95
H: 5 8 W: 12 03 b.Liverpool 15-4-86

2003–04	Tranmere R	10	1	
2004–05	Tranmere R	23	6	
2005–06	Tranmere R	6	0	39 7
2005–06	Rochdale	21	3	
2006–07	Rochdale	37	17	
2007–08	Rochdale	14	7	
2008–09	Rochdale	40	7	
2009–10	Rochdale	45	20	157 54
2010–11	Scunthorpe U	37	5	
2011–12	Scunthorpe U	23	4	60 9
2011–12	Barnsley	9	0	
2011–12	*Bradford C*	7	1	7 1
2012–13	Barnsley	36	5	
2013–14	Barnsley	8	1	53 6
2013–14	*Coventry C*	6	1	6 1
2013–14	Leyton Orient	20	6	
2014–15	Leyton Orient	38	11	58 17

DOSSENA, Andrea (D) 317 10
H: 5 11 W: 11 08 b.Lodi 11-9-81
Internationals: Italy U20, Full caps.

2001–02	Verona	2	0	
2002–03	Verona	21	1	
2003–04	Verona	37	1	
2004–05	Verona	39	1	99 3
2005–06	Treviso	21	0	21 0
2006–07	Udinese	28	0	
2007–08	Udinese	35	2	63 2
2008–09	Liverpool	16	1	
2009–10	Liverpool	2	0	18 1
2009–10	Napoli	10	0	
2010–11	Napoli	33	1	
2011–12	Napoli	33	2	
2012–13	Napoli	7	0	83 3
2012–13	*Palermo*	11	0	11 0
2013–14	Sunderland	7	0	7 0
2014–15	Leyton Orient	15	1	15 1

GRAINGER, Charlie (G) 0 0
b. 31-7-96
Internationals: England U18.

2012–13	Leyton Orient	0	0	
2013–14	Leyton Orient	0	0	
2014–15	Leyton Orient	0	0	

HENDERSON, Darius (F) 419 116
H: 6 3 W: 14 03 b.Sutton 7-9-81

1999–2000	Reading	6	0	
2000–01	Reading	4	0	
2001–02	Reading	38	7	
2002–03	Reading	22	4	
2003–04	Reading	1	0	71 11
2003–04	*Brighton & HA*	10	2	10 2
2003–04	Gillingham	4	0	
2004–05	Gillingham	32	9	36 9
2004–05	*Swindon T*	6	5	6 5
2005–06	Watford	30	14	
2006–07	Watford	35	3	
2007–08	Watford	40	12	105 29
2008–09	Sheffield U	32	6	
2009–10	Sheffield U	32	12	
2010–11	Sheffield U	8	2	72 20
2011–12	Millwall	31	15	
2012–13	Millwall	20	7	51 22
2012–13	Nottingham F	11	2	
2013–14	Nottingham F	34	8	45 10
2014–15	Leyton Orient	23	8	23 8

JAMES, Lloyd (M) 211 7
H: 5 11 W: 11 01 b.Bristol 16-2-88
Internationals: Wales U17, U19, U21.

2005–06	Southampton	0	0	
2006–07	Southampton	0	0	
2007–08	Southampton	0	0	
2008–09	Southampton	41	0	
2009–10	Southampton	30	2	71 2
2010–11	Colchester U	28	0	
2011–12	Colchester U	23	1	51 1
2011–12	*Crawley T*	6	0	6 0
2012–13	Leyton Orient	28	0	
2013–14	Leyton Orient	42	3	
2014–15	Leyton Orient	13	1	83 4

KASHKET, Scott (M) 1 0
H: 5 9 W: 10 06 b.London 6-7-95

2014–15	Leyton Orient	1	0	1 0

LEE, Harry (M) 3 0
H: 6 0 W: 11 09 b.Hackney 20-3-95

2012–13	Leyton Orient	1	0	
2013–14	Leyton Orient	0	0	
2014–15	Leyton Orient	2	0	3 0

LEGZDINS, Adam (G) 99 0
H: 6 1 W: 14 02 b.Penkridge 28-11-86

2006–07	Birmingham C	0	0	
2007–08	Birmingham C	0	0	

2008–09	Crewe Alex	0	0	
2009–10	Crewe Alex	6	0	6 0
2010–11	Burton Alb	46	0	
2011–12	Derby Co	4	0	
2011–12	*Burton Alb*	1	0	47 0
2012–13	Derby Co	31	0	
2013–14	Derby Co	0	0	35 0
2014–15	Leyton Orient	11	0	11 0

LISBIE, Kevin (F) 437 108
H: 5 10 W: 11 06 b.Hackney 17-10-78
Internationals: England Youth. Jamaica Full caps.

1996–97	Charlton Ath	25	1	
1997–98	Charlton Ath	17	1	
1998–99	Charlton Ath	1	0	
1998–99	*Gillingham*	7	4	7 4
1999–2000	Charlton Ath	0	0	
1999–2000	*Reading*	2	0	2 0
2000–01	Charlton Ath	18	0	
2000–01	*QPR*	2	0	2 0
2001–02	Charlton Ath	22	5	
2002–03	Charlton Ath	32	4	
2003–04	Charlton Ath	9	4	
2004–05	Charlton Ath	17	1	
2005–06	Charlton Ath	6	0	
2005–06	*Norwich C*	6	1	6 1
2005–06	*Derby Co*	7	1	7 1
2006–07	Charlton Ath	8	0	155 16
2007–08	Colchester U	42	17	
2008–09	Ipswich T	41	6	
2009–10	Ipswich T	0	0	
2009–10	*Colchester U*	41	13	83 30
2010–11	Ipswich T	0	0	41 6
2010–11	*Millwall*	20	4	20 4
2011–12	Leyton Orient	37	12	
2012–13	Leyton Orient	38	16	
2013–14	Leyton Orient	39	16	
2014–15	Leyton Orient	7	2	111 46
2014–15	*Stevenage*	3	0	3 0

LOWRY, Shane (D) 158 2
H: 6 1 W: 13 01 b.Perth 12-6-89
Internationals: Republic of Ireland U17, U21.

2007–08	Aston Villa	0	0	
2008–09	Aston Villa	0	0	
2009–10	Aston Villa	0	0	
2009–10	*Plymouth Arg*	13	0	13 0
2009–10	*Leeds U*	11	0	11 0
2010–11	Aston Villa	0	0	
2010–11	*Sheffield U*	17	0	17 0
2011–12	Aston Villa	0	0	
2011–12	*Millwall*	22	1	
2012–13	Millwall	39	1	
2013–14	Millwall	22	0	83 2
2014–15	Leyton Orient	34	0	34 0

McANUFF, Jobi (M) 532 51
H: 5 11 W: 11 05 b.Edmonton 9-11-81
Internationals: Jamaica Full caps.

2000–01	Wimbledon	0	0	
2001–02	Wimbledon	38	4	
2002–03	Wimbledon	31	4	
2003–04	Wimbledon	27	5	96 13
2003–04	West Ham U	12	1	
2004–05	West Ham U	1	0	13 1
2004–05	*Cardiff C*	43	2	43 2
2005–06	Crystal Palace	41	8	
2006–07	Crystal Palace	34	5	75 13
2007–08	Watford	39	2	
2008–09	Watford	40	3	
2009–10	Watford	3	0	82 5
2009–10	Reading	36	3	
2010–11	Reading	40	4	
2011–12	Reading	40	5	
2012–13	Reading	38	0	
2013–14	Reading	35	2	189 14
2014–15	Leyton Orient	34	3	34 3

MOONEY, David (F) 320 98
H: 6 2 W: 12 06 b.Dublin 30-10-84
Internationals: Republic of Ireland U23.

2005	Longford T	13	4	
2005	Shamrock R	14	2	14 2
2006	Longford T	3	0	
2007	Longford T	32	19	66 26
2008	Cork C	22	15	22 15
2008–09	Reading	0	0	
2008–09	*Stockport Co*	2	0	2 0
2008–09	*Norwich C*	9	3	9 3
2009–10	Reading	0	0	
2009–10	*Charlton Ath*	28	5	28 5
2010–11	Reading	0	0	
2010–11	*Colchester U*	39	9	39 9
2011–12	Leyton Orient	37	5	
2012–13	Leyton Orient	32	5	
2013–14	Leyton Orient	38	19	
2014–15	Leyton Orient	33	9	140 38

NIKOLAOU, Andis (D) 0 0
b. 10-3-96

2014–15	Leyton Orient	0	0	

OMOZUSI, Elliot (D) 158 0
H: 5 11 W: 12 09 b.Hackney 15-12-88
Internationals: England U16, U17, U18, U19.

2005–06	Fulham	0	0	
2006–07	Fulham	0	0	
2007–08	Fulham	8	0	
2008–09	Fulham	0	0	
2008–09	*Norwich C*	21	0	21 0
2009–10	Fulham	0	0	8 0
2009–10	*Charlton Ath*	9	0	9 0
2010–11	Leyton Orient	40	0	
2011–12	Leyton Orient	10	0	
2012–13	Leyton Orient	6	0	
2013–14	Leyton Orient	39	0	
2014–15	Leyton Orient	25	0	120 0

PLASMATI, Gianvito (F) 140 23
H: 6 6 W: 13 05 b.Matera 28-1-83

2006–07	Catania	1	0	
2007–08	Catania	0	0	
2007–08	Foggia	15	2	15 2
2008–09	Catania	13	2	
2008–09	*Atalanta*	12	3	12 3
2009–10	Catania	13	0	
2010–11	Catania	0	0	27 2
2011–12	Nocerina	15	3	15 3
2011–12	*Varese*	9	2	9 2
2012–13	Vicenza	16	2	16 2
2012–13	Lanciano	14	4	
2013–14	Lanciano	16	3	30 7
2013–14	Siena	2	0	2 0
2014–15	Leyton Orient	14	2	14 2

PRITCHARD, Bradley (M) 110 3
H: 6 1 W: 14 02 b.Zimbabwe 19-12-85

2011–12	Charlton Ath	20	0	
2012–13	Charlton Ath	42	3	
2013–14	Charlton Ath	17	0	79 3
2014–15	Leyton Orient	31	0	31 0

SARGEANT, Sam (G) 0 0

2014–15	Leyton Orient	0	0	

SAWYER, Gary (D) 227 6
H: 6 0 W: 11 08 b.Bideford 5-7-85

2004–05	Plymouth Arg	0	0	
2005–06	Plymouth Arg	0	0	
2006–07	Plymouth Arg	22	0	
2007–08	Plymouth Arg	31	1	
2008–09	Plymouth Arg	13	3	
2009–10	Plymouth Arg	29	1	95 5
2009–10	*Bristol C*	2	0	2 0
2010–11	Bristol R	37	0	
2011–12	Bristol R	24	0	61 0
2012–13	Leyton Orient	34	1	
2013–14	Leyton Orient	22	0	
2014–15	Leyton Orient	13	0	69 1

SIMPSON, Jay (F) 236 41
H: 5 11 W: 13 04 b.Enfield 1-12-88
Internationals: England U17.

2007–08	Arsenal	0	0	
2007–08	*Millwall*	41	6	
2008–09	Arsenal	0	0	
2008–09	*WBA*	13	1	13 1
2009–10	Arsenal	0	0	
2009–10	*QPR*	39	12	39 12
2010–11	Hull C	32	6	
2011–12	Hull C	3	0	
2011–12	*Millwall*	16	4	57 10
2012–13	Hull C	43	6	
2013–14	Hull C	0	0	78 12
2014–15	Buriram United	21	1	21 1
2014–15	Leyton Orient	28	5	28 5

VINCELOT, Romain (M) 226 19
H: 5 9 W: 11 02 b.Poitiers 29-10-85

2004–05	Chamois Niortais	0	0	3 0
2005–06	Chemois Niortais	28	1	
2006–07	Chemois Niortais	9	0	
2007–08	Chemois Niortais	6	0	43 1
2008–09	Gueugnon	20	0	20 0
2009–10	Dagenham & R	9	1	
2010–11	Dagenham & R	46	12	55 13
2011–12	Brighton & HA	15	1	
2012–13	Brighton & HA	0	0	15 1
2012–13	*Gillingham*	9	1	9 1
2013–14	Leyton Orient	15	1	
2013–14	Leyton Orient	39	0	
2014–15	Leyton Orient	27	2	81 3

WOODS, Gary (G) 90 0
H: 6 1 W: 11 00 b.Kettering 1-10-90
Internationals: England U18.

2008–09	Doncaster R	1	0	
2009–10	Doncaster R	5	0	

Season	Club				
2010–11	Doncaster R	16	0		
2011–12	Doncaster R	14	0		
2012–13	Doncaster R	42	0		
2013–14	Doncaster R	0	0	73	0
2013–14	Watford	0	0		
2014–15	Leyton Orient	17	0	17	0

WRIGHT, Josh (M) 196 4
H: 6 1 W: 11 07 b.Bethnal Green 6-11-89
Internationals: England U16, U17, U18, U19.

2007–08	Charlton Ath	0	0		
2007–08	*Barnet*	32	1	32	1
2008–09	Charlton Ath	2	0	2	0
2008–09	*Brentford*	5	0	5	0
2008–09	*Gillingham*	5	0	5	0
2009–10	Scunthorpe U	35	0		
2010–11	Scunthorpe U	36	0	71	0
2011–12	Millwall	18	1		
2012–13	Millwall	24	0		
2013–14	Millwall	3	0		
2013–14	*Leyton Orient*	2	0		
2014–15	Millwall	1	0	46	1
2014–15	*Crawley T*	4	0	4	0
2014–15	Leyton Orient	29	2	31	2

Scholars
Adams, Kane James Arthur Peter; Adeboyejo, Ayomide Victor; Agyemang, Montel Kofi Owusu; Bridle-Card, Benjamin William Daniel; Brown, Nicholas Joseph; Clark, Michael Albert; Humphrey, Jack Peter; Kashket, Scott Connor; Ling, Samuel Jack; Moncur, Freddy Daniel; Oladipo, Oluwanishola Kelvin Amusa; Owusu-Agyeman, Christian; Pollock, Aron Dean; Sargeant, Sam Joseph Dennis;

LIVERPOOL (45)

ALBERTO, Luis (M) 31 2
H: 6 0 b.San Jose Del Valle 28-9-92
Internationals: Spain U18, U19, U21.

2009–10	Sevilla	0	0		
2010–11	Sevilla	2	0		
2011–12	Sevilla	5	0		
2012–13	Sevilla	0	0	7	0
2013–14	Liverpool	9	0		
2014–15	Liverpool	0	0	9	0
2014–15	*Malaga*	15	2	15	2

ALLEN, Joe (M) 199 9
H: 5 6 W: 9 10 b.Carmarthen 14-3-90
Internationals: Wales U17, U19, U21. Full caps. Great Britain.

2006–07	Swansea C	1	0		
2007–08	Swansea C	6	0		
2008–09	Swansea C	23	1		
2009–10	Swansea C	21	0		
2010–11	Swansea C	40	2		
2011–12	Swansea C	36	4		
2012–13	Swansea C	0	0	127	7
2012–13	Liverpool	27	0		
2013–14	Liverpool	24	1		
2014–15	Liverpool	21	1	72	2

ASPAS, Iago (F) 164 48
H: 5 9 W: 10 11 b.Moana 1-8-87

2008–09	Celta Vigo	3	2		
2009–10	Celta Vigo	36	4		
2010–11	Celta Vigo	28	4		
2011–12	Celta Vigo	33	24		
2012–13	Celta Vigo	34	12	134	46
2013–14	Liverpool	14	0		
2014–15	Liverpool	0	0	14	0

Transferred to Celta Vigo June 2015.

2014–15	*Sevilla*	16	2	16	2

ASSAIDI, Oussama (F) 131 33
H: 5 10 W: 10 13 b.Beni Boughari 15-8-88
Internationals: Holland U20. Morocco Full caps.

2007–08	Almere City FC	3	3	3	3
2008–09	De Graafschap	13	1		
2009–10	De Graafschap	3	5	16	6
2009–10	Heerenveen	21	1		
2010–11	Heerenveen	31	9		
2011–12	Heerenveen	27	10		
2012–13	Heerenveen	1	0	80	20
2012–13	Liverpool	4	0		
2013–14	Liverpool	0	0		
2013–14	*Stoke C*	19	4		
2014–15	Liverpool	0	0	4	0
2014–15	*Stoke C*	9	0	28	4

Transferred to Al-Ahly Dubai January 2015.

BALOTELLI, Mario (F) 174 67
H: 6 2 W: 13 08 b.Palermo 12-8-90
Internationals: Italy U21, Full caps.

2005–06	Lumezzane	2	0	2	0
2006–07	Internazionale	0	0		
2007–08	Internazionale	11	3		
2008–09	Internazionale	22	8		
2009–10	Internazionale	26	9	59	20
2010–11	Manchester C	17	6		
2011–12	Manchester C	23	13		
2012–13	Manchester C	14	1	54	20
2012–13	AC Milan	13	12		
2013–14	AC Milan	30	14	43	26
2014–15	Liverpool	16	1	16	1

BORINI, Fabio (F) 94 24
H: 5 10 W: 11 08 b.Bentivoglio 23-3-91
Internationals: Italy U17, U19, U21, Full caps.

2008–09	Chelsea	0	0		
2009–10	Chelsea	4	0		
2010–11	Chelsea	0	0	4	0
2010–11	Swansea C	9	6	9	6
2011–12	Roma	24	9	24	9
2012–13	Liverpool	13	1		
2013–14	Liverpool	0	0		
2013–14	*Sunderland*	32	7	32	7
2014–15	Liverpool	12	1	25	2

BRANNAGAN, Cameron (M) 0 0
H: 5 11 W: 11 03 b.Manchester 9-5-96
Internationals: England U18.

2013–14	Liverpool	0	0		
2014–15	Liverpool	0	0	0	0

CAN, Emre (M) 60 5
H: 6 1 W: 11 09 b.Frankfurt 12-1-94
Internationals: Germany U16, U17, U19, U21.

2011–12	Bayern Munich	0	0		
2012–13	Bayern Munich	4	1	4	1
2013–14	Bayer Leverkusen	29	3	29	3
2014–15	Liverpool	27	1	27	1

COATES, Sebastian (D) 77 5
H: 6 5 W: 13 12 b.Montevideo 7-10-90
Internationals: Uruguay U20, U23, Full caps.

2008–09	Nacional	6	1		
2009–10	Nacional	21	2		
2010–11	Nacional	27	1		
2011–12	Nacional	1	0	55	4
2011–12	Liverpool	7	1		
2012–13	Liverpool	5	0		
2013–14	Liverpool	0	0		
2014–15	Liverpool	0	0	12	1
2014–15	*Sunderland*	10	0	10	0

COUTINHO, Phillippe (M) 131 22
H: 5 7 W: 10 09 b.Rio de Janeiro 12-6-92
Internationals: Brazil U17, U20, Full caps.

2009–10	Vasco da Gama	7	1	7	1
2010–11	Inter Milan	12	1		
2011–12	Inter Milan	5	1		
2011–12	*Espanyol*	16	5	16	5
2012–13	Inter Milan	10	1	27	3
2012–13	Liverpool	13	3		
2013–14	Liverpool	33	5		
2014–15	Liverpool	35	5	81	13

DUNN, Jack (M) 6 3
H: 6 0 W: 11 11 b.Liverpool 19-11-94
Internationals: England U17, U18, U19.

2011–12	Liverpool	0	0		
2012–13	Liverpool	0	0		
2013–14	Liverpool	0	0		
2014–15	Liverpool	0	0		
2014–15	*Cheltenham T*	5	3	5	3
2014–15	*Burton Alb*	1	0	1	0

FLANAGAN, John (D) 35 1
H: 5 11 W: 12 06 b.Liverpool 1-1-93
Internationals: England U19, U20, U21, Full caps.

2010–11	Liverpool	7	0		
2011–12	Liverpool	5	0		
2012–13	Liverpool	0	0		
2013–14	Liverpool	23	1		
2014–15	Liverpool	0	0	35	1

GERRARD, Steven (M) 504 120
H: 6 0 W: 12 05 b.Huyton 30-5-80
Internationals: England U21, Full caps.

1997–98	Liverpool	0	0		
1998–99	Liverpool	12	0		
1999–2000	Liverpool	29	1		
2000–01	Liverpool	33	7		
2001–02	Liverpool	28	3		
2002–03	Liverpool	34	5		
2003–04	Liverpool	34	4		
2004–05	Liverpool	30	7		
2005–06	Liverpool	32	10		
2006–07	Liverpool	36	7		
2007–08	Liverpool	34	11		
2008–09	Liverpool	31	16		
2009–10	Liverpool	33	9		
2010–11	Liverpool	21	4		
2011–12	Liverpool	18	5		
2012–13	Liverpool	36	9		
2013–14	Liverpool	34	13		
2014–15	Liverpool	29	9	504	120

Transferred to LA Galaxy.

HENDERSON, Jordan (M) 220 22
H: 6 0 W: 10 07 b.Sunderland 17-6-90
Internationals: England U19, U20, U21, Full caps.

2008–09	Sunderland	1	0		
2008–09	*Coventry C*	10	1	10	1
2009–10	Sunderland	33	1		
2010–11	Sunderland	37	3	71	4
2011–12	Liverpool	37	2		
2012–13	Liverpool	30	5		
2013–14	Liverpool	35	4		
2014–15	Liverpool	37	6	139	17

IBE, Jordan (F) 52 7
H: 5 9 W: 11 00 b.Southwark 8-12-95
Internationals: England U18, U19, U20.

2011–12	Wycombe W	7	1	7	1
2011–12	Liverpool	0	0		
2012–13	Liverpool	1	0		
2013–14	Liverpool	1	0		
2013–14	*Birmingham C*	11	1	11	1
2014–15	Liverpool	12	0	14	0
2014–15	*Derby Co*	20	5	20	5

JOHNSON, Glen (D) 309 15
H: 6 0 W: 13 04 b.Greenwich 23-8-84
Internationals: England U20, U21, Full caps.

2001–02	West Ham U	0	0		
2002–03	West Ham U	15	0	15	0
2002–03	*Millwall*	8	0	8	0
2003–04	Chelsea	19	3		
2004–05	Chelsea	17	0		
2005–06	Chelsea	0	0		
2006–07	Chelsea	2	0	42	3
2006–07	*Portsmouth*	26	0		
2007–08	Chelsea	2	0		
2007–08	Portsmouth	29	1		
2008–09	Portsmouth	29	3		
2009–10	Portsmouth	0	0	84	4
2009–10	Liverpool	25	3		
2010–11	Liverpool	28	2		
2011–12	Liverpool	23	1		
2012–13	Liverpool	36	1		
2013–14	Liverpool	29	0		
2014–15	Liverpool	19	1	160	8

JONES, Brad (G) 111 0
H: 6 3 W: 12 01 b.Armidale 19-3-82
Internationals: Australia U20, U23, Full caps.

1998–99	Middlesbrough	0	0		
1999–2000	Middlesbrough	0	0		
2000–01	Middlesbrough	0	0		
2001–02	Middlesbrough	0	0		
2002	*Shelbourne*	2	0	2	0
2002–03	Middlesbrough	0	0		
2002–03	*Stockport Co*	1	0	1	0
2003–04	Middlesbrough	1	0		
2003–04	*Blackpool*	5	0		
2003–04	*Rotherham U*	0	0		
2004–05	Middlesbrough	0	0		
2004–05	*Blackpool*	12	0	17	0
2005–06	Middlesbrough	9	0		
2006–07	Middlesbrough	2	0		
2006–07	*Sheffield W*	15	0	15	0
2007–08	Middlesbrough	1	0		
2008–09	Middlesbrough	16	0		
2009–10	Middlesbrough	24	0	58	0
2010–11	Liverpool	0	0		
2010–11	*Derby Co*	7	0	7	0
2011–12	Liverpool	1	0		
2012–13	Liverpool	7	0		
2013–14	Liverpool	0	0		
2014–15	Liverpool	3	0	11	0

JONES, Lloyd (D) 17 1
H: 6 3 W: 11 11 b.Plymouth 7-10-95
Internationals: Wales U17, U18. England U19, U20.

2012–13	Liverpool	0	0		
2013–14	Liverpool	0	0		
2014–15	Liverpool	0	0		
2014–15	*Cheltenham T*	6	0	6	0
2014–15	*Accrington S*	11	1	11	1

JOSE ENRIQUE (D) 251 4
H: 6 0 W: 12 00 b.Valencia 23-1-86
Internationals: Spain U16, U20, U21.

2004–05	Levante	19	1	19	1
2005–06	Valencia	0	0		

2005–06 Celta Vigo 14 0 **14 0**
2006–07 Villarreal 23 0 **23 0**
2007–08 Newcastle U 23 0
2008–09 Newcastle U 26 0
2009–10 Newcastle U 34 1
2010–11 Newcastle U 36 0 **119 1**
2011–12 Liverpool 35 0
2012–13 Liverpool 29 2
2013–14 Liverpool 8 0
2014–15 Liverpool 4 0 **76 2**

LALLANA, Adam (M) **265 53**
H: 5 8 W: 11 06 b.St Albans 10-5-88
Internationals: England U18, U19, U21, Full caps.
2005–06 Southampton 0 0
2006–07 Southampton 1 0
2007–08 Southampton 5 1
2007–08 Bournemouth 3 0 **3 0**
2008–09 Southampton 40 1
2009–10 Southampton 44 15
2010–11 Southampton 36 8
2011–12 Southampton 41 11
2012–13 Southampton 30 3
2013–14 Southampton 38 9 **235 48**
2014–15 Liverpool 27 5 **27 5**

LAMBERT, Ricky (F) **569 214**
H: 6 2 W: 14 08 b.Liverpool 16-2-82
Internationals: England Full caps.
1999–2000 Blackpool 2 0
2000–01 Blackpool 0 0 **3 0**
2000–01 Macclesfield T 9 0
2001–02 Macclesfield T 35 8 **44 8**
2001–02 Stockport Co 0 0
2002–03 Stockport Co 29 2
2003–04 Stockport Co 40 12
2004–05 Stockport Co 29 4 **98 18**
2004–05 Rochdale 15 6
2005–06 Rochdale 46 22
2006–07 Rochdale 3 0 **64 28**
2006–07 Bristol R 36 8
2007–08 Bristol R 46 14
2008–09 Bristol R 45 29
2009–10 Bristol R 1 1 **128 52**
2009–10 Southampton 45 30
2010–11 Southampton 45 21
2011–12 Southampton 42 27
2012–13 Southampton 38 15
2013–14 Southampton 37 13 **207 106**
2014–15 Liverpool 25 2 **25 2**

LOVREN, Dejan (D) **216 6**
H: 6 2 W: 13 02 b.Karlovac 5-7-89
Internationals: Croatia U17, U18, U19, U20, U21, Full caps.
2005–06 Dinamo Zagreb 1 0
2006–07 Dinamo Zagreb 0 0
2006–07 Inter Zapresic 21 0
2007–08 Dinamo Zagreb 0 0
2007–08 Inter Zapresic 29 1 **50 1**
2008–09 Dinamo Zagreb 22 1
2009–10 Dinamo Zagreb 14 0 **37 1**
2009–10 Lyon 8 0
2010–11 Lyon 28 0
2011–12 Lyon 18 1
2012–13 Lyon 18 1 **72 2**
2013–14 Southampton 31 2 **31 2**
2014–15 Liverpool 26 0 **26 0**

LUCAS (M) **229 5**
H: 5 10 W: 11 09 b.Dourados 9-1-87
Internationals: Brazil U20, U23, Full caps.
2005 Gremio 3 0
2006 Gremio 30 4 **33 4**
2007–08 Liverpool 18 0
2008–09 Liverpool 25 1
2009–10 Liverpool 35 0
2010–11 Liverpool 33 0
2011–12 Liverpool 12 0
2012–13 Liverpool 26 0
2013–14 Liverpool 27 0
2014–15 Liverpool 20 0 **196 1**

MANQUILLO, Javier (D) **16 0**
H: 5 11 W: 12 04 b.Madrid 5-5-94
Internationals: Spain U16, U17, U18, U19, U20, U21.
2012–13 Atletico Madrid 3 0
2013–14 Atletico Madrid 3 0
2014–15 Atletico Madrid 0 0 **6 0**
On loan from Atletico Madrid.
2014–15 Liverpool 10 0 **10 0**

MARKOVIC, Lazar (F) **91 20**
H: 5 9 W: 10 03 b.Cacak 2-3-94
Internationals: Serbia U17, U21, Full caps.
2010–11 Partizan Belgrade 1 0
2011–12 Partizan Belgrade 26 6

2012–13 Partizan Belgrade 19 7 **46 13**
2013–14 Benfica 26 5 **26 5**
2014–15 Liverpool 19 2 **19 2**

McLAUGHLIN, Ryan (D) **9 0**
H: 5 9 W: 10 12 b.Belfast 30-9-94
Internationals: Northern Ireland U16, U17, U19, U21, Full caps.
2011–12 Liverpool 0 0
2013–14 Liverpool 0 0
2013–14 Barnsley 9 0 **9 0**
2014–15 Liverpool 0 0

MIGNOLET, Simon (G) **286 1**
H: 6 4 W: 13 10 b.St Truiden 6-3-88
Internationals: Belgium U16, U17, U18, U19, U20, U21, Full caps.
2006–07 St Truiden 2 0
2007–08 St Truiden 25 0
2008–09 St Truiden 35 1
2009–10 St Truiden 37 0
2010–11 St Truiden 23 0 **122 1**
2010–11 Sunderland 23 0
2011–12 Sunderland 29 0
2012–13 Sunderland 38 0 **90 0**
2013–14 Liverpool 38 0
2014–15 Liverpool 36 0 **74 0**

MORENO, Alberto (D) **83 5**
H: 5 7 W: 10 01 b.Seville 5-7-92
Internationals: Spain U21, Full caps.
2011–12 Sevilla 11 0
2012–13 Sevilla 15 0
2013–14 Sevilla 29 3 **55 3**
2014–15 Liverpool 28 2 **28 2**

OJO, Sheyi (M) **11 0**
H: 5 10 W: 10 01 b.Hemel Hempstead 19-6-97
Internationals: England U16, U17, U18.
2014–15 Liverpool 0 0
2014–15 Wigan Ath 11 0 **11 0**

PELOSI, Marc (D) **0 0**
b.Bad Sackingen 17-6-94
Internationals: USA U17, U23.
2011–12 Liverpool 0 0
2012–13 Liverpool 0 0
2013–14 Liverpool 0 0
2014–15 Liverpool 0 0

PHILLIPS, Adam (M) **0 0**
b. 15-1-98
2014–15 Liverpool 0 0

RANDALL, Connor (D) **1 0**
b. 21-10-95
Internationals: England U17.
2014–15 Liverpool 0 0
2014–15 Shrewsbury T 1 0 **1 0**

ROSSITER, Jordan (M) **1 0**
H: 5 8 W: 10 10 b.Liverpool 24-3-97
Internationals: England U16, U17, U18.
2013–14 Liverpool 0 0
2014–15 Liverpool 0 0

SAKHO, Mamadou (D) **185 8**
H: 6 2 W: 12 07 b.Paris 13-2-90
Internationals: France U16, U17, U18, U19, U21, Full caps.
2006–07 Paris St Germain 0 0
2007–08 Paris St Germain 12 0
2008–09 Paris St Germain 23 1
2009–10 Paris St Germain 32 0
2010–11 Paris St Germain 35 4
2011–12 Paris St Germain 22 0
2012–13 Paris St Germain 27 2 **151 7**
2013–14 Liverpool 18 1
2014–15 Liverpool 16 0 **34 1**

SAMA, Stephen (D) **0 0**
H: 6 2 W: 13 01 b.Cameroon 5-3-93
Internationals: Germany U17, U18, U19, U20.
2009–10 Liverpool 0 0
2010–11 Liverpool 0 0
2011–12 Liverpool 0 0
2012–13 Liverpool 0 0
2013–14 Liverpool 0 0
2014–15 Liverpool 0 0

SINCLAIR, Jerome (F) **3 0**
H: 5 8 W: 12 06 b.Birmingham 20-9-96
Internationals: England U16, U17.
2012–13 Liverpool 0 0
2013–14 Liverpool 0 0
2014–15 Liverpool 2 0 **2 0**
2014–15 Wigan Ath 1 0 **1 0**

SKRTEL, Martin (D) **329 18**
H: 6 3 W: 12 10 b.Handlova 15-12-84
Internationals: Slovakia Full caps.
2002–03 Trencin 1 0
2003–04 Trencin 34 0 **35 0**
2004 Zenit 7 0
2005 Zenit 18 1
2006 Zenit 26 1
2007 Zenit 23 1 **74 3**
2007–08 Liverpool 14 0
2008–09 Liverpool 21 0
2009–10 Liverpool 19 1
2010–11 Liverpool 38 2
2011–12 Liverpool 34 2
2012–13 Liverpool 25 2
2013–14 Liverpool 36 7
2014–15 Liverpool 33 1 **220 15**

SMITH, Bradley (D) **8 0**
H: 5 10 W: 11 00 b.New South Wales 9-4-94
Internationals: England U17, U19, U20. Australia U23, Full caps.
2011–12 Liverpool 0 0
2012–13 Liverpool 0 0
2013–14 Liverpool 1 0
2014–15 Liverpool 0 0 **1 0**
2014–15 Swindon T 7 0 **7 0**

STERLING, Raheem (F) **95 18**
H: 5 7 W: 10 00 b.Kingston 8-12-94
Internationals: England U16, U17, U19, U21, Full caps.
2011–12 Liverpool 3 0
2012–13 Liverpool 24 2
2013–14 Liverpool 33 9
2014–15 Liverpool 35 7 **95 18**

STEWART, Kevin (D) **15 3**
H: 5 7 W: 11 06 b.Enfield 7-9-93
2012–13 Tottenham H 0 0
2012–13 Crewe Alex 4 0
2013–14 Crewe Alex 0 0
2014–15 Liverpool 0 0
2014–15 Cheltenham T 4 1 **4 1**
2014–15 Burton Alb 7 2 **7 2**

STURRIDGE, Daniel (F) **151 61**
H: 6 2 W: 12 00 b.Birmingham 1-9-89
Internationals: England U16, U17, U18, U19, U20, U21, Full caps. Great Britain.
2006–07 Manchester C 2 0
2007–08 Manchester C 3 1
2008–09 Manchester C 16 4
2009–10 Manchester C 0 0 **21 5**
2009–10 Chelsea 13 1
2010–11 Chelsea 13 0
2010–11 Bolton W 12 8 **12 8**
2011–12 Chelsea 30 11
2012–13 Chelsea 7 1 **63 13**
2012–13 Liverpool 14 10
2013–14 Liverpool 29 21
2014–15 Liverpool 12 4 **55 35**

TEIXEIRA, Joao Carlos (M) **35 6**
H: 5 9 W: 11 05 b.Braga 18-1-93
Internationals: Portugal U16, U17, U18, U19, U20, U21.
2011–12 Liverpool 0 0
2012–13 Liverpool 0 0
2013–14 Liverpool 1 0
2013–14 Brentford 2 0 **2 0**
2014–15 Liverpool 0 0 **1 0**
2014–15 Brighton & HA 32 6 **32 6**

TOURE, Kolo (D) **339 11**
H: 5 10 W: 13 08 b.Sokuora Bouake 19-3-81
Internationals: Ivory Coast Full caps.
2001–02 Arsenal 0 0
2002–03 Arsenal 26 2
2003–04 Arsenal 37 1
2004–05 Arsenal 35 0
2005–06 Arsenal 33 0
2006–07 Arsenal 35 3
2007–08 Arsenal 30 2
2008–09 Arsenal 29 1
2009–10 Arsenal 0 0 **225 9**
2009–10 Manchester C 31 1
2010–11 Manchester C 22 1
2011–12 Manchester C 14 0
2012–13 Manchester C 15 0 **82 2**
2013–14 Liverpool 20 0
2014–15 Liverpool 12 0 **32 0**

WARD, Danny (G) **5 0**
H: 5 11 W: 13 12 b.Wrexham 22-6-93
Internationals: Wales U17, U19, U21.
2011–12 Liverpool 0 0

2012–13 Liverpool 0 0
2013–14 Liverpool 0 0
2014–15 Liverpool 0 0
2014–15 *Morecambe* 5 0 **5 0**

WILLIAMS, Jordan (M)   **8 0**
H: 6 0 W: 12 02 b.Bangor 6-11-95
Internationals: Wales U21.
2014–15 Liverpool 0 0
2014–15 *Notts Co* 8 0 **8 0**

WISDOM, Andre (D)   **72 0**
H: 6 1 W: 12 04 b.Leeds 9-5-93
Internationals: England U16, U17, U19, U21.
2009–10 Liverpool 0 0
2010–11 Liverpool 0 0
2011–12 Liverpool 0 0
2012–13 Liverpool 12 0
2013–14 Liverpool 2 0
2013–14 *Derby Co* 34 0 **34 0**
2014–15 Liverpool 0 0 **14 0**
2014–15 *WBA* 24 0 **24 0**

YESIL, Samed (F)   **1 0**
H: 5 10 W: 10 13 b.Dusseldorf 25-5-94
Internationals: Germany U16, U17, U18, U19.
2011–12 Bayer Leverkusen 1 0 **1 0**
2012–13 Liverpool 0 0
2013–14 Liverpool 0 0
2014–15 Liverpool 0 0

Players retained or with offer of contract
Brewitt, Tom; Canos, Tenes Sergi; Chirivella, Burgos Pedro; Cleary, Daniel; Ejaria, Oviemuno; Fulton, Ryan; Gomes Aju, Madger Antonio; Ilori, Tiago; Kent, Ryan; Maguire, Joseph; Marsh, William George; O'Hanlon, Alex Joseph; Origi, Divock Okoth; Paez, Rafael; Polgar, Kristof; Smith, Bradley Shaun; Trickett-Smith, Daniel Thomas; Vigouroux, Lawrence; Wilson, Harry.

Scholars
Brimmer, Jake; Dobie, Joshua; Firth, Andrew; Griffin, Liam; Hart, Samuel James; Jackson, Benjamin Edward Alan; Lewis, Kane; Maxwell, Wade; Nicholas, Lewis; Quigley, Conor; Sheron, Nathan; Travis, Lewis; Virtue, Thick Matthew; Watts, Jack Thomas; Wheeler, Owen; Whelan, Corey.

LUTON T (46)

ANGOL, Lee (M)   **3 0**
H: 5 10 W: 11 04 b. 4-8-94
2012–13 Wycombe W 3 0
2013–14 Wycombe W 0 0 **3 0**
2014–15 Luton T 0 0

BANTON, Zane (F)   **0 0**
b. 6-6-96
2014–15 Luton T 0 0

BENSON, Paul (F)   **211 69**
H: 6 1 W: 11 01 b.Southend 12-10-79
Internationals: England C.
2007–08 Dagenham & R 22 6
2008–09 Dagenham & R 33 17
2009–10 Dagenham & R 45 17
2010–11 Dagenham & R 3 0 **103 40**
2010–11 Charlton Ath 32 10
2011–12 Charlton Ath 1 0 **33 10**
2011–12 Swindon T 22 11
2012–13 Swindon T 9 1
2012–13 *Portsmouth* 7 2 **7 2**
2012–13 *Cheltenham T* 16 4 **16 4**
2013–14 Swindon T 0 0 **31 12**
2014–15 Luton T 21 1 **21 1**

CONNOLLY, Paul (D)   **322 2**
H: 6 0 W: 11 09 b.Liverpool 29-9-83
2000–01 Plymouth Arg 1 0
2001–02 Plymouth Arg 0 0
2002–03 Plymouth Arg 2 0
2003–04 Plymouth Arg 29 0
2004–05 Plymouth Arg 19 0
2005–06 Plymouth Arg 31 0
2006–07 Plymouth Arg 38 0
2007–08 Plymouth Arg 42 1 **162 1**
2008–09 Derby Co 40 1
2009–10 Derby Co 21 0
2009–10 *Sheffield U* 7 0 **7 0**
2010–11 Leeds U 30 0
2011–12 Leeds U 28 0
2012–13 Leeds U 0 0 **58 0**
2012–13 *Portsmouth* 4 0 **4 0**

2012–13 *Preston NE* 15 0 **15 0**
2013–14 Millwall 4 0 **4 0**
2013–14 *Crawley T* 7 0 **7 0**
2014–15 Luton T 4 0 **4 0**

CULLEN, Mark (F)   **84 15**
H: 5 9 W: 11 11 b.Ashington 21-4-92
2009–10 Hull C 3 1
2010–11 Hull C 17 0
2010–11 *Bradford C* 4 0 **4 0**
2011–12 Hull C 4 0
2011–12 *Bury* 4 0
2012–13 Hull C 0 0
2012–13 Hull C 0 0 **24 1**
2012–13 *Bury* 10 1 **14 1**
2014–15 Luton T 42 13 **42 13**

DOYLE, Nathan (M)   **259 4**
H: 5 11 W: 12 06 b.Derby 12-1-87
Internationals: England U16, U17, U18, U19.
2003–04 Derby Co 2 0
2004–05 Derby Co 3 0
2005–06 Derby Co 4 0
2005–06 *Notts Co* 12 0 **12 0**
2006–07 Derby Co 0 0 **9 0**
2006–07 *Bradford C* 28 0
2006–07 Hull C 1 0
2007–08 Hull C 1 0
2008–09 Hull C 3 0
2009–10 Hull C 0 0 **5 0**
2009–10 Barnsley 34 0
2010–11 Barnsley 43 2
2011–12 Barnsley 21 0 **98 2**
2011–12 *Preston NE* 5 0 **5 0**
2012–13 Bradford C 37 2
2013–14 Bradford C 38 0 **103 2**
2014–15 Luton T 27 0 **27 0**

DRURY, Andy (M)   **151 12**
H: 5 11 W: 12 06 b.Sittingbourne 28-11-83
2010–11 Ipswich T 12 0
2011–12 Ipswich T 21 2
2011–12 *Crawley T* 13 3
2012–13 Ipswich T 29 0 **62 2**
2013–14 Crawley T 41 5 **54 8**
2014–15 Luton T 35 2 **35 2**

FITZSIMONS, Danny (D)   **0 0**
H: 6 1 W: 11 02 b. 5-5-92
2014–15 Luton T 0 0

FRANKS, Fraser (D)   **17 0**
H: 6 0 W: 10 12 b.Hammersmith 22-11-90
Internationals: England C.
2009–10 Brentford 0 0
2011–12 AFC Wimbledon 4 0 **4 0**
2014–15 Luton T 13 0 **13 0**

GOOCH, Liam (G)   **0 0**
2014–15 Luton T 0 0

GRIFFITHS, Scott (D)   **203 6**
H: 5 9 W: 11 08 b.Westminster 27-11-85
Internationals: England C.
2007–08 Dagenham & R 41 0
2008–09 Dagenham & R 44 0
2009–10 Dagenham & R 13 1 **98 1**
2009–10 Peterborough U 20 0
2010–11 Peterborough U 0 0
2010–11 *Chesterfield* 29 0
2011–12 Peterborough U 0 0
2011–12 *Crawley T* 6 0 **6 0**
2011–12 *Chesterfield* 3 0 **32 0**
2011–12 *Rotherham U* 8 0 **8 0**
2012–13 Peterborough U 0 0 **20 0**
2012–13 *Plymouth Arg* 4 0 **4 0**
2014–15 Luton T 35 2 **35 2**

GUTTRIDGE, Luke (M)   **424 48**
H: 5 6 W: 9 07 b.Barnstaple 27-3-82
1999–2000 Torquay U 1 0
2000–01 Torquay U 0 0 **1 0**
2000–01 *Cambridge U* 1 1
2001–02 Cambridge U 29 2
2002–03 Cambridge U 43 3
2003–04 Cambridge U 46 11
2004–05 Cambridge U 17 0 **136 17**
2004–05 Southend U 5 0
2005–06 Southend U 41 5
2006–07 Southend U 17 0 **63 5**
2006–07 *Leyton Orient* 17 1 **17 1**
2007–08 Colchester U 14 0 **14 0**
2008–09 Northampton T 25 2
2009–10 Northampton T 31 4
2010–11 Aldershot T 41 8
2011–12 Aldershot T 25 4 **66 12**
2011–12 *Northampton T* 19 3
2012–13 Northampton T 25 1
2013–14 Northampton T 0 0 **100 10**
2014–15 Luton T 27 3 **27 3**

HALL, Ryan (M)   **132 23**
H: 5 10 W: 10 04 b.Dulwich 4-1-88
Internationals: England C.
2005–06 Crystal Palace 0 0
2006–07 Crystal Palace 0 0
2007–08 Crystal Palace 1 0 **1 0**
2007–08 *Dagenham & R* 8 2 **8 2**
From Bromley.
2010–11 Southend U 41 9
2011–12 Southend U 43 10
2012–13 Southend U 2 0 **86 19**
2012–13 Leeds U 8 0
2013–14 Leeds U 0 0 **8 0**
2013–14 *Sheffield U* 4 0 **4 0**
2013–14 Milton Keynes D 11 1 **11 1**
2014–15 Rotherham U 3 1 **3 1**
2014–15 *Notts Co* 4 0 **4 0**
2014–15 Luton T 7 0 **7 0**

HOWELLS, Jake (D)   **36 4**
H: 5 9 W: 11 09 b.Hemel Hempstead 18-4-91
Internationals: England C. Wales U21.
2014–15 Luton T 36 4 **36 4**

ISAAC, Kynan (M)   **0 0**
H: 5 10 W: 10 06 b. 21-12-92
2014–15 Luton T 0 0

JUSTHAM, Elliot (G)   **15 0**
H: 6 3 W: 12 06 b. 18-7-90
2014–15 Luton T 15 0 **15 0**

LACEY, Alex (D)   **18 0**
b.Milton Keynes 31-5-93
2014–15 Luton T 18 0 **18 0**

LAFAYETTE, Ross (F)   **11 0**
b.London 11-4-87
2014–15 Luton T 11 0 **11 0**

LAWLESS, Alex (M)   **29 3**
H: 5 11 W: 10 08 b.Llwynupion 5-2-83
Internationals: Wales U19, U21.
2003–04 Fulham 0 0
2004–05 Fulham 0 0
2005–06 Torquay U 14 0 **14 0**
2014–15 Luton T 15 3 **15 3**

LONGDEN, Brett (D)   **0 0**
b. 8-5-94
2014–15 Luton T 0 0

McNULTY, Steve (D)   **57 2**
H: 6 1 W: 13 11 b.Liverpool 26-9-83
2012–13 Fleetwood T 16 2 **16 2**
2014–15 Luton T 41 0 **41 0**

MILLER, Ricky (F)   **12 1**
b. 13-3-89
2014–15 Luton T 12 1 **12 1**

ONYEMAH, Mark (D)   **0 0**
b. 9-4-96
2014–15 Luton T 0 0

PARRY, Andy (D)   **0 0**
H: 5 10 W: 11 07 b.Liverpool 13-9-91
2014–15 Luton T 0 0

REES, Ian (M)   **0 0**
2014–15 Luton T 0 0

ROBINSON, Matt (M)   **9 0**
H: 6 2 W: 12 08 b. 1-6-94
2014–15 Luton T 9 0 **9 0**

ROONEY, Luke (F)   **105 11**
H: 5 8 W: 11 07 b.Southwark 28-12-90
2009–10 Gillingham 13 2
2010–11 Gillingham 23 1
2011–12 Gillingham 17 3 **53 6**
2011–12 *Swindon T* 20 2
2012–13 Swindon T 11 0
2012–13 *Burton Alb* 3 0 **3 0**
2012–13 *Rotherham U* 3 0 **3 0**
2013–14 Swindon T 0 0 **31 2**
2013–14 *Crawley T* 4 0 **4 0**
2014–15 Luton T 11 3 **11 3**

RUDDOCK, Pelly (M)   **16 1**
H: 5 9 W: 9 13 b.Hendon 17-7-93
2011–12 West Ham U 0 0
2014–15 West Ham U 0 0
2014–15 Luton T 16 1 **16 1**

SMITH, Charlie (M)   **0 0**
b. 7-9-95
2014–15 Luton T 0 0

SMITH, Jonathan (M)   85   5
H: 6 3   W: 11 02   b.Preston 17-10-86

2011–12	Swindon T	38	3	38 3
2012–13	York C	12	0	12 0
2014–15	Luton T	35	2	35 2

STEVENSON, Jim (M)   11   1
H: 5 11   W: 9 06   b.Luton 17-5-92

2014–15	Luton T	11	1	11 1

TROTMAN, Luke (D)   0   0

2014–15	Luton T	0	0	

TYLER, Mark (G)   455   0
H: 6 0   W: 12 09   b.Norwich 2-4-77
Internationals: England U18.

1994–95	Peterborough U	5	0	
1995–96	Peterborough U	0	0	
1996–97	Peterborough U	3	0	
1997–98	Peterborough U	46	0	
1998–99	Peterborough U	27	0	
1999–2000	Peterborough U	32	0	
2000–01	Peterborough U	40	0	
2001–02	Peterborough U	44	0	
2002–03	Peterborough U	29	0	
2003–04	Peterborough U	43	0	
2004–05	Peterborough U	46	0	
2005–06	Peterborough U	40	0	
2006–07	Peterborough U	41	0	
2007–08	Peterborough U	17	0	
2008–09	Peterborough U	0	0	413 0
2008–09	Bury	11	0	11 0
2014–15	Luton T	31	0	31 0

VIANA, David (M)   2   0
Internationals: Portugal U17, U18, U19.

2012–13	Real Salt Lake	2	0	2 0
2014–15	Luton T	0	0	

WALKER, Charlie (F)   3   0
b. 8-3-90

2014–15	Luton T	3	0	3 0

WALL, Alex (F)   7   1
H: 5 11   W: 12 06   b.Thatcham 22-9-90

2014–15	Luton T	7	1	7 1

WHALLEY, Shaun (M)   18   3
H: 5 9   W: 10 08   b.Whiston 7-8-87

2014–15	Luton T	18	3	18 3

WILKINSON, Luke (D)   107   10
H: 6 2   W: 11 09   b.Wells 2-12-92

2009–10	Portsmouth	0	0	
2010–11	Dagenham & R	0	0	
2011–12	Dagenham & R	0	0	
2012–13	Dagenham & R	43	6	
2013–14	Dagenham & R	22	0	65 6
2014–15	Luton T	42	4	42 4

WILLIAMS, Curtley (D)   3   0
H: 6 0   W: 11 11   b.Ipswich 19-3-90

2014–15	Luton T	3	0	3 0

Players retained or with offer of contract
Mpanzu, Pelly Ruddock.

Scholars
Allman, Osamu Quao; Amadi, Ekene; Atkinson, Alexander James; Craig, Geo Luca; Galliford, Isaac Nathanial; Gooch, Liam Reece; Hawkes, Lee; Justin, James Michael; King, Craig Ian; Maguraushe, Leeroy Takunda; McGhan-George, Kyran Devante; Musonda, Frankie Chisenga; Ndambi, Ngwala Ii Michel Archange Junior; Perry, Lucas Alexander; Tamplin, Harry Charles; Tayali, Tuki Nkole Mwenge Ifeanyi.

MANCHESTER C (47)

AGUERO, Sergio (F)   349   175
H: 5 8   W: 11 09   b.Buenos Aires 2-6-88
Internationals: Argentina U17, U20, U23, Full caps.

2002–03	Independiente	1	0	
2003–04	Independiente	5	0	
2004–05	Independiente	12	5	
2005–06	Independiente	36	18	54 23
2006–07	Atletico Madrid	38	6	
2007–08	Atletico Madrid	37	19	
2008–09	Atletico Madrid	37	17	
2009–10	Atletico Madrid	31	12	
2010–11	Atletico Madrid	32	20	175 74
2011–12	Manchester C	34	23	
2012–13	Manchester C	30	12	
2013–14	Manchester C	23	17	
2014–15	Manchester C	33	26	120 78

AMBROSE, Thierry (F)   0   0
H: 5 10   W: 11 00   b.Sens 28-3-97
Internationals: France U16, U17, U18.

2014–15	Manchester C	0	0	

BONY, Wilfried (F)   187   95
H: 6 0   W: 13 11   b.Bingerville 10-12-88
Internationals: Ivory Coast Full caps.

2008–09	Sparta Prague	16	3	
2009–10	Sparta Prague	29	9	
2010–11	Sparta Prague	13	10	58 22
2010–11	Vitesse	7	3	
2011–12	Vitesse	28	12	
2012–13	Vitesse	30	31	65 46
2013–14	Swansea C	34	16	
2014–15	Swansea C	20	9	54 25
2014–15	Manchester C	10	2	10 2

BOSSAERTS, Mathias (D)   0   0
H: 6 0   W: 11 12   b.Gooreind 10-7-96
Internationals: Belgium U16, U17, U19.

2013–14	Manchester C	0	0	
2014–15	Manchester C	0	0	

BOYATA, Dedryck (M)   32   1
H: 6 2   W: 12 00   b.Brussels 8-9-90
Internationals: Belgium U19, 21, Full caps.

2008–09	Manchester C	0	0	
2009–10	Manchester C	3	0	
2010–11	Manchester C	7	0	
2011–12	Manchester C	0	0	
2011–12	Bolton W	14	1	14 1
2012–13	Manchester C	0	0	
2012–13	FC Twente	5	0	5 0
2013–14	Manchester C	1	0	
2014–15	Manchester C	2	0	13 0

BUNN, Harry (F)   57   10
H: 5 9   W: 11 10   b.Oldham 25-11-92

2010–11	Manchester C	0	0	
2011–12	Manchester C	0	0	
2011–12	Rochdale	6	0	6 0
2011–12	Preston NE	1	1	1 1
2011–12	Oldham Ath	11	0	11 0
2012–13	Manchester C	0	0	
2012–13	Crewe Alex	4	0	4 0
2013–14	Manchester C	0	0	
2013–14	Sheffield U	2	0	2 0
2013–14	Huddersfield T	3	0	
2014–15	Manchester C	0	0	
2014–15	Huddersfield T	30	9	33 9

CABALLERO, Willy (G)   300   0
H: 6 1   W: 12 08   b.Santa Elena 28-9-81
Internationals: Argentina U20.

2001–04	Boca Juniors	15	0	15 0
2004–08	Elche	67	0	
2008–09	Elche	38	0	
2009–10	Elche	39	0	
2010–11	Elche	22	0	166 0
2010–11	Malaga	15	0	
2011–12	Malaga	28	0	
2012–13	Malaga	36	0	
2013–14	Malaga	38	0	117 0
2014–15	Manchester C	2	0	2 0

CELINA, Bersant (F)   0   0
H: 5 4   W: 9 06   b.Prizren 9-9-96
Internationals: Norway U16, U17. Kosovo Full caps.

2014–15	Manchester C	0	0	

CLICHY, Gael (D)   286   2
H: 5 9   W: 10 04   b.Toulouse 26-7-85
Internationals: France U15, U17, U18, U19, 21, B, Full caps.

2003–04	Arsenal	12	0	
2004–05	Arsenal	15	0	
2005–06	Arsenal	7	0	
2006–07	Arsenal	27	0	
2007–08	Arsenal	38	0	
2008–09	Arsenal	31	1	
2009–10	Arsenal	24	0	
2010–11	Arsenal	33	0	187 1
2011–12	Manchester C	28	0	
2012–13	Manchester C	20	0	
2013–14	Manchester C	20	0	
2014–15	Manchester C	23	1	99 1

COLE, Devante (F)   34   8
H: 6 1   W: 11 06   b.Alderley Edge 10-5-95
Internationals: England U16, U17, U18, U19.

2013–14	Manchester C	0	0	
2014–15	Manchester C	0	0	
2014–15	Barnsley	19	5	19 5
2014–15	Milton Keynes D	15	3	15 3

DEMICHELIS, Martin (D)   367   25
H: 6 0   W: 12 03   b.Cordoba 20-12-80
Internationals: Argentina Full caps.

2001	River Plate	0	0	
2002	River Plate	17	0	
2003	River Plate	35	1	52 1
2003–04	Bayern Munich	14	2	
2004–05	Bayern Munich	23	0	
2005–06	Bayern Munich	27	1	
2006–07	Bayern Munich	26	3	
2007–08	Bayern Munich	28	1	
2008–09	Bayern Munich	29	4	
2009–10	Bayern Munich	21	1	
2010–11	Bayern Munich	6	1	174 13
2010–11	Malaga	17	1	
2011–12	Malaga	35	3	
2012–13	Malaga	31	4	83 8
2013–14	Atletico Madrid	0	0	
2013–14	Manchester C	27	2	
2014–15	Manchester C	31	1	58 3

DENAYER, Jason (D)   29   5
H: 6 0   b.Brussels 28-6-95
Internationals: Belgium U19, U21, Full caps.

2013–14	Manchester C	0	0	
2014–15	Manchester C	0	0	
2014–15	Celtic	29	5	29 5

DRURY, Adam (M)   24   3
H: 5 10   W: 10 10   b.Grimsby 21-9-93

2010–11	Manchester C	0	0	
2011–12	Manchester C	0	0	
2012–13	Manchester C	0	0	
2012–13	Burton Alb	12	0	12 0
2013–14	Manchester C	0	0	
2014–15	Manchester C	0	0	
2014–15	St Mirren	12	3	12 3

DZEKO, Edin (F)   312   139
H: 6 3   W: 12 08   b.Doboj 17-3-86
Internationals: Bosnia & Herzegovina U19, U21, Full caps.

2004–05	Zeljeznicar	13	1	13 1
2005–06	Usti nad Labem	15	6	15 6
2005–06	Teplice	13	3	
2006–07	Teplice	30	13	43 16
2007–08	Wolfsburg	28	8	
2008–09	Wolfsburg	32	26	
2009–10	Wolfsburg	34	22	
2010–11	Wolfsburg	17	10	111 66
2010–11	Manchester C	15	2	
2011–12	Manchester C	30	14	
2012–13	Manchester C	32	14	
2013–14	Manchester C	31	16	
2014–15	Manchester C	22	4	130 50

EVANS, George (M)   39   2
H: 6 0   W: 11 12   b.Cheadle 13-1-96
Internationals: England U17, U19, U20.

2012–13	Manchester C	0	0	
2013–14	Manchester C	0	0	
2013–14	Crewe Alex	23	1	23 1
2014–15	Manchester C	0	0	
2014–15	Scunthorpe U	16	1	16 1

FERNANDINHO, Luis (M)   292   42
H: 5 10   W: 10 09   b.Londrina 4-5-85
Internationals: Brazil Full caps.

2003	Paranaense	29	5	
2004	Paranaense	41	9	
2005	Paranaense	2	0	72 14
2005–06	Shakhtar Donetsk	22	1	
2006–07	Shakhtar Donetsk	25	1	
2008–09	Shakhtar Donetsk	21	5	
2009–10	Shakhtar Donetsk	24	4	
2010–11	Shakhtar Donetsk	15	3	
2011–12	Shakhtar Donetsk	24	2	
2012–13	Shakhtar Donetsk	23	2	154 20
2013–14	Manchester C	33	5	
2014–15	Manchester C	33	3	66 8

FERNANDO, Francisco (M)   193   5
H: 6 1   W: 11 00   b.Brasilia 25-7-87
Internationals: Brazil U20.

2007–08	Porto	0	0	
2007–08	Estrella Amadora	26	1	26 1
2008–09	Porto	25	0	
2009–10	Porto	25	0	
2010–11	Porto	21	0	
2011–12	Porto	22	1	
2012–13	Porto	24	1	
2013–14	Porto	25	0	142 2
2014–15	Manchester C	25	2	25 2

FOFANA, Seko (M)   21   1
H: 6 0   W: 11 08   b.Paris 7-5-95
Internationals: France U16, U17, U18, U19.

2013–14	Manchester C	0	0	

| 2014–15 | Manchester C | 0 | 0 | | |
| 2014–15 | *Fulham* | 21 | 1 | **21** | **1** |

GLENDON, George (M)   **0 0**
H: 5 10   b.Manchester 3-5-95
Internationals: England U16, U17.

| 2013–14 | Manchester C | 0 | 0 | | |
| 2014–15 | Manchester C | 0 | 0 | | |

GUIDETTI, John (F)   **66 32**
H: 5 11   W: 12 06   b.Stockholm 15-4-92
Internationals: Sweden U17, U19, U21, Full caps.

2009–10	Manchester C	0	0		
2009–10	*Brommapojkana*	8	3	**8**	**3**
2010–11	Manchester C	0	0		
2010–11	*Burnley*	5	1	**5**	**1**
2011–12	Manchester C	0	0		
2011–12	*Feyenoord*	23	20	**23**	**20**
2012–13	Manchester C	0	0		
2013–14	Manchester C	0	0		
2013–14	*Stoke C*	6	0	**6**	**0**
2014–15	Manchester C	0	0		
2014–15	*Celtic*	24	8	**24**	**8**

GUNN, Angus (G)   **0 0**
H: 6 0   W: 12 02   b.Norwich 22-1-96
Internationals: England U16, U17, U18, U19.

| 2013–14 | Manchester C | 0 | 0 | | |
| 2014–15 | Manchester C | 0 | 0 | | |

HART, Joe (G)   **330 0**
H: 6 3   W: 13 03   b.Shrewsbury 19-4-87
Internationals: England U19, U21, Full caps.

2004–05	*Shrewsbury T*	6	0		
2005–06	*Shrewsbury T*	46	0	**52**	**0**
2006–07	Manchester C	1	0		
2006–07	*Tranmere R*	6	0	**6**	**0**
2006–07	*Blackpool*	5	0	**5**	**0**
2007–08	Manchester C	26	0		
2008–09	Manchester C	23	0		
2009–10	Manchester C	0	0		
2009–10	*Birmingham C*	36	0	**36**	**0**
2010–11	Manchester C	38	0		
2011–12	Manchester C	38	0		
2012–13	Manchester C	38	0		
2013–14	Manchester C	31	0		
2014–15	Manchester C	36	0	**231**	**0**

HIWULA, Jordy (F)   **27 9**
H: 5 10   W: 11 12   b.Manchester 24-9-94
Internationals: England U18, U19.

2013–14	Manchester C	0	0		
2014–15	Manchester C	0	0		
2014–15	*Yeovil T*	8	0	**8**	**0**
2014–15	*Walsall*	19	9	**19**	**9**

IHEANACHO, Kelechi (M)   **0 0**
b. 3-10-96
Internationals: Nigeria U17, U20.

| 2014–15 | Manchester C | 0 | 0 | | |

JESUS NAVAS, Gonzalez (M)   **350 27**
H: 5 7   W: 9 05   b.Los Palacios 21-11-85
Internationals: Spain U21, Full caps.

2003–04	*Sevilla*	5	0		
2004–05	*Sevilla*	23	2		
2005–06	*Sevilla*	34	2		
2006–07	*Sevilla*	29	1		
2007–08	*Sevilla*	36	4		
2008–09	*Sevilla*	35	4		
2009–10	*Sevilla*	34	4		
2010–11	*Sevilla*	15	1		
2011–12	*Sevilla*	37	5		
2012–13	*Sevilla*	37	0	**285**	**23**
2013–14	Manchester C	30	4		
2014–15	Manchester C	35	0	**65**	**4**

JOVETIC, Stevan (F)   **195 55**
H: 6 0   W: 12 05   b.Podgorica 2-11-89
Internationals: Montenegro U21, Full caps.

2005–06	*Partizan Belgrade*	2	0		
2006–07	*Partizan Belgrade*	22	1		
2007–08	*Partizan Belgrade*	27	12	**51**	**13**
2008–09	*Fiorentina*	29	2		
2009–10	*Fiorentina*	27	5		
2010–11	*Fiorentina*	0	0		
2011–12	*Fiorentina*	27	14		
2012–13	*Fiorentina*	31	13	**114**	**34**
2013–14	Manchester C	13	3		
2014–15	Manchester C	17	5	**30**	**8**

KOLAROV, Aleksandar (D)   **271 20**
H: 6 2   W: 13 05   b.Belgrade 10-11-85
Internationals: Serbia U21, Full caps.

2004–05	*Cukaricki*	27	2		
2005–06	*Cukaricki*	17	0	**44**	**2**
2005–06	*OFK Belgrade*	11	1		
2006–07	*OFK Belgrade*	24	7	**38**	**5**
2007–08	*Lazio*	24	1		
2008–09	*Lazio*	25	2		
2009–10	*Lazio*	33	3	**82**	**6**

2010–11	Manchester C	24	1		
2011–12	Manchester C	12	2		
2012–13	Manchester C	20	1		
2013–14	Manchester C	30	1		
2014–15	Manchester C	21	2	**107**	**7**

KOMPANY, Vincent (D)   **296 16**
H: 6 3   W: 13 05   b.Brussels 10-4-86
Internationals: Belgium U16, U17, Full caps.

2004–05	*Anderlecht*	29	2		
2005–06	*Anderlecht*	32	2	**61**	**4**
2006–07	*Hamburg*	6	0		
2007–08	*Hamburg*	22	1		
2008–09	*Hamburg*	1	0	**29**	**1**
2008–09	Manchester C	34	1		
2009–10	Manchester C	25	2		
2010–11	Manchester C	37	0		
2011–12	Manchester C	31	3		
2012–13	Manchester C	26	1		
2013–14	Manchester C	28	4		
2014–15	Manchester C	25	0	**206**	**11**

LAMPARD, Frank (M)   **618 178**
H: 6 0   W: 14 02   b.Romford 20-6-78
Internationals: England U21, B, Full caps.

1994–95	*West Ham U*	0	0		
1995–96	*West Ham U*	2	0		
1995–96	*Swansea C*	9	1	**9**	**1**
1996–97	*West Ham U*	13	0		
1997–98	*West Ham U*	31	5		
1998–99	*West Ham U*	38	5		
1999–2000	*West Ham U*	34	7		
2000–01	*West Ham U*	30	7	**148**	**24**
2001–02	*Chelsea*	37	5		
2002–03	*Chelsea*	38	6		
2003–04	*Chelsea*	38	10		
2004–05	*Chelsea*	38	13		
2005–06	*Chelsea*	35	16		
2006–07	*Chelsea*	37	11		
2007–08	*Chelsea*	24	10		
2008–09	*Chelsea*	37	12		
2009–10	*Chelsea*	36	22		
2010–11	*Chelsea*	24	10		
2011–12	*Chelsea*	30	11		
2012–13	*Chelsea*	29	15		
2013–14	*Chelsea*	26	6	**429**	**147**
2014–15	Manchester C	32	6	**32**	**6**

Transferred to New York City July 2015.

LAWLOR, Ian (G)   **0 0**
H: 6 4   W: 12 08   b.Dublin 27-10-94
Internationals: Republic of Ireland U17, U19, U21.

2011–12	Manchester C	0	0		
2012–13	Manchester C	0	0		
2013–14	Manchester C	0	0		
2014–15	Manchester C	0	0		

LEIGH, Greg (D)   **38 1**
H: 5 11   b.Manchester 30-9-94
Internationals: England U19.

2013–14	Manchester C	0	0		
2014–15	Manchester C	0	0		
2014–15	*Crewe Alex*	38	1	**38**	**1**

LOPES, Marcos (F)   **23 3**
H: 5 8   W: 10 09   b.Belem 28-12-95
Internationals: Portugal U16, U17, U18, U19, U20, U21.

2012–13	Manchester C	0	0		
2013–14	Manchester C	0	0		
2014–15	Manchester C	0	0		
2014–15	*Lille*	23	3	**23**	**3**

MANGALA, Eliaquim (D)   **153 8**
H: 6 2   W: 11 09   b.Colombes 13-2-91
Internationals: France U21, Full caps.

2008–09	*Standard Liege*	11	0		
2009–10	*Standard Liege*	31	1		
2010–11	*Standard Liege*	35	1	**77**	**2**
2011–12	*Porto*	7	0		
2012–13	*Porto*	23	4		
2013–14	*Porto*	21	2	**51**	**6**
2014–15	Manchester C	25	0	**25**	**0**

MILNER, James (M)   **395 38**
H: 5 9   W: 11 00   b.Leeds 4-1-86
Internationals: England U16, U17, U19, U20, U21, Full caps.

2002–03	*Leeds U*	18	2		
2003–04	*Leeds U*	30	3	**48**	**5**
2003–04	*Swindon T*	6	2	**6**	**2**
2004–05	*Newcastle U*	25	1		
2005–06	*Newcastle U*	3	0		
2005–06	*Aston Villa*	27	1		
2006–07	*Newcastle U*	35	3		
2007–08	*Newcastle U*	29	2		
2008–09	*Newcastle U*	2	0	**94**	**6**
2008–09	*Aston Villa*	36	3		
2009–10	*Aston Villa*	36	7		
2010–11	*Aston Villa*	1	1	**100**	**12**
2010–11	Manchester C	32	0		
2011–12	Manchester C	26	3		
2012–13	Manchester C	26	4		
2013–14	Manchester C	31	1		
2014–15	Manchester C	32	5	**147**	**13**

NASRI, Samir (M)   **323 45**
H: 5 9   W: 11 11   b.Marseille 26-6-87
Internationals: France U16, U17, U18, U19, U21, Full caps.

2004–05	*Marseille*	24	1		
2005–06	*Marseille*	30	1		
2006–07	*Marseille*	37	3		
2007–08	*Marseille*	30	6	**121**	**11**
2008–09	*Arsenal*	29	6		
2009–10	*Arsenal*	26	2		
2010–11	*Arsenal*	30	10		
2011–12	*Arsenal*	1	0	**86**	**18**
2011–12	Manchester C	30	5		
2012–13	Manchester C	28	2		
2013–14	Manchester C	34	7		
2014–15	Manchester C	24	2	**116**	**16**

NEGREDO, Alvaro (F)   **271 115**
H: 6 1   W: 12 11   b.Madrid 20-8-85
Internationals: Spain U21, Full caps.

2007–08	*Almeria*	36	13		
2008–09	*Almeria*	34	18	**70**	**31**
2009–10	*Sevilla*	35	11		
2010–11	*Sevilla*	38	20		
2011–12	*Sevilla*	30	14		
2012–13	*Sevilla*	36	25	**139**	**70**
2013–14	Manchester C	32	9		
2014–15	Manchester C	0	0	**32**	**9**
2014–15	*Valencia*	30	5	**30**	**5**

NTCHAM, Jules Olivier (M)   **0 0**
H: 5 11   W: 12 07   b.Longjumeau 9-2-96
Internationals: France U18.

| 2013–14 | Manchester C | 0 | 0 | | |
| 2014–15 | Manchester C | 0 | 0 | | |

PLUMMER, Ellis (D)   **9 0**
H: 5 11   b.Denton 2-9-94
Internationals: England U16, U17.

2011–12	Manchester C	0	0		
2012–13	Manchester C	0	0		
2013–14	Manchester C	0	0		
2013–14	*Oldham Ath*	3	0	**3**	**0**
2014–15	Manchester C	0	0		
2014–15	*St Mirren*	6	0	**6**	**0**

POZO, Jose (M)   **3 0**
H: 5 7   W: 9 06   b.Malaga 15-3-96
Internationals: Spain U17, U18, U19.

| 2013–14 | Manchester C | 0 | 0 | | |
| 2014–15 | Manchester C | 3 | 0 | **3** | **0** |

REKIK, Karim (D)   **68 2**
H: 6 0   W: 12 00   b.Den Haag 2-12-94
Internationals: Netherlands U16, U17, U19, U21, Full caps.

2011–12	Manchester C	0	0		
2011–12	*Portsmouth*	8	0	**8**	**0**
2012–13	Manchester C	1	0		
2012–13	*Blackburn R*	5	0	**5**	**0**
2013–14	Manchester C	0	0		
2013–14	*PSV Eindhoven*	25	1		
2014–15	Manchester C	0	0	**1**	**0**
2014–15	*PSV Eindhoven*	29	1	**54**	**2**

RICHARDS, Micah (D)   **189 7**
H: 5 11   W: 13 00   b.Birmingham 24-6-88
Internationals: England U16, U19, U21, Full caps. Great Britain.

2005–06	Manchester C	13	0		
2006–07	Manchester C	28	1		
2007–08	Manchester C	25	0		
2008–09	Manchester C	34	1		
2009–10	Manchester C	23	3		
2010–11	Manchester C	18	1		
2011–12	Manchester C	29	1		
2012–13	Manchester C	7	0		
2013–14	Manchester C	2	0		
2014–15	Manchester C	0	0	**179**	**7**
2014–15	*Fiorentina*	10	0	**10**	**0**

SAGNA, Bakari (D)   **309 4**
H: 5 10   W: 11 05   b.Sens 14-2-83
Internationals: France U21, Full caps.

2003–04	*Auxerre*	14	0		
2004–05	*Auxerre*	26	0		
2005–06	*Auxerre*	23	0		
2006–07	*Auxerre*	38	0	**87**	**0**
2007–08	*Arsenal*	29	1		
2008–09	*Arsenal*	35	0		
2009–10	*Arsenal*	35	0		
2010–11	*Arsenal*	33	1		
2011–12	*Arsenal*	21	1		

2012–13	Arsenal	25	0		
2013–14	Arsenal	35	1	213	4
2014–15	Manchester C	9	0	9	0

SILVA, David (F)   **364**   **63**
H: 5 7   W: 10 07   b.Arguineguin 8-1-86
Internationals: Spain U16, U17, U19, U20, U21, Full caps.

2003–04	Mestalla	14	1	14	1
2004–05	Eibar	35	5	35	5
2005–06	Celta Vigo	34	3	34	3
2006–07	Valencia	36	5		
2007–08	Valencia	34	4		
2008–09	Valencia	19	4		
2009–10	Valencia	30	8	119	21
2010–11	Manchester C	35	4		
2011–12	Manchester C	36	6		
2012–13	Manchester C	32	4		
2013–14	Manchester C	27	7		
2014–15	Manchester C	32	12	162	33

SINCLAIR, Scott (F)   **184**   **35**
H: 5 10   W: 10 00   b.Bath 26-3-89
Internationals: England U17, U18, U19, U20, U21. Great Britain.

2004–05	Bristol R	2	0	2	0
2005–06	Chelsea	0	0		
2006–07	Chelsea	2	0		
2006–07	Plymouth Arg	15	2	15	2
2007–08	Chelsea	1	0		
2007–08	QPR	9	1	9	1
2007–08	Charlton Ath	3	0	3	0
2007–08	Crystal Palace	6	2	6	2
2008–09	Chelsea	2	0		
2008–09	Birmingham C	14	0	14	0
2009–10	Chelsea	0	0	5	0
2009–10	Wigan Ath	18	1	18	1
2010–11	Swansea C	43	19		
2011–12	Swansea C	38	8		
2012–13	Swansea C	1	1	82	28
2012–13	Manchester C	11	0		
2013–14	Manchester C	0	0		
2013–14	WBA	8	0	8	0
2014–15	Manchester C	2	0	13	0
2014–15	Aston Villa	9	1	9	1

TASENDE, Jose (D)   **0**   **0**
H: 5 7   W: 10 10   b.Coristanco 4-1-97
Internationals: Spain U17.

2014–15	Manchester C	0	0		

TOURE, Yaya (M)   **387**   **69**
H: 6 3   W: 14 02   b.Sokoura Bouake 13-5-83
Internationals: Ivory Coast Full caps.

2001–02	Beveren	28	0		
2002–03	Beveren	30	3		
2003–04	Beveren	12	0	70	3
2003–04	Metalurgs Donetsk	11	1		
2004–05	Metalurgs Donetsk	22	2	33	3
2005–06	Olympiacos	20	3	20	3
2006–07	Monaco	27	5	27	5
2007–08	Barcelona	26	1		
2008–09	Barcelona	25	2		
2009–10	Barcelona	23	1	74	4
2010–11	Manchester C	35	8		
2011–12	Manchester C	32	6		
2012–13	Manchester C	32	7		
2013–14	Manchester C	35	20		
2014–15	Manchester C	29	10	163	51

WRIGHT, Richard (G)   **380**   **0**
H: 6 2   W: 14 04   b.Ipswich 5-11-77
Internationals: England U18, U21, Full caps.

1994–95	Ipswich T	3	0		
1995–96	Ipswich T	23	0		
1996–97	Ipswich T	40	0		
1997–98	Ipswich T	46	0		
1998–99	Ipswich T	46	0		
1999–2000	Ipswich T	46	0		
2000–01	Ipswich T	36	0		
2001–02	Arsenal	12	0	12	0
2002–03	Everton	33	0		
2003–04	Everton	4	0		
2004–05	Everton	7	0		
2005–06	Everton	15	0		
2006–07	Everton	1	0	60	0
2007–08	West Ham U	0	0		
2007–08	Southampton	7	0	7	0
2008–09	Ipswich T	46	0		
2009–10	Ipswich T	12	0		
2010–11	Ipswich T	0	0		
2010–11	Sheffield U	2	0	2	0
2011–12	Ipswich T	1	0	299	0
2012–13	Manchester C	0	0		
2013–14	Manchester C	0	0		
2014–15	Manchester C	0	0		

ZABALETA, Pablo (D)   **343**   **19**
H: 5 8   W: 10 12   b.Buenos Aires 16-1-85
Internationals: Argentina U20, U23, Full caps.

2002–03	San Lorenzo	11	0		
2003–04	San Lorenzo	27	3		
2004–05	San Lorenzo	28	5	66	8
2005–06	Espanyol	27	2		
2006–07	Espanyol	21	0		
2007–08	Espanyol	32	1	80	3
2008–09	Manchester C	29	1		
2009–10	Manchester C	27	0		
2010–11	Manchester C	26	2		
2011–12	Manchester C	21	1		
2012–13	Manchester C	30	2		
2013–14	Manchester C	35	1		
2014–15	Manchester C	29	1	197	8

Players retained or with offer of contract
Adarabioyo, Tosin; Adjei-Boateng, Bismark; Barker, Brandon Lee; Bryan, Kean Shay; Byrne, Jack; Bytyqi, Sinan; Facey, Shay; Godsway, Donyoh; Horsfield, James; Maffeo Becerra, Pablo; Naah, Divine Yelsarmba; Nwakali, Chidiebere Chikioke; O'Brien, Billy Thomas; Reges, Fernando Francisco; Smith-Brown, Ashley; Zuculini, Bruno.

Scholars
Albinson, Charlie; Boadu-Adjei, Denzeil; Buckley-ricketts, Isaac; Bullock, Callum; Dilrosun, Javairo Joreno Faustino; Faour, Zackarias; Fernandes, Cantin Paolo; Garcia, Alonso Manuel; Grimshaw, Daniel James; Haug, Christian Kjetil; Humphreys-Grant, Cameron; Kongolo, Rodney; Murray, Joshua; Nemane, Aaron Evans; Oliver, Charles William Corrigan; Oseni, Nathaniel Adeyemi Andrew; Tattum, Sam; Vasi, Emanuel; Wood, Marcus James.

MANCHESTER U (48)

AMOS, Ben (G)   **53**   **0**
H: 6 1   W: 13 00   b.Macclesfield 10-4-90
Internationals: England U16, U17, U18, U19, U20, U21.

2007–08	Manchester U	0	0		
2008–09	Manchester U	0	0		
2009–10	Manchester U	0	0		
2009–10	Peterborough U	1	0	1	0
2010–11	Manchester U	0	0		
2010–11	Oldham Ath	16	0	16	0
2011–12	Manchester U	1	0		
2012–13	Manchester U	0	0		
2012–13	Hull C	17	0	17	0
2013–14	Manchester U	0	0		
2013–14	Carlisle U	9	0	9	0
2014–15	Manchester U	0	0	1	0
2014–15	Bolton W	9	0	9	0

ANDER HERRERA, Aguera (M)   **186**   **18**
H: 6 0   W: 10 10   b.Bilbao 14-8-89
Internationals: Spain U20, U21, U23.

2008–09	Real Zaragoza	17	2		
2009–10	Real Zaragoza	30	2		
2010–11	Real Zaragoza	19	1	66	5
2011–12	Athletic Bilbao	32	1		
2012–13	Althetic Bilbao	29	1		
2013–14	Athletic Bilbao	33	5	65	6
2014–15	Manchester U	26	6	26	6

ANDERSON (M)   **135**   **8**
H: 5 8   W: 10 07   b.Porto Alegre 13-4-88
Internationals: Brazil U17, U23, Full caps.

2004–05	Gremio	5	1	5	1
2005–06	Porto	9	0		
2006–07	Porto	15	2	18	2
2007–08	Manchester U	24	0		
2008–09	Manchester U	17	0		
2009–10	Manchester U	14	1		
2010–11	Manchester U	18	1		
2011–12	Manchester U	10	2		
2012–13	Manchester U	17	1		
2013–14	Manchester U	4	0		
2013–14	Fiorentina	7	0	7	0
2014–15	Manchester U	1	0	105	5
Transferred to Internacional February 2015.

BLACKETT, Tyler (D)   **24**   **0**
H: 6 1   W: 11 12   b.Manchester 2-4-94
Internationals: England U16, U17, U18, U19, U21.

2012–13	Manchester U	0	0		
2013–14	Manchester U	0	0		
2013–14	Blackpool	5	0	5	0

2013–14	Birmingham C	8	0	8	0
2014–15	Manchester U	11	0	11	0

BLIND, Daley (M)   **144**   **5**
H: 5 11   W: 10 10   b.Amsterdam 9-3-90
Internationals: Netherlands U16, U17, U19, U21, Full caps.

2008–09	Ajax	5	0		
2009–10	Ajax	0	0		
2009–10	Groningen	17	0	17	0
2010–11	Ajax	10	0		
2011–12	Ajax	21	0		
2012–13	Ajax	34	2		
2013–14	Ajax	29	1		
2014–15	Ajax	3	0	102	3
2014–15	Manchester U	25	2	25	2

CARRICK, Michael (M)   **471**   **27**
H: 6 1   W: 11 10   b.Wallsend 28-7-81
Internationals: England U18, U21, B, Full caps.

1998–99	West Ham U	0	0		
1999–2000	West Ham U	8	1		
1999–2000	Swindon T	6	2	6	2
1999–2000	Birmingham C	2	0	2	0
2000–01	West Ham U	33	1		
2001–02	West Ham U	30	2		
2002–03	West Ham U	30	1		
2003–04	West Ham U	35	1		
2004–05	West Ham U	0	0	136	6
2004–05	Tottenham H	29	0		
2005–06	Tottenham H	35	2	64	2
2006–07	Manchester U	33	3		
2007–08	Manchester U	31	2		
2008–09	Manchester U	28	4		
2009–10	Manchester U	30	3		
2010–11	Manchester U	28	0		
2011–12	Manchester U	30	2		
2012–13	Manchester U	36	1		
2013–14	Manchester U	29	1		
2014–15	Manchester U	18	1	263	17

CLEVERLEY, Tom (M)   **159**   **22**
H: 5 9   W: 10 07   b.Basingstoke 12-8-89
Internationals: England U20, U21, Full caps. Great Britain.

2007–08	Manchester U	0	0		
2008–09	Manchester U	0	0		
2008–09	Leicester C	15	2	15	2
2009–10	Manchester U	0	0		
2009–10	Watford	33	11	33	11
2010–11	Manchester U	0	0		
2010–11	Wigan Ath	25	3	25	3
2011–12	Manchester U	10	0		
2012–13	Manchester U	22	2		
2013–14	Manchester U	22	1		
2014–15	Manchester U	1	0	55	3
2014–15	Aston Villa	31	3	31	3

DA SILVA, Rafael (D)   **109**   **5**
H: 5 8   W: 10 03   b.Rio de Janeiro 9-7-90
Internationals: Brazil U17, U23, Full caps.

2008–09	Manchester U	16	1		
2009–10	Manchester U	8	1		
2010–11	Manchester U	16	0		
2011–12	Manchester U	12	0		
2012–13	Manchester U	28	3		
2013–14	Manchester U	19	0		
2014–15	Manchester U	10	0	109	5

DE GEA, David (G)   **188**   **0**
H: 6 3   W: 12 13   b.Madrid 7-11-90
Internationals: Spain U15, U17, U19, U20, U21, U23, Full caps.

2009–10	Atletico Madrid	19	0		
2010–11	Atletico Madrid	38	0	57	0
2011–12	Manchester U	29	0		
2012–13	Manchester U	28	0		
2013–14	Manchester U	37	0		
2014–15	Manchester U	37	0	131	0

DI MARIA, Angel (M)   **261**   **38**
H: 5 10   W: 10 01   b.Rosario 14-2-88
Internationals: Argentina U20, U23, Full caps.

2005–06	Rosario Central	10	0		
2006–07	Rosario Central	24	6	34	6
2007–08	Benfica	24	2		
2008–09	Benfica	26	5	76	7
2009–10	Benfica	35	6		
2010–11	Real Madrid	32	6		
2011–12	Real Madrid	32	7		
2012–13	Real Madrid	34	4	124	22
2014–15	Manchester U	27	3	27	3

EVANS, Jonny (D)   **178**   **7**
H: 6 2   W: 12 02   b.Belfast 3-1-88
Internationals: Northern Ireland U16, U17, U21, Full caps.

2004–05	Manchester U	0	0		

2005–06	Manchester U	0	0		
2006–07	Manchester U	0	0		
2006–07	Antwerp	14	2	14	2
2006–07	Sunderland	18	1		
2007–08	Manchester U	0	0		
2007–08	Sunderland	15	0	33	1
2008–09	Manchester U	17	0		
2009–10	Manchester U	18	0		
2010–11	Manchester U	13	0		
2011–12	Manchester U	29	1		
2012–13	Manchester U	23	3		
2013–14	Manchester U	17	0		
2014–15	Manchester U	14	0	131	4

FALCAO, Radamel (F)   **255 142**
H: 5 10 W: 11 11 b.Santa Marta 10-2-86
Internationals: Colombia U20, Full caps.

2005–06	River Plate	11	7		
2006–07	River Plate	20	3		
2007–08	River Plate	27	11		
2008–09	River Plate	32	13	90	34
2009–10	Porto	28	25		
2010–11	Porto	22	16		
2011–12	Porto	1	0	51	41
2011–12	Atletico Madrid	34	24		
2012–13	Atletico Madrid	34	28	68	52
2013–14	Monaco	17	9		
2014–15	Monaco	3	2	20	11
On loan from Monaco.					
2014–15	Manchester U	26	4	26	4

FELLAINI, Marouane (M)   **246 37**
H: 6 4 W: 13 05 b.Brussels 22-11-87
Internationals: Belgium U18, U19, U21, Full caps.

2006–07	Standard Liege	29	0		
2007–08	Standard Liege	30	6		
2008–09	Standard Liege	3	0	62	6
2008–09	Everton	30	8		
2009–10	Everton	23	2		
2010–11	Everton	20	1		
2011–12	Everton	34	3		
2012–13	Everton	31	11		
2013–14	Everton	3	0	141	25
2013–14	Manchester U	16	0		
2014–15	Manchester U	27	6	43	6

HENRIQUEZ, Angelo (F)   **71 38**
H: 5 10 W: 10 11 b.Santiago 13-4-94
Internationals: Chile U15, U17, U20, Full caps.

2012	Univ de Chile	17	11	17	11
2012–13	Manchester U	0	0		
2012–13	Wigan Ath	4	1	4	1
2013–14	Manchester U	0	0		
2013–14	Real Zaragoza	25	6	25	6
2014–15	Manchester U	0	0		
2014–15	Dinamo Zagreb	25	20	25	20

HERNANDEZ, Javier (F)   **209 74**
H: 5 8 W: 9 11 b.Guadalajara 1-6-88
Internationals: Mexico U20, Full caps.

2005–06	Tapatio	11	0		
2006–07	Tapatio	12	3		
2006–07	Guadalajara	7	1		
2007–08	Guadalajara	5	0		
2007–08	Tapatio	15	6		
2008–09	Tapatio	7	2	45	11
2008–09	Guadalajara	22	4		
2009–10	Guadalajara	28	21	62	26
2010–11	Manchester U	27	13		
2011–12	Manchester U	28	10		
2012–13	Manchester U	22	10		
2013–14	Manchester U	24	4		
2014–15	Manchester U	1	0	102	37
2014–15	Real Madrid	0	0		

JAMES, Reece (M)   **14 1**
H: 5 6 b.Bacup 7-11-93

2012–13	Manchester U	0	0		
2013–14	Manchester U	0	0		
2013–14	Carlisle U	1	0	1	0
2014–15	Manchester U	0	0		
2014–15	Rotherham U	7	0	7	0
2014–15	Huddersfield T	6	1	6	1

JANKO, Saidy (D)   **10 1**
H: 5 10 W: 11 00 b.Zurich 22-10-95
Internationals: Switzerland U19.

2014–15	Manchester U	0	0		
2014–15	Bolton W	10	1	10	1

JANUZAJ, Adnan (M)   **45 4**
H: 5 11 W: 11 11 b.Brussels 5-2-95
Internationals: Belgium Full caps.

2011–12	Manchester U	0	0		
2012–13	Manchester U	0	0		
2013–14	Manchester U	27	4		
2014–15	Manchester U	18	0	45	4

JOHNSTONE, Samuel (G)   **70 0**
H: 6 0 W: 12 10 b.Preston 25-3-93
Internationals: England U16, U17, U19, U20.

2009–10	Manchester U	0	0		
2010–11	Manchester U	0	0		
2011–12	Manchester U	0	0		
2011–12	Scunthorpe U	12	0	12	0
2012–13	Manchester U	0	0		
2012–13	Walsall	7	0	7	0
2013–14	Manchester U	0	0		
2013–14	Yeovil T	1	0	1	0
2013–14	Doncaster R	18	0		
2014–15	Manchester U	0	0		
2014–15	Doncaster R	10	0	28	0
2014–15	Preston NE	22	0	22	0

JONES, Phil (D)   **129 2**
H: 5 11 W: 11 02 b.Preston 21-2-92
Internationals: England U19, U21, Full caps.

2009–10	Blackburn R	9	0		
2010–11	Blackburn R	26	0	35	0
2011–12	Manchester U	29	1		
2012–13	Manchester U	17	0		
2013–14	Manchester U	26	1		
2014–15	Manchester U	22	0	94	2

KEANE, Will (F)   **28 3**
H: 6 2 W: 11 05 b.Stockport 11-1-93
Internationals: England U16, U17, U19, U21.

2009–10	Manchester U	0	0		
2010–11	Manchester U	0	0		
2011–12	Manchester U	1	0		
2012–13	Manchester U	0	0		
2013–14	Manchester U	0	0		
2013–14	Wigan Ath	4	0	4	0
2013–14	QPR	10	0	10	0
2014–15	Manchester U	0	0	1	0
2014–15	Sheffield W	13	3	13	3

LINDEGAARD, Anders (G)   **91 0**
H: 6 4 W: 12 08 b.Odense 13-4-84
Internationals: Denmark U19, U20, Full caps.

2003–04	Odense	0	0		
2004–05	Odense	0	0		
2005–06	Odense	0	0		
2006–07	Odense	1	0		
2007–08	Odense	1	0		
2008–09	Kolding	10	0	10	0
2009	Aalesund	26	0		
2009	Odense	4	0	6	0
2010	Aalesund	30	0	56	0
2010–11	Manchester U	0	0		
2011–12	Manchester U	8	0		
2012–13	Manchester U	10	0		
2013–14	Manchester U	1	0		
2014–15	Manchester U	0	0	19	0

LINGARD, Jesse (M)   **48 11**
H: 5 3 W: 11 11 b.Warrington 15-12-92
Internationals: England U17, U21.

2011–12	Manchester U	0	0		
2012–13	Manchester U	0	0		
2012–13	Leicester C	5	0	5	0
2013–14	Manchester U	0	0		
2013–14	Birmingham C	13	6	13	6
2013–14	Brighton & HA	15	3	15	3
2014–15	Manchester U	1	0	1	0
2014–15	Derby Co	14	2	14	2

MATA, Juan (M)   **298 76**
H: 5 7 W: 11 00 b.Ocon de Villafranca 28-4-88
Internationals: Spain U16, U17, U19, U20, U21, U23, Full caps.

2006–07	Real Madrid B	39	10	39	10
2007–08	Valencia	24	5		
2008–09	Valencia	37	11		
2009–10	Valencia	35	9		
2010–11	Valencia	33	8	129	33
2011–12	Chelsea	34	6		
2012–13	Chelsea	35	12		
2013–14	Chelsea	13	0	82	18
2013–14	Manchester U	15	6		
2014–15	Manchester U	33	9	48	15

McNAIR, Paddy (D)   **16 0**
H: 5 8 W: 11 05 b.Ballyclare 27-4-95
Internationals: Northern Ireland U16, U17, U19, U21, Full caps.

2012–13	Manchester U	0	0		
2013–14	Manchester U	0	0		
2014–15	Manchester U	16	0	16	0

NANI (M)   **232 42**
H: 5 9 W: 10 04 b.Cape Verde 17-11-86
Internationals: Portugal U21, Full caps.

2005–06	Sporting Lisbon	29	4		
2006–07	Sporting Lisbon	29	5		

2007–08	Manchester U	26	3		
2008–09	Manchester U	13	1		
2009–10	Manchester U	23	4		
2010–11	Manchester U	33	9		
2011–12	Manchester U	29	8		
2012–13	Manchester U	11	1		
2013–14	Manchester U	11	0		
2014–15	Manchester U	1	0	147	26
2014–15	Sporting Lisbon	27	7	85	16

PEARSON, Ben (M)   **22 1**
H: 5 5 W: 11 03 b. 4-1-95
Internationals: England U16, U17, U18, U19, U21, Full caps.

2013–14	Manchester U	0	0		
2014–15	Manchester U	0	0		
2014–15	Barnsley	22	1	22	1

PEREIRA, Andreas (M)   **1 0**
H: 5 10 W: 10 06 b.Duffel 1-1-96
Internationals: Belgium U16, U17. Brazil U20.

2014–15	Manchester U	1	0	1	0

PETRUCCI, Davide (M)   **9 1**
H: 6 2 W: 13 10 b.Rome 5-10-91
Internationals: Italy U19.

2008–09	Manchester U	0	0		
2009–10	Manchester U	0	0		
2010–11	Manchester U	0	0		
2011–12	Manchester U	0	0		
2012–13	Peterborough U	4	1	4	1
2013–14	Manchester U	0	0		
2013–14	Charlton Ath	5	0	5	0
2014–15	Manchester U	0	0		

POWELL, Nick (F)   **91 22**
H: 6 0 W: 10 05 b.Crewe 23-3-94
Internationals: England U16, U17, U18, U19, U21.

2010–11	Crewe Alex	17	0		
2011–12	Crewe Alex	38	14	55	14
2012–13	Manchester U	2	1		
2013–14	Manchester U	0	0		
2013–14	Wigan Ath	31	7	31	7
2014–15	Manchester U	0	0	2	1
2014–15	Leicester C	3	0	3	0

ROJO, Marcos (D)   **122 8**
H: 6 2 W: 12 06 b.La Plata 20-3-90
Internationals: Argentina Full caps.

2008–09	Estudiantes	6	1		
2009–10	Estudiantes	18	0		
2010–11	Estudiantes	19	2	43	3
2011–12	Spartak Moscow	8	0	8	0
2012–13	Sporting Lisbon	24	1		
2013–14	Sporting Lisbon	25	4	49	5
2014–15	Manchester U	22	0	22	0

ROONEY, Wayne (F)   **407 185**
H: 5 10 W: 12 13 b.Liverpool 24-10-85
Internationals: England U15, U16, U19, Full caps.

2002–03	Everton	33	6		
2003–04	Everton	34	9	67	15
2004–05	Manchester U	29	11		
2005–06	Manchester U	36	16		
2006–07	Manchester U	35	14		
2007–08	Manchester U	27	12		
2008–09	Manchester U	30	12		
2009–10	Manchester U	32	26		
2010–11	Manchester U	28	11		
2011–12	Manchester U	34	27		
2012–13	Manchester U	27	12		
2013–14	Manchester U	29	17		
2014–15	Manchester U	33	12	340	170

ROTHWELL, Joe (M)   **3 0**
b.Manchester 11-1-95
Internationals: England U16, U17, U19, U20.

2014–15	Manchester U	0	0		
2014–15	Blackpool	3	0	3	0

SHAW, Luke (D)   **76 0**
H: 6 1 W: 11 11 b.Kingston 12-7-95
Internationals: England U16, U17, U21, Full caps.

2011–12	Southampton	0	0		
2012–13	Southampton	25	0		
2013–14	Southampton	35	0	60	0
2014–15	Manchester U	16	0	16	0

SMALLING, Chris (D)   **113 6**
H: 6 4 W: 14 02 b.Greenwich 22-11-89
Internationals: England U18, U20, U21, Full caps.

2008–09	Fulham	1	0		
2009–10	Fulham	12	0	13	0
2010–11	Manchester U	16	0		
2011–12	Manchester U	19	1		
2012–13	Manchester U	15	0		

2013–14	Manchester U	25	1		
2014–15	Manchester U	25	4	100	6

THORPE, Tom (D)   7   0
H: 6 0 W: 14 00 b.Manchester 13-1-93
Internationals: England U16, U17, U18, U19, U20, U21.

2010–11	Manchester U	0	0
2011–12	Manchester U	0	0
2012–13	Manchester U	0	0
2013–14	Manchester U	0	0
2013–14	Birmingham C	6	0	6	0
2014–15	Manchester U	1	0	1	0

VALDES, Victor (G)   389   0
H: 6 2 W: 12 04 b.L'Hospitalet de Llobregat 14-1-82
Internationals: Spain U18, U19, U20, U21, Full caps.

2002–03	Barcelona	14	0		
2003–04	Barcelona	33	0		
2004–05	Barcelona	35	0		
2005–06	Barcelona	35	0		
2006–07	Barcelona	38	0		
2007–08	Barcelona	35	0		
2008–09	Barcelona	35	0		
2009–10	Barcelona	38	0		
2010–11	Barcelona	32	0		
2011–12	Barcelona	35	0		
2012–13	Barcelona	31	0		
2013–14	Barcelona	26	0	387	0
2014–15	Manchester U	2	0	2	0

VALENCIA, Antonio (M)   335   31
H: 5 10 W: 12 04 b.Lago Agrio 5-8-85
Internationals: Ecuador U20, 21, U23, Full caps.

2002	El Nacional	1	0		
2003	El Nacional	26	2		
2004	El Nacional	42	5		
2005	El Nacional	14	4	83	11
2005–06	Villarreal	2	0	2	0
2005–06	*Recreativo*	4	0	4	0
2006–07	Wigan Ath	22	1		
2007–08	Wigan Ath	31	3		
2008–09	Wigan Ath	31	3	84	7
2009–10	Manchester U	34	5		
2010–11	Manchester U	10	1		
2011–12	Manchester U	27	4		
2012–13	Manchester U	30	1		
2013–14	Manchester U	29	2		
2014–15	Manchester U	32	0	162	13

VAN PERSIE, Robin (F)   341   158
H: 6 0 W: 11 00 b.Rotterdam 6-8-83
Internationals: Netherlands U17, U19, U21, Full caps.

2001–02	Feyenoord	10	0		
2002–03	Feyenoord	23	8		
2003–04	Feyenoord	28	6	61	14
2004–05	Arsenal	26	5		
2005–06	Arsenal	24	5		
2006–07	Arsenal	22	11		
2007–08	Arsenal	15	7		
2008–09	Arsenal	28	11		
2009–10	Arsenal	16	9		
2010–11	Arsenal	25	18		
2011–12	Arsenal	38	30		
2012–13	Arsenal	0	0	194	96
2012–13	Manchester U	38	26		
2013–14	Manchester U	21	12		
2014–15	Manchester U	27	10	86	48

VARELA, Guillermo (D)   0   0
H: 5 7 W: 10 11 b.Montevideo 24-3-93
Internationals: Uruguay U17, U20.

2013–14	Manchester U	0	0
2014–15	Manchester U	0	0

WILSON, James (F)   14   3
H: 6 0 W: 12 04 b.Biddulph 1-12-95
Internationals: England U16, U19, U20.

2013–14	Manchester U	1	2		
2014–15	Manchester U	13	1	14	3

YOUNG, Ashley (M)   345   59
H: 5 10 W: 10 03 b.Stevenage 9-7-85
Internationals: England U21, Full caps.

2002–03	Watford	5	3		
2003–04	Watford	5	3		
2004–05	Watford	34	0		
2005–06	Watford	39	13		
2006–07	Watford	20	3	98	19
2006–07	Aston Villa	13	2		
2007–08	Aston Villa	37	9		
2008–09	Aston Villa	36	7		
2009–10	Aston Villa	37	5		
2010–11	Aston Villa	34	7	157	30
2011–12	Manchester U	25	6		
2012–13	Manchester U	19	0		
2013–14	Manchester U	20	2		
2014–15	Manchester U	26	2	90	10

Players retained or with offer of contract
Almedia, Da Cunha Luis Carlos; Doughty, Joshua Anders; El-Fitouri, Sadik; Fletcher, Ashley Michael; Goss, Sean Richard; Grimshaw, Liam David; Harrop, Joshua Andrew; Love, Donald Alistair; O'Hara, Kieran Michael; Rashford, Marcus; Weir, James Michael; Willock, Matthew.

Scholars
Borthwick-Jackson, Cameron Jake; Byrne, Oliver Joseph; Dorrington, George Edward; Dunne, James Gerard; Fosu-Mensah, Evans Timothy Fosu; Henderson, Dean Bradley; Johnson, Travis Conroy; Mctominay, Scott; Mitchell, Demetri Karim; Redmond, Devonte Vincent; Reid, Tyler; Riley, Joe; Scott, Charlie Thomas; Tuanzebe, Axel.

MANSFIELD T (49)

BEEVERS, Lee (D)   357   14
H: 6 2 W: 11 07 b.Doncaster 4-12-83
Internationals: Wales U21.

2000–01	Ipswich T	0	0		
2001–02	Ipswich T	0	0		
2002–03	Ipswich T	0	0		
2002–03	*Boston U*	1	0		
2003–04	Boston U	40	2		
2004–05	Boston U	31	1	72	3
2004–05	Lincoln C	8	0		
2005–06	Lincoln C	33	1		
2006–07	Lincoln C	44	5		
2007–08	Lincoln C	37	1		
2008–09	Lincoln C	44	2	166	9
2009–10	Colchester U	4	0		
2010–11	Colchester U	19	0	23	0
2011–12	Walsall	35	0	35	0
2013–14	Mansfield T	26	0		
2014–15	Mansfield T	35	2	61	2

BINGHAM, Rakish (F)   33   7
H: 6 0 W: 12 00 b.Newham 25-10-93

2011–12	Wigan Ath	0	0		
2012–13	Wigan Ath	0	0		
2013–14	Wigan Ath	0	0		
2014–15	Mansfield T	28	6	28	6
2014–15	*Hartlepool U*	5	1	5	1

BISHOP, Adam (G)   0   0
b. 12-6-98

2014–15	Mansfield T	0	0

BLAIR, Matty (M)   84   10
H: 5 10 W: 11 09 b.Coventry 30-11-87
Internationals: England C.

2012–13	York C	44	6	44	6
2013–14	Fleetwood T	24	3		
2013–14	*Northampton T*	3	1	3	1
2014–15	Fleetwood T	8	0	32	3
2014–15	*Cambridge U*	2	0	2	0
2014–15	Mansfield T	3	0	3	0

BROWN, Junior (D)   109   15
H: 5 9 W: 10 09 b.Crewe 7-5-89

2006–07	Crewe Alex	0	0		
2007–08	Crewe Alex	1	0	1	0
2012–13	Fleetwood T	43	11		
2013–14	Fleetwood T	21	1	64	12
2013–14	*Tranmere R*	9	1	9	1
2014–15	Oxford U	11	0	11	0
2014–15	Mansfield T	24	2	24	2

CLEMENTS, Chris (M)   72   3
H: 5 9 W: 10 04 b.Birmingham 6-2-90

2008–09	Crewe Alex	0	0		
2009	*IBV*	15	1	15	1
2009–10	Crewe Alex	0	0		
2010–11	Crewe Alex	0	0		
2013–14	Mansfield T	23	1		
2014–15	Mansfield T	34	1	57	2

DEMPSTER, John (D)   119   5
H: 6 1 W: 11 07 b.Kettering 1-4-83
Internationals: Scotland U21.

2001–02	Rushden & D	2	0		
2002–03	Rushden & D	16	1		
2003–04	Rushden & D	19	0		
2004–05	Rushden & D	15	0		
2005–06	Rushden & D	14	3	66	4
2005–06	Oxford U	6	0	6	0
From Kettering T					
2011–12	Crawley T	7	1	7	1
2013–14	Mansfield T	36	0		
2014–15	Mansfield T	4	0	40	0

FISHER, Alex (F)   98   24
H: 6 2 W: 12 00 b. 30-6-90

2006–07	Oxford U	0	0		
2007–08	Oxford U	10	1		
2008–09	Oxford U	3	1	13	2
2009–10	Jerez Industrial	0	0		
2010–11	Jerez Industrial	21	11	21	11
2011–12	Tienen	7	1	7	1
2012–13	Racing Mechelen	27	7	27	7
2013–14	Heist	2	0	2	0
2013–14	Monza	14	2	14	2
2014–15	Mansfield T	14	1	14	1

FITZPATRICK, Joe (M)   3   0
b. 20-8-97

2014–15	Mansfield T	3	0	3	0

FLETCHER, Dan (F)   1   0
b. 4-3-97

2014–15	Mansfield T	1	0	1	0

HEARN, Liam (F)   3   0
H: 5 11 b. 27-8-85
Internationals: England C.

2014–15	Mansfield T	3	0	3	0

HESLOP, Simon (M)   152   10
H: 5 11 W: 11 00 b.York 1-5-87

2005–06	Barnsley	0	0		
2006–07	Barnsley	1	0		
2007–08	Barnsley	0	0		
2008–09	Barnsley	0	0		
2008–09	Grimsby T	8	0	8	0
2009–10	Barnsley	0	0	1	0
2010–11	Oxford U	38	3		
2011–12	Oxford U	29	3		
2012–13	Oxford U	24	1		
2013–14	Oxford U	0	0	91	7
2013–14	Stevenage	27	1	27	1
2014–15	Mansfield T	25	2	25	2

JONES, Luke (D)   48   0
H: 6 0 W: 13 04 b.Darwen 10-4-87

2005–06	Blackburn R	0	0		
2005–06	*Cercle Brugge*	8	0	8	0
2006–07	Shrewsbury T	0	0		
2007–08	Shrewsbury T	7	0	14	0
From Kidderminster H, Mansfield T, Forest Green R					
2013–14	Stevenage	26	0	26	0
2014–15	Mansfield T	0	0		

LAMBE, Reggie (M)   104   8
H: 5 7 W: 10 09 b.Bermuda 4-2-91
Internationals: Bermuda Full caps.

2009–10	Ipswich T	0	0		
2010–11	Ipswich T	2	0	2	0
2010–11	*Bristol R*	7	0	7	0
2012	Toronto	27	2		
2013	Toronto	27	0	54	2
2014	Nykoping	11	1	11	1
2014–15	Mansfield T	30	5	30	5

MARSDEN, Liam (D)   12   0
b.Creswell 21-11-94

2013–14	Mansfield T	2	0		
2014–15	Mansfield T	10	0	12	0

McGUIRE, Jamie (M)   93   4
H: 5 7 W: 10 13 b.Birkenhead 13-11-83

2001–02	Tranmere R	0	0		
2002–03	Tranmere R	0	0		
2003–04	Tranmere R	0	0		
From Northwich Vic (loan), Droylsden					
2012–13	Fleetwood T	37	1	37	1
2013–14	Mansfield T	27	2		
2014–15	Mansfield T	29	1	56	3

MURRAY, Adam (M)   250   18
H: 5 9 W: 10 01 b.Birmingham 30-9-81

1998–99	Derby Co	4	0		
1999–2000	Derby Co	8	0		
2000–01	Derby Co	14	0		
2001–02	Derby Co	6	0		
2001–02	*Mansfield T*	13	7		
2002–03	Derby Co	24	0	56	0
2003–04	Kidderminster H	22	3	22	3
From Burton Alb					
2003–04	Notts Co	3	0	3	0
2004–05	Mansfield T	32	5		
2005–06	Carlisle U	37	1	37	1
2006–07	Torquay U	21	0	21	0
2006–07	Macclesfield U	11	0		
2007–08	Macclesfield T	23	0	34	0
From Oxford U, Luton T					
2013–14	Mansfield T	18	1		
2014–15	Mansfield T	14	1	77	14

PALMER, Oliver (F)   54   5
b.London 21-1-92

2013–14	Mansfield T	38	4		
2014–15	Mansfield T	16	1	54	5

RAVENHILL, Ricky (M)   391   22
H: 5 10   W: 11 02   b.Doncaster 16-1-81

2003–04	Doncaster R	36	3		
2004–05	Doncaster R	35	3		
2005–06	Doncaster R	27	3	98	9
2006–07	Chester C	3	0	3	0
2006–07	Grimsby T	17	2	17	2
2006–07	Darlington	15	1		
2007–08	Darlington	35	3		
2008–09	Darlington	38	2	88	6
2008–09	Notts Co	0	0		
2009–10	Notts Co	40	3		
2010–11	Notts Co	34	0		
2011–12	Notts Co	5	0	79	3
2011–12	Bradford C	26	1		
2012–13	Bradford C	22	1		
2013–14	Bradford C	8	0	56	2
2013–14	Northampton T	25	0		
2014–15	Northampton T	12	0	37	0
2014–15	Mansfield T	13	0	13	0

RAYNES, Michael (D)   286   6
H: 6 4   W: 12 00   b.Wythenshawe 15-10-87

2004–05	Stockport Co	19	0		
2005–06	Stockport Co	25	1		
2006–07	Stockport Co	9	0		
2007–08	Stockport Co	27	0		
2008–09	Stockport Co	35	3		
2009–10	Stockport Co	25	1	140	5
2009–10	Scunthorpe U	12	0		
2010–11	Scunthorpe U	22	0	34	0
2011–12	Rotherham U	33	0	33	0
2012–13	Oxford U	38	1		
2013–14	Oxford U	27	0		
2014–15	Oxford U	4	0	69	1
2014–15	Mansfield T	10	0	10	0

RHEAD, Matt (F)   72   9
b.Stoke-on-Trent 31-5-84

2013–14	Mansfield T	40	6		
2014–15	Mansfield T	32	3	72	9

RILEY, Martin (D)   90   1
H: 6 2   W: 12 10   b.Wolverhampton 5-12-86
Internationals: England C.

2006–07	Wolverhampton W	0	0		
2007–08	Wolverhampton W	0	0		
From Kidderminster H					
2010–11	Cheltenham T	26	0	26	0
From Wrexham					
2013–14	Mansfield T	31	1		
2014–15	Mansfield T	33	0	64	1

SHIRES, Corbin (D)   1   0
b. 31-12-97

2014–15	Mansfield T	1	0	1	0

STUDER, Sascha (G)   17   0
H: 6 3   W: 11 09   b. 3-9-91
Internationals: Switzerland U17.

2014–15	Mansfield T	17	0	17	0

SUTTON, Ritchie (D)   81   0
H: 6 0   W: 11 04   b.Stoke-on-Trent 29-4-86

2005–06	Crewe Alex	0	0		
From Stafford R, Northwich Vic, FC Halifax T, Nantwich T					
2010–11	Port Vale	11	0	11	0
2013–14	Mansfield T	36	0		
2014–15	Mansfield T	34	0	70	0

TAFAZOLLI, Ryan (D)   60   3
H: 6 5   W: 12 03   b.Sutton 28-9-91

2010–11	Southampton	0	0		
From Salisbury, Cambridge C, Carshalton Ath					
2013–14	Mansfield T	24	2		
2014–15	Mansfield T	36	1	60	3

THOMAS, Jack (M)   13   1
H: 5 9   W: 10 10   b.Sutton-in-Ashfield 3-6-96

2013–14	Mansfield T	1	0		
2014–15	Mansfield T	12	1	13	1

Non-Contract
Bishop, Adam James.

MIDDLESBROUGH (50)

ADOMAH, Albert (F)   328   53
H: 6 1   W: 11 08   b.Lambeth 13-12-87
Internationals: Ghana Full caps.

2007–08	Barnet	22	5		
2008–09	Barnet	45	9		
2009–10	Barnet	45	5	112	19
2010–11	Bristol C	46	5		
2011–12	Bristol C	45	5		
2012–13	Bristol C	40	7		
2013–14	Bristol C	0	0	131	17
2013–14	Middlesbrough	42	12		
2014–15	Middlesbrough	43	5	85	17

ATKINSON, David (D)   7   0
b.Shildon 27-4-93

2010–11	Middlesbrough	0	0		
2011–12	Middlesbrough	0	0		
2012–13	Middlesbrough	0	0		
2013–14	Middlesbrough	0	0		
2014–15	Middlesbrough	0	0		
2014–15	Hartlepool U	0	0		
2014–15	Carlisle U	7	0	7	0

AYALA, Daniel (M)   102   9
H: 6 3   W: 13 03   b.Sevilla 7-11-90
Internationals: Spain U21.

2007–08	Liverpool	0	0		
2008–09	Liverpool	0	0		
2009–10	Liverpool	5	0		
2010–11	Liverpool	0	0	5	0
2010–11	Hull C	12	1	12	1
2010–11	Derby Co	17	0	17	0
2011–12	Norwich C	7	0		
2012–13	Norwich C	0	0		
2012–13	Nottingham F	12	1	12	1
2013–14	Norwich C	0	0	7	0
2013–14	Middlesbrough	19	3		
2014–15	Middlesbrough	30	4	49	7

BENNETT, Andre (D)   0   0
H: 5 8   W: 10 02   b.Houghton-le-spring 22-10-94

2012–13	Middlesbrough	0	0		
2013–14	Middlesbrough	0	0		
2014–15	Middlesbrough	0	0		

BROBBEL, Ryan (M)   34   4
b.Hartlepool 5-3-93
Internationals: Northern Ireland U17, U18, U19, U21.

2011–12	Middlesbrough	0	0		
2012–13	Middlesbrough	0	0		
2013–14	Middlesbrough	0	0		
2013–14	York C	19	4	19	4
2014–15	Middlesbrough	0	0		
2014–15	Hartlepool U	15	0	15	0

CARAYOL, Mustapha (F)   138   24
H: 5 11   W: 11 11   b.Gambia 10-6-89

2007–08	Milton Keynes D	0	0		
2009–10	Torquay U	20	6	20	6
2010–11	Lincoln C	33	3	33	3
2011–12	Bristol R	30	4		
2012–13	Bristol R	0	0	30	4
2012–13	Middlesbrough	18	3		
2013–14	Middlesbrough	32	8		
2014–15	Middlesbrough	0	0	50	11
2014–15	Brighton & HA	5	0	5	0

CLAYTON, Adam (M)   214   19
H: 5 9   W: 11 11   b.Manchester 14-1-89
Internationals: England U20.

2007–08	Manchester C	0	0		
2008–09	Manchester C	0	0		
2009–10	Manchester C	0	0		
2009–10	Carlisle U	28	1	28	1
2010–11	Leeds U	0	0		
2010–11	Peterborough U	7	0	7	0
2010–11	Milton Keynes D	6	1	6	1
2011–12	Leeds U	43	6	47	6
2012–13	Huddersfield T	43	4		
2013–14	Huddersfield T	42	7	85	11
2014–15	Middlesbrough	40	1	41	0

CODDINGTON, Luke (G)   0   0
b.Middlesbrough 6-6-95
Internationals: England U17, U18, U19.

2013–14	Middlesbrough	0	0
2014–15	Middlesbrough	0	0

DAMIA, Abella (M)   232   5
H: 6 2   W: 12 02   b.Figueres 15-4-82

2004–05	Barcelona	9	0		
2005–06	Barcelona	0	0	9	0
2005–06	Santander	18	3	18	3
2006–07	Real Betis	0	0		
2007–08	Real Betis	26	0		
2008–09	Real Betis	25	2		
2009–10	Real Betis	28	0	79	2
2010–11	Osasuna	27	0		
2011–12	Osasuna	30	0		
2012–13	Osasuna	29	0		
2013–14	Osasuna	34	0	120	0
2014–15	Middlesbrough	6	0	6	0

FEWSTER, Bradley (F)   0   0
H: 5 10   W: 11 00   b. 27-1-96
Internationals: England U16, U17, U18, U19.

2013–14	Middlesbrough	0	0
2014–15	Middlesbrough	0	0
2014–15	Preston NE	0	0

FORSHAW, Adam (M)   124   12
H: 6 1   W: 11 02   b.Liverpool 8-10-91

2009–10	Everton	0	0		
2010–11	Everton	1	0		
2011–12	Everton	0	0	1	0
2011–12	Brentford	7	0		
2012–13	Brentford	43	3		
2013–14	Brentford	39	8	89	11
2014–15	Wigan Ath	16	1	16	1
2014–15	Middlesbrough	18	0	18	0

FRIEND, George (D)   216   7
H: 6 2   W: 13 01   b.Barnstaple 19-10-87

2008–09	Exeter C	4	0		
2008–09	Wolverhampton W	6	0		
2009–10	Wolverhampton W	1	0	7	0
2009–10	Millwall	6	0	6	0
2009–10	Southend U	6	1	6	1
2009–10	Scunthorpe U	4	0	4	0
2009–10	Exeter C	13	1	17	1
2010–11	Doncaster R	32	1		
2011–12	Doncaster R	27	0		
2012–13	Doncaster R	0	0	59	1
2012–13	Middlesbrough	34	0		
2013–14	Middlesbrough	41	3		
2014–15	Middlesbrough	42	1	117	4

GARCIA, Enrique (F)   190   57
b.Motilla del Palancar 25-11-89
Internationals: Spain U20.

2008–09	Murcia	3	1		
2009–10	Murcia	30	3		
2010–11	Murcia	34	12		
2011–12	Murcia	2	1		
2012–13	Murcia	36	8		
2013–14	Murcia	43	23	148	48
2014–15	Murcia	42	9	42	9

GIBSON, Ben (D)   110   2
H: 6 1   W: 12 04   b.Nunthorpe 15-1-93
Internationals: England U17, U18, U21.

2010–11	Middlesbrough	1	0		
2011–12	Middlesbrough	0	0		
2011–12	Plymouth Arg	13	0	13	0
2012–13	Middlesbrough	1	0		
2012–13	Tranmere R	28	1	28	1
2013–14	Middlesbrough	31	1		
2014–15	Middlesbrough	36	0	69	1

HALLIDAY, Bradley (M)   24   1
b.Redcar 10-7-95

2013–14	Middlesbrough	0	0		
2014–15	York C	24	1	24	1

HINES, Seb (D)   95   3
H: 6 1   W: 12 02   b.Wetherby 29-5-88
Internationals: England U16, U17, U19.

2005–06	Middlesbrough	0	0		
2006–07	Middlesbrough	1	0		
2007–08	Middlesbrough	1	0		
2008–09	Middlesbrough	1	0		
2008–09	Derby Co	0	0		
2008–09	Oldham Ath	4	0	4	0
2009–10	Middlesbrough	14	1		
2010–11	Middlesbrough	23	1		
2012–13	Middlesbrough	21	1		
2013–14	Middlesbrough	4	0		
2014–15	Middlesbrough	3	0	69	3
2014–15	Coventry C	9	0	9	0
2015	Orlando C	13	0	13	0

HUSBAND, James (D)   72   4
H: 5 10   W: 10 00   b.Leeds 3-1-94

2011–12	Doncaster R	3	0		
2012–13	Doncaster R	33	3		
2013–14	Doncaster R	28	1	64	4
2014–15	Middlesbrough	3	0	3	0
2014–15	Fulham	5	0	5	0

JACKSON, Adam (D)   0   0
b.Darlington 18-5-94
Internationals: England U16, U17, U18, U19.

2011–12	Middlesbrough	0	0
2012–13	Middlesbrough	0	0
2013–14	Middlesbrough	0	0
2014–15	Middlesbrough	0	0

JONES, Jordan (M)   11   0
H: 5 8   W: 9 07   b.Kettering 24-10-94

2012–13	Middlesbrough	0	0
2013–14	Middlesbrough	0	0

| 2014–15 | Middlesbrough | 0 | 0 | | |
| 2014–15 | *Hartlepool U* | 11 | 0 | **11** | **0** |

KONSTANTOPOULOS, Dimitrios (G)266 0
H: 6 4   W: 14 02   b.Kalamata 29-11-78
Internationals: Greece U21, Full caps.

2003–04	Hartlepool U	0	0		
2004–05	Hartlepool U	25	0		
2005–06	Hartlepool U	46	0		
2006–07	Hartlepool U	46	0	**117**	**0**
2007–08	Coventry C	21	0		
2008–09	Coventry C	0	0		
2008–09	*Swansea C*	4	0	**4**	**0**
2008–09	*Cardiff C*	6	0	**6**	**0**
2009–10	Coventry C	3	0	**24**	**0**
2010–11	Kerkyra	30	0	**30**	**0**
2011–12	AEK Athens	9	0		
2012–13	AEK Athens	24	0	**33**	**0**
2013–14	Middlesbrough	12	0		
2014–15	Middlesbrough	40	0	**52**	**0**

LEADBITTER, Grant (M)   356 45
H: 5 9   W: 11 06   b.Chester-le-Street 7-1-86
Internationals: England U16, U17, U19, U20, U21.

2002–03	Sunderland	0	0		
2003–04	Sunderland	0	0		
2004–05	Sunderland	0	0		
2005–06	Sunderland	12	0		
2005–06	*Rotherham U*	5	1	**5**	**1**
2006–07	Sunderland	44	7		
2007–08	Sunderland	31	2		
2008–09	Sunderland	23	2		
2009–10	Sunderland	1	0	**111**	**01**
2009–10	Ipswich T	38	3		
2010–11	Ipswich T	44	5		
2011–12	Ipswich T	34	5		
2012–13	Ipswich T	0	0	**116**	**13**
2012–13	Middlesbrough	42	3		
2013–14	Middlesbrough	39	6		
2014–15	Middlesbrough	43	11	**124**	**20**

LEDESMA, Emmanuel (M)   131 17
H: 5 11   W: 12 02   b.Quilmes 24-5-88

2007–08	Genoa	1	0	**1**	**0**
2008–09	*Salernitana*	8	1	**8**	**1**
2008–09	*QPR*	17	1	**17**	**1**
2009–10	*Novara*	8	1	**8**	**1**
2010–11	*Crotone*	10	0	**10**	**0**
2010–11	Walsall	10	1		
2011–12	Walsall	10	4	**20**	**5**
2012–13	Middlesbrough	28	2		
2013–14	Middlesbrough	27	6		
2014–15	Middlesbrough	1	0	**56**	**8**
2014–15	*Rotherham U*	7	1	**7**	**1**
2014–15	*Brighton & HA*	4	0	**4**	**0**

MEJIAS, Tomas (G)   9 0
H: 6 5   W: 13 02   b.Madrid 30-1-89
Internationals: Spain U19, U20.

2010–11	Real Madrid	1	0		
2011–12	Real Madrid	0	0		
2012–13	Real Madrid	0	0		
2013–14	Real Madrid	0	0	**1**	**0**
2013–14	*Middlesbrough*	1	0		
2014–15	Middlesbrough	7	0	**8**	**0**

MORRIS, Bryn (M)   7 0
H: 6 0   W: 11 01   b.Hartlepool 25-4-96
Internationals: England U16, U17, U18, U19.

2012–13	Middlesbrough	1	0		
2013–14	Middlesbrough	0	0		
2014–15	Middlesbrough	0	0	**2**	**0**
2014–15	*Burton Alb*	5	0	**5**	**0**

NSUE, Emilio (F)   239 25
H: 5 10   W: 11 11   b.Palma 30-9-89
Internationals: Spain U16, U17, U19, U20, U21. Equatorial Guinea Full caps.

2007–08	Mallorca	2	0		
2008–09	Mallorca	0	0		
2008–09	*Castellon*	37	7	**37**	**7**
2009–10	Mallorca	0	0		
2009–10	*Real Sociedad*	34	5	**34**	**5**
2010–11	Mallorca	38	4		
2011–12	Mallorca	30	3		
2012–13	Mallorca	32	2		
2013–14	Mallorca	40	4	**142**	**13**
2014–15	Middlesbrough	26	0	**26**	**0**

REACH, Adam (M)   99 17
H: 6 1   W: 11 07   b.Gateshead 3-2-93
Internationals: England U19, U20.

2010–11	Middlesbrough	1	1		
2011–12	Middlesbrough	1	0		
2012–13	Middlesbrough	16	2		
2013–14	Middlesbrough	0	0		
2013–14	*Shrewsbury T*	22	3	**22**	**3**
2013–14	*Bradford C*	18	3	**18**	**3**
2014–15	Middlesbrough	39	2	**59**	**5**

RIPLEY, Connor (G)   17 0
H: 5 11   W: 11 13   b.Middlesbrough 13-2-93
Internationals: England U19, U20.

2010–11	Middlesbrough	1	0		
2011–12	Middlesbrough	1	0		
2011–12	*Oxford U*	1	0	**1**	**0**
2012–13	Middlesbrough	0	0		
2013–14	Middlesbrough	0	0		
2013–14	*Bradford C*	0	0		
2014	*Ostersunds*	14	0	**14**	**0**
2014–15	Middlesbrough	0	0	**2**	**0**

SMALLWOOD, Richard (M)   120 4
H: 5 11   W: 11 05   b.Redcar 29-12-90
Internationals: England U18.

2008–09	Middlesbrough	0	0		
2009–10	Middlesbrough	0	0		
2010–11	Middlesbrough	13	1		
2011–12	Middlesbrough	13	0		
2012–13	Middlesbrough	22	2		
2013–14	Middlesbrough	13	0		
2013–14	*Rotherham U*	18	0		
2014–15	Middlesbrough	0	0	**61**	**3**
2014–15	*Rotherham U*	41	1	**59**	**1**

STEELE, Jason (G)   175 0
H: 6 2   W: 12 07   b.Newton Aycliffe 18-8-90
Internationals: England U16, U17, U19, U21. Great Britain.

2007–08	Middlesbrough	0	0		
2008–09	Middlesbrough	0	0		
2009–10	Middlesbrough	0	0		
2009–10	*Northampton T*	13	0	**13**	**0**
2010–11	Middlesbrough	35	0		
2011–12	Middlesbrough	34	0		
2012–13	Middlesbrough	46	0		
2013–14	Middlesbrough	16	0		
2014–15	Middlesbrough	0	0	**131**	**0**
2014–15	*Blackburn R*	31	0	**31**	**0**

TOMLIN, Lee (F)   191 43
H: 5 11   W: 11 09   b.Leicester 12-1-89
Internationals: England C.

2010–11	Peterborough U	37	8		
2011–12	Peterborough U	37	8		
2012–13	Peterborough U	42	11		
2013–14	Peterborough U	19	5	**135**	**32**
2013–14	Middlesbrough	14	4		
2014–15	Middlesbrough	42	7	**56**	**11**

VOSSEN, Jelle (F)   243 90
H: 5 11   W: 11 00   b.Bilzen 22-3-89
Internationals: Belgium U16, U17, U18, U19, U20, U21, Full caps.

2006–07	Genk	8	1		
2007–08	Genk	17	3		
2008–09	Genk	20	4		
2009–10	Genk	3	0		
2009–10	*Cercle Brugge*	17	6	**17**	**6**
2010–11	Genk	37	20		
2011–12	Genk	36	20		
2012–13	Genk	32	17		
2013–14	Genk	38	12		
2014–15	Genk	2	0	**193**	**77**
On loan from Genk.
2014–15	Middlesbrough	33	7	**33**	**7**

WHITEHEAD, Dean (M)   494 26
H: 5 11   W: 12 06   b.Abingdon 12-1-82

1999–2000	Oxford U	1	0		
2000–01	Oxford U	20	0		
2001–02	Oxford U	40	1		
2002–03	Oxford U	18	1		
2003–04	Oxford U	44	7	**122**	**9**
2004–05	Sunderland	42	5		
2005–06	Sunderland	37	3		
2006–07	Sunderland	45	4		
2007–08	Sunderland	27	1		
2008–09	Sunderland	34	0		
2009–10	Sunderland	0	0	**185**	**13**
2009–10	Stoke C	36	0		
2010–11	Stoke C	37	2		
2011–12	Stoke C	33	0		
2012–13	Stoke C	26	1	**132**	**3**
2013–14	Middlesbrough	37	1		
2014–15	Middlesbrough	18	0	**55**	**1**

WILDSCHUT, Yanic (F)   134 15
H: 6 2   W: 13 08   b. 1-11-91
Internationals: Netherlands U21.

2010–11	Zwolle	33	3	**33**	**3**
2011–12	VVV	29	7		
2012–13	VVV	32	1	**61**	**8**
2013–14	Heerenveen	18	2		
2013–14	*Den Haag*	7	0	**7**	**0**
2014–15	Heerenveen	4	0	**22**	**2**
2014–15	Middlesbrough	11	2	**11**	**2**

WILLIAMS, Luke (F)   54 6
H: 6 1   W: 11 08   b.Middlesbrough 11-6-93
Internationals: England U17, U19, U20.

2009–10	Middlesbrough	4	0		
2010–11	Middlesbrough	6	0		
2011–12	Middlesbrough	0	0		
2012–13	Middlesbrough	11	2		
2013–14	Middlesbrough	9	0		
2013–14	*Hartlepool U*	7	2	**7**	**2**
2014–15	Middlesbrough	4	0	**34**	**2**
2014–15	*Scunthorpe U*	6	2	**6**	**2**
2014–15	*Coventry C*	5	0	**5**	**0**
2014–15	*Peterborough U*	2	0	**.2**	**0**

WILLIAMS, Rhys (M)   142 5
H: 6 2   W: 11 05   b.Perth 14-7-88
Internationals: Wales U21. Australia Full caps.

2006–07	Middlesbrough	0	0		
2007–08	Middlesbrough	0	0		
2008–09	Middlesbrough	0	0		
2008–09	*Burnley*	17	0	**17**	**0**
2009–10	Middlesbrough	32	2		
2010–11	Middlesbrough	12	1		
2011–12	Middlesbrough	35	2		
2012–13	Middlesbrough	23	0		
2013–14	Middlesbrough	22	0		
2014–15	Middlesbrough	1	0	**125**	**5**

WOODGATE, Jonathan (D)   309 8
H: 6 2   W: 12 06   b.Middlesbrough 22-1-80
Internationals: England U16, U18, U21, Full caps.

1996–97	Leeds U	0	0		
1997–98	Leeds U	0	0		
1998–99	Leeds U	25	2		
1999–2000	Leeds U	34	1		
2000–01	Leeds U	14	1		
2001–02	Leeds U	13	0		
2002–03	Leeds U	18	0	**104**	**4**
2002–03	Newcastle U	10	0		
2003–04	Newcastle U	18	0	**28**	**0**
2004–05	Real Madrid	0	0		
2005–06	Real Madrid	9	0	**9**	**0**
2006–07	Middlesbrough	30	0		
2007–08	Middlesbrough	16	0		
2007–08	Tottenham H	12	1		
2008–09	Tottenham H	34	1		
2009–10	Tottenham H	3	0		
2010–11	Tottenham H	0	0	**49**	**2**
2011–12	Stoke C	17	0	**17**	**0**
2012–13	Middlesbrough	24	1		
2013–14	Middlesbrough	25	0		
2014–15	Middlesbrough	7	1	**102**	**2**

Players retained or with offer of contract
Burn, Jonathan David; Chapman, Harrison James; Cooke, Callum James; Fry, Dael Jonathan; Fryer, Joseph Luke; Maloney, Lewis Terence James; Morelli, Joao Neto; Osorio, Tomas Mejias; Scoble, Lewis Clive.

Scholars
Coulson, Hayden Ross; Dawson, Thomas James; Elsdon, Matthew; Griffiths, Priestley David; Helm, Jonathan David; Hetherington, Lee; Jardine, Daniel Lachlan; Johnson, Callum Charles; Jowers, Jordan; McAloon, Thomas; McCarthy, Scott; McGinley, Nathan; McGoldrick, Niall Richard; Pattison, Alexander Antony; Pears, Aynsley Alan William; Plews, Nathan Paul; Tinkler, Robbie; Wheatley, Josef James.

MILLWALL (51)

ABDOU, Nadjim (M)   386 10
H: 5 10   W: 11 02   b.Martigues 13-7-84
Internationals: Comoros Full caps.

2002–03	Martigues	26	1	**26**	**1**
2003–04	Sedan	17	0		
2004–05	Sedan	32	2		
2005–06	Sedan	14	0		
2006–07	Sedan	17	0	**80**	**2**
2007–08	Plymouth Arg	31	1	**31**	**1**
2008–09	Millwall	36	3		
2009–10	Millwall	43	1		
2010–11	Millwall	34	0		
2011–12	Millwall	39	1		
2012–13	Millwall	39	1		
2013–14	Millwall	24	0		
2014–15	Millwall	33	1	**249**	**6**

BAILEY, Nicky (M) 356 51
H: 5 10 W: 12 06 b.Hammersmith 10-6-84
Internationals: England C.
2005–06 Barnet 45 7
2006–07 Barnet 44 5 89 12
2007–08 Southend U 44 9
2008–09 Southend U 1 0 45 9
2008–09 Charlton Ath 43 13
2009–10 Charlton Ath 44 12 87 25
2010–11 Middlesbrough 34 0
2011–12 Middlesbrough 37 2
2012–13 Middlesbrough 28 2 99 4
2013–14 Millwall 28 1
2014–15 Millwall 8 0 36 1

BEEVERS, Mark (D) 242 6
H: 6 4 W: 13 00 b.Barnsley 21-11-89
Internationals: England U19.
2006–07 Sheffield W 2 0
2007–08 Sheffield W 28 0
2008–09 Sheffield W 34 0
2009–10 Sheffield W 35 0
2010–11 Sheffield W 28 2
2011–12 Sheffield W 7 0
2011–12 Milton Keynes D 14 1 14 1
2012–13 Sheffield W 6 0 140 2
2012–13 Millwall 35 1
2013–14 Millwall 28 0
2014–15 Millwall 25 2 88 3

BRIGGS, Matthew (D) 56 1
H: 6 1 W: 11 12 b.Wandsworth 6-3-91
Internationals: England U16, U17, U19, U20, U21.
2006–07 Fulham 1 0
2007–08 Fulham 0 0
2008–09 Fulham 0 0
2009–10 Fulham 0 0
2009–10 Leyton Orient 1 0 1 0
2010–11 Fulham 3 0
2011–12 Fulham 2 0
2011–12 Peterborough U 5 0 5 0
2012–13 Fulham 5 0
2012–13 Bristol C 4 0 4 0
2012–13 Watford 7 1 7 1
2013–14 Fulham 2 0 13 0
2014–15 Millwall 8 0 8 0
2014–15 Colchester U 18 0 18 0

CASEY, Dylan (D) 0 0
b. 15-11-95
2014–15 Millwall 0 0

CHAPLOW, Richard (M) 285 26
H: 5 9 W: 9 03 b.Accrington 2-2-85
Internationals: England U19, U20, U21.
2002–03 Burnley 5 0
2003–04 Burnley 39 5
2004–05 Burnley 21 2 65 7
2004–05 WBA 4 0
2005–06 WBA 7 0
2005–06 Southampton 11 1
2006–07 WBA 28 1
2007–08 WBA 5 0 44 1
2007–08 Preston NE 12 3
2008–09 Preston NE 25 3
2009–10 Preston NE 31 2
2010–11 Preston NE 0 0 68 8
2010–11 Southampton 33 4
2011–12 Southampton 25 3
2012–13 Southampton 3 0 72 8
2012–13 Millwall 4 0
2013–14 Millwall 19 1
2014–15 Millwall 7 0 30 1
2014–15 Ipswich T 6 1 6 1

COWAN-HALL, Paris (F) 94 13
H: 5 8 W: 11 08 b.Portsmouth 5-10-90
2008–09 Portsmouth 0 0
2009–10 Portsmouth 0 0
2009–10 Grimsby T 3 0 3 0
2010–11 Portsmouth 0 0
2010–11 Scunthorpe U 1 0 1 0
2012–13 Plymouth Arg 40 3 40 3
2013–14 Wycombe W 25 4
2014–15 Wycombe W 20 6 45 10
2014–15 Millwall 5 0 5 0

CUMMINGS, Shaun (D) 124 1
H: 6 0 W: 11 10 b.Hammersmith 25-2-89
Internationals: Jamaica Full caps.
2007–08 Chelsea 0 0
2008–09 Chelsea 0 0
2008–09 Milton Keynes D 32 0 32 0
2009–10 Chelsea 0 0
2009–10 WBA 3 0 3 0
2009–10 Reading 8 0
2010–11 Reading 10 0
2011–12 Reading 34 0
2012–13 Reading 9 0
2013–14 Reading 11 0
2014–15 Reading 5 1 77 1
2014–15 Millwall 12 0 12 0

DUNNE, Alan (D) 341 17
H: 5 10 W: 10 13 b.Dublin 23-8-82
1999–2000 Millwall 0 0
2000–01 Millwall 0 0
2001–02 Millwall 1 0
2002–03 Millwall 4 0
2003–04 Millwall 8 0
2004–05 Millwall 19 3
2005–06 Millwall 40 0
2006–07 Millwall 32 6
2007–08 Millwall 19 3
2008–09 Millwall 24 0
2009–10 Millwall 32 2
2010–11 Millwall 39 0
2011–12 Millwall 30 0
2012–13 Millwall 25 1
2013–14 Millwall 29 0
2014–15 Millwall 39 2 341 17

EASTER, Jermaine (F) 348 78
H: 5 9 W: 12 02 b.Cardiff 15-1-82
Internationals: Wales Full caps.
2000–01 Wolverhampton W 0 0
2000–01 Hartlepool U 4 0
2001–02 Hartlepool U 12 2
2002–03 Hartlepool U 8 0
2003–04 Hartlepool U 3 0 27 2
2003–04 Cambridge U 15 2
2004–05 Cambridge U 24 6 39 8
2004–05 Boston U 9 3 9 3
2005–06 Stockport Co 19 8 19 8
2005–06 Wycombe W 15 2
2006–07 Wycombe W 38 17
2007–08 Wycombe W 6 2 59 21
2007–08 Plymouth Arg 32 6
2008–09 Plymouth Arg 4 0 36 6
2008–09 Millwall 5 1
2008–09 Colchester U 5 2 5 2
2009–10 Milton Keynes D 36 14
2010–11 Milton Keynes D 14 0 50 14
2010–11 Swansea C 6 1 6 1
2010–11 Crystal Palace 14 1
2011–12 Crystal Palace 33 5
2012–13 Crystal Palace 8 1 55 7
2012–13 Millwall 9 1
2013–14 Millwall 20 3
2014–15 Millwall 9 1 43 6

EDWARDS, Carlos (M) 482 46
H: 5 8 W: 11 02 b.Port of Spain 24-10-78
Internationals: Trinidad & Tobago Full caps.
2000–01 Wrexham 36 4
2001–02 Wrexham 26 5
2002–03 Wrexham 44 8
2003–04 Wrexham 42 5
2004–05 Wrexham 18 1 166 23
2005–06 Luton T 42 2
2006–07 Luton T 26 6 68 8
2006–07 Sunderland 15 5
2007–08 Sunderland 13 0
2008–09 Sunderland 22 0
2008–09 Wolverhampton W 6 0 6 0
2009–10 Sunderland 0 0 50 5
2009–10 Ipswich T 28 2
2010–11 Ipswich T 45 3
2011–12 Ipswich T 45 0
2012–13 Ipswich T 43 3
2013–14 Ipswich T 15 1 176 9
2013–14 Millwall 8 1
2014–15 Millwall 8 0 16 1

EL BEKRI, Sofiane (M) 0 0
b. 22-2-94
2014–15 Millwall 0 0

FORDE, David (G) 387 0
H: 6 3 W: 13 06 b.Galway 20-12-79
Internationals: Republic of Ireland Full caps.
2001–02 West Ham U 0 0
2002–03 West Ham U 0 0
2003–04 West Ham U 0 0
2004 Derry C 11 0
2005 Derry C 33 0
2006 Derry C 29 0 73 0
2006–07 Cardiff C 7 0
2007–08 Cardiff C 0 0 7 0
2007–08 Luton T 5 0 5 0
2007–08 Bournemouth 11 0 11 0
2008–09 Millwall 46 0
2009–10 Millwall 46 0
2010–11 Millwall 46 0
2011–12 Millwall 27 0
2012–13 Millwall 40 0
2013–14 Millwall 40 0
2014–15 Millwall 46 0 291 0

FULLER, Ricardo (F) 436 105
H: 6 3 W: 12 10 b.Kingston, Jamaica 31-10-79
Internationals: Jamaica Full caps.
2000–01 Crystal Palace 8 0 8 0
2001–02 Hearts 27 8 27 8
From Tivoli Gardens.
2002–03 Preston NE 18 9
2003–04 Preston NE 38 17
2004–05 Preston NE 2 1 58 27
2004–05 Portsmouth 31 1 31 1
2005–06 Southampton 30 9
2005–06 Ipswich T 3 2 3 2
2006–07 Southampton 1 0 31 9
2006–07 Stoke C 30 10
2007–08 Stoke C 42 15
2008–09 Stoke C 34 11
2009–10 Stoke C 35 3
2010–11 Stoke C 28 4
2011–12 Stoke C 13 0 182 43
2012–13 Charlton Ath 31 5
2013–14 Charlton Ath 0 0 31 5
2013–14 Blackpool 27 6 27 6
2014–15 Millwall 38 4 38 4

GERRARD, Denzel (G) 0 0
H: 6 0 W: 13 05 b. 19-9-94
2013–14 Millwall 0 0
2014–15 Millwall 0 0

GOODMAN, Jake (D) 14 1
H: 6 2 W: 11 05 b. 5-8-93
2012–13 Millwall 0 0
2013–14 Millwall 0 0
2014–15 AFC Wimbledon 14 1 14 1

GREGORY, Lee (F) 39 9
b. 26-8-88
2014–15 Millwall 39 9 39 9

GUEYE, Magaye (F) 90 15
H: 5 10 W: 11 07 b.Paris 6-7-90
Internationals: France U16, U19, U20, U21. Senegal U23.
2008–09 Strasbourg 3 0
2009–10 Strasbourg 24 9 27 9
2010–11 Everton 5 0
2011–12 Everton 17 1
2012–13 Everton 2 0
2012–13 Brest 7 0 7 0
2013–14 Everton 0 0 24 1
2014–15 Everton 32 5 32 5

HOYTE, Justin (D) 210 4
H: 5 11 W: 11 00 b.Waltham Forest 20-11-84
Internationals: England U16, U19, U20, U21. Trinidad and Tobago Full caps.
2002–03 Arsenal 1 0
2003–04 Arsenal 1 0
2004–05 Arsenal 5 0
2005–06 Sunderland 27 1 27 1
2006–07 Arsenal 22 1
2007–08 Arsenal 5 0 34 1
2008–09 Middlesbrough 22 0
2009–10 Middlesbrough 30 1
2010–11 Middlesbrough 17 0
2011–12 Middlesbrough 39 0
2012–13 Middlesbrough 31 1
2013–14 Middlesbrough 3 0 142 2
2013–14 Millwall 5 0
2014–15 Millwall 2 0 7 0

KING, Tom (G) 0 0
b.Plymouth 9-3-95
Internationals: England U17.
2011–12 Crystal Palace 0 0
2012–13 Crystal Palace 0 0
2014–15 Millwall 0 0

MAIERHOFER, Stefan (F) 286 112
H: 6 8 W: 14 11 b.Vienna 16-8-82
Internationals: Austria Full caps.
2002–03 First Vienna 0 0
2003–04 Langenrohr 28 10
2004–05 Langenrohr 25 16 53 26
2005–06 Bayern Munich II 28 10
2006–07 Bayern Munich II 14 11 42 21
2006–07 Bayern Munich 2 0 2 0
2006–07 Koblenz 3 14 3 14
2007–08 Furth 10 2 10 2
2007–08 Rapid Vienna 11 7
2008–09 Rapid Vienna 35 23
2009–10 Rapid Vienna 3 1 49 31
2009–10 Wolverhampton W 8 1

Season	Club				
2009–10	*Bristol C*	3	0	3	0
2010–11	Wolverhampton W	0	0		
2010–11	*Duisburg*	27	8	27	8
2011–12	Wolverhampton W	1	0	9	1
2011–12	Salzburg	29	14		
2012–13	Salzburg	10	1	39	15
2012–13	*Cologne*	13	1	13	1
2013–14	Millwall	11	2		
2014–15	*Wiener Neustadt*	4	1	4	1
2014–15	Millwall	10	1	21	3

MARQUIS, John (F)   **100 20**
H: 6 1   W: 11 03   b.Lewisham 16-5-92

Season	Club				
2009–10	Millwall	1	0		
2010–11	Millwall	11	4		
2011–12	Millwall	17	1		
2012–13	Millwall	10	0		
2013–14	Millwall	2	0		
2013–14	*Portsmouth*	5	1	5	1
2013–14	*Torquay U*	5	3	5	3
2013–14	*Northampton T*	14	2	14	2
2014–15	Millwall	1	0	42	5
2014–15	*Cheltenham T*	13	1	13	1
2014–15	*Gillingham*	21	8	21	8

MARTIN, Lee (M)   **225 14**
H: 5 10   W: 10 03   b.Taunton 9-2-87

Season	Club				
2004–05	Manchester U	0	0		
2005–06	Manchester U	0	0		
2006–07	Manchester U	0	0		
2006–07	*Rangers*	7	0	7	0
2006–07	*Stoke C*	13	1	13	1
2007–08	Manchester U	0	0		
2007–08	*Plymouth Arg*	12	2	12	2
2007–08	*Sheffield U*	6	0	6	0
2008–09	Manchester U	1	0		
2008–09	*Nottingham F*	13	1	13	1
2009–10	Manchester U	1	0	1	0
2009–10	Ipswich T	16	1		
2010–11	Ipswich T	16	0		
2010–11	*Charlton Ath*	20	2	20	2
2011–12	Ipswich T	34	5		
2012–13	Ipswich T	34	0		
2013–14	Ipswich T	0	0	100	6
2013–14	Millwall	26	1		
2014–15	Millwall	27	1	53	2

MARTINEZ, Angel (M)   **206 10**
H: 5 9   W: 11 13   b.Girona 31-1-86
Internationals: Spain U19, U21.

Season	Club				
2006–07	Espanyol B	27	5	27	5
2006–07	Espanyol	7	0		
2007–08	Espanyol	28	2		
2008–09	Espanyol	15	0	50	2
2009–10	*Rayo Vallecano*	27	2	27	2
2010–11	Girona	36	0	36	0
2011–12	Blackpool	15	1		
2012–13	Blackpool	21	0		
2013–14	Blackpool	26	0	62	1
2014–15	Millwall	4	0	4	0

McDONALD, Scott (F)   **396 138**
H: 5 7   W: 12 07   b.Melbourne 21-8-83
Internationals: Australia U17, U20, U23, Full caps.

Season	Club				
1998–99	Eastern Pride	3	0	3	0
1999–2000	Southampton	0	0		
2000–01	Southampton	0	0		
2001–02	Southampton	2	0		
2002–03	Southampton	0	0	2	0
2002–03	*Huddersfield T*	13	1	13	1
2002–03	*Bournemouth*	7	1	7	1
2003–04	*Wimbledon*	2	0	2	0
2003–04	Motherwell	15	2		
2004–05	Motherwell	27	15		
2005–06	Motherwell	35	11		
2006–07	Motherwell	32	15	109	43
2007–08	Celtic	36	25		
2008–09	Celtic	34	16		
2009–10	Celtic	18	10	88	51
2009–10	Middlesbrough	13	4		
2010–11	Middlesbrough	38	12		
2011–12	Middlesbrough	33	9		
2012–13	Middlesbrough	32	12	116	37
2013–14	Millwall	32	3		
2014–15	Millwall	24	2	56	5

Transferred to Motherwell January 2015.

NELSON, Sid (D)   **14 0**
b. 1-1-96

Season	Club				
2013–14	Millwall	0	0		
2014–15	Millwall	14	0	14	0

O'BRIEN, Aiden (F)   **31 2**
H: 5 8   W: 10 12   b.Islington 4-10-93
Internationals: Republic of Ireland U17, U19, U21.

Season	Club				
2010–11	Millwall	0	0		
2011–12	Millwall	0	0		
2012–13	Millwall	0	0		
2012–13	*Crawley T*	9	0	9	0
2013–14	Millwall	0	0		
2013–14	*Torquay U*	3	0	3	0
2014–15	Millwall	19	2	19	2

ONYEDINMA, Fred (M)   **31 8**
b. 24-11-96

Season	Club				
2013–14	Millwall	4	0		
2014–15	Millwall	2	0	6	0
2014–15	*Wycombe W*	25	8	25	8

PAVEY, Alfie (F)   **1 0**
b. 2-10-95

Season	Club				
2013–14	Millwall	0	0		
2014–15	Millwall	1	0	1	0

PHILPOT, Jamie (F)   **1 1**
b. 2-10-96

Season	Club				
2014–15	Millwall	1	1	1	1

POWELL, Jack (M)   **5 0**
b. 29-1-94

Season	Club				
2013–14	Millwall	0	0		
2014–15	Millwall	5	0	5	0

SHITTU, Dan (D)   **350 29**
H: 6 2   W: 16 03   b.Lagos 2-9-80
Internationals: Nigeria Full caps.

Season	Club				
1999–2000	Charlton Ath	0	0		
2000–01	Charlton Ath	0	0		
2000–01	*Blackpool*	17	2	17	2
2001–02	Charlton Ath	0	0		
2001–02	QPR	27	2		
2002–03	QPR	43	7		
2003–04	QPR	20	0		
2004–05	QPR	34	4		
2005–06	QPR	45	4		
2006–07	Watford	30	1		
2007–08	Watford	39	7	69	8
2008–09	Bolton W	10	0		
2009–10	Bolton W	0	0		
2010–11	Bolton W	0	0	10	0
2010–11	*Millwall*	9	0		
2010–11	QPR	7	0		
2011–12	QPR	0	0	176	17
2012–13	Millwall	39	0		
2013–14	Millwall	22	1		
2014–15	Millwall	8	1	78	2

SIAFA, Josh (D)   **0 0**
b. 7-10-94

Season	Club				
2013–14	Millwall	0	0		
2014–15	Millwall	0	0		

THOMPSON, Ben (M)   **0 0**
H: 5 11   W: 12 04   b. 3-10-95

Season	Club				
2014–15	Millwall	0	0		

UPSON, Edward (M)   **174 12**
H: 5 10   W: 11 07   b.Bury St Edmunds 21-11-89
Internationals: England U17, U19.

Season	Club				
2006–07	Ipswich T	0	0		
2007–08	Ipswich T	0	0		
2008–09	Ipswich T	0	0		
2009–10	Ipswich T	0	0		
2009–10	*Barnet*	9	1	9	1
2010–11	Yeovil T	23	0		
2011–12	Yeovil T	41	3		
2012–13	Yeovil T	41	2		
2013–14	Yeovil T	24	4	129	9
2013–14	Millwall	10	0		
2014–15	Millwall	26	2	36	2

WEBSTER, Byron (D)   **168 12**
H: 6 5   W: 12 07   b.Sherburn-in-Elmet 31-3-87

Season	Club				
2007–08	Siad Most	23	4		
2008–09	Siad Most	0	0	23	4
2009–10	Doncaster R	5	0		
2010–11	Doncaster R	7	0	12	0
2010–11	*Hereford U*	2	0	2	0
2010–11	*Northampton T*	8	0		
2011–12	Northampton T	13	0	21	0
2012–13	Yeovil T	44	5		
2013–14	Yeovil T	41	3		
2014–15	Millwall	11	0	11	0
2014–15	*Yeovil T*	14	0	99	8

WILLIAMS, Shaun (M)   **246 45**
H: 5 9   W: 11 11   b.Dublin 19-10-86
Internationals: Republic of Ireland U21, U23.

Season	Club				
2007	Drogheda U	0	0		
2007	Dundalk	19	9	19	9
2008	Drogheda U	4	0		
2008	Finn Harps	14	2	14	2
2009	Drogheda U	1	0	5	0
2009	Sporting Fingal	13	7		
2010	Sporting Fingal	32	5	45	12
2011–12	Milton Keynes D	39	8		
2012–13	Milton Keynes D	44	3		
2013–14	Milton Keynes D	25	8	108	19
2013–14	Millwall	17	1		
2014–15	Millwall	38	2	55	3

WOOD, Keaton (D)   **0 0**
b. 10-5-95

Season	Club				
2014–15	Millwall	0	0		

WOOLFORD, Martyn (M)   **251 30**
H: 6 0   W: 11 09   b.Castleford 13-10-85
Internationals: England C.

Season	Club				
2008–09	Scunthorpe U	39	4		
2009–10	Scunthorpe U	40	5		
2010–11	Scunthorpe U	24	6	103	15
2010–11	Bristol C	15	0		
2011–12	Bristol C	25	1		
2012–13	Bristol C	15	3	55	4
2012–13	Millwall	15	1		
2013–14	Millwall	40	7		
2014–15	Millwall	38	3	93	11

Players retained or with offer of contract
Romeo, Mahlon Beresford Baker.

Scholars
Bray, Rian Edward; Brown, James Dominic; Bryon, Zak Lewis; Chesmain, Noah Litchfield; Eze, Eberechi Oluchi; Farrell, Kyron Cassius Daniel; Fitzgerald, James Francis John; Girling, Harry Leonard; Goodman, Max John; Mulrooney-Skinner, Alexander Hugo; Mundle-Smith, Kyren Cassius; Ndjoli, Mikael Bongili; O'Donnell, Ronald Richard; Parr, Christopher John; Peter, Dexter Washington; Philpot, James Frederick; Rylah, John-Prince Timothy; Twardek, Kristopher David; Webb, Callum Michael.

MILTON KEYNES D (52)

ALLI, Bamidele (M)   **72 22**
H: 6 1   W: 11 12   b.Watford 11-4-96
Internationals: England U17, U18, U19.

Season	Club				
2012–13	Milton Keynes D	0	0		
2013–14	Milton Keynes D	33	6		
2014–15	Milton Keynes D	39	16	72	22

BAKER, Carl (M)   **276 52**
H: 6 2   W: 12 06   b.Prescot 26-12-82
Internationals: England C.

Season	Club				
2007–08	Morecambe	42	10	42	10
2008–09	Stockport Co	22	3		
2009–10	Stockport Co	20	9	42	12
2009–10	Coventry C	22	0		
2010–11	Coventry C	32	1		
2011–12	Coventry C	26	1		
2012–13	Coventry C	43	12		
2013–14	Coventry C	37	7	160	21
2014–15	Milton Keynes D	32	9	32	9

BALDOCK, George (M)   **69 3**
H: 5 9   W: 10 07   b.Buckingham 26-1-93

Season	Club				
2009–10	Milton Keynes D	1	0		
2010–11	Milton Keynes D	2	0		
2011–12	Milton Keynes D	0	0		
2011–12	*Northampton T*	5	0	5	0
2012–13	Milton Keynes D	2	0		
2013–14	Milton Keynes D	38	2		
2014–15	Milton Keynes D	9	0	52	2
2014–15	*Oxford U*	12	1	12	1

BOWDITCH, Dean (F)   **319 68**
H: 5 11   W: 11 05   b.Bishops Stortford 15-6-86
Internationals: England U16, U17, U19.

Season	Club				
2002–03	Ipswich T	5	0		
2003–04	Ipswich T	16	4		
2004–05	Ipswich T	21	3		
2004–05	*Burnley*	10	1	10	1
2005–06	Ipswich T	21	0		
2005–06	*Wycombe W*	11	1	11	1
2006–07	Ipswich T	9	1		
2006–07	*Brighton & HA*	3	1		
2007–08	Ipswich T	0	0		
2007–08	*Northampton T*	10	2	10	2
2007–08	*Brighton & HA*	5	0	8	1
2008–09	Ipswich T	1	0	73	8
2008–09	*Brentford*	9	2	9	2
2009–10	Yeovil T	30	10		
2010–11	Yeovil T	41	15	71	25
2011–12	Milton Keynes D	41	12		
2012–13	Milton Keynes D	39	6		
2013–14	Milton Keynes D	12	1		
2014–15	Milton Keynes D	35	7	127	28

BURNS, Charlie (G)   1   0
2012–13	Milton Keynes D	0	0	
2013–14	Milton Keynes D	1	0	
2014–15	Milton Keynes D	0	0	1 0

CARRUTHERS, Samir (F)   58   4
H: 5 8 W: 11 00 b.Islington 4-4-93
Internationals: Republic of Ireland U19, U21.
2011–12	Aston Villa	3	0	
2012–13	Aston Villa	0	0	
2013–14	Aston Villa	0	0	3 0
2013–14	Milton Keynes D	23	2	
2014–15	Milton Keynes D	32	2	55 4

COLLINGE, Danny (D)   0   0
Internationals: England U16, U17.
2013–14	Milton Keynes D	0	0
2014–15	Milton Keynes D	0	0

FLANAGAN, Tom (D)   65   4
H: 6 2 W: 11 05 b.Hammersmith 21-10-91
Internationals: Northern Ireland U21.
2009–10	Milton Keynes D	1	0	
2010–11	Milton Keynes D	0	0	
2011–12	Milton Keynes D	21	3	
2012–13	Milton Keynes D	0	0	
2012–13	Gillingham	13	1	13 1
2012–13	Barnet	9	0	9 0
2013–14	Milton Keynes D	7	0	
2013–14	Stevenage	2	0	2 0
2014–15	Milton Keynes D	6	0	37 3
2014–15	Plymouth Arg	4	0	4 0

GREEN, Danny (M)   168   29
H: 5 11 W: 12 00 b.Harlow 9-7-88
2006–07	Northampton T	0	0	
2007–08	Nottingham F	0	0	

From Bishop's Stortford.
2009–10	Dagenham & R	46	13	
2010–11	Dagenham & R	41	11	87 24
2011–12	Charlton Ath	32	3	
2012–13	Charlton Ath	17	1	
2013–14	Charlton Ath	13	0	62 4
2013–14	Milton Keynes D	5	0	
2014–15	Milton Keynes D	14	1	19 1

HICKFORD, Harry (D)   0   0
b. 23-6-95
2012–13	Milton Keynes D	0	0
2013–14	Milton Keynes D	0	0
2014–15	Milton Keynes D	0	0

HITCHCOCK, Tom (F)   61   13
H: 5 11 W: 12 08 b.Hemel Hempstead 1-10-92
2009–10	Blackburn R	0	0	
2010–11	Blackburn R	0	0	
2011–12	Blackburn R	0	0	
2011–12	Plymouth Arg	8	0	8 0
2011–12	QPR	0	0	
2012–13	QPR	0	0	
2012–13	Bristol R	17	3	17 3
2013–14	QPR	1	1	1 1
2013–14	Crewe Alex	6	3	6 3
2013–14	Rotherham U	11	5	11 5
2014–15	Milton Keynes D	12	0	12 0
2014–15	Fleetwood T	6	1	6 1

HODSON, Lee (D)   133   7
H: 5 11 W: 11 02 b.Boreham Wood 2-10-91
Internationals: Northern Ireland U19, U21, Full caps.
2008–09	Watford	1	0	
2009–10	Watford	31	0	
2010–11	Watford	29	1	
2011–12	Watford	20	0	
2012–13	Watford	2	0	83 1
2012–13	Brentford	13	0	13 0
2013–14	Milton Keynes D	23	1	
2014–15	Milton Keynes D	14	1	37 2

KAY, Antony (D)   459   42
H: 5 11 W: 11 08 b.Barnsley 21-10-82
Internationals: England Youth.
1999–2000	Barnsley	0	0	
2000–01	Barnsley	7	0	
2001–02	Barnsley	1	0	
2002–03	Barnsley	16	0	
2003–04	Barnsley	43	3	
2004–05	Barnsley	39	6	
2005–06	Barnsley	36	1	
2006–07	Barnsley	32	1	174 11
2007–08	Tranmere R	38	6	
2008–09	Tranmere R	44	11	82 17
2009–10	Huddersfield T	40	6	
2010–11	Huddersfield T	27	3	
2011–12	Huddersfield T	28	1	
2012–13	Huddersfield T	0	0	95 10
2012–13	Milton Keynes D	33	1	
2013–14	Milton Keynes D	30	2	
2014–15	Milton Keynes D	45	1	108 4

LEWINGTON, Dean (D)   498   19
H: 5 11 W: 11 07 b.Kingston 18-5-84
2002–03	Wimbledon	1	0	
2003–04	Wimbledon	28	1	29 1
2004–05	Milton Keynes D	43	2	
2005–06	Milton Keynes D	44	1	
2006–07	Milton Keynes D	45	1	
2007–08	Milton Keynes D	45	0	
2008–09	Milton Keynes D	40	2	
2009–10	Milton Keynes D	42	1	
2010–11	Milton Keynes D	42	3	
2011–12	Milton Keynes D	46	3	
2012–13	Milton Keynes D	38	1	
2013–14	Milton Keynes D	43	1	
2014–15	Milton Keynes D	41	3	469 18

MARTIN, David E (G)   256   0
H: 6 1 W: 13 04 b.Romford 22-1-86
Internationals: England U16, U17, U18, U19.
2003–04	Wimbledon	2	0	2 0
2004–05	Milton Keynes D	15	0	
2005–06	Milton Keynes D	0	0	
2005–06	Liverpool	0	0	
2006–07	Liverpool	0	0	
2006–07	Accrington S	10	0	10 0
2007–08	Liverpool	0	0	
2008–09	Liverpool	0	0	
2008–09	Leicester C	25	0	25 0
2009–10	Liverpool	0	0	
2009–10	Tranmere R	3	0	3 0
2009–10	Leeds U	0	0	
2009–10	Derby Co	2	0	2 0
2010–11	Milton Keynes D	43	0	
2011–12	Milton Keynes D	46	0	
2012–13	Milton Keynes D	31	0	
2013–14	Milton Keynes D	40	0	
2014–15	Milton Keynes D	39	0	214 0

McFADZEAN, Kyle (D)   137   9
H: 6 1 W: 13 04 b.Sheffield 20-2-87
Internationals: England C.
2004–05	Sheffield U	0	0	
2005–06	Sheffield U	0	0	
2006–07	Sheffield U	0	0	

From Alfreton T
2011–12	Crawley T	37	2	
2012–13	Crawley T	17	3	
2013–14	Crawley T	42	1	96 6
2014–15	Milton Keynes D	41	3	41 3

McLOUGHLIN, Ian (G)   56   0
H: 6 3 W: 13 08 b.Dublin 9-8-91
Internationals: Republic of Ireland U19, U21.
2008–09	Ipswich T	0	0	
2009–10	Ipswich T	0	0	
2010–11	Ipswich T	0	0	
2010–11	Stockport Co	5	0	5 0
2011–12	Milton Keynes D	1	0	
2011–12	Milton Keynes D	16	0	
2012–13	Walsall	6	0	6 0
2013–14	Milton Keynes D	8	0	
2013–14	Newport Co	12	0	12 0
2014–15	Milton Keynes D	8	0	33 0

POTTER, Darren (M)   189   16
H: 6 0 W: 10 08 b.Liverpool 21-12-84
Internationals: Republic of Ireland Full caps.
2001–02	Liverpool	0	0	
2002–03	Liverpool	0	0	
2003–04	Liverpool	0	0	
2004–05	Liverpool	2	0	
2005–06	Liverpool	0	0	
2005–06	Southampton	10	0	10 0
2006–07	Liverpool	0	0	2 0
2007–08	Wolverhampton W	38	0	
2007–08	Wolverhampton W	18	0	
2008–09	Wolverhampton W	0	0	56 0
2008–09	Sheffield W	17	2	
2009–10	Sheffield W	46	3	
2010–11	Sheffield W	33	3	96 8
2011–12	Milton Keynes D	40	2	
2012–13	Milton Keynes D	46	4	
2013–14	Milton Keynes D	29	0	
2014–15	Milton Keynes D	40	2	155 8

POWELL, Daniel (F)   189   33
H: 5 11 W: 13 03 b.Luton 12-3-91
2008–09	Milton Keynes D	7	1	
2009–10	Milton Keynes D	2	1	
2010–11	Milton Keynes D	29	9	
2011–12	Milton Keynes D	43	6	
2012–13	Milton Keynes D	34	7	
2013–14	Milton Keynes D	32	1	
2014–15	Milton Keynes D	42	8	189 33

RANDALL, Mark (M)   96   3
H: 6 0 W: 12 12 b.Milton Keynes 28-9-89
Internationals: England U17, U18.
2006–07	Arsenal	0	0	
2007–08	Arsenal	1	0	
2007–08	Burnley	10	0	10 0
2008–09	Arsenal	1	0	
2009–10	Arsenal	0	0	
2009–10	Milton Keynes D	16	0	
2010–11	Arsenal	0	0	2 0
2010–11	Rotherham U	10	1	10 1
2011–12	Chesterfield	16	1	
2012–13	Chesterfield	29	1	
2013–14	Chesterfield	0	0	45 2
2013–14	Milton Keynes D	4	0	
2014–15	Milton Keynes D	9	0	29 0

RASULO, Georgio (M)   9   0
b.Banbury 23-1-97
Internationals: England U16, U17.
2012–13	Milton Keynes D	1	0	
2013–14	Milton Keynes D	7	0	
2014–15	Milton Keynes D	0	0	8 0
2014–15	Oxford U	1	0	1 0

REEVES, Ben (D)   78   15
H: 5 10 W: 10 07 b.Verwood 19-11-91
Internationals: Northern Ireland Full caps.
2008–09	Southampton	0	0	
2009–10	Southampton	0	0	
2010–11	Southampton	0	0	
2011–12	Southampton	2	0	
2011–12	Dagenham & R	5	0	5 0
2012–13	Southampton	3	0	5 0
2012–13	Southend U	10	1	10 1
2013–14	Milton Keynes D	28	7	
2014–15	Milton Keynes D	30	7	58 14

SPENCE, Jordan (D)   128   2
H: 6 2 W: 12 07 b.Woodford 24-5-90
Internationals: England U16, U17, U18, U19, U21.
2007–08	West Ham U	0	0	
2008–09	West Ham U	0	0	
2008–09	Leyton Orient	20	0	20 0
2009–10	West Ham U	1	0	
2009–10	Scunthorpe U	9	0	9 0
2010–11	West Ham U	2	0	
2010–11	Bristol C	11	0	
2011–12	West Ham U	0	0	
2011–12	Bristol C	10	0	21 0
2012–13	West Ham U	4	0	
2013–14	West Ham U	0	0	7 0
2013–14	Sheffield W	4	0	4 0
2013–14	Milton Keynes D	29	2	
2014–15	Milton Keynes D	38	0	67 2

SUMMERFIELD, Will (M)   0   0
2013–14	Milton Keynes D	0	0
2014–15	Milton Keynes D	0	0

TILNEY, Ben (M)   0   0
2014–15	Milton Keynes D	0	0

TSHIMANGA, Kabongo (F)   0   0
b. 31-5-96
2014–15	Milton Keynes D	0	0

Scholars
Brittain, Callum James; Daffern, Jacob Bempton Lewis; Furlong, Connor Jason; Hadden-Becker, Jack; Hunt, Adam Matthew Samuel; McCorkell, Andrew Robert William; Okito, Gedeon; Owusu, Kevin; Palmiero, Dominic Antonio; Steele, Joseph James; Tingey, Luke Steven; Vaughan, Laurence Murcot; Weston, Aaran Charles; Wiltshire, Kyran Tonell; Wyant, Thomas Paul.

MORECAMBE (53)

AMOND, Padraig (F)   279   72
H: 5 11 W: 12 05 b.Carlow 15-4-88
Internationals: Republic of Ireland U21.
2006	Shamrock R	10	1	
2007	Shamrock R	6	1	
2007	Kildare Co	13	5	13 5
2008	Shamrock R	26	9	
2009	Shamrock R	20	4	62 15
2010	Sligo R	27	17	27 17
2010–11	Pacos	17	0	17 0
2011–12	Accrington S	42	7	
2012–13	Accrington S	36	9	
2013–14	Accrington S	0	0	78 16
2013–14	Morecambe	45	11	
2014–15	Morecambe	37	8	82 19

ARESTIDOU, Andreas (G)   33   0
H: 6 2   W: 13 00   b.Lambeth 6-12-89

Season	Club				
2007–08	Blackburn R	0	0		
2008–09	Blackburn R	0	0		
2009–10	Shrewsbury T	2	0	2	0
2010–11	Preston NE	0	0		
2011–12	Preston NE	7	0	7	0
2012–13	Morecambe	6	0		
2013–14	Morecambe	1	0		
2014–15	Morecambe	17	0	24	0

BEELEY, Shaun (D)   108   0
H: 5 10   W: 11 05   b.Stockport 21-11-88
Internationals: England C.

Season	Club				
2012–13	Fleetwood T	34	0	34	0
2013–14	Bury	20	0	20	0
2013–14	Morecambe	12	0		
2014–15	Morecambe	42	0	54	0

BELL, Will (D)   0   0
H: 6 1   W: 14 07   b.Isleworth 22-11-80

Season	Club		
2012–13	Morecambe	0	0
2013–14	Morecambe	0	0
2014–15	Morecambe	0	0

BONDSWELL, Nathan (M)   0   0
b.Nottingham 10-2-97

Season	Club		
2014–15	Morecambe	0	0

DEVITT, Jamie (F)   127   16
H: 5 10   W: 10 05   b.Dublin 6-7-90
Internationals: Republic of Ireland U21.

Season	Club				
2007–08	Hull C	0	0		
2008–09	Hull C	0	0		
2009–10	Hull C	0	0		
2009–10	Darlington	6	1	6	1
2009–10	Shrewsbury T	9	2	9	2
2009–10	Grimsby T	15	5	15	5
2010–11	Hull C	16	0		
2011–12	Hull C	0	0		
2011–12	Bradford C	7	1	7	1
2011–12	Accrington S	16	2	16	2
2012–13	Hull C	0	0	16	0
2012–13	Rotherham U	1	0	1	0
2013–14	Chesterfield	7	0	7	0
2013–14	Morecambe	14	2		
2014–15	Morecambe	36	3	50	5

DOYLE, Chris (D)   9   0
H: 6 2   W: 13 05   b.Liverpool 22-7-94

Season	Club				
2012–13	Morecambe	4	0		
2013–14	Morecambe	3	0		
2014–15	Morecambe	2	0	9	0

DRUMMOND, Stuart (M)   431   53
H: 6 2   W: 13 08   b.Preston 11-12-75

Season	Club				
2004–05	Chester C	45	6		
2005–06	. Chester C	42	6	87	12
2006–07	Shrewsbury T	44	4		
2007–08	Shrewsbury T	23	3	67	7
2007–08	Morecambe	18	2		
2008–09	Morecambe	44	10		
2009–10	Morecambe	43	9		
2010–11	Morecambe	41	6		
2011–12	Morecambe	38	5		
2012–13	Morecambe	44	2		
2013–14	Morecambe	35	0		
2014–15	Morecambe	14	0	277	34

EDWARDS, Ryan (D)   80   0
b.Liverpool 7-10-93

Season	Club				
2011–12	Blackburn R	0	0		
2012–13	Rochdale	26	0	26	0
2012–13	Blackburn R	0	0		
2012–13	Fleetwood T	9	0	9	0
2013–14	Blackburn R	0	0		
2013–14	Chesterfield	5	0	5	0
2013–14	Tranmere R	0	0		
2013–14	Morecambe	9	0		
2014–15	Morecambe	31	0	40	0

ELLISON, Kevin (M)   460   95
H: 6 0   W: 12 00   b.Liverpool 23-2-79

Season	Club				
2000–01	Leicester C	1	0		
2001–02	Leicester C	0	0	1	0
2001–02	Stockport Co	11	0		
2002–03	Stockport Co	23	1		
2003–04	Stockport Co	14	1	48	2
2003–04	Lincoln C	11	0	11	0
2004–05	Chester C	24	9		
2004–05	Hull C	16	1		
2005–06	Hull C	23	1	39	2
2006–07	Tranmere R	34	4	34	4
2007–08	Chester C	36	11		
2008–09	Chester C	39	8	99	28
2008–09	Rotherham U	0	0		
2009–10	Rotherham U	39	8		
2010–11	Rotherham U	23	3	62	11
2010–11	Bradford C	7	1	7	1
2011–12	Morecambe	34	15		
2012–13	Morecambe	40	11		
2013–14	Morecambe	42	10		
2014–15	Morecambe	43	11	159	47

FLEMING, Andy (M)   155   13
H: 6 1   W: 12 00   b.Liverpool 18-2-89
Internationals: England C.

Season	Club				
2006–07	Wrexham	2	0		
2007–08	Wrexham	4	0	6	0
2010–11	Morecambe	30	2		
2011–12	Morecambe	17	2		
2012–13	Morecambe	32	5		
2013–14	Morecambe	35	2		
2014–15	Morecambe	35	2	149	13

GOODALL, Alan (D)   288   16
H: 5 9   W: 11 06   b.Birkenhead 2-12-81

Season	Club				
2004–05	Rochdale	34	2		
2005–06	Rochdale	40	3		
2006–07	Rochdale	46	3		
2007–08	Luton T	29	1	29	1
2008–09	Chesterfield	17	0		
2009–10	Chesterfield	17	0	45	3
2010–11	Rochdale	5	0	125	8
2010–11	Stockport Co	13	0	13	0
2012–13	Fleetwood T	29	4		
2013–14	Fleetwood T	19	0	48	4
2014–15	Morecambe	28	0	28	0

HUGHES, Mark (D)   294   18
H: 6 1   W: 13 03   b.Liverpool 9-12-86

Season	Club				
2004–05	Everton	0	0		
2005–06	Everton	0	0		
2005–06	Stockport Co	3	1	3	1
2006–07	Everton	1	0	1	0
2006–07	Northampton T	17	2		
2007–08	Northampton T	35	1		
2008–09	Northampton T	41	1	93	4
2009–10	Walsall	26	1	26	1
2010–11	N Queensland F	30	4	30	4
2011–12	Bury	25	0		
2012–13	Bury	27	0	52	0
2012–13	Accrington S	5	0	5	0
2013–14	Morecambe	44	5		
2014–15	Morecambe	40	3	84	8

JONES, Lee (G)   250   0
H: 5 8   W: 12 02   b.Pontypridd 9-8-70

Season	Club				
1994–95	Swansea C	1	0		
1995–96	Swansea C	1	0		
1995–96	Crewe Alex	1	0	1	0
1996–97	Swansea C	1	0		
1997–98	Swansea C	2	0	6	0
1997–98	Bristol R	8	0		
1998–99	Bristol R	32	0		
1999–2000	Bristol R	36	0	76	0
2000–01	Stockport Co	27	0		
2001–02	Stockport Co	24	0		
2002–03	Stockport Co	24	0	75	0
2003–04	Blackpool	21	0		
2004–05	Blackpool	29	0		
2005–06	Blackpool	31	0		
2006–07	Blackpool	0	0	81	0
2006–07	Bury	2	0	2	0
2006–07	Darlington	9	0	9	0
2012–13	Morecambe	0	0		
2013–14	Morecambe	0	0		
2014–15	Morecambe	0	0		

KENYON, Alex (M)   76   3
H: 5 11   W: 11 12   b.Preston 17-7-92

Season	Club				
2012–13	Morecambe	39	0		
2014–15	Morecambe	37	3	76	3

MARSHALL, Marcus (F)   111   5
H: 5 10   W: 11 06   b.Hammersmith 7-10-89

Season	Club				
2007–08	Blackburn R	0	0		
2008–09	Blackburn R	0	0		
2009–10	Blackburn R	0	0		
2009–10	Rotherham U	22	0		
2010–11	Rotherham U	36	3		
2011–12	Rotherham U	15	1	73	4
2011–12	Macclesfield T	14	1	14	1
2012–13	Bury	9	0	9	0
2013–14	Morecambe	15	0		
2014–15	Morecambe	0	0	15	0

McGOWAN, Aaron (D)   11   1
b.Maghull 20-9-95

Season	Club				
2012–13	Morecambe	1	0		
2013–14	Morecambe	2	0		
2014–15	Morecambe	8	1	11	1

MULLIN, Paul (F)   42   8
H: 5 10   W: 11 01   b. 6-11-94

Season	Club				
2013–14	Huddersfield T	0	0		
2014–15	Morecambe	42	8	42	8

PARRISH, Andy (D)   279   2
H: 6 0   W: 11 00   b.Bolton 22-6-88

Season	Club				
2005–06	Bury	8	0		
2006–07	Bury	9	0		
2007–08	Bury	26	1	43	1
2008–09	Morecambe	13	0		
2009–10	Morecambe	35	0		
2010–11	Morecambe	41	0		
2011–12	Morecambe	38	0		
2012–13	Morecambe	25	1		
2013–14	Morecambe	39	0		
2014–15	Morecambe	45	0	236	1

REDSHAW, Jack (F)   122   36
H: 5 6   W: 10 00   b.Salford 20-11-90

Season	Club				
2009–10	Manchester C	0	0		
2010–11	Rochdale	2	0	2	0

From Salford C, Altrincham

Season	Club				
2011–12	Morecambe	11	2		
2012–13	Morecambe	40	15		
2013–14	Morecambe	29	8		
2014–15	Morecambe	40	11	120	36

ROCHE, Barry (G)   414   0
H: 6 5   W: 14 08   b.Dublin 6-4-82
Internationals: Republic of Ireland U17.

Season	Club				
1999–2000	Nottingham F	0	0		
2000–01	Nottingham F	2	0		
2001–02	Nottingham F	1	0		
2002–03	Nottingham F	8	0		
2003–04	Nottingham F	0	0		
2004–05	Nottingham F	2	0	13	0
2005–06	Chesterfield	41	0		
2006–07	Chesterfield	40	0		
2007–08	Chesterfield	45	0	126	0
2008–09	Morecambe	46	0		
2009–10	Morecambe	42	0		
2010–11	Morecambe	42	0		
2011–12	Morecambe	44	0		
2012–13	Morecambe	42	0		
2013–14	Morecambe	45	0		
2014–15	Morecambe	14	0	275	0

SAMPSON, Jack (F)   72   5
H: 6 2   W: 12 04   b.Wigan 14-4-93
Internationals: England U19.

Season	Club				
2010–11	Bolton W	0	0		
2011–12	Bolton W	0	0		
2011–12	Southend U	9	0	9	0
2012–13	Bolton W	0	0		
2012–13	Accrington S	5	0		
2013–14	Accrington S	0	0	5	0
2013–14	Morecambe	42	5		
2014–15	Morecambe	16	0	58	5

STEWART, Tom (G)   1   0
b. 17.4.96

Season	Club				
2014–15	Morecambe	1	0	1	0

WATSON, Declan (M)   0   0
b. 13-2-96

Season	Club		
2014–15	Morecambe	0	0

WILLIAMS, Ryan (F)   53   5
H: 5 8   W: 10 09   b.Birkenhead 8-4-91

Season	Club				
2012–13	Morecambe	16	2		
2013–14	Morecambe	25	3		
2014–15	Morecambe	12	0	53	5

WILSON, Laurence (D)   312   17
H: 5 10   W: 10 09   b.Huyton 10-10-86
Internationals: England U18, U19.

Season	Club				
2004–05	Everton	0	0		
2005–06	Everton	0	0		
2005–06	Mansfield T	15	1	15	1
2006–07	Chester C	41	1		
2007–08	Chester C	40	2		
2008–09	Chester C	34	1	115	4
2009–10	Morecambe	41	3		
2010–11	Morecambe	38	3		
2011–12	Morecambe	30	5		
2012–13	Rotherham U	5	0	5	0
2012–13	Accrington S	19	0		
2013–14	Accrington S	15	0	34	0
2014–15	Morecambe	34	1	143	12

WRIGHT, Andrew (M)   179   2
H: 6 1   W: 13 07   b.Formby 15-1-85
From West Virginia Univ, Cape Cod Crusaders.

Season	Club				
2007–08	Scunthorpe U	2	0		
2008–09	Scunthorpe U	28	0		
2009–10	Scunthorpe U	19	0		
2010–11	Scunthorpe U	20	0		
2011–12	Scunthorpe U	18	0	87	0
2012–13	Morecambe	40	0		
2013–14	Morecambe	35	0		
2014–15	Morecambe	17	0	92	0

Scholars
Bailey, Charlie Ellis; Cowley, Thomas David; Hilton, Ross Thomas George; Homson-Smith, Morgan; Kitchen, William George; Livingstone,

Matthew Richard; Masters, Lewis Robert; Povey, Maxwell Jordan; Preston, Jack; Reynolds, Adam Alexander; Roberts, James Peter; Smith, James Michael; Tomlinson, Lewis; Towers, Daniel Harry; Townsend, Jake Ryan.

NEWCASTLE U (54)

AARONS, Rolando (M)   4   1
H: 5 9 W: 10 08 b.Kingston 16-11-95
Internationals: England U20.

Season	Club				
2014–15	Newcastle U	4	1	4	1

ABEID, Mehdi (M)   72   10
H: 6 1 W: 12 08 b.Paris 6-8-92
Internationals: France U16, U17, U18. Algeria U23, Full caps.

Season	Club				
2008–09	Lens B	0	0		
2009–10	Lens B	8	0		
2010–11	Lens B	11	3	19	3
2011–12	Newcastle U	0	0		
2012–13	Newcastle U	0	0		
2012–13	St Johnstone	12	0	12	0
2013–14	Newcastle U	0	0		
2013–14	Panathinaikos	28	7	28	7
2014–15	Newcastle U	13	0	13	0

ALNWICK, Jak (G)   7   0
H: 6 2 W: 12 13 b.Hexham 17-6-93
Internationals: England U17, U18, U19, U20.

Season	Club				
2010–11	Newcastle U	0	0		
2011–12	Newcastle U	0	0		
2012–13	Newcastle U	0	0		
2013–14	Newcastle U	0	0		
2014–15	Newcastle U	6	0	6	0
2014–15	Bradford C	1	0	1	0

AMEOBI, Sam (F)   63   3
H: 6 3 W: 10 04 b.Newcastle 1-5-92
Internationals: Nigeria U20. England U21.

Season	Club				
2010–11	Newcastle U	1	0		
2011–12	Newcastle U	10	0		
2012–13	Newcastle U	8	0		
2012–13	Middlesbrough	9	1	9	1
2013–14	Newcastle U	10	0		
2014–15	Newcastle U	25	2	54	2

ANITA, Vurnon (M)   187   6
H: 5 5 W: 10 04 b.Willemstad 4-4-89
Internationals: Netherlands U15, U17, U19, U20, U21, Full caps.

Season	Club				
2005–06	Ajax	1	0		
2006–07	Ajax	1	0		
2008–09	Ajax	16	0		
2009–10	Ajax	26	0		
2010–11	Ajax	31	3		
2011–12	Ajax	33	2		
2012–13	Ajax	1	0	109	5
2012–13	Newcastle U	25	0		
2013–14	Newcastle U	34	1		
2014–15	Newcastle U	19	0	78	1

ARMSTRONG, Adam (F)   15   0
H: 5 8 W: 10 12 b.Newcastle 10-2-97
Internationals: England U16, U17, U18.

Season	Club				
2013–14	Newcastle U	4	0		
2014–15	Newcastle U	11	0	15	0

BIGIRIMANA, Gael (M)   39   1
H: 5 9 W: 11 09 b.Burundi 22-10-93
Internationals: England U20.

Season	Club				
2011–12	Coventry C	26	0	26	0
2012–13	Newcastle U	13	1		
2013–14	Newcastle U	0	0		
2014–15	Newcastle U	0	0	13	1
2014–15	Rangers	0	0		

CABELLA, Remy (M)   145   28
H: 5 7 W: 9 11 b.Ajaccio 8-3-90
Internationals: France U21, Full caps.

Season	Club				
2010–11	Montpellier	0	0		
2010–11	Avignon	17	3	17	3
2011–12	Montpellier	29	3		
2012–13	Montpellier	31	7		
2013–14	Montpellier	37	14	97	24
2014–15	Newcastle U	31	1	31	1

CAMPBELL, Adam (F)   19   2
H: 5 7 W: 11 07 b.North Shields 1-1-95
Internationals: England U16, U17, U19.

Season	Club				
2011–12	Newcastle U	0	0		
2012–13	Newcastle U	3	0		
2013–14	Newcastle U	0	0		
2013–14	Carlisle U	1	0	1	0
2013–14	St Mirren	11	2	11	2
2014–15	Newcastle U	0	0	3	0
2014–15	Fleetwood T	2	0	2	0
2014–15	Hartlepool U	2	0	2	0

CISSE, Papiss (F)   338   147
H: 6 0 W: 11 07 b.Dakar 3-6-85
Internationals: Senegal Full caps.

Season	Club				
2003–04	AS Douanes	26	23	26	23
2004–05	Metz B	10	3		
2005–06	Metz B	3	0	13	3
2005–06	Metz	1	0		
2005–06	Cherbourg	28	11	28	11
2006–07	Metz	32	12		
2007–08	Metz	9	0		
2007–08	Chateauroux	15	4	15	4
2008–09	Metz	37	15		
2009–10	Metz	16	8	95	35
2009–10	Freiburg	16	6		
2010–11	Freiburg	32	22		
2011–12	Freiburg	17	9	65	37
2011–12	Newcastle U	14	13		
2012–13	Newcastle U	36	8		
2013–14	Newcastle U	24	2		
2014–15	Newcastle U	22	11	96	34

COLBACK, Jack (M)   200   12
H: 5 9 W: 11 05 b.Killingworth 24-10-89
Internationals: England U20.

Season	Club				
2007–08	Sunderland	0	0		
2008–09	Sunderland	0	0		
2009–10	Sunderland	1	0		
2009–10	Ipswich T	37	4		
2010–11	Sunderland	11	0		
2010–11	Ipswich T	13	0	50	4
2011–12	Sunderland	35	1		
2012–13	Sunderland	35	0		
2013–14	Sunderland	33	3	115	4
2014–15	Newcastle U	35	4	35	4

COLOCCINI, Fabricio (D)   440   21
H: 6 0 W: 12 04 b.Cordoba 22-1-82
Internationals: Argentina Full caps.

Season	Club				
1998–99	Boca Juniors	1	1		
1999–2000	Boca Juniors	1	0	2	1
1999–2000	AC Milan	0	0		
2000–01	AC Milan	0	0		
2000–01	San Lorenzo	19	3	19	3
2001–02	Alaves	33	6	33	6
2002–03	Atletico Madrid	27	0	27	0
2003–04	Villarreal	31	1	31	1
2004–05	AC Milan	1	0	1	0
2004–05	La Coruna	15	1		
2005–06	La Coruna	26	0		
2006–07	La Coruna	26	0		
2007–08	La Coruna	38	4	105	5
2008–09	Newcastle U	34	0		
2009–10	Newcastle U	37	2		
2010–11	Newcastle U	35	2		
2011–12	Newcastle U	35	0		
2012–13	Newcastle U	22	0		
2013–14	Newcastle U	27	0		
2014–15	Newcastle U	32	1	222	5

DARLOW, Karl (G)   115   0
H: 6 1 W: 12 05 b.Northampton 8-10-90

Season	Club				
2009–10	Nottingham F	0	0		
2010–11	Nottingham F	1	0		
2011–12	Nottingham F	0	0		
2012–13	Nottingham F	20	0		
2012–13	Walsall	9	0	9	0
2013–14	Nottingham F	43	0		
2014–15	Newcastle U	0	0		
2014–15	Nottingham F	42	0	106	0

DE JONG, Siem (M)   170   58
H: 6 1 W: 12 00 b.Aigle 28-1-89
Internationals: Netherlands U17, U19, U21, B, Full caps.

Season	Club				
2007–08	Ajax	22	2		
2008–09	Ajax	10	1		
2009–10	Ajax	22	10		
2010–11	Ajax	32	12		
2011–12	Ajax	29	13		
2012–13	Ajax	33	12		
2013–14	Ajax	18	7	166	57
2014–15	Newcastle U	4	1	4	1

DUMMETT, Paul (D)   73   3
H: 5 10 W: 10 02 b.Newcastle 26-9-91
Internationals: Wales U21, Full caps.

Season	Club				
2010–11	Newcastle U	0	0		
2011–12	Newcastle U	0	0		
2012–13	Newcastle U	0	0		
2012–13	St Mirren	30	2	30	2
2013–14	Newcastle U	18	1		
2014–15	Newcastle U	25	0	43	1

ELLIOT, Rob (G)   122   0
H: 6 3 W: 14 10 b.Chatham 30-4-86
Internationals: Republic of Ireland U19, Full caps.

Season	Club				
2004–05	Charlton Ath	0	0		
2004–05	Notts Co	4	0	4	0
2005–06	Charlton Ath	0	0		
2006–07	Charlton Ath	0	0		
2006–07	Accrington S	7	0	7	0
2007–08	Charlton Ath	1	0		
2008–09	Charlton Ath	23	0		
2009–10	Charlton Ath	33	0		
2010–11	Charlton Ath	35	0		
2011–12	Charlton Ath	4	0	96	0
2011–12	Newcastle U	0	0		
2012–13	Newcastle U	10	0		
2013–14	Newcastle U	2	0		
2014–15	Newcastle U	3	0	15	0

FERGUSON, Shane (D)   52   1
H: 5 9 W: 10 01 b.Limavady 12-7-91
Internationals: Northern Ireland U17, U19, U21, B, Full caps.

Season	Club				
2008–09	Newcastle U	0	0		
2009–10	Newcastle U	0	0		
2010–11	Newcastle U	7	0		
2011–12	Newcastle U	7	0		
2012–13	Newcastle U	9	0		
2012–13	Birmingham C	11	1		
2013–14	Newcastle U	0	0		
2013–14	Birmingham C	18	0	29	1
2014–15	Newcastle U	0	0	23	0
2014–15	Rangers	0	0		

GILLIEAD, Alex (F)   0   0
H: 6 0 W: 11 00 b.Shotley Bridge 11-2-96
Internationals: England U16, U17, U18.

Season	Club				
2014–15	Newcastle U	0	0		

GOOD, Curtis (D)   31   2
H: 6 2 W: 13 05 b.Melbourne 23-3-93
Internationals: Australia U20, U23, Full caps.

Season	Club				
2011–12	Melbourne Heart	24	1	24	1
2012–13	Newcastle U	0	0		
2012–13	Bradford C	3	0	3	0
2013–14	Newcastle U	0	0		
2013–14	Dundee U	4	1	4	1
2014–15	Newcastle U	0	0		

GOUFFRAN, Yoan (F)   330   76
H: 5 9 W: 11 11
b.Villeneuve-Saint-Georges 25-5-86
Internationals: France U21.

Season	Club				
2004–05	Caen	8	0		
2005–06	Caen	29	8		
2006–07	Caen	37	15		
2007–08	Caen	36	10	110	33
2008–09	Bordeaux	32	3		
2009–10	Bordeaux	32	5		
2010–11	Bordeaux	34	14		
2011–12	Bordeaux	20	8	139	32
2012–13	Bordeaux	15	3		
2013–14	Newcastle U	35	6		
2014–15	Newcastle U	32	1	81	11

GUTIERREZ, Jonas (M)   385   17
H: 6 0 W: 11 07 b.Buenos Aires 5-7-82
Internationals: Argentina Full caps.

Season	Club				
2001–02	Velez Sarsfield	17	0		
2002–03	Velez Sarsfield	21	1		
2003–04	Velez Sarsfield	27	0		
2004–05	Velez Sarsfield	33	0	98	1
2005–06	Mallorca	30	2		
2006–07	Mallorca	36	3		
2007–08	Mallorca	30	0	96	5
2008–09	Newcastle U	30	0		
2009–10	Newcastle U	37	4		
2010–11	Newcastle U	37	3		
2011–12	Newcastle U	32	1		
2012–13	Newcastle U	34	1		
2013–14	Newcastle U	2	0		
2013–14	Norwich C	4	0	4	0
2014–15	Newcastle U	10	1	187	11

HAIDARA, Massadio (D)   74   0
H: 5 11 W: 11 10 b.Trappes 2-12-92
Internationals: France U19, U20, U21.

Season	Club				
2010–11	AS Nancy	8	0		
2011–12	AS Nancy	17	0		
2012–13	AS Nancy	17	0	44	0
2012–13	Newcastle U	4	0		
2013–14	Newcastle U	11	0		
2014–15	Newcastle U	15	0	30	0

JANMAAT, Daryl (D)   208   13
H: 6 1 W: 12 13 b.Leidschendam 22-7-89
Internationals: Netherlands U20, U21, Full caps.

Season	Club				
2007–08	Den Haag	25	2	25	2
2008–09	Heerenveen	10	0		
2009–10	Heerenveen	28	0		
2010–11	Heerenveen	24	3		
2011–12	Heerenveen	22	2	84	5
2012–13	Feyenoord	32	3		

2013–14	Feyenoord	30	2	62	5
2014–15	Newcastle U	37	1	37	1

KEMEN, Olivier (M) 0 0
H: 5 10 W: 12 04 b.Metz 20-7-96
Internationals: France U16, U17, U18.

2013–14	Newcastle U	0	0
2014–15	Newcastle U	0	0

KRUL, Tim (G) 183 0
H: 6 2 W: 11 08 b.Den Haag 3-4-88
Internationals: Netherlands U15, U16, U17, U19, U20, U21, Full caps.

2005–06	Newcastle U	0	0		
2006–07	Newcastle U	0	0		
2007–08	Falkirk	22	0	22	0
2007–08	Newcastle U	0	0		
2008–09	Newcastle U	0	0		
2008–09	Carlisle U	9	0	9	0
2009–10	Newcastle U	3	0		
2010–11	Newcastle U	21	0		
2011–12	Newcastle U	38	0		
2012–13	Newcastle U	24	0		
2013–14	Newcastle U	36	0		
2014–15	Newcastle U	30	0	152	0

LASCELLES, Jamaal (D) 65 4
H: 6 2 W: 13 01 b.Derby 11-11-93
Internationals: England U18, U19, U20, U21.

2010–11	Nottingham F	0	0		
2011–12	Nottingham F	1	0		
2011–12	Stevenage	7	1	7	1
2012–13	Nottingham F	2	0		
2013–14	Nottingham F	29	2		
2014–15	Newcastle U	0	0		
2014–15	Nottingham F	26	1	58	3

MARVEAUX, Sylvain (M) 164 18
H: 5 8 W: 10 05 b.Vannes 15-4-86
Internationals: France U21.

2006–07	Rennes	28	5		
2007–08	Rennes	24	0		
2008–09	Rennes	5	0		
2009–10	Rennes	35	10		
2010–11	Rennes	10	1	102	16
2011–12	Newcastle U	7	0		
2012–13	Newcastle U	22	1		
2013–14	Newcastle U	9	0		
2014–15	Newcastle U	0	0	38	1
2014–15	Guingamp	24	1	24	1

MBABU, Kevin (D) 1 0
H: 6 0 W: 12 03 b.Zurich 19-4-95
Internationals: Switzerland U16, U17, U18, U19.

2012–13	Servette	1	0	1	0
2012–13	Newcastle U	0	0		
2013–14	Newcastle U	0	0		
2014–15	Newcastle U	0	0		
2014–15	Rangers	0	0		

OBERTAN, Gabriel (F) 136 6
H: 6 1 W: 12 06 b.Paris 26-2-89
Internationals: France U16, U17, U18, U19, U21.

2006–07	Bordeaux	17	1		
2007–08	Bordeaux	26	2		
2008–09	Bordeaux	11	0	54	3
2008–09	Lorient	15	1	15	1
2009–10	Manchester U	7	0		
2010–11	Manchester U	7	0	14	0
2011–12	Newcastle U	23	1		
2012–13	Newcastle U	14	0		
2013–14	Newcastle U	3	0		
2014–15	Newcastle U	13	1	53	2

PEREZ, Ayoze (F) 82 24
H: 5 10 W: 10 06 b.Santa Cruz de Tenerife 23-7-93
Internationals: Spain U21.

2012–13	Tenerife	16	1		
2013–14	Tenerife	30	16	46	17
2014–15	Newcastle U	36	7	36	7

RIVIERE, Emmanuel (F) 184 41
H: 6 0 W: 12 00 b.Lamentin 3-3-90
Internationals: France U16, U17, U18, U19, U21.

2008–09	St Etienne	8	1		
2009–10	St Etienne	30	8		
2010–11	St Etienne	35	8	73	17
2011–12	Toulouse	26	5		
2012–13	Toulouse	18	4	44	9
2012–13	Monaco	14	4		
2013–14	Monaco	30	10	44	14
2014–15	Newcastle U	23	1	23	1

ROBERTS, Callum (M) 0 0
b. 1-4-97

2014–15	Newcastle U	0	0

SATKA, Lubomir (D) 0 0
H: 6 1 W: 11 05 b.Ilava 2-12-95
Internationals: Slovakia U19, U21.

2013–14	Newcastle U	0	0
2014–15	Newcastle U	0	0

SISSOKO, Moussa (M) 271 30
H: 6 2 W: 13 00 b.Le Blanc Mesnil 16-8-89
Internationals: France U16, U17, U18, U19, U21, Full caps.

2007–08	Toulouse	29	1		
2008–09	Toulouse	35	4		
2009–10	Toulouse	37	7		
2010–11	Toulouse	35	5		
2011–12	Toulouse	35	2		
2012–13	Toulouse	19	1	190	20
2012–13	Newcastle U	12	3		
2013–14	Newcastle U	35	3		
2014–15	Newcastle U	34	4	81	10

STERRY, Jamie (D) 0 0
b. 21-11-95

2014–15	Newcastle U	0	0

STREETE, Remie (D) 2 0
H: 6 2 W: 12 13 b.Boldon 2-11-94

2011–12	Newcastle U	0	0		
2012–13	Newcastle U	0	0		
2013–14	Newcastle U	0	0		
2014–15	Newcastle U	0	0		
2014–15	Port Vale	2	0	2	0

TAYLOR, Ryan (M) 246 26
H: 5 8 W: 10 04 b.Liverpool 19-8-84
Internationals: England U21.

2001–02	Tranmere R	0	0		
2002–03	Tranmere R	25	1		
2003–04	Tranmere R	30	5		
2004–05	Tranmere R	43	8	98	14
2005–06	Wigan Ath	11	0		
2006–07	Wigan Ath	16	1		
2007–08	Wigan Ath	17	3		
2008–09	Wigan Ath	12	2	56	6
2008–09	Newcastle U	10	0		
2009–10	Newcastle U	31	4		
2010–11	Newcastle U	5	0		
2011–12	Newcastle U	31	2		
2012–13	Newcastle U	1	0		
2013–14	Newcastle U	0	0		
2014–15	Newcastle U	14	0	92	6

TAYLOR, Steven (D) 211 13
H: 6 2 W: 13 01 b.Greenwich 23-1-86
Internationals: England U16, U17, U20, U21, B.

2002–03	Newcastle U	0	0		
2003–04	Newcastle U	1	0		
2003–04	Wycombe W	6	0	6	0
2004–05	Newcastle U	13	0		
2005–06	Newcastle U	12	0		
2006–07	Newcastle U	27	2		
2007–08	Newcastle U	31	1		
2008–09	Newcastle U	27	4		
2009–10	Newcastle U	21	1		
2010–11	Newcastle U	14	3		
2011–12	Newcastle U	14	0		
2012–13	Newcastle U	25	0		
2013–14	Newcastle U	10	1		
2014–15	Newcastle U	10	1	205	13

TIOTE, Cheik (M) 206 4
H: 5 11 W: 12 06 b.Yamoussoukro 21-6-86
Internationals: Ivory Coast Full caps.

2005–06	Anderlecht	2	0		
2006–07	Anderlecht	2	0	4	0
2007–08	Roda JC	26	2	26	2
2008–09	Twente	28	0		
2009–10	Twente	28	1		
2010–11	Twente	2	0	58	1
2010–11	Newcastle U	26	1		
2011–12	Newcastle U	24	0		
2012–13	Newcastle U	24	0		
2013–14	Newcastle U	33	0		
2014–15	Newcastle U	11	0	118	1

VUCKIC, Haris (F) 56 13
H: 6 2 W: 12 02 b.Ljubljana 21-8-92
Internationals: Slovenia U17, U19, U21, Full caps.

2007–08	Domzale	1	0		
2008–09	Domzale	4	0	5	0
2009–10	Newcastle U	2	0		
2010–11	Newcastle U	0	0		
2011–12	Newcastle U	4	0		
2011–12	Cardiff C	5	1	5	1
2012–13	Newcastle U	0	0		
2013–14	Newcastle U	0	0		
2013–14	Rotherham U	22	4	22	4

2014–15	Newcastle U	1	0	7	0
2014–15	Rangers	17	8	17	8

WILLIAMSON, Mike (D) 328 14
H: 6 4 W: 13 03 b.Stoke 8-11-83

2001–02	Torquay U	3	0		
2001–02	Southampton	0	0		
2002–03	Southampton	0	0		
2003–04	Southampton	0	0		
2003–04	Torquay U	11	0	14	0
2003–04	Doncaster R	0	0		
2004–05	Southampton	0	0		
2004–05	Wycombe W	37	2		
2005–06	Wycombe W	39	5		
2006–07	Wycombe W	33	1		
2007–08	Wycombe W	12	0		
2008–09	Wycombe W	22	3	143	11
2008–09	Watford	17	1		
2009–10	Watford	4	1	21	2
2009–10	Portsmouth	0	0		
2009–10	Newcastle U	16	0		
2010–11	Newcastle U	29	0		
2011–12	Newcastle U	22	0		
2012–13	Newcastle U	19	0		
2013–14	Newcastle U	33	0		
2014–15	Newcastle U	31	1	150	1

WOODMAN, Freddie (G) 0 0
H: 6 1 W: 10 12 b.London 4-3-97
Internationals: England U16, U17, U18, U19.

2014–15	Newcastle U	0	0
2014–15	Hartlepool U	0	0

Players retained or with offer of contract
Barlaser, Daniel Tan.

Scholars
Broccoli, Stefan; Cameron, Kyle Milne; Charman, Luke; Cobain, Jamie Anthony; Gibson, Liam Steven; Gillesphey, Macauley; Heardman, Tom; Holmes, Jamie Jason; Hunter, Jack David; Johnson, Louis James; Laidler, Adam; Longstaff, Sean David; Newberry, Michael; Pearson, Brendan Conor; Pollock, Ben; Smith, Ben Joseph; Smith, Liam Phillip; Sterry, Jamie Michael; Suddick, Lewis Ethan; Trodd, Allan Jake; Ward, Daniel John; Williams, Callum Dylan; Woolston, Paul Hudson.

NEWPORT CO (55)

BYRNE, Mark (M) 155 18
H: 5 9 W: 11 00 b.Dublin 9-11-88

2006–07	Nottingham F	0	0		
2007–08	Nottingham F	1	0		
2008–09	Nottingham F	1	0		
2009–10	Nottingham F	0	0		
2010–11	Nottingham F	0	0	2	0
2010–11	Barnet	28	6		
2011–12	Barnet	43	5		
2012–13	Barnet	40	3	111	14
2014–15	Newport Co	42	4	42	4

CHAPMAN, Adam (M) 115 6
H: 5 10 W: 11 00 b.Doncaster 29-11-89
Internationals: Northern Ireland U21.

2008–09	Sheffield U	0	0		
2009–10	Sheffield U	0	0		
2010–11	Oxford U	0	0		
2011–12	Oxford U	14	1		
2012–13	Oxford U	26	1	40	2
2013–14	Mansfield T	0	0		
2013–14	Newport Co	39	1		
2014–15	Newport Co	36	3	75	4

COLLINS, Aaron (F) 2 0
b. 27-5-97
Internationals: Wales U19.

2014–15	Newport Co	2	0	2	0

CROW, Danny (F) 133 30
H: 5 9 W: 13 02 b.Great Yarmouth 26-1-86

2004–05	Norwich C	3	0	3	0
2004–05	Northampton T	10	2	10	2
2005–06	Peterborough U	38	15		
2006–07	Peterborough U	35	6		
2007–08	Peterborough U	4	2	77	23
2007–08	Notts Co	14	2	14	2

From Cambridge U, Luton T

2013–14	Newport Co	27	3		
2014–15	Newport Co	2	0	29	3

FEELY, Kevin (D) 62 2
H: 5 10 W: 11 07 b.Dublin 30-8-92
Internationals: Republic of Ireland U21.

2011	Bohemians	5	0		
2012	Bohemians	23	1	28	1

2012–13 Charlton Ath 0 0
2013–14 Charlton Ath 0 0
2013–14 *Carlisle U* 2 0 **2 0**
2013–14 *AFC Wimbledon* 0 0
2013–14 Newport Co 10 1
2014–15 Newport Co 22 0 **32 1**

FLYNN, Michael (M) **328 42**
H: 5 10 W: 13 04 b.Newport 17-10-80
2002–03 Wigan Ath 17 1
2003–04 Wigan Ath 8 0
2004–05 Wigan Ath 13 1 **38 2**
2004–05 *Blackpool* 6 0
2004–05 Gillingham 16 3
2005–06 Gillingham 36 6
2006–07 Gillingham 45 10 **97 19**
2007–08 Blackpool 28 3 **34 3**
2008–09 Darlington 0 0
2008–09 Huddersfield T 25 4 **25 4**
2009–10 Bradford C 42 6
2010–11 Bradford C 19 0
2011–12 Bradford C 30 4 **91 10**
2013–14 Newport Co 32 4
2014–15 Newport Co 11 0 **43 4**

HOWE, Rene (F) **244 60**
H: 6 0 W: 14 03 b.Bedford 22-10-86
2007–08 Peterborough U 15 1
2007–08 *Rochdale* 20 9 **20 9**
2008–09 Peterborough U 0 0
2008–09 *Morecambe* 37 10 **37 10**
2009–10 Peterborough U 0 0
2009–10 *Lincoln C* 17 5 **17 5**
2009–10 *Gillingham* 18 2 **18 2**
2010–11 Peterborough U 0 0 **15 1**
2010–11 *Bristol R* 12 1 **12 1**
2011–12 Torquay U 39 12
2012–13 Torquay U 42 16 **81 28**
2013–14 *Burton Alb* 15 1 **15 1**
2013–14 Newport Co 15 3
2014–15 Newport Co 14 0 **29 3**

HUGHES, Andrew (D) **42 3**
b.Cardiff 5-6-92
Internationals: Wales U23.
2013–14 Newport Co 26 2
2014–15 Newport Co 16 1 **42 3**

JACKSON, Ryan (M) **70 0**
H: 5 9 W: 10 03 b.Streatham 31-7-90
Internationals: England C.
2011–12 AFC Wimbledon 7 0 **7 0**
2013–14 Newport Co 29 0
2014–15 Newport Co 34 0 **63 0**

JEFFERS, Shaun (F) **72 4**
H: 6 1 W: 11 03 b.Bedford 14-4-92
Internationals: England U19.
2009–10 Coventry C 4 0
2010–11 Coventry C 0 0
2010–11 Cheltenham T 22 1 **22 1**
2011–12 Coventry C 3 0
2012–13 Coventry C 0 0 **7 0**
2013–14 Peterborough U 8 1 **8 1**
2013–14 Newport Co 14 0
2014–15 Newport Co 21 2 **35 2**

JOLLEY, Christian (F) **89 9**
H: 6 0 W: 10 00 b.Fleet 12-5-88
Internationals: England C.
2011–12 AFC Wimbledon 37 7
2012–13 AFC Wimbledon 15 0 **52 7**
2013–14 Newport Co 32 2
2014–15 Newport Co 5 0 **37 2**

JONES, Darren (D) **256 11**
H: 6 0 W: 14 12 b.Newport 28-8-83
2000–01 Bristol C 0 0
2001–02 Bristol C 2 0
2002–03 Bristol C 0 0
2003–04 Bristol C 0 0 **2 0**
2003–04 Cheltenham T 14 1 **14 1**
From Forest Green R.
2009–10 Hereford U 41 3 **41 3**
2010–11 Aldershot T 43 1
2011–12 Aldershot T 42 0 **85 1**
2012–13 Shrewsbury T 38 1
2013–14 Shrewsbury T 15 0 **53 1**
2013–14 AFC Wimbledon 18 1 **18 1**
2014–15 Newport Co 43 4 **43 4**

KLUKOWSKI, Yan (M) **38 4**
H: 6 1 W: 13 05 b.Chippenham 1-1-87
2014–15 Newport Co 38 4 **38 4**

MINSHULL, Lee (M) **97 7**
H: 6 2 W: 14 07 b.Chatham 11-11-85
2011–12 AFC Wimbledon 0 18 0
2013–14 Newport Co 40 4
2014–15 Newport Co 39 3 **79 7**

O'CONNOR, Aaron (F) **46 11**
b.Nottingham 9-8-83
2002–03 Scunthorpe U 3 0 **3 0**
From Ilkeston T, Gresley, Grays Ath, Mansfield T, Rushden & D, Luton T
2013–14 Newport Co 4 1
2014–15 Newport Co 39 10 **43 11**

OWEN-EVANS, Tom (F) **1 0**
b. 18-3-97
2014–15 Newport Co 1 0 **1 0**

PARKER, Joe (F) **4 0**
b.Gloucester 11-3-95
2013–14 Newport Co 0 0
2014–15 Newport Co 4 0 **4 0**

PARSELLE, Kieran (D) **0 0**
b. 30-11-96
2014–15 Newport Co 0 0

PATTEN, Kyle (M) **1 0**
b. 21-7-94
2014–15 Newport Co 1 0 **1 0**

PIDGELEY, Lenny (G) **176 0**
H: 6 4 W: 14 09 b.Twickenham 7-2-84
Internationals: England U16, U18, U19, U20.
2003–04 Chelsea 0 0
2003–04 *Watford* 27 0 **27 0**
2004–05 Chelsea 1 0
2005–06 Chelsea 1 0 **2 0**
2005–06 *Millwall* 0 0
2006–07 Millwall 42 0
2007–08 Millwall 13 0
2008–09 Millwall 0 0 **55 0**
2009–10 Carlisle U 17 0 **17 0**
From Woking
2010–11 Bradford C 21 0 **21 0**
2011–12 Exeter C 10 0 **10 0**
2013–14 Newport Co 25 0
2014–15 Newport Co 4 0 **29 0**
2014–15 *Mansfield T* 15 0 **15 0**

POOLE, Regan (D) **11 0**
b.Cardiff 18-6-98
Internationals: Wales U17.
2014–15 Newport Co 11 0 **11 0**

PORTER, Max (M) **120 4**
H: 5 10 W: 12 04 b.Hornchurch 29-6-87
Internationals: England C.
2007–08 Barnet 30 1
2008–09 Barnet 26 0 **56 1**
From Rushden & D.
2011–12 AFC Wimbledon 15 1 **15 1**
2013–14 Newport Co 22 1
2014–15 Newport Co 27 1 **49 2**

REDMAN, Ellis (D) **0 0**
2013–14 Newport Co 0 0
2014–15 Newport Co 0 0

SANDELL, Andy (D) **198 21**
H: 5 11 W: 11 09 b.Calne 8-9-83
2005–06 Bristol R 0 0
2006–07 Bristol R 36 3
2008–09 Bristol R 0 0 **36 3**
From Salisbury C.
2008–09 Aldershot T 29 2
2009–10 Aldershot T 29 5 **58 7**
2010–11 Wycombe W 32 7
2011–12 Wycombe W 11 0 **43 7**
2013–14 Newport Co 23 3
2014–15 Newport Co 38 1 **61 4**

STEPHENS, Jamie (G) **22 0**
b.Wotton 24-8-93
2012–13 Liverpool 0 0
2012–13 *Airbus UK* 13 0 **13 0**
2013–14 Newport Co 2 0
2014–15 Newport Co 7 0 **9 0**

WILLMOTT, Robbie (M) **62 4**
H: 5 9 W: 12 00 b.Harlow 16-5-90
Internationals: England C.
2013–14 Newport Co 46 3
2014–15 Newport Co 16 1 **62 4**

YAKUBU, Ismail (D) **204 14**
H: 5 11 W: 11 12 b.Kano 8-4-85
Internationals: England C.
2005–06 Barnet 26 1
2006–07 Barnet 29 1
2007–08 Barnet 28 2
2008–09 Barnet 38 3
2009–10 Barnet 25 2 **146 9**
From AFC Wimbledon, Cambridge U
2013–14 Newport Co 25 3
2014–15 Newport Co 33 2 **58 5**

ZEBROSKI, Chris (F) **282 59**
H: 6 1 W: 11 08 b.Swindon 29-10-86
2005–06 Plymouth Arg 4 0
2006–07 Plymouth Arg 0 0 **4 0**
2006–07 Millwall 25 3
2007–08 Millwall 0 0 **25 3**
2008–09 Wycombe W 33 7
2009–10 Wycombe W 15 2 **48 9**
2009–10 Torquay U 30 6
2010–11 Torquay U 44 14 **74 20**
2011–12 Bristol R 39 3
2012–13 Bristol R 0 0 **39 3**
2012–13 Cheltenham T 25 5 **21 5**
2013–14 Newport Co 35 12
2014–15 Newport Co 36 7 **71 19**

Players retained or with offer of contract
Day, Joseph David.

Scholars
Bamford, Lewis Paul; Brooks, Ben; Gray, Nyall James Wade; Harries, Luke Michael; James, Samuel Evan; Jones, Dafydd Rhys; Keating, Jake Alexander; Mathias, Nathan; Mpadi, Cedrick Matondo; O'Kelly, Aidan Finlay; Owen-Evans, Thomas; Parselle, Kieran Richard Ferguson; Poole, Regan Leslie; Redman, Ellis Anthony David; Shephard, Corey John; Ward, Joseph Adam; Waterhouse, Harry James; Wood, Spencer; Zanotti, Alexander.

NORTHAMPTON T (56)

BODIN, Billy (M) **115 14**
H: 5 11 W: 11 00 b.Swindon 24-3-92
Internationals: Wales U17, U19, U21.
2009–10 Swindon T 0 0
2010–11 Swindon T 5 0
2011–12 Swindon T 11 3 **16 3**
2011–12 Torquay U 17 5
2011–12 Crewe Alex 8 0 **8 0**
2012–13 Torquay U 43 5
2013–14 Torquay U 27 1 **87 11**
2014–15 Northampton T 4 0 **4 0**

BROWN, Brendan (G) **0 0**
b. 15-11-96
2014–15 Northampton T 0 0

BYROM, Joel (M) **116 11**
H: 6 0 W: 12 04 b.Accrington 14-9-86
Internationals: England C.
2004–05 Blackburn R 0 0
2005–06 Blackburn R 0 0
2006–07 Accrington S 1 0 **1 0**
From Clitheroe, Southport, Clitheroe, Northwich Vic.
2010–11 Stevenage 7 0
2011–12 Stevenage 32 4 **39 4**
2012–13 Preston NE 22 2
2013–14 Preston NE 11 2 **33 4**
2013–14 *Oldham Ath* 4 0 **4 0**
2014–15 Northampton T 39 3 **39 3**

CARTER, Darren (M) **306 24**
H: 6 2 W: 12 03 b.Solihull 18-12-83
Internationals: England U19, U20.
2001–02 Birmingham C 13 1
2002–03 Birmingham C 12 0
2003–04 Birmingham C 5 0
2004–05 Birmingham C 15 2 **45 3**
2004–05 *Sunderland* 10 1 **10 1**
2005–06 WBA 20 1
2006–07 WBA 33 3 **53 4**
2007–08 Preston NE 39 4
2008–09 Preston NE 18 0
2009–10 Preston NE 23 0
2010–11 Preston NE 14 0 **94 4**
2010–11 *Millwall* 10 0 **10 0**
2012–13 Cheltenham T 34 6 **34 6**
2013–14 Northampton T 37 5
2014–15 Northampton T 23 1 **60 6**

CLIFTON, Danny (M) **0 0**
b.Northampton 8-11-96
2014–15 Northampton T 0 0

COLLINS, Lee (D) **247 5**
H: 6 1 W: 11 10 b.Telford 23-9-83
2006–07 Wolverhampton W 0 0
2007–08 Wolverhampton W 0 0
2007–08 *Hereford U* 16 0 **16 0**
2008–09 Wolverhampton W 0 0
2008–09 Port Vale 39 1
2009–10 Port Vale 45 1
2010–11 Port Vale 42 2

2011–12 Port Vale 16 0 142 4
2011–12 Barnsley 7 0
2012–13 Barnsley 0 0 7 0
2012–13 Shrewsbury T 8 0 8 0
2012–13 Northampton T 15 0
2013–14 Northampton T 22 1
2014–15 Northampton T 37 0 74 1

CRESSWELL, Ryan (D) 211 22
H: 5 9 W: 10 05 b.Rotherham 22-12-87
2006–07 Sheffield U 0 0
2007–08 Sheffield U 0 0
2007–08 Rotherham U 3 0
2007–08 Morecambe 2 0 2 0
2007–08 Macclesfield T 19 1 19 1
2008–09 Bury 25 1
2009–10 Bury 28 0 53 1
2010–11 Rotherham U 22 4
2011–12 Rotherham U 16 4 41 8
2012–13 Southend U 43 6 43 6
2013–14 Fleetwood T 20 1
2014–15 Fleetwood T 1 0 21 1
2014–15 Northampton T 32 5 32 5

D'ATH, Lawson (M) 86 11
H: 5 9 W: 12 02 b.Witney 24-12-92
2010–11 Reading 0 0
2011–12 Reading 0 0
2011–12 Yeovil T 14 1 14 1
2012–13 Reading 0 0
2012–13 Cheltenham T 2 1 2 1
2012–13 Exeter C 8 1 8 1
2013–14 Reading 0 0
2013–14 Dagenham & R 21 1 21 1
2014–15 Northampton T 41 7 41 7

DIAMOND, Zander (D) 309 25
H: 6 2 W: 11 07 b.Alexandria 3-12-85
Internationals: Scotland U21.
2003–04 Aberdeen 19 2
2004–05 Aberdeen 29 3
2005–06 Aberdeen 33 0
2006–07 Aberdeen 21 0
2007–08 Aberdeen 26 3
2008–09 Aberdeen 28 4
2009–10 Aberdeen 16 3
2010–11 Aberdeen 32 1 204 16
2011–12 Oldham Ath 23 2 23 2
2012–13 Burton Alb 37 4
2013–14 Burton Alb 10 1 47 5
2013–14 *Northampton T* 14 1
2014–15 Northampton T 21 1 35 2

DUKE, Matt (G) 185 0
H: 6 5 W: 13 04 b.Sheffield 16-7-77
1999–2000 Sheffield U 0 0
2000–01 Sheffield U 0 0
2001–02 Sheffield U 0 0
2004–05 Hull C 2 0
2005–06 Hull C 2 0
2005–06 *Stockport Co* 3 0 3 0
2005–06 Wycombe W 5 0 5 0
2006–07 Hull C 1 0
2007–08 Hull C 3 0
2008–09 Hull C 10 0
2009–10 Hull C 11 0
2010–11 Hull C 21 0 50 0
2011–12 Bradford C 18 0
2011–12 *Northampton T* 9 0
2012–13 Bradford C 24 0 42 0
2013–14 Northampton T 46 0
2014–15 Northampton T 30 0 85 0

HACKETT, Chris (M) 376 25
H: 6 0 W: 12 08 b.Oxford 1-3-83
1999–2000 Oxford U 2 0
2000–01 Oxford U 16 2
2001–02 Oxford U 15 0
2002–03 Oxford U 12 0
2003–04 Oxford U 22 1
2004–05 Oxford U 37 4
2005–06 Oxford U 21 2 125 9
2005–06 Hearts 2 0 2 0
2006–07 Millwall 33 3
2007–08 Millwall 6 0
2008–09 Millwall 22 0
2009–10 Millwall 40 2
2010–11 Millwall 16 0
2011–12 Millwall 3 0 120 5
2011–12 Exeter C 5 0 5 0
2011–12 Wycombe W 8 0 8 0
2012–13 Northampton T 41 6
2013–14 Northampton T 37 2
2014–15 Northampton T 38 3 116 11

HOLMES, Ricky (M) 165 22
H: 6 2 W: 11 11 b.Southend 19-6-87
Internationals: England C.
2010–11 Barnet 25 2

2011–12 Barnet 41 8
2012–13 Barnet 25 5 91 15
2013–14 Portsmouth 40 2
2014–15 Portsmouth 13 0 53 2
2014–15 Northampton T 21 5 21 5

HORNBY, Lewis (M) 25 0
H: 5 10 W: 10 13 b.Kettering 25-4-94
2012–13 Northampton T 25 0
2013–14 Northampton T 0 0
2014–15 Northampton T 0 0 25 0

HORWOOD, Evan (D) 295 6
H: 6 0 W: 10 06 b.Billingham 10-3-86
2004–05 Sheffield U 0 0
2004–05 *Stockport Co* 10 0 10 0
2005–06 Sheffield U 0 0
2005–06 Scunthorpe U 0 0
2005–06 *Chester C* 1 0 1 0
2006–07 Sheffield U 0 0
2006–07 *Darlington* 20 0 20 0
2007–08 Sheffield U 0 0
2007–08 Gretna 15 1 15 1
2007–08 Carlisle U 19 0
2008–09 Carlisle U 24 0
2009–10 Carlisle U 32 0 75 0
2010–11 Hartlepool U 45 2
2011–12 Hartlepool U 41 1
2012–13 Hartlepool U 37 2 123 5
2013–14 Tranmere R 18 0 18 0
2013–14 *Northampton T* 8 0
2014–15 Northampton T 25 0 33 0

JACKSON, Ben (D) 0 0
b. 19-10-96
2014–15 Northampton T 0 0

JALAL, Shwan (G) 179 0
H: 6 2 W: 14 02 b.Baghdad 14-8-83
Internationals: England C.
2001–02 Tottenham H 0 0
2002–03 Tottenham H 0 0
2003–04 Tottenham H 0 0
From Woking.
2006–07 *Sheffield W* 0 0
2006–07 Peterborough U 1 0
2007–08 Peterborough U 7 0
2007–08 *Morecambe* 12 0 12 0
2008–09 Peterborough U 0 0 8 0
2008–09 Bournemouth 41 0
2009–10 Bournemouth 44 0
2010–11 Bournemouth 43 0
2011–12 Bournemouth 3 0
2012–13 Bournemouth 17 0
2013–14 Bournemouth 0 0 148 0
2013–14 Oxford U 0 0
2013–14 *Leyton Orient* 2 0 2 0
2014–15 Bury 5 0 5 0
2014–15 Northampton T 4 0 4 0

LANGMEAD, Kelvin (D) 375 35
H: 6 1 W: 12 00 b.Coventry 23-3-85
2003–04 Preston NE 0 0
2003–04 *Carlisle U* 11 1 11 1
2004–05 Preston NE 1 0 1 0
2004–05 *Kidderminster H* 10 1 10 1
2004–05 Shrewsbury T 28 3
2005–06 Shrewsbury T 42 9
2006–07 Shrewsbury T 45 3
2007–08 Shrewsbury T 39 1
2008–09 Shrewsbury T 33 0
2009–10 Shrewsbury T 44 3 231 19
2010–11 Peterborough U 32 3
2011–12 Peterborough U 0 0 32 3
2011–12 Northampton T 41 4
2012–13 Northampton T 39 7
2013–14 Northampton T 3 0
2014–15 Northampton T 7 0 90 11

McWILLIAMS, Shaun (M) 0 0
b.Northampton 14-8-98
2014–15 Northampton T 0 0

MORRIS, Ian (D) 221 17
H: 6 0 W: 11 05 b.Dublin 27-2-87
Internationals: Republic of Ireland U19, U21.
2003–04 Leeds U 0 0
2004–05 Leeds U 0 0
2005–06 Leeds U 0 0
2005–06 *Blackpool* 30 3 30 3
2006–07 Leeds U 0 0
2006–07 Scunthorpe U 28 3
2007–08 Scunthorpe U 25 3
2008–09 Scunthorpe U 20 1
2008–09 *Carlisle U* 6 0 6 0
2009–10 Scunthorpe U 3 0
2009–10 *Chesterfield* 7 0
2010–11 Scunthorpe U 0 0 76 7
2010–11 *Chesterfield* 19 1 26 1
2011–12 Torquay U 37 2

2012–13 Torquay U 11 1 48 3
2013–14 Northampton T 33 3
2014–15 Northampton T 2 0 35 3

MOYO, David (F) 14 1
H: 6 0 W: 10 12 b.Harare 17-12-94
2012–13 Northampton T 5 0
2013–14 Northampton T 6 0
2014–15 Northampton T 3 1 14 1

NICHOLLS, Alex (M) 244 37
H: 5 10 W: 11 00 b.Stourbridge 9-12-87
2005–06 Walsall 8 0
2006–07 Walsall 0 0
2007–08 Walsall 19 2
2008–09 Walsall 45 6
2009–10 Walsall 37 4
2010–11 Walsall 37 5
2011–12 Walsall 45 7 191 24
2012–13 Northampton T 15 7
2013–14 Northampton T 0 0
2014–15 Northampton T 6 1 21 8
2014–15 Exeter C 32 5 32 5

O'TOOLE, John (M) 234 31
H: 6 2 W: 13 07 b.Harrow 30-9-88
Internationals: Republic of Ireland U21.
2007–08 Watford 35 3
2008–09 Watford 22 7
2008–09 *Sheffield U* 9 1 9 1
2009–10 Watford 0 0 57 10
2009–10 Colchester U 31 2
2010–11 Colchester U 11 0
2011–12 Colchester U 15 0
2012–13 Colchester U 15 0 72 2
2012–13 *Bristol R* 18 3
2013–14 Bristol R 41 13 59 16
2014–15 Northampton T 35 2 35 2
2014–15 *Southend U* 2 0 2 0

POTTER, Alfie (M) 162 21
H: 5 7 W: 9 06 b.Islington 9-1-89
2007–08 Peterborough U 2 0 2 0
From Kettering T.
2010–11 Oxford U 38 2
From Kettering T.
2011–12 Oxford U 25 2
2012–13 Oxford U 43 10
2013–14 Oxford U 24 4
2014–15 Oxford U 15 2 145 20
2014–15 AFC Wimbledon 15 1 15 1
2014–15 Northampton T 0 0

RICHARDS, Marc (F) 442 143
H: 6 2 W: 12 06 b.Wolverhampton 8-7-82
Internationals: England U18, U20.
1999–2000 Blackburn R 0 0
2000–01 Blackburn R 0 0
2001–02 Blackburn R 0 0
2001–02 *Crewe Alex* 4 0 4 0
2001–02 *Oldham Ath* 5 0 5 0
2001–02 *Halifax T* 5 0 5 0
2002–03 Blackburn R 0 0
2002–03 *Swansea C* 17 7 17 7
2003–04 Northampton T 41 8
2004–05 Northampton T 12 2
2004–05 *Rochdale* 5 2 5 2
2005–06 Northampton T 0 0
2005–06 Barnsley 38 12
2006–07 Barnsley 31 6 69 18
2007–08 Port Vale 29 5
2008–09 Port Vale 30 10
2009–10 Port Vale 46 20
2010–11 Port Vale 40 16
2011–12 Port Vale 36 17 181 68
2012–13 Chesterfield 34 9
2013–14 Chesterfield 38 8 72 20
2013–14 *Northampton T* 0 0
2014–15 Northampton T 31 18 84 28

ROBERTSON, Gregor (D) 273 4
H: 6 0 W: 12 04 b.Edinburgh 19-1-84
Internationals: Scotland U21.
2000–01 Nottingham F 0 0
2001–02 Nottingham F 0 0
2002–03 Nottingham F 0 0
2003–04 Nottingham F 16 0
2004–05 Nottingham F 0 0 36 0
2005–06 Rotherham U 35 1
2006–07 Rotherham U 18 0 53 1
2007–08 Chesterfield 35 1
2008–09 Chesterfield 10 0
2009–10 Chesterfield 10 0
2010–11 Chesterfield 12 0 116 3
2012–13 Crewe Alex 29 0
2013–14 Crewe Alex 3 0 32 0
2013–14 Northampton T 15 0
2014–15 Northampton T 21 0 36 0

TAYLOR, Jason (M) 331 19
H: 6 1 W: 11 03 b.Ashton-under-Lyne 28-1-87

2005–06	Oldham Ath	0	0		
2005–06	*Stockport Co*	9	0		
2006–07	Stockport Co	45	1		
2007–08	Stockport Co	42	4		
2008–09	Stockport Co	8	1	104	6
2008–09	Rotherham U	15	1		
2009–10	Rotherham U	2	0		
2009–10	*Rochdale*	23	1	23	1
2010–11	Rotherham U	42	5		
2011–12	Rotherham U	39	2		
2012–13	Rotherham U	20	2	118	10
2012–13	Cheltenham T	16	0		
2013–14	Cheltenham T	33	2		
2014–15	Cheltenham T	16	0	65	2
2014–15	Northampton T	21	0	21	0

TONEY, Ivan (F) 53 11
b.Northampton 16-3-96

2012–13	Northampton T	0	0		
2013–14	Northampton T	13	3		
2014–15	Northampton T	40	8	53	11

TOZER, Ben (D) 177 6
H: 6 1 W: 12 11 b.Plymouth 1-3-90

2007–08	Swindon T	2	0	2	0
2007–08	Newcastle U	0	0		
2008–09	Newcastle U	0	0		
2009–10	Newcastle U	1	0		
2010–11	Newcastle U	0	0	1	0
2010–11	*Northampton T*	31	3		
2011–12	Northampton T	45	3		
2012–13	Northampton T	46	0		
2013–14	Northampton T	29	0		
2013–14	*Colchester U*	1	0	1	0
2014–15	Northampton T	22	0	173	6

Players retained or with offer of contract
Moloney, Brendon Anthony.

Scholars
Agbenu, Dodzi; Andrews, Charlie Shaun; Brown, Brendan Thomas; Burt, Harvey Jeremiah Thomas; Carroll, Thomas Edward; Clifton, Daniel Paul; Cooke, Ryan Lewis; Forster, Matthew James Michael; Jackson, Ben Robert; Marsden, Ryan John; Master, Shaquille; McWilliams, Shaun Daniel; Mushata, Alex; Parker, Richard Jonathan; Parsons, Robert Tony; Warburton, Samuel Jake; Westwood, Callum Lee.

NORWICH C (57)

ANDREU, Tony (M) 174 42
b.Cagnes-Sur-Mer 22-5-88

2009–10	Nyon	29	2		
2010–11	Nyon	21	2		
2011–12	Nyon	27	6	77	10
2012–13	Livingston	33	7	33	7
2013–14	Hamilton A	35	13		
2014–15	Hamilton A	23	12	58	25
2014–15	Norwich C	6	0	6	0

AWUAH, Reiss (D) 0 0
b. 14-1-94

| 2014–15 | Norwich C | 0 | 0 | | |

BASSONG, Sebastien (D) 253 6
H: 6 2 W: 11 07 b.Paris 9-7-86
Internationals: France U21. Cameroon Full caps.

2005–06	Metz	23	0		
2006–07	Metz	37	1		
2007–08	Metz	19	0	79	1
2008–09	Newcastle U	30	0		
2009–10	Newcastle U	0	0	30	0
2009–10	Tottenham H	28	1		
2010–11	Tottenham H	12	1		
2011–12	Tottenham H	5	0		
2011–12	*Wolverhampton W*	9	0	9	0
2012–13	Tottenham H	0	0	45	2
2012–13	Norwich C	34	3		
2013–14	Norwich C	27	0		
2014–15	Norwich C	18	0	79	3
2014–15	*Watford*	11	0	11	0

BECCHIO, Luciano (F) 308 109
H: 6 2 W: 13 05 b.Cordoba 28-12-83

2003–04	Mallorca B	0	0		
2004–05	Mallorca B	0	0		
2004–05	Murcia	16	3	16	3
2005–06	Terrassa	24	2	24	2
2006–07	Barcelona Ath	10	0	10	0
2006–07	Merida	12	5		
2007–08	Merida	38	22	50	27
2008–09	Leeds U	45	15		
2009–10	Leeds U	37	15		
2010–11	Leeds U	41	19		
2011–12	Leeds U	41	11		
2012–13	Leeds U	26	15	190	75
2012–13	Norwich C	8	0		
2013–14	Norwich C	5	0		
2014–15	Norwich C	0	0	13	0
2014–15	*Rotherham U*	5	2	5	2

BENNETT, Elliott (M) 238 20
H: 5 9 W: 10 11 b.Telford 18-12-88

2006–07	Wolverhampton W	0	0		
2007–08	Wolverhampton W	0	0		
2007–08	*Crewe Alex*	9	1	9	1
2007–08	Bury	19	1		
2008–09	Wolverhampton W	0	0		
2008–09	Bury	46	3	65	4
2009–10	Brighton & HA	43	7		
2010–11	Brighton & HA	46	6		
2011–12	Norwich C	33	1		
2012–13	Norwich C	24	1		
2013–14	Norwich C	2	0		
2014–15	Norwich C	9	0	68	2
2014–15	*Brighton & HA*	7	0	96	13

BENNETT, Ryan (M) 237 14
H: 6 2 W: 11 00 b.Thurrock 6-3-90
Internationals: England U18, U21.

2006–07	Grimsby T	5	0		
2007–08	Grimsby T	40	1		
2008–09	Grimsby T	45	5		
2009–10	Grimsby T	13	0	103	6
2009–10	Peterborough U	22	1		
2010–11	Peterborough U	34	4		
2011–12	Peterborough U	32	1	88	6
2011–12	Norwich C	8	0		
2012–13	Norwich C	15	1		
2013–14	Norwich C	16	1		
2014–15	Norwich C	7	0	46	2

BUNN, Mark (G) 154 0
H: 6 0 W: 12 02 b.Southgate 16-11-84

2004–05	Northampton T	0	0		
2005–06	Northampton T	0	0		
2006–07	Northampton T	42	0		
2007–08	Northampton T	45	0		
2008–09	Northampton T	3	0	90	0
2008–09	Blackburn R	0	0		
2008–09	*Leicester C*	3	0	3	0
2009–10	Blackburn R	0	0		
2009–10	*Sheffield U*	32	0	32	0
2010–11	Blackburn R	3	0		
2011–12	Blackburn R	3	0		
2012–13	Blackburn R	0	0	6	0
2012–13	Norwich C	23	0		
2013–14	Norwich C	0	0		
2014–15	Norwich C	0	0	23	0

CALLAN-McFADDEN, Kyle (D) 0 0
H: 6 0 W: 12 04 b.20-4-95
Internationals: Republic of Ireland U16, U17, U19, U21.

| 2014–15 | Norwich C | 0 | 0 | | |

CUELLAR, Carlos (D) 328 13
H: 6 3 W: 13 03 b.Madrid 23-8-81

2000–01	Calahorra	27	0	27	0
2001–02	Numancia	23	1		
2002–03	Numancia	39	3	62	4
2003–04	Osasuna	5	0		
2004–05	Osasuna	14	0		
2005–06	Osasuna	29	1		
2006–07	Osasuna	23	1	71	2
2007–08	Rangers	36	4	36	4
2008–09	Aston Villa	28	0		
2009–10	Aston Villa	36	2		
2010–11	Aston Villa	12	0		
2011–12	Aston Villa	18	0	94	2
2012–13	Sunderland	26	1		
2013–14	Sunderland	4	0	30	1
2014–15	Norwich C	8	0	8	0

GARRIDO, Javier (D) 203 3
H: 5 10 W: 11 12 b.Irun, Spain 15-3-85
Internationals: Spain U17, U19, U20, U21.

2004–05	Real Sociedad	28	0		
2005–06	Real Sociedad	33	0		
2006–07	Real Sociedad	25	1	86	1
2007–08	Manchester C	27	0		
2008–09	Manchester C	13	1		
2009–10	Manchester C	9	1	49	2
2010–11	Lazio	10	0		
2011–12	Lazio	11	0		
2012–13	Lazio	0	0	21	0

On loan from Lazio

2012–13	Norwich C	34	0		
2013–14	Norwich C	6	0		
2014–15	Norwich C	7	0	47	0

GRABBAN, Lewis (F) 274 82
H: 6 0 W: 11 03 b.Croydon 12-1-88

2005–06	Crystal Palace	0	0		
2006–07	Crystal Palace	8	1		
2006–07	*Oldham Ath*	9	0	9	0
2007–08	Crystal Palace	2	0	10	1
2007–08	*Motherwell*	6	0	6	0
2007–08	Millwall	13	3		
2008–09	Millwall	31	6		
2009–10	Millwall	11	0		
2009–10	*Brentford*	7	2		
2010–11	Millwall	1	0	56	9
2010–11	Brentford	22	5	29	7
2011–12	Rotherham U	43	18	43	18
2012–13	Bournemouth	42	13		
2013–14	Bournemouth	44	22	86	35
2014–15	Norwich C	35	12	35	12

HALL-JOHNSON, Reece (M) 0 0
H: 5 8 W: 10 08 b.Aylesbury 9-5-95

| 2013–14 | Norwich C | 0 | 0 | | |
| 2014–15 | Norwich C | 0 | 0 | | |

HOOLAHAN, Wes (M) 434 57
H: 5 6 W: 10 03 b.Dublin 10-8-83
Internationals: Republic of Ireland U21, B, Full caps.

2001–02	Shelbourne	20	3		
2002–03	Shelbourne	23	0		
2004	Shelbourne	31	2		
2005	Shelbourne	29	4	103	9
2005–06	Livingston	16	0	16	0
2006–07	Blackpool	42	8		
2007–08	Blackpool	45	5	87	13
2008–09	Norwich C	32	2		
2009–10	Norwich C	37	11		
2010–11	Norwich C	41	10		
2011–12	Norwich C	33	4		
2012–13	Norwich C	33	3		
2013–14	Norwich C	16	1		
2014–15	Norwich C	36	4	228	35

HOOPER, Gary (F) 292 139
H: 5 9 W: 11 02 b.Loughton 26-1-88

2006–07	Southend U	19	0		
2006–07	*Leyton Orient*	4	2	4	2
2007–08	Southend U	13	2	32	2
2008–09	Hereford U	19	11	19	11
2008–09	Scunthorpe U	0	0		
2009–10	Scunthorpe U	35	19	80	43
2010–11	Celtic	26	20		
2011–12	Celtic	37	24		
2012–13	Celtic	32	19	95	63
2013–14	Norwich C	32	6		
2014–15	Norwich C	30	12	62	18

HOWSON, Jonathan (M) 287 36
H: 5 11 W: 12 01 b.Morley 21-5-88
Internationals: England U21.

2006–07	Leeds U	9	1		
2007–08	Leeds U	26	3		
2008–09	Leeds U	40	4		
2009–10	Leeds U	45	4		
2010–11	Leeds U	46	10		
2011–12	Leeds U	19	1	185	23
2011–12	Norwich C	11	1		
2012–13	Norwich C	30	2		
2013–14	Norwich C	27	2		
2014–15	Norwich C	34	8	102	13

JEROME, Cameron (F) 373 88
H: 6 1 W: 13 06 b.Huddersfield 14-8-86
Internationals: England U21.

2004–05	Cardiff C	29	6		
2005–06	Cardiff C	44	18	73	24
2005–06	Birmingham C	0	0		
2006–07	Birmingham C	38	7		
2007–08	Birmingham C	33	7		
2008–09	Birmingham C	43	9		
2009–10	Birmingham C	32	11		
2010–11	Birmingham C	34	3		
2011–12	Birmingham C	1	0	181	37
2011–12	Stoke C	23	4		
2012–13	Stoke C	26	3		
2013–14	Stoke C	1	0	50	7
2013–14	*Crystal Palace*	28	2	28	2
2014–15	Norwich C	41	18	41	18

JOHNSON, Brad (M) 319 48
H: 6 0 W: 11 00 b.Hackney 28-4-87

2004–05	Cambridge U	0	0	1	0
2005–06	Northampton T	3	0		
2006–07	Northampton T	27	5		
2007–08	Northampton T	23	2	53	7
2007–08	Leeds U	21	3		
2008–09	Leeds U	15	1		
2008–09	*Brighton & HA*	10	4	10	4

2009–10	Leeds U	36	7		
2010–11	Leeds U	45	5	117	16
2011–12	Norwich C	28	2		
2012–13	Norwich C	37	1		
2013–14	Norwich C	32	3		
2014–15	Norwich C	41	15	138	21

KING, Cameron (M)   0 0
b. 5-10-95
Internationals: Scotland U19, U21.
2014–15	Norwich C	0	0		

LAFFERTY, Kyle (F)   287 63
H: 6 4   W: 11 00   b.Northern Ireland 16-9-87
Internationals: Northern Ireland U17, U19.
2005–06	Burnley	11	1		
2005–06	Darlington	9	3	9	3
2006–07	Burnley	35	4		
2007–08	Burnley	37	5	83	10
2008–09	Rangers	25	6		
2009–10	Rangers	28	7		
2010–11	Rangers	31	11		
2011–12	Rangers	20	7	104	31
2012–13	Sion	25	5	25	5
2013–14	Palermo	34	11	34	11
2014–15	Norwich C	18	1	18	1
2014–15	Caykur Rizespor	14	2	14	2

LOZA, Jamar (F)   19 2
H: 5 10   W: 11 01   b.Kingston 10-5-94
Internationals: Jamaica Full caps.
2013–14	Norwich C	1	0		
2013–14	Coventry C	1	0	1	0
2013–14	Leyton Orient	3	0	3	0
2013–14	Southend U	7	1	7	1
2014–15	Norwich C	2	1	3	1
2014–15	Yeovil T	5	0	5	0

MARTIN, Russell (M)   384 18
H: 6 0   W: 11 08   b.Brighton 4-1-86
Internationals: Scotland Full caps.
2004–05	Wycombe W	7	0		
2005–06	Wycombe W	23	3		
2006–07	Wycombe W	42	2		
2007–08	Wycombe W	44	0	116	5
2008–09	Peterborough U	46	1		
2009–10	Peterborough U	10	0	56	1
2009–10	Norwich C	26	0		
2010–11	Norwich C	46	5		
2011–12	Norwich C	33	2		
2012–13	Norwich C	31	3		
2013–14	Norwich C	31	0		
2014–15	Norwich C	45	2	212	12

MATTHEWS, Remi (G)   0 0
b.Gorleston 10-2-94
2014–15	Norwich C	0	0		
2014–15	Burton Alb	0	0		

McGEEHAN, Cameron (M)   19 6
H: 5 11   W: 11 03   b.Kingston upon Thames 6-4-95
Internationals: Northern Ireland U21.
2013–14	Norwich C	0	0		
2014–15	Norwich C	0	0		
2014–15	Luton T	15	3	15	3
2014–15	Cambridge U	4	3	4	3

McGRANDLES, Conor (M)   66 7
H: 6 0   W: 10 00   b.Falkirk 24-9-95
2012–13	Falkirk	26	2		
2013–14	Falkirk	36	5		
2014–15	Falkirk	3	0	65	7
2014–15	Norwich C	1	0	1	0

MIQUEL, Ignasi (D)   12 0
H: 6 4   W: 13 05   b.Barcelona 28-9-92
Internationals: Spain U16, U19, U21.
2009–10	Arsenal	0	0		
2010–11	Arsenal	0	0		
2011–12	Arsenal	4	0		
2012–13	Arsenal	1	0		
2013–14	Arsenal	0	0		
2013–14	Leicester C	7	0	7	0
2014–15	Arsenal	0	0	5	0
2014–15	Norwich C	0	0		

MORRIS, Carlton (F)   16 0
H: 6 1   W: 13 05   b.Cambridge 16-12-95
Internationals: England U19.
2014–15	Norwich C	1	0	1	0
2014–15	Oxford U	7	0	7	0
2014–15	York C	8	0	8	0

MURPHY, Jacob (M)   36 7
b.Wembley 24-2-95
Internationals: England U18, U19, U20.
2013–14	Norwich C	0	0		
2013–14	Swindon T	6	0	6	0
2013–14	Southend U	7	1	7	1

MURPHY, Josh (F)   27 1
H: 5 8   W: 10 07   b.London 24-2-95
Internationals: England U18, U19, U20.
2012–13	Norwich C	0	0		
2013–14	Norwich C	9	0		
2014–15	Norwich C	13	1	22	1
2014–15	Wigan Ath	5	0	5	0

O'NEIL, Gary (M)   398 29
H: 5 10   W: 11 00   b.Beckenham 18-5-83
Internationals: England U19, U20, U21.
1999–2000	Portsmouth	1	0		
2000–01	Portsmouth	10	1		
2001–02	Portsmouth	33	1		
2002–03	Portsmouth	31	3		
2003–04	Portsmouth	3	2		
2003–04	Walsall	7	0	7	0
2004–05	Portsmouth	24	2		
2004–05	Cardiff C	9	1	9	1
2005–06	Portsmouth	36	6		
2006–07	Portsmouth	35	1		
2007–08	Portsmouth	2	0	175	16
2007–08	Middlesbrough	26	0		
2008–09	Middlesbrough	29	4		
2009–10	Middlesbrough	36	4		
2010–11	Middlesbrough	18	0	109	8
2010–11	West Ham U	8	0		
2011–12	West Ham U	16	2		
2012–13	West Ham U	24	1	48	3
2013–14	QPR	29	1	29	1
2014–15	Norwich C	21	0	21	0

ODDJIDJA-OFOE, Vadis (M)   191 23
H: 5 11   W: 10 08   b.Gent 21-2-89
Internationals: Belgium U18, U19, U21, Full caps.
2007–08	Anderlecht	3	1	3	1
2008–09	Hamburg	2	0	2	0
2008–09	Club Brugge	16	0		
2009–10	Club Brugge	35	4		
2010–11	Club Brugge	37	6		
2011–12	Club Brugge	29	4		
2012–13	Club Brugge	31	5		
2013–14	Club Brugge	30	3		
2014–15	Club Brugge	3	0	181	22
2014–15	Norwich C	5	0	5	0

OLSSON, Martin (D)   193 4
H: 5 7   W: 12 12   b.Gavle 17-5-88
Internationals: Sweden U19, U21, Full caps.
2005–06	Blackburn R	0	0		
2006–07	Blackburn R	0	0		
2007–08	Blackburn R	2	0		
2008–09	Blackburn R	9	0		
2009–10	Blackburn R	21	1		
2010–11	Blackburn R	29	2		
2011–12	Blackburn R	27	0		
2012–13	Blackburn R	29	0	117	3
2013–14	Norwich C	34	0		
2014–15	Norwich C	42	1	76	1

REDMOND, Nathan (M)   139 12
H: 5 8   W: 11 11   b.Birmingham 6-3-94
Internationals: England U16, U17, U18, U19, U21.
2011–12	Birmingham C	24	5		
2012–13	Birmingham C	38	2	62	7
2013–14	Norwich C	34	~1		
2014–15	Norwich C	43	4	77	5

RUDD, Declan (G)   70 0
H: 6 3   W: 12 06   b.Diss 16-1-91
Internationals: England U16, U17, U19, U20, U21.
2008–09	Norwich C	0	0		
2009–10	Norwich C	7	0		
2010–11	Norwich C	1	0		
2011–12	Norwich C	2	0		
2012–13	Norwich C	0	0		
2012–13	Preston NE	14	0		
2013–14	Norwich C	0	0		
2013–14	Preston NE	46	0	60	0
2014–15	Norwich C	0	0	10	0

RUDDY, John (G)   315 0
H: 6 3   W: 12 07   b.St Ives 24-10-86
Internationals: England Full caps.
2003–04	Cambridge U	1	0		
2004–05	Cambridge U	38	0	39	0
2005–06	Everton	1	0		
2005–06	Walsall	5	0	5	0
2005–06	Rushden & D	3	0	3	0
2005–06	Chester C	4	0	4	0
2006–07	Everton	0	0		
2006–07	Stockport Co	11	0		
2006–07	Wrexham	5	0	5	0
2006–07	Bristol C	1	0	1	0
2007–08	Everton	0	0		
2007–08	Stockport Co	12	0	23	0
2008–09	Everton	0	0		
2008–09	Crewe Alex	19	0	19	0
2009–10	Everton	0	0	1	0
2009–10	Motherwell	34	0	34	0
2010–11	Norwich C	45	0		
2011–12	Norwich C	37	0		
2012–13	Norwich C	15	0		
2013–14	Norwich C	38	0		
2014–15	Norwich C	46	0	181	0

TETTEY, Alexander (M)   229 17
H: 5 11   W: 10 09   b.Accra 4-4-86
Internationals: Norway U18, U19, U21, Full caps.
2004–05	Rosenborg	0	0		
2005–06	Rosenborg	10	1		
2006–07	Rosenborg	21	1		
2007–08	Rosenborg	25	4		
2008–09	Rosenborg	28	6		
2009–10	Rosenborg	1	0	85	12
2009–10	Rennes	24	0		
2010–11	Rennes	17	1		
2011–12	Rennes	19	1	60	2
2012–13	Norwich C	27	0		
2013–14	Norwich C	21	1		
2014–15	Norwich C	36	2	84	3

THOMPSON, Louis (M)   64 4
H: 5 11   W: 11 10   b.Bristol 19-12-94
Internationals: Wales U19.
2012–13	Swindon T	4	0		
2013–14	Swindon T	28	2		
2014–15	Norwich C	0	0		
2014–15	Swindon T	32	2	64	4

TOFFOLO, Harry (D)   28 1
H: 6 0   W: 11 03   b. 19-8-95
Internationals: England U18, U19, U20.
2014–15	Norwich C	0	0		
2014–15	Swindon T	28	1	28	1

TURNER, Michael (D)   375 23
H: 6 4   W: 13 05   b.Lewisham 9-11-83
2001–02	Charlton Ath	0	0		
2002–03	Charlton Ath	0	0		
2002–03	Leyton Orient	7	1	7	1
2003–04	Charlton Ath	0	0		
2004–05	Brentford	45	1		
2005–06	Brentford	46	2	91	3
2006–07	Hull C	43	3		
2007–08	Hull C	44	5		
2008–09	Hull C	38	4		
2009–10	Hull C	4	0	129	12
2009–10	Sunderland	29	2		
2010–11	Sunderland	15	0		
2011–12	Sunderland	24	0	68	2
2012–13	Norwich C	26	3		
2013–14	Norwich C	22	0		
2014–15	Norwich C	23	1	71	4
2014–15	Fulham	9	1	9	1

VAN WOLFSWINKEL, Ricky (F)   204 68
H: 6 1   W: 10 13   b.Amersfoort 27-1-89
Internationals: Netherlands U19, U21, Full caps.
2007–08	Vitesse	1	0		
2008–09	Vitesse	32	8	33	8
2009–10	FC Utrecht	35	11		
2010–11	FC Utrecht	29	15	64	26
2011–12	Sporting Lisbon	25	14		
2012–13	Sporting Lisbon	29	14	54	28
2013–14	Norwich C	25	1		
2014–15	Norwich C	0	0	25	1
2014–15	St Etienne	28	5	28	5

WHITTAKER, Steven (D)   361 27
H: 6 1   W: 13 07   b.Edinburgh 16-6-84
Internationals: Scotland U21, Full caps.
2001–02	Hibernian	1	0		
2002–03	Hibernian	6	0		
2003–04	Hibernian	28	1		
2004–05	Hibernian	37	1		
2005–06	Hibernian	34	1		
2006–07	Hibernian	35	1	141	4
2007–08	Rangers	30	4		
2008–09	Rangers	24	2		
2009–10	Rangers	35	7		
2010–11	Rangers	36	4		
2011–12	Rangers	25	2	150	19
2012–13	Norwich C	13	1		
2013–14	Norwich C	20	1		
2014–15	Norwich C	37	2	70	4

Schoiars
Beauchamp, Marcus Andrew; Black, Harley Stuart; Boateng, Isaac Kofi; Burgess, Ben; Byrne-Hewitt, Lewis Christopher; Cantwell, Todd Owen; Cole, Oliver; Couzens, George Daniel; Crowe, Joe; Eaton-Collins, Jamie; Efete, Michee; Fox, Nathan Ross; Grant, Raymond Michael; Lewis, Jamal; Oxborough, Aston Jay; Ramsay, Louis Mark; Simpson, Jake Mark; Walters, Thomas Harvey.

NOTTINGHAM F (58)

ANTONIO, Michael (M)   204 39
H: 6 0   W: 11 11   b.Wandsworth 28-3-90

2008–09	Reading	0	0	
2008–09	*Cheltenham T*	9	0	9 0
2009–10	Reading	1	0	
2009–10	*Southampton*	28	3	28 3
2010–11	Reading	21	1	
2011–12	Reading	6	0	
2011–12	*Colchester U*	15	4	15 4
2011–12	*Sheffield W*	14	5	
2012–13	Reading	0	0	28 1
2012–13	Sheffield W	37	8	
2013–14	Sheffield W	27	4	78 17
2014–15	Nottingham F	46	14	46 14

ASSOMBALONGA, Britt (F)   119 53
H: 5 9   W: 11 13   b.Kinshasa 6-12-92

2010–11	Watford	0	0	
2011–12	Watford	4	0	
2012–13	Watford	0	0	
2012–13	*Southend U*	43	15	43 15
2013–14	Watford	0	0	4 0
2013–14	Peterborough U	43	23	43 23
2014–15	Nottingham F	29	15	29 15

BLACKSTOCK, Dexter (F)   306 80
H: 6 2   W: 13 00   b.Oxford 20-5-86
Internationals: England U18, U19, U20, U21. Antigua and Barbuda Full caps.

2004–05	Southampton	9	1	
2004–05	*Plymouth Arg*	14	4	14 4
2005–06	Southampton	19	3	28 4
2005–06	*Derby Co*	9	3	9 3
2006–07	QPR	39	13	
2007–08	QPR	35	6	
2008–09	QPR	36	11	110 30
2008–09	*Nottingham F*	6	2	
2009–10	Nottingham F	39	12	
2010–11	Nottingham F	17	5	
2011–12	Nottingham F	22	8	
2012–13	Nottingham F	37	6	
2013–14	Nottingham F	1	0	
2013–14	*Leeds U*	4	1	4 1
2014–15	Nottingham F	19	5	141 38

BLAKE, Jack (M)   3 0
b.Scotland 22-9-94
Internationals: Scotland U19.

2011–12	Nottingham F	0	0	
2012–13	Nottingham F	0	0	
2013–14	Nottingham F	0	0	
2013–14	*Mansfield T*	3	0	3 0
2014–15	Nottingham F	0	0	

BURKE, Chris (M)   369 56
H: 5 9   W: 10 10   b.Glasgow 2-12-83
Internationals: Scotland U21, B, Full caps.

2001–02	Rangers	2	1	
2002–03	Rangers	20	3	
2003–04	Rangers	20	3	
2004–05	Rangers	12	0	
2005–06	Rangers	27	3	
2006–07	Rangers	22	2	
2007–08	Rangers	11	2	
2008–09	Rangers	1	0	95 11
2008–09	Cardiff C	14	1	
2009–10	Cardiff C	44	9	
2010–11	Cardiff C	44	5	102 15
2011–12	Birmingham C	46	12	
2012–13	Birmingham C	41	8	
2013–14	Birmingham C	44	4	131 24
2014–15	Nottingham F	41	6	41 6

BURKE, Oliver (M)   4 0
H: 5 9   W: 11 11   b.Melton Mowbray 7-4-97

2014–15	Nottingham F	2	0	2 0
2014–15	*Bradford C*	2	0	2 0

COHEN, Chris (M)   327 19
H: 5 11   W: 10 11   b.Norwich 5-3-87

2003–04	West Ham U	7	0	
2004–05	West Ham U	11	0	
2005–06	West Ham U	0	0	18 0
2005–06	*Yeovil T*	30	1	

2006–07	*Yeovil T*	44	6	74 7
2007–08	Nottingham F	41	2	
2008–09	Nottingham F	41	2	
2009–10	Nottingham F	44	3	
2010–11	Nottingham F	42	2	
2011–12	Nottingham F	7	0	
2012–13	Nottingham F	38	2	
2013–14	Nottingham F	16	1	
2014–15	Nottingham F	6	0	235 12

COLLINS, Danny (D)   309 10
H: 6 2   W: 11 13   b.Buckley 6-8-80
Internationals: England C. Wales Full caps.

2004–05	Chester C	12	1	12 1
2004–05	Sunderland	14	0	
2005–06	Sunderland	23	1	
2006–07	Sunderland	38	0	
2007–08	Sunderland	36	1	
2008–09	Sunderland	35	1	
2009–10	Sunderland	3	0	149 3
2009–10	Stoke C	25	0	
2010–11	Stoke C	25	0	
2011–12	Stoke C	0	0	50 0
2011–12	*Ipswich T*	16	3	16 3
2011–12	*West Ham U*	11	1	11 1
2012–13	Nottingham F	40	0	
2013–14	Nottingham F	23	1	
2014–15	Nottingham F	8	1	71 2

DE VRIES, Dorus (G)   357 0
H: 6 1   W: 12 08   b.Bewerwijk 29-12-80

1999–2000	Telstar	1	0	
2000–01	Telstar	27	0	
2001–02	Telstar	27	0	
2002–03	Telstar	26	0	81 0
2003–04	Den Haag	18	0	
2004–05	Den Haag	32	0	
2005–06	Den Haag	0	0	50 0
2006–07	Dunfermline Ath	27	0	27 0
2007–08	Swansea C	46	0	
2008–09	Swansea C	40	0	
2009–10	Swansea C	46	0	
2010–11	Swansea C	46	0	178 0
2011–12	Wolverhampton W	4	0	
2012–13	Wolverhampton W	10	0	14 0
2013–14	Nottingham F	3	0	
2014–15	Nottingham F	4	0	7 0

DURRANT, Ross (G)   0 0
b. 12-11-95

2014–15	Nottingham F	0	0	

EVTIMOV, Dimitar (G)   11 0
H: 6 3   W: 13 00   b.Plevan 7-9-93
Internationals: Bulgaria U19, U21.

2012–13	Nottingham F	1	0	
2013–14	Nottingham F	0	0	1 0
2014–15	*Mansfield T*	10	0	10 0

FENTON, Kieran (D)   0 0
b. 25-11-94
Internationals: England U19.

2013–14	Nottingham F	0	0	
2014–15	Nottingham F	0	0	

FOX, Danny (D)   337 15
H: 5 11   W: 12 06   b.Winsford 29-5-86
Internationals: England U21. Scotland Full caps.

2004–05	Everton	0	0	
2004–05	*Stranraer*	11	1	11 1
2005–06	Walsall	33	0	
2006–07	Walsall	44	3	
2007–08	Walsall	22	3	99 6
2007–08	Coventry C	18	1	
2008–09	Coventry C	39	5	
2009–10	Coventry C	0	0	57 6
2009–10	Celtic	15	0	15 0
2009–10	Burnley	14	1	
2010–11	Burnley	35	0	
2011–12	Burnley	1	0	50 1
2011–12	Southampton	41	0	
2012–13	Southampton	20	1	
2013–14	Southampton	3	0	64 1
2013–14	Nottingham F	14	0	
2014–15	Nottingham F	27	0	41 0

FRYATT, Matty (F)   364 116
H: 5 10   W: 11 00   b.Nuneaton 5-3-86
Internationals: England U19.

2002–03	Walsall	0	0	
2003–04	Walsall	11	1	
2003–04	*Carlisle U*	10	1	10 1
2004–05	Walsall	36	15	
2005–06	Walsall	23	11	70 27
2005–06	Leicester C	19	6	
2006–07	Leicester C	32	3	
2007–08	Leicester C	30	2	
2008–09	Leicester C	46	27	

2009–10	Leicester C	29	11	
2010–11	Leicester C	12	2	168 51
2010–11	Hull C	22	9	
2011–12	Hull C	46	16	
2012–13	Hull C	4	0	
2013–14	Hull C	10	2	82 27
2013–14	*Sheffield W*	9	4	9 4
2014–15	Nottingham F	25	6	25 6

GARDNER, Gary (M)   58 7
H: 6 2   W: 12 13   b.Solihull 29-6-92
Internationals: England U17, U19, U20, U21.

2009–10	Aston Villa	0	0	
2010–11	Aston Villa	0	0	
2011–12	Aston Villa	14	0	
2011–12	*Coventry C*	4	1	4 1
2012–13	Aston Villa	2	0	
2013–14	Aston Villa	3	0	
2013–14	*Sheffield W*	3	0	3 0
2014–15	Aston Villa	0	0	16 0
2014–15	*Brighton & HA*	17	2	17 2
2014–15	Nottingham F	18	4	18 4

GNAHORE, Wilfried (M)   0 0
b. 30-12-95
Internationals: Ivory Coast U19.

2013–14	Nottingham F	0	0	
2014–15	Nottingham F	0	0	

GRANT, Jorge (M)   1 0
H: 5 9   W: 11 07   b.Oxford 26-9-94

2013–14	Nottingham F	0	0	
2014–15	Nottingham F	1	0	1 0

HALFORD, Greg (D)   388 43
H: 6 4   W: 12 10   b.Chelmsford 8-12-84
Internationals: England U20.

2002–03	Colchester U	1	0	
2003–04	Colchester U	18	4	
2004–05	Colchester U	44	4	
2005–06	Colchester U	45	7	
2006–07	Colchester U	28	3	136 18
2006–07	Reading	3	0	3 0
2007–08	Sunderland	8	0	
2007–08	*Charlton Ath*	16	2	16 2
2008–09	Sunderland	0	0	
2008–09	*Sheffield U*	41	4	41 4
2009–10	Sunderland	0	0	8 0
2009–10	*Wolverhampton W*	15	0	
2010–11	*Wolverhampton W*	2	0	17 0
2010–11	Portsmouth	33	5	
2011–12	Portsmouth	42	7	75 12
2012–13	Nottingham F	37	3	
2013–14	Nottingham F	36	4	
2014–15	Nottingham F	0	0	73 7
2014–15	*Brighton & HA*	19	0	19 0

HARDING, Dan (D)   354 7
H: 6 0   W: 11 11   b.Gloucester 23-12-83
Internationals: England U21.

2002–03	Brighton & HA	1	0	
2003–04	Brighton & HA	23	0	
2004–05	Brighton & HA	43	1	67 1
2005–06	Leeds U	20	0	20 0
2006–07	Ipswich T	42	0	
2007–08	Ipswich T	30	1	
2008–09	Ipswich T	0	0	73 1
2008–09	*Southend U*	19	1	19 1
2008–09	*Reading*	3	0	3 0
2009–10	Southampton	42	3	
2010–11	Southampton	36	0	
2011–12	Southampton	20	1	98 4
2012–13	Nottingham F	27	0	
2013–14	Nottingham F	19	0	
2014–15	Nottingham F	8	0	54 0
2014–15	*Millwall*	20	0	20 0

HOBBS, Jack (D)   245 4
H: 6 3   W: 13 05   b.Portsmouth 18-8-88
Internationals: England U19.

2004–05	Lincoln C	1	0	1 0
2005–06	Liverpool	0	0	
2006–07	Liverpool	0	0	
2007–08	Liverpool	2	0	
2007–08	*Scunthorpe U*	9	1	9 1
2008–09	Liverpool	0	0	2 0
2008–09	Leicester C	44	1	
2009–10	Leicester C	44	0	
2010–11	Leicester C	26	0	114 1
2010–11	*Hull C*	13	0	
2011–12	Hull C	40	1	
2012–13	Hull C	22	0	75 1
2013–14	Nottingham F	27	1	
2014–15	Nottingham F	17	0	44 1

LAING, Louis (D)   33 1
H: 5 11   W: 12 00   b.Newcastle 6-3-93
Internationals: England U16, U17, U18, U19.

2009–10	Sunderland	0	0	
2010–11	Sunderland	0	0	

2011–12 Sunderland 0 0
2011–12 *Wycombe W* 11 0 11 0
2012–13 Sunderland 0 0 1 0
2014–15 Nottingham F 0 0
2014–15 *Notts Co* 10 0 10 0
2014–15 *Motherwell* 11 1 11 1

LANSBURY, Henri (M) 201 36
H: 6 0 W: 13 06 b.Enfield 12-10-90
Internationals: England U16, U17, U19, U21.
2007–08 Arsenal 0 0
2008–09 Arsenal 0 0
2008–09 *Scunthorpe U* 16 4 16 4
2009–10 Arsenal 1 0
2009–10 *Watford* 37 5 37 5
2010–11 Arsenal 0 0
2010–11 *Norwich C* 23 4 23 4
2011–12 Arsenal 2 0
2011–12 *West Ham U* 22 1 22 1
2012–13 Arsenal 0 0 3 0
2012–13 Nottingham F 32 5
2013–14 Nottingham F 29 7
2014–15 Nottingham F 39 10 100 22

LICHAJ, Eric (D) 129 2
H: 5 11 W: 12 07 b.Chicago 17-11-88
Internationals: USA U17, U20, Full caps.
2007–08 Aston Villa 0 0
2008–09 Aston Villa 0 0
2009–10 Aston Villa 0 0
2009–10 *Lincoln C* 6 0 6 0
2009–10 *Leyton Orient* 9 1 9 1
2010–11 Aston Villa 5 0
2010–11 *Leeds U* 16 0 16 0
2011–12 Aston Villa 10 1
2012–13 Aston Villa 17 0 32 1
2013–14 Nottingham F 24 0
2014–15 Nottingham F 42 0 66 0

MAJEWSKI, Radoslaw (M) 223 21
H: 5 7 W: 10 06 b.Pruszkow 15-12-86
Internationals: Poland U21, U23, Full caps.
2006–07 Groclin 14 0
2007–08 Groclin 28 4 42 4
2008–09 Polonia Warsaw 29 1 29 1
2009–10 Nottingham F 35 3
2010–11 Nottingham F 26 2
2011–12 Nottingham F 28 6
2012–13 Nottingham F 31 5
2013–14 Nottingham F 24 0
2014–15 Nottingham F 0 0 144 16
2014–15 *Huddersfield T* 8 0 8 0

MANCIENNE, Michael (D) 203 0
H: 6 0 W: 11 09 b.Isleworth 8-1-88
Internationals: England U16, U17, U18, U19, U21.
2005–06 Chelsea 0 0
2006–07 Chelsea 0 0
2006–07 *QPR* 28 0
2007–08 Chelsea 0 0
2007–08 *QPR* 30 0 58 0
2008–09 Chelsea 4 0
2008–09 *Wolverhampton W* 10 0
2009–10 Chelsea 30 0
2009–10 *Wolverhampton W* 30 0
2010–11 Chelsea 0 0 4 0
2010–11 *Wolverhampton W* 16 0 56 0
2011–12 Hamburg 16 0
2012–13 Hamburg 21 0
2013–14 Hamburg 12 0 49 0
2014–15 Nottingham F 36 0 36 0

McLAUGHLIN, Stephen (M) 90 14
H: 5 9 W: 11 12 b.Derry 14-6-90
2011 Derry C 33 3
2012 Derry C 24 10 57 13
2012–13 Nottingham F 0 0
2013–14 Nottingham F 3 0
2013–14 *Bristol C* 5 0 5 0
2014–15 Nottingham F 6 0 9 0
2014–15 *Notts Co* 13 0 13 0
2014–15 *Southend U* 6 1 6 1

OSBORN, Ben (D) 45 3
H: 5 11 W: 11 11 b.Derby 5-8-94
Internationals: England U18, U19, U20.
2011–12 Nottingham F 0 0
2012–13 Nottingham F 0 0
2013–14 Nottingham F 8 0
2014–15 Nottingham F 37 3 45 3

PATERSON, Jamie (F) 147 24
H: 5 9 W: 10 07 b.Coventry 20-12-91
2010–11 Walsall 14 0
2011–12 Walsall 34 3
2012–13 Walsall 46 12 94 15
2013–14 Nottingham F 32 8
2014–15 Nottingham F 21 1 53 9

REID, Andy (M) 409 51
H: 5 9 W: 12 08 b.Dublin 29-7-82
Internationals: Republic of Ireland U21, Full caps.
1999–2000 Nottingham F 0 0
2000–01 Nottingham F 14 2
2001–02 Nottingham F 29 0
2002–03 Nottingham F 30 1
2003–04 Nottingham F 46 13
2004–05 Nottingham F 25 5
2004–05 *Tottenham H* 13 1
2005–06 *Tottenham H* 13 0 26 1
2006–07 *Charlton Ath* 16 2
2007–08 *Charlton Ath* 22 5 38 7
2007–08 Sunderland 13 1
2008–09 Sunderland 32 1
2009–10 Sunderland 21 2
2010–11 Sunderland 2 0 68 4
2010–11 *Sheffield U* 9 2 9 2
2010–11 *Blackpool* 5 0 5 0
2011–12 Nottingham F 39 2
2012–13 Nottingham F 42 5
2013–14 Nottingham F 32 9
2014–15 Nottingham F 6 0 263 37

RIERA, Roger (D) 0 0
b.El Masnou 17-2-95
2014–15 Nottingham F 0 0

SMITH, Jordan (G) 0 0
b. 8-8-94
Internationals: Costa Rica U17, U20, Full caps.
2013–14 Nottingham F 0 0
2014–15 Nottingham F 0 0

TESCHE, Robert (M) 159 11
H: 5 11 W: 11 03 b.Wismar 27-5-87
2006–07 Arminia Bielefeld 7 0
2007–08 Arminia Bielefeld 15 1 22 1
2008–09 Arminia Beilefeld 26 2 26 2
2009–10 Hamburg 16 2
2010–11 Hamburg 11 0
2011–12 Hamburg 23 2
2012–13 Hamburg 4 0
2012–13 *Fortuna Dusseldorf* 14 0 14 0
2013–14 Hamburg 9 0 63 4
2014–15 Nottingham F 22 2 22 2
2014–15 *Birmingham C* 12 2 12 2

VAUGHAN, David (M) 372 26
H: 5 7 W: 11 00 b.Abergele 18-2-83
Internationals: Wales U19, U21, Full caps.
2000–01 Crewe Alex 1 0
2001–02 Crewe Alex 13 0
2002–03 Crewe Alex 32 3
2003–04 Crewe Alex 31 0
2004–05 Crewe Alex 44 6
2005–06 Crewe Alex 34 5
2006–07 Crewe Alex 29 4
2007–08 Crewe Alex 1 0 185 18
2007–08 *Real Sociedad* 7 1 7 1
2008–09 Blackpool 33 1
2009–10 Blackpool 41 1
2010–11 Blackpool 35 2 109 4
2011–12 Sunderland 22 2
2012–13 Sunderland 24 1
2013–14 Sunderland 3 0 49 3
2013–14 *Nottingham F* 9 0
2014–15 *Nottingham F* 13 0 22 0

VELDWIJK, Lars (F) 87 44
H: 6 5 W: 14 13 b. 21-8-91
2010–11 Voldendam 2 0 2 0
2011–12 Utrecht 5 0 5 0
2012–13 Dordrecht 31 14 31 14
2013–14 Excelsior 38 30 38 30
2014–15 Nottingham F 11 0 11 0

WALKER, Tyler (F) 7 1
H: 5 10 W: 9 13 b. 17-10-96
2013–14 Nottingham F 0 0
2014–15 Nottingham F 7 1 7 1

WILSON, Kelvin (D) 307 4
H: 6 2 W: 12 01 b.Nottingham 3-9-85
2003–04 Notts Co 3 0
2004–05 Notts Co 41 2
2005–06 Notts Co 34 1 78 3
2005–06 *Preston NE* 5 0
2006–07 *Preston NE* 21 1 27 1
2007–08 Nottingham F 42 0
2008–09 Nottingham F 36 0
2009–10 Nottingham F 35 0
2010–11 Nottingham F 10 0
2011–12 Celtic 15 0
2012–13 Celtic 32 0 47 0
2013–14 *Nottingham F* 9 0
2014–15 *Nottingham F* 23 0 155 0

Players retained or with offer of contract
Abdoun, Djamal; Cash, Matthew; Petravicius, Deimantas; Rees, Joshua David; Todorov, Nikolay.

Scholars
Adams, Liam; Arrowsmith, David James; Austin, Aidan Jerry; Boyd, Joseph Alexander; Burns, Dylan John; Crookes, Adam Mark; Dearle, Richard Alexander; Diallo, Ismael; Gamblen, Thomas Anthony; Garcia, Worthington Jermaine Ramon; Iacovitti, Alexander; Karo, Antreas; Kelly, Jack Brent; McDonagh, Gerry Luke; Nielsen, Frederik Fisker; Otim, Elvis Apota; Thomas, Luke Washington; Walton, Kasheme Emmanuel; Worrall, Joseph Adrian; Yates, Ryan James.

NOTTS CO (59)

ADAMS, Blair (D) 115 1
H: 5 11 W: 11 05 b.South Shields 8-9-91
Internationals: England U20.
2010–11 Sunderland 0 0
2011–12 Sunderland 0 0
2011–12 *Brentford* 7 0 7 0
2011–12 *Northampton T* 22 0 22 0
2012–13 Sunderland 0 0
2012–13 *Coventry C* 16 0
2013–14 *Coventry C* 36 0 52 0
2014–15 *Notts Co* 34 1 34 1

ANDREWS, Zac (D) 0 0
b.Bristol 14-2-96
2011–12 Bristol C 0 0
2013–14 Notts Co 0 0
2014–15 Notts Co 0 0

BAJNER, Balint (F) 62 18
H: 6 5 W: 13 12 b.Szombathely 19-11-90
Internationals: Hungary U19.
2009–10 Honved 13 3
2010–11 Honved 6 1 19 4
2011–12 Sulmona 18 11 18 11
2012–13 Borussia Dortmund 1 0 1 0
2014–15 Ipswich T 5 0 5 0
2014–15 Notts Co 19 3 19 3

BISHOP, Colby (M) 3 0
H: 5 11 W: 11 05 b. 14-11-94
2013–14 Notts Co 0 0
2014–15 Notts Co 3 0 3 0

CARROLL, Roy (G) 416 0
H: 6 2 W: 12 09 b.Enniskillen 30-9-77
1995–96 Hull C 23 0
1996–97 Hull C 23 0 46 0
1996–97 *Wigan Ath* 29 0
1997–98 *Wigan Ath* 29 0
1998–99 *Wigan Ath* 43 0
1999–2000 *Wigan Ath* 34 0
2000–01 *Wigan Ath* 29 0 135 0
2001–02 Manchester U 7 0
2002–03 Manchester U 10 0
2003–04 Manchester U 6 0
2004–05 Manchester U 26 0 49 0
2005–06 West Ham U 19 0
2006–07 West Ham U 12 0 31 0
2007–08 Rangers 14 0
2007–08 *Derby Co* 14 0
2008–09 *Derby Co* 16 0 30 0
2009–10 Odense 28 0
2010–11 Odense 18 0 46 0
2011–12 OFI Crete 16 0 16 0
2012–13 Olympiacos 2 0
2012–13 Olympiacos 16 0
2013–14 Olympiacos . 0 0 18 0
2014–15 Notts Co 45 0 45 0

CRANSTON, Jordan (D) 9 0
H: 5 11 W: 13 01 b. 11-3-93
Internationals: Wales U19.
2012–13 Wolverhampton W 0 0
2013–14 Wolverhampton W 0 0
2014–15 Notts Co 9 0 9 0

DANIELS, Billy (F) 29 4
H: 6 0 W: 11 07 b.Bristol 3-7-94
2012–13 Coventry C 4 0
2013–14 Coventry C 18 3
2013–14 *Cheltenham T* 0 0 2 0
2014–15 *Coventry C* 2 0 24 3
2014–15 *Notts Co* 3 1 3 1

DUMBUYA, Mustapha (D)　129　0
H: 5 7　W: 11 00　b.Sierra Leone 7-8-87
Internationals: Sierra Leone Full caps.

Season	Club	Apps	Gls	Tot	Gls
2009–10	Doncaster R	3	0		
2010–11	Doncaster R	23	0		
2011–12	Doncaster R	10	0		
2011–12	Crystal Palace	2	0	2	0
2012–13	Doncaster R	0	0	36	0
2012–13	Portsmouth	23	0	23	0
2012–13	Crawley T	15	0	15	0
2013–14	Notts Co	24	0		
2014–15	Notts Co	29	0	53	0

EDWARDS, Mike (D)　527　30
H: 6 0　W: 12 10　b.Hessle 25-4-80

Season	Club	Apps	Gls	Tot	Gls
1997–98	Hull C	21	0		
1998–99	Hull C	30	0		
1999–2000	Hull C	40	1		
2000–01	Hull C	42	4		
2001–02	Hull C	39	1		
2002–03	Hull C	6	0	178	6
2002–03	Colchester U	5	0	5	0
2003–04	Grimsby T	33	1	33	1
2004–05	Notts Co	9	0		
2005–06	Notts Co	46	7		
2006–07	Notts Co	45	3		
2007–08	Notts Co	19	1		
2008–09	Notts Co	43	2		
2009–10	Notts Co	40	5		
2010–11	Notts Co	37	1		
2011–12	Notts Co	30	1		
2012–13	Carlisle U	23	0		
2013–14	Carlisle U	1	0	24	0
2014–15	Notts Co	18	3	287	23

HARRAD, Shaun (F)　216　54
H: 5 10　W: 12 04　b.Nottingham 11-12-84
Internationals: England C. Scotland Full caps.

Season	Club	Apps	Gls	Tot	Gls
2002–03	Notts Co	5	0		
2003–04	Notts Co	8	0		
2004–05	Notts Co	16	1		
2009–10	Burton Alb	42	21		
2010–11	Burton Alb	20	10	62	31
2010–11	Northampton T	18	6		
2011–12	Northampton T	0	0	18	6
2011–12	Bury	26	2		
2011–12	Rotherham U	8	3	8	3
2012–13	Bury	0	0		
2012–13	Cheltenham T	31	8		
2013–14	Bury	18	0	44	2
2014–15	Notts Co	12	2	41	3
2014–15	Cheltenham T	12	1	43	9

HAYHURST, Will (M)　66　5
H: 5 10　W: 11 02　b.Longridge 24-2-94
Internationals: Republic of Ireland U17, U19, U21.

Season	Club	Apps	Gls	Tot	Gls
2011–12	Preston NE	1	0		
2012–13	Preston NE	21	4		
2013–14	Preston NE	6	0		
2013–14	York C	18	1	18	1
2014–15	Preston NE	7	0	36	4
2014–15	Notts Co	12	0	12	0

HOLLIS, Haydn (D)　58　4
H: 6 4　W: 13 01　b.Selston 14-10-92

Season	Club	Apps	Gls	Tot	Gls
2011–12	Notts Co	1	0		
2012–13	Notts Co	6	0		
2013–14	Notts Co	10	4		
2014–15	Notts Co	41	0	58	4

JONES, Gary (M)　661　87
H: 5 11　W: 12 05　b.Birkenhead 3-6-77

Season	Club	Apps	Gls	Tot	Gls
1997–98	Swansea C	8	0	8	0
1997–98	Rochdale	17	2		
1998–99	Rochdale	20	0		
1999–2000	Rochdale	39	7		
2000–01	Rochdale	44	8		
2001–02	Rochdale	20	5		
2001–02	Barnsley	25	1		
2002–03	Barnsley	31	1		
2003–04	Barnsley	0	0	56	2
2003–04	Rochdale	26	4		
2004–05	Rochdale	39	8		
2005–06	Rochdale	42	4		
2006–07	Rochdale	27	3		
2007–08	Rochdale	43	7		
2008–09	Rochdale	28	0		
2009–10	Rochdale	34	4		
2010–11	Rochdale	46	17		
2011–12	Rochdale	45	5	470	74
2012–13	Bradford C	39	2		
2013–14	Bradford C	45	6	84	8
2014–15	Notts Co	43	3	43	3

KEANE, Cieron (D)　2　0
H: 5 10　W: 10 08　b.Nottingham 14-8-96
Internationals: Republic of Ireland U19.

Season	Club	Apps	Gls	Tot	Gls
2014–15	Notts Co	2	0	2	0

McGOWAN, Brad (D)　0　0
H: 6 1　W: 10 12　b. 30-4-96

Season	Club	Apps	Gls	Tot	Gls
2014–15	Notts Co	0	0		

McKENZIE, Taylor (D)　4　0
H: 6 2　W: 12 11　b.30-5-94

Season	Club	Apps	Gls	Tot	Gls
2013–14	Sheffield W	0	0		
2014–15	Notts Co	4	0	4	0

MULLINS, Hayden (D)　607　28
H: 5 11　W: 11 12　b.Reading 27-3-79
Internationals: England U21.

Season	Club	Apps	Gls	Tot	Gls
1996–97	Crystal Palace	0	0		
1997–98	Crystal Palace	0	0		
1998–99	Crystal Palace	40	5		
1999–2000	Crystal Palace	45	10		
2000–01	Crystal Palace	41	1		
2001–02	Crystal Palace	43	0		
2002–03	Crystal Palace	43	2		
2003–04	Crystal Palace	10	0	222	18
2003–04	West Ham U	27	0		
2004–05	West Ham U	37	1		
2005–06	West Ham U	35	0		
2006–07	West Ham U	30	2		
2007–08	West Ham U	34	0		
2008–09	West Ham U	17	1	180	4
2008–09	Portsmouth	17	0		
2009–10	Portsmouth	18	0		
2010–11	Portsmouth	45	2		
2011–12	Portsmouth	34	1	114	3
2011–12	Reading	7	0	7	0
2012–13	Birmingham C	28	2		
2013–14	Birmingham C	8	0	36	2
2013–14	Notts Co	16	1		
2014–15	Notts Co	32	0	48	1

MURRAY, Ronan (F)　93　13
H: 5 7　W: 11 00　b.Mayo 12-9-91
Internationals: Republic of Ireland U17, U19, U21.

Season	Club	Apps	Gls	Tot	Gls
2010–11	Ipswich T	8	0		
2010–11	Torquay U	7	1	7	1
2011–12	Ipswich T	0	0		
2011–12	Swindon T	20	3	20	3
2012–13	Ipswich T	1	0	9	0
2012–13	Plymouth Arg	13	1		
2013–14	Plymouth Arg	0	0	13	1
2013–14	Notts Co	24	7		
2014–15	Notts Co	20	1	44	8

NEWTON, Sean (D)　8　0
H: 6 1　W: 13 10　b.Liverpool 23-9-88
Internationals: England C.
From Droylsden, Barrow, AFC Telford U, Stockport Co, Lincoln C.

Season	Club	Apps	Gls	Tot	Gls
2014–15	Notts Co	8	0	8	0

NOBLE, Liam (M)　163　25
H: 5 9　W: 10 05　b.Newcastle 8-5-91

Season	Club	Apps	Gls	Tot	Gls
2009–10	Sunderland	0	0		
2010–11	Sunderland	0	0		
2010–11	Carlisle U	21	3		
2011–12	Sunderland	0	0		
2011–12	Carlisle U	40	6		
2012–13	Carlisle U	35	6		
2013–14	Carlisle U	34	5	130	20
2014–15	Carlisle U	33	5	33	5

PILKINGTON, Kevin (G)　363　0
H: 6 1　W: 13 08　b.Hitchin 8-3-74

Season	Club	Apps	Gls	Tot	Gls
1992–93	Manchester U	0	0		
1993–94	Manchester U	0	0		
1994–95	Manchester U	1	0		
1995–96	Manchester U	3	0		
1995–96	Rochdale	6	0	6	0
1996–97	Manchester U	6	0		
1996–97	Rotherham U	17	0	17	0
1997–98	Manchester U	2	0		
1998–99	Port Vale	8	0		
1999–2000	Port Vale	15	0	23	0
2000–01	Mansfield T	2	0		
2001–02	Mansfield T	45	0		
2002–03	Mansfield T	32	0		
2003–04	Mansfield T	46	0		
2004–05	Mansfield T	42	0	167	0
2005–06	Notts Co	45	0		
2006–07	Notts Co	39	0		
2007–08	Notts Co	32	0		
2008–09	Notts Co	25	0		
From Luton T, Mansfield T					
2012–13	Notts Co	1	0		
2013–14	Notts Co	1	0		
2014–15	Notts Co	1	0	144	0

SMITH, Alan (F)　407　47
H: 5 10　W: 12 04　b.Rothwell 28-10-80
Internationals: England U21, B, Full caps.

Season	Club	Apps	Gls	Tot	Gls
1997–98	Leeds U	0	0		
1998–99	Leeds U	22	7		
1999–2000	Leeds U	26	4		
2000–01	Leeds U	33	11		
2001–02	Leeds U	23	4		
2002–03	Leeds U	33	3		
2003–04	Leeds U	35	9	172	38
2004–05	Manchester U	31	6		
2005–06	Manchester U	21	1		
2006–07	Manchester U	9	0	61	7
2007–08	Newcastle U	33	0		
2008–09	Newcastle U	6	0		
2009–10	Newcastle U	32	0		
2010–11	Newcastle U	11	0		
2011–12	Newcastle U	2	0	84	0
2011–12	Milton Keynes D	16	1		
2012–13	Milton Keynes D	27	1		
2013–14	Milton Keynes D	24	0	67	2
2014–15	Notts Co	23	0	23	0

SPENCER, James (F)　111　25
H: 6 1　W: 13 00　b.Leeds 13-12-91

Season	Club	Apps	Gls	Tot	Gls
2008–09	Huddersfield T	0	0		
2009–10	Huddersfield T	0	0		
2010–11	Huddersfield T	0	0		
2010–11	Morecambe	32	8	32	8
2011–12	Huddersfield T	0	0		
2011–12	Cheltenham T	41	10	41	10
2012–13	Huddersfield T	1	0		
2012–13	Brentford	2	0	2	0
2013–14	Huddersfield T	0	0	1	0
2013–14	Scunthorpe U	13	1	13	1
2014–15	Notts Co	13	5		
2014–15	Notts Co	9	1	22	6

SPIESS, Fabian (G)　8　0
H: 6 2　W: 12 09　b.Germany 30-11-93

Season	Club	Apps	Gls	Tot	Gls
2011–12	Notts Co	0	0		
2012–13	Notts Co	7	0		
2013–14	Notts Co	1	0		
2014–15	Notts Co	0	0	8	0

TEMPEST, Greg (M)　17　0
H: 6 0　W: 11 04　b.Nottingham 28-12-95
Internationals: Northern Ireland U21.

Season	Club	Apps	Gls	Tot	Gls
2012–13	Notts Co	3	0		
2013–14	Notts Co	14	0		
2014–15	Notts Co	0	0	17	0

THOMPSON, Curtis (M)　44　0
H: 5 10　W: 12 06　b.Nottingham 2-9-93

Season	Club	Apps	Gls	Tot	Gls
2011–12	Notts Co	2	0		
2012–13	Notts Co	2	0		
2013–14	Notts Co	11	0		
2014–15	Notts Co	31	0	44	0

THOMPSON, Gary (M)　277　47
H: 6 0　W: 14 02　b.Kendal 24-11-80

Season	Club	Apps	Gls	Tot	Gls
2007–08	Morecambe	40	7	40	7
2008–09	Scunthorpe U	24	3		
2009–10	Scunthorpe U	36	9		
2010–11	Scunthorpe U	12	1		
2011–12	Scunthorpe U	39	7	111	20
2012–13	Bradford C	41	6		
2013–14	Bradford C	44	2	85	8
2014–15	Notts Co	41	12	41	12

TRAORE, Drissa (M)　9　0
H: 5 9　W: 11 11　b. 25-3-92

Season	Club	Apps	Gls	Tot	Gls
2012–13	Le Havre	5	0		
2013–14	Le Havre	0	0	5	0
2014–15	Notts Co	4	0	4	0

WHITEHOUSE, Elliott (M)　25　1
H: 5 11　W: 12 08　b.Worksop 27-10-93

Season	Club	Apps	Gls	Tot	Gls
2012–13	Sheffield U	3	0		
2013–14	Sheffield U	0	0	3	0
2013–14	York C	15	0	15	0
2014–15	Notts Co	7	1	7	1

WROE, Nicky (M)　258　30
H: 5 11　W: 10 02　b.Sheffield 28-9-85
Internationals: England C.

Season	Club	Apps	Gls	Tot	Gls
2002–03	Barnsley	1	0		
2003–04	Barnsley	2	1		
2004–05	Barnsley	31	0		
2005–06	Barnsley	12	0		
2006–07	Barnsley	3	0	49	1
2006–07	Bury	5	0	5	0
From York C.					
2009–10	Torquay U	45	9		
2010–11	Torquay U	20	3	65	12
2010–11	Shrewsbury T	18	3		
2011–12	Shrewsbury T	38	4		
2012–13	Preston NE	38	8		
2013–14	Preston NE	5	0	43	8
2013–14	Shrewsbury T	10	0	66	7
2013–14	Oxford U	18	2	18	2
2014–15	Notts Co	12	0	12	0

Scholars
Beraki, Paulos; Blaney, Kieran James;
Brown, Elliot George; Browne, Benjamin
James Peter; Duncan, Kieran McKenzie;
Fyfe, Reece Terence; Kelleher, Gino James T
J; Kenlock, Alexander James; Layton,
Keenan; McMillan, Jack Louie; Myers, Rhys
Anthony; Parkes, Monty Joshua; Payling,
Jake; Richards, Jordan Elijah; Sarpong, Nana
Owiredu Lartey; Symons, Kyle Sean; Wildin,
Luther Ash.

Non-Contract
Pilkington, Kevin William.

OLDHAM ATH (60)

BOVE, Jordan (F)   5 0
H: 5 9   W: 11 00 b.Manchester 12-12-95
2013–14   Oldham Ath   0   0
2014–15   Oldham Ath   5   0   5   0

BROWN, Connor (D)   84 1
H: 5 8   W: 10 12 b.Sheffield 2-10-91
2010–11   Sheffield U   0   0
2011–12   Sheffield U   0   0
2012–13   Oldham Ath   25   0
2013–14   Oldham Ath   27   1
2014–15   Oldham Ath   24   0   76   1
2014–15   Carlisle U   8   0   8   0

BYRNES, Danny (F)   0 0
b. 17-1-97
2013–14   Oldham Ath   0   0
2014–15   Oldham Ath   0   0

COLEMAN, Joel (G)   11 0
H: 6 6   W: 12 13 b.Bolton 26-9-95
2013–14   Oldham Ath   0   0
2014–15   Oldham Ath   11   0   11   0

DAYTON, James (M)   132 11
H: 5 8   W: 10 00 b.Enfield 12-12-88
2007–08   Crystal Palace 0   0
2008–09   Crystal Palace 0   0
2008–09   Yeovil T   2   0   2   0
From Bishop's Stortford, Bromley
2010–11   Kilmarnock   10   2
2011–12   Kilmarnock   29   3
2012–13   Kilmarnock   27   1   66   6
2013–14   Oldham Ath   34   3
2014–15   Oldham Ath   17   1   51   4
2014–15   St Mirren   13   1   13   1

DIENG, Timothee (M)   28 0
H: 5 11   W: 12 00   b. 9-4-92
2011–12   Brest   0   0
2012–13   Brest   2   0
2013–14   Brest   4   0   6   0
2014–15   Oldham Ath   22   0   22   0

ELOKOBI, George (D)   166 7
H: 5 10   W: 13 02   b.Cameroon 31-1-86
2004–05   Colchester U   0   0
2004–05   Chester C   5   0   5   0
2005–06   Colchester U   12   1
2006–07   Colchester U   10   0
2007–08   Colchester U   17   1   39   2
2007–08   Wolverhampton 15   0
2008–09   Wolverhampton   4   0
2009–10   Wolverhampton 22   0
2010–11   Wolverhampton 27   2
2011–12   Wolverhampton   9   0
2011–12   Nottingham F   12   0   12   0
2012–13   Wolverhampton   2   0
2012–13   Bristol C   1   0   1   0
2013–14   Wolverhampton   6   0   85   2
2014–15   Oldham Ath   24   3   24   3

FORTE, Jonathan (M)   293 57
H: 6 0   W: 12 02 b.Sheffield 25-7-86
Internationals: England Youth. Barbados Full
caps.
2003–04   Sheffield U   7   0
2004–05   Sheffield U   22   1
2005–06   Sheffield U   1   0
2005–06   Doncaster R   13   4
2005–06   Rotherham U   11   4   11   4
2006–07   Sheffield U   0   0
2006–07   Doncaster R   41   5   54   9
2007–08   Scunthorpe U   38   4
2008–09   Scunthorpe U   8   0
2008–09   Notts Co   18   8
2009–10   Scunthorpe U   28   2
2010–11   Scunthorpe U   24   3   98   9
2010–11   Southampton   10   2
2011–12   Southampton   1   0
2011–12   Preston NE   3   0   3   0

2011–12   Notts Co   10   5   28 13
2012–13   Southampton   0   0
2012–13   Crawley T   12   3   12   3
2012–13   Sheffield U   12   1   42   2
2013–14   Southampton   0   0   11   2
2014–15   Oldham Ath   34 15   34 15

GROS, William (F)   51 2
b. 31-3-92
2010–11   Kilmarnock   11   1
2011–12   Kilmarnock   8   0
2012–13   Kilmarnock   17   1
2013–14   Kilmarnock   14   0   50   2
2014–15   Oldham Ath   1   0   1   0

JACOBS, Devante (F)   2 0
b. 1-1-98
2014–15   Oldham Ath   2   0   2   0

JONES, Mike (M)   313 32
H: 5 11   W: 12 04   b.Birkenhead 15-8-87
2005–06   Tranmere R   1   0
2006–07   Tranmere R   0   0
2006–07   Shrewsbury T   13   1   13   1
2007–08   Tranmere R   9   1   10   1
2008–09   Bury   46   4
2009–10   Bury   41   5
2010–11   Bury   42   8
2011–12   Bury   24   3   153 20
2011–12   Sheffield W   10   0
2012–13   Sheffield W   0   0   10   0
2012–13   Crawley T   40   1
2013–14   Crawley T   42   3   82   4
2014–15   Oldham Ath   45   6   45   6

KELLY, Liam (M)   158 16
H: 6 2   W: 13 11   b.Milton Keynes 10-2-90
Internationals: Scotland U18, U21, Full caps.
2009–10   Kilmarnock   15   1
2010–11   Kilmarnock   32   7
2011–12   Kilmarnock   34   1
2012–13   Kilmarnock   19   6   100 15
2012–13   Bristol C   19   0
2013–14   Bristol C   2   0   21   0
2014–15   Oldham Ath   37   1   37   1

KUSUNGA, Genseric (D)   68 2
H: 6 1   W: 12 00   b.Lobamba 12-3-88
Internationals: Switzerland U21. Angola Full
caps.
2010–11   Basle   7   0
2011–12   Basle   6   0   13   0
2012–13   Servette   19   0   19   0
2013–14   Oldham Ath   18   1
2014–15   Oldham Ath   18   1   36   2

LOCKWOOD, Adam (D)   282 18
H: 6 0   W: 12 07   b.Wakefield 26-10-81
2003–04   Yeovil T   43   4
2004–05   Yeovil T   10   0
2005–06   Yeovil T   20   0   73   4
2005–06   Torquay U   9   3   9   3
2006–07   Doncaster R   44   2
2007–08   Doncaster R   39   3
2008–09   Doncaster R   22   0
2009–10   Doncaster R   16   2
2010–11   Doncaster R   16   1
2011–12   Doncaster R   14   0   151   8
2012–13   Bury   17   1
2013–14   Bury   1   0   18   1
2013–14   Oldham Ath   19   2
2014–15   Oldham Ath   12   0   31   2

MELLOR, David (D)   48 1
H: 5 9   W: 11 09 b.Oldham 10-7-91
2011–12   Oldham Ath   21   1
2012–13   Oldham Ath   5   0
2013–14   Oldham Ath   20   0
2014–15   Oldham Ath   2   0   48   1

MILLS, Joseph (D)   137 2
H: 5 9   W: 11 00 b.Swindon 30-10-89
Internationals: England U17, U18.
2006–07   Southampton   0   0
2007–08   Southampton   0   0
2008–09   Southampton   8   0
2008–09   Scunthorpe U   14   0   14   0
2009–10   Southampton   16   0
2010–11   Southampton   2   0
2010–11   Doncaster R   18   2   18   2
2011–12   Southampton   0   0   26   0
2011–12   Reading   15   0
2012–13   Reading   0   0   15   0
2012–13   Burnley   10   0
2013–14   Burnley   0   0   10   0
2013–14   Oldham Ath   11   0
2013–14   Shrewsbury T   13   0   13   0
2014–15   Oldham Ath   30   0   41   0

MORGAN-SMITH, Amari (M)   14 2
H: 6 0   W: 13 06 b.Wolverhampton 3-4-89
2007–08   Stockport Co   1   0   1   0
From Ilkeston T, Luton T, Macclesfield T,
Kidderminster H.
2014–15   Oldham Ath   13   2   13   2

MURPHY, Rhys (F)   88 22
H: 6 1   W: 11 13 b.Shoreham 6-11-90
Internationals: England U16, U17, U19.
Republic of Ireland U21.
2007–08   Arsenal   0   0
2008–09   Arsenal   0   0
2009–10   Arsenal   0   0
2009–10   Brentford   5   0   5   0
2010–11   Arsenal   0   0
2011–12   Arsenal   0   0
2011–12   Preston NE   5   0   5   0
2012–13   Arsenal   0   0
2012–13   Stormvogels Telstar 26 8   26   8
2013–14   Dagenham & R   32 13
2014–15   Dagenham & R   9   1   41 14
2014–15   Oldham Ath   11   0   11   0

PHILLISKIRK, Daniel (M)   91 8
H: 5 10   W: 11 05   b.Oldham 10-4-91
Internationals: England U17.
2008–09   Chelsea   0   0
2009–10   Chelsea   0   0
2010–11   Chelsea   0   0
2010–11   Oxford U   1   0
2010–11   Sheffield U   3   0
2011–12   Sheffield U   0   0
2011–12   Oxford U   4   0   5   0
2012–13   Sheffield U   1   0   4   0
2012–13   Coventry C   1   0
2013–14   Coventry C   0   0   1   0
2013–14   Oldham Ath   38   4
2014–15   Oldham Ath   43   4   81   8

POLEON, Dominic (F)   78 9
H: 6 3   W: 12 13   b.Newham 7-9-93
2012–13   Leeds U   6   2
2012–13   Bury   7   2   7   2
2012–13   Sheffield U   7   0   7   0
2013–14   Leeds U   19   1
2014–15   Leeds U   4   0   29   3
2014–15   Oldham Ath   35   4   35   4

TRUELOVE, Jack (D)   1 0
H: 5 11   W: 12 00   b.Burnley 27-12-95
2012–13   Oldham Ath   1   0
2013–14   Oldham Ath   0   0
2014–15   Oldham Ath   0   0   1   0

TUOHY, Jack (M)   1 0
b.Oldham
2014–15   Oldham Ath   1   0   1   0

TURNER, Rhys (F)   16 3
b.Preston 22-7-95
2013–14   Oldham Ath   2   0
2014–15   Oldham Ath   14   3   16   3

WILSON, Brian (D)   375 16
H: 5 10   W: 11 00   b.Manchester 9-5-83
2001–02   Stoke C   1   0
2002–03   Stoke C   3   0
2003–04   Stoke C   2   0   6   0
2003–04   Cheltenham T   14   0
2004–05   Cheltenham T   43   3
2005–06   Cheltenham T   43   9
2006–07   Cheltenham T   25   2   125 14
2006–07   Bristol C   19   0
2007–08   Bristol C   18   1
2008–09   Bristol C   30   0
2009–10   Bristol C   3   0   60   1
2010–11   Colchester U   26   1
2011–12   Colchester U   46   0
2012–13   Colchester U   41   0
2013–14   Colchester U   38   0   151   1
2014–15   Oldham Ath   33   0   33   0

WILSON, James (D)   119 2
H: 6 2   W: 11 05   b.Chepstow 26-2-89
Internationals: Wales U19. U21, Full caps.
2005–06   Bristol C   0   0
2006–07   Bristol C   0   0
2007–08   Bristol C   2   0
2008–09   Brentford   14   0
2009–10   Bristol C   0   0
2009–10   Brentford   13   0   27   0
2010–11   Bristol C   2   0
2011–12   Bristol C   21   0
2012–13   Bristol C   6   0
2013–14   Bristol C   0   0   31   0
2013–14   Cheltenham T   4   0   4   0
2014–15   Oldham Ath   16   1
2014–15   Oldham Ath   41   1   57   2

WINCHESTER, Carl (D)   80   6
H: 5 10   W: 11 08   b.Belfast 12-4-93
Internationals: Northern Ireland U16, U17, U18, U19, U21, Full caps.

2010–11	Oldham Ath	6	1		
2011–12	Oldham Ath	12	0		
2012–13	Oldham Ath	9	0		
2013–14	Oldham Ath	12	1		
2014–15	Oldham Ath	41	4	80	6

Scholars
Byrnes, Daniel Aaron; Edmundson, Samuel George Alan; Ellison, Ryan Henry; Etches, Callum Christopher; Fulwood, Edward-Paul Mugabe; Hargreaves, Jake Paul; Knight, Lee David; Mantack, Kallum Kevin; Murray, Rio Dennis; Parmar, Rahul; Read, Alexander Douglas Eldred; Renshaw, Christopher Thomas; Scullion, Callum Patrick; Stott, Jamie Garry; Tansinda, Emil Denzel; Tuohy, Jack Samuel; Tyson, Paul Stephen; Walters, Jordache Dave Akyme.

Non-Contract
Jacobs, Devante Rogea.

OXFORD U (61)

ASHBY, Josh (M)   2   0
b.Oxford 3-5-96

| 2013–14 | Oxford U | 0 | 0 | | |
| 2014–15 | Oxford U | 2 | 0 | 2 | 0 |

ASHDOWN, Jamie (G)   159   0
H: 6 1   W: 13 05   b.Reading 30-11-80

1999–2000	Reading	0	0		
2000–01	Reading	1	0		
2001–02	Reading	0	0		
2001–02	Arsenal	0	0		
2002–03	Reading	1	0		
2002–03	Bournemouth	2	0	2	0
2003–04	Reading	10	0	13	0
2003–04	Rushden & D	19	0	19	0
2004–05	Portsmouth	16	0		
2005–06	Portsmouth	17	0		
2006–07	Portsmouth	0	0		
2006–07	Norwich C	2	0	2	0
2007–08	Portsmouth	3	0		
2008–09	Portsmouth	0	0		
2009–10	Portsmouth	6	0		
2010–11	Portsmouth	46	0		
2011–12	Portsmouth	21	0	109	0
2012–13	Leeds U	0	0		
2013–14	Leeds U	0	0		
2014–15	Crawley T	9	0	9	0
2014–15	Oxford U	5	0	5	0

BALMY, Jeremy (M)   2   0
H: 5 8   W: 10 10   b. 19-4-94

2013–14	Notts Co	1	0		
2014–15	Notts Co	1	0	2	0
2014–15	Oxford U	0	0		

BEVANS, Matt (D)   10   0
b.Oxford 19-9-93

| 2013–14 | Oxford U | 10 | 0 | | |
| 2014–15 | Oxford U | 0 | 0 | 10 | 0 |

CAMPBELL, John (F)   3   1
b. 23-11-88

| 2014–15 | Oxford U | 3 | 1 | 3 | 1 |

CAVANAGH, Eddie (G)   0   0
b.Oxford 30-3-97

| 2014–15 | Oxford U | 0 | 0 | | |

CLARKE, Ryan (G)   219   0
H: 6 3   W: 13 00   b.Bristol 30-4-82

2001–02	Bristol R	1	0		
2002–03	Bristol R	2	0		
2003–04	Bristol R	2	0		
2004–05	Bristol R	18	0	23	0
2004–05	Southend U	1	0	1	0
2004–05	Kidderminster H	6	0	6	0

From Salisbury C.

2010–11	Oxford U	46	0		
2011–12	Oxford U	42	0		
2012–13	Oxford U	24	0		
2013–14	Oxford U	46	0		
2014–15	Oxford U	31	0	189	0

COLLINS, Michael (M)   300   23
H: 6 0   W: 11 00   b.Halifax 30-4-86
Internationals: Republic of Ireland U18, U19, U21.

2004–05	Huddersfield T	8	0		
2005–06	Huddersfield T	17	1		
2006–07	Huddersfield T	43	4		
2007–08	Huddersfield T	41	2		
2008–09	Huddersfield T	36	9		
2009–10	Huddersfield T	28	3	173	19
2010–11	Scunthorpe U	32	1		
2011–12	Scunthorpe U	1	0		
2012–13	Scunthorpe U	29	1		
2013–14	Scunthorpe U	17	0	79	2
2013–14	AFC Wimbledon	9	0	9	0
2014–15	Oxford U	39	2	39	2

CROCOMBE, Max (G)   4   0
H: 6 4   b.Auckland 12-8-93
Internationals: New Zealand U20, U23, Full caps.

2012–13	Oxford U	4	0		
2013–14	Oxford U	0	0		
2014–15	Oxford U	0	0	4	0

DUNKLEY, Cheyenne (D)   9   0
H: 6 2   W: 11 11   b.Wolverhampton 13-2-92
From Kidderminster H.

| 2014–15 | Oxford U | 9 | 0 | 9 | 0 |

HAWTIN, Aidan (M)   1   0
b. 13-6-95

| 2014–15 | Oxford U | 1 | 0 | 1 | 0 |

HOBAN, Patrick (F)   20   1
b.Galway 28-7-91

| 2014–15 | Oxford U | 20 | 1 | 20 | 1 |

HOSKINS, Will (F)   222   52
H: 5 11   W: 11 02   b.Nottingham 6-5-86
Internationals: England Youth, U18, U19.

2003–04	Rotherham U	4	2		
2004–05	Rotherham U	22	2		
2005–06	Rotherham U	23	4		
2006–07	Rotherham U	24	15		
2006–07	Watford	9	0		
2007–08	Watford	1	0		
2007–08	Millwall	10	2	10	2
2007–08	Nottingham F	2	0	2	0
2008–09	Watford	32	4		
2009–10	Watford	18	3	60	7
2010–11	Bristol R	43	17	43	17
2011–12	Brighton & HA	7	1		
2011–12	Sheffield U	12	2	12	2
2011–12	Rotherham U	0	0	73	23
2012–13	Brighton & HA	11	0		
2013–14	Brighton & HA	0	0	18	1
2014–15	Oxford U	4	0	4	0

HOWARD, Brian (M)   333   41
H: 5 8   W: 11 00   b.Winchester 23-1-83
Internationals: England U16, U17, U19, U20.

1999–2000	Southampton	0	0		
2000–01	Southampton	0	0		
2001–02	Southampton	0	0		
2002–03	Southampton	0	0		
2003–04	Swindon T	35	4		
2004–05	Swindon T	35	5	70	9
2005–06	Barnsley	31	5		
2006–07	Barnsley	42	8		
2007–08	Barnsley	41	13		
2008–09	Barnsley	7	1	121	27
2008–09	Sheffield U	26	2		
2009–10	Sheffield U	4	0	30	2
2009–10	Reading	34	2		
2010–11	Reading	24	0		
2011–12	Reading	1	0	59	2
2011–12	Millwall	12	0	12	0
2012–13	Portsmouth	23	0	23	0
2012–13	Bristol C	0	0		
2013–14	Bristol C	0	0	6	0
2013–14	Birmingham C	5	1	5	1
2014–15	Oxford U	7	0	7	0

HUMPHREYS, Sam (M)   1   0
b.Oxford 3-11-95

| 2014–15 | Oxford U | 1 | 0 | 1 | 0 |

HUNT, David (M)   315   11
H: 5 11   W: 11 09   b.Dulwich 10-9-82

2002–03	Crystal Palace	2	0	2	0
2003–04	Leyton Orient	38	1		
2004–05	Leyton Orient	27	0	65	1
2004–05	Northampton T	4	0		
2005–06	Northampton T	40	3		
2006–07	Northampton T	29	0	73	3
2007–08	Shrewsbury T	27	2		
2008–09	Shrewsbury T	2	0	29	2
2008–09	Brentford	20	2		
2009–10	Brentford	24	3		
2010–11	Brentford	3	0	47	5
2011–12	Crawley T	27	0		
2012–13	Crawley T	23	0	50	0
2013–14	Oxford U	46	0		
2014–15	Oxford U	3	0	49	0

HYLTON, Danny (F)   223   49
H: 6 0   W: 11 13   b.Camden 25-2-89

2008–09	Aldershot T	29	5		
2009–10	Aldershot T	21	3		
2010–11	Aldershot T	33	5		
2011–12	Aldershot T	44	13		
2012–13	Aldershot T	27	4	154	30
2013–14	Rotherham U	1	0	1	0
2013–14	Bury	7	2	7	2
2013–14	AFC Wimbledon	17	3	17	3
2014–15	Oxford U	44	14	44	14

LONG, Sam (D)   14   1
H: 5 10   W: 11 11   b.Oxford 16-1-95

2012–13	Oxford U	1	0		
2013–14	Oxford U	3	0		
2014–15	Oxford U	10	1	14	1

MACDONALD, Alex (F)   152   17
H: 5 7   W: 11 04   b.Warrington 14-4-90
Internationals: Scotland U19, U21.

2007–08	Burnley	2	0		
2008–09	Burnley	3	0		
2009–10	Burnley	0	0		
2009–10	Falkirk	11	1	11	1
2010–11	Burnley	0	0		
2010–11	Inverness CT	10	1	10	1
2011–12	Burnley	5	0		
2011–12	Plymouth Arg	18	4		
2012–13	Burnley	1	0	11	0
2012–13	Plymouth Arg	16	1	34	5
2012–13	Burton Alb	15	1		
2013–14	Burton Alb	35	0		
2014–15	Burton Alb	21	6	71	7
2014–15	Oxford U	15	3	15	3

MEADES, Jonathan (M)   33   1
H: 6 1   W: 13 00   b.Cardiff 2-3-92
Internationals: Wales U17, U21.

2010–11	Cardiff C	0	0		
2011–12	Cardiff C	0	0		
2012–13	Bournemouth	0	0		
2012–13	AFC Wimbledon	26	1	26	1
2013–14	Oxford U	0	0		
2014–15	Oxford U	7	0	7	0

MULLINS, John (D)   362   24
H: 5 11   W: 12 07   b.Hampstead 6-11-85

2004–05	Reading	0	0		
2004–05	Kidderminster H	21	2	21	2
2005–06	Reading	0	0		
2006–07	Mansfield T	43	2		
2007–08	Mansfield T	43	2	86	4
2008–09	Stockport Co	33	3		
2009–10	Stockport Co	36	1	69	4
2010–11	Rotherham U	35	1		
2011–12	Rotherham U	35	2		
2012–13	Rotherham U	29	4	99	7
2012–13	Oxford U	8	2		
2013–14	Oxford U	35	3		
2014–15	Oxford U	44	2	87	7

NEWEY, Tom (D)   428   8
H: 5 10   W: 10 02   b.Sheffield 31-10-82

2000–01	Leeds U	0	0		
2001–02	Leeds U	0	0		
2002–03	Leeds U	0	0		
2002–03	Cambridge U	6	0		
2002–03	Darlington	7	1	7	1
2003–04	Leyton Orient	34	2		
2004–05	Leyton Orient	20	1	54	3
2004–05	Cambridge U	16	0	22	0
2005–06	Grimsby T	38	1		
2006–07	Grimsby T	43	1		
2007–08	Grimsby T	42	1		
2008–09	Grimsby T	24	0		
2008–09	Rochdale	2	0	2	0
2009–10	Grimsby T	0	0	147	3
2009–10	Bury	32	0	32	0
2010–11	Rotherham U	38	0		
2011–12	Rotherham U	20	0	58	0
2012–13	Scunthorpe U	45	0	45	0
2013–14	Oxford U	40	1		
2014–15	Oxford U	12	0	52	1
2014–15	Northampton T	9	0	9	0

O'DOWDA, Callum (M)   49   4
H: 5 11   W: 11 11   b.Oxford 23-4-95
Internationals: Republic of Ireland U21.

2012–13	Oxford U	0	0		
2013–14	Oxford U	10	0		
2014–15	Oxford U	39	4	49	4

ROBERTS, James (F)   25   3
b.Stoke Mandeville 21-6-96

2012–13	Oxford U	0	0		
2013–14	Oxford U	0	0		
2014–15	Oxford U	25	3	25	3

ROSE, Danny (M) 103 8
H: 5 7 W: 10 04 b.Bristol 21-2-88
Internationals: England C.

| 2006–07 | Manchester U | 0 | 0 | | |
| 2007–08 | Manchester U | 0 | 0 | | |

From Oxford U, Newport Co

2012–13	Fleetwood T	0	0		
2012–13	*Aldershot T*	34	2	**34**	**2**
2013–14	Oxford U	40	4		
2014–15	Oxford U	29	2	**69**	**6**

RUFFELS, Joshua (M) 63 1
H: 5 10 W: 11 11 b.Oxford 23-10-93

2011–12	Coventry C	1	0		
2012–13	Coventry C	0	0	**1**	**0**
2013–14	Oxford U	29	1		
2014–15	Oxford U	33	0	**62**	**1**

SHAMA, Josh (M) 0 0
b. 14-10-94

| 2013–14 | Oxford U | 0 | 0 | | |
| 2014–15 | Oxford U | 0 | 0 | | |

SKARZ, Joe (D) 309 7
H: 5 10 W: 11 04 b.Huddersfield 13-7-89

2006–07	Huddersfield T	17	0		
2007–08	Huddersfield T	27	0		
2008–09	Huddersfield T	9	1		
2008–09	*Hartlepool U*	7	0	**7**	**0**
2009–10	Huddersfield T	15	0	**68**	**1**
2009–10	*Shrewsbury T*	20	0	**20**	**0**
2010–11	Bury	46	1		
2011–12	Bury	45	1		
2012–13	Bury	39	2	**130**	**4**
2012–13	Rotherham U	8	0		
2013–14	Rotherham U	41	2		
2014–15	Rotherham U	17	0	**66**	**2**
2014–15	Oxford U	18	0	**18**	**0**

STEPHENS, Jack (G) 0 0

| 2014–15 | Oxford U | 0 | 0 | | |

WHING, Andrew (D) 346 6
H: 6 0 W: 12 00 b.Birmingham 20-9-84

2002–03	Coventry C	14	0		
2003–04	Coventry C	28	1		
2004–05	Coventry C	16	1		
2005–06	Coventry C	32	0		
2006–07	Coventry C	16	0	**106**	**2**
2006–07	*Brighton & HA*	12	0		
2007–08	Brighton & HA	42	0		
2008–09	Brighton & HA	40	0		
2009–10	Brighton & HA	9	0		
2009–10	*Chesterfield*	11	0	**11**	**0**
2010–11	Brighton & HA	0	0	**103**	**0**
2010–11	*Leyton Orient*	24	2	**24**	**2**
2011–12	Oxford U	41	0		
2012–13	Oxford U	22	2		
2013–14	Oxford U	18	0		
2014–15	Oxford U	21	0	**102**	**2**

WRIGHT, Jake (D) 200 0
H: 5 10 W: 11 07 b.Keighley 11-3-86

| 2005–06 | Bradford C | 1 | 0 | **1** | **0** |

From Halifax T, Crawley T

2009–10	Brighton & HA	6	0	**6**	**0**
2010–11	Oxford U	35	0		
2011–12	Oxford U	43	0		
2012–13	Oxford U	42	0		
2013–14	Oxford U	31	0		
2014–15	Oxford U	42	0	**193**	**0**

Players retained or with offer of contract
Roofe, Kemar.

Scholars
Andrews, Kieran Mark; Cavanagh, Edward Roger; Conte, Muctaru; Cundy, Robbie David; Diaz-Benitez, Kieran Mark; George, Adriel Jared; Grant, Freddie Tom; Hastings, Luke Paul; Hayden, Lewis Scott; Humphries, Seth William Osborne; Jeacock, George Edward; McCormack, Cian Anthony; Ricketts, Drew Anthony; Stevens, Jack Anthony; Welch-Hayes, Miles Winfield.

PETERBOROUGH U (62)

ALNWICK, Ben (G) 109 0
H: 6 2 W: 13 12 b.Prudhoe 1-1-87
Internationals: England U16, U17, U18, U19, U21.

2003–04	Sunderland	0	0		
2004–05	Sunderland	3	0		
2005–06	Sunderland	5	0		
2006–07	Sunderland	11	0	**19**	**0**
2006–07	Tottenham H	0	0		
2007–08	Tottenham H	0	0		
2007–08	*Luton T*	4	0	**4**	**0**
2007–08	*Leicester C*	8	0	**8**	**0**
2008–09	Tottenham H	0	0		
2008–09	*Carlisle U*	6	0	**6**	**0**
2009–10	Tottenham H	1	0		
2009–10	*Norwich C*	3	0	**3**	**0**
2010–11	Tottenham H	0	0		
2010–11	*Leeds U*	0	0		
2010–11	*Doncaster R*	0	0		
2011–12	Tottenham H	0	0		
2011–12	*Leyton Orient*	6	0		
2012–13	Tottenham H	0	0	**1**	**0**
2012–13	Barnsley	10	0		
2013–14	Barnsley	0	0	**10**	**0**
2013–14	Charlton Ath	10	0	**10**	**0**
2013–14	*Leyton Orient*	1	0	**7**	**0**
2014–15	Peterborough U	41	0	**41**	**0**

ANDERSON, Harry (F) 10 0
H: 5 6 W: 9 11 b. 9-1-97

| 2014–15 | Peterborough U | 10 | 0 | **10** | **0** |

ANDERSON, Jermaine (M) 38 1
b. 16-5-96
Internationals: England U18.

2012–13	Peterborough U	1	0		
2013–14	Peterborough U	13	0		
2014–15	Peterborough U	24	1	**38**	**1**

BALDWIN, Jack (D) 99 4
H: 6 1 W: 11 00 b.Barking 30-6-93

2011–12	Hartlepool U	17	0		
2012–13	Hartlepool U	32	2		
2013–14	Hartlepool U	28	2	**77**	**4**
2013–14	Peterborough U	11	0		
2014–15	Peterborough U	11	0	**22**	**0**

BEAUTYMAN, Harry (M) 18 2
H: 5 10 W: 11 09 b.Newham 1-4-92
Internationals: England C.

| 2010–11 | Leyton Orient | 0 | 0 | | |

From Sutton U, Welling U.

| 2014–15 | Peterborough U | 18 | 2 | **18** | **2** |

BOSTWICK, Michael (D) 203 25
H: 6 4 W: 14 00 b.Eltham 17-5-88
Internationals: England C.

| 2006–07 | Millwall | 0 | 0 | | |

From Rushden & D, Ebbsfleet U

2010–11	Stevenage	41	2		
2011–12	Stevenage	43	7	**84**	**9**
2012–13	Peterborough U	39	5		
2013–14	Peterborough U	42	4		
2014–15	Peterborough U	38	7	**119**	**16**

BRISLEY, Shaun (D) 207 7
H: 6 2 W: 12 02 b.Macclesfield 6-5-90

2007–08	Macclesfield T	10	2		
2008–09	Macclesfield T	38	0		
2009–10	Macclesfield T	33	1		
2010–11	Macclesfield T	14	0		
2011–12	Macclesfield T	29	3	**124**	**6**
2011–12	Peterborough U	11	0		
2012–13	Peterborough U	28	0		
2013–14	Peterborough U	22	0		
2014–15	Peterborough U	15	1	**76**	**1**
2014–15	*Scunthorpe U*	7	0	**7**	**0**

BURGESS, Christian (D) 72 2
H: 6 5 W: 13 02 b. 7-10-91

2012–13	Middlesbrough	1	0		
2013–14	Middlesbrough	0	0	**1**	**0**
2013–14	*Hartlepool U*	41	0	**41**	**0**
2014–15	Peterborough U	30	2	**30**	**2**

DA SILVA LOPES, Leonardo (M) 2 0
b. 30-11-98

| 2014–15 | Peterborough U | 2 | 0 | **2** | **0** |

DAY, Joe (G) 40 0
H: 6 1 W: 12 00 b.Brighton 13-8-90

2011–12	Peterborough U	0	0		
2012–13	Peterborough U	0	0		
2013–14	Peterborough U	4	0		
2014–15	Peterborough U	0	0	**4**	**0**
2014–15	*Newport Co*	36	0	**36**	**0**

EDWARDS, Jonathan (M) 3 0
H: 5 11 W: 10 01 b.Luton 24-11-96

| 2014–15 | Peterborough U | 3 | 0 | **3** | **0** |

FERDINAND, Kane (D) 127 11
H: 6 1 W: 13 07 b.Newham 7-10-92
Internationals: Republic of Ireland U18, U19, U21.

2010–11	Southend U	22	2		
2011–12	Southend U	36	7		
2012–13	Southend U	3	1	**61**	**10**
2012–13	Peterborough U	32	1		
2013–14	Peterborough U	2	0		
2013–14	*Northampton T*	4	0	**4**	**0**
2014–15	Peterborough U	12	0	**46**	**1**
2014–15	*Cheltenham T*	16	0	**16**	**0**

HENRY, Dion (G) 0 0
H: 5 11 W: 10 03 b.Ipswich 12-9-97

| 2014–15 | Peterborough U | 0 | 0 | | |

JAMES, Luke (M) 123 20
H: 6 0 W: 12 08 b.Amble 4-11-94

2011–12	Hartlepool U	19	3		
2012–13	Hartlepool U	26	3		
2013–14	Hartlepool U	42	13		
2014–15	Hartlepool U	4	0	**91**	**19**
2014–15	Peterborough U	32	1	**32**	**1**

LUTO, Oliver (M) 0 0
H: 6 1 W: 12 00 b.Kinshasa 13-2-96

| 2014–15 | Peterborough U | 0 | 0 | | |

MADDISON, Marcus (M) 29 7
H: 5 9 W: 11 03 b.Sedgefield 26-9-93
Internationals: England C.

| 2014–15 | Peterborough U | 29 | 7 | **29** | **7** |

MARSHALL, Liam (D) 0 0
H: 5 10 W: 10 10 b.Leicester 17-9-96

| 2013–14 | Peterborough U | 0 | 0 | | |
| 2014–15 | Peterborough U | 0 | 0 | | |

McCANN, Grant (M) 499 85
H: 5 10 W: 11 00 b.Belfast 14-4-80
Internationals: Northern Ireland U21, Full caps.

1998–99	West Ham U	0	0		
1999–2000	West Ham U	0	0		
2000–01	West Ham U	1	0		
2000–01	*Notts Co*	2	0	**2**	**0**
2000–01	*Cheltenham T*	30	3		
2001–02	West Ham U	3	0		
2002–03	West Ham U	0	0	**4**	**0**
2002–03	Cheltenham T	27	6		
2003–04	Cheltenham T	43	8		
2004–05	Cheltenham T	39	4		
2005–06	Cheltenham T	39	8		
2006–07	Cheltenham T	15	5	**193**	**34**
2006–07	Barnsley	22	1		
2007–08	Barnsley	19	3	**41**	**4**
2007–08	Scunthorpe U	14	1		
2008–09	Scunthorpe U	43	9		
2009–10	Scunthorpe U	42	8	**99**	**18**
2010–11	Peterborough U	38	9		
2011–12	Peterborough U	41	8		
2012–13	Peterborough U	40	8		
2013–14	Peterborough U	35	4		
2014–15	Peterborough U	6	0	**160**	**29**

MENDEZ-LAING, Nathaniel (M) 117 11
H: 5 10 W: 11 12 b.Birmingham 15-4-92
Internationals: England U16, U17.

2009–10	Wolverhampton W	0	0		
2010–11	Wolverhampton W	0	0		
2010–11	*Peterborough U*	33	5		
2011–12	Wolverhampton W	0	0		
2011–12	*Sheffield U*	8	1	**8**	**1**
2012–13	Peterborough U	21	3		
2012–13	*Portsmouth*	8	0	**8**	**0**
2013–14	Peterborough U	16	1		
2013–14	*Shrewsbury T*	6	0	**6**	**0**
2014–15	Peterborough U	14	0	**84**	**9**
2014–15	*Cambridge U*	11	1	**11**	**1**

NEWELL, Joe (M) 96 3
H: 5 11 W: 11 02 b.Tamworth 15-3-93

2010–11	Peterborough U	2	0		
2011–12	Peterborough U	14	1		
2012–13	Peterborough U	30	0		
2013–14	Peterborough U	11	0		
2014–15	Peterborough U	39	2	**96**	**3**

NORRIS, David (M) 416 52
H: 5 7 W: 11 06 b.Stamford 22-2-81

1999–2000	Bolton W	0	0		
2000–01	Bolton W	0	0		
2001–02	Bolton W	0	0		
2001–02	*Hull C*	6	1	**6**	**1**
2002–03	Bolton W	0	0		
2002–03	Plymouth Arg	33	6		
2003–04	Plymouth Arg	45	5		
2004–05	Plymouth Arg	35	3		
2005–06	Plymouth Arg	45	2		
2006–07	Plymouth Arg	41	6		
2007–08	Plymouth Arg	27	5	**226**	**27**
2007–08	Ipswich T	9	1		
2008–09	Ipswich T	37	3		
2009–10	Ipswich T	24	1		
2010–11	Ipswich T	36	8	**106**	**13**
2011–12	Portsmouth	40	8	**40**	**8**
2012–13	Leeds U	30	3		
2013–14	Leeds U	0	0		
2014–15	Leeds U	0	0	**30**	**3**
2014–15	Peterborough U	8	0	**8**	**0**

NTLHE, Kgosietsile (D) 69 4
H: 5 9 W: 10 05 b.Pretoria 21-2-94
Internationals: South Africa U20, Full caps.
2010–11	Peterborough U	0	0		
2011–12	Peterborough U	2	0		
2012–13	Peterborough U	12	1		
2013–14	Peterborough U	27	2		
2014–15	Peterborough U	28	1	69	4

OLEJNIK, Robert (G) 265 0
H: 6 0 W: 15 06 b.Vienna 26-11-86
Internationals: Austria U21.
2004–05	Aston Villa	0	0		
2005–06	Aston Villa	0	0		
2006–07	Aston Villa	0	0		
2006–07	Lincoln C	0	0		
2007–08	Falkirk	13	0		
2008–09	Falkirk	15	0		
2009–10	Falkirk	38	0		
2010–11	Falkirk	36	0	102	0
2011–12	Torquay U	46	0	46	0
2012–13	Peterborough U	46	0		
2013–14	Peterborough U	42	0		
2014–15	Peterborough U	0	0	88	0
2014–15	Scunthorpe U	13	0	13	0
2014–15	York C	16	0	16	0

OZTUMER, Erhun (M) 20 1
H: 5 6 b.Greenwich 29-5-91
2014–15	Peterborough U	20	1	20	1

PAYNE, Jack (M) 188 10
H: 5 9 W: 9 02 b.Gravesend 5-12-91
2008–09	Gillingham	2	0		
2009–10	Gillingham	19	0		
2010–11	Gillingham	31	1		
2011–12	Gillingham	30	2		
2012–13	Gillingham	19	2	101	5
2012–13	Peterborough U	14	0		
2013–14	Peterborough U	32	1		
2014–15	Peterborough U	41	3	87	5

RICHENS, Michael (D) 2 0
H: 5 10 W: 11 09 b.Bedford 28-2-95
2012–13	Peterborough U	0	0		
2013–14	Peterborough U	0	0		
2014–15	Peterborough U	0	0		
2014–15	Stevenage	2	0	2	0

SANTOS, Ricardo (D) 25 0
H: 6 5 W: 12 02 b.Almada 18-6-95
2012–13	Dagenham & R	0	0		
2013–14	Dagenham & R	0	0		
2013–14	Peterborough U	1	0		
2014–15	Peterborough U	24	0	25	0

SMITH, Michael (D) 319 18
H: 5 11 W: 11 02 b.Ballyclare 4-9-88
Internationals: Northern Ireland U23.
2005–06	Ballyclare Com	1	0		
2006–07	Ballyclare Com	25	2		
2007–08	Ballyclare Com	39	1		
2008–09	Ballyclare Com	27	7	92	10
2008–09	Ballymena U	12	1		
2009–10	Ballymena U	37	2		
2010–11	Ballymena U	34	3	83	6
2011–12	Bristol R	20	0		
2012–13	Bristol R	38	1		
2013–14	Bristol R	43	0	101	1
2014–15	Peterborough U	43	1	43	1

TAYLOR, Jon (M) 157 26
H: 5 11 W: 12 04 b.Liverpool 23-12-89
2009–10	Shrewsbury T	2	0		
2010–11	Shrewsbury T	20	6		
2011–12	Shrewsbury T	33	0		
2012–13	Shrewsbury T	37	7		
2013–14	Shrewsbury T	41	9	133	22
2014–15	Peterborough U	24	3	24	3

VASSELL, Kyle (F) 29 6
H: 6 0 W: 12 04 b.Milton Keynes 7-2-93
2013–14	Peterborough U	6	0		
2014–15	Peterborough U	17	5	23	5
2014–15	Oxford U	6	1	6	1

WALKER, Jim (G) 482 0
H: 5 11 W: 13 04 b.Sutton-in-Ashfield 9-7-73
1991–92	Notts Co	0	0	
1992–93	Notts Co	0	0	
1993–94	Walsall	31	0	
1994–95	Walsall	4	0	
1995–96	Walsall	26	0	
1996–97	Walsall	36	0	
1997–98	Walsall	46	0	
1998–99	Walsall	46	0	
1999–2000	Walsall	43	0	
2000–01	Walsall	44	0	
2001–02	Walsall	43	0	
2002–03	Walsall	41	0	
2003–04	Walsall	43	0	
2004–05	West Ham U	10	0	
2005–06	West Ham U	3	0	
2006–07	West Ham U	0	0	
2007–08	West Ham U	0	0	
2008–09	West Ham U	0	0	
2008–09	Colchester U	16	0	16 0
2009–10	West Ham U	0	0	13 0
2010–11	Walsall	26	0	
2011–12	Walsall	24	0	
2012–13	Walsall	0	0	
2013–14	Walsall	0	0	453 0
2014–15	Peterborough U	0	0	

WASHINGTON, Conor (F) 81 21
H: 5 10 W: 11 09 b.Chatham 18-5-92
2013–14	Newport Co	24	4	24	4
2013–14	Peterborough U	17	4		
2014–15	Peterborough U	40	13	57	17

ZAKUANI, Gaby (D) 332 10
H: 6 1 W: 12 13 b.DR Congo 31-5-86
Internationals: DR Congo Full caps.
2002–03	Leyton Orient	1	0		
2003–04	Leyton Orient	10	2		
2004–05	Leyton Orient	33	0		
2005–06	Leyton Orient	43	1	87	3
2006–07	Fulham	0	0		
2006–07	Stoke C	9	0		
2007–08	Fulham	0	0		
2007–08	Stoke C	19	0	28	0
2008–09	Fulham	0	0		
2008–09	Peterborough U	32	1		
2009–10	Peterborough U	29	0		
2010–11	Peterborough U	30	2		
2011–12	Peterborough U	41	1		
2012–13	Peterborough U	33	1		
2013–14	Peterborough U	15	0		
2013–14	Kalloni	15	1	15	1
2014–15	Peterborough U	22	1	202	6

Scholars
Anderson, Harry John; Edwards, Jonathan Dvonte; Friend, Jack Peter; Hood, Joseph; Humphrey, Oliver James Victor; Keating, Ben Alex; Lee, Ethan; Luto, Oliver; Marshall, Liam Samuel Hugh; Maslen-Jones, Bradley; Phillips, Tye Gregory; Robinson, Keano Ricardo Reane; Ward, James Christopher.

PLYMOUTH ARG (63)

ALESSANDRA, Lewis (F) 235 33
H: 5 9 W: 11 07 b.Heywood 8-2-89
2007–08	Oldham Ath	15	2		
2008–09	Oldham Ath	32	5		
2009–10	Oldham Ath	1	0		
2010–11	Oldham Ath	19	1	67	8
2011–12	Morecambe	42	4		
2012–13	Morecambe	40	3	82	7
2013–14	Plymouth Arg	42	7		
2014–15	Plymouth Arg	44	11	86	18

ALLEN, River (M) 3 0
H: 6 2 W: 12 00 b.Plymouth 7-11-95
2014–15	Plymouth Arg	3	0	3	0

BANTON, Jason (F) 64 9
H: 5 10 W: 11 05 b.Tottenham 15-12-92
Internationals: England U17.
2009–10	Blackburn R	0	0		
2010–11	Blackburn R	0	0		
2010–11	Liverpool	0	0		
2011–12	Liverpool	0	0		
2011–12	Burton Alb	1	0	1	0
2012–13	Crystal Palace	0	0		
2012–13	Plymouth Arg	14	6		
2013–14	Crystal Palace	0	0		
2013–14	Milton Keynes D	11	2	11	2
2013–14	Plymouth Arg	13	1		
2014–15	Plymouth Arg	25	0	52	7

BENTLEY, Aaron (D) 3 0
H: 5 11 W: 11 00 b.Plymouth 8-11-95
2014–15	Plymouth Arg	3	0	3	0

BITTNER, James (G) 1 0
H: 6 2 W: 12 09 b.Devizes 2-2-82
2001–02	Bournemouth	0	0		
2005–06	Torquay U	0	0		
2013–14	Newport Co	0	0		
2014–15	Plymouth Arg	1	0	1	0

BLIZZARD, Dominic (M) 253 13
H: 6 2 W: 12 04 b.High Wycombe 2-9-83
2001–02	Watford	0	0		
2002–03	Watford	0	0		
2003–04	Watford	2	1		
2004–05	Watford	17	1		
2005–06	Watford	10	0		
2006–07	Watford	0	0	29	2
2006–07	Stockport Co	7	0		
2006–07	Milton Keynes D	8	0	8	0
2007–08	Stockport Co	27	1		
2008–09	Stockport Co	31	3	65	4
2009–10	Bristol R	34	1		
2010–11	Bristol R	5	0	39	1
2010–11	Port Vale	1	0	1	0
2011–12	Yeovil T	30	3		
2012–13	Yeovil T	24	1	54	4
2013–14	Plymouth Arg	26	1		
2014–15	Plymouth Arg	31	1	57	2

BRUNT, Ryan (F) 89 11
H: 6 1 W: 11 11 b.Birmingham 26-5-93
2011–12	Stoke C	0	0		
2011–12	Tranmere R	15	1	15	1
2012–13	Stoke C	0	0		
2012–13	Leyton Orient	18	3	18	3
2012–13	Bristol R	18	5		
2013–14	Bristol R	11	0		
2014–15	Bristol R	0	0	29	5
2014–15	York C	6	0	6	0
2014–15	Stevenage	5	0	5	0
2014–15	Plymouth Arg	16	2	16	2

COX, Lee (M) 137 4
H: 6 1 W: 12 02 b.Leicester 26-6-90
2007–08	Leicester C	0	0		
2008–09	Leicester C	0	0		
2008–09	Yeovil T	0	0		
2009–10	Inverness CT	35	2		
2010–11	Inverness CT	27	1		
2011–12	Inverness CT	7	0	69	3
2011–12	Swindon T	7	0		
2012–13	Swindon T	0	0		
2012–13	Oxford U	14	0	14	0
2012–13	Plymouth Arg	10	0		
2013–14	Plymouth Arg	0	0		
2013–14	Swindon T	5	1	12	1
2014–15	Plymouth Arg	32	0	42	0

HANNAH, Andrew (G) 0 0
2013–14	Plymouth Arg	0	0
2014–15	Plymouth Arg	0	0

HARTLEY, Peter (D) 249 16
H: 6 0 W: 12 06 b.Hartlepool 3-4-88
2006–07	Sunderland	1	0		
2007–08	Sunderland	0	0		
2007–08	Chesterfield	12	0	12	0
2008–09	Sunderland	0	0	1	0
2009–10	Hartlepool U	38	2		
2010–11	Hartlepool U	40	2		
2011–12	Hartlepool U	44	4		
2012–13	Hartlepool U	43	2		
2013–14	Hartlepool U	1	0	166	10
2013–14	Stevenage	31	2	31	2
2014–15	Plymouth Arg	39	4	39	4

HARVEY, Tyler (F) 44 3
H: 5 10 W: 11 05 b.Plymouth 29-6-95
2012–13	Plymouth Arg	10	1		
2013–14	Plymouth Arg	21	1		
2014–15	Plymouth Arg	13	1	44	3

LANE, Ryan (M) 0 0
2013–14	Plymouth Arg	0	0
2014–15	Plymouth Arg	0	0

LECOINTE, Matt (F) 25 2
H: 5 10 W: 10 07 b.Plymouth 28-10-94
Internationals: England U18.
2011–12	Plymouth Arg	19	2		
2012–13	Plymouth Arg	6	0		
2013–14	Plymouth Arg	0	0		
2014–15	Plymouth Arg	0	0	25	2

McCORMICK, Luke (G) 88 0
H: 6 0 W: 13 12 b.Coventry 15-8-83
2012–13	Oxford U	15	0	15	0
2013–14	Plymouth Arg	27	0		
2014–15	Plymouth Arg	46	0	73	0

McHUGH, Carl (D) 74 4
H: 5 11 W: 11 05 b.Co. Donegal 5-2-93
Internationals: Republic of Ireland U17, U19, U21.
2011–12	Reading	0	0		
2012–13	Bradford C	16	0		
2013–14	Bradford C	14	1	30	2
2014–15	Plymouth Arg	44	2	44	2

MELLOR, Kelvin (D)   113   3
H: 5 10 W: 11 09 b.Copenhagen 25-1-91

2007–08	Crewe Alex	0	0
2008–09	Crewe Alex	0	0
2009–10	Crewe Alex	0	0
2010–11	Crewe Alex	1	0
2011–12	Crewe Alex	12	1
2012–13	Crewe Alex	35	0
2013–14	Crewe Alex	28	1	76	2
2014–15	Plymouth Arg	37	1	37	1

MORGAN, Marvin (F)   227   44
H: 6 4 W: 12 08 b.Manchester 13-4-83

2008–09	Aldershot T	32	6
2009–10	Aldershot T	40	15
2010–11	Aldershot T	19	5	91	26
2010–11	Dagenham & R	12	0	12	0
2011–12	Shrewsbury T	42	8
2012–13	Shrewsbury T	40	7	82	15
2013–14	Plymouth Arg	21	1
2014–15	Plymouth Arg	16	1	37	2
2014–15	*Hartlepool U*	5	1	5	1

NELSON, Curtis (D)   165   5
H: 6 0 W: 11 07 b.Newcastle-u-Lyme 21-5-93
Internationals: England U18.

2010–11	Plymouth Arg	35	0
2011–12	Plymouth Arg	17	0
2012–13	Plymouth Arg	27	3
2013–14	Plymouth Arg	44	1
2014–15	Plymouth Arg	42	1	165	5

NORBURN, Oliver (M)   70   3
H: 6 1 W: 12 13 b.Leicester 26-10-92

2011–12	Leicester C	0	0
2011–12	*Bristol R*	5	0
2012–13	Bristol R	35	3
2013–14	Bristol R	16	0	56	3
2014–15	Plymouth Arg	14	0	14	0

O'CONNOR, Anthony (D)   117   3
H: 6 2 W: 12 06 b.Cork 25-10-92
Internationals: Republic of Ireland U17, U19, U21.

2010–11	Blackburn R	0	0
2011–12	Blackburn R	0	0
2012–13	Blackburn R	0	0
2012–13	*Burton Alb*	46	0	46	0
2013–14	Blackburn R	0	0
2013–14	*Torquay U*	31	0	31	0
2014–15	Plymouth Arg	40	3	40	3

PURRINGTON, Ben (D)   20   0
H: 5 9 W: 11 07 b.Exeter 5-5-96

2013–14	Plymouth Arg	12	0
2014–15	Plymouth Arg	8	0	20	0

REID, Reuben (F)   277   73
H: 6 0 W: 12 02 b.Bristol 26-7-88

2005–06	Plymouth Arg	1	0
2006–07	Plymouth Arg	6	0
2006–07	*Rochdale*	2	0	2	0
2006–07	*Torquay U*	7	2	7	2
2007–08	Plymouth Arg	0	0
2007–08	*Wycombe W*	11	1	11	1
2007–08	*Brentford*	10	1	10	1
2008–09	Rotherham U	41	18	41	18
2009–10	WBA	4	0
2009–10	*Peterborough U*	13	0	13	0
2010–11	WBA	0	0	4	0
2010–11	*Walsall*	18	3	18	3
2010–11	Oldham Ath	19	2
2011–12	Oldham Ath	20	5	39	7
2012–13	Yeovil T	19	4	19	4
2012–13	*Plymouth Arg*	18	2
2013–14	Plymouth Arg	46	17
2014–15	Plymouth Arg	42	18	113	37

RICHARDS, Jamie (D)   17   0
H: 6 0 b.Newton Abbot 24-6-94

2011–12	Plymouth Arg	0	0
2012–13	Plymouth Arg	1	0
2013–14	Plymouth Arg	1	0
2014–15	Plymouth Arg	0	0	2	0
2014–15	*Linfield*	15	0	15	0

SMALLEY, Deane (M)   246   36
H: 6 0 W: 11 10 b.Chadderton 5-9-88

2006–07	Oldham Ath	2	0
2007–08	Oldham Ath	37	2
2008–09	Oldham Ath	34	5
2009–10	Oldham Ath	29	3
2010–11	Oldham Ath	3	0	105	10
2010–11	*Rochdale*	3	0	3	0
2010–11	*Chesterfield*	28	12	28	12
2011–12	Oxford U	22	1
2011–12	*Bradford C*	13	0	13	0
2012–13	Oxford U	27	5

2013–14	Oxford U	32	7	81	13
2014–15	Plymouth Arg	16	1	16	1

THOMAS, Nathan (F)   19   1
H: 5 10 W: 12 08 b.Barwick 27-9-94

2013–14	Plymouth Arg	10	0
2014–15	Plymouth Arg	9	1	19	1

Transferred to Motherwell February 2015.

WOTTON, Paul (D)   552   61
H: 5 11 W: 12 00 b.Plymouth 17-8-77

1994–95	Plymouth Arg	7	0
1995–96	Plymouth Arg	1	0
1996–97	Plymouth Arg	9	1
1997–98	Plymouth Arg	34	1
1998–99	Plymouth Arg	36	1
1999–2000	Plymouth Arg	23	0
2000–01	Plymouth Arg	42	4
2001–02	Plymouth Arg	46	5
2002–03	Plymouth Arg	43	8
2003–04	Plymouth Arg	38	9
2004–05	Plymouth Arg	40	12
2005–06	Plymouth Arg	45	8
2006–07	Plymouth Arg	22	4
2007–08	Plymouth Arg	8	1
2008–09	Southampton	29	0
2009–10	Southampton	26	0
2010–11	Southampton	2	0	57	0
2010–11	*Oxford U*	4	0	4	0
2010–11	Yeovil T	23	2
2011–12	Yeovil T	22	2	45	4
2011–12	Plymouth Arg	18	1
2012–13	Plymouth Arg	19	2
2013–14	Plymouth Arg	15	0
2014–15	Plymouth Arg	0	0	446	57

Scholars
Calver, Jack Lee; Hall, Callum James; Hannah, Andrew James; Harvey, Cory Henri; Hughes, Mason Richard; Jones, Owen Martyn; Knowles, Liam Michael; Lane, Ryan Alan John; Miller-Medway, Jake; Moxham, Thomas Neal; Palfrey, William Harry; Roberts, Jamil; Rooney, Louis John; Sargent, William Michael; Steer, Benjamin George; Vincent, Jason James.

PORT VALE (64)

ANDOH, Ebo (M)   37   1
b. 1-1-93
Internationals: Ghana U20.

2012–13	AEL Limassol	20	0	20	0
2013–14	AEL Limassol	17	1	17	1
2014–15	Port Vale	0	0

BIRCHALL, Chris (M)   276   16
H: 6 2 W: 12 07 b.Liverpool 5-5-84
Internationals: Trinidad & Tobago Full caps.

2001–02	Port Vale	1	0
2002–03	Port Vale	2	0
2003–04	Port Vale	10	0
2004–05	Port Vale	34	6
2005–06	Port Vale	31	1
2006–07	Coventry C	28	2
2007–08	Coventry C	1	0
2007–08	*St Mirren*	9	0	9	0
2008–09	Coventry C	0	0	29	2
2008–09	*Carlisle U*	2	0	2	0
2008–09	*Brighton & HA*	9	0	9	0
2009	LA Galaxy	11	0
2010	LA Galaxy	28	0
2011	LA Galaxy	27	1	66	1
2012	Columbus Crew	18	1	18	1
2012–13	Port Vale	11	1
2013–14	Port Vale	27	1
2014–15	Port Vale	27	3	143	12

BOOT, Ryan (G)   0   0
H: 6 1 W: 11 03 b.Rocester 9-11-94

2012–13	Port Vale	0	0
2013–14	Port Vale	0	0
2014–15	Port Vale	0	0

BROWN, Michael (M)   546   42
H: 5 9 W: 12 04 b.Hartlepool 25-1-77
Internationals: England U21.

1994–95	Manchester C	1	0
1995–96	Manchester C	21	0
1996–97	Manchester C	11	0
1996–97	*Hartlepool U*	6	1	6	1
1997–98	Manchester C	26	0
1998–99	Manchester C	31	2
1999–2000	Manchester C	0	0	89	2
1999–2000	*Portsmouth*	4	0
1999–2000	Sheffield U	24	3
2000–01	Sheffield U	36	1

2001–02	Sheffield U	36	5
2002–03	Sheffield U	40	16
2003–04	Sheffield U	15	2	151	27
2003–04	Tottenham H	17	1
2004–05	Tottenham H	24	1
2005–06	Tottenham H	9	0	50	2
2005–06	Fulham	7	0
2006–07	Fulham	34	0	41	0
2007–08	Wigan Ath	31	0
2008–09	Wigan Ath	25	0
2009–10	Wigan Ath	2	0	58	0
2009–10	Portsmouth	24	2
2010–11	Portsmouth	21	2	49	4
2011–12	Leeds U	24	1
2012–13	Leeds U	24	1
2013–14	Leeds U	18	0	66	2
2014–15	Port Vale	36	4	36	4

CAMPION, Achille (F)   18   2
H: 6 2 W: 14 05 b.Levallois-Perret 10-3-90

2014	Norrby	6	1	6	1
2014–15	Port Vale	12	1	12	1

DANIEL, Colin (M)   195   20
H: 5 11 W: 11 06 b.Eastwood 15-2-88

2006–07	Crewe Alex	0	0
2007–08	Crewe Alex	1	0
2008–09	Crewe Alex	13	1	14	1
2008–09	Macclesfield T	8	0
2009–10	Macclesfield T	38	3
2010–11	Macclesfield T	43	8
2011–12	Macclesfield T	36	2	125	13
2013–14	Mansfield T	28	2	28	2
2014–15	Port Vale	28	4	28	4

DEEN-CONTEH, Aziz (D)   7   0
H: 5 9 W: 11 00 b.Sierra Leone 14-1-93
Internationals: England U16, U19.

2010–11	Chelsea	0	0
2011–12	Chelsea	0	0
2013–14	Ergotelis	7	0	7	0
2014–15	Port Vale	0	0

DICKINSON, Carl (D)   267   4
H: 6 1 W: 12 04 b.Swadlincote 31-3-87

2004–05	Stoke C	1	0
2005–06	Stoke C	5	0
2006–07	Stoke C	13	0
2006–07	*Blackpool*	7	0	7	0
2007–08	Stoke C	27	0
2008–09	Stoke C	5	0
2008–09	*Leeds U*	7	0	7	0
2009–10	Stoke C	0	0
2009–10	*Barnsley*	28	1	28	1
2010–11	Stoke C	0	0	51	0
2010–11	*Portsmouth*	36	0
2011–12	Watford	39	2
2012–13	Watford	4	0	43	2
2012–13	Portsmouth	6	0	42	0
2012–13	*Coventry C*	6	0	6	0
2013–14	Port Vale	40	0
2014–15	Port Vale	43	1	83	1

DODDS, Louis (M)   305   54
H: 5 10 W: 12 04 b.Sheffield 8-10-86

2005–06	Leicester C	0	0
2006–07	Leicester C	0	0
2006–07	*Rochdale*	12	2	12	2
2007–08	Leicester C	0	0
2007–08	*Lincoln C*	41	9	41	9
2008–09	Port Vale	44	7
2009–10	Port Vale	44	6
2010–11	Port Vale	33	7
2011–12	Port Vale	35	8
2012–13	Port Vale	30	7
2013–14	Port Vale	29	4
2014–15	Port Vale	37	4	252	43

DUFFY, Richard (D)   313   6
H: 5 9 W: 10 03 b.Swansea 30-8-85
Internationals: Wales U17, U19, U21, Full caps.

2002–03	Swansea C	0	0
2003–04	Swansea C	18	1
2003–04	Portsmouth	1	0
2004–05	Portsmouth	0	0
2004–05	*Burnley*	7	1	7	1
2004–05	Coventry C	14	0
2005–06	Portsmouth	0	0
2005–06	*Coventry C*	32	0
2006–07	Portsmouth	0	0
2006–07	*Coventry C*	13	0
2006–07	*Swansea C*	11	0	29	1
2007–08	Portsmouth	0	0
2007–08	*Coventry C*	2	0	61	0
2008–09	Portsmouth	0	0	1	0
2008–09	Millwall	12	0	12	0
2009–10	Exeter C	42	1
2010–11	Exeter C	42	2

2011–12	Exeter C	28	0	112 3
2012–13	Port Vale	36	0	
2013–14	Port Vale	28	0	
2014–15	Port Vale	27	1	91 1

JOHNSON, Sam (G)   23 0
H: 6 6 W: 12 04 b.Newcastle-under-Lyme 1-12-92

2011–12	Port Vale	0	0	
2012–13	Port Vale	0	0	
2013–14	Port Vale	16	0	
2014–15	Port Vale	7	0	23 0

LINES, Chris (M)   292 26
H: 6 2 W: 12 00 b.Bristol 30-11-88

2005–06	Bristol R	4	0	
2006–07	Bristol R	7	0	
2007–08	Bristol R	27	3	
2008–09	Bristol R	45	4	
2009–10	Bristol R	42	10	
2010–11	Bristol R	42	3	
2011–12	Bristol R	1	0	168 20
2011–12	Sheffield W	41	3	
2012–13	Sheffield W	6	0	47 3
2012–13	*Milton Keynes D*	16	0	16 0
2013–14	Port Vale	34	1	
2014–15	Port Vale	27	·2	61 3

LLOYD, Ryan (M)   12 0
H: 5 10 W: 10 03 b.Newcastle-u-Lyme 1-2-94

2010–11	Port Vale	1	0	
2011–12	Port Vale	2	0	
2012–13	Port Vale	6	0	
2013–14	Port Vale	3	0	
2014–15	Port Vale	0	0	12 0

MARSHALL, Mark (M)   158 14
H: 5 7 W: 10 07 b.Jamaica 9-5-86

2008–09	Swindon T	12	0	
2009–10	Swindon T	7	0	19 0
2009–10	Hereford U	8	0	8 0
2010–11	Barnet	46	6	
2011–12	Barnet	25	1	71 7
2013–14	Coventry C	14	0	14 0
2014–15	Port Vale	46	7	46 7

McGIVERN, Ryan (D)   149 2
H: 5 10 W: 11 07 b.Newry 8-1-90
Internationals: Northern Ireland U16, U17, U19, U21, B, Full caps.

2007–08	Manchester C	0	0	
2008–09	Manchester C	0	0	
2008–09	Morecambe	5	1	5 1
2009–10	Manchester C	0	0	
2009–10	Leicester C	12	0	12 0
2010–11	Manchester C	1	0	
2010–11	Walsall	15	0	15 0
2011–12	Manchester C	0	0	
2011–12	Crystal Palace	5	0	5 0
2011–12	*Bristol C*	31	0	31 0
2012–13	Manchester C	0	0	1 0
2012–13	Hibernian	27	1	
2013–14	Hibernian	33	0	60 1
2014–15	Port Vale	20	0	20 0

MOHAMED, Kaid (F)   257 55
H: 5 11 W: 12 06 b.Cardiff 23-7-84

2003–04	Cwmbran T	29	3	
2004–05	Cwmbran T	15	2	
2004–05	Llanelli	3	1	
2005–06	Carmarthen T	14	4	
2005–06	Carmarthen T	11	7	55 12
2006–07	Llanelli	5	0	8 1
2006–07	Carmarthen T	30	15	44 19
2007–08	Swindon T	11	0	11 0

From Forest Green R, Bath C, AFC Wimbledon.

2011–12	Cheltenham T	45	11	
2012–13	Cheltenham T	39	4	84 15
2013–14	Port Vale	6	0	
2013–14	*AFC Wimbledon*	5	0	5 0
2013–14	*Bristol R*	21	4	21 4
2014–15	Port Vale	0	0	6 0
2014–15	*Northampton T*	23	4	23 4

MOORE, Byron (M)   277 31
H: 6 0 W: 10 06 b.Stoke 24-8-88

2006–07	Crewe Alex	1	0	
2007–08	Crewe Alex	33	3	
2008–09	Crewe Alex	36	3	
2009–10	Crewe Alex	32	3	
2010–11	Crewe Alex	38	6	
2011–12	Crewe Alex	42	8	
2012–13	Crewe Alex	41	4	
2013–14	Crewe Alex	40	3	262 30
2014–15	Port Vale	15	1	15 1

N'GUESSAN, Dany (M)   226 40
H: 6 0 W: 12 13 b.Paris 11-8-87

2006–07	Boston U	23	5	23 5
2006–07	Lincoln C	9	0	
2007–08	Lincoln C	37	7	
2008–09	Lincoln C	45	8	91 15
2009–10	Leicester C	27	3	
2010–11	Leicester C	5	0	32 3
2010–11	*Scunthorpe U*	3	1	3 1
2010–11	*Southampton*	6	0	6 0
2011–12	Millwall	15	1	
2011–12	*Charlton Ath*	7	4	7 4
2012–13	Millwall	13	1	
2013–14	Millwall	1	0	29 2
2013–14	Swindon T	24	8	24 8
2014–15	Port Vale	11	2	11 2

NEAL, Chris (G)   182 0
H: 6 2 W: 12 04 b.St Albans 23-10-85

2004–05	Preston NE	1	0	
2005–06	Preston NE	0	0	
2006–07	Preston NE	0	0	
2006–07	Shrewsbury T	0	0	
2007–08	Morecambe	0	0	
2007–08	Preston NE	0	0	
2008–09	Preston NE	0	0	1 0
2009–10	Shrewsbury T	7	0	
2010–11	Shrewsbury T	22	0	
2011–12	Shrewsbury T	35	0	64 0
2012–13	Port Vale	46	0	
2013–14	Port Vale	31	0	
2014–15	Port Vale	40	0	117 0

NIMELY, Alex (F)   30 1
H: 5 11 W: 11 03 b.Monrovia 11-5-91
Internationals: Liberia Youth. England U20.

2008–09	Manchester C	0	0	
2009–10	Manchester C	1	0	
2010–11	Manchester C	0	0	
2011–12	Manchester C	0	0	
2011–12	*Middlesbrough*	9	0	9 0
2011–12	*Coventry C*	17	1	17 1
2012–13	Manchester C	0	0	
2012–13	*Crystal Palace*	2	0	2 0
2013–14	Manchester C	0	0	1 0
2014–15	Port Vale	1	0	1 0

O'CONNOR, Michael (M)   292 29
H: 6 1 W: 11 08 b.Belfast 6-10-87
Internationals: Northern Ireland U21, B, Full caps.

2005–06	Crewe Alex	2	0	
2006–07	Crewe Alex	29	0	
2007–08	Crewe Alex	23	0	
2008–09	Crewe Alex	23	3	77 3
2008–09	*Lincoln C*	10	1	10 1
2009–10	Scunthorpe U	32	2	
2010–11	Scunthorpe U	32	8	
2011–12	Scunthorpe U	33	1	97 11
2012–13	Rotherham U	35	6	
2013–14	Rotherham U	29	2	64 8
2014–15	Port Vale	44	6	44 6

POPE, Tom (F)   285 80
H: 6 3 W: 11 03 b.Stoke 27-8-85

2005–06	Crewe Alex	0	0	
2006–07	Crewe Alex	4	0	
2007–08	Crewe Alex	26	7	
2008–09	Crewe Alex	26	10	56 17
2009–10	Rotherham U	35	3	
2010–11	Rotherham U	18	1	53 4
2010–11	*Port Vale*	13	3	
2011–12	Port Vale	41	5	
2012–13	Port Vale	46	31	
2013–14	Port Vale	43	12	
2014–15	Port Vale	33	8	176 59

ROBERTSON, Chris (D)   223 10
H: 6 3 W: 11 08 b.Dundee 11-10-85

2005–06	Sheffield U	0	0	
2005–06	*Chester C*	1	0	1 0
2006–07	Torquay U	9	1	
2009–10	Torquay U	45	2	
2010–11	Torquay U	43	2	
2011–12	Torquay U	25	1	122 6
2011–12	Preston NE	18	1	
2012–13	Preston NE	21	0	39 1
2013–14	Port Vale	37	3	
2014–15	Port Vale	24	0	61 3

SMITH, Nathan (D)   0 0
H: 6 0 W: 11 05 b.Madeley 3-4-96

2013–14	Port Vale	0	0	
2014–15	Port Vale	0	0	0 0

VESELI, Frederic (D)   55 1
H: 6 0 W: 12 08 b.Kosovo 20-11-92
Internationals: Switzerland U16, U17, U18, U19, U20, U21.

2009–10	Manchester C	0	0	
2010–11	Manchester C	0	0	
2011–12	Manchester C	0	0	
2011–12	Manchester U	0	0	
2012–13	Manchester U	0	0	
2013–14	Ipswich T	0	0	
2013–14	*Bury*	18	0	18 0
2014–15	Port Vale	37	1	37 1

WILLIAMSON, Ben (F)   165 29
H: 5 11 W: 11 13 b.Lambeth 25-12-88

2010–11	Jerez Industrial	12	8	12 8
2010–11	Bournemouth	4	0	
2011–12	Bournemouth	0	0	4 0
2011–12	Port Vale	35	3	
2012–13	Port Vale	33	8	
2013–14	Port Vale	38	4	
2014–15	Port Vale	43	6	149 21

YATES, Adam (D)   277 4
H: 5 10 W: 10 07 b.Stoke 28-5-83
Internationals: England C.

2000–01	Crewe Alex	0	0	
2001–02	Crewe Alex	0	0	
2002–03	Crewe Alex	0	0	
2003–04	Crewe Alex	0	0	
2004–05	Crewe Alex	0	0	
2005–06	Crewe Alex	0	0	
2006–07	Crewe Alex	0	0	
2007–08	Morecambe	44	0	
2008–09	Morecambe	32	0	76 0
2009–10	Port Vale	32	0	
2010–11	Port Vale	46	0	
2011–12	Port Vale	38	2	
2012–13	Port Vale	26	0	
2013–14	Port Vale	34	1	
2014–15	Port Vale	25	1	201 4

Scholars
Ashton, Thomas Michael; Attrell, Taylor Thomas; Bergin, Lewis Thomas; Clarke, Kyle Benito; Ede, Brad Michael; Faulkner, Mackenzie; Ferrie, Calum John; Gibbons, James Andrew; Haughton, Omar Raheen Samuel; Kapend, Jonathan; Lewis, Luke Charles; Morris, Alex William; Pickering, Harry Thomas; Reeves, Calum David; Steele, Chekaine Craig; Turner, Daniel Graham; Wakeham, Daniel James.

PORTSMOUTH (65)

AGYEMANG, Patrick (F)   467 72
H: 6 1 W: 12 00 b.Walthamstow 29-9-80
Internationals: Ghana Full caps.

1998–99	Wimbledon	0	0	
1999–2000	Wimbledon	0	0	
1999–2000	*Brentford*	12	0	12 0
2000–01	Wimbledon	29	4	
2001–02	Wimbledon	33	4	
2002–03	Wimbledon	33	5	
2003–04	Wimbledon	26	7	121 20
2003–04	Gillingham	20	6	
2004–05	Gillingham	13	2	33 8
2004–05	Preston NE	27	4	
2005–06	Preston NE	42	6	
2006–07	Preston NE	31	7	
2007–08	Preston NE	22	4	122 21
2007–08	QPR	17	8	
2008–09	QPR	20	2	
2009–10	QPR	17	3	
2009–10	*Bristol C*	7	0	7 0
2010–11	QPR	19	2	
2011–12	QPR	2	0	75 15
2011–12	*Millwall*	2	0	2 0
2011–12	Stevenage	13	1	
2012–13	Stevenage	14	0	27 1
2012–13	Portsmouth	15	3	
2013–14	Portsmouth	41	4	
2014–15	Portsmouth	8	0	64 7
2014–15	*Dagenham & R*	4	0	4 0

ATANGANA, Nigel (M)   30 1
b.Corbeil-Essonnes 9-9-89

2014–15	Portsmouth	30	1	30 1

AWFORD, Nick (M)   2 0
b.Portsmouth 14-4-95

2012–13	Portsmouth	1	0	
2013–14	Portsmouth	0	0	
2014–15	Portsmouth	1	0	2 0

BARCHAM, Andy (F)   244 33
H: 5 8   W: 11 10   b.Basildon 16-12-86
Internationals: England U16.

Season	Club				
2005–06	Tottenham H	0	0		
2006–07	Tottenham H	0	0		
2007–08	Tottenham H	0	0		
2007–08	*Leyton Orient*	25	1	25	1
2008–09	Tottenham H	0	0		
2008–09	Gillingham	33	6		
2009–10	Gillingham	42	7		
2010–11	Gillingham	24	6	99	19
2011–12	Scunthorpe U	41	9		
2012–13	Scunthorpe U	34	0	75	9
2013–14	Portsmouth	0	0		
2014–15	Portsmouth	19	1	45	4

BASS, Alex (G)   0 0
b.Southampton 1-1-97

Season	Club		
2014–15	Portsmouth	0	0

BUTLER, Dan (D)   48 0
b.Cowes 26-8-94

Season	Club				
2012–13	Portsmouth	17	0		
2013–14	Portsmouth	1	0		
2014–15	Portsmouth	30	0	48	0

CHAPLIN, Conor (M)   9 1
b. 16-2-97

Season	Club				
2014–15	Portsmouth	9	1	9	1

CHORLEY, Ben (D)   401 15
H: 6 3   W: 13 02   b.Sidcup 30-9-82

Season	Club				
2001–02	Arsenal	0	0		
2002–03	Arsenal	0	0		
2002–03	*Brentford*	2	0	2	0
2002–03	Wimbledon	10	0		
2003–04	Wimbledon	35	2	45	2
2004–05	Milton Keynes D	41	2		
2005–06	Milton Keynes D	26	0		
2006–07	Milton Keynes D	13	1	80	3
2006–07	*Gillingham*	27	1	27	1
2007–08	Tranmere R	31	1		
2008–09	Tranmere R	45	1	76	2
2009–10	Leyton Orient	42	1		
2010–11	Leyton Orient	29	3		
2011–12	Leyton Orient	32	1		
2012–13	Leyton Orient	28	2	131	7
2012–13	Stevenage	8	0		
2013–14	Stevenage	4	0	12	0
2013–14	Portsmouth	12	0		
2014–15	Portsmouth	16	0	28	0

CLOSE, Ben (M)   6 0
b.Portsmouth 8-8-96

Season	Club				
2013–14	Portsmouth	0	0		
2014–15	Portsmouth	6	0	6	0

CRADDOCK, Tom (F)   124 37
H: 5 11   W: 11 10   b.Durham 14-10-86

Season	Club				
2005–06	Middlesbrough	1	0		
2006–07	Middlesbrough	0	0		
2006–07	*Wrexham*	1	1	1	1
2007–08	Middlesbrough	3	0		
2007–08	*Hartlepool U*	4	0	4	0
2008–09	Middlesbrough	0	0	4	0
2008–09	Luton T	27	10	27	10
2010–11	Oxford U	39	14		
2011–12	Oxford U	9	1		
2012–13	Oxford U	32	10	80	25
2013–14	Portsmouth	8	1		
2014–15	Portsmouth	0	0	8	1

DEVERA, Joe (D)   302 5
H: 6 2   W: 12 00   b.Southgate 6-2-87

Season	Club				
2005–06	Barnet	0	0		
2006–07	Barnet	26	0		
2007–08	Barnet	41	0		
2008–09	Barnet	34	1		
2009–10	Barnet	33	0		
2010–11	Barnet	43	1	177	2
2011–12	Swindon T	28	2		
2012–13	Swindon T	25	0	53	2
2013–14	Swindon T	33	0		
2014–15	Portsmouth	39	1	72	1

DUNNE, James (M)   214 12
H: 5 11   W: 10 12   b.Bromley 18-9-89

Season	Club				
2007–08	Arsenal	0	0		
2008–09	Arsenal	0	0		
2008–09	*Nottingham F*	0	0		
2009–10	Exeter C	23	3		
2010–11	Exeter C	42	1		
2011–12	Exeter C	45	2	110	6
2012–13	Stevenage	42	4		
2013–14	Stevenage	13	1	55	5
2013–14	*St Johnstone*	13	0	13	0
2014–15	Portsmouth	36	1	36	1

EAST, Danny (D)   35 1
H: 5 10   W: 11 03   b.Hessle 26-12-91

Season	Club				
2011–12	Hull C	0	0		
2012–13	Hull C	0	0		
2012–13	*Northampton T*	14	0	14	0
2012–13	*Gillingham*	2	0	2	0
2013–14	Portsmouth	15	1		
2014–15	Portsmouth	4	0	19	1

ERTL, Johannes (D)   277 8
H: 6 2   W: 12 08   b.Graz 13-11-82
Internationals: Austria Full caps.

Season	Club				
2003–04	*Kalzdorf*	11	3	11	3
2004–05	Sturm Graz	26	0		
2005–06	Sturm Graz	27	0		
2006–07	Sturm Graz	5	0	58	0
2006–07	FK Austria	24	1		
2007–08	FK Austria	24	2	48	3
2008–09	Crystal Palace	12	0		
2009–10	Crystal Palace	33	0	45	0
2010–11	Sheffield U	28	0		
2011–12	Sheffield U	7	0		
2012–13	Sheffield U	0	0	35	0
2012–13	Portsmouth	37	0		
2013–14	Portsmouth	29	1		
2014–15	Portsmouth	14	1	80	2

FOGDEN, Wes (F)   84 6
H: 5 8   W: 10 04   b.Brighton 12-4-88

Season	Club				
2006–07	Brighton & HA	0	0		
2007–08	Brighton & HA	3	0	3	0

From Dorchester T, Havant & Waterlooville.

Season	Club				
2011–12	Bournemouth	27	3		
2012–13	Bournemouth	26	1		
2013–14	Bournemouth	0	0	53	4
2013–14	Portsmouth	19	2		
2014–15	Portsmouth	9	0	28	2

HOLLANDS, Danny (M)   338 41
H: 6 0   W: 11 11   b.Ashford (Middlesex)
6-11-85

Season	Club				
2003–04	Chelsea	0	0		
2004–05	Chelsea	0	0		
2005–06	Chelsea	0	0		
2005–06	*Torquay U*	10	1	10	1
2006–07	Bournemouth	33	1		
2007–08	Bournemouth	37	4		
2008–09	Bournemouth	42	6		
2009–10	Bournemouth	39	6		
2010–11	Bournemouth	42	7	193	24
2011–12	Charlton Ath	43	7		
2012–13	Charlton Ath	14	0		
2012–13	*Swindon T*	10	2	10	2
2013–14	Charlton Ath	0	0	57	7
2013–14	*Gillingham*	17	1	17	1
2013–14	Portsmouth	7	5		
2014–15	Portsmouth	44	1	51	6

JONES, Paul (G)   264 0
H: 6 3   W: 13 00   b.Maidstone 28-6-86

Season	Club				
2008–09	Exeter C	46	0		
2009–10	Exeter C	26	0		
2010–11	Exeter C	18	0	90	0
2010–11	Peterborough U	1	0		
2011–12	Peterborough U	35	0	36	0
2012–13	Crawley T	46	0		
2013–14	Crawley T	46	0	92	0
2014–15	Portsmouth	46	0	46	0

MAY, Adam (M)   1 0
b. 6-12-97

Season	Club				
2014–15	Portsmouth	1	0	1	0

POKE, Michael (G)   98 0
H: 6 1   W: 13 12   b.Staines 21-11-85

Season	Club				
2003–04	Southampton	0	0		
2004–05	Southampton	0	0		
2005–06	Southampton	0	0		
2005–06	Oldham Ath	0	0		
2005–06	*Northampton T*	0	0		
2006–07	Southampton	0	0		
2007–08	Southampton	4	0		
2008–09	Southampton	0	0		
2009–10	Southampton	0	0	4	0
2009–10	*Torquay U*	29	0		
2010–11	Brighton & HA	0	0		
2011–12	Brighton & HA	0	0		
2011–12	*Bristol R*	8	0	8	0
2012–13	Torquay U	43	0		
2013–14	Torquay U	14	0	86	0
2014–15	Portsmouth	0	0		

ROBINSON, Paul (D)   349 18
H: 6 1   W: 11 09   b.Barnet 7-1-82

Season	Club				
2000–01	Millwall	3	0		
2001–02	Millwall	0	0		
2002–03	Millwall	14	0		
2003–04	Millwall	9	0		
2004–05	Millwall	0	0		
2004–05	*Torquay U*	12	0	12	0
2005–06	Millwall	32	0		
2006–07	Millwall	38	3		
2007–08	Millwall	45	3		
2008–09	Millwall	26	2		
2009–10	Millwall	34	4		
2010–11	Millwall	37	3		
2011–12	Millwall	41	1		
2012–13	Millwall	3	0		
2013–14	Millwall	25	0	304	16
2014–15	Portsmouth	33	2	33	2

SHOREY, Nicky (D)   449 12
H: 5 9   W: 10 08   b.Romford 19-2-81
Internationals: England B, Full caps.

Season	Club				
1999–2000	Leyton Orient	7	0		
2000–01	Leyton Orient	8	0	15	0
2000–01	Reading	0	0		
2001–02	Reading	32	0		
2002–03	Reading	43	2		
2003–04	Reading	35	2		
2004–05	Reading	44	3		
2005–06	Reading	40	2		
2006–07	Reading	37	1		
2007–08	Reading	36	2		
2008–09	Aston Villa	21	0		
2009–10	Aston Villa	3	0	24	0
2009–10	*Nottingham F*	9	0	9	0
2009–10	*Fulham*	9	0	9	0
2010–11	WBA	28	0		
2011–12	WBA	25	0	53	0
2012–13	Reading	17	0	284	12
2013–14	Bristol C	14	0	14	0
2013–14	Portsmouth	21	0		
2014–15	Portsmouth	20	0	41	0

TARBUCK, Bradley (F)   2 0
H: 5 9   W: 11 11   b.Emsworth 6-11-95

Season	Club				
2012–13	Portsmouth	0	0		
2013–14	Portsmouth	0	0		
2014–15	Portsmouth	2	0	2	0

TAYLOR, Ryan (F)   233 38
H: 6 2   W: 10 10   b.Rotherham 4-5-88

Season	Club				
2005–06	Rotherham U	1	0		
2006–07	Rotherham U	10	0		
2007–08	Rotherham U	35	6		
2008–09	Rotherham U	33	4		
2009–10	Rotherham U	19	0		
2009–10	*Exeter C*	7	0	7	0
2010–11	Rotherham U	34	11	132	21
2011–12	Bristol C	7	1		
2012–13	Bristol C	25	1		
2013–14	Bristol C	7	0	39	2
2013–14	Portsmouth	18	6		
2014–15	Portsmouth	37	9	55	15

TUBBS, Matt (F)   150 50
H: 5 9   W: 11 00   b.Salisbury 15-7-84
Internationals: England C.

Season	Club				
2008–09	Bournemouth	8	1		
2009–10	Bournemouth	0	0		
2011–12	Crawley T	24	12		
2011–12	Bournemouth	7	1		
2012–13	Bournemouth	31	6		
2013–14	Bournemouth	0	0		
2013–14	*Rotherham U*	17	1	17	1
2013–14	*Crawley T*	18	8	42	20
2014–15	Bournemouth	0	0	46	8
2014–15	*AFC Wimbledon*	22	12	22	12
2014–15	Portsmouth	23	9	23	9

WALLACE, Jed (M)   110 27
H: 6 0   b.Reading 15-12-93
Internationals: England U19.

Season	Club				
2011–12	Portsmouth	0	0		
2012–13	Portsmouth	22	6		
2013–14	Portsmouth	44	7		
2014–15	Portsmouth	44	14	110	27

WEBSTER, Adam (D)   40 3
H: 6 1   W: 11 11   b.West Wittering 4-1-95
Internationals: England U18, U19.

Season	Club				
2011–12	Portsmouth	0	0		
2012–13	Portsmouth	18	0		
2013–14	Portsmouth	4	2		
2014–15	Portsmouth	15	1	40	3

WESTCARR, Craig (F)   273 58
H: 5 11   W: 11 04   b.Nottingham 29-1-85
Internationals: England U18.

Season	Club				
2001–02	Nottingham F	8	0		
2002–03	Nottingham F	11	1		
2003–04	Nottingham F	3	0		
2004–05	Nottingham F	1	0	23	1
2004–05	*Lincoln C*	6	1	6	1
2004–05	*Milton Keynes D*	0	0	4	0

From Cambridge U, Kettering T.

Season	Club		
2009–10	Notts Co	42	9
2010–11	Notts Co	41	12

2011–12	Notts Co	4	0	87	21
2011–12	Chesterfield	38	8		
2012–13	Chesterfield	15	2	53	10
2012–13	*Walsall*	24	5		
2013–14	Walsall	43	14	67	19
2014–15	Portsmouth	33	6	33	6

WHATMOUGH, Jack (D)   34 0
b.Gosport 19-8-96
Internationals: England U18, U21.

2012–13	Portsmouth	0	0		
2013–14	Portsmouth	12	0		
2014–15	Portsmouth	22	0	34	0

Scholars
Bass, Alexander Michael; Davies, Calvin Jack; Field, Chad Paul; Gill, Lewis James; Granger, James John Keith; Haitham, Kaleem; Haunstrup, Brandon Neil; Joseph-Buadi, Brandon Yaw; May, Adam John; Nilsen, Snorre; Oxlade-Chamberlain, Christian Benjamin; Rwakarambwe, Fahad Ali; Sayers, Liam James; Yates, Dory Sean.

PRESTON NE (66)

ANDERTON, Nick (D)   0 0
H: 6 2 W: 12 06 b. 22-4-96

2014–15	Preston NE	0	0

BROWNE, Alan (M)   28 4
H: 5 8 W: 11 03 b.Cork 15-4-95
Internationals: Republic of Ireland U19.

2013–14	Preston NE	8	1		
2014–15	Preston NE	20	3	28	4

BROWNHILL, Josh (M)   42 5
H: 5 10 W: 10 12 b.Warrington 19-12-95

2013–14	Preston NE	24	3		
2014–15	Preston NE	18	2	42	5

BUCHANAN, David (M)   324 2
H: 5 7 W: 11 03 b.Rochdale 6-5-86
Internationals: Northern Ireland U19, U21.

2004–05	Bury	3	0		
2005–06	Bury	23	0		
2006–07	Bury	41	0		
2007–08	Bury	35	0		
2008–09	Bury	46	0		
2009–10	Bury	38	0	186	0
2010–11	Hamilton A	28	1	28	1
2011–12	Tranmere R	41	1	41	1
2012–13	Preston NE	33	0		
2013–14	Preston NE	19	0		
2014–15	Preston NE	17	0	69	0

CLARKE, Tom (D)   197 8
H: 6 0 W: 11 02 b.Sowerby Bridge 21-12-87
Internationals: England U18, U19.

2004–05	Huddersfield T	12	0		
2005–06	Huddersfield T	17	1		
2006–07	Huddersfield T	9	0		
2007–08	Huddersfield T	3	0		
2008–09	Huddersfield T	15	1		
2008–09	*Bradford C*	6	0	6	0
2009–10	Huddersfield T	21	0		
2010–11	Huddersfield T	5	1		
2011–12	Huddersfield T	14	0		
2011–12	*Leyton Orient*	10	0	10	0
2012–13	Huddersfield T	0	0	96	3
2013–14	Preston NE	42	4		
2014–15	Preston NE	43	1	85	5

DAVIES, Ben (D)   54 0
H: 6 1 W: 11 09 b.Barrow 11-8-95

2012–13	Preston NE	0	0		
2013–14	Preston NE	0	0		
2013–14	*York C*	44	0	44	0
2014–15	Preston NE	4	0	7	0
2014–15	*Tranmere R*	3	0	3	0

DAVIES, Kevin (F)   689 122
H: 6 0 W: 12 10 b.Sheffield 26-3-77
Internationals: England U18, U21, Full caps.

1993–94	Chesterfield	24	4		
1994–95	Chesterfield	41	11		
1995–96	Chesterfield	30	4		
1996–97	Chesterfield	34	3	129	22
1996–97	Southampton	0	0		
1997–98	Southampton	25	9		
1998–99	Blackburn R	21	1		
1999–2000	Blackburn R	2	0	23	1
1999–2000	Southampton	23	6		
2000–01	Southampton	27	1		
2001–02	Southampton	23	2		
2002–03	Southampton	9	1	107	19
2002–03	*Millwall*	9	3	9	3

2003–04	Bolton W	38	9		
2004–05	Bolton W	35	8		
2005–06	Bolton W	37	7		
2006–07	Bolton W	30	8		
2007–08	Bolton W	32	3		
2008–09	Bolton W	38	11		
2009–10	Bolton W	37	7		
2010–11	Bolton W	38	8		
2011–12	Bolton W	31	6		
2012–13	Bolton W	35	6	351	73
2013–14	Preston NE	38	3		
2014–15	Preston NE	32	1	70	4

EBANKS-BLAKE, Sylvan (F)   261 83
H: 5 10 W: 13 04 b.Cambridge 29-3-86
Internationals: England U21.

2004–05	Manchester U	0	0		
2005–06	Manchester U	0	0		
2006–07	Plymouth Arg	41	10		
2007–08	*Plymouth Arg*	25	11	66	21
2007–08	Wolverhampton W	20	12		
2008–09	Wolverhampton W	41	25		
2009–10	Wolverhampton W	23	2		
2010–11	Wolverhampton W	30	7		
2011–12	Wolverhampton W	23	1		
2012–13	Wolverhampton W	40	14	177	61
2013–14	*Ipswich T*	9	0	9	0
2014–15	Preston NE	9	1	9	1

GARNER, Joe (F)   257 85
H: 5 10 W: 12 04 b.Blackburn 12-4-88
Internationals: England U16, U17, U19.

2004–05	Blackburn R	0	0		
2005–06	Blackburn R	0	0		
2006–07	Blackburn R	0	0		
2006–07	*Carlisle U*	18	5		
2007–08	*Carlisle U*	31	14		
2008–09	Nottingham F	28	7		
2009–10	Nottingham F	18	2		
2010–11	Nottingham F	0	0		
2010–11	*Huddersfield T*	16	0	16	0
2010–11	*Scunthorpe U*	18	6	18	6
2011–12	Nottingham F	2	0	48	9
2011–12	Watford	22	1		
2012–13	Watford	2	0	24	1
2012–13	*Carlisle U*	16	7	65	26
2013–14	Preston NE	35	18		
2014–15	Preston NE	37	25	86	43

HOLMES, Lee (M)   215 17
H: 5 8 W: 10 06 b.Mansfield 2-4-87
Internationals: England U16, U17, U19.

2002–03	Derby Co	2	0		
2003–04	Derby Co	23	2		
2004–05	*Swindon T*	15	1		
2005–06	Derby Co	18	0		
2006–07	Derby Co	0	0		
2006–07	*Bradford C*	16	0	16	0
2007–08	Derby Co	0	0	46	2
2007–08	*Walsall*	19	4	19	4
2008–09	Southampton	11	0		
2009–10	Southampton	5	0		
2010–11	Southampton	7	0		
2011–12	Southampton	6	1	29	1
2011–12	*Oxford U*	7	2	7	2
2011–12	*Swindon T*	10	1	25	2
2012–13	Preston NE	28	3		
2013–14	Preston NE	32	3		
2014–15	Preston NE	0	0	60	6
2014–15	*Portsmouth*	5	0	5	0
2014–15	*Exeter C*	8	0	8	0

HUDSON, Matthew (G)   0 0
b. 29-7-98

2014–15	Preston NE	0	0

HUGILL, Jordan (F)   37 9
H: 6 0 W: 10 01 b.Middlesbrough 4-6-92

2013–14	Port Vale	20	4	20	4
2014–15	Preston NE	3	0	3	0
2014–15	*Tranmere R*	6	1	6	1
2014–15	*Hartlepool U*	8	4	8	4

HUMPHREY, Chris (M)   292 16
H: 5 11 W: 11 07 b.Walsall 19-9-87
Internationals: Jamaica Full caps.

2006–07	Shrewsbury T	12	0		
2007–08	Shrewsbury T	25	0		
2008–09	Shrewsbury T	37	2	74	2
2009–10	Motherwell	28	0		
2010–11	Motherwell	36	3		
2011–12	Motherwell	35	2		
2012–13	Motherwell	33	3	132	8
2013–14	Preston NE	42	2		
2014–15	Preston NE	44	4	86	6

HUNTINGTON, Paul (D)   227 20
H: 6 3 W: 12 08 b.Carlisle 17-9-87
Internationals: England U18.

2005–06	Newcastle U	0	0		
2006–07	Newcastle U	11	1		
2007–08	Newcastle U	0	0	11	1
2007–08	Leeds U	17	2		
2008–09	Leeds U	4	0		
2009–10	Leeds U	0	0	21	2
2009–10	*Stockport Co*	26	0	26	0
2010–11	Yeovil T	40	5		
2011–12	Yeovil T	37	2	77	7
2012–13	Preston NE	37	3		
2013–14	Preston NE	23	2		
2014–15	Preston NE	32	5	92	10

JAMES, Steven (G)
H: 6 2 W: 11 11 b.Southport 19-12-95

2012–13	Preston NE	0	0
2013–14	Preston NE	0	0
2014–15	Preston NE	0	0

JOHNSON, Daniel (M)   42 11
H: 5 8 W: 10 07 b.Kingston, Jam 8-10-92

2010–11	Aston Villa	0	0		
2011–12	Aston Villa	0	0		
2012–13	Aston Villa	0	0		
2012–13	*Yeovil T*	5	0	5	0
2013–14	Aston Villa	0	0		
2014–15	*Chesterfield*	11	0	11	0
2014–15	*Oldham Ath*	6	3	6	3
2014–15	Preston NE	20	8	20	8

JONES, Jamie (G)   185 0
H: 6 2 W: 14 05 b.Kirkby 18-2-89

2007–08	Everton	0	0		
2008–09	Leyton Orient	20	0		
2009–10	Leyton Orient	36	0		
2010–11	Leyton Orient	35	0		
2011–12	Leyton Orient	6	0		
2012–13	Leyton Orient	26	0		
2013–14	Leyton Orient	28	0	151	0
2014–15	Preston NE	17	0	17	0
2014–15	*Coventry C*	4	0	4	0
2014–15	*Rochdale*	13	0	13	0

KEANE, Keith (M)   212 7
H: 5 9 W: 11 01 b.Luton 20-11-86
Internationals: Republic of Ireland U19, U21.

2003–04	Luton T	15	1		
2004–05	Luton T	17	0		
2005–06	Luton T	10	1		
2006–07	Luton T	19	1		
2007–08	Luton T	28	1		
2008–09	Luton T	40	0	129	4
2012–13	Preston NE	26	1		
2013–14	Preston NE	38	2		
2014–15	Preston NE	0	0	64	3
2014–15	*Crawley T*	12	0	12	0
2014–15	*Stevenage*	7	0	7	0

KILKENNY, Neil (M)   321 16
H: 5 8 W: 10 08 b.Enfield 19-12-85
Internationals: England U18, U20. Australia U23, Full caps.

2003–04	Birmingham C	0	0		
2004–05	Birmingham C	0	0		
2004–05	*Oldham Ath*	27	4		
2005–06	Birmingham C	18	0		
2006–07	Birmingham C	8	0		
2007–08	Birmingham C	0	0	26	0
2007–08	*Oldham Ath*	20	1	47	5
2007–08	Leeds U	16	1		
2008–09	Leeds U	30	4		
2009–10	Leeds U	35	2		
2010–11	Leeds U	37	1	118	8
2011–12	Bristol C	41	1		
2012–13	Bristol C	0	0		
2013–14	Bristol C	3	0	68	1
2013–14	Preston NE	27	2		
2014–15	Preston NE	35	0	62	2

KING, Jack (M)   78 7
H: 6 0 W: 11 11 b.Oxford 20-8-85

2012–13	Preston NE	36	4		
2013–14	Preston NE	24	2		
2014–15	Preston NE	18	1	78	7

LAIRD, Scott (D)   174 17
H: 5 11 W: 11 05 b.Taunton 15-5-88
Internationals: Scotland U16. England C.

2006–07	Plymouth Arg	0	0		
2007–08	Plymouth Arg	0	0		
2010–11	Stevenage	44	4		
2011–12	Stevenage	46	8	90	12
2012–13	Preston NE	19	4		
2013–14	Preston NE	34	1		
2014–15	Preston NE	31	0	84	5

LITTLE, Andrew (M)   84 34
H: 6 0 W: 12 00 b.Enniskillen 12-5-89
Internationals: Northern Ireland Youth, U21, B, Full caps.
2008–09 Rangers   0 0
2009–10 Rangers   6 1
2010–11 Rangers   0 0
2011–12 Rangers   10 5
2011–12 Port Vale   7 0   7 0
2012–13 Rangers   28 22
2013–14 Rangers   21 5   65 33
On loan from Rangers.
2014–15 Preston NE   12 1   12 1

REID, Kyel (M)   212 18
H: 5 10 W: 12 05 b.Deptford 26-11-87
Internationals: England U17, U18, U19.
2004–05 West Ham U   0 0
2005–06 West Ham U   2 0
2006–07 West Ham U   0 0
2006–07 Barnsley   26 2   26 2
2007–08 West Ham U   1 0
2007–08 Crystal Palace   2 0   2 0
2008–09 West Ham U   0 0   3 0
2008–09 Blackpool   7 0   7 0
2008–09 Wolverhampton W 8 1   8 1
2009–10 Sheffield U   7 0   7 0
2009–10 Charlton Ath   17 4
2010–11 Charlton Ath   32 1   49 5
2011–12 Bradford C   37 4
2012–13 Bradford C   33 2
2013–14 Bradford C   26 4   96 10
2014–15 Preston NE   14 0   14 0

RYAN, Jack (F)   1 0
H: 6 0 W: 12 06 b.Barrow-in-Furness 5-4-96
2013–14 Preston NE   0 0
2014–15 Preston NE   1 0   1 0

SAMPSON, Josh (D)   0 0
b. 16-9-96
2014–15 Preston NE   0 0

STUCKMANN, Thorsten (G)   338 0
H: 6 6 W: 14 11 b.Gutersloh 17-3-81
2000–01 Pr Munster   25 0
2001–02 Pr Munster   19 0
2002–03 Pr Munster   30 0   74 0
2003–04 E Braunschweig 21 0
2004–05 E Braunschweig 36 0
2005–06 E Braunschweig 34 0
2006–07 E Braunschweig 34 0 125 0
2007–08 A Aachen   16 0
2008–09 A Aachen   34 0
2009–10 A Aachen   31 0
2010–11 A Aachen   1 0   82 0
2011–12 Preston NE   28 0
2012–13 Preston NE   22 0
2013–14 Preston NE   0 0
2014–15 Preston NE   7 0   57 0

WELSH, John (M)   303 17
H: 5 7 W: 12 02 b.Liverpool 10-1-84
Internationals: England U20, U21.
2000–01 Liverpool   0 0
2001–02 Liverpool   0 0
2002–03 Liverpool   0 0
2003–04 Liverpool   1 0
2004–05 Liverpool   3 0
2005–06 Liverpool   0 0   4 0
2005–06 Hull C   32 2
2006–07 Hull C   18 1
2007–08 Hull C   0 0
2007–08 Chester C   6 0   6 0
2008–09 Hull C   0 0   50 3
2008–09 Carlisle U   4 0   4 0
2008–09 Bury   5 0   5 0
2009–10 Tranmere R   45 4
2010–11 Tranmere R   41 4
2011–12 Tranmere R   44 3 130 11
2012–13 Preston NE   36 1
2013–14 Preston NE   36 2
2014–15 Preston NE   32 0 104 3

WISEMAN, Scott (D)   297 5
H: 6 0 W: 11 06 b.Hull 9-10-85
Internationals: England U20. Gilbraltar Full caps.
2003–04 Hull C   2 0
2004–05 Hull C   3 0
2004–05 Boston U   2 0   2 0
2005–06 Hull C   11 0
2006–07 Hull C   0 0   16 0
2006–07 Rotherham U   18 1   18 1
2006–07 Darlington   10 0
2007–08 Darlington   7 0   17 0
2008–09 Rochdale   32 0
2009–10 Rochdale   36 1

2010–11 Rochdale   37 0 105 1
2011–12 Barnsley   43 1
2012–13 Barnsley   36 0
2013–14 Barnsley   23 0 102 1
2013–14 Preston NE   15 0
2014–15 Preston NE   22 2   37 2

WOODS, Calum (D)   218 11
H: 5 11 W: 11 07 b.Liverpool 5-2-87
2006–07 Dunfermline Ath 12 0
2007–08 Dunfermline Ath 25 0
2008–09 Dunfermline Ath 30 5
2009–10 Dunfermline Ath 29 2
2010–11 Dunfermline Ath 32 3 128 10
2011–12 Huddersfield T 26 0
2012–13 Huddersfield T 27 0
2013–14 Huddersfield T   1 0   72 1
2014–15 Preston NE   18 0   18 0

WRIGHT, Bailey (D)   123 8
H: 5 9 W: 13 05 b.Melbourne 28-7-92
Internationals: Australia U17, Full caps.
2010–11 Preston NE   2 0
2011–12 Preston NE   13 1
2012–13 Preston NE   38 2
2013–14 Preston NE   43 4
2014–15 Preston NE   27 1 123 8

Players retained or with offer of contract
Wilmer-Anderton, Nicholas Jack.

Scholars
Boyd, James Thomas William; Dalton, Ross Anthony; Dsane, Eddie-Louis Kweku; Hagon, Harold Jack; Hudson, Mathew Anthony; Jagne, Lamin; Livesey, Sam Anthony; Lunney, Jonathan michael; Magolis, Lyle Daleroy; Pritchard, Luke Gerard; Quigley, James Alan; Roberts, Ben James; Robinson, Adam James; Robinson, Adam Joseph Thomas; Roscoe, Bradley Samuel; Sampson, Joshua William; Smith, Clive Reece; Whelan, Sean Kenneh; Wicks, Bradley Dalton.

QPR (67)

ANDRADE, Bruno (M)   55 3
H: 5 9 W: 11 09 b.Aveiro 2-10-93
2010–11 QPR   1 0
2011–12 QPR   1 0
2011–12 Aldershot T   1 0   1 0
2012–13 QPR   0 0
2012–13 Wycombe W   23 2   23 2
2013–14 QPR   0 0
2013–14 Stevenage   13 0
2014–15 QPR   0 0   2 0
2014–15 Stevenage   16 1   29 1

AUSTIN, Charlie (F)   202 107
H: 6 2 W: 13 03 b.Hungerford 5-7-89
2009–10 Swindon T   33 19
2010–11 Swindon T   21 12   54 31
2010–11 Burnley   4 0
2011–12 Burnley   41 16
2012–13 Burnley   37 25   82 41
2013–14 QPR   31 17
2014–15 QPR   35 18   66 35

BARTON, Joey (M)   329 29
H: 5 11 W: 12 05 b.Huyton 2-9-82
Internationals: England U21, Full caps.
2001–02 Manchester C   0 0
2002–03 Manchester C   7 1
2003–04 Manchester C   28 1
2004–05 Manchester C   31 6
2005–06 Manchester C   31 6
2006–07 Manchester C   33 6 130 15
2007–08 Newcastle U   23 1
2008–09 Newcastle U   9 1
2009–10 Newcastle U   15 1
2010–11 Newcastle U   32 4
2011–12 Newcastle U   2 0   81 7
2011–12 QPR   31 3
2012–13 QPR   0 0
2012–13 Marseille   25 0   25 0
2013–14 QPR   34 3
2014–15 QPR   28 1   93 7

CAULKER, Steven (D)   190 10
H: 6 3 W: 12 00 b.Feltham 29-12-91
Internationals: England U19 U21, Full caps. Great Britain.
2009–10 Tottenham H   0 0
2009–10 Yeovil T   44 0   44 0
2010–11 Tottenham H   0 0
2010–11 Bristol C   29 2   29 2

2011–12 Tottenham H   0 0
2011–12 Swansea C   26 0   26 0
2012–13 Tottenham H   18 2   18 2
2013–14 Cardiff C   38 5   38 5
2014–15 QPR   35 1   35 1

COMLEY, Brandon (M)   1 0
b.Islington 18-11-95
2014–15 QPR   1 0   1 0

DIAKITE, Samba (M)   131 2
H: 6 1 W: 11 13 b.Montfermeil 24-1-89
Internationals: Mali Full caps.
2007–08 Valenciennes B   7 0   7 0
2008–09 Olympique N-le-Sec 28 0 28 0
2009–10 Nancy B   19 0   19 0
2009–10 Nancy   3 0
2010–11 Nancy   23 0
2011–12 Nancy   15 0   41 0
2011–12 QPR   9 1
2012–13 QPR   14 0
2013–14 QPR   0 0
2013–14 Watford   6 0   6 0
2014–15 QPR   0 0   23 1
2014–15 Al-Ittihad   7 1   7 1

DONALDSON, Coll (D)   1 0
H: 6 2 W: 12 13 b.Edinburgh 9-4-95
2013–14 QPR   0 0
2014–15 QPR   0 0   1 0

DOUGHTY, Michael (M)   74 2
H: 6 1 W: 12 10 b.Westminster 20-11-92
Internationals: Wales U19, U21.
2010–11 QPR   0 0
2011–12 QPR   0 0
2011–12 Crawley T   16 0   16 0
2011–12 Aldershot T   5 0   5 0
2012–13 QPR   0 0
2012–13 St Johnstone   5 0   5 0
2013–14 QPR   0 0
2013–14 Stevenage   36 2   36 2
2014–15 QPR   3 0   3 0
2014–15 Gillingham   9 0   9 0

DUNNE, Richard (D)   515 13
H: 6 2 W: 15 10 b.Dublin 21-9-79
Internationals: Republic of Ireland U21, B, Full caps.
1996–97 Everton   7 0
1997–98 Everton   3 0
1998–99 Everton   16 0
1999–2000 Everton   31 0
2000–01 Everton   3 0   60 0
2000–01 Manchester C   25 0
2001–02 Manchester C   43 1
2002–03 Manchester C   25 0
2003–04 Manchester C   29 0
2004–05 Manchester C   35 2
2005–06 Manchester C   32 3
2006–07 Manchester C   38 1
2007–08 Manchester C   36 0
2008–09 Manchester C   31 1
2009–10 Manchester C   2 0 296 8
2009–10 Aston Villa   35 3
2010–11 Aston Villa   32 0
2011–12 Aston Villa   28 1
2012–13 Aston Villa   0 0   95 4
2013–14 QPR   41 1
2014–15 QPR   23 0   64 1

EHMER, Max (M)   106 3
H: 6 2 W: 11 00 b.Frankfurt 3-2-92
2009–10 QPR   0 0
2010–11 QPR   0 0
2010–11 Yeovil T   27 0
2011–12 QPR   0 0
2011–12 Yeovil T   24 0   51 0
2011–12 Preston NE   9 0   9 0
2012–13 QPR   0 0
2012–13 Stevenage   6 1   6 1
2013–14 QPR   1 0
2013–14 Carlisle U   12 1   12 1
2014–15 QPR   0 0   1 0
2014–15 Gillingham   27 1   27 1

FAURLIN, Alejandro (M)   195 13
H: 6 1 W: 12 06 b.Argentina 9-8-86
Internationals: Argentina U17.
2004 Rosario Central   1 0
2005 Rosario Central   0 0
2006 Rosario Central   0 0   1 0
2007 Atletico Rafaela   40 1   40 1
2008–09 Instituto   27 7   27 7
2009–10 QPR   41 1
2010–11 QPR   40 3
2011–12 QPR   20 1
2012–13 QPR   11 0
2012–13 Palermo   6 0   6 0

2013–14	QPR	7	0	
2014–15	QPR	2	0	121 5

FER, Leroy (M) 213 36
H: 6 2 W: 12 05 b.Zortermeer 5-1-90
Internationals: Netherlands U16, U17, U19, U21, Full caps.

2007–08	Feyenoord	13	1	
2008–09	Feyenoord	31	6	
2009–10	Feyenoord	31	2	
2010–11	Feyenoord	23	3	
2011–12	Feyenoord	4	2	102 14
2011–12	FC Twente	26	8	
2012–13	FC Twente	26	5	52 13
2013–14	Norwich C	29	3	
2014–15	Norwich C	1	0	30 3
2014–15	QPR	29	6	29 6

FERDINAND, Rio (D) 514 11
H: 6 2 W: 13 12 b.Peckham 7-11-78
Internationals: England U18, U21, B, Full caps.

1995–96	West Ham U	1	0	
1996–97	West Ham U	15	2	
1996–97	Bournemouth	10	0	10 0
1997–98	West Ham U	35	0	
1998–99	West Ham U	31	0	
1999–2000	West Ham U	33	0	
2000–01	West Ham U	12	0	127 2
2000–01	Leeds U	23	2	
2001–02	Leeds U	31	0	54 2
2002–03	Manchester U	28	0	
2003–04	Manchester U	20	0	
2004–05	Manchester U	31	0	
2005–06	Manchester U	37	3	
2006–07	Manchester U	33	1	
2007–08	Manchester U	35	2	
2008–09	Manchester U	24	0	
2009–10	Manchester U	13	0	
2010–11	Manchester U	19	0	
2011–12	Manchester U	30	0	
2012–13	Manchester U	28	1	
2013–14	Manchester U	14	0	312 7
2014–15	QPR	11	0	11 0

FURLONG, Darnell (D) 3 0
b. 31-10-95

2014–15	QPR	3	0	3 0

GIBBONS, Jordan (M) 1 0
H: 5 10 W: 10 12 b.London 18-11-93

2011–12	QPR	0	0	
2012–13	QPR	0	0	
2012–13	Inverness CT	1	0	1 0
2013–14	QPR	0	0	
2014–15	QPR	0	0	

GREEN, Rob (G) 539 0
H: 6 3 W: 14 09 b.Chertsey 18-1-80
Internationals: England U16, U18, B, Full caps.

1997–98	Norwich C	0	0	
1998–99	Norwich C	2	0	
1999–2000	Norwich C	3	0	
2000–01	Norwich C	5	0	
2001–02	Norwich C	41	0	
2002–03	Norwich C	46	0	
2003–04	Norwich C	46	0	
2004–05	Norwich C	38	0	
2005–06	Norwich C	42	0	223 0
2006–07	West Ham U	26	0	
2007–08	West Ham U	38	0	
2008–09	West Ham U	38	0	
2009–10	West Ham U	38	0	
2010–11	West Ham U	37	0	
2011–12	West Ham U	42	0	219 0
2012–13	QPR	16	0	
2013–14	QPR	45	0	
2014–15	QPR	36	0	97 0

GREGO-COX, Reece (F) 4 0
b. 12-11-96
Internationals: Republic of Ireland U19.

2014–15	QPR	4	0	4 0

HARRIMAN, Michael (D) 91 2
H: 5 6 W: 11 10 b.Chichester 23-10-92
Internationals: Republic of Ireland U18, U19, U21.

2010–11	QPR	0	0	
2011–12	QPR	1	0	
2012–13	QPR	1	0	
2012–13	Wycombe W	20	0	20 0
2013–14	QPR	0	0	
2013–14	Gillingham	34	1	34 1
2014–15	QPR	0	0	2 0
2014–15	Luton T	35	1	35 1

HENRY, Karl (M) 439 9
H: 6 0 W: 12 00 b.Wolverhampton 26-11-82
Internationals: England U20.

1999–2000	Stoke C	0	0	
2000–01	Stoke C	0	0	
2001–02	Stoke C	24	0	
2002–03	Stoke C	18	1	
2003–04	Stoke C	31	0	
2003–04	Cheltenham T	9	1	9 1
2004–05	Stoke C	34	0	
2005–06	Stoke C	24	0	120 1
2006–07	Wolverhampton W	34	3	
2007–08	Wolverhampton W	40	3	
2008–09	Wolverhampton W	43	0	
2009–10	Wolverhampton W	34	0	
2010–11	Wolverhampton W	29	0	
2011–12	Wolverhampton W	31	0	
2012–13	Wolverhampton W	39	0	250 6
2013–14	QPR	27	1	
2014–15	QPR	33	0	60 1

HILL, Clint (D) 512 29
H: 6 0 W: 11 06 b.Liverpool 19-10-78

1997–98	Tranmere R	14	0	
1998–99	Tranmere R	33	4	
1999–2000	Tranmere R	29	5	
2000–01	Tranmere R	34	5	
2001–02	Tranmere R	30	2	140 16
2002–03	Oldham Ath	17	1	17 1
2003–04	Stoke C	12	0	
2004–05	Stoke C	32	1	
2005–06	Stoke C	13	0	
2006–07	Stoke C	18	2	
2007–08	Stoke C	9	0	80 3
2007–08	Crystal Palace	28	3	
2008–09	Crystal Palace	43	1	
2009–10	Crystal Palace	43	1	114 5
2010–11	QPR	44	2	
2011–12	QPR	22	0	
2011–12	Nottingham F	5	0	5 0
2012–13	QPR	31	0	
2013–14	QPR	40	1	
2014–15	QPR	19	1	156 4

HOILETT, Junior (M) 197 24
H: 5 8 W: 11 00 b.Ottowa 5-6-90

2007–08	Blackburn R	0	0	
2007–08	Paderborn	12	1	12 1
2008–09	Blackburn R	0	0	
2008–09	St Pauli	21	6	21 6
2009–10	Blackburn R	23	0	
2010–11	Blackburn R	24	5	
2011–12	Blackburn R	34	7	81 12
2012–13	QPR	26	1	
2013–14	QPR	35	4	
2014–15	QPR	22	0	83 5

ISLA, Mauricio (M) 182 6
H: 5 9 W: 11 05 b.Buin 12-6-88
Internationals: Chile U20, Full caps.

2007–08	Udinese	10	0	
2008–09	Udinese	32	0	
2009–10	Udinese	30	1	
2010–11	Udinese	34	2	
2011–12	Udinese	21	3	127 6
2012–13	Juventus	11	0	
2013–14	Juventus	18	0	
2014–15	Juventus	0	0	29 0
On loan from Juventus.
2014–15	QPR	26	0	26 0

KPEKAWA, Cole (D) 7 0
b. 20-5-96

2014–15	QPR	1	0	1 0
2014–15	Colchester U	4	0	4 0
2014–15	Portsmouth	2	0	2 0

KRANJCAR, Niko (M) 331 59
H: 6 1 W: 12 13 b.Zagreb 13-8-84
Internationals: Croatia U17, U19, U21, Full caps.

2001–02	Dynamo Zagreb	24	3	
2002–03	Dynamo Zagreb	21	4	
2003–04	Dynamo Zagreb	24	10	
2004–05	Dynamo Zagreb	16	2	85 19
2004–05	Hajduk Split	13	1	
2005–06	Hajduk Split	32	10	
2006–07	Hajduk Split	5	3	50 14
2006–07	Portsmouth	24	2	
2007–08	Portsmouth	34	4	
2008–09	Portsmouth	21	3	
2009–10	Portsmouth	4	0	83 9
2009–10	Tottenham H	24	6	
2010–11	Tottenham H	13	2	
2011–12	Tottenham H	12	1	49 9
2012–13	Dynamo Kiev	13	4	
2013–14	Dynamo Kiev	0	0	
2013–14	QPR	29	2	
2014–15	Dynamo Kiev	0	0	13 4
On loan from Dynamo Kiev.
2014–15	QPR	22	2	51 4

LENNOX, Aaron (G) 0 0
b.Sydney 19-2-93
Internationals: Australia U23.

2011–12	QPR	0	0	
2012–13	QPR	0	0	
2013–14	QPR	0	0	
2014–15	QPR	0	0	

LUMLEY, Joe (G) 5 0
b. 15-2-95

2013–14	QPR	0	0	
2014–15	QPR	0	0	
2014–15	Accrington S	5	0	5 0
2014–15	Morecambe	0	0	

McCARTHY, Alex (G) 140 0
H: 6 4 W: 11 12 b.Guildford 3-12-89
Internationals: England U21.

2008–09	Reading	0	0	
2008–09	Aldershot T	4	0	4 0
2009–10	Reading	0	0	
2009–10	Yeovil T	44	0	44 0
2010–11	Reading	13	0	
2010–11	Brentford	3	0	3 0
2011–12	Reading	0	0	
2011–12	Leeds U	6	0	6 0
2011–12	Ipswich T	10	0	10 0
2012–13	Reading	13	0	
2013–14	Reading	44	0	70 0
2014–15	QPR	3	0	3 0

MITCHELL, Aaron (M) 0 0
b. 14-4-96

2014–15	QPR	0	0	

MURPHY, Brian (G) 133 0
H: 6 0 W: 13 00 b.Waterford 7-5-83
Internationals: Republic of Ireland U16.

2000–01	Manchester C	0	0	
2001–02	Manchester C	0	0	
2002–03	Manchester C	0	0	
2002–03	Oldham Ath	0	0	
2002–03	Peterborough U	1	0	1 0
From Waterford
2003–04	Swansea C	11	0	
2004–05	Swansea C	2	0	
2005–06	Swansea C	0	0	
2006–07	Swansea C	0	0	13 0
2007	Bohemians	29	0	
2008	Bohemians	33	0	
2009	Bohemians	35	0	97 0
2009–10	Ipswich T	16	0	
2010–11	Ipswich T	4	0	
2011–12	Ipswich T	0	0	20 0
2011–12	QPR	0	0	
2012–13	QPR	0	0	
2013–14	QPR	2	0	
2014–15	QPR	0	0	2 0

ONUOHA, Nedum (D) 214 6
H: 6 2 W: 12 04 b.Warri 12-11-86
Internationals: England U20, U21.

2004–05	Manchester C	17	0	
2005–06	Manchester C	10	0	
2006–07	Manchester C	18	0	
2007–08	Manchester C	16	1	
2008–09	Manchester C	23	1	
2009–10	Manchester C	10	1	
2010–11	Manchester C	0	0	
2010–11	Sunderland	31	1	31 1
2011–12	Manchester C	1	0	95 3
2011–12	QPR	16	0	
2012–13	QPR	23	0	
2013–14	QPR	23	0	
2014–15	QPR	23	0	88 2

PETRASSO, Michael (M) 30 5
H: 5 6 W: 10 01 b.Toronto 9-7-95
Internationals: Canada U17, U20.

2013–14	QPR	0	0	
2013–14	Oldham Ath	11	1	11 1
2013–14	Coventry C	7	1	7 1
2014–15	QPR	0	0	1 0
2014–15	Leyton Orient	3	0	3 0
2014–15	Notts Co	8	3	8 3

PHILLIPS, Matthew (M) 224 31
H: 6 0 W: 12 10 b.Aylesbury 13-3-91
Internationals: England U19, U20. Scotland Full caps.

2007–08	Wycombe W	2	0	
2008–09	Wycombe W	37	3	
2009–10	Wycombe W	36	5	
2010–11	Wycombe W	3	0	78 8
2010–11	Blackpool	27	1	
2011–12	Blackpool	33	7	

2011–12	Sheffield U	6	5	6	5
2012–13	Blackpool	34	4		
2013–14	Blackpool	0	0	94	12
2013–14	QPR	21	3		
2014–15	QPR	25	3	46	6

ROBINSON, Jack (D)   78   0
H: 5 11 W: 10 08 b.Warrington 1-9-93
Internationals: England U16, U17, U18, U19, U21.

2009–10	Liverpool	1	0		
2010–11	Liverpool	2	0		
2011–12	Liverpool	0	0		
2012–13	Liverpool	0	0		
2012–13	Wolverhampton W	11	0	11	0
2013–14	Liverpool	0	0	3	0
2013–14	Blackpool	34	0	34	0
2014–15	QPR	0	0		
2014–15	Huddersfield T	30	0	30	0

SANDRO (M)   141   8
H: 6 2 W: 11 11 b.Riachinho 15-3-89
Internationals: Brazil U20, U23, Full caps.

2008	Internacional	7	2		
2009	Internacional	27	1		
2010	Internacional	9	1	43	4
2010–11	Tottenham H	19	1		
2011–12	Tottenham H	23	0		
2012–13	Tottenham H	22	1		
2013–14	Tottenham H	17	1	81	3
2014–15	QPR	17	1	17	1

SENDLES-WHITE, Jamie (D)   7   0
H: 6 2 W: 13 05 b.Kingston 10-4-94
Internationals: Northern Ireland U19, U21.

2011–12	QPR	0	0		
2012–13	QPR	0	0		
2013–14	QPR	0	0		
2013–14	Colchester U	0	0		
2014–15	QPR	0	0		
2014–15	Mansfield T	7	0	7	0

SUTHERLAND, Frankie (M)   8   1
H: 5 9 W: 10 00 b.Hillingdon 6-12-93
Internationals: Republic of Ireland U17, U19, U21.

2010–11	QPR	0	0		
2011–12	QPR	0	0		
2012–13	QPR	0	0		
2012–13	Portsmouth	1	0	1	0
2013–14	QPR	0	0		
2013–14	Leyton Orient	0	0		
2014–15	QPR	0	0		
2014–15	AFC Wimbledon	7	1	7	1

TAARABT, Adel (M)   193   38
H: 5 9 W: 10 12 b.Marseille 24-5-89
Internationals: France Youth. Morocco Full caps.

2006–07	Lens	1	0	1	0
2006–07	Tottenham H	2	0		
2007–08	Tottenham H	6	0		
2008–09	Tottenham H	1	0		
2008–09	QPR	7	1		
2009–10	Tottenham H	0	0	9	0
2009–10	QPR	41	7		
2010–11	QPR	44	19		
2011–12	QPR	27	2		
2012–13	QPR	31	5		
2013–14	QPR	0	0		
2013–14	Fulham	12	0	12	0
2013–14	AC Milan	14	4	14	4
2014–15	QPR	7	0	157	34

TRAORE, Armand (D)   129   3
H: 6 1 W: 12 12 b.Paris 8-10-89
Internationals: France U19, U21. Senegal Full caps.

2006–07	Arsenal	0	0		
2007–08	Arsenal	3	0		
2008–09	Arsenal	0	0		
2008–09	Portsmouth	19	1	19	1
2009–10	Arsenal	9	0		
2010–11	Arsenal	0	0		
2010–11	Juventus	10	0	10	0
2011–12	Arsenal	1	0	13	0
2011–12	QPR	23	0		
2012–13	QPR	26	0		
2013–14	QPR	22	2		
2014–15	QPR	16	0	87	2

VARGAS, Eduardo (F)   183   40
H: 5 9 W: 11 00 b.Santiago 20-11-89
Internationals: Chile U20, Full caps.

2006	Cobreloa	3	0		
2007	Cobreloa	5	0		
2008	Cobreloa	21	4		
2009	Cobreloa	24	6	53	10
2010	Univ de Chile	18	1		
2011	Univ de Chile	37	17	55	18

2011–12	Napoli	10	0		
2012–13	Napoli	9	0		
2013	Gremio	18	6	18	6
2013–14	Napoli	0	0		
2013–14	Valencia	17	3	17	3
2014–15	Napoli	0	0	19	0

On loan from Napoli.

2014–15	QPR	21	3	21	3

WRIGHT-PHILLIPS, Shaun (M)   366   40
H: 5 5 W: 10 01 b.Lewisham 25-10-81
Internationals: England U21, Full caps.

1998–99	Manchester C	0	0		
1999–2000	Manchester C	4	0		
2000–01	Manchester C	15	0		
2001–02	Manchester C	35	8		
2002–03	Manchester C	31	1		
2003–04	Manchester C	34	7		
2004–05	Manchester C	34	10		
2005–06	Chelsea	27	0		
2006–07	Chelsea	27	2		
2007–08	Chelsea	27	2		
2008–09	Chelsea	1	0	82	4
2008–09	Manchester C	27	5		
2009–10	Manchester C	30	4		
2010–11	Manchester C	7	0		
2011–12	Manchester C	0	0	217	35
2011–12	QPR	32	0		
2012–13	QPR	20	1		
2013–14	QPR	11	0		
2014–15	QPR	4	0	67	1

YUN, Suk-Young (D)   113   6
H: 6 0 W: 11 09 b.Suwon 13-2-90
Internationals: South Korea U17, U20, U23, Full caps.

2009	Jeonnam Dragons	20	1		
2010	Jeonnam Dragons	16	0		
2011	Jeonnam Dragons	19	1		
2012	Jeonnam Dragons	25	3	80	5
2012–13	QPR	0	0		
2013–14	QPR	7	1		
2013–14	Doncaster R	3	0	3	0
2014–15	QPR	23	0	30	1

ZAMORA, Bobby (F)   449   138
H: 6 1 W: 11 11 b.Barking 16-1-81
Internationals: England U21, Full caps.

1999–2000	Bristol R	4	0	4	0
1999–2000	Brighton & HA	6	6		
2000–01	Brighton & HA	43	28		
2001–02	Brighton & HA	41	28		
2002–03	Brighton & HA	35	14	125	76
2003–04	Tottenham H	16	0	16	0
2003–04	West Ham U	17	5		
2004–05	West Ham U	34	7		
2005–06	West Ham U	34	6		
2006–07	West Ham U	32	11		
2007–08	West Ham U	13	1	130	30
2008–09	Fulham	35	2		
2009–10	Fulham	27	8		
2010–11	Fulham	14	5		
2011–12	Fulham	15	5	91	20
2011–12	QPR	14	2		
2012–13	QPR	21	4		
2013–14	QPR	17	3		
2014–15	QPR	31	3	83	12

Players retained or with offer of contract
Butler, George Douglas; Cordiero, Sandro Raniere Guimaraes; Corkery, Nathan Ryan; Kakay, Osman Jovan; Manning, Ryan Phelim; Mulraney, Jake David; Pattie, Ben; Shodipo, Olamide Oluwatimilehin; Sukyoung, Yun; Sutherland, Frankie Jay; Wise, Harly John.

Scholars
Adams, Brandon Lea; Arthur, Jeremy Bernard; Clarke, Ruudi Leon; Crichlow, Gianni Dimitri; Darbyshire, Daniel Richard; Donnellan, Leo James; Garnett, Addison Righteous Adam; Hamalainen, Nicholas Antero; Herdman, Martin John; Hudnott, Conor John James; Komodikis, Andreas; Matthews, Thomas William; O'Sullivan, Callum Liam; Williams, Jack.

READING (68)

AKPAN, Hope (M)   107   6
H: 6 0 W: 10 08 b.Liverpool 14-8-91
Internationals: Nigeria Full caps.

2007–08	Everton	0	0		
2008–09	Everton	0	0		
2009–10	Everton	0	0		
2010–11	Everton	0	0		
2010–11	Hull C	2	0	2	0
2011–12	Crawley T	26	1		
2012–13	Crawley T	21	4	47	5
2012–13	Reading	9	0		
2013–14	Reading	29	1		
2014–15	Reading	20	0	58	1

ANDERSEN, Mikkel (G)   95   0
H: 6 5 W: 12 08 b.Copenhagen 17-12-88
Internationals: Denmark U19, U20, U21.

2006–07	Reading	0	0		
2007–08	Reading	0	0		
2008–09	Reading	0	0		
2008–09	Brentford	1	0	1	0
2008–09	Brighton & HA	5	0	5	0
2009–10	Reading	0	0		
2009–10	Bristol R	39	0		
2010–11	Reading	0	0		
2010–11	Bristol R	19	0	58	0
2011–12	Reading	0	0		
2012–13	Reading	0	0		
2012–13	Portsmouth	18	0	18	0
2013–14	Reading	0	0		
2013–14	Randers FC	10	0	10	0
2014–15	Reading	3	0	3	0

BLACKMAN, Nick (F)   169   33
H: 6 2 W: 11 08 b.Whitefield 11-11-89

2006–07	Macclesfield T	1	0		
2007–08	Macclesfield T	11	1		
2008–09	Macclesfield T	0	0	12	1
2008–09	Blackburn R	0	0		
2008–09	Blackpool	5	1	5	1
2009–10	Blackburn R	0	0		
2009–10	Oldham Ath	12	1	12	1
2010–11	Blackburn R	0	0		
2010–11	Motherwell	18	10	18	10
2010–11	Aberdeen	15	2	15	2
2011–12	Blackburn R	1	0		
2012–13	Blackburn R	0	0	1	0
2012–13	Sheffield U	28	11	28	11
2012–13	Reading	11	0		
2013–14	Reading	30	4		
2014–15	Reading	37	3	78	7

COOPER, Jake (D)   15   2
H: 6 4 W: 13 05 b.Bracknell 3-2-95
Internationals: England U18, U19.

2013–14	Reading	0	0		
2014–15	Reading	15	2	15	2

COX, Simon (F)   279   78
H: 5 10 W: 10 12 b.Reading 28-4-87
Internationals: Republic of Ireland Full caps.

2005–06	Reading	2	0		
2006–07	Reading	0	0		
2006–07	Brentford	13	0	13	0
2006–07	Northampton T	8	3	8	3
2007–08	Reading	0	0		
2007–08	Swindon T	36	15		
2008–09	Swindon T	45	29	81	44
2009–10	WBA	28	9		
2010–11	WBA	19	1		
2011–12	WBA	0	0		
2012–13	WBA	0	0	65	10
2012–13	Nottingham F	39	5		
2013–14	Nottingham F	34	8	73	13
2014–15	Reading	37	8	39	8

DRENTHE, Royston (M)   154   15
H: 5 6 W: 10 07 b.Rotterdam 8-4-87
Internationals: Netherlands U18, U19, U21, B, Full caps.

2005–06	Feyenoord	3	0		
2006–07	Feyenoord	26	0	29	0
2007–08	Real Madrid	18	2		
2008–09	Real Madrid	20	0		
2009–10	Real Madrid	8	0	46	2
2010–11	Hercules	14	4	14	4
2011–12	Everton	21	3	21	3
2012–13	Alania Vladikavkaz	6	3	6	3
2013–14	Reading	23	2		
2014–15	Reading	0	0	23	2
2014–15	Sheffield W	15	1	15	1

Transferred to Kayseri Erciyesspor January 2015.

EDWARDS, Ryan (M)   7   0
H: 5 7 W: 11 07 b.Sydney 17-11-93
Internationals: Australia U20, U23.

2011–12	Reading	0	0		
2012–13	Reading	0	0		
2012–13	Rochdale	0	0		
2013–14	Reading	0	0		
2014–15	Reading	7	0	7	0

FEDERICI, Adam (G)   219   1
H: 6 2   W: 14 02   b.Nowra 31-1-85
Internationals: Australia U20, U23, Full caps.

2005–06	Reading	0	0	
2006–07	Reading	2	0	
2007–08	Reading	0	0	
2008–09	Reading	15	1	
2008–09	*Southend U*	10	0	10 0
2009–10	Reading	46	0	
2010–11	Reading	34	0	
2011–12	Reading	46	0	
2012–13	Reading	21	0	
2013–14	Reading	2	0	
2014–15	Reading	43	0	209 1

FERDINAND, Anton (D)   279   5
H: 6 2   W: 11 00   b.Peckham 18-2-85
Internationals: England U18, U20, U21.

2002–03	West Ham U	0	0	
2003–04	West Ham U	20	0	
2004–05	West Ham U	29	1	
2005–06	West Ham U	33	2	
2006–07	West Ham U	31	0	
2007–08	West Ham U	25	2	
2008–09	West Ham U	0	0	138 5
2008–09	Sunderland	31	0	
2009–10	Sunderland	24	0	
2010–11	Sunderland	27	0	
2011–12	Sunderland	3	0	85 0
2011–12	QPR	31	0	
2012–13	QPR	13	0	
2012–13	*Bursaspor*	7	0	7 0
2013–14	QPR	0	0	44 0
2013–14	*Antalyaspor*	3	0	3 0
2014–15	Reading	2	0	2 0

FOSU, Tarique (M)   1   0
b. 5-11-95
Internationals: England U18.

2013–14	Reading	0	0	
2014–15	Reading	1	0	1 0

GRIFFIN, Shane (D)   0   0
b. 8-9-94
Internationals: Republic of Ireland U19, U21.

2013–14	Reading	0	0
2014–15	Reading	0	0

GUNTER, Chris (D)   276   2
H: 5 11   W: 11 02   b.Newport 21-7-89
Internationals: Wales U17, U19, U21, Full caps.

2006–07	Cardiff C	15	0	
2007–08	Cardiff C	13	0	28 0
2007–08	Tottenham H	2	0	
2008–09	Tottenham H	3	0	5 0
2008–09	*Nottingham F*	8	0	
2009–10	Nottingham F	44	1	
2010–11	Nottingham F	43	0	
2011–12	Nottingham F	46	1	141 2
2012–13	Reading	20	0	
2013–14	Reading	44	0	
2014–15	Reading	38	0	102 0

GUTHRIE, Danny (M)   198   12
H: 5 9   W: 11 06   b.Shrewsbury 18-4-87
Internationals: England U16.

2004–05	Liverpool	0	0	
2005–06	Liverpool	0	0	
2006–07	Liverpool	3	0	
2006–07	*Southampton*	10	0	10 0
2007–08	Liverpool	0	0	3 0
2007–08	*Bolton W*	25	0	25 0
2008–09	Newcastle U	24	2	
2009–10	Newcastle U	38	4	
2010–11	Newcastle U	14	0	
2011–12	Newcastle U	16	1	92 7
2012–13	Reading	21	1	
2013–14	Reading	32	4	
2014–15	Reading	9	0	62 5
2014–15	Fulham	6	0	6 0

HECTOR, Michael (D)   142   10
H: 6 4   W: 12 13   b.Newham 19-7-92
Internationals: Jamaica Full caps.

2009–10	Reading	0	0	
2010–11	Reading	0	0	
2011	*Dundalk*	11	2	11 2
2011–12	Reading	0	0	
2011–12	*Barnet*	27	2	27 2
2012–13	Reading	0	0	
2012–13	*Shrewsbury T*	8	0	8 0
2012–13	*Aldershot T*	8	1	8 1
2012–13	*Cheltenham T*	18	1	18 1
2013–14	Reading	9	0	
2013–14	*Aberdeen*	20	1	20 1
2014–15	Reading	41	3	50 3

HENLY, Jonathan (G)   0   0
H: 6 3   W: 13 00   b.Reading 7-6-94
Internationals: Scotland U19, U21.

2012–13	Reading	0	0
2013–14	Reading	0	0
2013–14	*Oxford U*	0	0
2014–15	Reading	0	0

KARACAN, Jem (M)   175   12
H: 5 10   W: 11 13   b.Lewisham 21-2-89
Internationals: Turkey U17, U18, U19, U21.

2007–08	Reading	0	0	
2007–08	*Bournemouth*	13	1	13 1
2007–08	*Millwall*	7	0	7 0
2008–09	Reading	15	1	
2009–10	Reading	27	0	
2010–11	Reading	40	3	
2011–12	Reading	37	3	
2012–13	Reading	21	1	
2013–14	Reading	7	2	
2014–15	Reading	8	1	155 11

KELLY, Liam (M)   0   0
b. 22-11-95
Internationals: Republic of Ireland U19, U21.

2014–15	Reading	0	0

KELLY, Stephen (D)   242   3
H: 6 0   W: 12 04   b.Dublin 6-9-83
Internationals: Republic of Ireland U16, U20, U21, Full caps.

2000–01	Tottenham H	0	0	
2001–02	Tottenham H	0	0	
2002–03	Tottenham H	0	0	
2002–03	*Southend U*	10	0	10 0
2002–03	*QPR*	7	0	7 0
2003–04	Tottenham H	11	0	
2003–04	*Watford*	13	0	13 0
2004–05	Tottenham H	17	2	
2005–06	Tottenham H	9	0	37 2
2006–07	Birmingham C	36	0	
2007–08	Birmingham C	38	0	
2008–09	Birmingham C	5	0	
2008–09	*Stoke C*	6	0	6 0
2009–10	Birmingham C	8	0	79 0
2010–11	Fulham	10	0	
2011–12	Fulham	24	0	
2012–13	Reading	16	0	
2012–13	Fulham	2	0	44 0
2013–14	Reading	15	1	
2014–15	Reading	15	0	46 1

KEOWN, Niall (D)   2   0
b. 5-4-95

2013–14	Reading	0	0	
2014–15	Reading	2	0	2 0

KNIGHT, Zat (D)   372   9
H: 6 6   W: 15 02   b.Solihull 2-5-80
Internationals: England U21, Full caps.

1998–99	Fulham	0	0	
1999–2000	Fulham	0	0	
1999–2000	*Peterborough U*	8	0	8 0
2000–01	Fulham	0	0	
2001–02	Fulham	10	0	
2002–03	Fulham	17	0	
2003–04	Fulham	31	0	
2004–05	Fulham	35	1	
2005–06	Fulham	30	0	
2006–07	Fulham	23	2	
2007–08	Fulham	4	0	150 3
2007–08	Aston Villa	27	1	
2008–09	Aston Villa	13	1	
2009–10	Aston Villa	0	0	40 2
2009–10	Bolton W	35	1	
2010–11	Bolton W	34	1	
2011–12	Bolton W	25	0	
2012–13	Bolton W	43	0	
2013–14	Bolton W	31	2	168 4
2014	*Colorado Rapids*	4	0	4 0
2014–15	Reading	2	0	2 0

KUHL, Aaron (M)   6   0
H: 5 8   W: 10 06   b.Paulton 30-1-96
Internationals: England U19.

2014–15	Reading	6	0	6 0

LONG, Sean (D)   0   0
H: 5 10   W: 11 00   b.Dublin 2-5-95
Internationals: Republic of Ireland U19, U21.

2013–14	Reading	0	0
2014–15	Reading	0	0

MACKIE, Jamie (F)   276   43
H: 5 8   W: 11 00   b.Dorking 22-9-85
Internationals: Scotland Full caps.

2003–04	Wimbledon	13	0	13 0
2004–05	Milton Keynes D	3	0	3 0
From Exeter C				
2007–08	Plymouth Arg	13	3	
2008–09	Plymouth Arg	43	5	
2009–10	Plymouth Arg	42	8	98 16
2010–11	QPR	25	9	
2011–12	QPR	31	7	
2012–13	QPR	29	2	85 18
2013–14	Nottingham F	45	4	45 4
2014–15	Reading	32	5	32 5

McCLEARY, Garath (M)   210   22
H: 5 10   W: 12 06   b.Oxford 15-5-87
Internationals: Jamaica Full caps.

2007–08	Nottingham F	8	1	
2008–09	Nottingham F	39	1	
2009–10	Nottingham F	24	0	
2010–11	Nottingham F	18	2	
2011–12	Nottingham F	22	9	111 13
2011–12	Reading	0	0	
2012–13	Reading	31	3	
2013–14	Reading	42	5	
2014–15	Reading	26	1	99 9

MOORE, Stuart (G)   0   0
b. 8-9-94

2013–14	Reading	0	0
2014–15	Reading	0	0

NORWOOD, Oliver (M)   157   12
H: 5 11   W: 11 13   b.Burnley 12-4-91
Internationals: England U16, U17. Northern Ireland U19, U21, B, Full caps.

2009–10	Manchester U	0	0	
2010–11	Manchester U	0	0	
2010–11	*Carlisle U*	6	0	6 0
2011–12	Manchester U	0	0	
2011–12	*Scunthorpe U*	15	1	15 1
2011–12	*Coventry C*	18	2	18 2
2012–13	Huddersfield T	39	3	
2013–14	Huddersfield T	40	5	
2014–15	Huddersfield T	1	0	80 8
2014–15	Reading	38	1	38 1

NOVAKOVICH, Andrija (F)   2   0
b. 21-9-96
Internationals: USA U18, U20.

2014–15	Reading	2	0	2 0

OBITA, Jordan (M)   104   5
H: 5 11   W: 11 08   b.Oxford 8-12-93
Internationals: England U18, U19, U21.

2010–11	Reading	0	0	
2011–12	Reading	0	0	
2011–12	*Barnet*	5	0	5 0
2011–12	*Gillingham*	6	3	6 3
2012–13	Reading	0	0	
2012–13	*Portsmouth*	8	1	8 1
2012–13	*Oldham Ath*	8	0	8 0
2013–14	Reading	34	1	
2014–15	Reading	43	0	77 1

PEARCE, Alex (D)   258   17
H: 6 0   W: 11 10   b.Wallingford 9-11-88
Internationals: Scotland U19, U21, Full caps.

2006–07	Reading	0	0	
2006–07	*Northampton T*	15	1	15 1
2007–08	Reading	0	0	
2007–08	*Bournemouth*	11	0	11 0
2007–08	*Norwich C*	11	0	11 0
2008–09	Reading	16	1	
2008–09	*Southampton*	9	2	9 2
2009–10	Reading	25	4	
2010–11	Reading	21	1	
2011–12	Reading	46	5	
2012–13	Reading	19	0	
2013–14	Reading	45	3	
2014–15	Reading	40	0	212 14

POGREBNYAK, Pavel (F)   351   107
H: 6 2   W: 14 05   b.Moscow 8-11-83
Internationals: Russia Full caps.

2002	*Spartak Moscow*	2	0	
2003	*Baltika*	40	15	40 15
2004	*Spartak Moscow*	16	2	18 2
2004	*Khimki*	12	6	12 6
2005	*Shinnik*	23	4	23 4
2006	*Tomsk*	26	13	26 13
2007	*Zenit*	24	11	
2008	*Zenit*	19	6	
2009	*Zenit*	15	5	58 22
2009–10	*Stuttgart*	28	6	
2010–11	*Stuttgart*	26	8	
2011–12	*Stuttgart*	14	1	68 15
2011–12	Fulham	12	6	12 6
2012–13	Reading	29	5	
2013–14	Reading	39	13	
2014–15	Reading	26	6	94 24

ROBSON-KANU, Hal (F)   212 30
H: 5 7   W: 11 08   b.Acton 21-5-89
Internationals: England U19, U20. Wales U21, Full caps.

2007–08	Reading	0	0		
2007–08	Southend U	8	3		
2008–09	Reading	0	0		
2008–09	Southend U	14	2	22	5
2008–09	Swindon T	20	4	20	4
2009–10	Reading	17	0		
2010–11	Reading	27	5		
2011–12	Reading	36	4		
2012–13	Reading	25	7		
2013–14	Reading	36	4		
2014–15	Reading	29	1	170	21

SAMUEL, Dominic (F)   17 6
H: 6 0   W: 14 00   b.Southwark 1-4-94
Internationals: England U19.

2011–12	Reading	0	0		
2012–13	Reading	1	0		
2012–13	Colchester U	2	0	2	0
2013–14	Reading	0	0		
2013–14	Dagenham & R	1	0	1	0
2014–15	Reading	0	0	1	0
2014–15	Coventry C	13	6	13	6

STACEY, Jack (M)   6 0
H: 6 4   W: 13 05   b.Bracknell 6-4-96

2014–15	Reading	6	0	6	0

SWEENEY, Pierce (D)   0 0
H: 5 10   W: 12 07   b. 11-9-94
Internationals: Republic of Ireland U17, U19, U21.

2012–13	Reading	0	0
2013–14	Reading	0	0
2014–15	Reading	0	0

TANNER, Craig (F)   22 0
H: 5 7   W: 11 05   b.Reading 27-10-94

2011–12	Reading	0	0		
2012–13	Reading	0	0		
2013–14	Reading	0	0		
2014–15	Reading	3	0	3	0
2014–15	AFC Wimbledon	19	0	19	0

TAYLOR, Jake (M)   79 6
H: 5 10   W: 12 01   b.Ascot 1-12-91 caps.

2010–11	Reading	1	0		
2011–12	Reading	0	0		
2011–12	Aldershot T	3	0	3	0
2011–12	Exeter C	30	3	30	3
2012–13	Reading	0	0		
2012–13	Cheltenham T	8	1	8	1
2012–13	Crawley T	4	0	4	0
2013–14	Reading	8	0		
2014–15	Reading	22	2	31	2
2014–15	Leyton Orient	3	0	3	0

TRAVNER, Jure (D)   266 9
H: 5 11   W: 12 08   b.Celje 28-9-85

2004–05	Celje	2	0		
2004–05	Smartno	20	1	20	1
2005–06	Celje	25	0		
2005–06	Dravograd	6	0	6	0
2006–07	Celje	31	0		
2007–08	Celje	28	0		
2008–09	Celje	29	1	115	1
2009–10	Watford	0	0		
2010–11	Watford	0	0		
2010–11	St Mirren	37	1	37	1
2011–12	Ludogorets	3	0	3	0
2011–12	Mura 05	14	1		
2012–13	Mura 05	28	1	42	2
2013–14	Baku	35	3		
2014–15	Baku	7	1	42	4
2014–15	Reading	1	0	1	0

TSHIBOLA, Aaron (M)   24 0
H: 6 3   W: 11 01   b.Newham 2-1-95
Internationals: England U18.

2011–12	Reading	0	0		
2012–13	Reading	0	0		
2013–14	Reading	0	0		
2014–15	Reading	1	0	1	0
2014–15	Hartlepool U	23	0	23	0

VASTSUK, Bogdan (F)   0 0
b. 4-10-95
Internationals: Estonia U16, U17, U19, U21.

2013–14	Reading	0	0

WILLIAMS, Daniel (M)   113 5
H: 6 0   W: 11 12   b.Karlsruhe 8-3-89
Internationals: USA Full caps.

2009–10	SC Freiburg	5	0		
2010–11	SC Freiburg	7	0		
2011–12	SC Freiburg	1	0	13	0
2011–12	Hoffenheim	24	0		
2012–13	Hoffenheim	21	1	45	1
2013–14	Reading	30	3		
2014–15	Reading	25	1	55	4

YAKUBU, Ayegbeni (F)   403 162
H: 6 0   W: 14 07   b.Benin City 22-11-82
Internationals: Nigeria U21, U23, Full caps.

1999–2000	Gil Vicente	0	0		
1999–2000	Hapoel Kfar-Sava	23	6	23	6
2000–01	Maccabi Haifa	14	3		
2001–02	Maccabi Haifa	22	13	36	16
2002–03	Portsmouth	14	7		
2003–04	Portsmouth	37	16		
2004–05	Portsmouth	30	12	81	35
2005–06	Middlesbrough	34	13		
2006–07	Middlesbrough	37	12		
2007–08	Middlesbrough	2	0	73	25
2007–08	Everton	29	15		
2008–09	Everton	14	4		
2009–10	Everton	25	5		
2010–11	Everton	14	1		
2010–11	Leicester C	20	11	20	11
2011–12	Everton	0	0	82	25
2011–12	Blackburn R	30	17	30	17
2012–13	Guangzhou R&F	43	24	43	24
2013–14	Al Rayyan	8	3	8	3
2014–15	Reading	7	0	7	0

Players retained or with offer of contract
Andresson, Axel Oskar; Cardwell, Harry James; Dickie, Robert Joseph Andrew; Fridjonsson, Samuel Kari; Husin, Noor; Hyam, Dominic John; Lawal, Hammed; Legg, George Jack Adam; Owusu, Nana; Shaughnessy, Conor Glynn; Urbancic, Tomas Ingi; Ward, Lewis Moore; Watson, Tennai Rosharne.

Scholars
Akinwunmi, Daniel Oladapo Ayoola; Barrett, Joshua Lee; Bennett, Harrison George; Chatee, Joshua William; Collings, Billy Paul; Collins, Lewis James; Davis, Conor Florin; East, Ryan Henry; Ethelston, Marc Connor; Ismajli, Shpat; Jules, Zak Kennedy; Osho, Gabriel Jeremiah Adedayo; Richards, Omar Tyrell Crawford; Scheving, Sindri; Sheppard, Jake Edwin; Smith, Samuel Toby; Southwood, Luke Kevin; Thompson-Lee, Justin Nathan; Tupper, Joe Daniel; Waritay, Amadu; Williams, Daniel Olamide Cecil.

ROCHDALE (69)

ALLEN, Jamie (M)   60 6
H: 5 11   W: 11 05   b.Rochdale 29-1-95

2012–13	Rochdale	0	0		
2013–14	Rochdale	25	6		
2014–15	Rochdale	35	0	60	6

ANDREW, Calvin (F)   228 17
H: 6 0   W: 12 11   b.Luton 19-12-86

2004–05	Luton T	8	0		
2005–06	Luton T	1	1		
2005–06	Grimsby T	8	1	8	1
2005–06	Bristol C	3	0	3	0
2006–07	Luton T	7	0		
2007–08	Luton T	39	2	55	4
2008–09	Crystal Palace	7	0		
2008–09	Brighton & HA	9	2	9	2
2009–10	Crystal Palace	27	1		
2010–11	Crystal Palace	13	0		
2010–11	Millwall	10	1	10	1
2010–11	Swindon T	10	1	10	1
2011–12	Crystal Palace	6	0	53	1
2011–12	Leyton Orient	10	0	10	0
2012–13	Port Vale	22	1		
2013–14	Port Vale	0	0	22	1
2013–14	Mansfield T	15	1	15	1
2013–14	York C	8	1	8	1
2014–15	Rochdale	32	5	32	5

BARRY-MURPHY, Brian (M)   457 17
H: 5 10   W: 13 01   b.Cork 27-7-78
Internationals: Republic of Ireland U21.

1995–96	Cork C	13	0		
1996–97	Cork C	25	0		
1997–98	Cork C	15	1		
1998–99	Cork C	27	1	80	2
1999–2000	Preston NE	1	0		
2000–01	Preston NE	14	0		
2001–02	Preston NE	4	0		
2001–02	Southend U	8	1	8	1
2002–03	Preston NE	2	0	21	0
2002–03	Hartlepool U	7	0	7	0
2002–03	Sheffield W	17	0		
2003–04	Sheffield W	41	0	58	0
2004–05	Bury	45	6		
2005–06	Bury	40	3		
2006–07	Bury	14	0		
2007–08	Bury	31	1		
2008–09	Bury	42	2		
2009–10	Bury	46	1	218	13
2010–11	Rochdale	32	0		
2011–12	Rochdale	22	1		
2012–13	Rochdale	8	0		
2013–14	Rochdale	3	0		
2014–15	Rochdale	0	0	65	1

BELL, Nyal (D)   3 0
b.Manchester 17-1-97

2014–15	Rochdale	3	0	3	0

BENNETT, Rhys (D)   80 2
H: 6 3   W: 12 00   b.Manchester 1-9-91

2011–12	Bolton W	0	0		
2011–12	Falkirk	19	0	19	0
2013–14	Rochdale	22	0		
2014–15	Rochdale	39	2	61	2

BRANDY, Febian (F)   145 20
H: 5 6   W: 9 13   b.Manchester 4-2-89
Internationals: England U16, U17, U18, U19, U20.

2006–07	Manchester U	0	0		
2007–08	Manchester U	0	0		
2007–08	Swansea C	19	3		
2008–09	Manchester U	0	0		
2008–09	Swansea C	14	0	33	3
2008–09	Hereford U	15	4	15	4
2009–10	Manchester U	0	0		
2009–10	Gillingham	7	1	7	1
2010–11	Notts Co	9	0	9	0
2012–13	Walsall	34	7		
2013–14	Sheffield U	14	0	14	0
2013–14	Walsall	20	4	54	11
2014–15	Rotherham U	1	0	1	0
2014–15	Crewe Alex	8	1	8	1
2014–15	Rochdale	4	0	4	0

BUNNEY, Joe (F)   41 6
H: 6 1   W: 11 00   b.Manchester 26-9-93

2012–13	Rochdale	1	1		
2013–14	Rochdale	21	3		
2014–15	Rochdale	19	2	41	6

CAMPS, Callum (M)   14 1
b.Stockport 30-11-95
Internationals: Northern Ireland U18.

2012–13	Rochdale	2	0		
2013–14	Rochdale	0	0		
2014–15	Rochdale	12	1	14	1

CANNON, Andy (M)   18 0
H: 5 9   W: 11 09   b. 14-3-96

2014–15	Rochdale	18	0	18	0

COLLIS, Steve (G)   88 0
H: 6 3   W: 12 05   b.Harrow 18-3-81

1999–2000	Barnet	0	0		
2000–01	Nottingham F	0	0		
2001–02	Nottingham F	0	0		
2003–04	Yeovil T	11	0		
2004–05	Yeovil T	9	0		
2005–06	Yeovil T	23	0	43	0
2006–07	Southend U	1	0		
2007–08	Southend U	20	0	21	0
2008–09	Crewe Alex	18	0		
2009–10	Crewe Alex	1	0	19	0
2009–10	Bristol C	0	0		
2009–10	Torquay U	1	0	1	0
2010–11	Peterborough U	0	0		
2010–11	Northampton T	4	0	4	0
2011–12	Macclesfield T	0	0		
2012–13	Rochdale	0	0		
2013–14	Rochdale	0	0		
2014–15	Rochdale	0	0		

DAWSON, Stephen (M)   376 18
H: 5 9   W: 11 09   b.Dublin 4-12-85
Internationals: Republic of Ireland U21.

2003–04	Leicester	0	0		
2004–05	Leicester	0	0		
2005–06	Mansfield T	40	1		
2006–07	Mansfield T	34	1		
2007–08	Mansfield T	43	2	117	4
2008–09	Bury	43	2		
2009–10	Bury	45	4	88	6

2010–11 Leyton Orient 40 2
2011–12 Leyton Orient 20 1 **60 3**
2011–12 Barnsley 12 0
2012–13 Barnsley 32 4
2013–14 Barnsley 37 1 **81 5**
2014–15 Rochdale 30 0 **30 0**

DIBA MUSANGU, Jonathan (G) **1 0**
H: 6 0 W: 11 09 b.Mbuji-Mayi 12-10-97
2014–15 Rochdale 1 0 **1 0**

EASTHAM, Ashley (D) **135 4**
H: 6 3 W: 12 06 b.Preston 22-3-91
2009–10 Blackpool 1 0
2009–10 Cheltenham T 20 0
2010–11 Blackpool 0 0
2010–11 Cheltenham T 9 0 **29 0**
2010–11 Carlisle U 0 0
2011–12 Blackpool 0 0
2011–12 Bury 25 2
2012–13 Blackpool 0 0 **1 0**
2012–13 Fleetwood T 1 0 **1 0**
2012–13 Notts Co 4 0 **4 0**
2012–13 Bury 19 0 **44 2**
2013–14 Rochdale 15 0
2014–15 Rochdale 41 2 **56 2**

HASLER-CREGG, Billy (F) **0 0**
H: 5 8 W: 9 08 b.Accrington 11-9-96
2014–15 Rochdale 0 0

HENDERSON, Ian (F) **351 68**
H: 5 10 W: 11 06 b.Thetford 25-1-85
Internationals: England U18, U20.
2002–03 Norwich C 20 1
2003–04 Norwich C 19 4
2004–05 Norwich C 3 0
2005–06 Norwich C 24 1
2006–07 Norwich C 2 0 **68 6**
2006–07 *Rotherham U* 18 1 **18 1**
2007–08 Northampton T 23 0
2008–09 Northampton T 3 0 **26 0**
2008–09 Luton T 19 1 **19 1**
2009–10 Colchester U 13 2
2009–10 Ankaragucu 2 0 **2 0**
2010–11 Colchester U 36 10
2011–12 Colchester U 46 9
2012–13 Colchester U 22 3 **117 24**
2012–13 Rochdale 12 3
2013–14 Rochdale 45 11
2014–15 Rochdale 44 22 **101 36**

HERY, Bastien (M) **33 2**
b.Brou sur Chantereine 23-3-92
Internationals: France U18.
2012–13 Sheffield W 0 0
2013–14 Rochdale 12 1
2014–15 Rochdale 21 1 **33 2**

HOOPER, James (D) **0 0**
2014–15 Rochdale 0 0

KENNEDY, Tom (D) **409 15**
H: 5 10 W: 11 01 b.Bury 24-6-85
2002–03 Bury 0 0
2003–04 Bury 27 0
2004–05 Bury 46 1
2005–06 Bury 33 4
2006–07 Bury 37 0
2007–08 Rochdale 43 2
2008–09 Rochdale 45 4
2009–10 Rochdale 44 3
2010–11 Leicester C 1 0
2010–11 *Rochdale* 6 0
2010–11 Peterborough U 14 0
2011–12 Leicester C 5 0
2011–12 *Peterborough U* 10 0 **24 0**
2012–13 Leicester C 0 0 **6 0**
2012–13 Barnsley 24 0
2013–14 Barnsley 44 1 **68 1**
2014–15 Rochdale 23 0 **161 9**
2014–15 Bury 2 0 **145 5**
2014–15 Blackpool 5 0 **5 0**

KISIMBA, Kisimba (M) **0 0**
H: 5 9 W: 11 11 b. 23-10-97
2014–15 Rochdale 0 0

LANCASHIRE, Oliver (D) **158 2**
H: 6 1 W: 11 10 b.Basingstoke 13-12-88
2006–07 Southampton 0 0
2007–08 Southampton 0 0
2008–09 Southampton 1 0
2009–10 Southampton 2 0 **13 0**
2009–10 *Grimsby T* 25 1 **25 1**
2010–11 Walsall 29 0
2011–12 Walsall 20 1 **49 1**
2012–13 Aldershot T 12 0 **12 0**
2013–14 Rochdale 38 0
2014–15 Rochdale 21 0 **59 0**

LILLIS, Josh (G) **178 0**
H: 6 0 W: 12 08 b.Derby 24-6-87
2006–07 Scunthorpe U 1 0
2007–08 Scunthorpe U 3 0
2008–09 Scunthorpe U 5 0
2008–09 Notts Co 5 0 **5 0**
2009–10 Scunthorpe U 8 0
2009–10 Grimsby T 4 0 **4 0**
2009–10 *Rochdale* 1 0
2010–11 Scunthorpe U 15 0
2010–11 *Rochdale* 23 0
2011–12 Scunthorpe U 6 0 **38 0**
2012–13 Rochdale 46 0
2013–14 Rochdale 45 0
2014–15 Rochdale 16 0 **131 0**

LOGAN, Joel (F) **13 0**
H: 5 11 W: 11 00 b.Manchester 25-1-95
2012–13 Rochdale 5 0
2013–14 Rochdale 0 0
2014–15 Rochdale 8 0 **13 0**

LUND, Matthew (M) **102 15**
H: 6 0 W: 11 13 b.Manchester 21-11-90
Internationals: Northern Ireland U21.
2009–10 Stoke C 0 0
2010–11 Stoke C 0 0
2010–11 Hereford U 2 0 **2 0**
2011–12 Stoke C 0 0
2011–12 Oldham Ath 3 0 **3 0**
2011–12 Bristol R 13 2
2012–13 Stoke C 0 0
2012–13 Bristol R 18 2 **31 4**
2012–13 Southend U 12 1 **12 1**
2013–14 Rochdale 40 8
2014–15 Rochdale 14 2 **54 10**

McDERMOTT, Donal (F) **63 7**
H: 6 6 W: 12 00 b.Co. Meath 19-10-89
2007–08 Manchester C 0 0
2008–09 Manchester C 0 0
2008–09 Milton Keynes D 1 0 **1 0**
2009–10 Manchester C 0 0
2009–10 Chesterfield 15 5 **15 5**
2009–10 Scunthorpe U 9 0 **9 0**
2010–11 Manchester C 0 0
2010–11 Bournemouth 9 1
2011–12 Huddersfield T 9 0 **9 0**
2011–12 Bournemouth 14 1
2012–13 Bournemouth 6 0
2013–14 Bournemouth 0 0 **29 2**
2014–15 Rochdale 0 0

McGINTY, Sean (D) **13 0**
H: 6 0 W: 11 09 b.Maidstone 11-8-93
Internationals: Republic of Ireland U17, U19, U21.
2010–11 Manchester U 0 0
2011–12 Manchester U 0 0
2011–12 Morecambe 4 0 **4 0**
2012–13 Manchester U 0 0
2012–13 Oxford U 0 0
2012–13 Carlisle U 1 0 **1 0**
2012–13 Tranmere R 3 0 **3 0**
2013–14 Sheffield U 2 0 **2 0**
2013–14 *Northampton T* 2 0 **2 0**
2013–14 Rochdale 1 0
2014–15 Rochdale 0 0 **1 0**

MULDOON, Jack (F) **3 0**
b.Scunthorpe 19-5-89
2014–15 Rochdale 3 0 **3 0**

NOBLE-LAZARUS, Reuben (F) **69 4**
H: 5 11 W: 13 07 b.Huddersfield 16-8-93
2008–09 Barnsley 2 0
2009–10 Barnsley 2 0
2010–11 Barnsley 7 1
2011–12 Barnsley 8 0
2012–13 Barnsley 14 1
2013–14 Barnsley 12 1
2013–14 Scunthorpe U 4 0 **4 0**
2014–15 Barnsley 1 0 **46 3**
2014–15 Rochdale 19 1 **19 1**

RAFFERTY, Joe (D) **83 1**
H: 6 0 W: 11 11 b.Liverpool 6-10-93
Internationals: Republic of Ireland U18, U19.
2012–13 Rochdale 21 0
2013–14 Rochdale 31 0
2014–15 Rochdale 31 1 **83 1**

ROSE, Michael (D) **334 22**
H: 5 11 W: 12 04 b.Salford 28-7-82
Internationals: England C.
1999–2000 Manchester U 0 0
2000–01 Manchester U 0 0
2001–02 Manchester U 0 0
From Hereford U
2004–05 Yeovil T 40 1

2005–06 Yeovil T 1 0 **41 1**
2005–06 *Cheltenham T* 3 0 **3 0**
2005–06 *Scunthorpe U* 15 0 **15 0**
2006–07 Stockport Co 25 3
2007–08 Stockport Co 28 3
2008–09 Stockport Co 27 0
2009–10 Stockport Co 24 2 **104 8**
2009–10 Norwich C 12 1 **12 1**
2010–11 Swindon T 35 3 **35 3**
2010–11 Colchester U 0 0
2011–12 Colchester U 14 0
2012–13 Colchester U 22 2 **36 2**
2012–13 Rochdale 14 2
2013–14 Rochdale 42 4
2014–15 Rochdale 32 1 **88 7**

TANSER, Scott (D) **31 1**
b.Blackpool 23-10-94
2012–13 Rochdale 1 0
2013–14 Rochdale 0 0
2014–15 Rochdale 30 1 **31 1**

VINCENTI, Peter (F) **188 33**
H: 6 2 W: 11 13 b.St Peter 7-7-86
2007–08 Millwall 0 0
2010–11 Stevenage 5 1 **5 1**
2010–11 Aldershot T 23 6
2011–12 Aldershot T 42 6
2012–13 Aldershot T 39 2 **104 14**
2013–14 Rochdale 42 5
2014–15 Rochdale 37 13 **79 18**

Scholars
Bell, Nyal Aston Nathanial; Berry, Tyler James; Cowan-Thompson, Connor Richard; Coyne, Louis Patrick; Hasler-Cregg, William David; Hooper, James; Kisimba, Kisimba Arnon; Lovett, Rhys Christian; Pratt, Harry Partick; Reid, Dominic Michael; Samuels, Abayomi Jonathan Akinwale; Schorah, Callum Patrick; Sinclair, Omar Jermaine Kareem; Smalley, Brandon Joe.

ROTHERHAM U (70)

ARNASON, Kari (M) **356 17**
H: 6 3 W: 13 06 b.Reykjavik 13-10-82
Internationals: Iceland Full caps.
2001 Vikingur 5 2
2002 Vikingur 5 1
2003 Vikingur 16 0
2004 Vikingur 15 0 **41 3**
2005 Djurgarden 21 0
2006 Djurgarden 14 0 **35 0**
2006–07 Aarhus 14 2
2007–08 Aarhus 25 0
2008–09 Aarhus 12 1 **51 3**
2008–09 Esbjerg 8 0 **8 0**
2009–10 Plymouth Arg 32 2
2010–11 Plymouth Arg 40 1 **72 3**
2011–12 Aberdeen 33 3 **33 3**
2012–13 Rotherham U 33 2
2013–14 Rotherham U 40 0
2014–15 Rotherham U 43 3 **116 5**

BOWERY, Jordan (F) **138 15**
H: 6 1 W: 12 00 b.Nottingham 2-7-91
2008–09 Chesterfield 3 0
2009–10 Chesterfield 10 0
2010–11 Chesterfield 27 1
2011–12 Chesterfield 40 8
2012–13 Chesterfield 3 1 **83 10**
2012–13 Aston Villa 10 0
2013–14 Aston Villa 9 0 **19 0**
2013–14 *Doncaster R* 3 0 **3 0**
2014–15 Rotherham U 33 5 **33 5**

BRADLEY, Mark (D) **187 9**
H: 6 0 W: 11 05 b.Dudley 14-1-88
Internationals: Wales Youth, U21, Full caps.
2004–05 Walsall 1 0
2005–06 Walsall 3 0
2006–07 Walsall 1 0
2007–08 Walsall 35 3
2008–09 Walsall 28 2
2009–10 Walsall 28 0 **96 5**
2010–11 Rotherham U 21 0
2011–12 Rotherham U 21 1
2012–13 Rotherham U 27 1
2013–14 Rotherham U 22 2
2014–15 Rotherham U 0 0 **91 4**

BRINDLEY, Richard (D) **44 0**
H: 5 10 W: 11 09 b.Coventry 30-11-87
2012–13 Chesterfield 12 0 **12 0**
2013–14 Rotherham U 16 0
2014–15 Rotherham U 2 0 **18 0**

2014–15	Scunthorpe U	3	0	3	0
2014–15	Oxford U	3	0	3	0
2014–15	Colchester U	8	0	8	0

BROADFOOT, Kirk (D)   322 16
H: 6 3   W: 13 13   b.Irvine 8-8-84
Internationals: Scotland U21, B, Full caps.

2002–03	St Mirren	23	1		
2003–04	St Mirren	31	3		
2004–05	St Mirren	36	4		
2005–06	St Mirren	27	2		
2006–07	St Mirren	37	3	154	13
2007–08	Rangers	15	1		
2008–09	Rangers	27	0		
2009–10	Rangers	12	0		
2010–11	Rangers	8	0		
2011–12	Rangers	16	0	78	1
2012–13	Blackpool	32	2		
2013–14	Blackpool	33	0	65	2
2014–15	Rotherham U	25	0	25	0

CLARKE-HARRIS, Jonson (F)   89 15
H: 6 0   W: 11 01   b.Leicester 21-7-94

2012–13	Peterborough U	0	0		
2012–13	Southend U	3	0	3	0
2012–13	Bury	12	4	12	4
2013–14	Oldham Ath	40	6		
2014–15	Oldham Ath	5	1	45	7
2014–15	Rotherham U	15	3	15	3
2014–15	Milton Keynes D	5	0	5	0
2014–15	Doncaster R	9	1	9	1

COLLIN, Adam (G)   203 0
H: 6 2   W: 12 00   b.Penrith 9-12-84

| 2003–04 | Newcastle U | 0 | 0 | | |
| 2003–04 | Oldham Ath | 0 | 0 | | |

From Workington

2009–10	Carlisle U	29	0		
2010–11	Carlisle U	46	0		
2011–12	Carlisle U	46	0		
2012–13	Carlisle U	12	0	133	0
2013–14	Rotherham U	34	0		
2014–15	Rotherham U	36	0	70	0

DERBYSHIRE, Matt (F)   238 52
H: 5 10   W: 11 01   b.Gt Harwood 14-4-86
Internationals: England U21.

2003–04	Blackburn R	0	0		
2004–05	Blackburn R	1	0		
2005–06	Blackburn R	0	0		
2005–06	*Plymouth Arg*	12	0	12	0
2005–06	*Wrexham*	16	10	16	10
2006–07	Blackburn R	22	5		
2007–08	Blackburn R	23	3		
2008–09	Blackburn R	17	2	63	10
2008–09	*Olympiacos*	7	5		
2009–10	*Olympiacos*	19	6		
2010–11	*Olympiacos*	0	0	26	11
2010–11	*Birmingham C*	13	0	13	0
2011–12	Nottingham F	15	1		
2012–13	Nottingham F	0	0		
2012–13	*Oldham Ath*	18	4	18	4
2012–13	*Blackpool*	12	0		
2013–14	Blackpool	0	0	12	0
2013–14	Nottingham F	29	7	44	8
2014–15	Rotherham U	34	9	34	9

FRECKLINGTON, Lee (M)   316 47
H: 5 8   W: 11 00   b.Lincoln 8-9-85
Internationals: Republic of Ireland B.

2003–04	Lincoln C	0	0		
2004–05	Lincoln C	3	0		
2005–06	Lincoln C	18	2		
2006–07	Lincoln C	42	8		
2007–08	Lincoln C	34	4		
2008–09	Lincoln C	27	7	124	21
2008–09	Peterborough U	7	0		
2009–10	Peterborough U	35	2		
2010–11	Peterborough U	9	1		
2011–12	Peterborough U	37	5		
2012–13	Peterborough U	5	0	93	8
2012–13	*Rotherham U*	31	6		
2013–14	Rotherham U	39	10		
2014–15	Rotherham U	29	2	99	18

GREEN, Paul (M)   415 42
H: 5 9   W: 10 02   b.Pontefract 10-4-83
Internationals: Republic of Ireland Full caps.

2003–04	Doncaster R	43	8		
2004–05	Doncaster R	42	7		
2005–06	Doncaster R	34	3		
2006–07	Doncaster R	41	2		
2007–08	Doncaster R	38	5	198	25
2008–09	Derby Co	29	3		
2009–10	Derby Co	33	2		
2010–11	Derby Co	36	2		
2011–12	Derby Co	27	1	125	8
2012–13	Leeds U	32	4		
2013–14	Leeds U	9	0	41	4

| 2013–14 | Ipswich T | 14 | 2 | 14 | 2 |
| 2014–15 | Rotherham U | 37 | 3 | 37 | 3 |

LOACH, Scott (G)   219 0
H: 6 1   W: 13 01   b.Nottingham 27-5-88
Internationals: England U21.

2006–07	Watford	0	0		
2007–08	Watford	0	0		
2007–08	Morecambe	2	0	2	0
2007–08	*Bradford C*	20	0	20	0
2008–09	Watford	31	0		
2009–10	Watford	46	0		
2010–11	Watford	46	0		
2011–12	Watford	31	0	154	0
2012–13	Ipswich T	22	0		
2013–14	Ipswich T	6	0	28	0
2014–15	Rotherham U	2	0	2	0
2014–15	Bury	2	0	2	0
2014–15	*Peterborough U*	5	0	5	0
2014–15	*Yeovil T*	6	0	6	0

LUCAS, Reece (D)   0 0
b. 28-9-95

| 2014–15 | Rotherham U | 0 | 0 | | |

MILSOM, Robert (M)   117 3
H: 5 10   W: 11 04   b.Redhill 2-1-87

2005–06	Fulham	0	0		
2006–07	Fulham	0	0		
2007–08	Fulham	0	0		
2007–08	Brentford	6	0	6	0
2008–09	Fulham	1	0		
2008–09	Southend U	6	0	6	0
2009–10	Fulham	0	0		
2010	TPS Turku	14	0	14	0
2010–11	Fulham	0	0	1	0
2010–11	Aberdeen	18	1		
2011–12	Aberdeen	22	1		
2012–13	Aberdeen	13	0	53	2
2013–14	Rotherham U	27	1		
2014–15	Rotherham U	8	0	35	1
2014–15	Bury	2	0	2	0

MORGAN, Craig (D)   362 9
H: 6 0   W: 11 04   b.Flint 18-6-85
Internationals: Wales U17, U19, U21, Full caps.

2001–02	Wrexham	9	0		
2002–03	Wrexham	6	1		
2003–04	Wrexham	18	0		
2004–05	Wrexham	26	0		
2005–06	Milton Keynes D	9	0		
2006–07	Milton Keynes D	3	0	43	0
2006–07	*Wrexham*	1	0	53	1
2006–07	Peterborough U	23	1		
2007–08	Peterborough U	41	2		
2008–09	Peterborough U	27	0		
2009–10	Peterborough U	34	1	125	4
2010–11	Preston NE	31	2		
2011–12	Preston NE	19	1		
2012–13	Preston NE	0	0	50	3
2012–13	*Rotherham U*	21	1		
2013–14	Rotherham U	35	0		
2014–15	Rotherham U	35	0	91	1

NEWTON, Conor (M)   29 2
H: 5 11   W: 11 00   b.Whickham 17-10-91

2010–11	Newcastle U	0	0		
2011–12	Newcastle U	0	0		
2012–13	Newcastle U	0	0		
2012–13	*St Mirren*	16	2	16	2
2014–15	Rotherham U	13	0	13	0

PRINGLE, Ben (M)   172 19
H: 5 8   W: 11 10   b.Whitley Bay 25-7-88

2009–10	Derby Co	5	0		
2010–11	Derby Co	15	0	20	0
2010–11	*Torquay U*	5	0	5	0
2011–12	Rotherham U	21	4		
2012–13	Rotherham U	41	7		
2013–14	Rotherham U	45	5		
2014–15	Rotherham U	40	3	147	19

RICHARDSON, Frazer (D)   301 5
H: 5 11   W: 11 12   b.Rotherham 29-10-82

1999-2000	Leeds U	0	0		
2000–01	Leeds U	0	0		
2001–02	Leeds U	0	0		
2002–03	Leeds U	0	0		
2002–03	*Stoke C*	7	0		
2003–04	Leeds U	0	0		
2003–04	*Stoke C*	6	1	13	1
2004–05	Leeds U	38	1		
2005–06	Leeds U	23	1		
2006–07	Leeds U	22	0		
2007–08	Leeds U	39	1		
2008–09	Leeds U	23	0	149	3
2009–10	Charlton Ath	38	1	38	1
2010–11	Southampton	21	0		
2011–12	Southampton	34	0		

2012–13	Southampton	5	0	60	0
2013–14	Middlesbrough	11	0	11	0
2013–14	*Ipswich T*	7	0	7	0
2014–15	Rotherham U	23	0	23	0

ROSE, Mitchell (M)   6 0
H: 5 9   W: 12 03   b. 4-7-94

2012–13	Rotherham U	5	0		
2013–14	Rotherham U	0	0		
2014–15	Rotherham U	0	0	5	0
2014–15	*Crawley T*	1	0	1	0

ROWE, Daniel (D)   23 0
H: 6 2   W: 12 08   b.Middlesbrough 24-10-95

2012–13	Rotherham U	0	0		
2013–14	Rotherham U	0	0		
2013–14	*Wycombe W*	7	0		
2014–15	Rotherham U	0	0		
2014–15	*Wycombe W*	16	0	23	0

THOMPSON, Tony (G)   0 0
H: 6 0   W: 13 01   b.Liverpool 4-11-94

2012–13	Rotherham U	0	0		
2013–14	Rotherham U	0	0		
2014–15	Rotherham U	0	0		

TIDSER, Michael (M)   32 0
H: 6 0   W: 11 13   b.Glasgow 15-1-90
Internationals: Scotland U18, U19.

2013–14	Rotherham U	10	0		
2013–14	*Ross Co*	16	0	16	0
2014–15	Rotherham U	1	0	11	0
2014–15	*Oldham Ath*	5	0	5	0

WOOD, Richard (D)   325 18
H: 6 3   W: 12 13   b.Ossett 5-7-85

2002–03	Sheffield W	3	1		
2003–04	Sheffield W	12	0		
2004–05	Sheffield W	34	1		
2005–06	Sheffield W	30	1		
2006–07	Sheffield W	12	0		
2007–08	Sheffield W	27	2		
2008–09	Sheffield W	42	0		
2009–10	Sheffield W	11	2	171	7
2009–10	Coventry C	24	3		
2010–11	Coventry C	40	1		
2011–12	Coventry C	17	1		
2012–13	Coventry C	36	3	117	8
2013–14	Charlton Ath	21	0	21	0
2014–15	Rotherham U	6	0	6	0
2014–15	*Crawley T*	10	3	10	3

YATES, Jerry (M)   1 0
H: 5 9   W: 10 10   b.Doncaster 10-11-96

| 2014–15 | Rotherham U | 1 | 0 | 1 | 0 |

Players retained or with offer of contract
Smallwood, Richard; Ward, Daniel Carl.

Scholars
Bailey, Fabian Paul Richard; Bailey-King, Darnelle; Bilboe, Laurence Sidney; Denton, Peter Richard; Dickinson, Ross; Fenton, Jake; Gibson, Luke; Hallatt, Max; Johnson, Adam; Muskwe, Kudakwashe; Norfolk, Andrew Brian; Peace-McDonald, Bradley William; Potts, Brandon Russell; Rose, Thomas Andrew; Smalley, Daniel Matthew; Warren, Mason Rhys; Wiles, Alexander Peter; Yates, Jerry Arron.

SCUNTHORPE U (71)

ADELAKUN, Hakeeb (F)   62 8
H: 6 3   W: 11 11   b.Hackney 11-6-96

2012–13	Scunthorpe U	2	0		
2013–14	Scunthorpe U	28	2		
2014–15	Scunthorpe U	32	6	62	8

ANYON, Joe (G)   11 0
H: 6 4   W: 14 01   b.Blackpool 29-12-86
Internationals: England U16.

2006–07	Port Vale	0	0		
2010–11	Lincoln C	0	0		
2010–11	Morecambe	0	0		
2012–13	Shrewsbury T	0	0		
2013–14	Shrewsbury T	11	0		
2014–15	Shrewsbury T	0	0	11	0
2014–15	Scunthorpe U	0	0		

BISHOP, Neil (M)   321 19
H: 6 1   W: 12 10   b.Stockton 7-8-81
Internationals: England C.

2007–08	Barnet	39	2		
2008–09	Barnet	44	1	83	3
2009–10	Notts Co	43	1		
2010–11	Notts Co	43	1		
2011–12	Notts Co	41	2		
2012–13	Notts Co	41	7	168	11

2013–14	Blackpool	35	1	35	1
2014–15	Scunthorpe U	35	4	35	4

BOYCE, Andrew (D) 31 1
H: 6 3 W: 12 08 b.Doncaster 5-11-89

2013–14	Scunthorpe U	2	0		
2014–15	Scunthorpe U	29	1	31	1

BURDETT, Noel (F) 0 0
b. 13-11-97

2013–14	Scunthorpe U	0	0		
2014–15	Scunthorpe U	0	0		

BURTON, Deon (F) 593 140
H: 5 10 W: 11 08 b.Ashford 25-10-76
Internationals: Jamaica Full caps.

1993–94	Portsmouth	2	0		
1994–95	Portsmouth	7	2		
1995–96	Portsmouth	32	7		
1996–97	Portsmouth	21	1		
1996–97	Cardiff C	5	2	5	2
1997–98	Derby Co	29	3		
1998–99	Derby Co	21	9		
1998–99	Barnsley	3	0	3	0
1999–2000	Derby Co	19	4		
2000–01	Derby Co	32	5		
2001–02	Derby Co	17	1		
2001–02	Stoke C	12	2	12	2
2002–03	Derby Co	7	3	125	25
2002–03	Portsmouth	15	4		
2003–04	Portsmouth	1	0	78	14
2003–04	Walsall	3	0	3	0
2003–04	Swindon T	4	1	4	1
2004–05	Brentford	40	10	40	10
2005–06	Rotherham U	24	12	24	12
2005–06	Sheffield W	17	3		
2006–07	Sheffield W	42	12		
2007–08	Sheffield W	40	7		
2008–09	Sheffield W	17	1	116	23
2008–09	Charlton Ath	20	5		
2009–10	Charlton Ath	39	13	59	18
2010–11	Gabala	28	9		
2011–12	Gabala	21	6	49	15
2012–13	Gillingham	40	12	40	12
2013–14	Scunthorpe U	29	6		
2014–15	Scunthorpe U	5	0	34	6
2014–15	York C	1	0	1	0

CANAVAN, Niall (D) 147 15
H: 6 3 W: 12 00 b.Guiseley 11-4-91
Internationals: Republic of Ireland U21.

2009–10	Scunthorpe U	7	1		
2010–11	Scunthorpe U	8	0		
2010–11	Shrewsbury T	3	0	3	0
2011–12	Scunthorpe U	12	1		
2012–13	Scunthorpe U	40	6		
2013–14	Scunthorpe U	45	4		
2014–15	Scunthorpe U	32	3	144	15

CLARKE, Jordan (D) 153 6
H: 6 0 W: 11 02 b.Coventry 19-11-91
Internationals: England U19, U20.

2009–10	Coventry C	12	0		
2010–11	Coventry C	21	1		
2011–12	Coventry C	19	1		
2012–13	Coventry C	20	0		
2013–14	Coventry C	41	1		
2014–15	Coventry C	11	1	124	4
2014–15	Yeovil T	5	2	5	2
2014–15	Scunthorpe U	24	0	24	0

DANIELS, Luke (G) 120 0
H: 6 1 W: 12 10 b.Bolton 5-1-88
Internationals: England U19.

2006–07	WBA	0	0		
2007–08	Motherwell	2	0	2	0
2007–08	WBA	0	0		
2008–09	WBA	0	0		
2008–09	Shrewsbury T	38	0	38	0
2009–10	WBA	0	0		
2009–10	Tranmere R	37	0	37	0
2010–11	WBA	0	0		
2010–11	Charlton Ath	0	0		
2010–11	Rochdale	1	0	1	0
2010–11	Bristol R	9	0	9	0
2011–12	WBA	0	0		
2011–12	Southend U	9	0	9	0
2012–13	WBA	0	0		
2013–14	WBA	1	0		
2014–15	Scunthorpe U	23	0	23	0

DAWSON, Andy (D) 509 16
H: 5 9 W: 11 02 b.Leyburn 20-10-78

1995–96	Nottingham F	0	0		
1996–97	Nottingham F	0	0		
1997–98	Nottingham F	0	0		
1998–99	Nottingham F	0	0		
1998–99	Scunthorpe U	24	0		
1999–2000	Scunthorpe U	43	2		

2000–01	Scunthorpe U	41	4		
2001–02	Scunthorpe U	44	0		
2002–03	Scunthorpe U	43	2		
2003–04	Hull C	33	3		
2004–05	Hull C	34	0		
2005–06	Hull C	18	0		
2006–07	Hull C	38	2		
2007–08	Hull C	29	1		
2008–09	Hull C	25	1		
2009–10	Hull C	35	1		
2010–11	Hull C	45	0		
2011–12	Hull C	32	0		
2012–13	Hull C	4	0	293	8
2013–14	Scunthorpe U	18	0		
2014–15	Scunthorpe U	3	0	216	8

DYCHE, Jack (D) 0 0

2014–15	Scunthorpe U	0	0		

FALLON, Rory (F) 402 75
H: 6 2 W: 11 09 b.Gisbourne 20-3-82
Internationals: England Youth. New Zealand Full caps.

1998–99	Barnsley	0	0		
1999–2000	Barnsley	0	0		
2001–02	Barnsley	1	0		
2001–02	Barnsley	9	0		
2001–02	Shrewsbury T	11	0	11	0
2002–03	Barnsley	26	7		
2003–04	Barnsley	16	4	52	11
2003–04	Swindon T	19	6		
2004–05	Swindon T	31	3		
2004–05	Yeovil T	6	1		
2005–06	Swindon T	25	12	75	21
2005–06	Swansea C	17	4		
2006–07	Swansea C	24	8	41	12
2006–07	Plymouth Arg	15	1		
2007–08	Plymouth Arg	29	7		
2008–09	Plymouth Arg	44	5		
2009–10	Plymouth Arg	33	5		
2010–11	Plymouth Arg	28	4	149	22
2010–11	Ipswich T	6	1	6	1
2011–12	Yeovil T	5	0	11	1
2011–12	Aberdeen	22	2		
2012–13	Aberdeen	15	1	37	3
2013–14	St Johnstone	8	1	8	1
2013–14	Crawley T	8	0	8	0
2014–15	Scunthorpe U	4	3	4	3

HARE, Taron (D) 0 0
H: 6 1 W: 11 00 b.Bottesford 4-10-96

2014–15	Scunthorpe U	0	0		

HAWKRIDGE, Terry (M) 61 1
H: 5 9 W: 11 00 b.Nottingham 23-2-90

2013–14	Scunthorpe U	45	1		
2014–15	Scunthorpe U	11	0	56	1
2014–15	Mansfield T	5	0	5	0

HOWE, Callum (D) 0 0
H: 6 0 W: 11 07 b.Doncaster 9-4-94

2012–13	Scunthorpe U	0	0		
2013–14	Scunthorpe U	0	0		
2014–15	Scunthorpe U	0	0		

KEE, Billy (F) 205 59
H: 5 9 W: 11 04 b.Loughborough 1-12-90
Internationals: Northern Ireland U19, U21.

2009–10	Leicester C	1	0		
2009–10	Accrington S	37	9	37	9
2010–11	Torquay U	40	9		
2011–12	Torquay U	4	0	44	9
2011–12	Burton Alb	20	12		
2012–13	Burton Alb	40	13		
2013–14	Burton Alb	37	12		
2014–15	Burton Alb	2	2	99	39
2014–15	Scunthorpe U	12	0	12	0
2014–15	Mansfield T	13	2	13	2

LLERA, Miguel (D) 235 24
H: 6 3 W: 13 12 b.Seville 7-8-79

2005–06	Gimnastic	27	3		
2006–07	Gimnastic	12	2	39	5
2007–08	Heracles	13	1	13	1
2008–09	Milton Keynes D	34	2	34	2
2009–10	Charlton Ath	25	4		
2010–11	Charlton Ath	15	1		
2011–12	Charlton Ath	0	0	40	5
2011–12	Brentford	11	0	11	0
2012–13	Sheffield W	20	4		
2012–13	Sheffield W	41	6		
2013–14	Sheffield W	22	0	83	10
2014–15	Scunthorpe U	15	1	15	1

MADDEN, Patrick (F) 210 63
H: 6 0 W: 11 13 b.Dublin 4-3-90
Internationals: Republic of Ireland U19, U21, U23, Full caps.

2008	Bohemians	18	4		
2009	Bohemians	2	0		

2009	Shelbourne	13	6	13	6
2010	Bohemians	34	10	54	14
2010–11	Carlisle U	13	0		
2011–12	Carlisle U	18	1		
2012–13	Carlisle U	1	1	32	2
2012–13	Yeovil T	35	22		
2013–14	Yeovil T	9	0	44	22
2013–14	Scunthorpe U	21	5		
2014–15	Scunthorpe U	46	14	67	19

McALLISTER, Sean (M) 174 5
H: 5 8 W: 10 07 b.Bolton 15-8-87

2005–06	Sheffield W	2	0		
2006–07	Sheffield W	6	1		
2007–08	Sheffield W	8	0		
2007–08	Mansfield T	7	0	7	0
2007–08	Bury	0	0		
2008–09	Sheffield W	40	3		
2009–10	Sheffield W	12	0	68	4
2010–11	Shrewsbury T	18	0		
2011–12	Shrewsbury T	17	1	35	1
2012–13	Port Vale	2	0	2	0
2013–14	Scunthorpe U	39	0		
2014–15	Scunthorpe U	23	0	62	0

McSHEFFREY, Gary (F) 435 97
H: 5 8 W: 10 06 b.Coventry 13-8-82
Internationals: England U18, U20.

1998–99	Coventry C	1	0		
1999–2000	Coventry C	3	0		
2000–01	Coventry C	0	0		
2001–02	Stockport Co	5	1	5	1
2001–02	Coventry C	8	1		
2002–03	Coventry C	29	4		
2003–04	Coventry C	19	11		
2003–04	Luton T	18	9		
2004–05	Coventry C	37	12		
2004–05	Luton T	5	1	23	10
2005–06	Coventry C	43	15		
2006–07	Coventry C	3	1		
2006–07	Birmingham C	40	13		
2007–08	Birmingham C	32	3		
2008–09	Birmingham C	6	0		
2008–09	Nottingham F	4	0	4	0
2009–10	Birmingham C	5	0	83	16
2009–10	Leeds U	10	1	10	1
2010–11	Coventry C	33	8		
2011–12	Coventry C	39	8		
2012–13	Coventry C	32	1		
2013–14	Coventry C	0	0	247	61
2013–14	Chesterfield	9	1	9	1
2013–14	Scunthorpe U	13	0		
2014–15	Scunthorpe U	41	7	54	7

MIRFIN, David (D) 367 16
H: 6 3 W: 13 00 b.Sheffield 18-4-85

2002–03	Huddersfield T	1	0		
2003–04	Huddersfield T	21	2		
2004–05	Huddersfield T	41	4		
2005–06	Huddersfield T	31	1		
2006–07	Huddersfield T	38	1		
2007–08	Huddersfield T	29	1	161	9
2008–09	Scunthorpe U	33	0		
2009–10	Scunthorpe U	37	1		
2010–11	Scunthorpe U	23	3		
2011–12	Watford	4	0	4	0
2011–12	Scunthorpe U	19	1		
2012–13	Scunthorpe U	30	0		
2013–14	Scunthorpe U	45	2		
2014–15	Scunthorpe U	0	0	187	7
2014–15	Hartlepool U	15	0	15	0

MYRIE-WILLIAMS, Jennison (F) 259 29
H: 5 11 W: 12 08 b.Lambeth 17-5-88
Internationals: England U18.

2005–06	Bristol C	1	0		
2006–07	Bristol C	25	2		
2007–08	Bristol C	0	0		
2007–08	Cheltenham T	12	0		
2007–08	Tranmere R	25	3		
2008–09	Bristol C	0	0		
2008–09	Cheltenham T	5	1	17	1
2008–09	Carlisle U	8	0	8	0
2008–09	Hereford U	15	2	15	2
2009–10	Bristol C	0	0	26	2
2009–10	Dundee U	24	1	24	1
2010–11	St Johnstone	6	0	6	0
2011–12	Stevenage	17	0	17	0
2011–12	Port Vale	6	1		
2012–13	Port Vale	44	9		
2013–14	Port Vale	38	7	88	17
2014–15	Scunthorpe U	15	0	15	0
2014–15	Tranmere R	18	3	43	6

NOLAN, Eddie (D)   191   2
H: 6 0   W: 13 05   b.Waterford 5-8-88
Internationals: Republic of Ireland U21, B, Full caps.

2005–06	Blackburn R	0	0	
2006–07	Blackburn R	0	0	
2006–07	Stockport Co	4	0	4 0
2007–08	Blackburn R	0	0	
2007–08	Hartlepool U	11	0	11 0
2008–09	Blackburn R	0	0	
2008–09	Preston NE	21	0	
2009–10	Preston NE	19	0	
2009–10	Sheffield W	14	1	14 1
2010–11	Preston NE	0	0	40 0
2010–11	Scunthorpe U	35	0	
2011–12	Scunthorpe U	30	1	
2012–13	Scunthorpe U	12	0	
2013–14	Scunthorpe U	39	0	
2014–15	Scunthorpe U	6	0	122 1

OSBOURNE, Isaiah (M)   156   3
H: 6 2   W: 12 06   b.Birmingham 5-11-87
Internationals: England U16.

2005–06	Aston Villa	0	0	
2006–07	Aston Villa	11	0	
2007–08	Aston Villa	8	0	
2008–09	Aston Villa	0	0	
2008–09	Nottingham F	8	0	8 0
2009–10	Aston Villa	0	0	
2009–10	Middlesbrough	9	0	9 0
2010–11	Aston Villa	0	0	19 0
2010–11	Sheffield W	10	0	10 0
2011–12	Hibernian	30	1	30 1
2012–13	Blackpool	28	1	
2013–14	Blackpool	24	1	52 2
2014–15	Scunthorpe U	28	0	28 0

SEVERN, James (G)   4   0
H: 6 4   W: 14 11   b.Nottingham 10-10-91
Internationals: England U17, U19, U20.

2010–11	Derby Co	1	0	
2011–12	Derby Co	0	0	1 0
2012–13	Scunthorpe U	1	0	
2013–14	Scunthorpe U	0	0	
2014–15	Scunthorpe U	2	0	3 0

SLOCOMBE, Sam (G)   115   0
H: 6 0   W: 11 11   b.Scunthorpe 5-6-88

2008–09	Scunthorpe U	0	0	
2009–10	Scunthorpe U	1	0	
2010–11	Scunthorpe U	2	0	
2011–12	Scunthorpe U	28	0	
2012–13	Scunthorpe U	29	0	
2013–14	Scunthorpe U	46	0	
2014–15	Scunthorpe U	9	0	115 0

SPARROW, Matt (M)   446   51
H: 5 11   W: 10 06   b.Wembley 3-10-81

1999–2000	Scunthorpe U	11	0	
2000–01	Scunthorpe U	11	4	
2001–02	Scunthorpe U	24	1	
2002–03	Scunthorpe U	42	9	
2003–04	Scunthorpe U	38	3	
2004–05	Scunthorpe U	44	5	
2005–06	Scunthorpe U	39	5	
2006–07	Scunthorpe U	29	4	
2007–08	Scunthorpe U	32	1	
2008–09	Scunthorpe U	36	4	
2009–10	Scunthorpe U	30	1	
2010–11	Brighton & HA	29	4	
2011–12	Brighton & HA	18	2	47 6
2012–13	Crawley T	17	3	17 3
2013–14	Scunthorpe U	26	3	
2014–15	Scunthorpe U	9	1	371 41
2014–15	Cheltenham T	11	1	11 1

SUTTON, Levi (M)   0   0
b. 24-3-96

2014–15	Scunthorpe U	0	0

SYERS, Dave (M)   132   23
H: 6 0   W: 11 07   b.Leeds 30-11-87

2010–11	Bradford C	37	8	
2011–12	Bradford C	18	2	55 10
2012–13	Doncaster R	32	3	
2013–14	Doncaster R	2	0	34 3
2013–14	Scunthorpe U	37	10	
2014–15	Scunthorpe U	6	0	43 10

TAYLOR, Lyle (F)   110   17
H: 6 2   W: 12 00   b.Greenwich 29-3-90
Internationals: Montserrat Full caps.

2007–08	Millwall	0	0	
2008–09	Millwall	0	0	
From Concord R				
2010–11	Bournemouth	11	0	
2011–12	Bournemouth	18	0	29 0
2011–12	Hereford U	8	2	8 2
2013–14	Sheffield U	20	2	20 2

2013–14	Partick Thistle	20	7	
2014–15	Scunthorpe U	18	3	18 3
2014–15	Partick Thistle	15	3	35 10

VAN VEEN, Kevin (F)   69   38
H: 6 1   W: 11 11   b.Eindhoven 1-6-91

2013–14	JVC Cuyk	29	20	29 20
2014–15	FC Oss	20	16	20 16
2014–15	Scunthorpe U	20	2	20 2

WATERFALL, Luke (D)   14   1
H: 6 2   W: 13 02   b.Sheffield 30-7-90

2008–09	Tranmere R	0	0	
From Ilkeston, Gainsborough T				
2013–14	Scunthorpe U	9	1	
2014–15	Scunthorpe U	0	0	9 1
2014–15	Mansfield T	5	0	5 0

WEAVER, Pat (G)   0   0
H: 6 0   W: 12 04   b.Kingston upon Hull 4-1-96

2014–15	Scunthorpe U	0	0

WILLIAMS, Marcus (D)   282   0
H: 5 8   W: 10 07   b.Doncaster 8-4-86

2003–04	Scunthorpe U	1	0	
2004–05	Scunthorpe U	4	0	
2005–06	Scunthorpe U	29	0	
2006–07	Scunthorpe U	35	0	
2007–08	Scunthorpe U	34	0	
2008–09	Scunthorpe U	26	0	
2009–10	Scunthorpe U	37	0	
2010–11	Reading	3	0	
2010–11	Peterborough U	3	0	3 0
2010–11	Scunthorpe U	5	0	
2011–12	Reading	0	0	3 0
2011–12	Sheffield U	19	0	
2012–13	Sheffield U	18	0	
2013–14	Sheffield U	2	0	39 0
2013–14	Scunthorpe U	26	0	
2014–15	Scunthorpe U	40	0	237 0

WOOTTON, Jamie (F)   2   0
b.Rotherham

2012–13	Scunthorpe U	1	0	
2013–14	Scunthorpe U	1	0	
2014–15	Scunthorpe U	0	0	2 0

WOOTTON, Kyle (M)   12   1
H: 6 2   W: 12 04   b.11-10-96

2014–15	Scunthorpe U	12	1	12 1

Scholars
Baker, Riley James; Burdett, Noel Stephen; Cleminshaw, Charles George; Dyche, Jack Leigh; Hare, Taron Jay; Hood, Jacob Sebastian; Ledger, Ben David; Mawson, Jack Lewis; Mosanya, Reece Olusola James; Oliver-Stothard, Emilio Austin; Purdue, Connor; Shilling, Joseph Sonny; Stockill, Matthew Thomas; Sutton, Jack Levi; Watkis, De'Andre Michael; Weaver, Patrick Anthony.

SHEFFIELD U (72)

ADAMS, Che (F)   10   0
b.Leicester 13-7-96
Internationals: England C.

2014–15	Sheffield U	10	0	10 0

ALCOCK, Craig (D)   227   3
H: 5 8   W: 11 00   b.Cornwall 8-12-87

2006–07	Yeovil T	1	0	
2007–08	Yeovil T	8	0	
2008–09	Yeovil T	30	1	
2009–10	Yeovil T	42	1	
2010–11	Yeovil T	26	1	107 3
2011–12	Peterborough U	41	0	
2012–13	Peterborough U	27	0	
2013–14	Peterborough U	28	0	96 0
2014–15	Sheffield U	24	0	24 0

BANTON, Julian (D)   0   0
b. 10-10-95

2014–15	Sheffield U	0	0

BASHAM, Chris (M)   154   6
H: 5 11   W: 12 08   b.Hebburn 20-7-88

2007–08	Bolton W	0	0	
2007–08	Rochdale	13	0	13 0
2008–09	Bolton W	11	1	
2009–10	Bolton W	8	0	19 1
2010–11	Blackpool	2	0	
2011–12	Blackpool	17	1	
2012–13	Blackpool	26	1	
2013–14	Blackpool	40	2	85 5
2014–15	Sheffield U	37	0	37 0

BAXTER, Jose (F)			133	34

BAXTER, Jose (F)   133   34
H: 5 10   W: 11 07   b.Bootle 7-2-92
Internationals: England U16, U17.

2008–09	Everton	3	0	
2009–10	Everton	2	0	
2010–11	Everton	1	0	
2011–12	Everton	1	0	
2011–12	Tranmere R	14	3	14 3
2012–13	Everton	0	0	7 0
2012–13	Crystal Palace	0	0	
2012–13	Oldham Ath	39	13	
2013–14	Oldham Ath	4	2	43 15
2013–14	Sheffield U	35	6	
2014–15	Sheffield U	34	10	69 16

BRAYFORD, John (D)   253   6
H: 5 8   W: 11 02   b.Stoke 29-12-87
Internationals: England C.

2008–09	Crewe Alex	36	2	
2009–10	Crewe Alex	45	0	81 2
2010–11	Derby Co	46	1	
2011–12	Derby Co	23	0	
2012–13	Derby Co	40	1	109 2
2013–14	Cardiff C	0	0	
2013–14	Sheffield U	15	1	
2014–15	Cardiff C	26	0	26 0
2014–15	Sheffield U	22	1	37 2

CALVERT-LEWIN, Dominic (M)   2   0
b. 16-3-97

2013–14	Sheffield U	0	0	
2014–15	Sheffield U	2	0	2 0

CAMPBELL-RYCE, Jamal (M)   387   34
H: 5 7   W: 12 03   b.Lambeth 6-4-83
Internationals: Jamaica Full caps.

2002–03	Charlton Ath	1	0	
2002–03	Leyton Orient	17	2	
2003–04	Charlton Ath	2	0	
2003–04	Wimbledon	4	0	4 0
2004–05	Charlton Ath	0	0	3 0
2004–05	Chesterfield	14	0	14 0
2004–05	Rotherham U	24	0	
2005–06	Rotherham U	7	0	31 0
2005–06	Southend U	13	0	
2005–06	Colchester U	4	0	4 0
2006–07	Southend U	43	2	
2007–08	Southend U	2	0	58 2
2007–08	Barnsley	37	3	
2008–09	Barnsley	40	9	
2009–10	Barnsley	13	0	90 12
2010–11	Bristol C	14	0	
2011–12	Bristol C	31	2	
2011–12	Bristol C	17	0	62 2
2011–12	Leyton Orient	8	1	25 3
2012–13	Notts Co	37	8	
2013–14	Notts Co	36	3	
2014–15	Sheffield U	19	4	19 4
2014–15	Notts Co	4	0	77 11

COLLINS, Neill (D)   426   23
H: 6 3   W: 12 07   b.Irvine 2-9-83
Internationals: Scotland U21, B.

2000–01	Queen's Park	4	0	
2001–02	Queen's Park	28	0	32 0
2002–03	Dumbarton	33	2	
2003–04	Dumbarton	30	2	63 4
2004–05	Sunderland	11	0	
2005–06	Sunderland	0	0	
2005–06	Hartlepool U	22	0	22 0
2005–06	Sheffield U	2	0	
2006–07	Sunderland	7	1	18 1
2006–07	Wolverhampton W	22	2	
2007–08	Wolverhampton W	39	3	
2008–09	Wolverhampton W	23	4	
2009–10	Wolverhampton W	0	0	84 9
2009–10	Preston NE	21	1	21 1
2009–10	Leeds U	9	0	
2010–11	Leeds U	21	0	30 0
2010–11	Sheffield U	14	0	
2011–12	Sheffield U	42	2	
2012–13	Sheffield U	39	3	
2013–14	Sheffield U	44	2	
2014–15	Sheffield U	8	1	149 8
2014–15	Port Vale	7	0	7 0

COUTTS, Paul (M)   209   7
H: 5 9   W: 11 11   b.Aberdeen 22-7-88
Internationals: Scotland U21.

2008–09	Peterborough U	37	0	
2009–10	Peterborough U	16	0	53 0
2009–10	Preston NE	13	1	
2010–11	Preston NE	23	1	
2011–12	Preston NE	41	2	77 4
2012–13	Derby Co	44	3	
2013–14	Derby Co	8	0	
2013–14	Derby Co	7	0	59 3
2014–15	Sheffield U	20	0	20 0

CUVELIER, Florent (M) 50 7
H: 6 0　W: 11 05　b.Brussels 12-9-92
Internationals: Belgium U16, U17, U18, U19, U20, U21.

2009-10	Portsmouth	0	0	
2010-11	Stoke C	0	0	
2011-12	Stoke C	0	0	
2011-12	Walsall	18	4	
2012-13	Stoke C	0	0	
2012-13	Walsall	19	2	37 6
2012-13	Peterborough U	1	0	1 0
2013-14	Stoke C	0	0	
2013-14	Sheffield U	7	0	
2013-14	Port Vale	1	0	1 0
2014-15	Sheffield U	3	0	10 0
2014-15	Burton Alb	1	1	1 1

DAVIES, Ben (M) 387 73
H: 5 7　W: 12 03　b.Birmingham 27-5-81

2000-01	Kidderminster H	3	1	
2001-02	Kidderminster H	9	0	12 0
2004-05	Chester C	44	2	
2005-06	Chester C	45	7	89 9
2006-07	Shrewsbury T	43	12	
2007-08	Shrewsbury T	27	6	
2008-09	Shrewsbury T	42	12	112 30
2009-10	Notts Co	45	15	
2010-11	Notts Co	22	5	67 20
2010-11	Derby Co	13	1	
2011-12	Derby Co	35	2	
2012-13	Derby Co	23	4	
2013-14	Derby Co	4	0	75 7
2013-14	Sheffield U	18	3	
2014-15	Sheffield U	14	4	32 7

DE GIROLAMO, Diago (F) 20 4
H: 5 10　W: 11 00　b.Chesterfield 5-10-95
Internationals: Italy U18, U19, U20.

2012-13	Sheffield U	2	0	
2013-14	Sheffield U	0	0	
2014-15	Sheffield U	0	0	2 0
2014-15	York C	12	4	12 4
2014-15	Northampton T	6	0	6 0

DIMAIO, Connor (D) 3 0
H: 5 10　W: 11 05　b.Chesterfield 28-1-96
Internationals: Republic of Ireland U16, U17, U19.

2013-14	Sheffield U	3	0	
2014-15	Sheffield U	0	0	3 0

DONE, Matt (M) 282 27
H: 5 10　W: 10 04　b.Oswestry 22-6-88

2005-06	Wrexham	6	0	
2006-07	Wrexham	34	1	
2007-08	Wrexham	26	0	66 1
2008-09	Hereford U	36	0	
2009-10	Hereford U	20	0	56 0
2010-11	Rochdale	33	5	
2011-12	Barnsley	31	4	
2012-13	Barnsley	13	0	44 4
2012-13	Hibernian	7	0	7 0
2013-14	Rochdale	38	0	
2014-15	Rochdale	23	10	94 15
2014-15	Sheffield U	15	7	15 7

DOYLE, Micky (M) 495 29
H: 5 10　W: 11 00　b.Dublin 8-7-81
Internationals: Republic of Ireland U21, Full caps.

2003-04	Coventry C	40	5	
2004-05	Coventry C	44	2	
2005-06	Coventry C	44	0	
2006-07	Coventry C	40	3	
2007-08	Coventry C	42	7	
2008-09	Coventry C	37	2	
2009-10	Coventry C	0	0	
2009-10	Leeds U	42	0	42 0
2010-11	Coventry C	18	1	265 20
2011-12	Sheffield U	16	0	
2011-12	Sheffield U	43	3	
2012-13	Sheffield U	43	3	
2013-14	Sheffield U	43	2	
2014-15	Sheffield U	43	1	188 9

FLYNN, Ryan (M) 195 21
H: 5 8　W: 10 00　b.Falkirk 4-9-88
Internationals: Scotland U19.

2006-07	Liverpool	0	0	
2007-08	Hereford U	0	0	
2007-08	Liverpool	0	0	
2008-09	Liverpool	0	0	
2009-10	Liverpool	0	0	
2009-10	Falkirk	36	5	
2010-11	Falkirk	33	5	69 10
2011-12	Sheffield U	26	2	
2012-13	Sheffield U	36	3	
2013-14	Sheffield U	32	5	
2014-15	Sheffield U	32	1	126 11

FREEMAN, Kieron (D) 102 2
H: 5 10　W: 12 05　b.Nottingham 21-3-92
Internationals: Wales U17, U19, U21.

2010-11	Nottingham F	0	0	
2011-12	Nottingham F	0	0	
2011-12	Notts Co	19	1	
2012-13	Derby Co	19	0	
2013-14	Derby Co	6	0	
2013-14	Notts Co	16	0	35 1
2013-14	Sheffield U	12	0	
2014-15	Derby Co	0	0	25 0
2014-15	Mansfield T	11	0	11 0
2014-15	Sheffield U	19	1	31 1

HARRIS, Robert (D) 224 14
H: 5 8　W: 10 00　b.Glasgow 28-8-87

2004-05	Clyde	1	0	
2005-06	Clyde	20	0	
2006-07	Clyde	24	0	45 0
2007-08	Queen of the South	26	2	
2008-09	Queen of the South	21	2	
2009-10	Queen of the South	32	4	
2010-11	Queen of the South	31	2	110 10
2011-12	Blackpool	5	0	
2012-13	Blackpool	4	0	
2012-13	Rotherham U	5	1	5 1
2013-14	Blackpool	4	0	13 0
2013-14	Sheffield U	11	0	
2014-15	Sheffield U	40	3	51 3

HIGDON, Michael (F) 310 94
H: 6 1　W: 12 08　b.Liverpool 2-9-83

2000-01	Crewe Alex	0	0	
2001-02	Crewe Alex	0	0	
2002-03	Crewe Alex	0	0	
2003-04	Crewe Alex	10	1	
2004-05	Crewe Alex	20	3	
2005-06	Crewe Alex	26	3	
2006-07	Crewe Alex	25	3	
2007-08	Crewe Alex	0	0	81 10
2007-08	Falkirk	24	4	
2008-09	Falkirk	27	7	51 11
2009-10	St Mirren	33	3	
2010-11	St Mirren	28	14	61 17
2011-12	Motherwell	35	14	
2012-13	Motherwell	37	26	72 40
2013-14	NEC	32	14	32 14
2014-15	Sheffield U	13	2	13 2

HODDER, Jordan (D) 0 0

2013-14	Sheffield U	0	0
2014-15	Sheffield U	0	0

HOLT, Jason (M) 83 13
H: 5 5　W: 11 00　b.Edinburgh 19-2-93
Internationals: Scotland U19, U20, U21.

2010-11	Hearts	1	0	
2011-12	Hearts	2	1	
2011-12	Raith R	5	1	5 1
2012-13	Hearts	21	3	
2013-14	Hearts	23	1	
2014-15	Hearts	15	2	62 7

On loan from Hearts.

2014-15	Sheffield U	16	5	16 5

HOWARD, Mark (G) 131 0
H: 6 0　W: 11 13　b.Southwark 21-9-86

2005-06	Falkirk	8	0	8 0
2006-07	Cardiff C	0	0	
2006-07	Swansea C	0	0	
2007-08	St Mirren	10	0	
2008-09	St Mirren	33	0	
2009-10	St Mirren	2	0	45 0
2010-11	Aberdeen	9	0	9 0
2011-12	Blackpool	4	0	4 0
2011-12	Sheffield U	0	0	
2012-13	Sheffield U	11	0	
2013-14	Sheffield U	19	0	
2014-15	Sheffield U	35	0	65 0

IRONSIDE, Joe (F) 20 1
H: 5 11　W: 11 11　b.Middlesbrough 16-10-93

2012-13	Sheffield U	12	0	
2013-14	Sheffield U	4	0	
2014-15	Sheffield U	0	0	16 0
2014-15	Hartlepool U	4	1	4 1

KENNEDY, Terry (D) 18 0
H: 5 10　W: 12 04　b.Barnsley 14-11-93

2010-11	Sheffield U	0	0	
2011-12	Sheffield U	0	0	
2012-13	Sheffield U	1	0	
2013-14	Sheffield U	5	0	
2014-15	Sheffield U	11	0	18 0

KHAN, Otis (M) 2 0
H: 5 9　W: 11 03　b.Ashton-under-Lyme 5-9-95

2013-14	Sheffield U	2	0	
2014-15	Sheffield U	0	0	2 0

LONG, George (G) 89 0
H: 6 0　W: 12 05　b.Sheffield 5-11-93
Internationals: England U18.

2010-11	Sheffield U	1	0	
2011-12	Sheffield U	2	0	
2012-13	Sheffield U	36	0	
2013-14	Sheffield U	27	0	
2014-15	Sheffield U	0	0	66 0
2014-15	Oxford U	10	0	10 0
2014-15	Motherwell	13	0	13 0

McEVELEY, James (D) 304 8
H: 6 1　W: 13 03　b.Liverpool 11-2-85
Internationals: England U20, U21. Scotland B, Full caps.

2002-03	Blackburn R	9	0	
2003-04	Blackburn R	0	0	
2003-04	Burnley	4	0	4 0
2004-05	Blackburn R	5	0	
2004-05	Gillingham	10	1	10 1
2005-06	Blackburn R	0	0	
2005-06	Ipswich T	19	1	19 1
2006-07	Blackburn R	4	0	18 0
2006-07	Derby Co	15	0	
2007-08	Derby Co	29	2	
2008-09	Derby Co	15	0	
2008-09	Preston NE	7	0	7 0
2008-09	Charlton Ath	6	0	6 0
2009-10	Derby Co	33	2	92 4
2010-11	Barnsley	17	1	
2011-12	Barnsley	29	0	46 1
2011-12	Swindon T	8	0	
2012-13	Swindon T	28	0	
2013-14	Swindon T	32	0	68 0
2014-15	Sheffield U	34	1	34 1

McFADZEAN, Callum (D) 35 2
b.Sheffield 16-1-94
Internationals: England U16. Scotland U21.

2010-11	Sheffield U	0	0	
2011-12	Sheffield U	0	0	
2012-13	Sheffield U	8	0	
2013-14	Sheffield U	7	0	
2013-14	Chesterfield	4	0	4 0
2013-14	Burton Alb	7	1	
2014-15	Sheffield U	0	0	15 0
2014-15	Burton Alb	9	1	16 2

McGAHEY, Harrison (D) 23 0
b.Preston 26-9-95

2013-14	Blackpool	4	0	4 0
2014-15	Sheffield U	15	0	15 0
2014-15	Tranmere R	4	0	4 0

McGINN, Stephen (M) 172 12
H: 5 9　W: 10 01　b.Glasgow 2-12-88
Internationals: Scotland U19, U21.

2006-07	St Mirren	4	1	
2007-08	St Mirren	25	2	
2008-09	St Mirren	26	1	
2009-10	St Mirren	18	3	73 7
2009-10	Watford	9	0	
2010-11	Watford	29	2	
2011-12	Watford	0	0	
2012-13	Watford	0	0	38 2
2012-13	Shrewsbury T	18	2	18 2
2013-14	Sheffield U	30	0	
2014-15	Sheffield U	0	0	30 0
2014-15	Dundee	13	1	13 1

Transferred to Dundee January 2015.

McNULTY, Marc (M) 136 46
H: 5 10　W: 11 00　b.Edinburgh 14-9-92

2009-10	Livingston	5	1	
2010-11	Livingston	5	1	
2011-12	Livingston	30	11	
2012-13	Livingston	26	7	
2013-14	Livingston	35	17	105 37
2014-15	Sheffield U	31	9	31 9

MURPHY, Jamie (F) 270 51
H: 6 0　W: 12 00　b.Glasgow 28-8-89
Internationals: Scotland U19, U21.

2006-07	Motherwell	2	0	
2007-08	Motherwell	16	1	
2008-09	Motherwell	30	2	
2009-10	Motherwell	35	6	
2010-11	Motherwell	35	6	
2011-12	Motherwell	36	9	
2012-13	Motherwell	22	10	176 34
2012-13	Sheffield U	17	2	
2013-14	Sheffield U	34	4	
2014-15	Sheffield U	43	11	94 17

REED, Louis (M) 20 0
b. 25-7-97
Internationals: England U18.

2013–14	Sheffield U	1	0		
2014–15	Sheffield U	19	0	20	0

SCOUGALL, Stefan (M) 40 3
H: 5 7 W: 8 13 b.Edinburgh 7-12-92
Internationals: Scotland U21.

2013–14	Sheffield U	15	2		
2014–15	Sheffield U	25	1	40	3

TURNER, Iain (G) 89 1
H: 6 3 W: 12 10 b.Stirling 26-1-84
Internationals: Scotland Youth, U21, B.

2002–03	Stirling Alb	14	0	14	0
2002–03	Everton	0	0		
2003–04	Everton	0	0		
2004–05	Everton	0	0		
2004–05	Doncaster R	8	0	8	0
2005–06	Everton	3	0		
2005–06	Wycombe W	3	0	3	0
2006–07	Everton	1	0		
2006–07	Crystal Palace	5	0	5	0
2006–07	*Sheffield W*	11	0	11	0
2007–08	Everton	0	0		
2008–09	Everton	0	0		
2008–09	*Nottingham F*	3	0	3	0
2009–10	Everton	0	0		
2010–11	Everton	0	0	4	0
2010–11	*Coventry C*	2	0	2	0
2010–11	*Preston NE*	17	0		
2011–12	Preston NE	11	1	28	1
2013–14	Barnsley	0	0		
2014–15	Sheffield U	11	0	11	0

WALLACE, James (M) 82 7
H: 5 11 W: 12 08 b.Fazakerly 19-12-91
Internationals: England U19, U20.

2008–09	Everton	0	0		
2009–10	Everton	0	0		
2010–11	Everton	0	0		
2010–11	*Stockport Co*	14	1	14	0
2010–11	Bury	0	0		
2011–12	Everton	0	0		
2011–12	*Shrewsbury T*	3	0	3	0
2011–12	Stevenage	0	0		
2011–12	Tranmere R	18	2		
2012–13	Tranmere R	19	2		
2013–14	Everton	0	0		
2013–14	Tranmere R	18	2	55	6
2014–15	Sheffield U	10	0	10	0

WALLACE, Kieran (M) 4 0
b. 26-1-95
Internationals: England U16, U17.

2014–15	Sheffield U	4	0	4	0

WHITEMAN, Ben (M) 0 0
b.Rochdale 17-6-96

2014–15	Sheffield U	0	0

WILLIS, George (G) 0 0
H: 5 11 W: 11 05 b.Rotherham 30-7-95
Internationals: England U16, U17, U19.

2012–13	Sheffield U	0	0
2013–14	Sheffield U	0	0
2014–15	Sheffield U	0	0

Players retained or with offer of contract
Berry, Samuel Dean; Coustrain, Joel; Hamilton, Christopher; McDonagh, Jamie-Dean Cantona; Scarisbrick, Kyle Roy.

Scholars
Adebowale, Emmanuel; Brooks, David Robert; Cheeseman, Joe; Cockerline, Daniel; Eastwood, Jake; Evans, Ioan Thomas; Fixter, Robbie Ian; Giraud-Hutchinson, O'Shaye Samuel; Gordon, Shea Martin; Heh, Kler Low Eh Hmoo; Hinchcliffe, Jamie Sidebottom; Ismael, Fahad Abdisamad; Kedman, Michael Junior Wells; Kelly, Graham; Ramsdale, Aaron Christopher; Ramsey, Daniel Christopher; Slew, Jerome Anthony; Wright, Jake David.

SHEFFIELD W (73)

BETRA, Franck (F) 0 0
b. 18-12-96

2013–14	Sheffield W	0	0
2014–15	Sheffield W	0	0

BUS, Sergiu (F) 110 31
H: 6 1 W: 12 13 b.Cluj-Napoca 2-11-92
Internationals: Romania U21.

2009–10	CFR Cluj	1	0		
2010–11	CFR Cluj	12	1		
2010–11	Unirea Albu Iulia	12	2	12	2
2011–12	CFR Cluj	0	0		
2011–12	Targu Mures	22	6	22	6
2012–13	CFR Cluj	6	2		
2012–13	Gaz Metan Medias	3	0	3	0
2013–14	CFR Cluj	0	0	19	3
2013–14	Corona Brasov	28	9	28	9
2014–15	CSKA Sofia	19	10	19	10
2014–15	Sheffield W	7	1	7	1

BUXTON, Lewis (D) 326 7
H: 6 1 W: 13 11 b.Newport (IW) 10-12-83

2000–01	Portsmouth	1	0		
2001–02	Portsmouth	29	0		
2002–03	Portsmouth	1	0		
2002–03	*Exeter C*	4	0	4	0
2002–03	Bournemouth	17	0		
2003–04	Portsmouth	0	0		
2003–04	Bournemouth	26	0	43	0
2004–05	Portsmouth	0	0	30	0
2004–05	Stoke C	16	0		
2005–06	Stoke C	32	1		
2006–07	Stoke C	1	0		
2007–08	Stoke C	4	0		
2008–09	Stoke C	0	0	53	1
2008–09	Sheffield W	32	1		
2009–10	Sheffield W	28	0		
2010–11	Sheffield W	30	1		
2011–12	Sheffield W	37	1		
2012–13	Sheffield W	40	0		
2013–14	Sheffield W	20	3		
2014–15	Sheffield W	9	0	196	6

COKE, Giles (M) 276 26
H: 6 0 W: 11 11 b.Westminster 3-6-86

2004–05	Mansfield T	9	0		
2005–06	Mansfield T	40	4		
2006–07	Mansfield T	21	1	70	5
2007–08	Northampton T	20	5		
2008–09	Northampton T	32	2	52	7
2009–10	Motherwell	32	2	32	2
2010–11	Sheffield W	27	4		
2011–12	Bury	30	6	30	6
2012–13	Sheffield W	16	0		
2012–13	*Swindon T*	4	0	4	0
2013–14	Sheffield W	28	1		
2014–15	Sheffield W	13	1	84	6
2014–15	*Bolton W*	4	0	4	0

CORRY, Paul (M) 100 8
H: 6 2 W: 11 12 b.Dublin 3-2-91

2010	UCD	28	4		
2011	UCD	36	2		
2012	UCD	17	1	81	7
2012–13	Sheffield W	6	0		
2012–13	*Tranmere R*	6	0	6	0
2013–14	Sheffield W	1	0		
2014–15	Sheffield W	0	0	7	0
2014–15	*Carlisle U*	6	1	6	1

CROASDALE, Ryan (M) 0 0
b. 26-9-94

2013–14	Preston NE	0	0
2014–15	Sheffield W	0	0

DAWSON, Cameron (G) 0 0
H: 6 0 W: 10 12 b.Sheffield 7-7-95
Internationals: England U18, U19.

2013–14	Sheffield W	0	0
2013–14	*Plymouth Arg*	0	0
2014–15	Sheffield W	0	0

DE HAVILLAND, Will (D) 0 0
H: 6 0 W: 11 00 b.Huntingdon 8-11-94

2013–14	Millwall	0	0
2014–15	Sheffield W	0	0

DIELNA, Claude (D) 132 4
H: 6 0 W: 12 08 b.Clichy-la-Garenne 14-12-87

2006–07	Lorient	0	0		
2007–08	Lorient	0	0		
2009–10	Istres	21	0		
2010–11	Istres	24	1		
2011–12	Istres	17	0	62	1
2012–13	Olympiacos	3	0		
2012–13	Sedan	25	2	25	2
2013–14	Olympiacos	0	0		
2013–14	AC Ajaccio	22	0	22	0
2014–15	Sheffield W	23	1	23	1

DIESERUVWE, Emmanuel (F) 13 0
b. 5-1-94

2014–15	Sheffield W	0	0

2013–14	*Fleetwood T*	4	0	4	0
2014–15	Sheffield W	0	0		
2014–15	*Chesterfield*	9	0	9	0

FILIPE MELO, Silva (M) 143 5
H: 6 2 W: 12 13 b. 3-11-89

2006–07	Uniao Lamas	0	0		
2007–08	Uniao Lamas	0	0		
2008–09	Uniao Lamas	0	0		
2009–10	Beira-Mar	1	0		
2009–10	Avanca	21	1	21	1
2010–11	Beira-Mar	0	0		
2010–11	Espinho	23	0	23	0
2011–12	Beira-Mar	0	0	1	0
2011–12	Arouca	11	1	11	1
2012–13	Naval	29	1	29	1
2013–14	Moreirense	35	2		
2014–15	Moreirense	17	0	52	2
2014–15	Sheffield W	6	0	6	0

FLORO, Rafael (D) 1 0
H: 5 9 W: 11 07 b.Quarteira 19-1-94
Internationals: Portugal U18, U20.

2013–14	Sheffield W	1	0		
2014–15	Sheffield W	0	0	1	0

HELAN, Jeremy (M) 114 4
H: 5 11 W: 12 00 b.Paris 9-5-92
Internationals: France U19.

2009–10	Manchester C	0	0		
2010–11	Manchester C	0	0		
2011–12	Manchester C	0	0		
2011–12	*Carlisle U*	2	0	2	0
2012–13	Manchester C	0	0		
2012–13	*Shrewsbury T*	3	0	3	0
2013–14	*Sheffield W*	28	1		
2013–14	Sheffield W	43	2		
2014–15	Sheffield W	38	1	109	4

HUTCHINSON, Sam (M) 45 2
H: 6 0 W: 11 07 b.Windsor 3-8-89
Internationals: England U18, U19.

2006–07	Chelsea	1	0		
2007–08	Chelsea	0	0		
2008–09	Chelsea	0	0		
2009–10	Chelsea	2	0		
2010–11	Chelsea	0	0		
2011–12	Chelsea	2	0		
2012–13	Chelsea	0	0		
2012–13	*Nottingham F*	9	1	9	1
2013–14	Chelsea	0	0	5	0
2013–14	*Vitesse*	1	0	1	0
2013–14	*Sheffield W*	10	1		
2014–15	Sheffield W	20	0	30	1

KELHAR, Dejan (D) 221 4
H: 6 2 W: 13 05 b.5-4-84
Internationals: Slovenia Full caps.

2003–04	Celje	15	0		
2003–04	Krsko	15	0	15	0
2004–05	Celje	6	0		
2004–05	Olimpija Ljubljana	15	0	15	0
2005–06	Celje	23	0	35	0
2006–07	Greuther Furth	8	0	8	0
2007–08	NK Celje	13	0		
2008–09	NK Celje	18	2	31	2
2008–09	Cercle Brugge	7	0		
2009–10	Cercle Brugge	26	1		
2010–11	Cercle Brugge	9	0	42	1
2010–11	Legia Warsaw	2	0	2	0
2011–12	Hapoel Haifa	9	0	9	0
2011–12	Samsunspor	14	0	14	0
2012–13	Gabala	28	1		
2013–14	Gabala	7	0	35	1
2014–15	Red Star Belgrade	15	0	15	0
2014–15	Sheffield W	0	0		

KIRKLAND, Chris (G) 279 0
H: 6 5 W: 14 08 b.Barwell 2-5-81
Internationals: England U21, Full caps.

1997–98	Coventry C	0	0		
1998–99	Coventry C	0	0		
1999–2000	Coventry C	0	0		
2000–01	Coventry C	23	0		
2001–02	Coventry C	1	0	24	0
2001–02	Liverpool	7	0		
2002–03	Liverpool	8	0		
2003–04	Liverpool	10	0		
2004–05	Liverpool	10	0		
2005–06	Liverpool	0	0		
2005–06	*WBA*	10	0	10	0
2006–07	Liverpool	0	0	25	0
2006–07	Wigan Ath	26	0		
2007–08	Wigan Ath	37	0		
2008–09	Wigan Ath	32	0		
2009–10	Wigan Ath	32	0		
2010–11	Wigan Ath	4	0		
2010–11	*Leicester C*	3	0	3	0
2011–12	Wigan Ath	0	0	131	0

2011–12	*Doncaster R*	1	0	**1**	**0**
2012–13	Sheffield W	46	0		
2013–14	Sheffield W	35	0		
2014–15	Sheffield W	4	0	**85**	**0**

LAVERY, Caolan (F) **53** **12**
H: 5 11 W: 11 12 b.Red Deer 22-10-92
Internationals: Canada U17. Northern Ireland U19, U21.

2012–13	Sheffield W	0	0		
2012–13	*Southend U*	3	0	**3**	**0**
2013–14	Sheffield W	21	4		
2013–14	*Plymouth Arg*	8	3	**8**	**3**
2014–15	Sheffield W	13	2	**34**	**6**
2014–15	*Chesterfield*	8	3	**8**	**3**

LEE, Kieran (D) **207** **12**
H: 6 1 W: 12 00 b.Stalybridge 22-6-88

2006–07	Manchester U	1	0		
2007–08	Manchester U	0	0	**1**	**0**
2007–08	*QPR*	7	0	**7**	**0**
2008–09	Oldham Ath	7	0		
2009–10	Oldham Ath	24	1		
2010–11	Oldham Ath	43	2		
2011–12	Oldham Ath	43	2	**117**	**5**
2012–13	Sheffield W	23	0		
2013–14	Sheffield W	26	1		
2014–15	Sheffield W	33	6	**82**	**7**

LEES, Tom (D) **251** **7**
H: 6 1 W: 12 04 b.Warwick 28-11-90
Internationals: England U21.

2008–09	Leeds U	0	0		
2009–10	Leeds U	0	0		
2009–10	*Accrington S*	39	0	**39**	**0**
2010–11	Leeds U	0	0		
2010–11	*Bury*	45	4	**45**	**4**
2011–12	Leeds U	42	2		
2012–13	Leeds U	40	1		
2013–14	Leeds U	41	0	**123**	**3**
2014–15	Sheffield W	44	0	**44**	**0**

LOOVENS, Glenn (D) **292** **13**
H: 5 10 W: 11 08 b.Doetrinchem 22-10-83
Internationals: Netherlands U21, Full caps.

2001–02	Feyenoord	8	0		
2002–03	Feyenoord	12	0		
2003–04	Feyenoord	1	0		
2003–04	Excelsior	24	2	**24**	**2**
2004–05	Feyenoord	6	0	**27**	**0**
2004–05	De Graafschap	11	0	**11**	**0**
2005–06	Cardiff C	33	2		
2006–07	Cardiff C	30	1		
2007–08	Cardiff C	36	0		
2008–09	Cardiff C	1	0	**100**	**3**
2008–09	Celtic	17	3		
2009–10	Celtic	20	3		
2010–11	Celtic	13	1		
2011–12	Celtic	11	1	**61**	**8**
2012–13	Real Zaragoza	21	0	**21**	**0**
2013–14	Sheffield W	22	0		
2014–15	Sheffield W	26	0	**48**	**0**

MADINE, Gary (F) **214** **47**
H: 6 1 W: 12 00 b.Gateshead 24-8-90

2007–08	Carlisle U	11	0		
2008–09	Carlisle U	14	1		
2008–09	*Rochdale*	3	0	**3**	**0**
2009–10	Carlisle U	20	4		
2009–10	*Coventry C*	9	0		
2009–10	*Chesterfield*	4	0	**4**	**0**
2010–11	Carlisle U	21	8		
2010–11	Sheffield W	22	5		
2011–12	Sheffield W	38	18		
2012–13	Sheffield W	30	3		
2013–14	Sheffield W	1	0		
2013–14	*Carlisle U*	5	2	**71**	**15**
2014–15	Sheffield W	10	0	**101**	**26**
2014–15	*Coventry C*	11	3	**20**	**3**
2014–15	*Blackpool*	15	3	**15**	**3**

MAGHOMA, Jacques (M) **212** **28**
H: 5 9 W: 11 06 b.Lubumbashi 23-10-87
Internationals: DR Congo Full caps.

2005–06	Tottenham H	0	0		
2006–07	Tottenham H	0	0		
2007–08	Tottenham H	0	0		
2008–09	Tottenham H	0	0		
2009–10	Burton Alb	35	3		
2010–11	Burton Alb	41	4		
2011–12	Burton Alb	36	4		
2012–13	Burton Alb	43	15	**155**	**26**
2013–14	Sheffield W	25	2		
2014–15	Sheffield W	32	0	**57**	**2**

MAGUIRE, Chris (F) **245** **44**
H: 5 7 W: 10 05 b.Bellshill 16-1-89
Internationals: Scotland U16, U19, U21, Full caps.

2005–06	Aberdeen	1	0		
2006–07	Aberdeen	19	1		
2007–08	Aberdeen	28	4		
2008–09	Aberdeen	31	3		
2009–10	Aberdeen	17	1		
2009–10	*Kilmarnock*	14	4	**14**	**4**
2010–11	Aberdeen	35	7	**131**	**16**
2011–12	Derby Co	7	1	**7**	**1**
2011–12	*Portsmouth*	11	3	**11**	**3**
2012–13	Sheffield W	10	1		
2013–14	Sheffield W	27	9		
2013–14	*Coventry C*	3	2	**3**	**2**
2014–15	Sheffield W	42	8	**79**	**18**

MATTOCK, Joe (D) **187** **4**
H: 5 11 W: 12 05 b.Leicester 15-5-90
Internationals: England U17, U19, U21.

2006–07	Leicester C	4	0		
2007–08	Leicester C	31	0		
2008–09	Leicester C	31	1		
2009–10	Leicester C	0	0	**66**	**1**
2009–10	WBA	29	0		
2010–11	WBA	0	0		
2010–11	*Sheffield U*	13	0	**13**	**0**
2011–12	WBA	0	0	**29**	**0**
2011–12	*Portsmouth*	7	0	**7**	**0**
2011–12	*Brighton & HA*	15	1	**15**	**1**
2012–13	Sheffield W	7	0		
2013–14	Sheffield W	23	2		
2014–15	Sheffield W	27	0	**57**	**2**

MAY, Stevie (F) **156** **74**
H: 5 3 W: 9 07 b.Perth 3-11-92
Internationals: Scotland U20, U21, Full caps.

2008–09	St Johnstone	1	1		
2009–10	St Johnstone	0	0		
2010–11	St Johnstone	19	2		
2011–12	St Johnstone	1	0		
2011–12	*Alloa Ath*	22	19	**22**	**19**
2012–13	St Johnstone	3	0		
2012–13	*Hamilton A*	33	25	**33**	**25**
2013–14	St Johnstone	38	20	**62**	**23**
2014–15	Sheffield W	39	7	**39**	**7**

McCABE, Rhys (M) **43** **1**
H: 5 10 W: 11 08 b.Polbeth 24-7-92
Internationals: Scotland U21.

2011–12	Rangers	9	0	**9**	**0**
2012–13	Sheffield W	22	1		
2013–14	Sheffield W	7	0		
2013–14	*Portsmouth*	4	0	**4**	**0**
2014–15	Sheffield W	1	0	**30**	**1**

McELROY, Paul (M) **0** **0**
b. 7-7-94

2014–15	Sheffield W	0	0		

NUHIU, Atdhe (F) **214** **39**
H: 6 6 W: 13 05 b.Prishtina 29-7-89
Internationals: Austria U19, U20, U21.

2008–09	Austria Karnten	16	2		
2009–10	Austria Karnten	3	0	**19**	**2**
2009–10	SV Ried	27	6	**27**	**6**
2010–11	Rapid Vienna	28	5		
2011–12	Rapid Vienna	31	8	**59**	**13**
2012–13	Eskisehirspor	28	2	**28**	**2**
2013–14	Sheffield W	38	8		
2014–15	Sheffield W	43	8	**81**	**16**

PALMER, Liam (M) **140** **1**
H: 6 2 W: 12 10 b.Worksop 19-9-91
Internationals: Scotland U19, U21.

2010–11	Sheffield W	9	0		
2011–12	Sheffield W	14	1		
2012–13	Sheffield W	0	0		
2012–13	*Tranmere R*	43	0		
2013–14	*Tranmere R*	0	0	**43**	**0**
2013–14	Sheffield W	39	0		
2014–15	Sheffield W	35	0	**97**	**1**

PRUTTON, David (M) **439** **25**
H: 5 10 W: 13 00 b.Hull 12-9-81
Internationals: England U21.

1998–99	Nottingham F	0	0		
1999–2000	Nottingham F	34	2		
2000–01	Nottingham F	42	1		
2001–02	Nottingham F	43	3		
2002–03	Nottingham F	24	1		
2002–03	Southampton	12	0		
2003–04	Southampton	27	1		
2004–05	Southampton	23	1		
2005–06	Southampton	17	0		
2006–07	Southampton	3	1	**82**	**3**
2006–07	*Nottingham F*	12	2	**155**	**9**
2007–08	Leeds U	43	4		
2008–09	Leeds U	16	0		
2009–10	Leeds U	6	0	**65**	**4**
2009–10	Colchester U	19	3	**19**	**3**
2010–11	Swindon T	41	3	**41**	**3**
2011–12	Sheffield W	25	2		
2012–13	Sheffield W	22	0		
2012–13	*Scunthorpe U*	13	0	**13**	**0**
2013–14	Sheffield W	9	1		
2013–14	*Coventry C*	8	0	**8**	**0**
2014–15	Sheffield W	0	0	**56**	**3**

SANDERS, Ed (D) **0** **0**
b.Isle of Wight 11-10-95

2014–15	Sheffield W	0	0		

SEMEDO, Jose (D) **314** **5**
H: 6 0 W: 12 08 b.Setubal 11-1-85
Internationals: Portugal U17, U18, U19, U20, U21, B.

2004–05	Sporting Lisbon	0	0		
2004–05	*Casa Pia*	34	2	**34**	**2**
2005–06	*Feirense*	18	0	**18**	**0**
2006–07	*Cagliari*	3	0	**3**	**0**
2007–08	Charlton Ath	37	0		
2008–09	Charlton Ath	18	0		
2009–10	Charlton Ath	38	1		
2010–11	Charlton Ath	42	1	**135**	**2**
2011–12	Sheffield W	46	1		
2012–13	Sheffield W	26	0		
2013–14	Sheffield W	22	0		
2014–15	Sheffield W	30	0	**124**	**1**

STOBBS, Jack (M) **1** **0**
b. 27-2-97

2013–14	Sheffield W	1	0		
2014–15	Sheffield W	0	0	**1**	**0**

VERMIJL, Marnick (D) **39** **3**
H: 5 11 W: 11 12 b.Overpelt 13-1-92
Internationals: Belgium U17, U18, U19, U21.

2010–11	Manchester U	0	0		
2011–12	Manchester U	0	0		
2012–13	Manchester U	0	0		
2013–14	Manchester U	0	0		
2013–14	*NEC*	28	3	**28**	**3**
2014–15	Manchester U	0	0		
2014–15	Sheffield W	11	0	**11**	**0**

WESTWOOD, Keiren (G) **320** **0**
H: 6 1 W: 13 10 b.Manchester 23-10-84
Internationals: Republic of Ireland Full caps.

2001–02	Manchester C	0	0		
2002–03	Manchester C	0	0		
2003–04	Manchester C	0	0		
2003–04	*Oldham Ath*	0	0		
2004–05	Manchester C	0	0		
2005–06	Manchester C	0	0		
2005–06	Carlisle U	35	0		
2006–07	Carlisle U	46	0		
2007–08	Carlisle U	46	0	**127**	**0**
2008–09	Coventry C	46	0		
2009–10	Coventry C	44	0		
2010–11	Coventry C	41	0	**131**	**0**
2011–12	Sunderland	9	0		
2012–13	Sunderland	0	0		
2013–14	Sunderland	10	0	**19**	**0**
2014–15	Sheffield W	43	0	**43**	**0**

WILDSMITH, Joe (G) **2** **0**
H: 6 0 W: 10 03 b. 28-12-95

2013–14	Sheffield W	0	0		
2014–15	Sheffield W	0	0		
2014–15	*Barnsley*	2	0	**2**	**0**

YOUNG, Matt (D) **20** **0**
H: 5 11 W: 11 00 b. 26-1-94

2012–13	Southampton	0	0		
2013–14	Southampton	0	0		
2014–15	Sheffield W	0	0		
2014–15	*Carlisle U*	20	0	**20**	**0**

ZAYATTE, Kamil (D) **196** **9**
H: 6 2 W: 13 08 b.Conakry 7-3-85
Internationals: Guinea Full caps.

2005–06	Lens	0	0		
2006–07	Lens	1	0	**1**	**0**
2006–07	Young Boys	18	0		
2007–08	Young Boys	23	1		
2008–09	Young Boys	6	1	**47**	**2**
2008–09	Hull C	32	1		
2009–10	Hull C	23	2		
2010–11	Hull C	16	0	**71**	**3**
2010–11	Konyaspor	13	1	**13**	**1**
2011–12	Istanbul Buyuksehir	17	0		
2012–13	Istanbul Buyuksehir	25	1	**42**	**1**
2013–14	Sheffield W	11	2		
2014–15	Sheffield W	11	0	**22**	**2**

Players retained or with offer of contract
Meadows, Ryan Walter.

Scholars
Beatson, Bradley Lewis; Brown, Spencer Joseph; Clarke, Warren Eliott; Conneh, Mike Keita; Duffy, Mason; Ellam, Jake James; Foster, Seanan James; Fusco, Jonathan Nicholas; Kanteh, Emmanuel Saah; Law,

Glenn Jonathan; McDonagh, Bradley Michael; Nicholson, Jake Thomas; O'Grady, Connor Joseph; Penney, Matthew Luke; Rodney, Devante Darrius; Smith, Luke Adam; Stachini, Josh; Tracey, Frederick William Robert.

SHREWSBURY T (74)

AKPA AKPRO, Jean-Louis (F) 282 43
H: 6 0 W: 10 12 b.Toulouse 4-1-85

2004–05	Toulouse	13	0		
2005–06	Toulouse	14	3	**27**	**3**
2006–07	*Brest*	15	2	**15**	**2**
2007–08	FC Brussels	3	0	**3**	**0**
2008–09	Grimsby T	20	3		
2009–10	Grimsby T	36	5	**56**	**8**
2010–11	Rochdale	32	4		
2011–12	Rochdale	41	7	**73**	**11**
2012–13	Tranmere R	28	8		
2013–14	Tranmere R	25	2	**53**	**10**
2013–14	*Bury*	10	0	**10**	**0**
2014–15	Shrewsbury T	45	9	**45**	**9**

ANDERSON, Kayman (F) 0 0

2013–14	Shrewsbury T	0	0		
2014–15	Shrewsbury T	0	0		

BARNETT, Tyrone (F) 177 47
H: 6 3 W: 13 05 b.Stevenage 28-10-85

2010–11	Macclesfield T	45	13	**45**	**13**
2011–12	Crawley T	26	14	**26**	**14**
2011–12	Peterborough U	13	4		
2012–13	Peterborough U	18	1		
2012–13	*Ipswich T*	3	0	**3**	**0**
2013–14	Peterborough U	21	6		
2013–14	*Bristol C*	17	1	**17**	**1**
2014–15	Peterborough U	4	0	**56**	**11**
2014–15	*Oxford U*	12	4	**12**	**4**
2014–15	Shrewsbury T	18	4	**18**	**4**

BURTON, Callum (G) 0 0
H: 6 2 W: 12 00 b.Newport, Shropshire 15-8-96
Internationals: England U16, U17, U18.

2013–14	Shrewsbury T	0	0		
2014–15	Shrewsbury T	0	0		

CATON, James (M) 6 0
H: 5 8 W: 10 12 b.Bolton 4-1-94

2012–13	Blackpool	0	0		
2013–14	Blackpool	2	0	**2**	**0**
2013–14	*Accrington S*	2	0	**2**	**0**
2014–15	Shrewsbury T	2	0	**2**	**0**

CLARK, Jordan (F) 36 3
H: 6 0 W: 11 07 b.Barnsley 22-9-93

2010–11	Barnsley	4	0		
2011–12	Barnsley	2	0		
2012–13	Barnsley	0	0		
2012–13	*Chesterfield*	2	0	**2**	**0**
2013–14	Barnsley	0	0	**6**	**0**
2013–14	*Scunthorpe U*	1	0	**1**	**0**
2014–15	Shrewsbury T	27	3	**27**	**3**

COLLINS, James S (F) 209 64
H: 6 2 W: 13 08 b.Coventry 1-12-90
Internationals: Republic of Ireland U19, U21.

2008–09	Aston Villa	0	0		
2009–10	Aston Villa	0	0		
2009–10	*Darlington*	7	2	**7**	**2**
2010–11	Aston Villa	0	0		
2010–11	*Burton Alb*	10	4	**10**	**4**
2010–11	Shrewsbury T	24	8		
2011–12	Shrewsbury T	42	14		
2012–13	Swindon T	45	15	**45**	**15**
2013–14	Hibernian	36	6	**36**	**6**
2014–15	Shrewsbury T	45	15	**111**	**37**

DEMETRIOU, Mickey (D) 42 3
b.Durrington 12-3-90
Internationals: England C.

2014–15	Shrewsbury T	42	3	**42**	**3**

ELLIS, Mark (D) 202 16
H: 6 2 W: 12 04 b.Kingsbridge 30-9-88

2007–08	Bolton W	0	0		
2009–10	Torquay U	27	3		
2010–11	Torquay U	27	2		
2011–12	Torquay U	35	3	**89**	**8**
2012–13	Crewe Alex	44	5		
2013–14	Crewe Alex	37	1	**81**	**6**
2014–15	Shrewsbury T	32	2	**32**	**2**

FLETCHER, Alex (M) 0 0

2013–14	Shrewsbury T	0	0		
2014–15	Shrewsbury T	0	0		

FLINT, Niall (M) 0 0

2013–14	Shrewsbury T	0	0		
2014–15	Shrewsbury T	0	0		

GAYLE, Cameron (D) 49 1
H: 5 11 W: 11 00 b.Birmingham 22-11-92

2010–11	WBA	0	0		
2011–12	WBA	0	0		
2012–13	WBA	0	0		
2012–13	*Shrewsbury T*	18	1		
2013–14	WBA	0	0		
2013–14	*Shrewsbury T*	3	0		
2014–15	Shrewsbury T	28	0	**49**	**1**

GINNELLY, Josh (M) 3 0
b.Coventry 24-3-97

2013–14	Shrewsbury T	0	0		
2014–15	Shrewsbury T	3	0	**3**	**0**

GOLDSON, Connor (D) 108 8
H: 6 3 W: 13 05 b.York 18-12-92

2010–11	Shrewsbury T	3	0		
2011–12	Shrewsbury T	4	0		
2012–13	Shrewsbury T	17	1		
2013–14	Shrewsbury T	36	0		
2013–14	*Cheltenham T*	4	0	**4**	**0**
2014–15	Shrewsbury T	44	7	**104**	**8**

GRANDISON, Jermaine (D) 144 5
H: 6 4 W: 13 03 b.Birmingham 15-12-90

2008–09	Coventry C	2	0		
2009–10	Coventry C	3	0		
2010–11	Coventry C	0	0	**5**	**0**
2010–11	*Tranmere R*	8	0	**8**	**0**
2010–11	Shrewsbury T	13	0		
2011–12	Shrewsbury T	38	2		
2012–13	Shrewsbury T	30	1		
2013–14	Shrewsbury T	14	0		
2014–15	Shrewsbury T	36	2	**131**	**5**

HALSTEAD, Mark (G) 4 0
H: 6 3 W: 14 00 b.Blackpool 1-9-90

2009–10	Blackpool	0	0		
2010–11	Blackpool	1	0		
2011–12	Blackpool	0	0		
2012–13	Blackpool	2	0		
2013–14	Blackpool	0	0	**3**	**0**
2014–15	Shrewsbury T	1	0	**1**	**0**

KNIGHT-PERCIVAL, Nathaniel (M) 74 2
H: 6 0 W: 11 06 b.Cambridge 31-3-87

2012–13	Peterborough U	31	0		
2013–14	Peterborough U	15	1	**46**	**1**
2014–15	Shrewsbury T	28	1	**28**	**1**

LAWRENCE, Liam (M) 460 84
H: 5 11 W: 12 06 b.Retford 14-12-81
Internationals: Republic of Ireland Full caps.

1999–2000	Mansfield T	2	0		
2000–01	Mansfield T	18	4		
2001–02	Mansfield T	32	2		
2002–03	Mansfield T	43	10		
2003–04	Mansfield T	41	18	**136**	**34**
2004–05	Sunderland	32	7		
2005–06	Sunderland	29	3		
2006–07	Sunderland	12	0	**73**	**10**
2006–07	Stoke C	27	5		
2007–08	Stoke C	41	14		
2008–09	Stoke C	20	3		
2009–10	Stoke C	25	1		
2010–11	Stoke C	0	0	**113**	**23**
2010–11	Portsmouth	31	7		
2011–12	Portsmouth	23	0	**54**	**7**
2011–12	*Cardiff C*	13	1	**13**	**1**
2012–13	PAOK Salonika	22	3		
2013–14	PAOK Salonika	2	0	**24**	**3**
2013–14	Barnsley	14	1	**14**	**1**
2014–15	Shrewsbury T	33	5	**33**	**5**

LEUTWILER, Jayson (G) 49 0
H: 6 3 W: 12 07 b.Basel 25-4-89
Internationals: Switzerland U16, U17, U18, U19, U20, U21.

2012–13	Middlesbrough	0	0		
2013–14	Middlesbrough	3	0	**3**	**0**
2014–15	Shrewsbury T	46	0	**46**	**0**

MANGAN, Andy (F) 105 21
H: 6 0 W: 11 09 b.Liverpool 30-8-86
Internationals: England C.

2003–04	Blackpool	2	0		
2004–05	Blackpool	0	0	**2**	**0**
From Hyde					
2006–07	Accrington S	34	4		
2007–08	Bury	20	4	**20**	**4**
2007–08	*Accrington S*	7	1	**41**	**5**
From Forest Green R, Wrexham					
2012–13	Fleetwood T	12	4	**12**	**4**
From Forest Green R.					
2014–15	Shrewsbury T	30	8	**30**	**8**

ROBINSON, Andy (M) 329 63
H: 5 8 W: 11 04 b.Birkenhead 3-11-79

2002–03	Tranmere R	0	0		
2003–04	Swansea C	37	8		
2004–05	Swansea C	37	8		
2005–06	Swansea C	39	12		
2006–07	Swansea C	39	7		
2007–08	Swansea C	40	8	**192**	**43**
2008–09	Leeds U	32	2		
2009–10	Leeds U	6	0		
2009–10	*Tranmere R*	5	1		
2010–11	Leeds U	0	0	**38**	**2**
2010–11	Tranmere R	15	0		
2011–12	Tranmere R	25	4		
2012–13	Tranmere R	33	10		
2013–14	Tranmere R	19	3	**97**	**18**
2014–15	Shrewsbury T	2	0	**2**	**0**

SADLER, Matthew (D) 310 3
H: 5 11 W: 11 08 b.Birmingham 26-2-85
Internationals: England U17, U18, U19.

2001–02	Birmingham C	0	0		
2002–03	Birmingham C	2	0		
2003–04	Birmingham C	0	0		
2003–04	*Northampton T*	7	0	**7**	**0**
2004–05	Birmingham C	0	0		
2005–06	Birmingham C	8	0		
2006–07	Birmingham C	36	0		
2007–08	Birmingham C	5	0	**51**	**0**
2007–08	Watford	15	0		
2008–09	Watford	15	0		
2009–10	Watford	0	0		
2009–10	*Stockport Co*	20	0	**20**	**0**
2010–11	Watford	0	0	**30**	**0**
2010–11	*Shrewsbury T*	46	0		
2011–12	Walsall	46	1	**46**	**1**
2012–13	Crawley T	46	1		
2013–14	Crawley T	46	1		
2014–15	Rotherham U	0	0		
2014–15	*Crawley T*	10	0	**102**	**2**
2014–15	*Oldham Ath*	8	0	**8**	**0**
2014–15	Shrewsbury T	0	0	**46**	**0**

SMITH, Dominic (D) 0 0
H: 6 0 W: 11 11 b.Shewsbury 9-2-96
Internationals: Wales U19.

2012–13	Shrewsbury T	0	0		
2013–14	Shrewsbury T	0	0		
2014–15	Shrewsbury T	0	0		

VERNON, Scott (F) 387 88
H: 6 1 W: 11 06 b.Manchester 13-12-83

2002–03	Oldham Ath	8	1		
2003–04	Oldham Ath	45	12		
2004–05	Oldham Ath	22	7	**75**	**20**
2004–05	*Blackpool*	4	3		
2005–06	Blackpool	17	1		
2005–06	*Colchester U*	7	1		
2006–07	Blackpool	38	11		
2007–08	Blackpool	15	4	**74**	**19**
2007–08	Colchester U	17	5		
2008–09	Colchester U	33	4		
2008–09	*Northampton T*	6	1	**6**	**1**
2009–10	Colchester U	7	3	**64**	**13**
2009–10	*Gillingham*	1	0	**1**	**0**
2009–10	*Southend U*	17	4	**17**	**4**
2010–11	Aberdeen	33	10		
2011–12	Aberdeen	35	11		
2012–13	Aberdeen	35	3		
2013–14	Aberdeen	25	6	**128**	**30**
2014–15	Shrewsbury T	22	1	**22**	**1**

VINCENT, Ashley (M) 241 27
H: 5 10 W: 11 08 b.Oldbury 26-5-85

2004–05	Cheltenham T	26	1		
2005–06	Cheltenham T	13	2		
2006–07	Cheltenham T	5	0		
2007–08	Cheltenham T	37	2		
2008–09	Cheltenham T	29	3		
2008–09	Colchester U	6	1		
2009–10	Colchester U	19	3		
2010–11	Colchester U	37	5		
2011–12	Colchester U	9	1	**71**	**10**
2012–13	Port Vale	34	7	**34**	**7**
2013–14	Cheltenham T	18	2	**128**	**10**
2014–15	Shrewsbury T	8	0	**8**	**0**

WESOLOWSKI, James (M) 233 14
H: 5 8 W: 11 11 b.Sydney 25-8-87
Internationals: Australia U20.

2004–05	Leicester C	0	0		
2005–06	Leicester C	5	0		
2006–07	Leicester C	19	0		
2007–08	Leicester C	22	0		
2008–09	Leicester C	0	0		
2008–09	*Dundee U*	8	0	**8**	**0**
2008–09	*Cheltenham T*	4	0	**4**	**0**
2009–10	Leicester C	0	0	**46**	**0**
2009–10	*Hamilton A*	29	4	**29**	**4**

2010–11	Peterborough U	32	2	32	2
2011–12	Oldham Ath	21	3		
2012–13	Oldham Ath	33	0		
2013–14	Oldham Ath	39	4	93	7
2014–15	Shrewsbury T	21	1	21	1

WILDIG, Aaron (M)   89 7
H: 5 9   W: 11 02   b.Hereford 15-4-92
Internationals: Wales U16.

2009–10	Cardiff C	11	1		
2010–11	Cardiff C	2	0		
2010–11	*Hamilton A*	3	0	3	0
2011–12	Cardiff C	0	0	13	1
2011–12	Shrewsbury T	12	2		
2012–13	Shrewsbury T	21	1		
2013–14	Shrewsbury T	30	2		
2014–15	Shrewsbury T	1	0	64	5
2014–15	*Morecambe*	9	1	9	1

WOODS, Ryan (M)   86 1
H: 5 8   b.Norton Canes 13-12-93

2012–13	Shrewsbury T	2	0		
2013–14	Shrewsbury T	41	1		
2014–15	Shrewsbury T	43	0	86	1

Players retained or with offer of contract
Lewis, Harry Charles John.

Scholars
Anderson, Kaiman Selern; Ashton,
Alexander Neil; Astley, Thomas Ryan;
Burton, Benjamin Kenneth; Butts, Jack
Thomas; Carta, Joel Sebastian; Fletcher,
Alexander John; Flint, Niall Daniel; Ginnelly,
Joshua Lloyd; Hickman, Ryan Luke; Jones,
Ethan Anthony; Kenton, Joseph Lewis; King,
Thomas James William; Millis, Nathan David;
Rowley, Shaun Keith; Watkins, Jeff Trevor;
Wilson, Jordan Reece Keith.

SOUTHAMPTON (75)

ALDERWEIRELD, Toby (D)   165 9
H: 6 1   W: 11 11   b.Wilrijk 2-3-89
Internationals: Belgium U26, U17, U18, U19, U21, Full caps.

2008–09	Ajax	5	0		
2009–10	Ajax	31	2		
2010–11	Ajax	26	2		
2011–12	Ajax	29	1		
2012–13	Ajax	32	2		
2013–14	Ajax	4	0	127	7
2013–14	*Atletico Madrid*	12	1	12	1
2014–15	Southampton	26	1	26	1

BARNARD, Lee (F)   223 73
H: 5 10   W: 10 10   b.Romford 18-7-84

2002–03	Tottenham H	0	0		
2002–03	*Exeter C*	3	0	3	0
2003–04	Tottenham H	0	0		
2004–05	Tottenham H	0	0		
2004–05	*Leyton Orient*	8	0	8	0
2004–05	*Northampton T*	5	0	5	0
2005–06	Tottenham H	3	0		
2006–07	Tottenham H	0	0		
2007–08	Tottenham H	0	0	3	0
2007–08	*Crewe Alex*	10	3	10	3
2007–08	Southend U	15	9		
2008–09	Southend U	35	11		
2009–10	Southend U	25	15		
2009–10	Southampton	20	9		
2010–11	Southampton	36	14		
2011–12	Southampton	6	0		
2012–13	Southampton	0	0		
2012–13	*Bournemouth*	15	4	15	4
2012–13	*Oldham Ath*	14	3	14	3
2013–14	Southampton	0	0		
2013–14	*Southend U*	13	1		
2014–15	Southampton	0	0	62	23
2014–15	*Southend U*	9	1	97	37
2014–15	*Stevenage*	6	3	6	3

BERTRAND, Ryan (D)   223 3
H: 5 10   W: 11 00   b.Southwark 5-8-89
Internationals: England U17, U18, U19, U20, U21, Full caps. Great Britain.

2006–07	Chelsea	0	0		
2006–07	*Bournemouth*	5	0	5	0
2007–08	Chelsea	0	0		
2007–08	*Oldham Ath*	21	0	21	0
2007–08	*Norwich C*	18	0		
2008–09	Chelsea	0	0		
2008–09	*Norwich C*	38	0	56	0
2009–10	Chelsea	0	0		
2009–10	*Reading*	44	1	44	1
2010–11	Chelsea	0	0		
2010–11	*Nottingham F*	19	0	19	0
2011–12	Chelsea	7	0		
2012–13	Chelsea	19	0		
2013–14	Chelsea	1	0	28	0
2013–14	*Aston Villa*	16	0	16	0
2014–15	Southampton	34	2	34	2

BORUC, Artur (G)   310 0
H: 6 4   W: 13 08   b.Siedlce 20-2-80
Internationals: Poland Full caps.

2005–06	Celtic	34	0		
2006–07	Celtic	36	0		
2007–08	Celtic	30	0		
2008–09	Celtic	34	0		
2009–10	Celtic	28	0	162	0
2010–11	Fiorentina	26	0		
2011–12	Fiorentina	36	0	62	0
2012–13	Southampton	20	0		
2013–14	Southampton	29	0		
2014–15	Southampton	0	0	49	0
2014–15	*Bournemouth*	37	0	37	0

CLYNE, Nathaniel (D)   216 4
H: 5 9   W: 10 07   b.Stockwell 5-4-91
Internationals: England U19, U21, Full caps.

2008–09	Crystal Palace	26	0		
2009–10	Crystal Palace	22	1		
2010–11	Crystal Palace	46	0		
2011–12	Crystal Palace	28	0	122	1
2012–13	Southampton	34	1		
2013–14	Southampton	25	0		
2014–15	Southampton	35	2	94	3

CROPPER, Cody (G)   0 0
H: 6 3   W: 14 05   b.Atlanta 16-2-93
Internationals: USA U20, U23.

2011–12	Ipswich T	0	0		
2012–13	Ipswich T	0	0		
2012–13	Southampton	0	0		
2013–14	Southampton	0	0		
2014–15	Southampton	0	0		

DAVIS, Kelvin (G)   613 0
H: 6 1   W: 11 05   b.Bedford 29-9-76
Internationals: England U21.

1993–94	Luton T	1	0		
1994–95	Luton T	9	0		
1994–95	*Torquay U*	2	0	2	0
1995–96	Luton T	6	0		
1996–97	Luton T	0	0		
1997–98	Luton T	32	0		
1997–98	*Hartlepool U*	2	0	2	0
1998–99	Luton T	44	0	92	0
1999–2000	Wimbledon	0	0		
2000–01	Wimbledon	45	0		
2001–02	Wimbledon	40	0		
2002–03	Wimbledon	46	0	131	0
2003–04	Ipswich T	45	0		
2004–05	Ipswich T	39	0	84	0
2005–06	Sunderland	33	0	33	0
2006–07	Southampton	38	0		
2007–08	Southampton	35	0		
2008–09	Southampton	46	0		
2009–10	Southampton	40	0		
2010–11	Southampton	46	0		
2011–12	Southampton	45	0		
2012–13	Southampton	10	0		
2013–14	Southampton	2	0		
2014–15	Southampton	7	0	269	0

DAVIS, Steven (M)   366 27
H: 5 8   W: 11 04   b.Ballymena 1-1-85
Internationals: Northern Ireland U15, U16, U17, U19, U21, U23, Full caps.

2004–05	Aston Villa	28	1		
2005–06	Aston Villa	35	4		
2006–07	Aston Villa	28	0	91	5
2007–08	*Fulham*	22	0	22	0
2007–08	*Rangers*	12	0		
2008–09	Rangers	34	6		
2009–10	Rangers	36	3		
2010–11	Rangers	37	4		
2011–12	Rangers	33	5	152	18
2012–13	Southampton	32	2		
2013–14	Southampton	34	2		
2014–15	Southampton	35	0	101	4

DJURICIC, Filip (M)   130 20
H: 5 9   W: 11 05   b.Obrenovac 30-1-92
Internationals: Serbia U21, Full caps.

2009–10	Heerenveen	9	1		
2010–11	Heerenveen	24	2		
2011–12	Heerenveen	34	10		
2012–13	Heerenveen	32	7	99	20
2013–14	Benfica	11	0		
2014–15	Benfica	0	0	11	0
2014–15	*Mainz*	11	0	11	0

On loan from Benfica.

| 2014–15 | Southampton | 9 | 0 | 9 | 0 |

ELIA, Eljero (M)   261 30
H: 5 9   W: 11 00   b.Voorburg 13-2-87
Internationals: Netherlands U21, B, Full caps.

2004–05	Den Haag	4	1		
2005–06	Den Haag	30	2		
2006–07	Den Haag	25	3	59	6
2007–08	FC Twente	30	2		
2008–09	FC Twente	34	9	64	11
2009–10	Hamburg	24	5		
2010–11	Hamburg	24	2		
2011–12	Hamburg	4	0	52	7
2011–12	Juventus	4	0	4	0
2012–13	Werder Bremen	24	0		
2013–14	Werder Bremen	33	4		
2014–15	Werder Bremen	9	0	66	4

On loan from Werder Bremen.

| 2014–15 | Southampton | 16 | 2 | 16 | 2 |

FLANNIGAN, Jake (M)   0 0
b. 2-2-96

| 2014–15 | Southampton | 0 | 0 | | |

FONTE, Jose (D)   368 22
H: 6 2   W: 12 08   b.Penafiel 22-12-83
Internationals: Portugal U21, B, Full caps.

2004–05	Felgueiros	28	1	28	1
2005–06	Setubal	15	0	15	0
2005–06	Benfica	1	0	1	0
2005–06	Pacos	0	0	11	1
2006–07	Amadora	25	1	25	1
2007–08	Crystal Palace	22	1		
2008–09	Crystal Palace	38	4		
2009–10	Crystal Palace	22	1	82	6
2009–10	Southampton	21	0		
2010–11	Southampton	43	7		
2011–12	Southampton	42	1		
2012–13	Southampton	27	2		
2013–14	Southampton	36	3		
2014–15	Southampton	37	0	206	13

FORSTER, Fraser (G)   218 0
H: 6 0   W: 12 00   b.Hexham 17-3-88

2007–08	Newcastle U	0	0		
2008–09	Newcastle U	0	0		
2008–09	*Stockport Co*	6	0	6	0
2009–10	Newcastle U	0	0		
2009–10	*Bristol R*	4	0	4	0
2009–10	*Norwich C*	38	0	38	0
2010–11	Newcastle U	0	0		
2010–11	*Celtic*	36	0		
2011–12	Newcastle U	0	0		
2011–12	*Celtic*	33	0		
2012–13	*Celtic*	34	0		
2013–14	*Celtic*	37	0	140	0
2014–15	Southampton	30	0	30	0

GALLAGHER, Sam (F)   18 1
H: 6 4   b.Crediton 15-9-95
Internationals: Scotland U19, England U19.

| 2013–14 | Southampton | 18 | 1 | | |
| 2014–15 | Southampton | 0 | 0 | 18 | 1 |

GAPE, Dominic (M)   1 0
H: 5 11   W: 10 13   b.Southampton 9-9-94

2012–13	Southampton	0	0		
2013–14	Southampton	0	0		
2014–15	Southampton	1	0	1	0

GARDOS, Florin (D)   143 4
H: 6 4   W: 10 10   b.Satu Mare 29-10-88
Internationals: Romania U19, U21, Full caps.

2008–09	Concordia Chiajna	22	0		
2009–10	Concordia Chiajna	29	1	51	1
2010–11	Steau Bucharest	23	0		
2011–12	Steau Bucharest	8	0		
2012–13	Steau Bucharest	21	1	52	1
2013–14	Steaua Bucuresti	29	2	29	2
2014–15	Southampton	11	0	11	0

GAZZANIGA, Paulo (G)   39 0
H: 6 5   W: 14 02   b.Santa Fe 2-1-92

2011–12	Gillingham	20	0	20	0
2012–13	Southampton	9	0		
2013–14	Southampton	8	0		
2014–15	Southampton	2	0	19	0

HESKETH, Jake (M)   2 0
H: 5 6   W: 9 13   b. 27-3-96

| 2014–15 | Southampton | 2 | 0 | 2 | 0 |

HOOIVELD, Jos (D)   246 15
H: 6 3   W: 11 11   b.Zeijen 22-4-83
Internationals: Netherlands U19.

2002–03	Heerenveen	1	0		
2003–04	Heerenveen	12	0	13	0
2004–05	Zwolle	14	2		
2005–06	Zwolle	30	1	44	3
2006–07	Kapfenberger	14	0	14	0
2007	Inter Turku	26	0		
2008	Inter Turku	26	4	52	4

2009	AIK Stockholm	28	0	28	0
2009–10	Celtic	2	0		
2010–11	Celtic	5	0	7	0
2011–12	Southampton	39	7		
2012–13	Southampton	25	0		
2013–14	Southampton	3	0		
2014–15	Southampton	0	0	67	7
2014–15	*Norwich C*	6	0	6	0
2014–15	*Millwall*	15	1	15	1

ISGROVE, Lloyd (M)   17   1
H: 5 10   W: 11 05   b.Yeovil 12-1-93
Internationals: Wales U21.

2011–12	Southampton	0	0		
2012–13	Southampton	0	0		
2013–14	Southampton	0	0		
2013–14	*Peterborough U*	8	1	8	1
2014–15	Southampton	1	0	1	0
2014–15	*Sheffield W*	8	0	8	0

LONG, Shane (F)   303   72
H: 5 10   W: 11 02   b.Co. Tipperary 22-1-87
Internationals: Republic of Ireland B, U21, Full caps.

2005	Cork C	1	0	1	0
2005–06	Reading	11	3		
2006–07	Reading	21	2		
2007–08	Reading	29	3		
2008–09	Reading	37	9		
2009–10	Reading	31	6		
2010–11	Reading	44	21		
2011–12	Reading	1	0	174	44
2011–12	WBA	32	8		
2012–13	WBA	34	8		
2013–14	WBA	15	3	81	19
2013–14	Hull C	15	4	15	4
2014–15	Southampton	32	5	32	5

MANE, Sadio (F)   115   43
H: 5 9   b.Sedhiou 10-4-92
Internationals: Senegal Full caps.

2011–12	Metz	19	1		
2012–13	Metz	3	1	22	2
2012–13	Red Bull Salzburg	26	16		
2013–14	Red Bull Salzburg	33	13		
2014–15	Red Bull Salzburg	4	2	63	31
2014–15	Southampton	30	10	30	10

MAYUKA, Emmanuel (F)   166   39
H: 5 9   W: 11 01   b.Kabwe 21-11-90
Internationals: Zambia Full caps.

2006	Kabwe Warriors	1	0		
2007	Kabwe Warriors	16	4		
2008	Kabwe Warriors	9	3	26	7
2008–09	Maccabi Tel Aviv	12	1		
2009–10	Maccabi Tel Aviv	29	7	41	8
2010–11	Young Boys	27	9		
2011–12	Young Boys	28	9		
2012–13	Young Boys	7	2	62	20
2012–13	Southampton	11	0		
2013–14	Southampton	0	0		
2013–14	*Sochaux*	21	4	21	4
2014–15	Southampton	5	0	16	0

McCARTHY, Jason (D)   1   0
H: 6 1   W: 12 08   b.Southampton 7-11-95

2013–14	Southampton	0	0		
2014–15	Southampton	1	0	1	0

McQUEEN, Sam (M)   0   0
H: 5 9   W: 11 00   b.Southampton 6-2-95

2011–12	Southampton	0	0		
2012–13	Southampton	0	0		
2013–14	Southampton	0	0		
2014–15	Southampton	0	0		

OSVALDO, Pablo (F)   259   87
H: 6 0   W: 11 06   b.Buenos Aires 12-1-86
Internationals: Italy U21, Full caps.

2005–06	Huracan	33	11	33	11
2005–06	Atalanta	3	1		
2006–07	Atalanta	0	0	3	1
2006–07	Lecce	31	8	31	8
2007–08	Fiorentina	13	5		
2008–09	Fiorentina	8	0	21	5
2008–09	Bologna	12	0		
2009–10	Bologna	13	3	25	3
2009–10	Espanyol	20	7		
2010–11	Espanyol	24	13	44	20
2011–12	Roma	26	11		
2012–13	Roma	29	16	55	27
2013–14	Southampton	13	3		
2013–14	*Juventus*	11	1	11	1
2014–15	Southampton	0	0	13	3
2014–15	*Inter Milan*	12	5	12	5
2014–15	*Boca Juniors*	11	3	11	3

PELLE, Graziano (F)   278   97
H: 6 4   W: 13 03   b.Lecce 15-7-85
Internationals: Italy U20, U21, U23, Full caps.

2003–04	Leece	1	0		
2004–05	Leece	0	0		
2004–05	Catania	15	0	15	0
2005–06	Leece	10	0		
2005–06	Crotone	17	6	17	6
2006–07	Leece	0	0	11	0
2006–07	Cesena	38	10	38	10
2007–08	AZ Alkmaar	27	3		
2008–09	AZ Alkmaar	20	3		
2009–10	AZ Alkmaar	13	2		
2010–11	AZ Alkmaar	18	6	78	14
2011–12	Parma	11	1		
2011–12	*Sampdoria*	12	4	12	4
2012–13	Parma	1	0	12	1
2012–13	Feyenoord	29	27		
2013–14	Feyenoord	28	23	57	50
2014–15	Southampton	38	12	38	12

RAMIREZ, Gaston (M)   124   19
H: 6 0   W: 12 00   b.Montevideo 2-12-90
Internationals: Uruguay U20, U23, Full caps.

2010–11	Bologna	24	4		
2011–12	Bologna	33	8	57	12
2012–13	Southampton	26	5		
2013–14	Southampton	18	1		
2014–15	Southampton	1	0	45	6
2014–15	*Hull C*	22	1	22	1

REED, Harrison (M)   13   0
H: 5 9   W: 11 09   b.Worthing 27-1-95
Internationals: England U19, U20.

2011–12	Southampton	0	0		
2012–13	Southampton	0	0		
2013–14	Southampton	4	0		
2014–15	Southampton	9	0	13	0

RODRIGUEZ, Jay (F)   190   56
H: 6 0   W: 12 00   b.Burnley 29-7-89
Internationals: England U21, Full caps.

2007–08	Burnley	1	0		
2007–08	*Stirling Alb*	11	3	11	3
2008–09	Burnley	25	2		
2009–10	Burnley	0	0		
2009–10	*Barnsley*	6	1	6	1
2010–11	Burnley	42	14		
2011–12	Burnley	37	15	105	31
2012–13	Southampton	35	6		
2013–14	Southampton	33	15		
2014–15	Southampton	0	0	68	21

ROWE, Omar (M)   0   0
H: 5 8   W: 11 00   b.Southampton 30-10-94

2013–14	Southampton	0	0		
2014–15	Southampton	0	0		

SCHNEIDERLIN, Morgan (M)   236   14
H: 5 11   W: 11 11   b.Obernai 8-11-89
Internationals: France U16, U17, U18, U19, U20, U21, Full caps.

2007–08	Strasbourg	5	0	5	0
2008–09	Southampton	30	0		
2009–10	Southampton	37	1		
2010–11	Southampton	27	0		
2011–12	Southampton	42	2		
2012–13	Southampton	36	5		
2013–14	Southampton	33	2		
2014–15	Southampton	26	4	231	14

SEAGER, Ryan (F)   1   0
H: 5 11   W: 11 00   b.Southampton 5-2-96
Internationals: England U17.

2014–15	Southampton	1	0	1	0

SINCLAIR, Jake (F)   3   0
H: 5 7   W: 11 00   b.Bath 29-11-94

2011–12	Southampton	0	0		
2012–13	Southampton	0	0		
2013–14	Southampton	0	0		
2014–15	Southampton	0	0		
2014–15	*Hibernian*	3	0	3	0

STEPHENS, Jack (D)   52   1
H: 6 1   W: 13 03   b.Torpoint 27-1-94
Internationals: England U18, U19, U20.

2010–11	Plymouth Arg	5	0	5	0
2010–11	Southampton	0	0		
2011–12	Southampton	0	0		
2012–13	Southampton	0	0		
2013–14	Southampton	0	0		
2013–14	*Swindon T*	10	0		
2014–15	Southampton	0	0		
2014–15	*Swindon T*	37	1	47	1

TADIC, Dusan (M)   272   75
H: 5 11   W: 12 00   b.Backa Topola 20-11-88
Internationals: Serbia Full caps.

2006–07	Vojvodina	23	3		
2007–08	Vojvodina	28	7		
2008–09	Vojvodina	29	9		
2009–10	Vojvodina	27	10	107	29
2010–11	Groningen	34	7		
2011–12	Groningen	34	7	68	14
2012–13	FC Twente	33	12		
2013–14	FC Twente	33	16	66	28
2014–15	Southampton	31	4	31	4

TARGETT, Matt (D)   6   0
b.Edinburgh 18-9-95
Internationals: Scotland U19, England U19, U20, U21.

2013–14	Southampton	0	0		
2014–15	Southampton	6	0	6	0

TURNBULL, Jordan (D)   44   1
H: 6 1   W: 11 05   b.Trowbridge 30-10-94
Internationals: England U19, U20.

2014–15	Southampton	0	0		
2014–15	*Swindon T*	44	1	44	1

WANYAMA, Victor (M)   165   15
H: 6 2   W: 11 12   b.Nairobi 25-6-91
Internationals: Kenya Full caps.

2009–10	Beerschot	19	0		
2010–11	Beerschot	30	2	49	2
2011–12	Celtic	29	4		
2012–13	Celtic	32	6	61	10
2013–14	Southampton	23	0		
2014–15	Southampton	32	3	55	3

WARD-PROWSE, James (M)   74   1
H: 5 8   W: 10 06   b.Portsmouth 1-11-94
Internationals: England U17, U19, U20, U21.

2011–12	Southampton	0	0		
2012–13	Southampton	15	0		
2013–14	Southampton	34	0		
2014–15	Southampton	25	1	74	1

YOSHIDA, Maya (D)   116   7
H: 6 2   W: 12 03   b.Nagasaki 24-8-88
Internationals: Japan U23, Full caps.

2010–11	VVV	30	5		
2011–12	VVV	32	5		
2012–13	VVV	2	0	54	5
2012–13	Southampton	32	0		
2013–14	Southampton	8	1		
2014–15	Southampton	22	1	62	2

Players retained on with offer of contract
Barnes, Marcus Thomas; Britt, William David; Debayo, Joshua Akinkunmi; Isted, Harvey James Duke; Mugabi, Bevis Kristofer Kizito; Sims, Joshua Samuel; Turnbull, Jordan Robert; Willard, Harley Bryn.

Scholars
Bakary, Mohamed Richard; Clinton, Kyle; Cook, Oliver David Paul; Cvjeticanin, Oskar; Hallett, Jake; Jones, Alfie; Kayembe, Carel; Lea, Joseph William; Little, Armani; Olomola, Olufela; Wilkin, Stuart John; Wood, William Nicholas.

SOUTHEND U (76)

ATKINSON, Will (M)   218   17
H: 5 10   W: 10 07   b.Beverley 14-10-88

2006–07	Hull C	0	0		
2007–08	Hull C	0	0		
2007–08	*Port Vale*	4	0	4	0
2007–08	*Mansfield T*	12	0	12	0
2008–09	Hull C	0	0		
2009–10	Hull C	2	1		
2009–10	*Rochdale*	15	3		
2010–11	Hull C	4	0		
2010–11	*Rotherham U*	3	1	3	1
2010–11	*Rochdale*	21	2	36	5
2011–12	Hull C	0	0	6	1
2011–12	*Plymouth Arg*	22	4	22	4
2011–12	*Bradford C*	12	1		
2012–13	Bradford C	42	1	54	2
2013–14	Southend U	45	2		
2014–15	Southend U	36	2	81	4

BANTON, Josh (D)   0   0

2013–14	Southend U	0	0		
2014–15	Southend U	0	0		

BARRETT, Adam (D)   589   41
H: 5 10   W: 12 00   b.Dagenham 29-11-79

1998–99	Plymouth Arg	1	0		
1999–2000	Plymouth Arg	42	3		

2000–01	Plymouth Arg	9	0	52	3
2000–01	Mansfield T	8	1		
2001–02	Mansfield T	29	0	37	1
2002–03	Bristol R	45	1		
2003–04	Bristol R	45	4	90	5
2004–05	Southend U	43	11		
2005–06	Southend U	45	3		
2006–07	Southend U	28	3		
2007–08	Southend U	45	6		
2008–09	Southend U	45	2		
2009–10	Southend U	41	2		
2010–11	Crystal Palace	7	0	7	0
2010–11	*Leyton Orient*	14	0	14	0
2011–12	Bournemouth	21	1	21	1
2012–13	Gillingham	43	1		
2013–14	Gillingham	45	2		
2014–15	Gillingham	0	0	88	3
2014–15	*AFC Wimbledon*	23	1	23	1
2014–15	Southend U	10	0	257	27

BENTLEY, Daniel (G)   98   0
H: 6 2   W: 11 05   b.Wickford 13-7-93

2011–12	Southend U	1	0		
2012–13	Southend U	9	0		
2013–14	Southend U	46	0		
2014–15	Southend U	42	0	98	0

BOLGER, Cian (D)   76   3
H: 6 4   W: 12 05   b.Co. Kildare 12-3-92
Internationals: Republic of Ireland U21.

2009–10	Leicester C	0	0		
2010–11	Leicester C	0	0		
2010–11	*Bristol R*	6	0		
2011–12	Leicester C	0	0		
2011–12	*Bristol R*	39	2		
2012–13	Leicester C	0	0		
2012–13	*Bristol R*	3	0	48	2
2012–13	Bolton W	0	0		
2013–14	Bolton W	0	0		
2013–14	*Colchester U*	4	0	4	0
2013–14	*Southend U*	1	0		
2014–15	Southend U	23	1	24	1

BRIDGE, Jack (M)   0   0
H: 5 10   W: 11 07   b. 21-9-95

2013–14	Southend U	0	0		
2014–15	Southend U	0	0		

BROWN, Ellis (F)   0   0
b. 23-10-95

2014–15	Southend U	0	0		

CLIFFORD, Conor (M)   61   4
H: 5 8   W: 10 08   b.Dublin 1-10-91
Internationals: Republic of Ireland U17, U19, U21.

2008–09	Chelsea	0	0		
2009–10	Chelsea	0	0		
2010–11	Chelsea	0	0		
2010–11	*Plymouth Arg*	7	0	7	0
2010–11	Notts Co	9	0	9	0
2011–12	Chelsea	0	0		
2011–12	*Yeovil T*	7	0	7	0
2012–13	Chelsea	0	0		
2012–13	Portsmouth	2	1	2	1
2012–13	*Crawley T*	1	0	1	0
2012–13	Leicester C	0	0		
2013–14	Southend U	23	1		
2014–15	Southend U	12	3	35	3

COKER, Ben (D)   118   3
H: 5 11   W: 11 09   b.Hatfield 17-6-89

2010–11	Colchester U	20	0		
2011–12	Colchester U	20	0		
2012–13	Colchester U	1	0	41	0
2013–14	Southend U	45	2		
2014–15	Southend U	32	1	77	3

CORR, Barry (F)   245   63
H: 6 3   W: 12 07   b.Co Wicklow 2-4-85

2001–02	Leeds U	0	0		
2002–03	Leeds U	0	0		
2003–04	Leeds U	0	0		
2004–05	Leeds U	0	0		
2005–06	Sheffield W	16	0		
2006–07	Sheffield W	1	0	17	0
2006–07	*Bristol C*	3	0	3	0
2006–07	*Swindon T*	8	3		
2007–08	Swindon T	17	5		
2008–09	Swindon T	11	2	36	10
2009–10	Exeter C	34	3	34	3
2010–11	Southend U	41	18		
2011–12	Southend U	0	0		
2012–13	Southend U	32	6		
2013–14	Southend U	43	12		
2014–15	Southend U	39	14	155	50

DEEGAN, Gary (M)   211   18
H: 5 9   W: 11 11   b.Dublin 28-9-87

2005–06	Shelbourne	0	0		
2006	*Kilkenny City*	18	4	18	4
2007	*Longford Town*	30	3	30	3
2008	*Galway U*	17	0	17	0
2008	Bohemians	12	3	12	3
2009	Bohemains	23	2	23	2
2009–10	Coventry C	17	2		
2010–11	Coventry C	1	0		
2011–12	Coventry C	24	3	42	5
2012–13	Hibernian	20	0	20	0
2013–14	Northampton T	27	1	27	1
2014–15	Southend U	22	0	22	0

HURST, Kevan (M)   354   35
H: 5 10   W: 11 07   b.Chesterfield 27-8-85

2003–04	*Boston U*	7	1	7	1
2004–05	Sheffield U	1	0		
2004–05	*Stockport Co*	14	1	14	1
2005–06	Sheffield U	0	0		
2005–06	*Chesterfield*	37	4		
2006–07	Sheffield U	0	0	1	0
2006–07	*Chesterfield*	25	3	62	7
2006–07	*Scunthorpe U*	13	0		
2007–08	Scunthorpe U	33	1		
2008–09	Scunthorpe U	20	2	66	3
2009–10	Carlisle U	33	2		
2010–11	Carlisle U	2	0	35	2
2010–11	*Morecambe*	21	2	21	2
2011–12	Walsall	34	2	34	2
2012–13	Southend U	44	5		
2013–14	Southend U	42	11		
2014–15	Southend U	28	1	114	17

IBENFELDT, Mads (D)   93   4
H: 6 5   W: 13 10   b. 26-1-85

2010–11	Bronshoj	25	1		
2011–12	Bronshoj	24	1		
2012–13	Bronshoj	29	2	78	4
2013–14	AB Copenhagen	14	0	14	0
2014–15	Southend U	1	0	1	0

LEONARD, Ryan (D)   124   11
H: 6 0   W: 11 01   b.Plympton 24-5-92

2009–10	Plymouth Arg	1	0		
2010–11	Plymouth Arg	0	0	1	0
2011–12	Southend U	17	1		
2012–13	Southend U	22	2		
2013–14	Southend U	43	5		
2014–15	Southend U	41	3	123	11

MATSUZAKA, Daniel (D)   0   0

2014–15	Southend U	0	0		

PAYNE, Jack (M)   45   6
H: 5 5   W: 9 06   b.Tower Hamlets 25-10-94

2013–14	Southend U	11	0		
2014–15	Southend U	34	6	45	6

PROSSER, Luke (D)   151   7
H: 6 2   W: 12 04   b.Waltham Cross 28-5-88

2005–06	Port Vale	0	0		
2006–07	Port Vale	0	0		
2007–08	Port Vale	5	0		
2008–09	Port Vale	26	1		
2009–10	Port Vale	2	1	33	2
2010–11	Southend U	17	1		
2011–12	Southend U	21	1		
2012–13	Southend U	25	0		
2013–14	Southend U	25	3		
2014–15	Southend U	30	0	118	5

SMITH, Paul (G)   266   0
H: 6 3   W: 14 00   b.Epsom 17-12-79

1998–99	Charlton Ath	0	0		
1998–99	*Brentford*	0	0		
1999–2000	Charlton Ath	0	0		

From Carshalton Ath.

2000–01	Brentford	2	0		
2001–02	Brentford	18	0		
2002–03	Brentford	43	0		
2003–04	Brentford	24	0	87	0
2003–04	Southampton	0	0		
2004–05	Southampton	6	0		
2005–06	Southampton	9	0	15	0
2006–07	Nottingham F	45	0		
2007–08	Nottingham F	46	0		
2008–09	Nottingham F	28	0		
2009–10	Nottingham F	1	0		
2010–11	Nottingham F	0	0		
2010–11	*Middlesbrough*	10	0	10	0
2011–12	Nottingham F	0	0	120	0
2012–13	Southend U	34	0		
2013–14	Southend U	0	0		
2014–15	Southend U	0	0	34	0

SMITH, Ted (G)   4   0
b.Benfleet 18-1-96
Internationals: England U18, U19.

2012–13	Southend U	0	0		
2013–14	Southend U	0	0		
2014–15	Southend U	4	0	4	0

THOMPSON, Adam (D)   81   1
H: 6 2   W: 12 10   b.Harlow 28-9-92
Internationals: Northern Ireland U17, U19, U21, Full caps.

2010–11	Watford	10	1		
2011–12	Watford	0	0		
2011–12	*Brentford*	20	0	20	0
2012–13	Watford	4	0		
2012–13	*Wycombe W*	2	0	2	0
2012–13	*Barnet*	1	0	1	0
2013–14	Watford	0	0	14	1
2013–14	*Southend U*	16	0		
2014–15	Southend U	28	0	44	0

TIMLIN, Michael (M)   263   16
H: 5 8   W: 11 08   b.New Cross 19-3-85
Internationals: Republic of Ireland U21.

2002–03	Fulham	0	0		
2003–04	Fulham	0	0		
2004–05	Fulham	0	0		
2005–06	Fulham	0	0		
2005–06	*Scunthorpe U*	1	0	1	0
2005–06	*Doncaster R*	3	0	3	0
2006–07	Fulham	0	0		
2006–07	*Swindon T*	24	1		
2007–08	Fulham	0	0		
2007–08	*Swindon T*	10	1		
2008–09	Swindon T	41	2		
2009–10	Swindon T	21	0		
2010–11	Swindon T	22	2		
2010–11	*Southend U*	8	1		
2011–12	Swindon T	1	0	119	6
2011–12	Southend U	39	4		
2012–13	Southend U	25	0		
2013–14	Southend U	36	2		
2014–15	Southend U	32	3	140	10

WESTON, Myles (M)   291   27
H: 5 11   W: 12 05   b.Lewisham 12-3-88
Internationals: England U16, U17, U18, U19. Antigua and Barbuda Full caps.

2006–07	Charlton Ath	0	0		
2006–07	Notts Co	4	0		
2007–08	Notts Co	25	0		
2008–09	Notts Co	44	3	73	3
2009–10	Brentford	40	8		
2010–11	Brentford	42	3		
2011–12	Brentford	26	1	108	12
2012–13	Gillingham	37	8		
2013–14	Gillingham	39	2	76	10
2014–15	Southend U	34	2	34	2

WHITE, John (D)   315   1
H: 6 0   W: 12 01   b.Maldon 26-7-86

2004–05	Colchester U	20	0		
2005–06	Colchester U	35	0		
2006–07	Colchester U	16	0		
2007–08	Colchester U	21	0		
2008–09	Colchester U	26	0		
2009–10	Colchester U	39	0		
2009–10	*Southend U*	5	0		
2010–11	Colchester U	22	0		
2011–12	Colchester U	26	0		
2012–13	Colchester U	22	0	227	0
2013–14	Southend U	41	1		
2014–15	Southend U	42	0	88	1

WILLIAMS, Jason (F)   4   0
H: 6 0   W: 12 06   b. 1-11-95

2013–14	Southend U	2	0		
2014–15	Southend U	2	0	4	0

WORRALL, David (M)   235   19
H: 6 0   W: 11 03   b.Manchester 12-6-90

2006–07	Bury	1	0		
2007–08	Bury	0	0		
2007–08	WBA	0	0		
2008–09	*Accrington S*	4	0	4	0
2008–09	*Shrewsbury T*	9	0	9	0
2009–10	WBA	0	0		
2009–10	Bury	40	4		
2010–11	Bury	40	2		
2011–12	Bury	41	3		
2012–13	Bury	41	2	163	11
2013–14	Rotherham U	3	1	3	1
2013–14	*Oldham Ath*	18	1	18	1
2014–15	Southend U	38	6	38	6

Scholars
Adeyeye, Emmanuel Adekunle; Alawode-Williams, Jordan; Batlokwa, Wedu Reneilwe; Bedford, Joseph; Bexon, Josh Andrew; Cotton, Nico Lewis; Coutts, Sonny Joseph; Farrell, Kane Stephen William; Gard, Frederick Jack; Johnson, Ross Anthony; Keating, Macauley Anthony; Macree, James Terence; Matsuzaka, Daniel Lewis; Norman, Harry Alan; Phillips, Harry; Pitoula, Wabo Fotsing Norman Arthur; Salami, Abdus-Salam Efosa; Scott, Brandon Montel.

STEVENAGE (77)

AKINYEMI, Dipo (F) **0 0**
2014–15 Stevenage 0 0

ALLEN, George (D) **0 0**
2012–13 Stevenage 0 0
2013–14 Stevenage 0 0
2014–15 Stevenage 0 0

ASHTON, Jon (D) **254 3**
H: 6 2 W: 13 12 b.Nuneaton 4-10-82
Internationals: England C.
2000–01 Leicester C 0 0
2001–02 Leicester C 7 0
2002–03 *Notts Co* 4 0 **4 0**
2003–04 Leicester C 0 0 **7 0**
2003–04 Oxford U 34 0
2004–05 Oxford U 30 0
2005–06 Oxford U 33 1 **97 1**
From Rushden & D, Grays Ath.
2010–11 Stevenage 38 1
2011–12 Stevenage 43 1
2012–13 Stevenage 8 0
2013–14 Stevenage 40 0
2014–15 Stevenage 17 0 **146 2**

BEARDSLEY, Chris (F) **188 20**
H: 6 0 W: 12 12 b.Derby 28-2-84
2002–03 Mansfield T 5 0
2003–04 Mansfield T 15 1
2004–05 Doncaster R 4 0 **4 0**
2004–05 Kidderminster H 25 5 **25 5**
2005–06 Mansfield T 3 0
2006–07 Mansfield T 10 0 **33 1**
From Rushden & D, York C, Kettering T.
2010–11 Stevenage 23 1
2011–12 Stevenage 31 7
2012–13 Preston NE 19 1
2013–14 Preston NE 0 0 **19 1**
2013–14 *Bristol R* 24 1 **24 1**
2014–15 Stevenage 29 4 **83 12**

BEASANT, Sam (G) **8 0**
H: 6 5 W: 12 13 b.Denham 8-4-88
2014–15 Stevenage 8 0 **8 0**

BOND, Andy (M) **147 11**
H: 5 10 W: 11 07 b.Wigan 16-3-86
Internationals: England C.
2010–11 Colchester U 43 7
2011–12 Colchester U 40 3
2012–13 Colchester U 27 0
2012–13 *Crewe Alex* 4 0 **4 0**
2013–14 Colchester U 8 1 **118 11**
2013–14 *Bristol R* 5 0 **5 0**
2014–15 Stevenage 20 0 **20 0**

CALCUTT, Connor (F) **8 1**
H: 6 2 W: 12 13 b. 10-10-93
2014–15 Stevenage 8 1 **8 1**

CASEY, George (M) **0 0**
H: 6 0 W: 11 00 b. 8-9-97
2014–15 Stevenage 0 0

CHARLES, Darius (M) **181 14**
H: 6 1 W: 13 05 b.Ealing 10-12-87
Internationals: England C.
2004–05 Brentford 1 0
2005–06 Brentford 2 0
2006–07 Brentford 17 1
2007–08 Brentford 17 0 **37 1**
From Ebbsfleet U.
2010–11 Stevenage 28 2
2011–12 Stevenage 28 4
2012–13 Stevenage 37 1
2013–14 Stevenage 22 4
2014–15 Stevenage 29 2 **144 13**

COMMINGES, Miguel (D) **192 0**
H: 6 3 W: 12 07 b.Martinique 16-3-82
Internationals: Guadeloupe Full caps.
2002–03 Amiens 12 0 **12 0**
2003–04 Reims 29 0
2004–05 Reims 21 0
2005–06 Reims 11 0
2006–07 Reims 13 0 **74 0**
2007–08 Swindon T 40 0 **40 0**
2008–09 Cardiff C 30 0
2009–10 Cardiff C 1 0 **31 0**
2010–11 Southend U 7 0 **7 0**
2011 Colorado Rapids 7 0 **7 0**
2012–13 Stevenage 21 0
2013–14 Stevenage 0 0
2014–15 Stevenage 0 0 **21 0**

CONLON, Tom (M) **14 0**
H: 5 8 W: 9 11 b.Stoke-on-Trent 3-2-96
2013–14 Peterborough U 1 0 **1 0**
2014–15 Stevenage 13 0 **13 0**

DAY, Chris (G) **371 0**
H: 6 2 W: 13 07 b.Whipps Cross 28-7-75
Internationals: England U18, U21.
1992–93 Tottenham H 0 0
1993–94 Tottenham H 0 0
1994–95 Tottenham H 0 0
1995–96 Tottenham H 0 0
1996–97 Crystal Palace 24 0 **24 0**
1997–98 Watford 0 0
1998–99 Watford 0 0
1999–2000 Watford 11 0
2000–01 Watford 0 0 **11 0**
2000–01 *Lincoln C* 14 0 **14 0**
2001–02 QPR 16 0
2002–03 QPR 12 0
2003–04 QPR 29 0
2004–05 QPR 30 0 **87 0**
2004–05 *Preston NE* 6 0 **6 0**
2005–06 Oldham Ath 30 0 **30 0**
2006–07 Millwall 5 0
2007–08 Millwall 5 0 **10 0**
2010–11 Stevenage 46 0
2011–12 Stevenage 44 0
2012–13 Stevenage 17 0
2013–14 Stevenage 44 0
2014–15 Stevenage 38 0 **189 0**

DEACON, Roarie (M) **48 1**
H: 5 7 W: 10 10 b.London 12-10-91
Internationals: England U19.
2012–13 Stevenage 1 0
2013–14 Stevenage 23 0
2014–15 Stevenage 24 1 **48 1**

DEMBELE, Bira (D) **82 4**
H: 6 2 W: 11 10 b. 22-3-88
Internationals: France U21.
2007–08 Rennes 7 0
2008–09 Rennes 2 0
2009–10 Rennes 0 0
2009–10 *Boulogne* 23 1 **23 1**
2010–11 Rennes 0 0 **9 0**
2011–12 Sedan 1 0
2011–12 *Red Star 93* 9 0 **9 0**
2012–13 Sedan 0 0 **1 0**
2013–14 Stevenage 13 1
2014–15 Stevenage 27 2 **40 3**

GORDAN, Rohdell (M) **3 0**
2013–14 Stevenage 3 0
2014–15 Stevenage 0 0 **3 0**

GORMAN, Dale (D) **0 0**
H: 5 11 W: 11 00 b.Letterkenny 28-6-96
Internationals: Northern Ireland U19.
2014–15 Stevenage 0 0

HENRY, Ronnie (D) **123 0**
H: 5 11 W: 11 10 b.Hemel Hempstead 2-1-84
Internationals: England C.
2002–03 Tottenham H 0 0
2002–03 *Southend U* 3 0 **3 0**
2004 Dublin C 12 0 **12 0**
2010–11 Stevenage 42 0
2011–12 Stevenage 32 0
2014–15 Stevenage 34 0 **108 0**

JOHNSON, Ryan (D) **5 0**
H: 6 2 W: 13 05 b. 2-10-96
2013–14 Stevenage 1 0
2014–15 Stevenage 4 0 **5 0**

KENNEDY, Ben (F) **15 4**
H: 5 10 W: 11 00 b. 12-1-97
2014–15 Stevenage 15 4 **15 4**

LANCASTER, Cameron (F) **10 1**
H: 6 0 W: 11 09 b.Camden 5-11-92
2010–11 Tottenham H 0 0
2010–11 *Dagenham & R* 4 0 **4 0**
2011–12 Tottenham H 1 0
2012–13 Tottenham H 0 0 **1 0**
2014–15 Stevenage 5 1 **5 1**

LEE, Charlie (M) **301 34**
H: 5 11 W: 11 07 b.Whitechapel 5-1-87
2005–06 Tottenham H 0 0
2006–07 Tottenham H 0 0
2006–07 *Millwall* 5 0 **5 0**
2007–08 Peterborough U 42 6
2008–09 Peterborough U 44 5
2009–10 Peterborough U 33 2
2010–11 Peterborough U 34 1 **153 14**
2010–11 *Gillingham* 4 1
2011–12 Gillingham 33 6
2012–13 Gillingham 31 2
2013–14 Gillingham 31 2 **99 11**
2014–15 Stevenage 44 9 **44 9**

MARRIOTT, Adam (F) **13 3**
H: 5 9 W: 11 03 b.Brandon 14-4-91
2014–15 Stevenage 13 3 **13 3**

MARTIN, David J (M) **157 15**
H: 5 9 W: 10 10 b.Erith 3-6-85
2006–07 Crystal Palace 5 0
2007–08 Crystal Palace 9 0 **14 0**
2007–08 Millwall 11 2
2008–09 Millwall 44 4
2009–10 Millwall 20 3 **75 9**
2009–10 *Derby Co* 11 1
2010–11 Derby Co 2 0
2010–11 *Notts Co* 10 0 **10 0**
2011–12 Derby Co 0 0 **13 1**
2011–12 *Walsall* 4 0 **4 0**
2011–12 Southend U 17 3
2012–13 Southend U 14 1 **31 4**
2014–15 Stevenage 10 1 **10 1**

McALLISTER, David (M) **170 30**
H: 5 10 W: 11 09 b.Dublin 29-12-88
2008 Drogheda U 0 0
2008 *Shelbourne* 16 7
2009 Shelbourne 30 16 **46 23**
2010 St Patrick's Ath 32 3 **32 3**
2010–11 Sheffield U 2 1
2011–12 Sheffield U 4 0
2011–12 *Shrewsbury T* 15 0
2012–13 Sheffield U 14 1 **20 2**
2012–13 Shrewsbury T 15 1
2013–14 Shrewsbury T 26 1 **56 2**
2014–15 Stevenage 16 0 **16 0**

MILLARD, Ross (D) **0 0**
2014–15 Stevenage 0 0

N'GUESSAN, Joseph (M) **9 1**
H: 5 9 W: 11 00 b.Lewisham 15-7-95
2012–13 Stevenage 1 0
2013–14 Stevenage 5 1
2014–15 Stevenage 3 0 **9 1**

OKENABIRHIE, Fejiri (F) **3 0**
b. 25-2-96
2013–14 Stevenage 3 0
2014–15 Stevenage 0 0 **3 0**

OKIMO, Jerome (D) **29 0**
H: 6 0 W: 12 00 b. 8-6-88
2014–15 Stevenage 29 0 **29 0**

PARRETT, Dean (M) **76 8**
H: 5 10 W: 11 04 b.Hampstead 16-11-91
Internationals: England U16, U17, U19, U20.
2008–09 Tottenham H 0 0
2009–10 Tottenham H 0 0
2009–10 *Aldershot T* 4 0 **4 0**
2010–11 Tottenham H 0 0
2010–11 *Plymouth Arg* 8 1 **8 1**
2010–11 *Charlton Ath* 9 1 **9 1**
2011–12 Tottenham H 0 0
2011–12 *Yeovil T* 10 1 **10 1**
2012–13 Tottenham H 0 0
2012–13 *Swindon T* 3 0 **3 0**
2013–14 Stevenage 12 1
2014–15 Stevenage 30 4 **42 5**

PETT, Tom (M) **34 7**
H: 5 8 W: 11 00 b. 3-12-91
2014–15 Stevenage 34 7 **34 7**

READING, Tyler (G) **0 0**
H: 5 10 W: 11 11 b. 21-5-97
2014–15 Stevenage 0 0

STORER, Jack (F) **0 0**
2014–15 Stevenage 0 0

WALTON, Simon (M) **269 25**
H: 6 1 W: 13 05 b.Sherburn-in-Elmet 13-9-87
Internationals: England U16, U17, U19.
2004–05 Leeds U 30 3
2005–06 Leeds U 4 0 **34 3**
2006–07 Charlton Ath 0 0

```
2006-07   Ipswich T        19   3   19   3
2006-07   Cardiff C         6   0    6   0
2007-08   QPR               5   0    5   0
2007-08   Hull C           10   0   10   0
2008-09   Plymouth Arg     13   0
2008-09   Blackpool         1   0    1   0
2009-10   Plymouth Arg      0   0
2009-10   Crewe Alex       31   1   31   1
2010-11   Plymouth Arg      7   1
2010-11   Sheffield U       0   0
2011-12   Plymouth Arg     41   8   61   9
2012-13   Hartlepool U     34   1
2013-14   Hartlepool U     39   3   73   4
2014-15   Stevenage        29   5   29   5
```

WELLS, Dean (D) 　　43 4
H: 6 1　W: 13 03　b.Isleworth 25-5-85
```
2014-15   Stevenage        43   4   43   4
```

WHELPDALE, Chris (M) 　　272 42
H: 6 0　W: 12 08　b.Harold Wood 27-1-87
```
2007-08   Peterborough U   35   3
2008-09   Peterborough U   39   7
2009-10   Peterborough U   29   1
2010-11   Peterborough U   22   1  125  12
2010-11   Gillingham        4   3
2011-12   Gillingham       39  12
2012-13   Gillingham       41   7
2013-14   Gillingham       24   1  108  23
2014-15   Stevenage        39   7   39   7
```

WORLEY, Harry (D) 　　135 7
H: 6 3　W: 13 00　b.Warrington 25-11-88
```
2005-06   Chelsea           0   0
2006-07   Chelsea           0   0
2006-07   Doncaster R      10   0   10   0
2007-08   Chelsea           0   0
2007-08   Carlisle U        1   0    1   0
2007-08   Leicester C       2   0
2008-09   Leicester C       0   0
2008-09   Luton T           8   0    8   0
2009-10   Leicester C       0   0    2   0
2009-10   Crewe Alex       23   1   23   1
2010-11   Oxford U         43   1
2011-12   Oxford U         10   0
2012-13   Oxford U          9   1
2013-14   Oxford U          0   0   62   2
2013-14   Newport Co       26   4   26   4
2014-15   Stevenage         3   0    3   0
```

YAMFAM, Louis (F) 　　0 0
```
2014-15   Stevenage         0   0
```

ZOLA, Calvin (F) 　　300 71
H: 6 3　W: 14 06　b.Kinshasa 31-12-84
```
2001-02   Newcastle U       0   0
2002-03   Newcastle U       0   0
2003-04   Newcastle U       0   0
2003-04   Oldham Ath       25   5   25   5
2004-05   Tranmere R       15   2
2005-06   Tranmere R       22   4
2006-07   Tranmere R       29   5
2007-08   Tranmere R       30   5   96  16
2008-09   Crewe Alex       27   5
2009-10   Crewe Alex       34  15
2010-11   Crewe Alex        6   1   67  21
2010-11   Burton Alb       18   3
2011-12   Burton Alb       36  12
2012-13   Burton Alb       31  11   85  26
2013-14   Aberdeen         20   3   20   3
2014-15   Stevenage         7   0    7   0
```

Scholars
Bruce-de-Rouche, Morgan Michael Leyland; Casey, George James; Jackson, Edward Tom Charles; Jones, Jack Lewis; Kanda-Botaka, Norley; Kerr, Nathan; Millard, Ross Alan; Reading, Tyler Joel; Smyth, Matthew Mervyn; Storer, Jack Frederick Wendell; Sweeney, Robbie-Lee; Yamfam, Louis-Michel.

STOKE C (78)

ADAM, Charlie (M) 　　304 69
H: 6 1　W: 12 00　b.Dundee 10-12-85
Internationals: Scotland U21, B, Full caps.
```
2004-05   Rangers           1   0
2004-05   Ross Co          10   2   10   2
2005-06   Rangers           1   0
2005-06   St Mirren        29   5   29   5
2006-07   Rangers          32  11
2007-08   Rangers          16   2
2008-09   Rangers           9   0   59  13
2008-09   Blackpool        13   2
2009-10   Blackpool        43  16
2010-11   Blackpool        35  12   91  30
```

```
2011-12   Liverpool        28   2   28   2
2012-13   Stoke C          27   3
2013-14   Stoke C          31   7
2014-15   Stoke C          29   7   87  17
```

ALABI, James (F) 　　13 1
b.London 8-11-94
```
2012-13   Stoke C           0   0
2012-13   Scunthorpe U      9   1
2013-14   Stoke C           0   0
2013-14   Mansfield T       1   0    1   0
2013-14   Scunthorpe U      1   0   10   1
2014-15   Stoke C           0   0
2014-15   Accrington S      2   0    2   0
```

ARNAUTOVIC, Marko (F) 　　178 31
H: 6 4　W: 13 00　b.Floridsdorf 19-4-89
Internationals: Austria U18, U19, U21, Full caps.
```
2006-07   FC Twente         2   0
2007-08   FC Twente        14   0
2008-09   FC Twente        28  12
2009-10   FC Twente         0   0   44  12
2009-10   Inter Milan       3   0    3   0
2010-11   Werder Bremen    25   3
2011-12   Werder Bremen    19   6
2012-13   Werder Bremen    26   5
2013-14   Werder Bremen     2   0   72  14
2013-14   Stoke C          30   4
2014-15   Stoke C          29   1   59   5
```

BACHMANN, Daniel (G) 　　0 0
H: 6 3　W: 12 11　b.Vienna 9-7-94
Internationals: Austria U17, U18, U19, U21.
```
2011-12   Stoke C           0   0
2012-13   Stoke C           0   0
2013-14   Stoke C           0   0
2014-15   Stoke C           0   0
```

BARDSLEY, Phillip (D) 　　247 8
H: 5 11　W: 11 13　b.Salford 28-6-85
Internationals: Scotland Full caps.
```
2003-04   Manchester U      0   0
2004-05   Manchester U      0   0
2005-06   Manchester U      8   0
2005-06   Burnley           6   0    6   0
2006-07   Manchester U      0   0
2006-07   Rangers           5   1    5   1
2006-07   Aston Villa      13   0   13   0
2007-08   Manchester U      0   0    8   0
2007-08   Sheffield U      16   0   16   0
2007-08   Sunderland       11   0
2008-09   Sunderland       28   0
2009-10   Sunderland       26   0
2010-11   Sunderland       34   3
2011-12   Sunderland       31   1
2012-13   Sunderland       18   1
2013-14   Sunderland       26   2  174   7
2014-15   Stoke C          25   0   25   0
```

BEGOVIC, Asmir (G) 　　204 1
H: 6 5　W: 13 01　b.Trebinje 20-6-87
Internationals: Canada U20. Bosnia & Herzogovina Full caps.
```
2006-07   Portsmouth        0   0
2006-07   Macclesfield T    3   0    3   0
2007-08   Portsmouth        0   0
2007-08   Bournemouth       8   0    8   0
2007-08   Yeovil T          2   0
2008-09   Portsmouth        2   0
2008-09   Yeovil T         14   0   16   0
2009-10   Portsmouth        9   0   11   0
2009-10   Ipswich T         6   0    6   0
2009-10   Stoke C           4   0
2010-11   Stoke C          28   0
2011-12   Stoke C          23   0
2012-13   Stoke C          38   0
2013-14   Stoke C          32   1
2014-15   Stoke C          35   0  160   1
```

BOJAN, Krkic (F) 　　196 43
H: 5 8　W: 10 03　b.Linyola 28-8-90
Internationals: Spain U17, U21, Full caps.
```
2007-08   Barcelona        31  10
2008-09   Barcelona        23   2
2009-10   Barcelona        23   8
2010-11   Barcelona        27   6
2011-12   Roma             33   7
2012-13   Roma              0   0   33   7
2012-13   AC Milan         19   3   19   3
2013-14   Barcelona         0   0  104  26
2013-14   Ajax             24   3   24   3
2014-15   Stoke C          16   4   16   4
```

BUTLAND, Jack (G) 　　111 0
H: 6 4　W: 12 00　b.Clevedon 10-3-93
Internationals: England U16, U17, U19, U20, U21, Full caps.
```
2009-10   Birmingham C      0   0
2010-11   Birmingham C      0   0
```

```
2011-12   Birmingham C      0   0
2011-12   Cheltenham T     24   0   24   0
2012-13   Birmingham C     46   0   46   0
2012-13   Stoke C           0   0
2013-14   Stoke C           3   0
2013-14   Barnsley         13   0   13   0
2013-14   Leeds U          16   0   16   0
2014-15   Stoke C           3   0    6   0
2014-15   Derby Co          6   0    6   0
```

CAMERON, Geoff (D) 　　223 13
H: 6 3　W: 13 02　b.Attleboro 11-7-85
Internationals: USA Full caps.
```
2008      Houston D        24   1
2009      Houston D        32   2
2010      Houston D        16   3
2011      Houston D        37   5
2012      Houston D        15   0  124  11
2012-13   Stoke C          35   0
2013-14   Stoke C          37   2
2014-15   Stoke C          27   0   99   2
```

CAMPBELL, James (D) 　　0 0
b.Welwyn Garden City 1-11-93
Internationals: Scotland U19.
```
2013-14   Stoke C           0   0
2014-15   Stoke C           0   0
```

CROUCH, Peter (F) 　　487 128
H: 6 7　W: 13 03　b.Macclesfield 30-1-81
Internationals: England U20, U21, B, Full caps.
```
1998-99     Tottenham H     0   0
1999-2000   Tottenham H     0   0
2000-01     QPR            42  10   42  10
2001-02     Portsmouth     37  18
2001-02     Aston Villa     7   2
2002-03     Aston Villa    14   0
2003-04     Aston Villa    15   4   37   6
2003-04     Norwich C      15   4   15   4
2004-05     Southampton    27  12   27  12
2005-06     Liverpool      32   8
2006-07     Liverpool      32   9
2007-08     Liverpool      21   5   85  22
2008-09     Portsmouth     38  11
2009-10     Portsmouth      0   0   75  29
2009-10     Tottenham H    38   8
2010-11     Tottenham H    34   4
2011-12     Tottenham H     1   0   73  12
2011-12     Stoke C        32  10
2012-13     Stoke C        34   7
2013-14     Stoke C        34   8
2014-15     Stoke C        33   8  133  33
```

DIONATAN, Teixeira (D) 　　38 3
H: 6 4　W: 12 04　b. 24-7-92
Internationals: Brazil U17. Slovakia U21.
```
2009-10   Kosice            2   0
2010-11   Kosice            0   0
2011-12   Kosice            0   0    2   0
2012-13   Duckla           13   0   13   0
2013-14   Dukla            22   3   22   3
2014-15   Stoke C           1   0    1   0
```

DIOUF, Mame (F) 　　195 73
H: 6 1　W: 12 00　b.Dakar 16-12-87
Internationals: Senegal Full caps.
```
2007      Molde            21   9
2008      Molde            23   7
2009      Molde            29  16   73  32
2009-10   Manchester U      5   1
2010-11   Manchester U      0   0
2010-11   Blackburn R      26   3   26   3
2011-12   Manchester U      0   0    5   1
2011-12   Hannover 96      10   6
2012-13   Hannover 96      28  12
2013-14   Hannover 96      19   8   57  26
2014-15   Stoke C          34  11   34  11
```

GRANT, Alex (D) 　　0 0
H: 5 11　W: 11 11　b.Perth 23-1-94
Internationals: Australia U17.
```
2011-12   Portsmouth        0   0
2013-14   Stoke C           0   0
2014-15   Stoke C           0   0
```

IRELAND, Stephen (F) 　　229 19
H: 5 8　W: 10 07　b.Cork 22-8-86
Internationals: Republic of Ireland U21, Full caps.
```
2005-06   Manchester C     21   4
2006-07   Manchester C     24   1
2007-08   Manchester C     33   4
2008-09   Manchester C     35   9
2009-10   Manchester C     22   2
2010-11   Manchester C      0   0  138  16
2010-11   Aston Villa      10   0
2010-11   Newcastle U       2   0    2   0
2011-12   Aston Villa      24   1
2012-13   Aston Villa      13   0
```

2013–14	Aston Villa	0 0	**47** **1**
2013–14	Stoke C	25 2	
2014–15	Stoke C	17 0	**42** **2**

LECYGNE, Eddy (M)   **0** **0**
b.Pabu 6-8-96
Internationals: France U19.

2013–14	Stoke C	0 0	
2014–15	Stoke C	0 0	

MUNIESA, Marc (D)   **34** **0**
H: 5 10   W: 11 04   b.Lloret de Mar 27-3-92
Internationals: Spain U16, U17, U19, U21.

2008–09	Barcelona	1 0	
2009–10	Barcelona	0 0	
2010–11	Barcelona	0 0	
2011–12	Barcelona	1 0	
2012–13	Barcelona	0 0	**2** **0**
2013–14	Stoke C	13 0	
2014–15	Stoke C	19 0	**32** **0**

NESS, Jamie (M)   **63** **4**
H: 6 2   W: 10 13   b.Irvine 2-3-91
Internationals: Scotland U17, U19, U21.

2010–11	Rangers	11 0	
2011–12	Rangers	5 1	**16** **1**
2012–13	Stoke C	0 0	
2013–14	Stoke C	0 0	
2013–14	Leyton Orient	13 1	**13** **1**
2014–15	Stoke C	0 0	
2014–15	Crewe Alex	34 2	**34** **2**

NZONZI, Steven (M)   **232** **12**
H: 6 3   W: 11 11   b.Paris 15-12-88
Internationals: France U21.

2007–08	Amiens	3 0	
2008–09	Amiens	34 1	**37** **1**
2009–10	Blackburn R	33 2	
2010–11	Blackburn R	21 1	
2011–12	Blackburn R	32 2	**86** **5**
2012–13	Stoke C	35 1	
2013–14	Stoke C	36 2	
2014–15	Stoke C	38 3	**109** **6**

ODEMWINGIE, Peter (F)   **318** **89**
H: 6 0   W: 11 09   b.Tashkent 15-7-81
Internationals: Nigeria Full caps.

2002–03	La Louviere	14 2	
2003–04	La Louviere	27 5	
2004–05	La Louviere	3 2	**44** **9**
2004–05	Lille	20 4	
2005–06	Lille	26 14	
2006–07	Lille	29 5	**75** **23**
2007	Loko Moscow	14 4	
2008	Loko Moscow	26 10	
2009	Loko Moscow	25 7	
2010	Loko Moscow	10 0	**75** **21**
2010–11	WBA	32 15	
2011–12	WBA	30 10	
2012–13	WBA	25 5	**87** **30**
2013–14	Cardiff C	15 1	**15** **1**
2013–14	Stoke C	15 5	
2014–15	Stoke C	7 0	**22** **5**

PALACIOS, Wilson (D)   **147** **1**
H: 5 10   W: 11 11   b.La Ceiba 29-7-84
Internationals: Honduras Full caps.

2007–08	Birmingham C	7 0	**7** **0**
2007–08	Wigan Ath	16 0	
2008–09	Wigan Ath	21 0	**37** **0**
2008–09	Tottenham H	11 0	
2009–10	Tottenham H	33 1	
2010–11	Tottenham H	21 0	
2011–12	Tottenham H	0 0	**65** **1**
2011–12	Stoke C	18 0	
2012–13	Stoke C	4 0	
2013–14	Stoke C	16 0	
2014–15	Stoke C	0 0	**38** **0**

PIETERS, Erik (D)   **211** **3**
H: 6 0   W: 13 00   b.Tiel 7-8-88
Internationals: Netherlands U17, U19, U21,
Full caps.

2006–07	FC Utrecht	20 0	
2007–08	FC Utrecht	31 2	**51** **2**
2008–09	PSV Eindhoven	17 0	
2009–10	PSV Eindhoven	27 0	
2010–11	PSV Eindhoven	31 0	
2011–12	PSV Eindhoven	16 0	
2012–13	PSV Eindhoven	2 0	**93** **0**
2013–14	Stoke C	36 1	
2014–15	Stoke C	31 0	**67** **1**

SHAWCROSS, Ryan (D)   **277** **19**
H: 6 3   W: 13 13   b.Buckley 4-10-87
Internationals: England U21, Full caps.

2006–07	Manchester U	0 0	
2007–08	Manchester U	0 0	
2007–08	Stoke C	41 7	
2008–09	Stoke C	30 3	

2009–10	Stoke C	28 2	
2010–11	Stoke C	36 1	
2011–12	Stoke C	36 2	
2012–13	Stoke C	37 1	
2013–14	Stoke C	37 1	
2014–15	Stoke C	32 2	**277** **19**

SHEA, Brek (M)   **120** **17**
H: 6 3   W: 12 11   b.College Station, Texas
28-2-90
Internationals: USA U17, U20, U23, Full
caps.

2008	FC Dallas	2 0	
2009	FC Dallas	19 0	
2010	FC Dallas	29 5	
2011	FC Dallas	32 11	
2012	FC Dallas	21 3	**103** **19**
2012–13	Stoke C	2 0	
2013–14	Stoke C	1 0	
2013–14	Barnsley	8 0	**8** **0**
2014–15	Stoke C	0 0	**3** **0**
2014–15	Birmingham C	6 0	**6** **0**
Transferred to Orlando C January 2015.

SHENTON, Oliver (M)   **1** **0**
b. 6-11-97

2014–15	Stoke C	1 0	**1** **0**

SIDWELL, Steve (M)   **374** **55**
H: 5 10   W: 11 00   b.Wandsworth 14-12-82
Internationals: England U20, U21.

2001–02	Arsenal	0 0	
2001–02	Brentford	30 4	**30** **4**
2002–03	Arsenal	0 0	
2002–03	Brighton & HA	12 5	**12** **5**
2002–03	Reading	13 2	
2003–04	Reading	43 8	
2004–05	Reading	44 5	
2005–06	Reading	33 10	
2006–07	Reading	35 4	**168** **29**
2007–08	Chelsea	15 0	**15** **0**
2008–09	Aston Villa	16 3	
2009–10	Aston Villa	25 0	
2010–11	Aston Villa	4 0	**45** **3**
2010–11	Fulham	12 2	
2011–12	Fulham	14 1	
2012–13	Fulham	28 4	
2013–14	Fulham	38 7	**92** **14**
2014–15	Fulham	12 0	**12** **0**

SORENSEN, Thomas (G)   **409** **0**
H: 6 4   W: 13 10   b.Fredericia 12-6-76
Internationals: Denmark U19, U21, B, Full
caps.

1998–99	Sunderland	45 0	
1999–2000	Sunderland	37 0	
2000–01	Sunderland	34 0	
2001–02	Sunderland	34 0	
2002–03	Sunderland	21 0	**171** **0**
2003–04	Aston Villa	38 0	
2004–05	Aston Villa	36 0	
2005–06	Aston Villa	36 0	
2006–07	Aston Villa	29 0	
2007–08	Aston Villa	0 0	**139** **0**
2008–09	Stoke C	36 0	
2009–10	Stoke C	33 0	
2010–11	Stoke C	10 0	
2011–12	Stoke C	16 0	
2012–13	Stoke C	0 0	
2013–14	Stoke C	4 0	
2014–15	Stoke C	0 0	**99** **0**

THOMAS, Adam (M)   **0** **0**
b.Wiral 4-2-94

2013–14	Stoke C	0 0	
2014–15	Stoke C	0 0	

WALTERS, Jon (F)   **439** **85**
H: 6 0   W: 12 06   b.Birkenhead 20-9-83
Internationals: Republic of Ireland U21, B,
Full caps.

2001–02	Bolton W	0 0	
2002–03	Bolton W	4 0	
2002–03	Hull C	11 5	
2003–04	Bolton W	0 0	**4** **0**
2003–04	Crewe Alex	0 0	
2003–04	Barnsley	8 0	**8** **0**
2003–04	Hull C	16 1	
2004–05	Hull C	21 1	**48** **7**
2004–05	Scunthorpe U	3 0	**3** **0**
2005–06	Wrexham	38 5	
2006–07	Chester C	26 9	**26** **9**
2006–07	Ipswich T	16 4	
2007–08	Ipswich T	40 13	
2008–09	Ipswich T	36 5	
2009–10	Ipswich T	43 8	
2010–11	Ipswich T	1 0	**136** **30**
2010–11	Stoke C	36 6	
2011–12	Stoke C	38 7	

2012–13	Stoke C	38 8	
2013–14	Stoke C	32 5	
2014–15	Stoke C	32 8	**176** **34**

WARD, Charlie (M)   **0** **0**
H: 5 10   W: 11 09   b.Stoke 19-2-96

2013–14	Stoke C	0 0	
2014–15	Stoke C	0 0	

WARING, George (F)   **19** **6**
b.Chester 2-2-94

2013–14	Stoke C	0 0	
2014–15	Stoke C	0 0	
2014–15	Barnsley	19 6	**19** **6**

WATKINS-CLARK, Mason (D)   **0** **0**
b.Dublin 1-1-95
Internationals: Republic of Ireland U21.

2013–14	Stoke C	0 0	
2014–15	Stoke C	0 0	

WHEELER, Elliot (D)   **0** **0**
H: 5 11   W: 11 10   b.Stoke 19-12-93

2013–14	Stoke C	0 0	
2014–15	Stoke C	0 0	

WHELAN, Glenn (M)   **379** **17**
H: 5 11   W: 12 07   b.Dublin 13-1-84
Internationals: Republic of Ireland U16, U21,
B, Full caps.

2000–01	Manchester C	0 0	
2001–02	Manchester C	0 0	
2002–03	Manchester C	0 0	
2003–04	Manchester C	0 0	
2003–04	Bury	13 0	**13** **0**
2004–05	Sheffield W	36 2	
2005–06	Sheffield W	43 1	
2006–07	Sheffield W	38 7	
2007–08	Sheffield W	25 2	**142** **12**
2007–08	Stoke C	14 1	
2008–09	Stoke C	26 1	
2009–10	Stoke C	33 2	
2010–11	Stoke C	29 0	
2011–12	Stoke C	30 1	
2012–13	Stoke C	32 0	
2013–14	Stoke C	32 0	
2014–15	Stoke C	28 0	**224** **5**

WILKINSON, Andy (D)   **185** **0**
H: 5 11   W: 11 00   b.Stone 6-8-84

2001–02	Stoke C	0 0	
2002–03	Stoke C	0 0	
2003–04	Stoke C	3 0	
2004–05	Stoke C	1 0	
2004–05	Shrewsbury T	9 0	**9** **0**
2005–06	Stoke C	6 0	
2006–07	Stoke C	4 0	
2006–07	Blackpool	7 0	**7** **0**
2007–08	Stoke C	23 0	
2008–09	Stoke C	22 0	
2009–10	Stoke C	25 0	
2010–11	Stoke C	22 0	
2011–12	Stoke C	23 0	
2012–13	Stoke C	24 0	
2013–14	Stoke C	5 0	
2014–15	Stoke C	0 0	**160** **0**
2014–15	Millwall	9 0	**9** **0**

WILSON, Marc (M)   **209** **4**
H: 6 2   W: 12 07   b.Lisburn 17-8-87
Internationals: Republic of Ireland U18, U19,
U21, Full caps.

2005–06	Portsmouth	0 0	
2005–06	Yeovil T	2 0	**2** **0**
2006–07	Portsmouth	0 0	
2006–07	Bournemouth	19 3	
2007–08	Bournemouth	7 0	**26** **3**
2007–08	Luton T	4 0	**4** **0**
2008–09	Portsmouth	3 0	
2009–10	Portsmouth	28 0	
2010–11	Portsmouth	4 0	**35** **0**
2010–11	Stoke C	28 1	
2011–12	Stoke C	35 0	
2012–13	Stoke C	19 0	
2013–14	Stoke C	33 0	
2014–15	Stoke C	27 0	**142** **1**

WOLLSCHEID, Philipp (D)   **185** **11**
H: 6 4   W: 13 03   b.Wadern 6-3-89
Internationals: Germany U20, Full caps.

2006–07	Noswendel-Wadern	8 2	**8** **2**
2007–08	Hasborn-Dautweiler	18 0	**18** **0**
2007–08	Saarbrucken	7 1	
2008–09	Saarbrucken	23 2	**30** **3**
2009–10	Nuremberg II	26 1	
2010–11	Nuremberg II	14 0	**40** **1**
2010–11	Nuremberg	19 3	
2011–12	Nuremberg	2 0	**21** **3**
2012–13	Bayer Leverkusen	31 2	

2013–14	Bayer Leverkusen	20	0	
2014–15	Bayer Leverkusen	0	0	51 2
2014–15	*Mainz*	5	0	5 0
2014–15	Stoke C	12	0	12 0

Players retained or with offer of contract
Barber, Benjamin Thomas; Dryden, Edward; Eve, Dale Donald; O'Reilly, Ryan; Skapetis, Petros; Taylor, Joel.

Scholars
Banks, Lewis; Brierley, Theodore Tobias Clifford; Coban, Yusuf; Edwards, Liam; Gyollai, Daniel; Jarvis, Daniel Adam; Kurasik, Dominic; Marques, Christopher; Ngoy, Bin Cibambi Julien Fontaine; Renee-Pringle, Johnville Isaacs Joseph; Roberts, Oliver James; Shepherd, Thomas Roy; Smith, Liam James; Wells, Toby; Williams, Josh Aston; Yao, Abodje Freddy Bruce.

SUNDERLAND (79)

AGNEW, Liam (M) 0 0
H: 5 10 W: 11 05 b.Sunderland 9-12-93
2013–14	Sunderland	0	0
2014–15	Sunderland	0	0

ALTIDORE, Jozy (F) 195 57
H: 5 10 W: 12 07 b.Florida 6-11-89
Internationals: USA U17, U20, U23, Full caps.
2006	NY Red Bulls	7	3	
2007	NY Red Bulls	22	9	
2008	NY Red Bulls	8	3	37 15
2008–09	Villarreal	6	1	
2009–10	Villarreal	0	0	
2009–10	*Hull C*	28	1	28 1
2010–11	Villarreal	3	0	9 1
2010–11	*Bursaspor*	12	1	12 1
2011–12	AZ	34	15	
2012–13	AZ	33	23	67 38
2013–14	Sunderland	31	1	
2014–15	Sunderland	11	0	42 1
Transferred to Toronto January 2015.

ALVAREZ, Ricardo (M) 128 16
H: 6 2 W: 11 07 b.Capital Federal 12-4-88
Internationals: Argentina Full caps.
2007–08	Velez Sarsfield	1	0	
2008–09	Velez Sarsfield	1	0	
2009–10	Velez Sarsfield	11	1	
2010–11	Velez Sarsfield	29	4	42 5
2011–12	Inter Milan	21	2	
2012–13	Inter Milan	23	5	
2013–14	Inter Milan	29	4	
2014–15	Inter Milan	0	0	73 11
On loan from Inter Milan.
2014–15	Sunderland	13	0	13 0

BA, El-Hadji (M) 21 1
H: 6 0 W: 11 08 b.Paris 5-3-93
Internationals: France U18, U19, U20.
2011–12	Le Havre	1	0	
2012–13	Le Havre	12	1	13 1
2013–14	Sunderland	1	0	
2014–15	Sunderland	0	0	1 0
2014–15	*Bastia*	7	0	7 0

BEADLING, Tom (D) 0 0
H: 6 1 W: 12 08 b.Barrow-in-Furness 16-1-96
2014–15	Sunderland	0	0

BRIDCUTT, Liam (M) 192 2
H: 5 9 W: 11 07 b.Reading 8-5-89
Internationals: Scotland Full caps.
2007–08	Chelsea	0	0	
2007–08	*Yeovil T*	9	0	9 0
2008–09	Chelsea	0	0	
2008–09	*Watford*	6	0	6 0
2009–10	Chelsea	0	0	
2009–10	*Stockport Co*	15	0	15 0
2010–11	Chelsea	0	0	
2010–11	Brighton & HA	37	2	
2011–12	Brighton & HA	43	0	
2012–13	Brighton & HA	41	0	
2013–14	Brighton & HA	11	0	132 2
2013–14	Sunderland	12	0	
2014–15	Sunderland	18	0	30 0

BROWN, Wes (D) 302 4
H: 6 1 W: 13 08 b.Manchester 13-10-79
Internationals: England U21, Full caps.
1996–97	Manchester U	0	0
1997–98	Manchester U	2	0
1998–99	Manchester U	14	0
1999–2000	Manchester U	0	0
2000–01	Manchester U	28	0
2001–02	Manchester U	17	0
2002–03	Manchester U	22	0
2003–04	Manchester U	17	0
2004–05	Manchester U	21	1
2005–06	Manchester U	19	0
2006–07	Manchester U	22	0
2007–08	Manchester U	36	1
2008–09	Manchester U	8	1
2009–10	Manchester U	19	0
2010–11	Manchester U	7	0	232 3
2011–12	Sunderland	20	1
2012–13	Sunderland	0	0
2013–14	Sunderland	25	0
2014–15	Sunderland	25	0	70 1

BUCKLEY, Will (F) 216 37
H: 6 0 W: 13 00 b.Oldham 12-8-88
2007–08	Rochdale	7	0	
2008–09	Rochdale	37	10	
2009–10	Rochdale	15	3	59 13
2009–10	Watford	6	1	
2010–11	Watford	33	4	39 5
2011–12	Brighton & HA	29	8	
2012–13	Brighton & HA	36	8	
2013–14	Brighton & HA	30	3	
2014–15	Brighton & HA	1	0	96 19
2014–15	Sunderland	22	0	22 0

CATTERMOLE, Lee (M) 232 6
H: 5 10 W: 11 13 b.Stockton 21-3-88
Internationals: England U16, U17, U18, U19, U21.
2005–06	Middlesbrough	14	1	
2006–07	Middlesbrough	31	1	
2007–08	Middlesbrough	24	1	69 3
2008–09	Wigan Ath	33	1	
2009–10	Wigan Ath	0	0	33 1
2009–10	Sunderland	22	0	
2010–11	Sunderland	23	0	
2011–12	Sunderland	23	0	
2012–13	Sunderland	10	0	
2013–14	Sunderland	24	1	
2014–15	Sunderland	28	1	130 2

DEFOE, Jermain (F) 465 168
H: 5 7 W: 10 04 b.Beckton 7-10-82
Internationals: England U16, U18, U21, B, Full caps.
1999–2000	West Ham U	0	0	
2000–01	West Ham U	0	0	
2000–01	*Bournemouth*	29	18	29 18
2001–02	West Ham U	35	10	
2002–03	West Ham U	38	8	
2003–04	West Ham U	19	11	93 29
2003–04	Tottenham H	15	7	
2004–05	Tottenham H	35	13	
2005–06	Tottenham H	36	9	
2006–07	Tottenham H	34	10	
2007–08	Tottenham H	19	4	
2007–08	Portsmouth	12	8	
2008–09	Portsmouth	19	7	31 15
2008–09	Tottenham H	8	3	
2009–10	Tottenham H	34	18	
2010–11	Tottenham H	22	4	
2011–12	Tottenham H	25	11	
2012–13	Tottenham H	34	11	
2013–14	Tottenham H	14	1	276 91
2014	Toronto	19	11	19 11
2014–15	Sunderland	17	4	17 4

FLETCHER, Steven (F) 330 92
H: 6 0 W: 12 00 b.Shrewsbury 26-3-87
Internationals: Scotland U20, U21, B, Full caps.
2003–04	Hibernian	5	0	
2004–05	Hibernian	20	5	
2005–06	Hibernian	34	8	
2006–07	Hibernian	31	6	
2007–08	Hibernian	32	13	
2008–09	Hibernian	34	11	156 43
2009–10	Burnley	35	8	35 8
2010–11	Wolverhampton W	9	0	
2011–12	Wolverhampton W	32	12	61 22
2012–13	Sunderland	28	11	
2013–14	Sunderland	20	3	
2014–15	Sunderland	30	5	78 19

GIACCHERINI, Emanuele (M) 169 28
H: 5 3 W: 10 07 b.Forli 5-5-85
Internationals: Italy Full caps.
2008–09	Cesena	29	5	
2009–10	Cesena	32	8	
2010–11	Cesena	36	7	97 20
2011–12	Juventus	23	1	
2012–13	Juventus	17	3	40 4
2013–14	Sunderland	24	4	
2014–15	Sunderland	8	0	32 4

GOMEZ, Jordi (M) 223 33
H: 5 10 W: 11 09 b.Barcelona 24-5-85
Internationals: Spain U17.
2006–07	Espanyol B	21	0	21 0
2007–08	Espanyol	2	0	2 0
2008–09	Swansea C	44	12	44 12
2009–10	Wigan Ath	23	1	
2010–11	Wigan Ath	13	1	
2011–12	Wigan Ath	28	5	
2012–13	Wigan Ath	32	3	
2013–14	Wigan Ath	31	7	127 17
2014–15	Sunderland	29	4	29 4

GRAHAM, Danny (F) 358 101
H: 5 11 W: 12 05 b.Gateshead 12-8-85
Internationals: England U20.
2003–04	Middlesbrough	0	0	
2003–04	*Darlington*	9	2	9 2
2004–05	Middlesbrough	11	1	
2005–06	Middlesbrough	3	0	
2005–06	*Derby Co*	14	0	14 0
2005–06	*Leeds U*	3	0	3 0
2006–07	Middlesbrough	0	0	
2006–07	*Blackpool*	4	1	4 1
2006–07	*Carlisle U*	11	7	
2007–08	Carlisle U	45	14	
2008–09	Carlisle U	44	15	100 36
2009–10	Watford	46	14	
2010–11	Watford	45	23	91 37
2011–12	Swansea C	36	12	
2012–13	Swansea C	18	3	54 15
2012–13	Sunderland	13	0	
2013–14	Sunderland	0	0	
2013–14	*Hull C*	18	1	18 1
2013–14	*Middlesbrough*	18	6	33 7
2014–15	Sunderland	14	1	27 1
2014–15	*Wolverhampton W*	5	1	5 1

HARRISON, Scott (D) 43 1
b.Middlesbrough 3-9-93
2012–13	Sunderland	0	0	
2013–14	Sunderland	0	0	
2013–14	*Bury*	1	0	1 0
2014–15	Sunderland	0	0	
2014–15	*Hartlepool U*	6	0	
2014–15	*Hartlepool U*	36	1	42 1

HONEYMAN, George (M) 0 0
b. 8-9-94
2014–15	Sunderland	0	0

JOHNSON, Adam (M) 289 46
H: 5 8 W: 10 00 b.Sunderland 14-7-87
Internationals: England U19, U21, Full caps.
2004–05	Middlesbrough	0	0	
2005–06	Middlesbrough	13	1	
2005–06	Middlesbrough	12	0	
2006–07	*Leeds U*	5	0	5 0
2007–08	*Watford*	12	5	12 5
2007–08	Middlesbrough	19	1	
2008–09	Middlesbrough	26	0	
2009–10	Middlesbrough	26	11	96 13
2009–10	Manchester C	16	1	
2010–11	Manchester C	31	4	
2011–12	Manchester C	26	6	
2012–13	Manchester C	0	0	73 11
2012–13	Sunderland	35	5	
2013–14	Sunderland	36	4	
2014–15	Sunderland	34	2	103 17

JONES, Billy (M) 372 22
H: 5 11 W: 13 00 b.Shrewsbury 24-3-87
Internationals: England U16, U17, U19, U20.
2003–04	Crewe Alex	27	1	
2004–05	Crewe Alex	35	1	
2005–06	Crewe Alex	44	6	
2006–07	Crewe Alex	41	1	132 8
2007–08	Preston NE	29	0	
2008–09	Preston NE	44	3	
2009–10	Preston NE	44	5	
2010–11	Preston NE	43	6	160 13
2011–12	WBA	18	0	
2012–13	WBA	27	1	
2013–14	WBA	21	0	66 1
2014–15	Sunderland	14	0	14 0

LARSSON, Sebastian (M) 324 31
H: 5 11 W: 11 02 b.Eskilstuna 6-6-85
Internationals: Sweden U16, U17, U19, U21, Full caps.
2002–03	Arsenal	0	0	
2003–04	Arsenal	0	0	
2004–05	Arsenal	0	0	
2005–06	Arsenal	3	0	
2006–07	Arsenal	0	0	3 0
2006–07	Birmingham C	43	4	
2007–08	Birmingham C	35	6	
2008–09	Birmingham C	38	1	
2009–10	Birmingham C	33	4	

2010–11	Birmingham C	35	4	184	19
2011–12	Sunderland	32	7		
2012–13	Sunderland	38	1		
2013–14	Sunderland	31	1		
2014–15	Sunderland	36	3	137	12

MANDRON, Mikael (F)   17   1
H: 6 3 W: 12 13 b.Boulogne 11-10-94

2011–12	Sunderland	0	0		
2012–13	Sunderland	2	0		
2013–14	Sunderland	0	0		
2013–14	*Fleetwood T*	11	1	11	1
2014–15	Sunderland	1	0	3	0
2014–15	*Shrewsbury T*	3	0	3	0

MANNONE, Vito (G)   87   0
H: 6 0 W: 11 08 b.Milan 2-3-88
Internationals: Italy U21.

2005–06	Arsenal	0	0		
2006–07	Arsenal	0	0		
2006–07	Barnsley	2	0	2	0
2007–08	Arsenal	0	0		
2008–09	Arsenal	1	0		
2009–10	Arsenal	5	0		
2010–11	Arsenal	0	0		
2010–11	*Hull C*	10	0		
2011–12	Arsenal	0	0		
2011–12	*Hull C*	21	0	31	0
2012–13	Arsenal	9	0	15	0
2013–14	Sunderland	29	0		
2014–15	Sunderland	10	0	39	0

MAVRIAS, Charis (M)   64   4
H: 5 10 W: 11 08 b.Zakynthos 21-2-94
Internationals: Greece U17, U19, U21, Full caps.

2010–11	Panathinaikos	4	0		
2011–12	Panathinaikos	21	1		
2012–13	Panathinaikos	26	2		
2013–14	Sunderland	4	0		
2014–15	Sunderland	0	0	4	0
2014–15	*Panathinaikos*	9	1	60	4

O'SHEA, John (D)   399   14
H: 6 3 W: 13 07 b.Waterford 30-4-81
Internationals: Republic of Ireland U21, Full caps.

1998–99	Manchester U	0	0		
1999–2000	Manchester U	0	0		
1999–2000	*Bournemouth*	10	1	10	1
2000–01	Manchester U	0	0		
2001–02	Manchester U	9	0		
2002–03	Manchester U	32	0		
2003–04	Manchester U	33	2		
2004–05	Manchester U	23	2		
2005–06	Manchester U	34	1		
2006–07	Manchester U	32	4		
2007–08	Manchester U	28	0		
2008–09	Manchester U	30	0		
2009–10	Manchester U	15	1		
2010–11	Manchester U	20	0	256	10
2011–12	Sunderland	29	0		
2012–13	Sunderland	34	2		
2013–14	Sunderland	33	1		
2014–15	Sunderland	37	0	133	3

PANTILIMON, Costel (G)   137   0
H: 6 5 W: 15 02 b.Bacau 1-2-87
Internationals: Romania U17, U19, U21, Full caps.

2005–06	Aerostar Bacau	9	0	9	0
2006–07	Poli Timisoara	8	0		
2007–08	Poli Timisoara	5	0	13	0
2008–09	Timisoara	31	0		
2009–10	Timisoara	21	0		
2010–11	Timisoara	28	0	80	0
2011–12	*Manchester C*	0	0		
2012–13	*Manchester C*	0	0		
2013–14	*Manchester C*	7	0	7	0
2014–15	Sunderland	28	0	28	0

PICKFORD, Jordan (G)   63   0
H: 6 1 b.Washington 7-3-94
Internationals: England U16, U17, U18, U19, U20.

2010–11	Sunderland	0	0		
2011–12	Sunderland	0	0		
2012–13	Sunderland	0	0		
2013–14	Sunderland	0	0		
2013–14	*Burton Alb*	12	0	12	0
2013–14	*Carlisle U*	18	0	18	0
2014–15	Sunderland	0	0		
2014–15	*Bradford C*	33	0	33	0

REVEILLERE, Anthony (D)   473   7
H: 5 11 W: 12 02 b.Doue-la-Fontaine 10-11-79
Internationals: France U17, U18, U21, Full caps.

1997–98	Rennes	8	0		
1998–99	Rennes	32	0		
1999-2000	Rennes	16	0		
2000–01	Rennes	32	0		
2001–02	Rennes	32	1		
2002–03	Rennes	20	1	140	2
2002–03	*Valencia*	18	2	18	2
2003–04	Lyon	31	1		
2004–05	Lyon	33	0		
2005–06	Lyon	20	0		
2006–07	Lyon	30	0		
2007–08	Lyon	28	1		
2008–09	Lyon	19	0		
2009–10	Lyon	30	0		
2010–11	Lyon	35	0		
2011–12	Lyon	33	0		
2012–13	Lyon	27	1	286	3
2013–14	Napoli	13	0	13	0
2014–15	Sunderland	16	0	16	0

ROBERGE, Valentin (D)   123   2
H: 6 1 W: 11 06 b.Montreuil 9-6-87

2008–09	Aris Thessaloniki	20	0		
2009–10	Aris Thessaloniki	5	0	25	0
2010–11	Maritimo	25	1		
2011–12	Maritimo	25	0		
2012–13	Maritimo	27	1	77	2
2013–14	Sunderland	9	0		
2014–15	Sunderland	1	0	10	0
2014–15	*Reims*	11	0	11	0

ROBSON, Tom (M)   0   0
H: 5 10 W: 11 11 b.Stanley 9-11-95

2014–15	Sunderland	0	0		

RODWELL, Jack (D)   124   9
H: 6 2 W: 12 08 b.Southport 11-3-91
Internationals: England U16, U17, U19, U21, Full caps.

2007–08	Everton	2	0		
2008–09	Everton	19	0		
2009–10	Everton	26	2		
2010–11	Everton	24	0		
2011–12	Everton	14	2	85	4
2012–13	Manchester C	11	2		
2013–14	Manchester C	5	0	16	2
2014–15	Sunderland	23	3	23	3

SMITH, Martin (M)   0   0
H: 5 10 W: 11 00 b.Sunderland 25-1-96

2014–15	Sunderland	0	0		

STRYJEK, Maksymilian (G)   0   0
H: 6 2 W: 12 11 b.Warsaw 18-7-96
Internationals: Poland U17, U18, U19.

2014–15	Sunderland	0	0		

VAN AANHOLT, Patrick (D)   139   6
H: 5 9 W: 10 08 b.Den Bosch 3-7-88
Internationals: Netherlands U16, U17, U18, U19, U20, U21, Full caps.

2007–08	Chelsea	0	0		
2008–09	Chelsea	0	0		
2009–10	Chelsea	2	0		
2009–10	*Coventry C*	20	0	20	0
2009–10	*Newcastle U*	7	0	7	0
2010–11	Chelsea	0	0		
2010–11	*Leicester C*	12	1	12	1
2011–12	Chelsea	0	0		
2011–12	*Wigan Ath*	3	0	3	0
2011–12	*Vitesse*	9	0		
2012–13	*Vitesse*	0	0		
2012–13	*Vitesse*	31	1		
2013–14	Chelsea	0	0	2	0
2013–14	*Vitesse*	27	4	67	5
2014–15	Sunderland	28	0	28	0

VERGINI, Santiago (D)   144   6
H: 6 3 W: 13 00 b.Maximo Paz 3-8-88
Internationals: Argentina Full caps.

2008–09	Olimpia	0	0		
2009–10	Olimpia	0	0		
2010–11	Olimpia	4	0	4	0
2010–11	Verona	15	1	15	1
2011–12	Newell's Old Boys	32	3		
2012–13	Newell's Old Boys	34	1	66	4
2013–14	Estudiantes	17	1		
2013–14	*Sunderland*	11	0		
2014–15	Estudiantes	0	0	17	1

On loan from Estudiantes.

2014–15	Sunderland	31	0	42	0

WATMORE, Duncan (F)   9   1
H: 5 9 W: 11 05 b.Cheadle Hulme 8-3-94
Internationals: England U20.

2013–14	Sunderland	0	0		
2013–14	*Hibernian*	9	1	9	1
2014–15	Sunderland	0	0		

WICKHAM, Connor (F)   166   33
H: 6 0 W: 14 01 b.Hereford 31-3-93
Internationals: England U16, U17, U19, U21.

2008–09	Ipswich T	2	0		
2009–10	Ipswich T	26	4		
2010–11	Ipswich T	37	9	65	13
2011–12	Sunderland	16	1		
2012–13	Sunderland	12	0		
2012–13	*Sheffield W*	6	1		
2013–14	Sunderland	15	5		
2013–14	*Sheffield W*	11	8	17	9
2013–14	*Leeds U*	5	0	5	0
2014–15	Sunderland	36	5	79	11

Players retained or with offer of contract
Casey, Dan Patrick; Gooch, Lynden Jack; Greenwood, Rees; Lawson, Carl; Pybus, Daniel Joseph; Robson, Ethan; Talbot, James.

Scholars
Blinco, Jordan William; Ganiyu, Avis; Graham, Kieran; Hume, Denver Jay; Ledger, Michael; Lowrie, David James; McEvoy, Dylan James; Molyneux, Luke; Nelson, Andrew George Robert; Poame, Jean-Yves; Purvis, Greg Anthony; Robson, Joshua Paul; Wright, Daniel.

SWANSEA C (80)

ALFEI, Daniel (D)   27   0
H: 5 11 W: 12 02 b.Swansea 23-2-92
Internationals: Wales U17, U19, U21.

2010–11	Swansea C	1	0		
2011–12	Swansea C	0	0		
2012–13	Swansea C	0	0		
2013–14	Swansea C	0	0		
2013–14	*Portsmouth*	15	0	15	0
2014–15	Swansea C	0	0	1	0
2014–15	*Northampton T*	11	0	11	0

AMAT, Jordi (D)   95   1
H: 6 0 W: 12 03 b.Barcelona 21-3-92
Internationals: Spain U16, U17, U18, U19, U20, U21.

2009–10	Espanyol	6	0		
2010–11	Espanyol	26	0		
2011–12	Espanyol	9	0		
2012–13	Espanyol	0	0	41	0
2012–13	*Rayo Vallecano*	27	1	27	1
2013–14	Swansea C	17	0		
2014–15	Swansea C	10	0	27	0

BARROW, Modou (F)   103   40
H: 5 9 W: 9 13 b.Banjul 13-10-92
Internationals: Gambia Full caps.

2010	Mjolby Al	15	6	15	6
2011	Mjolby Sodra	19	23	19	23
2012	Norrkping	7	0	7	0
2013	Varbergs	28	2	28	2
2014	Ostersunds FK	19	9	19	9
2014–15	Swansea C	11	0	11	0
2014–15	*Nottingham F*	4	0	4	0

BARTLEY, Kyle (D)   87   4
H: 5 11 W: 11 00 b.Stockport 22-5-91
Internationals: England U16, U17.

2008–09	Arsenal	0	0		
2009–10	Arsenal	0	0		
2009–10	*Sheffield U*	14	0		
2010–11	Arsenal	0	0		
2010–11	*Sheffield U*	21	0	35	0
2010–11	*Rangers*	5	1		
2011–12	Arsenal	0	0		
2011–12	*Rangers*	19	0	24	1
2012–13	Arsenal	0	0		
2012–13	Swansea C	2	0		
2013–14	Swansea C	2	0		
2013–14	*Birmingham C*	17	3	17	3
2014–15	Swansea C	7	0	11	0

BRAY, Alex (M)   1   0
H: 5 10 W: 10 06 b.Bath 25-7-95
Internationals: Wales U19.

2013–14	Swansea C	0	0		
2014–15	Swansea C	0	0		
2014–15	*Plymouth Arg*	1	0	1	0

BRITTON, Leon (M)   439   11
H: 5 6 W: 10 00 b.Merton 16-9-82
Internationals: England U16.

1999–2000	West Ham U	0	0		
2000–01	West Ham U	0	0		
2001–02	West Ham U	0	0		
2002–03	West Ham U	0	0		
2002–03	*Swansea C*	25	0		

2003–04	Swansea C	42	3		
2004–05	Swansea C	30	1		
2005–06	Swansea C	38	4		
2006–07	Swansea C	41	2		
2007–08	Swansea C	40	0		
2008–09	Swansea C	43	0		
2009–10	Swansea C	36	0		
2010–11	Sheffield U	24	0	24	0
2010–11	Swansea C	17	1		
2011–12	Swansea C	36	0		
2012–13	Swansea C	33	0		
2013–14	Swansea C	25	0		
2014–15	Swansea C	9	0	415	11

CORK, Jack (D) 284 9
H: 6 0 W: 10 12 b.Carshalton 25-6-89
Internationals: England U17, U18, U19, U20, U21. Great Britain.

2006–07	Chelsea	0	0		
2006–07	Bournemouth	7	0	7	0
2007–08	Chelsea	0	0		
2007–08	*Scunthorpe U*	34	2	34	2
2008–09	Chelsea	0	0		
2008–09	Southampton	23	0		
2008–09	*Watford*	19	0	19	0
2009–10	Chelsea	0	0		
2009–10	*Coventry C*	21	0	21	0
2009–10	Burnley	11	1		
2010–11	Chelsea	0	0		
2010–11	*Burnley*	40	3	51	4
2011–12	Southampton	46	0		
2012–13	Southampton	28	0		
2013–14	Southampton	28	0		
2014–15	Southampton	12	2	137	2
2014–15	Swansea C	15	1	15	1

CORNELL, David (G) 30 0
H: 5 11 W: 11 07 b.Gorseinon 28-3-91
Internationals: Wales U17, U19, U21.

2009–10	Swansea C	0	0		
2010–11	Swansea C	0	0		
2011–12	Swansea C	0	0		
2011–12	*Hereford U*	25	0	25	0
2012–13	Swansea C	0	0		
2013–14	Swansea C	0	0		
2013–14	*St Mirren*	5	0	5	0
2014–15	Swansea C	0	0		
2014–15	*Portsmouth*	0	0		

DAVIES, Oliver (G) 0 0
H: 6 0 W: 12 00 b.Neath 31-12-94

2013–14	Swansea C	0	0		
2014–15	Swansea C	0	0		

DONNELLY, Rory (F) 69 25
H: 6 2 W: 12 10 b.Belfast 18-2-92
Internationals: Northern Ireland U21.

2010–11	Cliftonville	31	7		
2011–12	Cliftonville	18	13	49	20
2011–12	Swansea C	0	0		
2012–13	Swansea C	0	0		
2013–14	Swansea C	0	0		
2013–14	*Coventry C*	0	0		
2014–15	Swansea C	0	0		
2014–15	*Tranmere R*	20	5	20	5

DYER, Nathan (M) 301 27
H: 5 5 W: 9 00 b.Trowbridge 29-11-87

2005–06	Southampton	17	0		
2005–06	Burnley	5	2	5	2
2006–07	Southampton	18	0		
2007–08	Southampton	17	1		
2008–09	Southampton	4	0	56	1
2008–09	*Sheffield U*	7	1	7	1
2008–09	*Swansea C*	17	2		
2009–10	Swansea C	40	2		
2010–11	Swansea C	46	2		
2011–12	Swansea C	34	5		
2012–13	Swansea C	37	3		
2013–14	Swansea C	27	6		
2014–15	Swansea C	32	3	233	23

EMNES, Marvin (M) 226 36
H: 5 11 W: 10 06 b.Rotterdam 27-5-88
Internationals: Netherlands U16, U17, U19, U20, U21.

2005–06	Sparta Rotterdam	11	1		
2006–07	Sparta Rotterdam	16	0		
2007–08	Sparta Rotterdam	29	8	56	9
2008–09	Middlesbrough	15	0		
2009–10	Middlesbrough	16	1		
2010–11	Middlesbrough	23	3		
2010–11	*Swansea C*	4	2		
2011–12	Middlesbrough	42	14		
2012–13	Middlesbrough	24	5		
2013–14	Middlesbrough	22	1	142	24
2013–14	*Swansea C*	7	1		
2014–15	Swansea C	17	0	28	3

EVANS, Sam (M) 0 0
b.Swansea 12-5-95
Internationals: Wales U19.

2013–14	Swansea C	0	0		
2014–15	Swansea C	0	0		

FABIANSKI, Lukasz (G) 122 0
H: 6 3 W: 13 01 b.Costrzyn nad Odra 18-4-85
Internationals: Poland U21, Full caps.

2005–06	Legia	30	0		
2006–07	Legia	23	0	53	0
2007–08	Arsenal	3	0		
2008–09	Arsenal	6	0		
2009–10	Arsenal	4	0		
2010–11	Arsenal	14	0		
2011–12	Arsenal	0	0		
2012–13	Arsenal	4	0		
2013–14	Arsenal	1	0	32	0
2014–15	Swansea C	37	0	37	0

FERNANDEZ, Federico (D) 145 4
H: 6 3 W: 13 01 b.Tres Algarrobos 21-2-89
Internationals: Argentina U20, Full caps.

2008–09	Estudiantes	14	2		
2009–10	Estudiantes	12	0		
2010–11	Estudiantes	33	1	59	3
2011–12	Napoli	16	0		
2012–13	Napoli	2	0		
2012–13	*Getafe*	14	1	14	1
2013–14	Napoli	26	0	44	0
2014–15	Swansea C	28	0	28	0

FULTON, Jay (M) 4 0
H: 5 10 W: 10 08 b.Bolton 4-4-94
Internationals: Scotland U18, U19, U21.

2013–14	Swansea C	2	0		
2014–15	Swansea C	2	0	4	0

GOGIC, Alex (M) 0 0
H: 6 1 b.Nicosia 13-4-94
Internationals: Serbia U17. Cyprus U19.

2013–14	Swansea C	0	0		
2014–15	Swansea C	0	0		

GOMIS, Bafetimbi (F) 364 117
H: 6 0 W: 12 02 b.Seyne-sur-Mer 6-8-85
Internationals: France U17, Full caps.

2003–04	St Etienne	11	2		
2004–05	St Etienne	6	0		
2004–05	*Troyes*	13	6	13	6
2005–06	St Etienne	24	2		
2006–07	St Etienne	30	10		
2007–08	St Etienne	35	16		
2008–09	St Etienne	36	10	142	40
2009–10	Lyon	37	10		
2010–11	Lyon	35	10		
2011–12	Lyon	36	14		
2012–13	Lyon	37	16		
2013–14	Lyon	33	14	178	64
2014–15	Swansea C	31	7	31	7

GORRE, Kenji (M) 1 0
H: 5 10 W: 11 03 b.Paramaribo 29-9-94

2013–14	Swansea C	0	0		
2014–15	Swansea C	1	0	1	0

GRIMES, Matt (M) 61 5
H: 5 10 W: 11 00 b.Exeter 15-7-95
Internationals: England U20.

2013–14	Exeter C	35	1		
2014–15	Exeter C	23	4	58	5
2014–15	Swansea C	3	0	3	0

HANLEY, Raheem (D) 0 0
H: 5 8 W: 11 00 b.Blackburn 24-3-94
Internationals: England U19.

2011–12	Blackburn R	0	0		
2012–13	Blackburn R	0	0		
2013–14	Blackburn R	0	0		
2013–14	Swansea C	0	0		
2014–15	Swansea C	0	0		

HEDGES, Ryan (M) 17 2
b.Swansea 7-9-95
Internationals: Wales U19, U21.

2013–14	Swansea C	0	0		
2014–15	Swansea C	0	0		
2014–15	*Leyton Orient*	17	2	17	2

JONES, Henry (M) 0 0
H: 6 0 W: 13 02 b.Swansea 18-9-93

2012–13	Swansea C	0	0		
2013–14	Swansea C	0	0		
2014–15	Swansea C	0	0		

KI, Sung-Yeung (M) 156 20
H: 6 2 W: 11 10 b.Gwangju 24-1-89
Internationals: South Korea U17, U20, U23, Full caps.

2009–10	Celtic	10	0		
2010–11	Celtic	26	3		
2011–12	Celtic	30	6	66	9
2012–13	Swansea C	29	0		
2013–14	Swansea C	1	0		
2013–14	*Sunderland*	27	3	27	3
2014–15	Swansea C	33	8	63	8

KING, Adam (M) 2 0
H: 5 11 W: 11 10 b.Edinburgh 11-10-95
Internationals: Scotland U18, U19, U21.

2012–13	Hearts	0	0		
2013–14	Hearts	2	0	2	0
2013–14	Swansea C	0	0		
2014–15	Swansea C	0	0		

KINGSLEY, Stephen (D) 100 1
H: 5 10 W: 10 09 b.Stirling 23-7-94
Internationals: Scotland U18, U19, U21.

2010–11	Falkirk	3	0		
2011–12	Falkirk	15	0		
2012–13	Falkirk	35	0		
2013–14	Falkirk	35	1	88	1
2014–15	Swansea C	0	0		
2014–15	*Yeovil T*	12	0	12	0

LOVERIDGE, James (F) 14 0
H: 6 2 W: 13 04 b.Swansea 16-5-94
Internationals: Wales U17, U19.

2012–13	Swansea C	0	0		
2013–14	Swansea C	0	0		
2013–14	*Milton Keynes D*	7	0	7	0
2014–15	Swansea C	0	0		
2014–15	*Newport Co*	7	0	7	0

LUCAS, Lee (M) 4 0
H: 5 11 W: 11 08 b.Aberdare 10-6-92
Internationals: Wales U17, U19, U21.

2010–11	Swansea C	1	0		
2011–12	Swansea C	0	0		
2011–12	*Burton Alb*	1	0	1	0
2012–13	Swansea C	0	0		
2013–14	Swansea C	0	0		
2013–14	*Cheltenham T*	2	0	2	0
2014–15	Swansea C	0	0	1	0

MARCH, Kurtis (M) 0 0
H: 5 9 W: 11 03 b.Swansea 30-4-93
Internationals: Wales U19.

2011–12	Swansea C	0	0		
2012–13	Swansea C	0	0		
2013–14	Swansea C	0	0		
2014–15	Swansea C	0	0		

MEADE, Jernade (M) 0 0
H: 5 8 W: 11 03 b.Luton 25-10-92

2011–12	Arsenal	0	0		
2012–13	Arsenal	0	0		
2013–14	Swansea C	0	0		
2014–15	Swansea C	0	0		

MONTERO, Jefferson (M) 203 34
H: 5 8 W: 11 00 b.Babahoyo 1-9-89
Internationals: Ecuador Full caps.

2007	Emelec	22	2	22	2
2008	Independiente de Valle	25	8		
2008–09	*Dorados*	5	1	5	1
2009	Independiente de Valle	12	11	37	19
2010–11	Villareal	9	1		
2010–11	*Levante*	11	0	11	0
2010–11	Villareal	0	0	9	1
2011–12	*Real Betis*	32	1	32	1
2012–13	Morelia	32	4		
2013–14	Morelia	25	5	57	9
2014–15	Swansea C	30	1	30	1

NAUGHTON, Kyle (M) 191 6
H: 5 11 W: 11 07 b.Sheffield 11-11-88
Internationals: England U21.

2006–07	Sheffield U	0	0		
2007–08	*Gretna*	18	0	18	0
2007–08	Sheffield U	0	0		
2008–09	Sheffield U	40	1		
2009–10	Sheffield U	0	0	40	1
2009–10	Tottenham H	1	0		
2009–10	*Middlesbrough*	15	0	15	0
2010–11	Tottenham H	0	0		
2010–11	*Leicester C*	34	5	34	5
2011–12	Tottenham H	0	0		
2011–12	*Norwich C*	32	0	32	0
2012–13	Tottenham H	14	0		
2013–14	Tottenham H	22	0		
2014–15	Tottenham H	5	0	42	0
2014–15	Swansea C	10	0	10	0

NELSON OLIVEIRA, Miguel (F) 115 17
H: 6 1 W: 12 13 b.Barcelos 8-8-91
Internationals: Portugal U16, U17, U19, U20, U21, Full caps.

2009–10	Benfica	0	0		
2009–10	*Rio Ave*	10	0	10	0
2010–11	Benfica	0	0		

2010–11	*Pacos Ferreira*	23	4	23	4
2011–12	Benfica	12	0		
2012–13	Benfica	0	0		
2012–13	*La Coruna*	30	4	30	4
2013–14	Benfica	0	0		
2013–14	*Rennes*	30	8	30	8
2014–15	Benfica	0	0	12	0

On loan from Benfica.

2014–15	Swansea C	10	1	10	1

OBENG, Curtis (D) 29 0
H: 5 6 W: 10 05 b.Manchester 14-2-89
Internationals: England U19.

2007–08	Manchester C	0	0		
2008–09	Manchester C	0	0		

From Wrexham

2011–12	Swansea C	0	0		
2012–13	Swansea C	0	0		
2012–13	*Fleetwood T*	5	0	5	0
2012–13	*York C*	4	0	4	0
2013–14	Swansea C	0	0		
2013–14	*Stevenage*	15	0	15	0
2014–15	Swansea C	0	0		
2014–15	*Newport Co*	5	0	5	0

RANGEL, Angel (D) 317 10
H: 5 11 W: 11 09 b.Barcelona 28-10-82

2006–07	Terrassa	34	2	34	2
2007–08	Swansea C	43	2		
2008–09	Swansea C	40	1		
2009–10	Swansea C	38	0		
2010–11	Swansea C	38	2		
2011–12	Swansea C	34	0		
2012–13	Swansea C	33	3		
2013–14	Swansea C	30	0		
2014–15	Swansea C	27	0	283	8

RICHARDS, Ashley (M) 73 0
H: 6 1 W: 12 04 b.Swansea 12-4-91
Internationals: Wales U17, U19, U21, Full caps.

2009–10	Swansea C	15	0		
2010–11	Swansea C	6	0		
2011–12	Swansea C	8	0		
2012–13	Swansea C	0	0		
2012–13	*Crystal Palace*	11	0	11	0
2013–14	Swansea C	0	0		
2013–14	*Huddersfield T*	9	0	9	0
2014–15	Swansea C	10	0	39	0
2014–15	*Fulham*	14	0	14	0

ROUTLEDGE, Wayne (M) 389 34
H: 5 6 W: 11 02 b.Sidcup 7-1-85
Internationals: England U20, U21.

2001–02	Crystal Palace	2	0		
2002–03	Crystal Palace	26	4		
2003–04	Crystal Palace	44	6		
2004–05	Crystal Palace	38	0	110	10
2005–06	Tottenham H	3	0		
2005–06	Portsmouth	13	0	13	0
2006–07	Tottenham H	0	0		
2006–07	Fulham	24	0	24	0
2007–08	Tottenham H	2	0	5	0
2007–08	Aston Villa	1	0		
2008–09	Aston Villa	1	0	2	0
2008–09	*Cardiff C*	9	2	9	2
2008–09	QPR	19	1		
2009–10	QPR	25	2		
2009–10	Newcastle U	17	3		
2010–11	Newcastle U	17	0	34	3
2010–11	*QPR*	20	5	64	8
2011–12	Swansea C	28	1		
2012–13	Swansea C	36	5		
2013–14	Swansea C	35	2		
2014–15	Swansea C	29	3	128	11

SHEEHAN, Josh (M) 13 0
H: 6 0 W: 11 11 b.Pembrey 30-3-95
Internationals: Wales U19, U21.

2013–14	Swansea C	0	0		
2014–15	Swansea C	0	0		
2014–15	*Yeovil T*	13	0	13	0

SHELVEY, Jonjo (M) 162 24
H: 6 1 W: 11 02 b.Romford 27-2-92
Internationals: England U16, U17, U19, U21, Full caps.

2007–08	Charlton Ath	2	0		
2008–09	Charlton Ath	16	3		
2009–10	Charlton Ath	24	4	42	7
2010–11	Liverpool	15	0		
2011–12	Liverpool	13	1		
2011–12	*Blackpool*	10	6	10	6
2012–13	Liverpool	19	1	47	2
2013–14	Swansea C	32	6		
2014–15	Swansea C	31	3	63	9

SHEPHARD, Liam (D) 20 0
H: 5 10 W: 10 08 b.Rhondda 22-11-94

2013–14	Swansea C	0	0		
2014–15	Swansea C	0	0		
2014–15	*Yeovil T*	20	0	20	0

SIGURDSSON, Gylfi (M) 204 53
H: 6 1 W: 12 02 b.Reykjavik 9-9-89
Internationals: Iceland U17, U18, U19, U21, Full caps.

2007–08	Reading	0	0		
2008–09	Reading	0	0		
2008–09	*Shrewsbury T*	5	1	5	1
2008–09	*Crewe Alex*	15	3	15	3
2009–10	Reading	38	16		
2010–11	Reading	4	2	42	18
2010–11	Hoffenheim	28	9		
2011–12	Hoffenheim	6	0	34	9
2011–12	*Swansea C*	18	7		
2012–13	Tottenham H	33	3		
2013–14	Tottenham H	25	5	58	8
2014–15	Swansea C	32	7	50	14

TANCOCK, Scott (D) 4 0
H: 6 1 W: 11 10 b.Swansea 29-12-92
Internationals: Wales U21.

2012–13	Swansea C	0	0		
2013–14	Swansea C	0	0		
2014–15	Swansea C	0	0		
2014–15	*Newport Co*	4	0	4	0

TATE, Alan (D) 337 5
H: 6 1 W: 13 05 b.Seaham 2-9-82

2000–01	Manchester U	0	0		
2001–02	Manchester U	0	0		
2002–03	Manchester U	0	0		
2002–03	*Swansea C*	27	0		
2003–04	Manchester U	0	0		
2003–04	Swansea C	26	1		
2004–05	Swansea C	23	0		
2005–06	Swansea C	43	0		
2006–07	Swansea C	38	1		
2007–08	Swansea C	21	1		
2008–09	Swansea C	25	1		
2009–10	Swansea C	39	1		
2010–11	Swansea C	40	0		
2011–12	Swansea C	5	0		
2012–13	Swansea C	3	0		
2012–13	*Leeds U*	10	0	10	0
2013–14	Swansea C	0	0		
2013–14	*Yeovil T*	4	0	4	0
2013–14	*Aberdeen*	7	0	7	0
2014–15	Swansea C	0	0	290	5
2014–15	*Crewe Alex*	26	0	26	0

TAYLOR, Neil (D) 141 0
H: 5 9 W: 10 02 b.Ruthin 7-2-89
Internationals: Wales U17, U19, U21, Full caps. Great Britain.

2007–08	Wrexham	26	0	26	0
2010–11	Swansea C	29	0		
2011–12	Swansea C	36	0		
2012–13	Swansea C	6	0		
2013–14	Swansea C	10	0		
2014–15	Swansea C	34	0	115	0

TIENDALLI, Dwight (D) 188 5
H: 5 9 W: 11 08 b.Surinam 21-10-85
Internationals: Netherlands U21, Full caps.

2004–05	FC Utrecht	10	1		
2005–06	FC Utrecht	29	2		
2006–07	FC Utrecht	1	0	40	3
2006–07	Feyenoord	13	0		
2007–08	*S Rotterdam*	13	0	13	0
2008–09	Feyenoord	22	0	35	0
2009–10	FC Twente	26	1		
2010–11	FC Twente	18	0		
2011–12	FC Twente	27	0	71	1
2012–13	Swansea C	14	1		
2013–14	Swansea C	10	0		
2014–15	Swansea C	3	0	27	1
2014–15	*Middlesbrough*	2	0	2	0

TREMMEL, Gerhard (G) 122 0
H: 6 3 W: 14 00 b.Munich 16-11-78

2006–07	Energie Cottbus	24	0		
2007–08	Energie Cottbus	24	0		
2008–09	Energie Cottbus	34	0		
2009–10	Energie Cottbus	34	0	93	0
2011–12	Swansea C	1	0		
2012–13	Swansea C	14	0		
2013–14	Swansea C	12	0		
2014–15	Swansea C	2	0	29	0

WILLIAMS, Ashley (D) 448 15
H: 6 0 W: 11 02 b.Wolverhampton 23-8-84
Internationals: Wales Full caps.

2003–04	Stockport Co	10	0		
2004–05	Stockport Co	44	1		
2005–06	Stockport Co	36	1		
2006–07	Stockport Co	46	1		
2007–08	Stockport Co	26	0	162	3
2007–08	*Swansea C*	3	0		
2008–09	Swansea C	46	2		
2009–10	Swansea C	46	5		
2010–11	Swansea C	46	3		
2011–12	Swansea C	37	1		
2012–13	Swansea C	37	0		
2013–14	Swansea C	34	1		
2014–15	Swansea C	37	0	286	12

ZABRET, Gregor (G) 0 0
H: 6 2 W: 12 11 b.Ljubljana 18-8-95
Internationals: Slovenia U16, U17, U19, U21.

2013–14	Swansea C	0	0		
2014–15	Swansea C	0	0		

Players retained or with offer of contract
Davies, Keston Ellis; Demetriou, James Andreas; Hedges, Ryan Peter; James, Daniel; Maric, Adnan; Perez Cuesta, Miguel; Roberts, Connor Richard Jones; Samuel, Alexander Kinloch; Zaragoza, Angel Rangel.

Scholars
Copp, Kyle Thomas; Dyson, Thomas Jonathan; Evans, Jack; Fallon, Stephen; Griffiths, Brandon Lee; Harries, Ashleigh Mark; Jones, Ben Joseph; Jones, Owain Rhys; Lewis, Aaron James; Rodon, Joseph Peter; Thomas, Lewis Rhys.

SWINDON T (81)

AGOMBAR, Harry (M) 1 0
H: 5 10 b.London 12-7-92

2013–14	Swindon T	0	0		
2014–15	Swindon T	1	0	1	0

ANTONIO, Josue (D) 0 0
H: 5 10 W: 11 03 b.Merton 29-3-96

2014–15	Swindon T	0	0		

BARKER, George (F) 24 0
H: 5 8 W: 11 02 b.Portsmouth 26-9-91

2010–11	Brighton & HA	0	0		
2011–12	Brighton & HA	0	0		
2012–13	Brighton & HA	3	0		
2012–13	*Barnet*	1	0	1	0
2013–14	Brighton & HA	1	0	4	0
2013–14	*Newport Co*	2	0	2	0
2013–14	Swindon T	8	0		
2014–15	Swindon T	5	0	13	0
2014–15	*Tranmere R*	4	0	4	0

BARTHRAM, Jack (D) 16 0
H: 5 8 W: 11 09 b.Newham 13-10-93

2012–13	Tottenham H	0	0		
2013–14	Swindon T	11	0		
2014–15	Swindon T	5	0	16	0

BELFORD, Cameron (G) 101 0
H: 6 1 W: 11 10 b.Nuneaton 16-10-88

2007–08	Bury	1	0		
2008–09	Bury	1	0		
2009–10	Bury	7	0		
2010–11	Bury	39	0		
2011–12	Bury	23	0		
2011–12	*Southend U*	13	0		
2012–13	Bury	7	0		
2012–13	*Southend U*	4	0	17	0
2012–13	*Accrington S*	5	0	5	0
2013–14	Bury	0	0	78	0
2014–15	Swindon T	1	0	1	0

BELFORD, Tyrell (G) 7 0
H: 6 0 W: 12 00 b.Nuneaton 6-5-94
Internationals: England U16, U17.

2011–12	Liverpool	0	0		
2012–13	Liverpool	0	0		
2013–14	Swindon T	5	0		
2014–15	Swindon T	2	0	7	0

BRANCO, Raphael Rossi (D) 44 3
b. 25-7-90

2013–14	Swindon T	15	0		
2014–15	Swindon T	29	3	44	3

BYRNE, Nathan (D) 117 8
H: 5 10 W: 10 10 b.St Albans 5-6-92

2010–11	Tottenham H	0	0		
2010–11	*Brentford*	11	0	11	0
2011–12	Tottenham H	0	0		
2011–12	*Bournemouth*	9	0	9	0
2012–13	Tottenham H	0	0		
2012–13	*Crawley T*	12	1	12	1
2012–13	*Swindon T*	7	0		

2013–14	Swindon T	36	4		
2014–15	Swindon T	42	3	85	7

COOKE, Josh (F)   2   0
b. 4-2-97

2014–15	Swindon T	2	0	2	0

FODERINGHAM, Wesley (G)   164   0
H: 6 1 W: 12 00 b.Hammersmith 14-1-91
Internationals: England U16, U17, U19.

2009–10	Fulham	0	0		
2010–11	Crystal Palace	0	0		
2011–12	Crystal Palace	0	0		
2011–12	Swindon T	33	0		
2012–13	Swindon T	46	0		
2013–14	Swindon T	41	0		
2014–15	Swindon T	44	0	164	0

GLADWIN, Ben (D)   47   8
b.Reading 8-6-92

2013–14	Swindon T	13	0		
2014–15	Swindon T	34	8	47	8

HOLLAND, Tom (M)   0   0
Internationals: Republic of Ireland U17.

2014–15	Swindon T	0	0		

HYLTON, Jermaine (F)   11   1
H: 5 10 W: 11 00 b.Birmingham 28-6-93

2014–15	Swindon T	11	1	11	1

JOHNS, Connor (G)   0   0

2014–15	Swindon T	0	0		

JONES, Matthew (D)   1   0
b.Swindon

2012–13	Swindon T	0	0		
2013–14	Swindon T	1	0		
2014–15	Swindon T	0	0	1	0

KASIM, Yaser (M)   73   4
H: 5 11 W: 11 07 b.Bagdad 10-5-91
Internationals: Iraq U23, Iraq Full caps.

2010–11	Brighton & HA	1	0		
2011–12	Brighton & HA	0	0		
2012–13	Brighton & HA	0	0	1	0
2013–14	Swindon T	37	2		
2014–15	Swindon T	35	2	72	4

LUONGO, Massimo (F)   94   13
H: 5 8 W: 11 10 b.Sydney 25-9-92
Internationals: Australia Full caps.

2010–11	Tottenham H	0	0		
2011–12	Tottenham H	0	0		
2012–13	Tottenham H	0	0		
2012–13	Ipswich T	9	0	9	0
2012–13	Swindon T	7	1		
2013–14	Swindon T	44	6		
2014–15	Swindon T	34	6	85	13

MARSHALL, Lee (M)   2   0
H: 5 10 W: 11 03 b. 21-11-97

2014–15	Swindon T	2	0	2	0

OBIKA, Jonathan (F)   154   31
H: 6 0 W: 12 00 b.Enfield 12-9-90
Internationals: England U19, U20.

2008–09	Tottenham H	0	0		
2008–09	Yeovil T	10	4		
2009–10	Tottenham H	0	0		
2009–10	Yeovil T	22	6		
2009–10	Millwall	12	2	12	2
2010–11	Tottenham H	0	0		
2010–11	Crystal Palace	7	0	7	0
2010–11	Peterborough U	1	1	1	1
2010–11	Swindon T	5	0		
2010–11	Yeovil T	11	3		
2011–12	Tottenham H	0	0		
2011–12	Yeovil T	27	4	70	17
2012–13	Tottenham H	0	0		
2012–13	Charlton Ath	10	3		
2013–14	Tottenham H	0	0		
2013–14	Brighton & HA	5	0	5	0
2013–14	Charlton Ath	12	0	22	3
2014–15	Tottenham H	0	0		
2014–15	Swindon T	32	8	37	8

RANDALL, Will (M)   5   0
H: 5 11 W: 10 03 b.Swindon 2-5-97

2013–14	Swindon T	1	0		
2014–15	Swindon T	4	0	5	0

RODGERS, Anton (M)   19   2
H: 5 7 W: 10 02 b.Reading 26-1-93
Internationals: Republic of Ireland U21.

2011–12	Brighton & HA	0	0		
2012–13	Exeter C	2	0	2	0
2013–14	Oldham Ath	7	0	7	0
2014–15	Swindon T	10	2	10	2

SMITH, Michael (F)   97   34
H: 6 4 W: 11 02 b.Wallsend 17-10-91

2011–12	Charlton Ath	0	0		
2011–12	Accrington S	6	3	6	3
2012–13	Charlton Ath	0	0		
2012–13	Colchester U	8	1	8	1
2013–14	Charlton Ath	0	0		
2013–14	AFC Wimbledon	23	9	23	9
2013–14	Swindon T	20	8		
2014–15	Swindon T	40	13	60	21

SMITH, Tom (M)   1   0
H: 5 10 W: 11 00 b. 25-1-98

2014–15	Swindon T	1	0	1	0

STOREY, Miles (F)   73   8
H: 5 11 W: 11 00 b.West Bromwich 4-1-94
Internationals: England U19.

2010–11	Swindon T	2	0		
2011–12	Swindon T	4	0		
2012–13	Swindon T	8	1		
2013–14	Swindon T	18	3		
2013–14	Shrewsbury T	6	0	6	0
2014–15	Swindon T	0	0	32	4
2014–15	Portsmouth	17	2	17	2
2014–15	Newport Co	18	2	18	2

THOMPSON, Nathan (D)   110   1
H: 5 7 W: 11 02 b.Chester 9-11-90

2009–10	Swindon T	0	0		
2010–11	Swindon T	3	0		
2011–12	Swindon T	5	0		
2012–13	Swindon T	26	0		
2013–14	Swindon T	41	1		
2014–15	Swindon T	35	0	110	1

WALDON, Connor (F)   5   0
b.Swindon 13-2-95

2012–13	Swindon T	1	0		
2013–14	Swindon T	3	0		
2014–15	Swindon T	1	0	5	0

WARD, Darren (D)   520   17
H: 6 3 W: 11 04 b.Harrow 13-9-78

1995–96	Watford	1	0		
1996–97	Watford	7	0		
1997–98	Watford	0	0		
1998–99	Watford	1	0		
1999–2000	Watford	9	1		
1999–2000	QPR	14	0	14	0
2000–01	Watford	40	1		
2001–02	Watford	1	0		
2001–02	Millwall	14	0		
2002–03	Millwall	39	1		
2003–04	Millwall	46	3		
2004–05	Millwall	43	0		
2005–06	Crystal Palace	43	5		
2006–07	Crystal Palace	20	0	63	5
2007–08	Wolverhampton W	30	0		
2008–09	Wolverhampton W	1	0	31	0
2008–09	Watford	9	1	68	3
2008–09	Charlton Ath	16	0	16	0
2009–10	Millwall	31	1		
2010–11	Millwall	31	1		
2011–12	Millwall	30	0		
2012–13	Millwall	1	0	235	6
2012–13	Swindon T	39	2		
2013–14	Swindon T	36	0		
2014–15	Swindon T	0	0	75	2
2014–15	Crawley T	18	1	18	1

WILLIAMS, Andy (F)   325   72
H: 5 11 W: 11 09 b.Hereford 14-8-86

2006–07	Hereford U	41	8		
2007–08	Bristol R	41	4		
2008–09	Bristol R	4	1		
2008–09	Hereford U	26	2	67	10
2009–10	Bristol R	43	3	88	8
2010–11	Yeovil T	37	6		
2011–12	Yeovil T	35	16		
2012–13	Swindon T	40	11		
2013–14	Swindon T	3	0		
2013–14	Yeovil T	9	0	81	22
2014–15	Swindon T	46	21	89	32

WOOD, Ryan (D)   0   0

2013–14	Swindon T	0	0		
2014–15	Swindon T	0	0		

Scholars

Da-Costa, Claude; English, Joe; Evans, Jacob Finlay; Gied, Galib Amir; Holland, Tom; Johns, Connor Jason; Marks, Nathan James; Matthews, Luke Benjamin; McCormack, Callum Francis; Randall-Hurren, William; Smith, Thomas; Wood, Ryan Anthony.

TOTTENHAM H (82)

ADEBAYOR, Emmanuel (F)   366   134
H: 6 4 W: 11 08 b.Lome 26-2-84
Internationals: Togo Full caps.

2001–02	Metz	10	2		
2002–03	Metz	34	13	44	15
2003–04	Monaco	31	8		
2004–05	Monaco	34	9		
2005–06	Monaco	13	1	78	18
2005–06	Arsenal	13	4		
2006–07	Arsenal	29	8		
2007–08	Arsenal	36	24		
2008–09	Arsenal	26	10	104	46
2009–10	Manchester C	26	14		
2010–11	Manchester C	8	1		
2010–11	Real Madrid	14	5	14	5
2011–12	Manchester C	0	0		
2011–12	Tottenham H	33	17		
2012–13	Manchester C	0	0	34	15
2012–13	Tottenham H	25	5		
2013–14	Tottenham H	21	11		
2014–15	Tottenham H	13	2	92	35

ARCHER, Jordan (G)   40   0
H: 6 1 W: 12 08 b.Walthamstow 12-4-93
Internationals: Scotland U19, U20, U21.

2011–12	Tottenham H	0	0		
2012–13	Tottenham H	0	0		
2012–13	Wycombe W	27	0	27	0
2013–14	Tottenham H	0	0		
2014–15	Tottenham H	0	0		
2014–15	Northampton T	13	0	13	0
2014–15	Millwall	0	0		

BALL, Dominic (D)   11   0
b.Welwyn Garden City 2-8-95
Internationals: Northern Ireland U15, U16, U17, U18. England U19, U20.

2013–14	Tottenham H	0	0		
2014–15	Tottenham H	0	0		
2014–15	Cambridge U	11	0	11	0

BENTALEB, Nabil (M)   41   0
H: 6 2 W: 10 09 b.Lille, France 24-11-94
Internationals: France U18. Algeria Full caps.

2012–13	Tottenham H	0	0		
2013–14	Tottenham H	15	0		
2014–15	Tottenham H	26	0	41	0

CAPOUE, Etienne (M)   198   14
H: 6 2 W: 11 10 b.Niort 11-7-88
Internationals: France U18, U19, U21, Full caps.

2006–07	Toulouse	0	0		
2007–08	Toulouse	5	0		
2008–09	Toulouse	32	1		
2009–10	Toulouse	33	0		
2010–11	Toulouse	37	2		
2011–12	Toulouse	33	3		
2012–13	Toulouse	34	7	174	13
2013–14	Tottenham H	12	1		
2014–15	Tottenham H	12	0	24	1

CARROLL, Tommy (M)   70   1
H: 5 10 W: 10 00 b.Watford 28-5-92
Internationals: England U19, U21.

2010–11	Tottenham H	0	0		
2010–11	Leyton Orient	12	0	12	0
2011–12	Tottenham H	0	0		
2011–12	Derby Co	12	1	12	1
2012–13	Tottenham H	7	0		
2013–14	Tottenham H	0	0		
2013–14	QPR	26	0	26	0
2014–15	Tottenham H	0	0	7	0
2014–15	Swansea C	13	0	13	0

CEBALLOS, Cristian (M)   18   1
H: 5 8 W: 10 08 b.Barcelona 3-12-92

2011–12	Tottenham H	0	0		
2012–13	Tottenham H	0	0		
2013–14	Tottenham H	0	0		
2013–14	Arouca	18	1	18	1
2014–15	Tottenham H	0	0		

CHADLI, Nacer (M)   235   65
H: 6 2 W: 12 07 b.Liege 3-6-88
Internationals: Morocco Full caps. Belgium Full caps.

2007–08	AGOVV	19	2		
2008–09	AGOVV	34	9		
2009–10	AGOVV	39	17	92	28
2010–11	FC Twente	33	7		
2011–12	FC Twente	25	6		
2012–13	FC Twente	26	12	84	25
2013–14	Tottenham H	24	1		
2014–15	Tottenham H	35	11	59	12

CHIRICHES, Vlad (D) **149 3**
H: 6 0 W: 11 10 b.Bacau 14-11-89
Internationals: Romania U21, Full caps.

2008–09	Curtea-de-Arges	26	1		
2009–10	Curtea-de-Arges	15	0	**41**	**1**
2010–11	Pandurii T-J	24	0		
2011–12	Pandurii T-J	15	0	**39**	**0**
2011–12	Steaua Bucuresti	14	0		
2012–13	Steaua Bucuresti	26	1		
2013–14	Steaua Bucuresti	2	0	**42**	**1**
2013–14	Tottenham H	17	1		
2014–15	Tottenham H	10	0	**27**	**1**

COULTHIRST, Shaquile (F) **40 9**
H: 5 9 W: 12 02 b.Hackney 2-1-94
Internationals: England U19.

2012–13	Tottenham H	0	0		
2013–14	Tottenham H	0	0		
2013–14	*Leyton Orient*	1	1	**1**	**1**
2013–14	*Torquay U*	6	2	**6**	**2**
2014–15	Tottenham H	0	0		
2014–15	*Southend U*	22	4	**22**	**4**
2014–15	*York C*	11	2	**11**	**2**

DAVIES, Ben (D) **85 3**
H: 5 7 W: 12 00 b.Neath 24-4-93
Internationals: Wales U19, Full caps.

2011–12	Swansea C	0	0		
2012–13	Swansea C	37	1		
2013–14	Swansea C	34	2	**71**	**3**
2014–15	Tottenham H	14	0	**14**	**0**

DEMBELE, Mousa (F) **317 42**
H: 5 9 W: 10 01 b.Wilrijk 17-7-87
Internationals: Belgium U16, U17, U18, U19, Full caps.

2003–04	Beerschot	1	0		
2004–05	Beerschot	19	1	**20**	**1**
2005–06	Willem II	33	9	**33**	**9**
2006–07	AZ	33	6		
2007–08	AZ	33	4		
2008–09	AZ	23	10		
2009–10	AZ	29	4	**118**	**24**
2010–11	Fulham	24	3		
2011–12	Fulham	36	2		
2012–13	Fulham	2	0	**62**	**5**
2012–13	Tottenham H	30	1		
2013–14	Tottenham H	28	1		
2014–15	Tottenham H	26	1	**84**	**3**

DIER, Eric (D) **55 3**
H: 6 3 W: 13 08 b.Cheltenham 15-1-94
Internationals: England U18, U19, U20, U21.

2012–13	Sporting Lisbon	14	1		
2013–14	Sporting Lisbon	13	0	**27**	**1**

On loan from Sporting Lisbon.

2014–15	Tottenham H	28	2	**28**	**2**

ERIKSEN, Christian (M) **176 42**
H: 5 9 W: 10 02 b.Middelfart 14-2-92
Internationals: Denmark U17, U18, U19, U21, Full caps.

2009–10	Ajax	15	0		
2010–11	Ajax	28	6		
2011–12	Ajax	33	7		
2012–13	Ajax	33	10		
2013–14	Ajax	4	2	**113**	**25**
2013–14	Tottenham H	25	7		
2014–15	Tottenham H	38	10	**63**	**17**

FAZIO, Federico (D) **214 15**
H: 6 5 W: 13 05 b.Buenos Aires 17-3-87
Internationals: Argentina U20, U23, Full caps.

2005–06	Ferro Carill Oeste	31	3	**31**	**3**
2006–07	Ferro Carill Oeste	17	0	**17**	**0**
2007–08	Sevilla	20	3		
2008–09	Sevilla	16	0		
2009–10	Sevilla	10	1		
2010–11	Sevilla	19	1		
2011–12	Sevilla	28	2		
2012–13	Sevilla	26	3		
2013–14	Sevilla	27	2	**146**	**12**
2014–15	Tottenham H	20	0	**20**	**0**

FREDERICKS, Ryan (M) **35 1**
H: 5 8 W: 11 10 b.Potters Bar 10-10-92
Internationals: England U19.

2010–11	Tottenham H	0	0		
2011–12	Tottenham H	0	0		
2012–13	Tottenham H	0	0		
2012–13	*Brentford*	4	0	**4**	**0**
2013–14	Tottenham H	0	0		
2013–14	*Millwall*	14	1	**14**	**1**
2014–15	Tottenham H	0	0		
2014–15	*Middlesbrough*	17	0	**17**	**0**

FRIEDEL, Brad (G) **515 1**
H: 6 3 W: 14 00 b.Lakewood 18-5-71
Internationals: USA Full caps.

1996	Columbus Crew	9	0		
1997	Columbus Crew	29	0	**38**	**0**
1997–98	Liverpool	11	0		
1998–99	Liverpool	12	0		
1999–2000	Liverpool	2	0		
2000–01	Liverpool	0	0	**25**	**0**
2000–01	Blackburn R	27	0		
2001–02	Blackburn R	36	0		
2002–03	Blackburn R	37	0		
2003–04	Blackburn R	36	1		
2004–05	Blackburn R	38	0		
2005–06	Blackburn R	38	0		
2006–07	Blackburn R	38	0		
2007–08	Blackburn R	38	0	**288**	**1**
2008–09	Aston Villa	38	0		
2009–10	Aston Villa	38	0		
2010–11	Aston Villa	38	0	**114**	**0**
2011–12	Tottenham H	38	0		
2012–13	Tottenham H	11	0		
2013–14	Tottenham H	1	0		
2014–15	Tottenham H	0	0	**50**	**0**

HALL, Grant (D) **47 1**
H: 5 9 W: 11 02 b.Brighton 29-10-91

2009–10	Brighton & HA	0	0		
2010–11	Brighton & HA	0	0		
2011–12	Brighton & HA	1	0	**1**	**0**
2012–13	Tottenham H	0	0		
2013–14	Tottenham H	0	0		
2013–14	*Swindon T*	27	0	**27**	**0**
2014–15	Tottenham H	0	0		
2014–15	*Birmingham C*	7	0	**7**	**0**
2014–15	*Blackpool*	12	1	**12**	**1**

HOLTBY, Lewis (M) **170 26**
H: 5 8 W: 10 04 b.Erkelenz 18-9-90
Internationals: Germany U18, U19, U20, U21, Full caps.

2007–08	Alemania Aachen	2	0		
2008–09	Alemania Aachen	31	7	**33**	**7**
2009–10	Schalke 04	9	0		
2009–10	*VfL Bochum*	14	2	**14**	**2**
2010–11	*Mainz*	30	5	**30**	**5**
2011–12	Schalke 04	27	6		
2012–13	Schalke 04	19	4	**55**	**10**
2012–13	Tottenham H	11	0		
2013–14	Tottenham H	13	1		
2013–14	*Fulham*	13	1	**13**	**1**
2014–15	Tottenham H	1	0	**25**	**1**
2014–15	*Hamburg*	0	0		

KABOUL, Younes (D) **201 13**
H: 6 2 W: 13 07 b.Annemasse 4-1-86
Internationals: France U21, Full caps.

2004–05	Auxerre	12	1		
2005–06	Auxerre	9	0		
2006–07	Auxerre	31	2	**52**	**3**
2007–08	Tottenham H	21	3		
2008–09	Portsmouth	20	1		
2009–10	Portsmouth	19	3	**39**	**4**
2009–10	Tottenham H	10	0		
2010–11	Tottenham H	21	1		
2011–12	Tottenham H	33	1		
2012–13	Tottenham H	1	0		
2013–14	Tottenham H	13	1		
2014–15	Tottenham H	11	0	**110**	**6**

KANE, Harry (F) **101 38**
H: 6 0 W: 10 00 b.Chingford 28-7-93
Internationals: England U17, U19, U20, U21.

2010–11	Tottenham H	0	0		
2010–11	*Leyton Orient*	18	5	**18**	**5**
2011–12	Tottenham H	0	0		
2011–12	*Millwall*	22	7	**22**	**7**
2012–13	Tottenham H	1	0		
2012–13	*Norwich C*	3	0	**3**	**0**
2012–13	*Leicester C*	13	2	**13**	**2**
2013–14	Tottenham H	10	3		
2014–15	Tottenham H	34	21	**45**	**24**

KHUMALO, Bongani (D) **204 12**
H: 6 2 W: 12 13 b.Swaziland 6-1-87
Internationals: South Africa Full caps.

2005–06	Pretoria Univ	22	0		
2006–07	Pretoria Univ	28	4	**50**	**4**
2007–08	Supersport U	25	4		
2008–09	Supersport U	23	3		
2009–10	Supersport U	26	1		
2010–11	Supersport U	7	0	**81**	**8**
2010–11	Tottenham H	0	0		
2010–11	*Preston NE*	6	0	**6**	**0**
2011–12	Tottenham H	0	0		
2011–12	*Reading*	4	0	**4**	**0**
2012–13	Tottenham H	0	0		
2012–13	*PAOK Salonika*	23	0	**23**	**0**
2013–14	Tottenham H	0	0		
2013–14	*Doncaster R*	30	0	**30**	**0**
2014–15	Tottenham H	0	0		
2014–15	*Colchester U*	10	0	**10**	**0**

LAMELA, Erik (F) **137 25**
H: 6 0 W: 10 13 b.Buenos Aires 4-3-92
Internationals: Argentina U20, Full caps.

2008–09	River Plate	1	0		
2009–10	River Plate	1	0		
2010–11	River Plate	32	4	**34**	**4**
2011–12	Roma	29	4		
2012–13	Roma	32	15	**61**	**19**
2013–14	Tottenham H	9	0		
2014–15	Tottenham H	33	2	**42**	**2**

LENNON, Aaron (M) **318 29**
H: 5 6 W: 10 03 b.Leeds 16-4-87
Internationals: England U17, U19, U21, B, Full caps.

2003–04	Leeds U	11	0		
2004–05	Leeds U	27	1	**38**	**1**
2005–06	Tottenham H	27	2		
2006–07	Tottenham H	26	3		
2007–08	Tottenham H	29	2		
2008–09	Tottenham H	35	5		
2009–10	Tottenham H	22	3		
2010–11	Tottenham H	34	3		
2011–12	Tottenham H	23	3		
2012–13	Tottenham H	34	4		
2013–14	Tottenham H	27	1		
2014–15	Tottenham H	9	0	**266**	**26**
2014–15	*Everton*	14	2	**14**	**2**

LLORIS, Hugo (G) **317 0**
H: 6 2 W: 12 03 b.Nice 26-12-86
Internationals: France U18, U19, U20, U21, Full caps.

2005–06	Nice	5	0		
2006–07	Nice	37	0		
2007–08	Nice	30	0	**72**	**0**
2008–09	Lyon	35	0		
2009–10	Lyon	36	0		
2010–11	Lyon	37	0		
2011–12	Lyon	36	0		
2012–13	Lyon	2	0	**146**	**0**
2012–13	Tottenham H	27	0		
2013–14	Tottenham H	37	0		
2014–15	Tottenham H	35	0	**99**	**0**

MASON, Ryan (F) **101 12**
H: 5 9 W: 10 00 b.Enfield 13-6-91
Internationals: England U19, U20, Full caps.

2007–08	Tottenham H	0	0		
2008–09	Tottenham H	0	0		
2009–10	Tottenham H	0	0		
2009–10	*Yeovil T*	28	6	**28**	**6**
2010–11	Tottenham H	0	0		
2010–11	*Doncaster R*	15	0		
2011–12	Tottenham H	0	0		
2011–12	*Doncaster R*	4	0	**19**	**0**
2011–12	*Millwall*	5	0	**5**	**0**
2012–13	Tottenham H	0	0		
2012–13	*Lorient*	0	0		
2013–14	Tottenham H	0	0		
2013–14	*Swindon T*	18	5	**18**	**5**
2014–15	Tottenham H	31	1	**31**	**1**

McEVOY, Kenneth (M) **8 1**
H: 5 9 W: 10 01 b.Waterford 4-9-94
Internationals: Republic of Ireland U17, U19, U21.

2013–14	Tottenham H	0	0		
2014–15	Tottenham H	0	0		
2014–15	*Peterborough U*	7	1	**7**	**1**
2014–15	*Colchester U*	1	0	**1**	**0**

McGEE, Luke (G) **0 0**
b.Edgware 9-2-95

2014–15	Tottenham H	0	0

ODUWA, Nathan (F) **11 0**
b.London 5-3-96
Internationals: England U17, U18.

2013–14	Tottenham H	0	0		
2014–15	Tottenham H	0	0		
2014–15	*Luton T*	11	0	**11**	**0**

OGILVIE, Connor (D) **0 0**
b. 14-2-96
Internationals: England U16, U17.

2013–14	Tottenham H	0	0
2014–15	Tottenham H	0	0

ONOMAH, Joshua (M) **0 0**
H: 5 11 W: 10 01 b.Enfield 27-4-97
Internationals: England U16, U17, U18.

2013–14	Tottenham H	0	0
2014–15	Tottenham H	0	0

PAULINHO (M) **214 37**
H: 5 11 W: 12 00 b.Sao Paulo 25-7-88
Internationals: Brazil Full caps.

2006	FK Vilnius	17	2		
2007	FK Vilnius	21	3	**38**	**5**

2007–08	LKS Lodz	17	0	17	0
2009	Bragantino	28	6	28	6
2010	Corinthians	27	4		
2011	Corinthians	35	8		
2012	Corinthians	23	7		
2013	Corinthians	1	1	86	20
2013–14	Tottenham H	30	6		
2014–15	Tottenham H	15	0	45	6

PRITCHARD, Alex (M)   88 18
H: 5 7   W: 9 11   b.Grays 3-5-93
Internationals: England U20, U21.

2011–12	Tottenham H	0	0		
2012–13	Tottenham H	0	0		
2012–13	*Peterborough U*	6	0	6	0
2013–14	Tottenham H	1	0		
2013–14	*Swindon T*	36	6	36	6
2014–15	Tottenham H	0	0	1	0
2014–15	*Brentford*	45	12	45	12

ROSE, Danny (M)   117 6
H: 5 8   W: 11 11   b.Doncaster 2-6-90
Internationals: England U17, U19, U21. Great Britain.

2007–08	Tottenham H	0	0		
2008–09	Tottenham H	0	0		
2008–09	*Watford*	7	0	7	0
2009–10	Tottenham H	1	1		
2010–11	Tottenham H	4	0		
2010–11	*Bristol C*	17	0	17	0
2011–12	Tottenham H	11	0		
2012–13	Tottenham H	0	0		
2012–13	*Sunderland*	27	1	27	1
2013–14	Tottenham H	22	1		
2014–15	Tottenham H	28	3	66	5

SOLDADO, Roberto (F)   259 108
H: 5 9   W: 11 06   b.Valencia 27-5-85
Internationals: Spain U15, U17, U17, U19, U21, Full caps.

2005–06	Real Madrid	11	2		
2006–07	Real Madrid	0	0		
2006–07	Osasuna	30	11	30	11
2007–08	Real Madrid	5	0	16	2
2008–09	Getafe	34	13		
2009–10	Getafe	26	16	60	29
2010–11	Valencia	34	18		
2011–12	Valencia	32	17		
2012–13	Valencia	35	24	101	59
2013–14	Tottenham H	28	6		
2014–15	Tottenham H	24	1	52	7

SONUPE, Emmanuel (M)   4 0
Internationals: England U16, U18.

2014–15	Tottenham H	0	0		
2014–15	*St Mirren*	4	0	4	0

STAMBOULI, Benjamin (M)   121 3
H: 5 10   W: 11 11   b.Marseille 13-8-90
Internationals: France U21.

2010–11	Montpellier	26	0		
2011–12	Montpellier	26	0		
2012–13	Montpellier	18	1		
2013–14	Montpellier	37	2		
2014–15	Montpellier	2	0	109	3
2014–15	Tottenham H	12	0	12	0

TOWNSEND, Andros (M)   148 14
H: 6 0   W: 12 00   b.Chingford 16-7-91
Internationals: England U16, U17, U19, U21, Full caps.

2008–09	Tottenham H	0	0		
2008–09	*Yeovil T*	10	1	10	1
2009–10	Tottenham H	0	0		
2009–10	*Leyton Orient*	22	2	22	2
2009–10	*Milton Keynes D*	9	2	9	2
2010–11	Tottenham H	0	0		
2010–11	*Ipswich T*	13	1	13	1
2010–11	*Watford*	3	0	3	0
2010–11	*Millwall*	11	2	11	2
2011–12	Tottenham H	0	0		
2011–12	*Leeds U*	6	1	6	1
2011–12	*Birmingham C*	15	0	15	0
2012–13	Tottenham H	5	0		
2012–13	*QPR*	12	2	12	2
2013–14	Tottenham H	25	1		
2014–15	Tottenham H	17	2	47	3

VELJKOVIC, Milos (D)   8 0
H: 5 8   W: 10 12   b.Basel 26-9-95
Internationals: Switzerland U16. Serbia U17, U19, U20, U21.

2012–13	Tottenham H	0	0		
2013–14	Tottenham H	2	0		
2014–15	Tottenham H	0	0	2	0
2014–15	*Middlesbrough*	3	0	3	0
2014–15	*Charlton Ath*	3	0	3	0

VERTONGHEN, Jan (D)   256 30
H: 6 2   W: 12 05   b.Sint-Niklaas 24-4-87
Internationals: Belgium U16, U21, Full caps.

2006–07	Ajax	3	0		
2006–07	RKC	12	3	12	3
2007–08	Ajax	31	2		
2008–09	Ajax	26	4		
2009–10	Ajax	32	3		
2010–11	Ajax	32	6		
2011–12	Ajax	31	8	155	23
2012–13	Tottenham H	34	4		
2013–14	Tottenham H	23	0		
2014–15	Tottenham H	32	0	89	4

VORM, Michel (G)   264 0
H: 6 0   W: 13 03   b.Nieuwegein 20-10-83
Internationals: Netherlands Full caps.

2005–06	Den Bosch	35	0	35	0
2006–07	Utrecht	33	0		
2007–08	Utrecht	11	0		
2008–09	Utrecht	26	0		
2009–10	Utrecht	33	0		
2010–11	Utrecht	33	0	136	0
2011–12	Swansea C	37	0		
2012–13	Swansea C	26	0		
2013–14	Swansea C	26	0	89	0
2014–15	Tottenham H	4	0	4	0

WALKER, Kyle (D)   189 4
H: 5 10   W: 11 07   b.Sheffield 28-5-90
Internationals: England U19, U21, Full caps.

2008–09	Sheffield U	2	0		
2008–09	*Northampton T*	9	0	9	0
2009–10	Tottenham H	2	0		
2009–10	*Sheffield U*	26	0	28	0
2010–11	Tottenham H	1	0		
2010–11	*QPR*	20	0	20	0
2010–11	*Aston Villa*	15	1	15	1
2011–12	Tottenham H	37	2		
2012–13	Tottenham H	36	0		
2013–14	Tottenham H	26	1		
2014–15	Tottenham H	15	0	117	3

WARD, Grant (M)   34 1
H: 5-12-94

2013–14	Tottenham H	0	0		
2014	*Chicago Fire*	23	1	23	1
2014–15	Tottenham H	0	0		
2014–15	*Coventry C*	11	0	11	0

WINKS, Harry (M)   0 0
H: 5 10   W: 10 03   b.Hemel Hempstead 2-2-96
Internationals: England U17, U18, U19.

2013–14	Tottenham H	0	0		
2014–15	Tottenham H	0	0		

YEDLIN, DeAndre (D)   63 2
H: 5 9   W: 11 07   b.Seattle 9-7-93
Internationals: USA U20, Full caps.

2013	Seattle Sounders	33	2	33	2
2014	Seattle Sounders	29	0	29	0
2014–15	Tottenham H	1	0	1	0

Players retained or with offer of contract
Carter-Vickers, Cameron; Gomelt, Tomislav; Lesniak, Filip; Maghoma, Christian; Miller, William; Pritchard, Joe Cameron.

Scholars
Amos, Luke Ayodele; Azzaoui, Ismail; Daly, Armani; Georgiou, Anthony Michael; Glover, Thomas William; Goddard, Cy; Harrison, Shayon; Hayford, Charlie Garath; Loft, Ryan; Mcdermott, Thomas William; Muscatt, Joseph Luis; Owens, Charlie; Paul, Christopher David; Stylianides, Zenon; Voss, Harry William; Walkes, Anton.

TRANMERE R (83)

BELL-BAGGIE, Abdulai (F)   69 4
H: 5 6   W: 10 00   b.London 28-4-92
Internationals: England U16, U17. Sierra Leone Full caps.

2009–10	Reading	0	0		
2009–10	*Rotherham U*	11	0	11	0
2010–11	Reading	0	0		
2010–11	*Port Vale*	3	0	3	0
From Hayes & Y, Salisbury C					
2012–13	Tranmere R	31	1		
2013–14	Tranmere R	12	0		
2014–15	Tranmere R	12	3	55	4

BREZOVAN, Peter (G)   148 0
H: 6 6   W: 14 13   b.Bratislava 9-12-79
Internationals: Slovakia U21.

2002–03	Brno	10	0		
2003–04	Brno	2	0		
2004–05	Inter Bratislava	8	0	8	0
2005–06	Brno	7	0	19	0
2006–07	Swindon T	14	0		
2007–08	Swindon T	31	0		
2008–09	Swindon T	21	0	66	0
2009–10	Brighton & HA	20	0		
2010–11	Brighton & HA	2	0		
2011–12	Brighton & HA	20	0		
2012–13	Brighton & HA	1	0		
2013–14	Brighton & HA	4	0	47	0
2014–15	Tranmere R	8	0	8	0

DAVIES, Liam (M)   0 0
b. 22-10-92

2013–14	Tranmere R	0	0		
2014–15	Tranmere R	0	0		

DONNELLY, George (F)   161 31
H: 6 2   W: 13 03   b.Liverpool 28-5-88
Internationals: England C.

2008–09	Plymouth Arg	2	0		
2009–10	Plymouth Arg	0	0		
2009–10	*Stockport Co*	19	4		
2010–11	Plymouth Arg	0	0	2	0
2010–11	*Stockport Co*	23	8	42	12
From Fleetwood T					
2011–12	Macclesfield T	28	6	28	6
2011–12	Rochdale	43	8		
2012–13	Rochdale	43	8		
2013–14	Rochdale	32	5		
2014–15	Rochdale	3	0	78	13
2014–15	Tranmere R	11	0	11	0

DUGDALE, Adam (D)   142 7
H: 6 3   W: 12 07   b.Liverpool 12-9-87

2006–07	Crewe Alex	0	0		
2006–07	*Accrington S*	2	0	2	0
From Southport, Droylsden, Montagnee, Barrow, AFC Telford U.					
2010–11	Crewe Alex	20	1		
2011–12	Crewe Alex	43	3		
2012–13	Crewe Alex	18	0		
2013–14	Crewe Alex	21	1		
2013–14	*Tranmere R*	4	1		
2014–15	Crewe Alex	18	1	120	6
2014–15	Tranmere R	16	0	20	1

DUGGAN, Mitchell (M)   1 0
b. 20-3-97

2014–15	Tranmere R	1	0	1	0

FON WILLIAMS, Owain (G)   271 0
H: 6 1   W: 12 09   b.Penygroes 17-3-87
Internationals: Wales U17, U19, U21.

2005–06	Crewe Alex	0	0		
2006–07	Crewe Alex	0	0		
2007–08	Crewe Alex	0	0		
2008–09	Stockport Co	33	0		
2009–10	Stockport Co	44	0		
2010–11	Stockport Co	5	0	82	0
2010–11	*Bury*	6	0	6	0
2010–11	*Rochdale*	22	0	22	0
2011–12	Tranmere R	35	0		
2012–13	Tranmere R	45	0		
2013–14	Tranmere R	43	0		
2014–15	Tranmere R	38	0	161	0

GILL, Matthew (M)   352 16
H: 5 11   W: 11 10   b.Cambridge 8-11-80

1997–98	Peterborough U	2	0		
1998–99	Peterborough U	26	0		
1999–2000	Peterborough U	20	1		
2000–01	Peterborough U	17	1		
2001–02	Peterborough U	12	2		
2002–03	Peterborough U	41	1		
2003–04	Peterborough U	33	0		
2004–05	Notts Co	43	0		
2005–06	Notts Co	14	0	57	0
2008–09	Exeter C	43	9		
2009–10	Norwich C	8	0		
2010–11	Norwich C	4	0	12	0
2010–11	*Peterborough U*	4	0	155	5
2010–11	*Walsall*	8	2	8	2
2011–12	Bristol R	33	0		
2012–13	Bristol R	11	0		
2013–14	Bristol R	1	0	45	0
2013–14	*Exeter C*	24	0	67	9
2014–15	Tranmere R	8	0	8	0

GUMBS, Evan (M)   1 0
H: 5 10   W: 12 00   b.Runcorn 21-7-97

2014–15	Tranmere R	1	0	1	0

HILL, Matt (D) 450 8
H: 5 7 W: 12 06 b.Bristol 26-3-81
1998–99	Bristol C	3	0		
1999–2000	Bristol C	14	0		
2000–01	Bristol C	34	0		
2001–02	Bristol C	40	1		
2002–03	Bristol C	42	3		
2003–04	Bristol C	42	2		
2004–05	Bristol C	23	0	198	6
2004–05	Preston NE	14	0		
2005–06	Preston NE	26	0		
2006–07	Preston NE	38	0		
2007–08	Preston NE	26	0		
2008–09	Preston NE	1	0	105	0
2008–09	Wolverhampton W	13	0		
2009–10	Wolverhampton W	2	0		
2009–10	QPR	16	0	16	0
2010–11	Wolverhampton W	0	0	15	0
2010–11	Barnsley	23	2	23	2
2011–12	Blackpool	4	0	4	0
2011–12	Sheffield U	12	0		
2012–13	Sheffield U	34	0		
2013–14	Sheffield U	32	0	78	0
2014–15	Tranmere R	11	0	11	0

HOLMES, Danny (D) 192 7
H: 6 0 W: 11 13 b.Birkenhead 6-1-89
2007–08	Tranmere R	0	0		
2008–09	Tranmere R	1	0		
2009–10	The New Saints	32	0		
2010–11	The New Saints	26	3	58	3
2011–12	Tranmere R	26	0		
2012–13	Tranmere R	43	2		
2013–14	Tranmere R	28	0		
2014–15	Tranmere R	36	2	134	4

HOLNESS, Marcus (D) 164 5
H: 6 0 W: 12 02 b.Swinton 8-12-88
2007–08	Oldham Ath	0	0		
2007–08	Rochdale	19	0		
2008–09	Rochdale	8	0		
2009–10	Rochdale	11	0		
2010–11	Rochdale	46	1		
2011–12	Rochdale	24	3	108	4
2012–13	Burton Alb	22	1		
2013–14	Burton Alb	17	0	39	1
2014–15	Tranmere R	17	0	17	0

HUME, Iain (F) 467 109
H: 5 7 W: 11 02 b.Ontario 31-10-83
Internationals: Canada Youth, U20, Full caps.
1999–2000	Tranmere R	3	0		
2000–01	Tranmere R	10	0		
2001–02	Tranmere R	14	0		
2002–03	Tranmere R	35	6		
2003–04	Tranmere R	40	10		
2004–05	Tranmere R	42	15		
2005–06	Tranmere R	6	1		
2005–06	Leicester C	37	9		
2006–07	Leicester C	45	13		
2007–08	Leicester C	40	11	122	33
2008–09	Barnsley	15	4		
2009–10	Barnsley	35	5		
2010–11	Barnsley	1	0	51	9
2010–11	Preston NE	31	12		
2011–12	Preston NE	28	9		
2012–13	Preston NE	0	0		
2012–13	Doncaster R	33	6	33	6
2013–14	Preston NE	16	2	75	23
2013–14	Fleetwood T	8	1	8	1
2014–15	Kerala Blasters	16	5	16	5
2014–15	Tranmere R	12	0	162	32

IHIEKWE, Michael (D) 51 1
H: 6 1 W: 12 02 b.Liverpool 20-11-92
2011–12	Wolverhampton W	0	0		
2012–13	Wolverhampton W	0	0		
2013–14	Wolverhampton W	0	0		
2013–14	Cheltenham T	13	0	13	0
2014–15	Tranmere R	38	1	38	1

JAGO, Ben (M) 2 0
2014–15	Tranmere R	2	0	2	0

JENNINGS, Steven (M) 342 10
H: 5 5 W: 12 00 b.Liverpool 28-10-84
2003–04	Tranmere R	4	0		
2004–05	Tranmere R	11	0		
2005–06	Tranmere R	38	1		
2006–07	Tranmere R	2	0		
2006–07	Hereford U	11	0	11	0
2007–08	Tranmere R	41	2		
2008–09	Tranmere R	44	3		
2009–10	Motherwell	29	2		
2010–11	Motherwell	30	0		
2011–12	Motherwell	34	0	93	2
2012–13	Coventry C	39	0		
2013–14	Coventry C	0	0	39	0
2013–14	Tranmere R	25	1		
2014–15	Port Vale	4	0	4	0
2014–15	Tranmere R	30	1	195	8

KIRBY, Jake (M) 53 3
H: 5 11 W: 12 04 b.Liverpool 9-5-94
2011–12	Tranmere R	1	0		
2012–13	Tranmere R	4	0		
2013–14	Tranmere R	31	2		
2014–15	Tranmere R	17	1	53	3

KOUMAS, Jason (M) 422 67
H: 5 10 W: 11 07 b.Wrexham 25-9-79
Internationals: Wales Full caps.
1997–98	Tranmere R	0	0		
1998–99	Tranmere R	23	3		
1999–2000	Tranmere R	23	2		
2000–01	Tranmere R	39	10		
2001–02	Tranmere R	38	8		
2002–03	Tranmere R	4	2		
2002–03	WBA	32	4		
2003–04	WBA	42	10		
2004–05	WBA	10	0		
2005–06	WBA	0	0		
2005–06	Cardiff C	44	12		
2006–07	WBA	39	9	123	23
2007–08	Wigan Ath	30	1		
2008–09	Wigan Ath	16	0		
2009–10	Wigan Ath	8	1		
2010–11	Wigan Ath	0	0		
2010–11	Cardiff C	23	2	67	14
2011–12	Wigan Ath	0	0		
2012–13	Wigan Ath	0	0	54	2
2013–14	Tranmere R	31	3		
2014–15	Tranmere R	20	0	178	28

LAIRD, Marc (M) 200 12
H: 6 1 W: 10 07 b.Edinburgh 23-1-86
2003–04	Manchester C	0	0		
2004–05	Manchester C	0	0		
2005–06	Manchester C	0	0		
2006–07	Manchester C	0	0		
2006–07	Northampton T	6	0	6	0
2007–08	Manchester C	0	0		
2007–08	Port Vale	7	1	7	1
2007–08	Millwall	17	1		
2008–09	Millwall	38	5		
2009–10	Millwall	20	0		
2010–11	Millwall	1	0	76	6
2010–11	Brentford	4	1	4	1
2010–11	Walsall	8	0	8	0
2011–12	Leyton Orient	22	2		
2012–13	Leyton Orient	1	0		
2012–13	Southend U	23	1		
2013–14	Leyton Orient	0	0	23	2
2013–14	Southend U	19	0	42	1
2014–15	Tranmere R	34	1	34	1

MADJO, Guy (F) 109 32
H: 6 0 W: 13 05 b.Cameroon 1-6-84
Internationals: Cameroon U23.
2005–06	Bristol C	5	0	5	0

From Forest Green R, Stafford R, Crawley (loan)
2007–08	Cheltenham T	5	0	5	0
2008–09	Shrewsbury T	15	3		
2008–09	Shrewsbury T	0	0	15	3
2008–09	Guangdong S C	18	10	18	10
2009–10	Bylis Ballsh	15	2	15	2
2011–12	Stevenage	1	0	1	0
2011–12	Port Vale	6	4	6	4
2011–12	Aldershot T	20	8		
2012–13	Aldershot T	3	0	23	8
2012–13	Plymouth Arg	14	3	14	3
2013–14	Tuen Mun Progoal	5	2	5	2
2014–15	Tranmere R	2	0	2	0

McDONALD, Clayton (M) 103 1
H: 6 6 W: 16 05 b.Liverpool 26-12-88
2007–08	Manchester C	0	0		
2008–09	Manchester C	0	0		
2008–09	Macclesfield T	2	0	2	0
2008–09	Chesterfield	2	0	2	0
2009–10	Walsall	26	1		
2010–11	Walsall	14	0	40	1
2011–12	Port Vale	30	0		
2012–13	Port Vale	22	0	52	0
2012–13	Bristol R	6	0		
2013–14	Bristol R	0	0	6	0
2014–15	Tranmere R	1	0	1	0

MOLYNEUX, Lee (D) 103 15
H: 6 1 W: 12 09 b.Liverpool 24-2-89
Internationals: England U16, U17, U18.
2005–06	Everton	0	0		
2006–07	Everton	0	0		
2007–08	Everton	0	0		
2008–09	Southampton	4	0		
2009–10	Southampton	0	0	4	0
2010–11	Plymouth Arg	9	0	9	0
2012–13	Accrington S	39	8		
2013–14	Crewe Alex	7	0		
2013–14	Rochdale	5	0	3	0
2013–14	Accrington S	17	6		
2014–15	Crewe Alex	3	0	10	0
2014–15	Accrington S	10	1	66	15
2014–15	Tranmere R	11	0	11	0

ODEJAYI, Kayode (F) 461 70
H: 6 2 W: 12 02 b.Ibadon 21-2-82
Internationals: Nigeria Full caps.
1999–2000	Bristol C	3	0		
2000–01	Bristol C	3	0		
2001–02	Bristol C	0	0		
2002–03	Bristol C	0	0	6	0
2003–04	Cheltenham T	30	5		
2004–05	Cheltenham T	32	1		
2005–06	Cheltenham T	41	11		
2006–07	Cheltenham T	45	13	148	30
2007–08	Barnsley	39	3		
2008–09	Barnsley	28	1		
2008–09	Scunthorpe U	6	1	6	1
2009–10	Barnsley	5	0	72	4
2009–10	Colchester U	28	9		
2010–11	Colchester U	14	4		
2011–12	Colchester U	43	4	115	17
2012–13	Rotherham U	42	5		
2013–14	Rotherham U	0	0	42	5
2013–14	Accrington S	32	8	32	8
2014–15	Tranmere R	40	5	40	5

OMOTOLA, Tolani (F) 1 0
2014–15	Tranmere R	1	0	1	0

PILLING, Luke (G) 0 0
b. 25-7-97
Internationals: Wales U17.
2013–14	Tranmere R	0	0		
2014–15	Tranmere R	0	0		

POWER, Max (M) 109 12
H: 5 11 W: 11 13 b.Bebington 27-7-93
2010–11	Tranmere R	4	0		
2011–12	Tranmere R	4	0		
2012–13	Tranmere R	27	3		
2013–14	Tranmere R	33	2		
2014–15	Tranmere R	45	7	109	12

RAMSBOTTOM, Sam (G) 0 0
2012–13	Tranmere R	0	0		
2013–14	Tranmere R	0	0		
2014–15	Tranmere R	0	0		

RIDEHALGH, Liam (D) 139 2
H: 5 10 W: 11 05 b.Halifax 20-4-91
2009–10	Huddersfield T	0	0		
2010–11	Huddersfield T	20	0		
2011–12	Huddersfield T	0	0		
2011–12	Swindon T	11	0	11	0
2011–12	Chesterfield	20	1		
2012–13	Huddersfield T	0	0		
2012–13	Chesterfield	14	0	34	1
2012–13	Rotherham U	20	0	20	0
2013–14	Huddersfield T	0	0	20	0
2013–14	Tranmere R	36	1		
2014–15	Tranmere R	18	0	54	1

ROWE, James (M) 26 3
H: 5 11 W: 10 02 b. 21-10-91
2010–11	Reading	0	0		
2011–12	Reading	0	0		

From Forest Green R
2013–14	Tranmere R	19	1		
2014–15	Tranmere R	7	2	26	3

SHUKER, Chris (M) 355 37
H: 5 5 W: 9 03 b.Liverpool 9-5-82
1999–2000	Manchester C	0	0		
2000–01	Manchester C	0	0		
2000–01	Macclesfield T	9	1	9	1
2001–02	Manchester C	0	0		
2002–03	Manchester C	3	0		
2002–03	Walsall	5	0	5	0
2003–04	Manchester C	0	0	5	0
2003–04	Rochdale	14	1	14	1
2003–04	Hartlepool U	14	1	14	1
2004–05	Barnsley	9	0		
2004–05	Barnsley	45	7		
2005–06	Barnsley	46	10	100	17
2006–07	Tranmere R	46	6		
2007–08	Tranmere R	23	3		
2008–09	Tranmere R	28	3		
2009–10	Tranmere R	26	2		
2010–11	Morecambe	39	0		
2011–12	Morecambe	0	0	27	2
2011–12	Port Vale	16	1		
2012–13	Port Vale	29	0		
2013–14	Port Vale	10	0	55	1
2014–15	Tranmere R	3	0	126	14

STOCKTON, Cole (F) 75 9
H: 6 1 W: 11 11 b.Huyton 13-3-94
2011–12	Tranmere R	1	0	
2012–13	Tranmere R	31	3	
2013–14	Tranmere R	21	2	
2014–15	Tranmere R	22	4	75 9

TAYLOR, Rob (D) 191 15
H: 6 0 W: 12 08 b.Shrewsbury 16-1-85
2008–09	Port Vale	20	3	
2009–10	Port Vale	39	8	
2010–11	Port Vale	36	1	
2011–12	Port Vale	31	2	
2012–13	Port Vale	28	0	
2013–14	Port Vale	6	1	160 15
2014–15	Mansfield T	16	0	16 0
2014–15	Tranmere R	15	0	15 0

THOMPSON, Josh (D) 98 6
H: 6 4 W: 12 00 b.Bolton 25-2-91
Internationals: England U19.
2008–09	Stockport Co	9	0	9 0
2009–10	Celtic	18	3	18 3
2010–11	Rochdale	12	1	12 1
2011–12	Chesterfield	20	1	20 1
2012–13	Portsmouth	2	0	2 0
2012–13	Colchester U	22	1	
2013–14	Colchester U	0	0	22 1
2014–15	Tranmere R	15	0	15 0

WOODARDS, Danny (D) 225 5
H: 5 11 W: 11 01 b.Forest Gate 7-10-83
Internationals: England C.
2003–04	Chelsea	0	0	
2004–05	Chelsea	0	0	
2005–06	Chelsea	0	0	

From Exeter C.
2006–07	Crewe Alex	11	0	
2007–08	Crewe Alex	36	0	
2008–09	Crewe Alex	37	0	84 0
2009–10	Milton Keynes D	29	0	
2010–11	Milton Keynes D	37	1	66 1
2011–12	Bristol R	39	1	
2012–13	Bristol R	22	2	
2013–14	Bristol R	9	1	70 4
2014–15	Tranmere R	5	0	5 0

Scholars
Askew, Daren; Duggan, Mitchel James; Gumbs, Evan; Hulley, Jake Stephen; Hunter, James John; Ilesanmi, Samuel Oluwamayowa; Jago, Ben; Kubwalo, Gabriel Nikote; Lamb, Joe; Moynes, Lewis John; Omotola, Omotolani Daniel; Pilling, Luke Arthur; Rutter, Patrik Adam; Smith, Liam Alexander; Williams, Thomas James.

WALSALL (84)

BAKAYOKO, Amadou (F) 13 0
H: 6 4 W: 13 05 b. 1-1-96
2013–14	Walsall	6	0	
2014–15	Walsall	7	0	13 0

BAXENDALE, James (M) 103 7
H: 5 8 W: 10 03 b.Thorne 16-9-92
2011–12	Doncaster R	2	0	
2011–12	Hereford U	1	0	1 0
2012–13	Doncaster R	0	0	2 0
2012–13	Walsall	32	4	
2013–14	Walsall	40	2	
2014–15	Walsall	28	1	100 7

BENNING, Malvind (D) 55 2
H: 5 10 W: 12 00 b.Sandwell 2-11-93
2012–13	Walsall	10	0	
2013–14	Walsall	16	2	
2014–15	Walsall	20	0	46 2
2014–15	York C	9	0	9 0

BRADSHAW, Tom (F) 118 34
H: 5 5 W: 11 02 b.Shrewsbury 27-7-92
Internationals: Wales U19, U21.
2009–10	Shrewsbury T	6	3	
2010–11	Shrewsbury T	26	6	
2011–12	Shrewsbury T	8	1	
2012–13	Shrewsbury T	21	0	
2013–14	Shrewsbury T	28	7	89 17
2014–15	Walsall	29	17	29 17

CHAMBERS, Adam (D) 399 12
H: 5 10 W: 11 12 b.Sandwell 20-11-80
1998–99	WBA	0	0	
1999–2000	WBA	0	0	
2000–01	WBA	11	1	
2001–02	WBA	32	0	
2002–03	WBA	13	0	
2003–04	WBA	0	0	
2003–04	Sheffield W	11	0	11 0
2004–05	WBA	0	0	56 1
2004–05	Kidderminster H	2	0	2 0
2006–07	Leyton Orient	38	4	
2007–08	Leyton Orient	45	3	
2008–09	Leyton Orient	33	1	
2009–10	Leyton Orient	29	1	
2010–11	Leyton Orient	29	0	174 9
2011–12	Walsall	29	2	
2012–13	Walsall	37	0	
2013–14	Walsall	45	0	
2014–15	Walsall	45	0	156 2

CHAMBERS, James (D) 381 1
H: 5 10 W: 11 11 b.West Bromwich 20-11-80
1998–99	WBA	0	0	
1999–2000	WBA	12	0	
2000–01	WBA	31	0	
2001–02	WBA	5	0	
2002–03	WBA	8	0	
2003–04	WBA	17	0	
2004–05	WBA	0	0	73 0
2004–05	Watford	40	0	
2005–06	Watford	38	0	
2006–07	Watford	12	0	90 0
2006–07	Cardiff C	7	0	7 0
2007–08	Leicester C	24	0	24 0
2008–09	Doncaster R	37	0	
2009–10	Doncaster R	43	0	
2010–11	Doncaster R	7	0	
2011–12	Doncaster R	0	0	87 0
2011–12	Hereford U	7	0	7 0
2012–13	Walsall	22	0	
2013–14	Walsall	40	1	
2014–15	Walsall	31	0	93 1

CLIFFORD, Billy (M) 31 1
H: 5 7 W: 10 03 b.Slough 18-10-92
2010–11	Chelsea	0	0	
2011–12	Chelsea	0	0	
2012–13	Chelsea	0	0	
2012–13	Colchester U	18	1	18 1
2013–14	Chelsea	0	0	
2013–14	Yeovil T	0	0	
2014–15	Walsall	13	0	13 0

COOK, Jordan (F) 73 10
H: 5 10 W: 10 10 b.Hetton-le-Hole 20-3-90
2007–08	Sunderland	0	0	
2008–09	Sunderland	0	0	
2009–10	Sunderland	0	0	
2009–10	Darlington	5	0	5 0
2010–11	Sunderland	3	0	
2010–11	Walsall	8	1	
2011–12	Sunderland	0	0	3 0
2011–12	Carlisle U	14	4	14 4
2012–13	Charlton Ath	7	0	
2012–13	Yeovil T	1	0	1 0
2013–14	Charlton Ath	3	0	10 0
2014–15	Walsall	32	5	40 6

DOWNING, Paul (D) 142 3
H: 6 1 W: 12 06 b.Taunton 26-10-91
2009–10	WBA	0	0	
2009–10	Hereford U	6	0	
2010–11	WBA	0	0	
2010–11	Hereford U	0	0	6 0
2010–11	Swansea C	0	0	
2011–12	WBA	0	0	
2011–12	Barnet	26	0	26 0
2012–13	Walsall	31	1	
2013–14	Walsall	44	1	
2014–15	Walsall	35	1	110 3

FLANAGAN, Reece (M) 16 0
b. 19-10-94
2013–14	Walsall	0	0	
2014–15	Walsall	16	0	16 0

FORDE, Anthony (M) 66 3
H: 5 9 W: 10 10 b.Limerick 16-11-93
Internationals: Republic of Ireland U19, U21.
2011–12	Wolverhampton W	6	0	
2012–13	Wolverhampton W	12	0	
2012–13	Scunthorpe U	8	0	8 0
2013–14	Wolverhampton W	3	0	21 0
2014–15	Walsall	37	3	37 3

GRIMES, Ashley (M) 168 37
H: 6 0 W: 11 02 b.Swinton 9-12-86
2006–07	Manchester C	0	0	
2006–07	Swindon T	4	0	4 0
2007–08	Manchester C	0	0	
2008–09	Millwall	17	2	
2009–10	Millwall	4	0	
2010–11	Millwall	0	0	21 2
2010–11	Lincoln C	27	15	27 15
2011–12	Rochdale	36	8	
2012–13	Rochdale	38	10	74 18
2013–14	Bury	15	0	15 0
2014–15	Walsall	27	2	27 2

HEATH, Jake (M) 0 0
b. 9-3-95
2013–14	Walsall	0	0	
2014–15	Walsall	0	0	

HENRY, Rico (D) 9 0
b. 8-7-97
2014–15	Walsall	9	0	9 0

HOLDEN, Dean (D) 369 22
H: 6 1 W: 12 04 b.Swinton 15-9-79
1997–98	Bolton W	0	0	
1998–99	Bolton W	0	0	
1999–2000	Bolton W	12	0	
2000–01	Bolton W	1	1	13 1
2001	Valur	7	0	7 0
2001–02	Oldham Ath	23	2	
2002–03	Oldham Ath	6	2	
2003–04	Oldham Ath	39	4	
2004–05	Oldham Ath	40	2	108 10
2005–06	Peterborough U	35	3	
2006–07	Peterborough U	21	1	56 4
2006–07	Falkirk	9	1	
2007–08	Falkirk	20	0	
2008–09	Falkirk	19	1	48 2
2009–10	Shrewsbury T	37	0	
2010–11	Shrewsbury T	13	0	50 0
2010–11	Rotherham U	6	0	6 0
2010–11	Chesterfield	17	2	
2011–12	Chesterfield	14	1	31 3
2011–12	Rochdale	21	0	21 0
2012–13	Walsall	25	2	
2013–14	Walsall	0	0	
2014–15	Walsall	4	0	29 2

KINSELLA, Liam (M) 4 0
b.Colchester 23-2-96
2013–14	Walsall	0	0	
2014–15	Walsall	4	0	4 0

LEWIS, Shane (G) 0 0
b. 4-6-94
Internationals: England U17.
2013–14	Walsall	0	0	
2014–15	Walsall	0	0	

MACGILLIVRAY, Craig (G) 2 0
H: 6 2 W: 12 04 b.Harrogate 12-1-93
2014–15	Walsall	2	0	2 0

MANTOM, Sam (M) 103 10
H: 5 9 W: 11 00 b.Stourbridge 20-2-92
Internationals: England U17.
2010–11	WBA	0	0	
2010–11	Tranmere R	2	0	2 0
2010–11	Oldham Ath	4	0	4 0
2011–12	WBA	0	0	
2011–12	Walsall	13	3	
2012–13	WBA	0	0	
2012–13	Walsall	29	2	
2013–14	Walsall	43	5	
2014–15	Walsall	12	0	97 10

MORRIS, Kieron (M) 16 2
H: 5 10 W: 11 01 b.Hereford 3-6-94
2012–13	Walsall	2	0	
2013–14	Walsall	2	0	
2014–15	Walsall	14	2	16 2

MURPHY, Jordan (F) 2 0
H: 5 6 W: 10 01 b.Birmingham 5-6-96
2014–15	Walsall	2	0	2 0

O'CONNOR, James (D) 327 7
H: 5 10 W: 12 05 b.Birmingham 20-11-84
2003–04	Aston Villa	0	0	
2004–05	Aston Villa	0	0	
2004–05	Port Vale	13	0	13 0
2004–05	Bournemouth	6	0	
2005–06	Bournemouth	39	1	45 1
2006–07	Doncaster R	40	1	
2007–08	Doncaster R	40	0	
2008–09	Doncaster R	32	1	
2009–10	Doncaster R	38	0	
2010–11	Doncaster R	34	2	
2011–12	Doncaster R	28	0	212 4
2012–13	Derby Co	22	1	
2013–14	Walsall	0	0	22 1
2013–14	Bristol C	3	0	3 0
2014–15	Walsall	32	1	32 1

O'DONNELL, Richard (G) 138 0
H: 6 2 W: 13 05 b.Sheffield 12-9-88
2007–08	Sheffield W	0	0	
2007–08	Rotherham U	0	0	
2007–08	Oldham Ath	4	0	4 0
2008–09	Sheffield W	0	0	

2009–10	Sheffield W	0	0		
2010–11	Sheffield W	9	0		
2011–12	Sheffield W	6	0	**15**	**0**
2011–12	*Macclesfield T*	11	0	**11**	**0**
2012–13	Chesterfield	14	0	**14**	**0**
2013–14	Walsall	46	0		
2014–15	Walsall	44	0	**90**	**0**

PRESTON, Matt (D)   **1 0**
b. 16-3-95

2013–14	Walsall	0	0		
2014–15	Walsall	1	0	**1**	**0**

PURKISS, Ben (D)   **111 0**
H: 6 2   W: 10 13   b.Sheffield 1-4-84

2001–02	Sheffield U	0	0		
2002–03	Sheffield U	0	0		
From Gainsborough T, York C					
2010–11	Oxford U	23	0	**23**	**0**
2011–12	Hereford U	15	0	**15**	**0**
2012–13	Walsall	27	0		
2013–14	Walsall	14	0		
2014–15	Walsall	32	0	**73**	**0**

ROBERTS, Liam (G)   **0 0**
H: 6 0   W: 12 13   b.Walsall 24-11-94

2012–13	Walsall	0	0
2013–14	Walsall	0	0
2014–15	Walsall	0	0

ROWLEY, Kyle (M)   **0 0**
b. 4-5-97

2014–15	Walsall	0	0

SAWYERS, Romaine (M)   **98 10**
H: 5 9   W: 11 00   b.Birmingham 2-11-91
Internationals: St Kitts and Nevis U23, Full caps.

2009–10	WBA	0	0		
2010–11	WBA	0	0		
2010–11	*Port Vale*	1	0	**1**	**0**
2011–12	WBA	0	0		
2011–12	*Shrewsbury T*	7	0	**7**	**0**
2012–13	WBA	0	0		
2012–13	Walsall	4	0		
2013–14	Walsall	44	6		
2014–15	Walsall	42	4	**90**	**10**

TAYLOR, Andy (D)   **232 5**
H: 5 11   W: 11 07   b.Blackburn 14-3-86
Internationals: England U16, U17, U18, U19, U20.

2004–05	Blackburn R	0	0		
2005–06	Blackburn R	0	0		
2005–06	*QPR*	3	0	**3**	**0**
2005–06	*Blackpool*	3	0	**3**	**0**
2006–07	Blackburn R	0	0		
2006–07	*Crewe Alex*	4	0	**4**	**0**
2006–07	*Huddersfield T*	8	0	**8**	**0**
2007–08	Blackburn R	0	0		
2007–08	Tranmere R	30	2		
2008–09	Tranmere R	39	1	**69**	**3**
2009–10	Sheffield U	26	0		
2010–11	Sheffield U	9	0		
2011–12	Sheffield U	4	0		
2012–13	Sheffield U	0	0	**39**	**0**
2012–13	Nottingham F	0	0		
2012–13	Walsall	34	0		
2013–14	Walsall	33	1		
2014–15	Walsall	39	1	**106**	**2**

Scholars
Delaney, Luke; Jezeph, Daniel George Alfred; King, Kyle Malik Omar; Kouhyar, Qamaruddin Maziar; Lewis, Kane Michael; Oliver, Rory Benjamin; Owen, Nathan Paul; Pooni, Brendan Dharshan; Probert, Lewis Jon; Reid, Romario Rashaun; Roberts, Kory Paul; Rowley, Kyle Jake; Rowley, Levi James; Sangha, Jordon Phillip John; Shakespeare, Tevin McKoy Jhevon; Smith, Jamie Patrick; Smith, Raekwon Amari.

WATFORD (85)

ABDI, Almen (M)   **264 54**
H: 5 11   W: 12 11   b.Prizren 21-10-86
Internationals: Switzerland, U21, Full caps.

2003–04	FC Zurich	11	0		
2004–05	FC Zurich	5	0		
2005–06	FC Zurich	12	0		
2006–07	FC Zurich	28	5		
2007–08	FC Zurich	31	7		
2008–09	FC Zurich	32	19		
2009–10	FC Zurich	8	0	**127**	**31**
2009–10	*Le Mans*	13	0	**13**	**0**
2010–11	Udinese	19	0		

2011–12	Udinese	22	0	**41**	**0**
2012–13	*Watford*	38	12		
2013–14	Watford	13	2		
2014–15	Watford	32	9	**83**	**23**

ANGELLA, Gabriele (D)   **164 14**
H: 6 2   W: 12 05   b.Firenze 28-4-89
Internationals: Italy U21.

2008–09	Empoli	11	0		
2009–10	Empoli	35	0		
2010–11	Empoli	2	0	**48**	**0**
2010–11	Udinese	8	0		
2011–12	Udinese	0	0		
2011–12	Siena	0	0		
2011–12	*Reggina*	19	1	**19**	**1**
2012–13	Udinese	14	4	**22**	**4**
2013–14	Watford	40	7		
2014–15	Watford	35	2	**75**	**9**

ANYA, Ikechi (M)   **128 11**
H: 5 5   W: 11 04   b.Glasgow 3-1-88
Internationals: Scotland Full caps.

2004–05	Wycombe W	3	0		
2005–06	Wycombe W	2	0		
2006–07	Wycombe W	13	0		
2007–08	Wycombe W	0	0	**18**	**0**
2008–09	Northampton T	14	3	**14**	**3**
2010–11	Celta Vigo	1	0	**1**	**0**
From Cadiz					
2012–13	Watford	25	3		
2013–14	Watford	35	5		
2014–15	Watford	35	0	**95**	**8**

BATTOCCHIO, Cristian (M)   **85 6**
H: 5 10   W: 10 13   b.Buenos Aires 10-2-92
Internationals: Italy U20, U21.

2010–11	Udinese	1	0		
2011–12	Udinese	4	0		
2012–13	Udinese	1	0	**6**	**0**
2012–13	*Watford*	22	2		
2013–14	Watford	35	4		
2014–15	Watford	0	0	**57**	**6**
2014–15	*Virtus Entella*	22	0	**22**	**0**

BOND, Jonathan (G)   **33 0**
H: 6 3   W: 13 03   b.Hemel Hempstead 19-5-93
Internationals: Wales U17, U19. England U21.

2010–11	Watford	0	0		
2011–12	Watford	1	0		
2011–12	*Dagenham & R*	5	0	**5**	**0**
2011–12	*Bury*	6	0	**6**	**0**
2012–13	Watford	8	0		
2013–14	Watford	10	0		
2014–15	Watford	3	0	**22**	**0**

BYERS, George (M)   **1 0**
H: 5 11   W: 11 07   b. 29-5-96
Internationals: Scotland U17.

2014–15	Watford	1	0	**1**	**0**

CATHCART, Craig (D)   **197 9**
H: 6 2   W: 11 06   b.Belfast 6-2-89
Internationals: Northern Ireland U16, U17, U20, U21, Full caps.

2005–06	Manchester U	0	0		
2006–07	Manchester U	0	0		
2007–08	Manchester U	0	0		
2007–08	*Antwerp*	13	2	**13**	**2**
2008–09	Manchester U	0	0		
2008–09	*Plymouth Arg*	31	1	**31**	**1**
2009–10	Manchester U	0	0		
2009–10	*Watford*	12	0		
2010–11	Blackpool	30	1		
2011–12	Blackpool	27	0		
2012–13	Blackpool	25	1		
2013–14	Blackpool	30	1	**112**	**3**
2014–15	Watford	29	3	**41**	**3**

DEENEY, Troy (F)   **328 105**
H: 5 11   W: 12 00   b.Solihull 29-6-88

2006–07	Walsall	1	0		
2007–08	Walsall	35	1		
2008–09	Walsall	45	12		
2009–10	Walsall	42	14	**123**	**27**
2010–11	Watford	36	3		
2011–12	Watford	43	11		
2012–13	Watford	40	19		
2013–14	Watford	44	24		
2014–15	Watford	42	21	**205**	**78**

DOHERTY, Josh (M)   **1 0**
H: 5 10   W: 11 00   b. 15-3-96
Internationals: Northern Ireland U17, U19, U21.

2013–14	Watford	1	0		
2014–15	Watford	0	0	**1**	**0**

DOYLE, Lloyd (D)   **395 2**
H: 5 10   W: 12 13   b.Whitechapel 1-12-82
Internationals: Jamaica Full caps.

2000–01	Watford	0	0		
2001–02	Watford	20	0		
2002–03	Watford	22	0		
2003–04	Watford	9	0		
2004–05	Watford	29	0		
2005–06	Watford	44	0		
2006–07	Watford	21	0		
2007–08	Watford	36	0		
2008–09	Watford	37	0		
2009–10	Watford	44	1		
2010–11	Watford	36	0		
2011–12	Watford	33	0		
2012–13	Watford	34	1		
2013–14	Watford	24	0		
2014–15	Watford	6	0	**395**	**2**

DYER, Lloyd (M)   **403 51**
H: 5 8   W: 10 03   b.Birmingham 13-9-82

2001–02	WBA	0	0		
2002–03	WBA	0	0		
2003–04	WBA	17	2		
2003–04	*Kidderminster H*	7	1	**7**	**1**
2004–05	WBA	4	0		
2004–05	*Coventry C*	6	0	**6**	**0**
2005–06	WBA	0	0	**21**	**2**
2005–06	*QPR*	15	0	**15**	**0**
2005–06	*Millwall*	6	0	**6**	**0**
2006–07	Milton Keynes D	41	5		
2007–08	Milton Keynes D	45	11	**86**	**16**
2008–09	Leicester C	44	10		
2009–10	Leicester C	33	3		
2010–11	Leicester C	35	3		
2011–12	Leicester C	36	4		
2012–13	Leicester C	42	3		
2013–14	Leicester C	40	7	**230**	**30**
2014–15	Watford	14	1	**14**	**1**
2014–15	*Birmingham C*	18	1	**18**	**1**

EKSTRAND, Joel (D)   **175 3**
H: 6 2   W: 12 00   b.Lund 4-2-89
Internationals: Sweden U17, U19, U21, Full caps.

2007–08	Helsingborgs IF	12	0		
2008–09	Helsingborgs IF	24	0		
2009–10	Helsingborgs IF	25	1		
2010–11	Helsingborgs IF	12	0	**73**	**1**
2010–11	Udinese	1	0		
2011–12	Udinese	12	0	**13**	**0**
2012–13	*Watford*	32	1		
2013–14	Watford	33	0		
2014–15	Watford	24	1	**89**	**2**

FABBRINI, Diego (F)   **133 9**
H: 5 11   W: 11 12   b.San Giuliano terme 31-7-90
Internationals: Italy U21, Full caps.

2009–10	Empoli	29	1		
2010–11	Empoli	26	2	**55**	**3**
2011–12	Udinese	14	2		
2012–13	Udinese	6	0	**20**	**2**
2012–13	*Palermo*	8	1	**8**	**1**
2013–14	Watford	21	1		
2013–14	Siena	10	1	**10**	**1**
2014–15	Watford	2	0	**23**	**1**
2014–15	*Millwall*	12	1	**12**	**1**
2014–15	*Birmingham C*	5	0	**5**	**0**

FORESTIERI, Fernando (F)   **176 33**
H: 5 8   W: 10 07   b.Rosario 16-1-90
Internationals: Italy U17, U19, U20, U21.

2006–07	Genoa	1	1	**1**	**1**
2007–08	Siena	17	1		
2008–09	Siena	2	0	**19**	**1**
2008–09	*Vicenza*	13	5	**13**	**5**
2009–10	Malaga	19	1	**19**	**1**
2010–11	Empoli	17	3	**17**	**3**
2011–12	Bari	27	2	**27**	**2**
2012–13	Udinese	0	0		
2012–13	*Watford*	28	8		
2013–14	Watford	28	7		
2014–15	Watford	24	5	**80**	**20**

GILMARTIN, Rene (G)   **64 0**
H: 6 5   W: 13 06   b.Dublin 31-5-87
Internationals: Republic of Ireland U21.

2005–06	Walsall	2	0		
2006–07	Walsall	0	0		
2007–08	Walsall	0	0		
2008–09	Walsall	11	0		
2009–10	Walsall	22	0	**35**	**0**
2010–11	Watford	0	0		
2011–12	Watford	2	0		
2011–12	*Yeovil T*	8	0	**8**	**0**
2011–12	*Crawley T*	6	0	**6**	**0**
2012–13	Plymouth Arg	13	0		

2013–14	Plymouth Arg	0	0	13	0
2014–15	Watford	0	0	2	0

GOMES, Heurelho (G) 335 0
H: 6 3 W: 12 13 b.Minas Gerais 15-2-81
Internationals: Brazil U23, Full caps.

2001	Cruzeiro	0			
2002	Cruzeiro	14	0		
2003	Cruzeiro	40	0		
2004	Cruzeiro	5	0	59	0
2004–05	PSV Eindhoven	30	0		
2005–06	PSV Eindhoven	32	0		
2006–07	PSV Eindhoven	32	0		
2007–08	PSV Eindhoven	34	0	128	0
2008–09	Tottenham H	34	0		
2009–10	Tottenham H	31	0		
2010–11	Tottenham H	30	0		
2011–12	Tottenham H	0	0		
2012–13	Tottenham H	0	0		
2012–13	Hoffenheim	9	0	9	0
2013–14	Tottenham H	0	0	95	0
2014–15	Watford	44	0	44	0

HOBAN, Tommie (D) 54 2
H: 6 2 W: 11 13 b.Walthamstow 24-1-94
Internationals: Republic of Ireland U17, U19, U21.

2010–11	Watford	1	0		
2011–12	Watford	0	0		
2012–13	Watford	19	2		
2013–14	Watford	7	0		
2014–15	Watford	27	0	54	2

IGHALO, Odion Jude (F) 159 47
H: 6 2 W: 11 00 b.Lagos 16-6-89
Internationals: Nigeria U20, Full caps.

2007	Lyn	7	3		
2008	Lyn	13	6	20	9
2008–09	Udinese	6	1		
2009–10	Udinese	0	0		
2010–11	Udinese	0	0		
2010–11	Cesena	3	0	3	0
2010–11	Granada	21	4		
2011–12	Udinese	0	0		
2011–12	Granada	30	6		
2012–13	Udinese	0	0		
2012–13	Granada	28	5		
2013–14	Udinese	0	0		
2013–14	Granada	16	2	95	17
2014–15	Udinese	0	0	6	1

On loan from Udinese.

2014–15	Watford	35	20	35	20

IKPEAZU, Uche (F) 39 6
H: 6 3 W: 12 04 b.London 28-2-95

2013–14	Watford	0	0		
2013–14	Crewe Alex	15	4		
2014–15	Watford	0	0		
2014–15	Crewe Alex	17	2	32	6
2014–15	Doncaster R	7	0	7	0

JAKUBIAK, Alex (F) 33 5
H: 5 10 W: 10 06 b.Westminster 27-8-96
Internationals: Scotland U19.

2013–14	Watford	1	0		
2014–15	Watford	0	0		
2014–15	Oxford U	9	1	9	1
2014–15	Dagenham & R	23	4	23	4

JOHNSON, Jorell (D) 0 0
b.Hemel Hempstead 2-1-96

2014–15	Watford	0	0	

LAYUN, Miguel (D) 212 15
H: 5 10 W: 10 01 b.Cordoba 25-6-88
Internationals: Mexico Full caps.

2006–07	Veracruz	1	0		
2007–08	Veracruz	30	0		
2008–09	Veracruz	27	1	58	1
2009–10	Bergamo	2	0	2	0
2009–10	Club America	8	0		
2010–11	Club America	33	1		
2011–12	Club America	11	0		
2012–13	Club America	33	2		
2013–14	Club America	33	5		
2014–15	Club America	17	6	135	14
2014–15	Watford	17	0	17	0

McGUGAN, Lewis (M) 264 53
H: 5 9 W: 11 06 b.Long Eaton 25-10-88
Internationals: England U17, U19.

2006–07	Nottingham F	13	2		
2007–08	Nottingham F	33	6		
2008–09	Nottingham F	33	5		
2009–10	Nottingham F	18	3		
2010–11	Nottingham F	40	13		
2011–12	Nottingham F	35	3		
2012–13	Nottingham F	30	8	202	40
2013–14	Nottingham F	34	10		
2014–15	Watford	6	0	40	10
2014–15	Sheffield W	22	3	22	3

MENSAH, Bernard (F) 2 0
H: 5 8 W: 9 04 b.Hounslow 29-12-94

2011–12	Watford	0	0		
2012–13	Watford	0	0		
2013–14	Watford	1	0		
2014–15	Watford	1	0	2	0

MOTTA, Marco (D) 186 3
H: 5 11 W: 12 02 b.Bergamo 14-5-86
Internationals: Italy U16, U17, U18, u19, U20, U21, U23, Full caps.

2004–05	Atalanta	19	0	19	0
2005–06	Udinese	6	1		
2006–07	Udinese	16	0		
2007–08	Udinese	0	0		
2007–08	Torino	24	1	24	1
2008–09	Udinese	14	0	36	1
2008–09	Roma	13	0		
2009–10	Roma	16	0	29	0
2010–11	Juventus	22	0		
2011–12	Juventus	0	0		
2011–12	Catania	13	0	13	0
2012–13	Juventus	0	0		
2012–13	Bologna	19	1	19	1
2013–14	Juventus	2	0		
2013–14	Genoa	13	0	13	0
2014–15	Juventus	0	0	24	0
2014–15	Watford	9	0	9	0

MUNARI, Gianni (M) 307 33
H: 6 1 W: 12 08 b.Sassuolo 24-6-83

2004–05	Triestina	32	5		
2005–06	Triestina	1	0	33	5
2005–06	Verona	38	4	38	4
2006–07	Lecce	20	3		
2007–08	Lecce	38	2		
2008–09	Lecce	25	4		
2009–10	Lecce	26	6		
2010–11	Lecce	34	2	143	17
2011–12	Fiorentina	11	0	11	0
2011–12	Sampdoria	16	1		
2012–13	Sampdoria	27	3	43	4
2013–14	Parma	11	0		
2014–15	Parma	0	0	11	0

On loan from Parma.

2014–15	Watford	28	3	28	3

MURRAY, Sean (M) 75 11
H: 5 9 W: 10 10 b.Abbots Langley 11-10-93
Internationals: Republic of Ireland U17, U19, U21.

2010–11	Watford	2	0		
2011–12	Watford	18	7		
2012–13	Watford	15	1		
2013–14	Watford	34	3		
2014–15	Watford	6	0	75	11

O'NIEN, Luke (M) 1 0
b. 21-11-94

2013–14	Watford	1	0		
2014–15	Watford	0	0	1	0

PAREDES, Juan Carlos (D) 260 14
H: 5 10 W: 11 05 b.Esmeraldas 8-7-87
Internationals: Ecuador Full caps.

2006–07	Barcelona	5	0		
2007–08	Deportivo Cuena	19	1		
2007–08	Rocafuerte	22	3	29	2
2008–09	Deportivo Cuena	32	3	51	4
2009–10	Deportivo Quito	38	4		
2010–11	Deportivo Quito	36	3		
2011–12	Deportivo Quito	19	0	93	7
2012–13	Barcelona	35	1		
2013–14	Barcelona	8	0	48	1
2014–15	Watford	39	0	39	0

PUDIL, Daniel (D) 234 24
H: 6 1 W: 12 11 b.Prague 27-9-85
Internationals: Czech Republic U19, U21, Full caps.

2003–04	Blsany	2	2	2	2
2005–06	Liberec	3	4		
2006–07	Liberec	3	3	6	7
2007–08	Slavia Prague	16	6	16	6
2008–09	Genk	29	4		
2009–10	Genk	27	1		
2010–11	Genk	32	0		
2011–12	Cesena	7	1	7	1
2012–13	Watford	37	1		
2013–14	Watford	37	2		
2014–15	Watford	23	0	97	3

RANEGIE, Mathias (F) 166 56
H: 6 5 W: 14 07 b.Gothenburg 14-7-84
Internationals: Sweden Full caps.

2007	IFK Goteborg	5	0		
2008	IFK Goteborg	9	1	14	1
2008–09	Go Ahead Eagles	5	1	5	1
2009	BK Hacken	28	6		
2010	BK Hacken	30	12		
2011	BK Hacken	22	18	80	36
2011	Malmo FF	7	3		
2012	Malmo FF	19	10	26	13
2012–13	Udinese	20	1		
2013–14	Udinese	4	0	24	1
2013–14	Watford	10	4		
2014–15	Watford	0	0	10	4
2014–15	Millwall	7	0	7	0

SAVIC, Vujadin (D) 82 1
H: 6 4 W: 13 12 b.Belgrade 1-7-90
Internationals: Serbia U19, U21.

2007–08	Red Star Belgrade	4	0		
2007–08	Rad Beograd	6	0		
2008–09	Red Star Belgrade	0	0		
2008–09	Rad Beograd	12	0	18	0
2009–10	Red Star Belgrade	14	0	14	0
2010–11	Bordeaux	7	1		
2011–12	Bordeaux	1	0		
2011–12	Dynamo Dresden	13	0		
2012–13	Bordeaux	0	0		
2012–13	Dynamo Dresden	21	0	34	0
2013–14	Bordeaux	2	0	10	1
2013–14	Arminia Bielefeld	6	0	6	0
2014–15	Watford	0	0		

SMITH, Connor (M) 18 0
H: 5 11 W: 11 06 b.London 18-2-93
Internationals: Republic of Ireland U19, U21.

2012–13	Watford	7	0		
2013–14	Watford	1	0		
2013–14	Gillingham	10	0	10	0
2014–15	Watford	0	0	8	0

TAMAS, Gabriel (D) 283 12
H: 6 2 W: 12 02 b.Brasov 9-11-83
Internationals: Romania U16, U19, U21, Full caps.

1998–99	Brasov	1	0		
1999–2000	Brasov	0	0	1	0
2000–01	Tractorul	15	1		
2001–02	Tractorul	19	2	34	3
2002–03	Din Bucharest	19	4		
2003–04	Galatasaray	6	0	6	0
2004	Spartak Moscow	14	0		
2004–05	Din Bucharest	13	0		
2005–06	Din Bucharest	14	1		
2006	Spartak Moscow	3	0	17	0
2006–07	Celta Vigo	29	0	29	0
2007–08	Auxerre	27	0	27	0
2008–09	Din Bucharest	22	0		
2009–10	Din Bucharest	12	2	80	7
2009–10	WBA	23	2		
2010–11	WBA	26	0		
2011–12	WBA	8	0		
2012–13	WBA	11	0		
2013–14	WBA	0	0	68	2
2013–14	Doncaster R	14	0	14	0
2014–15	Watford	7	0	7	0

TOZSER, Daniel (M) 303 28
H: 6 1 W: 11 08 b.Szolnok 12-5-85
Internationals: Hungary U21, Full caps.

2002–03	Debrecen	0	0		
2003–04	Debrecen	1	0	1	0
2004–05	Ferencvaros	24	1		
2005–06	Ferencvaros	30	2	54	3
2006–07	AEK Athens	23	2		
2007–08	AEK Athens	12	1	35	3
2008–09	Genk	25	2		
2009–10	Genk	38	5		
2010–11	Genk	39	8		
2011–12	Genk	25	2	127	17
2012–13	Genoa	21	0		
2013–14	Genoa	0	0	21	0
2013–14	Watford	20	0		
2014–15	Parma	0	0		

On loan from Parma.

2014–15	Watford	45	5	65	5

VYDRA, Matej (F) 122 43
H: 5 10 W: 11 09 b.Chotebor 1-5-92
Internationals: Czech Republic U16, U17, U18, U19, U21, Full caps.

2009–10	Banik Ostrava	13	4	13	4
2010–11	Udinese	2	0		
2011–12	Udinese	0	0		
2011–12	Club Brugge	1	0	1	0
2012–13	Udinese	0	0		
2012–13	Watford	41	20		
2013–14	Udinese	0	0		

2013–14	WBA	23	3	**23 3**
2014–15	Udinese	0	0	**2 0**

On loan from Udinese.

2014–15	Watford	42	16	**83 36**

WATSON, Ben (M)   **323 34**
H: 5 10 W: 10 11 b.Camberwell 9-7-85
Internationals: England U21.

2002–03	Crystal Palace	5	0	
2003–04	Crystal Palace	16	1	
2004–05	Crystal Palace	21	0	
2005–06	Crystal Palace	42	4	
2006–07	Crystal Palace	25	3	
2007–08	Crystal Palace	42	5	
2008–09	Crystal Palace	18	5	**169 18**
2008–09	Wigan Ath	10	2	
2009–10	Wigan Ath	5	1	
2009–10	QPR	16	2	**16 2**
2009–10	WBA	7	1	**7 1**
2010–11	Wigan Ath	29	3	
2011–12	Wigan Ath	21	3	
2012–13	Wigan Ath	12	1	
2013–14	Wigan Ath	25	2	
2014–15	Wigan Ath	9	1	**111 13**
2014–15	Watford	20	0	**20 0**

Players retained or with offer of contract
Folivi, Michael Kwaku.

Scholars
Ammann, Arie Michael; Cook, Jacob
Thomas Samuel; Eleftheriou, Andrew;
Gartside, Nathan James; Hall, Matthew
Stuart; Kyprianou, Harry Kypros; Lewis,
Dennon Elliot; Makaka, Max; Martin,
Mahlando Javion; Mason, Brandon
Alexander; Obi, Ogochukwu Alexander;
Otudeko, Joseph Adekunle Ayodeji; Rowan,
Charles Alfred; Stevens, Connor John;
Young, Alfie Mac.

WBA (86)

ANICHEBE, Victor (F)   **176 23**
H: 6 1 W: 13 00 b.Nigeria 23-4-88
Internationals: Nigeria U23, Full caps.

2005–06	Everton	2	1	
2006–07	Everton	19	3	
2007–08	Everton	27	1	
2008–09	Everton	17	1	
2009–10	Everton	11	1	
2010–11	Everton	16	0	
2011–12	Everton	12	4	
2012–13	Everton	26	6	
2013–14	Everton	1	0	**131 17**
2013–14	WBA	24	3	
2014–15	WBA	21	3	**45 6**

ATKINSON, Wes (M)   **2 0**
b.West Bromwich 13-10-94

2014–15	WBA	0	0	
2014–15	Cambridge U	2	0	**2 0**

BAIRD, Chris (D)   **248 7**
H: 5 10 W: 11 11 b.Ballymoney 25-2-82
Internationals: Northern Ireland U18, U21,
Full caps.

2000–01	Southampton	0	0	
2001–02	Southampton	0	0	
2002–03	Southampton	3	0	
2003–04	Southampton	4	0	
2003–04	Walsall	10	0	**10 0**
2003–04	Watford	8	0	**8 0**
2004–05	Southampton	0	0	
2005–06	Southampton	17	0	
2006–07	Southampton	44	3	**68 3**
2007–08	Fulham	18	0	
2008–09	Fulham	10	0	
2009–10	Fulham	32	0	
2010–11	Fulham	29	2	
2011–12	Fulham	19	0	
2012–13	Fulham	19	2	**127 4**
2013–14	Reading	9	0	**9 0**
2013–14	Burnley	7	0	**7 0**
2014–15	WBA	19	0	**19 0**

BERAHINO, Saido (F)   **102 31**
H: 5 10 W: 11 13 b.Burundi 4-8-93
Internationals: England U16, U17, U18, U19,
U20, U21.

2010–11	WBA	0	0	
2011–12	WBA	0	0	
2011–12	Northampton T	14	6	**14 6**
2011–12	Brentford	8	4	**8 4**
2012–13	WBA	0	0	
2012–13	Peterborough U	10	2	**10 2**

2013–14	WBA	32	5	
2014–15	WBA	38	14	**70 19**

BLANCO, Sebastian (M)   **199 28**
b.Buenos Aires 15-3-88
Internationals: Argentina Full caps.

2006–07	Lanus	6	1	
2007–08	Lanus	24	3	
2008–09	Lanus	35	5	
2009–10	Lanus	34	7	
2010–11	Lanus	14	1	**113 17**
2011–12	Metalist Kharkiv	15	2	
2012–13	Metalist Kharkiv	26	2	
2013–14	Metalist Kharkiv	27	6	**68 10**
2014–15	WBA	3	0	**3 0**
2015	San Lorenzo	15	1	**15 1**

BRUNT, Chris (M)   **404 62**
H: 6 1 W: 13 04 b.Belfast 14-12-84
Internationals: Northern Ireland U19, U21,
U23, Full caps.

2002–03	Middlesbrough	0	0	
2003–04	Middlesbrough	0	0	
2003–04	Sheffield W	9	2	
2004–05	Sheffield W	42	4	
2005–06	Sheffield W	44	7	
2006–07	Sheffield W	44	11	
2007–08	Sheffield W	1	0	**140 24**
2007–08	WBA	34	4	
2008–09	WBA	34	8	
2009–10	WBA	40	13	
2010–11	WBA	34	4	
2011–12	WBA	29	2	
2012–13	WBA	31	2	
2013–14	WBA	28	3	
2014–15	WBA	34	2	**264 38**

DANIELS, Donervorn (D)   **44 3**
H: 6 1 W: 14 05 b.Montserrat 24-11-93
Internationals: England U20.

2011–12	WBA	0	0	
2012–13	WBA	0	0	
2012–13	Tranmere R	13	1	**13 1**
2013–14	WBA	0	0	
2013–14	Gillingham	3	1	**3 1**
2014–15	WBA	0	0	
2014–15	Blackpool	19	1	**19 1**
2014–15	Aberdeen	9	0	**9 0**

DAVIDSON, Jason (D)   **85 4**
H: 5 11 W: 11 05 b.Melbourne 29-6-91
Internationals: Australia U20, Full caps.

2009	Hume City	16	2	**16 2**
2009–10	Pacos de Ferreira	9	0	
2010–11	Pacos de Ferreira	0	0	**5 0**
2010–11	Sporting Covilha	14	0	**14 0**
2011–12	Heracles	6	0	
2012–13	Heracles	10	0	
2013–14	Heracles	32	2	**48 2**
2014–15	Heracles	2	0	**2 0**

DAWSON, Craig (D)   **153 25**
H: 6 0 W: 12 04 b.Rochdale 6-5-90
Internationals: England U21. Great Britain.

2008–09	Rochdale	0	0	
2009–10	Rochdale	42	9	
2010–11	WBA	0	0	
2010–11	Rochdale	45	10	**87 19**
2011–12	WBA	8	0	
2012–13	WBA	1	0	
2012–13	Bolton W	16	4	**16 4**
2013–14	WBA	14	0	
2014–15	WBA	29	2	**50 2**

DORRANS, Graham (F)   **272 45**
H: 5 9 W: 11 07 b.Glasgow 5-5-87
Internationals: Scotland U20, U21, Full caps.

2006–07	Livingston	8	0	
2006–07	Partick Thistle	5	5	**15 5**
2006–07	Livingston	34	5	
2007–08	Livingston	34	11	**76 16**
2008–09	WBA	8	0	
2009–10	WBA	45	13	
2010–11	WBA	21	1	
2011–12	WBA	31	3	
2012–13	WBA	26	1	
2013–14	WBA	14	2	
2014–15	WBA	21	1	**166 21**
2014–15	Norwich C	15	3	**15 3**

FLETCHER, Darren (M)   **238 19**
H: 6 0 W: 11 09 b.Edinburgh 1-2-84
Internationals: Scotland U20, U21, B, Full
caps.

2000–01	Manchester U	0	0	
2001–02	Manchester U	0	0	
2002–03	Manchester U	0	0	
2003–04	Manchester U	22	0	
2004–05	Manchester U	18	3	
2005–06	Manchester U	27	1	

2006–07	Manchester U	24	3	
2007–08	Manchester U	16	0	
2008–09	Manchester U	26	3	
2009–10	Manchester U	30	4	
2010–11	Manchester U	26	2	
2011–12	Manchester U	8	1	
2012–13	Manchester U	3	1	
2013–14	Manchester U	12	0	
2014–15	Manchester U	11	0	**223 18**
2014–15	WBA	15	1	**15 1**

FOSTER, Ben (G)   **261 0**
H: 6 2 W: 12 08 b.Leamington Spa 3-4-83
Internationals: England Full caps.

2000–01	Stoke C	0	0	
2001–02	Stoke C	0	0	
2002–03	Stoke C	0	0	
2003–04	Stoke C	0	0	
2004–05	Stoke C	0	0	
2004–05	Kidderminster H	2	0	**2 0**
2004–05	Wrexham	17	0	**17 0**
2005–06	Manchester U	0	0	
2005–06	Watford	44	0	
2006–07	Manchester U	0	0	
2006–07	Watford	29	0	**73 0**
2007–08	Manchester U	1	0	
2008–09	Manchester U	2	0	
2009–10	Manchester U	9	0	**12 0**
2010–11	Birmingham C	38	0	
2011–12	Birmingham C	0	0	**38 0**
2011–12	WBA	37	0	
2012–13	WBA	30	0	
2013–14	WBA	24	0	
2014–15	WBA	28	0	**119 0**

GAMBOA, Cristian (D)   **145 1**
H: 5 9 W: 10 08 b.Liberia 24-10-89
Internationals: Costa Rica Full caps.

2006–07	Municipal Liberia	16	0	**16 0**
2007–08	Liberia Mia	26	0	
2008–09	Liberia Mia	13	0	**39 0**
2009–10	Aguilas Guanacastercas	13	0	**13 0**
2010–11	Fredrikstad	11	1	
2011–12	Fredrikstad	16	0	**27 1**
2012	Rosenborg	10	0	
2013	Rosenborg	28	0	
2014	Rosenborg	2	0	**40 0**
2014–15	WBA	10	0	**10 0**

GARDNER, Craig (M)   **217 28**
H: 5 10 W: 11 13 b.Solihull 25-11-86
Internationals: England U21.

2004–05	Aston Villa	0	0	
2005–06	Aston Villa	8	0	
2006–07	Aston Villa	13	2	
2007–08	Aston Villa	23	3	
2008–09	Aston Villa	14	0	
2009–10	Aston Villa	1	0	**59 5**
2009–10	Birmingham C	13	1	
2010–11	Birmingham C	29	8	**42 9**
2011–12	Sunderland	30	3	
2012–13	Sunderland	33	6	
2013–14	Sunderland	18	2	**81 11**
2014–15	WBA	35	3	**35 3**

GARMSTON, Bradley (D)   **21 1**
H: 5 9 W: 10 12 b.Greenwich 18-1-94
Internationals: Republic of Ireland U19, U21.

2012–13	WBA	0	0	
2012–13	Colchester U	13	0	**13 0**
2013–14	WBA	0	0	
2014–15	WBA	0	0	
2014–15	Gillingham	8	1	**8 1**

IDEYE, Brown (F)   **237 94**
H: 5 11 W: 11 00 b.Yenagoa 10-10-88
Internationals: Nigeria U20, Full caps.

2005–06	Baysela United	19	6	**19 6**
2006–07	Ocean Boys	5	1	
2007–08	Ocean Boys	8	9	**13 10**
2007–08	Neuchatel Xamax	5	1	
2008–09	Neuchatel Xamax	33	10	
2009–10	Neuchatel Xamax	17	12	**55 23**
2009–10	Sochaux	12	2	
2010–11	Sochaux	35	15	**52 17**
2011–12	Dynamo Kiev	27	12	
2012–13	Dynamo Kiev	28	17	
2013–14	Dynamo Kiev	19	5	**74 34**
2014–15	WBA	24	4	**24 4**

JONES, Callum (M)   **0 0**
H: 6 0 W: 11 12 b.London 31-1-96
Internationals: England U16, U17.

2013–14	WBA	0	0	
2014–15	WBA	0	0	

LESCOTT, Jolean (D)   **466 35**
H: 6 2   W: 13 00   b.Birmingham 16-8-82
Internationals: England U17, U18, U20, U21, B, Full caps.

1999–2000	Wolverhampton W	0	0	
2000–01	Wolverhampton W	37	2	
2001–02	Wolverhampton W	44	5	
2002–03	Wolverhampton W	44	1	
2003–04	Wolverhampton W	0	0	
2004–05	Wolverhampton W	41	4	
2005–06	Wolverhampton W	46	1	**212 13**
2006–07	Everton	38	2	
2007–08	Everton	38	8	
2008–09	Everton	36	4	
2009–10	Everton	1	0	**113 14**
2009–10	Manchester C	18	1	
2010–11	Manchester C	22	3	
2011–12	Manchester C	31	2	
2012–13	Manchester C	26	1	
2013–14	Manchester C	10	0	**107 7**
2014–15	WBA	34	1	**34 1**

McAULEY, Gareth (D)   **385 28**
H: 6 3   W: 13 00   b.Larne 5-12-79
Internationals: Northern Ireland B, Full caps.

2004–05	Lincoln C	37	3	
2005–06	Lincoln C	35	5	**72 8**
2006–07	Leicester C	30	3	
2007–08	Leicester C	44	2	**74 5**
2008–09	Ipswich T	35	0	
2009–10	Ipswich T	41	5	
2010–11	Ipswich T	39	2	**115 7**
2011–12	WBA	32	2	
2012–13	WBA	36	3	
2013–14	WBA	32	2	
2014–15	WBA	24	1	**124 8**

McMANAMAN, Callum (F)   **101 12**
H: 5 9   W: 11 03   b.Huyton 25-4-91
Internationals: England U20.

2008–09	Wigan Ath	1	0	
2009–10	Wigan Ath	0	0	
2010–11	Wigan Ath	3	0	
2011–12	Wigan Ath	2	0	
2011–12	*Blackpool*	14	2	**14 2**
2012–13	Wigan Ath	20	2	
2013–14	Wigan Ath	30	3	
2014–15	Wigan Ath	23	5	**79 10**
2014–15	WBA	8	0	**8 0**

MORRISON, James (M)   **304 28**
H: 5 10   W: 10 06   b.Darlington 25-5-86
Internationals: England U17, U18, U19, U20. Scotland Full caps.

2003–04	Middlesbrough	1	0	
2004–05	Middlesbrough	14	0	
2005–06	Middlesbrough	24	1	
2006–07	Middlesbrough	28	2	**67 3**
2007–08	WBA	35	4	
2008–09	WBA	30	3	
2009–10	WBA	11	1	
2010–11	WBA	31	4	
2011–12	WBA	30	5	
2012–13	WBA	35	5	
2013–14	WBA	32	1	
2014–15	WBA	33	2	**237 25**

MULUMBU, Youssef (M)   **233 16**
H: 5 9   W: 10 03   b.Kinshasa 25-1-87
Internationals: France U20, U21. DR Congo Full caps.

2006–07	Paris St Germain	12	0	
2007–08	Paris St Germain	1	0	
2007–08	*Amiens*	23	1	**23 1**
2008–09	Paris St Germain	0	0	**13 0**
2008–09	WBA	6	0	
2009–10	WBA	40	3	
2010–11	WBA	34	7	
2011–12	WBA	35	1	
2012–13	WBA	28	2	
2013–14	WBA	37	2	
2014–15	WBA	17	0	**197 15**

MYHILL, Boaz (G)   **357 0**
H: 6 3   W: 14 06   b.California 9-11-82
Internationals: England U20. Wales Full caps.

2000–01	Aston Villa	0	0	
2001–02	Aston Villa	0	0	
2001–02	Stoke C	0	0	
2002–03	Aston Villa	0	0	
2002–03	Bristol C	0	0	
2002–03	*Bradford C*	2	0	**2 0**
2003–04	Aston Villa	0	0	
2003–04	*Macclesfield T*	15	0	**15 0**
2003–04	*Stockport Co*	2	0	**2 0**
2003–04	Hull C	23	0	
2004–05	Hull C	45	0	
2005–06	Hull C	45	0	
2006–07	Hull C	46	0	

2007–08	Hull C	43	0	
2008–09	Hull C	28	0	
2009–10	Hull C	27	0	**257 0**
2010–11	WBA	6	0	
2011–12	WBA	0	0	
2011–12	*Birmingham C*	42	0	**42 0**
2012–13	WBA	8	0	
2013–14	WBA	14	0	
2014–15	WBA	11	0	**39 0**

NABI, Adil (F)   **0 0**
H: 5 9   W: 10 10   b.Birmingham 28-2-94
Internationals: England U16, U17.

2010–11	WBA	0	0	
2011–12	WBA	0	0	
2012–13	WBA	0	0	
2013–14	WBA	0	0	
2014–15	WBA	0	0	

O'NEIL, Liam (D)   **39 2**
H: 6 0   W: 12 06   b.Cambridge 31-7-93

2011–12	WBA	0	0	
2011–12	*VPS*	14	0	**14 0**
2012–13	WBA	0	0	
2013–14	WBA	3	0	
2014–15	*Scunthorpe U*	22	2	**22 2**

O'SULLIVAN, Mani (M)   **0 0**
H: 6 0   W: 9 13   b.Aylesbury 18-9-93

2013–14	WBA	0	0	
2014–15	WBA	0	0	

OLSSON, Jonas (D)   **358 17**
H: 6 4   W: 12 08   b.Landskrona 10-3-83
Internationals: Sweden U21, Full caps.

2002	Landskrona	0	0	
2003	Landskrona	22	0	
2004	Landskrona	22	1	
2005	Landskrona	12	0	**56 1**
2005–06	NEC Nijmegen	34	0	
2006–07	NEC Nijmegen	32	2	
2007–08	NEC Nijmegen	27	3	**93 5**
2008–09	WBA	28	2	
2009–10	WBA	43	4	
2010–11	WBA	24	1	
2011–12	WBA	33	2	
2012–13	WBA	36	0	
2013–14	WBA	32	1	
2014–15	WBA	13	1	**209 11**

PALMER, Alex (G)   **0 0**
Internationals: England U16.

2014–15	WBA	0	0	

POCOGNOLI, Sebastien (D)   **240 8**
H: 5 11   W: 11 07   b.Liege 1-8-87
Internationals: Belgium U16, U17, U19, U21, U23.

2003–04	Genk	1	0	
2004–05	Genk	0	0	
2005–06	Genk	15	1	
2006–07	Genk	30	0	**46 1**
2007–08	AZ Alkmaar	28	2	
2008–09	AZ Alkmaar	25	2	
2009–10	AZ Alkmaar	11	1	**64 5**
2010–11	Standard Liege	10	1	
2011–12	Standard Liege	34	1	
2011–12	Standard Liege	32	0	
2012–13	Standard Liege	9	0	**85 2**
2012–13	Hannover 96	11	0	
2013–14	Hannover 96	19	0	**30 0**
2014–15	WBA	15	0	**15 0**

ROBERTS, Tyler (F)   **0 0**
Internationals: Wales U16, U17.

2014–15	WBA	0	0	

ROOFE, Kemar (M)   **33 7**
H: 5 10   W: 11 03   b.Walsall 6-1-93

2011–12	WBA	0	0	
2012–13	WBA	0	0	
2012–13	*Northampton T*	6	0	**6 0**
2013–14	WBA	0	0	
2013–14	*Cheltenham T*	9	1	**9 1**
2014–15	*Colchester U*	2	0	**2 0**
2014–15	*Oxford U*	16	6	**16 6**

ROSE, Jack (G)   **0 0**
H: 6 0   W: 11 11   b.Solihull 31-1-95

2014–15	WBA	0	0	
2014–15	*Accrington S*	4	0	**4 0**

SAMARAS, Georgios (F)   **325 86**
H: 6 3   W: 13 08   b.Heraklion 21-2-85
Internationals: Greece U21, Full caps.

2002–03	Heerenveen	15	4	
2003–04	Heerenveen	27	4	
2004–05	Heerenveen	31	11	
2005–06	Heerenveen	15	6	**88 25**

2005–06	Manchester C	14	4	
2006–07	Manchester C	36	4	
2007–08	Manchester C	5	0	**55 8**
2007–08	*Celtic*	16	5	
2008–09	Celtic	31	15	
2009–10	Celtic	32	10	
2010–11	Celtic	22	3	
2011–12	Celtic	26	4	
2012–13	Celtic	25	9	
2013–14	Celtic	20	7	**172 53**
2014–15	WBA	5	0	**5 0**
2014–15	*Al Hilal*	5	0	**5 0**

SESSEGNON, Stephane (M)   **349 47**
H: 5 8   W: 11 05   b.Allahe 1-6-84
Internationals: Benin Full caps.

2003–04	Requins	2	0	**2 0**
2004–05	Creteil	35	5	
2005–06	Creteil	33	5	**68 10**
2006–07	Le Mans	31	1	
2007–08	Le Mans	30	5	**61 6**
2008–09	Paris St Germain	34	5	
2009–10	Paris St Germain	29	3	
2010–11	Paris St Germain	14	0	**77 8**
2010–11	Sunderland	14	3	
2011–12	Sunderland	36	7	
2012–13	Sunderland	35	7	
2013–14	Sunderland	2	0	**87 17**
2013–14	WBA	26	5	
2014–15	WBA	28	1	**54 6**

VARELA, Silvestre (F)   **238 44**
H: 5 11   W: 11 11   b.Almada 2-2-85
Internationals: Portugal U21, Full caps.

2005–06	Sporting Lisbon	3	0	
2005–06	*Vitoria Setubal*	15	2	
2006–07	Sporting Lisbon	0	0	
2006–07	*Vitoria Setubal*	30	2	**45 4**
2007–08	Sporting Lisbon	0	0	**2 0**
2007–08	*Rec Huelva*	22	0	**22 0**
2008–09	Estrela Amadora	28	5	**28 5**
2009–10	Porto	18	8	
2010–11	Porto	26	10	
2011–12	Porto	21	3	
2012–13	Porto	25	5	
2013–14	Porto	25	5	
2014–15	Porto	0	0	**115 31**
On loan from Porto.				
2014–15	WBA	7	1	**7 1**
2014–15	*Parma*	19	3	**19 3**

YACOB, Claudio (M)   **202 5**
H: 5 11   W: 11 06   b.Carcarana 18-7-87
Internationals: Argentina U20, Full caps.

2006–07	Racing Club	12	0	
2007–08	Racing Club	24	0	
2008–09	Racing Club	25	1	
2009–10	Racing Club	26	0	
2010–11	Racing Club	21	2	
2011–12	Racing Club	17	1	**125 4**
2012–13	WBA	30	0	
2013–14	WBA	27	1	
2014–15	WBA	20	0	**77 1**

Players retained or with offer of contract
Elbouzedi, Zachary; Nabi, Samir.

Scholars
Barbir, Daniel; Campbell, Tahvon; Cleet, George Henry; Donnellan, Shaun; Edwards, Kyle Hakeem; Ezewele, Joshua Aizenose; Field, Samuel; Fitzwater, Jack Joseph; Hall, Matthew Raymond; Hallahan, Jack; Howkins, Kyle; McCourt, Robbie; Okoh, Ernest; Pritchatt, Callum George; Ross, Ethan Walker; Scrivens, Chay; Smith, James; Sweeney, Bradley Stuart; Ward, Joseph; Wright, Andre.

WEST HAM U (87)

ADRIAN (G)   **90 0**
H: 6 2   W: 12 00   b.Seville 3-1-87

2008–09	Real Betis	0	0	
2009–10	Real Betis	0	0	
2010–11	Real Betis	0	0	
2011–12	Real Betis	0	0	
2012–13	Real Betis	32	0	**32 0**
2013–14	West Ham U	20	0	
2014–15	West Ham U	38	0	**58 0**

AMALFITANO, Morgan (M)   **348 23**
H: 5 9   W: 10 09   b.Nice 20-3-85
Internationals: France Full caps.

2004–05	Sedan	26	0	
2005–06	Sedan	34	5	

2006–07	Sedan	31	0		
2007–08	Sedan	35	0	126	0
2008–09	Lorient	35	3		
2009–10	Lorient	37	6		
2010–11	Lorient	38	5	110	14
2011–12	Marseille	32	1		
2012–13	Marseille	26	1		
2013–14	Marseille	2	0	60	2
2013–14	*WBA*	28	4	28	4
2014–15	West Ham U	24	3	24	3

BURKE, Reece (D)   5   0
H: 6 2   W: 12 11   b.London 2-9-96
Internationals: England U18, U19.

2013–14	West Ham U	0	0		
2014–15	West Ham U	5	0	5	0

CARROLL, Andy (F)   188   52
H: 6 4   W: 11 00   b.Gateshead 6-1-89
Internationals: England U19, U21, Full caps.

2006–07	Newcastle U	4	0		
2007–08	Newcastle U	4	0		
2007–08	*Preston NE*	11	1	11	1
2008–09	Newcastle U	14	3		
2009–10	Newcastle U	39	17		
2010–11	Newcastle U	19	11	80	31
2010–11	Liverpool	7	2		
2011–12	Liverpool	35	4		
2012–13	Liverpool	2	0	44	6
2012–13	*West Ham U*	24	7		
2013–14	West Ham U	15	2		
2014–15	West Ham U	14	5	53	14

CHAMBERS, Leo (D)   0   0
H: 6 1   W: 13 00   b.London 5-8-95
Internationals: England U16, U17, U18, U19.

2012–13	West Ham U	0	0
2013–14	West Ham U	0	0
2014–15	West Ham U	0	0

COLE, Carlton (F)   336   67
H: 6 3   W: 14 02   b.Croydon 12-11-83
Internationals: England U19, U20, U21, Full caps.

2000–01	Chelsea	0	0		
2001–02	Chelsea	3	1		
2002–03	Chelsea	13	3		
2002–03	*Wolverhampton W*	7	1	7	1
2003–04	Chelsea	0	0		
2003–04	*Charlton Ath*	21	4	21	4
2004–05	Chelsea	0	0		
2004–05	*Aston Villa*	27	3	27	3
2005–06	Chelsea	9	0	25	4
2006–07	West Ham U	17	2		
2007–08	West Ham U	31	4		
2008–09	West Ham U	27	10		
2009–10	West Ham U	30	10		
2010–11	West Ham U	35	5		
2011–12	West Ham U	40	14		
2012–13	West Ham U	27	2		
2013–14	West Ham U	26	6		
2014–15	West Ham U	23	2	256	55

COLLINS, James M (D)   291   11
H: 6 2   W: 14 05   b.Newport 23-8-83
Internationals: Wales U19, U20, U21, Full caps.

2000–01	Cardiff C	3	0		
2001–02	Cardiff C	7	1		
2002–03	Cardiff C	2	0		
2003–04	Cardiff C	20	1		
2004–05	Cardiff C	34	1	66	3
2005–06	West Ham U	14	2		
2006–07	West Ham U	16	0		
2007–08	West Ham U	3	0		
2008–09	West Ham U	18	0		
2009–10	West Ham U	3	0		
2009–10	*Aston Villa*	27	1		
2010–11	Aston Villa	32	3		
2011–12	Aston Villa	32	1	91	5
2012–13	West Ham U	29	0		
2013–14	West Ham U	24	1		
2014–15	West Ham U	27	0	134	3

CRESSWELL, Aaron (D)   240   13
H: 5 7   W: 10 05   b.Liverpool 15-12-89

2008–09	Tranmere R	13	1		
2009–10	Tranmere R	14	0		
2010–11	Tranmere R	43	4	70	5
2011–12	Ipswich T	44	1		
2012–13	Ipswich T	46	3		
2013–14	Ipswich T	42	2	132	6
2014–15	West Ham U	38	2	38	2

CULLEN, Josh (M)   0   0
b.Southend-on-Sea 4-7-96
Internationals: England U16. Republic of Ireland U19.

2014–15	West Ham U	0	0

DEMEL, Guy (D)   281   12
H: 6 2   W: 13 12   b.Paris 13-6-81
Internationals: Ivory Coast Full caps.

1999–2000	Nimes	1	0	1	0
2000–01	Arsenal	0	0		
2001–02	Bor Dortmund II	16	3		
2002–03	Bor Dortmund II	24	6	40	9
2002–03	Bor Dortmund	4	0		
2003–04	Bor Dortmund	13	0		
2004–05	Bor Dortmund	16	0	33	0
2005–06	Hamburg	22	1		
2006–07	Hamburg	8	0		
2007–08	Hamburg	26	0		
2008–09	Hamburg	28	0		
2009–10	Hamburg	26	0		
2010–11	Hamburg	21	0	131	2
2011–12	West Ham U	30	0		
2012–13	West Ham U	31	0		
2013–14	West Ham U	32	1		
2014–15	West Ham U	6	0	76	1

DOWNING, Stewart (M)   385   39
H: 5 11   W: 10 04   b.Middlesbrough 22-7-84
Internationals: England U21, B, Full caps.

2001–02	Middlesbrough	3	0		
2002–03	Middlesbrough	2	0		
2003–04	Middlesbrough	20	0		
2003–04	*Sunderland*	7	3	7	3
2004–05	Middlesbrough	35	5		
2005–06	Middlesbrough	12	1		
2006–07	Middlesbrough	34	2		
2007–08	Middlesbrough	38	9		
2008–09	Middlesbrough	37	0	181	17
2009–10	Aston Villa	25	2		
2010–11	Aston Villa	38	7	63	9
2011–12	Liverpool	36	0		
2012–13	Liverpool	29	3		
2013–14	Liverpool	0	0	65	3
2013–14	*West Ham U*	32	1		
2014–15	West Ham U	37	6	69	7

FANIMO, Matthias (M)   1   0
H: 5 8   W: 11 03   b.Lambeth 28-1-94
Internationals: England U16, U17, U18.

2011–12	West Ham U	0	0		
2012–13	West Ham U	0	0		
2013–14	West Ham U	0	0		
2014–15	West Ham U	0	0		
2014–15	*Tranmere R*	1	0	1	0

HENRY, Doneil (D)   73   2
H: 6 2   W: 12 13   b.Brampton 20-4-93
Internationals: Canada U20, U23, Full caps.

2010	Toronto	1	0		
2011	Toronto	10	0		
2012	Toronto	18	1		
2013	Toronto	20	0	49	1
2014	Toronto FC	21	1	21	1
2014–15	West Ham U	0	0		
2014–15	*Blackburn R*	3	0	3	0

JAASKELAINEN, Jussi (G)   649   0
H: 6 3   W: 12 10   b.Vaasa 19-4-75
Internationals: Finland U21, Full caps.

1992	MP	6	0		
1993	MP	6	0		
1994	MP	26	0		
1995	MP	26	0	64	0
1996	VPS	27	0		
1997	VPS	27	0	54	0
1997–98	Bolton W	0	0		
1998–99	Bolton W	34	0		
1999–2000	Bolton W	34	0		
2000–01	Bolton W	27	0		
2001–02	Bolton W	34	0		
2002–03	Bolton W	38	0		
2003–04	Bolton W	38	0		
2004–05	Bolton W	36	0		
2005–06	Bolton W	38	0		
2006–07	Bolton W	28	0		
2007–08	Bolton W	28	0		
2008–09	Bolton W	38	0		
2009–10	Bolton W	38	0		
2010–11	Bolton W	38	0		
2011–12	Bolton W	18	0	474	0
2012–13	West Ham U	38	0		
2013–14	West Ham U	18	0		
2014–15	West Ham U	1	0	57	0

JARVIS, Matthew (M)   349   35
H: 5 8   W: 11 10   b.Middlesbrough 22-5-86
Internationals: England Full caps.

2003–04	Gillingham	10	0		
2004–05	Gillingham	30	3		
2005–06	Gillingham	35	3		
2006–07	Gillingham	35	6	110	12
2007–08	Wolverhampton W	26	1		
2008–09	Wolverhampton W	28	3		
2009–10	Wolverhampton W	34	3		

2010–11	Wolverhampton W	37	4		
2011–12	Wolverhampton W	37	8		
2012–13	Wolverhampton W	2	0	164	19
2012–13	West Ham U	32	2		
2013–14	West Ham U	32	2		
2014–15	West Ham U	11	0	75	4

KOUYATE, Cheikhou (M)   220   11
H: 6 3   W: 11 11   b.Dakar 21-12-89
Internationals: Senegal U20, Full caps.

2007–08	Brussels	10	0		
2008–09	Brussels	0	0	10	0
2008–09	Kortrijk	26	3	26	3
2009–10	Anderlecht	21	1		
2010–11	Anderlecht	23	1		
2011–12	Anderlecht	38	0		
2012–13	Anderlecht	33	1		
2013–14	Anderlecht	38	1	153	4
2014–15	West Ham U	31	4	31	4

LEE, Elliot (F)   17   4
H: 5 11   W: 11 05   b.Co. Durham 16-12-94

2011–12	West Ham U	0	0		
2012–13	West Ham U	0	0		
2013–14	West Ham U	0	0		
2013–14	*Colchester U*	4	1	4	1
2014–15	West Ham U	1	0	2	0
2014–15	*Southend U*	1	0		
2014–15	*Luton T*	11	3	11	3

MAGUIRE, Sean (F)   85   22
H: 5 9   W: 11 10   b.Luton 1-5-94
Internationals: Republic of Ireland U19, U21.

2010–11	West Ham U	0	0		
2011	*Waterford U*	8	1		
2011–12	West Ham U	0	0		
2012	*Waterford U*	26	13	34	14
2012–13	West Ham U	0	0		
2013–14	West Ham U	0	0		
2014	*Sligo R*	18	1	18	1
2014–15	West Ham U	0	0		
2014–15	*Accrington S*	33	7	33	7

McCALLUM, Paul (F)   36   10
H: 6 3   W: 12 00   b.Streatham 28-7-93

2010–11	West Ham U	0	0		
2011–12	West Ham U	0	0		
2011–12	*Rochdale*	0	0		
2012–13	West Ham U	0	0		
2012–13	*AFC Wimbledon*	9	4	9	4
2012–13	*Aldershot T*	9	3	9	3
2013–14	West Ham U	0	0		
2013–14	*Torquay U*	5	3	5	3
2013–14	*Hearts*	6	0	6	0
2014–15	West Ham U	0	0		
2014–15	*Portsmouth*	7	0	7	0

MORRISON, Ravel (M)   67   12
H: 5 9   W: 11 02   b.Wythenshawe 2-2-93
Internationals: England U16, U17, U18, U21.

2009–10	Manchester U	0	0		
2010–11	Manchester U	0	0		
2011–12	Manchester U	0	0		
2011–12	West Ham U	1	0		
2012–13	West Ham U	0	0		
2012–13	*Birmingham C*	27	3	27	3
2013–14	West Ham U	16	3		
2013–14	*QPR*	15	6	15	6
2014–15	West Ham U	1	0	18	3
2014–15	*Cardiff C*	7	0	7	0

NASHA, Amos (D)   0   0
b. 9-4-95

2014–15	West Ham U	0	0

NENE, Anderson (M)   449   149
H: 5 11   W: 11 00   b.Jundiai 19-7-81
Internationals: Brazil U23.

1999–01	Paulista	32	26	32	26
2001–02	Palmeiras	24	5	24	5
2002–03	Santos	22	8	22	8
2003–04	Mallorca	29	2	29	2
2004–05	Alaves	38	9		
2005–06	Alaves	38	12	76	21
2006–07	Celta Vigo	38	8	38	8
2007–08	Monaco	28	5		
2008–09	Monaco	1	0		
2008–09	Espanyol	35	4	35	4
2009–10	Monaco	34	14	63	19
2010–11	PSG	35	14		
2011–12	PSG	35	21		
2012–13	PSG	9	1	79	36
2012–13	Al Gharafa	6	3		
2013–14	Al Gharafa	23	10		
2014–15	Al Gharafa	14	7	43	20
2014–15	West Ham U	8	0	8	0

NOBLE, Mark (M) 298 32
H: 5 11 W: 12 00 b.West Ham 8-5-87
Internationals: England U16, U17, U18, U19, U21.

2004–05	West Ham U	13	0	
2005–06	West Ham U	5	0	
2005–06	*Hull C*	5	0	5 0
2006–07	West Ham U	10	2	
2006–07	*Ipswich T*	13	1	13 1
2007–08	West Ham U	31	3	
2008–09	West Ham U	29	3	
2009–10	West Ham U	27	2	
2010–11	West Ham U	26	4	
2011–12	West Ham U	45	8	
2012–13	West Ham U	28	4	
2013–14	West Ham U	38	3	
2014–15	West Ham U	28	2	280 31

NOLAN, Kevin (M) 520 99
H: 6 0 W: 14 00 b.Liverpool 24-6-82
Internationals: England U20, U21.

1999–2000	Bolton W	4	0	
2000–01	Bolton W	31	1	
2001–02	Bolton W	35	8	
2002–03	Bolton W	33	1	
2003–04	Bolton W	37	9	
2004–05	Bolton W	36	4	
2005–06	Bolton W	36	9	
2006–07	Bolton W	31	3	
2007–08	Bolton W	33	5	
2008–09	Bolton W	20	0	296 40
2008–09	Newcastle U	11	0	
2009–10	Newcastle U	44	17	
2010–11	Newcastle U	30	12	85 29
2011–12	West Ham U	42	12	
2012–13	West Ham U	35	10	
2013–14	West Ham U	33	7	
2014–15	West Ham U	29	1	139 30

O'BRIEN, Joey (M) 160 5
H: 5 11 W: 10 13 b.Dublin 17-2-86
Internationals: Republic of Ireland U19, U21, Full caps.

2004–05	Bolton W	1	0	
2004–05	*Sheffield W*	15	2	
2005–06	Bolton W	23	0	
2006–07	Bolton W	0	0	
2007–08	Bolton W	19	0	
2008–09	Bolton W	7	0	
2009–10	Bolton W	0	0	
2010–11	Bolton W	0	0	50 0
2010–11	*Sheffield W*	4	0	19 2
2011–12	West Ham U	32	1	
2012–13	West Ham U	33	2	
2013–14	West Ham U	17	0	
2014–15	West Ham U	9	0	91 3

ONARIASE, Manny (D) 0 0
b. 29-1-95

2014–15	West Ham U	0	0

OXFORD, Reece (D) 0 0
b. 16-12-98
Internationals: England U16, U17.

2014–15	West Ham U	0	0

PAGE, Lewis (D) 0 0
b. 20-5-96

2014–15	West Ham U	0	0

POTTS, Danny (D) 15 0
H: 5 8 W: 11 00 b.Barking 13-4-94
Internationals: USA U20. England U18, U19, U20.

2011–12	West Ham U	3	0	
2012–13	West Ham U	2	0	
2012–13	*Colchester U*	5	0	5 0
2013–14	West Ham U	0	0	
2013–14	*Portsmouth*	5	0	5 0
2014–15	West Ham U	0	0	5 0

POYET, Diego (M) 25 0
H: 6 0 W: 11 09 b. 8-4-95
Internationals: England U16, U17. Uruguay U20.

2011–12	Charlton Ath	0	0	
2012–13	Charlton Ath	5	0	
2013–14	Charlton Ath	20	0	20 0
2014–15	West Ham U	3	0	3 0
2014–15	*Huddersfield T*	2	0	2 0

REID, Winston (D) 206 8
H: 6 3 W: 13 10 b.North Shore 3-7-88
Internationals: Denmark U19, U20, U21. New Zealand Full caps.

2005–06	Midtjylland	9	0	
2006–07	Midtjylland	11	0	
2007–08	Midtjylland	9	0	
2008–09	Midtjylland	25	2	
2009–10	Midtjylland	29	0	83 2

2010–11	West Ham U	7	0	
2011–12	West Ham U	28	3	
2012–13	West Ham U	36	1	
2013–14	West Ham U	22	1	
2014–15	West Ham U	30	1	123 6

SAKHO, Diafra (F) 144 54
H: 6 0 W: 12 06 b.Guediaway 24-12-89
Internationals: Senegal Full caps.

2009–10	Metz	5	0	
2010–11	Metz	30	5	
2011–12	Metz	9	0	
2011–12	*Boulogne*	7	0	7 0
2012–13	Metz	33	19	
2013–14	Metz	37	20	114 44
2014–15	West Ham U	23	10	23 10

SONG, Alex (M) 217 8
H: 5 11 W: 12 04 b.Douala 9-9-87
Internationals: France Youth. Cameroon Youth, Full caps.

2005–06	Arsenal	5	0	
2006–07	Arsenal	2	0	
2006–07	*Charlton Ath*	12	0	12 0
2007–08	Arsenal	9	0	
2008–09	Arsenal	31	1	
2009–10	Arsenal	26	1	
2010–11	Arsenal	31	4	
2011–12	Arsenal	34	1	138 7
2012–13	Barcelona	20	1	
2013–14	Barcelona	19	0	

On loan from Barcelona.

2014–15	Barcelona	0	0	39 1
2014–15	West Ham U	28	0	28 0

SPIEGEL, Raphael (G) 19 0
H: 6 5 W: 15 00 b.Zurich 19-12-92
Internationals: Switzerland U17, U19, U21.

2011–12	Grasshoppers	0	0	
2011–12	*Bruhl*	17	0	17 0
2012–13	Grasshoppers	0	0	
2012–13	West Ham U	0	0	
2013–14	West Ham U	0	0	
2014–15	West Ham U	0	0	
2014–15	*Carlisle U*	2	0	2 0

TOMKINS, James (D) 190 8
H: 6 3 W: 11 10 b.Basildon 29-3-89
Internationals: England U16, U17, U18, U19, U20, U21. Great Britain.

2005–06	West Ham U	0	0	
2006–07	West Ham U	0	0	
2007–08	West Ham U	6	0	
2008–09	West Ham U	12	1	
2008–09	*Derby Co*	7	0	7 0
2009–10	West Ham U	23	0	
2010–11	West Ham U	19	1	
2011–12	West Ham U	44	4	
2012–13	West Ham U	26	1	
2013–14	West Ham U	31	0	
2014–15	West Ham U	22	1	183 8

VALENCIA, Enner (F) 185 49
H: 5 10 W: 11 05 b.San Lorenzo 11-4-89
Internationals: Ecuador Full caps.

2010	Emelec	25	1	
2011	Emelec	30	9	
2012	Emelec	40	13	
2013	Emelec	35	4	130 27
2013–14	Pachuca	23	18	23 18
2014–15	West Ham U	32	4	32 4

VAZ TE, Ricardo (F) 154 30
H: 6 2 W: 12 07 b.Lisbon 1-10-86
Internationals: Portugal U17, U19, U20, U21, U23.

2003–04	Bolton W	1	0	
2004–05	Bolton W	5	0	
2005–06	Bolton W	22	3	
2006–07	Bolton W	25	0	
2006–07	*Hull C*	6	0	6 0
2007–08	Bolton W	1	0	
2008–09	Bolton W	2	0	
2009–10	Bolton W	0	0	58 3
2010–11	*Panionios*	7	1	7 1
2010–11	*Hibernian*	10	1	10 1
2011–12	*Barnsley*	22	10	22 10
2011–12	West Ham U	15	10	
2012–13	West Ham U	24	3	
2013–14	West Ham U	8	2	
2014–15	West Ham U	4	0	51 15

Transferred to Akhisar Belediye January 2015.

ZARATE, Mauro (F) 269 74
H: 5 8 W: 10 10 b.Haedo 18-3-87
Internationals: Argentina U20.

2003–04	Velez Sarsfield	4	1
2004–05	Velez Sarsfield	14	2
2005–06	Velez Sarsfield	33	3

2006–07	Velez Sarsfield	32	16	
2007–08	Al-Sadd	6	0	6 0
2007–08	*Birmingham C*	14	4	14 4
2008–09	Al-Saad	0	0	
2008–09	Lazio	36	13	
2009–10	Lazio	32	3	
2010–11	Lazio	35	9	
2011–12	Lazio	0	0	
2011–12	*Inter Milan*	22	2	22 2
2012–13	Lazio	1	0	104 25
2013–14	Velez Sarsfield	29	19	112 41
2014–15	West Ham U	7	2	7 2
2014–15	*QPR*	4	0	4 0

Players retained or with offer of contract
Brown, Lionel Antonio; Gordon, Jaanai Derece; Howes, Samuel Scott; Maiga, Modibo; Makasi, Kusu Moses; Mavila, Nathan; Pask, Joshua David.

Scholars
Bogard, Clarke Ellis; Boness, Danny; Borg, Oscar Francis; Brown, Tim; Browne, Marcus Alexander; Carter, Matthew James; Diangana, Grady; Elsom, Ross; Knoyle, Kyle; Parfitt-Williams, Djair Terraii Carl; Pike, Alexander George; Sylvestre, Noha.

WIGAN ATH (88)

AL HABSI, Ali (G) 209 0
H: 6 4 W: 12 06 b.Oman 30-12-81
Internationals: Oman Full caps.

2003	Lyn	13	0	
2004	Lyn	24	0	
2005	Lyn	25	0	62 0
2005–06	Bolton W	0	0	
2006–07	Bolton W	0	0	
2007–08	Bolton W	10	0	
2008–09	Bolton W	0	0	
2009–10	Bolton W	0	0	
2010–11	Bolton W	0	0	10 0
2010–11	*Wigan Ath*	34	0	
2011–12	Wigan Ath	38	0	
2012–13	Wigan Ath	29	0	
2013–14	Wigan Ath	24	0	
2014–15	Wigan Ath	11	0	136 0
2014–15	*Brighton & HA*	1	0	1 0

BARNETT, Leon (D) 243 12
H: 6 0 W: 12 04 b.Stevenage 30-11-85

2003–04	Luton T	0	0	
2004–05	Luton T	0	0	
2005–06	Luton T	20	0	
2006–07	Luton T	39	3	59 3
2007–08	WBA	32	3	
2008–09	WBA	11	0	
2009–10	WBA	2	0	
2009–10	*Coventry C*	20	0	20 0
2010–11	WBA	0	0	45 3
2010–11	Norwich C	25	1	
2011–12	Norwich C	17	1	
2012–13	Norwich C	8	0	
2012–13	*Cardiff C*	8	0	8 0
2013–14	Norwich C	0	0	50 2
2013–14	*Wigan Ath*	41	4	
2014–15	Wigan Ath	20	0	61 4

BONG, Gaetan (D) 192 3
H: 6 0 W: 11 09 b.Sakbayeme 25-4-88
Internationals: France U21. Cameroon Full caps.

2005–06	Metz	3	0	
2006–07	Metz	2	0	
2007–08	Metz	11	0	
2008–09	Metz	0	0	16 0
2008–09	*Tours*	34	0	34 0
2009–10	Valenciennes	29	2	
2010–11	Valenciennes	22	1	
2011–12	Valenciennes	28	0	
2012–13	Valenciennes	29	0	
2013–14	Valenciennes	1	0	109 3
2013–14	*Olympiacos*	19	0	19 0
2014–15	Wigan Ath	14	0	14 0

BOYCE, Emmerson (D) 518 23
H: 6 0 W: 12 03 b.Aylesbury 24-9-79
Internationals: Barbados Full caps.

1997–98	Luton T	0	0	
1998–99	Luton T	1	0	
1999–2000	Luton T	30	1	
2000–01	Luton T	42	3	
2001–02	Luton T	37	0	
2002–03	Luton T	34	0	
2003–04	Luton T	42	4	186 8
2004–05	Crystal Palace	27	0	

2005–06	Crystal Palace	42	2	69	2
2006–07	Wigan Ath	34	0		
2007–08	Wigan Ath	25	0		
2008–09	Wigan Ath	27	1		
2009–10	Wigan Ath	24	3		
2010–11	Wigan Ath	22	0		
2011–12	Wigan Ath	26	3		
2012–13	Wigan Ath	36	4		
2013–14	Wigan Ath	42	2		
2014–15	Wigan Ath	27	0	263	13

CARSON, Scott (G) 310 0
H: 6 0 W: 13 06 b.Whitehaven 3-9-85
Internationals: England U18, U21, B, Full caps.

2002–03	Leeds U	0	0		
2003–04	Leeds U	3	0		
2004–05	Leeds U	0	0	3	0
2004–05	Liverpool	4	0		
2005–06	Liverpool	0	0		
2005–06	Sheffield W	9	0	9	0
2006–07	Liverpool	0	0		
2006–07	Charlton Ath	36	0	36	0
2007–08	Liverpool	0	0	4	0
2007–08	Aston Villa	35	0	35	0
2008–09	WBA	35	0		
2009–10	WBA	43	0		
2010–11	WBA	32	0	110	0
2011–12	Bursaspor	34	0		
2012–13	Bursaspor	29	0	63	0
2013–14	Wigan Ath	16	0		
2014–15	Wigan Ath	34	0	50	0

CHOW, Tim (M) 4 1
H: 5 11 W: 11 06 b.Wigan 18-1-94

2011–12	Wigan Ath	0	0		
2012–13	Wigan Ath	0	0		
2013–14	Wigan Ath	0	0		
2014–15	Wigan Ath	4	1	4	1

COSGROVE, Sam (F) 0 0
b.Beverley 2-12-96

2014–15	Wigan Ath	0	0		

COWIE, Don (M) 431 44
H: 5 5 W: 8 05 b.Inverness 15-2-83
Internationals: Scotland Full caps.

2000–01	Ross Co	1	0		
2001–02	Ross Co	18	0		
2002–03	Ross Co	30	1		
2003–04	Ross Co	23	0		
2004–05	Ross Co	34	5		
2005–06	Ross Co	32	4		
2006–07	Ross Co	28	7	166	17
2007–08	Inverness CT	37	9		
2008–09	Inverness CT	22	3	59	12
2008–09	Watford	10	3		
2009–10	Watford	41	2		
2010–11	Watford	37	4	88	9
2011–12	Cardiff C	43	4		
2012–13	Cardiff C	25	2		
2013–14	Cardiff C	18	0	86	6
2014–15	Wigan Ath	32	0	32	0

DELORT, Andy (F) 126 32
H: 6 0 W: 12 13 b.Nimes 9-10-91
Internationals: France U20.

2009–10	Nimes	3	0	3	0
2010–11	Ajaccio	24	4		
2011–12	Ajaccio	7	0		
2011–12	Metz	13	1	13	1
2012–13	Ajaccio	16	1	47	5
2013–14	Tours	36	24		
2014–15	Wigan Ath	0	11	0	
2014–15	Tours	16	2	52	26

ESPINOZA, Roger (M) 156 4
H: 5 10 W: 11 06 b.Puerto Cortes 25-10-86
Internationals: Honduras Full caps.

2008	Sporting Kansas C	24	1		
2009	Sporting Kansas C	10	0		
2010	Sporting Kansas C	25	0		
2011	Sporting Kansas C	27	1		
2012	Sporting Kansas C	28	0	114	2
2012–13	Wigan Ath	12	1		
2013–14	Wigan Ath	18	0		
2014–15	Wigan Ath	12	1	42	2

Transferred to Sporting Kansas City January 2015.

FLORES, Jordan (F) 1 0
b.Wigan 4-10-95

2014–15	Wigan Ath	1	0	1	0

FORTUNE, Marc-Antoine (F) 450 81
H: 6 0 W: 11 13 b.Cayenne 2-7-81

2000–01	Angouleme	18	3		
2001–02	Angouleme	36	12	54	15
2002–03	Nancy	12	1		
2002–03	Lille	15	0	15	0

2003–04	Rouen	34	10	34	10
2004–05	Brest	33	10	33	10
2005–06	Utrecht	31	6		
2006–07	Utrecht	22	5	53	11
2006–07	Nancy	15	5		
2007–08	Nancy	37	6		
2008–09	Nancy	19	1	90	13
2009–10	Celtic	30	10		
2010–11	Celtic	2	0	32	10
2010–11	WBA	25	2		
2011–12	WBA	17	2		
2011–12	Doncaster R	5	1	5	1
2012–13	WBA	21	2	63	6
2013–14	Wigan Ath	36	4		
2014–15	Wigan Ath	35	1	71	5

GARCIA, Juan (D) 133 5
Internationals: Honduras Full caps.

2007–08	Marathon	11	0		
2008–09	Marathon	22	1		
2009–10	Marathon	20	0	53	1
2010–11	Olimpia	30	0		
2011–12	Olimpia	27	2		
2012–13	Olimpia	23	2	80	4
2013–14	Wigan Ath	0	0		
2014–15	Wigan Ath	0	0		

HOLT, Grant (F) 443 152
H: 6 1 W: 14 02 b.Carlisle 12-4-81

1999–2000	Halifax T	4	0		
2000–01	Halifax T	2	0	6	0

From Sengkang, Barrow

2002–03	Sheffield W	7	1		
2003–04	Sheffield W	17	2	24	3
2003–04	Rochdale	14	4		
2004–05	Rochdale	40	17		
2005–06	Rochdale	21	14	75	35
2005–06	Nottingham F	19	4		
2006–07	Nottingham F	45	14		
2007–08	Nottingham F	32	3	96	21
2007–08	Blackpool	4	0	4	0
2008–09	Shrewsbury T	43	20	43	20
2009–10	Norwich C	39	24		
2010–11	Norwich C	45	21		
2011–12	Norwich C	36	15		
2012–13	Norwich C	34	8	154	68
2013–14	Wigan Ath	16	2		
2013–14	Aston Villa	10	1	10	1
2014–15	Wigan Ath	4	0		
2014–15	Huddersfield T	15	2	15	2

HUWS, Emyr (M) 43 2
H: 5 10 W: 11 07 b.Llanelli 30-9-93
Internationals: Wales U17, U19, U21, Full caps.

2010–11	Manchester C	0	0		
2011–12	Manchester C	0	0		
2012–13	Manchester C	0	0		
2012–13	Northampton T	10	0	10	0
2013–14	Manchester C	0	0		
2013–14	Birmingham C	17	2	17	2
2014–15	Wigan Ath	16	0	16	0

JENNINGS, Ryan (F) 0 0
b.Manchester 8-7-95

2013–14	Wigan Ath	0	0		
2014–15	Wigan Ath	0	0		
2014–15	Accrington S	0	0		

KIERNAN, Rob (D) 87 2
H: 6 1 W: 11 13 b.Rickmansworth 13-1-91
Internationals: Republic of Ireland U19, U21.

2008–09	Watford	0	0		
2009–10	Watford	0	0		
2009–10	Kilmarnock	4	0	4	0
2010–11	Watford	0	0		
2010–11	Yeovil T	3	0	3	0
2010–11	Bradford C	8	0	8	0
2010–11	Wycombe W	2	0	2	0
2011–12	Wigan Ath	0	0		
2011–12	Accrington S	3	0	3	0
2012–13	Wigan Ath	0	0		
2012–13	Burton Alb	6	0	6	0
2012–13	Brentford	8	0	8	0
2013–14	Wigan Ath	4	1		
2013–14	Southend U	12	0	12	0
2014–15	Wigan Ath	17	0	29	1
2014–15	Birmingham C	12	1	12	1

KIM, Bo-Kyung (M) 144 28
H: 5 10 W: 11 06 b.Oita 6-10-89
Internationals: South Korea U20, U23, Full caps.

2010	Oita Trinita	27	8	27	8
2011	Cerezo Osaka	26	8		
2012	Cerezo Osaka	15	7	41	15
2012–13	Cardiff C	28	2		
2013–14	Cardiff C	28	1		

2014–15	Cardiff C	2	0	58	3
2014–15	Wigan Ath	18	2	18	2

KVIST JORGENSEN, William (M) 281 8
H: 6 0 W: 12 07 b.Odder 24-2-85
Internationals: Denmark U16, U17, U18, U19, U20, U21, Full caps.

2004–05	Copenhagen	1	0		
2005–06	Copenhagen	20	0		
2006–07	Copenhagen	31	2		
2007–08	Copenhagen	32	0		
2008–09	Copenhagen	29	4		
2009–10	Copenhagen	33	2		
2010–11	Copenhagen	33	0	179	8
2011–12	Stuttgart	33	0		
2012–13	Stuttgart	23	0		
2013–14	Stuttgart	12	0	68	0
2013–14	Fulham	8	0	8	0
2014–15	Wigan Ath	26	0	26	0

MALONEY, Shaun (M) 268 58
H: 5 7 W: 10 01 b.Miri 24-1-83
Internationals: Scotland U20, U21, B, Full caps.

1999–2000	Celtic	0	0		
2000–01	Celtic	4	0		
2001–02	Celtic	16	5		
2002–03	Celtic	20	3		
2003–04	Celtic	17	5		
2004–05	Celtic	2	0		
2005–06	Celtic	36	13		
2006–07	Celtic	9	0		
2006–07	Aston Villa	8	1		
2007–08	Aston Villa	22	4	30	5
2008–09	Celtic	21	4		
2009–10	Celtic	10	4		
2010–11	Celtic	21	5		
2011–12	Celtic	3	0	159	39
2012–13	Wigan Ath	13	3		
2012–13	Wigan Ath	36	6		
2013–14	Wigan Ath	10	3		
2014–15	Wigan Ath	20	2	79	14

Transferred to Chicago Fire January 2015.

McCANN, Chris (M) 282 31
H: 6 1 W: 11 11 b.Dublin 21-7-87
Internationals: Republic of Ireland U19.

2005–06	Burnley	23	2		
2006–07	Burnley	38	5		
2007–08	Burnley	35	5		
2008–09	Burnley	44	6		
2009–10	Burnley	7	0		
2010–11	Burnley	4	1		
2011–12	Burnley	46	4		
2012–13	Burnley	41	4	238	27
2013–14	Wigan Ath	27	2		
2014–15	Wigan Ath	17	2	44	4

McCLEAN, James (M) 205 34
H: 5 11 W: 11 00 b.Derry 22-4-89
Internationals: Northern Ireland U21. Republic of Ireland Full caps.

2009	Derry C	27	1		
2010	Derry C	30	10		
2011	Derry C	16	7	73	18
2011–12	Sunderland	23	5		
2012–13	Sunderland	36	2		
2013–14	Sunderland	0	0	59	7
2013–14	Wigan Ath	37	3		
2014–15	Wigan Ath	36	6	73	9

McKAY, Billy (F) 204 67
H: 5 7 W: 10 10 b.Corby 22-10-88
Internationals: Northern Ireland U18, U20, U21, Full caps.

2007–08	Leicester C	0	0		
2008–09	Leicester C	0	0		
2009–10	Northampton T	40	8		
2010–11	Northampton T	34	5	74	13
2011–12	Inverness CT	22	3		
2012–13	Inverness CT	38	23		
2013–14	Inverness CT	38	18		
2014–15	Inverness CT	23	10	121	54
2014–15	Wigan Ath	9	0	9	0

NICHOLLS, Lee (G) 62 0
H: 6 3 W: 13 05 b.Huyton 5-10-92
Internationals: England U19.

2009–10	Wigan Ath	0	0		
2010–11	Wigan Ath	0	0		
2010–11	Hartlepool U	0	0		
2010–11	Shrewsbury T	0	0		
2011–12	Sheffield W	0	0		
2011–12	Wigan Ath	0	0		
2011–12	Accrington S	9	0	9	0
2012–13	Wigan Ath	0	0		
2012–13	Northampton T	46	0	46	0
2013–14	Wigan Ath	6	0		
2014–15	Wigan Ath	1	0	7	0

PEARCE, Jason (D) 320 13
H: 5 11 W: 12 00 b.Hillingdon 6-12-87

2006–07	Portsmouth	0	0		
2007–08	Bournemouth	33	1		
2008–09	Bournemouth	44	2		
2009–10	Bournemouth	39	1		
2010–11	Bournemouth	46	3	162	7
2011–12	Portsmouth	43	2	43	2
2011–12	Leeds U	0	0		
2012–13	Leeds U	33	0		
2013–14	Leeds U	45	2		
2014–15	Leeds U	21	0	99	2
2014–15	Wigan Ath	16	2	16	2

PENNANT, Jermaine (M) 312 19
H: 5 9 W: 10 06 b.Nottingham 15-1-83
Internationals: England U21.

1998–99	Notts Co	0	0		
1998–99	Arsenal	0	0		
1999–2000	Arsenal	0	0		
2000–01	Arsenal	0	0		
2001–02	Arsenal	9	2		
2002–03	Arsenal	5	3		
2002–03	*Watford*	12	0	21	2
2003–04	Arsenal	0	0		
2003–04	*Leeds U*	36	2	36	2
2004–05	Arsenal	7	0	12	3
2004–05	Birmingham C	12	0		
2005–06	Birmingham C	38	2	50	2
2006–07	Liverpool	34	1		
2007–08	Liverpool	18	2		
2008–09	Liverpool	3	0	55	3
2008–09	Portsmouth	13	0	13	0
2009–10	Zaragoza	25	0	25	0
2010–11	Stoke C	29	3		
2011–12	Stoke C	27	0		
2012–13	Stoke C	1	0		
2012–13	*Wolverhampton W*	15	0	15	0
2013–14	Stoke C	8	1	65	4
2014–15	Pune City	7	0	7	0
2014–15	Wigan Ath	13	3	13	3

PERCH, James (D) 336 16
H: 5 11 W: 11 05 b.Mansfield 29-9-85

2002–03	Nottingham F	0	0		
2003–04	Nottingham F	0	0		
2004–05	Nottingham F	22	0		
2005–06	Nottingham F	38	3		
2006–07	Nottingham F	46	5		
2007–08	Nottingham F	30	0		
2008–09	Nottingham F	37	3		
2009–10	Nottingham F	17	1	190	12
2010–11	Newcastle U	13	0		
2011–12	Newcastle U	25	0		
2012–13	Newcastle U	27	1	65	1
2013–14	Wigan Ath	40	0		
2014–15	Wigan Ath	41	3	81	3

POLLITT, Mike (G) 505 0
H: 6 4 W: 15 03 b.Farnworth 29-2-72

1990–91	Manchester U	0	0		
1990–91	*Oldham Ath*	0	0		
1991–92	Bury	0	0		
1992–93	Lincoln C	27	0		
1993–94	Lincoln C	30	0	57	0
1994–95	Darlington	40	0		
1995–96	Darlington	15	0	55	0
1995–96	Notts Co	0	0		
1996–97	Notts Co	8	0		
1997–98	Notts Co	2	0	10	0
1997–98	*Oldham Ath*	16	0	16	0
1997–98	*Gillingham*	6	0	6	0
1997–98	*Brentford*	5	0	5	0
1997–98	Sunderland	0	0		
1998–99	Rotherham U	46	0		
1999–2000	Rotherham U	46	0		
2000–01	*Chesterfield*	46	0	46	0
2001–02	Rotherham U	46	0		
2002–03	Rotherham U	41	0		
2003–04	Rotherham U	43	0		
2004–05	Rotherham U	45	0	267	0
2005–06	Wigan Ath	24	0		
2006–07	Wigan Ath	3	0		
2006–07	*Ipswich T*	1	0	1	0
2006–07	*Burnley*	4	0	4	0
2007–08	Wigan Ath	1	0		
2008–09	Wigan Ath	3	0		
2009–10	Wigan Ath	4	0		
2010–11	Wigan Ath	0	0		
2011–12	Wigan Ath	0	0		
2012–13	Wigan Ath	0	0		
2013–14	Wigan Ath	0	0		
2013–14	*Barnsley*	2	0	2	0
2014–15	Wigan Ath	0	0	36	0

POOLE, Declan (M) 0 0
H: 5 9 W: 10 10 b.Chester 5-9-95

2013–14	Wigan Ath	0	0		
2014–15	Wigan Ath	0	0		

RAMIS, Ivan (D) 240 13
H: 6 2 W: 12 11 b.Sa Pobla 25-10-84
Internationals: Spain U19, U21, U23.

2003–04	Mallorca	9	1		
2004–05	Mallorca	22	0		
2005–06	*Valladolid*	27	0	27	0
2006–07	Mallorca	7	0		
2007–08	Mallorca	14	3		
2008–09	Mallorca	19	0		
2009–10	Mallorca	26	0		
2010–11	Mallorca	33	3		
2011–12	Mallorca	34	2	164	9
2012–13	Wigan Ath	16	2		
2013–14	Wigan Ath	15	2		
2014–15	Wigan Ath	18	0	49	4

Transferred to Levante January 2015.

RIDGEWELL, Liam (D) 333 19
H: 5 10 W: 10 03 b.Bexley 21-7-84
Internationals: England U19, U20, U21.

2001–02	Aston Villa	0	0		
2002–03	Aston Villa	0	0		
2002–03	*Bournemouth*	5	0	5	0
2003–04	Aston Villa	11	0		
2004–05	Aston Villa	15	0		
2005–06	Aston Villa	32	5		
2006–07	Aston Villa	21	1	79	6
2007–08	Birmingham C	35	1		
2008–09	Birmingham C	36	1		
2009–10	Birmingham C	31	3		
2010–11	Birmingham C	36	4		
2011–12	Birmingham C	14	0	152	9
2011–12	WBA	13	1		
2012–13	WBA	30	0		
2013–14	WBA	33	1	76	2
2014	Portland Timbers	15	2	15	2
On loan from Portland Timbers.					
2014–15	Wigan Ath	6	0	6	0

RIERA, Oriol (F) 192 48
H: 6 1 W: 12 04 b.Vic 3-7-86

2009–10	Celta Vigo	5	0	5	0
2010–11	Cordoba	37	6	37	6
2011–12	Alcorcon	39	6		
2012–13	Alcorcon	40	18	79	24
2013–14	Osasuna	37	13	37	13
2014–15	Wigan Ath	13	1	13	1
2014–15	*La Coruna*	21	4	21	4

ROBLES, Louis (F) 1 0
b. 11-9-96

2014–15	Wigan Ath	1	0	1	0

TAVERNIER, James (D) 82 8
H: 5 9 W: 11 00 b.Bradford 31-10-91

2009–10	Newcastle U	0	0		
2010–11	Newcastle U	0	0		
2011–12	Newcastle U	0	0		
2011–12	*Carlisle U*	16	0	16	0
2011–12	*Sheffield W*	6	0	6	0
2011–12	*Milton Keynes D*	7	0	7	0
2012–13	Newcastle U	2	0		
2013–14	Newcastle U	0	0	2	0
2013–14	*Shrewsbury T*	1	0	1	0
2013–14	*Rotherham U*	27	5	27	5
2014–15	Wigan Ath	11	0	11	0
2014–15	*Bristol C*	12	3	12	3

TAYLOR, Andrew (D) 297 6
H: 5 10 W: 11 04 b.Hartlepool 1-8-86
Internationals: England U16, U17, U18, U19. U20, U21.

2003–04	Middlesbrough	0	0		
2004–05	Middlesbrough	0	0		
2005–06	Middlesbrough	13	0		
2005–06	*Bradford C*	24	0	24	0
2006–07	Middlesbrough	34	0		
2007–08	Middlesbrough	19	0		
2008–09	Middlesbrough	26	0		
2009–10	Middlesbrough	12	0		
2010–11	Middlesbrough	21	3	125	3
2010–11	*Watford*	19	1	19	1
2011–12	Cardiff C	42	1		
2012–13	Cardiff C	43	0		
2013–14	Cardiff C	18	0	103	1
2014–15	Wigan Ath	26	1	26	1

TAYLOR-SINCLAIR, Aaron (D) 160 9
H: 5 11 W: 11 07 b.Aberdeen 8-4-91

2008–09	Montrose	1	0		
2009–10	Montrose	30	2		
2010–11	Montrose	35	3	66	5
2011–12	Partick Thistle	30	1		
2012–13	Partick Thistle	28	1		
2013–14	Partick Thistle	36	2	94	4
2014–15	Wigan Ath	0	0		

WAGHORN, Martyn (F) 173 33
H: 5 9 W: 13 01 b.South Shields 23-1-90
Internationals: England U19, U21.

2007–08	Sunderland	3	0		
2008–09	Sunderland	1	0		
2008–09	*Charlton Ath*	7	1	7	1
2009–10	Sunderland	0	0		
2009–10	*Leicester C*	43	12		
2010–11	Sunderland	2	0	6	0
2010–11	Leicester C	30	4		
2011–12	Leicester C	4	1		
2011–12	*Hull C*	5	1	5	1
2012–13	Leicester C	24	3		
2013–14	Leicester C	2	0	103	20
2013–14	*Millwall*	14	3	14	3
2013–14	Wigan Ath	15	5		
2014–15	Wigan Ath	23	3	38	8

Players retained or with offer of contract
Hamilton, Matthew Lewis.

Scholars
Absalom, Kelland Ellis; Anson, Adam James;
Bannister, Lloyd Andrew; Barrigan, James
Patrick; Baxendale, Arnold Spencer; Burke,
Luke; Carey, Omar; Cosgrove, Sam
Benjamin; Evans, Owen Rhys; Foukamene,
Dieu Le Veut; Gregory, Joshua James;
Harrison, Sean Thomas; Lambert, Liam
James; Langford, Liam James; Lingard, Alex
Matthew; McNally, Reece Patrick; Purzycki,
Adrian Cyprian; Rimmer, Matthew Luke;
Robles, Louis Gabriel; Unsworth, Jordan
James.

WOLVERHAMPTON W (89)

AFOBE, Benik (F) 111 32
H: 5 10 W: 11 00 b.Leyton 12-2-93
Internationals: England U16, U17, U19, U21.

2009–10	Arsenal	0	0		
2010–11	Arsenal	0	0		
2010–11	*Huddersfield T*	28	5	28	5
2011–12	Arsenal	0	0		
2011–12	*Reading*	3	0	3	0
2012–13	Arsenal	0	0		
2012–13	*Bolton W*	20	2	20	2
2012–13	*Millwall*	5	0	5	0
2013–14	Arsenal	0	0		
2013–14	*Sheffield W*	12	2	12	2
2014–15	Arsenal	0	0		
2014–15	*Milton Keynes D*	22	10	22	10
2014–15	Wolverhampton W	21	13	21	13

BANCESSI, Eusebio (M) 4 0
b. 4-8-95

2014–15	Wolverhampton W	0	0		
2014–15	Wolverhampton W	0	0		
2014–15	*Cheltenham T*	4	0	4	0

BATTH, Danny (D) 174 10
H: 6 3 W: 13 05 b.Brierley Hill 21-9-90

2009–10	Wolverhampton W	0	0		
2009–10	*Colchester U*	17	1	17	1
2010–11	Wolverhampton W	0	0		
2010–11	*Sheffield U*	1	0	1	0
2010–11	*Sheffield W*	10	0		
2011–12	Wolverhampton W	0	0		
2011–12	*Sheffield W*	44	2	54	2
2012–13	Wolverhampton W	12	1		
2013–14	Wolverhampton W	46	2		
2014–15	Wolverhampton W	44	4	102	7

BOUKARI, Razak (M) 209 27
H: 6 0 W: 10 13 b.Lome 25-4-87
Internationals: France U21. Togo Full caps.

2004–05	Chateauroux	5	5		
2005–06	Chateauroux	35	3	40	8
2006–07	Lens	29	0		
2007–08	Lens	18	0		
2008–09	Lens	26	4		
2009–10	Lens	27	4		
2010–11	Lens	14	4	117	12
2010–11	*Rennes*	18	4		
2011–12	Rennes	20	3	38	7
2012–13	Wolverhampton W	4	0		
2013–14	*Sochaux*	10	0	10	0
2014–15	Wolverhampton W	0	0	4	0

CARTER, Ashley (D) 2 0
b. 12-9-95

2014–15	Wolverhampton W	0	0		
2014–15	*Chesterfield*	0	0	2	0

CASSIDY, Jake (F) — 108 20
H: 5 10 W: 11 02 b.Glan Conwy 9-2-93
Internationals: Wales U19, U21.

Season	Club	A	G	Tot A	Tot G
2010–11	Wolverhampton W	0	0		
2011–12	Wolverhampton W	0	0		
2011–12	Tranmere R	10	5		
2012–13	Wolverhampton W	6	0		
2012–13	Tranmere R	26	11		
2013–14	Wolverhampton W	14	0		
2013–14	Tranmere R	19	1		
2014–15	Wolverhampton W	0	0	20	0
2014–15	Tranmere R	0	0	55	17
2014–15	Notts Co	16	3	16	3
2014–15	Southend U	17	0	17	0

CLARKE, Leon (F) — 323 91
H: 6 2 W: 14 02 b.Birmingham 10-2-85

Season	Club	A	G	Tot A	Tot G
2003–04	Wolverhampton W	0	0		
2003–04	Kidderminster H	4	0	4	0
2004–05	Wolverhampton W	28	7		
2005–06	Wolverhampton W	24	1		
2005–06	QPR	1	0		
2005–06	Plymouth Arg	5	0	5	0
2006–07	Wolverhampton W	22	5		
2006–07	Sheffield W	10	1		
2006–07	Oldham Ath	5	3	5	3
2007–08	Sheffield W	8	3		
2007–08	Southend U	16	8	16	8
2008–09	Sheffield W	29	8		
2009–10	Sheffield W	36	6	83	18
2010–11	QPR	13	0	14	0
2010–11	Preston NE	6	1	6	1
2011–12	Swindon T	2	0	2	0
2011–12	Chesterfield	14	9	14	9
2011–12	Charlton Ath	7	0		
2011–12	Crawley T	4	1	4	1
2012–13	Charlton Ath	0	0	7	0
2012–13	Scunthorpe U	15	11	15	11
2012–13	Coventry C	12	8		
2013–14	Coventry C	23	15	35	23
2013–14	Wolverhampton W	13	1		
2014–15	Wolverhampton W	16	2	103	16
2014–15	Wigan Ath	10	1	10	1

DICKO, Nouha (M) — 142 53
H: 5 8 W: 11 00 b.Paris 14-5-92
Internationals: Mali Full caps.

Season	Club	A	G	Tot A	Tot G
2009–10	Strasbourg B	18	4		
2010–11	Strasbourg B	24	8	42	12
2010–11	Strasbourg	3	0	3	0
2011–12	Wigan Ath	0	0		
2011–12	Blackpool	10	4		
2012–13	Wigan Ath	0	0		
2012–13	Blackpool	22	5	32	9
2012–13	Wolverhampton W	4	1		
2013–14	Wigan Ath	0	0		
2013–14	Rotherham U	5	5	5	5
2013–14	Wolverhampton W	19	12		
2014–15	Wolverhampton W	37	14	60	27

DOHERTY, Matthew (M) — 95 5
H: 6 0 W: 12 08 b.Dublin 17-1-92
Internationals: Republic of Ireland U19, U21.

Season	Club	A	G	Tot A	Tot G
2010–11	Wolverhampton W	0	0		
2011–12	Wolverhampton W	1	0		
2011–12	Hibernian	13	2	13	2
2012–13	Wolverhampton W	13	1		
2012–13	Bury	17	1	17	1
2013–14	Wolverhampton W	18	1		
2014–15	Wolverhampton W	33	0	65	2

DOYLE, Kevin (F) — 373 107
H: 5 11 W: 12 06 b.Adamstown 18-9-83
Internationals: Republic of Ireland U21, Full caps.

Season	Club	A	G	Tot A	Tot G
2004	Cork C	32	13		
2005	Cork C	11	7	43	20
2005–06	Reading	45	18		
2006–07	Reading	32	13		
2007–08	Reading	36	6		
2008–09	Reading	41	18	154	55
2009–10	Wolverhampton W	34	9		
2010–11	Wolverhampton W	26	5		
2011–12	Wolverhampton W	33	4		
2012–13	Wolverhampton W	42	9		
2013–14	Wolverhampton W	23	3		
2013–14	QPR	9	2	9	2
2014–15	Wolverhampton W	6	0	164	30
2014–15	Crystal Palace	3	0	3	0

Transferred to Colorado Rapids May 2015.

DUTTON, Scott (G) — 0 0
b.Coventry 27-10-95

Season	Club	A	G	Tot A	Tot G
2014–15	Wolverhampton W	0	0		
2014–15	Crawley T	0	0		

EBANKS-LANDELL, Ethan (M) — 45 4
H: 5 6 W: 11 02 b.Oldbury 16-12-92

Season	Club	A	G	Tot A	Tot G
2009–10	Wolverhampton W	0	0		
2010–11	Wolverhampton W	0	0		
2011–12	Wolverhampton W	0	0		
2012–13	Wolverhampton W	0	0		
2012–13	Bury	24	0	24	0
2013–14	Wolverhampton W	7	2		
2014–15	Wolverhampton W	14	2	21	4

EDWARDS, Dave (M) — 332 42
H: 5 11 W: 11 04 b.Shrewsbury 3-2-86
Internationals: Wales U21, Full caps.

Season	Club	A	G	Tot A	Tot G
2002–03	Shrewsbury T	1	0		
2003–04	Shrewsbury T	0	0		
2004–05	Shrewsbury T	27	5		
2005–06	Shrewsbury T	30	2		
2006–07	Shrewsbury T	45	5	103	12
2007–08	Luton T	19	4	19	4
2007–08	Wolverhampton W	10	1		
2008–09	Wolverhampton W	44	3		
2009–10	Wolverhampton W	20	1		
2010–11	Wolverhampton W	15	1		
2011–12	Wolverhampton W	26	3		
2012–13	Wolverhampton W	24	2		
2013–14	Wolverhampton W	30	9		
2014–15	Wolverhampton W	41	6	210	26

ERDEI, Carlo (M) — 0 0
b.Satu Mare 22-3-96
Internationals: Romania U17.

Season	Club	A	G	Tot A	Tot G
2013–14	Wolverhampton W	0	0		
2014–15	Wolverhampton W	0	0		

EVANS, Lee (M) — 44 3
H: 6 1 W: 13 12 b.Newport 24-7-94
Internationals: Wales U21.

Season	Club	A	G	Tot A	Tot G
2012–13	Wolverhampton W	0	0		
2013–14	Wolverhampton W	26	2		
2014–15	Wolverhampton W	18	1	44	3

FLATT, Jonathan (G) — 0 0
H: 6 1 W: 13 12 b.Wolverhampton 12-9-94

Season	Club	A	G	Tot A	Tot G
2013–14	Wolverhampton W	0	0		
2014–15	Wolverhampton W	0	0		
2014–15	Chesterfield	0	0		

FOLEY, Kevin (D) — 354 8
H: 5 9 W: 11 11 b.Luton 1-11-84
Internationals: Republic of Ireland U21, B, Full caps.

Season	Club	A	G	Tot A	Tot G
2002–03	Luton T	2	0		
2003–04	Luton T	33	1		
2004–05	Luton T	39	2		
2005–06	Luton T	38	0		
2006–07	Luton T	39	0	151	3
2007–08	Wolverhampton W	44	1		
2008–09	Wolverhampton W	45	1		
2009–10	Wolverhampton W	25	0		
2010–11	Wolverhampton W	33	2		
2011–12	Wolverhampton W	16	0		
2012–13	Wolverhampton W	26	0		
2013–14	Wolverhampton W	5	1		
2013–14	Blackpool	5	0		
2014–15	Wolverhampton W	0	0	194	5
2014–15	Blackpool	4	0	9	0

Transferred to FC Copenhagen January 2015.

GOLBOURNE, Scott (D) — 281 6
H: 5 8 W: 11 08 b.Bristol 29-2-88
Internationals: England U17, U19

Season	Club	A	G	Tot A	Tot G
2004–05	Bristol C	9	0		
2005–06	Bristol C	5	0	14	0
2005–06	Reading	1	0		
2006–07	Reading	0	0		
2006–07	Wycombe W	34	1	34	1
2007–08	Reading	1	0		
2007–08	Bournemouth	5	0	5	0
2008–09	Reading	0	0	2	0
2008–09	Oldham Ath	8	0	8	0
2009–10	Exeter C	34	0		
2010–11	Exeter C	44	2		
2011–12	Exeter C	26	0	104	2
2011–12	Barnsley	12	1		
2012–13	Barnsley	31	1		
2013–14	Barnsley	4	0	47	2
2014–15	Wolverhampton W	27	0	67	1

GRAHAM, Jordan (M) — 3 0
H: 6 0 W: 10 10 b.Coventry 5-3-95
Internationals: England U16, U17.

Season	Club	A	G	Tot A	Tot G
2011–12	Aston Villa	0	0		
2012–13	Aston Villa	0	0		
2013–14	Aston Villa	0	0		
2013–14	Ipswich T	2	0	2	0
2013–14	Bradford C	1	0	1	0
2014–15	Wolverhampton W	0	0		

HAUSE, Kortney (D) — 54 3
H: 6 2 W: 13 03 b.Goodmayes 16-7-95
Internationals: England U20.

Season	Club	A	G	Tot A	Tot G
2012–13	Wycombe W	9	1		
2013–14	Wycombe W	14	1	23	2
2013–14	Wolverhampton W	0	0		
2014–15	Wolverhampton W	17	0	17	0
2014–15	Gillingham	14	1	14	1

HENRY, James (M) — 240 37
H: 6 1 W: 11 11 b.Reading 10-6-89
Internationals: Scotland U16, U19. England U18, U19.

Season	Club	A	G	Tot A	Tot G
2006–07	Reading	0	0		
2006–07	Nottingham F	1	0	1	0
2007–08	Reading	0	0		
2007–08	Bournemouth	11	4	11	4
2007–08	Norwich C	3	0	3	0
2008–09	Reading	7	0		
2008–09	Millwall	16	3		
2009–10	Reading	3	0	10	0
2009–10	Millwall	9	5		
2010–11	Millwall	42	5		
2011–12	Millwall	39	0		
2012–13	Millwall	35	5		
2013–14	Millwall	5	0	146	18
2013–14	Wolverhampton W	32	10		
2014–15	Wolverhampton W	37	5	69	15

HUNTE, Connor (M) — 0 0
b. 12-9-96
Internationals: England U16, U17.

Season	Club	A	G	Tot A	Tot G
2014–15	Wolverhampton W	0	0		

IKEME, Carl (G) — 188 0
H: 6 2 W: 13 09 b.Sutton Coldfield 8-6-86

Season	Club	A	G	Tot A	Tot G
2005–06	Wolverhampton W	0	0		
2005–06	Stockport Co	9	0	9	0
2006–07	Wolverhampton W	1	0		
2007–08	Wolverhampton W	0	0		
2008–09	Wolverhampton W	12	0		
2009–10	Wolverhampton W	0	0		
2009–10	Charlton Ath	4	0	4	0
2009–10	Sheffield U	2	0	2	0
2009–10	QPR	17	0	17	0
2010–11	Wolverhampton W	0	0		
2010–11	Leicester C	5	0	5	0
2011–12	Wolverhampton W	1	0		
2011–12	Middlesbrough	10	0	10	0
2011–12	Doncaster R	15	0	15	0
2012–13	Wolverhampton W	38	0		
2013–14	Wolverhampton W	41	0		
2014–15	Wolverhampton W	33	0	126	0

IORFA, Dominic (D) — 27 0
H: 6 2 W: 12 04 b.Southend-on-Sea 24-6-95
Internationals: England U18, U20.

Season	Club	A	G	Tot A	Tot G
2013–14	Wolverhampton W	0	0		
2013–14	Shrewsbury T	7	0	7	0
2014–15	Wolverhampton W	20	0	20	0

ISMAIL, Zeli (M) — 45 7
H: 5 8 W: 11 12 b.Kukes 12-12-93
Internationals: England U16, U17.

Season	Club	A	G	Tot A	Tot G
2010–11	Wolverhampton W	0	0		
2011–12	Wolverhampton W	0	0		
2012–13	Wolverhampton W	0	0		
2012–13	Milton Keynes D	7	0	7	0
2013–14	Wolverhampton W	9	0		
2013–14	Burton Alb	15	3	15	3
2014–15	Wolverhampton W	0	0	9	0
2014–15	Notts Co	14	4	14	4

JACOBS, Michael (M) — 175 22
H: 5 9 W: 11 08 b.Rothwell 23-3-92

Season	Club	A	G	Tot A	Tot G
2009–10	Northampton T	0	0		
2010–11	Northampton T	41	5		
2011–12	Northampton T	46	6	87	11
2012–13	Derby Co	38	2		
2013–14	Derby Co	3	0	41	2
2013–14	Wolverhampton W	30	8		
2014–15	Wolverhampton W	12	0	42	8
2014–15	Blackpool	5	1	5	1

KEITA, Ibrahim (F) — 0 0
b. 18-1-96
Internationals: France U16.

Season	Club	A	G	Tot A	Tot G
2013–14	Wolverhampton W	0	0		
2014–15	Wolverhampton W	0	0		

KELLERMANN, James (M) — 0 0
b. 10-11-97

Season	Club	A	G	Tot A	Tot G
2013–14	Wolverhampton W	0	0		
2014–15	Wolverhampton W	0	0		

KUSZCZAK, Tomasz (G) 173 0
H: 6 3 W: 13 03 b.Krosno Odrzansia
20-3-82
Internationals: Poland U16, U18, U21, Full caps.

2001–02	Hertha Berlin	0	0		
2002–03	Hertha Berlin	0	0		
2003–04	Hertha Berlin	0	0		
2004–05	WBA	3	0		
2005–06	WBA	28	0		
2006–07	WBA	0	0	31	0
2006–07	Manchester U	6	0		
2007–08	Manchester U	9	0		
2008–09	Manchester U	4	0		
2009–10	Manchester U	8	0		
2010–11	Manchester U	5	0		
2011–12	Manchester U	0	0	32	0
2011–12	Watford	13	0	13	0
2012–13	Brighton & HA	43	0		
2013–14	Brighton & HA	41	0	84	0
2014–15	Wolverhampton W	13	0	13	0

LEACOCK-McLEOD, Mekhi (M) 0 0
b. 15-9-96

2014–15	Wolverhampton W	0	0

MARGREITTER, Georg (D) 110 5
H: 6 1 W: 12 09 b.Schruns 7-11-88
Internationals: Austria U19, U20, U21.

2007–08	LASK Linz	7	0		
2009–10	LASK Linz	19	2	26	2
2010–11	FK Austria	25	1		
2011–12	FK Austria	29	1		
2012–13	FK Austria	3	0	57	2
2012–13	Wolverhampton W	1	0		
2013–14	Wolverhampton W	0	0		
2013–14	FC Copenhagen	13	0	13	0
2014–15	Wolverhampton W	0	0	1	0
2014–15	Chesterfield	13	1	13	1

McALINDEN, Liam (F) 42 8
H: 6 1 W: 11 10 b.Cannock 26-9-93
Internationals: Northern Ireland U21.
Republic of Ireland U21.

2010–11	Wolverhampton W	0	0		
2011–12	Wolverhampton W	0	0		
2012–13	Wolverhampton W	1	0		
2013–14	Wolverhampton W	7	1		
2013–14	Shrewsbury T	9	3	9	3
2014–15	Wolverhampton W	6	0	14	1
2014–15	Fleetwood T	19	4	19	4

McCAREY, Aaron (G) 24 0
H: 6 1 W: 11 09 b.Monaghan 14-1-92
Internationals: Republic of Ireland U17, U18,
U19, U21.

2009–10	Wolverhampton W	0	0		
2010–11	Wolverhampton W	0	0		
2011–12	Wolverhampton W	0	0		
2012–13	Wolverhampton W	0	0		
2012–13	Walsall	14	0	14	0
2013–14	Wolverhampton W	5	0		
2013–14	York C	5	0	5	0
2014–15	Wolverhampton W	0	0	5	0

McDONALD, Kevin (M) 322 27
H: 6 2 W: 13 03 b.Carnoustie 4-11-88
Internationals: Scotland U19, U21.

2005–06	Dundee	26	3		
2006–07	Dundee	31	2		
2007–08	Dundee	34	9	91	14
2008–09	Burnley	25	1		
2009–10	Burnley	26	1		
2010–11	Burnley	0	0	51	2
2010–11	Scunthorpe U	5	1	5	1
2011–12	Notts Co	11	0	11	0
2011–12	Sheffield U	31	3		
2012–13	Sheffield U	45	1		
2013–14	Sheffield U	1	1	77	5
2013–14	Wolverhampton W	41	5		
2014–15	Wolverhampton W	46	0	87	5

O'HANLON, Ben (D) 0 0
b. 22-2-96
Internationals: England U16, U17.

2014–15	Wolverhampton W	0	0

PRICE, Jack (M) 60 1
H: 6 3 W: 13 10 b.Shrewsbury 19-12-92

2011–12	Wolverhampton W	0	0		
2012–13	Wolverhampton W	0	0		
2013–14	Wolverhampton W	26	0		
2014–15	Wolverhampton W	23	1	49	1
2014–15	Yeovil T	6	0	6	0
2014–15	Leyton Orient	5	0	5	0

REID, Bradley (F) 0 0
b. 15-10-95
Internationals: Wales U19, U21.

2013–14	Wolverhampton W	0	0
2014–15	Wolverhampton W	0	0

RICKETTS, Sam (D) 397 6
H: 6 1 W: 12 01 b.Aylesbury 11-10-81
Internationals: England C. Wales Full caps.

1999–2000	Oxford U	0	0		
2000–01	Oxford U	14	0		
2001–02	Oxford U	29	1		
2002–03	Oxford U	2	0	45	1
From Telford U					
2004–05	Swansea C	42	0		
2005–06	Swansea C	44	1	86	1
2006–07	Hull C	40	1		
2007–08	Hull C	44	0		
2008–09	Hull C	29	0		
2009–10	Hull C	0	0	113	1
2009–10	Bolton W	27	0		
2010–11	Bolton W	17	0		
2011–12	Bolton W	20	1		
2012–13	Bolton W	32	0	96	1
2013–14	Wolverhampton W	44	2		
2014–15	Wolverhampton W	4	0	48	2
2014–15	Swindon T	9	0	9	0

ROWE, Tommy (M) 261 36
H: 5 11 W: 12 11 b.Manchester 1-5-89

2006–07	Stockport Co	4	0		
2007–08	Stockport Co	24	6		
2008–09	Stockport Co	44	7	72	13
2008–09	Peterborough U	0	0		
2009–10	Peterborough U	32	2		
2010–11	Peterborough U	35	5		
2011–12	Peterborough U	43	4		
2012–13	Peterborough U	31	5		
2013–14	Peterborough U	34	7	175	23
2014–15	Wolverhampton W	14	0	14	0

SAKO, Bakary (M) 288 59
H: 5 11 W: 11 12 b.Ivry Sur Seine 26-4-88
Internationals: France U21. Mali U17, Full
caps.

2006–07	Chateauroux	17	0		
2007–08	Chateauroux	12	1		
2008–09	Chateauroux	35	9	64	10
2009–10	St Etienne	30	1		
2010–11	St Etienne	38	7		
2011–12	St Etienne	36	5		
2012–13	St Etienne	2	0	106	13
2012–13	Wolverhampton W	37	9		
2013–14	Wolverhampton W	40	12		
2014–15	Wolverhampton W	41	15	118	36

SAVILLE, George (M) 57 4
H: 5 9 W: 11 07 b.Camberley 1-6-93

2010–11	Chelsea	0	0		
2011–12	Chelsea	0	0		
2012–13	Chelsea	0	0		
2012–13	Millwall	3	0	3	0
2013–14	Chelsea	0	0		
2013–14	Brentford	40	3	40	3
2014–15	Wolverhampton W	7	0	7	0
2014–15	Bristol C	7	1	7	1

SIGURDARSON, Bjorn (F) 154 28
H: 6 1 W: 12 09 b.Akranes 26-12-91
Internationals: Iceland U17, U19, U21, Full
caps.

2008–09	Lillestrom	5	0		
2009–10	Lillestrom	19	4		
2010–11	Lillestrom	22	4		
2011–12	Lillestrom	24	9	70	17
2012–13	Wolverhampton W	37	5		
2013–14	Wolverhampton W	18	2		
2014–15	Wolverhampton W	0	0	55	7
2014–15	Molde	15	3	15	3
2014–15	Copenhagen	14	1	14	1

STEARMAN, Richard (D) 339 12
H: 6 2 W: 10 08 b.Wolverhampton 19-8-87
Internationals: England U16, U17, U19, U21.

2004–05	Leicester C	8	1		
2005–06	Leicester C	34	3		
2006–07	Leicester C	35	1		
2007–08	Leicester C	39	2	116	7
2008–09	Wolverhampton W	37	1		
2009–10	Wolverhampton W	16	1		
2010–11	Wolverhampton W	31	0		
2011–12	Wolverhampton W	30	0		
2012–13	Wolverhampton W	12	1		
2012–13	Ipswich T	15	0	15	0
2013–14	Wolverhampton W	40	2		
2014–15	Wolverhampton W	42	0	208	5

SWANN, George (D) 0 0
H: 6 3 b.Plymouth 10-9-91

2012–13	Manchester C	0	0
2013–14	Manchester C	0	0
2013–14	Sheffield W	0	0
2014–15	Wolverhampton W	0	0

TORRAS, Albert (M) 0 0
b. 13-6-96

2013–14	Wolverhampton W	0	0
2014–15	Wolverhampton W	0	0

VAN LA PARRA, Rajiv (M) 142 16
H: 5 11 W: 11 05 b.Rotterdam 4-6-91
Internationals: Netherlands, U17, U19, U21.

2008–09	Caan	2	0		
2009–10	Caan	8	1		
2010–11	Caan	6	0	16	1
2011–12	Heerenveen	23	4		
2012–13	Heerenveen	31	5		
2013–14	Heerenveen	32	5	86	14
2014–15	Wolverhampton W	40	1	40	1

WEEKS, Declan (M) 0 0
b. 15-11-95
Internationals: Wales U19.

2014–15	Wolverhampton W	0	0

WILSON, Donovan (F) 0 0
b.Yate 14-3-97

2014–15	Wolverhampton W	0	0

Players retained or with offer of contract
Breslin, Anthony Patrick; Devers, Jesse
James; Div-Keita, Ibrahim; Harris, Callum
Lee; Ortega, Alcana Jordi; Rainey, Ryan
Gavin; Ronan, Connor Patrick; Simpson,
Aaron.

Scholars
Bills, Rhys Mason; Burgoyne, Harry James;
Carnat, Nicolae; Delacoe, Joseph Dennis
Leigh; Enobakhare, Bright; Finnie, Ross
Steven; Hayden, Aaron Edward-George;
Johnson, Connor William; Leak, Ryan David;
Levingston, Conor Thomas; Lindsey, Bradley
Carl; Matinyadze, Tendai Regis; Oaida,
Razvan Constantin; Upton, Regan David.

WYCOMBE W (90)

AMADI-HOLLOWAY, Aaron (D) 33 3
H: 6 2 W: 13 00 b.Newark 21-2-93
Internationals: Wales U17, U19.

2012–13	Bristol C	0	0		
2013–14	Bristol C	0	0		
2013–14	Newport Co	4	0	4	0
2014–15	Wycombe W	29	3	29	3

BEAN, Marcus (M) 355 25
H: 5 11 W: 11 06 b.Hammersmith 2-11-84
Internationals: Jamaica Full caps.

2002–03	QPR	7	0		
2003–04	QPR	31	1		
2004–05	QPR	20	1		
2004–05	Swansea C	8	0		
2005–06	QPR	9	0	67	2
2005–06	Swansea C	9	1	17	1
2005–06	Blackpool	17	1		
2006–07	Blackpool	6	0		
2007–08	Blackpool	0	0	23	1
2007–08	Rotherham U	12	1	12	1
2008–09	Brentford	44	9		
2009–10	Brentford	31	0		
2010–11	Brentford	37	3		
2011–12	Brentford	32	2	144	14
2012–13	Colchester U	31	0		
2013–14	Colchester U	35	5		
2014–15	Colchester U	3	0	69	5
2014–15	Portsmouth	6	1	6	1
2014–15	Wycombe W	17	0	17	0

BLOOMFIELD, Matt (M) 319 25
H: 5 9 W: 11 00 b.Felixstowe 8-2-84
Internationals: England U16, U17.

2001–02	Ipswich T	0	0		
2002–03	Ipswich T	0	0		
2003–04	Ipswich T	0	0		
2003–04	Wycombe W	12	1		
2004–05	Wycombe W	26	2		
2005–06	Wycombe W	39	5		
2006–07	Wycombe W	41	4		
2007–08	Wycombe W	35	4		
2008–09	Wycombe W	20	0		
2009–10	Wycombe W	14	2		
2010–11	Wycombe W	34	3		
2011–12	Wycombe W	31	2		
2012–13	Wycombe W	2	1		
2013–14	Wycombe W	32	0		
2014–15	Wycombe W	33	1	319	25

BULL, Nikki (G) 137 0
H: 6 2 W: 12 08 b.Hastings 2-10-81
Internationals: England C.
1999–2000	QPR	0	0		
2000–01	QPR	0	0		
2001–02	QPR	0	0		
2008–09	Aldershot T	30	0	30	0
2009–10	Brentford	6	0	6	0
2010–11	Wycombe W	46	0		
2011–12	Wycombe W	46	0		
2012–13	Wycombe W	9	0		
2013–14	Wycombe W	0	0		
2014–15	Wycombe W	0	0	101	0

CRAIG, Steven (F) 112 13
H: 5 11 W: 12 02 b.Preston 5-2-81
2002–03	Motherwell	13	2		
2003–04	Motherwell	24	3	37	5
2004–05	Aberdeen	14	2		
2005–06	Aberdeen	3	0	17	2

From Dundee, Livingston, Ross Co, Partick Thistle
2013–14	Wycombe W	27	4		
2014–15	Wycombe W	31	2	58	6

EPHRAIM, Hogan (F) 175 11
H: 5 9 W: 10 06 b.Islington 31-3-88
Internationals: England U16, U17, U18, U19.
2004–05	West Ham U	0	0		
2005–06	West Ham U	0	0		
2006–07	West Ham U	0	0		
2006–07	Colchester U	21	1	21	1
2007–08	West Ham U	0	0		
2007–08	QPR	29	3		
2008–09	QPR	27	1		
2009–10	QPR	22	0		
2009–10	Leeds U	3	0	3	0
2010–11	QPR	28	3		
2011–12	QPR	2	0		
2011–12	Charlton Ath	5	1	5	1
2011–12	Bristol C	5	1	5	1
2012–13	QPR	0	0		
2012–13	Toronto FC	11	0	11	0
2013–14	QPR	0	0	108	7
2013–14	Peterborough U	8	0	8	0
2014–15	Wycombe W	14	1	14	1

EVANS, Nathan (M) 0 0
H: 5 7 W: 10 03 b.Middlesbrough 9-7-94
2014–15	Wycombe W	0	0		

FLETCHER, Tommy (F) 0 0
H: 6 0 W: 12 00 b.Hoddesdon 1-8-95
2013–14	Wycombe W	0	0		
2014–15	Wycombe W	0	0		

HAYES, Paul (F) 457 107
H: 6 0 W: 12 12 b.Dagenham 20-9-83
2002–03	Scunthorpe U	18	8		
2003–04	Scunthorpe U	35	2		
2004–05	Scunthorpe U	46	18		
2005–06	Barnsley	45	6		
2006–07	Barnsley	30	5		
2006–07	Huddersfield T	4	1	4	1
2007–08	Scunthorpe U	40	8		
2008–09	Scunthorpe U	44	17		
2009–10	Scunthorpe U	45	9		
2010–11	Preston NE	23	2	23	2
2010–11	Barnsley	7	0	82	11
2011–12	Charlton Ath	19	3	19	3
2011–12	Wycombe W	6	6		
2012–13	Brentford	23	4		
2012–13	Crawley T	11	2	11	2
2013–14	Brentford	0	0	23	4
2013–14	Plymouth Arg	6	0	6	0
2013–14	Scunthorpe U	16	4	244	66
2014–15	Wycombe W	39	12	45	18

HORLOCK, Charlie (G) 0 0
H: 6 1 W: 12 06 b. 23-3-95
2012–13	Stevenage	0	0		
2013–14	Wycombe W	0	0		
2014–15	Wycombe W	0	0		

INGRAM, Matt (G) 100 0
H: 6 3 W: 12 13 b.Croydon 18-12-93
2011–12	Wycombe W	0	0		
2012–13	Wycombe W	8	0		
2013–14	Wycombe W	46	0		
2014–15	Wycombe W	46	0	100	0

JACOBSON, Joe (D) 274 14
H: 5 11 W: 12 06 b.Cardiff 17-11-86
Internationals: Wales U21.
2005–06	Cardiff C	1	0		
2006–07	Cardiff C	0	0	1	0
2006–07	Accrington S	6	1		
2006–07	Bristol R	11	0		
2007–08	Bristol R	40	1		
2008–09	Bristol R	22	0	73	1
2009–10	Oldham Ath	15	0		
2010–11	Oldham Ath	1	0	16	0
2010–11	Accrington S	26	2	32	3
2011–12	Shrewsbury T	39	1		
2012–13	Shrewsbury T	30	2		
2013–14	Shrewsbury T	41	4	110	7
2014–15	Wycombe W	42	3	42	3

JOMBATI, Sido (D) 151 4
H: 6 0 W: 11 11 b.Lisbon 20-8-87
2011–12	Cheltenham T	36	2		
2012–13	Cheltenham T	37	1		
2013–14	Cheltenham T	43	1	116	4
2014–15	Wycombe W	35	0	35	0

KRETZSCHMAR, Max (M) 51 6
H: 5 9 W: 11 03 b.Kingston upon Thames 12-10-93
2011–12	Wycombe W	0	0		
2012–13	Wycombe W	0	0		
2013–14	Wycombe W	35	6		
2014–15	Wycombe W	16	0	51	6

LEWIS, Stuart (M) 217 9
H: 5 10 W: 11 06 b.Welwyn 15-10-87
Internationals: England C, U16, U17.
2005–06	Tottenham H	0	0		
2006–07	Tottenham H	0	0		
2006–07	Barnet	4	0	4	0

From Stevenage B.
2007–08	Gillingham	10	0		
2008–09	Gillingham	21	0		
2009–10	Gillingham	20	1	51	1
2010–11	Dagenham & R	10	0	10	0
2010–11	Wycombe W	25	2		
2011–12	Wycombe W	41	1		
2012–13	Wycombe W	44	2		
2013–14	Wycombe W	36	3		
2014–15	Wycombe W	6	0	152	8

LYNCH, Alex (G) 1 0
H: 5 11 W: 9 08 b.Holyhead 4-4-95
Internationals: Wales U17.
2013–14	Peterborough U	0	0		
2014–15	Wycombe W	1	0	1	0

McCLURE, Matt (F) 110 24
H: 5 10 W: 11 00 b.Slough 17-11-91
Internationals: Northern Ireland U19, U21.
2010–11	Wycombe W	8	0		
2011–12	Wycombe W	12	1		
2012–13	Wycombe W	27	11		
2013–14	Wycombe W	36	7		
2014–15	Wycombe W	27	5	110	24

MURPHY, Peter (D) 197 25
H: 6 0 W: 11 10 b.Liverpool 13-2-90
2007–08	Accrington S	2	0		
2008–09	Accrington S	3	0		
2009–10	Accrington S	10	0		
2010–11	Accrington S	13	0		
2011–12	Accrington S	38	4		
2012–13	Accrington S	45	5		
2013–14	Accrington S	44	9	155	18
2014–15	Wycombe W	42	7	42	7

PIERRE, Aaron (D) 50 5
H: 6 1 W: 13 12 b.Southall 17-2-93
2011–12	Brentford	0	0		
2012–13	Brentford	0	0		
2013–14	Brentford	0	0		
2013–14	Wycombe W	8	1		
2014–15	Wycombe W	42	4	50	5

SAUNDERS, Sam (M) 210 39
H: 5 6 W: 11 04 b.Erith 29-8-83
2007–08	Dagenham & R	22	0		
2008–09	Dagenham & R	40	14	62	14
2009–10	Brentford	26	1		
2010–11	Brentford	21	2		
2011–12	Brentford	37	10		
2012–13	Brentford	31	3		
2013–14	Brentford	17	5		
2014–15	Brentford	5	0	137	23
2014–15	Wycombe W	11	2	11	2

SENIOR, Courtney (F) 1 0
b. 30-6-97
2014–15	Wycombe W	1	0	1	0

WOOD, Sam (M) 256 15
H: 6 0 W: 11 05 b.Sidcup 9-8-86
2008–09	Brentford	40	1		
2009–10	Brentford	43	2		
2010–11	Brentford	20	1		
2011–12	Brentford	5	0	108	4
2011–12	Rotherham U	26	1	26	1
2012–13	Wycombe W	35	3		
2013–14	Wycombe W	43	2		
2014–15	Wycombe W	44	5	122	10

YENNARIS, Nico (D) 26 1
H: 5 7 W: 10 03 b.Leytonstone 23-5-93
Internationals: England U17, U18, U19.
2010–11	Arsenal	0	0		
2011–12	Arsenal	1	0		
2011–12	Notts Co	2	0	2	0
2012–13	Arsenal	0	0		
2013–14	Arsenal	0	0	1	0
2013–14	Bournemouth	0	0		
2013–14	Brentford	8	0		
2014–15	Brentford	1	0	9	0
2014–15	Wycombe W	14	1	14	1

Non-Contract
Ainsworth, Gareth; Richardson, Barry.

YEOVIL T (91)

BELL, Fergus (M) 78 6
H: 6 0 W: 12 04 b.Wandsworth 25-1-91
2007–08	Hibernian	0	0		
2008–09	Hibernian	0	0		
2009–10	Hibernian	0	0		
2010–11	Jerez Industrial	26	5	26	5
2012–13	Mechelon	3	0	3	0
2013–14	Heist	29	0	29	0
2013–14	Monza	2	0	2	0
2014–15	Mansfield T	16	1	16	1
2014–15	Yeovil T	2	0	2	0

BERRETT, James (M) 233 26
H: 5 10 W: 10 13 b.Halifax 13-1-89
Internationals: Republic of Ireland U18, U19, U21.
2006–07	Huddersfield T	2	0		
2007–08	Huddersfield T	15	1		
2008–09	Huddersfield T	9	1		
2009–10	Huddersfield T	9	0	35	2
2010–11	Carlisle U	46	10		
2011–12	Carlisle U	42	9		
2012–13	Carlisle U	42	2		
2013–14	Carlisle U	40	2	170	23
2014–15	Yeovil T	28	1	28	1

BROOKS, Calvin (D) 0 0
H: 6 1 W: 12 04 b.Dortmund 1-6-94
2014–15	Yeovil T	0	0		

DAVIS, Liam (M) 199 12
H: 5 9 W: 11 07 b.Wandsworth 23-11-86
2005–06	Coventry C	2	0		
2006–07	Coventry C	3	0		
2006–07	Peterborough U	7	0	7	0
2007–08	Coventry C	6	0	11	0
2008–09	Northampton T	29	4		
2009–10	Northampton T	17	2		
2010–11	Northampton T	33	2	79	8
2011–12	Oxford U	44	2		
2012–13	Oxford U	23	1	67	3
2013–14	Yeovil T	27	1		
2014–15	Yeovil T	8	0	35	1

DAWSON, Kevin (M) 123 8
H: 5 10 W: 12 08 b.Dublin 30-6-90
Internationals: Republic of Ireland U18.
2011	Shelbourne	26	2		
2012	Shelbourne	25	2	51	4
2012–13	Yeovil T	20	2		
2013–14	Yeovil T	35	1		
2014–15	Yeovil T	17	1	72	4

EASTMOND, Craig (D) 86 7
H: 6 0 W: 11 11 b.Wandsworth 9-12-90
2009–10	Arsenal	4	0		
2010–11	Arsenal	0	0		
2010–11	Millwall	6	0	6	0
2011–12	Arsenal	0	0		
2011–12	Wycombe W	14	0	14	0
2012–13	Arsenal	0	0	4	0
2012–13	Colchester U	12	2		
2013–14	Colchester U	39	4		
2014–15	Colchester U	10	1	61	7
2014–15	Yeovil T	1	0	1	0

EDWARDS, Joe (D) 123 4
H: 5 8 W: 11 07 b.Gloucester 31-10-90
2009–10	Bristol C	5	0		
2010–11	Bristol C	2	0		
2011–12	Bristol C	2	0		
2011–12	Yeovil T	4	1		
2012–13	Bristol C	0	0	4	0
2012–13	Yeovil T	35	2		
2013–14	Yeovil T	46	1		
2014–15	Yeovil T	34	0	119	4

EMMANUEL-WILKINSON, Nelchi (F) 0 0
b. 8-8-94

Season	Club				
2012–13	Yeovil T	0	0		
2013–14	Yeovil T	0	0		
2014–15	Yeovil T	0	0		

FOLEY, Sam (M) 97 7
H: 6 0 W: 11 08 b.St Albans 17-10-86

Season	Club				
2012–13	Yeovil T	41	5		
2013–14	Yeovil T	7	0		
2013–14	Shrewsbury T	9	0	9	0
2014–15	Yeovil T	40	2	88	7

GILLETT, Simon (M) 219 9
H: 5 6 W: 11 07 b.Oxford 6-11-85

Season	Club				
2003–04	Southampton	0	0		
2004–05	Southampton	0	0		
2005–06	Southampton	0	0		
2005–06	Walsall	2	0	2	0
2006–07	Southampton	0	0		
2006–07	Blackpool	31	1	31	1
2006–07	Bournemouth	7	1	7	1
2007–08	Southampton	2	0		
2007–08	Yeovil T	4	0		
2008–09	Southampton	27	0		
2009–10	Southampton	2	0	31	0
2009–10	Doncaster R	11	0		
2010–11	Doncaster R	22	1		
2011–12	Doncaster R	46	3		
2012–13	Doncaster R	0	0	79	4
2012–13	Nottingham F	25	0		
2013–14	Nottingham F	0	0	25	0
2013–14	Bristol C	23	2	23	2
2014–15	Yeovil T	17	1	21	1

GRANT, Joel (F) 229 36
H: 6 0 W: 12 01 b.Acton 26-8-87
Internationals: Jamaica U20, Full caps.

Season	Club				
2005–06	Watford	7	0		
2006–07	Watford	0	0	7	0
From Aldershot T.					
2008–09	Crewe Alex	28	2		
2009–10	Crewe Alex	43	9		
2010–11	Crewe Alex	25	5	96	16
2011–12	Wycombe W	30	4		
2012–13	Wycombe W	41	10	71	14
2013–14	Yeovil T	34	3		
2014–15	Yeovil T	21	3	55	6

HAYTER, James (F) 639 152
H: 5 9 W: 10 13 b.Sandown 9-4-79

Season	Club				
1996–97	Bournemouth	2	0		
1997–98	Bournemouth	5	0		
1998–99	Bournemouth	20	2		
1999–2000	Bournemouth	31	2		
2000–01	Bournemouth	40	11		
2001–02	Bournemouth	44	7		
2002–03	Bournemouth	45	9		
2003–04	Bournemouth	44	14		
2004–05	Bournemouth	39	19		
2005–06	Bournemouth	46	20		
2006–07	Bournemouth	42	10	358	94
2007–08	Doncaster R	34	7		
2008–09	Doncaster R	27	4		
2009–10	Doncaster R	38	9		
2010–11	Doncaster R	32	9		
2011–12	Doncaster R	31	4	162	33
2012–13	Yeovil T	44	14		
2013–14	Yeovil T	37	6		
2014–15	Yeovil T	38	5	119	25

HOSKINS, Sam (F) 53 4
H: 5 8 W: 10 07 b.Dorchester 4-2-93

Season	Club				
2011–12	Southampton	0	0		
2011–12	Preston NE	0	0		
2011–12	Rotherham U	8	2	8	2
2012–13	Southampton	0	0		
2012–13	Stevenage	14	1	14	1
2013–14	Yeovil T	19	0		
2014–15	Yeovil T	12	1	31	1

KRYSIAK, Artur (G) 187 0
H: 6 1 W: 12 00 b.Lodz 11-8-89
Internationals: Poland U19.

Season	Club				
2006–07	Birmingham C	0	0		
2007–08	Gretna	4	0	4	0
2007–08	Birmingham C	0	0		
2008–09	Birmingham C	0	0		
2008–09	Motherwell	1	0	1	0
2008–09	Swansea C	2	0	2	0
2009–10	Birmingham C	0	0		
2009–10	Burton Alb	38	0	38	0
2010–11	Exeter C	10	0		
2011–12	Exeter C	38	0		
2012–13	Exeter C	42	0		
2013–14	Exeter C	37	0	127	0
2014–15	Yeovil T	15	0	15	0

LEITCH-SMITH, AJ (F) 154 26
H: 5 11 W: 12 04 b.Crewe 6-3-90

Season	Club				
2008–09	Crewe Alex	0	0		
2009	IBV	18	5	18	5
2009–10	Crewe Alex	1	0		
2010–11	Crewe Alex	16	5		
2011–12	Crewe Alex	38	8		
2012–13	Crewe Alex	28	4		
2013–14	Crewe Alex	20	2	103	19
2014–15	Yeovil T	33	2	33	2

MOLONEY, Brendan (M) 148 3
H: 6 1 W: 11 12 b.Killarney 18-1-89
Internationals: Republic of Ireland U21.

Season	Club				
2005–06	Nottingham F	0	0		
2006–07	Nottingham F	1	0		
2007–08	Nottingham F	2	0		
2007–08	Chesterfield	9	1	9	1
2008–09	Nottingham F	12	0		
2009–10	Nottingham F	0	0		
2009–10	Notts Co	18	1	18	1
2009–10	Scunthorpe U	3	0	3	0
2010–11	Nottingham F	6	0		
2011–12	Nottingham F	8	0		
2012–13	Nottingham F	13	0	42	0
2012–13	Bristol C	17	0		
2013–14	Bristol C	32	0	49	0
2014–15	Yeovil T	5	0	5	0
2014–15	Northampton T	22	1	22	1

MOORE, Kieffer (F) 50 7
H: 6 5 W: 13 01 b.Torquay 8-8-92

Season	Club				
2013–14	Yeovil T	20	4		
2014–15	Yeovil T	30	3	50	7

MORGAN, Adam (F) 24 1
H: 5 10 W: 11 03 b.Liverpool 21-4-94
Internationals: England U17, U19.

Season	Club				
2011–12	Liverpool	0	0		
2012–13	Liverpool	0	0		
2012–13	Rotherham U	1	0	1	0
2013–14	Liverpool	0	0		
2013–14	Yeovil T	12	0		
2014–15	Yeovil T	6	1	18	1
2014–15	St Johnstone	5	0	5	0

NANA OFORI-TWUMASI, Seth (D) 28 0
H: 5 8 W: 11 09 b.Accra 15-5-90
Internationals: England U16, U17, U18, U20.

Season	Club				
2009–10	Dagenham & R	0	0		
2010–11	Peterborough U	0	0		
2010–11	Northampton T	0	0		
2011–12	Northampton T	0	0		
2012–13	Northampton T	0	0		
2013–14	Yeovil T	3	0		
2014–15	Yeovil T	25	0	28	0

RALPH, Nathan (D) 35 1
H: 5 9 W: 11 00 b.Dunmow 14-2-93

Season	Club				
2011–12	Peterborough U	0	0		
2012–13	Yeovil T	14	1		
2013–14	Yeovil T	0	0		
2014–15	Yeovil T	21	0	35	1

SMITH, Alex (D) 17 1
H: 5 9 W: 8 09 b.Clapham 31-10-91

Season	Club				
2009–10	Fulham	0	0		
2010–11	Fulham	0	0		
2011–12	Fulham	0	0		
2012–13	Fulham	1	0	1	0
2012–13	Leyton Orient	2	0	2	0
2013–14	Swindon T	8	1	8	1
2014–15	Yeovil T	6	0	6	0

SMITH, Nathan (D) 222 1
H: 5 11 W: 12 00 b.Enfield 11-1-87
Internationals: Jamaica Full caps.

Season	Club				
2007–08	Yeovil T	7	0		
2008–09	Yeovil T	33	1		
2009–10	Yeovil T	34	0		
2010–11	Yeovil T	40	0		
2011–12	Chesterfield	25	0		
2012–13	Chesterfield	29	0		
2013–14	Chesterfield	13	0	67	0
2014–15	Yeovil T	41	0	155	1

SOKOLIK, Jakub (D) 22 0
H: 5 6 W: 12 02 b.Ostrava 28-8-93
Internationals: Czech Republic U16, U17.

Season	Club				
2010–11	Liverpool	0	0		
2011–12	Liverpool	0	0		
2012–13	Liverpool	0	0		
2013–14	Liverpool	0	0		
2013–14	Southend U	10	0		
2014–15	Yeovil T	11	0	11	0
2014–15	Southend U	1	0	11	0

STEWART, Gareth (G) 167 0
H: 6 0 W: 12 08 b.Preston 3-2-80

Season	Club				
1996–97	Blackburn R	0	0		
1997–98	Blackburn R	0	0		
1998–99	Blackburn R	0	0		
1999–2000	Bournemouth	3	0		
2000–01	Bournemouth	35	0		
2001–02	Bournemouth	45	0		
2002–03	Bournemouth	1	0		
2003–04	Bournemouth	0	0		
2004–05	Bournemouth	0	0		
2005–06	Bournemouth	42	0		
2006–07	Bournemouth	20	0		
2007–08	Bournemouth	18	0		
2008–09	Bournemouth	0	0	164	0
2011–12	Yeovil T	1	0		
2012–13	Yeovil T	0	0		
2013–14	Yeovil T	1	0		
2014–15	Yeovil T	1	0	3	0

UGWU, Chigozie (F) 64 16
H: 6 2 W: 12 00 b.Oxford 22-4-93

Season	Club				
2011–12	Reading	0	0		
2012–13	Reading	0	0		
2012–13	Yeovil T	15	3		
2012–13	Plymouth Arg	6	0	6	0
2013–14	Reading	0	0		
2013–14	Shrewsbury T	7	1	7	1
2014–15	Dunfermline Ath	14	7	14	7
2014–15	Yeovil T	22	5	37	8

WEALE, Chris (G) 286 1
H: 6 2 W: 13 03 b.Chard 9-2-82
Internationals: England C.

Season	Club				
2003–04	Yeovil T	35	0		
2004–05	Yeovil T	38	0		
2005–06	Yeovil T	25	0		
2006–07	Bristol C	1	0		
2007–08	Hereford U	1	0		
2007–08	Bristol C	3	0		
2008–09	Bristol C	5	0	9	0
2008–09	Hereford U	1	0	2	0
2008–09	Yeovil T	10	1		
2009–10	Leicester C	45	0		
2010–11	Leicester C	29	0		
2011–12	Leicester C	1	0	75	0
2011–12	Northampton T	3	0	3	0
2012–13	Shrewsbury T	46	0		
2013–14	Shrewsbury T	35	0	81	0
2014–15	Yeovil T	8	0	116	1
2014–15	Burton Alb	0	0		

YORK C (92)

CARSON, Josh (M) 89 11
H: 5 9 W: 11 00 b.Ballymena 3-6-93
Internationals: Northern Ireland U16, U17, U18, U19, U21, Full caps.

Season	Club				
2010–11	Ipswich T	9	3		
2011–12	Ipswich T	16	2		
2012–13	Ipswich T	6	0		
2012–13	York C	5	0		
2013–14	Ipswich T	0	0	31	5
2013–14	York C	31	4		
2014–15	York C	22	2	58	6

COULSON, Michael (F) 140 20
H: 5 10 W: 10 00 b.Scarborough 4-4-88
Internationals: England C.

Season	Club				
2006–07	Barnsley	2	0		
2007–08	Barnsley	12	0		
2008–09	Barnsley	2	0		
2009–10	Barnsley	0	0	16	0
2009–10	Grimsby T	29	5	29	5
2012–13	York	19	4		
2012–13	York C	33	7		
2014–15	York C	43	4	95	15

FLETCHER, Wes (F) 93 21
H: 5 11 W: 12 06 b.Ormskirk 28-2-91

Season	Club				
2009–10	Burnley	0	0		
2009–10	Grimsby T	6	1	6	1
2010–11	Burnley	0	0		
2010–11	Stockport Co	9	1	9	1
2011–12	Burnley	0	0		
2011–12	Accrington S	10	2	10	2
2011–12	Crewe Alex	6	1	6	1
2012–13	Burnley	0	0		
2012–13	Yeovil T	1	0	1	0
2013–14	York C	32	10		
2014–15	York C	29	6	61	16

GODFREY, Ben (M) 0 0
H: 6 0 W: 11 09 b.York 15-1-98

Season	Club				
2014–15	York C	0	0		

HIRST, Ben (F)   3   0
H: 6 0   W: 11 09   b.York 25-10-97

Season	Club				
2014–15	York C	3	0	**3**	**0**

HYDE, Jake (F)   143   38
H: 6 1   W: 13 02   b.Slough 1-7-90
Internationals: England C.

Season	Club				
2009–10	Barnet	34	6		
2010–11	Dundee	2	3		
2010–11	Dunfermline Ath	2	0	**2**	**0**
2011–12	Dundee	26	6	**28**	**9**
2012–13	Barnet	40	14	**74**	**20**
2014–15	York C	39	9	**39**	**9**

ILESANMI, Femi (D)   150   1
H: 6 1   W: 11 13   b.Southwark 18-4-91

Season	Club				
2010–11	Dagenham & R	25	0		
2011–12	Dagenham & R	17	0		
2012–13	Dagenham & R	46	1		
2013–14	Dagenham & R	29	0	**117**	**1**
2014–15	York C	33	0	**33**	**0**

INGHAM, Michael (G)   214   0
H: 6 4   W: 13 08   b.Preston 9-7-80
Internationals: Northern Ireland U18, U21, Full caps.

Season	Club				
1998–99	Cliftonville	18	0	**18**	**0**
1999–2000	Sunderland	0	0		
1999–2000	Carlisle U	7	0	**7**	**0**
2000–01	Sunderland	0	0		
2001–02	Sunderland	0	0		
2001–02	Stoke C	0	0		
2002–03	Sunderland	0	0		
2002–03	Darlington	3	0	**3**	**0**
2002–03	York C	17	0		
2003–04	Sunderland	0	0		
2003–04	Wrexham	11	0		
2004–05	Sunderland	2	0	**2**	**0**
2004–05	Doncaster R	1	0	**1**	**0**
2005–06	Wrexham	40	0		
2006–07	Wrexham	31	0	**82**	**0**
2012–13	York C	46	0		
2013–14	York C	19	0		
2014–15	York C	19	0	**101**	**0**

JARVIS, Ryan (F)   276   41
H: 6 1   W: 11 11   b.Fakenham 11-7-86
Internationals: England U16, U17, U19.

Season	Club				
2002–03	Norwich C	3	0		
2003–04	Norwich C	12	1		
2004–05	Norwich C	4	1		
2004–05	Colchester U	6	0	**6**	**0**
2005–06	Norwich C	4	1		
2006–07	Norwich C	5	0		
2006–07	Leyton Orient	14	6		
2007–08	Norwich C	1	0	**29**	**3**
2007–08	Kilmarnock	9	1	**9**	**1**
2007–08	Notts Co	17	2	**17**	**2**
2008–09	Leyton Orient	31	0		
2009–10	Leyton Orient	42	8		
2010–11	Leyton Orient	11	2	**98**	**16**
2010–11	Northampton T	3	0	**3**	**0**
2011–12	Walsall	19	2	**19**	**2**
2011–12	Torquay U	14	2		
2012–13	Torquay U	38	7	**52**	**9**
2013–14	York C	35	8		
2014–15	York C	8	0	**43**	**8**

LOWE, Keith (D)   284   19
H: 6 2   W: 13 03   b.Wolverhampton 13-9-85

Season	Club				
2004–05	Wolverhampton W	11	0		
2005–06	Wolverhampton W	3	0		
2005–06	Burnley	16	0	**16**	**0**
2005–06	QPR	1	0	**1**	**0**
2005–06	Swansea C	4	0	**4**	**0**
2006–07	Wolverhampton W	0	0		
2006–07	Brighton & HA	16	1		
2006–07	Cheltenham T	16	1		
2007–08	Wolverhampton W	0	0		
2007–08	Port Vale	28	3	**28**	**3**
2008–09	Wolverhampton W	0	0	**14**	**0**

(continued)

Season	Club				
2009–10	Hereford U	19	1	**19**	**1**
2010–11	Cheltenham T	36	1		
2011–12	Cheltenham T	30	1		
2012–13	Cheltenham T	31	4		
2013–14	Cheltenham T	13	1	**126**	**8**
2013–14	York C	30	1		
2014–15	York C	46	6	**76**	**7**

McCOMBE, John (D)   281   19
H: 6 2   W: 13 00   b.Pontefract 7-5-85

Season	Club				
2002–03	Huddersfield T	1	0		
2003–04	Huddersfield T	0	0		
2004–05	Huddersfield T	5	0		
2005–06	Huddersfield T	1	0		
2005–06	Torquay U	0	0		
2006–07	Huddersfield T	7	0	**14**	**0**
2007–08	Hereford U	27	0	**27**	**0**
2008–09	Port Vale	31	2		
2009–10	Port Vale	40	3		
2010–11	Port Vale	42	4		
2011–12	Port Vale	40	4		
2012–13	Port Vale	32	1		
2013–14	Port Vale	0	0	**185**	**14**
2013–14	Mansfield T	5	2	**5**	**2**
2013–14	York C	19	3		
2014–15	York C	31	0	**50**	**3**

McCOY, Marvin (D)   122   0
H: 5 11   W: 11 01   b.Walthamstow 2-10-88
Internationals: Antigua and Barbuda Full caps.

Season	Club				
2007–08	Hereford U	0	0		
From Leyton, Wealdstone.					
2010–11	Wycombe W	21	0		
2011–12	Wycombe W	28	0		
2012–13	Wycombe W	9	0		
2013–14	Wycombe W	33	0	**91**	**0**
2014–15	York C	31	0	**31**	**0**

MEIKLE, Lindon (F)   56   1
b.Nottingham 21-3-88
Internationals: England C.

Season	Club				
2013–14	Mansfield T	28	1	**28**	**1**
2014–15	York C	28	0	**28**	**0**

MONTROSE, Lewis (M)   171   10
H: 6 0   W: 12 00   b.Manchester 17-11-88

Season	Club				
2006–07	Wigan Ath	0	0		
2007–08	Wigan Ath	0	0		
2008–09	Wigan Ath	0	0		
2008–09	Cheltenham T	5	0	**5**	**0**
2008–09	Chesterfield	12	0	**12**	**0**
2009–10	Wycombe W	14	0		
2010–11	Wycombe W	36	4	**50**	**4**
2011–12	Gillingham	37	4		
2012–13	Gillingham	15	1	**52**	**5**
2012–13	Oxford U	5	0	**5**	**0**
2013–14	York C	33	1		
2014–15	York C	14	0	**47**	**1**

MOONEY, Jason (G)   8   0
H: 6 9   W: 14 00   b.Belfast 26-2-89

Season	Club				
2011–12	Wycombe W	0	0		
2012–13	Tranmere R	1	0		
2013–14	Tranmere R	3	0	**4**	**0**
2014–15	York C	4	0	**4**	**0**

PARSLOW, Daniel (D)   58   1
H: 5 11   W: 12 05   b.Cardiff 11-9-85
Internationals: Wales U17, U19, U21.

Season	Club				
2012–13	York C	45	1		
2013–14	York C	13	0		
2014–15	York C	0	0	**58**	**1**

PENN, Russ (M)   252   11
H: 5 11   W: 12 13   b.Dudley 8-11-85
Internationals: England C.

Season	Club				
2009–10	Burton Alb	40	4		
2010–11	Burton Alb	41	3	**81**	**7**
2011–12	Cheltenham T	43	1		
2012–13	Cheltenham T	43	1		
2013–14	Cheltenham T	19	0	**105**	**2**

(continued)

Season	Club				
2013–14	York C	21	0		
2014–15	York C	45	2	**66**	**2**

PLATT, Tom (M)   47   0
H: 6 1   W: 12 13   b.Pontefract 1-10-93

Season	Club				
2012–13	York C	7	0		
2013–14	York C	20	0		
2014–15	York C	20	0	**47**	**0**

SINCLAIR, Emile (F)   226   35
H: 6 0   W: 11 04   b.Leeds 29-12-87

Season	Club				
2007–08	Nottingham F	12	1		
2007–08	Brentford	4	0	**4**	**0**
2008–09	Nottingham F	3	0	**15**	**1**
2008–09	Macclesfield T	17	1		
2009–10	Macclesfield T	42	7		
2010–11	Macclesfield T	31	5		
2011–12	Macclesfield T	5	1	**95**	**14**
2011–12	Peterborough U	35	10		
2012–13	Peterborough U	12	3		
2012–13	Barnsley	4	0	**4**	**0**
2012–13	Doncaster R	4	0	**4**	**0**
2013–14	Peterborough U	0	0	**47**	**13**
2013–14	Crawley T	15	2	**15**	**2**
2013–14	Northampton T	20	2		
2014–15	Northampton T	10	1	**30**	**3**
2014–15	York C	12	2	**12**	**2**

STRAKER, Anthony (D)   246   8
H: 5 9   W: 11 01   b.Ealing 23-9-88
Internationals: England U18. Grenada Full caps.

Season	Club				
2008–09	Aldershot T	32	0		
2009–10	Aldershot T	37	2		
2010–11	Aldershot T	38	2		
2010–11	Wycombe W	4	0	**4**	**0**
2011–12	Aldershot T	44	2	**151**	**6**
2012–13	Southend U	28	0		
2013–14	Southend U	39	2	**67**	**2**
2014–15	York C	12	0	**12**	**0**
2014–15	Motherwell	12	0	**12**	**0**

SUMMERFIELD, Luke (M)   237   16
H: 6 0   W: 11 00   b.Ivybridge 6-12-87

Season	Club				
2004–05	Plymouth Arg	0	0		
2005–06	Plymouth Arg	0	0		
2006–07	Plymouth Arg	23	1		
2006–07	Bournemouth	8	1	**8**	**1**
2007–08	Plymouth Arg	7	0		
2008–09	Plymouth Arg	29	2		
2009–10	Plymouth Arg	12	0		
2009–10	Leyton Orient	14	0	**14**	**0**
2010–11	Plymouth Arg	7	1	**79**	**4**
2011–12	Cheltenham T	41	4	**41**	**4**
2012–13	Shrewsbury T	36	2		
2013–14	Shrewsbury T	28	1	**64**	**3**
2014–15	York C	31	4	**31**	**4**

WINFIELD, Dave (D)   160   10
H: 6 3   W: 13 08   b.Aldershot 24-3-88

Season	Club				
2008–09	Aldershot T	10	0		
2009–10	Aldershot T	25	2	**35**	**2**
2010–11	Wycombe W	37	2		
2011–12	Wycombe W	25	2		
2012–13	Wycombe W	29	2		
2013–14	Wycombe W	0	0	**91**	**6**
2013–14	Shrewsbury T	17	0	**17**	**0**
2014–15	York C	10	2	**10**	**2**
2014–15	AFC Wimbledon	7	0	**7**	**0**

Scholars
Bowkett, Joshua Vincent; Caulfield, Ryan Peter; Collis, Aaron Luke; Cooney, Robert James; De, Groot Richard Oshiro; Godfrey, Benjamin Matthew; Hardey, Liam Thomas; Jefferson, Sam David; Kennedy, Nicholas John Steve; Morley, Adam Alan; Parker, Matthew Keith; Price, Kieran Richard Roderick; Rzonca, Callum James; Salmon, Christopher; Wilson, Cameron James; Wilson, George Daniel; Wright, Daniel Mark.

ENGLISH LEAGUE PLAYERS – INDEX

NATIONAL LIST OF REFEREES FOR SEASON 2015–16

SELECT GROUP REFEREES

Atkinson, M (Martin) – West Yorkshire
Clattenburg, M (Mark) – County Durham
Dean, ML (Mike) – Wirral
Dowd, P (Phil) – Staffordshire
East, R (Roger) – Wiltshire
Friend, KA (Kevin) – Leicestershire
Jones, MJ (Michael) – Cheshire
Madley, RJ (Bobby) – West Yorkshire
Marriner, AM (André) – West Midlands
Mason, LS (Lee) – Lancashire
Moss, J (Jonathan) – West Yorkshire
Oliver, M (Michael) – Northumberland
Pawson, CL (Craig) – South Yorkshire
Probert, LW (Lee) – Wiltshire
Scott, GD (Graham) – Oxfordshire
Swarbrick, ND (Neil) – Lancashire
Taylor, A (Anthony) – Cheshire

NATIONAL GROUP REFEREES

Adcock, JG (James) – Nottinghamshire
Attwell, SB (Stuart) – Warwickshire
Bankes, P (Peter) – Merseyside
Berry, CJ (Carl) – Surrey
Bond, D (Darren) – Lancashire
Boyeson, C (Carl) – East Yorkshire
Bratt, S (Stephen) – West Midlands
Breakspear, C (Charles) – Surrey
Brown, M (Mark) – East Yorkshire
Bull, M (Michael) – Essex
Clark, R (Richard) – Northumberland
Collins, LM (Lee) – Surrey
Coote, D (David) – West Yorkshire
Davies, A (Andy) – Hampshire
Deadman, D (Darren) – Cambridgeshire
Drysdale, D (Darren) – Lincolnshire
Duncan, S (Scott) – Northumberland
Eltringham, G (Geoff) – Tyne & Wear
England, D (Darren) – South Yorkshire
Gibbs, PN (Phil) – West Midlands
Graham, F (Fred) – Essex
Haines, A (Andy) – Tyne & Wear
Handley, D (Darren) – Lancashire
Harrington, T (Tony) – Cleveland
Haywood, M (Mark) – West Yorkshire
Heywood, M (Mark) – Cheshire
Hill, K (Keith) – Hertfordshire
Hooper, SA (Simon) – Wiltshire
Horwood, G (Graham) – Bedfordshire
Ilderton, EL (Eddie) – Tyne & Wear
Johnson, K (Kevin) – Somerset
Joyce, R (Ross) – Cleveland
Kavanagh, (Chris) – Manchester
Kettle, TM (Trevor) – Leicestershire
Kinseley, N (Nick) – Essex
Langford, O (Oliver) – West Midlands
Lewis, RL (Rob) – Shropshire
Linington, JJ (James) – Isle of Wight
Madley, AJ (Andy) – West Yorkshire
Malone, BJ (Brendan) – Wiltshire
Martin, S (Stephen) – Staffordshire
Miller, NS (Nigel) – County Durham
Mohareb, D (Dean) – Cheshire
Naylor, MA (Michael) – South Yorkshire
Robinson, T (Tim) – West Sussex
Russell, MP (Mick) – Hertfordshire
Salisbury, G (Graham) – Lancashire
Sarginson, CD (Chris) – Staffordshire
Sheldrake, D (Darren) – Surrey
Simpson, J (Jeremy) – Lancashire
Stockbridge, S (Seb) – Tyne & Wear
Stroud, KP (Keith) – Hampshire
Sutton, GJ (Gary) – Lincolnshire
Swabey, L (Lee) – Devon
Tierney, P Paul) – Lancashire
Toner, B (Ben) – Lancashire
Ward, GL (Gavin) – Surrey
Webb, D (David) – County Durham
Whitestone, D (Dean) – Northamptonshire
Williamson, IG (Iain) – Berkshire
Woolmer, KA (Andy) – Northamptonshire
Wright, KK (Kevin) – Merseyside

ASSISTANT REFEREES

Akers, C (Chris) – South Yorkshire
Amey, JR (Justin) – Dorset
Amphlett, MJ (Marvyn) – Worcestershire
Atkin, R (Robert) – Lincolnshire
Atkin, RT (Ryan) – London
Avent, D (David) – Northamptonshire
Aylott, A (Andrew) – Bedfordshire
Backhouse, A (Anthony) – Cumbria
Barnard, N (Nicholas) – Cheshire
Barratt, W (Wayne) – Worcestershire
Barrow, SJ (Simon) – Staffordshire
Bartlett, R (Richard) – Cheshire
Beck, S (Simon) – Bedfordshire
Bell, J (James) – South Yorkshire
Bennett, A (Andrew) – Devon
Bennett, S (Simon) – Staffordshire
Benton, DK (David) – South Yorkshire
Beswick, G (Gary) – County Durham
Betts, L (Lee) – Norfolk
Blunden, D (Darren) – Kent
Bourne, D (Declan) – Nottinghamshire
Bramall, T (Thomas) – Sheffield
Bristow, M (Matthew) – Manchester
Bromley, A (Adam) – Devon
Brook, C (Carl) – East Sussex
Brooks, J (John) – Leicestershire
Bryan, D (Dave) – Lincolnshire
Bull, W (William) – Hampshire
Buonassisi, M (Mathew) – Northamptonshire
Burt, S (Stuart) – Northamptonshire
Busby, J (John) – Oxfordshire
Bushell, DD (David) – London
Butler, S (Stuart) – Kent
Byrne, H (Helen) – Liverpool
Cann, D (Darren) – Norfolk
Cheosiaua D-R (Dumitru-Ravel) – Worcestershire
Child, S (Stephen) – Kent
Clark, J (Joseph) – West Midlands
Clayton, A (Alan) – Cheshire
Clayton, S (Simon) – County Durham
Coggins, A (Anthony) – Oxfordshire
Collin, J (Jake) – Merseyside
Cook, D (Daniel) – Hampshire
Cooper, IJ (Ian) – Kent
Cooper, N (Nicholas) – Suffolk
Copeland, SJ (Steven) – Merseyside
Corlett, M (Matthew) – Liverpool
Coy, M (Martin) – County Durham
Cropp, B (Barry) – Lancashire
Crysell, A (Adam) – Essex
Dabbs, R (Robert) – Dorset
Da Costa, A (Anthony) – Cambridgeshire
D'aguilar, M (Michael) – Staffordshire
Dale, A (Alan) – Suffolk
Daly, SDJ (Stephen) – Middlesex
Davies, N (Neil) – London
Davison, P (Paul) – County Durham
Degnarain, A (Ashvin) – London
Denton, MJ (Michael) – Lancashire
Dermott, P (Philip) – Lancashire
Derrien, M (Mark) – Dorset
Dicicco, M (Matthew) – Cleveland
Donohue, M (Matthew) – Manchester
Dudley, IA (Ian) – Nottinghamshire
Duncan, M (Mark) – Cheshire
Durie, B (Brian) – Gloucestershire
Dwyer, MJ (Mark) – West Yorkshire
Eagland, S (Stuart) – Staffordshire
Eaton, D (Derek) – Gloucestershire
Edwards, M (Marc) – County Durham
Eva, M (Matt) – Surrey
Evans, K (Karl) – Lancashire

Farries, J (John) – Oxfordshire
Fearn, AE (Amy) – Leicestershire
Finch, S (Stephen) – Suffolk
Fissenden, I (Ian) – Kent
Fitch, C (Carl) – Suffolk
Flynn, J (John) – Wiltshire
Foley, MJ (Matt) – London
Ford, D (Declan) – Lincolnshire
Fox, A (Andrew) – Warwickshire
Fyvie, G (Graeme) – Tyne & Wear
Ganfield, R (Ron) – Somerset
Garratt, A (Andy) – West Midlands
Garratt, S (Sarah) – West Midlands
George, M (Mike) – Norfolk
Gibbons, P (Peter) – Cheshire
Gooch, P (Peter) – Lancashire
Gordon, B (Barry) – County Durham
Graham, P (Paul) – Manchester
Gratton, D (Danny) – Staffordshire
Greenhalgh, N (Nick) – Lancashire
Greenwood, AH (Alf) –
  North Yorkshire
Griffiths, M (Mark) –
  South Yorkshire
Grunnill, W (Wayne) –
  East Yorkshire
Hair, NA (Neil) – Cambridgeshire
Halliday, A (Andy) –
  North Yorkshire
Hanley, M (Michael) – Liverpool
Harris, P (Paul) – Kent
Hart, G (Glen) – County Durham
Hatzidakis, C (Constantine) – Kent
Haycock, KW (Ken) –
  South Yorkshire
Hendley, AR (Andy) –
  West Midlands
Hicks, C (Craig) – Surrey
Hillier, J (Jake) – Hertfordshire
Hilton, G (Gary) – Lancashire
Hobbis, N (Nick) – West Midlands
Hobday, P (Paul) – West Midlands
Hodges, R (Robert) –
  Buckinghamshire
Hodskinson, P (Paul) – Lancashire
Holderness, BC (Barry) – Essex
Holmes, A (Adrian) –
  West Yorkshire
Hopkins, AJ (Adam) – Devon
Hopton, N (Nicholas) – Derbyshire
Howard, P (Paul) – London
Howes, M (Mark) – Birmingham
Howson, A (Akil) – Leicestershire
Hudson, S (Shaun) – Tyne & Wear
Hull, J (Joe) – Cheshire
Hulme, R (Richard) – Somerset
Hunt, J (Jonathan) – Liverpool
Husband, C (Christopher) –
  Worcestershire
Hussin, I (Ian) – Merseyside
Huxtable, B (Brett) – Devon
Hyde, RA (Robert) – London
Isherwood, C (Chris) – Lancashire
Johnson, J (Joe) – Liverpool
Johnson, P (Paul) – Surrey
Johnson, RL (Ryan) – Manchester
Jones, M (Matthew) – Staffordshire
Jones, MT (Mark) – Nottinghamshire
Jones, RJ (Robert) – Merseyside
Kane, G (Graham) – East Sussex
Kaye, E (Elliott) – Essex

Kelly, P (Paul) – Kent
Kendall, R (Richard) – Bedfordshire
Kettlewell, PT (Paul) – Lancashire
Khatib, B (Billy) – County Durham
Kirk, T (Thomas) – Cheshire
Kirkup, P (Peter) – Northamptonshire
Knapp, SC (Simon) – Bristol
Laver, AA (Andrew) – Hampshire
Law, J (John) – Worcestershire
Leach, D (Daniel) – Oxfordshire
Ledger, S (Scott) – South Yorkshire
Lennard, H (Harry) – East Sussex
Liddle, G (Geoff) – County Durham
Linden, W (Wes) – Middlesex
Long, S (Simon) – Cornwall
Lucas, S (Simeon) – Lancashire
Lugg, N (Nigel) – Surrey
Lymer, C (Colin) – Hampshire
McDonough, M (Mick) –
  Northumberland
McGrath, M (Matt) – East Yorkshire
Mackay, R (Rob) – Bedfordshire
Magill, JP (John) – Essex
Mainwaring, J (James) – Lancashire
Markham, DR (Danny) –
  Tyne & Wear
Marsden, PR (Paul) – Lancashire
Martin, RJ (Richard) –
  Weston-super-Mare
Massey-Ellis, R (Rob) –
  West Midlands
Massey-Ellis, S (Sian) –
  West Midlands
Mather, S (Simon) – Manchester
Matthews, A (Adam) –
  Gloucestershire
Mattocks, KJ (Kevin) – Lancashire
Meeson, DP (Daniel) – Staffordshire
Mellor, G (Gareth) – West Yorkshire
Mellor, JM (Mark) – Hertfordshire
Merchant, R (Rob) – Staffordshire
Meredith, S (Steven) –
  Nottinghamshire
Metcalfe, RL (Lee) – Lancashire
Miller, A (Andrew) – County
  Durham
Moore, A (Anthony) – Manchester
Morris, K (Kevin) – Herefordshire
Muge, G (Gavin) – Bedfordshire
Mullarkey, M (Mike) – Devon
Mulraine, K (Kevin) – Cumbria
Newbold, AM (Andy) –
  Leicestershire
Nield, T (Tom) – West Yorkshire
Norcott, WG (Wade) – Essex
Nunn, A (Adam) – Wiltshire
O'Brien, J (John) – London
O'Donnell, CJ (Chris) – Bedfordshire
Oldham, SA (Scott) – Lancashire
Parry, MJ (Matthew) – Liverpool
Pashley, A (Alix) – Derbyshire
Peart, T (Tony) – North Yorkshire
Perry, M (Marc) – West Midlands
Plane, S (Steven) – Worcestershire
Plowright, DP (David) –
  Nottinghamshire
Pollard, C (Christopher) – Suffolk
Pottage, M (Mark) – Dorset
Powell, CI (Chris) – Dorset
Purkiss, S (Sam) – London
Quin, A (Andrew) – Devon

Radford, N (Neil) – Worcestershire
Ramsey, T (Thomas) – Essex
Rashid, L (Lisa) – Birmingham
Rathbone, I (Ian) –
  Northamptonshire
Rees, P (Paul) – Somerset
Richardson, D (David) –
  West Yorkshire
Robathan, DM (Daniel) – Surrey
Roberts, B (Bob) – Lancashire
Rock, DK (David) – Hertfordshire
Ross, SJ (Stephen) – Lincolnshire
Rushton, S (Steven) – Staffordshire
Russell, GR (Geoff) –
  Northamptonshire
Russell, M (Mark) – Somerset
Salisbury, M (Michael) – Lancashire
Saliy, O (Oleksandr) – Middlesex
Sannerude, A (Adrian) – Suffolk
Scholes, M (Mark) –
  Buckinghamshire
Scregg, AJ (Andrew) – Liverpool
Serrano, A (Anthony) –
  Hertfordshire
Sharp, N (Neil) – Cleveland
Siddall, I (Iain) – Lancashire
Simpson, J (Joe) – Manchester
Slaughter, A (Ashley) – West Sussex
Smallwood, W (William) – Cheshire
Smart, E (Eddie) – West Midlands
Smedley, I (Ian) – Derbyshire
Smith, J (Josh) – Lincolnshire
Smith, M (Michael) – Essex
Smith, N (Nigel) – Derbyshire
Smith, R (Rob) – Hertfordshire
Storrie, D (David) – West Yorkshire
Strain, D (Darren) – Cheshire
Street, DR (Duncan) –
  West Yorkshire
Stretton, GS (Guy) – Leicestershire
Tankard, A (Anthony) –
  South Yorkshire
Taylor, C (Craig) – Staffordshire
Thompson, PI (Paul) – Derbyshire
Tranter, A (Adrian) – Dorset
Treleaven, D (Dean) – West Sussex
Turner, A (Andrew) – Devon
Tyas, J (Jason) – West Yorkshire
Venamore, L (Lee) – Kent
Wade, C (Christopher) – Hampshire
Wade, S (Stephen) – East Yorkshire
Ward, C (Chris) – South Yorkshire
Waters, A (Adrian) – Hertfordshire
Webb, MP (Michael) – Surrey
West, R (Richard) – East Riding
Whiteley, J (Jason) – West Yorkshire
Whitton, RP (Rob) – Essex
Wigglesworth, RJ (Richard) –
  South Yorkshire
Wild, R (Richard) – Lancashire
Wilkes, M (Matthew) –
  West Midlands
Wilson, J (James) – Cheshire
Wilson, M (Marc) – Cambridgeshire
Wood, L (Lloyd) – Essex
Wood, T (Tim) – Gloucestershire
Wootton, R (Ricky) – West Yorkshire
Wright, P (Peter) – Merseyside
Yates, O (Oliver) – Staffordshire
Young, A (Alan) – Cambridgeshire

MANAGERS – IN AND OUT 2014–15

AUGUST 2014

10   Mark Robins leaves as manager of Huddersfield Town by mutual agreement after only one game of the Championship season. Academy manager, Mark Lillis appointed caretaker manager of Town for the third time following spells in charge in 2012 and 2013.

14   Tony Pulis leaves his post as manager of Crystal Palace by mutual consent less than 48 hour before the Eagles' season opener at Arsenal. Assistant manager Keith Millen takes temporary charge.

27   Neil Warnock appointed manager of Crystal Palace.

28   David Hockaday sacked as manager of Leeds United after only six games in charge. Academy manager, Neil Redfearn appointed caretaker manager.

31   Giuseppe Sannino resigns as manager of Watford.

SEPTEMBER 2014

1   Joe Dunne leaves as manager of Colchester United by mutual consent. Academy boss Tony Humes takes over as manager. Graham Kavanagh sacked as manager of Carlisle United. Club captain Paul Thirwell and goalkeeping coach Tony Caig take temporary charge.

2   Oscar Garcia appointed manager of Watford.

3   Chris Powell appointed manager of Huddersfield Town.

12   James Beattie leaves as manager of Accrington Stanley by mutual consent. Assistant manager Paul Stephenson takes temporary charge.

18   Ole Gunnar Solskaer sacked as manager Cardiff City after less than nine months in charge. Danny Gabbidon and Scott Young take temporary charge. Felix Magath sacked as manager of Fulham. Kit Symons appointed caretaker manager. John Coleman appointed manager of Accrington Stanley. Micky Adams resigns as manager of Port Vale. Assistant boss Robert Page takes temporary charge.

19   Keith Curle appointed manager of Carlisle United.

23   Darko Milanic appointed manager of Leeds United.

24   Russell Slade resigns as manager of Leyton Orient. Assistant manager Kevin Nugent appointed new manager.

29   Oscar Garcia steps down as manager of Watford because of ill health after only 27 days in charge. Billy McKinlay appointed the new manager after one week at the club as first-team coach.

OCTOBER 2014

3   Dougie Freedman leaves as manager of Bolton Wanderers by mutual consent. Academy director Jimmy Phillips takes temporary charge.

4   Colin Cooper resigns as manager of Hartlepool United. Assistant manager Sam Collins and coach Stephen Pears in temporary charge.

6   Russell Slade appointed manager of Cardiff City.

7   Slavisa Jokanovic appointed manager of Watford after Billy McKinlay left the Hornets having been in charge for only eight days.

8   Russ Wilcox sacked as manager of Scunthorpe United. Coach Tony Daws and full back Andy Dawson take temporary charge.

12   Neil Lennon appointed manager of Bolton Wanderers.

13   Nigel Worthington resigns as manager of York City. Assistant manager Steve Torpey takes temporary charge. Mark Robins appointed manager of Scunthorpe United. Rob Edwards sacked as manager of Tranmere Rovers after five months in charge.

15   Russ Wilcox appointed manager of York City.

16   Micky Adams appointed manager of Tranmere Rovers.

20   Lee Clark sacked as manager of Birmingham City. Chief Scout Malcolm Crosby and first-team coach Richard Beale take temporary charge.

23   Paul Murray appointed manager of Hartlepool United.

25   Darko Milanic sacked as manager of Leeds United after only 32 days in charge.

26   Mauro Milanese appointed manager of Leyton Orient, Kevin Nugent reverts to assistant coach.

27   Gary Rowett leaves Burton Albion and appointed manager of Birmingham City. Jose Riga sacked as manager of Blackpool.

29   Kit Symons appointed manager of Fulham having been in temporary charge. Robert Page appointed manager of Port Vale having been in temporary charge.

30   Lee Clark appointed manager of Blackpool.

NOVEMBER 2014

1   Neil Redfearn appointed manager of Leeds United, becoming the fourth man in charge in five months.

13   Uwe Rosler sacked as manager of Wigan Athletic. Assistant manager Graham Barrow takes temporary charge. Jimmy Floyd Hasselbaink appointed manager of Burton Albion.

19   Malky Mackay appointed manager of Wigan Athletic.

21   Paul Cox leaves as manager of Mansfield Town by mutal consent. Player and assistant manager Adam Murray takes temporary charge.

25   Mark Yates sacked as manager of Cheltenham Town.

26   Paul Buckle appointed manager of Cheltenham Town.

DECEMBER 2014

5   Adam Murray appointed manager of Mansfield Town having been in temporary charge.

6   Paul Murray sacked as manager of Hartlepool United after just six weeks in charge, Sam Collins takes temporary charge.

8   Mauro Milanese sacked as manager of Watford after only 6 weeks in charge. Fabio Liverani appointed manager.

15   Nigel Adkins sacked as manager of Reading.

16   Steve Clarke appointed manager of Reading. Ronnie Moore appointed manager of Hartlepool United.

22   Sami Hyypia resigns as manager of Brighton & Hove Albion. Assistant manager Nathan Jones takes temporary charge.

27   Neil Warnock sacked as manager of Crystal Palace and becomes the first Premier League manager to lose his job this season. Assistant manager Keith Millen takes temporary charge. John Gregory steps down as manager of Crawley Town to undergo heart surgery. Dean Saunders appointed interim manager.

29   Alan Irvine sacked as manager of WBA. Assistant head coaches Rob Kelly and Keith Downing take temporary charge.

31   Chris Hughton appointed manager of Brighton & Hove Albion. Peter Taylor sacked as manager of Gillingham. Assistant Andy Hessenthaler takes temporary charge.

JANUARY 2015

1   Tony Pulis appointed manager of WBA.
3   Alan Pardew resigns as manager of Newcastle United. Assistant manager John Carver takes temporary charge.
     Alan Pardew appointed manager of Crystal Palace.
5   Neil Adams resigns as manager of Norwich City. First-team coach Mike Phelan takes temporary charge.
9   Alex Neil appointed manager of Norwich City.
11   Bob Peeters sacked as manager of Charlton Athletic.
13   Guy Luzon appointed manager of Charlton Athletic
26   John Carver appointed manager of Newcastle United until the end of the season.

FEBRUARY 2015

1   Stuart Pearce sacked as manager of Nottingham Forest. Dougie Freedman appointed manager.
3   Harry Redknapp resigns as manager of Queens Park Rangers. Les Ferdinand and Chris Ramsey take temporary charge.
4   Gary Johnson sacked as manager of Yeovil Town.
5   Terry Skiverton appointed manager of Yeovil Town.
7   Justin Edinburgh resigns as manager of Newport County and is appointed manager of Gillingham. Assistant manager Jimmy Dack takes temporary charge.
11   Paul Lambert sacked as manager of Aston Villa. First team coach Scott Marshall and goalkeeping coach Andy Marshall take temporary charge.
12   Danny Wilson sacked as manager of Barnsley. Academy manager Mark Burton and coach Paul Heckingbottom take temporary charge. Chris Ramsey appointed manager of QPR.
13   Paul Buckle leaves as manager of Cheltenham Town after 79 days in charge by mutual consent. Academy coach Russell Milton takes temporary charge.
14   Tim Sherwood appointed manager of Aston Villa.
21   Darren Ferguson leaves as manager of Peterborough United by mutual consent. Youth team manager Dave Robertson takes temporary charge.
23   Steven Pressley sacked as manager of Coventry City. Assistant manager Neil MacFarlane and coach Dave Hockaday take temporary charge.
24   Jimmy Dack appointed manager of Newport County until the end of the season having been in temporary charge.
25   Lee Johnson leaves Oldham Athletic to become manager of Barnsley. First-team coach Dean Holden takes temporary charge.

MARCH 2015

3   Tony Mowbray appointed manager of Coventry City.
10   Ian Holloway sacked as manager of Millwall. Neil Harris appointed manager until the end of the season.
13   Dave Robertson appointed manager of Peterborough United having been in temporary charge. Dean Holden appointed manager of Oldham Athletic until the end of the season having been in temporary charge.
16   Gus Poyet sacked as manager of Sunderland.
17   Dick Advocaat appointed manager of Sunderland.
23   Shaun Derry sacked as manager of Notts County. Academy manager Paul Hart takes temporary charge.
30   Gary Johnson appointed manager of Cheltenham Town until the end of the season.

APRIL 2015

6   Malky Mackay sacked as manager of Wigan Athletic.
7   Gary Caldwell appointed manager of Wigan Athletic. Ricardo Moniz appointed manager of Notts County.
9   Paul Sturrock appointed manager of Yeovil Town. Terry Skiverton reverts to assistant manager.
15   Andy Awford leaves as manager of Portsmouth by mutual consent. Assistant manager Gary Waddock takes temporary charge.
19   Micky Adams leaves as manager of Tranmere Rovers by mutual consent. Coach Alan Rogers and academy manager Shaun Garnett take temporary charge.
29   Neil Harris appointed manager of Millwall having been in temporary charge.
30   Terry Butcher appointed manager of Newport County.

MAY 2015

4   Gary Brabin appointed manager of Tranmere Rovers.
5   Darren Kelly appointed manager of Oldham Athletic.
9   Lee Clark resigns as manager of Blackpool.
12   Paul Cook leaves Chesterfield to become manager of Portsmouth.
13   Dean Saunders appointed manager of Chesterfield. Fabio Liverani leaves as manager of Leyton Orient by mutal consent.
19   Mark Yates appointed manager of Crawley Town.
20   Neil Redfearn sacked as manager of Leeds United. Uwe Rosler appointed manager.
21   Graham Westley sacked as manager of Stevenage. Teddy Sheringham appointed manager.
24   Sam Allardyce leaves as manager of West Ham United by mutual consent.
25   Steve McClaren sacked as manager of Derby Co. Nigel Clough sacked as manager of Sheffield United.
28   John Sheridan leaves as manager of Plymouth Argyle by mutual consent. Ian Hendon appointed manager of Leyton Orient.

JUNE 2015

1   Paul Clement appointed manager of Derby County. Marinus Dijkhuizen appointed manager of Brentford.
2   Nigel Adkins appointed manager of Sheffield United. Neil McDonald appointed manager of Blackpool.
5   Quique Sanchez Flores appointed manager of Watford replacing Slavisa Jokanovic.
9   Slaven Bilic appointed manager of West Ham United. John Carver sacked as manager of Newcastle United.
10   Steve McClaren appointed manager of Newcastle United.
11   Derek Adams appointed manager of Plymouth Argyle. Stuart Gray sacked as manager of Sheffield Wednesday.
14   Chris Hargreaves leaves Torquay United.
17   Paul Cox appointed manager of Torquay United.
30   Nigel Pearson sacked as manager of Leicester City.

TRANSFERS 2014–15

JUNE 2014 TRANSFERS	From	To	Fee in £
20 Akinfenwa, Adebayo	Gillingham	AFC Wimbledon	Free
18 Akins, Lucas	Stevenage	Burton Alb	Undisclosed
6 Ansah, Zak	Arsenal	Charlton Ath	Free
26 Azeez, Adebayo	Charlton Ath	AFC Wimbledon	Free
24 Barnard, Lee	Southampton	Southend U	Free
5 Basham, Chris	Blackpool	Sheffield U	Free
7 Benayoun, Yossi	QPR	Maccabi Haifa	Free
19 Bishop, Neal	Blackpool	Scunthorpe U	Free
10 Bowery, Jordan	Aston Villa	Rotherham U	Undisclosed
17 Bradley, Sonny	Portsmouth	Crawley T	Undisclosed
23 Bradshaw, Tom	Shrewsbury T	Walsall	Undisclosed
27 Brandy, Febian	Sheffield U	Rotherham U	Free
9 Broadfoot, Kirk	Blackpool	Rotherham U	Free
23 Brown, Chris	Doncaster R	Blackburn R	Free
10 Bulman, Dannie	Crawley T	AFC Wimbledon	Free
5 Butler, Andy	Walsall	Sheffield U	Free
28 Buttner, Alexander	Manchester U	Dynamo Moscow	£4.4m
23 Carrico, Daniel	Reading	Sevilla	Undisclosed
30 Carson, Trevor	Bury	Cheltenham T	Free
24 Cathcart, Craig	Blackpool	Watford	Free
18 Caton, James	Blackpool	Shrewsbury T	Free
7 Chadwick, Luke	Milton Keynes D	Cambridge U	Free
19 Chambers, Ashley	Cambridge U	Dagenham & R	Free
27 Clarke, Billy	Crawley T	Bradford C	Free
9 Colback, Jack	Sunderland	Newcastle U	Free
10 Cole, Joe	West Ham U	Aston Villa	Free
24 Cotterill, David	Doncaster R	Birmingham C	Free
23 Cousins, Mark	Colchester U	Dagenham & R	Free
9 Croasdale, Ryan	Preston NE	Sheffield W	Free
13 Davies, Adam	Sheffield W	Barnsley	Free
9 Davies, Ben	Derby Co	Sheffield U	Free
30 Dickenson, Brennan	Brighton & HA	Gillingham	Free
27 Dicker, Gary	Crawley T	Carlisle U	Free
4 Dickson, Ryan	Colchester U	Crawley T	Free
12 Dikgacoi, Kagisho	Crystal Palace	Cardiff C	Free
25 Donaldson, Clayton	Brentford	Birmingham C	Free
30 Drury, Andy	Crawley T	Luton T	£100,000
10 Duff, Damien	Fulham	Melbourne City	Free
18 Duffy, Mark	Doncaster R	Birmingham C	Free
24 Dunne, James	Stevenage	Portsmouth	Free
12 Dyer, Lloyd	Leicester C	Watford	Free
12 Edgar, David	Burnley	Birmingham C	Free
25 Elliott, Wade	Birmingham C	Bristol C	Free
27 Etuhu, Kelvin	Barnsley	Bury	Free
7 Ferry, Simon	Portsmouth	Dundee	Free
26 Freeman, Luke	Stevenage	Bristol C	Undisclosed
9 Fryatt, Matt	Hull C	Nottingham F	Free
9 Gleeson, Stephen	Milton Keynes D	Birmingham C	Free
5 Grabban, Lewis	Bournemouth	Norwich C	Undisclosed
20 Grainger, Danny	Dunfermline Ath	Carlisle U	Free
27 Gray, Andre	Luton T	Brentford	Undisclosed
30 Green, Paul	Leeds U	Rotherham U	Free
2 Grounds, Jonathan	Oldham Ath	Birmingham C	Free
26 Hall, Ryan	Milton Keynes D	Rotherham U	Free
5 Halstead, Mark	Blackpool	Shrewsbury T	Free
27 Harrold, Matt	Bristol R	Crawley T	Free
19 Hartley, Peter	Stevenage	Plymouth Arg	Free
24 Haworth, Andy	Notts Co	Cheltenham T	Free
26 Henderson, Conor	Hull C	Crawley T	Free
30 Henry, Ronnie	Luton T	Stevenage	Free
27 Henshall, Alex	Manchester C	Ipswich T	Free
27 Holness, Marcus	Burton Alb	Tranmere R	Free
23 Hourihane, Conor	Plymouth Arg	Barnsley	Undisclosed
19 Hugill, Jordan	Port Vale	Preston NE	Undisclosed
11 Hunt, Johnny	Wrexham	Cambridge U	Compensation
6 Hylton, Danny	Rotherham U	Oxford U	Free
18 Ihiekwe, Michael	Wolverhampton W	Tranmere R	Free
5 Jalal, Shwan	Bournemouth	Bury	Free
7 Jervis, Jake	Portsmouth	Ross Co	Free
6 Jones, Jamie	Leyton Orient	Preston NE	Free
10 Jones, Mike	Crawley T	Oldham Ath	Free
4 Jones, Paul	Crawley T	Portsmouth	Free
2 Judge, Alan	Blackburn R	Brentford	Undisclosed
27 Kelly, Liam	Bristol C	Oldham Ath	Undisclosed
19 Kettings, Chris	Blackpool	Crystal Palace	Free
27 Kightly, Michael	Stoke C	Burnley	Undisclosed
30 Krysiak, Artur	Exeter C	Yeovil T	Free
20 Laing, Louis	Sunderland	Nottingham F	Free
2 Lambert, Rickie	Southampton	Liverpool	£4m
13 Legzdins, Adam	Derby Co	Leyton Orient	Free
27 Leitch-Smith, AJ	Crewe Alex	Yeovil T	Free
20 Lescott, Joleon	Manchester C	WBA	Free
11 Leutwiler, Jayson	Middlesbrough	Shrewsbury T	Free
9 Liddle, Gary	Notts Co	Bradford C	Free
25 Little, Mark	Peterborough U	Bristol C	Free
25 Livermore, Jake	Tottenham H	Hull C	£8m
5 Loach, Scott	Ipswich T	Rotherham U	Free
10 Loft, Doug	Port Vale	Gillingham	Free
13 Luiz, David	Chelsea	Paris Saint-Germain	£40m

4	Martin, Aaron	Birmingham C	Yeovil T	Free
24	McElroy, Paul	Hull C	Sheffield W	Free
20	McFadzean, Kyle	Crawley T	Milton Keynes D	Undisclosed
3	McGlashan, Jermaine	Cheltenham T	Gillingham	Free
16	McHugh, Carl	Bradford C	Plymouth Arg	Free
25	McLeod, Izale	Milton Keynes D	Crawley T	Free
26	Mellor, Kelvin	Crewe Alex	Plymouth Arg	Free
4	Mills, Joseph	Burnley	Oldham Ath	Free
4	Mitchell, Jonathan	Newcastle U	Derby Co	Free
6	Mousinho, John	Preston NE	Burton Alb	Free
5	Mullins, Hayden	Birmingham C	Notts Co	Free
17	Murphy, Joe	Coventry C	Huddersfield T	Free
20	Murphy, Peter	Accrington S	Wycombe W	Free
11	Myrie-Williams, Jennison	Port Vale	Scunthorpe U	Free
3	Noble, Liam	Carlisle U	Notts Co	Free
21	O'Connor, James	Derby Co	Walsall	Free
26	Odejayi, Kayode	Rotherham U	Tranmere R	Free
27	Odubajo, Moses	Leyton Orient	Brentford	£1m
4	Oyebanjo, Lanre	York C	Crawley T	Free
16	Pantilimon, Costel	Manchester C	Sunderland	Free
26	Parnaby, Stuart	Middlesbrough	Hartlepool U	Free
27	Paynter, Billy	Doncaster R	Carlisle U	Free
23	Peltier, Lee	Leeds U	Huddersfield T	Free
23	Phillips, Mark	Southend U	AFC Wimbledon	Free
24	Poke, Michael	Torquay U	Portsmouth	Free
17	Pritchard, Josh	Fulham	Gillingham	Free
24	Proctor, Jamie	Crawley T	Fleetwood T	Free
11	Redmond, Danny	Wigan Ath	Hamilton A	Free
24	Reid, Kyel	Bradford C	Preston NE	Free
27	Richardson, Frazer	Middlesbrough	Rotherham U	Free
25	Ridgewell, Liam	WBA	Portland Timbers	Free
26	Riether, Sascha	Fulham	SC Freiburg	Undisclosed
3	Rowe, Tommy	Peterborough U	Wolverhampton W	Free
17	Sadler, Mat	Crawley T	Rotherham U	Free
13	Sagna, Bacary	Arsenal	Manchester C	Free
3	Sanders, Ed	Stoke C	Sheffield W	Free
27	Shaw, Luke	Southampton	Manchester U	£27m (rising to £31m)
19	Sheehan, Alan	Notts Co	Bradford C	Free
9	Sidwell, Steve	Fulham	Stoke C	Free
9	Simpson, Robbie	Leyton Orient	Cambridge U	Free
27	Smith, Korey	Oldham Ath	Bristol C	Undisclosed
30	Snodgrass, Robert	Norwich C	Hull C	Undisclosed
30	Sokolik, Jakub	Liverpool	Yeovil T	Free
26	Southern, Keith	Huddersfield T	Fleetwood T	Free
26	Stanislas, Junior	Burnley	Bournemouth	Free
12	Straker, Anthony	Southend U	York C	Free
30	Summerfield, Luke	Shrewsbury T	York C	Free
30	Sweeney, Antony	Hartlepool U	Carlisle U	Free
28	Tavernier, James	Newcastle U	Wigan Ath	Undisclosed
3	Taylor, Andrew	Cardiff C	Wigan Ath	Free
4	Taylor, Jon	Shrewsbury T	Peterborough U	Undisclosed
30	Taylor, Lyle	Sheffield U	Scunthorpe U	Undisclosed
11	Thomas, Wes	Rotherham U	Birmingham C	Free
18	Tomlin, Gavin	Port Vale	Crawley T	Undisclosed
13	Wallace, James	Tranmere R	Sheffield U	Free
30	Walton, Simon	Hartlepool U	Stevenage	Free
30	Weale, Chris	Shrewsbury T	Yeovil T	Free
24	Webster, Byron	Yeovil T	Millwall	Free
6	Wesolowski, James	Oldham Ath	Shrewsbury T	Free
14	Weston, Myles	Gillingham	Southend U	Free
30	Whelpdale, Chris	Gillingham	Stevenage	Free
27	Whitbread, Zak	Leicester C	Derby Co	Free
10	Wilson, Brian	Colchester U	Oldham Ath	Free
26	Wood, Richard	Charlton Ath	Rotherham U	Free
9	Woods, Calum	Huddersfield T	Preston NE	Free
7	Worley, Harry	Newport Co	Stevenage	Free
30	Wroe, Nicky	Preston NE	Notts Co	Free
3	Young, Matt	Southampton	Sheffield W	Free

JULY 2014

25	Aanholt, Patrick van	Chelsea	Sunderland	Undisclosed
2	Akpro, Jean-Louis Akpa	Tranmere R	Shrewsbury T	Free
14	Alagui, Farid El	Brentford	Hibernian	Free
15	Alcock, Craig	Peterborough U	Sheffield U	Free
25	Andrew, Calvin	York C	Rochdale	Free
9	Angol, Lee	Wycombe W	Luton T	Free
2	Archibald-Henville, Troy	Swindon T	Carlisle U	Free
22	Atkinson, Chris	Huddersfield T	Crewe Alex	Free
8	Ayling, Luke	Yeovil T	Bristol C	Compensation
18	Ba, Demba	Chelsea	Besiktas	£4.7m
22	Bailey, James	Derby Co	Barnsley	Free
7	Baird, Chris	Burnley	WBA	Free
30	Ball, Callum	Derby Co	St Mirren	Free
8	Barry, Gareth	Manchester C	Everton	Free
25	Bawling, Bobson	Watford	Crawley T	Free
12	Beardsley, Chris	Preston NE	Stevenage	Free
25	Bebe	Manchester U	Benfica	£2.4m
22	Benson, Paul	Swindon T	Luton T	Free
3	Berrett, James	Carlisle U	Yeovil T	Free
29	Berry, Luke	Cambridge U	Barnsley	Undisclosed
15	Bialkowski, Bartosz	Notts Co	Ipswich T	Undisclosed
31	Brown, Junior	Fleetwood T	Oxford U	Free
31	Brown, Reece	Watford	Barnsley	Undisclosed
17	Buaben, Prince	Carlisle U	Hearts	Free
29	Burke, Chris	Birmingham C	Nottingham F	Free
20	Buxton, Adam	Wigan Ath	Accrington S	Free

22	Campana, Jose	Crystal Palace	Sampdoria	Undisclosed
24	Campbell, Fraizer	Cardiff C	Crystal Palace	£900,000
22	Caulker, Steven	Cardiff C	QPR	Undisclosed
28	Chambers, Calum	Southampton	Arsenal	£16m
10	Christie, Cyrus	Coventry C	Derby Co	Undisclosed
17	Clark, Jordan	Barnsley	Shrewsbury T	Free
28	Clarke, Peter	Huddersfield T	Blackpool	Free
7	Cole, Ashley	Chelsea	Roma	Free
15	Collins, Michael	Scunthorpe U	Oxford U	Free
11	Connolly, Mark	Crawley T	Kilmarnock	Free
5	Connolly, Paul	Crawley T	Luton T	Free
7	Cook, Jordan	Charlton Ath	Walsall	Free
10	Cowie, Don	Cardiff C	Wigan Ath	Free
3	Cresswell, Aaron	Ipswich T	West Ham U	Undisclosed
24	Cureton, Jamie	Cheltenham T	Dagenham & R	Free
28	Cywka, Tomasz	Barnsley	Blackpool	Free
23	Davies, Ben	Swansea C	Tottenham H	Undisclosed
17	Debuchy, Mathieu	Newcastle U	Arsenal	Undisclosed
29	Dejagah, Ashkan	Fulham	Al-Arabi	Undisclosed
29	Delfouneso, Nathan	Aston Villa	Blackpool	Free
11	Edwards, Gwion	Swansea C	Crawley T	Undisclosed
3	Egan, John	Sunderland	Gillingham	Free
23	Eisfeld, Thomas	Arsenal	Fulham	Undisclosed
2	Emnes, Marvin	Middlesbrough	Swansea C	Undisclosed
30	Evina, Cedric	Charlton Ath	Doncaster R	Free
21	Evra, Patrice	Manchester U	Juventus	£1.2m
18	Faraoni, Marco Davide	Watford	Udinese	Undisclosed
21	Fenlon, James	AFC Wimbledon	Ross Co	Free
17	Ferdinand, Rio	Manchester U	QPR	Free
18	Frempah, Ben	Leicester C	Ross Co	Free
16	Fuller, Ricardo	Blackpool	Millwall	Free
10	Gayle, Cameron	WBA	Shrewsbury T	Free
2	Gilks, Matt	Blackpool	Burnley	Free
15	Goodall, Alan	Fleetwood T	Morecambe	Free
7	Goodwillie, David	Blackburn R	Aberdeen	Free
28	Granero, Esteban	QPR	Real Sociedad	Undisclosed
25	Grimes, Ashley	Bury	Walsall	Free
25	Gueye, Magaye	Everton	Millwall	Free
31	Haber, Marcus	Stevenage	Crewe Alex	Free
28	Hemmings, Ashley	Walsall	Dagenham & R	Free
21	Henderson, Stephen	West Ham U	Charlton Ath	Free
1	Hitchcock, Tom	QPR	Milton Keynes D	Free
21	Hogan, Scott	Rochdale	Brentford	Undisclosed
2	Horwood, Evan	Tranmere R	Northampton T	Free
14	Hughes, Aaron	QPR	Brighton & HA	Free
22	Hughes, Andy	Charlton Ath	Bolton W	Free
30	Husband, James	Doncaster R	Middlesbrough	Undisclosed
8	Hutchinson, Sam	Chelsea	Sheffield W	Free
7	Ince, Tom	Blackpool	Hull C	Compensation
1	Jacobson, Joe	Shrewsbury T	Wycombe W	Free
4	Johnson, Reda	Sheffield W	Coventry C	Free
15	Jutkiewicz, Lukas	Middlesbrough	Burnley	£1.5m
9	Kasami, Pajtim	Fulham	Olympiacos	Undisclosed
11	Kearns, Danny	Peterborough U	Carlisle U	Free
8	Labadie, Joss	Torquay U	Dagenham & R	Free
10	Laird, Marc	Southend U	Tranmere R	Free
1	Lallana, Adam	Southampton	Liverpool	£25m
24	Lampard, Frank	Chelsea	New York C	Free
4	Lawrence, Liam	Barnsley	Shrewsbury T	Free
17	Leacock, Dean	Notts Co	Crawley T	Free
12	Lee, Charlie	Gillingham	Stevenage	Free
31	Lees, Tom	Leeds U	Sheffield W	Undisclosed
1	Lewington, Chris	Dagenham & R	Colchester U	Free
31	Llera, Miguel	Sheffield W	Scunthorpe U	Free
27	Lovren, Dejan	Southampton	Liverpool	£20m
21	Lowry, Shane	Millwall	Leyton Orient	Free
30	Lukaku, Romelu	Chelsea	Everton	£28m
2	Lynch, Alex	Peterborough U	Wycombe W	Free
29	Maguire, Harry	Sheffield U	Hull C	£2.5m
30	Main, Curtis	Middlesbrough	Doncaster R	Swap
15	Marrow, Alex	Blackburn R	Carlisle U	Free
2	Marshall, Mark	Coventry C	Port Vale	Free
26	McAnuff, Jobi	Reading	Leyton Orient	Free
8	McCormack, Ross	Leeds U	Fulham	£11m
18	McGahey, Harrison	Blackpool	Sheffield U	Compensation
23	McLaughlin, Jon	Bradford C	Burton Alb	Free
28	Mellis, Jacob	Barnsley	Blackpool	Free
1	Miller, Lee	Carlisle U	Kilmarnock	Free
16	Miller, Shaun	Sheffield U	Coventry C	Free
8	Moloney, Brendan	Bristol C	Yeovil T	Free
3	Moore, Byron	Crewe Alex	Port Vale	Free
21	Morgan-Smith, Amari	Kidderminster H	Oldham Ath	Free
2	Moussa, Franck	Coventry C	Charlton Ath	Free
2	Moxey, Dean	Crystal Palace	Bolton W	Free
28	Nasseri, Navid	Bury	Birmingham C	Free
22	Norburn, Oliver	Bristol R	Plymouth Arg	Free
3	Norris, Luke	Brentford	Gillingham	Compensation
16	Obadeyi, Tope	Bury	Kilmarnock	Free
4	O'Brien, Jim	Barnsley	Coventry C	Free
19	O'Grady, Chris	Barnsley	Brighton & HA	Undisclosed
31	Onovwigun, Michael	Brentford	Chesterfield	Free
23	Osman, Abdul	Crewe Alex	Partick Thistle	Free
7	Parr, Jonathan	Crystal Palace	Ipswich T	Free
8	Partridge, Matt	Reading	Dagenham & R	Free
8	Poyet, Diego	Charlton Ath	West Ham U	Compensation

24 Pozuelo, Alejandro	Swansea C	Rayo Vallecano	Undisclosed
10 Pritchard, Bradley	Charlton Ath	Leyton Orient	Free
16 Pugh, Danny	Leeds U	Coventry C	Free
7 Reid, Steven	WBA	Burnley	Free
11 Richardson, Kieran	Fulham	Aston Villa	Undisclosed
29 Robertson, Andrew	Dundee U	Hull C	£2.85m
17 Robinson, Andy	Tranmere R	Shrewsbury T	Free
17 Rodgers, Anton	Oldham Ath	Swindon T	Free
18 Rowley, Louis	Manchester U	Leicester C	Free
1 Santos, Alefe	Bristol R	Derby Co	Compensation
24 Scocco, Ignacio	Sunderland	Newell's Old Boys	£2.1m
2 Seabright, Jordan	Dagenham & R	Torquay U	Free
3 Shearer, Scott	Rotherham U	Crewe Alex	Free
23 Sigurdsson, Gylfi	Tottenham H	Swansea C	Undisclosed
8 Smith, Jack	Millwall	AFC Wimbledon	Free
25 Smith, Michael	Bristol R	Peterborough U	Undisclosed
4 Sordell, Marvin	Bolton W	Burnley	Undisclosed
21 Sow, Osman	Crystal Palace	Hearts	Free
18 Steele, Luke	Barnsley	Panathinaikos	Free
21 Sterling-James, Omari	Birmingham C	Cheltenham T	Free
1 Stewart, Cameron	Hull C	Ipswich T	Free
28 Stockdale, David	Fulham	Brighton & HA	Undisclosed
16 Suarez, Luis	Liverpool	Barcelona	£75m
3 Swanson, Danny	Peterborough U	Coventry C	Free
4 Taylor, Matt	West Ham U	Burnley	Free
25 Taylor, Matt	Bradford C	Cheltenham T	Free
28 Taylor, Quade	Crystal Palace	Bolton W	Free
3 Taylor, Stuart	Reading	Leeds U	Free
23 Thompson, Garry	Bradford C	Notts Co	Free
19 Thorne, George	WBA	Derby Co	Undisclosed
29 Tudgay, Marcus	Nottingham F	Coventry C	Free
23 Turnbull, Ross	Doncaster R	Barnsley	Free
28 Tyson, Nathan	Blackpool	Doncaster R	Free
22 Ulloa, Leonardo	Brighton & HA	Leicester C	£8m
1 Varney, Luke	Leeds U	Blackburn R	Free
23 Vorm, Michel	Swansea C	Tottenham H	Undisclosed
7 Westwood, Keiren	Sunderland	Sheffield W	Free
2 Wilbraham, Aaron	Crystal Palace	Bristol C	Free
7 Wilkinson, Luke	Dagenham & R	Luton T	Undisclosed
4 Wilson, Callum	Coventry C	Bournemouth	Undisclosed
16 Wilson, Laurence	Accrington S	Morecambe	Free
23 Winnall, Sam	Scunthorpe U	Barnsley	Undisclosed
28 Woodards, Danny	Bristol R	Tranmere R	Free
17 Woods, Gary	Watford	Leyton Orient	Free
23 Worrall, David	Rotherham U	Southend U	Free
14 Young, Lewis	Bury	Crawley T	Free
11 Zaliukas, Marius	Leeds U	Rangers	Free

AUGUST 2014

1 Acuna, Javier	Watford	Olimpia Asuncion	Undisclosed
7 Adeyemi, Tom	Birmingham C	Cardiff C	Undisclosed
21 Agard, Kieran	Rotherham U	Bristol C	Undisclosed
30 Agger, Daniel	Liverpool	Brondby	Undisclosed
5 Ajose, Nicky	Peterborough U	Leeds U	Undisclosed
9 Amadi-Holloway, Aaron	Newport Co	Wycombe W	Free
11 Ameobi, Shola	Newcastle U	Gaziantep BB	Free
6 Antonio, Michail	Sheffield W	Nottingham F	£1.5m
29 Ariyibi, Gboly	Leeds U	Chesterfield	Free
18 Armstrong, Luke	Middlesbrough	Birmingham C	Free
29 Ashdown, Jamie	Leeds U	Crawley T	Free
6 Assombalonga, Britt	Peterborough U	Nottingham F	£5.5m
27 Baldock, Sam	Bristol C	Brighton & HA	Undisclosed
7 Banya, Charles	Fulham	Crawley T	Free
15 Bendtner, Nicklas	Arsenal	Wolfsburg	Free
9 Boco, Romuald	Plymouth Arg	Chesterfield	Free
5 Bolger, Cian	Bolton W	Southend U	Undisclosed
7 Boucaud, Andre	Notts Co	Dagenham & R	Free
18 Brezovan, Peter	Brighton & HA	Portsmouth	Free
1 Briggs, Matthew	Fulham	Millwall	Free
9 Bruna, Gerardo	Blackpool	Tranmere R	Free
14 Buckley, Will	Brighton & HA	Sunderland	Undisclosed
13 Butterfield, Jacob	Middlesbrough	Huddersfield T	Swap
26 Carreiro, Dylan	QPR	Dundee	Free
6 Carruthers, Samir	Aston Villa	Milton Keynes D	Undisclosed
19 Cesar, Julio	QPR	Benfica	Free
9 Chantler, Chris	Carlisle U	Kilmarnock	Free
1 Charles-Cook, Reice	Bury	Coventry C	Free
13 Clayton, Adam	Huddersfield T	Middlesbrough	Swap
9 Clifford, Billy	Chelsea	Walsall	Free
6 Coady, Conor	Liverpool	Huddersfield T	Undisclosed
13 Cooper, Liam	Chesterfield	Leeds U	Undisclosed
7 Cox, Simon	Nottingham F	Reading	Undisclosed
1 Crainey, Stephen	Wigan Ath	Fleetwood T	Free
20 Cuellar, Carlos	Sunderland	Norwich C	Free
15 Cummins, Graham	Preston NE	Exeter C	Free
9 Darlow, Karl	Nottingham F	Newcastle U	Undisclosed
11 Davis, David	Wolverhampton W	Birmingham C	Undisclosed
26 Dawson, Michael	Tottenham H	Hull C	Undisclosed
13 Dawson, Stephen	Barnsley	Rochdale	Free
22 Deegan, Gary	Northampton T	Southend U	Free
29 Demetriou, James	Nottingham F	Swansea C	Free
29 Doumbia, Tongo	Wolverhampton W	Toulouse	Undisclosed
18 Edwards, Mike	Carlisle U	Notts Co	Free
9 Elokobi, George	Wolverhampton W	Oldham Ath	Free
26 Eto'o, Samuel	Chelsea	Everton	Free
1 Falque, Iago	Tottenham H	Genoa	Undisclosed

19	Featherstone, Nicky	Walsall	Scunthorpe U	Free
20	Fer, Leroy	Norwich C	QPR	£8m
11	Ferdinand, Anton	Antalyaspor	Reading	Free
9	Flores, Chico	Swansea C	Lekhwiya SC	Undisclosed
26	Fontaine, Liam	Bristol C	Hibernian	Free
12	Forde, Anthony	Wolverhampton W	Walsall	Undisclosed
9	Forster, Fraser	Celtic	Southampton	£10m
1	Forte, Jonathan	Southampton	Oldham Ath	Free
2	Galloway, Brendan	Milton Keynes D	Everton	Undisclosed
14	Garcia, Javi	Manchester C	Zenit St Petersburg	£13m
7	Gillett, Simon	Nottingham F	Yeovil T	Free
27	Griffith, Anthony	Port Vale	Shrewsbury T	Free
1	Hangeland, Brede	Fulham	Crystal Palace	Free
1	Henderson, Darius	Nottingham F	Leyton Orient	Free
9	Hill, Matt	Sheffield U	Tranmere R	Free
25	Hoskins, Will	Brighton & HA	Oxford U	Free
19	Hoyte, Gavin	Dagenham & R	Gillingham	Free
18	Jackson, Simeon	Millwall	Coventry C	Free
20	Jerome, Cameron	Stoke C	Norwich C	Undisclosed
7	Jones, Gary	Bradford C	Notts Co	Free
31	Kagawa, Shinji	Manchester U	Borussia Dortmund	Undisclosed
18	Kee, Billy	Burton Alb	Scunthorpe U	Undisclosed
14	Kelly, Martin	Liverpool	Crystal Palace	Undisclosed
14	Kennedy, Tom	Barnsley	Rochdale	Free
3	Koren, Robert	Hull C	Melbourne C	Free
28	Lanzoni, Matteo	Yeovil T	Cambridge U	Free
21	Lappin, Simon	Cardiff C	St Johnstone	Free
9	Lascelles, Jamaal	Nottingham F	Newcastle U	Undisclosed
9	Lita, Leroy	Swansea C	Barnsley	Free
14	Long, Shane	Hull C	Southampton	£12m
9	Lynch, Jay	Bolton W	Accrington S	Free
7	Marosi, Marko	Wigan Ath	Doncaster R	Free
28	Marquis, John	Millwall	Cheltenham T	Free
5	Martin, Connor	Rochdale	Accrington S	Free
29	McCarthy, Alex	Reading	QPR	Undisclosed
1	McDonald, Shaquille	York C	Derby Co	Free
15	McEveley, Jay	Swindon T	Sheffield U	Free
9	Medel, Gary	Cardiff C	Internazionale	£10m
6	Miller, Ishmael	Nottingham F	Blackpool	Free
9	Miller, Tommy	Bury	Hartlepool U	Free
9	Morais, Filipe	Stevenage	Bradford C	Free
15	Morrison, Sean	Reading	Cardiff C	Undisclosed
2	Mullin, Paul	Huddersfield T	Morecambe	Free
11	Mustoe, Jordan	Wigan Ath	Accrington S	Free
5	Mutch, Jordon	Cardiff C	QPR	£6m
15	Ngoo, Michael	Liverpool	Kilmarnock	Free
15	Noble, David	Rotherham U	Oldham Ath	Free
21	Norwood, Oliver	Huddersfield T	Reading	Undisclosed
5	O'Neil, Gary	QPR	Norwich C	Free
9	Orlandi, Andrea	Brighton & HA	Blackpool	Free
7	Parish, Elliot	Bristol C	Blackpool	Free
15	Pilkington, Anthony	Norwich C	Cardiff C	£1m
9	Poole, James	Hartlepool U	Bury	Free
4	Porter, George	Rochdale	Dagenham & R	Free
7	Proschwitz, Nick	Hull C	Brentford	Free
29	Reeves, Jake	Brentford	Swindon T	Free
9	Reina, Pepe	Liverpool	Bayern Munich	Undisclosed
31	Remy, Loic	QPR	Chelsea	£10.5m
21	Ribeiro, Christian	Scunthorpe U	Exeter C	Free
28	Robinson, Jack	Liverpool	QPR	Undisclosed
6	Rochina, Ruben	Blackburn R	Granada	Undisclosed
5	Rodwell, Jack	Manchester C	Sunderland	£10m
18	Rose, Danny	Barnsley	Bury	Undisclosed
22	Samaras, Georgios	Celtic	WBA	Free
26	Saville, George	Chelsea	Wolverhampton W	Undisclosed
11	Seaborne, Daniel	Coventry C	Partick Thistle	Free
5	Shariff, Mo	QPR	Bradford C	Free
13	Sharp, Billy	Southampton	Leeds U	Undisclosed
30	Simpson, Danny	QPR	Leicester C	Undisclosed
4	Simpson, Luke	Oldham Ath	Accrington S	Free
22	Smallwood, Richard	Middlesbrough	Rotherham U	Undisclosed
7	Smith, Tommy	Cardiff C	Brentford	Free
21	Spence, Jordan	West Ham U	Milton Keynes D	Free
5	Taylor, Rob	Port Vale	Mansfield T	Free
6	Thompson, Joe	Tranmere R	Bury	Free
15	Turner, Iain	Barnsley	Sheffield U	Free
5	Urwin, Matt	Blackburn R	Bradford C	Free
10	Vermaelen, Thomas	Arsenal	Barcelona	£15m
1	Wabara, Reece	Manchester C	Doncaster R	Free
15	Ward, Stephen	Wolverhampton W	Burnley	Undisclosed
6	Whitehouse, Elliott	Sheffield U	Notts Co	Free
14	Whittall, Sam	Wolverhampton W	Cambridge U	Free
6	Widdowson, Joe	Northampton T	Bury	Free
15	Zoko, Francois	Stevenage	Blackpool	Free

SEPTEMBER 2014

1	Adorjan, Krisztian	Liverpool	Novara Calcio	Undisclosed
1	Beavon, Stuart	Preston NE	Burton Alb	Undisclosed
1	Bingham, Rakish	Wigan Ath	Mansfield T	Free
1	Bird, Ryan	Portsmouth	Cambridge U	Free
1	Boyd, George	Hull C	Burnley	£3m
1	Brezovan, Peter	Portsmouth	Tranmere R	Free
1	Canas, Jose	Swansea C	Espanyol	Free
1	Clarke-Harris, Jonson	Oldham Ath	Rotherham U	Undisclosed
18	Clayton, Max	Crewe Alex	Bolton W	£300,000
1	Cresswell, Ryan	Fleetwood T	Northampton T	Undisclosed

1 Diame, Mohamed	West Ham U	Hull C	Undisclosed
1 Donnelly, George	Rochdale	Tranmere R	Undisclosed
1 Duffy, Shane	Everton	Blackburn R	Undisclosed
1 Eccleston, Nathan	Coventry C	Partick Thistle	Free
1 El Ahmadi, Karim	Aston Villa	Feyenoord	Undisclosed
1 Forshaw, Adam	Brentford	Wigan Ath	Undisclosed
1 Fryers, Zeki	Tottenham H	Crystal Palace	Undisclosed
1 Hudson, Mark	Cardiff C	Huddersfield T	Undisclosed
1 Huws, Emyr	Manchester C	Wigan Ath	Undisclosed
1 James, Luke	Hartlepool U	Peterborough U	Undisclosed
2 Lawrence, Byron	Ipswich T	Colchester U	Free
1 Lawrence, Tom	Manchester U	Leicester C	Undisclosed
2 Martinez, Angel	Blackpool	Millwall	Free
1 McArthur, James	Wigan Ath	Crystal Palace	£7m
1 Miquel, Ignasi	Arsenal	Norwich C	Undisclosed
1 Obika, Jonathan	Tottenham H	Swindon T	Undisclosed
1 Poleon, Dominic	Leeds U	Oldham Ath	Undisclosed
1 Procter, Andy	Bury	Accrington S	Free
1 Sandro,	Tottenham H	QPR	£6m
1 Scott, Kris	Swansea C	Leicester C	Free
1 Smith, Matt	Leeds U	Fulham	Undisclosed
1 Surman, Andrew	Norwich C	Bournemouth	Undisclosed
1 Thompson, Louis	Swindon T	Norwich C	Undisclosed
1 Welbeck, Danny	Manchester U	Arsenal	£16m

OCTOBER 2014

24 Ighalo, Odion	Udinese	Watford	Undisclosed

NOVEMBER 2014

18 Moncur, George	West Ham U	Colchester U	Undisclosed

DECEMBER 2014

31 Cowan-Hall, Paris	Wycombe W	Millwall	Undisclosed
22 Daehli, Mats Moller	Cardiff C	Freiburg	Undisclosed
29 Day, Joe	Peterborough U	Newport Co	Undisclosed
16 Morrison, Michael	Charlton Ath	Birmingham C	Undisclosed
27 Torres, Fernando	Chelsea	AC Milan	Undisclosed

JANUARY 2015

14 Afobe, Benik	Arsenal	Wolverhampton W	Undisclosed
16 Altidore, Jozy	Sunderland	Toronto	Swap
29 Ameobi, Shola	Gaziantep	Crystal Palace	Free
13 Assaidi, Oussama	Liverpool	Al Ahli Club	Undisclosed
20 Bajner, Balint	Ipswich T	Notts Co	Free
15 Barrett, Adam	Gillingham	Southend U	Free
9 Bean, Marcus	Colchester U	Wycombe W	Free
29 Bell, Fergus	Mansfield T	Yeovil T	Free
5 Ben Arfa, Hatem	Newcastle U	Nice	Free
13 Blair, Matty	Fleetwood T	Mansfield T	Free
20 Boco, Romuald	Chesterfield	Bharat FC	Free
14 Bony, Wilfried	Swansea C	Manchester C	£28m
12 Brandy, Febian	Rotherham U	Rochdale	Free
24 Brayford, John	Cardiff C	Sheffield U	Undisclosed
7 Brown, Junior	Oxford U	Mansfield T	Free
20 Brunt, Ryan	Bristol R	Plymouth Arg	Free
6 Butler, Andy	Sheffield U	Doncaster R	Undisclosed
8 Byrom, Joel	Preston NE	Northampton T	Free
16 Bywater, Stephen	Millwall	Doncaster R	Free
9 Clarke, Jordan	Coventry C	Scunthorpe U	Undisclosed
6 Conlon, Tom	Peterborough U	Stevenage	Undisclosed
15 Connolly, David	Portsmouth	AFC Wimbledon	Free
30 Cork, Jack	Southampton	Swansea C	Undisclosed
23 Coutts, Paul	Derby Co	Sheffield U	Undisclosed
12 Cummings, Shaun	Reading	Millwall	Undisclosed
15 Daniels, Billy	Coventry C	Notts Co	Undisclosed
22 Daniels, Luke	WBA	Scunthorpe U	Undisclosed
16 Defoe, Jermain	Toronto	Sunderland	Swap
23 Drenthe, Royston	Reading	Kayseri Erciyesspor	Undisclosed
29 Dugdale, Adam	Crewe Alex	Tranmere R	Free
30 El Fitouri, Sadiq	Salford C	Manchester U	Undisclosed
5 Etheridge, Neil	Oldham Ath	Charlton Ath	Free
27 Eto'o, Samuel	Everton	Sampdoria	Undisclosed
9 Ferguson, David	Sunderland	Blackpool	Undisclosed
12 Foley, Kevin	Wolverhampton W	FC Copenhagen	Free
29 Forshaw, Adam	Wigan Ath	Middlesbrough	Undisclosed
23 Freeman, Kieron	Derby Co	Sheffield U	Free
7 Gerrard, Steven	Liverpool	LA Galaxy To be completed in July 2015 Free
30 Gorkss, Kaspars	Colchester U	Ergotelis	Free
5 Graham, Jordan	Aston Villa	Wolverhampton W	Undisclosed
15 Griffith, Anthony	Shrewsbury T	Carlise U	Free
2 Grimes, Matt	Exeter C	Swansea C	£1.75m
22 Halliday, Andrew	Middlesbrough	Bradford C	Free
12 Harley, Ryan	Swindon T	Exeter C	Free
29 Harney, Jamie	West Ham U	Colchester U	Free
27 Harrison, Byron	Cheltenham T	Chesterfield	Undisclosed
13 Hayhurst, Will	Preston NE	Notts Co	Free
27 Holmes, Ricky	Portsmouth	Northampton T	Free
1 Hope, Hallam	Everton	Bury	Undisclosed
8 Hunt, Noel	Leeds U	Ipswich T	Free
8 Jennings, Steve	Port Vale	Tranmere R	Free
23 Johnson, Daniel	Aston Villa	Preston NE	Undisclosed
8 Keane, Michael	Manchester U	Burnley	Undisclosed
20 Kenny, Paddy	Bolton W	Ipswich T	Free
7 Malone, Scott	Millwall	Cardiff C	Undisclosed
25 Maloney, Shaun	Wigan Ath	Chicago Fire	Undisclosed
9 Martin, Aaron	Yeovil T	Coventry C	Free
20 McAllister, David	Shrewsbury T	Stevenage	Free

29	McManaman, Callum	Wigan Ath	WBA	£4.75m
13	Molyneux, Lee	Crewe Alex	Tranmere R	Free
29	Mutch, Jordon	QPR	Crystal Palace	Undisclosed
22	Naughton, Kyle	Tottenham H	Swansea C	£5m
27	Newey, Tom	Oxford U	Northampton T	Free
6	Nicholls, Alex	Northampton T	Exeter C	Free
6	Noble, David	Oldham Ath	Exeter C	Free
13	Noble-Lazarus, Reuben	Barnsley	Rochdale	Free
9	Nouble, Frank	Ipswich T	Coventry C	Free
29	O'Keefe, Stuart	Crystal Palace	Cardiff C	Undisclosed
9	Oliver, Connor	Sunderland	Blackpool	Undisclosed
30	Pearce, Jason	Leeds U	Wigan Ath	Undisclosed
24	Peltier, Lee	Huddersfield T	Cardiff C	Undisclosed
22	Porter, Chris	Sheffield U	Colchester U	Free
16	Potter, Alfie	Oxford U	AFC Wimbledon	Free
29	Ramis, Ivan	Wigan Ath	Levante	Free
7	Ravenhill, Ricky	Northampton T	Mansfield T	Free
9	Raynes, Michael	Oxford U	Mansfield T	Free
7	Reeves, Jake	Swindon T	AFC Wimbledon	Free
9	Revell, Alex	Rotherham U	Cardiff C	Undisclosed
6	Richens, Michael	Peterborough U	Stevenage	Undisclosed
14	Riley, Joe	Bolton W	Bury	Free
7	Robinson, Paul	Millwall	Portsmouth	Free
6	Schwarzer, Mark	Chelsea	Leicester C	Free
15	Scowen, Josh	Wycombe W	Barnsley	Undisclosed
16	Sears, Freddie	Colchester U	Ipswich T	Undisclosed
1	Shotton, Ryan	Stoke C	Derby Co	Undisclosed
20	Sinclair, Emile	Northampton T	York C	Free
24	Skarz, Joe	Rotherham U	Oxford U	Free
6	Stewart, Anthony	Wycombe W	Crewe Alex	Undisclosed
17	Suso	Liverpool	AC Milan	Undisclosed
7	Taylor, Jason	Cheltenham T	Northampton T	Free
13	Taylor, Rob	Mansfield T	Tranmere R	Undisclosed
29	Thompson, Josh	Colchester U	Tranmere R	Free
9	Trotta, Marcello	Fulham	Avellino	Undisclosed
8	Tubbs, Matt	Bournemouth	Portsmouth	Free
7	Veseli, Freddie	Ipswich T	Port Vale	Free
12	Ward, Danny	Huddersfield T	Rotherham U	Undisclosed
15	Warnock, Stephen	Leeds U	Derby Co	Undisclosed
23	Watson, Ben	Wigan Ath	Watford	Undisclosed
9	Widdowson, Joe	Bury	Dagenham & R	Free
6	Wright, Josh	Millwall	Leyton Orient	Free
23	Wyke, Charlie	Middlesbrough	Carlise U	Undisclosed
10	Wynter, Alex	Crystal Palace	Colchester U	Undisclosed
27	Yanga-Mbiwa, Mapou	Newcastle U	Roma	£5.5m

FEBRUARY 2015

2	Aldred, Tom	Accrington S	Blackpool	Undisclosed
2	Alli, Dele	Milton Keynes D	Tottenham H	£5m
			Loaned back to Milton Keynes D until the end of the season	
3	Anderson	Manchester U	Internazional	Free
2	Anderson, Keshi	Barton R	Crystal Palace	Undisclosed
2	Andreu, Tony	Hamilton A	Norwich C	Undisclosed
2	Armstrong, Stuart	Dundee U	Celtic	Undisclosed
2	Barnett, Tyrone	Peterborough U	Shrewsbury T	Undisclosed
2	Bertrand, Ryan	Chelsea	Southampton	Undisclosed
6	Bo-kyung, Kim	Cardiff C	Wigan Ath	Free
2	Chung-yong, Lee	Bolton W	Crystal Palace	Undisclosed
5	Connolly, Dylan	Shelbourne	Ipswich T	Free
2	Dieseruvwe, Mani	Sheffield W	Chesterfield	Undisclosed
2	Dixon, Paul	Huddersfield T	Dundee U	Free
2	Done, Matt	Rochdale	Sheffield U	Undisclosed
2	Doyle, Eoin	Chesterfield	Cardiff C	Undisclosed
2	Fletcher, Darren	Manchester U	WBA	Free
2	Fyvie, Fraser	Wigan Ath	Hibernian	Free
2	Gornell, Terry	Cheltenham T	Accrington S	Free
2	Harrison, Scott	Sunderland	Hartlepool U	Undisclosed
23	Hazard, Thorgan	Chelsea	Borussia Monchengladbach	Undisclosed
2	Johnson, Marvin	Kidderminster H	Motherwell	Undisclosed
3	Johnson, Roger	Wolverhampton W	Charlton Ath	Free
2	Kennedy, Matthew	Everton	Cardiff C	Undisclosed
2	MacDonald, Alex	Burton Alb	Oxford U	Undisclosed
2	Manset, Mathieu	Walsall	Cheltenham T	Free
14	Martin, David	Luton T	Stevenage	Free
2	McCready, Tom	Morecambe	Exeter C	Free
2	McGinn, Stephen	Sheffield U	Dundee	Free
2	Miller, Ishmael	Blackpool	Huddersfield T	Undisclosed
2	Moloney, Brendan	Yeovil T	Northampton T	Free
2	Murphy, Rhys	Dagenham & R	Oldham Ath	Undisclosed
14	Norris, David	Leeds U	Peterborough U	Free
2	O'Connell, Jack	Blackburn R	Brentford	Undisclosed
2	O'Connor, Anthony	Blackburn R	Plymouth Arg	Undisclosed
2	Priest, Ben	Wolverhampton W	Dundee	Free
20	Rachubka, Paul	Oldham Ath	Crewe Alex	Free
2	Richards, Eliot	Tranmere R	Cheltenham T	Free
2	Schurrle, Andre	Chelsea	Wolfsburg	£22m
6	Slew, Jordan	Blackburn R	Cambridge U	Free
2	Thomas, Nathan	Plymouth Arg	Motherwell	Free
2	Turgott, Blair	West Ham U	Coventry C	Free
2	Twardzik, Filip	Celtic	Bolton W	Undisclosed
2	Vermijl, Marnick	Manchester U	Sheffield W	Undisclosed
2	Wynter, Jordan	Bristol C	Cheltenham T	Free
2	Zaha, Wilfried	Manchester U	Crystal Palace	Undisclosed

MARCH 2015

20 Doyle, Kevin	Wolverhampton W	Colorado Rapids	Free
11 Nastasic, Matija	Manchester C	Schalke	Undisclosed

MAY 2015

22 Adams, Nicky	Bury	Northampton T	Free
9 Barkhuizen, Tom	Blackpool	Morecambe	Free
29 Barrow, Scott	Macclesfield T	Newport Co	Free
20 Bell, Amari'i	Birmingham C	Fleetwood T	Free
21 Bennett, Kyle	Doncaster R	Portsmouth	Free
27 Bennett, Scot	Exeter C	Notts Co	Free
22 Benning, Malvind	Walsall	Mansfield T	Free
20 Bingham, Rakish	Mansfield T	Hartlepool U	Free
26 Boruc, Artur	Southampton	Bournemouth	Free
28 Buchanan, David	Preston NE	Northampton T	Free
15 Chapman, Adam	Newport Co	Mansfield T	Free
29 Collison, Jack	Ipswich T	Peterborough U	Free
26 Cuthbert, Scott	Leyton Orient	Luton T	Free
26 Davies, Tom	Fleetwood T	Accrington S	Free
20 Dawson, Stephen	Rochdale	Scunthorpe U	Free
27 Dorrans, Graham	WBA	Norwich C	Undisclosed
23 Dsane, Eddie	Preston NE	Fleetwood T	Free
27 Federici, Adam	Reading	Bournemouth	Free
28 Gladwin, Ben	Swindon T	QPR	Undisclosed
22 Green, Matt	Birmingham	Mansfield T	Free
28 Holmes, Lee	Preston NE	Exeter C	Free
27 Hughes, Mark	Morecambe	Stevenage	Free
26 Jackson, Ryan	Newport Co	Gillingham	Free
29 John-Lewis, Lenell	Grimsby	Newport Co	Free
19 Jones, Alex	WBA	Birmingham C	Free
21 Joyce, Luke	Accrington S	Carlisle U	Free
27 Keane, Keith	Preston NE	Cambridge U	Free
19 Kennedy, Jason	Bradford C	Carlisle U	Free
26 King, Jack	Preston NE	Scunthorpe U	Free
28 King, Joshua	Blackburn R	Bournemouth	Free
19 Legge, Leon	Gillingham	Cambridge U	Free
29 Lisbie, Kevin	Leyton Orient	Barnet	Free
28 Luongo, Massimo	Swindon T	QPR	Undisclosed
20 Marriott, Jack	Ipswich T	Luton T	Free
15 McManus, Declan	Aberdeen	Fleetwood T	Free
28 Naismith, Kal	Accrington S	Portsmouth	Undisclosed
22 O'Donnell, Richard	Walsall	Wigan Ath	Free
20 Oliver, Vadaine	Crewe Alex	York C	Free
7 Oyeleke, Manny	Brentford	Exeter C	Free
20 Perkins, David	Blackpool	Wigan Ath	Free
20 Potter, Alfie	AFC Wimbledon	Northampton T	Free
29 Potts, Dan	West Ham U	Luton T	Free
30 Randolph, Darren	Birmingham C	West Ham U	Free
20 Raynes, Michael	Mansfield T	Carlisle U	Free
25 Roberts, Mark	Fleetwood T	Cambridge U	Free
12 Roofe, Kemar	WBA	Oxford U	Undisclosed
14 Sadler, Mat	Rotherham U	Shrewsbury U	Free
13 Sercombe, Liam	Exeter C	Oxford U	Free
19 Sinclair, Scott	Manchester C	Aston Villa	Undisclosed
29 Taylor, Rhys	Macclesfield T	Newport Co	Free
26 Taylor, Ryan	Portsmouth	Oxford U	Free
21 Wallace, Jed	Portsmouth	Wolverhampton W	Undisclosed
28 Walsh, Joe	Crawley T	Milton Keynes D	Undisclosed
29 Wimmer, Kevin	1. FC Cologne	Tottenham H	Undisclosed
28 Wiseman, Scott	Preston NE	Scunthorpe U	Free
27 Woods, Martin	Ross Co	Shrewsbury T	Free

THE NEW FOREIGN LEGION 2014–15

JUNE 2014

	From	To	Fee in £
10 Bunjaku, Alban	Sevilla	Derby Co	Free
21 Buyens, Yoni	Standard Liege	Charlton Ath	Loan
11 Diouf, Mame Biram	Hannover 96	Stoke C	Free
12 Fabregas, Cesc	Barcelona	Chelsea	£30m
26 Fernando	Porto	Manchester C	In region of £12m
4 Fisher, Alex	AC Monza	Mansfield T	Free
27 Gomis, Bafetimbi	Lyon	Swansea C	Free
26 Herrera, Ander	Athletic Bilbao	Manchester U	£29m
25 Hoogland, Tim	Schalke	Fulham	Free
5 Keita, Seydou	Valencia	Roma	Free
18 Kouyate, Cheikhou	Anderlecht	West Ham U	Undisclosed
10 La Parra, Rajiv van	Heerenveen	Wolverhampton W	Free
27 Lafferty, Kyle	Palermo	Norwich C	Undisclosed
6 Perez, Ayoze	Tenerife	Newcastle U	Undisclosed
25 Ramiro, Marcos Tebar	UD Almeria	Brentford	Free
28 Riera, Oriol	Osasuna	Wigan Ath	Undisclosed
5 Senderos, Philippe	Valencia	Aston Villa	Free
24 Taggart, Stuart	Newcastle U Jets	Fulham	Undisclosed
11 Teixeira, Dionatan	Banska Bystrica	Stoke C	Undisclosed
24 Vetokele, Igor	FC Copenhagen	Charlton Ath	Undisclosed
12 Veldwijk, Lars	Excelsior	Nottingham F	Undisclosed
26 Vydra, Matej	Udinese	Watford	Loan
8 Zakuani, Gabriel	Kalloni FC	Peterborough U	Free

JULY 2014

31 Bajner, Balint	Borussia Dortmund	Ipswich T	Free
18 Balk, Jordi	Utrecht	Ross Co	Free
19 Berardi, Gaetano	Sampdoria	Leeds U	Undisclosed
28 Besic, Muhamed	Ferencvaros	Everton	Undisclosed

13	Bianchi, Tommaso	Sassuolo	Leeds U	Undisclosed
9	Bikey, Andre	Panetolikos	Charlton Ath	Free
19	Bilate, Mario	Sparta Rotterdam	Dundee U	Free
31	Bru, Kevin	Levski Sofia	Ipswich T	Free
8	Caballero, Willy	Malaga	Manchester C	£4.4m, rising to £6m
13	Cabella, Remy	Montpellier	Newcastle U	Undisclosed
18	Calero, Ivan	Atletico Madrid	Derby Co	Free
3	Can, Emre	Bayer Leverkusen	Liverpool	£10m
23	Chihi, Adil	1. FC Cologne	Fulham	Free
15	Costa, Diego	Atletico Madrid	Chelsea	£32m
31	Cubero, Jose Miguel	Herediano	Blackpool	Undisclosed
14	Dieng, Timothee	Stade Brestois	Oldham Ath	Free
13	Doukara, Souleymane	Catania	Leeds U	Loan
18	Dreesen, Tim	Fortuna Sittard	Ross Co	Free
25	Drogba, Didier	Galatasaray	Chelsea	Free
14	Fojut, Jaroslaw	Tromso	Dundee U	Free
15	Garcia, Enrique 'Kike'	Real Murcia	Middlesbrough	Undisclosed
11	Gudmundsson, Johann Berg	AZ Alkmaar	Charlton Ath	Free
11	Haim, Tal Ben	Standard Liege	Charlton Ath	Free
14	Hanford, Dan	Floriana FC	Carlisle U	Free
18	Ideye, Brown	Dynamo Kiev	WBA	£10m
29	Ighalo, Odion	Udinese	Watford	Loan
17	Janmaat, Daryl	Feyenoord	Newcastle U	Undisclosed
1	Jong, Siem de	Ajax	Newcastle U	Undisclosed
21	Konrad, Thomas	Eintracht Trier	Dundee	Free
22	Krkic, Bojan	Barcelona	Stoke C	Undisclosed
18	Luis, Filipe	Atletico Madrid	Chelsea	£15.8m
16	Mancienne, Michael	Hamburg	Nottingham F	£1m
15	Markovic, Lazar	Benfica	Liverpool	£20m
4	Mejias, Tomas	Real Madrid	Middlesbrough	Undisclosed
24	Montero, Jefferson	Monarcas Morelia	Swansea C	Undisclosed
29	Origi, Divock	Lille	Liverpool	£10m
27	Ospina, David	Nice	Arsenal	£3m
17	Paredes, Jaun Carlos	Granada	Watford	Undisclosed
9	Pasalic, Mario	Hajduk Split	Chelsea	Undisclosed
12	Pelle, Graziano	Feyenoord	Southampton	Undisclosed
12	Pocognoli, Sebastien	Hannover 96	WBA	Undisclosed
15	Riera, Roger	Barcelona	Nottingham F	Free
16	Riviere, Emmanuel	Monaco	Newcastle U	Undisclosed
10	Sanchez, Alexis	Barcelona	Arsenal	£35m
9	Silvestri, Marco	Chievo	Leeds U	Undisclosed
31	Simpson, Jay	Buriram U	Leyton Orient	Free
9	Stafylidis, Konstantinos	Bayer Leverkusen	Fulham	Loan
24	Studer, Sascha	Winterthur	Mansfield T	Free
31	Szromnik, Michal	Arka Gydnia	Dundee U	Undisclosed
8	Tadic, Dusan	FC Twente	Southampton	£10.9m
21	Tankulic, Luka	Wolfsburg II	Dundee	Free
7	Tozser, Daniel	Parma	Watford	Loan
15	Tucudean, George	Standard Liege	Charlton Ath	Free
17	Valencia, Enner	Pachuca	West Ham U	£12m
2	Voser, Kay	FC Basel	Fulham	Undisclosed
4	Zenjov, Sergei	FC Karpaty Lviv	Blackpool	Free

AUGUST 2014

16	Abella, Damia	Osasuna	Middlesbrough	Free
30	Adryan	Flamengo	Leeds U	Loan
21	Antenucci, Mirco	Ternana	Leeds U	Undisclosed
25	Balotelli, Mario	AC Milan	Liverpool	£16m
4	Benedicic, Zan	AC Milan	Leeds U	Loan
30	Blanco, Sebastian	Metalist Kharkiv	WBA	Undisclosed
1	Bodurov, Nikolay	Litex Lovech	Fulham	Free
30	Bulot, Frederic	Standard Liege	Charlton Ath	Loan
28	Cambiasso, Esteban	Internazionale	Leicester C	Free
4	Carroll, Roy	Olympiakos	Notts Co	Free
22	Casasola, Tiago	Boca Juniors	Fulham	Undisclosed
6	Celcer, Uros	Parma	Ross Co	Free
9	Cissokho, Aly	Valencia	Aston Villa	Undisclosed
24	Colunga, Adrian	Getafe	Brighton & HA	Undisclosed
5	Davidson, Jason	Heracles	WBA	Undisclosed
5	Diallo, Issaga	Kaposvari RFC	Cambridge U	Free
30	Dielna, Claude	Olympiacos	Sheffield W	Free
12	Dielna, Joel	Vannes	Blackpool	Free
2	Dier, Eric	Sporting Lisbon	Tottenham H	£4m
21	Eckersley, Adam	Aarhus	Hearts	Free
31	Fabro, Dario Del	Cagliari	Leeds U	Free
27	Fazio, Federico	Sevilla	Tottenham H	Undisclosed
20	Fernandez, Federico	Napoli	Swansea C	Undisclosed
3	Ferreyra, Facundo	Shakhtar Donetsk	Newcastle U	Loan
5	Gamboa, Cristian	Rosenborg	WBA	Undisclosed
14	Gardos, Florin	Steaua Bucharest	Southampton	£6m
4	Higdon, Michael	NEC Nijmegen	Sheffield U	Free
18	Holla, Danny	Den Haag	Brighton & HA	Free
6	Isla, Mauricio	Juventus	QPR	Loan
15	Jota	Celta Vigo	Brentford	Undisclosed
6	Kelhar, Dejan	Red Star Belgrade	Sheffield W	Free
28	Kiraly, Gabor	1860 Munich	Fulham	Undisclosed
11	Mangala, Eliaquim	FC Porto	Manchester C	£32m
6	Manquillo, Javier	Atletico Madrid	Liverpool	Loan
27	Manset, Mathieu	Royal Antwerp	Walsall	Free
26	Maria, Angel Di	Real Madrid	Manchester U	£59.7m
6	Mascarell, Omar	Real Madrid	Derby Co	Loan
16	Moreno, Alberto	Sevilla	Liverpool	£12m
27	Mubarak, Wakaso	Rubin Kazan	Celtic	Loan
4	Munari, Gianni	Parma	Watford	Loan
1	Nsue, Emilio	Real Mallorca	Middlesbrough	Undisclosed
29	Odjidja-Ofoe, Vadis	Club Brugge	Norwich C	Undisclosed

14	Ojamaa, Henrik	Legia Warsaw	Motherwell	Loan
18	Oriol, Edu	AEL Limassol	Blackpool	Free
3	Oriol, Joan	Osasuna	Blackpool	Free
1	O'Shaughnessy, Daniel	FC Metz	Brentford	Free
12	Rentmeister, Jeffrey	Westerlo	Blackpool	Undisclosed
20	Rojo, Marcos	Sporting Lisbon	Man U	£16m
9	Routis, Christopher	Servette	Bradford C	Free
15	Sakho, Diafra	FC Metz	West Ham U	Undisclosed
15	Sanchez, Carlos	Elche	Aston Villa	Undisclosed
25	Sloth, Casper	AGF Aarhus	Leeds U	Undisclosed
30	Song, Alex	Barcelona	West Ham U	Loan
6	Taider, Saphir	Internazionale	Southampton	Loan
14	Tesche, Robert	Hamburg	Nottingham F	Free
7	Vergini, Santiago	Estudiantes	Sunderland	Loan
13	Yedlin, DeAndre	Seattle	Tottenham H	Undisclosed
9	Zuculini, Bruno	Racing Club	Manchester C	Undisclosed

SEPTEMBER 2014

1	Amalfitano, Morgan	Marseille	West Ham U	Undisclosed
1	Alvarez, Ricardo	Internazionale	Sunderland	Loan
1	Alderweireld	Atletico Madrid	Southampton	Loan
1	Barrow, Modu	Ostersunds	Swansea C	Undisclosed
1	Betinho	Sporting Lisbon	Brentford	Loan
1	Blind, Daley	Ajax	Man U	£13.8m
1	Campion, Achille	Norrby IF	Port Vale	Loan
1	Delort, Andy	FC Tours	Wigan Ath	Undisclosed
1	Doukara, Souleymane	Catania	Leeds U	Undisclosed
1	Falcao, Radamel	Monaco	Man U	Loan
2	Henen, David	Olympiacos	Everton	Loan
1	Hernandez, Abel	Palermo	Hull C	£10m
1	Koblenz, Tom	Hoffenheim	Derby Co	Free
1	Kranjcar, Niko	Dynamo Kyiv	QPR	Loan
1	Kvist, William	Stuttgart	Wigan Ath	Free
5	Malonga, Dominique	Cesena	Hibernian	Free
1	Mane, Sadio	Red Bull Salzburg	Southampton	£10m
1	Manga, Bruno Ecuele	Lorient	Cardiff C	£5m+
1	Montenegro, Brian	Nacional	Leeds U	Loan
1	Scepovic, Stefan	Sporting Gijon	Celtic	£2.3m
1	Stambouli, Benjamin	Montpellier	Tottenham H	Undisclosed
2	Traore, Drissa	Le Havre	Notts Co	Free
1	Vossen, Jelle	Genk	Middlesbrough	Loan
1	Wildschut, Yanic	Heerenveen	Middlesbrough	Undisclosed

OCTOBER 2014

24	Ighalo, Odion	Udinese	Watford	Undisclosed

DECEMBER 2014

31	Campion, Achille	Norrby IF	Port Vale	Undisclosed
23	Elia, Eljero	Werder Bremen	Southampton	Loan
23	Oliveira, Nelson	Benfica	Swansea C	Loan

JANUARY 2015

16	Albentosa, Raul	Eibar	Derby Co	Undisclosed
23	Bamba, Sol	Palermo	Leeds U	Loan
21	Bielik, Krystian	Legia Warsaw	Arsenal	£2.4m
6	Dmitrovic, Marko	Ujpest	Charlton Ath	Undisclosed
29	El Khayati, Abdenasser	Kozakken Boys	Burton Alb	Undisclosed
13	Gil, Carles	Valencia	Aston Villa	£3.2m
4	Henry, Doneil	Apollon Limassol	West Ham U	Undisclosed
29	Hume, Iain	Kerala Blasters	Tranmere R	Free
16	Kramaric, Andrej	HNK Rijeka	Leicester C	£9m
8	Lalkovic, Milan	FK Mlada Boleslav	Barnsley	Free
1	Layun, Miguel	Granada	Watford	Undisclosed
29	Lepoint, Christophe	KAA Gent	Charlton Ath	Undisclosed
9	Maierhofer, Stefan	SC Wiener Neustadt	Millwall	Free
8	Maletic, Stefan	Achilles '92	Burton Alb	Undisclosed
16	McAllister, Jamie	Kerala Blasters	Exeter C	Free
26	Ngoyi, Granddi	Palermo	Leeds U	Loan
29	Paulista, Gabriel	Villarreal	Arsenal	£11.2m
27	Rochinha	Benfica	Bolton W	Loan
9	Sene, Saer	New York Red Bulls	Blackpool	Free
30	Souare, Pape	Lille	Crystal Palace	Undisclosed
12	Ssewankambo, Isak	NAC Breda	Derby Co	Free
30	Tagliapietra, Lucas	Milsami Orhei	Hamilton	Free
22	Travner, Jure	FC Baku	Reading	Free
7	Valdes, Victor	Unattached	Manchester U	Free
30	Veen, Kevin van	FC Oss	Scunthorpe U	Undisclosed
6	Watt, Tony	Standard Liege	Charlton Ath	Undisclosed
7	Wollscheid, Philipp	Bayer Leverkusen	Stoke C	Loan

FEBRUARY 2015

2	Bong, Gaetan	Olympiacos	Wigan Ath	Free
2	Breimyr, Andreas	Bryne FK	Crystal Palace	Undisclosed
2	Bruna, Gerardo	Whitehawk	Accrington S	Free
2	Bus, Sergiu	CSKA Sofia	Sheffield W	Undisclosed
2	Cani, Edgar	Catania	Leeds U	Loan
2	Cuadrado, Juan	Fiorentina	Chelsea	£23.3m
2	Djuricic, Filip	Benfica	Southampton	Loan
2	N'Doye, Dame	Lokomotiv Moscow	Hull C	Undisclosed
4	Pogba, Mathias	Pescara	Crawley T	Free
2	Silva, Filipe Joaquim Melo	Moreirenses	Sheffield W	Undisclosed
2	Slavchev, Simeon	Sporting Lisbon	Bolton W	Loan

MAY 2015

16	Gogia, Akaki	Hallescher FC	Brentford	Free
27	Haugaard, Jakob	FC Midtjylland	Stoke C	Undisclosed
14	Nathan	Atletico Paranaense	Chelsea	Undisclosed
21	Wollscheid, Philipp	Bayer Leverkusen	Stoke C	Undisclosed

ENGLISH LEAGUE HONOURS 1888–2015

Won or placed on goal average (ratio), goal difference or most goals scored. ‡Not promoted after play-offs. No official competition during 1915–19 and 1939–46, regional leagues operated.

FOOTBALL LEAGUE (1888–89 to 1891–92) – TIER 1

MAXIMUM POINTS: a 44; b 60

1	1888–89a	Preston NE	40	Aston Villa	29	Wolverhampton W	28
1	1889–90a	Preston NE	33	Everton	31	Blackburn R	27
1	1890–91a	Everton	29	Preston NE	27	Notts Co	26
1	1891–92b	Sunderland	42	Preston NE	37	Bolton W	36

DIVISION 1 (1892–93 to 1991–92)

MAXIMUM POINTS: a 44; b 52; c 60; d 68; e 76; f 84; g 126; h 120; k 114.

1	1892–93c	Sunderland	48	Preston NE	37	Everton	36
1	1893–94c	Aston Villa	44	Sunderland	38	Derby Co	36
1	1894–95c	Sunderland	47	Everton	42	Aston Villa	39
1	1895–96c	Aston Villa	45	Derby Co	41	Everton	39
1	1896–97c	Aston Villa	47	Sheffield U*	36	Derby Co	36
1	1897–98c	Sheffield U	42	Sunderland	37	Wolverhampton W*	35
1	1898–99d	Aston Villa	45	Liverpool	43	Burnley	39
1	1899–1900d	Aston Villa	50	Sheffield U	48	Sunderland	41
1	1900–01d	Liverpool	45	Sunderland	43	Notts Co	40
1	1901–02d	Sunderland	44	Everton	41	Newcastle U	37
1	1902–03d	The Wednesday	42	Aston Villa*	41	Sunderland	41
1	1903–04d	The Wednesday	47	Manchester C	44	Everton	43
1	1904–05d	Newcastle U	48	Everton	47	Manchester C	46
1	1905–06e	Liverpool	51	Preston NE	47	The Wednesday	44
1	1906–07e	Newcastle U	51	Bristol C	48	Everton*	45
1	1907–08e	Manchester U	52	Aston Villa*	43	Manchester C	43
1	1908–09e	Newcastle U	53	Everton	46	Sunderland	44
1	1909–10e	Aston Villa	53	Liverpool	48	Blackburn R*	45
1	1910–11e	Manchester U	52	Aston Villa	51	Sunderland*	45
1	1911–12e	Blackburn R	49	Everton	46	Newcastle U	44
1	1912–13e	Sunderland	54	Aston Villa	50	Sheffield W	49
1	1913–14e	Blackburn R	51	Aston Villa	44	Middlesbrough*	43
1	1914–15e	Everton	46	Oldham Ath	45	Blackburn R*	43
1	1919–20f	WBA	60	Burnley	51	Chelsea	49
1	1920–21f	Burnley	59	Manchester C	54	Bolton W	52
1	1921–22f	Liverpool	57	Tottenham H	51	Burnley	49
1	1922–23f	Liverpool	60	Sunderland	54	Huddersfield T	53
1	1923–24f	Huddersfield T*	57	Cardiff C	57	Sunderland	53
1	1924–25f	Huddersfield T	58	WBA	56	Bolton W	55
1	1925–26f	Huddersfield T	57	Arsenal	52	Sunderland	48
1	1926–27f	Newcastle U	56	Huddersfield T	51	Sunderland	49
1	1927–28f	Everton	53	Huddersfield T	51	Leicester C	48
1	1928–29f	Sheffield W	52	Leicester C	51	Aston Villa	50
1	1929–30f	Sheffield W	60	Derby Co	50	Manchester C*	47
1	1930–31f	Arsenal	66	Aston Villa	59	Sheffield W	52
1	1931–32f	Everton	56	Arsenal	54	Sheffield W	50
1	1932–33f	Arsenal	58	Aston Villa	54	Sheffield W	51
1	1933–34f	Arsenal	59	Huddersfield T	56	Tottenham H	49
1	1934–35f	Arsenal	58	Sunderland	54	Sheffield W	49
1	1935–36f	Sunderland	56	Derby Co*	48	Huddersfield T	48
1	1936–37f	Manchester C	57	Charlton Ath	54	Arsenal	52
1	1937–38f	Arsenal	52	Wolverhampton W	51	Preston NE	49
1	1938–39f	Everton	59	Wolverhampton W	55	Charlton Ath	50
1	1946–47f	Liverpool	57	Manchester U*	56	Wolverhampton W	56
1	1947–48f	Arsenal	59	Manchester U*	52	Burnley	52
1	1948–49f	Portsmouth	58	Manchester U*	53	Derby Co	53
1	1949–50f	Portsmouth*	53	Wolverhampton W	53	Sunderland	52
1	1950–51f	Tottenham H	60	Manchester U	56	Blackpool	50
1	1951–52f	Manchester U	57	Tottenham H*	53	Arsenal	53
1	1952–53f	Arsenal*	54	Preston NE	54	Wolverhampton W	51
1	1953–54f	Wolverhampton W	57	WBA	53	Huddersfield T	51
1	1954–55f	Chelsea	52	Wolverhampton W*	48	Portsmouth*	48
1	1955–56f	Manchester U	60	Blackpool*	49	Wolverhampton W	49
1	1956–57f	Manchester U	64	Tottenham H*	56	Preston NE	56
1	1957–58f	Wolverhampton W	64	Preston NE	59	Tottenham H	51
1	1958–59f	Wolverhampton W	61	Manchester U	55	Arsenal*	50
1	1959–60f	Burnley	55	Wolverhampton W	54	Tottenham H	53
1	1960–61f	Tottenham H	66	Sheffield W	58	Wolverhampton W	57
1	1961–62f	Ipswich T	56	Burnley	53	Tottenham H	52
1	1962–63f	Everton	61	Tottenham H	55	Burnley	54
1	1963–64f	Liverpool	57	Manchester U	53	Everton	52
1	1964–65f	Manchester U*	61	Leeds U	61	Chelsea	56

1	1965–66f	Liverpool	61	Leeds U*	55	Burnley	55
1	1966–67f	Manchester U	60	Nottingham F*	56	Tottenham H	56
1	1967–68f	Manchester C	58	Manchester U	56	Liverpool	55
1	1968–69f	Leeds U	67	Liverpool	61	Everton	57
1	1969–70f	Everton	66	Leeds U	57	Chelsea	55
1	1970–71f	Arsenal	65	Leeds U	64	Tottenham H*	52
1	1971–72f	Derby Co	58	Leeds U*	57	Liverpool*	57
1	1972–73f	Liverpool	60	Arsenal	57	Leeds U	53
1	1973–74f	Leeds U	62	Liverpool	57	Derby Co	48
1	1974–75f	Derby Co	53	Liverpool*	51	Ipswich T	51
1	1975–76f	Liverpool	60	QPR	59	Manchester U	56
1	1976–77f	Liverpool	57	Manchester C	56	Ipswich T	52
1	1977–78f	Nottingham F	64	Liverpool	57	Everton	55
1	1978–79f	Liverpool	68	Nottingham F	60	WBA	59
1	1979–80f	Liverpool	60	Manchester U	58	Ipswich T	53
1	1980–81f	Aston Villa	60	Ipswich T	56	Arsenal	53
1	1981–82g	Liverpool	87	Ipswich T	83	Manchester U	78
1	1982–83g	Liverpool	82	Watford	71	Manchester U	70
1	1983–84g	Liverpool	80	Southampton	77	Nottingham F*	74
1	1984–85g	Everton	90	Liverpool*	77	Tottenham H	77
1	1985–86g	Liverpool	88	Everton	86	West Ham U	84
1	1986–87g	Everton	86	Liverpool	77	Tottenham H	71
1	1987–88h	Liverpool	90	Manchester U	81	Nottingham F	73
1	1988–89k	Arsenal*	76	Liverpool	76	Nottingham F	64
1	1989–90k	Liverpool	79	Aston Villa	70	Tottenham H	63
1	1990–91k	Arsenal[1]	83	Liverpool	76	Crystal Palace	69
1	1991–92g	Leeds U	82	Manchester U	78	Sheffield W	75

[1] *Arsenal deducted 2pts due to player misconduct in match on 20/10/1990 v Manchester U at Old Trafford.*

FA PREMIER LEAGUE (1992–93 to 2014–15)

MAXIMUM POINTS: *a* 126; *b* 114.

1	1992–93a	Manchester U	84	Aston Villa	74	Norwich C	72
1	1993–94a	Manchester U	92	Blackburn R	84	Newcastle U	77
1	1994–95a	Blackburn R	89	Manchester U	88	Nottingham F	77
1	1995–96b	Manchester U	82	Newcastle U	78	Liverpool	71
1	1996–97b	Manchester U	75	Newcastle U*	68	Arsenal*	68
1	1997–98b	Arsenal	78	Manchester U	77	Liverpool	65
1	1998–99b	Manchester U	79	Arsenal	78	Chelsea	75
1	1999–2000b	Manchester U	91	Arsenal	73	Leeds U	69
1	2000–01b	Manchester U	80	Arsenal	70	Liverpool	69
1	2001–02b	Arsenal	87	Liverpool	80	Manchester U	77
1	2002–03b	Manchester U	83	Arsenal	78	Newcastle U	69
1	2003–04b	Arsenal	90	Chelsea	79	Manchester U	75
1	2004–05b	Chelsea	95	Arsenal	83	Manchester U	77
1	2005–06b	Chelsea	91	Manchester U	83	Liverpool	82
1	2006–07b	Manchester U	89	Chelsea	83	Liverpool*	68
1	2007–08b	Manchester U	87	Chelsea	85	Arsenal	83
1	2008–09b	Manchester U	90	Liverpool	86	Chelsea	83
1	2009–10b	Chelsea	86	Manchester U	85	Arsenal	75
1	2010–11b	Manchester U	80	Chelsea*	71	Manchester C	71
1	2011–12b	Manchester C*	89	Manchester U	89	Arsenal	70
1	2012–13b	Manchester U	89	Manchester C	78	Chelsea	75
1	2013–14b	Manchester C	86	Liverpool	84	Chelsea	82
1	2014–15b	Chelsea	87	Manchester C	79	Arsenal	75

DIVISION 2 (1892–93 to 1991–92) – TIER 2

MAXIMUM POINTS: *a* 44; *b* 56; *c* 60; *d* 68; *e* 76; *f* 84; *g* 126; *h* 132; *k* 138.

2	1892–93a	Small Heath	36	Sheffield U	35	Darwen	30
2	1893–94b	Liverpool	50	Small Heath	42	Notts Co	39
2	1894–95c	Bury	48	Notts Co	39	Newton Heath*	38
2	1895–96c	Liverpool*	46	Manchester C	46	Grimsby T*	42
2	1896–97c	Notts Co	42	Newton Heath	39	Grimsby T	38
2	1897–98c	Burnley	48	Newcastle U	45	Manchester C	39
2	1898–99d	Manchester C	52	Glossop NE	46	Leicester Fosse	45
2	1899–1900d	The Wednesday	54	Bolton W	52	Small Heath	46
2	1900–01d	Grimsby T	49	Small Heath	48	Burnley	44
2	1901–02d	WBA	55	Middlesbrough	51	Preston NE*	42
2	1902–03d	Manchester C	54	Small Heath	51	Woolwich A	48
2	1903–04d	Preston NE	50	Woolwich A	49	Manchester U	48
2	1904–05d	Liverpool	58	Bolton W	56	Manchester U	53
2	1905–06e	Bristol C	66	Manchester U	62	Chelsea	53
2	1906–07e	Nottingham F	60	Chelsea	57	Leicester Fosse	48
2	1907–08e	Bradford C	54	Leicester Fosse	52	Oldham Ath	50
2	1908–09e	Bolton W	52	Tottenham H*	51	WBA	51
2	1909–10e	Manchester C	54	Oldham Ath*	53	Hull C*	53
2	1910–11e	WBA	53	Bolton W	51	Chelsea	49
2	1911–12e	Derby Co*	54	Chelsea	54	Burnley	52
2	1912–13e	Preston NE	53	Burnley	50	Birmingham	46

2	1913–14e	Notts Co	53	Bradford PA*	49	Woolwich A	49
2	1914–15e	Derby Co	53	Preston NE	50	Barnsley	47
2	1919–20f	Tottenham H	70	Huddersfield T	64	Birmingham	56
2	1920–21f	Birmingham*	58	Cardiff C	58	Bristol C	51
2	1921–22f	Nottingham F	56	Stoke C*	52	Barnsley	52
2	1922–23f	Notts Co	53	West Ham U*	51	Leicester C	51
2	1923–24f	Leeds U	54	Bury*	51	Derby Co	51
2	1924–25f	Leicester C	59	Manchester U	57	Derby Co	55
2	1925–26f	Sheffield W	60	Derby Co	57	Chelsea	52
2	1926–27f	Middlesbrough	62	Portsmouth*	54	Manchester C	54
2	1927–28f	Manchester C	59	Leeds U	57	Chelsea	54
2	1928–29f	Middlesbrough	55	Grimsby T	53	Bradford PA*	48
2	1929–30f	Blackpool	58	Chelsea	55	Oldham Ath	53
2	1930–31f	Everton	61	WBA	54	Tottenham H	51
2	1931–32f	Wolverhampton W	56	Leeds U	54	Stoke C	52
2	1932–33f	Stoke C	56	Tottenham H	55	Fulham	50
2	1933–34f	Grimsby T	59	Preston NE	52	Bolton W*	51
2	1934–35f	Brentford	61	Bolton W*	56	West Ham U	56
2	1935–36f	Manchester U	56	Charlton Ath	55	Sheffield U*	52
2	1936–37f	Leicester C	56	Blackpool	55	Bury	52
2	1937–38f	Aston Villa	57	Manchester U*	53	Sheffield U	53
2	1938–39f	Blackburn R	55	Sheffield U	54	Sheffield W	53
2	1946–47f	Manchester C	62	Burnley	58	Birmingham C	55
2	1947–48f	Birmingham C	59	Newcastle U	56	Southampton	52
2	1948–49f	Fulham	57	WBA	56	Southampton	55
2	1949–50f	Tottenham H	61	Sheffield W*	52	Sheffield U*	52
2	1950–51f	Preston NE	57	Manchester C	52	Cardiff C	50
2	1951–52f	Sheffield W	53	Cardiff C*	51	Birmingham C	51
2	1952–53f	Sheffield U	60	Huddersfield T	58	Luton T	52
2	1953–54f	Leicester C*	56	Everton	56	Blackburn R	55
2	1954–55f	Birmingham C*	54	Luton T*	54	Rotherham U	54
2	1955–56f	Sheffield W	55	Leeds U	52	Liverpool*	48
2	1956–57f	Leicester C	61	Nottingham F	54	Liverpool	53
2	1957–58f	West Ham U	57	Blackburn R	56	Charlton Ath	55
2	1958–59f	Sheffield W	62	Fulham	60	Sheffield U*	53
2	1959–60f	Aston Villa	59	Cardiff C	58	Liverpool*	50
2	1960–61f	Ipswich T	59	Sheffield U	58	Liverpool	52
2	1961–62f	Liverpool	62	Leyton Orient	54	Sunderland	53
2	1962–63f	Stoke C	53	Chelsea*	52	Sunderland	52
2	1963–64f	Leeds U	63	Sunderland	61	Preston NE	56
2	1964–65f	Newcastle U	57	Northampton T	56	Bolton W	50
2	1965–66f	Manchester C	59	Southampton	54	Coventry C	53
2	1966–67f	Coventry C	59	Wolverhampton W	58	Carlisle U	52
2	1967–68f	Ipswich T	59	QPR*	58	Blackpool	58
2	1968–69f	Derby Co	63	Crystal Palace	56	Charlton Ath	50
2	1969–70f	Huddersfield T	60	Blackpool	53	Leicester C	51
2	1970–71f	Leicester C	59	Sheffield U	56	Cardiff C*	53
2	1971–72f	Norwich C	57	Birmingham C	56	Millwall	55
2	1972–73f	Burnley	62	QPR	61	Aston Villa	50
2	1973–74f	Middlesbrough	65	Luton T	50	Carlisle U	49
2	1974–75f	Manchester U	61	Aston Villa	58	Norwich C	53
2	1975–76f	Sunderland	56	Bristol C*	53	WBA	53
2	1976–77f	Wolverhampton W	57	Chelsea	55	Nottingham F	52
2	1977–78f	Bolton W	58	Southampton	57	Tottenham H*	56
2	1978–79f	Crystal Palace	57	Brighton & HA*	56	Stoke C	56
2	1979–80f	Leicester C	55	Sunderland	54	Birmingham C*	53
2	1980–81f	West Ham U	66	Notts Co	53	Swansea C*	50
2	1981–82g	Luton T	88	Watford	80	Norwich C	71
2	1982–83g	QPR	85	Wolverhampton W	75	Leicester C	70
2	1983–84g	Chelsea*	88	Sheffield W	88	Newcastle U	80
2	1984–85g	Oxford U	84	Birmingham C	82	Manchester C*	74
2	1985–86g	Norwich C	84	Charlton Ath	77	Wimbledon	76
2	1986–87g	Derby Co	84	Portsmouth	78	Oldham Ath‡	75
2	1987–88h	Millwall	82	Aston Villa*	78	Middlesbrough	78
2	1988–89k	Chelsea	99	Manchester C	82	Crystal Palace	81
2	1989–90k	Leeds U*	85	Sheffield U	85	Newcastle U‡	80
2	1990–91k	Oldham Ath	88	West Ham U	87	Sheffield W	82
2	1991–92k	Ipswich T	84	Middlesbrough	80	Derby Co	78

FIRST DIVISION (1992–93 to 2003–04)

MAXIMUM POINTS: 138

2	1992–93	Newcastle U	96	West Ham U*	88	Portsmouth‡	88
2	1993–94	Crystal Palace	90	Nottingham F	83	Millwall‡	74
2	1994–95	Middlesbrough	82	Reading‡	79	Bolton W	77
2	1995–96	Sunderland	83	Derby Co	79	Crystal Palace‡	75
2	1996–97	Bolton W	98	Barnsley	80	Wolverhampton W‡	76
2	1997–98	Nottingham F	94	Middlesbrough	91	Sunderland‡	90
2	1998–99	Sunderland	105	Bradford C	87	Ipswich T‡	86

2	1999–2000	Charlton Ath	91	Manchester C	89	Ipswich T	87
2	2000–01	Fulham	101	Blackburn R	91	Bolton W	87
2	2001–02	Manchester C	99	WBA	89	Wolverhampton W‡	86
2	2002–03	Portsmouth	98	Leicester C	92	Sheffield U‡	80
2	2003–04	Norwich C	94	WBA	86	Sunderland‡	79

FOOTBALL LEAGUE CHAMPIONSHIP (2004–05 to 2014–15)

MAXIMUM POINTS: 138

2	2004–05	Sunderland	94	Wigan Ath	87	Ipswich T‡	85
2	2005–06	Reading	106	Sheffield U	90	Watford	81
2	2006–07	Sunderland	88	Birmingham C	86	Derby Co	84
2	2007–08	WBA	81	Stoke C	79	Hull C	75
2	2008–09	Wolverhampton W	90	Birmingham C	83	Sheffield U‡	80
2	2009–10	Newcastle U	102	WBA	91	Nottingham F‡	79
2	2010–11	QPR	88	Norwich C	84	Swansea C*	80
2	2011–12	Reading	89	Southampton	88	West Ham U	86
2	2012–13	Cardiff C	87	Hull C	79	Watford‡	77
2	2013–14	Leicester C	102	Burnley	93	Derby Co‡	85
2	2014–15	Bournemouth	90	Watford	89	Norwich C	86

DIVISION 3 (1920–1921) – TIER 3

MAXIMUM POINTS: a 84.

| 3 | 1920–21a | Crystal Palace | 59 | Southampton | 54 | QPR | 53 |

DIVISION 3—SOUTH (1921–22 to 1957–58)

MAXIMUM POINTS: a 84; b 92.

3	1921–22a	Southampton*	61	Plymouth Arg	61	Portsmouth	53
3	1922–23a	Bristol C	59	Plymouth Arg*	53	Swansea T	53
3	1923–24a	Portsmouth	59	Plymouth Arg	55	Millwall	54
3	1924–25a	Swansea T	57	Plymouth Arg	56	Bristol C	53
3	1925–26a	Reading	57	Plymouth Arg	56	Millwall	53
3	1926–27a	Bristol C	62	Plymouth Arg	60	Millwall	56
3	1927–28a	Millwall	65	Northampton T	55	Plymouth Arg	53
3	1928–29a	Charlton Ath*	54	Crystal Palace	54	Northampton T*	52
3	1929–30a	Plymouth Arg	68	Brentford	61	QPR	51
3	1930–31a	Notts Co	59	Crystal Palace	51	Brentford	50
3	1931–32a	Fulham	57	Reading	55	Southend U	53
3	1932–33a	Brentford	62	Exeter C	58	Norwich C	57
3	1933–34a	Norwich C	61	Coventry C*	54	Reading*	54
3	1934–35a	Charlton Ath	61	Reading	53	Coventry C	51
3	1935–36a	Coventry C	57	Luton T	56	Reading	54
3	1936–37a	Luton T	58	Notts Co	56	Brighton & HA	53
3	1937–38a	Millwall	56	Bristol C	55	QPR*	53
3	1938–39a	Newport Co	55	Crystal Palace	52	Brighton & HA	49
3	1946–47a	Cardiff C	66	QPR	57	Bristol C	51
3	1947–48a	QPR	61	Bournemouth	57	Walsall	51
3	1948–49a	Swansea T	62	Reading	55	Bournemouth	52
3	1949–50a	Notts Co	58	Northampton T*	51	Southend U	51
3	1950–51b	Nottingham F	70	Norwich C	64	Reading*	57
3	1951–52b	Plymouth Arg	66	Reading*	61	Norwich C	61
3	1952–53b	Bristol R	64	Millwall*	62	Northampton T	62
3	1953–54b	Ipswich T	64	Brighton & HA	61	Bristol C	56
3	1954–55b	Bristol C	70	Leyton Orient	61	Southampton	59
3	1955–56b	Leyton Orient	66	Brighton & HA	65	Ipswich T	64
3	1956–57b	Ipswich T*	59	Torquay U	59	Colchester U	58
3	1957–58b	Brighton & HA	60	Brentford*	58	Plymouth Arg	58

DIVISION 3—NORTH (1921–22 to 1957–58)

MAXIMUM POINTS: a 76; b 84; c 80; d 92.

3	1921–22a	Stockport Co	56	Darlington*	50	Grimsby T	50
3	1922–23a	Nelson	51	Bradford PA	47	Walsall	46
3	1923–24b	Wolverhampton W	63	Rochdale	62	Chesterfield	54
3	1924–25b	Darlington	58	Nelson*	53	New Brighton	53
3	1925–26b	Grimsby T	61	Bradford PA	60	Rochdale	59
3	1926–27b	Stoke C	63	Rochdale	58	Bradford PA	55
3	1927–28b	Bradford PA	63	Lincoln C	55	Stockport Co	54
3	1928–29b	Bradford C	63	Stockport Co	62	Wrexham	52
3	1929–30b	Port Vale	67	Stockport Co	63	Darlington*	50
3	1930–31b	Chesterfield	58	Lincoln C	57	Wrexham*	54
3	1931–32c	Lincoln C*	57	Gateshead	57	Chester	50
3	1932–33b	Hull C	59	Wrexham	57	Stockport Co	54
3	1933–34b	Barnsley	62	Chesterfield	61	Stockport Co	59
3	1934–35b	Doncaster R	57	Halifax T	55	Chester	54
3	1935–36b	Chesterfield	60	Chester*	55	Tranmere R	55
3	1936–37b	Stockport Co	60	Lincoln C	57	Chester	53
3	1937–38b	Tranmere R	56	Doncaster R	54	Hull C	53

3	1938–39*b*	Barnsley	67	Doncaster R	56	Bradford C	52
3	1946–47*b*	Doncaster R	72	Rotherham U	64	Chester	56
3	1947–48*b*	Lincoln C	60	Rotherham U	59	Wrexham	50
3	1948–49*b*	Hull C	65	Rotherham U	62	Doncaster R	50
3	1949–50*b*	Doncaster R	55	Gateshead	53	Rochdale*	51
3	1950–51*d*	Rotherham U	71	Mansfield T	64	Carlisle U	62
3	1951–52*d*	Lincoln C	69	Grimsby T	66	Stockport Co	59
3	1952–53*d*	Oldham Ath	59	Port Vale	58	Wrexham	56
3	1953–54*d*	Port Vale	69	Barnsley	58	Scunthorpe U	57
3	1954–55*d*	Barnsley	65	Accrington S	61	Scunthorpe U*	58
3	1955–56*d*	Grimsby T	68	Derby Co	63	Accrington S	59
3	1956–57*d*	Derby Co	63	Hartlepools U	59	Accrington S*	58
3	1957–58*d*	Scunthorpe U	66	Accrington S	59	Bradford C	57

DIVISION 3 (1958–59 to 1991–92)

MAXIMUM POINTS: 92; 138 FROM 1981–82.

3	1958–59	Plymouth Arg	62	Hull C	61	Brentford*	57
3	1959–60	Southampton	61	Norwich C	59	Shrewsbury T*	52
3	1960–61	Bury	68	Walsall	62	QPR	60
3	1961–62	Portsmouth	65	Grimsby T	62	Bournemouth*	59
3	1962–63	Northampton T	62	Swindon T	58	Port Vale	54
3	1963–64	Coventry C*	60	Crystal Palace	60	Watford	58
3	1964–65	Carlisle U	60	Bristol C*	59	Mansfield T	59
3	1965–66	Hull C	69	Millwall	65	QPR	57
3	1966–67	QPR	67	Middlesbrough	55	Watford	54
3	1967–68	Oxford U	57	Bury	56	Shrewsbury T	55
3	1968–69	Watford*	64	Swindon T	64	Luton T	61
3	1969–70	Orient	62	Luton T	60	Bristol R	56
3	1970–71	Preston NE	61	Fulham	60	Halifax T	56
3	1971–72	Aston Villa	70	Brighton & HA	65	Bournemouth*	62
3	1972–73	Bolton W	61	Notts Co	57	Blackburn R	55
3	1973–74	Oldham Ath	62	Bristol R*	61	York C	61
3	1974–75	Blackburn R	60	Plymouth Arg	59	Charlton Ath	55
3	1975–76	Hereford U	63	Cardiff C	57	Millwall	56
3	1976–77	Mansfield T	64	Brighton & HA	61	Crystal Palace*	59
3	1977–78	Wrexham	61	Cambridge U	58	Preston NE*	56
3	1978–79	Shrewsbury T	61	Watford*	60	Swansea C	60
3	1979–80	Grimsby T	62	Blackburn R	59	Sheffield W	58
3	1980–81	Rotherham U	61	Barnsley*	59	Charlton Ath	59
3	1981–82	Burnley*	80	Carlisle U	80	Fulham	78
3	1982–83	Portsmouth	91	Cardiff C	86	Huddersfield T	82
3	1983–84	Oxford U	95	Wimbledon	87	Sheffield U*	83
3	1984–85	Bradford C	94	Millwall	90	Hull C	87
3	1985–86	Reading	94	Plymouth Arg	87	Derby Co	84
3	1986–87	Bournemouth	97	Middlesbrough	94	Swindon T	87
3	1987–88	Sunderland	93	Brighton & HA	84	Walsall	82
3	1988–89	Wolverhampton W	92	Sheffield U*	84	Port Vale	84
3	1989–90	Bristol R	93	Bristol C	91	Notts Co	87
3	1990–91	Cambridge U	86	Southend U	85	Grimsby T*	83
3	1991–92	Brentford	82	Birmingham C	81	Huddersfield T‡	78

SECOND DIVISION (1992–93 to 2003–04)

MAXIMUM POINTS: 138

3	1992–93	Stoke C	93	Bolton W	90	Port Vale‡	89
3	1993–94	Reading	89	Port Vale	88	Plymouth Arg*‡	85
3	1994–95	Birmingham C	89	Brentford‡	85	Crewe Alex‡	83
3	1995–96	Swindon T	92	Oxford U	83	Blackpool‡	82
3	1996–97	Bury	84	Stockport Co	82	Luton T‡	78
3	1997–98	Watford	88	Bristol C	85	Grimsby T	72
3	1998–99	Fulham	101	Walsall	87	Manchester C	82
3	1999–2000	Preston NE	95	Burnley	88	Gillingham	85
3	2000–01	Millwall	93	Rotherham U	91	Reading‡	86
3	2001–02	Brighton & HA	90	Reading	84	Brentford*‡	83
3	2002–03	Wigan Ath	100	Crewe Alex	86	Bristol C*‡	83
3	2003–04	Plymouth Arg	90	QPR	83	Bristol C‡	82

FOOTBALL LEAGUE 1 (2004–05 to 2014–15)

MAXIMUM POINTS: 138

3	2004–05	Luton T	98	Hull C	86	Tranmere R‡	79
3	2005–06	Southend U	82	Colchester U	79	Brentford‡	76
3	2006–07	Scunthorpe U	91	Bristol C	85	Blackpool	83
3	2007–08	Swansea C	92	Nottingham F	82	Doncaster R*	80
3	2008–09	Leicester C	96	Peterborough U	89	Milton Keynes D‡	87
3	2009–10	Norwich C	95	Leeds U	86	Millwall	85
3	2010–11	Brighton & HA	95	Southampton	92	Huddersfield T‡	87
3	2011–12	Charlton Ath	101	Sheffield W	93	Sheffield U‡	90
3	2012–13	Doncaster R	84	Bournemouth	83	Brentford‡	79
3	2013–14	Wolverhampton W	103	Brentford	94	Leyton Orient‡	86
3	2014–15	Bristol C	99	Milton Keynes D	91	Preston NE	89

DIVISION 4 (1958–59 to 1991–92) – TIER 4

MAXIMUM POINTS: 92; 138 FROM 1981–82.

4	1958–59	Port Vale	64	Coventry C*	60	York C	60	Shrewsbury T	58
4	1959–60	Walsall	65	Notts Co*	60	Torquay U	60	Watford	57
4	1960–61	Peterborough U	66	Crystal Palace	64	Northampton T*	60	Bradford PA	60
4	1961–62[2]	Millwall	56	Colchester U	55	Wrexham	53	Carlisle U	52
4	1962–63	Brentford	62	Oldham Ath*	59	Crewe Alex	59	Mansfield T*	57
4	1963–64	Gillingham*	60	Carlisle U	60	Workington	59	Exeter C	58
4	1964–65	Brighton & HA	63	Millwall*	62	York C	62	Oxford U	61
4	1965–66	Doncaster R*	59	Darlington	59	Torquay U	58	Colchester U*	56
4	1966–67	Stockport Co	64	Southport*	59	Barrow	59	Tranmere R	58
4	1967–68	Luton T	66	Barnsley	61	Hartlepools U	60	Crewe Alex	58
4	1968–69	Doncaster R	59	Halifax T	57	Rochdale*	56	Bradford C	56
4	1969–70	Chesterfield	64	Wrexham	61	Swansea C	60	Port Vale	59
4	1970–71	Notts Co	69	Bournemouth	60	Oldham Ath	59	York C	56
4	1971–72	Grimsby T	63	Southend U	60	Brentford	59	Scunthorpe U	57
4	1972–73	Southport	62	Hereford U	58	Cambridge U	57	Aldershot*	56
4	1973–74	Peterborough U	65	Gillingham	62	Colchester U	60	Bury	59
4	1974–75	Mansfield T	68	Shrewsbury T	62	Rotherham U	59	Chester*	57
4	1975–76	Lincoln C	74	Northampton T	68	Reading	60	Tranmere R	58
4	1976–77	Cambridge U	65	Exeter C	62	Colchester U*	59	Bradford C	59
4	1977–78	Watford	71	Southend U	60	Swansea C*	56	Brentford	56
4	1978–79	Reading	65	Grimsby T*	61	Wimbledon*	61	Barnsley	61
4	1979–80	Huddersfield T	66	Walsall	64	Newport Co	61	Portsmouth*	60
4	1980–81	Southend U	67	Lincoln C	65	Doncaster R	56	Wimbledon	55
4	1981–82	Sheffield U	96	Bradford C*	91	Wigan Ath	91	Bournemouth	88
4	1982–83	Wimbledon	98	Hull C	90	Port Vale	88	Scunthorpe U	83
4	1983–84	York C	101	Doncaster R	85	Reading*	82	Bristol C	82
4	1984–85	Chesterfield	91	Blackpool	86	Darlington	85	Bury	84
4	1985–86	Swindon T	102	Chester C	84	Mansfield T	81	Port Vale	79
4	1986–87	Northampton T	99	Preston NE	90	Southend U	80	Wolverhampton W‡	79
4	1987–88	Wolverhampton W	90	Cardiff C	85	Bolton W	78	Scunthorpe U*‡	77
4	1988–89	Rotherham U	82	Tranmere R	80	Crewe Alex	78	Scunthorpe U*‡	77
4	1989–90	Exeter C	89	Grimsby T	79	Southend U	75	Stockport Co‡	74
4	1990–91	Darlington	83	Stockport Co*	82	Hartlepool U	82	Peterborough U	80
4	1991–92[3]	Burnley	83	Rotherham U*	77	Mansfield T	77	Blackpool	76

[2]*Maximum points:* 88 owing to Accrington Stanley's resignation.
[3]*Maximum points:* 126 owing to Aldershot being expelled (and only 23 teams started the competition).

THIRD DIVISION (1992–93 to 2003–04)

MAXIMUM POINTS: *a* 126; *b* 138.

4	1992–93a	Cardiff C	83	Wrexham	80	Barnet	79	York C	75
4	1993–94a	Shrewsbury T	79	Chester C	74	Crewe Alex	73	Wycombe W	70
4	1994–95a	Carlisle U	91	Walsall	83	Chesterfield	81	Bury‡	80
4	1995–96b	Preston NE	86	Gillingham	83	Bury	79	Plymouth Arg*	78
4	1996–97b	Wigan Ath*	87	Fulham	87	Carlisle U	84	Northampton T	72
4	1997–98b	Notts Co	99	Macclesfield T	82	Lincoln C	72	Colchester U*	74
4	1998–99b	Brentford	85	Cambridge U	81	Cardiff C	80	Scunthorpe U	74
4	1999–2000b	Swansea C	85	Rotherham U	84	Northampton T	82	Darlington‡	79
4	2000–01b	Brighton & HA	92	Cardiff C	82	Chesterfield[4]	80	Hartlepool U‡	77
4	2001–02b	Plymouth Arg	102	Luton T	97	Mansfield T	79	Cheltenham T	78
4	2002–03b	Rushden & D	87	Hartlepool U	85	Wrexham	84	Bournemouth	74
4	2003–04b	Doncaster R	92	Hull C	88	Torquay U*	81	Huddersfield T	81

[4]*Chesterfield deducted 9pts for irregularities.*

FOOTBALL LEAGUE 2 (2004–05 to 2014–15)

MAXIMUM POINTS: 138

4	2004–05	Yeovil T	83	Scunthorpe U*	80	Swansea C	80	Southend U	80
4	2005–06	Carlisle U	86	Northampton T	83	Leyton Orient	81	Grimsby T‡	78
4	2006–07	Walsall	89	Hartlepool U	88	Swindon T	85	Milton Keynes D‡	84
4	2007–08	Milton Keynes D	97	Peterborough U	92	Hereford U	88	Stockport Co	82
4	2008–09	Brentford	85	Exeter C	79	Wycombe W*	78	Bury‡	78
4	2009–10	Notts Co	93	Bournemouth	83	Rochdale	82	Morecambe*‡	73
4	2010–11	Chesterfield	86	Bury	81	Wycombe W	80	Shrewsbury T‡	79
4	2011–12	Swindon T	93	Shrewsbury T	88	Crawley T	84	Southend U‡	83
4	2012–13	Gillingham	83	Rotherham U	79	Port Vale	78	Burton Alb	76
4	2013–14	Chesterfield	84	Scunthorpe U*	81	Rochdale	81	Fleetwood T	76
4	2014–15	Burton Alb	94	Shrewsbury T	89	Bury	85	Wycombe W*‡	84

LEAGUE TITLE WINS

DIVISION 1 (1888–89 to 1991–92) – TIER 1
Liverpool 18, Arsenal 10, Everton 9, Aston Villa 7, Manchester U 7, Sunderland 6, Newcastle U 4, Sheffield W 4 (2 as The Wednesday), Huddersfield T 3, Leeds U 3, Wolverhampton W 3, Blackburn R 2, Burnley 2, Derby Co 2, Manchester C 2, Portsmouth 2, Preston NE 2, Tottenham H 2, Chelsea 1, Ipswich T 1, Nottingham F 1, Sheffield U 1, WBA 1.

FA PREMIER LEAGUE (1992–93 to 2014–15) – TIER 1
Manchester U 13, Chelsea 4, Arsenal 3, Manchester C 2, Blackburn R 1.

DIVISION 2 (1892–93 TO 1991–92) – TIER 2
Leicester C 6, Manchester C 6, Sheffield W 5 (1 as The Wednesday), Birmingham C 4 (1 as Small Heath), Derby Co 4, Liverpool 4, Ipswich T 3, Leeds U 3, Middlesbrough 3, Notts Co 3, Preston NE 3, Aston Villa 2, Bolton W 2, Burnley 2, Chelsea 2, Grimsby T 2, Manchester U 2, Norwich C 2, Nottingham F 2, Stoke C 2, Tottenham H 2, WBA 2, West Ham U 2, Wolverhampton W 2, Blackburn R 1, Blackpool 1, Bradford C 1, Brentford 1, Bristol C 1, Bury 1, Coventry C 1, Crystal Palace 1, Everton 1, Fulham 1, Huddersfield T 1, Luton T 1, Millwall 1, Newcastle U 1, Oldham Ath 1, Oxford U 1, QPR 1, Sheffield U 1, Sunderland 1.

FIRST DIVISION (1992–93 to 2003–04) – TIER 2
Sunderland , Bolton W, Charlton Ath 1, Crystal Palace 1, Fulham 1, Manchester C 1, Middlesbrough 1, Newcastle U 1, Norwich C 1, Nottingham F 1, Portsmouth 1.

FOOTBALL LEAGUE CHAMPIONSHIP (2004–05 to 2014–15) – TIER 2
Reading 2, Sunderland 2, Bournemouth 1, Cardiff C 1, Leicester C 1, Newcastle U 1, QPR 1, WBA 1, Wolverhampton W 1.

DIVISION 3—SOUTH (1920–21 to 1957–58) – TIER 3
Bristol C 3, Charlton Ath 2, Ipswich T 2, Millwall 2, Notts Co 2, Plymouth Arg 2, Swansea T 2, Brentford 1, Brighton & HA 1, Bristol R 1, Cardiff C 1, Coventry C 1, Crystal Palace 1, Fulham 1, Leyton Orient 1, Luton T 1, Newport Co 1, Norwich C 1, Nottingham F 1, Portsmouth 1, QPR 1, Reading 1, Southampton 1.

DIVISION 3—NORTH (1921–22 to 1957–58) – TIER 3
Barnsley 3, Doncaster R 3, Lincoln C 3, Chesterfield 2, Grimsby T 2, Hull C 2, Port Vale 2, Stockport Co 2, Bradford C 1, Bradford PA 1, Darlington 1, Derby Co 1, Nelson 1, Oldham Ath 1, Rotherham U 1, Scunthorpe U 1, Stoke C 1, Tranmere R 1, Wolverhampton W 1.

DIVISION 3 (1958–59 to 1991–92) – TIER 3
Oxford U 2, Portsmouth 2, Aston Villa 1, Blackburn R 1, Bolton W 1, Bournemouth 1, Bradford C 1, Brentford 1, Bristol R 1, Burnley 1, Bury 1, Cambridge U 1, Carlisle U 1, Coventry C 1, Grimsby T 1, Hereford U 1, Hull C 1, Mansfield T 1, Northampton T 1, Oldham Ath 1, Orient 1, Plymouth Arg 1, Preston NE 1, QPR 1, Reading 1, Rotherham U 1, Shrewsbury T 1, Southampton 1, Sunderland 1, Watford 1, Wolverhampton W 1, Wrexham 1.

SECOND DIVISION (1992–93 to 2003–04) – TIER 3
Birmingham C 1, Brighton & HA 1, Bury 1, Fulham 1, Millwall 1, Plymouth Arg 1, Preston NE 1, Reading 1, Stoke C 1, Swindon T 1, Watford 1, Wigan Ath 1.

FOOTBALL LEAGUE 1 (2004–05 to 2014–15) – TIER 3
Brighton & HA 1, Bristol C 1, Charlton Ath 1, Doncaster R 1, Leicester C 1, Luton T 1, Norwich C 1, Scunthorpe U 1, Southend U 1, Swansea C 1, Wolverhampton W 1.

DIVISION 4 (1958–59 to 1991–92) – TIER 4
Chesterfield 2, Doncaster R 2, Peterborough U 2, Brentford 1, Brighton & HA 1, Burnley 1, Cambridge U 1, Darlington 1, Exeter C 1, Gillingham 1, Grimsby T 1, Huddersfield T 1, Lincoln C 1, Luton T 1, Mansfield T 1, Millwall 1, Northampton T 1, Notts Co 1, Port Vale 1, Reading 1, Rotherham U 1, Sheffield U 1, Southend U 1, Southport 1, Stockport Co 1, Swindon T 1, Walsall 1, Watford 1, Wimbledon 1, Wolverhampton W 1, York C 1.

THIRD DIVISION (1992–93 to 2003–04) – TIER 4
Brentford 1, Brighton & HA 1, Cardiff C 1, Carlisle U 1, Doncaster R 1, Notts Co 1, Plymouth Arg 1, Preston NE 1, Rushden & D 1, Shrewsbury T 1, Swansea C 1, Wigan Ath 1.

FOOTBALL LEAGUE 2 (2004–05 to 2014–15) – TIER 4
Chesterfield 2, Brentford 1, Burton Alb 1, Carlisle U 1, Gillingham 1, Milton Keynes D 1, Notts Co 1, Swindon T 1, Walsall 1, Yeovil T 1.

PROMOTED AFTER PLAY-OFFS

1986–87	Charlton Ath to Division 1; Swindon T to Division 2; Aldershot to Division 3
1987–88	Middlesbrough to Division 1; Walsall to Division 2; Swansea C to Division 3
1988–89	Crystal Palace to Division 1; Port Vale to Division 2; Leyton Orient to Division 3
1989–90	Sunderland to Division 1; Notts Co to Division 2; Cambridge U to Division 3
1990–91	Notts Co to Division 1; Tranmere R to Division 2; Torquay U to Division 3
1991–92	Blackburn R to Premier League; Peterborough U to First Division; Blackpool to Second Division
1992–93	Swindon T to Premier League; WBA to First Division; York C to Second Division
1993–94	Leicester C to Premier League; Burnley to First Division; Wycombe W to Second Division
1994–95	Bolton W to Premier League; Huddersfield T to First Division; Wycome Wanderers to Second Division
1995–96	Leicester C to Premier League; Bradford C to First Division; Plymouth Arg to Second Division
1996–97	Crystal Palace to Premier League; Crewe Alex to First Division; Northampton T to Second Division
1997–98	Charlton Ath to Premier League; Grimsby T to First Division; Colchester U to Second Division
1998–99	Watford to Premier League; Manchester C to First Division; Scunthorpe U to Second Division
1999–2000	Ipswich to Premier League; Gillingham to First Division; Peterborough U to Second Division
2000–01	Bolton W to Premier league; Walsall to First Division; Blackpool to Second Division
2001–02	Birmingham C to Premier League; Stoke C to First Division; Cheltenham T to Second Division
2002–03	Wolverhampton W to Premier League; Cardiff C to First Division; Bournemouth to Second Division
2003–04	Crystal Palace to Premier League; Brighton & HA to First Division; Huddersfield T to Second Division
2004–05	West Ham U to Premier League; Sheffield W to Championship; Southend U to Football League 1
2005–06	Watford to Premier League; Barnsley to Championship; Cheltenham T to Football League 1
2006–07	Derby Co to Premier League; Blackpool to Championship; Bristol R to Football League 1
2007–08	Hull C to Premier League; Doncaster R to Championship; Stockport Co to Football League 1
2008–09	Burnley to Premier League; Scunthorpe U to Championship; Gillingham to Football League 1
2009–10	Blackpool to Premier League; Millwall to Championship; Dagenham & R to Football League 1
2010–11	Swansea C to Premier League; Peterborough U to Championship; Stevenage to Football League 1
2011–12	West Ham U to Premier League; Huddersfield T to Championship; Crewe Alex to Football League 1
2012–13	Crystal Palace to Premier League; Yeovil T to Championship; Bradford C to Football League 1
2013–14	QPR to Premier League; Rotherham U to Championship; Fleetwood T to Football League 1
2014–15	Norwich C to Premier League; Preston NE to Championship; Southend U to Football League 1

RELEGATED CLUBS

1891–92 League extended. Newton Heath, Sheffield W and Nottingham F admitted. *Second Division formed* including Darwen.
1892–93 In Test matches, Sheffield U and Darwen won promotion in place of Notts Co and Accrington S.
1893–94 In Tests, Liverpool and Small Heath won promotion. Newton Heath and Darwen relegated.
1894–95 After Tests, Bury promoted, Liverpool relegated.
1895–96 After Tests, Liverpool promoted, Small Heath relegated.
1896–97 After Tests, Notts Co promoted, Burnley relegated.
1897–98 Test system abolished after success of Stoke C and Burnley. League extended. Blackburn R and Newcastle U elected to First Division. *Automatic promotion and relegation introduced.*

DIVISION 1 TO DIVISION 2 (1898–99 to 1991–92)

1898–99 Bolton W and Sheffield W	1952–53 Stoke C and Derby Co
1899–1900 Burnley and Glossop	1953–54 Middlesbrough and Liverpool
1900–01 Preston NE and WBA	1954–55 Leicester C and Sheffield W
1901–02 Small Heath and Manchester C	1955–56 Huddersfield T and Sheffield U
1902–03 Grimsby T and Bolton W	1956–57 Charlton Ath and Cardiff C
1903–04 Liverpool and WBA	1957–58 Sheffield W and Sunderland
1904–05 League extended. Bury and Notts Co, two	1958–59 Portsmouth and Aston Villa
bottom clubs in First Division, re-elected.	1959–60 Luton T and Leeds U
1905–06 Nottingham F and Wolverhampton W	1960–61 Preston NE and Newcastle U
1906–07 Derby Co and Stoke C	1961–62 Chelsea and Cardiff C
1907–08 Bolton W and Birmingham C	1962–63 Manchester C and Leyton Orient
1908–09 Manchester C and Leicester Fosse	1963–64 Bolton W and Ipswich T
1909–10 Bolton W and Chelsea	1964–65 Wolverhampton W and Birmingham C
1910–11 Bristol C and Nottingham F	1965–66 Northampton T and Blackburn R
1911–12 Preston NE and Bury	1966–67 Aston Villa and Blackpool
1912–13 Notts Co and Woolwich Arsenal	1967–68 Fulham and Sheffield U
1913–14 Preston NE and Derby Co	1968–69 Leicester C and QPR
1914–15 Tottenham H and Chelsea*	1969–70 Sunderland and Sheffield W
1919–20 Notts Co and Sheffield W	1970–71 Burnley and Blackpool
1920–21 Derby Co and Bradford PA	1971–72 Huddersfield T and Nottingham F
1921–22 Bradford C and Manchester U	1972–73 Crystal Palace and WBA
1922–23 Stoke C and Oldham Ath	1973–74 Southampton, Manchester U, Norwich C
1923–24 Chelsea and Middlesbrough	1974–75 Luton T, Chelsea, Carlisle U
1924–25 Preston NE and Nottingham F	1975–76 Wolverhampton W, Burnley, Sheffield U
1925–26 Manchester C and Notts Co	1976–77 Sunderland, Stoke C, Tottenham H
1926–27 Leeds U and WBA	1977–78 West Ham U, Newcastle U, Leicester C
1927–28 Tottenham H and Middlesbrough	1978–79 QPR, Birmingham C, Chelsea
1928–29 Bury and Cardiff C	1979–80 Bristol C, Derby Co, Bolton W
1929–30 Burnley and Everton	1980–81 Norwich C, Leicester C, Crystal Palace
1930–31 Leeds U and Manchester U	1981–82 Leeds U, Wolverhampton W, Middlesbrough
1931–32 Grimsby T and West Ham U	1982–83 Manchester C, Swansea C, Brighton & HA
1932–33 Bolton W and Blackpool	1983–84 Birmingham C, Notts Co, Wolverhampton W
1933–34 Newcastle U and Sheffield U	1984–85 Norwich C, Sunderland, Stoke C
1934–35 Leicester C and Tottenham H	1985–86 Ipswich T, Birmingham C, WBA
1935–36 Aston Villa and Blackburn R	1986–87 Leicester C, Manchester C, Aston Villa
1936–37 Manchester U and Sheffield W	1987–88 Chelsea**, Portsmouth, Watford, Oxford U
1937–38 Manchester C and WBA	1988–89 Middlesbrough, West Ham U, Newcastle U
1938–39 Birmingham C and Leicester C	1989–90 Sheffield W, Charlton Ath, Millwall
1946–47 Brentford and Leeds U	1990–91 Sunderland and Derby Co
1947–48 Blackburn R and Grimsby T	1991–92 Luton T, Notts Co, West Ham U
1948–49 Preston NE and Sheffield U	***Relegated after play-offs.*
1949–50 Manchester C and Birmingham C	**Subsequently re-elected to Division 1 when League was*
1950–51 Sheffield W and Everton	*extended after the War.*
1951–52 Huddersfield T and Fulham	

FA PREMIER LEAGUE TO DIVISION 1 (1992–93 to 2003–04)

1992–93 Crystal Palace, Middlesbrough, Nottingham F	1998–99 Charlton Ath, Blackburn R, Nottingham F
1993–94 Sheffield U, Oldham Ath, Swindon T	1999–2000 Wimbledon, Sheffield W, Watford
1994–95 Crystal Palace, Norwich C, Leicester C, Ipswich T	2000–01 Manchester C, Coventry C, Bradford C
1995–96 Manchester C, QPR, Bolton W	2001–02 Ipswich T, Derby Co, Leicester C
1996–97 Sunderland, Middlesbrough, Nottingham F	2002–03 West Ham U, WBA, Sunderland
1997–98 Bolton W, Barnsley, Crystal Palace	2003–04 Leicester C, Leeds U, Wolverhampton W

FA PREMIER LEAGUE TO CHAMPIONSHIP (2004–05 to 2014–15)

2004–05 Crystal Palace, Norwich C, Southampton	2010–11 Birmingham C, Blackpool, West Ham U
2005–06 Birmingham C, WBA, Sunderland	2011–12 Bolton W, Blackburn R, Wolverhampton W
2006–07 Sheffield U, Charlton Ath, Watford	2012–13 Wigan Ath, Reading, QPR
2007–08 Reading, Birmingham C, Derby Co	2013–14 Norwich C, Fulham, Cardiff C
2008–09 Newcastle U, Middlesbrough, WBA	2014–15 Hull C, Burnley, QPR
2009–10 Burnley, Hull C, Portsmouth	

DIVISION 2 TO DIVISION 3 (1920–21 to 1991–92)

1920–21 Stockport Co	1923–24 Nelson and Bristol C
1921–22 Bradford PA and Bristol C	1924–25 Crystal Palace and Coventry C
1922–23 Rotherham Co and Wolverhampton W	1925–26 Stoke C and Stockport Co

1926–27 Darlington and Bradford C	1963–64 Grimsby T and Scunthorpe U
1927–28 Fulham and South Shields	1964–65 Swindon T and Swansea T
1928–29 Port Vale and Clapton Orient	1965–66 Middlesbrough and Leyton Orient
1929–30 Hull C and Notts Co	1966–67 Northampton T and Bury
1930–31 Reading and Cardiff C	1967–68 Plymouth Arg and Rotherham U
1931–32 Barnsley and Bristol C	1968–69 Fulham and Bury
1932–33 Chesterfield and Charlton Ath	1969–70 Preston NE and Aston Villa
1933–34 Millwall and Lincoln C	1970–71 Blackburn R and Bolton W
1934–35 Oldham Ath and Notts Co	1971–72 Charlton Ath and Watford
1935–36 Port Vale and Hull C	1972–73 Huddersfield T and Brighton & HA
1936–37 Doncaster R and Bradford C	1973–74 Crystal Palace, Preston NE, Swindon T
1937–38 Barnsley and Stockport Co	1974–75 Millwall, Cardiff C, Sheffield W
1938–39 Norwich C and Tranmere R	1975–76 Oxford U, York C, Portsmouth
1946–47 Swansea T and Newport Co	1976–77 Carlisle U, Plymouth Arg, Hereford U
1947–48 Doncaster R and Millwall	1977–78 Blackpool, Mansfield T, Hull C
1948–49 Nottingham F and Lincoln C	1978–79 Sheffield U, Millwall, Blackburn R
1949–50 Plymouth Arg and Bradford PA	1979–80 Fulham, Burnley, Charlton Ath
1950–51 Grimsby T and Chesterfield	1980–81 Preston NE, Bristol C, Bristol R
1951–52 Coventry C and QPR	1981–82 Cardiff C, Wrexham, Orient
1952–53 Southampton and Barnsley	1982–83 Rotherham U, Burnley, Bolton W
1953–54 Brentford and Oldham Ath	1983–84 Derby Co, Swansea C, Cambridge U
1954–55 Ipswich T and Derby Co	1984–85 Notts Co, Cardiff C, Wolverhampton W
1955–56 Plymouth Arg and Hull C	1985–86 Carlisle U, Middlesbrough, Fulham
1956–57 Port Vale and Bury	1986–87 Sunderland**, Grimsby T, Brighton & HA
1957–58 Doncaster R and Notts Co	1987–88 Huddersfield T, Reading, Sheffield U**
1958–59 Barnsley and Grimsby T	1988–89 Shrewsbury T, Birmingham C, Walsall
1959–60 Bristol C and Hull C	1989–90 Bournemouth, Bradford C, Stoke C
1960–61 Lincoln C and Portsmouth	1990–91 WBA and Hull C
1961–62 Brighton & HA and Bristol R	1991–92 Plymouth Arg, Brighton & HA, Port Vale
1962–63 Walsall and Luton T	

FIRST DIVISION TO SECOND DIVISION (1992–93 to 2003–04)

1992–93 Brentford, Cambridge U, Bristol R	1998–99 Bury, Oxford U, Bristol C
1993–94 Birmingham C, Oxford U, Peterborough U	1999–2000 Walsall, Port Vale, Swindon T
1994–95 Swindon T, Burnley, Bristol C, Notts Co	2000–01 Huddersfield T, QPR, Tranmere R
1995–96 Millwall, Watford, Luton T	2001–02 Crewe Alex, Barnsley, Stockport Co
1996–97 Grimsby T, Oldham Ath, Southend U	2002–03 Sheffield W, Brighton & HA, Grimsby T
1997–98 Manchester C, Stoke C, Reading	2003–04 Walsall, Bradford C, Wimbledon

FOOTBALL LEAGUE CHAMPIONSHIP TO FOOTBALL LEAGUE 1 (2004–05 to 2014–15)

2004–05 Gillingham, Nottingham F, Rotherham U	2010–11 Preston NE, Sheffield U, Scunthorpe U
2005–06 Crewe Alex, Millwall, Brighton & HA	2011–12 Portsmouth, Coventry C, Doncaster R
2006–07 Southend U, Luton T, Leeds U	2012–13 Peterborough U, Wolverhampton W, Bristol C
2007–08 Leicester C, Scunthorpe U, Colchester U	2013–14 Doncaster R, Barnsley, Yeovil T
2008–09 Norwich C, Southampton, Charlton Ath	2014–15 Millwall, Wigan Ath, Blackpool
2009–10 Sheffield W, Plymouth Arg, Peterborough U	

DIVISION 3 TO DIVISION 4 (1958–59 to 1991–92)

1958–59 Stockport Co, Doncaster R, Notts Co, Rochdale	1974–75 Bournemouth, Tranmere R, Watford, Huddersfield T
1959–60 York C, Mansfield T, Wrexham, Accrington S	1975–76 Aldershot, Colchester U, Southend U, Halifax T
1960–61 Tranmere R, Bradford C, Colchester U, Chesterfield	1976–77 Reading, Northampton T, Grimsby T, York C
1961–62 Torquay U, Lincoln C, Brentford, Newport Co	1977–78 Port Vale, Bradford C, Hereford U, Portsmouth
1962–63 Bradford PA, Brighton & HA, Carlisle U, Halifax T	1978–79 Peterborough U, Walsall, Tranmere R, Lincoln C
1963–64 Millwall, Crewe Alex, Wrexham, Notts Co	1979–80 Bury, Southend U, Mansfield T, Wimbledon
1964–65 Luton T, Port Vale, Colchester U, Barnsley	1980–81 Sheffield U, Colchester U, Blackpool, Hull C
1965–66 Southend U, Exeter C, Brentford, York C	1981–82 Wimbledon, Swindon T, Bristol C, Chester
1966–67 Swansea T, Darlington, Doncaster R, Workington	1982–83 Reading, Wrexham, Doncaster R, Chesterfield
1967–68 Grimsby T, Colchester U, Scunthorpe U, Peterborough U (demoted)	1983–84 Scunthorpe U, Southend U, Port Vale, Exeter C
1968–69 Northampton T, Hartlepool, Crewe Alex, Oldham Ath	1984–85 Burnley, Orient, Preston NE, Cambridge U
1969–70 Bournemouth, Southport, Barrow, Stockport Co	1985–86 Lincoln C, Cardiff C, Wolverhampton W, Swansea C
1970–71 Reading, Bury, Doncaster R, Gillingham	1986–87 Bolton W**, Carlisle U, Darlington, Newport Co
1971–72 Mansfield T, Barnsley, Torquay U, Bradford C	1987–88 Rotherham U**, Grimsby T, York C, Doncaster R
1972–73 Rotherham U, Brentford, Swansea C, Scunthorpe U	1988–89 Southend U, Chesterfield, Gillingham, Aldershot
1973–74 Cambridge U, Shrewsbury T, Southport, Rochdale	1989–90 Cardiff C, Northampton T, Blackpool, Walsall
	1990–91 Crewe Alex, Rotherham U, Mansfield T
	1991–92 Bury, Shrewsbury T, Torquay U, Darlington

*** Relegated after play-offs.*

SECOND DIVISION TO THIRD DIVISION (1992–93 to 2003–04)

1992–93 Preston NE, Mansfield T, Wigan Ath, Chester C	1996–97 Peterborough U, Shrewsbury T, Rotherham U, Notts Co
1993–94 Fulham, Exeter C, Hartlepool U, Barnet	1997–98 Brentford, Plymouth Arg, Carlisle U, Southend U
1994–95 Cambridge U, Plymouth Arg, Cardiff C, Chester C, Leyton Orient	1998–99 York C, Northampton T, Lincoln C, Macclesfield T
1995–96 Carlisle U, Swansea C, Brighton & HA, Hull C	

1999–2000 Cardiff C, Blackpool, Scunthorpe U,
             Chesterfield
2000–01 Bristol R, Luton T, Swansea C, Oxford U
2001–02 Bournemouth, Bury, Wrexham, Cambridge U

FOOTBALL LEAGUE 1 TO FOOTBALL LEAGUE 2 (2004–05 to 2014–15)

2004–05 Torquay U, Wrexham, Peterborough U,
             Stockport Co
2005–06 Hartlepool U, Milton Keynes D, Swindon T,
             Walsall
2006–07 Chesterfield, Bradford C, Rotherham U,
             Brentford
2007–08 Bournemouth, Gillingham, Port Vale, Luton T
2008–09 Northampton T, Crewe Alex, Cheltenham T,
             Hereford U
2009–10 Gillingham, Wycombe W, Southend U,
             Stockport Co

2002–03 Cheltenham T, Huddersfield T, Mansfield T
             Northampton T
2003–04 Grimsby T, Rushden & D, Notts Co, Wycombe W

2010–11 Dagenham & R, Bristol R, Plymouth Arg,
             Swindon T
2011–12 Wycombe W, Chesterfield, Exeter C, Rochdale
2012–13 Scunthorpe U, Bury, Hartlepool U, Portsmouth
2013–14 Tranmere R, Carlisle U, Shrewsbury T,
             Stevenage
2014–15 Notts Co, Crawley T, Leyton Orient, Yeovil T

LEAGUE STATUS FROM 1986–87

RELEGATED FROM LEAGUE

1986–87 Lincoln C	1987–88 Newport Co
1988–89 Darlington	1989–90 Colchester U
1990–91 —	1991–92 —
1992–93 Halifax T	1993–94 —
1994–95 —	1995–96 —
1996–97 Hereford U	1997–98 Doncaster R
1998–99 Scarborough	1999–2000 Chester C
2000–01 Barnet	2001–02 Halifax T
2002–03 Shrewsbury T, Exeter C	
2003–04 Carlisle U, York C	
2004–05 Kidderminster H, Cambridge U	
2005–06 Oxford U, Rushden & D	
2006–07 Boston U, Torquay U	
2007–08 Mansfield T, Wrexham	
2008–09 Chester C, Luton T	
2009–10 Grimsby T, Darlington	
2010–11 Lincoln C, Stockport Co	
2011–12 Hereford U, Macclesfield T	
2012–13 Barnet, Aldershot T	
2013–14 Bristol R, Torquay U	
2014–15 Cheltenham T, Tranmere R	

PROMOTED TO LEAGUE

1986–87 Scarborough	1987–88 Lincoln C
1988–89 Maidstone U	1989–90 Darlington
1990–91 Barnet	1991–92 Colchester U
1992–93 Wycombe W	1993–94 —
1994–95 —	1995–96 —
1996–97 Macclesfield T	1997–98 Halifax T
1998–99 Cheltenham T	1999–2000 Kidderminster H
2000–01 Rushden & D	2001–02 Boston U
2002–03 Yeovil T, Doncaster R	
2003–04 Chester C, Shrewsbury T	
2004–05 Barnet, Carlisle U	
2005–06 Accrington S, Hereford U	
2006–07 Dagenham & R, Morecambe	
2007–08 Aldershot T, Exeter C	
2008–09 Burton Alb, Torquay U	
2009–10 Stevenage B, Oxford U	
2010–11 Crawley T, AFC Wimbledon	
2011–12 Fleetwood T, York C	
2012–13 Mansfield T, Newport Co	
2013–14 Luton T, Cambridge U	
2014–15 Barnet, Bristol R	

APPLICATIONS FOR RE-ELECTION

FOURTH DIVISION

Eleven: Hartlepool U.
Seven: Crewe Alex.
Six: Barrow (lost League place to Hereford U 1972), Halifax T, Rochdale, Southport (lost League place to Wigan
      Ath 1978), York C.
Five: Chester C, Darlington, Lincoln C, Stockport Co, Workington (lost League place to Wimbledon 1977).
Four: Bradford PA (lost League place to Cambridge U 1970), Newport Co, Northampton T.
Three: Doncaster R, Hereford U.
Two: Bradford C, Exeter C, Oldham Ath, Scunthorpe U, Torquay U.
One: Aldershot, Colchester U, Gateshead (lost League place to Peterborough U 1960), Grimsby T, Swansea C,
      Tranmere R, Wrexham, Blackpool, Cambridge U, Preston NE.
Accrington S resigned and Oxford U were elected 1962.
Port Vale were forced to re-apply following expulsion in 1968.
Aldershot expelled March 1992. Maidstone U resigned August 1992.

THIRD DIVISIONS NORTH & SOUTH

Seven: Walsall.
Six: Exeter C, Halifax T, Newport Co.
Five: Accrington S, Barrow, Gillingham, New Brighton, Southport.
Four: Rochdale, Norwich C.
Three: Crystal Palace, Crewe Alex, Darlington, Hartlepool U, Merthyr T, Swindon T.
Two: Aberdare Ath, Aldershot, Ashington, Bournemouth, Brentford, Chester, Colchester U, Durham C, Millwall,
      Nelson, QPR, Rotherham U, Southend U, Tranmere R, Watford, Workington.
One: Bradford C, Bradford PA, Brighton & HA, Bristol R, Cardiff C, Carlisle U, Charlton Ath, Gateshead,
      Grimsby T, Mansfield T, Shrewsbury T, Torquay U, York C.

LEAGUE ATTENDANCES SINCE 1946–47

Season	Matches	Total	Div. 1	Div. 2	Div. 3 (S)	Div. 3 (N)
1946–47	1848	35,604,606	15,005,316	11,071,572	5,664,004	3,863,714
1947–48	1848	40,259,130	16,732,341	12,286,350	6,653,610	4,586,829
1948–49	1848	41,271,414	17,914,667	11,353,237	6,998,429	5,005,081
1949–50	1848	40,517,865	17,278,625	11,694,158	7,104,155	4,440,927
1950–51	2028	39,584,967	16,679,454	10,780,580	7,367,884	4,757,109
1951–52	2028	39,015,866	16,110,322	11,066,189	6,958,927	4,880,428
1952–53	2028	37,149,966	16,050,278	9,686,654	6,704,299	4,708,735
1953–54	2028	36,174,590	16,154,915	9,510,053	6,311,508	4,198,114
1954–55	2028	34,133,103	15,087,221	8,988,794	5,996,017	4,051,071
1955–56	2028	33,150,809	14,108,961	9,080,002	5,692,479	4,269,367
1956–57	2028	32,744,405	13,803,037	8,718,162	5,622,189	4,601,017
1957–58	2028	33,562,208	14,468,652	8,663,712	6,097,183	4,332,661

Season	Matches	Total	Div. 1	Div. 2	Div. 3	Div. 4
1958–59	2028	33,610,985	14,727,691	8,641,997	5,946,600	4,276,697
1959–60	2028	32,538,611	14,391,227	8,399,627	5,739,707	4,008,050
1960–61	2028	28,619,754	12,926,948	7,033,936	4,784,256	3,874,614
1961–62	2015	27,979,902	12,061,194	7,453,089	5,199,106	3,266,513
1962–63	2028	28,885,852	12,490,239	7,792,770	5,341,362	3,261,481
1963–64	2028	28,535,022	12,486,626	7,594,158	5,419,157	3,035,081
1964–65	2028	27,641,168	12,708,752	6,984,104	4,436,245	3,512,067
1965–66	2028	27,206,980	12,480,644	6,914,757	4,779,150	3,032,429
1966–67	2028	28,902,596	14,242,957	7,253,819	4,421,172	2,984,648
1967–68	2028	30,107,298	15,289,410	7,450,410	4,013,087	3,354,391
1968–69	2028	29,382,172	14,584,851	7,382,390	4,339,656	3,075,275
1969–70	2028	29,600,972	14,868,754	7,581,728	4,223,761	2,926,729
1970–71	2028	28,194,146	13,954,337	7,098,265	4,377,213	2,764,331
1971–72	2028	28,700,729	14,484,603	6,769,308	4,697,392	2,749,426
1972–73	2028	25,448,642	13,998,154	5,631,730	3,737,252	2,081,506
1973–74	2027	24,982,203	13,070,991	6,326,108	3,421,624	2,163,480
1974–75	2028	25,577,977	12,613,178	6,955,970	4,086,145	1,992,684
1975–76	2028	24,896,053	13,089,861	5,798,405	3,948,449	2,059,338
1976–77	2028	26,182,800	13,647,585	6,250,597	4,152,218	2,132,400
1977–78	2028	25,392,872	13,255,677	6,474,763	3,332,042	2,330,390
1978–79	2028	24,540,627	12,704,549	6,153,223	3,374,558	2,308,297
1979–80	2028	24,623,975	12,163,002	6,112,025	3,999,328	2,349,620
1980–81	2028	21,907,569	11,392,894	5,175,442	3,637,854	1,701,379
1981–82	2028	20,006,961	10,420,793	4,750,463	2,836,915	1,998,790
1982–83	2028	18,766,158	9,295,613	4,974,937	2,943,568	1,552,040
1983–84	2028	18,358,631	8,711,448	5,359,757	2,729,942	1,557,484
1984–85	2028	17,849,835	9,761,404	4,030,823	2,667,008	1,390,600
1985–86	2028	16,488,577	9,037,854	3,551,968	2,490,481	1,408,274
1986–87	2028	17,379,218	9,144,676	4,168,131	2,350,970	1,715,441
1987–88	2030	17,959,732	8,094,571	5,341,599	2,751,275	1,772,287
1988–89	2036	18,464,192	7,809,993	5,887,805	3,035,327	1,791,067
1989–90	2036	19,445,442	7,883,039	6,867,674	2,803,551	1,891,178
1990–91	2036	19,508,202	8,618,709	6,285,068	2,835,759	1,768,666
1991–92	2064*	20,487,273	9,989,160	5,809,787	2,993,352	1,694,974

Season	Matches	Total	FA Premier	Div. 1	Div. 2	Div. 3
1992–93	2028	20,657,327	9,759,809	5,874,017	3,483,073	1,540,428
1993–94	2028	21,683,381	10,644,551	6,487,104	2,972,702	1,579,024
1994–95	2028	21,856,020	11,213,168	6,044,293	3,037,752	1,560,807
1995–96	2036	21,844,416	10,469,107	6,566,349	2,843,652	1,965,308
1996–97	2036	22,783,163	10,804,762	6,931,539	3,195,223	1,851,639
1997–98	2036	24,692,608	11,092,106	8,330,018	3,503,264	1,767,220
1998–99	2036	25,435,542	11,620,326	7,543,369	4,169,697	2,102,150
1999–2000	2036	25,341,090	11,668,497	7,810,208	3,700,433	2,161,952
2000–01	2036	26,030,167	12,472,094	7,909,512	3,488,166	2,160,395
2001–02	2036	27,756,977	13,043,118	8,352,128	3,963,153	2,398,578
2002–03	2036	28,343,386	13,468,965	8,521,017	3,892,469	2,460,935
2003–04	2036	29,197,510	13,303,136	8,772,780	4,146,495	2,975,099

Season	Matches	Total	FA Premier	Championship	League 1	League 2
2004–05	2036	29,245,870	12,878,791	9,612,761	4,270,674	2,483,644
2005–06	2036	29,089,084	12,871,643	9,719,204	4,183,011	2,315,226
2006–07	2036	29,541,949	13,058,115	10,057,813	4,135,599	2,290,422
2007–08	2036	29,914,212	13,708,875	9,397,036	4,412,023	2,396,278
2008–09	2036	29,881,966	13,527,815	9,877,552	4,171,834	2,304,765
2009–10	2036	30,057,892	12,977,251	9,909,882	5,043,099	2,127,660
2010–11	2036	29,459,105	13,406,990	9,595,236	4,150,547	2,306,332
2011–12	2036	29,454,401	13,148,465	9,784,100	4,091,897	2,429,939
2012–13	2036	29,225,443	13,653,958	9,662,232	3,485,290	2,423,963
2013–14	2036	29,629,309	13,930,810	9,168,922	4,126,701	2,402,876
2014–15	2036	30,052,575	13,746,753	9,838,940	3,884,414	2,582,468

*Figures include matches played by Aldershot.
Football League official total for their three divisions in 2001–02 was 14,716,162.

ENGLISH LEAGUE ATTENDANCES 2014–15

BARCLAYS PREMIER LEAGUE ATTENDANCES

	Average Gate			Season 2014–15	
	2013–14	2014–15	+/–%	Highest	Lowest
Arsenal	60,013	59,992	–0.04	60,081	59,900
Aston Villa	36,081	34,133	–5.40	41,273	25,311
Burnley	13,722	19,131	+39.42	21,335	16,904
Chelsea	41,482	41,546	+0.16	41,629	41,098
Crystal Palace	24,377	24,421	+0.18	25,197	23,038
Everton	37,732	38,406	+1.79	39,621	34,035
Hull C	24,117	23,557	–2.32	24,877	21,275
Leicester C	24,995	31,693	+26.80	32,021	31,121
Liverpool	44,671	44,659	–0.03	44,736	44,405
Manchester C	47,080	45,365	–3.64	45,919	44,564
Manchester U	75,207	75,335	+0.17	75,454	75,112
Newcastle U	50,395	50,359	–0.07	52,315	46,884
QPR	16,656	17,809	+6.92	18,098	16,163
Southampton	30,212	30,652	+1.46	31,723	27,598
Stoke City	26,137	27,081	+3.61	27,602	26,332
Sunderland	41,090	43,157	+5.03	47,563	39,077
Swansea C	20,407	20,555	+0.73	20,828	20,145
Tottenham H	35,808	35,728	–0.23	36,130	34,008
WBA	25,194	25,064	–0.52	26,768	23,516
West Ham U	33,986	34,871	+2.60	34,977	34,125

TOTAL ATTENDANCES: 13,746,753 (380 games)
                              Average 36,176 (–1.32%)
HIGHEST: 75,454 Manchester U v WBA
LOWEST: 16,163 QPR v Stoke C
HIGHEST AVERAGE: 75,335 Manchester U
LOWEST AVERAGE: 17,809 QPR

SKY BET FOOTBALL LEAGUE: CHAMPIONSHIP ATTENDANCES

	Average Gate			Season 2014–15	
	2013–14	2014–15	+/–%	Highest	Lowest
Birmingham C	15,458	16,111	+4.23	23,851	13,837
Blackburn R	14,960	14,930	–0.20	22,340	12,852
Blackpool	14,217	10,928	–23.13	12,233	9,168
Bolton W	16,141	15,413	–4.51	23,203	12,790
Bournemouth	9,952	10,265	+3.15	11,318	8,480
Brentford	7,716	10,822	+40.26	12,255	8,765
Brighton & HA	27,283	25,660	–5.95	28,890	23,044
Cardiff C	27,430	21,124	–22.99	26,357	19,057
Charlton Ath	16,134	16,708	+3.56	25,545	13,433
Derby Co	24,933	29,232	+17.24	32,705	26,373
Fulham	24,977	18,276	–26.83	23,271	14,325
Huddersfield T	14,213	13,613	–4.22	20,029	10,282
Ipswich T	17,111	19,603	+14.56	26,157	15,726
Leeds U	25,088	24,052	–4.13	31,850	17,634
Middlesbrough	15,748	19,562	+24.22	33,381	14,970
Millwall	11,063	10,902	–1.46	16,205	8,250
Norwich C	26,805	26,343	–1.73	27,005	25,595
Nottingham F	22,630	23,492	+3.81	30,227	19,619
Reading	19,167	17,022	–11.19	20,048	13,775
Rotherham U	8,450	10,240	+21.19	11,707	8,534
Sheffield W	21,278	21,993	+3.36	29,848	16,881
Watford	15,512	16,664	+7.43	20,250	13,468
Wigan Ath	15,177	12,882	–15.12	16,810	10,016
Wolverhampton W	20,879	22,419	+7.38	28,132	17,744

TOTAL ATTENDANCES: 9,838,940 (552 games)
                              Average 17,857 (+7.50%)
HIGHEST: 33,381 Middlesbrough v Brighton & HA
LOWEST: 8,250 Millwall v Blackburn R
HIGHEST AVERAGE: 29,232 Derby Co
LOWEST AVERAGE: 10,240 Rotherham U

Premier League and Football League attendance averages and highest crowd figures for 2014–15 are unofficial.

SKY BET FOOTBALL LEAGUE: DIVISION 1 ATTENDANCES

	Average Gate			Season 2014–15	
	2013–14	*2014–15*	*+/–%*	*Highest*	*Lowest*
Barnsley	11,557	9,768	–15.48	17,532	8,328
Bradford C	14,121	13,353	–5.44	16,032	11,683
Bristol C	11,929	12,056	+1.07	13,731	10,719
Chesterfield	6,318	6,925	+9.61	9,723	4,804
Colchester U	3,735	3,886	+4.04	8,413	2,336
Coventry C	2,348	9,332	+297.44	27,306	2,279
Crawley T	3,486	2,709	–22.29	5,744	1,905
Crewe Alex	4,932	4,732	–4.07	7,608	3,495
Doncaster R	9,041	6,884	–23.85	11,520	5,197
Fleetwood T	2,819	3,522	+24.92	5,110	2,601
Gillingham	6,219	5,694	–8.44	8,443	4,632
Leyton Orient	5,468	5,042	–7.79	7,249	3,534
Milton Keynes D	9,047	9,452	+4.48	16,965	6,720
Notts Co	5,508	5,351	–2.85	7,746	3,159
Oldham Ath	4,415	4,349	–1.50	6,344	2,445
Peterborough U	6,340	6,227	–1.78	7,325	4,338
Port Vale	6,249	5,313	–14.98	8,524	3,590
Preston NE	10,234	10,852	+6.04	17,621	7,491
Rochdale	2,900	3,309	+14.10	7,269	1,914
Scunthorpe U	4,013	3,646	–9.13	5,550	2,773
Sheffield U	17,507	19,805	+13.13	26,078	17,030
Swindon T	8,130	7,940	–2.33	12,565	6,305
Walsall	4,807	4,392	–8.64	5,930	3,296
Yeovil T	6,616	4,346	–34.31	6,837	3,509

TOTAL ATTENDANCES: 3,884,414 (552 games)
Average 7,037 (–5.87%)
HIGHEST: 27,306 Coventry C v Gillingham
LOWEST: 1,905 Crawley T v Fleetwood T
HIGHEST AVERAGE: 19,805 Sheffield U
LOWEST AVERAGE: 2,709 Crawley T

SKY BET FOOTBALL LEAGUE: DIVISION 2 ATTENDANCES

	Average Gate			Season 2014–15	
	2013–14	*2014–15*	*+/–%*	*Highest*	*Lowest*
Accrington S	1,606	1,478	–7.92	2,274	919
AFC Wimbledon	4,135	4,073	–1.50	4,667	3,195
Burton Alb	2,720	3,237	+18.98	5,720	2,099
Bury	3,139	3,774	+20.23	8,396	2,638
Cambridge U	3,085	5,108	+65.56	7,109	3,152
Carlisle U	4,243	4,376	+3.12	8,105	3,116
Cheltenham T	2,989	2,864	–4.16	5,117	2,122
Dagenham & R	1,920	2,041	+6.28	3,393	1,529
Exeter C	3,701	3,873	+4.66	7,440	2,741
Hartlepool U	3,723	3,736	+0.34	5,393	2,792
Luton T	7,387	8,702	+17.81	10,071	7,666
Mansfield T	3,385	3,064	–9.48	4,614	2,185
Morecambe	1,939	1,998	+3.03	4,165	1,156
Newport Co	3,453	3,213	–6.96	5,020	2,327
Northampton T	4,548	4,599	+1.13	5,723	3,653
Oxford U	5,923	6,154	+3.88	9,406	4,111
Plymouth Arg	7,305	7,412	+1.47	11,418	5,657
Portsmouth	15,461	15,242	–1.42	17,558	13,281
Shrewsbury T	5,581	5,343	–4.26	8,963	3,833
Southend U	5,960	6,024	+1.08	10,730	5,013
Stevenage	2,964	3,180	+7.30	5,236	2,165
Tranmere R	5,113	5,192	+1.55	7,518	3,948
Wycombe W	3,681	4,044	+9.87	7,539	2,621
York C	3,773	3,555	–5.79	5,424	2,854

TOTAL ATTENDANCES: 2,582,468 (552 games)
Average 4,678 (+7.47%)
HIGHEST: 17,558 Portsmouth v AFC Wimbledon
LOWEST: 919 Accrington S v Burton Alb
HIGHEST AVERAGE: 15,242 Portsmouth
LOWEST AVERAGE: 1,478 Accrington S

LEAGUE CUP FINALS 1961–2015

Played as a two-leg final until 1966. All subsequent finals played at Wembley except between 2001 and 2007 (inclusive) which were played at Millennium Stadium, Cardiff.

FOOTBALL LEAGUE CUP

1961	Rotherham U v Aston Villa	2-0
	Aston Villa v Rotherham U	3-0*
	Aston Villa won 3-2 on aggregate.	
1962	Rochdale v Norwich C	0-3
	Norwich C v Rochdale	1-0
	Norwich C won 4-0 on aggregate.	
1963	Birmingham C v Aston Villa	3-1
	Aston Villa v Birmingham C	0-0
	Birmingham C won 3-1 on aggregate.	
1964	Stoke C v Leicester C	1-1
	Leicester C v Stoke C	3-2
	Leicester C won 4-3 on aggregate.	
1965	Chelsea v Leicester C	3-2
	Leicester C v Chelsea	0-0
	Chelsea won 3-2 on aggregate.	
1966	West Ham U v WBA	2-1
	WBA v West Ham U	4-1
	WBA won 5-3 on aggregate.	
1967	QPR v WBA	3-2
1968	Leeds U v Arsenal	1-0
1969	Swindon T v Arsenal	3-1*
1970	Manchester C v WBA	2-1*
1971	Tottenham H v Aston Villa	2-0
1972	Stoke C v Chelsea	2-1
1973	Tottenham H v Norwich C	1-0
1974	Wolverhampton W v Manchester C	2-1
1975	Aston Villa v Norwich C	1-0
1976	Manchester C v Newcastle U	2-1
1977	Aston Villa v Everton	0-0
Replay	Aston Villa v Everton	1-1*
	(at Hillsborough)	
Replay	Aston Villa v Everton	3-2*
	(at Old Trafford)	
1978	Nottingham F v Liverpool	0-0*
Replay	Nottingham F v Liverpool	1-0
	(at Old Trafford)	
1979	Nottingham F v Southampton	3-2
1980	Wolverhampton W v Nottingham F	1-0
1981	Liverpool v West Ham U	1-1*
Replay	Liverpool v West Ham U	2-1
	(at Villa Park)	

MILK CUP

1982	Liverpool v Tottenham H	3-1*
1983	Liverpool v Manchester U	2-1*
1984	Liverpool v Everton	0-0*
Replay	Liverpool v Everton	1-0
	(at Maine Road)	
1985	Norwich C v Sunderland	1-0
1986	Oxford U v QPR	3-0

LITTLEWOODS CUP

1987	Arsenal v Liverpool	2-1
1988	Luton T v Arsenal	3-2
1989	Nottingham F v Luton T	3-1
1990	Nottingham F v Oldham Ath	1-0

RUMBELOWS LEAGUE CUP

| 1991 | Sheffield W v Manchester U | 1-0 |
| 1992 | Manchester U v Nottingham F | 1-0 |

COCA-COLA CUP

1993	Arsenal v Sheffield W	2-1
1994	Aston Villa v Manchester U	3-1
1995	Liverpool v Bolton W	2-1
1996	Aston Villa v Leeds U	3-0
1997	Leicester C v Middlesbrough	1-1*
Replay	Leicester C v Middlesbrough	1-0*
	(at Hillsborough)	
1998	Chelsea v Middlesbrough	2-0*

WORTHINGTON CUP

1999	Tottenham H v Leicester C	1-0
2000	Leicester C v Tranmere R	2-1
2001	Liverpool v Birmingham C	1-1*
	Liverpool won 5-4 on penalties.	
2002	Blackburn R v Tottenham H	2-1
2003	Liverpool v Manchester U	2-0

CARLING CUP

2004	Middlesbrough v Bolton W	2-1
2005	Chelsea v Liverpool	3-2*
2006	Manchester U v Wigan Ath	4-0
2007	Chelsea v Arsenal	2-1
2008	Tottenham H v Chelsea	2-1*
2009	Manchester U v Tottenham H	0-0*
	Manchester U won 4-1 on penalties.	
2010	Manchester U v Aston Villa	2-1
2011	Birmingham C v Arsenal	2-1
2012	Liverpool v Cardiff C	2-2*
	Liverpool won 3-2 on penalties.	

CAPITAL ONE CUP

2013	Swansea C v Bradford C	5-0
2014	Manchester C v Sunderland	3-1
2015	Chelsea v Tottenham H	2-0

*After extra time.

LEAGUE CUP WINS

Liverpool 8, Aston Villa 5, Chelsea 5, Manchester U 4, Nottingham F 4, Tottenham H 4, Leicester C 3, Manchester C 3, Arsenal 2, Birmingham C 2, Norwich C 2, Wolverhampton W 2, Blackburn R 1, Leeds U 1, Luton T 1, Middlesbrough 1, Oxford U 1, QPR 1, Sheffield W 1, Stoke C 1, Swansea C 1, Swindon T 1, WBA 1.

APPEARANCES IN FINALS

Liverpool 11, Aston Villa 8, Manchester U 8, Tottenham H 8, Arsenal 7, Chelsea 7, Nottingham F 6, Leicester C 5, Manchester C 4, Norwich C 4, Birmingham C 3, Middlesbrough 3, WBA 3, Bolton W 2, Everton 2, Leeds U 2, Luton T 2, QPR 2, Sheffield W 2, Stoke C 2, Sunderland 2, West Ham U 2, Wolverhampton W 2, Blackburn R 1, Bradford C 1, Cardiff C 1, Newcastle U 1, Oldham Ath 1, Oxford U 1, Rochdale 1, Rotherham U 1, Southampton 1, Swansea C 1, Swindon T 1, Tranmere R 1, Wigan Ath 1.

APPEARANCES IN SEMI-FINALS

Liverpool 15, Arsenal 14, Aston Villa 14, Tottenham H 14, Manchester U 13, Chelsea 12, West Ham U 9, Manchester C 8, Blackburn R 6, Nottingham F 6, Birmingham C 5, Leeds U 5, Leicester C 5, Middlesbrough 5, Norwich C 5, Bolton W 4, Burnley 4, Crystal Palace 4, Everton 4, Ipswich T 4, Sheffield W 4, Sunderland 4, WBA 4, QPR 3, Swindon T 3, Wolverhampton W 3, Bristol C 2, Cardiff C 2, Coventry C 2, Derby Co 2, Luton T 2, Oxford U 2, Plymouth Arg 2, Sheffield U 2, Southampton 2, Stoke C 2, Tranmere R 2, Watford 2, Wimbledon 2, Blackpool 1, Bradford C 1, Bury 1, Carlisle U 1, Chester C 1, Huddersfield T 1, Newcastle U 1, Oldham Ath 1, Peterborough U 1, Rochdale 1, Rotherham U 1, Shrewsbury T 1, Stockport Co 1, Swansea C 1, Walsall 1, Wigan Ath 1, Wycombe W 1.

LEAGUE CUP FINAL TEAMS 1961–2015

First Leg: Millmoor, 22 August 1961   12,226
Rotherham United (0) 2 *(Webster, Kirkman)*
Aston Villa (0) 0

Rotherham United: Ironside; Perry, Morgan, Lambert, Madden, Waterhouse, Webster, Weston, Houghton, Kirkman, Bambridge.
Aston Villa: Sims; Lynn, Lee, Crowe, Dugdale, Deakin, MacEwan, Thomson, Brown, Wylie, McParland.

Second Leg: Villa Park, 5 September 1961   31,202
Aston Villa (0) 3 *(O'Neill, Burrows, McParland)*
Rotherham United (0) 0

Aston Villa: Sidebottom; Neal, Lee, Crowe, Dugdale, Deakin, MacEwan, O'Neill, McParland, Thomson, Burrows.
Rotherham United: Ironside; Perry, Morgan, Lambert, Madden, Waterhouse, Webster, Weston, Houghton, Kirkman, Bambridge.
aet.
Twenty-nine goal Villa played 12 games and defended title eight days after winning it!

First Leg: Spotland, 26 April 1962   11,123
Rochdale (0) 0
Norwich City (2) 3 *(Lythgoe 2, Punton)*

Rochdale: Burgin; Milburn, Winton, Bodell, Aspden, Thompson, Wragg, Hepton, Bimpson, Cairns, Whitaker.
Norwich City: Kennon; McCrohan, Ashman, Burton, Butler, Mullett, Mannion, Lythgoe, Scott, Hill, Punton.

Second Leg: Carrow Road, 1 May 1962   19,708
Norwich City (0) 1 *(Hill)*
Rochdale (0) 0

Norwich City: Kennon; McCrohan, Ashman, Burton, Butler, Mullett, Mannion, Lythgoe, Scott, Hill, Punton.
Rochdale: Burgin; Milburn, Winton, Bodell, Aspden, Thompson, Whyke, Richardson, Bimson, Cairns, Whittaker.
First big trophy for Norwich City; Rochdale from Division Four was lowest ranking finalist.

First Leg: St Andrew's, 23 May 1963   31,850
Birmingham City (1) 3 *(Leek 2, Bloomfield)*
Aston Villa (1) 1 *(Thomson)*

Birmingham City: Scofield; Lynn, Green, Hennessey, Smith, Beard, Hellawell, Bloomfield, Harris, Leek, Auld.
Aston Villa: Sims; Frazer, Aitken, Crowe, Sleeuwenhoek, Lee, Baker, Graham, Thomson, Wylie, Burrows.

Second Leg: Villa Park, 27 May 1963   37,921
Aston Villa (0) 0
Birmingham City (0) 0

Aston Villa: Sims; Frazer, Aitken, Crowe, Chatterley, Lee, Baker, Graham, Thomson, Wylie, Burrows.
Birmingham City: Scofield; Lynn, Green, Hennessey, Smith, Beard, Hellawell, Bloomfield, Harris, Leek, Auld.
Another initial such triumph for Birmingham City and Ken Leek who scored eight goals in eight games.

First Leg: Victoria Ground, 15 April 1964   22,309
Stoke City (0) 1 *(Bebbington)*
Leicester City (0) 1 *(Gibson)*

Stoke City: Leslie; Asprey, Allen, Palmer, Kinnell, Skeels, Dobing, Viollet, Ritchie, McIlroy, Bebbington.
Leicester City: Banks; Sjoberg, Appleton, Dugan, King, Cross, Riley, Heath, Keyworth, Gibson, Stringfellow.

Second Leg: Filbert Street, 22 April 1964   25,372
Leicester City (1) 3 *(Stringfellow, Gibson, Riley)*
Stoke City (0) 2 *(Viollet, Kinnell)*

Leicester City: Banks; Sjoberg, Norman, Cross, King, Appleton, Riley, Gibson, Keyworth, Sweenie, Stringfellow.
Stoke City: Irvine; Asprey, Allen, Palmer, Kinnell, Skeels, Dobing, Viollet, Ritchie, McIlroy, Bebbington.
Leicester City succeeded in keeping John Ritchie – ten goals in ten matches – quiet.

First Leg: Stamford Bridge, 15 March 1965   20,690
Chelsea (1) 3 *(Tambling, Venables (pen), McCreadie)*
Leicester City (0) 2 *(Appleton, Goodfellow)*

Chelsea: Bonetti; Hinton, Harris R, Hollins, Young, Boyle, Murray, Graham, McCreadie, Venables, Tambling.
Leicester City: Banks; Sjoberg, Norman, Chalmers, King, Appleton, Hodgson, Cross, Goodfellow, Gibson, Sweenie.

Second Leg: Filbert Street, 5 April 1965   26,958
Leicester City (0) 0
Chelsea (0) 0

Leicester City: Banks; Walker, Norman, Roberts, Sjoberg, Appleton, Hodgson, Cross, Goodfellow, Gibson, Stringfellow.
Chelsea: Bonetti; Hinton, McCreadie, Harris R, Mortimore, Upton, Murray, Boyle, Bridges, Venables, Tambling.
Holders beaten and tie remembered for fine Eddie McCreadie goal after 60-yard run.

First Leg: Upton Park, 9 March 1966   28,341
West Ham United (0) 2 *(Moore, Byrne)*
West Bromwich Albion (0) 1 *(Astle)*

West Ham United: Standen; Burnett, Burkett, Peters, Brown, Moore, Brabrook, Boyce, Byrne, Hurst, Dear.
West Bromwich Albion: Potter; Cram, Fairfax, Frazer, Campbell, Williams, Brown, Astle, Kaye, Lovett, Clark.

Second Leg: The Hawthorns, 23 March 1966   31,925
West Bromwich Albion (4) 4 *(Kay, Brown, Clark, Williams)*
West Ham United (0) 1 *(Peters)*

West Bromwich Albion: Potter; Cramb, Fairfax, Frazer, Campbell, Williams, Brown, Astle, Kay, Hope, Clark.
West Ham United: Standen; Burnett, Peters, Bovington, Brown, Moore, Brabrook, Boyce, Byrne, Hurst, Sissons.
Outstanding Baggies come back against Bobby Moore, Geoff Hurst and Martin Peters.

Final: Wembley, 4 March 1967   97,952
Queens Park Rangers (0) 3 *(Morgan R, Marsh, Lazarus)*
West Bromwich Albion (2) 2 *(Clark 2)*

Queens Park Rangers: Springett; Hazell, Langley, Sibley, Hunt, Keen, Lazarus, Sanderson, Allen, Marsh, Morgan R.
West Bromwich Albion: Sheppard; Cramb, Williams, Collard, Clark, Fraser, Brown, Astle, Kay, Hope, Clark.
Rodney Marsh solo for fight-back Rangers denied Fairs Cup entry as a Third Division team.

Wembley, 2 March 1968   97,887
Leeds United (1) 1 *(Cooper)*
Arsenal (0) 0

Leeds United: Sprake; Reaney, Cooper, Bremner, Charlton, Hunter, Greenhoff, Lorimer, Madeley, Giles, Gray E (Belfitt).
Arsenal: Furnell; Storey, McNab, McLintock, Simpson, Ure, Radford, Jenkins (Neill), Graham, Sammels, Armstrong.
First trophy for Don Revie at Leeds as United conceded only three goals in seven games.

Wembley, 15 March 1969   98,189
Swindon Town (1) 3 *(Smart, Rogers 2)*
Arsenal (0) 1 *(Gould)*

Swindon Town: Downsborough; Thomas, Trollope, Butler, Burrows, Harland, Heath, Smart, Smith, Noble (Penman), Rogers.
Arsenal: Wilson; Storey, McNab, McLintock, Ure, Simpson (Graham), Radford, Sammels, Court, Gould, Armstrong.
aet.
Third Division Swindon triumphed on pitch recently used for Horse of the Year Show.

Wembley, 7 March 1970   97,963
Manchester City (0) 2 *(Doyle, Pardew)*
West Bromwich Albion (1) 1 *(Astle)*

Manchester City: Corrigan; Book, Mann, Doyle, Booth, Oakes, Heslop, Bell, Summerbee (Bowyer), Lee, Pardew.
West Bromwich Albion: Osborne; Frazer, Wilson, Brown, Talbut, Kaye, Cantello, Suggett, Astle, Hartford (Krzywicki), Hope.
aet.
Jeff Astle was first to score in League and FA Cup finals plus another muddy surface.

Wembley, 27 February 1971   100,000
Tottenham Hotspur (0) 2 *(Chivers 2)*
Aston Villa (0) 0

Tottenham Hotspur: Jennings; Kinnear, Knowles, Mullery, Collins, Beal, Gilzean, Perryman, Chivers, Peters, Neighbour.
Aston Villa: Dunn; Bradley, Aitken, Godfrey, Turnbull, Tiler, McMahon, Rioch, Lochhead, Hamilton, Anderson.
Third Division Villa outplayed Spurs for long periods and should have taken the lead.

Wembley, 4 March 1972   100,000
Stoke City (1) 2 *(Conroy, Eastham)*
Chelsea (1) 1 *(Osgood)*

Stoke City: Banks; Marsh, Pejic, Bernard, Smith, Bloor, Conroy, Greenhough (Mahoney), Ritchie, Dobing, Eastham.
Chelsea: Bonetti; Mulligan (Baldwin), Harris R, Hollins, Dempsey, Webb, Cooke, Garland, Osgood, Hudson, Houseman.
First major trophy for Stoke City; veteran George Eastham, 35, scored the winner.

Wembley, 3 March 1973   100,000
Tottenham Hotspur (0) 1 *(Coates)*
Norwich City (0) 0

Tottenham Hotspur: Jennings; Kinnear, Knowles, Pratt (Coates), England, Beall, Gilzean, Perryman, Chivers, Peters, Pearce.
Norwich City: Keelan; Payne, Butler, Stringer, Forbes, Briggs, Livermore, Blair (Howard), Cross, Paddon, Anderson.
Two previous winners and Ralph Coates scored the 72nd minute winner for Tottenham.

Wembley, 2 March 1974   100,000
Wolverhampton Wanderers (1) 2 *(Hibbitt, Richards)*
Manchester City (0) 1 *(Bell)*

Wolverhampton Wanderers: Pierce; Palmer, Parkin, Bailey, Munro, McAlle, Sunderland, Hibbitt, Richards, Dougan, Wagstaffe (Powell).
Manchester City: MacRae; Pardoe, Donachie, Doyle, Booth, Towers, Summerbee, Bell, Lee, Law, Marsh.
Brilliant display by Gary Pierce in the Wolves goal as Wolves won first trophy since 1960.

Wembley, 1 March 1975   100,000
Aston Villa (0) 1 *(Graydon)*
Norwich City (0) 0

Aston Villa: Cumbes; Robson, Aitken, Ross, Nicholl, McDonald, Graydon, Little, Leonard, Hamilton, Carrodus.
Norwich City: Keelan; Machin, Sullivan, Morris, Forbes, Stringer, Miller, MacDougall, Boyer, Suggett, Powell.
Villa boss Ron Saunders led third different team in three finals – Norwich and Man City!

Wembley, 28 February 1976   100,000
Manchester City (1) 2 *(Barnes, Tueart)*
Newcastle United (1) 1 *(Gowling)*

Manchester City: Corrigan; Keegan, Donachie, Doyle, Watson, Oakes, Barnes, Booth, Royle, Hartford, Tueart.
Newcastle United: Mahoney; Nattrass, Kennedy, Barrowclough, Keeley, Howard, Burns, Cassidy, Macdonald, Gowling, Craig.
Overhead kick by Dennis Tueart won it and Joe Royle had a goal disallowed as well.

Wembley, 12 March 1977   100,000
Aston Villa (0) 0
Everton (0) 0

Aston Villa: Burridge; Gidman, Robson, Phillips, Nicholl, Mortimer, Deehan, Little, Gray, Cropley, Carrodus.
Everton: Lawson; Jones, Darracott, Lyons, McNaught, King, Hamilton, Dobson, Latchford, McKenzie, Goodlass.

Replay: Hillsborough, 16 March 1977   55,000
Aston Villa (0) 1 *(Kenyon (og))*
Everton (0) 1 *(Latchford)*

Aston Villa: Burridge; Gidman, Robson, Phillips, Nicholl, Mortimer, Deehan, Little, Gray, Cowans, Carradus.
Everton: Lawson; Bernard, Darracott, Lyons, McNaught, King, Hamilton (Pearson), Kenyon, Latchford, McKenzie, Goodlass.
aet.

Second Replay: Old Trafford, 13 April 1977   54,749
Aston Villa (0) 3 *(Little 2, Nicholl)*
Everton (1) 2 *(Latchford, Lyons)*

Aston Villa: Burridge; Gidman (Smith), Robson, Phillips, Nicholl, Mortimer, Graydon, Little, Deehan, Cropley, Cowans.
Everton: Lawson; Robinson, Darracott, Lyons, McNaught, King, Hamilton, Dobson, Latchford, Pearson (Seargeant), Goodlass.
aet.
Chris Nicholl 40-yard goal and two-goal Brian Little scoring the winner in the last seconds.

Wembley, 18 March 1978   100,000
Nottingham Forest (0) 0
Liverpool (0) 0

Nottingham Forest: Woods; Anderson, Clark, McGovern (O'Hare), Lloyd, Burns, O'Neill, Bowyer, Withe, Woodcock, Robertson.
Liverpool: Clemence; Neal, Kennedy (Fairclough), Smith, Thompson, Hughes, Dalglish, Case, Heighway, McDermott, Callaghan.
aet.

Replay: Old Trafford, 22 March 1978   54,375
Nottingham Forest (0) 1 *(Robertson (pen))*
Liverpool (0) 0

Nottingham Forest: Woods; Anderson, Clark, O'Hare, Lloyd, Burns, O'Neill, Bowyer, Withe, Woodcock, Robertson.
Liverpool: Clemence; Neal, Kennedy, Smith, Thompson, Hughes, Dalglish, Case (Fairclough), Heighway, McDermott, Callaghan.
Forest in another first: League and League Cup double but penalty awarded outside area.

Wembley, 17 March 1979 100,000

Nottingham Forest (0) 3 *(Birtles 2, Woodcock)*

Southampton (1) 2 *(Peach, Holmes)*

Nottingham Forest: Shilton; Barrett, Clark, McGovern, Lloyd, Needham, O'Neill, Gemmell, Birtles, Woodcock, Robertson.

Southampton: Gennoe; Golac, Peach, Williams, Nicholl, Waldron, Ball, Boyer, Hayes (Sealy), Holmes, Curran.

First Division title winners again but Forest had to come back to overturn the Saints.

Wembley, 15 March 1980 100,000

Wolverhampton Wanderers (0) 1 *(Gray)*

Nottingham Forest (0) 0

Wolverhampton Wanderers: Bradshaw; Palmer, Parkin, Daniel, Berry, Hughes, Carr, Hibbitt, Gray, Richards, Eaves.

Nottingham Forest: Shilton; Anderson, Gray, McGovern, Needham, Burns, O'Neill, Bowyer, Birtles, Francis, Robertson.

Defensive error cost Forest's cup run and Emlyn Hughes achieved every major honour.

Wembley, 14 March 1981 100,000

Liverpool (0) 1 *(Kennedy A)*

West Ham United (0) 1 *(Stewart (pen))*

Liverpool: Clemence; Neal, Kennedy A, Irwin, Kennedy R, Hansen, Dalglish, Lee, Heighway (Case), McDermott, Souness.

West Ham United: Parkes; Stewart, Lampard, Bonds, Martin, Devonshire, Neighbour, Goddard (Pearson), Cross, Brooking, Pike.

aet.

Replay: Villa Park, 1 April 1981 36,693

Liverpool (2) 2 *(Dalglish, Hansen)*

West Ham United (1) 1 *(Goddard)*

Liverpool: Clemence; Neal, Kennedy A, Thompson, Kennedy R, Hansen, Dalglish, Lee, Rush, McDermott, Case.

West Ham United: Parkes; Stewart, Lampard, Bonds, Martin, Devonshire, Neighbour, Goddard, Cross, Brooking, Pike (Pearson).

Rare goal indeed from Alan Hansen as Liverpool were forced to overhaul Hammers lead.

Wembley, 13 March 1982 100,000

Liverpool (0) 3 *(Whelan 2, Rush)*

Tottenham Hotspur (1) 1 *(Archibald)*

Liverpool: Grobbelaar; Neal, Kennedy A, Thompson, Whelan, Lawrenson, Dalglish, Lee, Rush, McDermott (Johnson), Souness.

Tottenham Hotspur: Clemence; Hughton, Miller, Price, Hazard (Villa), Perryman, Ardiles, Archibald, Galvin, Hoddle, Crooks.

aet.

Liverpool hit 25 goals in the run compared with Spurs scoring just eight in eight matches.

Wembley, 26 March 1983 100,000

Liverpool (0) 2 *(Kennedy A, Whelan)*

Manchester United (1) 1 *(Whiteside)*

Liverpool: Grobbelaar; Neal, Kennedy A, Lawrenson, Whelan, Hansen, Dalglish, Lee, Rush, Johnston (Fairclough), Souness.

Manchester United: Bailey; Duxbury, Albiston, Moses, Moran (Macari), McQueen, Wilkins, Muhren, Stapleton, Whiteside, Coppell.

aet.

Bob Paisley's last major honour with Liverpool and United led them for over an hour.

Wembley, 25 March 1984 100,000

Liverpool (0) 0

Everton (0) 0

Liverpool: Grobbelaar; Neal, Kennedy A, Lawrenson, Whelan, Hansen, Dalglish, Lee, Rush, Johnston (Robinson), Souness.

Everton: Southall; Stevens, Bailey, Ratcliffe, Mountfield, Reid, Irvine, Heath, Sharp, Richardson, Sheedy (Harper).

aet.

Replay: Maine Road, 28 March 1984 52,089

Liverpool (1) 1 *(Souness)*

Everton (0) 0

Liverpool: Grobbelaar; Neal, Kennedy A, Lawrenson, Whelan, Hansen, Dalglish, Lee, Rush, Johnston, Souness.

Everton: Southall; Stevens, Bailey, Ratcliffe, Mountfield, Reid, Irvine (King), Heath, Sharp, Richardson, Harper.

Four in a row for the Anfield team which had lost only one leg of a tie throughout the sequence.

Wembley, 24 March 1985 100,000

Norwich City (0) 1 *(Chisholm (og))*

Sunderland (0) 0

Norwich City: Woods; Haylock, Van Wyk, Bruce, Mendham, Watson, Barham, Channon, Deehan, Hartford, Donowa.

Sunderland: Turner; Venison, Pickering, Bennett, Chisholm, Corner (Gayle), Daniel, Wallace, Hodgson, Berry, Walker.

Deflected shot by Asa Hartford, Clive Walker missed a penalty and both reams relegated.

Wembley, 20 April 1986 90,396

Oxford United (1) 3 *(Hebberd, Houghton, Charles)*

Queens Park Rangers (0) 0

Oxford United: Judge; Langan, Trewick, Phillips, Briggs, Shotton, Houghton, Aldridge, Charles, Hebberd, Brock.

Queens Park Rangers: Barron; McDonald, Dawes, Neill, Wicks, Fenwick, Allen (Rosenior), James, Bannister, Byrne, Robinson.

One-sided final and the first big prize for Oxford United during a good run in the League.

Wembley, 5 April 1987 96,000

Arsenal (1) 2 *(Nicholas 2)*

Liverpool (1) 1 *(Rush)*

Arsenal: Lukic; Anderson, Sansom, Williams, O'Leary, Adams, Rocastle, Davis, Quinn (Groves), Nicholas, Hayes (Thomas).

Liverpool: Grobbelaar; Gillespie, Venison, Spackman, Whelan, Hansen, Walsh (Dalglish), Johnston, Rush, Molby, McMahon (Wark).

Firsts: Arsenal's such cup; Liverpool loss when talisman goal scorer Ian Rush had scored.

Wembley, 24 April 1988 95,732

Luton Town (1) 3 *(Stein B 2, Wilson)*

Arsenal (0) 2 *(Hayes, Smith)*

Luton Town: Dibble; Breacker, Johnson, Hill, Foster, Donaghy, Wilson, Black, Stein B, Harford (Stein M), Preece (Grimes).

Arsenal: Lukic; Winterburn, Sansom, Thomas, Caeser, Adams, Rocastle, Davis, Smith, Groves (Hayes), Richardson.

Andy Dibble saved penalty when Arsenal and Luton hit two goals in last seven minutes.

Wembley, 9 April 1989 76,130
Nottingham Forest (0) 3 *(Clough 2 (1 pen), Webb)*
Luton Town (1) 1 *(Harford)*

Nottingham Forest: Sutton; Laws, Pearce, Walker, Wilson, Hodge, Gaynor, Webb, Clough, Chapman, Parker.
Luton Town: Sealey; Breacker, Grimes (McDonough), Preece, Foster, Beaumont, Wilson, Wegerle, Harford, Hill, Black.
Giant-killers beaten and Forest had a goal disallowed and had also won the Simod Cup.

Wembley, 29 April 1990 74,343
Nottingham Forest (0) 1 *(Jemson)*
Oldham Athletic (0) 0

Nottingham Forest: Sutton; Laws, Pearce, Walker, Chettle, Hodge, Crosby, Parker, Clough, Jemson, Carr.
Oldham Athletic: Rhodes; Irwin, Barlow, Henry, Barrett, Warhurst, Adams, Ritchie, Bunn (Palmer), Milligan, Holden R.
Forest equalled the then Liverpool record of four wins against Second Division Oldham.

Wembley, 21 April 1991 80,000
Sheffield Wednesday (1) 1 *(Sheridan)*
Manchester United (0) 0

Sheffield Wednesday: Turner; Nilsson, King, Harkes (Madden), Shirtliff, Pearson, Wilson, Sheridan, Hirst, Williams, Worthington.
Manchester United: Sealey; Irwin, Blackmore, Bruce, Webb (Phelan), Pallister, Robson, Ince, McClair, Hughes, Sharpe.
Impressive Wednesday coupled this cup success with promotion to First Division.

Wembley, 12 April 1992 76,810
Manchester United (1) 1 *(McClair)*
Nottingham Forest (0) 0

Manchester United: Schmeichel; Parker, Irwin, Bruce, Phelan, Pallister, Kanchelskis (Sharpe), Ince, McClair, Hughes, Giggs.
Nottingham Forest: Marriott; Charles (Laws), Williams, Walker, Wassall, Keane, Crosby, Gemmill, Clough, Sheringham, Black.
United became the first losing team to win the next time; Brian Clough's last big trophy.

Wembley, 18 April 1993 74,007
Arsenal (1) 2 *(Merson, Morrow)*
Sheffield Wednesday (1) 1 *(Parkes)*

Arsenal: Seaman; O'Leary, Winterburn, Parlour, Adams, Linighan, Morrow, Merson, Wright, Campbell, Davis.
Sheffield Wednesday: Woods; Nilsson, King (Hyde), Palmer, Anderson, Parkes, Wilson (Hirst), Waddle, Warhurst, Bright, Sheridan.
First of three Wembley finals for these teams; squad numbering also made its appearance.

Wembley, 27 March 1994 77,231
Aston Villa (1) 3 *(Atkinson, Saunders 2 (1 pen))*
Manchester United (0) 1 *(Hughes)*

Aston Villa: Bosnich; Barrett, Staunton (Cox), Teale, McGrath, Richardson, Daley, Townsend, Saunders, Atkinson, Fenton.
Manchester United: Sealey; Parker, Irwin, Bruce (McClair), Kanchelskis, Pallister, Cantona, Ince, Keane, Hughes, Giggs (Sharpe).
Villa denied United of a treble after League and FA Cup; Andrei Kanchelskis was sent off.

Wembley, 2 April 1995 75,595
Liverpool (1) 2 *(McManaman 2)*
Bolton Wanderers (0) 1 *(Thompson)*

Liverpool: James; Jones, Bjornebye, Scales, Babb, Ruddock, McManaman, Redknapp, Rush, Barnes, Fowler.
Bolton Wanderers: Branagan; Green (Bergsson), Phillips, McAteer, Seagraves, Stubbs, Lee, Sneekes, Paatelainen, McGinlay, Thompson.
Steve McManaman was rightly awarded Man of the Match accolade for his two fine goals.

Wembley, 24 March 1996 77,056
Aston Villa (1) 3 *(Milosevic, Taylor, Yorke)*
Leeds United (0) 0

Aston Villa: Bosnich; Charles, Wright, Southgate, McGrath, Ehiogu, Taylor, Draper, Milosevic, Townsend, Yorke.
Leeds United: Lukic; Kelly, Radebe (Brolin), Parker, Wetherall, Pemberton, Gray, Ford (Deane), Yeboah, McAllister, Speed.
An emphatic victory for Villa levelled the Liverpool achievement of five such cup victories.

Wembley, 6 April 1997 76,757
Leicester City (0) 1 *(Heskey)*
Middlesbrough (0) 1 *(Ravanelli)*

Leicester City: Keller; Grayson, Whitlow (Robins), Kamark, Walsh, Prior, Lennon, Parker, Claridge, Izzet (Taylor), Heskey.
Middlesbrough: Schwarzer; Cox, Fleming, Mustoe, Pearson, Festa, Emerson, Hignett, Beck, Juninho, Ravanelli.
aet.

Replay: Hillsborough, 16 April 1997 39,428
Leicester City (0) 1 *(Claridge)*
Middlesbrough (0) 0

Leicester City: Keller; Grayson, Whitlow (Lawrence), Kamark, Walsh, Prior, Lennon, Parker, Claridge (Robins), Izzet, Heskey.
Middlesbrough: Roberts; Cox (Moore), Kinder, Festa (Vickers), Pearson, Blackmore, Emerson, Mustoe, Ravanelli, Juninho, Hignett (Beck).
aet.
The last final decided by a replay; Emile Heskey had equalised two minutes from time.

Wembley, 29 March 1998 77,698
Chelsea (0) 2 *(Sinclair, Di Matteo)*
Middlesbrough (0) 0

Chelsea: De Goey; Petrescu (Clarke), Le Saux, Sinclair, Leboeuf, Duberry, Newton, Di Matteo, Zola, Hughes M (Flo), Wise.
Middlesbrough: Schwarzer; Festa, Kinder, Vickers, Pearson, Mustoe, Ricard (Gascoigne), Townsend, Branca, Merson, Maddison (Beck).
aet.
Boro beaten again and Chelsea also went on to win the European Cup-Winners' Cup.

Wembley, 21 March 1999 77,892
Leicester C (0) 0
Tottenham H (0) 1 *(Nielsen 90)*

Leicester C: Keller; Ullathorne, Guppy, Elliott, Walsh, Taggart, Lennon, Izzet, Cottee, Savage (Zagorakis), Heskey (Marshall).
Tottenham H: Walker; Carr, Edinburgh, Freund, Vega, Campbell, Anderton, Nielsen, Iversen, Ferdinand, Ginola (Sinton).
Referee: T. Heilbron (Newton Aycliffe).
Last minute diving header by Allan Nielsen but Spurs had Justin Edinburgh sent off.

Wembley, 27 February 2000 74,313
Leicester C (1) 2 *(Elliott 29, 81)*
Tranmere R (0) 1 *(Kelly 77)*
Leicester C: Flowers; Savage, Guppy, Elliott, Taggart, Sinclair, Lennon, Izzet, Cottee (Marshall), Oakes (Impey), Heskey.
Tranmere R: Murphy; Hazell, Roberts, Henry, Hill, Challinor, Mahon, Parkinson (Yates), Jones G, Kelly, Taylor S.
Referee: A. Wilkie (Chester-le-Street).
(P. Richards (Preston) (substitute 57 minutes)).
Clint Hill had two yellow cards but Tranmere kept plugging away against Leicester City.

Millennium Stadium, 25 February 2001 73,500
Birmingham C (0) 1 *(Purse 90 (pen))*
Liverpool (1) 1 *(Fowler 30)*
Birmingham C: Bennett; Eaden, Grainger, Sonner (Hughes), Purse, Johnson M, McCarthy, O'Connor, Horsfield (Marcelo), Adebola (Johnson A), Lazaridis.
Liverpool: Westerveld; Babbel, Carragher, Hamann, Henchoz, Hyypia, Gerrard (McAllister), Smicer (Barmby), Heskey, Fowler, Biscan (Ziege).
aet; Liverpool won 5-4 on penalties.
Referee: D. Elleray (Harrow).
Birmingham also had penalty appeal turned down in extra time in first shoot-out final.
Penalties: McAllister scored; Grainger missed; Barmby scored; Purse scored; Ziege missed; Marcelo scored; Hamann missed; Lazaridis scored; Fowler scored, Hughes scored; Carragher scored; sub Johnson missed.

Millennium Stadium, 24 February 2002 72,500
Blackburn R (1) 2 *(Jansen 25, Cole 69)*
Tottenham H (1) 1 *(Ziege 33)*
Blackburn R: Friedel; Taylor, Bjornebye, Dunn, Berg, Johansson, Gillespie (Hignett), Jansen (Yordi), Cole, Hughes, Duff.
Tottenham H: Sullivan; Taricco (Davies), Ziege, Thatcher, Perry, King, Anderton, Sherwood, Ferdinand, Sheringham, Poyet (Iversen).
Referee: G. Poll.
Teddy Sheringham was denied a penalty in the last minute; Blackburn's first such cup win.

Millennium Stadium, 2 March 2003 74,500
Liverpool (1) 2 *(Gerrard 38, Owen 86)*
Manchester U (0) 0
Liverpool: Dudek; Carragher, Riise, Hamann, Henchoz, Hyypia, Gerrard, Diouf (Biscan), Heskey (Baros) (Smicer), Owen, Murphy.
Manchester U: Barthez; Neville G, Silvestre, Brown (Solskjaer), Keane, Ferdinand, Beckham, Veron, Van Nistelrooy, Scholes, Giggs.
Referee: P. Durkin (Portland).
Steven Gerrard's goal was a deflection off David Beckham; Michael Owen soloed the second.

Millennium Stadium, 29 February 2004 72,634
Middlesbrough (2) 2 *(Job 2, Zenden 7 (pen))*
Bolton W (1) 1 *(Davies 21)*
Middlesbrough: Schwarzer; Mills, Queudrue, Southgate, Ehiogu, Doriva, Mendieta, Boateng, Job (Ricketts), Juninho, Zenden.
Bolton W: Jaaskelainen; Hunt (Giannakopoulos), Charlton, Campo, N'Gotty, Emerson, Nolan (Javi Moreno), Frandsen (Pedersen), Davies, Djorkaeff, Okocha.
Referee: M. Riley (W. Yorkshire).
Fastest final goal and Boudewijn Zenden slipped taking the penalty as Boro finally won.

Millennium Stadium, 27 February 2005 78,000
Liverpool (1) 2 *(Riise 1, Nunez 113)*
Chelsea (0) 3 *(Gerrard 79 (og), Drogba 107, Kezman 112)*
Liverpool: Dudek; Finnan, Traore (Biscan), Hamann, Carragher, Hyypia, Kewell (Nunez), Gerrard, Luis Garcia, Morientes (Baros), Riise.
Chelsea: Cech; Paulo Ferreira, Gallas (Kezman), Makelele, Terry, Ricardo Carvalho, Jarosik (Gudjohnsen), Lampard, Drogba, Cole (Johnson), Duff.
aet.
Referee: S. Bennett (Orpington).
Even faster goal and the own goal came from a Paulo Ferreira free kick for Chelsea leveller.

Millennium Stadium, 26 February 2006 66,866
Manchester U (1) 4 *(Rooney 33, 61, Saha 55, Ronaldo 59)*
Wigan Ath (0) 0
Manchester U: Van der Sar; Neville, Silvestre (Evra), Park, Brown (Vidic), Ferdinand, Ronaldo (Richardson), O'Shea, Saha, Rooney, Giggs.
Wigan Ath: Pollitt (Filan); Chimbonda, Baines, Kavanagh (Ziegler), Henchoz (McCulloch), De Zeeuw, Teale, Bullard, Camara, Roberts, Scharner.
Referee: A. Wiley (Staffordshire).
Easy success for United whose ex-goalkeeper Mike Pollitt was injured after 14 minutes play.

Millennium Stadium, 25 February 2007 70,073
Chelsea (1) 2 *(Drogba 20, 84)*
Arsenal (1) 1 *(Walcott 12)*
Chelsea: Cech; Diarra, Bridge, Makelele (Robben), Terry (Mikel■), Ricardo Carvalho, Essien, Lampard, Drogba, Shevchenko (Kalou), Ballack.
Arsenal: Almunia; Hoyte, Traore (Eboue), Denilson, Toure■, Senderos, Walcott, Fabregas, Aliadiere (Adebayor■), Julio Baptista, Diaby (Hleb).
Referee: H. Webb (South Yorkshire).
First all-London final and first to have three players sent off in the dying minutes of the game.

Wembley, 24 February 2008 87,660
Tottenham H (0) 2 *(Berbatov 70 (pen), Woodgate 94)*
Chelsea (1) 1 *(Drogba 39)*
Tottenham H: Robinson; Hutton, Chimbonda (Huddlestone), Zokora, Woodgate, King, Lennon, Jenas, Berbatov, Keane (Kaboul), Malbranque (Tainio).
Chelsea: Cech; Belletti, Bridge, Mikel (Cole J), Terry, Ricardo Carvalho, Essien (Ballack), Lampard, Drogba, Anelka, Wright-Phillips (Kalou).
aet.
Referee: M. Halsey (Lancashire).
Didier Drogba was the first to score in three League Cup finals; Wayne Bridge hands for penalty.

Wembley, 1 March 2009 88,217
Manchester U (0) 0
Tottenham H (0) 0
Manchester U: Foster; O'Shea (Vidic), Evra, Gibson (Giggs), Ferdinand, Evans, Ronaldo, Scholes, Welbeck (Anderson), Tevez, Nani.
Tottenham H: Gomes; Corluka, Assou-Ekotto, Zokora, Dawson, King, Lennon (Bentley), Jenas (Bale), Pavlyuchenko (O'Hara), Bent, Modric.
aet; Manchester U won 4-1 on penalties: Giggs scored; O'Hara saved; Tevez scored; Corluka scored; Ronaldo scored; Bentley missed; Anderson scored.
Referee: C. Foy (Merseyside).
Penalties – though Carlos Tevez and Roman Pavlyuchenko had each scored six goals en route.

Wembley, 28 February 2010 88,596
Aston Villa (1) 1 *(Milner 5 (pen))*
Manchester U (1) 2 *(Owen 12, Rooney 74)*
Aston Villa: Friedel; Cuellar (Carew), Warnock, Collins JM, Dunne, Downing, Milner, Petrov, Agbonlahor, Heskey, Young A.
Manchester U: Kuszczak; Rafael (Neville), Evra, Carrick, Evans J, Vidic, Valencia, Fletcher, Berbatov, Owen (Rooney), Park (Gibson).
Referee: P. Dowd (Staffordshire).
Evenly contested final, fourth win for United and their third in five years after Villa lead early.

Wembley, Sunday, 27 February 2011 88,851
Birmingham C (1) 2 *(Zigic 28, Martins 89)*
Arsenal (1) 1 *(Van Persie 39)*
Arsenal: Szczesny; Sagna, Clichy, Song Billong, Djourou, Koscielny, Rosicky, Wilshere, Van Persie (Bendtner), Arshavin (Chamakh), Nasri.
Birmingham C: Foster; Carr, Ridgewell, Bowyer, Jiranek, Johnson, Larsson, Ferguson, Zigic (Jerome), Gardner (Beausejour), Fahey (Martins).
Referee: M. Dean (Wirral).
Birmingham upset form, win place in Europa League but find themselves relegated later on.

Wembley, Sunday, 26 February 2012 89,044
Liverpool (0) 2 *(Skrtel 60, Kuyt 108)*
Cardiff C (1) 2 *(Mason 19, Turner 118)*
Liverpool: Reina; Johnson, Jose Enrique, Skrtel, Agger (Carragher), Adam, Henderson (Bellamy), Gerrard, Carroll (Kuyt), Suarez, Downing.
Cardiff C: Heaton; McNaughton (Blake), Taylor, Gunnarsson, Hudson (Gerrard), Turner, Cowie, Whittingham, Miller, Gestede, Mason (Kiss).
aet; Liverpool won 3-2 on penalties.
Referee: M. Clattenburg (Tyne & Wear).
Liverpool miss the first two penalties in the shoot-out but still triumph over the Championship side.

Wembley, Sunday, 24 February 2013 82,597
Swansea C (2) 5 *(Dyer 16, 48, Michu 40, de Guzman 59 (pen), 90)*
Bradford C (0) 0
Swansea C: (451) Tremmel; Rangel, Williams, Ki (Monk 62), Davies (Tiendalli 84); Dyer (Lamah 77), Britton, de Guzman, Routledge, Hernandez; Michu.
Bradford C: (442) Duke; Darby, McHugh, McArdle, Good (Davies 46); Atkinson, Jones G, Doyle, Thompson (Hines 73); Wells (McLaughlin 57), Hanson.
Referee: Kevin Friend (Leicestershire).
First time a non-English club won the competition and the first time a fourth-tier club had played in the final.

Wembley, Sunday, 2 March 2014 84,697
Manchester C (0) 3 *(Toure 55, Nasri 56, Jesus Navas 90)*
Sunderland (1) 1 *(Borini 10)*
Manchester C: (442) Pantilimon; Zabaleta, Kompany, Demichelis, Kolarov; Nasri, Toure, Fernandinho, Silva (Javi Garcia 77); Dzeko (Negredo 88), Aguero (Jesus Navas 58).
Sunderland: (4141) Mannone; Bardsley, O'Shea, Brown, Alonso; Cattermole (Giaccherini 77); Johnson (Gardner 60), Larsson (Fletcher 60), Ki, Colback; Borini.
Referee: Martin Atkinson (West Yorkshire).
Pellegrini's men come from behind to lift trophy and keep faint hopes of quadruple alive, leaving Sunderland to concentrate on their relegation great escape.

Wembley, Sunday, 1 March 2015 89,294
Chelsea (1) 2 *(Terry 45, Walker 56 (og))*
Tottenham H (0) 0
Chelsea: (433) Cech; Ivanovic, Cahill, Terry, Azpilicueta; Ramires, Zouma, Fabregas (Oscar 88); Willian (Cuadrado 76), Costa (Drogba 90), Hazard.
Tottenham H: (4231) Lloris; Walker, Dier, Vertonghen, Rose; Bentaleb, Mason (Lamela 71); Townsend (Dembele 62), Eriksen, Chadli (Soldado 80); Kane.
Referee: Anthony Taylor (Cheshire).
A repeat of the 2008 final saw manager Jose Mourinho win his first trophy since his return to English football.

CAPITAL ONE CUP 2014–15

■ *Denotes player sent off.*

FIRST ROUND

Monday, 11 August 2014

Carlisle U (0) 0
Derby Co (0) 2 *(Hendrick 62, Martin 90)*   3481
Carlisle U: (532) Gillespie; Symington, O'Hanlon, Meppen-Walter, Thirlwell (Marrow 75), Robson; Dempsey, Potts, Sweeney; Paynter (Elliott 71), Kearns (Brough 81).
Derby Co: (433) Grant; Christie, Whitbread, Keogh, Forsyth; Bryson, Hughes, Hendrick; Dawkins (Best 70), Martin, Ward (Russell 70).
Referee: Darren Bond.

Tuesday, 12 August 2014

Barnsley (0) 0
Crewe Alex (1) 2 *(Waters 32, Tootle 84)*   4391
Barnsley: (442) Davies; Bree, Cranie, Brown, Nyatanga; Noble-Lazarus (Boakye-Yiadom 87), Bailey, Hourihane, Treacy (Mvoto 76); Lita (McHale 61), Winnall.
Crewe Alex: (451) Garratt; Tootle, Dugdale, Ray, Leigh (Guthrie 62); Turton, Inman (Molyneux 76), Grant, Nolan, Waters; Oliver (Haber 87).
Referee: Christopher Sarginson.

Birmingham C (1) 3 *(Donaldson 16, Caddis 96, Duffy 105)*
Cambridge U (1) 1 *(Donaldson 38)*   9816
Birmingham C: (442) Doyle; Caddis, Gunning (Edgar 38), Hall, Grounds; Cotterill, Davis, Spector, Gray (Duffy 75); Donaldson, Thomas (Novak 63).
Cambridge U: (442) Dunn; Tait, Bonner, Coulson, Taylor G; Donaldson, Champion, Hughes, Dunk (Chadwick 69); Cunnington (Sam-Yorke 46), Appiah (Simpson 83).
aet.
Referee: Tim Robinson.

Blackburn R (0) 0
Scunthorpe U (1) 1 *(Bishop 34)*   5352
Blackburn R: (4411) Kean; Lowe, O'Connell, Songo'o, Henley; Marshall (Conway 63), Taylor C (Cairney 78), Williamson, King; Dunn (Gestede 62); Varney.
Scunthorpe U: (442) Slocombe; Nolan, Canavan, Llera, Dawson; Myrie-Williams, Bishop, McAllister, McSheffrey; Madden, Taylor (Addison 85).
Referee: Seb Stockbridge.

Bolton W (0) 3 *(Davies C 90 (pen), Danns 93, 96)*
Bury (1) 2 *(Lowe 20, McNulty 97)*   9249
Bolton W: (442) Bogdan; Threlkeld, Dervite, Wheater, Ream; Hall (Lee 67), Pratley (Danns 78), Trotter, Feeney; Wilkinson (Davies C 67), Beckford.
Bury: (442) Jalal (Lainton 46); Tutte, Mills, McNulty, Hussey; Adams, Sedgwick, Soares, Cameron; Lowe (Thompson 85), Nardiello (Mayor 63).
aet.
Referee: Jeremy Simpson.

Brighton & HA (0) 2 *(Dunk 79, Mackail-Smith 90)*
Cheltenham T (0) 0   6595
Brighton & HA: (433) Stockdale; Saltor, Greer, Dunk, Calderon; Agustien (LuaLua 68), Ince, Chicksen (Maksimenko 90); Mackail-Smith, O'Grady (Fenelon 90), Forster-Caskey.
Cheltenham T: (451) Carson; Vaughan, Elliott, Brown T, Braham-Barrett; Taylor J, Hanks (Sterling-James 88), Gornell (Haworth 66), Deaman, Richards M; Harrison.
Referee: Michael Bull.

Bristol C (1) 1 *(Bryan 2)*
Oxford U (0) 2 *(Morris 55, Hylton 87)*   6145
Bristol C: (352) Fielding; Ayling, Osborne, El-Abd; Wagstaff, Wynter, Pack, Reid (Williams 62), Bryan (Burns 83); Baldock, Emmanuel-Thomas (Wilbraham 82).
Oxford U: (4411) Crocombe; Hunt, Mullins, Wright, Newey; Riley, Meades, Ruffels (Collins 19), Brown; Potter; Morris (Hylton 73).
Referee: Lee Collins.

Burton Alb (1) 2 *(Knowles 45, Beavon 52)*
Wigan Ath (1) 1 *(Fortune 27)*   2602
Burton Alb: (442) McLaughlin; Edwards, Sharps, Cansdell-Sherriff, Taft; Akins, Weir, Mousinho, MacDonald; Beavon (Kee 58), McGurk (Knowles 39).
Wigan Ath: (532) Al Habsi; Tavernier, Ramis, Rogne, Barnett, Taylor-Sinclair; Fyvie, Maloney (Holt 61), Espinoza; Waghorn, Fortune.
Referee: Pat Miller.

Charlton Ath (1) 4 *(Buyens 24 (pen), Wilson 54, 59, Church 89)*
Colchester U (0) 0   5752
Charlton Ath: (442) Henderson; Gomez, Morrison, Bikey, Fox; Wilson, Cousins, Buyens (Gudmundsson 64), Harriott; Moussa (Vetokele 60), Tucudean (Church 72).
Colchester U: (4231) Lewington; Clohessy, Okuonghae■, Eastman, Gordon; Gilbey, Moncur; Vose (Bean 29), Sears (Szmodics 63), Massey (Holman 46); Ibehre.
Referee: Charles Breakspear.

Chesterfield (2) 3 *(Humphreys 32, Banks 45, Doyle 71)*
Huddersfield T (0) 5 *(Wells 58, 84 (pen), 94, Stead 90, Lolley 98)*   4569
Chesterfield: (4231) Lee; Darikwa, Evatt, Hird, Jones; Morsy, Ryan (Gnanduillet 95); Boco (Johnson 57), Roberts, Humphreys (Banks 43); Doyle.
Huddersfield T: (442) Murphy; Peltier, Wallace, Smith, Dixon; Scannell (Majewski 66), Coady, Norwood (Hammill 81), Ward (Lolley 86); Wells, Stead.
aet.
Referee: Gary Sutton.

Crawley T (0) 1 *(McLeod 111)*
Ipswich T (0) 0   3043
Crawley T: (4411) Jensen; Oyebanjo, Walsh, Leacock, Bradley; Bawling (Dickson 63), Smith, Henderson (O'Connor 94), Edwards; Young (Banya 56); McLeod.
Ipswich T: (442) Bialkowski; Hewitt, Chambers, Berra, Clarke; Taylor (McQueen 80), Bru (Bishop 77), Wordsworth, Henshall; Marriott (Bajner 63), Nouble.
aet.
Referee: Andy Haines.

Dagenham & R (2) 6 *(Porter 17, Chambers 45, Boucaud 55, Hemmings 90, 113, Cureton 100)*
Brentford (3) 6 *(Dallas 5, 9, Proschwitz 32, Gray 83, Moore 91, Dean 117)*   1576
Dagenham & R: (433) O'Brien; Batt (Connors 59), Doe, Saah, Partridge; Labadie (Cureton 86), Ogogo, Boucaud (Howell 75); Hemmings, Chambers, Porter.
Brentford: (433) Lee; Yennaris (Bidwell 21), Dean, Craig, O'Connor; Diagouraga, Tebar (Judge 64); Dallas; Moore, Proschwitz (Gray 64), Smith.
aet; Brentford won 4-2 on penalties.
Referee: Keith Hill.

Exeter C (0) 0
Bournemouth (0) 2 *(Bennett 55 (og), Gosling 74)*   2648
Exeter C: (532) Pym; Wheeler (Dawson 76), Bennett, Tillson, Baldwin, Woodman (Riley-Lowe 60); Davies (Oakley 46), Butterfield, Grimes; Nichols, Keohane.
Bournemouth: (442) Flahavan; Smith, Ward, Cargill, Harte; Fraser (Arter 77), MacDonald, Gosling, Stanislas (Ritchie 90); Rantie (Wilson 77), Pitman.
Referee: Andy Davies.

Leeds U (2) 2 *(Doukara 19, 38)*
Accrington S (0) 1 *(Gray 84)*   13,407
Leeds U: (433) Taylor S; Berardi■, Wootton, Pearce, Taylor C; Tonge, Cook (Benedicic 66), Bianchi; Ajose (Hunt 63), Smith, Doukara (Poleon 79).
Accrington S: (442) Simpson; Buxton, Aldred, Winnard, Mustoe; Mingoia, Hunt (Hatfield 75), Windass, Naismith (Atkinson 46); Gray, Alabi.
Referee: Richard Clark.

Luton T (0) 1 *(Rooney 53 (pen))*
Swindon T (0) 2 *(Smith M 76 (pen), 81)*   4410
Luton T: (442) Tyler; Connolly, McNulty, Wilkinson, Griffiths; Rooney■, Franks, Robinson (Ruddock 78), Drury; Cullen (Guttridge 66), Benson (Lafayette 72).
Swindon T: (3511) Foderingham; Thompson N, Branco, Turnbull; Byrne, Luongo, Kasim, Thompson L (Marshall 90), Smith B (Barthram 46); Gladwin (Williams 54); Smith M.
Referee: Paul Tierney.

Millwall (1) 1 *(Briggs 27)*
Wycombe W (0) 0   3403
Millwall: (4231) Forde; Dunne, Shittu, Webster, Briggs■; Wright, Abdou; Gueye (Onyedinma 48), McDonald (Powell 63), Easter (Siafa 84); Gregory.
Wycombe W: (442) Ingram; Jombati, Pierre, Mawson (Craig 82), Jacobson; Cowan-Hall, Murphy, Kretzschmar (Bloomfield 82), Wood; Hayes, McClure (Amadi-Holloway 72).
Referee: Andy D'Urso.

Milton Keynes D (1) 3 *(McFadzean 19, Powell 49, Afobe 76)*
AFC Wimbledon (0) 1 *(Tubbs 90 (pen))*   7174
Milton Keynes D: (4231) Martin; Hodson, Kay, McFadzean, Lewington; Potter, Alli (Randall 68); Green (Baldock 81), Reeves (Hitchcock 61), Powell; Afobe.
AFC Wimbledon: (442) Shea; Fuller, Bennett, Phillips, Smith (Kennedy 14); Rigg (Arthur 74), Moore, Bulman, Francomb (Sainte-Luce 63); Akinfenwa, Tubbs.
Referee: Dean Whitestone.

Morecambe (0) 0
Bradford C (0) 1 *(Mclean 83)*   2395
Morecambe: (433) Roche; Wright, Parrish, Hughes, Devitt (Kenyon 85); Wilson, Goodall, Fleming; Ellison (Mullin 61), Redshaw, Williams (Amond 61).
Bradford C: (442) Williams; Darby, Sheehan, McArdle, Meredith; Morais (Knott 69), Kennedy, Dolan, Yeates (Mclean 69); Clarke (Shariff 78), Hanson.
Referee: Scott Duncan.

Oldham Ath (0) 0
Middlesbrough (1) 3 *(Williams L 30, Leadbitter 48, Garcia 60)*   4311
Oldham Ath: (352) Rachubka; Dieng, Wilson J, Elokobi; Wilson B, Philliskirk, Mellor (Dayton 46), Kelly, Mills (Brown 75); Clarke-Harris, Gros (Winchester 46).
Middlesbrough: (4411) Konstantopoulos; Hines, Woodgate, Ayala, Husband; Nsue, Leadbitter, Whitehead (Smallwood 70), Reach (Garcia 57); Williams L; Fewster (Adomah 73).
Referee: James Adcock.

Plymouth Arg (1) 3 *(Reid R 45, 64, McHugh 108)*
Leyton Orient (2) 3 *(Cox 13, Baudry 38, Vincelot 103)*   3343
Plymouth Arg: (442) McCormick; Mellor, Nelson, Hartley, McHugh; O'Connor, Cox (Allen 107), Norburn (Harvey 105), Banton; Reid R (Morgan 98), Alessandra.
Leyton Orient: (442) Woods; Omozusi, Baudry, Clarke, Sawyer; Batt (Cox 11), James (Vincelot 86), Bartley, McAnuff; Simpson J (Lisbie 77), Mooney.
aet; Leyton Orient won 6-5 on penalties.
Referee: Tony Harrington.

Port Vale (3) 6 *(Williamson 8, 14, 18, Brown 62, Pope 74, 84)*
Hartlepool U (1) 2 *(Franks 10, Austin 59 (pen))*   2824
Port Vale: (442) Johnson; Veseli, Robertson, McGivern, Dickinson; Birchall (Jennings 65), Lines, O'Connor (Brown 46), Marshall; Pope, Williamson (Dodds 73).
Hartlepool U: (433) Flinders; Duckworth, Bates, Collins, Austin; Woods (Harewood 60), Miller, Walker; Franks, James, Brobbel.
Referee: Graham Scott.

Portsmouth (1) 1 *(Storey 12)*
Peterborough U (0) 0   7726
Portsmouth: (352) Jones; Devera, Robinson, Chorley; Wynter (Webster 60), Dunne, Atangana, Hollands, Butler; Storey (Bird 59), Westcarr (Wallace 75).
Peterborough U: (442) Alnwick; Smith, Bostwick, Santos (McCann 78), Ntlhe; Mendez-Laing, Anderson J, Payne (Ferdinand 83), McEvoy; Washington, Vassell (Barnett 65).
Referee: Brendan Malone.

Reading (1) 3 *(Pogrebnyak 20, Blackman 87, Tanner 90)*
Newport Co (0) 1 *(Jeffers 90)*   6459
Reading: (442) McCarthy; Gunter, Morrison, Pearce, Cummings; Cox (Edwards 80), Taylor J (Akpan 67), Obita, Hector; Blackman (Tanner 90), Pogrebnyak.
Newport Co: (442) Pidgeley; Jackson, Jones D, Klukowski (Minshull 71); Howe (Jeffers 79), O'Connor (Jolley 71).
Referee: James Linington.

Rochdale (0) 0
Preston NE (1) 2 *(Little 43, Kilkenny 48)*   2348
Rochdale: (433) Lillis; Bennett, Lancashire, Tanser, Rose (Rafferty 61); Henderson, Lund, Hery; Vincenti, Andrew (Donnelly 59), Bunney (Logan J 59).
Preston NE: (433) Jones; Woods, Clarke, Wright, Davies B; Brownhill, Kilkenny, Browne; Little (Humphrey 74), Davies K (Hugill 80), Gallagher (Hayhurst 73).
Referee: Mark Brown.

Rotherham U (0) 0 *(Derbyshire 109 (pen))*
Fleetwood T (0) 0   4487
Rotherham U: (442) Loach; Broadfoot, Morgan, Wood, Skarz; Swift (Derbyshire 66), Tidser, Green, Hall (Pringle 91); Bowery (Revell 66), Agard.
Fleetwood T: (451) Maxwell; Hogan (Ball 113), Pond, Jordan, McLaughlin; Blair (Campbell 65), Sarcevic, Evans, Murdoch, Morris; Proctor.
aet.
Referee: Nigel Miller.

Sheffield W (2) 3 *(Maghoma 2, Madine 10, Nuhiu 65)*
Notts Co (0) 0   12,851
Sheffield W: (442) Kirkland; Palmer, Lees, Loovens (Zayatte 68), Mattock; Maguire, Coke (McCabe 75), Semedo, Maghoma (Corry 82); Nuhiu, Madine.
Notts Co: (433) Carroll; Thompson, Mullins, Hollis, Adams; Smith (Balmy 50), Wroe (Jones 50), Noble; Whitehouse (Dawson 51), Cassidy, Murray.
Referee: Eddie Ilderton.

Shrewsbury T (1) 1 *(Vernon 34)*
Blackpool (0) 0   4524
Shrewsbury T: (442) Leutwiler; Gayle, Ellis, Goldson, Knight-Percival; Clark, Wesolowski, Woods (Lawrence 88), Vincent (Caton 68); Collins, Vernon (Mangan 79).
Blackpool: (4231) Lewis; Mellis (Waddington 60), Lundstram, Clarke, Joan Oriol; Rentmeister, Perkins; Orlandi (Dielna 56), Cywka, Zenjov (Miller 46); Delfouneso.
Referee: Mark Heywood.

Southend U (0) 1 *(Leonard 68)*
Walsall (1) 2 *(Benning 25, Morris 87)*   3146
Southend U: (343) Smith; Thompson, Ibenfeldt, Prosser; Worrall (Weston 64), Leonard, Atkinson (Clifford 30), Coker; Coulthirst, Barnard, Payne (Hurst 81).
Walsall: (4231) O'Donnell; O'Connor, Downing, Chambers J, Taylor; Chambers A, Baxendale (Clifford 56); Grimes, Sawyers, Benning (Morris 76); Bradshaw.
Referee: Gavin Ward.

Stevenage (0) 0
Watford (0) 1 *(Dyer 52)*   3989
Stevenage: (352) Beasant; Wells, Worley, Dembele; Pett (Ashton 81), Whelpdale, Lee, Bond, Okimo (Deacon 56); Marriott (Calcutt 80), Charles.
Watford: (442) Bond; Doyley (Ekstrand 29), Pudil, Tamas, Munari; Dyer, Andrews, Hoban, Ighalo (Vydra 84); Forestieri, Fabbrini (Murray 81).
Referee: Carl Berry.

Tranmere R (0) 0

Nottingham F (1) 1 *(Antonio 12)* 4374

Tranmere R: (442) Fon Williams; Holmes, Ihiekwe, Hill, Woodards; Bell-Baggie (Bruna 74), Koumas, Gill (Power 84), Rowe (Stockton 79); Odejayi, Richards.
Nottingham F: (4231) Darlow; Lichaj (Grant 88), Hobbs, Fox, Harding; Mancienne■, Osborn; Burke C, Paterson (Hunt 57), Antonio (McLaughlin 81); Assombalonga.
Referee: David Webb.

Wolverhampton W (0) 2 *(Dicko 66, Ricketts 67)*

Northampton T (0) 3 *(D'Ath 58, 74, Toney 63)* 6171

Wolverhampton W: (442) McCarey; Doherty, Stearman, Ebanks-Landell, Ricketts; Jacobs, Evans, Price, Henry (Dicko 65); Clarke (Sako 64), McAlinden (Edwards 83).
Northampton T: (4411) Duke; Alfei (Tozer 69), Diamond, Collins, Robertson; Mohamed, Morris, Ravenhill, Horwood (D'Ath 56); O'Toole; Toney (Richards 83).
Referee: Stuart Attwell.

Yeovil T (0) 1 *(Gillett 56)*

Gillingham (1) 2 *(Dickenson 23, Morris A 59)* 2283

Yeovil T: (352) Krysiak; Sokolik, Martin, Nugent; Nana Ofori-Twumasi■, Edwards, Berrett (Leitch-Smith 52), Gillett, Smith; Hayter (Ralph 68), Moore (Hoskins 77).
Gillingham: (541) Morris G; Hare, Egan, Hause, Legge, Martin; Dack, Loft, Morris A, Dickenson (German 46); Norris (Kedwell 77).
Referee: Darren Sheldrake.

York C (0) 0

Doncaster R (0) 1 *(Forrester 90)* 3357

York C: (442) Mooney; McCoy, McCombe, Winfield, Ilesanmi; Meikle, Penn, Platt, Straker; Coulson, Jarvis (Hirst 78).
Doncaster R: (442) Steer; Wakefield, McCullough, McCombe (Jones 82), Evina; Coppinger, Furman, De Val Fernandez, Bennett (Forrester 66); Robinson, Main (Keegan 90).
Referee: Mark Haywood.

Wednesday, 13 August 2014

Coventry C (0) 1 *(Miller 83)*

Cardiff C (1) 2 *(Burgstaller 4, Haynes 81 (og))* 1382

Coventry C: (3511) Burge; Willis, Webster, Finch; Clarke, Daniels (Miller 62), O'Brien, Fleck, Pugh (Haynes 51); Swanson; McQuoid (Maddison 69).
Cardiff C: (4231) Moore; Barnum-Bobb (Harris 66), Theophile-Catherine, Connolly, John; Gunnarsson, Eikrem; Burgstaller (Daehli 66), Kim (O'Sullivan 84), Ralls; Maynard.
Referee: Simon Hooper.

Sheffield U (0) 2 *(Butler 53, McNulty 86)*

Mansfield T (0) 1 *(Fisher 57)* 7929

Sheffield U: (41212) Howard; Davies B, Butler, Collins, Harris; Doyle; Campbell-Ryce, Baxter; McGinn (Murphy 71); McNulty (McGahey 89), Porter (Higdon 73).
Mansfield T: (3412) Studer; Riley (Dempster 72), Tafazolli, Sutton; Taylor, McGuire (Bell F 68), Heslop, Beevers; Clements; Fisher, Hearn (Clucas 16).
Referee: Geoff Eltringham.

SECOND ROUND

Tuesday, 26 August 2014

Bournemouth (2) 3 *(Gosling 21, Pitman 30, Wilson 79)*

Northampton T (0) 0 5250

Bournemouth: (442) Camp; Smith, Cook, Cargill, Harte; Fraser, Gosling, O'Kane, Pugh (Ritchie 70); Rantie (Wilson 69), Pitman (Stanislas 82).
Northampton T: (442) Archer; Tozer, Diamond, Collins, Robertson; Mohamed, Byrom, Ravenhill (O'Toole 57), D'Ath (Nicholls 76); Richards, Sinclair (Moyo 73).
Referee: Carl Berry.

Brentford (0) 0

Fulham (0) 1 *(McCormack 68)* 7563

Brentford: (4411) Button; Odubajo, Dean, Tarkowski, Bidwell; Jota (Gray 74), Toral (Diagouraga 63), Tebar, Dallas; Smith; Proschwitz (Hogan 74).
Fulham: (4231) Bettinelli; Voser, Hutchinson, Burn, Stafylidis; Hoogland, Parker (Fotheringham 46 (Eisfeld 69)); David (Bodurov 87), Williams R, McCormack; Woodrow.
Referee: Scott Duncan.

Burnley (0) 0

Sheffield W (0) 1 *(Nuhiu 78 (pen))* 4979

Burnley: (442) Gilks; Trippier, Long, Shackell, Ward; Wallace, Jones (Taylor 60), Arfield, Kightly (Ings 82); Sordell (Jutkiewicz 83), Barnes.
Sheffield W: (4141) Kirkland; Palmer, Lees, Zayatte, Mattock; Semedo; Maguire (Nuhiu 73), Coke, Helan, Maghoma (May 63); Madine.
Referee: Geoff Eltringham.

Crewe Alex (1) 2 *(Inman 2, Haber 90)*

Bolton W (1) 3 *(Pratley 40, Beckford 90, 107)* 2642

Crewe Alex: (433) Garratt; Tootle, Dugdale, Ray (Leigh 77), Guthrie; Turton, Atkinson (Grant 87), Nolan; Waters, Oliver (Haber 69), Inman.
Bolton W: (442) Lonergan; Threlkeld, Mills, Dervite, Ream; Feeney, Pratley, Trotter (Danns 45), Lester (Lee 69); Wilkinson (Mason 68), Beckford.
aet.
Referee: Tony Harrington.

Derby Co (0) 1 *(Calero 87)*

Charlton Ath (0) 0 16,367

Derby Co: (433) Grant; Shotton, Keogh, Whitbread, Forsyth; Hendrick, Mascarell (Martin 69), Hughes; Dawkins (Calero 70), Best, Russell (Santos 70).
Charlton Ath: (442) Pope; Gomez, Morrison, Bikey, Fox; Wilson, Cousins, Jackson (Buyens 65), Harriott; Moussa (Gudmundsson 79), Tucudean (Vetokele 65).
Referee: Graham Salisbury.

Gillingham (0) 0

Newcastle U (1) 1 *(Egan 25 (og))* 10,204

Gillingham: (442) Bywater; Fish, Legge, Hause, Egan; Davies, Hessenthaler, Dack, Pritchard (Morris A 46); Kedwell (Norris 65), McDonald (German 65).
Newcastle U: (4231) Krul; Janmaat, Coloccini, Taylor S, Haidara; Sissoko, Abeid; Obertan, De Jong (Perez 68), Aarons (Cabella 60); Riviere (Gouffran 86).
Referee: Oliver Langford.

Huddersfield T (0) 0

Nottingham F (0) 2 *(Vaughan 72 (og), Lansbury 82)* 6509

Huddersfield T: (4141) Murphy; Smith (Holmes 73), Wallace, Lynch, Dixon; Coady; Ward, Hammill, Butterfield, Bunn (Vaughan 61); Stead (Scannell 78).
Nottingham F: (442) Darlow; Hunt, Mancienne, Lascelles, Lichaj; Antonio (Burke C 46), Tesche, Lansbury, Osborn; Veldwijk (Assombalonga 66), Paterson (Fryatt 79).
Referee: Mark Brown.

Leicester C (0) 0

Shrewsbury T (1) 1 *(Mangan 38)* 8017

Leicester C: (442) Hamer; Pearson, Wasilewski, Moore, Konchesky; Knockaert, Cain (King 58), Watson (Nugent 58), Mahrez (Schlupp 70); Taylor-Fletcher, Wood.
Shrewsbury T: (442) Leutwiler; Grandison, Woods, Goldson, Demetriou; Knight-Percival, Gayle, Wesolowski, Clark (Akpa Akpro 85); Collins (Robinson 85), Mangan (Vernon 40).
Referee: Simon Hooper.

Middlesbrough (0) 3 *(Tomlin 51, 66, Clarke 57 (og))*

Preston NE (0) 1 *(Hugill 54)* 10,727

Middlesbrough: (4231) Konstantopoulos; Husband, Ayala, Hines, Damia; Whitehead, Clayton, Nsue (Reach 41), Tomlin (Ledesma 68), Adomah (Carayol 87); Fewster.
Preston NE: (433) Jones; Wiseman, Clarke, King, Davies B; Welsh (Brownhill 64), Browne, Kilkenny; Hayhurst, Hugill (Davies K 68), Laird (Little 77).
Referee: Mark Haywood.

Millwall (0) 0
Southampton (0) 2 *(Cork 53, Pelle 90)*   6014
Millwall: (442) Forde; Hoyte, Williams, Webster, Briggs; Powell, Abdou (Thompson 76), Chaplow (O'Brien 63), Gueye (Onyedinma 63); Marquis, Easter.
Southampton: (442) Forster; Clyne, Yoshida, Fonte, Targett; Ward-Prowse, Davis, Wanyama (Cork 46), Isgrove (Tadic 29); Pelle, Long (Ramirez 90).
Referee: Dean Whitestone.

Milton Keynes D (1) 4 *(Grigg 25, 63, Afobe 70, 84)*
Manchester U (0) 0   26,969
Milton Keynes D: (451) Martin; Baldock, Kay, McFadzean, Lewington; Carruthers (Green 61), Potter, Reeves, Alli, Bowditch (Powell 56); Grigg (Afobe 68).
Manchester U: (442) De Gea; Vermijl, Evans, Keane, James; Janko (Pereira 46), Anderson, Kagawa (Januzaj 20), Powell (Wilson 57); Welbeck, Hernandez.
Referee: Stuart Attwell.

Norwich C (1) 3 *(Jerome 14, Josh Murphy 49, 90)*
Crawley T (0) 1 *(Cuellar 55 (og))*   14,414
Norwich C: (442) Rudd; Martin, Cuellar, Callan-McFadden, Whittaker; Josh Murphy, Bennett E, Surman, Jacob Murphy (Hall-Johnson 65); Jerome (Becchio 80), Loza.
Crawley T: (442) Jensen; Oyebanjo, Leacock, Walsh, Dickson; Edwards, Henderson, Smith, Bawling (O'Connor 64); Young (Tomlin 52), McLeod.
Referee: Darren Deadman.

Port Vale (1) 2 *(O'Connor 34, Brown 90)*
Cardiff C (1) 3 *(Ralls 26, Macheda 60, 79)*   4390
Port Vale: (433) Neal; Yates, Robertson, McGivern, Dickinson; O'Connor (Moore 70), Brown, Jennings (Lines 71); Dodds (Williamson 70), Pope, Daniel.
Cardiff C: (442) Moore; Barnum-Bobb, Oshilaja, Cala, John; Eikrem (Burgstaller 73), Ralls, Kim (Harris 61), Dikgacoi; Macheda, Guerra (Velikonja 81).
Referee: David Webb.

Scunthorpe U (0) 0
Reading (0) 1 *(Taylor J 85)*   2657
Scunthorpe U: (442) Olejnik; Nolan, Addison, Canavan, Williams M; Adelakun (Wootton K 88), McAllister, Bishop, Hawkridge; McSheffrey, Madden.
Reading: (442) Federici; Gunter, Cooper, Pearce, Cummings (Long 46); Blackman, Akpan, Kuhl, Mackie (Taylor J 74); Cox, Tanner (Edwards 74).
Referee: Kevin Wright.

Swansea C (1) 1 *(Gomis 22)*
Rotherham U (0) 0   12,987
Swansea C: (4231) Tremmel; Tiendalli, Fernandez, Bartley, Richards; Dyer, Fulton (Shelvey 46); Carroll, Montero, Sheehan (Sigurdsson 59); Gomis (Bony 74).
Rotherham U: (442) Loach; Broadfoot (Brindley 55), Wood, Morgan, Arnason; Tidser (Newton 58), Frecklington, Pringle, Sadler (Skarz 71); Bowery, Revell.
Referee: Stephen Martin.

Swindon T (0) 2 *(Thompson L 46, Kasim 112)*
Brighton & HA (1) 4 *(Ince 10, Adrian Colunga 95, Forster-Caskey 100 (pen), 120 (pen))*   5414
Swindon T: (352) Foderingham; Turnbull, Thompson N■, Branco; Byrne, Luongo (Gladwin 77 (Waldon 90)), Kasim, Thompson L, Smith B; Smith M, Williams (Barker 81).
Brighton & HA: (433) Ankergren; Calderon, Hughes, Dunk, Chicksen; Ince, Forster-Caskey, Crofts (Gardner 71); LuaLua (McCourt 72), Adrian Colunga, O'Grady (Teixeira 91).
aet.
Referee: Andrew Madley.

Walsall (0) 0
Crystal Palace (3) 3 *(Gayle 7, 25, 41)*   3987
Walsall: (4231) O'Donnell; Kinsella, Holden, Downing, Taylor; Chambers A, Clifford (Flanagan 61); Grimes, Forde (Benning 75), Sawyers (Baxendale 61); Bradshaw.

Crystal Palace: (442) Hennessey; Binnom-Williams, McCarthy, Delaney (Hangeland 46), Mariappa; Bannan, Guedioura, Williams (Garvan 75), Thomas; Gayle (Gray 62), Murray.
Referee: Darren Drysdale.

Watford (1) 1 *(Dyer 31)*
Doncaster R (1) 2 *(Tyson 12 (pen), Wakefield 52)*   7318
Watford: (352) Bond; Hoban, Doyley (Pudil 69), Tamas; Anya, Andrews, Murray (Fabbrini 75), McGugan (Munari 69), Dyer; Vydra, Ighalo.
Doncaster R: (442) Steer; Wakefield, McCullough, Wabara, Evina; Bennett, Keegan, De Val Fernandez (Wellens 79), Coppinger; Tyson, Furman.
Referee: Andy Woolmer.

WBA (1) 1 *(Mullins 29 (og))*
Oxford U (0) 1 *(Hylton 86)*   10,939
WBA: (4231) Myhill; Wisdom, McAuley, Dawson, Davidson; Baird (Gamboa 106), Brunt (Morrison 64); Sessegnon (Mulumbu 78), Berahino, Yacob; Ideye.
Oxford U: (4231) Crocombe; Rose (Jakubiak 70), Mullins, Wright, Newey; Collins, Riley (Hunt 46); Brown■, Ruffels, Hylton; Morris (Hoskins 81).
aet; WBA won 7-6 on penalties.
Referee: James Adcock.

West Ham U (1) 1 *(Sakho 40)*
Sheffield U (0) 1 *(Reid 58 (og))*   28,930
West Ham U: (433) Jaaskelainen; Demel, Reid, Burke, Potts; Morrison (Noble 98), Diame, Poyet; Vaz Te (Zarate 79), Valencia, Sakho (Downing 63).
Sheffield U: (4231) Howard; Alcock, Collins, McGahey, Harris (McEveley 73); Basham, Doyle; Davies B, Baxter (Wallace J 100), Flynn (Campbell-Ryce 84); McNulty.
aet; Sheffield U won 5-4 on penalties.
Referee: James Linington.

Wednesday, 27 August 2014

Aston Villa (0) 0
Leyton Orient (0) 1 *(Vincelot 87)*   17,918
Aston Villa: (4231) Given; Hutton, Senderos, Baker, Richardson; Westwood, Sanchez; Bacuna, Cole (Weimann 62), Grealish; Bent.
Leyton Orient: (442) Woods; Omozusi, Baudry, Lowry, Sawyer (Cuthbert 62); Pritchard, James, Bartley (Vincelot 83), Cox; Mooney (Dagnall 66), Simpson J.
Referee: Carl Boyeson.

Birmingham C (0) 0
Sunderland (0) 3 *(Gomez 77, Johnson 87, Wickham 88)*
     11,245
Birmingham C: (442) Doyle; Eardley (Spector 33), Edgar, Hall, Robinson; Duffy (Novak 61), Gleeson, Caddis, Cotterill; Donaldson, Thomas.
Sunderland: (4141) Pantilimon; Vergini, Brown, O'Shea, Jones; Bridcutt; Johnson, Larsson (Giaccherini 81), Gomez, Wickham; Altidore.
Referee: Darren Bond.

Bradford C (0) 2 *(Knott 84, Hanson 86)*
Leeds U (0) 1 *(Smith 82)*   18,750
Bradford C: (433) Williams; Darby, Sheehan, McArdle, Meredith; Liddle, Knott (Dolan 90), Kennedy; Mclean (McBurnie 70), Hanson, Clarke.
Leeds U: (41212) Taylor S; Wootton, Cooper, Pearce, Warnock; Murphy■; Bianchi, Tonge; Norris (Poleon 90); Sharp, Smith.
Referee: Graham Scott.

Burton Alb (0) 1 *(McGurk 77)*
QPR (0) 0   3999
Burton Alb: (442) McLaughlin; Edwards, Sharps, Cansdell-Sherriff, Taft; Harness, Mousinho (Weir 46), Palmer, MacDonald; Knowles (Blyth 78), McGurk (McFadzean 85).
QPR: (4411) Murphy; Simpson, Onuoha, Dunne, Hill; Hoilett, Faurlin (Fer 59), Henry (Mutch 81), Wright-Phillips (Zamora 78); Phillips; Taarabt.
Referee: Paul Tierney.

Stoke C (1) 3 *(Walters 16, 47, Crouch 90)*
Portsmouth (0) 0   10,312
Stoke C: (4231) Butland; Wilkinson, Shawcross, Huth,
Muniesa; Adam, Cameron (Sidwell 38); Odemwingie
(Shenton 81), Walters, Moses (Arnautovic 64); Crouch.
Portsmouth: (4231) Jones; Webster (Hollands 64),
Whatmough (Robinson 34), Devera, Butler; Ertl,
Awford; Holmes, Wallace, Barcham (Storey 71); Taylor.
Referee: Andy D'Urso.

THIRD ROUND

Tuesday, 23 September 2014
Arsenal (1) 1 *(Sanchez 13)*
Southampton (2) 2 *(Tadic 20 (pen), Clyne 39)*   59,621
Arsenal: (4231) Ospina; Bellerin (Akpom 86), Chambers,
Hayden, Coquelin; Wilshere, Diaby (Cazorla 67);
Sanchez, Rosicky, Campbell (Oxlade-Chamberlain 71);
Podolski.
Southampton: (433) Forster; Clyne, Gardos, Fonte,
Targett (Bertrand 85); Schneiderlin, Wanyama, Davis;
Mane (Long 72), Pelle, Tadic.
Referee: Keith Stroud.

Cardiff C (0) 0
Bournemouth (3) 3 *(Gosling 9, 33, Daniels 22)*   6491
Cardiff C: (442) Moore; Brayford, Cala, Gabbidon, John;
Le Fondre, Kim (Daehli 37), Gunnarsson, Adeyemi;
Guerra (Macheda 37), Maynard (Pilkington 81).
Bournemouth: (352) Boruc; Elphick, Smith (Francis 86),
Cargill; Gosling, Pugh, Daniels, MacDonald (Arter 75),
O'Kane; Pitman, Stanislas (Rantie 87).
Referee: Andrew Madley.

Derby Co (0) 2 *(Russell 67, Pearce 82 (og))*
Reading (0) 0   18,409
Derby Co: (433) Roos; Christie, Shotton, Keogh, Forsyth;
Bryson (Eustace 83), Mascarell, Hughes (Martin 64);
Russell, Best (Dawkins 76), Ibe.
Reading: (442) Andersen; Gunter, Pearce, Hector
(Cooper 87), Obita; Kuhl, Guthrie (Taylor J 72),
Edwards, Robson-Kanu (Cox 76); Pogrebnyak, Mackie.
Referee: Simon Hooper.

Fulham (2) 2 *(Ruiz 16, Burn 32)*
Doncaster R (0) 1 *(Coppinger 60)*   8070
Fulham: (442) Bettinelli; Hoogland, Bodurov, Burn,
Amorebieta (Kavanagh 69); Christensen, Hyndman, Ruiz
(Williams G 81), Stafylidis (Parker 72); McCormack,
Rodallega.
Doncaster R: (4231) Steer; Wakefield (McCombe 89),
Wabara, McCullough, Evina; Wellens (Robinson 46),
Keegan; Coppinger, Furman, Bennett (Forrester 46);
Tyson.
Referee: Kevin Friend.

Leyton Orient (0) 0
Sheffield U (1) 1 *(Higdon 2)*   3223
Leyton Orient: (442) Woods; Cuthbert (Pritchard 12),
Baudry, Clarke, Omozusi; McAnuff, Vincelot, James,
Petrasso (Cox 62); Mooney (Henderson 68), Simpson J.
Sheffield U: (433) Howard; Alcock, McGahey, Collins,
Harris; McGinn, Wallace J (Doyle 67), Reed; Flynn,
Higdon (Porter 77), Murphy.
Referee: James Adcock.

Liverpool (1) 2 *(Rossiter 10, Suso 109)*
Middlesbrough (0) 2 *(Reach 62, Bamford 120 (pen))*   41,857
Liverpool: (4231) Mignolet; Manquillo, Toure, Sakho,
Jose Enrique; Rossiter (Williams 79), Lucas; Markovic
(Suso 98), Sterling, Lallana; Lambert (Balotelli 74).
Middlesbrough: (4411) Blackman; Fredericks, Ayala,
Omeruo, Friend; Adomah, Clayton, Leadbitter (Bamford
112), Reach; Tomlin (Vossen 112); Garcia (Wildschut
76).
aet; Liverpool won 14-13 on penalties.
Referee: Mike Jones.

Milton Keynes D (1) 2 *(Afobe 5, 86)*
Bradford C (0) 0   5707
Milton Keynes D: (451) Martin; Spence, McFadzean,
Kay, Lewington; Carruthers (Grigg 78), Potter, Reeves
(Baldock 90), Alli, Bowditch (Powell 54); Afobe.
Bradford C: (442) Williams; Liddle, McArdle, Routis,
Meredith; Morais (Webb-Foster 85), Kennedy, McBurnie
(Mclean 65), Knott; Bennett (Urwin 65), Clarke.
Referee: Mick Russell.

Shrewsbury T (0) 1 *(Collins 54)*
Norwich C (0) 0   6187
Shrewsbury T: (352) Leutwiler; Grandison, Knight-
Percival, Goldson; Gayle, Woods, Lawrence (Vincent
89), Wesolowski, Demetriou; Collins (Mangan 85), Akpa
Akpro.
Norwich C: (442) Rudd; Whittaker, Cuellar, Miquel,
Garrido; Bennett E, Howson, O'Neil, Odjidja-Ofoe (Josh
Murphy 56); Hooper (Loza 61), Lafferty (King 79).
Referee: Scott Mathieson.

Sunderland (1) 1 *(Altidore 16)*
Stoke C (1) 2 *(Muniesa 31, 71)*   17,353
Sunderland: (451) Pantilimon; Jones, O'Shea, Coates
(Van Aanholt 46), Vergini; Johnson (Graham 88),
Rodwell (Alvarez 76), Gomez, Bridcutt, Buckley;
Altidore.
Stoke C: (442) Butland; Bardsley, Huth, Shawcross,
Muniesa; Assaidi (Crouch 87), Adam, Ireland, Nzonzi;
Diouf, Arnautovic (Moses 85).
Referee: Mike Dean.

Swansea C (1) 3 *(Dyer 28, Sigurdsson 64, Emnes 87)*
Everton (0) 0   20,397
Swansea C: (4231) Tremmel; Richards, Williams,
Fernandez, Taylor; Shelvey, Carroll (Ki 70); Dyer
(Routledge 68), Sigurdsson (Emnes 85), Montero;
Gomis.
Everton: (451) Howard; Hibbert, Oviedo (McCarthy 58),
Alcaraz, Distin; McGeady (Osman 81), Gibson, Garbutt,
Besic, Atsu; Eto'o (Lukaku 46).
Referee: Roger East.

Wednesday, 24 September 2014
Burton Alb (0) 0
Brighton & HA (2) 3 *(Ince 18, LuaLua 37,*
Mackail-Smith 66)   3253
Burton Alb: (442) McLaughlin; Edwards, Sharps (Slade
83), Taft, McFadzean; Harness, Weir, Palmer, McGurk
(Austin 78); Knowles, Blyth.
Brighton & HA: (41212) Stockdale; Calderon■, Dunk,
Hughes, Chicksen; Ince; McCourt (Toko 70), Gardner;
LuaLua (Adrian Colunga 78); O'Grady, Mackail-Smith.
Referee: Darren Bond.

Chelsea (1) 2 *(Zouma 25, Oscar 55)*
Bolton W (1) 1 *(Mills 31)*   40,988
Chelsea: (4231) Cech; Azpilicueta, Zouma, Cahill, Luis;
Mikel, Ake (Matic 90); Oscar, Schurrle, Salah (Hazard E
80); Remy (Drogba 72).
Bolton W: (442) Lonergan; Herd, Mills, Dervite, Moxey;
Feeney (Spearing 68), Danns (Mason 83), Pratley,
Kamara; Beckford, Davies C (Lee 52).
Referee: Graham Scott.

Crystal Palace (1) 2 *(Gayle 25 (pen), KaiKai 90)*
Newcastle U (1) 3 *(Riviere 36, 48 (pen), Dummett 112)*   13,773
Crystal Palace: (442) Hennessey; Mariappa, Hangeland,
McCarthy (Gray 90), Fryers; Bannan, Williams (KaiKai
80), Guedioura, Zaha; Doyle (Johnson 71), Gayle.
Newcastle U: (451) Elliot; Janmaat (Haidara 45),
Coloccini, Taylor S, Dummett; Colback, Abeid■;
Obertan, Armstrong, Sammy Ameobi (Sissoko 67);
Riviere (Perez 81).
aet.
Referee: Robert Madley.

Manchester C (0) 7 *(Lampard 47, 90, Dzeko 53, 77, Jesus Navas 54, Toure 60 (pen), Pozo 88)*
Sheffield W (0) 0   32,346
Manchester C: (4231) Caballero; Sagna, Demichelis, Mangala, Kolarov; Lampard, Fernandinho (Boyata 70); Jesus Navas, Toure (Pozo 64), Milner (Sinclair 73); Dzeko.
Sheffield W: (4141) Kirkland; Buxton, Lees, Zayatte[■], Mattock; Coke (Dielna 61); Maguire, Palmer (Helan 70), Maghoma, May; Madine (Nuhiu 61).
Referee: Paul Tierney.

Tottenham H (0) 3 *(Mason 72, Soldado 83, Kane 90)*
Nottingham F (0) 1 *(Grant 61)*   31,912
Tottenham H: (4231) Vorm; Naughton, Fazio, Vertonghen, Davies; Stambouli (Mason 65), Bentaleb; Lennon, Paulinho (Kane 64), Townsend; Soldado (Lamela 85).
Nottingham F: (451) De Vries; Harding, Lascelles, Wilson, Fox; Paterson, Grant (Burke O 86), Osborn, Vaughan (Tesche 46), McLaughlin; Veldwijk (Blackstock 74).
Referee: Andre Marriner.

WBA (1) 3 *(Ideye 15, McAuley 87, Berahino 88)*
Hull C (1) 2 *(Ince 41, Brady 50)*   10,496
WBA: (41212) Myhill; Gamboa, Olsson, McAuley, Davidson; O'Neil; Yacob, Mulumbu (Varela 75); Blanco; Ideye (Samaras 21), Anichebe (Berahino 59).
Hull C: (41212) Harper; Rosenior, Chester, McShane, Figueroa; Bruce (Livermore 64); Ben Arfa, Meyler (Maguire 85); Brady (Aluko 89); Ince, Sagbo.
Referee: Phil Dowd.

FOURTH ROUND
Tuesday, 28 October 2014
Bournemouth (0) 2 *(O'Kane 49, Wilson 86)*
WBA (0) 1 *(Elphick 85 (og))*   11,296
Bournemouth: (442) Camp; Smith, Elphick, Cargill, Harte; Fraser (Francis 75), Gosling, O'Kane, Stanislas; Kermorgant (MacDonald 88), Rantie (Wilson 69).
WBA: (4222) Myhill; Gamboa, Dawson, McAuley, Davidson; Mulumbu, O'Neil (Sessegnon 63); Baird, Blanco (Berahino 75); Ideye (Samaras 55), Anichebe.
Referee: Paul Tierney.

Fulham (2) 2 *(Dembele 27, 45)*
Derby Co (1) 5 *(Martin 45 (pen), Russell 47, Dawkins 54, 65, Hendrick 62)*   15,156
Fulham: (442) Kiraly; Hoogland, Hutchinson, Zverotic, Kavanagh; Hyndman, Roberts (McCormack 72); Williams G (David 72), Arthurworrey; Ruiz (Eisfeld 86), Dembele.
Derby Co: (433) Roos; Christie, Keogh, Buxton, Forsyth; Mascarell (Coutts 69), Hendrick, Bryson (Hughes 77); Russell, Martin, Dawkins (Ibe 75).
Referee: Graham Scott.

Liverpool (0) 2 *(Balotelli 86, Lovren 90)*
Swansea C (0) 1 *(Emnes 65)*   42,582
Liverpool: (4231) Jones; Manquillo, Toure, Lovren, Johnson; Lucas, Henderson; Markovic (Lallana 70), Coutinho, Borini; Lambert (Balotelli 79).
Swansea C: (442) Tremmel; Rangel, Fernandez[■], Williams, Taylor; Dyer (Routledge 67), Fulton (Carroll 88), Shelvey, Montero; Gomis (Bony 82), Emnes.
Referee: Keith Stroud.

Milton Keynes D (0) 1 *(Afobe 67 (pen))*
Sheffield U (0) 2 *(Higdon 86, 90)*   8520
Milton Keynes D: (4231) Martin; Spence, Flanagan, McFadzean, Lewington; Potter, Alli; Carruthers, Reeves (Grigg 61), Bowditch (Powell 61); Afobe.
Sheffield U: (451) Howard; Alcock, McGahey, McEveley, Harris; Davies B (Campbell-Ryce 76), Doyle, Scougall (Baxter 70), Reed, Murphy; McNulty (Higdon 55).
Referee: Roger East.

Shrewsbury T (0) 1 *(Mangan 77)*
Chelsea (0) 2 *(Drogba 48, Grandison 81 (og))*   10,210
Shrewsbury T: (352) Leutwiler; Goldson, Grandison, Knight-Percival; Grimmer, Grant (Clark 67), Woods, Lawrence, Demetriou; Collins (Mangan 75), Akpa Akpro.

Chelsea: (4231) Cech; Christensen, Zouma, Cahill, Luis; Mikel (Matic 80), Ake; Salah (Willian 80), Oscar (Hazard E 90), Schurrle; Drogba.
Referee: Neil Swarbrick.

Wednesday, 29 October 2014
Manchester C (0) 0
Newcastle U (1) 2 *(Aarons 6, Sissoko 75)*   40,752
Manchester C: (442) Caballero; Sagna, Demichelis, Mangala, Kolarov; Milner, Fernandinho, Toure (Jesus Navas 60), Silva (Nasri 9 (Aguero 70)); Jovetic, Dzeko.
Newcastle U: (433) Elliot; Janmaat (Sissoko 64), Coloccini, Dummett, Haidara; Taylor R, Abeid, Colback; Obertan, Armstrong (Riviere 65), Aarons (Sammy Ameobi 46).
Referee: Stuart Attwell.

Stoke C (0) 2 *(Nzonzi 49, Diouf 82)*
Southampton (2) 3 *(Pelle 6, 89, Long 30)*   16,340
Stoke C: (4231) Begovic; Bardsley, Shawcross, Wilson, Pieters; Cameron (Adam 73), Nzonzi; Walters, Krkic (Crouch[■] 73), Arnautovic; Diouf.
Southampton: (433) Forster; Clyne, Gardos (Alderweireld 90), Fonte, Targett; Schneiderlin, Davis (Cork 90), Wanyama; Long, Pelle, Tadic.
Referee: Lee Mason.

Tottenham H (0) 2 *(Lamela 54, Kane 74)*
Brighton & HA (0) 0   33,537
Tottenham H: (442) Vorm; Naughton, Fazio, Vertonghen, Davies; Lennon (Lamela 46), Stambouli, Dembele, Townsend (Chadli 81); Kane (Paulinho 85), Soldado.
Brighton & HA: (433) Walton; Calderon, Hughes, Dunk, Chicksen; Holla, Ince, Forster-Caskey (Gardner 65); McCourt (Teixeira 66), LuaLua (Mackail-Smith 88), Adrian Colunga.
Referee: Mark Clattenburg.

QUARTER-FINALS
Tuesday, 16 December 2014
Derby Co (0) 1 *(Bryson 71)*
Chelsea (1) 3 *(Hazard E 23, Luis 56, Schurrle 82)*   30,639
Derby Co: (433) Grant; Christie, Keogh, Buxton[■], Forsyth; Hughes (Hendrick 76), Mascarell (Best 84), Bryson; Russell, Martin, Dawkins (Ibe 57).
Chelsea: (4231) Cech; Azpilicueta, Zouma (Ivanovic 45), Terry, Luis; Mikel, Matic; Schurrle, Fabregas, Hazard E (Ramires 84); Drogba (Remy 63).
Referee: Jonathan Moss.

Sheffield U (0) 1 *(McNulty 63)*
Southampton (0) 0   21,906
Sheffield U: (4231) Howard; Flynn, Basham, McEveley, Harris; Reed (Wallace K 81), Doyle; Campbell-Ryce (Adams 46), Cuvelier (Baxter 73), Murphy; McNulty.
Southampton: (4231) Forster; Clyne, Fonte, Gardos[■], Targett (Isgrove 46); Schneiderlin, Wanyama (Alderweireld 74); Mane (Mayuka 71), Ward-Prowse, Bertrand; Long.
Referee: Chris Foy.

Wednesday, 17 December 2014
Bournemouth (0) 1 *(Gosling 57)*
Liverpool (2) 3 *(Sterling 20, 51, Markovic 27)*   11,347
Bournemouth: (4231) Boruc; Francis, Elphick, Cargill, Smith; O'Kane (Pitman 81), Gosling; Ritchie, Kermorgant (Arter 53), Stanislas (Fraser 54); Wilson.
Liverpool: (343) Jones; Toure, Skrtel, Lovren (Sakho 46); Henderson, Gerrard (Borini 90), Lucas, Markovic; Coutinho (Can 74), Sterling, Lallana.
Referee: Mark Clattenburg.

Tottenham H (1) 4 *(Bentaleb 18, Chadli 46, Kane 63, Soldado 70)*
Newcastle U (0) 0   34,677
Tottenham H: (4231) Vorm; Chiriches, Vertonghen, Fazio, Rose; Stambouli, Bentaleb (Capoue 80); Townsend, Eriksen, Chadli (Dembele 61); Kane (Soldado 69).
Newcastle U: (4231) Alnwick; Coloccini, Williamson, Haidara, Dummett; Colback, Cabella (Vuckic 80); Gouffran, Perez, Sissoko (Anita 73); Riviere (Armstrong 60).
Referee: Andre Marriner.

SEMI-FINALS FIRST LEG

Tuesday, 20 January 2015
Liverpool (0) 1 *(Sterling 59)*
Chelsea (1) 1 *(Hazard E 18 (pen))*   44,573
Liverpool: (3421) Mignolet; Can, Skrtel, Sakho; Markovic, Henderson, Lucas, Moreno; Gerrard (Lallana 70), Coutinho; Sterling.
Chelsea: (4231) Courtois; Ivanovic, Cahill, Terry, Luis; Mikel, Matic; Willian (Azpilicueta 89), Fabregas, Hazard E; Costa.
Referee: Martin Atkinson.

Wednesday, 21 January 2015
Tottenham H (0) 1 *(Townsend 74 (pen))*
Sheffield U (0) 0   35,323
Tottenham H: (4231) Vorm; Walker, Dier, Vertonghen, Davies; Stambouli (Paulinho 75), Mason (Dembele 65); Townsend, Kane, Eriksen; Adebayor (Soldado 65).
Sheffield U: (4231) Howard; Flynn, Basham, McEveley, Harris; Doyle, Reed; Campbell-Ryce, Scougall (Wallace K 87), Murphy; McNulty (Baxter 83).
Referee: Neil Swarbrick.

SEMI-FINALS SECOND LEG

Tuesday, 27 January 2015
Chelsea (0) 1 *(Ivanovic 94)*
Liverpool (0) 0   40,659
Chelsea: (4231) Courtois; Ivanovic, Zouma, Terry, Luis (Azpilicueta 78); Fabregas (Ramires 50), Matic; Willian (Drogba 119), Oscar, Hazard E; Costa.
Liverpool: (3421) Mignolet; Can, Skrtel, Sakho (Johnson 57); Markovic (Balotelli 70), Henderson, Lucas, Moreno (Lambert 106); Gerrard, Coutinho; Sterling.
aet; Chelsea won 2-1 on aggregate.
Referee: Michael Oliver.

Wednesday, 28 January 2015
Sheffield U (0) 2 *(Adams 77, 79)*
Tottenham H (1) 2 *(Eriksen 28, 88)*   30,236
Sheffield U: (4141) Howard; Flynn, Basham, McEveley, Harris; Doyle (Reed 65); Campbell-Ryce (Adams 74), Scougall, Baxter, Murphy; McNulty (Higdon 74).
Tottenham H: (4231) Vorm; Walker, Dier, Vertonghen, Davies; Stambouli, Mason (Rose 90); Lamela (Townsend 74), Dembele (Paulinho 66), Eriksen; Kane.
Tottenham H won 3-2 on aggregate.
Referee: Mike Dean.

CAPITAL ONE CUP FINAL 2015

Sunday, 1 March 2015

(at Wembley Stadium, attendance 89,294)

Chelsea (1) 2   Tottenham H (0) 0

Chelsea: (433) Cech; Ivanovic, Cahill, Terry, Azpilicueta; Ramires, Zouma, Fabregas (Oscar 88); Willian (Cuadrado 76), Costa (Drogba 90), Hazard E.
Scorers: Terry 45, Walker 56 (og).

Tottenham H: (4231) Lloris; Walker, Dier, Vertonghen, Rose; Bentaleb, Mason (Lamela 71); Townsend (Dembele 62), Eriksen, Chadli (Soldado 80); Kane.

Referee: Anthony Taylor.

Chelsea's Diego Costa celebrates his side's second goal in their 2-0 defeat of Tottenham Hotspur in the Capital One Cup final at Wembley on 1 March. (Suzanne Plunkett/Action Images via Reuters)

LEAGUE CUP ATTENDANCES

Season	Attendances	Games	Average
1960–61	1,204,580	112	10,755
1961–62	1,030,534	104	9,909
1962–63	1,029,893	102	10,097
1963–64	945,265	104	9,089
1964–65	962,802	98	9,825
1965–66	1,205,876	106	11,376
1966–67	1,394,553	118	11,818
1967–68	1,671,326	110	15,194
1968–69	2,064,647	118	17,497
1969–70	2,299,819	122	18,851
1970–71	2,035,315	116	17,546
1971–72	2,397,154	123	19,489
1972–73	1,935,474	120	16,129
1973–74	1,722,629	132	13,050
1974–75	1,901,094	127	14,969
1975–76	1,841,735	140	13,155
1976–77	2,236,636	147	15,215
1977–78	2,038,295	148	13,772
1978–79	1,825,643	139	13,134
1979–80	2,322,866	169	13,745
1980–81	2,051,576	161	12,743
1981–82	1,880,682	161	11,681
1982–83	1,679,756	160	10,498
1983–84	1,900,491	168	11,312
1984–85	1,876,429	167	11,236
1985–86	1,579,916	163	9,693
1986–87	1,531,498	157	9,755
1987–88	1,539,253	158	9,742
1988–89	1,552,780	162	9,585
1989–90	1,836,916	168	10,934
1990–91	1,675,496	159	10,538
1991–92	1,622,337	164	9,892
1992–93	1,558,031	161	9,677
1993–94	1,744,120	163	10,700
1994–95	1,530,478	157	9,748
1995–96	1,776,060	162	10,963
1996–97	1,529,321	163	9,382
1997–98	1,484,297	153	9,701
1998–99	1,555,856	153	10,169
1999–2000	1,354,233	153	8,851
2000–01	1,501,304	154	9,749
2001–02	1,076,390	93	11,574
2002–03	1,242,478	92	13,505
2003–04	1,267,729	93	13,631
2004–05	1,313,693	93	14,216
2005–06	1,072,362	93	11,531
2006–07	1,098,403	93	11,811
2007–08	1,332,841	94	14,179
2008–09	1,329,753	93	14,298
2009–10	1,376,405	93	14,800
2010–11	1,197,917	93	12,881
2011–12	1,209,684	93	13,007
2012–13	1,210,031	93	13,011
2013–14	1,362,360	93	14,649
2014–15	1,274,413	93	13,690

CAPITAL ONE CUP 2014–15

Round	Aggregate	Games	Average
One	177,512	35	5,072
Two	258,501	25	10,340
Three	320,083	16	20,005
Four	178,393	8	22,299
Quarter-finals	98,569	4	24,642
Semi-finals	150,791	4	37,698
Final	89,294	1	89,294
Total	1,274,413	93	13,690

FOOTBALL LEAGUE TROPHY
FINALS 1984–2015

The 1984 final was played at Boothferry Park, Hull. All subsequent finals played at Wembley except between 2001 and 2007 (inclusive) which were played at Millennium Stadium, Cardiff.

ASSOCIATE MEMBERS' CUP

1984	Bournemouth v Hull C	2-1

FREIGHT ROVER TROPHY

1985	Wigan Ath v Brentford	3-1
1986	Bristol C v Bolton W	3-0
1987	Mansfield T v Bristol C	1-1*
	Mansfield T won 5-4 on penalties	

SHERPA VANS TROPHY

1988	Wolverhampton W v Burnley	2-0
1989	Bolton W v Torquay U	4-1

LEYLAND DAF CUP

1990	Tranmere R v Bristol R	2-1
1991	Birmingham C v Tranmere R	3-2

AUTOGLASS TROPHY

1992	Stoke C v Stockport Co	1-0
1993	Port Vale v Stockport Co	2-1
1994	Swansea C v Huddersfield T	1-1*
	Swansea C won 3-1 on penalties	

AUTO WINDSCREENS SHIELD

1995	Birmingham C v Carlisle U	1-0*
1996	Rotherham U v Shrewsbury T	2-1
1997	Carlisle U v Colchester U	0-0*
	Carlisle U won 4-3 on penalties	
1998	Grimsby T v Bournemouth	2-1
1999	Wigan Ath v Millwall	1-0
2000	Stoke C v Bristol C	2-1

LDV VANS TROPHY

2001	Port Vale v Brentford	2-1
2002	Blackpool v Cambridge U	4-1
2003	Bristol C v Carlisle U	2-0
2004	Blackpool v Southend U	2-0
2005	Wrexham v Southend U	2-0*

FOOTBALL LEAGUE TROPHY

2006	Swansea C v Carlisle U	2-1

JOHNSTONE'S PAINT TROPHY

2007	Doncaster R v Bristol R	3-2*
2008	Milton Keynes D v Grimsby T	2-0
2009	Luton T v Scunthorpe U	3-2*
2010	Southampton v Carlisle U	4-1
2011	Carlisle U v Brentford	1-0
2012	Chesterfield v Swindon T	2-0
2013	Crewe Alex v Southend U	2-0
2014	Peterborough U v Chesterfield	3-1
2015	Bristol C v Walsall	2-0

*After extra time.

FOOTBALL LEAGUE TROPHY WINS

Bristol C 3, Birmingham C 2, Blackpool 2, Carlisle U 2, Port Vale 2, Stoke C 2, Swansea C 2, Wigan Ath 2, Bolton W 1, Bournemouth 1, Chesterfield 1, Crewe Alex 1, Doncaster R 1, Grimsby T 1, Luton T 1, Mansfield T 1, Milton Keynes D 1, Peterborough U 1, Rotherham U 1, Southampton 1, Tranmere R 1, Wolverhampton W 1, Wrexham 1.

APPEARANCES IN FINALS

Carlisle U 6, Bristol C 5, Brentford 3, Southend U 3, Birmingham C 2, Blackpool 2, Bolton W 2, Bournemouth 2, Bristol R 2, Chesterfield 2, Grimsby T 2, Port Vale 2, Stockport Co 2, Stoke C 2, Swansea C 2, Tranmere R 2, Wigan Ath 2, Burnley 1, Cambridge U 1, Colchester U 1, Crewe Alex 1, Doncaster R 1, Huddersfield T 1, Hull C 1, Luton T 1, Mansfield T 1, Millwall 1, Milton Keynes D 1, Peterborough U 1, Rotherham U 1, Scunthorpe U 1, Shrewsbury T 1, Southampton 1, Swindon T 1, Torquay U 1, Walsall 1, Wolverhampton W 1, Wrexham 1.

JOHNSTONE'S PAINT TROPHY 2014–15

■ *Denotes player sent off.*

NORTHERN SECTION FIRST ROUND

Tuesday, 2 September 2014

Accrington S (1) 1 *(Carver 21)*
Carlisle U (1) 3 *(Sweeney 24, Dempsey 49, Paynter 70)*
818
Accrington S: (442) Lumley; Buxton, Aldred, Atkinson, Mustoe; Naismith, Joyce, Windass, Carver (Mingoia 83); Hatfield, Bowerman (McCartan 65).
Carlisle U: (433) Gillespie; Symington, O'Hanlon, Grainger, Brough; Potts, Sweeney (Thirlwell 64), Dicker; Gillies (Marriott 86), Dempsey, Paynter (Elliott 71).
Referee: Lee Collins.

Barnsley (0) 2 *(Cole 63, Hemmings 80)*
York C (0) 0
4218
Barnsley: (442) Davies; Brown, Cranie, Nyatanga, Dudgeon; Bree (Berry 82), Abbott, Hourihane, Jennings; Winnall (Hemmings 65), Cole.
York C: (442) Ingham; McCoy, McCombe, Lowe, Ilesanmi; Meikle, Summerfield, Penn (Montrose 75), Straker; Fletcher (Hyde 46), Coulson (Hirst 65).
Referee: Peter Bankes.

Crewe Alex (0) 0
Rochdale (1) 3 *(Done 42, Vincenti 64, Andrew 88)* 1529
Crewe Alex: (451) Shearer; Turton, Dugdale, Guthrie, Tootle; Atkinson (Audel 46), Grant, Nolan, Inman (Cooper 71), Waters; Oliver (Saunders 87).
Rochdale: (442) Logan C; Rafferty, Eastham, O'Connell, Tanser; Dawson, Hery (Bennett 82), Allen, Vincenti; Done (Andrew 70), Fenelon (Camps 51).
Referee: Scott Duncan.

Fleetwood T (1) 1 *(Evans 12)*
Morecambe (2) 3 *(Amond 28, 80, Redshaw 34)* 2045
Fleetwood T: (352) Maxwell; Hogan, Roberts, Crainey (Andrew 67); Blair, Sarcevic, Murdoch, Evans (Proctor 72); Ball, Campbell (Dobbie 60).
Morecambe: (433) Roche; Beeley, Parrish (Doyle 30), Edwards (Wright 65), Wildowson; Williams (Mullin 76), Kenyon, Drummond; Amond, Sampson, Redshaw.
Referee: Christopher Sarginson.

Notts Co (1) 2 *(Murray 28, Cassidy 65)*
Mansfield T (0) 0
3701
Notts Co: (343) Spiess; Edwards, Mullins, Hollis; Thompson C, Noble (Wroe 83), Jones, Cranston; Brown, Cassidy (Harrad 76), Murray.
Mansfield T: (352) Evtimov; Sutton, Tafazolli, Riley; Clements (Bell F 73), Marsden (Beevers 87), Murray, Heslop, Taylor; Fisher (Palmer 66), Rhead.
Referee: Mark Haywood.

Oldham Ath (0) 1 *(Bove 88)*
Bradford C (0) 0
2535
Oldham Ath: (4411) Rachubka; Wilson B (Brown 89), Wilson J, Elokobi, Mills; Winchester, Kelly, Jones, Dayton (Bove 82); Philliskirk; Morgan-Smith (Dieng 82).
Bradford C: (442) Pickford; Darby, Routis, McArdle, Sheehan; Kennedy, Meredith (Clarke 74), Dolan, Yeates; Mclean (Hanson 69), McBurnie (Bennett 69).
Referee: Scott Mathieson.

Preston NE (0) 1 *(Hugill 59)*
Shrewsbury T (0) 0
4029
Preston NE: (433) Stuckmann; Woods, King, Huntington, Buchanan; Brownhill (Garner 82), Welsh, Browne; Hayhurst, Hugill (Davies K 67), Laird (Reid 72).
Shrewsbury T: (352) Leutwiler; Knight-Percival, Grandison, Ellis; Griffith, Woods (Wesolowski 72), Gayle, Caton (Vernon 60), Demetriou (Collins 69); Clark, Akpa Akpro.
Referee: Chris Kavanagh.

Scunthorpe U (2) 2 *(McAllister 15, McSheffrey 25)*
Chesterfield (0) 0
2004
Scunthorpe U: (442) Olejnik; O'Neill (Myrie-Williams 46), Llera, Canavan, Dawson; Hawkridge, McAllister, Bishop, Adelakun; Madden (Taylor 71), McSheffrey (Kee 71).
Chesterfield: (4411) Lee; Darikwa, Broadhead■, Raglan, Jones; Ariyibi (Onovwigun 77), Ryan, Johnson, Dawes (Beesley 74); Banks; Gnanduillet.
Referee: Darren Handley.

SOUTHERN SECTION FIRST ROUND

Tuesday, 2 September 2014

AFC Wimbledon (1) 2 *(Sainte-Luce 16, Barrett 88)*
Southend U (1) 2 *(Payne 5, 51)* 1495
AFC Wimbledon: (442) Shea; Fuller, Kennedy (Harrison 46), Nicholson, Barrett; Phillips, Rigg (Bulman 61), Pell■, Sainte-Luce (Tubbs 61); Azeez, Beere.
Southend U: (433) Bentley; White (Corr 90), Coker, Ibenfeldt, Prosser; Payne, Deegan (Leonard 81), Atkinson; Coulthirst, Weston (Barnard 84), Worrall.
AFC Wimbledon won 4-2 on penalties.
Referee: Charles Breakspear.

Cheltenham T (1) 2 *(Marquis 45, Arthur 78)*
Oxford U (0) 0
1424
Cheltenham T: (352) Carson; Brown T, Taylor M (Black 46), Deaman; Haworth, Taylor J (Richards M 80), Sterling-James, Hanks, Braham-Barrett; Arthur, Marquis (Gornell 74).
Oxford U: (4231) Long G; Riley, Raynes, Wright, Newey; Meades■, Ruffels (Rose 63 (O'Dowda 87)); Potter, Hylton, Brown; Hoskins (Morris 77).
Referee: Brendan Malone.

Crawley T (0) 2 *(Tait 54 (og), Banya 77)*
Cambridge U (0) 0
1252
Crawley T: (352) Ashdown; Oyebanjo, Bradley, Leacock; Smith, Young, O'Connor, Rose (Banya 46), Dickson (McLeod 62); Tomlin, Harrold (Richefond 71).
Cambridge U: (442) Dunn; Tait, Taylor, Coulson, Donaldson; Champion (Hughes 10), Simpson, Diallo, Chadwick; Stockley (Whittall 60), Lennon.
Referee: Gavin Ward.

Peterborough U (1) 2 *(Maddison 16, James 90)*
Leyton Orient (1) 3 *(Dagnall 4, 47, Pritchard 62)* 3149
Peterborough U: (442) Alnwick; Ferdinand (Barnett 80), Brisley, Burgess, Smith; Maddison, Payne (McCann 66), Anderson J, Newell; Vassell (James 61), Washington.
Leyton Orient: (442) Woods; Cuthbert, Baudry, Clarke, Lowry; Pritchard, James (McAnuff 61), Bartley, Vincelot■; Mooney, Dagnall (Lee 87).
Referee: Dean Whitestone.

Stevenage (0) 0
Gillingham (1) 1 *(Norris 17 (pen))* 1613
Stevenage: (442) Day; Henry (Ashton 87), Charles, Wells, Okimo; Whelpdale, Lee, Walton, Deacon (Zola 81); Lancaster, Calcutt (Marriott 80).
Gillingham: (442) Morris G; Martin (McKain 46), Legge, Dickenson, Hoyte■; Hessenthaler, Pritchard, Davies, Dack; McDonald (German 46), Norris.
Referee: Darren Deadman.

Wycombe W (0) 0
Coventry C (0) 1 *(McQuoid 66)* 1685
Wycombe W: (442) Ingram; Jombati, Pierre, Mawson, Jacobson; Rowe, Bloomfield, Lewis, Kretzschmar; Amadi-Holloway (Cowan-Hall 65), McClure (Craig 63).
Coventry C: (442) Burge; Willis, Thomas C, McQuoid (Maddison 68), Pugh; Swanson, Coulibaly (Spence 80), Daniels, Phillips; Clarke, Finch.
Referee: Mick Russell.

Yeovil T (0) 1 *(Ralph 84)*
Portsmouth (0) 3 *(Wallace 55, 72, Westcarr 74)* 2787
Yeovil T: (433) Weale; Moloney, Martin, Nugent, Smith; Nana Ofori-Twumasi (Price 56), Foley, Ralph; Leitch-Smith, Moore (Hayter 46), Hoskins (Dawson 71).
Portsmouth: (433) Jones; Wynter, Ertl, Robinson, Butler; Dunne (Agyemang 79), Awford (Barcham 67), Atangana (Close 43); Wallace, Storey, Westcarr.
Referee: Kevin Johnson.

Tuesday, 23 September 2014
Newport Co (0) 1 *(Klukowski 81)*
Swindon T (1) 2 *(Obika 45, Williams 62)* 1822
Newport Co: (442) Day; Jackson (Zebroski 59), Poole, Sandell, Willmott; Flynn (Collins 11 (Pigott 46)), Chapman, Minshull, Klukowski; Jolley, O'Connor.
Swindon T: (352) Belford; Lelan, Thompson N, Turnbull; Byrne (Barker 13), Barthram, Thompson L (Rodgers 58), Reeves, Smith B (Waldon 68); Williams, Obika.
Referee: Tim Robinson.

NORTHERN SECTION SECOND ROUND

Tuesday, 7 October 2014
Burton Alb (0) 0
Doncaster R (2) 3 *(Forrester 32, Tyson 41 (pen),*
Wellens 87) 1269
Burton Alb: (442) Lyness; Edwards, Sharps (Bell 46), Cansdell-Sherriff, McCrory (Taft 46); Akins, Palmer, Mousinho, MacDonald (Harness 71); Knowles, Blyth.
Doncaster R: (4141) Steer; Lund, Wabara, McCombe, Evina; Keegan (Middleton 86); Coppinger, De Val Fernandez, Wellens, Forrester (Whitehouse 90); Tyson (Robinson 73).
Referee: Mark Brown.

Bury (2) 3 *(Nardiello 14 (pen), 39, Lowe 90)*
Morecambe (0) 1 *(Beeley 74)* 1681
Bury: (442) Jalal; Jones, Mills, Cameron, Hussey; Adams (Holmes 63), Mayor, Sedgwick, Tutte (Soares 69); Nardiello (Lowe 73), Rose.
Morecambe: (442) Roche; Beeley, Hughes, Goodall, Edwards; Devitt, Kenyon (Sampson 69), Williams, Fleming; Amond (Mullin 86), Redshaw (McCready 69).
Referee: Graham Salisbury.

Hartlepool U (0) 1 *(Duckworth 50)*
Sheffield U (1) 2 *(Baxter 30, Campbell-Ryce 82)* 1856
Hartlepool U: (433) Flinders; Duckworth, Austin, Harrison, Jones; Miller, Woods, Green (Walker 74); Hawkins (Smith 86), Wyke, Brobbel.
Sheffield U: (442) Turner; Davies B, McGahey, Basham, Harris; Campbell-Ryce, McGinn, Reed, Baxter (McNulty 46); Porter (Collins 85), De Girolamo (Murphy 63).
Referee: Carl Boyeson.

Oldham Ath (2) 2 *(Poleon 22, Philliskirk 44)*
Barnsley (0) 2 *(Berry 53, Winnall 90)* 2502
Oldham Ath: (433) Rachubka; Wilson B, Wilson J, Dieng, Mills; Dayton (Winchester 81), Jones, Tidser (Kelly 87); Philliskirk, Poleon (Turner 79), Wilkinson.
Barnsley: (4411) Turnbull; Bree, Brown, Nyatanga, Dudgeon; Williams (Cole 36), Bailey (Abbott 85), Berry, Treacy (Hemmings 54); Hourihane; Winnall.
Oldham Ath won 4-2 on penalties.
Referee: Gary Sutton.

Preston NE (1) 3 *(Humphrey 13, Garner 63, Gallagher 69)*
Port Vale (0) 2 *(Pope 51, 89)* 3836
Preston NE: (4231) Stuckmann; King, Clarke, Huntington, Buchanan; Welsh (Brownhill 82), Kilkenny; Humphrey (Ryan 71), Gallagher (Holmes 82), Reid; Garner.
Port Vale: (451) Neal; Yates, Zubar, Duffy, Dickinson; Dodds, Brown (Moore 83), Marshall, Birchall (Williamson 70), Lines; Pope.
Referee: Peter Bankes.

Rochdale (0) 0
Walsall (1) 1 *(Manset 23)* 1156
Rochdale: (433) Logan C; Rafferty, Eastham, O'Connell, Kennedy; Hery (Andrew 76), Allen, Cannon (Muldoon 58); Vincenti, Done, Henderson.
Walsall: (433) O'Donnell; Purkiss, Downing, Chambers J, Taylor; Baxendale, Chambers A, Clifford (Flanagan 87); Grimes (Forde 84), Manset (Cook 73), Benning.
Referee: Mark Heywood.

Scunthorpe U (1) 1 *(Madden 14)*
Notts Co (2) 2 *(McLaughlin 23, Murray 32)* 1509
Scunthorpe U: (442) Olejnik; O'Neill, Boyce, Llera, Williams M; Hawkridge (Adelakun 81), Bishop, McAllister, McSheffrey (Myrie-Williams 81); Fallon, Madden (Kee 82).
Notts Co: (442) Spiess; Thompson C, Laing, Hollis, Adams (Cranston 65); Ismail, Traore (Wroe 82), Smith, McLaughlin; Murray, Harrad (Thompson G 66).
Referee: Andy Haines.

Tranmere R (1) 1 *(Power 40)*
Carlisle U (0) 1 *(Potts 76)* 2056
Tranmere R: (4231) Brezovan; Donacien (Davies 64), Ihiekwe, Holness, Holmes; Gill, Power; Bell-Baggie (Kirby 71), Koumas, Richards; Odejayi.
Carlisle U: (41212) Hanford; White, Thirlwell, O'Hanlon, Brough; Dicker; Symington, Gillies (Potts 68); Rigg; Elliott (Dempsey 68), Paynter (Beck 38).
Tranmere R won 5-4 on penalties.
Referee: Richard Clark.

SOUTHERN SECTION SECOND ROUND

Tuesday, 7 October 2014
Colchester U (2) 3 *(Drey Wright 17, Watt 38 (pen),*
Sears 87)
Gillingham (1) 3 *(Dickenson 24, Dack 55, German 74)* 1401
Colchester U: (433) Walker; Hewitt, Kent (David Wright 46), Eastman, Clohessy; Moncur, Eastmond, Massey (Szmodics 82); Watt, Healey (Sears 70), Drey Wright.
Gillingham: (433) Nelson; Fish, Legge, Davies, Martin (Hoyte 76); Dack, Hessenthaler, Linganzi; McGlashan, Dickenson, German (Millbank 76).
Gillingham won 4-2 on penalties.
Referee: Michael Bull.

Coventry C (2) 3 *(Phillips 35, 45, McQuoid 59)*
Exeter C (0) 1 *(Watkins 86)* 7273
Coventry C: (352) Burge; Willis, Webster (Clarke 46), Finch; Coulibaly, Phillips, Thomas C, Haynes, Fleck (Maddison 46); McQuoid (Thomas G 60), Jackson.
Exeter C: (352) Hamon; Ribeiro, Moore-Taylor (Tillson 38), Bennett (Pope 64); Oakley (Watkins 65), Butterfield, Dawson, Riley-Lowe, Davies; Keohane, Nichols.
Referee: Andrew Madley.

Dagenham & R (0) 0
Leyton Orient (1) 2 *(Simpson J 5, 69)* 2318
Dagenham & R: (433) O'Brien; Batt, Doe, Saah, Partridge; Bingham (Porter 76), Ogogo (Raymond 88), Labadie; Chambers, Doidge, Yusuff (Goldberg 66).
Leyton Orient: (433) Woods; Cuthbert, Baudry (Lowry 24), Clarke, Omozusi; Pritchard (Lee 79), Vincelot, Bartley; Batt (Cox 68), Henderson, Simpson J.
Referee: James Linington.

Luton T (0) 0
Crawley T (0) 1 *(Edwards 51)* 2186
Luton T: (442) Justham; Lacey, McNulty, Wilkinson, Griffiths (Lawless 46); Guttridge, Smith J (Robinson 46), Doyle, Howells; Benson, Wall (Walker 60).
Crawley T: (442) Jensen; Bawling, Bradley, Leacock, Sadler; Young, Keane, Elliott, Edwards (Smith 84); Harrold, Tomlin.
Referee: Andy Woolmer.

Milton Keynes D (2) 2 *(Powell 2, Afobe 40)*
AFC Wimbledon (1) 3 *(Azeez 26, Rigg 68, Akinfenwa 80)*
                                                      4407
Milton Keynes D: (4231) Martin; Randall, McFadzean, Spence, Lewington; Potter, Carruthers (Baker C 66); Powell, Hitchcock, Bowditch; Afobe.
AFC Wimbledon: (442) Shea; Fuller, Barrett, Frampton, Smith; Nicholson, Bulman, Moore (Tubbs 65), Francomb; Azeez (Akinfenwa 65), Beere (Rigg 65).
Referee: Tim Robinson.

Plymouth Arg (3) 3 *(Alessandra 4, 44, Smalley 23)*
Swindon T (0) 2 *(Smith M 72 (pen), Gladwin 87)*   2668
Plymouth Arg: (352) McCormick; Nelson, Hartley, McHugh; Mellor, Cox, Harvey, Norburn (Bentley 90), Thomas (O'Connor 34); Alessandra, Smalley (Reid R 68).
Swindon T: (352) Belford; Stephens, Thompson N, Turnbull; Barthram (Smith M 55), Thompson L (Gladwin 46), Rodgers, Reeves, Bell; Williams, Waldon (Barker 46).
Referee: Carl Berry.

Portsmouth (1) 1 *(Taylor 36)*
Northampton T (1) 2 *(Moyo 28, Mohamed 55)*   5853
Portsmouth: (442) Jones; Wynter, Ertl, Devera (Webster 8 (Shorey 60)); Butler; Holmes, Awford, Atangana, Wallace (Barcham 47); Taylor, Close.
Northampton T: (433) Archer; Tozer, Collins, Cresswell, Byrom; D'Ath, O'Toole, Carter; Nicholls, Richards (Mohamed 41), Moyo (Toney 78).
Referee: Graham Horwood.

Wednesday, 8 October 2014
Cheltenham T (0) 1 *(Gornell 64)*
Bristol C (1) 3 *(Burns 28, Smith K 56, 84)*   3599
Cheltenham T: (352) Carson; Taylor M, Deaman, Vaughan; Brown T, Hanks (Haworth 68), Braham-Barrett, Richards M, Taylor J; De Vita (Gornell 53), Harrison (Marquis 52).
Bristol C: (352) Fielding; Flint, Williams (El-Abd 87), Wagstaff; Ayling, Smith K, Emmanuel-Thomas, Cunningham, Pack; Burns, Wilbraham (Wynter 88).
Referee: Keith Stroud.

NORTHERN SECTION QUARTER-FINALS

Tuesday, 11 November 2014
Bury (1) 1 *(Cameron 35)*
Tranmere R (2) 2 *(Power 43, Johnson 45)*   1842
Bury: (352) Loach; Cameron, Mills, McNulty; Soares, Adams, Etuhu, Tutte (Duffus 62), Mayor; Rose (Thompson 46), Nardiello (Hope 46).
Tranmere R: (3142) Brezovan; Holness, Thompson, Ihiekwe; Rowe (Laird 80); Holmes, Power, Jennings, Ridehalgh; Bell-Baggie (Kirby 79), Johnson (Odejayi 79).
Referee: Oliver Langford.

Wednesday, 12 November 2014
Walsall (0) 1 *(Sawyers 55)*
Sheffield U (0) 0   2127
Walsall: (4411) O'Donnell; Purkiss, Chambers J, Downing, Taylor; Cook (Grimes 71), Chambers A, Cain (Mantom 72), Forde; Sawyers; Bradshaw (Manset 46).
Sheffield U: (433) Turner; Alcock, McGahey, Basham, Harris; Reed, Doyle, McGinn (Scougall 79); De Girolamo (Campbell-Ryce 83), Porter (Baxter 79), Flynn.
Referee: David Coote.

Tuesday, 25 November 2014
Oldham Ath (0) 2 *(Poleon 46, Philliskirk 59)*
Preston NE (1) 2 *(Laird 32, Clarke 80)*   3056
Oldham Ath: (41212) Etheridge; Kusunga, Wilson J, Dieng, Mills; Tidser (Kelly 46); Winchester (Wilson B 46), Jones; Dayton (Forte 46); Poleon, Philliskirk.
Preston NE: (352) Stuckmann; Clarke (Buchanan 86), King (Kilkenny 62), Huntington; Wiseman, Reid, Welsh, Brownhill (Hayhurst 62), Laird; Davies K, Beckford.
Preston NE won 10-9 on penalties.
Referee: Tony Harrington.

Tuesday, 9 December 2014
Doncaster R (0) 0
Notts Co (0) 1 *(Noble 74)*   2570
Doncaster R: (4132) Johnstone; Wakefield (McCombe 90), McCullough, Butler, Evina; De Val Fernandez; Forrester (Wellens 63), Whitehouse (Coppinger 63), Bennett; Main, Robinson.
Notts Co: (4231) Carroll; Dumbuya, Laing, Hollis, Adams; Noble, Smith (Thompson C 89); McLaughlin, Petrasso (Thompson G 75), Hall (Traore 75); Cassidy.
Referee: David Webb.

SOUTHERN SECTION QUARTER-FINALS

Tuesday, 11 November 2014
Bristol C (0) 2 *(Wilbraham 73, 77)*
AFC Wimbledon (0) 1 *(Francomb 84)*   4647
Bristol C: (352) Fielding; Flint, El-Abd (Ayling 63), Williams; Wagstaff, Smith K, Emmanuel-Thomas, Pack, Bryan (Cunningham 85); Wilbraham, Burns (Freeman 33).
AFC Wimbledon: (433) Shea; Fuller, Bennett, Barrett, Smith; Bulman (Sutherland 60), Moore, Nicholson; Tubbs (Akinfenwa 70), Azeez, Rigg (Francomb 54).
Referee: Stuart Attwell.

Crawley T (1) 1 *(McLeod 21 (pen))*
Gillingham (0) 2 *(McGlashan 68, Loft 87)*   1305
Crawley T: (442) Ashdown; Oyebanjo (Banya 84), Bradley, Walsh, Dickson (Sadler 54); Bawling, Smith, Keane, Edwards; McLeod, Tomlin (Young 61).
Gillingham: (442) Nelson; Fish (Dack 46), Egan, Legge, Martin■; Loft, Hessenthaler, Doughty, Dickenson; German (Kedwell 75), Norris (McGlashan 49).
Referee: Darren Sheldrake.

Leyton Orient (1) 2 *(Simpson J 28, Bartley 89)*
Northampton T (0) 0   1966
Leyton Orient: (442) Legzdins; Omozusi (Batt 69), Clarke, Lowry, Sawyer; Pritchard, Wright, Bartley, Cox; Dagnall (Baudry 90), Simpson J (Kashket 52).
Northampton T: (433) Duke; Alfei, Tozer, Cresswell (Langmead 57), Collins; O'Toole, Ravenhill (Hackett 57), Carter; Nicholls, Sinclair (Richards 56), Mohamed.
Referee: Andy Davies.

Wednesday, 12 November 2014
Coventry C (0) 2 *(Madine 61, Nouble 85)*
Plymouth Arg (0) 0   7121
Coventry C: (4411) Allsop; Phillips, Willis, Webster, Haynes; O'Brien, Barton, Finch, Fleck; Maddison (Nouble 60); Madine (Thomas C 77).
Plymouth Arg: (3412) McCormick; Nelson, McHugh (Morgan 68), Hartley; O'Connor, Cox, Blizzard (Norburn 86), Kellett; Alessandra; Smalley, Reid R (Thomas 80).
Referee: James Adcock.

NORTHERN SECTION SEMI-FINALS

Tuesday, 9 December 2014
Tranmere R (2) 2 *(Power 37, Odejayi 43)*
Walsall (0) 2 *(Forde 63, Cain 80)*   2355
Tranmere R: (532) Fon Williams; Holmes, Donacien, Ihiekwe, Holness, Ridehalgh; Rowe (Laird 76), Power, Jennings; Stockton (Donnelly G 82), Odejayi.
Walsall: (4231) O'Donnell; Purkiss, Chambers J (Grimes 90), Downing, Henry; Cain, Chambers A; Baxendale (Manset 54), Sawyers, Cook (Forde 46); Bradshaw.
Walsall won 5-4 on penalties.
Referee: Geoff Eltringham.

Tuesday, 16 December 2014
Notts Co (0) 0
Preston NE (1) 1 *(Huntington 20)*   2058
Notts Co: (343) Carroll; McKenzie (Murray 61), Edwards, Hollis; Thompson C, Smith, Jones, Adams (Hall 75); Petrasso, Thompson G, McLaughlin.
Preston NE: (433) Stuckmann; Wiseman, Clarke, Huntington, Laird; Browne, King, Brownhill; Little, Beckford (Humphrey 75), Reid.
Referee: Phil Gibbs.

SOUTHERN SECTION SEMI-FINALS

Saturday, 6 December 2014

Gillingham (0) 1 *(Egan 79)*

Leyton Orient (0) 0 3103

Gillingham: (442) Nelson; Egan, Legge, Ehmer, Chicksen; Loft (McGlashan 73), Hessenthaler, Doughty, Dack; Norris (McDonald 73), Dickenson.
Leyton Orient: (442) Legzdins; Omozusi, Cuthbert, Lowry, Sawyer; Pritchard (Kashket 89), Vincelot, Wright, McAnuff (Cox 79); Mooney, Plasmati (Batt 72).
Referee: Trevor Kettle.

Wednesday, 10 December 2014

Bristol C (1) 2 *(Williams 30, Wilbraham 75)*

Coventry C (0) 0 5019

Bristol C: (352) Fielding; Ayling, Flint, Williams; Little, Elliott W, Smith K, Freeman (Pack 90), Bryan; Smith M (Agard 68), Wilbraham (Emmanuel-Thomas 90).
Coventry C: (451) Allsop; Pennington, Willis, Webster, Johnson; O'Brien (Maddison 81), Fleck, McQuoid (Nouble 72), Barton, Swanson (Haynes 67); Madine.
Referee: Stephen Martin.

NORTHERN FINAL FIRST LEG

Wednesday, 7 January 2015

Preston NE (0) 0

Walsall (0) 2 *(Forde 84, Bradshaw 88)* 8561

Preston NE: (442) Stuckmann; Wiseman, Clarke, Huntington, Laird; Humphrey (Ebanks-Blake 74), Browne, Kilkenny, Gallagher; Beckford (King 74), Davies K (Reid 63).
Walsall: (442) O'Donnell; Taylor, O'Connor, Downing, Chambers J; Forde, Sawyers, Chambers A, Cain; Bradshaw (Grimes 90), Cook (Baxendale 78).
Referee: Simon Hooper.

NORTHERN FINAL SECOND LEG

Tuesday, 27 January 2015

Walsall (0) 0

Preston NE (0) 0 10,038

Walsall: (4231) O'Donnell; O'Connor, Downing, Chambers J (Purkiss 90), Taylor; Cain, Chambers A; Forde, Sawyers, Cook (Baxendale 88); Bradshaw.

Preston NE: (4231) Stuckmann; Woods, Clarke, Huntington, Buchanan; Welsh (Browne 70), Kilkenny; Humphrey (King 71), Gallagher, Reid; Davies K (Ebanks-Blake 60).
Walsall won 2-0 on aggregate.
Referee: Nigel Miller.

SOUTHERN FINAL FIRST LEG

Tuesday, 6 January 2015

Gillingham (1) 2 *(McDonald 6, 70)*

Bristol C (2) 4 *(Smith M 18, 27, 50, 77)* 2368

Gillingham: (41212) Nelson; Hoyte, Egan, Legge, Martin; Hessenthaler; Loft, Doughty (McGlashan 65); Dack; McDonald, Dickenson (Norris 59).
Bristol C: (352) Fielding; Ayling, Flint, Williams; Wagstaff (Little 78), Pack, Smith K, Freeman, Cunningham (Bryan 87); Emmanuel-Thomas (Elliott 81), Smith M.
Referee: Andy D'Urso.

SOUTHERN FINAL SECOND LEG

Thursday, 29 January 2015

Bristol C (1) 1 *(Smith M 17)*

Gillingham (1) 1 *(McGlashan 32)* 8469

Bristol C: (352) Fielding; Ayling, Flint, Williams; Tavernier (Elliott W 69), Smith K, Pack, Freeman (Wagstaff 90), Cunningham; Emmanuel-Thomas, Smith M (Agard 85).
Gillingham: (442) Nelson; Hoyte, Egan, Ehmer, Martin (Dickenson 74); Loft (Garmston 87), Hessenthaler, Dack, Pritchard; McGlashan (Norris 83), McDonald.
Bristol C won 5-3 on aggregate.
Referee: Graham Scott.

JOHNSTONE'S PAINT TROPHY FINAL 2015

Sunday, 22 March 2015

(at Wembley Stadium, attendance 72,315)

Bristol C (1) 2   Walsall (0) 0

Bristol C: (3511) Fielding; Ayling, Flint, Williams; Little, Smith K, Pack, Freeman (Elliott 90), Bryan (Cunningham 87); Wilbraham; Agard (Emmanuel-Thomas 89).
Scorers: Flint 15, Little 51.

Walsall: (4141) O'Donnell; Purkiss, Downing, Chambers J, Taylor; Mantom; Forde (Grimes 74), Sawyers, Chambers A, Cook (Baxendale 81); Bradshaw (Hiwula 62).

Referee: Mick Russell.

JOHNSTONE'S PAINT TROPHY
ATTENDANCES 2014–15

Round	Aggregate	Games	Average
One	36,106	16	2,257
Two	45,570	16	2,848
Area Quarter-finals	24,634	8	3,079
Area Semi-finals	12,535	4	3,134
Area finals	29,436	4	7,359
Final	72,315	1	72,315
Total	220,596	49	4,502

FA CUP FINALS 1872–2015

VENUES

1872 and 1874–92	Kennington Oval	1895–1914	Crystal Palace
1873	Lillie Bridge	1915	Old Trafford, Manchester
1893	Fallowfield, Manchester	1920–22	Stamford Bridge
1894	Everton	2001–2006	Millennium Stadium, Cardiff
1923–2000	Wembley Stadium (old)	2007 to date	Wembley Stadium (new)

THE FA CUP

1872	Wanderers v Royal Engineers	1-0
1873	Wanderers v Oxford University	2-0
1874	Oxford University v Royal Engineers	2-0
1875	Royal Engineers v Old Etonians	1-1*
Replay	Royal Engineers v Old Etonians	2-0
1876	Wanderers v Old Etonians	1-1*
Replay	Wanderers v Old Etonians	3-0
1877	Wanderers v Oxford University	2-1*
1878	Wanderers v Royal Engineers	3-1

Wanderers won the cup outright, but it was restored to the Football Association.

1879	Old Etonians v Clapham R	1-0
1880	Clapham R v Oxford University	1-0
1881	Old Carthusians v Old Etonians	3-0
1882	Old Etonians v Blackburn R	1-0
1883	Blackburn Olympic v Old Etonians	2-1*
1884	Blackburn R v Queen's Park, Glasgow	2-1
1885	Blackburn R v Queen's Park, Glasgow	2-0
1886	Blackburn R v WBA	0-0
Replay	Blackburn R v WBA	2-0
	(at Racecourse Ground, Derby Co)	

A special trophy was awarded to Blackburn R for third consecutive win.

1887	Aston Villa v WBA	2-0
1888	WBA v Preston NE	2-1
1889	Preston NE v Wolverhampton W	3-0
1890	Blackburn R v The Wednesday	6-1
1891	Blackburn R v Notts Co	3-1
1892	WBA v Aston Villa	3-0
1893	Wolverhampton W v Everton	1-0
1894	Notts Co v Bolton W	4-1
1895	Aston Villa v WBA	1-0

FA Cup was stolen from a shop window in Birmingham and never found.

1896	The Wednesday v Wolverhampton W	2-1
1897	Aston Villa v Everton	3-2
1898	Nottingham F v Derby Co	3-1
1899	Sheffield U v Derby Co	4-1
1900	Bury v Southampton	4-0
1901	Tottenham H v Sheffield U	2-2
Replay	Tottenham H v Sheffield U	3-1
	(at Burnden Park, Bolton W)	
1902	Sheffield U v Southampton	1-1
Replay	Sheffield U v Southampton	2-1
1903	Bury v Derby Co	6-0
1904	Manchester C v Bolton W	1-0
1905	Aston Villa v Newcastle U	2-0
1906	Everton v Newcastle U	1-0
1907	The Wednesday v Everton	2-1
1908	Wolverhampton W v Newcastle U	3-1
1909	Manchester U v Bristol C	1-0
1910	Newcastle U v Barnsley	1-1
Replay	Newcastle U v Barnsley	2-0
	(at Goodison Park, Everton)	
1911	Bradford C v Newcastle U	0-0
Replay	Bradford C v Newcastle U	1-0
	(at Old Trafford, Manchester U)	

Trophy was given to Lord Kinniard – he made nine FA Cup Final appearances – for services to football.

1912	Barnsley v WBA	0-0
Replay	Barnsley v WBA	1-0
	(at Bramall Lane, Sheffield U)	

1913	Aston Villa v Sunderland	1-0
1914	Burnley v Liverpool	1-0
1915	Sheffield U v Chelsea	3-0
1920	Aston Villa v Huddersfield T	1-0*
1921	Tottenham H v Wolverhampton W	1-0
1922	Huddersfield T v Preston NE	1-0
1923	Bolton W v West Ham U	2-0
1924	Newcastle U v Aston Villa	2-0
1925	Sheffield U v Cardiff C	1-0
1926	Bolton W v Manchester C	1-0
1927	Cardiff C v Arsenal	1-0
1928	Blackburn R v Huddersfield T	3-1
1929	Bolton W v Portsmouth	2-0
1930	Arsenal v Huddersfield T	2-0
1931	WBA v Birmingham	2-1
1932	Newcastle U v Arsenal	2-1
1933	Everton v Manchester C	3-0
1934	Manchester C v Portsmouth	2-1
1935	Sheffield W v WBA	4-2
1936	Arsenal v Sheffield U	1-0
1937	Sunderland v Preston NE	3-1
1938	Preston NE v Huddersfield T	1-0*
1939	Portsmouth v Wolverhampton W	4-1
1946	Derby Co v Charlton Ath	4-1*
1947	Charlton Ath v Burnley	1-0*
1948	Manchester U v Blackpool	4-2
1949	Wolverhampton W v Leicester C	3-1
1950	Arsenal v Liverpool	2-0
1951	Newcastle U v Blackpool	2-0
1952	Newcastle U v Arsenal	1-0
1953	Blackpool v Bolton W	4-3
1954	WBA v Preston NE	3-2
1955	Newcastle U v Manchester C	3-1
1956	Manchester C v Birmingham C	3-1
1957	Aston Villa v Manchester U	2-1
1958	Bolton W v Manchester U	2-0
1959	Nottingham F v Luton T	2-1
1960	Wolverhampton W v Blackburn R	3-0
1961	Tottenham H v Leicester C	2-0
1962	Tottenham H v Burnley	3-1
1963	Manchester U v Leicester C	3-1
1964	West Ham U v Preston NE	3-2
1965	Liverpool v Leeds U	2-1*
1966	Everton v Sheffield W	3-2
1967	Tottenham H v Chelsea	2-1
1968	WBA v Everton	1-0*
1969	Manchester C v Leicester C	1-0
1970	Chelsea v Leeds U	2-2*
Replay	Chelsea v Leeds U	2-1
	(at Old Trafford, Manchester U)	
1971	Arsenal v Liverpool	2-1*
1972	Leeds U v Arsenal	1-0
1973	Sunderland v Leeds U	1-0
1974	Liverpool v Newcastle U	3-0
1975	West Ham U v Fulham	2-0
1976	Southampton v Manchester U	1-0
1977	Manchester U v Liverpool	2-1
1978	Ipswich T v Arsenal	1-0
1979	Arsenal v Manchester U	3-2
1980	West Ham U v Arsenal	1-0
1981	Tottenham H v Manchester C	1-1*
Replay	Tottenham H v Manchester C	3-2

1982	Tottenham H v QPR	1-1*
Replay	Tottenham H v QPR	1-0
1983	Manchester U v Brighton & HA	2-2*
Replay	Manchester U v Brighton & HA	4-0
1984	Everton v Watford	2-0
1985	Manchester U v Everton	1-0*
1986	Liverpool v Everton	3-1
1987	Coventry C v Tottenham H	3-2*
1988	Wimbledon v Liverpool	1-0
1989	Liverpool v Everton	3-2*
1990	Manchester U v Crystal Palace	3-3*
Replay	Manchester U v Crystal Palace	1-0
1991	Tottenham H v Nottingham F	2-1*
1992	Liverpool v Sunderland	2-0
1993	Arsenal v Sheffield W	1-1*
Replay	Arsenal v Sheffield W	2-1*
1994	Manchester U v Chelsea	4-0

THE FA CUP SPONSORED BY LITTLEWOODS POOLS

1995	Everton v Manchester U	1-0
1996	Manchester U v Liverpool	1-0
1997	Chelsea v Middlesbrough	2-0
1998	Arsenal v Newcastle U	2-0

THE AXA-SPONSORED FA CUP

1999	Manchester U v Newcastle U	2-0
2000	Chelsea v Aston Villa	1-0
2001	Liverpool v Arsenal	2-1
2002	Arsenal v Chelsea	2-0

THE FA CUP

2003	Arsenal v Southampton	1-0
2004	Manchester U v Millwall	3-0
2005	Arsenal v Manchester U	0-0*
	Arsenal won 5-4 on penalties.	
2006	Liverpool v West Ham U	3-3*
	Liverpool won 3-1 on penalties.	

THE FA CUP SPONSORED BY E.ON

2007	Chelsea v Manchester U	1-0*
2008	Portsmouth v Cardiff C	1-0
2009	Chelsea v Everton	2-1
2010	Chelsea v Portsmouth	1-0
2011	Manchester C v Stoke C	1-0

THE FA CUP WITH BUDWEISER

2012	Chelsea v Liverpool	2-1
2013	Wigan Ath v Manchester C	1-0
2014	Arsenal v Hull C	3-2*

THE FA CUP

2015	Arsenal v Aston Villa	4-0

After extra time.

FA CUP WINS

Arsenal 12, Manchester U 11, Tottenham H 8, Aston Villa 7, Chelsea 7, Liverpool 7, Blackburn R 6, Newcastle U 6, Everton 5, Manchester C 5, The Wanderers 5, WBA 5, Bolton W 4, Sheffield U 4, Wolverhampton W 4, Sheffield W 3, West Ham U 3, Bury 2, Nottingham F 2, Old Etonians 2, Portsmouth 2, Preston NE 2, Sunderland 2, Barnsley 1, Blackburn Olympic 1, Blackpool 1, Bradford C 1, Burnley 1, Cardiff C 1, Charlton Ath 1, Clapham R 1, Coventry C 1, Derby Co 1, Huddersfield T 1, Ipswich T 1, Leeds U 1, Notts Co 1, Old Carthusians 1, Oxford University 1, Royal Engineers 1, Southampton 1, Wigan Ath 1, Wimbledon 1.

APPEARANCES IN FINALS

Arsenal 19, Manchester U 18, Liverpool 14, Everton 13, Newcastle U 13, Aston Villa 11, Chelsea 11, Manchester C 10, WBA 10, Tottenham H 9, Blackburn R 8, Wolverhampton W 8, Bolton W 7, Preston NE 7, Old Etonians 6, Sheffield U 6, Sheffield W 6, Huddersfield T 5, Portsmouth 5, *The Wanderers 5, West Ham U 5, Derby Co 4, Leeds U 4, Leicester C 4, Oxford University 4, Royal Engineers 4, Southampton 4, Sunderland 4, Blackpool 3, Burnley 3, Cardiff C 3, Nottingham F 3, Barnsley 2, Birmingham C 2, *Bury 2, Charlton Ath 2, Clapham R 2, Notts Co 2, Queen's Park (Glasgow) 2, *Blackburn Olympic 1, *Bradford C 1, Brighton & HA 1, Bristol C 1, *Coventry C 1, Crystal Palace 1, Fulham 1, Hull C 1, *Ipswich T 1, Luton T 1, Middlesbrough 1, Millwall 1, *Old Carthusians 1, QPR 1, Stoke C 1, Watford 1, *Wigan Ath 1, *Wimbledon 1.
* Denotes undefeated in final.

APPEARANCES IN SEMI-FINALS

Arsenal 28, Manchester U 27, Everton 25, Liverpool 24, Aston Villa 21, Chelsea 21, WBA 20, Tottenham H 19, Blackburn R 18, Newcastle U 17, Sheffield W 16, Bolton W 14, Sheffield U 14, Wolverhampton W 14, Derby Co 13, Manchester C 12, Nottingham F 12, Sunderland 12, Southampton 11, Preston NE 10, Birmingham C 9, Burnley 8, Leeds U 8, Huddersfield T 7, Leicester C 7, Portsmouth 7, West Ham U 7, Old Etonians 6, Fulham 6, Oxford University 6, Millwall 5, Notts Co 5, The Wanderers 5, Watford 5, Cardiff C 4, Luton T 4, Queen's Park (Glasgow) 4, Royal Engineers 4, Stoke C 4, Barnsley 3, Blackpool 3, Clapham R 3, Crystal Palace (professional club) 3, Ipswich T 3, Middlesbrough 3, Norwich C 3, Old Carthusians 3, Oldham Ath 3, The Swifts 3, Blackburn Olympic 2, Bristol C 2, Bury 2, Charlton Ath 2, Grimsby T 2, Hull C 2, Reading 2, Swansea T 2, Swindon T 2, Wigan Ath 2, Wimbledon 2, Bradford C 1, Brighton & HA 1, Cambridge University 1, Chesterfield 1, Coventry C 1, Crewe Alex 1, Crystal Palace (amateur club) 1, Darwen 1, Derby Junction 1, Glasgow R 1, Marlow 1, Old Harrovians 1, Orient 1, Plymouth Arg 1, Port Vale 1, QPR 1, Shropshire W 1, Wycombe W 1, York C 1.

FA CUP FINAL TEAMS 1872–2015

Denotes player sent off.

Kennington Oval, 16 March 1872   2000
The Wanderers (1) 1 *(Betts)*
Royal Engineers (0) 0
The Wanderers: Welch; Lubbock E., Thompson A.C., Alcock, Bowen, Bonsor, Betts, Crake, Hooman, Vidal, Wollaston.
Royal Engineers: Merriman; Marindin, Addison, Cresswell, Mitchell, Renny-Tailyour, Rich, Goodwyn, Muirhead, Cotter, Bogle.
Referee: A. Stair.
Lt Creswell broke collarbone 10 mins, soldiered on; A.H. Chequer was actually Betts.

Lillie Bridge, 29 March 1873   3000
The Wanderers (0) 2 *(Kinnaird, Wollaston)*
Oxford University (0) 0
The Wanderers: Welch; Howell, Bowen, Wollaston, Kingsford, Bonsor, Kenyon-Slaney, Thompson C.M., Sturgis, Kinnaird, Stewart.
Oxford University: Leach; Smith, Mackarness, Birley, Longman, Maddison, Dixon, Paton, Vidal, Sumner, Ottaway.
Referee: A. Stair.
Kick-off a.m. because of the Boat Race. Oxford even moved goalie Leach up front!

Kennington Oval, 14 March 1874   2000
Oxford University (2) 2 *(Mackarness, Patton)*
Royal Engineers (0) 0
Oxford University: Neapean; Mackarness, Birley, Green, Vidal, Ottoway, Benson, Patton, Rawson, Maddison, Johnson.
Royal Engineers: Merriman; Marindin, Addison, Onslow, Olivier, Digby, Renny-Tailyour, Rawson, Blackburn, Wood, von Donop.
Referee: A. Stair.
Engineers had undergone special training for the game. Oxford had four caps.

Kennington Oval, 13 March 1875   3000
Royal Engineers (1) 1 *(Renny-Tailyour)*
Old Etonians (1) 1 *(Bonsor)*
Royal Engineers: Merriman; Sim, Onslow, Ruck, von Donop, Wood, Rawson, Stafford, Renny-Tailyour, Mein, Wingfield-Stratford.
Old Etonians: Farmer; Wilson, Merysey-Thompson A.C., Lubbock E., Benson, Kenyon-Slaney, Patton, Bonsor, Ottoway, Kinnaird, Stronge.
aet.
Referee: C.W. Alcock.
Ottaway injured after 37 mins and did not return. Stiff breeze hindered play, too.

Replay: Kennington Oval, 16 March 1875   3000
Royal Engineers (0) 2 *(Renny-Tailyour 2)*
Old Etonians (0) 0
Royal Engineers: Merriman; Sim, Onslow, Ruck, von Donop, Wood, Rawson, Stafford, Renny-Tailyour, Mein, Wingfield-Stratford.
Old Etonians: Drummond-Moray; Farrer, Lubbock E, Wilson, Kinnaird, Stronge, Patton, Farmer, Bonsor, Lubbock A, Hammond.
Referee: C.W. Alcock.
Engineers had goal disallowed for offside, 20th unbeaten game; Bonsor injured.

Kennington Oval, 11 March 1876   3000
The Wanderers (1) 1 *(Edwards)*
Old Etonians (0) 1 *(Bonsor)*
The Wanderers: Greig; Stratford, Lindsay, Maddison, Birley, Wollaston, Heron H, Heron F, Edwards, Kenrick, Hughes.
Old Etonians: Hogg; Welldon, Lyttelton E, Meysey-Thompson A.C., Kinnaird, Meysey-Thompson C.M., Kenyon-Slaney, Lyttelton A, Sturgis, Bonsor, Allene.
aet.
Referee: W.S. Rawson.
Bonsor's goal cannot be confirmed in contemporary accounts; three pairs of brothers; Kinnaird and Meysey-Thompson carried on with injuries.

Replay: Kennington Oval, 18 March 1876   3500
The Wanderers (2) 3 *(Wollaston, Hughes 2)*
Old Etonians (0) 0
The Wanderers: Greig; Stratford, Lindsay, Maddison, Birley, Wollaston, Heron H, Heron F, Edwards, Kenrick, Hughes.
Old Etonians: Wilson; Lubbock E, Lyttelton E, Farrer, Kinnaird, Stronge, Kenyon-Slaney, Lyttelton A, Sturgis, Bonsor, Alleyne.
Referee: W.S. Rawson.
Wanderers benefited from being unchanged compared with their opponents.

Kennington Oval, 24 March 1877   3000
The Wanderers (0) 2 *(Lindsay, Kenrick)*
Oxford University (1) 1 *(Kinnaird (og))*
The Wanderers: Kinnaird; Lindsay, Stratford, Birley, Denton, Green, Heron H, Hughes, Kenrick, Wace, Wollaston.
Oxford University: Allington; Bain, Dunell, Savory, Todd, Waddington, Fernandez, Hills, Otter, Parry, Rawson.
aet.
Referee: S.H. Wright.
For years the score was given as 2-0 and Kinnaird's own goal was even annulled; the now accepted result is 2-1 after extra time, and Kinnaird's own goal is reinstated.

Kennington Oval, 23 March 1878   4500
The Wanderers (2) 3 *(Kenrick 2, Kinnaird)*
Royal Engineers (1) 1 *(unknown)*
The Wanderers: Kirkpatrick; Stratford, Lindsay, Kinnaird, Green, Wollaston, Heron H, Wylie, Wace, Denton, Kenrick.
Royal Engineers: Friend; Cowan, Morris, Mayne, Heath, Haynes, Lindsay, Hedley, Bond, Barnet, Ruck.
Referee: S.R. Bastard.
Kinnaird's goal cannot be confirmed in contemporary accounts; The Royal Engineers goal was scored "in a rush" and is therefore not credited to an individual player; Broken arm for Kirkpatrick 30 mins but carried on; Wanderers handed back cup.

Kennington Oval, 29 March 1879   5000
Old Etonians (0) 1 *(Clerke)*
Clapham Rovers (0) 0
Old Etonians: Hawtrey; Christian, Bury, Kinnaird, Lubbock E, Clerke, Pares, Goodhart, Whitfield, Chevalier, Beaufoy.
Clapham Rovers: Birkett; Ogilvie, Field, Bailey, Prinsep, Rawson, Stanley, Scott, Bevington, Growse, Keith-Falconer.
Referee: C.W. Alcock.
Prinsep at 17 years 245 days was the youngest finalist; Old Boys' stamina told.

Kennington Oval, 10 April 1880   6000
Clapham Rovers (0) 1 *(Lloyd-Jones)*
Oxford University (0) 0
Clapham Rovers: Birkett; Ogilvie, Field, Weston, Bailey, Brougham, Stanley, Barry, Sparks, Lloyd-Jones, Ram.
Oxford University: Parr; Wilson, King, Phillips, Rogers, Heygate, Childs, Eyre, Crowdy, Hill, Lubbock J.
Referee: Major Marindin.
Wind buffeted Oxford in the first half, but it abated for the favourites Clapham.

Kennington Oval, 9 April 1881   4500
Old Carthusians (1) 3 *(Wynyard, Parry, Todd)*
Old Etonians (0) 0
Old Carthusians: Gillett; Norris, Colvin, Prinsep, Vintcent, Hansell, Richards, Page, Wynyard, Parry, Tod.
Old Etonians: Rawlinson; Foley, French, Kinnaird, Farrer, Chevalier, Anderson, Goodhart, Macaulay, Whitfield, Novelli.
Referee: W. Pierce Dix.
The far-fitter, more organised Carthusians had Parry the first overseas-born winning captain.

Kennington Oval, 25 March 1882   6500
Old Etonians (1) 1 *(Anderson)*
Blackburn Rovers (0) 0
Old Etonians: Rawlinson; French, de Paravicini, Kinnaird, Foley, Novelli, Dunn, Macaulay, Goodhart, Anderson, Chevalier.
Blackburn Rovers: Howarth; McIntyre, Suter, Sharples, Hargreaves F, Duckworth, Douglas, Strachan, Brown, Avery, Hargreaves J.
Referee: J.C. Clegg.
Avery injured near the break but the favourites were held up by goalie Rawlinson.

Kennington Oval, 31 March 1883   8000
Blackburn Olympic (0) 2 *(Costley, Matthews)*
Old Etonians (1) 1 *(Goodhart)*
Blackburn Olympic: Hacking; Ward, Warburton, Gibson, Astley, Hunter, Dewhurst, Matthews, Wilson, Costley, Yates.
Old Etonians: Rawlinson; French, de Paravicini, Kinnaird, Foley, Chevalier, Anderson, Macaulay, Goodhart, Dunn, Bainbridge.
aet.
Referee: C. Crump.
Old Etonians suffered several injuries and the well-trained cotton workers prevailed.

Kennington Oval, 29 March 1884   12,000
Blackburn Rovers (2) 2 *(Sowerbutts, Forrest)*
Queen's Park (0) 1 *(Christie)*
Blackburn Rovers: Arthur; Beverley, Suter, McIntyre, Hargreaves J, Forrest, Lofthouse, Douglas, Sowerbutts, Inglis, Brown.
Queen's Park: Gillespie; Arnott, McDonald, Campbell, Gow, Anderson, Watt, Smith, Harrower, Allan, Christie.
Referee: Major Marindin.
Scottish finalists bowed to "professional" Rovers, both having two goals disallowed.

Kennington Oval, 4 April 1885   12,500
Blackburn Rovers (1) 2 *(Forrest, Brown)*
Queen's Park (0) 0
Blackburn Rovers: Arthur; Turner, Suter, McIntyre, Haworth, Forrest, Lofthouse, Douglas, Brown, Fecitt, Sowerbutts.
Queen's Park: Gillespie; Arnott, MacLeod, Campbell, McDonald, Hamilton, Anderson, Sellar, Gray, McWhannel, Allan.
Referee: Major Marindin.
Professionalism had arrived, but it was the last entry for amateur Queen's Park.

Kennington Oval, 3 April 1886   15,000
Blackburn Rovers (0) 0
West Bromwich Albion (0) 0
Blackburn Rovers: Arthur; Turner, Suter, Douglas, Forrest, McIntyre, Heyes, Strachan, Brown, Fecitt, Sowerbutts.
West Bromwich Albion: Roberts; Green H, Bell H, Horton, Perry, Timmins, Woodhall, Green T, Bayliss, Loach, Bell G.
Referee: Major Marindin.
Boat Race day kept crowd down yet fledgling Albion earned their replay chance.

Replay: County Ground, Derby, 10 April 1886   12,000
Blackburn Rovers (1) 2 *(Brown, Sowerbutts)*
West Bromwich Albion (0) 0
Blackburn Rovers: Arthur; Turner, Suter, Douglas, Forrest, McIntyre, Walton, Strachan, Brown, Fecitt, Sowerbutts.
West Bromwich Albion: Roberts; Green H, Bell H, Horton, Perry, Timmins, Woodhall, Green T, Bayliss, Loach, Bell G.
Referee: Major Marindin.
Rovers equalled the earlier feat of Wanderers and given a silver shield.

Kennington Oval, 2 April 1887   15,500
Aston Villa (0) 2 *(Hunter, Hodgetts)*
West Bromwich Albion (0) 0
Aston Villa: Warner; Coulton, Simmonds, Yates, Dawson, Burton, Davis, Brown, Hunter, Vaughton, Hodgetts.

West Bromwich Albion: Roberts; Green H, Aldridge, Horton, Perry, Timmins, Woodhall, Green T, Bayliss, Paddock, Pearson.
Referee: Major Marindin.
Aston Villa had gained the mastery over their midland rivals after the first 20 mins.

Kennington Oval, 24 March 1888   19,000
West Bromwich Albion (1) 2 *(Woodhall, Bayliss)*
Preston North End (0) 1 *(Dewhurst)*
West Bromwich Albion: Roberts; Aldridge, Green, Horton, Perry, Timmins, Bassett, Woodhall, Bayliss, Wilson, Pearson.
Preston North End: Mills-Roberts; Howarth, Ross N, Holmes, Russell, Graham, Gordon, Ross J, Goodall, Dewhurst, Drummond.
Referee: Major Marindin.
Triumph for the £5 total wage, all-English Albion against the Preston professionals.

Kennington Oval, 30 March 1889   22,000
Preston North End (2) 3 *(Dewhurst, Ross J, Thompson)*
Wolverhampton Wanderers (0) 0
Preston North End: Mills-Roberts; Howarth, Holmes, Drummond, Russell, Graham, Gordon, Ross J, Goodall, Dewhurst, Thompson.
Wolverhampton Wanderers: Baynton; Baugh, Mason, Fletcher, Allen, Lowder, Hunter, Wykes, Brodie, Wood, Knight.
Referee: Major Marindin.
Proud Preston completed the first League and Cup double, no goals conceded.

Kennington Oval, 29 March 1890   20,000
Blackburn Rovers (3) 6 *(Walton, John Southworth, Lofthouse, Townley 3)*
Sheffield Wednesday (0) 1 *(Mumford)*
Blackburn Rovers: Horne; James Southworth, Forbes, Barton, Dewar, Forrest, Lofthouse, Campbell, John Southworth, Walton, Townley.
Sheffield Wednesday: Smith; Brayshaw, Morley, Dungworth, Betts, Waller, Ingram, Woodhouse, Bennett, Mumford, Cawley.
Referee: Major Marindin.
Non-League Wednesday on the defensive and a goal down from the sixth minute.

Kennington Oval, 21 March 1891   23,000
Blackburn Rovers (3) 3 *(Dewar, John Southworth, Townley)*
Notts County (0) 1 *(Oswald)*
Blackburn Rovers: Pennington; Brandon, Forbes, Barton, Dewar, Forrest, Lofthouse, Walton, John Southworth, Hall, Townley.
Notts County: Thraves; Ferguson, Hendry, Osbourne, Calderhead, Shelton, McGregor, McInnes, Oswald, Locker, Daft.
Referee: C.J. Hughes.
Season of penalties. Rovers displayed the much better combination all-round.

Kennington Oval, 19 March 1892   32,810
West Bromwich Albion (2) 3 *(Geddes, Nicholls, Reynolds)*
Aston Villa (0) 0
West Bromwich Albion: Reader; Nicholson, McCulloch, Reynolds, Perry, Groves, Bassett, McLeod, Nicholls, Pearson, Geddes.
Aston Villa: Warner; Evans, Cox, Devey H, Cowan, Baird, Athersmith, Devey J, Dickson, Campbell, Hodgetts.
Referee: J.C. Clegg.
Fast moving, well-organised Albion, goal nets and crossbar featured.

Fallowfield, Manchester, 25 March 1893   45,000
Wolverhampton Wanderers (0) 1 *(Allen)*
Everton (0) 0
Wolverhampton Wanderers: Rose; Baugh, Swift, Malpass, Allen, Kinsey, Topham, Wykes, Butcher, Wood, Griffin.
Everton: Williams; Howarth, Kelso, Stewart, Holt, Boyle, Latta, Gordon, Maxwell, Chadwick, Milward.
Referee: C.J. Hughes.
Everton protested over the goal; good-natured crowd spilled near the touch-lines.

Goodison Park, Liverpool, 31 March 1894   37,000
Notts County (2) 4 *(Watson, Logan 3)*
Bolton Wanderers (0) 1 *(Cassidy)*
Notts County: Toone; Harper, Hendry, Bramley, Calderhead, Shelton, Watson, Donnelly, Logan, Bruce, Daft.
Bolton Wanderers: Sutcliffe; Somerville, Jones, Gardiner, Paton, Hughes, Dickenson, Wilson, Tannahill, Bentley, Cassidy.
Referee: C.J. Hughes.
Logan led his Second Division forwards in fine style and Bolton just had to be content.

Crystal Palace, 20 April 1895   42,560
Aston Villa (1) 1 *(Chatt)*
West Bromwich Albion (0) 0
Aston Villa: Wilkes; Spencer, Welford, Reynolds, James Cowan, Russell, Athersmith, Chatt, Devey J, Hodgetts, Smith.
West Bromwich Albion: Reader; Williams, Horton, Taggart, Higgins, Perry, Bassett, McLeod, Richards, Hutchinson, Banks.
Referee: J. Lewis.
A goal hit in 30 seconds, scorching heat and cup later stolen and never recovered.

Crystal Palace, 18 April 1896   48,836
Sheffield Wednesday (1) 2 *(Spiksley 2)*
Wolverhampton Wanderers (0) 1 *(Black)*
Sheffield Wednesday: Massey; Earp, Langley, Brandon, Crawshaw, Petrie, Brash, Brady, Bell, Davis, Spiksley.
Wolverhampton Wanderers: Tennant; Baugh, Dunn, Owen, Malpass, Griffiths, Tonks, Henderson, Beats, Wood, Black.
Referee: Captain W. Simpson.
Spiksley game, one goal in the first minute and the winning second in off the post.

Crystal Palace, 10 April 1897   65,891
Aston Villa (3) 3 *(Campbell, Wheldon, Crabtree)*
Everton (2) 2 *(Boyle, Bell)*
Aston Villa: Whitehouse; Spencer, Evans, Reynolds, James Cowan, Crabtree, Athersmith, Devey J, Campbell, Wheldon, John Cowan.
Everton: Menham; Meehan, Storrier, Boyle, Holt, Stewart, Taylor, Bell, Hartley, Chadwick, Milward.
Referee: J. Lewis.
Well-matched opponents, but Villa had the edge in midfield in their double season.

Crystal Palace, 16 April 1898   62,017
Nottingham Forest (2) 3 *(Capes 2, McPherson)*
Derby County (1) 1 *(Bloomer)*
Nottingham Forest: Allsop; Ritchie, Scott, Frank Forman, McPherson, Wragg, McInnes, Richards, Benbow, Capes, Spouncer.
Derby County: Fryer; Methven, Leiper, Cox, Goodall A, Turner, Goodall J, Bloomer, Boag, Stevenson, McQueen.
Referee: J. Lewis.
Forest found each other with more ease though their second goal was rather fortunate.

Crystal Palace, 15 April 1899   73,833
Sheffield United (0) 4 *(Bennett, Beers, Almond, Priest)*
Derby County (1) 1 *(Boag)*
Sheffield United: Foulke; Thickett, Boyle, Johnson, Morren, Needham, Bennett, Beers, Hedley, Almond, Priest.
Derby County: Fryer; Methvin, Staley, Cox, Paterson, May, Arkesden, Bloomer, Boag, McDonald, Allen.
Referee: A. Scragg.
United transformed in the second half and Thickett played on with broken ribs.

Crystal Palace, 21 April 1900   68,945
Bury (3) 4 *(McLuckie 2, Wood, Plant)*
Southampton (0) 0
Bury: Thompson; Darroch, Davidson, Pray, Leeming, Ross, Richards, Wood, McLuckie, Sagar, Plant.
Southampton: Robinson; Meehan, Durber, Meston, Chadwick, Petrie, Turner, Yates, Farrell, Wood, Milward.
Referee: A.G. Kingscott.
First southern professional team to reach the final beaten by Bury's superior fitness.

Crystal Palace, 20 April 1901   110,820
Tottenham Hotspur (1) 2 *(Brown 2)*
Sheffield United (1) 2 *(Bennett, Priest)*
Tottenham Hotspur: Clawley; Erentz, Tait, Morris, Hughes, Jones, Smith, Cameron, Brown, Copeland, Kirwan.
Sheffield United: Foulke; Thickett, Boyle, Johnson, Morren, Needham, Bennett, Field, Hedley, Priest, Lipsham.
Referee: A.G. Kingscott.
Spurs had to rally after going behind in a match which drew an unprecedented crowd.

Replay: Burnden Park, Bolton, 27 April 1901   20,470
Tottenham Hotspur (0) 3 *(Cameron, Smith, Brown)*
Sheffield United (1) 1 *(Priest)*
Tottenham Hotspur: Clawley; Erentz, Tait, Morris, Hughes, Jones, Smith, Cameron, Brown, Copeland, Kirwan.
Sheffield United: Foulke; Thickett, Boyle, Johnson, Morren, Needham, Bennett, Field, Hedley, Priest, Lipsham.
Referee: A.G. Kingscott.
Trailing a goal down, Spurs became the first southern professionals to win the cup.

Crystal Palace, 19 April 1902   76,914
Sheffield United (0) 1 *(Common)*
Southampton (0) 1 *(Wood)*
Sheffield United: Foulke; Thickett, Boyle, Needham, Wilkinson, Johnson, Bennett, Common, Hedley, Priest, Lipsham.
Southampton: Robinson; Fry, Molyneux, Meston, Bowman, Lee, Turner A, Wood, Brown, Chadwick, Turner J.
Referee: T. Kirkham.
Saints forced a replay with a goal three minutes from time in game of missed chances.

Replay: Crystal Palace, 26 April 1902   33,068
Sheffield United (1) 2 *(Hedley, Barnes)*
Southampton (0) 1 *(Brown)*
Sheffield United: Foulke; Thickett, Boyle, Needham, Wilkinson, Johnson, Barnes, Common, Hedley, Priest, Lipsham.
Southampton: Robinson; Fry, Molyneux, Meeston, Bowman, Lee, Turner A, Wood, Brown, Chadwick, Turner J.
Referee: T. Kirkham.
Both teams gave an improved display but United just had the advantage in the end.

Crystal Palace, 18 April 1903   63,102
Bury (1) 6 *(Ross, Sagar, Leeming 2, Wood, Plant)*
Derby County (0) 0
Bury: Monteith; Lindsey, McEwen, Johnstone, Thorpe, Ross, Richards, Wood, Sagar, Leeming, Plant.
Derby County: Fryer; Methven, Morris, Warren, Goodall A, May, Warrington, York, Boag, Richards, Davis.
Referee: J. Adams.
Bury, after a quiet start, equalled Preston's feat of not conceding a goal in the cup.

Crystal Palace, 23 April 1904   61,374
Manchester City (1) 1 *(Meredith)*
Bolton Wanderers (0) 0
Manchester City: Hillman; McMahon, Burgess, Frost, Hynds, Ashworth, Meredith, Livingstone, Gillespie, Turnbull A., Booth.
Bolton Wanderers: Davies; Brown, Struthers, Clifford, Greenhalgh, Freebairn, Stokes, Marsh, Yenson, White, Taylor.
Referee: A.J. Barker.
Disappointing match decided in 20 mins, the occasion proving too much for both.

Crystal Palace, 15 April 1905   101,117
Aston Villa (1) 2 *(Hampton 2)*
Newcastle United (0) 0
Aston Villa: George; Spencer, Miles, Pearson, Leake, Windmill, Brawn, Garraty, Hampton, Bache, Hall.

Newcastle United: Lawrence; McCombie, Carr, Gardner, Aitken, McWilliam, Rutherford, Howie, Appleyard, Veitch, Gosnell.
Referee: P.R. Harrower.
All out attacking play sparked by Hampton's goal in the third minute, first of two.

Crystal Palace, 21 April 1906   75,609
Everton (0) 1 *(Young)*
Newcastle United (0) 0
Everton: Scott; Balmer W, Crelley, Makepeace, Taylor, Abbott, Sharp, Bolton, Young, Settle, Hardman.
Newcastle United: Lawrence; McCombie, Carr, Gardner, Aitken, McWilliam, Rutherford, Howie, Veitch, Orr, Gosnell.
Referee: F. Kirkham.
Best move of the game produced the goal: Young finishing off a cross by Sharp.

Crystal Palace, 20 April 1907   84,584
Sheffield Wednesday (1) 2 *(Stewart, Simpson)*
Everton (1) 1 *(Sharp)*
Sheffield Wednesday: Lyall; Layton, Burton, Brittleton, Crawshaw, Bartlett, Chapman, Bradshaw, Wilson, Stewart, Simpson.
Everton: Scott; Balmer W, Balmer R, Makepeace, Taylor, Abbott, Sharp, Bolton, Young, Settle, Hardman.
Referee: N. Whittaker.
Defensive error gave Wednesday the first goal and a simple header for their second.

Crystal Palace, 25 April 1908   74,967
Wolverhampton Wanderers (2) 3 *(Hunt, Hedley, Harrison)*
Newcastle United (0) 1 *(Howie)*
Wolverhampton Wanderers: Lunn; Jones, Collins, Hunt, Wooldridge, Bishop, Harrison, Shelton, Hedley, Radford, Pedley.
Newcastle United: Lawrence; McCracken, Pudan, Gardner, Veitch, McWilliam, Rutherford, Howie, Appleyard, Speedie, Wilson.
Referee: T.P. Campbell.
Third defeat in four for Newcastle as the "H" men of Second Division Wolves prevailed.

Crystal Palace, 24 April 1909   71,401
Manchester United (1) 1 *(Turnbull A)*
Bristol City (0) 0
Manchester United: Moger; Stacey, Hayes, Duckworth, Roberts, Bell, Meredith, Halse, Turnbull J, Turnbull A, Wall.
Bristol City: Clay; Annan, Cottle, Hanlin, Wedlock, Spear, Staniforth, Hardy, Gilligan, Burton, Hilton.
Referee: J. Mason.
Turnbull scored after Halse hit the crossbar, United's experience proving the answer.

Crystal Palace, 23 April 1910   76,980
Newcastle United (0) 1 *(Rutherford)*
Barnsley (1) 1 *(Tufnell)*
Newcastle United: Lawrence; McCracken, Whitson, Veitch, Low, McWilliam, Rutherford, Howie, Shepherd, Higgins, Wilson.
Barnsley: Mearns; Downs, Ness, Glendinning, Boyle, Utley, Bartrop, Gadsby, Lillycrop, Tufnell, Forman.
Referee: J.T. Ibbotson.
Late on Newcastle showed their true worth and outstanding Rutherford earned replay.

Replay: Goodison Park, Liverpool, 28 April 1910 55,364
Newcastle United (0) 2 *(Shepherd 2 (1 pen))*
Barnsley (0) 0
Newcastle United: Lawrence; McCracken, Carr, Veitch, Low, McWilliam, Rutherford, Howie, Shepherd, Higgins, Wilson.
Barnsley: Mearns; Downs, Ness, Glendinning, Boyle, Utley, Bartrop, Gadsby, Lillycrop, Tufnell, Forman.
Referee: J.T. Ibbotson.
An improved United settled down quicker and Shepherd scored from a penalty.

Crystal Palace, 22 April 1911   69,098
Bradford City (0) 0
Newcastle United (0) 0
Bradford City: Mellors; Campbell, Taylor, Robinson, Gildea, McDonald, Logan, Speirs, O'Rourke, Devine, Thompson.
Newcastle United: Lawrence; McCracken, Whitson, Veitch, Low, Willis, Rutherford, Jobey, Stewart, Higgins, Wilson.
Referee: J.H. Pearson.
Evenly matched but neither able to raise their game sufficiently for a defining result.

Replay: Old Trafford, Manchester, 26 April 1911 58,000
Bradford City (1) 1 *(Speirs)*
Newcastle United (0) 0
Bradford City: Mellors; Campbell, Taylor, Robinson, Torrance, McDonald, Logan, Speirs, O'Rourke, Devine, Thompson.
Newcastle United: Lawrence; McCracken, Whitson, Veitch, Low, Willis, Rutherford, Jobey, Stewart, Higgins, Wilson.
Referee: J.H. Pearson.
Bradford with the new cup made locally earned victory after a defensive error.

Crystal Palace, 20 April 1912   54,556
Barnsley (0) 0
West Bromwich Albion (0) 0
Barnsley: Cooper; Downs, Taylor, Glendinning, Bratley, Utley, Bartrop, Tufnell, Lillycrop, Travers, Moore.
West Bromwich Albion: Pearson; Cook, Pennington, Baddeley, Buck, McNeal, Jephcott, Wright, Pailor, Bowser, Shearman.
Referee: J.R. Schumacher.
Dour game finishing with West Bromwich slightly the more enterprising team.

Replay: Bramall Lane, Sheffield, 24 April 1912 38,555
Barnsley (1) 1 *(Tufnell)*
West Bromwich Albion (0) 0
Barnsley: Cooper; Downs, Taylor, Glendinning, Bratley, Utley, Bartrop, Tufnell, Lillycrop, Travers, Moore.
West Bromwich Albion: Pearson; Cook, Pennington, Baddeley, Buck, McNeal, Jephcott, Wright, Pailor, Bowser, Shearman.
aet.
Referee: J.R. Schumacher.
Albion had the better of the first half but Barnsley's winner at the death.

Crystal Palace, 19 April 1913   121,919
Aston Villa (0) 1 *(Barber)*
Sunderland (0) 0
Aston Villa: Hardy; Lyons, Weston, Barber, Harrop, Leach, Wallace, Halse, Hampton, Stephenson, Bache.
Sunderland: Butler; Gladwin, Ness, Cuggy, Thomson, Low, Mordue, Buchan, Richardson, Holley, Martin.
Referee: A. Adams.
Attendance record for an erratic match with Villa having the edge in midfield.

Crystal Palace, 25 April 1914   72,778
Burnley (0) 1 *(Freeman)*
Liverpool (0) 0
Burnley: Sewell; Bamford, Taylor, Halley, Boyle, Watson, Nesbitt, Lindley, Freeman, Hodgson, Mosscrop.
Liverpool: Campbell; Longworth, Pursell, Fairfoul, Ferguson, McKinlay, Sheldon, Metcalf, Miller, Lacey, Nicholl.
Referee: H.S. Bamlett.
King George V present; even final decided by a ferocious shot in the 55th minute.

Old Trafford, Manchester, 24 April 1915   49,557
Sheffield United (1) 3 *(Simmons, Fazackerley, Kitchen)*
Chelsea (0) 0
Sheffield United: Gough; Cook, English, Sturgess, Brelsford, Utley, Simmons, Fazackerley, Kitchen, Masterman, Evans.
Chelsea: Molyneux; Bettridge, Harrow, Taylor, Logan, Walker, Ford, Halse, Thomson, Croal, McNeil.
Referee: H.H. Taylor.
The Khaki final; a low key occasion with United fairly comfortable winners.

Stamford Bridge, 24 April 1920   50,018
Aston Villa (0) 1 *(Kirton)*
Huddersfield Town (0) 0
Aston Villa: Hardy; Smart, Weston, Ducat, Barson, Moss, Wallace, Kirton, Walker, Stephenson, Dorrell.
Huddersfield Town: Mutch; Wood, Bullock, Slade, Wilson, Watson, Richardson, Mann, Taylor, Swann, Islip. *aet.*
Referee: J.T. Howcroft.
Extra time before a decision, Kirton's header taken a deflection off Wilson's back.

Stamford Bridge, 23 April 1921   72,805
Tottenham Hotspur (0) 1 *(Dimmock)*
Wolverhampton Wanderers (0) 0
Tottenham Hotspur: Hunter; Clay, McDonald, Smith, Walters, Grimsdell, Banks, Seed, Cantrell, Bliss, Dimmock.
Wolverhampton Wanderers: George; Woodward, Marshall, Gregory, Hodnett, Riley, Lea, Burrill, Edmonds, Potts, Brooks.
Referee: J. Davies.
Spurs favourite crossfield pass executed by Seed and a slick solo by Dimmock.

Stamford Bridge, 29 April 1922   53,000
Huddersfield Town (0) 1 *(Smith (pen))*
Preston North End (0) 0
Huddersfield Town: Mutch; Wood, Wadsworth, Slade, Wilson, Watson, Richardson, Mann, Islip, Stephenson, Smith.
Preston North End: Mitchell; Hamilton, Doolan, Duxbury, McCall, Williamson, Rawlings, Jefferis, Roberts, Woodhouse, Quinn.
Referee: J.W.D. Fowler.
Sixty-five minutes, Smith tripped, got up and then scored from the penalty spot.

Wembley, 28 April 1923   126,047
Bolton Wanderers (1) 2 *(Jack, Smith JR)*
West Ham United (0) 0
Bolton Wanderers: Pym; Haworth, Finney, Nuttall, Seddon, Jennings, Butler, Jack, Smith JR, Smith J, Vizard.
West Ham United: Hufton; Henderson, Young, Bishop, Kay, Tresadern, Richards, Brown, Watson, Moore, Ruffell.
Referee: D.H. Asson.
Huge crowd ringed the touchline; PC Scorey and his white horse (grey) in charge.

Wembley, 26 April 1924   91,695
Newcastle United (0) 2 *(Harris, Seymour)*
Aston Villa (0) 0
Newcastle United: Bradley; Hampson, Hudspeth, Mooney, Spencer, Gibson, Low, Cowan, Harris, McDonald, Seymour.
Aston Villa: Jackson; Smart, Mort, Moss, Milne, Blackburn, York, Kirton, Capewell, Walker, Dorrell.
Referee: W.E. Russell.
First all-ticket game; Newcastle produced a devastating two goals in 90 seconds.

Wembley, 25 April 1925   91,763
Sheffield United (1) 1 *(Tunstall)*
Cardiff City (0) 0
Sheffield United: Sutcliffe; Cook, Milton, Pantling, King, Green, Mercer, Boyle, Johnson, Gillespie, Tunstall.
Cardiff City: Farquharson; Nelson, Blair, Wake, Keenor, Hardy, Davies, Gill, Nicholson, Beadles, Evans.
Referee: G.N. Watson.
One error Cardiff missed chances; skipper Gillespie was outstanding for United.

Wembley, 24 April 1926   91,447
Bolton Wanderers (0) 1 *(Jack)*
Manchester City (0) 0
Bolton Wanderers: Pym; Haworth, Greenhalgh, Nuttall, Seddon, Jennings, Butler, Jack, Smith JR, Smith J, Vizard.
Manchester City: Goodchild; Cookson, McCloy, Pringle, Cowan, McMullan, Austin, Browell, Roberts, Johnson, Hicks.
Referee: I. Baker.
Both defences in command, the winning goal arriving 12 minutes from time.

Wembley, 23 April 1927   91,206
Cardiff City (0) 1 *(Ferguson)*
Arsenal (0) 0
Cardiff City: Farquharson; Nelson, Watson, Keenor, Sloan, Hardy, Curtis, Irving, Ferguson, Davies, McLachlan.
Arsenal: Lewis; Parker, Kennedy, Baker, Butler, John, Hulme, Buchan, Brain, Blyth, Hoar.
Referee: W.F. Bunnell.
Slip-up by Welsh goalkeeper Lewis and the cup goes with Cardiff to Wales.

Wembley, 21 April 1928   92,041
Blackburn Rovers (2) 3 *(Roscamp 2, McLean)*
Huddersfield Town (0) 1 *(Jackson)*
Blackburn Rovers: Crawford; Hutton, Jones, Healless, Rankin, Campbell, Thornewell, Puddefoot, Roscamp, McLean, Rigby.
Huddersfield Town: Mercer; Goodall, Barkas, Redfern, Wilson, Steele, Jackson, Kelly, Brown, Stephenson, Smith.
Referee: T.G. Bryan.
BBC Radio coverage; Roscamp bundling keeper and ball after a minute.

Wembley, 27 April 1929   92,576
Bolton Wanderers (0) 2 *(Butler, Blackmore)*
Portsmouth (0) 0
Bolton Wanderers: Pym; Haworth, Finney, Kean, Seddon, Nuttall, Butler, McClelland, Blackmore, Gibson, Cook.
Portsmouth: Gilfillan; Mackie, Bell, Nichol, McIlwaine, Thackeray, Forward, Smith, Weddle, Watson, Cook.
Referee: A. Josephs.
Portsmouth had the better of the first half but Bolton gradually got on top.

Wembley, 26 April 1930   92,488
Arsenal (1) 2 *(James, Lambert)*
Huddersfield Town (0) 0
Arsenal: Preedy; Parker, Hapgood, Baker, Seddon, John, Hulme, Jack, Lambert, James, Bastin.
Huddersfield Town: Turner; Goodall, Spence, Naylor, Wilson, Campbell, Jackson, Kelly, Davies, Raw, Smith.
Referee: T. Crew.
Arsenal weathered a comeback by Huddersfield, thanks to their stout defence.

Wembley, 25 April 1931   92,406
West Bromwich Albion (1) 2 *(Richardson WG 2)*
Birmingham (0) 1 *(Bradford)*
West Bromwich Albion: Pearson; Shaw, Trentham, Magee, Richardson W, Edwards, Glidden, Carter, Richardson WG, Sandford, Wood.
Birmingham: Hibbs; Liddell, Barkas, Cringan, Morrall, Leslie, Briggs, Crosbie, Bradford, Gregg, Curtis.
Referee: A.H. Kingscott.
A unique double for Albion – the cup and promotion from Division Two.

Wembley, 23 April 1932   92,298
Newcastle United (1) 2 *(Allen 2)*
Arsenal (1) 1 *(John)*
Newcastle United: McInroy; Nelson, Fairhurst, McKenzie, Davidson, Weaver, Boyd, Richardson J.R., Allen, McMenemy, Lang.
Arsenal: Moss; Parker, Hapgood, Jones, Roberts, Male, Hulme, Jack, Lambert, Bastin, John.
Referee: W.P. Harper.
Controversy! Richardson's cross was already over the line for the Allen goal.

Wembley, 29 April 1933   92,950
Everton (1) 3 *(Stein, Dean, Dunn)*
Manchester City (0) 0
Everton: Sagar; Cook, Cresswell, Britton, White, Thomson, Geldard, Dunn, Dean, Johnson, Stein.
Manchester City: Langford; Cann, Dale, Busby, Cowan, Bray, Toseland, Marshall, Herd, McMullan, Brook.
Referee: E. Wood.
Players numbered for the first time but strangely from 1 to Langford's 22!

Wembley, 28 April 1934 93,258
Manchester City (0) 2 *(Tilson 2)*
Portsmouth (1) 1 *(Rutherford)*
Manchester City: Swift; Barnett, Dale, Busby, Cowan, Bray, Toseland, Marshall, Tilson, Herd, Brook.
Portsmouth: Gilfillan; Mackie, Smith W, Nichol, Allen, Thackeray, Worrall, Smith J, Weddle, Easson, Rutherford.
Referee: S.F. Rous.
Tilson who had been left out in 1933 predicted his brace and ensured City's win.

Wembley, 27 April 1935 93,204
Sheffield Wednesday (1) 4 *(Rimmer 2, Palethorpe, Hooper)*
West Bromwich Albion (1) 2 *(Boyes, Sandford)*
Sheffield Wednesday: Brown; Nibloe, Catlin, Sharp, Millership, Burrows, Hooper, Surtees, Palethorpe, Starling, Rimmer.
West Bromwich Albion: Pearson; Shaw, Trentham, Murphy, Richardson W, Edwards, Glidden, Carter, Richardson W G, Sandford, Boyes.
Referee: A.E. Fogg.
Rimmer double kept his record of scoring in every round with lucky horseshoe.

Wembley, 25 April 1936 93,384
Arsenal (0) 1 *(Drake)*
Sheffield United (0) 0
Arsenal: Wilson; Male, Hapgood, Crayston, Roberts, Copping, Hulme, Bowden, Drake, James, Bastin.
Sheffield United: Smith; Hooper, Wilkinson, Jackson, Johnson, McPherson, Barton, Barclay, Dodds, Pickering, Williams.
Referee: H. Nattrass.
Drake shrugs off discomfiture of his heavily bandaged knee; ban on cameras!

Wembley, 1 May 1937 93,495
Sunderland (0) 3 *(Gurney, Carter, Burbanks)*
Preston North End (1) 1 *(O'Donnell F)*
Sunderland: Mapson; Gorman, Hall, Thomson, Johnson, McNab, Duns, Carter, Gurney, Gallacher, Burbanks.
Preston North End: Burns; Gallimore, Beattie A, Shankly, Tremelling, Milne, Dougal, Beresford, O'Donnell F, Fagan, O'Donnell H.
Referee: R.G. Rudd.
First for TV cameras and Sunderland's recently-wed local boy Carter inspires.

Wembley, 30 April 1938 93,497
Preston North End (0) 1 *(Mutch (pen))*
Huddersfield Town (0) 0
Preston North End: Holdcroft; Gallimore, Beattie A, Shankly, Smith, Batey, Watmough, Mutch, Maxwell, Beattie R, O'Donnell H.
Huddersfield Town: Hesford; Craig, Mountford, Willingham, Young, Boot, Hulme, Isaac, McFadyen, Barclay, Beasley.
aet.
Referee: A.J. Jewell.
Controversial Mutch penalty in off the crossbar in the 119th minute.

Wembley, 29 April 1939 99,370
Portsmouth (2) 4 *(Parker 2, Barlow, Anderson)*
Wolverhampton Wanderers (0) 1 *(Dorsett)*
Portsmouth: Walker; Morgan, Rochford, Guthrie, Rowe, Wharton, Worrall, McAlinden, Anderson, Barlow, Parker.
Wolverhampton Wanderers: Scott; Morris, Taylor, Galley, Cullis, Gardiner, Burton, McIntosh, Westcott, Dorsett, Maguire.
Referee: T. Thompson.
Barlow scores against his old club; odds-on favourites are decisively beaten.

Wembley, 27 April 1946 97,106
Derby County (0) 4 *(Turner H (og), Doherty, Stamps 2)*
Charlton Athletic (0) 1 *(Turner H)*
Derby County: Woodley; Nicholas, Howe, Bullions, Leuty, Musson, Harrison, Carter, Stamps, Doherty, Duncan.

Charlton Athletic: Bartram; Phipps, Shreeve, Turner H, Oakes, Johnson, Fell, Brown, Turner A, Welsh, Duffy.
aet.
Referee: E.D. Smith.
Turner H scores for both teams and Derby really turn on the style.

Wembley, 26 April 1947 98,215
Charlton Athletic (0) 1 *(Duffy)*
Burnley (0) 0
Charlton Athletic: Bartram; Croker, Shreeve, Johnson, Phipps, Whittaker, Hurst, Dawson, Robinson, Welsh, Duffy.
Burnley: Strong; Woodruff, Mather, Attwell, Brown, Bray, Chew, Morris, Harrison, Potts, Kippax.
aet.
Referee: J.M. Wiltshire.
Winner six minutes from the end; ball bursts for second year running.

Wembley, 24 April 1948 99,000
Manchester United (1) 4 *(Rowley 2, Pearson, Anderson)*
Blackpool (2) 2 *(Shimwell (pen), Mortensen)*
Manchester United: Crompton; Carey, Aston, Anderson, Chilton, Cockburn, Delaney, Morris, Rowley, Pearson, Mitten.
Blackpool: Robinson; Shimwell, Crosland, Johnston, Hayward, Kelly, Matthews, Munro, Mortensen, Dick, Rickett.
Referee: C.J. Barrick.
Exceptional, enthralling contest; Shimwell first full-back to score at Wembley.

Wembley, 30 April 1949 98,920
Wolverhampton Wanderers (2) 3 *(Pye 2, Smyth)*
Leicester City (0) 1 *(Griffiths)*
Wolverhampton Wanderers: Williams; Pritchard, Springthorpe, Crook, Shorthouse, Wright, Hancocks, Smyth, Pye, Dunn, Mullen.
Leicester City: Bradley; Jelly, Scott, Harrison W, Plummer, King, Griffiths, Lee, Harrison J, Chisholm, Adam.
Referee: R.A. Mortimer.
Leicester miss nosebleed victim Revie; Wolves' four capped forwards supreme.

Wembley, 29 April 1950 100,000
Arsenal (1) 2 *(Lewis 2)*
Liverpool (0) 0
Arsenal: Swindin; Scott, Barnes, Forbes, Compton L, Mercer, Cox, Logie, Goring, Lewis, Compton D.
Liverpool: Sidlow; Lambert, Spicer, Taylor, Hughes, Jones, Payne, Baron, Stubbins, Fagan, Liddell.
Referee: H. Pearce.
Arsenal, the oldest team to win the cup (average age 30 years 2 months), in control.

Wembley, 28 April 1951 100,000
Newcastle United (0) 2 *(Milburn 2)*
Blackpool (0) 0
Newcastle United: Fairbrother; Cowell, Corbett, Harvey, Brennan, Crowe, Walker, Taylor, Milburn, Robledo G, Mitchell.
Blackpool: Farm; Shimwell, Garrett, Johnston, Hayward, Kelly, Matthews, Mudie, Mortensen, Slater, Perry.
Referee: W. Ling.
Seymour (1924) first to play for and then manage a winning Cup Final team.

Wembley, 3 May 1952 100,000
Newcastle United (0) 1 *(Robledo G)*
Arsenal (0) 0
Newcastle United: Simpson; Cowell, McMichael, Harvey, Brennan, Robledo E, Walker, Foulkes, Milburn, Robledo G, Mitchell.
Arsenal: Swindin; Barnes, Smith, Forbes, Daniel, Mercer, Cox, Logie, Holton, Lishman, Roper.
Referee: A. Ellis.
Walley Barnes off with a split cartilage; Chilean Robledo scores in 84 minutes.

Wembley, 2 May 1953   100,000
Blackpool (1) 4 *(Mortensen 3, Perry)*
Bolton Wanderers (2) 3 *(Lofthouse, Moir, Bell)*
Blackpool: Farm; Shimwell, Garrett, Fenton, Johnston, Robinson, Matthews, Taylor, Mortensen, Mudie, Perry.
Bolton Wanderers: Hanson; Ball, Banks, Wheeler, Barrass, Bell, Holden, Moir, Lofthouse, Hassall, Langton.
Referee: M. Griffiths.
The Matthews Final; injury-ridden Bolton suffer heavily in last 20 minutes.

Wembley, 1 May 1954   100,000
West Bromwich Albion (1) 3 *(Allen 2 (1 pen), Griffin)*
Preston North End (1) 2 *(Morrison, Wayman)*
West Bromwich Albion: Sanders; Kennedy, Millard, Dudley, Dugdale, Barlow, Griffin, Ryan, Allen, Nicholls, Lee.
Preston North End: Thompson; Cunningham, Walton, Docherty, Marston, Forbes, Finney, Foster, Wayman, Baxter, Morrison.
Referee: A. Luty.
Finney disappoints for Preston and favourites Albion win in the last minute.

Wembley, 7 May 1955   100,000
Newcastle United (1) 3 *(Milburn, Mitchell, Hannah)*
Manchester City (1) 1 *(Johnstone)*
Newcastle United: Simpson; Cowell, Batty, Scoular, Stokoe, Casey, White, Milburn, Keeble, Hannah, Mitchell.
Manchester City: Trautmann; Meadows, Little, Barnes, Ewing, Paul, Spurdle, Hayes, Revie, Johnstone, Fagan.
Referee: R. Leafe.
Meadows out with a twisted knee and City hit by Milburn's 45 second goal.

Wembley, 5 May 1956   100,000
Manchester City (1) 3 *(Hayes, Dyson, Johnstone)*
Birmingham City (1) 1 *(Kinsey)*
Manchester City: Trautmann; Leivers, Little, Barnes, Ewing, Paul, Johnstone, Hayes, Revie, Dyson, Clarke.
Birmingham City: Merrick; Hall, Green, Newman, Smith, Boyd, Astall, Kinsey, Brown, Murphy, Govan.
Referee: A. Bond.
The Revie plan works; Trautmann plays the last 20 minutes with a broken neck.

Wembley, 4 May 1957   100,000
Aston Villa (0) 2 *(McParland 2)*
Manchester United (0) 1 *(Taylor T)*
Aston Villa: Sims; Lynn, Aldis, Crowther, Dugdale, Saward, Smith, Sewell, Myerscough, Dixon, McParland.
Manchester United: Wood; Foulkes, Byrne, Colman, Blanchflower, Edwards, Berry, Whelan, Taylor T, Charlton, Pegg.
Referee: F. Coultas.
Wood broken collarbone after challenge by McParland, Blanchflower in goal.

Wembley, 3 May 1958   100,000
Bolton Wanderers (1) 2 *(Lofthouse 2)*
Manchester United (0) 0
Bolton Wanderers: Hopkinson; Hartle, Banks, Hennin, Higgins, Edwards, Birch, Stevens, Lofthouse, Parry, Holden.
Manchester United: Gregg; Foulkes, Greaves, Goodwin, Cope, Crowther, Dawson, Taylor E, Charlton, Viollet, Webster.
Referee: J. Sherlock.
Post-Munich Final; United given dispensation for Taylor and Crowther to play.

Wembley, 2 May 1959   100,000
Nottingham Forest (2) 2 *(Dwight, Wilson)*
Luton Town (0) 1 *(Pacey)*
Nottingham Forest: Thomson; Whare, McDonald, Whitefoot, McKinlay, Burkitt, Dwight, Quigley, Wilson, Gray, Imlach.

Luton Town: Baynham; McNally, Hawkes, Groves, Owen, Pacey, Bingham, Brown, Morton, Cummins, Gregory.
Referee: J. Clough.
Dwight scores, breaks his leg and watches the final on TV from hospital bed.

Wembley, 7 May 1960   100,000
Wolverhampton Wanderers (1) 3 *(McGrath (og), Deeley 2)*
Blackburn Rovers (0) 0
Wolverhampton Wanderers: Finlayson; Showell, Harris, Clamp, Slater, Flowers, Deeley, .Stobart, Murray, Broadbent, Horne.
Blackburn Rovers: Leyland; Bray, Whelan, Clayton, Woods, McGrath, Bimpson, Dobing, Dougan, Douglas, MacLeod.
Referee: K. Howley.
Whelan breaks his leg and Wolves have an easy ride to winning their medals.

Wembley, 6 May 1961   100,000
Tottenham Hotspur (0) 2 *(Smith, Dyson)*
Leicester City (0) 0
Tottenham Hotspur: Brown; Baker, Henry, Blanchflower, Norman, Mackay, Jones, White, Smith, Allen, Dyson.
Leicester City: Banks; Chalmers, Norman, McLintock, King, Appleton, Riley, Walsh, McIlmoyle, Keyworth, Cheesebrough.
Referee: J. Kelly.
Blanchflower inspires Spurs to the first League and Cup double of the century.

Wembley, 5 May 1962   100,000
Tottenham Hotspur (1) 3 *(Greaves, Smith, Blanchflower (pen))*
Burnley (0) 1 *(Robson)*
Tottenham Hotspur: Brown; Baker, Henry, Blanchflower, Norman, Mackay, Medwin, White, Smith, Greaves, Jones.
Burnley: Blacklaw; Angus, Elder, Adamson, Cummings, Miller, Connelly, McIlroy, Pointer, Robson, Harris.
Referee: J. Finney.
Robson scores the 100th Cup Final goal but Spurs prove the ultimate masters.

Wembley, 25 May 1963   100,000
Manchester United (1) 3 *(Herd 2, Law)*
Leicester City (0) 1 *(Keyworth)*
Manchester United: Gaskell; Dunne, Cantwell, Crerand, Foulkes, Setters, Giles, Quixall, Herd, Law, Charlton.
Leicester City: Banks; Sjoberg, Norman, McLintock, King, Appleton, Riley, Cross, Keyworth, Gibson, Stringfellow.
Referee: K. Aston.
Harsh winter decides late date and United are in control in all departments.

Wembley, 2 May 1964   100,000
West Ham United (1) 3 *(Sissons, Hurst, Boyce)*
Preston North End (2) 2 *(Holden, Dawson)*
West Ham United: Standen; Bond, Burkett, Bovington, Brown, Moore, Brabrook, Boyce, Byrne, Hurst, Sissons.
Preston North End: Kelly; Ross, Smith, Lawton, Singleton, Kendall, Wilson, Ashworth, Dawson, Spavin, Holden.
Referee: A. Holland.
Kendall 17 years 345 days Wembley's youngest, Sissons the youngest scorer.

Wembley, 1 May 1965   100,000
Liverpool (0) 2 *(Hunt, St John)*
Leeds United (0) 1 *(Bremner)*
Liverpool: Lawrence; Lawler, Byrne, Strong, Yeats, Stevenson, Callaghan, Hunt, St John, Smith, Thompson.
Leeds United: Sprake; Reaney, Bell, Bremner, Charlton, Hunter, Giles, Storrie, Peacock, Collins, Johanneson.
aet.
Referee: W. Clements.
Byrne breaks his collarbone, extra time and Liverpool cry of "ee-ay-addio".

Wembley, 14 May 1966 100,000
Everton (0) 3 *(Trebilcock 2, Temple)*
Sheffield Wednesday (1) 2 *(McCalliog, Ford)*
Everton: West; Wright, Wilson, Gabriel, Labone, Harris,
Scott, Trebilcock, Young, Harvey, Temple.
Sheffield Wednesday: Springett; Smith, Megson, Eustace,
Ellis, Young, Pugh, Fantham, McCalliog, Ford, Quinn.
Referee: J.K. Taylor.
*Two down in 57 minutes but Trebilcock (not mentioned in
programme) wins it.*

Wembley, 20 May 1967 100,000
Tottenham Hotspur (1) 2 *(Robertson, Saul)*
Chelsea (0) 1 *(Tambling)*
Tottenham Hotspur: Jennings; Kinnear, Knowles,
Mullery, England, Mackay, Robertson, Greaves, Gilzean,
Venables, Saul.
Chelsea: Bonetti; Harris A, McCreadie, Hollins, Hinton,
Harris R, Cooke, Baldwin, Hateley, Tambling, Boyle.
Referee: K. Dagnall.
*First all-London final and all-action Spurs make it five
wins in five finals.*

Wembley, 18 May 1968 100,000
West Bromwich Albion (0) 1 *(Astle)*
Everton (0) 0
West Bromwich Albion: Osborne; Fraser, Williams,
Brown, Talbut, Kaye (Clarke), Lovett, Collard, Astle,
Hope, Clark.
Everton: West; Wright, Wilson, Kendall, Labone,
Harvey, Husband, Ball, Royle, Hurst, Morrissey.
aet.
Referee: L. Callaghan.
*Astle scores in every round with the scuffed winner in the
third minute of extra time.*

Wembley, 26 April 1969 100,000
Manchester City (1) 1 *(Young)*
Leicester City (0) 0
Manchester City: Dowd; Book, Pardoe, Doyle, Booth,
Oakes, Summerbee, Bell, Lee, Young, Coleman.
Leicester City: Shilton; Rodrigues, Nish, Roberts,
Woollett, Cross, Fern, Gibson, Lochhead, Clarke, Glover
(Manley).
Referee: G. McCabe.
*The double for fourth finalists Leicester – defeat and
relegation to Division Two.*

Wembley, 11 April 1970 100,000
Chelsea (1) 2 *(Houseman, Hutchinson)*
Leeds United (1) 2 *(Charlton, Jones)*
Chelsea: Bonetti; Webb, McCreadie, Hollins, Dempsey,
Harris R (Hinton), Baldwin, Houseman, Osgood,
Hutchinson, Cooke.
Leeds United: Sprake; Madeley, Cooper, Bremner,
Charlton, Hunter, Lorimer, Clarke, Jones, Giles, Gray E.
aet.
Referee: E. Jennings.
*Chelsea twice behind force a replay – first since 1912 –
against dominant Leeds.*

Replay: Old Trafford, Manchester, 29 April 1970 62,078
Chelsea (0) 2 *(Osgood, Webb)*
Leeds United (1) 1 *(Jones)*
Chelsea: Bonetti; Harris R, McCreadie, Hollins,
Dempsey, Webb, Baldwin, Cooke, Osgood (Hinton),
Hutchinson, Houseman.
Leeds United: Harvey; Madeley, Cooper, Bremner,
Charlton, Hunter, Lorimer, Clarke, Jones, Giles, Gray E.
aet.
Referee: E. Jennings.
*Chelsea out of town find a rarity – taking a late lead and
winning the cup.*

Wembley, 8 May 1971 100,000
Arsenal (0) 2 *(Kelly, George)*
Liverpool (0) 1 *(Heighway)*
Arsenal: Wilson; Rice, McNabb, Storey (Kelly),
McLintock, Simpson, Armstrong, Graham, Radford,
Kennedy, George.

Liverpool: Clemence; Lawler, Lindsay, Smith, Lloyd,
Hughes, Callaghan, Evans (Thompson), Heighway,
Toshack, Hall.
aet.
Referee: N. Burtenshaw.
*Drawn away in every round, Arsenal double winners and
Kelly first sub scorer.*

Wembley, 6 May 1972 100,000
Leeds United (0) 1 *(Clarke)*
Arsenal (0) 0
Leeds United: Harvey; Reaney, Madeley, Bremner,
Charlton, Hunter, Lorimer, Clarke, Jones, Giles, Gray E.
Arsenal: Barnett; Rice, McNab, Storey, McLintock,
Simpson, Armstrong, Ball, George, Radford (Kennedy),
Graham.
Referee: D.W. Smith.
*Centenary Final; goal provider Jones dislocates his elbow
in the last minute.*

Wembley, 5 May 1973 100,000
Sunderland (1) 1 *(Porterfield)*
Leeds United (0) 0
Sunderland: Montgomery; Malone, Guthrie, Horswill,
Watson, Pitt, Kerr, Hughes, Halom, Porterfield, Tueart.
Leeds United: Harvey; Reaney, Cherry, Bremner,
Madeley, Hunter, Lorimer, Clarke, Jones, Giles, Gray E
(Yorath).
Referee: K. Burns.
*First Second Division winners in 42 years and the
Montgomery double save.*

Wembley, 4 May 1974 100,000
Liverpool (0) 3 *(Keegan 2, Heighway)*
Newcastle United (0) 0
Liverpool: Clemence; Smith, Lindsay, Thompson,
Cormack, Hughes, Keegan, Hall, Heighway, Toshack,
Callaghan.
Newcastle United: McFaul; Clark, Kennedy, McDermott,
Howard, Moncur, Smith (Gibb), Cassidy, Macdonald,
Tudor, Hibbitt.
Referee: G.C. Kew.
*United's 11th final but suffer first Wembley defeat against
skilful Liverpool.*

Wembley, 3 May 1975 100,000
West Ham United (0) 2 *(Taylor A 2)*
Fulham (0) 0
West Ham United: Day; McDowell, Taylor T, Lock,
Lampard, Bonds, Paddon, Brooking, Jennings, Taylor A,
Holland.
Fulham: Mellor; Cutbush, Lacy, Moore, Fraser, Mullery,
Conway, Slough, Mitchell, Busby, Barrett.
Referee: P. Partridge.
*Hammers win is Taylor-made – striker signed in
November from Rochdale.*

Wembley, 1 May 1976 100,000
Southampton (0) 1 *(Stokes)*
Manchester United (0) 0
Southampton: Turner; Rodrigues, Peach, Holmes, Blyth,
Steele, Gilchrist, Channon, Osgood, McCalliog, Stokes.
Manchester United: Stepney; Forsyth, Houston, Daly,
Greenhoff B, Buchan, Coppell, McIlroy, Pearson,
Macari, Hill (McCreery).
Referee: C. Thomas.
*Third time lucky for the Second Division Saints, 83rd
minute winner.*

Wembley, 21 May 1977 100,000
Manchester United (0) 2 *(Pearson, Greenhoff J)*
Liverpool (0) 1 *(Case)*
Manchester United: Stepney; Nicholl, Albiston, McIlroy,
Greenhoff B, Buchan, Coppell, Greenhoff J, Pearson,
Macari, Hill (McCreery).
Liverpool: Clemence; Neal, Jones, Smith, Kennedy,
Hughes, Keegan, Case, Heighway, Johnson (Callaghan),
McDermott.
Referee: R. Matthewson.
*All three goals in a five minute spell after half-time in well-
fought display.*

Wembley, 6 May 1978   100,000
Ipswich Town (0) 1 *(Osborne)*
Arsenal (0) 0
Ipswich Town: Cooper; Burley, Mills, Osborne (Lambert), Hunter, Beattie, Talbot, Wark, Mariner, Geddis, Woods.
Arsenal: Jennings; Rice, Nelson, Price, Young, O'Leary, Brady (Rix), Hudson, Macdonald, Stapleton, Sunderland.
Referee: D.R.G. Nippard.
Wembley's 50th final, 40th different winners Osborne replaced – exhausted

Wembley, 12 May 1979   100,000
Arsenal (2) 3 *(Talbot, Stapleton, Sunderland)*
Manchester United (0) 2 *(McQueen, McIlroy)*
Arsenal: Jennings; Rice, Nelson, Talbot, O'Leary, Young, Brady, Sunderland, Stapleton, Price (Walford), Rix.
Manchester United: Bailey; Nicholl, Albiston, McIlroy, McQueen, Buchan, Coppell, Greenhoff J, Jordan, Macari, Thomas.
Referee: R. Challis.
Despite goals in 86 and 88 minutes to level, United are the ultimate losers.

Wembley, 10 May 1980   100,000
West Ham United (1) 1 *(Brooking)*
Arsenal (0) 0
West Ham United: Parkes; Stewart, Lampard, Bonds, Martin, Devonshire, Allen, Pearson, Cross, Brooking, Pike.
Arsenal: Jennings; Rice, Devine (Nelson), Talbot, O'Leary, Young, Brady, Sunderland, Stapleton, Price, Rix.
Referee: G. Courtney.
Allen at 17 years 256 days youngest Wembley finalist; Brooking header!

Wembley, 9 May 1981   100,000
Tottenham Hotspur (0) 1 *(Hutchison (og))*
Manchester City (1) 1 *(Hutchison)*
Tottenham Hotspur: Aleksic; Hughton, Miller, Roberts, Perryman, Villa (Brooke), Ardiles, Archibald, Galvin, Hoddle, Crooks.
Manchester City: Corrigan; Ranson, McDonald, Reid, Power, Caton, Bennett, Gow, MacKenzie, Hutchison (Henry), Reeves.
aet.
Referee: K. Hackett.
The 100th final, well-matched teams given another chance after own goal.

Replay: **Wembley, 14 May 1981**   92,000
Tottenham Hotspur (1) 3 *(Villa 2, Crooks)*
Manchester City (1) 2 *(MacKenzie, Reeves (pen))*
Tottenham Hotspur: Aleksic; Hughton, Miller, Roberts, Perryman, Villa, Ardiles, Archibald, Galvin, Hoddle, Crooks.
Manchester City: Corrigan; Ranson, McDonald (Tueart), Caton, Reid, Gow, Power, MacKenzie, Reeves, Bennett, Hutchison.
Referee: K. Hackett.
Villa caps an unforgettable final, beating three men in a 30 yard run.

Wembley, 22 May 1982   100,000
Tottenham Hotspur (0) 1 *(Hoddle)*
Queens Park Rangers (0) 1 *(Fenwick)*
Tottenham Hotspur: Clemence; Hughton, Miller, Price, Roberts, Perryman, Hazard (Brooke), Archibald, Galvin, Hoddle, Crooks.
Queens Park Rangers: Hucker; Fenwick, Gillard, Waddock, Hazell, Roeder, Currie, Flanagan, Allen (Micklewhite), Stainrod, Gregory.
aet.
Referee: C. White.
Spurs' Centenary year but forced to try again against a plucky Rangers.

Replay: **Wembley, 27 May 1982**   90,000
Tottenham Hotspur (1) 1 *(Hoddle (pen))*
Queens Park Rangers (0) 0
Tottenham Hotspur: Clemence; Hughton, Miller, Price, Roberts, Perryman, Hazard (Brooke), Archibald, Galvin, Hoddle, Crooks.
Queens Park Rangers: Hucker; Fenwick, Gillard, Waddock, Hazell, Neill, Currie, Flanagan, Micklewhite (Burke), Stainrod, Gregory.
Referee: C. White.
Hoddle's penalty makes it seven wins in seven for celebrating Spurs.

Wembley, 21 May 1983   100,000
Manchester United (0) 2 *(Stapleton, Wilkins)*
Brighton & Hove Albion (1) 2 *(Smith, Stevens)*
Manchester United: Bailey; Duxbury, Albiston, Wilkins, McQueen, Moran, Robson, Muhren, Stapleton, Whiteside, Davies.
Brighton & Hove Albion: Moseley; Ramsey (Ryan), Stevens, Gatting, Pearce, Smillie, Case, Grealish, Howlett, Robinson, Smith.
aet.
Referee: A.W. Grey.
Relegated Brighton and Smith misses easy chance in last minute.

Replay: **Wembley, 26 May 1983**   92,000
Manchester United (3) 4 *(Robson 2, Whiteside, Muhren (pen))*
Brighton & Hove Albion (0) 0
Manchester United: Bailey; Duxbury, Albiston, Wilkins, McQueen, Moran, Robson, Muhren, Stapleton, Whiteside, Davies.
Brighton & Hove Albion: Moseley; Gatting, Pearce, Grealish, Foster, Stevens, Case, Howlett, Robinson, Smith, Smillie.
Referee: A.W. Grey.
Whiteside youngest final scorer at 18 years 18 days in one-sided game.

Wembley, 19 May 1984   100,000
Everton (1) 2 *(Sharp, Gray)*
Watford (0) 0
Everton: Southall; Stevens, Bailey, Ratcliffe, Mountfield, Reid, Steven, Heath, Sharp, Gray, Richardson.
Watford: Sherwood; Bardsley, Price (Atkinson), Taylor, Terry, Sinnott, Callaghan, Johnston, Reilly, Jackett, Barnes.
Referee: J. Hunting.
Sharp via post and Gray header out of goalkeeper's hands see off Watford.

Wembley, 18 May 1985   100,000
Manchester United (0) 1 *(Whiteside)*
Everton (0) 0
Manchester United: Bailey; Gidman, Albiston (Duxbury), Whiteside, McGrath, Moran■, Robson, Strachan, Hughes, Stapleton, Olsen.
Everton: Southall; Stevens, Van Den Hauwe, Ratcliffe, Mountfield, Reid, Steven, Gray, Sharp, Bracewell, Sheedy.
aet.
Referee: P. Willis.
Policeman Willis makes Moran first finalist to be sent off. £1m gate.

Wembley, 10 May 1986   98,000
Liverpool (0) 3 *(Rush 2, Johnston)*
Everton (1) 1 *(Lineker)*
Liverpool: Grobbelaar; Lawrenson, Beglin, Nicol, Whelan, Hansen, Dalglish, Johnston, Rush, Molby, MacDonald.
Everton: Mimms; Stevens (Heath), Van Den Hauwe, Ratcliffe, Mountfield, Reid, Steven, Lineker, Sharp, Bracewell, Sheedy.
Referee: A. Robinson.
All-Mersey final and Liverpool with first non-English team.

Wembley, 16 May 1987 98,000
Coventry City (1) 3 *(Bennett, Houchen, Mabbutt (og))*
Tottenham Hotspur (2) 2 *(Allen C, Mabbutt)*
Coventry City: Ogrizovic; Phillips, Downs, McGrath, Kilcline (Rodger), Peake, Bennett, Gynn, Regis, Houchen, Pickering.
Tottenham Hotspur: Clemence; Hughton (Claeson), Thomas, Hodge, Gough, Mabbutt, Allen C, Allen P, Waddle, Hoddle, Ardiles (Stevens).
aet.
Referee: N. Midgley.
In their 104th year, twice in arrears Coventry achieve first major honour.

Wembley, 14 May 1988 98,203
Wimbledon (1) 1 *(Sanchez)*
Liverpool (0) 0
Wimbledon: Beasant; Goodyear, Phelan, Jones, Young, Thorn, Gibson (Scales), Cork (Cunningham), Fashanu, Sanchez, Wise.
Liverpool: Grobbelaar; Gillespie, Ablett, Nicol, Spackman (Molby), Hansen, Beardsley, Aldridge (Johnston), Houghton, Barnes, McMahon.
Referee: B. Hill.
Beasant saves an Aldridge penalty and the fledgling Dons cause a huge upset.

Wembley, 20 May 1989 82,500
Liverpool (1) 3 *(Aldridge, Rush 2)*
Everton (0) 2 *(McCall 2)*
Liverpool: Grobbelaar; Ablett, Staunton (Venison), Nicol, Whelan, Hansen, Beardsley, Aldridge (Rush), Houghton, Barnes, McMahon.
Everton: Southall; McDonald, Van Den Hauwe, Ratcliffe, Watson, Bracewell (McCall), Nevin, Steven, Sharp, Cottee, Sheedy (Wilson).
aet.
Referee: J. Worrall.
Poignant Merseyside final played in the aftermath of the Hillsborough disaster.

Wembley, 12 May 1990 80,000
Manchester United (1) 3 *(Robson, Hughes 2)*
Crystal Palace (1) 3 *(O'Reilly, Wright 2)*
Manchester United: Leighton; Ince, Martin (Blackmore), Bruce, Phelan, Pallister (Robins), Robson, Webb, McClair, Hughes, Wallace.
Crystal Palace: Martyn; Pemberton, Shaw, Gray (Madden), O'Reilly, Thorn, Barber (Wright), Thomas, Bright, Salako, Pardew.
aet.
Referee: A. Gunn.
Palace force a replay against much fancied United in a feast of goalscoring.

Replay: Wembley, 17 May 1990 80,000
Manchester United (0) 1 *(Martin)*
Crystal Palace (0) 0
Manchester United: Sealey; Ince, Martin, Bruce, Phelan, Pallister, Robson, Webb, McClair, Hughes, Wallace.
Crystal Palace: Martyn; Pemberton, Shaw, Gray, O'Reilly, Thorn, Barber (Wright), Thomas, Bright, Salako (Madden), Pardew.
Referee: A. Gunn.
Match-winner Martin's goal was his only one in the entire season.

Wembley, 18 May 1991 80,000
Tottenham Hotspur (0) 2 *(Stewart, Walker (og))*
Nottingham Forest (1) 1 *(Pearce)*
Tottenham Hotspur: Thorstvedt; Edinburgh, Van Den Hauwe, Sedgley, Howells, Mabbutt, Stewart, Gascoigne (Nayim), Samways (Walsh), Lineker, Allen.
Nottingham Forest: Crossley; Charles, Pearce, Walker, Chettle, Keane, Crosby, Parker, Clough, Glover (Laws), Woan (Hodge).
aet.
Referee: R. Milford.
Gascoigne self-inflicted injury and Spurs need extra time own goal to win.

Wembley, 9 May 1992 79,544
Liverpool (0) 2 *(Thomas, Rush)*
Sunderland (0) 0
Liverpool: Grobbelaar; Jones, Burrows, Nicol, Molby, Wright, Saunders, Houghton, Rush, McManaman, Thomas.
Sunderland: Norman; Owers, Ball, Bennett, Rogan, Rush (Hardyman), Bracewell, Davenport, Armstrong, Byrne, Atkinson (Hawke).
Referee: P. Don.
Fourth trophy but winning medals given to wrong team! Rush goal record.

Wembley, 15 May 1993 79,347
Arsenal (1) 1 *(Wright)*
Sheffield Wednesday (0) 1 *(Hirst)*
Arsenal: Seaman; Dixon, Winterburn, Davis, Linighan, Adams, Jensen, Wright (O'Leary), Campbell, Merson, Parlour (Smith).
Sheffield Wednesday: Woods; Nilsson, Worthington, Palmer, Anderson (Hyde), Warhurst, Harkes, Waddle (Bart-Williams), Hirst, Bright, Sheridan.
aet.
Referee: K. Barratt.
Squad numbers and names but the League Cup finalists pushed to replay.

Replay: Wembley, 20 May 1993 62,267
Arsenal (1) 2 *(Wright, Linighan)*
Sheffield Wednesday (0) 1 *(Waddle)*
Arsenal: Seaman; Dixon, Winterburn, Davis, Linighan, Adams, Jensen, Wright (O'Leary), Smith, Merson, Campbell.
Sheffield Wednesday: Woods; Nilsson (Bart-Williams), Worthington, Harkes, Palmer, Warhurst, Wilson (Hyde), Waddle, Hirst, Bright, Sheridan.
aet.
Referee: K. Barratt.
Penalty shoot-out avoided only by Linighan header 44 seconds from time.

Wembley, 14 May 1994 79,634
Manchester United (0) 4 *(Cantona 2 (2 pens), Hughes, McClair)*
Chelsea (0) 0
Manchester United: Schmeichel; Parker, Irwin (Sharpe), Bruce, Kanchelskis (McClair), Pallister, Cantona, Ince, Keane, Hughes, Giggs.
Chelsea: Kharine; Clarke, Sinclair, Kjeldbjerg, Johnsen, Burley (Hoddle), Spencer, Newton, Stein (Cascarino), Peacock, Wise.
Referee: D. Elleray.
United on the double again; Chelsea in contention for an hour.

Wembley, 20 May 1995 79,592
Everton (1) 1 *(Rideout)*
Manchester United (0) 0
Everton: Southall; Jackson, Ablett, Parkinson, Watson, Unsworth, Limpar (Amokachi), Horne, Stuart, Rideout (Ferguson), Hinchcliffe.
Manchester United: Schmeichel; Neville G, Irwin, Bruce (Giggs), Sharpe (Scholes), Pallister, Keane, Ince, McClair, Hughes, Butt.
Referee: G. Ashby.
It's the Littlewoods Pools Cup; Everton win after Stuart strikes the crossbar.

Wembley, 11 May 1996 79,007
Manchester United (0) 1 *(Cantona)*
Liverpool (0) 0
Manchester United: Schmeichel; Irwin, Neville P, May, Keane, Pallister, Cantona, Beckham (Neville G), Cole (Scholes), Butt, Giggs.
Liverpool: James; McAteer, Jones (Thomas), Scales, Wright, Babb, McManaman, Redknapp, Collymore (Rush), Barnes, Fowler.
Referee: D. Gallagher.
Liverpool lose a disappointing match to a classic from the edge of the area.

Wembley, 17 May 1997   79,160
Chelsea (1) 2 *(Di Matteo, Newton)*
Middlesbrough (0) 0
Chelsea: Grodas; Petrescu, Minto, Sinclair, Leboeuf,
Clarke, Zola (Vialli), Di Matteo, Newton, Hughes M,
Wise.
Middlesbrough: Roberts; Blackmore, Fleming, Stamp,
Pearson, Festa, Emerson, Mustoe (Vickers), Ravanelli
(Beck), Juninho, Hignett (Kinder).
Referee: S. Lodge.
*Middlesbrough already relegated and on the back foot
after 42 seconds goal.*

Wembley, 16 May 1998   79,183
Arsenal (0) 2 *(Overmars, Anelka)*
Newcastle U (0) 0
Arsenal: Seaman; Dixon, Winterburn, Vieira, Keown,
Adams, Parlour, Anelka, Petit, Wreh (Platt), Overmars.
Newcastle U: Given; Pistone, Pearce (Andersson), Batty,
Dabizas, Howey, Lee, Barton (Watson), Shearer,
Ketsbaia (Barnes), Speed.
Referee: P. Durkin.
*Arsenal, League title secured, achieve their second League
and Cup double.*

Wembley, 22 May 1999   79,101
Manchester U (1) 2 *(Sheringham 11, Scholes 53)*
Newcastle U (0) 0
Manchester U: Schmeichel; Neville G, Neville P, May,
Keane (Sheringham), Johnsen, Beckham, Scholes
(Stam), Cole (Yorke), Solskjaer, Giggs.
Newcastle U: Harper; Griffin, Domi, Dabizas, Charvet,
Solano (Maric), Lee, Hamann (Ferguson), Shearer,
Ketsbaia (Glass), Speed.
Referee: P. Jones (Loughborough).
*Manchester United on way to an historic treble home plus
European, win a one-sided affair.*

Wembley, 20 May 2000   78,217
Chelsea (0) 1 *(Di Matteo 72)*
Aston Villa (0) 0
Chelsea: De Goey; Melchiot, Babayaro, Deschamps,
Leboeuf, Desailly, Poyet, Di Matteo, Weah (Flo), Zola
(Morris), Wise.
Aston Villa: James; Delaney, Wright (Hendric),
Southgate, Ehiogu, Barry, Taylor (Stone), Boateng,
Dublin, Carbone (Joachim), Merson.
Referee: G. Poll (Tring).
*After a poor first half the game decided by a 73rd minute
goalkeeping error.*

Millennium Stadium, 12 May 2001   74,200
Liverpool (0) 2 *(Owen 83, 88)*
Arsenal (0) 1 *(Ljungberg 72)*
Liverpool: Westerveld; Babbel, Carragher, Hamann
(McAllister), Henchoz, Hyypia, Murphy (Berger),
Gerrard, Heskey, Owen, Smicer (Fowler).
Arsenal: Seaman; Dixon (Bergkamp), Cole, Vieira,
Keown, Adams, Pires, Grimandi, Wiltord (Parlour),
Henry, Ljungberg (Kanu).
Referee: S. Dunn (Bristol).
*First final played outside of England, Liverpool gain
second of three trophies.*

Millennium Stadium, 4 May 2002   73,963
Arsenal (0) 2 *(Parlour 70, Ljungberg 80)*
Chelsea (0) 0
Arsenal: Seaman; Lauren, Cole, Vieira, Campbell,
Adams, Wiltord (Keown), Parlour, Henry (Kanu),
Bergkamp (Edu), Ljungberg.
Chelsea: Cudicini; Melchiot (Zenden), Babayaro (Terry),
Petit, Gallas, Desailly, Gronkjaer, Lampard, Hasselbaink
(Zola), Gudjohnsen, Le Saux.
Referee: M. Riley (Leeds).
*For double Gunners, Ljungberg first to score in straight
finals for 40 years.*

Millennium Stadium, 17 May 2003   73,726
Arsenal (1) 1 *(Pires 38)*
Southampton (0) 0
Arsenal: Seaman; Lauren, Cole, Silva, Luzhny, Keown,
Ljungberg, Parlour, Henry, Bergkamp (Wiltord), Pires.

Southampton: Niemi (Jones); Baird (Fernandez), Bridge,
Marsden, Lundekvam, Svensson M, Telfer, Oakley,
Beattie, Ormerod, Svensson A (Tessem).
Referee: G. Barber (Hertfordshire).
*Goalkeeper substitute for the first time and Seaman even
captains Arsenal.*

Millennium Stadium, 22 May 2004   72,350
Manchester U (1) 3 *(Ronaldo 42, Van Nistelrooy 64
(pen), 80)*
Millwall (0) 0
Manchester U: Howard (Carroll); Neville G, O'Shea,
Brown, Keane, Silvestre, Ronaldo (Solskjaer), Fletcher
(Butt), Van Nistelrooy, Scholes, Giggs.
Millwall: Marshall; Elliott, Ryan (Cogan), Cahill,
Lawrence, Ward, Ifill, Wise (Weston), Harris
(McCammon), Livermore, Sweeney.
Referee: J. Winter (Stockton).
*First non-Premier team and Weston 17 years 119 days is
youngest ever.*

Millennium Stadium, 21 May 2005   71,896
Arsenal (0) 0
Manchester U (0) 0
Arsenal: Lehmann; Lauren, Cole, Vieira, Toure,
Senderos, Fabregas (Van Persie), Silva, Reyes■,
Bergkamp (Ljungberg), Pires (Edu).
Manchester U: Carroll; Brown, O'Shea (Fortune),
Ferdinand, Keane, Silvestre, Fletcher (Giggs), Scholes,
Van Nistelrooy, Rooney, Ronaldo.
*aet; Arsenal won 5-4 on penalties: Van Nistelrooy scored;
Lauren scored; Scholes saved; Ljungberg scored; Ronaldo
scored; Van Persie scored; Rooney scored; Cole scored;
Keane scored; Vieira scored.*
Referee: R. Styles (Waterlooville).
*First Final unhappily decided on penalties; Reyes sent off
in extra time.*

Millennium Stadium, 13 May 2006   74,000
Liverpool (1) 3 *(Cisse 32, Gerrard 54, 90)*
West Ham U (2) 3 *(Carragher 21 (og), Ashton 28,
Konchesky 64)*
Liverpool: Reina; Finnan, Riise, Xabi Alonso
(Kromkamp), Carragher, Hyypia, Sissoko, Gerrard,
Crouch (Hamann), Cisse, Kewell (Morientes).
West Ham U: Hislop; Scaloni, Konchesky, Gabbidon,
Ferdinand, Fletcher (Dailly), Benayoun, Reo-Coker,
Harewood, Ashton (Zamora), Etherington
(Sheringham).
*aet; Liverpool won 3-1 on penalties: Hamann scored;
Zamora saved; Hyypia saved; Sheringham scored;
Gerrard scored; Konchesky saved; Riise scored;
Ferdinand saved.*
Referee: A. Wiley (Staffordshire).
*Excellent contest, Gerrard rescuing Liverpool with a
lightning strike.*

Wembley, 19 May 2007   89,826
Chelsea (0) 1 *(Drogba 116)*
Manchester U (0) 0
Chelsea: Cech; Paulo Ferreira, Bridge, Makelele, Terry,
Essien, Wright-Phillips (Kalou), Lampard, Drogba,
Mikel, Cole J (Robben) (Cole A).
Manchester U: Van der Sar; Brown, Heinze, Carrick
(O'Shea), Ferdinand, Vidic, Ronaldo, Scholes, Rooney,
Fletcher (Smith), Giggs (Solskjaer).
aet.
Referee: S. Bennett (Kent).
*Eighth in-a-row final with at least one London club;
defence dominated.*

Wembley, 17 May 2008   89,874
Portsmouth (1) 1 *(Kanu 37)*
Cardiff C (0) 0
Portsmouth: James; Johnson, Hreidarsson, Diarra,
Campbell, Distin, Utaka (Nugent), Pedro Mendes
(Diop), Kranjcar, Kanu (Baros), Muntari.
Cardiff C: Enckelman; McNaughton, Capaldi, Rae
(Sinclair), Johnson, Loovens, Ledley, McPhail,
Hasselbaink (Thompson), Whittingham (Ramsey), Parry.
Referee: M. Dean (Wirral).
*Portsmouth gifted by goalkeeping error – shades of 1927
for Cardiff.*

Wembley, 30 May 2009   89,391
Chelsea (1) 2 *(Drogba 21, Lampard 72)*
Everton (1) 1 *(Saha 1)*
Chelsea: Cech; Bosingwa, Cole A, Mikel, Terry, Alex, Essien (Ballack), Lampard, Anelka, Drogba, Malouda.
Everton: Howard; Hibbert (Jacobsen), Baines, Yobo, Lescott, Neville, Osman (Gosling), Fellani, Saha (Vaughan), Cahill, Pienaar.
Referee: H. Webb (South Yorkshire).
Fastest FA Cup final goal for Everton's Louis Saha after 25 seconds not enough as Chelsea win the cup for 5th time.

Wembley, 15 May 2010   88,335
Chelsea (0) 1 *(Drogba 59)*
Portsmouth (0) 0
Chelsea: Cech; Ivanovic, Cole A, Ballack (Belletti), Terry, Alex, Kalou (Cole J), Lampard, Anelka (Sturridge), Drogba, Malouda.
Portsmouth: James; Finnan, Mullins (Belhadj), Boateng (Utaka), Ricardo Rocha, Mokoena, Brown, Diop (Kanu), Piquionne, Dindane, O'Hara.
Referee: C. Foy (Merseyside).
Chelsea complete their first domestic double. First final in which both clubs miss penalties.

Wembley, 14 May 2011   88,643
Manchester C (0) 1 *(Toure Y 74)*
Stoke C (0) 0
Manchester C: Hart; Richards, Kolarov, De Jong, Lescott, Kompany, Barry (Johnson A), Toure Y, Balotelli, Tevez (Zabaleta), Silva (Vieira).
Stoke C: Sorensen; Wilkinson, Wilson, Huth, Shawcross, Whelan (Pugh), Pennant, Delap (Carew), Jones, Walters, Etherington (Whitehead).
Referee: M. Atkinson (West Yorkshire).
City end 35-year major trophy drought, successful winners for the 5th time. Stoke's first FA Cup final appearance.

Wembley, 5 May 2012   89,102
Chelsea (1) 2 *(Ramires 11, Drogba 52)*
Liverpool (0) 1 *(Carroll 64)*
Chelsea: Cech; Bosingwa, Cole, Mikel, Terry, Ivanovic, Ramires (Raul Meireles), Lampard, Kalou, Drogba, Mata (Malouda).
Liverpool: Reina; Johnson, Jose Enrique, Spearing (Carroll), Agger, Skrtel, Henderson, Gerrard, Suarez, Bellamy (Kuyt), Downing.
Referee: P. Dowd (Staffordshire).
Chelsea claim fourth final victory in six years with Drogba's strike his fourth in FA Cup finals.

Wembley, 11 May 2013   86,254
Wigan Ath (0) 1 *(Watson B 90)*
Manchester C (0) 0
Wigan Ath: (442) Robles; Boyce, Scharner, Alcaraz, Espinoza; McCarthy, McArthur, Gomez (Watson B 81), McManaman; Kone, Maloney.
Manchester C: (442) Hart; Zabaleta■, Kompany, Nastasic, Clichy; Silva, Toure Y, Barry (Dzeko 90), Nasri (Milner 54); Aguero, Tevez (Rodwell 69).
Referee: Andre Marriner (West Midlands).
Pablo Zabaletta third player to be sent off in the final only minutes before Wigan's injury-time winner. City manager Mancini paid with his job two days later. Wigan failed to avoid relegation.

Wembley, 17 May 2014   89,345
Arsenal (1) 3 *(Cazorla 17, Koscielny 71, Ramsey 109)*
Hull C (2) 2 *(Chester 4, Davies 9)*
Arsenal: (4231) Fabianski; Sagna, Mertesacker, Koscielny, Gibbs; Arteta, Ramsey; Cazorla (Wilshere 106), Ozil (Rosicky 106), Podolski (Sanogo 61); Giroud.
Hull C: (3511) McGregor; Chester, Bruce (McShane 67), Davies; Elmohamady, Livermore, Huddlestone, Meyler, Rosenior (Boyd 102); Quinn (Aluko 75); Fryatt.
aet.
Referee: Lee Probert (Wiltshire).
Joint-record 11th FA Cup victory for the Gunners after being two goals down after only 9 minutes.

Wembley, 30 May 2015   89,283
Arsenal (1) 4 *(Walcott 40, Sanchez 50, Mertesacker 62, Giroud 90)*
Aston Villa (0) 0
Arsenal: (4231) Szczesny; Bellerin, Mertesacker, Koscielny, Monreal; Coquelin, Cazorla; Ramsey, Ozil (Wilshere 77), Sanchez (Oxlade-Chamberlain 90); Walcott (Giroud 77).
Aston Villa: (433) Given; Hutton, Okore, Vlaar, Richardson (Bacuna 68); Cleverley, Westwood (Sanchez 71), Delph; N'Zogbia (Agbonlahor 53), Benteke, Grealish.
Referee: Jon Moss (West Yorkshire).
Arsene Wenger became first post-war manager to win the FA Cup six times. Gunners lift the trophy for record-breaking 12th time.

Per Mertesacker heads Arsenal's third goal in the 2015 FA Cup final. (Alastair Grant/AP/Press Association Images)

FA CUP ATTENDANCES 1969–2015

	1st Round	2nd Round	3rd Round	4th Round	5th Round	6th Round	Semi-finals & Final	Total	No. of matches	Average per match
1969–70	345,229	195,102	925,930	651,374	319,893	198,537	390,700	3,026,765	170	17,805
1970–71	329,687	230,942	956,683	757,852	360,687	304,937	279,644	3,220,432	162	19,879
1971–72	277,726	236,127	986,094	711,399	486,378	230,292	248,546	3,158,562	160	19,741
1972–73	259,432	169,114	938,741	735,825	357,386	241,934	226,543	2,928,975	160	18,306
1973–74	214,236	125,295	840,142	747,909	346,012	233,307	273,051	2,779,952	167	16,646
1974–75	283,956	170,466	914,994	646,434	393,323	268,361	291,369	2,968,903	172	17,261
1975–76	255,533	178,099	867,880	573,843	471,925	206,851	205,810	2,759,941	161	17,142
1976–77	379,230	192,159	942,523	631,265	373,330	205,379	258,216	2,982,102	174	17,139
1977–78	258,248	178,930	881,406	540,164	400,751	137,059	198,020	2,594,578	160	16,216
1978–79	243,773	185,343	880,345	537,748	243,683	263,213	249,897	2,604,002	166	15,687
1979–80	267,121	204,759	804,701	507,725	364,039	157,530	355,541	2,661,416	163	16,328
1980–81	246,824	194,502	832,578	534,402	320,530	288,714	339,250	2,756,800	169	16,312
1981–82	236,220	127,300	513,185	356,987	203,334	124,308	279,621	1,840,955	160	11,506
1982–83	191,312	150,046	670,503	452,688	260,069	193,845	291,162	2,209,625	154	14,348
1983–84	192,276	151,647	625,965	417,298	181,832	185,382	187,000	1,941,400	166	11,695
1984–85	174,604	137,078	616,229	320,772	269,232	148,690	242,754	1,909,359	157	12,162
1985–86	171,142	130,034	486,838	495,526	311,833	184,262	192,316	1,971,951	168	11,738
1986–87	209,290	146,761	593,520	349,342	263,550	119,396	195,533	1,877,400	165	11,378
1987–88	204,411	104,561	720,121	443,133	281,461	119,313	177,585	2,050,585	155	13,229
1988–89	212,775	121,326	690,199	421,255	206,781	176,629	167,353	1,966,318	164	12,173
1989–90	209,542	133,483	683,047	412,483	351,423	123,065	277,420	2,190,463	170	12,885
1990–91	194,195	121,450	594,592	530,279	276,112	124,826	196,434	2,038,518	162	12,583
1991–92	231,940	117,078	586,014	372,576	270,537	155,603	201,592	1,935,340	160	12,095
1992–93	241,968	174,702	612,494	377,211	198,379	149,675	293,241	2,047,670	161	12,718
1993–94	190,683	118,031	691,064	430,234	172,196	134,705	228,233	1,965,146	159	12,359
1994–95	219,511	125,629	640,017	438,596	257,650	159,787	174,059	2,015,249	161	12,517
1995–96	185,538	115,669	748,997	391,218	274,055	174,142	156,500	2,046,199	167	12,252
1996–97	209,521	122,324	651,139	402,293	199,873	67,035	191,813	1,843,998	151	12,211
1997–98	204,803	130,261	629,127	455,557	341,290	192,651	172,007	2,125,696	165	12,883
1998–99	191,954	132,341	609,486	431,613	359,398	181,005	202,150	2,107,947	155	13,599
1999–2000	181,485	127,728	514,030	374,795	182,511	105,443	214,921	1,700,913	158	10,765
2000–01	171,689	122,061	577,204	398,241	256,899	100,663	177,778	1,804,535	151	11,951
2001–02	198,369	119,781	566,284	330,434	249,190	173,757	171,278	1,809,093	148	12,224
2002–03	189,905	104,103	577,494	404,599	242,483	156,244	175,498	1,850,326	150	12,336
2003–04	162,738	117,967	624,732	347,964	292,521	156,780	167,401	1,870,103	149	12,551
2004–05	161,197	98,702	602,152	477,472	339,082	127,914	193,233	1,999,752	146	13,697
2005–06	188,876	107,456	654,570	388,339	286,225	163,449	177,723	1,966,638	160	12,291
2006–07	168,884	113,924	708,628	478,924	340,612	230,064	177,810	2,218,846	158	14,043
2007–08	175,195	99,528	704,300	356,404	276,903	142,780	256,210	2,011,320	152	13,232
2008–09	161,526	96,923	631,070	529,585	297,364	149,566	264,635	2,131,669	163	13,078
2009–10	147,078	100,476	613,113	335,426	288,604	144,918	254,806	1,884,421	151	12,480
2010–11	169,259	101,291	637,202	390,524	284,311	164,092	250,256	1,996,935	150	13,313
2011–12	155,858	92,267	640,700	391,214	250,666	194,971	262,064	1,987,740	151	13,164
2012–13	135,642	115,965	645,676	373,892	288,509	221,216	234,210	2,015,110	156	12,917
2013–14	144,709	75,903	668,242	346,706	254,084	156,630	243,350	1,889,624	149	12,682
2014–15	156,621	111,434	609,368	515,229	208,908	233,341	258,780	2,093,681	153	13,684

THE FA CUP 2014–15
PRELIMINARY AND QUALIFYING ROUNDS

EXTRA PRELIMINARY ROUND

Whickham v Bacup & Rossendale Bor	5-0
Guisborough T v Armthorpe Welfare	1-1, 2-2
aet; Armthorpe Welfare won 3-2 on penalties.	
Seaham Red Star v Liversedge	2-1
Jarrow Roofing Boldon CA v Eccleshill U	4-1
Bridlington T v Whitley Bay	1-1, 1-0
North Shields v Pontefract Collieries	1-0
Silsden v Consett	0-2
Shildon v Crook T	7-0
Billingham Synthonia v Durham C	1-2
Thackley v Albion Sports	1-2
Holker Old Boys v Ashington	2-2, 0-3
Northallerton T v Colne	3-0
Hebburn T v West Allotment Celtic	2-2, 0-2
Glasshoughton Welfare v Knaresborough T	1-2
Pickering T v Washington	0-6
Newton Aycliffe v Garforth T	1-2
Bishop Auckland v Sunderland RCA	1-1, 2-0
Nelson v West Auckland T	1-2
Newcastle Benfield v Penrith	2-1
Marske U v Billingham T	7-1
Tadcaster Alb v Barnoldswick T	5-0
Morpeth T v Dunston UTS	0-2
Cammell Laird v West Didsbury & Chorlton	
Walkover for West Didsbury & Chorlton – Cammell Laird removed.	
Nostell MW v Stockport Sports	1-2
Parkgate v Congleton T	1-3
1874 Northwich v Maine Road	2-1
Glossop North End v AFC Blackpool	3-0
St Helens T v Atherton Collieries	2-5
Rochdale T v Runcorn Linnets	0-6
Bootle v Runcorn T	0-1
AFC Liverpool v Squires Gate	0-3
Barton T Old Boys v Abbey Hey	7-0
AFC Emley v Ashton Ath	2-1
Alsager T v Winterton Rangers	2-3
Wigan Robin Park v Maltby Main	1-2
Winsford U v Athersley Recreation	0-1
Rocester v Stafford T	1-1, 1-2
Walsall Wood v Heath Hayes	1-0
Blaby & Whetstone Ath v Harborough T	2-2, 6-1
Heather St Johns v Coventry Sphinx	0-2
Kirby Muxloe v Wolverhampton Casuals	3-0
Stourport Swifts v Lye T	2-0
Causeway U v Cradley T	4-1
Bolehall Swifts v Dudley T	1-2
St Andrews v Tipton T	2-2, 1-2
Bromsgrove Sporting v Bewdley T	2-0
Boldmere St Michaels v Desborough T	4-3
Shawbury U v Continental Star	2-1
Ellistown & Ibstock U v Studley	2-0
Black Country Rangers v Lichfield C	1-3
AFC Wulfrunians v Alvechurch	3-2
Coleshill T v Nuneaton Griff	10-0
Sporting Khalsa v Pegasus Juniors	0-0, 2-1
Wellington v Ellesmere Rangers	2-1
Atherstone T v Brocton	1-1, 1-2
Gornal Ath v Westfields	1-2
Heanor T v Long Eaton U	1-0
Shirebrook T v Loughborough University	2-2, 1-2
Quorn v Bottesford T	3-1
Cleethorpes T v Borrowash Vic	4-1
Shepshed Dynamo v Dunkirk	1-1, 2-2
aet; Shepshed Dynamo won 3-0 on penalties.	
Clipstone v Harrowby U	2-0
Holwell Sports v Graham St Prims	3-0
Thurnby Nirvana v Lincoln Moorlands Railway	5-1
Arnold T v Basford U	1-4
Retford U v Stapenhill	2-2, 3-1
Handsworth Parramore v Oadby T	5-1
Staveley MW v Worksop T	2-0
Peterborough Northern Star v Team Bury	3-0
Mildenhall T v Gorleston	3-0
Kirkley & Pakefield v Ely C	3-0
Boston T v Walsham Le Willows	1-1, 3-1
Norwich U v Deeping Rangers	1-0
Great Yarmouth T v Huntingdon T	1-0

Sleaford T v Wisbech T	1-3
Thetford T v Swaffham T	1-0
Newmarket T v Fakenham T	1-1, 1-0
Yaxley v Godmanchester R	0-3
Diss T v Holbeach U	1-5
Clapton v Bowers & Pitsea	1-1, 3-3
aet; Bowers & Pitsea won 4-3 on penalties.	
Colney Heath v Southend Manor	3-2
Halstead T v St Margaretsbury	0-0, 2-6
First attempt at replay abandoned after 45 minutes due to floodlight failure, 0-1.	
Brantham Ath v Codicote	1-1, 0-5
FC Romania v Haverhill R	0-0, 3-0
Stansted v Ipswich W	0-2
Takeley v London Tigers	2-2, 0-4
Whitton U v Eton Manor	2-0
London Colney v Woodbridge T	6-0
Wivenhoe T v Enfield 1893	3-0
Sporting Bengal U v FC Clacton	1-2
Waltham Forest v Hoddesdon T	1-2
Ilford v Saffron Walden T	1-2
Tower Hamlets v Felixstowe & Walton U	0-1
Haverhill Bor v Barking	1-0
Basildon U v Stanway R	3-2
Hadleigh U v Sawbridgeworth T	3-2
Cockfosters v Hullbridge Sports	5-4
Haringey Bor v Hertford T	0-3
Welwyn Garden C v Hadley	1-1, 2-1
Hatfield T v Baldock T	0-3
Sileby Rangers v Hillingdon Bor	3-0
Tring Ath v Holmer Green	3-4
Staines Lammas v Bedfont Sports	3-2
Harefield U v Crawley Green	2-1
Cogenhoe U v Wembley	1-1, 3-1
Northampton Spencer v AFC Kempston R	0-2
Ashford T (Middlesex) v Berkhamsted	3-1
Wellingborough T v Bedfont & Feltham	2-4
Long Buckby v Hanworth Villa	1-1, 0-4
AFC Dunstable v Ampthill T	2-0
Bedford v Kings Langley	2-3
AFC Rushden & Diamonds v Oxhey Jets	5-1
Stotfold v Biggleswade U	1-3
Leverstock Green v Newport Pagnell T	2-1
Hartley Wintney v Frimley Green	2-1
First match abandoned after 45 minutes, 1-2.	
Kidlington v Newbury	3-0
Cove v Thame U	0-1
Fairford T v Knaphill	1-3
Brimscombe & Thrupp v Windsor	1-2
Ardley U v Ash U	5-1
Holyport v Abingdon U	2-2, 0-4
Slimbridge v Thatcham T	1-1, 2-1
Reading T v Shrivenham	0-1
Cheltenham Saracens v Camberley T	1-0
Flackwell Heath v Bracknell T	4-0
Chertsey T v Milton U	1-1, 1-1
aet; Milton U won 4-1 on penalties.	
Ascot U v Tadley Calleva	1-1, 4-2
Badshot Lea v Binfield	3-0
Farnham T v Highmoor Ibis	1-4
Pagham v Woodstock Sports	2-0
Erith T v St Francis Rangers	1-2
Horsham YMCA v Alton T	3-2
Sevenoaks T v East Preston	1-2
Ringmer v Corinthian	2-1
Guildford C v Ashford U	0-2
Chichester C v Mole Valley SCR	2-3
Deal T v Phoenix Sports	2-2, 3-3
aet; Deal T won 9-7 on penalties.	
Molesey v Haywards Heath T	11-0
Westfield v Horley T	3-2
Dorking W v Crowborough Ath	0-0, 7-0
Colliers Wood U v Lordswood	0-1
Holmesdale v Tunbridge Wells	4-1
Chessington & Hook U v Worthing U	1-0
Canterbury C v Lingfield	2-1
Greenwich Bor v Lancing	2-1
Arundel v Croydon	0-1
Shoreham v Crawley Down Gatwick	1-1, 3-1

Epsom Ath v Littlehampton T	2-5
Eastbourne U v Hailsham T	5-2
Erith & Belvedere v AFC Croydon Ath	2-0
Hassocks v Epsom & Ewell	1-3
Beckenham T v Eastbourne T	1-3
Selsey v Fisher	0-3
Cray Valley (PM) v Raynes Park Vale	1-3
Newport (IW) v Hamworthy U	2-0
Whitchurch U v Hallen	1-1, 1-2
Winterbourne U v Hythe & Dibden	3-2
Bemerton Heath Harlequins v Totton & Eling	1-0
Bridport v Highworth T	2-3
Longwell Green Sports v Melksham T	1-1, 1-0
Bitton v Blackfield & Langley	1-2
Pewsey Vale v Sherborne T	0-1
Folland Sports v Downton	5-1
Alresford T v Christchurch	1-1, 3-1
Bournemouth v Verwood T	4-2
AFC Portchester v Fawley	2-1
Cadbury Heath v Cribbs	3-4
Brockenhurst v Wootton Bassett T	0-3
Bradford T v Moneyfields	4-3
Gillingham T v Almondsbury UWE	4-1
Corsham T v Horndean	2-3
Petersfield T v Bristol Manor Farm	2-3
Romsey T v Fareham T	1-3
Lymington T v Winchester C	2-5
Cowes Sports v Team Solent	1-0
Hengrove Ath v Bodmin T	0-1
Barnstaple T v Witheridge	0-1
Saltash U v Welton R	2-1
AFC St Austell v Bishop Sutton	5-0
Willand R v Radstock T	3-1
Brislington v Street	2-2, 2-1

aet; 0-0 at the end of normal time.

Shepton Mallet v Ilfracombe T	

Walkover for Shepton Mallet – Ilfracombe T removed.

Torpoint Ath v Odd Down	2-4
Plymouth Parkway v Buckland Ath	4-1

PRELIMINARY ROUND

Newcastle Benfield v Kendal T	0-0, 4-0
Dunston UTS v Durham C	3-0
West Auckland T v Darlington 1883	1-1, 1-3
Garforth T v Harrogate Railway Ath	1-2
Knaresborough T v West Allotment Celtic	0-1
Tadcaster Alb v Spennymoor T	0-2
Consett v Whickham	2-0
Bishop Auckland v Jarrow Roofing Boldon CA	4-4, 4-3

aet; 3-3 at the end of normal time.

Albion Sports v Ashington	1-2
Washington v Lancaster C	0-7
Bridlington T v Northallerton T	3-0
Padiham v Shildon	0-1
Armthorpe Welfare v Marske U	1-4
Clitheroe v Seaham Red Star	3-2
Scarborough Ath v North Shields	1-1, 4-4

aet; Scarborough Ath won 4-2 on penalties.

New Mills v Squires Gate	2-3
Stockport Sports v Ossett T	1-5
Northwich Vic v AFC Emley	4-0
Winterton Rangers v Ossett Alb	0-3
Farsley v Athersley Recreation	4-1
Stocksbridge Park Steels v Bamber Bridge	0-2
Warrington T v Barton T Old Boys	4-1
Runcorn T v Goole	1-1, 1-0
West Didsbury & Chorlton v Brighouse T	0-3
Burscough v Mossley	1-1, 2-1

aet; 1-1 at the end of normal time.

1874 Northwich v Prescot Cables	3-3, 1-2
Congleton T v Salford C	0-0, 3-6

aet; 3-3 at the end of normal time.

Radcliffe Bor v Atherton Colleries	2-2, 2-2

aet; Radcliffe Bor won 3-2 on penalties.

Droylsden v Runcorn Linnets	4-0
Maltby Main v Glossop North End	0-7
Sporting Khalsa v Tipton T	0-1
Newcastle T v Chasetown	1-1, 1-2
Walsall Wood v Stafford Rangers	0-3
AFC Wulfrunians v Boldmere St Michaels	1-2
Shawbury U v Tividale	3-3, 2-5
Leek T v Lichfield C	5-1
Sutton Coldfield T v Brocton	3-3, 1-0

aet; 0-0 at the end of normal time.

Coleshill T v Bromsgrove Sporting	2-2, 3-2

aet; 1-1 at the end of normal time.

Dudley T v Market Drayton T	0-6
Stafford T v Norton U	1-4
Westfields v Rugby T	0-2
Coventry Sphinx v Bedworth U	0-0, 1-3

aet; 1-1 at the end of normal time.

Blaby & Whetstone Ath v Stratford T	1-0
Evesham U v Kidsgrove Ath	3-1
Wellington v Stourport Swifts	2-3
Romulus v Causeway U	3-1
Ellistown & Ibstock U v Kirby Muxloe	1-0
Lincoln U v Brigg T	4-0
Rainworth MW v Staveley MW	0-3
Spalding U v Heanor T	1-0
Basford U v Sheffield	3-3, 1-2

aet; 1-1 at the end of normal time.

Mickleover Sports v Thurnby Nirvana	3-1
Gresley v Cleethorpes T	0-0, 4-5

aet; 3-3 at the end of normal time.

Clipstone v Loughborough University	2-1
Loughborough Dynamo v Coalville T	0-2
Carlton T v Handsworth Parramore	2-1
Shepshed Dynamo v Quorn	2-0
Retford U v Holwell Sports	1-3
Dereham T v St Ives T	2-2, 3-3

aet; Dereham T won 3-0 on penalties.

Needham Market v Soham T Rangers	1-0
Peterborough Northern Star v Mildenhall T	0-2
Godmanchester R v Newmarket T	2-3
Thetford T v Norwich U	0-3
Holbeach U v Boston T	2-4
Wisbech T v Kirkley & Pakefield	2-1
Wroxham v Great Yarmouth T	4-1
Royston T v Brightlingsea Regent	2-3
Cheshunt v Thurrock	0-1
Baldock T v Harlow T	0-3
Barkingside v Wivenhoe T	5-0
Brentwood T v Potters Bar T	1-0
Ware v Felixstowe & Walton U	0-3
London Tigers v FC Clacton	2-0
Ipswich W v Hoddesdon T	2-1
Burnham Ramblers v Hadleigh U	1-3
Redbridge v AFC Sudbury	1-1, 2-3

aet; 2-2 at the end of normal time.

FC Romania v Heybridge Swifts	2-1
Maldon & Tiptree v London Colney	1-2
Aveley v Basildon U	2-0
Codicote v Tilbury	1-1, 0-2
Bowers & Pitsea v Colney Heath	1-0
Whitton U v Haverhill Bor	0-2
Waltham Abbey v Cockfosters	6-3
Hertford T v Great Wakering R	3-2
St Margaretsbury v Romford	0-4
Saffron Walden T v Welwyn Garden C	1-1, 0-1

aet; 0-0 at the end of normal time.

Harefield U v Leverstock Green	1-2
AFC Rushden & Diamonds v Bedford T	1-1, 3-0
Hanworth Villa v North Greenford U	1-1, 1-2
Staines Lammas v Barton R	1-8
Northwood v Kings Langley	1-1, 3-1

aet; 1-1 at the end of normal time.

Aylesbury U v Aylesbury	2-3
AFC Kempston R v Sileby Rangers	4-0

Tie awarded to Sileby Rangers – Kempston R removed.

Cogenhoe v Kettering T	1-4
Bedfont & Feltham v Leighton T	3-2
AFC Hayes v Holmer Green	1-1, 4-0
AFC Dunstable v Uxbridge	2-3
Hanwell T v Biggleswade U	1-2
Ashford T (Middlesex) v Daventry T	1-1, 1-2
Knaphill v Badshot Lea	2-1
Milton U v Marlow	2-1
Shrivenham v Shortwood U	1-6
Thame U v Highmoor Ibis	3-2
North Leigh v Flackwell Heath	1-2
Beaconsfield SYCOB v Didcot T	5-1
Ardley U v Hartley Wintney	1-1, 0-0

aet; Ardley U won 5-4 on penalties.

Windsor v Godalming T	0-2
Slimbridge v Chalfont St Peter	0-1
Wantage T v Kidlington	3-2
Cheltenham Saracens v Fleet T	1-3
Bishop's Cleeve v Ascot U	1-0
Abingdon U v Egham T	1-0
Chatham T v Whyteleafe	1-2
Greenwich Bor v St Francis Rangers	5-2

Lordswood v Hythe T	2-2, 0-2
Faversham T v Westfield	2-1
Worthing v Guernsey	2-0
Cray W v Molesey	3-1
East Preston v Holmesdale	2-1
Burgess Hill T v Eastbourne T	1-0
Ashford U v Chipstead	0-1
Redhill v Horsham YMCA	0-0, 2-0
Epsom & Ewell v Croydon	1-1, 1-4
Mole Valley SCR v Carshalton Ath	1-5
Sittingbourne v Dorking W	0-3
Walton & Hersham v Herne Bay	1-2
Littlehampton T v Shoreham	4-2
Eastbourne U v Hastings U	2-3
Deal T v Chessington & Hook U	1-1, 1-2
Walton Casuals v Whitstable T	1-1, 1-3
Tooting & Mitcham U v Three Bridges	0-0, 4-1
Erith & Belvedere v Folkestone Invicta	2-2, 1-3
aet; 1-1 at the end of normal time.	
Fisher v Ramsgate	2-4
East Grinstead T v Raynes Park Vale	2-2, 1-2
aet; 1-1 at the end of normal time.	
South Park v Thamesmead T	2-1
Ringmer v Merstham	0-4
Canterbury C v Pagham	0-2
Horsham v Corinthian Casuals	1-0
Bashley v Winchester C	0-2
Alresford T v Sherborne T	2-2, 0-4
Cowes Sports v Yate T	0-1
Fareham T v Longwell Green Sports	0-3
Cinderford T v Horndean	1-2
Swindon Supermarine v Hallen	1-0
Bradford T v Wootton Bassett T	2-1
AFC Totton v Gillingham T	2-0
Sholing v Bristol Manor Farm	3-1
Newport (IW) v Winterbourne U	5-2
Bemerton Heath Harlequins v Bournemouth	0-0, 3-2
Mangotsfield U v Cribbs	4-1
Blackfield & Langley v Highworth T	4-0
AFC Portchester v Folland Sports	1-4
Taunton T v Clevedon T	4-1
Merthyr T v Larkhall Ath	0-1
Bodmin T v Witheridge	4-1
Tiverton T v Plymouth Parkway	1-0
Odd Down v Willand R	0-2
Wimborne T v AFC St Austell	3-2
Shepton Mallet v Saltash U	0-0, 0-1
Bridgwater T v Brislington	1-0

FIRST QUALIFYING ROUND

Marske U v Dunston UTS	2-2, 0-2
West Allotment Celtic v Lancaster C	0-5
Darlington 1883 v Blyth Spartans	0-0, 0-3
Newcastle Benfield v Bridlington T	3-1
Ashington v Scarborough Ath	2-2, 0-1
Shildon v Whitby T	1-1, 2-1
Workington v Consett	2-0
Harrogate Railway Ath v Clitheroe	3-1
Bishop Auckland v Spennymoor T	2-3
Ossett Alb v Droylsden	0-4
Salford C v Nantwich T	2-0
Brighouse T v Ashton U	1-2
Northwich Vic v Glossop North End	0-0, 2-2
aet; Glossop North End won 4-2 on penalties.	
FC United of Manchester v Prescot Cables	4-1
Buxton v Ramsbottom U	3-2
Bamber Bridge v Squires Gate	2-2, 3-2
aet; 2-2 at the end of normal time.	
Farsley v Frickley Ath	2-1
Runcorn v Witton Alb	5-3
Marine v Ossett T	2-1
Burscough v Curzon Ashton	0-1
Skelmersdale U v Radcliffe Bor	4-3
Warrington T v Trafford	1-0
Rugby T v Chasetown	1-1, 3-1
aet; 1-1 at the end of normal time.	
Evesham U v Redditch U	0-0, 1-0
Market Drayton T v Stourbridge	1-3
Boldmere St Michaels v Bedworth U	0-3
Halesowen T v Sutton Coldfield T	3-0
Coleshill T v Barwell	1-2
Blaby & Whetstone Ath v Tipton T	4-1
Rushall Olympic v Romulus	3-2
Ellistown & Ibstock U v Hereford U	3-2
Stafford Rangers v Tividale	0-0, 0-4

Corby T v Norton U	3-3, 1-2
Leek T v Stourport Swifts	2-1
Lincoln U v Stamford	2-3
Mickleover Sports v Staveley MW	3-0
Matlock T v Ilkeston	1-2
Sheffield v Shepshed Dynamo	3-2
Spalding U v Holwell Sports	4-0
Belper T v Coalville T	3-3, 0-2
Cleethorpes T v Carlton T	3-2
Grantham T v Clipstone	4-1
Mildenhall T v Wroxham	1-3
St Neots T v Dereham T	1-1, 1-1
aet; Dereham T won 4-2 on penalties.	
Newmarket T v Histon	0-3
King's Lynn T v Boston T	7-0
Cambridge C v Needham Market	2-4
Norwich U v Wisbech T	1-0
Romford v Bury T	1-0
Billericay T v Hadleigh U	4-0
Hertford T v Canvey Island	1-4
Haverhill Bor v Leiston	0-2
Tilbury v Aveley	0-4
AFC Hornchurch v East Thurrock U	1-1, 2-2
aet; East Thurrock U won 4-3 on penalties.	
London Tigers v Brightlingsea Regent	1-0
Waltham Abbey v Barkingside	3-1
AFC Sudbury v FC Romania	1-3
Bowers & Pitsea v Witham T	0-4
Brentwood T v London Colney	1-0
Wingate & Finchley v Ipswich W	2-2, 4-3
Thurrock v Welwyn Garden C	2-0
Grays Ath v Harlow T	2-2, 4-2
Enfield T v Felixstowe & Walton U	5-0
Barton R v Northwood	1-1, 3-2
Aylesbury v Kettering T	1-2
Bedfont & Feltham v Uxbridge	0-6
Biggleswade U v Leverstock Green	1-2
AFC Hayes v Harrow Bor	2-3
Hitchin T v Daventry T	2-1
Sileby Rangers v North Greenford U	1-3
Biggleswade T v Arlesey T	2-1
Dunstable T v Chesham U	2-2, 2-1
Hendon v AFC Rushden & Diamonds	1-0
Abingdon U v Milton U	3-0
Flackwell Heath v Wantage T	3-3, 2-1
aet; 1-1 at the end of normal time.	
Shortwood U v Cirencester T	1-1, 1-0
aet; 0-0 at the end of normal time.	
Knaphill v Fleet T	1-2
Chalfont St Peter v Hungerford T	2-1
Bishop's Cleeve v Banbury U	0-1
Slough T v Ardley U	1-2
Thame U v Burnham	1-2
Godalming T v Beaconsfield SYCOB	0-0, 1-2
Leatherhead v Faversham T	1-2
Hythe T v Whitstable T	4-0
Ramsgate v Raynes Park Vale	1-2
Horsham v Kingstonian	0-4
Peacehaven & Telscombe v East Preston	0-0, 0-2
Redhill v Carshalton Ath	1-0
Dorking W v Pagham	4-2
South Park v Metropolitan Police	2-2, 0-3
Dulwich Hamlet v Worthing	0-3
Whyteleafe v Hastings U	1-2
Folkestone Invicta v Margate	0-0, 1-3
Tonbridge Angels v Herne Bay	6-0
Croydon v Burgess Hill T	2-3
Greenwich Bor v Chessington & Hook U	1-0
Cray W v Tooting & Mitcham U	1-2
Merstham v Chipstead	2-2, 4-3
aet; 2-2 at the end of normal time.	
Maidstone U v Littlehampton T	10-0
VCD Ath v Hampton & Richmond Bor	3-2
Bognor Regis T v Lewes	0-0, 0-1
Blackfield & Langley v Sherborne T	3-2
Horndean v Newport (IW)	0-1
Yate T v Dorchester T	1-2
Winchester C v Bemerton Heath Harlequins	3-0
Sholing v Chippenham T	0-1
Mangotsfield U v Weymouth	0-3
Poole T v Bradford T	4-0
Longwell Green Sports v Folland Sports	0-1
AFC Totton v Swindon Supermarine	0-2
Bodmin T v Bridgwater T	3-3, 1-2
Paulton R v Taunton T	3-1
Tiverton T v Bideford	0-0, 0-1

Frome T v Wimborne T	2-0
Truro C v Larkhall Ath	0-2
Willand R v Saltash U	2-1

SECOND QUALIFYING ROUND

Bradford (Park Avenue) v AFC Fylde	2-2, 1-2
aet; 0-0 at the end of normal time.	
Curzon Ashton v Scarborough Ath	1-0
Droylsden v Guiseley	0-1
Barrow v Runcorn T	0-1
Workington v Bamber Bridge	0-1
Harrogate T v Stockport Co	1-2
Warrington T v Sheffield	0-0, 3-1
Shildon v Stalybridge Celtic	1-0
Colwyn Bay v Harrogate Railway Ath	3-2
Buxton v Newcastle Benfield	2-0
Hyde v Marine	4-5
Skelmersdale U v Blyth Spartans	1-4
Gainsborough Trinity v Farsley	4-1
Ashton U v Salford C	1-1, 1-0
Chorley v Glossop North End	1-0
FC United Of Manchester v Lancaster C	0-1
Cleethorpes T v North Ferriby U	1-2
Dunston UTS v Spennymoor T	1-4
Norton U v Spalding U	2-1
Bedworth U v Mickleover Sports	1-1, 0-3
Worcester C v Rugby T	3-1
Ellistown & Ibstock U v Halesowen T	1-7
Histon v Evesham U	0-0, 1-3
Boston U v Dereham T	3-1
Barwell v Norwich U	0-0, 2-0
Ilkeston v Solihull Moors	1-0
Blaby & Whetstone Ath v Stourbridge	1-1, 1-4
Leamington v Wroxham	4-1
Coalville T v Lowestoft T	0-0, 0-5
Tamworth v Rushall Olympic	2-1
Stamford v Grantham T	1-2
King's Lynn T v Hednesford T	1-0
Tividale v Leek T	2-2, 0-1
Redhill v Tonbridge Angels	2-1
VCD Ath v Harrow Bor	0-4
Ebbsfleet U v Hythe T	7-1
Needham Market v London Tigers	5-2
Hendon v Leiston	4-1
Hemel Hempstead T v Dunstable T	2-0
Hitchin T v Wingate & Finchley	0-3
Chelmsford C v Worthing	6-0
Dorking W v Biggleswade T	2-2, 0-1
Staines T v Leverstock Green	5-0
Bromley v Uxbridge	5-1
Maidstone U v Brentwood T	2-1
Bishop's Stortford v Tooting & Mitcham U	0-0, 1-3
Eastbourne Bor v Enfield T	1-1, 4-4
aet; Eastbourne Bor won 4-3 on penalties.	
Hayes & Yeading U v St Albans C	0-1
Boreham Wood v East Preston	3-2
Brackley T v Farnborough	2-2, 1-0
Witham T v Lewes	4-2
Margate v Barton R	1-2
Whitehawk v Merstham	2-1
FC Romania v Sutton U	2-3
Burnham v Canvey Island	0-1
Billericay T v Raynes Park Vale	2-1
Grays Ath v Hastings U	1-0
Maidenhead U v Faversham T	4-0
Thurrock v Aveley	0-2
Fleet T v Burgess Hill T	0-4
Wealdstone v Concord Rangers	1-1, 0-2
Waltham Abbey v North Greenford U	1-0
Kettering T v Chalfont St Peter	0-1
Beaconsfield SYCOB v Greenwich Bor	1-3
Romford v Kingstonian	0-0, 3-5
aet; 2-2 at the end of normal time.	
Metropolitan Police v East Thurrock U	3-4
Winchester C v Newport (IW)	3-3, 1-0
Paulton R v Gloucester C	1-1, 1-2
Folland Sports v Frome T	1-1, 0-1
Bridgwater T v Basingstoke T	0-2
Larkhall Ath v Gosport Bor	3-3, 0-7
Havant & Waterlooville v Swindon Supermarine	3-0
Weston-super-Mare v Banbury U	3-0
Blackfield & Langley v Willand R	0-0, 0-1
Abingdon U v Dorchester T	0-2
Shortwood U v Oxford C	2-1
Bath C v Poole T	1-1, 2-0

Weymouth v Bideford	4-1
Chippenham T v Ardley U	1-0
Flackwell Heath v Salisbury C	
Walkover for Flackwell Heath – Salisbury C removed.	

THIRD QUALIFYING ROUND

North Ferriby U v Grantham T	2-1
Tamworth v Lowestoft T	1-0
Leamington v Worcester C	1-1, 0-2
Guiseley v Halesowen T	3-0
Runcorn T v Norton U	2-5
Shildon v Stourbridge	0-0, 2-0
AFC Fylde v Buxton	1-0
Mickleover Sports v Blyth Spartans	1-2
Stockport Co v Ilkeston	1-0
Barwell v Curzon Ashton	2-1
Colwyn Bay v Warrington T	1-1, 0-1
Leek T v Boston U	2-0
Bamber Bridge v Chorley	1-4
King's Lynn T v Lancaster C	3-2
Gainsborough Trinity v Marine	4-0
Spennymoor T v Ashton U	1-0
Grays Ath v Bromley	0-0, 0-5
Dorchester T v Hendon	1-0
Barton R v Canvey Island	0-1
Frome T v Boreham Wood	2-2, 0-1
Biggleswade T v Maidstone U	0-2
Evesham U v Chalfont St Peter	4-1
Staines T v Gloucester C	1-1, 2-3
Chippenham T v Hemel Hempstead T	0-5
Concord Rangers v Winchester C	3-2
Willand R v Aveley	3-2
East Thurrock U v Tooting & Mitcham U	2-1
Billericay T v Weymouth	0-1
Wingate & Finchley v Havant & Waterlooville	0-2
Maidenhead U v Gosport Bor	1-1, 0-3
Needham Market v Witham T	1-2
Kingstonian v Eastbourne Bor	2-3
Flackwell Heath v Weston-super-Mare	1-4
Greenwich Bor v Redhill	1-0
Bath C v Shortwood U	2-2, 3-1
Ebbsfleet U v Basingstoke T	1-2
Harrow Bor v Waltham Abbey	2-1
St Albans C v Brackley T	2-0
Sutton U v Burgess Hill T	1-3
Whitehawk v Chelmsford C	4-4, 1-4

FOURTH QUALIFYING ROUND

Spennymoor T v AFC Telford U	2-2, 0-3
King's Lynn T v AFC Fylde	3-4
Grimsby T v Guiseley	3-0
Norton U v Shildon	1-1, 2-1
Warrington T v North Ferriby U	1-0
Alfreton T v Lincoln C	1-1, 1-5
Macclesfield T v Wrexham	1-1, 2-5
Chorley v FC Halifax T	0-0, 0-5
Barwell v Altrincham	0-3
Leek T v Blyth Spartans	3-4
Stockport Co v Chester FC	2-4
Gateshead v Gainsborough Trinity	4-0
Tamworth v Southport	1-1, 1-1
aet; Southport won 4-2 on penalties.	
Dorchester T v Bristol R	1-7
East Thurrock U v Bath C	7-1
Gloucester C v Forest Green R	1-4
Dartford v Burgess Hill T	3-1
Maidstone U v Welling U	2-1
Willand R v Gosport Bor	1-3
Witham T v Weston-super-Mare	1-2
Eastbourne Bor v Dover Ath	0-0, 0-1
Weymouth v Braintree T	0-0, 3-5
aet; 3-3 at the end of normal time.	
Worcester C v Greenwich Bor	2-1
Canvey Island v Havant & Waterlooville	0-0, 0-3
St Albans C v Concord Rangers	0-1
Basingstoke T v Harrow Bor	1-1, 4-1
aet; 1-1 at the end of normal time.	
Aldershot T v Torquay U	2-0
Kidderminster H v Eastleigh	0-1
Evesham U v Bromley	1-2
Chelmsford C v Barnet	0-0, 1-4
Nuneaton T v Hemel Hempstead T	0-0, 0-2
aet; 0-0 at the end of normal time.	
Woking v Boreham Wood	2-1

THE FA CUP 2014–15
COMPETITION PROPER

■ *Denotes player sent off.*

FIRST ROUND

Friday, 7 November 2014
Warrington T (1) 1 *(Robinson 7)*
Exeter C (0) 0 2400
Warrington T: (352) Wills; McCarten, Robinson, Hardwick; Field, Burke, Mannix, Roberts (Corrigan 88), Doughty (Davies 59); Wharton (Foster 90), Metcalfe.
Exeter C: (433) Pym; Ribeiro (Keohane 67), Butterfield, Oakley, Woodman; Sercombe, Noble (Davies 59), Grimes; Cummins (Nichols 74), Bennett, Wheeler.
Referee: David Coote.

Saturday, 8 November 2014
Barnet (1) 1 *(Akinde 3)*
Wycombe W (1) 3 *(Hayes 34 (pen), Pierre 59, Wood 74)* 2410
Barnet: (442) Stack; Yiadom■, Stephens, N'Gala, Johnson; Villa (Mensah 61), Weston, Togwell■, Cook (Gambin 70); MacDonald (Hunt 46), Akinde.
Wycombe W: (442) Ingram; Scowen, Jombati, Pierre, Jacobson; Bloomfield (Lewis 80), Kretzschmar, Murphy, Wood; McClure (Ephraim 83), Hayes (Cowan-Hall 75).
Referee: Oliver Langford.

Barnsley (2) 5 *(Winnall 40, 42, 74, Hourihane 56, Cole 83)*
Burton Alb (0) 0 5158
Barnsley: (4321) Turnbull; Cranie, Ramage, Nyatanga, Dudgeon; Berry, Bailey, Hourihane; Winnall (Lita 75), Williams (Treacy 61); Trotta (Cole 79).
Burton Alb: (442) Lyness; Edwards, Sharps, Cansdell-Sherriff, McCrory; Bell (Knowles 46), Weir, Palmer, MacDonald (McGurk 67); Akins, Beavon (Harness 59).
Referee: David Webb.

Basingstoke T (0) 1 *(Flood 50)*
AFC Telford U (1) 1 *(McDonald 18)* 1251
Basingstoke T: (451) Moore; Rice, Ray, Gasson, Bird; Dunn, McAuley, Harper, Soares, Brown; Flood.
AFC Telford U: (532) Hedge; Higgins, Byrne, Parry, McDonald, Clancy; Grogan, Cooke (Todd 79), Poku; Smith (Hancock 79), Farrell.
Referee: Richard Martin.

Bromley (1) 3 *(Dennis 1, Ademola 56, Waldren 73)*
Dartford (0) 4 *(Harris 48, Hayes 55, Bradbrook E 65, Bradbrook T 81)* 4105
Bromley: (442) Brown; Holland, Anderson, Fuseini (Pinnock 86), Swaine; McNaughton, Joseph-Dubois (Scannell 78), Waldren, Robertson (Culley 73); Ademola, Dennis.
Dartford: (442) Brown; Bender, Collier, McAuley, Burns; Sweeney, Cornhill, Bradbrook E, Hayes (Noble 90); Harris, Bradbrook T (Crawford 84).
Referee: Steven Rushton.

Bury (1) 3 *(Tutte 16, Cameron 88, Nardiello 90)*
Hemel Hempstead T (1) 1 *(Potton 10)* 2944
Bury: (352) Lainton; Cameron, Mills, McNulty (Thompson 80); Adams, Tutte, Mayor, Etuhu, Kennedy (Hussey 64); Rose, Duffus (Nardiello 46).
Hemel Hempstead T: (442) Walker; Asafu-Adjaye, Johnson (Toomey 46 (Simmonds 57)), Diarra, Connolly; Talbot, Daly, Parkes, Potton (Lowe 66); Hawkins, Thorne.
Referee: Andy Haines.

Cambridge U (0) 1 *(Appiah 80)*
Fleetwood T (0) 0 2870
Cambridge U: (442) Dunn; Tait, Nelson, Coulson, Taylor G; Hughes, Champion, Naylor (Chadwick 54), Dunk (Bird 79); Elliott (Simpson 65), Appiah.
Fleetwood T: (442) Maxwell; McLaughlin, Pond, Jordan, Crainey; Evans (Sarcevic 87), Schumacher, Southern (Proctor■ 61), Hughes J; Dobbie, Hitchcock.
Referee: Gary Sutton.

Cheltenham T (2) 5 *(Harrison 10, 53, 84, Gornell 36, Richards M 72)*
Swindon T (0) 0 3470
Cheltenham T: (352) Carson; Brown T, Elliott, Black; Vaughan, De Vita (Hanks 85), Taylor J, Richards M, Braham-Barrett (Kotwica 90); Harrison, Gornell (Marquis 77).
Swindon T: (352) Foderingham; Stephens (Branco 62), Thompson N■, Turnbull; Byrne, Kasim (Gladwin 81), Luongo, Thompson L, Toffolo; Williams, Obika (Smith M 56).
Referee: Carl Boyeson.

Crewe Alex (0) 0
Sheffield U (0) 0 3222
Crewe Alex: (3511) Garratt; Davis, Dugdale, Guthrie; Baillie, Turton, Grant, Atkinson (Jones 46), Leigh (Inman 80); Cooper (Waters 85); Haber.
Sheffield U: (442) Howard; Alcock, Basham, McEveley, Harris; Flynn (De Girolamo 69), Doyle, Reed, Campbell-Ryce; Murphy, Baxter (Scougall 61).
Referee: Mick Russell.

Dagenham & R (0) 0
Southport (0) 0 1172
Dagenham & R: (451) Cousins; Batt, Saah, Partridge, Green; Chambers, Ogogo (Boucaud 61), Howell (Hemmings 75), Bingham, Porter (Murphy 46); Cureton.
Southport: (442) Raya; Collins, Foster, Connor, Fitzpatrick; Rutherford, Kay, George, Austin; Hattersley, Brodie (Marsden 69).
Referee: Keith Hill.

Dover Ath (1) 1 *(Payne 45)*
Morecambe (0) 0 1609
Dover Ath: (442) Rafferty; Francis (Raggett 90), Essam, Bonner, Orlu; Deverdics (Wynter 86), Kinnear, Taiwo, Sterling; Payne, Murphy (Bellamy 75).
Morecambe: (442) Lumley; Wright, Parrish, Edwards, Wilson; Beeley (Sampson 79), Fleming, Kenyon (Williams 84), Ellison; Mullin, Redshaw (Amond 57).
Referee: Michael Bull.

Eastleigh (1) 2 *(McAllister 9, Strevens 90)*
Lincoln C (0) 1 *(Sam-Yorke 73)* 873
Eastleigh: (352) Flitney; Spence, Reid, Green; Strevens, Reason (Todd 90), Evans, Stanley, McAllister; Constable (Odubade 73), Fleetwood (Wright 84).
Lincoln C: (442) Farman; Miller, Brown, Audel, Newton; Power, Bencherif, Mendy, Robinson (Kabba 88); Burrow (Sam-Yorke 70), Marshall.
Referee: Nick Kinseley.

Gillingham (0) 1 *(Kedwell 81 (pen))*
Bristol C (1) 2 *(Cunningham 40, Emmanuel-Thomas 77)* 2654
Gillingham: (352) Nelson; Legge (McGlashan 46), Egan, Hause; Hoyte (Dickenson 75), Doughty, Loft, Hessenthaler, Martin; Kedwell, McDonald (German 67).
Bristol C: (352) Fielding; Ayling, Flint, El-Abd; Wagstaff (Burns 74), Elliott W, Freeman, Pack, Cunningham; Emmanuel-Thomas (Wilbraham 86), Agard (Bryan 90).
Referee: Pat Miller.

Grimsby T (0) 1 *(Pearson 80)*
Oxford U (2) 3 *(Roberts 35, 42, Rose 51)* 3241
Grimsby T: (442) McKeown; Parslow, Nsiala, Pearson, Thomas; Mackreth, Disley (McLaughlin 59), Clay, Arnold (Neilson 64); Pittman, John-Lewis (Hannah 70).
Oxford U: (442) Clarke; Riley (Meades 75), Mullins, Wright, Holmes-Dennis; O'Dowda (Barnett 85), Whing, Rose, Potter; Roberts (Brown 85), Howard.
Referee: Chris Kavanagh.

Hartlepool U (1) 2 *(Franks 32, 86)*
East Thurrock U (0) 0 2800
Hartlepool U: (442) Flinders; Duckworth, Collins, Jones, Austin; Richards, Featherstone, Walker, Franks; Harewood, Schmeltz (Woods 73).
East Thurrock U: (4411) Hughes; Peddie, Goodacre, Wood, Stephen; Bryant (Sammons 80), Parmenter, Witherspoon (Symons 87), Gilbey (Harris 65); Smith; Higgins.
Referee: Ben Toner.

Luton T (1) 4 *(Guttridge 40, Benson 58, Miller 77, Howells 86)*
Newport Co (0) 2 *(Klukowski 51, O'Connor 64)* 3656
Luton T: (442) Tyler; Harriman, McNulty, Wilkinson, Lacey; Guttridge, Smith J, Doyle, Howells; Cullen (Miller 71), Benson.
Newport Co: (352) Day; Hughes, Jones D, Yakubu; Klukowski, Flynn, Minshull (Jackson 67), Byrne (Loveridge 81), Obeng; Zebroski, O'Connor.
Referee: Christopher Sarginson.

Northampton T (0) 0
Rochdale (0) 0 2790
Northampton T: (352) Duke; Tozer, Cresswell, Collins; Alfei (Carter 46), Byrom (Nicholls 80), Murdoch, D'Ath (Mohamed 16), Newey; Sinclair, Toney.
Rochdale: (41212) Logan C; Bennett, Eastham, Lancashire, Tanser; Rose (Bunney 63 (Andrew 87)); Lund, Hery (Rafferty 59); Dawson; Done, Henderson■.
Referee: Kevin Johnson.

Oldham Ath (1) 1 *(Jones 38)*
Leyton Orient (0) 0 3034
Oldham Ath: (41212) Rachubka; Wilson B, Wilson J, Kusunga, Mills; Kelly; Winchester, Jones; Philliskirk; Poleon (Dayton 74), Forte.
Leyton Orient: (442) Woods; Cuthbert, Baudry (Sawyer 82), Clarke, Lowry; Batt (Bartley 57), Wright, Pritchard, Cox; Dagnall, Simpson J.
Referee: Seb Stockbridge.

Peterborough U (1) 2 *(Burgess 42, 90)*
Carlisle U (1) 1 *(Asamoah 8)* 3168
Peterborough U: (442) Alnwick; Smith, Santos, Burgess, Newell; Mendez-Laing (Oztumer 66), Payne, Bostwick, Taylor; Vassell, Washington.
Carlisle U: (451) Hanford; Brown, Anderson, Meppen-Walter, Grainger; Potts, Sweeney (Beck 90), Dicker, Robson (Amoo 75), Dempsey; Asamoah (Kearns 87).
Referee: Scott Mathieson.

Plymouth Arg (1) 2 *(Hartley 28, Morgan 69)*
AFC Fylde (0) 0 5153
Plymouth Arg: (352) McCormick; Nelson, McHugh, Hartley; Mellor (O'Connor 46), Cox, Harvey (Thomas 73), Norburn, Kellett; Reid R (Alessandra 61), Morgan.
AFC Fylde: (451) Hinchliffe; Denson, Langley, Hannigan, Sumner; Barnes M, Hughes, Allen J (Lloyd 66), Rowe (Potts 58), Tomsett (Booth 77); Allen R.
Referee: James Linington.

Port Vale (2) 3 *(Williamson 11, N'Guessan 44, 85)*
Milton Keynes D (2) 4 *(Afobe 31, 59 (pen), Baker C 40, Green 81)* 4120
Port Vale: (442) Neal; Yates (Dodds 80), Duffy, Streete, McGivern; Birchall (Moore 64), Lines, O'Connor, Marshall; Williamson (Daniel 64), N'Guessan.
Milton Keynes D: (4231) Martin; Spence, Flanagan, McFadzean, Lewington; Reeves, Randall; Carruthers (Green 73), Grigg, Baker C; Afobe (Tshimanga 90).
Referee: Charles Breakspear.

Southend U (1) 1 *(Corr 31 (pen))*
Chester FC (1) 2 *(Heneghan 5, Mahon 51)* 4047
Southend U: (442) Bentley; White, Sokolik, Prosser, Binnom-Williams; Worrall (Hurst 60), Leonard, Deegan (Coulthirst 60), Timlin; Corr (Payne 71), Weston.
Chester FC: (4411) Worsnop; Heneghan, Brown, Charnock, Roberts; Mahon (Menagh 86), James, Rooney, Winn (Touray 67); McConville; Hobson.
Referee: Graham Horwood.

Tranmere R (0) 1 *(Power 54 (pen))*
Bristol R (0) 0 3559
Tranmere R: (352) Fon Williams; Ihiekwe, Holness, Thompson; Donacien, Jennings, Laird, Power, Ridehalgh; Donnelly G■, Richards (Odejayi 64).
Bristol R: (442) Mildenhall; Lockyer, McChrystal (Cunnington 81), Parkes, Brown; Gosling (Della Verde 58), Mansell, Sinclair, Martin (Harrison 68); Brunt, Taylor.
Referee: Darren England.

Walsall (0) 2 *(Bradshaw 56, 90)*
Shrewsbury T (1) 2 *(Ellis 5, Collins 61)* 3546
Walsall: (4231) O'Donnell; Purkiss, Downing, Chambers J, Taylor; Cain, Chambers A; Baxendale (Manset 65), Sawyers (Grimes 81), Forde (Mantom 71); Bradshaw.
Shrewsbury T: (442) Leutwiler (Halstead 71); Gayle, Goldson, Ellis, Knight-Percival; Woods, Lawrence, Grant (Clark 65), Demetriou (Wesolowski 46); Collins, Mangan.
Referee: Darren Deadman.

Yeovil T (1) 1 *(Hiwula 7)*
Crawley T (0) 0 2355
Yeovil T: (451) Steer; Clarke, Nugent, Arthurworrey, Davis; Dawson, Edwards, Foley, Berrett, Leitch-Smith (Gillett 81); Hiwula.
Crawley T: (442) Ashdown; Oyebanjo, Leacock, Walsh, Dickson; Simpson, Smith, Keane, Edwards (Young 61); McLeod, Harrold (Tomlin 62).
Referee: Phil Gibbs.

York C (1) 1 *(Hyde 8)*
AFC Wimbledon (1) 1 *(Frampton 22)* 2085
York C: (442) Ingham; McCoy, McCombe (Zubar 27), Lowe, Ilesanmi; Meikle, Penn, Montrose (Summerfield 75), Coulson; Burton (Fletcher 54), Hyde.
AFC Wimbledon: (442) Shea; Fuller, Barrett, Frampton (Bennett 59), Smith; Francomb, Sutherland, Bulman, Rigg; Azeez (Oakley 76), Akinfenwa (Tubbs 76).
Referee: Mark Brown.

Sunday, 9 November 2014
Blyth Spartans (1) 4 *(Dale 4 (pen), 84, Maguire 61, 88)*
Altrincham (0) 1 *(Perry 72)* 1763
Blyth Spartans: (442) Jeffries; Nicholson (Dixon 49), Hutchinson, Buddle, Watson; Rivers, Turnbull (Hooks 57), Hawkins, Dale; Maguire, Wade (Mullen 76).
Altrincham: (4411) Coburn; Densmore, Havern, Marshall, Leather; Richman, Moult, Williams (Perry 46), Griffin; Lawrie (Wilkinson 80); Reeves.
Referee: Martin Coy.

Braintree T (0) 0
Chesterfield (3) 6 *(Doyle 20, 90, O'Shea 30, Clucas 45, Roberts 53, Clerima 74 (og))* 1206
Braintree T: (451) Hamann; Peters, Sowunmi (Clerima 62), Massey, Habergham; Mulley, Isaac, Davis, Brundle (Strutton 46), Akinola; Marks (Cox 46).
Chesterfield: (4231) Lee; Darikwa, Evatt, Raglan, Jones (Humphreys 78); Morsy, Ryan; O'Shea (Gardner 78), Clucas, Roberts (Boco 78); Doyle.
Referee: Brendan Malone.

Coventry C (0) 1 *(Johnson 81)*
Worcester C (1) 2 *(Geddes 41 (pen), 55)* 8439
Coventry C: (442) Burge■; Willis (McQuoid 58), Martin, Johnson, Haynes; O'Brien, Barton (Tudgay 67), Finch, Maddison; Jackson, Nouble (Allsop 40).
Worcester C: (451) Vaughan; Williams, Hutchison, Thomas, Weir; Nti (Dunkley 75), Deeney, Geddes (Gater 73), Jackson, Murphy; Symons (Wright 52).
Referee: Ross Joyce.

FC Halifax T (1) 1 *(Maynard 3)*
Bradford C (0) 2 *(Stead 50, Morais 53)* 8042
FC Halifax T: (352) Glennon; Ainge, Roberts M, Williams (Smith 54); Roberts K, Pearson, Maynard, Marshall (Jackson 74), McManus; Peniket, Boden.
Bradford C: (4411) Williams; Darby, Davies, Sheehan, Meredith; Morais, Kennedy, Halliday (Clarke 46), Yeates (McArdle 87); Knott (Dolan 90); Stead.
Referee: Andy D'Urso.

Forest Green R (0) 0
Scunthorpe U (1) 2 *(McSheffrey 20, 60)* 1791
Forest Green R: (442) Russell; Bennett, Oshodi, Coles, Kelly; Norwood, Sinclair, Wedgbury (Kamdjo 81), Frear (Jolley 65); Parkin (Hughes 65), Guthrie.
Scunthorpe U: (442) Slocombe; Nolan, Boyce, Llera, Williams M; Adelakun (Myrie-Williams 46), Bishop, Osbourne (McAllister 74), McSheffrey (Kee 71); Madden, Taylor.
Referee: Graham Scott.

Gosport Bor (1) 3 *(Bennett 39, 53, Wort 90)*
Colchester U (4) 6 *(Massey 14, Watt 21, Sears 26 (pen), 78, Gilbey 45, Szmodics 90)* 2013
Gosport Bor: (41212) Ashmore; Forbes, Gerring (Molyneaux 68), Poate, Williams; Smith; Carter, Wooden; Ramsey (Wilde 46); Bennett, Paterson (Wort 82).
Colchester U: (433) Walker; Clohessy, Okuonghae, Eastman, Gordon; Gilbey (Szmodics 81), Fox, Moncur (Eastmond 60); Massey (Roofe 85), Sears, Watt.
Referee: Lee Collins.

Norton U (0) 0
Gateshead (3) 4 *(Rodman 11, Ramshaw 39, 43, 74)* 1762
Norton U: (442) Roberts; Green, Clarkson (Smith 75), Beaumont, Fogg; Blackhurst, Winkle (Skellern 61), McDonald (Hawthorne 75), Baker; Cropper, Lennon.
Gateshead: (433) Bartlett; Baxter, Curtis, Clark, Anderton; Oster, Turnbull, Pattison (Jones 55); Ramshaw, Wright (Rankine 55), Rodman (Guy 75).
Referee: Lee Swabey.

Notts Co (0) 0
Accrington S (0) 0 3661
Notts Co: (442) Carroll; Dumbuya, Edwards, Mullins (McKenzie 37), Adams; Ismail, Jones (Wroe 77), Noble, Petrasso; Murray (Harrad 69), Thompson G.
Accrington S: (4231) Rose; Winnard, Aldred, Atkinson, Liddle; Procter, Joyce; McCartan (Roddan 86), Windass (Naismith 68), Molyneux (Carver 77); Gray.
Referee: Darren Bond.

Portsmouth (1) 2 *(Wallace 16 (pen), Hollands 81)*
Aldershot T (1) 2 *(Roberts 45, Molesley 68)* 11,095
Portsmouth: (442) Jones; Wynter, Robinson■, Devera, Shorey; Wallace, Atangana (Taylor 72), Hollands, Holmes (Chorley 83); Storey, Westcarr (Close 66).
Aldershot T: (442) Smith; Gibbs, Wilson, Barker, Phillips (Forbes 45); Derry (Hatton 37), Molesley, Oastler, Roberts; Williams, Holman.
Referee: Paul Tierney.

Stevenage (0) 0
Maidstone U (0) 0 2935
Stevenage: (442) Day; Henry, Ashton, Wells, Charles; Whelpdale, McAllister (Walton 60), Barnard, Pett (Beardsley 85); Lee, Adams (Deacon 60).
Maidstone U: (442) Worgan; Coyle (Simpson 89), Miles, Watt, Mills; Bodkin, Parkinson, Rogers, Flisher; Collin (Brown 86), May (Greenhalgh 73).
Referee: Brett Huxtable.

Wrexham (3) 3 *(Ashton 19, York 36, Bishop 43)*
Woking (0) 0 2253
Wrexham: (442) Coughlin; Pearson, Hudson, Smith, Ashton; Durrell (Keates 85), Carrington, Clarke, Hunt; York (Jennings 71), Bishop (Moult 81).
Woking: (442) Cole; Clarke (Newton 54), McNerney, Cestor, Arthur; Lewis, Payne, Jones (Goddard 63), Betsy; Rendell (Taylor 68), Marriott.
Referee: Simon Bennett.

Monday, 10 November 2014

Havant and Waterlooville (0) 0
Preston NE (2) 3 *(Robinson 7, 30, 81 (pen))* 2382
Havant and Waterlooville: (442) Young; Strugnell, Dutton, Harris, Cummings■; Swallow (Ryan 63), Stock■, Donnelly, Huggins; Hooper (Connell 73), Bubb (Mullings 63).
Preston NE: (4141) Jones; Wiseman, Clarke, Huntington, Buchanan; King; Gallagher (Reid 72), Browne, Brownhill (Kilkenny 72), Robinson (Laird 87); Davies K.
Referee: Stephen Martin.

Tuesday, 18 November 2014
Mansfield T (1) 1 *(Glozier 17 (og))*
Concord Rangers (1) 1 *(Chiedozie 18)* 2023
Mansfield T: (352) Studer; Riley, Waterfall, Tafazolli; Marsden, Murray, Bell F (Lambe 73), Clements, Beevers; Rhead (Palmer 58), Bingham.
Concord Rangers: (4411) Vickers; Walker, Lampe, Fry, Glozier; Collins (Ogilvie 72), Woodyard, White, Cawley (Miles 85); Stokes (Gardner 55); Chiedozie.
Referee: Kevin Wright.

Weston-super-Mare (0) 1 *(Monelle 90)*
Doncaster R (3) 4 *(Main 16, 36, Coppinger 45, Wellens 64)* 2949
Weston-super-Mare: (442) Purnell; Jordan, Barnes, Fortune, Brown; McClennan (Teale 80), Mawford, Ash (Monelle 71), Grubb; Cane, Bath (Harris 71).
Doncaster R: (433) Johnstone; Wabara, Butler, McCullough, Stevens; Keegan (De Val Fernandez 71), Wellens, Coppinger (Forrester 70); Robinson, Main, Bennett (Whitehouse 79).
Referee: Tim Robinson.

FIRST ROUND REPLAYS
Tuesday, 18 November 2014
Accrington S (1) 2 *(Joyce 45, Carver 49)*
Notts Co (1) 1 *(Murray 12)* 1026
Accrington S: (4231) Rose; Liddle, Aldred, Atkinson, Winnard; Joyce, Procter; Mingoia, McCartan, Molyneux; Carver (Gray 79).
Notts Co: (442) Carroll; Cranston, McKenzie, Hollis, Thompson C; Adams (Cassidy 57), Wroe (Noble 64), Traore, Petrasso; Thompson G, Murray (Harrad 72).
Referee: Eddie Ilderton.

AFC Telford U (2) 2 *(Parry 11, Gray 33)*
Basingstoke T (0) 1 *(Soares 52)* 1006
AFC Telford U: (532) Hedge; Higgins, Akrigg, Parry, McDonald, Cooke (Todd 62); Grogan■, Poku (Farrell 90), Hancock; Gray (Barnett 62), Smith.
Basingstoke T: (442) Moore; Smart, Ray, Gasson, Bird; Harper, Brown■, Soares, Dunn (Macklin 63); Flood, Williams (Charlick 75).
Referee: Carl Berry.

AFC Wimbledon (0) 3 *(Smith 71, Tubbs 81, 90)*
York C (1) 1 *(Fletcher 5)* 2048
AFC Wimbledon: (442) Shea; Fuller, Bennett, Barrett, Smith; Francomb (Moore 61), Bulman, Sutherland, Rigg (Azeez 61); Tubbs, Akinfenwa.
York C: (442) Ingham; McCoy, Zubar, Lowe, Ilesanmi; Meikle, Penn, Montrose (Platt 78), Coulson; Fletcher (Carson 64), Hyde.
Referee: Peter Bankes.

Rochdale (0) 2 *(Noble-Lazarus 85, Lancashire 90)*
Northampton T (1) 1 *(Toney 4)* 1717
Rochdale: (433) Logan C; Rafferty (Allen 68), Eastham, Lancashire, Rose; Dawson, Lund, Hery (Noble-Lazarus 55); Bennett, Muldoon (Andrew 68), Done.
Northampton T: (433) Archer; Tozer, Collins, Cresswell (Langmead 68), Robertson; Murdoch, Carter, O'Toole (Hackett 78); Toney, Richards, Sinclair (Byrom 72).
Referee: Richard Clark.

Sheffield U (1) 2 *(Flynn 19, 77)*
Crewe Alex (0) 0 5987
Sheffield U: (4411) Howard; Alcock, Basham, McEveley, Harris; Campbell-Ryce (Baxter 69), Reed, Doyle, Flynn; Scougall (Whiteman 88); Murphy (De Girolamo 81).
Crewe Alex: (433) Garratt; Turton, Dugdale, Davis, Guthrie (Leigh 83); Ness, Grant, Atkinson (Jones 71); Inman, Saunders, Cooper (Waters 65).
Referee: Geoff Eltringham.

Shrewsbury T (0) 1 *(Lawrence 53)*
Walsall (0) 0 4222
Shrewsbury T: (442) Leutwiler; Goldson, Grandison, Knight-Percival, Demetriou; Woods, Wesolowski, Lawrence, Grant (Vernon 77); Akpa Akpro, Collins.
Walsall: (4231) O'Donnell; Purkiss, Chambers J, Downing, Taylor; Chambers A■, Cain; Cook, Sawyers (Baxendale 72), Forde (Benning 57); Manset (Grimes 65).
Referee: Gavin Ward.

Southport (0) 2 *(Marsden 50, Hattersley 58 (pen))*
Dagenham & R (0) 0   1472
Southport: (442) Raya; Mitchell, McDonald, Connor, Fitzpatrick; Rutherford, George, Joyce, Austin (Challoner 90); Hattersley, Marsden (Evans 90).
Dagenham & R: (442) Cousins; Batt, Saah, Partridge, Hemmings (Porter 62); Chambers, Labadie, Howell■, Bingham; Cureton (Doidge 82), Murphy (Goldberg 71).
Referee: Scott Duncan.

Wednesday, 19 November 2014
Aldershot T (0) 1 *(Molesley 81)*
Portsmouth (0) 0   5374
Aldershot T: (442) Smith; Gibbs, Wilson, Oastler, Barker (Diallo 37); Molesley, Oyeleke, Forbes, Roberts; Williams, Holman.
Portsmouth: (442) Jones; Wynter, Robinson, Whatmough (Chorley 76), Shorey; Wallace, Atangana, Hollands, Holmes; Taylor (Agyemang 82), Westcarr (Storey 82).
Referee: Stuart Attwell.

Thursday, 20 November 2014
Maidstone U (1) 2 *(Collin 2, 87)*
Stevenage (0) 1 *(Charles 47)*   2226
Maidstone U: (442) Worgan; Simpson, Miles, Coyle, Mills; Bodkin (Greenhalgh 79), Parkinson, Rogers, Flisher; May, Collin (Brown 89).
Stevenage: (4411) Day; Henry, Wells, Charles, Okimo (Dembele 81); Whelpdale, McAllister (Jebb 90), Walton, Deacon (Adams 81); Lee; Barnard.
Referee: Simon Hooper.

Tuesday, 25 November 2014
Concord Rangers (0) 0
Mansfield T (0) 1 *(Palmer 61)*   1537
Concord Rangers: (442) Vickers; Walker, Lampe, Fry, Glozier (Miles 80); Woodyard, White, Cawley (Stokes 75); Collins; Chiedozie, Taaffe (Gardner 71).
Mansfield T: (433) Studer; Marsden, Riley, Tafazolli, Beevers; Heslop, Sendles-White (Bell F 46), Clements; Lambe, Palmer (Rhead 81), Taylor (Bingham 68).
Referee: Andy Davies.

SECOND ROUND

Friday, 5 December 2014
Hartlepool U (1) 1 *(Franks 31)*
Blyth Spartans (0) 2 *(Turnbull 56, Rivers 90)*   3735
Hartlepool U: (433) Flinders; Austin, Lanzoni, Bates, Jones; Walker, Featherstone, Woods; Franks, Harewood, Schmeltz (Compton 75).
Blyth Spartans: (4231) Jeffries; Nicholson, Buddle, Hutchinson, Watson; Hawkins (Mullen 67), Turnbull; Rivers, Wade (Richardson 76), Dale (Wearmouth 90); Maguire.
Referee: Andrew Madley.

Saturday, 6 December 2014
Accrington S (0) 1 *(Aldred 64)*
Yeovil T (1) 1 *(Clarke 30)*   1440
Accrington S: (4231) Rose; Winnard, Atkinson, Aldred, Liddle; Joyce, Procter (Windass 43); Mingoia, McCartan, Naismith (Molyneux 79); Crooks (Carver 75).
Yeovil T: (442) Steer; Clarke, Nugent, Arthurworrey, Smith; Dawson, Edwards, Berrett (Gillett 78), Foley; Leitch-Smith (Nana Ofori-Twumasi 89), Hayter.
Referee: Seb Stockbridge.

Bury (0) 1 *(Nardiello 90)*
Luton T (0) 1 *(Cullen 51)*   2790
Bury: (442) Lainton; Jones, Mills, Cameron, McNulty (Hussey 71); Adams (Lowe 61), Mayor, Soares, Tutte; Rose, Hope (Nardiello 83).
Luton T: (352) Tyler; Franks, McNulty, Wilkinson; Harriman, Smith J, Drury, Doyle, Griffiths (Howells 76); Walker (Miller 59), Cullen.
Referee: Nigel Miller.

Cambridge U (1) 2 *(Chadwick 10, Appiah 90)*
Mansfield T (1) 2 *(Bingham 3, Champion 81 (og))*   3869
Cambridge U: (442) Dunn; Tait, Coulson, Nelson, Taylor G; KaiKai (Blair 53), Champion, Hughes, Chadwick (Donaldson 67); Appiah, Bird (Simpson 75).
Mansfield T: (442) Studer; Sutton, Riley, Tafazolli, Beevers; Lambe, Clements (McGuire 72), Heslop, Taylor; Oliver (Bell F 62), Bingham (Palmer 56).
Referee: Darren Bond.

Milton Keynes D (0) 0
Chesterfield (0) 1 *(Gnanduillet 53)*   5591
Milton Keynes D: (4411) Martin; Spence (Baldock 71), McFadzean (Flanagan 76), Kay, Lewington; Baker C, Potter, Alli, Powell; Grigg (Rasulo 71); Aube.
Chesterfield: (442) Lee; Darikwa, Raglan, Margreitter, Clucas; O'Shea (Boco 64), Morsy, Ryan, Roberts (Hird 87); Gnanduillet (Humphreys 81), Doyle.
Chesterfield fielded an ineligible player. Match replayed on 2 January.
Referee: Keith Stroud.

Oldham Ath (0) 0
Doncaster R (0) 1 *(Elokobi 86 (og))*   3242
Oldham Ath: (4132) Kenny; Wilson B, Kusunga, Elokobi, Mills; Kelly; Winchester (Poleon 69), Philliskirk, Johnson (Morgan-Smith 89); Ibehre, Forte.
Doncaster R: (442) Johnstone; Wabara, McCullough, Butler, Stevens; Coppinger (Furman 67), Keegan, Wellens, Bennett (Forrester 76); Robinson, Main.
Referee: Lee Collins.

Oxford U (0) 2 *(Barnett 59, 64)*
Tranmere R (1) 2 *(Stockton 33, Koumas 76)*   4681
Oxford U: (451) Clarke; Riley, Wright, Mullins, Holmes-Dennis; Hylton, Collins, Rose, Whing, O'Dowda (Potter 84); Barnett.
Tranmere R: (442) Fon Williams; Donacien, Ihiekwe, Holness, Ridehalgh; Jahraldo-Martin (Madjo 66), Holmes (Koumas 73), Jennings; Power; Stockton (Odejayi 72), Fenelon.
Referee: Mark Haywood.

Preston NE (1) 1 *(Huntington 19)*
Shrewsbury T (0) 0   6011
Preston NE: (4231) Stuckmann; Wiseman, Clarke, Huntington, Buchanan; Welsh, Kilkenny (Brownhill 61); Humphrey (Browne 70), Gallagher, Reid (Davies K 61); Beckford.
Shrewsbury T: (352) Leutwiler; Goldson, Grandison (Demetriou 46), Knight-Percival; Passley, Grant, Wesolowski (Clark 16), Woods, Lawrence; Akpa Akpro (Mangan 59), Collins.
Referee: David Webb.

Sheffield U (0) 3 *(Baxter 55 (pen), 62 (pen), McNulty 90)*
Plymouth Arg (0) 0   7348
Sheffield U: (433) Howard; Flynn, Basham, McEveley, Harris; Baxter (Cuvelier 85), Doyle, Scougall (Reed 76); Campbell-Ryce (McNulty 46), Higdon, Murphy.
Plymouth Arg: (433) McCormick; Mellor, Nelson, Hartley, Purrington (Norburn 72); Blizzard (Harvey 80), O'Connor, Kellett; Alessandra, Reid R, Banton (Cox 72).
Referee: Gary Sutton.

Wrexham (1) 3 *(Smith 19, Bishop 57 (pen), 87)*
Maidstone U (0) 1 *(Flisher 63)*   3093
Wrexham: (442) Flatt; White (Pearson 85), Smith, Hudson, Ashton; Carrington, Clarke, Harris (Durrell 90), Jennings; York (Moult 76), Bishop.
Maidstone U: (442) Worgan; Simpson■, Miles, Coyle, Mills; Bodkin (Brown 78), Parkinson, Rogers, Flisher; May (Davies 60), Collin (Lovell 76).
Referee: Scott Mathieson.

Sunday, 7 December 2014
Aldershot T (0) 0
Rochdale (0) 0   3143
Aldershot T: (442) Smith; Gibbs, Oastler, Wilson, Barker; Molesley (Plummer 74), Forbes (Hatton 90), Oyeleke, Roberts; Williams, Holman.

Rochdale: (4231) Logan C; Rose, Lancashire, Eastham, Tanser; Allen, Dawson; Vincenti, Hery (Cywka 71), Henderson; Andrew (Muldoon 74).
Referee: Phil Gibbs.

Barnsley (0) 0
Chester FC (0) 0   7227
Barnsley: (433) Turnbull; Cranie, Ramage (Brown 20), Nyatanga, Dudgeon; Berry, Abbott (Jennings 57), Hourihane; Lita (Treacy 76), Hemmings, Trotta.
Chester FC: (4231) Worsnop; Kay, Brown, Charnock, Roberts; Rooney, James; Heneghan, McConville, Mahon; Hobson.
Referee: Darren Handley.

Bradford C (2) 4 *(Clarke 10, Stead 31, Morais 58, Yeates 59)*
Dartford (0) 1 *(Noble 64)*   5373
Bradford C: (442) Williams; Darby (Routis 60), Davies, McArdle, Meredith; Morais, Liddle, Knott, Yeates; Clarke (Zoko 80), Stead (Hanson 84).
Dartford: (352) Brown; Bradbrook E, McAuley, Mitchel-King; Hayes (Daley 68), Cornhill, Sweeney, Collier (Bender 66), Noble; Harris, Bradbrook T (Tarbuck 71).
Referee: Andy Woolmer.

Bristol C (0) 1 *(Agard 90)*
AFC Telford U (0) 0   6678
Bristol C: (352) Fielding; Ayling, Flint, Williams (Smith K 77); Kane, Pack, Emmanuel-Thomas (Freeman 65), Wagstaff, Cunningham (Bryan 69); Agard, Wilbraham.
AFC Telford U: (3511) Hedge; Akrigg, McDonald, Parry; Higgins, Platt (Gray 90), Poku, Grogan, Todd; Hancock (Cooke 90); Farrell (Smith 81).
Referee: Jeremy Simpson.

Cheltenham T (0) 0
Dover Ath (0) 1 *(Essam 83)*   3552
Cheltenham T: (442) Carson; Deaman, Taylor M, Brown T, Braham-Barrett; Ferdinand, Taylor J, Richards M, De Vita (Kotwica 90); Harrison, Gornell (Williams 88).
Dover Ath: (532) Rafferty; Essam, Bonner, Francis, Orlu, Sterling; Kinnear, Davies (Wynter 40), Deverdics; Murphy, Payne.
Referee: Dean Whitestone.

Colchester U (0) 1 *(Moncur 90)*
Peterborough U (0) 0   2905
Colchester U: (433) Walker; Hewitt, Eastman, Gorkss, Kpekawa; Moncur, Fox, Eastmond; Massey (Healey 81), Sears, Watt (Clohessy 90).
Peterborough U: (41212) Alnwick; Bostwick, Zakuani (Vassell 90), Burgess, Ntlhe; Payne (James 90); Anderson J, Newell; Oztumer; Washington, Mclean.
Referee: Tony Harrington.

Gateshead (1) 2 *(Pattison 8, Wright 90)*
Warrington T (0) 0   2874
Gateshead: (4411) Bartlett; Baxter, Curtis, Clark, Allan (O'Donnell 57); Pattison, Turnbull, Chandler, Rodman; Oster (Wright 76); Ramshaw.
Warrington T: (3511) Wills; McCarten, Robinson, Hardwick (Foster 69); Field, Mannix, Burke, Corrigan, Doughty (Colbeck 58); Metcalfe; Gaskell (Ruane 76).
Referee: James Adcock.

Scunthorpe U (1) 1 *(Madden 35)*
Worcester C (0) 1 *(Nti 46)*   5606
Scunthorpe U: (433) Slocombe; Hawkridge, Davey, Llera, Williams M; McAllister, Bishop, McSheffrey (Myrie-Williams 37 (Adelakun 46)); Madden, Kee (Sparrow 69), Taylor.
Worcester C: (4231) Vaughan; Williams, Hutchison, Thomas, Weir; Deeney, Gater (Jackman 72); Nti, Geddes, Murphy (Dunkley 79); Symons (Wright 69).
Referee: Graham Salisbury.

Southport (1) 2 *(Brodie 45, Evans 71)*
Eastleigh (1) 1 *(Constable 41)*   2169
Southport: (4231) Raya; Collins, Foster, Connor, Fitzpatrick; Kay, George; Rutherford, Austin, Evans (Joyce 86); Brodie.

Eastleigh: (442) Flitney; Evans, Beckwith■, Reid, Green; Reason, Strevens, Stanley (Odubade 82), Collins (Spence 70); Constable, McAllister (Fleetwood 58).
Referee: Geoff Eltringham.

Wycombe W (0) 0
AFC Wimbledon (0) 1 *(Rigg 56)*   3196
Wycombe W: (442) Ingram; Scowen, Jombati, Pierre, Jacobson; Kretzschmar (Ephraim 70), Bloomfield, Murphy, Wood (McClure 83); Hayes, Craig (Amadi-Holloway 66).
AFC Wimbledon: (442) Shea; Fuller, Goodman, Barrett, Kennedy (Harrison 89); Francomb (Pell 77), Moore, Bulman, Rigg (Azeez 77); Tubbs, Akinfenwa.
Referee: Chris Kavanagh.

Friday, 2 January 2015

Milton Keynes D (0) 0
Chesterfield (1) 1 *(Roberts 43)*   8040
Milton Keynes D: (451) Martin; Baldock, Spence, McFadzean, Lewington; Green (Carruthers 60), Randall (Reeves 46), Potter, Bowditch, Powell (Grigg 60); Afobe.
Chesterfield: (442) Lee; Darikwa, Raglan, Morsy, Clucas; Boco, Hird, Humphreys, Roberts; Doyle, Gnanduillet.
Referee: Stephen Martin.

SECOND ROUND REPLAYS

Tuesday, 16 December 2014

Chester FC (0) 0
Barnsley (1) 3 *(Hemmings 16, Jennings 63, 88)*   3534
Chester FC: (4231) Worsnop; Kay, Brown, Charnock, Roberts; James, Rooney; Heneghan (Greenop 67), McConville, Mahon; Hobson (Winn 89).
Barnsley: (433) Turnbull; Holgate, Ramage, Cranie, Brown; Bailey (Digby 89), Berry, Hourihane; Cole (Lita 84), Hemmings, Jennings (Boakye-Yiadom 90).
Referee: Keith Hill.

Luton T (0) 1 *(Rooney 48)*
Bury (0) 0   2923
Luton T: (451) Tyler; Harriman, Franks, Wilkinson, Griffiths; Rooney, Smith J, Drury (Howells 78), Doyle, Whalley (Robinson 84); Cullen (Lafayette 79).
Bury: (352) Jalal; Cameron, O'Brien (Rose 78), McNulty; Soares, Etuhu, Adams, Tutte (Jones 70); Mayor; Lowe, Nardiello (Hope 59).
Referee: Oliver Langford.

Mansfield T (0) 0
Cambridge U (0) 1 *(KaiKai 10)*   1920
Mansfield T: (343) Studer; Sutton, Tafazolli, Waterfall; Beevers (Fletcher 81), Heslop, Clements, Taylor; Palmer (Lambe 55), Oliver (Rhead 70), Bingham.
Cambridge U: (442) Dunn; Tait, Coulson, Miller, Taylor G; Hughes, Champion, Chadwick (Naylor 74), Blair (Bird 58); Appiah, KaiKai (Taylor B 70).
Referee: Carl Boyeson.

Rochdale (1) 4 *(Done 31, 81, 88, Vincenti 75)*
Aldershot T (0) 1 *(Fitchett 73)*   2077
Rochdale: (4141) Logan C; Rafferty, Eastham, Lancashire, Rose; Bennett (Andrew 82); Done, Dawson, Lund (Hery 78), Vincenti; Henderson.
Aldershot T: (442) Smith; Gibbs, Oastler, Wilson, Barker; Molesley (Plummer 79), Roberts, Hatton, Forbes; Holman (Fitchett 66), Williams.
Referee: Mark Brown.

Tranmere R (1) 2 *(Odejayi 36, Power 76)*
Oxford U (1) 1 *(Potter 29)*   3296
Tranmere R: (532) Fon Williams; Holmes (Jahraldo-Martin 66), Donacien, Ihiekwe, Holness, Ridehalgh; Rowe (Fenelon 66), Power, Jennings; Stockton (Laird 75), Odejayi.
Oxford U: (4231) Clarke; Riley, Mullins, Wright, Holmes-Dennis; Ruffels, Rose; Potter, Collins, O'Dowda; Hylton.
Referee: Mick Russell.

Yeovil T (0) 2 *(Gillett 84, Moore 88)*
Accrington S (0) 0 6373
Yeovil T: (4231) Steer; Moloney, Arthurworrey, Nugent, Smith; Foley, Edwards; Nana Ofori-Twumasi, Gillett, Eaves (Leitch-Smith 90); Hayter (Moore 69).
Accrington S: (442) Rose; Winnard, Atkinson, Aldred, Liddle; McCartan, Joyce, Procter, Mingoia (Molyneux 67); Carver (Windass 46), Crooks.
Referee: James Linington.

Wednesday, 17 December 2014
Worcester C (0) 1 *(Geddes 69)*
Scunthorpe U (1) 1 *(Madden 45)* 4339
Worcester C: (4231) Vaughan; Williams, Hutchison, Thomas, Weir; Gater (Jackman 106), Deeney; Nti, Geddes, Murphy (Wright 96); Symons (Dunkley 65).
Scunthorpe U: (451) Slocombe; Davey, Boyce, Llera, Williams M; Madden, Bishop, McAllister (Hawkridge 101), Osbourne (Sparrow 79), McSheffrey (Adelakun 68); Taylor.
aet; Scunthorpe U won 14-13 on penalties.
Referee: Stephen Martin.

THIRD ROUND

Friday, 2 January 2015
Cardiff C (1) 3 *(Ralls 34, Harris 53, Jones 60)*
Colchester U (0) 1 *(Sears 74)* 4194
Cardiff C: (442) Moore; Brayford, Turner, Connolly, John; Harris, Adeyemi, Whittingham (Le Fondre 69); Noone (Da Silva 85); Macheda (Jones 60), Ralls.
Colchester U: (352) Walker; Gorkss, Clohessy, Kpekawa; Eastman, Moncur (Lapslie 64), Szmodics, Fox, Hewitt (Sembie-Ferris 85); Sears, Massey (Watt 62).
Referee: James Linington.

Saturday, 3 January 2015
Barnsley (0) 0
Middlesbrough (0) 2 *(Vossen 48, Ayala 84)* 9473
Barnsley: (442) Turnbull; Holgate, Ramage, Nyatanga, Smith; Berry (Boakye-Yiadom 82), Digby, Hourihane, Jennings; Hemmings (Oates 69), Lita.
Middlesbrough: (4231) Mejias; Williams R (Veljkovic 5), Ayala, Omeruo, Husband; Clayton[■], Whitehead; Tomlin (Leadbitter 80), Vossen, Bamford; Garcia (Reach 66).
Referee: Dean Whitestone.

Blyth Spartans (2) 2 *(Dale 35, 41)*
Birmingham C (0) 3 *(Novak 52, Thomas 55, 58)* 3644
Blyth Spartans: (433) Jeffries; Dixon (Nicholson 90), Hutchinson (Parker 85), Buddle, Watson; Turnbull, Hawkins, Mullen (Richardson 66); Rivers, Maguire, Dale.
Birmingham C: (442) Doyle; Eardley, Edgar, Morrison, Hancox; Novak, Reilly, Moussi, Duffy (Arthur 82); Zigic, Thomas.
Referee: Mike Jones.

Bolton W (0) 1 *(Clough 76)*
Wigan Ath (0) 0 16,788
Bolton W: (442) Bogdan; Vela, Wheater, Dervite, Ream; Trotter, Danns, Pratley, Feeney; Heskey (Davies C 62), Clough (Gudjohnsen 88).
Wigan Ath: (532) Al Habsi; Tavernier (Boyce 64), Perch, Ramis, Kiernan, Taylor; McCann, Watson (Cowie 53), Forshaw; Fortune (Maloney 66), McClean.
Referee: Phil Dowd.

Brentford (0) 0
Brighton & HA (0) 2 *(Dunk 88, O'Grady 90)* 8542
Brentford: (442) Bonham; Odubajo, Dean, Tarkowski, Bidwell; Jota, Diagouraga, Toral (Dallas 78), Judge (Yennaris 88); Gray, Smith (Saunders 62).
Brighton & HA: (433) Stockdale; Calderon, Greer, Dunk, Chicksen; Baldock, Ince, March; Teixeira (Halford 68), Mackail-Smith (O'Grady 67), Holla.
Referee: David Coote.

Cambridge U (1) 2 *(Simpson 27, Donaldson 66)*
Luton T (0) 1 *(Harriman 74)* 7063
Cambridge U: (442) Dunn; Tait, Coulson, Nelson, Taylor G; Chadwick (KaiKai 89), Champion, Hughes, Donaldson (Dunk 79); Simpson, Elliott (Bird 84).
Luton T: (451) Tyler; Connolly (Ruddock 59), Franks, Wilkinson, Howells; Harriman, Smith J, Drury, Stevenson, Miller (Walker 65); Cullen (Lafayette 59).
Referee: Tony Harrington.

Charlton Ath (0) 1 *(Gudmundsson 55)*
Blackburn R (1) 2 *(Taylor C 4, 59)* 8727
Charlton Ath: (442) Etheridge; Wilson, Ben Haim, Bikey, Fox; Gudmundsson (Gomez 84), Buyens[■], Jackson, Cousins; Tucudean (Pigott 89), Church (Ahearne-Grant 63).
Blackburn R: (451) Eastwood; Henley, Duffy, Kilgallon, Taylor C; Marshall, Cairney, Williamson, Dunn (Varney 72), Conway; Brown.
Referee: Keith Stroud.

Derby Co (0) 1 *(Martin 90 (pen))*
Southport (0) 0 20,201
Derby Co: (433) Roos; Shotton (Russell 63), Keogh, Buxton, Naylor; Coutts, Mascarell, Bryson; Dawkins, Best (Martin 63), Ward (Ibe 62).
Southport: (442) Raya; Austin (Bakayoko 82), Collins, Foster, Fitzpatrick; George, Kay, Smith, Rutherford; Joyce, Brodie (Hattersley 70).
Referee: Graham Scott.

Doncaster R (0) 1 *(McCullough 50)*
Bristol C (0) 1 *(Smith M 75)* 5671
Doncaster R: (433) Johnstone; Wabara, McCullough, Butler, Stevens; Keegan, Furman (Tyson 88), Wellens; Coppinger, Robinson (Main 79), Forrester (Bennett 78).
Bristol C: (3511) Fielding; Ayling, Flint, Williams; Little, Elliott W, Smith K (Freeman 89), Kane (Pack 83), Bryan; Emmanuel-Thomas; Smith M.
Referee: Scott Duncan.

Fulham (0) 0
Wolverhampton W (0) 0 11,879
Fulham: (4231) Bettinelli; Grimmer, Bodurov, Hutchinson, Stafylidis; Parker, Fofana; Christensen (Kavanagh 32), Woodrow (Dembele 71), McCormack; Rodallega.
Wolverhampton W: (442) Ikeme; Iorfa, Stearman, Batth, Doherty; Henry, Evans, Price, Edwards; Clarke (Dicko 63), Sako.
Referee: Lee Probert.

Huddersfield T (0) 0
Reading (0) 1 *(Blackman 69)* 7980
Huddersfield T: (442) Smithies; Smith (Lolley 86), Hudson, Wallace (Gerrard 46), Robinson; Hammill (Scannell 66), Coady, Hogg[■], Bunn; Vaughan, Wells.
Reading: (433) Andersen; Gunter, Pearce, Hector, Obita; Guthrie (Samuel 77), Norwood, Williams; Mackie (Blackman 46), Cox (Cooper 90), Robson-Kanu.
Referee: Phil Gibbs.

Leicester C (1) 1 *(Ulloa 39)*
Newcastle U (0) 0 23,212
Leicester C: (442) Hamer; De Laet, Morgan, Moore, Konchesky; Knockaert, Cambiasso (Albrighton 26), James, Lawrence; Ulloa (Wood 59), Nugent (Vardy 70).
Newcastle U: (433) Alnwick; Santon (Satka 59), Williamson, Dummett, Haidara; Tiote, Anita, Vuckic (Roberts 79); Armstrong, Riviere, Cabella.
Referee: Lee Mason.

Millwall (1) 3 *(McDonald 36, Fuller 66, 83)*
Bradford C (1) 3 *(Knott 6, 76, Nelson 70 (og))* 5470
Millwall: (442) Forde; Dunne, Nelson, Shittu, Briggs; Upson (Woolford 89), Abdou, Chaplow (Gueye 81), Martin; McDonald, Fuller.
Bradford C: (41212) Williams; Darby, McArdle, Sheehan, Meredith; Liddle; Morais, Halliday (Kennedy 77); Knott (McBurnie 90); Stead (Zoko 89), Hanson.
Referee: David Webb.

Preston NE (0) 2 *(Gallagher 71, 84)*
Norwich C (0) 0 9807
Preston NE: (433) Stuckmann; Woods, Huntington, Wright, Buchanan; Brownhill (Humphrey 63), King, Browne; Reid (Ebanks-Blake 86), Little (Beckford 63), Gallagher.
Norwich C: (41212) Ruddy; Whittaker, Turner, Bennett R, Miquel (Loza 84); O'Neil; Howson, Redmond; Johnson; Hoolahan (Josh Murphy 71), Hooper (Lafferty 68).
Referee: Stuart Attwell.

Rochdale (1) 1 *(Vincenti 12 (pen))*
Nottingham F (0) 0 6791
Rochdale: (41212) Lillis; Rafferty, Eastham, Lancashire, Tanser; Bennett; Camps (Cywka 83), Logan J (Bunney 70); Allen (Andrew 90); Vincenti, Done.
Nottingham F: (442) De Vries; Lichaj, Hobbs, Wilson, Fox (McLaughlin 74); Burke C (Paterson 89), Tesche, Vaughan, Antonio; Assombalonga, Veldwijk.
Referee: Gary Sutton.

Rotherham U (1) 1 *(Brindley 10)*
Bournemouth (1) 5 *(MacDonald 44, Stanislas 58, Fraser 63, Kermorgant 67, 71)* 5875
Rotherham U: (4312) Collin; Brindley, Morgan, Arnason, James; Green, Smallwood, Frecklington; Pringle (Skarz 63); Bowery, Clarke-Harris (Derbyshire 62).
Bournemouth: (451) Camp; Smith, Cook, Cargill, Harte; Stanislas (Cornick 71), Gosling, MacDonald (Pitman 82), O'Kane, Fraser (Ritchie 88); Kermorgant.
Referee: Neil Swarbrick.

Tranmere R (0) 2 *(Power 70, Stockton 83)*
Swansea C (1) 6 *(Dyer 34, Carroll 49, Barrow 58, Gomis 77, 90, Routledge 85)* 10,007
Tranmere R: (532) Fon Williams; Donacien, Holness, Thompson (Kirby 56), Ihiekwe, Holmes; Power, Jennings, Laird (Rowe 72); Fenelon (Bell-Baggie 72), Stockton.
Swansea C: (4231) Tremmel; Richards, Bartley, Amat, Tiendalli; Fulton (King 71), Carroll; Barrow, Emnes, Dyer (Routledge 78); Gomis.
Referee: Paul Tierney.

WBA (2) 7 *(Berahino 42, 46, 53, 90, Anichebe 45, Brunt 55, Morrison 79)*
Gateshead (0) 0 16,593
WBA: (442) Myhill; Baird, McAuley, Dawson, Pocognoli; Sessegnon (Varela 67), Morrison, Brunt, Dorrans (Samaras 54); Anichebe (Yacob 54), Berahino.
Gateshead: (4411) Bartlett; Baxter, Curtis, Clark, Jones; Pattison (Ramshaw 56), Turnbull, Gjokaj (Chandler 60), Rodman; Oster; Rankine (Wright 68).
Referee: Andrew Madley.

Sunday, 4 January 2015

Arsenal (0) 2 *(Mertesacker 20, Sanchez 82)*
Hull C (0) 0 59,439
Arsenal: (4231) Ospina; Bellerin, Chambers, Mertesacker, Monreal; Rosicky, Coquelin; Walcott (Oxlade-Chamberlain 76), Cazorla, Campbell (Maitland-Niles 90); Sanchez (Akpom 84).
Hull C: (442) Harper; McShane, Maguire, Davies, Figueroa; Ince, Huddlestone, Quinn, Brady; Sagbo (Hernandez 67), Aluko (Elmohamady 62).
Referee: Robert Madley.

Aston Villa (0) 1 *(Benteke 88)*
Blackpool (0) 0 21,837
Aston Villa: (4411) Given; Hutton, Okore, Clark, Cissokho; Cleverley (N'Zogbia 63), Westwood, Sanchez, Grealish (Weimann 75); Cole (Bacuna 90); Benteke.
Blackpool: (41212) Lewis; McMahon, Clarke, O'Dea, Dunne; O'Hara; Waddington (Telford 90), Perkins; Orlandi (Barkhuizen 87); Davies (Miller 63), Delfouneso.
Referee: Chris Foy.

Chelsea (0) 3 *(Willian 58, Remy 70, Zouma 72)*
Watford (0) 0 41,010
Chelsea: (4132) Cech; Azpilicueta, Zouma, Cahill, Luis; Mikel; Ramires, Oscar (Costa 46); Schurrle (Willian 46); Drogba (Ake 80), Remy.

Watford: (442) Bond; Paredes, Hoban, Cathcart, Angella; Munari (Murray 83), Tozser (Abdi 73), Pudil, Ighalo (Vydra 65); Deeney, Forestieri.
Referee: Kevin Friend.

Dover Ath (0) 0
Crystal Palace (2) 4 *(Dann 10, 34, Gayle 68, Doyle 87)* 5645
Dover Ath: (532) Rafferty; Essam, Raggett (Nanetti 57), Bonner, Orlu, Sterling; Bellamy (Wynter 70), Cogan, Deverdics; Murphy (Modeste 82), Payne.
Crystal Palace: (433) Hennessey; Ward, Dann, Delaney, Kelly; Ledley (Mariappa 76), O'Keefe, Bannan; Zaha, Murray (Doyle 46), Gayle (Thomas 73).
Referee: Andre Marriner.

Manchester C (0) 2 *(Milner 66, 90)*
Sheffield W (1) 1 *(Nuhiu 14)* 44,309
Manchester C: (4231) Caballero; Sagna, Boyata, Mangala, Kolarov (Clichy 75); Toure, Fernando; Jesus Navas, Lampard (Silva 61), Milner; Jovetic (Nasri 61).
Sheffield W: (442) Kirkland; Palmer, Lees, Loovens, Dielna (McCabe 85); Maghoma, Semedo, Lee, Helan; May (Lavery 66), Nuhiu (Maguire 75).
Referee: Michael Oliver.

QPR (0) 0
Sheffield U (1) 3 *(McNulty 36, Campbell-Ryce 49, 90)* 12,972
QPR: (442) McCarthy; Onuoha, Caulker (Isla 61), Ferdinand, Traore; Fer, Henry (Vargas 61), Mutch, Phillips; Austin, Hoilett (Zamora 46).
Sheffield U: (4231) Howard; McNulty (Murphy 82), McEveley, Kennedy, Harris; Doyle (Higdon 90), Reed; Flynn, Scougall, Campbell-Ryce; Baxter (Wallace J 90).
Referee: Mark Clattenburg.

Southampton (1) 1 *(Schneiderlin 33)*
Ipswich T (1) 1 *(Ambrose 19)* 31,201
Southampton: (442) Forster; Ward-Prowse, Fonte, Gardos, Bertrand; Davis, Schneiderlin, Wanyama, Tadic (Isgrove 66); Long, Pelle.
Ipswich T: (442) Gerken; Chambers, Smith, Berra, Mings; Hyam, Bru (Sammon 87), Ambrose (Skuse 70), Hunt S (Stewart 63); McGoldrick, Murphy.
Referee: Martin Atkinson.

Stoke C (0) 3 *(Arnautovic 80, Ireland 88, 90)*
Wrexham (0) 1 *(Carrington 73)* 19,423
Stoke C: (4231) Butland; Bardsley, Shawcross, Huth, Wilson; Cameron (Ireland 76), Sidwell (Crouch 62); Arnautovic, Adam, Assaidi; Diouf (Walters 61).
Wrexham: (442) Flatt; Pearson, Smith, Hudson, Ashton; Carrington (Moult 90), Harris, Hunt, Evans (Clarke 82); Jennings, York (Bishop 71).
Referee: Simon Hooper.

Sunderland (1) 1 *(Van Aanholt 33)*
Leeds U (0) 0 30,302
Sunderland: (433) Pantilimon; Vergini, Coates, O'Shea, Van Aanholt; Rodwell (Larsson 37), Bridcutt, Gomez; Giaccherini (Johnson 74), Fletcher, Alvarez (Wickham 46).
Leeds U: (41212) Silvestri; Berardi, Del Fabro, Cooper, Taylor C; Sloth; Austin, Murphy; Adryan (Sharp 62); Antenucci, Montenegro (Doukara 85).
Referee: Mike Dean.

Yeovil T (0) 0
Manchester U (0) 2 *(Ander Herrera 64, Di Maria 90)* 9264
Yeovil T: (4411) Steer; Nana Ofori-Twumasi, Arthurworrey, Nugent, Smith; Dawson (Berrett 88), Foley (Hayter 88), Edwards, Ralph (Eaves 69); Gillett; Moore.
Manchester U: (3412) De Gea; McNair, Smalling, Blackett; Da Silva (Mata 46), Ander Herrera, Fletcher, Shaw (Evans 46); Rooney; Falcao (Di Maria 60), Wilson.
Referee: Craig Pawson.

Monday, 5 January 2015
AFC Wimbledon (1) 1 *(Akinfenwa 36)*
Liverpool (1) 2 *(Gerrard 12, 62)* 4784
AFC Wimbledon: (442) Shea; Fuller, Goodman, Barrett, Kennedy; Francomb (Sutherland 86), Moore (Pell 86), Bulman, Rigg (Azeez 79); Tubbs, Akinfenwa.
Liverpool: (343) Mignolet; Can, Skrtel, Sakho; Manquillo (Jose Enrique 71), Henderson, Lucas, Markovic (Toure 86); Gerrard, Lambert (Balotelli 79), Coutinho.
Referee: Jonathan Moss.

Burnley (0) 1 *(Vokes 73)*
Tottenham H (0) 1 *(Chadli 56)* 9348
Burnley: (4411) Heaton; Trippier, Mee, Keane, Lafferty; Boyd (Wallace 79), Arfield, Kightly, Marney; Ings (Sordell 78); Barnes (Vokes 61).
Tottenham H: (4231) Vorm; Chiriches, Fazio, Vertonghen, Davies; Stambouli (Kane 46), Dembele; Paulinho, Eriksen, Chadli; Soldado (Townsend 68).
Referee: Roger East.

Tuesday, 6 January 2015
Everton (0) 1 *(Lukaku 90)*
West Ham U (0) 1 *(Collins 56)* 22,236
Everton: (4231) Robles; Coleman, Jagielka, Distin (Stones 71), Oviedo; Besic (McGeady 85), Barry; Mirallas (Eto'o 65), Naismith, Barkley; Lukaku.
West Ham U: (4231) Adrian; Jenkinson, Collins, Reid, Cresswell; Noble, Downing; Amalfitano (O'Brien 78), Nolan, Jarvis (Poyet 68); Valencia (Cole C 60).
Referee: Anthony Taylor.

Scunthorpe U (2) 2 *(Davey 18, Taylor 44)*
Chesterfield (0) 2 *(Doyle 71 (pen), O'Shea 85)* 4307
Scunthorpe U: (442) Slocombe; Davey (Canavan 72), Boyce, Llera, Williams M; Adelakun (Nolan 61), Bishop, McAllister, McSheffrey; Madden, Taylor (Wootton K 79).
Chesterfield: (442) Lee; Darikwa, Raglan, Morsy, Clucas; Boco (Gardner 67), Hird, Humphreys (O'Shea 67), Roberts; Gnanduillet, Doyle.
Referee: Mark Haywood.

THIRD ROUND REPLAYS

Tuesday, 13 January 2015
Bristol C (1) 2 *(Emmanuel-Thomas 36, 79)*
Doncaster R (0) 0 6951
Bristol C: (352) Fielding; Williams, Flint, Ayling, Cunningham, Smith K, Pack, Wagstaff (Freeman 76), Little; Smith M (Osborne 88), Emmanuel-Thomas.
Doncaster R: (4141) Marosi; Wabara, McCullough, Butler, Stevens; Keegan (Bennett 78); Coppinger, Wellens, Middleton (Tyson 62), Forrester (Robinson 62); Main.
Referee: Darren Bond.

Chesterfield (0) 2 *(Clucas 105, 116)*
Scunthorpe U (0) 0 6815
Chesterfield: (442) Lee; Darikwa, Hird, Raglan, Clucas; Boco (Jones 91), Morsy, Humphreys (Ryan 82); Roberts; Gnanduillet, Doyle.
Scunthorpe U: (433) Slocombe; Nolan (Sparrow 48), Bishop, Llera, Davey; Boyce, Williams M, Osbourne (Hawkridge 94); Taylor, Madden, McSheffrey (Adelakun 56).
aet.
Referee: Keith Hill.

West Ham U (0) 2 *(Valencia 51, Cole C 113)*
Everton (0) 2 *(Mirallas 82, Lukaku 97)* 25,301
West Ham U: (4231) Adrian; Jenkinson, Collins (Cole C 111), Tomkins, Cresswell; Noble, Song (Nolan 61); Jarvis (Amalfitano 69), Downing, Valencia; Carroll.
Everton: (4231) Robles; Coleman, Stones, Jagielka, Baines; Besic (Mirallas 67), Barry; McGeady*, Barkley (Oviedo 67), Naismith; Lukaku.
aet; West Ham U won 9-8 on penalties.
Referee: Neil Swarbrick.

Wolverhampton W (0) 3 *(Edwards 71, 109, van La Parra 73)*
Fulham (1) 3 *(Woodrow 27, 76, McCormack 120 (pen))* 8148
Wolverhampton W: (4231) Ikeme; Iorfa, Batth, Stearman, Doherty; Price, McDonald; Henry (Edwards 46), Evans, van La Parra; McAlinden (Dicko 46 (Clarke 118)).
Fulham: (4321) Bettinelli; Grimmer, Hutchinson, Bodurov, Stafylidis; Fofana, Parker (Zverotic 106), Kavanagh (Roberts 78); Woodrow, Dembele (Rodallega 78); McCormack.
aet; Fulham won 5-3 on penalties.
Referee: David Coote.

Wednesday, 14 January 2015
Bradford C (3) 4 *(Hanson 8, Stead 17, Halliday 39, Knott 57)*
Millwall (0) 0 11,859
Bradford C: (4312) Williams; Darby, McArdle, Davies, Meredith; Morais, Liddle, Halliday; Knott (Yeates 73); Hanson (Routis 80), Stead (Zoko 69).
Millwall: (352) Forde; Dunne, Shittu, Beevers*; Martin (Gueye 62), Abdou, Chaplow, Upson (Webster 46), Briggs; Gregory, Fuller (Woolford 23).
Referee: James Adcock.

Ipswich T (0) 0
Southampton (1) 1 *(Long 19)* 27,933
Ipswich T: (442) Bialkowski; Chambers, Smith, Berra, Parr; Ambrose (Stewart 82), Hyam, Bru, Hunt S (Mings 55); McGoldrick (Bajner 63), Murphy.
Southampton: (352) Forster; Gardos, Fonte, Bertrand; Clyne, Ward-Prowse, Wanyama (Davis 46), Reed, Targett; Long, Tadic (Pelle 67).
Referee: Graham Scott.

Tottenham H (2) 4 *(Paulinho 10, Capoue 45, Chiriches 49, Rose 52)*
Burnley (2) 2 *(Sordell 3, Wallace 7)* 24,367
Tottenham H: (4231) Vorm; Chiriches (Dier 80), Kaboul, Vertonghen, Davies; Capoue, Stambouli; Townsend (Onomah 76), Paulinho, Rose (Chadli 59); Soldado.
Burnley: (442) Heaton; Trippier (Reid 68), Duff, Keane, Mee; Kightly, Arfield, Jones (Marney 76), Wallace (Boyd 89); Sordell, Vokes.
Referee: Craig Pawson.

FOURTH ROUND

Friday, 23 January 2015
Cambridge U (0) 0
Manchester U (0) 0 7987
Cambridge U: (4231) Dunn; Tait, Nelson, Coulson, Taylor G; Champion, Hughes (Chadwick 76); Donaldson, McGeehan, KaiKai (Dunk 53); Elliott.
Manchester U: (41212) De Gea; Valencia, Jones, Rojo, Blind (Shaw 86); Carrick; Fellaini (Ander Herrera 67), Januzaj; Di Maria; Wilson (van Persie 67), Falcao.
Referee: Chris Foy.

Saturday, 24 January 2015
Birmingham C (1) 1 *(Grounds 45)*
WBA (2) 2 *(Anichebe 25, 35)* 28,438
Birmingham C: (4231) Randolph; Caddis, Morrison, Robinson, Grounds; Davis (Thomas 86), Gleeson; Cotterill, Shinnie, Dyer (Gray 70); Novak (Zigic 75).
WBA: (442) Myhill (Foster 62); Wisdom, McAuley, Dawson, Lescott; Gardner, Brunt, Yacob, Sessegnon (Baird 68); Berahino, Anichebe (Ideye 81).
Referee: Mark Clattenburg.

Blackburn R (1) 3 *(Taylor C 23, Gestede 78, Conway 89)*
Swansea C (1) 1 *(Sigurdsson 21)* 5928
Blackburn R: (4411) Eastwood; Henley, Duffy, Kilgallon, Olsson; Taylor C, Williamson (Dunn 41 (Rhodes 77)), Lowe, Conway; Cairney; King (Gestede 60).
Swansea C: (4231) Fabianski; Rangel, Amat, Bartley*, Tiendalli; Carroll (Fernandez 9), Shelvey; Dyer, Sigurdsson*, Barrow (Montero 62); Gomis (Nelson Oliveira 77).
Referee: Craig Pawson.

Cardiff C (1) 1 *(Jones 25)*
Reading (0) 2 *(Norwood 64, Robson-Kanu 88)*   11,750
Cardiff C: (442) Moore; Da Silva, Morrison, Turner (Connolly 43), Malone; Harris (Macheda 85), Gunnarsson, Whittingham, Noone; Jones, Revell (Adeyemi 71).
Reading: (442) Federici; Gunter (Kelly 35), Pearce, Hector, Obita; McCleary, Norwood (Cooper 89), Chalobah, Williams; Blackman (Robson-Kanu 82), Pogrebnyak.
Referee: Lee Probert.

Chelsea (2) 2 *(Cahill 21, Ramires 38)*
Bradford C (1) 4 *(Stead 41, Morais 75, Halliday 82, Yeates 90)*   41,014
Chelsea: (442) Cech; Christensen, Zouma, Cahill, Azpilicueta; Ramires, Oscar, Mikel (Fabregas 70), Salah (Willian 70); Drogba, Remy (Hazard E 76).
Bradford C: (442) Williams; Darby, McArdle, Davies, Meredith; Knott (Yeates 80), Liddle, Morais (Clarke 89), Halliday (Routis 87); Hanson, Stead.
Referee: Andre Marriner.

Derby Co (1) 2 *(Bent 20, Hughes 82)*
Chesterfield (0) 0   28,392
·*Derby Co:* (352) Roos; Albentosa (Russell 46 (Ward 65)), Keogh, Buxton; Christie, Hendrick, Mascarell, Hughes, Forsyth; Martin (Dawkins 70), Bent.
Chesterfield: (442) Lee; Darikwa, Hird, Raglan, Jones; Clucas, Morsy, Ryan (Banks 75), O'Shea (Gardner 75); Gnanduillet (Dieseruvwe 88), Doyle.
Referee: David Webb.

Liverpool (0) 0
Bolton W (0) 0   43,847
Liverpool: (3421) Mignolet; Johnson, Can, Sakho; Manquillo (Borini 68), Henderson, Allen (Lucas 67), Jose Enrique (Markovic 46); Lallana, Coutinho; Sterling.
Bolton W: (3511) Bogdan; Dervite, Mills (Spearing 73), Ream; Feeney, Danns, Pratley, Vela, Moxey (Wheater 83); Gudjohnsen; Heskey (Wilkinson 56).
Referee: Kevin Friend.

Manchester C (0) 0
Middlesbrough (0) 2 *(Bamford 53, Garcia 90)*   44,836
Manchester C: (4231) Caballero; Zabaleta, Boyata, Kompany, Kolarov; Milner, Fernando (Dzeko 79); Jesus Navas (Lampard 67), Silva, Jovetic (Fernandinho 70); Aguero.
Middlesbrough: (4231) Mejias; Whitehead, Ayala, Gibson, Friend; Clayton, Leadbitter; Bamford (Wildschut 90), Tomlin (Reach 81), Adomah; Vossen (Garcia 87).
Referee: Phil Dowd.

Preston NE (1) 1 *(Gallagher 19)*
Sheffield U (0) 1 *(De Girolamo 68)*   10,770
Preston NE: (4231) Stuckmann; Woods, Clarke, Huntington, Buchanan; Welsh (Davies K 74), Kilkenny (King 62); Humphrey, Gallagher, Reid (Browne 85); Ebanks-Blake.
Sheffield U: (451) Howard; Alcock, McGahey, Kennedy, Davies B (Harris 82); Dimaio (Murphy 56), Basham, De Girolamo (McNulty 78), Reed, Baxter; Higdon.
Referee: Keith Stroud.

Southampton (2) 2 *(Pelle 9, Dann 16 (og))*
Crystal Palace (3) 3 *(Chamakh 11, 39, Sanogo 21)*   31,320
Southampton: (4231) Forster; Clyne, Gardos (Targett 46), Fonte, Bertrand; Cork (Long 59 (Seager 73)), Davis; Ward-Prowse, Elia, Tadic; Pelle.
Crystal Palace: (433) Hennessey; Ward, Dann, Delaney, Kelly; Zaha, Ledley, McArthur; Campbell (Murray 82), Chamakh (Puncheon 65), Sanogo (Mariappa 78).
Referee: Jonathan Moss.

Sunderland (0) 0
Fulham (0) 0   22,961
Sunderland: (352) Mannone; Vergini, O'Shea, Coates; Jones (Buckley 76), Larsson, Bridcutt, Rodwell■, Van Aanholt; Fletcher (Wickham 66), Defoe.
Fulham: (442) Bettinelli; Stafylidis, Hutchinson, Bodurov, Grimmer; Christensen, Dembele (McCormack 61), Tunnicliffe, Fofana (Kacaniklic 75); Ruiz, Woodrow (Rodallega 76).
Referee: Anthony Taylor.

Tottenham H (1) 1 *(Townsend 19 (pen))*
Leicester C (0) 2 *(Ulloa 83, Schlupp 90)*   35,548
Tottenham H: (4231) Vorm; Chiriches, Fazio, Kaboul, Rose; Capoue, Dembele (Kane 87); Townsend (Eriksen 64), Paulinho, Lamela; Soldado (Adebayor 71).
Leicester C: (433) Schwarzer; Simpson, Moore (Wasilewski 26), Morgan, De Laet; King, Drinkwater, Schlupp; Kramaric (Albrighton 73), Ulloa, Vardy (Nugent 72).
Referee: Robert Madley.

Sunday, 25 January 2015
Aston Villa (0) 2 *(Gil 51, Weimann 71)*
Bournemouth (0) 1 *(Wilson 90)*   27,415
Aston Villa: (433) Given; Hutton, Okore, Clark, Richardson; Bacuna (Grealish 90), Gil (Westwood 87), Sanchez; Cleverley, Benteke, Weimann.
Bournemouth: (451) Camp; Smith, Elphick, Cook, Harte (Francis 60); Stanislas (Ritchie 79), MacDonald, O'Kane, Arter, Fraser; Kermorgant (Wilson 60).
Referee: Mike Dean.

Brighton & HA (0) 2 *(O'Grady 50, Baldock 75)*
Arsenal (2) 3 *(Walcott 2, Ozil 24, Rosicky 59)*   30,278
Brighton & HA: (4231) Stockdale; Saltor (March 63), Greer, Dunk, Bennett J; Holla, Ince; Calderon, Forster-Caskey (Adrian Colunga 82), Baldock; O'Grady.
Arsenal: (4141) Szczesny; Chambers, Koscielny, Monreal, Gibbs; Flamini; Walcott (Sanchez 70), Rosicky, Ramsey, Ozil (Coquelin 80); Giroud (Akpom 70).
Referee: Michael Oliver.

Bristol C (0) 0
West Ham U (0) 1 *(Sakho 81)*   12,682
Bristol C: (3412) Fielding; Ayling, Flint, Williams; Little (Wagstaff 75), Saville (Pack 83), Smith K, Bryan; Freeman (Agard 82); Emmanuel-Thomas, Smith M.
West Ham U: (41212) Adrian; Jenkinson, Tomkins, Reid, Cresswell; Song (Amalfitano 57); Noble, Nolan (Demel 88); Downing; Carroll, Valencia (Sakho 57).
Referee: Lee Mason.

Monday, 26 January 2015
Rochdale (0) 1 *(Bennett 78)*
Stoke C (1) 4 *(Krkic 4, Ireland 52, Moses 61, Walters 90)*   7443
Rochdale: (4141) Lillis; Rafferty, Eastham, Lancashire, Tanser; Bennett; Vincenti (Noble-Lazarus 58), Dawson, Camps (Allen 63), Henderson; Done (Andrew 55).
Stoke C: (4231) Butland; Bardsley, Shawcross, Wollscheid, Wilson; Nzonzi (Sidwell 46), Whelan; Arnautovic, Krkic (Ireland 32), Moses (Adam 75); Walters.
Referee: Martin Atkinson.

FOURTH ROUND REPLAYS
Tuesday, 3 February 2015
Fulham (1) 1 *(Rodallega 28)*
Sunderland (0) 3 *(Bettinelli 61 (og), Alvarez 75, Gomez 90 (pen))*   14,777
Fulham: (41212) Bettinelli; Grimmer, Hutchinson, Bodurov, Stafylidis; Tunnicliffe; Fofana (Christensen 83), Kacaniklic (Roberts 83); McCormack; Woodrow, Rodallega.
Sunderland: (41212) Mannone; Reveillere, O'Shea, Vergini, Van Aanholt; Bridcutt; Gomez, Giaccherini (Brown 90); Alvarez (Agnew 87); Fletcher (Graham 74), Defoe.
Referee: Paul Tierney.

Manchester U (2) 3 *(Mata 25, Rojo 32, Wilson 73)*
Cambridge U (0) 0   74,511
Manchester U: (41212) De Gea; McNair, Smalling, Evans,
Rojo (Young 81); Blind; Rooney, Di Maria (Ander
Herrera 71); Mata; van Persie (Wilson 66), Fellaini.
Cambridge U: (442) Dunn; Tait, Nelson (Miller 87),
Coulson, Taylor G; Donaldson, McGeehan, Champion,
Chadwick (Morrissey 51); Elliott, Simpson (KaiKai 61).
Referee: Jonathan Moss.

Sheffield U (1) 1 *(Murphy 38)*
Preston NE (0) 3 *(Gallagher 63, 73 (pen), Huntington 69)*
       13,161
Sheffield U: (4411) Howard; Flynn, Basham, McEveley,
Harris; Campbell-Ryce, Scougall (Reed 64), Doyle (De
Girolamo 80), Murphy; Baxter; McNulty.
Preston NE: (352) Stuckmann; Huntington, Clarke,
Woods; Wiseman, Brownhill, Kilkenny, Gallagher, Laird
(Welsh 88); Davies K (Garner 88), Humphrey (Reid 83).
Referee: Lee Probert.

Wednesday, 4 February 2015
Bolton W (0) 1 *(Gudjohnsen 59 (pen))*
Liverpool (0) 2 *(Sterling 86, Coutinho 90)*   22,171
Bolton W: (343) Lonergan; Wheater, Dervite, Ream;
Feeney, Vela, Danns■, Moxey; Gudjohnsen, Mills,
Clough (Trotter 72).
Liverpool: (3421) Mignolet; Can, Skrtel, Sakho;
Markovic (Borini 65), Allen (Sturridge 70), Gerrard,
Moreno; Lallana (Henderson 54); Coutinho; Sterling.
Referee: Roger East.

FIFTH ROUND
Saturday, 14 February 2015
Blackburn R (2) 4 *(King 36, 50, 55, Gestede 45 (pen))*
Stoke C (1) 1 *(Crouch 10)*   13,934
Blackburn R: (442) Eastwood; Henley, Duffy, Kilgallon,
Olsson; Taylor C, Cairney, Williamson (Evans 46),
Marshall (Conway 11); Gestede, King (Varney 78).
Stoke C: (4231) Butland; Cameron■, Wollscheid, Muniesa
(Sidwell 52); Bardsley; Nzonzi, Whelan; Arnautovic
(Wilkinson 46), Diouf, Moses (Adam 67); Crouch.
Referee: Anthony Taylor.

Crystal Palace (1) 1 *(Campbell 15)*
Liverpool (0) 2 *(Sturridge 49, Lallana 58)*   20,391
Crystal Palace: (4411) Speroni; Kelly (Guedioura 63),
Dann, Hangeland, Souare; Bolasie (Zaha 72), Ward,
Ledley, Gayle; Chamakh (Puncheon 46); Campbell.
Liverpool: (343) Mignolet; Can, Skrtel, Sakho; Markovic
(Balotelli 46), Henderson, Allen, Moreno; Lallana,
Sturridge (Lambert 78), Coutinho (Lovren 79).
Referee: Robert Madley.

Derby Co (0) 1 *(Bent 61)*
Reading (0) 2 *(Robson-Kanu 53, Yakubu 82)*   21,337
Derby Co: (433) Roos; Christie, Keogh, Shotton,
Warnock■; Hendrick, Mascarell (Forsyth 44), Bryson
(Thomas 83); Lingard, Bent, Dawkins (Ward 67).
Reading: (442) Federici; Kelly, Hector, Pearce, Obita;
Mackie (Yakubu 71), Williams, Chalobah (Akpan 79),
Robson-Kanu; Cox, Pogrebnyak (Blackman 71).
Referee: Craig Pawson.

WBA (2) 4 *(Ideye 20, 57, Morrison 42, Berahino 72)*
West Ham U (0) 0   19,956
WBA: (4411) Foster; Dawson, McAuley, Lescott, Brunt;
Gardner (Gamboa 90), Morrison, Yacob, Sessegnon
(McManaman 78); Berahino; Ideye (Baird 86).
West Ham U: (4312) Adrian; Jenkinson, Kouyate,
Tomkins, Cresswell; Noble, Song (O'Brien 68), Nolan
(Amalfitano■ 60); Downing; Sakho (Cole C 68), Valencia.
Referee: Martin Atkinson.

Sunday, 15 February 2015
Arsenal (2) 2 *(Giroud 27, 29)*
Middlesbrough (0) 0   59,823
Arsenal: (4231) Szczesny; Chambers (Gabriel, Koscielny,
Gibbs; Flamini, Cazorla; Sanchez (Rosicky 72), Ozil,
Welbeck (Walcott 72); Giroud (Akpom 83).

Middlesbrough: (4231) Mejias; Fredericks, Omeruo,
Gibson; Friend; Clayton, Leadbitter; Bamford (Reach
54), Tomlin (Vossen 54), Adomah; Garcia.
Referee: Mike Dean.

Aston Villa (0) 2 *(Bacuna 68, Sinclair 89)*
Leicester C (0) 1 *(Kramaric 90)*   28,098
Aston Villa: (433) Given; Hutton, Vlaar, Clark, Cissokho;
Cleverley, Westwood, Delph; Bacuna (Sinclair 77),
Benteke, Weimann (Grealish 83).
Leicester C: (541) Schwarzer; Simpson, Wasilewski
(Ulloa 65), Morgan, Upson, Konchesky; Mahrez, James,
Cambiasso, Schlupp; Kramaric.
Referee: Mark Clattenburg.

Bradford C (1) 2 *(O'Shea 3 (og), Stead 61)*
Sunderland (0) 0   24,021
Bradford C: (4312) Williams; Darby, McArdle, Davies,
Meredith; Morais, Liddle, Knott (Halliday 79); Clarke
(Yeates 86); Stead (Zoko 89), Hanson.
Sunderland: (442) Mannone; Jones (Vergini 86), O'Shea,
Brown, Van Aanholt; Alvarez (Honeyman 86), Larsson,
Bridcutt, Johnson; Graham (Wickham 46), Fletcher.
Referee: Kevin Friend.

Monday, 16 February 2015
Preston NE (0) 1 *(Laird 47)*
Manchester U (0) 3 *(Ander Herrera 65, Fellaini 72,*
Rooney 88 (pen))   21,348
Preston NE: (352) Stuckmann; Clarke, Huntington, Wright
(Wiseman 75); Humphrey, Kilkenny (Reid 75), Welsh,
Gallagher, Laird; Davies K (Robinson 75), Garner.
Manchester U: (41212) De Gea; Valencia, Smalling, Rojo,
Shaw; Blind; Ander Herrera, Di Maria; Fellaini; Falcao
(Young 60), Rooney.
Referee: Phil Dowd.

SIXTH ROUND
Saturday, 7 March 2015
Aston Villa (0) 2 *(Delph 51, Sinclair 85)*
WBA (0) 0   39,592
Aston Villa: (433) Given; Bacuna, Okore, Clark, Lowton;
Cleverley (Sanchez 65), Westwood, Delph; N'Zogbia
(Grealish■ 74), Agbonlahor (Gil 89), Sinclair.
WBA: (442) Myhill; Dawson, McAuley, Olsson
(McManaman 68), Lescott; Gardner (Mulumbu 85),
Yacob■, Morrison, Brunt; Ideye, Berahino.
Referee: Anthony Taylor.

Bradford C (0) 0
Reading (0) 0   24,321
Bradford C: (41212) Williams; Darby, McArdle, Davies,
Meredith; Liddle; Morais (Halliday 76), Knott (Yeates
83); Clarke (Zoko 83); Stead, Hanson.
Reading: (451) Federici; Kelly, Pearce, Hector, Obita;
Mackie (Yakubu 80), Williams, Chalobah (Akpan 83),
Norwood, Robson-Kanu (McCleary 66); Pogrebnyak.
Referee: Lee Mason.

Sunday, 8 March 2015
Liverpool (0) 0
Blackburn R (0) 0   43,820
Liverpool: (343) Mignolet; Johnson, Skrtel (Toure 11),
Lovren; Markovic (Balotelli 59), Can, Henderson,
Sterling; Lallana, Sturridge, Coutinho.
Blackburn R: (4231) Eastwood; Henley, Baptiste,
Kilgallon, Olsson; Williamson, Evans; Conway, Cairney,
Marshall (Taylor C 68); Gestede.
Referee: Andre Marriner.

Monday, 9 March 2015
Manchester U (1) 1 *(Rooney 29)*
Arsenal (1) 2 *(Monreal 25, Welbeck 61)*   74,285
Manchester U: (4141) De Gea; Valencia, Smalling, Rojo
(Januzaj 73), Shaw (Jones 46); Blind; Di Maria■, Ander
Herrera (Carrick 46), Fellaini, Young; Rooney.
Arsenal: (4231) Szczesny; Bellerin (Chambers 66),
Mertesacker, Koscielny, Monreal; Coquelin, Cazorla;
Oxlade-Chamberlain (Ramsey 51), Ozil, Sanchez;
Welbeck (Giroud 74).
Referee: Michael Oliver.

SIXTH ROUND REPLAYS

Monday, 16 March 2015

Reading (2) 3 *(Robson-Kanu 6, McCleary 9, Mackie 68)*
Bradford C (0) 0   22,908

Reading: (442) Federici; Gunter, Pearce, Hector, Obita; McCleary (Norwood 86), Williams, Chalobah, Robson-Kanu (Blackman 83); Mackie, Pogrebnyak (Yakubu 89).
Bradford C: (41212) Williams; Darby, McArdle, Sheehan, Meredith; Liddle; Morais*, Halliday (Yeates 59); Knott (Dolan 74); Hanson, Stead (Clarke 59).
Referee: Mike Jones.

Wednesday, 8 April 2015

Blackburn R (0) 0
Liverpool (0) 1 *(Coutinho 70)*   28,415

Blackburn R: (4231) Eastwood; Henley, Baptiste (Spurr 80), Kilgallon, Olsson; Evans, Williamson; Conway (Gestede 65), Cairney, Marshall; Rhodes.
Liverpool: (433) Mignolet; Johnson, Lovren, Sakho (Toure 28), Moreno; Henderson, Lucas, Allen; Coutinho, Sturridge (Lambert 85), Sterling.
Referee: Kevin Friend.

SEMI-FINALS (at Wembley)

Saturday, 18 April 2015

Reading (0) 1 *(McCleary 54)*
Arsenal (1) 2 *(Sanchez 39, 105)*   84,081

Reading: (442) Federici; Gunter, Hector, Pearce, Obita; McCleary, Williams, Chalobah (Cox 106), Robson-Kanu (Karacan 90); Mackie, Pogrebnyak (Yakubu 111).
Arsenal: (4231) Szczesny; Debuchy, Mertesacker (Gabriel 63), Koscielny, Gibbs; Coquelin (Walcott 101), Cazorla; Ramsey, Ozil, Sanchez; Welbeck (Giroud 72).
aet.
Referee: Martin Atkinson.

Sunday, 19 April 2015

Aston Villa (1) 2 *(Benteke 36, Delph 54)*
Liverpool (1) 1 *(Coutinho 30)*   85,416

Aston Villa: (433) Given; Bacuna, Vlaar, Baker (Okore 26), Richardson; Cleverley, Westwood, Delph; N'Zogbia (Sinclair 75), Benteke, Grealish (Cole 84).
Liverpool: (3421) Mignolet; Can, Skrtel, Lovren; Markovic (Balotelli 46), Henderson, Allen (Johnson 78); Moreno (Lambert 90); Gerrard, Coutinho; Sterling.
Referee: Michael Oliver.

THE FA CUP FINAL 2015

Saturday, 30 May 2015

(at Wembley Stadium, attendance 89,283)

Arsenal (1) 4   **Aston Villa (0) 0**

Arsenal: (4231) Szczesny; Bellerin, Mertesacker, Koscielny, Monreal; Coquelin, Cazorla; Ramsey, Ozil (Wilshere 77), Sanchez (Oxlade-Chamberlain 90); Walcott (Giroud 77).
Scorers: Walcott 40, Sanchez 50, Mertesacker 62, Giroud 90.

Aston Villa: (433) Given; Hutton, Okore, Vlaar, Richardson (Bacuna 68); Cleverley, Westwood (Sanchez 71), Delph; N'Zogbia (Agbonlahor 53), Benteke, Grealish.

Referee: Jonathan Moss.

Arsenal's Theo Walcott volleys home the London club's opening goal in their 4-0 demolition of Aston Villa in the FA Cup final at Wembley on 30 May. (Anthony Devlin/PA Wire/Press Association Images)

VANARAMA CONFERENCE PREMIER 2014-15

(P) *Promoted into division at end of 2013–14 season.*   (R) *Relegated into division at end of 2013–14 season.*

			Total				Home				Away					
		P	W	D	L	F	A	W	D	L	F	A	W	D	L	F	A	GD	Pts
1	Barnet	46	28	8	10	94	46	16	2	5	54	21	12	6	5	40	25	48	92
2	Bristol R (R)¶	46	25	16	5	73	34	17	4	2	47	14	8	12	3	26	20	39	91
3	Grimsby T	46	25	11	10	74	40	12	4	7	36	20	13	7	3	38	20	34	86
4	Eastleigh (P)	46	24	10	12	87	61	12	6	5	45	28	12	4	7	42	33	26	82
5	Forest Green R*	46	22	16	8	80	54	12	7	4	42	27	10	9	4	38	27	26	79
6	Macclesfield T	46	21	15	10	60	46	14	7	2	34	14	7	8	8	26	32	14	78
7	Woking	46	21	13	12	77	52	11	7	5	39	24	10	6	7	38	28	25	76
8	Dover Ath (P)	46	19	11	16	69	58	13	4	6	38	18	6	7	10	31	40	11	68
9	FC Halifax T	46	17	15	14	60	54	11	7	5	38	27	6	8	9	22	27	6	66
10	Gateshead	46	17	15	14	66	62	10	6	7	38	34	7	9	7	28	28	4	66
11	Wrexham	46	17	15	14	56	52	9	8	6	27	22	8	7	8	29	30	4	66
12	Chester FC	46	19	6	21	64	76	11	3	9	35	36	8	3	12	29	40	–12	63
13	Torquay U (R)	46	16	13	17	64	60	10	7	6	35	26	6	6	11	29	34	4	61
14	Braintree T	46	18	5	23	56	57	10	4	9	28	25	8	1	14	28	32	–1	59
15	Lincoln C	46	16	10	20	62	71	11	4	8	35	28	5	6	12	27	43	–9	58
16	Kidderminster H	46	15	12	19	51	60	9	6	8	31	30	6	6	11	20	30	–9	57
17	Altrincham (P)	46	16	8	22	54	73	9	5	9	29	34	7	3	13	25	39	–19	56
18	Aldershot T	46	14	11	21	51	61	8	5	10	27	28	6	6	11	24	33	–10	53
19	Southport	46	13	12	21	47	72	6	6	11	21	33	7	6	10	26	39	–25	51
20	Welling U	46	11	12	23	52	73	7	8	8	29	27	4	4	15	23	46	–21	45
21	Alfreton T	46	12	9	25	49	90	6	8	9	33	40	6	1	16	16	50	–41	45
22	AFC Telford U (P)	46	10	9	27	58	84	3	5	15	27	44	7	4	12	31	40	–26	39
23	Dartford	46	8	15	23	44	74	4	9	10	26	34	4	6	13	18	40	–30	39
24	Nuneaton T	46	10	9	27	38	76	7	6	10	25	33	3	3	17	13	43	–38	39

*Forest Green R deducted 3 points for fielding an ineligible player. ¶Bristol R promoted via play-offs.

VANARAMA CONFERENCE PREMIER PLAY-OFFS 2014-15

■ *Denotes player sent off.*

SEMI-FINALS FIRST LEG

Wednesday, 29 April 2015

Forest Green R (0) 0
Bristol R (1) 1 *(Taylor 17)*   3336
Forest Green R: (442) Arnold; Pipe, Racine, Clough, Bennett; Frear (Marwood 89), Sinclair, Wedgbury, Fleetwood (Norwood 65); Guthrie, Parkin.
Bristol R: (442) Puddy; Lockyer, McChrystal, Parkes, Brown; Gosling (Blissett 81), Mansell (Clarke 90), Lines, Monkhouse; Harrison■, Taylor.
Referee: Lee Swabey.

Thursday, 30 April 2015

Eastleigh (0) 1 *(Odubade 62)*
Grimsby T (1) 2 *(Arnold 3, 72)*   3251
Eastleigh: (532) Flitney; Evans, Turley, Strevens, Partington, Spence; Stanley (Howard 78), Reason, McAllister; Constable, Midson (Odubade 59).
Grimsby T: (442) McKeown; Nsiala, Gowling, Pearson, Magnay; Mackreth, Disley, Brown (Clay 76), Arnold; John-Lewis, Palmer (Pittman 76).
Referee: Simon Bennett.

SEMI-FINALS SECOND LEG

Sunday, 3 May 2015

Bristol R (1) 2 *(Lines 24, Taylor 88)*
Forest Green R (0) 0   10,563
Bristol R: (442) Puddy; Lockyer, McChrystal, Parkes, Brown; Gosling, Mansell (Clarke 86), Lines, Monkhouse; Taylor (Balanta 90), Blissett.

Forest Green R: (442) Arnold; Bennett (Wedgbury 27), Coles (Clough 70), Racine, Jennings; Marwood, Pipe, Sinclair, Frear (Norwood 63); Guthrie, Parkin.
Referee: Darren England.
Bristol R won 3-0 on aggregate.

Grimsby T (2) 3 *(Palmer 35, 71, John-Lewis 44)*
Eastleigh (0) 0   6286
Grimsby T: (442) McKeown; Nsiala, Pearson, Gowling, Magnay; Mackreth, Brown (Clay 68), Disley, Arnold (Hannah 85); John-Lewis, Palmer (Pittman 79).
Eastleigh: (442) Flitney; Partington, Turley, Evans, Green; Howard (Walker 46), Pell (Burton 46), Strevens, Reason; McAllister, Constable (Odubade 46).
Referee: Ben Toner.
Grimsby T won 5-1 on aggregate.

FINAL

Sunday, 17 May 2015

Bristol R (1) 1 *(Harrison 29)*
Grimsby T (1) 1 *(John-Lewis 2)*   47,029
Bristol R: (442) Puddy (Mildenhall 120); Lockyer, Parkes, McChrystal, Brown; Gosling (Balanta 75), Lines, Mansell, Monkhouse; Harrison (Blissett 79), Taylor.
Grimsby T: (442) McKeown; Robertson (Parslow 73), Nsiala, Pearson, Magnay; Mackreth, Disley, Brown (Clay 99), Arnold; Palmer (Pittman 70), John-Lewis.
aet; Bristol R won 5-3 on penalties.
Referee: Ross Joyce.

VANARAMA CONFERENCE PREMIER PROMOTED TEAMS ROLL CALL 2014–15

BARNET

Player	H	W	DOB
Akinde, John (F)	6 2	13 10	08/07/1989
Allen, Iffy (M)	5 9	10 12	15/03/1994
Cook, Lee (M)	5 9	10 12	03/08/1982
Cowler, Sam (G)	6 3	11 00	26/10/1992
Gambin, Luke (M)	5 6	11 00	16/03/1993
Gash, Michael (F)	5 10	12 02	03/09/1986
Gater, Joe (D)	6 3		24/03/1987
Johnson, Elliot (D)	5 10	12 02	17/08/1994
MacDonald, Charlie (F)	5 9	11 00	13/02/1981
Marsh-Brown, Keanu (M)	5 11	12 04	10/08/1992
McKenzie-Lyle, Kai (G)	6 5	13 08	30/11/1997
Muggleton, Sam (D)	5 11	11 03	17/11/1995
N'Gala, Bondz (D)	6 2	14 02	13/09/1989
Nurse, Jon (F)	5 9	12 04	01/03/1981
Saville, Jack (D)	6 3	12 00	02/04/1991
Stack, Graham (G)	6 2	12 07	26/09/1981
Stephens, David (D)	6 4	14 06	08/07/1991
Stevens, Mathew (F)	5 11	11 09	12/02/1998
Taylor, Harry (D)	6 2		04/05/1997
Togwell, Sam (M)	5 11	12 03	14/10/1984
Vilhete, Mauro (M)	5 9	11 09	10/05/1993
Villa, Luisma (M)	5 10	10 03	11/08/1989
Weston, Curtis (M)	5 11	11 09	24/01/1987
Yiadom, Andy (M)	5 11	11 11	09/12/1991

BRISTOL ROVERS

Player	H	W	DOB
Balanta, Angelo (F)	5 10	11 11	01/07/1990
Bell-Baggie, Abdulai (F)	5 6	10 01	28/04/1992
Brown, Lee (D)	6 0	12 06	10/08/1990
Clarke, Ollie (M)	5 11	11 11	29/06/1992
Easter, Jermaine (F)	5 9	13 05	15/01/1982
Gosling, Jake (M)	5 9	10 10	11/08/1993
Greenslade, Danny (F)			29/01/1994
Harrison, Ellis (F)	5 11	12 06	29/01/1994
Leadbitter, Daniel (D)	6 0	11 00	07/10/1990
Lockyer, Tom (D)	6 0	11 05	30/12/1994
Lucas, Jamie (F)	6 2	13 01	06/12/1995
Mansell, Lee (M)	5 9	10 10	23/09/1982
McChrystal, Mark (D)	6 1	13 08	26/06/1984
Mildenhall, Steve (G)	6 4	14 00	13/05/1978
Monkhouse, Andy (M)	6 2	13 01	23/10/1980
Parkes, Tom (D)	6 2	12 06	15/01/1992
Preston, Kieran (G)			04/10/1996
Puddy, Will (G)	6 1	13 00	04/10/1987
Sinclair, Stuart (M)	5 7	10 08	29/11/1987
Taylor, Matt (F)	5 9	11 05	30/03/1990
Thomas, Dominic (M)	6 1	11 00	23/11/1995
Trotman, Neal (D)	6 2	13 08	11/03/1987
Ward-Baptiste, Aaron (F)			06/12/1995

VANARAMA CONFERENCE PREMIER ATTENDANCES BY CLUB 2014–15

	Aggregate 2014–15	Average 2014–15	Highest Attendance 2014–15
Bristol R	152,469	6,629	11,085 v Alfreton T
Grimsby T	84,717	3,683	7,136 v Lincoln C
Wrexham	74,403	3,235	8,163 v Grimsby T
Lincoln C	58,941	2,563	5,209 v Grimsby T
Chester FC	50,336	2,189	3,183 v Wrexham
Barnet	45,093	1,961	5,233 v Gateshead
Torquay U	44,829	1,949	3,755 v Bristol R
Woking	43,975	1,912	3,853 v Bristol R
Kidderminster H	43,941	1,910	4,229 v Bristol R
Aldershot T	40,446	1,759	3,567 v Woking
Eastleigh	40,295	1,752	4,126 v Macclesfield T
Macclesfield T	37,103	1,613	2,786 v Grimsby T
AFC Telford U	35,849	1,559	2,860 v Bristol R
Forest Green R	34,537	1,502	3,781 v Bristol R
FC Halifax T	33,859	1,472	2,369 v Lincoln C
Altrincham	28,279	1,230	1,881 v Grimsby T
Gateshead	27,127	1,179	1,782 v Grimsby T
Dartford	25,584	1,112	1,832 v Bristol R
Southport	24,619	1,070	1,968 v Grimsby T
Dover Ath	22,151	963	2,351 v Bristol R
Nuneaton T	19,914	866	1,661 v Bristol R
Braintree T	19,183	834	2,115 v AFC Telford U
Alfreton T	18,466	803	3,327 v Grimsby T
Welling U	16,846	732	1,306 v Dartford

VANARAMA CONFERENCE PREMIER LEADING GOALSCORERS 2014–15

Player	Club	League	FA Cup	FA Trophy	Play-Offs	Total
John Akinde	Barnet	31	2	0	0	33
Jon Parkin	Forest Green R	25	1	4	0	30
Scott Rendell	Woking	24	0	2	0	26
Louis Moult	Wrexham	16	0	7	0	23
Damian Reeves	Altrincham	18	1	2	0	21
Matty Taylor	Bristol R	18	1	0	2	21
Lenell John-Lewis	Grimsby T	16	2	0	2	20
James Constable	Eastleigh	18	1	0	0	19
Ryan Bowman	Torquay U	13	0	6	0	19
Tony Gray	AFC Telford U	18	1	0	0	19
Stefan Payne	Dover Ath	15	1	2	0	18
Ellis Harrison	Bristol R	13	3	0	1	17
Brett Williams	Aldershot T	15	0	0	0	15
Villa, Luisma	Barnet	13	1	0	0	14
Richard Brodie	Southport	12	2	0	0	14
Ben Tomlinson	Lincoln C	14	0	0	0	14
Daniel Wright	Kidderminster H	11	2	1	0	14

(Includes 7 League goals and 2 FA Cup goals and 1 FA Trophy goal for Gateshead.)

Harry Beautyman	Welling U	13	0	0	0	13

(Includes 2 League goals for Peterborough U.)

James Norwood	Forest Green R	11	2	0	0	13
Lois Maynard	FC Halifax T	11	1	0	0	12
Tom Murphy	Dover Ath	11	0	1	0	12
Craig McAllister	Eastleigh	10	1	0	0	11
Jack Midson	Eastleigh	11	0	0	0	11
John Rooney	Chester	11	0	0	0	11

VANARAMA CONFERENCE NORTH 2014–15

(P) *Promoted into division at end of 2013–14 season.*   (R) *Relegated into division at end of 2013–14 season.*

			Total					Home					Away					
		P	W	D	L	F	A	W	D	L	F	A	W	D	L	F	A	GD	Pts
1	Barrow	42	26	9	7	81	43	16	3	2	45	16	10	6	5	36	27	38	87
2	AFC Fylde (P)	42	25	10	7	93	43	14	5	2	51	23	11	5	5	42	20	50	85
3	Boston U	42	20	12	10	75	51	12	5	4	47	25	8	7	6	28	26	24	72
4	Chorley (P)	42	20	11	11	76	55	11	8	2	42	19	9	3	9	34	36	21	71
5	Guiseley¶	42	20	10	12	68	49	12	2	7	40	27	8	8	5	28	22	19	70
6	Oxford C	42	20	9	13	81	67	9	7	5	29	32	11	2	8	52	35	14	69
7	Tamworth (R)	42	19	12	11	66	57	13	4	4	40	23	6	8	7	26	34	9	69
8	Hednesford T	42	17	10	15	63	50	9	5	7	34	28	8	5	8	29	22	13	61
9	Worcester C	42	16	12	14	54	54	9	6	6	32	30	7	6	8	22	24	0	60
10	North Ferriby U	42	14	16	12	65	63	8	8	5	38	31	6	8	7	27	32	2	58
11	Stockport Co	42	16	9	17	56	59	12	2	7	37	28	4	7	10	19	31	-3	57
12	Solihull Moors	42	16	7	19	68	63	6	4	11	31	36	10	3	8	37	27	5	55
13	Bradford PA	42	14	11	17	52	66	8	6	7	27	31	6	5	10	25	35	-14	53
14	Gloucester C	42	14	10	18	63	75	8	6	7	26	28	6	4	11	37	47	-12	52
15	Harrogate T	42	14	10	18	50	62	9	6	6	30	27	5	4	12	20	35	-12	52
16	Lowestoft T (P)	42	12	15	15	54	66	8	9	4	31	24	4	6	11	23	42	-12	51
17	Gainsborough Trinity	42	14	8	20	59	67	8	6	7	33	27	6	2	13	26	40	-8	50
18	Brackley T	42	13	8	21	39	62	9	4	8	17	23	4	4	13	22	39	-23	47
19	Stalybridge Celtic	42	12	9	21	54	70	6	4	11	31	39	6	5	10	23	31	-16	45
20	Colwyn Bay	42	11	12	19	59	82	4	3	14	22	43	7	9	5	37	39	-23	45
21	Leamington	42	10	10	22	59	74	7	5	9	33	35	3	5	13	26	39	-15	40
22	Hyde (R)	42	3	12	27	49	106	3	8	10	31	42	0	4	17	18	64	-57	21

¶*Guiseley promoted via play-offs.*

VANARAMA CONFERENCE NORTH PLAY-OFFS 2014–15

▪ *Denotes player sent off.*

SEMI-FINALS FIRST LEG
Wednesday 29 April 2015
Guiseley (1) 1 *(Lawlor 42)*
AFC Fylde (0) 0   1025
Guiseley: Drench; Toulson, Lowe, Holdsworth, Hall, Lawlor, Brooksby, Boshell D, Boyes (Boshell N 90), Johnson O (Dickinson L 67), Rothery.
AFC Fylde: Hinchliffe; Denson, Sumner, Langley, Hannigan, Barnes B, Baker (Tomsett 86), Wilson (Blinkhorn 76), Rowe, McGoldrick, Barnes M (Allen R 55).
Referee: A. Tankard.

Chorley (0) 0
Boston U (0) 0   2022
Chorley: Ashton; Ross, Jarvis, Teague, Doyle, Roscoe, Hine, Whitham, Dean, Winter (Cottrell 67), Dorney (Almond 78).
Boston U: Stryjek; Marrs, Steer (Dixon 77), Roberts, Garner, Piergianni, Felix, Mills, Southwell, Jones, Walker.
Referee: K. Mulraine.

SEMI-FINALS SECOND LEG
Saturday 2 May 2015
AFC Fylde (1) 1 *(Allen R 1)*
Guiseley (1) 2 *(Boshell D 36, Holdsworth 57)*   950
AFC Fylde: Hinchliffe; Denson (Barnes M 76), Sumner, Langley, Hannigan, Barnes B, Baker (Tomsett 70), Wilson (Blinkhorn 59), Rowe, Lloyd, Allen R.
Guiseley: Drench; Toulson, Lowe, Holdsworth, Hall, Lawlor, Brooksby, Boshell D (Boshell N 90), Boyes (Dickinson L 90), Johnson O, Rothery.
Referee: O. Yates.
Guiseley won 3-1 on aggregate.

Boston U (1) 2 *(Garner 43, Felix 49)*
Chorley (0) 2 *(Doyle 56, Roscoe 90)*   3174
Boston U: Stryjek; Marrs, Steer, Dixon (Roberts 47), Garner, Piergianni, Felix (Hall 90), Mills, Southwell, Jones, Walker (McGhee 111).
Chorley: Ashton; Ross, Jarvis, Teague (Flynn 58), Doyle, Roscoe▪, Hine (Burns 64), Whitham, Dean, Winter (Almond 56), Dorney.
Referee: T. Nield.
aet; 2-2 on aggregate, Chorley won 5-4 on penalties.

FINAL
Chorley, Saturday 9 May 2015
Chorley (2) 2 *(Teague 5, Jarvis 24)*
Guiseley (0) 3 *(Boyes 56, Dickinson L 73, Boshell N 79)*   3418
Chorley: Ashton (Grundy 66); Ross, Jarvis (Mather 53), Teague (Flynn 47), Doyle, Winter, Hine, Whitham, Dean, Dorney, Cottrell.
Guiseley: Drench; Toulson, Lowe, Holdworth, Hall, Lawlor, Brooksby, Boshell D, Boyes, Johnson O (Dickinson L 64), Rothery (Bushell N 65).
Referee: J. Johnson.

VANARAMA CONFERENCE SOUTH 2014–15

(P) *Promoted into division at end of 2013–14 season.*   (R) *Relegated into division at end of 2013–14 season.*

				Total				Home					Away						
		P	W	D	L	F	A	W	D	L	F	A	W	D	L	F	A	GD	Pts
1	Bromley	40	23	8	9	79	46	11	2	7	33	23	12	6	2	46	23	33	77
2	Boreham Wood¶	40	23	6	11	79	44	12	4	4	39	20	11	2	7	40	24	35	75
3	Basingstoke T	40	22	7	11	67	43	10	4	6	27	22	12	3	5	40	21	24	73
4	Whitehawk	40	22	6	12	62	47	12	3	5	32	18	10	3	7	30	29	15	72
5	Havant & Waterlooville	40	21	7	12	61	41	12	3	5	34	21	9	4	7	27	20	20	70
6	Gosport Bor	40	19	10	11	63	40	9	7	4	30	19	10	3	7	33	21	23	67
7	Concord Rangers	40	18	11	11	60	44	10	5	5	39	24	8	6	6	21	20	16	65
8	Ebbsfleet U	40	17	9	14	60	41	9	5	6	29	20	8	4	8	31	21	19	60
9	Hemel Hempstead T (P)	40	16	12	12	64	60	6	8	6	30	33	10	4	6	34	27	4	60
10	Chelmsford C	40	17	5	18	65	71	8	4	8	36	34	9	1	10	29	37	-6	56
11	Eastbourne Bor	40	14	13	13	51	50	11	5	4	33	21	3	8	9	18	29	1	55
12	Wealdstone (P)	40	14	12	14	56	56	5	5	10	22	32	9	7	4	34	24	0	54
13	St Albans C (P)	40	16	6	18	53	53	9	4	7	29	25	7	2	11	24	28	0	54
14	Bath C	40	15	8	17	59	57	9	4	7	31	26	6	4	10	28	31	2	53
15	Sutton U	40	13	11	16	50	54	7	4	9	25	28	6	7	7	25	26	-4	50
16	Bishop's Stortford	40	12	10	18	55	69	4	8	8	29	38	8	2	10	26	31	-14	46
17	Weston-super-Mare	40	13	5	22	55	86	6	3	11	30	45	7	2	11	25	41	-31	44
18	Maidenhead U	40	10	13	17	54	70	5	4	11	24	35	5	9	6	30	35	-16	43
19	Hayes & Yeading U	40	11	9	20	39	58	6	3	11	21	29	5	6	9	18	29	-19	42
20	Farnborough	40	8	6	26	42	101	4	3	13	19	46	4	3	13	23	55	-59	30
21	Staines T	40	7	4	29	39	82	3	1	16	18	44	4	3	13	21	38	-43	25

¶*Boreham Wood promoted via play-offs.*

VANARAMA CONFERENCE SOUTH PLAY-OFFS 2014–15

SEMI-FINALS FIRST LEG
Wednesday 29 April 2015
Whitehawk (0) 1 *(Robinson 50)*
Basingstoke T (1) 1 *(Flood 11)*   629
Whitehawk: Ross; Arnold, Hills, Hamilton, Sankofa, Kissock, Deering, Torres, Robinson (Gargan 90), Mills (Abdulla 90), Neilson.
Basingstoke T: Moore, Smart, Bird, Dickie, Gasson, Ray, Brown (Dunn 66), Harper, Macklin (Bignall 75), Flood, Soares.
Referee: D. Eaton.

Havant & Waterlooville (0) 0
Boreham Wood (2) 2 *(Morias 3, Montgomery 39)*   1296
Havant & Waterlooville: Young; Huggins, Cummings, Carmichael, Dutton, Strugnell, Swallow (Ciardini 81), Donnelly, Hooper, Bubb (Mullings 75), Cornick.
Boreham Wood: Russell, Nunn, Herd, Cox, Hill, Reynolds, Thomas, Shakes, Angol (Whichelow 85), Morias (Walker 88), Montgomery.
Referee: A. Young.

SEMI-FINALS SECOND LEG
Saturday 2 May 2015
Basingstoke T (0) 0
Whitehawk (0) 1 *(Robinson 51)*   1749
Basingstoke T: Moore, Smart, Bird, Harper, Dickie, Ray, Soares (McAuley 61), Dunn (Brown 81), Enver-Marum, Flood, Williams (Macklin 51).
Whitehawk: Ross; Arnold, Hills, Hamilton, Sankofa, Kissock (Ijaha 53), Deering (Guyonnet 81), Torres, Robinson, Mills (Gargan 76), Neilson.
Referee: C. Hatzidakis.
Whitehawk won 2-1 on aggregate.

Boreham Wood (0) 2 *(Shakes 64, Angol 67)*
Havant & Waterlooville (1) 2 *(Dutton 16 Mullings 83)* 906
Boreham Wood: Russell, Nunn, Herd, Cox, Hill (Martin 86), Reynolds, Thomas, Shakes, Angol, Morias (Whichelow 90), Montgomery.
Havant & Waterlooville: Young; Strugnell, Cummings (Ciardini 69), Stock, Dutton, Harris, Swallow (Mullings 69), Donnelly, Wright (Hooper 69), Cornick, Huggins.
Referee: L. Betts.
Boreham Wood won 4-2 on aggregate.

FINAL
Boreham Wood, Saturday 9 May 2015
Boreham Wood (0) 2 *(Angol 67, Morias 91)*
Whitehawk (0) 1 *(Deering 82 (pen))*   2201
Boreham Wood: Russell; Nunn, Herd, Cox, Hill, Reynolds, Thomas, Shakes, Angol, Morias (Walker 120), Montgomery (Whichelow 80).
Whitehawk: Ross; Arnold, Hills, Hamilton Sankofa, Kissock, Deering, Torres (Gargan 79), Robinson, Mills (Abdulla 88), Neilson (Ijaha 61).
Referee: A. Coggins.
aet; 1-1 after 90 minutes.

AFC TELFORD UNITED

Ground: The New Bucks Head Stadium, Watling Street, Wellington, Telford, Shropshire TF1 2TU.
Tel: (01952) 640 064. *Fax:* (01952) 640 021. *Website:* www.telfordunited.com. *Year Formed:* 2004.
Record Gate: 5,710 (2007 v Burscough). *Nickname:* 'The Bucks' or 'Lillywhites'. *Manager:* Steve Kittrick.
Colours: White shirts with black trim, white shorts, white socks with black trim.

AFC TELFORD UNITED – VANARAMA PREMIER 2014–15 LEAGUE RECORD

Match No.	Date	Venue	Opponents	Result	H/T Score	Lg Pos.	Goalscorers	Attendance
1	Aug 9	A	Welling U	D	1-1	1-0	10	Platt [36]	611
2	12	H	Macclesfield T	L	2-3	1-3	15	Owens [32], Akrigg [81]	1655
3	17	H	Aldershot T	L	0-2	0-2	18		1619
4	23	A	Bristol R	L	0-1	0-0	22		5450
5	25	H	Southport	D	3-3	1-2	20	Phenix 2 [30, 89], Gray [53]	1421
6	30	A	Dartford	L	1-2	1-0	23	Gray [35]	923
7	Sept 6	H	Dover Ath	L	1-4	1-1	23	Phenix [19]	1515
8	9	A	Gateshead	L	1-4	1-3	23	Clancy [2]	1093
9	13	H	Barnet	D	2-2	1-0	24	Gray (pen) [39], Phenix [90]	1492
10	16	A	Alfreton T	L	2-3	1-3	24	Gray [17], Byrne [71]	519
11	20	A	FC Halifax T	L	0-5	0-2	24		1519
12	27	H	Torquay U	W	4-3	2-2	24	Grogan [7], McDonald [45], Akrigg [66], Farrell [82]	1669
13	30	H	Chester FC	L	1-2	1-1	24	Grogan [19]	1871
14	Oct 4	A	Kidderminster H	D	1-1	0-1	24	Todd [79]	2117
15	7	H	Forest Green R	L	0-1	0-0	24		1361
16	11	H	Lincoln C	L	0-2	0-0	24		2529
17	18	A	Woking	W	3-1	1-1	24	Phenix 2 [10, 47], Smith [60]	1817
18	Nov 1	H	Bristol R	L	0-1	0-0	24		2860
19	12	H	Altrincham	W	2-1	1-0	24	Smith [25], Farrell [90]	1417
20	15	A	Barnet	L	1-3	1-2	24	Cooke [35]	1671
21	22	A	Braintree T	L	1-3	0-3	24	Gray [53]	1523
22	29	H	Grimsby T	D	1-1	1-0	24	Parry [34]	1849
23	Dec 2	A	Chester FC	L	0-2	0-0	24		1860
24	9	H	Welling U	L	1-2	0-0	24	Ledsham [63]	1011
25	20	H	Eastleigh	L	3-4	2-2	24	Gray 3 [9, 25, 89]	1265
26	26	A	Nuneaton T	D	4-4	1-1	24	Smith 2 [6, 90], Farrell [52], Cooke [90]	1017
27	Jan 1	H	Nuneaton T	D	0-0	0-0	24		1797
28	4	A	Aldershot T	W	2-1	1-0	24	Byrne [28], Oastler (og) [64]	1410
29	17	A	Wrexham	W	4-0	2-0	24	Smith [2], Gray 2 [8, 58], Byrne [73]	3194
30	27	H	FC Halifax T	L	0-1	0-0	24		1248
31	Feb 7	A	Eastleigh	D	3-3	1-1	23	Gray [42], Farrell [56], Smith [59]	1219
32	14	H	Dartford	L	2-3	1-1	24	Gray 2 (1 pen) [32 (p), 82]	1653
33	21	A	Forest Green R	L	0-3	0-0	24		1300
34	24	A	Grimsby T	L	0-1	0-0	24		3047
35	28	H	Alfreton T	L	0-1	0-0	24		1561
36	Mar 7	A	Torquay U	W	1-0	1-0	24	Gray [11]	1647
37	10	A	Macclesfield T	L	0-1	0-1	24		1225
38	14	H	Woking	L	1-3	0-0	24	McDonald [64]	1265
39	17	H	Gateshead	L	0-1	0-1	24		657
40	24	A	Braintree T	W	2-0	0-0	24	Gray (pen) [59], Ventre [64]	2115
41	28	A	Dover Ath	L	0-1	0-1	24		795
42	Apr 4	H	Kidderminster H	D	1-1	0-0	24	Gray [61]	1773
43	6	A	Southport	W	3-0	1-0	24	Reid [43], Gray [47], Smith [58]	1092
44	11	H	Lincoln C	W	1-0	0-0	24	Byrne [83]	1243
45	18	A	Altrincham	W	2-1	1-0	22	Gray [39], Farrell [53]	1265
46	25	H	Wrexham	L	1-2	0-0	22	Jennings (og) [67]	2124

Final League Position: 22

GOALSCORERS

League (58): Gray 18 (3 pens), Smith 7, Phenix 5, Farrell 5, Byrne 4, Akrigg 2, Cooke 2, Grogan 2, McDonald 2, Clancy 1, Ledsham 1, Owens 1, Parry 1, Platt 1, Reid 1, Todd 1, Ventre 1, own goals 2.
FA Cup (8): Farrell 3, Gray 1, Grogan 2, McDonald 1, Parry 1.
FA Trophy (2): Deacey 1, Smith 1.

Hedge 18	Platt 8+5	Owens 13+3	Byrne 38	Akrigg 18	Phenix 12+2	Grogan 29+3	Clancy 28+7	Poku 36+2	Smith 29+5	Farrell 33+11	Barnett 9+7	Cooke 6+15	Deacey 4+11	Baynes 6+1	Gray 36+6	McDonald 20+2	Lever 3	O'Keefe 5	Todd 12+4	Higgins 16	Parry 10	Hall 21	Hancock 4+6	Ledsham 5	Brownhill 6+2	Rea 4+1	Dixon —+2	Disney 11+3	McLaughlin 7	Ventre 16+1	Sharps 15	Matthews 8+4	Dyer 5+9	Reid 8+1	Montgomery 7	Match No.
1	2	3	4	5	6*	7	8¹	9*	10	11	12																									1
1	2³	5	4	3		7	12		11¹	9	6²	8	10	13	14																					2
1	2	5	4	3	8	7	10¹	6	11³	13		14	9²	12																						3
1		2	5	4	13		7³	9	10²	11	14	8¹	12	6		3																				4
1		8	2³	3	10	7	13	6*	11¹	12			14	5	9²	4																				5
1	7	9²	2	3	11		8³		12	6		14	13	5	10¹	4																				6
1	13		4	6²		7¹		10	8³	12		9	11	2	3	5	14																			7
1	14	9²	2	3		8		11	7	13*	12	10³	4	5¹	6																					8
1	12	6	3	4	11	14		13	7		2³	10¹	5		8	9²																				9
1		8	4	2	9	14	13		12	6²		5	10		3³	7	11¹																			10
1		2	4	6	12	9¹	8		11		10	5		7		3																				11
1		2	3	10	7³	6	8		13	12	14		11²	4		9¹	5																			12
1		4	5	9²	8	3¹	7		11	14	13	12		10³	6			2																		13
1	12		2	3²		6	8	7		11	4³	10¹	13		14				9	5																14
1	13		3²		14	7	6	8	10	12			9¹		11³	4			5	2																15
1	6		2¹		10	8	7	11	12		13			4				9²	5	3																16
	7		2		11	6	9	8	10¹					4					12	5	3	1														17
	9¹		3²			7	6	8	10³	11		13			12	5			2	4	1	14														18
		3				7²	6	9	10	11		13			12	5			14	2	4	1	8³													19
		4¹					7	10	11	13	6				5				9²	2	3	1		8	12											20
			3					6	13	11²	14	8²			9	5				2	4	1	10¹	7	12											21
	7²		3					8	11	13	12				10³	5				2	4	1	14	9	6											22
		4³			7¹			8	11	14		13			10²	5				2	3	1	12	9	6											23
		3¹			6			7	12	11		4	13		10					5	2	1		8²	9											24
1	4			3		7³	13	11	6	12	9¹				10				8	2					5											25
1	9	4		3				11	10	7	12				6¹				8	2					5											26
	9	3		4				11¹	6	8	12				10				7				1	2	5											27
	9³	4		3			8	11	6		14	13			10				5				1	2²		7¹	12									28
	12	3		4			8	10¹	6		13				11				7³				1			9	14	2	5							29
	13	3		4			7	10¹	6						11				9³				1	14		8²		2	5	12						30
		3			5		6²	7	11¹	10					9				13				1	12				2	4	8						31
	13	3					12	9³	7*	11	6²				10								1	14				2	5	8	4					32
		3					8	13	7	11	12				9²								1					2	6	4	5	10				33
		3					7³	13	14	10¹					9								1			8³		2	5	6	4	12	11			34
		4					11³	14	7	9	13				8								1					2	3¹	6	5	12	10²			35
		4					2	9	8	10¹	6				11²								1							7	3	5	12			36
							2	9²	7	6			12		10	4							1			13	14		8³	3	5	11¹			37
							3	9	8	6¹					10	5²							1					12		7	4	2	13	11		38
		2					4	10²	7	11			13		8								1							6	3	5	12	9¹		39
		2					7	8	5¹	11²					10													12		6	3	4	13	9	1	40
		3					2	9	7	13	6				11															8¹	4	5²	12	10	1	41
		4					14	5	7¹	10²	6				9													2		8	3	12	13	11¹	1	42
		3					8		9	6					11													2		7	4	5¹	12	10	1	43
		3					5	7	11²	6					10													2		8	4	12	13	9¹	1	44
		4					5	8	9¹	6					11	13												2		7	3	10²	12		1	45
		3					5	7	9	6					10	12												2		8²	4		13	11¹	1	46

FA Cup

Fourth Qualifying	Spennymoor U	(a)	2-2	
Replay	Spennymoor U	(h)	3-0	
First Round	Basingstoke	(a)	1-1	
Replay	Basingstoke	(h)	2-1	
Second Round	Bristol C	(a)	0-1	

FA Trophy

First Round	Chester	(h)	1-1	
Replay	Chester	(a)	1-1	
(aet; AFC Telford U won 4-3 on penalties)				
Second Round	AFC Fylde	(a)	0-4	

ALDERSHOT TOWN

Ground: The ESS Stadium at the Recreation Ground, High Street, Aldershot, Hampshire GU11 1TW.
Tel: (01252) 320211. *Fax:* (01252) 324347. *Website:* www.theshots.co.uk *Year Formed:* 1926.
Record Attendance: 19,138 v Carlisle U, FA Cup 4th rd (replay), 28 January 1970. *Nickname:* 'The Shots'.
Manager: Barry Smith. *Colours:* Red shirts with white trim, blue shorts with white trim, red socks.

ALDERSHOT TOWN – VANARAMA PREMIER 2014–15 LEAGUE RECORD

Match No.	Date		Venue	Opponents	Result	H/T Score	Lg Pos.	Goalscorers	Atten- dance
1	Aug	9	H	Altrincham	W 3-1	2-0	3	Williams [10], Roberts [34], Scott [50]	1964
2		14	A	Eastleigh	L 0-1	0-0	12		1914
3		17	A	AFC Telford U	W 2-0	2-0	9	Oastler [5], Williams (pen) [26]	1619
4		22	H	Forest Green R	D 1-1	1-0	6	Williams (pen) [37]	2006
5		25	A	Torquay U	D 1-1	0-1	12	N'Guessan [71]	2135
6		30	H	Grimsby T	W 2-1	0-0	8	Williams 2 [56, 64]	1998
7	Sept	6	A	FC Halifax T	L 0-1	0-0	13		1837
8		9	H	Woking	L 0-1	0-0	14		3567
9		13	A	Nuneaton T	D 1-1	0-1	15	Hatton [66]	803
10		16	H	Braintree T	L 1-3	0-1	15	Lathrope [90]	1295
11		20	H	Lincoln C	W 1-0	1-0	14	Williams [31]	1582
12		27	A	Gateshead	D 1-1	1-0	14	N'Guessan [39]	1451
13		30	A	Dover Ath	L 0-3	0-1	15		797
14	Oct	4	H	Alfreton T	W 2-0	1-0	14	Hatton [33], Gibbs [63]	1476
15		7	A	Chester FC	L 0-1	0-0	15		1776
16		11	H	Bristol R	D 2-2	1-1	15	Williams (pen) [16], Roberts [77]	3466
17		18	A	Dartford	D 1-1	1-0	15	Scott [24]	1310
18	Nov	1	H	Gateshead	L 1-2	0-0	16	Holman [66]	1679
19		12	A	Kidderminster H	W 2-0	0-0	13	Williams (pen) [48], Molesley [73]	1577
20		15	H	Nuneaton T	W 1-0	0-0	13	Holman [53]	1658
21		22	H	Eastleigh	L 0-2	0-1	14		1737
22		25	A	Southport	W 3-1	2-1	12	McCollin [17], Hatton [24], Williams [71]	843
23		29	A	Wrexham	L 1-3	1-1	15	Holman [14]	2464
24	Dec	10	A	Macclesfield T	L 0-1	0-0	16		966
25		20	A	Welling U	L 1-3	0-1	18	Wilson [66]	756
26		26	H	Barnet	L 1-3	0-1	19	Roberts [48]	1940
27		28	A	Woking	W 2-1	2-0	17	McCollin [7], Williams [28]	3559
28	Jan	1	H	Barnet	L 0-1	0-1	18		2088
29		4	H	AFC Telford U	L 1-2	0-1	18	Williams [69]	1410
30		17	A	Lincoln C	L 0-3	0-2	18		3022
31		20	H	Kidderminster H	L 0-1	0-0	18		1035
32	Feb	7	A	Altrincham	L 0-1	0-1	18		925
33		14	H	Welling U	W 2-1	1-1	18	Stevenson [41], Jarvis (pen) [90]	1541
34		21	A	Alfreton T	W 3-2	2-1	18	Hatton 2 (1 pen) [39 (p), 50], Williams [40]	692
35		28	H	Dartford	D 1-1	0-1	18	Plummer [60]	1787
36	Mar	3	H	Dover Ath	W 3-1	0-0	16	Stevenson 2 [53, 68], McCollin [85]	1154
37		7	A	Macclesfield T	D 0-0	0-0	18		1671
38		10	H	FC Halifax T	D 1-1	1-0	18	German [27]	1167
39		14	H	Southport	L 1-2	0-2	18	Williams [58]	1646
40		20	A	Bristol R	L 1-3	1-1	18	Williams [32]	7416
41	Apr	3	A	Forest Green R	W 3-1	0-1	18	Williams [61], Plummer [64], Roberts [69]	2247
42		6	H	Torquay U	W 2-0	1-0	18	Plummer [5], Wilson [74]	2033
43		11	A	Braintree T	D 1-1	1-0	18	Hatton [29]	621
44		18	H	Chester FC	L 0-1	0-1	18		1953
45		21	H	Wrexham	D 1-1	1-1	18	McCollin [45]	1386
46		25	A	Grimsby T	L 1-3	0-2	18	Roberts [86]	3364

Final League Position: 18

GOALSCORERS

League (51): Williams 15 (4 pens), Hatton 6 (1 pen), Roberts 5, McCollin 4, Holman 3, Plummer 3, Stevenson 3, N'Guessan 2, Scott 2, Wilson 2, German 1, Gibbs 1, Jarvis 1 (1 pen), Lathrope 1, Molesley 1, Oastler 1.
FA Cup (6): Molesley 2, Fitchett 1, Roberts 1, Scott 2.
FA Trophy (0).

Smith 45	Oastler 33	Wilson 4 + 1	Barker 31 + 1	Gibbs 34	Molesley 15 + 4	Lathrope 19 + 5	Forbes 28 + 1	Roberts 28 + 1	Williams 44 + 2	Scott 12 + 11	N'Guessan 5 + 13	Fitchett 6 + 16	Derry 3 – 13	Hatton 34 + 7	Tonkin 9 + 2	Plummer 9 + 10	Diallo 6 + 4	Phillips 5	Oyeleke 8	McCollin 16 + 12	Holman 12	Thomas 1 + 1	East 5 + 1	Saunders 8	Jarvis 6 + 6	Stevenson 13 + 1	Tshimanga — + 2	McGinty 13	German 4 + 2	Richards 2 + 7	Rasulo — + 4	Alexander 2 + 2	Match No.
1	2	3	4	5	6[1]	7	8	9[3]	10[2]	11	12	13	14																				1
1	2	3	4	7	6[2]	5	9	8[3]	10[1]	11	14	13		12																			2
1	4	3	5	2			8	7	9[4]	11	10	6[1]	13	12																			3
1	2	3	4[2]	5	6[1]	7	8		10[3]	11	13	14		9	12																		4
1	3	4		2	14	9	8	7	10[2]	11[3]	13	12		6	5[1]																		5
1	4	3		2	5[3]	6	7	9	10		13	11[2]	14	8[1]	12																		6
1	3	4		2			8[1]	7	9	10	11	13[3]	12	14	6	5[2]																	7
1	2	3	4					7	8	9	10	11[3]		12	13	6[1]	5[2]	14															8
1	2		4	7		5	6[3]	8	10	13		11[2]	14	12		3[1]	9																9
1	2		4	7		6	9[1]	8	10	11	12	13		5	3[2]																		10
1	3	4		2			7	8[1]	9	10	13	6[3]	11[2]	12	14	5																	11
1	4	3		2			7	8[1]	9	10		6[2]	11[3]	12	13	5			14														12
1	4	3		2			7	8[3]	9	10		6[2]	11	12	13	5[1]			14														13
1	2				6		13	7	8	10	14	9[3]		11[1]	5	4[2]	12		3														14
1	2	3		5	9[1]	6	7	10[2]	13		14	11[1]	8		12		4																15
1	5	3		2	13	12	8	9[4]	10	11[1]	14		6[3]	7[2]			4																16
1	3	2	4[1]	7	5[2]		8		11	9	13		12			14				6	10[3]												17
1	3	4	5[3]	2	7		8[1]	9	10	6[2]	13			12							14	11											18
1	3	4	5		6[2]		8		10[1]					14	13	7[3]	12			2	9	11											19
1	3	4	5		6			9[1]	14	12	13	2							8[3]		7[2]	11	10										20
1	2	3		6	5		7		10	13				4					8[2]		9[1]	12	11										21
1	4	3		2	6		7		9	12[2]	13			5					8[1]		10	11											22
1	3	4	12	2	7[2]		8[3]		10		13	14	6	5							11			9[1]									23
1		4	5	2			8	12	10[3]		14			7		13	6[2]	3		9[1]	11												24
1	2	3	5[2]				8	9	13	10[3]				7		12	6	4[1]		14	11												25
1[1]	3	4[1]	5	2			7	9	10[3]		13			6						8[2]	12	11	14										26
	3	4		2			7	5	9		12			6						8	10[1]	11	1										27
1	3		4	2			7	5	10[1]		13			8		12				6[2]	11	9											28
1	3	4	5[1]	2			7[2]	9	11					8		12				6	13	10											29
1	3	4	6	2			12	9	10	13				5[2]						14					7[1]	8		11[3]					30
1	3	4	5	2				9	10[2]	12										13				6	7	11[1]	8						31
1	3	4	5	2				9	10[2]	12										11[1]				6	7	14	8[2]	13					32
1	3[1]	4	5	2				9	11[3]											10[2]				6	7	13	8	14					33
1	3	4		2[3]				9	12	13[4]				6		14				11[3]				8	10[1]	7		5					34
1	3	4		2				9[1]	11					6[2]		13				10[3]				7	8	5		12	14				35
1	3	4		2[3]	13				10					6		9[1]				14					7[2]	8		5	11	12			36
1	3	4		2[3]		14			9	11				7		6[2]				10[1]			12			8		5	13				37
1	3		5		13			7[1]	10[1]	14				6		9[3]								4		8		2	11	12			38
1	3	4			6[2]	12			9	10				2										7[1]	14	8[3]		5	11	13			39
1	3[3]	13	4[1]		6[2]	7			9	11	12			2						14						8		5	10				40
1	3	4			8				9[1]	10	14			2		6[2]				11[3]						13		7	5	12			41
1	3	4			9			8	10					7		11[1]				13						2[2]		6	5	12	14		42
1	3[3]	4	12	7					9	11				2		6				14						10[2]	8[1]	5				13	43
1	4				7			5	10	9[3]				2		6				13						11[2]		3	12	14	8[1]		44
1	3	4			8	7[1]			10					6		9[2]				11[1]						13		5	2	14	12		45
1	3[3]		5		9			8	10[2]					6						11[1]						14	13	4	2	12	7		46

FA Cup

Fourth Qualifying	Torquay U	(h)	2-0	
First Round	Portsmouth	(a)	2-2	
Replay	Portsmouth	(h)	1-0	
Second Round	Rochdale	(h)	0-0	
Replay	Rochdale	(a)	1-4	

FA Trophy

First Round	Burgess Hill T	(h)	0-1

ALFRETON TOWN

Ground: The Impact Arena, North Street, Alfreton, Derbyshire DE55 7FZ. *Tel:* (01773) 830 277.
Fax: (01773) 836 164. *Website:* www.alfretontownfc.com *Year Formed:* 1959.
Record Attendance: 5,023 v Matlock T, Central Alliance League, 23 April 1960. *Nickname:* 'The Reds'.
Manager: Nicky Law. *Colours:* Red shirts with white trim, red shorts with white trim, red socks.

ALFRETON TOWN – VANARAMA PREMIER 2014–15 LEAGUE RECORD

Match No.	Date	Venue	Opponents	Result	H/T Score	Lg Pos.	Goalscorers	Atten- dance
1	Aug 9	H	Woking	L	1-3	1-1	20	Stevenson [14]	613
2	12	A	Kidderminster H	L	0-3	0-1	23		1686
3	16	A	Forest Green R	L	0-2	0-1	24		956
4	23	H	Wrexham	L	2-3	1-3	24	Ironside [5], Clayton [74]	916
5	25	A	Grimsby T	L	0-7	0-3	24		3619
6	30	H	Braintree T	L	0-2	0-0	24		442
7	Sept 6	A	Barnet	L	1-2	0-0	24	McDonald [47]	1815
8	9	H	Altrincham	D	1-1	1-0	24	Ironside [42]	562
9	13	A	Southport	W	2-0	2-0	23	Ironside [2], Hawley [9]	832
10	16	H	AFC Telford U	W	3-2	3-1	23	Thanoj [11], Shaw [19], Ironside [45]	519
11	20	H	Nuneaton T	W	1-0	0-0	18	Mellor [62]	600
12	27	A	Dover Ath	L	0-1	0-1	20		715
13	30	H	FC Halifax T	L	0-2	0-1	22		705
14	Oct 4	A	Aldershot T	L	0-2	0-1	23		1476
15	7	A	Gateshead	L	0-2	0-2	23		1259
16	11	H	Torquay U	W	4-2	2-1	23	Hawley 2 [18, 77], Shaw [45], Clayton [70]	736
17	18	A	Chester FC	L	1-2	1-1	23	Shaw [15]	2084
18	Nov 1	A	Altrincham	W	1-0	1-0	22	Graham [20]	960
19	11	H	Bristol R	D	0-0	0-0	22		880
20	15	H	Dover Ath	L	2-3	1-0	22	Shaw 2 [40, 90]	650
21	22	A	Macclesfield T	L	0-2	0-1	22		1471
22	29	A	FC Halifax T	L	0-2	0-0	23		1198
23	Dec 2	H	Gateshead	L	1-2	0-1	23	Clayton [90]	454
24	6	A	Nuneaton T	W	1-0	1-0	22	Wood (pen) [15]	727
25	10	H	Eastleigh	W	3-2	1-1	21	Byrne [7], Hawley [78], Bradley [89]	442
26	20	H	Macclesfield T	L	1-5	1-3	22	Wood (pen) [8]	664
27	26	A	Lincoln C	L	2-3	0-1	22	Hawley [57], Bradley [90]	2685
28	Jan 4	A	Torquay U	D	1-1	0-0	21	Thanoj [90]	2028
29	17	A	Welling U	W	3-2	2-0	21	Wood 2 (2 pens) [10, 40], Hawley [74]	572
30	31	H	Woking	L	0-3	0-1	21		1526
31	Feb 7	H	Southport	W	4-2	0-1	21	Wood (pen) [47], Hawley [50], Howe [64], Connor (og) [87]	529
32	10	H	Forest Green R	D	2-2	0-0	21	Johnston [67], Rowe-Turner [90]	458
33	14	A	Braintree T	L	1-2	0-0	21	Howell [90]	468
34	21	H	Aldershot T	L	2-3	1-2	21	Johnston [4], Hawley [53]	692
35	28	A	AFC Telford U	W	1-0	0-0	19	Graham [57]	1561
36	Mar 7	H	Kidderminster H	W	2-0	1-0	20	Johnston [11], Hawley [70]	604
37	14	A	Dartford	W	1-0	0-0	20	Shaw [89]	913
38	17	H	Lincoln C	D	0-0	0-0	20		744
39	21	H	Chester FC	D	1-1	1-0	20	Shaw [22]	857
40	24	H	Dartford	D	0-0	0-0	20		490
41	28	H	Barnet	D	1-1	0-1	20	Wood (pen) [90]	989
42	Apr 4	A	Wrexham	L	0-4	0-3	20		2468
43	6	H	Grimsby T	L	0-2	0-0	20		3327
44	11	A	Eastleigh	L	1-3	1-2	20	Hawley [26]	1441
45	18	H	Welling U	D	2-2	1-1	21	Bradley (pen) [16], McDonald [70]	1593
46	25	A	Bristol R	L	0-7	0-3	21		11,085

Final League Position: 21

GOALSCORERS

League (49): Hawley 10, Shaw 7, Wood 6 (6 pens), Ironside 4, Bradley 3 (1 pen), Clayton 3, Johnston 3, Graham 2, McDonald 2, Thanoj 2, Byrne 1, Howe 1, Howell 1, Mellor 1, Rowe-Turner 1, Stevenson 1, own goal 1.
FA Cup (2): Hawley 1, Wood 1.
FA Trophy (5): Graham 1, Shaw 2, Stevenson 1, Wood 1.

Match No.	Stewart 3	Gray 6+1	Graham 45	Smith 8	Rowe-Turner 44	Bradley 34+4	Wood 44	Howell 28+8	Shaw 34+8	Clayton 8+10	Stevenson 8+6	Sheridan 5+9	McDonald 4+10	Hicks 6+9	Keane 16+5	Courtney 13+1	Ironside 22+7	Dawson 17	Thanoj 18+6	Gorman —+1	Igiehon —+3	Hawley 33+1	Mellor 7	Davies 9	Lamb 2+2	Johnson 4	Byrne 7	Johnston 21+2	Willis 4	Mooney 13	Howe 13	Leesley 1+10	Heaton 6+4	Bentley 2	Lenighan 9	Speight 4+4	Phillips 3+2	Flynn 5
1	1	2	3	4	5	6	7[3]	8	9[2]	10	11[1]	12	13	14																								
2	1	2[2]	3	4	5	8	7	9[3]		11[1]	12	10	13	14	6																							
3	1		3	4	5	8[1]	2	9	14	13	10					12	7[2]	6[3]	11																			
4			3[1]	4[2]	5	6[3]	2	8	14	10	13	9[1]				12	7		11	1																		
5	12			5	6[2]	2	7[1]	8	11[1]	13	14		9	3		4[2]		10	1																			
6		3		5	7	2		6	14	11[1]	9	12	13	4		10[3]	1	8[2]																				
7	4	3		5[4]	6[1]	2		8			12	10[3]		7		11[2]	1	9	13	14																		
8	5	3			2		7		12	9	11[2]	6[1]	4		10	1	8											13										
9			4	3	5	2	9	8[2]	13	12	6	11[1]	1	7			10																					
10			3	4	5	2	7	6	13	12			10[1]	1	8	11	9[2]																					
11			4	5	3	13	2	7	6			12	10[1]	1	8[2]	11[1]	9											9[2]										
12		3	4	5	2	7[1]	8	14	6	11[3]	1	13	12	10	9[2]																							
13		3[2]	5	6	2	13	14	7	4	11[1]	1	8	12	10[3]	9																							
14		3	5	6	2	12	13	14	7	4	11	1	8[2]	10[3]	9[1]																							
15	9	5	3	6	2	7	12	14	13	8[3]	4	10[1]	1	11[2]																								
16	5[1]	3	4	14	2	8	6	10[3]		12	7	13	1	11	9[2]																							
17		3	5	12	2	8	6		13	14	7	11[1]	1	10[3]	9[2]	4																						
18		4	5	6	2	7	8	10	13	11[1]	9[2]	12	1															3										
19		3	5	7	2	9	8	10	11[1]	6[2]	13		1															4	12									
20		3	5	7	2	9	8	11[3]	13	14	6[2]		12	1														4	10[1]									
21		4		6	2	7	9	12			13	8[1]		10								3	11[2]	1	5													
22		5		8	6	2	10[2]	9	12		7					11	4			1	3	13																
23		3	5	10			8	12		6[2]	7					11[1]	4	13	1	2	9																	
24		5	3	7	4	10	9									11	6	1	2	8																		
25		3	5	10	7	9	8									11	4		2	6	1																	
26		3	6	4	7[3]	9	10[1]	12	13	14	5					11			2	8[3]	1																	
27		4	5	10	7	9[3]	8[2]	12	14	13	3					11			2	6[1]	1																	
28		4	5	9[3]	2	8[2]	7	10[1]	14	13	3		12			11			6	1																		
29		4	5	2	10	7	8[1]	12	9				11			6			1	3																		
30		3	5	12	2	10	7[2]	9[1]	8	11[3]	6		1	4	13	14																						
31		3	5	10	2[2]	12	8	9[1]	13	11	6		1	4	7																							
32		3	4	9	2	13	7	10[1]	8				11	6[2]	1	12	5																					
33		3	4	9[2]	7	12	8[1]	10	2	14	11	6[3]	1	13	5																							
34		3	4	7[1]	6	9[2]	13	10	12	11	8[3]	1	14	5[1]	2																							
35		3	5	7	2	10	8	9	11[1]	1	12	4	6																									
36		2	4	8	5[2]	13	12	10[3]	7	11	6[1]	1	3	14	9																							
37		2	4	7[1]	5	14	13	11[3]	9	10	6[2]	1	3	12	8																							
38		2	4	5	6	11[1]	8	10	9[2]	1	3	12	13	7																								
39		2	4	5	9	10	8	11	6[1]	1	3	7	12																									
40		2	3	5	13	8	14	7	11[1]	9[3]	1	4	12	6	10[2]																							
41		2	4	10	5	9[2]		13	7				1	3	14	12	8[1]	11	6[1]																			
42		2	4	6	5	14	10[1]	8[3]	11	9[2]			3				7	13	12	1																		
43		2	3	6	5	9[2]	8[1]	14	12	11	13	4					10	7[3]	1																			
44		3	6	7	2[4]	8	13					4	10[3]					5[2]	11	12	9[1]	14	1																
45		2[1]	5	9	7			13	8	10[2]	11	6[3]	3	4	14	12	10[2]	11	1																			
46		4	6	8	2	7	3	13	12	9[1]	5	10[2]	11	1																								

FA Cup

Fourth Qualifying	Lincoln C	(h)	1-1
Replay	Lincoln C	(a)	1-5

FA Trophy

First Round	Lincoln C	(a)	2-0
Second Round	FC Halifax T	(a)	3-5

ALTRINCHAM

Ground: J. Davidson Stadium, Moss Lane, Altrincham WA15 8AP.   *Tel:* (0161) 928 1045.   *Fax:* (0161) 926 9934.
Website: altrinchamfc.co.uk   *Year Formed:* 1903.
Record Attendance: 10,275 (1991 Altrincham Boys v Sunderland Boys, ESFA Shield).   *Nickname:* The Robins.
Manager: Lee Sinnott.   *Colours:* Red and white striped shirts, red shorts with black trim, red socks with black and white trim.

ALTRINCHAM – VANARAMA PREMIER 2014–15 LEAGUE RECORD

Match No.	Date	Venue	Opponents	Result	H/T Score	Lg Pos.	Goalscorers	Attendance
1	Aug 9	A	Aldershot T	L	1-3	0-2	20	Clee [58]	1964
2	12	H	Lincoln C	L	1-2	0-1	20	Reeves [90]	996
3	16	H	Bristol R	W	2-1	1-0	15	Reeves [18], McChrystal (og) [65]	1463
4	23	A	Southport	L	1-2	0-1	18	Gillespie [61]	1082
5	25	H	Gateshead	L	0-1	0-1	19		1089
6	30	A	Nuneaton T	L	1-2	0-1	21	Reeves [87]	774
7	Sept 6	H	Dartford	W	2-1	1-0	18	Reeves 2 [41, 47]	1571
8	9	A	Alfreton T	D	1-1	0-1	17	Perry [89]	562
9	13	H	Eastleigh	D	3-3	2-2	16	Reeves 2 [11, 65], Griffin [35]	945
10	16	A	Kidderminster H	L	0-4	0-2	19		1451
11	20	A	Barnet	L	0-5	0-4	21		1516
12	27	H	Welling U	L	0-4	0-3	23		850
13	30	H	Macclesfield T	W	1-0	0-0	21	Lawrie [90]	1317
14	Oct 4	A	FC Halifax T	W	3-1	1-0	20	Clee [34], Lawrie [77], Perry [81]	1727
15	7	A	Grimsby T	D	0-0	0-0	18		2535
16	11	H	Woking	L	0-3	0-0	21		1218
17	18	H	Braintree T	W	1-0	1-0	19	Clee [27]	894
18	Nov 1	H	Alfreton T	L	0-1	0-1	20		960
19	4	A	Lincoln C	W	2-1	1-0	17	Richman [45], Reeves [51]	1953
20	12	A	AFC Telford U	L	1-2	0-1	18	Perry [90]	1417
21	15	H	Grimsby T	D	1-1	0-0	18	Leather [90]	1881
22	22	A	Wrexham	W	3-2	0-2	18	Reeves 2 [74, 79], Lawrie [83]	3002
23	29	H	Kidderminster H	W	2-1	0-0	17	Lawrie [57], Reeves [86]	1019
24	Dec 2	H	Woking	L	0-2	0-0	17		1056
25	6	A	Forest Green R	D	1-1	0-1	17	Marshall [49]	1261
26	20	H	Dover Ath	D	2-2	0-0	19	Crowther [74], Lawrie [90]	870
27	26	A	Chester FC	W	2-0	1-0	17	Marshall [25], Havern [59]	2569
28	28	H	Nuneaton T	L	0-1	0-0	19		1025
29	Jan 1	H	Chester FC	W	4-1	2-1	16	Clee 2 [10, 67], Reeves 2 [17, 61]	1840
30	4	A	Eastleigh	W	2-0	1-0	15	Midson (og) [39], Densmore [86]	1204
31	17	H	Torquay U	W	2-1	1-0	14	Reeves [37], Crowther [62]	1333
32	Feb 7	A	Aldershot T	W	1-0	0-0	14	Barker (og) [74]	925
33	10	A	Macclesfield T	L	1-2	0-1	24	Perry [63]	1962
34	14	H	Forest Green R	D	2-2	2-1	25	Perry [9], Reeves [43]	1071
35	21	A	Bristol R	L	0-1	0-1	25		6765
36	28	H	Barnet	L	1-3	0-2	25	Reeves [48]	1450
37	Mar 8	A	Welling U	W	1-0	0-0	13	Crowther [75]	1009
38	14	H	Wrexham	L	1-4	0-3	15	Lawrie [51]	1525
39	17	A	Dover Ath	L	1-2	0-1	16	Havern [79]	550
40	21	H	FC Halifax T	D	0-0	0-0	16		1371
41	28	A	Dartford	W	2-1	1-0	14	Reeves 2 [7, 50]	982
42	Apr 3	H	Southport	W	2-0	1-0	12	Clee [37], Sinnott [71]	1401
43	6	A	Gateshead	L	0-1	0-1	14		957
44	11	A	Torquay U	L	0-2	0-2	15		1462
45	18	H	AFC Telford U	L	1-2	0-1	17	Clee [82]	1265
46	25	A	Braintree T	L	2-4	1-1	17	Lawrie [39], Perry [78]	535

Final League Position: 17

GOALSCORERS

League (54): Reeves 18, Clee 7, Lawrie 7, Perry 6, Crowther 3, Havern 2, Marshall 2, Densmore 1, Gillespie 1, Griffin 1, Leather 1, Richman 1, Sinnott 1, own goals 3.
FA Cup (4): Lawrie 1, Perry 2, Reeves 1.
FA Trophy (2): Reeves 2.

Coburn 32+1	Densmore 28+1	Haven 45	Williams M 1	Griffin 43	Lawrie 37+5	Richman 34+4	Cavanagh 28+6	Clee 29+5	Gillespie 8+14	Reeves 40+5	Marshall 36+2	Leather 31+5	Perry 18+25	Williams S 22+10	Crowther 16+17	Moult 35+6	Wilkinson 1+9	Parton 14+1	Sinnott 8+5	Swift —+1	Match No.
1	2	3	4^1	5^3	6	7	8	9	10^2	11	12	13	14								1
1	2^1	4		3	9		6	14	10	13	5		11^2	7	8^3	12					2
1		3		5	12	7	6	9^1	10^1	11	2	4	13	8^2	14						3
1		3		5	12	6		11^2	10^1	4	2	13	8	9^1	7	14					4
		3		5	10^2	8	9		12	11	2	4	14	6^1		7^1	13	1			5
		3		5^1		6^2	7	9	10^3	11	4	2	13	8	12	14		1			6
		3		5	12	14	8	9^2		11	4	2	10	7^1	6^3	13		1			7
		3		5^2	9	6^1	7		12	11	4	2	10	8^3		13	14	1			8
		3		5	9	8	6	12	13	10^2	4	2	11	7^1				1			9
		3		5^3	9^2	8^4	6	13	12	10^1	4	2	11			7	14	1			10
12	13	4		5	6^3		7	9^2	14	10	3	2	11			8			11^1		11
1	2			5	6^2		8	9	13	11	3^4	4	10^1	7^3			12	14			12
1	2	3		5	6	7		10^2		11		4		8^1	12	9	13				13
1	2	3		5	10	6	13	9^1		11^2		4	12	8^3	14	7					14
1	2	3		5		6	12	9^3		11		4	13	8^2	14	7	10^1				15
1	2	4		3^4	11		6^2	14	9^1	10		5	13	7^2	12	8					16
1	5	3		10	8	6	9^1	13	11^2	2	4	12			7						17
1	2	3		6	12	7^2	9^3	14	10	4	5	11^1	13		8						18
	2	3		5	10	8	13		11^1	6	4	12	9^2		7		1				19
1	2	3		5	9^2	6^1	7		10^3	12		4	11	8	14		13				20
1	2	3		5	6^2	8	7		10^1	13		4	11	12	14	9^2					21
1	2	3		5	10	6	8		9^3	13	12	4^4	11^2		14	7^1					22
1	2	3		5	10^3	6	8		11	4		14	13	9^2	7^4	12					23
1	2	3		5	11^2	7	8^1		12	10	4		13	14	9^3	6					24
	2	3		5	6^3	7	11		12	10^1	4		13	14	9^2	8		1			25
	2	3		5	10	6	8^3	9^2		11	4		12	7	13	14		1			26
1	2	3		5	10	6	4	12		9	13	11^1		8^2	7						27
1		3		5	10		9^1	14	11	4	2	13	7^1	6^2	8	12					28
1	2	4		5		6	7	9		11	3		12	10	8^1						29
1	2	3		5		7	8^1	9	14	10^3	4	12	13		11^2	6					30
1	2^1	3		5	13	6		9^2		11	4	12	14	7^4	10^1	8					31
1	2	3		5	12	10		8	14	11^1	4		13	7^3	6^2	9					32
1	2	3		5	11	7		13	10	4		12	8^1	9^2	6						33
1	2	3		5	8	6		9^1		10	4		11			7			12		34
1	2	3		5	7	8		9		10	4		11^1			6			12		35
1	2	3		5	6^2	7	14	9^3		11	4	4^4	12	10^1					13		36
1	2	3		5	9	7^2	12		10^1		4	11	14	13	8				6^2		37
1	4^1	2		5	9		6	13		11		3	10^3	12	8^2	7			14		38
	5			10		4	9		12	2	3	11		8^1	7		1	6			39
1		3		5	9	7^2	8^1	10^3		11	4	2		14	13	6			12		40
1		4		5	10		7^4	9^3		11^1	3	2	13	12	14	6			6^2		41
1		3		5	9	12		10^2		11	4	2	13	7^3	14	6			8^1		42
	4			5	10	12^6	6	9^1		11^2	3	2	13		14	8		1	7^3		43
1^3		3		5	10	7^1		9^2		11	4	2	13		14	8^4		12	6		44
		3		5	9^3	7^2		8		11^1	4	2	12	6	13			1	10	14	45
		4		5	9			8		11	3	2	12		10^1	6		1	7		46

FA Cup

Fourth Qualifying	Barwell	(a)	3-0	
First Round	Blyth Spartans	(a)	1-4	

FA Trophy

First Round	Macclesfield T	(h)	1-0	
Second Round	Kidderminster H	(a)	1-0	
Third Round	Bath C	(a)	0-1	

BARNET

Ground: The Hive Stadium, Camrose Avenue, Edgware HA8 6AG. *Tel:* (020) 831 3800. *Fax:* (020) 8447 0655.
Website: www.barnetfc.com *Year Formed:* 1888. *Record Attendance:* 11,026 v Wycombe W, FA Amateur Cup, 1951–52.
Nickname: 'The Bees'. *Manager:* Martin Allen. *Colours:* Amber and black striped shirts, black shorts, black socks.

BARNET – VANARAMA PREMIER 2014–15 LEAGUE RECORD

Match No.	Date		Venue	Opponents	Result		H/T Score	Lg Pos.	Goalscorers	Attendance
1	Aug	9	A	Chester FC	W	5-0	3-0	1	Yiadom [4], Cook 2 [19, 52], MacDonald (pen) [31], Marsh-Brown [57]	2514
2		12	H	Bristol R	W	2-0	2-0	1	Akinde [22], MacDonald [43]	2027
3		16	H	Lincoln C	L	1-2	0-2	8	Marsh-Brown [56]	1529
4		23	A	Nuneaton T	W	2-0	2-0	4	MacDonald 2 (1 pen) [8 (p), 13]	863
5		25	H	Dartford	W	4-0	1-0	2	Akinde [43], Cook 3 (1 pen) [49, 59, 86 (p)]	1605
6		30	A	Southport	W	2-0	2-0	1	Cook [25], Akinde [39]	909
7	Sept	6	H	Alfreton T	W	2-1	0-0	1	MacDonald (pen) [62], Villa [90]	1815
8		10	A	Dover Ath	W	3-0	2-0	1	Villa [17], Gambin 2 [44, 61]	1023
9		13	A	AFC Telford U	D	2-2	0-1	1	Cook [69], Johnson [80]	1492
10		16	H	Wrexham	L	0-1	0-0	1		1336
11		20	H	Altrincham	W	5-0	4-0	1	Villa [13], Akinde 3 (2 pens) [30 (p), 45, 45 (p)], Hoskins [49]	1516
12		27	A	Forest Green R	W	2-1	1-0	1	Yiadom [13], N'Gala [90]	1424
13		30	A	Braintree T	D	1-1	1-1	1	Akinde [12]	1167
14	Oct	4	H	Eastleigh	W	1-0	1-0	1	Hoskins [37]	1610
15		7	A	Macclesfield T	L	1-2	0-0	1	Akinde [78]	1209
16		11	H	Kidderminster H	D	3-3	3-0	1	Villa [32], Cook [38], Akinde [43]	1689
17		18	A	Gateshead	W	2-0	2-0	1	Weston [4], Villa [7]	1747
18		21	H	Braintree T	W	3-0	2-0	1	Villa 2 [26, 34], Gambin [58]	1074
19	Nov	1	A	Welling U	W	2-1	1-1	1	Akinde 2 [25, 90]	906
20		11	H	Torquay U	L	2-3	0-2	1	Villa [49], Mensah [64]	1745
21		15	H	AFC Telford U	W	3-1	2-1	1	Akinde 3 (2 pens) [1, 19 (p), 83 (p)]	1671
22		22	A	Woking	D	1-1	1-0	1	Villa [2]	2617
23		25	A	Bristol R	L	1-2	1-1	1	Villa [37]	6012
24		29	H	Macclesfield T	W	3-1	0-1	1	Yiadom [57], Akinde [60], Weston [90]	1610
25	Dec	6	A	Torquay U	W	2-1	2-0	1	Vilhete [15], Akinde (pen) [40]	1933
26		20	H	Chester FC	W	3-0	1-0	1	Akinde [28], MacDonald [58], Weston [81]	1946
27		26	A	Aldershot T	W	3-1	1-0	1	Akinde 3 (1 pen) [41, 49, 90 (p)]	1940
28		28	H	Dover Ath	D	2-2	0-2	1	Weston [46], Akinde [75]	2048
29	Jan	1	H	Aldershot T	W	1-0	1-0	1	MacDonald [19]	2088
30		4	A	Lincoln C	L	1-4	0-2	1	Gambin [86]	2759
31		17	A	Grimsby T	L	1-3	1-2	1	Akinde (pen) [6]	3116
32		24	A	Southport	W	4-0	1-0	1	MacDonald [20], Villa [82], Akinde [88], Muggleton [90]	1833
33	Feb	7	H	Woking	W	2-1	1-0	1	Akinde (pen) [28], Jones (og) [50]	2036
34		14	A	Wrexham	L	0-1	0-1	1		2727
35		21	H	Grimsby T	L	1-3	0-1	1	Clifford [56]	2756
36		28	H	Altrincham	W	3-1	2-0	2	Akinde (pen) [6], Gash 2 [29, 61]	1450
37	Mar	7	H	Forest Green R	L	1-3	1-1	2	Akinde (pen) [7]	2070
38		14	A	Eastleigh	W	2-1	1-0	1	Weston [29], Akinde [46]	2034
39		17	A	FC Halifax T	D	1-1	0-0	1	Weston [67]	1127
40		21	H	Welling U	W	5-0	3-0	1	Vilhete [17], Akinde 2 (1 pen) [22, 40 (p)], Gash [60], Villa [82]	1700
41		28	A	Alfreton T	D	1-1	1-0	1	Weston [18]	989
42	Apr	4	H	Nuneaton T	W	1-0	0-0	1	Akinde [69]	2006
43		6	A	Dartford	W	1-0	1-0	1	Weston [30]	1579
44		11	H	FC Halifax T	W	3-0	2-0	1	Vilhete [2], Akinde [44], Weston [61]	2150
45		18	A	Kidderminster H	D	1-1	0-1	1	Villa [74]	2540
46		25	H	Gateshead	W	2-0	1-0	1	Vilhete 2 [25, 49]	5233

Final League Position: 1

GOALSCORERS

League (94): Akinde 31 (11 pens), Villa 13, Weston 9, Cook 8 (1 pen), MacDonald 8 (3 pens), Vilhete 5, Gambin 4, Gash 3, Yiadom 3, Hoskins 2, Marsh-Brown 2, Clifford 1, Johnson 1, Mensah 1, Muggleton 1, N'Gala 1, own goal 1.
FA Cup (5): Akinde 2, Villa 1, Stephens 1, Weston 1.
FA Trophy (2): Mensah 1 (pen), Stevens 1 (pen).

Stack 45	Yiadom 41	N'Gala 43 + 1	Stephens 37 + 5	Johnson 42	Vilhete 26 + 4	Weston 46	Togwell 38 + 4	Cook 32 + 7	Akinde 45	MacDonald 24 + 6	Saville 14 + 12	Marsh-Brown 2 + 8	Villa 22 + 11	Nurse 6 + 5	Muggleton 7 + 9	Gambin 4 + 22	Lowe — + 2	Mekki 3 + 6	Stevens — + 1	Hoskins 5 + 1	Pavey — + 3	Hunt 4 + 6	Mensah 1 + 7	Spiegel 1	Gash 8 + 7	Clifford 10 + 3	Match No.
1	2	3³	4	5	6¹	7	8	9²	10	11	12	13	14														1
1	2	3	4	5	9	6	7	8	10	11¹					12												2
1	5	3	4	2³	12	8	7²	6¹	10	11			9		13	14											3
1	6	3	2	4	5	7	8	9¹	10²	11³			12		13		14										4
1	6	4	3			7	8	12	11	10²	2	13	9³			14		5¹									5
1	2	3	4	5	8³	6	7	9²	11	10¹	13				12	14											6
1	6	3	4			7	5³	9	10	11	2²		13		12	8¹			14								7
1	2	3	4	5		7	8	9²	11¹	10³			6		13	12	14										8
1	2	3	4	5			7³	9	10				6²	13	14	11¹		12									9
1	2	3	4	5¹		7	8	9	10			12	6²	11³	13	14											10
1	2	4¹	3	6		7	12		11²				8	10	5	14		9³		13							11
1	2	4	5	3		6	8	7²	10					11	12				9¹	13							12
1	2	4	3	9²	13	7	8		10				14	6³	5¹	12			11								13
1	2	4	3	7	5	8	14	9¹	10						6³		12		11²	13							14
1	2	3		5	9¹	8	7	12	10		4³		14	6²			13	11									15
1	2	4	3	5		8	7	9	10³		14	13	6²						11¹	12							16
1	2	3	4	5	11	7¹	8	9	10		14		6²		13³	12											17
1	2	3	4	5		7	8	9²	10				6	11¹	12	13											18
1	5	3	2	4	6³	10	7¹	8	11	12			9²		14					13							19
1		4	3	5	6¹	8		13	10	11			12		7²	9³				2	14						20
1		3	8	5	7		9¹	10	12	4			6²		13	14				2	11¹						21
1		3	4	2	5	7		9	10³	11²	13		6¹	14						8	12						22
	2	3	4	5²	12	8	7	6¹	11	10			9³		14					13	1						23
1	2	3	14	5		7	8	9¹	10	11¹	4		6³							12	13						24
1	2	4¹	12	5	6	7	8	9²	10²	11¹	3			14					13								25
1	2	4	14	5	12	7	8	9¹	11¹	10³	3		6						13								26
1	2	13	4¹	5	6	8³	7	9²	10	11	3								12	14							27
1	2	3	14	5¹		7	8	9²	10	11	4	12	6³						13								28
1	2	3	4	8	5	7	9	13	10²	11¹	14	6³						12									29
1	2	3	4	5		7	8³	9¹	10	11		14	6¹		12				13								30
1	2	3	4		9	8¹	7	6	10	11²	12	14							5³			13					31
1	2	3		5	7	8	9¹	10	11³	4		6²	12	14					13								32
1	2	4	14	5		7	8	9²	10	11¹	3		6³							13	12						33
1	2	4		5		7	8	9²	10¹	11	3		13			14			12	6³							34
1	2	4	3³	5		8	7²	9¹		10	14		6		13				11	12							35
1		3³	4	9	2	7		14	10	13	12		6²	5¹						11	8						36
1	2		3	5		7¹	13	9	10		4		6²	14	12					11³	8						37
1	2	3	4	5¹	10	9	6		11		12			8							7						38
1	2	3	4¹	6	10	8	9	13	11¹		14		5³							12	7²						39
1	2	4		5	8¹	7³	9	6	10²		3		13		14					11	12						40
1	2	3	4	5	6	10	7	13	11				9¹							12	8²						41
1	2	3	4	5	6³	7	8		10¹	11²	14		9		13					12							42
1		4	3	9	2	7	12	6²	10					5¹	13					11	8						43
1	2	4	3	5	6³	8¹	7		10¹	12			14		13					11	9						44
1	2	4	3	5	6¹	8	7²		10	12			14		13					11³	9						45
1	2	3	4	5	9³	7	8		10¹	14	12		13							11	6²						46

FA Cup

Fourth Qualifying	Chelmsford C	(a)	0-0	
Replay	Chelmsford C	(h)	4-1	
First Round	Wycombe W	(h)	1-3	

FA Trophy

First Round	Concord Rangers	(a)	0-0	
Replay	Concord Rangers	(h)	2-6	

BRAINTREE TOWN

Ground: The Amlin Stadium, Clockhouse Way, Braintree, Essex CM7 3RD. *Tel:* (01376) 345 617. *Fax:* (01376) 330 976.
Website: www.braintreetownfc.org.uk *Year Formed:* 1898.
Record Attendance: 4,000 v Tottenham H, Friendly, 8 May 1952. *Nickname:* 'The Iron'. *Manager:* Danny Cowley.
Colours: Orange shirts with white trim, blue shorts, blue socks.

BRAINTREE TOWN – VANARAMA PREMIER 2014–15 LEAGUE RECORD

Match No.	Date	Venue	Opponents	Result	H/T Score	Lg Pos.	Goalscorers	Attendance
1	Aug 9	A	Macclesfield T	L 0-1	0-1	17		1309
2	12	H	Dover Ath	W 3-0	2-0	10	Massey 2 [14, 85], Mulley [25]	786
3	16	H	Chester FC	L 1-3	1-0	13	Davis (pen) [24]	800
4	23	A	Lincoln C	L 2-3	0-2	17	Davis (pen) [49], Brundle [90]	2231
5	25	H	Nuneaton T	W 2-0	0-0	13	Brundle [79], Bakare [88]	658
6	30	A	Alfreton T	W 2-0	0-0	13	Davis [64], Sparkes [80]	442
7	Sept 6	H	Bristol R	W 2-0	1-0	10	Davis (pen) [31], Sparkes [59]	1621
8	9	A	Welling U	L 1-2	1-0	12	Cox [15]	506
9	13	H	Kidderminster H	W 2-0	1-0	8	Mulley [14], Davis [48]	751
10	16	A	Aldershot T	W 3-1	1-0	7	Sparkes [17], Cox 2 [52, 78]	1295
11	20	A	Eastleigh	L 0-1	0-1	11		1131
12	27	H	FC Halifax T	D 0-0	0-0	11		909
13	30	H	Barnet	D 1-1	1-1	10	Cox [36]	1167
14	Oct 4	A	Gateshead	L 1-3	1-0	12	Cox [35]	1244
15	11	H	Southport	L 0-2	0-0	14		810
16	18	A	Altrincham	L 0-1	0-1	16		894
17	21	A	Barnet	L 0-3	0-2	16		1074
18	Nov 1	H	Woking	D 0-0	0-0	15		876
19	4	H	Grimsby T	L 0-1	0-0	15		875
20	11	A	Dover Ath	L 0-1	0-1	16		696
21	15	H	Wrexham	W 1-0	1-0	15	Strutton [26]	840
22	22	A	AFC Telford U	W 3-1	3-0	13	Strutton 2 [14, 38], Marks [43]	1523
23	25	H	Welling U	L 0-1	0-0	16		580
24	29	A	Woking	L 0-1	0-1	18		1622
25	Dec 20	H	Torquay U	W 2-0	2-0	17	Marks [20], Akinola [45]	818
26	26	A	Dartford	W 2-0	1-0	15	Strutton (pen) [8], Akinola [76]	1201
27	28	H	Eastleigh	L 1-5	1-1	16	Brundle (pen) [44]	748
28	Jan 1	H	Dartford	W 3-0	0-0	15	Isaac [78], Akinola [80], Sparkes [90]	934
29	4	A	Chester FC	W 3-2	0-1	14	Davis [52], Cox 2 [56, 77]	1690
30	17	H	Forest Green R	L 1-2	0-0	15	Marks [84]	661
31	Feb 14	A	Alfreton T	W 2-1	0-0	16	Marks [62], Isaac [70]	468
32	21	A	FC Halifax T	L 0-1	0-0	16		1268
33	24	A	Bristol R	L 1-2	1-1	16	Akinola [38]	6471
34	28	A	Grimsby T	L 0-1	0-0	16		3339
35	Mar 3	H	Macclesfield T	L 0-1	0-1	17		445
36	7	H	Gateshead	W 1-0	0-0	16	Davis (pen) [69]	515
37	14	A	Forest Green R	D 1-1	1-1	17	Brundle [45]	1313
38	17	A	Torquay U	W 5-1	2-1	16	Sparkes 3 [4, 40, 71], Paine [75], Peters [82]	1103
39	24	H	AFC Telford U	L 0-2	0-0	17		2115
40	28	A	Kidderminster H	L 1-3	0-3	17	Davis [46]	1317
41	Apr 3	H	Lincoln C	L 1-3	1-2	17	Sparkes [44]	650
42	6	A	Nuneaton T	W 1-0	0-0	17	Sparkes [81]	636
43	11	H	Aldershot T	D 1-1	0-1	17	Sparkes [56]	621
44	14	A	Southport	W 2-0	0-0	15	Cox [56], Isaac [84]	748
45	18	A	Wrexham	L 0-3	0-0	16		2766
46	25	H	Altrincham	W 4-2	1-1	14	Mulley [36], Cox 2 [51, 56], Mensah [82]	535

Final League Position: 14

GOALSCORERS

League (56): Cox 10, Sparkes 10, Davis 8 (4 pens), Akinola 4, Brundle 4 (1 pen), Marks 4, Strutton 4 (1 pen), Isaac 3, Mulley 3, Massey 2, Bakare 1, Mensah 1, Paine 1, Peters 1.
FA Cup (5): Akinola 2, Cox 1, Walker 2.
FA Trophy (4): Akinola 1, Cox 1, Davis 2 (1 pen).

Hamann 44	Peters 27+4	Clerima 27	Massey 46	Habergham 44	Mulley 31+7	Isaac 43+1	Paine 26	Davis 35+5	Sparkes 27+14	Marks 23+11	Bakare 2+9	Cox 24+11	Walker 13+7	Brundle 38+5	Maybanks 1+7	Case —+6	Smith 1+7	Akinola 33+5	Sowunmi 3	Strutton 7+4	Mensah 9+4	Moore —+1	Pentney 2	Pullen —+1	Match No
1	2	3	4	5	6	7²	8	9	10¹	11³	12	13	14												1
1	2		4	5	6³	7	8	9	10²		12	13	11¹	3				14							2
1	2		4	5	6	8		7	9	10¹	12	13	11²	3											3
1	2		4	5³	6¹	7	8	9	14	11²		10	13			3	12								4
1	2	3	4	5		7³		9	8	13	12	10¹	11²	6				14							5
1		3	4	5	6	8		7	9	13			11¹	10²		2		12							6
1		3	4	5	6	8		7	9³	14			11¹	12		2	13	10²							7
1	3²		4	5	6	7	8		13	14			11³	9¹		2	12	10							8
1	2		4	5	6	8	7¹	9³			12		11²	3		14	13	10¹							9
1	11³		4	3	7	5	6	8²	10¹			12	2	13	14	9									10
1	2		4	5	6²	7		8	9¹			13	11	12		3		10							11
1	2		4	5	6	8		7				12	11	9¹		3		10							12
1	2		4	5	6	8		7					11	9		3		10							13
1	2		4	5	6³	7		8²		12			11¹	9		13	14	10							14
1	2		4	5	6	8		7	9²	12			11²	10		3		13							15
1	2		4	5	7	9¹		8	12	13			11	10²	3			6							16
1	2		3		6	7		8¹	11⁴		9²	10	4	12		5	13								17
1	2		4	5	6	8				11			9	7				10	3						18
1			4	5	7³	9²	8	12	10¹	11			14	6		2				3	13				19
1	5	9	4		6²	14	3¹	8	12	11³			7			2		10		13					20
1	2	3	4	5	6	8	7			12		10		13				9¹		11²					21
1	2³	4	3	5	6	7	8		12	14		10		13				9¹		11²					22
1	2	3	4	5	6¹	8	7		12	14		10		13				9²		11²					23
1		3	4	5	6	8¹	7		12			10		13				9		11²					24
1	2³	3	4	5	6	8	7		12	11		13	14					9¹		10²					25
1	2²	3	4	5	6	8	7		13	10	14	12						9¹		11³					26
1		3	4	5	6	8²	7	13	9	11¹	12			2				10³		14					27
1		3	4	5	6	7	8	13	14	10³		12		2				9¹		11²					28
1		3	4	5	9	8²	7	6	12	13		10¹	14	2				11³							29
1	2	3	4	5	6²	8	7¹	9	12	13		11³		10	14										30
1		3	6	4		5	8	9	7¹	12	11²			2		13		10							31
1		2	6		4	7	5	9	8¹		10	3		11		12									32
1			4	3	12	5	6¹	7	8	9		2	13	10¹		11²									33
1	13		3	4	5	6¹	8²	7	9		10		2	12²	11										34
1	9¹		4	5	3		6	8	7	11		2	12	10											35
1	13		4	3	2	8	7	9	11		5	12		10¹		6²									36
1	12		4	3	2	9	8	7	13	10		5		6¹		11²									37
1	13		4	3	5	14	6	7	8	9¹	10³	2		12		11²									38
1		3	4	5	7	6¹	8	11	12	2		9		10		10³									39
1	2		4	5	14	6¹	7	8	13	11²	12	3		9		10³									40
1	2		4	5	12	6³	7	8	9	10¹	3²	11		13	14										41
1	2		6	5	13	7	4	8	11	10¹	12	9		3²											42
	2²	3	4	5		7	8	11	12	10	6	13		9¹		12		1					1		43
1	8		4	5	14	6	3	7	9¹	13	11²	2		12		10³									44
	4	3	5	14	7²	6³	8	9	10¹	12	2	13		11		1							1		45
1			4	5	8³	3	7	10¹	14	11	2	9²		6		12						13			46

FA Cup

Fourth Qualifying	Weymouth		(a)	0-0
Replay	Weymouth		(h)	5-3
(aet; 3-3 at end of normal time)				
First Round	Chesterfield		(h)	0-6

FA Trophy

First Round	AFC Sudbury		(h)	1-0
Second Round	Gosport Bor		(a)	2-0
Third Round	Ebbsfleet U		(h)	1-1
Replay	Ebbsfleet U		(a)	0-2

BRISTOL ROVERS

Ground: The Memorial Stadium, Filton Avenue, Horfield, Bristol BS7 0BF. *Tel:* (0117) 909 6648. *Fax:* (0117) 907 4312.
Website: www.bristolrovers.co.uk   *Year Formed:* 1883.   *Record Attendance:* 38,472 v Preston NE, FA Cup 4th rd,
30 January 1960 (at Eastville); 9,464 v Liverpool, FA Cup 4th rd, 8 February 1992 (at Twerton Park); 12,011 v WBA,
FA Cup 6th rd, 9 March 2008 (at Memorial Stadium).   *Nickname:*   'The Pirates', 'The Gas'.
Manager: Darrell Clarke.   *Colours:* Blue and white quarters, white shorts with blue trim, blue socks with white trim.

BRISTOL ROVERS – VANARAMA PREMIER 2014–15 LEAGUE RECORD

Match No.	Date		Venue	Opponents	Result		H/T Score	Lg Pos.	Goalscorers	Atten- dance
1	Aug	9	H	Grimsby T	D	0-0	0-0	12		7019
2		12	A	Barnet	L	0-2	0-2	17		2027
3		16	A	Altrincham	L	1-2	0-1	19	Mansell 76	1463
4		23	H	AFC Telford U	W	1-0	0-0	15	Clarke 55	5450
5		25	A	Forest Green R	D	1-1	0-0	16	Monkhouse 55	3781
6		30	H	FC Halifax T	W	2-1	1-0	15	Cunnington 27, Harrison 90	5394
7	Sept	6	A	Braintree T	L	0-2	0-1	15		1621
8		9	H	Wrexham	W	1-0	1-0	15	Monkhouse 34	5082
9		13	A	Lincoln C	W	3-2	2-2	12	Sinclair 13, Leadbitter 22, Harrison 90	2933
10		16	H	Nuneaton T	W	3-1	1-0	10	Parkes 2, Taylor 48, Gosling 78	4861
11		20	H	Woking	W	2-0	1-0	7	Cunnington 3, Mansell 86	6028
12		27	A	Southport	W	1-0	1-0	4	Gosling 13	1202
13		30	A	Eastleigh	D	1-1	0-1	6	Clarke 52	2621
14	Oct	4	H	Dover Ath	D	1-1	1-0	6	Cunnington 35	6162
15		7	H	Dartford	W	1-0	1-0	4	Taylor (pen) 37	5112
16		11	A	Aldershot T	D	2-2	1-1	4	Monkhouse 42, Taylor (pen) 68	3466
17		18	H	Forest Green R	L	0-1	0-1	6		7014
18	Nov	1	A	AFC Telford U	W	1-0	0-0	4	Clarke 50	2860
19		11	A	Alfreton T	D	0-0	0-0	4		880
20		15	H	Kidderminster H	D	1-1	0-0	4	Taylor 83	5848
21		22	A	Chester FC	D	2-2	0-0	6	Blissett 51, Parkes 58	2936
22		25	H	Barnet	W	2-1	1-1	4	Taylor 4, Balanta 90	6012
23		29	H	Welling U	W	2-0	0-0	3	Blissett 53, Taylor (pen) 73	5791
24	Dec	2	A	Wrexham	D	0-0	0-0	3		2608
25		6	A	Welling U	D	0-0	0-0	2		1176
26		19	H	Gateshead	W	3-2	0-1	2	Clarke 59, Mansell 69, Sinclair 72	5367
27		26	A	Torquay U	W	2-1	2-1	2	Taylor 8, Trotman 31	3755
28		28	H	Macclesfield T	W	4-0	1-0	2	Monkhouse 44, Blissett 65, Taylor 76, Harrison (pen) 83	6943
29	Jan	1	H	Torquay U	D	1-1	0-1	2	Taylor (pen) 83	8044
30		4	A	Nuneaton T	W	2-0	1-0	2	Mansell 40, Blissett 49	1661
31		17	A	Woking	D	0-0	0-0	2		3853
32		31	A	Dartford	D	2-2	1-1	2	Taylor 28, Harrison 77	1832
33	Feb	7	H	Lincoln C	W	2-0	2-0	2	Brown 36, Blissett 40	6528
34		14	A	Grimsby T	W	1-0	0-0	2	Lockyer 67	4073
35		21	H	Altrincham	W	1-0	1-0	2	Parkes 45	6765
36		24	H	Braintree T	W	2-1	1-1	1	Taylor (pen) 31, Harrison 83	6471
37		28	A	Gateshead	W	1-0	0-0	1	Harrison 71	1668
38	Mar	7	H	Eastleigh	L	1-2	0-1	2	Taylor 79	7371
39		14	A	FC Halifax T	D	2-2	0-2	2	Brown 83, Harrison 89	2248
40		20	H	Aldershot T	W	3-1	1-1	2	Easter 13, Monkhouse 59, Taylor 61	7416
41		28	A	Macclesfield T	D	0-0	0-0	3		2591
42	Apr	3	H	Chester FC	W	5-1	3-0	1	Taylor 15, Heneghan (og) 26, Monkhouse 2 33, 83, Harrison 88	8455
43		6	A	Kidderminster H	W	3-0	0-0	2	Harrison 2 50, 83, Taylor 90	4229
44		11	H	Southport	W	2-0	1-0	2	Harrison 11, Taylor 50	8251
45		18	A	Dover Ath	D	1-1	0-0	2	Harrison 64	2351
46		25	H	Alfreton T	W	7-0	3-0	2	Gosling 20, Harrison 29, Taylor 2 45, 48, Mansell 79, Monkhouse 82, Parkes 90	11,085

Final League Position: 2

GOALSCORERS

League (73): Taylor 18 (5 pens), Harrison 13 (1 pen), Monkhouse 8, Blissett 5, Mansell 5, Clarke 4, Parkes 4, Cunnington 3, Gosling 3, Brown 2, Sinclair 2, Balanta 1, Easter 1, Leadbitter 1, Lockyer 1, Trotman 1, own goal 1.
FA Cup (7): Harrison 3, Mansell 1, Monkhouse 2, Taylor 1.
FA Trophy (0).
Vanarama Premier Play-Offs (4): Taylor 2, Harrison 1, Lines 1.

Mildenhall 29	Lockyer 44	McChrystal 28 + 5	Parkes 45 + 1	Leadbitter 20 + 4	Mansell 44	Sinclair 24 + 3	Monkhouse 36 + 3	Brown 43	Brunt 4 + 2	Taylor 41 + 4	Gosling 15 + 8	Clarke 15 + 12	White 5 + 6	Puddy 14 + 1	Trotman 17 + 2	Martin 13 + 4	Cunnington 12 + 3	Harrison 7 + 28	Della Verde 4 + 2	Bissett 17 + 5	Goldberg 1 + 5	Balanta 3 + 13	Wall 2 + 3	Spiess 3	Easter 4 + 1	Dawson 8 + 4	Lines 8	Match No.
1	2	3	4	5¹	6	7	8³	9	10²	11	12	13	14															1
	2¹	3	12	13	7	8	6	5	14	10	9²	11		1		4³												2
1		4	3	2³	7	6⁴	13	5	10²	11	12	8¹	14					9										3
1	2	3			7		6	5		11¹		8				4		9	10	12								4
1	2	4		8	13	6	5		11¹		7	14				3	9³	10³	12									5
1	2	4		8	13	6	5			7	11²					3	9¹	10	12									6
1	2	3¹		8	13	9	5	14	12		7	10³				4	6	11²										7
1	2	4		8	7	6	5		11	12						3	9¹	10										8
1	5		6	3²	7	10	9³	4		11¹		8				2	13	14	12									9
1	2	3		8	7		5		10²	6¹	13	14				4	9	11³	12									10
1	4		5	2	6	9		3		10³	7²	12	14				8	11¹	13									11
1	2	14	4		5	10		3		6	7²	12				8	9¹	11³	13									12
1¹	2		4		7	9		5		10³	6¹	8⁴		12		3	14	13	11²									13
	2	3		8	7	13	5		11		6²			1		4	9	10¹	12									14
1	3		4		6	8	12	2		10¹		7				5	9²	11	13									15
1	2	14	3¹	12	7		6³	5		11		8				4	9	10²	13									16
1		4	2⁴	8		6³	5		11¹	9	7²	14				3	12	10	13									17
	2	12	3		7	9⁴	5		10	6	8			1		4¹		13	11²									18
1	2	3	4	5²	6	7		8	9³	10				11¹		14			12	13								19
1	2	3	4		7	8		5	10¹	12		13	11²			9³	14	6										20
1		3	4	5		6	8	7	2	10³	12					13	11²	9¹	14									21
1	2	3	4		8	7	6³	5		10¹						13	9	11¹	14	12								22
1	2	3	4		8	7	6	5		10¹	9³					14	13			12	11²							23
1²	2	3	4	8	9	5			11				13			6³	10¹	12	14									24
	2	3	4		6	5		8		14	13	7								10¹	11³	9³	12	1				25
	2	3¹	4		7	6	8	5		10		12				13		14			9³	11²	1					26
	5		3	2	7	9	8			11¹	6					4				10²	13		12	1				27
	5	3	4	2	7	8	6			10²	9³	12	1			14		11¹	13									28
	5	12	3	2	8	9	6			10	13	7²		1		4³		14		11¹								29
	2	3	4		8¹	7	9	5		10²	6	14	1			13		11³	12									30
	2	3	4	12	7		6	5		11²	9	8¹	1			13	10											31
1	7	3	4	2³	6		8	5		9						13		11²	12						10¹	14		32
1	6	3	4	2	7		9	5		10²	14					12		11¹	13							8¹		33
1	7	2	3	4	6		8	5		10						11										9		34
1	7	3	4	2	8		9	5		10³	13					12		11¹	14							6²		35
1	6²	4	5	2	7		9	3		10	8³					13		11¹	12							14		36
1	6	3	4	2	9¹		8	5		10²						13		11								12		37
1	6	4	5	2	7²		8	3		10		14				11		12	13							9²		38
1	2³	4	3	5	7		10	6		11²	9¹					12			14				13	8				39
	7	3	4	2		9	5			10³	14		1			12			13			11²	6	8¹				40
	7	3	4	2		6	5			10			1			12	13	9²		11¹	12	8						41
	3	13	4	2	7	9	5			11¹			1			12	14			10²	6³	8						42
	2	4	3		6		8	5		12		13	1			11¹	10					9	7²					43
	2	6	3		7		10	5		8			1			9²	12	13			11¹	4						44
	2	3	4		8		6	5		10			1			9¹	11	12				7						45
	2³	3	4	14	8	9	5			10	6	13	1			11¹						7²						46

FA Cup

Fourth Qualifying	Dorchester T		(a)	7-1
First Round	Tranmere R		(a)	0-1

FA Trophy

First Round	Bath C		(h)	0-2

Vanarama Premier Play-Offs

Semi-Finals 1st leg	Forest Green R		(a)	1-0
Semi-Finals 2nd leg	Forest Green R		(h)	2-0
Final	Grimsby T	Wembley		1-1

(aet; Bristol R won 5-3 on penalties)

CHESTER FC

Ground: Swansway Chester Stadium, Bumpers Lane, Chester CH1 4LT. *Tel:* (01244) 371376.
Website: www.chesterfc.com   *Year Formed:* 1885, renamed Chester City 1983, reformed as Chester FC 2010.
Record Attendance: 20,500 v Chelsea, FA Cup 3rd rd (replay), 16 January 1952 (at Sealand Road).
Nickname: 'The Blues'.   *Manager:* Steve Burr.   *Colours:* Blue shirts with white sleeves, blue shorts with white trim,
white socks with blue trim.

CHESTER FC – VANARAMA PREMIER 2014–15 LEAGUE RECORD

Match No.	Date	Venue	Opponents	Result	H/T Score	Lg Pos.	Goalscorers	Atten-dance
1	Aug 9	H	Barnet	L 0-5	0-3	24		2514
2	12	A	Forest Green R	L 1-2	0-1	24	Winn [79]	1083
3	16	A	Braintree T	W 3-1	0-1	16	McConville 2 [48, 67], Iwelumo [64]	800
4	23	H	FC Halifax T	L 0-3	0-1	19		2501
5	25	A	Kidderminster H	D 2-2	0-2	17	Hobson [81], Riley [83]	2304
6	30	A	Gateshead	L 1-2	1-0	19	Hobson [28]	1138
7	Sept 6	H	Macclesfield T	W 1-0	1-0	17	Rooney [13]	2612
8	9	H	Torquay U	L 0-2	0-0	19		1954
9	13	A	Woking	L 0-1	0-0	19		1629
10	16	H	Southport	W 2-0	2-0	16	Charnock [3], Hobson [14]	1790
11	22	H	Wrexham	W 2-1	0-1	16	Hobson [74], Heneghan [90]	3183
12	27	A	Grimsby T	L 0-3	0-1	17		3245
13	30	A	AFC Telford U	W 2-1	1-1	16	Rooney [28], McConville [66]	1871
14	Oct 4	H	Welling U	D 1-1	1-0	16	Mahon [10]	1997
15	7	H	Aldershot T	W 1-0	0-0	14	Hughes [80]	1776
16	11	A	Dover Ath	L 0-2	0-0	16		1009
17	18	H	Alfreton T	W 2-1	1-1	13	Hughes [29], Mahon [90]	2084
18	Nov 1	A	Eastleigh	L 2-3	0-1	14	McConville [78], James [90]	1306
19	11	A	Macclesfield T	L 1-3	0-2	14	Heneghan [54]	1951
20	15	H	Gateshead	W 1-0	0-0	14	Rooney [68]	2308
21	22	H	Bristol R	D 2-2	0-0	16	Oates [68], Hughes [70]	2936
22	25	A	Dartford	W 4-2	0-1	14	Mahon 2 [50, 54], Hughes [60], Oates [86]	904
23	29	A	Nuneaton T	L 2-3	0-2	16	Hobson 2 [50, 88]	973
24	Dec 2	H	AFC Telford U	W 2-0	0-0	13	Brown [52], Parry (og) [76]	1860
25	20	A	Barnet	L 0-3	0-1	15		1946
26	26	H	Altrincham	L 0-2	0-1	16		2569
27	28	A	FC Halifax T	W 2-0	1-0	15	Brown [7], Peers [84]	1901
28	Jan 1	A	Altrincham	L 1-4	1-2	17	Rooney [28]	1840
29	4	H	Braintree T	L 2-3	1-0	17	McConville [40], Brown [76]	1690
30	17	A	Southport	D 0-0	0-0	17		1894
31	24	H	Kidderminster H	W 1-0	1-0	15	Mahon [30]	2111
32	27	H	Lincoln C	W 4-0	3-0	13	Rooney [5], McConville [12], Higgins [24], Abbott [66]	1569
33	31	A	Welling U	W 3-1	2-1	13	McBurnie [37], Rooney 2 (1 pen) [45 (p), 47]	619
34	Feb 14	A	Lincoln C	W 1-0	1-0	10	McConville [41]	4568
35	21	H	Eastleigh	L 0-1	0-0	10		2294
36	Mar 7	A	Wrexham	L 0-1	0-1	12		6336
37	10	A	Torquay U	W 1-0	1-0	11	Thomson [29]	1221
38	14	A	Grimsby T	D 2-2	0-1	10	Heneghan [75], Rooney (pen) [84]	2916
39	17	H	Dartford	L 1-2	0-0	11	McBurnie [54]	1603
40	21	A	Alfreton T	D 1-1	0-1	11	Heneghan [88]	857
41	28	H	Woking	L 2-3	1-1	12	Mahon [44], Heneghan [79]	1899
42	Apr 3	A	Bristol R	L 1-5	0-3	14	McBurnie [60]	8455
43	6	H	Forest Green R	L 1-4	1-3	15	Rooney [45]	1911
44	11	A	Dover Ath	W 3-1	0-1	13	McBurnie [46], Hobson [58], Rooney [73]	1645
45	18	A	Aldershot T	W 1-0	1-0	13	Rooney (pen) [14]	1953
46	25	H	Nuneaton T	W 5-3	1-2	12	McBurnie [44], James [62], McConville 2 [69, 75], Thomson [84]	2614

Final League Position: 12

GOALSCORERS

League (64): Rooney 11 (3 pens), McConville 9, Hobson 7, Mahon 6, Heneghan 5, McBurnie 5, Hughes 4, Brown 3, James 2, Oates 2, Thomson 2, Abbott 1, Charnock 1, Higgins 1, Iwelumo 1, Peers 1, Riley 1, Winn 1, own goal 1.
FA Cup (6): Heneghan 2, Hughes 1, Mahon 1, McConville 2.
FA Trophy (2): Heneghan 1, James 1 (pen).

Worsnop 42	Taylor 4	Brown 21 + 2	Charnock 33 + 4	Roberts 40 + 2	Harrison 7 + 6	James 37 + 3	Rooney 43 + 3	Mahon 38 + 6	Hobson 24 + 11	Winn 6 + 6	Menagh 3 + 9	Iwelumo 4 + 6	McConville 35 + 6	Hall F 4	Disney 1	Heneghan 34 + 4	Kay 31 + 2	Riley — + 6	Hall J 7 + 1	Morris — + 2	Touray 7 + 12	Hughes 24 + 1	Oates 5 + 1	O'Keefe 2 + 1	Peers 1 + 9	Richards 5 + 7	Higgins 17	Abbott 15 + 1	Green — + 2	McBurnie 14	Thomson 2 + 6	Viscosi — + 1	Match No.
1	2[1]	3	4	5	6[8]	7	8	9	10[2]	11[3]	12	13	14																				1
	2	3	4	5		7	8	6[1]	11[2]	9	13	12	10		1																		2
		3	4	5		7	8	6	13	9[4]	14	11[3]	10		1		2[1]	12															3
		3	4	5[2]		7	8	6[3]	14	10[1]	13	11	9		1		12	2															4
	2	3		5	7	8[6]	6		9	12		10[1]	11		1		4	13															5
1	2			5	6	8[1]	7[3]		10[2]	13		14	9			4	3	12	11														6
1		3		5	8	7	6	12	10				11			2	4		9[1]														7
1		3		5	8[3]	7	6	12	10				11[2]			2	4	14	9[1]	13													8
1		3		5	7[2]	8	10	12	11[1]			14	6[3]			2	4		9	13													9
1			4	5	13	8	6	9	10[2]				7			2	3	11[1]		12													10
1		3		5		7	6	8[8]	10[3]			14	11			2	4	13	9[1]	12													11
1			4	2[1]	13	7	8	6	11[2]				10			9	3[3]	12	14	5													12
1		3	9	14	6[3]	7	5	10[2]				13	8			2	4	11[1]		12													13
1			4	5	12	8	7	6[1]	13			10[2]	11			2	3			9													14
1			4	5	13	8	7	6[2]		9[2]	14		10[1]			2	3			12	11												15
1			4	5[1]		8	7	6	13	9[2]	14		11[3]			2	3			12	10												16
1			4	5		8	7	6	10[1]		12		9			2	3			11													17
1		3	4	5		6	9	10[2]	11[1]	12	13		7			2				8[4]													18
1		3	4	5		7	8	6	11[2]		9[1]		10[3]			2				12		13	14											19
1		3	4[2]	5		6	7	8	9[1]							2	13			12		11	10											20
1		3	4	5		6	7	8	13				12			2				14	9[2]	11[3]	10[1]										21
1		3	5	2		8	7	6[1]	12				9[1]				4			13	10	11[3]		14										22
1		3	4	5[2]	7[1]		6	8	13				9				2			12	10	11											23
1		3	4	5	12	6	8	7[1]					9[2]				2			13	11	10		14									24
1		3	4	5[1]		7	8	6	11[1]				10			2				12				9									25
1		3	4[2]			7	8	6[1]	10		13		11[3]			12	2	14		5				9									26
1		3	4			8	7	13	10[1]	6			9			5				2				12	11[2]								27
1		4	3	13		7	6	14	11[3]		9[2]		10[1]			2				5[1]				12	8								28
1		3	4	5		7	8	9	10[1]				11			6	2[2]							12	13								29
1		3		5		7[8]	13	8[1]					6			4				10				11[12]	12	2	9[3]	14					30
1		4[2]		5		6[3]	9						7			12	3			11					2	8[1]	13	10	14				31
1		14		5[1]		6	9						7[2]			4	3			11				12	2	8	10	13					32
1		12	2			7	8[1]						9			3	4[2]			10				14	5	6[1]		11	13				33
1		12	3		14	8	7[2]						9			2[1]	4			6[2]				13	11	5		10					34
1		4	5		12	7[1]	6	11[2]					10[3]			3				9				13	2	8			14				35
1	12	4[1]	5		13	7	6	14					10[2]			3				9					2	8[3]	11						36
1	14		5			7	6	9	13							4	3[1]			12					2	8		11[2]	10[3]				37
1						8	13	12	14							4	3			5	9			6[1]	2	7[2]		11	10[3]				38
1						8	11[1]	6					12			4	3			5	9			13	2	7[2]		10					39
1		13	5[2]			6	7[3]	9					12			4	3			10				14	2	8[1]		11					40
1	3	5[1]	13			8	9	6	12				11			4	14			10[1]					2[1]	7[2]							41
1			5			7	8[3]	6	14				10[1]			3	4			9[2]		13			2	12		11					42
1		3[2]		5		7	13	6					12			4	8[1]			10					2	9		11					43
1			4	5		8	6[1]	11[2]	13							3				9		12			2	7		10					44
1			4	5		8	9[1]	10[2]	14								3			6[3]		13			2	7		11	12				45
1[2]			4	5		7	8	6[3]	11				12			3				9					2			10[1]	13	14			46

FA Cup

Fourth Qualifying	Stockport Co	(a)	4-2	
First Round	Southend U	(a)	2-1	
Second Round	Barnsley	(a)	0-0	
Replay	Barnsley	(h)	0-3	

FA Trophy

First Round	AFC Telford U	(a)	1-1
Replay	AFC Telford U	(h)	1-1
(aet; AFC Telford U won 4-3 on penalties)			

DARTFORD

Ground: Princes Park, Grassbanks, Darenth Road, Dartford, Kent DA1 1RT.
Tel: (01322) 299 991. *Website:* www.dartfordfconline.co.uk *Year Formed:* 1888.
Record Attendance: 4,097 v Horsham YMCA, Ryman League, 11 November 2006.
Nickname: 'The Darts'. *Manager:* Tony Burman.
Colours: White shirts with black trim, black shorts, black socks with white trim.

DARTFORD – VANARAMA PREMIER 2014–15 LEAGUE RECORD

Match No.	Date	Venue	Opponents	Result	H/T Score	Lg Pos.	Goalscorers	Attendance
1	Aug 9	H	Wrexham	L	1-2	0-1	16	Bradbrook, T [51]	1561
2	12	A	Woking	D	1-1	0-0	16	McAuley [48]	1538
3	16	A	Kidderminster H	L	0-1	0-1	18		1626
4	23	H	Torquay U	D	0-0	0-0	20		1163
5	25	A	Barnet	L	0-4	0-1	21		1605
6	30	H	AFC Telford U	W	2-1	0-1	17	Daley [52], Pugh [64]	923
7	Sept 6	A	Altrincham	L	1-2	0-1	20	Bradbrook, E [83]	1571
8	9	H	Eastleigh	D	2-2	0-2	21	Bradbrook, E [55], Crawford [90]	806
9	13	A	Gateshead	L	0-1	0-0	21		1336
10	16	H	Dover Ath	W	2-1	0-1	17	Crawford [72], Bradbrook, T [85]	1103
11	20	H	Forest Green R	L	1-2	0-0	19	Cornhill [90]	1003
12	27	A	Nuneaton T	W	2-1	0-1	18	Bradbrook, E (pen) [78], Harris [80]	759
13	30	A	Welling U	D	2-2	2-2	18	Sweeney [9], Bradbrook, E [36]	1306
14	Oct 4	H	Grimsby T	D	1-1	0-0	18	Bradbrook, T [61]	1285
15	7	A	Bristol R	L	0-1	0-1	19		5112
16	11	H	Macclesfield T	D	1-1	0-0	19	Hayes [85]	1063
17	18	H	Aldershot T	D	1-1	0-1	21	Pugh [67]	1310
18	Nov 1	A	Grimsby T	L	0-3	0-2	21		3116
19	11	H	Welling U	W	2-1	1-0	19	Cornhill [33], Crawford [52]	1512
20	15	H	Southport	D	1-1	0-1	19	Crawford [90]	1163
21	22	A	Lincoln C	L	0-1	0-1	21		2483
22	25	H	Chester FC	L	2-4	1-0	21	Noble [15], Bradbrook, E [47]	904
23	29	A	Forest Green R	L	1-2	0-1	21	Oshodi (og) [82]	1148
24	Dec 2	A	Eastleigh	L	0-2	0-1	21		1765
25	20	A	Wrexham	W	3-1	1-0	21	Bradbrook, E [6], McAuley [63], Bradbrook, T [90]	2662
26	26	H	Braintree T	L	0-2	0-1	21		1201
27	Jan 1	A	Braintree T	L	0-3	0-0	21		934
28	4	A	Kidderminster H	L	1-2	1-0	22	Hayes [1]	902
29	13	H	FC Halifax T	L	1-2	1-1	22	Crawford [9]	811
30	17	A	Dover Ath	L	1-6	1-2	22	Crawford [21]	1042
31	31	H	Bristol R	D	2-2	1-1	22	Hayes 2 [32, 79]	1832
32	Feb 14	A	AFC Telford U	W	3-2	1-1	22	Pugh 2 [24, 79], Ventre (og) [90]	1653
33	28	A	Aldershot T	D	1-1	1-0	23	Bradbrook, E [16]	1787
34	Mar 3	H	Woking	L	1-3	1-1	23	Green, N [43]	884
35	7	A	FC Halifax T	D	0-0	0-0	23		1253
36	14	H	Alfreton T	L	0-1	0-0	23		913
37	17	A	Chester FC	W	2-1	0-0	22	Green, N [55], James (og) [89]	1603
38	21	A	Southport	L	0-2	0-0	23		850
39	24	A	Alfreton T	D	0-0	0-0	23		490
40	28	H	Altrincham	L	1-2	0-1	23	Hayes [68]	982
41	31	H	Gateshead	D	1-1	1-1	23	Chiedozie [9]	602
42	Apr 4	A	Torquay U	D	1-1	0-0	23	Chiedozie [82]	1754
43	6	H	Barnet	L	0-1	0-1	23		1579
44	11	H	Nuneaton T	W	3-1	0-1	22	Bradbrook, E (pen) [63], Bradbrook, T [78], Crawford [83]	808
45	18	A	Macclesfield T	L	0-2	0-1	24		1756
46	25	H	Lincoln C	D	0-0	0-0	23		1274

Final League Position: 23

GOALSCORERS

League (44): Bradbrook, E 8 (2 pens), Crawford 7, Bradbrook, T 5, Hayes 5, Pugh 4, Chiedozie 2, Cornhill 2, Green, N 2, McAuley 2, Daley 1, Harris 1, Noble 1, Sweeney 1, own goals 3.
FA Cup (8): Bradbrook, E 2 (1 pen), Bradbrook, T 1, Crawford 2, Harris 1, Hayes 1, Noble 1.
FA Trophy (7): Bradbrook, E 1, Bradbrook, T 1, Burns 1, Crawford 1 (pen), Harris 1, McAuley 1, Pugh 1.

Brown 30	Burns 19+1	McAuley 45	Mitchel-King 28	Green A 11	Noble 30+6	Collier 23+5	Bradbrook E 42	Daley 21+10	Pugh 19+10	Bradbrook T 19+13	Crawford 28+12	Harris 21+18	Sweeney 29+7	Cornhill 16+7	Hayes 21+16	Bender 15+1	Driver 19+3	Tarbuck —+2	Ibrahim 16	Green N 14+1	Doidge 6+1	Richards 16	Dallison 12	Chiedozie 4	Adams 1+3	Vint 1	Dembele —+1	Match No.
1	2	3	4	5	6	7	8	9	10³	11²	12	13	14															1
1	8¹	4	2	3	12	7	5	11	10					9	6													2
1		4	3	5		2	7	9²	10	12	11¹	14	6³	8	13													3
1		4	3	5		2	8	12	11¹	10	13		9²	7	6													4
1		4	3	5	10³	2	7	9	11¹	6	13	12	8²	14														5
1		4	3	5	13	2	8	9	10¹	11³	14	12	7	6²														6
1		4	3	5	6³	2	8	9	11¹	12	13	10²	7	14														7
1	2	4	3	5²	12	13	8	9	11¹	10	14	7	6³															8
1	6	2	3	4³	8²	5	7	10	14	13	11	9¹	12															9
1	5³	4	3	9	7¹	2	8	11	12	10²	6	14	13															10
1	2	4	3	5			8	9¹	10³	11		12	7	13	6													11
1	2	4	3	5		7	9²	10	11³	12		8	14	6¹	13													12
1	2	4	3	6		9	10¹	13	11²	12		7¹	8	14	5													13
1	7¹	3	2	5	8	13	14	11	10²	6	9	12³	4															14
1		4		5	3²	6	8	13	11¹	10	9	7	12	2														15
1		4	3	13		2	8	9²	14	10¹	11³	12	7	6	5													16
1	3	2	12	5	6		8⁴	10¹	11	14	13	7	9	4														17
1		4		5	8	7	3	11³	10¹	14	6²	12	9	13	2													18
1	2³	3		9	4	13		11²	12	10	8	7	6¹	5	14													19
1		3		9	4	13	12	11	10²	8	7	6	5	2														20
1		4	3			7	8				12	10	9¹	2	6	5	11											21
1	3	4			8³	12	6	14	11	13	9	7¹	10	2	5²													22
1		4	3		10	8	14	11	6²	7	9	13	5¹	2³	12													23
1		3	14		7	4	11²	10³	12	9	8	6¹	2	5	13													24
1		3	4		6	13	7	9	11	10²	12	8		5	2¹													25
1		4	3		6	2	8	9¹	10	11²	13	7³	14	12	5													26
	2	4	3		6		8	9¹	10	11	12	7²			13	5	1											27
	2	4	3		13		8	10²	11¹	12		7			6	5	1		9									28
	2	4	3				8	13	10	11	12	7²			6	5¹	1		9									29
	2¹	4	3				8³	7	6	14	10	5²		13		12	1		9	11								30
1	2	3			8	4	7		13		10²	12		6								9	11¹	5				31
1	2	3			8		7	11	13	6	12			9								10²	5	4				32
1	2	3			8		7		11	6	12	13		9¹								10²	5	4				33
1	2	3			8		7		11²	12	13	14		6¹								9	10	5	4			34
	2	4			8			14	10¹		13³	6	7				12		1			9	11²	5	3			35
		3			6¹		8		11		10	7		12		2			2			1	9²	13	5	4		36
		3			6¹		8		6	12		10¹	11	9		2			2		1	7	5	4				37
		3			9		6	12	13		11¹	8	7³		14	2			2		1	10²	5	4				38
13		3			8²		5		11		9	10	6	12		4			1			2¹	7					39
		3			7	12	4	11³		13		6²	8		12	2			1	9¹			5	10				40
		3			7		4	9²	12	10		13	8	6¹		2			1				5	11				41
		3			4			13	14	8¹	9²	7	6³			2			1			5	10	11	12			42
		3			7	4		12	13	9	10³		6			2¹			1			5	8	11²	14			43
		3			9		7²	8	11	13	10		6³			2¹			1		12		5	4		14		44
		3			7²		8	10	12	11¹	13					2			1	9			5	4	6			45
		3			7		8	10²	12	13	9³		6			2			1	11¹			5		4		14	46

FA Cup

Fourth Qualifying	Burgess Hill T	(h)	3-1
First Round	Bromley	(a)	4-3
Second Round	Bradford C	(a)	1-4

FA Trophy

First Round	Solihull Moors	(h)	2-0
Second Round	Burgess Hill T	(a)	2-1
Third Round	FC Halifax T	(h)	2-2
Replay	FC Halifax T	(a)	1-3

DOVER ATHLETIC

Ground: Crabbie Athletic Ground, Lewisham Road, River, Dover, Kent CT17 0JB. *Tel:* (01304) 822373.
Fax: (01304) 821383. *Website:* doverathletic.com *Year Formed:* 1894 as Dover FC, reformed as Dover Ath 1983.
Record Attendance: 7,000 v Folkestone, 13 October 1951. *Nickname:* The Whites. *Manager:* Chris Kinnear.
Colours: White shirts with black trim, black shorts with white trim, black socks.

DOVER ATHLETIC – VANARAMA PREMIER 2014–15 LEAGUE RECORD

Match No.	Date	Venue	Opponents	Result	H/T Score	Lg Pos.	Goalscorers	Attendance
1	Aug 9	H	FC Halifax T	L 0-1	0-0	17		1321
2	12	A	Braintree T	L 0-3	0-2	22		786
3	16	A	Grimsby T	D 1-1	0-0	21	Lock [86]	3548
4	23	H	Eastleigh	W 2-1	1-1	16	Payne [43], Elder [78]	787
5	25	A	Woking	L 1-6	1-3	18	Payne [30]	1454
6	30	H	Kidderminster H	L 0-1	0-0	20		833
7	Sept 6	A	AFC Telford U	W 4-1	1-1	16	Bonner [38], Reid 2 [76, 90], Miller [87]	1515
8	10	H	Barnet	L 0-3	0-2	18		1023
9	13	H	Macclesfield T	L 0-1	0-0	19		754
10	16	A	Dartford	L 1-2	1-0	22	Miller [8]	1103
11	20	A	Torquay U	L 0-2	0-1	23		2363
12	27	H	Alfreton T	W 1-0	1-0	19	Miller [38]	715
13	30	H	Aldershot T	W 3-0	1-0	19	Sterling [22], Nanetti [54], Miller [69]	797
14	Oct 4	A	Bristol R	D 1-1	0-1	19	Murphy [90]	6162
15	7	A	Nuneaton T	L 2-3	1-2	20	Miller [37], Payne [51]	753
16	11	H	Chester FC	W 2-0	0-0	18	Heneghan (og) [47], Essam [64]	1009
17	18	A	Macclesfield T	L 0-1	0-0	20		1439
18	Nov 1	A	Southport	D 2-2	1-2	19	Payne [1], Francis [70]	1398
19	11	H	Braintree T	W 1-0	1-0	17	Deverdics [45]	696
20	15	A	Alfreton T	W 3-2	0-1	17	Deverdics 2 [53, 65], Payne [73]	650
21	22	H	Forest Green R	D 0-0	0-0	17		916
22	25	H	Nuneaton T	W 5-0	3-0	15	Murphy [21], Essam [24], Deverdics [32], Payne 2 [59, 82]	727
23	29	A	Gateshead	W 2-1	2-0	13	Payne [21], Francis [43]	1111
24	Dec 2	H	Torquay U	D 2-2	0-1	14	Essam [75], Sterling [90]	795
25	20	A	Altrincham	D 2-2	0-0	14	Densmore (og) [50], Payne [79]	870
26	26	H	Welling U	W 4-0	2-0	13	Payne [20], Murphy 2 [37, 47], Poole (pen) [90]	1509
27	28	A	Barnet	D 2-2	2-0	13	Murphy [9], Payne [18]	2048
28	Jan 1	A	Welling U	W 2-0	0-0	12	Raggett [63], Cogan [78]	906
29	17	H	Dartford	W 6-1	2-1	12	Deverdics [5], Orlu [45], Murphy 2 [53, 79], Bellamy [55], Cogan (pen) [77]	1042
30	20	H	Wrexham	W 2-0	2-0	8	Murphy [12], Raggett [36]	793
31	31	A	Lincoln C	L 0-1	0-0	12		2509
32	Feb 14	A	FC Halifax T	L 2-3	1-2	13	Murphy [34], Holman [77]	1151
33	21	H	Southport	D 2-2	1-0	12	Raggett [13], Holman [73]	1008
34	Mar 3	A	Aldershot T	L 1-3	0-0	13	Francis [76]	1154
35	7	H	Lincoln C	L 1-2	1-2	13	Modeste [6]	1016
36	14	A	Kidderminster H	W 2-0	1-0	13	Murphy 2 [7, 79]	1484
37	17	H	Altrincham	W 2-1	1-0	10	Deverdics 2 [11, 85]	550
38	21	H	Gateshead	W 1-0	0-0	10	Essam [54]	725
39	24	H	Grimsby T	L 0-1	0-1	10		911
40	28	H	AFC Telford U	W 1-0	1-0	10	Payne [4]	795
41	31	A	Wrexham	D 1-1	0-1	10	Modeste [60]	1831
42	Apr 4	A	Eastleigh	W 1-0	0-0	9	Raggett [71]	1703
43	6	H	Woking	W 2-1	0-1	9	Payne 2 (1 pen) [49, 89 (p)]	1078
44	11	A	Chester FC	L 1-3	1-0	8	Payne [35]	1645
45	18	H	Bristol R	D 1-1	0-0	8	Modeste [88]	2351
46	25	A	Forest Green R	D 0-0	0-0	8		2674

Final League Position: 8

GOALSCORERS

League (69): Payne 15 (1 pen), Murphy 11, Deverdics 7, Miller 5, Essam 4, Raggett 4, Francis 3, Modeste 3, Cogan 2 (1 pen), Holman 2, Reid 2, Sterling 2, Bellamy 1, Bonner 1, Elder 1, Lock 1, Nanetti 1, Orlu 1, Poole 1 (1 pen), own goals 2.
FA Cup (3): Deverdics 1, Essam 1, Payne 1.
FA Trophy (12): Deverdics 2, Essam 1, Modeste 1, Murphy 1, Orlu 1, Payne 2, Poole 1, Reid 1, Sterling 2.

Walker 20	Stone 18	Raggett 26 + 5	Sterling 42	Orfa 45	Wynter 14 + 11	Kinnear 25 + 2	Bellamy 10 + 7	Cogan 12 + 8	Modeste 15 + 7	Elder 7 + 3	Reid 4 + 15	Deverdics 37 + 6	Nanetti 7 + 12	Payne 37 + 5	Lock 13	Francis 21 + 1	Mambo 1	Murphy 31 + 5	Bonner 22	Essam 38	Taiwo 21 + 2	Miller 8 + 2	Rafferty 25	Saunders — + 1	Rutherford — + 3	Poole 1 + 16	Davies 1 + 1	Hook 1	Holman 4 + 2	Mekki — + 1	Match No.
1	2	3	4	5	6	7	8¹	9²	10³	11	12	13	14																		1
1	2¹	3	5	4	6	7	8	9²	10	13	11³			14	12																2
1	2	4	11	3	5²	8¹			6	10	12	13	14	7³		9															3
1			6	5¹	3	2		7		9¹	10			12	11	8	4														4
1		5		3	2	9²	7			11³	14	12	8	10	6¹			4	13												5
1		6	9	2	3²	5¹	14	8		10¹	13			12	11	7			4												6
1		8	4	2	14			-		10¹	12	9²		11¹	3			6	5	7	13										7
1		6	5	2¹				10²	12	9	14	11³	8			3	4	7	13												8
1		6	5	2		7²		13	10²	9¹	12	14	8			3	4	11													9
1³	5	14	9	2		7		11²	8	13	12	6¹				3	4	10													10
	6		5	2		7²		10²	9	12	14	8¹				3	4	11		1	13										11
	2		5	6				12	14	9³	11²	7		13	3	4	8	10¹		1											12
	5	14	8	3				13	9³	11²	6		12	4	2	7¹	10			1											13
	5		8	2				12	13	9	10²	6		14	4¹	3	7³	11		1											14
	5	12	8²	2				13	7	9	10¹	6		14	4	3		11		1											15
	5	13		3	8	6	12		14		7	9³		11²	4	2		10¹		1											16
	8			4	7	6	12			14	5¹¹	10³		9	3¹	2	13			1											17
	2¹		3	5		9			13	6	11²		12	10	4	7	8			1											18
	9	5			7	12		6		10²	3	11¹		4	2	8		1	13												19
	6²	5	13	8	14			12	7¹		11²	3	10¹	4	2	9	1														20
		4	5	7	9			12	6	13	10²	3	11¹	2	8		1														21
	14	9	5		7³			6¹	13	10	3	11²	4	2	8		1	12													22
	6	4	7					9¹		11²	5	10	3	2	8		1	12	13												23
	4	9			7¹			6²		10	3	11	5	2	8		1	13	12	3											24
		11	2	12	7	6¹		8	10		3	9	4	5			1														25
	3	9	5	13	7	8		6³	14	11²		10¹	4	2		1	12														26
	3	2	4	13	7	8¹		9	10²		11	5	6		1	12															27
	4	6	5	12	9	8		7¹	11²		10	3	2		1	13															28
	3	9	7			6	8¹⁴	13	5²	11¹	4	10	2	12	1																29
	5	6	4	12	7	8¹	13	14	10³	11²	3	9	2	1																	30
	4	6	3	5²		9	12	8	2¹	7	11	10	1	13																	31
1	3	6	4		14		12	8¹	7⁴		2	10	5	9³		11	13														32
1	4	5	6		9	12		7²		3	10¹	2	8		13	11															33
1	3	9	4		6	13		7	12	2¹	10³	5	8²		14	11															34
	4	6	2	7³		14	9²		8	10¹	3	11	5		12		13														35
	4	9	5	12	8		6²		7	10¹	3	11	2		13																36
	3	6	4	14	7		13	10³		9	11²	5	8¹	2	12																37
1	6	5	3		7			8		9	11	4	10	2																	38
1	6	5	3	7¹		14	8		9	11²	4	10¹	2		13	12															39
1	8	2	3	5	6		14	13	9	11²	4	10¹		12	7¹																40
1	2	6	3	5	7		13	12	8	10¹	4	11		9²																	41
1	3	5	4	13		12	7	8	11¹	2	10	6	9²																		42
1	6	5	3	12		9	7	11	4	10¹	2	8																			43
1	3	6	4	5¹	12	14	9	8	10	11³	2	7²		13																	44
1	4	3	5³	14	6²	13	7	9	11¹	10	8	12																			45
	3	6	4	2		10		7	11	8¹	5	9	1	12																	46

FA Cup

Fourth Qualifying	Eastbourne Bor	(a)	0-0
Replay	Eastbourne Bor	(h)	1-0
First Round	Morecambe	(h)	1-0
Second Round	Cheltenham T	(a)	1-0
Third Round	Crystal Palace	(h)	0-4

FA Trophy

First Round	Lowestoft T	(a)	3-1
Second Round	Havant & Waterlooville	(a)	1-0
Third Round	Woking	(a)	3-3
Replay	Woking	(h)	1-0
Fourth Round	Bath C	(h)	3-3
Replay	Bath C	(a)	1-2

EASTLEIGH

Ground: The Silverlake Stadium, Stoneham Lane, Eastleigh, Hampshire SO50 9HT. *Tel:* (02380) 613361.
Fax: (02380) 612379. *Website:* eastleighfc.com *Year Formed:* 1946. *Record Attendance:* 4,216 v Macclesfield,
Vanarama Conference, 28 February 2015. *Nickname:* Spitfires. *Manager:* Richard Hill. *Colours:* Blue shirts with
white trim, white shorts, blue socks.

EASTLEIGH – VANARAMA PREMIER 2014–15 LEAGUE RECORD

Match No.	Date		Venue	Opponents	Result	H/T Score	Lg Pos.	Goalscorers	Attendance
1	Aug	9	A	Nuneaton T	W 3-0	1-0	2	Reason [19], Stanley [57], Strevens [74]	935
2		14	H	Aldershot T	W 1-0	0-0	3	Wright [90]	1914
3		16	H	Gateshead	D 2-2	2-1	4	Strevens [40], Midson [44]	1081
4		23	A	Dover Ath	L 1-2	1-1	8	Midson [16]	787
5		25	H	Welling U	W 3-1	1-1	4	Constable 2 [26, 48], Evans [87]	953
6		30	A	Macclesfield T	L 0-2	0-1	9		1284
7	Sept	6	H	Southport	W 2-1	0-0	5	Reason [49], Collins (og) [90]	1309
8		9	A	Dartford	D 2-2	2-0	7	Collins (pen) [13], Constable [22]	806
9		13	A	Altrincham	D 3-3	2-2	9	Reid [16], McAllister [43], Reason [79]	945
10		16	H	Forest Green R	D 2-2	0-1	11	Midson [57], Constable [73]	2108
11		20	H	Braintree T	W 1-0	1-0	8	Fleetwood [35]	1131
12		27	A	Wrexham	L 0-3	0-2	13		2692
13		30	H	Bristol R	D 1-1	1-0	12	Collins [33]	2621
14	Oct	4	A	Barnet	L 0-1	0-1	13		1610
15		11	H	FC Halifax T	W 4-1	1-1	12	Reason [22], Green [53], Fleetwood [76], Strevens [90]	1498
16		18	H	Nuneaton T	W 2-1	1-0	11	McAllister [19], Collins [56]	1009
17	Nov	1	H	Chester FC	W 3-2	1-0	8	Strevens [26], Fleetwood (pen) [60], McAllister [65]	1306
18		11	A	Forest Green R	D 1-1	0-0	10	Constable [85]	967
19		22	A	Aldershot T	W 2-0	1-0	8	McAllister [45], Fleetwood (pen) [65]	1737
20		29	A	Torquay U	L 0-2	0-1	11		1862
21	Dec	2	H	Dartford	W 2-0	1-0	11	Midson [44], Green [87]	1765
22		10	A	Alfreton T	L 2-3	1-1	11	Reason [25], McAllister [80]	442
23		20	A	AFC Telford U	W 4-3	2-2	9	Stanley [18], Midson [45], Constable 2 [66, 69]	1265
24		26	H	Woking	D 2-2	2-2	8	Evans [22], McAllister [43]	1752
25		28	H	Braintree T	W 5-1	1-1	5	Stanley [31], Constable 3 [54, 55, 77], Midson [75]	748
26	Jan	1	A	Woking	D 1-1	0-0	5	McAllister [69]	1383
27		4	H	Altrincham	L 0-2	0-1	8		1204
28		10	H	Lincoln C	W 4-0	1-0	5	Midson 2 [40, 56], Constable [54], McAllister [90]	1492
29		27	H	Grimsby T	L 0-1	0-1	7		1515
30	Feb	7	H	AFC Telford U	D 3-3	1-1	8	Evans [8], Reason [71], Constable [82]	1219
31		10	A	Southport	W 2-1	0-0	6	Partington [83], Reason [86]	727
32		14	A	Torquay U	L 1-2	1-1	6	Burton [17]	1844
33		21	A	Chester FC	W 1-0	0-0	6	Walker [65]	2294
34		28	H	Macclesfield T	W 4-0	1-0	6	Audel (og) [12], Constable [54], Reason [61], Burton [78]	4126
35	Mar	7	A	Bristol R	W 2-1	1-0	6	Green [7], Midson [63]	7371
36		10	A	Kidderminster H	W 3-1	0-1	6	Walker [59], Midson [66], Reason [70]	1225
37		14	H	Barnet	L 1-2	0-1	6	Strevens (pen) [78]	2034
38		17	A	Wrexham	D 2-2	1-2	6	Strevens (pen) [17], Constable [85]	1246
39		21	A	Grimsby T	L 1-2	0-1	6	Turley [90]	4034
40		28	A	Gateshead	W 3-2	1-1	7	Constable 2 [25, 83], McAllister [74]	1231
41	Apr	4	A	Dover Ath	L 0-1	0-0	7		1703
42		6	A	Welling U	W 2-1	1-1	6	Reason [6], Turley [75]	700
43		11	H	Alfreton T	W 3-1	2-1	6	Partington [21], Strevens (pen) [32], Stanley [88]	1441
44		14	A	FC Halifax T	W 2-0	1-0	4	Roberts, M (og) [8], Constable [60]	852
45		18	A	Lincoln C	W 2-1	1-0	4	Midson [38], McAllister [62]	2132
46		25	H	Kidderminster H	W 2-1	0-1	4	Stanley [54], Constable [74]	4024

Final League Position: 4

GOALSCORERS

League (87): Constable 18, Midson 11, McAllister 10, Reason 10, Strevens 7 (3 pens), Stanley 5, Fleetwood 4 (2 pens),
Collins 3 (1 pen), Evans 3, Green 3, Burton 2, Partington 2, Turley 2, Walker 2, Reid 1, Wright 1, own goals 3.
FA Cup (4): Constable 1, McAllister 1, Reason 1, Strevens 1.
FA Trophy (0).
Vanarama Premier Play-Offs (1): Odubade 1.

Fitney 46	Spence 34 + 2	Beckwith 25 + 1	Reid 29	Green 31 + 3	Reason 42 + 1	Stanley 29 + 3	Strevens 44 + 1	Fleetwood 15 + 10	Constable 41 + 2	Midson 38 + 3	McAllister 24 + 18	Evans 30 + 5	Wright 1 + 9	Odubade 1 + 13	Collins 17 + 5	Todd 4 + 5	Fry 3	Lee — + 1	Turley 12	Partington 16 + 1	Howard 9 + 9	Pell 13	Walker 1 + 12	Burton 1 + 11	Match No.
1	2	3	4	5	6	7¹	8	9	10³	11²	12	13	14												1
1	2	4	5	3	6		8	12	10	11¹	13	7¹	14	9¹											2
1	2	3³	4	5*	7		8	9	10	11¹	12	13	14		6²										3
1	2²	4		7			8	9	10	11¹	12	13	14		6³	3	5								4
1		4		6		9	8	10²	11¹	12	7	13			5	2	3								5
1		3	4		9		7	8¹	11	10²	14	2	12	13	6³		5								6
1	2	4	3	5	6		7	12	11	10²	9¹				13	14	8³								7
1	2	3¹	4	5	9		7	12	11	8¹	10²				6	14		13							8
1	2		3	4	6		8	12	10	9²	11¹	5			13	7									9
1	2		3	4	7		8	12	10	11	9¹	5			6										10
1	2		4		11	12	7	9	10	6¹	13	3			8²				5						11
1	2		4	5	9	12	7²	6	11¹	10	13	3			8										12
1		4	3	5	11	6	7	12		10¹	9	2			8										13
1	2	5	4	6	9	8	11²	12		10					13	7	3¹								14
1		3	2	4	8	6	9	11		10¹	5				12	7									15
1		3	4	5	10¹	8	7	6²	12		11	2			9	13									16
1	2	4*		3	7	6	11³	10	9²		8¹	5	13	14		12									17
1	2		4	5	8	7	6	11²	10	12	13	3	9¹												18
1	3		2	4	6	7	11	10¹	8²	12	9³	5			14	13									19
1	5	4	3		7	8¹	9³	10	11²	13	2	14	12	6											20
1	2	4		12	6	7¹	8	9³	10²	11	13	5			14	3									21
1	2		4	12	6	7¹	8	9	11¹	10	13				5	3									22
1	2	12	4	3³	6	5	9		11	10¹	8²	7			13	14									23
1	2²	3	4	13	7	6	8	12	9	11¹	10³	5			14										24
1		3¹	4	2	7	6²	8	14	10¹	9	11	5			13	12									25
1	2		4	5	11²	7³	6	14	10	8	9¹	3			13	12									26
1	2²		4	5*	6	8¹	7		10	11²	9	12			14					3	13				27
1	2		3		6¹	7	4		10	11	13	8			12					5	9²				28
1	2			6	7²	4		11	10	13	5	12								3	8	9¹			29
1	12		3	5		11		9	10¹		6									2³	4	7²	8	13	14	30
1	12		4²	3	7		8		10	6¹	11³	2								5		9	14	13	31
1		4		5	6³	8			13	14	10	7								3	9²	2	12	11¹	32
1	2	3		5	9	7	6		10¹	11²					4	14				8³	12	13			33
1	2	3		5	6³	8	7²		11		10¹				4	14				9	12	13			34
1	2	4		3	7	6	8		10¹	11²	12				5					9		13			35
1	2	3		5	9	7²	13		11	10²	14				4	12	8			6¹					36
1	2	4		5	6	8²	9		10	11	14				3	13	7³			12					37
1	3		2	6¹		7			10	11³	9²	4			5				13	8	12	14			38
1	6	3	2		7	4			9³	8¹	13				5				10²	11	12	14*			39
1	3	2			6				10	11	7	4			5				9	8					40
1	5		2¹	12	7		11		10³	8	3				4	14	9²	6	13						41
1	5	4		9	8	7			10²	11	12				3	2	6¹	13							42
1	4	3		6	5	9			10	11¹					2	7	8²	13	12						43
1	5		6¹	7	8		11		9	10²	2				4	3	13		12						44
1	2			9	12	7	11	6²	10¹	5					3	4	13	8²	14						45
1	2			9	6²	8	10³	5	11¹	7					4	3	12		14	13					46

FA Cup

Fourth Qualifying	Kidderminster H	(a)	1-0
First Round	Lincoln C	(h)	2-1
Second Round	Southport	(a)	1-2

FA Trophy

First Round	Woking	(a)	0-2

Vanarama Premier Play-Offs

Semi-Finals 1st leg	Grimsby T	(h)	1-2
Semi-Finals 2nd leg	Grimsby T	(a)	0-3

FOREST GREEN ROVERS

Ground: The New Lawn, Another Way, Nailsworth, Gloucestershire GL6 0FG.   *Tel:* (01453) 834 860.
Fax: (01453) 835 291.   *Website:* www.forestgreenroversfc.com   *Year Formed:* 1890.
Record Attendance: 4,836 v Derby Co, FA Cup 3rd rd, 3 January 2009.
Nickname: 'The Rovers'.   *Manager:* Adrian Pennock.
Colours: Green shirts with black trim, green shorts with black trim, black socks with green trim.

FOREST GREEN ROVERS – VANARAMA PREMIER 2014–15 LEAGUE RECORD

Match No.	Date		Venue	Opponents	Result	H/T Score	Lg Pos.	Goalscorers	Atten- dance
1	Aug	9	A	Southport	W 1-0	0-0	7	Hughes [47]	1023
2		12	H	Chester FC	W 2-1	1-0	5	Kamdjo [11], Parkin [55]	1083
3		16	H	Alfreton T	W 2-0	1-0	2	Hughes [31], Kamdjo [70]	956
4		22	A	Aldershot T	D 1-1	0-1	1	Hughes [58]	2006
5		25	H	Bristol R	D 1-1	0-0	3	Parkin [68]	3781
6		30	A	Welling U	D 1-1	1-1	6	Norwood [45]	501
7	Sept	6	H	Wrexham	L 0-1	0-0	11		1401
8		9	A	Nuneaton T	L 0-1	0-0	13		789
9		13	H	FC Halifax T	W 2-0	2-0	10	Norwood [20], Parkin [29]	1005
10		16	A	Eastleigh	D 2-2	1-0	12	Norwood [30], Parkin [85]	2108
11		20	A	Dartford	W 2-1	0-0	9	Kelly [56], Hughes [69]	1003
12		27	H	Barnet	L 1-2	0-1	12	Sinclair [88]	1424
13		30	A	Torquay U	W 2-1	1-1	8	Parkin [36], Norwood [80]	1365
14	Oct	4	A	Macclesfield T	D 2-2	1-0	8	Frear [11], Hughes [78]	1329
15		7	A	AFC Telford U	W 1-0	0-0	7	Hughes [71]	1361
16		11	H	Gateshead	D 1-1	0-0	7	Parkin [71]	1217
17		18	A	Bristol R	W 1-0	1-0	5	Coles [15]	7014
18	Nov	1	H	Lincoln C	D 3-3	0-2	6	Norwood 2 (1 pen) [69 (p), 71], Bennett [90]	1379
19		11	H	Eastleigh	D 1-1	0-0	7	Kamdjo [58]	967
20		15	A	Torquay U	D 3-3	1-2	6	Guthrie 2 [38, 79], Norwood [75]	2117
21		22	A	Dover Ath	D 0-0	0-0	7		916
22		29	H	Dartford	W 2-1	1-0	6	Oshodi [5], Norwood [70]	1148
23	Dec	2	A	FC Halifax T	L 0-1	0-1	9		1030
24		6	H	Altrincham	D 1-1	1-0	8	Guthrie [7]	1261
25		9	H	Woking	W 2-1	2-1	6	Parkin [35], Oliver [42]	970
26		19	A	Grimsby T	L 1-2	0-1	9	Stokes [63]	3204
27		26	H	Kidderminster H	L 2-3	2-2	11	Hughes [29], Norwood [39]	2044
28	Jan	1	A	Kidderminster H	W 4-2	3-0	10	Parkin 2 [22, 59], Kamdjo [37], Guthrie [39]	2182
29		4	H	Welling U	W 4-1	1-1	7	Parkin 2 [22, 55], Guthrie [65], Norwood [78]	1147
30		17	A	Braintree T	W 2-1	0-0	6	Parkin 2 [68, 87]	661
31		31	H	Nuneaton T	W 1-0	1-0	5	Parkin [19]	1333
32	Feb	7	A	Grimsby T	W 2-1	1-1	5	Frear [37], Norwood [84]	1586
33		10	A	Alfreton T	D 2-2	0-0	5	Marwood [64], Parkin [85]	458
34		14	A	Altrincham	D 2-2	1-2	5	Parkin [7], Sinclair [61]	1071
35		21	H	AFC Telford U	W 3-0	0-0	5	Parkin [65], Clough [82], Frear [90]	1300
36		24	A	Wrexham	D 0-0	0-0	5		2044
37		28	H	Southport	W 5-3	3-1	5	Parkin (pen) [15], Racine [34], Guthrie [44], Kelly [55], Kamdjo [61]	1222
38	Mar	7	A	Barnet	W 3-1	1-1	5	Bennett [25], Parkin [67], Guthrie [74]	2070
39		14	H	Braintree T	D 1-1	1-1	5	Clough [22]	1313
40		21	A	Woking	L 0-1	0-0	5		1436
41		28	A	Lincoln C	W 2-1	2-0	5	Frear [7], Parkin (pen) [14]	1938
42	Apr	3	H	Aldershot T	L 1-3	1-0	5	Frear [9]	2247
43		6	A	Chester FC	W 4-1	3-1	5	Parkin 2 (1 pen) [5 (p), 16], Frear [23], Racine [47]	1911
44		11	H	Macclesfield T	W 3-1	2-1	4	Racine [6], Parkin [22], Bennett [59]	1714
45		18	A	Gateshead	W 4-2	2-1	5	Parkin 2 (1 pen) [26 (p), 80], Guthrie [33], Sinclair [73]	1203
46		25	H	Dover Ath	D 0-0	0-0	5		2674

Final League Position: 5

GOALSCORERS

League (80): Parkin 25 (4 pens), Norwood 11 (1 pen), Guthrie 8, Hughes 7, Frear 6, Kamdjo 5, Bennett 3, Racine 3, Sinclair 3, Clough 2, Kelly 2, Coles 1, Marwood 1, Oliver 1, Oshodi 1, Stokes 1.
FA Cup (4): Norwood 2, Parkin 1, Rodgers 1.
FA Trophy (5): Kelly 1, Parkin 4.
Vanarama Premier Play-Offs (0).

Russell 34	Pipe 30 + 4	Oliver 20	Coles 29	Stokes 15 + 3	Sinclair 40 + 1	Kamdjo 26 + 9	Wedgbury 32 + 5	Frear 38 + 4	Hughes 13 + 8	Parkin 40 + 5	Rodgers 4 + 6	Kelly 37 + 4	Norwood 26 + 11	Guthrie 26 + 13	Oshodi 10 + 2	Jolley 4 + 3	Bennett 20 + 3	Racine 16 + 1	Fleetwood 11 + 5	Clough 17	Marwood 4 + 10	Arnold 12	Bender 2 + 6	Moore — + 1	Match No.
1	2	3	4	5	6	7	8	9^3	10^2	11^1	12	13	14												1
1	2	3	4	5	6^3	8	7	9	10^2	11	14		12	13											2
1	2	3	4	5^2	6^1	8	7	9	11	10^3	12	14	13												3
1	6	4	2	5	8^1	3	7	9	11	10			12												4
1	2	3	4	5	6^3	8	7	9^1	10^1	11	14	12	13												5
1	7	3	4	2		5	6	13	11^2	10	12		8^1	9^3	14										6
1	2	3	4	5	6	7		9^2	12	11		8^1	10	13											7
1	2	3	4	5		9^2	8	7	6^1	11	13	10	12												8
1	2	4	5	3		9^2	7	8	10^1	6		11	13	12											9
1	7	3	4	5	6	2^2	8	12	11	9^1		10	13												10
1	2	3	4	5	8^1	11	7	12	10				9	6											11
1	2	4	5	3		9	7	13	10^3	14		8^1	6	12	11^1										12
1	2	3^1	4			7	8	9	13	10^3			5	6	14	12	11^2								13
1	4	3		7	6	8	13	11	5	10^2			12	2	9^1										14
1	4	3		6	7	8^3	10^2	14	13	5			11	12	2	9^1									15
1	2^3	3					8^2	14	7	13			11	10^1	5	9	6	4	12						16
1		3					8^2	14	6	12		10	11^1	5	9^3	7	4	13	2						17
1			4	7	5		8	9^2	11^1	6		10	12	3	13	2									18
1	2	4	5	13		7	8	9	10^2	14			11^3	12	6^1	3									19
1		3				8	7	9^1	10				5	6	11		4			12	2				20
1		3	5			8	7	12	10^2	13			9^1	6	11						4	2			21
1			4			7	8	9^1	11	12			5	6	10		3					2			22
1			4		8^1	12	7	9	10				5	6	11		3					2			23
1	5	2	3	6	4		8	9^1	12	11						7	10								24
1	2	4	3	12	6	7	8	9^1	10							5	11								25
1	2^1	3	4	5			7	9	12	11		8	6^2	10			13								26
1	2	4	3^1			7	8	9	10	11			5	6					12						27
1			4	12		8	7	9	10^1				5	6	11					2	3				28
1			4			8	7	14	9	13	10^1		5	6^3	11^2				2	3	12				29
1	13					8	2^2	7	9	10			5	12	6		4	11^1	3						30
1	14					8^2	2	7	9	11			5	13	6^1		4	10^3	3	12					31
1	2		4			8	14	7	9^1	10			5	12	6^2		11^1	3	13						32
1	2		4			8	13	7	9^1	10			5	12	6^2		12	3	11^2						33
1	2		4			7	14	8	9^1	11			5^1	12	10^2		13	3	6						34
	13						7	8	9	10^3			5	6	14		2^1	3	12	4	11^3	1			35
	8						12	7^2	9	10			5	6^1	13		2	4	14	3	11^3	1			36
	8						7	9^1	11				5	6^2	2		4	10	3	1		12	13		37
	14						7	3^1	8	9			6	10^1	2		5	11^2	4	12	1	13			38
	7^1						8	6	10	2			13	9^2	5		3	11^3	4	14	1	12			39
	14						8	7^1	9	11			5	6^2	2		4	10^3	3	12	1	13			40
	7						8	9^1	10				5	6	11		2	4	3	1	12				41
	7						8^1	14	9	10			5	6^3	11^2		2	3	13	4	12	1			42
	8						7^3	14	9^1	10			5	6^2	2		4	11	3	12	1	13			43
	8						7	6	10	2			11	5	3		9^1	4	12	1					44
	7						8^3	14	13	9^1	10		11^2	2	4		6	3	12	1	5				45
	6						7	12	8	10			11	2	4		9^2	3	13	1	5^1				46

FA Cup

Fourth Qualifying	Gloucester C	(a)	4-1
First Round	Scunthorpe U	(h)	0-2

FA Trophy

First Round	Didcot T	(h)	2-2
Replay	Didcot T	(a)	3-0
Second Round	Ebsfleet U	(a)	0-1

Vanarama Premier Play-Offs

Semi-Finals 1st leg	Bristol R	(h)	0-1
Semi-Finals 2nd leg	Bristol R	(a)	0-2

GATESHEAD

Ground: Gateshead International Stadium, Neilson Road, Gateshead NE10 0EF. *Tel:* (0191) 478 3883.
Fax: (0191) 440 0404. *Website:* www.gateshead-fc.com *Year Formed:* 1889 (Reformed 1977).
Record Attendance: 20,752 v Lincoln C, Division 3N (at Redheugh Park), 25 September 1937.
Nickname: 'The Tynesiders', 'The Heed'. *Manager:* Malcolm Crosby.
Colours: White shirts, black shorts, white socks with black trim.

GATESHEAD – VANARAMA PREMIER 2014–15 LEAGUE RECORD

Match No.	Date	Venue	Opponents	Result	H/T Score	Lg Pos.	Goalscorers	Attendance
1	Aug 9	H	Torquay U	W 3-1	2-0	3	Guy [18], Maddison 2 [33, 74]	1765
2	12	A	Wrexham	W 3-0	1-0	2	Chandler [26], Maddison [64], Shaw [67]	4068
3	16	A	Eastleigh	D 2-2	1-2	3	Beckwith (og) [21], Rodman [54]	1081
4	23	H	Grimsby T	L 1-6	0-3	10	Maddison [55]	1782
5	25	A	Altrincham	W 1-0	1-0	6	Chandler [44]	1089
6	30	H	Chester FC	W 2-1	0-1	3	Shaw (pen) [67], Chandler [80]	1138
7	Sept 6	A	Kidderminster H	L 1-2	0-0	6	Shaw [64]	2607
8	9	H	AFC Telford U	W 4-1	3-1	4	Akrigg (og) [10], Turnbull [13], Wright [35], Guy [52]	1093
9	13	H	Dartford	W 1-0	0-0	4	Wright [53]	1336
10	16	A	Macclesfield T	D 1-1	0-1	5	Wright [66]	1110
11	20	A	Welling U	D 1-1	0-1	5	Finnigan [50]	536
12	27	H	Aldershot T	D 1-1	0-1	5	Wright [88]	1451
13	30	A	Lincoln C	D 1-1	0-0	7	Wright [63]	2394
14	Oct 4	H	Braintree T	W 3-1	0-1	5	Finnigan [69], Turnbull [72], Shaw [75]	1244
15	7	H	Alfreton T	W 2-0	2-0	2	Shaw 2 [8, 13]	1259
16	11	A	Forest Green R	D 1-1	0-0	3	Howe [77]	1217
17	18	H	Barnet	L 0-2	0-2	4		1747
18	Nov 1	A	Aldershot T	W 2-1	0-0	2	Ramshaw 2 [49, 90]	1679
19	11	H	Lincoln C	D 3-3	1-1	3	Wright (pen) [29], Rodman [59], Pattison [81]	1211
20	15	A	Chester FC	L 0-1	0-0	3		2308
21	22	H	Torquay U	D 2-2	0-1	5	Rodman (pen) [86], Ramshaw [89]	1947
22	29	H	Dover Ath	L 1-2	1-2	9	Rodman [37]	1111
23	Dec 2	A	Alfreton T	W 2-1	1-0	7	Pattison 2 [31, 68]	454
24	10	H	Southport	D 1-1	0-0	8	Rodman [76]	808
25	19	A	Bristol R	L 2-3	1-0	7	Pattison [18], Rodman [62]	5367
26	26	H	FC Halifax T	D 2-2	2-2	9	Oster [12], Wright (pen) [39]	1216
27	Jan 7	H	Woking	D 0-0	0-0	12		772
28	17	A	Nuneaton T	W 2-0	2-0	11	Campbell 2 [16, 33]	637
29	31	A	Southport	W 1-0	1-0	11	Ramshaw [8]	904
30	Feb 14	H	Nuneaton T	L 1-2	1-1	12	Campbell (pen) [31]	1047
31	24	H	Kidderminster H	W 2-0	1-0	10	Rodman [42], Finnigan [90]	620
32	28	H	Bristol R	L 0-1	0-0	10		1668
33	Mar 3	H	Wrexham	W 3-1	1-1	9	Rodman [20], Gooch [47], Tomassen (og) [66]	705
34	7	A	Braintree T	L 0-1	0-0	9		515
35	10	A	Welling U	D 1-1	1-0	9	Rodman [2]	711
36	14	H	Macclesfield T	W 2-1	1-1	9	Chandler [21], Rankine [67]	1052
37	17	A	AFC Telford U	W 1-0	1-0	7	Rankine [5]	657
38	21	A	Dover Ath	L 0-1	0-0	9		725
39	24	A	FC Halifax T	D 2-2	1-1	9	Finnigan [25], Gillies [69]	1073
40	28	H	Eastleigh	L 2-3	1-1	9	Rankine [32], Shaw [90]	1231
41	31	A	Dartford	D 1-1	1-1	9	Allan [18]	602
42	Apr 4	A	Grimsby T	D 2-2	1-0	10	Sainte-Luce 2 [34, 73]	5958
43	6	H	Altrincham	W 1-0	1-0	10	Rankine [40]	957
44	11	A	Woking	L 0-3	0-2	10		1889
45	18	H	Forest Green R	L 2-4	1-2	10	Sainte-Luce [21], Shaw (pen) [90]	1203
46	25	A	Barnet	L 0-2	0-1	10		5233

Final League Position: 10

GOALSCORERS

League (66): Rodman 9 (1 pen), Shaw 8 (2 pens), Wright 7 (2 pens), Chandler 4, Finnigan 4, Maddison 4, Pattison 4, Ramshaw 4, Rankine 4, Campbell 3 (1 pen), Sainte-Luce 3, Guy 2, Turnbull 2, Allan 1, Gillies 1, Gooch 1, Howe 1, Oster 1, own goals 3.
FA Cup (10): Allan 1, Ramshaw 3, Pattison 1, Rodman 2, Shaw 1, Wright 2.
FA Trophy (8): Campbell 1, Chandler 1, Curtis 1, Gjokaj 1, Guy 1, Rankine 1, Shaw 1, Wright 1.

Bartlett 38	Baxter 33+2	Curtis 43	Clark 32+1	Wilson 4+2	Oster 35	Turnbull 28	Guy 6+7	Maddison 5	Shaw 21+9	Rodman 37+2	Chandler 28+2	O'Donnell 10+4	Brown 3+6	Jones 17+3	Baird 2	Allan 10+10	Ramshaw 24+13	Wright 17+3	Rankine 15+14	Finnigan 13+9	Howe 2	Pattison 28	McDermott 1	Anderton 3	Heardman 1+2	Gjokaj 16+3	Robson 3	Sainte-Luce 6+7	Campbell 4+4	Roberts 3	Gooch 7	Orrell —+6	Gillies 5	Dixon 6	Match No.
1	2	3	4	5	6^3	7	8^1	9	10^2	11	12	13	14																						1
1	2	3	4	5	6	7		9^1	10^1	11	8^2	13	14	12																					2
1	2	3	4	5	6^2	8	11^3	9^1		10	7	12	14	13																					3
	2	3	4	5^2	6	7	11^1	9	10	8^2	13	12			1	14																			4
14	3	4		8	6^2		11^3	10	9	7	5^1		2	1	13	12																			5
1	14	3	4		6^3	7	13	10	11^2	8	5		2			12	9^1																		6
1		2	3		6^2	8^1	13	10	9^3	7	5		4		14	12	11																		7
1		3	4		8	7	12	10^1	11	6^3	5^2		2		14	13	9																		8
1		2	3		8^3	7	11^1		9^2	6	5		4		14	13	10	12																	9
1		3			8	7	12		11	6^1	5	10	2		4	9																			10
1		2	3		8	5			9	7^1	6	11	4			10^2	13	12																	11
1		3	4		7	8			9	13	5	10^2	2^1		14	11	12	6^3																	12
1		3	4		8	7	12		9^1		2				5	10	11	6																	13
1		3	4		8	7	10^2		13	11^3	2				5	6^1	9	14	12																14
1	10	2	3		4	5	7^3		6^2	12		13			9	14	11^1	8																	15
1		4			6	8			9^1	11		14	3		5	10^2	13	12	2	7^3															16
1		4	14		8^2	7			10	11			2		5^1	13	9	12	3	6^3															17
1	2	3	4		6	7			10^1					14		13	9	11^2	12^3		8	5													18
1	3	4	5		6^1	7			9							8	11^2	13		10			2	12											19
1	7	3^4	4		6^3	8			14	9						2^1	11^2		13	10		5	12												20
1	2		3		6^1	7			13	11						14	9^2	12		8		5	10^3	4^4											21
1	2	3	4		6^2	7	14		13	11						5	12	9^1	10^3		8														22
1	2	3^2	4		9	7				6	8					5	11^1		13		10		12												23
1	2	4	3		7	8			13	11	6^3	5				10^1	12	14		9^2															24
1	2	3	4		7	8			11	6^2	5					10^1	13	12		9															25
1	8	2	3		4	5	12									7	6	11		9^1		10													26
1		3	4		6^2	7			10^3	11^1	8				2	9	14	12				13	5												27
1	2	3	4		6	7					8				5	13				8^1		12		9^2	10	11									28
1	2	3	4		6^2					8				14	10^1		13			11		7^3	5	12	9	11									29
1	2	3	4		7				13	12						6^2	14		11			8	5		9^3	10^1									30
1	2	3	4		7					11				5		9		12	6			8			10^1										31
1	2	3	4^2		8^1				10				6		12	14		11		9		5^3		13	7										32
1	2	3			7				11	8			5			6		10				4			9										33
1	2	3			10				14	7	4					8^1		11^2	5			9		12	13	6^3									34
1	2	3			7^2				12	11^3	8					6	13	10^1	5			4		14		9^1										35
1	2	3^1	4						4	8						7	10	11	6			5				9	12								36
1	3	4			9				5							6	11	10^1	7			2		12		8									37
1	2	4			3				7							8^2	10^1		5			6		13		11	12	9							38
	2	3	12		4				10^1	7						8	11	6	5							9						9^4	1		39
	2^1	3			4				9^2	6						8	10	11	5					7		13		12					1		40
	2	3			9				11^2	4	8					10^1	6^3	5						7		13	12	14					1		41
	2	3	4		9					6						7^1	10		5			8^4		11		12^2	13						1		42
	2	3			10				8	5						7	11		4					9								6	1		43
	2	4	12^4		3				11^2	7		14				6	10	13	5					9^1								8^3	1		44
1	2	3	4						11^3	8		14				6	10	12	5^1			7^2		9				13							45
1	2	3	4						13	11^1	6					12	9	8	5					10								7^2			46

FA Cup

Fourth Qualifying	Gainsborough Trinity	(h)	4-0
First Round	Norton U	(a)	4-0
Second Round	Warrington T	(h)	2-0
Third Round	WBA	(a)	0-7

FA Trophy

First Round	Halesowen T	(h)	2-0
Second Round	Grimsby T	(a)	0-0
Replay	Grimsby T	(h)	3-2
(aet; 2-2 at end of normal time)			
Third Round	Wrexham	(a)	1-1
Replay	Wrexham	(h)	2-2
(aet; Wrexham won 5-3 on penalties)			

GRIMSBY TOWN

Ground: Blundell Park, Cleethorpes, NE Lincolnshire DN35 7PY. *Tel:* (01472) 605 050. *Fax:* (01472) 693 665.
Website: www.grimsby-townfc.co.uk *Year Formed:* 1878. *Record Attendance:* 31,651 v Wolverhampton W, FA Cup
5th rd, 20 February 1937. *Nickname:* 'The Mariners'. *Team Manager:* Paul Hurst.
Colours: Black and white striped shirts, black shorts with white trim, red socks with black trim.

GRIMSBY TOWN – VANARAMA PREMIER 2014–15 LEAGUE RECORD

Match No.	Date		Venue	Opponents	Result	H/T Score	Lg Pos.	Goalscorers	Attendance
1	Aug	9	A	Bristol R	D	0-0	0-0	12		7019
2		12	H	Nuneaton T	D	0-0	0-0	14		3710
3		16	H	Dover Ath	D	1-1	0-0	14	Pittman [74]	3548
4		23	A	Gateshead	W	6-1	3-0	11	Baxter (og) [6], Neilson 2 [15, 46], John-Lewis [42, 90], Disley [84]	1782
5		25	H	Alfreton T	W	7-0	3-0	8	John-Lewis [10], Dawson (og) [31], Pittman [43], Clay 2 [46, 88], Brown [79], Neilson [90]	3619
6		30	A	Aldershot T	L	1-2	0-0	11	Neilson [77]	1998
7	Sept	6	H	Welling U	W	2-0	1-0	8	Pittman [39], Hannah (pen) [71]	3785
8		9	A	Lincoln C	L	2-3	1-1	11	Disley [43], Pittman [59]	5209
9		13	H	Torquay U	L	0-2	0-2	14		3300
10		16	A	FC Halifax T	D	1-1	1-1	13	Neilson [15]	1867
11		20	A	Kidderminster H	W	1-0	0-0	13	Oates [85]	2093
12		27	H	Chester FC	W	3-0	1-0	10	Pearson [18], Hannah [49], Arnold [90]	3245
13		30	H	Southport	L	0-1	0-0	13		3353
14	Oct	4	A	Dartford	D	1-1	0-0	11	John-Lewis (pen) [84]	1285
15		7	H	Altrincham	D	0-0	0-0	11		2535
16		11	A	Wrexham	W	1-0	1-0	11	John-Lewis (pen) [28]	8163
17		18	A	Torquay U	W	3-2	2-1	8	John-Lewis 2 [38, 70], Disley [45]	2353
18	Nov	1	H	Dartford	W	3-0	2-0	7	Magnay [13], Arnold [38], John-Lewis (pen) [87]	3116
19		4	A	Braintree T	W	1-0	0-0	2	John-Lewis [66]	875
20		11	H	FC Halifax T	W	1-0	1-0	2	Pearson [41]	3443
21		15	A	Altrincham	D	1-1	0-0	2	Arnold [67]	1881
22		22	H	Kidderminster H	L	0-2	0-1	2		3446
23		25	H	Woking	W	3-1	1-0	2	Disley [14], John-Lewis 2 [54, 89]	2663
24		29	A	AFC Telford U	D	1-1	0-1	2	Mackreth [57]	1849
25	Dec	19	H	Forest Green R	W	2-1	1-0	4	John-Lewis [24], Disley [73]	3204
26		26	A	Macclesfield T	W	1-0	1-0	4	Mackreth [4]	2786
27		28	H	Lincoln C	L	1-3	1-2	4	Disley [21]	7136
28	Jan	1	H	Macclesfield T	L	1-2	1-1	4	Pittman [37]	3545
29		17	H	Barnet	W	3-1	2-1	4	Palmer [11], John-Lewis (pen) [15], Mackreth [52]	3116
30		24	A	Nuneaton T	W	2-0	0-0	4	Pittman [53], Hannah [88]	989
31		27	A	Eastleigh	W	1-0	1-0	4	Palmer [38]	1515
32	Feb	7	A	Forest Green R	L	1-2	1-1	4	Guthrie (og) [41]	1586
33		14	H	Bristol R	L	0-1	0-0	4		4073
34		21	A	Barnet	W	3-1	1-0	4	Jolley [27], Disley [90], Pittman [90]	2756
35		24	H	AFC Telford U	W	1-0	0-0	4	Arnold [47]	3047
36		28	H	Braintree T	W	1-0	0-0	3	Disley [47]	3339
37	Mar	7	A	Woking	W	2-1	1-0	3	Palmer [41], Pittman [65]	2653
38		14	A	Chester FC	D	2-2	1-0	4	Palmer [21], Pittman [67]	2916
39		21	H	Eastleigh	W	2-1	1-0	3	Palmer [13], John-Lewis [78]	4034
40		24	A	Dover Ath	W	1-0	1-0	3	John-Lewis [6]	911
41		28	A	Welling U	W	2-0	2-0	2	Palmer [9], Pearson [43]	1042
42	Apr	4	H	Gateshead	D	2-2	0-1	3	Mackreth [54], Disley [90]	5958
43		6	A	Alfreton T	W	2-0	0-0	3	Gowling [69], John-Lewis [87]	3327
44		11	H	Wrexham	L	0-1	0-1	3		4138
45		18	A	Southport	D	2-2	1-0	3	Chapell [24], Pearson [85]	1968
46		25	H	Aldershot T	W	3-1	2-0	3	Hannah 2 [14, 16], Pittman [56]	3364

Final League Position: 3

GOALSCORERS

League (74): John-Lewis 16 (4 pens), Pittman 10, Disley 9, Palmer 6, Hannah 5 (1 pen), Neilson 5, Arnold 4, Mackreth 4, Pearson 4, Clay 2, Brown 1, Chapell 1, Gowling 1, Jolley 1, Magnay 1, Oates 1, own goals 3.
FA Cup (4): Arnold 1, John-Lewis 2, Pearson 1.
FA Trophy (4): Mackreth 2, McLaughlin 1, Pittman 1.
Vanarama Premier Play-Offs (6): Arnold 2, John-Lewis 2, Palmer 2.

McKeown 46	Magnay 42	Boyce 6	Thomas 13	Mackreth 30 + 10	Brown 29 + 4	Disley 35 + 5	Doig 3 + 1	McLaughlin 11 + 12	Connell 3	John-Lewis 36 + 3	Clay 30 + 9	Nsiala 40	Winfarrah —+ 2	Pearson 42	Pittman 20 + 11	Neilson 17 + 3	Bignot 5 + 8	Hannah 6 + 16	Arnold 26 + 5	Parslow 21 + 5	Oates 1 + 5	Pell 5	Watson —+ 4	Palmer 12 + 1	Robertson 14	Jolley 8 + 3	Chapell 2 + 4	Gowling 3	Sunter —+ 1	Match No.
1	2	3	4	5	6	7	8	9		10¹	11	12																		1
1	2	3	4¹		6	7		9		10	11	5		8	12															2
1	5¹	3		13	6	7		9		11²	10	8	4	2	12															3
1	5	2		12	7	13		9		10	8	3⁴		4	11¹	6³	14													4
1	5¹	4		13	8			9		11	7	2¹	14	3	10²	6	12													5
1	4	5		14	2			7²		10⁴	8	6²		3	11¹	9	12	13												6
1	4			10¹	2	14		7²			8	6		3	11³	9	5	12	13											7
1	4			6	7	12	13			10	8¹	5		3³	11	9²	2	14												8
1	5			13	8	7²		9¹		10	14	4		3	11²	6	2	12												9
1	4			6¹	8	7	2	12			9	5		3	10		11													10
1	5			6¹	9	7		13			8	2		3	10²		11		4	12										11
1	5			6	7			13		12	8	4		3	9¹		11³	14	2	10²										12
1	5			6	7	13		14		11¹	8³	4		3	9		10		2¹	12										13
1	5			6¹	7	8		9		10		4		3	12		11²		2	13										14
1	4	5		6	7			9²		10¹	8			3	11		13		2	12										15
1	2	5		6	7	12				10	8¹	11		3	9²				13	4										16
1	2	5	9	6³	7	3	13			11²		4			10¹				12	8	14									17
1	2	5	6¹		7¹	13		10		8	3			4	12		14	11²		9										18
1	2²	5	9¹		7			10		6	3			4	12	13		11		8										19
1	8¹	5	13		7			11		12	3			4	10²			9	2	6										20
1	2	5	14	12	7¹			11		13	4			3	10³			6	8	9²										21
1	2	5		7	14			10¹			3			4	12	11		13	9	6²	8³									22
1	5			8	6¹	7		10¹	13		3			4	9²			12	11	2			14							23
1	5			6²	7	8		10			4			3	11¹	12		13	9	2										24
1	4¹			6	2³	7		10	12	11				3	9²	13	14		8	5										25
1		5	6	8¹	7			13		11	12	3		4	10²				9	2										26
1	5¹	3	12		8			14		10	7³			4	11	9²	13		6	2										27
1		5	6	8				14		11³	7²			3	10¹		2	12	9	4		13								28
1	5			6	7¹	8				10	12	3		4	13			9	2			11²								29
1	5			6		7		13			8	4		3	11¹			12	9²	2		14	10³							30
1	5				7					10	8	4		3			6	12				11	2	9¹						31
1	2			12	8			10		7	4			3			13	9				11¹	5	6²						32
1	2			6	7	13		11		8¹	4			3	12		9		14			5²	10³							33
1	2			6	7			11		8²	4			3	12		9	13				5	10¹							34
1	2			6	13	7		10		8²	4			3	12		9					5	11¹							35
1	2			6	13	7		11²		8¹	4			3	10		9³	14				5	12							36
1	2			6	8			7			4			3	11²		12	9	13			10¹	5							37
1	2			6	7					8	3			4	10		9²	12				11¹	5	13						38
1	2				7			12		8	3			4	11¹		9					10	5	6						39
1	2			13	7			11		8¹	3			4	12	14	9					10³	5	6²						40
1	2			6²	8	7		10¹			3			4	13		9					11	5	12						41
1	2			6	7	8		10¹			4			3³	13		9³					11	5	12	14					42
1				6¹	7			10	8		3			11²			13	2				12	5	9¹	14	4				43
1	2			6²	8	7		10			4			3	14		13	9				11³	5¹	12						44
1	3			13	6			7²		8				2	10	14	12	4¹				11³			9	5				45
1				9¹	7	8		12		14	3¹			10²		2	11	4						6	5	13				46

FA Cup

Fourth Qualifying	Guiseley	(h)	3-0
First Round	Oxford U	(h)	1-3

FA Trophy

First Round	Nuneaton T	(a)	2-0
Second Round	Gateshead	(h)	0-0
Replay	Gateshead	(a)	2-3

(aet; 2-2 at end of normal time)

Vanarama Premier Play-Offs

Semi-Finals 1st leg	Eastleigh	(a)	2-1
Semi-Finals 2nd leg	Eastleigh	(h)	3-0
Final	Bristol R	Wembley	1-1

(aet; Bristol R won 5-3 on penalties)

FC HALIFAX TOWN

Ground: The Shay Stadium, Halifax, West Yorkshire HX1 2 YT. *Tel:* (01422) 341222. *Fax:* (01422) 349487.
Website: www.halifaxafc.co.uk *Year Formed:* 1911.
Record Attendance: 36,855 v Tottenham H, FA Cup 5th rd, 15 February 1953. *Nickname:* 'The Shaymen'.
Manager: Neil Aspin. *Colours:* Blue shirts with white trim, blue shorts with white trim, blue socks with white trim.

FC HALIFAX TOWN – VANARAMA PREMIER 2014–15 LEAGUE RECORD

Match No.	Date	Venue	Opponents	Result	H/T Score	Lg Pos.	Goalscorers	Attendance
1	Aug 9	A	Dover Ath	W 1-0	0-0	7	McManus [47]	1321
2	12	H	Southport	W 3-1	1-1	3	Bolton [15], Roberts, M [59], Jackson [90]	1463
3	16	H	Welling U	W 3-0	0-0	1	Roberts, M [47], Peniket 2 [51, 78]	1337
4	23	A	Chester FC	W 3-0	1-0	1	Peniket [34], Boden [70], Pearson [83]	2501
5	25	H	Lincoln C	W 3-2	2-1	1	Roberts, M [29], Boden (pen) [45], Williams [76]	2369
6	30	A	Bristol R	L 1-2	0-1	2	Boden [62]	5394
7	Sept 6	H	Aldershot T	W 1-0	0-0	2	Dyer [72]	1837
8	9	A	Macclesfield T	D 1-1	0-0	1	Boden [51]	1509
9	13	A	Forest Green R	L 0-2	0-2	3		1005
10	16	H	Grimsby T	D 1-1	1-1	4	Marshall [4]	1867
11	20	H	AFC Telford U	W 5-0	2-0	3	Smith [12], Hattersley 2 [16, 90], Boden [69], Marshall [86]	1519
12	27	A	Braintree T	D 0-0	0-0	2		909
13	30	A	Alfreton T	W 2-0	1-0	2	Ainge [12], Boden [53]	705
14	Oct 4	H	Altrincham	L 1-3	0-1	2	Boden [87]	1727
15	7	H	Wrexham	D 2-2	1-0	3	Schofield [6], Hattersley [61]	1617
16	11	A	Eastleigh	L 1-4	1-1	5	Boden (pen) [16]	1498
17	18	H	Kidderminster H	W 2-0	2-0	2	Maynard [34], Peniket [39]	1437
18	Nov 1	A	Wrexham	D 0-0	0-0	3		3421
19	11	A	Grimsby T	L 0-1	0-1	5		3443
20	16	H	Woking	L 1-3	0-2	8	Marshall (pen) [72]	1415
21	22	A	Welling U	L 1-2	1-1	11	Maynard [45]	500
22	29	H	Alfreton T	W 2-0	0-0	8	Maynard [61], Jackson [82]	1198
23	Dec 2	H	Forest Green R	W 1-0	1-0	6	Boden [5]	1030
24	9	A	Torquay U	L 1-2	0-2	8	Maynard [80]	1470
25	20	A	Nuneaton T	W 2-0	0-0	6	Bolton [74], Maynard [90]	1227
26	26	A	Gateshead	D 2-2	2-2	7	Maynard 2 [10, 25]	1216
27	28	H	Chester FC	L 0-2	0-1	8		1901
28	Jan 13	A	Dartford	W 2-1	1-1	8	Pearson [33], Boden (pen) [69]	811
29	27	A	AFC Telford U	W 1-0	0-0	6	Pearson [58]	1248
30	Feb 14	A	Dover Ath	W 3-2	2-1	7	Maynard [5], Peniket [19], Jackson [66]	1151
31	21	H	Braintree T	W 1-0	0-0	7	Jackson [90]	1268
32	28	A	Kidderminster H	D 0-0	0-0	7		1766
33	Mar 3	A	Southport	L 0-1	0-0	8		715
34	7	H	Dartford	D 0-0	0-0	8		1253
35	10	A	Aldershot T	D 1-1	0-1	7	Peniket [59]	1167
36	14	H	Bristol R	D 2-2	2-0	8	Maynard [25], Roberts, M [39]	2248
37	17	H	Barnet	D 1-1	0-0	9	Maynard [90]	1127
38	21	A	Altrincham	D 0-0	0-0	8		1371
39	24	H	Gateshead	D 2-2	1-1	8	Bolton 2 [29, 69]	1073
40	28	A	Nuneaton T	W 2-1	1-0	8	Muldoon 2 [3, 60]	947
41	Apr 3	H	Macclesfield T	D 2-2	1-2	8	Audel (og) [3], Hatfield [75]	1768
42	6	A	Lincoln C	D 1-1	0-1	8	Maynard [90]	2263
43	11	A	Barnet	L 0-3	0-2	9		2150
44	14	H	Eastleigh	L 0-2	0-1	9		852
45	18	H	Torquay U	L 0-2	0-0	9		1175
46	25	A	Woking	L 2-3	1-1	9	McManus [9], Hatfield (pen) [47]	2175

Final League Position: 9

GOALSCORERS

League (60): Maynard 11, Boden 10 (3 pens), Peniket 6, Bolton 4, Jackson 4, Roberts, M 4, Hattersley 3, Marshall 3 (1 pen), Pearson 3, Hatfield 2 (1 pen), McManus 2, Muldoon 2, Ainge 1, Dyer 1, Schofield 1, Smith 1, Williams 1, own goal 1.
FA Cup (6): Boden 1, Maynard 1, Peniket 2, Smith 2.
FA Trophy (11): Boden 2, Pearson 1, Peniket 4, Roberts, M 1, Williams 2, own goal 1.

Glennon 46	Bolton 31 + 3	McManus 46	Roberts K 21 + 3	Roberts M 45	Ainge 13 + 3	Maynard 35 + 3	Pearson 36 + 5	Schofield 20 + 15	Dyer 8 + 5	Boden 31 + 7	Smith 28 + 12	Marshall 33 + 3	Peniket 24 + 10	Williams 25 + 1	Jackson 12 + 26	Hattersley 14 + 5	Hibbs — + 1	McGinty 2	Hatfield 12 + 5	Hillhouse — + 2	Killock 1	Hutchison 15	Muldoon 8 + 4	Match No.
1	2	3	4^2	5	6^4	7	8	9^3	10^1	11	12	13	14											1
1	2	5	3			8	7	12	10^2	11^1	6^3	9	13	4	14									2
1	2	5	4			9	7	8^2		11	6^1	10	13	3	12									3
1	2	5	3			7	6	12	13	10		8	9^2	4	11^1									4
1	2	5	3			8	7	12		11	6^2	9	10	4	13									5
1	2	5	14	3		9	6^1	12	13	11		7	10^2	4	8^3									6
1	2	5	3			7	6	13	12	10	9^2	8		4	11^1									7
1	2	5	3	14		8^1	6	11	10^2	9	13	7		4	12^3									8
1	2	3	4	12		8^1	5	10^2		11	13	6	9	7										9
1	2^2	5	12	3		8^3	4	13	14	10	9^1	7	11	6										10
1	6	3	4	13	2^1	12	10	7^2	8	9^3	5			11	14									11
1	9	5	2	3^3		6^2	14	10	7^1	8	13	4	12	11										12
1	5	2	3	7		6		11	9^1	8	12	4	13	10^2										13
1	5	2	3	8^2		6		11	9^1	7	12	4	13	10										14
1	5	2	3^4	7	14	12	9^2	10^1	6^3	8	13	4		11										15
1	2	6^2	3	4	12		8^1	10	7	9		5	13	11										16
1	5	2	3	6	7	8		10^2	12	9^1	11	4	13											17
1	8	5	2	3	7	6^1		11	12	9	10	4												18
1	9	5	3	4	8	12	14	6^1	11^3	13	7	10		2^2										19
1	9	2	3	4	8		12		10^2	6	7	11		13					5^1					20
1	12	5	2	3	4	6	7^4	11^2	13	9^1	8	10^3	14											21
1	5	2	3	4	6		9	11	12	7	10^1		13						8^2					22
1	13	5	2	3	4	6		12	11^2	10^1	9^3	8	14						7					23
1	12	5	2	4^3	7			10^1	11	6	9	14		13					8^2					24
1	4	5	2	3		7	14	6^1	13	10	9^2		11^3	12					8					25
1	3	2		4		10	5^1	8		6^2	12		13	9	7				11					26
1	2	3	5	4		6	14	8		11	7^3	13	12	9^2					9^2					27
1	2^4	5	12	3		6^4	7	10		13	9^2	8^1	11	4										28
1	5	2	3			7	6	12		9^1	13^3	10	4	11^2					8	14				29
1	2	5	3			8	7	9		6^1	10		12	11^2					13		4			30
1	2	5	3			6	7^1			9^2	8	11		12	10^3				14			4	13	31
1	2	5	4			7	8	6^1		12	9^2	11		13	10^3							3	14	32
1	2	5	3			7	6^1	8		10	12		11^2	13					14			4	9^3	33
1	2	5	3			13	8^1	7		10	9		12	11^2					14			4	6^3	34
1	2	5	3			10	6	8^1			7	9	11	12								4		35
1	2	5	3			8	6			13	9^2	7	10		11^1					12		4		36
1	2	5	3			9	8			6^1	7^3	11		10	13							4	12	37
1	2	3	4			10^1	5	13	14	6	7^3	9^2		8	12				11					38
1	2	5	3			6	7^2	8		12	9		11	10^1								4	13	39
1	2	6	3			8	7	9^1		10^1	13		4	12								5	11	40
1	5	8	3			6	7^3			11	13		4	9^1	14				12			2^2	10	41
1	2^2	6	3			7	8			10^1			4	12	13				9			5	11	42
1	2	6	3			8	7	13		14			4	12	11^3				9^1			5^2	10	43
1	6	5	2	4		8^2	13			9		3^1	11	12					7				10	44
1	3^1	6	2	5		12	14			9	8		13	10^3					7		4		11^2	45
1		5	2	4^1		7	6			9^2	11		13	12	10				8			3		46

FA Cup

Fourth Qualifying	Chorley	(a)	0-0
Replay	Chorley	(h)	5-0
First Round	Bradford C	(h)	1-2

FA Trophy

First Round	Worcester C	(a)	1-0
Second Round	Alfreton T	(h)	5-3
Third Round	Dartford	(a)	2-2
Replay	Dartford	(h)	3-1
Fourth Round	Wrexham	(h)	0-1

KIDDERMINSTER HARRIERS

Ground: Aggborough Stadium, Hoo Road, Kidderminster DY10 1NB.   *Tel:* (01562) 823 931.   *Fax:* (01562) 827 329.
Website: www.harriers.co.uk   *Year Formed:* 1886.   *Record Attendance:* 9,155 v Hereford U, FA Cup 1st rd, 27 November 1948.
Nickname: 'The Harriers'.   *Manager:* Gary Whild.   *Colours:* Red shirts with white trim, red shorts with white trim,
white socks.

KIDDERMINSTER HARRIERS – VANARAMA PREMIER 2014–15 LEAGUE RECORD

Match No.	Date	Venue	Opponents	Result	H/T Score	Lg Pos.	Goalscorers	Attendance
1	Aug 9	A	Lincoln C	D 0-0	0-0	12		2598
2	12	H	Alfreton T	W 3-0	1-0	6	Dunkley 2 [24, 61], Johnson [84]	1686
3	16	H	Dartford	W 1-0	1-0	5	Storer [41]	1626
4	23	A	Macclesfield T	D 0-0	0-0	6		1407
5	25	H	Chester FC	D 2-2	2-0	10	Gittings [6], Dunkley [9]	2304
6	30	A	Dover Ath	W 1-0	0-0	5	Byrne [51]	833
7	Sept 6	H	Gateshead	W 2-1	0-0	4	Reid [46], Blissett [49]	2607
8	9	A	Southport	L 0-1	0-1	6		769
9	13	A	Braintree T	L 0-2	0-1	11		751
10	16	H	Altrincham	W 4-0	2-0	8	Gash [37], Reid [40], Johnson [72], Styche [90]	1451
11	20	H	Grimsby T	L 0-1	0-0	12		2093
12	27	A	Woking	W 3-2	3-0	8	Styche [21], Gash [26], Storer [29]	1524
13	30	A	Wrexham	L 0-1	0-0	9		3149
14	Oct 4	H	AFC Telford U	D 1-1	1-0	9	Verma [45]	2117
15	8	H	Welling U	W 2-1	2-0	9	Hodgkiss [14], Dunkley [39]	1560
16	11	A	Barnet	D 3-3	0-3	8	Gash [58], Blissett 2 [80, 82]	1689
17	18	A	FC Halifax T	L 0-2	0-2	12		1437
18	Nov 1	H	Torquay U	W 2-1	2-0	9	Johnson [4], Nicholson [26]	2081
19	12	H	Aldershot T	L 0-2	0-0	11		1577
20	15	A	Bristol R	D 1-1	0-0	11	Blissett [67]	5848
21	22	A	Grimsby T	W 2-0	1-0	9	Johnson [2], Byrne [49]	3446
22	25	H	Wrexham	D 1-1	1-0	8	Verma [2]	1645
23	29	A	Altrincham	L 1-2	0-0	10	Johnson [50]	1019
24	Dec 2	H	Nuneaton T	W 3-1	2-0	8	Reid [6], Storer [40], Byrne [72]	1377
25	20	H	Lincoln C	W 2-1	0-1	7	Johnson [51], Obeng [90]	1784
26	26	A	Forest Green R	W 3-2	2-2	6	Verma 2 [34, 81], Byrne [44]	2044
27	28	H	Southport	L 0-1	0-0	7		1883
28	Jan 1	H	Forest Green R	L 2-4	0-3	7	Reid (pen) [70], Johnson [73]	2182
29	4	A	Dartford	W 2-1	0-1	5	Johnson 2 [79, 85]	902
30	17	H	Macclesfield T	L 0-2	0-0	8		1761
31	20	A	Aldershot T	W 1-0	0-0	5	Byrne [74]	1035
32	24	A	Chester FC	L 0-1	0-1	5		2111
33	Feb 14	H	Woking	D 1-1	1-0	9	Hughes [39]	1646
34	21	A	Nuneaton T	D 0-0	0-0	8		983
35	24	A	Gateshead	L 0-2	0-1	8		620
36	28	H	FC Halifax T	D 0-0	0-0	9		1766
37	Mar 7	A	Alfreton T	L 0-2	0-1	10		604
38	10	H	Eastleigh	L 1-3	1-0	10	Partington (og) [9]	1225
39	14	H	Dover Ath	L 0-2	0-1	11		1484
40	21	A	Torquay U	L 1-2	0-1	13	Hughes [62]	1607
41	28	H	Braintree T	W 3-1	3-0	11	Wright 2 [8, 39], Hughes [13]	1317
42	Apr 4	A	AFC Telford U	D 1-1	0-0	11	Gittings [78]	1773
43	6	H	Bristol R	L 0-3	0-0	13		4229
44	11	A	Welling U	L 0-3	0-2	14		505
45	18	H	Barnet	D 1-1	1-0	14	Wright [39]	2540
46	25	A	Eastleigh	L 1-2	1-0	16	Wright [1]	4024

Final League Position: 16

GOALSCORERS

League (51): Johnson 9, Byrne 5, Blissett 4, Dunkley 4, Reid 4 (1 pen), Verma 4, Wright 4, Gash 3, Hughes 3, Storer 3, Gittings 2, Styche 2, Hodgkiss 1, Nicholson 1, Obeng 1, own goal 1.
FA Cup (0).
FA Trophy (4): Gittings 1, Gowling 1, Johnson 1, Reid 1.

Lewis 45	Hodgkiss 44	Dunkley 19	Gowling 30	Nicholson 41+2	Gittings 17+17	Verma 30+5	Storer 23	Obeng 6+14	Blissett 13+5	Reid 23+8	Johnson 30+2	Gash 7+9	Styche 10+9	Byrne 40	Grimes 36+3	Green 12+10	O'Keefe 2+1	Robinson 6	Hales 3+3	Asante 1+9	Tunnicliffe 10	Maxwell 5+3	Spencer 1+7	Reffell 4+7	Singh 1	Wildig 4	Wright 15+1	Knowles 3+3	Hughes 12+1	Digie 1+1	Kelly 5+1	Fry 4	Harrison 1	Boyle 2	Match No.
1	2	3	4	5	6	7	8	9^1	10^3	11^2	12	13	14																						1
1	2	3	4	5	13	7	8		10^3	11	9^2	12	14		6^1																				2
1	2	3	4	5	14	7	8		11^3	10	9^1	13			6^2	12																			3
1	2	3	4	5		7	8	12	9^2	10^1	11^3	14	13		6																				4
1	2	4^1	3	5	8	13	7	9^1	10^2	11^2	14				6	12																			5
1	2		3	5	14	8	7	9^3	10^1	11^2	12	13			6	4																			6
1	2	4	3	5		7		9^2	10^1	11	13	12			8	6																			7
1	2	3	4	5	14	13	7		12	10	11		9^3	8^1	6^2																				8
1	2	3	4	5		7^1	6	13	11^2	14	9	12	10^1	8																					9
1		3	4	5	12	7^1	14		11^3	9	10^2	13			6	8	2																		10
1	2^1	4	3	5	14	7		12	13	9	10^2	11^3			6	8																			11
1	2	4	3	5	14	8	7		13	12	10^3	11^2	9^1		6																				12
1	2	3	4	5		8	7		12	9	10	11^1			6																				13
1	2	3	4	5	13	8	7		14	12	9^1	10^1	11^2		6																				14
1	2	3		5	12	8^1	6		13	11	9	10^1		7	4																				15
1	2	5	4^2	3	8		6	14	9	10^1	11^3	13		7	12																				16
1	2	3		5	8^3	6^2		11	9^1		12	10	14	7	4		13																		17
1	2	3		5	14	12		6^1	10	11	9^3			7	4	13		8^2																	18
1	2^4	4	3	5	13			9^2	10	11^3	6			7^1	12			8	14																19
1		3	4	5		8		11	10^1	7				6	2				9	12															20
1	2	3		5	13	6		12	11^1	9^2				8	4	14				7		10^1													21
1	2	3		5	12	6		13	11^2	9				8	4					7		10^1													22
1	2	4		5	14	7		13	10^4	9	12			6	3					8^1		11^3													23
1	2	3		5	8	9	6		11^1	10				7	4					12															24
1	2	3		5	9	7	13		10^1	6				11^2	8	4					12														25
1	2		5		6^3	10	7	12	9					11^1	8^2	4			14		13	3													26
1	2		5		8	13	10^1	6						11^1	7	4			14		12	3	9^2												27
1	2		5		7	6		9	11					10^1	8^2	4		13			3		12												28
1	2		5		8	7		9^1	11^2	14				6	3	13					10^3	4	12												29
1	2		5		13	11^1	7		10					8	4	6						3	12	9^2											30
	2		5		13	8		10						6	3							4	12	7^2	1	9^1	11								31
	2^1		5			8		11						6	4	13						3	12	9^2			7	10							32
1	2	3		5		8	12							7	4								14				13	6^1	11	9^2	10^1				33
1	3	2	4		14	7^1		13						6	5												12	8^1	11	9^3	10				34
1	2	4		5	8^2	6								7	3	12											13		11	10^1	9				35
1	2	4		5	9	7								8	3	6^1											12		11^2	13	10				36
1	5	2		12	6^1	8								7	3	9						4^3	14				11^2	13	10						37
1	2	3		5	14				11^2	7				4	6								9	12			13		10^2	8^1					38
1	2	3		5	12	8		6						7^1	4	9^2							11^1	14			10	13							39
1	2	3		5	8	7		9^1						4	6	13						14	12	10^3			11								40
1	2		6	8	14	7^2		4	9					13	12								11^1	10^3				3	5						41
1	5		7	8^1		3		9^2	13	6				14					10					12				4	2	11^1					42
1	5		7		12	3		9^1	13	6				11	10^2									4	2				8						43
1	2		13	7^1		12		4	9					8^1	14				10	11								3	6^3		5^2				44
1	2		5		13	7		8	6^2	9^3				4	14	12						10	11^1								14				45
1	2^3		5		8	13		6	4	12	7			3	9^2							10	11^1								14				46

FA Cup
Fourth Qualifying   Eastleigh   (h)   0-1

FA Trophy
First Round   Bradford (Park Avenue)   (a)   4-1
Second Round   Altrincham   (h)   0-1

LINCOLN CITY

Ground: Gelder Group Sincil Bank Stadium, Sincil Bank, Lincoln LN5 8LD.   *Tel:* (01522) 880 011.   *Fax:* (01522) 880 020.
Website: www.redimps.com   *Year Formed:* 1884.   *Record Attendance:* 23,196 v Derby Co, League Cup 4th rd (replay),
15 November 1967.   *Nickname:* 'The Red Imps'.   *Manager:* Chris Moyses.
Colours: Red and white striped shirts, black shorts, red and white hooped socks.

LINCOLN CITY – VANARAMA PREMIER 2014–15 LEAGUE RECORD

Match No.	Date		Venue	Opponents	Result	H/T Score	Lg Pos.	Goalscorers	Atten- dance
1	Aug	9	H	Kidderminster H	D 0-0	0-0	12		2598
2		12	A	Altrincham	W 2-1	1-0	8	Burrow [12], Robinson [81]	996
3		16	A	Barnet	W 2-1	2-0	6	Burrow [15], Bencherif [22]	1529
4		23	H	Braintree T	W 3-2	2-0	3	Newton [7], Bencherif [21], Tomlinson [61]	2231
5		25	A	FC Halifax T	L 2-3	1-2	5	Bencherif [10], Tomlinson (pen) [50]	2369
6		30	H	Torquay U	L 1-3	1-1	10	Tomlinson (pen) [14]	2373
7	Sept	6	A	Woking	L 1-3	0-2	14	Burrow [64]	2160
8		9	H	Grimsby T	W 3-2	1-1	9	Burrow [8], Newton (pen) [57], Bencherif [88]	5209
9		13	H	Bristol R	L 2-3	2-2	13	Newton (pen) [37], Burrow [45]	2933
10		16	A	Welling U	L 0-2	0-1	14		504
11		20	A	Aldershot T	L 0-1	0-1	15		1582
12		27	H	Macclesfield T	W 2-0	2-0	15	Miller [9], Tomlinson [19]	2265
13		30	H	Gateshead	D 1-1	0-0	14	Anderson [55]	2394
14	Oct	4	A	Nuneaton T	L 1-2	1-1	15	Miller [39]	920
15		7	A	Southport	D 3-3	3-2	16	Sam-Yorke [11], Tomlinson [17], Brodie (og) [36]	746
16		11	H	AFC Telford U	W 2-0	0-0	13	Newton (pen) [63], Tomlinson [76]	2529
17		18	H	Wrexham	D 1-1	0-1	14	Power [83]	2360
18	Nov	1	A	Forest Green R	D 3-3	2-0	13	Sam-Yorke [9], Ledsham [40], Burrow [62]	1379
19		4	H	Altrincham	L 1-2	0-1	13	Robinson [66]	1953
20		11	A	Gateshead	D 3-3	1-1	13	Power 2 (2 pens) [17, 90], Sam-Yorke [54]	1211
21		22	H	Dartford	W 1-0	1-0	15	Miller [27]	2483
22		29	H	Southport	W 1-0	0-0	14	Miller [62]	2034
23	Dec	9	H	Nuneaton T	W 3-1	2-0	13	Burrow 2 [6, 60], Tomlinson [17]	1421
24		20	A	Kidderminster H	L 1-2	1-0	13	Sam-Yorke [45]	1784
25		26	H	Alfreton T	W 3-2	1-0	14	Bencherif [6], Tomlinson [70], Marshall [73]	2685
26		28	A	Grimsby T	W 3-1	2-1	11	Adams [43], Power [45], Marshall [69]	7136
27	Jan	4	H	Barnet	W 4-1	2-0	11	Tomlinson [17], Power [24], Nolan [56], Robinson [84]	2759
28		10	A	Eastleigh	L 0-4	0-1	11		1492
29		17	A	Aldershot T	W 3-0	2-0	10	Adams [31], Tomlinson [40], Mendy [48]	3022
30		24	H	Macclesfield T	L 0-3	0-1	11		1974
31		27	A	Chester FC	L 0-4	0-3	11		1569
32		31	H	Dover Ath	W 1-0	0-0	9	Tomlinson [47]	2509
33	Feb	7	A	Bristol R	L 0-2	0-2	10		6528
34		14	A	Chester FC	L 0-1	0-1	11		4568
35		28	H	Woking	L 0-2	0-2	12		2347
36	Mar	7	H	Dover Ath	W 2-1	2-1	11	Sam-Yorke [36], Power [40]	1016
37		14	H	Welling U	L 0-2	0-2	12		1935
38		17	A	Alfreton T	D 0-0	0-0	13		744
39		21	A	Wrexham	D 1-1	1-1	12	Tomlinson [15]	2650
40		28	H	Forest Green R	L 1-2	0-2	13	Power (pen) [79]	1938
41	Apr	3	A	Braintree T	W 3-1	2-1	11	Tomlinson [26], Burrow 2 [32, 49]	650
42		6	H	FC Halifax T	D 1-1	1-0	11	Bencherif [12]	2263
43		11	A	AFC Telford U	L 0-1	0-0	12		1243
44		14	A	Torquay U	L 0-1	0-0	13		1249
45		18	H	Eastleigh	L 1-2	0-1	15	Tomlinson [59]	2132
46		25	A	Dartford	D 0-0	0-0	15		1274

Final League Position: 15

GOALSCORERS

League (62): Tomlinson 14 (2 pens), Burrow 10, Power 7 (3 pens), Bencherif 6, Sam-Yorke 5, Miller 4, Newton 4 (3 pens), Robinson 3, Adams 2, Marshall 2, Anderson 1, Ledsham 1, Mendy 1, Nolan 1, own goal 1.
FA Cup (7): Sam-Yorke 3, Newton 4 (2 pens).
FA Trophy (0).

Townsend 17	Caprice 34 + 3	Diagne 15 + 3	Brown 36	Newton 32	Nolan 28 + 6	Power 33 + 4	Bencherif 41	Marshall 24 + 8	Burrow 28 + 11	Tomlinson 39 + 7	Mendy 26 + 4	Robinson 9 + 10	Ledsham 7 + 6	Kabba — + 2	Jordan 1 + 1	Sam-Yorke 24 + 9	Miller 26 + 1	Anderson 6	Audel 3	Farman 28	Adams 14	Simmons 1 + 6	Waite 2 + 4	Everington 5 + 2	Davies — + 1	Cranston 11	Marsden 2 + 4	Keane 7	Wallace 6	Grant 1	Hodge — + 1	Match No.
1	2	3	4	5	6	7^1	8	9	10	11	12																					1
1	4	3	5	2	8	7^2	6	9^1	10	11^1	12	13	14																			2
1	4	5	3	2	7	9^1	8	12	10	11	6																					3
1	2	3^4	4	5	6	8	7	12	10^1	11	9																					4
1	2	3	4	5	6^3	7^4	9^8	12	10^1	11	8	13	14																			5
1	2^3	4	3^6	5	6^1	8		9^2	10	11	7	14	12			13																6
1	2^1	4		5	8	6^2	3	12	9	11	7	13	14				10^3															7
1	2	3	4	5	6^1		8	9	10	11	7						12															8
1	2	3	4	5	6^1		8	9	10	11	7						12															9
1	5	4	3^1	2	9^2	7	8	14	11^3	10	6						13															10
1	12	3^3		5	9^1	8	7	6^2	11	10		13					14	2	4													11
1	13	3		5		7	12	11	9	6						8^2	10^1	2	4													12
1	5	3		12	8	9		10	6	7						11^1		2	4													13
1	12	3		5	6^2	13	8		10	7		9				11		2	4^1													14
1	4	3	5		9	8		10	6	7						8	11	2														15
1		3	5	7		9		11	6	8						10	2	4														16
1		3	6	8	13		12	9	11	7						10^2	2	4	5^1													17
	4	5	8^1		7	11^3	12	13	6	14	9^2	10						2	3	1												18
14		3	5	8	7	10	12	6^2	13	9	11^3							2	4^1	1												19
3		2	5	13	8	7	6^3	14	12	9^1	11^2	10						4		1												20
2		4	5		7	8	9^1	12	11								10^4			1	6											21
2		5	8	7	4	9^1	10	11								3				1	6	12										22
2		5	7	8	4	9	11^3	10	12	13						3				1	6^2	14										23
2		5	6^1	8^4	4	9		13	12		10					3				1	7	11^2										24
2		3	5	13	4	9	14	12	8	7^3		11^1				1	6	10^2														25
2		3	4	12	6	5	9	13	11^1	7^2	10					1	8															26
2		3	5	7	8	4	11^1	12	9	13	10^2					1	6															27
4		3	5	9^8	8	7	6^1	13	11	12	10^2					1	2															28
2		3^2	5		8	4	13	10	7	9^1	11^1	12				1	6	14														29
2		4	5		7	3	9	13	11	8	12	10^1				1	6^2															30
2		4	5	7^4		6^2	9	10	8	11^1		3^4	13			1		12														31
2		3	4	7		5	9		11	8		10				1	6															32
3		4	2^2	8		5	6^3	13	10	9	11^1	1	7	14	12																	33
		3		8^2		4	9	11	10^1	7	2	1	6	13		5	12															34
2		3		8^2	7	4	9	11	12	10^1	13	1	6	5																		35
2		4		8^1	6	7	12	9	10^2	11	3	1	5	13																		36
2^1		4		7	8	6^3	14	10	9^3	11^8	3	1	12	5	13																	37
2		4		9	6		11	10	7^1	3	1	13	12	5	8^2																	38
2		4		8	6	7		10	11	12	3	1	5	9^1																		39
12		4		7	3		10	11	6^1	2	1	5	13	8	9^2																	40
2	14			12	7	4	10	9^1	3	1	13	6^2	5	8	11^3																	41
2				12	7	3	11	10^2	13	4	1	6^1	5^1	8	9																	42
2	5			8^2	4	10^1	11	12	3	1	13	6	7	9																		43
2				12	4	9	10	11	3	1	13	6^1	5	7	8^2																	44
2				13	9	3	10	12	11	4	1	7^2	5	6	8^1																	45
	5	3		8	6	4	7^2	12	9^3	14	2	10^1	11	1	13																	46

FA Cup

Fourth Qualifying	Alfreton T	(a)	1-1
Replay	Alfreton T	(h)	5-1
First Round	Eastleigh	(a)	1-2

FA Trophy

First Round	Alfreton T	(h)	0-2

MACCLESFIELD TOWN

Ground: Moss Rose Stadium, London Road, Macclesfield, Cheshire SK11 7SP. *Tel:* (01625) 264 686.
Fax: (01625) 264 692. *Website:* www.mtfc.co.uk *Year Formed:* 1874.
Record Attendance: 9,008 v Winsford U, Cheshire Senior Cup 2nd rd, 4 February 1948.
Nickname: 'The Silkmen'. *Manager:* John Askey. *Colours:* Blue shirts with white trim, white shorts, blue socks with white trim.

MACCLESFIELD TOWN – VANARAMA PREMIER 2014–15 LEAGUE RECORD

Match No.	Date	Venue	Opponents	Result	H/T Score	Lg Pos.	Goalscorers	Attendance
1	Aug 9	H	Braintree T	W 1-0	1-0	7	Holroyd [15]	1309
2	12	A	AFC Telford U	W 3-2	3-1	4	Moke [4], Fairhurst 2 [38, 43]	1655
3	16	A	Woking	D 0-0	0-0	6		1340
4	23	H	Kidderminster H	D 0-0	0-0	7		1407
5	25	A	Wrexham	D 2-2	1-1	11	Fairhurst [40], Turnbull [74]	4012
6	30	H	Eastleigh	W 2-0	1-0	6	Rouse [32], Lewis [60]	1284
7	Sept 6	A	Chester FC	L 0-1	0-1	11		2612
8	9	H	FC Halifax T	D 1-1	0-0	8	Gnahoua [56]	1509
9	13	A	Dover Ath	W 1-0	0-0	6	Holroyd [77]	754
10	16	H	Gateshead	D 1-1	1-0	9	Gnahoua [34]	1110
11	20	H	Southport	W 3-0	3-0	6	Waterfall 2 [9, 42], Turnbull [22]	1450
12	27	A	Lincoln C	L 0-2	0-2	9		2265
13	30	A	Altrincham	L 0-1	0-0	11		1317
14	Oct 4	H	Forest Green R	D 2-2	0-1	10	Lewis [52], Fairhurst [73]	1329
15	7	H	Barnet	W 2-1	0-0	9	Barrow [50], Holroyd [66]	1209
16	11	A	Dartford	D 1-1	0-0	10	Barnes-Homer [87]	1063
17	18	H	Dover Ath	W 1-0	0-0	7	Lewis [66]	1439
18	Nov 1	A	Nuneaton T	D 1-1	0-0	10	Turnbull [50]	853
19	11	H	Chester FC	W 3-1	2-0	6	Fairhurst 2 (1 pen) [39 (p), 42], Barnes-Homer [52]	1951
20	15	A	Welling U	D 0-0	0-0	5		508
21	22	H	Alfreton T	W 2-0	1-0	4	Barrow [14], Fairhurst [85]	1471
22	25	H	Torquay U	W 1-0	0-0	3	Whitaker [56]	1234
23	29	A	Barnet	L 1-3	1-0	5	Moke [41]	1610
24	Dec 6	H	Woking	W 2-1	1-0	4	Barnes-Homer [13], Turnbull [89]	1383
25	10	A	Aldershot T	W 1-0	0-0	2	Whitaker [56]	966
26	20	A	Alfreton T	W 5-1	3-1	2	Barnes-Homer 2 [17, 27], Whitaker [36], Holroyd [55], Johnstone [82]	664
27	26	H	Grimsby T	L 0-1	0-1	3		2786
28	28	A	Bristol R	L 0-4	0-1	3		6943
29	Jan 1	H	Grimsby T	W 2-1	1-1	3	Johnstone [30], Whitaker [84]	3545
30	17	A	Kidderminster H	W 2-0	0-0	3	Grant [66], Fairhurst [69]	1761
31	24	H	Lincoln C	W 3-0	1-0	2	Johnstone [37], Lewis [52], Barnes-Homer [90]	1974
32	Feb 7	H	Welling U	W 3-2	1-1	3	Fairhurst (pen) [30], Barnes-Homer 2 [75, 83]	1489
33	10	H	Altrincham	W 2-1	1-0	2	Barnes-Homer [29], Moke [49]	1962
34	14	A	Southport	D 1-1	0-0	3	Whitaker [67]	1207
35	28	A	Eastleigh	L 0-4	0-1	4		4126
36	Mar 3	A	Braintree T	W 1-0	1-0	3	Grant [38]	445
37	7	H	Aldershot T	D 0-0	0-0	4		1671
38	10	H	AFC Telford U	W 1-0	1-0	3	Audel [18]	1225
39	14	A	Gateshead	L 1-2	1-1	3	Pilkington [22]	1052
40	21	H	Nuneaton T	L 0-1	0-0	4		1514
41	28	H	Bristol R	D 0-0	0-0	4		2591
42	Apr 3	A	FC Halifax T	D 2-2	2-1	4	Sampson 2 [15, 31]	1768
43	6	H	Wrexham	D 2-2	1-1	4	Whitaker [14], Bell [57]	2050
44	11	A	Forest Green R	L 1-3	1-2	5	Bell [24]	1714
45	18	H	Dartford	W 2-0	1-0	6	Bell [22], Audel [80]	1756
46	25	A	Torquay U	D 1-1	0-1	6	Fairhurst [71]	2260

Final League Position: 6

GOALSCORERS

League (60): Fairhurst 10 (2 pens), Barnes-Homer 9, Whitaker 6, Holroyd 4, Lewis 4, Turnbull 4, Bell 3, Johnstone 3, Moke 3, Audel 2, Barrow 2, Gnahoua 2, Grant 2, Sampson 2, Waterfall 2, Pilkington 1, Rouse 1.
FA Cup (3): Fairhurst 1, Grant 1, Turnbull 1.
FA Trophy (0).

Taylor 46	Halls 36 + 1	Waterfall 17	Pilkington 44	Barrow 37 + 1	Moke 31 + 8	Lewis 25 + 2	Turnbull 36 + 1	Whitaker 29	Holroyd 29 + 8	Fairhurst 36 + 6	Gnahoua 17 + 4	Lavelle-Moore 1 + 4	Gonzalez 9 + 2	Rouse 3 + 2	Haining 8 + 4	Cowan 10 + 7	Thomas — + 2	Grant 22 + 3	Barnes-Homer 23 + 7	Hogan 9	Bailey 1 + 1	Johnstone 5 + 4	Rowe 5 + 5	Bell 9 + 1	Audel 12	Bailey-Jones 3 + 2	Phenix — + 3	Sampson 3 + 1	Match No.
1	2	3	4	5	6	7	8	9	10	11^1	12																		1
1	2	3	4	5	6	8	7	9	11^1	10			12																2
1	2	3	4	5	6	7	8	9		10	11																		3
1	2	3	4	5	6	8	9			11	10	12	7^1																4
1	2	3	4	5	6	8	9			11	10		7^1		12														5
1	2	3	4	5	6	7	8		11	9			10																6
1	3	2	4	5	6^1	7	8		12	11	9		10^2		13														7
1	2	3	4	5			6^1	8^3	9	10	11		13	12	7^2	14													8
1	2	3	4	5				8	9^2	11			6	10^1	7	13	12												9
1	2	3	4	5	12		6		10	11	9		7^2		6^1	13													10
1	2	3	4	5	12		8		11^2	10	9		7		6^1	13													11
1	2		3	5	9	8	7		12	10^2	11	14	6^3			4^1	13												12
1	2	3	4	5	9^1	8	7		10^2	11	6	13			12														13
1	2	3	4	5	12	8			10^1	11	9		7		6														14
1		3	4	5		8	12		10	11	9		7		6^1	2													15
1	2		4	3	5	13	6	8		9	10	11^1		7^2				12											16
1	2	3		4^1	5	9	7	8		6	11							12	10										17
1	2		4	3	5			7	6	8	11^1	9	12						10										18
1	2		4	5	12	8	7	6		10^1	9							11	3										19
1	2		4	3	12			8		10			5^2		13	7^1	11	6	9										20
1	2^1		5	3	8		6	7	11	9						12	10	4											21
1			3	5	9		8	7	6	11		10				4	2												22
1			5	3	7		6^1	8	9^2	10^1	12				4	11	2	14	13										23
1	2		5	3	7		6	8	9^2	10^1	12					11	4	13											24
1	2		5	3	7		6	8	9	12						11	4	10^1											25
1	2		3	4	7		8	6	11	9^1						10	5	12											26
1	3		4	5	8^1		6	7	9	10^2	14				12	11	2^2	13											27
1	2		4	3	7			9	6	12				8		5	10	11^1											28
1	2		3	5	9		7	8		10^2	11^3			14		4	13	6^1	12										29
1	2		3	5	8	7	6	9		10					9^1	4	12	11^1											30
1	2		3	5	8	7	6		10^2					9^1		4	13	11	12										31
1	2		4	5	11	7	8^1		13	9^2						3	10		12	6									32
1			4	5	6	9		7	12					2		3	11		10^1	8									33
1			4	5	11	7^2		6	13	12				2		3	10		9^1	8									34
1	2		4		6^2	7^1		9	13	12						5	11		10^3	8	3	14							35
1	4		6		7^1	8		9		10					3	2	11		12	5									36
1	2^2		4		9		8^3	7	6^1	11				12		5	10		13	3	14								37
1			5		6^3	12	8	9	13	14				2		4	11		7^1	3	10^2								38
1	14		4		12	7	8	6^1	13	10^1				2^2		5	11			3	9								39
1	2		4		7^1	13	6^1	9^2		14						5	11			8	3	10	12						40
1	2		4		11	7	8	6^1	9^1	10^3						5	12			3		13	14						41
1	2		4			6	7	9	10	8^4						5	12			3			11^1						42
1			4^1	12		8	9	7					13	2		5	10			6	3		11^2						43
1			2			6	8	9					4^1			5	11		12	7	3	13	10^2						44
1			4^4	5	12		9	8	7^2				13			2	11		10^1	6	3								45
1	2			5	6		7	8	10	11						3	12			9^1	4								46

FA Cup
Fourth Qualifying   Wrexham   (h)   1-1
Replay   Wrexham   (a)   2-5

FA Trophy
First Round   Altrincham   (a)   0-1

NUNEATON TOWN

Ground: James Parnell Stadium, Liberty Way, Nuneaton, Warwickshire CV11 6RR.
Tel: (0247) 638 5738. *Fax:* (0247) 637 2995. *Website:* nuneatontownfc.com *Year Formed:* 1889.
Record Attendance: 22,114 v Rotherham U, FA Cup 3rd rd, 28 January 1967 (at Manor Park).
Nickname: 'Boro', 'The Nuns'. *Manager:* Kevin Wilson. *Colours:* Blue and white striped shirts, white shorts, white
socks.

NUNEATON TOWN – VANARAMA PREMIER 2014–15 LEAGUE RECORD

Match No.	Date	Venue	Opponents	Result	H/T Score	Lg Pos.	Goalscorers	Atten- dance
1	Aug 9	H	Eastleigh	L	0-3	0-1	23		935
2	12	A	Grimsby T	D	0-0	0-0	19		3710
3	16	A	Wrexham	L	0-1	0-1	22		3292
4	23	H	Barnet	L	0-2	0-2	23		863
5	25	A	Braintree T	L	0-2	0-0	23		658
6	30	H	Altrincham	W	2-1	1-0	18	Brown, Andy 36, Dyer 67	774
7	Sept 6	A	Torquay U	L	0-4	0-3	21		2177
8	9	H	Forest Green R	W	1-0	0-0	20	John 75	789
9	13	H	Aldershot T	D	1-1	1-0	18	Brown, Andy 19	803
10	16	A	Bristol R	L	1-3	0-1	21	Dean 68	4861
11	20	A	Alfreton T	L	0-1	0-0	22		600
12	27	H	Dartford	L	1-2	1-0	22	Curran 35	759
13	30	A	Woking	L	0-1	0-0	23		1313
14	Oct 4	H	Lincoln C	W	2-1	1-1	22	Fowler 30, Dawson, A 67	920
15	7	H	Dover Ath	W	3-2	2-1	21	Sodje 16, Armson 33, Franklin 77	753
16	11	A	Welling U	L	1-4	1-2	22	Dean 23	614
17	18	A	Eastleigh	L	1-2	0-1	22	Fowler 68	1009
18	Nov 1	H	Macclesfield T	D	1-1	0-0	23	Dawson, A 90	853
19	15	A	Aldershot T	L	0-1	0-0	23		1658
20	22	H	Southport	L	2-3	1-2	23	Sodje 38, Smith 49	743
21	25	A	Dover Ath	L	0-5	0-3	23		727
22	29	H	Chester FC	W	3-2	2-0	22	Armson 20, Fowler 23, Barrington 79	973
23	Dec 2	A	Kidderminster H	L	1-3	0-2	22	Gowling (og) 62	1377
24	6	H	Alfreton T	L	0-1	0-1	23		727
25	9	A	Lincoln C	L	1-3	0-2	23	Cowan 90	1421
26	20	A	FC Halifax T	L	0-2	0-0	23		1227
27	26	H	AFC Telford U	D	4-4	1-1	23	Armson 2 (1 pen) 41 (pl), 75, Dawson, A 60, Sodje 80	1017
28	28	A	Altrincham	W	1-0	0-0	23	Gash 69	1025
29	Jan 1	A	AFC Telford U	D	0-0	0-0	23		1797
30	4	H	Bristol R	L	0-2	0-1	23		1661
31	17	H	Gateshead	L	0-2	0-2	23		637
32	24	H	Grimsby T	L	0-2	0-0	23		989
33	31	A	Forest Green R	L	0-1	0-1	23		1333
34	Feb 14	A	Gateshead	W	2-1	1-1	23	Brown, Andy 45, Streete 64	1047
35	21	H	Kidderminster H	D	0-0	0-0	23		983
36	28	H	Welling U	W	1-0	0-0	22	Walker 50	763
37	Mar 7	A	Southport	D	0-0	0-0	22		1040
38	14	H	Torquay U	D	0-0	0-0	22		862
39	21	A	Macclesfield T	W	1-0	0-0	22	Sodje 90	1514
40	24	H	Wrexham	W	2-0	1-0	21	Walker 36, Ogleby 63	818
41	28	H	FC Halifax T	L	1-2	0-1	21	Brown, Andy 68	947
42	Apr 4	A	Barnet	L	0-1	0-0	22		2006
43	6	H	Braintree T	L	0-1	0-0	22		636
44	11	A	Dartford	L	1-3	1-0	23	Brown, Andy 22	808
45	18	H	Woking	D	1-1	1-0	23	Gordon, J 18	709
46	25	A	Chester FC	L	3-5	2-1	24	Brown, Andy 20, Cowan 28, Rees 46	2614

Final League Position: 24

GOALSCORERS

League (38): Brown, Andy 6, Armson 4 (1 pen), Sodje 4, Dawson, A 3, Fowler 3, Cowan 2, Dean 2, Walker 2,
Barrington 1, Curran 1, Dyer 1, Franklin 1, Gash 1, Gordon, J 1, John 1, Ogleby 1, Rees 1, Smith 1, Streete 1, own goal
1.
FA Cup (0).
FA Trophy (0).

Charles-Cook 17	Dean 34+1	Cowan 16+3	Streete 42	John 5+7	Amson 30+8	Dyer 8+3	Walker 29+12	Franklin 45	Brown Andy 25+1	Maris 8+1	Vieira 1+1	Hutchinson 5+6	Brown Anton 27+7	Gordon D 2+2	Wheeler 11	Waite 1+2	Quinn —+8	Crocombe 10	Geoghaghon 8	Smith 21+6	Starosta 8+3	Cranston 1	Rees 8	Curran 11+2	Fowler 20+1	Lincoln 2	McSweeney 4	Charles 10	Dawson L 5+2	Dawson A 13	Sodje 18+11	Griffiths 3+1	Hogarth-Wren 4+1	Gash 11	Gordon J 4+1	Stankevicius 1+4	Dibile 10	Barrington 1+3	Burton 3	Baker-Richardson —+2	Ogleby 11+2	Mafuta 6	Nardiello 2+5	Whitehouse 5	Match No.
1	2	3^2	4	5	6	7^3	8	9^1	10	11		12	13		14																														1
1	2	3	4	5^1	12	7	8	9	10							11^2			6	13																									2
1	2	3^1	4	5^2	12	7	8	9	11			13	10		6																													3
1	2		4	5	6^1	8^2	12	9	10	7		3	11		13																													4
1	3^2		6	10^1	8	13	9	5		11^4			2	12		4	7																											5
1		4	13	8^1	7	12	5	11		14						3	6^2	2	9	10^3																									6
1		3				12	9	5^1	10			7^4			13	4	6	2		11	8^2																								7
1	4		2	12		7	8	5	10						3	9^1		11	6																									8
1	4		9^2	12	8^3		7	2^1	11			13		14	3	5		10	6																									9
1	3		9^3	13	12		2		10			14	7^1		4	6^2		11	8	5																								10
1	3		7	14	13		9	5	11			12			4	6^3		10^1	8	2^2																								11
1	4		7	14	6^2		9	5	10^3			12	13		3			11	8	2^1																								12
1	4		3	12	9		10	5				11	6					8^1	7	2																								13
1	3		6		7	8^1	12	4				10	13					11	5^2		2	9																						14
1	3		6		7	8^2	4	12									13	10^1	5		2	9	11																					15
1^1	3			9	8	5						14						2	13	6^3		4	7^1	11	10^2	12																		16
	4		2	6^2	14		5					13	7						12	8		3	9	11^3	10^1	1																		17
1	2	3	6^1			13	5					7						12	14		11^2	8		4^3	9	10																		18
	4	3	2	7	9	5						8^2	13					6	14								11	12^3	1	10													19
3^4	4	2^1	7^3	9	5							14						6	13		8						11^2	1	10	12													20
	4	2	7	14	5							9^2						13	6		8^3		3	11^1	1	10	12																21
	4		7				3					9						13	2		8^2		5	6	11^1		10		1	12														22
	3		6^1	13	5		9					2									8^2		4	7	10		11	1	12															23
	7		5		3		8					2									9		4	6^3	13	10^1	12	1	11															24
	12	8^1	6	13	3		9											4^1	2		10^2		5^3	7	14	11	1																	25
	3^2	4	8^1	9	5							7						14	2^1		6	11^3		10	13	1	12																	26
	4	3	7	9	5							8					12	2		6^1	11		10			1										1								27
	12	3	4	7	9^1	5						8					13	2^2		6	11		10			1										1								28
	3	4	8	9	5							7						2		6	11		10			1										1								29
	3	4	2	8	9^2	5	10^2					7^1			14	6					12			11^2			10		1	13							1		13					30
	3	4	12	9	5	10^2												2		7				13												1				6	8	11^1		31
	3	13	4^1		5	11						7						2		8^2				6												1				10	9	12		32
	3	4	12	14	5	9	11^3									2															8^1					1			7^2	6	13	10	33
	3	4	12	9^1	13	5	10	8					2																							1			11^2	7		6	34
	3	4	6	5^2		8^1	2	9	10				4				1													13										11	12	7	35
	3	4	6		9	5	10	11					2				1													13										8^1	12	7	36
	3	5	6^2		9^1	4	10	11		8			1	2																13										12		7	37
	3	4	6		8	5	11	10		7		2	1																	12										9^1			38
	4	14	7^2	5		2	9^1	10		6	3		1							11										13								12	8^3				39
	3	9	12	6^1	2	8^3	10^2	5		4										11	1		14	13													7						40
	3	5	8^2	7^1	4	13				6	2									10	1	14	12			11											9^3						41
	3	6	5^3	13	4	11				7	2^2			1						9			8	12		10^1											14						42
		4	3		10	5	11				2	1	8^1							6			9	13		12											7^2						43
	3	4			9	5	11			7^1	2	1	12							8			6	10																			44
	4	3			13	2		12			5	1	14							9			6	11		8^1												7^1		10^3				45
2	3^1				13	4	11				12	1	8							7			5	9^2		10											6^1		14				46

FA Cup
Fourth Qualifying   Hemel Hempstead T   (h)   0-0
Replay   Hemel Hempstead T   (a)   0-2
(aet; 0-0 at end of normal time)

FA Trophy
First Round   Grimsby T   (h)   0-2

SOUTHPORT

Ground: Merseyrail Community Stadium, Haig Avenue, Southport PR8 6JZ.   *Tel:* (01704) 533 422.
Website: southportfc.net   *Year Formed:* 1881.   *Record Attendance:* 20,010 v Newcastle U, FA Cup 4th rd (replay),
26 January 1932.   *Nickname:* 'The Sandgrounders'.   *Manager:* Paul Carden.   *Colours:* Yellow and black striped
shirts, black shorts, black socks.

SOUTHPORT – VANARAMA PREMIER 2014–15 LEAGUE RECORD

Match No.	Date		Venue	Opponents	Result	H/T Score	Lg Pos.	Goalscorers	Atten- dance
1	Aug	9	H	Forest Green R	L 0-1	0-0	17		1023
2		12	A	FC Halifax T	L 1-3	1-1	21	Hattersley [43]	1463
3		16	A	Torquay U	D 0-0	0-0	19		1997
4		23	H	Altrincham	W 2-1	1-0	14	Brodie [20], Foster [90]	1082
5		25	A	AFC Telford U	D 3-3	2-1	15	Gorman [21], Brodie 2 [44, 71]	1421
6		30	H	Barnet	L 0-2	0-2	16		909
7	Sept	6	A	Eastleigh	L 1-2	0-0	19	Connor [63]	1309
8		9	H	Kidderminster H	W 1-0	1-0	16	Connor [26]	769
9		13	H	Alfreton T	L 0-2	0-2	17		832
10		16	A	Chester FC	L 0-2	0-2	20		1790
11		20	A	Macclesfield T	L 0-3	0-3	20		1450
12		27	H	Bristol R	L 0-1	0-1	21		1202
13		30	A	Grimsby T	W 1-0	0-0	20	Brodie [82]	3353
14	Oct	4	H	Woking	L 2-5	0-1	21	Fitzpatrick [55], Foster [81]	730
15		7	H	Lincoln C	D 3-3	2-3	22	Joyce [33], Brodie [38], Marsden [86]	746
16		11	A	Braintree T	W 2-0	0-0	20	George [69], Bakayoko [84]	810
17		18	H	Welling U	W 1-0	0-0	18	Connor [90]	1007
18	Nov	1	H	Dover Ath	D 2-2	2-1	17	Marsden [11], Connor [17]	1398
19		15	A	Dartford	D 1-1	1-0	20	Marsden [45]	1163
20		22	A	Nuneaton T	W 3-2	2-1	19	Marsden [15], Brodie [23], Bakayoko [79]	743
21		25	H	Aldershot T	L 1-3	1-2	20	Brodie [45]	843
22		29	A	Lincoln C	L 0-1	0-0	20		2034
23	Dec	10	A	Gateshead	D 1-1	0-0	20	Brodie [66]	808
24		20	A	Woking	W 2-1	1-0	20	Joyce [12], Collins [67]	1688
25		26	H	Wrexham	L 0-1	0-0	20		1912
26		28	A	Kidderminster H	W 1-0	0-0	20	George [66]	1883
27	Jan	17	H	Chester FC	D 0-0	0-0	20		1894
28		24	A	Barnet	L 0-4	0-1	20		1833
29		31	H	Gateshead	L 0-1	0-1	20		904
30	Feb	7	A	Alfreton T	L 2-4	1-0	20	Brodie [12], Rutherford [66]	529
31		10	H	Eastleigh	L 1-2	0-0	20	Marsden [76]	727
32		14	H	Macclesfield T	D 1-1	0-0	20	Brodie [77]	1207
33		21	A	Dover Ath	D 2-2	0-1	20	Brodie [70], Rutherford [75]	1008
34		28	A	Forest Green R	L 3-5	1-3	21	Fitzpatrick [4], Foster [62], McCarthy [82]	1222
35	Mar	3	H	FC Halifax T	W 1-0	0-0	19	Kay [81]	715
36		7	H	Nuneaton T	D 0-0	0-0	19		1040
37		10	A	Wrexham	D 0-0	0-0	19		2188
38		14	A	Aldershot T	W 2-1	2-0	19	Smith [19], Donnelly [25]	1646
39		21	H	Dartford	W 2-0	0-0	19	Brodie [64], Rutherford [90]	850
40		28	H	Torquay U	W 2-1	1-0	18	Kay [10], Smith [86]	1021
41	Apr	3	A	Altrincham	L 0-2	0-1	19		1401
42		6	H	AFC Telford U	L 0-3	0-1	19		1092
43		11	A	Bristol R	L 0-2	0-1	19		8251
44		14	A	Braintree T	L 0-2	0-0	19		748
45		18	H	Grimsby T	D 2-2	0-1	19	Almond [46], Foster [54]	1968
46		25	A	Welling U	W 1-0	0-0	19	Hewitt [78]	1015

Final League Position: 19

GOALSCORERS

League (47): Brodie 12, Marsden 5, Connor 4, Foster 4, Rutherford 3, Bakayoko 2, Fitzpatrick 2, George 2, Joyce 2, Kay
2, Smith 2, Almond 1, Collins 1, Donnelly 1, Gorman 1, Hattersley 1, Hewitt 1, McCarthy 1.
FA Cup (6): Brodie 2, Evans 1, George 1, Hattersley 1 (1 pen), Marsden 1.
FA Trophy (1): Mitchell 1.

Lloyd-Weston 12	Mitchell 7+3	Collins 32+1	Foster 35	Fitzpatrick 35+2	Rutherford 29+11	George 38+1	Kay 29+2	Brogan 10+1	Marsden 16+15	Hattersley 12+4	Whitehall —+3	Lynch 4+2	Joyce 30+2	Connor 25+3	Evans 8+8	Brodie 34+2	Smith 17+7	Gorman 3+2	McDonald 10+2	Porter 1	Raya 16	Dyer 5+1	Challoner 14+3	Bakayoko 4+7	Austin 6+2	Burton 4	Symes —+2	Parry 4	Caton 3+1	Donnelly 14+2	Beesley 12+1	Thompson J 3+1	McCarthy 4+10	Brezovan 6	Almond 3+4	Davies 8+1	Thompson T 7	Hewitt 6+1	Match No.
1	2	3	4	5	6^3	7^2	8	9^1	10	11	12	13	14																										1
1	2^3	3	4	5	13	7	6	9	11^2	10	12		14	8																									2
1	2	3	4	5		8	6^2	9^1	10^1	11		13				7	12	14																					3
1	2	3	4	5	13	8	7	9^2	10^1				14	6^3	11				12																				4
1		3	4	5		8	7		13	10^1			2	6	11	12	9^2																						5
1	14	3	4^2	5	12	7	8		13	10^1			2	6^3	11		9																						6
1		3	4	5	12	8	7	9	11				2	6^1	10																								7
1			4	5	12^3	7	9	8^2	11	14			2	6^1	10^4	13	3																						8
1	12	3		5	8	7	6		9	10^2	11	14	2			13			4^3																				9
13		3		5	6	8^2	7		11	14			2^1			10	12	9^1	4	1																			10
	2^1	4		5	9^2	8	7	14	12				3			11	6^3				1	10	13																11
	2	5	12	13	7	8^2	6	14				3^1				9			4^3		1	10	11																12
	2	5	3			8	6^2	12							13	10^1	7		11		1	9	4																13
	2	5	4	12	14	3^1	10	13							9	6^3	11^2		7		1	8																	14
		3	2	5^1	9	7			12				6	8^2	13	10			4		1	11^3	14																15
		2	3	9	6	8		11				5	7	4			10				1		12																16
		4	5	6	7	8		13				3^1	9	2	10^2						1	14	11^1	12															17
2		4	3	6			8^1	11	10			9	5		13						1	12	7^2																18
	2	3	5	6	8	7		10^2	11			4									1	12	13	9^1															19
		4	5	6	8		10					7	2	11^1	3						1	12	9																20
2			5	9	7		10					8^1	4	12	11						3	1	13	6^2															21
	2	3	5	9	7	8		11^1				4	6	10							1	12																	22
		4	5	10^3	7	6						9	3	14	11^1		12				1	2	13	8^2															23
		3	4	5	6	7						8	2^2	10^1	9		12				1	11																	24
	2	3	5	6^1	8		13	10^2				7		11	4		1				9	12																	25
		4	3	5	6	8		7	12			10		11^1	9		1				2																		26
		4	5	3	10	6	7		13	11		9^1	12^4	8^2	1	2																							27
		4	5	8^2	13		14	11		6	3	12	9	1	2^3	10																							28
		3	5	8^1	9	13	10^2	6	4	14	12	1	2^3	7	11																								29
		3	4	5	12	7	2	13	10	6	1	8^1	9^1	11																									30
1		4	5	3	6	8		13				9	12	10	2															11^2	7^1								31
1		4	3	5	13	7		8	10			2	12	11^2	9^1	6^1	14																						32
1		4	3	5	9^1	7		8	10			2	11	12	6																								33
		3	4	5	9	7	12	8^2	10^1	2	11		6^2	14	1	13																							34
		3		7^1	8	6	9^2	8	4	11	5^2	2	12	10			13	1																					35
		3		10^1	6	9^2	8	4	11	13	2	7	5			12	1																						36
		3			8	7	9	4^1	11	10	2	6^2	5			13	1	12																					37
		3			9	8	7	11^2	6^1	2	10	5				12	13	1	4																				38
		3	12	9	8	7^1	11^2	6	2	10	5					13		1	4																				39
	2			7^1	6	8	10^2	9	5	11	4	12							3	1	13																		40
	12		5	2	3	6^2	8	7^3	2	10	11	5^1	14						13	1	9																		41
	12		9^1	3	8	6	11^3	2	10	5^1	13	14	4	7^2	9																								42
12		5	2	3	6^2	8	7															13								10	11	4	1	9				43
	2^1	3	5^3	7	6^2	8	14		13																					10	11	12	4	1	9				44
		3		7	6	4	12	10														2								5	11	9^1	1	8				45
		3		7^1	6	8	11^3	14														2								13	5^1	12	10	4	1	9		46

FA Cup

Fourth Qualifying	Tamworth	(a)	1-1
Replay	Tamworth	(h)	1-1
(aet; Southport won 4-2 on penalties)			
First Round	Dagenham & R	(a)	0-0
Replay	Dagenham & R	(h)	2-0
Second Round	Eastleigh	(h)	2-1
Third Round	Derby Co	(a)	0-1

FA Trophy

First Round	Wrexham	(h)	1-1
Replay	Wrexham	(a)	0-2

TORQUAY UNITED

Ground: Plainmoor Ground, Torquay, Devon TQ1 3PS. *Tel:* (01803) 328666. *Fax:* (01803) 323976.
Website: www.torquayunited.com *Year Formed:* 1899. *Record Attendance:* 21,908 v Huddersfield T, FA Cup 4th rd,
29 January 1955. *Nickname:* The Gulls. *Manager:* Chris Hargreaves. *Colours:* Yellow shirts with blue trim, yellow
shorts with blue trim, yellow socks.

TORQUAY UNITED – VANARAMA PREMIER 2014–15 LEAGUE RECORD

Match No.	Date		Venue	Opponents	Result	H/T Score	Lg Pos.	Goalscorers	Atten- dance
1	Aug	9	A	Gateshead	L 1-3	0-2	20	Briscoe [89]	1765
2		12	H	Welling U	W 3-0	2-0	12	Bowman [15], Cameron (pen) [43], Ajala [67]	1895
3		16	H	Southport	D 0-0	0-0	11		1997
4		23	A	Dartford	D 0-0	0-0	13		1163
5		25	A	Aldershot T	D 1-1	1-0	14	Cameron [3]	2135
6		30	A	Lincoln C	W 3-1	1-1	14	Ofori-Acheampong 2 [33, 72], Richards [62]	2373
7	Sept	6	H	Nuneaton T	W 4-0	3-0	9	Young 2 [21, 29], Downes [39], Bowman [58]	2177
8		9	A	Chester FC	W 2-0	0-0	5	Downes [61], Bowman [78]	1954
9		13	A	Grimsby T	W 2-0	2-0	5	Richards [14], Young [37]	3300
10		16	H	Woking	W 1-0	0-0	2	Young [90]	2144
11		20	H	Dover Ath	W 2-0	1-0	2	Downes [35], Essam (og) [90]	2363
12		27	A	AFC Telford U	L 3-4	2-2	2	MacDonald [19], Bowman [31], Wakefield [71]	1669
13		30	A	Forest Green R	L 1-2	1-1	4	Ofori-Acheampong [22]	1365
14	Oct	4	H	Wrexham	W 2-1	0-1	2	Briscoe [62], Young [84]	2350
15		11	A	Alfreton T	L 2-4	1-2	6	Briscoe 2 [30, 54]	736
16		18	H	Grimsby T	L 2-3	1-2	9	Young [43], Downes [61]	2353
17	Nov	1	A	Kidderminster H	L 1-2	0-2	12	Downes [89]	2081
18		11	A	Barnet	W 3-2	2-0	9	Briscoe 2 [24, 50], Stack (og) [41]	1745
19		15	H	Forest Green R	D 3-3	2-1	9	Bowman [4], Ajala 2 [19, 63]	2117
20		22	H	Gateshead	D 2-2	1-0	10	Bowman 2 (1 pen) [8 (pl), 90]	1947
21		25	A	Macclesfield T	L 0-1	0-0	10		1234
22		29	H	Eastleigh	W 2-0	1-0	7	Ajala [6], Bowman [86]	1862
23	Dec	2	A	Dover Ath	D 2-2	1-0	10	Pearce [23], Yeoman [80]	795
24		6	H	Barnet	L 1-2	0-2	10	Richards [90]	1933
25		9	H	FC Halifax T	W 2-1	2-0	7	Bowman [36], Ofori-Acheampong [43]	1470
26		20	H	Braintree T	L 0-2	0-2	8		818
27		26	H	Bristol R	L 1-2	1-2	10	Spiess (og) [34]	3755
28		28	A	Welling U	D 0-0	0-0	9		808
29	Jan	1	A	Bristol R	D 1-1	1-0	9	Ofori-Acheampong [10]	8044
30		4	H	Alfreton T	D 1-1	0-0	10	Chapell [72]	2028
31		17	A	Altrincham	L 1-2	0-1	13	Briscoe [66]	1333
32		31	A	Wrexham	D 0-0	0-0	14		2655
33	Feb	14	A	Eastleigh	W 2-1	1-1	14	Gueguen [45], Bowman [76]	1844
34	Mar	7	A	AFC Telford U	L 0-1	0-1	14		1647
35		10	H	Chester FC	L 0-1	0-1	15		1221
36		14	A	Nuneaton T	D 0-0	0-0	16		862
37		17	H	Braintree T	L 1-5	1-2	17	Campbell [22]	1103
38		21	H	Kidderminster H	W 2-1	1-0	15	Bowman 2 [23, 65]	1607
39		24	H	Woking	L 2-3	2-0	15	Downes [17], Briscoe [19]	1506
40		28	A	Southport	L 1-2	0-1	16	Ajala [78]	1021
41	Apr	4	H	Dartford	D 1-1	0-0	16	McQuilkin [67]	1754
42		6	A	Aldershot T	L 0-2	0-1	17		2033
43		11	A	Altrincham	W 2-0	2-0	16	Daniel [22], Bowman (pen) [27]	1462
44		14	H	Lincoln C	W 1-0	0-0	12	Yeoman [80]	1249
45		18	A	FC Halifax T	W 2-0	0-0	12	Campbell [71], Daniel [74]	1175
46		25	H	Macclesfield T	D 1-1	1-0	13	Briscoe [24]	2260

Final League Position: 13

GOALSCORERS

League (64): Bowman 13 (2 pens), Briscoe 9, Downes 6, Young 6, Ajala 5, Ofori-Acheampong 5, Richards 3, Cameron
2 (1 pen), Campbell 2, Daniel 2, Yeoman 2, Chapell 1, Gueguen 1, MacDonald 1, McQuilkin 1, Pearce 1, Wakefield 1,
own goals 3.
FA Cup (0).
FA Trophy (13): Ajala 1, Bowman 6 (1 pen), Chapell 1, Downes 1, Harding 1, Ofori-Acheampong 1, Yeoman 1,
Young 1.

Rice 35	Tonge 17	Downes 39	MacDonald 23+3	Cruise 23+1	Briscoe 32+7	Young 38+1	Harding 15+2	Cameron 23+4	Bowman 35+2	Benyon 1+5	Ajala 37+8	Ofori-Acheampong 16+14	Richards 28+10	Yeoman 7+22	Wakefield 3+7	Ives 20	Chapell 17+6	Sullivan —+1	Pearce 28+4	Seabright 6	Thompson 1+2	Berry 12	McQuilkin 13+4	Dawson 14	Prynn —+4	Gueguen 7	Campbell 5+4	Reid 1+1	Daniel 5+2	Lavercombe 5	Match No.
1	2	3	4	5	6	7	8³	9¹	10	11²	12	13	14																		1
1	2	3	4	5	6²	7	8	9	10		12	13		11¹																	2
1	2	3	4	5	6³	8	7²	9	11■		13	12	14	10¹																	3
1	2	4	3	5	6¹	7		9			14	10³	11²	8	12	13															4
1	2	3	5	12	7		6				11³	10¹	8²		13		4		9		14										5
1	2	4	3	5	10¹	8		9			12	11²	7	14	6³		13														6
1	2	3	4	5		7		9¹	11		6	10²	8³	13	14		12														7
1	2	3	4	5		7			10		9	11	8				6														8
1	2	3	4	5		7			11¹		9	10²	8	12	13		6³		14												9
1	2	3	4	5		8		12	10		9	11	7				6¹														10
1	2	4	3	5		7		12	10		9¹	11	8		13		6²														11
1	2	4■	5	3		6		13	10		7■	11²	9		12		8¹														12
1	2	3	5	6¹	7			9	10		11²	8³	13	12					4												13
1	2		4	5	6¹	7		9	10		11		12	8					3												14
1	2		5	9	7			6²	10¹		11	12	4	13	8				3												15
1	2	3	4	5	6	7		9¹	10		11²	12	8				13														16
	2²	4	3	5		7		9¹	11		14	13	8	10³					12	1	6										17
1		4		5	11²	6		8¹	10		9	12	7						3	13	2										18
1		3		5	11³	7		9¹	10²		6	12	8	14					4	13	2										19
1		3		5	10²	7		9¹	11	13	6	14	8¹						4		2	12									20
1		4			11²	8		6¹	10	12	9	13	7			5			3		2										21
1		3	12		11¹	7			10		9		8			5	6²		4		2	13									22
1		3	13		10³	7			11		9²		8	12		5	6¹		4		2	14									23
1		3■	12		10²	7			11³		9	13	8	14		5	6¹		4		2										24
1			4		6¹	7	13		10		9	11²	8	12		5	14		3		2³										25
1			4	12	6²		7		11		9	10³	8	14		5	13		3		2¹										26
			4		12	7			9	10	13	6²	11¹	8³	14	5			3	1	2										27
			4	5	3	10	7²	6			11	14	12		13	9¹			8³		1	2									28
		3	4■	2	12	7	9		10		8	11¹				6²		13	1	5											29
		3			5	12	8	7²	10		9	11¹	13	14		6³		4	1	2											30
		3			5	12	8	7³	9²		11	10¹	14	13		6		4	1	2											31
1		3		9²					11	12	7	10¹		5	6		4				8	2	13								32
1		2		10³	8			12	11		9²	13	7		4	6¹				14		5									33
1		3		13	7			11		12			14		5	6	4			8²	2			9¹	10³						34
1		3		10¹	7	8³		11			9	12	13		6		4			5²			2	14							35
1		2	3³	11²	6			10			12	7		9			13			5		4	8¹	14							36
1		4		14	7			11²			8	6		9	12	3³				5	13	2	10¹								37
1		3		11²	7			9	12		6²	14	13	5			8			2	4	10¹									38
1		4		10¹	8			9	11²		6	13				5				7	2	12	3								39
1		3		10²	5■	12	7	11¹			6	14				4				8	9³	2					13				40
1		4		10	7	9		6			12					5				3	8	2					11¹				41
		7		11¹	4	6³		10²			8	14		5						3	9	2	13				12	1			42
		4		11²	8		10¹	6			13			5						3	7	2			12		9	1			43
		3		10	13	7		6			12			5						4	8¹	2			11²		9	1			44
		3		11¹	7			9			13	10		5						4	8²	2			12		6	1			45
		4		11³	8		12	6			14	10²		5						3	7¹	2			13		9	1			46

FA Cup
Fourth Qualifying   Aldershot T   (a)   0-2

FA Trophy

First Round	Bishop's Stortford	(a)	5-0
Second Round	Bromley	(h)	4-0
Third Round	Hemel Hempstead T	(a)	2-0
Fourth Round	FC United of Manchester	(h)	1-0
Semi-Finals 1st leg	Wrexham	(a)	1-2
Semi-Finals 2nd leg	Wrexham	(h)	0-3

(Wrexham won 5-1 on aggregate)

WELLING UNITED

Ground: Park View Road, Welling, Kent DA16 1SY.   *Tel:* (0208) 3011196.   *Fax:* (0208) 3015676.
Website: www.wellingunited.com   *Year Formed:* 1963.
Record Attendance: 4,100 v Gillingham, FA Cup 1st rd (replay), 22 November 1989.
Nickname: 'The Wings'.   *Manager:* Loui Fazakerley.   *Colours:* Red shirts with white trim, red shorts, white socks.

WELLING UNITED – VANARAMA PREMIER 2014–15 LEAGUE RECORD

Match No.	Date	Venue	Opponents	Result	H/T Score	Lg Pos.	Goalscorers	Attendance
1	Aug 9	H	AFC Telford U	D 1-1	0-1	10	Beautyman [67]	611
2	12	A	Torquay U	L 0-3	0-2	18		1895
3	16	A	FC Halifax T	L 0-3	0-0	23		1337
4	23	H	Woking	D 1-1	1-0	21	Beautyman [33]	634
5	25	A	Eastleigh	L 1-3	1-1	22	Hudson [23]	953
6	30	H	Forest Green R	D 1-1	1-1	22	Fagan [36]	501
7	Sept 6	A	Grimsby T	L 0-2	0-1	22		3785
8	9	H	Braintree T	W 2-1	0-1	22	Bush [48], Beautyman [79]	506
9	13	A	Wrexham	L 1-2	1-0	22	Beautyman [33]	2857
10	16	H	Lincoln C	W 2-0	1-0	18	Gallagher [25], Marsh [78]	504
11	20	H	Gateshead	D 1-1	1-0	16	Beautyman [5]	536
12	27	A	Altrincham	W 4-0	3-0	16	Beautyman [13], Marsh [34], Gallagher [45], Bush [86]	850
13	30	H	Dartford	D 2-2	2-2	17	Beautyman [6], Fyfield [14]	1306
14	Oct 4	A	Chester FC	D 1-1	0-1	17	Marsh [90]	1997
15	8	A	Kidderminster H	L 1-2	0-2	17	Beautyman [53]	1560
16	11	H	Nuneaton T	W 4-1	2-1	17	Beautyman 2 [19, 45], Marsh 2 [72, 74]	614
17	18	A	Southport	L 0-1	0-0	17		1007
18	Nov 1	H	Barnet	L 1-2	1-1	18	Healy [44]	906
19	11	A	Dartford	L 1-2	0-1	21	Beautyman [86]	1512
20	15	H	Macclesfield T	D 0-0	0-0	21		508
21	22	H	FC Halifax T	W 2-1	1-1	20	Bassele [42], Penny [50]	500
22	25	A	Braintree T	W 1-0	0-0	18	Penny [61]	580
23	29	A	Bristol R	L 0-2	0-0	19		5791
24	Dec 6	H	Bristol R	D 0-0	0-0	19		1176
25	9	A	AFC Telford U	W 2-1	0-0	17	Marsh [48], Bassele [67]	1011
26	20	H	Aldershot T	W 3-1	1-0	16	Marsh 2 [45, 81], St Aimie [53]	756
27	26	A	Dover Ath	L 0-4	0-2	18		1509
28	28	H	Torquay U	D 0-0	0-0	18		808
29	Jan 1	H	Dover Ath	L 0-2	0-0	19		906
30	4	A	Forest Green R	L 1-4	1-1	19	Healy [19]	1147
31	17	H	Alfreton T	L 2-3	0-2	19	Vine (pen) [87], Bush [90]	572
32	31	H	Chester FC	L 1-3	1-2	19	Harris [15]	619
33	Feb 7	A	Macclesfield T	L 2-3	1-1	19	Vose [20], Williams, J [68]	1489
34	14	A	Aldershot T	L 1-2	1-1	19	Vose [45]	1541
35	28	A	Nuneaton T	L 0-1	0-0	20		763
36	Mar 8	H	Altrincham	L 0-1	0-0	21		1009
37	10	A	Gateshead	D 1-1	0-1	21	Vose [81]	711
38	14	A	Lincoln C	W 2-0	2-0	21	Vose [20], Williams, J [31]	1935
39	21	A	Barnet	L 0-5	0-3	21		1700
40	28	H	Grimsby T	L 0-2	0-2	22		1042
41	Apr 4	A	Woking	D 2-2	1-0	21	Lafayette [9], Adeyinka [77]	2819
42	6	H	Eastleigh	L 1-2	1-1	21	Osborne [30]	700
43	11	H	Kidderminster H	W 3-0	2-0	21	Gallagher [26], St Aimie [35], Corne [71]	505
44	14	H	Wrexham	W 2-1	2-0	21	Berry [7], Vose [20]	612
45	18	A	Alfreton T	D 2-2	1-1	20	Lafayette [45], Bush [57]	1593
46	25	H	Southport	L 0-1	0-0	20		1015

Final League Position: 20

GOALSCORERS

League (52): Beautyman 11, Marsh 8, Vose 5, Bush 4, Gallagher 3, Bassele 2, Healy 2, Lafayette 2, Penny 2, St Aimie 2, Williams, J 2, Adeyinka 1, Berry 1, Corne 1, Fagan 1, Fyfield 1, Harris 1, Hudson 1, Osborne 1, Vine 1 (1 pen).
FA Cup (1): Gallagher 1.
FA Trophy (3): Marsh 1, St Aimie 2 (2 pens).

Butcher 5	Jefford 27 + 2	Bush 31 + 2	Fyfield 32 + 2	Fazakerley 11 + 5	Gallagher 34 + 1	Young 3 + 4	Beautyman 21	Berry 9 + 1	Gorman 1 + 3	Obafemi 4 + 1	Akinde — + 3	Marsh 18 + 2	Healy 28 + 6	Ouani — + 5	Williams B 33 + 2	Fagan 26 + 7	Corne 23 + 10	St Aimie 18 + 12	Noubie 6 + 6	Hudson 13 + 12	Turner 5	Lafayette 7	Day 12	Sho-Silva 3	Adeyinka 2 + 1	Bassele 16 + 6	Henly 26 + 1	McEntegart 2	Buchel 8	Penny 10 + 3	Chambers 15 + 1	Taylor 1 + 1	Klassos — + 1	Osborne 8	Carmichael 2 + 2	Harris 13 + 2	Purse 5	Vose 15 + 1	Vine 1 + 1	Duguid 3	Jeffrey 2	Williams J 7	Match No.
1	2	3	4	5¹	6	7²	8	9¹	10	11	12	13	14																														1
1	5	4	3	2	7	6¹	8²	13	10	11	9	12																															2
1		4	2	5¹	6	13	7	12	10	11	9¹				8	3																											3
1		4	5³	2	8	9	6¹	10²							12	3	7	11	13	14																							4
1	4	3		5	6	13	8	12	9³						2	7²	11	14		10¹																							5
	4	2	5		6	8	12	3							13	9	11¹	10²			1	7																					6
	4	2¹	13	5	6	8	12	3							9¹	11	10				1	7																					7
5	4	13	2	7	6	11³		3	8¹	10²	14				9	12					1																						8
5	4		6	7	8²	11¹	12	2	3³	10⁸	14				9	13					1																						9
6	5	2	14	9	7	8	12	4	3¹	13		10³			11²						1																						10
5	3	4	13	8	7	9	12	2	6¹	10³	11²				14												1																11
5	4	3	13	6	9	11	8³	2	7²	14	12	10¹															1																12
5	4	3	12	7	6	10	11	2	8²	13		9¹															1																13
5	3	4	2	7	8	11	10		6¹	12		9															1																14
5	3	4	6²	10	11	9		2	7¹	13	8	12															1																15
5		4	3		6		10	8	2	14	13	12	11¹									7²	9³				1																16
2		4	6		8		11	7	3	9¹	1⁸	5⁸	10	12																													17
5	4	3		7	8		10	2	11	12	6¹	9															1																18
5²	3⁸	4		9⁸	7		10¹	2			11	13			8											6	12					1											19
		2			6		10	5	3	8	12				9	11¹						7	4				1																20
		2			6		3	5	8	12	11				9	10						7¹	4				1																21
			7		11		2	3	8	13		12			6	10¹						9	4	5²			1																22
14		2	7⁸		10²		4	6	8	12	13				9	11¹						6³		5³	3		1																23
5	14	3		11	9¹		2	7	8	12	13				6³	10²	4										1																24
5¹	12	4		10	8		2	6	7	9		11					3										1																25
	5	3		10	8	13	2	4	7	6		11²			9¹										12		1																26
	5	3	6		8²	12	2	4	7³	9¹		11			10	13	14										1⁸																27
7	5	2	3		11	14	9³	4	12	13		10²			8¹	6											1																28
4	5	2		6		8	3	7	12	11¹	10	9															1																29
5	4	3	6	13			10³	7²	14	11¹	9	2	8	12													1																30
3	5	6		7	14		9³	10²	2	8¹	13	4	11	12													1					2		8	13	4	11	12					31
4	5		7⁸		6³		2	12	14																		1							13	10	3	11²	9¹	8			32
3	5	12			9		2	7²	13	14																	1							10	4	5	10²	7	6⁸	8¹		33
3		6	2		8		9¹	14	13																		1							12	4	5	10²	7	11³			34
	5				3		13	8	2	12																	1							11	4	6²	7¹	9	10			35
5					10³	4	7⁸	2	14																	13	1					3		9	8					11²		36
5					7⁸	4		2	14	6¹	12				2	7	6	11								12	1					3		9	8					10¹		37
	5				7	13		4							2	12	6	10								1						3		9	8¹					11²		38
	2⁸				7³	13		4							6	14	9	11								1						3	12	5¹	8					10²		39
					7							10			2	9¹	12	8	11							1						3		6	4	5						40
9					7			2				8			5	13	11	10	12							1						3		4	2	6¹						41
5					7²			3				6			2	12	9	10¹	11							1						4		8	13							42
5					7¹			13				2			12	9	10	11¹								1					4		3	8	6							43
12	4				13			2			14				8³	6	11	10²								1					3		5	9¹	7							44
11	4				6			12				13			5	14	7¹	9²	10							1					3		2⁸	8³							45
9	4				8³			2²			14				5	12	6	11		10¹						1					13		3		7							46

FA Cup
Fourth Qualifying   Maidstone U   (a)   1-2

FA Trophy
First Round   Ebbsfleet U   (a)   1-1
Replay   Ebbsfleet U   (h)   2-3
(aet; 2-2 at end of normal time)

WOKING

Ground: Kingfield Stadium, Kingfield, Woking, Surrey GU22 9AA. *Tel:* (01483) 722 470. *Fax:* (01483) 888 423.
Website: wokingfc.co.uk   *Year Formed:* 1889. *Record Attendance:* 6,064 v Coventry C, FA Cup 3rd rd, 4 February 1997.
Nickname: 'The Cardinals'.   *Manager:* Garry Hill.   *Colours:* Red and white halved shirts, black shorts with white trim,
white socks with black and red trim.

WOKING – VANARAMA PREMIER 2014–15 LEAGUE RECORD

Match No.	Date		Venue	Opponents	Result	H/T Score	Lg Pos.	Goalscorers	Attendance
1	Aug	9	A	Alfreton T	W 3-1	1-1	3	Morgan [27], Rendell 2 [60, 68]	613
2		12	H	Dartford	D 1-1	0-0	7	Sole [90]	1538
3		16	H	Macclesfield T	D 0-0	0-0	10		1340
4		23	A	Welling U	D 1-1	0-1	12	Newton [81]	634
5		25	H	Dover Ath	W 6-1	3-1	9	Sole 2 [10, 20], Rendell 4 (1 pen) [25, 52, 60 (p), 72]	1454
6		30	A	Wrexham	W 2-1	1-1	4	Rendell [24], Morgan [66]	3154
7	Sept	6	H	Lincoln C	W 3-1	2-0	3	Morgan 2 [15, 73], Payne [44]	2160
8		9	A	Aldershot T	W 1-0	0-0	3	Sole [70]	3567
9		13	H	Chester FC	W 1-0	0-0	2	Sole [52]	1629
10		16	A	Torquay U	L 0-1	0-0	3		2144
11		20	A	Bristol R	L 0-2	0-1	4		6028
12		27	H	Kidderminster H	L 2-3	0-3	7	Rendell [49], Marriott [88]	1524
13		30	A	Nuneaton T	W 1-0	0-0	5	Sole [90]	1313
14	Oct	4	A	Southport	W 5-2	1-0	4	Rendell 3 (1 pen) [5, 83, 87 (p)], Lewis [53], Sole [65]	730
15		11	A	Altrincham	W 3-0	0-0	2	Rendell [52], Morgan [66], Payne [90]	1218
16		18	H	AFC Telford U	L 1-3	1-1	3	Goddard [34]	1817
17	Nov	1	A	Braintree T	D 0-0	0-0	5		876
18		12	H	Wrexham	D 1-1	0-1	5	Rendell [47]	1418
19		16	A	FC Halifax T	W 3-1	2-0	3	Sole [24], Newton 2 [44, 59]	1415
20		22	H	Barnet	D 1-1	0-1	3	Cestor [57]	2617
21		25	A	Grimsby T	L 1-3	0-1	5	Morgan [67]	2663
22		29	H	Braintree T	W 1-0	1-0	4	Goddard [38]	1622
23	Dec	2	H	Altrincham	W 2-0	0-0	2	Marriott [48], Rendell [65]	1056
24		6	A	Macclesfield T	L 1-2	0-1	3	Morgan [51]	1383
25		9	A	Forest Green R	L 1-2	1-2	3	Morgan [22]	970
26		20	H	Southport	L 1-2	0-1	5	Sole [87]	1688
27		26	A	Eastleigh	D 2-2	2-2	5	Morgan [8], Lewis [34]	1752
28		28	H	Aldershot T	L 1-2	0-2	6	Marriott [88]	3559
29	Jan	1	H	Eastleigh	D 1-1	0-0	6	Marriott [90]	1383
30		7	A	Gateshead	D 0-0	0-0	6		772
31		17	H	Bristol R	D 0-0	0-0	7		3853
32		31	H	Alfreton T	W 3-0	1-0	6	Rendell (pen) [18], Lafayette [59], Banya [63]	1526
33	Feb	7	A	Barnet	L 1-2	0-1	6	Odubade [79]	2036
34		14	A	Kidderminster H	D 1-1	0-1	8	Odubade [68]	1646
35		28	A	Lincoln C	W 2-0	2-0	8	Rendell [20], Payne [45]	2347
36	Mar	3	A	Dartford	W 3-1	1-1	7	Odubade [5], Goddard 2 [52, 60]	884
37		7	H	Grimsby T	L 1-2	0-1	7	Goddard [83]	2653
38		14	A	AFC Telford U	W 3-1	0-0	7	Rendell (pen) [48], Betsy [81], Sole [86]	1265
39		21	A	Forest Green R	W 1-0	0-0	7	Rendell (pen) [49]	1436
40		24	H	Torquay U	W 3-2	0-2	6	Odubade [52], Payne [63], Rendell [81]	1506
41		28	A	Chester FC	W 3-2	1-1	6	Rendell 2 [29, 69], Payne [84]	1899
42	Apr	4	H	Welling U	D 2-2	0-1	5	Rendell (pen) [52], Odubade [68]	2819
43		6	A	Dover Ath	L 1-2	1-0	7	Odubade [37]	1078
44		11	H	Gateshead	W 3-0	2-0	7	Payne 2 (1 pen) [7, 67 (p)], Rendell [20]	1889
45		18	A	Nuneaton T	D 1-1	0-1	7	Betsy [53]	709
46		25	H	FC Halifax T	W 3-2	1-1	7	Payne [17], Rendell (pen) [90], Odubade [90]	2175

Final League Position: 7

GOALSCORERS

League (77): Rendell 24 (7 pens), Sole 10, Morgan 9, Payne 8 (1 pen), Odubade 7, Goddard 5, Marriott 4, Newton 3, Betsy 2, Lewis 2, Banya 1, Cestor 1, Lafayette 1.
FA Cup (2): Sole 2.
FA Trophy (9): Arthur 1, Betsy 1, Goddard 2, Marriott 1, Payne 2, Rendell 2 (1 pen).

Howe 7 + 2	Newton 22 + 13	McNerney 33	Jones 37 + 6	Nutter 3 + 2	Lewis 19 + 5	Payne 42	Murtagh 24 + 10	Goddard 28 + 13	Morgan 23 + 2	Rendell 37 + 3	Cestor 18 + 3	Clarke 28 + 2	Sole 14 + 30	Ricketts 22	Beckles — + 3	Arthur 41 + 2	Cole 19	Arnold — + 2	Little — + 1	Worner 16	Marriott 15 + 4	Betsy 25 + 9	Lafayette 3 + 1	Banya 3 + 6	Odubade 12 + 3	Thomas 2	Saah 8	Crowe 4	Oyeleke 1 + 4	Match No.
1	2	3	4	5^2	6	7	8	9^1	10^3	11	12	13	14																	1
1	2^1	4	12		8^3	6	7^2	9	11	10	5	13	3	14																2
1	3	7	5	6^3	8	13	9	11^2	10	4	14			2	12															3
1	14	3	8^3		5^1	7	12	9^2	11	10		4	13	2		6														4
14	2	3	13		12	8^3	6		7	10		9^1	11	4		5	1^2													5
1	4^3	2	13		12	5	6^2	14	9	10		3	11^1	8		7														6
1		4	7		8^3	6		12	9	11	13	2	10^2	3			5	14												7
1^2		3	5		6	8		14	2	10	12	4	11^1	7^3		9			13											8
	12	3	7		5^3	6	14	13	9^1	10	2	4	11^2			8				1										9
	12	4	8		14	6	7^2	13	11	9	3	2^1	10^3			5				1										10
	2^2	4	7		6	13	8^3	11	9	3		10^1		14	5	12		1												11
	14	4	2		12	7	8^1	9^1	11^2	10	5			13		6					1	3								12
	12	4	7		2^1		6	8	9^3	11	3			14		5					1	10^2 13								13
	14	3	9		7	4	5	10^2		6	2^3		12			11					1	8^1 13								14
	13		4		9	5		6^2 10^3 11	2	3	14			7							1	8^1 12								15
		3	2		7^1	6		8	5^2	10	4			13		9					1	11 12								16
	2	4	13		9^1	7	8^3 14		11		3		10^2	5							1	12 6								17
	2		7	13	8^1		9		10	4	3	12		5	1							11^2 6								18
	2	3			6	7		12		10	4	5	11^1	8	1							9								19
	6	4	12		8^1	7			10	3	2	11^2		5	1							13 9								20
12	6		4		8	7		13	10^3	3	2	14		5	1^1							11^2 9								21
	4	12	8		7^1	6	10^3 14		3	2	13			5							1	11^2 9								22
	14	3			7	8	9	12	11^1	4^3	2	13		5							1	10^2 6								23
	13	4	5		7		9^1 10^1 11		3	2^2	12		6							1	14 8								24
	6^3	3	8		7	14	13	10		4	2	11^2		5^1							1	12 9								25
	4	3	2^4	9	6	7	12	11		5^1		13		14							1	10 8^3								26
	3	2	6^1	7	8	12	11		4	9		5									1	10^2 13								27
12	3	2^2		7	8	6^3 11 14			4	9^1		5									1	10 13								28
	2	3	8		7^1	6		11		4	12			5	1							10 9								29
	2	3	6		7	8	13	10^2		4	12			5	1							11^1 9								30
	2^3	3	4		9	14	8		13	5	12		6	1							11^1	7 10^2								31
	2	4	6		9			10^1		8	14	3^3		5	1						13	11^2 7 12								32
	2	3^4	6		8		13	10		4^1			9	1							12	11^2 7^3 14 5								33
	2		4		7		9		11^3	3	13	8		5	1						12	14 6^1 10^2								34
13	3	4		7	14	9		11		2	12	8^2		5	1						6^2	10^1								35
12	3^3	9		5^2 14 10		6		4	13	2				5	1	1					7	8^1								36
		3			7	12	8		11		4	14	6^1	5	1						9^3	13 10^2		2						37
	2		7			8	9		11			13	3^3	12	1						6	14 10^1 5^2 4								38
	2	4	14			9	7^2		10		12	8^3		5	1						6	13 11^1		3						39
	2				6^1	7	8		11		13	4		3	4						9	12 10^2	5 1							40
	2				7	8	6^1		10		13	4		5							9	12 11^2	3 1							41
12	2				6	7^1	8		11		14	4		3							9^3	10^3	5 1	13						42
	2				6	7	12		11		13	4		3							9	10^1	5^1 1	8^2						43
	2	4			7	8	9^2		11^3	12				6							6	14 10^1			13					44
	3	2^3			7	12	8^1		11		13	6		5	1						9	10^2		4	14					45
	2^1	3	14		7^4	8^3	6		11			10^2	4	5	1						9	13			12					46

FA Cup

Fourth Qualifying	Boreham Wood	(h)	2-1
First Round	Wrexham	(a)	0-3

FA Trophy

First Round	Eastleigh	(h)	2-0
Second Round	Oxford C	(a)	2-2
Replay	Oxford C	(h)	2-1
Third Round	Dover Ath	(h)	3-3
Replay	Dover Ath	(a)	0-1

WREXHAM

Ground: Racecourse Ground, Mold Road, Wrexham LL11 2AH.   *Tel:* (01978) 891 864.   *Fax:* (01978) 357 821.
Website: wrexhamafc.co.uk   *Year Formed:* 1872.
Record Attendance: 34,445 v Manchester U, FA Cup 4th rd, 26 January 1957.
Nickname: 'Red Dragons'.   *Manager:* Gary Mills.
Colours: Red and black hooped shirts, black shorts, red socks.

WREXHAM – VANARAMA PREMIER 2014–15 LEAGUE RECORD

Match No.	Date	Venue	Opponents	Result	H/T Score	Lg Pos.	Goalscorers	Attendance
1	Aug 9	A	Dartford	W 2-1	1-0	6	York 2 [30, 78]	1561
2	12	H	Gateshead	L 0-3	0-1	13		4068
3	16	H	Nuneaton T	W 1-0	1-0	9	Moult [4]	3292
4	23	A	Alfreton T	W 3-2	3-1	5	Moult [13], Hudson [27], Jennings [45]	916
5	25	H	Macclesfield T	D 2-2	1-1	7	Jennings [45], Hudson [61]	4012
6	30	H	Woking	L 1-2	1-1	11	Moult [38]	3154
7	Sept 6	A	Forest Green R	W 1-0	0-0	7	Moult [54]	1401
8	9	A	Bristol R	L 0-1	0-1	10		5082
9	13	H	Welling U	W 2-1	0-1	7	Moult [84], Clarke [86]	2857
10	16	A	Barnet	W 1-0	0-0	6	Evans [49]	1336
11	22	A	Chester FC	L 1-2	1-0	10	Hudson [2]	3183
12	27	H	Eastleigh	W 3-0	2-0	6	Durrell [12], York [27], Bishop [71]	2692
13	30	H	Kidderminster H	W 1-0	0-0	3	Durrell [84]	3149
14	Oct 4	A	Torquay U	L 1-2	1-0	7	Moult [29]	2350
15	7	A	FC Halifax T	D 2-2	0-1	8	Moult 2 [59, 84]	1617
16	11	H	Grimsby T	L 0-1	0-1	9		8163
17	18	A	Lincoln C	D 1-1	1-0	10	Durrell [35]	2360
18	Nov 1	H	FC Halifax T	D 0-0	0-0	11		3421
19	12	A	Woking	D 1-1	1-0	12	Bishop [45]	1418
20	15	A	Braintree T	L 0-1	0-1	12		840
21	22	H	Altrincham	L 2-3	2-0	12	Durrell [14], Moult [45]	3002
22	25	A	Kidderminster H	D 1-1	0-1	13	Jennings [66]	1645
23	29	H	Aldershot T	W 3-1	1-1	12	Carrington [26], Bishop [48], Moult (pen) [71]	2464
24	Dec 2	H	Bristol R	D 0-0	0-0	12		2608
25	20	H	Dartford	L 1-3	0-1	12	Moult [67]	2662
26	26	A	Southport	W 1-0	0-0	12	Harris [46]	1912
27	Jan 17	H	AFC Telford U	L 0-4	0-2	16		3194
28	20	A	Dover Ath	L 0-2	0-2	16		793
29	31	H	Torquay U	D 0-0	0-0	17		2655
30	Feb 14	H	Barnet	W 1-0	1-0	17	Evans [24]	2727
31	24	H	Forest Green R	D 0-0	0-0	17		2044
32	Mar 3	A	Gateshead	L 1-3	1-1	18	Ramshaw (og) [26]	705
33	7	H	Chester FC	W 1-0	1-0	17	Morris [7]	6336
34	10	H	Southport	D 0-0	0-0	16		2188
35	14	A	Altrincham	W 4-1	3-0	14	Morris [7], White [40], Moult [44], Jennings [85]	1525
36	17	A	Eastleigh	D 2-2	2-1	14	Moult [18], Ashton [35]	1246
37	21	H	Lincoln C	D 1-1	1-1	14	Storer [40]	2650
38	24	A	Nuneaton T	L 0-2	0-1	14		818
39	31	H	Dover Ath	D 1-1	1-0	15	Harris [38]	1831
40	Apr 4	H	Alfreton T	W 4-0	3-0	14	Jennings [19], Harris [32], Bishop 2 [40, 66]	2468
41	6	A	Macclesfield T	D 2-2	1-1	12	Jennings [43], Evans [90]	2050
42	11	A	Grimsby T	W 1-0	1-0	11	Clarke [17]	4138
43	14	A	Welling U	L 1-2	0-2	11	Bishop [82]	612
44	18	H	Braintree T	W 3-0	0-0	11	Moult 2 [62, 78], Bishop [90]	2766
45	21	A	Aldershot T	D 1-1	1-1	11	Moult [10]	1386
46	25	A	AFC Telford U	W 2-1	0-0	11	Keates (pen) [61], Waterfall [75]	2124

Final League Position: 11

GOALSCORERS
League (56): Moult 16 (1 pen), Bishop 7, Jennings 6, Durrell 4, Evans 3, Harris 3, Hudson 3, York 3, Clarke 2, Morris 2, Ashton 1, Carrington 1, Keates 1 (1 pen), Storer 1, Waterfall 1, White 1, own goal 1.
FA Cup (13): Bishop 5 (1 pen), Ashton 1, Carrington 1, Hunt 1, Jennings 1, Rushton 1, Smith 1, York 2.
FA Trophy (23): Ashton 2, Bishop 3, Clarke 1, Harris 1, Jennings 2, Morris 2, Moult 7, Smith 1, Tomassen 1, York 3.

Bachmann 15	Carrington 27 + 3	Smith 46	Hudson 35	Ashton 39	Harris 23 + 7	Clarke 37 + 6	Durrell 19 + 8	Jennings 35 + 6	Moult 32 + 7	York 29 + 11	Bailey-Jones — + 8	Bishop 24 + 15	Coughlin 28	Rushton — + 2	Evans 16 + 10	White 11 + 1	Hunt 6 + 4	Keates 15 + 4	Holman — + 4	Pearson 5	Flatt 3	Tancock 2	Tomassen 17 + 2	Waterfall 7 + 2	Storer 11 + 2	Morris 8 + 1	Stephens 5 + 2	Finley 11 + 3	Roper — + 3	Match No.
1	2	3	4	5	6	7	8¹	9	10	11	12																			1
1	2	3	4	5	8	6	7¹	9²	10	11	12	13																		2
	2	3	4	5	8	6	7¹	9	10	11	12			1																3
		6	2	3	4	7	5	8²	10	11		9¹	12	1	13															4
	2	3	4	5	6²	7	8¹	9	10	11			13	1	12															5
1	14	3	4	5		8	6³	9	11	10²	13	12			7	2¹														6
1	2	3	4	5		7		11	10¹	6		12			8	9														7
1	2¹	3	4	5	13	8	12	11	10¹	6					7²		9													8
1		3	4²	5	7	6	12	11¹	10	9	13	14			2		8³													9
1		3	4	5		6	8	10	11¹	9	12				7	2														10
1		3	4	5		7	9¹	11	10	6³	13				8²	2		12	14											11
1	2	3	4	5		7		9	11¹	10²	6³	12					14	8	13											12
1	2	3	4	5		7		9¹	11	10	6²	12					13	8												13
1	2	3	4	5		7		9¹	11	10²	6	12						8	13											14
	2	4	3	5	6	7	13	11²	10	9	12	1						8¹												15
	2	3	4³	5	8	6	12	13	10⁴	9	11²	1						7¹	14											16
	2	3	4	5	7	8	6¹	10		9	11	1					12													17
	6	4	5	3		7	8	12		11²	10	1					9¹	13		2										18
	6	3	4	5		7	8¹			9	10	1			13	11			2²											19
	8	3	4⁴			7	9²	11	13	6¹		10	1		14	2³	5	12												20
	8	3		5	14	7	6³	12	10⁴	9¹		11⁴			13	2²							1	4						21
	8	3	4	5	13	7	6³	11	10¹	9					14	12							1	2²						22
	6	3		5	13	7³		9	12	11¹		10			8	2							4²	1	14					23
1	6	3	4	5		7	12	9	13	11³		10²			8²	2														24
1	6¹	3	4	5	7²	8¹	14	9	13	10		11			12							2								25
1	6	4	3	5	8			9	10²	13		11¹			7	12						2								26
	2	3		5	7	14		9¹	10	6³		11	1		8²	4¹									13	12				27
	8	4		3		5			10	9	12	11	1				7¹								2	6				28
	12	3			5	8	7¹		10²	13		11	1				9¹								2	4	6	14		29
		3		5	12	7		9	10¹	13		14	1		6²										2	4	8	11³		30
	6¹	3	4			12		13	9²			10	1					7³							2	4	13	10		31
		3		5	6²	9		8¹	11	14		12	1					7³							2	4	13	10		32
		3	4	5		6		9	10³	14		13	1		8			12							2		7²	11¹		33
		3	4			6	13	9²		12		10	1		8										2		7¹	11³	5 14	34
	2	3	4		12	5		9²	11	14			1		7²	8									6¹	10		13		35
		4	3²	5	9	13			11³	7¹			14	1		2									12	8	10	6		36
1	14		3		5	6¹	13	9³		10²			12												2	4	7	11	8	37
	2	4		3		5	6	10¹	13			7	1		14			8³							9	11²		12		38
		3	4	5²	8			11	10¹	13		9	1					7							2		12	6		39
	2	4			7²	11³		10				9	1		12			8¹					3	13	5	6	14			40
	4	3				8¹	7²	11		12		10	1		13			6					2			5	9			41
		4	3		11	7		9		14		10¹	1		12			13					2		6²		5	8¹ 13		42
		3	4	5	6¹	9²		10	12			11	1		13								2		7			8		43
		3	4	5	14	13		9²	10			11	1		8								2			12	6¹			44
		3		2	7	13		12	10			11²	1		6³			8					4	5			9¹	14		45
		3		5	6¹	13		12	10	14		11⁷	1		9³			7					2	4			8			46

FA Cup

Fourth Qualifying	Macclesfield T	(a)	1-1
Replay	Macclesfield T	(h)	5-2
First Round	Woking	(h)	3-0
Second Round	Maidstone U	(h)	3-1
Third Round	Stoke C	(a)	1-3

FA Trophy

First Round	Southport	(a)	1-1
Replay	Southport	(h)	2-0
Second Round	Stockport Co	(a)	2-2

Replay	Stockport Co	(h)	6-1
Third Round	Gateshead	(h)	1-1
Replay	Gateshead	(a)	2-2

(aet; Wrexham won 5-3 on penalties)

Fourth Round	FC Halifax T	(a)	1-0
Semi-Finals 1st leg	Torquay U	(h)	2-1
Semi-Finals 2nd leg	Torquay U	(a)	3-0

(Wrexham won 5-1 on aggregate)

Final	North Ferriby U	Wembley	3-3

(aet; 2-2 at the end of normal time, North Ferriby U won 5-4 on penalties)

SCOTTISH LEAGUE TABLES 2014–15

(P) *Promoted into division at end of 2013–14 season.*   (R) *Relegated into division at end of 2013–14 season.*

SPFL SCOTTISH PREMIERSHIP 2014–15

			Total				Home					Away						
		P	W	D	L	F	A	W	D	L	F	A	W	D	L	F	A	GD	Pts
1	Celtic	38	29	5	4	84	17	15	2	2	50	8	14	3	2	34	9	67	92
2	Aberdeen	38	23	6	9	57	33	12	3	4	32	15	11	3	5	25	18	24	75
3	Inverness CT	38	19	8	11	52	42	10	6	3	29	19	9	2	8	23	23	10	65
4	St Johnstone	38	16	9	13	34	34	8	5	6	19	17	8	4	7	15	17	0	57
5	Dundee U	38	17	5	16	58	56	12	2	5	32	20	5	3	11	26	36	2	56
6	Dundee (P)*	38	11	12	15	46	57	5	8	7	25	27	6	4	8	21	30	–11	45
7	Hamilton A (P)	38	15	8	15	50	53	8	6	5	30	20	7	2	10	20	33	–3	53
8	Partick Thistle	38	12	10	16	48	44	8	4	7	32	22	4	6	9	16	22	4	46
9	Ross Co	38	12	8	18	46	63	7	0	12	21	31	5	8	6	25	32	–17	44
10	Kilmarnock	38	11	8	19	44	59	7	1	10	23	27	4	7	9	21	32	–15	41
11	Motherwell	38	10	6	22	38	63	7	5	7	23	21	3	1	15	15	42	–25	36
12	St Mirren	38	9	3	26	30	66	3	2	14	14	30	6	1	12	16	36	–36	30

Top 6 teams split after 33 games, teams in the bottom six cannot pass teams in the top six after the split. Motherwell not relegated after play-offs.

SPFL SCOTTISH CHAMPIONSHIP 2014–15

			Total				Home					Away						
		P	W	D	L	F	A	W	D	L	F	A	W	D	L	F	A	GD	Pts
1	Hearts (R)	36	29	4	3	96	26	15	2	1	57	12	14	2	2	39	14	70	91
2	Hibernian (R)	36	21	7	8	70	32	9	6	3	33	15	12	1	5	37	17	38	70
3	Rangers (P)	36	19	10	7	69	39	10	5	3	43	21	9	5	4	26	18	30	67
4	Queen of the South	36	17	9	10	58	41	13	1	4	32	14	4	8	6	26	27	17	60
5	Falkirk	36	14	11	11	48	48	7	6	5	22	19	7	5	6	26	29	0	53
6	Raith R	36	12	7	17	42	65	6	3	9	25	40	6	4	8	17	25	–23	43
7	Dumbarton	36	9	7	20	36	79	5	4	9	18	37	4	3	11	18	42	–43	34
8	Livingston*	36	8	8	20	41	53	4	4	10	18	26	4	4	10	23	27	–12	27
9	Alloa Ath	36	6	9	21	34	56	4	5	9	21	25	2	4	12	13	31	–22	27
10	Cowdenbeath	36	7	4	25	31	86	3	2	13	13	34	4	2	12	18	52	–55	25

*No team promoted via play-offs. Alloa Ath not relegated after play-offs. *Livingston deducted 5 points.*

SPFL SCOTTISH LEAGUE ONE 2014–15

			Total				Home					Away						
		P	W	D	L	F	A	W	D	L	F	A	W	D	L	F	A	GD	Pts
1	Greenock Morton (R)	36	22	3	11	65	40	12	1	5	33	16	10	2	6	32	24	25	69
2	Stranraer	36	20	7	9	59	38	12	2	4	34	17	8	5	5	25	21	21	67
3	Forfar Ath	36	20	6	10	59	41	13	2	3	32	14	7	4	7	27	27	18	66
4	Brechin C	36	15	14	7	58	46	7	7	4	30	26	8	7	3	28	20	12	59
5	Airdrieonians	36	16	10	10	53	39	10	4	4	35	20	6	6	6	18	19	14	58
6	Peterhead (P)	36	14	9	13	51	54	8	5	5	25	20	6	4	8	26	34	–3	51
7	Dunfermline Ath	36	13	9	14	46	48	8	5	5	28	20	5	4	9	18	28	–2	48
8	Ayr U	36	9	7	20	45	60	4	5	9	22	28	5	2	11	23	32	–15	34
9	Stenhousemuir	36	8	5	23	42	63	5	4	9	22	30	3	1	14	20	33	–21	29
10	Stirling Alb (P)	36	4	8	24	35	84	2	4	12	19	42	2	4	12	16	42	–49	20

No team promoted via play-offs. Stenhousemuir not relegated after play-offs.

SPFL SCOTTISH LEAGUE TWO 2014–15

			Total				Home					Away						
		P	W	D	L	F	A	W	D	L	F	A	W	D	L	F	A	GD	Pts
1	Albion R	36	22	5	9	61	33	10	3	5	27	18	12	2	4	34	15	28	71
2	Queen's Park	36	17	10	9	51	34	10	4	4	27	13	7	6	5	24	21	17	61
3	Arbroath (R)	36	16	8	12	65	46	9	5	4	35	19	7	3	8	30	27	19	56
4	East Fife (R)	36	15	8	13	56	48	8	6	4	28	22	7	2	9	28	26	8	53
5	Annan Ath	36	14	8	14	56	56	11	2	5	37	28	3	6	9	19	28	0	50
6	Clyde	36	13	8	15	40	50	6	4	8	22	27	7	4	7	18	23	–10	47
7	Elgin C	36	12	9	15	55	58	7	4	7	28	29	5	5	8	27	29	–3	45
8	Berwick Rangers	36	11	10	15	60	57	5	8	5	30	23	6	2	10	30	34	3	43
9	East Stirlingshire	36	13	4	19	40	66	7	1	10	22	31	6	3	9	18	35	–26	43
10	Montrose	36	9	6	21	42	78	6	1	11	24	36	3	5	10	18	42	–36	33

No team promoted via play-offs. Montrose not relegated after play-offs.

SCOTTISH LEAGUE ATTENDANCES 2014–15

SPFL SCOTTISH PREMIERSHIP ATTENDANCES

	Average Gate			Season 2014–15	
	2013–14	*2014–15*	*+/–%*	*Highest*	*Lowest*
Aberdeen	13,085	13,359	+2.09	19,051	10,330
Celtic	47,079	44,585	–5.30	55,638	40,633
Dundee	4,738	6,966	+47.03	11,447	5,017
Dundee U	7,599	8,113	+6.76	12,964	5,243
Hamilton A	1,436	2,877	+100.35	6,007	1,544
Inverness CT	3,558	3,733	+4.91	6,614	2,426
Kilmarnock	4,250	4,076	–4.08	5,329	2,793
Motherwell	5,175	4,286	–17.18	7,740	3,193
Partick Thistle	5,003	3,586	–28.32	5,776	2,138
Ross Co	3,787	3,525	–6.92	5,693	2,790
St Johnstone	3,806	4,592	+20.64	7,384	2,531
St Mirren	4,511	3,869	–14.23	5,784	2,511

SPFL SCOTTISH CHAMPIONSHIP ATTENDANCES

	Average Gate			Season 2014–15	
	2013–14	*2014–15*	*+/–%*	*Highest*	*Lowest*
Alloa Ath	876	1,429	+63.06	3,067	535
Cowdenbeath	623	1,462	+134.67	3,919	505
Dumbarton	938	1,072	+14.26	1,850	663
Falkirk	3,114	4,661	+49.68	7,735	3,021
Hearts	14,123	15,985	+13.18	17,280	14,848
Hibernian	11,027	10,170	–7.77	15,261	7,857
Livingston	1,157	2,364	+104.31	8,178	723
Queen of the South	1,724	2,778	+61.16	6,185	1,597
Raith R	1,659	2,598	+56.64	6,250	1,100
Rangers	42,657	32,798	–23.11	43,683	28,053

SPFL SCOTTISH LEAGUE ONE ATTENDANCES

	Average Gate			Season 2014–15	
	2013–14	*2014–15*	*+/–%*	*Highest*	*Lowest*
Airdrieonians	1,586	830	–47.68	1,109	642
Ayr U	1,905	1,123	–41.08	1,617	646
Brechin C	900	552	–38.64	835	407
Dunfermline Ath	3,331	2,523	–24.24	3,342	1,574
Forfar Ath	865	735	–15.05	1,916	489
Greenock Morton	1,686	1,728	+2.51	6,024	1,037
Peterhead	573	580	+1.25	743	428
Stenhousemuir	826	584	–29.27	1,177	221
Stirling Alb	616	770	+24.98	1,623	442
Stranraer	802	546	–31.86	1,321	329

SPFL SCOTTISH LEAGUE TWO ATTENDANCES

	Average Gate			Season 2014–15	
	2013–14	*2014–15*	*+/–%*	*Highest*	*Lowest*
Albion R	403	552	+36.82	1,100	333
Annan Ath	409	393	–3.95	578	251
Arbroath	1,054	721	–31.63	1,395	539
Berwick R	468	466	–0.27	598	347
Clyde	519	525	+1.20	739	402
East Fife	1,249	557	–55.39	806	342
East Stirling	343	315	–8.29	470	224
Elgin C	574	544	–5.33	828	328
Montrose	363	419	+15.43	1,143	233
Queen's Park	425	608	+43.17	2,027	304

ABERDEEN

Year Formed: 1903. *Ground & Address:* Pittodrie Stadium, Pittodrie St, Aberdeen AB24 5QH. *Telephone:* 01224 650400. *Fax:* 01224 644173. *E-mail:* feedback@afc.co.uk *Website:* www.afc.co.uk
Ground Capacity: all seated: 22,199. *Size of Pitch:* 105m × 66m.
Chairman: Stewart Milne. *Chief Executive:* Duncan Fraser.
Manager: Derek McInnes. *Assistant Manager:* Tony Docherty. *U-20 Coach:* Paul Sheerin.
Club Nicknames: 'The Dons', 'The Reds', 'The Dandies'.
Previous Grounds: None.
Record Attendance: 45,061 v Hearts, Scottish Cup 4th rd, 13 Mar 1954.
Record Transfer Fee received: £1.75 million for Eoin Jess to Coventry C (February 1996).
Record Transfer Fee paid: £1m+ for Paul Bernard from Oldham Ath (September 1995).
Record Victory: 13-0 v Peterhead, Scottish Cup 3rd rd, 10 Feb 1923.
Record Defeat: 0-9 v Celtic, Premier League, 6 Nov 2010.
Most Capped Player: Alex McLeish, 77 (Scotland).
Most League Appearances: 556: Willie Miller, 1973-90.
Most League Goals in Season (Individual): 38: Benny Yorston, Division I, 1929-30.
Most Goals Overall (Individual): 199: Joe Harper, 1969-72; 1976-81.

ABERDEEN – SCOTTISH PREMIER LEAGUE 2014–15 LEAGUE RECORD

Match No.	Date		Venue	Opponents	Result	H/T Score	Lg Pos.	Goalscorers	Atten- dance
1	Aug	10	H	Dundee U	L 0-3	0-2	12		16,471
2		13	A	Kilmarnock	W 2-0	1-0	7	Pawlett [45], Jack [71]	5079
3		23	A	St Johnstone	L 0-1	0-0	9		6377
4		30	H	Partick Thistle	W 2-0	0-0	8	Low [47], McGinn [66]	11,003
5	Sept	13	A	Celtic	L 1-2	0-1	9	Goodwillie [60]	43,640
6		20	H	Ross Co	W 3-0	2-0	7	Rooney [20], Goodwillie [26], Pawlett [50]	10,865
7		27	H	Inverness CT	W 3-2	2-1	6	Rooney [24], Logan [40], Hayes [59]	11,414
8		30	H	St Mirren	D 2-2	1-0	6	Reynolds [45], Pawlett [56]	10,373
9	Oct	4	A	Dundee	W 3-2	2-1	5	Considine [5], McPake (og) [28], Goodwillie [64]	8784
10		17	A	Hamilton A	L 0-3	0-1	5		4093
11		24	H	Motherwell	W 1-0	1-0	5	Hayes [2]	11,149
12	Nov	3	A	Ross Co	W 1-0	0-0	5	Quinn (og) [56]	3745
13		9	H	Celtic	L 1-2	1-1	5	Rooney [27]	19,051
14		23	A	Partick Thistle	W 1-0	1-0	5	Rooney (pen) [34]	4145
15	Dec	6	H	Hamilton A	W 3-0	1-0	4	Taylor [28], McGinn [51], Rooney (pen) [55]	10,330
16		13	A	Dundee U	W 2-0	2-0	4	Rooney 2 [19, 33]	11,196
17		20	H	Kilmarnock	W 1-0	0-0	2	Pawlett [69]	11,282
18		28	A	Inverness CT	W 1-0	1-0	2	Pawlett [12]	6614
19	Jan	1	H	St Johnstone	W 2-0	1-0	1	Goodwillie [6], Smith [90]	15,263
20		4	A	Motherwell	W 2-0	1-0	1	Rooney 2 (1 pen) [36, 89 (p)]	4805
21		10	A	St Mirren	W 2-0	2-0	1	McGinn [31], Logan [33]	4977
22		17	H	Dundee	D 3-3	1-2	1	Goodwillie [7], Hayes (pen) [87], Jack [90]	16,796
23		23	A	St Johnstone	D 1-1	0-1	2	Rooney [57]	4845
24	Feb	7	H	Ross Co	W 4-0	0-0	2	Rooney [12], Pawlett [50], Logan [61], Goodwillie [85]	12,036
25		15	A	Hamilton A	W 3-0	2-0	2	Considine [6], Jack [8], McGinn [88]	3095
26		21	H	St Mirren	W 3-0	1-0	2	Rooney 2 [21, 48], Reynolds [66]	14,720
27	Mar	1	A	Celtic	L 0-4	0-1	2		50,256
28		13	H	Motherwell	W 2-1	0-1	2	Taylor [50], Rooney [52]	13,267
29		21	A	Dundee	D 1-1	1-0	2	Rooney [36]	7014
30	Apr	4	H	Partick Thistle	D 0-0	0-0	2		12,727
31		8	H	Inverness CT	W 1-0	0-0	2	Taylor [47]	11,319
32		12	A	Kilmarnock	W 2-1	1-0	2	Rooney [40], Smith [69]	3525
33		18	H	Dundee U	W 1-0	1-0	2	Rooney [39]	12,619
34		25	A	Inverness CT	W 2-1	0-0	2	Raven (og) [69], McGinn [74]	4530
35	May	2	A	Dundee U	L 0-1	0-1	2		8686
36		10	H	Celtic	L 0-1	0-0	2		16,742
37		16	A	Dundee	D 1-1	0-1	2	Rooney [90]	6434
38		24	H	St Johnstone	L 0-1	0-0	2		16,389

Final League Position: 2

Scottish League Clubs – Aberdeen

Honours
League Champions: Division I 1954-55. Premier Division 1979-80, 1983-84, 1984-85; *Runners-up:* Premiership 2014-15. Division I 1910-11, 1936-37, 1955-56, 1970-71, 1971-72. Premier Division 1977-78, 1980-81, 1981-82, 1988-89, 1989-90, 1990-91, 1992-93, 1993-94.
Scottish Cup Winners: 1947, 1970, 1982, 1983, 1984, 1986, 1990; *Runners-up:* 1937, 1953, 1954, 1959, 1967, 1978, 1993, 2000.
League Cup Winners: 1955-56, 1976-77, 1985-86, 1989-90, 1995-96, 2013-14; *Runners-up:* 1946-47, 1978-79, 1979-80, 1987-88, 1988-89, 1992-93, 1999-2000.
Drybrough Cup Winners: 1971, 1980.

European: *European Cup:* 12 matches (1980-81, 1984-85, 1985-86); *Cup Winners' Cup:* 39 matches (1967-68, 1970-71, 1978-79, 1982-83 winners, 1983-84 semi-finals, 1986-87, 1990-91, 1993-94); *UEFA Cup:* 56 matches (*Fairs Cup:* 1968-69. *UEFA Cup:* 1971-72, 1972-73, 1973-74, 1977-78, 1979-80, 1981-82, 1987-88, 1988-89, 1989-90, 1991-92, 1994-95, 1996-97, 2000-01, 2002-03, 2007-08). *Europa League:* 8 matches (2009-10, 2014-15).

Club colours: All red with white trim.

Goalscorers: *League (57):* Rooney 18 (3 pens), Goodwillie 6, Pawlett 6, McGinn 5, Hayes 3 (1 pen), Jack 3, Logan 3, Taylor 3, Considine 2, Reynolds 2, Smith 2, Low 1, own goals 3.
William Hill Scottish FA Cup (1): own goal 1.
Scottish League Cup (6): Rooney 4, Daniels 1, Taylor 1.
UEFA Europa League (12): Rooney 6 (2 pens), McGinn 2, Hayes 1, Logan 1, Pawlett 1, Reynolds 1.

Langfield J 13	Logan S 35	Taylor A 31+1	Reynolds M 37	Considine A 36+1	McGinn N 34+2	Flood W 22+3	Jack R 30+2	Robson B 9+11	Pawlett P 28+8	Goodwillie D 21+10	Rooney A 32+5	Low N 3+4	Hayes J 32	Shaughnessy J 1+2	Smith C 5+19	Anderson R 2	Monakana J —+10	Shankland L 2+15	Murray C 1+1	Brown S 25	Gibbons K —+1	Daniels D 7+2	McLean K 11+2	Robertson C —+1	Driver A 1	Ross F —+2	Wright S —+1	Match No.
1	2	3	4	5^1	6	7	8	9^2	10	11	12	13																1
1	2	3^1	4	5	8	6	7		9^1	11	12		10^1	13	14													2
1	2		4	5	6	8	7	13	9^3	12	10^1	11	14			3^2												3
1	2	3	4	5	11		7	12	6^3	10	14	8^1	9^2	13														4
1	2	3	4	5^1	10	9	7	6	11	13	8^3							12										5
1	2	3	4	6^2	7	8	14	9^1	10	11^3	5							13	12									6
1	2	3	4	5		7	8	6^1	10^1	11^2	9			13				12	14									7
1	2	3	4	12	6^1	7	8	9^2	11	10					5			13										8
1	2	3	4	5	6^1	7	8	9^3	10^2	11					12			14	13									9
1	5	2	3	4^3	13	6	7	8^1	12	11	10^2	9			14													10
	2	3	4	5	8	6	7	13	9^2	11^3	12		10^1		14					1								11
	2	3	4	5	8	7	6	13	9^2	12	11^1	10^3			14					1								12
	2	3	4	5	8	7^1	6	12	9^3	13	11^2	10			14					1								13
	2	3	4	9^1	6	7	11^2	10	5	8^2					14		12		13	1								14
	2	3	4	5	9	7	8^1		10^1	11^2	6				14		13	12		1								15
	2	3	4	5	6^2	7	8^1		10^3	11	9				14		13	12		1								16
	2	3	4	5	6	8	7		10^1	11	9							12		1								17
		3	4	5	6	7	8		10^1	11	9							12		1	2							18
	2	3	4	5	6^1	8	7^2		10^3	11	9				13		14	12		1								19
	2	3	4	5	8	6	13	7^2	11	10^3	9				14		12			1								20
	2	3	4	5	9	7		12	6^2	10	11^3	8			13		14			1								21
	2	3^1	4	5	6	8	13	7^2	10	11^3	9						14	12		1								22
	2	3	4	9	8^2	7	14	6^3	10^1	11	5				13			12		1								23
	2		4	5	8^2	6	13	14	11	10	12	7^1								1		3^2	9					24
	2		4	5	8	6	12	14	9^3	13	11^1	7^2								1		3	10					25
	2	14	4	5	9	7^1	8	6^1	12	11^3	13									1		3	10					26
	2	14	4	5	9^3	7	8	12	13	11^1	6^2									1		3	10					27
1	6	2	4	9	5	7	13	12^3	11^2	10							14					3^1		8				28
1	2	3	4	5	11^2	7	6		12	10								13				8		9^1				29
1	2	3	4	5	12	7^3	8	13	11	9							14					6^2	10^1					30
	2	3	4	5	6	7	8		10^1	11	9									1								31
	2		4	5	8	6^1	12		11^2	10	7^3				13		14			1		3	9					32
	2	3	4	5	9^2	7^1	12	8^4	11	6										1		10	13					33
	2	3	4	5	6^3	7	8	13	11^1	9					12					1		14	10^2					34
	2	3	4	5^1	6	7	8^2		10^1	11	9				14			12		1			13					35
	2	3	4	5	9	7^1	8^2	13	12	11^3	6						14			1			10					36
	2	3		5	8	6	10^1	12		9	7		11^3		13					1				4^2		14		37
	2	4^2			9	11	10	6^1	8	5	7^3				3			12		1						14	13	38

AIRDRIEONIANS

Year Formed: 2002. *Ground & Address:* Excelsior Stadium, New Broomfield, Craigneuk Avenue, Airdrie ML6 8QZ.
Telephone: (Stadium) 01236 622000. *Fax:* 01236 626002. *Postal Address:* 60 St Enoch Square, Glasgow G1 4AG.
E-mail: annmarie@ballantyneand.co.uk *Website:* www.airdriefc.com
Ground Capacity: 10,171 (all seated). *Size of Pitch:* 105m × 67m.
Chairman: Tom Wotherspoon. *Secretary:* Ann Marie Ballantyne.
Manager: Gary Bollan. *Assistant Manager:* Stuart Balmer.
Club Nickname: 'The Diamonds'.
Record Attendance: 9,044 v Rangers, League 1, 23 Aug 2013.
Record Victory: 11-0 v Gala Fairydean, Scottish Cup 3rd rd, 19 Nov 2011.
Record Defeat: 0-7 v Partick Thistle, First Division, 20 Oct 2012.
Most League Appearances: 222, Paul Lovering 2004-12.
Most League Goals in Season (Individual): 21: Ryan Donnelly, 2011-12.
Most Goals Overall (Individual): 33: Stephen McKeown, 2002-08.

AIRDRIEONIANS – SCOTTISH LEAGUE ONE 2014–15 LEAGUE RECORD

Match No.	Date	Venue	Opponents	Result	H/T Score	Lg Pos.	Goalscorers	Attendance
1	Aug 9	A	Stenhousemuir	L	0-1	0-0	9		728
2	16	H	Peterhead	L	0-2	0-0	10		810
3	23	A	Dunfermline Ath	L	0-3	0-2	10		2653
4	30	H	Stirling Alb	D	0-0	0-0	10		825
5	Sept 13	A	Greenock Morton	L	1-2	1-0	10	Watt [15]	1482
6	20	H	Stranraer	D	3-3	2-1	10	Boyle, P [21], Prunty [32], Gasparotto [77]	864
7	27	A	Ayr U	W	3-2	1-0	10	Lister [30], Gasparotto [87], Bain [90]	1185
8	Oct 4	H	Forfar Ath	L	1-2	1-0	10	Lister [21]	710
9	11	H	Brechin C	W	4-0	2-0	8	Fraser [3], Proctor [21], Lister [57], Blockley [76]	718
10	18	A	Peterhead	D	1-1	1-1	9	Parker (pen) [41]	467
11	25	A	Stirling Alb	D	2-2	0-1	9	Fraser [57], Fitzpatrick [87]	847
12	Nov 8	H	Stenhousemuir	W	2-0	2-0	8	Fraser [8], Parker [32]	743
13	15	H	Greenock Morton	L	0-1	0-1	9		949
14	22	A	Stranraer	L	0-1	0-0	9		445
15	Dec 6	A	Brechin C	D	1-1	0-0	8	Lister [85]	437
16	13	H	Dunfermline Ath	W	3-1	1-0	7	Prunty [3], Blockley [55], Fitzpatrick [64]	878
17	20	A	Forfar Ath	D	1-1	0-0	7	Boyle, P [57]	572
18	27	H	Ayr U	W	3-0	2-0	7	Prunty 2 [8, 20], McKinlay (og) [79]	1023
19	Jan 3	A	Greenock Morton	W	1-0	0-0	6	Lister [47]	1712
20	10	H	Peterhead	L	1-3	1-2	7	Fraser [10]	642
21	17	A	Dunfermline Ath	D	2-2	1-1	7	Lister [10], Gilfillan [56]	2589
22	24	H	Stranraer	D	1-1	0-0	7	Lister [89]	712
23	31	H	Brechin C	D	1-1	0-0	7	Bain [69]	676
24	Feb 14	H	Forfar Ath	W	3-1	2-0	7	Fitzpatrick [5], Prunty (pen) [22], Fraser [76]	839
25	21	A	Stenhousemuir	W	2-0	1-0	7	Prunty 2 [38, 58]	524
26	28	H	Stirling Alb	W	4-1	0-1	5	Prunty 2 (1 pen) [58 (p), 83], Lister 2 [59, 80]	779
27	Mar 7	A	Brechin C	D	0-0	0-0	6		603
28	10	A	Ayr U	W	1-0	0-0	5	Fitzpatrick [52]	835
29	14	H	Greenock Morton	W	2-1	0-0	5	Prunty [56], Blockley [66]	1109
30	21	A	Stranraer	L	0-1	0-0	6		498
31	28	H	Stenhousemuir	W	2-1	1-0	5	Prunty 2 (1 pen) [32, 65 (p)]	722
32	Apr 4	A	Stirling Alb	W	2-0	0-0	5	Prunty 2 (2 pens) [53, 79]	942
33	11	A	Forfar Ath	L	0-2	0-1	5		772
34	18	H	Ayr U	W	2-0	0-0	5	McHugh 2 [79, 86]	881
35	25	A	Peterhead	W	1-0	0-0	5	Lindsay [83]	678
36	May 2	H	Dunfermline Ath	W	3-2	1-1	5	Morton [45], McHugh 2 [47, 90]	1055

Final League Position: 5

Honours
League Champions: Second Division 2003-04; *Runners-up:* Second Division 2007-08.
League Challenge Cup Winners: 2008-09; *Runners-up:* 2003-04.

Club colours: Shirt: White with red diamond. Shorts: Red. Socks: White.

Goalscorers: *League (53):* Prunty 14 (5 pens), Lister 9, Fraser 5, Fitzpatrick 4, McHugh 4, Blockley 3, Bain 2, Boyle, P 2, Gasparotto 2, Parker 2 (1 pen), Gilfillan 1, Lindsay 1, Morton 1, Proctor 1, Watt 1, own goal 1.
William Hill Scottish FA Cup (0).
Scottish League Cup (1): Kirwan 1.
Petrofac Training Cup (2): Blockley 1, Watt 1.

McNeil A 35	Bain J 25 + 5	Hamill J 2	Proctor D 7	Boyle P 32	Gray S 11 + 13	Stewart S 4 + 3	Fitzpatrick M 35	Watt L 12 + 16	O'Neil C 23 + 1	Lister J 24 + 1	Haggerty J — + 1	Boyle J 1 + 14	Parker K 8 + 7	Kirwan J 1 + 3	Richards-Everton B 18	Wilson R — + 1	Blockley N 17 + 5	Gasparotto L 26	Richford K 1 + 4	Prunty B 27 + 3	Fraser S 28	Cadden N 1 + 3	Docherty R 22	Gilfillan B 9	Lindsay L 13	Morton J 8 + 1	McHugh B 5	Ferguson R 1	McCue J — + 1	Match No.
1	2	3¹	4	5	6²	7	8	9	10	11	12	13																		1
1	9	3		5	6²	8	4	7	2¹	10	12				11⁵	13														2
1	9	10¹	3²	5	6²	13	4	7	2	11					14	8	12													3
1	6			5	13	3¹	4	9	2	10					12	11²	8	7												4
1	9			5	12		8	7²	2						13	14	4			6	3	10¹	11³							5
1	6			5	13	12	3	9	2	10²					4		7³	8	14	11¹										6
1	13		8	5	6²	7	9		2	10	12				4		3	11¹												7
1		3¹	5	6		8	9	2	10	12					4		7	13	11²											8
1	13	3²	5	6³	8	7	2	10		11		4	12					9¹	14											9
1	12		5	6	13	8¹	9	2	10²	11		3	4				7													10
1			5	6		7	9²	2	11¹	10	4				3		13	8	12											11
1	13		5	6		7	9¹	2	10²	14	11³	4			3		12	8												12
1	9		5			4		2	12	11		3	7				10	8	6¹											13
1	5			14		4	13	2	12	9¹	11				7	3	10³	6	8¹											14
1			5	12		8		2	10	11²	4				6¹	3	13	9	7											15
1			5	13		8		2	11¹	12	4				6	3	10²	9	7											16
1	12		5			8		2	10	13	3				6	4	11²	9¹	7											17
1			5	12		8³	14	2	10¹	13	4				6	3	11	9²	7											18
1	5			13		9	12	2	10		4				6	3	11	8¹	7²											19
1	6¹		5			8		2	10	12	4		7				9	11	3											20
1	2		5	14	9³		12		10	13		4	6				11²	8¹		7	3									21
1	2		5				3¹	12	10			4	8				11	9		6	7									22
1	2		5	12		8¹		11				6	3				10	9		7	4									23
1	2		5	12		8		11		14			4				10²	9		6³	7¹		3	13						24
1	2		5			7	12	10					3				11	9¹		6	8		6³	9¹	4					25
1	2		5	13		7	12	10²		14			3				11	8		6³	9¹		4							26
1	2		5			7		11*				12	3	13	10¹	8²				6	9		4							27
1	2		5			8	12			13		14	3				11²	9¹		6	7		4	10³						28
1	2		5			9	14			13		12	3				11²	8		6	7³		4	10¹						29
1	2		5			8	12	5		13			7	3	14		11²	9¹		6			4	10³						30
1	2		3	6³		8	13	5		12							11²	10	14	7			4	9¹						31
1	2		5	6²		7	13			14			12	3			10¹	9			4		11³	8						32
1	2		5¹			7	13	12					8	3			11	10¹		6			4	9						33
1	2			12		8	13	5					3				10	9¹		7			4	6¹	11					34
1	2		5			8	12						3				10	9		7			4	6¹	11					35
	2		5			8	12			14			3				11¹	9		7²			4	6¹	10			1	13	36

ALBION ROVERS

Year Formed: 1882. *Ground & Address:* Cliftonhill Stadium, Main St, Coatbridge ML5 3RB. *Telephone/Fax:* 01236 606334.
E-mail: info@albionroversfc.com *Website:* albionroversfc.com
Ground capacity: 1,249 (seated: 489). *Size of Pitch:* 101m × 66m.
Chairman John Devlin. *Secretary:* Paul Reilly.
Manager: Darren Young. *Assistant Manager:* Billy Stark.
Club Nickname: 'The Wee Rovers'.
Previous Grounds: Cowheath Park, Meadow Park, Whifflet.
Record Attendance: 27,381 v Rangers, Scottish Cup 2nd rd, 8 Feb 1936.
Record Transfer Fee received: £40,000 from Motherwell for Bruce Cleland.
Record Transfer Fee paid: £7000 for Gerry McTeague to Stirling Alb, September 1989.
Record Victory: 12-0 v Airdriehill, Scottish Cup 1st rd, 3 Sept 1887.
Record Defeat: 1-11 v Partick Thistle, League Cup 2nd rd, 11 Aug 1993.
Most Capped Player: Jock White, 1 (2), Scotland.
Most League Appearances: 399: Murdy Walls, 1921-36.
Most League Goals in Season (Individual): 41: Jim Renwick, Division II, 1932-33.
Most Goals Overall (Individual): 105: Bunty Weir, 1928-31.

ALBION ROVERS – SCOTTISH LEAGUE TWO 2014–15 LEAGUE RECORD

Match No.	Date	Venue	Opponents	Result	H/T Score	Lg Pos.	Goalscorers	Attendance
1	Aug 9	H	Annan Ath	W 2-1	0-1	2	Black (og) [49], Dunlop, M [51]	530
2	16	A	Arbroath	L 0-1	0-0	5		598
3	23	H	East Fife	W 2-0	2-0	4	Pollock [22], Gemmell [45]	532
4	30	H	Queen's Park	W 1-0	0-0	3	McKenzie [80]	577
5	Sept 13	A	Montrose	W 2-0	1-0	1	McNeil [29], McGuigan [80]	348
6	20	A	Berwick R	D 1-1	1-1	2	McGuigan [42]	489
7	27	H	East Stirling	L 1-2	1-2	2	Reid [11]	566
8	Oct 18	H	Clyde	D 2-2	1-2	3	Chaplain [27], McGuigan [65]	715
9	25	H	Berwick R	W 2-1	0-0	3	Young [47], Gemmell [77]	425
10	28	A	Elgin C	W 4-0	3-0	2	Chaplain 2 [5, 31], Dunlop, M [10], Phillips [56]	352
11	Nov 8	A	East Fife	D 0-0	0-0	3		446
12	15	H	Arbroath	W 2-1	1-1	3	McKenzie [10], Gemmell [79]	658
13	22	A	Queen's Park	W 1-0	0-0	2	Chaplain [55]	484
14	Dec 2	A	Annan Ath	L 1-2	0-1	3	Chaplain [70]	251
15	6	H	Elgin C	W 3-0	1-0	3	Chaplain 2 [35, 53], McKenzie [90]	333
16	13	A	Clyde	W 1-0	1-0	3	Cusack [14]	422
17	20	H	Montrose	D 0-0	0-0	3		386
18	27	A	East Stirling	W 4-1	3-1	2	McGuigan 2 [3, 82], Chaplain 2 [15, 35]	300
19	Jan 3	H	Annan Ath	W 2-0	0-0	2	McKenzie [51], Mullin [90]	677
20	24	A	Montrose	W 4-3	2-2	2	McGuigan 2 [19, 32], Davidson [51], McCluskey [90]	352
21	31	H	Queen's Park	W 2-1	1-0	2	Chaplain [17], Phillips [52]	509
22	Feb 7	A	Elgin C	L 0-2	0-1	2		625
23	10	H	East Fife	L 2-3	1-0	2	McKenzie [24], Gemmell (pen) [83]	403
24	14	H	Clyde	L 0-2	0-1	2		714
25	21	H	East Stirling	L 0-1	0-0	3		429
26	28	A	Berwick R	W 2-0	1-0	1	Dunlop, R [33], McGuigan [59]	475
27	Mar 7	A	Annan Ath	W 3-1	3-1	1	Love 2 [20, 26], McGuigan [43]	374
28	14	H	Montrose	W 3-0	1-0	1	Love [37], Davidson [61], Ferns [67]	389
29	18	A	Arbroath	W 2-0	1-0	1	Love [4], Fisher [65]	754
30	21	A	Queen's Park	W 1-0	1-0	1	Fisher [35]	821
31	28	H	Elgin C	L 0-3	0-2	1		546
32	Apr 4	H	Berwick R	W 2-0	0-0	1	Cadden [62], McGuigan [71]	439
33	11	A	East Fife	L 0-1	0-1	1		707
34	18	A	Clyde	W 3-2	1-2	1	Cadden [40], Gemmell [62], Fisher [74]	739
35	25	H	Arbroath	D 1-1	0-0	1	Love [90]	1100
36	May 2	A	East Stirling	W 5-1	2-0	1	McGuigan [9], Dunlop, M (pen) [43], Love 2 [55, 66], McKenzie [84]	340

Final League Position: 1

Honours
League Champions: Division II 1933-34, Second Division 1988-89. League Two 2014-15; *Runners-up:* Division II 1913-14, 1937-38, 1947-48. *Promoted to Second Division:* 2010-11 (play-offs).
Scottish Cup Runners-up: 1920.

Club colours: Shirt: Yellow with red trim. Shorts: Red. Socks: Red.

Goalscorers: *League (61):* McGuigan 11, Chaplain 10, Love 7, McKenzie 6, Gemmell 5 (1 pen), Dunlop, M 3 (1 pen), Fisher 3, Cadden 2, Davidson 2, Phillips 2, Cusack 1, Dunlop, R 1, Ferns 1, McCluskey 1, McNeil 1, Mullin 1, Pollock 1, Reid 1, Young 1, own goal 1.
William Hill Scottish FA Cup (7): Gemmell 2, Chaplain 1, Donnelly 1, Dunlop, M 1, McKenzie 1, Young 1.
Scottish League Cup (0).
Petrofac Training Cup (3): Gemmell 2 (1 pen), Love 1.

Parry N 35	Reid A 25	Dunlop R 35	Dunlop M 34	Turnbull K 24 + 1	Mullin J 22 + 9	Young D 19	Fisher G 25 + 4	Phillips G 24 + 7	Gemmell J 16 + 10	McGuigan M 29 + 3	McKenzie M 22 + 10	Donnelly C 2 + 5	Maguire M 1	Cusack L 5 + 11	Love A 12 + 10	Pollock J 5 + 5	McNeil R 3 + 2	Dallas C — + 1	Chaplain S 16 + 6	Davidson R 25 + 1	McCluskey T 1 + 5	Ferns E 9	Cadden C 5 + 5	Stevenson S 1	Hughes K 1	Match No.
1	2	3	4	5	6^2	7	8^1	9	10	11	12	13														1
1	2	3		5	6^2	7	8^1	9^3	10	11	12			4	13	14										2
1	2	3	4	5	6	7	13	9	10^3		12		14	11^1	8^2											3
1	2	4	3	5	6^3	7		9		10	13			11^1	8^2	12	14									4
1	2	3	4	5	12	7	8^1	9		10	6			13			11^2									5
1	2	3	4	5	13	6	7^2	10		11	8			12			9^1									6
1	2*	4	3	5	13	7		9		10	6			8^1	12	14	11^2									7
1		4	5	2	7^2	13	9	10^3	8	6	3^4			12	14		11^1									8
1	2	3	4	5	12	7		9	11	10	6								8^1							9
1	2	3	4	5	14	7^1		9	10	11^3	6^2	12		13					8							10
1	2	3	4	5	13		9	11	10	6	7^1								8^3	12						11
1	2	3	4	5	12		9	11	10	6				13					8^1	7^2						12
1	2	3	4	5			9	10	11	6				12					8^1	7						13
1	2	3	4		5^2		11	9	10	13	6^3			14	8^1				12	7						14
1	2	4	3		5		11^3	12	13	10	6			9^1		14			7^2	8						15
1	2	4	8		5		11	12	10^2	13	6	14		9^1					7^3	3						16
1	2	3	4		5		11	9	10	12	13			6^1		14			8^3	7^1						17
1	2	3	4		5		11^3	12	10^1	9	13			14		6^4			7^2	8						18
1	2	3	4		5		10	6	13	11	9^2			12					8^1	7						19
1	2	4	7		5		11	9	14	10^5	6^2			12					8^1	3	13					20
1	2	3	4		5		11^3	9	12	10^2	6			13	14				8^1	7						21
1	2	3	4		5		11^2	9	12	10^1	6			13	14				8^3	7						22
1	2^2	4	3		5		13	9	11	6	10^1			12	14				8^1	7						23
1		3	4	5^2	2		9	8	11		10			6^1					13	7	12					24
1		3	4	5	2^1		9	12		11	10			14	8^3	7^2			13	6						25
1	2	3	4	5		8^1	6	12		10	13			9^3							7	14	11^2			26
1	2	3	4	5	13	8	7		10		9^2								11			6^1	12			27
1	2	4	3	5^1		7^2	8		12	9^1	14								11		10		6	13		28
		3	4	5	2	7	8^3	13		9	14			11^2					10			6^1	12			29
1		3	4	5	2	6^3	9	13	14	11^3				7^1					8			10	12			30
1		4	3	5	2^3	7	8		12	9				11^2		14			10			6^1	13			31
1		4	3	5	12	8^1	7		10	9^3				14					11	13		6^1	2			32
1		4	3		8^1	7	5	12	10	9^2				14					13	11		6^1	2			33
1		3		4		7	2	5	12	11	13			9^2					8^1	6		10				34
1		3	4	5	8		12		10		14			13					7	11^3	9^1	6	2^1			35
	4	3	12	2		6	5^1		11^3	8		10^2							13	9	14		7		1	36

ALLOA ATHLETIC

Year Formed: 1878. *Ground & Address:* Indodrill Stadium, Recreation Park, Clackmannan Rd, Alloa FK10 1RY.
Telephone: 01259 722695. *Fax:* 01259 210886. *E-mail:* fcadmin@alloaatheltic.co.uk *Website:* www.alloaathletic.co.uk
Ground Capacity: 3,100 (seated: 919). *Size of Pitch:* 102m × 69m.
Honorary President: George Ormiston. *Chairman:* Mike Mulraney. *Secretary:* Ewen G. Cameron.
Manager: Danny Lennon. *Assistant Manager:* Paddy Connolly. *Physio:* Jim Law.
Club Nicknames: 'The Wasps', 'The Hornets'.
Previous Grounds: West End Public Park, Gabberston Park, Bellevue Park.
Record Attendance: 13,000 v Dunfermline Ath, Scottish Cup 3rd rd replay, 26 Feb 1939.
Record Transfer Fee received: £100,000 for Martin Cameron to Bristol R.
Record Transfer Fee paid: £26,000 for Ross Hamilton from Stenhousemuir.
Record Victory: 9-0 v Selkirk, Scottish Cup 1st rd, 28 November 2005.
Record Defeat: 0-10 v Dundee, Division II, 8 Mar 1947 v Third Lanark, League Cup, 8 Aug 1953.
Most Capped Player: Jock Hepburn, 1, Scotland.
Most League Appearances: 239: Peter Smith 1960-69.
Most League Goals in Season (Individual): 49: 'Wee' Willie Crilley, Division II, 1921-22.
Most Goals Overall (Individual): 91: Willie Irvine, 1996-2001.

ALLOA ATHLETIC – SCOTTISH CHAMPIONSHIP 2014–15 LEAGUE RECORD

Match No.	Date	Venue	Opponents	Result	H/T Score	Lg Pos.	Goalscorers	Attendance
1	Aug 9	A	Queen of the South	L	0-2	0-2	10		1635
2	16	H	Raith R	L	0-1	0-1	9		858
3	23	A	Cowdenbeath	W	3-0	1-0	7	Cawley [38], Spence [48], Buchanan [54]	549
4	30	H	Hibernian	W	2-1	0-1	5	Buchanan [56], Flannigan [85]	2476
5	Sept 13	A	Livingston	L	0-4	0-2	7		1150
6	20	H	Rangers	D	1-1	1-0	6	Tiffoney [35]	2793
7	27	A	Dumbarton	L	1-3	0-1	8	Simmons [90]	758
8	Oct 4	A	Falkirk	L	1-2	1-1	9	Buchanan (pen) [42]	3037
9	11	H	Hearts	L	0-1	0-0	9		3067
10	18	H	Cowdenbeath	L	2-3	0-1	9	Buchanan [59], Spence [78]	643
11	25	A	Raith R	D	1-1	1-1	9	Buchanan [14]	1541
12	Nov 8	H	Livingston	W	1-0	0-0	7	Buchanan [48]	586
13	15	A	Rangers	D	1-1	0-0	8	Buchanan [78]	29,548
14	22	H	Falkirk	L	2-3	1-2	8	Docherty [31], Buchanan (pen) [86]	1026
15	Dec 6	H	Dumbarton	L	0-1	0-1	8		666
16	13	A	Hibernian	L	0-2	0-1	8		8031
17	20	A	Hearts	L	0-2	0-2	9		15,224
18	27	H	Queen of the South	D	1-1	0-1	9	Cawley [75]	921
19	Jan 3	A	Falkirk	L	0-1	0-1	9		3690
20	10	H	Rangers	L	0-1	0-1	9		3012
21	24	H	Raith R	D	0-0	0-0	9		914
22	31	H	Hearts	L	1-4	0-2	9	Spence [61]	2592
23	Feb 3	A	Livingston	D	0-0	0-0	8		723
24	14	A	Queen of the South	L	0-1	0-0	9		1673
25	21	A	Cowdenbeath	W	2-0	0-0	8	Docherty [65], Cawley [78]	505
26	28	H	Hibernian	L	0-1	0-1	8		2024
27	Mar 7	A	Dumbarton	L	0-1	0-1	9		791
28	14	H	Falkirk	L	1-3	0-1	9	Cawley [57]	855
29	17	A	Rangers	D	2-2	0-0	8	Gordon [53], Buchanan [82]	28,902
30	21	A	Raith R	L	1-2	1-1	8	Buchanan [33]	1100
31	28	H	Livingston	D	2-2	0-0	8	Buchanan 2 [53, 73]	706
32	Apr 8	A	Hearts	L	0-3	0-1	9		15,156
33	11	H	Dumbarton	W	3-0	2-0	9	Flannigan [7], Cawley [21], Spence [71]	535
34	18	H	Queen of the South	D	2-2	1-0	9	Gordon [40], Buchanan [66]	822
35	25	A	Hibernian	L	1-4	0-2	10	Flannigan [63]	8328
36	May 2	H	Cowdenbeath	W	3-0	1-0	9	Chopra [12], Armstrong (og) [53], Buchanan [74]	1219

Final League Position: 9

Honours
League Champions: Division II 1921-22; Third Division 1997-98, 2011-12; *Runners-up:* Division II 1938-39.
Second Division 1976-77, 1981-82, 1984-85, 1988-89, 1999-2000, 2001-02, 2009-10; *Runners-up:* 2012-13 (promoted via play-offs).
League Challenge Cup Winners: 1999-2000; *Runners-up:* 2001-02, 2014-15.

Club colours: Shirt: Gold with black trim. Shorts: Black. Socks: Black.

Goalscorers: *League (34):* Buchanan 14 (2 pens), Cawley 5, Spence 4, Flannigan 3, Docherty 2, Gordon 2, Chopra 1, Simmons 1, Tiffoney 1, own goal 1.
William Hill Scottish FA Cup (6): Buchanan 2, Docherty 2, Meggatt 2.
Scottish League Cup (2): Spence 2.
Petrofac Training Cup (10): Spence 7, McCord 2, Simmons 1.
Championship Play-Offs (6): Benedictus 2, Chopra 2, Buchanan 1, Meggatt 1.

Gibson J 9	Doyle M 35	Marr J 12 + 1	Gordon B 35	Meggatt D 29 + 1	Holmes G 30 + 1	Simmons S 20	McCord R 34 + 1	Buchanan L 31 + 2	Cawley K 32 + 2	Spence G 17 + 11	Flannigan I 5 + 6	Fens E 2 + 14	Docherty M 30 + 2	Hetherington S 3 + 4	McDowall C 27	Benedictus K 22 + 4	Tiffoney J 7 + 3	Weatherston D 1 + 1	Jahraldo-Martin C — + 2	Layne I 5 + 5	Rutherford G — + 8	Roberts P 5 + 2	Chopra M 3 + 5	Ferguson D 2 + 2	Asghar A — + 1		Match No.
1	2	3	4	5	6	7	8¹	9	10	11	12																1
1	2	4	3	5	9	7	8²	10¹	6	11	12	13															2
1	2		3	4	9	8	7²	11	6³	10¹	13	12	5	14													3
	2		3	4	9	8⁴	7	11¹	6	10	12		5	13	1												4
	2		3	4	9	8	7¹	11	6	10		12	5		1												5
1	2		3		10	7	9		6	11			5	12		4	8¹										6
1	2		3		10	8	9	12	6	11²		13	5			4	7¹										7
	2		3		7	6	10	11	8			12	5		1	4	9¹										8
	2		3		9	7	8	10	6	11¹		12	5		1	4											9
	2		3	14	9	8²	7³	11	6¹	10		13	5		1	4		12									10
2	13		3	5	10	8¹	9	11²	7			12	6		1	4¹											11
5	4	3	9	6³	7	13	11	8¹				12	14	1		2	10²										12
2	4	3	5		6	8²	11¹	10		12	9			1	13	7											13
5	7³	3	4	8⁹		6	10	11	12		14	2	9²	1	13												14
	2		3	5		7	8			11		6	9	10	1	4											15
	2		3	5	13	6	7		12	10		11²	8	9¹	1	4											16
	2		3	5¹	9	7	6	11	12	10²		13	8		1	4											17
	2		3	5	8		7	11	6	10		12	9¹		1	4											18
	2		3	5	8		7	11²	6	10		13	9¹		1	4	12										19
	2		3	5	8	6¹	10	11	7	12		13	9²		1	4											20
	2		4	5	8¹	6	10	11	7	12			9		1	3											21
	2		3	5	6¹	7	8	11²		10			9		1	4			12	13							22
	2		3	5	9	7¹	8	11²	6	10¹			12		1	4				13	14						23
	2	3¹		5	7			8²	6	13			9		1	4¹			12	11	14	10¹					24
	2	4	3	5			7	10²	6	12			8		1		13			11¹		9					25
	2	4	3	5²	10		9	12	8	13			7		1					11²	14	6¹					26
	2¹	4	3	5			8	10	6	13			7		1		12			11²	14	9²					27
	2	4	3	5	8²		9	10	7	12³			6		1					11¹	13	14					28
	2	4	3	5	7		9	11¹	10		12		8²		1	13	6³						14				29
	2	4³	3	5	6		7	11	9				10²		1	12					14	8¹	13				30
	2		3	5	6		9²	11	8	12	13		7		1	4							10¹				31
		3		9¹			7	11²	10		8		5⁴		1	4	2³		13		12	14	6				32
1	2		3	5	7		6	11²	9	12	8³					4			14			10¹	13				33
1	2		3	5¹	7		8	11	6	10²	9³					4							12	13	14		34
1	6		3		8		9³	11¹	10		7		5			4				13	12		14	2²			35
1	2		3	5			7	10²	9	13	8		6			4						12		11¹			36

ANNAN ATHLETIC

Year Formed: 1942. *Ground & Address:* Galabank, North Street, Annan DG12 5DQ. *Telephone:* 01461 204108.
E-mail: enquiries@annanathleticfc.com *Website:* www.annanathleticfc.com
Ground capacity: 2,517 (seated: 500). *Size of Pitch:* 100m × 62m.
Chairman: Henry McClelland.
Secretary: Alan Irving.
Manager: Jim Chapman.
Assistant Manager: John Joyce.
Coaches: Peter Weatherson and Bill Bentley.
Club Nicknames: 'Galabankies', 'Black and Golds'.
Record attendance: 2,517, v Rangers, Third Division, 15 Sept 2012.
Most League Appearances: 180: Steven Sloan, 2008-15.
Most League Goals in Season (Individual): 22: Peter Weatherson, 2014-15.
Most Goals Overall (Individual): 28: Peter Weatherson, 2013-15.

ANNAN ATHLETIC – SCOTTISH LEAGUE TWO 2014–15 LEAGUE RECORD

Match No.	Date	Venue	Opponents	Result	H/T Score	Lg Pos.	Goalscorers	Atten- dance
1	Aug 9	A	Albion R	L 1-2	1-0	6	Hopkirk (pen) [30]	530
2	16	H	Queen's Park	L 0-1	0-1	10		401
3	23	A	Montrose	L 0-2	0-2	10		341
4	30	H	Elgin C	D 3-3	2-1	10	Todd [1], Mackay [33], Carcary [77]	341
5	Sept 13	H	Berwick R	W 2-0	0-0	10	McColm [64], Mackay [67]	422
6	20	A	East Stirling	W 1-0	0-0	6	Weatherson [64]	224
7	27	A	Clyde	D 1-1	0-1	8	Weatherson (pen) [52]	605
8	Oct 18	A	East Fife	D 1-1	0-1	7	Weatherson [78]	544
9	21	H	Arbroath	L 0-1	0-1	7		313
10	25	H	East Stirling	W 4-3	3-1	5	Weatherson 2 [2, 33], Hopkirk [18], Flynn [77]	373
11	Nov 11	A	Elgin C	D 0-0	0-0	6		328
12	15	H	Montrose	D 2-2	1-1	6	Weatherson 2 (1 pen) [26, 90 (p)]	394
13	22	A	Berwick R	L 0-2	0-0	8		412
14	Dec 2	H	Albion R	W 2-1	1-0	5	Hopkirk [8], Todd [85]	251
15	6	A	Arbroath	L 2-3	0-1	6	McStay [79], Davidson [87]	577
16	13	H	East Fife	W 2-1	0-0	5	Weatherson [50], Davidson (pen) [90]	426
17	20	A	Queen's Park	D 0-0	0-0	4		320
18	27	H	Clyde	W 2-1	1-1	4	Hopkirk [4], Todd [61]	578
19	Jan 3	A	Albion R	L 0-2	0-0	4		677
20	10	H	Elgin C	L 2-3	1-1	5	Hopkirk [5], McStay [50]	411
21	17	A	East Stirling	W 3-1	1-1	5	Weatherson 3 [8, 74, 89]	276
22	24	H	Berwick R	W 4-2	3-0	4	McColm 2 [3, 35], Todd [8], Weatherson (pen) [89]	370
23	31	A	Montrose	L 1-2	0-0	4	Omar [63]	244
24	Feb 14	H	Queen's Park	W 2-0	0-0	4	Todd [50], Weatherson [59]	451
25	21	H	Arbroath	W 2-0	0-0	4	Swinglehurst [60], Weatherson [90]	362
26	28	A	East Fife	L 1-2	1-0	4	Logan [27]	499
27	Mar 3	A	Clyde	L 0-1	0-1	5		402
28	7	H	Albion R	L 1-3	1-3	5	Weatherson [41]	374
29	14	A	Berwick R	D 2-2	0-1	5	Todd [52], Ogen [77]	356
30	21	H	East Stirling	W 3-2	1-1	5	Swinglehurst [2], Weatherson 2 [68, 87]	322
31	28	H	Clyde	L 0-1	0-0	7		485
32	Apr 4	A	Arbroath	D 1-1	0-0	7	Mackay [51]	539
33	11	A	Queen's Park	L 0-2	0-2	7		462
34	18	H	East Fife	W 2-1	1-1	6	McStay [2], McNiff [90]	419
35	25	A	Elgin C	W 5-4	3-3	5	Andrew Mitchell [21], Ogen [22], Weatherson 3 [43, 66, 88]	758
36	May 2	H	Montrose	W 4-3	2-0	5	Weatherson 2 [18, 22], Ogen [66], McNiff [85]	386

Final League Position: 5

Honours
League Two Runners-up: 2013-14.
East of Scotland Premier League: Winners (4).
East of Scotland League Cup: Winners (1).
East of Scotland Div 1: Winners (1).
South of Scotland League: Winners (2).
South of Scotland League Cup: Winners (4).
Scottish Challenge Cup South: Winners (1).
Scottish Qualifying Cup South: Winners (1).

Club colours: Shirt: Gold with black trim. Shorts: Black. Socks: Gold with black and white rings.

Goalscorers: League (56): Weatherson 22 (3 pens), Todd 6, Hopkirk 5 (1 pen), Mackay 3, McColm 3, McStay 3, Ogen 3, Davidson 2 (1 pen), McNiff 2, Swinglehurst 2, Carcary 1, Flynn 1, Logan 1, Andrew Mitchell 1, Omar 1.
William Hill Scottish FA Cup (8): Weatherson 3 (1 pen), McColm 2, Davidson 1, Flynn 1, Hopkirk 1.
Scottish League Cup (1): Hopkirk 1.
Petrofac Training Cup (1): Davidson 1.

Mitchell Alex 27	Black S 28+1	Watson P 34	Swinglehurst S 17+2	Bradley P 1+1	Sloan S 22+4	Logan S 14+7	McStay R 25+3	Hopkirk D 22	Todd J 33+3	Carcary D 2+4	Flynn M 18+4	McNiff M 34	Chisholm I 20+2	Liddell C —+1	Brannan K 11+5	Mackay K 6+3	McColm S 23+1	Omar R 3+14	Weatherson P 26+2	Davidson S 1+10	McAnespie M 1	Gemmell J 1	Wood D —+1	Dickinson C —+4	Allan J —+1	Ogen J 4+6	Mitchell Andrew 12	Hart J 8+1	Breslin J 3+2	Cook C —+1	Wadge D —+1	Match No.
1	2	3	4	5¹	6	7	8	9	10	11	12																					1
1	2	3⁴	4¹		6	13	7³	9	11	10	8²	5	12	14																		2
1	4		14		5²	7	6¹	11	10		12	8³	3	2		9	13															3
1	3	2			13	8	11	6	12	7	4	5				9¹	10²															4
1	4	3			12	7¹	11	6³	13	8	5	2				10	9²14															5
1	2	4			9	13		8	6³	7	3	5			11¹	10²14	12															6
1	2	4				7²10	9¹	6	12	3	5	13		8³		11	14															7
1	2	4			12	8	7¹	9	6³	3	5			10²	14	11	13															8
1	3	4	12		8	10²	6¹	7		2		9	13	11	5																	9
1	3	4			6	8		10	12	7	5	2		9¹		11²13																10
1	2	4			6	8		11	12	7¹	3	5		9²	13	10																11
1	3	4			7²	6¹13	10	12	8	5	2		9		11																	12
1	4	3			7¹	6²14	9	11		8³	5	2	12			10	13															13
1	3	4			7		8	10	6	9¹	5	2				11	12															14
1	3	4	14		7		8	6¹	9	11²	5	2	13			10³	12															15
1	2	3	4²		8¹		7	10	6	12	5	13	9		11³14																	16
1	2¹	3			8	11	6	7	4	5		12	9²			10	13															17
		3			7	10	6	8	4	5	2¹	9²	13	11	12			1														18
1		4			8	7²11	6			3	5	2	9	12		10¹			13													19
1		3			7²	8³10	6	12	4	5		2¹	9		11	14			13													20
1		4	5		8	11	6	7	3		2	9¹	10							12												21
1		3	4		8	10	6	7	5		2	9¹	12	11																		22
1		3	4		14	8²	6	7³	5		2	9¹	10	11					12		13											23
1¹	7³	3	5				10	8	4	2²	9	13	11			11³14							14	6	12							24
	7	3	4		12			11	8¹	5	13	2²	9³14	10										6	1							25
	7	3	5¹		13	8		11		4	9	2²14		12	10³									6	1							26
	7	4			5¹	8		11		3	2	12		9¹	10²								13	6	1	14						27
	3	4			7²	8³13		9		5	2¹			14	11	10							6	1	12							28
	3²	4			8	7		9		5¹				11³12	10								14	6	1	2	13					29
	12	3	4¹		7		8²	11		5				9	10								13	6	1	2						30
1		3	4		7		8	6		5			10	9									11		2							31
1	2	4	5		7	13	8²	9		3				10³	11¹								14	12	6							32
1	2	3	4		6	14	8¹	10		5				11	9²	12								13	7³							33
	2	3	4		7	12	8	9		5				11										10	6¹	1						34
	2	4	5²		7		8¹	11		3				12	10									9	6	1			13			35
1	3	2	4		7¹		8	9		13	5²			12	10									11	6							36

ARBROATH

Year Formed: 1878. *Ground & Address:* Gayfield Park, Arbroath DD11 1QB. *Telephone:* 01241 872157. *Fax:* 01241 431125. *E-mail:* afc@gayfield.fsnet.co.uk *Website:* www.arbroathfc.co.uk
Ground Capacity: 5,940 (seated: 860). *Size of Pitch:* 105m × 65m.
Chairman: John Christison. *Secretary:* Dr Gary Callon. *Administrator:* Mike Cargill.
Manager: Todd Lumsden. *Assistant Manager:* Steven Hislop. *Physio:* Becky Dunphy.
Club Nickname: 'The Red Lichties'.
Previous Grounds: Lesser Gayfield.
Record Attendance: 13,510 v Rangers, Scottish Cup 3rd rd, 23 Feb 1952.
Record Transfer Fee received: £120,000 for Paul Tosh to Dundee (Aug 1993).
Record Transfer Fee paid: £20,000 for Douglas Robb from Montrose (1981).
Record Victory: 36-0 v Bon Accord, Scottish Cup 1st rd, 12 Sept 1885.
Record Defeat: 1-9 v Celtic, League Cup 3rd rd, 25 Aug 1993.
Most Capped Player: Ned Doig, 2 (5), Scotland.
Most League Appearances: 445: Tom Cargill, 1966-81.
Most League Goals in Season (Individual): 45: Dave Easson, Division II, 1958-59.
Most Goals Overall (Individual): 120: Jimmy Jack, 1966-71.

ARBROATH – SCOTTISH LEAGUE TWO 2014–15 LEAGUE RECORD

Match No.	Date	Venue	Opponents	Result	H/T Score	Lg Pos.	Goalscorers	Atten- dance
1	Aug 9	A	Berwick R	W 2-1	0-1	2	Buchan [53], McManus [60]	590
2	16	H	Albion R	W 1-0	0-0	1	McManus [66]	598
3	23	A	Queen's Park	W 2-0	0-0	1	McBride [69], Smith [90]	520
4	30	H	Montrose	W 3-1	2-0	1	Linn [14], Buchan [22], Murray, S [61]	1137
5	Sept 13	H	East Fife	L 0-2	0-0	2		829
6	20	A	Clyde	W 5-2	2-2	1	McManus [25], McBride [38], Carreiro 2 [68, 76], Murray, S [78]	614
7	27	H	Elgin C	W 1-0	0-0	1	Murray, S [75]	601
8	Oct 18	A	East Stirling	W 4-0	2-0	1	El-Zubaidi [20], Linn [33], Buchan [74], Murray, S [80]	614
9	21	A	Annan Ath	W 1-0	1-0	1	Carreiro [11]	313
10	25	A	Montrose	W 5-1	1-0	1	Murray, S [17], Carreiro [52], Crawford [78], McManus 2 (1 pen) [86 (p), 90]	1143
11	Nov 8	H	Queen's Park	L 1-2	0-1	1	McManus [82]	737
12	15	A	Albion R	L 1-2	1-1	1	McBride [30]	658
13	22	H	Clyde	W 4-0	4-0	1	McManus (pen) [16], Murray, S 2 [18, 45], Linn [42]	656
14	Dec 2	A	Elgin C	D 1-1	1-0	1	Murray, S [33]	425
15	6	H	Annan Ath	W 3-2	1-0	1	Linn [15], Smith [56], Carreiro [58]	577
16	13	A	East Stirling	W 3-2	1-0	1	Murray, S [20], McManus 2 [73, 82]	289
17	20	H	Berwick R	W 2-0	1-0	1	Murray, S [28], Linn [52]	641
18	27	A	East Fife	W 5-1	1-1	1	Murray, S 3 [10, 60, 65], McManus [58], Smith [88]	806
19	Jan 3	H	Montrose	D 2-2	1-0	1	Hunter [44], Murray, S [54]	1395
20	17	A	Queen's Park	L 1-2	0-2	1	Linn [90]	729
21	24	A	Clyde	D 1-1	0-1	1	Whatley [67]	598
22	31	H	East Fife	D 1-1	1-0	1	Murray, S [36]	695
23	Feb 14	A	Berwick R	L 1-3	0-0	1	Grant [63]	462
24	21	A	Annan Ath	L 0-2	0-0	2		362
25	28	H	Elgin C	D 3-3	0-1	3	McManus [66], Little [82], Linn [88]	701
26	Mar 4	H	East Stirling	L 0-1	0-0	3		584
27	7	A	Montrose	L 0-3	0-1	3		970
28	14	H	Clyde	W 3-1	2-0	3	Linn 3 [2, 34, 52]	673
29	18	H	Albion R	L 0-2	0-1	3		754
30	21	A	East Fife	L 0-2	0-1	3		567
31	28	A	East Stirling	L 0-1	0-1	3		332
32	Apr 4	H	Annan Ath	D 1-1	0-0	3	Murray, S [67]	539
33	11	A	Elgin C	L 1-2	0-0	3	Linn [58]	828
34	18	H	Queen's Park	D 1-1	1-0	3	Murray, S [25]	680
35	25	A	Albion R	D 1-1	0-0	3	Linn [86]	1100
36	May 2	H	Berwick R	W 5-0	0-0	3	Linn [52], Murray, S 2 [59, 67], Grant [84], Little [89]	564

Final League Position: 3

Honours
League Champions: Third Division 2010-11; *Runners-up:* Division II 1934-35, 1958-59, 1967-68, 1971-72; Second Division 2000-01; Third Division 1997-98, 2007-08. *Promoted to Second Division:* 2007-08 (play-offs).
Scottish Cup: Quarter-finals 1993.

Club colours: Shirt: Maroon with white trim. Shorts: Maroon. Socks: Maroon with white tops.

Goalscorers: *League (65):* Murray, S 19, Linn 13, McManus 11 (2 pens), Carreiro 5, Buchan 3, McBride 3, Smith 3, Grant 2, Little 2, Crawford 1, El-Zubaidi 1, Hunter 1, Whatley 1.
William Hill Scottish FA Cup (13): McManus 7 (1 pen), Murray, S 3, Hunter 1, McBride 1, Stewart 1.
Scottish League Cup (1): Buchan 1.
Petrofac Training Cup (1): own goal 1.
League One Play-Offs (2): Murray, S 2.

Crawford D 10	Travis M 3+1	Little R 23+2	Fisher R 1	Murray E 1	Linn R 36	Nicoll K 28	Whatley M 36	McBride S 27+1	Hunter A 22+1	McManus P 26+5	Buchan K 6+24	Stewart K 22+4	Murray S 27+9	El-Zubaidi A 15	Johnstone C 20+1	Smith J 4+15	Morrison S 1+1	Carreiro D 12+6	McWalter K 5+1	Lowdon J 13+6	Lindsay J 4+1	McCallum M 25	Easton D 1+2	McGeever R 8+2	Rowan L 7+2	Grant T 3+8	Gordon L 10	Match No.
1	2	3^2	4	5^1	6	7	8	9	10	11^1	12	13	14															1
1	2				6	3	5	9	7	10	11^1	8	12	4														2
1		2^2			6	3	5	9	8	10^1	11^1	7	12	4	13	14												3
1^1					6	3	2	9	7	10^1	11^2	8	13	4	5	14	12											4
1					6	8	2	9	7	10	11^2	4^1	12	3	5^3							13	14					5
1	13				6^2	3	2	9		10	12	8	11^1	4	5							7						6
1					6	3	2	9	12	10	13	8	11^2	4	5							7						7
1	12				6	3	2	5		8^1	10^3	14	7	11	4							13	9^2					8
1	2				6	4	7	5		10	12	8	11	3								9^2	13					9
1	2				6^2	3	9	5^3		10	12	7	11^1	4								8	13	14				10
	2^2				6	3	8	5	7	10	12		11^1	4		13	1	9										11
	2				6^1	7	4	5	8	10^2	11	9	13	3		12							1					12
	3				6		2	5	8	10^3	13	7	11^2	4		14		12		9^1	1							13
	2				6^1	3	7	9	8	10^3			11	4	5^2	14		12	13		1							14
	2				6	3	8		7	14	13		10^3	4	5	11^2		9^1	12		1							15
	2				6	8	4	13	7	12	14		11	3^2	5	10^1		9^3			1							16
	2				6	7	4	3	8	10^2	12		11		5	13			9^1		1							17
	2				6	3	8	4	7	10^3	14		11^2		5	13			9^1		1	12						18
	2				6	3	7	4	8	10			11			9^1	5	1	12									19
	2				6		8	4	7		12	14	11^3		5^2	10^1		13		1	9	3						20
	4				6		7		8	10	14	12	11^2					9^1	5^3	1		3	2	13				21
					6		8		7	10^1	12	9	11^2					5	1		3	2	13	4				22
	4				7		6			10	14	9	11^3			8^2		5^1	1	12	2	13	3					23
					6		7		8	10	13		12	5				9^2		1	4	2	11^1	3				24
	12				6		7		8	10			11	5	14	13		9^2	1		4^1	2^3		3				25
					6	3	2	5	8^2	10^3	14	7	11^1		12			9		1				13	4			26
					6	3	2	5	8	10^3	13	7	12		11^1			9		1		14			4^3			27
	2				6^1	3	8	9		12	14	7	11^3	5		10^2			1			4	13					28
	2				6	3	8	9^2		12		7	10	5^3				13		1		4	11^1	14				29
	2				6	3	8			10	14	7^1	11^2	5	13			9		1		4^1	12					30
	2				6		8	3		10	11^2	7	14	5				9^3		1		12	13	4^1				31
					6	3	4	7		12^3	13		10	5	14		11	9^2		1			2^1	8				32
	2^3				6	3	4			12	13	10	5	14			8	9^1		1			11^2					33
	2				10	3	7	9			8	11	5			6				1					4			34
	3				7	6	2	10^1		9	11^2		5	13	12	8		1							4			35
	2				6^2	3	7		12	9	10^1		13		8^3	11	5		1					14	4			36

AYR UNITED

Year Formed: 1910. *Ground & Address:* Somerset Park, Tryfield Place, Ayr KA8 9NB. *Telephone:* 01292 263435.
Fax: 01292 281314. *E-mail:* info@ayrunitedfc.co.uk *Website:* ayrunitedfc.co.uk
Ground Capacity: 10,185 (seated: 1,597). *Size of Pitch:* 101m × 66m.
Chairman: Lachlan Cameron.
Managing Director: Lewis Grant.
Manager: Ian McCall. *Assistant Manager:* John Henry. *Physio:* Steven Maguire.
Club Nickname: 'The Honest Men'.
Previous Grounds: None.
Record Attendance: 25,225 v Rangers, Division I, 13 Sept 1969.
Record Transfer Fee received: £300,000 for Steven Nicol to Liverpool (Oct 1981).
Record Transfer Fee paid: £90,000 for Mark Campbell from Stranraer (March 1999).
Record Victory: 11-1 v Dumbarton, League Cup, 13 Aug 1952.
Record Defeat: 0-9 in Division I v Rangers (1929); v Hearts (1931); B Division v Third Lanark (1954).
Most Capped Player: Jim Nisbet, 3, Scotland.
Most League Appearances: 459: John Murphy, 1963-78.
Most League League and Cup Goals in Season (Individual): 66: Jimmy Smith, 1927-28.
Most League and Cup Goals Overall (Individual): 213: Peter Price, 1955-61.

AYR UNITED – SCOTTISH LEAGUE ONE 2014–15 LEAGUE RECORD

Match No.	Date	Venue	Opponents	Result	H/T Score	Lg Pos.	Goalscorers	Atten-dance
1	Aug 9	H	Greenock Morton	W 1-0	0-0	1	Donnelly [79]	1617
2	16	A	Stirling Alb	W 3-1	1-0	1	Forrest 2 [5, 56], Gilmour [69]	823
3	23	H	Forfar Ath	W 2-0	0-0	1	McLaughlin 2 (1 pen) [85, 89 (p)]	1156
4	30	A	Stenhousemuir	D 1-1	1-1	1	Donnelly [12]	669
5	Sept 13	H	Stranraer	L 0-2	0-0	2		1414
6	20	A	Brechin C	W 4-2	0-0	1	McLaughlin 2 (2 pens) [53, 86], Beattie 2 [73, 90]	537
7	27	H	Airdrieonians	L 2-3	0-1	3	Murphy [51], Beattie [80]	1185
8	Oct 4	A	Peterhead	L 0-2	0-0	3		506
9	10	H	Dunfermline Ath	L 0-1	0-1	3		1457
10	18	A	Greenock Morton	W 1-0	1-0	3	McLaughlin [36]	1744
11	25	H	Brechin C	L 0-2	0-2	4		1060
12	Nov 8	A	Stranraer	L 1-3	1-1	5	McGovern [9]	630
13	22	A	Forfar Ath	L 0-2	0-1	7		562
14	Dec 6	A	Dunfermline Ath	L 2-4	1-3	7	McLaughlin [27], Forrest [56]	2509
15	13	H	Stenhousemuir	L 2-3	1-2	9	McLaughlin [28], Forrest [89]	646
16	20	H	Stirling Alb	D 2-2	0-0	8	Forrest [55], Beattie [90]	880
17	27	A	Airdrieonians	L 0-3	0-2	9		1023
18	Jan 3	A	Stranraer	L 0-2	0-1	9		1235
19	10	A	Brechin C	L 1-2	0-1	9	Forrest [90]	504
20	17	H	Greenock Morton	D 1-1	1-0	9	Neill [37]	1217
21	24	A	Stenhousemuir	D 1-1	1-1	9	Forrest [33]	651
22	31	H	Dunfermline Ath	L 0-2	0-0	9		1149
23	Feb 14	A	Stirling Alb	W 4-1	2-0	8	Robertson [12], Smith (og) [15], Beattie [74], Preston [83]	785
24	21	A	Peterhead	L 0-2	0-0	8		560
25	28	H	Forfar Ath	W 1-0	1-0	8	Preston [35]	1017
26	Mar 3	H	Peterhead	D 3-3	2-1	8	Devlin [3], Beattie [30], Preston [88]	693
27	7	A	Dunfermline Ath	L 1-2	0-0	9	Crawford [86]	2467
28	10	H	Airdrieonians	L 0-1	0-0	9		835
29	14	H	Stenhousemuir	D 0-0	0-0	9		1055
30	21	A	Greenock Morton	L 1-2	0-0	9	McGovern [53]	1552
31	28	H	Brechin C	D 2-2	0-0	8	Gilmour [49], McGovern (pen) [53]	986
32	Apr 4	A	Stranraer	L 0-1	0-0	8		1010
33	11	H	Peterhead	L 2-4	2-1	8	Forrest [18], Preston [21]	998
34	18	A	Airdrieonians	L 0-2	0-0	9		881
35	25	H	Stirling Alb	W 4-0	2-0	8	McKenna [6], Blakeman 2 [21, 87], McGovern (pen) [73]	1608
36	May 2	H	Forfar Ath	W 3-1	2-1	8	McGovern (pen) [35], Preston [41], Forrest [65]	1916

Final League Position: 8

Honours
League Champions: Division II 1911-12, 1912-13, 1927-28, 1936-37, 1958-59, 1965-66. Second Division 1987-88, 1996-97;
Runners-up: Division II 1910-11, 1955-56, 1968-69. Second Division 2008-09. *Promoted to First Division:* 2008-09
(play-offs). *Promoted to First Division:* 2010-11 (play-offs).
Scottish Cup: Semi-finals 2002.
League Cup: Runners-up: 2001-02.
B&Q Cup Runners-up: 1990-91, 1991-92.

Club colours: Shirt: White with black trim. Shorts: Black. Socks: White.

Goalscorers: *League (45):* Forrest 9, McLaughlin 7 (3 pens), Beattie 6, McGovern 5 (3 pens), Preston 5, Blakeman 2,
Donnelly 2, Gilmour 2, Crawford 1, Devlin 1, McKenna 1, Murphy 1, Neill 1, Robertson 1, own goal 1.
William Hill Scottish FA Cup (1): Donnelly 1.
Scottish League Cup (4): Donnelly 2, Gilmour 1, McLaughlin 1 (1 pen).
Petrofac Training Cup (0).

Hutton D 36	Devlin N 36	Murphy P 25	Campbell M 11+2	Donald M 33+1	Forrest A 23+8	Gilmour B 24+7	McLaughlin S 21+1	McGill P 4+2	McGovern J 35+1	Donnelly R 19+5	Shirkie D 1+15	McKenzie S 1+3	McKinlay K 13+1	Slane P 7+5	Beattie C 14+14	Muir A 1+5	Crawford R 18+5	Rutkiewicz K 1	Nisbet R —+10	Cummins A 4	Keenan D 2	McArthur J —+1	Neill M 6+1	McCracken C 1+1	Murray C 13+1	Blakeman A 12+2	Robertson D 9+3	Preston J 14	McKenna S 12	Match No.
1	2	3	4¹	5	6	7	8	9²	10	11	12	13																		1
1	2		3	5	6	8	7	9¹	11	10	12		4																	2
1	2	4		5	9	6¹	7	11²	8	10	12	13	3																	3
1	2	4	3²	9	6	8	7	12	10	11	13		5¹																	4
1	2	4	3	5	6	8³	7	9¹	11	10¹	14				12	13														5
1	2	3	4²	9		6³	7	8	11	10	13		5¹		12	14														6
1	2	4¹	3²	9			7	8	10	11	12		5	6	13															7
1	2		5²	6	7	3	13	8	11²	12			4	9	10¹	14														8
1	2	3	10	6²	9³	4		7	11¹	13			5	8	12		14													9
1	2	4	3	9	12		8	7	11²	14			5	6³	10¹		13													10
1	2	3	4	9¹	6	13	7	8	11³	12			5²		10	14														11
1	2	4³		6	7	8	11	10	12	14			9²		5¹		3	13												12
1	2	4		9	6¹	7	8	11	12	13			10²						3	5										13
1	2¹	4	5²	12	7	8		9	13				6	10	11³	14			3											14
1	2	4		14	13	7¹	8	10	12				9	6²	11				3	5³										15
1	2	3		9	6	7¹	8	10	11				12		5		4													16
1	2	4³		5	9²	7¹	3	8	11				12	13⁴	10	14	6													17
1	2		8	6		7		9	10	13	4¹	3		11³		5			12											18
1	2		8	5	13	6		7	11²		9¹		12		10							3	4							19
1	3		5	10¹	9	8²		6	11	14			13		7							4	12	2³						20
1	2		9	10²	3	13		7	11³				14	12	6							4			5	8¹				21
1	2		9	10	8	7²		3	11¹				14	12	13							4			6	5³				22
1	2		9	10³		4		12	13	8¹	14			3											6	5	7²	11		23
1	2		9	14	13	3		10²		7¹			4												6	12	8³	11	5	24
1	2	3	9	10¹		7	14	12	13																6	5	8³	11²	4	25
1	2	3	9²	12	13	6		11	7				5¹	8												10			4	26
1	2		9		7³			14	12				11²	3			13								6¹	5	8	10	4	27
1	2	3	9			13		6		12	7	14													5²	8⁴	10¹	11³	4	28
1	2	3	5	12	13	7		11²	8	14															6		9¹	10³	4	29
1	2	3	5		11	7																			6		9	10¹	4	30
1	2	4	13	9	14	8		7		11	6¹														5²	12	3³	10		31
1	2	4	3	9		12		7³		11¹	6	13													8	14	10	5²		32
1	5	3²	2	9	10¹			7		13	8³	14													6	12	11	4		33
1	2	3		8	14	9²		6		11¹	13	12													5	7³	10	4		34
1	2	3		5²	10	6¹		8		13	7	14													9	12	11²	4		35
1	2	3	12		11²	6³		8		13	7														14	5	9¹	10	4	36

BERWICK RANGERS

Year Formed: 1884. *Ground & Address:* Shielfield Park, Tweedmouth, Berwick-upon-Tweed TD15 2EF. *Telephone:* 01289 307424. *Fax:* 01289 309424. *Email:* club@berwickrangersfc.co.uk *Website:* berwickrangersfc.com
Ground Capacity: 4,131 (seated: 1,366). *Size of Pitch:* 101m × 64m.
Chairman: Brian Porteous. *Vice-Chairman:* John Bell. *Football Secretary:* Dennis McCleary.
Manager: Colin Cameron Dods. *Assistant Manager:* Robbie Horn. *Physio:* Steven Shaw.
Club Nicknames: 'The Borderers', 'Black and Gold', 'The Wee Gers'.
Previous Grounds: Bull Stob Close, Pier Field, Meadow Field, Union Park, Old Shielfield.
Record Transfer Fee received: £80,000 for John Hughes to Swansea C (Nov 1989).
Record Transfer Fee paid: £27,000 for Sandy Ross from Cowdenbeath (Mar 1991).
Record Attendance: 13,283 v Rangers, Scottish Cup 1st rd, 28 Jan 1967.
Record Victory: 8-1 v Forfar Ath, Division II, 25 Dec 1965; v Vale of Leithen, Scottish Cup, Dec 1966.
Record Defeat: 1-9 v Hamilton A, First Division, 9 Aug 1980.
Most League Appearances: 439: Eric Tait, 1970-87.
Most League Goals in Season (Individual): 33: Ken Bowron, Division II, 1963-64.
Most Goals Overall (Individual): 114: Eric Tait, 1970-87.

BERWICK RANGERS – SCOTTISH LEAGUE TWO 2014–15 LEAGUE RECORD

Match No.	Date	Venue	Opponents	Result	H/T Score	Lg Pos.	Goalscorers	Atten- dance
1	Aug 9	H	Arbroath	L 1-2	1-0	6	Willis [6]	590
2	16	A	East Fife	W 3-2	2-0	4	Currie, P [37], Walker (og) [43], Gold [89]	645
3	23	H	East Stirling	W 5-0	1-0	2	Currie, L [34], Cameron [64], Lavery [74], Dalziel [81], Fairbairn [87]	509
4	30	A	Clyde	D 3-3	2-1	3	Fairbairn [9], Currie, L [44], Gold [67]	511
5	Sept 13	A	Annan Ath	L 0-2	0-0	3		422
6	20	H	Albion R	D 1-1	1-1	4	Currie, P [15]	489
7	27	A	Queen's Park	L 0-2	0-2	7		351
8	Oct 15	H	Montrose	D 2-2	2-1	6	Lavery [13], Gray [28]	347
9	18	H	Elgin C	D 1-1	1-1	6	Currie, P [31]	410
10	25	A	Albion R	L 1-2	0-0	8	Lavery [71]	425
11	Nov 8	H	East Stirling	W 2-0	1-0	5	Lavery 2 [26, 88]	273
12	15	H	East Fife	L 2-3	0-0	8	Lavery 2 [78, 90]	490
13	22	H	Annan Ath	W 2-0	0-0	4	Lavery [63], Currie, L [88]	412
14	Dec 2	A	Montrose	L 1-2	1-1	7	Russell [30]	233
15	6	H	Clyde	W 4-0	1-0	5	Russell [27], Currie, L [47], Willis [64], Gray [84]	407
16	20	A	Arbroath	L 0-2	0-1	6		641
17	27	A	Queen's Park	D 0-0	0-0	5		598
18	Jan 3	H	East Stirling	W 3-0	2-0	5	Maxwell [31], Notman [34], Drummond [47]	474
19	10	A	Clyde	W 3-0	0-0	4	Lavery 2 [66, 82], Notman [76]	414
20	17	H	Montrose	D 3-3	2-1	4	Russell [38], Willis 2 (1 pen) [45, 84 (p)]	423
21	24	A	Annan Ath	L 2-4	0-3	5	Willis [80], Henderson [86]	370
22	31	H	Elgin C	L 0-2	0-0	5		371
23	Feb 14	H	Arbroath	W 3-1	0-0	5	Currie, L [66], Willis [72], Russell [90]	462
24	21	A	Queen's Park	L 1-2	0-0	5	Russell [78]	966
25	24	A	Elgin C	L 1-2	0-1	6	Willis (pen) [67]	411
26	28	H	Albion R	L 0-2	0-1	7		475
27	Mar 14	A	Annan Ath	D 2-2	1-0	9	Russell 2 [45, 51]	356
28	21	A	Montrose	W 2-0	0-0	8	Currie, L [74], Henderson [75]	320
29	24	A	East Fife	W 4-1	1-0	7	Willis [14], Wilkie [53], Henderson [70], Gold [90]	487
30	28	H	Queen's Park	D 1-1	1-1	8	Willis (pen) [40]	550
31	31	H	Elgin C	D 3-3	1-0	8	Henderson 2 [37, 75], Gold [85]	423
32	Apr 4	A	Albion R	L 0-2	0-0	9		439
33	11	H	Clyde	D 0-0	0-0	9		506
34	18	A	East Stirling	W 4-0	1-0	7	Russell [5], Wilkie [54], Henderson [60], Currie, L [83]	261
35	25	H	East Fife	L 0-3	0-1	8		523
36	May 2	A	Arbroath	L 0-5	0-0	8		564

Final League Position: 8

Honours
League Champions: Second Division 1978-79. Third Division 2006-07; *Runners-up:* Second Division 1993-94. Third Division 1999-2000, 2005-06 (not promoted).
Scottish Cup: Quarter-finals 1953-54, 1979-80.
League Cup: Semi-finals 1963-64.
League Challenge Cup: Quarter-finals 2004-05.

Club colours: Shirt: Black with gold vertical stripe. Shorts: Black. Socks: Black.

Goalscorers: *League (60):* Lavery 10, Willis 9 (3 pens), Russell 8, Currie, L 7, Henderson 6, Gold 4, Currie, P 3, Fairbairn 2, Gray 2, Notman 2, Wilkie 2, Cameron 1, Dalziel 1, Drummond 1, Maxwell 1, own goal 1.
William Hill Scottish FA Cup (9): Lavery 3, Dargo 2, Currie, L 1 (1 pen), Gold 1, Russell 1, Willis 1.
Scottish League Cup (1): Currie, L 1 (1 pen).
Petrofac Training Cup (3): Currie, L 1, Lavery 1, Maxwell 1.

Baird W 19	Jacobs D 30+2	Fairbairn J 28+1	Tulloch S 13	Hoskins D 12+1	Gold D 17+13	Notman S 24	Maxwell S 23+5	Willis P 31+3	Dalziel S 3+9	Lavery D 24+4	Russell A 21+6	Miller B 1+7	Horribine D 1+1	Currie P 8+3	Currie L 30+1	Cameron C 12+2	Dargo C 7+12	Andrews M 17+1	Young K 28	Gray R 10+16	Drummond R 14+1	Henderson B 10+3	Bauld E 2+1	Wilkie K 9	Dillon C 1+1	Martyniuk N 1+2	Match No.
2^3	3	4	5	6^2	7	8	9	10	11^1	12	13	14															1
1	2	3	4	5	14	7^1	9	6^2		11		12		8^1	10	13											2
1	5	3		4	6	2^1	11^2	9	13	10		12			8	7^3	14										3
1	5	3		4	6	2	11	9^2	12	10^1		13			8^4	7											4
12	13	4	5^1	8	2	9^3	6	11	10						7^2	14	1	3									5
5		4		8	2	11	14	12	10^3			6			7^2	9^1	1	3	13								6
5		4		6^2	2	10^1	8	14		13		9			7	11^3	1	3	12								7
		4	5	9	2			12	10^1	11		7	8	13			1	3	6^2								8
1	2		4	5	11^1	7	12			10				6^2	8				13	3	9						9
1	5^3	2	4		14			11		10				9^1	13	8	7^2	12		3	6						10
1			4^1	12	13	2		9		11	14			8	7		10^3			3	6^2	5					11
1				4		2		9	13	11	12			7	8		10^1			3	6	5^2					12
	2	3		5	13	7		6	12	11^1				8			10^2	1	4			9					13
	2	3		9		7	12	6^2	13	10				8			11^2	1	4	14		5^1					14
	2	3		5	6^1	7	13	9		11^3	10			12	8^2			1	4			14					15
	2	4		5^3	6^1	7		9	13	11	10^2			12	8			1	3			14					16
1	2	4			6	8	9	13		11^3	10^1			7			12			3		5					17
1	2	4			14	6	8	9^2		11^1	10			7^3			12			3		13	5				18
1	2	4			14	6	8^1	9		11^3	10^2			7			13			3		12	5				19
1	2	4				6	8^1	9		11^3	10^2			7			12			3^1	13	5	14				20
1	2^3	3	4			6	8^1	9		11	10^2			7			13				12	5	14				21
1	2^1	4■				6		9		11	13			7			10^2			3	8	5	12				22
1	2					12	3	13	9	11^3	14			8			7^2			4	6	5	10^1				23
1	2	4				8		10^1	7		12	11^3			9	6^2	14			3	13	5					24
1	2	4				10^2		9^1	8			11			6	7^2	12			3	13	5					25
1			4			6^3		12	9	11^2	10			8	7^1	13				3	14	5		2			26
1^1			4			9^3	8	5	7			11			13	6^2	3			12	3	14					27
	2	4				12	7	5	6						10^2	13		8^3			1	3	14	11	9^1		28
	2^3	4				12		5	6						10	13		7			1	3	8^1	11	14	9^2	29
	2	4				13		5	9						10^2	12		8			1	3	6^1	11	7		30
	2	4				12		5	9						10			8			1	3	6^1	11	7		31
	2	7				9^3		5	8						10^1			4			1	3^2	13	11	6	12 14	32
	2	4				12		5	6						13	9^1		7			1			10	8	11^2 3	33
12	3	4				9		5^3							13	10		8	7^2		1		14	11	2^1	6	34
2^2	3	4				9^1		5	12						13	10		8■		6	1			11	7		35
	2	3	4■			13			8^2					9^3	10^1	7		1	5	12			11		6	14	36

BRECHIN CITY

Year Formed: 1906. *Ground & Address:* Glebe Park, Trinity Rd, Brechin, Angus DD9 6BJ. *Telephone:* 01356 622856.
Fax: 01382 206331. *E-mail:* secretary@brechincityfc.com *Website:* www.brechincity.com
Ground Capacity: 3,960 (seated: 1,519). *Size of Pitch:* 101m × 61m.
Chairman: Kenneth Ferguson. *Vice-Chairman:* Martin Smith. *Secretary:* Gus Fairlie.
Manager: Darren Dods. *Assistant Manager:* Grant Johnson. *Coach:* Darren Taylor.
Club Nicknames: 'The City', 'The Hedgemen'.
Previous Grounds: Nursery Park.
Record Attendance: 8,122 v Aberdeen, Scottish Cup 3rd rd, 3 Feb 1973.
Record Transfer Fee received: £100,000 for Scott Thomson to Aberdeen (1991) and Chris Templeman to Morton (2004).
Record Transfer Fee paid: £16,000 for Sandy Ross from Berwick R (1991).
Record Victory: 12-1 v Thornhill, Scottish Cup 1st rd, 28 Jan 1926.
Record Defeat: 0-10 v Airdrieonians, Albion R and Cowdenbeath, all in Division II, 1937-38.
Most League Appearances: 459: David Watt, 1975-89.
Most League Goals in Season (Individual): 26: Ronald McIntosh, Division II, 1959-60.
Most Goals Overall (Individual): 131: Ian Campbell, 1977-85.

BRECHIN CITY – SCOTTISH LEAGUE ONE 2014–15 LEAGUE RECORD

Match No.	Date	Venue	Opponents	Result	H/T Score	Lg Pos.	Goalscorers	Attendance
1	Aug 9	A	Dunfermline Ath	D 0-0	0-0	7		2875
2	16	H	Stenhousemuir	W 1-0	1-0	4	Trouten [43]	418
3	23	A	Stranraer	D 2-2	2-0	3	Hamilton [16], Molloy [24]	432
4	30	H	Peterhead	D 1-1	0-0	5	McLean [49]	465
5	Sept 13	A	Stirling Alb	W 5-0	1-0	4	Jackson, A 2 [14, 63], Trouten 2 (1 pen) [67 (p), 89], Barr [77]	601
6	20	H	Ayr U	L 2-4	0-0	5	Trouten [49], Masson [59]	537
7	27	A	Forfar Ath	L 1-3	1-2	5	Hamilton [44]	628
8	Oct 4	H	Greenock Morton	W 3-1	2-0	4	Trouten (pen) [11], Thomson [33], McAusland [62]	557
9	11	A	Airdrieonians	L 0-4	0-2	5		718
10	18	H	Stranraer	L 1-2	1-1	7	Thomson [36]	407
11	25	A	Ayr U	W 2-0	2-0	5	Thomson [8], McAusland [26]	1060
12	Nov 11	H	Stirling Alb	W 2-1	1-0	5	Thomson [27], McLean [56]	408
13	15	H	Forfar Ath	D 3-3	2-1	5	Jackson, A [20], Barr [33], Trouten [82]	749
14	22	A	Peterhead	D 1-1	0-0	5	Trouten [64]	613
15	Dec 6	H	Airdrieonians	D 1-1	0-0	5	Barr [81]	437
16	13	A	Greenock Morton	D 2-2	2-0	5	Jackson, A [9], Masson [18]	1108
17	20	A	Stenhousemuir	W 2-0	1-0	5	Trouten (pen) [32], Thomson [90]	320
18	Jan 3	A	Forfar Ath	W 2-0	1-0	5	Masson [13], Trouten [81]	1110
19	10	H	Ayr U	W 2-1	1-0	4	McLean [16], Thomson [80]	504
20	17	A	Stranraer	W 2-0	1-0	4	Wighton 2 [44, 73]	470
21	31	A	Airdrieonians	D 1-1	0-0	4	Trouten [59]	676
22	Feb 14	H	Greenock Morton	D 1-1	0-0	5	Thomson [79]	602
23	21	A	Stirling Alb	W 1-0	0-0	4	Trouten (pen) [61]	568
24	24	A	Dunfermline Ath	W 1-0	0-0	4	Trouten [73]	1574
25	28	H	Stenhousemuir	W 2-1	1-1	3	Jackson, A [18], McLean [59]	506
26	Mar 3	H	Dunfermline Ath	D 1-1	0-1	3	McLean [58]	615
27	7	A	Airdrieonians	D 0-0	0-0	4		603
28	14	A	Peterhead	L 0-3	0-1	4		618
29	21	H	Forfar Ath	L 2-3	1-2	4	McLean [6], Jackson, A [84]	835
30	24	H	Peterhead	D 2-2	1-2	4	Hamilton [43], Barr (pen) [90]	519
31	28	A	Ayr U	D 2-2	1-0	4	Jackson, A [36], McLean [75]	986
32	Apr 4	A	Greenock Morton	W 2-0	0-0	4	Barr (pen) [79], Masson [88]	1823
33	11	H	Stirling Alb	W 2-1	1-0	4	Jackson, A 2 [12, 90]	427
34	18	H	Dunfermline Ath	W 3-0	2-0	4	Trouten 2 [25, 29], Jackson, A [64]	808
35	25	A	Stenhousemuir	D 2-2	2-2	4	Jackson, A [12], Trouten [20]	577
36	May 2	H	Stranraer	L 1-3	1-2	4	Ferguson [22]	538

Final League Position: 4

Honours
League Champions: Second Division 1982-83, 1989-90, 2004-05. Third Division 2001-02. C Division 1953-54;
Runners-up: Second Division 1992-93, 2002-03. Third Division 1995-96.
League Challenge Cup Runners-up: 2002-03.

Club colours: Shirt: Red with white trim. Shorts: White. Socks: Red.

Goalscorers: *League (58):* Trouten 15 (4 pens), Jackson, A 11, McLean 7, Thomson 7, Barr 5 (2 pens), Masson 4, Hamilton 3, McAusland 2, Wighton 2, Ferguson 1, Molloy 1.
William Hill Scottish FA Cup (8): Jackson, A 3, Hamilton 2, Barr 1 (1 pen), McAusland 1, Trouten 1 (1 pen).
Scottish League Cup (0).
Petrofac Training Cup (3): Ferguson 1, Thomson 1, Trouten 1.
Championship Play-Offs (1): Trouten 1.

Smith G 35	McCormack J 9+1	McCormack D 34	McLean P 32+1	Hamilton C 32	Ferguson R 9+12	Fusco G 26+7	Molloy C 26+5	Tapping C 6+7	Jackson A 31+3	Thomson R 23+11	Barr R 30+4	Cameron G 5+4	Trouten A 21+5	McLauchlan G 23+2	Masson J 21	McAusland K 7+1	McNeil E 14+4	Riordan D —+1	Wighton C 3+1	Storie C 6+3	Durojaiye O 1+2	Jackson S 1+1	O'Neil P 1	Match No.
1	2	3	4	5	6[1]	7	8	9[2]	10	11	12	13												1
1	2	3	4	5	9[3]	13	7	6[2]	10	11[1]	12	14	8											2
1	2	3	4	5		6[2]	7		9	11	12	10[3]	14	8[1]	13									3
1	2	3	4	5	13	12	7	8	9	11	10[1]	6[2]												4
1	2	4	3	5	14	13	7	8[3]	11		10[1]	6[2]	12			9								5
1	3	4	2	5		13	7		10	12	11[2]	8*	9[1]	8										6
1	2	4	3	5	7[1]	6[2]			11	13	9		8	10	12									7
1	2	4	3	5		12	7[1]	13	11[3]	10	14	8	9[2]	6										8
1	2[3]	4	3	5		12	7	13	10	11	6[1]	14	9	8[2]										9
1	12	3		5		9[2]	7		10	11	6		4	8	2[1]	13								10
1		3		5		12	7		10	11	6[1]		4	9	8	2								11
1	3	12	5*			7	13		10[2]	11[3]	6	8[1]	14	4	9	2								12
1			4	5		7	12		10	11[2]	6	8[1]	13	3	9	2								13
1	4[2]	2	5			9	11[3]	8	12	3	10		6		13									14
1		3		5	14	13	6[3]		9	11[2]	12	8[1]	4	10	7	2								15
1	3	2	5		7[1]	12	11[2]	13	9	6	4	10	8											16
1	3	2	5		8[2]	13	11	14	10	6[1]	4	9[3]	7				12							17
1	3	2	5		13	6	12	11	14	10	7[1]	4	8[3]				9[2]							18
1	4	2	5		13	7	8		10	12	9[1]	6	3				11[2]							19
1	4	2	5			7	8		10	12	9	6	3				11[1]							20
1	3	2	5			7	8		10	11[3]	9	6	4				12							21
1	3	2	5		8[1]	6	7	13	10	11	4						12		9[2]					22
1	3	2	5		8[1]	7	10[2]	11	9	6	4						12		13					23
1	3[2]	2	5		8[1]	14	7[3]	13	11	9	10	4					12		6					24
1		2	5		10[1]	12	7		9	11	8		4	3			6							25
1	3	2	5		8[1]	6	7		9	11	10		4				12							26
1	3	2	5			7	9		11	10	8		4				6							27
1	3	5*			12		13	9	11[1]	10	8	4	2				7				6[2]			28
1	3	5			12	6[3]	7	13	10	9	11[2]	4	2				8[1]				14			29
1	3	2	5		6[2]	7	13		11	12	10	4	9		8[1]									30
1	3		5		6[1]	7	8[2]	13*	10	11	4		9	2			12							31
1	3	2	5		13	7	8		10	11	6[2]		4[1]	9	12									32
1	4	3	5		6	7	12		9	11[1]	8		10	2										33
1	4	3	5		14	7	8[3]	13	10	12	9		11[1]	6[2]	2									34
1	3	2	5		8	7	12		10	11	6			9[1]	4									35
	3*	4			8	6	7	9[2]		11	12	13	10[1]	2								5	1	36

CELTIC

Year Formed: 1888. *Ground & Address:* Celtic Park, Glasgow G40 3RE. *Telephone:* 0871 226 1888. *Fax:* 0141 551 4223.
E-mail: customerservices@celticfc.co.uk *Website:* www.celticfc.net
Ground Capacity: 60,355 (all seated). *Size of Pitch:* 105m × 68m.
Chairman: Ian Bankier. *Chief Executive:* Peter Lawwell. *Secretary:* Michael Nicholson.
Manager: Ronny Deila. *Assistant Manager:* John Collins. *First Team Coach:* John Kennedy. *Physio:* Graham Parsons.
Club Nicknames: 'The Bhoys', 'The Hoops', 'The Celts'. *Previous Grounds:* None.
Record Attendance: 92,000 v Rangers, Division I, 1 Jan 1938.
Record Transfer Fee received: £6,500,000 for Stilian Petrov to Aston Villa (August 2007).
Record Transfer Fee paid: £6,000,000 for Chris Sutton from Chelsea (July 2000).
Record Victory: 11-0 Dundee, Division I, 26 Oct 1895.
Record Defeat: 0-8 v Motherwell, Division I, 30 Apr 1937.
Most Capped Player: Pat Bonner 80, Republic of Ireland.
Most League Appearances: 486: Billy McNeill, 1957-75.
Most League Goals in Season (Individual): 50: James McGrory, Division I, 1935-36.
Most Goals Overall (Individual): 397: James McGrory, 1922-39.

Honours
League Champions: (46 times) Division I 1892-93, 1893-94, 1895-96, 1897-98, 1904-05, 1905-06, 1906-07, 1907-08, 1908-09, 1909-10, 1913-14, 1914-15, 1915-16, 1916-17, 1918-19, 1921-22, 1925-26, 1935-36, 1937-38, 1953-54, 1965-66, 1966-67, 1967-68, 1968-69, 1969-70, 1970-71, 1971-72, 1972-73, 1973-74. Premier Division 1976-77, 1978-79, 1980-81, 1981-82, 1985-86, 1987-88, 1997-98, 2000-01, 2001-02, 2003-04, 2005-06, 2006-07, 2007-08, 2011-12, 2012-13; Premiership 2013-14, 2014-15. *Runners-up:* 31 times.
Scottish Cup Winners: (36 times) 1892, 1899, 1900, 1904, 1907, 1908, 1911, 1912, 1914, 1923, 1925, 1927, 1931, 1933, 1937, 1951, 1954, 1965, 1967, 1969, 1971, 1972, 1974, 1975, 1977, 1980, 1985, 1988, 1989, 1995, 2001, 2004, 2005, 2007, 2011, 2013. *Runners-up:* 18 times.

CELTIC – SCOTTISH PREMIER LEAGUE 2014–15 LEAGUE RECORD

Match No.	Date	Venue	Opponents	Result	H/T Score	Lg Pos.	Goalscorers	Attendance
1	Aug 13	A	St Johnstone	W 3-0	0-0	4	Stokes [55], Biton (pen) [76], McGregor [84]	6890
2	16	H	Dundee U	W 6-1	3-0	2	Denayer [4], Commons [27], Johansen [34], Stokes [54], Berget 2 [62, 90]	44,484
3	23	A	Inverness CT	L 0-1	0-0	5		5862
4	31	A	Dundee	D 1-1	0-1	5	Griffiths [55]	9276
5	Sept 13	H	Aberdeen	W 2-1	1-0	4	Denayer [7], Commons [46]	43,640
6	21	H	Motherwell	D 1-1	0-1	4	Commons (pen) [68]	41,719
7	27	A	St Mirren	W 2-1	1-0	4	Guidetti 2 [42, 63]	5280
8	Oct 5	H	Hamilton A	L 0-1	0-0	6		42,412
9	18	A	Ross Co	W 5-0	4-0	5	Guidetti [11], McGregor [14], Stokes 2 [29, 56], Denayer [35]	5693
10	26	H	Kilmarnock	W 2-0	1-0	4	Guidetti [35], Scepovic [64]	42,800
11	Nov 1	H	Inverness CT	W 1-0	0-0	3	Guidetti [49]	42,553
12	9	A	Aberdeen	W 2-1	1-1	1	Johansen [38], van Dijk [90]	19,051
13	22	H	Dundee	W 2-1	1-0	1	Stokes [45], Guidetti [54]	43,787
14	Dec 3	H	Partick Thistle	W 1-0	0-0	1	van Dijk [60]	40,633
15	6	A	Motherwell	W 1-0	1-0	1	Stokes [6]	7740
16	14	H	St Mirren	W 4-1	3-1	1	Brown 2 [4, 18], Forrest [15], Stokes [67]	44,827
17	21	A	Dundee U	L 1-2	0-1	1	Griffiths [87]	12,098
18	27	H	Ross Co	D 0-0	0-0	1		45,798
19	Jan 5	A	Kilmarnock	W 2-0	1-0	2	Izaguirre [36], Scepovic [72]	5329
20	17	A	Hamilton A	W 2-0	1-0	2	Matthews [33], Henderson [50]	6007
21	21	H	Motherwell	W 4-0	2-0	1	van Dijk [26], Griffiths [42], Lustig 2 [76, 81]	42,296
22	24	A	Ross Co	W 1-0	0-0	1	Commons [52]	5289
23	Feb 11	A	Partick Thistle	W 3-0	2-0	1	Mackay-Steven [1], Armstrong [30], Johansen [66]	5776
24	14	A	St Johnstone	W 2-1	1-0	1	Griffiths [1], Johansen [52]	6727
25	22	H	Hamilton A	W 4-0	0-0	1	Commons 2 [57, 82], Johansen [64], Guidetti [78]	47,989
26	Mar 1	H	Aberdeen	W 4-0	1-0	1	Denayer [37], Griffiths (pen) [63], Mackay-Steven [69], Johansen [80]	50,256
27	4	H	St Johnstone	L 0-1	0-0	1		41,849
28	21	H	Dundee U	W 3-0	3-0	1	Mackay-Steven [16], Guidetti [33], Denayer [45]	45,884
29	Apr 3	A	St Mirren	W 2-0	0-0	1	Forrest [64], Johansen (pen) [79]	5784
30	8	H	Partick Thistle	W 2-0	1-0	1	Commons (pen) [45], Johansen [63]	43,784
31	11	A	Inverness CT	D 1-1	1-1	1	Griffiths [3]	6059
32	15	H	Kilmarnock	W 4-1	0-0	1	Commons [58], Griffiths 3 [66, 80, 85]	42,464
33	22	A	Dundee	W 2-1	1-0	1	Mackay-Steven [32], van Dijk [63]	8908
34	26	A	Dundee U	W 3-0	0-0	1	Griffiths 3 (1 pen) [47, 65, 84 (p)]	8329
35	May 1	H	Dundee	W 5-0	2-0	1	Griffiths [30], Brown [37], Commons (pen) [71], Forrest [77], Biton [88]	44,299
36	10	A	Aberdeen	W 1-0	0-0	1	Brown [49]	16,742
37	15	A	St Johnstone	D 0-0	0-0	1		6984
38	24	H	Inverness CT	W 5-0	2-0	1	Scepovic 2 [5, 70], Johansen [18], Griffiths [80], Commons [90]	55,638

Final League Position: 1

League Cup Winners: (15 times) 1956-57, 1957-58, 1965-66, 1966-67, 1967-68, 1968-69, 1969-70, 1974-75, 1982-83, 1997-98, 1999-2000, 2000-01, 2005-06, 2008-09, 2014-15; *Runners-up:* 15 times.

European: *European Cup/Champions League:* 170 matches (1966-67 winners, 1967-68, 1968-69, 1969-70 runners-up, 1970-71, 1971-72, 1972-73, 1973-74 semi-finals, 1974-75, 1977-78, 1979-80, 1981-82, 1982-83, 1986-87, 1988-89, 1998-99, 2001-02, 2002-03, 2003-04, 2004-05, 2005-06, 2006-07, 2007-08, 2008-09, 2009-10, 2010-11, 2012-13, 2013-14, 2014-15). *Cup Winners' Cup:* 38 matches (1963-64 semi-finals, 1965-66 semi-finals, 1975-76, 1980-81, 1984-85, 1985-86, 1989-90, 1995-96). *UEFA Cup:* 75 matches (*Fairs Cup:* 1962-63, 1964-65. *UEFA Cup:* 1976-77, 1983-84, 1987-88, 1991-92, 1992-93, 1993-94, 1996-97, 1997-98, 1998-99, 1999-2000, 2000-01, 2001-02, 2002-03 runners-up, 2003-04 quarter-finals). *Europa League:* 24 matches (2009-10, 2010-11, 2011-12, 2014-15).

Club colours: Shirt: Green and white hoops. Shorts: White. Socks: White with green hoops.

Goalscorers: *League (84):* Griffiths 14 (2 pens), Commons 10 (3 pens), Johansen 9 (1 pen), Guidetti 8, Stokes 7, Denayer 5, Brown 4, Mackay-Steven 4, Scepovic 4, van Dijk 4, Forrest 3, Berget 2, Biton 2 (1 pen), Lustig 2, McGregor 2, Armstrong 1, Henderson 1, Izaguirre 1, Matthews 1.
William Hill Scottish FA Cup (13): van Dijk 4, Griffiths 3, Guidetti 2 (1 pen), Commons 1, Denayer 1, Johansen 1, Stokes 1.
Scottish League Cup (13): Guidetti 4 (1 pen), Commons 3 (1 pen), Griffiths 3, Forrest 1, Izaguirre 1, own goal 1.
UEFA Champions League (7): McGregor 3, Pukki 2, van Dijk 2.
UEFA Europa League (13): Johansen 3, Commons 2, Scepovic 2, Armstrong 1, Brown 1, Guidetti 1, Wakaso 1, own goals 2.

Gordon C 33	Matthews A 24+5	Lustig M 3+2	van Dijk V 35	Izaguirre E 34+1	Forrest J 12+7	Biton N 24+7	Commons K 20+9	McGregor C 8+10	Stokes A 18+3	Johansen S 33+1	Boerrigter D —+1	Berget J 2+2	Kayal B 2+4	Ambrose E 21+6	Denayer J 29	Mulgrew C 7+3	Griffiths L 14+10	Zaluska L 5	O'Connell E 2+1	McGeouch D 1	Henderson L 4+5	Twardzik F 1	Pukki T 1	Brown S 31+1	Tonev A 3+3	Scepovic S 4+14	Guidetti J 19+5	Wakaso M 4+1	Fisher D 1+4	Mackay-Steven G 10+3	Armstrong S 12+3	Tierney K 1+1	Match No.
1	2	3	4	5	6³	7	8¹	9	10²	11		12	13	14																			1
1		3	5	13		9	8¹	11²	6³	10		12	2	4	7	14																	2
					7	9	12	14	13			2		4	10³	1	3	5	6	8²	11¹												3
1	2¹		5		14	10	6	11	7		9³	8²	3	4		12	13																4
1		4	5	14	10	6		8		13	2	3			1									7²	9³	11¹	12						5
		4	5	8	12	6	11			7²	2	3			1									13	9¹	14	10³						6
1		3	5	14		9	11¹	8	13	2				4										7		12	10³	6²					7
1		4	5		9	10	7			3	13													6	12	11²	8¹						8
1	12	2¹	4	5³	13		6	10	8	3	9													7		14	11²						9
1	2		4	5		6		8¹		3	12	13												7	14	11³	10	9²					10
12	2³	4	5			13	10	9		3	7	14	1											6		11²	8¹						11
	2³	14	4	5	8¹			12	9²	7					3	10	13	1						6•		11							12
1	2		4	5	8¹		9³	14	10	7				13	12	3²	6									11							13
1	2		4	5	12	13		10	9					3			7³							6	8²	14	11¹						14
1	2		4	5	8³	7	14	10¹	9					3										6	12	13	11²						15
1	2		4	5	8³	7¹		12	10	9				3			14							6		13	10²						16
1	2		4	5	6	7¹	12	11³	9					3			14							8		13	10²						17
1	2		4	5		6	13	12²	8² 10					3			9							7		14	11¹						18
1	2¹		4	5		7	9	14		8				3								10²		6		11³ 13		12					19
1		2	3	5		8	10¹	12		9					4		11						6²	7		13							20
1	2² 12	3	5	13	6	9		8³	10⁵					4		11							7		14								21
1	2		3	5		7	8² 13			14				4	10¹		9							6		12	11³						22
1	2¹		4	5	7		14	9³		3							12							6		11		13	8² 10				23
1	2		4	5	7		12 10			14	3			11¹		13								6		11			8²	9³			24
1	12		4	5	10¹	7	9			2	3⁰				14									6		11			13				25
1	5		4		6	9¹	14	8		2	3			11²										7		13		10	12³				26
1	2²	4		13 14				10³ 9		5	3			11										7		12		8¹ 6					27
1		4	5	6	12		9			2	3			11			14							7	13	11²		8¹ 10³					28
1	2³	3	5	8	13	9²	11	7		12				4			11							7		14		10¹					29
1	2³		4	5	12	6	9²			7				3	14									11¹		13	8 10						30
1	13	4	5		7	12		9		2³	3			11³			6							14		10² 8							31
1	2		4	5	10³	7	8¹			9²	3			12			6							11		14 13							32
1		3	5³	8¹	6 12			2		4				11²			7							13		10 9 14							33
1	2²	3	5	14	6	8		9³		13	4			11			7							12		10¹							34
1		4	5	12	6	8		9³		2³	3			11¹			7							14		13 10							35
1	12	4	5	13	6	8²		9		14	3			11			7							2³		10¹							36
	2		13	8	9²					4¹ 12	11	1		6			14							10	7	5³							37
1	2¹	4	5	10	6	13		9		3	12			14			7							11³		8²							38

CLYDE

Year Formed: 1877. *Ground & Address:* Broadwood Stadium, Cumbernauld, G68 9NE. *Telephone:* 01236 451511.
Fax: 01236 733490. *E-mail:* info@clydefc.co.uk *Website:* www.clydefc.co.uk
Ground Capacity: 8,006 (all seated). *Size of Pitch:* 100m × 68m.
Chairman: John Alexander. *Secretary:* Gordon Thomson.
Manager: Barry Ferguson. *Assistant Manager:* Robert Malcolm. *Physio:* Iain McKinlay.
Club Nickname: 'The Bully Wee'.
Previous Grounds: Barrowfield Park 1877-98, Shawfield Stadium 1898-1986, Firhill Stadium 1986-91, Douglas Park 1991-94.
Record Attendance: 52,000 v Rangers, Division I, 21 Nov 1908.
Record Transfer Fee received: £200,000 from Blackburn R for Gordon Greer (May 2001).
Record Transfer Fee paid: £14,000 for Harry Hood from Sunderland (1966).
Record Victory: 11-1 v Cowdenbeath, Division II, 6 Oct 1951.
Record Defeat: 0-11 v Dumbarton, Scottish Cup 4th rd, 22 Nov, 1879; v Rangers, Scottish Cup 4th rd, 13 Nov 1880.
Most Capped Player: Tommy Ring, 12, Scotland.
Most League Appearances: 420: Brian Ahern, 1971-81; 1987-88.
Most League Goals in Season (Individual): 32: Bill Boyd, 1932-33.
Most Goals Overall (Individual): 124: Tommy Ring, 1950-60.

CLYDE – SCOTTISH LEAGUE TWO 2014–15 LEAGUE RECORD

Match No.	Date		Venue	Opponents	Result		H/T Score	Lg Pos.	Goalscorers	Atten- dance
1	Aug	9	A	Queen's Park	W	2-1	0-0	2	McKinnon (pen) [78], Daly [89]	685
2		23	A	Elgin C	L	0-1	0-1	6		603
3		30	H	Berwick R	D	3-3	1-2	6	McManus 2 (1 pen) [34, 76 (p)], Daly [80]	511
4	Sept	13	A	East Stirling	L	0-1	0-0	9		470
5		20	H	Arbroath	L	2-5	2-2	10	Ferguson, S 2 [36, 45]	614
6		23	H	Montrose	L	1-2	1-1	10	Watt [11]	459
7		27	H	Annan Ath	D	1-1	1-0	10	Smith [39]	605
8	Oct	11	A	East Fife	W	1-0	1-0	9	McManus [38]	596
9		18	A	Albion R	D	2-2	2-1	8	McManus 2 (2 pens) [4, 44]	715
10		25	H	Elgin C	W	2-1	1-0	6	Watt 2 [29, 60]	419
11	Nov	8	A	Montrose	W	3-0	2-0	4	Ferguson, S [1], Murray, E [27], McIlduff [72]	405
12		15	H	East Stirling	L	0-1	0-1	5		456
13		22	A	Arbroath	L	0-4	0-4	6		656
14		29	H	Queen's Park	L	0-2	0-1	7		589
15	Dec	6	A	Berwick R	L	0-4	0-1	9		407
16		13	H	Albion R	L	0-1	0-1	9		422
17		20	H	East Fife	W	3-1	0-1	7	McQueen [55], Smith [66], Traynor [80]	456
18		27	A	Annan Ath	L	1-2	1-1	7	Sinclair [32]	578
19	Jan	3	A	Queen's Park	D	1-1	0-0	7	Gray, I [54]	2027
20		10	H	Berwick R	L	0-3	0-0	7		414
21		24	H	Arbroath	D	1-1	1-0	7	Fisher [20]	598
22		31	A	East Stirling	W	2-1	0-0	6	O'Donnell [53], McManus [80]	362
23	Feb	14	A	Albion R	W	2-0	1-0	7	McDougall [14], Ferguson, S [79]	714
24		21	A	East Fife	D	1-1	0-0	8	McQueen [65]	551
25		28	H	Montrose	W	2-0	0-0	8	Wood (og) [57], Ferguson, S [80]	447
26	Mar	3	A	Annan Ath	W	1-0	1-0	6	Roberts [45]	402
27		7	H	East Stirling	D	1-1	1-1	6	McQueen [33]	593
28		10	A	Elgin C	L	0-2	0-1	7		403
29		14	A	Arbroath	L	1-3	0-2	8	Parker [90]	673
30		21	H	Elgin C	L	0-2	0-1	9		448
31		28	A	Annan Ath	W	1-0	0-0	9	Pollock [87]	485
32	Apr	4	H	East Fife	W	1-0	0-0	8	McManus [70]	620
33		11	A	Berwick R	D	0-0	0-0	8		506
34		18	A	Albion R	L	2-3	2-1	9	McQueen [20], Marsh [28]	739
35		25	A	Montrose	W	1-0	0-0	7	Marsh [52]	338
36	May	2	H	Queen's Park	W	2-0	1-0	6	McDougall [34], McQueen [70]	664

Final League Position: 6

Honours
League Champions: Division II 1904-05, 1951-52, 1956-57, 1961-62, 1972-73. Second Division 1977-78, 1981-82, 1992-93, 1999-2000; *Runners-up:* Division II 1903-04, 1905-06, 1925-26, 1963-64. First Division 2002-03, 2003-04.
Scottish Cup Winners: 1939, 1955, 1958; *Runners-up:* 1910, 1912, 1949.
League Challenge Cup Runners-up: 2006-07.

Club colours: Shirt: White with black trim. Shorts: Black. Socks: Red.

Goalscorers: *League (40):* McManus 7 (3 pens), Ferguson, S 5, McQueen 5, Watt 3, Daly 2, Marsh 2, McDougall 2, Smith 2, Fisher 1, Gray, I 1, McIlduff 1, McKinnon 1 (1 pen), Murray, E 1, O'Donnell 1, Parker 1, Pollock 1, Roberts 1, Sinclair 1, Traynor 1, own goal 1.
William Hill Scottish FA Cup (3): Ferguson, S 1, McManus 1, Watt 1.
Scottish League Cup (1): Gray 1.
Petrofac Training Cup (3): McManus 1, Sweeney 1 (1 pen), Watt 1.

The following is a players' appearance and goalscorer grid. Player names with appearances (+ substitute appearances) appear as column headings; each cell shows the shirt number worn with goals scored as a superscript. The right-hand column shows the Match Number (1–36).

Column headings (left to right): Barclay J 5 · Durie S 36 · Marsh D 26 + 1 · McQueen B 23 + 7 · McKinnon R 4 · Capuano G 1 · Gray D 16 + 8 · Sinclair D 8 + 3 · Ferguson S 22 + 5 · McManus S 21 + 4 · Watt K 9 + 6 · McColm S — + 2 · Young G — + 3 · Pollock J 4 + 3 · Daly M 5 + 8 · Lynass C 1 + 1 · Frances R 6 · Sweeney J 1 · O'Donnell S 21 + 5 · Gibson A 9 + 1 · Halkett C 10 · Robb B 3 · McIlduff A 10 + 1 · Smith E 15 · McLeish C 2 + 2 · Murray E 3 + 4 · Martin A 31 · Ferguson B 1 · McGhee F 3 + 3 · Currie J — + 3 · Gray 14 + 1 · McBrearty C — + 1 · Traynor G 19 · Fisher R 12 + 2 · Murray H 17 · McDougall S 12 + 4 · McLaughlin M 13 · Roberts M 4 + 6 · McLaughlin S 4 · Parker K 9 + 1 · Slane P 6 + 2 · Match No.

COWDENBEATH

Year Formed: 1882. *Ground & Address:* Central Park, Cowdenbeath KY4 9QQ. *Telephone:* 01383 610166. *Fax:* 01383 512132.
E-mail: office@cowdenbeathfc.com *Website:* www.cowdenbeathfc.com
Ground Capacity: 4,370 (seated: 1,431). *Size of Pitch:* 98m × 59m.
Chairman: Donald Findlay QC. *Vice-Chairman:* John Lints. *Operations:* John Cameron.
Club Nicknames: 'The Blue Brazil', 'Cowden', 'The Miners'.
Manager: Colin Nish. *Assistant Manager:* Lee Makel. *Physio:* Grant McLeod.
Previous Grounds: North End Park.
Record Attendance: 25,586 v Rangers, League Cup quarter-final, 21 Sept 1949.
Record Transfer Fee received: £30,000 for Nicky Henderson to Falkirk (March 1994).
Record Victory: 12-0 v Johnstone, Scottish Cup 1st rd, 21 Jan 1928.
Record Defeat: 1-11 v Clyde, Division II, 6 Oct 1951.
Most Capped Player: Jim Paterson, 3, Scotland.
Most League and Cup Appearances: 491, Ray Allan 1972-75, 1979-89.
Most League Goals in Season (Individual): 54, Rab Walls, Division II, 1938-39.
Most Goals Overall (Individual): 127, Willie Devlin, 1922-26, 1929-30.

COWDENBEATH – SCOTTISH CHAMPIONSHIP 2014–15 LEAGUE RECORD

Match No.	Date		Venue	Opponents	Result		H/T Score	Lg Pos.	Goalscorers	Atten- dance
1	Aug	9	H	Falkirk	D	2-2	1-0	4	Milne [34], Higgins [57]	1074
2		16	A	Livingston	L	1-2	0-0	7	Milne [89]	1147
3		23	H	Alloa Ath	L	0-3	0-1	9		549
4		30	H	Raith R	L	1-3	0-1	10	Milne [90]	1216
5	Sept	13	A	Hibernian	L	2-3	0-1	10	Higgins [50], Robertson [56]	11,021
6		20	A	Hearts	L	1-5	1-1	10	Gallagher [21]	15,594
7		27	H	Queen of the South	W	2-1	2-0	10	Oyenuga [28], Gallagher [41]	674
8	Oct	4	A	Dumbarton	D	0-0	0-0	10		851
9		18	A	Alloa Ath	W	3-2	1-0	8	Oyenuga 2 [34, 60], Gallagher [65]	643
10		25	A	Falkirk	L	0-6	0-4	10		3466
11	Nov	4	H	Rangers	L	0-3	0-1	10		3919
12		8	H	Hibernian	L	1-2	0-2	10	Robertson [63]	2563
13		15	A	Raith R	L	1-2	1-0	10	Oyenuga [35]	1779
14		22	H	Livingston	W	1-0	0-0	9	Gallagher [54]	542
15	Dec	6	A	Rangers	L	0-1	0-0	9		28,137
16		20	A	Queen of the South	W	2-1	1-0	8	Gallagher [41], Higgins [90]	1717
17		23	H	Hearts	L	0-2	0-1	8		3718
18		27	H	Dumbarton	L	1-3	0-1	8	Sutherland [66]	556
19	Jan	3	H	Raith R	L	0-1	0-0	8		1265
20		10	A	Livingston	D	1-1	1-1	8	Mensing (og) [26]	829
21		17	A	Hibernian	L	0-5	0-2	8		8240
22		31	H	Queen of the South	L	0-5	0-1	8		569
23	Feb	14	A	Dumbarton	W	2-1	0-1	8	Brownlie [70], Oyenuga [73]	756
24		21	A	Alloa Ath	L	0-2	0-0	9		505
25		28	A	Hearts	L	0-10	0-5	9		15,180
26	Mar	7	H	Rangers	D	0-0	0-0	9		3244
27		14	H	Hibernian	L	0-2	0-2	8		1822
28		21	A	Queen of the South	L	1-4	0-1	9	Higgins [60]	1671
29		24	H	Falkirk	L	0-1	0-0	9		565
30		28	A	Rangers	L	1-4	0-0	9	Oyenuga [76]	32,682
31		31	A	Falkirk	L	0-1	0-1	9		3220
32	Apr	4	H	Dumbarton	W	3-0	1-0	8	Toshney [44], Higgins [48], Nish [79]	515
33		8	A	Raith R	W	3-1	1-0	8	Nish 3 [33, 61, 90]	1350
34		11	H	Livingston	L	1-2	0-0	8	Wedderburn [48]	624
35		25	H	Hearts	L	1-2	1-1	8	Marshall [14]	2394
36	May	2	A	Alloa Ath	L	0-3	0-1	10		1219

Final League Position: 10

Honours
League Champions: Division II 1913-14, 1914-15, 1938-39. Second Division 2011-12. Third Division 2005-06. *Runners-up:* Division II 1921-22, 1923-24, 1969-70. Second Division 1991-92. Third Division 2000-01, 2008-09. *Promoted to First Division:* 2009-10 (play-offs).
Scottish Cup: Quarter-finals 1931.
League Cup: Semi-finals 1959-60, 1970-71.

Club colours: Shirt: Royal blue. Shorts: White. Socks: Red.

Goalscorers: *League (31):* Oyenuga 6, Gallagher 5, Higgins 5, Nish 4, Milne 3, Robertson 2, Brownlie 1, Marshall 1, Sutherland 1, Toshney 1, Wedderburn 1, own goal 1.
William Hill Scottish FA Cup (3): Higgins 1, Hughes 1, Milne 1.
Scottish League Cup (2): Miller 1, Milne 1.
Petrofac Training Cup (1): Higgins 1.

Flynn T 4	Armstrong J 16 + 1	O'Brien T 28 + 3	Wedderburn N 28 + 1	Brett D 12 + 3	Miller K 21 + 4	Milne L 22 + 5	Robertson J 29 + 2	Adamson K 10 + 4	Johnston C 3 + 11	Higgins S 30 + 2	Sutherland C 2 + 10	Kane C 12 + 4	Jurisic D — + 4	Campbell I 9 + 4	Brownlie D 19 + 4	Oyenuga K 24 + 4	Thomson R 32	Fraser M 11	Gallagher C 10	Hughes D 10 + 3	Scullion P — + 3	Marshall C 23	Halsman J 8	Gallaghan L 1	Buchanan R 4 + 6	Herron J 5	Nish C 11 + 2	Toshney L 12 + 1	Match No.
1	2	3	4	5	6	7	8	9	10¹	11	12																		1
1	3	7	4	2	10²	9	8	5¹		11	12	6¹	13	14															2
1	2	8	4	5	6	7	9	12²	10	11¹		13			3														3
1	12	3²	2	9¹	7	6	13	11	8	5	4	10																	4
	3	4	14	7	6	13	11	8³						5	12	10¹	1	2	9²										5
	4	7²	3		6	13	11	14		5¹	12	10¹					1	2	9	8									6
	2		5		6		12	10¹		7²		8	4	9	1	3	11		13										7
	2		5		6		10¹	12	7	8	4	9	1	3	11														8
	7	14	12	2		8	13	10		6		5²	3	11³	1	4	9¹												9
	2³		12	5	13	7		11	14	6¹		8²	4	10	1	3	9												10
	4	2¹	5	9	8		14	11	13	12			10	1	3		7²		6³										11
	4	5	2	8	6			11	12		13		10²	1	3	9		7¹											12
	6	4	5¹	2	9			11	12³	14		13		10	1	3	8²		7										13
	10¹	4		2	9²	6		13	11¹			12	7	1	3	8		14	5										14
	4		2	8	7		12	11				10	1	3		9¹		6	5										15
	4	3	2	7	6²			10	12	14		13		1		11¹	9		8¹	5									16
	3	4	2	9		8²	11	12	6¹	14	13		1				7	5	10³										17
	3⁴	4	2	8	9		11	10	6¹			1					12	7	5										18
	6	4	2	9¹	10		11	13		7²	3		1		12		8	5											19
	2	3	5	12	8		11¹			4	10	1		6	7	9													20
	3	4	2	7	6		10			11	1			8¹		9	5	12											21
	3	4	2	8		13	12			7	1			6	5²	11¹	9	10											22
	3		8			5	12	7		4	10¹	1		6			9	11	2										23
	2		12	5³	14	13	9²		6		3	11	1		7¹		8	10	4										24
12	3	4	5		13	6	9			7¹		1		8			10²	11	2⁴										25
	3	7	4	5		6		9		10¹			2	12	1		8		8	11									26
	3	7	4	5³		10	12	8	14	9²			2¹	11	1		6						13						27
	3	7	4			8³	6¹	5	9					13	1		14	11²	10	12	2								28
	3	6	4			8	5⁴	10						12	1		9²	7¹	13	11	2								29
	3	14	4		12	8²	7		11¹				2	10	1		9³	6	13		5								30
	4	13	5		8²	7	6¹						3	11	1		9		10	12	2								31
	4	9	5			7	12	11¹					3	8²	1		6		13	11	5								32
	3³	4	8		14	7	12	10¹					2	9¹	1		6		13	11	5								33
	3	7	4			8	14	9²	12				2	11	1		6¹		13	10³	5								34
	4	6	5²		12	7¹	8	13					3	11	1		9		10	2									35
	4	6³			12	8		9²					5	3	13	1		14	7¹	10	11	2							36

DUMBARTON

Year Formed: 1872. *Ground:* Dumbarton Football Stadium, Castle Road, Dumbarton G82 1JJ. *Telephone/Fax:* 01389 762569. *E-mail:* enquiries@dumbartonfc.com *Website:* www.dumbartonfootballclub.com
Ground Capacity: total: 2,025. *Size of Pitch:* 104m × 69m.
Chairman: Alan Jardine. *Vice-Chairman:* Colin Hosie. *Chief Executive Officer:* Gilbert Lawrie.
Manager: Stephen Aitken. *Assistant Manager:* Stephen Farrell. *Physio:* Douglas Fyffe.
Club Nickname: 'The Sons', 'Sons of the Rock'.
Previous Grounds: Broadmeadow, Ropework Lane, Townend Ground, Boghead Park, Cliftonhill Stadium.
Record Attendance: 18,000 v Raith R, Scottish Cup, 2 Mar 1957.
Record Transfer Fee received: £125,000 for Graeme Sharp to Everton (March 1982).
Record Transfer Fee paid: £50,000 for Charlie Gibson from Stirling Alb (1989).
Record Victory: 13-1 v Kirkintilloch Central, Scottish Cup 1st rd, 1 Sept 1888.
Record Defeat: 1-11 v Albion R, Division II, 30 Jan 1926: v Ayr U, League Cup, 13 Aug 1952.
Most Capped Player: James McAulay, 9, Scotland.
Most League Appearances: 298: Andy Jardine, 1957-67.
Most Goals in Season (Individual): 38: Kenny Wilson, Division II, 1971-72. *(League and Cup):* 46 Hughie Gallacher, 1955-56.
Most Goals Overall (Individual): 202: Hughie Gallacher, 1954-62

DUMBARTON – SCOTTISH CHAMPIONSHIP 2014–15 LEAGUE RECORD

Match No.	Date	Venue	Opponents	Result	H/T Score	Lg Pos.	Goalscorers	Atten- dance
1	Aug 9	A	Raith R	L 1-3	0-0	9	Agnew [90]	1642
2	16	H	Queen of the South	L 0-4	0-1	10		958
3	23	A	Rangers	L 1-4	0-2	10	Mohsni (og) [81]	31,175
4	30	H	Livingston	W 1-0	0-0	9	Kane [88]	814
5	Sept 13	H	Hearts	D 0-0	0-0	9		1757
6	20	A	Falkirk	D 1-1	0-1	9	Kane [90]	3503
7	27	H	Alloa Ath	W 3-1	1-0	5	Campbell [39], Kirkpatrick [54], Nish [78]	758
8	Oct 4	H	Cowdenbeath	D 0-0	0-0	7		851
9	11	A	Hibernian	D 0-0	0-0	7		7923
10	18	A	Hearts	L 1-5	0-2	7	Fleming [73]	15,522
11	25	H	Rangers	L 0-3	0-1	7		1850
12	Nov 8	A	Queen of the South	L 0-3	0-1	8		1677
13	15	A	Livingston	W 2-1	0-1	7	Fleming [62], Megginson [70]	1020
14	22	H	Hibernian	L 3-6	0-3	7	Kane [50], Graham [61], Fleming [71]	1409
15	Dec 6	A	Alloa Ath	W 1-0	1-0	7	Kane [9]	666
16	13	H	Raith R	W 2-1	1-0	6	Agnew 2 (1 pen) [20, 88 (p)]	764
17	20	H	Falkirk	L 0-3	0-1	6		663
18	27	A	Cowdenbeath	W 3-1	1-0	6	Nish [36], Mair [68], Fleming [73]	556
19	Jan 3	A	Rangers	L 1-3	1-2	7	Graham [15]	30,031
20	10	H	Hearts	L 1-5	0-2	7	Kane [63]	1537
21	17	A	Raith R	L 1-2	0-2	7	Megginson [81]	1474
22	24	H	Livingston	L 1-5	0-1	7	McCallum [87]	793
23	31	A	Falkirk	D 3-3	1-2	7	Taggart [19], Petrie [63], Campbell [71]	3703
24	Feb 14	H	Cowdenbeath	L 1-2	1-0	7	Taggart [34]	756
25	21	A	Hibernian	L 0-3	0-2	7		8370
26	28	H	Queen of the South	D 0-0	0-0	7		904
27	Mar 7	H	Alloa Ath	W 1-0	1-0	7	Fleming (pen) [42]	791
28	14	A	Hearts	L 0-4	0-0	7		15,631
29	21	A	Livingston	W 2-1	0-1	7	Agnew [80], Fleming [88]	831
30	28	H	Falkirk	W 1-0	0-0	7	Campbell [81]	1016
31	Apr 4	A	Cowdenbeath	L 0-3	0-1	7		515
32	8	H	Hibernian	L 1-2	0-1	7	Megginson [55]	1110
33	11	A	Alloa Ath	L 0-3	0-2	7		535
34	18	H	Rangers	L 1-3	1-1	7	Wilson [2]	1766
35	25	A	Queen of the South	L 1-2	0-0	7	McCallum [90]	1865
36	May 2	H	Raith R	D 2-2	1-0	7	Kirkpatrick [21], Agnew [78]	801

Final League Position: 7

Honours

League Champions: Division I 1890-91 (shared with Rangers), 1891-92. Division II 1910-11, 1971-72. Second Division 1991-92. Third Division 2008-09; *Runners-up:* First Division 1983-84. Division II 1907-08. Second Division 1994-95. Third Division 2001-02.
Scottish Cup Winners: 1883; *Runners-up:* 1881, 1882, 1887, 1891, 1897.

Club colours: Shirt: White with yellow and black horizontal stripe. Shorts: White. Socks: White.

Goalscorers: *League (36):* Fleming 6 (1 pen), Agnew 5 (1 pen), Kane 5, Campbell 3, Megginson 3, Graham 2, Kirkpatrick 2, McCallum 2, Nish 2, Taggart 2, Mair 1, Petrie 1, Wilson 1, own goal 1.
William Hill Scottish FA Cup (0).
Scottish League Cup (3): Gilhaney 1, Graham 1, Megginson 1.
Petrofac Training Cup (2): Gilhaney 1, Kirkpatrick 1.

Rogers D 34	van Zanten D 19	Graham A 34	Mair L 12+1	Linton S 24+4	Kirkpatrick J 15+5	Turner C 20+5	Agnew S 35+1	Megginson M 26+10	Nish C 14+6	Campbell A 20+14	Gilhaney M 27+6	Fleming G 29+3	Prunty B —+2	Taggart S 28+5	Murray H —+1	MacDonald K 4+9	Kane C 8+2	McDougall S 2+6	McLaughlin M 2+1	Ewings J 2	McCallum D —+5	Findlay S 15	Easton D 8+5	Petrie D 5+3	Wilson M 9+2	Duggan C 4+3	Clark R —+2	Match No.
1	2¹	3	4	5	6	7	8	9²	10	11³	12	13	14															1
1	2	3	4	5	6	7	8²	9	10³	11¹	12	13	14															2
1	2	3	4²	5	9³	6¹	12	13	11	10	8			7	14													3
1	2²	4		5		7	8	9	10¹	14	6	11³		3		12	13											4
1	2²	3		5	9		8³	7	10¹	14	6	13		4		12	11											5
1	2	3		5	9³		8	7²	12	13	6	11¹		4			10	14										6
1	2	3		5	7		8	9¹	13	10	6²	11³		4		12		14										7
1	2³	3		5	7¹		8²	9	12	10	6	11		4		13		14										8
1	2	3		5	10		7¹	8²	11	13	6	9³		4		12			14									9
1	2	3		5	9³		7¹	8	11²	13	6	10		4		12		14										10
1	2¹	3	4	5	9²	14	8	7¹	11	13	6	10		4		12													11
	2	4			13	7	10	12	11	6²	8¹		5		9		14	3³	1									12
	2	4		13	6	7	8²	9	12	5	10¹		3		14		11³		1									13
1		2	3		14	6	7	10³	11		5	9		8²		13	12		4¹									14
1	4	3			12	7³	8	11	13	14	5	9²		2		6	10¹											15
1	2	3			7¹		8	9²	12	14	6³	10		4		5	11	13										16
1	2³	3		14		12	7	9¹	11	13		6		4		5	10	8²										17
1	2	3	4	5		8¹	7	12	10	6³	13	9²		14			11											18
1	2³	3	4	5		8	6	13	11	9¹	12	7²		14			10											19
1	2	3	4	5		7	8	12	11³	9²	6			13			10¹					14						20
1	2	3	4	5¹		8	7	10		11		9		12										6				21
1	5²	2	4	9		6¹	7	8		13		10		12								14	3	11³				22
1		3	13	5¹			7	10		11²	8			2								12	4	9	6			23
1		3		5²		12	6	8		11	7¹	10		2									4	9		13		24
1			5²		13	7	10			11	6³	8		3									4	9¹	14	2	12	25
1		4		5		8	7¹	13		12	6²	10³		2									3	9		14	11	26
1		4		5		7²	8	14		13	6	10²		2									3	9¹	12		11	27
1		3	5¹			8	7	14		13	10			4									9	12	6	2³	11²	28
1		3				7	8	11¹		14	6	10		2²									4	12	9¹	5	13	29
1		3				7¹	8	9		11	6²	10		2									4	13		5	12	30
1		3		13			7	10		11	6	8		4										5¹	12	2	9²	31
1		3	13	12	7⁴	8	9²			11³	5¹	10		6									4	14		2		32
1		3	13	8		7	14			10	5³	11		6¹									4	12	9²	2		33
1		3	13	8			7	12		11	2¹	10		9									4	6²		5		34
1		5		9³	4	7	8²			10	12			6								14	3		11¹	2	13	35
1		4		5	9³	7¹	8	12		11	6²	10		2									13	3			14	36

DUNDEE

Year Formed: 1893. *Ground & Address:* Dens Park Stadium, Sandeman St, Dundee DD3 7JY. *Telephone:* 01382 889966.
Fax: 01382 832284. *E-mail:* reception@dundeefc.co.uk *Website:* www.dundeefc.co.uk
Ground Capacity: 11,850 (all seated). *Size of Pitch:* 101m × 66m.
Chairmain: Bill Covlin. *Managing Director:* John Nelms.
Manager: Paul Hartley. *Assistant Manager:* Gerry McCabe. *Youth Development Coach:* Gerry Creaney.
Physio: Karen Gibson.
Club Nicknames: 'The Dark Blues' or 'The Dee'.
Previous Grounds: Carolina Port 1893-98.
Record Attendance: 43,024 v Rangers, Scottish Cup 2nd rd, 7 Feb 1953.
Record Transfer Fee received: £1,200,000 for Robert Douglas to Celtic (2000).
Record Transfer Fee paid: £600,000 for Fabian Caballero from Sol de América (Paraguay) (July 2000).
Record Victory: 10-0 Division II v Alloa Ath, 9 Mar 1947 and v Dunfermline Ath, 22 Mar 1947.
Record Defeat: 0-11 v Celtic, Division I, 26 Oct 1895.
Most Capped Player: Alex Hamilton, 24, Scotland.
Most League Appearances: 400: Barry Smith, 1995-2006.
Most League Goals in Season (Individual): 52: Alan Gilzean, 1960-64.
Most Goals Overall (Individual): 113: Alan Gilzean 1960-64.

DUNDEE – SCOTTISH PREMIER LEAGUE 2014–15 LEAGUE RECORD

Match No.	Date	Venue	Opponents	Result	H/T Score	Lg Pos.	Goalscorers	Attendance
1	Aug 9	H	Kilmarnock	D 1-1	1-1	3	Harkins (pen) [17]	7588
2	13	A	Inverness CT	D 0-0	0-0	9		3082
3	16	A	Partick Thistle	D 1-1	0-1	7	Wighton [54]	6453
4	23	A	St Mirren	W 1-0	0-0	6	MacDonald [80]	4517
5	31	H	Celtic	D 1-1	1-0	6	McPake [1]	9276
6	Sept 13	A	St Johnstone	W 1-0	1-0	5	Konrad [28]	6562
7	21	H	Dundee U	L 1-4	0-1	6	Stewart [90]	11,447
8	27	A	Ross Co	L 1-2	0-1	7	Clarkson [69]	3118
9	Oct 4	H	Aberdeen	L 2-3	1-2	8	Harkins [6], Clarkson (pen) [55]	8784
10	18	A	Motherwell	W 3-1	2-0	7	Clarkson [3], Harkins [30], Stewart [59]	4061
11	25	H	Hamilton A	W 2-0	0-0	7	Clarkson [69], Stewart [73]	6035
12	Nov 1	A	Kilmarnock	W 3-1	1-0	6	Stewart 2 [44, 90], Clarkson [51]	4481
13	8	H	St Johnstone	D 1-1	1-0	6	Clarkson [41]	6931
14	22	A	Celtic	L 1-2	0-1	6	Clarkson [58]	43,787
15	Dec 6	H	Inverness CT	L 1-2	1-0	7	Stewart [21]	5400
16	13	A	Hamilton A	L 1-2	0-2	8	Stewart [61]	2636
17	20	A	Partick Thistle	D 1-1	0-0	7	Balatoni (og) [90]	3203
18	27	H	St Mirren	L 1-3	0-1	8	Irvine [84]	6447
19	Jan 1	A	Dundee U	L 2-6	1-4	8	Stewart [24], Tankulic [90]	12,964
20	4	H	Ross Co	D 1-1	0-0	8	McAlister [52]	5017
21	10	H	Motherwell	W 4-1	3-1	8	Harris [3], Stewart [8], Irvine [34], O'Brien (og) [70]	5105
22	17	A	Aberdeen	D 3-3	2-1	8	Irvine [38], Stewart [40], Harkins [48]	16,796
23	21	H	Kilmarnock	W 1-0	1-0	7	Stewart (pen) [19]	5141
24	24	A	St Mirren	W 2-1	0-1	7	Irvine [53], Davidson [69]	4010
25	31	H	Hamilton A	D 1-1	0-0	7	Stewart [88]	5618
26	Feb 14	H	Partick Thistle	W 1-0	0-0	6	McGowan [90]	5560
27	21	A	Motherwell	W 1-0	1-0	6	McGinn, P [12]	4282
28	28	A	Ross Co	L 0-1	0-0	6		3413
29	Mar 21	H	Aberdeen	D 1-1	0-1	7	McGinn, S [69]	7014
30	Apr 4	A	Inverness CT	D 1-1	0-0	7	Clarkson [53]	3362
31	8	H	Dundee U	W 3-1	2-1	6	Stewart [14], McPake [23], Heffernan [68]	10,510
32	11	A	St Johnstone	L 0-1	0-1	6		6386
33	22	H	Celtic	L 1-2	0-1	6	McAlister [87]	8908
34	25	H	St Johnstone	L 0-2	0-0	6		6530
35	May 1	A	Celtic	L 0-5	0-2	6		44,299
36	9	H	Inverness CT	L 0-1	0-1	6		5123
37	16	H	Aberdeen	D 1-1	1-0	6	Tankulic [43]	6434
38	24	A	Dundee U	L 0-3	0-2	6		10,812

Final League Position: 6

Honours
League Champions: Division I 1961-62. First Division 1978-79, 1991-92, 1997-98. Division II 1946-47; Championship 2013-14.
Runners-up: Division I 1902-03, 1906-07, 1908-09, 1948-49. First Division 1980-81, 2007-08, 2009-10, 2011-12.
Scottish Cup Winners: 1910; *Runners-up:* 1925, 1952, 1964, 2003.
League Cup Winners: 1951-52, 1952-53, 1973-74; *Runners-up:* 1967-68, 1980-81, 1995-96.
League Challenge Cup Winners: 1990-91, 2009-10.
B&Q (Centenary) Cup Winners: 1990-91; *Runners-up:* 1994-95.

European: *European Cup:* 8 matches (1962-63 semi-finals). *Cup Winners' Cup:* 2 matches: (1964-65).
UEFA Cup: 22 matches: (*Fairs Cup:* 1967-68 semi-finals. *UEFA Cup:* 1971-72, 1973-74, 1974-75, 2003-04).

Club colours: Shirt: Navy blue. Shorts: White. Socks: Navy blue.

Goalscorers: *League (46):* Stewart 13 (1 pen), Clarkson 8 (1 pen), Harkins 4 (1 pen), Irvine 4, McAlister 2, McPake 2, Tankulic 2, Davidson 1, Harris 1, Heffernan 1, Konrad 1, MacDonald 1, McGinn, S 1, McGinn, P 1, McGowan 1, Wighton 1, own goals 2.
William Hill Scottish FA Cup (2): Clarkson 1, Konrad 1.
Scottish League Cup (8): MacDonald 2, Stewart 2, Boyle 1, Ferry 1, McGinn, P 1, Tankulic 1.

Letheren K 15	McGinn P 34	McPake J 34	Konrad T 30 + 3	Dyer W 18 + 3	Thomson K 20 + 4	McGowan P 30	Ferry S 14 + 5	Harkins G 21 + 7	Stewart G 32 + 2	Tankulic L 12 + 14	McAlister J 34 + 3	MacDonald P 2 + 5	Wighton C 1 + 15	Boyle M 6 + 12	Irvine G 25 + 1	McBride K 4 + 2	Davidson 18 + 5	Roberts P 4 + 4	Kerr C — + 2	Clarkson D 18 + 5	Bain S 22	Schenk A 1	Carreiro D — + 1	Harris A 11 + 5	Gadzhalov K 6 + 2	McGinn S 11 + 2	Heffernan P 4 + 3	Black A — + 1	Colquhoun C 1 + 1	Match No.
1	2	3	4	5	6	7		8³	9	10²	11¹	12	13	14																1
1	2	3	4	5	8¹	9	6	7	10²	11³	12	13		14																2
1	2	3	4	5²		8	7	9¹		10³	6	11	13	14	12															3
1	5	4	3			10		9¹		11²	6	12	8	14	2	7³	13													4
1	2	4	3			7	13	8²	11	12	9	10³		14	5			6¹												5
1	2	3	4			6	9²	8	11³	13	10			12	5	14		7¹												6
1	2	3	4¹			6	9²	8³	11	12	10			13	14	5		7¹												7
1	2	3				8	6³	10	9	11²	5¹			13	7	4				12	14									8
1	2	3	4			9		10	6¹		8	14	12	13	5	7³				11²										9
1	2¹		4	13	7			9³	11²		8			14	5	6	3		12	10										10
	2	3	4	13	6		7²	10¹		9			12	5	8¹		14	11	1											11
	2	4	3		12	6		8¹	11		7			9	5			13		10²	1									12
	2	4	3		12	9		8	10		6			7¹	5					11	1									13
	2	4	3		7³	8	13	9²	10¹	14	6			12	5					11	1									14
	2	4	3		6²		12	9	10¹	13	7			8³	5	14				11	1									15
	2	4	3			7	9¹⁰	12	13	6		14	8³	5					10¹	11	1									16
1	8¹	3	4	5	6²		7³		9	13	10			12	2					14	11									17
1	2⁴	3	4²		7			13	9	11¹	8	14		6³	5					12	10									18
	3	4¹	5		7			8²	9	13	6			12	2	10				11³		1	14							19
	2	3²	13		6	9¹		14	10	12	7			5		4				11³	1			8						20
	2		13	6¹	9			12	10	14	7²				5³		4			11	1			8	3					21
	2		13	14	6²			12	9	10	11¹	7			5		4			11¹	1			8	3³					22
	3²		5			6		9²	10	11¹	7		14		2		4			12	1			8	13					23
	4	14	5	7	8			9³	11	13	10				2		6²				1			12	3¹					24
	4		5	6³	8			7	12	9		14			2					11²	1			10¹	3	13				25
	2	3	6	12		10		13			9			14	5³						1			8	4¹	7	11²			26
	2	4	3	5	7	11¹		12	10²	8										13	1			9		6				27
	2	4	3	5	7¹		13	10	11³		9			12							1			6²		8	14			28
	2	3	4	5	8	9	10²		12				14							11¹	1			6²		7	13			29
	2	3²	4	5	6	8	9²		10		13					12				11¹	1			14	7					30
	2	3	4	5	7	9			10²		6³					12				14	1			13	8	11¹				31
	2		3	5	8	7³		10		6²	12				4					11¹	1			14		9	13			32
	2	4	3	5			6¹		10	12	7						13				1			8²		9	11			33
	2	4	3³	5	7	8			6⁸	13	9		14				12			11²	1						10¹			34
	2	4	3	5	9		8²			11	10									14	1			6¹		7	13³	12		35
1	2	3	4	5	8¹	7		13	10	11	9		12													6²				36
1	2	3			7	9			10	11²	8¹				5									13	4	12		6		37
1	2	3	4¹			6	8²	13	9	11	7		14		5											12	10³			38

DUNDEE UNITED

Year Formed: 1909 (1923). *Ground & Address:* Tannadice Park, Tannadice St, Dundee DD3 7JW. *Telephone:* 01382
833166. *Fax:* 01382 889398. *E-mail:* enquiries@dundeeunited.co.uk *Website:* www.dufc.co
Ground Capacity: 14,223 (all seated). *Size of Pitch:* 100m × 66m.
Chairman: Stephen Thompson, OBE. *Vice-Chair:* Justine Mitchell. *Secretary:* Spence Anderson.
Manager: Jackie McNamara. *Assistant Manager:* Simon Donnelly. *First Team Coach:* Darren Jackson. *Physio:* Jeff Clarke.
Club Nicknames: 'The Terrors', 'The Arabs'.
Previous Grounds: None.
Record Attendance: 28,000 v Barcelona, Fairs Cup, 16 Nov 1966.
Record Transfer Fee received: £4,000,000 for Duncan Ferguson from Rangers (July 1993).
Record Transfer Fee paid: £750,000 for Steven Pressley from Coventry C (July 1995).
Record Victory: 14-0 v Nithsdale Wanderers, Scottish Cup 1st rd, 17 Jan 1931.
Record Defeat: 1-12 v Motherwell, Division II, 23 Jan 1954.
Most Capped Player: Maurice Malpas, 55, Scotland.
Most League Appearances: 618, Maurice Malpas, 1980-2000.
Most Appearances in European Matches: 76, Dave Narey (record for Scottish player).
Most League Goals in Season (Individual): 40: John Coyle, Division II, 1955-56.
Most Goals Overall (Individual): 199: Peter McKay, 1947-54.

DUNDEE UNITED – SCOTTISH PREMIER LEAGUE 2014–15 LEAGUE RECORD

Match No.	Date	Venue	Opponents	Result	H/T Score	Lg Pos.	Goalscorers	Atten- dance
1	Aug 10	A	Aberdeen	W 3-0	2-0	1	Dow [29], Mackay-Steven [45], Erskine [90]	16,471
2	13	H	Motherwell	W 1-0	0-0	1	Bilate [83]	8367
3	16	A	Celtic	L 1-6	0-3	4	Rankin [71]	44,484
4	23	H	Ross Co	W 2-1	1-0	3	Ciftci [19], Erskine [86]	7179
5	30	A	St Mirren	W 3-0	0-0	3	Erskine [47], Fojut [69], Spittal [86]	4245
6	Sept 13	H	Hamilton A	D 2-2	2-2	3	Ciftci [17], Fojut [45]	7109
7	21	A	Dundee	W 4-1	1-0	1	Bilate (pen) [25], Dow [54], Morris [59], Watson [79]	11,447
8	27	H	St Johnstone	W 2-0	1-0	1	Erskine [23], Paton [72]	7161
9	Oct 3	A	Kilmarnock	L 0-2	0-0	1		3953
10	18	H	Partick Thistle	W 1-0	0-0	2	Ciftci (pen) [84]	6756
11	25	A	Inverness CT	L 0-1	0-1	3		3508
12	Nov 1	H	St Mirren	W 3-0	1-0	1	Paton [45], Ciftci [56], Telfer [73]	6808
13	7	A	Motherwell	L 0-1	0-0	1		3961
14	22	H	Kilmarnock	W 3-1	2-1	3	Ciftci [6], Armstrong [42], Connolly [90]	6664
15	Dec 6	A	Ross Co	W 3-2	1-0	2	Ciftci 2 [21, 58], Armstrong [48]	2922
16	13	H	Aberdeen	L 0-2	0-2	3		11,196
17	21	H	Celtic	W 2-1	1-0	2	Ciftci [5], Armstrong [65]	12,098
18	27	A	St Johnstone	L 1-2	1-0	2	Butcher [43]	7384
19	Jan 1	H	Dundee	W 6-2	4-1	3	Armstrong [1], Mackay-Steven 2 [27, 42], Erskine [31], Fojut [64], Telfer [83]	12,964
20	4	A	Partick Thistle	D 2-2	1-2	4	Mackay-Steven [10], Ciftci [73]	3761
21	12	A	Hamilton A	W 3-2	1-0	3	Armstrong [38], Mackay-Steven [46], Dillon [77]	2384
22	21	H	St Mirren	D 1-1	1-1	4	Armstrong [43]	2511
23	24	A	Motherwell	W 3-1	0-0	4	Telfer 2 [61, 90], Fojut [69]	7176
24	Feb 14	A	Kilmarnock	L 2-3	2-1	4	Ciftci (pen) [3], Anier [13]	3788
25	21	H	St Johnstone	L 0-2	0-2	4		7623
26	24	H	Inverness CT	D 1-1	0-1	4	McGowan [74]	7276
27	28	A	Partick Thistle	L 0-2	0-2	4		6517
28	Mar 21	A	Celtic	L 0-3	0-3	4		45,884
29	Apr 4	H	Ross Co	L 1-2	1-1	4	Ciftci (pen) [20]	6187
30	8	A	Dundee	L 1-3	1-2	4	Ciftci (pen) [16]	10,510
31	11	H	Hamilton A	W 1-0	0-0	4	Erskine [70]	5243
32	18	A	Aberdeen	L 0-1	0-1	4		12,619
33	26	H	Celtic	L 0-3	0-0	5		8329
34	May 2	H	Aberdeen	W 1-0	1-0	4	Muirhead [13]	8686
35	5	A	Inverness CT	L 1-2	1-2	4	Muirhead [2]	2426
36	9	A	St Johnstone	D 1-1	0-0	4	Rankin [68]	4862
37	16	A	Inverness CT	L 0-3	0-0	5		3508
38	24	H	Dundee	W 3-0	2-0	5	Ciftci 2 (1 pen) [8, 31 (p)], Spittal [50]	10,812

Final League Position: 5

Honours: *League Champions:* Premier Division 1982-83. Division II 1924-25, 1928-29.
Runners-up: Division II 1930-31, 1959-60. First Division 1995-96.
Scottish Cup Winners: 1994, 2010; *Runners-up:* 1974, 1981, 1985, 1987, 1988, 1991, 2005, 2014.
League Cup Winners: 1979-80, 1980-81; *Runners-up:* 1981-82, 1984-85, 1997-98, 2007-08, 2014-15.
League Challenge Cup Runners-up: 1995-96.

European: *European Cup:* 8 matches (1983-84, semi-finals). *Cup Winners' Cup:* 10 matches (1974-75, 1988-89, 1994-95). *UEFA Cup (Fairs Cup:* 1966-67, 1969-70, 1970-71. *UEFA Cup:* 1975-76, 1977-78, 1978-79, 1979-80, 1980-81, 1981-82, 1982-83, 1984-85, 1985-86, 1986-87 runners-up, 1987-88, 1989-90, 1990-91, 1993-94, 1997-98, 2005-06). *Europa League:* 6 matches (2010-2011, 2011-12, 2012-13).

Club colours: Shirt: Tangerine with black trim. Shorts: Black. Socks: Tangerine with black hoop.

Goalscorers: *League (58):* Ciftci 14 (5 pens), Armstrong 6, Erskine 6, Mackay-Steven 5, Fojut 4, Telfer 4, Bilate 2 (1 pen), Dow 2, Muirhead 2, Paton 2, Rankin 2, Spittal 2, Anier 1, Butcher 1, Connolly 1, Dillon 1, McGowan 1, Morris 1, Watson 1.
William Hill Scottish FA Cup (6): Dow 2, Ciftci 1 (1 pen), Erskine 1, Souttar 1, Watson 1.
Scottish League Cup (6): Ciftci 1, Connolly 1, Dow 1, Erskine 1, Fojut 1, Morris 1.

Cierzniak R 36+1	Watson K 14	Fojut J 36	Morris C 23+2	Townsend C 16+1	Dow R 17+7	Armstrong S 17+3	Paton P 22+2	Rankin J 29+1	Mackay-Steven G 14+7	Ciftci N 34+2	Erskine C 27+7	Bilate M 6+8	Telfer C 13+8	Spittal B 13+12	Graham B —+1	Spark E —+2	Dillon S 26+1	Smith S —+3	Connolly A 8+10	Butcher C 15	Souttar J 13	Anier H 4+8	McGowan R 12	Dixon P 15	Muirhead R 6+7	Szromnik M 2+2	Coote A —+3	Johnson J —+1	Match No.
1	2	3	4	5	6	7[2]	8	9	10[3]	11[1]	12	13	14																1
1	2[2]	3	4	5	8	9	6	7	10[1]	11[12]	13	12	14																2
1	2	4	3	5	10[3]	9[2]	6	7	8[1]	11	13	12		14															3
1	2[3]	3	4	5	8		7	6	10[1]	9	12	11[12]	14	13															4
1	2[2]	4	3	5	10		6	7	8[1]	9[1]	12		14	13															5
1	2	4	3		6	7	8	10[4]	9	11[1]	12						5												6
1	2	3		10	12	6[1]	7	9	8[2]	11[13]	14						5		14										7
1	2	4	3	10[1]	12	6	7	13	9	8[3]	11[12]	14					5												8
1	2	4	3	8	9[1]	6	7	12	11	10							5												9
1	2	3	4	12	9[1]	6[2]	7	10	11	8[3]		13					5		14										10
1	2[2]	4	3	12	6	10[1]	7	9	11	8	14		13				5[3]												11
1		4	3	5	13	12	6			10[3]	14	11[1]	8				2		7	9[2]									12
1		4	14	5	9	8	2	7	12	13	6		10[3]						11[1]		3[2]								13
1		4	3	5	13	7	6		11[1]	10[4]	9[2]		8	12			2		14										14
1		4		5	7[2]	10	8	14	12	11	9[4]						2		13	6[1]	3								15
1		4	12	5	8[1]	9	6	7[4]	13	11	10						2		14		3[3]								16
1		4	3	5	12	9		7	11[1]	10			8				2		6										17
1		4	3[1]	5		9		6	12	11	10		8				2		6										18
1	2	3		5	12	9		7	10	11[1]	8[3]	13					4		14	6[4]									19
1	2[1]	4		5	14	9		7[3]	8	11	10[2]						3		6										20
1		4		5		8	13		9	11	12		6[2]	2			3		10[1]	7									21
1	3	4		5		9	6	7[2]	8	11	10[1]	13		2					12										22
1		4	3		11	8[1]	14		13	12			6	2			5		9[3]	7		10[2]							23
1		4[3]		10		6		11	9[1]		7	13	12	12	3							8[2]	2	5	14				24
	4			9		7	8[2]	10		13	12			3			14	6[1]		11[3]	2	5		1					25
12	3			10		6		11	9[2]					4			8[3]	7[1]		14	2	5	13	1[*]					26
1		4		10		6		11	9[2]	13	7[1]	8		2					12	3	5								27
1		4		12		7	8	11			6[2]	10[3]					9[1]	3	13	12	2	5	14						28
1		4				6[1]	7	11	9	13	10[2]			2			8[3]		3	14		5	12						29
1		4					7		9	10	13		12	3			8[3]	6[2]		11[1]	2	5	14						30
1			4				7		11	9[2]	12	8	10[1]				6	3		2	5	9							31
1	2	3						10	8	11[1]	7								4[2]	6	5	9	12		13				32
1	3	4				7		10[1]		9[2]	8[3]			13			6	14	2	5	11		12						33
1	3	4				7		11		9	6[1]		13	12			8		2	5	10[2]								34
1	3	4				7		10	13		6[1]	9[3]		12					8	14	2[2]	5	11						35
1	3	4				7		9	10				2	13			6[2]	6	12		5	11[1]							36
1[1]	3					7		10	9[2]	6			5		13	8[3]	4			2	11	14		12					37
1[1]	3					7		10	9		6[2]		2		12		4		8	5	11[2]	14	13						38

DUNFERMLINE ATHLETIC

Year Formed: 1885. *Ground & Address:* East End Park, Halbeath Road, Dunfermline KY12 7RB.
Telephone: 01383 724295. *Fax:* 01383 745 959. *E-mail:* enquiries@dafc.co.uk
Website: www.dafc.co.uk
Ground Capacity: 11,380 (all seated). *Size of Pitch:* 105m × 65m.
Chairman: Bob Garmony. *Football matters:* Kip McBay.
Manager: Allan Johnston. *Assistant Manager:* Sandy Clark. *Head Coach:* John Potter. *Physio:* Kenny Murray.
Club Nickname: 'The Pars'.
Previous Grounds: None.
Record Attendance: 27,816 v Celtic, Division I, 30 Apr 1968.
Record Transfer Fee received: £650,000 for Jackie McNamara to Celtic (Oct 1995).
Record Transfer Fee paid: £540,000 for Istvan Kozma from Bordeaux (Sept 1989).
Record Victory: 11-2 v Stenhousemuir, Division II, 27 Sept 1930.
Record Defeat: 1-13 v St. Bernard's, Scottish Cup, 1st rd; 15 Sept 1883.
Most Capped Player: Colin Miller 16 (61), Canada.
Most League Appearances: 497: Norrie McCathie, 1981-96.
Most League Goals in Season (Individual): 53: Bobby Skinner, Division II, 1925-26.
Most Goals Overall (Individual): 212: Charles Dickson, 1954-64.

DUNFERMLINE ATHLETIC – SCOTTISH LEAGUE ONE 2014–15 LEAGUE RECORD

Match No.	Date		Venue	Opponents	Result	H/T Score	Lg Pos.	Goalscorers	Atten- dance
1	Aug	9	H	Brechin C	D 0-0	0-0	7		2875
2		16	A	Forfar Ath	L 0-2	0-0	8		1003
3		23	H	Airdrieonians	W 3-0	2-0	5	Ugwu 2 24, 80, Moffat 41	2653
4		30	A	Stranraer	W 2-1	1-1	2	Ugwu 6, Moffat 63	573
5	Sept	13	H	Stenhousemuir	W 2-0	0-0	1	Thomson 54, Moffat (pen) 84	2671
6		20	A	Greenock Morton	L 1-2	0-1	4	Millen (pen) 72	1934
7		27	H	Peterhead	W 3-0	0-0	2	Falkingham 59, Ugwu 71, Thomas 88	2409
8	Oct	4	A	Stirling Alb	W 2-0	0-0	2	Byrne 80, El Bakhtaoui 90	1623
9		10	A	Ayr U	W 1-0	1-0	1	El Bakhtaoui 29	1457
10		18	H	Forfar Ath	D 0-0	0-0	2		2923
11		25	H	Greenock Morton	L 1-2	0-0	2	El Bakhtaoui 52	3342
12	Nov	8	A	Peterhead	D 1-1	1-0	2	El Bakhtaoui 19	740
13		15	A	Stenhousemuir	L 0-1	0-0	4		1177
14		22	H	Stirling Alb	W 4-0	2-0	3	Ugwu 3 5, 18, 60, Stirling 71	2451
15	Dec	6	H	Ayr U	W 4-2	3-1	2	Stirling 19, Smith 2 22, 57, Byrne 30	2509
16		13	A	Airdrieonians	L 1-3	0-1	4	Buchanan 84	878
17		20	H	Stranraer	L 0-1	0-0	4		2572
18	Jan	3	H	Peterhead	D 1-1	1-0	4	Forbes 20	2729
19		10	A	Stirling Alb	D 2-2	1-0	5	Smith 42, Martin 90	1152
20		17	H	Airdrieonians	D 2-2	1-1	5	Millen (pen) 34, Moffat 75	2589
21		24	A	Greenock Morton	L 0-2	0-0	5		1447
22		31	A	Ayr U	W 2-0	0-0	5	Geggan 66, Hopkirk 90	1149
23	Feb	14	H	Stenhousemuir	W 3-2	1-2	4	Barrowman 2 45, 90, McAusland 74	2393
24		21	A	Forfar Ath	L 0-1	0-0	5		1134
25		24	H	Brechin C	L 0-1	0-0	5		1574
26		28	A	Stranraer	L 1-5	1-3	6	Geggan 26	498
27	Mar	3	H	Brechin C	D 1-1	1-0	5	Falkingham 1	615
28		7	H	Ayr U	W 2-1	0-0	5	Devlin (og) 63, Geggan 76	2467
29		14	H	Stirling Alb	D 1-1	0-0	7	Geggan 75	2318
30		21	A	Stenhousemuir	W 1-0	0-0	5	El Bakhtaoui 47	983
31		28	H	Greenock Morton	L 0-4	0-1	6		2732
32	Apr	4	A	Peterhead	D 1-1	1-0	6	Moffat 18	668
33		11	H	Stranraer	W 1-0	0-0	6	El Bakhtaoui 83	1951
34		18	A	Brechin C	L 0-3	0-2	7		808
35		25	H	Forfar Ath	L 1-3	0-3	7	El Bakhtaoui 77	2262
36	May	2	A	Airdrieonians	L 2-3	1-1	7	Geggan 33, Falkingham 59	1055

Final League Position: 7

Honours
League Champions: First Division 1988-89, 1995-96, 2010-11. Division II 1925-26. Second Division 1985-86;
Runners-up: First Division 1986-87, 1993-94, 1994-95, 1999-2000. Division II 1912-13, 1933-34, 1954-55, 1957-58, 1972-73.
Second Division 1978-79. League One 2013-14.
Scottish Cup Winners: 1961, 1968; *Runners-up:* 1965, 2004, 2007.
League Cup Runners-up: 1949-50, 1991-92, 2005-06.
League Challenge Cup Runners-up: 2007-08.

European: *Cup Winners' Cup:* 14 matches (1961-62, 1968-69 semi-finals). *UEFA Cup:* 32 matches (*Fairs Cup:* 1962-63, 1964-65, 1965-66, 1966-67, 1969-70. *UEFA Cup:* 2004-05, 2007-08).

Club colours: Shirt: White with black stripes. Shorts: Black. Socks: Black.

Goalscorers: *League (46):* El Bakhtaoui 7, Ugwu 7, Geggan 5, Moffat 5 (1 pen), Falkingham 3, Smith 3, Barrowman 2, Byrne 2, Millen 2 (2 pens), Stirling 2, Buchanan 1, Forbes 1, Hopkirk 1, Martin 1, McAusland 1, Thomas 1, Thomson 1, own goal 1.
William Hill Scottish FA Cup (7): El Bakhtaoui 2, Millen 2 (2 pens), Buchanan 1, Byrne 1, Geggan 1.
Scottish League Cup (6): Buchanan 1, Martin 1, Moffat 1, Spence 1, Wallace 1, Whittle 1.
Petrofac Training Cup (2): Geggan 1, Millen 1.

Scully R 34	Millen R 27	Martin L 27 + 1	Buchanan G 30	Drummond R 4 + 1	Spence L 20 + 6	Geggan A 29 + 3	Forbes R 7 + 5	Byrne S 20 + 2	El Bakhtaoui F 12 + 11	Moffat M 29 + 5	Page J 2 + 1	Wallace R 1 + 3	Ugwu G 9 + 5	Whittle A 20 + 4	Falkingham J 26 + 6	Thomson R 10 + 8	Williamson R 12 + 2	Urquhart S 10 + 2	Stirling A 7 + 8	Smith A 8 + 5	Thomas J — + 2	Chemin S — + 2	Goodfellow R — + 2	Paterson J 5 + 1	McAusland K 13 + 1	Barrowman A 9 + 4	Hopkirk D 10 + 2	George P 3 + 1	Allan L 5 + 3	O'Kane D 1 + 3	Graham F 4	Wilson J 2	Match No.
1	2	3	4²	5	6	7	8¹	9	10³	11	12	13	14																				1
1	2	3	12	8	7		6²	14	10	4			11¹	5³	9	13																	2
1	2	3	4	5¹	8	7³	13		6²	10			11		9	14	12																3
1	5¹	4	3		7	9			10¹				11²		6	8²	2	12	13	14													4
1		3	4	5	7	6			10				11		8	9¹	2		12														5
1	2	3	4	9	6³	8	14		10				11²		7	12	5¹		13														6
1	5	4	3		7¹		9	14	10				11		8²	6²	2		12	13													7
1	5		4	13				8²	7	12	10		9¹	11		2	3	6³		14													8
1	5		3	6	14		7	8	11²	13	12	9		2	4³	10¹																	9
1	5²	3	4		6	7¹	12		10³	11			14	13	9		2	8															10
1	2	3	4		6	7	14	8²	11	10³			5	9¹	12			13															11
1	2	14	3		7	8³	9¹	6	11²	10			12	5		13	4																12
1²	2		3		8¹	7	9³	6	11	10			5	12		4	13			14													13
1	4	3				14		6³	12	13			11¹	5	7	8	2		9²	10													14
1	3	4		12	2	14	6			11³		5	7	8		9¹	10²	13															15
1	2		4	13	7		6¹	14	11	3	12	5	8		9²	10³																	16
1	2	4	3	7²	9		6	10		13			5	8	11¹		12																17
1	5	4	3		2⁴	8¹	7	12	10³	11²			9	6		13	14																18
1	2	3	4	9³		8²	6	13	10¹				7	14	12	11		5															19
1	2	3	4			7		14		13			9	6		12³	11¹			5²	8	10											20
1	2	3		13	8	7²	12	11		5	6		9¹							4	10												21
1¹		3	4	7	2	8²		10		12	13				14	5⁵	6	11	9														22
1		4	3¹	8	2		14	11³		5	6		12			7	10	9²	13														23
1		4	9	2		11¹	14		5¹	8		3				12	7	10		6³	13												24
1		3		13	7³		11²		12	8	2¹	4				5	6	14	9		10												25
1		4	3⁴	12	6		13		14	8	2²	5				7	10³	9¹		11													26
1	2	3		6³	8		9		7				14			5	4	10¹	12		11²	13											27
1	2	4		3	6		12		11			5				7	13	9	8¹	10²													28
1	2	4		8²	7		11		14	12		5				3	13	9	6²	10¹													29
1	2	4	3	13	7³		11²		5	6						8	10	9¹	12	14													30
1	2		3	7			11	12		5	6				4²	8³	10¹	9	13	14													31
1	2	3	4	7			14	10²		5	8		12			11¹		6³	13	9													32
1	2	4	3	8		7³	13	11		5			9			10¹		12				6											33
1	2⁴	4	3	8		6³	13	10		5	12	9²	11¹			14					7												34
	3			7		6¹	11	10		5	9	12	2						4	8	1												35
	3	4		7¹			11	10²		5	6	13	2			12			9			8	1										36

EAST FIFE

Year Formed: 1903. *Ground & Address:* Bayview Stadium, Harbour View, Methil, Fife KY8 3RW. *Telephone:* 01333 426323. *Fax:* 01333 426376. *E-mail:* office@eastfifefc.info. *Website:* www.eastfifefc.info
Ground Capacity: 1,992. *Size of Pitch:* 105m × 65m.
Chairman: Jim Stevenson. *Vice-Chairman:* David Marshall.
Manager: Gary Naysmith. *Coach:* Douglas Anderson.
Club Nickname: 'The Fifers'.
Previous Ground: Bayview Park.
Record Attendance: 22,515 v Raith Rovers, Division I, 2 Jan 1950 (Bayview Park); 4,700 v Rangers, League One, 26 Oct 2013 (Bayview Stadium).
Record Transfer Fee received: £150,000 for Paul Hunter from Hull C (March 1990).
Record Transfer Fee paid: £70,000 for John Sludden from Kilmarnock (July 1991).
Record Victory: 13-2 v Edinburgh C, Division II, 11 Dec 1937.
Record Defeat: 0-9 v Hearts, Division I, 5 Oct 1957.
Most Capped Player: George Aitken, 5 (8), Scotland.
Most League Appearances: 517: David Clarke, 1968-86.
Most League Goals in Season (Individual): 41: Jock Wood, Division II; 1926-27 and Henry Morris, Division II, 1947-48.
Most Goals Overall (Individual): 225: Phil Weir, 1922-35.

EAST FIFE – SCOTTISH LEAGUE TWO 2014–15 LEAGUE RECORD

Match No.	Date	Venue	Opponents	Result	H/T Score	Lg Pos.	Goalscorers	Atten-dance
1	Aug 9	A	Elgin C	L 0-1	0-0	9		654
2	16	H	Berwick R	L 2-3	0-2	9	Cook (pen) 56, Campbell, S 77	645
3	23	A	Albion R	L 0-2	0-2	9		532
4	30	H	East Stirling	W 3-1	2-0	7	McShane 21, Smith, K 45, Maskrey 51	603
5	Sept13	A	Arbroath	W 2-0	0-0	6	Walker 51, Smith, K 57	829
6	20	H	Queen's Park	D 2-2	1-1	5	McAleer 14, Smith, L 82	678
7	27	A	Montrose	W 4-0	3-0	4	Mullen 24, Brown 28, McShane 43, Smith, K 85	465
8	Oct 11	H	Clyde	L 0-1	0-1	5		596
9	18	H	Annan Ath	D 1-1	1-0	5	McAleer 9	544
10	25	A	Queen's Park	L 0-3	0-2	7		408
11	Nov 8	H	Albion R	D 0-0	0-0	7		446
12	15	A	Berwick R	W 3-2	0-0	4	Walker 69, Smith, K 85, Page 90	490
13	22	H	Elgin C	D 1-1	1-1	4	Smith, K 26	505
14	29	A	East Stirling	D 1-1	1-0	4	Walker 45	339
15	Dec 6	H	Montrose	W 3-0	1-0	4	Campbell, R 43, Smith, K 61, McShane (pen) 90	419
16	13	A	Annan Ath	L 1-2	0-0	4	Cook 74	426
17	20	A	Clyde	L 1-3	1-0	5	Austin 5	456
18	27	H	Arbroath	L 1-5	1-1	6	McShane (pen) 17	806
19	Jan 10	H	Queen's Park	D 0-0	0-0	6		498
20	31	A	Arbroath	D 1-1	0-1	8	Walker 84	695
21	Feb 10	A	Albion R	W 3-2	0-1	6	Smith, K 2 56, 85, Austin 80	403
22	14	A	Montrose	W 3-0	1-0	6	Dickson 31, Brown 63, Mullen 86	371
23	21	H	Clyde	D 1-1	0-0	6	Mullen 90	551
24	24	H	East Stirling	W 2-1	1-0	5	Dickson 2 43, 67	342
25	28	H	Annan Ath	W 2-1	0-1	5	Austin 67, Riordan 89	499
26	Mar 3	A	Elgin C	W 5-3	4-1	4	Austin 4 25, 27, 35, 53, Riordan 45	463
27	7	A	Queen's Park	L 0-1	0-1	4		678
28	14	A	East Stirling	L 0-2	0-1	4		386
29	21	H	Arbroath	W 2-0	1-0	4	Riordan 44, McAleer 90	567
30	24	H	Berwick R	L 1-4	0-1	4	Dickson 88	487
31	28	H	Montrose	W 3-0	2-0	4	Austin 2 24, 59, Watson (og) 35	439
32	Apr 4	A	Clyde	L 0-1	0-0	4		620
33	11	H	Albion R	W 1-0	1-0	4	Phillips (og) 30	707
34	18	A	Annan Ath	L 1-2	1-1	4	Austin 31	419
35	25	A	Berwick R	W 3-0	1-0	4	Smith, K 2 35, 83, Page 71	523
36	May 2	H	Elgin C	W 3-1	1-0	4	Smith, K 2 35, 60, Riordan 72	697

Final League Position: 4

Honours
League Champions: Division II 1947-48. Third Division 2007-08.
Runners-up: Division II 1929-30, 1970-71. Second Division 1983-84, 1995-96. Third Division 2002-03.
Scottish Cup Winners: 1938; *Runners-up:* 1927, 1950.
League Cup Winners: 1947-48, 1949-50, 1953-54.

Club colours: Shirt: Gold and black stripes. Shorts: White. Socks: Black with gold hoops.

Goalscorers: *League (56):* Smith, K 12, Austin 10, Dickson 4, McShane 4 (2 pens), Riordan 4, Walker 4, McAleer 3, Mullen 3, Brown 2, Cook 2 (1 pen), Page 2, Campbell, S 1, Campbell, R 1, Maskrey 1, Smith, L 1, own goals 2.
William Hill Scottish FA Cup (9): Austin 3, McShane 2, Campbell, R 1, McAleer 1, Smith, S 1, Walker 1.
Scottish League Cup (0).
Petrofac Training Cup (5): McShane 3 (1 pen), Austin 1, Moyes 1.
League One Play-Offs (2): Brown 1, Page 1.

Fleming A 26+1	Mullen F 31+1	Campbell S 32	Moyes E 8	Smith S 22+4	Beaton J 2+3	Brown R 33+2	Walker R 32+1	Cook A 6+18	McShane J 10+8	Campbell R 10+7	Austin N 20+10	Barr L 10+13	Maskrey D 1+2	McAleer C 10+6	Smith K 23+3	Smith L 20+1	Page J 28	Naysmith G 21	Millar J 8	Falconer D ——+2	Exxabeguren Leanizbarrutia J 13	Dickson S 12+5	Adeyemo D 4+7	Riordan D 8+3	Leyden J 4	Match No.
1	2	3	4	5	6¹	7	8	9¹	10	11²	12	13	14													1
1	2	3	4	5	6¹	14	8	9	10²	13	11	12		7³												2
1	2	3	4	5		7	6	13	10	12	11³	8¹		14	9²											3
1	2	3	4	5	13		6		11¹	12	14		7²	8	9³	10										4
1	7	3		9		12	8	13	14		11²			6¹	10³	2	4	5								5
1	8	3		5		6¹	7	12	13	14	10²			9	11³	2	4									6
1	8	4		5		9	7²		10¹	12	6³	13		14	11	2	3									7
1	2	3	4*			8	7¹		10	14	9²	13		12	11³	6	5									8
1	2	3			13	8	7		10	11¹	12	9		6²		5	4									9
12	2	3			13	8	7		11	10	6²			9³	14	5	4		1¹							10
1	2	3¹	9			8	7		12	10²		13		11		6	4	5								11
1	7	3	11¹			8	6³		14	9²	13	12		10		2	4	5								12
1	2	3	9²		8¹	7		13	10³	12		14	11	6		4	5									13
1	2²	4		9	8	7		12	10¹	13	6			11		3	5									14
1	8	3		9¹		6	7	13	12	10²		2		11		4	5									15
1	2	3	4	9		6	8	13	12	10¹		7²		11			5⁴									16
1	2	4	3³	5		7	8		10¹	11	9²	6		14	12				13							17
1	2	3		5¹		7	8	13	10³	12⁴	6	4		9²	11				14							18
	9	4	3			8	7	11¹		12	13			6²	10	5			1	2						19
	2		14			8	7	9²		13				6¹	10	11	3	5¹	1		4	12				20
1	14	6				7	8³			12	13			9	2	4	5				3	10²	11¹			21
1	8	4		14		7		12		13				10¹	2	5	6³				3	9	11²			22
1	8	6				7	9¹	12		11²					2	4	5				3	10	13			23
1	8	6				7	9³	13			14				2	4	5				3	10²	11¹	12		24
1	8¹	6				7	12	10²		11³					2	4	5				3	9	14	13		25
1		7		13		6	8	14		10²	12				2	4	5				3	9¹		11³		26
1		6¹		5		9	8	13		11⁴	12			2²	3	4						10	14	7³		27
1		4		5		2	8	6			12				3	9					7	10¹	11			28
	8	3		13		2	7	14		11³	6		12		4	5	1				9¹		10²			29
	2	3		5		6	7³	14		10	8²		9¹	13		4	1				12		11			30
	2	3				6	7³	12		9	8			11¹		4	5	1				14	13	10²		31
	7	2¹				6	8²	13		9				10³	12	4	5	1			3	14		11		32
	7			8		2				10				11¹		4	5	1			3	9²	12	13	6	33
1	7			2		8		12		11	13			10		4	5²				3	6¹			9	34
1	6			2		8	9³	14		11²				10	5¹	4					3	12	13		7	35
1	8			5¹		2⁴	7	12			13			11³		4					3	9	14	10	6	36

EAST STIRLINGSHIRE

Year Formed: 1880. *Grounds:* Ochilview Park (with Stenhousemuir). *Contact address:* 81d Main Street, Bainsford, Falkirk FK2 7NZ. *Telephone/Fax:* 01324 629 942.
E-mail: fceaststirlingshire@gmail.com *Website:* www.eaststirlingshirefc.com
Ground Capacity: 3,776 (626 seated). *Size of Pitch:* 100m × 66m.
Chairman: Tony Ford. *Secretary:* Tadek Kopszywa.
Head Coach: Craig Tully. *Assistant Head Coach:* George Shaw.
Club Nickname: 'The Shire'.
Previous Grounds: Burnhouse, Randyford Park, Merchiston Park, New Kilbowie Park, Firs Park.
Record Attendance: 12,000 v Partick Thistle, *Scottish Cup* 3rd rd, 21 Feb 1921.
Record Transfer Fee received: £35,000 for Jim Docherty to Chelsea (1978).
Record Transfer Fee paid: £6,000 for Colin McKinnon from Falkirk (March 1991).
Record Victory: 11-2 v Vale of Bannock, *Scottish Cup* 2nd rd, 22 Sept 1888.
Record Defeat: 1-12 v Dundee U, Division II, 13 Apr 1936.
Most Capped Player: Humphrey Jones, 5 (14), Wales.
Most League Appearances: 415: Gordon Russell, 1983-2001.
Most League Goals in Season (Individual): 36: Malcolm Morrison, Division II, 1938-39.

EAST STIRLINGSHIRE – SCOTTISH LEAGUE TWO 2014–15 LEAGUE RECORD

Match No.	Date	Venue	Opponents	Result	H/T Score	Lg Pos.	Goalscorers	Atten- dance
1	Aug 9	A	Montrose	L 1-4	0-1	10	Wright [83]	315
2	16	H	Elgin C	W 2-1	1-0	8	Townsley [23], McKenna [66]	293
3	23	A	Berwick R	L 0-5	0-1	8		509
4	30	A	East Fife	L 1-3	0-2	9	Tapping [82]	603
5	Sept 13	H	Clyde	W 1-0	0-0	8	Doyle [79]	470
6	20	H	Annan Ath	L 0-1	0-0	9		224
7	27	A	Albion R	W 2-1	2-1	6	McKenna [20], McKenzie (og) [38]	566
8	Oct 11	H	Queen's Park	L 1-3	0-2	6	Greene [65]	351
9	18	A	Arbroath	L 0-4	0-2	9		614
10	25	A	Annan Ath	L 3-4	1-3	9	McCabe [24], McKenna [85], Brennan [88]	373
11	Nov 8	H	Berwick R	L 0-2	0-1	9		273
12	15	A	Clyde	W 1-0	1-0	9	McQueen (og) [7]	456
13	22	H	Montrose	W 4-0	2-0	7	McKenna 2 [19, 81], Donnelly [28], Wright [59]	241
14	29	H	East Fife	D 1-1	0-1	6	Greenhill [55]	339
15	Dec 6	A	Queen's Park	L 0-3	0-1	8		322
16	13	H	Arbroath	L 2-3	0-1	8	McKenna [55], McCabe [56]	289
17	27	H	Albion R	L 1-4	1-3	9	McKenna (pen) [19]	300
18	Jan 3	A	Berwick R	L 0-3	0-2	9		474
19	10	A	Montrose	W 1-0	0-0	9	Greenhill [59]	269
20	17	H	Annan Ath	L 1-3	1-1	9	McKenna [33]	276
21	31	H	Clyde	L 1-2	0-0	10	McCabe [61]	362
22	Feb 14	H	Elgin C	W 1-0	0-0	10	McKenna (pen) [86]	256
23	21	A	Albion R	W 1-0	0-0	9	Gilmour [78]	429
24	24	A	East Fife	L 1-2	0-1	9	Vidler [89]	342
25	28	H	Queen's Park	W 3-1	1-0	9	Nisbet 2 [12, 87], McKenna [66]	367
26	Mar 4	A	Arbroath	W 1-0	0-0	8	Gilmour [72]	584
27	7	A	Clyde	D 1-1	1-1	7	Brisbane [9]	593
28	14	H	East Fife	W 2-0	1-0	6	Townsley [19], Nisbet [47]	386
29	17	H	Elgin C	W 2-1	1-1	5	McKenna [32], Nisbet [90]	363
30	21	A	Annan Ath	L 2-3	1-1	6	McKenna [41], Townsley [54]	322
31	28	H	Arbroath	W 1-0	1-0	5	Nisbet [25]	332
32	Apr 4	A	Elgin C	D 0-0	0-0	6		704
33	11	H	Montrose	L 0-1	0-1	6		305
34	18	H	Berwick R	L 0-4	0-1	8		261
35	25	A	Queen's Park	D 1-1	0-1	9	Nisbet [65]	507
36	May 2	H	Albion R	L 1-5	0-2	9	Bates [73]	340

Final League Position: 9

Honours
League Champions: Division II 1931-32; C Division 1947-48.
Runners-up: Division II 1962-63. Second Division 1979-80. Division Three 1923-24.

Club colours: Shirt: Black and white hoops. Shorts: Black. Socks: Red.

Goalscorers: *League (40):* McKenna 12 (2 pens), Nisbet 6, McCabe 3, Townsley 3, Gilmour 2, Greenhill 2, Wright 2, Bates 1, Brennan 1, Brisbane 1, Donnelly 1, Doyle 1, Greene 1, Tapping 1, Vidler 1, own goals 2.
William Hill Scottish FA Cup (2): Greenhill 1, McKenna 1.
Scottish League Cup (0).
Petrofac Training Cup (1): McKenna 1.

Barnard R 36	Greene C 31 + 1	Bolochoweckyj M 13 + 2	Townsley C 27 + 1	Kinnaird L 30	Greenhill D 31 + 3	Brisbane S 17 + 10	MacGregor G 17 + 7	Shepherd N 7 + 1	Wright M 17 + 7	Doyle J 4 + 4	Vidler W 9 + 19	McMullan P — + 1	Shield M 7 + 3	McKenna D 34 + 1	Gilmour R 21 + 5	McCabe N 33	Tully C 1	Tapping J 5 + 2	Brennan P — + 6	Kay A 2 + 2	Donnelly L 14 + 3	Bates D 16 + 1	Brown G 2 + 3	Wallace M 7 + 7	Boyle R — + 1	Tully J 2 + 1	Nicholson J — + 2	Nisbet K 11	Asghar A 2	Match No.
1	2	3	4	5¹	6	7	8⁰	9	10	11¹	12	13	14																	1
1		2	3	5	9		7	8	4	10¹	13	6		11²	12															2
1	14	2⁴	3	5		7	8	4	10³	12	6²		13	11		9¹														3
1	8		4¹		9	7²	10³	5		14	6		13	11	2		3	12												4
1	3				12	9¹	2	6	11³	13		7²	10	5	8		4	14												5
1	3	14		5	13		8		6²	10³	12	9¹	11	2	7		4													6
1	2	3		9	10	12		14	13	6³	8¹	11²	5	7		4														7
1	2		4	6	13	12		10²	9²	8¹	11	5	7		3	14														8
1	2	3	14		10	6¹	13		9	8²	11	5	7		4³	12														9
1	4		3	5	10	9	6		11	2¹	8		12	7																10
1	2	3	4	5	9²	12⁴	8¹	14	13		11	7		6³	10															11
1	2	3	4	5	9		7	11¹	12	10	8		6																	12
1	2	3²	4	5	9		8	10¹	12	11³		13	14	6																13
1	2	3	4	5	9		7	10	13	11²	6¹		12	8																14
1	2	4	3	5	8	13	6	10¹	12	11	7²		9																	15
1	2	3	4	5	9¹	7²		12	10	11	8		13	6																16
1	2¹	3	4	5²	9	14	8	13	10³	11	12	7	6																	17
1	4	3	8				14	11	9³	6		12	7¹	2	5²	10	13													18
1	2	13	4²	5	7		6	14	10³	12	8	3	9¹	11																19
1	2		4	5	9		6	13	10	8¹	7	3⁴	11²	12																20
1	2²	3	4	5	9		8¹	12	10³	11	7	13	6	14																21
1	4		3	5	10	2	13	12	11	9	7	8¹	6²																	22
1	2		3	5	8	6²	12	10	11³	7	13	4	14	9¹																23
1	2		3	5	8⁵	6	9²	13	10	11¹	7	4	14	12																24
1	4¹		3	5	9	8	6	10	12	7	2	11																		25
1	2		4²	5	14	6	9³	10¹	13	8	3	12	11	7																26
1	3		5	10	6	9¹	12	2	7	4	11	8																		27
1		3	5	9²	7	12	6¹	11	4	8	13	2	14	10³																28
1	2		5	9²	7¹	13	6³	11	3	8	12	4	14	10																29
1	2	3	5	8²	12	13	9³	11	7	6¹	4	14	10																	30
1	2	3	8	6	12	13	11²	5	7	9¹	4	10																		31
1	4	3	5	9³	14	10¹	13	8²	2	6	7	12	11																	32
1	7	3	9	8³	13	12	14	11	2	6	5¹	4²	10																	33
1	4⁴	3¹	5	9	8	6	13	11	2²	7	12	14	10³																	34
1	2	9¹	8	5	12	13	10³	7²	6	3	14	4	11																	35
1	13	12	14	5	10	7	11	2	6³	8²	3	9¹	4																	36

ELGIN CITY

Year Formed: 1893. *Ground and Address:* Borough Briggs, Borough Briggs Road, Elgin IV30 1AP.
Telephone: 01343 551114. *Fax:* 01343 547921. *E-mail:* office@elgincity.com *Website:* www.elgincity.com
Ground Capacity: 3,927 (seated: 478). *Size of pitch:* 102m × 68m.
Chairman: Graham Tatters. *Secretary:* Kate Taylor.
Manager: Jim Weir. *Assistant Manager:* Gavin Price. *Physio:* Kerry Hendry.
Previous names: 1893-1900 Elgin City, 1900-03 Elgin City United, 1903- Elgin City.
Club Nicknames: 'City', 'The Black & Whites'.
Previous Grounds: Association Park 1893-95; Milnfield Park 1895-1909; Station Park 1909-19; Cooper Park 1919-21.
Record Attendance: 12,608 v Arbroath, Scottish Cup, 17 Feb 1968.
Record Transfer Fee received: £32,000 for Michael Teasdale to Dundee (Jan 1994).
Record Transfer Fee paid: £10,000 for Russell McBride from Fraserburgh (July 2001).
Record Victory: 18-1 v Brora Rangers, North of Scotland Cup, 6 Feb 1960.
Record Defeat: 1-14 v Hearts, Scottish Cup, 4 Feb 1939.
Most League Appearances: 224: David Hind, 2001-09.
Most League Goals in Season (Individual): 19: Martin Johnston, 2005-06.
Most Goals Overall (Individual): 89: Craig Gunn, 2009-15.

ELGIN CITY – SCOTTISH LEAGUE TWO 2014–15 LEAGUE RECORD

Match No.	Date	Venue	Opponents	Result	H/T Score	Lg Pos.	Goalscorers	Attendance
1	Aug 9	H	East Fife	W 1-0	0-0	5	Gunn 71	654
2	16	A	East Stirling	L 1-2	0-1	5	Andrews 90	293
3	23	H	Clyde	W 1-0	1-0	5	Gunn 28	603
4	30	A	Annan Ath	D 3-3	1-2	4	Andrews 5, Gunn (pen) 53, MacPhee 73	341
5	Sept 13	A	Queen's Park	L 1-2	1-0	4	Sutherland 34	304
6	20	H	Montrose	L 0-1	0-0	6		580
7	27	A	Arbroath	L 0-1	0-0	9		601
8	Oct 18	A	Berwick R	D 1-1	1-1	10	Gunn 43	410
9	25	A	Clyde	L 1-2	0-1	10	Nicolson 66	419
10	28	H	Albion R	L 0-4	0-3	10		352
11	Nov 11	H	Annan Ath	D 0-0	0-0	9		328
12	15	H	Queen's Park	L 1-4	0-3	10	Gunn 46	552
13	22	A	East Fife	D 1-1	1-1	10	Wyness 34	505
14	Dec 2	H	Arbroath	D 1-1	0-1	10	Gunn 77	425
15	6	A	Albion R	L 0-3	0-1	10		333
16	27	A	Montrose	W 3-2	2-0	10	Wyness 16, Graham (og) 23, Gunn 88	385
17	Jan 10	A	Annan Ath	W 3-2	1-1	10	Gunn 30, Moore 65, Gilchrist 74	411
18	24	A	Queen's Park	D 1-1	1-1	10	Quinn (og) 3	538
19	31	A	Berwick R	W 2-0	0-0	9	MacPhee (pen) 70, Moore 90	371
20	Feb 7	H	Albion R	W 2-0	1-0	6	Wyness 39, Sutherland 90	625
21	14	A	East Stirling	L 0-1	0-0	8		256
22	21	H	Montrose	W 4-0	3-0	7	Gilchrist 23, Sutherland 40, Nicolson 45, Duff 77	611
23	24	H	Berwick R	W 2-1	1-0	7	Sutherland 2 9, 73	411
24	28	A	Arbroath	D 3-3	1-0	6	Sutherland 2 40, 48, Cameron 62	701
25	Mar 3	H	East Fife	L 3-5	1-4	7	Gunn 40, Cameron 46, Moore 90	463
26	10	H	Clyde	W 2-0	1-0	6	McHardy 11, Cameron 83	403
27	14	H	Queen's Park	L 1-2	1-1	7	Gilchrist 2	704
28	17	H	East Stirling	L 1-2	1-1	7	Sutherland 4	363
29	21	A	Clyde	W 2-0	1-0	7	Cameron 2, Reid 65	448
30	28	A	Albion R	W 3-0	2-0	6	McHardy 5, Reid 2 26, 76	546
31	31	H	Berwick R	D 3-3	0-1	5	Gunn 3 52, 58, 69	423
32	Apr 4	H	East Stirling	D 0-0	0-0	5		704
33	11	H	Arbroath	W 2-1	0-0	5	Gunn 61, Sutherland 73	828
34	18	A	Montrose	L 1-2	1-1	5	McHardy 37	320
35	25	H	Annan Ath	L 4-5	3-3	6	Duff 16, McHardy 3 26, 45, 90	758
36	May 2	A	East Fife	L 1-3	0-1	7	Reid 89	697

Final League Position: 7

Honours
Scottish Cup: Quarter-finals 1968.
Highland League Champions: winners 15 times.
Scottish Qualifying Cup (North): winners 7 times.
North of Scotland Cup: winners 17 times.
Highland League Cup: winners 5 times.
Inverness Cup: winners twice.

Club colours: Shirt: Black and white stripes. Shorts: Black. Socks: White.

Goalscorers: *League (55):* Gunn 13 (1 pen), Sutherland 9, McHardy 6, Cameron 4, Reid 4, Gilchrist 3, Moore 3, Wyness 3, Andrews 2, Duff 2, MacPhee 2 (1 pen), Nicolson 2, own goals 2.
William Hill Scottish FA Cup (11): Cameron 3, Sutherland 3 (1 pen), Gunn 2 (1 pen), Nicolson 2, Andrews 1.
Scottish League Cup (0).
Petrofac Training Cup (0).

Fraser M 16	Beveridge G 10 + 5	Cooper M 31 + 2	Andrews M 13	Finlayson G 12 + 1	Nicolson M 30 + 2	MacPhee A 29 + 4	Cameron B 28 + 4	Sutherland S 29 + 5	Moore D 27 + 8	Gunn C 30 + 6	McKenzie A — + 7	Wyness D 9 + 20	Bayne G 2 + 7	McHardy D 29 + 1	MacEwan R 3 + 2	McLean C 6 + 3	Duff J 26	Gilchrist A 21	Thomson C 17 + 3	Black S 5	Laidlaw R 15	Reid J 8 + 7	Match No.
1	2	3	4	5	6	7	8¹	9	10	11²	12	13											1
1	2¹	3	4	5²	8	7	10	11	9	6²	14	13	12										2
1	2	3	4	5	7	8	6	11³	9²	10¹	13	14	12										3
1	8	3	4	5	2	7	6	10	9²	11¹	13			12									4
1	2²	4	3	5¹	7	8	10³	11	9	6		13		12		14							5
1	13	3	4	2²	7	8¹	6	11	9	10			14	12		5¹							6
1	12	3¹	4	2	7	8	6	9	10³	13			14	11²		5							7
1	6	13	4	2	3	8	7	9	12	10²				11¹		5							8
1	12	3	4	2	7³	8	11	9	6²	10		13	14	5¹									9
1	2²	3	4	5	7	8	6	9	13	10	11¹			12									10
1		3			7	8	6	11	9¹	10	12			5				2	4				11
1		3			7	8	6	11	9	10³		13	14	5¹				12	2¹	4			12
1	2	3	4		7	5	6	11	13	12	10¹				9²	8							13
1	9¹		4		2	7	6	11	10	12				5				8	3				14
1	9	12	3	2		8	11	6¹	10				14	13		5¹		7²	4				15
1	13	2			7	9	8	11¹	14	12		10²		5				4	3	6³			16
	12	2			8		9	10¹	13	11²				5				7	4	3	6	1	17
	2				7	8	12	9	11²	13	10¹			5				3	4	6	1		18
	2				7	9	12	8	11²	10¹				5			13	3	4	6	1		19
	2				7	9	13	12	8	11²	10¹			5				4	3	6	1		20
	2				8	9	14	12	7³	11²	10¹			5				4	3	6	1	13	21
	2				8¹	9	12	11	7²	10²				5			13	4	3	6	1	14	22
	2¹				7	8	12	11	9	10²				5			13	4	3	6	1		23
	2				2²	9	11	10¹	8	12				5			7	4	3	6	1	13	24
	2				2	9	7	11	8	10²	13			5¹				4	3	6	1	12	25
	2				7	12	8	11	9¹	10²	14			5				3	4	6³	1	13	26
	2				7¹	12	9	10	8	11²	14			5				4	3	6³	1	13	27
	2					13	11	8²	10¹	12				5				4	3	6	1	9	28
	2				9	8	13	12	10					5			7²	4	3	6¹	1	11	29
	2				13	9	7	11	4²	10¹	14			5				3	8	12	1	6³	30
	2				12	9	7	11	8¹	6				5				3	4		1	10	31
	2				7	9³	8	10¹	14	11	13			5				3	4	12	1	6²	32
	2	14			7		6	11³	9	10²	13			5¹				3	4	12	1	8	33
	2				7	13	6		9	11	12			5				4	3	10¹	1	8²	34
	2				7	10²	6	11	13	12	14			5				3	4	8¹	1	9¹	35
	2				7	10¹	6	11	13	9²	14			5				3	4	8³	1	12	36

FALKIRK

Year Formed: 1876. *Ground & Address:* The Falkirk Stadium, 4 Stadium Way, Falkirk FK2 9EE. *Telephone:* 01324 624121. *Fax:* 01324 612418. *Email:* feedback@falkirkfc.co.uk *Website:* www.falkirkfc.co.uk
Ground Capacity: 8,750 (all seated). *Size of Pitch:* 105m × 68m.
Chairman: Doug Henderson. *Secretary:* Robert Bateman.
Manager: Peter Houston. *Assistant Manager:* Dale Brooks.
Club Nickname: 'The Bairns'.
Previous Grounds: Randyford 1876-81; Blinkbonny Grounds 1881-83; Brockville Park 1883-2003.
Record Attendance: 23,100 v Celtic, Scottish Cup 3rd rd, 21 Feb 1953.
Record Transfer Fee received: £380,000 for John Hughes to Celtic (Aug 1995).
Record Transfer Fee paid: £225,000 to Chelsea for Kevin McAllister (Aug 1991).
Record Victory: 11-1 v Tillicoultry, Scottish Cup 1st rd, 7 Sep 1889.
Record Defeat: 1-11 v Airdrieonians, Division I, 28 Apr 1951.
Most Capped Player: Alex Parker, 14 (15), Scotland.
Most League Appearances: 451: Tom Ferguson, 1919-32.
Most League Goals in Season (Individual): 43: Evelyn Morrison, Division I, 1928-29.
Most Goals Overall (Individual): 154: Kenneth Dawson, 1935-51.

FALKIRK – SCOTTISH CHAMPIONSHIP 2014–15 LEAGUE RECORD

Match No.	Date		Venue	Opponents	Result	H/T Score	Lg Pos.	Goalscorers	Atten- dance
1	Aug	9	A	Cowdenbeath	D 2-2	0-1	4	Loy [47], Bia Bi [77]	1074
2		15	H	Rangers	L 0-2	0-0	7		6927
3		23	A	Hibernian	W 1-0	1-0	6	Loy [13]	9153
4		30	A	Hearts	L 1-4	0-3	7	Bia Bi [86]	16,369
5	Sept	13	H	Queen of the South	D 1-1	0-0	8	Higgins (og) [83]	3793
6		20	H	Dumbarton	D 1-1	1-0	8	Sibbald [5]	3503
7		27	A	Raith R	D 0-0	0-0	7		1871
8	Oct	4	H	Alloa Ath	W 2-1	1-1	6	Grant, P [16], Leahy [70]	3037
9		18	A	Queen of the South	L 0-3	0-2	6		2038
10		21	H	Livingston	D 0-0	0-0	6		3021
11		25	H	Cowdenbeath	W 6-0	4-0	6	Loy [4], Smith [19], Cooper [35], Grant, P [38], McCracken [52], Vaulks [90]	3466
12	Nov	8	A	Rangers	L 0-4	0-1	6		33,359
13		15	H	Hearts	L 1-2	0-2	6	Bia Bi [71]	7003
14		22	A	Alloa Ath	W 3-2	2-1	6	Cooper [10], Loy [43], Alston [56]	1026
15	Dec	6	H	Hibernian	W 1-0	0-0	5	McCracken [90]	4983
16		13	A	Livingston	W 1-0	1-0	5	Alston [28]	1176
17		20	A	Dumbarton	W 3-0	1-0	5	Loy [11], Alston [80], Sibbald [83]	663
18		27	H	Raith R	L 0-1	0-0	5		3358
19	Jan	3	H	Alloa Ath	W 1-0	1-0	5	Loy [23]	3690
20		10	A	Hibernian	D 3-3	1-3	5	Baird [18], Craig (og) [59], Grant, P [65]	9498
21		17	H	Queen of the South	D 1-1	1-0	5	Loy (pen) [16]	3478
22		24	A	Hearts	W 3-2	1-1	4	Baird (pen) [33], Loy [52], Sibbald [80]	16,206
23		31	H	Dumbarton	D 3-3	2-1	5	Sibbald [21], Leahy [35], Smith [80]	3703
24	Feb	14	A	Raith R	D 2-2	1-0	5	Baird (pen) [23], McCracken [68]	2092
25		21	H	Livingston	W 2-0	2-0	5	Duffie [8], Vaulks [16]	3780
26		27	H	Rangers	D 1-1	1-1	4	Loy [22]	7492
27	Mar	14	A	Alloa Ath	W 3-1	1-0	5	Leahy [17], Baird [79], Cooper [87]	855
28		21	H	Hearts	L 0-3	0-1	5		7735
29		24	A	Cowdenbeath	W 1-0	0-0	5	Baird [50]	565
30		28	A	Dumbarton	L 0-1	0-0	5		1016
31		31	H	Cowdenbeath	W 1-0	1-0	4	McCracken [45]	3220
32	Apr	4	H	Raith R	W 1-0	0-0	4	Vaulks [62]	4032
33		8	A	Livingston	L 1-2	1-1	4	Baird (pen) [44]	1047
34		12	A	Queen of the South	L 0-1	0-1	5		2057
35		25	A	Rangers	D 2-2	0-0	5	Baird [57], Taiwo [61]	35,566
36	May	2	H	Hibernian	L 0-3	0-2	5		7672

Final League Position: 5

Honours
League Champions: Division II 1935-36, 1969-70, 1974-75. First Division 1990-91, 1993-94, 2002-03, 2004-05. Second Division 1979-80;
Runners-up: Division I 1907-08, 1909-10. First Division 1985-86, 1988-89, 1997-98, 1998-99. Division II 1904-05, 1951-52, 1960-61.
Scottish Cup Winners: 1913, 1957; *Runners-up:* 1997, 2009, 2015. *League Cup Runners-up:* 1947-48. *B&Q Cup Winners:* 1993-94. *League Challenge Cup Winners:* 1997-98, 2004-05, 2011-12.

European: *Europa League:* 2 matches (2009-10).

Club colours: Shirt: Navy blue. Shorts: White. Socks: Navy blue and white.

Goalscorers: *League (48):* Loy 9 (1 pen), Baird 7 (3 pens), McCracken 4, Sibbald 4, Alston 3, Bia Bi 3, Cooper 3, Grant, P 3, Leahy 3, Vaulks 3, Smith 2, Duffie 1, Taiwo 1, own goals 2.
William Hill Scottish FA Cup (6): Sibbald 3, Grant, P 1, McCracken 1, Smith 1.
Scottish League Cup (4): Alston 1 (1 pen), Cooper 1, Loy 1, Shepherd 1.
Petrofac Training Cup (9): Alston 2, Loy 2 (1 pen), Taiwo 2, Bia Bi 1, Cooper 1, Vaulks 1.

MacDonald A J 36	Mayberry A 5 + 1	McCracken D 32	Vaulks W 33 + 1	Dick L 5 + 2	Alston B 29 + 7	Durojaiye O 4 + 1	Taiwo T 28 + 3	Cooper A 10 + 14	McGrandles C 3	Loy R 26	Bia Bi B 9 + 13	Sibbald C 34 + 2	Leahy L 31 + 2	Boulding R 1 + 3	Rowan L — + 1	Shaughnessy J 9	Tudur Jones O 4	Smith D 10 + 16	Shepherd S — + 12	Grant P 30	Duffie K 18	Grant T — + 1	Bowman G — + 1	Kerr M 16 + 2	Baird J 17	Morgan T 3 + 7	Muirhead A 3	O'Hara K — + 1	Match No.
1	2	3	4	5	6	7[1]	8	9[1]	10	11	12	13																	1
1	2	4	3	5	8	6[2]	7	9[1]	10	11	12	13																	2
1	2	3	4	5	8[3]	7	6[1]	12	10	11[2]		9	13	14															3
1	2[2]	3	4	5[9]	8	7	6	10[1]		11	13	9	12			14													4
1		4	3	12	8		10	2[1]		6	9							5	7[2]	11	13								5
1		4	3		9		6[2]	13		11[3]	14	8	2					5	7	10[1]	12								6
1		3	9[1]	12	6[2]		11[3]	13				8	5	14				2	7	10	4								7
1		4	14		8[2]		6[1]	12		11	9	5	13					2	7	10[3]	3								8
1		3	8		13		7[2]	6[3]		10	9	5	11[1]					2	14	12	4								9
1	2	3	7		6			9[2]		11	12	8[1]	5							10	13	4							10
1		3	7		9[3]		13	6[1]		11	14	8	5					2	10[2]	12	4								11
1		3	4		9[1]		6	12		11	13	10[2]	8					2	7	5									12
1		3	6		8		9[1]	12		11	13	10	5					2	7[2]	14	4[3]								13
1	12	3	8		7	14	9[1]	11		10[3]		6	5					2[2]	13	4									14
1		4	3		6[3]		7[2]	13		10	11[1]	8	5					12	14	9	2								15
1		3	7		9		6[1]	12		11	10[2]	8	5					13		4	2								16
1		3	7		9[2]		6	12		11[3]	10[1]	8	5					13	14	4	2								17
1		3	8		6[3]		7[1]	11		10[2]	9	5						13	12	4	2		14						18
1[1]		3	6		10		7[2]	11		8[3]	9	5						14		4	2			12	13				19
1		3	7				9	13		10			6					5		4	2			8[2]	11[1]	12			20
1		3	8[1]				9	12		10			6					5		4	2			7	11[2]	13			21
1		3		13	9		7[1]			10[3]	14		6					5	12	4	2			8	11[2]				22
1	7	3			9[1]		10	13					6					5	12	4	2			8[2]	11				23
1		3	7		12		8			10[3]			6[1]					5	14	4	2			9	11[2]	13			24
1		3	6		14		7[1]			10	9[1]		5					13		4	2			8	11[2]	12			25
1		3	7		12		6[3]			10	9		5					14		4	2			8	11[2]	13			26
1		3	6		8[1]		9[2]	14		10			5					7[3]		4	2			13	11	12			27
1		3	6[3]		14		7[2]	13		9			5					12		4	2			8	11	10[1]			28
1		3	8		7			12		10	9		5							4	2			6[1]	11				29
1		3	6		7[2]		13			9			5					12		4	2			8	10	11[1]			30
1		4	8		13		2			9[2]			6					5		12	3			7	10	11[1]			31
1		4	7		9[2]		12			10[1]			6					5		13	3			8	11	2			32
1		3	8		6					10[1]	9		5					12		4	2			7[1]	11	13	2		33
1		4	7[1]		6		13			9			5					10		3	2			8[2]	11			12	34
1		3	7		13		9			8								12	10[1]	5	4			6	11[12]	2			35
1		3	7[2]	5			9			8			10					13	12	4	2			6[1]	11				36

FORFAR ATHLETIC

Year Formed: 1885. *Ground & Address:* Station Park, Carseview Road, Forfar DD8 3BT. *Telephone:* 01307 463576.
Fax: 01307 466956. *E-mail:* pat@ramsayladders.co.uk *Website:* www.forfarathletic.co.uk
Ground Capacity: 6,777 (seated: 739). *Size of Pitch:* 103m × 64m.
Chairman: Alastair Donald. *Vice-Chairman:* Jim Farquhar. *Secretary:* David McGregor.
Manager: Dick Campbell. *Coaches:* John Young and Barry Sellars. *Physios:* Duncan Sangster and Donald Ritchie.
Club Nicknames: 'The Loons', 'The Sky Blues'.
Previous Grounds: None.
Record Attendance: 10,780 v Rangers, Scottish Cup 2nd rd, 2 Feb 1970.
Record Transfer Fee received: £65,000 for David Bingham to Dunfermline Ath (September 1995).
Record Transfer Fee paid: £50,000 for Ian McPhee from Airdrieonians (1991).
Record Victory: 14-1 v Lindertis, Scottish Cup 1st rd, 1 Sept 1888.
Record Defeat: 2-12 v King's Park, Division II, 2 Jan 1930.
Most League Appearances: 463: Ian McPhee, 1978-88 and 1991-98.
Most League Goals in Season (Individual): 46: Dave Kilgour, Division II, 1929-30.
Most Goals Overall: 125: John Clark, 1978-91.

FORFAR ATHLETIC – SCOTTISH LEAGUE ONE 2014–15 LEAGUE RECORD

Match No.	Date	Venue	Opponents	Result	H/T Score	Lg Pos.	Goalscorers	Attendance
1	Aug 9	A	Stranraer	D	1-1	0-1	3	Malcolm [64]	409
2	16	H	Dunfermline Ath	W	2-0	0-0	2	Hilson [58], Dods [73]	1003
3	23	A	Ayr U	L	0-2	0-0	6		1156
4	30	H	Greenock Morton	W	3-2	1-1	3	Swankie 2 [19, 71], Denholm [53]	704
5	Sept 13	H	Peterhead	W	1-0	1-0	3	Denholm [43]	502
6	20	A	Stirling Alb	D	2-2	1-0	3	Kader [12], Swankie [71]	567
7	27	H	Brechin C	W	3-1	2-1	1	Denholm [12], Hilson 2 (1 pen) [34, 81 (p)]	628
8	Oct 4	A	Airdrieonians	W	2-1	0-1	1	Hilson [67], Swankie [90]	710
9	11	A	Stenhousemuir	W	3-0	1-0	1	Hilson [4], Swankie [50], Fotheringham [77]	489
10	18	A	Dunfermline Ath	D	0-0	0-0	1		2923
11	25	H	Stranraer	D	1-1	1-1	1	Hilson [42]	548
12	Nov 8	A	Greenock Morton	L	0-2	0-1	1		1244
13	15	A	Brechin C	D	3-3	1-2	2	Kader [40], Swankie [71], Templeman [76]	749
14	22	H	Ayr U	W	2-0	1-0	2	Smith, S [4], Kader [56]	562
15	Dec 6	A	Stenhousemuir	W	2-0	1-0	1	Dunlop [11], Husband [71]	434
16	13	H	Stirling Alb	W	2-1	1-1	1	Dods [26], Fotheringham [80]	495
17	20	A	Airdrieonians	D	1-1	0-0	2	Dunlop [81]	572
18	Jan 3	H	Brechin C	L	0-2	0-1	2		1110
19	10	A	Stranraer	L	2-4	0-2	3	Hilson [47], Malin [90]	475
20	17	H	Stenhousemuir	W	1-0	0-0	2	Denholm [77]	515
21	24	A	Stirling Alb	W	1-0	1-0	2	Malin [38]	571
22	31	H	Greenock Morton	L	1-2	0-1	3	Denholm [66]	595
23	Feb 7	H	Peterhead	W	3-1	1-0	2	Templeman [33], Swankie 2 [54, 90]	535
24	14	A	Airdrieonians	L	1-3	0-2	3	Travis [86]	839
25	21	H	Dunfermline Ath	W	1-0	0-0	3	Husband [58]	1134
26	28	A	Ayr U	L	0-1	0-1	4		1017
27	Mar 7	A	Greenock Morton	W	2-0	1-0	3	Dale [25], Malin [78]	1560
28	10	A	Peterhead	L	2-3	1-2	3	Swankie [2], Denholm [82]	491
29	14	H	Stranraer	W	1-0	1-0	2	Swankie [20]	545
30	21	A	Brechin C	W	3-2	2-1	3	Young [13], Templeman [15], Dods [65]	835
31	28	H	Stirling Alb	W	4-0	2-0	3	Hilson [20], Smith (og) [22], Kader [71], Templeman [89]	606
32	Apr 4	A	Stenhousemuir	W	3-1	0-0	2	Fotheringham 2 [71, 78], Swankie [90]	518
33	11	H	Airdrieonians	W	2-0	1-0	1	Fotheringham [30], Dunlop [89]	772
34	18	A	Peterhead	L	0-1	0-1	3		743
35	25	A	Dunfermline Ath	W	3-1	3-0	2	Fotheringham [8], Templeman [19], Hilson (pen) [36]	2262
36	May 2	H	Ayr U	L	1-3	1-2	3	Hilson (pen) [7]	1916

Final League Position: 3

Honours
League Champions: Second Division 1983-84. Third Division 1994-95; C Division 1948-49.
Runners-up: Third Division 1996-97, 2009-10. *Promoted to Second Division:* 2009-10 (play-offs).
Scottish Cup: Semi-finals 1982.
League Cup: Semi-finals 1977-78.
League Challenge Cup: Semi-finals 2004-05.

Club colours: Shirt: Sky blue and navy hoops. Shorts: Navy. Socks: Navy.

Goalscorers: *League (59):* Swankie 11, Hilson 10 (3 pens), Denholm 6, Fotheringham 6, Templeman 5, Kader 4, Dods 3, Dunlop 3, Malin 3, Husband 2, Dale 1, Malcolm 1, Smith, S 1, Travis 1, Young 1, own goal 1.
William Hill Scottish FA Cup (1): Hilson 1.
Scottish League Cup (2): Denholm 2.
Petrofac Training Cup (1): Hilson 1.
Championship Play-Offs (7): Kader 2, Swankie 2 (1 pen), Hay 1, Templeman 1, Travis 1.

Douglas R 36	Dunlop M 18+2	James A 4	Malcolm S 25+2	Steeves A 1	Hilson D 30+4	Dale J 7+19	Young D 21	Denholm D 24+9	Templeman C 22+9	Malin G 11+13	Kader O 23+13	Smith C —+6	Dods D 35	Husband S 22+10	Swankie G 34	Fotheringham M 11+13	Baxter M 20+1	Paterson J 11+1	Smith S 8	Travis M 18+1	Campbell I 15	Hay K —+1	Match No.
1	2	3	4	5¹	6²	7	8	9	10	11	12	13											1
1	2	5	3		10³	12	8	6¹	11		13		4		7²	9	14						2
1	2	5²	3		6¹	14	8	9	10³		13		4		7	11	12						3
1	2		3		10	12	8	9¹			6²	13	4		7³	11	14	5					4
1	2		3		10	12	8	6³			9¹	13	4		7²	11		5	14				5
1			3		10⁹	12	7	9²	14		6		4		8¹	11	13	2	5				6
1			4		10	12	8²	9¹	14	13	6		3		7	11	2³	5					7
1			4		10		8³	9²	13	12	6		3		7¹	11	14	2	5				8
1	14		4²		10		8¹	9		12	6³		3		7	11	13	2	5				9
1			3		10		8	9		12	6		4		7¹	11		2	5				10
1			3		10		8¹	6	11³	12	9²	13	4		7		14	2	5				11
1	2		3		11	14		12	7³		6²	13	4		8¹	10			5⁴	9			12
1	2	5²	4		10	12			11	13	6		3		7¹	8				9³	14		13
1			3		11	13		12	10²	14	6¹		4	8	9		2			7³	5		14
1			3		12	10			9¹	13	6³		4	7	11	14		2	8	5⁴			15
1			3		13	10			9¹	12	6²		4	7	11	14		2	8	5¹			16
1			3		10³			9	14	13	12		4	7¹	11	6²	2			5	8		17
1			3		10³			9	12	13	6¹		4	8	11	14	2			5	7²		18
1	2³		4		11	12			10	14	13		3	7²	9		5			6¹	8		19
1			3		11²	13	7			8³	6		4	14	9	10¹				2	5		20
1			3			13	7³	9	12	8	6¹		4	14	11	10²				2	5		21
1			3			14	7	9	12	8	6³		4	13	10	11¹				2²	5		22
1			3		12	14	7³	9	10	8²	6¹		4	13	11					2	5		23
1			3		12	14	7²	9¹	11	8⁴	6¹		4	13	10					2	5		24
1			3		9²	14	7¹	12	11		6³		4	8	10	13				2	5		25
1			3		11		7	12	10	14	6²		4	8	9³	13				2¹	5		26
1			3			6¹	7	13	10²	9	12		4		11³	14	5			2	8		27
1			3⁴		14	6³	7	12	10¹	9²	13		4		11		5			2	8		28
1					11		7	6²	10		12		4	8¹	9	13	2			3	5		29
1					11	12	7¹	6¹	10		14		4	13	9	8⁰	2			3	5		30
1	3				11	13		6¹	10	7¹	12		4	14	9	8¹	2				5		31
1	12				11	14	7³		10		6		4	13	9	8²	2¹			3	5		32
1	2				11	13	7¹	12	10		6²		4	14	9	8³				3	5		33
1	2				11		7²	12	10¹	13	6³		4	14	9	8				3	5		34
1	2	5			11			6¹	10	13	12	14	4	8	9³	7²					3		35
1	2⁴	3			11³			6¹	10¹	8	12	13	4		9	7			5			14	36

GREENOCK MORTON

Year Formed: 1874. *Ground & Address:* Cappielow Park, Sinclair St, Greenock PA15 2TY. *Telephone:* 01475 723571.
Fax: 01475 781084. *E-mail:* info@gmfc.net *Website:* www.gmfc.net
Ground Capacity: 11,612 (seated: 6,062). *Size of Pitch:* 100m × 65m.
Chairman: Douglas Rae. *Chief Executive:* Gillian Donaldson. *Company Secretary:* Mary Davidson.
Manager: Jim Duffy. *Assistant Manager:* Craig McPherson. *Physio:* Alyson Hendry.
Club Nickname: 'The Ton'.
Previous Grounds: Grant Street 1874, Garvel Park 1875, Cappielow Park 1879, Ladyburn Park 1882, Cappielow Park 1883.
Record Attendance: 23,500 v Celtic, 29 April 1922.
Record Transfer Fee received: £500,000 for Derek Lilley to Leeds U (March 1997).
Record Transfer Fee paid: £250,000 for Janne Lindberg and Marko Rajamäki from MyPa, Finland (Nov 1994).
Record Victory: 11-0 v Carfin Shamrock, Scottish Cup 4th rd, 13 Nov 1886.
Record Defeat: 1-10 v Port Glasgow Ath, Division II, 5 May, 1894 and v St Bernards, Division II, 14 Oct 1933.
Most Capped Player: Jimmy Cowan, 25, Scotland.
Most League Appearances: 534: Derek Collins, 1987-98, 2001-05.
Most League Goals in Season (Individual): 58: Allan McGraw, Division II, 1963-64.
Most Goals Overall (Individual): 136: Andy Ritchie, 1976-83.

GREENOCK MORTON – SCOTTISH LEAGUE ONE 2014–15 LEAGUE RECORD

Match No.	Date	Venue	Opponents	Result	H/T Score	Lg Pos.	Goalscorers	Attendance
1	Aug 9	A	Ayr U	L	0-1	0-0	9		1617
2	16	H	Stranraer	W	4-0	3-0	5	McManus 2 (1 pen) [19 (p), 45], McCluskey, J [32], Pepper [56]	1314
3	23	A	Peterhead	W	2-1	0-0	2	Milojevic [47], O'Ware [90]	708
4	30	A	Forfar Ath	L	2-3	1-1	4	McManus [37], Hands [89]	704
5	Sept 13	H	Airdrieonians	W	2-1	0-1	5	Barrowman [51], Crawford [69]	1482
6	20	H	Dunfermline Ath	W	2-1	1-0	2	McManus [29], Pepper [76]	1934
7	27	A	Stenhousemuir	L	1-2	1-1	4	McManus [31]	692
8	Oct 4	A	Brechin C	L	1-3	0-2	5	O'Ware [69]	557
9	11	H	Stirling Alb	W	2-0	1-0	3	Barrowman [33], McNeil [85]	1225
10	18	A	Ayr U	L	0-1	0-1	4		1744
11	25	A	Dunfermline Ath	W	2-1	0-0	3	O'Ware [79], McManus [90]	3342
12	Nov 8	H	Forfar Ath	W	2-0	1-0	3	Scullion [15], Barrowman [62]	1244
13	15	A	Airdrieonians	W	1-0	1-0	1	McCluskey, J [40]	949
14	22	H	Stenhousemuir	W	3-1	2-0	1	Kilday 2 [15, 35], McCluskey, S [87]	1315
15	Dec 6	A	Stranraer	L	0-2	0-1	4		415
16	13	H	Brechin C	D	2-2	0-2	3	McCluskey, J [64], McManus (pen) [90]	1108
17	20	H	Peterhead	L	0-1	0-0	3		1098
18	27	A	Stirling Alb	W	4-3	1-2	3	McKee [28], McManus 2 [75, 81], Wedderburn (og) [79]	931
19	Jan 3	H	Airdrieonians	L	0-1	0-0	3		1712
20	10	A	Stenhousemuir	W	3-2	0-0	2	McCluskey, S [52], O'Ware [59], Caldwell [63]	508
21	17	A	Ayr U	D	1-1	0-1	3	MacDonald [47]	1217
22	24	H	Dunfermline Ath	W	2-0	0-0	3	Caldwell [67], MacDonald [81]	1447
23	31	A	Forfar Ath	W	2-1	1-0	2	McKee [34], MacDonald [71]	595
24	Feb 14	A	Brechin C	D	1-1	0-0	2	Caldwell (pen) [54]	602
25	21	H	Stranraer	W	2-0	1-0	2	McManus [44], Russell [90]	1921
26	28	A	Peterhead	W	3-1	0-0	2	McManus 2 [61, 87], Caldwell [90]	659
27	Mar 3	H	Stirling Alb	W	4-0	1-0	1	McCluskey, S 3 [35, 62, 79], McManus [82]	1037
28	7	H	Forfar Ath	L	0-2	0-1	1		1560
29	14	A	Airdrieonians	L	1-2	0-0	1	McCluskey, J [90]	1109
30	21	H	Ayr U	W	2-1	0-0	2	Forbes [90], McManus [90]	1552
31	28	A	Dunfermline Ath	W	4-0	1-0	2	McCluskey, S [45], Kilday [50], McManus [76], Russell [90]	2732
32	Apr 4	H	Brechin C	L	0-2	0-0	3		1823
33	11	H	Stenhousemuir	W	3-2	0-1	3	MacDonald [78], McManus [87], McCluskey, S [90]	1568
34	18	A	Stirling Alb	W	2-0	0-0	2	McCluskey, J [53], McManus [59]	963
35	25	A	Stranraer	W	2-0	2-0	1	McManus 2 (1 pen) [40 (p), 44]	1321
36	May 2	H	Peterhead	W	3-1	2-1	1	Miller [36], Russell [39], McManus [83]	6024

Final League Position: 1

Honours

League Champions: First Division 1977-78, 1983-84, 1986-87. League One: 2014–15. Division II 1949-50, 1963-64, 1966-67. Second Division 1994-95, 2006-07. Third Division 2002-03.
Runners-up: Division 1 1916-17. First Division 2012-13. Division II 1899-1900, 1928-29, 1936-37.
Scottish Cup Winners: 1922; *Runners-up:* 1948. *League Cup Runners-up:* 1963-64.
B&Q Cup Runners-up: 1992-93.

European: *UEFA Cup:* 2 matches (*Fairs Cup:* 1968-69).

Club colours: Shirt: Blue and white hoops. Shorts: White with blue trim. Socks: White.

Goalscorers: *League (65):* McManus 20 (3 pens), McCluskey, S 7, McCluskey, J 5, Caldwell 4 (1 pen), MacDonald 4, O'Ware 4, Barrowman 3, Kilday 3, Russell 3, McKee 2, Pepper 2, Crawford 1, Forbes 1, Hands 1, McNeil 1, Miller 1, Milojevic 1, Scullion 1, own goal 1.
William Hill Scottish FA Cup (3): Barrowman 3.
Scottish League Cup (2): McKee 2.
Petrofac Training Cup (6): McManus 3, McCluskey, J 1, O'Neil 1, O'Ware 1.

Gaston D 31	Kilday L 36	Crighton S 29+1	Milojevic S 19+2	Lamie R 25+4	McKee J 20+4	Pepper C 21+4	Miller M 18+5	Allan J 1+2	McCluskey J 21+6	McManus D 32	O'Ware T 31+3	McNeil D —+5	Hands R 3+5	Russell M 26+3	Orr T —+2	McCluskey S 16+8	Crawford R 9+1	Barrowman A 15	Scullion J 3+6	Caraux N 1	Cairnie J —+1	McGowan J —+1	Adam G 4	Caldwell R 10+7	MacDonald P 10+5	Ferris A —+3	Forbes R 15+1	Match No.
1	2	3	4	5	6	7¹	8³		9¹	10²	11	12	13	14														1
1	2	3	4¹	5		7	8²		6³	10	11	12	13	9	14													2
1	2	3	4	5	6	8	7		9¹	10	11			12														3
1	2	3	4	5	6	8	7³		10	11¹	14	13	12	9²														4
1	2	3			6	7	12		11²	4	9¹			5		13	8	10										5
1	2	3		5	8	7	12		6¹	10	4			13		9²	11											6
1	2	3		5²	7	8	6		11	4				12		9¹	10	13										7
2²	3	12		5	7	8¹	6		11	4				13		9	10						1					8
1	2		4		6	7	12		11	3	13			8		5	9¹	10²										9
1	2		4	13	8	6			11	3	7²			5		9¹	10	12										10
1	2	4		7	5	8	6²		11	3	13			9¹		12	10											11
1	2	3	4	13		7			12	11	6			5		8³	10¹	9²	14									12
1	2	3	4	5		7	12		6¹	11	8			5		13	9³	11										13
1²	2	3	4	14		7			6¹	10	8			5		13	9³	11		12								14
	2	3⁴	4	5	6	7⁴	8	12	11					9¹		10						1						15
1	2		3	4¹	6		7		8	10				5		12	11	9										16
1	2	3	4	5	6¹	13	7		8	10	14			12		11³	9²											17
1	2	3	4¹	5	6	7²			9	11	8			13		12	10											18
	2	3	4		7	9¹			8	11	6			5	12	10						1						19
	2	3		5	8	7			6	4				9		10²				1				11¹	12		13	20
	2		4	8		7			6²	3				5		11							1	12	10¹	13	9	21
1	2	13		4	6	12	7¹		3					5		9								11²	10		8	22
1	2	4		8	9¹	12	13		3					5		6								11	10²	14	7³	23
1	2	3		12		6	7²		11	4				5		8			13					9¹			10	24
1	2	3		4	13	6			9¹	11	7			5		12								10			8²	25
1	2	3	4		6	13			9¹	11	7			5										12	10²		8	26
1	2²	3	4		7³		14		12	10	8			5		6								11¹	13		9	27
1	2	3	4		7¹				6	11	8			5		9²			14					10¹	13		12	28
1	2		4	5¹		7			13	11²	3			9		6								12	10		8	29
1	2		4		6				8¹	9	3			5		12			13					10¹	11		7	30
1	2	3	13	4		9			14	10¹	7			5		8¹								12	11²		6	31
1	2	3	4¹			7			12	11	8			5		6								13	10²		9	32
1	2	3²	4	14					9³	11	7			5		6			13					10¹	12		8	33
1	2	3	4			7			6²	11	12			5		9								10³	13		8	34
1	2	3	4¹	12		7¹			11	6				5		6²								13	10²		8	35
1	2	3		13	14	7			9³	11	4			5		6²								12	10		8¹	36

HAMILTON ACADEMICAL

Year Formed: 1874. *Ground:* New Douglas Park, Cadzow Avenue, Hamilton ML3 0FT. *Telephone:* 01698 368652.
Fax: 01698 285422. *E-mail:* office@acciesfc.co.uk *Website:* www.acciesfc.co.uk
Ground Capacity: 6,078 (all seated). *Size of Pitch:* 105m × 68m.
Chairman: Les Gray. *Secretary:* Scott Struthers.
Player Manager: Martin Canning. *Assistant Manager:* Chris Swailes. *Physio:* Victoria McIntyre.
Club Nickname: 'The Accies'.
Previous Grounds: Bent Farm, South Avenue, South Haugh, Douglas Park, Cliftonhill Stadium, Firhill Stadium.
Record Attendance: 28,690 v Hearts, Scottish Cup 3rd rd, 3 Mar 1937 (at Douglas Park); 5,895 v Rangers, 28 Feb 2009
(at New Douglas Park).
Record Transfer Fee received: £1,200,000 for James McCarthy to Wigan Ath (July 2009).
Record Transfer Fee paid: £180,000 for Tomas Cerny from Sigma Olomouc (July 2009).
Record Victory: 10-2 v Greenock Morton, Scottish Championship, 3 May 2014.
Record Defeat: 1-11 v Hibernian, Division I, 6 Nov 1965.
Most Capped Player: Colin Miller, 29 (61), Canada, 1988-94.
Most League Appearances: 452: Rikki Ferguson, 1974-88.
Most League Goals in Season (Individual): 35: David Wilson, Division I; 1936-37.
Most Goals Overall (Individual): 246: David Wilson, 1928-39.

HAMILTON ACADEMICAL – SCOTTISH PREMIER LEAGUE 2014–15 LEAGUE RECORD

Match No.	Date	Venue	Opponents	Result	H/T Score	Lg Pos.	Goalscorers	Atten- dance
1	Aug 9	H	Inverness CT	L 0-2	0-2	12		1622
2	13	A	St Mirren	W 2-0	1-0	5	Crawford 2 [19, 51]	3635
3	16	H	St Johnstone	W 1-0	1-0	3	MacKinnon [16]	1577
4	23	A	Partick Thistle	W 2-1	0-0	2	Andreu [87], Scotland [90]	3578
5	30	H	Ross Co	W 4-0	0-0	2	Canning [47], Antoine-Curier 2 (2 pens) [56, 63], Scotland [90]	2684
6	Sept 13	A	Dundee U	D 2-2	2-2	1	Antoine-Curier [28], Andreu [34]	7109
7	20	H	Kilmarnock	D 0-0	0-0	2		2604
8	27	A	Motherwell	W 4-0	2-0	2	Andreu [34], Crawford 2 [45, 90], Antoine-Curier (pen) [63]	4125
9	Oct 5	A	Celtic	W 1-0	0-0	1	Crawford [49]	42,412
10	17	H	Aberdeen	W 3-0	1-0	1	Andreu 2 [15, 53], Antoine-Curier [90]	4093
11	25	H	Dundee	L 0-2	0-0	1		6035
12	Nov 1	H	Partick Thistle	D 3-3	2-1	2	MacKinnon [22], Redmond [23], Andreu [90]	2855
13	8	A	Inverness CT	L 2-4	1-1	3	Andreu 2 [17, 72]	3022
14	22	H	St Mirren	W 3-0	1-0	4	Andreu [40], Antoine-Curier [67], Crawford [74]	2195
15	Dec 6	A	Aberdeen	L 0-3	0-1	5		10,330
16	13	H	Dundee	W 2-1	2-0	5	Andreu [3], Antoine-Curier [14]	2636
17	20	A	Ross Co	W 1-0	1-0	3	Canning [6]	2966
18	27	A	Kilmarnock	L 0-1	0-0	4		3921
19	Jan 1	H	Motherwell	W 5-0	2-0	4	Imrie [8], Crawford [29], Antoine-Curier [64], Andreu [69], Redmond [87]	3926
20	4	A	St Johnstone	W 1-0	1-0	3	Andreu [34]	3202
21	12	H	Dundee U	L 2-3	0-1	5	Garcia Tena [57], Crawford [70]	2384
22	17	H	Celtic	L 0-2	0-1	5		6007
23	21	A	Partick Thistle	L 0-5	0-2	5		2138
24	24	H	Inverness CT	L 0-2	0-0	5		5089
25	31	A	Dundee	D 1-1	0-0	5	Canning [86]	5618
26	Feb 7	H	Kilmarnock	D 0-0	0-0	5		2245
27	15	A	Aberdeen	L 0-3	0-2	5		3095
28	22	A	Celtic	L 0-4	0-0	5		47,989
29	28	A	St Mirren	L 0-1	0-0	5		3503
30	Mar 14	H	Ross Co	D 2-2	2-1	5	Scotland [2], Imrie [18]	1544
31	20	A	Motherwell	L 0-4	0-0	5		4250
32	Apr 4	H	St Johnstone	D 1-1	1-0	6	Crawford [7]	2032
33	11	A	Dundee U	L 0-1	0-0	7		5243
34	24	H	Motherwell	W 2-0	1-0	6	Scotland [21], Crawford [52]	3301
35	May 2	A	Kilmarnock	W 3-2	1-0	6	Scotland [24], MacKinnon [65], Hasselbaink [70]	3450
36	9	H	Partick Thistle	D 1-1	0-0	6	Docherty [85]	2342
37	16	A	Ross Co	L 1-2	1-0	6	Tagliapietra [27]	3381
38	23	H	St Mirren	W 1-0	0-0	6	Crawford [83]	2425

Final League Position: 6

Honours
League Champions: Division II 1903-04. First Division 1985-86, 1987-88, 2007-08; Third Division 2000-01.
Runners-up: Division II 1952-53, 1964-65; Second Division 1996-97, 2003-04; Championship 2013-14 (promoted via play-offs).
Scottish Cup Runners-up: 1911, 1935. *League Cup:* Semi-finalists three times. *League Challenge Cup Runners-up:* 2005-06, 2011-12. *B&Q Cup Winners:* 1991-92, 1992-93.

Club colours: Shirt: Red and white hoops. Shorts: White. Socks: White.

Goalscorers: *League (50):* Andreu 12, Crawford 11, Antoine-Curier 8 (3 pens), Scotland 5, Canning 3, MacKinnon 3, Imrie 2, Redmond 2, Docherty 1, Garcia Tena 1, Hasselbaink 1, Tagliapietra 1.
William Hill Scottish FA Cup (0).
Scottish League Cup (6): Longridge 2, Andreu 1, Brophy 1, Canning 1, Imrie 1.

McGovern M 38	Gordon Z 24	Devlin M 25+3	Canning M 22+1	Hendrie S 26+4	Imrie D 33+1	Gillespie G 36	Neil A 7	Longridge L 9+23	Scotland J 12+12	Redmond D 26+3	Crawford A 37+1	Antoine-Curier M 20+2	Ryan A —+7	Garcia Tena J 25+1	MacKinnon D 27+3	Andreu T 21+2	Docherty G 1+6	Lyon D 8+6	Brophy E 2+14	Routledge J 12+3	Watson C —+2	Sumsky N —+1	Hasselbaink N 4+6	Tagliapietra L 2+4	MacDonald K 7+1	McMann S —+1	Boyd S —+1	Match No.
1	2	3	4	5¹	6	7	8	9³	10²	11	12	13	14															1
1	5		3	12	9	2	7²		14	6¹	11	10³	11	13		4	8											2
1	2		3	5	7¹	6			10³	9²	11	13		4	8	12	14											3
1	2		3		7²	6		5¹	12	10	9	11³	14	4	8	13												4
1	2	12	3		9¹	5		13	14	11	8	10²		4³	6	7												5
1	2	12	3	13	6	5		14		10²	8	11		4³	7⁸	9¹												6
1	2	3		5	7¹	4	6³	13	11²	10	8			9		12	14											7
1	2	3		5	7	6		12		9¹	8	11²		4		10³	14	13										8
1	2	3		5	6	8		12		9³	10	11²	14	4		7¹	13											9
1	2	3		5	8	7		13		10¹	6	11²	14	4	12	9³												10
1	5	3		4	10	6		13	12	9³	8¹	11²		2	14	7												11
1	2	12³	3	14	6	5			9¹	7	11			4⁸	8	10			13									12
1	2	3		5	12			14	9³	6	10²	13		4	8	11			7¹									13
1	2		3	5	10	6		12	14	8²	9	11¹		4	13	7³												14
1	2	4	3	5				7²		12	11¹			9	13		6	8		10⁸								15
1		4	3	5	10	2	7¹	12	13		9²	11		6	8													16
1		4	3	5	6	2	7¹	12	13		9	11²		8	10³		14											17
1		4	3	5	6	2	7¹	14	13		9	11²		8	10³				12									18
1		4	3	5	8	2	6²		14	10	11¹			7	9³			13	12									19
1		4	3	5	7	2		13		10¹	11³			6²	9	14		12	8									20
1		4	14	5²	6	2		12		9	11		3²	8	10			13	7¹									21
1		4	3	5	9¹	2		12		14	7	11		6³	10			13	8²									22
1	3¹		5	8	2			12		10	11³		4	6	9		14	7²	13									23
1		3	5	10³	2			13		9¹	8		4	7²	11	14		12	6									24
1	2		3	5	7⁸	6²		12	11¹		8			4		9			13	10								25
1	2		3	5¹		6		12	10²	11	8			4	7³			14	13	9								26
1	2		3	5		7³			11²	10	9¹			4⁸	6			13	8	12	14							27
1	2²	4	3³	5	10	7¹		12		9				6		13		8		11	14							28
1	2	3	4		7			13	10²	9		8¹			12	6			11			5						29
1	2	3			7	6		12	11²	10¹	8			4		9			13			5						30
1	2	3		6³	9			13	10²	8	11			4		7⁸	14		12			5						31
1	2	3	4⁸	5¹		6		8		9³	10			12	7			14		11²	13							32
1	2	3		5	9	7		6²	12	13	11			8³		4	14		10¹									33
1		3		5	10	8		6	11²		9			4¹	7		2						13	12				34
1		3	13	8²	6			10	11¹		9			4	7		2						12	14	5³			35
1	3²			6	8			9	11¹	10				4	7³	14	2						13	12	5			36
1				10	6			7²	12		8			4	9³	13	2	11¹					14	3	5			37
1				7²	6			10	14		9			4		8¹	2	11					3	5³	12	13		38

HEART OF MIDLOTHIAN

Year Formed: 1874. *Ground & Address:* Tynecastle Stadium, McLeod Street, Edinburgh EH11 2NL. *Telephone:* 0871 663 1874. *Fax:* 0131 200 7222. *E-mail:* supporterservices@homplc.co.uk *Website:* www.heartsfc.co.uk
Ground Capacity: 17,529. *Size of Pitch:* 100m × 64m.
Chairman: Brian Cormack. *Chief Executive:* Ann Budge.
Head Coach: Robbie Neilson. *Assistant Head Coach:* Stevie Crawford. *Physio:* Rob Marshall.
Club Nicknames: 'Hearts', 'Jambos'.
Previous Grounds: The Meadows 1874, Powderhall 1878, Old Tynecastle 1881 Tynecastle Park, 1886.
Record Attendance: 53,396 v Rangers, Scottish Cup 3rd rd, 13 Feb 1932 (57,857 v Barcelona, 28 July 2007 at Murrayfield).
Record Transfer Fee received: £9,000,000 for Craig Gordon to Sunderland (August 2008).
Record of Transfer paid: £850,000 for Mirsad Beslija to Genk (January 2006).
Record Victory: 15-0 v King's Park, Scottish Cup 2nd rd, 13 Feb 1937 (21-0 v Anchor, EFA Cup, 30 Oct 1880).
Record Defeat: 1-8 v Vale of Leven, Scottish Cup 3rd rd, 1883.
Most Capped Player: Steven Pressley, 32, Scotland.
Most League Appearances: 515: Gary Mackay, 1980-97.
Most League Goals in Season (Individual): 44: Barney Battles, 1930-31.
Most Goals Overall (Individual): 214: John Robertson, 1983-98.

HEART OF MIDLOTHIAN – SCOTTISH CHAMPIONSHIP 2014–15 LEAGUE RECORD

Match No.	Date	Venue	Opponents	Result	H/T Score	Lg Pos.	Goalscorers	Attendance
1	Aug 10	A	Rangers	W 2-1	0-0	3	Wilson [53], Sow [90]	43,683
2	17	H	Hibernian	W 2-1	0-0	3	Nicholson [76], Buaben (pen) [80]	17,280
3	23	A	Raith R	W 4-0	2-0	1	Keatings 3 [13, 28, 58], Oliver [90]	6105
4	30	H	Falkirk	W 4-1	3-0	1	McGhee [17], King 2 [25, 37], Sow (pen) [78]	16,369
5	Sept 13	A	Dumbarton	D 0-0	0-0	1		1757
6	20	H	Cowdenbeath	W 5-1	1-1	1	King [15], Walker [48], Sow (pen) [55], Carrick 2 [79, 87]	15,594
7	28	H	Livingston	W 5-0	3-0	1	El Hassnaoui [14], Walker [30], Sow 2 [43, 90], Keatings [87]	14,848
8	Oct 4	A	Queen of the South	W 3-0	2-0	1	Sow [39], Buaben [42], McGhee [59]	5534
9	11	A	Alloa Ath	W 1-0	0-0	1	Eckersley [87]	3067
10	18	H	Dumbarton	W 5-1	2-0	1	Sow [26], Buaben (pen) [40], Holt [56], Paterson [84], King [88]	15,522
11	26	A	Hibernian	D 1-1	0-1	1	Ozturk [90]	14,562
12	Nov 8	H	Raith R	W 1-0	1-0	1	Ozturk [5]	16,372
13	15	A	Falkirk	W 2-1	2-0	1	McHattie [27], El Hassnaoui [37]	7003
14	22	H	Rangers	W 2-0	0-0	1	Holt [56], Walker (pen) [88]	17,004
15	Dec 6	H	Queen of the South	W 4-1	1-0	1	Keatings [19], Wilson [67], Buaben [74], Eckersley [79]	15,459
16	20	H	Alloa Ath	W 2-0	2-0	1	Keatings [16], Paterson [29]	15,224
17	23	A	Cowdenbeath	W 2-0	1-0	1	Keatings [25], Paterson [62]	3718
18	27	A	Livingston	W 1-0	1-0	1	Keatings [25]	8178
19	Jan 3	H	Hibernian	D 1-1	1-1	1	Walker [40]	17,279
20	10	A	Dumbarton	W 5-1	2-0	1	Nicholson 2 [8, 57], Walker [26], Zeefuik 2 [52, 62]	1537
21	24	H	Falkirk	L 2-3	1-1	1	Zeefuik [2], Keatings [73]	16,206
22	31	A	Alloa Ath	W 4-1	2-0	1	Pallardo [5], Keatings [12], Walker [66], Paterson [90]	2592
23	Feb 7	A	Livingston	W 3-2	1-0	1	Zeefuik [4], Anderson [82], Walker [84]	5352
24	14	A	Livingston	W 1-0	1-0	1	Walker [40]	15,463
25	21	A	Queen of the South	W 2-1	1-1	1	King [32], Zeefuik [85]	5100
26	28	H	Cowdenbeath	W 10-0	5-0	1	Zeefuik 3 (2 pens) [26 (p), 27, 29 (p)], Nicholson [33], Walker [39], Gomis (pen) [57], Ozturk [61], Wilson [68], Sow 2 [70, 74]	15,180
27	Mar 14	H	Dumbarton	W 4-0	0-0	1	Sow [53], Wilson [69], King 2 [86, 90]	15,631
28	17	A	Raith R	W 3-1	1-1	1	McHattie [27], Walker [79], King [85]	4760
29	21	A	Falkirk	W 3-0	1-0	1	Walker [28], Zeefuik [47], Keatings [82]	7735
30	28	H	Queen of the South	W 2-0	1-0	1	Sow [6], Ozturk [67]	16,855
31	Apr 5	A	Rangers	L 1-2	0-2	1	Zeefuik [83]	40,521
32	8	H	Alloa Ath	W 3-0	1-0	1	Paterson [43], Wilson [49], El Hassnaoui [69]	15,156
33	12	A	Hibernian	L 0-2	0-1	1		13,530
34	18	H	Raith R	W 2-1	1-0	1	Nicholson [34], El Hassnaoui [56]	15,405
35	25	A	Cowdenbeath	W 2-1	1-1	1	Paterson [32], McKay (pen) [90]	2394
36	May 2	H	Rangers	D 2-2	0-2	1	Zeefuik 2 [82, 90]	16,874

Final League Position: 1

Honours
League Champions: Division I 1894-95, 1896-97, 1957-58, 1959-60. First Division 1979-80. Championship 2014-15.
Runners-up: Division I 1893-94, 1898-99, 1903-04, 1905-06, 1914-15, 1937-38, 1953-54, 1956-57, 1958-59, 1964-65. Premier Division 1985-86, 1987-88, 1991-92, 2005-06. First Division 1977-78, 1982-83.
Scottish Cup Winners: 1891, 1896, 1901, 1906, 1956, 1998, 2006, 2012; *Runners-up:* 1903, 1907, 1968, 1976, 1986, 1996.
League Cup Winners: 1954-55, 1958-59, 1959-60, 1962-63; *Runners-up:* 1961-62, 1996-97, 2012-13.

European: *European Cup:* 8 matches (1958-59, 1960-61, 2006-07). *Cup Winners' Cup:* 10 matches (1976-77, 1996-97, 1998-99). *UEFA Cup:* 46 matches (*Fairs Cup:* 1961-62, 1963-64, 1965-66. *UEFA Cup:* 1984-85, 1986-87, 1988-89, 1990-91, 1992-93, 1993-94, 2000-01, 2003-04, 2004-05, 2006-07). *Europa League:* 8 matches (2010-11, 2011-12, 2012-13).

Club colours: Shirt: Maroon with white trim. Shorts: White with maroon trim. Socks: Maroon with white trim.

Goalscorers: *League (96):* Zeefuik 12 (2 pens), Keatings 11, Sow 12 (2 pens), Walker 11 (1 pen), King 8, Paterson 6, Nicholson 5, Wilson 5, Buaben 4 (2 pens), El Hassnaoui 4, Ozturk 4, Carrick 2, Eckersley 2, Holt 2, McGhee 2, McHattie 2, Anderson 1, Gomis 1 (1 pen), McKay 1 (1 pen), Oliver 1, Pallardo 1.
William Hill Scottish FA Cup (0).
Scottish League Cup (2): McHattie 1, Oliver 1.
Petrofac Training Cup (4): King 1, Paterson 1, Sow 1, own goal 1.

Alexander N 29	McGhee J 14+4	Ozturk A 33	Wilson D 31	McHattie K 14	King B 22+9	Gomis M 33+1	Buaben P 21	Nicholson S 21+8	Sow O 20+2	Carrick D 2+2	McKay B 6+4	Gallacher S 2+1	Holt J 5+10	Hamilton J 5	Walker J 26+6	Oliver G —+9	Keatings J 15+14	Robinson S 2+3	Roy A —+1	Eckersley A 22+2	El Hassnaoui S 10+8	Paterson C 27+2	Pallardo M 18+5	Buchanan R 1+3	Flanagan N —+1	Zeefuik G 13+2	Anderson K 4+5	McKirdy S —+1	Match No.
1[2]	2[1]	3	4	5	6	7	8	9	10	11[3]	12	13	14																1
1	2	3	4	5	8[1]	7	6	10[3]	11[8]						9[2]	1	12	13	14										2
1	2	3	4	5	8	7[1]	6[2]	10							9	1	13	11[3]	12	14									3
1	2	3[3]	4	5	9[2]	7	8	6	11						12	14	1	13		10									4
1	2	3	4	5[1]	6[2]	8		9	11				7		13		10[3]			12	14								5
1		3	4		9[3]	8[1]		10	13				14		6		11[2]	7		5	12	2							6
1		3	4	5	13	7	8	9[1]	10	12					6[2]		14			5	11[3]	2							7
1	2	3[1]	4		9	8	7[3]	12	11						6					5	10[2]	14	13						8
1	2[3]	3	4		6	7	8	12	10	11[2]					9[1]					5	14	13							9
1		4	3		6	8	7[2]	9[2]	10[1]				12		14					5	11	2	13						10
1	13	3	4[1]		9[2]	8	7	6	10				12							5	11[3]	2[4]	14						11
1	2	4			6	8	7	9[1]		3			13		11[2]		12			5	10[3]		14						12
1	2	4		5	6	8	7[1]			3			13		11		12			5	10[2]	9							13
1	14	3		5[1]	9	8							4		10[3]		6			13	12	11[2]	2	7					14
1	13	3	4		6	8		8							9[3]		11[2]	12		5		2	7	10[1]	14				15
1		3	4		9		7	13					12		10[2]	14	11[3]	6[1]		5		2	8						16
1	2		4		8	6[1]	12		3				13		11[2]		10[3]			5		9	7	14					17
1		4	3		10	6	7	8					9[2]				13			11[1]		5	2	12					18
1		3	4		12	8	9[2]	6	10[3]				14		11[1]		13			5		2	7						19
1		3	4		14	8[3]	7[2]	6					12		9		10			5		2	13			11[1]			20
1	3	4			8[1]	7	9	10[2]					13		6		12			5		2				11			21
1		3	4		13	7	9		11[2]						6[3]	14	10[1]			5		2	8			12			22
1	5	3	4		13	8		6[2]			14				9							2	7			11[3]	12		23
1		3	4		12	13	8		6[2]						7	14	10[1]			5		2	8			11[3]	9[3]		24
1		3	4		10[2]	6	8[3]		13				14		9					5		2	7			11[3]	12		25
1		3	4		10[3]	7		8	12						9[2]		13			5	14	2	6			11[1]			26
1		3	4		12	8		6	10[1]						9[2]		13			5	14	2	7			11[3]			27
1		3	4	5	6[2]	7		9							12		10[3]			13	2	8				11[3]	14		28
1		3	4		6	8		12	10[1]						9[2]		13			5		2	7			11[3]	14		29
1		4	3		6[1]	8		12	10[3]						9		13			5	14	2	7			11[2]			30
1		3	4	5[2]	12	8[1]		6	10						9		13				2	7				11			31
		14	4		9	8[1]		6				3[3]		1	12	11[2]				5	10	2	13				7		32
1		3	4		9[1]	13	8		12	10					6					5		2	7			11[2]			33
		5	4	2		7		9[2]	10[1]			1			6	14	13			11	3					8[3]	12		34
2[1]		3	5		8	12	9		4			1			6		13			14	10					11[3]	7[2]		35
		3	4	5		8	9[2]	11				1			6		14			10[1]	2	7[3]				12	13		36

HIBERNIAN

Year Formed: 1875. *Ground & Address:* Easter Road Stadium, 12 Albion Place, Edinburgh EH7 5QG. *Telephone:* 0131 661 2159. *Fax:* 0131 659 6488. *E-mail:* club@hibernianfc.co.uk *Website:* www.hibernianfc.co.uk
Ground Capacity: 20,421 (all seated). *Size of Pitch:* 102m × 67m.
Chairman: Rod Petrie. *Chief Executive:* Leean Dempster. *Club Secretary:* Garry O'Hagan.
Head Coach: Alan Stubbs. *Assistant Head Coach:* Andy Holden. *Physio:* John Porteous.
Club Nickname: 'Hibs', 'Hibees'.
Previous Grounds: Meadows 1875-78, Powderhall 1878-79, Mayfield 1879-80, First Easter Road 1880-92, Second Easter Road 1892-.
Record Attendance: 65,860 v Hearts, Division I, 2 Jan 1950.
Record Transfer Fee received: £4,400,000 for Scott Brown from Celtic (2007).
Record of Transfer paid: £700,000 for Ulises de la Cruz to LDU Quito (2001).
Record Victory: 15-1 v Pebbles Rovers, Scottish Cup 2nd rd, 11 Feb 1961.
Record Defeat: 0-10 v Rangers, Division I, 24 Dec 1898.
Most Capped Player: Lawrie Reilly, 38, Scotland.
Most League Appearances: 446: Arthur Duncan.
Most League Goals in Season (Individual): 42: Joe Baker, 1959-60.
Most Goals Overall (Individual): 233: Lawrie Reilly, 1945-58.

HIBERNIAN – SCOTTISH CHAMPIONSHIP 2014–15 LEAGUE RECORD

Match No.	Date	Venue	Opponents	Result	H/T Score	Lg Pos.	Goalscorers	Atten- dance
1	Aug 9	H	Livingston	W 2-1	2-0	3	El Alagui [16], Oxley [19]	9390
2	17	A	Hearts	L 1-2	0-0	5	El Alagui [90]	17,280
3	23	H	Falkirk	L 0-1	0-1	8		9153
4	30	A	Alloa Ath	L 1-2	1-0	8	Cummings [15]	2476
5	Sept 13	H	Cowdenbeath	W 3-2	1-0	6	Forster [26], Malonga (pen) [78], Cummings [90]	11,021
6	20	A	Queen of the South	L 0-1	0-1	7		3083
7	29	A	Rangers	W 3-1	3-0	5	Cummings 2 [25, 39], Gray [31]	31,619
8	Oct 4	H	Raith R	D 1-1	1-0	5	Robertson [44]	9954
9	11	H	Dumbarton	D 0-0	0-0	5		7923
10	18	A	Livingston	W 4-0	1-0	4	Malonga [31], Handling [53], McGeouch (pen) [70], Heffernan [86]	2666
11	26	H	Hearts	D 1-1	1-0	4	Malonga [44]	14,562
12	Nov 8	A	Cowdenbeath	W 2-1	2-0	4	Hanlon [25], Cummings [41]	2563
13	15	H	Queen of the South	D 0-0	0-0	4		10,069
14	22	A	Dumbarton	W 6-3	3-0	4	Allan, S [23], Malonga 3 [27, 64, 85], Hanlon [30], Stanton [83]	1409
15	Dec 6	A	Falkirk	L 0-1	0-0	4		4983
16	13	A	Alloa Ath	W 2-0	1-0	4	Handling [28], Malonga [73]	8031
17	20	A	Raith R	W 3-1	1-1	3	Cummings [44], Fontaine [78], Malonga [81]	3166
18	27	H	Rangers	W 4-0	2-0	3	Gray [8], Cummings [12], Robertson [63], Craig [70]	15,261
19	Jan 3	A	Hearts	D 1-1	1-1	3	Cummings [23]	17,279
20	10	H	Falkirk	D 3-3	3-1	3	Cummings 2 [12, 42], Leahy (og) [39]	9498
21	17	A	Cowdenbeath	W 5-0	2-0	3	Hanlon [9], Cummings [24], Robertson [74], Booth [84], Stevenson [90]	8240
22	24	A	Queen of the South	W 2-0	0-0	3	McGeouch (pen) [63], Robertson [75-]	3677
23	31	H	Raith R	D 1-1	0-0	3	Boyle [46]	9024
24	Feb 13	A	Rangers	W 2-0	1-0	2	Robertson [19], Stevenson [82]	29,769
25	21	H	Dumbarton	W 3-0	2-0	2	Dja Djedje [29], Malonga 2 [32, 56]	8370
26	28	A	Alloa Ath	W 1-0	1-0	2	Allan, S [26]	2024
27	Mar 11	H	Livingston	W 2-1	1-0	2	Cummings [31], Dja Djedje [89]	7857
28	14	A	Cowdenbeath	W 2-0	2-0	2	Fyvie [32], Cummings [34]	1822
29	22	H	Rangers	L 0-2	0-1	2		14,075
30	28	A	Raith R	L 1-2	0-0	2	Fyvie [56]	3183
31	Apr 4	H	Queen of the South	L 0-1	0-0	2		8773
32	8	A	Dumbarton	W 2-1	1-0	2	Hanlon [42], Cummings [66]	1110
33	12	H	Hearts	W 2-0	1-0	2	Cummings [30], El Alagui [90]	13,530
34	22	A	Livingston	W 3-1	2-1	3	Robertson [6], Cummings [15], Malonga [82]	2301
35	25	H	Alloa Ath	W 4-1	2-0	2	Boyle [31], Craig [42], Cummings [61], Malonga [71]	8328
36	May 2	A	Falkirk	W 3-0	2-0	2	Boyle [5], Cummings [40], Malonga [77]	7672

Final League Position: 2

Honours

League Champions: Division I 1902-03, 1947-48, 1950-51, 1951-52. First Division 1980-81, 1998-99. Division II 1893-94, 1894-95, 1932-33; *Runners-up:* Division I 1896-97, 1946-47, 1949-50, 1952-53, 1973-74, 1974-75. Championship 2014-15.
Scottish Cup Winners: 1887, 1902; *Runners-up:* 1896, 1914, 1923, 1924, 1947, 1958, 1972, 1979, 2001, 2012, 2013.
League Cup Winners: 1972-73, 1991-92, 2006-07; *Runners-up:* 1950-51, 1968-69, 1974-75, 1985-86, 1993-94, 2003-04.
Drybrough Cup Winners: 1972-73, 1973-74.

European: *European Cup:* 6 matches (1955-56 semi-finals). *Cup Winners' Cup:* 6 matches (1972-73). *UEFA Cup:* 64 matches (*Fairs Cup:* 1960-61 semi-finals, 1961-62, 1962-63, 1965-66, 1967-68, 1968-69, 1970-71. *UEFA Cup:* 1973-74, 1974-75, 1975-76, 1976-77, 1978-79, 1989-90, 1992-93, 2001-02, 2005-06. *Europa League:* 4 matches 2010-11, 2013-14).

Club colours: Shirt: Green with white sleeves. Shorts: White. Socks: Green.

Goalscorers: *League (70):* Cummings 18, Malonga 13 (1 pen), Robertson 6, Hanlon 4, Boyle 3, El Alagui 3, Allan, S 2, Craig 2, Dja Djedje 2, Fyvie 2, Gray 2, Handling 2, McGeouch 2 (2 pens), Stevenson 2, Booth 1, Fontaine 1, Forster 1, Heffernan 1, Oxley 1, Stanton 1, own goal 1.
William Hill Scottish FA Cup (9): Craig 1, Cummings 1, Dja Djedje 1, Fontaine 1, Gray 1, McGeouch 1, Stanton 1, Stevenson 1, own goal 1.
Scottish League Cup (8): Malonga 3, El Alagui 2, Cummings 1, Kennedy 1, Stanton 1.
Petrofac Training Cup (1): Handling 1.
Premiership Play-Offs (1): Cummings 1.

Oxley M 35	Gray D 23+2	Forster J 14+3	Hanlon P 31	Stevenson L 35	Robertson S 32	Craig L 22+2	Harris A 4+8	Heffernan P 4+7	Stanton S 8+14	El Alagui F 7+2	Kennedy M 5+8	Cummings J 27+6	Nelson M 2	Handling D 12+8	Allan S 29+3	Booth C 6+5	Fontaine L 29	McGeouch D 17+3	Malonga D 20+4	Sinclair J 1+2	Perntreou K 1+1	Allan L —+1	Martin S —+3	Boyle M 10+7	Dja Djedje F 5+6	Watson K 8+1	Fyvie F 9+3	Duthie C —+1	Match No.
1	2	3	4	5	6	7	8	9[2]	10[1]	11	12	13																	1
1	2	3		5	6[8]	7	8		10[1]	11	12			4	9[2]	13													2
1	2	3					8	6[2]	11[1]	13	10	9	12	4	14	7[3]	5												3
1	2	3		5		7	13	12	9	11[2]	10[1]	8[3]		14	6		4												4
1	2	3	4	5	6			11[1]	10[2]			8	14		7[3]			9	12	13									5
1	2	3	4	6	8[2]			5[1]		9	12		13	14		7	10	11[3]											6
1	6[2]	2	3	9	7	5	13			11[1]				8	12	4		10											7
1		2	3	5	6	8[1]	13	14		10				7[1]	9	4	12	11[2]											8
1	5	2	3	9	6	8[1]		13		12	11			14		4[2]	7	10[1]											9
1	2		3	5	7			13	14	12		11[2]		9[1]	8	4		6	10[3]										10
1	2		4	5	8			13	12			14	11[2]	9[3]	7[1]		3	6	10										11
1[3]	2		3	5	6	8	14			13	11			7[2]	9		4	10[1]	12										12
	2		4	5		7		8[3]	12	14		10	11[1]		9[2]	6		3		13	1								13
	2		4	5	8		7	14		12		13	10[1]		9[2]	6[3]		3		11									14
1	2		4	5	7			13	10[3]	6[1]			11[2]		9	8		3					12	14					15
1	2[3]		3	5	7	8		14				13	11[1]		9[2]	6	12	4						10					16
1	2[2]		3	5	7	8			14	12			11		9[1]	6	13	4						10[3]					17
1	2[1]		3	5	7	8				14		13	10[3]		9[2]	6	12	4						11					18
1	2[1]		3	5	7	8						10[3]		9[2]	6	12	4	13	11					14					19
1			3	5	8	9						11		13	6[2]	2	4	7						10[1]	12				20
1		13	3	5	8	9		12				11		14	6[1]	2	4	7[3]						10[3]					21
1		13	3	5	6	8		12				11[1]		14	9[2]	2	4	7						10[3]					22
1			4	5	7[2]	8						11[3]		12	6		3	9[1]					14	10	13	2			23
1	5		3	9	6							11[1]		7[3]	4		8	10[2]						12	14	2	13		24
1	13		3	5[2]	6							7[1]			4		8	10[3]						12	11	2	9	14	25
1	2		4	5	6	14						12		9[3]	4		8	10[2]						13	11[1]	3	7		26
1			3	9	7	8[2]						13		10[1]	4		12							5	11	2	6		27
1	2	14		5	7							13		11[3]	6[2]	4	8							12	10[1]	3	9		28
1	2[2]		3	5	7[3]							14		9	4		8	10						13	11[1]	12	6		29
1	2		5	8								10[2]	13	12	7		4	9	11[3]					14		3	6[1]		30
1			3	5	7							6	12	11[1]	8		4	10						13	2	9[2]			31
1		2	3	9	7[2]	8						10		11[1]	6		4		13					5			12		32
1		2	3	9								10		11[1]	7		4	6	12[2]					5	13		8		33
1		2	3	9	7	14						10[1]		11[1]			4	6	12					5	13		8[2]		34
1		2	3	9	7[2]	8						12		11[3]	13	6[1]	4		10				14	5					35
1	12	2[3]	3	9	7	8						13		10[3]		6	4		11					5[1]			14		36

INVERNESS CALEDONIAN THISTLE

Year Formed: 1994. *Ground & Address:* Tulloch Caledonian Stadium, Stadium Road, Inverness IV1 1FF. *Telephone:*
01463 222880. *Fax:* 01463 227479. *E-mail:* info@ictfc.co.uk *Website:* www.ictfc.co.uk
Ground Capacity: 7,780 (all seated). *Size of Pitch:* 105m × 68m.
Chairman: Kenny Cameron. *Club Secretary:* Ian MacDonald.
Club Nicknames: 'Caley Thistle', 'Caley Jags', 'ICT'.
Manager: John Hughes. *Assistant Manager:* Russell Latapy. *Physio:* John McCreadie.
Record Attendance: 7,753 v Rangers, SPL, 20 January 2008.
Record Transfer Fee received: £400,000 for Marius Niculae to Dinamo Bucharest (July 2008).
Record of Transfer paid: £65,000 for John Rankin from Ross Co (July 2006).
Record Victory: 8-1 v Annan Ath, Scottish Cup 3rd rd, 24 January 1998.
Record Defeats: 0-6 v Airdrieonians, First Division, 21 Sep 2000; 0-6 v Celtic, League Cup 3rd rd, 22 Sep 2010; 0-6 v
Celtic, Scottish Premiership, 27 April 2014.
Most Capped Player: Richard Hastings, 38 (59), Canada.
Most League Appearances: 490: Ross Tokely, 1995-2012.
Most League Goals in Season: 27: Iain Stewart, 1996-97; Denis Wyness, 2002-03.
Most Goals Overall (Individual): 118: Denis Wyness, 2000-03, 2005-08.

INVERNESS CALEDONIAN THISTLE –
SCOTTISH PREMIER LEAGUE 2014–15 LEAGUE RECORD

Match No.	Date	Venue	Opponents	Result	H/T Score	Lg Pos.	Goalscorers	Atten-dance
1	Aug 9	A	Hamilton A	W 2-0	2-0	1	McKay [10], Christie [25]	1622
2	13	H	Dundee	D 0-0	0-0	2		3082
3	16	A	Motherwell	W 2-0	1-0	1	Tansey [42], Doran [89]	3732
4	23	H	Celtic	W 1-0	0-0	1	O'Connell (og) [65]	5862
5	30	H	Kilmarnock	W 2-0	0-0	1	Doran [76], Samson (og) [80]	3830
6	Sept 13	A	Partick Thistle	L 1-3	1-2	2	Doran [13]	2917
7	20	H	St Johnstone	W 2-1	0-0	1	Watkins [61], Christie [66]	2770
8	27	A	Aberdeen	L 2-3	1-2	3	Meekings [16], Watkins [50]	11,414
9	Oct 5	A	Ross Co	D 1-1	0-1	3	Watkins [49]	3741
10	18	A	St Mirren	W 1-0	1-0	2	Tansey (pen) [43]	3109
11	25	H	Dundee U	W 1-0	1-0	2	Watkins [10]	3508
12	Nov 1	A	Celtic	L 0-1	0-0	4		42,553
13	8	H	Hamilton A	W 4-2	1-1	1	McKay 2 [25, 68], Warren [59], Vincent [78]	3022
14	22	H	Motherwell	W 3-1	1-1	2	McKay [29], Watkins [71], Meekings [78]	3037
15	Dec 6	A	Dundee	W 2-1	0-1	2	McKay [55], Christie [88]	5400
16	13	H	Partick Thistle	L 0-4	0-2	2		2723
17	20	A	St Johnstone	L 0-1	0-0	4		2891
18	28	H	Aberdeen	L 0-1	0-1	5		6614
19	Jan 1	A	Ross Co	W 3-1	1-0	5	Doran 2 [27, 58], McKay [73]	4887
20	4	H	St Mirren	W 1-0	0-0	5	McKay [77]	2751
21	10	A	Kilmarnock	W 2-1	0-0	3	McKay 2 [53, 81]	2793
22	20	H	St Johnstone	W 2-0	2-0	3	McKay [34], Watkins [41]	3161
23	24	A	Hamilton A	W 2-0	0-0	3	Gillespie (og) [53], Ross [76]	5089
24	31	H	Ross Co	D 1-1	1-0	3	Watkins [38]	4021
25	Feb 14	A	St Mirren	W 2-1	1-0	3	Tansey [3], Christie [60]	3154
26	21	H	Kilmarnock	D 3-3	2-2	3	Shinnie [18], Ross [33], Williams [52]	2912
27	24	A	Dundee U	D 1-1	1-0	3	Tansey (pen) [9]	7276
28	28	A	Motherwell	L 1-2	0-0	3	Ofere [76]	3508
29	Mar 21	A	Partick Thistle	L 0-1	0-0	3		2603
30	Apr 4	H	Dundee	D 1-1	0-0	3	Shinnie [55]	3362
31	8	A	Aberdeen	L 0-1	0-0	3		11,319
32	11	H	Celtic	D 1-1	1-1	3	Ofere [4]	6059
33	25	H	Aberdeen	L 1-2	0-0	3	Ofere [48]	4530
34	May 2	A	St Johnstone	D 1-1	0-0	3	Doran [55]	2986
35	5	H	Dundee U	W 2-1	2-1	3	Ofere [38], Williams [43]	2426
36	9	A	Dundee	W 1-0	1-0	3	Ofere [8]	5123
37	16	H	Dundee U	W 3-0	0-0	3	Meekings [55], Ross [80], Warren [83]	3508
38	24	A	Celtic	L 0-5	0-2	3		55,638

Final League Position: 3

Honours
League Champions: First Division 2003-04, 2009-10. Third Division 1996-97.
Scottish Cup Winners: 2015; Semi-finals 2003, 2004; Quarter-finals 1996; *Runners-up:* Second Division 1998-99.
League Cup Runners-up: 2013-14.
League Challenge Cup Winners: 2003-04; *Runners-up:* 1999-2000, 2009-10.

Club colours: Shirt: Blue with red trim. Shorts: Blue. Socks: Blue.

Goalscorers: *League (52):* McKay 10, Watkins 7, Doran 6, Ofere 5, Christie 4, Tansey 4 (2 pens), Meekings 3, Ross 3, Shinnie 2, Warren 2, Williams 2, Vincent 1, own goals 3.
William Hill Scottish FA Cup (13): Tansey 3 (2 pens), Watkins 2, Devine 1, Meekings 1, Ofere 1, Raven 1, Shinnie 1, Vincent 1, Warren 1, Williams 1.
Scottish League Cup (0).

Brill D 24	Raven D 33	Warren G 36	Meekings J 37	Shinnie G 37	Draper R 31+1	Tansey G 36	Williams D 27+7	Christie R 26+9	Vincent J 13+7	McKay B 22+1	Watkins M 29+4	Doran A 15+18	Ross N 13+13	Horner L 1+1	Polworth L 1+4	Tremarco C 9+2	Sekajja I —+4	Sutherland A —+2	Esson R 14+2	Ferguson C —+2	Devine D 6+2	Ofere E 7+3	Kink T 1+4	Mackay C —+1	Match No.
1	2	3	4	5	6	7	8^2	9^1	10^1	11	12	13	14												1
1	2^1	3	4	5	7	8	9^2	10	6^3	11	12	13	14												2
1	2	3	4	5	6	7	9^3	10^2	11^1	8	12	14			13										3
1	2	3	4	5	8	7	9	10^2	11^1	6^2	14	12			13										4
1	2		3	5	4	7	8	10^1	11	6	9	12													5
1	2	3	4	5	7^1	8	12	9^2	10	6	11				13										6
1	2	3	4	5	7	8	12	10^2	11	6	9^1	13													7
1	2	3	4	5	7	8	12	10^2	11	6	9^1	13													8
1	2	3	4	5	8	9	12	10	11	6	7^1														9
1	2	3	4	5	6	7	10^2	8^4	12	11^3	9^1				13	14									10
1	2	3	4	5	6	7	8	9	11^{10}	10		12													11
1	5	2	3	9	8^1	6	11^3	13	7^2	12	10	14			4										12
1	2	3	4	5	6	7	10^1	13	8^2	11	9	12													13
1	2	4	3	5		7	8	6^3	9^2	11^1	10	12	13		14										14
1	2	4	3	5	7^2	8	9	13	6^1	11^3	10	12	14												15
1	2	3	4	5	8^2	7	9	13	6^1	11	10	12													16
1	2	4	3	5	9^4	6	14	8^3	7^2	11	12	10^1	13												17
1	2	3	4	7		6		9		11	8	10^1			5	12									18
1	2	3	4	7		6		9^2	12	11^4	8^1	10	13		5	14									19
1	2	3	4	8	13	7	12	10^1	14	11		9^2	6^3		5										20
1	2^8	3	4	7		9	6	12	13	11		8^1	10^2		5										21
1		3	4	2	7		8^3	12	13	11^4	6^1	9	10		5	14									22
1^1	2	3	9	5	7	8	6^2		11		12	10			4				13						23
	5	3	4	8	7	6^2	10	12		11	13	9^1			2				1						24
	2	4	3	5	6	8	7^1	9		10		11		12					1						25
	2	3	4	5	7	6	10	9		11		8^1							1		12				26
	2^3	4	5	7	8	9	10			11		6							1						27
	2		4	5	7	8	6^1	11		13		9^2							1		12	3	10		28
	2^2	3	4	5	8	9	7^3	10^1		11	13								1		6	14	12		29
	2	3	4	5	7	8		10^2		11	6	9^1							1		12	13			30
	2^2	3	4	5	7	9^1	8	13		11	6	10^3							1		14	12			31
1^2	2	3	4	5	6	7	10^3	9^1	13	8	14								12			11			32
	2^3	3	4	5		7	9	8^1	12	11	13	6^2							1			10	14		33
	2^4	3	4	5		8	9		7	11		6^1							1		12	10			34
	3	2	5	6	7	10^1	12	9^3		8^2	14	13							1		4	11			35
	3	2	5	7	8^3	9^1	6	12		10^2	13		14						1		4	11			36
	3	2	5	6	7		9^2	8		12	10^3	13							1		4	11^1	14		37
	3				8	11^2	4			12	6	2	9	5		14	1^3		7			10^1	13		38

KILMARNOCK

Year Formed: 1869. *Ground & Address:* Rugby Park, Kilmarnock KA1 2DP. *Telephone:* 01563 545300. *Fax:* 01563 522181. *Email:* kirstencallaghan@kilmarnockfc.co.uk *Website:* www.kilmarnockfc.co.uk
Ground Capacity: 18,128 (all seated). *Size of Pitch:* 102m × 67m.
Chairman: Jim Mann. *Secretary:* Michael Johnston.
Manager: Gary Locke. *U-20 Coach:* Alan Robertson. *Physio:* Alex MacQueen.
Club Nickname: 'Killie'.
Previous Grounds: Rugby Park (Dundonald Road); The Grange; Holm Quarry; Rugby Park 1899.
Record Attendance: 35,995 v Rangers, Scottish Cup Quarter-final, 10 Mar 1962.
Record Transfer Fee received: £1,900,000 for Steven Naismith to Rangers (2007).
Record Transfer Fee paid: £340,000 for Paul Wright from St Johnstone (1995).
Record Victory: 11-1 v Paisley Academical, Scottish Cup 1st rd, 18 Jan 1930.
Record Defeat: 1-9 v Celtic, Division I, 13 Aug 1938.
Most Capped Player: Joe Nibloe, 11, Scotland.
Most League Appearances: 481: Alan Robertson, 1972-88.
Most League Goals in Season (Individual): 34: Harry 'Peerie' Cunningham 1927-28; Andy Kerr 1960-61.
Most Goals Overall (Individual): 148: Willy Culley, 1912-23.

KILMARNOCK – SCOTTISH PREMIER LEAGUE 2014–15 LEAGUE RECORD

Match No.	Date	Venue	Opponents	Result	H/T Score	Lg Pos.	Goalscorers	Attendance
1	Aug 9	A	Dundee	D	1-1	1-1	3	Slater [24]	7588
2	13	H	Aberdeen	L	0-2	0-1	10		5079
3	16	A	Ross Co	W	2-1	1-0	6	Magennis [39], Obadeyi [56]	2790
4	23	H	Motherwell	W	2-0	1-0	4	Muirhead [9], Clingan [78]	4146
5	30	A	Inverness CT	L	0-2	0-0	5		3830
6	Sept13	H	St Mirren	W	2-1	0-0	6	Muirhead [63], Connolly [82]	4417
7	20	A	Hamilton A	D	0-0	0-0	4		2604
8	27	H	Partick Thistle	W	3-0	1-0	5	Obadeyi 2 [25, 57], Pascali [51]	3980
9	Oct 3	H	Dundee U	W	2-0	0-0	3	Obadeyi [63], Connolly [65]	3953
10	18	A	St Johnstone	W	2-1	2-1	3	Magennis 2 [19, 22]	3115
11	26	A	Celtic	L	0-2	0-1	5		42,800
12	Nov 1	H	Dundee	L	1-3	0-1	5	Eremenko [76]	4481
13	8	H	Ross Co	L	0-3	0-3	7		3684
14	22	A	Dundee U	L	1-3	1-2	7	Pascali [38]	6664
15	Dec 6	A	Partick Thistle	D	1-1	1-1	6	Obadeyi [11]	3054
16	13	H	St Johnstone	L	0-1	0-0	7		3220
17	20	H	Aberdeen	L	0-1	0-0	8		11,282
18	27	H	Hamilton A	W	1-0	0-0	7	Eremenko [90]	3921
19	Jan 1	A	St Mirren	W	2-1	0-0	7	Eremenko (pen) [54], Slater (pen) [85]	3912
20	5	H	Celtic	L	0-2	0-1	7		5329
21	10	H	Inverness CT	L	1-2	0-0	7	Eremenko (pen) [47]	2793
22	21	A	Dundee	L	0-1	0-1	8		5141
23	24	H	Partick Thistle	D	2-2	1-1	8	Magennis [33], Pascali [79]	4130
24	Feb 7	A	Hamilton A	D	0-0	0-0	8		2245
25	14	H	Dundee U	W	3-2	1-2	8	Magennis [10], Johnston [52], Clingan [90]	3788
26	21	A	Inverness CT	D	3-3	2-2	8	Eccleston [20], Slater [45], Obadeyi [61]	2912
27	28	A	St Johnstone	D	0-0	0-0	8		3170
28	Mar 7	A	Motherwell	D	1-1	1-1	8	Obadeyi [20]	4192
29	14	H	St Mirren	W	1-0	0-0	8	Miller [87]	4721
30	21	A	Ross Co	L	1-2	0-1	8	Ashcroft [88]	3389
31	Apr 4	H	Motherwell	L	1-2	1-1	8	Straker (og) [17]	4532
32	12	H	Aberdeen	L	1-2	0-1	9	Slater [47]	3525
33	15	A	Celtic	L	1-4	0-0	9	Westlake [50]	42,464
34	25	A	St Mirren	L	1-4	0-2	9	Magennis [53]	3205
35	May 2	H	Hamilton A	L	2-3	1-1	9	Ashcroft [8], Kiltie [78]	3450
36	8	A	Motherwell	L	1-3	0-2	9	Magennis [53]	3986
37	16	A	Partick Thistle	W	4-1	2-0	9	Hamill [25], Obadeyi 2 [37, 63], Magennis [71]	4503
38	23	H	Ross Co	L	1-2	1-0	10	Kiltie [36]	4226

Final League Position: 10

Honours
League Champions: Division I 1964-65. Division II 1897-98, 1898-99; *Runners-up:* Division I 1959-60, 1960-61, 1962-63, 1963-64. First Division 1975-76, 1978-79, 1981-82, 1992-93. Division II 1953-54, 1973-74. Second Division 1989-90.
Scottish Cup Winners: 1920, 1929, 1997; *Runners-up:* 1898, 1932, 1938, 1957, 1960.
League Cup Winners: 2011-12; *Runners-up:* 1952-53, 1960-61, 1962-63, 2000-01, 2006-07.

European: *European Cup:* 4 matches (1965-66). *Cup Winners' Cup:* 4 matches (1997-98). *UEFA Cup:* 32 matches (*Fairs Cup:* 1964-65, 1966-67 semi-finals, 1969-70, 1970-71. *UEFA Cup:* 1998-99, 1999-2000, 2001-02).

Club colours: Shirts: White and blue stripes. Shorts: Blue. Socks: Blue with yellow tops.

Goalscorers: *League (44):* Obadeyi 9, Magennis 8, Eremenko 4 (2 pens), Slater 4 (1 pen), Pascali 3, Ashcroft 2, Clingan 2, Connolly 2, Kiltie 2, Muirhead 2, Eccleston 1, Hamill 1, Johnston 1, Miller 1, Westlake 1, own goal 1.
William Hill Scottish FA Cup (0).
Scottish League Cup (1): McKenzie 1.

Samson C 35	Barbour R 28 + 2	Ashcroft L 20 + 2	Connolly M 25 + 1	Chandler C 26	Johnston C 19 + 11	Pascali M 29 + 2	Slater C 23 + 3	Obadeyi T 28 + 1	Magennis J 38	McKenzie R 21 + 7	Eremenko A 17 + 10	Clingan S 22 + 2	Hamill J 20 + 1	Cairney P 3 + 13	Ngoo M 3 + 3	O'Hara M 14 + 4	Miller L 9 + 10	Westlake D 16 + 1	Brennan C 3 + 1	Eccleston N 6 + 4	Syme D 3 + 2	Kiltie G 2 + 6	Splaine A 1	Match No.
1	2	3	4	5	6^2	7	8^1	9	10	11	12	13												1
1	2		3	5	9^1	8	7	10^1	11	6^2	13		4	12	14									2
1	2		3	5	4	7	9^2	10^1	6		13	8	12	11										3
1	2		3	5	4		9^2	10	6	13	8^3	11^1	14	12		7								4
1	2		3	5	12	4	9	11	6^1	13	8^1	7		10^2		14								5
1	2		3	5	14	4	9^2	11	6^1	13	8	7	12	10^1										6
1	2		3	5	13	4	10^1	11^2	9	12	7	6	8^4		14									7
1	2		3		8	4	14	10^1	11^2		9^3	7	6	13	12		5							8
11^1	2		3	5	8	4		11	10		9^2	7	6	13				12						9
	2		3	5	9^1	4		10	11	7		8	6	12				1						10
	2	12	3	5	4^a		9	11^2	6	10^1	7	8		13				1						11
1	2^1	4	3	5	6^3		9	11	13	10	8^2	7	14			12								12
1	2		4	5	9^2	3	14	11	6	10^1	7	8^3	12			13								13
1	2		4	5	12	3		11^2	6	10^3	7	8	9^1	14		13								14
1			3	5	13	4		9	10	6^2		8	7	12		11^1	2							15
1			3	5		4	12	9	11	13		7^1	8	6		10^1	2							16
1	12	8		4	14	3	6	10	9^4		7	5	13			11^1	2^3							17
1	2	3	4	5^1	12		8	9	6	13	7	10^1		14	11^3									18
1	2	3	4	5	14	13	7^4	9	6^2	10^3	12		8	11^1										19
1	2	3	4	5		9^2	13	11	6	10	8^1	12	7											20
1	2	4	3	5	13		8	9	6	10^1		12	14	7^3	11^2									21
1	2	4		5	9^2	3	8	11^2	6		10	7		13	12									22
1	4^1		5	13	3	8	11^2	9	6		7		10^3		14	12	2							23
1		4	5	12	3	9	10^1	11	7	6^2	8		13				2							24
1		3	5	6^1	4	8^2	9	11		10^3	7	12	13				2	14						25
1	5		3^1		8	4	7	10	11					6			2		9^2	12	13			26
1	3		5	8	4	7	10^1	11	12					6			2	9						27
1	12	3		5	10^3	4	9	6^1	11	13				7	14	2^a		8^2						28
1	2	3	6		4	7	9^1	11	8^3		12		5	13			10^2		14					29
1	5	3	6		4	8	11^2	10		13		2^3	12	9			7^1		14					30
1	3	4		6^2			9	11	13			8^1		7	10^3	2	12	5	14					31
1	3		6		7		9^2	11	13	10^1	8^3		2			12	5	14	4					32
1	3				7	9	10^2	12		8		6^1	2	11	5	13	4							33
1	5	4	6	3	8^2	9^1	10	14	13	7			2	12	11^3									34
1	5	3		9^3	4	8^1	11	6^2	10	7		14	2	13			12							35
1	2	3	14		4^1		12	10	9^2		8^5	7	6			11	5		13					36
1	2	12	3		4^2	8	9	11	13	10^1	7		14	5					6^3					37
	5	3	4^3		7	10^1	11	13	8		14		2			1		12	6	9^2				38

LIVINGSTON

Year Formed: 1974. *Ground:* The Energy Assets Arena Stadium, Almondvale Stadium, Alderstone Road, Livingston EH54 7DN. *Telephone:* 01506 417000. *Fax:* 01506 429 948.
Email: lfcreception@livingstonfc.co.uk *Website:* www.livingstonfc.co.uk
Ground Capacity: 9,865 (all seated). *Size of Pitch:* 98m × 69m.
Chairman: Gordon McDougall. *Secretary:* Carolyn Sumner.
Manager: Mark Burchill. *Assistant Manager:* David Hopkin. *Physio:* Andy Mackenzie.
Club Nickname: 'Livi Lions'.
Previous Grounds: Meadowbank Stadium (as Meadowbank Thistle).
Record Attendance: 10,024 v Celtic, Premier League, 18 Aug 2001.
Record Transfer Fee received: £1,000,000 for David Fernandez to Celtic (June 2002).
Record Transfer Fee paid: £120,000 for Wes Hoolahan from Shelbourne (December 2005).
Record Victory: 7-0 v Queen of the South, Scottish Cup, 29 Jan 2000.
Record Defeat: 0-8 v Hamilton A. Division II, 14 Dec 1974.
Most Capped Player (under 18): Ian Little.
Most League Appearances: 446: Walter Boyd, 1979-89.
Most League Goals in Season (Individual): 22: Leigh Griffiths, 2008-09; Iain Russell, 2010-11.
Most Goals Overall (Individual): 64: David Roseburgh, 1986-93.

LIVINGSTON – SCOTTISH CHAMPIONSHIP 2014–15 LEAGUE RECORD

Match No.	Date	Venue	Opponents	Result	H/T Score	Lg Pos.	Goalscorers	Attendance
1	Aug 9	A	Hibernian	L 1-2	0-2	8	Gallacher [60]	9390
2	16	H	Cowdenbeath	W 2-1	0-0	6	Mullen [46], White [74]	1147
3	23	A	Queen of the South	D 1-1	0-1	5	White (pen) [66]	1805
4	30	A	Dumbarton	L 0-1	0-0	6		814
5	Sept 13	H	Alloa Ath	W 4-0	2-0	5	Fordyce [27], White 3 [33, 63, 77]	1150
6	20	H	Raith R	L 0-1	0-1	5		1309
7	28	A	Hearts	L 0-5	0-3	6		14,848
8	Oct 4	H	Rangers	L 0-1	0-1	8		5924
9	18	H	Hibernian	L 0-4	0-1	10		2666
10	21	A	Falkirk	D 0-0	0-0	8		3021
11	25	H	Queen of the South	D 2-2	0-1	8	Mullen [81], Glen [88]	1099
12	Nov 8	A	Alloa Ath	L 0-1	0-0	9		586
13	15	H	Dumbarton	L 1-2	1-0	9	Mullen [29]	1020
14	22	A	Cowdenbeath	L 0-1	0-0	10		542
15	Dec 6	A	Raith R	W 5-1	3-1	10	White (pen) [3], Burchill [23], Glen [44], Mullen [78], McKenna [88]	1385
16	13	A	Falkirk	L 0-1	0-0	10		1176
17	20	A	Rangers	L 0-2	0-1	10		28,053
18	27	H	Hearts	L 0-1	0-1	10		8178
19	Jan 3	A	Queen of the South	L 1-3	1-1	10	White [39]	1940
20	10	H	Cowdenbeath	D 1-1	1-1	10	Mullen [4]	829
21	24	A	Dumbarton	W 5-1	1-0	10	White 2 [5, 82], Mullen 2 [63, 73], Keaghan Jacobs [79]	793
22	Feb 3	H	Alloa Ath	D 0-0	0-0	10		723
23	7	H	Hearts	L 2-3	0-1	10	Sives [52], Kyle Jacobs (pen) [90]	5352
24	14	A	Hearts	L 0-1	0-1	10		15,463
25	21	A	Falkirk	L 0-2	0-2	10		3780
26	28	H	Raith R	L 0-2	0-2	10		972
27	Mar 11	A	Hibernian	L 1-2	0-1	10	Sekajja [88]	7857
28	14	A	Rangers	D 1-1	1-1	10	Sekajja [45]	35,066
29	21	H	Dumbarton	L 1-2	1-0	10	Sives [14]	831
30	28	A	Alloa Ath	D 2-2	0-0	10	Gordon (og) [59], Boulding [88]	706
31	Apr 8	H	Falkirk	W 2-1	1-1	10	Mullen 2 [9, 54]	1047
32	11	A	Cowdenbeath	W 2-1	0-0	10	White 2 [63, 80]	624
33	15	H	Rangers	D 1-1	0-0	10	Hippolyte [47]	4345
34	22	H	Hibernian	L 1-3	1-2	10	Hippolyte [14]	2301
35	25	A	Raith R	W 4-0	1-0	9	Fordyce [19], Sives [49], Mullen [55], Barr (og) [71]	1766
36	May 2	H	Queen of the South	W 1-0	0-0	8	Kyle Jacobs [78]	2475

Final League Position: 8

Honours
League Champions: First Division 2000-01. Second Division 1986-87, 1998-99, 2010-11. Third Division 1995-96, 2009-10;
Runners-up: Second Division 1982-83. First Division 1987-88.
Scottish Cup: Semi-finals 2001, 2004.
League Cup Winners: 2003-04. Semi-finals 1984-85. *B&Q Cup:* Semi-finals 1992-93, 1993-94, 2001.
League Challenge Cup Winners: 2014-15. *Runners-up:* 2000-01.

European: *UEFA Cup:* 4 matches (2002-03).

Club colours: Shirt: Yellow with black trim. Shorts: Black with yellow trim. Socks: Yellow.

Goalscorers: *League (41):* White 11 (2 pens), Mullen 10, Sives 3, Fordyce 2, Glen 2, Hippolyte 2, Kyle Jacobs 2 (1 pen),
Sekajja 2, Boulding 1, Burchill 1, Gallacher 1, Keaghan Jacobs 1, McKenna 1, own goals 2.
William Hill Scottish FA Cup (2): Keaghan Jacobs 1, Mullen 1.
Scottish League Cup (1): Hippolyte 1.
Petrofac Training Cup (14): White 4, Hippolyte 3, Robertson 2, Fordyce 1, Glen 1, Mullen 1, Pitman 1, Sives 1.

Jamieson D 36	White J 28 + 7	Fordyce C 35	Gallacher D 28	Talbot J 28	O'Brien B 28	Jacobs Kyle 34	Jacobs Keaghan 32	Mullen D 26 + 7	McKenna M 12 + 13	Glen G 18 + 11	Hippolyte M 12 + 21	Burchill M 4 + 7	Robertson D 6 + 7	Sives C 20 + 1	Ogleby R 1 + 11	Rutherford S 10 + 1	Mensing S 6	Beaumont J 1 + 2	Praprotnik N 4 + 5	Sekajja 18 + 3	Pitman S 10 + 2	Cole D 8 + 1	Boulding R — + 4	Donaldson B 1 + 2	Match No.
1	2¹	3	4	5	6	7	8	9²	10	11³	12	13	14												1
1	11	4	3	5⁴	8	2	7	6²	9	10⁵		13	14	12											2
1	10	3	5	2	7²	4	6	13	8	12	11¹¹	14	9²												3
1	10	4	3	5	7	2	6	11¹	9²	8³	14		13		12										4
1	10³	4		5	8	2	7		6²	11	12	13	9¹	3	14										5
1	10	4		5	8	2	7		6³	11²	12	13	9¹	3	14										6
1	8	3		5¹	7	6	2	13	14	9	10²	11²	12	4											7
1	10	4		5	8³	2	7	9²	6	12	13			3¹	14	11									8
1	10	2		4	7	8	6¹		5²	9	14	11¹¹		3	13	12									9
1	11	4		5	6	2		14	7	9³	13		12	3²	10¹	8									10
1	10	3		5	7²	2	8	13	6¹¹	11	12		14	4		9³									11
1	10	4	3⁴	5	7¹	2	8	9	12	11²	14	13	6³												12
1	12	3		4	8	2	7	11		9	10		6²		13	5¹									13
1	12	3	8	4		2	7	11	14	10²	9³		6¹	5	13										14
1	10	4	2			7¹	6	5	14	9²		11¹		13	8	3	12								15
1	10	2	3			7	11	12	6²	14	9¹			13	5	4	8								16
1	11	3	5		9	2²	7	8³	14	10¹	12				6	4		13							17
1	10	2	4		7	8⁴		11	6¹	9	12			14	5²	3		13							18
1	10	2	4		8¹	7		11		9²	6²	12		13	5	3		14							19
1	10	2	3	5	7²	8	6	11		9¹	12				4	13								·	20
1	10	4	5	7	6¹	9	11²	12		14		3			8³	13									21
1	11	2	3	5	7	8	6¹	10		13		4			9²	12									22
1	10³	2	3	5	7²	9	6	8		12		4			13	11¹	14								23
1	10	2	3		7²	9	6	8¹	13	12		4				14	5⁴	11³							24
1	9	2	3		7		6	8	12	11¹¹	13		4		5²			10¹	14						25
1	10²		4	5	7³	2	6	8	12	14	13		3				9	11¹							26
1		4	6	5¹		7	8	12	9²	14	13		2				10	11³	3						27
1	13	2	3	5		6	8	9¹	14		12		4				11³	10²	7						28
1	14	2	4	5		7	6³	9¹	12		13		3				11	10²	8						29
1	9	3⁴	4	5		7	6	12			13		2				11³	10	8¹	14					30
1	12	2	4	5	7	9	6	10²		13	11¹							8³	3				14		31
1	10	2	3	5		7	6	11¹		12	9²							8³	4	13	14				32
1	10²	2	3	5	7	9	6	13		12	11³							8¹	4	14					33
1	10¹	5	3		7	6		11		13	9³						14	8	4⁴	12	2²				34
1	13	2	3	5⁴	7	9	6¹	11	14	12	10²		4					8							35
1	12	2	3	5	7	9	6²	11		14	10³		4					8¹	13						36

MONTROSE

Year Formed: 1879. *Ground & Address:* Links Park, Wellington St, Montrose DD10 8QD. *Telephone:* 01674 673200.
Fax: 01674 677311. *E-mail:* office@montrosefc.co.uk *Website:* www.montrosefc.co.uk
Ground Capacity: total: 4,936, (seated: 1,338). *Size of Pitch:* 100m × 64m.
Chairman: Derek Sim. *Vice-Chairman:* John Crawford. *Secretary:* Brian Petrie.
Manager: Paul Hegarty. *Assistant Manager:* John Holt.
Club Nickname: 'The Gable Endies'.
Previous Grounds: None.
Record Attendance: 8,983 v Dundee, Scottish Cup 3rd rd, 17 Mar 1973.
Record Transfer Fee received: £50,000 for Gary Murray to Hibernian (Dec 1980).
Record Transfer Fee paid: £17,500 for Jim Smith from Airdrieonians (Feb 1992).
Record Victory: 12-0 v Vale of Leithen, Scottish Cup 2nd rd, 4 Jan 1975.
Record Defeat: 0-13 v Aberdeen, 17 Mar 1951.
Most Capped Player: Alexander Keillor, 2 (6), Scotland.
Most League Appearances: 432: David Larter, 1987-98.
Most League Goals in Season (Individual): 28: Brian Third, Division II, 1972-73.

MONTROSE – SCOTTISH LEAGUE TWO 2014–15 LEAGUE RECORD

Match No.	Date		Venue	Opponents	Result	H/T Score	Lg Pos.	Goalscorers	Atten- dance
1	Aug	9	H	East Stirling	W 4-1	1-0	1	Campbell, A [36], Masson [48], Wood 2 (1 pen) [70, 90 (p)]	315
2		23	H	Annan Ath	W 2-0	2-0	3	Harkins [32], Watson [39]	341
3		30	A	Arbroath	L 1-3	0-2	5	Webster [82]	1137
4	Sept	13	H	Albion R	L 0-2	0-1	5		348
5		20	A	Elgin C	W 1-0	0-0	3	Watson [71]	580
6		23	A	Clyde	W 2-1	1-1	3	Wood [6], Masson [59]	459
7		27	H	East Fife	L 0-4	0-3	3		465
8	Oct	15	A	Berwick R	D 2-2	1-2	4	McIntosh [45], Watson [90]	347
9		18	A	Queen's Park	L 0-2	0-2	4		321
10		25	H	Arbroath	L 1-5	0-1	4	Wood (pen) [57]	1143
11	Nov	8	H	Clyde	L 0-3	0-2	6		405
12		15	A	Annan Ath	D 2-2	1-1	7	Day [11], McIntosh [76]	394
13		22	A	East Stirling	L 0-4	0-2	9		241
14	Dec	2	H	Berwick R	W 2-1	1-1	6	Deasley [45], Watson [77]	233
15		6	A	East Fife	L 0-3	0-1	7		419
16		13	H	Queen's Park	L 1-2	0-2	7	Wood (pen) [64]	353
17		20	A	Albion R	D 0-0	0-0	8		386
18		27	H	Elgin C	L 2-3	0-2	8	Wood [50], McCord [90]	385
19	Jan	3	A	Arbroath	D 2-2	0-1	8	McBride (og) [69], Day [72]	1395
20		10	H	East Stirling	L 0-1	0-0	8		269
21		17	A	Berwick R	D 3-3	1-2	7	Johnston, S [31], Wood [59], Andrews [90]	423
22		24	H	Albion R	L 3-4	2-2	8	O'Neill [6], Banjo 2 [15, 59]	352
23		31	H	Annan Ath	W 2-1	0-0	7	Alex Mitchell (og) [64], Wood [66]	244
24	Feb	7	A	Queen's Park	L 1-4	0-2	8	Campbell, R [76]	505
25		14	H	East Fife	L 0-3	0-1	9		371
26		21	A	Elgin C	L 0-4	0-3	10		611
27		28	A	Clyde	L 0-2	0-0	10		447
28	Mar	7	H	Arbroath	W 3-0	1-0	10	Webster [28], Campbell, R 2 [48, 53]	970
29		14	A	Albion R	L 0-3	0-1	10		389
30		21	H	Berwick R	L 0-2	0-0	10		320
31		28	A	East Fife	L 0-3	0-2	10		439
32	Apr	4	H	Queen's Park	D 2-2	1-0	10	Watson [35], Wood [81]	367
33		11	A	East Stirling	W 1-0	1-0	10	Campbell, R [21]	305
34		18	H	Elgin C	W 2-1	1-1	10	Allan [33], Webster [69]	320
35		25	H	Clyde	L 0-1	0-0	10		338
36	May	2	A	Annan Ath	L 3-4	0-2	10	Wood [60], Campbell, R 2 [80, 82]	386

Final League Position: 10

Honours
League Champions: Second Division 1984-85; *Runners-up:* Second Division 1990-91. Third Division 1994-95.
Scottish Cup: Quarter-finals 1973, 1976.
League Cup: Semi-finals 1975-76.
B&Q Cup: Semi-finals 1992-93.
League Challenge Cup: Semi-finals 1996-97.

Club colours: Shirt: Blue with white trim. Shorts: Blue. Socks: Blue.

Goalscorers: *League (42):* Wood 10 (3 pens), Campbell, R 6, Watson 5, Webster 3, Banjo 2, Day 2, Masson 2, McIntosh 2, Allan 1, Andrews 1, Campbell, A 1, Deasley 1, Harkins 1, Johnston, S 1, McCord 1, O'Neill 1, own goals 2.
William Hill Scottish FA Cup (3): Harkins 1, Watson 1, Wood 1.
Scottish League Cup (1): Wood 1.
Petrofac Training Cup (0).
League Two Play-Offs (3): Andrews 1, Johnston, S 1, Wood 1.

McKenzie S 29	Masson T 25+4	Campbell A 12+1	O'Kane D 3	Graham R 22+2	McCord R 23+2	Watson P 25+3	Robb S 6+2	Harkins P 11+7	Wood G 35	Johnston S 27+5	O'Neill S 10+7	Day S 7+11	Crawford J 30+1	Deasley B 16+3	Webster G 13+3	Cavanagh D 2+6	McCafferty J —+1	Birnstingl L 4+1	McIntosh L 11+5	Bell C 3	Harwood A 10+1	McGovern J 3	Nowosielski L —+1	Travis M 3	Andrews M 12	Banjo D 6+3	Davidson S —+1	Moyes E 8+1	Cameron G 10	Allan J 9+4	Campbell R 11+1	Johnston C 1+3	Steeves A 8	Milne D 1+4	Match No.
1	2	3	4	5	6■	7	8¹	9²	10	11	12	13																							1
1	2	3¹	4	5		6	14	9²	11	10	7³	8	12	13																					2
1	2	3*		5		7		9¹	6³	11	8	13	4	10²	12	14																			3
1■	2	3				7	8	5³	11²	10	13		9¹	4	6			14	12																4
	2		4		6³	7	5	8¹	10	13	14	11²	3	9				1	12																5
	2		4			7	8	5¹	11²	10³	12	13	3	6				1	14	9															6
	2		4	5	6²		8		10¹	12	7	13	3	11				1	9■																7
1	14		4	5		7³	8	11¹	3	6²	12	2	9	13					10																8
1■	2			5³				9	13	4	6	8²	14	3	10¹	7		12	11																9
13	3²			5		7	8²		10	9	14	2	11¹	6				1■	12		4														10
7	12			5			3	11	8²	9	2	6¹	13						10		4	1													11
6						7	12	3	8	9²	2	13	11¹						10		5	4	1												12
6				12		7		13	3	8	9¹	2	11						10		5²	4	1												13
1	6			5		7	8	12		4	10	13	3¹	9²	2				11																14
1	6¹			5		7	8			4	9²	14	3	11³	2	13			10						12										15
1	8		4	5	6¹	7				13	10	12	3	11²					9					2											16
1	8		2	5¹				9		4	6	13	3	11²					10		12			7											17
1	6		3	5		7	8			10	12	13	2	9²					11¹						4										18
1	12			5	6	7			9¹	11	8	10	2												4	3									19
1	7			5	6		8		11	10	2	12	9¹												3	4									20
1	8¹			5		7²			10	11	12	2	9	6	13										3	4									21
1	12			5		8			10	11	6³	2	9²	14											3¹	4			7	13					22
1				5		12			10	11	6¹	2													4	7			3	8	9				23
1				5		12		14	10	11	7²														2	3		6³	4	8¹	9	13			24
1				5		7²		12	10	6³	13		2¹													3		8	4	9	11	14			25
1				4		7			9	10	6		2													3*■		8	5	11	12				26
1	2		4	5					10	8	12		3	6											13			7	9²	11¹					27
1	2					8			10	9			3	6¹												4		12	7	13	11²		5		28
1	8³					13			10	9	14		4	6									2			3			7	12	11²		5		29
1	2■					8			9	10	11³		4	6²												3		12	7	13	14		5		30
1				5		8			11	10			4	7												3		6¹		12	9²		2	13	31
1	2					8			10	6			4													3¹		12	7	9	11²		5	13	32
1	2					7			10	6	8		12													4			3	11	9²		5	13	33
1	2							8²	10	6	13		4	7											12				3	11	9¹		5		34
1	2							7¹	13	10	6		4	8															3	11	9²		5	12	35
1	14			12	7³	4			10	6²	8		13																3¹	2	9		5	11	36

MOTHERWELL

Year Formed: 1886. *Ground & Address:* Fir Park Stadium, Motherwell ML1 2QN. *Telephone:* 01698 333333. *Fax:* 01698 338001.
E-mail: mfcenquiries@motherwellfc.co.uk *Website:* www.motherwellfc.co.uk
Ground Capacity: 13,742 (all seated). *Size of Pitch:* 100m × 68m.
Chairman: Brian McCafferty. *Vice-Chairman:* Les Hutchinson. *Secretary:* Graham Keys.
Manager: Ian Baraclough. *Assistant Manager:* Stephen Robinson. *Physio:* Aileen Anderson.
Club Nicknames: 'The Well', 'The Steelmen'.
Previous Grounds: The Meadows, Dalziel Park.
Record Attendance: 35,632 v Rangers, Scottish Cup 4th rd replay, 12 Mar 1952.
Record Transfer Fee received: £1,750,000 for Phil O'Donnell to Celtic (September 1994).
Record Transfer Fee paid: £500,000 for John Spencer from Everton (Jan 1999).
Record Victory: 12-1 v Dundee U, Division II, 23 Jan 1954.
Record Defeat: 0-8 v Aberdeen, Premier Division, 26 Mar 1979.
Most Capped Player: Stephen Craigan, 54, Northern Ireland.
Most League Appearances: 626: Bobby Ferrier, 1918-37.
Most League Goals in Season (Individual): 52: Willie McFadyen, Division I, 1931-32.
Most Goals Overall (Individual): 283: Hugh Ferguson, 1916-25.

MOTHERWELL – SCOTTISH PREMIER LEAGUE 2014–15 LEAGUE RECORD

Match No.	Date	Venue	Opponents	Result	H/T Score	Lg Pos.	Goalscorers	Attendance
1	Aug 9	H	St Mirren	W 1-0	0-0	2	Erwin [64]	4620
2	13	A	Dundee U	L 0-1	0-0	6		8367
3	16	H	Inverness CT	L 0-2	0-1	9		3732
4	23	A	Kilmarnock	L 0-2	0-1	10		4146
5	30	H	St Johnstone	L 0-1	0-0	10		3700
6	Sept 13	A	Ross Co	W 2-1	0-0	10	Vigurs [49], Sutton [54]	3012
7	21	A	Celtic	D 1-1	1-0	10	Sutton [19]	41,719
8	27	H	Hamilton A	L 0-4	0-2	10		4125
9	Oct 4	A	Partick Thistle	L 1-3	0-1	11	Ainsworth [72]	3405
10	18	H	Dundee	L 1-3	0-2	11	Ojamaa [62]	4061
11	24	A	Aberdeen	L 0-1	0-1	11		11,149
12	31	A	St Johnstone	L 1-2	1-1	11	Ainsworth [13]	2531
13	Nov 7	H	Dundee U	W 1-0	0-0	10	Vigurs [52]	3961
14	22	A	Inverness CT	L 1-3	1-1	10	Ojamaa [31]	3037
15	Dec 6	H	Celtic	L 0-1	0-1	10		7740
16	13	H	Ross Co	D 2-2	0-1	10	Sutton [53], Ojamaa [59]	3193
17	20	A	St Mirren	W 1-0	0-0	10	Sutton [72]	3909
18	27	H	Partick Thistle	W 1-0	1-0	10	Sutton (pen) [14]	5236
19	Jan 1	A	Hamilton A	L 0-5	0-2	10		3926
20	4	H	Aberdeen	L 0-2	0-1	10		4805
21	10	A	Dundee	L 1-4	1-3	10	Sutton [19]	5105
22	21	A	Celtic	L 0-4	0-2	10		42,296
23	24	A	Dundee U	L 1-3	0-0	10	Ramsden [78]	7176
24	31	H	St Johnstone	D 1-1	0-1	11	Sutton [75]	3449
25	Feb 14	A	Ross Co	L 2-3	0-1	11	Grant [53], Kerr [78]	2982
26	21	H	Dundee	L 0-1	0-1	12		4282
27	28	H	Inverness CT	W 2-1	0-0	12	Laing [48], Ainsworth [84]	3508
28	Mar 7	H	Kilmarnock	D 1-1	1-1	11	McDonald [45]	4192
29	13	A	Aberdeen	L 1-2	1-0	11	McDonald [37]	13,267
30	20	H	Hamilton A	W 4-0	0-0	11	Ainsworth 2 [49, 50], Sutton 2 (1 pen) [80, 83 (p)]	4250
31	Apr 4	A	Kilmarnock	W 2-1	1-1	11	Pearson [38], Erwin [77]	4532
32	7	H	St Mirren	W 5-0	3-0	11	Erwin 2 [7, 25], McDonald [45], Sutton 2 [74, 79]	4596
33	11	A	Partick Thistle	L 0-2	0-0	11		5003
34	24	A	Hamilton A	L 0-2	0-1	11		3301
35	May 2	H	Ross Co	D 1-1	1-1	11	McDonald [19]	4281
36	8	H	Kilmarnock	W 3-1	2-0	11	McDonald [28], Erwin [39], Ainsworth [90]	3986
37	16	A	St Mirren	L 1-2	0-0	11	Sutton (pen) [75]	3912
38	23	H	Partick Thistle	D 0-0	0-0	11		3711

Final League Position: 11

Honours
League Champions: Division I 1931-32. First Division 1981-82, 1984-85. Division II 1953-54, 1968-69.
Runners-up: Premier Division 1994-95, 2012-13. Premiership 2013-14. Division I 1926-27, 1929-30, 1932-33, 1933-34.
Division II 1894-95, 1902-03.
Scottish Cup: 1952, 1991; *Runners-up:* 1931, 1933, 1939, 1951, 2011.
League Cup Winners: 1950-51; *Runners-up:* 1954-55, 2004-05.

European: *Champions League:* 2 matches (2012-13). *Cup Winners' Cup:* 2 matches (1991-92). *UEFA Cup:* 8 matches (1994-95, 1995-96, 2008-09). *Europa League:* 18 matches (2009-10, 2010-11, 2012-13, 2013-14, 2014-15).

Club colours: Shirt: Amber with maroon band. Shorts: Maroon. Socks: Amber.

Goalscorers: *League (38):* Sutton 12 (3 pens), Ainsworth 6, Erwin 5, McDonald 5, Ojamaa 3, Vigurs 2, Grant 1, Kerr 1, Laing 1, Pearson 1, Ramsden 1.
William Hill Scottish FA Cup (1): Ojamaa 1.
Scottish League Cup (0).
Premiership Play-Offs (6): Ainsworth 2, Erwin 1, Johnson 1, McManus 1, Sutton 1 (1 pen).
UEFA Europa League (4): Law 2, Ainsworth 1, Hammell 1.

Twardzik D 25	Reid C 19+1	Kerr F 16+5	McManus S 36	Francis-Angol Z 10+1	Ainsworth L 19+15	Lasley K 33	Carswell S 14+5	Law J 28+6	Sutton J 27+11	Erwin L 20+14	Leitch J 4+3	Ferguson D 3+3	McHugh B 1+3	Ojamaa H 16+2	Vigurs I 10+1	O'Brien M 17+2	Lawson P 3	Ramsden S 20+2	Hammell S 8	Cadden C —+3	Thomas D 2+13	Watt L 5	MacLean R —+1	Pearson S 13	Moore C 2+7	Laing L 11	Straker A 11+1	Long G 13	Thomas N 1+1	Grant C 10+1	Johnson M 10+1	McDonald S 11	Match No.
1	2	3	4	5	6	7	8	9¹	10	11	12																						1
1	2	3	4	5³	14	6	7	10	11¹	9	8²	12	13																				2
1	2	3	4	6³	8²	7	9	10¹	11	14	5		12	13																			3
1	2	3¹	4		12	8	7	9	10		5		11¹	6																			4
1	2		4	5¹	6	8		9²	11	12		13	10³		3	7	14																5
1	2		4		8	12	9	11	10²				13	6	5	7¹	3																6
1	8	2	4	9		6	12	10	11¹	13				7²	3		5																7
1	12	2	4²	5¹		7	14	13	9	8	11	10		6³	3																	8
1		2	4	14	12	7	8	6²	10	13				11	9³	3		5¹															9
1		12	4³	5¹	6	7	13	14	10				8²	11	9	3		2															10
1	4	7	3	6²	14	8		9¹	11	12		13	10¹					2	5														11
1	7	3	2³	6	8		14	11	12				10	9¹	13			4	5²														12
1	6	2	4	7¹	8			12	11				10	9	5	3																	13
1	5	2	3	6²	8			12	11	13			10	9	4	7¹																	14
1		2⁴	4	5	13	7	6	9	11³	14		12	10	8¹			3⁴																15
1		4	5	12	7	8	6²	11	13		2		10²	9¹	3				14														16
1	5	12	4	9³	7	8	6	10	13		2¹	11		3²					14														17
1	8	13	4	6	7			9	10³	12		14	11		3²			2	5¹														18
1	2	3	4	6³	7			10	11	12			9					8¹	5²	13	14												19
1	5	8¹	4⁴	6	7			9	10²	12				11	3						13	2											20
1	2		4	6²	7	3	8	10¹	13					11⁴	5						14	9³	12										21
1	6		4	10¹	7	8		11³	13					3²	2						12	5		9	14								22
1	6	2	4	13		7²	8	11	10					3							5			9	12								23
1	2	12			7³	6	10	11						4²	8						13	5¹		14	3⁴	9							24
	2	5	3		14	8¹		11	10						4							13		9	1		6¹	7³	12				25
	4	14	7					10²	11						2						13			9³	3	5	1	12	6	8¹			26
	4	14	7			5	12	11⁴							2⁴									9	13	3		1		6	8¹	10²	27
	4	12	7			2	13	10³													14			8		3	5	1		6²	9¹	11	28
	4	12	7			2	13	11³													14			8		3	5	1		6²	9¹	10	29
	4	6¹	7			2	12	11													14			8	13	3	5	1		9²	10⁴		30
	4	6²	7	13		2	12	11¹							14									8		3	5	1		9³	10		31
	4	6³	7			2	13	11¹										14						8²		3	5	1		12	9	10	32
	4	6³	7	14⁴		2	11²	9													12			8	13	3	5	1				10	33
	12	4	6	7		2	14	10							13									8		3¹	5	1		9	9	11²	34
	3	12	7			2	13	10³				4					5			14			8				1		9²	6¹	11		35
	4	12	8				14	10³				3			2		5²				7				13	1		6¹	9	11		36
	4	12	7				13	11				3			2		5				8					1		6²	9	10⁴		37
1		6¹		7	14	10		12						13	4³			9	2		11	3⁴	5			8							38

PARTICK THISTLE

Year Formed: 1876. *Ground & Address:* Firhill Stadium, 80 Firhill Rd, Glasgow G20 7AL. *Telephone:* 0141 579 1971.
Fax: 0141 945 1525. *E-mail:* mail@ptfc.co.uk *Website:* www.ptfc.co.uk
Ground Capacity: 10,102 (all seated). *Size of Pitch:* 105m × 69m.
Chairman: David Beattie. *General Manager:* Ian Maxwell.
Manager: Alan Archibald. *Assistant Manager:* Scott Paterson. *Head of Youth Development:* Gerry Britton.
Club Nickname: 'The Jags'.
Previous Grounds: Overnewton Park; Jordanvale Park; Muirpark; Inchview; Meadowside Park.
Record Attendance: 49,838 v Rangers, Division I, 18 Feb 1922. *Ground Record:* 54,728, Scotland v Ireland, 25 Feb 1928.
Record Transfer Fee received: £200,000 for Mo Johnston to Watford (July 1981).
Record Transfer Fee paid: £85,000 for Andy Murdoch from Celtic (Feb 1991).
Record Victory: 16-0 v Royal Albert, Scottish Cup 1st rd, 17 Jan 1931.
Record Defeat: 0-10 v Queen's Park, Scottish Cup 5th rd, 3 Dec 1881.
Most Capped Player: Alan Rough, 51 (53), Scotland.
Most League Appearances: 410: Alan Rough, 1969-82.
Most League Goals in Season (Individual): 41: Alex Hair, Division I, 1926-27.
Most Goals Overall (Individual): 229: Willie Sharp, 1939-57.

PARTICK THISTLE – SCOTTISH PREMIER LEAGUE 2014–15 LEAGUE RECORD

Match No.	Date	Venue	Opponents	Result	H/T Score	Lg Pos.	Goalscorers	Atten- dance
1	Aug 13	H	Ross Co	W 4-0	1-0	3	Bannigan [40], Frempah (og) [55], Fraser [73], O'Donnell [90]	3261
2	16	A	Dundee	D 1-1	1-0	5	Fraser [4]	6453
3	23	H	Hamilton A	L 1-2	0-0	8	Higginbotham [85]	3578
4	30	A	Aberdeen	L 0-2	0-0	9		11,003
5	Sept 13	H	Inverness CT	W 3-1	2-1	8	Lawless [19], Osman [23], Higginbotham [72]	2917
6	19	H	St Mirren	L 1-2	1-0	8	Doolan [22]	3821
7	27	A	Kilmarnock	L 0-3	0-1	9		3980
8	Oct 4	H	Motherwell	W 3-1	1-0	7	Bannigan [16], Doolan [63], O'Donnell [82]	3405
9	18	A	Dundee U	L 0-1	0-0	8		6756
10	25	H	St Johnstone	D 0-0	0-0	8		3090
11	Nov 1	A	Hamilton A	D 3-3	1-2	9	McMillan [32], Craigen [68], Elliot [72]	2855
12	8	A	St Mirren	W 1-0	0-0	8	Elliot [75]	4636
13	23	H	Aberdeen	L 0-1	0-1	9		4145
14	Dec 3	A	Celtic	L 0-1	0-0	9		40,633
15	6	H	Kilmarnock	D 1-1	1-1	9	Seaborne [19]	3054
16	13	A	Inverness CT	W 4-0	2-0	9	Stevenson 2 [12, 40], Fraser [49], Balatoni [56]	2723
17	20	H	Dundee	D 1-1	0-0	9	Craigen [58]	3203
18	27	A	Motherwell	L 0-1	0-1	9		5236
19	Jan 4	H	Dundee U	D 2-2	2-1	9	Stevenson [24], Doolan [32]	3761
20	17	A	St Johnstone	L 0-2	0-1	9		2994
21	21	H	Hamilton A	W 5-0	2-0	9	Doolan 4 [29, 44, 60, 62], Eccleston [89]	2138
22	24	A	Kilmarnock	D 2-2	1-1	9	Stevenson [2], Frans [84]	4130
23	30	H	St Mirren	L 0-1	0-1	9		3864
24	Feb 11	H	Celtic	L 0-3	0-2	9		5776
25	14	A	Dundee	L 0-1	0-0	9		5560
26	21	H	Ross Co	L 1-3	0-1	9	Taylor [68]	2951
27	28	A	Dundee U	W 2-0	2-0	9	O'Donnell [34], McGowan (og) [41]	6517
28	Mar 7	A	Ross Co	L 0-1	0-1	9		3358
29	14	H	St Johnstone	W 3-0	2-0	9	Doolan [3], Balatoni [9], Bannigan [65]	3196
30	21	H	Inverness CT	W 1-0	0-0	9	Lawless [84]	2603
31	Apr 4	H	Aberdeen	D 0-0	0-0	9		12,727
32	8	A	Celtic	L 0-2	0-1	9		43,784
33	11	H	Motherwell	W 2-0	0-0	8	Taylor 2 [54, 61]	5003
34	25	A	Ross Co	W 2-1	1-1	8	Frans [26], O'Donnell [54]	3315
35	May 2	A	St Mirren	W 3-0	0-0	7	Stevenson [66], Doolan [82], Lawless [90]	3865
36	9	A	Hamilton A	D 1-1	0-0	7	O'Donnell [72]	2342
37	16	H	Kilmarnock	L 1-4	0-2	7	Balatoni [67]	4503
38	23	A	Motherwell	D 0-0	0-0	8		3711

Final League Position: 8

Honours
League Champions: First Division 1975-76, 2001-02, 2012-13; Division II 1896-97, 1899-1900, 1970-71; Second Division 2000-01; *Runners-up:* First Division 1991-92, 2008-09. Division II 1901-02. *Promoted to First Division:* 2005-06 (play-offs).
Scottish Cup Winners: 1921; *Runners-up:* 1930.
League Cup Winners: 1971-72; *Runners-up:* 1953-54, 1956-57, 1958-59.
League Challenge Cup Runners-up: 2012-13.

European: *Fairs Cup:* 4 matches (1963-64). *UEFA Cup:* 2 matches (1972-73). *Intertoto Cup:* 4 matches (1995-96).

Club colours: Shirt: Yellow and red stripes. Shorts: Black. Socks: Red.

Goalscorers: *League (48):* Doolan 9, O'Donnell 5, Stevenson 5, Balatoni 3, Bannigan 3, Fraser 3, Lawless 3, Taylor 3, Craigen 2, Elliot 2, Frans 2, Higginbotham 2, Eccleston 1, McMillan 1, Osman 1, Seaborne 1, own goals 2.
William Hill Scottish FA Cup (3): Stevenson 2, Taylor 1.
Scottish League Cup (2): Doolan 1, Eccleston 1.

Fox S 22	O'Donnell S 34	Balatoni C 32	Seaborne D 18	McMillan J 11	Osman A 34	Fraser G 13+10	Lawless S 28+5	Higginbotham K 24+6	Bannigan S 34+2	Stevenson R 28+4	Elliot C 18+8	Craigen J 19+7	Doolan K 18+17	Keenan D 4+1	Gallacher P 16+2	Muirhead A 3+2	Carroll J 8+2	McDaid D 5+11	Eccleston N —+9	Frans F 20	Welsh S 1+2	Wilson D 1+5	Lindsay L 1	Booth C 14	Taylor L 10+5	Richards-Everton B 1+1	Hendry J 1	McLaughlin N —+1	Match No.
	2	3	4	5	6	7	8¹	9²	10³	11	12	13	14																1
1ª	2	3	4	5¹	6	8	9²	7¹	11	10	14	12	13																2
	2	3			7	6	8³	9	10¹	11²	12	14	13	5	1	4													3
	2	3¹	4		6	9	14	10	7	11²	8³	12		1	13	5													4
1	4	3	2		8	9³	6¹	7	11²	13	12	10		5	14														5
1	4		2		6	8¹	10	7	9³	14	12	11²		3	5	13													6
1	3	4¹	2		6	8²	10³	7	9	13	11	12		5	14														7
1	2	3	4	5	6	8³		7	10¹	9	11²		12	14	13														8
1	2	4	3¹	5²	7		9¹	6	12	10	8	11³		13	14														9
1	2		4	5	8	9²		6	11	7	10¹			13	12	3													10
1	4	3	2	6		9	12	8	10	7	11²		5¹			13													11
1	2		4	5	7	12	9³		11¹	10	8	13		14		3	6²												12
	2		4		6	12	10¹	13	7	14	8²	9²	11	1	5		3												13
	2		4		9	8	13	11³	7²	10¹		6		12	1	3	5	14											14
	2	3	4		6	12	13	10³	7	11²	8	9	14	1	5¹														15
	2	3	4	5	6	9	12	10¹	7³	11²	8			1	13			14											16
	2	4	3		7	8		9	5	11³	10	6	12	1	14														17
	2	3	4		7	6¹	12	10	5	11²	9	8³	13	1	14														18
	2	3			6	8	7¹	9	12	11	5	1	10			4													19
	2³	4	3		7	8²	12	6	9	11¹	5	1	10	13		14													20
	2	4	6¹		8	10³	9	5	7	11²	1	13	14	3	12														21
	2	4	6	13	8¹	10	12	9³	5³	7	11	1	14	3															22
	2	4	6¹	12	8	10³	7	9	11²	1	13	14	3	5															23
1	2	4	6	14	12	7¹	9	10²	13	8				3										5	11³				24
1²	2	3	6	9¹	7	14	10	13	12	8	4			3										5	11³				25
	2	3	6³	7	14	13	9	10	12	1	8¹	4		5²	11														26
	5	4	9	7	6²	2	10	8	13	1	12	3	11¹																27
	2	3	6	8¹	10⁴	7	13	9²	12	5	1	4	14	11²															28
1	2	5	6	14	9²	8³	11	7	10¹	4	12	3	13																29
1	2	4	6	9²	8	11	7	10¹	3			5	12	13															30
1	2	4	7	9²	13	8	11	6	10¹	3			5	12															31
1	2	4	8	14	9²	10	7³	11³	6⁴	13	3		5	12															32
1	2	4	7	9	6	8	10	12	3			5	11¹																33
1	2	4	6	8	9¹	7	11	12	13	3			5	10²															34
1	2	4	7	13	8	10²	6	9	12	3			5	11¹															35
1	2	3	12	8	10	7	9²	6	13	4			5	11¹															36
1	2	4	6¹	8	10	7	12	14	9	3	13		5²	11¹															37
1	2		7	9³	8	11	13	10²					6¹											5	12	4	3	14	38

PETERHEAD

Year Formed: 1891. *Ground and Address:* Balmoor Stadium, Balmoor Terrace, Peterhead AB42 1EQ.
Telephone: 01779 478256. *Fax:* 01779 490682. *E-mail:* office@peterheadfc.co.uk *Website:* www.peterheadfc.com
Ground Capacity: 4,000 (seated: 1,000). *Size of Pitch:* 101m × 64m.
Chairman: Rodger Morrison. *Vice-Chairman:* Ian Grant. *Secretary:* Brian McCombie.
Manager: Jim McInally. *Assistant coach:* David Nicholls. *Physio:* Greig Smith.
Club Nickname: 'Blue Toon'.
Previous Ground: Recreation Park.
Record Attendance: 8,643 v Raith R, Scottish Cup 4th rd replay, 25 Feb 1987 (Recreation Park); 4,855 v Rangers, Third
Division, 19 Jan 2013 (at Balmoor).
Record Victory: 8-0 v Forfar Athletic, Second Division, 30 Sep 2006.
Record Defeat: 0-13 v Aberdeen, Scottish Cup 3rd rd, 10 Feb 1923.
Most League Appearances: 275: Martin Bavidge, 2003-13.
Most League Goals in Season (Individual): 32: Rory McAllister, 2013-14.
Most Goals Overall (Individual): 98: Martin Bavidge, 2003-13.

PETERHEAD – SCOTTISH LEAGUE ONE 2014–15 LEAGUE RECORD

Match No.	Date	Venue	Opponents	Result	H/T Score	Lg Pos.	Goalscorers	Atten- dance
1	Aug 9	H	Stirling Alb	D 1-1	0-0	3	McAllister [85]	539
2	16	A	Airdrieonians	W 2-0	0-0	2	Rodgers [73], Cox [77]	810
3	23	H	Greenock Morton	L 1-2	0-0	4	McAllister (pen) [66]	708
4	30	A	Brechin C	D 1-1	0-0	6	Brown [86]	465
5	Sept 13	A	Forfar Ath	L 0-1	0-1	6		502
6	20	H	Stenhousemuir	W 1-0	1-0	6	Noble [3]	486
7	27	A	Dunfermline Ath	L 0-3	0-0	7		2409
8	Oct 4	H	Ayr U	W 2-0	0-0	6	Stevenson [56], Strachan [62]	506
9	18	H	Airdrieonians	D 1-1	1-1	6	McAllister [33]	467
10	25	A	Stenhousemuir	W 2-1	0-0	6	McAllister 2 (1 pen) [72, 90 (p)]	423
11	28	A	Stranraer	L 0-5	0-1	7		329
12	Nov 8	H	Dunfermline Ath	D 1-1	0-1	6	Stevenson [88]	740
13	22	H	Brechin C	D 1-1	0-0	6	Gilfillan [88]	613
14	Dec 6	A	Stirling Alb	W 3-2	1-0	6	Gilfillan [30], Johnston (og) [51], Kerr [73]	515
15	13	H	Stranraer	L 1-4	1-1	6	Stevenson [4]	428
16	20	A	Greenock Morton	W 1-0	0-0	6	Stevenson [46]	1098
17	Jan 3	A	Dunfermline Ath	D 1-1	0-1	7	McAllister (pen) [63]	2729
18	10	A	Airdrieonians	W 3-1	2-1	6	Strachan [6], Fitzpatrick (og) [42], Stevenson [47]	642
19	17	H	Stirling Alb	W 2-1	0-1	6	McAllister (pen) [73], Stevenson [75]	566
20	31	H	Stenhousemuir	W 2-0	1-0	6	Kerr [32], Dzierzawski [58]	454
21	Feb 7	A	Forfar Ath	L 1-3	0-1	6	Kerr [60]	535
22	14	A	Stranraer	L 0-2	0-1	6		371
23	21	H	Ayr U	W 2-0	0-0	6	McDonald [79], Rodgers (pen) [86]	560
24	28	H	Greenock Morton	L 1-3	0-0	7	Rodgers (pen) [56]	659
25	Mar 3	A	Ayr U	D 3-3	1-2	6	McDonald [12], Noble [71], Brown [87]	693
26	7	A	Stenhousemuir	L 1-2	1-1	7	Redman [41]	436
27	10	H	Forfar Ath	W 3-2	2-1	7	Redman [39], Rodgers [41], McDonald [87]	491
28	14	H	Brechin C	W 3-0	1-0	6	McDonald [32], Cox [71], Brown [90]	618
29	21	A	Stirling Alb	L 1-2	1-1	7	McAllister [4]	479
30	24	A	Brechin C	D 2-2	2-1	6	McDonald [26], Noble [30]	519
31	28	H	Stranraer	L 1-2	1-0	7	Rodgers [34]	516
32	Apr 4	H	Dunfermline Ath	D 1-1	0-1	7	Rodgers [78]	668
33	11	A	Ayr U	W 4-2	1-2	7	Rodgers [42], Brown 2 [53, 59], McDonald [76]	998
34	18	H	Forfar Ath	W 1-0	1-0	6	Redman [37]	743
35	25	H	Airdrieonians	L 0-1	0-0	6		678
36	May 2	A	Greenock Morton	L 1-3	1-2	6	McDonald [17]	6024

Final League Position: 6

Honours
League Champions League Two: 2013-14.
Third Division Runners up: 2004-05, 2012-13.
Scottish Cup: Quarter-finals 2001.

Club colours: Shirt: Royal blue shirts with white trim. Shorts: White. Socks: Royal blue.

Goalscorers: *League (51):* McAllister 8 (4 pens), McDonald 7, Rodgers 7 (2 pens), Stevenson 6, Brown 5, Kerr 3, Noble 3, Redman 3, Cox 2, Gilfillan 2, Strachan 2, Dzierzawski 1, own goals 2.
William Hill Scottish FA Cup (0).
Scottish League Cup (0).
Petrofac Training Cup (5): McAllister 1, Noble 1, Redman 1, Rodgers 1, Stevenson 1.

Smith G 36	Smith R 18+2	Strachan R 30+3	Ross S 31+1	Donaldson R 19+2	Redman J 33	Stevenson J 28+2	Gilfillan B 5+10	Noble S 33	McAllister R 29+2	Cox D 21+12	Brown J 7+21	McCann R —+4	Sharp G 7	Millar M 9+1	Rodgers A 14+18	Cowie D 9+7	Riley N 14+6	Richardson D 1+3	Tait J —+1	Lawrence M —+1	Kerr C 22	Dzierzawski K 16+1	McLaren F —+3	McDonald G 14+1	Match No.
1	2^1	3	4	5	6	7	8	9	10	11^2	12	13													1
1	2^1	12	3	4	7	9	14	8	11^3	13			5	6	10^2										2
1	4	13	3	2^1	6	8	14	9	11	12			5		10^2	7^1									3
1	2^1	3	4		6	8	14	9	10^2	13			5	7^3	11	12									4
1	2^1	12	3^2	4	6	8	14	9	11	13			5		10^3	7									5
1	4	2	3		6	7^3	13	9	11	12		14	5		10^2	8^1									6
1	7	10^2	3	4	8	9^1		5	11^3	12	6	14									2	13			7
1	5	4	3		6	7		9^2	11	12							10	13^1			2	8^1		14	8
1	3	7	4	5	11	10	6	8	9												2^1	12			9
1	14	9	3	2^3	8	11	4	10	5	6^2				12			7^1	13							10
1	3	9		4	7^1	11	5	10	2	6^2				8			12					13			11
1		4	3		6	11	12	5	10	9				7^2			8	13			2^1				12
1		3	4^3	2^1	6	9	13	8	10	11^2					7	14	12					5			13
1		4	3		7	9	8^3	5	11^2	10^1	14				6	13	12					2			14
1		4	13	3	9	11^2	5	10	6^1	14					8^3	12	7					2			15
1		8	3	6	10	9^2	13	5	11^3	12					7^1	14	4					2			16
1		6	4	3	8	11	13	5	10^3	9^1	12					14	7^1					2			17
1		3	2	4	8	7^2	13	9	10	11^1					14	6	12					5			18
1	14	3	2	4^3	7	9	8	10^1	11^2	13					12	6						5			19
1		4	3		8	11		5	10^2	6^1	12				9^3		13				2	7	14		20
1		3	4	12	8	11^2		5	10	6	13				9^3		14				2	7^1			21
1	6	3	4	5^3	8				11^2	13	12				9^1						2	7	14	10	22
1	4	3		5	6				11^2	12					9^1	10					2	8	13	7	23
1	4	3		5	6	12			11^1	13					9^2	10					2	8		7	24
1	8	3		5	9	6^3			11^1	12	14				10		13				2	7^2		4	25
1	4	3		5		7^2		11	10	13					9^1		14				2	6^3		8	26
1	4	3		5		7		10^1	11^2	13	12				9^1		14				2	6		8	27
1		3	4	5		8^3		9	10	12	13				11^1		14				2	6		7	28
1	3^3	4		5		7		9^1	10	12	13				11		14				2	6^2		8	29
1		3	4	5		8		9	10^3	13	12				11^2		14				2	6^1		7	30
1	4	8	3^2	5		7^3		9^1	10	13					11		14				2	6		12	31
1	4	3		5		8^3		10	11^2	12	13				9^1		14				2	6		7	32
1	4	3	12	2^1	6			10		11				5	9^3		13	14				7^2		8	33
1	2	4	3	6				8	10^1	11^2	12			5	9^3		14	13						7	34
1		3	4	5		8^1		9	10	12	13				11^3		14				2^2	6		7	35
1	2	4	3	5	6^2	13		10	12		14				11							9^3	8^1	7	36

QUEEN OF THE SOUTH

Year Formed: 1919. *Ground & Address:* Palmerston Park, Dumfries DG2 9BA. *Telephone:* 01387 254853.
Fax: 01387 240470. *E-mail:* admin@qosfc.com *Website:* www.qosfc.com
Ground Capacity: 8,690 (seated: 3,377) *Size of Pitch:* 102m × 66m.
Chairman: Billy Hewitson. *Vice-Chairman:* Craig Paterson. *Football Administration:* Ewan Lithgow.
Manager: James Fowler. *Coach:* Paul Burns. *Physio:* Ross Goodwin.
Club Nickname: 'The Doonhamers'.
Previous Grounds: None.
Record Attendance: 26,552 v Hearts, Scottish Cup 3rd rd, 23 Feb 1952.
Record Transfer Fee received: £250,000 for Andy Thomson to Southend U (July 1994).
Record Transfer Fee paid: £30,000 for Jim Butter from Alloa Ath (1995).
Record Victory: 11-1 v Stranraer, Scottish Cup 1st rd, 16 Jan 1932.
Record Defeat: 2-10 v Dundee, Division I, 1 Dec 1962.
Most Capped Player: Billy Houliston, 3, Scotland.
Most League Appearances: 731: Allan Ball, 1963-82.
Most League Goals in Season (Individual): 37: Jimmy Gray, Division II, 1927-28.
Most Goals in Season: 41: Jimmy Rutherford, 1931-32; Nicky Clark, 2012-13.
Most Goals Overall (Individual): 251: Jim Patterson, 1949-63.

QUEEN OF THE SOUTH – SCOTTISH CHAMPIONSHIP 2014–15 LEAGUE RECORD

Match No.	Date	Venue	Opponents	Result	H/T Score	Lg Pos.	Goalscorers	Atten- dance
1	Aug 9	H	Alloa Ath	W 2-0	2-0	2	Lyle [8], Reilly [40]	1635
2	16	A	Dumbarton	W 4-0	1-0	1	Lyle [20], Reilly [50], Fowler [88], Russell [77]	958
3	23	H	Livingston	D 1-1	1-0	2	Kyle Jacobs (og) [34]	1805
4	30	A	Rangers	L 2-4	2-1	4	Reilly [22], Russell [36]	31,851
5	Sept 13	A	Falkirk	D 1-1	0-0	4	Reilly [70]	3793
6	20	H	Hibernian	W 1-0	1-0	4	McShane [29]	3083
7	27	A	Cowdenbeath	L 1-2	0-2	4	Lyle [62]	674
8	Oct 4	H	Hearts	L 0-3	0-2	4		5534
9	10	A	Raith R	W 4-3	1-0	3	Baird [7], Reilly [50], Lyle [74], Russell [90]	1552
10	18	H	Falkirk	W 3-0	2-0	3	Dowie [38], Reilly [42], Kerr [72]	2038
11	25	A	Livingston	D 2-2	1-0	3	Russell [31], Reilly [69]	1099
12	Nov 8	H	Dumbarton	W 3-0	1-0	3	Baird (pen) [32], Durnan [69], Lyle [71]	1677
13	15	A	Hibernian	D 0-0	0-0	3		10,069
14	22	H	Raith R	W 2-0	1-0	3	Baird [22], Reilly [80]	1597
15	Dec 6	A	Hearts	L 1-4	0-1	3	Russell (pen) [56]	15,459
16	12	H	Rangers	W 2-0	1-0	3	Holt [22], Reilly [67]	6185
17	20	H	Cowdenbeath	L 1-2	0-1	4	Lyle [86]	1717
18	27	A	Alloa Ath	D 1-1	1-0	4	Lyle [41]	921
19	Jan 3	H	Livingston	W 3-1	1-1	4	Dowie [31], Lyle [65], Russell [76]	1940
20	17	A	Falkirk	D 1-1	0-1	4	Reilly [56]	3478
21	24	H	Hibernian	L 0-2	0-0	5		3677
22	31	A	Cowdenbeath	W 5-0	1-0	4	Lyle 3 (1 pen) [45, 58, 81 (p)], Reilly [56], McShane [61]	569
23	Feb 14	A	Alloa Ath	W 1-0	0-0	4	Holt [76]	1673
24	21	H	Hearts	L 1-2	1-1	4	Carmichael [24]	5100
25	28	A	Dumbarton	D 0-0	0-0	4		904
26	Mar 10	A	Rangers	D 1-1	0-0	4	Smith, A [86]	35,018
27	14	H	Raith R	W 2-1	2-1	4	Russell [9], Reilly [39]	1656
28	21	H	Cowdenbeath	W 4-1	1-0	4	Russell [27], Paton [51], Durnan [75], Lyle [89]	1671
29	24	A	Raith R	L 0-3	0-1	4		1152
30	28	A	Hearts	L 0-2	0-1	4		16,855
31	Apr 4	A	Hibernian	W 1-0	0-0	5	Durnan [47]	8773
32	9	H	Rangers	W 3-0	1-0	4	Lyle [33], Wallace (og) [46], Reilly [69]	5093
33	12	H	Falkirk	W 1-0	1-0	4	Lyle [22]	2057
34	18	A	Alloa Ath	D 2-2	0-1	4	Lyle (pen) [51], Millar [53]	822
35	25	H	Dumbarton	W 2-1	0-0	4	Holt [55], McKenna [72]	1865
36	May 2	A	Livingston	L 0-1	0-0	4		2475

Final League Position: 4

Honours
League Champions: Division II 1950-51. Second Division 2001-02, 2012-13.
Runners-up: Division II 1932-33, 1961-62, 1974-75. Second Division 1980-81, 1985-86.
Scottish Cup Runners-up: 2007-08.
League Cup: semi-finals 1950-51, 1960-61.
League Challenge Cup Winners: 2002-03, 2012-13; *Runners-up:* 1997-98, 2010-11. *B&Q Cup:* semi-finals 1991-92.

European: *UEFA Cup:* 2 matches (2008-09).

Club colours: Shirt: Royal blue with white trim. Shorts: White. Socks: Royal blue.

Goalscorers: *League (58):* Lyle 15 (2 pens), Reilly 13, Russell 8 (1 pen), Baird 3 (1 pen), Durnan 3, Holt 3, Dowie 2, McShane 2, Carmichael 1, Fowler 1, Kerr 1, McKenna 1, Millar 1, Paton 1, Smith, A 1, own goals 2.
William Hill Scottish FA Cup (6): Lyle 2, Reilly 2, Kidd 1, Russell 1.
Scottish League Cup (5): Russell 3, Lyle 2.
Petrofac Training Cup (3): Dowie 1, Paton 1, Russell 1.
Premiership Play-Offs (2): Lyle 2.

Clark A 33	Dowie A 34	Durnan M 29+1	Higgins C 34	Holt K 33	Carmichael D 30+3	McShane I 32+1	Fowler J 7+1	Russell I 24+8	Lyle D 26+8	Reilly G 30+2	Kidd L 23+12	Baird J 8+10	Dzierzawski K 2+14	Smith D —+3	Kerr M 10+2	Kiltie G 3	McKenna S 7+6	Hooper S 2+5	Paton M 13+7	Atkinson J 3+1	Millar M 10+3	Burns P 2+3	Pickard J —+11	Smith A 1+4	Mitchell C —+1	Match No.
1	2	3	4	5	6^3	7	8	9	10^1	11^2	12	13	14													1
1	2	3	4	5	6^3	8	7	9	11^2	10^1	14	13	12													2
1	2	3	4	5	6^3	8	7*	9	10^1	11^2	12	13	14													3
1	2	3	4	5		7			10	11^2	9^1	8	12	6	13											4
1	2	3	4	5	9^1	7	6^3	8	10	11^2	13	14	12													5
1	2	3	4	5	6	8	7^2	9	11^3	10^1	13	14	12													6
1	2	3	4	5		8^1	9^3	11	10^2	7	6	12	14	13												7
1	4	3		5		8	7^2	9	10^3	11	2	14	13	12	6^1											8
1	3		4	5^5	6	8	13	9	12	11	2	10^2	14		7^3											9
1	3	4^3		5	6	7		9	12	11^1	2	10	8^2				13	14								10
1	5	3^4	4		6	8		9		11^1	2	10	14		7		13^3	12								11
1	2	3	4	5	9	8		12	11^2	13	10	14			7^3	6^1										12
1	2	3	4	5	8	6		10^1	9^3	12	13	11^2	14		7											13
1	2	3	4	5	6^2	8		9	12	11	13	10^1			7											14
1	2	3	4	5	14	8		10	12	11^2	6	13	7^1		9^3											15
1	2	3	4	5	6^1	8		9^2	12	11	13	10^3			7		14									16
1		3	4	5	9^1	8^2		13	11	2	10	14			7	6^2		12								17
1		3		5	6	8		9	11^1	10^3	2	12	14		7^2		4	13								18
1^2	2	3	4	5	9	7	8^3	11^1	10		6	14			13		12									19
	2	3^b	4	5	6	7		9^3	11^2	10	8^1				14		13		1		12					20
	3		4	5	7	6^b		8	11^1	10	2		12		1		9^2	13	14							21
1	2	4	3		9	6^2		13	10^3	11^1	5	8			7		12	14								22
1	3	2	4		8	14		7	12	11	10^3	5			9^2		13	6^1								23
1	3	2	4		8	9		13	11^1	5	12	10^3			7^2		6	14								24
1	5	2	3	4	9^2	8		12	11*	6		10^3			7^1		13	14								25
1	3		4	5	7	6		9	11^2	8		12	10^3		2^1		14	13								26
1	3		5	6	7			9^1	12	11^2	2	4	10		8^3		14	13								27
1	3	13	4	8	5	7		10^1	12	11^2	2		14		9		6^3									28
1	2	3^b	4	5	9	7^3		11	12	6^1		14	10		8			13								29
1	2	3	4	5	6	12		11^1	7	13		10^3			8		9^2	14								30
1	2	3	4	5	6	7		10^1	11	12		14		8^2	9^2		13									31
1	3	2^1	4	9	7	6		14	10^3	11^2	5		8		12		13									32
1	3		4	5	6	8		14	11^2	10^3	2^1		7		12		9	13								33
1	3	4	6	5	9			12	10^3	11^1	2		8^2		7*		14	13								34
	3	2	4	5	6	8		9	11^3	10^3	13		7		12		1	14								35
1	2^1	3		5	14	8		9^3	11^2	7		13			4		6		12	10						36

QUEEN'S PARK

Year Formed: 1867. *Ground & Address:* Hampden Park, Mount Florida, Glasgow G42 9BA. *Telephone:* 0141 632 1275.
Fax: 0141 636 1612. *E-mail:* secretary@queensparkfc.co.uk *Website:* queensparkfc.co.uk
Ground Capacity: 52,025 (all seated). *Size of Pitch:* 105m × 68m.
President: Ron Jack. *Secretary:* Christine Wright. *Treasurer:* David Gordon.
Head Coach: Gus MacPherson. *Assistant Head Coach:* Chris Hillcoat.
Club Nickname: 'The Spiders'.
Previous Grounds: 1st Hampden (Recreation Ground); (Titwood Park was used as an interim measure between 1st & 2nd Hampdens); 2nd Hampden (Cathkin); 3rd Hampden.
Record Attendance: 95,772 v Rangers, Scottish Cup 1st rd, 18 Jan 1930.
Record for Ground: 149,547 Scotland v England, 1937.
Record Transfer Fee received: Not applicable due to amateur status.
Record Transfer Fee paid: Not applicable due to amateur status.
Record Victory: 16-0 v St. Peter's, Scottish Cup 1st rd, 12 Sep 1885.
Record Defeat: 0-9 v Motherwell, Division I, 26 Apr 1930.
Most Capped Player: Walter Arnott, 14, Scotland.
Most League Appearances: 532: Ross Caven, 1982-2002.
Most League Goals in Season (Individual): 30: William Martin, Division I, 1937-38.
Most Goals Overall (Individual): 163: James B. McAlpine, 1919-33.

QUEEN'S PARK – SCOTTISH LEAGUE TWO 2014–15 LEAGUE RECORD

Match No.	Date	Venue	Opponents	Result	H/T Score	Lg Pos.	Goalscorers	Atten- dance
1	Aug 9	H	Clyde	L	1-2	0-0	6	Miller [58]	685
2	16	A	Annan Ath	W	1-0	1-0	5	Fraser [41]	401
3	23	H	Arbroath	L	0-2	0-0	7		520
4	30	A	Albion R	L	0-1	0-0	8		577
5	Sept 13	H	Elgin C	W	2-1	0-1	7	Woods 2 [54, 55]	304
6	20	A	East Fife	D	2-2	1-1	8	Miller [45], Woods [63]	678
7	27	H	Berwick R	W	2-0	2-0	5	Wharton [19], Burns [29]	351
8	Oct 11	A	East Stirling	W	3-1	2-0	3	Fraser 2 [5, 25], Woods [90]	351
9	18	H	Montrose	W	2-0	2-0	2	Duggan (pen) [4], MacGregor [45]	321
10	25	H	East Fife	W	3-0	2-0	2	Fraser (pen) [15], McElroy [39], Miller [81]	408
11	Nov 8	A	Arbroath	W	2-1	1-0	2	Fraser [2], Fotheringham [79]	737
12	15	A	Elgin C	W	4-1	3-0	2	Woods [24], Rooney [28], Miller (pen) [43], Carter [66]	552
13	22	H	Albion R	L	0-1	0-0	3		484
14	29	A	Clyde	W	2-0	1-0	2	Rooney [4], Fraser [66]	589
15	Dec 6	H	East Stirling	W	3-0	1-0	2	Wharton [7], Carter [58], Miller [82]	322
16	13	A	Montrose	W	2-1	2-0	2	Carter [24], Woods [37]	353
17	20	H	Annan Ath	D	0-0	0-0	2		320
18	27	A	Berwick R	D	0-0	0-0	3		598
19	Jan 3	H	Clyde	D	1-1	0-0	3	Miller (pen) [90]	2027
20	10	A	East Fife	D	0-0	0-0	3		498
21	17	H	Arbroath	W	2-1	2-0	2	Woods [4], Burns [19]	729
22	24	A	Elgin C	D	1-1	1-1	3	Fraser (pen) [15]	538
23	31	A	Albion R	L	1-2	0-1	3	Carter [50]	509
24	Feb 7	H	Montrose	W	4-1	2-0	3	Miller [24], Woods [34], Moore 2 (1 pen) [82 (p), 87]	505
25	14	A	Annan Ath	L	0-2	0-0	3		451
26	21	H	Berwick R	W	2-0	0-0	1	McPherson [75], Woods [96]	966
27	28	A	East Stirling	L	1-3	0-1	2	Berry [76]	367
28	Mar 7	H	East Fife	W	1-0	1-0	2	McElroy [11]	678
29	14	A	Elgin C	W	2-1	1-1	2	Nicolson (og) [37], Moore [90]	704
30	21	H	Albion R	L	0-1	0-1	2		821
31	28	A	Berwick R	D	1-1	1-1	2	Carter [19]	550
32	Apr 4	A	Montrose	D	2-2	0-1	2	Steeves (og) [57], Rooney [59]	367
33	11	H	Annan Ath	W	2-0	2-0	2	Burns [37], Rooney [45]	462
34	18	A	Arbroath	D	1-1	0-1	2	Burns [90]	680
35	25	H	East Stirling	D	1-1	1-0	2	Slattery [28]	507
36	May 2	A	Clyde	L	0-2	0-1	2		664

Final League Position: 2

Honours
League Champions: Division II 1922-23. B Division 1955-56. Second Division 1980-81. Third Division 1999-2000.
Runners-up: Third Division 2011-12. League Two 2014-15. *Promoted to Second Division:* 2006-07 (play-offs).
Scottish Cup Winners: 1874, 1875, 1876, 1880, 1881, 1882, 1884, 1886, 1890, 1893; *Runners-up:* 1892, 1900.
FA Cup Runners-up: 1884, 1885.
FA Charity Shield: 1899 (shared with Aston Villa).

Club colours: Shirt: Black and white thin hoops. Shorts: White. Socks: Black.

Goalscorers: *League (51):* Woods 9, Fraser 7 (2 pens), Miller 7 (2 pens), Carter 5, Burns 4, Rooney 4, Moore 3 (1 pen), McElroy 2, Wharton 2, Berry 1, Duggan 1 (1 pen), Fotheringham 1, MacGregor 1, McPherson 1, Slattery 1, own goals 2.
William Hill Scottish FA Cup (2): Burns 1, Miller 1.
Scottish League Cup (1): Quinn 1.
Petrofac Training Cup (1): McPherson 1.
League One Play-Offs (4): Fraser 2, Quinn 1, Wharton 1.

Muir W 36	Quinn A 30+1	Mitchell G 15+3	MacGregor D 16+2	Gallacher R 9	Berry V 27+1	Miller D 30	Woods P 35	Fraser S 26+5	Fotheringham K 3+14	McPherson R 12+15	Baty J —+1	Carter J 14+15	McElroy C 22+11	Gibson S 11+3	Wharton B 25+7	Burns S 26+7	McVey C 7+5	Rooney S 23+1	Duggan C 5	Chalmers K —+1	Biggart S —+1	Slattery P 16	Wylie G —+1	Hynes R 3+6	Moore J 4+4	Mortimer W 1+1	Marr J 1	Gallagher J —+1	Match No.
1	2	3	4	5	6	7	8	9^1	10^3	11^{12}	12	13	14																1
1	3	2	4	5	7	8	6	9	11^{11}	10		12																	2
1	2	5	3		7^2	9	8	6		11^1		10^3	14	12	4	13													3
1	3	2	4	5	7^3	8	6	11		10^2		13	12			9^1	14												4
1	3^3	13	4	5	7	6	9	12				11^1	14	8			2^2	10											5
1	4	14	3	5^1	7	8	11			13		9	12^1	6		2	10^2												6
1		4	5	7	6	9^1	13	14		10^3		3	8^2	2	11	12													7
1		4		7	8	6	10			13		9^1	5	3	12	2	11^2												8
1		4		7	6	8^1	9			14		10^3	5^2	3	12	2	11	13											9
1	14	4		7	6	8^2	9			11^1		12	10^3	5	3	13	2												10
1		4			8	9^2	7	12	14			10^1	13	5	3	11^1	2		6										11
1	4				8	9	7^2	12				10		5	3	11^1	13	2	6										12
1	3				7	8^2	9	14	12			11	13	5^1	4	10^3	2		6										13
1	4		5		8	6^7	11^3	13				10	9^1	7	12	2		3	14										14
1	3				7	8	9^1	14	13			11^2	10^1	4	12	6	2		5										15
1	3				8^2	7	9	13	14			11^3	10^1	4	12	5	2		6										16
1	3				12	7	8^3	9	13	14		11	10^2	5	4		6^1	2											17
1	3				6		8^3		14	12		11^2	13	5	4	10	9^1	2			7								18
1	3				6	7	8	9	12	13		11^1	10^2	4	14		2				5^3								19
1	4	2			7	6^4	8	13	12	11^3		14	10	3	9						5^1								20
1	3				6	7	8	9^2	13	11^{11}			4	10		2					5	12							21
1	3				7	6	8	9^2	14			13	12	4	10		2				5^1	11^2							22
1	3	12	5		7^3	8	6	11^2				10	13	4^8	9^1		2					14							23
1	3	2	4		7	6^2	8	9^1	10^1			14			5	13							12	11					24
1	4		3		7	8^2	6	11		14			12^1		5		2						13	10^3					25
1	3	12	4		7	6	8	9		14			13		5		2^1						10^1	11^3					26
1	3	2	4		8		6	11		12		14	9^3	5^2	7								13^1	10^1					27
1	3	2			6	7	8	9^1		11^2		13	10^1	12	4	5	14												28
1	3	2			6	7	8	9^1		11^2		12	10^3	14	4	5								13					29
1	3	2			7	6	8	9^{12}		11^3			10^1		4	5								13	14				30
1	3	2			7^1	6	13	12		11			9^3		4	5	10	8^2							14				31
1	3	2			8	7^1	6			11^2			10	13	4	5		12				9							32
1	3	2			7		9	13		12			11^1	8	4	5		6^2				10							33
1	3	2^2			6^3		8			11			10		4	5	12	7^1				9		14					34
1	3^1	2	12		6		8			11^2			13	10	4	5	9^3					7				14			35
1		3					9^1			12			13	10	4		5	6				7^1		11^2		8	2	14	36

RAITH ROVERS

Year Formed: 1883. *Ground & Address:* Stark's Park, Pratt St, Kirkcaldy KY1 1SA. *Telephone:* 01592 263514. *Fax:* 01592 642833. *E-mail:* info@raithrovers.net *Website:* www.raithrovers.net
Ground Capacity: 8,473 (all seated). *Size of Pitch:* 103m × 64m.
Chairman: Alan Young. *Chief Executive:* Eric Drysdale.
Manager: Ray McKinnon. *Coach:* Laurie Ellis.
Club Nickname: 'Rovers'.
Previous Grounds: Robbie's Park.
Record Attendance: 31,306 v Hearts, Scottish Cup 2nd rd, 7 Feb 1953.
Record Transfer Fee received: £900,000 for Steve McAnespie to Bolton W (Sept 1995).
Record Transfer Fee paid: £225,000 for Paul Harvey from Airdrieonians (July 1996).
Record Victory: 10-1 v Coldstream, Scottish Cup 2nd rd, 13 Feb 1954.
Record Defeat: 2-11 v Morton, Division II, 18 Mar 1936.
Most Capped Player: David Morris, 6, Scotland.
Most League Appearances: 430: Willie McNaught, 1946-51.
Most League Goals in Season (Individual): 38: Norman Haywood, Division II, 1937-38.
Most Goals Overall (Individual): 154: Gordon Dalziel (League), 1987-94.

RAITH ROVERS – SCOTTISH CHAMPIONSHIP 2014–15 LEAGUE RECORD

Match No.	Date	Venue	Opponents	Result	H/T Score	Lg Pos.	Goalscorers	Attendance
1	Aug 9	H	Dumbarton	W 3-1	0-0	1	Watson [56], Conroy [78], Nade [81]	1642
2	16	A	Alloa Ath	W 1-0	1-0	2	Conroy [4]	858
3	23	H	Hearts	L 0-4	0-2	4	°	6105
4	30	A	Cowdenbeath	W 3-1	1-0	3	Stewart [29], Vaughan [71], Conroy [77]	1216
5	Sept 12	H	Rangers	L 0-4	0-3	3		6250
6	20	A	Livingston	W 1-0	1-0	3	Scott [18]	1309
7	27	H	Falkirk	D 0-0	0-0	3		1871
8	Oct 4	A	Hibernian	D 1-1	0-1	3	Nade [68]	9954
9	10	A	Queen of the South	L 3-4	0-1	4	Stewart 2 [59, 78], Nade [62]	1552
10	18	A	Rangers	L 1-6	0-2	5	Scott [54]	33,956
11	25	H	Alloa Ath	D 1-1	1-1	4	Anderson [34]	1541
12	Nov 8	A	Hearts	L 0-1	0-1	5		16,372
13	15	H	Cowdenbeath	W 2-1	0-1	5	Moon [58], Nade [71]	1779
14	22	A	Queen of the South	L 0-2	0-1	5		1597
15	Dec 6	H	Livingston	L 1-5	1-3	6	Anderson [45]	1385
16	13	A	Dumbarton	L 1-2	0-1	7	Stewart [63]	764
17	20	H	Hibernian	L 1-3	1-1	7	McKay [40]	3166
18	27	A	Falkirk	W 1-0	0-0	7	Conroy [79]	3358
19	Jan 3	A	Cowdenbeath	W 1-0	0-0	6	Nade [89]	1265
20	17	H	Dumbarton	W 2-1	2-0	6	Conroy (pen) [29], Anderson [32]	1474
21	24	A	Alloa Ath	D 0-0	0-0	6		914
22	31	A	Hibernian	D 1-1	0-0	6	Nade [90]	9024
23	Feb 14	H	Falkirk	D 2-2	0-1	6	Vaulks (og) [60], Callachan [90]	2092
24	20	H	Rangers	L 1-2	0-1	6	Conroy [70]	4604
25	28	A	Livingston	W 2-0	2-0	6	Callachan [15], Vaughan [21]	972
26	Mar 14	A	Queen of the South	L 1-2	1-2	6	Vaughan [20]	1656
27	17	H	Hearts	L 1-3	1-1	6	Barr [43]	4760
28	21	A	Alloa Ath	W 2-1	1-1	6	Stewart [29], Vaughan [47]	1100
29	24	A	Queen of the South	W 3-0	1-0	6	Stewart 2 [23, 78], Vaughan [82]	1152
30	28	H	Hibernian	W 2-1	0-0	6	Stewart [53], Vaughan [84]	3183
31	Apr 4	A	Falkirk	L 0-1	0-0	6		4032
32	8	H	Cowdenbeath	L 1-3	0-1	6	Stewart [88]	1350
33	12	A	Rangers	L 0-4	0-2	6		31,427
34	18	H	Hearts	L 1-2	0-1	6	Elliot [66]	15,405
35	25	H	Livingston	L 0-4	0-1	6		1766
36	May 2	A	Dumbarton	D 2-2	0-1	6	Stewart [53], Vaughan [60]	801

Final League Position: 6

Honours
League Champions: First Division 1992-93, 1994-95. Second Division 2002-03, 2008-09. Division II 1907-08, 1909-10 (shared), 1937-38, 1948-49; *Runners-up:* Division II 1908-09, 1926-27, 1966-67. Second Division 1975-76, 1977-78, 1986-87.
Scottish Cup Runners-up: 1913.
League Cup Winners: 1994-95. *Runners-up:* 1948-49.
League Challenge Cup Winners: 2013-14.

European: *UEFA Cup:* 6 matches (1995-96).

Club colours: Shirt: Navy with white sleeves. Shorts: White with navy trim. Socks: Navy.

Goalscorers: *League (42):* Stewart 10, Vaughan 7, Conroy 6 (1 pen), Nade 6, Anderson 3, Callachan 2, Scott 2, Barr 1, Elliot 1, McKay 1, Moon 1, Watson 1, own goal 1.
William Hill Scottish FA Cup (6): Conroy 2 (1 pen), Anderson 1, McKay 1, Nade 1, Watson 1.
Scottish League Cup (4): Elliot 2 (1 pen), Conroy 1, own goal 1.
Petrofac Training Cup (0).

Cuthbert K 7	Thomson J 36	Watson P 36	Perry R 10+1	McKeown R 36	Anderson G 22+9	Fox L 22+3	Scott M 21+5	Conroy R 29+6	Nade C 16+11	Elliot C 11+6	Stewart M 26+7	Moon K 18+5	Callachan R 21+4	Vaughan L 12+9	Laidlaw R 7	Ellis L 5+1	McKay B 16+7	McGurn D 22	Hill D 10+1	Carrick D —+1	Barr C 12	Matthews R 1	Robertson C —+1	Match No.
1	2	3	4	5	6[2]	7[1]	8	9	10	11[1]	12	13	14											1
1	2	3	4	5	6[2]	7	8	9	11		10[1]	12		13										2
1	2	3	4	5	6	8[1]	7	9	11		10[2]	12		13										3
	2	3	4[3]	5	14	7[2]	8	9		13	11	6		10[1]	1	12								4
	2	3	4	5	12	9[2]	8	10		13	11	7		6[1]	1									5
	2	3		5		7	8	9	10[3]	11[2]	13	6[1]	14		1	4	12							6
	2	3		5		7	8	9	11[1]	12	6[2]	13			1	4	10							7
	2	3		5		9	10	8	11	12	7	13			1	4	6[1]							8
	2	3		5	12	7	10	6	11[1]	13	8[1]		14		1	4	9[2]							9
	2	3	14	5	9	7[2]	10	6[1]	11	8	12	13			1	4[3]								10
	2	3	4	5	9[1]	8	11	12	10	7[3]	14	13		6[2]				1						11
	2	4	3	5	9	8	11	13	10	12	7[2]			6[1]				1						12
	2	3	4	5	6	8	11[1]	12	10	7	9							1						13
	2	3	4	5	6[1]	8[3]	13	14	11	10[2]	12	7	9					1						14
	2	4	3[b]	5	6	13	10	14	11[2]	8[1]	7	9					1			12[9]				15
	2	4		5	6	11	10	7	8	9								1			3			16
	2	3		5	12	8	6[1]	11[2]	13	10	7	9						1	4					17
	2	3		5	12	11	9[2]	13	10	7[1]	8	6						1	4					18
	2	3		5	6	8	9	12	11[1]	10	7							1	4					19
	2	3		5	6[1]	8[2]	9	13	11	10[3]	12	7	14					1	4					20
	2	3		5	6	8	9[2]	12	11[1]	10	7	13						1	4					21
	2	3		5	6[2]	13	11	10[1]	8	7	9							1	4	12				22
	2	3		5	6	13	9[1]	11	10	7[2]	8	12						1	4					23
	2	3		5	6[2]	12	9	11	10	8[1]	7	13						1	4					24
	2	4		5	6	8	13	12	10	7	11[2]						9[1]	1			3			25
	2	3		5	12	8[1]	9[2]	6	10	13	7	11						1	4					26
	2	3		5	6	8	9	11[1]	12	7	10[5]							1	4					27
	2	4		5	6	8	9	10	7	11								1			3			28
	2	4		5	6[3]	7	12	9	14	10	8[1]	11[2]	13					1			3			29
	2	4		5	6[1]	7	9	13	11[2]	8	10	12						1			3			30
	2	3		5	13	8	12	6[1]	14	10	7	11[2]					9[1]	1	4					31
1	2	3		5	9	14	6[2]	8	13	10	12	7	11[1]						4[7]					32
	2	3		5	6	8	9	13	12	11[1]	7	10[5]						1	4					33
1	2	4		5	12	9	13	10	11[2]	7[3]	8	14					6[1]				3			34
1	2	4		5	13	7	6	12	10[2]	11[1]	8	14					9[3]				3			35
	2	3		5	6[2]	13	9	10[3]	7	11	12							1	4			8[1]	14	36

RANGERS

Year Formed: 1873. *Ground & Address:* Ibrox Stadium, 150 Edmiston Drive, Glasgow G51 2XD.
Telephone: 0871 702 1972. *Fax:* 0870 600 1978. *Website:* www.rangers.co.uk
Ground Capacity: 51,082 (all seated). *Size of Pitch:* 105m × 68m.
Chairman: Dave King. *Secretary:* James Blair.
Manager: Mark Warburton. *Assistant Manager:* David Weir. *Managing Director:* Stewart Robinson.
Club Nickname: 'The Gers', 'The Teddy Bears'.
Previous Grounds: Flesher's Haugh, Burnbank, Kinning Park, Old Ibrox.
Record Attendance: 118,567 v Celtic, Division I, 2 Jan 1939.
Record Transfer Fee received: £8,500,000 for Giovanni van Bronckhorst to Arsenal (July 2001).
Record Transfer Fee paid: £12,000,000 for Tore Andre Flo from Chelsea (November 2000).
Record Victory: 14-2 v Blairgowrie, Scottish Cup 1st rd, 20 Jan, 1934.
Record Defeat: 1-7 v Celtic, League Cup Final, 19 Oct 1957.
Most Capped Player: Ally McCoist, 60, Scotland.
Most League Appearances: 496: John Greig, 1962-78.
Most League Goals in Season (Individual): 44: Sam English, Division I, 1931-32.
Most Goals Overall (Individual): 355: Ally McCoist; 1985-98.

Honours
League Champions: (54 times) Division I 1890-91 (shared), 1898-99, 1899-1900, 1900-01, 1901-02, 1910-11, 1911-12, 1912-13, 1917-18, 1919-20, 1920-21, 1922-23, 1923-24, 1924-25, 1926-27, 1927-28, 1928-29, 1929-30, 1930-31, 1932-33, 1933-34, 1934-35, 1936-37, 1938-39, 1946-47, 1948-49, 1949-50, 1952-53, 1955-56, 1956-57, 1958-59, 1960-61, 1962-63, 1963-64, 1974-75. Premier Division: 1975-76, 1977-78, 1986-87, 1988-89, 1989-90, 1990-91, 1991-92, 1992-93, 1993-94, 1994-95, 1995-96, 1996-97, 1998-99, 1999-2000, 2002-03, 2004-05, 2008-09, 2009-10, 2010-11. Third Division 2012-13. League One 2013-14. *Runners-up:* 30 times.
Scottish Cup Winners: (33 times) 1894, 1897, 1898, 1903, 1928, 1930, 1932, 1934, 1935, 1936, 1948, 1949, 1950, 1953, 1960, 1962, 1963, 1964, 1966, 1973, 1976, 1978, 1979, 1981, 1992, 1993, 1996, 1999, 2000, 2002, 2003, 2008, 2009; *Runners-up:* 17 times.

RANGERS – SCOTTISH CHAMPIONSHIP 2014–15 LEAGUE RECORD

Match No.	Date	Venue	Opponents	Result	H/T Score	Lg Pos.	Goalscorers	Atten-dance
1	Aug 10	H	Hearts	L 1-2	0-0	7	Law [90]	43,683
2	15	A	Falkirk	W 2-0	0-0	3	Macleod [78], Clark [84]	6927
3	23	H	Dumbarton	W 4-1	2-0	3	McCulloch [15], McGregor [30], Clark [54], Turner (og) [76]	31,175
4	30	H	Queen of the South	W 4-2	1-2	2	Zaliukaš [27], Templeton [46], Mohsni [64], Miller [86]	31,851
5	Sept 12	A	Raith R	W 4-0	3-0	1	Clark [16], Black [38], Law [39], McCulloch (pen) [73]	6250
6	20	A	Alloa Ath	D 1-1	0-1	2	Templeton [84]	2793
7	29	H	Hibernian	L 1-3	0-3	2	Law [55]	31,619
8	Oct 4	A	Livingston	W 1-0	1-0	2	Macleod [8]	5924
9	18	H	Raith R	W 6-1	2-0	2	McCulloch [8], Law [36], Miller [55], Boyd [63], Daly 2 [84, 90]	33,956
10	25	A	Dumbarton	W 3-0	1-0	2	Miller [26], Wallace [61], Boyd [72]	1850
11	Nov 1	A	Cowdenbeath	W 3-0	1-0	2	Law [3], Miller (og) [55], Templeton [85]	3919
12	8	H	Falkirk	W 4-0	1-0	2	Law [25], Macleod [69], Miller [75], Clark [82]	33,359
13	15	H	Alloa Ath	D 1-1	0-0	2	McCulloch [72]	29,548
14	22	A	Hearts	L 0-2	0-0	2		17,004
15	Dec 6	H	Cowdenbeath	W 1-0	0-0	2	Shiels [58]	28,137
16	12	A	Queen of the South	L 0-2	0-1	2		6185
17	20	H	Livingston	W 2-0	1-0	2	Aird [10], Mensing (og) [74]	28,053
18	27	A	Hibernian	L 0-4	0-2	2		15,261
19	Jan 3	H	Dumbarton	W 3-1	2-1	2	Daly [22], Wallace [41], Shiels [90]	30,031
20	10	A	Alloa Ath	W 1-0	1-0	2	Law [16]	3012
21	Feb 13	H	Hibernian	L 0-2	0-1	3		29,769
22	20	A	Raith R	W 2-1	1-0	2	Murdoch [35], Boyd [54]	4604
23	27	A	Falkirk	D 1-1	1-1	3	McGregor [20]	7492
24	Mar 7	A	Cowdenbeath	D 0-0	0-0	3		3244
25	10	H	Queen of the South	D 1-1	0-0	3	Vuckic [77]	35,018
26	14	H	Livingston	D 1-1	1-1	3	Vuckic [9]	35,066
27	17	H	Alloa Ath	D 2-2	0-0	3	Clark 2 [72, 77]	28,902
28	22	H	Hibernian	W 2-0	1-0	3	Wallace [44], Miller [80]	14,075
29	28	H	Cowdenbeath	W 4-1	0-0	3	Clark [49], McGregor [83], Vuckic 2 [88, 90]	32,682
30	Apr 5	H	Hearts	W 2-1	2-0	2	Miller [28], Vuckic [38]	40,521
31	9	A	Queen of the South	L 0-3	0-1	3		5093
32	12	H	Raith R	W 4-0	2-0	3	Clark [6], Vuckic [27], Law 2 [72, 88]	31,427
33	15	A	Livingston	D 1-1	0-0	2	Zaliukas [49]	4345
34	18	A	Dumbarton	W 3-1	1-1	2	Hardie 2 [10, 48], Vuckic [52]	1766
35	25	H	Falkirk	D 2-2	0-0	3	Vuckic [83], Law [90]	35,566
36	May 2	A	Hearts	D 2-2	2-0	3	McGregor [32], Miller [40]	16,874

Final League Position: 3

League Cup Winners: (27 times) 1946-47, 1948-49, 1960-61, 1961-62, 1963-64, 1964-65, 1970-71, 1975-76, 1977-78, 1978-79, 1981-82, 1983-84, 1984-85, 1986-87, 1987-88, 1988-89, 1990-91, 1992-93, 1993-94, 1996-97, 1998-99, 2001-02, 2002-03, 2004-05, 2007-08, 2009-10, 2010-11; *Runners-up:* 7 times.
League Challenge Cup Runners-up: 2013-14.

European: *European Cup:* 161 matches (1956-57, 1957-58, 1959-60 semi-finals, 1961-62, 1963-64, 1964-65, 1975-76, 1976-77, 1978-79, 1987-88, 1989-90, 1990-91, 1991-92, 1992-93 final pool, 1993-94, 1994-95, 1995-96; 1996-97, 1997-98, 1999-2000, 2000-01, 2001-02, 2003-04, 2004-05, 2005-06, 2007-08, 2008-09, 2009-10, 2010-11, 2011-12).
Cup Winners' Cup: 54 matches (1960-61 runners-up, 1962-63, 1966-67 runners-up, 1969-70, 1971-72 winners, 1973-74, 1977-78, 1979-80, 1981-82, 1983-84).
UEFA Cup: 88 matches (*Fairs Cup:* 1967-68, 1968-69 semi-finals, 1970-71. *UEFA Cup:* 1982-83, 1984-85, 1985-86, 1986-87, 1988-89, 1997-98, 1998-99, 1999-2000, 2000-01, 2001-02, 2002-03, 2004-05, 2006-07, 2007-08 runners-up). *Europa League:* 6 matches (2010-11, 2011-12).

Club colours: Shirt: Royal blue with red trim. Shorts: White. Socks: Black with red tops.

Goalscorers: *League (69):* Law 10, Clark 8, Vuckic 8, Miller 7, McCulloch 4 (1 pen), McGregor 4, Boyd 3, Daly 3, Macleod 3, Templeton 3, Wallace 3, Hardie 2, Shiels 2, Zaliukas 2, Aird 1, Black 1, Mohsni 1, Murdoch 1, own goals 3.
William Hill Scottish FA Cup (5): Boyd 2, Law 2, Vuckic 1.
Scottish League Cup (7): Boyd 2, Macleod 2, Black 1, Shiels 1, own goal 1.
Petrofac Training Cup (14): Boyd 3, Macleod 3, McCulloch 2, Aird 1, Black 1, Daly 1, Law 1, Miller 1, Shiels 1.
Premiership Play-Offs (6): Clark 1, McGregor 1, Miller 1, Shiels 1, Smith 1, Wallace 1.

Bell C 11	Foster R 14+1	McCulloch L 31+1	Zaliukas M 18+1	Wallace L 31	Templeton D 9+13	Black I 14+8	Law N 36	Macleod 13	Miller K 25+2	Boyd K 19+10	Hutton K 8+2	Shiels D 10+10	McGregor D 33+3	Mohsni B 13+2	Clark N 21+12	Aird F 9+4	Simonsen S 18	Peralta A 2+2	Daly J 5+14	Smith S 11+2	Faure S 4+1	Robinson L 7	Murdoch A 14	Vuckic H 13+2	Walsh T 4+4	Hardie R 2+3	Crawford R 1+3	Gallagher C —+1	Match No.
	2³	3	4	5	6²	7¹	8	9	10	11	12	13	14																1
1	6	3		5	10¹			9	8	11²	7			2	4	12	13												2
	7	3		5	9²	14	8³	6¹		11	12			2	4	10	1	6⁴											3
	7	3¹		5	12³	13	8	9	14	11				2	4	10	1	6²											4
		3		5	12	8	7	9¹		11¹		13		2	4	10²	6	1	14										5
		4			12	7	8	9²		10			2	3	11³	6¹	1	14	13	5									6
		4		5	14	7	8			10		11²	2	3		1	6³	13	9¹										7
2	4	3¹	5	14	8	7	9			11²			12		10	6³	1		13										8
2	4		5	14	7	8	9²	10²	11¹			3		13	6	1		12											9
2	4		5	12	7	8	11¹		10²			3		14	6	1		13	9²										10
2	4		5	12	8	7	6		10		11¹	3			1	13	9²												11
2	4		5	6¹	7	8	9	10²	11³			3		14	1	12	13												12
2¹	4			9³	7	8	6	11	10²			3		14	1	12	5	13											13
12	3	5			7	8	6¹	10²	13			2	4	14	1	11¹	9⁴												14
5	3				7	8	11¹	10²	9			2	4	13	6	1		12											15
5	3			12	8	6	10¹	13	9¹			2	4	14	7	1	11²												16
2	4		5	13	7²	8	10¹	12	14			3	11	6	1	9³													17
2	4		5	7¹	8	11²	13	12	14			3	10	6²	1	9													18
2	4		5	6³	8	10²	7	14				3	12	13	1	11	9¹												19
2	4		5	6³	8	10²	12	7				3	14	13	1	11¹	9												20
		3	5		6	11³	10²	8	14	4		12		13	2	1								7	9¹				21
	3⁴	4	5		6		11¹	8	13	12		10³	14	2	1								7	9					22
			13		6	12	11	7	4	3		10	5	2	1					8²		9¹							23
	3	4	5		6	9²	10³	7	12	2	11			13	14	1				8¹									24
	3	4	5²		9		13	6	2	14	8			11¹	1					7²	10	12							25
	4	12	5	13	7	11¹	14	8	3	10				2²	1					9²	6								26
1	4	3²	5	12	6		11¹	10	2			9		13						7	8								27
1	3	2	8		12	7	9²	11¹	5	4	10			6	13					7									28
1	3	5		9²	14	8	10	6¹	2	4	11³			7	12	13													29
1	4⁴	3	5		14	7	11³	6¹	2	12	10			8	9²	13													30
	3	5	6¹		7		10³	14	2	4	11²	1	8	9		13	12												31
1	3	5		14	7	11²	13	9¹	4	10³		8	6	2						8	6	9	2						32
1	3	4	5		9		10¹	12	7²	2	11³	8	6	14	13														33
1	3	4	5	12	8		2	11		7	6¹	9	10²	13															34
1	3	4³	5		8	11¹	13	2	14	7	9	6	10²	12															35
1	2³	12	4	5	14	8	10²	6	3	11		7	9¹	13															36

ROSS COUNTY

Year Formed: 1929. *Ground & Address:* The Global Energy Stadium, Victoria Park, Dingwall IV15 9QZ. *Telephone:* 01349 860860. *Fax:* 01349 866277. *E-mail:* info@rosscountyfootballclub.co.uk
Website: www.rosscountyfootballclub.co.uk
Ground Capacity: 6,700 (all seated). *Size of Ground:* 105 × 68m.
Chairman: Rory MacGregor. *Secretary:* Donnie MacBean.
Manager: Jim McIntyre. *Assistant Manager:* Billy Dodds. *Director of Football:* George Adams.
Club Nickname: 'The Staggies'.
Record Attendance: 6,110 v Celtic, Premier League, 18 August 2012.
Record Transfer Fee received: £200,000 for Neil Tarrant to Aston Villa (April 1999).
Record Transfer Fee paid: £50,000 for Derek Holmes from Hearts (1999).
Record Victory: 11-0 v St Cuthbert Wanderers, Scottish Cup 1st rd, 11 Dec 1993.
Record Defeat: 0-7 v Kilmarnock, Scottish Cup 3rd rd, 17 Feb 1962.
Most League Appearances: 230: Mark McCulloch, 2002-09.
Most League Goals in Season: 24: Andrew Barrowman, 2007-08.
Most League Goals (Overall): 47: Sean Higgins, 2002-09.

ROSS COUNTY – SCOTTISH PREMIER LEAGUE 2014–15 LEAGUE RECORD

Match No.	Date	Venue	Opponents	Result		H/T Score	Lg Pos.	Goalscorers	Attendance
1	Aug 10	H	St Johnstone	L	1-2	0-1	9	Jervis [55]	3287
2	13	A	Partick Thistle	L	0-4	0-1	12		3261
3	16	H	Kilmarnock	L	1-2	0-1	12	Boyce [81]	2790
4	23	A	Dundee U	L	1-2	0-1	12	Jervis [51]	7179
5	30	A	Hamilton A	L	0-4	0-0	12		2684
6	Sept 13	H	Motherwell	L	1-2	0-0	12	Boyce [78]	3012
7	20	A	Aberdeen	L	0-3	0-2	12		10,865
8	27	H	Dundee	W	2-1	1-0	12	Gardyne [27], Maatsen [90]	3118
9	Oct 5	A	Inverness CT	D	1-1	1-0	12	Arquin [21]	3741
10	18	H	Celtic	L	0-5	0-4	12		5693
11	25	A	St Mirren	D	2-2	1-1	12	Quinn, P [11], Carey [58]	3459
12	Nov 3	H	Aberdeen	L	0-1	0-0	12		3745
13	8	A	Kilmarnock	W	3-0	3-0	12	Carey [33], Gardyne [40], Quinn, P [45]	3684
14	22	A	St Johnstone	L	1-2	0-1	12	Jervis [75]	2776
15	Dec 5	H	Dundee U	L	2-3	0-1	12	Arquin [76], Maatsen [89]	2922
16	13	A	Motherwell	D	2-2	1-0	11	Dingwall 2 [45, 90]	3193
17	20	H	Hamilton A	L	0-1	0-1	11		2966
18	27	A	Celtic	D	0-0	0-0	12		45,798
19	Jan 1	H	Inverness CT	L	1-3	0-1	12	Irvine [60]	4887
20	4	A	Dundee	D	1-1	0-0	12	Curran [65]	5017
21	17	H	St Mirren	L	1-2	0-1	12	Boyce [82]	3005
22	24	H	Celtic	L	0-1	0-0	12		5289
23	31	A	Inverness CT	D	1-1	0-1	12	Jervis [76]	4021
24	Feb 7	A	Aberdeen	L	0-4	0-1	12		12,036
25	14	H	Motherwell	W	3-2	1-0	12	Woods [34], Quinn, P [58], De Vita [62]	2982
26	21	A	Partick Thistle	W	3-1	1-0	10	Curran [11], De Vita [65], Fraser [71]	2951
27	28	H	Dundee	W	1-0	0-0	10	Reckord [66]	3413
28	Mar 7	H	Partick Thistle	W	1-0	1-0	10	Curran [33]	3358
29	14	A	Hamilton A	D	2-2	1-0	10	Curran [28], Gardyne [72]	1544
30	21	H	Kilmarnock	W	2-1	1-0	10	Gardyne [23], Curran [59]	3389
31	Apr 4	A	Dundee U	W	2-1	1-1	10	Irvine [12], De Vita [72]	6187
32	7	H	St Johnstone	W	1-0	0-0	10	Boyce [84]	3319
33	13	A	St Mirren	W	3-0	1-0	10	Boyce 3 [30, 75, 90]	3033
34	25	H	Partick Thistle	L	1-2	1-1	10	Gardyne [21]	3315
35	May 2	A	Motherwell	D	1-1	1-1	10	Boyce [41]	4281
36	9	H	St Mirren	L	1-2	1-1	10	Woods (pen) [31]	3098
37	16	H	Hamilton A	W	2-1	0-1	10	Gardyne [58], Boyce [85]	3381
38	23	A	Kilmarnock	W	2-1	0-1	9	Boyce [63], Quinn, R [76]	4226

Final League Position: 9

Honours
League Champions: First Division 2011-12. Second Division 2007-08. Third Division 1998-99.
Scottish Cup Runners-up: 2009-10.
League Challenge Cup Winners: 2006-07, 2010-11; *Runners-up:* 2004-05, 2008-09.

Club colours: Shirt: Navy blue with red trim. Shorts: Navy blue. Socks: Navy blue.

Goalscorers: *League (46):* Boyce 10, Gardyne 6, Curran 5, Jervis 4, De Vita 3, Quinn, P 3, Arquin 2, Carey 2, Dingwall 2, Irvine 2, Maatsen 2, Woods 2 (1 pen), Fraser 1, Quinn, R 1, Reckord 1.
William Hill Scottish FA Cup (1): Jervis 1.
Scottish League Cup (2): Boyce 1, de Leeuw 1.

Reguero A 16	Fenlon J 4	Boyd S 31+1	Dreesen T 3	Celcer U 5	Brittain R 18+3	Kiss F 21+10	Quinn R 8+5	Carey G 17+5	Jervis J 10+17	Arquin Y 14+3	de Leeuw M 3+3	Cardle J 1+11	Boyce L 17+13	Frempah B 4+2	Balk J 4	Maatsen D —+8	Brown M 22	Dingwall T 10+9	Irvine J 27+1	Barr D 5+1	Gardyne M 22+2	Toshney L 7+2	Dunfield T 4	Quinn P 28+1	Woods M 26+1	Reckord J 26	Ross S 2+3	Saunders S 6+1	Curran C 17+2	Fraser M 16	Palazuelos R 1+4	De Vita R 13+1	Sernas D —+5	Match No.
1	2	3	4	5	6	7^4	8^1	9	10^3	11	12	13	14																					1
1	11	3^2	2	5	7	10	8	8^2	9	4^1	14	13				12																		2
1		3	4	5	12	7^2	8	9	11	6^3	10^1	13	14			2																		3
1	4	3		5	7^1	6	12	10	8^2	11		9^1	14			2	13																	4
	3	5^8	8	9	7		13	12	10^2	6^3	11^1	4	2			1	14																	5
1	3			6	8	11^3	12	10^2	7	13		2	14				4	5	9^1															6
2	3^2			7	12	9	8	13	11^3	10^1			14		1		4	5	6															7
				7	9^3	6	5	11	14	10	13	4		12	1		3		8^1	2^2														8
	3			6	10^3	8^2	5	12	11^1	9	14	7		1		4	13		2															9
	3^3			6	10		5	14	11^2	9				4	1			8^1	12	2	7	13												10
	3			8	10^1		9	13	11^2					1	14	7	5	6^3	2		4	12												11
	4			8			9	13	11^3	12	14			1		7^2	5	6^1	2		3	10												12
	3			8	12		9	11^3	13					1	10	2	6^1	14		4	7^2	5												13
	3			7	13		9	11			12	14		1	10^3	2	6^1			4	8^2	5												14
		2					11^1	14	10^3	12^8		13	1	8	6		3		4	9	5	7^2												15
1		7^1				9^1	10^2	11	12			14	6	3	13		4	8	5		2													16
1		2				13	12	11	9			14	10^1	8^2		6^3		4	7	5		3												17
1	9	2	8			13	11^3						10^2	12	6^1	4	7	5	14	3														18
1	3	7^1	6			10	14	11^2	12			13				9^3	4	8	5	2														19
1	12	7	8			14		6^3	10^3				2			9^4	4		5	13	3	11^2												20
1		6				10	14	9^3	12		13		8				5^2	2	7	4	3	11^1												21
1	4		6			9^1	14		12		13	8^2					3	7^3	5	10	11	2												22
1	4		7^1	13	14		10				6^1	8				3	9	5	11^2	2	12													23
1	4^1		7	13			11				6^2	9				3	10	5	12	14	2	8^3												24
	3		13			11		1	12	7	9^2		4	6	5	10^1	2	8^3	14															25
	4		13	12		11^2		1	14	6	8		3	7^1	5	10^3	2	9																26
	3		14			13	12	11^3		1	8	6^2		4	7	5	10^1	2	9															27
	3		13	14	12	11^3		1	8	6^2		4	7	5	10^1	2	9																	28
	4		8	10^3	14		1	6		3	7	5	13	11^2	2	9^1	12																	29
	3		2	13	12	11^3		1	7	6^1	4	8	5	10^2	14	9																		30
	3		6			11^1		1	12	7	4	8	5	10^3	13	2	9^2	14																31
	3		13	12	10		1	7^2	6^3	4	8	5	11	14	2	9^1																		32
	5		13	10		1	12	4	7	6	8^2	3	9^3	2	11^1	14																		33
	3		7^2	12	14	10	1	13		6	4	8	5	11^3	2	9^1																		34
	4		14	13	11	1	12	8	6^3	3	7	5	10^1	2	9^2																			35
	3			14	10^3	1^4	6^2	8	9	4	7	5	11^3	2	12	13																		36
1		14	2^3	13	11		12	8	6^1	4	7	5	10^3	3	9^2																			37
1	3		14	12		11		10^1	8	6	4	7^2	5	13	2	9^3																		38

ST JOHNSTONE

Year Formed: 1884. *Ground & Address:* McDiarmid Park, Crieff Road, Perth PH1 2SJ. *Telephone:* 01738 459090. *Fax:* 01738 625 771. *Email:* enquiries@perthsaints.co.uk *Website:* www.perthstjohnstonefc.co.uk
Ground Capacity: 10,673 (all seated). *Size of Pitch:* 105m × 68m.
Chairman: Steve Brown. *Football Administrator:* Paul Smith.
Manager: Tommy Wright. *U20 Coach:* Alec Cleland. *Youth Coach:* Alistair Stevenson. *Physio:* Nick Summersgill.
Club Nickname: 'Saints'.
Previous Grounds: Recreation Grounds, Muirton Park.
Record Attendance: 29,972 v Dundee, Scottish Cup 2nd rd, 10 Feb 1951 (Muirton Park): 10,545 v Dundee, Premier Division, 23 May 1999 (McDiarmid Park).
Record Transfer Fee received: £1,750,000 for Callum Davidson to Blackburn R (March 1998).
Record Transfer Fee paid: £400,000 for Billy Dodds from Dundee (1994).
Record Victory: 9-0 v Albion R, League Cup, 9 Mar 1946.
Record Defeat: 1-10 v Third Lanark, Scottish Cup 1st rd, 24 Jan 1903.
Most Capped Player: Nick Dasovic, 26, Canada.
Most League Appearances: 298: Drew Rutherford, 1976-85.
Most League Goals in Season (Individual): 36: Jimmy Benson, Division II, 1931-32.
Most Goals Overall (Individual): 140: John Brogan, 1977-83.

ST JOHNSTONE – SCOTTISH PREMIER LEAGUE 2014–15 LEAGUE RECORD

Match No.	Date	Venue	Opponents	Result	H/T Score	Lg Pos.	Goalscorers	Atten- dance
1	Aug 10	A	Ross Co	W 2-1	1-0	3	O'Halloran 31, MacLean 48	3287
2	13	H	Celtic	L 0-3	0-0	8		6890
3	16	A	Hamilton A	L 0-1	0-1	10		1577
4	23	H	Aberdeen	W 1-0	0-0	7	MacLean 80	6377
5	30	A	Motherwell	W 1-0	0-0	4	Graham 86	3700
6	Sept 13	H	Dundee	L 0-1	0-1	7		6562
7	20	A	Inverness CT	L 1-2	0-0	8	Graham 78	2770
8	27	A	Dundee U	L 0-2	0-1	8		7161
9	Oct 4	A	St Mirren	L 1-2	0-1	9	Anderson 68	3400
10	18	H	Kilmarnock	L 1-2	1-2	9	Davidson 10	3115
11	25	A	Partick Thistle	D 0-0	0-0	9		3090
12	31	H	Motherwell	W 2-1	1-1	8	O'Halloran 2 40, 80	2531
13	Nov 8	A	Dundee	D 1-1	0-1	9	Graham (pen) 53	6931
14	22	H	Ross Co	W 2-1	1-0	8	McFadden 39, O'Halloran 73	2776
15	Dec 6	A	St Mirren	W 1-0	1-0	8	O'Halloran 8	2720
16	13	A	Kilmarnock	W 1-0	0-0	6	Graham (pen) 82	3220
17	20	H	Inverness CT	W 1-0	0-0	6	Graham (pen) 62	2891
18	27	H	Dundee U	W 2-1	0-1	6	O'Halloran 76, Millar 86	7384
19	Jan 1	A	Aberdeen	L 0-2	0-1	6		15,263
20	4	H	Hamilton A	L 0-1	0-1	6		3202
21	17	H	Partick Thistle	W 2-0	1-0	6	Mackay 4, Anderson 49	2994
22	20	A	Inverness CT	L 0-2	0-2	6		3161
23	23	H	Aberdeen	D 1-1	1-0	6	Lappin 30	4845
24	31	A	Motherwell	D 1-1	1-0	6	Davidson 8	3449
25	Feb 14	H	Celtic	L 1-2	0-1	7	O'Halloran 72	6727
26	21	A	Dundee U	W 2-0	2-0	7	O'Halloran 2 9, 44	7623
27	28	H	Kilmarnock	D 0-0	0-0	7		3170
28	Mar 4	A	Celtic	W 1-0	0-0	6	Swanson 54	41,849
29	14	A	Partick Thistle	L 0-3	0-2	6		3196
30	21	H	St Mirren	W 2-0	1-0	5	Graham 33, Anderson 62	3166
31	Apr 4	A	Hamilton A	D 1-1	0-1	5	Graham 72	2032
32	7	A	Ross Co	L 0-1	0-0	5		3319
33	11	H	Dundee	W 1-0	1-0	5	Graham 26	6386
34	25	A	Dundee	W 2-0	0-0	4	Swanson 53, Wotherspoon 67	6530
35	May 2	H	Inverness CT	D 1-1	0-0	5	Graham 82	2986
36	9	H	Dundee U	D 1-1	0-0	5	Davidson 77	4862
37	15	H	Celtic	D 0-0	0-0	4		6984
38	24	A	Aberdeen	W 1-0	0-0	4	Kane 70	16,389

Final League Position: 4

Honours
League Champions: First Division 1982-83, 1989-90, 1996-97, 2008-09. Division II 1923-24, 1959-60, 1962-63; *Runners-up:* Division II 1931-32. First Division 2005-06, 2006-07. Second Division 1987-88.
Scottish Cup Winners: 2014.
League Cup Runners-up: 1969-70, 1998-99.
League Challenge Cup Winners: 2007-08; *Runners-up:* 1996-97.

European: *UEFA Cup:* 20 matches (1971-72, 1999-2000, 2012-13, 2013-14, 2014-15).

Club colours: Shirt: Blue with white trim. Short: White. Socks: Blue.

Goalscorers: *League (34):* Graham 9 (3 pens), O'Halloran 9, Anderson 3, Davidson 3, MacLean 2, Swanson 2, Kane 1, Lappin 1, Mackay 1, McFadden 1, Millar 1, Wotherspoon 1.
William Hill Scottish FA Cup (2): McFadden 1, O'Halloran 1.
Scottish League Cup (1): Graham 1.
UEFA Europa League (4): May 2 (1 pen), Mackay 1, MacLean 1.

Mannus A 38	Mackay D 34	Wright F 23+1	Anderson S 37	Scobbie T 17+3	Millar C 32	McDonald G 10+6	Wotherspoon D 30+5	Brown S 8+2	O'Halloran M 30+8	MacLean S 23+1	Caddis L 6+9	Croft L 17+10	Kane C 4+11	Easton B 31	Morgan A 1+4	Miller G 8+11	Lappin S 19+8	Graham B 17+7	Davidson M 17+6	McFadden J 8+9	Swanson D 8+3	Match No.
1	2	3	4	5	6	7	8^1	9	10^2	11^3	12	13	14									1
1	2^*	3	4		7	8^2	12		10^1	11	9^3	6		5			13	14				2
1	2	3	4	7	13	9	8^1	6^3	10		12	14		5			11^2					3
1	2	3	4	7	11	9^2	8^3	12	10		6^1			5			14	13				4
1	2	3	4	7	8	10	9^2	12	11^1		6^1			5			13	14				5
1	2	4	3		6	9^1	10	7^3	8^2			14		5	13		12	11				6
1	2	4	3		6	8^4	7^1		12		9			5	13		10^2	11	14			7
1	2	3	4		7^2	10		11	9	8^1				5	12		13		6			8
1		3	4			6^3	8^2	11^1	14	13				5	2	9	10	7	12			9
1	2		4			12	11^3	13		14	6^1			5	9	8^2	3	7	10			10
1	2	3	4		8		13		12			6^1		5			9	11	7	10^2		11
1	2	4	3		7	8		9	12	6^2				5	13		10		11^1			12
1	2	3	4		7	8^2	13	11		9^3	6^1			5	14	12	10					13
1	2	4	3		7			9		13	6^3			5	14	8^1	11	12	10^2			14
1	2	4	3		8	6		9						5	13	7^1	11	12	10^2			15
1	2	4	3		7		6^2	9		12				5		8	10	13	11^1			16
1	2	4	3		7^3	13	10^1	9		6^2				5	14	8	11	12				17
1	2	4	3		7	12	10	9	11	6^4				5	13	8^1						18
1	2	4	3		7^2	12	10	9	11^1	6^3				5	8		14	13				19
1	2	3	5		7	8^2	13	9	12	14	6^1				4	10^3		11^*				20
1	2	3	4	14	8^3	13	6	12	10^1	11	9			5^2		7						21
1	2	4^2	3	5	13	10	7^3	6^1	9		12			14	8	11						22
1		14	3	4		9	13	11	12	6^1	10^2	5		2^9	8	7						23
1		3	4		10	14	11^1	9^1	7^3	5	2	6	13	8	12							24
1	2	3	4	7		10	11^1	6^3	12	5		9	14	8^2	13							25
1	2	3	4	6		8	9	11	12	10^2	5		13	7^1								26
1	2	3^2	4	13	6	7	9	10^1		11^3	5		12	8		14						27
1	2		4	5	6	7	9^2	11		12	3		13		8		10^1					28
1	2	3	4	7		6^3	10	11^1	13	14	5			8	12	9^2						29
1	2	4	3	7	6		9^2	11		13	5			10^1	8	12						30
1	2	3	4	7		6^1		13	14	5		12	11	8^3		9^2						31
1	2	3	4		6	8	9^3	11^2	12	14	5			7	13	10^1						32
1	2	3	4	14	6	8	9^3	11		12	5^2			7	10^1		13					33
1	2	3		4	8		5	13	12	11	14		9	10^3	7^1		6^2					34
1	2	3	4	8		10	9	11^3		5		13	7^1	12	6							35
1	2	3	4	5	7		6^3	11	10^2		12	14		8	13	9^1						36
1		3	4	7	6		11	10^2	12				5	2^1	14	8	13	9^3				37
1		2	3	6	5		10^2	11^3	7^1	14	4			12	8	13	9					38

ST MIRREN

Year Formed: 1877. *Ground & Address:* St Mirren Park, Greenhill Road, Paisley PA3 1RU. *Telephone:* 0141 889 2558.
Fax: 0141 848 6444. *E-mail:* info@saintmirren.net *Website:* www.saintmirren.net
Ground Capacity: 8,023 (all seated). *Size of Pitch:* 100m × 64m.
Chairman: Stewart Gilmour. *Vice-Chairman:* George Campbell. *Secretary:* Chris Stewart.
Manager: Ian Murray. *Youth Development Officer:* David Longwell. *Physio:* Gerry Docherty.
Club Nickname: 'The Buddies'.
Previous Grounds: Shortroods 1877-79, Thistle Park Greenhill 1879-83, Westmarch 1883-94, Love Street 1894-2009.
Record Attendance: 47,438 v Celtic, League Cup, 20 Aug 1949.
Record Transfer Fee received: £850,000 for Ian Ferguson to Rangers (Feb 1988).
Record Transfer Fee paid: £400,000 for Thomas Stickroth from Bayer Uerdingen (March 1990).
Record Victory: 15-0 v Glasgow University, Scottish Cup 1st rd, 30 Jan 1960.
Record Defeat: 0-9 v Rangers, Division I, 4 Dec 1897.
Most Capped Player: Godmundur Torfason, 29, Iceland.
Most League Appearances: 399: Hugh Murray, 1997-2012.
Most League Goals in Season (Individual): 45: Dunky Walker, Division I, 1921-22.
Most Goals Overall (Individual): 221: David McCrae, 1923-34.

ST MIRREN – SCOTTISH PREMIER LEAGUE 2014–15 LEAGUE RECORD

Match No.	Date	Venue	Opponents	Result	H/T Score	Lg Pos.	Goalscorers	Atten- dance
1	Aug 9	A	Motherwell	L	0-1	0-0	11		4620
2	13	H	Hamilton A	L	0-2	0-1	11		3635
3	23	H	Dundee	L	0-1	0-0	11		4517
4	30	H	Dundee U	L	0-3	0-0	11		4245
5	Sept13	A	Kilmarnock	L	1-2	0-0	11	Drury [71]	4417
6	19	A	Partick Thistle	W	2-1	0-1	11	Ball [60], McLean (pen) [90]	3821
7	27	H	Celtic	L	1-2	0-1	11	McLean [49]	5280
8	30	A	Aberdeen	D	2-2	0-1	11	Ball [57], McLean (pen) [86]	10,373
9	Oct 4	A	St Johnstone	W	2-1	1-0	10	Naismith [28], Drury [87]	3400
10	18	H	Inverness CT	L	0-1	0-1	10		3109
11	25	H	Ross Co	D	2-2	1-1	10	Drury [44], Tesselaar [60]	3459
12	Nov 1	A	Dundee U	L	0-3	0-1	10		6808
13	8	H	Partick Thistle	L	0-1	0-0	11		4636
14	22	A	Hamilton A	L	0-3	0-1	11		2195
15	Dec 6	H	St Johnstone	L	0-1	0-1	11		2720
16	14	A	Celtic	L	1-4	1-3	12	Kelly [10]	44,827
17	20	H	Motherwell	L	0-1	0-0	12		3909
18	27	A	Dundee	W	3-1	1-0	11	McLean 2 (1 pen) [28, 79 (p)], Mallan [68]	6447
19	Jan 1	H	Kilmarnock	L	1-2	0-0	11	Wylde (pen) [90]	3912
20	4	A	Inverness CT	L	0-1	0-0	11		2751
21	10	H	Aberdeen	L	0-2	0-2	11		4977
22	17	A	Ross Co	W	2-1	1-0	11	Kelly [16], Mallan [87]	3005
23	21	A	Dundee U	D	1-1	1-1	11	McLean [39]	2511
24	24	H	Dundee	L	1-2	1-0	11	McLean [40]	4010
25	30	A	Partick Thistle	W	1-0	1-0	10	Dayton [6]	3864
26	Feb 14	H	Inverness CT	L	1-2	0-1	10	Goodwin [68]	3154
27	21	A	Aberdeen	L	0-3	0-1	11		14,720
28	28	H	Hamilton A	W	1-0	0-0	11	Thompson [63]	3503
29	Mar 14	A	Kilmarnock	L	0-1	0-0	12		4721
30	21	A	St Johnstone	L	0-2	0-1	12		3166
31	Apr 3	H	Celtic	L	0-2	0-0	12		5784
32	7	A	Motherwell	L	0-5	0-3	12		4596
33	13	H	Ross Co	L	0-3	0-1	12		3033
34	25	H	Kilmarnock	W	4-1	2-0	12	Kelly [8], Sadlier [33], Thompson 2 (2 pens) [57, 65]	3205
35	May 2	A	Partick Thistle	L	0-3	0-0	12		3865
36	9	A	Ross Co	W	2-1	1-1	12	Mallan [39], Thompson (pen) [90]	3098
37	16	H	Motherwell	W	2-1	0-0	12	Naismith [84], Mallan [90]	3912
38	23	A	Hamilton A	L	0-1	0-0	12		2425

Final League Position: 12

Honours
League Champions: First Division 1976-77, 1999-2000, 2005-06. Division II 1967-68; *Runners-up:* First Division 2004-05; Division II 1935-36.
Scottish Cup Winners: 1926, 1959, 1987; *Runners-up:* 1908, 1934, 1962.
League Cup Winners: 2012-13; *Runners-up:* 1955-56, 2009-10.
League Challenge Cup Winners: 2005-06.
B&Q Cup Runners-up: 1993-94. *Anglo-Scottish Cup:* 1979-80.

European: *Cup Winners' Cup:* 4 matches (1987-88). *UEFA Cup:* 10 matches (1980-81, 1983-84, 1985-86).

Club colours: Shirt: Thin black and white vertical stripes with yellow trim. Shorts: White. Socks: Black with yellow tops.

Goalscorers: *League (30):* McLean 7 (3 pens), Mallan 4, Thompson 4 (3 pens), Drury 3, Kelly 3, Ball 2, Naismith 2, Dayton 1, Goodwin 1, Sadlier 1, Tesselaar 1, Wylde 1 (1 pen).
William Hill Scottish FA Cup (1): McAusland 1.
Scottish League Cup (2): Caldwell 2.

Kello M 15	Naismith J 38	Plummer E 6	McAusland M 28+1	Tesselaar J 32	McGinn J 30	Goodwin J 28	McLean K 25	Wylde G 11+16	Ball C 11+9	Marwood J 10+3	Caldwell R 2+11	Brown A 1+6	Teale G 3+2	Reilly T 14+6	Drury A 10+2	Thompson S 15+3	Osbourne I 13+1	Kelly S 29+3	Morgan L 1+7	Ridgers M 23	Baird J 7+1	Mallan S 24+1	McLear L 6+5	Arquin Y 8+4	Dayton J 13	Sonupe E —+4	Genev V 6	Gow A 5+3	Sadlier K 5+6	Cuddihy B —+3	Stewart J —+1	Match No.
1	2	3	4	5	6	7*	8	9	10¹	11	12																					1
1	2	4	3	5	7		8	9¹	11¹	10	12		6²	13	14																	2
1	2	4	3	5	8	6	9	14	11²	10¹	12					7³	13															3
1	2	4	3²	5	7		9	12	10	11				13	6³	8¹	14															4
1	2	3	4	5	10¹	6²	8	12	11	13							9	7														5
1	2	4¹	14	5	8	3	10	9¹	13	11³	6	12						7														6
1	2	4	5²	8	3	7	12	11	10³	13	6¹						9	14														7
1	2	3		9	4	8	6	10	11	12				7¹				5														8
1	2	3		7	4	8	9¹	11	10²	14	13				6²	12		5														9
1	2	3		8	4	9	11	10	12	13						7²	6¹	5														10
1	2	3	4	8	7	9	11¹	12	10						6			5														11
1	2	3	4	7	8		11²	13	12					6¹	10			9	5													12
1	2	3	5		6		11²	9¹	12	10						7	8	4	13													13
	2		4	5			9	13	12	11¹			14		7	6³		10		1		3	8²									14
	2	3		5	9		10		12								6¹	11²	8	1	13	4	7									15
	2	3	4	10	8	9		13	12				14			6³	11²	7¹	5	1												16
	2	3	5	9²	4	7	12	13					14			11*	6³		1			10	8¹									17
	2	3	10	11	4	9¹	13	12					14			7²	5		1			8	6³									18
6	2		9	11	4	10*	14	12								5³	8²	13	1			3	7¹									19
	2	3	5	8	4	10	13						14		6³	11		9¹	1			7²	12									20
	2		4	9	3	11	10³	13					14			7²	5	12	1			6	8¹									21
	2	10	4	9	3	8										7	5		1			6	11*									22
	2		3	5	10	4	11									8¹	9		1			6	12	7								23
	2		3	5²	10	4	11	12	14							13	9³		1			6	8¹	7*								24
	2		3	5	6	4	10	14								11³	7²	12	1			8	13	9²								25
	2		3	7¹	4		14									11	8	5	1			9	12	10³	6²	13							26
	2	3¹	9	10	4		13									5		1			12	8	7³	11	13	14							27
	2		5	8	4		13									11	9		1			6²	14		3³	10¹	12					28
	2		5¹	7	3		13									11	10³		1			6	14	8²	4	9	12					29
	2		5	8	3		10	9									7³	13	1			12	6²	4	11¹	14						30
	2	3	5	9	6								14				12	1				8³	11	7¹	13	4	10²					31
	2	3		10	6¹		13						14			12	5		1			9	11	7²	4	8³						32
	2	5³		4	8		11					12	9²	3		1	7		10¹			6¹	14	13								33
	2	4			9				12	6²		11³	5		1	3	8		7¹			13	10	14								34
	2	5			10			12	7¹	11³	4		1	3	6		13	8				14	9²									35
	2	5			9³		8		11	4		13	1	3	7³		6		10¹			14	12									36
1	2	4			9¹		10		11²	5		13	3	7		14	6		8³	12												37
1	2	5¹			13				7	10	4	9²	3	8		6			11³	12	14											38

STENHOUSEMUIR

Year Formed: 1884. *Ground & Address:* Ochilview Park, Gladstone Rd, Stenhousemuir FK5 4QL. *Telephone:* 01324 562992. *Fax:* 01324 562980. *E-mail:* info@stenhousemuirfc.com *Website:* www.stenhousemuirfc.com
Ground Capacity: 3,776 (seated: 626). *Size of Pitch:* 101m × 66m.
Chairman: Gordon Thompson. *Vice-Chairman:* David Reid. *Secretary/General Manager:* Margaret Kilpatrick.
Manager: Brown Ferguson. *First-Team Coach:* David Irons. *Physio:* Melanie Stewart.
Club Nickname: 'The Warriors'.
Previous Grounds: Tryst Ground 1884-86, Goschen Park 1886-90.
Record Attendance: 12,500 v East Fife, Scottish Cup Quarter-final, 11 Mar 1950.
Record Transfer Fee received: £70,000 for Euan Donaldson to St Johnstone (May 1995).
Record Transfer Fee paid: £20,000 to Livingston for Ian Little (June 1995); £20,000 to East Fife for Paul Hunter (September 1995).
Record Victory: 9-2 v Dundee U, Division II, 16 Apr 1937.
Record Defeat: 2-11 v Dunfermline Ath, Division II, 27 Sept 1930.
Most League Appearances: 434: Jimmy Richardson, 1957-73.
Most League Goals in Season (Individual): 32: Robert Taylor, Division II, 1925-26.

STENHOUSEMUIR – SCOTTISH LEAGUE ONE 2014–15 LEAGUE RECORD

Match No.	Date		Venue	Opponents	Result	H/T Score	Lg Pos.	Goalscorers	Atten-dance
1	Aug	9	H	Airdrieonians	W 1-0	0-0	1	Grehan [87]	728
2		16	A	Brechin C	L 0-1	0-1	6		418
3		23	H	Stirling Alb	L 4-5	2-1	8	Hodge 2 [16, 65], Dickson [37], Comrie (og) [90]	613
4		30	H	Ayr U	D 1-1	1-1	8	Grehan [26]	669
5	Sept	13	A	Dunfermline Ath	L 0-2	0-0	9		2671
6		20	A	Peterhead	L 0-1	0-1	9		486
7		27	H	Greenock Morton	W 2-1	1-1	8	Grehan [32], Dickson [48]	692
8	Oct	4	H	Stranraer	D 2-2	0-1	8	McMenamin 2 [57, 90]	453
9		11	A	Forfar Ath	L 0-3	0-1	9		489
10		18	A	Stirling Alb	W 4-0	1-0	8	Faulds [17], Oliver 2 [51, 66], Walsh [76]	689
11		25	H	Peterhead	L 1-2	0-0	8	McMenamin [60]	423
12	Nov	8	A	Airdrieonians	L 0-2	0-2	9		743
13		15	H	Dunfermline Ath	W 1-0	0-0	8	Faulds [71]	1177
14		22	A	Greenock Morton	L 1-3	0-2	8	Dickson [68]	1315
15	Dec	6	H	Forfar Ath	L 0-2	0-1	9		434
16		13	A	Ayr U	W 3-2	2-1	8	McMenamin 3 [12, 41, 53]	646
17		20	H	Brechin C	L 0-2	0-1	9		320
18		27	A	Stranraer	W 2-0	1-0	8	Walsh [12], McMenamin [72]	573
19	Jan	3	H	Stirling Alb	L 1-2	1-2	8	McMenamin [35]	586
20		10	H	Greenock Morton	L 2-3	0-0	8	McMenamin 2 (1 pen) [50, 88 (p)]	508
21		17	A	Forfar Ath	L 0-1	0-0	8		515
22		24	H	Ayr U	D 1-1	1-1	8	McMullan [20]	651
23		31	A	Peterhead	L 0-2	0-1	8		454
24	Feb	14	A	Dunfermline Ath	L 2-3	2-1	9	McMullan [18], McMenamin [44]	2393
25		21	H	Airdrieonians	L 0-2	0-1	9		524
26		28	A	Brechin C	L 1-2	1-1	9	McMenamin [3]	506
27	Mar	3	H	Stranraer	W 1-0	1-0	9	Watt [20]	221
28		7	H	Peterhead	W 2-1	1-1	8	McMenamin [6], Watt [56]	436
29		14	A	Ayr U	D 0-0	0-0	8		1055
30		21	H	Dunfermline Ath	L 0-1	0-0	8		983
31		28	A	Airdrieonians	L 1-2	0-1	9	Grehan [81]	722
32	Apr	4	H	Forfar Ath	L 1-3	0-0	9	McMenamin [48]	518
33		11	A	Greenock Morton	L 2-3	1-0	9	Meechan [35], McMullan [55]	1568
34		18	A	Stranraer	L 2-3	0-2	8	Grehan [65], Summers [88]	552
35		25	H	Brechin C	D 2-2	2-2	9	Grehan [2], Lithgow [11]	577
36	May	2	A	Stirling Alb	L 2-3	1-1	9	McMenamin [13], Sutherland [76]	766

Final League Position: 9

Honours
League Champions: Third Division runners-up: 1998-99. *Promoted to Second Division:* 2008-09 (play-offs).
Scottish Cup: Semi-finals 1902-03. Quarter-finals 1948-49, 1949-50, 1994-95.
League Cup: Quarter-finals 1947-48, 1960-61, 1975-76.
League Challenge Cup Winners: 1995-96.

Club colours: Shirt: Maroon with white trim. Shorts: White. Socks: Maroon.

Goalscorers: *League (42):* McMenamin 15 (1 pen), Grehan 6, Dickson 3, McMullan 3, Faulds 2, Hodge 2, Oliver 2, Walsh 2, Watt 2, Lithgow 1, Meechan 1, Summers 1, Sutherland 1, own goal 1.
William Hill Scottish FA Cup (1): own goal 1.
Scottish League Cup (4): Lithgow 1, McMenamin 1, Millar, K 1, Sludden 1.
Petrofac Training Cup (1): Grehan 1 (1 pen).
League One Play-Offs (6): McCormack 2, Lithgow 1, McMenamin 1, Millar, K 1, Sutherland 1.

Hamilton J 1	Meechan R 30	Lithgow A 32+2	Summers C 30+1	Greacen S 11	Faulds K 27+5	Hodge B 21+1	Sludden P 3+4	Reid J 10+2	Grehan M 17+8	Watt J 14+12	McMenamin C 27+6	Dickson S 14+4	Millar R 2+6	Fleming G 35	McMillan R 29	Millar K 29+1	Oliver G 11	Walsh T 6+3	Fotheringham G 3+14	Duncan R 7+2	Eddington F 3+8	Shaw D —+1	Gallacher L 3+5	McCormack J 6+1	McMullan P 14	Sutherland C 2+5	Marenghi A 9+3	Moutinho P —+2	Match No.
1	2	3	4	5	6³	7	8	9²	10	11¹	12	13	14																1
	2	3	5		14	7			13	10	12	11	6¹	9²	1	4	8³												2
	2	5	4		6	7	14		9³	10	11²	13	8	12	1	3													3
	5	2	9¹	4	6²	7			10	12	11³	13	14	1	3	8													4
	2		5	3	7	8²	9¹		10	14	13⁸	12⁴		1	4	6	11												5
	2	14	5¹	3	6²				13	10	9³			12	1	4	7	11	8										6
	2		5	3	7				11³	10²	12	13	8³	1	4	6	9		14										7
	2	14	5	3	8				11³	10²		12	7	13	1	4¹	6	9											8
	2	3	5⁸		8³			14	11²	13		10¹	7		1	4	6	9	12										9
		5		3	8				6²		10¹			1	4	7	11	9	12	2	13								10
		5³	14	3	6		13	9		10¹				1	4	7	11²	8		2		12							11
	2	3	5		6	10		11¹		8	12		1	9	4			13		7²									12
2¹	5		3	7				6²		10	9³		1	4	8	11	14	13	12										13
	2	4		5	8¹			6²	12	11²	10		1	3	9	7	13		14										14
3	4	5³		7¹		14	6²		12	10	9		1	8	11	13		2											15
	5	3		14	7				10³	8¹	9	4		11	6²	12	2	13											16
	5	4		6¹	7			13	10	9		1	3⁸	8		11⁷	14	2³	12										17
	5	4	3	6²	7			14	10	9¹		1		8	11³	13	2	12											18
3	4	5		6	7²			13	14	10	9¹		1		8		2	12	11³										19
3	2	5		7	8			12	13	10	9²		1	4			11	6¹											20
2	3	5		13	8			14	7²	10	9²		1	4	6			11¹		12									21
	3	5			7				9¹	10			1	4	8		13		12	2	6	11²							22
3	4	5		6²	8			12		10			1		7		13			2	9	11¹							23
2	3	5		7	6			11²	8¹	10¹			1	4		13	14				9		12						24
	3	5		13	8			11²	9¹	10			1	4	7³					2	6	14	12						25
	3	5			7			11¹	12	10			1	4	8²				14	2	6	13	9³						26
2	3	5			8			13	9	10¹			1	4	7		12				6		11						27
2	3	5		12	8³			14	9¹	10²			1	4	7		13				11		6						28
3	4	5		8				6¹	11				1		7		13			12	2	10	9²						29
3	4	5		7				13	9¹	10			1		8²		12			14	2	6	11³						30
2	4	5		8		11	13		12⁸	1	3	9		7²			10³			14	6¹								31
2	3	5		7		11¹			10			1	4	8²	12					6	9⁸	13							32
2	3	5		7				10²	9³			1	4	8		6				11	13	12							33
2	3	5		8³	12			10	9³	13			1	4	7		6¹				11	14							34
2	4	5		7	8			11⁸		10			1	3							6	9							35
2	3	5		7²	8				9¹	11			1	4	12					14	10	13	6³						36

STIRLING ALBION

Year Formed: 1945. *Ground & Address:* Forthbank Stadium, Springkerse, Stirling FK7 7UJ. *Telephone:* 01786 450399.
Fax: 01786 448592. *Email:* office@stirlingalbionfc.co.uk *Website:* www.stirlingalbionfc.co.uk
Ground Capacity: 3,808 (seated: 2,508). *Size of Pitch:* 101m × 68m.
Chairman: Stuart Brown.
Manager: Stuart McLaren. *Assistant Manager:* Martyn Corrigan.
Club Nickname: 'The Binos'.
Previous Grounds: Annfield 1945-92.
Record Attendance: 26,400 v Celtic, Scottish Cup 4th rd, 14 Mar 1959 (Annfield); 3,808 v Aberdeen, Scottish Cup 4th rd,
15 February 1996 (Forthbank).
Record Transfer Fee received: £90,000 for Stephen Nicholas to Motherwell (Mar 1999).
Record Transfer Fee paid: £25,000 for Craig Taggart from Falkirk (Aug 1994).
Record Victory: 20-0 v Selkirk, Scottish Cup 1st rd, 8 Dec 1984.
Record Defeat: 0-9 v Dundee U, Division I, 30 Dec 1967; 0-9 v Ross Co, Scottish Cup 5th rd, 6 Feb 2010.
Most League Appearances: 504: Matt McPhee, 1967-81.
Most League Goals in Season (Individual): 27: Joe Hughes, Division II, 1969-70.
Most Goals Overall (Individual): 129: Billy Steele, 1971-83.

STIRLING ALBION – SCOTTISH LEAGUE ONE 2014–15 LEAGUE RECORD

Match No.	Date	Venue	Opponents	Result	H/T Score	Lg Pos.	Goalscorers	Atten- dance
1	Aug 9	A	Peterhead	D 1-1	0-0	3	Smith, G [55]	539
2	16	H	Ayr U	L 1-3	0-1	7	Smith, G (pen) [66]	823
3	23	A	Stenhousemuir	W 5-4	1-2	7	Wedderburn [31], Smith, G 2 [54, 69], Cunningham [55], Darren L Smith [62]	613
4	30	A	Airdrieonians	D 0-0	0-0	7		825
5	Sept 13	H	Brechin C	L 0-5	0-1	8		601
6	20	H	Forfar Ath	D 2-2	0-1	8	Cunningham 2 [73, 86]	567
7	27	A	Stranraer	L 0-2	0-2	9		446
8	Oct 4	H	Dunfermline Ath	L 0-2	0-0	9		1623
9	11	A	Greenock Morton	L 0-2	0-1	10		1225
10	18	H	Stenhousemuir	L 0-4	0-1	10		689
11	25	H	Airdrieonians	D 2-2	1-0	10	Fulton [20], Smith, G [85]	847
12	Nov 11	A	Brechin C	L 1-2	0-1	10	Weir [85]	408
13	15	H	Stranraer	D 1-1	1-1	10	Johnston [23]	589
14	22	A	Dunfermline Ath	L 0-4	0-2	10		2451
15	Dec 6	H	Peterhead	L 2-3	0-1	10	Doris [70], Cunningham [79]	515
16	13	A	Forfar Ath	L 1-2	1-1	10	Doris [45]	495
17	20	A	Ayr U	D 2-2	0-0	10	Doris 2 [66, 80]	880
18	27	H	Greenock Morton	L 3-4	2-1	10	Cunningham [3], McGeachie [30], Beith [59]	931
19	Jan 3	A	Stenhousemuir	W 2-1	2-1	10	Comrie [24], Smith, G [30]	586
20	10	H	Dunfermline Ath	D 2-2	0-1	10	Smith, C [60], Wedderburn [79]	1152
21	17	A	Peterhead	L 1-2	1-0	10	Wedderburn [41]	566
22	24	H	Forfar Ath	L 0-1	0-1	10		571
23	31	A	Stranraer	L 0-1	0-0	10		387
24	Feb 14	H	Ayr U	L 1-4	0-2	10	Johnston [54]	785
25	21	H	Brechin C	L 0-1	0-0	10		568
26	28	A	Airdrieonians	L 1-4	1-0	10	McGeachie [3]	779
27	Mar 3	A	Greenock Morton	L 0-4	0-1	10		1037
28	14	A	Dunfermline Ath	D 1-1	0-0	10	Smith, G [71]	2318
29	17	H	Stranraer	L 0-1	0-0	10		442
30	21	H	Peterhead	W 2-1	1-1	10	Coult [5], Stirling [84]	479
31	28	A	Forfar Ath	L 0-4	0-2	10		606
32	Apr 4	H	Airdrieonians	L 0-2	0-0	10		942
33	11	A	Brechin C	L 1-2	0-1	10	Cunningham [86]	427
34	18	H	Greenock Morton	L 0-2	0-0	10		963
35	25	A	Ayr U	L 0-4	0-2	10		1608
36	May 2	H	Stenhousemuir	W 3-2	1-1	10	Smith, G [19], Forsyth [89], Stirling [90]	766

Final League Position: 10

Honours
League Champions: Division II 1952-53, 1957-58, 1960-61, 1964-65. Second Division 1976-77, 1990-91, 1995-96, 2009-10; *Runners-up:* Division II 1948-49, 1950-51. Second Division 2006-07. Third Division 2003-04. *Promoted to First Division:* 2006-07 (play-offs). *Promoted to League One:* 2013-14 (play-offs).
League Cup: Semi-finals 1961-62.

Club colours: Shirt: White with red trim. Shorts: Red. Socks: Red and white hoops.

Goalscorers: *League (35):* Smith, G 8 (1 pen), Cunningham 6, Doris 4, Wedderburn 3, Johnston 2, McGeachie 2, Stirling 2, Beith 1, Comrie 1, Coult 1, Forsyth 1, Fulton 1, Darren L Smith 1, Smith, C 1, Weir 1.
William Hill Scottish FA Cup (3): Doris 2, Smith, C 1.
Scottish League Cup (0).
Petrofac Training Cup (4): Darren L Smith 2, Smith, G 2 (1 pen).

Paterson G 12	Hamilton L 21+10	Wedderburn C 16	Smith C 29+1	Johnston P 21+5	Weir G 10+5	Doris S 14+1	Comrie C 24+2	Creaney J 13+5	Smith G 32+4	Coult L 13+7	Forsyth R 19+3	Smith Darren L 6+8	Cunningham A 23+13	Robertson W 16+1	Smith Darren 4+2	McClune D 9+2	Reidford C 21	Fulton D 7+4	McGeachie R 27+1	Beith A 18	Small L 1+3	Shepherd S 3+5	McKinlay K 10	Paton C 1+6	Cummins A 10	Stirling A 10	Binnie C 3+1	Sinclair J 1+3	Hurst G —+2	Davidson S 2	Match No.
1	2	3	4	5¹	6	7	8	9	10²	11¹	12	13	14																		1
1	2	3	4	14	7			6³	9	11	10²		5	13	8	12															2
1	2	4	8	9³		7	13	10²	14	5	6	11¹		3	12																3
	2	3	4			8¹	12	11		5	6	10		7	1	9															4
	2	3	4		6	13		10²	12	5	9²	11		14	7¹	1	8														5
	2	3	4		6	11		5	10³	14	13	12	9¹	8	7²	1															6
	2	3	4			11		5	10²	13		9	12	6²	8³	7	1	14													7
2²	4⁸	3		10	6		5	13	11¹		14	8	7²		9	1		12													8
	2		4	10¹	9		5	12	11²		8	13	7	6³	1	14	3														9
9	3	4			11		5	10¹		12	13	6⁸	7³	8²	1	14	2														10
	2	3	4	12	8	11		9	10	5¹		6		1	7																11
	2		4	12	6	10		13	11	5³	14	9²	7		1	8⁸	3														12
13		4	6²	9³	10	14	11		5	12	8		2¹	1	7	3															13
13		4	6	12	11	14		10³	5		9¹	8⁸	2¹	1	7	3															14
	2		4	6²	12	10	13		11³	5		9		1	8³	3	7	14													15
	2		4	6²	14	10	8¹	12	11		5²	9		1		3	7	13													16
	2		4	6¹	12	11	8	5	9²			10		1		3	7	13													17
		3	4	6²	12	10	7	5	11³	14		9¹	13	1⁸		2	8														18
1	14	3	4	6		7	5	11³	12			9²		13		2	8	10¹													19
1	13	3	4	8²		9	5	11¹	7⁸	14		10³				2	6	12													20
1		3	4	6		8	5	11		9¹				12	2	7	10														21
1	12	3	4⁸	6²		7		9			11			2	8	10¹	5	13													22
1	2	3		6		7		11	10	12		9		4	8²		5¹	13													23
1	2		4	6		7		9	10		12			3	8	11¹	5														24
1	13		4	6²		7		8¹	11	5		10		2	3	12	9														25
1			6²			8³	11	10¹	4	14	13		2	7	12	5		3	9												26
1	14		4	6³		7¹	11	13	5	12	9²		2	8		3	10														27
12		4	8			7	10¹	11²	9	6		1	2	13	5	3															28
12		4	6²			7	11¹	10	13	3		1	2	14	5	8	9²														29
6		4				7	12	10²	5	11¹	8		1	2	13	3	9														30
6¹		4	13			8	14	10	5	11²	7	1³	2		3	9	12														31
6		12				10³	4	9	8²	1	2	7	5	13	3	11¹	14														32
12		6		8		10²	4	13	7²	1	2	9¹	5	3	11	14															33
		9¹		7		11²	6	13	2	3	5	10³	4	8	1	14	12														34
6⁸	13		8	10²	7	12	11	2	3	14	9¹	1	5³	4																	35
	6		7	10¹	5	12	9³	2	8²	13	3	11	1	14	4																36

STRANRAER

Year Formed: 1870. *Ground & Address:* Stair Park, London Rd, Stranraer DG9 8BS. *Telephone and Fax:* 01776 703271.
E-mail: secretary@stranraerfc.org *Website:* www.stranraerfc.org
Ground Capacity: 6,250 (seated: 1,830). *Size of Pitch:* 103m × 64m.
Chairman: Robert Rice. *Vice-Chairman:* Iain Dougan. *Secretary:* David Broadfoot.
Manager: Brian Reid. *Assistant Manager:* Lee Mair. *Physio:* Matthew Wallace.
Club Nicknames: 'The Blues', 'The Clayholers'.
Previous Grounds: None.
Record Attendance: 6,500 v Rangers, Scottish Cup 1st rd, 24 Jan 1948.
Record Transfer Fee received: £90,000 for Mark Campbell to Ayr U (1999).
Record Transfer Fee paid: £35,000 for Michael Moore from St Johnstone (Mar 2005).
Record Victory: 9-0 v St Cuthbert Wanderers, Scottish Cup 2nd rd, 23 Oct 2010; 9-0 v Wigtown & Bladnoch, Scottish Cup 2nd rd, 22 Oct 2011.
Record Defeat: 1-11 v Queen of the South, Scottish Cup 1st rd, 16 Jan 1932.
Most League Appearances: 301: Keith Knox, 1986-90; 1999-2001.
Most League Goals in Season (Individual): 27: Derek Frye, 1977-78.
Most Goals Overall (Individual): 115: Jim Campbell, 1965-75.

STRANRAER – SCOTTISH LEAGUE ONE 2014–15 LEAGUE RECORD

Match No.	Date	Venue	Opponents	Result	H/T Score	Lg Pos.	Goalscorers	Atten- dance
1	Aug 9	H	Forfar Ath	D 1-1	1-0	3	Longworth [17]	409
2	16	A	Greenock Morton	L 0-4	0-3	9		1314
3	23	H	Brechin C	D 2-2	0-2	9	Forde [56], Stirling [90]	432
4	30	H	Dunfermline Ath	L 1-2	1-1	9	Gibson [35]	573
5	Sept 13	A	Ayr U	W 2-0	0-0	7	Gallagher [65], Longworth [81]	1414
6	20	A	Airdrieonians	D 3-3	1-2	7	Longworth [8], Malcolm [59], Forde [90]	864
7	27	H	Stirling Alb	W 2-0	2-0	6	Longworth [3], Stirling [25]	446
8	Oct 4	A	Stenhousemuir	D 2-2	1-0	7	Longworth [26], Winter [76]	453
9	18	A	Brechin C	W 2-1	1-1	5	McKeown [28], Winter [73]	407
10	25	A	Forfar Ath	D 1-1	1-1	7	Winter [1]	548
11	28	H	Peterhead	W 5-0	1-0	4	Gibson [20], Longworth 2 [59, 81], Aitken (pen) [68], Stoney [90]	329
12	Nov 8	H	Ayr U	W 3-1	1-1	4	Malcolm 2 [36, 51], Stoney [82]	630
13	15	A	Stirling Alb	D 1-1	1-1	3	Bell [35]	589
14	22	H	Airdrieonians	W 1-0	0-0	4	Stirling (pen) [68]	445
15	Dec 6	H	Greenock Morton	W 2-0	1-0	3	Malcolm 2 [30, 47]	415
16	13	A	Peterhead	W 4-1	1-1	2	McKeown [14], Gallagher [61], Malcolm [69], Aitken [74]	428
17	20	A	Dunfermline Ath	W 1-0	0-0	1	McKeown [59]	2572
18	27	H	Stenhousemuir	L 0-2	0-1	1		573
19	Jan 3	A	Ayr U	W 2-0	1-0	1	Malcolm [40], Longworth [74]	1235
20	10	H	Forfar Ath	W 4-2	2-0	1	Malcolm 2 [34, 70], Bell [38], Longridge [90]	475
21	17	H	Brechin C	L 0-2	0-1	1		470
22	24	A	Airdrieonians	D 1-1	0-0	1	McShane [87]	712
23	31	A	Stirling Alb	W 1-0	0-0	1	McKeown [86]	387
24	Feb 14	H	Peterhead	W 2-0	1-0	1	Longworth [28], McShane [46]	371
25	21	A	Greenock Morton	L 0-2	0-1	1		1921
26	28	H	Dunfermline Ath	W 5-1	3-1	1	Gallagher [10], Aitken [31], Gibson [44], Longworth [49], McShane [83]	498
27	Mar 3	A	Stenhousemuir	L 0-1	0-1	2		221
28	14	A	Forfar Ath	L 0-1	0-1	3		545
29	17	H	Stirling Alb	W 1-0	0-0	1	Gibson [68]	442
30	21	H	Airdrieonians	W 1-0	0-0	1	Gibson [83]	498
31	28	H	Peterhead	W 2-1	0-1	1	Gibson [57], Longworth [82]	516
32	Apr 4	H	Ayr U	W 1-0	0-0	1	Malcolm [64]	1010
33	11	A	Dunfermline Ath	L 0-1	0-0	2		1951
34	18	A	Stenhousemuir	W 3-2	2-0	1	Gibson [13], Winter [41], Pettigrew [58]	552
35	25	H	Greenock Morton	L 0-2	0-2	3		1321
36	May 2	A	Brechin C	W 3-1	2-1	2	Stirling [20], Gibson 2 (2 pens) [43, 76]	538

Final League Position: 2

Honours
League Champions: Second Division 1993-94, 1997-98. Third Division 2003-04.
Runners-up: Second Division 2004-05, Third Division 2007-08. League One: 2014-15. Promoted to Second Division 2011-12 (play-offs).
Scottish Cup: Quarter-finals 2003
League Challenge Cup Winners: 1996-97.
Qualifying Cup Winners: 1937.

Club colours: Shirt: Blue with white trim. Shorts: White. Socks: Blue.

Goalscorers: *League (59):* Longworth 11, Malcolm 10, Gibson 9 (2 pens), McKeown 4, Stirling 4 (1 pen), Winter 4, Aitken 3 (1 pen), Gallagher 3, McShane 3, Bell 2, Forde 2, Stoney 2, Longridge 1, Pettigrew 1.
William Hill Scottish FA Cup (6): Longworth 2, Gibson 1, Malcolm 1, Stirling 1, Winter 1.
Scottish League Cup (2): Malcolm 1, Winter 1.
Petrofac Training Cup (7): McKeown 2, Longworth 1, Malcolm 1, Marenghi 1, Rumsby 1, Winter 1.
Championship Play-Offs (1): Aitken 1 (1 pen).

Mitchell D 35	Rumsby S 31	Pettigrew C 29	McKeown F 35	Robertson S 11 + 4	Gallagher G 32 + 2	Winter S 29 + 3	Stirling S 18 + 11	Longridge J 32 + 2	Malcolm C 32 + 2	Longworth J 30 + 5	Marenghi A 3 + 7	Aitken C 22 + 7	Forde A — + 7	Russell B 4 + 12	Fahey C 1 + 1	McCloskey S — + 2	Gibson W 27 + 1	Stoney D 4 + 23	Bell S 17 + 6	McShane J 4 + 8	Match No.
1	2	3	4	5	6	7¹	8²	9	10	11³	12	13	14								1
1*		8	3	5	6	7³	9	4	10	11³	14	13		2*			12				2
	2	3	4	5	6¹	9	13		10	11	8³	7²	12				1	14			3
1	3³	5	4	2	8²		7	9¹	10*	11	12	13	14				6				4
1	3	5	4	2*	7	13	8	12	11	9¹							6²	10			5
1	8³	2	3		4	6²	7	5	10	11¹		13					14	9	12		6
1	3	2	4		8	9	7³	5	10	11¹ 12			14				6²	13			7
1	3	2³	4		8	6	7¹	5	10	11	9² 12		13				14				8
1	3		4		2	6	8	5	10¹	11²		7	14 13				9³	12			9
1	3		4		2	6	8²	5	10¹	12		7	14				9	11³	13		10
1	3		4		2	6	7	5	10²	11		8¹	14				9³	13	12		11
1	3		4		2	6		5²	10	11¹ 14		8	13				9	12	7³		12
1	3		4		2	6		5	10	11¹		7	13				9²	12	8		13
1	3		4		2	6	12	5	10			8²	13				9	11¹	7		14
1	3	2	4		6	9	7³	5²	10	11³ 13		12					14		8		15
1	3	2	4		6	10¹	7²	5	11³	12 13		8					14		9		16
1	3	2	4		6	9		5	10	11²		7	12				13	8¹			17
1	3	2	4		6	9	12	5	10	11³		8² 14					13	7¹			18
1	3	2	4		7	6	10²	9¹ 11¹ 12				8		5			13 14				19
1	3	2	4		7	6		5	10³ 11²			13					9¹ 14	8	12		20
1	3	2	4		7¹	6	14		10² 12					5			9	13	8	11³	21
1	3	2	4		6		8²	5	10³ 11¹			7					9	13	12	14	22
1	3	2	4		6		7³	5	10 11¹			8					9²	13	12	14	23
1	3	2	4		12	6		5	13 11¹			8					9	14	7²	10³	24
1		2	4	3	6		13	5	12 11¹			7					9¹		8	10²	25
1		2	4	3	6	14	13	5	10² 11¹			8²					9		7	12	26
1		2	4	3	6²	13	8³	5	10 11¹			7					9		12	14	27
1		2	4	3	13	6		5	10¹ 14			7³					9	12	8	11²	28
1	3	2	4		7	6	14	5	10¹ 11³			8²					9	13	12		29
1	3	2	4	14	7	6²		5	10³	13		9¹					12	8			30
1	3	2	4	14	8	6²	12	5	10³ 11			7¹					9	13			31
1	3	2	4	14	7	6³	13	5	10³ 11²			8					9	12			32
1	3	2	4		8	6	13	5	10³ 11²			7¹					9	12		14	33
1	3	2	4	12	6		7³	5	10² 11¹			9					13	8	14		34
1	3		4	2	7¹	6³	13	5	10² 11			12*					9	14	8		35
1	3	2		4		6	8¹	13		11²				5			9	10	7	12	36

SCOTTISH LEAGUE HONOURS 1890–2015

=Until 1921–22 season teams were equal if level on points, unless a play-off took place. §Not promoted after play-offs.
*Won or placed on goal average (ratio), goal difference or most goals scored (goal average from 1921–22 until 1971–72 when it was replaced by goal difference). No official competition during 1939–46; Regional Leagues operated.

DIVISION 1 (1890–91 to 1974–75) – TIER 1

Tier	Season	Max Pts	First	Pts	Second	Pts	Third	Pts
1	1890–91	36	Dumbarton=	29	Rangers=	29	Celtic	21

Dumbarton and Rangers held title jointly after indecisive play-off ended 2-2. Celtic deducted 4 points for fielding an ineligible player.

Tier	Season	Max Pts	First	Pts	Second	Pts	Third	Pts
1	1891–92	44	Dumbarton	37	Celtic	35	Hearts	34
1	1892–93	36	Celtic	29	Rangers	28	St Mirren	20
1	1893–94	36	Celtic	29	Hearts	26	St Bernard's	23
1	1894–95	36	Hearts	31	Celtic	26	Rangers	22
1	1895–96	36	Celtic	30	Rangers	26	Hibernian	24
1	1896–97	36	Hearts	28	Hibernian	26	Rangers	25
1	1897–98	36	Celtic	33	Rangers	29	Hibernian	22
1	1898–99	36	Rangers	36	Hearts	26	Celtic	24
1	1899–1900	36	Rangers	32	Celtic	25	Hibernian	24
1	1900–01	40	Rangers	35	Celtic	29	Hibernian	25
1	1901–02	36	Rangers	28	Celtic	26	Hearts	22
1	1902–03	44	Hibernian	37	Dundee	31	Rangers	29
1	1903–04	52	Third Lanark	43	Hearts	39	Celtic / Rangers=	38
1	1904–05	52	Celtic=	41	Rangers=	41	Third Lanark	35

Celtic won title after beating Rangers 2-1 in play-off.

Tier	Season	Max Pts	First	Pts	Second	Pts	Third	Pts
1	1905–06	60	Celtic	49	Hearts	43	Airdrieonians	38
1	1906–07	68	Celtic	55	Dundee	48	Rangers	45
1	1907–08	68	Celtic	55	Falkirk	51	Rangers	50
1	1908–09	68	Celtic	51	Dundee	50	Clyde	48
1	1909–10	68	Celtic	54	Falkirk	52	Rangers	46
1	1910–11	68	Rangers	52	Aberdeen	48	Falkirk	44
1	1911–12	68	Rangers	51	Celtic	45	Clyde	42
1	1912–13	68	Rangers	53	Celtic	49	Hearts / Airdrieonians=	41
1	1913–14	76	Celtic	65	Rangers	59	Hearts / Morton=	54
1	1914–15	76	Celtic	65	Hearts	61	Rangers	50
1	1915–16	76	Celtic	67	Rangers	56	Morton	51
1	1916–17	76	Celtic	64	Morton	54	Rangers	53
1	1917–18	68	Rangers	56	Celtic	55	Kilmarnock / Morton=	43
1	1918–19	68	Celtic	58	Rangers	57	Morton	47
1	1919–20	84	Rangers	71	Celtic	68	Motherwell	57
1	1920–21	84	Rangers	76	Celtic	66	Hearts	50
1	1921–22	84	Celtic	67	Rangers	66	Raith R	51
1	1922–23	76	Rangers	55	Airdrieonians	50	Celtic	46
1	1923–24	76	Rangers	59	Airdrieonians	50	Celtic	46
1	1924–25	76	Rangers	60	Airdrieonians	57	Hibernian	52
1	1925–26	76	Celtic	58	Airdrieonians*	50	Hearts	50
1	1926–27	76	Rangers	56	Motherwell	51	Celtic	49
1	1927–28	76	Rangers	60	Celtic*	55	Motherwell	55
1	1928–29	76	Rangers	67	Celtic	51	Motherwell	50
1	1929–30	76	Rangers	60	Motherwell	55	Aberdeen	53
1	1930–31	76	Rangers	60	Celtic	58	Motherwell	56
1	1931–32	76	Motherwell	66	Rangers	61	Celtic	48
1	1932–33	76	Rangers	62	Motherwell	59	Hearts	50
1	1933–34	76	Rangers	66	Motherwell	62	Celtic	47
1	1934–35	76	Rangers	55	Celtic	52	Hearts	50
1	1935–36	76	Celtic	66	Rangers*	61	Aberdeen	61
1	1936–37	76	Rangers	61	Aberdeen	54	Celtic	52
1	1937–38	76	Celtic	61	Hearts	58	Rangers	49
1	1938–39	76	Rangers	59	Celtic	48	Aberdeen	46
1	1946–47	60	Rangers	46	Hibernian	44	Aberdeen	39
1	1947–48	60	Hibernian	48	Rangers	46	Partick Thistle	36
1	1948–49	60	Rangers	46	Dundee	45	Hibernian	39
1	1949–50	60	Rangers	50	Hibernian	49	Hearts	43
1	1950–51	60	Hibernian	48	Rangers*	38	Dundee	38
1	1951–52	60	Hibernian	45	Rangers	41	East Fife	37
1	1952–53	60	Rangers*	43	Hibernian	43	East Fife	39
1	1953–54	60	Celtic	43	Hearts	38	Partick Thistle	35
1	1954–55	60	Aberdeen	49	Celtic	46	Rangers	41
1	1955–56	68	Rangers	52	Aberdeen	46	Hearts*	45
1	1956–57	68	Rangers	55	Hearts	53	Kilmarnock	42
1	1957–58	68	Hearts	62	Rangers	49	Celtic	46
1	1958–59	68	Rangers	50	Hearts	48	Motherwell	44
1	1959–60	68	Hearts	54	Kilmarnock	50	Rangers*	42
1	1960–61	68	Rangers	51	Kilmarnock	50	Third Lanark	42
1	1961–62	68	Dundee	54	Rangers	51	Celtic	46

1	1962–63	68	Rangers	57	Kilmarnock	48	Partick Thistle	46
1	1963–64	68	Rangers	55	Kilmarnock	49	Celtic*	47
1	1964–65	68	Kilmarnock*	50	Hearts	50	Dunfermline Ath	49
1	1965–66	68	Celtic	57	Rangers	55	Kilmarnock	45
1	1966–67	68	Celtic	58	Rangers	55	Clyde	46
1	1967–68	68	Celtic	63	Rangers	61	Hibernian	45
1	1968–69	68	Celtic	54	Rangers	49	Dunfermline Ath	45
1	1969–70	68	Celtic	57	Rangers	45	Hibernian	44
1	1970–71	68	Celtic	56	Aberdeen	54	St Johnstone	44
1	1971–72	68	Celtic	60	Aberdeen	50	Rangers	44
1	1972–73	68	Celtic	57	Rangers	56	Hibernian	45
1	1973–74	68	Celtic	53	Hibernian	49	Rangers	48
1	1974–75	68	Rangers	56	Hibernian	49	Celtic*	45

PREMIER DIVISION (1975–76 to 1997–98)

1	1975–76	72	Rangers	54	Celtic	48	Hibernian	43
1	1976–77	72	Celtic	55	Rangers	46	Aberdeen	43
1	1977–78	72	Rangers	55	Aberdeen	53	Dundee U	40
1	1978–79	72	Celtic	48	Rangers	45	Dundee U	44
1	1979–80	72	Aberdeen	48	Celtic	47	St Mirren	42
1	1980–81	72	Celtic	56	Aberdeen	49	Rangers*	44
1	1981–82	72	Celtic	55	Aberdeen	53	Rangers	43
1	1982–83	72	Dundee U	56	Celtic*	55	Aberdeen	55
1	1983–84	72	Aberdeen	57	Celtic	50	Dundee U	47
1	1984–85	72	Aberdeen	59	Celtic	52	Dundee U	47
1	1985–86	72	Celtic*	50	Hearts	50	Dundee U	47
1	1986–87	88	Rangers	69	Celtic	63	Dundee U	60
1	1987–88	88	Celtic	72	Hearts	62	Rangers	60
1	1988–89	72	Rangers	56	Aberdeen	50	Celtic	46
1	1989–90	72	Rangers	51	Aberdeen*	44	Hearts	44
1	1990–91	72	Rangers	55	Aberdeen	53	Celtic*	41
1	1991–92	88	Rangers	72	Hearts	63	Celtic	62
1	1992–93	88	Rangers	73	Aberdeen	64	Celtic	60
1	1993–94	88	Rangers	58	Aberdeen	55	Motherwell	54
1	1994–95	108	Rangers	69	Motherwell	54	Hibernian	53
1	1995–96	108	Rangers	87	Celtic	83	Aberdeen*	55
1	1996–97	108	Rangers	80	Celtic	75	Dundee U	60
1	1997–98	108	Celtic	74	Rangers	72	Hearts	67

PREMIER LEAGUE (1998–99 to 2012–13)

1	1998–99	108	Rangers	77	Celtic	71	St Johnstone	57
1	1999–2000	108	Rangers	90	Celtic	69	Hearts	54
1	2000–01	114	Celtic	97	Rangers	82	Hibernian	66
1	2001–02	114	Celtic	103	Rangers	85	Livingston	58
1	2002–03	114	Rangers*	97	Celtic	97	Hearts	63
1	2003–04	114	Celtic	98	Rangers	81	Hearts	68
1	2004–05	114	Rangers	93	Celtic	92	Hibernian*	61
1	2005–06	114	Celtic	91	Hearts	74	Rangers	73
1	2006–07	114	Celtic	84	Rangers	72	Aberdeen	65
1	2007–08	114	Celtic	89	Rangers	86	Motherwell	60
1	2008–09	114	Rangers	86	Celtic	82	Hearts	59
1	2009–10	114	Rangers	87	Celtic	81	Dundee U	63
1	2010–11	114	Rangers	93	Celtic	92	Hearts	63
1	2011–12	114	Celtic	93	Rangers	73	Motherwell	62

Rangers deducted 10 points for entering administration.

| 1 | 2012–13 | 114 | Celtic | 79 | Motherwell | 63 | St Johnstone | 56 |

SPFL SCOTTISH PREMIERSHIP

Tier	Season	Max Pts	First	Pts	Second	Pts	Third	Pts
1	2013–14	114	Celtic	99	Motherwell	70	Aberdeen	68
1	2014–15	114	Celtic	92	Aberdeen	75	Inverness CT	65

DIVISION 2 (1893–93 to 1974–75) – TIER 2

2	1893–94	36	Hibernian	29	Cowlairs	27	Clyde	24
2	1894–95	36	Hibernian	30	Motherwell	22	Port Glasgow Ath	20
2	1895–96	36	Abercorn	27	Leith Ath	23	Renton / Kilmarnock=	21
2	1896–97	36	Partick Thistle	31	Leith Ath	27	Airdrieonians / Kilmarnock=	21
2	1897–98	36	Kilmarnock	29	Port Glasgow Ath	25	Morton	22
2	1898–99	36	Kilmarnock	32	Leith Ath	27	Port Glasgow Ath	25
2	1899–1900	36	Partick Thistle	29	Morton	28	Port Glasgow Ath	20
2	1900–01	36	St Bernard's	26	Airdrieonians	23	Abercorn	21
2	1901–02	44	Port Glasgow Ath	32	Partick Thistle	30	Motherwell	26
2	1902–03	44	Airdrieonians	35	Motherwell	28	Ayr U / Leith Ath=	27
2	1903–04	44	Hamilton A	37	Clyde	29	Ayr U	28

2	1904–05	44	Clyde	32	Falkirk	28	Hamilton A	27
2	1905–06	44	Leith Ath	34	Clyde	31	Albion R	27
2	1906–07	44	St Bernard's	32	Vale of Leven=	27	Arthurlie=	27
2	1907–08	44	Raith R	30	Dumbarton=	27	Ayr U=	27

Dumbarton deducted 2 points for registration irregularities.

2	1908–09	44	Abercorn	31	Raith R=	28	Vale of Leven=	28
2	1909–10	44	Leith Ath=	33	Raith R=	33	St Bernard's	27

Leith Ath and Raith R held title jointly, no play-off game played.

2	1910–11	44	Dumbarton	31	Ayr U	27	Albion R	25
2	1911–12	44	Ayr U	35	Abercorn	30	Dumbarton	27
2	1912–13	52	Ayr U	34	Dunfermline Ath	33	East Stirling	32
2	1913–14	44	Cowdenbeath	31	Albion R	27	Dunfermline Ath / Dundee U=	26
2	1914–15	52	Cowdenbeath=	37	St Bernard's=	37	Leith Ath=	37

Cowdenbeath won title after a round robin tournament between the three tied clubs.

2	1921–22	76	Alloa Ath	60	Cowdenbeath	47	Armadale	45
2	1922–23	76	Queen's Park	57	Clydebank	50	St Johnstone	48

Clydebank and St Johnstone both deducted 2 points for fielding an inelligible player.

2	1923–24	76	St Johnstone	56	Cowdenbeath	55	Bathgate	44
2	1924–25	76	Dundee U	50	Clydebank	48	Clyde	47
2	1925–26	76	Dunfermline Ath	59	Clyde	53	Ayr U	52
2	1926–27	76	Bo'ness	56	Raith R	49	Clydebank	45
2	1927–28	76	Ayr U	54	Third Lanark	45	King's Park	44
2	1928–29	72	Dundee U	51	Morton	50	Arbroath	47
2	1929–30	76	Leith Ath*	57	East Fife	57	Albion R	54
2	1930–31	76	Third Lanark	61	Dundee U	50	Dunfermline Ath	47
2	1931–32	76	East Stirling*	55	St Johnstone	55	Raith R*	46
2	1932–33	68	Hibernian	54	Queen of the South	49	Dunfermline Ath	47

Armadale and Bo'ness were expelled for failing to meet match guarantees. Their records were expunged.

2	1933–34	68	Albion R	45	Dunfermline Ath*	44	Arbroath	44
2	1934–35	68	Third Lanark	52	Arbroath	50	St Bernard's	47
2	1935–36	68	Falkirk	59	St Mirren	52	Morton	48
2	1936–37	68	Ayr U	54	Morton	51	St Bernard's	48
2	1937–38	68	Raith R	59	Albion R	48	Airdrieonians	47
2	1938–39	68	Cowdenbeath	60	Alloa Ath*	48	East Fife	48
2	1946–47	52	Dundee	45	Airdrieonians	42	East Fife	31
2	1947–48	60	East Fife	53	Albion R	42	Hamilton A	40
2	1948–49	60	Raith R*	42	Stirling Alb	42	Airdrieonians*	41
2	1949–50	60	Morton	47	Airdrieonians	44	Dunfermline Ath*	36
2	1950–51	60	Queen of the South*	45	Stirling Alb	45	Ayr U*	36
2	1951–52	60	Clyde	44	Falkirk	43	Ayr U	39
2	1952–53	60	Stirling Alb	44	Hamilton A	43	Queen's Park	37
2	1953–54	60	Motherwell	45	Kilmarnock	42	Third Lanark*	36
2	1954–55	60	Airdrieonians	46	Dunfermline Ath	42	Hamilton A	39
2	1955–56	72	Queen's Park	54	Ayr U	51	St Johnstone	49
2	1956–57	72	Clyde	64	Third Lanark	51	Cowdenbeath	45
2	1957–58	72	Stirling Alb	55	Dunfermline Ath	53	Arbroath	47
2	1958–59	72	Ayr U	60	Arbroath	51	Stenhousemuir	46
2	1959–60	72	St Johnstone	53	Dundee U	50	Queen of the South	49
2	1960–61	72	Stirling Alb	55	Falkirk	54	Stenhousemuir	50
2	1961–62	72	Clyde	54	Queen of the South	53	Morton	44
2	1962–63	72	St Johnstone	55	East Stirling	49	Morton	48
2	1963–64	72	Morton	67	Clyde	53	Arbroath	46
2	1964–65	72	Stirling Alb	59	Hamilton A	50	Queen of the South	45
2	1965–66	72	Ayr U	53	Airdrieonians	50	Queen of the South	47
2	1966–67	76	Morton	69	Raith R	58	Arbroath	57
2	1967–68	72	St Mirren	62	Arbroath	53	East Fife	49
2	1968–69	72	Motherwell	64	Ayr U	53	East Fife*	48
2	1969–70	72	Falkirk	56	Cowdenbeath	55	Queen of the South	50
2	1970–71	72	Partick Thistle	56	East Fife	51	Arbroath	46
2	1971–72	72	Dumbarton*	52	Arbroath	52	Stirling Alb*	50
2	1972–73	72	Clyde	56	Dumfermline Ath	52	Raith R*	47
2	1973–74	72	Airdrieonians	60	Kilmarnock	58	Hamilton A	55
2	1974–75	76	Falkirk	54	Queen of the South*	53	Montrose	53

Elected to First Division: 1894 Clyde; 1895 Hibernian; 1896 Abercorn; 1897 Partick Thistle; 1899 Kilmarnock; 1900 Morton and Partick Thistle; 1902 Port Glasgow and Partick Thistle; 1903 Airdrieonians and Motherwell; 1905 Falkirk and Aberdeen; 1906 Clyde and Hamilton A; 1910 Raith R; 1913 Ayr U and Dumbarton.

FIRST DIVISION (1975–76 to 2012–13)

2	1975–76	52	Partick Thistle	41	Kilmarnock	35	Montrose	30
2	1976–77	78	St Mirren	62	Clydebank	58	Dundee	51
2	1977–78	78	Morton*	58	Hearts	58	Dundee	57
2	1978–79	78	Dundee	55	Kilmarnock*	54	Clydebank	54
2	1979–80	78	Hearts	53	Airdrieonians	51	Ayr U*	44
2	1980–81	78	Hibernian	57	Dundee	52	St Johnstone	51
2	1981–82	78	Motherwell	61	Kilmarnock	51	Hearts	50

2	1982–83	78	St Johnstone	55	Hearts	54	Clydebank	50
2	1983–84	78	Morton	54	Dumbarton	51	Partick Thistle	46
2	1984–85	78	Motherwell	50	Clydebank	48	Falkirk	45
2	1985–86	78	Hamilton A	56	Falkirk	45	Kilmarnock*	44
2	1986–87	88	Morton	57	Dunfermline Ath	56	Dumbarton	53
2	1987–88	88	Hamilton A	56	Meadowbank Thistle	52	Clydebank	49
2	1988–89	78	Dunfermline Ath	54	Falkirk	52	Clydebank	48
2	1989–90	78	St Johnstone	58	Airdrieonians	54	Clydebank	44
2	1990–91	78	Falkirk	54	Airdrieonians	53	Dundee	52
2	1991–92	88	Dundee	58	Partick Thistle*	57	Hamilton A	57
2	1992–93	88	Raith R	65	Kilmarnock	54	Dunfermline Ath	52
2	1993–94	88	Falkirk	66	Dunfermline Ath	65	Airdrieonians	54
2	1994–95	108	Raith R	69	Dunfermline Ath*	68	Dundee	68
2	1995–96	108	Dunfermline Ath	71	Dundee U*	67	Greenock Morton	67
2	1996–97	108	St Johnstone	80	Airdieonians	60	Dundee*	58
2	1997–98	108	Dundee	70	Falkirk	65	Raith R*	60
2	1998–99	108	Hibernian	89	Falkirk	66	Ayr U	62
2	1999–2000	108	St Mirren	76	Dunfermline Ath	71	Falkirk	68
2	2000–01	108	Livingston	76	Ayr U	69	Falkirk	56
2	2001–02	108	Partick Thistle	66	Airdrieonians	56	Ayr U*	52
2	2002–03	108	Falkirk	81	Clyde	72	St Johnstone	67
2	2003–04	108	Inverness CT	70	Clyde	69	St Johnstone	57
2	2004–05	108	Falkirk	75	St Mirren*	60	Clyde	60
2	2005–06	108	St Mirren	76	St Johnstone	66	Hamilton A	59
2	2006–07	108	Gretna	66	St Johnstone	65	Dundee*	53
2	2007–08	108	Hamilton A	76	Dundee	69	St Johnstone	58
2	2008–09	108	St Johnstone	65	Partick Thistle	55	Dunfermline Ath	51
2	2009–10	108	Inverness CT	73	Dundee	61	Dunfermline Ath	58
2	2010–11	108	Dunfermline Ath	70	Raith R	60	Falkirk	58
2	2011–12	108	Ross Co	79	Dundee	55	Falkirk	52
2	2012–13	108	Partick Thistle	78	Greenock Morton	67	Falkirk	53

SPFL SCOTTISH CHAMPIONSHIP

Tier	Season	Max Pts	First	Pts	Second	Pts	Third	Pts
2	2013–14	108	Dundee	69	Hamilton A	67	Falkirk§	66
2	2014–15	108	Hearts	91	Hibernian§	70	Rangers§	67

SECOND DIVISION (1975–76 to 2012–13) – TIER 3

3	1975–76	52	Clydebank*	40	Raith R	40	Alloa Ath	35
3	1976–77	78	Stirling Alb	55	Alloa Ath	51	Dunfermline Ath	50
3	1977–78	78	Clyde*	53	Raith R	53	Dunfermline Ath*	48
3	1978–79	78	Berwick R	54	Dunfermline Ath	52	Falkirk	50
3	1979–80	78	Falkirk	50	East Stirling	49	Forfar Ath	46
3	1980–81	78	Queen's Park	50	Queen of the South	46	Cowdenbeath	45
3	1981–82	78	Clyde	59	Alloa Ath*	50	Arbroath	50
3	1982–83	78	Brechin C	55	Meadowbank Thistle	54	Arbroath	49
3	1983–84	78	Forfar Ath	63	East Fife	47	Berwick R	43
3	1984–85	78	Montrose	53	Alloa Ath	50	Dunfermline Ath	49
3	1985–86	78	Dunfermline Ath	57	Queen of the South	55	Meadowbank Thistle	49
3	1986–87	78	Meadowbank Thistle	55	Raith R*	52	Stirling Alb*	52
3	1987–88	78	Ayr U	61	St Johnstone	59	Queen's Park	51
3	1988–89	78	Albion R	50	Alloa Ath	45	Brechin C	43
3	1989–90	78	Brechin C	49	Kilmarnock	48	Stirling Alb	47
3	1990–91	78	Stirling Alb	54	Montrose	46	Cowdenbeath	45
3	1991–92	78	Dumbarton	52	Cowdenbeath	51	Alloa Ath	50
3	1992–93	78	Clyde	54	Brechin C*	53	Stranraer	53
3	1993–94	78	Stranraer	56	Berwick R	48	Stenhousemuir*	47
3	1994–95	108	Greenock Morton	64	Dumbarton	60	Stirling Alb	58
3	1995–96	108	Stirling Alb	81	East Fife	67	Berwick R	60
3	1996–97	108	Ayr U	77	Hamilton A	74	Livingston	64
3	1997–98	108	Stranraer	61	Clydebank	60	Livingston	59
3	1998–99	108	Livingston	77	Inverness CT	72	Clyde	53
3	1999–2000	108	Clyde	65	Alloa Ath	64	Ross Co	62
3	2000–01	108	Partick Thistle	75	Arbroath	58	Berwick R*	54
3	2001–02	108	Queen of the South	67	Alloa Ath	59	Forfar Ath	53
3	2002–03	108	Raith R	59	Brechin C	55	Airdrie U	54
3	2003–04	108	Airdrie U	70	Hamilton A	62	Dumbarton	60
3	2004–05	108	Brechin C	72	Stranraer	63	Greenock Morton	62
3	2005–06	108	Gretna	88	Greenock Morton§	70	Peterhead*§	57
3	2006–07	108	Greenock Morton	77	Stirling Alb	69	Raith R§	62
3	2007–08	108	Ross Co	73	Airdrie U	66	Raith R§	60
3	2008–09	108	Raith R	76	Ayr U	74	Brechin C§	62
3	2009–10	108	Stirling Alb*	65	Alloa Ath§	65	Cowdenbeath	59
3	2010–11	108	Livingston	82	Ayr U*	59	Forfar Ath§	59
3	2011–12	108	Cowdenbeath	71	Arbroath§	63	Dumbarton	58
3	2012–13	108	Queen of the South	92	Alloa Ath	67	Brechin C	61

SPFL SCOTTISH LEAGUE ONE

Tier	Season	Max Pts	First	Pts	Second	Pts	Third	Pts
3	2013–14	108	Rangers	102	Dunfermline Ath§	63	Stranraer§	51
3	2014–15	108	Greenock Morton	69	Stranraer§	67	Forfar Ath	66

THIRD DIVISION (1994–95 to 2012–13) – TIER 4

Tier	Season	Max Pts	First	Pts	Second	Pts	Third	Pts
4	1994–95	108	Forfar Ath	80	Montrose	67	Ross Co	60
4	1995–96	108	Livingston	72	Brechin C	63	Inverness CT	57
4	1996–97	108	Inverness CT	76	Forfar Ath*	67	Ross Co	67
4	1997–98	108	Alloa Ath	76	Arbroath	68	Ross Co	67
4	1998–99	108	Ross Co	77	Stenhousemuir	64	Brechin C	59
4	1999–2000	108	Queen's Park	69	Berwick R	66	Forfar Ath	61
4	2000–01	108	Hamilton A*	76	Cowdenbeath	76	Brechin C	72
4	2001–02	108	Brechin C	73	Dumbarton	61	Albion R	59
4	2002–03	108	Greenock Morton	72	East Fife	71	Albion R	70
4	2003–04	108	Stranraer	79	Stirling Alb	77	Gretna	68
4	2004–05	108	Gretna	98	Peterhead	78	Cowdenbeath	51
4	2005–06	108	Cowdenbeath*	76	Berwick R§	76	Stenhousemuir§	73
4	2006–07	108	Berwick R	75	Arbroath§	70	Queen's Park	68
4	2007–08	108	East Fife	88	Stranraer	65	Montrose§	59
4	2008–09	108	Dumbarton	67	Cowdenbeath	63	East Stirling§	61
4	2009–10	108	Livingston	78	Forfar Ath	63	East Stirling§	61
4	2010–11	108	Arbroath	66	Albion R	61	Queen's Park*§	59
4	2011–12	108	Alloa Ath	77	Queen's Park§	63	Stranraer	58
4	2012–13	108	Rangers	83	Peterhead§	59	Queen's Park§	56

SPFL SCOTTISH LEAGUE TWO

Tier	Season	Max Pts	First	Pts	Second	Pts	Third	Pts
4	2013–14	108	Peterhead	76	Annan Ath§	63	Stirling Alb	57
3	2014–15	108	Albion R	71	Queen's Park§	61	Arbroath§	56

RELEGATED CLUBS

RELEGATED FROM DIVISION I (1921–22 to 1973–74)

1921–22 *Dumbarton, Queen's Park, Clydebank
1922–23 Albion R, Alloa Ath
1923–24 Clyde, Clydebank
1924–25 Ayr U, Third Lanark
1925–26 Raith R, Clydebank
1926–27 Morton, Dundee U
1927–28 Bo'ness, Dunfermline Ath
1928–29 Third Lanark, Raith R
1929–30 Dundee U, St Johnstone
1930–31 Hibernian, East Fife
1931–32 Dundee U, Leith Ath
1932–33 Morton, East Stirling
1933–34 Third Lanark, Cowdenbeath
1934–35 St Mirren, Falkirk
1935–36 Airdrieonians, Ayr U
1936–37 Dunfermline Ath, Albion R
1937–38 Dundee, Morton
1938–39 Queen's Park, Raith R
1946–47 Kilmarnock, Hamilton A
1947–48 Airdrieonians, Queen's Park
1948–49 Morton, Albion R
1949–50 Queen of the South, Stirling Alb
1950–51 Clyde, Falkirk

1951–52 Morton, Stirling Alb
1952–53 Motherwell, Third Lanark
1953–54 Airdrieonians, Hamilton A
1954–55 *No clubs relegated as league extended to 18 teams*
1955–56 Clyde, Stirling Alb
1956–57 Dunfermline Ath, Ayr U
1957–58 East Fife, Queen's Park
1958–59 Falkirk, Queen of the South
1959–60 Stirling Alb, Arbroath
1960–61 Clyde, Ayr U
1961–62 St Johnstone, Stirling Alb
1962–63 Clyde, Raith R
1963–64 Queen of the South, East Stirling
1964–65 Airdrieonians, Third Lanark
1965–66 Morton, Hamilton A
1966–67 St Mirren, Ayr U
1967–68 Motherwell, Stirling Alb
1968–69 Falkirk, Arbroath
1969–70 Raith R, Partick Thistle
1970–71 St Mirren, Cowdenbeath
1971–72 Clyde, Dunfermline Ath
1972–73 Kilmarnock, Airdrieonians
1973–74 East Fife, Falkirk

Season 1921–22 – only 1 club promoted, 3 clubs relegated.

RELEGATED FROM PREMIER DIVISION (1974–75 to 1997–98)

1974–75 *No relegation due to League reorganization*
1975–76 Dundee, St Johnstone
1976–77 Hearts, Kilmarnock
1977–78 Ayr U, Clydebank
1978–79 Hearts, Motherwell
1979–80 Dundee, Hibernian
1980–81 Kilmarnock, Hearts
1981–82 Partick Thistle, Airdrieonians
1982–83 Morton, Kilmarnock
1983–84 St Johnstone, Motherwell
1984–85 Dumbarton, Morton
1985–86 *No relegation due to League reorganization*

1986–87 Clydebank, Hamilton A
1987–88 Falkirk, Dunfermline Ath, Morton
1988–89 Hamilton A
1989–90 Dundee
1990–91 *No clubs relegated*
1991–92 St Mirren, Dunfermline Ath
1992–93 Falkirk, Airdrieonians
1993–94 *See footnote.* St Johnstone, Raith R, Dundee
1994–95 Dundee U
1995–96 Partick Thistle, Falkirk
1996–97 Raith R
1997–98 Hibernian

RELEGATED FROM PREMIER LEAGUE (1998–99 to 2012–13)

1998–99 Dunfermline Ath
1999–2000 *No relegation due to League reorganization*
2000–01 St Mirren
2001–02 St Johnstone
2002–03 *No clubs relegated*
2003–04 Partick Thistle
2005–06 Livingston
2006–07 Dunfermline Ath

2007–08 Gretna
2008–09 Inverness CT
2009–10 Hamilton A
2010–11 Hamilton A
2011–12 Dunfermline Ath, Rangers (demoted to third division)
2012–13 Dundee

RELEGATED FROM SPFL SCOTTISH PREMIERSHIP (2013–14 to 2014–15)

2013–14　Hibernian, Hearts　　　　　　　　　2014–15　St Mirren

RELEGATED FROM FIRST DIVISION (1975–76 to 2013–14)

1975–76　Dunfermline Ath, Clyde	1994–95　Ayr U, Stranraer
1976–77　Raith R, Falkirk	1995–96　Hamilton A, Dumbarton
1977–78　Alloa Ath, East Fife	1996–97　Clydebank, East Fife
1978–79　Montrose, Queen of the South	1997–98　Partick Thistle, Stirling Alb
1979–80　Arbroath, Clyde	1998–99　Hamilton A, Stranraer
1980–81　Stirling Alb, Berwick R	1999–2000　Clydebank
1981–82　East Stirling, Queen of the South	2000–01　Morton, Alloa Ath
1982–83　Dunfermline Ath, Queen's Park	2001–02　Raith R
1983–84　Raith R, Alloa Ath	2002–03　Alloa Ath, Arbroath
1984–85　Meadowbank Thistle, St Johnstone	2003–04　Ayr U, Brechin C
1985–86　Ayr U, Alloa Ath	2004–05　Partick Thistle, Raith R
1986–87　Brechin C, Montrose	2005–06　Stranraer, Brechin C
1987–88　East Fife, Dumbarton	2006–07　Airdrie U, Ross Co
1988–89　Kilmarnock, Queen of the South	2007–08　Stirling Alb
1989–90　Albion R, Alloa Ath	2008–09　Livingstone *(for breaching rules)*, Clyde
1990–91　Clyde, Brechin C	2009–10　Airdrie U, Ayr U
1991–92　Montrose, Forfar Ath	2010–11　Cowdenbeath, Stirling Alb
1992–93　Meadowbank Thistle, Cowdenbeath	2011–12　Ayr U, Queen of the South
1993–94　*See footnote.* Dumbarton, Stirling Alb, Clyde, Morton, Brechin C	2012–13　Dunfermline Ath, Airdrie U

RELEGATED FROM SPFL SCOTTISH CHAMPIONSHIP (2013–14 to 2014–15)

2013–14　Greenock Morton　　　　　　　　　2014–15　Cowdenbeath

RELEGATED FROM SECOND DIVISION (1993–94 to 2012–13)

1993–94　*See footnote.* Alloa Ath, Forfar Ath, East Stirlingshire, Montrose, Queen's Park, Arbroath, Albion R, Cowdenbeath

1994–95　Meadowbank Thistle, Brechin C	2004–05　Arbroath, Berwick R
1995–96　Forfar Ath, Montrose	2005–06　Dumbarton
1996–97　Dumbarton, Berwick R	2006–07　Stranraer, Forfar Ath
1997–98　Stenhousemuir, Brechin C	2007–08　Cowdenbeath, Berwick R
1998–99　East Fife, Forfar Ath	2008–09　Queen's Park, Stranraer
1999–2000　Hamilton A *(after being deducted 15 points)*	2009–10　Arbroath, Clyde
2000–01　Queen's Park, Stirling Alb	2010–11　Alloa Ath, Peterhead
2001–02　Morton	2011–12　Stirling Alb
2002–03　Stranraer, Cowdenbeath	2012–13　Albion R
2003–04　East Fife, Stenhousemuir	

RELEGATED FROM SPFL SCOTTISH LEAGUE ONE (2013–14 to 2014-15)

2013–14　East Fife, Arbroath　　　　　　　　2014–15　Stirling Alb

SCOTTISH LEAGUE CHAMPIONSHIP WINS

Rangers 54, Celtic 46, Aberdeen 4, Hearts 4, Hibernian 4, Dumbarton 2, Dundee 1, Dundee U 1, Kilmarnock 1, Motherwell 1, Third Lanark 1.

The totals for Rangers and Dumbarton each include the shared championship of 1890–91.

Since the formation of the Scottish Football League in 1890, there have been periodic reorganisations of the leagues to allow for expansion, improve competition and commercial aspects of the game. The table below lists the league names by tier and chronology. This table can be used to assist when studying the records.

Tier	Division		Tier	Division	
1	Scottish League Division I	1890–1939	3	Scottish League Division III	1923–1926
	Scottish League Division A	1946–1956		Scottish League Division C	1946–1949
	Scottish League Division I	1956–1975		Second Division	1975–2013
	Premier Division	1975–1998		SPFL League One	2013–
	Scottish Premier League	1998–2013	4	Third Division	1994–2013
	SPFL Premiership	2013–		SPFL League Two	2013–
2	Scottish League Division II	1893–1939			
	Scottish League Division B	1946–1956			
	Scottish League Division II	1956–1975			
	First Division	1975–2013			
	SPFL Championship	2013–			

In 2013–14 the SPFL introduced play-offs to determine a second promotion/relegation place for the Premiership, Championship and League One.

In each division, the team finishing second bottom plays two legs against the team from the lower division that won the eliminator games played between the teams finishing second, third and fourth.

In 2014–15 a play-off was introduced for promotion/relegation from League Two. The team finishing bottom of League Two plays two legs against the victors of the eliminator games between the winners of the Highland and Lowland leagues.

SCOTTISH LEAGUE PLAY-OFFS 2014–15

■ *Denotes player sent off.*

SCOTTISH PREMIER QUARTER-FINAL FIRST LEG

Saturday, 9 May 2015

Queen of the South (0) 1 *(Lyle 64)*

Rangers (1) 2 *(Smith 44, Shiels 75)* 5224

Queen of the South: (442) Clark; Dowie, Durnan, Higgins, Holt; Kidd (Russell 83), McKenna (Millar 59), McShane, Carmichael; Reilly, Lyle (Paton 76).
Rangers: (442) Bell; Foster, Zaliukas, McGregor, Wallace; Shiels, Law, Murdoch, Smith (Crawford 62); Miller, Vuckic (Clark 82).
Referee: Alan Muir.

SCOTTISH PREMIER QUARTER-FINAL SECOND LEG

Sunday, 17 May 2015

Rangers (0) 1 *(Wallace 60)*

Queen of the South (1) 1 *(Lyle 35)* 48,035

Rangers: (4132) Bell; Foster, McGregor, Zaliukas, Wallace; Murdoch; Shiels (Smith 86), Vuckic, Law; Miller, Clark (Mohsni 86).
Queen of the South: (352) Clark; Durnan (Russell 69), Dowie, Higgins; Kidd, McShane, Carmichael, Millar (McKenna 62), Holt; Lyle, Reilly (Smith A 73).
Rangers won 3-2 on aggregate.
Referee: Kevin Clancy.

SCOTTISH PREMIER SEMI-FINAL FIRST LEG

Wednesday, 20 May 2015

Rangers (1) 2 *(Clark 44, Miller 63)*

Hibernian (0) 0 41,236

Rangers: (41212) Bell; Foster, McGregor, Zaliukas, Wallace; Murdoch; Shiels (Black 76), Law; Vuckic; Miller (Boyd 78), Clark (Smith 74).
Hibernian: (41212) Oxley; Gray, Hanlon, Fontaine, Stevenson; Robertson (McGeouch 65); Fyvie, Craig; Allan S; Cummings, Malonga.
Referee: Calum Murray.

SCOTTISH PREMIER SEMI-FINAL SECOND LEG

Saturday, 23 May 2015

Hibernian (0) 1 *(Cummings 90)*

Rangers (0) 0 14,742

Hibernian: (41212) Oxley; Gray, Hanlon, Fontaine, Stevenson (Dja Djedje 70); Craig (El Alagui 54); McGeouch, Fyvie; Allan S; Cummings, Malonga.
Rangers: (352) Bell; McGregor, McCulloch, Zaliukas; Foster, Shiels (Black 82), Murdoch, Law, Wallace; Vuckic (Clark 74), Miller (Mohsni 88).
Rangers won 2-1 on aggregate.
Referee: John Beaton.

SCOTTISH PREMIER FINAL FIRST LEG

Thursday, 28 May 2015

Rangers (0) 1 *(McGregor 82)*

Motherwell (2) 3 *(Erwin 27, McManus 40, Ainsworth 47)* 49,200

Rangers: (41212) Bell; Foster, McGregor, Zaliukas (Ferguson 67), Wallace; Murdoch; Shiels (Walsh 54), Law; Vuckic; Miller, Clark (Boyd 55).
Motherwell: (442) Long; Law, Laing, McManus, Hammell (Straker 70); Ainsworth, Lasley, Pearson (Ramsden 82), Johnson; McDonald, Erwin (Moore 88).
Referee: Bobby Madden.

SCOTTISH PREMIER FINAL SECOND LEG

Sunday, 31 May 2015

Motherwell (0) 3 *(Johnson 52, Ainsworth 70, Sutton 90 (pen))*

Rangers (0) 0 9220

Motherwell: (4411) Long; Law, Laing, McManus, Hammell; Ainsworth (Sutton 76), Lasley, Pearson (Grant 74), Johnson (Ramsden 84); McDonald; Erwin.
Rangers: (442) Bell; Foster, McCulloch, Zaliukas (Mohsni 72), Wallace; Vuckic, Murdoch, Law, Ferguson (Walsh 55); Miller, Boyd (Clark 59).
Motherwell won 6-1 on aggregate.
Referee: Craig Thomson.

SCOTTISH CHAMPIONSHIP SEMI-FINALS FIRST LEG

Wednesday, 6 May 2015

Brechin C (0) 0

Alloa Ath (0) 2 *(Chopra 56, Benedictus 90)* 505

Brechin C: (442) Smith; McNeil, McLean, McLauchlan, Hamilton; Masson, Molloy, Fusco (Tapping 72), Barr; Jackson A (Thomson 64), Trouten (Ferguson 86).
Alloa Ath: (442) Gibson; Doyle, Gordon, Benedictus, Meggatt; Cawley, McCord (Holmes 80), Flannigan, Docherty; Chopra (Layne 72), Buchanan (Spence 88).
Referee: Brian Colvin.

Forfar Ath (0) 3 *(Kader 61, Swankie 87, Hay 90)*

Stranraer (0) 0 717

Forfar Ath: (442) Douglas; Travis (Malin 89), Malcolm, Dods, Kennedy; Kader (Hay 72), Young, Fotheringham, Denholm; Templeman (Smith C 74), Swankie.
Stranraer: (4231) Mitchell; Pettigrew, Rumsby, McKeown (McShane 75); Longridge; Bell, Robertson; Winter, Stirling (Malcolm 69), Gibson; Longworth (Stoney 68).
Referee: Stephen Finnie.

SCOTTISH CHAMPIONSHIP SEMI-FINALS SECOND LEG

Saturday, 9 May 2015

Alloa Ath (0) 0

Brechin C (0) 1 *(Trouten 80)* 606

Alloa Ath: (442) Gibson; Doyle (Ferguson 10), Gordon, Benedictus, Meggatt; Flannigan (Hetherington 88), McCord, Docherty, Cawley; Buchanan, Chopra (Holmes 46).
Brechin C: (442) Smith; McLean, McLauchlan, McCormack D, Hamilton; Trouten, Masson, Tapping (Molloy 70), Barr; Jackson A, Thomson.
Alloa Ath won 2-1 on aggregate.
Referee: Crawford Allan.

Stranraer (1) 1 *(Aitken 41 (pen))*

Forfar Ath (0) 1 *(Swankie 53 (pen))* 519

Stranraer: (442) Mitchell; Pettigrew, Robertson, McKeown, Longridge; Winter, Bell, Aitken (Stoney 63); Gibson; Malcolm (Stirling 69), McShane (Longworth 54).
Forfar Ath: (442) Douglas; Travis, Dunlop, Dods, Kennedy; Kader, Young, Fotheringham (Denholm 46), Dale (Malin 59); Templeman (Smith C 73), Swankie.
Forfar Ath won 4-1 on aggregate.
Referee: Bobby Madden.

SCOTTISH CHAMPIONSHIP FINAL FIRST LEG

Wednesday, 13 May 2015

Forfar Ath (1) 3 *(Kader 10, Templeman 57, Travis 90)*

Alloa Ath (0) 1 *(Benedictus 82)* 1212

Forfar Ath: (442) Douglas; Travis, Malcolm, Dods, Kennedy; Kader, Young (Dale 84), Fotheringham (Malin 77), Denholm; Templeman (Smith C 86), Swankie.
Alloa Ath: (442) Gibson; Hetherington, Gordon, Benedictus, Docherty; Cawley, McCord, Flannigan, Holmes (Spence 80); Buchanan, Chopra.
Referee: Kevin Graham.

SCOTTISH CHAMPIONSHIP FINAL SECOND LEG

Sunday, 17 May 2015
Alloa Ath (1) 3 *(Chopra 45, Buchanan 67, Meggatt 84)*
Forfar Ath (0) 0 1423
Alloa Ath: (442) Gibson; Doyle (Holmes■ 33), Gordon, Benedictus, Meggatt; Flannigan, McCord, Docherty, Cawley (Hetherington 71); Buchanan, Chopra (Asghar 87).
Forfar Ath: (4411) Douglas; Travis, Malcolm, Dods, Kennedy (Hay 86); Kader, Young, Fotheringham (Malin 78), Denholm; Templeman; Hilson (Smith C 86).
Alloa Ath won 4-3 on aggregate.
Referee: William Collum.

SCOTTISH LEAGUE ONE SEMI-FINALS FIRST LEG

Wednesday, 6 May 2015
Arbroath (1) 2 *(Murray S 43, 64)*
Queen's Park (2) 2 *(Wharton 18, Fraser 36)* 837
Arbroath: (442) McCallum; Little, Nicoll, Gordon, Lowdon (Johnstone 46); Linn, Whatley, Carreiro (McBride 46), Stewart; McWalter■, Murray S (Buchan 86).
Queen's Park: (451) Muir; Mitchell, Quinn, Wharton, Burns; Berry, Slattery, Woods, Fraser (McPherson 66), Rooney; Carter.
Referee: Craig Charleston.

East Fife (1) 1 *(Brown 3)*
Stenhousemuir (0) 1 *(Lithgow 61)* 679
East Fife: (451) Fleming; Brown, Page, Etxabeguren Leanizbarrutia, Smith S; Dickson (Smith L 60), Mullen, Walker, Leyden (Riordan 74), Smith K (Cook 82); Austin.
Stenhousemuir: (451) Fleming; McCormack, Lithgow, McMillan, Summers; McMullan, Millar K, Meechan, Hodge, Watt (Faulds 85); McMenamin (Grehan 88).
Referee: Euan Anderson.

SCOTTISH LEAGUE ONE SEMI-FINALS SECOND LEG

Saturday, 9 May 2015
Queen's Park (0) 1 *(Quinn 118)*
Arbroath (0) 0 1026
Queen's Park: (4231) Muir; Mitchell, Quinn, Wharton, Burns; Berry (McVey 90), Slattery; Rooney (McPherson 99), Fraser (McElroy 70), Woods; Carter.
Arbroath: (4141) McCallum; Whatley, Little, Gordon, Johnstone (Lowdon 92); Nicoll; Linn, Stewart, Carreiro (Grant 85), McBride; Murray S.
aet; Queen's Park won 3-2 on aggregate.
Referee: Andrew Dallas.

Stenhousemuir (1) 3 *(Millar K 2, McCormack 94, Sutherland 116)*
East Fife (0) 1 *(Page 87)* 799
Stenhousemuir: (442) Fleming; McCormack, Lithgow, McMillan, Summers; Meechan, Millar K, Hodge, Watt (Marenghi 70); McMullan (Sutherland 115), McMenamin (Faulds 85).
East Fife: (451) Fleming; Smith L (Dickson 74), Etxabeguren Leanizbarrutia, Page, Smith S (Cook 62); Mullen (Adeyemo 83), Brown, Walker, Smith K, Riordan; Austin.
aet; Stenhousemuir won 4-2 on aggregate.
Referee: John McKendrick.

SCOTTISH LEAGUE ONE FINAL FIRST LEG

Wednesday, 13 May 2015
Queen's Park (0) 0
Stenhousemuir (0) 1 *(McCormack 55)* 811
Queen's Park: (4231) Muir; Mitchell (McElroy 67), Quinn, Wharton, Burns; Berry (McPherson 80), Slattery; Rooney, Fraser, Woods; Carter.
Stenhousemuir: (442) Fleming; McCormack, McMillan, Lithgow, Summers (Faulds 65); McMullan, Hodge, Meechan, Watt (Marenghi 60); McMenamin, Millar K (Fotheringham 82).
Referee: Barry Cook.

SCOTTISH LEAGUE ONE FINAL SECOND LEG

Saturday, 16 May 2015
Stenhousemuir (1) 1 *(McMenamin 3)*
Queen's Park (0) 1 *(Fraser 59)* 1165
Stenhousemuir: (442) Fleming; McCormack, Meechan, Lithgow, Summers; McMullan, Faulds, Hodge, Marenghi (Fotheringham 90); Grehan (Watt 76), McMenamin.
Queen's Park: (4231) Muir; Mitchell, Quinn, Wharton, Burns; Berry (Rooney 55), Slattery; Woods, McElroy (Carter 55), Fraser; McPherson (Hynes 81).
Stenhousemuir won 2-1 on aggregate.
Referee: Don Robertson.

SCOTTISH LEAGUE TWO SEMI-FINALS FIRST LEG

Saturday, 25 April 2015
Edinburgh C (0) 1 *(Deniran 58)*
Brora R (0) 1 *(Martin Maclean 80)*
Edinburgh C: (442) Stobie; Caddow, McKee, Mbu, Harrison; McFarland, James, Gair (MacDonald 83), Dunn; Allum (Vanson 77), Deniran (McConnell 71).
Brora R: (442) Malin; Houston, McKeown, Munro, Morrison; Martin Maclean, Gillespie, Greig (Macdonald 65), Graham (Maclean C 75); Sutherland, Mackay S.
Referee: David Munro.

SCOTTISH LEAGUE TWO SEMI-FINALS SECOND LEG

Saturday, 2 May 2015
Brora R (0) 1 *(Graham 65)*
Edinburgh C (1) 1 *(Allum 5)*
Brora R: (442) Malin; Houston, Macdonald, McKeown, Kettlewell; Morrison, Martin Maclean, Maclean C, Greig; Mackay S, Graham.
Edinburgh C: (442) Stobie; Caddow, Harrison, McKee■, Mbu; Gibson (MacDonald 81), James, McFarland, Gair (McConnell 65); Allum (Deniran 108), Dunn.
Brora R won 4-2 on penalties.
Referee: Mike Roncone.

SCOTTISH LEAGUE TWO FINAL FIRST LEG

Saturday, 9 May 2015
Brora R (1) 1 *(Andrews 38 (og))*
Montrose (0) 0 525
Brora R: (442) Malin; Houston, Macdonald, McKeown, Munro; Gillespie, Martin Maclean, Morrison, Richardson; Mackay S, Sutherland.
Montrose: (442) McKenzie; Cameron (Allan 54), Steeves, Andrews, Crawford; Masson, Johnston S (Campbell R 70), Watson, Webster; McIntosh (Milne 76), Wood.
Referee: Greg Aitken.

SCOTTISH LEAGUE TWO FINAL SECOND LEG

Saturday, 16 May 2015
Montrose (1) 3 *(Johnston S 37, Andrews 76, Wood 77)*
Brora R (0) 1 *(Maclean C 47)* 2132
Montrose: (442) McKenzie; Masson, Steeves, Andrews, Crawford (Moyes 77); Cameron (McIntosh 72), Webster, Watson, Johnston S; Campbell R (McCord 72), Wood.
Brora R: (442) Malin; Kettlewell, Macdonald, Munro, Gillespie; Martin Maclean, Greig, Richardson, Maclean C (Michael Maclean 71); Sutherland, Mackay S■.
Montrose won 3-2 on aggregate.
Referee: John McKendrick.

SCOTTISH LEAGUE CUP
PRESENTED BY QTS 2014–15

■ *Denotes player sent off.*

FIRST ROUND

Saturday, 2 August 2014
Airdrieonians (0) 1 *(Kirwan 90)*
Stenhousemuir (2) 3 *(Lithgow 8, Sludden 20,*
McMenamin 90)   501
Airdrieonians: (41212) McNeil; Bain, Proctor, Fitzpatrick,
Boyle P; Hamill (Boyle J 80); Stewart (Gray 76), Watt;
Blockley; Lister, Parker (Kirwan 67).
Stenhousemuir: (433) Hamilton; Duncan (Dickson 60),
Lithgow, McMillan, Summers; Faulds, Hodge, Sludden
(Meechan 59); Reid, Grehan (McMenamin 79), Watt.
Referee: Nick Walsh.

Albion R (0) 0
Livingston (0) 0   536
Albion R: (442) Parry; Reid, Dunlop R, Dunlop M,
Turnbull; McKenzie (Pollock 105), Young, McGuigan,
Phillips; Love (Mullin 67), Gemmell.
Livingston: (4231) Jamieson; Sives, Fordyce, Gallacher,
Rutherford; Kyle Jacobs, O'Brien; Glen (Robertson 66),
Mullen (Hippolyte 105), McKenna; Ogleby (White 26).
aet; Livingston won 4-3 on penalties.
Referee: Des Roache.

Alloa Ath (1) 1 *(Spence 27)*
Stirling Alb (0) 0   684
Alloa Ath: (442) Gibson; Doyle, Gordon, Docherty,
Meggatt; Holmes, Simmons, Cawley (Flannigan 70),
McCord; Buchanan (Hetherington 86), Spence.
Stirling Alb: (442) Reidford; Hamilton, Fulton
(Robertson 63), Wedderburn, Creaney; Johnston (Coult
73), Comrie, Smith C, Darren L Smith; Smith G
(Cunningham 80), Doris.
Referee: Colin Steven.

Brechin C (0) 0
Dumbarton (0) 1 *(Graham 59)*   379
Brechin C: (4231) Smith; McCormack J, McLean,
McLauchlan, Hamilton; Fusco, Molloy (Cameron 75);
Trouten, Jackson A, Tapping (Barr 62); Thomson
(Ferguson 62).
Dumbarton: (4231) Rogers; van Zanten, Mair, Graham,
Linton; Agnew, Turner (Kirkpatrick 68); Gilhaney
(McDougall 88), Megginson, Prunty (Campbell 56); Nish.
Referee: Kevin Clancy.

Clyde (1) 1 *(Gray D 45)*
Cowdenbeath (0) 2 *(Milne 51, Miller 90)*   503
Clyde: (442) Barclay; Durie, Marsh, McQueen,
McKinnon; Ferguson S (McColm 61), Gray D (Young
59), Sweeney, Watt; McManus, Sinclair.
Cowdenbeath: (442) Flynn; Brett, Armstrong,
Wedderburn, Adamson (Campbell 46); Miller, O'Brien,
Robertson, Stewart (Johnston 34); Milne, Higgins.
Referee: Matt Northcroft.

Dundee (2) 4 *(Ferry 22, Stewart 45, MacDonald 78,*
Tankulic 82)
Peterhead (0) 0   3079
Dundee: (41212) Letheren; McGinn, Konrad, Benedictus,
Dyer; Thomson; McGowan, Ferry (McBride 63);
Harkins; Stewart (MacDonald 63), Tankulic (Boyle 85).
Peterhead: (352) Smith G; Smith R, Ross, Donaldson;
Sharp, Redman, Stevenson (Brown 85), Strachan
(Gilfillan 71), Noble; McAllister, Rodgers (Cox 53).
Referee: William Collum.

Dunfermline Ath (2) 5 *(Whittle 24, Buchanan 36,*
Moffat 47, Wallace 71, Martin 89)
Annan Ath (0) 1 *(Hopkirk 57)*   1544
Dunfermline Ath: (442) Scully; Williamson, Martin,
Buchanan, Whittle; Falkingham (Thomson 75), Geggan,
Spence, Forbes (Wallace 65); Moffat, El Bakhtaoui
(Smith 75).
Annan Ath: (442) Alex Mitchell; Chisholm, Swinglehurst,
Black, McNiff; McStay, Sloan (Davidson 64 (Brannan
82)), Logan (Flynn 68), Carcary; Todd, Hopkirk.
Referee: John McKendrick.

East Stirling (0) 0
Ayr U (0) 4 *(Donnelly 50, 77, McLaughlin 63 (pen),*
Gilmour 90)   295
East Stirling: (442) Barnard; Kinnaird, Greene,
Bolochoweckyj, Shepherd; Greenhill, Brisbane (Doyle
68), MacGregor (Shield 84), Wright; McKenna■, Vidler
(McMullan 66).
Ayr U: (442) Hutton; Devlin, Campbell, Murphy,
McKinlay (Muir 75); Forrest, McLaughlin, Gilmour,
Donald (McGill 40); Donnelly, McGovern.
Referee: Greg Aitken.

Greenock Morton (1) 2 *(McKee 27, 64)*
Berwick R (0) 1 *(Currie L 63 (pen))*   931
Greenock Morton: (4411) Caraux; Kilday, Crighton,
McCluskey S, Lamie; McKee, Hands (McCluskey J 66),
Miller, Russell (Allan 76); Pepper (O'Neil 84); O'Ware.
Berwick R: (4141) Bald; Jacobs (Russell 65), Fairbairn,
Tulloch, Maxwell; Notman; Willis (Hoskins 76), Currie L,
Currie P■, Lavery; Dalziel (Gold 66).
Referee: Calum Murray.

Hamilton A (1) 2 *(Imrie 3, Longridge 69)*
Arbroath (0) 1 *(Buchan 90)*   730
Hamilton A: (4411) McGovern; Gordon, Devlin,
Canning, Gillespie; Imrie (Lyon 78), MacKinnon,
Crawford (Antoine-Curier 70), Longridge; Redmond;
Scotland (Brophy 78).
Arbroath: (442) Crawford; Travis, Fisher, Nicoll, Lindsay
(Stewart 25); Linn (Murray S 70), Whittle, Hunter,
McBride; McManus (Buchan 76), Whatley.
Referee: Craig Thomson.

Montrose (1) 1 *(Wood 24)*
Falkirk (2) 3 *(Alston 30 (pen), Cooper 45, Shepherd 88)*
                                                   584
Montrose: (442) McKenzie; Masson, Graham, Campbell
A, Bell; Robb (Harkins 73), McCord, Watson, Day
(O'Neill 84); Johnston S, Wood (Deasley 76).
Falkirk: (442) MacDonald; Maybury, McCracken,
Vaulks, Dick; Alston (Sibbald 77), Durojaiye, Taiwo,
McGrandles; Bia Bi (Shepherd 84), Cooper.
Referee: John Beaton.

Queen of the South (2) 5 *(Russell 6, 61, 86, Lyle 35, 90)*
Elgin C (0) 0   939
Queen of the South: (442) Clark; Dowie (Kidd 37),
Durnan, Higgins, Holt; Carmichael, McShane, Fowler
(Dzierzawski 54), Russell; Lyle, Reilly (Smith D 70).
Elgin C: (442) Fraser; McLean, Nicolson, Cooper,
Finlayson; Sutherland, MacPhee, Beveridge (MaCaulay
85), Moore (MacKenzie 65); Cameron (McHardy 75),
Gunn.
Referee: Crawford Allan.

Raith R (1) 4 *(Conroy 34, Elliot 65 (pen), 103, Young 118 (og))*
Forfar Ath (1) 2 *(Denholm 25, 75)* 1143
Raith R: (433) Cuthbert; Thomson, Perry, Watson, McKeown; Scott, Fox (Vaughan 106), Conroy; Stewart (Anderson 72), Nade (Callachan 119), Elliot.
Forfar Ath: (442) Douglas; Dunlop, James, Dods, Steeves (Malin 73); Hilson, Husband (Kader 73), Young, Denholm; Templeman (Dale 73), Swankie.
aet.
Referee: Brian Colvin.

Stranraer (0) 1 *(Malcolm 90)*
East Fife (0) 0 275
Stranraer: (352) Mitchell; Rumsby, Pettigrew, McKeown; Robertson (Aitken 72), Gallagher, Winter, Stirling (Marenghi 66), Longridge; Malcolm, Longworth (Forde 90).
East Fife: (442) Fleming; Mullen, Campbell S, Moyes, Smith S; McAleer, Walker, Beaton, Cook (Brown 46); McShane (Austin 84), Smith K■.
Referee: Andrew Dallas.

Tuesday, 26 August 2014
Queen's Park (1) 1 *(Quinn 31)*
Rangers (1) 2 *(Boyd 7, 53)* 3674
Queen's Park: (451) Muir; Mitchell, Quinn, MacGregor, Gallacher; Woods (McElroy 83), Miller, Fraser, Berry (Carter 88), Fotheringham (Burns 27); McPherson.
Rangers: (442) Simonsen; McGregor, Zaliukas, Mohsni, Wallace; Peralta, McCulloch, Law (Black 76), Macleod; Boyd, Clark.
Referee: Alan Muir.

SECOND ROUND

Tuesday, 26 August 2014
Dundee (2) 4 *(Stewart 3, McGinn P 43, MacDonald 59, Boyle 70)*
Raith R (0) 0 2645
Dundee: (442) Bain; McGinn P, Konrad (McGowan 46), McPake, Irvine; Roberts, Davidson, McAlister (Harkins 67), Boyle; Stewart, MacDonald (Tankulic 71).
Raith R: (451) Cuthbert; Thomson, Watson, Perry (Ellis 84), McKeown; Moon (Callachan 77), Scott, Stewart, Vaughan, Conroy; Nade (Anderson 57).
Referee: Kevin Clancy.

Falkirk (0) 0
Cowdenbeath (0) 0 1128
Falkirk: (4231) MacDonald; Rowan, Grant, Vaulks, Dick; Durojaiye, Taiwo; Alston (Shepherd 78), Sibbald, Cooper (Loy 62); Bia Bi (Boulding 62).
Cowdenbeath: (442) Flynn; Brett, Armstrong (Brownlie 107), Wedderburn, Campbell; Robertson, Milne, Miller, Johnston; Higgins, Oyenuga (Kane 74).
aet; Falkirk won 4-3 on penalties.
Referee: Greg Aitken.

Greenock Morton (0) 0
Partick Thistle (1) 1 *(Doolan 45)* 2005
Greenock Morton: (4411) Caraux; Kilday, Crighton, Milojevic, Lamie; Pepper (McNeil 85), Miller, Hands (McKee 67), Russell; McCluskey S (O'Ware 73); McManus.
Partick Thistle: (4231) Gallacher; O'Donnell, Balatoni, Muirhead, Keenan; Craigen (Stevenson 59), Osman; Lawless (Elliot 73), Fraser, Higginbotham (Bannigan 85); Doolan.
Referee: Stephen Finnie.

Hamilton A (1) 4 *(Andreu 17, Canning 66, Longridge 81, Brophy 87)*
Alloa Ath (1) 1 *(Spence 40)* 649
Hamilton A: (442) McGovern; Gordon, Canning, Devlin, Hendrie (MacKinnon 57); Redmond, Andreu, Gillespie, Longridge; Ryan (Crawford 57), Scotland (Brophy 82).
Alloa Ath: (442) Gibson; Doyle, Gordon, Meggatt, Docherty; Cawley (Flannigan 86), Simmons, McCord, Holmes; Spence (Asghar 86), Buchanan (Ferns 76).
Referee: Crawford Allan.

Hibernian (0) 3 *(El Alagui 78, 84, Stanton 90)*
Dumbarton (0) 2 *(Megginson 52, Gilhaney 59)* 5066
Hibernian: (4411) Oxley; Gray, Forster, Fontaine, Booth; Harris (Cummings 57), Robertson, Allan S, Kennedy; Handling (Stanton 70); El Alagui.
Dumbarton: (4231) Rogers; van Zanten (Prunty 90), Graham, Fleming (Campbell 82), Linton; Taggart, Turner; Gilhaney, Agnew, Megginson; Nish (Kirkpatrick 72).
Referee: Don Robertson.

Kilmarnock (0) 1 *(McKenzie 69)*
Ayr U (0) 0 8877
Kilmarnock: (442) Samson; Barbour, Connolly, Pascali, Chantler; McKenzie, Hamill, Clingan, Obadeyi (Eremenko 37); Magennis (Miller 90), Muirhead (Johnston 55).
Ayr U: (433) Hutton; Devlin, Campbell, Murphy, McKinlay; McLaughlin, Gilmour (McGill 70), McGovern; Forrest (Shirkie 76), Donnelly, Donald.
Referee: Craig Thomson.

Livingston (0) 1 *(Hippolyte 119)*
Queen of the South (0) 0 620
Livingston: (442) Jamieson; Kyle Jacobs (Sives 61), Gallacher, Fordyce, Talbot; McKenna, Keaghan Jacobs, O'Brien, Mullen (Hippolyte 70); White, Glen (Burchill 106).
Queen of the South: (4411) Clark; Holt, Higgins, Durnan, Dowie; Kidd (Smith D 97), Fowler, McShane (Lyle 34), Russell; Dzierzawski; Baird (Carmichael 75).
aet.
Referee: John McKendrick.

St Mirren (0) 2 *(Caldwell 50, 80)*
Dunfermline Ath (1) 1 *(Spence 9)* 1931
St Mirren: (433) Kello; Naismith, McAusland, Plummer, Tesselaar; McGinn, Osbourne (Caldwell 46), McLean; Drury, Thompson (Ball 46), Wylde.
Dunfermline Ath: (41212) Scully; Williamson, Buchanan, Martin, Millen; Spence; Falkingham, Geggan (Forbes 87); Thomson (Stirling 82); Ugwu, Moffat.
Referee: Steven McLean.

Stenhousemuir (1) 1 *(Millar K 38)*
Hearts (2) 2 *(Oliver 6, McHattie 31)* 1768
Stenhousemuir: (352) Fleming; Greacen, Summers, McMillan; Meechan, Dickson (Lithgow 46), Faulds, Hodge, Millar K (Sludden 76); Grehan, Millar R (McMenamin 46).
Hearts: (4231) Hollis; McGhee (Gordon 30), McKay, Smith D, McHattie (Eckersley 88); Smith L, Oliver; Walker, Robinson, Holt; Keatings (Sow 39).
Referee: Calum Murray.

Stranraer (1) 1 *(Winter 3)*
Ross Co (1) 2 *(de Leeuw 15, Boyce 69)* 297
Stranraer: (451) Mitchell; Robertson, Pettigrew, McKeown, Rumsby; Winter, Gallagher, Aitken (Forde 80), Stirling (Marenghi 74), Longridge (Longworth 74); Malcolm.
Ross Co: (4231) Brown; Balk, Boyd, Fenlon (Frempah 33), Celcer; Kiss, Brittain; Carey (Quinn R 80), de Leeuw, Cardle; Jervis (Boyce 59).
Referee: Craig Charleston.

Tuesday, 16 September 2014
Rangers (0) 1 *(Macleod 78)*
Inverness CT (0) 0   15,208
Rangers: (442) Simonsen; McGregor, McCulloch, Mohsni, Wallace; Aird (Templeton 73), Black, Law, Macleod; Clark, Boyd (Daly 72).
Inverness CT: (4231) Brill; Raven, Warren, Meekings, Tremarco; Tansey, Williams (Christie 73); Watkins, Polworth, Doran; McKay.
Referee: Crawford Allan.

THIRD ROUND

Tuesday, 23 September 2014
Aberdeen (1) 4 *(Taylor 8, Rooney 61, 74, 87)*
Livingston (0) 0   6454
Aberdeen: (442) Brown; Logan, Taylor, Reynolds, Hayes; Pawlett, Flood, Jack (Robson 71), Low (Considine 61); Rooney, Goodwillie (Smith 71).
Livingston: (433) Jamieson; Kyle Jacobs, Sives, Fordyce, Talbot; Robertson (Hippolyte 57), O'Brien, Keaghan Jacobs; McKenna (Mullen 79), White, Glen (Ogleby 78).
Referee: Andrew Dallas.

Falkirk (1) 1 *(Loy 5)*
Rangers (1) 3 *(Tudur Jones 7 (og), Shiels 65, Black 90)*
                                                        5259
Falkirk: (451) MacDonald; Shaughnessy, McCracken, Vaulks, Dick (Cooper 80); Leahy, Taiwo (Durojaiye 76), Alston, Tudur Jones (Bia Bi 69), Sibbald; Loy.
Rangers: (442) Simonsen; McGregor, McCulloch, Mohsni, Wallace; Aird (Templeton 56), Law, Black, Smith; Boyd (Daly 78), Shiels (Hardie 86).
Referee: Alan Muir.

Kilmarnock (0) 0
St Johnstone (0) 1 *(Graham 54)*   2550
Kilmarnock: (4411) Samson; Barbour, Connolly, Pascali, Chantler (Westlake 51); Johnston (Miller 67), Clingan (Ngoo 63), Hamill, Obadeyi; Eremenko■; Magennis.
St Johnstone: (4231) Mannus; Miller, Mackay, Anderson, Easton; Millar, Lappin (Wotherspoon 76); Croft (Caddis 86), Davidson, O'Halloran; Graham.
Referee: Steven McLean.

Partick Thistle (0) 1 *(Eccleston 100)*
St Mirren (0) 0   1879
Partick Thistle: (4231) Fox; McMillan, Seaborne, Balatoni, Carroll; Osman, Bannigan; Lawless, Craigen (Stevenson 63), Higginbotham (Elliot 98); Doolan (Eccleston 63).
St Mirren: (4411) Kello; Drury (Kelly 90), McAusland, Goodwin, Tesselaar; Teale (Reilly 26), Osbourne, McLean, Wylde (Caldwell 62); Marwood; Ball.
aet.
Referee: Calum Murray.

Ross Co (0) 0
Hibernian (2) 2 *(Malonga 22, 36)*   1819
Ross Co: (4411) Brown; Fenlon (Brittain 41), Frempah, Dreesen, Carey; Cardle, Irvine, Kiss (Boyce 58), Quinn R; de Leeuw (Gardyne 53); Arquin.
Hibernian: (352) Oxley; Forster, Hanlon, Fontaine; Gray, McGeouch■, Robertson, Craig, Stevenson; Malonga (Heffernan 86), Cummings (Allan S 83).
Referee: Stephen Finnie.

Wednesday, 24 September 2014
Celtic (1) 3 *(Guidetti 24, Commons 57 (pen), Eckersley 61 (og))*
Hearts (0) 0   15,522
Celtic: (4231) Gordon; Ambrose, Denayer (O'Connell 46), van Dijk, Izaguirre; Brown, Johansen; McGregor (Tonev 72), Commons, Stokes; Guidetti (Scepovic 64).
Hearts: (4231) Alexander; Paterson, Wilson, Ozturk, Eckersley; Gomis, Buaben; Walker (Keatings 78), Carrick (Holt 64), Nicholson; Sow (El Hassnaoui 78).
Referee: William Collum.

Dundee U (0) 1 *(Fojut 90)*
Dundee (0) 0   13,041
Dundee U: (4231) Cierzniak; Watson, Morris, Fojut, Dillon; Paton, Rankin (Bilate 57); Spittal (Erskine 77), Armstrong, Dow (Mackay-Steven 54); Ciftci.
Dundee: (442) Letheren; McGinn P, McPake, Konrad, Irvine; Boyle■, McGowan, Ferry, McAlister; Stewart, Tankulic (Roberts 58).
Referee: Craig Thomson.

Hamilton A (0) 0
Motherwell (0) 0   3631
Hamilton A: (4141) McGovern; Gillespie, Gordon, Devlin, Hendrie■; Neil (Lyon 79); Longridge, Crawford, Andreu (Watson 70), Redmond (Imrie 84); Brophy.
Motherwell: (442) Twardzik; Reid, O'Brien■, McManus, Kerr; Ainsworth (Ramsden 105), Lasley, Leitch, Vigurs (Ojamaa 80); Law, Sutton.
aet; Hamilton A won 6-5 on penalties.
Referee: Craig Charleston.

QUARTER-FINALS

Tuesday, 28 October 2014
Rangers (0) 1 *(Macleod 86)*
St Johnstone (0) 0   13,023
Rangers: (442) Simonsen (Robinson 54); Foster, McGregor, McCulloch, Wallace; Aird (Smith 90), Black, Law, Macleod; Miller, Boyd (Daly 74).
St Johnstone: (4411) Mannus; Mackay, Wright, Anderson, Easton; Millar, Davidson (McDonald 23), Lappin (Caddis 75), Croft (McFadden 90); O'Halloran; Graham.
Referee: Steven McLean.

Wednesday, 29 October 2014
Aberdeen (1) 1 *(Rooney 24)*
Hamilton A (0) 0   9311
Aberdeen: (4231) Brown; Logan, Taylor, Reynolds, Considine; Flood, Jack; McGinn (Robson 90), Pawlett (Smith 66), Hayes; Rooney.
Hamilton A: (451) McGovern; Gordon, Canning, Devlin, Gillespie; Imrie, MacKinnon (Ryan 85), Andreu, Crawford, Longridge (Routledge 52); Antoine-Curier.
Referee: Bobby Madden.

Celtic (1) 6 *(Guidetti 31, 52, 56 (pen), Izaguirre 48, Griffiths 62, 68)*
Partick Thistle (0) 0   16,805
Celtic: (4231) Gordon; Lustig, Denayer, van Dijk, Izaguirre; Brown, Mulgrew; McGregor (Wakaso 46), Johansen, Stokes (Griffiths 58); Guidetti (Scepovic 63).
Partick Thistle: (442) Fox; O'Donnell, Balatoni, Seaborne, McMillan; Bannigan■, Craigen, Osman, Lawless (Higginbotham 57); Elliot (Carroll 64), Eccleston (Doolan 59).
Referee: Kevin Clancy.

Hibernian (1) 3 *(Malonga 16, Cummings 57, Kennedy 78)*
Dundee U (2) 3 *(Erskine 12, Connolly 19, Dow 61)*   8689
Hibernian: (442) Oxley; Gray, Hanlon, Fontaine, Stevenson; Robertson (Stanton 119), Craig, Allan S, Handling (Kennedy 68); Malonga, Cummings (Harris 84).
Dundee U: (352) Cierzniak; Souttar, Fojut, Townsend; Spittal, Connolly (Armstrong 67), Paton (Smith 67), Rankin, Mackay-Steven (Ciftci 20); Dow, Erskine.
aet; Dundee U won 7-6 on penalties.
Referee: John Beaton.

SEMI-FINALS (at Hampden Park)

Saturday, 31 January 2015

Dundee U (0) 2 *(Morris 60, Ciftci 84)*

Aberdeen (0) 1 *(Daniels 49)*   29,608

Dundee U: (4231) Cierzniak; McGowan, Morris, Fojut, Dillon; Paton, Butcher; Telfer (Dow 58), Armstrong, Mackay-Steven; Ciftci (Anier 90).

Aberdeen: (4231) Brown; Logan, Daniels, Reynolds, Considine; Jack, Hayes; McGinn, Pawlett (Smith 85), Rooney; Goodwillie.

Referee: Steven McLean.

Sunday, 1 February 2015

Celtic (2) 2 *(Griffiths 10, Commons 31)*

Rangers (0) 0   50,925

Celtic: (4231) Gordon; Lustig (Matthews 84), Denayer, van Dijk, Izaguirre; Brown, Biton; Commons, Johansen, Stokes (Forrest 74); Griffiths (Guidetti 68).

Rangers: (4141) Simonsen; Foster, McGregor, McCulloch, Wallace; Black; Aird (Daly 46), Law, Hutton, Smith; Miller (Clark 81).

Referee: Craig Thomson.

SCOTTISH LEAGUE CUP PRESENTED BY QTS FINAL 2015

Sunday, 15 March 2015

(at Hampden Park, attendance 49,259)

Celtic (1) 2   Dundee U (0) 0

Celtic: (4231) Gordon; Ambrose, Denayer, van Dijk, Izaguirre; Brown, Biton (Henderson 82); Commons (Forrest 69), Johansen, Stokes; Griffiths (Guidetti 69).

Scorers: Commons 28, Forest 79.

Dundee U: (4411) Cierzniak; Dillon▪, Morris, Fojut, Dixon; McGowan, Butcher, Paton (Erskine 72), Rankin; Dow; Bilate (Anier 59).

Referee: Bobby Madden.

Celtic skipper Scott Brown and team-mates celebrate their 2-0 victory over Dundee United in the QTS Scottish League Cup final at Hampden on 15 March. (Danny Lawson/PA Wire/Press Association Images)

SCOTTISH LEAGUE CUP FINALS 1946–2015

SCOTTISH LEAGUE CUP

1946–47	Rangers v Aberdeen	4-0
1947–48	East Fife v Falkirk	0-0*
Replay	East Fife v Falkirk	4-1
1948–49	Rangers v Raith R	2-0
1949–50	East Fife v Dunfermline Ath	3-0
1950–51	Motherwell v Hibernian	3-0
1951–52	Dundee v Rangers	3-2
1952–53	Dundee v Kilmarnock	2-0
1953–54	East Fife v Partick Thistle	3-2
1954–55	Hearts v Motherwell	4-2
1955–56	Aberdeen v St Mirren	2-1
1956–57	Celtic v Partick Thistle	0-0*
Replay	Celtic v Partick Thistle	3-0
1957–58	Celtic v Rangers	7-1
1958–59	Hearts v Partick Thistle	5-1
1959–60	Hearts v Third Lanark	2-1
1960–61	Rangers v Kilmarnock	2-0
1961–62	Rangers v Hearts	1-1*
Replay	Rangers v Hearts	3-1
1962–63	Hearts v Kilmarnock	1-0
1963–64	Rangers v Morton	5-0
1964–65	Rangers v Celtic	2-1
1965–66	Celtic v Rangers	2-1
1966–67	Celtic v Rangers	1-0
1967–68	Celtic v Dundee	5-3
1968–69	Celtic v Hibernian	6-2
1969–70	Celtic v St Johnstone	1-0
1970–71	Rangers v Celtic	1-0
1971–72	Partick Thistle v Celtic	4-1
1972–73	Hibernian v Celtic	2-1
1973–74	Dundee v Celtic	1-0
1974–75	Celtic v Hibernian	6-3
1975–76	Rangers v Celtic	1-0
1976–77	Aberdeen v Celtic	2-1*
1977–78	Rangers v Celtic	2-1*
1978–79	Rangers v Aberdeen	2-1

BELL'S LEAGUE CUP

1979–80	Dundee U v Aberdeen	0-0*
Replay	Dundee U v Aberdeen	3-0
1980–81	Dundee U v Dundee	3-0

SCOTTISH LEAGUE CUP

1981–82	Rangers v Dundee U	2-1
1982–83	Celtic v Rangers	2-1
1983–84	Rangers v Celtic	3-2*

SKOL CUP

1984–85	Rangers v Dundee U	1-0
1985–86	Aberdeen v Hibernian	3-0
1986–87	Rangers v Celtic	2-1
1987–88	Rangers v Aberdeen	3-3*
	Rangers won 5-3 on penalties.	
1988–89	Rangers v Aberdeen	3-2
1989–90	Aberdeen v Rangers	2-1*
1990–91	Rangers v Celtic	2-1*
1991–92	Hibernian v Dunfermline Ath	2-0
1992–93	Rangers v Aberdeen	2-1*

SCOTTISH LEAGUE CUP

1993–94	Rangers v Hibernian	2-1

COCA-COLA CUP

1994–95	Raith R v Celtic	2-2*
	Raith R won 6-5 on penalties.	
1995–96	Aberdeen v Dundee	2-0
1996–97	Rangers v Hearts	4-3
1997–98	Celtic v Dundee U	3-0

SCOTTISH LEAGUE CUP

1998–99	Rangers v St Johnstone	2-1

CIS INSURANCE CUP

1999–2000	Celtic v Aberdeen	2-0
2000–01	Celtic v Kilmarnock	3-0
2001–02	Rangers v Ayr U	4-0
2002–03	Rangers v Celtic	2-1
2003–04	Livingston v Hibernian	2-0
2004–05	Rangers v Motherwell	5-1
2005–06	Celtic v Dunfermline Ath	3-0
2006–07	Hibernian v Kilmarnock	5-1
2007–08	Rangers v Dundee U	2-2*
	Rangers won 3-2 on penalties.	

CO-OPERATIVE INSURANCE CUP

2008–09	Celtic v Rangers	2-0*
2009–10	Rangers v St Mirren	1-0
2010–11	Rangers v Celtic	2-1*

SCOTTISH COMMUNITIES LEAGUE CUP

2011–12	Kilmarnock v Celtic	1-0
2012–13	St Mirren v Hearts	3-2
2013–14	Aberdeen v Inverness CT	0-0*
	Aberdeen won 4-2 on penalties.	

SCOTTISH LEAGUE CUP PRESENTED BY QTS

2014–15	Celtic v Dundee U	2-0

After extra time.

SCOTTISH LEAGUE CUP WINS

Rangers 27, Celtic 15, Aberdeen 6, Hearts 4, Dundee 3, East Fife 3, Hibernian 3, Dundee U 2, Kilmarnock 1, Livingston 1, Motherwell 1, Partick Thistle 1, Raith R 1, St Mirren 1.

APPEARANCES IN FINALS

Rangers 34, Celtic 30 Aberdeen 13, Hibernian 9, Dundee U 7, Hearts 7, Dundee 6, Kilmarnock 6, Partick Thistle 4, Dunfermline Ath 3, East Fife 3, Motherwell 3, St Mirren 3, Raith R 2, St Johnstone 2, Ayr U 1, Falkirk 1, Inverness CT 1, Livingston 1, Morton 1, Third Lanark 1.

PETROFAC TRAINING SCOTTISH LEAGUE CHALLENGE CUP 2014-15

■ *Denotes player sent off.*

FIRST ROUND NORTH

Saturday, 26 July 2014

Arbroath (0) 1 *(Tiffoney 89 (og))*

Alloa Ath (1) 4 *(Simmons 9, Spence 54, 70, 83)*   560

Arbroath: (442) Crawford; Travis, Fisher, Whittle, Johnstone; Linn, Hunter (McWalter 87), Nicoll (Whatley 57), McBride (Buchan 67); McManus, Murray S.
Alloa Ath: (442) Gibson; Doyle (Tiffoney 87), Gordon, Meggatt, Docherty; Cawley, McCord, Simmons (Asghar 82), Holmes; Spence, Buchanan (Flannigan 67).
Referee: Don Robertson.

Brora R (1) 3 *(Sutherland 32, 92, 104)*

Stenhousemuir (0) 1 *(Grehan 52 (pen))*   250

Brora R: (442) Malin; Tokely (Porritt 114), Munro, Houston, Williamson; Graham, Morrison, Martin Maclean (Gillespie 91), Greig (MacKay J 63); Mackay S, Sutherland.
Stenhousemuir: (433) Hamilton; Duncan, McMillan, Lithgow, Summers; Hodge, Faulds (McMenamin 99), Dickson (Sludden 85); Reid (Millar R 85), Grehan, Watt.
aet.
Referee: Matt Northcroft.

Cowdenbeath (1) 1 *(Higgins 13)*

Brechin C (0) 3 *(Thomson 64, Trouten 93, Ferguson 108)*   294

Cowdenbeath: (352) Thomson; Armstrong, O'Brien (Johnston 73), Wedderburn; Robertson, Miller, Stewart, Kane (Campbell 97), Adamson; Sutherland (Brownlie 86), Higgins.
Brechin C: (451) Smith; McLean, McCormack J, McCormack D, Hamilton; Trouten, Molloy, Barr (Ferguson 71), Fusco (Thomson 63), Tapping (Brash 76); Jackson A.
aet.
Referee: Gavin Duncan.

East Fife (2) 2 *(McShane 15, Moyes 43)*

Forfar Ath (0) 1 *(Hilson 72)*   449

East Fife: (442) Fleming; Mullen, Moyes, Campbell S, Smith S; McAleer (Barr 75), Walker, Beaton, Cook; McShane (Austin 82), Smith K.
Forfar Ath: (442) Douglas; Baxter (James 46), Dunlop, Malcolm, Steeves; Kader (Dale 65), Young, Husband (Templeman 66), Denholm; Hilson, Swankie.
Referee: Alan Newlands.

East Stirling (0) 1 *(McKenna 71)*

Falkirk (1) 7 *(Vaulks 29, Cooper 62, Loy 67 (pen), 73, Bia Bi 81, Alston 85, 87)*   933

East Stirling: (442) Shaw; Kinnaird, Greene, Bolochoweckyj, Shepherd; Greenhill, Brisbane, MacGregor, Vidler (Glasgow 59); Wright (McMullan 84), McKenna.
Falkirk: (442) MacDonald; Maybury (Rowan 84), McCracken, Vaulks, Dick; Taiwo, Durojaiye (Alston 65), McGrandles, Cooper; Shepherd (Bia Bi 55), Loy.
Referee: Andrew Dallas.

Elgin C (0) 0

Stirling Alb (0) 3 *(Darren L Smith 48, Smith G 59 (pen), 78)*   470

Elgin C: (442) Fraser; Beveridge, Cooper■, Nicolson, Finlayson (Cook 66); MacKenzie (Cameron 73), McLean, MacPhee, Moore; Gunn, Sutherland (Bayne 66).
Stirling Alb: (442) Paterson; Hamilton, Wedderburn, Smith C, Creaney (Coult 62); Johnston (Cunningham 73), Comrie, Fulton (Robertson 66), Darren L Smith; Smith G, Doris.
Referee: Nick Walsh.

Montrose (0) 0

Peterhead (3) 3 *(Rodgers 5, McAllister 17, Stevenson 27)*   347

Montrose: (442) McKenzie; Webster■, Graham, Campbell A, Bell; O'Neill (Masson 62), Robb (Cavanagh 77), McCord, Watson; Wood■, Johnston S (Deasley 83).
Peterhead: (352) Smith G; Smith R, Ross (Brown 55), Donaldson (Cox 51); Sharp, Redman, Stevenson, Strachan, Noble; Rodgers (McCann 77), McAllister.
Referee: Colin Steven.

Tuesday, 5 August 2014

Dunfermline Ath (0) 1 *(Millen 82)*

Raith R (0) 0   4230

Dunfermline Ath: (4411) Scully; Millen, Martin, Buchanan, Drummond; Geggan, Falkingham, Spence, Byrne (Thomson 87); El Bakhtaoui (Ugwu 88); Moffat.
Raith R: (451) Cuthbert; Thomson, Perry, Watson, McKeown; Stewart, Fox (Callachan 78), Vaughan, Scott, Conroy; Nade.
Referee: Alan Muir.

FIRST ROUND SOUTH

Friday, 25 July 2014

Queen's Park (1) 1 *(McPherson 33)*

Berwick R (1) 1 *(Lavery 3)*   245

Queen's Park: (4231) Muir; Mitchell, Gallacher, McPherson (Carter 63), Miller; Quinn, MacGregor; Berry, Fraser■, Fotheringham (McElroy 71); Woods (Davison 111).
Berwick R: (41212) Bald; Notman, Fairbairn, Tulloch, Maxwell; Cameron (Jacobs 70); Willis, Gold (Hoskins 76); Currie P; Russell, Lavery (Dalziel 87).
aet; Berwick won 4-3 on penalties
Referee: Kevin Graham.

Saturday, 26 July 2014

Airdrieonians (1) 2 *(Watt 6, Blockley 63)*

Albion R (1) 2 *(Love 39, Gemmell 87)*   851

Airdrieonians: (442) McNeil (Birnstingl 46); Bain, Proctor, Fitzpatrick, Boyle P; Gray (Stewart 71), Hamill, Blockley (Boyle J 111), Watt; Lister, Parker.
Albion R: (433) Parry; Reid, Dunlop R, Dunlop M, Turnbull; Young, Fisher (Mullin 63), McKenzie (Cusack 80); Love (Pollock 84), Gemmell, Phillips.
aet; Albion won 4-2 on penalties.
Referee: Bobby Madden.

Clyde (2) 2 *(McManus 8, Sweeney 29 (pen))*

Ayr U (0) 0   689

Clyde: (433) Barclay; Durie, Marsh, McQueen, McKinnon (Frances 77); Sweeney, Gray D, Sinclair; Ferguson S, McManus (McColm 63), Watt.
Ayr U: (442) Hutton; Devlin, Murphy, McLaughlin, Donald; Forrest, Gilmour (McKinlay 71), McArthur, McGill; Donnelly, McGovern.
Referee: Stephen Finnie.

Greenock Morton (1) 1 *(O'Neil 27)*

Spartans (0) 0   928

Greenock Morton: (4411) Gaston; Kilday, O'Ware, Milojevic, Lamie; O'Neil (Stevenson 83), McKee, Miller, Russell; McNeil (Scullion 78); Barrowman (Allan 29).
Spartans: (451) Swain; O'Donnell (MacKinnon 80), Bruce, Sivewright, Cennerazzo; Henretty, Beesley, Muhsin (McLeod 66); Bremner, Stevenson; Herd.
Referee: Gavin Ross.

Hearts (3) 3 *(King 8, Sow 19, Paterson 40)*
Annan Ath (0) 1 *(Davidson 90)*   6708
Hearts: (442) Alexander; Paterson (McGhee 46), Ozturk, Wilson, McHattie; Nicholson, Gomis, Buaben (Holt 64), King; Carrick, Sow (Oliver 75).
Annan Ath: (442) Alex Mitchell; Watson, McNiff, Black, Chisholm; McStay, Swinglehurst, Flynn (Logan 56), Carcary (Sloan 68); Todd (Davidson 84), Hopkirk.
Referee: Calum Murray.

Queen of the South (1) 3 *(Dowie 24, Russell 56, Paton 107)*
Livingston (0) 4 *(Sives 58, Mullen 65, Hippolyte 98, Robertson 115)*   1196
Queen of the South: (4231) Clark; Kidd, Durnan, Dowie, Holt; Fowler, McShane (Dzierzawski 73); Carmichael, Paton, Russell (Smith D 78); Reilly (Lyle 73).
Livingston: (4231) Jamieson; Fordyce, Sives, Gallacher, Rutherford; McKenna, O'Brien; Kyle Jacobs, Mullen (Robertson 105), Glen (Hippolyte 70); Ogleby (White 69).
aet.
Referee: Craig Charleston.

Stranraer (0) 3 *(McKeown 64, 77, Winter 90)*
Dumbarton (2) 2 *(Kirkpatrick 4, Gilhaney 45)*   355
Stranraer: (442) Mitchell; Rumsby, Pettigrew, McKeown, Longridge; Robertson, Gallagher, Stirling (Marenghi 79), Winter; Malcolm, Longworth (Forde 72).
Dumbarton: (442) Grindlay; van Zanten, Graham, Taggart, Linton; Murray, Gilhaney (Nish 46), Agnew, Kirkpatrick (Prunty 63); Fleming (Campbell 46), Megginson.
Referee: Des Roache.

Tuesday, 5 August 2014
Rangers (1) 2 *(Macleod 14, Law 101)*
Hibernian (0) 1 *(Handling 59)*   18,138
Rangers: (352) Bell; McGregor (Templeton 67), McCulloch, Zaliukas; Foster, Black, Law, Macleod (Aird 109), Wallace; Miller, Boyd.
Hibernian: (4231) Oxley; Gray, Forster, Hanlon, Stevenson; Robertson (Tudur Jones 103), Craig; Harris, Handling■, Stanton (Heffernan 74); El Alagui (Allan 97).
aet.
Referee: John Beaton.

SECOND ROUND NORTH

Tuesday, 19 August 2014
Brechin C (0) 0
Peterhead (1) 2 *(Redman 8, Noble 58)*   328
Brechin C: (4231) Smith; McCormack J, McLean, McCormack D, Hamilton; Fusco (Cameron 64), Molloy; Trouten, Jackson A, Barr (Tapping 64); Thomson (Ferguson 64).
Peterhead: (442) Smith G; Donaldson, Ross, Smith R, Noble; Sharp, Redman, Stevenson (McCann 79 (Gilfillan 83)), Cowie; Cox (Millar 63), McAllister.
Referee: Craig Charleston.

Brora R (2) 2 *(Mackay S 29, Sutherland 38)*
East Fife (2) 3 *(McShane 34 (pen), 42, Austin 86)*   395
Brora R: (442) Malin; Tokely, Houston, Munro, Ross; Maclean, Gillespie, Morrison, Greig; Sutherland, Mackay S.
East Fife: (442) Fleming; Mullen, Campbell S, Moyes, Smith S; McAleer (Brown 46), Smith K (Cook 67), Walker, Austin; McShane, Barr (Beaton 53).
Referee: John McKendrick.

Dunfermline Ath (0) 1 *(Geggan 68)*
Falkirk (0) 2 *(Taiwo 55, 60)*   2810
Dunfermline Ath: (442) Scully; Millen, Martin, Page (Williamson 65), Drummond; Geggan, Spence, Falkingham, Forbes (Ugwu 65); El Bakhtaoui, Moffat.
Falkirk: (433) MacDonald; Maybury, Vaulks, McCracken, Dick; Durojaiye, McGrandles (Leahy 85), Taiwo; Alston (Bia Bi■ 52), Loy, Cooper (Sibbald 52).
Referee: George Salmond.

Stirling Alb (0) 1 *(Darren L Smith 82)*
Alloa Ath (0) 2 *(Spence 49, 69)*   537
Stirling Alb: (442) Reidford; Hamilton, Wedderburn, Smith C, Forsyth; Darren L Smith, Comrie, Robertson (Darren Smith 76), Weir; Smith G (Coult 71), Cunningham (Fulton 77).
Alloa Ath: (41212) Gibson; Doyle, Marr (Docherty 43), Gordon, Meggatt; Hetherington; Cawley, Holmes; McCord (Simmons 85); Spence, Buchanan (Ferns 71).
Referee: Euan Anderson.

SECOND ROUND SOUTH

Monday, 18 August 2014
Rangers (5) 8 *(Boyd 16, 33, 79, Aird 24, McCulloch 38, 77, Macleod 45, 65)*
Clyde (0) 1 *(Watt 90)*   11,190
Rangers: (442) Simonsen; McGregor, Zaliukas (Faure 65), Mohsni, Wallace; Aird, Law (Templeton 72), McCulloch, Macleod; Clark (Shiels 61), Boyd.
Clyde: (451) Barclay; Durie, Marsh, McQueen, McKinnon; Ferguson S, Sweeney (Young 46), Watt, Gray D (Daly 46), Sinclair; McManus (Frances 46).
Referee: Andrew Dallas.

Tuesday, 19 August 2014
Greenock Morton (2) 5 *(McCluskey J 14, O'Ware 45, McManus 105, 114, 117)*
Berwick R (1) 2 *(Maxwell 9, Currie L 90)*   906
Greenock Morton: (442) Caraux; Miller (Hands 77), Crighton, Milojevic, Lamie; McCluskey S (Kilday 64), McKee (Russell 87), Pepper, McCluskey J■; McManus, O'Ware.
Berwick R: (4411) Bald; Jacobs (Dargo 79), Fairbairn, Hoskins, Maxwell; Willis, Notman, Cameron (Dalziel 87), Gold; Currie L; Lavery (Russell 74).
aet.
Referee: Barry Cook.

Stra\nraer (2) 2 *(Malcolm 19, Rumsby 37)*
Albion R (0) 1 *(Gemmell 72 (pen))*   236
Stranraer: (352) Mitchell; Rumsby, Pettigrew, McKeown; Robertson, Gallagher, Aitken (Longridge 90), Marenghi (Stirling 81), Winter; Malcolm, Longworth (Forde 89).
Albion R: (541) Parry; Reid, Dunlop R, Donnelly, Dunlop M, Turnbull; Love, Pollock, Fisher (Mullin 47), Cusack (Phillips 72); McGuigan (Gemmell 65).
Referee: Stephen Finnie.

Wednesday, 20 August 2014
Livingston (1) 4 *(White 6, 76, Hippolyte 81, Robertson 84)*
Hearts (0) 1 *(Talbot 90 (og))*   3807
Livingston: (4411) Jamieson; Kyle Jacobs, Gallacher, Fordyce, Talbot; McKenna, Keaghan Jacobs, O'Brien (Beaumont 85), Mullen (Hippolyte 78); Glen (Robertson 37); White.
Hearts: (451) Hollis; Smith L, McGhee, McKay, Gordon (Roy 65); Keatings, Henderson, Beith (McKirdy 85), Robinson, Smith D; Oliver (Buchanan 56).
Referee: Crawford Allan.

QUARTER-FINALS

Saturday, 6 September 2014
Greenock Morton (0) 0
Alloa Ath (0) 1 *(McCord 89)*   1273
Greenock Morton: (41212) Caraux; Kilday, Crighton, Milojevic (Allan 46), Lamie (Hands 46); Miller (McNeil 71); McKee, Pepper; Crawford; McCluskey S, O'Ware.
Alloa Ath: (4231) McDowall; Doyle, Gordon, Meggatt, Docherty; Simmons (Ferns 77), Holmes; Cawley (Flannigan 60), Buchanan, McCord; Spence.
Referee: Des Roache.

Peterhead (0) 0

Livingston (0) 1 *(Hippolyte 113)* 695

Peterhead: (352) Smith G; Donaldson, Strachan (Rodgers■ 65), Ross; Sharp, Redman, Cowie, Brown (Cox 55), Noble; Stevenson, McAllister (Gilfillan 75).

Livingston: (442) Jamieson; Kyle Jacobs, Sives, Fordyce, Talbot; Keaghan Jacobs, O'Brien, Robertson (Hippolyte 80), Glen (Burchill 81); White, McKenna (Ogleby 105). *aet.*

Referee: Brian Colvin.

Stranraer (1) 1 *(Marenghi 41)*

Falkirk (0) 0 551

Stranraer: (451) Mitchell; Robertson, Rumsby, McKeown, Pettigrew (Longridge 82); Gibson, Gallagher, Aitken (Longworth 72), Stirling, Marenghi (Winter 69); Malcolm.

Falkirk: (352) MacDonald; Vaulks, McCracken, Shaughnessy; Alston (Boulding 68), Sibbald, Taiwo, Leahy, Cooper (Shepherd 50); Blair, Loy.

Referee: Euan Anderson.

Tuesday, 21 October 2014

East Fife (0) 0

Rangers (1) 2 *(Daly 29, Black 57)* 1827

East Fife: (442) Fleming; Brown, Moyes, Campbell S, Barr; McAleer (Campbell R 72), Walker, Beaton; McShane (Maskrey 87), Austin (Falconer 81).

Rangers: (442) Simonsen; Foster, McGregor, McCulloch, Wallace; Aird, Black, Law (Shiels 71), Templeton; Daly (Miller 72), Clark (Boyd 83).

Referee: George Salmond.

SEMI-FINALS

Sunday, 12 October 2014

Livingston (0) 1 *(Glen 66)*

Stranraer (1) 1 *(Longworth 45)* 845

Livingston: (442) Jamieson; Kyle Jacobs, Fordyce, Sives, Talbot; McKenna (Burchill 98), O'Brien, Keaghan Jacobs, Rutherford (Hippolyte 46); White, Mullen (Glen 60).

Stranraer: (442) Mitchell; Gallagher, Rumsby, McKeown, Longridge (Russell 105); Winter, Aitken, Stirling 80), Gibson (Marenghi 69); Malcolm, Longworth.

aet; Livingston won 5-4 on penalties.

Referee: George Salmond.

Wednesday, 3 December 2014

Alloa Ath (0) 3 *(Spence 72, 89, McCord 74)*

Rangers (0) 2 *(Miller 49, Shiels 64)* 2443

Alloa Ath: (442) McDowall; Doyle, Benedictus, Gordon, Meggatt; Asghar (Ferns 69), Hetherington, McCord, Docherty; Spence, Buchanan.

Rangers: (442) Simonsen; McGregor, McCulloch, Mohsni, Foster; Aird (Templeton 81), Law, Black, Macleod (Shiels 13); Boyd (Daly 68), Miller.

Referee: John McKendrick.

PETROFAC TRAINING SCOTTISH LEAGUE CHALLENGE CUP FINAL 2015

Sunday, 5 April 2015

(at McDiarmid Park, attendance 2869)

Livingston (1) 4   Alloa Ath (0) 0

Livingston: (442) Jamieson; Cole, Gallacher, Fordyce, Talbot; Mullen (White 69), Keaghan Jacobs, Kyle Jacobs (Beaumont 88), O'Brien; Hippolyte (Glen 84), Pitman.

Scorers: Pitman 21, Fordyce 61, White 86, 90.

Alloa Ath: (4231) McDowall; Doyle, Gordon, Benedictus, Meggatt; Holmes, Docherty (Flannigan 69); Cawley, McCord (Spence 82), Chopra (Layne 69); Buchanan.

Referee: John Beaton.

LEAGUE CHALLENGE FINALS 1991–2015

B&Q CENTENARY CUP

1990–91	Dundee v Ayr U	3-2*

B&Q CUP

1991–92	Hamilton A v Ayr U	1-0
1992–93	Hamilton A v Morton	3-2
1993–94	Falkirk v St Mirren	3-0
1994–95	Airdrieonians v Dundee	3-2*

SCOTTISH LEAGUE CHALLENGE CUP

1995–96	Stenhousemuir v Dundee U	0-0*
	Stenhousemuir won 5-4 on penalties.	
1996–97	Stranraer v St Johnstone	1-0
1997–98	Falkirk v Queen of the South	1-0
1998–99	*No competition.*	
	Suspended due to lack of sponsorship.	

BELL'S CHALLENGE CUP

1999–2000	Alloa Ath v Inverness CT	4-4*
	Alloa Ath won 5-4 on penalties.	
2000–01	Airdrieonians v Livingston	2-2*
	Airdrieonians won 3-2 on penalties.	
2001–02	Airdrieonians v Alloa Ath	2-1

BELL'S CUP

2002–03	Queen of the South v Brechin C	2-0
2003–04	Inverness CT v Airdrie U	2-0
2004–05	Falkirk v Ross Co	2-1
2005–06	St Mirren v Hamilton A	2-1

SCOTTISH LEAGUE CHALLENGE CUP

2006–07	Ross Co v Clyde	1-1*
	Ross Co won 5-4 on penalties.	
2007–08	St Johnstone v Dunfermline Ath	3-2

ALBA CHALLENGE CUP

2008–09	Airdrie U v Ross Co	2-2*
	Airdrie U won 3-2 on penalties.	
2009–10	Dundee v Inverness CT	3-2
2010–11	Ross Co v Queen of the South	2-0

RAMSDENS CUP

2011–12	Falkirk v Hamilton A	1-0
2012–13	Queen of the South v Partick Thistle	1-1*
	Queen of the South won 6-5 on penalties.	
2013–14	Raith R v Rangers	1-0*

PETROFAC TRAINING SCOTTISH LEAGUE CHALLENGE CUP

2014–15	Livingston v Alloa Athletic	4-0

*After extra time.

SCOTTISH CUP FINALS 1874–2015

SCOTTISH FA CUP

1874	Queen's Park v Clydesdale	2-0
1875	Queen's Park v Renton	3-0
1876	Queen's Park v Third Lanark	1-1
Replay	Queen's Park v Third Lanark	2-0
1877	Vale of Leven v Rangers	1-1
Replay	Vale of Leven v Rangers	1-1
2nd Replay	Vale of Leven v Rangers	3-2
1878	Vale of Leven v Third Lanark	1-0
1879	Vale of Leven v Rangers	1-1
	Vale of Leven awarded cup, Rangers failing to appear for replay.	
1880	Queen's Park v Thornliebank	3-0
1881	Queen's Park v Dumbarton	2-1
Replay	Queen's Park v Dumbarton	3-1
	After Dumbarton protested the first game.	
1882	Queen's Park v Dumbarton	2-2
Replay	Queen's Park v Dumbarton	4-1
1883	Dumbarton v Vale of Leven	2-2
Replay	Dumbarton v Vale of Leven	2-1
1884	Queen's Park v Vale of Leven	
	Queen's Park awarded cup, Vale of Leven failing to appear.	
1885	Renton v Vale of Leven	0-0
Replay	Renton v Vale of Leven	3-1
1886	Queen's Park v Renton	3-1
1887	Hibernian v Dumbarton	2-1
1888	Renton v Cambuslang	6-1
1889	Third Lanark v Celtic	3-0
Replay	Third Lanark v Celtic	2-1
	Replay by order of Scottish FA because of playing conditions in first match.	
1890	Queen's Park v Vale of Leven	1-1
Replay	Queen's Park v Vale of Leven	2-1
1891	Hearts v Dumbarton	1-0
1892	Celtic v Queen's Park	1-0
Replay	Celtic v Queen's Park	5-1
	After mutually protested first match.	
1893	Queen's Park v Celtic	0-1
Replay	Queen's Park v Celtic	2-1
	Replay by order of Scottish FA because of playing conditions in first match.	
1894	Rangers v Celtic	3-1
1895	St Bernard's v Renton	2-1
1896	Hearts v Hibernian	3-1
1897	Rangers v Dumbarton	5-1
1898	Rangers v Kilmarnock	2-0
1899	Celtic v Rangers	2-0
1900	Celtic v Queen's Park	4-3
1901	Hearts v Celtic	4-3
1902	Hibernian v Celtic	1-0
1903	Rangers v Hearts	1-1
Replay	Rangers v Hearts	0-0
2nd Replay	Rangers v Hearts	2-0
1904	Celtic v Rangers	3-2
1905	Third Lanark v Rangers	0-0
Replay	Third Lanark v Rangers	3-1
1906	Hearts v Third Lanark	1-0
1907	Celtic v Hearts	3-0
1908	Celtic v St Mirren	5-1
1909	Celtic v Rangers	2-2
Replay	Celtic v Rangers	1-1
	Owing to riot, the cup was withheld.	
1910	Dundee v Clyde	2-2
Replay	Dundee v Clyde	0-0*
2nd Replay	Dundee v Clyde	2-1
1911	Celtic v Hamilton A	0-0
Replay	Celtic v Hamilton A	2-0
1912	Celtic v Clyde	2-0
1913	Falkirk v Raith R	2-0
1914	Celtic v Hibernian	0-0
Replay	Celtic v Hibernian	4-1
1920	Kilmarnock v Albion R	3-2
1921	Partick Thistle v Rangers	1-0
1922	Morton v Rangers	1-0

1923	Celtic v Hibernian	1-0
1924	Airdrieonians v Hibernian	2-0
1925	Celtic v Dundee	2-1
1926	St Mirren v Celtic	2-0
1927	Celtic v East Fife	3-1
1928	Rangers v Celtic	4-0
1929	Kilmarnock v Rangers	2-0
1930	Rangers v Partick Thistle	0-0
Replay	Rangers v Partick Thistle	2-1
1931	Celtic v Motherwell	2-2
Replay	Celtic v Motherwell	4-2
1932	Rangers v Kilmarnock	1-1
Replay	Rangers v Kilmarnock	3-0
1933	Celtic v Motherwell	1-0
1934	Rangers v St Mirren	5-0
1935	Rangers v Hamilton A	2-1
1936	Rangers v Third Lanark	1-0
1937	Celtic v Aberdeen	2-1
1938	East Fife v Kilmarnock	1-1
Replay	East Fife v Kilmarnock	4-2*
1939	Clyde v Motherwell	4-0
1947	Aberdeen v Hibernian	2-1
1948	Rangers v Morton	1-1*
Replay	Rangers v Morton	1-0*
1949	Rangers v Clyde	4-1
1950	Rangers v East Fife	3-0
1951	Celtic v Motherwell	1-0
1952	Motherwell v Dundee	4-0
1953	Rangers v Aberdeen	1-1
Replay	Rangers v Aberdeen	1-0
1954	Celtic v Aberdeen	2-1
1955	Clyde v Celtic	1-1
Replay	Clyde v Celtic	1-0
1956	Hearts v Celtic	3-1
1957	Falkirk v Kilmarnock	1-1
Replay	Falkirk v Kilmarnock	2-1*
1958	Clyde v Hibernian	1-0
1959	St Mirren v Aberdeen	3-1
1960	Rangers v Kilmarnock	2-0
1961	Dunfermline Ath v Celtic	0-0
Replay	Dunfermline Ath v Celtic	2-0
1962	Rangers v St Mirren	2-0
1963	Rangers v Celtic	1-1
Replay	Rangers v Celtic	3-0
1964	Rangers v Dundee	3-1
1965	Celtic v Dunfermline Ath	3-2
1966	Rangers v Celtic	0-0
Replay	Rangers v Celtic	1-0
1967	Celtic v Aberdeen	2-0
1968	Dunfermline Ath v Hearts	3-1
1969	Celtic v Rangers	4-0
1970	Aberdeen v Celtic	3-1
1971	Celtic v Rangers	1-1
Replay	Celtic v Rangers	2-1
1972	Celtic v Hibernian	6-1
1973	Rangers v Celtic	3-2
1974	Celtic v Dundee U	3-0
1975	Celtic v Airdrieonians	3-1
1976	Rangers v Hearts	3-1
1977	Celtic v Rangers	1-0
1978	Rangers v Aberdeen	2-1
1979	Rangers v Hibernian	0-0
Replay	Rangers v Hibernian	0-0*
2nd Replay	Rangers v Hibernian	3-2*
1980	Celtic v Rangers	1-0*
1981	Rangers v Dundee U	0-0*
Replay	Rangers v Dundee U	4-1
1982	Aberdeen v Rangers	4-1*
1983	Aberdeen v Rangers	1-0*
1984	Aberdeen v Celtic	2-1*
1985	Celtic v Dundee U	2-1
1986	Aberdeen v Hearts	3-0
1987	St Mirren v Dundee U	1-0*
1988	Celtic v Dundee U	2-1
1989	Celtic v Rangers	1-0

TENNENTS SCOTTISH CUP

1990	Aberdeen v Celtic	0-0*
	Aberdeen won 9-8 on penalties.	
1991	Motherwell v Dundee U	4-3*
1992	Rangers v Airdrieonians	2-1
1993	Rangers v Aberdeen	2-1
1994	Dundee U v Rangers	1-0
1995	Celtic v Airdrieonians	1-0
1996	Rangers v Hearts	5-1
1997	Kilmarnock v Falkirk	1-0
1998	Hearts v Rangers	2-1
1999	Rangers v Celtic	1-0
2000	Rangers v Aberdeen	4-0
2001	Celtic v Hibernian	3-0
2002	Rangers v Celtic	3-2
2003	Rangers v Dundee	1-0
2004	Celtic v Dunfermline Ath	3-1
2005	Celtic v Dundee U	1-0
2006	Hearts v Gretna	1-1*
	Hearts won 4-2 on penalties.	
2007	Celtic v Dunfermline Ath	1-0

SCOTTISH FA CUP

2008	Rangers v Queen of the South	3-2

HOMECOMING SCOTTISH CUP

2009	Rangers v Falkirk	1-0

ACTIVE NATION SCOTTISH CUP

2010	Dundee U v Ross Co	3-0

SCOTTISH FA CUP

2011	Celtic v Motherwell	3-0

WILLIAM HILL SCOTTISH CUP

2012	Hearts v Hibernian	5-1
2013	Celtic v Hibernian	3-0
2014	St Johnstone v Dundee U	2-0
2015	Inverness CT v Falkirk	2-1

After extra time.

SCOTTISH CUP WINS

Celtic 36, Rangers 33, Queen's Park 10, Hearts 8, Aberdeen 7, Clyde 3, Kilmarnock 3, St Mirren 3, Vale of Leven 3, Dundee U 2, Dunfermline Ath 2, Falkirk 2, Hibernian 2, Motherwell 2, Renton 2, Third Lanark 2, Airdrieonians 1, Dumbarton 1, Dundee 1, East Fife 1, Inverness CT 1, Morton 1, Partick Thistle 1, St Bernard's 1, St Johnstone 1.

APPEARANCES IN FINAL

Celtic 54, Rangers 50, Aberdeen 15, Hearts 14, Hibernian 13, Queen's Park 12, Dundee U 10, Kilmarnock 8, Motherwell 7, Vale of Leven 7, Clyde 6, Dumbarton 6, St Mirren 6, Third Lanark 6, Dundee 5, Dunfermline Ath 5, Falkirk 5, Renton 5, Airdrieonians 4, East Fife 3, Hamilton A 2, Morton 2, Partick Thistle 2, Albion R 1, Cambuslang 1, Clydesdale 1, Gretna 1, Inverness CT 1, Queen of the South 1, Raith R 1, Ross Co 1, St Bernard's 1, St Johnstone 1, Thornliebank 1.

WILLIAM HILL SCOTTISH CUP 2014–15

■ *Denotes player sent off.*

FIRST ROUND

Auchinleck Talbot v Buckie Thistle	5-0
Clachnacuddin v Hurlford U	1-7
Cove R v Hawick Royal Albert	9-0
Culter v Strathspey Thistle	4-2
Deveronvale v Nairn Co	0-1
Edinburgh C v Coldstream	2-1
Forres Mech v Civil Service Strollers	4-1
Fraserburgh v Linlithgow Rose	0-0, 1-2
Golspie Sutherland v Dalbeattie Star	1-4
Gretna 2008 v Gala Fairydean	2-1
Huntly v Wick Academy	2-1
Keith v Formartine U	1-3
Lossiemouth v Turriff U	0-4
Lothian Thistle v East Kilbride	0-1
Preston Ath v Threave R	1-2
Rothes v Banks O'Dee	0-4
Selkirk v Bo'ness U	0-4
Whitehill Welfare v Girvan	3-1

SECOND ROUND

Arbroath v Montrose	2-2, 3-1
Berwick R v Formartine U	2-0
Bo'ness U v Culter	7-1
Brora R v Banks O'Dee	5-0
Cove R v Annan Ath	1-2
East Fife v Threave R	7-0
Edinburgh C v Auchinleck Talbot	2-1
Elgin C v Forres Mech	0-0, 3-1
Gretna 2008 v Queen's Park	0-1
Inverurie Loco Works v Hurlford U	0-3
Linlithgow Rose v Dalbeattie Star	5-1
Nairn Co v Huntly	2-1
Spartans v East Kilbride	3-3, 5-1
Turriff U v Clyde	0-3
Whitehill Welfare v East Stirling	0-1
Stirling Univ v Albion R	1-4

THIRD ROUND

Saturday, 1 November 2014

Annan Ath (2) 3 *(Weatherson 20, 41, McColm 58)*
Livingston (1) 2 *(Keaghan Jacobs 13, Mullen 83)*   560
Annan Ath: (4411) Alex Mitchell; Chisholm, Black, Watson, McNiff; Logan, Sloan, Flynn, McColm; Hopkirk; Weatherson (Todd 81).
Livingston: (442) Jamieson; Sives, Fordyce, Mensing (Mullen 64), Talbot; Keaghan Jacobs (McKenna 64), Kyle Jacobs, O'Brien, Hippolyte (Robertson 73); White, Glen.
Referee: Euan Anderson.

Arbroath (1) 2 *(McManus 22 (pen), McBride 66)*
Nairn Co (0) 1 *(Webb 88)*   682
Arbroath: (442) Crawford (Morrison 71); Little, Nicoll, El-Zubaidi, McBride; Linn, Whatley, Stewart, Lowdon (Johnstone 63); McManus (Buchan 78), Murray S.
Nairn Co: (352) Antell; Webb, Macdonald, Morrison; Halsman, Wilkie (Naismith 82), Pollock, Mackintosh, Main; Duncanson (Urquhart 73), Gethins.
Referee: Gavin Duncan.

Ayr U (1) 1 *(Donnelly 34)*
Alloa Ath (1) 1 *(Buchanan 29)*   784
Ayr U: (442) Hutton; Devlin, Campbell (Shirkie 33), Murphy, Muir; Forrest (Beattie 71), Gilmour, McLaughlin, Slane; Donnelly (McKenzie 80), McGovern.
Alloa Ath: (442) McDowall; Doyle, Benedictus, Gordon, Meggatt; McCord (Weatherston 56), Simmons, Docherty (Ferns 81), Holmes; Cawley, Buchanan.
Referee: Don Robertson.

Dumbarton (0) 0
Rangers (1) 1 *(Boyd 45)*   1878
Dumbarton: (352) Ewings; Graham, Mair, McLaughlin; Gilhaney, Megginson (McDougall 81), Fleming, Agnew, Linton (van Zanten 84); Nish, Campbell (Turner 69).
Rangers: (442) Robinson; Foster, McGregor, McCulloch, Wallace; Macleod, Law, Black, Smith; Boyd (Daly 75), Miller.
Referee: Bobby Madden.

East Fife (2) 2 *(Smith S 12, Walker 45)*
Berwick R (2) 3 *(Dargo 10, 36, Currie L 56 (pen))*   477
East Fife: (442) Millar; Campbell R, Moyes, Naysmith (Beaton■ 57), Smith S; Barr, Mullen (McShane 69), Walker■, Brown; Austin (McAleer■ 78), Smith K.
Berwick R: (433) Bald; Notman, Young, Tulloch, Drummond; Gray (Hoskins 82), Currie L, Currie P; Lavery (Russell 87), Willis (Gold 78), Dargo.
Referee: Craig Charleston.

Edinburgh C (1) 2 *(McFarland 2, Dunn 72)*
Brora R (3) 3 *(Williamson 6, Morrison 23, Greig 43)*   601
Edinburgh C: (352) Stobie; Paterson (Osborne 32), Mbu, Donaldson; Caddow (Wilson 86), McFarland, Vanson (Deniran 69), MacDonald, Gair; Allum■, Dunn.
Brora R: (442) Malin; Houston, Tokely, Ross, Williamson; Martin Maclean (Kettlewell 78), Morrison, Gillespie, Greig; Sutherland (Graham 78), Mackay S.
Referee: Ryan Milne.

Elgin C (3) 4 *(Nicolson 16, Cameron 25, 36, Sutherland 71)*
Bo'ness U (0) 4 *(Anderson 53, Walker 59, Gribben 61, Scott 82)*   858
Elgin C: (442) Fraser; Finlayson, Cooper, Andrews (Duff 74), MacPhee; Cameron, Nicolson, Beveridge, Sutherland; Gunn, Wyness (Moore 64).
Bo'ness U: (451) Peat; Snowden, Murphy, Leiper, Hunter (Anderson 46); Scott, Nimmo, Gribben (Cowan 81), Pitman, Philp; Donnelly (Walker 46).
Referee: David Munro.

Forfar Ath (1) 1 *(Hilson 30)*
Cowdenbeath (2) 3 *(Hughes 11, Higgins 26, Milne 64)*   592
Forfar Ath: (442) Douglas; Malin, Dunlop, Dods, Paterson (Steeves 68); Kader, Dale (Templeman 60), Husband, Denholm (Smith 75); Hilson, Swankie.
Cowdenbeath: (343) Thomson; Marshall, Fraser, Wedderburn; Milne, Robertson, Brett, Miller; Oyenuga (Sutherland 80), Hughes (Brownlie 80), Higgins (Johnston 88).
Referee: Barry Cook.

Greenock Morton (0) 0
Airdrieonians (0) 0   1420
Greenock Morton: (442) Gaston; Kilday, Crighton, Milojevic, Lamie; Pepper, McKee■, O'Ware, McCluskey J (Russell 69); McCluskey S (Crawford 77), Barrowman.
Airdrieonians: (4411) McNeil; O'Neil, Gasparotto, Fitzpatrick, Boyle P; Gray (Boyle J 90), Fraser, Blockley, Watt; Parker (Prunty 90); Lister.
Referee: George Salmond.

Hurlford U (1) 1 *(Kean 10)*
Stirling Alb (0) 1 *(Smith C 78)*   551
Hurlford U: (442) Brown A; Cameron, McGregor (Robertson R 46), Mitchell G, Byrne (Brown M 73); McKenzie, Masterton (Wilson 68), Cochrane, Chisholm; Kean, Robertson C.
Stirling Alb: (442) Reidford; Hamilton (McGeachie 62), Wedderburn■, Smith C, Forsyth; Weir, Fulton, McClune, Creaney (Johnston 53); Smith G, Doris.
Referee: Alan Newlands.

Linlithgow Rose (0) 0
Raith R (0) 2 *(Conroy 68 (pen), Watson 86)*   2250
Linlithgow Rose: (451) McKinven; Thom (Kelbie 85), O'Byrne, Ovenstone, McKillen; Smith, Bachelor, MacLennan, Nelson (Shirra 88), Coyne; Strickland.
Raith R: (442) McGurn; Thomson, Watson, Perry, McKeown; Anderson, Fox, Scott, Conroy (Moon 78); Stewart (Vaughan 73), Elliot.
Referee: John McKendrick.

Peterhead (0) 0
Stranraer (0) 1 *(Longworth 61)*   430
Peterhead: (352) Smith G; Smith R (Rodgers 71), Donaldson■, Ross; Redman, Strachan, Stevenson, Millar (Gilfillan 80), Noble (Brown 88); McAllister, Riley.
Stranraer: (442) Mitchell; Gallagher, Rumsby, McKeown, Russell (Longridge 76); Winter, Aitken, Bell (Stirling 77), Gibson (Stoney 84); Longworth, Malcolm.
Referee: Kevin Graham.

Queen's Park (0) 1 *(Burns 90)*
Albion R (1) 2 *(Gemmell 45, 51)*   438
Queen's Park: (4231) Muir; Rooney, Wharton, MacGregor, Gibson; Berry (Quinn 35), Miller; McElroy, Fraser (Mortimer 75), Burns; McPherson (Carter 65).
Albion R: (442) Parry; Reid, Dunlop R, Dunlop M, Turnbull; McKenzie, Donnelly, Chaplain, Phillips; Gemmell, McGuigan.
Referee: Des Roache.

Spartans (1) 2 *(Motion 14 (pen), 72 (pen))*
Clyde (0) 0   611
Spartans: (41212) Swain; Nixon, Sivewright■, MacKinnon, Cennerazzo; Stevenson; Beesley (Henretty 88), Motion (Douglas 75); Grant; Bremner, McLeod (Brown 66).
Clyde: (442) Martin; Durie, McQueen, Frances (Ferguson S 46), McIlduff; Sinclair (Halkett 47), O'Donnell (Gibson 59), Gray D, Smith; McManus, Watt.
Referee: Steven Kirkland.

Stenhousemuir (1) 1 *(McCormack D 34 (og))*
Brechin C (0) 2 *(McAusland 52, Barr 83 (pen))*   451
Stenhousemuir: (442) Fleming; Duncan, Greacen, McMillan (Summers 68), Lithgow; Reid (Dickson 66), Faulds, Millar K (Hodge 11), Eddington; McMenamin, Walsh.
Brechin C: (442) Smith; McNeil, McLauchlan, McCormack D, Hamilton; Barr, Fusco, McAusland, Ferguson (McLean 89); Jackson A, Thomson.
Referee: Colin Steven.

Sunday, 2 November 2014
East Stirling (0) 1 *(Greenhill 79)*
Dunfermline Ath (1) 4 *(El Bakhtaoui 37, 62, Byrne 76, Millen 84 (pen))*   991
East Stirling: (442) Barnard; Greene, Townsley, Bolochoweckyj, Kinnaird; Kay, McCabe, MacGregor (Brisbane 62), Greenhill; McKenna, Tahin (Brennan 71).
Dunfermline Ath: (442) Scully; Millen, Buchanan, Urquhart, Whittle; Byrne, Spence, Geggan, Forbes (Thomson 77); Moffat (Ugwu 73), El Bakhtaoui (Thomas 72).
Referee: Alan Muir.

THIRD ROUND REPLAYS

Saturday, 8 November 2014
Bo'ness U (3) 5 *(Gribben 4, 31, Snowden 17, Campbell 65, Walker 77)*
Elgin C (2) 4 *(Sutherland 11 (pen), 42, Nicolson 72, Andrews 88)*   1280
Bo'ness U: (442) Peat; Philp, Campbell, Leiper, Snowden; Walker, Scott (Donnelly 69), Murphy, Gribben (Gibb 90); Pitman, Anderson (Cowan 84).
Elgin C: (442) Fraser; Finlayson (Moore 46), Cooper, Andrews, McHardy (MacEwan 78); Beveridge, Nicolson, MacPhee, Cameron; Wyness (Gunn 62), Sutherland.
Referee: Nick Walsh.

Stirling Alb (0) 2 *(Doris 77, 116)*
Hurlford U (1) 2 *(Robertson R 15, Kean 111)*   567
Stirling Alb: (442) Reidford; Hamilton, McGeachie, Smith C, Forsyth; Johnston (Weir 72), Robertson, Darren L Smith (Fulton 63), Cunningham (Creaney 104); Smith G, Doris.
Hurlford U: (442) Brown A; Cameron, Mitchell G, Robertson C, Byrne; McKenzie, Masterton (Mitchell D 53), Cochrane (Wilson 107), Chisholm; Kean, Robertson R (Dempster 66).
aet; Stirling won 13-12 on penalties.
Referee: Gavin Ross.

Tuesday, 11 November 2014
Airdrieonians (0) 0
Greenock Morton (1) 2 *(Barrowman 36, 77)*   668
Airdrieonians: (442) McNeil; O'Neil, Bain, Fitzpatrick, Boyle P; Gray (Cadden 58), Fraser, Blockley, Watt (Stewart 73); Parker, Lister (Prunty 73).
Greenock Morton: (4411) Gaston; Kilday, Crighton, Milojevic, Lamie; McCluskey J (Miller 89), O'Ware, Pepper, McNeil (Allan 64); Scullion (McCluskey S 79); Barrowman.
Referee: George Salmond.

Alloa Ath (3) 4 *(Buchanan 24, Meggatt 28, Docherty 33, 60)*
Ayr U (0) 0   420
Alloa Ath: (343) McDowall; Doyle, Gordon, Marr; Tiffoney, Simmons (Asghar 72), Meggatt, Docherty; Cawley, Buchanan (Ferns 64), Weatherston (McCord 42).
Ayr U: (4411) Hutton; Devlin, McArthur (McGill 47), McLaughlin, Muir; Forrest (McCracken 47), Gilmour, McGovern, Slane; Shirkie; Donnelly (Beattie 46).
Referee: Don Robertson.

FOURTH ROUND

Saturday, 29 November 2014
Alloa Ath (1) 1 *(Meggatt 15)*
Hibernian (2) 2 *(Craig 28, Gray 37)*   2138
Alloa Ath: (442) McDowall; Doyle, Gordon, Benedictus, Meggatt; Docherty, Hetherington (Ferns 76), McCord, Cawley; Spence, Buchanan.
Hibernian: (442) Oxley; Gray, Hanlon, Fontaine, Stevenson; Robertson, Handling, Craig (Harris 79), Allan S (Kennedy 84); Malonga■, Cummings (Stanton 76).
Referee: John Beaton.

Annan Ath (0) 1 *(Flynn 60)*
Brechin C (1) 1 *(Hamilton 42)*   440
Annan Ath: (4411) Alex Mitchell; Chisholm, Black, Watson, McNiff; Sloan, Flynn, McStay (Logan 76), Todd; Hopkirk; Weatherson.
Brechin C: (442) Smith; McLean, McLauchlan, McCormack D, Hamilton; Trouten, McAusland, Fusco, Barr; Jackson A, Thomson.
Referee: Barry Cook.

Berwick R (1) 1 *(Lavery 9)*
Albion R (0) 1 *(Dunlop M 84)*   439
Berwick R: (442) Andrews; Jacobs, Fairbairn, Young, Drummond; Willis, Currie L, Notman, Hoskins; Dargo (Gold 82), Lavery (Russell 54).
Albion R: (4411) Parry; Reid, Dunlop R, Dunlop M, Turnbull; McKenzie, Davidson, Chaplain (Love 58), Phillips (Fisher 80); McGuigan (Mullin 72); Gemmell.
Referee: Matt Northcroft.

Bo'ness U (0) 0
Arbroath (1) 5 *(Murray S 27, 69, 75 McManus 68, 76)*   1769
Bo'ness U: (433) Peat; Philp, Campbell, Hunter, Snowden; Nimmo, Donnelly (Scott 60), Pitman; Walker, Anderson (Cowan 63), Gribben.
Arbroath: (442) McCallum; Little, Nicoll, El-Zubaidi, McBride; Linn, Whatley, Hunter, Lowdon (Johnstone 53); McManus (Buchan 81), Murray S (Smith 77).
Referee: Craig Charleston.

Dundee (1) 2 *(Konrad 4, Clarkson 90)*
Aberdeen (1) 1 *(Konrad 17 (og))* 5956
Dundee: (4231) Bain; McGinn P (Dyer 73), Konrad, McPake, Irvine; Thomson, McAlister; Boyle (Tankulic 85), Harkins (Ferry 71), Stewart; Clarkson.
Aberdeen: (4411) Brown; Logan, Taylor, Reynolds, Considine; Hayes, Jack, Pawlett (Smith 84), McGinn; Rooney; Goodwillie.
Referee: Steven McLean.

Falkirk (0) 1 *(Sibbald 73)*
Cowdenbeath (0) 0 1237
Falkirk: (442) MacDonald; Duffie, Grant P, Vaulks, Leahy; Cooper (Smith 64), Taiwo, Alston, Sibbald (Durojaiye 90); Bia Bi (Shepherd 67), Loy.
Cowdenbeath: (4411) Thomson; Marshall (Johnston 82), Fraser, Wedderburn, Miller; Hughes, Brownlie (Scullion 83), Oyenuga, Milne; O'Brien; Higgins.
Referee: John McKendrick.

Motherwell (1) 1 *(Ojamaa 7)*
Dundee U (0) 2 *(Souttar 66, Watson 82)* 4827
Motherwell: (442) Twardzik; Ramsden, O'Brien, McManus, Francis-Angol (Kerr 84); Lawson (Reid 48), Lasley, Vigurs, Law (Erwin 76); Sutton, Ojamaa.
Dundee U: (4231) Cierzniak; Dillon, Souttar, Watson, Townsend; Paton, Telfer (Butcher 46); Erskine (Adeyemo 84), Armstrong, Mackay-Steven (Connolly 62); Dow.
Referee: Craig Thomson.

Partick Thistle (1) 2 *(Stevenson 19, 54)*
Hamilton A (0) 0 2467
Partick Thistle: (4231) Gallacher; O'Donnell, Frans, Seaborne, Carroll; Osman, Bannigan; Elliot, Stevenson (Doolan 68), Fraser (Craigen 77); Higginbotham (Lawless 83).
Hamilton A: (4231) McGovern; Gordon (Antoine-Curier 72), Canning, Garcia Tena, Hendrie; MacKinnon, Gillespie (Routledge 57); Imrie■, Crawford, Redmond (Longridge 57); Scotland.
Referee: Kevin Clancy.

Queen of the South (1) 4 *(Lyle 3, Reilly 61, Russell 71, Kidd 80)*
Brora R (0) 1 *(Greig 65)* 1434
Queen of the South: (442) Atkinson; Dowie, Durnan, Higgins, Holt; Carmichael (Kidd 60), McShane, Kerr, Russell; Reilly (Baird 70), Lyle (Pickard 86).
Brora R: (4411) Malin; Ross, Houston, Gillespie, Williamson (Kettlewell 46); Graham (Maclean C 85), Martin Maclean, Morrison, Greig (Michael MacLean 88); Sutherland; Mackay.
Referee: Alan Muir.

Spartans (0) 2 *(Bremner 71, Beesley 90)*
Greenock Morton (1) 1 *(Barrowman 25)* 1288
Spartans: (442) Swain; Nixon, MacKinnon, Bruce (Brown 44), Cennerazzo; Beesley, Grant (Douglas 79), Stevenson, Motion; Bremner, McLeod (Beacher 85).
Greenock Morton: (442) McGowan; Kilday, Crighton, Milojevic, Lamie; McCluskey J (Allan 86), O'Ware, McKee, Russell (Orr 79); McCluskey S■, Barrowman.
Referee: Euan Anderson.

St Johnstone (2) 2 *(O'Halloran 7, McFadden 12)*
Ross Co (0) 1 *(Jervis 63)* 2383
St Johnstone: (442) Mannus; Mackay, Anderson, Wright, Easton; Croft (Miller 89), Millar, Lappin, O'Halloran (Davidson 64); Graham, McFadden (Wotherspoon 71).
Ross Co: (4231) Brown; Brittain, Boyd, Quinn P, Reckord; Woods (Boyce 46), Irvine; Cardle, Carey, Dingwall (Gardyne 79); Jervis (Arquin 75).
Referee: John Beaton.

St Mirren (1) 1 *(McAusland 17)*
Inverness CT (0) 1 *(Meekings 63)* 1957
St Mirren: (442) Ridgers; Naismith, McAusland, Kelly, Tesselaar; Reilly, Osbourne (Teale 81), McLean, McGinn (Drury 61); Thompson (Ball 75), Marwood.
Inverness CT: (4231) Brill; Raven, Meekings, Warren, Shinnie; Draper, Williams; Christie, Ross (Doran 74), Vincent; McKay.
Referee: Calum Murray.

Stirling Alb (0) 0
Raith R (1) 2 *(McKay 44, Anderson 54)* 912
Stirling Alb: (442) Reidford; Hamilton, McGeachie, Smith C, Forsyth (Creaney 82); Johnston, McClune (Fulton 57), Beith, Cunningham (Comrie 68); Doris, Smith G.
Raith R: (442) McGurn; Thomson, Watson, McKeown, Perry; Anderson (Conroy 79), Moon, McKay, Scott (Callachan 90); Nade, Stewart.
Referee: Greg Aitken.

Stranraer (0) 2 *(Gibson 80, Malcolm 90)*
Dunfermline Ath (1) 2 *(Geggan 14, Buchanan 61)* 489
Stranraer: (442) Mitchell; Gallagher, Rumsby, McKeown, Longridge; Winter, Bell (Russell 73), Aitken (Stirling 67), Gibson; Malcolm, Stoney (Longworth 58).
Dunfermline Ath: (442) Scully; Millen, Buchanan, Martin, Whittle; Byrne, Geggan, Thomson, Stirling (El Bakhtaoui 67); Smith (Moffat 67), Falkingham.
Referee: Des Roache.

Sunday, 30 November 2014

Hearts (0) 0
Celtic (1) 4 *(van Dijk 29, 61, Guidetti 52 (pen), Stokes 54)* 12,676
Hearts: (4231) Alexander; Paterson, McKay, Ozturk, Eckersley; Pallardo, Gomis■; King, Walker (Buchanan 69), Holt (Buaben 58); Keatings (Robinson 77).
Celtic: (4231) Gordon; Matthews, Ambrose, van Dijk, Izaguirre; Brown, Biton; Forrest (Tonev 57), Johansen (Commons 67), Stokes (Griffiths 67); Guidetti.
Referee: William Collum.

Rangers (1) 3 *(Law 19, 84, Boyd 72)*
Kilmarnock (0) 0 14,412
Rangers: (442) Simonsen; McGregor, McCulloch, Mohsni, Foster; Aird, Law, Black, Macleod (Shiels 87); Daly (Boyd 70), Miller (Clark 70).
Kilmarnock: (4411) Samson; Barbour, Connolly, Pascali, Chantler; McKenzie, Clingan, Slater (Hamill 62), Obadeyi (Magennis 83); Eremenko (Muirhead 62); Miller.
Referee: Brian Colvin.

FOURTH ROUND REPLAYS

Tuesday, 2 December 2014

Inverness CT (2) 4 *(Warren 20, Tansey 23 (pen), Williams 67, Shinnie 90)*
St Mirren (0) 0 1326
Inverness CT: (4411) Brill; Raven, Meekings, Warren, Shinnie; Vincent, Draper, Tansey, Williams (Doran 76); Watkins (Christie 74); McKay (Ross 84).
St Mirren: (4141) Ridgers; Naismith, McAusland (Brown 63), Tesselaar, Kelly; Goodwin; Reilly (Drury 53), Osbourne (Ball 73), McLean, McGinn; Thompson.
Referee: Calum Murray.

Tuesday, 9 December 2014

Albion R (0) 0
Berwick R (0) 1 *(Russell 80)* 311
Albion R: (442) Parry; Reid, Dunlop R, Dunlop M, Mullin■; McKenzie (Pollock 86), Davidson (Phillips 73), Chaplain, Cusack (Gemmell 58); McGuigan, Fisher.
Berwick R: (442) Andrews; Jacobs, Notman, Young, Hoskins; Willis, Fairbairn, Currie L, Lavery (Drummond 88); Russell (Dalziel 89), Gold (Gray 46).
Referee: Matt Northcroft.

Brechin C (3) 4 *(Jackson A 4, 11, 27, Hamilton 72)*
Annan Ath (0) 2 *(Davidson 68, Hopkirk 76)* 224
Brechin C: (442) Smith; McNeil, McLean, McLauchlan, Hamilton; Barr, Fusco, McAusland (Cameron 89), Masson (Molloy 86); Jackson A (Thomson 70), Trouten.
Annan Ath: (442) Alex Mitchell; Chisholm, Black, Watson, McNiff; Hopkirk, Sloan (Davidson 66), Logan (McStay 46), Todd; Weatherson, Swinglehurst (McColm 46).
Referee: Barry Cook.

Dunfermline Ath (0) 1 *(Millen 62 (pen))*
Stranraer (1) 3 *(Winter 32, Stirling 57, Longworth 90)* 1436
Dunfermline Ath: (442) Scully; Millen, Urquhart, Buchanan, Whittle; Geggan, Byrne, Falkingham, Stirling (Chemin 69); Thomson (El Bakhtaoui 63), Smith (Moffat 63).
Stranraer: (451) Mitchell; Pettigrew, Rumsby, McKeown, Longridge; Gallagher (Stoney 77), Stirling (Russell 79), Aitken, Bell, Winter; Malcolm (Longworth 77).
Referee: Des Roache.

FIFTH ROUND

Saturday, 7 February 2015
Dundee (0) 0
Celtic (1) 2 *(Griffiths 7, Johansen 47)* 7525
Dundee: (442) Bain; Irvine, Gadzhalov, McPake, Dyer; Stewart (McGinn P 36), McGowan, McAlister, McGinn S; Tankulic (Black 90), Wighton (Clarkson 58).
Celtic: (4411) Gordon; Lustig (Matthews 55), van Dijk, Denayer, Izaguirre; Forrest (Guidetti 74), Brown, Biton, Commons (Stokes 46); Johansen; Griffiths.
Referee: John Beaton.

Falkirk (1) 2 *(McCracken 11, Smith 79)*
Brechin C (0) 1 *(Trouten 55 (pen))* 2083
Falkirk: (442) MacDonald; Duffie, McCracken, Grant P, Leahy; Sibbald, Vaulks, Taiwo, Alston (Smith 60); Loy, Morgan (Bia Bi 90).
Brechin C: (4411) Smith; McLean, McCormack D, McLauchlan, Hamilton; Trouten, Fusco, Molloy (Storie 72), Barr (McNeil 87); Ferguson (Thomson 65); Jackson A.
Referee: John McKendrick.

Hibernian (1) 3 *(Dja Djedje 42, Gordon 60 (og), McGeouch 68)*
Arbroath (1) 1 *(Stewart 17)* 9065
Hibernian: (442) Oxley; Gray, Hanlon, Fontaine, Stevenson; Robertson, Allan S (Stanton 77), Fyvie, Craig (McGeouch 59); Dja Djedje, Cummings.
Arbroath: (442) McCallum; Rowan, Gordon, Whatley, Lindsay; Carreiro (Lowdon 88), Little, Hunter (Linn 59), Stewart; McManus, Murray S (Buchan 78).
Referee: Andrew Dallas.

Partick Thistle (0) 1 *(Taylor 67)*
Inverness CT (2) 2 *(Watkins 16, Tansey 27)* 2915
Partick Thistle: (4231) Gallacher; O'Donnell, Seaborne, Frans, Elliot; Osman, Fraser (Craigen 46); Lawless (Doolan 63), Bannigan, Higginbotham (Taylor 46); Stevenson.
Inverness CT: (4231) Esson; Raven, Meekings, Warren, Shinnie; Tansey, Draper; Vincent, Williams, Ross (Christie 76); Watkins (Devine 89).
Referee: William Collum.

Queen of the South (0) 2 *(Lyle 48, Reilly 90)*
St Johnstone (0) 0 3043
Queen of the South: (3412) Atkinson; Dowie, Durnan, Higgins; Kidd, McShane, Burns (Carmichael 80), Holt; Paton (McKenna 86); Lyle (Russell 75), Reilly.
St Johnstone: (442) Mannus; Mackay, Anderson, Scobbie, Easton; Wotherspoon, Lappin, Davidson, Swanson (O'Halloran 59); McFadden, Kane (Graham 64).
Referee: Steven McLean.

Spartans (0) 1 *(MacKinnon 90)*
Berwick R (1) 1 *(Willis 4)* 2500
Spartans: (442) Swain; Nixon, Malone, MacKinnon, Cennerazzo; Beesley, Thomson (Brown 46), Motion (Douglas 63), Stevenson; Bremner, Sludden (Beacher 80).
Berwick R: (433) Bald; Jacobs, Young, Fairbairn, Drummond; Notman, Currie L, Gray (Miller 72); Lavery, Henderson (Russell 81), Willis.
Referee: Don Robertson.

Sunday, 8 February 2015
Rangers (0) 1 *(Vuckic 62)*
Raith R (0) 2 *(Conroy 54, Nade 75)* 11,422
Rangers: (4231) Simonsen; Foster, Streete (McGregor 44), McCulloch, Wallace; Black (Murdoch 74), Hutton; Law, Miller, Vuckic; Daly (Boyd 65).
Raith R: (442) McGurn; Thomson, Watson, Hill, McKeown; Anderson, Moon, Callachan, Conroy; Carrick (Stewart 51), Nade (Scott 86).
Referee: Bobby Madden.

Stranraer (0) 0
Dundee U (3) 3 *(Erskine 21, Dow 27, 31)* 1491
Stranraer: (451) Mitchell; Pettigrew, Rumsby, McKeown, Longridge; Winter, Stirling (Longworth 63), Aitken (Robertson 83), Gallagher, Gibson; Malcolm (Stoney 72).
Dundee U: (4231) Cierzniak; McGowan, Morris, Fojut, Dillon; Butcher, Paton; Erskine (Spittal 74), Anier (Telfer 79), Dow; Ciftci.
Referee: Kevin Clancy.

FIFTH ROUND REPLAY

Tuesday, 17 February 2015
Berwick R (1) 1 *(Lavery 29)*
Spartans (0) 0 2003
Berwick R: (433) Bald; Jacobs, Young, Fairbairn, Drummond; Notman (Gold 27), Cameron, Currie L; Gray (Henderson 68), Lavery (Maxwell 81), Willis.
Spartans: (442) Carswell; Nixon, MacKinnon, Malone, Cennerazzo; Brown, Grant, Bremner, Motion (McLeod 59); Beesley (Stevenson 74), Sludden (Douglas 59).
Referee: Greg Aitken.

QUARTER-FINALS

Friday, 6 March 2015
Queen of the South (0) 0
Falkirk (1) 1 *(Sibbald 34)* 2833
Queen of the South: (3421) Clark; Durnan (Mitchell 76), Dowie, Higgins; Kidd, Burns (Carmichael 64), McShane, Holt; Paton, Russell; Reilly (Smith A 79).
Falkirk: (442) MacDonald; Duffie, McCracken, Grant P, Leahy (Muirhead 89); Alston (Dick 82), Taiwo, Vaulks, Sibbald; Smith, Loy (Morgan 84).
Referee: Kevin Clancy.

Sunday, 8 March 2015
Dundee U (1) 1 *(Ciftci 45 (pen))*
Celtic (0) 1 *(Griffiths 71)* 10,504
Dundee U: (433) Cierzniak; McGowan, Dillon, Fojut, Dixon■; Paton■, Butcher, Rankin; Dow (Erskine 64), Ciftci, Connolly (Souttar 51).
Celtic: (4231) Gordon; Ambrose, Denayer, van Dijk■, Izaguirre; Brown, Biton (Fisher 90); Forrest, Johansen, Stokes (Guidetti 64); Griffiths (Scepovic 87).
Referee: Craig Thomson.

Hibernian (2) 4 *(Cummings 26, Stevenson 28, Stanton 66, Fontaine 82)*
Berwick R (0) 0 11,259
Hibernian: (442) Oxley; Gray, Fontaine, Hanlon, Stevenson; Robertson, Allan S (Stanton 64), McGeouch (Craig 74); Fyvie; Cummings, Malonga (Dja Djedje 80).
Berwick R: (442) Bald; Jacobs, Young, Fairbairn, Drummond; Gray (Lavery 64), Currie L (Maxwell 74), Notman, Willis; Russell (Henderson 86), Gold.
Referee: Bobby Madden.

Tuesday, 10 March 2015
Inverness CT (0) 1 *(Devine 63)*
Raith R (0) 0 2276
Inverness CT: (4231) Esson; Raven, Devine, Meekings, Shinnie; Tansey, Draper; Watkins, Christie (Ross 90), Williams (Kink 79); Ofere (Doran 79).
Raith R: (4411) McGurn; Thomson, Watson, Barr, McKeown; Anderson (Vaughan 76), Fox (Conroy 88), Callachan, McKay; Stewart; Nade.
Referee: Crawford Allan.

QUARTER-FINAL REPLAY

Wednesday, 18 March 2015

Celtic (1) 4 *(Denayer 17, Griffiths 57, Commons 79, van Dijk 90)*

Dundee U (0) 0   28,847

Celtic: (4231) Gordon; Ambrose (Fisher 72), Denayer, van Dijk, Izaguirre; Biton, Brown; Forrest, Commons (Henderson 80), Stokes■; Griffiths (Guidetti 58).
Dundee U: (442) Cierzniak; McGowan■, Fojut, Morris, Rankin; Spittal (Connolly 74), Paton, Butcher, Erskine (Anier 70); Dow (Telfer 70), Ciftci.
Referee: Calum Murray.

Sunday, 19 April 2015

Inverness CT (0) 3 *(Tansey 58 (pen), Ofere 96, Raven 117)*

Celtic (1) 2 *(van Dijk 18, Guidetti 103)*   28,643

Inverness CT: (4231) Esson; Raven, Warren, Meekings, Shinnie; Draper, Tansey; Watkins, Christie, Williams (Ross 74); Ofere.
Celtic: (4231) Gordon■; Matthews, van Dijk, Denayer, Izaguirre; Brown, Biton; Forrest (Zaluska 56), Johansen, Commons (Tonev 90); Griffiths (Guidetti 98).
aet.
Referee: Steven McLean.

SEMI-FINALS

Saturday, 18 April 2015

Hibernian (0) 0

Falkirk (0) 1 *(Sibbald 75)*   21,227

Hibernian: (352) Oxley; Forster, Hanlon, Fontaine; McGeouch, Allan S, Robertson (Dja Djedje 80), Fyvie, Stevenson; El Alagui, Cummings (Malonga 87).
Falkirk: (433) MacDonald; Duffie, McCracken, Grant P, Leahy; Taiwo, Vaulks, Sibbald; Smith (Bia Bi 46), Morgan (Muirhead 77), Alston.
Referee: John Beaton.

WILLIAM HILL SCOTTISH CUP FINAL 2015

Saturday, 30 May 2015

(at Hampden Park, attendance 37,149)

Falkirk (0) 1   Inverness CT (1) 2

Falkirk: (4411) MacDonald; Duffie, McCracken, Grant P, Leahy; Alston, Vaulks, Taiwo, Sibbald; Smith (Bia Bi 63); Loy (Morgan 90).
Scorer: Grant P 80.
Inverness CT: (4231) Esson; Shinnie, Devine, Meekings, Tremarco■; Tansey, Draper; Watkins (Ross 90), Doran (Williams 78), Christie (Vincent 72); Ofere.
Scorers: Watkins 38, Vincent 86.
Referee: William Collum.

James Vincent's late winner for ten-man Inverness Caledonian Thistle clinched a 2-1 victory over Falkirk in the William Hill Scottish Cup final at Hampden on 30 May. (Jeff Holmes/PA Wire/Press Association Images)

SCOTTISH JUNIOR FOOTBALL 2014–15

PRESS & JOURNAL HIGHLAND LEAGUE

	P	W	D	L	F	A	GD	Pts
Brora Rangers	34	30	4	0	134	13	121	94
Turriff U*	34	27	2	5	90	40	50	80
Cove Rangers	34	22	7	5	103	40	63	73
Wick Academy	34	23	3	8	94	43	51	72
Fraserburgh	34	19	8	7	91	48	43	65
Formartine U	34	19	7	8	85	59	26	64
Inverurie Loco Works	34	20	3	11	93	51	42	63
Nairn County	34	18	3	13	88	43	45	57
Forres Mechanics	34	18	3	13	71	59	12	57
Buckie Thistle	34	15	5	14	71	66	5	50
Clachnacuddin	34	14	3	17	63	74	–11	45
Deveronvale	34	9	9	16	53	82	–29	36
Fort William	34	8	3	23	52	98	–46	27
Keith	34	7	3	24	42	97	–55	24
Lossiemouth	34	7	2	25	50	105	–55	23
Huntly	34	5	5	24	37	100	–63	20
Strathspey Thistle	34	3	5	26	36	125	–89	14
Rothes	34	2	5	27	32	142	–110	11

*Turriff U deducted 3 points for playing an ineligible player.

THE SCOTTISH SUN LOWLAND FOOTBALL LEAGUE

	P	W	D	L	F	A	GD	Pts
Edinburgh C	26	22	3	1	65	14	51	69
East Kilbride	26	15	5	6	63	25	38	50
Gretna 2008	26	13	6	7	62	32	30	45
Dalbeattie	26	11	9	6	51	39	12	42
Spartans	26	11	9	6	45	34	11	42
Stirling University	26	12	6	8	46	38	8	42
Whitehill Welfare	26	11	7	8	57	38	19	40
Gala Fairydean R	26	9	7	10	48	54	–6	34
Vale of Leithen	26	9	6	11	39	53	–14	33
BSC Glasgow	26	7	9	10	39	52	–13	30
Edinburgh University	26	8	4	14	40	52	–12	28
Selkirk	26	6	5	15	53	74	–21	23
Preston Ath	26	3	5	18	31	75	–44	14
Threave R	26	2	5	19	21	80	–59	11

JUNIOR FOOTBALL WEST REGION
STAGECOACH WEST OF SCOTLAND
SUPER LEAGUE PREMIER DIVISION

	P	W	D	L	F	A	GD	Pts
Auchinleck Talbot	22	18	2	2	53	12	41	56
Hurlford United	22	16	4	2	54	22	32	52
Irvine Meadow XI	22	12	4	6	42	25	17	40
Glenafton Athletic	22	9	5	8	47	37	10	32
Petershill	22	10	2	10	33	38	–5	32
Beith Juniors	22	8	5	9	35	45	–10	29
Troon	22	7	7	8	35	38	–3	28
Kilbirnie Ladeside	22	7	4	11	38	41	–3	25
Arthurlie	22	7	4	11	28	41	–13	25
Shotts Bon Accord	22	8	1	13	24	45	–21	25
Cumnock Juniors	22	3	7	12	28	45	–17	16
Clydebank	22	2	5	15	17	45	–28	11

MCBOOKIE.COM EAST SUPERLEAGUE

	P	W	D	L	F	A	GD	Pts
Kelty Hearts	28	20	5	3	63	23	40	65
Bo'ness U	28	18	5	5	55	21	34	59
Linlithgow Rose	28	17	5	6	65	36	29	56
Newtongrange Star	28	16	7	5	52	29	23	55
Sauchie Juniors	28	12	8	8	46	48	–2	44
Penicuik Ath	28	11	7	10	41	43	–2	40
Bonnyrigg Rose	28	11	4	13	50	48	2	37
Broxburn Thistle	28	8	12	8	39	42	–3	36
Hill of Beath Hawthorn	28	10	4	14	47	50	–3	34
Fauldhouse U	28	8	9	11	46	52	–6	33
Musselburgh Ath	28	9	6	13	53	60	–7	33
Camelon Juniors	28	9	4	15	38	58	–20	31
Carnoustie Panmure	28	5	7	16	33	56	–23	22
Armadale Thistle	28	5	6	17	36	61	–25	21
Lochee U	28	4	5	19	40	77	–37	17

JUNIOR FOOTBALL NORTH REGION
PMAC GROUP SUPERLEAGUE

	P	W	D	L	F	A	GD	Pts
Hermes	26	22	2	2	74	16	58	68
Maud	26	18	4	4	90	46	44	58
Banks O' Dee	26	17	5	4	84	27	57	56
Culter	26	16	4	6	67	42	25	52
Deveronside	26	13	4	9	50	49	1	43
FC Stoneywood	26	11	3	12	49	53	–4	36
Inverness City	26	10	6	10	46	57	–11	36
Dyce Juniors	26	10	4	12	50	57	–7	34
Stonehaven	26	9	6	11	52	53	–1	33
Banchory St Ternan*	26	11	2	13	50	59	–9	27
Hall Russell U	26	5	6	15	35	49	–14	21
Ellon U	26	5	3	18	32	64	–32	18
Cruden Bay	26	3	5	18	23	64	–41	14
New Elgin	26	3	4	19	27	93	–66	13

*Banchory St Ternan deducted 8 points.

DYSLEXIA SCOTLAND JUNIOR CUP
SEMI-FINALS

Hurlford United v Auchinleck Talbot	2-5
Musselburgh Ath v Linlithgow Rose	5-4

FINAL

Rugby Park, Kilmarnock, Sunday 7 June 2015
Auchinleck Talbot (1) 2 *(Hislop 30, Pope 60 (pen))*
Musselburgh Ath (1) 1 *(Sheerin 41)*   5186

WELSH FOOTBALL 2014–15

CORBETT SPORTS WELSH PREMIER LEAGUE 2014–15

		Total					Home					Away					
		P	W	D	L	F	A	W	D	L	F	A	W	D	L	F	A	GD	Pts
1	The New Saints	32	23	8	1	90	24	12	4	0	46	10	11	4	1	44	14	66	77
2	Bala T	32	18	5	9	67	42	9	3	4	42	19	9	2	5	25	23	25	59
3	Airbus UK Broughton	32	18	4	10	62	34	12	1	3	44	16	6	3	7	18	18	28	58
4	Aberystwyth T	32	14	10	8	69	61	8	4	4	33	28	6	6	4	36	33	8	52
5	Port Talbot T	32	13	4	15	54	59	10	1	5	33	20	3	3	10	21	39	−5	43
6	Newtown	32	10	8	14	52	65	6	4	6	30	29	4	4	8	22	36	−13	38
7	Connah's Quay Nomads	32	11	10	11	44	53	4	6	6	20	27	7	4	5	24	26	−9	43
8	Rhyl	32	11	9	12	41	49	4	7	5	20	23	7	2	7	21	26	−8	42
9	Carmarthen T	32	12	6	14	48	57	7	3	6	29	27	5	3	8	19	30	−9	42
10	Bangor C	32	9	8	15	48	62	5	3	8	25	32	4	5	7	23	30	−14	35
11	Cefn Druids	32	7	6	19	38	64	4	2	10	15	29	3	4	9	23	35	−26	27
12	Prestatyn T	32	4	6	22	43	86	3	4	9	23	36	1	2	13	20	50	−43	18

Top 6 teams split after 22 games.

PREVIOUS WELSH LEAGUE WINNERS

1993	Cwmbran Town	1999	Barry Town	2005	TNS	2011	Bangor C
1994	Bangor City	2000	TNS	2006	TNS	2012	The New Saints
1995	Bangor City	2001	Barry Town	2007	TNS	2013	The New Saints
1996	Barry Town	2002	Barry Town	2008	Llanelli	2014	The New Saints
1997	Barry Town	2003	Barry Town	2009	Rhyl	2015	The New Saints
1998	Barry Town	2004	Rhyl	2010	The New Saints		

NATHANIEL CARS WELSH LEAGUE 2014–15

		Total					Home					Away					
		P	W	D	L	F	A	W	D	L	F	A	W	D	L	F	A	GD	Pts
1	Caerau (Ely)	30	21	5	4	75	39	11	2	2	42	20	10	3	2	33	19	36	68
2	Haverfordwest Co	30	19	6	5	69	32	10	4	1	36	13	9	2	4	33	19	37	63
3	Cardiff Met University	30	19	6	5	57	20	10	4	1	33	9	9	2	4	24	11	37	63
4	Goytre U	30	16	8	6	74	41	10	2	3	38	16	6	6	3	36	25	33	56
5	Penybont	30	17	5	8	73	52	9	1	5	35	26	8	4	3	38	26	21	56
6	Monmouth T	30	16	3	11	57	35	9	2	4	26	13	7	1	7	31	22	22	51
7	Briton Ferry Llansawel	30	13	9	8	52	37	6	7	2	31	20	7	2	6	21	17	15	48
8	Taffs Well	30	15	2	13	61	45	9	0	6	33	16	6	2	7	28	29	16	47
9	Ton Pentre	30	12	4	14	44	54	7	2	6	18	17	5	2	8	26	37	−10	40
10	Goytre	30	11	3	16	46	47	9	1	5	35	20	2	2	11	11	27	−1	36
11	Aberdare T	30	10	5	15	48	68	4	4	7	24	36	6	1	8	24	32	−20	35
12	Garden Village	30	8	10	12	49	61	4	5	6	27	31	4	5	6	22	30	−12	34
13	Afan Lido	30	9	6	15	40	60	5	2	8	21	29	4	4	7	19	31	−20	33
14	Cambrian & Clydach Vale	30	7	7	16	45	46	5	3	7	27	18	2	4	9	18	28	−1	28
15	Pontardawe T	30	4	6	20	28	66	1	4	10	12	35	3	2	10	16	31	−38	18
16	AFC Porth	30	0	1	29	16	131	0	0	15	13	64	0	1	14	3	67	−115	1

HUWS GRAY CYMRU ALLIANCE LEAGUE 2014–15

		Total					Home					Away					
		P	W	D	L	F	A	W	D	L	F	A	W	D	L	F	A	GD	Pts
1	Llandudno	30	22	5	3	96	27	13	1	1	57	12	9	4	2	39	15	69	71
2	Caernarfon T	30	20	6	4	82	25	11	2	2	43	10	9	4	2	39	15	57	66
3	Guilsfield	30	19	6	5	68	33	9	3	3	34	18	10	3	2	34	15	35	63
4	Buckley T	30	15	7	8	69	47	8	4	3	32	22	7	3	5	37	25	22	52
5	Holyhead Hotspur	30	15	6	9	49	38	9	4	2	27	13	6	2	7	22	25	11	51
6	Porthmadog	30	15	5	10	63	35	9	2	4	35	14	6	3	6	28	21	28	50
7	Denbigh T	30	14	6	10	54	51	7	4	4	28	25	7	2	6	26	26	3	48
8	Caersws	30	13	8	9	61	47	6	6	3	29	18	7	2	6	32	29	14	47
9	Mold Alexandra	30	13	5	12	57	48	8	1	6	35	24	5	4	6	22	24	9	44
10	Flint Town U	30	13	5	12	39	45	6	3	6	20	20	7	2	6	19	25	−6	44
11	Conwy Bor	30	12	5	13	52	46	6	1	8	24	24	6	4	5	28	22	6	41
12	Rhayader T	30	8	6	16	41	53	6	3	6	28	27	2	3	10	13	26	−12	30
13	Llanidloes T	30	8	5	17	56	78	6	2	7	27	32	2	3	10	29	46	−22	29
14	Penycae	30	6	4	20	46	78	2	3	10	22	42	4	1	10	24	36	−32	22
15	Llandrindod Wells	30	5	3	22	32	103	2	2	11	18	47	3	1	11	14	56	−71	18
16	Rhydymwyn*	30	1	0	29	21	132	1	0	14	15	64	0	0	15	6	68	−111	0

* *Rhydymwyn deducted 3 points for breaking league rules.*

WELSH CUP 2014–15

After extra time.

FIRST QUALIFYING ROUND – CENTRAL

Builth Wells v Kerry	0-1
Four Crosses v Welshpool T	2-4
Hay St Mary v Borth U	7-2
Montgomery T v Llanuwchllyn	1-2
Presteigne St Andrews v Newbridge on Wye	4-3
Knighton T v Machynlleth	2-1

FIRST QUALIFYING ROUND – NORTH

Amlwch T v Trearddur Bay U	1-2
Brickfield Rangers v Brymbo	2-1
Caerwys v Llangollen T	2-4
Castell Alun Colts v Greenfield	1-3
Flint Mountain v Brynford U	2-6
Gaerwen v Llanllyfni	6-2
Halkyn U v Coedpoeth U	2-6
Lex Glyndwr v Llandyrnog U	0-2
Llandudno Junction v Llannerch ym Medd	3-4*
Llangefni T v Llanystumdwy	3-2
Mynydd Llandegai v Pwllheli	1-2
Nefyn U v Dyffryn Nantlle Vale	1-4
Penmaenmawr Phoenix v Pentraeth	2-1
Penrhyndeudraeth v Llanfairpwll	6-4
Queens Park v FC Nomads of Connah's Quay	3-4
St Asaph C v New Brighton Villa	8-1
Talysarn Celts v Kinmel Bay Sports	1-4
Venture (withdrawn) v Meliden (walkover)	

FIRST QUALIFYING ROUND – SOUTH

Newport Civil Service v Dynamo Aber	3-4
Aber Valley YMCA v Tiger Bay	3-5
AFC Butetown v Carnetown	4-2
Albion R v Cwmbran T	4-2
Ammanford v Trostre	3-2*
Bettws v Ynysgerwn	3-0
Bridgend Street v Llantwit Fardre	5-4*
Caerau v Treforest	3-3*
Caerau won 4-1 on penalties.	
Cwm Rhondda v Trelewis Welfare	10-0
Cwm Welfare v Cardiff Grange Harlequins	6-0
FC Tredegar v Newport YMCA	0-2
Garw v Cornelly U	3-3*
Cornelly won 8-7 on penalties.	
Kenfig Hill v Trefelin	0-3
Llantwit Major v Cardiff Corinthians	1-2
Lliswerry v Risca U	1-2
Malpas U v Llanwern	3-2
Merthyr Saints v Cwmaman Institute	0-1
Newcastle Emlyn v Llanelli T	1-2
Penrhiwceiber Constitutional Ath v Canton Liberal	5-6*
Penrhiwfer v Dinas Powys	1-1*
Dinas Powys won 3-1 on penalties.	
Pontyclun v Sporting Marvels	1-1*
Pontyclun won 4-3 on penalties.	
Porthcawl T Ath v Cwmamman U	1-2
Rhoose v Cardiff Hibernian	7-2
RTB Ebbw Vale v Marshfield	3-4
Splott Alb v Barry Town U	0-8
STM Sports v Pontypridd T	3-2
Sully Sports v Llanharry	10-1
Tredegar T v Cefn Fforest	2-0
Treharris Ath Western v Aberfan	2-1*
Treowen Stars v Trethomas Bluebirds	5-1
Ynysddu Welfare v Blaenavon Blues	0-1
Ystradgynlais v Dafen Welfare	4-2

SECOND QUALIFYING ROUND – CENTRAL

Berriew v Penrhyncoch	0-1*
Bow Street v Waterloo R	1-2
Carno v Llansantffraid Village	2-1*
Hay St Mary v Barmouth & Dyffryn U	5-0
Kerry v Aberaeron	3-2
Llanfair U v Knighton T	3-1
Llanrhaeadr ym Mochnant v Presteigne St Andrews	3-0
Tywyn Bryncrug v Welshpool T	2-3

SECOND QUALIFYING ROUND – NORTH

Llanberis v Llannerch ym Medd	5-3
AFC Brynford v Greenfield	4-0
Corwen v Gaerwen	1-1*
Gaerwen won 3-1 on penalties.	
Dyffryn Nantlle Vale v Trearddur Bay U	1-0
Glan Conwy v Hawarden Rangers	1-0
Glantraeth v FC Nomads of Connah's Quay	2-4
Gwalchmai v Brickfield Rangers	2-3
Kinmel Bay Sports v Gresford Ath	2-4
Llangefni T v Llandyrnog U	3-1*
Llangollen T v Llanrwst U	3-0
Llanrug U v Coedpoeth U	1-3
Llay Miners Welfare v Penmaenmawr Phoenix	3-0
Meliden (walkover) v Bodedern Ath (withdrawn)	
Pwllheli v St Asaph C	1-4
Rhos Aelwyd v Llanuwchllyn	1-3
Ruthin T v Chirk AAA	3-2
Saltney T v Penrhyndeudraeth	1-2

SECOND QUALIFYING ROUND – SOUTH

Trefelin v Rhoose	3-2
AFC Butetown v Tredegar T	1-0
Albion R v Pontyclun	3-2
Barry Town U v Ystradgynlais	5-2
Bettws v Cardiff Corinthians	0-1
Blaenavon Blues v Cwmbran Celtic	0-2
Caerleon v Dinas Powys	0-4
Canton Liberal v Cwmaman Institute	3-1
Chepstow T v Bridgend Street	3-0
Cwm Welfare v Cornelly U	1-2
Cwmamman U v Ammanford	1-2*
Dynamo Aber v Newport YMCA	3-1
Ely Rangers v Aberbargoed Buds	3-5
Llanelli T v Caldicot T	2-0
Marshfield v Croesyceiliog	3-0
Penrhiwceiber Rangers v Sully Sports	2-3
Risca U v Treowen Stars	5-1
Tata Steel v Caerau	3-0
Tiger Bay v Cwm Rhondda	5-2
Treharris Ath Western v STM Sports	1-4
Undy Ath v Malpas U	8-1
West End v AFC Llwydcoed	3-5*

FIRST ROUND – NORTH

Caernarfon T v Porthmadog	4-0
Caersws v Llandudno	1-0
Carno v Rhayader T	0-1
Coedpoeth U v Denbigh T	0-3
Dyffryn Nantlle Vale v Llanberis	5-5*
Llanberis won 4-2 on penalties.	
FC Nomads of Connah's Quay v AFC Brynford	1-0*
Guilsfield Ath v Penycae	3-1
Holyhead Hotspur v Conwy Borough	0-2
Holywell T v Hay St Mary	4-2
Kerry v Brickfield Rangers	1-2
Llandrindod Wells v Llangollen T	2-3*
Llangefni T v St Asaph C	3-6
Llanidloes T v Gaerwen	4-0
Llanrhaeadr ym Mochnant v Glan Conwy	4-2
Llay Miners Welfare v Gresford Ath	1-3
Mold Alexandra v Welshpool T	4-0
Penrhyncoch v Flint Town U	2-1*
Penrhyndeudraeth v Llanfair U	0-3
Rhydymwyn v Meliden	0-3
Ruthin T v Buckley T	2-3
Waterloo R v Llanuwchllyn	2-1

FIRST ROUND – SOUTH

Aberdare T v Barry Town U	4-2*
Albion R v Cardiff Corinthians	3-1
Ammanford v Sully Sports	5-2
Briton Ferry Llansawel v Aberbargoed Buds	4-1
Cambrian & Clydach Vale v Undy Ath	0-2
Canton Liberal v Risca U	1-2
Cardiff Metropolitan Univ v AFC Llwydcoed	9-0
Cornelly U v Pontardawe T	1-0
Cwmbran Celtic v Llanelli T	2-1
Dinas Powys v Pen-y-Bont	0-1*
Dynamo Aber v AFC Butetown	4-2
Garden Village v AFC Porth	9-0

Goytre (Gwent) v Goytre U	0-4
Monmouth T v Ton Pentre	3-0
STM Sports v Haverfordwest Co	0-2
Tata Steel v Marshfield	1-1
Marshfield won 3-1 on penalties.	
Tiger Bay v Trefelin	3-2
Afan Lido v Chepstow T	4-0
Taffs Well v Caerau (Ely)	0-3

SECOND ROUND – NORTH

Brickfield Rangers v Llanrhaeadr ym Mochnant	1-2*
Buckley T v Waterloo R	6-0
Caernarfon T v Guilsfield Ath	1-0
Conwy Bor v Denbigh T	5-0
FC Nomads of Connah's Quay v Llangollen T	5-2
Gresford Ath v Llanfair U	2-1
Llanberis v Caersws	0-3
Llanidloes T v Penrhyncoch	0-2
Mold Alexandra v Holywell T	0-1
St Asaph C v Meliden	1-0

SECOND ROUND – SOUTH

Albion R v Undy Ath	0-2
Briton Ferry Llansawel v Aberdare T	5-1
Cwmbran Celtic v Caerau (Ely)	0-2
Dynamo Aber v Tiger Bay	2-3
Monmouth T v Pen-y-Bont	3-1
Risca U v Garden Village	1-2
Ammanford v Cardiff Metropolitan Univ	2-3
Cornelly U v Goytre U	1-5
Haverfordwest Co v Rhayader T	2-1
Afan Lido v Marshfield	4-1

THIRD ROUND

Caernarfon T v The New Saints	2-3
Undy Ath v Carmarthen T	2-4
Afan Lido v Llanrhaeadr ym Mochnant	0-3
Airbus UK Broughton v Haverfordwest Co	5-0
Bala T v Port Talbot T	2-1
Bangor C v Garden Village	1-0
Buckley T v Holywell T	0-1
Cardiff Metropolitan Univ v Prestatyn T	4-1
Cefn Druids v Aberystwyth T	1-5
Conwy Bor v Briton Ferry Llansawel	4-3

Connah's Quay Nomads v Monmouth T	5-3
Gresford Ath v St Asaph C	5-0
Newtown v FC Nomads of Connah's Quay	2-0
Penrhyncoch v Caerau (Ely)	0-5
Rhyl v Goytre U	2-1
Tiger Bay v Caersws	0-4

FOURTH ROUND

Caersws v Newtown	2-3
The New Saints v Gresford Ath	3-0
Bangor C v Conwy Bor	3-0
Caerau (Ely) v Carmarthen T	0-4*
Cardiff Metropolitan Univ v Airbus UK Broughton	1-4
Connah's Quay Nomads v Bala T	2-2*
Connah's Quay Nomads won 4-2 on penalties.	
Holywell T v Aberystwyth T	0-0*
Aberystwyth T won 3-2 on penalties.	
Llanrhaeadr ym Mochnant v Rhyl	2-4

QUARTER-FINAL

Carmarthen T v Rhyl	1-2
Aberystwyth T v Airbus UK Broughton	1-1
Airbus UK Broughton won 4-2 on penalties.	
Bangor C v Newtown	1-2
Connah's Quay Nomads v The New Saints	0-1

SEMI-FINAL

The New Saints v Airbus UK Broughton	4-2
Newtown v Rhyl	2-1

FAW WELSH CUP FINAL 2015

Newtown, Saturday 2 May 2015

The New Saints (0) 2 *(Williams 53, 84 (pen))*

Newtown (0) 0　　　　　　　　　　　　　　1579

The New Saints: Harrison; Spender, Marriott, Baker, Edwards K, Williams, Mullan, Rawlinson (Seargeant 10), Wilde (Draper 87), Cieslewicz (Quigley 71), Edwards A. *Newtown:* Jones; Edwards, Owen, Mills-Evans, Sutton ■, Cook (Hearsey 88), Boundford, Oswell, Mitchell (Evans 78), Williams, Goodwin. *Referee:* D. John.

PREVIOUS WELSH CUP WINNERS

1878	Wrexham	1910	Wrexham	1952	Rhyl	1984	Shrewsbury Town
1879	Newtown White Star	1911	Wrexham	1953	Rhyl	1985	Shrewsbury Town
1880	Druids	1912	Cardiff City	1954	Flint Town United	1986	Wrexham
1881	Druids	1913	Swansea Town	1955	Barry Town	1987	Merthyr Tydfil
1882	Druids	1914	Wrexham	1956	Cardiff City	1988	Cardiff City
1883	Wrexham	1915	Wrexham	1957	Wrexham	1989	Swansea City
1884	Oswestry White Stars	1920	Cardiff City	1958	Wrexham	1990	Hereford United
1885	Druids	1921	Wrexham	1959	Cardiff City	1991	Swansea City
1886	Druids	1922	Cardiff City	1960	Wrexham	1992	Cardiff City
1887	Chirk	1923	Cardiff City	1961	Swansea Town	1993	Cardiff City
1888	Chirk	1924	Wrexham	1962	Bangor City	1994	Barry Town
1889	Bangor	1925	Wrexham	1963	Borough United	1995	Wrexham
1890	Chirk	1926	Ebbw Vale	1964	Cardiff City	1996	TNS
1891	Shrewsbury Town	1927	Cardiff City	1965	Cardiff City	1997	Barry Town
1892	Chirk	1928	Cardiff City	1966	Swansea Town	1998	Bangor City
1893	Wrexham	1929	Connah's Quay	1967	Cardiff City	1999	Inter Cable-Tel
1894	Chirk	1930	Cardiff City	1968	Cardiff City	2000	Bangor City
1895	Newtown	1931	Wrexham	1969	Cardiff City	2001	Barry Town
1896	Bangor	1932	Swansea Town	1970	Cardiff City	2002	Barry Town
1897	Wrexham	1933	Chester	1971	Cardiff City	2003	Barry Town
1898	Druids	1934	Bristol City	1972	Wrexham	2004	Rhyl
1899	Druids	1935	Tranmere Rovers	1973	Cardiff City	2005	TNS
1900	Aberystwyth Town	1936	Crewe Alexandra	1974	Cardiff City	2006	Rhyl
1901	Oswestry United	1937	Crewe Alexandra	1975	Wrexham	2007	Carmarthen Town
1902	Wellington Town	1938	Shrewsbury Town	1976	Cardiff City	2008	Bangor City
1903	Wrexham	1939	South Liverpool	1977	Shrewsbury Town	2009	Bangor City
1904	Druids	1940	Wellington Town	1978	Wrexham	2010	Bangor City
1905	Wrexham	1947	Chester	1979	Shrewsbury Town	2011	Llanelli
1906	Wellington Town	1948	Lovell's Athletic	1980	Newport County	2012	The New Saints
1907	Oswestry United	1949	Merthyr Tydfil	1981	Swansea City	2013	Prestatyn Town
1908	Chester	1950	Swansea Town	1982	Swansea City	2014	The New Saints
1909	Wrexham	1951	Merthyr Tydfil	1983	Swansea City	2015	The New Saints

WELSH THEWORD LEAGUE CUP 2014–15

After extra time.

FIRST ROUND – NORTHERN SECTION
Bangor C v Newtown	3-1
Caersws v Llandudno	3-5
Denbigh T v Cefn Druids	0-1
Connah's Quay Nomads v Rhyl	0-2
Guilsfield v Caernarfon T	2-3
Porthmadog v The New Saints	0-2
Prestatyn T v Conwy Bor	4-2

FIRST ROUND – SOUTHERN SECTION
Aberdare T v Port Talbot T	1-5
Barry T v Merthyr T	1-7
Haverfordwest Co v Afan Lido	4-0
Pen-y-Bont v Llanidloes T	4-0
Taff's Well v Aberystwyth T	0-2

SECOND ROUND – NORTHERN SECTION
Aberystwyth T v Bala T	0-1*
Bangor C v Cefn Druids	2-1
Llandudno v Rhyl	1-1*
Llandudno won 4-2 on penalties.	
Prestatyn T v Caernarfon T	6-5*
The New Saints v Airbus UK Broughton	2-1

SECOND ROUND – SOUTHERN SECTION
Carmarthen T v Pen-y-Bont	2-3*
Cambrian & Clydach Vale v Merthyr T	1-2
Port Talbot T v Haverfordwest Co	1-0

QUARTER-FINALS – NORTHERN SECTION
Bala T v Llandudno	3-1
Prestatyn T v Bangor C	1-0

QUARTER-FINALS – SOUTHERN SECTION
Port Talbot T v Merthyr T	2-1
The New Saints v Pen-y-Bont	3-0

SEMI-FINALS
Bala T v Prestatyn T	2-0
The New Saints v Port Talbot T	2-1*

WELSH THEWORD LEAGUE CUP FINAL 2015
Newtown, 25 January 2015

The New Saints (1) 3 *(Quigley 29, 80, Seargeant 41)*
Bala T (0) 0   697

The New Saints: Mullock; Spender, Marriott, Baker, Edwards K, Cieslewicz, Quigley, Seargeant (Rawlinson 85), Draper (Reed 70), Williams (Finley 63), Edwards A.
Bala T: Morris; Valentine, Smith S, Artell, Bell, Murtagh, Connolly, Jones (Lunt 73) Pearson, Sheridan (Brown 73), Smith K (Hayes 73).
Referee: Mark Whitby.

THE FAW TROPHY 2014–15

THIRD ROUND – NORTH
Bethesda Ath v Rhos Aelwyd	3-5
Bow Street v Berriew	4-2
Caerwys v Llandudno Junction	0-4
Castell Alun Colts v Penrhyndeudraeth	0-2
Chirk AAA v Greenfield	1-2
Coedpoeth U v FC Nomads of Connah's Quay	1-4
Corwen v Borth U	4-0
Four Crosses v Dyffryn Banw	2-0
Gaerwen v Brickfield Rangers	0-2
Holywell T v Dyffryn Nantlle Vale	4-0
Llanberis v Cefn Alb	3-3
Llanberis won 4-3 on penalties.	
Llannerch y Medd v Glantraeth	1-2
Llanrug U v Hawarden Rangers	3-2
Llanrwst U v Llangefni T	0-2
Llanystumdwy v Gwalchmai	2-2
Gwalchmai won 4-2 on penalties.	
Machynlleth v Llanrhaeadr ym Mochnant	1-3*
Meliden v Kinmel Bay Sports	1-2
Mynydd Llandegai v Gresford Ath	4-6
Penrhyncoch v Ruthin T	3-2
Tywyn Bryncrug v Llangollen T	3-1

THIRD ROUND – SOUTH
Abergavenny T v Johnston	10-0
Blaenavon Blues v CRC Rangers	2-3
Cwmfelin Press v Ystradgynlais	4-2
Garw (walkover) v Abercynon	
Abercynon failed to fulfil fixture. Garw receive a bye.	
Hakin U v Penrhiwceiber Constitutional Ath	6-1
Maerdy Social v STM Sports	0-4
Maltsters Sports v Ynystawe Ath	3-0
Merthyr Saints v Ragged School	3-4
Pencoed Ath Amateur v Carnetown	7-4
Penlan v Sully Sports	4-2
Sporting Marvels v Cwmbach Royal Stars	2-1
Ton & Gelli v Marshfield	2-1

FOURTH ROUND – NORTH
Llanrhaeadr ym Mochnant v Kinmel Bay Sports	3-2
Bow Street v Glantraeth	4-5
Greenfield v FC Nomads of Connah's Quay	1-4
Gresford Ath v Rhos Aelwyd	4-2
Gwalchmai v Llanrug U	0-2
Llanberis v Four Crosses	4-1
Llandudno Junction v Brickfield Rangers	6-0
Penrhyncoch v Llangefni T	1-1
Penrhyncoch won 4-2 on penalties.	

Penrhyndeudraeth v Corwen	1-1
Penrhyndeudraeth won 4-2 on penalties.	
Tywyn Bryncrug v Holywell T	1-4

FOURTH ROUND – SOUTH
Garw v Cwmfelin Press	3-1
Hakin U v Pencoed Ath Amateur	5-1
Ragged School v Maltsters Sports	1-2
Sporting Marvels v CRC Rangers	9-0
STM Sports v Penlan	2-3*
Ton & Gelli v Abergavenny T	1-3

FIFTH ROUND – NORTH
FC Nomads of Connah's Quay v Penrhyndeudraeth	1-2
Llanrug U v Llanberis	2-2
Llanberis won 5-4 on penalties.	
Gresford Ath v Holywell T	1-5
Llanrhaeadr ym Mochnant v Glantraeth	1-3
Penrhyncoch v Llandudno Junction	2-2*
Llandudno Junction won 3-2 on penalties.	

FIFTH ROUND – SOUTH
Abergavenny T v Sporting Marvels	4-0
Hakin U v Garw	3-0
Penlan v Maltsters Sports	3-0

QUARTER-FINAL
Glantraeth v Penlan	3-0
Hakin U v Holywell T	3-4
Llandudno Junction v Abergavenny T	1-4
Penrhyndeudraeth v Llanberis	5-1

SEMI-FINAL
Glantraeth v Penrhyndeudraeth	2-3
Holywell T v Abergavenny T	1-0

THE FAW TROPHY FINAL 2014–15
Llandudno, Saturday 18 April 2015

Holywell T (1) 4 *(Lloyd 12, 70, Thomas 55, Jones 80)*
Penrhyndeudraeth (1) 2 *(Roberts 45, Hughes T 64)*   510

Holywell: Platt; Harvey, Emberton (Williams G 81), McElmeel, Griffith, D'Arcy, Williams P, Roebuck (Leonard 28), Lloyd, Jones, Thomas (Roberts 81).
Penrhyndeudraeth: Watson, Jones J (Jones R 84), Watson, Price, Foster, Lane, Griffiths (Price 80), Jones S, Hughes M, Roberts, Hughes T.

NORTHERN IRISH FOOTBALL 2014–15

NORTHERN IRISH DANSKE BANK PREMIERSHIP 2014–15

		Total					Home					Away						
		P	W	D	L	F	A	W	D	L	F	A	W	D	L	F	A	GD	Pts
1	Crusaders	38	25	7	6	93	43	14	2	3	49	19	11	5	3	44	24	50	82
2	Linfield	38	21	9	8	67	46	11	3	5	37	24	10	6	3	30	22	21	72
3	Glenavon	38	20	6	12	82	65	9	3	7	38	35	11	3	5	44	30	17	66
4	Portadown	38	17	11	10	65	56	10	6	3	38	25	7	5	7	27	31	9	62
5	Cliftonville	38	16	13	9	71	47	8	7	4	42	21	8	6	5	29	26	24	61
6	Glentoran	38	16	10	12	67	51	11	2	6	37	22	5	8	6	30	29	16	58
7	Ballymena U	38	15	6	17	62	75	9	3	7	35	35	6	3	10	27	40	–13	51
8	Coleraine*	38	14	7	17	48	55	6	6	9	21	32	8	1	8	27	23	–7	46
9	Ballinamallard U	38	10	9	19	40	71	8	6	6	28	28	2	3	13	12	43	–31	39
10	Dungannon Swifts	38	8	13	17	38	56	4	7	8	20	29	4	6	9	18	27	–18	37
11	Warrenpoint T†	38	6	12	20	50	76	5	5	8	29	35	1	7	12	21	41	–26	30
12	Institute*	38	4	9	25	36	84	2	6	9	15	28	2	3	16	21	56	–48	21

*Coleraine and Institute each deducted 3 points for fielding an ineligible player. Top 6 split after 33 games.
†Warrenpoint T not relegated after play-off against Bangor.

LEADING GOALSCORERS (League goals only)

31	Joe Gormley	Cliftonville
27	Paul Heatley	Crusaders
26	Jordan Owens	Crusaders
17	Aaron Burns	Linfield
17	Daniel Hughes	Warrenpoint T
16	Kevin Braniff	Glenavon
15	Curtis Allen	Glentoran
15	Andy Waterworth	Linfield
13	Eoin Bradley	Glenavon
13	Darren Murray	Portadown
13	Jordan Stewart	Glentoran
13	Gary Twigg	Portadown
12	Ciaran Martyn	Glenavon
12	Neil McCafferty	Coleraine
10	Allan Jenkins	Ballymena U
10	Mark McAllister	Portadown
10	David McDaid	Cliftonville
10	Stephen O'Flynn	Crusaders
10	David Scullion	Glentoran
10	Matthew Tipton	Ballymena U

IRISH LEAGUE CHAMPIONSHIP WINNERS

1891	Linfield	1913	Glentoran	1940	Belfast Celtic	1970	Glentoran	1993	Linfield
1892	Linfield	1914	Linfield	1948	Belfast Celtic	1971	Linfield	1994	Linfield
1893	Linfield	1915	Belfast Celtic	1949	Linfield	1972	Glentoran	1995	Crusaders
1894	Glentoran	1920	Belfast Celtic	1950	Linfield	1973	Crusaders	1996	Portadown
1895	Linfield	1921	Glentoran	1951	Glentoran	1974	Coleraine	1997	Crusaders
1896	Distillery	1922	Linfield	1952	Glenavon	1975	Linfield	1998	Cliftonville
1897	Glentoran	1923	Linfield	1953	Glentoran	1976	Crusaders	1999	Glentoran
1898	Linfield	1924	Queen's Island	1954	Linfield	1977	Glentoran	2000	Linfield
1899	Distillery	1925	Glentoran	1955	Linfield	1978	Linfield	2001	Linfield
1900	Belfast Celtic	1926	Belfast Celtic	1956	Linfield	1979	Linfield	2002	Portadown
1901	Distillery	1927	Belfast Celtic	1957	Glentoran	1980	Linfield	2003	Glentoran
1902	Linfield	1928	Belfast Celtic	1958	Ards	1981	Glentoran	2004	Linfield
1903	Distillery	1929	Belfast Celtic	1959	Linfield	1982	Linfield	2005	Glentoran
1904	Linfield	1930	Linfield	1960	Glenavon	1983	Linfield	2006	Linfield
1905	Glentoran	1931	Glentoran	1961	Linfield	1984	Linfield	2007	Linfield
1906	Cliftonville/	1932	Linfield	1962	Linfield	1985	Linfield	2008	Linfield
	Distillery (shared)	1933	Belfast Celtic	1963	Distillery	1986	Linfield	2009	Glentoran
1907	Linfield	1934	Linfield	1964	Glentoran	1987	Linfield	2010	Linfield
1908	Linfield	1935	Linfield	1965	Derry City	1988	Glentoran	2011	Linfield
1909	Linfield	1936	Belfast Celtic	1966	Linfield	1989	Linfield	2012	Linfield
1910	Cliftonville	1937	Belfast Celtic	1967	Glentoran	1990	Portadown	2013	Cliftonville
1911	Linfield	1938	Belfast Celtic	1968	Glentoran	1991	Portadown	2014	Cliftonville
1912	Glentoran	1939	Belfast Celtic	1969	Linfield	1992	Glentoran	2015	Crusaders

BELFAST TELEGRAPH CHAMPIONSHIP ONE 2014–15

		Total					Home					Away						
		P	W	D	L	F	A	W	D	L	F	A	W	D	L	F	A	GD	Pts
1	Carrick Rangers	26	19	5	2	54	22	12	1	0	29	9	7	4	2	25	13	32	62
2	Bangor*	26	18	6	2	71	32	9	3	1	39	17	9	3	1	32	15	39	60
3	Ards	26	16	8	2	61	30	9	4	0	32	13	7	4	2	29	17	31	56
4	H&W Welders	26	15	5	6	59	37	8	1	4	27	18	7	4	2	32	19	22	50
5	Larne	26	13	3	10	52	36	6	1	6	21	19	7	2	4	31	17	16	42
6	Dergview	26	8	9	9	40	43	8	3	2	26	17	0	6	7	14	26	–3	33
7	Armagh C	26	9	5	12	38	48	6	2	5	23	19	3	3	7	15	29	–10	32
8	Knockbreda	26	9	3	14	31	43	6	2	5	23	23	3	1	9	8	20	–12	30
9	Ballyclare Comrades	26	8	4	14	46	48	4	3	6	19	17	4	1	8	27	31	–2	28
10	Lisburn Distillery	26	8	4	14	38	58	3	4	6	17	28	5	0	8	21	30	–20	28
11	Loughgall	26	7	6	13	36	54	3	4	6	21	30	4	2	7	15	24	–18	27
12	Donegal Celtic	26	5	9	12	35	42	3	4	6	17	20	2	5	6	18	22	–7	24
13	PSNI	26	6	5	15	27	64	3	3	7	15	33	3	2	8	12	31	–37	23
14	Dundela	26	3	4	19	34	65	3	3	7	21	29	0	1	12	13	36	–31	13

*Bangor not promoted after play-off against Warrenpoint T.

BELFAST TELEGRAPH CHAMPIONSHIP (Previously First Division)

1996	Coleraine	2003	Dungannon Swifts	2010	Loughgall
1997	Ballymena United	2004	Loughgall	2011	Carrick Rangers
1998	Newry Town	2005	Armagh City	2012	Ballinamallard U
1999	Distillery	2006	Crusaders	2013	Ards
2000	Omagh Town	2007	Institute	2014	Institute
2001	Ards	2008	Loughgall	2015	Carrick Rangers
2002	Lisburn Distillery	2009	Portadown		

BELFAST TELEGRAPH CHAMPIONSHIP TWO 2014–15

		Total					Home					Away						
		P	W	D	L	F	A	W	D	L	F	A	W	D	L	F	A	GD	Pts
1	Lurgan Celtic	28	19	6	3	68	21	11	1	2	39	9	8	5	1	29	12	47	63
2	Annagh U	28	18	4	6	73	46	7	2	5	33	31	11	2	1	40	15	27	58
3	Limavady U	28	17	5	6	67	32	9	3	2	34	14	8	2	4	33	18	35	56
4	Sport & Leisure Swifts	28	16	5	7	50	34	8	2	4	28	14	8	3	3	22	20	16	53
5	Newington YC	28	15	5	8	40	29	8	2	4	20	16	7	3	4	20	13	11	50
6	Moyola Park	28	14	6	8	58	44	9	3	2	33	21	5	3	6	25	23	14	48
7	Dollingstown	28	12	7	9	53	39	6	5	3	28	18	6	2	6	25	21	14	43
8	Portstewart	28	12	6	10	43	40	5	4	5	25	22	7	2	5	18	18	3	42
9	Queen's Universith	28	11	7	10	48	34	7	3	4	26	15	4	4	6	22	19	14	40
10	Tobermore U	28	9	7	12	48	45	6	3	5	24	15	3	4	7	24	30	3	34
11	Banbridge T	28	7	7	14	38	70	5	3	6	21	28	2	4	8	17	42	–32	28
12	Glebe Rangers	28	6	6	16	45	64	5	3	6	29	25	1	3	10	16	39	–19	24
13	Wakehurst	28	6	4	18	28	68	3	3	8	17	29	3	1	10	11	39	–40	22
14	Coagh U	28	3	6	19	29	72	2	4	8	14	28	1	2	11	15	44	–43	15
15	Ballymoney U	28	2	5	21	26	76	2	2	10	19	39	0	3	11	7	37	–50	11

IFA YOUTH LEAGUE 2014–15

SECTION A

	P	W	D	L	F	A	GD	Pts
Linfield Rangers	20	17	2	1	62	14	48	53
Cliftonville Strollers	20	16	0	4	64	27	37	48
Crusaders Colts	20	11	3	6	46	34	12	36
Ballymena U III	20	11	2	7	40	39	1	35
Glentoran Colts	20	8	3	9	50	48	2	27
Institute Colts	20	5	6	9	40	51	–11	21
Dungannon Swifts Youth	20	6	2	12	44	77	–33	20
Glenavon III	20	6	3	11	56	56	0	21
Lisburn Distillery III	20	6	1	13	28	52	–24	19
Coleraine Colts	20	4	5	11	40	51	–11	17
Ballinamallard U III	20	4	5	11	36	57	–21	17

SECTION B

	P	W	D	L	F	A	GD	Pts
Portadown III	18	13	1	4	72	23	49	40
Ballyclare Comrades Colts	18	9	6	3	53	30	23	33
Newington YC U18	18	10	2	6	43	32	11	32
St Oliver Plunkett	18	9	0	9	32	33	–1	27
Knockbreda Youth	18	7	4	7	41	44	–3	25
Newry C AFC Youth	18	7	4	7	36	39	–3	25
Carrick Rangers Colts	18	7	3	8	47	46	1	24
Carniny Youth	18	6	2	10	31	62	–31	20
Annagh U Youth	18	5	1	12	25	64	–39	16
Ards Youth	18	4	3	11	36	43	–7	15

IFA RESERVE LEAGUE 2014–15

	P	W	D	L	F	A	GD	Pts
Linfield Swifts	33	24	6	3	112	35	77	78
Coleraine Res	33	24	3	6	92	46	46	75
Cliftonville Olympic	33	22	3	8	85	31	54	69
Dungannon Swifts Res	33	16	6	11	61	65	–4	54
Glentoran II	33	14	6	13	71	69	2	48
Ballymena U Res	33	15	3	15	59	64	–5	48
Institute Res	33	14	3	16	64	67	–3	45
Glenavon Res	33	14	2	17	70	77	–7	44
Crusaders Res	33	11	7	15	44	53	–9	40
Ballinamallard U II	33	9	4	20	51	78	–27	31
Portadown Res	33	6	5	22	46	95	–49	23
Warrenpoint T Res	33	3	4	26	31	106	–75	13

IRISH CUP 2014–15

After extra time. ■ *Denotes player sent off.*

FIRST ROUND

Albert Foundry v Portaferry R	1-0
Ardglass v Fivemiletown U	4-3*
Ards Rangers v Islandmagee	3-2
Ballymacash Rangers v Dromara Village	2-1
Ballynahinch Olympic v Grove U	3-1
Ballynahinch U v Lisburn Rangers	2-3
Ballywalter Rec v Bryansburn Rangers	2-0
Banbridge Rangers (walkover) v	
Draperstown Celtic (withdrawn)	
Bangor Amateurs v Dundonald	2-1
Chimney Corner v Malachians	2-3*
Comber Rec v Hanover	1-2
Crewe U v St. Mary's	0-7
Crumlin Star v Larne Tech. OB	2-1
Crumlin U v Orangefield OB	5-1
Derriaghy CC v Newcastle	3-1
Drumaness Mills v Downshire YM	2-1
Dungiven v Donard Hospital	0-1
Dunloy v Ballysillan Swifts	2-0
Dunmurry Rec v Downpatrick	3-0
East Belfast v Lower Maze	3-2
Groomsport v 1st Bangor OB	0-4
Immaculata v St. Patrick's YM	2-0
Killyleagh YC v Barn U	2-2*
Killyleagh YC won 3-2 on penalties.	
Killymoon Rangers v Newtowne	2-5
Kilmore Rec v Brantwood	2-5*
Kilroot Rec v Sirocco Works	0-8
Lisanally Rangers (withdrawn) v Abbey Villa (walkover)	
Lurgan T v UUJ	2-3*
Magherafelt Sky Blues v Dromore Amateurs	4-2
Moneyslane v Colin Valley	1-4
Mountjoy U (withdrawn) v Holywood (walkover)	
Nortel v Shankill U	2-2*
Shankill U won 3-2 on penalties.	
Newbuildings U v Desertmartin	1-3
Oxford Sunnyside v Ardstraw	1-3
Rathfern Rangers v Iveagh U	3-1
Rathfriland Rangers v Seagoe	4-0
Richhill v Oxford U Stars	0-2
Roe R v Broomhill	1-3*
Saintfield U v Shorts	2-2*
Shorts won 9-8 on penalties.	
Strabane Athletic v Newry City AFC	1-4*
Tandragee R v Dunmyrry YM	4-1
Valley Rangers v Bloomfield	2-3
Wellington Rec v Ballynure OB	3-2*
Bye: Markethill Swifts	

SECOND ROUND

1st Bangor OB v Colin Valley	2-0
Abbey Villa v Ardstraw	2-0
Ardglass v Ards Rangers	2-4
Ballynahinch Olympic v Immaculata	3-3*
Immaculata won 5-4 on penalties.	
Ballywalter Rec v Shankill U	4-5
Banbridge Rangers v Shorts	4-3*
Bloomfield v St. Mary's	2-3
Brantwood v Bangor Amateurs	4-2
Crumlin U v Broomhill	7-0
Derriaghy CC v Holywood	3-2
Desertmartin v Newtowne	1-3
Dunmurry Rec v Oxford U Stars	0-2
Hanover v Magherafelt Sky Blues	3-3*
Hanover won 5-4 on penalties.	
Killyleagh YC v Drumaness Mills	0-3
Malachians v Crumlin Star	1-4*
Markethill Swifts v East Belfast	1-5
Newry City AFC v Donard Hospital	1-0
Rathfern Rangers v Albert Foundry	2-5
Rathfriland Rangers v Dunloy	3-0
Sirocco Works v Lisburn Rangers	1-1*
Lisburn Rangers won 3-1 on penalties.	
Tandragee R v Ballymacash Rangers	5-1
UUJ v Wellington Rec	2-0

THIRD ROUND

1st Bangor OB v Rathfriland Rangers	1-1*
1st Bangor OB won 6-5 on penalties.	
Abbey Villa v Shankill U	1-2

Albert Foundry v St. Mary's	6-1
Banbridge Rangers v Tandragee R	0-2
Crumlin U v UUJ	3-0
Derriaghy CC v Oxford U Stars	4-2*
Drumaness Mills v Brantwood	1-2
East Belfast v Newtowne	3-5
Immaculata v Crumlin Star	0-2
Lisburn Rangers v Ards Rangers	2-7*
Newry City AFC v Hanover	4-0

FOURTH ROUND

Annagh U v 1st Bangor OB	3-0
Armagh C v Shankill U	2-0
Banbridge T v Ards	1-4
Bangor v Lurgan Celtic	2-1
Carrick Rangers v Albert Foundry	4-1
Coagh U v Brantwood	0-2
Dergview v Larne	0-1
Derriaghy CC v Wakehurst	3-2
Donegal Celtic v Ballyclare Comrades	2-3*
Dundela v Ballymoney U	4-1
H&W Welders v Dollingstown	2-0
Limavady U v Tobermore U	1-3*
Lisburn Distillery v Crumlin Star	0-1
Loughgall v Tandragee R	6-2
Moyola Park v Glebe Rangers	3-2
Newtowne v Crumlin U	4-1
Portstewart v Newry City AFC	2-1
PSNI v Knockbreda	2-1
Queen's University v Newington YC	2-3
Sport & Leisure Swifts v Ards Rangers	2-6

FIFTH ROUND

Annagh U v Ballyclare Comrades	1-3
Armagh C v Newtowne	3-0
Ballymena U v Crumlin Star	4-0
Bangor v Brantwood	4-0
Cliftonville v Ards Rangers	6-0
Coleraine v Warrenpoint T	1-3
Crusaders v Newington YC	6-0
Dungannon Swifts v Ballinamallard U	4-2*
Glentoran v Ards	2-0
H&W Welders v Derriaghy CC	2-0
Institute v Loughgall	5-1
Larne v Carrick Rangers	1-2
Moyola Park v Glenavon	2-3
Portstewart v Dundela	3-2
PSNI v Portadown	1-2*
Tobermore U v Linfield	0-2

SIXTH ROUND

Ballyclare Comrades v Dungannon Swifts	0-0*
Dungannon Swifts won 5-4 on penalties.	
Bangor v Crusaders	0-2
Carrick Rangers v Institute	3-1*
Cliftonville v Ballymena U	1-2
Glentoran v Armagh C	4-1
H&W Welders v Glenavon	2-0
Linfield v Warrenpoint T	5-0
Portstewart v Portadown	0-2

QUARTER-FINALS

Crusaders v Carrick Rangers	4-1
Glentoran v Dungannon Swifts	3-0
H&W Welders v Ballymena U	2-3
Portadown v Linfield	3-2

SEMI-FINALS

Ballymena U v Portadown	1-3
Crusaders v Glentoran	0-1

NORTHERN IRISH FA CUP FINAL 2014–15

Windsor Park, Belfast, Saturday 2 May 2015

Glentoran (0) 1 *(Scullion 54)*

Portadown (0) 0

Glentoran: Morris; Holland, Birney, Garrett, Kane, McAlorum, Henderson (Addis 89), Gordon, Scullion (McCaffrey 89), Stewart (Nelson 90), Allan.
Portadown: Miskelly; Casement, Redman, O'Hara, Breen, McMahon; Mackle, McAllister (Murray 72), Gault, Twigg, Garrett.
Referee: Ross Dunlop.

IRISH CUP FINALS (from 1946–47)

1946–47 Belfast Celtic 1, Glentoran 0	1982–83 Glentoran 1:2, Linfield 1:1
1947–48 Linfield 3, Coleraine 0	1983–84 Ballymena U 4, Carrick Rangers 1
1948–49 Derry City 3, Glentoran 1	1984–85 Glentoran 1:1, Linfield 1:0
1949–50 Linfield 2, Distillery 1	1985–86 Glentoran 2, Coleraine 1
1950–51 Glentoran 3, Ballymena U 1	1986–87 Glentoran 1, Larne 0
1951–52 Ards 1, Glentoran 0	1987–88 Glentoran 1, Glenavon 0
1952–53 Linfield 5, Coleraine 0	1988–89 Ballymena U 1, Larne 0
1953–54 Derry City 1, Glentoran 0	1989–90 Glentoran 3, Portadown 0
1954–55 Dundela 3, Glenavon 0	1990–91 Portadown 2, Glenavon 1
1955–56 Distillery 1, Glentoran 0	1991–92 Glenavon 2, Linfield 1
1956–57 Glenavon 2, Derry City 0	1992–93 Bangor 1:1:1, Ards 1:1:0
1957–58 Ballymena U 2, Linfield 0	1993–94 Linfield 2, Bangor 0
1958–59 Glenavon 2, Ballymena U 0	1994–95 Linfield 3, Carrick Rangers 1
1959–60 Linfield 5, Ards 1	1995–96 Glentoran 1, Glenavon 0
1960–61 Glenavon 5, Linfield 1	1996–97 Glenavon 1, Cliftonville 0
1961–62 Linfield 4, Portadown 0	1997–98 Glentoran 1, Glenavon 0
1962–63 Linfield 2, Distillery 1	1998–99 *Portadown awarded trophy after Cliftonville*
1963–64 Derry City 2, Glentoran 0	*were eliminated for using an ineligible player in*
1964–65 Coleraine 2, Glenavon 1	*semi-final.*
1965–66 Glentoran 2, Linfield 0	1999–2000 Glentoran 1, Portadown 0
1966–67 Crusaders 3, Glentoran 1	2000–01 Glentoran 1, Linfield 0
1967–68 Crusaders 2, Linfield 0	2001–02 Linfield 2, Portadown 1
1968–69 Ards 4, Distillery 2	2002–03 Coleraine 1, Glentoran 0
1969–70 Linfield 2, Ballymena U 1	2003–04 Glentoran 1, Coleraine 0
1970–71 Distillery 3, Derry City	2004–05 Portadown 5, Larne 1
1971–72 Coleraine 2, Portadown 1	2005–06 Linfield 2, Glentoran 1
1972–73 Glentoran 3, Linfield 2	2006–07 Linfield 2, Dungannon Swifts 2
1973–74 Ards 2, Ballymena U 1	*(aet; Linfield won 3-2 on penalties).*
1974–75 Coleraine 1:0:1, Linfield 1:0:0	2007–08 Linfield 2, Coleraine 1
1975–76 Carrick Rangers 2, Linfield 1	2008–09 Crusaders 1, Cliftonville 0
1976–77 Coleraine 4, Linfield 1	2009–10 Linfield 2, Portadown 1
1977–78 Linfield 3, Ballymena U 1	2010–11 Linfield 2, Crusaders 1
1978–79 Cliftonville 3, Portadown 2	2011–12 Linfield 4, Crusaders 1
1979–80 Linfield 2, Crusaders 0	2012–13 Glentoran 3, Cliftonville 1
1980–81 Ballymena U 1, Glenavon 0	2013–14 Glenavon 2, Ballymena U 1
1981–82 Linfield 2, Coleraine 1	2014–15 Glentoran 1, Portadown 0

ULSTER CUP WINNERS

1949 Linfield	1978 Linfield
1950 Larne	1979 Linfield
1951 Glentoran	1980 Ballymena U
1952 *No competition*	1981 Glentoran
1953 Glentoran	1982 Glentoran
1954 Crusaders	1983 Glentoran
1955 Glenavon	1984 Linfield
1956 Linfield	1985 Coleraine
1957 Linfield	1986 Coleraine
1958 Distillery	1987 Larne
1959 Glenavon	1988 Glentoran
1960 Linfield	1989 Glentoran
1961 Ballymena U	1990 Portadown
1962 Linfield	1991 Bangor
1963 Crusaders	1992 Linfield
1964 Linfield	1993 Crusaders
1965 Coleraine	1994 Bangor
1966 Glentoran	1995 Portadown
1967 Linfield	1996 Portadown
1968 Coleraine	1997 Coleraine
1969 Coleraine	1998 Ballyclare Comrades
1970 Linfield	1999 Distillery
1971 Linfield	2000 *No competition*
1972 Coleraine	2001 *No competition*
1973 Ards	2002 *No competition*
1974 Linfield	2003 Dungannon Swifts
1975 Coleraine	*(Confined to First Division clubs)*
1976 Glentoran	2004–15 *No competition*
1977 Linfield	

SETANTA SPORTS CUP WINNERS

2004–05 Linfield	2010–11 Shamrock R
2005–06 Drogheda U	2011–12 Crusaders
2006–07 Drogheda U	2012–13 Shamrock R
2007–08 Cork C	2013–14 Sligo R
2009–10 Bohemians	2014–15 *No competition*

ROLL OF HONOUR SEASON 2014–15

Competition	Winner	Runner-up
Northern Irish Danske Bank Premier League	Crusaders	Linfield
Northern Irish FA Cup	Glentoran	Portadown
Belfast Telegraph Irish Championship Division One	Carrick Rangers	Bangor
Belfast Telegraph Irish Championship Division Two	Lurgan Celtic	Annagh U
Wasp Solutions League Cup	Cliftonville	Ballymena U
County Antrim Shield	Cliftonville	Bangor
Steel & Sons Cup	Carrick Rangers	H&W Welders
Co Antrim Junior Shield	Tullycarnet	Kelvin OB
Coca-Cola Irish Junior Cup	Harryville Homers	Rosemount Rec
Mid Ulster Cup (Senior)	Dungannon Swifts	Armagh C
Harry Cavan Youth Cup	Glenavon Youth	Linfield Rangers
George Wilson Memorial Cup	Crusaders Reserves	Cliftonville Olympic
North West Senior Cup	Institute	Moyala Park
The Fermanagh Mulhern Cup	Strathroy Harps	Enniskillen Town
Britton Rose Bowl	Northern Irish AFL	Scottish AFA
Intermediate Cup	Carrick Rangers	H&W Welders

NORTHERN IRELAND FOOTBALL WRITERS ASSOCIATION AWARDS

MANAGER OF THE YEAR
Stephen Baxter (Crusaders)

PLAYER OF THE YEAR
Paul Heatley (Crusaders)

CHAMPIONSHIP PLAYER OF THE YEAR
Jordan Forsythe (Bangor)

YOUNG PLAYER OF THE YEAR
Gavin Whyte (Crusaders)

INTERNATIONAL PERSONALITY OF THE YEAR
Kyle Lafferty (Norwich C)

NON-SENIOR TEAM OF THE YEAR
Carrick Rangers

MERIT AWARD
Ruth McCreery (Glentoran)

DR MALCOLM BRODIE HALL OF FAME
Gerry Armstrong

TEAM OF THE SEASON
Sean O'Neil (Crusaders)
Billy Joe Burns (Crusaders)
Mark Haughey (Linfield)
Colin Coates (Crusaders)
Craig McClean (Crusaders)
Gavin Whyte (Crusaders)
Richard Clarke (Crusaders)
Declan Caddell (Crusaders)
Paul Heatley (Crusaders)
Joe Gormley (Cliftonville)
Jordan Owens (Crusaders)

NIFWA @BTSPORT PREMIERSHIP PLAYER OF THE MONTH 2014–15

Month	Player	Team
August	Davy McDaid	Cliftonville
September	Johnny Taylor	Ballymena U
October	Jude Winchester	Cliftonville
November	Joe Gormley	Cliftonville
December	Mark McAllister	Portadown
January	Richard Clarke	Crusaders
February	Gavin Whyte	Crusaders
March	Curtis Allen	Glentoran
April	Billy Joe Burns	Crusaders

NIFWA MANAGER OF THE MONTH 2014–15

August	Glenn Ferguson	Ballymena U
September	Ronnie McFall	Portadown
October	Tommy Breslin	Cliftonville
November	Ronnie McFall	Portadown
December	Warren Feeney	Linfield
January	Stephen Baxter	Crusaders
February	Stephen Baxter	Crusaders
March	Eddie Patterson	Glentoran
April	Gary Hamilton	Glenavon

NIFWA CHAMPIONSHIP PLAYER OF THE MONTH 2014–15

August	Richard Gibson	Bangor
September	Michael McLellan	H&W Welders
October	Jordan Forsythe	Bangor
November	Ciaran Murray	Larne
December	Conor McCluskey	Carrick Rangers
January	David Rainey	H&W Welders
February	Mark Magennis	H&W Welders

EUROPEAN CUP FINALS

EUROPEAN CUP FINALS 1956–1992

Year	Winners v Runners-up		Venue	Attendance	Referee
1956	Real Madrid v Reims	4-3	Paris	38,239	A. Ellis (England)
1957	Real Madrid v Fiorentina	2-0	Madrid	124,000	L. Horn (Netherlands)
1958	Real Madrid v AC Milan	3-2*	Brussels	67,000	A. Alsteen (Belgium)
1959	Real Madrid v Reims	2-0	Stuttgart	72,000	A. Dutsch (West Germany)
1960	Real Madrid v Eintracht Frankfurt	7-3	Glasgow	127,621	J. Mowat (Scotland)
1961	Benfica v Barcelona	3-2	Berne	26,732	G. Dienst (Switzerland)
1962	Benfica v Real Madrid	5-3	Amsterdam	61,257	L. Horn (Netherlands)
1963	AC Milan v Benfica	2-1	Wembley	45,715	A. Holland (England)
1964	Internazionale v Real Madrid	3-1	Vienna	71,333	J. Stoll (Austria)
1965	Internazionale v Benfica	1-0	Milan	89,000	G. Dienst (Switzerland)
1966	Real Madrid v Partizan Belgrade	2-1	Brussels	46,745	R. Kreitlein (West Germany)
1967	Celtic v Internazionale	2-1	Lisbon	45,000	K. Tschenscher (West Germany)
1968	Manchester U v Benfica	4-1*	Wembley	92,225	C. Lo Bello (Italy)
1969	AC Milan v Ajax	4-1	Madrid	31,782	J. Ortiz de Mendibil (Spain)
1970	Feyenoord v Celtic	2-1*	Milan	53,187	C. Lo Bello (Italy)
1971	Ajax v Panathinaikos	2-0	Wembley	90,000	J. Taylor (England)
1972	Ajax v Internazionale	2-0	Rotterdam	61,354	R. Helies (France)
1973	Ajax v Juventus	1-0	Belgrade	89,484	M. Guglovic (Yugoslavia)
1974	Bayern Munich v Atletico Madrid	1-1	Brussels	48,722	V. Loraux (Belgium)
Replay	Bayern Munich v Atletico Madrid	4-0	Brussels	23,325	A. Delcourt (Belgium)
1975	Bayern Munich v Leeds U	2-0	Paris	48,374	M. Kitabdjian (France)
1976	Bayern Munich v St Etienne	1-0	Glasgow	54,864	K. Palotai (Hungary)
1977	Liverpool v Moenchengladbach	3-1	Rome	52,078	R. Wurtz (France)
1978	Liverpool v FC Brugge	1-0	Wembley	92,500	C. Corver (Netherlands)
1979	Nottingham F v Malmo	1-0	Munich	57,500	E. Linemayr (Austria)
1980	Nottingham F v Hamburg	1-0	Madrid	51,000	A. Garrido (Portugal)
1981	Liverpool v Real Madrid	1-0	Paris	48,360	K. Palotai (Hungary)
1982	Aston Villa v Bayern Munich	1-0	Rotterdam	46,000	G. Konrath (France)
1983	Hamburg v Juventus	1-0	Athens	73,500	N. Rainea (Romania)
1984	Liverpool v Roma	1-1*	Rome	69,693	E. Fredriksson (Sweden)
	(Liverpool won 4-2 on penalties)				
1985	Juventus v Liverpool	1-0	Brussels	58,000	A. Daina (Switzerland)
1986	Steaua Bucharest v Barcelona	0-0*	Seville	70,000	M. Vautrot (France)
	(Steaua won 2-0 on penalties)				
1987	Porto v Bayern Munich	2-1	Vienna	57,500	A. Ponnet (Belgium)
1988	PSV Eindhoven v Benfica	0-0*	Stuttgart	68,000	L. Agnolin (Italy)
	(PSV won 6-5 on penalties)				
1989	AC Milan v Steaua Bucharest	4-0	Barcelona	97,000	K.-H. Tritschler (West Germany)
1990	AC Milan v Benfica	1-0	Vienna	57,500	H. Kohl (Austria)
1991	Red Star Belgrade v Marseille	0-0*	Bari	56,000	T. Lanese (Italy)
	(Red Star won 5-3 on penalties)				
1992	Barcelona v Sampdoria	1-0*	Wembley	70,827	A. Schmidhuber (Germany)

UEFA CHAMPIONS LEAGUE FINALS 1993–2015

Year	Winners v Runners-up		Venue	Attendance	Referee
1993	Marseille† v AC Milan	1-0	Munich	64,400	K. Rothlisberger (Switzerland)
1994	AC Milan v Barcelona	4-0	Athens	70,000	P. Don (England)
1995	Ajax v AC Milan	1-0	Vienna	49,730	I. Craciunescu (Romania)
1996	Juventus v Ajax	1-1*	Rome	70,000	M. D. Vega (Spain)
	(Juventus won 4-2 on penalties)				
1997	Borussia Dortmund v Juventus	3-1	Munich	59,000	S. Puhl (Hungary)
1998	Real Madrid v Juventus	1-0	Amsterdam	48,500	H. Krug (Germany)
1999	Manchester U v Bayern Munich	2-1	Barcelona	90,245	P. Collina (Italy)
2000	Real Madrid v Valencia	3-0	Paris	80,000	S. Braschi (Italy)
2001	Bayern Munich v Valencia	1-1*	Milan	79,000	D. Jol (Netherlands)
	(Bayern Munich won 5-4 on penalties)				
2002	Real Madrid v Leverkusen	2-1	Glasgow	50,499	U. Meier (Switzerland)
2003	AC Milan v Juventus	0-0*	Manchester	62,315	M. Merk (Germany)
	(AC Milan won 3-2 on penalties)				
2004	Porto v Monaco	3-0	Gelsenkirchen	53,053	K. M. Nielsen (Denmark)
2005	Liverpool v AC Milan	3-3*	Istanbul	65,000	M. M. González (Spain)
	(Liverpool won 3-2 on penalties)				
2006	Barcelona v Arsenal	2-1	Paris	79,610	T. Hauge (Norway)
2007	AC Milan v Liverpool	2-1	Athens	74,000	H. Fandel (Germany)
2008	Manchester U v Chelsea	1-1*	Moscow	67,310	L. Michel (Slovakia)
	(Manchester U won 6-5 on penalties)				
2009	Barcelona v Manchester U	2-0	Rome	62,467	M. Busacca (Switzerland)
2010	Internazionale v Bayern Munich	2-0	Madrid	73,490	H. Webb (England)
2011	Barcelona v Manchester U	3-1	Wembley	87,695	V. Kassai (Hungary)
2012	Chelsea v Bayern Munich	1-1*	Munich	62,500	P. Proença (Portugal)
	(Chelsea won 4-3 on penalties)				
2013	Bayern Munich v Borussia Dortmund	2-1	Wembley	86,298	N. Rizzoli (Italy)
2014	Real Madrid v Atletico Madrid	4-1*	Lisbon	60,000	B. Kuipers (Netherlands)
2015	Barcelona v Juventus	3-1	Berlin	70,442	C. Cakir (Turkey)

†*Subsequently stripped of title.*
After extra time.

UEFA CHAMPIONS LEAGUE 2014–15

■ *Denotes player sent off.*

FIRST QUALIFYING ROUND FIRST LEG

Tuesday, 1 July 2014

La Fiorita (0) 0
Levadia Tallinn (0) 1 *(Tamm 90)* 438
La Fiorita: (4141) Montanari; Angeletti, Bugli, Bollini, Calzolari (Confalone 53); Rinaldi; Mazzola, Pensalfini, Cangini, Ceci; Selva (Gualtieri 35 (Scarponi 87)).
Levadia Tallinn: (442) Smishko; Pikk, Podholjuzin, Raudsepp (Aallikko 79), Artjunin; Subbotin, Tipuric, Ivanov (Tamm 59), Vukobratovic; Teever, Antonov.

FC Santa Coloma (1) 1 *(Pujol 5)*
Banants Yerevan (0) 0 323
FC Santa Coloma: (442) Casals; Wagner, Ramos A, Lima, Ramos R; Pujol, Rebes (Martinez J 58), Juvenal, Juanfer (Mercade 63); Martinez C, Parra (Romero 19).
Banants Yerevan: (433) Toroyan; Fofana, Usanov (Ayvazyan 73), Shakhnazaryan, Daghbashyan; Loretsyan, Arakelyan, Hovsepyan; Nranyan, Karapetyan (Muradyan 78), Azatyan (Poghosyan 59).

Wednesday, 2 July 2014

Lincoln (1) 1 *(Chipolina J 18 (pen))*
HB Torshavn (0) 1 *(Hanssen 71)* 1821
Lincoln: (442) Perez J; Casciaro K, Casciaro R, Casciaro L, Gulling (Cabrera 68); Duarte D (Payas 77), Chipolina R, Duarte J (Perez B 83), Clarke; Chipolina J, Garcia.
HB Torshavn: (442) Gestsson; dos Santos, Holm, Johan Davidsen, Vatnsdal; Benjaminsen, Edmundsson, Hanssen, Mouritsen (Ingason 84); Joensen R, Jensen.

FIRST QUALIFYING ROUND SECOND LEG

Tuesday, 8 July 2014

Banants Yerevan (1) 3 *(Hovsepyan 11, 56 (pen), Mashumyan 47)*
FC Santa Coloma (1) 2 *(Lima 20, Casals 90)* 1500
Banants Yerevan: (442) Toroyan; Fofana, Usanov (Karapetyan 25 (Muradyan 90)), Arakelyan, Daghbashyan; Loretsyan, Poghosyan, Hovsepyan, Ayvazyan; Azatyan (Mashumyan 46), Nranyan■.
FC Santa Coloma: (442) Casals; Wagner (Martinez J 82), Lima (Blanco 58), Ramos A, Ramos R; Pujol, Rebes, Juvenal, Juanfer (Toscano 67); Martinez C, Parra.
FC Santa Coloma won on away goals.

HB Torshavn (3) 5 *(Hanssen 11, 81, Jensen 25, Edmundsson 34, Benjaminsen 88)*
Lincoln (0) 2 *(Cabrera 50, Duarte J 77)* 1068
HB Torshavn: (442) Gestsson; Hanssen, Jensen (Flotum 58), Edmundsson, Alex; Holm, Johan Davidsen, Vatnsdal, Benjaminsen; Mouritsen (Joensen P 90), Joensen R (Jogvan Davidsen 90).
Lincoln: (442) Perez J; Casciaro K (Casciaro L 46), Casciaro R, Perez B, Chipolina R; Payas (Gulling 86), Cabrera, Clarke, Pons (Duarte J 68); Chipolina J, Garcia.

Levadia Tallinn (2) 7 *(Kulinits 7, Subbotin 30, 72, Elhussieny 48, Artjunin 75, 90, Tipuric 85)*
La Fiorita (0) 0 1455
Levadia Tallinn: (442) Smishko; Artjunin, Pikk, Kulinits, Podholjuzin; Subbotin, Tamm (Elhussieny 46), Tipuric, Vukobratovic (Kaljumae 60); Antonov, Teever (Marin 71).
La Fiorita: (442) Montanari; Angeletti, Rinaldi, Bugli, Mazzola; Pensalfini, Confalone, Cangini (Cavalli 55), Bollini (Scarponi 75); Ceci (Forcellini 64), Selva.

SECOND QUALIFYING ROUND FIRST LEG

Tuesday, 15 July 2014

BATE Borisov (0) 0
Skenderbeu (0) 0 12,671
BATE Borisov: (433) Chernik; Filipenko, Palyakow, Khagush (Gordeichuk 70), Hayduchyk; Karnitskiy, Valadzko M, Aleksiyevich; Krivets (Pavlov 70), Signevich, Rodionov.

Skenderbeu: (4411) Shehi; Radas, Vangjeli, Osmani, Ademir (Nimaga 74); Arapi, Lilaj, Progni (Jashanica 90), Orelesi; Shkembi; Sefa (Ribaj 90).

Cliftonville (0) 0
Debrecen (0) 0 1750
Cliftonville: (442) Devlin; McGovern, Scannell, Flynn, Seydak (McMullan 83); Cosgrove, Johnston, Curran, Donnelly (Garrett 63); Catney, Gormley (Murray 90).
Debrecen: (442) Novakovic; Lazar, Meszaros, Mate, Korhut; Jovanovic (Zsidai 86), Bouadla, Bodi (Mihelic 79), Varga; Sidibe, Tisza (Seydi 46).

Dinamo Zagreb (0) 2 *(Soudani 58, Antolic 70)*
Zalgiris (0) 0 4211
Dinamo Zagreb: (451) Eduardo; Sigali, Ibanez, Simunic, Ivo Pinto; Antolic (Goncalo 85), Paulo Machado (Andrijasevic 78), Ademi, Brozovic, Cop; Soudani (Pjaca 73).
Zalgiris: (4411) Vitkauskas; Vaitkunas, Kerla, Semberas, Freidgeimas; Zulpa (Janusauskas 67), Wilk, Svrljuga, Kuklys (Pilibaitis 67); Adi; Nyuiadzi (Silenas 85).

KR Reykjavik (0) 0
Celtic (0) 1 *(McGregor 84)* 2781
KR Reykjavik: (442) Magnusson; Hauksson, Josepsson, Sigurdsson G, Gudmundur Gunnarsson; Atlason (Ormarsson 88), Saevarsson, Sigurdsson B, Lorenzo (Zato 58); Finnbogason, Martin (Ragnarsson 81).
Celtic: (4411) Forster; Lustig, van Dijk, Ambrose, Izaguirre; Griffiths (Boerrigter 74), Johansen, Mulgrew, McGregor; Commons; Stokes (Pukki 74).

Partizan Belgrade (1) 3 *(Lazovic 14, 64, Skuletic 71)*
HB Torshavn (0) 0 11,758
Partizan Belgrade: (442) Lukac; Trajkovic, Vulicevic, Petrovic, Stankovic; Brasanac, Pantic (Ilic S 72), Grbic (Zivkovic 54), Drincic; Lazovic (Ninkovic 83), Skuletic.
HB Torshavn: (442) Gestsson; Joensen R (Wardum 63), Alex, Holm, Johan Davidsen; Vatnsdal, Benjaminsen, Edmundsson, Jogvan Davidsen (Flotum 77); Mouritsen (Ingason 66), Hanssen.

Rabotnicki Kometal (0) 0
HJK Helsinki (0) 0 1000
Rabotnicki Kometal: (442) Siskovski; Najdoski, Siljanovski, Milushev, Ilievski; Vujcic (Bojku 90), Petrovic, Sulejmanov, Markoshi; Avramovski (Trajcevski 77), Anene (Todorovski 53).
HJK Helsinki: (442) Tornes; Lampi, Sorsa, Moren, Vayrynen; Savage, Heikkinen, Tainio, Alho (Schuller 70); Lod, Kandji.

FC Santa Coloma (0) 0
Maccabi Tel Aviv (0) 1 *(Prica 64)* 494
FC Santa Coloma: (433) Casals; Ramos R, Ramos A, Martinez C, Rebes; Pujol, Juvenal, Mercade (Romero 71); Martinez J (Blanco 70), Parra, Toscano (Juanfer 58).
Maccabi Tel Aviv: (433) Juan Pablo; Tibi, Carlos Garcia, Ben Haroush, Yeyni; Alberman, Radi (Einbinder 64), Mikha; Ben Haim (Badash 85), Prica (Margolis 85), Zahavi.

Sheriff (0) 2 *(Muresan 71, Isa 87)*
Sutjeska (0) 0 6351
Sheriff: (442) Degra; Ligger, Metoua, Luvannor, Muresan; Ernandes, Blanco, Cadu (Galvao 75), Ginsari; Potiguar (Benson 52), Ricardinho (Isa 61).
Sutjeska: (541) Janjusevic; Lukic (Krivokapic 39), Igumanovic (Fukui 76), Jovanovic, Cukovic, Stefanovic; Jovovic, Nikolic, Nikola, Pejovic (Kovacevic 63); Vujovic G.

Slovan Bratislava (0) 1 *(Cikos 52)*
The New Saints (0) 0 4828
Slovan Bratislava: (442) Pernis; Ninaj, Hudak, Cikos, Jablonsky; Zofcak (Peltier 70), Milinkovic, Soumah, Lasik; Fort, Halenar (Grendel 80).
The New Saints: (442) Harrison; Spender, Marriott, Edwards K, Rawlinson; Finley (Ruscoe 89), Fraughan (Darlington 46), Seargeant, Edwards A (Draper 84); Williams, Wilde.

Sparta Prague (3) 7 *(Lafata 22, 44, 45 (pen), 57, 60,*
Tipuric 55 (og), Prikryl 84)
Levadia Tallinn (0) 0 10,152
Sparta Prague: (433) Bicik; Nhamoinesu, Kaderabek,
Svejdik, Holek; Vacha, Matejovsky, Dockal; Husbauer
(Marecek 69), Krejci (Prikryl 79), Lafata (Bednar 73).
Levadia Tallinn: (4231) Smishko; Artjunin, Podholjuzin,
Pikk, Kulinits (Teever 58); Tipuric, Vukobratovic;
Subbotin, Raudsepp, Antonov (Kaljumae 82); Elhussieny
(Penic 63).

Valletta (0) 0
Qarabag (1) 1 *(Chumbinho 18)* 1200
Valletta: (433) Vella; Caruana, Azzopardi, Camilleri■,
Dimech; Faria, Bajada (Arab 90), Briffa; Nafti (Zammit
85), Fenech, Elford-Alliyu (Kooh Sohna 72).
Qarabag: (433) Sehic; Qarayev (Yusifov 79), Teli, Agolli,
Huseynov; Reynaldo, Muarem (Danilo Dias 72),
Almeida; Qurbanov, George (Nadirov 87), Chumbinho.

Zrinjski Mostar (0) 0
Maribor (0) 0 5100
Zrinjski Mostar: (442) Dujkovic; Graovac, Muminovic■,
Pehar, Scepanovic; Stojkic, Zlatic, Stojanovic (Durak 66),
Nikolic (Kordic 82); Katanec, Djuric (Simeunovic 65).
Maribor: (442) Handanovic; Suler, Filipovic, Ibraimi
(Bohar 81), Mendy (Tavares 67); Fajic, Dervisevic, Vrsic,
Rajcevic; Viler, Stojanovic.

Wednesday, 16 July 2014
Dinamo Tbilisi (0) 0
Aktobe (0) 1 *(Danilo Neco 51)* 10,100
Dinamo Tbilisi: (4411) Loria; Totadze, Janelidze (Xisco
46), Merebashvilli (Martsvaladze 66), Grigalashvili;
Papava, Dosoudil, Gvelesiani, Shergelashvili; Dzaria;
Vouho (Jorda 79).
Aktobe: (4411) Sidelnikov; Tsarikayev, Miroshnichenko,
Pizzelli (Zenkovich 61), Khairullin; Danilo Neco
(Shabalin 81), Arzumanyan, Korobkin, Logvinenko;
Mineiro; Antonov (Kapadze 72).

Legia Warsaw (0) 1 *(Radovic 90)*
Saint Patrick's Ath (1) 1 *(Fagan 38)* 11,075
Legia Warsaw: (442) Kuciak; Jodlowiec, Astiz,
Rzezniczak, Broz; Pinto (Vrdoljak 66), Brzyski, Radovic,
Kosecki (Duda 77); Zyro, Orlando Sa (Saganowski 16).
Saint Patrick's Ath: (442) Clarke; O'Brien, Bermingham,
Oman, Browne; Bolger, Byrne, Fahey, Brennan
(Chambers 76); Forrester (Quigley 49), Fagan (Lynch
85).

Ludogorets Razgrad (2) 4 *(Dani Abalo 35, Bezjak 43,*
Abel 65, Fabio Espinho 68)
F91 Dudelange (0) 0 4104
Ludogorets Razgrad: (4411) Stoyanov; Barthe, Fabio
Espinho (Wanderson 82), Bezjak, Dani Abalo; Dyakov
(Zlatinski 73), Minev, Moti, Junior Caicara; Marcelinho
(Abel 63); Misidjan.
F91 Dudelange: (4411) Joubert; Moreira, Ney, Schnell,
Karapetian (Turpel 78); Benzouien, Pedro, Sylla (Malget
88), Prempeh; Schulz (Stelvio Cruz 52); Benajiba.

Malmo (0) 0
Ventspils (0) 0 8831
Malmo: (442) Olsen; Concha, Hammar, Ricardinho,
Johansson E; Nazari (Rakip 85), Forsberg, Halsti,
Rosenberg; Thelin (Cibicki 69), Eriksson.
Ventspils: (442) Uvarenko; Dubra, Kurakins, Barinovs,
Freidgeimas; Timofejevs, Paulius (Tarkhnishvili 52),
Ulimbashevs (Karlsons 64), Recickis; Mujeci,
Abdultaofik (Tidenbergs 63).

Stromsgodset (0) 0
Steaua Bucharest (0) 1 *(Iancu 49)* 5056
Stromsgodset: (442) Kwarasey; Storbaek, Abu,
Hoibraten, Junior; Fossum, Vilsvik (Odegaard 85),
Storflor, Ogunjimi (Sorum 61); Hamoud, Kastrati
(Wikheim 69).
Steaua Bucharest: (442) Arlauskis; Rapa, Szukala,
Latovlevici, Varela; Chipciu, Iancu (Filip 75), Tanase,
Prepelita; Sanmartean (Vilceanu 90), Parvulescu (Stanciu
58).

SECOND QUALIFYING ROUND SECOND LEG
Tuesday, 22 July 2014
Celtic (3) 4 *(van Dijk 14, 20, Pukki 27, 71)*
KR Reykjavik (0) 0 36,000
Celtic: (4411) Forster; Lustig, Ambrose, van Dijk,
Izaguirre (Matthews 61); Griffiths (Kayal 61), Johansen,
Mulgrew, McGregor; Commons; Pukki (Henderson 72).
KR Reykjavik: (4411) Magnusson; Hauksson, Josepsson,
Sigurdsson G, Gunnar Thor Gunnarsson; Finnbogason,
Saevarsson (Zato-Arouna 57), Sigurdsson B, Atlason
(Ormarsson 46); Lorenzo (Jonsson 72); Martin.

Debrecen (0) 2 *(Mihelic 55, Sidibe 79)*
Cliftonville (0) 0 9457
Debrecen: (442) Novakovic; Meszaros, Mate, Korhut,
Jovanovic; Mihelic, Bodi (Zsidai 80), Varga, Szakaly
(Vadnai 72); Volas, Sidibe (Tisza 83).
Cliftonville: (442) Devlin; McGovern■, Scannell, Flynn,
Seydak; Cosgrove (Smyth 56), Johnston, Curran,
Donnelly; Catney (Caldwell 81), Garrett (Winchester 62).

F91 Dudelange (0) 1 *(Turpel 81)*
Ludogorets Razgrad (0) 1 *(Bezjak 51)* 842
F91 Dudelange: (442) Joubert; Moreira, Prempeh,
Benzouien (Malget 68), Schnell; Ney, Turpel (Schulz 82),
Stelvio Cruz, Benajiba; Sylla (Karapetian 60), Pedro.
Ludogorets Razgrad: (433) Stoyanov; Barthe (Mantyla
73), Moti, Minev, Choco; Zlatinski, Fabio Espinho,
Marcelinho (Wanderson 65); Bezjak, Misidjan
(Aleksandrov M 64), Lumu.

HB Torshavn (1) 1 *(Wardum 35)*
Partizan Belgrade (0) 3 *(Ninkovic 49, Lazovic 75,*
Grbic 90) 1151
HB Torshavn: (442) Gestsson; Johan Davidsen, Holm,
Vatnsdal (Wardum 22), Joensen P; Benjaminsen, Jogvan
Davidsen, Jensen (Ingason 75), Edmundsson; Mouritsen
(Flotum 82), Hanssen.
Partizan Belgrade: (442) Lukac; Ilic B, Volkov,
Stankovic, Ostojic; Drincic, Luka (Grbic 66), Brasanac,
Ninkovic; Lazovic (Fofana 78), Skuletic (Ilic S 73).

Levadia Tallinn (0) 1 *(Teever 68)*
Sparta Prague (1) 1 *(Marecek 38)* 1150
Levadia Tallinn: (4411) Pikker; Penic (Marin 81),
Artjunin, Antonov (Kaljumae 84), Subbotin; Teever,
Podholjuzin, Tipuric, Pikk; Ivanov (Elhussieny 61);
Raudsepp.
Sparta Prague: (433) Stech; Brabec, Vacha, Dockal
(Lafata 78), Marecek; Nespor (Holek 84), Kovac,
Kaderabek; Konate, Hybs, Breznanik (Prikryl 76).

Maccabi Tel Aviv (0) 2 *(Zahavi 62 (pen), Ben Haim 90)*
FC Santa Coloma (0) 0 100
Maccabi Tel Aviv: (433) Juan Pablo; Tibi, Carlos Garcia,
Ben Haroush, Yeyni; Mikha (Lugasi 80), Einbinder (Radi
68), Alberman; Prica (Badash■ 65), Zahavi, Ben Haim.
FC Santa Coloma: (433) Casals; Martinez C, Ramos A,
Rebes, Juanfer (Ramos R 52); Pujol, Juvenal, Mercade■;
Parra, Toscano (Garcia 82), Martinez J (Blanco 49).
Played in Larnaca.

Qarabag (1) 4 *(Reynaldo 15, Chumbinho 48,*
Danilo Dias 56, George 80)
Valletta (0) 0 23,350
Qarabag: (4231) Sehic; Teli, Qarayev, Huseynov,
Qurbanov; Chumbinho, Agolli (Guliyev 81); Reynaldo
(Nadirov 46), Almeida (Yusifov 75); George; Danilo Dias.
Valletta: (4411) Vella; Caruana■, Dimech, Azzopardi, Nafti
(Al Kamali 85); Faria, Bajada, Briffa, Fenech■; Zammit
(Montebello 69); Elford-Alliyu (Kooh Sohna 57).

Skenderbeu (0) 1 *(Radas 67)*
BATE Borisov (1) 1 *(Alyakhnovich 29)* 6200
Skenderbeu: (433) Shehi; Radas, Vangjeli, Osmani
(Jashanica 66), Arapi; Progni, Lilaj, Orelesi; Shkembi,
Berisha (Ribaj 60), Sefa.
BATE Borisov: (442) Chernik; Khagush (Hayduchyk 62),
Palyakow, Filipenko, Valadzko A; Aleksiyevich
(Karnitskiy 85), Alyakhnovich, Valadzko M, Gordeichuk
(Pavlov 90); Signevich, Rodionov.
BATE Borisov won on away goals.

Sutjeska (0) 0
Sheriff (2) 3 *(Benson 5, Luvannor 35, Isa 55)*   6351
Sutjeska: (442) Janjusevic; Ognjanovic, Stefanovic, Jovovic (Djajic 90), Nikolic; Nikola (Vujovic J 81), Vujovic G■, Cukovic, Igumanovic; Lukic, Fukui (Kovacevic 66).
Sheriff: (442) Degra; Ginsari (Leonel 46), Metoua, Benson, Cadu; Blanco (Galvao 85), Ernandes, Isa, Muresan; Ligger, Luvannor (Ricardinho 66).

The New Saints (0) 0
Slovan Bratislava (0) 2 *(Milinkovic 74, 89)*   1140
The New Saints: (442) Harrison; Spender, Marriott, Baker, Edwards K; Finley, Seargeant (Quigley 75), Edwards A, Draper; Williams (Darlington 59), Wilde (Evans 80).
Slovan Bratislava: (442) Pernis; Ninaj, Cikos, Hudak, Jablonsky; Grendel (Jakubek 90), Zofcak (Meszaros 66), Milinkovic, Soumah (Halenar 69); Lasik, Fort.

Zalgiris (0) 0
Dinamo Zagreb (0) 2 *(Soudani 47, Simunic 49)*   4000
Zalgiris: (4231) Vitkauskas; Freidgeimas, Vaitkunas, Kerla, Semberas (Janusauskas 76); Wilk (Silenas 78), Pilibaitis (Zulpa 65); Svrljuga, Adi, Komolov; Nyuiadzi.
Dinamo Zagreb: (4321) Eduardo; Simunic, Ibanez, Ivo Pinto, Simunovic; Paulo Machado, Ademi (Coric 56), Antolic; Brozovic (Goncalo 67), Pjaca; Radonjic (Soudani 46).

Wednesday, 23 July 2014

Aktobe (0) 3 *(Antonov 75, Zenkovich 82, Aimbetov 90)*
Dinamo Tbilisi (0) 0   12,100
Aktobe: (442) Sidelnikov; Muldarov, Tsarikayev, Miroshnichenko, Antonov (Zenkovich 81); Pizzelli (Tagybergen 84), Khairullin, Danilo Neco (Aimbetov 86), Arzumanyan; Korobkin, Anderson Mineiro.
Dinamo Tbilisi: (442) Loria; Khurtsilava, Totadze, Merebashvili (Martsvaladze 63), Jorda; Grigalashvili, Papava (Vouho 77), Xisco, Dosoudil; Gvelesiani, Dzaria.

HJK Helsinki (2) 2 *(Lod 22, Moren 26)*
Rabotnicki Kometal (0) 1 *(Vujcic 47)*   10,153
HJK Helsinki: (4411) Tornes; Sorsa, Moren, Heikkinen, Lampi; Alho, Tainio, Schuller, Savage (Baah 90); Lod; Kandji (Vayrynen 88).
Rabotnicki Kometal: (433) Siskovski; Siljanovski, Najdoski, Ilievski, Milushev (Trajcevski 68); Vujcic, Velkovski (Avramovski 59), Petrovic; Todorovski, Markoshi (Anene 38), Sulejmanov.

Maribor (1) 2 *(Vrsic 45, Ibraimi 57 (pen))*
Zrinjski Mostar (0) 0   7500
Maribor: (442) Handanovic; Vrsic, Ibraimi, Suler, Filipovic; Tavares (Bohar 72), Mendy (Fajic 87), Dervisevic (Mertelj 81), Viler; Rajcevic, Stojanovic.
Zrinjski Mostar: (442) Dujkovic; Graovac, Pehar (Simeunovic 60), Scepanovic, Blaic; Radulovic, Stojanovic (Radeljic 75), Stojkic, Nikolic; Katanec, Djuric (Kordic 68).

Saint Patrick's Ath (0) 0
Legia Warsaw (1) 5 *(Radovic 25, 82, Zyro 69, Saganowski 87, Byrne 90 (og))*   4213
Saint Patrick's Ath: (4231) Clarke; O'Brien (Hoare 62), Foran, Browne (Lynch 74), Bermingham; Fahey, Bolger; Byrne, Brennan, Forrester (Quigley 46); Fagan.
Legia Warsaw: (442) Kuciak; Broz, Rzezniczak, Astiz, Brzyski; Kucharczyk (Kosecki 85), Vrdoljak, Jodlowiec, Zyro; Duda (Saganowski 84), Radovic (Piech 88).

Steaua Bucharest (0) 2 *(Rapa 72, Stanciu 84)*
Stromsgodset (0) 0   1000
Steaua Bucharest: (442) Arlauskis; Rapa, Szukala, Varela, Latovlevici; Filip, Prepelita, Popa (Gradinaru 71), Sanmartean (Stanciu 60); Tanase, Chipciu (Vilceanu 87).
Stromsgodset: (442) Kwarasey; Vilsvik (Wikheim 61), Storbaek, Hoibraten, Hamoud; Storflor (Kovacs 75), Junior (Sorum 75), Abu, Kastrati; Ogunjimi, Fossum.

Ventspils (0) 0
Malmo (1) 1 *(Thelin 19)*   3000
Ventspils: (442) Uvarenko; Dubra, Kurakins, Timofejevs, Freidgeimas (Mujeci 72); Barinovs, Tarkhnishvili, Ulimbashevs (Zigajevs 73), Recickis; Abdultaofik (Tidenbergs 86), Karlsons.
Malmo: (442) Olsen; Ricardinho, Johansson E, Hammar, Concha; Forsberg, Halsti, Kroon (Cibicki 83), Nazari; Rosenberg (Johansson P 90), Thelin (Eriksson 62).

THIRD QUALIFYING ROUND FIRST LEG

Tuesday, 29 July 2014

Debrecen (0) 1 *(Sidibe 56 (pen))*
BATE Borisov (0) 0   10,000
Debrecen: (442) Novakovic; Jovanovic, Mate, Meszaros, Korhut; Mihelic (Bodi 32), Zsidai, Varga, Szakaly (Bouadla 80); Volas (Seydi 62), Sidibe.
BATE Borisov: (442) Chernik; Valadzko M, Filipenko, Khagush, Palyakow; Valadzko A (Karnitskiy 81), Alyakhnovich, Gordeichuk (Krivets 61), Aleksiyevich (Pawlaw 59); Rodionov, Signevich.

Slovan Bratislava (1) 2 *(Zofcak 42 (pen), Meszaros 85)*
Sheriff (0) 1 *(Ricardinho 74)*   6711
Slovan Bratislava: (4411) Pernis; Cikos, Hudak, Ninaj, Jablonsky; Milinkovic, Lasik■, Grendel, Zofcak (Meszaros 58); Soumah (Halenar 65), Fort (Peltier 81).
Sheriff: (442) Degra; Balima, Metoua, Muresan, Joaozinho; Isa (Potiguar 84), Blanco, Cadu, Luvannor (Ricardinho 72); Galvao (Ginsari 56), Benson.

Sparta Prague (1) 4 *(Lafata 23, 51, 70, Kovac 52)*
Malmo (2) 2 *(Forsberg 17, Thelin 27)*   12,833
Sparta Prague: (4321) Bicik; Kaderabek, Kovac, Holek, Nhamoinesu; Dockal, Vacha, Prikryl (Breznanik 71); Matejovsky (Vacek 84), Lafata (Bednar 87); Husbauer.
Malmo: (442) Olsen; Concha (Nazari 53), Hammar, Helander, Ricardinho; Tinnerholm, Halsti (Kroon 85), Adu, Forsberg; Rosenberg, Thelin (Mehmeti 75).

Wednesday, 30 July 2014

Aalborg (0) 0
Dinamo Zagreb (0) 1 *(Brozovic 49)*   9438
Aalborg: (442) Larsen; Kristensen, Petersen, Thelander, Mathiasen; Wichmann, Risgard (Thomsen 46), Augustinussen, Enevoldsen (Helenius 73); Jacobsen, Spalvis (Bruhn 73).
Dinamo Zagreb: (442) Eduardo; Ivo Pinto, Sigali, Simunic, Pivaric; Antolic (Goncalo Santos 70), Ademi, Brozovic, Paulo Machado; Soudani (Andrijasevic 79), Cop (Pjaca 46).

AEL Limassol (0) 1 *(Gikiewicz 64)*
Zenit St Petersburg (0) 0   6700
AEL Limassol: (4231) Fegrouch; Carlitos Tavares, Cadu, Sielis, Edmar; Guidilleye, Nicolaou; Sardinero (Tagbajumi 69), Zezinho (Bebe 60), Danielzinho (Eleftheriou 76); Gikiewicz.
Zenit St Petersburg: (442) Lodygin; Aniukov (Smolnikov 73), Garay, Luis Neto, Criscito; Witsel■, Fayzulin, Tymoschuk, Danny (Shatov 69); Hulk, Kerzhakov (Rondon 60).

Aktobe (0) 2 *(Korobkin 57, Arzumanyan 88)*
Steaua Bucharest (1) 2 *(Keseru 44, Prepelita 78)*   12,500
Aktobe: (433) Sidelnikov; Muldarov, Miroshnichenko, Arzumanyan, Anderson Mineiro; Korobkin, Khairullin (Kapadze 55), Tsarikaev; Pizzelli, Danilo Neco, Antonov (Zenkovich 75).
Steaua Bucharest: (4231) Arlauskis; Rapa, Szukala, Filip, Latovlevici; Varela, Popa (Stanciu 84); Chipciu (Iancu 89), Tanase, Prepelita; Keseru (Lemnaru 72).

Dnipro Dnipropetrovsk (0) 0
FC Copenhagen (0) 0   23,410
Dnipro Dnipropetrovsk: (4231) Boyko; Leo Matos, Mazuch, Douglas, Fedetskiy; Kankava (Kravchenko 55), Politylo; Matheus, Seleznyov (Bruno Gama 63), Konoplyanka; Kalinic.
FC Copenhagen: (442) Andersen; Hogli, Nilsson, Jorgensen M, Bengtsson; Amankwaa (Toutouh 78), Amartey, Delaney, Kadrii (Remmer 71); Cornelius, Jorgensen N (De Ridder 87).

Feyenoord (0) 1 *(Te Vrede 90 (pen))*
Besiktas (1) 2 *(Pektemek 13, Boulahrouz 71 (og))* 50,000
Feyenoord: (442) Mulder; Mathijsen, Kongolo, van Beek, Clasie; Immers, Trindade de Vilhena, Boetius, Verhoek (Manu 65); Te Vrede, Schaken (Boulahrouz 61).
Besiktas: (442) Zengin; Kurtulus, Franco, Gulum, Ramon; Hutchinson, Ozyakup (Ba 59), Uysal, Frei (Tosun 89); Sahan (Koybasi 75), Pektemek.

Grasshoppers (0) 0
Lille (1) 2 *(Corchia 30, Ryan Mendes 49)* 15,000
Grasshoppers: (442) Davari; Grichting (Kahraba 46), Jahic, Lang, Pavlovic; Dingsdag, Salatic, Sinkala (Merkel 61), Abrashi; Ravet (Tarashaj 74), Dabbur.
Lille: (442) Elana; Corchia, Kjaer, Beria, Souare; Basa, Balmont, Gueye, Delaplace (Meite 80); Rodelin (Sidibe 90), Ryan Mendes (Roux 71).

HJK Helsinki (2) 2 *(Savage 11, 45 (pen))*
APOEL Nicosia (0) 2 *(De Vincenti 71, Sheridan 74)* 10,300
HJK Helsinki: (4411) Tornes; Sorsa, Heikkila, Lampi, Moren; Savage, Tainio, Alho (Baah 77), Schuller (Vayrynen 76); Lod (Mannstrom 87); Kandji■.
APOEL Nicosia: (442) Urko; Joao Guilherme, Carlao, Morais, Antoniades (Ioannou 75); Mario Sergio, Gomes, Charalambidis (Efrem 63), Vinicius; De Vincenti, Sheridan (Adorno 79).

Legia Warsaw (2) 4 *(Radovic 10, 36, Zyro 84, Kosecki 90)*
Celtic (1) 1 *(McGregor 7)* 25,000
Legia Warsaw: (4411) Kuciak; Broz, Rzezniczak, Astiz, Brzyski; Zyro (Saganowski 87), Jodlowiec, Vrdoljak, Kucharczyk (Kosecki 74); Duda; Radovic.
Celtic: (4231) Forster; Matthews, Ambrose■, van Dijk, Lustig; Johansen, Mulgrew; McGregor, Commons (Griffiths 74), Berget (Izaguirre 62); Pukki (Kayal 46).

Ludogorets Razgrad (0) 0
Partizan Belgrade (0) 0 6000
Ludogorets Razgrad: (4411) Stoyanov; Aleksandrov A, Moti, Vitinha (Angulo 47), Junior Caicara; Aleksandrov M (Abel 75), Fabio Espinho, Dyakov, Marcelinho; Bezjak; Dani Abalo (Misidjan 62).
Partizan Belgrade: (442) Lukac; Volkov, Vulicevic, Stankovic, Trajkovic; Zivkovic (Grbic 67), Brasanac, Drincic, Ilic S (Luka 81); Lazovic (Ninkovic 54), Skuletic.

Maribor (0) 1 *(Bohar 90)*
Maccabi Tel Aviv (0) 0 8500
Maribor: (4231) Handanovic; Stojanovic, Rajcevic, Suler, Viler; Vrsic, Dervisevic; Filipovic, Bohar, Ibraimi (Sallalich 78); Mendy (Tavares 63).
Maccabi Tel Aviv: (433) Juan Pablo; Yeyni, Tibi, Carlos Garcia, Spungin; Radi, Alberman (Ben Haroush 46), Igiebor (Einbinder 58); Ben Haim (Margolis 89), Ben Basat, Zahavi.

Qarabag (1) 2 *(Danilo Dias 2, Reynaldo 86)*
Red Bull Salzburg (0) 1 *(Soriano 77)* 30,000
Qarabag: (4231) Sehic; Medvedev, Huseynov, Teli■, Agolli; Garayev (Gurbanov 46), Almeida; George (Sadygov 57), Chumbinho, Danilo Dias (Yusifov 70); Reynaldo■.
Red Bull Salzburg: (442) Gulacsi; Schwegler■, Ramalho Silva, Hinteregger, Ulmer; Kampl, Keita (Ankersen 38), Leitgeb (Quaschner 90), Mane; Sabitzer (Bruno 61), Soriano.

Standard Liege (0) 0
Panathinaikos (0) 0 16,721
Standard Liege: (442) Kawashima; Teixeira, Ciman (M'Poku 61), Stam (Milec 88), Arslanagic; Van Damme, Carcela-Gonzalez, Marquet, Mujangi Bia (Mbombo 82); de Camargo, Ezekiel.
Panathinaikos: (442) Kotsolis; Koutroubis, Triantafyllopoulos, Schildenfeld, Mendes Da Silva (Karelis 71); Lagos, Zeca, Ajagun (Klonaridis 85), Nano; Berg, Petric (Pranjic 64).

THIRD QUALIFYING ROUND SECOND LEG
Tuesday, 5 August 2014
BATE Borisov (1) 3 *(Valadzko A 39, Rodionov 66, Krivets 90)*
Debrecen (1) 1 *(Sidibe 20 (pen))* 12,788
BATE Borisov: (442) Chernik; Hayduchyk (Signevich 42), Khagush (Pawlaw 69), Filipenko, Mladenovic; Palyakow, Likhtarovich (Alyakhnovich 55), Valadzko A, Krivets; Gordeichuk, Rodionov.
Debrecen: (442) Novakovic; Meszaros (Brkovic 84), Mate, Korhut, Jovanovic; Zsidai (Ludanszki 65), Bouadla■, Varga, Szakaly (Bodi 71); Sidibe, Seydi.

Lille (1) 1 *(Balmont 19)*
Grasshoppers (1) 1 *(Abrashi 33)* 20,000
Lille: (442) Enyeama; Beria (Origi 83), Kjaer, Basa, Souare; Corchia, Balmont, Gueye, Meite (Delaplace 56); Ryan Mendes (Kalou 76), Rodelin.
Grasshoppers: (433) Vasic; Pavlovic■, Jahic, Grichting, Lang; Ravet (Tarashaj 68), Salatic, Kahraba (Bauer 75); Abrashi, Dabbur, Sinkala.

Maccabi Tel Aviv (1) 2 *(Ben Haim 42, Ben Basat 54)*
Maribor (1) 2 *(Ibraimi 36, 55)* 875
Maccabi Tel Aviv: (442) Juan Pablo; Yeyni, Carlos Garcia (Prica 46), Tibi, Spungin; Mikha, Radi, Ben Haroush (Igiebor 63), Ben Haim (Einbinder 71); Zahavi, Ben Basat.
Maribor: (442) Handanovic; Stojanovic, Suler, Rajcevic, Viler (Bohar, Filipovic, Dervisevic (Mertelj 73), Vrsic (Sallalich 85); Tavares (Mendy 67), Ibraimi.
Played in Larnaca.

Panathinaikos (1) 1 *(Arslanagic 17 (og))*
Standard Liege (2) 2 *(Mbombo 36, M'Poku 41)* 20,000
Panathinaikos: (442) Kotsolis; Koutroubis, Triantafyllopoulos, Schildenfeld, Pranjic; Mendes Da Silva (Karelis 56), Zeca, Ajagun, Nano; Berg, Petric (Klonaridis 56 (Dinas 66)).
Standard Liege: (442) Kawashima; Teixeira, Ciman, Stam, Arslanagic; Van Damme, Carcela-Gonzalez (Watt 54), Mujangi Bia (M'Poku 20), Lumanza-Lembi; de Camargo, Mbombo (Ajdarevic 71).

Wednesday, 6 August 2014
APOEL Nicosia (2) 2 *(Sheridan 19, De Vincenti 43 (pen))*
HJK Helsinki (0) 0 16,500
APOEL Nicosia: (433) Urko; Mario Sergio, Joao Guilherme, Carlao, Antoniades; Vinicius, Morais, Gomes; De Vincenti (Sotiriou 76), Charalambidis (Efrem 68), Sheridan (Papazoglou 81).
HJK Helsinki: (442) Tornes; Sorsa (Mannstrom 78), Moren, Heikkinen, Lampi; Alho, Tainio (Forssell 74), Schuller, Savage; Vayrynen (Baah 46), Lod.

Besiktas (1) 3 *(Ba 28, 80, 86)*
Feyenoord (0) 1 *(Manu 74)* 55,000
Besiktas: (4411) Zengin; Uysal, Franco, Gulum, Ramon; Frei (Koybasi 74), Hutchinson, Kavlak, Sahan; Ba (Tosun 87); Pektemek (Ozyakup 85).
Feyenoord: (433) Mulder; van Beek, Mathijsen, Kongolo, Nelom (Vormer 57); Immers, Clasie (Karsdorp 69), Trindade de Vilhena; Schaken, Te Vrede (Manu 57), Boetius.

Celtic (0) 0
Legia Warsaw (1) 2 *(Zyro 36, Kucharczyk 61)* 20,000
Celtic: (442) Forster; Matthews, Izaguirre, van Dijk, Mulgrew; Lustig (Griffiths 57), Biton, Commons (Pukki 70), McGregor; Stokes (Forrest 70), Johansen.
Legia Warsaw: (442) Kuciak; Vrdoljak, Jodlowiec, Astiz, Rzezniczak; Broz, Duda (Pinto 87), Brzyski, Radovic; Zyro (Bereszynski 87), Kucharczyk (Kosecki 74).
Match awarded to Celtic 3-0 – Legia Warsaw fielded an ineligible player. Celtic won on away goals.

Dinamo Zagreb (0) 0
Aalborg (1) 2 *(Jacobsen 36, 85)* 5000
Dinamo Zagreb: (451) Eduardo; Ivo Pinto, Simunovic, Simunic, Pivaric; Soudani, Brozovic, Ademi, Paulo Machado (Wilson Eduardo 88), Antolic (Pjaca 66); Cop.
Aalborg: (442) Larsen; Kristensen, Thelander, Petersen, Mathiasen; Wichmann (Enevoldsen 57), Wurtz (Augustinussen 88); Risgard, Thomsen; Spalvis (Helenius 62), Jacobsen.

FC Copenhagen (1) 2 *(Cornelius 36, Kadrii 52)*
Dnipro Dnipropetrovsk (0) 0 18,875
FC Copenhagen: (442) Andersen; Hogli, Bengtsson, Nilsson, Jorgensen M; Delaney (Antonsson 90), Amartey, Jorgensen N, Cornelius; Amankwaa, Kadrii (Toutouh 70).
Dnipro Dnipropetrovsk: (4411) Boyko; Leo Matos, Mazuch, Polevoy, Douglas; Fedetskiy (Bruno Gama 75), Kankava, Bartulovic (Seleznyov 46), Politylo; Konoplyanka; Matheus (Kalinic 54).

Malmo (1) 2 *(Rosenberg 35, 55)*
Sparta Prague (0) 0 19,322
Malmo: (442) Olsen; Tinnerholm, Helander, Johansson E, Ricardinho; Kroon (Mehmeti 65), Halsti, Adu, Forsberg; Rosenberg (Cibicki 90), Thelin (Eriksson 83).
Sparta Prague: (4141) Bicik; Kaderabek, Kovac, Svejdik, Nhamoinesu (Breznanik 85); Vacha■; Dockal, Husbauer, Matejovsky (Bednar 74), Prikryl (Krejci 60); Lafata.
Malmo won on away goals.

Partizan Belgrade (2) 2 *(Skuletic 30, 35)*
Ludogorets Razgrad (2) 2 *(Marcelinho 19, 21)* 25,000
Partizan Belgrade: (442) Lukac; Volkov, Vulicevic, Stankovic, Trajkovic■; Brasanac (Ninkovic 83), Zivkovic (Luka 70), Drincic, Ilic S (Ilic B 46); Lazovic, Skuletic.
Ludogorets Razgrad: (442) Stoyanov; Aleksandrov A, Angulo, Moti, Junior Caicara; Dyakov, Zlatinski, Marcelinho (Fabio Espinho 85), Aleksandrov M (Abel 78); Dani Abalo (Misidjan 46), Bezjak.
Ludogorets Razgrad won on away goals.

Red Bull Salzburg (2) 2 *(Hinteregger 18, 34)*
Qarabag (0) 0 20,716
Red Bull Salzburg: (442) Gulacsi; Ankersen, Ulmer, Hinteregger, Ramalho Silva; Ilsanker (Keita 73), Leitgeb, Kampl (Bruno 86), Soriano; Mane, Alan (Sabitzer 79).
Qarabag: (442) Sehic; Garayev, Medvedev (Guliyev 60), Sadygov, Huseynov; Agolli, Gurbanov (Yusifov 20), Almeida, George; Nadirov, Danilo Dias (Chumbinho 55).

Sheriff (0) 0
Slovan Bratislava (0) 0 11,000
Sheriff: (4141) Degra; Balima, Metoua, Muresan, Joaozinho; Blanco■; Isa, Ginsari (Luvannor 46), Cadu, Ricardinho (Leonel 58); Benson (Potiguar 61).
Slovan Bratislava: (4231) Pernis; Cikos, Hudak, Ninaj, Jablonsky; Kolcak (Halenar 85), Grendel; Zofcak, Fort (Vittek 59), Milinkovic; Soumah (Jakubek 90).

Steaua Bucharest (2) 2 *(Chipciu 2, Stanciu 38)*
Aktobe (0) 1 *(Kapadze 85)* 35,000
Steaua Bucharest: (4231) Arlauskis; Rapa, Szukala, Varela, Latovlevici; Prepelita, Sanmartean (Filip 12); Popa, Stanciu (Iancu 48), Tanase (Parvulescu 82); Chipciu.
Aktobe: (442) Sidelnikov; Miroshnichenko, Arzumanyan, Logvinenko■, Anderson Mineiro; Danilo Neco, Korobkin, Tsarikaev, Khairullin (Kapadze 61); Antonov (Aimbetov 68), Pizzelli (Shabalin 80).

Zenit St Petersburg (0) 3 *(Rondon 55, Danny 88, Kerzhakov 90 (pen))*
AEL Limassol (0) 0 17,600
Zenit St Petersburg: (4231) Lodygin; Smolnikov (Kerzhakov 46), Garay, Lombaerts, Criscito; Tymoschuk (Ryazantsev 75), Fayzulin; Hulk, Danny, Shatov (Solovyev 85); Rondon.
AEL Limassol: (4231) Fegrouch; Carlitos Tavares, Sielis, Cadu, Edmar; Guidilleye, Nicolaou; Sardinero (Eleftheriou 58), Zezinho (Diego Barcelos 18), Danielzinho■; Gikiewicz (Tagbajumi 86).

PLAY-OFF ROUND FIRST LEG

Tuesday, 19 August 2014

Besiktas (0) 0
Arsenal (0) 0 52,000
Besiktas: (4141) Zengin; Koybasi, Franco, Gulum, Ramon; Uysal; Pektemek (Tosun 88), Ozyakup (Frei 81), Kavlak, Sahan (Tore 73); Ba.

Arsenal: (4231) Szczesny; Debuchy, Chambers, Koscielny, Monreal; Arteta (Flamini 50), Wilshere; Sanchez (Oxlade-Chamberlain 72), Ramsey■, Cazorla (Rosicky 90); Giroud.

FC Copenhagen (2) 2 *(Jorgensen M 9, Amartey 13)*
Bayer Leverkusen (3) 3 *(Kiessling 5, Bellarabi 31, Son 42)* 18,221
FC Copenhagen: (442) Andersen; Hogli, Bengtsson, Nilsson, Jorgensen M; Claudemir (De Ridder 54), Delaney, Amartey, Cornelius; Amankwaa, Kadrii.
Bayer Leverkusen: (442) Leno; Castro, Spahic, Boenisch, Toprak; Donati (Jedvaj 45), Rolfes, Calhanoglu (Drmic 88), Bellarabi; Son, Kiessling.

Napoli (0) 1 *(Higuain 68)*
Athletic Bilbao (1) 1 *(Muniain 41)* 42,000
Napoli: (442) Rafael Cabral; Britos, Koulibaly, Albiol, Jorginho; Hamsik (Michu 78), Insigne (Mertens 60), Maggio, Gargano; Higuain, Callejon.
Athletic Bilbao: (442) Iraizoz; Laporte, Balenziaga, Benat (San Jose 74), Iturraspe (Moran 89); Susaeta (Ibai 80), Mikel Rico, Gurpegi, Muniain; Aduriz, De Marcos.

Red Bull Salzburg (1) 2 *(Schiemer 16, Soriano 54)*
Malmo (0) 1 *(Forsberg 90)* 29,110
Red Bull Salzburg: (442) Gulacsi; Schwegler, Ramalho Silva, Schiemer, Ulmer; Kampl, Leitgeb (Keita 87), Ilsanker, Mane (Bruno 80); Soriano, Sabitzer (Alan 85).
Malmo: (442) Olsen; Tinnerholm, Johansson E, Helander, Ricardinho; Kroon (Cibicki 87), Adu, Halsti, Forsberg; Thelin (Eriksson 61), Rosenberg.

Steaua Bucharest (0) 1 *(Chipciu 88)*
Ludogorets Razgrad (0) 0 25,000
Steaua Bucharest: (4231) Arlauskis; Rapa, Szukala, Varela, Latovlevici; Prepelita, Breeveld; Popa (Iancu 83), Sanmartean (Filip 90), Stanciu (Keseru 57); Chipciu.
Ludogorets Razgrad: (4231) Stoyanov; Junior Caicara, Moti, Terziev, Minev; Zlatinski (Fabio Espinho 46); Dyakov; Aleksandrov M, Marcelinho (Abel 85), Misidjan; Younes.

Wednesday, 20 August 2014

Aalborg (1) 1 *(Thomsen 16)*
APOEL Nicosia (0) 1 *(Vinicius 54)* 9000
Aalborg: (442) Larsen; Kristensen (Dalsgaard 76), Petersen, Thelander, Blabjerg; Wichmann, Wurtz, Risgard, Thomsen (Thrane 86); Jacobsen, Helenius (Ahlmann 76).
APOEL Nicosia: (433) Urko; Mario Sergio, Joao Guilherme, Carlao, Antoniades; Gomes, Morais, Vinicius; Charalambidis (Alexandrou 66), Sheridan (Manduca 90), De Vincenti (Papazoglou 82).

Lille (0) 0
Porto (0) 1 *(Herrera 61)* 35,000
Lille: (442) Enyeama; Corchia, Kjaer, Beria, Souare; Basa, Balmont (Lopes 62), Gueye, Mavuba; Kalou (Roux 76), Origi (Ryan Mendes 71).
Porto: (442) Fabiano; Danilo, Martins Indi, Maicon, Alex Sandro; Casemiro, Brahimi (Tello 60), Herrera, Torres (Quaresma 89); Ruben Neves (Evandro 73), Martinez.

Maribor (1) 1 *(Bohar 14)*
Celtic (1) 1 *(McGregor 5)* 11,500
Maribor: (442) Handanovic; Stojanovic, Rajcevic, Suler, Viler; Vrsic (Mendy 72), Filipovic, Dervisevic (Mertelj 80), Bohar (Sallaich 78); Tavares, Ibraimi.
Celtic: (4231) Gordon; Lustig, Denayer, van Dijk, Izaguirre; Johansen, Mulgrew; McGregor, Kayal (Biton 86), Berget (Ambrose 72); Stokes (Griffiths 80).

Slovan Bratislava (0) 1 *(Vittek 80)*
BATE Borisov (1) 1 *(Jablonsky 44 (og))* 8461
Slovan Bratislava: (4411) Pernis; Cikos, Hudak, Gorosito, Jablonsky; Zofcak (Halenar 59), Stefanik (Lasik 46), Grendel, Milinkovic; Soumah; Fort (Vittek 72).
BATE Borisov: (433) Chernik; Khagush, Palyakow, Filipenko, Mladenovic; Valadzko A, Likhtarovich, Alyakhnovich; Gordeichuk, Rodionov (Signevich 87), Krivets.

Standard Liege (0) 0
Zenit St Petersburg (1) 1 *(Shatov 16)*   14,735
Standard Liege: (442) Kawashima; Ciman, Arslanagic, Teixeira, Van Damme; M'Poku, Faty, Louis, Lumanza-Lembi (Mbombo 71); Watt (Mujangi Bia 65), de Camargo.
Zenit St Petersburg: (442) Lodygin; Smolnikov, Garay, Lombaerts, Criscito; Shatov (Ryazantsev 82), Fayzulin, Tymoschuk, Danny; Rondon, Hulk (Solovyev 90).

PLAY-OFF ROUND SECOND LEG

Tuesday, 26 August 2014
APOEL Nicosia (2) 4 *(Vinicius 29, De Vincenti 43, Aloneftis 64, Sheridan 75)*
Aalborg (0) 0   18,476
APOEL Nicosia: (442) Urko; Joao Guilherme, Morais, Carlao, Antoniades; Mario Sergio, Gomes, Vinicius, De Vincenti (Efrem 82); Manduca (Aloneftis 62), Sheridan (Djebbour 79).
Aalborg: (442) Larsen; Kristensen (Dalsgaard 46), Petersen, Thelander, Blabjerg (Gorter 62); Enevoldsen, Wurtz, Risgard, Thomsen; Boersting (Helenius 46), Jacobsen.

BATE Borisov (1) 3 *(Gordeichuk 41, Krivets 84, Rodionov 85)*
Slovan Bratislava (0) 0   12,970
BATE Borisov: (433) Chernik; Khagush, Palyakow, Filipenko, Mladenovic; Alyakhnovich, Likhtarovich (Aleksiyevich 61), Valadzko A; Gordeichuk (Yakovlev 68), Rodionov (Signevich 87), Krivets.
Slovan Bratislava: (442) Pernis; Cikos, Hudak, Gorosito, Jablonsky; Kolcak, Grendel (Peltier 83), Zofcak (Stefanik 46), Fort (Vittek 62); Halenar, Soumah■.

Celtic (0) 0
Maribor (0) 1 *(Tavares 75)*   58,000
Celtic: (451) Gordon; Lustig (Boerrigter 71), Ambrose, van Dijk, Izaguirre; McGregor, Mulgrew, Johansen, Kayal (Commons 46), Berget (Matthews 66); Stokes.
Maribor: (442) Handanovic; Stojanovic, Rajcevic, Suler, Viler; Vrsic (Bohar 82), Mertelj, Filipovic, Ibraimi; Mendy, Tavares (Dervisevic 90).

Porto (0) 2 *(Brahimi 49, Martinez 68)*
Lille (0) 0   45,208
Porto: (442) Fabiano; Danilo, Maicon, Martins Indi, Alex Sandro (Reyes 39); Torres, Herrera, Casemiro (Ricardo Pereira 84), Ruben Neves (Evandro 62); Brahimi, Martinez.
Lille: (433) Enyeama; Beria, Rozehnal, Kjaer, Souare; Gueye (Delaplace 78), Mavuba, Balmont; Corchia (Lopes 71), Roux (Ryan Mendes 67), Origi.

Zenit St Petersburg (1) 3 *(Rondon 30, Hulk 54 (pen), 58)*
Standard Liege (0) 0   16,017
Zenit St Petersburg: (4411) Lodygin; Smolnikov, Garay, Lombaerts, Criscito; Hulk (Arshavin 90), Fayzulin■, Witsel, Danny; Shatov (Aniukov 83); Rondon (Tymoschuk 46).

Standard Liege: (442) Kawashima; Ciman, Teixeira, Faty■, Van Damme; M'Poku, Louis (Ajdarevic 69), Trebel, Mujangi Bia (Mbombo 59); de Camargo, Watt (Ono 59).

Wednesday, 27 August 2014
Arsenal (1) 1 *(Sanchez 45)*
Besiktas (0) 0   59,946
Arsenal: (4231) Szczesny; Debuchy■, Mertesacker, Koscielny, Monreal; Wilshere, Flamini; Oxlade-Chamberlain, Ozil (Chambers 76), Cazorla; Sanchez.
Besiktas: (451) Zengin; Koybasi, Franco, Gulum, Ramon; Hutchinson, Kavlak (Uysal 76), Ozyakup, Pektemek (Tosun 87), Sahan (Tore 63); Ba.

Athletic Bilbao (0) 3 *(Aduriz 61, 69, Ibai 74)*
Napoli (0) 1 *(Hamsik 47)*   51,000
Athletic Bilbao: (4231) Iraizoz; De Marcos, Gurpegi, Laporte, Balenziaga; Iturraspe, Mikel Rico; Susaeta (Lopez 72), Muniain (San Jose 85), Benat (Ibai 58); Aduriz.
Napoli: (4231) Rafael Cabral; Maggio, Albiol, Koulibaly, Ghoulam (Britos 56); Jorginho, Gargano; Callejon, Mertens (Zapata 77), Hamsik (Insigne 70); Higuain.

Bayer Leverkusen (3) 4 *(Son 2, Calhanoglu 7, Kiessling 21 (pen), 65)*
FC Copenhagen (0) 0   23,321
Bayer Leverkusen: (4231) Leno; Jedvaj, Spahic, Toprak (Papadopoulos 54), Castro; Rolfes (Reinartz 65), Boenisch; Bellarabi, Calhanoglu, Son; Kiessling (Drmic 73).
FC Copenhagen: (4231) Andersen; Hogli, Antonsson, Jorgensen M, Bengtsson; Delaney, Claudemir; Amankwaa (Pourie 75), Kadrii, Toutouh (Gislason 58); Cornelius (De Ridder 46).

Ludogorets Razgrad (0) 1 *(Wanderson 89)*
Steaua Bucharest (0) 0   25,000
Ludogorets Razgrad: (4411) Stoyanov■; Junior Caicara, Terziev, Moti, Minev; Misidjan (Wanderson 83), Dyakov, Fabio Espinho, Aleksandrov M (Dani Abalo 76); Marcelinho; Bezjak (Younes 76).
Steaua Bucharest: (4231) Arlauskis; Rapa, Szukala, Varela, Latovlevici (Parvulescu 66); Prepelita, Breeveld; Popa, Sanmartean (Filip 82), Tanase (Stanciu 3); Keseru. *aet; Ludogorets Razgrad won 6-5 on penalties.*

Malmo (2) 3 *(Rosenberg 10 (pen), 84, Eriksson 19)*
Red Bull Salzburg (0) 0   21,000
Malmo: (442) Olsen; Tinnerholm, Johansson E, Helander, Konate; Thelin (Mehmeti 72), Adu, Halsti, Forsberg; Rosenberg, Eriksson (Kroon 73).
Red Bull Salzburg: (442) Gulacsi; Schwegler, Ramalho Silva, Ilsanker, Hinteregger; Kampl, Leitgeb (Lazaro 78), Keita (Ankersen 46); Bruno (Sabitzer 66); Soriano, Alan.

GROUP STAGE

GROUP A
Tuesday, 16 September 2014
Juventus (0) 2 *(Tevez 59, 89)*
Malmo (0) 0   25,000
Juventus: (352) Buffon; Caceres, Bonucci, Chiellini; Lichtsteiner (Giovinco 90), Pogba, Marchisio, Asamoah, Evra; Llorente (Morata 85), Tevez (Romulo 90).
Malmo: (523) Olsen; Tinnerholm, Johansson E, Halsti, Helander, Konate; Eriksson (Rakip 82), Forsberg; Rosenberg (Mehmeti 53), Adu, Thelin (Kroon 73).

Olympiacos (2) 3 *(Masuaku 13, Afellay 31, Mitroglou 73)*
Atletico Madrid (1) 2 *(Mandzukic 38, Griezmann 86)*   31,946
Olympiacos: (4411) Roberto; Elabdellaoui, Botia, Abidal, Masuaku; Maniatis, Kasami (Giannoulis 84), Milivojevic, Afellay (Ndinga 69); Dominguez (David Fuster 57); Mitroglou.
Atletico Madrid: (4411) Oblak; Juanfran, Godin, Miranda, Ansaldi; Turan, Mario Suarez (Saul 75), Gabi (Griezmann 56), Koke; Raul Garcia (Cerci 66); Mandzukic.

Wednesday, 1 October 2014
Atletico Madrid (0) 1 *(Turan 75)*
Juventus (0) 0   45,000
Atletico Madrid: (442) Moya; Juanfran, Godin, Miranda, Ansaldi; Turan (Siqueira 89), Koke, Tiago, Saul (Griezmann 53); Raul Garcia, Mandzukic (Mario Suarez 83).
Juventus: (352) Buffon; Caceres (Pereyra 77), Bonucci, Chiellini; Lichtsteiner (Giovinco 88), Vidal (Morata 82), Marchisio, Pogba, Evra; Tevez, Llorente.

Malmo (1) 2 *(Rosenberg 42, 82)*
Olympiacos (0) 0   24,000
Malmo: (442) Olsen; Tinnerholm, Johansson E, Helander, Ricardinho; Thelin, Adu, Halsti, Forsberg (Rakip 90); Rosenberg, Eriksson (Cibicki 74).
Olympiacos: (433) Roberto; Elabdellaoui, Botia, Abidal, Masuaku; Ndinga (Dominguez 57), Milivojevic, Maniatis; Kasami (Durmaz 69), Mitroglou, Afellay (Diamantakos 79).

Wednesday, 22 October 2014
Atletico Madrid (0) 5 *(Koke 48, Mandzukic 61, Griezmann 63, Godin 87, Cerci 90)*
Malmo (0) 0   50,000
Atletico Madrid: (451) Moya; Juanfran, Miranda, Godin, Siqueira; Turan (Raul Garcia 68), Saul, Mario Suarez, Koke, Griezmann (Rodriguez 72); Mandzukic (Cerci 77).
Malmo: (532) Olsen; Tinnerholm, Johansson E, Halsti, Helander, Ricardinho (Konate 90); Eriksson (Thern 87), Adu, Forsberg (Kroon 66); Thelin, Rosenberg.

Olympiacos (1) 1 *(Kasami 35)*
Juventus (0) 0   30,000
Olympiacos: (442) Roberto; Masuaku, Abidal, Botia, Elabdellaoui; Ndinga, Kasami (Giannoulis 90), Maniatis, Milivojevic; Dominguez (David Fuster 84), Mitroglou (Afellay 68).
Juventus: (352) Buffon; Chiellini, Bonucci, Ogbonna (Pereyra 77); Asamoah, Pogba (Giovinco 87), Pirlo (Marchisio 57), Vidal, Lichtsteiner; Morata, Tevez.

Tuesday, 4 November 2014
Juventus (1) 3 *(Pirlo 21, Roberto 65 (og), Pogba 66)*
Olympiacos (1) 2 *(Botia 24, Ndinga 61)*   36,000
Juventus: (4312) Buffon; Lichtsteiner, Bonucci, Chiellini, Asamoah (Pereyra 82); Vidal, Pirlo, Marchisio (Padoin 70); Pogba; Morata (Llorente 58), Tevez.
Olympiacos: (4321) Roberto; Elabdellaoui, Botia, Abidal, Masuaku; Maniatis (Diamantakos 82), Ndinga (Kasami 74); Milivojevic; Afellay, Dominguez (David Fuster 71); Mitroglou.

Malmo (0) 0
Atletico Madrid (1) 2 *(Koke 30, Raul Garcia 78)* 20,000
Malmo: (442) Olsen; Tinnerholm, Johansson E (Kroon 64), Helander, Ricardinho; Eriksson, Adu, Halsti, Forsberg (Thern 86); Rosenberg, Thelin.
Atletico Madrid: (442) Moya; Juanfran, Miranda, Godin, Siqueira; Koke, Gabi, Mario Suarez, Turan (Rodriguez 76); Mandzukic (Griezmann 69), Raul Garcia.

Wednesday, 26 November 2014
Atletico Madrid (2) 4 *(Raul Garcia 9, Mandzukic 38, 62, 65)*
Olympiacos (0) 0   51,000
Atletico Madrid: (4411) Moya; Juanfran, Gimenez, Godin, Ansaldi; Raul Garcia, Tiago (Mario Suarez 46), Gabi, Koke; Turan (Jimenez 66); Mandzukic (Griezmann 69).
Olympiacos: (4411) Roberto; Elabdellaoui, Botia, Abidal, Masuaku; Milivojevic, Ndinga, Maniatis (David Fuster 46); Dominguez (Bouchalakis 82); Afellay (Kasami 46); Mitroglou.

Malmo (0) 0
Juventus (0) 2 *(Llorente 49, Tevez 88)*   24,000
Malmo: (442) Olsen; Tinnerholm (Rakip 85), Johansson E■, Helander, Ricardinho; Eriksson, Halsti, Adu, Forsberg; Thelin (Cibicki 70), Rosenberg.
Juventus: (4312) Buffon; Lichtsteiner, Bonucci, Chiellini, Padoin; Marchisio (Pereyra 83), Pirlo, Pogba, Vidal; Llorente (Morata 72), Tevez.

Tuesday, 9 December 2014
Juventus (0) 0
Atletico Madrid (0) 0   39,219
Juventus: (433) Buffon; Lichtsteiner, Chiellini, Bonucci, Evra; Pogba, Pirlo, Vidal; Tevez, Llorente, Pereyra.
Atletico Madrid: (4231) Moya; Juanfran, Gimenez, Godin, Siqueira; Mario Suarez, Gabi; Turan, Raul Garcia, Koke; Mandzukic.

Olympiacos (1) 4 *(David Fuster 23, Dominguez 63, Mitroglou 87, Afellay 90)*
Malmo (0) 2 *(Kroon 59, Rosenberg 81)* 27,562
Olympiacos: (442) Roberto; Elabdellaoui, Botia, Abidal, Masuaku; David Fuster (Afellay 77), Ndinga, Maniatis, Kasami; Dominguez (Siovas 89), Mitroglou (Benitez 88).
Malmo: (442) Olsen; Ricardinho, Halsti, Helander, Konate (Kroon 56); Tinnerholm, Eriksson (Thern 74), Adu■, Forsberg; Rosenberg, Thelin (Cibicki 80).

Group A Table	P	W	D	L	F	A	GD	Pts
Atletico Madrid	6	4	1	1	14	3	11	13
Juventus	6	3	1	2	7	4	3	10
Olympiacos	6	3	0	3	10	13	–3	9
Malmo	6	1	0	5	4	15	–11	3

GROUP B

Tuesday, 16 September 2014
Liverpool (0) 2 *(Balotelli 82, Gerrard 90 (pen))*
Ludogorets Razgrad (0) 1 *(Dani Abalo 90)* 45,000
Liverpool: (433) Mignolet; Manquillo, Lovren, Sakho, Moreno; Gerrard, Henderson, Lallana (Borini 68); Coutinho (Lucas 68), Sterling, Balotelli.
Ludogorets Razgrad: (4411) Borjan; Junior Caicara, Moti, Aleksandrov A, Minev; Dyakov (Fabio Espinho 84), Abel, Misidjan (Dani Abalo 73); Marcelinho; Bezjak (Younes 86).

Real Madrid (4) 5 *(Suchy 14 (og), Bale 30, Ronaldo 31, Rodriguez 36, Benzema 80)*
FC Basel (1) 1 *(Gonzalez 38)*   80,454
Real Madrid: (442) Casillas; Pepe, Sergio Ramos (Varane 66), Marcelo, Nacho; Kroos, Rodriguez, Bale, Modric (Illarramendi 73); Ronaldo, Benzema (Hernandez 82).
FC Basel: (442) Vaclik; Samuel (Kakitani 64), Schar, Suchy, Safari; Zuffi, Frei (Delgado 83), El-Nenny, Xhaka; Streller (Embolo 73), Gonzalez.

Wednesday, 1 October 2014
FC Basel (0) 1 *(Streller 52)*
Liverpool (0) 0   36,000
FC Basel: (4321) Vaclik; Xhaka, Schar, Suchy, Safari (Gonzalez 10); Die, Frei, El-Nenny; Embolo (Calla 81), Hamoudi (Zuffi 90); Streller.
Liverpool: (433) Mignolet; Manquillo, Lovren, Skrtel, Jose Enrique; Henderson, Gerrard, Markovic (Lambert 81); Sterling, Balotelli, Coutinho (Lallana 70).

Ludogorets Razgrad (1) 1 *(Marcelinho 7)*
Real Madrid (1) 2 *(Ronaldo 24 (pen), Benzema 77)* 7500
Ludogorets Razgrad: (433) Stoyanov; Junior Caicara, Moti, Aleksandrov A, Minev; Dyakov, Marcelinho (Wanderson 70), Fabio Espinho (Abel 82); Dani Abalo, Bezjak, Aleksandrov M (Misidjan 82).
Real Madrid: (442) Casillas; Arbeloa, Sergio Ramos, Varane, Marcelo; Bale, Modric (Kroos 73), Illarramendi, Isco (Rodriguez 76); Hernandez (Benzema 67), Ronaldo.

Wednesday, 22 October 2014
Liverpool (0) 0
Real Madrid (3) 3 *(Ronaldo 23, Benzema 30, 41)* 45,000
Liverpool: (451) Mignolet; Johnson, Skrtel, Lovren, Moreno; Sterling, Allen, Henderson (Can 67), Coutinho (Markovic 67); Balotelli (Lallana 46).
Real Madrid: (442) Casillas; Arbeloa, Varane, Pepe, Marcelo (Nacho 84); Rodriguez, Kroos (Illarramendi 81), Modric, Isco; Benzema, Ronaldo (Khedira 75).

Ludogorets Razgrad (0) 1 *(Minev 90)*
FC Basel (0) 0   3500
Ludogorets Razgrad: (4231) Stoyanov; Junior Caicara, Terziev, Moti, Minev; Dyakov, Fabio Espinho; Dani Abalo (Misidjan 77), Marcelinho, Aleksandrov M (Wanderson 81); Bezjak (Younes 68).

FC Basel: (451) Vaclik; Xhaka, Schar, Suchy, Aliji (Ajeti 75); Calla (Hamoudi 84), El-Nenny, Frei, Die▪, Gonzalez (Sio 87); Embolo.

Tuesday, 4 November 2014

FC Basel (2) 4 *(Embolo 34, Gonzalez 41, Gashi 58, Suchy 65)*

Ludogorets Razgrad (0) 0   35,272

FC Basel: (451) Vaclik; Xhaka, Schar, Suchy, Safari; Gonzalez (Calla 69), El-Nenny, Frei (Diaz 80), Zuffi, Gashi (Delgado 73); Embolo.
Ludogorets Razgrad: (4231) Stoyanov; Junior Caicara, Moti (Aleksandrov A 21), Terziev, Angulo; Dyakov, Fabio Espinho (Abel 63); Dani Abalo, Marcelinho, Aleksandrov M; Bezjak (Younes 46).

Real Madrid (1) 1 *(Benzema 27)*

Liverpool (0) 0   75,000

Real Madrid: (442) Casillas; Arbeloa (Nacho 83), Varane, Sergio Ramos, Marcelo; Rodriguez (Bale 62), Modric, Kroos, Isco; Benzema (Hernandez 87), Ronaldo.
Liverpool: (4231) Mignolet; Moreno, Toure, Skrtel, Manquillo; Can (Coutinho 75), Lucas (Gerrard 69); Lallana, Allen, Markovic (Sterling 69); Borini.

Wednesday, 26 November 2014

FC Basel (0) 0

Real Madrid (1) 1 *(Ronaldo 35)*   38,500

FC Basel: (4141) Vaclik; Degen (Hamoudi 76), Schar, Suchy, Safari; Frei (Diaz 83); Gonzalez, El-Nenny, Zuffi (Kakitani 86), Gashi; Embolo.
Real Madrid: (4231) Navas; Arbeloa, Varane, Sergio Ramos, Fabio Coentrao; Isco (Nacho 90), Kroos; Bale, Rodriguez (Marcelo 89), Ronaldo; Benzema (Illarramendi 71).

Ludogorets Razgrad (1) 2 *(Dani Abalo 3, Terziev 88)*

Liverpool (2) 2 *(Lambert 8, Henderson 37)*   30,000

Ludogorets Razgrad: (4411) Stoyanov; Junior Caicara, Moti, Terziev, Minev; Misidjan, Dyakov, Fabio Espinho (Younes 80), Aleksandrov M (Wanderson 72); Marcelinho; Dani Abalo (Quixada 69).
Liverpool: (433) Mignolet; Johnson, Skrtel, Toure, Manquillo; Henderson, Gerrard, Lucas; Lambert, Allen, Sterling (Moreno 82).

Tuesday, 9 December 2014

Liverpool (0) 1 *(Gerrard 81)*

FC Basel (1) 1 *(Frei 25)*   43,290

Liverpool: (451) Mignolet; Johnson, Lovren, Skrtel, Jose Enrique (Moreno 47); Allen, Lucas (Coutinho 74), Gerrard, Henderson, Sterling; Lambert (Markovic▪ 47).
FC Basel: (3412) Vaclik; Schar, Suchy, Safari; Xhaka, El-Nenny (Diaz 83), Frei, Gashi; Zuffi (Samuel 87); Streller (Embolo 75), Gonzalez.

Real Madrid (2) 4 *(Ronaldo 21 (pen), Bale 38, Arbeloa 80, Medran 88)*

Ludogorets Razgrad (0) 0   58,393

Real Madrid: (442) Navas; Arbeloa, Varane, Nacho, Fabio Coentrao (Marcelo 60); Bale (Medran 83), Illarramendi, Kroos (Jese 60), Isco; Ronaldo, Hernandez.
Ludogorets Razgrad: (4231) Stoyanov; Junior Caicara, Terziev, Moti, Minev; Dyakov, Fabio Espinho (Abel 63); Aleksandrov M (Wanderson 60), Marcelinho▪, Misidjan (Quixada 71); Dani Abalo.

Group B Table

	P	W	D	L	F	A	GD	Pts
Real Madrid	6	6	0	0	16	2	14	18
FC Basel	6	2	1	3	7	8	–1	7
Liverpool	6	1	2	3	5	9	–4	5
Ludogorets Razgrad	6	1	1	4	5	14	–9	4

GROUP C

Tuesday, 16 September 2014

Benfica (0) 0

Zenit St Petersburg (2) 2 *(Hulk 5, Witsel 22)*   20,000

Benfica: (442) Artur Moraes▪; Maxi Pereira, Luisao, Jardel, Eliseu; Salvio, Perez, Samaris (Andre Almeida 73), Gaitan; Lima (Derley 73), Anderson Talisca (Paulo Lopes 20).

Zenit St Petersburg: (433) Lodygin; Smolnikov (Aniukov 46), Lombaerts, Garay, Criscito; Shatov, Javi Garcia, Witsel; Hulk (Arshavin 85), Danny, Rondon (Mogilevets 76).

Monaco (0) 1 *(Joao Moutinho 61)*

Bayer Leverkusen (0) 0   12,000

Monaco: (433) Subasic; Fabinho, Ricardo Carvalho, Raggi, Kurzawa; Kondogbia (Wallace Santos 90), Toulalan, Joao Moutinho; Carrasco (Dirar 86), Berbatov, Ocampos (Bernardo Silva 57).
Bayer Leverkusen: (4231) Leno; Jedvaj (Donati 65), Toprak (Reinartz 71), Spahic, Boenisch; Bender (Drmic 76), Castro; Bellarabi, Calhanoglu, Son; Kiessling.

Wednesday, 1 October 2014

Bayer Leverkusen (2) 3 *(Kiessling 25, Son 34, Calhanoglu 64 (pen))*

Benfica (0) 1 *(Salvio 61)*   27,000

Bayer Leverkusen: (442) Leno; Hilbert, Toprak, Spahic, Wendell; Bellarabi (Oztunali 69), Reinartz, Bender (Donati 81), Son; Calhanoglu, Kiessling (Drmic 75).
Benfica: (4411) Julio Cesar; Andre Almeida, Luisao, Jardel, Eliseu; Salvio, Perez (Samaris 77), Cristante (Maxi Pereira 46); Gaitan; Anderson Talisca (Lima 46); Derley.

Zenit St Petersburg (0) 0

Monaco (0) 0   13,000

Zenit St Petersburg: (4231) Lodygin; Aniukov (Arshavin 88), Garay, Lombaerts, Criscito; Javi Garcia, Fayzulin; Hulk, Shatov (Smolnikov 66), Danny; Rondon (Kerzhakov 75).
Monaco: (433) Subasic; Fabinho, Raggi, Ricardo Carvalho, Kurzawa; Kondogbia, Toulalan, Joao Moutinho (Bakayoko 90); Dirar, Berbatov (Carrasco 52), Ocampos (Germain 79).

Wednesday, 22 October 2014

Bayer Leverkusen (0) 2 *(Donati 58, Papadopoulos 63)*

Zenit St Petersburg (0) 0   27,254

Bayer Leverkusen: (442) Leno; Donati, Toprak, Spahic (Papadopoulos 60), Wendell▪; Bellarabi (Brandt 85), Bender, Reinartz, Son; Calhanoglu (Jedvaj 81), Kiessling.
Zenit St Petersburg: (4231) Lodygin; Aniukov, Garay, Lombaerts, Criscito; Javi Garcia, Witsel (Kerzhakov 82); Danny, Fayzulin (Shatov 62), Hulk; Rondon.

Monaco (0) 0

Benfica (0) 0   10,000

Monaco: (433) Subasic; Fabinho, Raggi, Ricardo Carvalho, Kurzawa; Joao Moutinho (Bernardo Silva 82), Toulalan, Kondogbia; Dirar, Berbatov (Martial 33), Ocampos (Carrasco 62).
Benfica: (433) Artur Moraes; Maxi Pereira, Luisao, Lopez▪, Eliseu; Salvio, Andre Almeida, Gaitan (Cesar 79); Perez (Samaris 87), Lima, Anderson Talisca (Bebe 68).

Tuesday, 4 November 2014

Benfica (0) 1 *(Anderson Talisca 82)*

Monaco (0) 0   60,000

Benfica: (433) Julio Cesar; Maxi Pereira, Luisao, Jardel, Andre Almeida; Samaris (Lima 63), Perez; Derley (Cristante 86), Gaitan (Bebe 90), Anderson Talisca.
Monaco: (433) Subasic; Fabinho, Raggi, Ricardo Carvalho, Kurzawa; Joao Moutinho, Toulalan, Kondogbia (Germain 87); Ocampos (Dirar 62), Traore (Martial 71), Carrasco.

Zenit St Petersburg (0) 1 *(Rondon 89)*

Bayer Leverkusen (0) 2 *(Son 68, 73)*   21,000

Zenit St Petersburg: (4231) Lodygin; Aniukov, Garay, Lombaerts, Criscito; Javi Garcia, Witsel; Hulk, Danny (Ryazantsev 79), Shatov (Arshavin 87); Kerzhakov (Rondon 79).
Bayer Leverkusen: (4231) Leno; Donati, Toprak, Spahic, Jedvaj (Boenisch 65); Calhanoglu, Bender; Bellarabi, Brandt (Drmic 53), Son; Kiessling (Kruse 90).

Wednesday, 26 November 2014
Bayer Leverkusen (0) 0
Monaco (0) 1 *(Ocampos 72)*   26,000
Bayer Leverkusen: (442) Leno; Wendell, Spahic, Toprak, Donati; Son (Drmic 59), Castro, Bender (Rolfes 77), Bellarabi (Brandt 76); Calhanoglu, Kiessling.
Monaco: (433) Subasic; Elderson, Abdennour, Ricardo Carvalho, Raggi; Bakayoko, Toulalan, Joao Moutinho; Carrasco (Ocampos 70), Berbatov (Traore 90), Dirar (Fabinho 83).

Zenit St Petersburg (0) 1 *(Danny 79)*
Benfica (0) 0   18,000
Zenit St Petersburg: (4231) Lodygin; Aniukov, Garay, Lombaerts (Luis Neto 23), Criscito; Javi Garcia (Fayzulin 58), Witsel; Hulk, Ryazantsev (Shatov 64), Danny; Rondon.
Benfica: (433) Julio Cesar; Maxi Pereira, Luisao■, Jardel, Andre Almeida; Perez, Samaris (John 81), Anderson Talisca (Derley 70); Salvio, Lima, Gaitan.

Tuesday, 9 December 2014
Benfica (0) 0
Bayer Leverkusen (0) 0   17,564
Benfica: (433) Artur Moraes; Andre Almeida, Lopez, Cesar, Benito; Bebe (Joao Teixeira 87), Cristante, John; Lima (Anderson Talisca 63), Pizzi, Derley (Nelson Oliveira 76).
Bayer Leverkusen: (4411) Leno; Hilbert, Toprak■, Spahic, Boenisch; Bellarabi, Castro, Rolfes (Kiessling 83), Kruse (Brandt 46); Calhanoglu; Drmic (Son 71).

Monaco (0) 2 *(Abdennour 63, Fabinho 89)*
Zenit St Petersburg (0) 0   11,319
Monaco: (451) Subasic; Fabinho, Wallace Santos, Abdennour, Raggi; Dirar (Bernardo Silva 90), Bakayoko, Toulalan, Joao Moutinho, Carrasco (Ocampos 90); Berbatov (Martial 56).
Zenit St Petersburg: (4411) Lodygin; Smolnikov (Ryazantsev 79), Garay, Lombaerts, Criscito; Hulk, Fayzulin (Shatov 68), Javi Garcia, Witsel; Danny; Rondon.

Group C Table

	P	W	D	L	F	A	GD	Pts
Monaco	6	3	2	1	4	1	3	11
Bayer Leverkusen	6	3	1	2	7	4	3	10
Zenit St Petersburg	6	2	1	3	4	6	-2	7
Benfica	6	1	2	3	2	6	-4	5

GROUP D

Tuesday, 16 September 2014
Borussia Dortmund (1) 2 *(Immobile 45, Aubameyang 48)*
Arsenal (0) 0   70,000
Borussia Dortmund: (451) Weidenfeller; Durm, Subotic, Papastathopoulos, Schmelzer (Jojic 79); Aubameyang, Bender, Kehl (Ginter 46), Grosskreutz, Mkhitaryan; Immobile (Ramos 85).
Arsenal: (4231) Szczesny; Bellerin, Mertesacker, Koscielny, Gibbs; Arteta (Podolski 77), Sanchez; Ramsey (Cazorla 62), Wilshere, Ozil (Oxlade-Chamberlain 61); Welbeck.

Galatasaray (0) 1 *(Yilmaz 90)*
Anderlecht (0) 1 *(Praet 52)*   40,000
Galatasaray: (4312) Muslera; Sari, Kaya, Chedjou, Alex (Camdal 79); Inan (Bulut 72), Felipe Melo, Dzemaili; Sneijder; Yilmaz, Pandev (Bruma 57).
Anderlecht: (4411) Roef; Najar, Mbemba, Nuytinck (Suarez 22), Deschacht; Defour, Tielemans, Conte, Praet (Dendoncker 78); Acheampong; Mitrovic (Kljestan 66).

Wednesday, 1 October 2014
Anderlecht (0) 0
Borussia Dortmund (1) 3 *(Immobile 3, Ramos 69, 79)*   25,800
Anderlecht: (442) Proto; Najar, Mbemba, Nuytinck, Deschacht; Conte (Acheampong 73), Defour, Tielemans, Praet; Suarez (Cyriac 83), Mitrovic (Kabasele 82).
Borussia Dortmund: (4231) Weidenfeller; Schmelzer, Papastathopoulos, Subotic, Piszczek; Kehl, Bender (Hummels 82); Grosskreutz (Ramos 65), Kagawa, Aubameyang; Immobile (Durm 72).

Arsenal (3) 4 *(Welbeck 22, 30, 52, Sanchez 41)*
Galatasaray (0) 1 *(Yilmaz 63 (pen))*   52,000
Arsenal: (4231) Szczesny■; Chambers, Mertesacker, Koscielny, Gibbs; Flamini, Cazorla; Oxlade-Chamberlain (Rosicky 68), Ozil (Wilshere 76), Sanchez (Ospina 61); Welbeck.
Galatasaray: (352) Muslera; Kaya, Felipe Melo, Chedjou; Sari (Bulut 68), Kurtulus (Altintop 46), Sneijder, Dzemaili, Alex; Yilmaz, Pandev (Bruma 68).

Wednesday, 22 October 2014
Anderlecht (0) 1 *(Najar 71)*
Arsenal (0) 2 *(Gibbs 89, Podolski 90)*   25,000
Anderlecht: (4231) Proto; Vanden Borre, Mbemba, Deschacht, Acheampong; Tielemans, Defour; Najar, Praet (Dendoncker 88), Conte; Cyriac (Suarez 83).
Arsenal: (4141) Chambers, Mertesacker, Monreal, Gibbs; Flamini (Oxlade-Chamberlain 74); Sanchez, Ramsey, Wilshere (Podolski 84), Cazorla; Welbeck (Campbell 74).

Galatasaray (0) 0
Borussia Dortmund (3) 4 *(Aubameyang 6, 18, Reus 41, Ramos 83)*   48,000
Galatasaray: (4312) Muslera; Camdal, Kaya, Chedjou, Alex (Oztekin 62); Altintop (Dzemaili 61), Felipe Melo, Inan; Sneijder; Pandev (Colak 77), Yilmaz.
Borussia Dortmund: (4411) Weidenfeller; Piszczek, Subotic, Hummels (Gundogan 69), Papastathopoulos; Mkhitaryan, Bender (Ginter 55), Kehl, Reus; Kagawa (Ramos 82); Aubameyang.

Tuesday, 4 November 2014
Arsenal (2) 3 *(Arteta 25 (pen), Sanchez 29, Oxlade-Chamberlain 58)*
Anderlecht (0) 3 *(Vanden Borre 61, 73 (pen), Mitrovic 90)*   60,000
Arsenal: (4141) Szczesny; Chambers, Mertesacker, Monreal, Gibbs; Arteta (Flamini 62); Ramsey, Chamberlain (Rosicky 81), Cazorla, Sanchez; Welbeck (Podolski 81).
Anderlecht: (352) Proto; Deschacht, Mbemba (Dendoncker 54), Vanden Borre; Praet, Kljestan, Tielemans, Najar, Conte (Kawaya 46); Cyriac (Mitrovic 62), Acheampong.

Borussia Dortmund (1) 4 *(Reus 39, Papastathopoulos 56, Immobile 74, Kaya 85 (og))*
Galatasaray (0) 1 *(Balta 70)*   78,000
Borussia Dortmund: (4231) Weidenfeller; Piszczek, Subotic, Papastathopoulos, Durm; Bender (Ramos 84), Kehl; Mkhitaryan, Kagawa (Gundogan 62), Reus (Immobile 70); Aubameyang.
Galatasaray: (4141) Muslera; Balta, Chedjou, Kaya, Camdal; Felipe Melo; Altintop (Oztekin 81), Dzemaili, Inan, Sneijder; Bulut (Yilmaz 83).

Wednesday, 26 November 2014
Anderlecht (1) 2 *(Mbemba 44, 86)*
Galatasaray (0) 0   21,500
Anderlecht: (451) Proto; Vanden Borre, Mbemba, Deschacht, Acheampong; Najar, Defour (Kawaya 46), Praet (Kljestan 84), Tielemans, Conte; Mitrovic (Cyriac 89).
Galatasaray: (451) Muslera; Camdal, Chedjou, Kaya, Alex; Altintop (Ozcal 90), Inan■, Sneijder, Felipe Melo, Bruma (Bulut 75); Yilmaz.

Arsenal (1) 2 *(Sanogo 2, Sanchez 57)*
Borussia Dortmund (0) 0   59,902
Arsenal: (451) Martinez; Chambers, Mertesacker, Monreal, Gibbs; Arteta (Flamini 66), Oxlade-Chamberlain (Campbell 89), Ramsey, Cazorla, Sanchez; Sanogo (Podolski 79).
Borussia Dortmund: (4411) Weidenfeller; Piszczek, Subotic, Ginter, Schmelzer; Mkhitaryan, Bender, Gundogan, Grosskreutz (Jojic 78); Immobile (Kagawa 60); Aubameyang (Ramos 60).

Tuesday, 9 December 2014

Borussia Dortmund (0) 1 *(Immobile 58)*

Anderlecht (0) 1 *(Mitrovic 84)* 65,851

Borussia Dortmund: (4231) Langerak; Durm, Subotic, Ginter, Schmelzer (Aubameyang 75); Gundogan (Kirch 65), Sahin; Mkhitaryan, Kagawa (Blaszczykowski 85), Grosskreutz; Immobile.

Anderlecht: (4231) Proto; Vanden Borre, Mbemba, Deschacht, N'Sakala; Dendoncker, Kljestan (Tielemans 69); Conte (Cyriac 79), Praet, Acheampong; Mitrovic (Heylen 89).

Galatasaray (0) 1 *(Sneijder 88)*

Arsenal (3) 4 *(Podolski 3, 90, Ramsey 11, 29)* 20,590

Galatasaray: (442) Bolat; Alex, Balta, Kaya, Camdal (Altintop 46); Felipe Melo, Sneijder, Bruma (Adin 77), Colak; Bulut, Yilmaz (Oztekin 46).

Arsenal: (433) Szczesny; Debuchy (O'Connor 76), Mertesacker, Chambers, Bellerin; Oxlade-Chamberlain, Flamini (Zelalem 46), Ramsey (Maitland-Niles 46); Campbell, Sanogo, Podolski.

Group D Table	P	W	D	L	F	A	GD	Pts
Borussia Dortmund	6	4	1	1	14	4	10	13
Arsenal	6	4	1	1	15	8	7	13
Anderlecht	6	1	3	2	8	10	-2	6
Galatasaray	6	0	1	5	4	19	-15	1

GROUP E

Wednesday, 17 September 2014

Bayern Munich (0) 1 *(Boateng 89)*

Manchester C (0) 0 68,000

Bayern Munich: (433) Neuer; Rafinha (Pizarro 84), Boateng, Benatia (Dante 85), Bernat; Lahm, Alonso, Alaba; Muller (Robben 76), Lewandowski, Gotze.

Manchester C: (4411) Hart; Clichy, Demichelis, Kompany, Sagna; Nasri (Milner 58), Fernandinho, Toure, Jesus Navas (Kolarov 87); Silva; Dzeko (Aguero 74).

Roma (4) 5 *(Iturbe 6, Gervinho 10, 31, Maicon 20, Ignashevich 50 (og))*

CSKA Moscow (0) 1 *(Musa 82)* 40,000

Roma: (433) De Sanctis; Maicon, Manolas (Yanga-Mbiwa 76), Astori, Torosidis; Pjanic, Keita, Nainggolan; Gervinho (Ljajic 71), Totti, Iturbe (Florenzi 26).

CSKA Moscow: (4411) Akinfeev; Mario Fernandes, Berezutski V, Ignashevich, Nababkin (Shchennikov 46); Tosic (Efremov 53), Natcho, Milanov, Musa; Eremenko (Panchenko 66); Doumbia.

Tuesday, 30 September 2014

CSKA Moscow (0) 0

Bayern Munich (1) 1 *(Muller 22 (pen))*

CSKA Moscow: (4141) Akinfeev; Mario Fernandes, Berezutski V, Ignashevich, Shchennikov; Berezutski A; Tosic (Efremov 78), Natcho (Doumbia 66), Eremenko, Milanov; Musa.

Bayern Munich: (3511) Neuer; Benatia, Dante, Alaba; Robben (Rafinha 81), Lahm, Alonso, Bernat, Gotze (Shaqiri 77); Muller; Lewandowski (Pizarro 90).

Behind closed doors.

Manchester C (1) 1 *(Aguero 4 (pen))*

Roma (1) 1 *(Totti 23)* 46,000

Manchester C: (442) Hart; Zabaleta, Kompany, Demichelis, Clichy; Jesus Navas (Milner 45), Fernandinho, Toure, Silva; Dzeko (Lampard 57), Aguero (Jovetic 84).

Roma: (451) Skorupski; Maicon (Torosidis 89), Manolas, Yanga-Mbiwa, Cole; Florenzi (Holebas 82), Pjanic, Keita, Nainggolan, Gervinho; Totti (Iturbe 71).

Tuesday, 21 October 2014

CSKA Moscow (0) 2 *(Doumbia 64, Natcho 86 (pen))*

Manchester C (2) 2 *(Aguero 29, Milner 37)*

CSKA Moscow: (541) Akinfeev; Mario Fernandes, Berezutski V, Berezutski A (Doumbia 46 (Cauna 90)), Ignashevich, Shchennikov; Tosic (Efremov 69), Natcho, Milanov, Eremenko; Musa.

Manchester C: (442) Hart; Zabaleta, Kompany, Mangala, Kolarov; Milner, Toure, Fernando (Jovetic 86), Silva (Fernandinho 78); Dzeko (Jesus Navas 72), Aguero.

Behind closed doors.

Roma (0) 1 *(Gervinho 66)*

Bayern Munich (5) 7 *(Robben 9, 30, Gotze 23, Lewandowski 25, Muller 36 (pen), Ribery 78, Shaqiri 80)* 65,000

Roma: (433) De Sanctis; Torosidis, Yanga-Mbiwa, Manolas, Cole (Holebas 46); Nainggolan, De Rossi, Pjanic (Ljajic 79); Iturbe, Totti (Florenzi 46), Gervinho.

Bayern Munich: (4231) Neuer; Bernat, Boateng, Benatia, Alaba; Lahm, Alonso; Robben, Muller (Rafinha 60), Gotze (Shaqiri 79); Lewandowski (Ribery 68).

Wednesday, 5 November 2014

Bayern Munich (1) 2 *(Ribery 38, Gotze 64)*

Roma (0) 0 68,000

Bayern Munich: (3421) Neuer; Benatia, Boateng, Alaba (Rode 80); Rafinha, Lahm (Hojbjerg 88), Alonso (Shaqiri 72), Bernat; Gotze, Ribery; Lewandowski.

Roma: (433) Skorupski; Torosidis, Manolas, Yanga-Mbiwa, Holebas (Cole 46); Nainggolan, De Rossi, Keita; Florenzi (Pjanic 58), Destro, Iturbe (Gervinho 74).

Manchester C (1) 1 *(Toure 8)*

CSKA Moscow (2) 2 *(Doumbia 2, 34)* 42,000

Manchester C: (442) Hart; Zabaleta, Kompany, Demichelis, Clichy; Jesus Navas (Nasri 46), Toure▪, Fernando (Dzeko 65), Milner; Aguero, Jovetic (Fernandinho▪ 46).

CSKA Moscow: (451) Akinfeev; Mario Fernandes, Berezutski V, Ignashevich, Shchennikov; Musa, Wernbloom, Eremenko, Natcho, Dzagoev (Efremov 86); Doumbia (Milanov 66).

Tuesday, 25 November 2014

CSKA Moscow (0) 1 *(Berezutski V 90)*

Roma (1) 1 *(Totti 43)*

CSKA Moscow: (4141) Akinfeev; Mario Fernandes, Ignashevich, Berezutski V, Shchennikov; Dzagoev; Cauna (Milanov 64), Eremenko, Natcho, Musa (Tosic 81); Doumbia.

Roma: (433) De Sanctis; Manolas, Astori, Holebas, Nainggolan (Strootman 83); De Rossi, Keita, Florenzi; Ljajic (Pjanic 87), Totti, Gervinho (Iturbe 77).

Behind closed doors.

Manchester C (1) 3 *(Aguero 22 (pen), 85, 90)*

Bayern Munich (2) 2 *(Alonso 40, Lewandowski 45)* 44,510

Manchester C: (4231) Hart; Sagna (Zabaleta 68), Kompany, Mangala, Clichy; Fernando, Milner (Jovetic 66); Jesus Navas, Lampard, Nasri; Aguero (Demichelis 90).

Bayern Munich: (433) Neuer; Rafinha, Benatia▪, Boateng, Bernat; Hojbjerg, Alonso, Rode (Dante 25); Robben, Lewandowski (Shaqiri 84), Ribery (Schweinsteiger 80).

Wednesday, 10 December 2014

Bayern Munich (1) 3 *(Muller 18 (pen), Rode 83, Gotze 90)*

CSKA Moscow (0) 0 68,000

Bayern Munich: (343) Neuer; Boateng, Dante, Bernat; Hojbjerg, Rode, Schweinsteiger, Gaudino (Weiser 73); Muller (Robben 46), Gotze, Ribery (Lewandowski 46).

CSKA Moscow: (4231) Akinfeev; Mario Fernandes, Berezutski V, Ignashevich, Nababkin; Wernbloom, Natcho (Tosic 65); Dzagoev, Eremenko (Milanov 82), Musa (Efremov 90); Doumbia.

Roma (0) 0

Manchester C (0) 2 *(Nasri 60, Zabaleta 86)* 54,119

Roma: (4411) De Sanctis; Maicon (Florenzi 79), Manolas, Yanga-Mbiwa, Holebas; Ljajic (Iturbe 67), Nainggolan, Keita, Gervinho; Pjanic; Totti (Destro 70).

Manchester C: (4411) Hart; Zabaleta, Demichelis, Mangala, Clichy; Jesus Navas (Silva 67), Fernandinho, Fernando, Milner; Nasri (Kolarov 83); Dzeko (Jovetic 78).

Group E Table	P	W	D	L	F	A	GD	Pts
Bayern Munich	6	5	0	1	16	4	12	15
Manchester C	6	2	2	2	9	8	1	8
Roma	6	1	2	3	8	14	-6	5
CSKA Moscow	6	1	2	3	6	13	-7	5

GROUP F

Wednesday, 17 September 2014

Ajax (0) 1 *(Schone 74)*

Paris Saint-Germain (1) 1 *(Cavani 14)* 50,430

Ajax: (4231) Cillessen; Van Rhijn, Veltman, Moisander, Boilesen; Viergever (Zimling 46), Klaassen; Schone (Milik 82), Serero, Andersen; Sigthorsson (El Ghazi 61).
Paris Saint-Germain: (433) Sirigu; van der Wiel, Marquinhos, Luiz, Maxwell; Matuidi, Verratti (Pastore 81), Thiago Motta; Lucas Moura (Lavezzi 81), Ibrahimovic, Cavani.

Barcelona (1) 1 *(Pique 28)*

APOEL Nicosia (0) 0 62,832

Barcelona: (433) ter Stegen; Dani Alves, Pique, Bartra, Adriano; Xavi (Iniesta 60), Samper, Sergi Roberto (Rafinha 79); Messi, Munir (Sandro 68), Neymar.
APOEL Nicosia: (442) Urko; Mario Sergio, Joao Guilherme, Carlao, Antoniades; Morais, Vinicius, Aloneftis; De Vincenti (Charalambidis 79), Sheridan (Djebbour 75).

Tuesday, 30 September 2014

APOEL Nicosia (1) 1 *(Manduca 32 (pen))*

Ajax (1) 1 *(Andersen 28)* 20,000

APOEL Nicosia: (442) Urko; Morais, Joao Guilherme, Carlao, Antoniades; Mario Sergio, Gomes (De Vincenti 71), Vinicius, Aloneftis; Sheridan (Djebbour 82), Manduca (Efrem 79).
Ajax: (442) Cillessen; Van Rhijn, Veltman, Moisander, Boilesen; Viergever, Klaassen, Schone (El Ghazi 74), Serero; Andersen (Kishna 74), Sigthorsson.

Paris Saint-Germain (2) 3 *(Luiz 10, Verratti 26, Matuidi 54)*

Barcelona (1) 2 *(Messi 11, Neymar 56)* 48,000

Paris Saint-Germain: (433) Sirigu; van der Wiel, Marquinhos, Luiz, Maxwell; Verratti (Cabaye 70), Thiago Motta, Matuidi; Lucas Moura (Bahebeck 90), Cavani, Pastore (Chantome 86).
Barcelona: (433) ter Stegen; Dani Alves (Sandro 83), Mascherano, Mathieu, Jordi Alba; Rakitic (Xavi 69), Busquets, Iniesta; Messi, Neymar, Pedro (Munir 62).

Tuesday, 21 October 2014

APOEL Nicosia (0) 0

Paris Saint-Germain (0) 1 *(Cavani 87)* 20,000

APOEL Nicosia: (442) Urko; Mario Sergio, Joao Guilherme, Carlao, Antoniades (Riise 41); Gomes, Vinicius, Morais (De Vincenti 79), Efrem; Manduca, Sheridan (Djebbour 67).
Paris Saint-Germain: (433) Sirigu; van der Wiel, Thiago Silva, Luiz, Maxwell; Verratti (Bahebeck 70), Thiago Motta, Matuidi; Lucas Moura (Chantome 88), Cavani, Pastore (Cabaye 70).

Barcelona (2) 3 *(Neymar 7, Messi 24, Sandro 90)*

Ajax (0) 1 *(El Ghazi 88)* 79,357

Barcelona: (433) ter Stegen; Dani Alves, Bartra, Pique, Jordi Alba; Rakitic, Mascherano, Iniesta (Rafinha 76); Pedro, Messi (Munir 66), Neymar (Sandro 61).
Ajax: (433) Cillessen; Van Rhijn, Veltman, Moisander, Viergever; Klaassen, Zimling (Riedewald 56), Andersen; Schone, Sigthorsson (El Ghazi 73), Kishna (Milik 46).

Wednesday, 5 November 2014

Ajax (0) 0

Barcelona (1) 2 *(Messi 36, 76)* 52,116

Ajax: (433) Cillessen; Van Rhijn, Veltman[■], Moisander, Boilesen; Klaassen, Serero (Denswil 80), Andersen (Riedewald 72); El Ghazi, Sigthorsson (Milik 62), Schone.
Barcelona: (433) ter Stegen; Dani Alves (Adriano 83), Bartra, Mascherano, Jordi Alba; Rakitic (Rafinha 80), Busquets, Xavi; Suarez, Messi, Neymar (Pedro 74).

Paris Saint-Germain (1) 1 *(Cavani 1)*

APOEL Nicosia (0) 0 42,000

Paris Saint-Germain: (433) Sirigu; van der Wiel, Thiago Silva, Luiz, Maxwell; Pastore, Thiago Motta, Matuidi; Lucas Moura (Cabaye 86), Cavani, Lavezzi (Bahebeck 77).

Tuesday, 25 November 2014

APOEL Nicosia (0) 0

Barcelona (2) 4 *(Suarez 27, Messi 38, 58, 87)* 22,000

APOEL Nicosia: (442) Urko; Mario Sergio, Joao Guilherme[■], Carlao, Antoniades; Gomes, Morais, Vinicius (Djebbour 74), Aloneftis (Efrem 46); Manduca (De Vincenti 62), Sheridan.
Barcelona: (433) ter Stegen; Dani Alves, Bartra, Pique, Jordi Alba (Adriano 63); Rakitic (Xavi 62), Mascherano, Rafinha[■]; Suarez (Busquets 76), Messi, Pedro.

Paris Saint-Germain (1) 3 *(Cavani 33, 83, Ibrahimovic 79)*

Ajax (0) 1 *(Klaassen 67)* 45,000

Paris Saint-Germain: (433) Sirigu; Marquinhos, Maxwell, van der Wiel, Luiz; Matuidi, Rabiot (Chantome 75), Pastore; Cavani, Ibrahimovic (Digne 86), Lavezzi (Lucas Moura 68).
Ajax: (433) Cillessen; Van Rhijn, Boilesen (Viergever 10), van der Hoorn, Denswil; Klaassen, Schone, Serero (Zimling 68); Andersen, Milik, Kishna.

Wednesday, 10 December 2014

Ajax (1) 4 *(Schone 45 (pen), 50, Klaassen 53, Milik 74)*

APOEL Nicosia (0) 0 51,796

Ajax: (433) Cillessen; Van Rhijn, Veltman, Moisander, Viergever; Klaassen, Serero, Andersen (Riedewald 68); Schone (El Ghazi 75), Milik (Zivkovic 84), Kishna.
APOEL Nicosia: (4231) Urko; Mario Sergio, Papazoglou, Carlao, Antoniades; Vinicius, Morais (Artymatas 72); Gomes, Efrem (Aloneftis 65), Alexandrou; Sheridan (Sotiriou 65).

Barcelona (2) 3 *(Messi 19, Neymar 42, Suarez 77)*

Paris Saint-Germain (1) 1 *(Ibrahimovic 15)* 82,570

Barcelona: (433) ter Stegen; Bartra (Adriano 90), Pique, Mascherano, Mathieu; Busquets, Pedro (Rakitic 67), Iniesta (Xavi 73); Messi, Suarez, Neymar.
Paris Saint-Germain: (433) Sirigu; van der Wiel, Luiz, Thiago Silva, Maxwell; Verratti (Pastore 62), Thiago Motta, Matuidi (Lavezzi 75); Lucas Moura, Ibrahimovic, Cavani.

Group F Table	P	W	D	L	F	A	GD	Pts
Barcelona	6	5	0	1	15	5	10	15
Paris Saint-Germain	6	4	1	1	10	7	3	13
Ajax	6	1	2	3	8	10	–2	5
APOEL Nicosia	6	0	1	5	1	12	–11	1

GROUP G

Wednesday, 17 September 2014

Chelsea (1) 1 *(Fabregas 11)*

Schalke 04 (0) 1 *(Huntelaar 62)* 39,500

Chelsea: (4411) Courtois; Ivanovic, Cahill, Terry, Luis; Ramires (Oscar 67), Fabregas, Matic, Hazard E; Willian (Remy 74); Drogba (Costa 74).
Schalke 04: (4411) Fahrmann; Hoger, Ayhan, Neustadter, Fuchs; Sam (Barnetta 78), Boateng, Aogo, Draxler (Obasi Ogbuke 86); Meyer (Choupo-Moting 73); Huntelaar.

Maribor (0) 1 *(Zahovic 90)*

Sporting Lisbon (0) 1 *(Nani 80)* 12,500

Maribor: (442) Handanovic; Stojanovic, Rajcevic, Arghus, Viler; Sallalich (Bohar 58), Mertelj, Filipovic, Vrsic (Zahovic 82); Tavares (Mendy 84), Ibraimi.
Sporting Lisbon: (433) Rui Patricio; Cedric Soares, Mauricio, Sarr, Jefferson; Andre Martins (Joao Mario 46), William Carvalho, Adrien Silva; Nani, Slimani (Montero 90), Carrillo (Carlos Mane 66).

Tuesday, 30 September 2014

Schalke 04 (0) 1 *(Huntelaar 56)*

Maribor (1) 1 *(Bohar 37)* 70,000

Schalke 04: (4231) Fahrmann; Ayhan (Uchida 45), Matip, Neustadter, Fuchs; Boateng (Meyer 79), Aogo; Choupo-Moting (Obasi Ogbuke 66), Barnetta, Draxler; Huntelaar.
Maribor: (442) Handanovic; Mejac, Rajcevic, Suler, Viler; Filipovic, Mertelj (N'Diaye 80), Bohar (Sallalich 83), Vrsic (Mendy 67); Ibraimi, Tavares.

Sporting Lisbon (0) 0
Chelsea (1) 1 *(Matic 34)* 50,000
Sporting Lisbon: (451) Rui Patricio; Mauricio (Paulo Oliveira 63), Sarr, Silva, Cedric Soares; William Carvalho, Joao Mario, Adrien Silva (Montero 81), Slimani, Carrillo (Diego Capel 81); Nani.
Chelsea: (4411) Courtois; Ivanovic, Cahill, Terry, Luis; Fabregas, Oscar (Mikel 71), Hazard E (Salah 84), Matic; Schurrle (Willian 57); Costa.

Tuesday, 21 October 2014
Chelsea (3) 6 *(Remy 13, Drogba 23 (pen), Terry 31, Viler 54 (og), Hazard E 77 (pen), 90)*
Maribor (0) 0 41,126
Chelsea: (4411) Cech; Ivanovic, Zouma, Terry, Luis; Willian, Fabregas (Ake 60), Matic, Hazard E; Oscar (Solanke 73); Remy (Drogba 16).
Maribor: (442) Handanovic; Stojanovic, Rajcevic, Suler, Viler (Vrsic 56); Mejac, Mertelj, Filipovic, Bohar; Ibraimi (Zahovic 68), Tavares (Mendy 72).

Schalke 04 (1) 4 *(Obasi Ogbuke 34, Huntelaar 51, Howedes 60, Choupo-Moting 90 (pen))*
Sporting Lisbon (1) 3 *(Nani 16, Adrien Silva 64 (pen), 78)* 49,943
Schalke 04: (4411) Fahrmann; Uchida, Howedes, Ayhan, Aogo; Obasi Ogbuke (Meyer 65), Neustadter, Hoger, Draxler (Sam 82); Boateng (Choupo-Moting 46); Huntelaar.
Sporting Lisbon: (4321) Rui Patricio; Cedric Soares, Paulo Oliveira, Mauricio■, Silva; Joao Mario (Sarr 38), William Carvalho, Adrien Silva; Nani, Carrillo (Diego Capel 89); Slimani (Montero 25).

Wednesday, 5 November 2014
Maribor (0) 1 *(Ibraimi 50)*
Chelsea (0) 1 *(Matic 73)* 12,500
Maribor: (442) Handanovic; Viler, Arghus, Rajcevic, Stojanovic; Sallalich (N'Diaye 90), Filipovic, Mertelj, Ibraimi (Bohar 89); Tavares, Zahovic (Mendy 72).
Chelsea: (4411) Cech; Luis (Ramires 55), Terry, Zouma, Ivanovic; Hazard E, Matic, Fabregas, Willian (Oscar 46); Schurrle (Costa 46); Drogba.

Sporting Lisbon (1) 4 *(Sarr 26, Jefferson 52, Nani 72, Slimani 90)*
Schalke 04 (1) 2 *(Slimani 17 (og), Aogo 87)* 35,473
Sporting Lisbon: (4141) Rui Patricio; Cedric Soares, Sarr, Paulo Oliveira, Jefferson; William Carvalho; Nani (Diego Capel 89), Adrien Silva, Joao Mario (Rosell 82), Carlos Mane (Carrillo 68); Slimani.
Schalke 04: (4231) Fahrmann; Uchida, Howedes, Neustadter, Fuchs (Kirchhoff 78); Hoger, Aogo; Choupo-Moting, Meyer (Boateng 65), Obasi Ogbuke (Sam 69); Huntelaar.

Tuesday, 25 November 2014
Schalke 04 (0) 0
Chelsea (3) 5 *(Terry 2, Willian 29, Kirchhoff 44 (og), Drogba 76, Ramires 78)* 46,500
Schalke 04: (4411) Fahrmann; Uchida, Howedes, Felipe Santana, Aogo; Hoger, Neustadter, Kirchhoff (Clemens 46), Choupo-Moting; Boateng (Meyer 63); Huntelaar.
Chelsea: (451) Courtois; Ivanovic, Terry, Cahill, Azpilicueta; Willian, Fabregas (Schurrle 78), Matic, Oscar (Ramires 75); Hazard E; Costa (Drogba 66).

Sporting Lisbon (2) 3 *(Carlos Mane 10, Nani 35, Slimani 65)*
Maribor (1) 1 *(Jefferson 42 (og))* 44,000
Sporting Lisbon: (433) Rui Patricio; Cedric Soares, Mauricio, Paulo Oliveira, Jefferson; Joao Mario (Andre Martins 82), William Carvalho, Adrien Silva; Carlos Mane (Carrillo 67), Slimani (Montero 75), Nani.
Maribor: (442) Handanovic; Stojanovic, Rajcevic, Arghus, Mejac; Vrsic (Ibraimi 46), Mertelj, Filipovic, Sallalich (Bohar 70); Tavares, Zahovic (Mendy 76).

Wednesday, 10 December 2014
Chelsea (2) 3 *(Fabregas 8 (pen), Schurrle 16, Mikel 57)*
Sporting Lisbon (0) 1 *(Silva 50)* 41,089
Chelsea: (433) Cech; Azpilicueta, Cahill, Zouma, Luis; Fabregas (Loftus-Cheek 83), Mikel, Matic; Salah (Remy 71), Costa, Schurrle (Ramires 74).

Sporting Lisbon: (451) Rui Patricio; Ricardo Esgaio, Mauricio, Paulo Oliveira, Silva; Joao Mario (Andre Martins 69), William Carvalho (Montero 60), Adrien Silva, Carrillo, Slimani; Diego Capel (Carlos Mane 60).

Maribor (0) 0
Schalke 04 (0) 1 *(Meyer 62)* 12,516
Maribor: (442) Handanovic; Stojanovic (Vrsic 76), Rajcevic, Arghus, Viler; Sallalich (Mendy 65), Mertelj, Filipovic, Bohar; Tavares, Ibraimi (Zahovic 82).
Schalke 04: (532) Fahrmann; Uchida, Neustadter, Kirchhoff, Howedes, Fuchs; Barnetta (Meyer 56), Aogo, Hoger (Ayhan 88); Choupo-Moting, Huntelaar (Friedrich 90).

Group G Table	P	W	D	L	F	A	GD	Pts
Chelsea	6	4	2	0	17	3	14	14
Schalke 04	6	2	2	2	9	14	–5	8
Sporting Lisbon	6	2	1	3	12	12	0	7
Maribor	6	0	3	3	4	13	–9	3

GROUP H

Wednesday, 17 September 2014
Athletic Bilbao (0) 0
Shakhtar Donetsk (0) 0 48,000
Athletic Bilbao: (4411) Iraizoz; De Marcos, Gurpegi, Laporte, Balenziaga; Ibai, Mikel Rico, Iturraspe, Muniain (Aketxe 74); Benat (Susaeta 64); Aduriz (Guillermo 77).
Shakhtar Donetsk: (4411) Pyatov; Srna, Kucher, Rakitskiy, Azevedo; Douglas Costa, Fernando (Fred 73), Stepanenko, Taison (Marlos 80); Alex Teixeira; Adriano (Gladkiy 89).

Porto (3) 6 *(Brahimi 5, 32, 57, Martinez 37, Adrian 61, Aboubakar 76)*
BATE Borisov (0) 0 20,000
Porto: (451) Fabiano; Danilo, Maicon, Martins Indi, Alex Sandro; Quaresma, Herrera (Tello 68), Casemiro, Brahimi (Evandro 59), Adrian; Martinez (Aboubakar 63).
BATE Borisov: (433) Chernik; Khagush, Palyakow, Filipenko, Mladenovic; Olekhnovich (Karnitskiy 62), Likhtarovich (Yakovlev 53), Valadzko A; Gordeichuk, Aleksiyevich, Rodionov (Signevich 70).

Tuesday, 30 September 2014
BATE Borisov (2) 2 *(Palyakow 19, Karnitskiy 41)*
Athletic Bilbao (1) 1 *(Aduriz 45)* 12,000
BATE Borisov: (4411) Chernik; Khagush, Palyakow, Filipenko, Mladenovic; Gordeichuk (Olekhnovich 90), Yablonskiy, Valadzko A, Valadzko M (Yakovlev 80); Karnitskiy (Rodionov 86); Signevich.
Athletic Bilbao: (433) Iraizoz; Iraola (Toquero 77), San Jose, Laporte, Balenziaga; Benat, Iturraspe, Mikel Rico (Susaeta 46); Muniain, Aduriz, Ibai (De Marcos 46).

Shakhtar Donetsk (0) 2 *(Alex Teixeira 52, Luiz Adriano 85)*
Porto (0) 2 *(Martinez 89 (pen), 90)* 30,000
Shakhtar Donetsk: (4231) Pyatov; Srna, Kucher, Rakitskiy, Azevedo; Fernando, Stepanenko; Douglas Costa (Bernard 79), Alex Teixeira, Taison (Ilsinho 75); Luiz Adriano.
Porto: (4231) Fabiano; Danilo, Maicon, Martins Indi, Alex Sandro; Marcano (Quintero 65), Herrera; Brahimi (Adrian 77), Torres, Tello; Aboubakar (Martinez 65).

Tuesday, 21 October 2014
BATE Borisov (0) 0
Shakhtar Donetsk (6) 7 *(Alex Teixeira 11, Luiz Adriano 28 (pen), 37, 40, 44, 82 (pen), Douglas Costa 35)* 20,000
BATE Borisov: (4411) Chernik; Khagush, Palyakow, Tubic (Hayduchyk 46), Mladenovic; Gordeichuk, Yablonskiy, Likhtarovich (Aleksiyevich 46), Valadzko M; Karnitskiy; Signevich (Baha 74).
Shakhtar Donetsk: (4411) Pyatov; Srna, Kucher, Rakitskiy, Shevchuk; Douglas Costa (Marlos 46), Fernando (Fred 46), Stepanenko, Taison (Bernard 46); Alex Teixeira; Luiz Adriano.

Porto (1) 2 *(Herrera 45, Quaresma 75)*
Athletic Bilbao (0) 1 *(Guillermo 58)* 　　　45,000
Porto: (433) Fabiano; Danilo, Maicon, Martins Indi, Alex Sandro; Herrera, Casemiro (Quaresma 70), Brahimi; Quintero (Ruben Neves 64), Tello (Torres 82), Martinez.
Athletic Bilbao: (4231) Iraizoz; De Marcos, Etxeita, Laporte, Balenziaga; San Jose (Benat 46), Iturraspe; Guillermo, Mikel Rico (Gurpegi 73), Susaeta; Aduriz (Muniain 46).

Wednesday, 5 November 2014
Athletic Bilbao (0) 0
Porto (0) 2 *(Martinez 55, Brahimi 73)* 　　　44,000
Athletic Bilbao: (4411) Iraizoz; De Marcos, Gurpegi, Laporte, Balenziaga; Ibai (Viguera 73), Mikel Rico, San Jose, Susaeta (Muniain 46); Benat (Iraola 46); Guillermo.
Porto: (451) Fabiano; Danilo, Maicon, Martins Indi, Alex Sandro; Tello (Quaresma 60), Torres (Ruben Neves 82), Casemiro, Herrera, Brahimi (Adrian 90); Martinez.

Shakhtar Donetsk (1) 5 *(Srna 19, Alex Teixeira 48, Luiz Adriano 58 (pen), 83, 90)*
BATE Borisov (0) 0 　　　33,000
Shakhtar Donetsk: (4411) Pyatov; Srna, Ordets, Rakitskiy, Shevchuk (Marlos 64); Douglas Costa, Fernando (Fred 66), Stepanenko, Taison (Bernard 73); Alex Teixeira; Luiz Adriano.
BATE Borisov: (4231) Chernik; Khagush[■], Hayduchyk, Polyakov, Mladenovic; Yablonskiy (Valadzko M 59), Valadzko A; Yakovlev (Olekhnovich 46), Karnitskiy, Gordeichuk; Signevich (Rodionov 70).

Tuesday, 25 November 2014
BATE Borisov (0) 0
Porto (0) 3 *(Herrera 56, Martinez 65, Tello 89)* 　　　6000
BATE Borisov: (4231) Chernik; Olekhnovich, Hayduchyk, Tubic, Mladenovic (Aleksiyevich 71); Valadzko A, Yablonskiy; Gordeichuk, Karnitskiy (Baha 66), Valadzko M; Rodionov (Signevich 75).
Porto: (433) Fabiano; Danilo, Marcano, Martins Indi, Alex Sandro; Herrera, Casemiro, Torres; Quaresma (Tello 71), Martinez (Quintero 90), Brahimi (Adrian 83).

Shakhtar Donetsk (0) 0
Athletic Bilbao (0) 1 *(San Jose 68)* 　　　50,000
Shakhtar Donetsk: (442) Pyatov; Srna, Kucher, Rakitskiy, Shevchuk; Douglas Costa (Marlos 67), Fernando (Fred 77), Stepanenko, Taison (Bernard 71); Alex Teixeira, Luiz Adriano.
Athletic Bilbao: (4231) Iraizoz; De Marcos, Etxeita (Gurpegi 32), San Jose, Balenziaga; Iturraspe, Mikel Rico; Susaeta (Aduriz 65), Benat, Muniain (Lopez 88); Viguera.

Wednesday, 10 December 2014
Athletic Bilbao (0) 2 *(San Jose 47, Susaeta 88)*
BATE Borisov (0) 0 　　　42,852
Athletic Bilbao: (4411) Iraizoz; Iraola (Lopez 75), San Jose, Laporte, Balenziaga; Susaeta, Iturraspe, Mikel Rico, Ibai (Viguera 87); De Marcos; Guillermo (Aduriz 78).
BATE Borisov: (4411) Soroko; Olekhnovich, Filipenko, Tubic, Khagush; Gordeichuk, Valadzko A (Signevich 60), Yablonskiy (Baha 77), Valadzko M; Karnitskiy; Rodionov (Likhtarovich 83).

Porto (0) 1 *(Aboubakar 87)*
Shakhtar Donetsk (0) 1 *(Stepanenko 50)* 　　　28,010
Porto: (433) Fernandez; Ricardo Pereira, Marcano, Maicon, Alex Sandro; Quintero (Torres 69), Ruben Neves (Martins Indi 41), Evandro; Quaresma, Aboubakar, Adrian (Kelvin 53).
Shakhtar Donetsk: (442) Pyatov; Ilsinho, Kryvtsov, Rakitskiy, Shevchuk; Douglas Costa (Marlos 66), Fred, Stepanenko (Fernando 86), Bernard (Taison 66); Alex Teixeira, Gladkiy.

Group H Table	P	W	D	L	F	A	GD	Pts
Porto	6	4	2	0	16	4	12	14
Shakhtar Donetsk	6	2	3	1	15	4	11	9
Athletic Bilbao	6	2	1	3	5	6	–1	7
BATE Borisov	6	1	0	5	2	24	–22	3

KNOCK-OUT STAGE

ROUND OF 16 FIRST LEG
Tuesday, 17 February 2015
Paris Saint-Germain (0) 1 *(Cavani 54)*
Chelsea (1) 1 *(Ivanovic 36)* 　　　45,713
Paris Saint-Germain: (433) Sirigu; van der Wiel, Marquinhos, Thiago Silva, Maxwell; Verratti, Luiz, Matuidi; Lavezzi (Pastore 81), Ibrahimovic, Cavani.
Chelsea: (4231) Courtois; Ivanovic, Cahill, Terry, Azpilicueta; Ramires, Matic; Willian (Cuadrado 79), Fabregas (Oscar 84), Hazard E; Costa (Remy 81).

Shakhtar Donetsk (0) 0
Bayern Munich (0) 0 　　　34,915
Shakhtar Donetsk: (4231) Pyatov; Srna, Kucher, Rakitskiy, Shevchuk; Fernando, Fred; Douglas Costa (Marlos 78), Alex Teixeira, Taison (Nem 84); Luiz Adriano (Gladkiy 89).
Bayern Munich: (3331) Neuer; Rafinha, Boateng, Alaba; Schweinsteiger, Alonso[■], Bernat; Robben, Gotze (Lewandowski 75), Ribery; Muller (Badstuber 70).

Wednesday, 18 February 2015
FC Basel (1) 1 *(Gonzalez 11)*
Porto (0) 1 *(Danilo 79 (pen))* 　　　34,464
FC Basel: (451) Vaclik; Xhaka, Suchy, Samuel, Safari; Gonzalez (Calla 25), El-Nenny, Frei, Zuffi, Gashi (Hamoudi 83); Streller (Embolo 63).
Porto: (433) Fabiano; Danilo, Maicon, Marcano, Alex Sandro; Herrera, Casemiro, Torres (Ruben Neves 68); Tello (Quintero 81), Martinez, Brahimi (Quaresma 63).

Schalke 04 (0) 0
Real Madrid (1) 2 *(Ronaldo 26, Marcelo 79)* 　　　54,442
Schalke 04: (532) Wellenreuther; Uchida, Howedes, Matip, Nastasic, Aogo; Hoger (Meyer 80), Neustadter (Kirchhoff 57); Boateng; Choupo-Moting, Huntelaar (Platte 33).

Real Madrid: (433) Casillas; Carvajal (Arbeloa 82), Varane, Pepe, Marcelo; Lucas Silva, Kroos, Isco (Illarramendi 85); Bale, Benzema (Hernandez 78), Ronaldo.

Tuesday, 24 February 2015
Juventus (2) 2 *(Tevez 13, Morata 43)*
Borussia Dortmund (1) 1 *(Reus 18)* 　　　41,182
Juventus: (442) Buffon; Lichtsteiner, Bonucci, Chiellini, Evra; Marchisio, Pirlo (Pereyra 37), Pogba, Vidal (Padoin 86); Tevez (Coman 89), Morata.
Borussia Dortmund: (4312) Weidenfeller; Piszczek (Ginter 32), Papastathopoulos (Kirch 46), Hummels, Schmelzer; Gundogan, Sahin, Aubameyang; Mkhitaryan; Reus, Immobile (Blaszczykowski 76).

Manchester C (0) 1 *(Aguero 69)*
Barcelona (2) 2 *(Suarez 16, 30)* 　　　45,550
Manchester C: (442) Hart; Zabaleta, Kompany, Demichelis, Clichy[■]; Nasri (Fernandinho 62), Milner, Fernando, Silva (Sagna 78); Dzeko (Bony 68), Aguero.
Barcelona: (433) ter Stegen; Dani Alves (Adriano 75), Pique, Mascherano, Jordi Alba; Rakitic (Mathieu 71), Busquets, Iniesta; Messi, Suarez, Neymar (Pedro 80).

Wednesday, 25 February 2015
Arsenal (0) 1 *(Oxlade-Chamberlain 90)*
Monaco (1) 3 *(Kondogbia 38, Berbatov 53, Carrasco 90)* 　　　59,868
Arsenal: (4231) Ospina; Bellerin, Mertesacker, Koscielny, Gibbs; Coquelin (Oxlade-Chamberlain 68), Cazorla (Rosicky 82); Sanchez, Ozil, Welbeck; Giroud (Walcott 60).
Monaco: (451) Subasic; Toure, Wallace Santos, Abdennour, Elderson; Dirar (Kurzawa 82), Kondogbia, Fabinho, Joao Moutinho; Martial (Bernardo Silva 84); Berbatov (Carrasco 76).

Bayer Leverkusen (0) 1 *(Calhanoglu 57)*
Atletico Madrid (0) 0 30,210
Bayer Leverkusen: (4231) Leno; Hilbert, Papadopoulos, Spahic, Wendell; Castro, Bender (Rolfes 68); Bellarabi, Calhanoglu (Brandt 87), Son; Drmic (Kiessling 80).
Atletico Madrid: (433) Moya; Juanfran, Miranda, Godin, Siqueira (Jesus Gamez 38); Gabi, Tiago■, Saul (Raul Garcia 42); Turan (Torres 64), Mandzukic, Griezmann.

ROUND OF 16 SECOND LEG
Tuesday, 10 March 2015
Porto (1) 4 *(Brahimi 14, Herrera 47, Casemiro 56, Aboubakar 76)*
FC Basel (0) 0 40,000
Porto: (433) Fabiano; Danilo (Martins Indi 22), Maicon, Marcano, Alex Sandro; Herrera, Casemiro, Evandro (Quaresma 79); Tello, Aboubakar, Brahimi (Ruben Neves 74).
FC Basel: (433) Vaclik; Xhaka, Schar (Embolo 57), Samuel■, Safari; El-Nenny, Frei (Kakitani 63), Zuffi ; Gonzalez, Streller, Gashi (Calla 77).

Real Madrid (2) 3 *(Ronaldo 25, 45, Benzema 53)*
Schalke 04 (2) 4 *(Fuchs 20, Huntelaar 40, 84, Sane 57)* 58,393
Real Madrid: (433) Casillas; Arbeloa (Nacho 83), Varane, Pepe, Fabio Coentrao (Marcelo 58); Khedira (Modric 58), Kroos, Isco; Ronaldo, Benzema, Bale.
Schalke 04: (442) Wellenreuther; Howedes, Nastasic, Matip, Fuchs; Meyer, Neustadter, Hoger (Goretzka 57), Barnetta (Uchida 81); Choupo-Moting (Sane 29), Huntelaar.

Wednesday, 11 March 2015
Bayern Munich (2) 7 *(Muller 4 (pen), 51, Boateng 34, Ribery 49, Badstuber 63, Lewandowski 75, Gotze 87)*
Shakhtar Donetsk (0) 0 70,000
Bayern Munich: (4141) Neuer; Rafinha, Boateng, Badstuber (Dante 67), Alaba; Schweinsteiger, Robben (Rode 19), Gotze, Muller, Ribery (Bernat 59); Lewandowski.
Shakhtar Donetsk: (442) Pyatov; Srna, Kucher■, Rakitskiy, Shevchuk; Taison (Kryvtsov 9), Fred, Stepanenko, Douglas Costa (Nem 79); Alex Teixeira (Illsinho 70), Luiz Adriano.

Chelsea (0) 2 *(Cahill 81, Hazard E 96 (pen))*
Paris Saint-Germain (0) 2 *(Luiz 86, Thiago Silva 114)* 37,692
Chelsea: (4231) Courtois; Ivanovic, Cahill, Terry, Azpilicueta; Matic (Zouma 84), Ramires (Drogba 90); Fabregas, Oscar (Willian 46), Hazard E; Costa.
Paris Saint-Germain: (433) Sirigu; Marquinhos, Thiago Silva, Luiz, Maxwell; Thiago Motta, Matuidi (Rabiot 82), Verratti (Levezzi 82); Pastore (van der Wiel 118), Cavani, Ibrahimovic■.
aet; Paris Saint-Germain won on away goals.

Tuesday, 17 March 2015
Atletico Madrid (1) 1 *(Mario Suarez 27)*
Bayer Leverkusen (0) 0 48,273
Atletico Madrid: (442) Moya (Oblak 23); Juanfran, Miranda, Gimenez, Jesus Gamez; Cani (Raul Garcia 46), Mario Suarez, Koke, Turan; Griezmann, Mandzukic (Torres 83).
Bayer Leverkusen: (4411) Leno; Hilbert, Toprak, Spahic, Wendell; Bellarabi, Castro, Bender (Papadopoulos 104), Son (Rolfes 77); Calhanoglu; Drmic (Kiessling 69).
aet; Atletico Madrid won 3-2 on penalties.

Monaco (0) 0
Arsenal (1) 2 *(Giroud 36, Ramsey 79)* 17,263
Monaco: (433) Subasic; Fabinho, Wallace Santos, Abdennour, Kurzawa; Toulalan, Kondogbia, Joao Moutinho; Dirar (Elderson 86), Martial (Carrasco 60), Berbatov (Bernardo Silva 70).
Arsenal: (4231) Ospina; Bellerin, Mertesacker, Koscielny, Monreal (Gibbs 83); Coquelin (Ramsey 63), Cazorla; Ozil, Welbeck (Walcott 72), Sanchez; Giroud.
Monaco won on away goals.

Wednesday, 18 March 2015
Barcelona (1) 1 *(Rakitic 31)*
Manchester C (0) 0 92,551
Barcelona: (433) ter Stegen; Dani Alves (Adriano 90), Pique, Mathieu, Jordi Alba; Rakitic (Rafinha 84), Mascherano, Iniesta; Messi, Suarez, Neymar.

Manchester C: (4411) Hart; Sagna, Kompany, Demichelis, Kolarov; Nasri (Jesus Navas 46), Toure (Bony 72), Fernandinho, Milner (Lampard 87); Silva; Aguero.

Borussia Dortmund (0) 0
Juventus (1) 3 *(Tevez 3, 79, Morata 70)* 65,851
Borussia Dortmund: (4411) Weidenfeller; Papastathopoulos, Subotic, Hummels, Schmelzer (Kirch 46); Kampl, Bender (Ramos 63), Gundogan, Reus; Mkhitaryan (Blaszczykowski 63); Aubameyang.
Juventus: (433) Buffon; Lichtsteiner, Bonucci, Chiellini, Evra; Vidal, Marchisio, Pogba (Barzagli 27); Tevez (Pepe 81), Pereyra, Morata (Matri 78).

QUARTER-FINALS FIRST LEG
Tuesday, 14 April 2015
Atletico Madrid (0) 0
Real Madrid (0) 0 52,553
Atletico Madrid: (4411) Oblak; Juanfran, Miranda, Godin, Siqueira; Turan, Mario Suarez, Gabi, Koke (Torres 83); Griezmann (Raul Garcia 77); Mandzukic.
Real Madrid: (433) Casillas; Carvajal (Arbeloa 85), Varane, Sergio Ramos, Marcelo; Modric, Kroos, Rodriguez; Bale, Benzema (Isco 76), Ronaldo.

Juventus (0) 1 *(Vidal 57 (pen))*
Monaco (0) 0 40,801
Juventus: (433) Buffon; Lichtsteiner, Bonucci, Chiellini, Evra; Vidal, Pirlo (Barzagli 74), Marchisio; Tevez, Pereyra (Sturaro 87), Morata (Matri 83).
Monaco: (433) Subasic; Raggi (Berbatov 71), Ricardo Carvalho, Abdennour, Kurzawa; Joao Moutinho, Fabinho, Kondogbia; Dirar (Bernardo Silva 51), Martial (Mattheu Carvalho 87), Carrasco.

Wednesday, 15 April 2015
Paris Saint-Germain (0) 1 *(van der Wiel 82)*
Barcelona (1) 3 *(Neymar 18, Suarez 67, 79)* 45,713
Paris Saint-Germain: (433) Sirigu; van der Wiel, Thiago Silva (Luiz 21), Marquinhos, Maxwell; Rabiot (Lucas Moura 65), Cabaye, Matuidi; Lavezzi, Cavani, Pastore.
Barcelona: (433) ter Stegen; Montoya (Adriano 80), Pique, Mascherano, Jordi Alba; Rakitic (Mathieu 74), Busquets, Iniesta (Xavi 53); Messi, Suarez, Neymar.

Porto (2) 3 *(Quaresma 3 (pen), 10, Martinez 65)*
Bayern Munich (1) 1 *(Thiago 28)* 50,092
Porto: (433) Fabiano; Danilo, Maicon, Martins Indi, Alex Sandro; Herrera, Casemiro, Torres (Ruben Neves 75); Quaresma (Evandro 84), Martinez, Brahimi (Hernani 80).
Bayern Munich: (433) Neuer; Rafinha, Boateng, Dante, Bernat; Lahm, Alonso (Badstuber 74), Thiago; Muller, Lewandowski, Gotze (Rode 56).

QUARTER-FINALS SECOND LEG
Tuesday, 21 April 2015
Barcelona (2) 2 *(Neymar 14, 34)*
Paris Saint-Germain (0) 0 84,477
Barcelona: (433) ter Stegen; Dani Alves, Pique, Mascherano, Jordi Alba; Rakitic, Busquets (Sergi Roberto 55), Iniesta (Xavi 46); Messi, Suarez (Pedro 75), Neymar.
Paris Saint-Germain: (433) Sirigu; van der Wiel, Marquinhos, Luiz, Maxwell; Verratti, Cabaye (Lucas Moura 66), Matuidi (Rabiot 80); Cavani (Lavezzi 80), Ibrahimovic, Pastore.

Bayern Munich (5) 6 *(Thiago 14, Boateng 22, Lewandowski 27, 40, Muller 36, Alonso 88)*
Porto (0) 1 *(Martinez 73)* 70,000
Bayern Munich: (433) Neuer; Rafinha (Rode 72), Boateng, Badstuber, Bernat; Lahm, Alonso, Thiago (Dante 90); Muller, Lewandowski, Gotze (Weiser 86).
Porto: (433) Fabiano; Reyes (Ricardo Pereira 33), Maicon, Marcano■, Martins Indi; Herrera, Casemiro, Torres; Quaresma (Ruben Neves 46), Martinez, Brahimi (Evandro 67).

Wednesday, 22 April 2015
Monaco (0) 0
Juventus (0) 0   16,889
Monaco: (433) Subasic; Fabinho, Raggi , Abdennour, Kurzawa; Joao Moutinho, Toulalan (Berbatov 46), Kondogbia; Bernardo Silva, Martial (Germain 76), Carrasco (Mattheu Carvalho 87).
Juventus: (532) Buffon; Lichtsteiner, Barzagli, Bonucci, Chiellini, Evra (Padoin 90); Marchisio, Pirlo, Vidal (Pereyra 77); Tevez, Morata (Llorente 69).

Real Madrid (0) 1 *(Hernandez 88)*
Atletico Madrid (0) 0   78,300
Real Madrid: (442) Casillas; Carvajal, Varane, Sergio Ramos, Fabio Coentrao (Arbeloa 88); Rodriguez, Pepe, Kroos, Isco (Illarramendi 90); Hernandez (Jese 88), Ronaldo.
Atletico Madrid: (442) Oblak; Juanfran, Miranda, Godin, Jesus Gamez; Turan■, Tiago (Gimenez 86), Koke, Saul (Gabi 46); Mandzukic, Griezmann (Raul Garcia 65).

SEMI-FINALS FIRST LEG

Tuesday, 5 May 2015
Juventus (1) 2 *(Morata 8, Tevez 57 (pen))*
Real Madrid (1) 1 *(Ronaldo 27)*   41,011
Juventus: (433) Buffon; Evra, Lichtsteiner, Chiellini, Bonucci; Pirlo, Marchisio, Vidal; Sturaro (Barzagli 64), Morata (Llorente 78), Tevez (Pereyra 86).
Real Madrid: (4141) Casillas; Carvajal, Marcelo, Varane, Sergio Ramos; Pepe; Kroos, Isco (Hernandez 63), Rodriguez, Bale (Jese 86); Ronaldo.

Wednesday, 6 May 2015
Barcelona (0) 3 *(Messi 77, 80, Neymar 90)*
Bayern Munich (0) 0   95,639
Barcelona: (433) ter Stegen; Dani Alves, Pique, Mascherano (Bartra 89), Jordi Alba; Rakitic (Xavi 82), Busquets, Iniesta (Rafinha 87); Messi, Suarez, Neymar.
Bayern Munich: (4141) Neuer; Rafinha, Benatia, Boateng, Bernat; Alonso; Muller (Gotze 79), Lahm, Schweinsteiger, Thiago; Lewandowski.

SEMI-FINALS SECOND LEG

Tuesday, 12 May 2015
Bayern Munich (1) 3 *(Benatia 7, Lewandowski 59, Muller 74)*
Barcelona (2) 2 *(Neymar 15, 29)*   70,000
Bayern Munich: (442) Neuer; Rafinha, Benatia, Boateng, Bernat; Lahm (Rode 68), Schweinsteiger (Martinez 87), Alonso, Thiago; Muller (Gotze 87), Lewandowski.
Barcelona: (433) ter Stegen; Dani Alves, Pique, Mascherano, Jordi Alba; Rakitic (Mathieu 72), Busquets, Iniesta (Xavi 75); Messi, Suarez (Pedro 46), Neymar.

Wednesday, 13 May 2015
Real Madrid (1) 1 *(Ronaldo 23 (pen))*
Juventus (0) 1 *(Morata 57)*   78,153
Real Madrid: (433) Casillas; Carvajal, Sergio Ramos, Varane, Marcelo; Rodriguez, Kroos, Isco; Bale, Benzema (Hernandez 67), Ronaldo.
Juventus: (4312) Buffon; Lichtsteiner, Bonucci, Chiellini, Evra; Pogba (Pereyra 89), Pirlo (Barzagli 79), Marchisio; Vidal; Tevez, Morata (Llorent 84).

CHAMPIONS LEAGUE FINAL 2015

Saturday, 6 June 2015
(in Berlin, 70,442)

Juventus (0) 1 *(Morata 55)*   **Barcelona (1) 3** *(Rakitic 4, Suarez 68, Neymar 90)*

Juventus: (4312) Buffon; Lichtsteiner, Barzagli, Bonucci, Evra (Coman 89); Marchisio, Pirlo, Pogba; Vidal (Pereyra 79); Tevez, Morata (Llorente 85).

Barcelona: (433) ter Stegen; Dani Alves, Pique, Mascherano, Jordi Alba; Rakitic (Mathieu 90), Busquets, Iniesta (Xavi 78); Messi, Suarez (Pedro 90), Neymar.

Referee: Cuneyt Cakir.

Luis Suarez puts Barcelona ahead again in the UEFA Champions League final in Berlin on 6 June. Barcelona clinched their fifth Champions League trophy with a 3-1 defeat of Italian giants Juventus.
(Dylan Martinez/Action Images via Reuters)

EUROPEAN CUP-WINNERS' CUP
FINALS 1961–99

Year	Winners v Runners-up		Venue	Attendance	Referee
1961	1st Leg Fiorentina v Rangers	2-0	Glasgow	80,000	C. E. Steiner (Austria)
	2nd Leg Fiorentina v Rangers	2-1	Florence	50,000	V. Hernadi (Hungary)
1962	Atletico Madrid v Fiorentina	1-1	Glasgow	27,389	T. Wharton (Scotland)
Replay	Atletico Madrid v Fiorentina	3-0	Stuttgart	38,000	K. Tschenscher (West Germany)
1963	Tottenham Hotspur v Atletico Madrid	5-1	Rotterdam	49,000	A. van Leuwen (Netherlands)
1964	Sporting Lisbon v MTK Budapest	3-3*	Brussels	3,208	L. van Nuffel (Belgium)
Replay	Sporting Lisbon v MTK Budapest	1-0	Antwerp	13,924	G. Versyp (Belgium)
1965	West Ham U v Munich 1860	2-0	Wembley	7,974	I. Zsolt (Hungary)
1966	Borussia Dortmund v Liverpool	2-1*	Glasgow	41,657	P. Schwinte (France)
1967	Bayern Munich v Rangers	1-0*	Nuremberg	69,480	C. Lo Bello (Italy)
1968	AC Milan v Hamburg	2-0	Rotterdam	53,000	J. Ortiz de Mendibil (Spain)
1969	Slovan Bratislava v Barcelona	3-2	Basle	19,000	L. van Ravens (Netherlands)
1970	Manchester C v Gornik Zabrze	2-1	Vienna	7,968	P. Schiller (Austria)
1971	Chelsea v Real Madrid	1-1*	Athens	45,000	R. Scheurer (Switzerland)
Replay	Chelsea v Real Madrid	2-1*	Athens	19,917	R. Scheurer (Switzerland)
1972	Rangers v Moscow Dynamo	3-2	Barcelona	24,701	J. Ortiz de Mendibil (Spain)
1973	AC Milan v Leeds U	1-0	Salonika	40,154	C. Mihas (Greece)
1974	Magdeburg v AC Milan	2-0	Rotterdam	4,641	A. van Gemert (Netherlands)
1975	Dynamo Kyiv v Ferencvaros	3-0	Basle	13,000	R. Davidson (Scotland)
1976	Anderlecht v West Ham U	4-2	Brussels	51,296	R. Wurtz (France)
1977	Hamburg v Anderlecht	2-0	Amsterdam	66,000	P. Partridge (England)
1978	Anderlecht v Austria/WAC	4-0	Paris	48,679	H. Adlinger (West Germany)
1979	Barcelona v Fortuna Dusseldorf	4-3*	Basle	58,000	K. Palotai (Hungary)
1980	Valencia v Arsenal	0-0*	Brussels	40,000	V. Christov (Czechoslovakia)
	(Valencia won 5-4 on penalties)				
1981	Dinamo Tbilisi v Carl Zeiss Jena	2-1	Dusseldorf	4,750	R. Lattanzi (Italy)
1982	Barcelona v Standard Liege	2-1	Barcelona	80,000	W. Eschweiler (West Germany)
1983	Aberdeen v Real Madrid	2-1*	Gothenburg	17,804	G. Menegali (Italy)
1984	Juventus v Porto	2-1	Basle	55,000	A. Prokop (Egypt)
1985	Everton v Rapid Vienna	3-1	Rotterdam	38,500	P. Casarin (Italy)
1986	Dynamo Kyiv v Atletico Madrid	3-0	Lyon	50,000	F. Wohrer (Austria)
1987	Ajax v Lokomotiv Leipzig	1-0	Athens	35,107	L. Agnolin (Italy)
1988	Mechelen v Ajax	1-0	Strasbourg	39,446	D. Pauly (West Germany)
1989	Barcelona v Sampdoria	2-0	Berne	42,707	G. Courtney (England)
1990	Sampdoria v Anderlecht	2-0*	Gothenburg	20,103	B. Galler (Switzerland)
1991	Manchester U v Barcelona	2-1	Rotterdam	43,500	B. Karlsson (Sweden)
1992	Werder Bremen v Monaco	2-0	Lisbon	16,000	P. D'Elia (Italy)
1993	Parma v Antwerp	3-1	Wembley	37,393	K.-J. Assenmacher (Germany)
1994	Arsenal v Parma	1-0	Copenhagen	33,765	V. Krondl (Czech Republic)
1995	Zaragoza v Arsenal	2-1	Paris	42,424	P. Ceccarini (Italy)
1996	Paris Saint-Germain v Rapid Vienna	1-0	Brussels	37,000	P. Pairetto (Italy)
1997	Barcelona v Paris Saint-Germain	1-0	Rotterdam	52,000	M. Merk (Germany)
1998	Chelsea v Stuttgart	1-0	Stockholm	30,216	S. Braschi (Italy)
1999	Lazio v Mallorca	2-1	Villa Park	33,021	G. Benko (Austria)

INTER-CITIES FAIRS CUP FINALS 1958–71

Year	1st Leg		Attendance	2nd Leg	Attendance	Agg	Winner
1958	London XI v Barcelona	2-2	45,466	0-6	70,000	2-8	Barcelona
1960	Birmingham C v Barcelona	0-0	40,524	1-4	70,000	1-4	Barcelona
1961	Birmingham C v Roma	2-2	21,005	0-2	60,000	2-4	Roma
1962	Valencia v Barcelona	6-2	65,000	1-1	60,000	7-3	Valencia
1963	Dinamo Zagreb v Valencia	1-2	40,000	0-2	55,000	1-4	Valencia
1964	Real Zaragoza v Valencia	2-1	50,000 (in Barcelona, one match only)				Real Zaragoza
1965	Ferencvaros v Juventus	1-0	25,000 (in Turin, one match only)				Ferencvaros
1966	Barcelona v Real Zaragoza	0-1	70,000	4-2*	70,000	4-3	Barcelona
1967	Dinamo Zagreb v Leeds U	2-0	40,000	0-0	35,604	2-0	Dynamo Zagreb
1968	Leeds U v Ferencvaros	1-0	25,368	0-0	70,000	1-0	Leeds U
1969	Newcastle U v Ujpest Dozsa	3-0	60,000	3-2	37,000	6-2	Newcastle U
1970	Anderlecht v Arsenal	3-1	37,000	0-3	51,612	3-4	Arsenal
1971	Juventus v Leeds U	0-0	*(abandoned 51 minutes)*		42,000		
	Juventus v Leeds U	2-2	42,000	1-1	42,483	3-3	Leeds U
	Leeds U won on away goals rule.						

Trophy Play-Off – *between first and last winners to decide who would have possession of the original trophy*
| | | | | | | | |
| 1971 | Barcelona v Leeds U | 2-1 | 50,000 (in Barcelona, one match only) | | | | |

*After extra time.

UEFA CUP FINALS 1972–97

Year	1st Leg		Attendance	2nd Leg	Attendance	Agg	Winner
1972	Wolverhampton W v Tottenham H	1-2	38,562	1-1	54,303	2-3	Tottenham H
1973	Liverpool v Moenchengladbach	0-0	*(abandoned after 27 minutes)*		44,967		
	Liverpool v Moenchengladbach	3-0	41,169	0-2	35,000	3-2	Liverpool
1974	Tottenham H v Feyenoord	2-2	46,281	0-2	59,317	2-4	Feyenoord
1975	Moenchengladbach v Twente	0-0	42,368	5-1	21,767	5-1	Moenchengladbach
1976	Liverpool v Club Brugge	3-2	49,981	1-1	29,423	4-3	Liverpool
1977	Juventus v Athletic Bilbao	1-0	66,000	1-2	39,700	2-2	Juventus
	Juventus won on away goals rule.						
1978	Bastia v PSV Eindhoven	0-0	8,006	0-3	28,000	0-3	PSV Eindhoven
1979	RS Belgrade v Moenchengladbach	1-1	65,000	0-1	45,000	1-2	Moenchengladbach
1980	Moenchengladbach v E. Frankfurt	3-2	25,000	0-1	59,000	3-3	E. Frankfurt
	Eintracht Frankfurt won on away goals rule.						
1981	Ipswich T v AZ 67 Alkmaar	3-0	27,532	2-4	22,291	5-4	Ipswich T
1982	IFK Gothenburg v Hamburg	1-0	42,548	3-0	57,312	4-0	Gothenburg
1983	Anderlecht v Benfica	1-0	55,000	1-1	70,000	2-1	Anderlecht
1984	Anderlecht v Tottenham H	1-1	33,000	1-1*	46,258	2-2	Tottenham H
	Tottenham H won 4-3 on penalties.						
1985	Videoton v Real Madrid	0-3	30,000	1-0	80,000	1-3	Real Madrid
1986	Real Madrid v Cologne	5-1	60,000	0-2	22,000	5-3	Real Madrid
1987	IFK Gothenburg v Dundee U	1-0	48,614	1-1	20,900	2-1	Gothenburg
1988	Espanol v Bayer Leverkusen	3-0	31,180	0-3*	21,600	3-3	B. Leverkusen
	Bayer Leverkusen won 3-2 on penalties.						
1989	Napoli v Stuttgart	2-1	81,093	3-3	64,000	5-4	Napoli
1990	Juventus v Fiorentina	3-1	47,519	0-0	30,999	3-1	Juventus
1991	Internazionale v Roma	2-0	68,887	0-1	70,901	2-1	Internazionale
1992	Torino v Ajax	2-2	65,377	0-0	40,000	2-2	Ajax
	Ajax won on away goals rule.						
1993	Borussia Dortmund v Juventus	1-3	37,000	0-3	62,781	1-6	Juventus
1994	Salzburg v Internazionale	0-1	43,000	0-1	80,345	0-2	Internazionale
1995	Parma v Juventus	1-0	22,057	1-1	80,000	2-1	Parma
1996	Bayern Munich v Bordeaux	2-0	63,000	3-1	30,000	5-1	Bayern Munich
1997	Schalke v Internazionale	1-0	57,000	0-1*	81,675	1-1	Schalke
	Schalke won 4-1 on penalties.						

UEFA CUP FINALS 1998–2009

Year	Winners v Runners-up		Venue	Attendance	Referee
1998	Internazionale v Lazio	3-0	Paris	44,412	A. L. Nieto (Spain)
1999	Parma v Marseille	3-0	Moscow	61,000	H. Dallas (Scotland)
2000	Galatasaray v Arsenal	0-0*	Copenhagen	38,919	A. L. Nieto (Spain)
	Galatasaray won 4-1 on penalties.				
2001	Liverpool v Alaves	5-4*	Dortmund	48,050	G. Veissiere (France)
	Liverpool won on sudden death 'golden goal'.				
2002	Feyenoord v Borussia Dortmund	3-2	Rotterdam	45,611	V. M. M. Pereira (Portugal)
2003	Porto v Celtic	3-2*	Seville	52,140	L. Michel (Slovakia)
2004	Valencia v Marseille	2-0	Gothenburg	39,000	P. Collina (Italy)
2005	CSKA Moscow v Sporting Lisbon	3-1	Lisbon	47,085	G. Poll (England)
2006	Sevilla v Middlesbrough	4-0	Eindhoven	32,100	H. Fandel (Germany)
2007	Sevilla v Espanyol	2-2*	Glasgow	47,602	M. Busacca (Switzerland)
	Sevilla won 3-1 on penalties.				
2008	Zenit St Petersburg v Rangers	2-0	Manchester	43,878	P. Fröjdfeldt (Sweden)
2009	Shakhtar Donetsk v Werder Bremen	2-1*	Istanbul	37,357	L. M. Chantalejo (Spain)

UEFA EUROPA LEAGUE FINALS 2010–15

Year	Winners v Runners-up		Venue	Attendance	Referee
2010	Atletico Madrid v Fulham	2-1*	Hamburg	49,000	N. Rizzoli (Italy)
2011	Porto v Braga	1-0	Dublin	45,391	V. Carballo (Spain)
2012	Atletico Madrid v Athletic Bilbao	3-0	Bucharest	52,347	W. Stark (Germany)
2013	Chelsea v Benfica	2-1	Amsterdam	46,163	B. Kuipers (Netherlands)
2014	Sevilla v Benfica	0-0*	Turin	33,120	F. Brych (Germany)
	Sevilla won 4-2 on penalties.				
2015	Sevilla v Dnipro Dnipropetrovsk	3-2	Warsaw	45,000	M. Atkinson (England)

*After extra time.

UEFA EUROPA LEAGUE 2014–15

■ *Denotes player sent off.*

FIRST QUALIFYING ROUND FIRST LEG
Tuesday, 1 July 2014

Jeunesse Esch (0) 0
Dundalk (0) 2 *(Towell 59 (pen), 71)* 759
Jeunesse Esch: (433) Oberweis; Kintziger, Vitali, Hoffmann, Portier; Dragovic (Todorovic 46), Da Graca, Zydko (Albanese 67); Melisse (De Sousa 81), Corral, Ibrahimovic.
Dundalk: (433) Cherrie; Gannon, Gartland, Boyle, Massey; Shields, Horgan (Mountney 85), Towell; Meenan, Byrne (Higgins 70), McMillan (Hoban 79).

Skendija Tetovo (1) 2 *(Vrucina 45, Mitrov 47)*
Zimbru Chisinau (0) 1 *(Grossu 50 (pen))* 2720
Skendija Tetovo: (442) Jovanovski; Bejtulai, Berisha (Kavdanski 34), Murati, Miliev; Selmani (Kurtishi 51), Polozani, Mitrov, Huseini; Vrucina, Junior (Fazliu 81).
Zimbru Chisinau: (442) Rusu; Erhan, Bologan, Klimovich, Pavlyuchek; Amani (Damascan 86), Vremea, Cheptine (Anton 73), Jardan; Dedov (Pascenco 53), Grossu.

Sliema Wanderers (1) 1 *(Ohawuchi 39)*
Ferencvaros (0) 1 *(Nalepa 77)* 525
Sliema Wanderers: (442) Zammit; Muscat A, Scozzese, Potezica, Mintoff; Scerri, Mifsud, Ohawuchi, Barbetti; Muscat G (Cilia 68), Bianciardi.
Ferencvaros: (442) Dibusz; Bonig, Lauth, Bode, Kukuruzovic (Holman 82); Gyomber, Busai (Cukic 46), Nagy (Somalia 46), Nalepa; Bosnjak, Mateos.

Thursday, 3 July 2014

Aberdeen (1) 5 *(Logan 33, McGinn 49, Rooney 52 (pen), 90, Hayes 73)*
Daugava Riga (0) 0 15,184
Aberdeen: (4231) Langfield; Logan, Anderson, Reynolds, Hayes; Flood, Jack; Pawlett (Smith 50), Robson (Wright 78), McGinn (McManus 89); Rooney.
Daugava Riga: (433) Zubas; Borovskij (Markevicius 83), Ribokas (Blanks 57), Tomkevicius, Mendy; Knapsis, Savenas, Kucys■; Joksts, Zils■, Flora (Abdelaziz 58).

Airbus UK Broughton (1) 1 *(Johnson 29)*
Haugesund (1) 1 *(Bamberg 43)* 595
Airbus UK Broughton: (442) Coates; Pearson, Kearney, Owens, Short; Field (Barrow 90), Jones, Wignall (Wade 59), Rule; Budrys, Johnson.
Haugesund: (442) Bratveit; Myrestam, Elsner, Nilsen, Skjerve; Andreassen, Fevang, Stolas, Bamberg; Sema (Haraldseid 72), Gytkjaer.

B36 Torshavn (0) 1 *(Lawal 72)*
Linfield (1) 2 *(Mulgrew 38, Carvill 88)* 786
B36 Torshavn: (4321) Thomsen; Faero (Joensen 63), Eriksen, Thorleifsson (Sorensen 90), Eysturoy; Askham, Jakobsen, Matras; Cieslewicz A (Poulsen 89), Cieslewicz L; Lawal.
Linfield: (433) Tuffey; Richards, Hegarty, Clarke M, Haughey (Callacher 30); Sproule, Lowry, Burns; Mulgrew, Waterworth (Thompson 74), Carvill (Morrow 90).

Banga (0) 0
Sligo R (0) 0 2000
Banga: (442) Jurevicius; Urbaitis, Khablov, Karkusov, Epifanov; Butkus, Shevchuk, Grigaitis, Arlauskis; Zagurskas (Tsalagov 78), Staponka.
Sligo R: (3421) Rogers; Conneely, Keane (Ledwith 89), McMillan; Cawley, O'Conor, Russell, Djilali; Cretaro (Greene 74), Gaynor; North.

Botev Plovdiv (1) 4 *(Ognyanov 25, 51, Tsvetkov 58, Pedro 72)*
Libertas (0) 0 2400
Botev Plovdiv: (442) Stachowiak; Terziev, Minev, Hristov, Filipov; Curtean, Sarmov, Jirsak (Vasev 69), Ognyanov (Yusein 81); Tsvetkov, Kortzorg (Pedro 56).
Libertas: (442) Simoncini A; Molinari, Benvenuti, Rocchetti, Facondini (Zavoli 88); Morelli, Antonelli, Zennaro (Golinucci 61), Righi; Torelli, Rosti (Angeli 74).

Celik Niksic (0) 0
Koper (2) 5 *(Palcic 21, Halilovic 37, Covilo 50, 86, Guberac 87)* 250
Celik Niksic: (433) Giljen; Vukovic, Adrovic, Ivanovic (Nikolic 79), Bubanja (Bulatovic 52); Jovovic■, Kalezic (Bozovic 83), Brnovic; Djalac, Prtenjak, Vidakanic.
Koper: (352) Radosevic; Hadzic, Halilovic, Blazic; Guberac, Ivetic, Galesic (Lotric 68), Crnigoj (Zibert 80), Palcic; Stromajer (Pucko 61), Covilo.

Crusaders (2) 3 *(Cockcroft 23, Owens 43, Coates 58)*
Ekranas (0) 1 *(Susnjar 88)* 998
Crusaders: (442) O'Neill; Burns, Coates, Morrow, Robinson; McClean, Clarke, Caddell, Heatley; Owens (Adamson 85), Cockcroft (O'Carroll 78).
Ekranas: (442) Timofejevas; Meskinis (Tamulevicius 69), Pilotas, Girdvainis, Susnjar; Salamanavicius (Stanulevicius 45), Norvilas, Petrauskas, Baranauskas (Dapkus 78); Elivelto, Kochanauskas.

Cukaricki (1) 4 *(Mirosavljevic 8, Bojic 49, Srnic S 89, Stojiljkovic 90 (pen))*
Sant Julia (0) 0 2120
Cukaricki: (442) Ristic; Brezancic, Piasentin, Ostojic, Todorovich; Matic, Srnic S (Mandic 90), Stojkovic, Bojic (Srnic D 58); Stojiljkovic, Mirosavljevic (Pavlovic A 77).
Sant Julia: (442) Coca; Estepa, Rodrìguez, Ruis, Perez; Serra, Fontan (Puente 76), Soto, Spano; Varela, Cabezas Jurado.

Derry C (2) 4 *(McEleney P 15, Patterson 25 (pen), Timlin 47, McNamee 86)*
Aberystwyth T (0) 0 1980
Derry C: (433) Doherty; McBride, Byrne, Barry, Jarvis; Molloy, Timlin (Tracey 68), McNamee; Duffy, Patterson (Boyle 82), McEleney P (Lowry 76).
Aberystwyth T: (433) Lewis■; Chris Davies (Morgan 66), Jones S, Thomas, Cledan Davies; Corbisiero, Venables, Sherbon; Kellaway, Jones M, Williams (Draper 25).

Differdange 03 (0) 1 *(Er Rafik 87)*
Atlantas (0) 0 821
Differdange 03: (442) Weber; Martin, May, Ribeiro (Caron 68), Er Rafik; Bettmer (Kettenmeyer 64), Janisch, Lebresne, Franzoni; Luisi (Meligner 78), Caillet.
Atlantas: (442) Galdikas; Bartkus, Razulis, Kazlauskas D, Eliosius (Papsys 67); Navikas (Krusnauskas 90), Beneta (Joksas 25), Gnedojus, Jemelins; Kazlauskas M, Zukauskas.

Diosgyor (1) 2 *(Barczi 34, Bacsa 90)*
Birkirkara (1) 1 *(Bissi 36)* 6205
Diosgyor: (433) Rados; Husic (Marjanovic 67), Kadar, William, Okuka; Elek, Gosztonyi (Bori 55), Grumic; Nikhazi, Bacsa, Barczi.
Birkirkara: (442) Adrian Murcia; Herrera, Camenzuli (Scicluna 59), Vucanac, Bissi■; Sciberras (Agius 74), Fenech, Zerafa, Muscat; Moreno, Vella (Ledesma 81).

FH Hafnarfjordur (0) 3 *(Oskarsson I 82, Gudnason 90, 90)*
Glenavon (0) 0 643
FH Hafnarfjordur: (442) Oskarsson R; Jonsson (Palsson 70), Doumbia, Vidarsson P, Bodvarsson; Snorrason, Vidarsson D, Hewson, Gudnason; Bjornsson, Emilsson (Oskarsson I 70).
Glenavon: (442) McGrath; McCabe, Dillon, Lindsay, Neill; McGrory, McIlveen, Marshall, Bradley; Braniff (Hamilton 86), Bates (Rainey 86).

Folgore/Falciano (0) 1 *(Perrotta 55)*
Buducnost Podgorica (2) 2 *(Raspopovic 30, Raickovic 36)* 378
Folgore/Falciano: (4141) Bicchiarelli; Muraccini, Sartori, Nucci, Pacini; Della (Vagnetti 84); Loiodice (Berretti 81), Paglialonga, Muccini, Ceschi; Perrotta (Berardi 88).
Buducnost Podgorica: (4231) Ljuljanovic; Tomkovic, Kopitovic, Raspopovic, Vukcevic; Rogosic, Raickovic; Hocko, Ilincic (Burzanovic 81), Vujacic (Milosevic 90); Raicevic.

Fram Reykjavík (0) 0
Nomme Kalju (0) 1 *(Prates 61)*   607
Fram Reykjavík: (442) Kristinsson; Bjarnason, Briem, Atlason, Arnason; Gudjonsson, Gudmundsson, Marteinsson (Albertsson 63), Arnarsson V; Gunnarsson, Takefusa (Thorarinson 72).
Nomme Kalju: (442) Teles; Reintam, Sisov, Kallaste, Barengrub; Quintieri (Mbu Alidor 85), Vunk, Toomet (Kirss 74), Prates; Wakui, Kimbaloula.

Gabala (0) 0
Siroki Brijeg (0) 2 *(Wagner 74, 89)*   4200
Gabala: (442) Agayev; Jamalov (Cristea 56), Levin, Hajiyev, Mendi; Dodo, Abisov, Taghizade, Ropotan; Allahverdiyev, Dos Santos.
Siroki Brijeg: (442) Bilobrk; Markovic (Barisic 27), Lastro, Brekalo, Coric; Pehar, Zakaric (Kozul 90), Landeka, Wagner; Peko (Ivankovic 90), Maric.

Hibernians (0) 2 *(Cohen 49, Failla 50)*
Spartak Trnava (3) 4 *(Sabo 11 (pen), 13, Vlasko 36,*
Mikinic 88)   616
Hibernians: (334) Balzan; Desira, Gracia Gomes, Pearson[■]; Soares, Dias (Muscat 65), Cohen; Kristensen, Failla (Degabriele 81), Bezzina, Farrugia (Mbongo 90).
Spartak Trnava: (4321) Strapak; Siva (Bortel 58), Janecka, Mikovic (Mikinic 74), Vlasko; Chovanec, Toth, Conka; Sabo, Kuzma; Spalek (Schranz 55).

IFK Gothenburg (0) 0
Fola Esch (0) 0   5919
IFK Gothenburg: (4411) Sandberg; Salomonsson, Waehler (Jonsson 17), Svensson, Johansson J; Larsson, Mane (Soder 56), Johansson A (Allansson 60), Mahlangu; Vibe; Bjarsmyr.
Fola Esch: (4321) Hym; Keita, Payal, Hornuss (Klapp 83), Hadji; Rani (Skrijelj 88), Jans, Laterza (Lukic 77); Kirch, Ronny; Klein.

Kairat Almaty (0) 1 *(Darabayev 89)*
Kukesi (0) 0   14,000
Kairat Almaty: (4231) Khomich; Pliev, Gorman, Kislitsyn, Smakov; Islamkhan, Bakaev; Michalik (Baitana 82), Yedigaryan (Knezevic 66), Gohou; Barbosa (Darabayev 66).
Kukesi: (4411) Halili; Smajlaj, Shameti, Dushkaj, Lushtaku (Catarina 86); Cikalleshi, Hallaci, Allmuca (Lopes 18), Bicaj; Hoxha; Musolli.

Myllykosken Pallo-47 (0) 1 *(Abdulahi 76)*
IF Fuglafjordur (0) 0   1306
Myllykosken Pallo-47: (442) Iiskola; Vesala (Salmikivi 90), Dema (Minkenen 72), Abdulahi, Pirinen; Sihvola, Bah, Soiri (Ristola 63), Koskinen; Aho, Nongotamba.
IF Fuglafjordur: (433) Mikkelsen J; Petersen A, Mikkelsen P, Lambanum, Lokin; Lakjuni, Petersen B (Jakobsen 77), Ellingsgaard A (Joensen 90); Zachariasen, Ellingsgaard J, Eliasen.

Pyunik (0) 1 *(Papikyan 68)*
Astana (1) 4 *(Nuserbaev 40, Dzholchiev 67,*
Kethevoama 67, Kurdov 84)   1380
Pyunik: (4231) Harutyunyan; Haroyan (Ghukas Poghosyan 74), Hovhannisyan G, Hovhannisyan K, Gagik Poghosyan; Malakyan, Yuspashyan; Papikyan (Aslanyan 72), Minasyan, Hakobyan (Baloyan 60); Voskanyan.
Astana: (4411) Eric; Dmitrenko, Anicic, Nurdauletov (Kurdov 46), Kethevoama; Pikalkin, Nuserbaev (Shakhmetov 59), Zhukov, Dzholchiev (Beissebekov 90); Shomko; Canas.

RNK Split (1) 2 *(Glumac 39, Vojnovic 87)*
Mika (0) 0   1500
RNK Split: (442) Zagorac; Glavina (Roce 63), Glumac, Vojnovic, Bilic (Galic 86); Erceg, Vidovic, Rugasevic, Galovic; Ibriks, Belle (Bagaric 46).
Mika: (4321) Kasparov; Petrosyan, Voskanyan A, Karapetyan, Satunyan; Arakelyan (Grigoryan 67), Barseghyan, Poghosian (Poghosyan 22); Movsisyan, Beglaryan (Voskanyan H 83); Alex.

Rosenborg (2) 4 *(Pedersen 23, Soderlund 44, 54 (pen),*
Jensen 73)
Jelgava (0) 0   2700
Rosenborg: (442) Hansen; Dorsin (Skjelvik 71), Reginiussen, Strandberg, Jensen; Pedersen (Berntsen 80), Selnaes, Svensson, Riski; Helland (Sormo 88), Soderlund.
Jelgava: (442) Ikstens; Petrenko, Oss, Redjko, Bogdaskins; Zulevs, Bespalovs (Medeckis 81), Lazdins, Freimanis; Kozlovs (Malasenoks 66), Danilovs (Eriba 57).

Rudar Velenje (1) 1 *(Klinar 13)*
Laci (0) 1 *(Adeniyi 89)*   1150
Rudar Velenje: (442) Rozman; Buksek, Stjepanovic (Kocic 45), Roser (Bolha 75), Firer; Krefl (Jahic 60), Crncic, Tolimir, Eterovic; Klinar, Knezovic.
Laci: (4321) Vujadinovic; Adeniyi, Ofoyen, Cela, Owoeye (Ndreca 39); Nimani, Zefi, Veliaj; Sheta, Sefa; Teqja.

UE Santa Coloma (0) 0
Metalurg Skopje (2) 3 *(Krstev 3, Stojanovski 15,*
Simonovski 83)   252
UE Santa Coloma: (442) Godswill; Jesus Rubio, Maneiro, Martinez, Roca; Anton, Vall, Bernat, Crespo; Jordi Rubio, Rodriguez.
Metalurg Skopje: (442) Efremov; Ristovski, Gjorgievski, Leskarovski, Dalceski; Simonovski, Mitrev, Radeski, Dodevski; Krstev, Stojanovski.

Santos Tartu (0) 0
Tromso (4) 7 *(Andersen 14, 44, Johansen J 22,*
Moldskred 24, Drage 56, Norbye 75, Johnsen 79)   1169
Santos Tartu: (442) Saesk; Teniste, Alve (Vidaja 83), Vellemaa, Sonn; Laas K, Laas M (Kartsep 75), Roops, Eessaar; Flyak (Kallandi 86), Vereshchak.
Tromso: (442) Lekstrom (Herlofsen 46); Moldskred, Koppinen, Bendiksen, Drage; Johansen J (Nilsen 77), Norbye, Andersen, Johansen R (Johnsen 62); Frantzen, Wangberg.

Shirak (0) 1 *(Deble 85 (pen))*
Shakhter Karagandy (0) 2 *(Topcagic 71, Maliy 83)*   2500
Shirak: (4411) Beglaryan; Deble, Aleksanyan, Hakobyan (Muradyan A 78), Marikyan; Muradyan K, Yoro (Diarrassouba 67), Hovanisian, Diop (Barikian 46); Davtyan; Kpodo.
Shakhter Karagandy: (532) Mokin; Vicius, Topcagic (Murzoev 89), Konysbayev (Salomov 79), Finonchenko, Dzidic; Maliy, Maslo, Simcevic; Pokrivac (Baizhanov 90), Kirov.

Sillamae Kalev (1) 2 *(Ratnikov 32, Kabaev 72)*
Honka Espoo (0) 1 *(Kabashi 82)*   425
Sillamae Kalev: (4141) Starodubtsev; Dudarev, Silich, Cheminava (Baguzis 78), Volodin; Ratnikov; Mashichev, Tjapkin, Sidorenkov, Murikhin (Kvasov 54); Kabaev.
Honka Espoo: (442) Viitala; Aalto, Anyamele (Mombilo 68), Makijarvi, Aijala; Vaisanen, Hatakka, Levanen (jokinen 46), Porokara; Hetemaj, Kabashi.

Sioni Bolnisi (2) 2 *(Isiani 27, 30)*
Flamurtari Vlore (1) 3 *(Veliu 20, Kuqi 74, Lika G 90)*   3254
Sioni Bolnisi: (4411) Merlani; Tskhadaia, Svanadze, Kakhelishvili, Lobjanidze (Ugulava 54); Aptsiauri (Samkharadze 74), Isiani, Kandelaki, Imedashvili; Popkhadze; Gureshidze (Adamia 85).
Flamurtari Vlore: (4411) Lika I; Mici, Lena, Veliu, Arberi (Idrizaj 90); Telushi, Zeqiri (Shehaj 83), Kuqi, Abulaliaj; Muzaka (Meto 87); Lika G.

Stjarnan (2) 4 *(Finsen 14 (pen), 54, Gunnarson 16,*
Bjorgvinsson 70)
Bangor C (0) 0   908
Stjarnan: (433) Jonsson; Arnason, Praest, Vemmelund, Rauschenberg; Johannsson, Laxdal D, Punyed; Gunnarson (Johannesson 62), Bjorgvinsson (Palsson 76), Finsen (Asgeirsson 89).
Bangor C: (4141) Cudworth; Roberts, Johnston, Edwards R (Culshaw 90), Walker; Hart[■]; Miley, Edwards S (Jones R 80), Allen, Chris Jones (McDaid 71); Davies.

Tiraspol (0) 2 *(Novikov 78, Karaneychev 88)*
Inter Baku (2) 3 *(Tskhadadze 8 (pen), Mammadov E 10,*
Novikov 71 (og)) 2223
Tiraspol: (442) Georgiev; Barroso, Novikov, Zarichinyuk, Shapoval; Molla, Boghiu (Karaneychev 63), Rata (Bulat 58), Japaridze; Ademar Xavier (Ovseanicov 81), Sydorenko.
Inter Baku: (442) Lomaia; Salukvadze, Amisulashvili, Georgievski, Mammadov E (Alvaro 72); Mammadov A (Guseynpur 90), Bocognano, Dashdemirov, Tskhadadze (Madrigal 82); Spicic, Meza.

Turnovo (0) 0
Chikhura Sachkhere (1) 1 *(Kutchukhidze 31)* 380
Turnovo: (442) Dimovski; Tasev, Iliev (Kochoski 62), Mutafchyiski, Mecinovikj; Dolapchiev (Curlinov 54), Pandev, Varelovski, Najdenov (Stoilov 54); Pandovski, Georgiev.
Chikhura Sachkhere: (442) Somkhishvili; Tchelidze, Kashia, Rekhviashvili, Kutchukhidze (Mumladze 86); Chikvaidze■, Datunaishvili, Bechvaia, Odikadze; Dekanoidze (Koripadze 79), Gabedava.

VPS Vaasa (0) 2 *(Strandvall 53, Parikka 54)*
Brommapojkarna (1) 1 *(Kouakou 33)* 1025
VPS Vaasa: (523) Henriksson; Koskimaa, Brown, Honkaniemi, Strandvall, Engstrom; Nganbe, Bjork; Dafaa, Parikka (Linjaja 82), Stewart (Seabrook 69).
Brommapojkarna: (433) Blazevic; Starfelt (Ozkan 73), Une-Larsson, Segerstrom, Bjorkstrom; Jonsson, Karlstrom, Sandberg-Magnusson; Kouakou, Rexhepi (Soderstrom 75), Barkroth.

Vaduz (2) 3 *(Sutter 6, Schurpf 8, 72)*
College Europa (0) 0 1135
Vaduz: (442) Jehle; Grippo, Lang (Pak 77), Ciccone, Sutter (Abbeglen 57); Burgmeier (Niederhausen 64), Schurpf, Untersee, Stahel; Neumayr, Muntwiler.
College Europa: (442) Cafer; Soto, Coombes L, Pereyra, Tamayo (Molina 59); Toncheff (Montovio 81), Mouelhi, Saavedra (Coombes J 67), Juanse; Juanca, Bosio.

Veris (0) 0
Litex Lovech (0) 0 1900
Veris: (442) Gaiduchevici; Cascaval, Cojocari, Cucerenco, Josan (Zasavitchi 64); Frunza (Cemirtan 53), Ivanov (Turcan 46), Mocanu, Pisla; Racu, Bogdanovic.
Litex Lovech: (442) Pirgov; Bodurov, Mendy, Jordan (Minchev 84), Bozhikov; Vajushi (Rumenov 80), Popov, Zlatinov, Tsvetanov; Kossoko, Kolev (Tsvetkov 69).

Vikingur (1) 2 *(Justinussen 23, Olsen A 59)*
Daugava Daugavpils (0) 1 *(Kokins 56)* 342
Vikingur: (4141) Turi; Jacobsen H, Gregersen, Joensen (Olsen A 46 (Vatnhamar G 88)), Hansen H (Sorensen 73); Djordjevic; Hansson, Hansen B, Jacobsen E, Djurhuus; Justinussen.
Daugava Daugavpils: (433) Vlasovs; Chikhradze, Solovjovs, Jaliashvili, Vladimirs; Kokins, Sevelovs, Zaikins (Gryshchenko 18); Kozlovs, Kosmacovs, Oginskis.

Zeljeznicar Sarajevo (0) 0
Lovcen (0) 0 6250
Zeljeznicar Sarajevo: (4141) Antolovic; Colic, Zeljkovic, Kvesic, Bogdanovic; Bucan; Stanic, Sadikovic (Svraka 85), Tomic, Hasanovic (Jamak 59); Turkovic (Bajic 70).
Lovcen: (433) Perovic; Bozovic, Simovic, Tatar, Martinovic (Djurovic 65); Radunovic, Brnovic, Bogdanovic; Radovic, Kosovic, Merdovic (Draganic 67).

FIRST QUALIFYING ROUND SECOND LEG

Tuesday, 8 July 2014
Linfield (1) 1 *(Carvill 17)*
B36 Torshavn (0) 1 *(Lawal 48 (pen))* 1150
Linfield: (451) Tuffey; Richards, Hegarty, Haughey, Clarke M; Lowry, Burns (Clarke R 72), Mulgrew, Sproule, Waterworth (Thompson 86); Carvill (Callacher 86).
B36 Torshavn: (433) Thomsen; Faero, Eysturoy, Thorleifsson (Cieslewicz A 56), Askham; Jakobsen, Mellemgaard, Matras (Sorensen 84); Poulsen, Cieslewicz L, Lawal.

Thursday, 10 July 2014
Aberystwyth T (0) 0
Derry C (2) 5 *(Duffy 11, McNamee 14,*
Patterson 60, 84, 86 (pen)) 1046
Aberystwyth T: (4411) Draper; Corbisiero, Jones S, Atyeo, Cledan Davies (James 87); Kellaway, Morgan (Chris Davies 61), Sherbon (Davies R 87), Williams; Venables; Jones M.
Derry C: (433) Doherty; McBride, Byrne, Barry (Ventre 46), Jarvis; Molloy (McEleney S 69), Timlin, McNamee; Duffy, Patterson, McEleney P (Lowry 61).

Astana (1) 2 *(Dzholchiev 13, Shomko 79)*
Pyunik (0) 0 7200
Astana: (442) Eric; Beissebekov, Shomko, Anicic, Postnikov; Kojasevic (Kethevoama 46), Pikalkin, Dzholchiev, Nuserbaev; Kurdov (Zhukov 57), Canas (Muzhikov 82).
Pyunik: (442) Ohanyan; Haroyan, Hovhannisyan G, Gagik Poghosyan (Aslanyan 46), Malakyan; Hovhannisyan K, Yuspashyan, Papikyan, Minasyan; Hakobyan (Ghukas Poghosyan 64), Voskanyan.

Atlantas (1) 3 *(Gnedojus 10, Papsys 62 (pen), Maksimov 89)*
Differdange 03 (0) 1 *(Caillet 81)* 2000
Atlantas: (442) Galdikas; Bartkus, Kazlauskas D, Papsys, Eliosius (Maksimov 87); Joksas, Gnedojus (Krusa 65), Jemelins, Kazlauskas M; Zukauskas, Krusnauskas (Baranauskas 78).
Differdange 03: (442) Weber; Martin■, Rodrigues (Bukvic 21), Ribeiro (Luisi 70), Er Rafik; Caron, Bettmer, Janisch, Lebresne (Arthur 90); Franzoni, Caillet.

Bangor C (0) 0
Stjarnan (0) 4 *(Rauschenberg 53, Bjorgvinsson 68, 81,*
Johannsson 85) 805
Bangor C: (442) Cudworth; Walker, Johnston (Hughes 56), Miley, Roberts; McDaid, Allen, Edwards R (Corey Jones 82), Edwards S; Chris Jones (Culshaw 71), Davies.
Stjarnan: (4231) Jonsson; Sturluson, Rauschenberg, Laxdal D, Arnason; Johannsson, Praest; Palsson (Bjorgvinsson 55), Punyed, Finsen (Gunnarson 46); Johannesson (Blondal 71).

Birkirkara (1) 1 *(Camenzuli 44)*
Diosgyor (1) 4 *(Elek 30, Husic 62, Barczi 66,*
Marjanovic 90) 1200
Birkirkara: (424) Adrian Murcia; Agius (Ledesma 46), Herrera, Camenzuli, Grech (Omerou 64); Fenech, Vukanac; Zerafa, Scicluna, Moreno, Vella (Zammit 84).
Diosgyor: (442) Antal; Husic, Kadar, William, Okuka; Bacsa (Barczi 61), Bori (Nikhazi 71), Elek, Dedeceni (Marjanovic 71); Gosztonyi, Grumic.

Brommapojkarna (0) 2 *(Une-Larsson 64, Petrovic 79)*
VPS Vaasa (0) 0 777
Brommapojkarna: (442) Blazevic; Segerstrom, Jonsson, Bjorkstrom, Une-Larsson, Falkenborn (Asbrink 63), Karlstrom (Soderstrom 90), Petrovic, Sandberg-Magnusson; Martinsson-Ngouali, Barkroth.
VPS Vaasa: (442) Henriksson; Koskimaa, Honkaniemi, Brown (Simpson 50), Nganbe; Strandvall, Engstrom, Bjork, Dafaa; Parikka (Seabrook 46), Stewart (Linjaja 81).

Buducnost Podgorica (1) 3 *(Tomkovic 14, Raicevic 58,*
Vujacic 72)
Folgore/Falciano (0) 0 2077
Buducnost Podgorica: (451) Ljuljanovic; Banovic, Tomkovic, Raspopovic, Kopitovic; Ilincic (Burzanovic 69), Hocko, Rogosic (Vukcevic 73), Raickovic, Raicevic (Milosevic 84); Vujacic.
Folgore/Falciano: (541) Bicchiarelli; Nucci, Muraccini, Sartori, Magnani (Della 49), Pacini (Casadei 72); Loiodice, Paglialonga, Muccini (Ottaviani 88), Perrotta; Ceschi.

Chikhura Sachkhere (1) 3 *(Gabedava 7, 67,*
Rekhviashvili 75)
Turnovo (1) 1 *(Pandovski 45)* 1500
Chikhura Sachkhere: (442) Somkhishvili; Rekhviashvili, Kashia, Tchelidze, Kutchukhidze (Mumladze 79); Kimadze, Datunaishvili, Bechvaia, Odikadze; Dekanoidze, Gabedava (Koripadze 80).

Turnovo: (442) Dimovski; Tasev, Mutafchyiski, Harizanov (Kovacev 53), Mavrov (Dolapchiev 60); Curlinov, Pandev, Varelovski, Najdenov; Pandovski (Naumchevski 49), Georgiev.

College Europa (0) 0
Vaduz (0) 1 *(Hasler 89)*   824
College Europa: (361) Robba; Coombes L■, Mouelhi, Jolley; Molina (Marquez 79), Pereyra, Coombes J (Saavedra 52), Bakkari, Juanse, Bosio (Martin 63); Ferberovich.
Vaduz: (442) Jehle; Grippo, Niederhausen, Stahel, Kaufmann; Abbeglen (Sutter 56), Kryeziu, Neumayr (Hasler 72), Polverino; Pak (Lang 65), Schurpf.

Daugava Daugavpils (0) 1 *(Zaikins 60)*
Vikingur (0) 1 *(Olsen A 88)*   200
Daugava Daugavpils: (433) Vlasovs; Ostrovskis, Oginskis, Sevelovs, Chikhradze; Solovjovs■, Zaikins (Sikorskiy 64), Kosmacovs; Kokins, Kozlovs, Vladimirs.
Vikingur: (4411) Turi; Djurhuus (Olsen A 73), Jacobsen E, Hansen B, Jacobsen H; Gregersen, Djordjevic (Sorensen 90), Vatnhamar S, Hansson; Justinussen; Hansen H.

Daugava Riga (0) 0
Aberdeen (3) 3 *(Rooney 22, 40, 45)*   600
Daugava Riga: (4411) Krumins; Kacanovs, Ribokas (Vitolnieks 62), Tomkevicius, Mendy; Savenas, Knapsis, Abdelaziz, Solovich; Flora (Karklins 55); Blanks (Markevicius 66).
Aberdeen: (4231) Langfield; Logan, Considine, Reynolds, Hayes (Smith 62); Jack, Robson (Low 80); Taylor, Flood, McGinn (Wright 80); Rooney.

Dundalk (3) 3 *(Gartland 8, Byrne 37, Mountney 45)*
Jeunesse Esch (0) 1 *(Zydko 55)*   2534
Dundalk: (4411) Cherrie; Gannon, Gartland (Kelly 80), Boyle, Massey; Mountney, Higgins, Towell, Horgan (Griffin 46); Byrne (Hoban 62); McMillan.
Jeunesse Esch: (4141) Oberweis; Da Graca, Portier, Hoffmann, Vitali; Todorovic (Delgado 46); Corral (Albanese 46), Zydko (Agovic 78), Kintziger, Melisse; Ibrahimovic.

Ekranas (0) 1 *(Kochanauskas 60)*
Crusaders (0) 2 *(Heatley 56, 71)*   1400
Ekranas: (442) Zukauskas; Duda, Susnjar, Pilotas, Girdvainis; Petrauskas, Salamanavicius (Tamulevicius 59), Elivelton, Baranauskas (Norvilas 52); Umeh, Kochanauskas (Meskinis 65).
Crusaders: (442) O'Neill; Burns, Leeman, Robinson, McClean; Morrow (Magowan 90), Caddell, Clarke, Heatley (Snoddy 73); Cockcroft (O'Carroll 55), Owens.

Ferencvaros (1) 2 *(Ugrai 14 (pen), Busai 56)*
Sliema Wanderers (0) 1 *(Scozzese 60)*   4724
Ferencvaros: (442) Dibusz; Lauth (Nagy 73), Kukuruzovic (Cukic 88), Gyomber, Busai (Bode 70); Nalepa, Bosnjak, Mateos, Dilaver; Ugrai, Somalia.
Sliema Wanderers: (442) Zammit; Muscat A, Scozzese, Potezica, Mintoff; Scerri, Mifsud, Ohawuchi, Barbetti■; Muscat G (Cilia 80), Bianciardi.

Flamurtari Vlore (0) 1 *(Shehaj 85)*
Sioni Bolnisi (0) 2 *(Ugulava 56, Kuqi 83 (og))*   2500
Flamurtari Vlore: (442) Lika I; Mici, Veliu, Lena, Arberi; Muzaka (Licaj 89), Telushi, Kuqi, Lika G (Meto 78); Zeqiri (Shehaj 67), Abulaliaj.
Sioni Bolnisi: (442) Merlani; Kandelaki, Svanadze, Imedashvili, Popkhadze (Adamia 81); Goboberishvili, Ganugrava (Samkharadze 65), Lobjanidze, Aptsiauri; Gureshidze (Ugulava 54), Isiani.
Flamurtari won on away goals.

Fola Esch (0) 0
IFK Gothenburg (0) 2 *(Vibe 76, Mahlangu 81)*   1516
Fola Esch: (4231) Hym; Laterza, Keita, Payal (Dallevedove 81), Skrijelj (Francoise 64); Rani, Jans; Ronny, Klein, Hornuss (Lukic 81); Hadji.
IFK Gothenburg: (442) Sandberg; Salomonsson, Jonsson (Engvall 85), Bjarsmyr, Augustinsson (Johansson A 79); Smedberg-Dalence (Svensson 62), Soder, Johansson J, Mahlangu; Larsson, Vibe.

Glenavon (0) 2 *(Braniff 58, Bradley 60)*
FH Hafnarfjordur (2) 3 *(Oskarsson I 3, Emilsson 37, 69 (pen))*   1634
Glenavon: (442) Blayney; Lindsay (McKeown 55), Dillon, Marshall, McCabe; Martyn (Sykes 83), Neill, Bradley, Hamilton (Rainey 78); Bates, Braniff.
FH Hafnarfjordur: (442) Oskarsson R; Reynolds, Emilsson, Doumbia, Bodvarsson (Gudmundsson 70); Hewson (Ingason 75), Palsson, Runarsson, Oskarsson I; Snorrason (Gudnason 46), Jonsson.

Haugesund (1) 2 *(Agdestein 7, Sema 56)*
Airbus UK Broughton (1) 1 *(Pearson 14)*   3079
Haugesund: (442) Bratveit; Myrestam, Cvetinovic, Andreassen, Haraldseid; Mawejje, Anyora, Bamberg (Nilsen 71), Sema (Fevang 87); Agdestein, Aasheim (Stolas 46).
Airbus UK Broughton: (442) Coates; Pearson, Kearney, Owens, Short; Field (Roddy 80), Jones, Rule, Budrys (Barrow■ 52); Johnson (Hassall 61), Wade.

Honka Espoo (1) 3 *(Aijala 45, Mombilo 90, Porokara 105)*
Sillamae Kalev (1) 2 *(Sidorenkov 25, Kabaev 120)*   1102
Honka Espoo: (442) Kollar; Hatakka, Aijala, Vaisanen, Aalto; Makijarvi, Anyamele (Mombilo 46), Hetemaj, Kabashi (Levanen 81); Porokara, Tuomela (Saarinen 52).
Sillamae Kalev: (442) Starodubtsev; Dudarev, Sidorenkov, Cheminava, Volodin (Baguzis 25); Silich (Kvasov 46), Ratnikov, Mashichev (Vnukov 67), Tjapkin; Murikhin, Kabaev.
aet; Sillamae Kalev won on away goals.

IF Fuglafjordur (0) 0
Myllykosken Pallo-47 (0) 0   228
IF Fuglafjordur: (4321) Mikkelsen J; Ellingsgaard J, Mikkelsen P, Eliasen, Lokin; Petersen B, Zachariasen, Joensen; Saric, Jakobsen (Jokladal 88); Ellingsgaard A (Poulsen 80).
Myllykosken Pallo-47: (4321) Iiskola; Vesala (Hoivala 90), Koskinen, Aho, Nongotamba; Dema, Abdulahi, Pirinen; Minkenen, Salmikivi (Motta 72); Soiri (Ristola 77).

Inter Baku (0) 3 *(Dashdemirov 79, Tskhadadze 83 (pen), Guseynpur 90)*
Tiraspol (1) 1 *(Bulat 6)*   3120
Inter Baku: (532) Lomaia; Salukvadze, Amisulashvili, Spicic, Bocognano, Georgievski; Alvaro, Mammadov A (Tskhadadze 41), Dashdemirov; Meza, Madrigal (Guseynpur 78).
Tiraspol: (532) Georgiev■; Novikov, Hausi, Japaridze■, Vidovic, Sydorenko (Shapoval 46); Zarichinyuk (Ovseanicov 71), Bulat, Ademar Xavier; Molla, Karaneychev (Boghiu 56).

Jelgava (0) 0
Rosenborg (1) 2 *(Jensen 30, Diskerud 73)*   1500
Jelgava: (532) Ikstens; Petrenko, Redjko, Zulevs (Eriba 64), Bespalovs, Medeckis (Petersons 84); Kozlovs, Oss, Gubins; Freimanis, Malasenoks (Jaudzems 77).
Rosenborg: (3511) Orlund; Reginiussen (Svensson 70), Ronning, Jensen (Selnaes 46); Riski, Mikkelsen, Soderlund (Pedersen 57), Skjelvik, Berntsen; Strandberg; Diskerud.

Koper (2) 4 *(Stromajer 10, Galesic 17 (pen), 90, Pucko 90)*
Celik Niksic (0) 0   700
Koper: (442) Radosevic; Gregoric, Blazic, Guberac, Halilovic; Ivetic, Crnigoj, Palcic (Stulac 52), Covilo (Pucko 52); Galesic, Stromajer (Zibert 89).
Celik Niksic: (442) Giljen; Vukovic, Bubanja (Nikolic 81), Bulatovic (Delibasic 16), Vidakanic; Kalezic, Adrovic, Ivanovic (Vujovic 89), Brnovic; Djalac, Prtenjak.

Kukesi (0) 0
Kairat Almaty (0) 0   2000
Kukesi: (4411) Halili; Smajlaj, Dushkaj, Lushtaku (Hysa 59), Cikalleshi; Hallaci, Allmuca (Shameti 72), Bicaj, Hoxha (Perich 80); Pejic; Musolli.
Kairat Almaty: (433) Khomich; Michalik, Pliev, Gorman, Kislitsyn; Smakov, Islamkhan (Li 90), Knezevic (Lunin 46); Bakaev, Yedigaryan (Barbosa 63), Gohou.

Laci (0) 1 *(Adeniyi 58)*

Rudar Velenje (0) 1 *(Eterovic 90)* 1200

Laci: (442) Vujadinovic; Ofoyen, Cela, Sheta, Sefa (Sefgjinaj 46); Vucaj, Nimani (Kastrati 82), Teqja, Zefi; Veliaj (Ndreca 46), Adeniyi.
Rudar Velenje: (442) Rozman; Roser, Jahic (Krefl 58), Knezovic, Crncic; Tolimir, Klinar, Dedic (Plesec 82), Radujko; Firer (Kocic 32), Eterovic.
aet; Laci won 3-2 on penalties.

Libertas (0) 0

Botev Plovdiv (0) 2 *(Benga 64, Filipov 88)* 412

Libertas: (442) Simoncini A; Molinari (Angeli 79), Rocchetti, Simoncini D (Rossi 70 (Zennaro 72)), Facondini; Golinucci, Antonelli, Righi, Rocchi; Morelli, Rosti.
Botev Plovdiv: (442) Stachowiak; Benga, Filipov, Hristov, Terziev; Sarmov (Chunchukov 71), Ognyanov, Curtean (Vasev 46), Jirsak; Pedro (Yusein 86), Tsvetkov.

Lovcen (0) 0

Zeljeznicar Sarajevo (0) 1 *(Sadikovic 57)* 1200

Lovcen: (442) Perovic; Bozovic, Tatar, Martinovic, Simovic; Radovic, Bogdanovic[■], Brnovic, Kosovic (Djurovic 73); Draganic (Vujanovic 66), Radunovic.
Zeljeznicar Sarajevo: (541) Antolovic; Colic (Memija 72), Kvesic, Sadikovic, Zeljkovic (Jamak 46), Stanic; Turkovic, Bucan (Bajic 56), Bogdanovic, Hasanhodzic; Tomic.

Metalurg Skopje (2) 2 *(Gjorgievski 19, Simonovski 34)*

EU Santa Coloma (0) 0 480

Metalurg Skopje: (442) Efremov; Ristovski, Gjorgievski, Leskaroski, Naumoski; Simonovski, Mitrev, Radeski, Dodevski; Angelov, Stojanovski.
EU Santa Coloma: (442) Godswill; Maneiro, Martinez, Roca, Anton; Salvat, Bernat, Lopez, Crespo; Jordi Rubio, Rodriguez.

Mika (1) 1 *(Karapetyan 45)*

RNK Split (0) 1 *(Bilic 88)* 1600

Mika: (442) Kasparov; Alex, Petrosyan, Voskanyan A, Poghosyan; Grigoryan (Ghazaryan 55), Satunyan, Barseghyan, Movsisyan (Hakobyan 77); Voskanyan H (Beglaryan 61), Karapetyan.
RNK Split: (442) Zagorac; Rugasevic, Ibriks, Galovic, Glavina (Rog 70); Glumac, Vojnovic (Dujmovic 80), Erceg, Vidovic; Bilic, Bagaric (Belle 59).

Nomme Kalju (1) 2 *(Felipe Nunes 10, Wakui 53)*

Fram Reykjavĺk (1) 2 *(Omarsson 25, Bjarnason 64)* 842

Nomme Kalju: (433) Teles; Reintam, Barengrub, Kallaste, Mbu Alidor; Vunk, Toomet (Kirss 57), Prates; Wakui, Quintieri (Rodrigues 89), Felipe Nunes (Jevdokimov 61).
Fram Reykjavĺk: (442) Kristinsson; Traustason (Thorlaksson 61), Bjarnason, Gunnarsson, Atlason; Omarsson, Gudjonsson (Arnarsson H 81), Marteinsson (Albertsson 57), Arnarsson V; Baldvinsson, Takefusa.

Sant Julia (0) 0

Cukaricki (0) 0 150

Sant Julia: (433) Coca (Rivas 84); Estepa, Yael, Ruis, Rodrĺguez; Varela, Girau (Cabezas Jurado 74), Soto; Spano, Perez (Barba 88), Serra.
Cukaricki: (451) Ristic; Piasentin, Stojkovic, Ostojic, Brezancic (Boljevic 86); Todorovich, Matic, Bojic (Srnic D 71), Stojiljkovic (Pavlovic A 81), Srnic S; Mirosavljevic.

Shakhter Karagandy (3) 4 *(Kpodo 12 (og), Konysbayev 29, Pokrivac 45, Finonchenko 49)*

Shirak (0) 0 11,200

Shakhter Karagandy: (541) Mokin; Dzidic (Baizhanov 62), Maliy, Maslo, Kirov, Simcevic; Vicius, Konysbayev (Murzoev 78), Pokrivac, Topcagic (Murtazaev 71); Finonchenko.
Shirak: (442) Ermakov; Kpodo, Marikyan (Darbinyan 53), Hovanisian, Hakobian; Aleksanyan, Muradyan K, Yoro (Barikian 46), Diop; Deble, Bougouhi (Davtyan 46).

Siroki Brijeg (2) 3 *(Zakaric 17, Maric 29, 56)*

Gabala (0) 0 1500

Siroki Brijeg: (442) Soldo; Barisic, Brekalo, Lastro, Coric (Kozulj 78); Pehar (Ivankovic 60), Zakaric, Landeka, Wagner; Peko (Corluka 34), Maric.
Gabala: (442) Agayev; Levin (Guliyev 83), Abisov, Tagizada (Amirjanov 46), Abbasov; Dos Santos, Hajiyev, Ropotan, Mendi; Dodo, Cristea (Jamalov 65).

Sligo R (1) 4 *(Keane 45, Greene 72, North 83, Cawley 89)*

Banga (0) 0 2169

Sligo R: (442) Rogers (Brush 84); Keane (Peers 87), McMillan, Spillane (Gaynor 23), Conneely; Cawley, Greene, Russell, Djilali; North, Cretaro.
Banga: (442) Jurevicius; Urbaitis[■], Karkusov (Stezhka 25), Epifanov, Arlauskis; Grigaitis, Butkus (Siryk 74), Khablov (Makiev 71), Zagurskas; Shevchuk, Staponka.

Spartak Trnava (3) 5 *(Mikovic 12, Sabo 21, 90, Vlasko 28, Mikinic 85)*

Hibernians (0) 0 2220

Spartak Trnava: (442) Strapak; Bortel, Conka, Toth (Banovic 46), Janecka; Chovanec, Sabo, Schranz (Spalek 59), Kuzma; Mikovic (Mikinic 64), Vlasko.
Hibernians: (433) Balzan; Muscat (Degabriele 65), Desira, Gomes, Soares; Kristensen, Failla, Bezzina; Farrugia, Dias, Cohen.

Tromso (3) 6 *(Espejord 13, Drage 23, Andersen 28, 57, Wangberg 54, 79)*

Santos Tartu (1) 1 *(Alve 39)* 760

Tromso: (4321) Herlofsen; Moldskred, Bendiksen (Johnsen 46), Drage, Norbye; Andersen (Andreassen 76), Johansen R (Ingebrigtsen 61), Frantzen; Wangberg, Nilsen; Espejord.
Santos Tartu: (442) Kohler; Teniste, Kallandi, Alve, Vellemaa (Laurson 34); Sonn, Laas K, Laas M (Eessaar 79), Roops; Flyak, Vereshchak (Vidaja 85).

Zimbru Chisinau (1) 2 *(Amani 6, Pascenco 87)*

Skendija Tetovo (0) 0 4500

Zimbru Chisinau: (442) Rusu; Erhan, Bologan (Burghiu 57), Dedov, Klimovich; Pavlyuchek, Amani (Pascenco 68), Vremea, Grossu; Cheptine (Spataru 46), Jardan.
Skendija Tetovo: (442) Jovanovski; Bejtulai, Polozani, Vrucina, Nurisi (Imeri 51); Murati (Kavdanski 86), Junior, Mitrov (Selmani 65), Huseini[■]; Berisha, Miliev.

Friday, 11 July 2014

Litex Lovech (1) 3 *(Mendy 27, Jordan 63, 74)*

Veris (0) 0 400

Litex Lovech: (433) Pirgov; Bodurov, Popov, Mendy (Nedyalkov 83), Bozhikov; Vajushi, Zlatinov, Karakolev (Rumenov 66); Jordan, Moreno Asprilla (Tsvetanov 79), Kossoko.
Veris: (451) Gaiduchevici; Cascaval, Racu, Bacal[■], Cojocari; Cucerenco, Bogdanovic (Bugneac 71), Mocanu, Josan, Zasavitchi (Pisla 49); Frunza (Milinceanu 59).

SECOND QUALIFYING ROUND FIRST LEG

Thursday, 17 July 2014

Aberdeen (0) 0

FC Groningen (0) 0 16,523

Aberdeen: (4231) Langfield; Logan, Anderson, Reynolds, Hayes; Jack, Flood; Robson, Pawlett (Low 89), McGinn; Rooney (Goodwillie 76).
FC Groningen: (433) Padt; Hateboer, Botteghin, Kappelhof, Burnet; Lindgren, Kieftenbeld, Chery; Van der Velden (Ivanschitz 82), Hoesen (Antonia 65), Kostic.

Astana (1) 3 *(Canas 16 (pen), Nuserbaev 58, Beissebekov 69)*

Hapoel Tel Aviv (0) 0 10,800

Astana: (442) Eric; Akhnetov, Dmitrenko, Kethevoama (Muzhikov 85), Beissebekov; Nuserbaev (Kurdov 80), Zhukov, Canas, Dzholchiev (Kojasevic 90); Essame, Postnikov.
Hapoel Tel Aviv: (442) Amos; Cohen (Chekoll 70), Colin, Zaguri, Lucas Sasha; Dgani[■], Vermouth, Abutbul, Gerzycich; Shrem (Fadida 66), Malka (Levi 20).

Atlantas (0) 0
Shakhter Karagandy (0) 0　　　　　　　3000
Atlantas: (4231) Galdikas; Joksas, Gnedojus, Jemelins, Kazlauskas M; Bartkus, Kazlauskas D; Papsys, Zukauskas, Eliosius (Maksimov 80); Krusnauskas (Baranauskas 70).
Shakhter Karagandy: (3421) Mokin; Dzidic, Maliy, Maslo; Kirov, Simcevic, Vicius, Konysbayev (Salomov 89); Pokrivac, Topcagic (Murzoev 84); Finonchenko (Murtazaev 90).

Botev Plovdiv (1) 2 *(Tsvetko 39 (pen), Chunchukov 86)*
SKN St Polten (0) 1 *(Segovia 55)*　　　　2200
Botev Plovdiv: (442) Stachowiak; Luchin, Benga, Ognyanov, Curtean (Gamakov 64); Hristov, Tsvetkov, Chunchukov, Jirsak; Filipov, Vasev (Marin 76 (Yusein 90)).
SKN St Polten: (433) Kostner; Huber, Wisio, Parada, Harti (Stec 73); Kerschbaumer, Segovia (Noel 77), Ambichl; Hofbauer (Schibany 88), Grasegger, Holzmann.

Brommapojkarna (2) 4 *(Rexhepi 9, Albornoz 27, Une-Larsson 62, Barkroth 65 (pen))*
Crusaders (0) 0　　　　　　　　　　524
Brommapojkarna: (442) Blazevic; Segerstrom (Karlstrom 45), Jonson, Bjorkstrom, Une-Larsson; Albornoz (Starfelt 45), Petrovic, Martinsson-Ngouali, Rexhepi (Sandberg-Magnusson 50); Kouakou, Barkroth.
Crusaders: (442) O'Neill; Burns, Coates, Robinson, McClean; Morrow, Caddell, Clarke (Leeman 76), Heatley; O'Carroll (Cockcroft 58), Owens (Adamson 82).

Buducnost Podgorica (0) 0
Omonia Nicosia (1) 2 *(Roberto 36, Lobjanidze 79)*　　1000
Buducnost Podgorica: (442) Ljuljanovic; Tomkovic, Kopitovic, Ilincic (Burzanovic 72), Vujacic; Vukcevic, Rogosic (Cetkovic 46), Raickovic, Raspopovic; Raicevic, Hocko.
Omonia Nicosia: (442) Moreira; Roberto (Pote 86), Lobjanidze, Rodri, Grigalashvili (Alex Rubio 77); Alipio, Cristovao, Scaramozzino (Fylaktou 82), Kyriakou; Serginho, Acquistapace.

Bursaspor (0) 0
Chikhura Sachkhere (0) 0　　　　　17,300
Bursaspor: (442) Tekin; Civelli, Belluschi, Eraltay, Traore; Karabulut (Kiraz 46), Fernandao (Unal 56), Sen, Ozbayrakli; Ozturk, Yilmaz (Tufan 82).
Chikhura Sachkhere: (442) Kvilitaia; Jigauri, Kimadze, Gabedava, Kutchukhidze; Datunaishvili, Bechvaia, Kashia, Odikadze; Dekanoidze (Koripadze 90), Rekhviashvili.

Cluj-Napoca (0) 0
Jagodina (0) 0　　　　　　　　5600
Cluj-Napoca: (442) Mario Felgueiras; Susic, Larie, Deac, Sulley; Costea (Jakolis 58), Chuka, Negrut (Christian 75), Lopes; Rada, Monroy (Paun 88).
Jagodina: (433) Djuricic; Djuric (Martinovic 77), Susnjar, Mihajlovic (Gasic 54), Cvetkovic; Arsenijevic, Simac, Filipovic; Mitosevic, Milinkovic, Jakimovski (Lepovic 84).

CSKA Sofia (1) 1 *(Karachanakov 41)*
Zimbru Chisinau (1) 1 *(Alexeev 31)*　　　5000
CSKA Sofia: (442) Divis; Sunny (Kamburov 46), Krachunov, Silva (Karachanakov 36), Marquinhos; Bergonsi, Joachim, Popov, Vasilev; Supusepa, Stoyanov (Galchev 62).
Zimbru Chisinau: (442) Rusu; Burghiu, Erhan, Anton (Potirniche 45), Dedov; Klimovich, Alexeev (Grossu 81), Pavlyuchek, Vremea; Cheptine (Spataru 60), Jardan.

Cukaricki (0) 0
Grodig (1) 4 *(Nutz 37, 90, Schutz 80, 85)*　　1500
Cukaricki: (442) Ristic; Piasentin■, Srnic D, Todorovich, Jankovic (Bojic 62); Stojiljkovic, Matic (Pavlovic A 80), Srnic S, Ostojic; Mirosavljevic (Boljevic 46), Brezancic.
Grodig: (442) Stankovic; Karner, Handle, Reyna (Wallner 78), Brauer; Tomi Correa, Strobl, Huspek (Schutz 29), Boller (Martschinko 84); Nutz, Maak.

Derry C (0) 0
Shakhtyor Soligorsk (1) 1 *(Yanush 28)*　　1837
Derry C: (4411) Doherty; McEleney S, Byrne, McBride, Barry; Timlin, Molloy, McNamee, Duffy (Dooley 63); McEleney P (Boyle 86); Patterson.
Shakhtyor Soligorsk: (343) Kotenko; Kuzmyanok, Yanushkevich, Kashewski; Matsveychyk, Starhorodskyi, Halyuza, Yurevich; Balanovich (Guruli 77), Yanush (Osipenko 67), Ryas (Tsevan 88).

Dinamo Minsk (1) 3 *(Udoji 25, Stasevich 61 (pen), Nikolic 86)*
Myllykosken Pallo-47 (0) 0　　　　　2600
Dinamo Minsk: (451) Hutar; Veretilo, Palitsevich, Zaleski, Nikolic; Simovic, Voronkov (Bykov 66), Udoji, Bangura, Stasevich (Figueredo 81); Adamovic (Diomande 73).
Myllykosken Pallo-47: (442) Iiskola; Aho, Koskinen, Vesala (Ristola 70), William; Abdulahi, Pirinen, Minkenen (Motta 62), Bah; Nongotamba, Soiri (Salmikivi 84).

Dundalk (0) 0
Hajduk Split (1) 2 *(Caktas 9, Vlasic 73)*　　3014
Dundalk: (4411) Cherrie; Gannon, Gartland, Boyle, Massey; Shields (Higgins 71), Mountney (McDermott 56), Horgan (McMillan 81), Towell; Meenan; Hoban.
Hajduk Split: (433) Stipica; Milic, Milovic, Vrsajevic, Maloca; Vlasic, Caktas, Bradaric (Maloku 80); Maglica (Andjelkovic 57), Gotal, Kouassi (Basic 78).

Elfsborg (0) 0
Inter Baku (1) 1 *(Georgievski 29)*　　2393
Elfsborg: (433) Hassan; Jonsson, Larsson, Holmen, Klarstrom (Lundqvist 62); Svensson, Rohden, Claesson (Hedlund 86); Beckmann, Frick (Nilsson 69), Prodell.
Inter Baku: (442) Lomaia; Salukvadze, Amisulashvili, Bocognano, Spicic; Georgievski, Mikel Alvaro (Ivan Benitez 90), Dashdemirov, Meza; Madrigal (Mammadov A 74), Tskhadadze (Guseynpur 63).

Gyori ETO (0) 0
IFK Gothenburg (1) 3 *(Vibe 8, Johansson J 56, Mahlangu 83)*　　3000
Gyori ETO: (442) Kamenar; Kamber, Had, Svec (Varga 45), Dinjar; Dudas, Kronaveter (Koltai 57), Patkai, Windecker (Trajkovic 59); Andric, Rudolf.
IFK Gothenburg: (442) Sandberg; Augustinsson, Jonsson, Johansson A, Bjarsmyr; Smedberg-Dalence (Daniel Sobralense 80), Svensson, Mahlangu (Allansson 87), Johansson J; Larsson, Vibe (Soder 70).

Kairat Almaty (0) 1 *(Knezevic 50 (pen))*
Esbjerg (0) 1 *(Fellah 90)*　　　　19,000
Kairat Almaty: (442) Khomich; Pliev, Michalik, Kislitsyn, Smakov; Islamkhan (Gorman 90), Knezevic (Barbosa 86), Kuantayev, Bakaev; Yedigaryan (Lunin 62), Gohou.
Esbjerg: (442) Dubravka; Jakobsen, Lucena, Laursen, Gomes (Berthel Askou 81); Lekven, Andersen, Ankersen, Fellah; van Buren (Nielsen 84), Lyng (Vestergaard 66).

Laci (0) 0
Zorya Luhansk (1) 3 *(Sheta 23 (og), Ljubenovic 47, Boli 75)*　　1200
Laci: (442) Vujadinovic; Teqja, Sheta (Veliaj 69), Ofoyen, Cela; Adeniyi, Vucaj, Sefgjinaj (Buljan 27), Nimani; Zefi, Morina (Sela 40).
Zorya Luhansk: (442) Shevchenko; Vernydub, Gritsay (Borodai 75), Ignjatijevic (Yarmash 46), Chaykovsky; Kamenyuka, Ljubenovic (Lipartia 60), Beliy, Khomchenovskiy; Boli, Karavayev.

Linfield (0) 1 *(Waterworth 87)*
AIK Solna (0) 0　　　　　　　1741
Linfield: (442) Tuffey; Glendinning (Callacher 80), Hegarty, Richards, Clarke M; Sproule, Mulgrew (Ward 21), Lowry, Burns; Thompson (Waterworth 74), Carvill.
AIK Solna: (352) Carlgren; Lorentzson, Karlsson, Johansson; Pavey (Ofori 70), Sundberg, Borges, Saletros, Bahoui; Igboananike (Moro 87), Goitom.

Litex Lovech (0) 0
Diosgyor (0) 2 *(Nemeth 83, Grumic 90)*   1300
Litex Lovech: (451) Vinicius; Bodurov, Mendy, Bozhikov, Popov; Boumal (Rumenov 60), Jordan, Vajushi, Zlatinov, Moreno Asprilla (Tsvetanov 82); Kossoko (Tsvetkov 77).
Diosgyor: (532) Antal; Husic, Kadar, Okuka, Dedreceni, Nemeth; Egerszegi, Gosztonyi (Grumic 59), Elek; Barczi (Bognar 50), Bacsa (Marjanovic 78).

Lucerne (0) 1 *(Schneuwly 68)*
St Johnstone (0) 1 *(MacLean 48)*   10,000
Lucerne: (4231) Zibung, Rogulj, Lustenberger, Thiesson, Affolter; Wiss (Lezcano 60), Doubai (Bento 60); Hyka (Bozanic 75), Winter, Freuler; Schneuwly.
St Johnstone: (4231) Mannus; Mackay, Wright, Caddis (O'Halloran 75), Miller; Easton, Millar; Wotherspoon, Brown, Croft (Scobbie 89); MacLean.

Metalurg Skopje (0) 0
Zeljeznicar Sarajevo (0) 0   3010
Metalurg Skopje: (4231) Efremov; Ristovski (Tanturovski 86), Gjorgievski, Leskaroski, Dodevski; Dalceski (Naumoski 46), Mitrev (Angelov 46); Krstev, Simonovski, Radeski; Stojanovski.
Zeljeznicar Sarajevo: (4231) Antolovic; Kosoric, Colic, Bogdanovic, Kvesic; Bucan, Stanic (Nuspahic 53); Sadikovic, Tomic (Jamak 63), Hasanovic; Turkovic (Bajic 72).

MFK Kosice (0) 0
Slovan Liberec (0) 1 *(Jarolim 83 (pen))*   7055
MFK Kosice: (442) Tofiloski; Sekulic, Singlar (Skvasik 90), Korijkov, Kavka; Basista, Viazanko (Ostojic 85), Bukata, Pacinda (Diaby 80); Redzic, Novak.
Slovan Liberec: (433) Hroso; Karisik, Coufal, Rajnoch, Fleisman; Pavelka, Sackey, Jarolim (Pimpara 90); Hadascok (Hamulak 65), Sural (Obzera 78), Dubek.

Mlada Boleslav (0) 2 *(Skalak 68, Duris 76)*
Siroki Brijeg (0) 1 *(Zakaric 51)*   4127
Mlada Boleslav: (4411) Hruska; Rosa, Smejkal, Hulka, Milla (Sultes 69); Skalak, Stohanzl (Vukadinovic 59), Scuk, Sisler; Boril (Bartl 75); Duris.
Siroki Brijeg: (4231) Soldo; Barisic (Markovic 81), Brekalo, Lastro, Coric; Pehar (Kozulj 56), Zakaric; Landeka, Wagner, Zadro (Ivankovic 56); Maric.

Molde (3) 4 *(Toivio 16, Forren 37, 41 (pen), Hoseth 88)*
Gorica (0) 1 *(Majcen 70 (pen))*   5837
Molde: (442) Nyland; Linnes (Rindaroy K 70), Flo, Forren, Toivio; Singh, Hussain (Berg Hestad 80), Mostrom (Hoseth 57), Agnaldo; Elyounoussi, Chukwa.
Gorica: (433) Simcic; Modolo, Sirok, Jogan, Vanin; Vetrih, Kolenc (Enow 46), Johnson; Zigon (Dzuzdanovic 66), Majcen, Arcon.

Motherwell (2) 2 *(Law 9, 19)*
Stjarnan (1) 2 *(Finsen 35 (pen), 90 (pen))*   4877
Motherwell: (442) Twardzik; Reid, Hammell, Ramsden, McManus; Carswell, Vigurs, Lasley, Law (Kerr 70); Ainsworth (Erwin 69), Sutton.
Stjarnan: (442) Jonsson; Vemmelund, Laxdal D, Arnason, Rauschenberg; Praest, Johannsson, Punyed, Gunnarson (Toft 88); Bjorgvinsson, Finsen.

Neftchi (1) 1 *(Abdullayev 45)*
Koper (2) 2 *(Galesic 24, Palcic 41)*   9500
Neftchi: (4231) Stamenkovic; Carlos Cardoso, Isayev, Bertucci, Yunuszade; Abdullayev (Masimov 78), Flavinho; Wobay, Ramos, Caue (Seyidov 59); Nfor (Gurbanov 73).
Koper: (3331) Radosevic; Blazic, Guberac, Ivetic; Galesic (Lotric 83), Halilovic, Crnigoj; Hadzic, Palcic (Gregoric 87), Zibert; Stromajer (Pucko 66).

Neman Grodno (0) 1 *(Savitskiy 66 (pen))*
FH Hafnarfjordur (0) 1 *(Emilsson 55)*   4800
Neman Grodno: (451) Rapalis; Rakhmanaw, Rawneyka (Veselinov 69), Denisevich, Rekish (Lyavitski 76); Zubovich (Kavalyonak 76), Rybak, Vitus, Tarasovs, Legchilin; Savitskiy.

FH Hafnarfjordur: (451) Oskarsson R; Vidarsson P, Hewson (Reynolds 70), Vidarsson D, Gudnason (Oskarsson I 82); Emilsson, Jonsson, Doumbia, Snorrason, Runarsson (Palsson 84); Hendrickx[■].

Nomme Kalju (0) 1 *(Wakui 81)*
Lech Poznan (0) 0   2280
Nomme Kalju: (451) Teles; Purg (Toomet 64), Kallaste, Barengrub, Rodrigues; Mbu Alidor, Mool, Quintieri (Ainsalu 77), Wakui, Vunk; Felipe Nunes (Kirss 62).
Lech Poznan: (442) Buric; Kedziora, Wolakiewicz, Henriquez, Wilusz; Tralka, Linetty (Kotorowski 60), Pawlowski, Jevtic; Hamalainen, Lovrencsics.

Petrolul Ploiesti (0) 2 *(Nepomuceno 77, Tamuz 84)*
Flamurtari Vlore (0) 0   8714
Petrolul Ploiesti: (442) Pecanha; Geraldo Alves, Fanchone, Teixeira, Hoban; Alcenat, Marinescu (Nkoyi 72), De Lucas, Tamuz (Morar 85); Albin (Nepomuceno 46), Mutu.
Flamurtari Vlore: (442) Lika I; Mici, Lena, Telushi, Abulaliaj (Shehaj 66); Arberi, Veliu, Zeqiri (Gerxho 90), Kuqi; Lika G (Meto 75), Muzaka.

Rijeka (0) 1 *(Krstanovic 85 (pen))*
Ferencvaros (0) 0   9000
Rijeka: (442) Vargic; Jajalo (Kramaric 57), Sharbini (Kvrzic 66), Tomecak, Mitrovic; Samardzic, Leovac, Brezovec, Moises; Jugovic (Jahovic 82), Krstanovic.
Ferencvaros: (442) Dibusz; Havojic, Kukuruzovic, Gyomber, Nalepa (Busai 90); Bosnjak, Pavlovic, Mateos, Dilaver; Ugrai (Lauth 79), Somalia.

RNK Split (0) 2 *(Dujmovic 78, Bilic 86 (pen))*
Hapoel Beer Sheva (1) 1 *(Buzaglo 31)*   2000
RNK Split: (442) Vukovic; Glavina, Glumac, Vojnovic (Dujmovic 46), Bilic; Erceg, Bagaric (Belle 70), Vidovic, Rugasevic (Rog 60); Galovic, Ibriks.
Hapoel Beer Sheva: (442) Ejide; Bitton, Harael, Barda, Buzaglo (Nasser 80); Davidadze, Gabay (Melikson 63), Pajovic, William Soares; Arbeitman (Malul 74), Gordana.

RoPS Rovaniemi (1) 1 *(Lahdenmaki 2)*
Asteras Tripolis (1) 1 *(Sankare 10)*   3424
RoPS Rovaniemi: (442) Sahlgren; Obilor, Lahdenmaki, Saxman, Okkonen; Makitalo, Majava, Nyassi (Emenike 90), Otaru (Virtanen 88); Kokko (Lahtinen 23), Gay.
Asteras Tripolis: (442) Bantis; Panteliadis, Goian, Sankare, Usero; Rolle (Munafo 73), Kourbelis, Lluy, De Blasis (Zisopoulos 90); Barrales, Bakasetas (Badibanga 65).

Rosenborg (0) 1 *(Diskerud 81)*
Sligo R (0) 2 *(Keane 56, North 70)*   2902
Rosenborg: (442) Hansen; Dorsin, Reginiussen, Helland (Sorloth 82), Skjelvik; Jensen (Diskerud 71), Pedersen, Berntsen (Selnaes 57), Riski; Mikkelsen, Soderlund.
Sligo R: (442) Rogers; Keane, McMillan, Spillane, Conneely; Ledwith, Cawley, Russell, Djilali (Maguire 85); North (Keating 82), Gaynor.

Ruch Chorzow (2) 3 *(Zienczuk 19, Stawarczyk 24, 74)*
Vaduz (1) 2 *(Muntwiler 16, Stahel 59)*   999
Ruch Chorzow: (442) Kaminski; Stawarczyk, Dziwniel, Konczkowski, Surma; Zienczuk, Kowalski, Starzynski (Efir 69), Babiarz; Malinowski, Kuswik.
Vaduz: (442) Jehle; Untersee, Grippo, Stahel, Burgmeier (Niederhausen 77); Ciccone (Polverino 62), Schurpf, Neumayr, Muntwiler; Sutter (Lang 70), Pak.

Sarajevo (0) 0
Haugesund (0) 1 *(Bamberg 85)*   13,000
Sarajevo: (433) Bandovic; Tatomirovic (Kovacevic 89), Berberovic, Dupovac, Stojcev; Cimirot, Puzigaca, Okic; Velkoski, Radovac, Bilbija (Duljevic 68).
Haugesund: (4411) Bratveit; Myrestam, Elsner, Andreassen, Bjornbakk; Haraldseid, Cvetinovic, Ekpo (Fevang 68), Anyora; Agdestein (Nilsen 84); Aasheim (Bamberg 64).

Sillamae Kalev (0) 0
Krasnodar (2) 4 *(Ari 9, Gazinski 39, Wanderson 68,*
Bystrov 86) 2130
Sillamae Kalev: (4411) Starodubtsev; Dudarev,
Sidorenkov, Cheminava, Vnukov (Kvasov 81); Ratnikov,
Mashichev (Silich 53), Tjapkin, Baguzis; Murikhin
(Novikov 90); Kabaev.
Krasnodar: (442) Sinitsyn; Jedrzejczyk, Granqvist,
Gazinski, Ari (Wanderson 56); Ahmedov, Kaleshin,
Laborde (Bystrov 46), Joaozinho; Sigurdsson, Pereyra
(Pomerko 69).

Trencin (1) 4 *(Moses 20, 53, 60, Jairo 72)*
Vojvodina (0) 0 3725
Trencin: (433) Volesak; Misak (Hajradinovic 69), Baez
(Rundic 85), Kubik, Jairo (Mondek 79); Holubek,
Cogley, Ramon; Lobotka, Klescik, Moses.
Vojvodina: (442) Jovanic; Radoja, Ivanic, Makaric
(Stojanovic 57), Pekaric; Alivodic, Puskaric (Zivkovic
58), Veselinovic (Popara 80), Nastic; Poletanovic, Baric.

Vikingur (0) 0
Tromso (0) 0 447
Vikingur: (4321) Turi; Jacobsen H, Gregersen, Olsen S
(Sorensen 90), Djordjevic (Olsen A 68); Vatnhamar S
(Hansen H 76), Hansson, Hansen B; Jacobsen E,
Djurhuus; Justinussen.
Tromso: (433) Lekstrom; Moldskred, Bendiksen, Drage
(Johnsen 83), Johansen J (Espejord 71); Norbye,
Andersen, Johansen R; Frantzen, Wangberg, Nilsen.

Zestafoni (0) 0
Spartak Trnava (0) 0 2537
Zestafoni: (442) Pavlovic; Chelidze, Santos, Guruli,
Gagoshidze; Kukhianidze (Chanturishvili 84),
Sharikadze, Getsadze, Dolidze; Dvali (Pantsulaia 78),
Gelashvili (Tatanashvili 65).
Spartak Trnava: (451) Rusov; Janecka, Bortel, Toth,
Conka; Sabo, Chovanec (Siva 87), Vlasko (Spalek 78),
Schranz (Casado 73), Mikovic; Kuzma.

Zulte Waregem (2) 2 *(Colpaert 8, Plet 45)*
Zawisza Bydgoszcz (1) 1 *(Drygas 15)* 8543
Zulte Waregem: (433) Bostyn; Cissako, Colpaert,
Verboom, Plet; N'Diaye (Ekangamene 86), Skulason,
Conte (Caceres 82); D'Haene, Aneke, Bongonda (Sylla
83).
Zawisza Bydgoszcz: (4231) Sandomierski; Silva (Petasz
46), Micael, Vasconcelos, Wojcicki (Kadu 56); Ziajka,
Drygas; Luis, Sochan (Gevorgyan 76), Wagner;
Nawotczynski.

SECOND QUALIFYING ROUND SECOND LEG

Tuesday, 22 July 2014

Zeljeznicar Sarajevo (1) 2 *(Dodevski 16 (og), Bajic 54)*
Metalurg Skopje (0) 2 *(Radeski 62, Krstev 90)* 10,262
Zeljeznicar Sarajevo: (433) Antolovic; Colic, Kvesic,
Kosoric, Bajic (Turkovic 82); Stanic, Sadikovic
(Hasanovic 77), Bogdanovic; Jamak, Tomic, Nuspahic
(Bucan 64).
Metalurg Skopje: (4411) Efremov; Ristovski (Naumoski
53), Gjorgievski, Leskaroski, Dalceski; Mitrev, Radeski,
Dodevski (Angelov 69), Krstev; Stojanovski; Tanturovski
(Simonovski 32).
Metalurg Skopje won on away goals.

Thursday, 24 July 2014

AIK Solna (0) 2 *(Igboananike 56, Goitom 72)*
Linfield (0) 0 9570
AIK Solna: (442) Carlgren; Karlsson, Johansson,
Milosevic, Lorentzson; Ofori (Saletros 75), Moro,
Borges, Bahoui; Igboananike (Pavey 84), Goitom.
Linfield: (442) Tuffey; Richards, Hegarty, Ward, Clarke
M; Glendinning (Mulgrew 58), Lowry, Burns, Sproule
(Clarke R 62); Waterworth, Carvill (Thompson 75).

Asteras Tripolis (2) 4 *(Kourbelis 12, De Blasis 45 (pen), 73,
Bakasetas 81)*
RoPS Rovaniemi (0) 2 *(Makitalo 53, Lahdenmaki 62)*
2867
Asteras Tripolis: (442) Bantis; Panteliadis, Sankare,
Goian, Usero; Rolle, Kourbelis (Bakasetas 72), Lluy, De
Blasis; Mazza (Munafo 75), Barrales (Badibanga 69).
RoPS Rovaniemi: (433) Sahlgren■; Obilor, Lahdenmaki,
Okkonen, Makitalo; Saxman, Majava, Nyassi (Lahtinen
84); Otaru (Forsman 45), Kokko (Emenike 71), Gay.

Chikhura Sachkhere (0) 0
Bursaspor (0) 0 13,000
Chikhura Sachkhere: (442) Kvilitaia; Jigauri, Kashia,
Rekhviashvili, Kutchukhidze (Mumladze 119); Kimadze
(Chikvaidze 117), Datunaishvili, Bechvaia, Odikadze;
Dekanoidze (Koripadze 90), Gabedava.
Bursaspor: (442) Tekin; Civelli, Cinaz, Eraltay,
Ozbayrakli■; Ozturk, Sen, Yilmaz (Tufan 53), Traore;
Unal (Altintas 80), Kiraz.
aet; Chikhura Sachkhere won 4-1 on penalties.

Crusaders (1) 1 *(Coates 17)*
Brommapojkarna (1) 1 *(Rexhepi 27)* 798
Crusaders: (442) O'Neill; Burns, Leeman, Coates
(Magowan 81), McClean; Morrow (Snoddy 57), Clarke,
Heatley, O'Carroll; Owens, Cockcroft (McCutcheon 63).
Brommapojkarna: (442) Blazevic; Jonsson, Bjorkstrom,
Starfelt, Une-Larsson; Karlstrom (Albornoz 68),
Petrovic, Asbrink (Vecchia 64), Sandberg-Magnusson
(Soderstrom 79); Martinsson-Ngouali, Rexhepi.

Diosgyor (1) 1 *(Gosztonyi 38 (pen))*
Litex Lovech (0) 2 *(Moreno Asprilla 80, Jordan 85 (pen))*
4260
Diosgyor: (433) Antal; Husic, Kadar, Okuka, Dedreceni;
Elek, Bognar (Marjanovic 63), Egerszegi; Bacsa,
Gosztonyi (Bori 73), Grumic (Nemeth 82).
Litex Lovech: (343) Vinicius; Nedyalkov, Bodurov,
Mendy; Tsvetkov (Angelov 66), Malinov (Rumenov 77),
Vajushi, Boumal; Jordan, Popov (Bozhikov 86), Moreno
Asprilla.

Esbjerg (1) 1 *(Ankersen 38)*
Kairat Almaty (0) 0 5522
Esbjerg: (442) Dubravka; Jakobsen, Gomes, Laursen,
Bergvold (Brinch 67); Lekven, Andersen, Nielsen
(Rasmussen 72), Ankersen; Fellah, Pusic (Lyng 62).
Kairat Almaty: (442) Khomich; Pliev, Kislitsyn, Michalik,
Smakov; Islamkhan, Kuantayev (Sito Riera 78), Baitana
(Knezevic 32), Bakaev; Gohou, Barbosa (Lunin 86).

FC Groningen (1) 1 *(Kieftenbeld 44)*
Aberdeen (2) 2 *(Rooney 26 (pen), McGinn 33)* 22,550
FC Groningen: (433) Padt; Kappelhof, Botteghin, Burnet
(van Nieff 62), Hateboer; Kieftenbeld (De Leeuw 46),
Van der Velden, Lindgren; Kostic, Hoesen (Antonia 46),
Chery.
Aberdeen: (532) Langfield; Logan, Reynolds, Anderson,
Considine, Hayes; Jack, Flood (Low 90), Pawlett
(Robson 66); Rooney (Goodwillie 73), McGinn.

Ferencvaros (0) 1 *(Ugrai 65 (pen))*
Rijeka (2) 2 *(Krstanovic 20 (pen), Samardzic 37)* 5127
Ferencvaros: (442) Dibusz; Nalepa (Kukuruzovic 66),
Bosnjak, Dilaver, Mateos; Pavlovic, Gera (Bode 61),
Gyomber, Ugrai (Busai 79); Somalia, Lauth.
Rijeka: (442) Vargic; Leovac, Samardzic, Jajalo (Kvrzic
69), Sharbini (Mitrovic 87); Tomecak, Leskovic,
Brezovec, Jugovic; Kramaric (Zlomislic 59), Krstanovic■.

FH Hafnarfjordur (1) 2 *(Gudnason 42, Bjornsson 80)*
Neman Grodno (0) 0 1438
FH Hafnarfjordur: (433) Oskarsson R; Jonsson,
Doumbia, Bodvarsson, Vidarsson P; Runarsson, Hewson
(Bjornsson 57), Vidarsson D; Gudnason, Snorrason
(Oskarsson I 76), Palsson.
Neman Grodno: (433) Rapalis; Yasinski, Rybak,
Tarasovs, Vitus, Veselinov, Denisevich, Legchilin
(Kavalyonak 64); Zubovich (Lyavitski 64), Savitskiy,
Rekish.

Flamurtari Vlore (1) 1 *(Lena 37)*
Petrolul Ploiesti (1) 3 *(Teixeira 39, De Lucas 84,*
Priso 90) 3650
Flamurtari Vlore: (451) Lika I; Mendes, Mici, Lena,
Arberi, Muzaka (Meto 86), Telushi (Gerxho 62), Zeqiri,
Kuqi, Lika G; Shehaj (Licai 67).
Petrolul Ploiesti: (352) Pecanha; Geraldo Alves, Gerson
Guimaraes, Fanchone (Beta 76); Teixeira, Alcenat,
Hoban, De Lucas, Tamuz (Albin 72); Mutu,
Nepomuceno (Priso 59).

Gorica (0) 1 *(Jogan 63)*
Molde (0) 1 *(Agnaldo 49)* 607
Gorica: (442) Simcic; Enow, Modolo (Kavcic 58), Sirok,
Vetrih■; Johnson, Osuji (Dzuzdanovic 41), Zigon, Jogan;
Majcen, Arcon.
Molde: (442) Nyland; Linnes, Forren, Toivio, Diouf;
Singh (Hestad 60), Agnaldo (Svendsen 66), Hoseth,
Hussain; Hoiland, Flo (Rindaroy O 82).

Grodig (1) 1 *(Karner 29)*
Cukaricki (0) 2 *(Bojic 61, Stojiljkovic 65)* 2129
Grodig: (442) Stankovic; Karner, Strobl, Maak, Brauer;
Handle, Tomi Correa (Djuric 85), Schutz (Huspek 46),
Reyna; Nutz, Boller (Wallner 62).
Cukaricki: (442) Ristic; Pavlovic D (Jankovic 79),
Stojkovic, Brezancic, Srnic D; Todorovich, Bojic,
Boljevic, Stojiljkovic; Pavlovic A (Matic 85), Srnic S
(Radovanovic 89).

Hajduk Split (1) 1 *(Kouassi 25)*
Dundalk (0) 2 *(Hoban 66, Byrne 74)* 15,000
Hajduk Split: (442) Stipica; Milovic, Jozinovic, Maloca,
Nizic; Andjelkovic, Vlasic (Maloku 76), Caktas (Bradaric
46), Bencun; Gotal, Kouassi (Maglica 62).
Dundalk: (442) Sava; Gannon, Gartland, Boyle, Massey;
Shields, Towell, Mountney, Higgins (Meenan 87);
McDermott (Hoban 57), McMillan (Byrne 68).

Hapoel Beer Sheva (0) 0
RNK Split (0) 0 5000
Hapoel Beer Sheva: (442) Ejide; Bitton (Malul 86),
Davidadze, Pajovic, William Soares; Harael (Gabay 67),
Buzaglo (Nasser 83), Melikson, Gordana; Barda,
Arbeitman.
RNK Split: (442) Vukovic; Glavina, Galovic, Ibriks,
Glumac; Vojnovic (Kvesic 50), Erceg, Roce (Rog 79),
Vidovic; Bilic, Bagaric.

Hapoel Tel Aviv (0) 1 *(Lucas Sasha 57 (pen))*
Astana (0) 0 200
Hapoel Tel Aviv: (4411) Al-Madon; Chekoll (Dado 77),
Levi, Cohen, Colin; Zaguri, Lucas Sasha (Fadida 89),
Vermouth, Malka; Abutbul; Gozlan (Lazmi 69).
Astana: (451) Eric; Beissebekov, Akhnetov, Dmitrenko,
Kethevoama (Twumasi 89); Pikalkin, Zhukov, Essame
(Muzhikov 90), Postnikov, Nuserbaev (Shomko 88);
Canas.

Haugesund (0) 1 *(Sema 47 (pen))*
Sarajevo (2) 3 *(Stojcev 21, Okic 36, 82)* 3879
Haugesund: (442) Kristiansen; Myrestam, Cvetinovic,
Bjorkkjaer (Andreassen 56), Ekpo (Nilsen 46); Anyora,
Haraldseid, Sema, Stolas (Gytkjaer 49); Bamberg,
Agdestein.
Sarajevo: (433) Bandovic; Tatomirovic, Puzigaca,
Berberovic■, Dupovac; Stojcev (Kovacevic 82), Duljevic
(Radovac 46), Cimirot; Velkoski, Okic, Bilbija (Protic
90).

IFK Gothenburg (0) 0
Gyori ETO (0) 1 *(Andric 68)* 6112
IFK Gothenburg: (442) Sandberg; Augustinsson, Jonsson,
Johansson A, Bjarsmyr; Johansson J, Smedberg-Dalence
(Soder 79), Mahlangu, Allansson; Vibe, Larsson (Daniel
Sobralense 69).
Gyori ETO: (442) Kocic; Lang, Svec, Wolfe, Dudas;
Kronaveter (Koltai 71), Volgyi, Andric, Patkai
(Windecker 75); Kamber, Rudolf■.

Inter Baku (0) 0
Elfsborg (1) 1 *(Holmen 45)* 3420
Inter Baku: (442) Lomaia; Salukvadze■, Amisulashvili,
Bocognano, Spicic; Georgievski, Mikel Alvaro,
Dashdemirov, Meza; Madrigal (Mammadov A 70
(Guseynpur 105)), Tskhadadze.
Elfsborg: (442) Stuhr-Ellegaard; Larsson (Klarstrom 71),
Mobaeck, Holmen, Svensson; Lundqvist, Claesson
(Beckmann 16), Hauger, Rohden; Nilsson, Frick (Prodell
110).
aet; Elfsborg won 4-3 on penalties.

Jagodina (0) 0
Cluj-Napoca (0) 1 *(Guima 81)* 6500
Jagodina: (433) Djuricic; Simac, Gasic, Filipovic, Djuric
(Martinovic 85); Susnjar (Stoicev 85), Mitosevic, Cvetkovic;
Milinkovic, Jakimovski (Lepovic 62), Arsenijevic.
Cluj-Napoca: (4411) Mario Felgueiras; Susic, Sulley,
Larie, Rada; Camora, Monroy, Deac (Jakolis 90), Costea
(Guima 69); Tade; Negrut (da Silva Fiel 85).

Koper (0) 0
Neftchi (1) 2 *(Seyidov 21, Carlos Cardoso 84)* 1800
Koper: (352) Radosevic; Hadzic (Lotric 89), Halilovic,
Blazic (Pucko 63); Guberac, Ivetic, Galesic, Crnigoj
(Gregoric 73), Palcic; Stromajer■, Covilo.
Neftchi: (4411) Stamenkovic; Bertucci (Gurbanov 68),
Carlos Cardoso, Yunuszade, Abdullayev (Masimov 72);
Flavinho, Wobay, Ramos, Caue; Seyidov; Nfor (Badalov
90).

Krasnodar (1) 5 *(Joaozinho 28, Laborde 65,*
Wanderson 67, 74 (pen), Burmistrov 76)
Sillamae Kalev (0) 0 12,200
Krasnodar: (451) Dykan; Sigurdsson, Martynovich,
Gazinski (Ahmedov 46), Wanderson; Pomerko, Bystrov
(Markov 68), Joaozinho (Laborde 57), Pereyra, Petrov;
Burmistrov.
Sillamae Kalev: (4411) Starodubtsev; Baguzis, Dudarev,
Sidorenkov, Cheminava; Vnukov (Ratnikov 70), Silich
(Kvasov 72), Mashichev (Novikov 83), Tjapkin;
Murikhin; Kabaev.

Lech Poznan (2) 3 *(Kedziora 33, Hamalainen 43,*
Kownacki 90)
Nomme Kalju (0) 0 20,263
Lech Poznan: (4411) Buric; Kedziora, Tralka, Pawlowski
(Keita 74), Lovrencsics; Ubiparip (Teodorczyk 85),
Jevtic, Hamalainen (Kownacki 68), Wolakiewicz;
Henriquez; Kaminski.
Nomme Kalju: (4411) Teles; Purg (Ainsalu 46), Barengrub,
Rodrigues, Mbu Alidor; Mool, Quintieri, Kallaste, Kirss
(Jevdokimov 68); Felipe Nunes (Ahjupera 75); Wakui.

Myllykosken Pallo-47 (0) 0
Dinamo Minsk (0) 0 1060
Myllykosken Pallo-47: (4231) Iiskola; Hoivala, Abdulahi
(Minkenen 62), Salmikivi, Sihvola; Bah, Soiri (Ristola
72); Koskinen, Motta (Dema 58), Aho; Nongotamba.
Dinamo Minsk: (442) Hutar; Voronkov (Udoji 67), Simovic,
Palitsevich, Nikolic; Diomande (Adamovic 46), Karpovich,
Veretilo, Figueredo (Nikitin 76); Stasevich, Kantsavy.

Omonia Nicosia (0) 0
Buducnost Podgorica (0) 0 11,661
Omonia Nicosia: (352) Moreira; Lobjanidze, Rodri,
Roberto; Grigalashvili (Pote 78), Alipio (Nuno Assis 69),
Cristovao (Alex Rubio 46), Kakubava, Kyriakou;
Serginho, Acquistapace.
Buducnost Podgorica: (4321) Ljubjanovic; Tomkovic,
Kopitovic, Ilincic (Burzanovic 86), Vujacic; Cetkovic,
Vukcevic, Rogosic; Raspopovic, Raicevic; Hocko.

Shakhter Karagandy (0) 3 *(Topcagic 46, Konysbayev 61,*
Murtazaev 90)
Atlantas (0) 0 12,200
Shakhter Karagandy: (442) Mokin; Dzidic, Maliy, Maslo,
Kirov; Simcevic, Vicius, Konysbayev, Pokrivac (Baizhanov
68); Topcagic (Murzoev 84), Finonchenko (Murtazaev 89).
Atlantas: (442) Galdikas; Joksas, Gnedojus, Jemelins,
Kazlauskas M; Bartkus, Kazlauskas D, Papsys,
Zukauskas (Rakauskas 80); Eliosius (Maksimov 62),
Krusnauskas (Baranauskas 72).

Shakhtyor Soligorsk (2) 5 *(Balanovich 9, Guruli 28, Osipenko 68, Yanush 81, Halyuza 90)*
Derry C (1) 1 *(Duffy 6)* 2900
Shakhtyor Soligorsk: (442) Kotenko; Yanushkevich, Kashewski, Yurevich, Kuzmyanok; Matsveychyk, Guruli (Ryas 73), Starhorodskyi, Balanovich (Lyavonchyk 85); Yanush, Osipenko (Halyuza 79).
Derry C: (442) Doherty; McBride, Ventre, Byrne, Barry; Molloy, McNamee, McEleney P, Dooley (Timlin 61); Patterson (Boyle 79), Duffy (Lowry 73).

Siroki Brijeg (0) 0
Mlada Boleslav (1) 4 *(Skalak 19, Duris 55, 85, Rosa 75)* 3500
Siroki Brijeg: (442) Soldo; Brekalo, Lastro, Markovic, Coric; Pehar (Kozulj 78), Zakaric, Landeka (Mihaljevic 61), Wagner; Peko (Ljubic 61), Maric.
Mlada Boleslav: (442) Hruska; Navratil, Rosa, Smejkal, Skalak; Stohanzl (Vukadinovic 61), Scuk, Sisler (Milla 70), Boril; Duris, Magera (Sultes 78).

SKN St Polten (1) 2 *(Segovia 6, 55)*
Botev Plovdiv (0) 0 4250
SKN St Polten: (442) Kostner; Huber, Wisio, Hofbauer (Ambichl 90), Grasegger; Holzmann, Stec, Parada, Kerschbaumer; Noel (Fucik 68), Segovia (Hartl 86).
Botev Plovdiv: (442) Stachowiak; Luchin, Filipov, Kolev, Ognyanov (Marin 77); Hristov, Jirsak, Chunchukov, Vasev (Curtean 59); Gamakov (Yusein 83), Tsvetkov.

Sligo R (1) 1 *(North 13)*
Rosenborg (1) 3 *(Helland 16, Jensen 48, 64)* 3792
Sligo R: (442) Rogers; Keane, McMillan, Spillane, Conneely; Cawley, O'Conor (Keating 70), Russell, Djilali (Ledwith 84); North, Gaynor (Maguire 70).
Rosenborg: (442) Hansen; Dorsin, Reginiussen, Strandberg, Jensen; Pedersen, Selnaes, Helland (Svensson 27), Riski; Mikkelsen, Soderlund (Sorloth 78).

Slovan Liberec (0) 3 *(Dubek 54, Delarge 81, Sural 90)*
MFK Kosice (0) 0 7100
Slovan Liberec: (433) Hroso; Karisik, Coufal, Pavelka, Sackey; Hamulak (Luckassen 75), Rajnoch, Sural; Fleisman, Dubek (Hadascok 84), Delarge (Kolar 87).
MFK Kosice: (433) Tofiloski; Sekulic, Ostojic, Skvasik (Haskic 68), Singlar (Novak 77); Diaby, Korijkov, Kavka; Viazanko (Pacinda 67), Bukata, Basista.

Spartak Trnava (2) 3 *(Janecka 4, 43, Sabo 60 (pen))*
Zestafoni (0) 0 2940
Spartak Trnava: (442) Rusov; Siva, Janecka (Chovanec 84), Mikovic (Mikinic 80), Vlasko; Bortel, Casado, Toth, Conka; Sabo, Schranz (Spalek 76).
Zestafoni: (442) Pavlovic; Gongadze (Grigalashvili 72), Gelashvili, Kukhianidze, Dvali (Gvalia 46); Sharikadze, Guruli, Dolidze, Santos; Chelidze, Getsadze (Pantsulaia 53).

St Johnstone (1) 1 *(May 23 (pen))*
Luzern (0) 1 *(Schneuwly 59)* 8486
St Johnstone: (442) Mannus; Mackay, Wright, Miller (Scobbie 114), Easton; Millar, Wotherspoon (Caddis 97), Brown, MacLean; May, O'Halloran (Croft 73).
Luzern: (442) Zibung; Rogulj, Lustenberger, Affolter, Sarr; Freuler, Bozanic (Wiss 15), Hyka (Thiesson 91), Winter; Hochstrasser (Schneuwly 54), Lezcano.
aet; St Johnstone won 5-4 on penalties.

Stjarnan (1) 3 *(Finsen 37 (pen), Toft 85, Johannsson 113)*
Motherwell (1) 2 *(Hammell 11, Ainsworth 66)* 1021
Stjarnan: (4231) Jonsson; Vemmelund, Rauschenberg, Laxdal D, Arnason; Johannsson, Praest; Bjorgvinsson (Palsson 105), Punyed, Finsen; Gunnarson (Toft 25 (Aegisson 107)).
Motherwell: (442) Twardzik; Reid, Ramsden, McManus, Hammell; Ainsworth (Francis-Angol 77), Carswell (Leitch 95), Lasley, Vigurs; Law (Kerr 76), Sutton.
aet.

Tromso (0) 1 *(Wangberg 51)*
Vikingur (0) 2 *(Hansen B 60, Hansson 77)* 1281
Tromso: (451) Lekstrom; Moldskred (Espejord 46), Koppinen, Drage, Johansen J[■]; Andersen, Johnsen (Bendiksen 46), Johansen R, Frantzen, Wangberg; Nilsen (Norbye 46).

Vikingur: (451) Turi; Olsen A (Djordjevic 63), Jacobsen H, Gregersen, Olsen S (Hansen H 78); Vatnhamar S (Sorensen 90), Hansson, Hansen B, Jacobsen E, Djurhuus; Justinussen.

Vaduz (0) 0
Ruch Chorzow (0) 0 2036
Vaduz: (442) Jehle; Grippo, Lang (Schurpf 59), Sutter, Burgmeier (Cecchini 68); Pak, Untersee, Kryeziu (Abbeglen 83), Stahel; Neumayr, Muntwiler[■].
Ruch Chorzow: (442) Kaminski; Stawarczyk, Dziwniel (Konczkowski 90), Surma, Szewczyk (Efir 66); Kowalski (Wlodyka 89), Kuswik, Starzynski, Babiarz; Malinowski, Helik.

Vojvodina (1) 3 *(Ivanic 17, Alivodic 52, Stojanovic 68)*
Trencin (0) 0 5414
Vojvodina: (451) Jovanic; Radoja, Ivanic, Makaric (Grgic 66), Pekaric; Alivodic, Puskaric, Pankov, Nastic, Poletanovic; Stojanovic.
Trencin: (433) Volesak; Rundic, Misak (Madu 46), Kubik (Mondek 55), Jairo (Hajradinovic 11); Holubek, Cogley, Ramon; Moses, Lobotka, Klescik.

Zawisza Bydgoszcz (0) 1 *(Petasz 52)*
Zulte Waregem (1) 3 *(Plet 1, Aneke 48, Skulason 76)* 5997
Zawisza Bydgoszcz: (451) Sandomierski; Araujo, Petasz, Vasconcelos[■], Alvarinho; Nawotczynski (Micael 53), Ziajka, Drygas (Wojcicki 73), Strak, Luis; Wagner (Kadu 58).
Zulte Waregem: (451) Bostyn; Cissako (Mendy 34), Colpaert, Verboom, Plet; N'Diaye, Skulason, Conte (Trajkovski 73), D'Haene, Aneke; Bongonda (Sylla 64).

Zimbru Chisinau (0) 0
CSKA Sofia (0) 0 8505
Zimbru Chisinau: (442) Rusu; Burghiu, Erhan, Dedov, Klimovich (Potirniche 60); Pavlyuchek, Amani (Alexeev 46), Vremea, Grossu; Cheptine (Spataru 59), Jardan.
CSKA Sofia: (442) Divis; Tunchev, Krachunov, Silva, Galchev (Joachim 51); Kamburov (Bus 51), Popov, Vasilev (Supusepa 42), Bergonsi[■]; Marquinhos, Stoyanov.
Zimbru Chisinau won on away goals.

Zorya Luhansk (0) 2 *(Ignjatijevic 74, Budkivskiy 87)*
Laci (0) 1 *(Nimani 85)* 4200
Zorya Luhansk: (442) Shevchenko; Chaykovsky, Kamenyuka, Lipartia (Ljubenovic 46), Vernydub; Yarmash, Ignjatijevic, Budkivskiy, Petryak (Karavayev 61); Gritsay (Beliy 65), Khomchenovskiy.
Laci: (442) Vujadinovic; Ofoyen, Cela (Sefgjinaj 69), Sheta, Adeniyi (Veliaj 81); Sefa, Vucaj, Buljan, Nimani (Ndreca 90); Teqja, Zefi.

THIRD QUALIFYING ROUND FIRST LEG

Thursday, 31 July 2014
Astana (1) 1 *(Nuserbaev 42)*
AIK Solna (1) 1 *(Bahoui 8)* 13,500
Astana: (442) Eric; Akhnetov, Dmitrenko, Beissebekov, Postnikov; Kethevoama, Zhukov (Twumasi 46), Essame, Dzholchiev (Muzhikov 82); Canas, Nuserbaev.
AIK Solna: (3142) Carlgren; Lorentzson, Karlsson, Johansson; Milosevic; Pavey, Moro, Saletros, Karikari; Goitom, Bahoui.

Astra Giurgiu (1) 3 *(Fatai 4, 74, 81)*
Slovan Liberec (0) 0 5000
Astra Giurgiu: (4411) Lung Jr; Pliatsikas, Gaman, Ben Youssef, Junior Morais; Enache (Rus 85), Yahaya, Laban, William Amorim (Cristescu 87); Budescu; Fatai (Bukari 82).
Slovan Liberec: (433) Hroso; Coufal, Karisik (Pimpara 63), Rajnoch, Fleisman; Pavelka, Sackey, Delarge (Frydek 75); Sural, Luckassen (Hamulak 71), Dubek.

Brommapojkarna (0) 0
Torino (1) 3 *(Larrondo 45 (pen), 53, Barreto 58)* 2043
Brommapojkarna: (442) Blazevic; Segerstrom[■], Bjorkstrom, Falkenborn, Une-Larsson; Jonsson, Karlstrom, Petrovic (Albornoz 63), Martinsson-Ngouali (Asbrink 76); Rexhepi (Sandberg-Magnusson 63), Barkroth.

Torino: (442) Padelli; Molinaro, Moretti, Glik, Bovo; El Kaddouri (Ruben Perez 84), Vives*, Nocerino, Vesovic (Benassi 74); Larrondo, Barreto (Martinez 70).

Club Brugge (2) 3 *(Duarte 14, Castillo 30, Vazquez 63)*
Brondby (0) 0 24,217
Club Brugge: (442) Ryan; Duarte, De Bock, Engels, Simons; Menegazzo, Vazquez (Jorgensen 89), Rafaelov (Storm 72), Lestienne; Meunier, Castillo (Sobota 83).
Brondby: (442) Hradecky; Almeback, Semb Berge, Albrechtsen, Durmisi; Ornskov Nielsen (Norgaard 86), Kahlenberg, Thygesen (Rashani 76), Phiri; Makienok Christoffersen, Hasani (Holst 85).

Dinamo Minsk (0) 1 *(Adamovic 54)*
Cluj-Napoca (0) 0 5281
Dinamo Minsk: (451) Hutar; Zaleski (Karpovich 46), Palitsevich, Bangura, Veretilo; Udoji, Voronkov (Figueredo 62), Simovic, Nikolic, Stasevich; Adamovic.
Cluj-Napoca: (4411) Mario Felgueiras; Susic, Larie, Rada, Camora; Deac (Japones 76), Sulley, Negrut (Guima 59), Monroy; Costea (Jakolis 55); Tade.

Diosgyor (0) 1 *(Bacsa 49)*
Krasnodar (2) 5 *(Ari 28, Ahmedov 40, Pereyra 51, Joaozinho 88 (pen), Bystrov 90)* 4000
Diosgyor: (442) Antal (Rados 80); Husic, Kadar, William, Debreceni (Grumic 46); Nemeth, Eperjesi (Bognar 46), Egerszegi, Elek; Gosztonyi, Bacsa.
Krasnodar: (4231) Sinitsyn; Martynovich, Jedrzejczyk, Kaleshin, Sigurdsson; Gazinski, Ahmedov; Laborde (Bystrov 58), Joaozinho, Pereyra (Pomerko 81); Ari (Wanderson 58).

Dynamo Moscow (0) 1 *(Kuranyi 71)*
Ironi Kiryat Shmona (0) 1 *(Kola 63)* 10,000
Dynamo Moscow: (4411) Gabulov; Manolev, Samba, Granat, Buttner; Ionov, Vainqueur, Denisov, Dzsudzsak; Noboa (Kokorin 54); Kuranyi.
Ironi Kiryat Shmona: (4231) Haimov; Kassio, Tzedek, Dilmoni, Elkayami; Brown, Manga (Rochet 71); Panka, Kahat, Abed (Mizrachi 85); Kola (Mayo 90).

Elfsborg (0) 4 *(Holmen 55 (pen), Frick 70, Rohden 81, Hedlund 89 (pen))*
FH Hafnarfjordur (0) 1 *(Lennon 62)* 3889
Elfsborg: (433) Stuhr-Ellegaard; Larsson, Mobaeck, Holmen, Lundqvist; Rohden, Svensson, Claesson; Beckmann (Hedlund 36), Prodell (Frick 68), Nilsson.
FH Hafnarfjordur: (451) Oskarsson R; Jonsson, Vidarsson P, Doumbia, Hendrickx; Snorrason, Runarsson (Hewson 79), Palsson, Vidarsson D, Gudnason (Oskarsson I 79); Lennon.

Grodig (0) 1 *(Tomi Correa 89)*
Zimbru Chisinau (1) 2 *(Alexeev 35, Handle 59 (og))* 1926
Grodig: (442) Stankovic; Karner, Strobl (Martschinko 63), Maak, Handle; Huspek, Nutz (Djuric 74), Boller (Schutz 63), Brauer; Tomi Correa, Reyna.
Zimbru Chisinau: (442) Rusu; Erhan, Potirniche, Pavlyuchek, Vremea; Jardan, Burghiu, Pascenco (Amani 78), Cheptine (Sfataru 54); Dedov (Grossu 63), Alexeev.

IFK Gothenburg (0) 0
Rio Ave (1) 1 *(Koka 22)* 7137
IFK Gothenburg: (442) Alvbage; Johansson A (Salomonsson 80), Bjarsmyr, Jonsson, Augustinsson; Svensson, Johansson J (Engvall 66), Vibe, Mahlangu; Larsson, Smedberg-Dalence (Daniel Sobralense 66).
Rio Ave: (433) Cassio; Lionn, Marcelo, Gouano, Tiago Pinto; Tarantini, Pedro Moreira, Filipe Augusto (Diego Lopes 75); Ukra (Vilas Boas 88), Koka, Del Valle (Boateng 64).

Kardemir Karabukspor (0) 0
Rosenborg (0) 0 4400
Kardemir Karabukspor: (4411) Waterman; Gungor, Mabiala, Ozgenc, Kayhan; Kas, Incedemir, Traore (Ozer 69), Ozek; Sow; Kumbela (Ayik 76).
Rosenborg: (433) Hansen; Dorsin, Reginiussen, Strandberg (Ronning 84), Skjelvik; Mikkelsen, Jensen, Pedersen; Selnaes, Diskerud (Berntsen 84), Riski.

Mainz 05 (1) 1 *(Okazaki 45)*
Asteras Tripolis (0) 0 18,287
Mainz 05: (4231) Karius; Jara, Noveski, Bell, Park (Diaz 70); Moritz, Malli; Geis, Koo (Zimling 77), Baumgartlinger (Brosinski 61); Okazaki.
Asteras Tripolis: (442) Theodoropoulos; Panteliadis, Lluy, Goian, Munafo (Tsokanis 71); Rolle (Sankare 64), Zisopoulos, Kourbelis, De Blasis; Mazza, Badibanga (Kitoko 81).

Mlada Boleslav (0) 1 *(Rosa 66)*
Lyon (2) 4 *(Yattara 9, 47, Gonalons 36, Umtiti 67)* 4800
Mlada Boleslav: (433) Hruska; Boril, Navratil, Smejkal, Rosa; Milla, Scuk, Stohanzl (Vukadinovic 60); Skalak, Magera (Sultes 46), Duris (Sisler 71).
Lyon: (442) Lopes; Jallet, Bisevac, Kone (Bedimo 71), Umtiti; Gonalons, Ferri, Mvuemba, Malbranque (Fekir 64); Lacazette, Yattara (Benzia 70).

Neftchi (0) 0
Chikhura Sachkhere (0) 0 8500
Neftchi: (433) Stamenkovic; Carlos Cardoso, Yunuszade, Bertucci, Abdullayev (Masimov 67); Flavinho, Wobay, Ramos; Caue, Seyidov (Imamverdiyev 82), Nfor (Qurbanov 72).
Chikhura Sachkhere: (442) Kvilitaia; Kashia, Rekhviashvili, Jigauri, Dekanoidze (Chikvaidze 90); Koripadze (Tchelidze 81), Kimadze, Datunaishvili, Odikadze; Gabedava, Kutchukhidze.

Omonia Nicosia (2) 3 *(Cristovao 9, 57, Pote 14)*
Metalurg Skopje (0) 0 15,000
Omonia Nicosia: (343) Moreira; Lobjanidze, Stepanov, Acquistapace; Rodri, Cristovao, Nuno Assis (Grigalashvili 59), Serginho (Fylaktou 72); Fofana (Alex Rubio 64), Pote, Roberto.
Metalurg Skopje: (451) Efremov; Krstev, Ristovski (Naumovski 58), Gjorgievski, Leskaroski; Dalceski, Mitrev (Tanturovski 65), Radeski, Angelov (Dodevski 29), Stojanovski; Simonovski.

Petrolul Ploiesti (0) 1 *(Mutu 77)*
Viktoria Plzen (0) 1 *(Kolar 90)* 11,244
Petrolul Ploiesti: (442) Pecanha; Geraldo Alves, Gerson Guimaraes, Fanchone, Alcenat; Hoban, Teixeira, De Lucas, Tamuz (Nkoyi 87); Nepomuceno (Priso 72), Albin (Mutu 76).
Viktoria Plzen: (442) Kozacik; Hubnik, Limbersky, Reznik, Prochazka; Pilar (Kovarik 83), Horava (Kolar 86), Horvath, Petrzela (Hrosovsky 75); Vanek, Bakos.

PSV Eindhoven (0) 1 *(De Jong 56)*
SKN St Polten (0) 0 35,000
PSV Eindhoven: (442) Zoet; Bruma, Brenet, Tamata, Hendrix; Maher, Ritzmaier (Vloet 79), Hiljemark, De Jong; Narsingh (Jozefzoon* 72), Locadia.
SKN St Polten: (442) Kostner; Huber, Wisio, Grasegger, Holzmann (Ambichl 65); Stec, Hofbauer, Parada, Kerschbaumer; Fucik (Hartl 46), Segovia (Noel 76).

Real Sociedad (0) 2 *(Zurutuza 53, Canales 68)*
Aberdeen (0) 0 15,000
Real Sociedad: (433) Zubikarai; Zaldua, Elustondo, Martinez, De la Bella; Pardo (Granero 83), Markel, Zurutuza; Finnbogason, Prieto (Agirretxe 74), Castro (Canales 64).
Aberdeen: (352) Langfield; Logan, Anderson, Reynolds; Jack, Flood, Pawlett (Considine 62), Robson (Low 71), Hayes; McGinn, Rooney (Goodwillie 71).

RNK Split (1) 2 *(Rog 24, Belle 49)*
Chornomorets Odesa (0) 0 2000
RNK Split: (442) Vukovic; Glavina (Erceg 74), Radotic, Rugasevic, Galovic; Rog, Glumac, Dujmovic, Vidovic; Bilic (Roce 88), Belle (Bagaric 65).
Chornomorets Odesa: (442) Bezotosny; Shinder (Didenko 44), Opanasenko, Teikeu, Kutas; Kovalchuk (Grechyshkin 76), Sivakov, Gai, Arzhanov; Fomin, Balashov (Danchenko 44).

Ruch Chorzow (0) 0
Esbjerg (0) 0 6000
Ruch Chorzow: (442) Kaminski; Helik, Malinowski, Stawarczyk, Dziwniel; Zienczuk, Surma, Babiarz, Kowalski (Efir 83); Kuswik (Szewczyk 75), Starzynski.
Esbjerg: (442) Dubravka; Laursen, Berthel Askou, Jakobsen, Stenderup (Gomes 79); Andreasen (Lekven 46), Andersen (Ankersen 63), Nielsen, Fellah; Pusic, van Buren.

Sarajevo (1) 1 *(Puzigaca 26)*
Atromitos (1) 2 *(Fitanidis 11, Nastos 74)* 15,000
Sarajevo: (442) Bandovic; Baric, Tatomirovic, Dupovac, Puzigaca; Cimirot, Radovac (Kovacevic 88), Stojcev, Okic (Puric 81); Velkoski, Bilbija (Duljevic 71).
Atromitos: (442) Cennamo; Lazaridis, Tavlaridis, Fitanidis, Nastos; Giannoulis, Dimoutsos (Mpalas 90), Pitu, Brito (Fabio 68); Napoleoni (Tatos 62), Karamanos.

Shakhter Karagandy (2) 4 *(Topcagic 10, Finonchenko 21, Dzidic 70, Zhanglyshbay 90)*
Hajduk Split (1) 2 *(Gotal 19, Caktas 78 (pen))* 13,000
Shakhter Karagandy: (541) Mokin; Poryvaev, Maslo, Dzidic, Kirov, Konysbayev; Maliy, Pokrivac (Baizhanov 60), Vicius, Finonchenko (Murzoev 85); Topcagic (Zhanglyshbay 83).
Hajduk Split: (442) Stipica; Mikanovic, Milic, Jozinovic, Maloca; Andjelkovic, Vlasic (Maloku 88), Caktas, Bradaric; Gotal, Kouassi (Bencun 71).

St Johnstone (0) 1 *(Mackay 90)*
Spartak Trnava (1) 2 *(Schranz 34, 64)* 7001
St Johnstone: (451) Mannus; Miller, Mackay, Wright, Easton; Brown, Millar (McDonald 29), Croft, Wotherspoon, O'Halloran (Kane 76); MacLean.
Spartak Trnava: (4231) Rusov; Siva, Bortel, Toth, Conka; Janecka, Sabo; Jose Casado, Schranz (Mikinic 88), Vlasko (Chovanec 78); Mikovic (Vyskocil 61).

Stjarnan (0) 1 *(Toft 48)*
Lech Poznan (0) 0 1021
Stjarnan: (442) Jonsson; Vemmelund, Laxdal D, Arnason, Rauschenberg; Praest, Punyed (Aegisson 90), Johannsson, Bjorgvinsson (Laxdal J 84); Finsen, Toft.
Lech Poznan: (442) Buric; Kedziora, Wolakiewicz, Henriquez, Kaminski; Tralka, Jevtic, Hamalainen (Keita 70), Pawlowski; Lovrencsics (Douglas 87), Ubiparip.

Trencin (0) 0
Hull C (0) 0 8254
Trencin: (451) Volesak; Cogley, Ramon, Klescik, Rundic; Kubik (Malek 67), Hajradinovic (Opatovsky 87), Lobotka, Misak (Mondek 83), Moses; Holubek.
Hull C: (3511) McGregor; Chester, Davies, Bruce; Elmohamady, Meyler (Snodgrass 65), Huddlestone, Livermore, Rosenior; Aluko (Ince 65); Long (Jelavic 86).

Vikingur (1) 1 *(Hansson 35)*
Rijeka (2) 5 *(Leskovic 14, Kvrzic 45, 76, Jahovic 51, Kramaric 81 (pen))* 1203
Vikingur: (442) Turi; Olsen A (Sorensen 76), Gregersen, Hansen B, Djurhuus (Djordjevic 45); Jacobsen E, Jacobsen H, Olsen S, Vatnhamar S; Hansson (Hansen H 64), Justinussen.
Rijeka: (442) Vargic; Mitrovic, Leovac, Tomecak, Leskovic; Jajalo (Zlomislic 68), Kvrzic, Brezovec, Jugovic (Goodness 64); Jahovic, Kramaric (Canadija 82).

Young Boys (0) 1 *(Nuzzolo 58)*
Ermis Aradippou (0) 0 7346
Young Boys: (4231) Mvogo; Sutter, Wuthrich, Rochat, Lecjaks; Costanzo, Gajic; Steffen (Zarate 70), Kubo (Affum 23), Nuzzolo; Frey (Nikci 87).
Ermis Aradippou: (4411) Bogatinov; Belusso, Ouon (Paulinho 46), Pina, China; Packer, Zarkovic, Taralidis, Palazuelos; Moran (Iluridze 66); Axente (Araba 78).

Zorya Luhansk (0) 1 *(Kamenyuka 62)*
Molde (0) 1 *(Svendsen 89)* 3250
Zorya Luhansk: (433) Santini; Vernydub, Ignjatijevic, Gritsay, Beliy; Chaykovsky, Kamenyuka, Khomchenovskiy; Khudzik (Malinovsky 59), Karavayev (Pysko 76), Budkivskiy (Ljubenovic 46).

Molde: (433) Nyland; Ruben Grabrielsen, Forren, Toivio, Berg Hestad; Singh, Agnaldo (Linnes 84), Diouf (Svendsen 68); Flo, Elyounoussi, Chukwa (Hoiland 75).

Zulte Waregem (1) 2 *(Plet 40, Conte 75)*
Shakhtyor Soligorsk (3) 5 *(Galyuza 4, Matsveychyk 12, Starhorodskyi 45, Yanush 78, Guruli 90)* 4474
Zulte Waregem: (4411) Bossut; Mendy (Bongonda 24), D'Haene, Colpaert, Ekangamene (Trajkovski 77); Conte, Skulason, N'Diaye (Isci 25), Sylla; Aneke; Plet**.
Shakhtyor Soligorsk: (541) Kotenko; Matsveychyk, Kuzmyanok (Vasilewski 45), Yanushkevich, Kashewski, Yurevich; Balanovich, Starhorodskyi, Galyuza, Ryas (Guruli 69); Osipenko (Yanush 61).

THIRD QUALIFYING ROUND SECOND LEG

Thursday, 7 August 2014
Aberdeen (1) 2 *(Pawlett 44, Reynolds 57)*
Real Sociedad (1) 3 *(Prieto 28, 86 (pen), Markel 90)* 17,676
Aberdeen: (433) Langfield; Logan, Reynolds, Anderson, Considine (Low 71); Flood, Jack, Hayes; McGinn, Goodwillie (Taylor 82), Pawlett (Rooney 65).
Real Sociedad: (4141) Zubikarai; Zaldua, Markel, Elustondo, De la Bella; Prieto; Castro (Canales 64), Zurutuza (Granero 42), Pardo, Martinez; Finnbogason (Agirretxe 58).

AIK Solna (0) 0
Astana (1) 3 *(Kethevoama 36, Shomko 54, Dzholchiev 71)* 12,314
AIK Solna: (442) Carlgren; Lorentzson (Atakora 75), Karlsson, Milosevic, Johansson; Lundholm, Moro, Borges**, Saletros (Igboananike 46); Goitom (Nikolic 75), Karikari.
Astana: (343) Eric; Dmitrenko, Postnikov, Anicic; Beissebekov, Zhukov, Essame, Shomko; Dzholchiev (Kurdov 85), Nuserbaev (Twumasi 63), Kethevoama (Muzhikov 87).

Asteras Tripolis (1) 3 *(De Blasis 30, Mazza 68, 86)*
Mainz 05 (1) 1 *(Koo 39)* 3659
Asteras Tripolis: (442) Theodoropoulos; Panteliadis (Sankare 83), Goian, Munafo (Bakasetas 59), Rolle; Zisopoulos, Kourbelis, Lluy, De Blasis; Mazza, Badibanga (Usero 28).
Mainz 05: (442) Karius; Noveski, Bell, Brosinski, Park (Jara 73); Moritz, Malli (Soto 85), Geis, Koo (Diaz 69); Baumgartlinger, Okazaki.

Atromitos (0) 0 *(Tavlaridis 86)*
Sarajevo (1) 3 *(Duljevic 24, Bilbija 81, 105)* 2300
Atromitos: (442) Cennamo; Tavlaridis, Fitanidis, Nastos (Napoleoni 46); Giannoulis; Lazaridis, Dimoutsos, Pitu (Mpalas 75), Brito; Fabio (Tatos 46), Karamanos.
Sarajevo: (442) Bandovic; Baric (Protic 99), Tatomirovic, Dupovac, Puzigaca; Stojcev, Duljevic, Cimirot, Radovac (Kovacevic 99); Okic (Bilbija 69), Velkoski.
aet.

Brondby (0) 0
Club Brugge (2) 2 *(Castillo 38, Menegazzo 45)* 10,046
Brondby: (442) Hradecky; Semb Berge (Albrechtsen 46), Holst, Durmisi, Dumic; Ornskov Nielsen, Kahlenberg (Nunez 74), Phiri, Szymanowski; Rashani (Thygesen 63), Makienok Christoffersen.
Club Brugge: (442) Ryan; De Fauw, Duarte (Mechele 46), De Bock, Engels; Simons, Menegazzo, Jorgensen (Rafaelov 61), Sobota; Castillo (Lestienne 73), Storm.

Chikhura Sachkhere (1) 2 *(Gabedava 29, 50)*
Neftchi (3) 3 *(Nfor 16, 27, 38)* 21,359
Chikhura Sachkhere: (442) Kvilitaia; Kimadze, Kashia, Rekhviashvili, Jigauri; Koripadze (Mumladze 79), Datunaishvili, Odikadze, Gabedava; Kutchukhidze, Dekanoidze.
Neftchi: (442) Stamenkovic; Carlos Cardoso, Yunuszade, Bertucci, Abdullayev (Masimov 72); Flavinho, Wobay (Imamverdiyev 83), Ramos, Caue; Seyidov (Isayev 64), Nfor.

Chornomorets Odesa (0) 0
RNK Split (0) 0 11,422

Chornomorets Odesa: (4231) Bezotosny; Zubeyko (Grechyshkin 89), Teikeu, Sivakov, Slinkin; Gai, Kovalchuk (Kabayev 89); Arzhanov, Didenko (Nazarenko 83), Shinder; Fomin.
RNK Split: (442) Vukovic; Radotic (Ibriks 82), Galovic, Glumac, Glavina; Belle, Vidovic, Dujmovic, Roce (Erceg 71); Rog, Bilic (Bagaric 82).

Cluj-Napoca (0) 0
Dinamo Minsk (0) 2 *(Stasevich 71, Udoji 81 (pen))* 5137

Cluj-Napoca: (442) Mario Felgueiras; Susic, Larie, Rada■, Camora; Monroy, Sulley, Negrut (Guima 46), Deac; Costea (Jazvic 46), Tade (Ivanovski 67).
Dinamo Minsk: (442) Hutar; Palitsevich, Karpovich, Bangura, Veretilo; Voronkov (Diomande 5), Simovic, Nikolic, Udoji; Stasevich (Kantsavy 90), Adamovic (Figueredo 84).

Ermis Aradippou (0) 0
Young Boys (1) 2 *(Steffen 36, Frey 65)* 1000

Ermis Aradippou: (4141) Bogatinov; Zarkovic (Papathanasiou 46), Taralidis (Demetriou 66), Ouon, Pina; Palazuelos; Paulinho■, Packer, Belusso, China; Axente (Iluridze 76).
Young Boys: (451) Mvogo; Sutter (Affum 66), Wuthrich, Rochat, Lecjaks; Nuzzolo, Costanzo, Sanogo, Gajic (Bertone 62), Steffen (Nikci 58); Frey.

Esbjerg (1) 2 *(Nielsen 29, Pusic 85)*
Ruch Chorzow (1) 2 *(Starzynski 13 (pen), Surma 90)* 7008

Esbjerg: (442) Dubravka; Jakobsen, Stenderup (Laursen 72), Gomes, Knudsen; Lekven (Rasmussen 64), Ankersen, Fellah, Nielsen (Andersen 64); van Buren, Pusic.
Ruch Chorzow: (442) Kaminski; Stawarczyk, Dziwniel (Kus 87), Helik, Surma; Zienczuk, Kowalski, Starzynski, Babiarz; Malinowski, Kuswik (Efir 68).
Ruch Chorzow won on away goals.

FH Hafnarfjordur (1) 2 *(Gudnason 17, Bjornsson 76)*
Elfsborg (0) 1 *(Beckmann 90)* 1543

FH Hafnarfjordur: (433) Oskarsson R; Vidarsson P, Doumbia, Hendrickx, Palsson (Bjornsson 68); Vidarsson D, Runarsson (Hewson 85), Gudnason; Snorrason (Oskarsson I 74), Jonsson, Lennon.
Elfsborg: (433) Stuhr-Ellegaard; Jonsson (Mobaeck 25), Holmen, Klarstrom, Hedlund (Zeneli 61); Lundqvist, Hauger, Rohden; Beckmann, Claesson, Frick (Larsson 85).

Hajduk Split (2) 3 *(Susic 14, Maglica 34, Gotal 90)*
Shakhter Karagandy (0) 0 28,000

Hajduk Split: (442) Kalinic; Milic (Nizic 66), Maloca, Milovic, Vrsajevic (Vasilj 73); Andjelkovic, Vlasic (Kouassi 82), Caktas, Susic; Maglica, Gotal.
Shakhter Karagandy: (442) Mokin; Simcevic, Kirov, Poryvaev (Murtazaev 53), Dzidic; Maslo (Zhanglyshbay 60), Maliy, Vicius, Konysbayev; Pokrivac, Topcagic.

Hull C (1) 2 *(Elmohamady 27, Aluko 80)*
Trencin (1) 1 *(Malek 2)* 21,156

Hull C: (352) McGregor; Bruce (Ince 65), Chester, Davies; Elmohamady, Huddlestone, Snodgrass, Livermore, Brady (Rosenior 56); Long (Aluko 74), Sagbo.
Trencin: (451) Volesak; Cogley, Ramon, Klescik, Malek; Kubik, Hajradinovic (Opatovsky 74), Lobotka, Misak (Mondek 81), Moses (Rundic 90); Holubeka.

Ironi Kiryat Shmona (1) 1 *(Kahat 11)*
Dynamo Moscow (2) 2 *(Kuranyi 22 (pen), Ionov 30)* 250

Ironi Kiryat Shmona: (4231) Haimov; Elkayami, Kassio, Tzedek, Dilmoni (Pinas 72); Panka (Mizrachi 74), Brown; Manga, Kahat, Abed (Rochet 84); Kola.
Dynamo Moscow: (442) Berezovsky; Kozlov, Samba, Granat, Buttner; Ionov (Smolov 62), Vainqueur, Denisov, Dzsudzsak (Zhirkov 68); Kokorin, Kuranyi (Noboa 58).

Krasnodar (1) 3 *(Konate 30, 55, Ari 86)*
Diosgyor (0) 0 8800

Krasnodar: (442) Sinitsyn; Markov, Martynovich, Granqvist, Izmailov; Pomerko, Laborde (Joaozinho 61), Petrov, Wanderson (Ari 61); Burmistrov, Konate (Ageev 76).
Diosgyor: (433) Rados; Kadar, Okuka, Debreceni, Nemeth; Egerszegi (Bognar 39), Bori, Takacs; Gosztonyi (Csirszki 70), Nikhazi, Marjanovic (Bacsa 70).

Lech Poznan (0) 0
Stjarnan (0) 0 35,000

Lech Poznan: (4411) Kotorowski; Kedziora (Kownacki 76), Wolakiewicz, Kaminski, Henriquez; Pawlowski, Jevtic, Tralka, Keita (Lovrencsics 59); Hamalainen (Teodorczyk 54); Ubiparip.
Stjarnan: (3200) Jonsson; Vemmelund, Rauschenberg, Laxdal D, Arnason; Praest (Runarsson 74), Johannsson; Bjorgvinsson (Laxdal J 79), Punyed, Finsen; Toft (Aegisson 22).

Lyon (0) 2 *(Lacazette 56, N'Jie 89)*
Mlada Boleslav (0) 1 *(Milla 72 (pen))* 22,717

Lyon: (442) Lopes; Bedimo (Kone 36), Rose (Ferri 53), Umtiti, Malbranque; Fekir, Jallet, Gonalons, Tolisso; Lacazette (N'Jie 73), Benzia.
Mlada Boleslav: (442) Hruska; Boril, Navratil, Rosa (Magera 70), Smejkal; Milla, Stohanzl, Scuk, Sisler; Duris (Sultes 68), Skalak (Bartl 79).

Metalurg Skopje (0) 0
Omonia Nicosia (0) 1 *(Nuno Assis 54)* 1000

Metalurg Skopje: (4231) Efremov; Ristovski, Leskaroski, Dodevski, Gjorgievski; Mitrev, Mitrov (Krstev 46); Tanturovski (Radeski 46), Dalceski, Stojanovski; Angelov (Chavoli 66).
Omonia Nicosia: (4231) Moreira; Kyriakou (Nuno Assis 46), Stepanov, Acquistapace, Lobjanidze; Serginho (Roushias 64), Rodri; Fofana (Alex Rubio 74), Grigalashvili, Cristovao; Pote.

Molde (1) 1 *(Gulbrandsen 43)*
Zorya Luhansk (1) 2 *(Kamenyuka 2, Forren 89 (og))* 4438

Molde: (442) Nyland; Linnes, Toivio, Forren, Flo; Diouf (Elyounoussi 63), Singh, Berg Hestad, Mostrom (Agnaldo 90); Gulbrandsen (Hoiland 73), Chukwa.
Zorya Luhansk: (442) Shevchenko; Malyshev (Malinovsky 46), Vernydub, Ignjatijevic, Gritsay; Beliy, Kamenyuka, Ljubenovic (Lipartia 90), Khomchenovskiy; Karavayev, Budkivskiy (Khudzik 60).

Rijeka (1) 4 *(Jahovic 39, 49, 64, Jacobsen E 77 (og))*
Vikingur (0) 0 5036

Rijeka: (442) Prskalo; Mitrovic, Samardzic, Bertosa, Sharbini; Jajalo (Canadija 46), Kvrzic (Kramaric 46), Boras, Zlomislic (Jugovic 71); Jahovic, Goodness.
Vikingur: (442) Turi; Djurhuus, Gregersen, Hansen B, Jacobsen E; Jacobsen H, Olsen S, Vatnhamar S, Hansson (Hansen H 80); Djordjevic (Sorensen 81), Justinussen (Olsen A 71).

Rio Ave (0) 0
IFK Gothenburg (0) 0 7000

Rio Ave: (451) Cassio; Lionn, Gouano, Marcelo, Tiago Pinto; Ukra (Roderick Miranda 90), Tarantini, Pedro Moreira, Filipe Augusto (Wakaso 86), Del Valle; Koka (Boateng 79).
IFK Gothenburg: (4231) Alvbage; Augustinsson, Bjarsmyr, Waehler, Johansson A (Allansson 76); Mahlangu, Svensson; Vibe, Johansson J, Larsson; Soder (Daniel Sobralense 60).

Rosenborg (1) 1 *(Helland 8)*
Kardemir Karabukspor (1) 1 *(Ozmert 35)* 6313

Rosenborg: (433) Hansen; Dorsin, Reginiussen, Strandberg, Jensen; Selnaes, Skjelvik (Sorloth 89), Svensson; Diskerud (Pedersen 75), Riski (Soderlund 60), Helland.
Kardemir Karabukspor: (433) Waterman; Gungor, Mabiala, Ozgenc, Kayhan; Traore (Kas 66), Incedemir, Ozmert (Aydin 81); Ozek, Sow, Kumbela (Akca 86).
Kardemir Karabukspor won on away goals.

Shakhtyor Soligorsk (2) 2 *(Balanovich 7, 42)*
Zulte Waregem (1) 2 *(Sylla 41, 74)*   4200
Shakhtyor Soligorsk: (442) Kotenko; Galyuza, Yanushkevich, Kashewski, Yurevich; Lyavonchyk, Balanovich (Guruli 66), Matsveychyk, Starhorodskyi (Vasilewski 71); Ryas, Osipenko (Yanush 66).
Zulte Waregem: (442) Bossut; Aneke (Caceres 69), Conte (Hazard 69), D'Haene, Tiago Ferreira; Paye, N'Diaye, Ekangamene, Isci (Skulason 46); Trajkovski, Sylla.

SKN St Polten (0) 2 *(Segovia 56, Kerschbaumer 90)*
PSV Eindhoven (1) 3 *(Locadia 28, Depay 69,*
De Jong 70)   8000
SKN St Polten: (352) Riegler; Huber, Wisio, Grasegger; Holzmann, Stec (Hartl 77), Hofbauer, Parada (Ambichl 46), Kerschbaumer; Noel (Fucik 73), Segovia.
PSV Eindhoven: (442) Zoet; Bruma, Brenet, Tamata, Hendrix; Maher, Ritzmaier (Vloet 81), Hiljemark, De Jong; Narsingh (Depay 62), Locadia (Arias 74).

Slovan Liberec (2) 2 *(Obrocnik 45, Sural 45)*
Astra Giurgiu (1) 3 *(Enache 38, Rus 83, Bukari 89)*   2500
Slovan Liberec: (442) Hroso; Mudra, Rajnoch, Pimpara, Fleisman; Sackey, Frydek (Luckassen 73), Obrocnik (Delarge 65), Sural; Dubek, Hamulak (Hadascok 53).
Astra Giurgiu: (442) Lung Jr; Gaman, Oros, Junior Morais, Laban (Seto 37); Pliatsikas, Yahaya, Enache (Rus 74), William Amorim; Budescu, Fatai (Bukari 78).

Spartak Trnava (0) 1 *(Mikovic 82)*
St Johnstone (1) 1 *(May 42)*   4000
Spartak Trnava: (433) Rusov; Siva, Janecka, Bortel, Toth; Conka, Mikovic (Spalek 90), Vlasko (Vyskocil 59); Jose Casado, Sabo, Schranz (Grabez 87).
St Johnstone: (442) Mannus; Mackay, Scobbie, Caddis (Croft 64), Miller; Easton, Millar, McDonald (O'Halloran 79), Wotherspoon; MacLean, May.

Torino (2) 4 *(Jonsson 4 (og), Darmian 37,*
Quagliarella 80 (pen), Martinez 90)
Brommapojkarna (0) 0   22,931
Torino: (442) Padelli; Molinaro, Bovo, Moretti, Glik (Jansson 81); Darmian, Ruben Perez, Nocerino, Benassi; Larrondo (Quagliarella 55), Barreto (Martinez 63).
Brommapojkarna: (442) Blazevic; Jonsson, Bjorkstrom, Starfelt (Soderstrom 77), Falkenborn; Albornoz (Petrovic 46), Karlstrom, Asbrink, Martinsson-Ngouali; Rexhepi (Sandberg-Magnusson 61), Barkroth.

Viktoria Plzen (1) 1 *(Pilar 40)*
Petrolul Ploiesti (3) 4 *(Teixeira 20, Mutu 38, De Lucas 43,*
Tamuz 69)   10,521
Viktoria Plzen: (442) Kozacik; Reznik, Hubnik, Prochazka, Limbersky; Horava (Vanek 73), Horvath, Petrzela (Tecl 66), Kolar; Pilar, Bakos (Chramosta 53).
Petrolul Ploiesti: (442) Pecanha; Geraldo Alves, Gerson Guimaraes, Fanchone, De Lucas; Hoban, Alcenat, Teixeira (Marinescu 83), Tamuz; Mutu (Albin 73), Nepomuceno (Mustivar 64).

Zimbru Chisinau (0) 0
Grodig (0) 1 *(Djuric 84)*   10,000
Zimbru Chisinau: (442) Rusu; Klimovich (Potirniche 76), Erhan, Pavlyuchek, Vremea; Jardan, Cheptine (Spataru 60), Burghiu, Amani (Pascenco 66); Dedov, Alexeev.
Grodig: (442) Stankovic; Karner, Strobl, Maak (Wallner 58), Brauer; Handle, Schutz (Djuric 78), Huspek, Nutz; Tomi Correa, Reyna.
Zimbru Chisinau won on away goals.

PLAY-OFF ROUND FIRST LEG

Wednesday, 20 August 2014

Dnipro Dnipropetrovsk (0) 2 *(Kalinic 50, Shakhov 88)*
Hajduk Split (0) 1 *(Susic 47)*   10,320
Dnipro Dnipropetrovsk: (442) Boyko; Fedetskiy (Leo Matos 70), Mazuch, Douglas, Strinic; Zozulya, Rotan, Kravchenko, Bruno Gama (Shakhov 59); Kalinic, Seleznyov (Bartulovic 78).
Hajduk Split: (433) Kalinic; Vrsajevic, Maloca, Milovic, Milic; Caktas, Andjelkovic (Mezga 71), Susic; Maglica (Milevskiy 77), Gotal (Vlasic 46), Kouassi.

Stjarnan (0) 0
Internazionale (1) 3 *(Icardi 41, Dodo 48, D'Ambrosio 89)*   9829
Stjarnan: (4231) Jonsson; Vemmelund, Laxdal D, Rauschenberg, Arnason; Runarsson (Toft 69), Johannsson; Bjorgvinsson, Punyed, Finsen; Gunnarson (Johannesson 69).
Internazionale: (3511) Handanovic; Juan Jesus, Vidic, Ranocchia; Jonathan (D'Ambrosio 75), Kovacic, M'Vila, Hernanes (Kuzmanovic 88), Dodo; Botta (Osvaldo 60); Icardi.

Thursday, 21 August 2014

AEL Limassol (1) 1 *(Sardinero 14)*
Tottenham H (0) 2 *(Soldado 74, Kane 80)*   8350
AEL Limassol: (4231) Fegrouch; Nicolaou, Sielis, Carlitos Tavares, Cadu; Edmar, Bebe; Guidilleye, Sardinero (Carlitos Miguel 81), Gikiewicz (Tagbajumi 73); Diego Barcelos (Eleftheriou 67).
Tottenham H: (433) Lloris; Vertonghen, Dier, Naughton, Davies; Paulinho (Chadli 59), Holtby (Dembele 66), Townsend (Lamela 72); Bentaleb, Soldado, Kane.

Aktobe (0) 0
Legia Warsaw (0) 1 *(Duda 48)*   12,000
Aktobe: (442) Sidelnikov; Korobkin, Muldarov, Miroshnichenko (Tsarikaev 32), Arzumanyan; Anderson Mineiro, Khairullin (Aimbetov 66), Tagybergen, Danilo Neco; Antonov (Zenkovich 56), Pizzelli.
Legia Warsaw: (442) Kuciak; Broz, Rzezniczak, Vrdoljak, Dossa Junior; Jodlowiec, Brzyski, Duda, Radovic; Zyro, Kucharczyk.

Apollon Limassol (0) 1 *(Guie Guie 80)*
Lokomotiv Moscow (1) 1 *(Kasaev 39)*   7146
Apollon Limassol: (4411) Bruno Vale; Stylianou (Mulder 70), Joao Paulo, Merkis, Vasiliou; Papoulis, Hamdani, Gullon, Robert; Meriem (Rezek 69); Guie Guie.
Lokomotiv Moscow: (4411) Guilherme; Shishkin, Corluka, Durica, Denisov[■]; Samedov, Tarasov (Mykhalyk 65), Tigorev[■], Kasaev (Maicon 62); Fernandes; Niasse (N'Doye 46).

Astana (0) 0
Villarreal (1) 3 *(Cani 33, Giovani 48, Mario 84)*   25,000
Astana: (4411) Eric; Beissebekov, Anicic[■], Postnikov, Shomko; Dzholchiev (Akhnetov 64), Canas, Zhukov, Kethevoama; Essame (Twumasi 57); Nuserbaev (Muzhikov 80).
Villarreal: (442) Sergio Asenjo; Mario, Musacchio, Gabriel Paulista (Victor Ruiz 31), Jaume; Cani, Trigueros, Bruno, Cheryshev (Espinosa 74); Uche (Vietto 65), Giovani.

Asteras Tripolis (1) 2 *(Mazza 29, Zisopoulos 47)*
Maccabi Tel Aviv (0) 0   7500
Asteras Tripolis: (433) Theodoropoulos; Lluy (Tie Bi 88), Goian, Zisopoulos, Panteliadis; Usero, Kourbelis, Munafo; Rolle (Sankare 70), De Blasis, Mazza.
Maccabi Tel Aviv: (433) Juan Pablo; Yeyni, Tibi, Carlos Garcia, Spungin; Alberman, Igiebor, Radi (Lugasi 86); Zahavi, Mikha (Ben Haim 76), Ben Basat (Prica 66).

Dinamo Minsk (1) 2 *(Stasevich 44 (pen), Nikolic 55)*
Nacional (0) 0   7500
Dinamo Minsk: (4411) Hutar; Karpovich, Kantsavy, Palitsevich, Veretilo; Udoji (Nikitin 89), Bangura, Nikolic, Stasevich (Molosh 90); Figueredo (Diomande 65); Adamovic.
Nacional: (451) Gottardi; Zainadine Junior (Lucas Joao 60), Miguel Rodrigues, Ezzat, Marcal; Rondon, Joao Aurelio, Ghazal, Gomaa, Marco Matias; Suk (Reginaldo 57).

Dynamo Moscow (1) 2 *(Samba 33, Buttner 72)*
Omonia Nicosia (1) 2 *(Lobjanidze 2, Fofana 59)*   6000
Dynamo Moscow: (343) Berezovsky; Samba, Douglas, Granat; Vainqueur, Dzsudzsak, Ionov (Buttner 36), Valbuena (Manolev 90); Denisov, Kokorin[■], Kuranyi.
Omonia Nicosia: (4321) Moreira; Acquistapace, Lobjanidze; Stepanov, Margaca; Rodri, Cristovao, Nuno Assis (Grigalashvili 77); Serginho, Fofana (Kyriakou 86); Pote (Roberto 71).

Elfsborg (2) 2 *(Prodell 27, Mobaeck 38)*
Rio Ave (0) 1 *(Marcelo 65)*   4189
Elfsborg: (433) Stuhr-Ellegaard; Holmen, Mobaeck, Larsson, Lundqvist; Claesson, Svensson, Hauger; Rohden, Prodell (Frick 79), Beckmann (Hedlund 75).
Rio Ave: (433) Cassio; Gouano, Marcelo, Tiago Pinto, Lionn; Filipe Augusto, Pedro Moreira (Bressan 46), Tarantini; Del Valle (Diego Lopes 46), Boateng (Koka 81), Ukra.

Grasshoppers (1) 1 *(Lang 8)*
Club Brugge (2) 2 *(Jahic 14 (og), Vazquez 15)*   18,000
Grasshoppers: (4141) Vasic; Lang, Jahic, Grichting, Garcia Lopes; Salatic; Kahraba, Dabbur, Abrashi, Ravet (Merkel 73); Ngamukol (Tarashaj 62).
Club Brugge: (442) Ryan; Meunier, Engels, Duarte, De Bock; Jorgensen (Odjidja-Ofoe 70), Menegazzo, Simons, Vazquez (Lestienne 81); Storm (Rafaelov 59), Sobota.

HJK Helsinki (0) 2 *(Lod 65, Vayrynen 73)*
Rapid Vienna (0) 1 *(Schaub 58)*   7000
HJK Helsinki: (4411) Doblas; Sorsa (Baah 75), Moren, Heikkinen, Lampi; Alho (Zeneli 71), Perovuo, Lod, Savage; Vayrynen (Heikkila 90); Kandji.
Rapid Vienna: (4141) Novota; Pavelic, Dibon (Hofmann M 64), Sonnleitner, Schrammel; Behrendt; Hofmann S (Starkl 77), Wydra, Schwab (Kainz 90), Schaub; Beric.

Kardemir Karabukspor (0) 1 *(Kumbela 60)*
Saint-Etienne (0) 0   10,250
Kardemir Karabukspor: (4231) Waterman; Ozgenc, Gungor, Mabiala, Kayhan; Incedemir, Sow; Ozek (Viola 72), Traore (Ozmert 79), Kas; Kumbela (Akpala 89).
Saint-Etienne: (4141) Ruffier; Brison, Bayal Sall, Perrin, Tabanou; Clement; Hamouma (Monnet-Paquet 57), Lemoine (Corgnet 80), Cohade, Gradel; Erdinc.

Lokeren (0) 1 *(Vanaken 58)*
Hull C (0) 0   7935
Lokeren: (4141) Verhulst; Galitsios, Maric, Scholz, Odoi; Overmeire; De Pauw (Abdurahimi 88), Persoons, Vanaken, Remacle (De Man 76); Junior Dutra (Harbaoui 83).
Hull C: (433) McGregor; Rosenior, Maguire, McShane, Figueroa; Meyler, Chester, Boyd (Elmohamady 81); Aluko, Sagbo (Jelavic 72), Brady (Ince 72).

Lyon (1) 1 *(Malbranque 26)*
Astra Giurgiu (0) 2 *(Fatai 72, Budescu 81 (pen))*   20,001
Lyon: (433) Lopes; Jallet, Kone, Rose■, Tolisso; Ferri, Gonalons, Malbranque (Grenier 76); Bahlouli (Mvuemba 68), Lacazette, Yattara (Ghezzal 82).
Astra Giurgiu: (442) Lung Jr; Pliatsikas, Ben Youssef, Oros, Junior Morais; Enache, Laban (Rus 86), Yahaya, Budescu; Seto (William Amorim 46), Fatai (Bukari 82).

Panathinaikos (3) 4 *(Berg 21 (pen), 24, 45, Lauridsen 89 (og))*
Midtjylland (1) 1 *(Lauridsen 13)*   7500
Panathinaikos: (4321) Kotsolis; Triantafyllopoulos■, Mendes Da Silva, Schildenfeld, Nano; Zeca, Lagos (Bouy 78), Pranjic; Dinas (Ajagun 67), Karelis (Petric 78); Berg.
Midtjylland: (451) Haugaard; Jensen, Sviatchenko■, Dickoh, Lauridsen; Sisto, Hassan (Larsen J 60), Uzochukwu, Poulsen, Igboun Emeka; Rasmussen (Onuachu 22 (Janssen 85)).

Partizan Belgrade (2) 3 *(Silva 29 (og), Grbic 32, Yunuszade 69 (og))*
Neftchi (2) 2 *(Silva 11, 17)*   4000
Partizan Belgrade: (442) Lukac; Vulicevic, Ilic B, Stankovic, Petrovic; Ninkovic (Zivkovic 61), Brasanac, Drincic, Grbic (Ilic S 71); Skuletic (Fofana 80), Lazovic.
Neftchi: (343) Stamenkovic; Caue, Silva, Yunuszade; Abdullayev (Canales 72), Seyidov (Imamverdiyev 90), Ramos, Bertucci; Wobay, Nfor, Flavinho (Masimov 82).

Petrolul Ploiesti (1) 1 *(Tamuz 45)*
Dinamo Zagreb (1) 1 *(Cop 29 (pen), 80, Paulo Machado 90)*   13,460
Petrolul Ploiesti: (4231) Pecanha; Alcenat, Geraldo Alves■, Gerson Guimaraes, Fanchone; De Lucas, Hoban (Mustivar 50); Priso (Albin 63), Mutu (Nepomuceno 83), Teixeira; Tamuz.

Dinamo Zagreb: (4231) Eduardo; Ivo Pinto, Simunovic, Simunic, Pivaric; Ademi, Brozovic; Soudani (Paulo Machado 46), Antolic (Vukojevic 73), Wilson Eduardo (Pjaca 63); Cop.

PSV Eindhoven (0) 1 *(Maher 59)*
Shakhtyor Soligorsk (0) 0   15,000
PSV Eindhoven: (433) Pasveer; Brenet, Bruma, Rekik, Tamata; Wijnaldum, Hiljemark (Hendrix 51), Maher (Ritzmaier 88); Locadia (Narsingh 63), De Jong, Depay.
Shakhtyor Soligorsk: (343) Kotenko; Yanushkevich, Kuzmyanok, Kashewski; Matsveychyk, Starhorodskyi, Galyuza (Lyavonchyk 88), Yurevich; Ryas, Yanush (Osipenko 85), Guruli (Kovalev 89).

Qarabag (0) 0
FC Twente (0) 0   28,000
Qarabag: (4231) Sehic; Medvedev, Sadygov, Huseynov, Agolli; Almeida, Garayev; Danilo Dias (Tagiyev 56), Muarem (Alaskarov 67), George (Nadirov 29); Reynaldo.
FC Twente: (4231) Marsman; Martina, Bengtsson, Lachman, Schilder; Ebecilio, Mokotjo; Kusk (Holscher 69), Ziyech (Eghan 77), Mokhtar; Castaignos.

Real Sociedad (0) 1 *(Prieto 71)*
Krasnodar (0) 0   22,245
Real Sociedad: (4312) Zubikarai; Zaldua, Elustondo, Martinez, De la Bella; Pardo (Granero 67), Markel, Canales; Prieto; Castro (Zurutuza 67), Agirretxe (Vela 76).
Krasnodar: (451) Dykan; Jedrzejczyk, Sigurdsson, Granqvist, Petrov; Pereyra (Laborde 81), Izmailov, Gazinski, Ahmedov, Joaozinho (Bystrov 81); Ari (Wanderson 59).

Rijeka (0) 1 *(Leovac 85)*
Sheriff (0) 0   9020
Rijeka: (442) Vargic; Leovac, Samardzic, Tomecak, Leskovic; Jajalo, Kvrzic (Cvijanovic 87), Brezovec, Jugovic (Sharbini 62); Jahovic (Moises 76), Kramaric.
Sheriff: (442) Degra; Metoua, Joaozinho, Ernandes, Muresan; Ligger, Balima, Leonel, Cadu (Ginsari 79); Galvao (Ricardinho 66), Potiguar (Isa 46).

RNK Split (0) 0
Torino (0) 0   5000
RNK Split: (442) Vukovic; Ibriks, Galovic, Glumac, Rugasevic; Bagaric, Vidovic, Dujmovic (Kvesic 87), Belle (Roce 63); Rog (Novovic 71), Bilic.
Torino: (3142) Padelli; Bovo, Glik, Moretti; Vives; Darmian, Nocerino (Benassi 62), El Kaddouri, Molinaro; Barreto (Quagliarella 68), Larrondo.

Ruch Chorzow (0) 0
Metalist Kharkiv (0) 0   6100
Ruch Chorzow: (451) Kaminski; Stawarczyk, Dziwniel, Kus (Helik 90), Surma; Zienczuk (Gigolaev 73), Kowalski, Starzynski, Babiarz, Malinowski; Kuswik (Efir 76).
Metalist Kharkiv: (4141) Shust; Villagra, Yussuf, Gueye, Osman; Torres (Krasnopyorov 52); Kulakov, Edmar, Cleiton Xavier, Rebenok; Jaja (Homenyuk 63).

Sarajevo (1) 2 *(Puzigaca 26, Duljevic 59)*
Borussia Moenchengladbach (2) 3 *(Hahn 11, Hrgota 41, 73)*   28,000
Sarajevo: (442) Bandovic; Tatomirovic, Berberovic, Dupovac, Puzigaca (Protic 76); Stojcev, Cimirot, Radovac (Kovacevic 76), Okic (Duljevic 52); Velkoski, Bilbija.
Borussia Moenchengladbach: (442) Sommer; Dominguez, Johnson, Jantschke, Stranzl; Traore (Herrmann 46), Nordtveit, Hahn (Korb 65), Xhaka; Raffael (Hazard 82), Hrgota.

Spartak Trnava (1) 1 *(Vlasko 14 (pen))*
FC Zurich (2) 3 *(Chermiti 4, 45, 58)*   21,000
Spartak Trnava: (4411) Rusov; Janecka, Toth, Bortel, Conka; Schranz (Spalek 72), Kuzma, Jose Casado, Vlasko (Vyskocil 85); Silva Nascimento (Chovanec 76); Jendrisek.
FC Zurich: (352) Da Costa; Koch, Kecojevic, Djimsiti; Buff, Yapi Yapo, Chiumiento, Rikan (Rossini 83), Schonbachler; Chikhaoui, Chermiti (Etoundi 73).

Trabzonspor (1) 2 *(Medjani 37, Cardozo 73)*

Rostov (0) 0 7000

Trabzonspor: (4231) Kivrak; Bosingwa, Belkalem, Yumlu, Nizam; Medjani, Constant (Dursun 77); Yilmaz S, Aydogdu, Erdogan (Atik 67); Cardozo (Yilmaz D 77).
Rostov: (442) Pletikosa; Goreux, Dyakov, Bastos, Milic; Kalachev, Gatcan, Grigorev (Bukharov 64), Torbinski; Poloz (Doumbia 68), Kanga.

Young Boys (1) 3 *(Nuzzolo 26, Steffen 67, Frey 87)*

Debrecen (1) 1 *(Sidibe 39)* 7927

Young Boys: (4231) Mvogo; Hadergjonaj, von Bergen, Rochat, Lecjaks; Steffen (Nikci 86), Bertone; Sanogo, Nuzzolo, Costanzo (Kubo 77); Frey (Affum 90).
Debrecen: (442) Poleksic; Korhut, Meszaros, Mate, Jovanovic; Szakaly, Zsidai, Varga, Bodi; Seydi (Kulcsar 74), Sidibe.

Zimbru Chisinau (0) 1 *(Burghiu 80)*

PAOK Salonika (0) 0 8530

Zimbru Chisinau: (4411) Rusu; Jardan, Burghiu, Pavlyuchek, Erhan; Cheptine (Diallo 82), Klimovich, Vremea, Spataru (Visnakovs 61); Amani (Alexeev 69); Grossu.
PAOK Salonika: (433) Glykos; Kitsiou (Spyropoulos 79), Skondras, Katsikas, Rat; Tziolis (Pereyra 67), Maduro, Mak (Martens 67); Kace, Salpingidis, Athanasiadis.

Zorya Luhansk (1) 1 *(Beliy 27)*

Feyenoord (1) 1 *(Te Vrede 38)* 3700

Zorya Luhansk: (4231) Shevchenko; Kamenyuka, Beliy, Ignjatijevic, Pysko; Karavayev, Chaykovsky; Malyshev (Gritsay 46), Khomchenovskiy, Segbefia (Malinovsky 56); Budkivskiy.
Feyenoord: (433) Mulder; Kongolo, van Beek, Mathijsen, Wilkshire (Karsdorp 82); Trindade de Vilhena, Clasie (Vormer 72), Immers; Boetius (Basacikoglu 62), Te Vrede, Schaken.

Zwolle (0) 1 *(Lukoki 77)*

Sparta Prague (0) 1 *(Krejci 82)* 12,130

Zwolle: (4231) Boer; Van Polen, Van der Werff, Sainsbury, Van Hintum; Saymak, Rienstra; Drost, Ioannidis (Lukoki 49), Thomas (Nijland 65); Necid.
Sparta Prague: (4141) Bicik; Nhamoinesu, Brabec, Kovac, Kaderabek; Marecek; Krejci, Matejovsky, Husbauer (Prikryl 66), Dockal (Vacek 76); Lafata (Bednar 92).

PLAY-OFF ROUND SECOND LEG

Thursday, 28 August 2014

Astra Giurgiu (0) 0

Lyon (1) 1 *(Ferri 23)* 7200

Astra Giurgiu: (4231) Lung Jr; Ben Youssef, Junior Morais, Oros, Pliatsikas; Yahaya, Enache; Laban (Seto 85), Bukari (Grandin 90), William Amorim; Budescu (Rus 89).
Lyon: (4231) Lopes; Zeffane (Bahlouli 72), Kone, Jallet, Ghezzal (Danic 64); Ferri, Malbranque (Mvuemba 80); Gonalons, Tolisso, Lacazette; N'Jie.
Astra Giurgiu won on away goals.

Borussia Moenchengladbach (3) 7 *(Hahn 20, Xhaka 24, Hrgota 34, 67, 82, Hazard 74 (pen), 90)*

Sarajevo (0) 0 44,152

Borussia Moenchengladbach: (442) Sommer; Korb, Stranzl, Jantschke, Dominguez; Hahn (Herrmann 64), Kramer (Dahoud 55), Xhaka, Johnson; Raffael (Hazard 70), Hrgota.
Sarajevo: (4231) Bandovic; Berberovic, Dupovac, Tatomirovic*, Puzigaca (Protic 46); Radovac, Cimirot; Duljevic, Stojcev (Bilbija 46), Okic; Velkoski.

Club Brugge (0) 1 *(Vazquez 62)*

Grasshoppers (0) 0 23,743

Club Brugge: (4231) Ryan; Meunier, Engels, Duarte, De Bock; Menegazzo, Simons; Storm (Jorgensen 79), Vazquez (Bolingoli Mbombo 86), Sobota (Dierckx 90); Castillo.
Grasshoppers: (4231) Davari; Lang, Jahic, Grichting, Gulen; Abrashi, Sinkala (Merkel 67); Ravet (Kahraba 67), Dabbur, Ngamukol; Tarashaj (Al Abbadie 83).

Debrecen (0) 0

Young Boys (0) 0 6393

Debrecen: (541) Novakovic; Korhut, Meszaros (Morozov 45), Mate, Jovanovic, Vadnai (Ferenczi 79); Zsidai, Varga, Bodi, Sidibe; Kulcsar (Seydi* 65).
Young Boys: (4411) Mvogo; Hadergjonaj, Rochat, von Bergen, Lecjaks; Steffen, Bertone, Sanogo, Nuzzolo (Sutter 90); Costanzo (Wuthrich 67); Frey (Kubo 81).

Dinamo Zagreb (1) 2 *(Cop 22, Antolic 90)*

Petrolul Ploiesti (0) 1 *(Albin 59)* 8000

Dinamo Zagreb: (433) Eduardo; Ivo Pinto, Simunovic, Simunic, Pivaric; Brozovic, Ademi (Coric 90), Antolic; Paulo Machado (Vukojevic 64), Cop, Wilson Eduardo (Soudani 71).
Petrolul Ploiesti: (4141) Cobrea; Alcenat, Hoban, Gerson Guimaraes, Satli; De Lucas (Nkoyi 74); Albin, Mutu (Nepomuceno 67), Teixeira, Mustivar (Marinescu 79); Tamuz.

FC Twente (1) 1 *(Castaignos 37)*

Qarabag (0) 1 *(Muarem 51)* 20,200

FC Twente: (442) Marsman; Martina, Bjelland, Lachman, Schilder; Ebecilio (Eghan 64), Kusk, Mokotjo, Mokhtar (Ould-Chikh 90); Ziyech (Borven 79), Castaignos.
Qarabag: (442) Sehic; Huseynov, Garayev, Medvedev, Sadygov; Agolli, Reynaldo, Muarem (Danilo Dias 71), Almeida; Chumbinho (Yusifov 79), Nadirov (Teli 85).
Qarabag won on away goals.

FC Zurich (0) 1 *(Chikhaoui 48)*

Spartak Trnava (0) 1 *(Spalek 90)* 12,000

FC Zurich: (343) Da Costa; Koch, Kecojevic, Djimsiti; Buff (Rodriguez 78), Yapi Yapo, Rikan, Schonbachler (Brunner M 82); Chermiti, Chiumiento, Chikhaoui (Etoundi 69).
Spartak Trnava: (4411) Rusov; Siva, Bortel (Soungole 74), Toth, Conka; Schranz (Kuzma 51), Janecka, Jose Casado, Jendrisek; Silva Nascimento (Spalek 56); Mikovic.

Feyenoord (2) 4 *(Te Vrede 18, Schaken 26, Beliy 48 (og), Manu 90)*

Zorya Luhansk (0) 3 *(Malinovsky 56, Beliy 71, Malinovsky 80)* 32,500

Feyenoord: (442) Mulder; Wilkshire, Mathijsen (Achahbar 84), van Beek, Kongolo; Clasie (Manu 84), Immers, Trindade de Vilhena, Basacikoglu (Nelom 78); Te Vrede, Schaken.
Zorya Luhansk: (442) Shevchenko; Pylyavskyi, Ignjatijevic (Pysko 72), Chaykovsky (Gritsay 79), Kamenyuka; Malinovsky, Beliy, Khomchenovskiy, Budkivskiy; Karavayev, Segbefia (Ljubenovic 66).

Hajduk Split (0) 0

Dnipro Dnipropetrovsk (0) 0 38,000

Hajduk Split: (442) Kalinic; Vrsajevic, Milovic, Maloca, Milic; Mezga, Susic (Nizic 84), Andjelkovic (Bencun 60), Caktas; Maglica, Kouassi (Gotal 60).
Dnipro Dnipropetrovsk: (4411) Boyko; Fedetskiy, Mazuch, Douglas, Strinic; Leo Matos, Rotan (Kravchenko 40), Kankava, Bruno Gama (Bartulovic 90); Shakhov (Kalinic 72); Zozulya.

Hull C (1) 2 *(Brady 6, 56 (pen))*

Lokeren (1) 1 *(Remacle 49)* 18,149

Hull C: (4411) McGregor; Rosenior (Jelavic 66), Chester (Ince 75), Davies, Figueroa; Elmohamady, Livermore, Meyler (Huddlestone 75), Brady; Aluko; Sagbo*.
Lokeren: (451) Verhulst; Galitsios, Scholz, Maric, Odoi; De Pauw (Mertens 90), Persoons, Overmeire, Remacle (Ngolok 88), Vanaken; Junior Dutra (Leye 76).
Lokeren won on away goals.

Internazionale (2) 6 *(Kovacic 28, 33, 51, Osvaldo 47, Icardi 69, 80)*

Stjarnan (0) 0 35,000

Internazionale: (3511) Carrizo; Andreolli, Ranocchia, Juan Jesus; D'Ambrosio, Hernanes (Jonathan 65), M'Vila, Obi (Kuzmanovic 59), Nagatomo; Kovacic (Icardi 53); Osvaldo.
Stjarnan: (442) Jonsson; Vemmelund, Rauschenberg, Laxdal D, Arnason; Bjorgvinsson, Johannsson (Runarsson 63), Punyed, Finsen (Aegisson 63); Gunnarson (Johannesson 59), Toft.

Krasnodar (0) 3 *(Joaozinho 71 (pen), Pereyra 88, Ari 90)*
Real Sociedad (0) 0 32,500
Krasnodar: (433) Dykan; Jedrzejczyk, Granqvist, Sigurdsson, Kaleshin; Pereyra (Adzhindzhal 90), Gazinski (Laborde 64), Ahmedov; Joaozinho■, Ari, Izmailov (Wanderson 53).
Real Sociedad: (433) Rulli (Zubikarai 85); Zaldua, Elustondo, Martinez, De la Bella; Pardo (Granero 63), Markel■, Zurutuza (Vela 80); Agirretxe, Prieto, Canales.

Legia Warsaw (1) 2 *(Kucharczyk 26, Vrdoljak 66 (pen))*
Aktobe (0) 0 18,549
Legia Warsaw: (451) Kuciak; Dossa Junior, Jodlowiec, Vrdoljak, Rzezniczak; Broz, Duda (Saganowski 88), Brzyski, Radovic, Zyro; Kucharczyk (Kosecki 66).
Aktobe: (433) Sidelnikov; Muldarov, Miroshnichenko, Logvinenko, Anderson Mineiro; Korobkin (Kapadze 42), Khairullin, Tagybergen; Tsarikaev (Aimbetov 71), Danilo Neco, Antonov (Zenkovich 57).

Lokomotiv Moscow (0) 1 *(Pavlyuchenko 85)*
Apollon Limassol (1) 4 *(Rezek 20, Papoulis 51, Thuram 78, Lopez 83)* 6520
Lokomotiv Moscow: (4411) Guilherme; Pejcinovic, Corluka, Durica, Shishkin; Seraskhov, Kasaev (Samedov 67), Fernandes (Miranchuk 53), Tarasov; Maicon; Niasse (Pavlyuchenko 53).
Apollon Limassol: (4411) Bruno Vale; Merkis, Robert, Stylianou, Joao Paulo; Gullon (Charalambous 87), Meriem (Thuram 64), Hamdani, Sangoy; Rezek; Papoulis (Lopez 81).

Maccabi Tel Aviv (1) 3 *(Badash 27, Zahavi 54 (pen), Prica 75)*
Asteras Tripolis (1) 1 *(Goian 23)* 350
Maccabi Tel Aviv: (442) Juan Pablo; Tibi, Ben Haroush, Carlos Garcia, Alberman; Mikha, Yeyni, Igiebor (Ben Haim 62), Ben Basat (Prica 72); Badash (Radi 85), Zahavi.
Asteras Tripolis: (442) Theodoropoulos; Goian, Panteliadis, Lluy, Munafo; Usero, Rolle (Sankare 77), Zisopoulos, Kourbelis; De Blasis, Mazza.
Asteras Tripolis won on away goals.

Metalist Kharkiv (0) 1 *(Cleiton Xavier 105 (pen))*
Ruch Chorzow (0) 0 2548
Metalist Kharkiv: (442) Shust; Pshenichnikh, Yussuf, Gueye, Edmar; Cleiton Xavier, Kulakov, Krasnopyorov, Rebenok (Radchenko 68); Homenyuk, Jaja (Villagra 62).
Ruch Chorzow: (442) Kaminski■; Stawarczyk, Dziwniel (Gigolaev 83), Kus, Surma; Zienczuk (Lech 105), Kowalski (Wlodyka 81), Starzynski, Babiarz; Malinowski, Kuswik. *aet.*

Midtjylland (0) 1 *(Igboun Emeka 73 (pen))*
Panathinaikos (0) 2 *(Nano 55, Klonaridis 74)* 6039
Midtjylland: (442) Haugaard; Romer, Jensen, Larsen J, Lauridsen; Sisto, Poulsen, Sparv (Uzochukwu 76), Hassan; Andersson (Igboun Emeka 59), Larsen M (Onuachu 46).
Panathinaikos: (4141) Kotsolis; Bourbos, Risvanis, Schildenfeld, Nano; Mendes Da Silva (Donis 79); Lagos (Bouy 59), Zeca, Ajagun, Pranjic; Karelis (Klonaridis 66).

Nacional (1) 2 *(Marco Matias 30 (pen), Ghazal 53)*
Dinamo Minsk (2) 3 *(Udoji 32, 63, Simovic 40)* 4000
Nacional: (433) Gottardi; Zainadine Junior, Miguel Rodrigues, Rui Correia, Marcal; Ghazal, Ayala (Suk 46), Joao Aurelio (Fofana 67); Gomaa (Reginaldo 67), Rondon, Marco Matias.
Dinamo Minsk: (451) Hutar; Veretilo, Kantsavy, Karpovich, Palitsevich; Simovic, Bangura, Nikolic, Udoji (Rassadkin 85), Stasevich; Adamovic (Voronkov 89).

Neftchi (0) 1 *(Wobay 58)*
Partizan Belgrade (1) 2 *(Skuletic 24, 90)* 20,000
Neftchi: (4231) Stamenkovic; Caue■, Yunuszade, Carlos Cardoso, Silva; Seyidov (Canales 54), Ramos■; Abdullayev, Wobay (Masimov 83), Flavinho (Bertucci 54); Nfor■.
Partizan Belgrade: (4231) Lukac; Vulicevic, Ilic B, Stankovic, Petrovic; Brasanac, Drincic; Zivkovic (Ostojic 90), Lazovic (Pantic 84), Grbic (Ilic S 59); Skuletic■.

Omonia Nicosia (1) 1 *(Pote 23)*
Dynamo Moscow (1) 2 *(Stepanov 11 (og), Samba 90)* 20,500
Omonia Nicosia: (433) Moreira; Lobjanidze, Stepanov, Acquistapace, Margaca; Nuno Assis (Grigalashvili 90), Rodri, Serginho; Fofana (Kyriakou 86), Pote (Roberto 74), Cristovao.
Dynamo Moscow: (442) Berezovsky; Manolev, Douglas, Samba, Buttner (Prudnikov 83); Ionov (Zhirkov 68), Vainqueur■, Denisov, Dzsudzsak (Noboa 75); Kuranyi, Valbuena.

PAOK Salonika (2) 4 *(Pereyra 11, Athanasiadis 45, Mak 79, Martens 84)*
Zimbru Chisinau (0) 0 20,000
PAOK Salonika: (433) Glykos; Kitsiou, Skondras, Tzavelas, Rat; Pereyra, Tziolis, Maduro (Kace 52); Mak (Pozoglou 83), Athanasiadis, Salpingidis (Martens 62).
Zimbru Chisinau: (442) Rusu; Jardan (Spataru 80), Burghiu, Pavlyuchek, Erhan; Cheptine, Vremea, Klimovich, Dedov; Amani■, Grossu (Alexeev 46).

Rapid Vienna (2) 3 *(Schaub 10, 13, Wydra 90)*
HJK Helsinki (1) 3 *(Kandji 15, Alho 77, Savage 88 (pen))* 21,100
Rapid Vienna: (4411) Novota; Schrammel, Hofmann M, Sonnleitner, Pavelic; Kainz (Starkl 79), Schwab, Behrendt (Wydra 46), Schaub; Hofmann S (Petsos 72); Beric.
HJK Helsinki: (4411) Doblas; Sorsa, Moren, Heikkinen, Lampi; Alho (Heikkila 90), Tainio, Schuller (Zeneli 68), Savage; Lod; Kandji (Perovuo 88).

Rio Ave (0) 1 *(Goncalves 90)*
Elfsborg (0) 0 8730
Rio Ave: (442) Cassio; Gouano, Lionn (Goncalves 79), Tiago Pinto, Marcelo; Filipe Augusto, Tarantini, Diego Lopes (Jebor 70), Bressan (Boateng 57); Koka, Ukra.
Elfsborg: (433) Stuhr-Ellegaard; Larsson, Holmen, Lans, Svensson; Lundqvist, Hauger, Rohden; Beckmann (Klarstrom 75), Claesson (Frick 90), Prodell.
Rio Ave won on away goals.

Rostov (0) 0
Trabzonspor (0) 0 8000
Rostov: (4231) Pletikosa; Goreux, Djakov, Bastos, Milic; Torbinski (Bukharov 69), Gatcan; Kalachev, Kanga, Poloz (Doumbia 60); Grigorev (Yoo 78).
Trabzonspor: (4231) Kivrak; Yavru, Demir (Yumlu 20), Belkalem, Nizam; Dursun, Medjani; Yilmaz S (Cardozo 71), Aydogdu (Artarslan 80), Atik; Yilmaz D.

Saint-Etienne (1) 1 *(Monnet-Paquet 13)*
Kardemir Karabukspor (0) 0 27,280
Saint-Etienne: (442) Ruffier; Theophile-Catherine, Bayal Sall, Perrin (Pogba 46), Tabanou; Monnet-Paquet, Lemoine, Clement, Gradel; Erdinc (van Wolfswinkel 66), Hamouma (Cohade 77).
Kardemir Karabukspor: (4231) Waterman; Ozgenc, Gungor, Mabiala, Kayhan; Incedemir, Sow; Ozek, Traore (Akgun 103), Kas (Commert 46); Kumbela (Akpala 46).
aet; Saint-Etienne won 4-3 on penalties.

Shakhtyor Soligorsk (0) 0
PSV Eindhoven (0) 2 *(Depay 89, 90)* 5500
Shakhtyor Soligorsk: (451) Kotenko; Matsveychyk, Yanushkevich, Kuzmyanok, Yurevich; Ryas, Galyuza (Yanush 62), Lyavonchyk, Starhorodskyi, Guruli (Wojciechowski 54); Osipenko.
PSV Eindhoven: (451) Zoet; Brenet, Bruma, Rekik, Tamata; Locadia (Narsingh 66), Hendrix, Hiljemark, Maher (Ritzmaier 78); Depay; De Jong.

Sheriff (0) 0
Rijeka (2) 3 *(Ligger 29 (og), Kramaric 44, Moises 61)* 5000
Sheriff: (451) Degra; Metoua (Paireli 18), Muresan, Ligger, Joaozinho; Balima, Galvao, Leonel (Ricardinho 53), Cadu, Ernandes; Isa (Potiguar 75).
Rijeka: (442) Vargic; Tomecak, Leskovic, Samardzic, Leovac; Jugovic (Cvijanovic 81), Jajalo, Brezovec, Sharbini (Kvrzic 54); Moises (Zlomislic 68), Kramaric.

Sparta Prague (2) 3 *(Krejci 10, Dockal 44, Brabec 62)*
Zwolle (0) 1 *(Nijland 83 (pen))*   16,612
Sparta Prague: (4231) Bicik; Kaderabek, Kovac, Brabec, Nhamoinesu; Marecek, Matejovsky; Dockal, Vacek (Konate 83), Krejci (Breznanik 90); Lafata (Nespor 90).
Zwolle: (433) Boer; Van Polen, Sainsbury, Van der Werff, Van Hintum; Drost, Saymak, Rienstra; Lukoki (Dekker 77), Necid (Nijland 54), Thomas (Moro 69).

Torino (1) 1 *(El Kaddouri 22 (pen))*
RNK Split (0) 0   30,000
Torino: (352) Padelli; Maksimovic, Glik, Moretti; Darmian, Benassi (Nocerino 58), Vives, El Kaddouri (Gazzi 90), Molinaro; Barreto (Martinez 64), Quagliarella.
RNK Split: (451) Vukovic; Ibriks (Roce 84), Galovic, Glumac, Rugasevic; Bagaric, Vidovic (Kvesic 63), Dujmovic, Rog, Glavina (Radotic 63); Bilic.

Tottenham H (1) 1 *(Kane 45, Paulinho 49, Townsend 66 (pen))*
AEL Limassol (0) 0   29,976
Tottenham H: (4141) Lloris; Naughton, Chiriches (Veljkovic 86), Kaboul, Davies; Sandro (Holtby 77); Lennon, Paulinho, Dembele, Townsend; Kane.
AEL Limassol: (352) Fegrouch (Pulpo 13); Cadu, Sielis, Carlitos Tavares; Diego Barcelos, Sardinero (Tagbajumi 80), Edmar, Guidilleye, Bebe; Gikiewicz, Nicolaou (Danielzinho 45).

Villarreal (1) 4 *(Vietto 21, 54, Bruno 60 (pen), Nahuel 67)*
Astana (0) 0   12,000
Villarreal: (442) Juan Carlos; Mario, Musacchio, Gabriel Paulista, Jaume (Marin 56); Moi Gomez (Nahuel 62), Pina, Trigueros (Bruno 46), Espinosa; Vietto, Moreno.
Astana: (4231) Loginovskiy; Beissebekov, Postnikov, Dmitrenko, Shomko; Canas, Zhukov; Dzholchiev, Twumasi (Kurdov 71), Kethevoama (Kojasevic 76); Nuserbaev (Essame 62).

GROUP STAGE

GROUP A

Thursday, 18 September 2014
Apollon Limassol (2) 3 *(Papoulis 9, Gullon 40, Koch 87 (og))*
FC Zurich (0) 2 *(Rikan 50, Yapi Yapo 53)*   7000
Apollon Limassol: (433) Bruno Vale; Merkis, Robert, Stylianou (Charalambous 90), Joao Paulo; Gullon■, Meriem, Hamdani (Thuram 67); Sangoy (Lopez 77), Rezek, Papoulis.
FC Zurich: (352) Da Costa; Djimsiti, Koch, Kecojevic; Chiumiento (Rossini 90), Chikhaoui■, Kukeli, Schonbachler (Buff 73), Yapi Yapo; Rikan, Chermiti (Etoundi 68).

Borussia Moenchengladbach (1) 1 *(Herrmann 21)*
Villarreal (0) 1 *(Uche 68)*   37,000
Borussia Moenchengladbach: (442) Sommer; Jantschke, Stranzl, Dominguez, Wendt; Herrmann (Traore 74), Kramer, Xhaka, Johnson (Hahn 62); Hrgota (Raffael 77), Kruse.
Villarreal: (4321) Sergio Asenjo; Gabriel Paulista, Victor Ruiz, Musacchio, Mario; Cani, Bruno, Pina (Trigueros 60); Cheryshev, Vietto (Uche 67 (Jonathan 73)); Moi Gomez.

Thursday, 2 October 2014
FC Zurich (1) 1 *(Etoundi 23)*
Borussia Moenchengladbach (1) 1 *(Nordtveit 25)*   18,422
FC Zurich: (3412) Da Costa; Djimsiti, Kecojevic, Nef; Schonbachler (Koch 84), Kukeli, Yapi Yapo, Rikan (Rodriguez 20); Chiumiento; Etoundi, Chermiti (Rossini 90).
Borussia Moenchengladbach: (442) Sommer; Korb, Stranzl, Jantschke, Dominguez (Wendt 85); Hahn (Herrmann 73), Nordtveit, Xhaka, Hazard (Traore 67); Hrgota, Kruse.

Villarreal (2) 4 *(Moreno 8, 82, Espinosa 44, 51)*
Apollon Limassol (0) 0   13,000
Villarreal: (442) Juan Carlos; Rukavina (Mario 15), Gabriel Paulista, Victor Ruiz, Marin; Espinosa, Jonathan (Trigueros 62), Bruno, Cani; Moreno, Vietto (Giovani 72).
Apollon Limassol: (442) Bruno Vale; Stylianou, Merkis, Joao Paulo, Vasiliou (Rezek 47); Papoulis (Thuram 83), Hamdani, Meriem, Robert; Lopez (Guie Guie 46), Sangoy.

Thursday, 23 October 2014
Borussia Moenchengladbach (1) 5 *(Traore 11, 66, Hrgota 56, Herrmann 83, Charalambous 90 (og))*
Apollon Limassol (0) 0   40,000
Borussia Moenchengladbach: (442) Sommer; Korb, Stranzl, Jantschke, Wendt; Traore, Nordtveit, Xhaka (Dahoud 70), Hazard; Hrgota (Herrmann 78), Kruse (Raffael 46).
Apollon Limassol: (442) Bruno Vale; Mulder, Charalambous, Merkis, Robert; Sangoy, Gullon (Grigore 50 (Joao Paulo 65)), Hamdani, Lopez; Guie Guie (Meriem 70), Rezek.

Villarreal (1) 4 *(Cani 6, Vietto 57, Bruno 60, Giovani 77)*
FC Zurich (1) 1 *(Schonbachler 43)*   14,092
Villarreal: (442) Juan Carlos; Mario, Gabriel Paulista, Victor Ruiz, Marin; Cani (Cheryshev 73), Jonathan, Bruno (Pina 69), Espinosa; Moreno, Vietto (Giovani 65).
FC Zurich: (3412) Da Costa; Koch, Nef, Djimsiti (Elvedi 83); Buff (Rodriguez 73), Kukeli, Yapi Yapo, Schonbachler; Chiumiento; Chikhaoui, Chermiti (Etoundi 74).

Thursday, 6 November 2014
Apollon Limassol (0) 0
Borussia Moenchengladbach (0) 2 *(Raffael 56, Herrmann 90)*   5000
Apollon Limassol: (433) Bruno Vale; Mulder (Papoulis 67), Merkis, Charalambous, Wheeler; Meriem, Hamdani, Robert; Thuram, Guie Guie (Stylianou 60 (Lopez 65)), Rosa.
Borussia Moenchengladbach: (442) Sommer; Johnson, Stranzl, Jantschke, Wendt; Hazard (Brouwers 90), Kramer, Nordtveit, Traore (Hahn 80); Hrgota (Herrmann 72), Raffael.

FC Zurich (3) 3 *(Etoundi 21, Buff 28, Chikhaoui 29)*
Villarreal (2) 2 *(Pina 19, Moreno 24)*   19,000
FC Zurich: (3421) Da Costa; Elvedi, Nef, Djimsiti; Rodriguez (Brunner M 82), Kukeli, Yapi Yapo, Schonbachler; Chikhaoui, Buff (Rossini 71); Etoundi (Chermiti 53).
Villarreal: (442) Juan Carlos; Rukavina, Gabriel Paulista, Victor Ruiz, Marin; Moi Gomez (Vietto 59), Jonathan, Pina (Bruno 65), Espinosa (Cheryshev 68); Moreno, Giovani.

Thursday, 27 November 2014
FC Zurich (2) 3 *(Djimsiti 31, Chikhaoui 38 (pen), 60 (pen))*
Apollon Limassol (1) 1 *(Rosa 23)*   10,000
FC Zurich: (343) Da Costa; Nef, Kecojevic, Djimsiti (Elvedi 80); Rodriguez (Koch 72), Buff, Kajevic, Schonbachler; Chikhaoui, Chiumiento, Etoundi (Chermiti 76).
Apollon Limassol: (442) Bruno Vale; Lopez, Charalambous, Joao Paulo, Robert; Papoulis (Olinga 55), Hamdani, Meriem (Gullon 46), Rosa; Thuram, Guie Guie (Sangoy 80).

Villarreal (1) 2 *(Vietto 26, Cheryshev 63)*
Borussia Moenchengladbach (0) 2 *(Raffael 55, Xhaka 67)*   16,000
Villarreal: (442) Sergio Asenjo; Mario, Gabriel Paulista, Victor Ruiz, Jaume; Cani (Jonathan 57), Trigueros (Espinosa 86), Bruno, Cheryshev; Uche (Pina 71), Vietto.
Borussia Moenchengladbach: (442) Sommer; Korb, Brouwers, Jantschke, Dominguez; Traore (Herrmann 71), Nordtveit, Xhaka, Hazard; Raffael, Hrgota (Kruse 70).

Thursday, 11 December 2014
Apollon Limassol (0) 0
Villarreal (2) 2 *(Moreno 35, Vietto 40)*   4200
Apollon Limassol: (4141) Hidi; Mulder, Merkis, Charalambous, Vasiliou; Hamdani (Kyriakou 75); Olinga (Sangoy 59), Gullon, Rosa, Papoulis (Rezek 66); Thuram.
Villarreal: (442) Sergio Asenjo; Mario (Espinosa 46), Gabriel Paulista, Dorado, Jaume; Rukavina, Pina, Bruno (Trigueros 46), Moi Gomez; Vietto (Uche 59), Moreno.

Borussia Moenchengladbach (1) 3 *(Herrmann 31, Hrgota 58, 64)*
FC Zurich (0) 0   44,323
Borussia Moenchengladbach: (442) Sommer; Jantschke, Brouwers, Dominguez, Wendt; Traore (Johnson 78), Kramer, Xhaka, Herrmann (Hazard 67); Hrgota, Raffael (Kruse 66).
FC Zurich: (3412) Da Costa; Koch, Kecojevic (Brunner C 25), Elvedi; Rodriguez (Brunner M 69), Buff, Kukeli, Schonbachler; Chiumiento; Etoundi (Chermiti 69), Chikhaoui.

Group A Table	P	W	D	L	F	A	GD	Pts
Borussia M'gladbach	6	3	3	0	14	4	10	12
Villarreal	6	3	2	1	15	7	8	11
FC Zurich	6	2	1	3	10	14	–4	7
Apollon Limassol	6	1	0	5	4	18	–14	3

GROUP B

Thursday, 18 September 2014
Club Brugge (0) 0
Torino (0) 0   17,000
Club Brugge: (442) Ryan; Meunier, Mechele, Duarte, Bolingoli Mbombo (De Bock 80); Menegazzo (Vormer 66), Silva, Simons, Vazquez (Storm 66); Felipe Gedoz, Izquierdo.
Torino: (352) Gillet; Darmian, Benassi (El Kaddouri 65), Gazzi, Sanchez Mino (Nocerino 84), Molinaro; Quagliarella (Martinez 69), Amauri.

FC Copenhagen (0) 2 *(Jorgensen N 68, 81)*
HJK Helsinki (0) 0   1371
FC Copenhagen: (442) Andersen; Amartey, Jorgensen M, Nilsson (Antonsson 82), Bengtsson; Gislason (Amankwaa 58), Claudemir, Toutouh, Kacaniklic; Kadrii (Jorgensen N 58), Cornelius.
HJK Helsinki: (433) Doblas; Sorsa, Moren, Heikkinen, Lampi; Savage (Zeneli 77), Tainio, Lod; Annan, Bance, Porokara (Kandji 71).

Thursday, 2 October 2014
HJK Helsinki (0) 0
Club Brugge (1) 3 *(Heikkinen 19 (og), De Sutter 70, De Bock 78)*   7000
HJK Helsinki: (451) Doblas; Sorsa, Heikkinen, Baah, Lampi; Lod (Kandji 43), Annan, Vayrynen (Zeneli 46), Tainio, Savage; Bance (Porokara 66).
Club Brugge: (442) Ryan; Meunier, Mechele, Duarte, De Bock; Felipe Gedoz (Izquierdo 80), Menegazzo, Silva, Vazquez (Simons 73); Oulare (De Sutter 64), Rafaelov.

Torino (0) 1 *(Quagliarella 90 (pen))*
FC Copenhagen (0) 0   15,000
Torino: (352) Gillet; Maksimovic, Glik, Moretti; Darmian, Benassi, Gazzi, Sanchez Mino (El Kaddouri 69), Molinaro; Martinez (Quagliarella 72), Amauri (Larrondo 78).
FC Copenhagen: (442) Andersen; Bengtsson, Antonsson, Jorgensen M, Hogli; Toutouh, Claudemir (Delaney 82), Amartey, Gislason (Kacaniklic 68); Kadrii (Jorgensen N 58), Cornelius.

Thursday, 23 October 2014
Club Brugge (0) 1 *(Vazquez 90)*
FC Copenhagen (0) 1 *(Amartey 89)*   20,000
Club Brugge: (433) Ryan; De Fauw, Mechele, Duarte, De Bock; Silva (Izquierdo 79), Simons, Vazquez; Felipe Gedoz, Castillo (De Sutter 69), Sobota (Rafaelov 56).

FC Copenhagen: (442) Andersen; Hogli, Jorgensen M, Antonsson, Bengtsson; Kacaniklic (Gislason 64), Amankwaa (Claudemir 82), Amartey, Delaney; Cornelius, Jorgensen N (De Ridder 68).

Torino (1) 2 *(Molinaro 35, Amauri 58)*
HJK Helsinki (0) 0   10,000
Torino: (352) Padelli; Maksimovic, Jansson, Silva; Darmian, Benassi (Nocerino 71), Vives, El Kaddouri, Molinaro; Martinez (Barreto 76), Amauri (Quagliarella 67).
HJK Helsinki: (442) Doblas (Eriksson 46); Sorsa, Heikkinen, Baah, Lampi; Savage, Tainio (Vayrynen 76), Annan, Zeneli (Alho 66); Lod, Kandji.

Thursday, 6 November 2014
FC Copenhagen (0) 0
Club Brugge (3) 4 *(Rafaelov 7, 30, 36, Vormer 60)*   14,000
FC Copenhagen: (442) Andersen; Hogli, Bengtsson (Toutouh 62), Antonsson, Jorgensen M; Claudemir, Kacaniklic, Amartey (Delaney 46), Gislason; Jorgensen N (Amankwaa 33), De Ridder.
Club Brugge: (433) Ryan; De Fauw, Duarte, Meunier, Mechele; Simons, Vazquez (Menegazzo 65), Rafaelov; Vormer, Felipe Gedoz (Sobota 77), De Sutter (Castillo 46).

HJK Helsinki (0) 2 *(Baah 60, Moren 81)*
Torino (0) 1 *(Quagliarella 90)*   10,000
HJK Helsinki: (4411) Doblas; Sorsa, Moren, Baah, Lampi; Savage, Annan, Lod, Zeneli (Alho 86); Vayrynen (Perovuo 75); Kandji (Heikkila 89).
Torino: (352) Padelli; Jansson, Glik, Silva; Masiello (Molinaro 71), Sanchez Mino, Gazzi, Benassi (El Kaddouri 64), Darmian; Martinez (Larrondo 55), Quagliarella.

Thursday, 27 November 2014
HJK Helsinki (1) 2 *(Baah 28, Kandji 90)*
FC Copenhagen (0) 1 *(Nilsson 90)*   10,000
HJK Helsinki: (433) Doblas; Sorsa, Moren, Heikkinen, Baah; Tainio (Schuller 53), Vayrynen (Heikkila 70), Lod; Alho, Kandji, Zeneli (Perovuo 80).
FC Copenhagen: (4411) Andersen; Hogli (Amankwaa 71), Nilsson, Antonsson, Bengtsson; Gislason, Amartey, Delaney (Toutouh 71), Kacaniklic (Jorgensen N 46); De Ridder; Cornelius.

Torino (0) 0
Club Brugge (0) 0   10,000
Torino: (352) Padelli; Bovo, Jansson, Moretti; Darmian, Benassi (Vives 78), Gazzi, El Kaddouri, Molinaro; Martinez (Larrondo 87), Amauri.
Club Brugge: (433) Ryan; Meunier, Mechele, Duarte, De Bock; Silva (Vormer 62), Simons, Menegazzo; Felipe Gedoz, Vazquez (Rafaelov 62), Castillo (De Sutter 87).

Thursday, 11 December 2014
Club Brugge (1) 2 *(Felipe Gedoz 28 (pen), Rafaelov 88)*
HJK Helsinki (0) 1 *(Kandji 51)*   11,894
Club Brugge: (442) Ryan; Mechele, Storm, Duarte, De Fauw; Felipe Gedoz, Menegazzo (Rafaelov 71), Simons, Vormer; Coopman (Vazquez 71), De Sutter (Oulare 79).
HJK Helsinki: (4231) Doblas; Sorsa, Moren, Heikkinen, Baah; Annan, Schuller; Lod, Vayrynen (Perovuo 83), Zeneli (Porokara 63); Kandji.

FC Copenhagen (1) 1 *(Amartey 6)*
Torino (2) 5 *(Martinez 15, 47, Amauri 41 (pen), Darmian 49, Silva 53)*   9202
FC Copenhagen: (442) Andersen; Amartey, Jorgensen M*, Antonsson*, Hogli; Amankwaa, Delaney, Claudemir (Lindberg 76), Toutouh; Jorgensen N (Felfel 83), De Ridder (Olsen 63).
Torino: (532) Padelli; Maksimovic (Jansson 60), Darmian, Glik, Moretti; Silva; Bovo, Gazzi, El Kaddouri (Graziano 66); Martinez (Quagliarella 58), Amauri.

Group B Table	P	W	D	L	F	A	GD	Pts
Club Brugge	6	3	3	0	10	2	8	12
Torino	6	3	2	1	9	3	6	11
HJK Helsinki	6	2	0	4	5	11	–6	6
FC Copenhagen	6	1	1	4	5	13	–8	4

GROUP C

Thursday, 18 September 2014
Besiktas (1) 1 *(Tore 33)*
Asteras Tripolis (0) 1 *(Parra 88)*   7760
Besiktas: (4231) Zengin; Uysal, Sivok, Franco, Ramon; Kavlak, Hutchinson; Tore, Ozyakup (Sosa 69), Sahan (Frei 85); Pektemek (Tosun 30).
Asteras Tripolis: (4141) Kosicky; Lluy, Goian, Sankare, Panteliadis (Munafo 76); Zisopoulos; Badibanga (Parra 69), Usero, Rolle, Mazza; Barrales (Gianniotas 84).

Partizan Belgrade (0) 0
Tottenham H (0) 0   21,000
Partizan Belgrade: (451) Lukac; Vulicevic, Ilic B, Stankovic, Volkov (Petrovic 54); Grbic (Luka 84), Drincic, Cirkovic (Markovic 68), Pantic, Ilic S; Lazovic.
Tottenham H: (451) Lloris; Naughton, Fazio, Vertonghen, Davies; Lennon, Bentaleb, Paulinho (Soldado 59), Stambouli (Capoue 72), Townsend (Lamela 59); Kane.

Thursday, 2 October 2014
Asteras Tripolis (1) 2 *(Usero 22, Parra 52)*
Partizan Belgrade (0) 0   3500
Asteras Tripolis: (442) Kosicky; Panteliadis, Goian, Sankare, Lluy; Usero, Rolle (Munafo 89), Zisopoulos, Gianniotas (Kitoko 73); Mazza, Parra (Barrales 59).
Partizan Belgrade: (442) Lukac; Volkov, Vulicevic, Stankovic, Cirkovic; Ilic B, Grbic (Ninkovic 63), Zivkovic (Fofana 46), Ilic S (Kojic 77); Pantic, Lazovic.

Tottenham H (1) 1 *(Kane 27)*
Besiktas (0) 1 *(Ba 89 (pen))*   32,000
Tottenham H: (433) Lloris; Dier, Chiriches, Fazio, Davies; Stambouli (Dembele 64), Paulinho (Lennon 60), Bentaleb; Townsend, Soldado (Adebayor 78), Kane.
Besiktas: (433) Zengin; Kurtulus, Sivok, Franco, Ramon; Sosa, Tore (Koyunlu 82), Kavlak (Ozyakup 65); Hutchinson, Ba, Sahan (Pektemek 72).

Thursday, 23 October 2014
Partizan Belgrade (0) 0
Besiktas (2) 4 *(Kavlak 18, Ba 44, Ozyakup 52, Tore 54)*   17,500
Partizan Belgrade: (4411) Lukac; Stevanovic, Cirkovic, Stankovic, Volkov; Zivkovic (Grbic 67), Ilic B, Drincic (Markovic 61), Pantic; Lazovic (Ninkovic 61); Skuletic.
Besiktas: (451) Zengin; Uysal, Franco, Sivok, Ramon; Tore (Koyunlu 64), Ozyakup (Koybasi 78), Kavlak, Hutchinson, Sahan; Ba (Tosun 69).

Tottenham H (2) 5 *(Kane 13, 75, 81, Lamela 29, 66)*
Asteras Tripolis (0) 1 *(Barrales 89)*   21,000
Tottenham H: (442) Lloris■; Dier, Fazio, Vertonghen, Davies; Lamela (Eriksen 76), Capoue, Dembele, Townsend (Lennon 83); Kane, Adebayor (Chadli 76).
Asteras Tripolis: (4141) Kosicky; Lluy, Sankare, Zisopoulos, Panteliadis; Munafo; Mazza, Usero, Rolle (Barrales 72), Tsokanis; Parra (Fernandez 80).

Thursday, 6 November 2014
Asteras Tripolis (0) 1 *(Barrales 90 (pen))*
Tottenham H (2) 2 *(Townsend 37 (pen), Kane 42)*   6500
Asteras Tripolis: (4231) Kosicky; Lluy, Sankare, Zisopoulos, Panteliadis; Usero, Munafo (Gianniotas 81); Mazza, Rolle, Tsokanis (Badibanga 60); Parra (Barrales 84).
Tottenham H: (4231) Vorm; Dier, Fazio■, Vertonghen, Davies; Stambouli, Dembele; Townsend, Lamela (Soldado 46), Eriksen (Mason 63); Kane (Paulinho 76).

Besiktas (0) 2 *(Ba 57 (pen), 62)*
Partizan Belgrade (0) 1 *(Markovic 78)*   12,000
Besiktas: (4231) Gonen; Koybasi, Franco, Sivok, Ramon; Kavlak, Hutchinson; Tore (Uysal 90), Ozyakup (Sosa 69), Sahan (Pektemek 72); Ba.
Partizan Belgrade: (4231) Lukac; Stevanovic, Cirkovic, Stankovic, Volkov; Markovic, Drincic; Grbic (Zivkovic 67), Pantic (Ilic S 65), Ninkovic; Skuletic (Lazovic 67).

Thursday, 27 November 2014
Asteras Tripolis (0) 2 *(Barrales 72, Parra 83)*
Besiktas (1) 2 *(Ba 15, Tore 61 (pen))*   14,000
Asteras Tripolis: (433) Kosicky; Lluy, Sankare, Goian, Panteliadis; Kourbelis (Usero 62), Zisopoulos, Fernandez (Bakasetas 77); Mazza, Gianniotas (Barrales 46), Parra.
Besiktas: (4231) Gonen; Kurtulus, Franco, Gulum, Ramon; Hutchinson■, Sosa (Ozyakup 71); Tore (Uysal 86), Kavlak, Sahan (Koyunlu 64); Ba.

Tottenham H (0) 1 *(Stambouli 49)*
Partizan Belgrade (0) 0   30,000
Tottenham H: (4411) Lloris; Naughton, Vertonghen, Chiriches, Davies; Lennon, Stambouli, Dembele (Bentaleb 56), Lamela; Paulinho (Winks 87); Soldado (Kane 65).
Partizan Belgrade: (451) Lukac; Ilic B, Cirkovic, Stankovic, Volkov; Lazovic, Ninkovic (Zivkovic 62), Markovic, Ilic S (Marinkovic 74), Grbic; Skuletic (Kojic 78).

Thursday, 11 December 2014
Besiktas (0) 1 *(Tosun 59)*
Tottenham H (0) 0   19,511
Besiktas: (4141) Zengin; Kurtulus, Franco, Gulum (Nukan 46), Ramon; Uysal; Tore (Koybasi 84), Koyunlu (Yaman 90), Sosa, Sahan; Tosun.
Tottenham H: (4231) Vorm; Walker (Capoue 76), Kaboul, Chiriches, Rose; Stambouli, Dembele; Townsend, Paulinho (Lennon 69), Chadli; Soldado (Lamela 69).

Partizan Belgrade (0) 0
Asteras Tripolis (0) 0   8500
Partizan Belgrade: (4411) Lukac; Petrovic, Ilic B, Stankovic, Volkov; Grbic (Ilic S 74), Markovic, Drincic, Zivkovic; Ninkovic (Luka 81); Skuletic (Kojic 89).
Asteras Tripolis: (451) Theodoropoulos; Sankare, Zisopoulos, Lluy, Panteliadis; Bakasetas (Badibanga 72), Tie Bi (Mazza 75), Munafo, Tsokanis, Gianniotas (Fernandez 63); Barrales.

Group C Table	P	W	D	L	F	A	GD	Pts
Besiktas	6	3	3	0	11	5	6	12
Tottenham H	6	3	2	1	9	4	5	11
Asteras Tripolis	6	1	3	2	7	10	–3	6
Partizan Belgrade	6	0	2	4	1	9	–8	2

GROUP D

Thursday, 18 September 2014
Dinamo Zagreb (3) 5 *(Soudani 16, 23, 45, Henriquez 70, Coric 90)*
Astra Giurgiu (0) 1 *(Chitu 82)*   15,000
Dinamo Zagreb: (4231) Eduardo; Ivo Pinto (Paulo Machado 72), Sigali, Simunic, Pivaric; Brozovic, Ademi; Soudani, Antolic (Coric 77), Wilson Eduardo; Cop (Henriquez 67).
Astra Giurgiu: (4231) Lung Jr; Pliatsikas, Ben Youssef, Oros, Junior Morais; Yahaya (Florescu 74), Laban; Enache (Chitu 57), Budescu, William Amorim; Fatai (Bukari 65).

Red Bull Salzburg (1) 2 *(Alan 36, Soriano 78)*
Celtic (1) 2 *(Wakaso 14, Brown 60)*   17,886
Red Bull Salzburg: (442) Gulacsi; Schwegler, Ramalho Silva, Hinteregger, Ulmer (Ankersen 82); Kampl, Leitgeb, Ilsanker, Sabitzer; Alan, Soriano.
Celtic: (451) Gordon; Ambrose, Denayer, van Dijk, Izaguirre; Commons (Tonev 75), McGregor, Brown, Johansen (Kayal 90), Wakaso; Scepovic (Stokes 67).

Thursday, 2 October 2014
Astra Giurgiu (1) 1 *(Seto 15)*
Red Bull Salzburg (2) 2 *(Kampl 36, Soriano 42)*   3000
Astra Giurgiu: (4411) Lung Jr; Pliatsikas, Ben Youssef, Oros, Junior Morais; Enache, Laban (Florescu 73), Seto, William Amorim; Budescu; Bukari.
Red Bull Salzburg: (442) Gulacsi; Lazaro, Ramalho Silva, Hinteregger, Ulmer; Kampl, Ilsanker, Leitgeb, Sabitzer; Soriano (Quaschner 73), Alan (Bruno 83).

Celtic (1) 1 *(Commons 6)*
Dinamo Zagreb (0) 0   37,000
Celtic: (4411) Gordon; Denayer, Ambrose, van Dijk, Izaguirre; Tonev (Berget 87), Johansen, Brown, Wakaso (Griffiths 77); Commons (Kayal 68); Stokes.
Dinamo Zagreb: (433) Eduardo; Ivo Pinto, Sigali, Simunic, Pivaric; Ademi, Brozovic, Antolic (Coric 75); Soudani, Cop (Henriquez 60), Wilson Eduardo (Pjaca 84).

Thursday, 23 October 2014

Celtic (0) 2 *(Scepovic 73, Johansen 79)*
Astra Giurgiu (0) 1 *(Enache 81)*   28,182
Celtic: (433) Gordon; Lustig, Denayer, van Dijk, Izaguirre; Brown, Mulgrew (Wakaso 66), Johansen; McGregor (Tonev 57), Scepovic, Stokes (Kayal 77).
Astra Giurgiu: (4231) Lung Jr; Pliatsikas, Ben Youssef, Oros, Junior Morais; Laban (Florescu 88), Yahaya; Enache, Seto (Fatai 78), William Amorim (Rus 87); Budescu.

Red Bull Salzburg (2) 4 *(Alan 13, 45, 52, Ramalho Silva 49)*
Dinamo Zagreb (0) 2 *(Ademi 81, Henriquez 89)*   12,872
Red Bull Salzburg: (442) Gulacsi; Ankersen, Ramalho Silva, Hinteregger, Ulmer (Lazaro 69); Kampl, Ilsanker, Leitgeb (Keita 83), Bruno; Alan (Sabitzer 70), Soriano.
Dinamo Zagreb: (433) Eduardo; Ivo Pinto (Simunovic 64), Sigali, Simunic, Pivaric (Vukojevic 64); Paulo Machado (Pjaca 54), Ademi, Brozovic; Soudani, Henriquez, Antolic.

Thursday, 6 November 2014

Astra Giurgiu (0) 1 *(William Amorim 79)*
Celtic (1) 1 *(Johansen 32)*   2500
Astra Giurgiu: (4231) Lung Jr; Pliatsikas, Ben Youssef, Oros, Junior Morais; Laban*, Yahaya (Seto 81); Enache, Budescu (Florescu 62), Joaozinho (William Amorim 46); Bukari.
Celtic: (4231) Gordon; Lustig, Denayer, van Dijk, Izaguirre; Brown, Mulgrew; McGregor, Johansen, Wakaso (Matthews 81); Scepovic (Griffiths 73).

Dinamo Zagreb (0) 1 *(Henriquez 60)*
Red Bull Salzburg (1) 5 *(Soriano 40, 64, 85, Kampl 59, Bruno 72)*   10,000
Dinamo Zagreb: (451) Eduardo; Ivo Pinto, Simunovic, Taravel, Ibanez; Soudani, Brozovic, Ademi, Antolic (Andrijasevic 69), Cop (Fernandes 61); Henriquez.
Red Bull Salzburg: (442) Gulacsi; Ankersen, Ramalho Silva, Hinteregger (Schiemer 87), Ulmer; Keita (Laimer 77), Ilsanker, Leitgeb, Kampl; Sabitzer (Bruno 32), Soriano.

Thursday, 27 November 2014

Astra Giurgiu (0) 1 *(Bukari 50)*
Dinamo Zagreb (0) 0   1000
Astra Giurgiu: (433) Lung Jr; Rus, Oros, Ben Youssef, Junior Morais; Florescu, Yahaya, Seto; Enache, Bukari (Chitu 90), Budescu (William Amorim 76).
Dinamo Zagreb: (433) Eduardo; Ivo Pinto, Simunovic, Taravel, Pivaric; Brozovic, Vukojevic (Paulo Machado 54), Antolic; Soudani, Henriquez (Cop 68), Wilson Eduardo (Fernandes 54).

Celtic (1) 1 *(Johansen 30)*
Red Bull Salzburg (2) 3 *(Alan 8, 13, Keita 90)*   32,414
Celtic: (4231) Gordon; Matthews, Ambrose, van Dijk, Izaguirre; Mulgrew (Tonev 74), Brown; McGregor (Forrest 67), Johansen, Stokes (Commons 67); Griffiths.
Red Bull Salzburg: (442) Gulacsi; Ankersen (Schwegler 80), Ramalho Silva, Hinteregger, Schmitz; Kampl, Bruno (Keita 71), Ilsanker, Leitgeb; Alan, Soriano (Sabitzer 74).

Thursday, 11 December 2014

Dinamo Zagreb (2) 4 *(Pjaca 14, 39, 50, Brozovic 48)*
Celtic (2) 3 *(Commons 23, Scepovic 30, Pivaric 82 (og))*   4054
Dinamo Zagreb: (451) Eduardo; Ivo Pinto, Sigali, Taravel (Simunovic 11), Pivaric; Soudani (Fernandes 82), Brozovic, Ademi, Antolic, Pjaca; Henriquez (Cop 65).
Celtic: (4411) Gordon; Matthews (Fisher 56), Ambrose, van Dijk, Izaguirre; McGregor (Henderson 63), Biton, Johansen, Wakaso (Stokes 77); Commons; Scepovic.

Red Bull Salzburg (2) 5 *(Sabitzer 9, Kampl 34, 90, Alan 46, 70)*
Astra Giurgiu (0) 1 *(Florescu 51)*   8258
Red Bull Salzburg: (442) Walke; Ankersen (Schwegler 78), Caleta-Car, Hinteregger (Schiemer 82), Schmitz; Bruno (Soriano 74), Keita, Laimer, Kampl; Sabitzer, Alan.
Astra Giurgiu: (451) Lung Jr; Rus, Oros, Ben Youssef, Junior Morais; William Amorim (Grandin 79), Pliatsikas, Florescu, Chitu (Yahaya 57), Seto; Budescu (Fatai 90).

Group D Table	P	W	D	L	F	A	GD	Pts
Red Bull Salzburg	6	5	1	0	21	8	13	16
Celtic	6	2	2	2	10	11	–1	8
Dinamo Zagreb	6	2	0	4	12	15	–3	6
Astra Giurgiu	6	1	1	4	6	15	–9	4

GROUP E

Thursday, 18 September 2014

Panathinaikos (0) 1 *(Dinas 64)*
Dynamo Moscow (1) 2 *(Kokorin 40, Ionov 50)*   11,000
Panathinaikos: (4312) Kotsolis; Triantafyllopoulos, Mendes Da Silva, Schildenfeld, Nano; Zeca, Lagos (Petric 76), Pranjic (Koutroubis 80); Dinas; Klonaridis (Donis 58), Karelis.
Dynamo Moscow: (442) Gabulov; Manolev, Samba, Douglas, Buttner (Granat 69); Noboa, Yusupov, Ionov, Dzsudzsak; Kuranyi (Prudnikov 90), Kokorin (Hubocan 89).

PSV Eindhoven (1) 1 *(De Jong 26 (pen))*
Estoril Praia (0) 0   18,000
PSV Eindhoven: (433) Zoet; Brenet, Bruma, Rekik, Willems; Hendrix, Wijnaldum, Maher (Ritzmaier 74); Narsingh, De Jong, Locadia (Jozefzoon 65).
Estoril Praia: (433) Kieszek; Mano, Tavares, Bruno Miguel, Emidio Rafael; Diogo Amado, Toze (Babanco 73), Filipe Goncalves; Kuca, Bruno Lopes (Arthuro 73), Seba (Ricardo Vaz 88).

Thursday, 2 October 2014

Dynamo Moscow (0) 1 *(Zhirkov 90)*
PSV Eindhoven (0) 0   7872
Dynamo Moscow: (4411) Gabulov; Hubocan, Douglas, Samba, Buttner; Ionov (Valbuena 73), Yusupov, Vainqueur, Dzsudzsak (Zhirkov 61); Noboa (Kuranyi 68); Kokorin.
PSV Eindhoven: (433) Zoet; Arias, Bruma, Rekik, Willems; Wijnaldum, Hendrix, Maher (Ritzmaier 85); Narsingh, Locadia, Jozefzoon (Vloet 84).

Estoril Praia (0) 2 *(Kleber 52, Diogo Amado 66)*
Panathinaikos (0) 0   4000
Estoril Praia: (451) Vagner; Anderson Luis, Bruno, Tavares, Emidio Rafael; Toze (Kuca 62), Diogo Amado (Filipe Goncalves 78), Esiti, Cabrera, Seba; Bruno Lopes (Kleber 46).
Panathinaikos: (4411) Kotsolis; Bourbos, Schildenfeld, Triantafyllopoulos, Nano; Bajrami (Karelis 46), Zeca, Pranjic (Lagos 75), Dinas (Donis 57); Ajagun; Petric.

Thursday, 23 October 2014

Estoril Praia (0) 1 *(Tavares 90)*
Dynamo Moscow (0) 2 *(Kokorin 52, Zhirkov 81)*   2164
Estoril Praia: (4231) Vagner; Anderson Luis, Bruno Miguel, Tavares, Ruben Fernandes; Diogo Amado, Esiti; Seba (Ricardo Vaz 85), Toze (Arthuro 77), Kuca; Kleber (Cabrera 81).
Dynamo Moscow: (4231) Gabulov; Kozlov, Douglas, Samba, Buttner; Denisov, Vainqueur; Ionov (Zhirkov 56), Noboa, Valbuena (Rotenberg 90); Kokorin (Kuranyi 75).

PSV Eindhoven (1) 1 *(Depay 43)*
Panathinaikos (0) 1 *(Karelis 87)*   22,000
PSV Eindhoven: (433) Pasveer; Brenet, Bruma*, Rekik, Willems; Maher, Hendrix (Isimat-Mirin 90), Guardado; Narsingh (Ritzmaier 75); De Jong, Depay (Jozefzoon 67).
Panathinaikos: (433) Steele; Triantafyllopoulos, Koutroubis, Schildenfeld, Nano; Zeca, Donis, Pranjic (Karelis 60); Dinas (Ajagun 24), Klonaridis (Petric 75), Bouy.

Thursday, 6 November 2014

Dynamo Moscow (0) 1 *(Kuranyi 78)*

Estoril Praia (0) 0 5374

Dynamo Moscow: (4411) Gabulov; Hubocan, Douglas, Samba, Buttner; Ionov, Denisov, Vainqueur, Dzsudzsak (Zhirkov 76); Valbuena (Yusupov 86); Kokorin (Kuranyi 74).
Estoril Praia: (433) Kieszek; Anderson Luis (Ricardo Vaz 87), Tavares, Ruben Fernandes, Emidio Rafael; Diogo Amado, Esiti, Toze; Kuca, Kleber (Bruno Lopes 73), Seba.

Panathinaikos (2) 2 *(Ajagun 11, Petric 43)*

PSV Eindhoven (1) 3 *(Depay 27, De Jong 65, Wijnaldum 78)* 19,500

Panathinaikos: (4141) Steele; Triantafyllopoulos, Mendes Da Silva, Schildenfeld, Nano; Lagos (Donis 45); Zeca, Pranjic, Ajagun (Bouy 72), Karelis; Petric (Berg 63).
PSV Eindhoven: (4141) Zoet; Arias, Rekik, Isimat-Mirin, Willems (Hendrix 90); Guardado; Wijnaldum, Maher, Narsingh (Jozefzoon 90), Depay; De Jong.

Thursday, 27 November 2014

Dynamo Moscow (0) 2 *(Triantafyllopoulos 55 (og), Ionov 61)*

Panathinaikos (1) 1 *(Berg 14)* 4207

Dynamo Moscow: (4411) Gabulov; Rotenberg, Douglas, Samba, Buttner; Ionov (Dzsudzsak 81), Noboa, Vainqueur, Zhirkov (Yusupov 72); Valbuena; Kuranyi (Prudnikov 88).
Panathinaikos: (433) Kotsolis; Bourbos (Koutroubis 56), Triantafyllopoulos, Schildenfeld, Nano; Lagos, Mendes Da Silva (Pranjic 86), Donis; Bajrami, Berg (Klonaridis 78), Petric.

Friday, 28 November 2014

Estoril Praia (3) 3 *(Toze 12, Kuca 30, Diogo Amado 39)*

PSV Eindhoven (2) 3 *(Depay 6, Narsingh 14, Wijnaldum 82)* 3700

Estoril Praia: (4321) Kieszek; Anderson Luis, Tavares, Ruben Fernandes (Arthuro 86), Emidio Rafael; Diogo Amado, Esiti, Toze; Kuca, Seba; Kleber.
PSV Eindhoven: (433) Zoet; Arias, Bruma, Rekik, Willems; Wijnaldum, Guardado, Maher (Hendrix 78); Narsingh (Locadia 83), De Jong (Isimat-Mirin 88), Depay.

Thursday, 11 December 2014

Panathinaikos (0) 1 *(Karelis 55)*

Estoril Praia (0) 1 *(Kleber 87)* 8200

Panathinaikos: (433) Steele; Bourbos (Triantafyllopoulos 28), Risvanis, Koutroubis, Chouchoumis; Donis, Lagos, Bouy; Ajagun (Pranjic 60), Karelis, Dinas (Berg 67).
Estoril Praia: (433) Vagner; Mano, Bruno, Tavares, Emidio Rafael; Babanco (Diogo Amado 72), Esiti, Cabrera; Kuca (Balboa 68), Arthuro (Kleber 61), Seba.

PSV Eindhoven (0) 0

Dynamo Moscow (0) 1 *(Ionov 90)* 20,400

PSV Eindhoven: (433) Pasveer; Brenet, Rekik, Isimat-Mirin, Willems; Maher (Wijnaldum 81), Hendrix (Ritzmaier 67), Guardado; Jozefzoon, Locadia, Depay (De Jong 67).
Dynamo Moscow: (4411) Shunin; Kozlov, Douglas, Hubocan, Manolev; Valbuena, Noboa, Vainqueur (Ionov 59), Dzsudzsak (Aleksandr 90); Yusupov; Kuranyi (Prudnikov 68).

Group E Table	P	W	D	L	F	A	GD	Pts
Dynamo Moscow	6	6	0	0	9	3	6	18
PSV Eindhoven	6	2	2	2	8	8	0	8
Estoril Praia	6	1	2	3	7	8	–1	5
Panathinaikos	6	0	2	4	6	11	–5	2

GROUP F

Thursday, 18 September 2014

Dnipro Dnipropetrovsk (0) 0

Internazionale (0) 1 *(D'Ambrosio 71)* 14,000

Dnipro Dnipropetrovsk: (442) Boyko; Fedetskiy, Mazuch, Douglas, Strinic; Bruno Gama, Kankava, Rotan[a], Konoplyanka; Kravchenko (Shakhov 67 (Luchkevych 74)), Zozulya (Kalinic 78).

Internazionale: (352) Handanovic; Campagnaro, Vidic, Juan Jesus; D'Ambrosio, Kuzmanovic (Osvaldo 62), M'Vila, Hernanes (Jonathan 76), Dodo; Icardi, Guarin.

Qarabag (0) 0

Saint-Etienne (0) 0 28,786

Qarabag: (442) Sehic; Garayev, Medvedev, Sadygov, Huseynov; Agolli, Almeida, Muarem (Danilo Dias 80), Reynaldo; Chumbinho (Nadirov 46), George (Alaskarov 70).
Saint-Etienne: (442) Ruffier; Baysse, Pogba, Bayal Sall, Clement; Corgnet (Saint-Maximin 49), Cohade (Diomande 87), Brison, Gradel; Erdinc (Lemoine 74), Monnet-Paquet.

Thursday, 2 October 2014

Internazionale (1) 2 *(D'Ambrosio 18, Icardi 85)*

Qarabag (0) 0 70,000

Internazionale: (352) Carrizo; Andreolli, Ranocchia, Juan Jesus; D'Ambrosio, Hernanes (Obi 71), M'Vila, Kuzmanovic (Medel 58), Nagatomo; Guarin (Osvaldo 63), Icardi.
Qarabag: (4411) Sehic; Gurbanov (Sadygov 68), Teli, Huseynov, Agolli; Muarem, Garayev, Yusifov (Nadirov 54), George (Tagiyev 62); Almeida; Reynaldo.

Saint-Etienne (0) 0

Dnipro Dnipropetrovsk (0) 0 28,207

Saint-Etienne: (442) Ruffier; Clerc, Bayal Sall, Clement, Cohade (Corgnet 75); Lemoine, Perrin, Tabanou, Gradel; van Wolfswinkel, Monnet-Paquet.
Dnipro Dnipropetrovsk: (442) Boyko; Mazuch, Strinic, Douglas, Fedetskiy; Kravchenko, Kankava (Shakhov 80), Bruno Gama, Politylo; Kalinic (Konoplyanka 56), Zozulya (Seleznyov 73).

Thursday, 23 October 2014

Dnipro Dnipropetrovsk (0) 0

Qarabag (1) 1 *(Muarem 21)* 3120

Dnipro Dnipropetrovsk: (4231) Boyko; Fedetskiy, Mazuch, Douglas, Strinic; Bruno Gama, Kravchenko; Rotan, Konoplyanka, Shakhov (Seleznyov 46); Kalinic.
Qarabag: (4411) Sehic; Agolli, Sadygov, Huseynov, Medvedev; Muarem (Alaskarov 89), Yusifov, Qarayev, Nadirov (Tagiyev 72); Almeida (Teli 82); Reynaldo.

Internazionale (0) 0

Saint-Etienne (0) 0 30,000

Internazionale: (352) Carrizo; Andreolli, Vidic, Juan Jesus; Mbaye, Kuzmanovic (Krhin 85), M'Vila (Hernanes 53), Kovacic, Dodo; Guarin (Palacio 70), Icardi.
Saint-Etienne: (433) Ruffier; Theophile-Catherine, Bayal Sall, Perrin, Pogba (Baysse 77); Lemoine, Clement, Diomande (Cohade 85); Hamouma, van Wolfswinkel (Monnet-Paquet 64), Tabanou.

Thursday, 6 November 2014

Qarabag (1) 1 *(George 36)*

Dnipro Dnipropetrovsk (1) 2 *(Kalinic 15, 73)* 31,000

Qarabag: (4141) Sehic; Medvedev, Sadygov, Huseynov, Agolli; Qarayev; George (Nadirov 65), Yusifov (Tagiyev 77), Almeida, Muarem; Reynaldo.
Dnipro Dnipropetrovsk: (4141) Boyko; Fedetskiy, Douglas, Mazuch, Strinic (Kankava 46); Cheberyachko; Zozulya, Bruno Gama (Shakhov 85), Rotan (Kravchenko 90), Konoplyanka; Kalinic.

Saint-Etienne (0) 1 *(Bayal Sall 50)*

Internazionale (1) 1 *(Dodo 33)* 36,411

Saint-Etienne: (343) Ruffier; Perrin, Bayal Sall, Pogba; Theophile-Catherine, Lemoine, Clement, Tabanou; Hamouma (van Wolfswinkel 68), Erdinc (Diomande 56), Gradel.
Internazionale: (352) Carrizo; Andreolli, Vidic, Juan Jesus; Dodo, Mbaye, Medel, Kuzmanovic (Palazzi 83), Kovacic (Osvaldo 74); Palacio, Bonazzoli (Obi 66).

Thursday, 27 November 2014
Internazionale (1) 2 *(Kuzmanovic 30, Osvaldo 50)*
Dnipro Dnipropetrovsk (1) 1 *(Rotan 16)* 25,000
Internazionale: (4312) Handanovic; Nagatomo (Campagnaro 37), Ranocchia▪, Juan Jesus, Dodo; Guarin, Medel, Kuzmanovic; Hernanes (Obi 61); Icardi (Andreolli 55), Osvaldo.
Dnipro Dnipropetrovsk: (4231) Boyko; Fedetskiy (Matheus 70), Douglas, Mazuch (Seleznyov 82), Vlad; Kravchenko (Bruno Gama 73), Cheberyachko; Luchkevych, Rotan, Kalinic; Konoplyanka.

Saint-Etienne (1) 1 *(van Wolfswinkel 21)*
Qarabag (1) 1 *(Nadirov 15)* 29,769
Saint-Etienne: (4411) Ruffier; Theophile-Catherine, Bayal Sall, Perrin, Brison; Hamouma (Monnet-Paquet 63), Lemoine, Clement, Gradel; Cohade (Mollo 67); van Wolfswinkel (Pogba 90).
Qarabag: (4321) Sehic; Medvedev, Huseynov, Sadygov, Agolli; George (Gurbanov 63), Qarayev, Muarem; Yusifov (Teli 75), Nadirov (Alaskarov 80); Almeida.

Thursday, 11 December 2014
Dnipro Dnipropetrovsk (0) 1 *(Fedetskiy 66)*
Saint-Etienne (0) 0 2579
Dnipro Dnipropetrovsk: (4231) Boyko; Fedetskiy, Douglas, Cheberyachko, Vlad; Rotan (Politylo 87), Kravchenko; Zozulya (Bruno Gama 67), Shakhov (Matheus 67), Konoplyanka; Kalinic.
Saint-Etienne: (442) Ruffier; Theophile-Catherine, Perrin, Pogba, Brison (Tabano 83); Monnet-Paquet (Cohade 80), Lemoine, Diomande, Gradel; Mollo (Hamouma 61), van Wolfswinkel.

Qarabag (0) 0
Internazionale (0) 0 31,200
Qarabag: (4411) Sehic; Medvedev, Huseynov, Sadygov, Agolli; Alaskarov (Gurbanov 60), Qarayev, Almeida, Muarem; George; Nadirov (Yusifov 43).
Internazionale: (442) Carrizo; Donkor, Campagnaro, Andreolli, D'Ambrosio (Dimarco 84); M'Vila, Mbaye, Obi (Baldini 90), Krhin; Osvaldo, Bonazzoli.

Group F Table

	P	W	D	L	F	A	GD	Pts
Internazionale	6	3	3	0	6	2	4	12
Dnipro Dnipropetrovsk	6	2	1	3	4	5	−1	7
Qarabag	6	1	3	2	3	5	−2	6
Saint-Etienne	6	0	5	1	2	3	−1	5

GROUP G

Thursday, 18 September 2014
Sevilla (2) 2 *(Krychowiak 8, Mbia 31)*
Feyenoord (0) 0 35,000
Sevilla: (433) Sergio Rico; Fernando Navarro, Diogo Figueiras, Kolodzieczak, Carrico; Krychowiak (Suarez 60), Banega, Mbia; Bacca (Aspas 60), Reyes, Deulofeu.
Feyenoord: (442) Vermeer; Wilkshire, Mathijsen, van Beek, Nelom; Clasie (Te Vrede 73), El Ahmadi, Trindade de Vilhena, Toornstra; Schaken (Basacikoglu 64), Manu (Boetius 82).

Standard Liege (0) 2 *(Ciman 74, Vinicius Araujo 87)*
Rijeka (0) 0 5000
Standard Liege: (442) Kawashima; Teixeira, Ciman, Van Damme, Milec; De Sart, Trebel, Louis (Vinicius Araujo 84), Carcela-Gonzalez (Viera 56); Mujangi Bia (M'Poku 16), de Camargo.
Rijeka: (4411) Vargic; Samardzic, Leovac, Tomecak, Leskovic; Jajalo, Cvijanovic, Kvrzic (Vesovic 66), Jugovic (Ivancic 81); Kramaric (Moises 63); Krstanovic.

Thursday, 2 October 2014
Feyenoord (0) 2 *(van Beek 47, Manu 83)*
Standard Liege (0) 1 *(Viera 63)* 42,000
Feyenoord: (4312) Vermeer; Wilkshire, van Beek, Kongolo, Nelom; El Ahmadi, Clasie, Toornstra; Immers (Basacikoglu 75); Manu (Trindade de Vilhena 88), Kazim-Richards.
Standard Liege: (4411) Kawashima; Milec, Ciman, Arslanagic, Van Damme; Viera (Ono 75), Trebel (de Camargo 86), Faty, M'Poku; Louis; Vinicius Araujo (Watt 68).

Rijeka (0) 2 *(Kramaric 52 (pen), Kvrzic 66)*
Sevilla (1) 2 *(Aspas 26, Mbia 90)* 10,000
Rijeka: (442) Vargic; Tomecak, Mitrovic, Leskovic, Leovac; Jajalo, Cvijanovic, Jugovic, Moises (Vesovic 87); Kramaric (Krstanovic 80), Kvrzic (Zlomislic 73).
Sevilla: (4231) Beto; Coke, Carrico, Kolodzieczak▪, Fernando Navarro; Iborra, Krychowiak; Alex Vidal, Banega (Mbia 56), Reyes (Tremoulinas 56); Aspas (Bacca 71).

Thursday, 23 October 2014
Rijeka (0) 3 *(Kramaric 63, 70, 76 (pen))*
Feyenoord (0) 1 *(Toornstra 66)* 11,200
Rijeka: (442) Vargic; Tomecak, Mitrovic, Leskovic (Samardzic 65), Leovac; Jugovic (Kvrzic 84), Jajalo, Cvijanovic, Moises (Krstanovic 88), Kramaric.
Feyenoord: (451) Vermeer; Steenvoorden, Kongolo, Nelom, Wilkshire (Karsdorp 46); Toornstra, El Ahmadi, Immers, Clasie, Manu (Boetius 80); Kazim-Richards (Te Vrede 80).

Standard Liege (0) 0
Sevilla (0) 0 8000
Standard Liege: (451) Thuram-Ulien; Milec, Ciman, Teixeira, Van Damme; M'Poku, Trebel, Faty, Enoh (Louis 67), Mujangi Bia (Viera 79); de Camargo (Vinicius Araujo 90).
Sevilla: (4231) Beto; Diogo Figueiras, Arribas, Carrico, Fernando Navarro; Iborra, Krychowiak; Alex Vidal (Deulofeu 78), Banega, Reyes (Suarez 64); Gameiro (Bacca 63).

Thursday, 6 November 2014
Feyenoord (2) 2 *(El Ahmadi 8, Immers 20)*
Rijeka (0) 0 30,000
Feyenoord: (442) Vermeer; Wilkshire (Boulahrouz 72), van Beek, Kongolo, Nelom; El Ahmadi, Clasie, Immers, Toornstra; Kazim-Richards, Manu (Boetius 62).
Rijeka: (442) Vargic; Tomecak (Vesovic 79), Samardzic, Leskovic, Leovac; Jugovic, Jajalo, Cvijanovic, Moises (Krstanovic 61); Sharbini (Kvrzic 50), Kramaric.

Sevilla (2) 3 *(Gameiro 19, Reyes 42, Bacca 90)*
Standard Liege (1) 1 *(M'Poku 32)* 35,000
Sevilla: (442) Beto (Sergio Rico 50); Diogo Figueiras, Pareja, Carrico, Tremoulinas; Deulofeu (Bacca 71), Krychowiak, Mbia, Reyes (Vitolo 57); Suarez, Gameiro.
Standard Liege: (442) Thuram-Ulien; Milec, Arslanagic, Ciman, Andrade; M'Poku, Enoh, Trebel (Lumanza-Lembi 82), Van Damme (Mujangi Bia 63); de Camargo, Louis (Watt 67).

Thursday, 27 November 2014
Feyenoord (0) 2 *(Toornstra 55, El Ahmadi 83)*
Sevilla (0) 0 51,117
Feyenoord: (4411) Vermeer; Boulahrouz, van Beek, Kongolo, Nelom; Toornstra, El Ahmadi, Clasie, Boetius; Immers; Kazim-Richards.
Sevilla: (4411) Sergio Rico; Coke, Arribas, Carrico, Kolodzieczak; Suarez (Deulofeu 61), Mbia, Krychowiak, Reyes (Vitolo 81); Aspas (Bacca 60); Gameiro.

Rijeka (2) 2 *(Moises 25, Kramaric 34 (pen))*
Standard Liege (0) 0 11,000
Rijeka: (4411) Vargic; Vesovic, Mitrovic, Leskovic, Tomecak; Jugovic, Mocinic, Jajalo (Cvijanovic 77), Sharbini (Kvrzic 66); Moises (Krstanovic 89); Kramaric.
Standard Liege: (442) Thuram-Ulien; Milec, Ciman, Arslanagic▪, Van Damme; Mujangi Bia (Ono 68), Trebel, De Sart, M'Poku; Vinicius Araujo (Watt 58), de Camargo (Lumanza-Lembi 46).

Thursday, 11 December 2014
Sevilla (1) 1 *(Suarez 20)*
Rijeka (0) 0 24,967
Sevilla: (4231) Beto; Coke (Diogo Figueiras 77), Pareja, Carrico, Fernando Navarro; Mbia, Banega; Reyes, Suarez (Arribas 60), Vitolo; Bacca (Gameiro 66).
Rijeka: (4231) Vargic; Vesovic, Samardzic, Mitrovic, Tomecak; Mocinic (Cvijanovic 71), Jajalo, Kvrzic (Jugovic 67); Moises (Ivancic 76), Sharbini; Kramaric.

Standard Liege (0) 0
Feyenoord (1) 3 *(Toornstra 16, Boetius 60, Manu 89)*
                          11,913
Standard Liege: (442) Kawashima; Stam, Ciman, Fiore, Andrade; Ono (Milosevic 73), Mujangi Bia (de Camargo 61), Faty (De Sart 61), Lumanza-Lembi; Watt, Louis.
Feyenoord: (442) Vermeer; Boulahrouz (Wilkshire 26), van Beek, Kongolo (Dammers 67), Woudenberg; Clasie, Immers, Trindade de Vilhena, Boetius (Manu 82); Toornstra, Kazim-Richards.

Group G Table	P	W	D	L	F	A	GD	Pts
Feyenoord	6	4	0	2	10	6	4	12
Sevilla	6	3	2	1	8	5	3	11
Rijeka	6	2	1	3	7	8	–1	7
Standard Liege	6	1	1	4	4	10	–6	4

GROUP H

Thursday, 18 September 2014
Everton (2) 4 *(Rodriguez 15 (og), Coleman 45, Baines 48 (pen), Mirallas 89)*
Wolfsburg (0) 1 *(Rodriguez 90)*   29,593
Everton: (4231) Howard; Coleman (Osman 90), Stones, Jagielka, Baines; Barry, McCarthy; McGeady, Naismith (Gibson 81), Mirallas; Lukaku (Eto'o 68).
Wolfsburg: (4231) Benaglio; Jung, Knoche, Naldo, Rodriguez; Gustavo (Guilavogui 76), Malanda (Hunt 46); De Bruyne, Arnold, Caligiuri (Bendtner 60); Olic.

Lille (0) 1 *(Kjaer 63)*
Krasnodar (1) 1 *(Laborde 35)*   27,000
Lille: (442) Enyeama; Corchia, Kjaer, Souare, Basa; Balmont (Ryan Mendes 77), Gueye, Mavuba (Delaplace 46), Lopes; Roux (Frey 46), Origi.
Krasnodar: (4411) Dykan; Jedrzejczyk, Granqvist, Sigurdsson, Kaleshin; Gazinski, Ahmedov, Izmailov (Bystrov 69 (Burmistrov 86)), Laborde (Wanderson 70); Pereyra; Ari.

Thursday, 2 October 2014
Krasnodar (1) 1 *(Ari 43)*
Everton (0) 1 *(Eto'o 82)*   31,050
Krasnodar: (451) Dykan; Jedrzejczyk, Sigurdsson, Granqvist, Kaleshin; Izmailov (Wanderson 64), Ahmedov, Gazinski, Pereyra (Petrov 84), Laborde (Mamaev 71); Ari.
Everton: (4231) Howard; Hibbert, Stones, Jagielka, Baines; Gibson, Barry; McGeady, Atsu (Lukaku 46), Osman; Eto'o.

Wolfsburg (0) 1 *(De Bruyne 82)*
Lille (0) 1 *(Origi 77 (pen))*   16,097
Wolfsburg: (4231) Benaglio; Jung (Vieirinha 62), Naldo, Knoche (Caligiuri 79), Rodriguez; Gustavo, Guilavogui; Perisic, Hunt, De Bruyne; Olic (Bendtner 62).
Lille: (451) Enyeama; Beria, Kjaer, Basa, Souare (Sidibe 43); Gueye, Corchia, Rozehnal, Ryan Mendes (Roux 46); Balmont; Origi (Rodelin 85).

Thursday, 23 October 2014
Krasnodar (0) 2 *(Granqvist 51 (pen), Wanderson 86)*
Wolfsburg (1) 4 *(Granqvist 38 (og), De Bruyne 46, 79, Gustavo 64)*   18,000
Krasnodar: (451) Dykan; Jedrzejczyk, Granqvist, Sigurdsson, Kaleshin; Laborde, Ahmedov, Gazinski (Petrov 80), Pereyra (Wanderson 68), Mamaev (Adzhindzhal 68); Ari.
Wolfsburg: (4231) Benaglio; Jung, Naldo, Knoche, Schafer; Gustavo, Guilavogui; Perisic (Vieirinha 61), De Bruyne (Arnold 86), Caligiuri; Olic (Dost 77).

Lille (0) 0
Everton (0) 0   42,000
Lille: (433) Enyeama; Beria, Basa, Kjaer, Souare; Balmont, Gueye, Mavuba (Martin 85); Corchia, Rodelin (Ryan Mendes 73), Origi.
Everton: (4231) Howard; Hibbert, Jagielka, Distin, Baines; Barkley (McCarthy 90), Barry; McGeady (Atsu 82), Pienaar (Lukaku 63), Besic; Eto'o.

Thursday, 6 November 2014
Everton (2) 3 *(Osman 27, Jagielka 42, Naismith 61)*
Lille (0) 0   32,000
Everton: (4231) Howard; Hibbert, Jagielka, Distin, Baines; McCarthy (Besic 84), Barry (Gibson 67); Osman, Naismith, McGeady (Atsu 66); Lukaku.
Lille: (433) Enyeama; Corchia (Rodelin 75), Kjaer, Basa, Souare; Gueye, Mavuba, Balmont; Ryan Mendes (Beria 64), Origi, Frey (Roux 63).

Wolfsburg (0) 5 *(Hunt 47, 57, Guilavogui 73, Bendtner 89 (pen), 90)*
Krasnodar (0) 1 *(Wanderson 72)*   16,674
Wolfsburg: (4231) Benaglio; Trasch, Naldo, Knoche, Schafer (Klose 39); Gustavo, Guilavogui; Vieirinha, De Bruyne, Perisic (Hunt 46); Dost (Bendtner 74).
Krasnodar: (4411) Dykan; Jedrzejczyk, Sigurdsson, Granqvist, Kaleshin (Petrov 29); Gazinski; Wanderson (Mamaev 80), Pereyra, Ahmedov, Laborde; Ari (Izmailov 71).

Thursday, 27 November 2014
Krasnodar (1) 1 *(Ari 35)*
Lille (0) 1 *(Roux 79)*   15,000
Krasnodar: (451) Dykan; Petrov, Jedrzejczyk (Martynovich 45), Sigurdsson, Kaleshin; Mamaev (Wanderson 82), Izmailov (Laborde 46), Gazinski, Pereyra, Joaozinho; Ari.
Lille: (4312) Enyeama; Corchia, Basa, Rozehnal, Beria; Delaplace (Mavuba 62), Balmont, Gueye; Martin (Rodelin 67); Frey (Ryan Mendes 80), Roux.

Wolfsburg (0) 0
Everton (1) 2 *(Lukaku 43, Mirallas 75)*   23,625
Wolfsburg: (4411) Benaglio; Vieirinha, Naldo, Knoche, Schafer; De Bruyne, Gustavo, Malanda (Caligiuri 63), Perisic; Hunt (Arnold 76); Bendtner (Olic 77).
Everton: (4231) Howard; Hibbert, Distin, Jagielka, Garbutt; Besic, McCarthy (Osman 31); McGeady, Eto'o (Barkley 72), Mirallas (Atsu 83); Lukaku.

Thursday, 11 December 2014
Everton (0) 0
Krasnodar (1) 1 *(Laborde 30)*   20,260
Everton: (4411) Robles; Browning (Jones 90), Alcaraz, Barry, Garbutt; Atsu (Dowell 10), Oviedo, Ledson, Pienaar; McAleny (Long 80); Kone.
Krasnodar: (451) Sinitsyn; Petrov, Sigurdsson, Granqvist, Kaleshin; Laborde (Burmistrov 73), Izmailov, Gazinski, Pereyra, Joaozinho (Ageev 90); Wanderson.

Lille (0) 0
Wolfsburg (1) 3 *(Vieirinha 45, Rodriguez 65, 89 (pen))*   33,559
Lille: (442) Enyeama; Sidibe, Kjaer, Basa, Souare; Corchia (Rodelin 67), Mavuba, Gueye (Meite 83), Balmont; Ryan Mendes (Roux 67), Origi.
Wolfsburg: (4231) Benaglio; Jung, Naldo, Knoche, Rodriguez; Gustavo, Guilavogui■; Vieirinha (Malanda 58), De Bruyne (Caligiuri 85), Perisic; Olic (Dost 46).

Group H Table	P	W	D	L	F	A	GD	Pts
Everton	6	3	2	1	10	3	7	11
Wolfsburg	6	3	1	2	14	10	4	10
Krasnodar	6	1	3	2	7	12	–5	6
Lille	6	0	4	2	3	9	–6	4

GROUP I

Thursday, 18 September 2014
Napoli (1) 3 *(Higuain 23 (pen), Mertens 51, 81)*
Sparta Prague (1) 1 *(Husbauer 14)*   18,000
Napoli: (4231) Rafael Cabral; Henrique, Albiol, Koulibaly, Britos; Gargano, Inler; Callejon (David Lopez 83), Hamsik (Zuniga 81), Mertens; Higuain (Michu 69).
Sparta Prague: (442) Bicik; Kaderabek, Kovac, Brabec, Nhamoinesu; Dockal (Konate 75), Matejovsky, Marecek, Krejci; Husbauer (Bednar 78), Lafata (Schick 84).

Young Boys (2) 5 *(Lecjaks 5, Steffen 29, Nuzzolo 63, Nikci 80, Hoarau 90)*
Slovan Bratislava (0) 0 9900
Young Boys: (4231) Mvogo; Hadergjonaj, von Bergen, Rochat, Lecjaks; Bertone, Sanogo; Steffen (Nikci 79), Costanzo (Kubo 66), Nuzzolo; Affum (Hoarau 70).
Slovan Bratislava: (433) Pernis; Cikos, Hudak, Gorosito, Kolcak; Grendel (Milinkovic 62), Lasik, Halenar (Jakubek 77); Meszaros (Zofcak 71), Peltier, Kubik.

Thursday, 2 October 2014
Slovan Bratislava (0) 0
Napoli (1) 2 *(Hamsik 35, Higuain 74)* 10,738
Slovan Bratislava: (4231) Pernis; Cikos, Ninaj, Gorosito, Jablonsky; Grendel (Milinkovic 46), Lasik (Kolcak 85); Kubik (Zofcak 71), Halenar, Peltier; Soumah.
Napoli: (4231) Rafael Cabral; Maggio, Koulibaly, Britos, Ghoulam; David Lopez, Inler; de Guzman (Callejon 63), Hamsik (Mesto 80), Mertens; Zapata (Higuain 73).

Sparta Prague (2) 3 *(Vacha 26, Lafata 28, 85)*
Young Boys (0) 1 *(Hoarau 52)* 10,205
Sparta Prague: (433) Bicik; Kaderabek, Brabec, Holek, Nhamoinesu; Konate (Marecek 80), Vacha, Krejci (Kovac 89); Dockal, Lafata, Matejovsky (Vacek 64).
Young Boys: (433) Mvogo; Sutter (Hadergjonaj 66), Wuthrich (Affum 69), von Bergen, Rochat; Nuzzolo, Sanogo, Lecjaks; Gajic, Hoarau, Steffen (Nikci 89).

Thursday, 23 October 2014
Slovan Bratislava (0) 0
Sparta Prague (0) 3 *(Lafata 56, Konate 61, Krejci 81)* 6891
Slovan Bratislava: (451) Pernis; Bagayoko, Gorosito, Kolcak, Cikos; Zofcak, Halenar (Fort 79), Lasik, Grendel (Hudak 76), Jablonsky (Kubik 59); Soumah.
Sparta Prague: (451) Bicik; Kaderabek, Brabec, Holek, Nhamoinesu; Konate, Matejovsky (Vacek 80), Vacha, Dockal (Marecek 90), Krejci; Lafata (Prikryl 87).

Young Boys (0) 2 *(Hoarau 52, Bertone 90)*
Napoli (0) 0 28,000
Young Boys: (4411) Mvogo; Sutter, Vilotic, von Bergen, Lecjaks; Steffen (Nikci 90), Sanogo, Gajic, Nuzzolo (Rochat 86); Kubo (Bertone 71); Hoarau.
Napoli: (451) Rafael Cabral; Maggio, Albiol, Henrique, Ghoulam; de Guzman (Higuain 84), Jorginho (Callejon 75), Inler, Mertens, Michu (Hamsik 62); Zapata.

Thursday, 6 November 2014
Napoli (1) 3 *(de Guzman 45, 65, 83)*
Young Boys (0) 0 25,000
Napoli: (442) Rafael Cabral; Mesto, Henrique, Koulibaly, Britos (Ghoulam 37); Insigne (Callejon 73), Gargano, Inler, Mertens; de Guzman, Zapata (Higuain 79).
Young Boys: (4141) Mvogo; Hadergjonaj, von Bergen, Vilotic, Rochat; Sanogo; Steffen, Gajic (Kubo 60), Bertone, Nuzzolo (Nikci 61); Hoarau (Affum 68).

Sparta Prague (2) 4 *(Lafata 39, 84, Krejci 32, Nhamoinesu 75)*
Slovan Bratislava (0) 0 13,805
Sparta Prague: (4141) Bicik; Kaderabek, Brabec, Holek, Nhamoinesu; Vacha (Marecek 79); Konate, Dockal (Vacek 72), Matejovsky, Krejci; Lafata (Bednar 89).
Slovan Bratislava: (4231) Pernis; Bagayoko, Kolcak, Ninaj, Cikos; Lasik, Grendel (Stefanik 82); Zofcak, Milinkovic, Kubik (Vittek 73); Peltier (Soumah 46).

Thursday, 27 November 2014
Slovan Bratislava (1) 1 *(Soumah 12)*
Young Boys (2) 3 *(Hoarau 9 (pen), Kubo 18, 63)* 2000
Slovan Bratislava: (4411) Pernis; Kolcak, Hudak, Gorosito, Cikos; Peltier, Grendel (Zofcak 80), Stefanik, Kubik (Milinkovic 83); Halenar; Soumah.
Young Boys: (4411) Mvogo; Sutter, Vilotic, von Bergen, Lecjaks; Steffen (Nuzzolo 71), Sanogo, Bertone, Zarate (Hadergjonaj 80); Kubo; Hoarau (Affum 67).

Sparta Prague (0) 0
Napoli (0) 0 16,111
Sparta Prague: (433) Stech; Kaderabek, Brabec, Holek, Nhamoinesu; Husbauer (Prikryl 72), Marecek, Matejovsky (Vacek 90); Dockal, Lafata, Krejci.

Napoli: (4231) Rafael Cabral; Mesto, Albiol, Koulibaly, Britos; Gargano, David Lopez; Callejon, Jorginho (Ghoulam 77), Hamsik; Higuain (Zapata 68).

Thursday, 11 December 2014
Napoli (2) 3 *(Mertens 6, Hamsik 16, Zapata 75)*
Slovan Bratislava (0) 0 6490
Napoli: (4231) Andujar; Maggio, Koulibaly, Britos, Ghoulam; Inler, Gargano; Callejon (Mesto 74), Hamsik, Mertens (de Guzman 62); Zapata (Higuain 78).
Slovan Bratislava: (4231) Pernis; Cikos, Hudak, Gorosito, Jablonsky; Kolcak, Stefanik; Zofcak (Duris 62), Milinkovic (Halenar 72), Kubik (Gasparovic 87); Peltier.

Young Boys (0) 2 *(Hoarau 76 (pen), Steffen 90)*
Sparta Prague (0) 0 15,150
Young Boys: (4411) Mvogo; Hadergjonaj, Vilotic, von Bergen, Lecjaks; Steffen, Gajic (Rochat 89), Sanogo, Nuzzolo (Zarate 63); Kubo (Bertone 82); Hoarau.
Sparta Prague: (451) Stech; Kaderabek, Brabec, Holek, Nhamoinesu (Schick 81); Dockal, Matejovsky, Marecek, Husbauer (Bednar 86), Krejci; Prikryl (Konate 60).

Group I Table	P	W	D	L	F	A	GD	Pts
Napoli	6	4	1	1	11	3	8	13
Young Boys	6	4	0	2	13	7	6	12
Sparta Prague	6	3	1	2	11	6	5	10
Slovan Bratislava	6	0	0	6	1	20	−19	0

GROUP J

Thursday, 18 September 2014
Rio Ave (0) 0
Dynamo Kyiv (2) 3 *(Yarmolenko 20, Belhanda 25, Kravets 71)* 2315
Rio Ave: (442) Cassio; Gouano, Lionn, Tiago Pinto, Marcelo; Tarantini, Diego Lopes (Wakaso 78), Bressan (Jebor 65), Pedro Moreira; Boateng, Ukra (Goncalves 81).
Dynamo Kyiv: (442) Rybka; Dragovic, Vida, Burda (Selin 87), Makarenko; Sydorchuk (Veloso 67), Rybalka, Belhanda, Lens (Kalitvintsev 79); Yarmolenko, Kravets.

Steaua Bucharest (0) 6 *(Sanmartean 51, Rusescu 60 (pen), 73, Keseru 61, 65, 72)*
Aalborg (0) 0 24
Steaua Bucharest: (442) Arlauskis; Rapa (Rusescu 50), Szukala, Latovlevici, Varela; Chipciu, Prepelita, Sanmartean, Breeveld (Papp 67); Popa, Keseru (Iancu 74).
Aalborg: (442) Larsen■; Petersen, Gorter (Frederiksen 15), Thelander, Enevoldsen (Christensen 59); Wurtz, Wichmann, Risgard, Thomsen; Jacobsen (Helenius 63), Dalsgaard.
(Behind closed doors)

Thursday, 2 October 2014
Aalborg (0) 1 *(Helenius 47)*
Rio Ave (0) 0 6000
Aalborg: (442) Christensen; Dalsgaard, Petersen, Thelander, Gorter; Boersting (Bruhn 66), Wurtz, Risgard, Thomsen; Helenius (Augustinussen 78), Jacobsen (Enevoldsen 90).
Rio Ave: (451) Cassio; Nuno Lopes, Marcelo, Gouano (Vilas Boas 43), Tiago Pinto; Ukra, Tarantini, Wakaso, Pedro Moreira (Koka 64), Diego Lopes; Boateng (Bressan 75).

Dynamo Kyiv (1) 3 *(Yarmolenko 40, Kravets 66, Teodorczyk 90)*
Steaua Bucharest (0) 1 *(Rusescu 89)* 28,280
Dynamo Kyiv: (4231) Rybka; Vida, Danilo Silva, Dragovic, Burda; Sydorchuk (Buyalsky 75), Rybalka; Yarmolenko, Belhanda, Lens (Kalitvintsev 83); Kravets (Teodorczyk 90).
Steaua Bucharest: (4231) Arlauskis; Papp, Varela, Szukala, Latovlevici; Prepelita, Sanmartean; Chipciu, Tanase, Iancu (Stanciu 58 (Rusescu 81)); Keseru.

Thursday, 23 October 2014
Aalborg (2) 3 *(Enevoldsen 11, Thomsen 39, 90)*
Dynamo Kyiv (0) 0 6043
Aalborg: (442) Larsen; Gorter, Thelander, Petersen, Dalsgaard; Thomsen, Wurtz (Augustinussen 82), Risgard, Bruhn; Helenius (Jacobsen 70), Enevoldsen (Frederiksen 86).
Dynamo Kyiv: (4411) Rybka; Burda, Dragovic, Danilo Silva, Vida; Sydorchuk, Rybalka (Veloso 46), Lens (Gusev 76), Belhanda (Teodorczyk 67); Yarmolenko; Kravets.

Steaua Bucharest (2) 2 *(Rusescu 17, 45)*
Rio Ave (0) 1 *(Del Valle 48)* 12,000
Steaua Bucharest: (4411) Arlauskis; Rapa, Szukala, Papp, Latovlevici; Prepelita, Sanmartean (Filip 89), Popa (Breeveld 66), Tanase; Rusescu (Stanciu 69); Keseru.
Rio Ave: (433) Cassio; Nuno Lopes, Marcelo, Gouano, Tiago Pinto; Wakaso, Diego Lopes, Tarantini; Ukra (Boateng 69), Goncalves (Koka 75), Del Valle (Bressan 81).

Thursday, 6 November 2014
Dynamo Kyiv (0) 2 *(Vida 70, Gusev 90)*
Aalborg (0) 0 25,230
Dynamo Kyiv: (442) Shovkovskiy; Danilo Silva, Khacheridi, Dragovic■, Vida; Yarmolenko (Gusev 84), Rybalka, Sydorchuk (Veloso 77), Lens (Burda 72); Belhanda, Kravets.
Aalborg: (442) Larsen; Dalsgaard, Petersen, Thelander, Gorter; Bruhn (Frederiksen 83), Wurtz (Ahlmann 83), Risgard, Thomsen; Enevoldsen (Augustinussen 66), Helenius.

Rio Ave (1) 2 *(Diego Lopes 35, 77 (pen))*
Steaua Bucharest (0) 2 *(Keseru 60, Filip 90)* 3000
Rio Ave: (4231) Ederson Moraes; Nuno Lopes, Marcelo, Gouano■, Tiago Pinto; Wakaso, Tarantini; Ukra, Diego Lopes (Vilas Boas 80), Del Valle (Bressan 59); Goncalves (Koka 68).
Steaua Bucharest: (4231) Arlauskis; Papp, Szukala, Varela, Filip; Prepelita, Sanmartean; Popa (Bourceanu 74), Chipciu, Tanase; Keseru.

Thursday, 27 November 2014
Aalborg (0) 1 *(Enevoldsen 72)*
Steaua Bucharest (0) 0 7515
Aalborg: (442) Larsen; Dalsgaard, Petersen, Thelander, Gorter; Bruhn (Wichmann 77), Wurtz, Risgard, Thomsen; Enevoldsen (Jacobsen 74), Helenius (Augustinussen 87).
Steaua Bucharest: (4411) Arlauskis; Luchin, Papp, Varela, Filip; Popa, Bourceanu (Breeveld 65), Sanmartean, Tanase (Stanciu 77); Chipciu; Keseru.

Dynamo Kyiv (0) 2 *(Lens 53, Veloso 78)*
Rio Ave (0) 0 14,054
Dynamo Kyiv: (4231) Shovkovskiy; Burda, Danilo Silva, Khacheridi, Vida; Sydorchuk (Veloso 62), Rybalka; Yarmolenko, Belhanda, Lens (Gusev 81), Kravets (Mbokani 69).
Rio Ave: (4231) Ederson Moraes; Lionn (Marcelo 80), Vilas Boas, Roderick Miranda, Tiago Pinto; Pedro Moreira, Luis Gustavo; Boateng (Ukra 61), Bressan (Diego Lopes 62), Del Valle; Koka.

Thursday, 11 December 2014
Rio Ave (0) 2 *(Del Valle 59, 79)*
Aalborg (0) 0 2672
Rio Ave: (4231) Cassio; Lionn, Roderick Miranda, Vilas Boas, Tiago Pinto; Pedro Moreira, Luis Gustavo (Wakaso 77); Boateng (Ukra 67), Bressan (Tarantini 75), Del Valle; Koka.
Aalborg: (442) Larsen; Dalsgaard, Petersen, Thelander, Gorter (Blabjerg 11); Bruhn (Jacobsen 63), Wurtz, Risgard (Frederiksen 73), Thomsen; Enevoldsen, Helenius.

Steaua Bucharest (0) 0
Dynamo Kyiv (0) 2 *(Yarmolenko 71, Lens 90)* 5000
Steaua Bucharest: (4231) Arlauskis; Papp, Szukala, Varela, Filip (Latovlevici 78); Prepelita, Bourceanu (Rusescu 61); Chipciu, Sanmartean (Popa 78); Keseru.

Dynamo Kyiv: (4231) Shovkovskiy; Gusev, Dragovic, Khacheridi, Burda; Veloso (Sydorchuk 65), Rybalka; Yarmolenko, Belhanda (Buyalsky 81), Lens; Kravets (Mbokani 79).

Group J Table

	P	W	D	L	F	A	GD	Pts
Dynamo Kyiv	6	5	0	1	12	4	8	15
Aalborg	6	3	0	3	5	10	–5	9
Steaua Bucharest	6	2	1	3	11	9	2	7
Rio Ave	6	1	1	4	5	10	–5	4

GROUP K

Thursday, 18 September 2014
Fiorentina (1) 3 *(Vargas 34, Cuadrado 67, Bernarderschi 88)*
Guingamp (0) 0 32,000
Fiorentina: (442) Tatarusanu; Savic (Richards 57), Basanta, Pasqual, Tomovic; Vargas, Pizarro, Cuadrado (Bernarderschi 71), Kurtic; Valero (Badelj 46), Gomez.
Guingamp: (442) Samassa; Angoua, Sankoh, Kerbrat, Diallo■; Leveque, Beauvue, Mathis, Pied (Giresse 61); Mandanne (Douniama 71), Marveaux (Yatabare 52).

PAOK Salonika (4) 6 *(Nikolic 4 (og), Athanasiadis 11, 16, 27, Papadopoulos 50, Tzandaris 90)*
Dinamo Minsk (0) 1 *(Nikolic 80)* 21,000
PAOK Salonika: (442) Glykos; Skondras, Katsikas, Rat (Spyropoulos 72), Miguel Vitor; Tziolis, Mak (Papadopoulos 46), Kace, Tzandaris; Salpingidis, Athanasiadis (Golasa 67).
Dinamo Minsk: (4411) Hutar; Palitsevich, Karpovich, Veretilo, Bangura; Voronkov (Figueredo 57), Simovic■, Nikolic, Udoji (Rassadkin 88); Stasevich; Dja Djedje (Adamovic 33).

Thursday, 2 October 2014
Dinamo Minsk (0) 0
Fiorentina (1) 3 *(Aquilani 33, Ilicic 61, Bernarderschi 67)* 5500
Dinamo Minsk: (4411) Ignatovich; Veretilo, Kontsevoi, Bangura, Molosh; Adamovic (Rassadkin 86), Nikolic, Voronkov, Stasevich (Yarotsky 88); Figueredo (Dja Djedje 62); Diomande.
Fiorentina: (433) Tatarusanu; Tomovic, Basanta, Richards (Alonso 41), Pasqual; Aquilani (Pizarro 46), Badelj, Vargas; Ilicic, Valero (Lazzari 60), Bernarderschi.

Guingamp (0) 2 *(Marveaux 47, 50)*
PAOK Salonika (0) 0 8783
Guingamp: (4231) Lossl; Jacobsen, Sorbon, Kerbrat, Leveque; Sankhare, Beauvue; Mathis, Pied (Yatabare 54), Marveaux (Giresse 78); Schwartz (Mandanne 72).
PAOK Salonika: (433) Glykos; Skondras (Golasa 74), Katsikas, Rat, Miguel Vitor; Tziolis (Martens 55), Mak (Papadopoulos 62), Kace; Tzandaris, Salpingidis, Athanasiadis.

Thursday, 23 October 2014
Dinamo Minsk (0) 0
Guingamp (0) 0 5000
Dinamo Minsk: (4411) Ignatovich; Karpovich, Kontsevoi, Palitsevich, Veretilo; Stasevich, Voronkov (Simovic 62), Nikolic, Dja Djedje (Diomande 54); Figueredo (Korzun 78); Adamovic.
Guingamp: (451) Lossl; Jacobsen, Angoua, Sorbon, Dos Santos; Beauvue, Yatabare, Mathis, Sankhare (Diallo 78); Marveaux (Mandanne 69); Alioui.

PAOK Salonika (0) 0
Fiorentina (1) 1 *(Vargas 38)* 20,000
PAOK Salonika: (433) Glykos; Skondras (Kitsiou 11), Miguel Vitor, Katsikas, Rat; Tzandaris, Tziolis, Kace; Salpingidis (Papadopoulos 81), Athanasiadis, Pereyra (Golasa 54).
Fiorentina: (433) Tatarusanu; Richards, Tomovic, Basanta, Pasqual; Badelj, Kurtic, Valero (Lazzari 66); Ilicic (Marin 78), Vargas, Bernarderschi (Cuadrado 57).

Thursday, 6 November 2014

Fiorentina (0) 1 *(Pasqual 88)*

PAOK Salonika (0) 1 *(Martens 81)* 10,000

Fiorentina: (433) Tatarusanu; Tomovic (El Babacar 86), Basanta, Rodriguez, Pasqual; Kurtic, Pizarro, Lazzari (Marin 57); Cuadrado, Gomez, Vargas (Valero 70).
PAOK Salonika: (433) Glykos; Kitsiou, Miguel Vitor, Katsikas, Spyropoulos (Tzavelas 90); Tzandaris, Golasa, Tziolis; Salpingidis (Martens 71), Athanasiadis, Pereyra (Maduro 46).

Guingamp (1) 2 *(Beauvue 44, Mandanne 86)*

Dinamo Minsk (0) 0 17,000

Guingamp: (433) Lossl; Sankoh, Kerbrat, Angoua, Dos Santos (Baca 83); Diallo (Pied 74), Mathis, Marveaux (Sankhare 64); Beauvue, Mandanne, Yatabare.
Dinamo Minsk: (451) Hutar; Veretilo, Kantsavy, Palitsevich, Molosh; Udoji (Adamovic 75), Voronkov (Figueredo 46), Simovic, Nikolic, Dja Djedje (Stasevich 46); Diomande.

Thursday, 27 November 2014

Dinamo Minsk (0) 0

PAOK Salonika (0) 2 *(Athanasiadis 82, 88)* 2000

Dinamo Minsk: (4231) Ignatovich; Karpovich, Kantsavy, Palitsevich, Veretilo; Nikolic, Simovic; Adamovic, Udoji (Yarotsky 73), Stasevich; Dja Djedje (Diomande 80).
PAOK Salonika: (4231) Glykos; Skondras, Miguel Vitor, Katsikas (Tzavelas 27), Rat; Tziolis, Kace; Salpingidis (Golasa 46), Pereyra, Tzandaris; Athanasiadis (Papadopoulos 89).

Guingamp (1) 1 *(Beauvue 45 (pen))*

Fiorentina (2) 2 *(Marin 6, El Babacar 13)* 5519

Guingamp: (451) Lossl; Jacobsen, Kerbrat, Sorbon, Sankoh; Yatabare, Diallo, Mathis, Pied (Schwartz 78), Beauvue; Marveaux (Giresse 90).
Fiorentina: (352) Tatarusanu; Richards, Tomovic, Basanta■; Vargas, Badelj (Alonso 70), Lazzari (Cuadrado 53), Aquilani, Kurtic; El Babacar, Marin (Savic 52).

Thursday, 11 December 2014

Fiorentina (0) 1 *(Marin 87)*

Dinamo Minsk (1) 2 *(Kantsavy 39, Nikolic 55)* 7562

Fiorentina: (352) Tatarusanu; Richards, Rodriguez (Pizarro 59), Tomovic; Cuadrado (Minelli 24), Kurtic, Badelj, Lazzari, Vargas; Marin, Gomez (Ilicic 46).
Dinamo Minsk: (4231) Hutar; Veretilo■, Kantsavy, Palitsevich, Molosh; Voronkov (Udoji 77), Simovic; Stasevich, Nikolic, Dja Djedje (Karpovich 90); Adamovic (Bykov 68).

PAOK Salonika (1) 1 *(Athanasiadis 22 (pen))*

Guingamp (1) 2 *(Beauvue 8, 83)* 12,101

PAOK Salonika: (433) Glykos; Skondras, Miguel Vitor, Tzavelas, Rat; Golasa (Martens 53), Tzandaris, Kace (Maduro 77); Salpingidis, Athanasiadis, Pereyra (Papadopoulos 61).
Guingamp: (433) Lossl; Jacobsen, Sorbon, Angoua, Leveque; Sankhare, Mathis, Giresse (Dos Santos 86); Yatabare (Pied 46), Mandanne (Kerbrat 75), Beauvue.

Group K Table	P	W	D	L	F	A	GD	Pts
Fiorentina	6	4	1	1	11	4	7	13
Guingamp	6	3	1	2	7	6	1	10
PAOK Salonika	6	2	1	3	10	7	3	7
Dinamo Minsk	6	1	1	4	3	14	–11	4

GROUP L

Thursday, 18 September 2014

Legia Warsaw (0) 1 *(Radovic 58)*

Lokeren (0) 0 20,000

Legia Warsaw: (4411) Kuciak; Broz, Rzezniczak, Dossa Junior, Brzyski; Zyro, Vrdoljak, Jodlowiec, Kucharczyk; Duda (Saganowski 90); Radovic.
Lokeren: (433) Barry; Galitsios, Maric, Scholz, Odoi; Persoons, Vanaken, Overmeire; De Pauw (Patosi 81), Leye (Junior Dutra 73), Remacle (Abdurahimi 65).

Metalist Kharkiv (0) 1 *(Homenyuk 61)*

Trabzonspor (1) 2 *(Constant 25, Papadopoulos 90)* 6834

Metalist Kharkiv: (442) Goryainov; Villagra, Torsiglieri, Cleiton Xavier (Kulakov 90), Bolbat (Radchenko 79); Pshenichnikh, Gueye, Krasnopyorov, Kobin; Homenyuk, Jaja (Rebenok 82).
Trabzonspor: (442) Kivrak; Nizam, Belkalem, Papadopoulos, Medjani; Yilmaz S, Constant, Dursun (Ekici 71), Yavru; Cardozo (Yatabare 57), Waris (Erdogan 82).

Thursday, 2 October 2014

Lokeren (0) 1 *(De Pauw 74)*

Metalist Kharkiv (0) 0 6000

Lokeren: (4231) Barry; Galitsios, Scholz, Maric, Odoi; Persoons, Overmeire; De Pauw, Vanaken (Ngolok 87), Abdurahimi (Remacle 79); Leye (Dessers 70).
Metalist Kharkiv: (4231) Disljenkovic; Villagra, Yussuf, Gueye, Pshenichnikh (Berezovchuk 85); Kobin (Radchenko 60), Edmar; Krasnopyorov, Cleiton Xavier, Bolbat (Kulakov 69); Homenyuk.

Trabzonspor (0) 0

Legia Warsaw (1) 1 *(Kucharczyk 17)* 8000

Trabzonspor: (4231) Kivrak (Ozturk 62); Bosingwa, Belkalem, Papadopoulos, Nizam; Medjani, Constant; Atik (Yilmaz S 46), Ekici (Yatabare 76), Waris; Cardozo.
Legia Warsaw: (4231) Kuciak; Broz, Rzezniczak, Dossa Junior, Brzyski; Jodlowiec, Vrdoljak; Zyro■, Duda, Kucharczyk (Kosecki 90); Radovic (Saganowski 90).

Wednesday, 22 October 2014

Metalist Kharkiv (0) 0

Legia Warsaw (1) 1 *(Duda 28)* 2374

Metalist Kharkiv: (433) Goryainov; Villagra, Torsiglieri, Yussuf (Berezovchuk 73), Pshenichnikh (Kulakov 61); Edmar, Torres, Krasnopyorov (Kobin 57); Jaja, Homenyuk, Bolbat.
Legia Warsaw: (442) Kuciak; Broz, Rzezniczak, Astiz, Guilherme; Kosecki, Jodlowiec, Vrdoljak, Kucharczyk; Duda, Orlando Sa (Saganowski 81).

Thursday, 23 October 2014

Trabzonspor (0) 2 *(Yatabare 55, Constant 87)*

Lokeren (0) 0 9500

Trabzonspor: (4411) Ozturk; Bosingwa, Belkalem, Papadopoulos, Yavru; Yatabare, Medjani, Constant (Aydogdu 88), Waris; Ekici (Dursun 73); Cardozo (Yilmaz S 82).
Lokeren: (433) Barry; Galitsios (Mertens 60), Maric, Scholz, Odoi; De Pauw, Persoons (Remacle 76), Overmeire; Abdurahimi (Junior Dutra 63), Leye, Vanaken.

Thursday, 6 November 2014

Legia Warsaw (1) 2 *(Saganowski 29, Duda 84)*

Metalist Kharkiv (1) 1 *(Kobin 22)* 26,000

Legia Warsaw: (442) Kuciak; Jodlowiec, Astiz, Rzezniczak, Broz; Guilherme, Duda, Vrdoljak, Saganowski (Orlando Sa 75); Kucharczyk (Kosecki 80), Zyro.
Metalist Kharkiv: (442) Disljenkovic; Villagra, Berezovchuk, Torsiglieri, Cleiton Xavier; Torres (Homenyuk 90), Radchenko (Kulakov 50); Kobin, Rebenok; Jaja, Krasnopyorov (Edmar 80).

Lokeren (1) 1 *(Patosi 4)*

Trabzonspor (1) 1 *(Waris 45)* 8400

Lokeren: (433) Barry; Galitsios, Maric, Scholz, Odoi; Persoons, Junior Dutra, Overmeire (Ngolok 53); De Pauw (Abdurahimi 79), Leye, Patosi.
Trabzonspor: (4231) Ozturk; Bosingwa, Belkalem, Papadopoulos, Nizam; Medjani, Constant; Ekici (Dursun 76), Atik (Yilmaz S 85), Waris; Yatabare (Cardozo 76).

Thursday, 27 November 2014

Lokeren (1) 1 *(Vanaken 7)*

Legia Warsaw (0) 0 6592

Lokeren: (433) Barry; Galitsios, Maric, Scholz, Odoi; Vanaken, Overmeire, Persoons; De Pauw (Leye 74), Junior Dutra (Dessers 90), Patosi (Remacle 86).
Legia Warsaw: (4231) Kuciak; Broz, Rzezniczak, Astiz, Guilherme; Vrdoljak, Jodlowiec; Orlando Sa (Saganowski 63), Duda, Kucharczyk; Kosecki (Zyro 46).

Trabzonspor (1) 3 *(Belkalem 37, Ekici 86, Yilmaz S 90)*
Metalist Kharkiv (0) 1 *(Homenyuk 68)* 6250
Trabzonspor: (4141) Ozturk; Bosingwa, Papadopoulos, Belkalem, Erdogan; Medjani■; Yatabare, Ekici, Aydogdu (Atik 58), Waris (Nizam 88); Cardozo (Yilmaz S 59).
Metalist Kharkiv: (4411) Goryainov; Villagra (Bolbat 84), Gueye, Torsiglieri, Pshenichnikh; Krasnopyorov, Tkachuk, Kobin (Kulakov 69), Jaja; Rebenok (Osman 88); Homenyuk.

Thursday, 11 December 2014
Legia Warsaw (1) 2 *(Ozturk 22 (og), Orlando Sa 55)*
Trabzonspor (0) 0 200
Legia Warsaw: (4411) Kuciak; Broz, Lewczuk, Astiz, Guilherme; Zyro (Kosecki 34), Vrdoljak, Jodlowiec, Kucharczyk (Saganovski 86); Duda (Bielik 87); Orlando Sa.
Trabzonspor: (4411) Ozturk; Bosingwa, Belkalem, Demir, Nizam; Yilmaz S (Dogan 85), Ekici■, Dursun (Atik 46), Constant; Yatabare; Cardozo.

Metalist Kharkiv (0) 0
Lokeren (1) 1 *(Leye 16)* 1386
Metalist Kharkiv: (4411) Goryainov; Kobin, Berezovchuk, Pshenichnikh, Osman; Bolbat, Tkachuk, Krasnopyorov, Rebenok; Radchenko (Barvinko 88); Homenyuk.
Lokeren: (433) Barry; Odoi, Mertens, Maric, Corryn; Remacle, Ngolok (Scholz 90), Overmeire (Persoons 79); Dessers (Ansah 78), Leye, De Pauw.

Group L Table	P	W	D	L	F	A	GD	Pts
Legia Warsaw	6	5	0	1	7	2	5	15
Trabzonspor	6	3	1	2	8	6	2	10
Lokeren	6	3	1	2	4	4	0	10
Metalist Kharkiv	6	0	0	6	3	10	-7	0

KNOCKOUT STAGE

ROUND OF 32 FIRST LEG
Thursday, 19 February 2015
Aalborg (0) 1 *(Helenius 71 (pen))*
Club Brugge (2) 3 *(Oulare 25, Rafaelov 29, Petersen 61 (og))* 8115
Aalborg: (442) Larsen; Dalsgaard, Petersen, Thelander, Blabjerg; Boersting (Kristensen 80), Wurtz, Thomsen, Bruhn (Augustinussen 46); Helenius, Jacobsen (Enevoldsen 62).
Club Brugge: (442) Ryan; Meunier, Duarte, Mechele, De Fauw; Vormer, Simons, Rafaelov (De Sutter 80), Bolingoli Mbombo; Felipe Gedoz (Silva 57), Oulare (Vazquez 67).

Ajax (1) 1 *(Milik 34)*
Legia Warsaw (0) 0 46,761
Ajax: (433) Cillessen; Van Rhijn, van der Hoorn, Viergever, Boilesen; Klaassen (Sinkgraven 82), Serero (Riedewald 71), Bazoer; El Ghazi, Milik, Kishna (Schone 74).
Legia Warsaw: (451) Kuciak; Broz, Rzezniczak, Dossa Junior, Guilherme; Vrdoljak, Zyro, Jodlowiec, Kucharczyk, Maslowski; Orlando Sa.

Anderlecht (0) 0
Dynamo Moscow (0) 0 17,317
Anderlecht: (433) Proto; Vanden Borre (Iseka 83), Rolando, Deschacht, N'Sakala; Defour (Colin 67), Tielemans, Dendoncker; Najar, Mitrovic, Acheampong (Kabasele 86).
Dynamo Moscow: (4231) Gabulov; Kozlov, Hubocan, Samba, Buttner■; Vainqueur, Yusupov; Kokorin, Valbuena (Ionov 80), Dzsudzsak (Zhirkov 69); Kuranyi (Denisov 51).

Celtic (2) 3 *(Armstrong 24, Campagnaro 26 (og), Guidetti 90)*
Internazionale (3) 3 *(Shaqiri 4, Palacio 13, 45)* 58,500
Celtic: (4231) Gordon; Matthews (Ambrose 81), Denayer, van Dijk, Izaguirre; Brown, Biton; Mackay-Steven, Johansen, Armstrong (Henderson 75); Griffiths (Guidetti 75).
Internazionale: (4312) Carrizo; Santon, Ranocchia, Juan Jesus, Campagnaro; Kuzmanovic (Dodo 79), Guarin, Medel; Shaqiri; Palacio, Icardi (Kovacic 75).

Dnipro Dnipropetrovsk (0) 2 *(Kankava 50, Rotan 55)*
Olympiacos (0) 0 5837
Dnipro Dnipropetrovsk: (4411) Boyko; Luchkevych, Douglas, Cheberyachko, Egidio; Kankava, Rotan, Matheus (Bruno Gama 88), Bezus (Kalinic 45); Konoplyanka; Zozulya (Fedorchuk 69).
Olympiacos: (4411) Roberto; Maniatis, Felipe Santana (Milivojevic 57), Siovas, Masuaku; Dossevi (Durmaz 71), Elabdellaoui, Kasami, Afellay; Dominguez (Fortounis 58); Mitroglou.

Guingamp (0) 2 *(Beauvue 72, Diallo 75)*
Dynamo Kyiv (1) 1 *(Veloso 20)* 16,191
Guingamp: (451) Lossl; Jacobsen, Sorbon, Kerbrat, Leveque; Beauvue, Pied, Mathis (Diallo 75), Sankhare, Yatabare (Giresse 68); Mandanne (Marveaux 46).
Dynamo Kyiv: (4231) Shovkovskiy; Vida, Dragovic, Danilo Silva, Antunes; Sydorchuk (Belhanda■ 41), Rybalka; Yarmolenko■, Veloso, Lens (Gusev 7); Kravets.

Liverpool (0) 1 *(Balotelli 85 (pen))*
Besiktas (0) 0 43,353
Liverpool: (343) Mignolet; Can, Skrtel, Sakho; Ibe, Henderson, Allen (Lovren 63), Moreno; Lallana (Sterling 77), Sturridge, Coutinho (Balotelli 63).
Besiktas: (4231) Gonen; Kurtulus, Franco, Gulum, Ramon; Hutchinson, Kavlak; Tore, Sosa (Ozyakup 60), Sahan (Frei 71); Ba.

PSV Eindhoven (0) 0
Zenit St Petersburg (0) 1 *(Hulk 64)* 20,000
PSV Eindhoven: (433) Zoet; Arias (Brenet 74), Bruma, Isimat-Mirin, Willems; Wijnaldum, Hiljemark (Maher 85), Guardado; Narsingh (Locadia 74), de Jong, Depay.
Zenit St Petersburg: (442) Lodygin; Smolnikov, Luis Neto, Criscito, Garay; Witsel (Tymoschuk 86), Javi Garcia, Shatov, Danny; Hulk (Arshavin 90), Rondon (Ryazantsev 76).

Roma (1) 1 *(Gervinho 22)*
Feyenoord (0) 1 *(Kazim-Richards 55)* 29,292
Roma: (433) Skorupski; Yanga-Mbiwa, Holebas, Torosidis, Manolas; Nainggolan, Pjanic, De Rossi (Keita 65); Totti (Doumbia 65), Gervinho, Verde (Florenzi 75).
Feyenoord: (433) Vermeer; Wilkshire (Karsdorp 30), Kongolo, Nelom, Boulahrouz; Clasie, El Ahmadi, Immers; Trindade de Vilhena, Toornstra, Kazim-Richards.

Sevilla (0) 1 *(Iborra 70)*
Borussia Moenchengladbach (0) 0 26,850
Sevilla: (4231) Sergio Rico; Aleix Vidal (Deulofeu 90), Pareja, Carrico, Fernando Navarro; Iborra, Krychowiak; Vitolo, Banega (Suarez 88), Reyes (Diogo Figueiras 54); Bacca.
Borussia Moenchengladbach: (442) Sommer; Jantschke, Stranzl, Dominguez, Wendt; Hazard, Kramer, Xhaka, Johnson; Raffael (Kruse 79), Hrgota (Herrmann 69).

Torino (2) 2 *(Maxi Lopez 18, 43)*
Athletic Bilbao (1) 2 *(Williams 9, Gurpegi 73)* 25,725
Torino: (352) Padelli; Maksimovic, Glik, Moretti; Darmian, Benassi, Gazzi, El Kaddouri (Farnerud 76), Molinaro; Martinez (Quagliarella 58), Maxi Lopez (Amauri 72).
Athletic Bilbao: (4231) Herrerin; De Marcos, Etxeita, Laporte, Aurtenetxe (Iraola 57); San Jose, Benat; Viguera (Gurpegi 58), Mikel Rico, Muniain; Williams (Kike Sola 72).

Tottenham H (1) 1 *(Soldado 6)*
Fiorentina (1) 1 *(Basanta 36)* 34,235
Tottenham H: (451) Lloris; Walker, Fazio, Vertonghen, Davies; Townsend (Lamela 73), Paulinho (Mason 84), Bentaleb, Chadli (Kane 66), Eriksen; Soldado.
Fiorentina: (442) Tatarusanu; Savic, Rodriguez, Pizarro, Basanta; Joaquin, Fernandez, Valero (Badelj 78), Pasqual (Alonso 65); Salah, Gomez (Ilicic 84).

Trabzonspor (0) 0
Napoli (3) 4 *(Henrique 6, Higuain 20, Gabbiadini 27, Zapata 90)* 23,760
Trabzonspor: (451) Arikan; Dogan, Medjani, Demir, Bosingwa; Aydogdu (Yavru 84), Zengin, Atik (Dursun 90), Hurmaci (Nizam 90), Yilmaz S; Cardozo.
Napoli: (442) Andujar; Ghoulam, Koulibaly, Albiol, Henrique; Mertens, Gargano (David Lopez 46), Inler, Gabbiadini; de Guzman (Callejon 70), Higuain (Zapata 80).

Villarreal (1) 2 *(Uche 32, Cheryshev 54)*
Red Bull Salzburg (0) 1 *(Soriano 49 (pen))* 16,000
Villarreal: (442) Sergio Asenjo; Mario, Musacchio, Victor Ruiz, Jaume; Jonathan (Campbell 66), Trigueros, Pina, Cheryshev; Uche (Giovani 69), Vietto.
Red Bull Salzburg: (442) Gulacsi; Schwegler, Ramalho Silva, Hinteregger, Ulmer; Sabitzer, Leitgeb (Keita 63), Ilsanker, Bruno (Pires 63); Djuricin (Berisha 76), Soriano.

Wolfsburg (0) 2 *(Dost 46, 63)*
Sporting Lisbon (0) 0 19,207
Wolfsburg: (4141) Benaglio; Jung, Naldo, Knoche, Rodriguez; Trasch; Vieirinha (Schafer 89), Hunt (Arnold 41), De Bruyne, Schurrle (Caligiuri 79); Dost.
Sporting Lisbon: (4141) Rui Patricio; Cedric Soares, Figueiredo, Paulo Oliveira, Jefferson; Rosell (Andre Martins 80); Nani, Adrien Silva, Joao Mario, Montero (Tanaka 79); Carrillo (Carlos Mane 70).

Young Boys (1) 1 *(Hoarau 10)*
Everton (3) 4 *(Lukaku 24, 39, 58, Coleman 28)* 25,000
Young Boys: (4231) Mvogo; Hadergjonaj, Vilotic, von Bergen, Lecjaks; Sanogo (Bertone 90), Gajic (Gerndt 70); Steffen (Sulejmanov 78), Kubo, Nuzzolo; Hoarau.
Everton: (4231) Howard; Coleman, Stones, Jagielka, Oviedo (Garbutt 58); McCarthy (Alcaraz 69), Barry; Mirallas, Barkley, Naismith; Lukaku (Atsu 85).

ROUND OF 32 SECOND LEG
Thursday, 26 February 2015

Athletic Bilbao (1) 2 *(Iraola 44, De Marcos 61)*
Torino (2) 3 *(Quagliarella 16 (pen), Maxi Lopez 45, Darmian 67)* 36,000
Athletic Bilbao: (532) Herrerin; Iraola, Etxeita, Gurpegi (Williams 41), Laporte, De Marcos; Benat (Susaeta 70), San Jose, Mikel Rico (Lopez 80); Muniain, Aduriz.
Torino: (352) Padelli; Maksimovic, Glik, Moretti; Darmian, Vives, Gazzi, El Kaddouri (Farnerud 84), Molinaro; Maxi Lopez (Martinez 73), Quagliarella.

Besiktas (0) 1 *(Arslan 72)*
Liverpool (0) 0 63,000
Besiktas: (4231) Gonen; Opare, Franco, Uysal, Kurtulus; Hutchinson, Kavlak; Tore, Sosa (Arslan 61), Sahan (Frei 105); Ba.
Liverpool: (442) Mignolet; Toure, Lovren, Skrtel, Moreno; Can, Allen, Sterling, Ibe (Manquillo 76); Sturridge (Lambert 106), Balotelli (Lallana 82).
aet; Besiktas won 5-4 on penalties.

Borussia Moenchengladbach (2) 2 *(Xhaka 19, Hazard 29)*
Sevilla (2) 3 *(Bacca 8, Vitolo 26, 79)* 45,337
Borussia Moenchengladbach: (442) Sommer; Jantschke (Johnson 78), Stranzl, Dominguez (Hrgota 77), Wendt; Herrmann (Traore 72), Xhaka■, Kramer, Hazard; Raffael, Kruse.
Sevilla: (4231) Sergio Rico; Diogo Figueiras, Carrico, Kolodziezcak, Tremoulinas (Fernando Navarro 82); Krychowiak, Iborra; Aleix Vidal, Banega (Mbia 65), Vitolo; Bacca (Gameiro 77).

Club Brugge (1) 3 *(Vazquez 11, Oulare 64, Bolingoli Mbombo 74)*
Aalborg (0) 0 11,804
Club Brugge: (4141) Ryan; Meunier (De Bock 78), Mechele, Duarte, De Fauw; Simons; Rafaelov, Vormer, Vazquez (Silva 75), Bolingoli Mbombo; Oulare (Dierckx 75).
Aalborg: (442) Larsen; Dalsgaard (Thrane 69), Petersen, Thelander, Kristensen; Bruhn, Wurtz (Augustinussen 58), Risgard, Thomsen; Enevoldsen (Jacobsen 62), Helenius.

Dynamo Kyiv (1) 3 *(Teodorczyk 31, Buyalsky 46, Gusev 75 (pen))*
Guingamp (0) 1 *(Mandanne 66)* 54,308
Dynamo Kyiv: (4411) Shovkovskiy; Vida, Dragovic, Danilo Silva, Antunes; Gusev (Kalitvintsev 90), Buyalsky (Chumak 72), Rybalka, Lens; Veloso (Teodorczyk 10); Kravets.
Guingamp: (451) Lossl; Jacobsen, Sorbon, Angoua, Leveque; Beauvue, Giresse (Yatabare 77), Mathis (Diallo 60), Pied, Sankhare; Mandanne.

Dynamo Moscow (0) 3 *(Kozlov 47, Yusupov 63, Kuranyi 90)*
Anderlecht (1) 1 *(Mitrovic 28)* 12,316
Dynamo Moscow: (451) Gabulov; Kozlov (Douglas 53), Hubocan, Samba, Zhirkov; Valbuena (Kuranyi 84), Denisov, Vainqueur, Dzsudzsak (Ionov 67), Yusupov; Kokorin.
Anderlecht: (4321) Proto; Vanden Borre, Rolando, Deschacht, N'Sakala; Conte (Iseka 83), Defour, Dendoncker (Cyriac 82); Acheampong, Tielemans (Najar 71); Mitrovic.

Everton (3) 3 *(Lukaku 25 (pen), 30, Mirallas 42)*
Young Boys (1) 1 *(Sanogo 13)* 25,058
Everton: (433) Howard; Coleman, Jagielka, Alcaraz, Garbutt; McCarthy (Besic 61), Gibson, Barry; Naismith (Osman 80), Lukaku (Kone 48), Mirallas.
Young Boys: (442) Wolfli; Sutter, Vilotic, Rochat, Lecjaks (Burki 57); Zarate, Sanogo, Bertone, Nuzzolo (Gerndt 68); Hoarau, Kubo (Affum 76).

Feyenoord (0) 1 *(Manu 57)*
Roma (1) 2 *(Ljajic 45, Gervinho 60)* 42,000
Feyenoord: (433) Vermeer; Boulahrouz (Manu 56), van Beek, Kongolo, Nelom; El Ahmadi, Toornstra, Clasie; Karsdorp, Kazim-Richards (Te Vrede■ 30), Trindade de Vilhena (Achahbar 84).
Roma: (433) Skorupski; Manolas, Torosidis, Yanga-Mbiwa, Holebas; Keita, De Rossi, Pjanic (Nainggolan 74); Ljajic (Iturbe 74), Totti (Paredes 82), Gervinho.

Fiorentina (0) 2 *(Gomez 54, Salah 71)*
Tottenham H (0) 0 29,886
Fiorentina: (433) Neto; Richards, Basanta (Rodriguez 57), Savic, Alonso; Fernandez (Aquilani 25), Pizarro, Badelj; Joaquin (Pasqual 84), Salah, Gomez.
Tottenham H: (4411) Lloris; Chiriches, Fazio, Vertonghen (Walker 75), Davies; Lamela, Stambouli, Bentaleb (Kane 63), Chadli (Townsend 63); Eriksen; Soldado.

Internazionale (0) 1 *(Guarin 88)*
Celtic (0) 0 39,711
Internazionale: (433) Carrizo; Santon, Ranocchia, Juan Jesus, D'Ambrosio (Campagnaro 80); Guarin, Medel, Hernanes (Kovacic 80); Palacio (Puscas 89), Shaqiri, Icardi.
Celtic: (4411) Gordon; Matthews, Denayer, van Dijk■, Izaguirre; Mackay-Steven (Ambrose 40), Brown, Biton, Armstrong (Commons 78); Johansen (Guidetti Forrest 59).

Legia Warsaw (0) 0
Ajax (3) 3 *(Milik 11, 42, Viergever 13)* 0
Legia Warsaw: (4231) Kuciak; Dossa Junior, Jodlowiec, Rzezniczak, Broz; Guilherme, Maslowski (Pinto 71); Vrdoljak, Zyro (Kosecki 59), Kucharczyk; Orlando Sa (Saganowski 59).
Ajax: (433) Cillessen; Van Rhijn, Veltman (van der Hoorn 71), Boilesen, Viergever; Klaassen (Sinkgraven 46), Serero, Bazoer; Kishna (Andersen 79), Milik, El Ghazi.
(Behind closed doors)

Napoli (1) 1 *(de Guzman 19)*
Trabzonspor (0) 0   20,000
Napoli: (4411) Rafael Cabral; Mesto, Henrique, Britos, Ghoulam; Callejon (Hamsik 76), Jorginho, Inler, Mertens; de Guzman (Gabbiadini 69); Higuain (Zapata 63).
Trabzonspor: (433) Arikan; Dursun (Yavru 88), Bosingwa, Demir, Dogan; Ekici, Atik (Aydogdu 77), Medjani; Hurmaci, Cardozo, Zengin (Yilmaz S 84).

Olympiacos (1) 2 *(Mitroglou 14, Dominguez 89 (pen))*
Dnipro Dnipropetrovsk (1) 2 *(Fedetskiy 23, Kalinic 90)*
           24,854
Olympiacos: (451) Roberto; Elabdellaoui, Felipe Santana, Siovas, Masuaku; Durmaz (Dossevi 65), Dominguez, Milivojevic▪, Kasami, Afellay (Fortounis 65); Mitroglou.
Dnipro Dnipropetrovsk: (4411) Boyko; Egidio, Cheberyachko, Douglas, Fedetskiy; Konoplyanka, Fedorchuk (Bezus 83), Kankava, Matheus (Bruno Gama 76); Rotan; Zozulya (Kalinic 62).

Red Bull Salzburg (1) 1 *(Djuricin 18)*
Villarreal (1) 3 *(Vietto 33, 76, Giovani 79)*   26,020
Red Bull Salzburg: (442) Gulacsi; Schwegler, Ramalho Silva, Hinteregger, Ulmer; Minamino (Pires 46), Keita, Laimer (Bruno 70), Sabitzer; Soriano, Djuricin (Berisha 84).
Villarreal: (442) Sergio Asenjo; Mario, Musacchio, Victor Ruiz, Jaume; Jonathan, Trigueros, Pina (Campbell 86), Cheryshev; Vietto (Moi Gomez 81), Uche (Giovani 68).

Sporting Lisbon (0) 0
Wolfsburg (0) 0   23,097
Sporting Lisbon: (451) Rui Patricio; Cedric Soares, Paulo Oliveira, Figueiredo, Silva; Carrillo (Montero 78), Joao Mario, William Carvalho, Adrien Silva (Slimani 64); Nani; Tanaka (Carlos Mane 78).
Wolfsburg: (433) Benaglio; Trasch, Naldo, Knoche, Rodriguez; Gustavo, Guilavogui, Vieirinha (Schafer 76); De Bruyne (Arnold 90); Schurrle (Caligiuri 62), Dost.

Zenit St Petersburg (1) 3 *(Rondon 28, 67, Hulk 48)*
PSV Eindhoven (0) 0   17,194
Zenit St Petersburg: (442) Lodygin; Smolnikov, Luis Neto, Garay, Aniukov; Hulk (Mogilevets 85), Shatov, Javi Garcia, Danny (Ryazantsev 81); Witsel (Tymoschuk 72), Rondon.
PSV Eindhoven: (4141) Zoet; Brenet (Tamata 69), Bruma, Isimat-Mirin, Willems; Guardado (Hendrix 81); Narsingh (Locadia 63), Wijnaldum, Maher, Depay; de Jong.

ROUND OF 16 FIRST LEG

Thursday, 12 March 2015
Club Brugge (0) 2 *(De Sutter 62, Rafaelov 79 (pen))*
Besiktas (0) 1 *(Tore 46)*   12,977
Club Brugge: (4132) Ryan; De Fauw (Oulare 61), Duarte, De Bock, Mechele; Simons; Rafaelov, Vormer, Meunier; Bolingoli Mbombo (Felipe Gedoz 46), De Sutter (Dierckx 87).
Besiktas: (433) Gonen; Kurtulus, Gulum, Opare, Tore; Kavlak, Ozyakup (Frei 72), Arslan; Uysal, Ba, Sahan (Pektemek 83).

Dnipro Dnipropetrovsk (1) 1 *(Zozulya 30)*
Ajax (0) 0   10,581
Dnipro Dnipropetrovsk: (4411) Boyko; Fedetskiy, Douglas, Cheberyachko, Egidio; Zozulya, Fedorchuk, Rotan, Konoplyanka (Shakhov 82); Bezus (Bruno Gama 58); Seleznyov (Kalinic 75).
Ajax: (433) Cillessen; Van Rhijn, Veltman, Viergever, Boilesen; Bazoer, Klaassen, Serero (Sinkgraven 60); El Ghazi, Milik (Zivkovic 77), Schone (Kishna 60).

Everton (1) 2 *(Naismith 39, Lukaku 82 (pen))*
Dynamo Kyiv (1) 1 *(Gusev 14)*   26,150
Everton: (433) Howard; Coleman, Alcaraz, Jagielka, Garbutt; McCarthy, Barkley (Osman 74), Barry; Naismith, Lukaku, Mirallas (Kone 63).
Dynamo Kyiv: (4231) Shovkovskiy; Vida, Dragovic, Danilo Silva, Antunes; Veloso (Chumak 84), Sydorchuk; Gusev (Kravets 76), Buyalsky (Garmash 67), Yarmolenko; Mbokani.

Fiorentina (1) 1 *(Ilicic 17)*
Roma (0) 1 *(Keita 77)*   23,557
Fiorentina: (433) Neto; Tomovic, Rodriguez, Basanta, Alonso; Badelj, Pizarro (Fernandez 45), Valero (Aquilani 71); Joaquin, Ilicic (El Babacar 81), Salah.
Roma: (433) Skorupski; Torosidis, Holebas, Yanga-Mbiwa, Manolas (Astori 26); Nainggolan, De Rossi (Pjanic 22); Keita; Florenzi, Ljajic (Gervinho 75), Iturbe.

Napoli (2) 3 *(Higuain 25, 32 (pen), 54)*
Dynamo Moscow (1) 1 *(Kuranyi 2)*   17,727
Napoli: (4411) Andujar; Henrique, Koulibaly (Albiol 8), Britos, Ghoulam; Jorginho, Inler, Callejon (Zuniga 82), de Guzman (Hamsik 70); Mertens; Higuain.
Dynamo Moscow: (4411) Gabulov; Kozlov, Hubocan, Samba, Zhirkov; Valbuena (Ionov 72), Zobnin▪, Vainqueur, Dzsudzsak (Tashaev 90); Kuranyi (Buttner 61); Kokorin.

Villarreal (0) 1 *(Vietto 49)*
Sevilla (2) 3 *(Vitolo 1, Mbia 26, Gameiro 50)*   19,930
Villarreal: (442) Sergio Asenjo; Mario, Musacchio (Dorado 84), Bailly, Jaume; Moi Gomez (Campbell 46), Trigueros, Jonathan, Cheryshev; Uche (Moreno 68), Vietto.
Sevilla: (4411) Sergio Rico; Diogo Figueiras, Pareja, Carrico, Tremoulinas; Aleix Vidal, Mbia, Krychowiak, Vitolo (Reyes 78); Iborra (Banega 75); Gameiro (Bacca 64).

Wolfsburg (1) 3 *(Naldo 28, De Bruyne 63, 75)*
Internazionale (1) 1 *(Palacio 5)*   25,374
Wolfsburg: (4411) Benaglio; Vieirinha (Perisic 87), Naldo, Knoche, Rodriguez; Caligiuri, Guilavogui, Gustavo, Schurrle (Trasch 46); De Bruyne; Dost (Bendtner 70).
Internazionale: (433) Carrizo; D'Ambrosio, Juan Jesus, Ranocchia, Santon (Kuzmanovic 82); Medel, Guarin, Hernanes (Vidic 58); Palacio, Shaqiri (Kovacic 82), Icardi.

Zenit St Petersburg (1) 2 *(Witsel 38, Criscito 53)*
Torino (0) 0   21,400
Zenit St Petersburg: (451) Lodygin; Smolnikov, Luis Neto, Garay, Criscito; Hulk, Witsel (Tymoschuk 90), Javi Garcia, Danny, Shatov (Ryazantsev 81); Rondon.
Torino: (352) Padelli; Maksimovic, Glik, Moretti; Darmian, Benassi▪, Gazzi, El Kaddouri, Molinaro; Quagliarella (Maxi Lopez 74); Martinez (Vives 33).

ROUND OF 16 SECOND LEG

Thursday, 19 March 2015
Ajax (0) 2 *(Bazoer 60, van der Hoorn 117)*
Dnipro Dnipropetrovsk (0) 1 *(Konoplyanka 97)*   51,756
Ajax: (433) Cillessen; Van Rhijn, Veltman, Viergever, Boilesen (van der Hoorn 100); Bazoer, Klaassen, Sinkgraven (Serero 87); El Ghazi, Milik, Kishna (Sigthorsson 78).
Dnipro Dnipropetrovsk: (4411) Boyko; Leo Matos, Douglas, Cheberyachko, Egidio; Luchkevych (Bruno Gama 90), Kankava, Fedorchuk, Konoplyanka (Seleznyov 108); Bezus (Shakhov 85); Kalinic.
aet; Dnipro won on away goals.

Besiktas (0) 1 *(Ramon 48)*
Club Brugge (0) 3 *(De Sutter 61,*
Bolingoli Mbombo 80, 90) 65,110
Besiktas: (442) Zengin; Opare (Frei 71), Uysal, Franco, Ramon; Arslan, Kavlak, Tore, Sahan■; Pektemek (Tosun 74), Ba.
Club Brugge: (41212) Ryan; Mechele, Izquierdo (Bolingoli Mbombo 65), De Fauw (Felipe Gedoz 60), Duarte; De Bock; Vormer, Simons; Rafaelov; Meunier, De Sutter (Oulare 81).

Dynamo Kyiv (3) 5 *(Yarmolenko 21, Teodorczyk 35, Veloso 37, Gusev 56, Antunes 76)*
Everton (1) 2 *(Lukaku 29, Jagielka 82)* 67,553
Dynamo Kyiv: (4231) Shovkovskiy; Danilo Silva, Khacheridi, Dragovic, Antunes; Rybalka, Veloso; Yarmolenko, Sydorchuk (Buyalsky 64), Gusev (Kalitvintsev 90); Teodorczyk (Kravets 74).
Everton: (4231) Howard; Coleman, Alcaraz, Jagielka, Baines; McCarthy (Besic 78), Barry; Naismith (Kone 64), Barkley, Atsu (Osman 65); Lukaku.

Dynamo Moscow (0) 0
Napoli (0) 0 17,356
Dynamo Moscow: (451) Gabulov; Kozlov, Samba, Hubocan, Buttner (Ionov 84); Kokorin, Vainqueur, Valbuena, Zhirkov, Dzsudzsak; Kuranyi.
Napoli: (4231) Andujar; Maggio, Albiol, Britos, Ghoulam; Jorginho, David Lopez; Callejon, Gabbiadini (Hamsik 71), Mertens (de Guzman 63); Higuain (Zuniga 81).

Internazionale (0) 1 *(Palacio 71)*
Wolfsburg (1) 2 *(Caligiuri 24, Bendtner 89)* 38,800
Internazionale: (433) Carrizo; Santon, Ranocchia, Juan Jesus, Campagnaro (D'Ambrosio 68); Hernanes, Medel, Guarin; Kovacic (Kuzmanovic 55), Icardi, Palacio.
Wolfsburg: (4411) Benaglio; Trasch, Knoche, Klose, Rodriguez; Vieirinha (Arnold 85), Guilavogui, Gustavo, Caligiuri (Perisic 73); De Bruyne; Dost (Bendtner 64).

Roma (0) 0
Fiorentina (3) 3 *(Rodriguez 10 (pen), Alonso 18, Basanta 21)* 30,591
Roma: (433) Skorupski; Yanga-Mbiwa (Astori 58), Holebas, Torosidis (Iturbe 27), Manolas; Pjanic, De Rossi, Keita (Verde 44); Florenzi, Ljajic■, Gervinho.
Fiorentina: (352) Neto; Rodriguez, Savic (Tomovic 41), Basanta; Alonso, Badelj, Fernandez, Joaquin, Valero (Aquilani 79); El Babacar (Vargas 63), Salah.

Sevilla (0) 2 *(Iborra 69, Suarez 82)*
Villarreal (0) 1 *(Giovani 73)* 28,784
Sevilla: (4411) Sergio Rico; Diogo Figueiras, Pareja, Kolodzieczak, Tremoulinas; Aleix Vidal (Reyes 74), Mbia, Carrico, Vitolo; Iborra (Suarez 79); Gameiro (Bacca 65).
Villarreal: (442) Sergio Asenjo; Mario, Musacchio, Bailly■, Rukavina; Jonathan, Pina, Trigueros, Campbell (Moreno 70); Uche (Giovani 46), Vietto (Dorado 85).

Torino (0) 1 *(Glik 90)*
Zenit St Petersburg (0) 0 24,736
Torino: (352) Padelli; Maksimovic, Glik, Moretti; Darmian, El Kaddouri (Martinez 76), Gazzi, Farnerud (Bovo 64), Molinaro (Amauri 82); Maxi Lopez, Quagliarella.
Zenit St Petersburg: (442) Lodygin; Smolnikov, Luis Neto, Garay, Criscito; Hulk, Tymoschuk, Witsel, Shatov (Ryazantsev 81); Rondon, Danny (Lombaerts 87).

QUARTER-FINALS FIRST LEG

Thursday, 16 April 2015
Club Brugge (0) 0
Dnipro Dnipropetrovsk (0) 0 29,000
Club Brugge: (442) Ryan; De Fauw, De Bock, Mechele, Simons; Izquierdo (Dierckx 79), Silva, Vazquez, Rafaelov (Coopman 89); Vormer, Oulare (De Sutter 72).

Dnipro Dnipropetrovsk: (442) Boyko; Douglas, Luchkevych (Bruno Gama 80), Fedetskiy, Kankava; Leo Matos, Cheberyachko, Fedorchuk, Rotan (Bezus 88); Kalinic (Seleznyov 78), Konoplyanka.

Dynamo Kyiv (1) 1 *(Lens 36)*
Fiorentina (0) 1 *(El Babacar 90)* 65,535
Dynamo Kyiv: (4411) Shovkovskiy; Danilo Silva, Antunes (Vida 24), Dragovic, Khacheridi; Sydorchuk (Belhanda 68), Rybalka, Buyalsky (Chumak 79), Lens; Yarmolenko; Teodorczyk.
Fiorentina: (433) Neto; Rodriguez, Savic, Alonso, Tomovic; Badelj, Fernandez, Joaquin (Vargas 68); Valero (Aquilani 83), Gomez (El Babacar 77), Salah.

Sevilla (0) 2 *(Bacca 73, Suarez 88)*
Zenit St Petersburg (1) 1 *(Ryazantsev 30)* 28,450
Sevilla: (4231) Sergio Rico; Coke (Suarez 46), Pareja, Kolodzieczak, Tremoulinas; Krychowiak, Iborra (Mbia 46); Aleix Vidal, Banega, Reyes; Gameiro (Bacca 64).
Zenit St Petersburg: (4231) Lodygin; Luis Neto, Garay, Lombaerts, Aniukov; Javi Garcia, Witsel; Shatov (Khodzhaniyazov 76), Ryazantsev (Tymoschuk 82), Rodic (Mogilevets 64); Rondon.

Wolfsburg (0) 1 *(Bendtner 80)*
Napoli (2) 4 *(Higuain 15, Hamsik 23, 64, Gabbiadini 77)* 25,112
Wolfsburg: (4411) Benaglio; Vieirinha, Naldo, Knoche, Rodriguez; Caligiuri, Guilavogui (Arnold 70), Gustavo, Schurrle (Perisic 64); De Bruyne; Dost (Bendtner 57).
Napoli: (4411) Andujar; Maggio, Albiol, Britos, Ghoulam; Callejon, David Lopez, Inler, Mertens (Insigne 60); Hamsik (Gabbiadini 75); Higuain (Henrique 86).

QUARTER-FINALS SECOND LEG

Thursday, 23 April 2015
Dnipro Dnipropetrovsk (0) 1 *(Shakhov 82)*
Club Brugge (0) 0 16,234
Dnipro Dnipropetrovsk: (4231) Boyko; Fedetskiy, Douglas, Cheberyachko, Leo Matos; Kankava, Rotan; Luchkevych (Bruno Gama 90), Bezus (Shakhov 46), Konoplyanka; Seleznyov (Kalinic 72).
Club Brugge: (451) Ryan; De Fauw, Duarte, Mechele, De Bock; Rafaelov, Vormer, Simons, Storm (Vazquez 86), Izquierdo (Dierckx 86); De Sutter (Oulare 70).

Fiorentina (1) 2 *(Gomez 43, Vargas 90)*
Dynamo Kyiv (0) 0 28,058
Fiorentina: (433) Neto; Tomovic, Rodriguez, Savic, Alonso; Fernandez, Pizarro (Aquilani 84), Valero (Badelj 79); Salah (Vargas 88), Gomez, Joaquin.
Dynamo Kyiv: (4411) Shovkovskiy; Danilo Silva, Vida, Khacheridi, Antunes; Yarmolenko, Rybalka, Buyalsky (Sydorchuk 69), Lens■; Belhanda (Kalitvintsev 63); Teodorczyk (Gusev 45).

Napoli (0) 2 *(Callejon 49, Mertens 65)*
Wolfsburg (0) 2 *(Klose 71, Perisic 73)* 30,000
Napoli: (4411) Andujar; Mesto, Albiol, Britos, Ghoulam; Callejon, David Lopez, Inler, Mertens (Henrique 82); Hamsik (Insigne 60); Higuain (Zapata 68).
Wolfsburg: (4411) Benaglio; Trasch (Dost 79), Naldo, Klose, Rodriguez (Schafer 89); Perisic, Guilavogui (Jung 75), Gustavo, Caligiuri; Arnold; Bendtner.

Zenit St Petersburg (0) 2 *(Rondon 48, Hulk 72)*
Sevilla (1) 2 *(Bacca 6 (pen), Gameiro 86)* 21,050
Zenit St Petersburg: (4231) Lodygin; Smolnikov, Luis Neto, Lombaerts, Criscito; Javi Garcia, Witsel; Hulk, Danny, Shatov; Rondon (Kerzhakov 83).
Sevilla: (4231) Beto; Coke, Pareja (Iborra 22), Carrico, Tremoulinas; Krychowiak, Mbia; Aleix Vidal, Banega, Vitolo (Suarez 90); Bacca (Gameiro 75).

SEMI-FINALS FIRST LEG

Thursday, 7 May 2015

Napoli (0) 1 *(David Lopez 50)*

Dnipro Dnipropetrovsk (0) 1 *(Seleznyov 81)*   41,095

Napoli: (4231) Andujar; Maggio, Albiol, Britos, Ghoulam; Jorginho, David Lopez (Gargano 71); Callejon (Gabbiadini 76), Hamsik, Insigne (Mertens 82); Higuain.
Dnipro Dnipropetrovsk: (4231) Boyko; Fedetskiy, Douglas, Cheberyachko, Leo Matos; Kankava (Bezus 69), Fedorchuk; Luchkevych (Bruno Gama 57), Rotan, Konoplyanka; Kalinic (Seleznyov 79).

Sevilla (1) 3 *(Aleix Vidal 17, 52, Gameiro 75)*

Fiorentina (0) 0   35,840

Sevilla: (4231) Sergio Rico; Aleix Vidal, Carrico, Kolodzieczak, Tremoulinas; Krychowiak, Mbia (Iborra 73); Reyes (Coke 58), Banega, Vitolo; Bacca (Gameiro 75).
Fiorentina: (433) Neto; Tomovic (Richards 46), Savic, Rodriguez, Alonso; Fernandez, Badelj (Pizarro 68), Valero; Joaquin, Gomez (Ilicic 80), Salah.

SEMI-FINALS SECOND LEG

Thursday, 14 May 2015

Dnipro Dnipropetrovsk (0) 1 *(Seleznyov 58)*

Napoli (0) 0   62,344

Dnipro Dnipropetrovsk: (4231) Boyko; Fedetskiy, Douglas, Cheberyachko, Leo Matos; Kankava, Fedorchuk; Luchkevych (Matheus 67), Rotan, Konoplyanka (Bruno Gama 85); Seleznyov (Kalinic 75).
Napoli: (4231) Andujar; Maggio, Albiol, Britos, Ghoulam; David Lopez (Henrique 79), Inler; Callejon, Gabbiadini (Hamsik 55), Insigne (Mertens 61); Higuain.

Fiorentina (0) 0

Sevilla (2) 2 *(Bacca 22, Carrico 27)*   32,466

Fiorentina: (433) Neto; Alonso, Basanta (Pasqual 46), Rodriguez, Savic; Valero (Lazzari 85), Pizarro, Fernandez (Badelj 67); Salah, Ilicic, Joaquin.
Sevilla: (4231) Sergio Rico; Coke, Carrico, Kolodzieczak, Tremoulinas; Mbia, Krychowiak; Aleix Vidal, Banega (Iborra 55), Vitolo (Reyes 74); Bacca (Gameiro 69).

EUROPA LEAGUE FINAL 2015

Wednesday, 27 May 2015

(in Warsaw, 45,000)

Dnipro Dnipropetrovsk (2) 2 *(Kalinic 7, Rotan 44)*   **Sevilla (2) 3** *(Krychowiak 28, Bacca 31, 73)*

Dnipro Dnipropetrovsk: (4231) Boyko; Fedetskiy, Douglas, Cheberyachko, Leo Matos; Kankava (Shakhov 85), Fedorchuk (Bezus 68); Matheus, Rotan, Konoplyanka; Kalinic (Seleznyov 78).

Sevilla: (4231) Sergio Rico; Aleix Vidal, Carrico, Kolodzieczak, Tremoulinas; Mbia, Krychowiak; Reyes (Coke 58), Banega (Iborra 87), Vitolo; Bacca (Gameiro 82).

Referee: Martin Atkinson (England).

Sevilla's Carlos Bacca scores the Spanish side's third goal in a 3-2 victory over Ukrainian side Dnipro Dnipropetrovsk in Warsaw on 27 May. This was Sevilla's fourth Europa League trophy in 10 years. (Adam Davy/EMPICS Sport)

UEFA CHAMPIONS LEAGUE 2015–16

PARTICIPATING CLUBS
The list below is provisional and is subject to pending legal proceedings and final confirmation from UEFA.

UEFA CHAMPIONS LEAGUE GROUP STAGE
Barcelona (ESP)
Bayern Munich (GER)
Chelsea (ENG)
Benfica (POR)
Paris Saint-Germain (FRA)
Juventus (ITA)
Zenit St Petersburg (RUS)
PSV Eindhoven (NED)
Real Madrid (ESP)
Atletico Madrid (ESP)
Porto (POR)
Arsenal (ENG)
Manchester City (ENG)
Sevilla (ESP)
Olympique Lyonnais (FRA)
Dynamo Kyiv (UKR)
Olympiacos (GRE)
Galatasaray (TUR)
Roma (ITA)
Borussia Moenchengladbach (GER)
Wolfsburg (GER)
KAA Gent (BEL)

UEFA CHAMPIONS LEAGUE PLAY-OFF – LEAGUE ROUTE
Manchester United (ENG)
Valencia (ESP)
Bayer Leverkusen (GER)
Sporting Lisbon (POR)
Lazio (ITA)

UEFA CHAMPIONS LEAGUE THIRD QUALIFYING ROUND – CHAMPIONS ROUTE
Basel (SUI)
Salzburg (AUT)
Viktoria Plzen (CZE)

UEFA CHAMPIONS LEAGUE THIRD QUALIFYING ROUND – LEAGUE ROUTE
Shakhtar Donetsk (UKR)
Ajax (NED)
CSKA Moscow (RUS)
Club Brugge (BEL)
Monaco (FRA)

Young Boys (SUI)
Sparta Prague (CZE)
Fenerbahce SK (TUR)
Panathinaikos FC (GRE)
Rapid Vienna (AUT)

UEFA CHAMPIONS LEAGUE SECOND QUALIFYING ROUND
Steaua Bucharest (ROU)
Celtic (SCO)
APOEL (CYP)
BATE Borisov (BLR)
Ludogorets Razgrad (BUL)
Dinamo Zagreb (CRO)
Maribor (SVN)
Maccabi Tel Aviv (ISR)
Lech Poznan (POL)
FK Partizan (SRB)
Malmo (SWE)
Qarabag FK (AZE)
Helsinki (FIN)
Molde (NOR)
Midtjylland (DEN)
Videoton (HUN)
Skenderbeu (ALB)
Sarajevo (BIH)
Ventspils (LVA)
Dila Gori (GEO)
Trencin (SVK)
Zalgiris Vilnius (LTU)
Astana (KAZ)
Milsami Orhei (MDA)
Rudar Pljevlja (MNE)
Vardar (MKD)
Stjarnan (ISL)
Fola Esch (LUX)
Dundalk (IRL)
Hibernians (MLT)

UEFA CHAMPIONS LEAGUE FIRST QUALIFYING ROUND
The New Saints (WAL)
Levadia Tallinn (EST)
Pyunik (ARM)
Santa Coloma (AND)
Crusaders (NIR)
Torshavn (FRO)
Lincoln (GIB)
Folgore (SMR)

UEFA EUROPA LEAGUE 2015–16

PARTICIPATING CLUBS
The list below is provisional and is subject to pending legal proceedings and final confirmation from UEFA.

UEFA EUROPA LEAGUE GROUP STAGE
Schalke 04 (GER)
Napoli (ITA)
Tottenham Hotspur (ENG)
Villarreal (ESP)
Olympique Marseille (FRA)
Dnipro Dnipropetrovsk (UKR)
Braga (POR)
Fiorentina (ITA)
Anderlecht (BEL)
Liverpool (ENG)
Besiktas (TUR)

Lokomotiv Moscow (RUS)
Augsburg (GER)
Asteras Tripolis (GRE)
Groningen (NED)
Sion (SUI)

UEFA EUROPA LEAGUE THIRD QUALIFYING ROUND
Borussia Dortmund (GER)
Athletic Bilbao (ESP)
AZ Alkmaar (NED)
Dinamo Moscow (RUS)
Standard Liege (BEL)
Bordeaux (FRA)
Sampdoria (ITA)
Vitoria (POR)

Saint-Etienne (FRA)
Zurich (SUI)
Slovan Liberec (CZE)
Southampton (ENG)
Krasnodar (RUS)
Os Belenenses (POR)
Vorksla Poltava (UKR)
Atromitos (GRE)
Zorya Luhansk (UKR)
Vitesse (NED)
Jablonec (CZE)
Sturm Graz (AUT)
AEK Larnaca (CYP)
Hapoel Kiryat Shmona (ISR)
Istanbul Basaksehir (TUR)
Targu Mures (ROU)
SCR Altach (AUT)

**UEFA EUROPA LEAGUE
SECOND QUALIFYING ROUND**
Copenhagen (DEN)
PAOK (GRE)
Trabzonspor (TUR)
Legia Warsaw (POL)
HNK Rijeka (CRO)
Thun (SUI)
Astra Giurgiu (ROU)
Dinamo Minsk (BLR)
Mlada Boleslav (CZE)
Charleroi (BEL)
IFK Gothenburg (SWE)
Wolfsburger (AUT)
Hapoel Beer Sheva FC (ISR)
Inverness Caledonian Thistle (SCO)
Cherno More Varna (BUL)

UEFA EUROPA LEAGUE FIRST QUALIFYING ROUND
West Ham United* (ENG)
Sheriff (MDA)
Rosenborg (NOR)
Elfsborg (SWE)
Hajduk Split (CRO)
Apollon Limassol FC (CYP)
Omonia (CYP)
Slovan Bratislava (SVK)
AIK Solna (SWE)
Neftci PFK (AZE)
Slask Wroclaw (POL)
Zilina (SVK)
Aktobe (KAZ)
Go Ahead Eagles* (NED)
Crvena Zvezda (SRB)
Debreceni (HUN)
Brondby (DEN)
Shakhtyor Soligorsk (BLR)
Dinamo Tbilisi (GEO)
Litex Lovech (BUL)
Vojvodina (SRB)
Spartak Trnava (SVK)
Hafnarfjordur (ISL)
St Johnstone (SCO)
FK Zeljeznicar (BIH)
Randers (DEN)
Stromsgodset (NOR)
KR Reykjavik (ISL)
Jagiellonia Bialystok (POL)
FC Botosani (ROU)
Lokomotive Zagreb (CRO)
Shamrock Rovers (IRL)
F91 Dudelange (LUX)

Inter Baku (AZE)
Linfield (NIR)
Beroe Stara Zagora (BUL)
Valletta (MLT)
Differdange 03 (LUX)
Rabotnicki (MKD)
Torpedo Zhodino (BLR)
Aberdeen (SCO)
Dacia Chisinau (MDA)
Koper (SVN)
St Patrick's Athletic (IRL)
Beitar Jerusalem (ISL)
Zrinjski (CRO)
Torshavn (FRO)
Buducnost Podgorica (MNE)
Birkirkara (MLT)
Domzale (SVN)
Vaduz (LIE)
Cukaricki (SRB)
Celje (SVN)
Ferencvarosi TC (HUN)
Nomme Kalju FC (EST)
Flora Tallinn (EST)
Sutjeska (MNE)
Skonto (LVA)
Víkingur (FRO)
Renova (MNE)
Odds (NOR)
Kukesi (ALB)
Qabala (AZE)
Shkendija (MKD)
Kairat Almaty (KAZ)
Ordabasy Shymkent (KAZ)
MTK Budapest (HUN)
Shirak (ARM)
Mladost Podgorica (MNE)
Laci (ALB)
Ulisses (ARM)
Saxan (MDA)
Glentoran (NIR)
VPS Vaasa (FIN)
Dinamo Batumi (GEO)
Tskhinvali (GEO)
Sillamae Kalev (EST)
Lusitans (AND)
Seinajoki (FIN)
Lahti (FIN)
Víkingur Reykjavik (ISL)
Jelgava (LVA)
Olimpic Sarajevo (BIH)
NSI Runavik (FRO)
UE Sant Julia (AND)
Atlantas Klaipeda (LTU)
Glenavon (NIR)
Cork City (IRL)
University College Dublin* (IRL)
Kruoja Pakruojis (LTU)
La Fiorita (SMR)
AUK Broughton (WAL)
Partizani (ALB)
Progres Niederkorn (LUX)
Trakai (LTU)
Spartaks Jurmala (LVA)
Balzan (MLT)
Bala Town (WAL)
Juvenes/Dogana (SMR)
Newtown (WAL)
Alashkert (ARM)
College Europa (GIB)

Respect Fair Play entrants.

BRITISH AND IRISH CLUBS IN EUROPE

SUMMARY OF APPEARANCES

EUROPEAN CUP AND CHAMPIONS LEAGUE (1955–2015)

(Winners in brackets) (SE = seasons entered).

ENGLAND	SE	P	W	D	L	F	A
Manchester U (3)	25	253	141	62	50	469	240
Liverpool (5)	21	185	100	41	40	322	153
Arsenal	19	185	94	41	50	299	187
Chelsea (1)	13	144	73	42	29	242	123
Manchester C	5	30	10	7	13	46	44
Leeds U	4	40	22	6	12	76	41
Nottingham F (2)	3	20	12	4	4	32	14
Newcastle U	3	24	11	3	10	33	33
Everton	3	10	2	5	3	14	10
Tottenham H	2	20	9	4	7	46	32
Aston Villa (1)	2	15	9	3	3	24	10
Derby Co	2	12	6	2	4	18	12
Wolverhampton W	2	8	2	2	4	12	16
Ipswich T	1	4	3	0	1	16	5
Burnley	1	4	2	0	2	8	8
Blackburn R	1	6	1	1	4	5	8

SCOTLAND	SE	P	W	D	L	F	A
Rangers	30	161	62	40	59	232	218
Celtic (1)	29	170	81	27	62	251	189
Aberdeen	3	12	5	4	3	14	12
Hearts	3	8	2	1	5	8	16
Dundee U	1	8	5	1	2	14	5
Dundee	1	8	5	0	3	20	14
Hibernian	1	6	3	1	2	9	5
Kilmarnock	1	4	1	2	1	4	7
Motherwell	1	2	0	0	2	0	5

WALES	SE	P	W	D	L	F	A
The New Saints	8	18	2	2	14	12	35
Barry T	6	14	4	1	9	11	38

	SE	P	W	D	L	F	A
Rhyl	2	4	0	0	4	1	19
Cwmbran T	1	2	1	0	1	4	4
Llanelli	1	2	1	0	1	1	4
Bangor C	1	2	0	0	2	0	13

NORTHERN IRELAND	SE	P	W	D	L	F	A
Linfield	27	63	6	22	35	55	112
Glentoran	12	28	3	7	18	20	59
Portadown	3	6	0	1	5	3	24
Crusaders	3	6	0	0	6	2	27
Cliftonville	3	6	0	1	5	1	20
Glenavon	1	2	0	1	1	0	3
Lisburn Distillery	1	2	0	1	1	3	8
Ards	1	2	0	0	2	3	10
Coleraine	1	2	0	0	2	1	11

REPUBLIC OF IRELAND	SE	P	W	D	L	F	A
Shamrock R	9	20	1	6	13	9	33
Dundalk	7	18	3	4	11	13	41
Shelbourne	6	20	4	8	8	21	31
Bohemians	6	18	4	4	10	13	29
Waterford U	6	14	3	0	11	15	47
Derry C	4	9	1	1	7	9	26
St Patrick's Ath	4	8	0	3	5	2	23
Dublin C	3	6	1	0	5	3	25
Cork C	2	8	2	1	5	7	12
Athlone T	2	4	0	2	2	7	14
Sligo R	2	4	0	0	4	0	9
Limerick	2	4	0	0	4	4	16
Drogheda U	1	4	2	1	1	6	5
Cork Hibernians	1	2	0	0	2	1	7
Cork Celtic	1	2	0	0	2	1	7

UEFA CUP AND EUROPA LEAGUE 1971–2015

ENGLAND	SE	P	W	D	L	F	A
Aston Villa	13	56	24	14	18	77	60
Tottenham H (2)	13	128	73	33	22	259	106
Liverpool (3)	12	107	59	27	21	166	80
Ipswich T (1)	10	52	30	10	12	98	53
Newcastle U	8	72	42	17	13	123	60
Manchester C	8	52	28	13	11	84	51
Leeds U	8	46	20	10	16	66	48
Everton	8	42	23	6	13	75	48
Manchester U	7	24	7	10	7	25	23
Arsenal	6	25	12	4	9	45	32
Blackburn R	6	22	7	8	7	27	26
Southampton	5	12	2	6	4	11	14
Chelsea (1)	4	17	10	2	5	28	20
Wolverhampton W	4	20	13	3	4	41	23
Fulham	3	39	21	10	8	64	31
Nottingham F	3	20	10	5	5	18	16
Stoke C	3	16	8	4	4	21	16
WBA	3	12	5	2	5	15	13
West Ham U	2	6	2	1	3	6	7
Leicester C	2	4	0	1	3	3	8
Middlesbrough	2	25	13	4	8	36	24
Bolton W	2	18	6	10	2	18	14
QPR	2	12	8	1	3	39	18
Derby Co	2	10	5	2	3	32	17
Birmingham C	1	8	4	2	2	11	8
Norwich C	1	6	2	2	2	6	4
Portsmouth	1	6	2	2	2	11	10
Watford	1	6	2	1	3	10	12
Wigan Ath	1	6	1	2	3	6	7
Sheffield W	1	4	2	1	1	13	7
Millwall	1	2	0	1	1	2	4
Hull C	1	4	2	1	1	4	3

SCOTLAND	SE	P	W	D	L	F	A
Dundee U	19	82	33	25	24	134	89
Celtic	18	93	40	22	31	147	100
Aberdeen	17	60	18	19	23	75	83
Rangers	16	76	31	23	22	99	77
Hearts	13	46	19	9	18	54	57
Hibernian	11	32	11	9	12	40	51
Motherwell	8	26	8	2	16	33	34
St Johnstone	5	20	6	7	7	22	25
Dundee	4	14	6	0	8	24	24

	SE	P	W	D	L	F	A
Kilmarnock	3	12	4	2	6	7	14
St Mirren	3	10	2	3	5	9	12
Dunfermline Ath	2	4	0	2	2	4	6
Raith R	1	6	2	1	3	10	8
Livingston	1	4	1	2	1	7	9
Falkirk	1	2	1	0	1	1	2
Gretna	1	2	0	1	1	3	7
Queen of the South	1	2	0	0	2	2	4
Partick Thistle	1	2	0	0	2	0	4

WALES	SE	P	W	D	L	F	A
Bangor C	9	20	2	2	16	10	57
The New Saints	8	18	1	2	15	12	49
Llanelli	5	12	3	3	6	12	24
Rhyl	3	8	2	1	5	9	12
UWIC Inter Cardiff	3	6	1	0	5	1	18
Cwmbran T	3	6	0	0	6	0	21
Barry T	2	8	2	2	4	10	16
Carmarthen T	2	6	1	0	5	8	21
Newtown	2	4	0	1	3	1	14
Air UK Broughton	2	4	0	3	1	3	4
Prestatyn T	1	4	1	0	3	3	11
Bala T	1	2	1	0	1	2	3
Afan Lido	1	2	0	1	1	1	2
Cefn Druids	1	2	0	1	1	0	5
Port Talbot T	1	2	0	0	2	1	7
Neath	1	2	0	0	2	1	6
Haverfordwest Co	1	2	0	0	2	1	4
Swansea C	1	12	4	4	4	17	10
Aberystwith T	1	2	0	0	2	0	9

NORTHERN IRELAND	SE	P	W	D	L	F	A
Glentoran	17	38	3	8	27	21	90
Portadown	11	28	3	7	18	16	62
Linfield	10	28	8	7	13	29	52
Crusaders	8	18	3	3	12	16	45
Coleraine	7	14	1	3	10	8	36
Glenavon	6	14	1	2	11	5	30
Cliftonville	4	10	2	2	6	4	22
Ards	1	2	1	0	1	4	8
Ballymena U	1	2	1	0	1	2	4
Dungannon Swifts	1	2	1	0	1	1	4
Lisburn Distillery	1	2	0	0	2	1	11
Bangor	1	2	0	0	2	0	6

REPUBLIC OF IRELAND

Bohemians	14	30	3	9	18	16	56
St Patrick's Ath	8	32	9	6	17	30	49
Derry C	7	22	6	5	11	26	32
Cork C	6	16	2	4	10	8	26
Shelbourne	6	12	0	2	10	8	28
Dundalk	6	16	4	2	10	12	35
Shamrock R	5	20	4	2	14	17	43
Drogheda U	4	12	3	4	5	10	24

Sligo R	4	10	2	4	4	11	13
Longford T	3	6	1	1	4	6	12
Finn Harps	3	6	0	0	6	3	33
Athlone T	1	4	1	2	1	4	5
Limerick	1	2	0	1	1	1	4
Sporting Fingal	1	2	0	0	2	4	6
Galway U	1	2	0	0	2	2	8
Bray W	1	2	0	0	2	0	8

EUROPEAN CUP WINNERS' CUP 1960–1999

ENGLAND	SE	P	W	D	L	F	A
Tottenham H (1)	6	33	20	5	8	65	34
Chelsea (2)	5	39	23	10	6	81	28
Liverpool	5	29	16	5	8	57	29
Manchester U (1)	5	31	16	9	6	55	35
West Ham U (1)	4	30	15	6	9	58	42
Arsenal (1)	3	27	15	10	2	48	20
Everton (1)	3	17	11	4	2	25	9
Manchester C (1)	2	18	11	2	5	32	13
Ipswich T	1	6	3	2	1	6	3
Leeds U	1	9	5	3	1	13	3
Leicester C	1	4	2	1	1	8	5
Newcastle U	1	2	1	0	1	2	2
Southampton	1	6	4	0	2	16	8
Sunderland	1	4	3	0	1	5	3
WBA	1	6	2	2	2	8	5
Wolverhampton W	1	4	1	1	2	6	5

SCOTLAND							
Rangers (1)	10	54	27	11	16	100	62
Aberdeen (1)	8	39	22	5	12	79	37
Celtic	8	38	21	4	13	75	37
Dundee U	3	10	3	3	4	9	10
Hearts	3	10	3	3	4	16	14
Dunfermline Ath	2	14	7	2	5	34	14
Airdrieonians	1	2	0	0	2	1	3
Dundee	1	2	0	1	1	3	4
Hibernian	1	6	3	1	2	19	10
Kilmarnock	1	4	1	2	1	5	6
Motherwell	1	2	1	0	1	3	3
St Mirren	1	4	1	2	1	1	2

WALES							
Cardiff C	14	49	16	14	19	67	61
Wrexham	8	28	10	8	10	34	35
Swansea C	7	18	3	4	11	32	37
Bangor C	3	9	1	2	6	5	12
Barry T	1	2	0	0	2	0	7
Borough U	1	4	1	1	2	2	4
Cwmbran T	1	2	0	0	2	2	12
Merthyr Tydfil	1	2	1	0	1	2	3
Newport Co	1	6	2	3	1	12	3
The New Saints (Llansantfraid)	1	2	0	1	1	1	6

NORTHERN IRELAND							
Glentoran	9	22	3	7	12	18	46
Glenavon	5	10	1	3	6	11	25
Ballymena U	4	8	0	0	8	1	25
Coleraine	4	8	0	1	7	7	34
Crusaders	3	6	0	2	4	5	18
Derry C	3	6	1	1	4	1	11
Linfield	3	6	2	0	4	6	11
Ards	2	4	0	1	3	2	17
Bangor	2	4	0	1	3	2	8
Carrick Rangers	1	4	1	0	3	7	12
Cliftonville	1	2	0	0	2	0	8
Distillery	1	2	0	0	2	1	7
Portadown	1	2	0	1	1	4	7

REPUBLIC OF IRELAND							
Shamrock R	6	16	5	2	9	19	27
Shelbourne	4	10	1	1	8	9	20
Bohemians	3	8	2	2	4	6	13
Dundalk	3	8	2	1	5	7	14
Limerick U	3	6	0	1	5	2	11
Waterford U	3	8	1	1	6	6	14
Cork C	2	4	1	0	3	2	9
Cork Hibernians	2	6	2	1	3	7	8
Galway U	2	4	0	0	4	2	11
Sligo R	2	6	1	1	4	5	11
Bray W	1	2	0	1	1	1	3
Cork Celtic	1	2	0	1	1	1	3
Finn Harps	1	2	0	1	1	2	4
Home Farm	1	2	0	1	1	1	7
St Patrick's Ath	1	2	0	0	2	1	8
University College Dublin	1	2	0	1	1	0	1

INTER-CITIES FAIRS CUP 1955–1970

ENGLAND	SE	P	W	D	L	F	A
Leeds U (2)	5	53	28	17	8	92	40
Birmingham C	4	25	14	6	5	51	38
Liverpool	4	22	12	4	6	46	15
Arsenal (1)	3	24	12	5	7	46	19
Chelsea	3	20	10	5	5	33	24
Everton	3	12	7	2	3	22	15
Newcastle U (1)	3	24	13	6	5	37	21
Nottingham F	2	6	3	0	3	8	9
Sheffield W	2	10	5	0	5	25	18
Burnley	1	8	4	3	1	16	5
Coventry C	1	4	3	0	1	9	8
London XI	1	8	4	1	3	14	13
Manchester U	1	11	6	3	2	29	10
Southampton	1	6	2	3	1	11	6
WBA	1	4	1	1	2	7	9

SCOTLAND							
Hibernian	7	36	18	5	13	66	60
Dunfermline Ath	5	28	16	3	9	49	31
Kilmarnock	4	20	8	3	9	34	32
Dundee U	3	10	5	1	4	11	12
Hearts	3	12	4	4	4	20	20
Rangers	3	18	8	4	6	27	17
Celtic	2	6	1	3	2	9	10
Aberdeen	1	4	2	1	1	4	4
Dundee	1	8	5	1	2	14	9
Morton	1	2	0	0	2	3	9
Partick Thistle	1	4	3	0	1	10	7

NORTHERN IRELAND							
Glentoran	4	8	1	1	6	7	22
Coleraine	2	8	2	1	5	15	23
Linfield	2	4	1	0	3	3	11

REPUBLIC OF IRELAND							
Drumcondra	2	6	2	0	4	8	19
Dundalk	2	6	1	1	4	4	25
Shamrock R	2	4	0	2	2	4	6
Cork Hibernians	1	2	0	0	2	1	6
Shelbourne	1	5	1	2	2	3	4
St Patrick's Ath	1	2	0	0	2	4	9

FIFA CLUB WORLD CUP 2014

Formerly known as the FIFA Club World Championship, this tournament is played annually between the champion clubs from all 6 continental confederations, although since 2007 the champions of Oceania must play a qualifying play-off against the champion club of the host country.

(Finals in Morocco)

■ *Denotes player sent off.*

PLAY-OFF FOR QUARTER FINALS
Wednesday 10 December 2014
Moghreb Tetouan (0) 0
Auckland City (0) 0   35,247
Moghreb Tetouan: Lyousfi; Abarhoun, Fall, Khallati, Maimouni (Grada 98), Iajour (Krouch 46), Faouzi (Ould El Haj 94), Naim, Jahouh, Hardoumi, Akhadrouf.
Auckland City: Williams; Takuya, Bilen, Berlanga, Irving, Payne, De Vries, Vicelich, Dordevic, Tade (White 68), Tavano (Issa 107).
aet; Auckland City won 4-3 on penalties.
Referee: Walter Lopez (Guatemala).

QUARTER-FINALS
Saturday 13 December 2014
ES Setif (0) 0
Auckland City (0) 1 *(Irving 52)*   22,153
ES Setif: Khedairia; Arroussi, Megatli, Gasmi (Ziaya 65), Benyettou, Boukria, Mellouli, Belameiri (Younes 69), Lagraa, Zerara, Dagoulou (Djahnit 46).
Auckland City: Williams; Takuya, Bilen, Berlanga, Irving, Payne, De Vries (White 90), Vicelich, Dordevic, Tade, Tavano (Issa 86).
Referee: Pedro Proenca (Portugal).

Cruz Azul (0) 3 *(Torrado 89 (pen), 118 (pen), Pavone 108)*
WS Wanderers (0) 1 *(La Rocca 65)*   22,153
Cruz Azul: Corona; Pinto, (Valadez 78), Rodriguez, Dominguez, Torrado, Fabian (Vela 106), Pavone, Gimenez, Flores, Baez (Rojas 69), Formica.
WS Wanderers: Covic; Topor-Stanley■, Hamill, Haliti (Juric 68), Poljak, Rukavytsya, Spiranovic■, Castelen (Cole 78), La Rocca, Bridge, Adeleke (Golec 72).
aet. (1-1 after 90 minutes)
Referee: Noumandiez Doue (Ivory Coast).

SEMI-FINALS
Tuesday 16 December 2014
Cruz Azul (0) 0
Real Madrid (2) 4 *(Sergio Ramos 15, Benzema 36, Bale 50, Isco 72)*   34,862
Cruz Azul: Corona; Pinto, Rodriguez, Dominguez, Torrado, Pavone (Barrera 65), Gimenez (Fabian 65), Rojas (Valadez 76), Flores, Bernardello, Formica.
Real Madrid: Casillas; Pepe, Sergio Ramos (Varane 64), Ronaldo, Kroos (Khedira 73), Benzema, Bale, Marcelo, Carvajal, Isco (Jese 76), Illarra.
Referee: Enrique Osses (Chile).

Wednesday 17 December 2014
San Lorenzo (1) 2 *(Barrientos 45, Matos 93)*
Auckland City (0) 1 *(Berlanga 67)*   18,458
San Lorenzo: Torrico; Yepes, Mercier, Buffarini, Kalinski (Matos 77), Cauteruccio, Barrientos, Kannemann, Ortigoza (Quignon 109), Mas E, Veron (Romagnoli 68).
Auckland City: Williams; Takuya, Bilen, Berlanga, Irving, Payne, De Vries, Vicelich, Dordevic (Issa 96), Tade (Browne 90), Tavano (Burfoot 100).
aet. (1-1 after 90 minutes)
Referee: Benjamin Williams (Australia).

MATCH FOR FIFTH PLACE
Wednesday 17 December 2014
ES Setif (0) 2 *(Mullen 50 (og), Ziaya 57)*
WS Wanderers (1) 2 *(Castelen 5, Saba 89)*   18,458
ES Setif: Khedairia; Younes (Belameiri 77), Arroussi, Megatli, Gasmi, Djahnit, Lamri (Lagraa 64), Ze Ondo, Ziaya, Mellouli, Zerara.
WS Wanderers: Bouzanis; Mullen, Golec, Haliti, Poljak (Fofanah 79), Sotirio (Juric 67), Castelen, Adeleke, Trifiro, Alessi, Baccus (Saba 67).
aet. (2-2 after 90 minutes), ES Setif won 5-4 on penalties.
Referee: Norbert Hauata (Tahiti).

MATCH FOR THIRD PLACE
Saturday 20 December 2014
Cruz Azul (0) 1 *(Rojas 57)*
Auckland City (1) 1 *(De Vries 45)*   38,345
Cruz Azul: Corona; Rodriguez, Dominguez, Torrado, Fabian (Pavone 85), Rojas, Flores, Valadez, Vela, Baez (Gimenez 46), Formica.
Auckland City: Spoonley; Takuya, Bilen, Irving, Payne, White, De Vries, Vicelich (Lindsay 80), Tade (Pritchett 90), Burfoot (Issa 57), Tavano.
aet. (1-1 after 90 minutes), Auckland City won 4-2 on penalties.
Referee: Pedro Proenca (Portugal).

FIFA CLUB WORLD CUP FINAL 2014
Marrakesh, Saturday 20 December 2014 (attendance 38,345)

Real Madrid (1) 2 *(Sergio Ramos 37, Bale 51)*   **San Lorenzo (0) 0**

Real Madrid: Casillas; Pepe, Sergio Ramos (Varane 89), Ronaldo, Kroos, Benzema, James, Bale, Marcelo (Fabio Coentrao 44), Carvajal (Arbeloa 73), Isco.
San Lorenzo: Torrico; Yepes (Cetto 61), Mercier, Buffarini, Kalinski, Cauteruccio (Matos 68), Barrientos, Kannemann, Ortigoza, Mas E, Veron (Romagnoli 57).
Referee: Walter Lopez (Guatemala).

PREVIOUS FINALS
2000 Corinthians beat Vaso de Gama 4-3 on penalties after 0-0 draw	2009 Barcelona beat Estudiantes 2-1
2001–04 Not contested	2010 Internazionale beat TP Mazembe Englebert 3-0
2005 Sao Paulo beat Liverpool 1-0	2011 Barcelona beat Santos 4-0
2006 Internacional beat Barcelona 1-0	2012 Corinthians beat Chelsea 1-0
2007 AC Milan beat Boca Juniors 4-2	2013 Bayern Munich beat Raja Casablanca 2-0
2008 Manchester U beat Liga De Quito 1-0	2014 Real Madrid beat San Lorenzo 2-0

WORLD CLUB CHAMPIONSHIP

Played annually up to 1974 and intermittently since then between the winners of the European Cup and the winners of the South American Champions Cup — known as the Copa Libertadores. In 1980 the winners were decided by one match arranged in Tokyo in February 1981 which remained the venue until 2004, when the match was superseded by the FIFA Club World Championship. AC Milan replaced Marseille who had been stripped of their European Cup title in 1993.

1960 Real Madrid beat Penarol 0-0, 5-1
1961 Penarol beat Benfica 0-1, 5-0, 2-1
1962 Santos beat Benfica 3-2, 5-2
1963 Santos beat AC Milan 2-4, 4-2, 1-0
1964 Inter-Milan beat Independiente 0-1, 2-0, 1-0
1965 Inter-Milan beat Independiente 3-0, 0-0
1966 Penarol beat Real Madrid 2-0, 2-0
1967 Racing Club beat Celtic 0-1, 2-1, 1-0
1968 Estudiantes beat Manchester United 1-0, 1-1
1969 AC Milan beat Estudiantes 3-0, 1-2
1970 Feyenoord beat Estudiantes 2-2, 1-0
1971 Nacional beat Panathinaikos* 1-1, 2-1
1972 Ajax beat Independiente 1-1, 3-0
1973 Independiente beat Juventus* 1-0
1974 Atlético Madrid* beat Independiente 0-1, 2-0
1975 Independiente and Bayern Munich could not agree dates; no matches.
1976 Bayern Munich beat Cruzeiro 2-0, 0-0
1977 Boca Juniors beat Borussia Moenchengladbach* 2-2, 3-0
1978 Not contested
1979 Olimpia beat Malmö* 1-0, 2-1
1980 Nacional beat Nottingham Forest 1-0
1981 Flamengo beat Liverpool 3-0
1982 Penarol beat Aston Villa 2-0
1983 Gremio Porto Alegre beat SV Hamburg 2-1
1984 Independiente beat Liverpool 1-0

1985 Juventus beat Argentinos Juniors 4-2 on penalties after a 2-2 draw
1986 River Plate beat Steaua Bucharest 1-0
1987 FC Porto beat Penarol 2-1 after extra time
1988 Nacional (Uru) beat PSV Eindhoven 7-6 on penalties after 1-1 draw
1989 AC Milan beat Atletico Nacional (Col) 1-0 after extra time
1990 AC Milan beat Olimpia 3-0
1991 Red Star Belgrade beat Colo Colo 3-0
1992 Sao Paulo beat Barcelona 2-1
1993 Sao Paulo beat AC Milan 3-2
1994 Velez Sarsfield beat AC Milan 2-0
1995 Ajax beat Gremio Porto Alegre 4-3 on penalties after 0-0 draw
1996 Juventus beat River Plate 1-0
1997 Borussia Dortmund beat Cruzeiro 2-0
1998 Real Madrid beat Vasco da Gama 2-1
1999 Manchester U beat Palmeiras 1-0
2000 Boca Juniors beat Real Madrid 2-1
2001 Bayern Munich beat Boca Juniors 1-0 after extra time
2002 Real Madrid beat Olimpia 2-0
2003 Boca Juniors beat AC Milan 3-1 on penalties after 1-1 draw
2004 Porto beat Once Caldas 8-7 on penalties after 0-0 draw

*European Cup runners-up; winners declined to take part.

EUROPEAN SUPER CUP 2014

Played annually between the winners of the European Champions' Cup and the European Cup-Winners' Cup (UEFA Cup from 2000; UEFA Europa League from 2010). AC Milan replaced Marseille in 1993–94.

Cardiff City Stadium, Cardiff, Tuesday 12 August 2014, attendance 30,854

Real Madrid (1) 2 *(Ronaldo 30, 49)*   **Sevilla (0)**

Real Madrid: (433) Casillas; Carvajal, Pepe, Ramos, Fabio Coentrao (Marcelo 84); Kroos, Rodriguez (Isco 72), Modric (Illarramendi 86); Bale, Benzema, Ronaldo.

Sevilla: (4411) Beto; Coke (Figueiras 84), Pareja, Fazio, Navarro; Vidal (Aspas 66), Krychowiak, Carrico, Vitolo; Suarez (Reyes 79); Bacca.

Referee: Mark Clattenburg.

PREVIOUS MATCHES

1972 Ajax beat Rangers 3-1, 3-2
1973 Ajax beat AC Milan 0-1, 6-0
1974 Not contested
1975 Dynamo Kyiv beat Bayern Munich 1-0, 2-0
1976 Anderlecht beat Bayern Munich 4-1, 1-2
1977 Liverpool beat Hamburg 1-1, 6-0
1978 Anderlecht beat Liverpool 3-1, 1-2
1979 Nottingham F beat Barcelona 1-0, 1-1
1980 Valencia beat Nottingham F 1-0, 1-2
1981 Not contested
1982 Aston Villa beat Barcelona 0-1, 3-0
1983 Aberdeen beat Hamburg 0-0, 2-0
1984 Juventus beat Liverpool 2-0
1985 Juventus v Everton not contested due to UEFA ban on English clubs
1986 Steaua Bucharest beat Dynamo Kyiv 1-0
1987 FC Porto beat Ajax 1-0, 1-0
1988 KV Mechelen beat PSV Eindhoven 3-0, 0-1
1989 AC Milan beat Barcelona 1-1, 1-0
1990 AC Milan beat Sampdoria 1-1, 2-0
1991 Manchester U beat Red Star Belgrade 1-0
1992 Barcelona beat Werder Bremen 1-1, 2-1
1993 Parma beat AC Milan 0-1, 2-0

1994 AC Milan beat Arsenal 0-0, 2-0
1995 Ajax beat Zaragoza 1-1, 4-0
1996 Juventus beat Paris St Germain 6-1, 3-1
1997 Barcelona beat Borussia Dortmund 2-0, 1-1
1998 Chelsea beat Real Madrid 1-0
1999 Lazio beat Manchester U 1-0
2000 Galatasaray beat Real Madrid 2-1
2001 Liverpool beat Bayern Munich 3-2
2002 Real Madrid beat Feyenoord 3-1
2003 AC Milan beat Porto 1-0
2004 Valencia beat Porto 2-1
2005 Liverpool beat CSKA Moscow 3-1
2006 Sevilla beat Barcelona 3-0
2007 AC Milan beat Sevilla 3-1
2008 Zenit beat Manchester U 2-1
2009 Barcelona beat Shakhtar Donetsk 1-0
2010 Atletico Madrid beat Internazionale 2-0
2011 Barcelona beat Porto 2-0
2012 Atletico Madrid beat Chelsea 4-1
2013 Bayern Munch beat Chelsea 5-4 on penalties after 2-2 draw
2014 Real Madrid beat Sevilla 2-0

INTERNATIONAL DIRECTORY

The latest available information has been given regarding numbers of clubs and players registered with FIFA, the world governing body. Where known, official colours are listed. With European countries, League tables show a number of signs: * team relegated, *+ team relegated after play-offs, + team not relegated after play-offs.

There are 209 member associations in the six FIFA Confederations, indicated in brackets after the regional heading. The four home countries, England, Scotland, Northern Ireland and Wales, are dealt with elsewhere in the Yearbook; but basic details appear in this directory. Gibraltar was admitted to full UEFA membership in 2013; Kosovo and Northern Cyprus are not members of FIFA or UEFA and are the subject of international territorial disputes; since March 2014 FIFA has permitted Kosovo to play friendlies against full member nations. Gozo is included for its close links with Maltese football. *N.B. In this edition international results for 2014–15 include matches played from 14 July 2014 to 4 July 2015.*

There are a number of associate members and others who have affiliation to their confederations; the most recent admission to full membership was South Sudan in 2011. The current associate members are as follows: AFC: Northern Mariana Islands; CAF: Reunion, Zanzibar; CONCACAF: Bonaire, French Guiana, Guadeloupe, Martinique, Saint-Martin, Sint Maarten; OFC: Kiribati, Niue, Tuvalu. Matches between full members and associate members are indicated with †; matches between full members and Kosovo are indicated with ‡.

EUROPE (UEFA)

ALBANIA

Football Association of Albania, Rruga e Elbasanit, 1000 Tirana.
Founded: 1930. *FIFA:* 1932; *UEFA:* 1954. *National Colours:* Red shirts with white trim, black shorts, red socks.

International matches 2014–15
Portugal (a) 1-0, Denmark (h) 1-1, Serbia (a) 0-3, France (a) 1-1, Italy (a) 0-1, Armenia (h) 2-1, France (h) 1-0.

League Championship wins (1930–37; 1945–2015)
KF Tirana 24 (formerly SK Tirana; includes 17 Nentori 8); Dinamo Tirana 18; Partizani Tirana 15; Vllaznia 9; Skenderbeu 6; Elbasani 2 (including Labinoti 1); Flamurtari 1; Teuta 1.

Cup wins (1948–2015)
Partizani Tirana 15; KF Tirana 15 (formerly SK Tirana; includes 17 Nentori 8); Dinamo Tirana 13; Vllaznia 6; Flamurtari 4; Teuta 3; Elbasani 2 (including Labinoti 1); Besa 2; Laci 2; Apolonia 1.

Final League Table 2014–15

	P	W	D	L	F	A	GD	Pts
Skenderbeu	36	24	7	5	58	18	40	79
Kukesi	36	23	6	7	59	27	32	75
Partizani	36	22	7	7	42	24	18	73
KF Tirana	36	21	8	7	47	27	20	71
Laci	36	20	9	7	46	19	27	69
Flamurtari	36	10	8	18	29	37	–8	38
Vllaznia (–3)	36	11	5	20	27	41	–14	35
Teuta	36	9	2	25	31	54	–23	29
Apolonia*	36	7	4	25	19	56	–37	25
Elbasani*	36	4	2	30	19	74	–55	14

Top scorer: Pejic (Kukesi) 31.
Cup Final: Laci 2, Kukesi 1.

ANDORRA

Federacio Andorrana de Futbol, Avda Carlemany 67, 3er Pis, Apartado postal 65, Escaldes-Engordany.
Founded: 1994. *FIFA:* 1996; *UEFA:* 1996. *National Colours:* All red.

International matches 2014–15
Wales (h) 1-2, Belgium (a) 0-6, Israel (h) 1-4, Cyprus (a) 0-5, Bosnia-Herzogovina (h) 0-3, Equatorial Guinea (h) 0-1, Cyprus (h) 1-3.

League Championship wins (1996–2015)
FC Santa Coloma 7; Principat 3; Encamp 2; Sant Julia 2; Ranger's 2; Lusitanos 2; Constel-lacio 1.

Cup wins (1991, 1994–2015)
FC Santa Coloma 9*; Principat 6*; Sant Julia 5; Constel-lacio 1; Lusitanos 1; UE Santa Coloma 1.
*Includes one unofficial title.

Qualifying League Table 2014–15

	P	W	D	L	F	A	GD	Pts
FC Santa Coloma	14	10	1	3	53	7	46	31
Lusitanos	14	10	1	3	45	17	28	31
UE Santa Coloma	14	9	2	3	23	8	15	29
Sant Julia	14	8	3	3	35	13	22	27
Ordino	14	6	2	6	22	22	0	20
Encamp	14	4	1	9	13	28	–15	13
Engordany	14	2	1	11	11	62	–51	7
Inter Club	14	1	1	12	7	52	–45	4

Championship Round

	P	W	D	L	F	A	GD	Pts
FC Santa Coloma	20	13	3	4	64	14	50	42
Lusitans	20	12	3	5	53	26	27	39
UE Santa Coloma	20	12	2	6	33	17	16	38
Sant Julia	20	9	5	6	41	23	18	32

Relegation Round

	P	W	D	L	F	A	GD	Pts
Ordino	20	10	3	7	36	29	7	33
Encamp (–3)	20	7	3	10	21	34	–13	21
Engordany+	20	5	2	13	21	72	–51	17
Inter Club d'Escaldes*	20	1	1	18	9	63	–54	4

Top scorer: Dos Reis (Lusitanos) 13.
Cup Final: Sant Julia 1, FC Santa Coloma 1.
aet; Sant Julia won 5-4 on penalties.

ARMENIA

Football Federation of Armenia, Khanjyan Street 27, 0010 Yerevan.
Founded: 1992. *FIFA:* 1992; *UEFA:* 1993. *National Colours:* Red shirts with white trim, red shorts, red socks.

International matches 2014–15
Latvia (a) 0-2, Denmark (a) 1-2, Serbia (h) 1-1, France (h) 0-3, Portugal (a) 0-1, Albania (a) 1-2, Portugal (h) 2-3.

League Championship wins (1992–2015)
Pyunik 14 (including Homenetmen); Shirak 5*; Ararat Yerevan 2*; Araks 2 (including Tsement); FC Yerevan 1; Ulisses 1; Banants 1.
*Includes one unofficial shared title.

Cup wins (1992–2015)
Pyunik 7; Mika 6; Ararat Yerevan 5; Banants 2; Tsement 2; Pyunik (including Homenetmen) 1; Shirak 1.

Final League Table 2014–15

	P	W	D	L	F	A	GD	Pts
Pyunik	28	19	4	5	58	26	32	61
Ulisses	28	15	5	8	43	32	11	50
Shirak	28	14	7	7	51	32	19	49
Alashkert	28	10	8	10	32	35	–3	38
Mika	28	9	10	9	33	34	–1	37
Banants	28	8	8	12	42	46	–4	32
Gandzasar	28	7	8	13	31	44	–13	29
Ararat	28	3	4	21	28	69	–41	13

Top scorers (equal): Boughoui (Shirak), Romero (Pyunik) 21.
Cup Final: Pyunik 3, Mika 1.

AUSTRIA

Oesterreichischer Fussball-Bund, Ernst-Happel Stadion, Sektor A/F, Meierstrasse 7, Wien 1021.
Founded: 1904. *FIFA:* 1905; *UEFA:* 1954. *National Colours:* Red shirts, white shorts, red socks.

International matches 2014–15
Sweden (h) 1-1, Moldova (a) 2-1, Montenegro (h) 1-0, Russia (h) 1-0, Brazil (h) 1-2, Liechtenstein (a) 5-0, Bosnia-Herzegovina (h) 1-1, Russia (a) 1-0.

League Championship wins (1912–2015)
Rapid Vienna 32; FK Austria Vienna (formerly Amateure) 24; Wacker Innsbruck 14 (incl. Svarowski Tirol 2, Tirol Innsbruck 3); Admira Vienna (now Admira

Wacker Modling) 9 (incl. Wacker Vienna 1); Red Bull Salzburg 9 (incl. Austria Salzburg 3); First Vienna 6; Wiener Sportklub 3; Sturm Graz 3; WAF 1; WAC 1; Florisdorfer 1; Hakoah 1; Linz ASK 1; Voest Linz 1; Graz 1.

Cup wins (1919–2015)
FK Austria Vienna (formerly Amateure) 27; Rapid Vienna 14; Wacker Innsbruck 7 (incl. Tirol 1, Tirol Innsbruck); Admira Vienna 6 (including Wacker Vienna 1); Graz 4; Sturm Graz 4; First Vienna 3; Red Bull Salzburg 3; WAC 2; Ried 2; Linz ASK 1; WAF 1; Wiener Sportklub 1; Kremser 1; Stockerau 1; Karnten 1; Kremser 1; Horn 1; Pasching 1.

Final League Table 2014–15

	P	W	D	L	F	A	GD	Pts
Red Bull Salzburg	36	22	7	7	99	42	57	73
Rapid Vienna	36	19	10	7	68	38	30	67
Altach	36	17	8	11	50	49	1	59
Sturm Graz	36	16	10	10	57	41	16	58
Wolfsberger	36	16	4	16	44	50	–6	52
Ried	36	12	8	16	49	51	–2	44
Austria Vienna	36	10	13	13	45	51	–6	43
Grodig	36	10	7	19	46	65	–19	37
Admira Wacker Modling	36	7	13	16	32	61	–29	34
Wiener Neustadt*	36	7	8	21	37	79	–42	29

Top scorer: Soriano (Red Bull Salzburg) 31.
Cup Final: Red Bull Salzburg 2, Austria Vienna 0 (aet).

AZERBAIJAN

Association of Football Federations of Azerbaijan, 2208 Nobel prospekti, 1025 Baku.
Founded: 1992. *FIFA:* 1994; *UEFA:* 1994. *National Colours:* All red.

International matches 2014–15
Uzbekistan (h) 0-0, Russia (a) 0-4, Bulgaria (h) 1-2, Italy (a) 1-2, Croatia (h) 0-6, Norway (h) 0-1, Malta (h) 2-0, Serbia (n) 1-4, Norway (a) 0-0.

League Championship wins (1992–2015)
Neftchi 8; Qarabag 3; Kapaz 3; Shamkir 3; FK Baku 2; Inter Baku 2; Turan 1; Khazar Lankaran 1.
Includes one unofficial title for Shamkir in 2002.

Cup wins (1992–2015)
Neftchi 7; Qarabag 4; Kapaz 4; FK Baku 3; Khazar Lankaran 2; Inshatchi 1; Shafa 1.
Includes one title awarded by forfeit to Neftchi in 2002.

Final League Table 2014–15

	P	W	D	L	F	A	GD	Pts
Qarabag	32	20	8	4	51	28	23	68
Inter Baku	32	17	12	3	55	20	35	63
Gabala	32	15	9	8	46	35	11	54
Neftchi	32	13	10	9	38	33	5	49
Simurq	32	11	6	15	41	39	2	39
AZAL-Olimpik Suvalan	32	10	9	13	37	42	–5	39
Khazar Lankaran	32	8	8	16	35	46	–11	32
Sumqayit	32	7	10	15	32	43	–11	31
Baku	32	3	8	21	19	68	–49	17
Araz Naxcivan†	0	0	0	0	0	0	0	0

† *Araz Naxcivan withdrew from league.*
Top scorer: Novruzov (Baku) 15.
Cup Final: Qarabag 3, Neftchi 1.

BELARUS

Belarus Football Federation, Prospekt Pobeditelei 20/3, 220020 Minsk.
Founded: 1989. *FIFA:* 1992; *UEFA:* 1993. *National Colours:* All red with white trim.

International matches 2014–15
Tajikistan (h) 6-1, Luxembourg (a) 1-1, Ukraine (h) 0-2, Slovakia (h) 1-3, Spain (a) 0-3, Mexico (h) 3-2, FYR Macedonia (a) 2-1, Gabon (n) 0-0, Russia (a) 2-4, Spain (h) 0-1.

League Championship wins (1992–2014)
BATE Borisov 9; Dinamo Minsk 7; Slavia Mozyr (formerly MPKC Mozyr) 2; Shakhtyor Soligorsk 2; Dnepr Mogilev 1; Belshina Bobruisk 1; Gomel 1.

Cup wins (1992–2015)
Dinamo Minsk 3; Belshina Bobruisk 3; BATE Borisov 3; Slavia Mozyr (formerly MPKC Mozyr) 2; Gomel 2; Shakhtyor Soligorsk 2; MTZ-RIPA 2; Naftan Novopolotsk 2; Neman Grodno 1; Dinamo 93 Minsk 1; Lokomotiv 96 1; Dinamo Brest 1; FC Minsk 1.

Qualifying League Table 2014

	P	W	D	L	F	A	GD	Pts
BATE Borisov	22	15	6	1	46	12	34	51
Dinamo Minsk	22	15	4	3	33	8	25	49
Naftan Novopolotsk	22	10	7	5	30	20	10	37
Gomel	22	8	8	6	21	21	0	32
Shakhtyor Soligorsk	22	9	5	8	20	20	0	32
Torpedo Zhodino	22	8	7	7	21	20	1	31
Neman Grodno	22	7	6	9	25	24	1	27
FC Minsk	22	8	2	12	23	26	–3	26
Slutsk	22	7	4	11	15	26	–11	25
Dinamo Brest	22	6	4	12	23	52	–29	22
Belshina Bobruisk	22	4	6	12	28	38	–10	18
Dnepr Mogilev	22	1	9	12	11	29	–18	12

Championship Round

	P	W	D	L	F	A	GD	Pts
BATE Borisov	32	20	11	1	68	21	47	71
Dinamo Minsk	32	18	7	7	44	21	23	61
Shakhtyor Soligorsk	32	14	8	10	35	28	7	50
Torpedo Zhodino	32	13	11	8	38	30	8	50
Naftan Novopolotsk	32	11	10	11	40	43	–3	43
Gomel	32	10	8	14	29	41	–12	38

Relegation Round

	P	W	D	L	F	A	GD	Pts
FC Minsk	32	16	4	12	45	36	9	52
Neman Grodno	32	11	9	12	41	36	5	42
Slutsk	32	11	7	14	26	34	–8	40
Belshina Bobruisk	32	8	8	16	42	56	–14	32
Dinamo Brest	32	7	5	20	29	68	–39	26
Dnepr Mogilev*+	32	2	14	16	19	42	–23	20

Top scorer: Yanush (Shakhtyor Soligorsk) 15.
Cup Final: BATE Borisov 4, Shakhtyor Soligorsk 1.

BELGIUM

Union Royale Belge des Societes de Football-Association, 145 Avenue Houba de Strooper, B-1020 Bruxelles.
Founded: 1895. *FIFA:* 1904; *UEFA:* 1954. *National Colours:* All red.

International matches 2014–15
Australia (h) 2-0, Andorra (h) 6-0, Bosnia-Herzegovina (a) 1-1, Iceland (h) 3-1, Wales (h) 0-0, Cyprus (h) 5-0, Israel (a) 1-0, France (a) 4-3, Wales (a) 0-1.

League Championship wins (1896–2015)
Anderlecht 33; Club Brugge 13; Union St Gilloise 11; Standard Liege 10; Beerschot VAC (became Germinal) 7; RC Brussels 6; RFC Liege 5; Daring Brussels 5; Antwerp 4; Lierse 4; Mechelen 4; Cercle Brugge 3; Genk 3; Beveren 2; RWD Molenbeek 1; Gent 1.

Cup wins (1912–14; 1927; 1935; 1954–2015)
Club Brugge 11; Anderlecht 9; Standard Liege 6; Genk 4; KAA Gent 3; Union St Gilloise 2; Beerschot VAC (became Germinal) 2; Waterschei (became Racing Genk) 2; Beveren 2; Cercle Brugge 2; Antwerp 2; Lierse 2; Beerschot Antwerpen Club (incl. Germinal Ekeren) 2; Lokeren 2; Racing 1; Daring 1; Tournai 1; Waregem 1; Mechelen 1; FC Liege 1; Westerlo 1; La Louviere 1; Zulte-Waregem 1.

Qualifying League Table 2014–15

	P	W	D	L	F	A	GD	Pts
Club Brugge	30	17	10	3	69	28	41	66
Gent	30	16	9	5	52	29	23	57
Anderlecht	30	16	9	5	51	30	21	57
Standard Liege	30	16	5	9	49	39	10	53
Kortrijk	30	16	3	11	54	35	19	51
Charleroi	30	14	7	9	44	31	13	49
Genk	30	13	10	7	38	28	10	49
Lokeren	30	10	12	8	38	32	6	42
Mechelen	30	10	11	9	37	39	–2	41
Oostende	30	11	5	14	40	52	–12	38
Westerlo	30	8	9	13	42	63	–21	33
Zulte Waregem	30	8	7	15	41	54	–13	31
Mouscron Peruwelz	30	7	5	18	32	51	–19	26
Waasland-Beveren	30	7	5	18	30	49	–19	26
Cercle Brugge	30	6	6	18	21	45	–24	24
Lierse	30	5	7	18	30	63	–33	22

NB: Points earned in Qualifying phase are halved and rounded up at start of Championship play-off phase.

Championship Play-off

	P	W	D	L	F	A	GD	Pts
Gent	10	6	2	2	18	11	7	49
Club Brugge	10	5	1	4	16	16	0	47

	P	W	D	L	F	A	GD	Pts
Anderlecht	10	5	2	3	18	13	5	46
Standard Liege	10	4	1	5	14	13	1	40
Charleroi	10	3	2	5	13	15	-2	36
Kortrijk	10	2	2	6	11	22	-11	34

Europa League Qualifying Table A

	P	W	D	L	F	A	GD	Pts
Mechelen	6	5	0	1	14	3	11	15
Genk	6	5	0	1	14	7	7	15
Zulte Waregem	6	1	1	4	6	10	-4	4
Waasland-Beveren	6	0	1	5	5	19	-14	1

Europa League Qualifying Table B

	P	W	D	L	F	A	GD	Pts
Lokeren	6	4	1	1	19	9	10	13
Mouscron Peruwelz	6	3	1	2	9	8	1	10
Oostende	6	2	0	4	6	12	-6	6
Westerlo	6	1	2	3	7	12	-5	5

Europa League Qualifying Play-off
Lokeren 2, 1, Mechelen 2, 2 (agg 3-4)

Europa League Testmatch
Played between Europa League play-off winners and fifth-placed team in Championship play-off.
Mechelen 2, 0, Charleroi 1, 2 (agg 2-3)

Relegation Table

	P	W	D	L	F	A	GD	Pts
Lierse*+	4	3	0	1	8	4	4	9
Cercle Brugge*	4	1	0	3	4	8	-4	6

Top scorer: Mitrovic (Anderlecht) 20.
Cup Final: Club Brugge 2, Anderlecht 1.

BOSNIA-HERZEGOVINA
Football Federation of Bosnia & Herzegovina, Ferhadija 30, 71000 Sarajevo.
Founded: 1992. *FIFA:* 1996; *UEFA:* 1998. *National Colours:* Blue shirts, blue shorts, blue socks with white tops.

International matches 2014–15
Liechtenstein (h) 3-0, Cyprus (h) 1-2, Wales (a) 0-0, Belgium (h) 1-1, Israel (a) 0-3, Andorra (a) 3-0, Austria (a) 1-1, Israel (h) 3-1.

League Championship wins (1998–2015)
Zeljeznicar 6; FK Sarajevo 3; Zrinjski 3; Siroki Brijeg 2; Brotnjo 1; Leotar 1; Modrica 1; Borac Banja Luka 1.

Cup wins (1998; 2000–15)
Zeljeznicar 5; FK Sarajevo 4; Siroki Brijeg 2; Modrica 1; Orasje 1; Zrinjski 1; Slavija 1; Borac Banja Luka 1; Olimpic Sarajevo 1 .

Final League Table 2014–15

	P	W	D	L	F	A	GD	Pts
FK Sarajevo	30	19	9	2	55	17	38	66
Zeljeznicar	30	18	9	3	52	22	30	63
Zrinjski	30	16	11	3	41	13	28	59
Siroki Brijeg	30	15	11	4	46	23	23	56
Borac Banja Luka	30	14	7	9	26	26	0	49
Olimpic Sarajevo	30	13	7	10	41	34	7	46
Celik Zenica	30	10	11	9	34	35	-1	41
Sloboda Tuzla	30	11	7	12	33	28	5	40
Velez	30	10	8	12	32	33	-1	38
Radnik Bijeljina	30	7	10	13	29	39	-10	31
Travnik	30	8	7	15	22	42	-20	31
Slavija Sarajevo	30	7	7	16	30	44	-14	28
Drina Zvornik	30	6	9	15	26	40	-14	27
Vitez	30	7	5	18	21	43	-22	26
Mladost Velika Obarska*	30	6	8	16	18	44	-26	26
Zvijezda*	30	5	10	15	30	53	-23	25

Top scorer: Bajic (Zeljeznicar) 15.
Cup Final: Siroki Brijeg 1, 1, Olimpic Sarajevo 1, 1 (agg. 2-2).
Olimpic Sarajevo won 5-4 on penalties.

BULGARIA
Bulgarian Football Union, 26 Tzar Ivan Assen II Str., 1124 Sofia.
Founded: 1923. *FIFA:* 1992; *UEFA:* 1954. *National Colours:* White shirts, green shorts, red socks.

International matches 2014–15
Azerbaijan (a) 2-1, Croatia (h) 0-1, Norway (a) 1-2, Malta (h) 1-1, Romania (n) 0-0, Italy (h) 2-2, Turkey (a) 0-4, Malta (a) 1-0.

League Championship wins (1925–2015)
CSKA Sofia 31; Levski Sofia 26; Slavia Sofia 7;
Lokomotiv Sofia 4; Litex Lovech 4; Ludogorets Razgrad 4; Vladislav Varna 3; Botev Plovdiv (includes Trakija) 2; AC 23 Sofia 1; Sokol (Spartak) Varna 1; Sportklub Sofia 1; Ticha Varna 1; Spartak Plovdiv 1; Beroe Stara Zagora 1; Etar 1; Lokomotiv Plovdiv 1.

Cup wins (1946–2015)
Levski Sofia 24; CSKA Sofia 19; Slavia Sofia 7; Lokomotiv Sofia 4; Litex Lovech 4; Botev Plovdiv (includes Trakija) 2; Beroe Stara Zagora 2; Ludogorets Razgrad 2; Spartak Plovdiv 1; Septemvri Sofia 1; Spartak Sofia 1; Marek Dupnica 1; Sliven 1; Cherno More Varna 1.

Qualifying League Table 2014–15

	P	W	D	L	F	A	GD	Pts
Ludogorets Razgrad	22	14	5	3	46	14	32	47
Beroe Stara Zagora	22	13	5	4	39	15	24	44
Lokomotiv Sofia	22	12	3	7	29	24	5	39
Litex Lovech	22	12	3	7	37	24	13	39
CSKA Sofia	22	11	5	6	34	21	13	38
Botev Plovdiv	22	11	3	8	32	26	6	36
Levski Sofia	22	10	4	8	36	25	11	34
Cherno More Varna	22	9	4	9	26	24	2	31
Slavia Sofia	22	6	5	11	24	30	-6	23
Lokomotiv Plovdiv	22	5	5	12	13	36	-23	20
Marek Dupnitsa	22	3	5	14	8	45	-37	14
Haskovo	22	2	1	19	12	52	-40	7

Championship Round

	P	W	D	L	F	A	GD	Pts
Ludogorets Razgrad	32	18	9	5	63	24	39	63
Beroe Stara Zagora	32	15	10	7	46	30	16	55
Lokomotiv Sofia	32	16	7	9	39	31	8	55
Litex Lovech	32	16	6	10	49	36	13	54
CSKA Sofia	32	14	10	8	45	27	18	52
Botev Plovdiv	32	12	6	14	38	39	-1	42

Relegation Round

	P	W	D	L	F	A	GD	Pts
Levski Sofia	32	17	5	10	66	33	33	56
Cherno More Varna	32	15	5	12	42	36	6	50
Slavia Sofia	32	12	7	13	40	38	2	43
Lokomotiv Plovdiv	32	9	5	18	28	52	-24	32
Marek Dupnitsa*	32	5	5	22	14	71	-57	20
Haskovo*	32	4	3	25	18	71	-53	15

Top scorer: Anete (Levski Sofia) 14.
Cup Final: Cherno More Varna 2, Levski Sofia 1 (aet).

CHANNEL ISLANDS
Guernsey

League Championship wins (1894–2015)
Northerners 31; Guernsey Rangers 17; Vale Recreation 15; St Martin's 13; Sylvans 10; Belgrave Wanderers 8; 2nd Bn Manchesters 3; 2nd Bn Royal Irish Regt 2; 2nd Bn Wiltshires 2; 10th Comp W Div Royal Artillery 1; 2nd Bn Leicesters 1; 2nd Bn PA Somerset Light Infantry 1; 2nd Middlesex Regt 1; Athletics 1; Band Comp 2nd Bn Royal Fusiliers 1; G&H Comp Royal Fusiliers 1; Grange 1; Yorkshire Regt (Green Howards) 1.

Final League Table 2014–15

	P	W	D	L	F	A	GD	Pts
Northerners	18	12	2	4	59	35	24	38
Sylvans	18	11	2	5	52	36	16	35
Vale Recreation	18	8	5	5	39	33	6	29
Rovers	18	8	4	6	43	32	11	28
Belgrave Wanderers	18	7	2	9	40	42	-2	23
Guernsey Rangers	18	4	2	12	32	66	-34	14
St Martins	18	1	7	10	25	46	-21	10

Jersey

League Championship wins (1894–2015)
Jersey Wanderers 20; First Tower United 19; St Paul's 16; Jersey Scottish 10; Beeches Old Boys 5; Bn King's Own Regt 3; Oaklands 3; St Peter 3; 1st Batt Devon Regt 2; 1st Bn East Surrey Regt 2; Georgetown 2; Mechanics 2; YMCA 2; 2nd Bn East Surrey Regt 1; 20th Comp Royal Garrison Artillery 1; National Rovers 1; Sporting Academics 1; Trinity 1.

Final League Table 2014–15

	P	W	D	L	F	A	GD	Pts
St Paul's	18	14	3	1	60	10	50	45
Jersey Scottish	18	14	2	2	75	16	59	44
Jersey Wanderers	18	12	1	5	36	26	10	37
St Ouen	18	8	6	4	29	25	4	30
Trinity	18	9	2	7	32	38	-6	29

St Peter	18	4	5	9	19	33	–14	17
Rozel Rovers	18	4	4	10	23	37	–14	16
St Brelade	18	4	2	12	22	39	–17	14
St Lawrence	18	4	2	12	16	52	–36	14
St Clement	18	3	1	14	15	51	–36	10

Upton Park Trophy 2015 (For Guernsey & Jersey League Champions)
St Paul's 9, Northerners 0

Upton Park Trophy wins (1907–2015)
Northerners 18; First Tower United 12; Jersey Wanderers 11; St Martin's 11; St Paul's 8; Jersey Scottish 6; Guernsey Rangers 5; Vale Recreation 4; Belgrave Wanderers 4; Beeches Old Boys 3; Old St Paul's 3; Magpies 3; Sylvans 3; St Peter 2; Jersey Mechanics 1; Jersey YMCA 1; National Rovers 1; Sporting Academics 1; Trinity 1.

CROATIA

Croatian Football Federation, Vukovarska 269A, 10000 Zagreb.
Founded: 1912. *FIFA:* 1992; *UEFA:* 1993. *National Colours:* Red and white check shirts, white shorts, blue socks.

International matches 2014–15
Cyprus (h) 2-0, Malta (h) 2-0, Bulgaria (a) 1-0, Azerbaijan (h) 6-0, Argentina (n) 1-2, Italy (a) 1-1, Norway (h) 5-1, Gibraltar (h) 4-0, Italy (h) 1-1.

League Championship wins (1941–46; 1992–2015)
Dinamo Zagreb (formerly Croatia Zagreb) 17; Hajduk Split 8; Concordia 1; Gradjanski 1; NK Zagreb 1.

Cup wins (1992–2015)
Dinamo Zagreb (formerly Croatia Zagreb) 13; Hajduk Split 6; Rijeka 3; Inter Zapresic 1; Osijek 1.

Final League Table 2014–15

	P	W	D	L	F	A	GD	Pts
Dinamo Zagreb	36	26	10	0	85	21	64	88
Rijeka	36	22	9	5	76	29	47	75
Hajduk Split (–3)	36	15	8	13	59	56	3	50
Lokomotiva Zagreb	36	13	7	16	59	68	–9	46
Zagreb	36	13	7	16	45	54	–9	46
Slaven Koprivnica	36	11	9	16	38	49	–11	42
RNK Split	36	9	14	13	42	49	–7	41
Osijek	36	10	6	20	42	59	–17	36
Istra 1961	36	7	14	15	36	59	–23	35
Zadar*	36	8	8	20	37	75	–38	32

Top scorer: Henriquez (Dinamo Zagreb) 21.
Cup Final: Dinamo Zagreb 0, RNK Split 0.
aet; Dinamo Zagreb won 4-2 on penalties.

CYPRUS

Cyprus Football Association, 10 Achaion Street, 2413 Engomi, PO Box 25071, 1306 Nicosia.
Founded: 1934. *FIFA:* 1948; *UEFA:* 1962. *National Colours:* All blue with white trim.

International matches 2014–15
Croatia (a) 0-2, Bosnia-Herzegovina (a) 2-1, Israel (h) 1-2, Wales (a) 1-2, Andorra (h) 5-0, Belgium (a) 0-5, Andorra (a) 3-1.

League Championship wins (1935–2015)
APOEL 24; Omonia 20; Anorthosis 13; AEL Limassol 6; EPA Larnaca 3; Olympiakos Nicosia 3; Apollon Limassol 3; Pezoporikos Larnaca 2; Trast 1; Cetinkaya 1.

Cup wins (1935–2015)
APOEL 21; Omonia 14; Anorthosis 10; Apollon Limassol 7; AEL Limassol 6; EPA Larnaca 5; Trast 3; Cetinkaya 2; Pezoporikos Larnaca 1; Olympiakos Nicosia 1; Nea Salamis 1; AEK Larnaca 1; APOP Kinyras 1.

Qualifying League Table 2014–15

	P	W	D	L	F	A	GD	Pts
Apollon Limassol	22	15	3	4	49	26	23	48
APOEL	22	13	7	2	34	13	21	46
Omonia	22	13	3	7	32	22	10	39
AEK Larnaca	22	11	6	5	41	23	18	39
Anorthosis Famagusta	22	12	2	8	32	22	10	38
Ermis Aradippou	22	10	5	7	29	28	1	35
AEL Limassol	22	7	9	6	33	26	7	30
Ethnikos Achnas	22	5	7	10	18	37	–19	22
Nea Salamis Famagusta	22	4	7	11	16	29	–13	19
Ayia Napa	22	3	7	12	21	42	–21	16
Othellos Athienou	22	3	7	12	13	26	–13	16
Doxa Katokopia	22	3	5	14	14	38	–24	14

Championship Round

	P	W	D	L	F	A	GD	Pts
APOEL	32	17	11	4	52	26	26	62
AEK Larnaca	32	17	8	7	56	31	25	59
Apollon Limassol	32	18	5	9	59	41	18	59
Omonia	32	17	5	10	52	34	18	56
Anorthosis Famagusta	32	16	4	12	50	37	13	52
Ermis Aradippou	32	11	7	14	38	55	–17	40

Relegation Round

	P	W	D	L	F	A	GD	Pts
Ethnikos Achnas	32	11	8	13	36	49	–13	41
AEL Limassol	32	9	12	11	42	42	0	39
Nea Salamis Famagusta	32	9	9	14	31	37	–6	36
Ayia Napa	32	6	12	14	32	54	–22	30
Doxa Katokopia	32	7	7	18	29	55	–26	28
Othellos Athienou	32	5	10	17	26	42	–16	25

Top scorer: Pote (Omonia) 17.
Cup Final: APOEL 4, AEL Limassol 2.

CZECH REPUBLIC

Fotbalova Asociace Ceske Republiky, Diskarska 2431/4, PO Box 11, Praha 6 16017.
Founded: 1901. *FIFA:* 1907; *UEFA:* 1954. *National Colours:* All red.

International matches 2014–15
USA (h) 0-1, Netherlands (h) 2-1, Turkey (a) 2-1, Kazakhstan (a) 4-2, Iceland (h) 2-1, Latvia (h) 1-1, Slovakia (a) 0-1, Iceland (a) 1-2.

League Championship wins – Czechoslovakia (1925–93)
Sparta Prague 21; Slavia Prague 13; Dukla Prague (prev. UDA, now Marila Pribram) 11; Slovan Bratislava (formerly NV Bratislava) 8; Spartak Trnava 5; Banik Ostrava 3; Viktoria Zizkov 1; Inter-Bratislava 1; Spartak Hradec Kralove 1; Zbrojovka Brno 1; Bohemians 1; Vitkovice 1.

Cup wins – Czechoslovakia (1961–93)
Dukla Prague 8; Sparta Prague 8; Slovan Bratislava 5; Spartak Trnava 4; Banik Ostrava 3; Lokomotiva Kosice 2; TJ Gottwaldov 1; Lokomotiva Kosice 1; Dunajska Streda 1.

League Championship wins – Czech Republic (1994–2015)
Sparta Prague 12; Slavia Prague 3; Slovan Liberec 3; Viktoria Plzen 3; Banik Ostrava 1.

Cup wins – Czech Republic (1994–2015)
Sparta Prague 6; Slavia Prague 3; Viktoria Zizkov 2; Jablonec 2; Teplice 2; Slovan Liberec 2; Hradec Kralove (formerly Spartak) 1; Banik Ostrava 1; Viktoria Plzen 1; Mlada Boleslav 1; Sigma Olomouc 1.

Final League Table 2014–15

	P	W	D	L	F	A	GD	Pts
Viktoria Plzen	30	23	3	4	70	24	46	72
Sparta Prague	30	21	4	5	57	20	37	67
Jablonec	30	19	7	4	58	22	36	64
Mlada Boleslav	30	13	7	10	43	34	9	46
Pribram	30	12	7	11	40	45	–5	43
Dukla Prague	30	11	8	11	34	40	–6	41
Teplice	30	9	11	10	41	37	4	38
Bohemians Prague	30	10	8	12	35	41	–6	38
Slovacko	30	10	7	13	43	46	–3	37
Vysocina Jihlava	30	10	6	14	33	38	–5	36
Slavia Prague	30	9	7	14	40	45	–5	34
Slovan Liberec	30	7	12	11	39	43	–4	33
Banik Ostrava	30	8	9	13	23	41	–18	33
Zbrojovka Brno	30	9	6	15	34	45	–11	33
Hradec Kralove*	30	6	7	17	26	52	–26	25
Dynamo Ceske Budejovice*	30	5	7	18	29	72	–43	22

Top scorer: Lafata (Sparta Prague) 20.
Cup Final: Jablonec 1, Slovan Liberec 1.
Slovan Liberec won 3-1 on penalties.

DENMARK

Dansk Boldspil-Union, Idraettens Hus, DBU Alle 1, DK-2605, Brondby.
Founded: 1889. *FIFA:* 1904; *UEFA:* 1954. *National Colours:* Red shirts, white shorts, red socks.

International matches 2014–15
Turkey (h) 1-2, Armenia (h) 2-1, Albania (a) 1-1, Portugal (h) 0-1, Serbia (a) 3-1, Romania (a) 0-2, USA (h) 3-2, France (a) 0-2, Montenegro (h) 2-1, Serbia (h) 2-0.

League Championship wins (1913–2015)

KB Copenhagen 15; Brondby 10; FC Copenhagen 10; B 93 Copenhagen 9; AB (Akademisk) 9; B 1903 Copenhagen 7; Frem 6; AGF Aarhus 5; Vejle 5; Esbjerg 5; AaB Aalborg 4; Hvidovre 3; OB Odense 3; Koge 2; B 1909 Odense 2; Lyngby 2; Silkeborg 1; Herfolge 1; Nordsjaelland 1; Midtjylland 1.

Cup wins (1955–2015)

AGF Aarhus 9; Vejle 6; Brondby 6; FC Copenhagen 6; OB Odense 5; Esbjerg 3; AaB Aalborg 3; Randers Freja 3; Lyngby 3; B 1909 Odense 2; Frem 2; B 1903 Copenhagen 2; Nordsjaelland 2; B 1913 Odense 1; KB Copenhagen 1; Vanlose 1; Hvidovre 1; B 93 Copenhagen 1; AB (Akademisk) 1; Viborg 1; Silkeborg 1; Randers 1.

Final League Table 2014–15

	P	W	D	L	F	A	GD	Pts
Midtjylland	33	22	5	6	64	34	30	71
FC Copenhagen	33	20	7	6	40	22	18	67
Brondby	33	16	7	10	43	29	14	55
Randers	33	14	10	9	39	28	11	52
AaB Aalborg	33	13	9	11	39	31	8	48
Nordsjaelland	33	13	5	15	39	44	–5	44
Hobro	33	11	10	12	40	47	–7	43
Esbjerg	33	10	10	13	47	45	2	40
OB Odense	33	11	7	15	35	43	–8	40
SonderjyskE	33	7	16	10	35	44	–9	37
Vestsjaelland*	33	9	6	18	31	52	–21	33
Silkeborg*	33	2	8	23	26	59	–33	14

Top scorers (equal): Hvilsom (Hobro), Pusic (Midtjylland, inc. 8 for Esbjerg) 16.
Cup Final: FC Copenhagen 3,Vestsjaelland 2 (aet).

ENGLAND

The Football Association, Wembley Stadium, PO Box 1966, London SW1P 9EQ.
Founded: 1863. *FIFA:* 1905; *UEFA:* 1954. *National Colours:* All white.

ESTONIA

Eesti Jalgpalli Liit, A. Le Coq Arena, Asula 4c, 11312 Tallinn.
Founded: 1921. *FIFA:* 1923; *UEFA:* 1992. *National Colours:* Blue shirts, black shorts, white socks.

International matches 2014–15

Sweden (a) 0-2, Slovenia (h) 1-0, Lithuania (a) 0-1, England (h) 0-1, Norway (a) 1-0, San Marino (a) 0-0, Jordan (h) 1-0, Qatar (a) 0-3, Switzerland (a) 0-3, Iceland (h) 1-1, Finland (a) 2-0, San Marino (h) 2-0.

League Championship wins (1921–40; 1992–2014)

Sport 9; Flora 9; Levadia Tallinn (formerly Levadia Maardu) 9; Estonia 5; Tallinn JK 2; Norma 2; Lantana (formerly Nikol) 2; Sillamae Kalev 2; Olimpia Tartu 1; TVMK Tallinn 1; Nomme Kalju 1.

Cup wins (1993–2015)

Levadia Tallinn (formerly Levadia Maardu) 8; Flora 6; Sadam 2; TVMK Tallinn 2; Lantana (formerly Nikol) 1; Norma 1; Narva Trans 1; Levadia Tallinn (pre-2004) 1, Nomme Kalju 1.

Final League Table 2014

	P	W	D	L	F	A	GD	Pts
Levadia Tallinn	36	26	6	4	112	19	93	84
Sillamae Kalev	36	25	4	7	108	34	74	79
Flora Tallinn	36	24	7	5	88	36	52	79
Nomme Kalju	36	24	6	6	85	19	66	78
Infonet Tallinn	36	19	9	8	80	44	36	66
Paide Linnameeskond	36	9	8	19	39	67	–28	35
Tammeka Tartu	36	7	7	22	37	83	–46	28
Narva Trans	36	6	10	20	37	79	–42	28
Lokomotiv+	36	4	6	26	35	115	–80	18
Tallinna Kalev*	36	3	3	30	21	146	–125	12

Top scorer: Kabaev (Sillamae Kalev) 36.
Cup Final: Nomme Kalju 2, Paide Linnameeskond 0.

FAROE ISLANDS

Fotboltssamband Foroya, Gundadalur, PO Box 3028, 110 Torshavn.
Founded: 1979. *FIFA:* 1988; *UEFA:* 1990. *National Colours:* White shirts with blue trim, white shorts, white socks.

International matches 2014–15

Finland (h) 1-3, Northern Ireland (a) 0-2, Hungary (h) 0-1, Greece (a) 1-0, Romania (a) 0-1, Greece (h) 2-1.

League Championship wins (1942–2014)

HB Torshavn 22; KI Klaksvik 17; B36 Torshavn 10; TB Tvoroyri 7; GI Gota 6; B68 Toftir 3; EB/Streymur 2; SI Sorvagur 1; IF Fuglafjordur 1; B71 Sandur 1; VB Vagur 1; NSI Runavik 1.

Cup wins (1955–2014)

HB Torshavn 26; GI Gota 6; TB Tvoroyri 5; B36 Torshavn 5; KI Klaksvik 5; EB/Streymur 4; Vikingur 4; NSI Runavik 3; VB Vagur 1; B71 Sandur 1.

Final League Table 2014

	P	W	D	L	F	A	GD	Pts
B36 Torshavn	27	19	4	4	53	25	28	61
HB Torshavn	27	18	6	3	59	20	39	60
Vikingur	27	13	10	4	60	30	30	49
NSI Runavik	27	12	4	11	53	42	11	40
EB/Streymur	27	11	7	9	41	33	8	40
KI Klaksvik	27	10	6	11	41	38	3	36
IF Fuglafjordur	27	7	7	13	36	52	–16	28
AB Argir	27	6	7	14	30	61	–31	25
Skala*	27	3	8	16	19	54	–35	17
B68 Toftir*	27	4	5	18	23	60	–37	17

Top scorer: Olsen (NSI Runavik) 22.
Cup Final: Víkingur 1, HB Torshavn 0.

FINLAND

Suomen Palloliitto Finlands Bollfoerbund, Urheilukatu 5, PO Box 191, 00251 Helsinki.
Founded: 1907. *FIFA:* 1908; *UEFA:* 1954. *National Colours:* White shirts with blue trim, white shorts, white socks.

International matches 2014–15

Faroe Islands (a) 3-1, Greece (h) 1-1, Romania (h) 0-2, Hungary (a) 0-1, Slovakia (a) 1-2, Sweden (n) 1-0, Yemen (n) 0-0, Northern Ireland (a) 1-2, Estonia (h) 0-2, Hungary (h) 0-1.

League Championship wins (1908–2014)

HJK Helsinki 27; Haka Valkeakoski 9; HPS Helsinki 9; TPS Turku 8; HIFK Helsinki 7; Tampere United (includes Ilves) 5; KuPS Kuopio 5; Kuusysi Lahti 5; KIF Helsinki 4; AIFK Turku 3; Reipas Lahti 3; VIFK Vaasa 3; Jazz Pori 2; KTP Kotka 2; OPS Oulu 2; VPS Vaasa 2; Unitas Helsinki 1; PUS Helsinki 1; Sudet Viipuri 1; HT Helsinki 1; Pyrkiva Turku 1; KPV Kokkola 1; TPV Tampere 1; MyPa Anjalankoski (renamed MYPA-47) 1; Inter Turku 1.

Cup wins (1955–2014)

Haka Valkeakoski 12; HJK Helsinki 12; Reipas Lahti 7; KTP Kotka 4; Tampere United (includes Ilves) 3; TPS Turku 3; MyPa Anjalankoski (renamed MYPA-47) 3; KuPS Kuopio 2; Mikkeli 2; Kuusysi Lahti 2; RoPS Rovaniemi 2; Pallo-Pojat 1; Drott (renamed Jaro) 1; HPS Helsinki 1; AIFK Turku 1; Jokerit (formerly PK-35) 1; Allianssi (formerly Atlantis) 1; Inter Turku 1; FC Honka 1.

Final League Table 2014

	P	W	D	L	F	A	GD	Pts
HJK Helsinki	33	21	9	3	65	22	43	72
SJK Seinajoki	33	16	11	6	40	26	14	59
Lahti	33	15	13	5	45	23	22	58
VPS Vaasa	33	13	9	11	39	34	5	48
IFK Mariehamn	33	14	6	13	49	55	–6	48
FF Jaro	33	12	8	13	47	47	0	44
KuPS Kuopio	33	11	11	11	44	44	0	44
MYPA-47†	33	10	9	14	41	54	–13	39
Inter Turku	33	8	12	13	42	47	–5	36
RoPS Rovaniemi	33	10	5	18	34	44	–10	35
FC Honka†	33	6	13	14	38	57	–19	31
TPS Turku*	33	6	6	21	29	60	–31	24

† *MYPA-47 folded after failing to regain licence. FC Honka denied licence and demoted to third tier.*
Top scorers (equal): Emet (FF Jaro), Solignac (IFK Mariehamn) 14.
Cup Final: HJK Helsinki 0, Inter Turku 0.
aet; HJK Helsinki won 5-3 on penalties.

FRANCE

Federation Francaise de Football, 87 Boulevard de Grenelle, 75738 Paris Cedex 15.
Founded: 1919. *FIFA:* 1904; *UEFA:* 1954. *National Colours:* Blue shirts, white shorts, red socks.

International matches 2014–15

Spain (h) 1-0, Serbia (a) 1-1, Portugal (h) 2-1, Armenia

(a) 3-0, Albania (h) 1-1, Sweden (h) 1-0, Brazil (h) 1-3, Denmark (h) 2-0, Belgium (h) 3-4, Albania (a) 0-1.

League Championship wins (1933–2015)
Saint-Etienne 10; Olympique Marseille 9; Nantes 8; AS Monaco 7; Olympique Lyonnais 7; Stade de Reims 6; Bordeaux 6; Paris Saint-Germain 5; OGC Nice 4; Lille OSC (includes Olympique Lillois) 4; FC Sete 2; Sochaux 2; Racing Club Paris 1; Roubaix-Tourcoing 1; Strasbourg 1; Auxerre 1; Lens 1; Montpellier 1.

Cup wins (1918–2015)
Olympique Marseille 10; Paris Saint-Germain 9; Lille OSC 6; Saint-Etienne 6; Red Star 5; Racing Club Paris 5; AS Monaco 5; Olympique Lyonnais 5; Bordeaux 4; Auxerre 4; Strasbourg 3; OGC Nice 3; Nantes 3; CAS Genereaux 2; Montpellier 2; FC Sete 2; Sochaux 2; Stade de Reims 2; Sedan 2; Stade Rennais 2; Metz 2; Guingamp 2; Olympique de Pantin 1; CA Paris 1; Club Français 1; AS Cannes 1; Excelsior Roubaix 1; EF Nancy-Lorraine 1; Toulouse 1; Le Havre 1; AS Nancy 1; Bastia 1; Lorient 1.

Final League Table 2014–15

	P	W	D	L	F	A	GD	Pts
Paris Saint-Germain	38	24	11	3	83	36	47	83
Olympique Lyonnais	38	22	9	7	72	33	39	75
AS Monaco	38	20	11	7	51	26	25	71
Olympique Marseille	38	21	6	11	76	42	34	69
Saint-Etienne	38	19	12	7	51	30	21	69
Bordeaux	38	17	12	9	47	44	3	63
Montpellier	38	16	8	14	46	39	7	56
Lille OSC	38	16	8	14	43	42	1	56
Stade Rennais	38	13	11	14	35	42	–7	50
Guingamp	38	15	4	19	41	55	–14	49
Nice	38	13	9	16	44	53	–9	48
Bastia	38	12	11	15	37	46	–9	47
Caen	38	12	10	16	54	55	–1	46
Nantes	38	11	12	15	29	40	–11	45
Stade de Reims	38	12	8	18	47	66	–19	44
Lorient	38	12	7	19	44	50	–6	43
Toulouse	38	12	6	20	43	64	–21	42
Evian Thonon Gaillard*	38	11	4	23	41	62	–21	37
Metz*	38	7	9	22	31	61	–30	30
Lens*	38	7	8	23	32	61	–29	29

Top scorer: Lacazette (Olympique Lyonnais) 27.
Cup Final: Paris Saint-Germain 1, Auxerre 0.

FYR MACEDONIA

Football Federation of the Former Yugoslav Republic of Macedonia, 8-ma Udarna Brigada 31-A, PO Box 84, 1000 Skopje.
Founded: 1948. *FIFA:* 1994; *UEFA:* 1994. *National Colours:* All red.

International matches 2014–15
Spain (a) 1-5, Luxembourg (h) 3-2, Ukraine (a) 0-1, Slovakia (h) 0-2, Belarus (h) 1-2, Australia (h) 0-0, Slovakia (a) 1-2.

League Championship wins (1992–2015)
Vardar 8; Rabotnicki 4; Sileks 3; Sloga Jugomagnat 3; Pobeda 2; Renova 1; Makedonija 1; Shkendija 1.

Cup wins (1992–2015)
Vardar 5; Rabotnicki 4; Sloga Jugomagnat 3; Sileks 2; Teteks 2; Pelister 1; Pobeda 1; Cementarnica 55 1; Bashkimi 1; Makedonija 1; Metalurg 1; Renova 1.

Final League Table 2014–15

	P	W	D	L	F	A	GD	Pts
Vardar	32	20	9	3	56	21	35	69
Rabotnicki	32	20	6	6	55	30	25	66
Shkendija	32	18	5	9	58	31	27	59
Renova	32	13	9	10	41	39	2	48
Sileks	32	10	11	11	33	42	–9	41
Metalurg Skopje	32	8	9	15	34	42	–8	33
Bregalnica Stip	33	13	9	11	33	29	4	48
Turnovo+	33	9	9	15	26	37	–11	36
Pelister*	33	7	9	17	21	35	–14	30
Teteks*	33	3	6	24	22	73	–51	15

Top scorer: Emini (Renova) 20.
Cup Final: Rabotnicki 2, Teteks 1.

GEORGIA

Georgian Football Federation, 76A Chavchavadze Avenue, 0179 Tbilisi.
Founded: 1990. *FIFA:* 1992; *UEFA:* 1992. *National Colours:* All white with red trim.

International matches 2014–15
Republic of Ireland (h) 1-2, Scotland (h) 0-1, Gibraltar (n) 3-0, Poland (h) 0-4, Malta (h) 2-0, Germany (h) 0-2, Ukraine (n) 1-2, Poland (a) 0-4.

League Championship wins (1990–2015)
Dinamo Tbilisi 15; Torpedo Kutaisi 3; WIT Georgia 2; Metalurgi Rustavi (formerly Olimpi) 2; Zestafoni 2; Sioni 1; Dila Gori 1.

Cup wins (1990–2015)
Dinamo Tbilisi 12; Lokomotivi 3; Torpedo Kutaisi 2; Ameri 2; Guria Lanchkhuti 1; Dinamo Batumi 1; Zestafoni 1; WIT Georgia 1; Gagra 1; Dila Gori 1.

Final League Table 2014–15

	P	W	D	L	F	A	GD	Pts
Dila Gori	30	19	7	4	50	21	29	64
Dinamo Batumi	30	18	4	8	40	24	16	58
Dinamo Tbilisi	30	17	7	6	56	28	28	58
Tskhinvali	30	16	5	9	47	37	10	53
Chikhura Sachkhere	30	13	7	10	39	36	3	46
Samtredia	30	13	6	11	40	31	9	45
Shukura Kobuleti	30	11	8	11	36	38	–2	41
Torpedo Kutaisi	30	10	11	9	39	33	6	41
Guria Lanchkhuti	30	10	9	11	38	43	–5	39
Kolkheti Poti	30	9	10	11	31	31	0	37
Merani Martvili	30	9	9	12	29	33	–4	36
Zugdidi	30	8	9	13	24	45	–21	33
Sioni Bolnisi	30	9	5	16	32	46	–14	32
Metalurgi Rustavi*+	30	6	8	16	25	46	–21	26
WIT Georgia*	30	7	5	18	27	40	–13	26
Zestafoni*†	30	6	8	16	40	61	–21	26

† *Zestafoni expelled for failing to fulfil a fixture.*
Top scorer: Modebadze (Dila Gori) 16.
Cup Final: Dinamo Tbilisi 5, Samtredia 0.

GERMANY

Deutscher Fussball-Bund, Hermann-Neuberger-Haus, Otto-Fleck-Schneise 6, 60528 Frankfurt Am Main.
Founded: 1900. *FIFA:* 1904; *UEFA:* 1954. *National Colours:* White shirts with red and black trim, white shorts, white socks with red tops.

International matches 2014–15
Argentina (h) 2-4, Scotland (h) 2-1, Poland (a) 0-2, Republic of Ireland (h) 1-1, Gibraltar (h) 4-0, Spain (a) 1-0, Australia (h) 2-2, Georgia (a) 2-0, USA (h) 1-2, Gibraltar (n) 7-0.

League Championship wins (1903–2015)
Bayern Munich 25; 1.FC Nuremberg 9; Borussia Dortmund 8; Schalke 04 7; Hamburger SV 6; VfB Stuttgart 5; Borussia Moenchengladbach 5; 1.FC Kaiserslautern 4; Werder Bremen 4; 1.FC Lokomotive Leipzig 3; SpVgg Greuther Furth 3; 1.FC Cologne 3; Viktoria Berlin 2; Hertha Berlin 2; Hannover 96 2; Dresden SC 2; Union Berlin 1; Freiburger FC 1; Phoenix Karlsruhe 1; Karlsruher FV 1; Holstein Kiel 1; Fortuna Dusseldorf 1; Rapid Vienna 1; VfR Mannheim 1; Rot-Weiss Essen 1; Eintracht Frankfurt 1; Munich 1860 1; Eintracht Braunschweig 1; VfL Wolfsburg 1.

Cup wins (1935–2015)
Bayern Munich 17; Werder Bremen 6; Schalke 04 5; 1.FC Nuremberg 4; 1.FC Cologne 4; Eintracht Frankfurt 4; Hamburger SV 3; VfB Stuttgart 3; Borussia Moenchengladbach 3; Borussia Dortmund 3; Dresden SC 2; Munich 1860 2; Fortuna Dusseldorf 2; Karlsruhe SC 2; 1.FC Kaiserslautern 2; 1.FC Lokomotive Leipzig 1; Rapid Vienna 1; First Vienna 1; Rot-Weiss Essen 1; SW Essen 1; Kickers Offenbach 1; Bayer Uerdingen 1; Hannover 96 1; Bayer Leverkusen 1; VfLWolfsburg 1.

Final League Table 2014–15

	P	W	D	L	F	A	GD	Pts
Bayern Munich	34	25	4	5	80	18	62	79
VfL Wolfsburg	34	20	9	5	72	38	34	69
Borussia M'gladbach	34	19	9	6	53	26	27	66
Bayer Leverkusen	34	17	10	7	62	37	25	61
Augsburg	34	15	4	15	43	43	0	49
Schalke 04	34	13	9	12	42	40	2	48
Borussia Dortmund	34	13	7	14	47	42	5	46
TSG 1899 Hoffenheim	34	12	8	14	49	55	–6	44
Eintracht Frankfurt	34	11	10	13	56	62	–6	43
Werder Bremen	34	11	10	13	50	65	–15	43
1.FSV Mainz 05	34	9	13	12	45	47	–2	40
1.FC Cologne	34	9	13	12	34	40	–6	40
Hannover 96	34	9	10	15	40	56	–16	37

VfB Stuttgart	34	9	9	16	42	60	–18	36
Hertha Berlin	34	9	8	17	36	52	–16	35
Hamburger SV+	34	9	8	17	25	50	–25	35
Freiburg*	34	7	13	14	36	47	–11	34
Paderborn 07*	34	7	10	17	31	65	–34	31

Top scorer: Meier (Eintracht Frankfurt) 19.
Cup Final: VfLWolfsburg 3, Borussia Dortmund 1.

GIBRALTAR

Gibraltar Football Association, Bayside Sports Complex, PO Box 513, Gibraltar GX11 1AA.
Founded: 1895. *UEFA:* 2013. *National Colours:* Red shirts with white trim, red shorts, red socks.

International matches 2014–15
Poland (n) 0-7, Republic of Ireland (a) 0-7, Georgia (n) 0-3, Germany (a) 0-4, Scotland (a) 1-6, Croatia (a) 0-4, Germany (n) 0-7.

League Championship wins (1896–2015)
Lincoln 21 (incl. Newcastle United 5; 1 title shared); Prince of Wales 19; Glacis United 17 (incl. 1 shared); Britannia (now Britannia XI) 14; Gibraltar United 11; Manchester United (now Manchester 62) 7; Europa 6; St Theresa's 3; Chief Construction 2; Jubilee 2; Exiles 2; South United 2; Gibraltar FC 2; Albion 1; Athletic 1; Royal Sovereign 1; Commander of the Yard 1; St Joseph's 1.

Cup wins (1895–2015)
Lincoln (incl. Newcastle United 4) 16; St Joseph's 9; Europa 5; Glacis United 5; Britannia (now Britannia XI) 3; Gibraltar United 3; Manchester United (now Manchester 62) 3; Gibraltar FC 1; HMS Hood 1; 2nd Bn The King's Regt 1; AARA 1; RAF New Camp 1; 4th Bn Royal Scots 1; Prince of Wales 1; Manchester United Reserves 1; 2nd Bn Royal Green Jackets 1; RAF Gibraltar 1; St Theresa's 1.

Final League Table 2014–15

	P	W	D	L	F	A	GD	Pts
Lincoln	21	19	1	1	80	12	68	58
College Europa	21	12	6	3	42	14	28	42
Lynx	21	10	8	3	36	18	18	38
St Joseph's	21	12	2	7	36	18	18	38
Manchester 62	21	7	6	8	22	25	–3	27
Glacis United	21	4	3	14	14	50	–36	15
Britannia XI	21	2	3	16	13	67	–54	9
Lions Gibraltar	21	1	5	15	9	48	–39	8

No relegation as league to expand to 10 teams.
Top scorer: Casciaro (Lincoln) 20.
Cup Final: Lincoln 4, Lynx 0.

GOZO

Gozo Football Association, GFA Headquarters, Mgarr Road, Xewkija, XWK 9014, Malta. (Not a member of FIFA or UEFA.)
Founded: 1936.

League Championship wins (1938–2015)
Victoria Hotspurs 11; Nadur Youngsters 11; Sannat Lions 10; Xewkija Tigers 7; Xaghra United 6 (incl. Xaghra Blue Stars 1, Xaghra Young Stars 1); Salesian Youths (renamed Oratory Youths) 6; Ghajnsielem 6; Victoria Athletics 4; Victoria Stars 1; Victoria City 1; Calypcians 1; Kercem Ajax 1; Victoria United (renamed Victoria Wanderers) 1; Zebbug Rovers 1.

Cup wins (1972–2015)
Sannat Lions 9; Xewkija Tigers 9; Nadur Youngsters 8; Ghajnsielem 4; Xaghra United 4; Kercem Ajax 2; Calypsians 1; Calypsians Bosco Youths 1; Victoria Hotspurs 1; Qala St Joseph 1; Victoria Wanderers 1.

Qualifying League Table 2014–15

	P	W	D	L	F	A	GD	Pts
Xewkija Tigers	14	11	2	1	40	12	28	35
Nadur Youngsters	14	11	1	2	32	10	22	34
Victoria Hotspurs	14	6	3	5	30	18	12	21
Kercem Ajax	14	6	2	6	24	24	0	20
Oratory Youths	14	4	4	6	22	33	–11	16
St Lawrence Spurs	14	4	3	7	21	38	–17	15
Victoria Wanderers	14	3	3	8	17	26	–9	12
Sannat Lions	14	0	4	10	6	31	–25	4

Championship Round

	P	W	D	L	F	A	GD	Pts
Xewkija Tigers	20	16	2	2	57	19	28	50
Nadur Youngsters†	20	16	1	3	51	17	34	49
Victoria Hotspurs	20	7	4	9	35	33	2	25
Kercem Ajax	20	6	3	11	30	42	–12	21

Relegation Round

	P	W	D	L	F	A	GD	Pts
Victoria Wanderers	20	8	3	9	27	30	–3	27
Oratory Youths	20	7	5	8	31	39	–8	26
St Lawrence Spurs+	20	6	4	10	31	48	–17	22
Sannat Lions*	20	0	6	14	9	43	–34	6

† *Nadur Youngsters relegated following match-fixing charges.*
Top scorer: Antunes (Nadur Youngsters) 23.
Cup Final: Xewkija Tigers 2, Oratory Youths 1.

GREECE

Hellenic Football Federation, Parko Goudi, PO Box 14161, 11510 Athens.
Founded: 1926. *FIFA:* 1927; *UEFA:* 1954. *National Colours:* All white.

International matches 2014–15
Romania (h) 0-1, Finland (a) 1-1, Northern Ireland (h) 0-2, Faroe Islands (h) 0-1, Serbia (h) 0-2, Hungary (a) 0-0, Faroe Islands (a) 1-2, Poland (a) 0-0.

League Championship wins (1928–2015)
Olympiacos 42; Panathinaikos 20; AEK Athens 11; Aris Salonika 3; PAOK Salonika 2; Larissa 1.

Cup wins (1932–2015)
Olympiacos 27; Panathinaikos 18; AEK Athens 14; PAOK Salonika 4; Panionios 2; Larissa 2; Ethnikos 1; Aris Salonika 1; Iraklis 1; Kastoria 1; OFI Crete 1.

Final League Table 2014–15

	P	W	D	L	F	A	GD	Pts
Olympiacos	34	24	6	4	79	23	56	78
Panathinaikos (–3)	34	21	6	7	59	31	28	66
PAOK	34	20	5	9	57	42	15	65
Asteras Tripolis	34	17	8	9	52	37	15	59
Atromitos	34	14	12	8	43	27	16	54
PAS Giannina	34	13	14	7	47	33	14	53
Panetolikos	34	14	10	10	41	28	13	52
Xanthi	34	12	11	11	44	41	3	47
Platanias	34	12	8	14	32	30	2	44
Kerkyra	34	12	8	14	39	38	1	44
Kalloni	34	11	11	12	34	39	–5	44
Panthrakikos	34	11	10	13	35	44	–9	43
Panionios	34	11	10	13	43	42	1	43
Veria	34	12	7	15	45	54	–9	43
Levadiakos*	34	12	7	15	41	34	7	43
Ergotelis*	34	8	8	18	35	60	–25	32
OFI Crete*† (–29)	34	7	2	25	26	72	–46	–6
Niki Volou*† (–13)	34	2	1	31	7	84	–77	–6

† *OFI Crete deducted 29 points for financial irregularities. Niki Volou demoted to second tier with a 6-point deduction in 2015–16.*
Top scorer: Barrales (Asteras Tripolis) 17.
Cup Final: Olympiacos 3, Xanthi 1.

HUNGARY

Magyar Labdarugo Szovetseg, Kanai ut 2. D, 1112 Budapest.
Founded: 1901. *FIFA:* 1907; *UEFA:* 1954. *National Colours:* Red shirts, white shorts, green socks.

International matches 2014–15
Northern Ireland (h) 1-2, Romania (a) 1-1, Faroe Islands (a) 1-0, Finland (h) 1-0, Russia (h) 1-2, Greece (h) 0-0, Lithuania (h) 4-0, Finland (a) 1-0.

League Championship wins (1901–2015)
Ferencvaros 28; MTK-Hungaria Budapest 23; Ujpest 20; Budapest Honved 13 (incl. Kispest Honved); Debrecen 7; Vasas Budapest 6; Csepel 4; Gyor 4; Budapesti TC 2; Videoton 2; Nagyvarad 1; Vac 1; Dunaferr (renamed Dunaujvaros) 1; Zalaegerszeg 1.

Cup wins (1910–2015)
Ferencvaros 21; MTK-Hungaria Budapest 12; Ujpest 9; Budapest Honved 7 (inc. Kispest Honved); Debrecen 6; Vasas Budapest 4; Gyor 4; Diosgyor 2; Bocskai 1; III Ker 1; Soroksar 1; Szolnoki MAV 1; Siofoki Banyasz 1; Bekescsaba 1; Pecsi 1; Sopron 1; Fehervar (renamed Videoton) 1; Kecskemet 1.
Cup not regularly held until 1964.

Final League Table 2014–15

	P	W	D	L	F	A	GD	Pts
Videoton	30	22	5	3	64	14	50	71
Ferencvaros	30	19	7	4	49	19	30	64
MTK Budapest	30	18	3	9	39	25	14	57
Debrecen	30	15	9	6	44	19	25	54

Paks	30	14	9	7	44	27	17	51
Ujpest	30	14	9	7	40	28	12	51
Diosgyor	30	13	9	8	43	36	7	48
Gyor †	30	10	8	12	41	44	–3	38
Kecskemet†	30	10	8	12	30	39	–9	38
Puskas Akademia	30	10	5	15	35	40	–5	35
Pecs†	30	8	7	15	32	51	–19	31
Nyiregyhaza Spartacus†	30	8	6	16	33	49	–16	30
Budapest Honved	30	6	10	14	26	36	–10	28
Szombathelyi Haladas	30	7	4	19	26	53	–27	25
Dunaujvaros* (–1)	30	5	8	17	26	49	–23	22
Lombard-Papa*	30	4	7	19	14	57	–43	19

† *Demoted for various financial and licence irregularities.*
Top scorer: Nikolic (Videoton) 21.
Cup Final: Ferencvaros 4, Videoton 0.

ICELAND

Knattspyrnusamband Islands, Laugardal, 104 Reykjavik.
Founded: 1947. *FIFA:* 1947; *UEFA:* 1954. *National Colours:* All blue.

International matches 2014–15
Turkey (h) 3-0, Latvia (a) 3-0, Netherlands (h) 2-0, Belgium (a) 1-3, Czech Republic (a) 1-2, Canada (n) 2-1, Canada (n) 1-1, Kazakhstan (a) 3-0, Estonia (a) 1-1, Czech Republic (h) 2-1.

League Championship wins (1912–2014)
KR Reykjavik 26; Valur 20; Fram 18; IA Akranes 18; FH Hafnarfjordur 6; Vikingur 5; IBK Keflavik 4; IBV Vestmannaeyjar 3; KA Akureyri 1; Breidablik 1; Stjarnan 1.

Cup wins (1960–2014)
KR Reykjavik 14; Valur 9; IA Akranes 9; Fram 8; IBV Vestmannaeyjar 4; IBK Keflavik 4; Fylkir 2; FH Hafnarfjordur 2; IBA Akureyri 1; Vikingur 1; Breidablik 1.

Final League Table 2014

	P	W	D	L	F	A	GD	Pts
Stjarnan	22	15	7	0	42	21	21	52
FH Hafnarfjordur	22	15	6	1	46	17	29	51
KR Reykjavik	22	13	4	5	40	24	16	43
Vikingur Reykjavik	22	9	3	10	25	29	–4	30
Valur	22	8	4	10	31	36	–5	28
Fylkir	22	8	4	10	34	40	–6	28
Breidablik	22	5	12	5	36	33	3	27
Keflavik	22	6	7	9	29	32	–3	25
Fjolnir	22	5	8	9	33	36	–3	23
IBV Vestmannaeyjar	22	5	7	10	28	38	–10	22
Fram*	22	6	3	13	30	48	–18	21
Thor*	22	3	3	16	24	44	–20	12

Top scorer: Martin (KR) 13.
Cup Final: KR Reykjavik 2, Keflavik 1.

ISRAEL

Israel Football Association, Ramat Gan Stadium, 299 Aba Hilell Street, PO Box 3591, Ramat Gan 52134.
Founded: 1928. *FIFA:* 1929; *UEFA:* 1994. *National Colours:* Blue shirts with white trim, blue shorts, blue socks.

International matches 2014–15
Cyprus (a) 2-1, Andorra (a) 4-1, Bosnia-Herzegovina (h) 3-0, Wales (h) 0-3, Belgium (h) 0-1, Bosnia-Herzegovina (a) 1-3.

League Championship wins (1932–2015)
Maccabi Tel Aviv 21; Hapoel Tel Aviv 13; Maccabi Haifa 12; Hapoel Petah Tikva 6; Beitar Jerusalem 6; Maccabi Netanya 5; Hakoah Ramat Gan 2; Hapoel Be'er Sheba 2; British Police 1; Hapoel Ramat Gan 1; Hapoel Kfar Saba 1; Bnei Yehuda 1; Hapoel Haifa 1; Ironi Kiryat Shmona 1.

Cup wins (1928–2015)
Maccabi Tel Aviv 23; Hapoel Tel Aviv 15; Beitar Jerusalem 7; Maccabi Haifa 5; Hapoel Haifa 3; Hapoel Kfar Saba 3; Maccabi Petah Tikva 2; Beitar Tel Aviv 2; Hapoel Petah Tikva 2; Bnei Yehuda 2; Hakoah Amidar Ramat Gan 2; Hapoel Ramat Gan 2; Maccabi Hashmonai Jerusalem 1; British Police 1; Hapoel Jerusalem 1; Maccabi Netanya 1; Hapoel Yehud 1; Hapoel Lod 1; Hapoel Be'er Sheba 1; Bnei Sakhnin 1; Ironi Kiryat Shmona 1.

Qualifying League Table 2014–15

	P	W	D	L	F	A	GD	Pts
Maccabi Tel Aviv (–2)	26	17	5	4	53	20	33	54
Hapoel Be'er Sheva	26	14	7	5	47	24	23	49
Ironi Kiryat Shmona	26	13	8	5	40	27	13	47
Beitar Jerusalem	26	10	10	6	38	29	9	40
Maccabi Petach Tikva	26	10	9	7	28	30	–2	39
Maccabi Haifa	26	11	4	11	38	29	9	37
Hapoel Ra'anana	26	9	7	10	24	23	1	34
Maccabi Netanya	26	9	6	11	37	45	–8	33
Bnei Sakhnin	26	7	9	10	32	37	–5	30
Hapoel Tel Aviv (–2)	26	8	7	11	27	33	–12	29
FC Ashdod	26	6	9	11	29	41	–14	27
Hapoel Haifa	26	7	5	14	20	41	–21	26
Hapoel Petahh Tikva	26	5	8	13	28	43	–15	23
Hapoel Acre	26	4	10	12	20	39	–19	22

Championship Round

	P	W	D	L	F	A	GD	Pts
Maccabi Tel Aviv	36	21	9	6	67	32	35	72
Ironi Kiryat Shmona	36	18	10	8	53	38	15	64
Hapoel Be'er Sheva	36	17	11	8	63	40	23	62
Beitar Jerusalem (–1)	36	13	13	10	48	43	5	51
Maccabi Haifa	36	14	8	14	51	37	14	50
Maccabi Petah Tikva	36	12	12	12	34	41	–7	48

Relegation Round

	P	W	D	L	F	A	GD	Pts
Bnei Sakhnin	33	11	11	11	43	44	–1	44
Hapoel Tel Aviv (–2)	33	12	8	13	36	40	–4	42
Maccabi Netanya	33	11	8	14	46	54	–8	41
Hapoel Ra'anana	33	10	9	14	35	36	–1	39
Hapoel Acre	33	9	11	13	28	42	–14	38
Hapoel Haifa	33	9	7	17	25	47	–22	34
Hapoel Petach Tikva*	33	8	8	17	43	59	–16	32
FC Ashdod*	33	6	14	13	32	51	–19	31

Top scorer: Zahavi (Maccabi Tel Aviv) 27.
Cup Final: Maccabi Tel Aviv 6, Hapoel Be'er Sheva 2

ITALY

Federazione Italiana Giuoco Calcio, Via Gregorio Allegri 14, 00198 Roma.
Founded: 1898. *FIFA:* 1905; *UEFA:* 1954. *National Colours:* Blue shirts, white shorts, blue socks with white tops.

International matches 2014–15
Netherlands (h) 2-0, Norway (a) 2-0, Azerbaijan (h) 2-1, Malta (a) 1-0, Croatia (h) 1-1, Albania (h) 1-0, Bulgaria (a) 2-2, England (h) 1-1, Croatia (a) 1-1, Portugal (n) 0-1.

League Championship wins (1898–2015)
Juventus 31 (excludes two titles revoked); AC Milan 18; Internazionale 18 (includes one title awarded); Genoa 9; Pro Vercelli 7; Bologna 7; Torino 7 (excludes one title revoked); Roma 3; Fiorentina 2; Lazio 2; Napoli 2; Casale 1; Novese 1; Cagliari 1; Verona 1; Sampdoria 1.

Cup wins (1928–2015)
Juventus 10; Roma 9; Internazionale 7; Fiorentina 6; Lazio 6; Torino 5; Napoli 5; AC Milan 5; Sampdoria 4; Parma 3; Bologna 2; Vado 1; Genoa 1; Venezia 1; Atalanta 1; Vicenza 1.

Final League Table 2014–15

	P	W	D	L	F	A	GD	Pts
Juventus	38	26	9	3	72	24	48	87
Roma	38	19	13	6	54	31	23	70
Lazio	38	21	6	11	71	38	33	69
Fiorentina	38	18	10	10	61	46	15	64
Napoli	38	18	9	11	70	54	16	63
Genoa	38	16	11	11	62	47	15	59
Sampdoria	38	13	17	8	48	42	6	56
Internazionale	38	14	13	11	59	48	11	55
Torino	38	14	12	12	48	45	3	54
AC Milan	38	13	13	12	56	50	6	52
Palermo	38	12	13	13	53	55	–2	49
Sassuolo	38	12	13	13	49	57	–8	49
Hellas Verona	38	11	13	14	49	65	–16	46
Chievo Verona	38	10	13	15	28	41	–13	43
Empoli	38	8	18	12	46	52	–6	42
Udinese	38	10	11	17	43	56	–13	41
Atalanta	38	7	16	15	38	57	–19	37
Cagliari*	38	8	10	20	48	68	–20	34
Cesena*	38	4	12	22	36	73	–37	24
Parma*† (–7)	38	6	8	24	33	75	–42	19

†*Parma deducted 7 points for non-payment of wages.*
Top scorers (equal): Icardi (Internazionale), Toni (Verona) 22.
Cup Final: Juventus 2, Lazio 3 (aet).

KAZAKHSTAN

Football Federation of Kazakhstan, 29 Syganak Street, 9th floor, 010000 Astana.
Founded: 1914. *FIFA:* 1994; *UEFA:* 2002. *National Colours:* All yellow.

International matches 2014–15
Tajikistan (h) 2-1, Kyrgyzstan (h) 7-1, Latvia (h) 0-0, Netherlands (a) 1-3, Czech Republic (h) 2-4, Turkey (a) 1-3, Moldova (n) 1-1, Iceland (h) 0-3, Russia (a) 0-0, Burkina Faso (h) 0-0, Turkey (h) 0-1.

League Championship wins (1992–2014)
Irtysh (includes Ansat) 5; Aktobe 5; Yelimay (renamed Spartak Semey) 3; FC Astana-64 (incl. Zhenis) 3; Kairat 2; Shakhter Karagandy 2; Taraz 1; Tobol 1; Astana 1.

Cup wins (1992–2014)
Kairat 6; FC Astana-64 (incl. Zhenis) 3; Astana (incl. Lokomotiv) 2; Dostyk 1; Vostok 1; Yelimay (renamed Spartak Semey) 1; Irtysh 1; Kaisar 1; Taraz 1; Almaty 1; Tobol 1; Aktobe 1; Atirau 1; Ordabasy 1; Shakhter Karagandy 1.

Qualifying League Table 2014

	P	W	D	L	F	A	GD	Pts
Aktobe	22	12	7	3	34	17	17	43
Kairat	22	13	3	6	41	20	21	42
Astana	22	10	9	3	34	17	17	39
Shakhter Karagandy	22	11	3	8	33	27	6	36
Ordabasy	22	10	5	7	24	22	2	35
Kaisar	22	8	8	6	23	23	0	32
Zhetysu	22	7	6	9	15	18	–3	27
Tobol	22	6	8	8	22	29	–7	26
Irtysh	22	6	6	10	28	35	–7	24
Atyrau	22	6	6	10	19	27	–8	24
Taraz	22	5	4	13	21	34	–13	19
Spartak Semey	22	3	5	14	16	41	–25	14

NB: Points earned in Qualifying phase are halved at start of Championship and Relegation phase.

Championship Round

	P	W	D	L	F	A	GD	Pts
Astana	32	18	10	4	63	26	37	45
Aktobe	32	17	10	5	52	31	21	40
Kairat	32	18	5	9	58	31	27	38
Ordabasy	32	13	5	14	34	44	–10	27
Kaisar	32	10	13	9	30	34	–4	27
Shakhter Karagandy	32	11	6	15	41	49	–8	21

Relegation Round

	P	W	D	L	F	A	GD	Pts
Tobol (–3)	32	10	12	10	35	35	0	26
Zhetysu	32	10	8	14	21	31	–10	25
Atyrau	32	10	7	15	30	43	–13	25
Irtysh	32	9	10	13	39	44	–5	25
Taraz+	32	9	7	16	32	45	–13	25
Spartak Semey*	32	7	7	18	30	52	–22	21

Top scorer: Kethevoama (Astana) 15.
Cup Final: Kairat 4, Aktobe 1.

KOSOVO

Football Federation of Kosovo, Rruga Agim Ramadani 45, Prishtina, Kosovo 10000. (Not a member of FIFA or UEFA.)
Founded: 1946; *National Colours:* All blue.

International matches 2014–15
Haiti (h) 0-0*, Turkey (h) 1-6*, Senegal (h) 1-1*, Oman (h) 1-0.
* *Played in 2013–14, results omitted from last edition.*

League Championship wins (1945–2015)
Prishtina 14; Vellaznimi 9; KF Trepca 7; Liria 5; Buduqnosti 4; Rudari 3; Red Star 3; Besa 3; Jedinstvo 2; Kosova Prishtina 2; Slloga 2; Obiliqi 2; Fushe-Kosova 2; Proletari 1; KXEK Kosova 1; Rudniku 1; KNI Ramiz Sadiku 1; Dukagjini 1; Besiana 1; Drita 1; Hysi 1; Kosova Vushtrri 1; Feronikeli.

Cup wins (1992–2015)
Prishtina 3; Liria 3; Flamurtari 2; Besa 2; Feronikeli 2; KF Trepca 1; KF 2 Korriku 1; Gjilani 1; Drita 1; Besiana 1; KEK-u 1; Kosova Prishtina 1; Vellaznimi 1; Hysi 1; Trepca'89 1.

Final League Table 2014–15

	P	W	D	L	F	A	GD	Pts
Feronikeli	33	19	10	4	51	25	26	67
Besa Peje	33	20	6	7	51	37	14	66
Prishtina	33	15	11	7	43	28	15	56
Hajvalia	33	15	9	9	46	32	14	54
Kosova Vushtrri	33	13	11	9	36	27	9	50
Trepca'89	33	12	12	9	36	36	16	48
Drenica Skenderaj	33	12	8	13	39	35	4	44
Istogu	33	12	7	14	41	45	–4	43
Drita+	33	10	9	14	30	38	–8	39

Vellaznimi*+	33	8	10	15	24	38	–14	34
Ferizaj*	33	5	6	22	22	55	–33	21
Trepca Mitrovice*	33	4	7	22	18	57	–39	19

Top scorer: Zenkovich (Shakhter Karagandy) 15.
Cup Final: Feronikeli 1, Trepca '89 1.
aet; Feronikeli won 5-4 on penalties.

LATVIA

Latvijas Futbola Federacija, Olympic Sports Centre, Grostonas Street 6B, 1013 Riga.
Founded: 1921. *FIFA:* 1922; *UEFA:* 1992. *National Colours:* All carmine red.

International matches 2014–15
Armenia (h) 2-0, Kazakhstan (a) 0-0, Iceland (h) 0-3, Turkey (h) 1-1, Netherlands (a) 0-6, Czech Republic (a) 1-1, Ukraine (a) 1-1, Netherlands (h) 0-2.

League Championship wins (1922–2014)
Skonto Riga 15; ASK Riga (incl. AVN 2) 11; RFK Riga 8; Sarkanais Metalurgs Liepaja 7; Olympija Liepaya 7; VEF Riga 6; Ventspils 6; Energija Riga (incl. ESR Riga 2) 4; Elektrons Riga (incl. Alfa 1) 4; Torpedo Riga 3; Keisermezhs Riga 2; Khimikis Daugavpils 2; RAF Yelgava 2; Daugava Liepaja 2; Liepajas Metalurgs 2; Dinamo Riga 1; Zhmilyeva Team 1; Darba Rezervi 1; RER Riga 1; Starts Brotseni 1; Venta Ventspils 1; Jumieks Riga 1; Gauja Valmiera 1; Daugava Daugavpils 1.

Cup wins (1937–2015)
Skonto Riga 8; Elektrons Riga 7; Ventspils 6; Sarkanais Metalurgs Liepaja 5; VEF Riga 3; ASK Riga 3; Tseltnieks Riga 3; RAF Yelgava 3; Jelgava 3; RFK Riga 2; Daugava Liepaja 2; Starts Brotseni 2; Selmash Liepaya 2; Yurnieks Riga 2; Khimikis Daugavpils 2; Rigas Vilki 1; Dinamo Liepaya 1; Dinamo Riga 1; RER Riga 1; Voulkan Kouldiga 1; Baltika Liepaja 1; Venta Ventspils 1; Pilots Riga 1; Lielupe Yurmala 1; Energija Riga (formerly ESR Riga)1; Torpedo Riga 1; Daugava SKIF Riga 1; Tseltnieks Daugavpils 1; Olympija Riga 1; FK Riga 1; Liepajas Metalurgs 1; Daugava Daugavpils 1.

Final League Table 2014

	P	W	D	L	F	A	GD	Pts
Ventspils	36	26	5	5	75	20	55	83
Skonto	36	25	1	10	77	34	43	71
Jelgava	36	20	10	6	57	27	30	70
Liepaja	36	21	3	12	72	45	27	66
Daugava Daugavpils†	36	19	8	9	53	39	14	65
Spartaks	36	14	9	13	38	42	6	51
Daugava Riga†	36	13	4	19	48	64	–16	43
BFC Daugavpils	36	8	5	23	30	65	–35	29
Metta/LU+	36	3	7	26	26	69	–43	16
FC Jurmala* (–5)	36	2	6	28	29	110	–81	7

† *Daugava Daugavpils demoted pending match-fixing inquiry. Daugava Riga folded in 2015.*
Top scorer: Gutkovskis (Skonto) 28.
Cup Final: Jelgava 2, Ventspils 0.

LIECHTENSTEIN

Liechtensteiner Fussballverband, Landstrasse 149, 9494 Schaan.
Founded: 1934. *FIFA:* 1974; *UEFA:* 1974. *National Colours:* Blue shirts, red shorts, blue socks.

International matches 2014–15
Bosnia-Herzegovina (a) 0-3, Russia (a) 0-4, Montenegro (h) 0-0, Sweden (a) 0-2, Moldova (a) 1-0, Austria (h) 0-5, San Marino (h) 1-0, Switzerland (a) 0-3, Moldova (h) 1-1.
Liechtenstein has no national league. Teams compete in Swiss regional leagues.

Cup wins (1937–2015)
Vaduz 43; Balzers 11; Triesen 8; 5; Schaan 3.
Cup Final: Vaduz 5, FC Triesenberg 0.

LITHUANIA

Lietuvos Futbolo Federacija, Stadiono g. 2, 02106 Vilnius.
Founded: 1922. *FIFA:* 1923; *UEFA:* 1992. *National Colours:* Yellow shirts, green shorts, yellow socks.

International matches 2014–15
UAE (n) 1-1, San Marino (a) 2-0, Estonia (h) 1-0, Slovenia (h) 0-2, Switzerland (a) 0-4, Ukraine (a) 0-0, England (a) 0-4, Hungary (a) 0-4, Malta (a) 0-2, Switzerland (h) 1-2.

League Championship wins (1990–2014)

FBK Kaunas 8 (including Zalgiris Kaunas 1); Ekranas 7; Zalgiris Vilnius 5; Inkaras Kaunas 2; Kareda 2; Sirijus Klaipeda 1; Mazeikiai 1.

Cup wins (1990–2015)

Zalgiris Vilnius 9; Ekranas 4; FBK Kaunas 4; Kareda 2; Atlantas 2; Suduva 2; Sirijus Klaipeda 1; Lietuvos Makabi Vilnius 1; Inkaras Kaunas 1.

Final League Table 2014

	P	W	D	L	F	A	GD	Pts
Zalgiris	36	25	9	2	92	17	75	84
Kruoja	36	19	9	8	67	34	33	66
Atlantas	36	19	8	9	76	36	40	65
Trakai	36	18	9	9	65	38	27	63
Suduva	36	17	11	8	70	38	32	62
Ekranas	36	12	9	15	51	58	−7	45
Siauliai	36	12	4	20	50	63	−13	40
Granitas Klaipeda	36	9	10	17	47	67	−20	37
Banga*	36	8	6	22	29	65	−36	30
Dainava*	36	2	3	31	12	143	−131	9

Top scorer: Tokic (Siauliai) 19.
Cup Final: Zalgiris 2, Atlantas 0.

LUXEMBOURG

Federation Luxembourgeoise de Football, BP 5 Rue de Limpach, 3932 Mondercange.
Founded: 1908. *FIFA:* 1910; *UEFA:* 1954. *National Colours:* White shirts with blue trim, white shorts, white socks.

International matches 2014–15

Belarus (h) 1-1, FYR Macedonia (a) 2-3, Spain (h) 0-4, Ukraine (h) 0-3, Slovakia (a) 0-3, Turkey (h) 1-2, Moldova (h) 0-0, Ukraine (a) 0-3.

League Championship wins (1910–2015)

Jeunesse Esch 28; Spora Luxembourg 11; F91 Dudelange 11; Stade Dudelange 10; Fola Esch 7; Red Boys Differdange 6; Union Luxembourg 6; Avenir Beggen 6; US Hollerich-Bonnevoie 5; Progres Niedercorn 3; Aris Bonnevoie 3; Sporting Club 2; Racing Club 1; National Schifflange 1; Grevenmacher 1.

Cup wins (1922–2015)

Red Boys Differdange 15; Jeunesse Esch 13; Union Luxembourg 10; Spora Luxembourg 8; Avenir Beggen 7; F91 Dudelange 5; Progres Niedercorn 4; Stade Dudelange 4; Grevenmacher 4; Differdange 03 4; Fola Esch 3; Alliance Dudelange 2; US Rumelange 2; Racing Club 1; US Dudelange 1; SC Tetange 1; National Schifflange 1; Aris Bonnevoie 1; Jeunesse Hautcharage 1; Swift Hesperange 1; Etzella Ettelbruck 1; CS Petange 1.

Final League Table 2014–15

	P	W	D	L	F	A	GD	Pts
Fola Esch	26	19	4	3	63	21	42	61
Differdange 03	26	18	5	3	61	31	30	59
F91 Dudelange	26	16	6	4	55	20	35	54
Progres Niederkorn	26	15	5	6	51	29	22	50
Jeunesse Esch	26	12	8	6	46	34	12	44
Victoria Rosport	26	8	7	11	36	46	−10	31
Etzella Ettelbruck	26	9	3	14	36	50	−14	30
Mondorf-les-Bains	26	8	5	13	30	40	−10	29
Grevenmacher	26	8	5	13	24	48	−24	29
Rumelange	26	7	7	12	29	38	−9	28
Wiltz	26	7	6	13	29	38	−9	27
UN Kaerjeng 97*+	26	8	3	15	33	52	−19	27
Hostert*	26	5	8	13	35	52	−17	23
Jeunesse Canach*	26	3	6	17	16	45	−29	15

Top scorer: Ibrahimovic (Jeunesse Esch) 21.
Cup Final: Differdange 03 1, F91 Dudelange 1.
aet; Differdange 03 won 3-2 on penalties.

MALTA

Malta Football Association, Millennium Stand, Floor 2, National Stadium, Ta'Qali ATD4000.
Founded: 1900. *FIFA:* 1959; *UEFA:* 1960. *National Colours:* Red shirts, white shorts, red socks.

International matches 2014–15

Slovakia (a) 0-1, Croatia (a) 0-2, Norway (h) 0-3, Italy (h) 0-1, Bulgaria (h) 1-1, Georgia (h) 0-2, Azerbaijan (a) 0-2, Lithuania (h) 2-0, Bulgaria (h) 0-1.

League Championship wins (1910–2015)

Sliema Wanderers 26; Floriana 25; Valletta 22; Hibernians 11; Hamrun Spartans 7; Birkirkara 4; Rabat Ajax 2; St George's 1; KOMR 1; Marsaxlokk 1.

Cup wins (1935–2015)

Sliema Wanderers 20; Floriana 19; Valletta 13; Hibernians 10; Hamrun Spartans 6; Birkirkara 5; Melita 1; Gzira United 1; Zurrieq 1; Rabat Ajax 1.

Qualifying League Table 2014–15

	P	W	D	L	F	A	GD	Pts
Hibernians	22	19	3	0	68	13	55	60
Valletta	22	14	2	6	51	17	34	44
Birkirkara	22	13	4	5	41	22	19	43
Balzan	22	9	7	6	35	33	2	34
Floriana	22	7	8	7	38	41	−3	29
Sliema Wanderers	22	7	6	9	26	31	−5	27
Mosta	22	7	4	11	24	43	−19	25
Naxxar Lions	22	5	7	10	26	34	−8	22
Tarxien Rainbows	22	4	9	9	22	38	−16	21
Pieta Hotspurs	22	5	6	11	19	36	−17	21
Qormi	22	4	6	12	22	38	−16	18
Zebbug Rangers	22	4	6	12	25	51	−26	18

NB: Points earned in first phase are halved at start of second round during which teams play each other once.

Second Round

	P	W	D	L	F	A	GD	Pts
Hibernians	33	27	5	1	97	24	73	56
Valletta	33	22	3	8	74	30	44	47
Birkirkara	33	19	7	7	59	31	28	43
Balzan	33	17	8	8	59	45	14	42
Floriana	33	13	11	9	58	51	7	36
Sliema Wanderers	33	10	9	14	50	56	−6	26
Naxxar Lions	33	9	9	15	40	51	−11	25
Qormi	33	8	9	16	40	55	−15	24
Tarxien Rainbows	33	8	9	16	35	60	−25	23
Mosta+	33	9	6	18	38	72	−34	21
Pieta Hotspurs*	33	8	3	19	30	58	−28	16
Zebbug Rangers*	33	5	6	22	37	84	−47	12

Top scorer: Pereira (Hibernians) 25.
Cup Final: Birkirkara 2, Hibernians 0.

MOLDOVA

Federatia Moldoveneasca de Fotbal, Str. Tricolorului 39, 2012 Chisinau.
Founded: 1990. *FIFA:* 1994; *UEFA:* 1993. *National Colours:* All blue.

International matches 2014–15

Ukraine (a) 0-1, Montenegro (a) 0-2, Austria (h) 1-2, Russia (a) 1-1, Liechtenstein (h) 0-1, Romania (h) 1-2, Kazakhstan (n) 1-1, Sweden (h) 0-2, Luxembourg (a) 0-0, Liechtenstein (a) 1-1.

League Championship wins (1992–2015)

Sheriff 13; Zimbru Chisinau 8; Constructorul 1; Dacia Chisinau 1; Milsami Orhei 1.

Cup wins (1992–2015)

Sheriff 8; Zimbru Chisinau 5; Tiligul 3; Tiraspol 3 (incl. Constructorul 2); Comrat 1; Nistru Otaci 1; Iskra-Stal 1; Milsami Orhei 1.

Final League Table 2014–15

	P	W	D	L	F	A	GD	Pts
Milsami Orhei	24	17	4	3	50	15	35	55
Dacia Chisinau	24	17	4	3	48	13	35	55
Sheriff	24	17	4	3	56	16	40	55
Tiraspol†	24	14	2	8	49	28	21	44
Saxan	24	8	6	10	20	30	−10	30
Zimbru Chisinau	24	7	6	11	23	19	4	27
Academia Chisinau	24	5	2	17	18	47	−29	17
Dinamo-Auto	24	4	2	18	23	63	−40	14
Zaria Balti	24	4	0	20	10	66	−56	12

† *Tiraspol folded at end of season. Costuleni and Veris withdrew.*
Top scorer: Ricardinho (Sheriff) 19.
Cup Final: Sheriff 3, Dacia Chisinau 2 (aet).

MONTENEGRO

Fudbalski Savez Crne Gore, Ulica 19. Decembar 13, PO Box 275, 81000 Podgorica.
Founded: 1931 *FIFA:* 2007; *UEFA:* 2007. *National Colours:* All red with gold trim.

International matches 2014–15

Moldova (h) 2-0, Liechtenstein (a) 0-0, Austria (a) 0-1, Sweden (h) 1-1, Russia (h) 0-3, Denmark (a) 1-2, Sweden (a) 1-3.

League Championship wins (2006–15)

Buducnost Podgorica 2; Mogren 2; Rudar Pljevlja 2; Sutjeska 2; Zeta 1.

Cup wins (2006-15)
Rudar Pljevlja 3; Mogren 1; Petrovac 1; Celik 1; Buducnost Podgorica 1; Lovcen 1: Mladost Podgorica 1.

Final League Table 2014-15

	P	W	D	L	F	A	GD	Pts
Rudar Pljevlja	33	22	6	5	58	18	40	72
Sutjeska	33	20	9	4	58	23	35	69
Buducnost Podgorica	33	18	9	6	46	20	26	63
Mladost Podgorica	33	16	9	8	53	36	17	57
Grbalj	33	15	7	11	52	44	8	52
Lovcen	33	15	5	13	42	32	10	50
Petrovac	33	12	7	14	30	35	-5	43
Bokelj	33	11	8	14	38	45	-7	41
Zeta	33	11	7	15	48	44	4	40
Mornar+	33	9	5	19	32	63	-31	32
Mogren*+	33	5	6	22	26	70	-44	21
Berane*	33	3	4	26	25	78	-53	13

Top scorer: Vujovic (Sutjeska) 21.
Cup Final: Mladost Podgorica 2, Petrovac 1 (aet).

NETHERLANDS

Koninklijke Nederlandse Voetbalbond, Woudenbergseweg 56-58, Postbus 515, 3700 AM Zeist.
Founded: 1889. *FIFA:* 1904; *UEFA:* 1954. *National Colours:* Orange shirts, white shorts, orange socks.

International matches 2014-15
Italy (h) 0-2, Czech Republic (a) 1-2, Kazakhstan (h) 3-1, Netherlands (a) 1-3, Iceland (a) 0-2, Mexico (h) 2-3, Latvia (h) 6-0, Turkey (h) 1-1, Spain (h) 2-0, USA (h) 3-4, Latvia (a) 2-0.

League Championship wins (1889-2015)
Ajax Amsterdam 33; PSV Eindhoven 22; Feyenoord 14; HVV The Hague 10; Sparta Rotterdam 6; RAP Amsterdam 5; Go Ahead Eagles Deventer 4; HFC Haarlem 3; HBS Craeyenhout 3; Willem II Tilburg 3; RCH Heemstede 2; Heracles 2; ADO The Hague 2; AZ 67 Alkmaar 2; VV Concordia 1; Quick The Hague 1; Be Quick Groningen 1; NAC Breda 1; SC Enschede 1; Volewijckers Amsterdam 1; Haarlem 1; BVV Den Bosch 1; Schiedam 1; Limburgia 1; EVV Eindhoven 1; SVV Rapid JC Den Heerlen 1; DOS Utrecht 1; DWS Amsterdam 1; FC Twente 1.

Cup wins (1899-2015)
Ajax Amsterdam 18; Feyenoord 11; PSV Eindhoven 9; Quick The Hague 4; AZ 67 Alkmaar 4; HFC Haarlem 3; Sparta Rotterdam 3; Twente 3; Utrecht 3; Haarlem 2; VOC 2; HBS Craeyenhout 2; DFC 2; RCH Haarlem 2; Wageningen 2; Willem II Tilburg 2; Fortuna 54 2; FC Den Haag (includes ADO) 2; Roda JC 2; RAP Amsterdam 1; Velocitas Breda 1; HVV The Hague 1; Concordia Delft 1; CVV 1; Schoten 1; ZFC Zaandam 1; Longa 1; VUC 1; Velocitas Groningen 1; Roermond 1; FC Eindhoven 1; VSV 1; Quick 1888 Nijmegen 1; VVV Groningen 1; NAC Breda 1; Heerenveen 1; PEC Zwolle 1; FC Groningen 1.

Final League Table 2014-15

	P	W	D	L	F	A	GD	Pts
PSV Eindhoven	34	29	1	4	92	31	61	88
Ajax	34	21	8	5	69	29	40	71
AZ Alkmaar	34	19	5	10	63	56	7	62
Feyenoord	34	17	8	9	56	39	17	59
Vitesse	34	16	10	8	66	43	23	58
PEC Zwolle	34	16	5	13	59	43	16	53
Heerenveen	34	13	11	10	53	46	7	50
FC Groningen	34	11	13	10	49	53	-4	46
Willem II	34	13	7	14	46	50	-4	46
FC Twente† (-6)	34	13	10	11	56	51	5	43
Utrecht	34	11	8	15	60	62	-2	41
Cambuur	34	11	8	15	46	56	-10	41
ADO Den Haag	34	9	10	15	44	53	-9	37
Heracles Almelo	34	11	4	19	47	64	-17	37
SBV Excelsior	34	6	14	14	47	63	-16	32
NAC Breda*+	34	6	10	18	36	68	-32	28
Go Ahead Eagles*+	34	7	6	21	29	59	-30	27
Dordrecht*	34	4	8	22	24	76	-52	20

† *FC Twente deducted 6 points for financial reasons.*
Top scorer: Depay (PSV Eindhoven) 22.
Cup Final: FC Groningen 2, PEC Zwolle 0.

NORTHERN CYPRUS

Cyprus Turkish Football Federation, 7 Memduh Asaf Street, 107 Koskluciftlik, Lefkosa. (Not a member of FIFA or UEFA.)

Founded: 1955; *National Colours:* Red shirts with white trim, red shorts, red socks.

League Championship wins (1956-63; 1969-74; 1976-2015)
Cetinkaya 14; Gonyeli 9; Magusa 7; Dogan 7; Yenicami Agdelen 7; Baf Ulku 4; Kucuk Kaymakli 4; Akincilar Genclik 1; Binatli 1.

Cup wins (1956-2015)
Cetinkaya 17; Gonyeli 8; Yenicami Agdelen 7; Kucuk Kaymakli 6; Magusa 5; Turk Ocagi 4; Dogan 2; Lefke 2; Akincilar Genclik 1; Yalova 1; Binatli 1.

Final League Table 2014-15

	P	W	D	L	F	A	GD	Pts
Yenicami Agdelen	26	22	2	2	86	20	66	68
Kucuk Kaymakli	26	17	4	5	58	26	32	55
Mormenekse	26	14	6	6	42	24	18	48
Dogan	26	14	4	8	50	37	13	46
Lefke	26	13	1	12	60	40	20	40
Cihangir	26	11	6	9	46	43	3	39
Magusa	26	11	4	11	42	37	5	37
Yeni Bogazici	26	9	10	7	22	26	-4	37
Serdarli	26	8	11	7	40	35	5	35
Bostanci Bagcil	26	9	7	10	59	39	20	34
Gencler Birligi	26	9	6	11	36	32	4	33
Cetinkaya	26	7	5	14	53	55	-22	26
Gonyeli	26	1	3	22	28	107	-79	6
Lapta	26	1	3	22	12	93	-81	6

Top scorer: Tagman (Lefke) 28.
Cup Final: Yenicami Agdelen 4, Mormenekse 2 (aet).

NORTHERN IRELAND

Irish Football Association, 20 Windsor Avenue, Belfast BT9 6EG.
Founded: 1880. *FIFA:* 1911; *UEFA:* 1954. *National Colours:* Green shirts, white shorts, green socks.

NORWAY

Norges Fotballforbund, Ullevaal Stadion, Serviceboks 1, 0840 Oslo.
Founded: 1902. *FIFA:* 1908; *UEFA:* 1954. *National Colours:* Red shirts, white shorts, red socks.

International matches 2014-15
UAE (h) 0-0, Italy (h) 0-2, Malta (a) 3-0, Bulgaria (h) 2-1, Estonia (h) 0-1, Azerbaijan (a) 1-0, Croatia (a) 1-5, Sweden (h) 0-0, Azerbaijan (h) 0-0.

League Championship wins (1938-2014)
Rosenborg 22; Fredrikstad 9; Viking Stavanger 8; Lillestrom 5; Valerenga 5; Larvik Turn 3; Brann 3; Molde 3; Lyn Oslo 2; Stromsgodset 2; IK Start 2; Freidig 1; Fram 1; Skeid 1; Moss 1; Stabaek 1.

Cup wins (1902-2014)
Odd Grenland 12; Fredrikstad 11; Rosenborg 9; Lyn Oslo 8; Skeid 8; Sarpsborg 6; Brann 6; Viking Stavanger 5; Stromsgodset 5; Lillestrom 5; Orn-Horten 4; Valerenga 4; Molde 4; Frigg 3; Mjondalen 3; Mercantile 2; Bodo/Glimt 2; Tromso 2; Aalesund 2; Grane Nordstrand 1; Kvik Halden 1; Sparta 1; Gjovik/Lyn 1; Moss 1; Bryne 1; Stabaek 1; Hodd 1.
(Known as the Norwegian Championship for HM The King's Trophy.)

Final League Table 2014

	P	W	D	L	F	A	GD	Pts
Molde	30	22	5	3	62	24	38	71
Rosenborg	30	18	6	6	64	43	21	60
Odd	30	17	7	6	52	32	20	58
Stromsgodset	30	15	5	10	48	42	6	50
Lillestrom	30	13	7	10	49	35	14	46
Valerenga	30	11	9	10	59	53	6	42
Aalesund	30	11	8	11	40	39	1	41
Sarpsborg 08	30	10	10	10	41	48	-7	40
Stabaek	30	11	6	13	44	52	-8	39
Viking	30	8	12	10	42	42	0	36
Haugesund	30	10	6	14	43	49	-6	36
Start	30	10	5	15	47	60	-13	35
Bodo/Glimt	30	10	5	15	45	60	-15	35
Brann*+	30	8	5	17	41	54	-13	29
Sogndal*	30	6	6	18	31	49	-18	24
Sandnes Ulf*	30	4	10	16	27	53	-26	22

Top scorer: Kjartansson (Valerenga) 25.
Cup Final: Molde 2, Odd 0.

POLAND

Polski Zwiazek Pilki Noznej, ul. Bitwy Warszawskiej 1920r. 7, 02-366 Warszawa.
Founded: 1919. *FIFA:* 1923; *UEFA:* 1954. *National Colours:* White shirts with red vertical band, red shorts, white socks.

International matches 2014–15
Gibraltar (n) 7-0, Germany (h) 2-0, Scotland (h) 2-2, Georgia (a) 4-0, Switzerland (h) 2-2, Republic of Ireland (a) 1-1, Georgia (h) 4-0, Greece (h) 0-0.

League Championship wins (1921–2015)
Gornik Zabrze 14; Ruch Chorzow 14; Wisla Krakow 13; Legia Warsaw 10; Lech Poznan 7; Cracovia 5; Pogon Lwow 4; Widzew Lodz 4; Warta Poznan 2; Polonia Warsaw 2; Polonia Bytom 2; LKS Lodz 2; Stal Mielec 2; Slask Wroclaw 2; Zaglebie Lubin 2; Garbarnia Krakow 1; Szombierki Bytom 1.

Cup wins (1926; 1951–2015)
Legia Warsaw 17; Gornik Zabrze 6; Lech Poznan 5; Wisla Krakow 4; Zaglebie Sosnowiec 4; Ruch Chorzow 3; GKS Katowice 3; Amica Wronki 3; Polonia Warsaw 2; Slask Wroclaw 2; Dyskobolia Grodzisk 2; Gwardia Warsaw 1; LKS Lodz 1; Stal Rzeszow 1; Arka Gdynia 1; Lechia Gdansk 1; Widzew Lodz 1; Miedz Legnica 1; Wisla Plock 1; Jagiellonia Bialystok 1; Zawisza Bydgoszcz 1.

Qualifying League Table 2014–15

	P	W	D	L	F	A	GD	Pts
Legia Warsaw	30	17	5	8	57	30	27	56
Lech Poznan	30	14	12	4	52	27	25	54
Jagiellonia Bialystok	30	14	7	9	43	35	8	49
Slask Wroclaw	30	12	10	8	43	36	7	46
Wisla Krakow	30	11	10	9	47	39	8	43
Gornik Zabrze	30	11	10	9	43	43	0	43
Pogon Szczecin	30	11	8	11	40	38	2	41
Lechia Gdansk	30	11	8	11	36	37	-1	41
Korona Kielce	30	10	9	11	34	42	-8	39
GKS Piast Gliwice	30	11	6	13	38	43	-5	39
Podbeskidzie Bielsko-Biala	30	10	9	11	40	48	-8	39
Cracovia Krakow	30	10	7	13	35	41	-6	37
Gornik Leczna	30	8	10	12	31	37	-6	34
Ruch Chorzow	30	8	9	13	33	38	-5	33
GKS Belchatow	30	8	7	15	24	42	-18	31
Zawisza Bydgoszcz	30	8	5	17	32	52	-20	29

Championship Round

	P	W	D	L	F	A	GD	Pts
Lech Poznan	37	19	13	5	67	33	34	43
Legia Warsaw	37	21	7	9	64	33	31	42
Jagiellonia Bialystok	37	19	8	10	59	44	15	41
Slask Wroclaw	37	15	13	9	50	43	7	35
Lechia Gdansk	37	13	10	14	45	47	-2	29
Wisla Krakow	37	12	13	12	56	48	8	28
Gornik Zabrze	37	12	11	14	50	60	-10	26
Pogon Szczecin	37	11	9	17	45	52	-7	22

Relegation Round

	P	W	D	L	F	A	GD	Pts
Cracovia Krakow	37	15	9	13	50	44	6	36
Ruch Chorzow	37	12	10	15	44	46	-2	30
Korona Kielce	37	12	11	14	44	55	-11	28
GKS Piast Gliwice	37	13	8	16	50	56	-6	28
Podbeskidzie Bielsko-Biala	37	12	10	15	47	60	-13	27
Gornik Leczna	37	11	11	15	39	46	-7	27
Zawisza Bydgoszcz*	37	10	8	19	45	63	-18	24
GKS Belchatow*	37	9	9	19	35	60	-25	21

Top scorer: Wilczek (GKS Piast Gliwice) 20.
Cup Final: Legia Warsaw 2, Lech Poznan 1.

PORTUGAL

Federacao Portuguesa de Futebol, Rua Alexandre Herculano No. 58, Apartado postal 24013, Lisboa 1250-012.
Founded: 1914. *FIFA:* 1923; *UEFA:* 1954. *National Colours:* Carmine shirts with , red shorts, red and green socks.

International matches 2014–15
Albania (h) 0-1, France (a) 1-2, Denmark (a) 1-0, Armenia (h) 1-0, Argentina (n) 1-0, Serbia (h) 2-1, Cape Verde Islands (h) 0-2, Armenia (a) 3-2, Italy (n) 1-0.

League Championship wins (1935–2015)
Benfica 34; FC Porto 27; Sporting Lisbon 18; Belenenses 1; Boavista 1.

Cup wins (1939–2015)
Benfica 25; Sporting Lisbon 16; FC Porto 16; Boavista 5; Belenenses 3; Vitoria de Setubal 3; Academica de Coimbra 2; Vitoria de Guimaraes 1; Leixoes 1; Braga 1; Estrela da Amadora 1; Beira-Mar 1.

Final League Table 2014–15

	P	W	D	L	F	A	GD	Pts
Benfica	34	27	4	3	86	16	70	85
FC Porto	34	25	7	2	74	13	61	82
Sporting Lisbon	34	22	10	2	67	29	38	76
Braga	34	17	7	10	55	28	27	58
Vitoria	34	15	10	9	50	35	15	55
Os Belenenses	34	12	12	10	34	35	-1	48
Nacional	34	13	8	13	45	46	-1	47
Pacos de Ferreira	34	12	11	11	40	45	-5	47
Maritimo	34	12	8	14	46	45	1	44
Rio Ave	34	10	13	11	38	42	-4	43
Moreirense	34	11	10	13	33	42	-9	43
Estoril Praia	34	9	13	12	38	56	-18	40
Boavista	34	9	7	18	27	50	-23	34
Vitoria	34	7	8	19	24	56	-32	29
Academica de Coimbra	34	4	17	13	26	46	-20	29
Arouca	34	7	7	20	26	50	-24	28
Gil Vicente*	34	4	11	19	25	60	-35	23
Penafiel*	34	5	7	22	29	69	-40	22

Top scorer: Jackson Martinez (FC Porto) 21.
Cup Final: Sporting Lisbon 2, Braga 2.
aet; Sporting Lisbon won 3-1 on penalties.

REPUBLIC OF IRELAND

Football Association of Ireland (Cumann Peile na hEireann), National Sports Campus, Abbotstown, Dublin 15.
Founded: 1921. *FIFA:* 1923; *UEFA:* 1954. *National Colours:* Green shirts, green shorts, green socks with white tops.

League Championship wins (1922–2014)
Shamrock Rovers 17; Shelbourne 13; Bohemians 11; Dundalk 10; St Patrick's Athletic 8; Cork Athletic (formerly Cork United) 7; Waterford United 6; Drumcondra 5; Sligo Rovers 3; St James's Gate 2; Limerick 2; Athlone Town 2; Derry City 2; Cork City 2; Dolphin 1; Cork Hibernians 1; Cork Celtic 1; Drogheda United 1.

Cup wins (1922–2014)
Shamrock Rovers 24; Dundalk 9; Bohemians 7; Shelbourne 7; Drumcondra 5; Sligo Rovers 5; Derry City 5; St Patrick's Athletic 3; St James's Gate 2; Cork (incl. Fordsons 1) 2; Waterford United 2; Cork United 2; Cork Athletic 2; Limerick 2; Cork Hibernians 2; Bray Wanderers 2; Cork City 2; Longford Town 2; Alton United 1; Athlone Town 1; Transport 1; Finn Harps 1; Home Farm 1; UC Dublin 1; Galway United 1; Drogheda United 1; Sporting Fingal 1.

Final League Table 2014

	P	W	D	L	F	A	GD	Pts
Dundalk	33	22	8	3	73	24	49	74
Cork City	33	22	6	5	51	25	26	72
St Patrick's Athletic	33	19	8	6	66	37	29	65
Shamrock Rovers	33	18	8	7	43	26	17	62
Sligo Rovers	33	12	7	14	44	36	8	43
Limerick	33	12	5	16	37	45	-8	41
Bohemians	33	9	13	11	42	43	-1	40
Derry City	33	9	11	13	42	41	1	38
Drogheda United	33	10	6	17	40	63	-23	36
Bray Wanderers	33	5	11	17	28	61	-33	26
UCD*+	33	6	7	20	27	71	-44	25
Athlone Town*	33	4	10	19	35	56	-21	22

Top scorers (equal): Fagan (St Patrick's Athletic), Hoban (Dundalk) 20.
Cup Final: St Patrick's Athletic 2, Derry City 0.

ROMANIA

Federatia Romana de Fotbal, House of Football, Str. Sergent Serbanica Vasile 12, 22186 Bucuresti.
Founded: 1909. *FIFA:* 1923; *UEFA:* 1954. *National Colours:* All yellow.

International matches 2014–15
Greece (a) 1-0, Hungary (h) 1-1, Finland (a) 2-0, Northern Ireland (h) 2-0, Denmark (h) 2-0, Bulgaria (n) 0-0, Moldova (n) 2-1, Faroe Islands (h) 1-0, Northern Ireland (0) 0-0.

League Championship wins (1910–2015)
Steaua Bucharest 26; Dinamo Bucharest 18; Venus Bucharest 8; Chinezul Timisoara 6; UTA Arad 6; Petrolul

Ploiesti 4; Ripensia Timisoara 4; Universitatea Craiova 4; Rapid Bucharest 3; CFR Cluj 3; Olimpia Bucharest 2; Colentina Bucharest 2; Arges Pitesti 2; United Ploiesti 1; Romano-Americana Bucharest 1; Prahova Ploiesti 1; Coltea Brasov 1; Metalochimia Resita 1; Unirea Tricolor 1; CA Oradea 1; Unirea Urziceni 1; Otelul Galati 1.

Cup wins (1934–2015)
Steaua Bucharest 23; Rapid Bucharest 13; Dinamo Bucharest 13; Universitatea Craiova 6; Petrolul Ploiesti 3; CFR Cluj 3; Ripensia Timisoara 2; UTA Arad 2; Politehnica Timisoara 2; CFR Turnu Severin 1; Metalochimia Resita 1; Universitatea Cluj (includes Stiinta) 1; Progresul Oradea (formerly ICO) 1; Progresul Bucharest 1; Ariesul Turda 1; Chimia Ramnicu Vilcea 1; Jiul Petrosani 1; Gloria Bistrita 1; Astra Giurgiu 1.

Final League Table 2014–15
	P	W	D	L	F	A	GD	Pts
Steaua Bucharest	34	22	5	7	59	23	36	71
Targu Mures	34	20	8	6	51	25	26	68
Astra Giurgiu	34	15	12	7	53	27	26	57
CFR Cluj	34	16	9	9	46	29	17	57
Universitatea Craiova	34	14	11	9	40	34	6	53
Petrolul Ploiesti	34	14	10	10	42	30	12	52
Dinamo Bucharest	34	13	9	12	47	44	3	48
Botosani	34	12	11	11	40	43	–3	47
Pandurii Targu Jiu	34	12	9	13	47	42	5	45
CSMS Iasi	34	11	10	13	31	39	–8	43
Viitorul Constanta	34	11	10	13	44	54	–10	43
Concordia Chiajna	34	9	14	11	39	44	–5	41
Gaz Metan Medias*	34	8	15	11	29	34	–5	39
Brasov*	34	9	9	16	33	46	–13	36
Universitatea Cluj*	34	8	11	15	29	41	–12	35
Rapid Bucharest*	34	8	9	17	21	42	–21	33
Otelul Galati*	34	7	11	16	24	45	–21	32
Ceahlaul Piatra Neamt*	34	6	9	19	25	58	–33	27

Top scorer: Tade (CFR Cluj) 18.
Cup Final: Steaua Bucharest 3, Universitatea Cluj 0.

RUSSIA
Russian Football Union, Ulitsa Narodnaya 7, 115 172 Moscow.
Founded: 1912. *FIFA:* 1912; *UEFA:* 1954. *National Colours:* All brick red.

International matches 2014–15
Azerbaijan (h) 4-0, Liechtenstein (h) 4-0, Sweden (a) 1-1, Moldova (h) 1-1, Austria (a) 0-1, Hungary (a) 2-1, Montenegro (a) 3-0, Kazakhstan (h) 0-0, Belarus (h) 4-2, Austria (h) 0-1.

League Championship wins (1936–2015)
Spartak Moscow 21; Dynamo Kyiv 13; CSKA Moscow 12; Dynamo Moscow 11; Zenit St Petersburg (formerly Zenit Leningrad) 5; Torpedo Moscow 3; Dinamo Tbilisi 2; Dnepr Dnepropetrovsk 2; Lokomotiv Moscow 2; Rubin Kazan 2; Saria Voroshilovgrad 1; Ararat Erevan 1; Dynamo Minsk 1; Spartak Vladikavkaz (renamed Alania) 1.

Cup wins (1936–2015)
Spartak Moscow 13; CSKA Moscow 12; Dynamo Kyiv 9; Lokomotiv Moscow 8; Torpedo Moscow 7; Dynamo Moscow 7; Shakhtar Donetsk 4; Zenit St Petersburg (formerly Zenit Leningrad) 3; Dinamo Tbilisi 2; Ararat Erevan 2; Karpaty Lvov 1; SKA Rostov-on-Don 1; Metalist Kharkov 1; Dnepr 1; Terek Grozny 1; Rubin Kazan 1; Rostov 1.

Final League Table 2014–15
	P	W	D	L	F	A	GD	Pts
Zenit St Petersburg	30	20	7	3	58	17	41	67
CSKA Moscow	30	19	3	8	67	27	40	60
Krasnodar	30	17	9	4	52	27	25	60
Dinamo Moscow	30	14	8	8	53	36	17	50
Rubin Kazan	30	13	9	8	39	33	6	48
Spartak Moscow	30	12	8	10	42	42	0	44
Lokomotiv Moscow	30	11	10	9	31	25	6	43
Mordovia Saransk	30	11	5	14	22	43	–21	38
Terek Grozny	30	10	7	13	30	30	0	37
Kuban Krasnodar	30	8	12	10	32	36	–4	36
Amkar Perm	30	8	8	14	25	42	–17	32
Ufa	30	8	7	15	26	39	–13	31
Ural Sverdlovsk Oblast+	30	9	3	18	31	44	–13	30
Rostov+	30	7	8	15	27	51	–24	29
Torpedo Moscow*	30	7	8	15	13	28	45	–17	29
Arsenal Tula*	30	7	4	19	20	46	–26	25

Top scorer: Hulk (Zenit St Petersburg) 15.
Cup Final: Lokomotiv Moscow 3, Kuban Krasnodar 1.

SAN MARINO
Federazione Sammarinese Giuoco Calcio, Strada di Montecchio 17, 47890 San Marino.
Founded: 1931. *FIFA:* 1988; *UEFA:* 1988. *National Colours:* Cobalt blue shirts with white trim, white shorts, cobalt blue socks.

International matches 2014–15
Lithuania (h) 0-2, England (a) 0-5, Switzerland (h) 0-4, Estonia (h) 0-0, Slovenia (a) 0-6, Liechtenstein (a) 0-1, Estonia (a) 0-2.

League Championship wins (1986–2015)
Tre Fiori 7; Domagnano 4; Folgore/Falciano 4; Faetano 3; La Fiorita 3; Murata 3;Tre Penne 2; Montevito 1; Libertas 1; Cosmos 1; Pennarossa 1.

Cup wins (1937–2015)
Libertas 11; Domagnano 8; Tre Fiori 6; Juvenes 5; Tre Penne 5; Cosmos 4; La Fiorita 3; Faetano 3; Murata 3; Dogana 2; Pennarossa 2; Juvenes/Dogana 2; Folgore/Falciano 1.

Qualifying League Table 2014–15
Group A
	P	W	D	L	F	A	GD	Pts
Juvenes/Dogana	20	12	4	4	35	15	20	40
Tre Fiori	20	12	2	6	36	17	19	38
Faetano	20	9	5	6	26	21	5	32
Cailungo	20	8	4	8	28	29	–1	28
Virtus	20	8	4	8	27	28	–1	28
Murata	20	5	5	10	26	34	–8	20
Cosmos	20	0	5	15	13	48	–35	5

Group B
	P	W	D	L	F	A	GD	Pts
Folgore/Faetano	21	13	5	3	41	19	22	44
La Fiorita	21	11	5	5	37	25	12	38
Domagnano	21	11	3	7	28	23	5	36
Libertas	21	8	8	5	23	16	7	32
Fiorentino	21	9	5	7	24	22	2	32
Pennarossa	21	9	3	9	33	26	7	30
Tre Penne	21	5	3	13	24	43	–19	18
San Giovanni	21	2	3	16	21	56	–35	9

Play-offs
(Double-elimination format; Group winners receive byes in first two rounds.)
Rnd 1: Tre Fiori 1, Domagnano 0; La Fiorita 3, Faetano 1
Rnd 2: Domagnano 0, Faetano 2; Tre Fiori 0, La Fiorita 1
Rnd 3: Folgore 2, Juvenes/Dogana 1; Faetano 3, Tre Fiore 5 (aet)
Rnd 4: Folgore 2, La Fiorita 1 (aet); Tre Fiore 0, Juvenes/Dogana 3
Rnd 5: Juvenes/Dogana 0, La Fiorita 0 (aet; 4-2p)
Final: Folgore 3, Juvenes/Dogana 1
Top scorer: Frigulietti (San Giovanni) 16.
Cup Final: Folgore/Falciano 5, Murata 0.

SCOTLAND
Scottish Football Association, Hampden Park, Glasgow G42 9AY.
Founded: 1873. *FIFA:* 1910; *UEFA:* 1954. *National Colours:* Dark blue shirts, dark blue shorts, red socks.

SERBIA
Football Association of Serbia, Terazije 35, PO Box 263, 11000 Beograd.
Founded: 1919. *FIFA:* 1921; *UEFA:* 1954. *National Colours:* Red shirts, blue shorts, white socks.

International matches 2014–15
France (h) 1-1, Armenia (a) 1-1, Albania (h) 3-0, Denmark (h) 1-3, Greece (a) 2-0, Portugal (a) 1-2, Azerbaijan (a) 4-1, Denmark (a) 0-2.

League Championship wins (1923–2015)
Partizan Belgrade 26; Red Star Belgrade 26; Hajduk Split 9; Gradjanski Zagreb 5; BSK Belgrade (renamed OFK) 5; Dinamo Zagreb 4; Jugoslavija Belgrade 2; Concordia Zagreb 2; FC Sarajevo 2; Vojvodina Novi Sad 2; HASK Zagreb 1; Zeljeznicar 1; Obilic 1.

Cup wins (1947–2015)
Red Star Belgrade 24; Partizan Belgrade 12; Hajduk Split 9; Dinamo Zagreb 8; OFK Belgrade (incl. BSK 3) 5; Rijeka 2; Velez Mostar 2; Vardar Skopje 1; Borac Banjaluka 1; Sartid 1; Zeleznik 1; Jagodina 1; Vojvodina 1; Cukaricki 1.

Final League Table 2014–15

	P	W	D	L	F	A	GD	Pts
Partizan Belgrade	30	21	8	1	67	22	45	71
Red Star Belgrade	30	19	7	4	46	20	26	64
Cukaricki	30	16	9	5	48	24	24	57
Vojvodina	30	16	4	10	44	36	8	52
Novi Pazar	30	13	8	9	39	28	11	47
Rad	30	13	4	13	33	38	–5	43
Mladost Lucani	30	11	7	12	41	47	–6	40
OFK Belgrade	30	10	9	11	35	43	–8	39
Radnicki Nis	30	9	10	11	25	31	–6	37
Jagodina	30	10	5	15	38	45	–7	35
Spartak Subotica	30	9	7	14	23	33	–10	34
Vozdovac	30	9	7	14	24	37	–13	34
Borac Cacak	30	8	9	13	29	35	–6	33
Napredak Krusevac*+	30	8	7	15	23	34	–11	31
Donji Srem*	30	6	8	16	25	42	–17	26
Radnicki 1923*	30	4	7	19	17	42	–25	19

Top scorer: Eze (Mladost Lucani) 15.
Cup Final: Cukaricki 1, Partizan Belgrade 0.

SLOVAKIA

Slovensky Futbalovy Zvaz, Trnavska cesta 100, 821 01 Bratislava.
Founded: 1938. *FIFA:* 1994; *UEFA:* 1993. *National Colours:* White shirts with blue trim, white shorts, white socks.

International matches 2014–15
Malta (h) 1-0, Ukraine (a) 1-0, Spain (h) 2-1, Belarus (a) 3-1, FYR Macedonia (a) 2-0, Finland (h) 2-1, Luxembourg (h) 3-0, Czech Republic (h) 1-0, FYR Macedonia (h) 2-1.

League Championship wins (1939–44; 1994–2015)
Slovan Bratislava 12; Zilina 6; Kosice 2; Inter Bratislava 2; Artmedia Petrzalka 2; Bystrica 1; OAP Bratislava 1; Ruzomberok 1; Trencin 1.
See also Czech Republic section for Slovak club honours in Czechoslovak era 1925–93.

Cup wins (1994–2015)
Slovan Bratislava 6; Inter Bratislava 3; Artmedia Petrzalka 2; Kosice 2; Humenne 1; Spartak Trnava 1; Koba Senec 1; Matador Puchov 1; Bystrica 1; Ruzomberok 1; ViOn Zlate Moravce 1; Zilina 1; Trencin 1.

Final League Table 2014–15

	P	W	D	L	F	A	GD	Pts
Trencin	33	23	5	5	67	28	39	74
Zilina	33	20	9	4	68	25	43	69
Slovan Bratislava	33	18	3	12	49	42	7	57
Spartak Trnava	33	16	8	9	53	31	22	56
Senica	33	12	11	10	52	50	2	47
Kosice	33	11	8	14	43	48	–5	41
Ruzomberok	33	10	10	13	41	45	–4	40
DAC Dunajska Streda	33	9	12	12	32	44	–12	39
Spartak Myjava	33	11	6	16	38	53	–15	39
ViOn Zlate Moravce	33	8	8	17	27	54	–27	32
Sport Podbrezova	33	7	8	18	32	54	–22	29
Dukla Banska Bystrica*	33	4	10	19	29	57	–28	22

Top scorers (equal): Jelic (Zilina), Kalabiska (Senica) 19.
Cup Final: Trencin 2, Senica 2.
aet; Trencin won 3-2 on penalties.

SLOVENIA

Nogometna Zveza Slovenije, Brnciceva 41g, PP 3986, 1001 Ljubljana.
Founded: 1920. *FIFA:* 1992; *UEFA:* 1992. *National Colours:* White shirts with blue trim, white shorts, white socks.

International matches 2014–15
Estonia (a) 0-1, Switzerland (h) 1-0, Lithuania (a) 2-0, England (a) 1-3, Colombia (h) 0-1, San Marino (h) 6-0, Qatar (a) 0-1, England (h) 2-3.

League Championship wins (1992–2015)
Maribor 13; Olimpija Ljubljana (pre-2005) 4; Gorica 4; Domzale 2; Koper 1.

Cup wins (1992–2015)
Maribor 8; Olimpija Ljubljana (pre-2005) 4; Gorica 3; Koper 3; Interblock 2; Mura (pre-2004) 1; Rudar Velenje 1; Celje 1; Domzale 1.

Final League Table 2014–15

	P	W	D	L	F	A	GD	Pts
Maribor	36	24	7	5	74	32	42	79
Celje	36	20	10	6	58	31	27	70
Domzale	36	21	5	10	52	22	30	68
Olimpija Ljubljana	36	17	10	9	55	32	23	61
Zavrc	36	15	4	17	38	52	–14	49
Rudar Velenje	36	12	10	14	44	43	1	46
Krka	36	11	7	18	38	54	–16	40
Koper	36	12	4	20	35	58	–23	40
Gorica+	36	10	7	19	40	46	–6	37
Radomlje*	36	4	4	28	21	85	–64	16

Top scorer: Tavares (Maribor) 17.
Cup Final: Koper 2, Celje 0.

SPAIN

Real Federacion Espanola de Futbol, Calle Ramon y Cajal s/n, Apartado postale 385, 28230 Las Rozas, Madrid.
Founded: 1913. *FIFA:* 1913; *UEFA:* 1954. *National Colours:* All red with yellow trim.

International matches 2014–15
France (a) 0-1, FYR Macedonia (h) 5-1, Slovakia (a) 1-2, Luxembourg (a) 4-0, Belarus (h) 3-0, Germany (h) 0-1, Ukraine (h) 1-0, Netherlands (a) 0-2, Costa Rica (h) 2-1, Belarus (a) 1-0.

League Championship wins (1929–36; 1940–2015)
Real Madrid 32; Barcelona 23; Atletico Madrid 10; Athletic Bilbao 8; Valencia 6; Real Sociedad 2; Real Betis 1; Sevilla 1; Deportivo La Coruna 1.

Cup wins (1903–2015)
Barcelona 27; Athletic Bilbao (includesVizcaya Bilbao 1) 23; Real Madrid 19; Atletico Madrid 10; Valencia 7; Real Zaragoza 6; Sevilla 5; Espanyol 4; Real Union de Irun 3; Real Betis 2; Real Sociedad (includes Ciclista) 2; Deportivo La Coruna 2; Arenas 1; Racing de Irun 1; Mallorca 1.

Final League Table 2014–15

	P	W	D	L	F	A	GD	Pts
Barcelona	38	30	4	4	110	21	89	94
Real Madrid	38	30	2	6	118	38	80	92
Atletico Madrid	38	23	9	6	67	29	38	78
Valencia	38	22	11	5	70	32	38	77
Sevilla	38	23	7	8	71	45	26	76
Villarreal	38	16	12	10	48	37	11	60
Athletic Bilbao	38	15	10	13	42	41	1	55
Celta Vigo	38	13	12	13	47	44	3	51
Malaga	38	14	8	16	42	48	–6	50
Espanyol	38	13	10	15	47	51	–4	49
Rayo Vallecano	38	15	4	19	46	68	–22	49
Real Sociedad	38	11	13	14	44	51	–7	46
Elche	38	11	8	19	35	62	–27	41
Levante	38	9	10	19	34	67	–33	37
Getafe	38	10	7	21	33	64	–31	37
Deportivo La Coruna	38	7	14	17	35	60	–25	35
Granada	38	7	14	17	29	64	–35	35
Eibar	38	9	8	21	34	55	–21	35
UD Almeria* (–3)	38	8	8	22	35	64	–29	29
Cordoba*	38	3	11	24	22	68	–46	20

Top scorer: Ronaldo (Real Madrid) 48.
Cup Final: Barcelona 3, Athletic Bilbao 1.

SWEDEN

Svenska Fotbollfoerbundet, Evenemangsgatan 31, PO Box 1216, SE-171 23 Solna.
Founded: 1904. *FIFA:* 1904; *UEFA:* 1954. *National Colours:* Yellow shirts with blue trim, blue shorts, yellow socks.

International matches 2014–15
Estonia (h) 2-0, Austria (a) 1-1, Russia (h) 1-1, Liechtenstein (h) 2-0, Montenegro (a) 1-1, France (a) 0-1, Ivory Coast (n) 2-0, Finland (n) 1-0, Moldova (a) 2-0, Iran (h) 3-1, Norway (a) 0-0, Montenegro (h) 3-1.

League Championship wins (1896–2014)
IFK Gothenburg 18; Malmo 18; Orgryte 12; IFK Norrkoping 12; AIK Stockholm 11; Djurgaarden 11; IF Elfsborg 6; Helsingborg 5; GAIS Gothenburg 4; Oster Vaxjo 4; Halmstad 4; Atvidaberg 2; IF Gothenburg 1; IFK Eskilstuna 1; Fassbergs 1; IF Gavic Brynas 1; IK Sleipner 1; Hammarby 1; Kalmar 1.

Cup wins (1941–2015)
Malmo 14; AIK Stockholm 8; IFK Gothenburg 7; IFK Norrkoping 6; Helsingborg 5; Djurgaarden 4; Kalmar 3; IF Elfsborg 3; Atvidaberg 2; GAIS Gothenburg 1; IF Raa 1;

Landskrona 1; Oster Vaxjo 1; Degerfors 1; Halmstad 1; Orgryte 1.

Final League Table 2014

	P	W	D	L	F	A	GD	Pts
Malmo	30	18	8	4	59	31	28	62
IFK Gothenburg	30	15	11	4	58	34	24	56
AIK Solna	30	15	7	8	59	42	17	52
Elfsborg	30	15	7	8	40	31	9	52
Hacken	30	13	7	10	58	45	13	46
Orebro	30	13	7	10	54	44	10	46
Djurgarden	30	11	10	9	47	33	14	43
Atvidaberg	30	12	7	11	39	46	–7	43
Helsingborg	30	10	9	11	41	44	–3	39
Halmstad	30	11	6	13	44	50	–6	39
Kalmar	30	10	9	11	36	45	–9	39
Norrkoping	30	9	9	12	39	50	–11	36
Falkenberg	30	9	6	15	37	49	–12	33
Gefle+	30	8	8	14	34	42	–8	32
Mjallby*	30	8	5	17	29	47	–18	29
Brommapojkarna*	30	2	6	22	28	69	–41	12

Top scorer: Vibe (IFK Gothenburg) 23.
Cup Final: IFK Gothenburg 2, Orebro 1.

SWITZERLAND

Schweizerisher Fussballverband, Worbstrasse 48, Postfach 3000, Bern 15.
Founded: 1895. *FIFA:* 1904; *UEFA:* 1954. *National Colours:* Red shirts, white shorts, red socks.

International matches 2014–15
England (h) 0-2, Slovenia (a) 0-1, San Marino (a) 4-0, Lithuania (h) 4-0, Poland (a) 2-2, Estonia (h) 3-0, USA (h) 1-1, Liechtenstein (h) 3-0, Lithuania (a) 2-1.

League Championship wins (1897–2015)
Grasshoppers 27; FC Basel 18; Servette 17; FC Zurich 12; Young Boys 11; Lausanne-Sport 7; Winterthur 3; Aarau 3; Lugano 3; La Chaux-de-Fonds 3; St Gallen 2; Neuchatel Xamax 2; Sion 2; Anglo-American Club 1; Brühl 1; Cantonal-Neuchatel 1; Etoile La Chaux-de-Fonds 1; Biel-Bienne 1; Bellinzona 1; Luzern 1.

Cup wins (1926–2015)
Grasshoppers 19; Sion 13; FC Basel 11; Lausanne-Sport 9; FC Zurich 8; Servette 7; Young Boys 6; La Chaux-de-Fonds 6; Lugano 3; Luzern 2; FC Grenchen 1; St Gallen 1; Urania Geneva 1; Young Fellows Zurich 1; Aarau 1; Wil 1.

Final League Table 2014–15

	P	W	D	L	F	A	GD	Pts
FC Basel	36	24	6	6	84	41	43	78
Young Boys	36	19	9	8	64	45	19	66
Zurich	36	15	8	13	55	48	7	53
Thun	36	13	13	10	47	45	2	52
Luzern	36	12	11	13	54	46	8	47
St Gallen	36	13	8	15	57	65	–8	47
Sion	36	12	9	15	47	48	–1	45
Grasshoppers	36	11	10	15	50	56	–6	43
Vaduz	36	7	10	19	28	59	–31	31
Aarau*	36	6	12	18	31	64	–33	30

Top scorer: Gashi (FC Basel) 22.
Cup Final: Sion 3, FC Basel 0.

TURKEY

Turkiye Futbol Federasyonu, Hasan Dogan Milli Takimlar, Kamp ve Egitim Tesisleri, Riva, Beykoz, Istanbul.
Founded: 1923. *FIFA:* 1923; *UEFA:* 1962. *National Colours:* All red.

International matches 2014–15
Denmark (a) 2-1, Iceland (a) 0-3, Czech Republic (h) 1-2, Latvia (a) 1-1, Brazil (a) 0-4, Kazakhstan (h) 3-1, Netherlands (a) 1-1, Luxembourg (a) 2-1, Bulgaria (h) 4-0, Kazakhstan (a) 1-0.

League Championship wins (1959–2015)
Galatasaray 20; Fenerbahce 19; Besiktas 11; Trabzonspor 6; Bursaspor 1.

Cup wins (1963–2015)
Galatasaray 16; Besiktas 9; Trabzonspor 8; Fenerbahce 6; Altay Izmir 2; Goztepe Izmir 2; Ankaragucu 2; Genclerbirligi 2; Kocaelispor 2; Eskisehirspor 1; Bursaspor 1; Sakaryaspor 1; Kayseri 1.

Final League Table 2014–15

	P	W	D	L	F	A	GD	Pts
Galatasaray	34	24	5	5	60	35	25	77
Fenerbahce	34	22	8	4	60	29	31	74
Besiktas	34	21	6	7	55	32	23	69
Istanbul Basaksehir	34	15	14	5	49	30	19	59
Trabzonspor	34	15	12	7	58	48	10	57
Bursaspor	34	16	9	9	69	44	25	57
Mersin Idman Yurdu	34	13	8	13	54	48	6	47
Konyaspor	34	12	10	12	30	39	–9	46
Genclerbirligi	34	10	10	14	46	44	2	40
Gaziantepspor	34	11	7	16	31	48	–17	40
Eskisehirspor	34	9	12	13	45	52	–7	39
Akhisar Belediyespor	34	9	11	14	41	51	–10	38
Kasimpasa	34	9	10	15	56	73	–17	37
Rizespor	34	9	9	16	41	55	–14	36
Sivasspor	34	9	9	16	43	50	–7	36
Kardemir Karabukspor*	34	7	7	20	44	64	–20	28
Kayseri Erciyesspor*	34	5	12	17	43	62	–19	27
Balikesirspor*	34	6	9	19	48	69	–21	27

Top scorer: Fernandao (Bursaspor) 22.
Cup Final: Galatasaray 3, Bursaspor 2.

UKRAINE

Football Federation of Ukraine, Provulok Laboratornyi 7-A, PO Box 55, 01133 Kyiv.
Founded: 1991. *FIFA:* 1992; *UEFA:* 1992. *National Colours:* All yellow with blue trim.

International matches 2014–15
Moldova (h) 1-0, Slovakia (h) 0-1, Belarus (a) 2-0, FYR Macedonia (h) 1-0, Luxembourg (a) 3-0, Lithuania (h) 0-0, Spain (a) 0-1, Latvia (h) 1-1, Georgia (n) 2-1, Luxembourg (h) 3-0.

League Championship wins (1992–2015)
Dynamo Kyiv 14; Shakhtar Donetsk 9; Tavriya Simferopol 1.

Cup wins (1992–2015)
Dynamo Kyiv 11; Shakhtar Donetsk 9; Chornomorets Odessa 2; Vorskla 1; Tavriya Simferopol 1.

Final League Table 2014–15

	P	W	D	L	F	A	GD	Pts
Dynamo Kyiv	26	20	6	0	65	12	53	66
Shakhtar Donetsk	26	17	5	4	71	21	50	56
Dnipro Dnipropetrovsk	26	16	6	4	47	17	30	54
Zorya Luhansk	26	13	6	7	40	31	9	45
Vorskla Poltava	26	11	9	6	35	22	13	42
Metalist Kharkiv	25	8	11	6	34	32	2	35
Metalurh Zaporizhya	26	6	8	12	20	40	–20	26
Olimpik Donetsk	26	7	5	14	24	64	–40	26
Volyn Lutsk (–9)	26	9	7	10	38	44	–6	25
Metalurh Donetsk (–6)	26	6	10	10	27	38	–11	22
Chornomorets Odessa	25	3	11	11	15	31	–16	20
Hoverla Uzhhorod	26	3	10	13	22	47	–25	19
Karpaty Lviv (–9)	26	5	9	12	22	31	–9	15
Illychivets Mariupil*	26	3	5	18	25	55	–30	14

Top scorers (equal): Bicfalvi (Volyn), Alex Teixera (Shakhtar Donetsk) 17.
Cup Final: Dynamo Kyiv 0, Shakhtar Donetsk 0.
aet; Dynamo Kyiv won 5-4 on penalties.

WALES

Football Association of Wales, 11/12 Neptune Court, Vanguard Way, Cardiff CF24 5PJ.
Founded: 1876. *FIFA:* 1910; *UEFA:* 1954. *National Colours:* All red with green trim.

SOUTH AMERICA (CONMEBOL)

ARGENTINA

Asociacion del Futbol Argentina, Viamonte 1366/76, Buenos Aires 1053.
Founded: 1893. *FIFA:* 1912; *CONMEBOL:* 1916. *National Colours:* Light blue and white vertical striped shirts, white shorts, white socks.
International matches 2014–15
Germany (a) 4-2, Brazil (n) 0-2, Hong Kong (a) 7-0, Croatia (n) 2-1, Portugal (n) 0-1, El Salvador (n) 2-0, Ecuador (n) 2-1, Bolivia (h) 5-0, Paraguay (n) 2-2, Uruguay (n) 1-0, Jamaica (n) 1-0, Colombia (n) 1-0 (5-4p), Paraguay (n) 6-1, Chile (a) 0-0 (1-4p).

BOLIVIA

Federacion Boliviana de Futbol, Avenida Libertador Bolivar 1168, Casilla 484, Cochabamba.
Founded: 1925. *FIFA:* 1926; *CONMEBOL:* 1926.
National Colours: Green shirts, white shorts, white socks.
International matches 2014–15
Ecuador (n) 0-4, Mexico (n) 0-1, Chile (a) 2-2, Venezuela (h) 3-2, Argentina (a) 0-5, Mexico (n) 0-0, Ecuador (n) 3-2, Chile (n) 0-5, Peru (n) 1-3.

BRAZIL

Confederacao Brasileira de Futebol, Avenida Luis Carlos Prestes 130, Barra da Tijuca, Rio de Janeiro 22775-055.
Founded: 1914. *FIFA:* 1923; *CONMEBOL:* 1916.
National Colours: Yellow shirts with green collar and cuffs, blue shorts, white socks.
International matches 2014–15
Colombia (n) 1-0, Ecuador (n) 1-0, Argentina (n) 2-0, Japan (n) 4-0, Turkey (a) 4-0, Austria (a) 2-1, France (a) 3-1, Chile (n) 1-0, Mexico (h) 2-0, Honduras (h) 1-0, Peru (n) 2-1, Colombia (n) 0-1, Venezuela (n) 2-1, Paraguay (n) 1-1 (3-4p).

CHILE

Federacion de Futbol de Chile, Avenida Quilin 5635, Comuna Penalolen, Casilla 3733, Santiago de Chile.
Founded: 1895. *FIFA:* 1913; *CONMEBOL:* 1916.
National Colours: Red shirts with blue collars, blue shorts, white socks.
International matches 2014–15
Mexico (n) 0-0, Haiti (n) 1-0, Peru (h) 3-0, Bolivia (h) 2-2, Venezuela (h) 5-0, Uruguay (h) 1-2, USA (h) 3-2, Iran (n) 0-2, Brazil (n) 0-1, El Salvador (h) 1-0, Ecuador (h) 2-0, Mexico (n) 3-3, Bolivia (h) 5-0, Uruguay (h) 1-0, Peru (h) 2-1, Argentina (h) 0-0 (4-1p).

COLOMBIA

Federacion Colombiana de Futbol, Avenida 32 No. 16–22, Bogota.
Founded: 1924. *FIFA:* 1936; *CONMEBOL:* 1936.
National Colours: Yellow shirts with blue trim, white shorts, white socks.
International matches 2014–15
Brazil (n) 0-1, El Salvador (n) 3-0, Canada (n) 1-0, USA (n) 2-1, Slovenia (a) 1-0, Bahrain (a) 6-0, Kuwait (n) 3-1, Costa Rica (n) 1-0, Venezuela (n) 0-1, Brazil (n) 1-0, Peru (n) 0-0, Argentina (n) 0-0 (4-5p).

ECUADOR

Federacion Ecuatoriana del Futbol, Avenida Las Aguas y Calle Alianza, PO Box 09-01-7447, Guayaquil 593.
Founded: 1925. *FIFA:* 1927; *CONMEBOL:* 1927.
National Colours: Yellow shirts, blue shorts, red socks.
International matches 2014–15
Bolivia (h) 4-0, Brazil (n) 0-1, USA (a) 1-1, El Salvador (n) 5-1, Mexico (n) 0-1, Argentina (n) 1-2, Panama (a) 1-1, Panama (h) 4-0, Chile (a) 0-2, Bolivia (n) 2-3, Mexico (n) 2-1.

PARAGUAY

Asociacion Paraguaya de Futbol, Calle Mayor Martinez 1393, Asuncion.
Founded: 1906. *FIFA:* 1925; *CONMEBOL:* 1921.
National Colours: Red and white stroped shirts, blue shorts, blue socks.
International matches 2014–15
UAE (n) 0-0, Korea Republic (a) 0-2, China PR (a) 1-2, Peru (h) 2-1, Peru (a) 1-2, Costa Rica (a) 0-0, Mexico (n) 0-1, Honduras (h) 2-2, Argentina (n) 2-2, Jamaica (n) 1-0, Uruguay (n) 1-1, Brazil (n) 1-1 (4-3p), Argentina (n) 1-6, Peru (n) 0-2.

PERU

Federacion Peruana de Futbol, Avenida Aviacion 2085, San Luis, Lima 30.
Founded: 1922. *FIFA:* 1924; *CONMEBOL:* 1925.
National Colours: White shirts with red sash, white shorts, white socks.
International matches 2014–15
Panama (h) 3-0, Iraq (n) 2-0, Qatar (a) 2-0, Chile (a) 0-3, Guatemala (h) 1-0, Paraguay (a) 1-2, Paraguay (h) 2-1, Venezuela (n) 1-0, Mexico (h) 1-1, Brazil (n) 1-2, Venezuela (n) 1-0, Colombia (n) 0-0, Bolivia (n) 3-1, Chile (a) 1-2, Paraguay (n) 2-0.

URUGUAY

Asociacion Uruguaya de Futbol, Guayabo 1531, Montevideo 11200.
Founded: 1900. *FIFA:* 1923; *CONMEBOL:* 1916.

National Colours: Sky blue shirts, black shorts, black socks with sky blue tops.
International matches 2014–15
Japan (a) 2-0, Korea Republic (a) 1-0, Saudi Arabia (a) 1-1, Oman (a) 3-0, Costa Rica (h) 3-3 (6-7p), Chile (a) 2-1, Morocco (a) 1-0, Guatemala (h) 5-1, Jamaica (n) 1-0, Argentina (n) 0-1, Paraguay (n) 1-1, Chile (a) 0-1.

VENEZUELA

Federacion Venezolana de Futbol, Avenida Santos Erminy 1ra Calle las Delicias, Torre Mega II, P.H.B. Sabana Grande, 1050 Caracas.
Founded: 1926. *FIFA:* 1952; *CONMEBOL:* 1952.
National Colours: All burgundy.
International matches 2014–15
Korea Republic (a) 1-3, Japan (a) 0-3 (after 2-2 draw; match awarded to Japan), Chile (a) 0-5, Bolivia (h) 2-3, Honduras (a) 3-2, Honduras (h) 2-1, Jamaica (a) 1-2, Peru (n) 1-0, Colombia (n) 1-0, Peru (n) 0-1, Brazil (n) 1-2.

ASIA (AFC)

AFGHANISTAN

Afghanistan Football Federation, PO Box 128, Kabul.
Founded: 1933. *FIFA:* 1948; *AFC:* 1954. *National Colours:* All red.
International matches 2014–15
Pakistan (h) 1-2, Laos (a) 2-0, Bangladesh (a) 1-1, Syria (n) 0-6, Cambodia (a) 1-0.

AUSTRALIA

Football Federation Australia Ltd, Locked Bag A4071, Sydney South, NSW 1235.
Founded: 1961. *FIFA:* 1963; *AFC:* 2006. *National Colours:* Gold shirts, green shorts, white socks.
International matches 2014–15
Belgium (a) 0-2, Saudi Arabia (n) 3-2, UAE (a) 0-0, Qatar (a) 0-1, Japan (a) 1-2, Kuwait (h) 4-1, Oman (h) 4-0, Korea Republic (h) 0-1, China PR (h) 2-0, UAE (n) 2-0, Korea Republic (a) 2-1, Germany (a) 2-2, FYR Macedonia (a) 0-0, Kyrgyzstan (a) 2-1.

BAHRAIN

Bahrain Football Association, PO Box 5464, Building 315, Road 2407, Block 934, East Riffa.
Founded: 1957. *FIFA:* 1968; *AFC:* 1969. *National Colours:* All red.
International matches 2014–15
Kuwait (n) 1-0, Uzbekistan (n) 0-0, Iraq (h) 0-0, Korea DPR (h) 2-2, Singapore (h) 2-0, Yemen (n) 0-0, Saudi Arabia (a) 0-3, Qatar (n) 0-0, Saudi Arabia (n) 4-1, Jordan (n) 1-0, Iran (n) 0-2, UAE (n) 1-2, Qatar (n) 2-1, Colombia (h) 0-6, Philippines (h) 2-1, Oman (h) 0-0, Thailand (a) 1-1, Philippines (a) 1-2.

BANGLADESH

Bangladesh Football Federation, BFF House, Motijheel Commercial Area, Dhaka 1000.
Founded: 1972. *FIFA:* 1976; *AFC:* 1974. *National Colours:* Green shirts, white shorts, green socks.
International matches 2014–15
Sri Lanka (h) 1-1, Sri Lanka (h) 1-0, Sri Lanka (h) 1-0, Singapore (h) 1-2, Afghanistan (h) 1-1, Kyrgyzstan (h) 1-3, Tajikistan (h) 1-1.

BHUTAN

Bhutan Football Federation, PO Box 365, Changiiji, Thimphu 11001.
Founded: 1983. *FIFA:* 2000; *AFC:* 2000. *National Colours:* Yellow and orange shirts, white shorts, orange socks.
International matches 2014–15
Sri Lanka (a) 1-0, Sri Lanka (h) 2-1, Sri Lanka (h) 1-0, Hong Kong (a) 0-7, China PR (h) 0-6.

BRUNEI

National Football Association of Brunei Darussalam, NFABD House, Jalan Pusat Persidangan, Bandar Seri Begawan BB4313.
Founded: 1959. *FIFA:* 1972; *AFC:* 1969. *National Colours:* Yellow and black shirts, white shorts, yellow socks.
International matches 2014–15
Timor-Leste (n) 2-4, Laos (a) 2-4, Myanmar (n) 1-3, Cambodia (n) 0-1, Chinese Taipei (a) 1-0, Chinese Taipei (h) 0-2, Singapore (a) 1-5.

CAMBODIA

Football Federation of Cambodia, National Football Centre, Road Kabsrov Sangkat Samrongkrom, Khan Dangkor, Phnom Penh 2327 PPT3.
Founded: 1933. *FIFA:* 1954; *AFC:* 1954. *National Colours:* Red and blue shirts, blue shorts, red socks.
International matches 2014–15
Malaysia (h) 1-4, Indonesia (a) 0-1, Chinese Taipei (a) 2-0, Laos (a) 2-3, Timor-Leste (n) 3-2, Myanmar (n) 0-1, Brunei (n) 1-0, Philippines (a) 0-3, Singapore (a) 2-4, Macao (h) 3-0, Macao (a) 1-1, Laos (h) 1-1, Myanmar (n) 0-0, Singapore (h) 0-4, Afghanistan (h) 0-1.

CHINA PR

Football Association of the People's Republic of China, Building A, Dongjiudasha Mansion, Xizhaosi Street, Dongcheng, Beijing 100061.
Founded: 1924. *FIFA:* 1931, rejoined 1980; *AFC:* 1974. *National Colours:* All red.
International matches 2014–15
Kuwait (h) 3-1, Jordan (h) 1-1, Thailand (h) 3-0, Paraguay (h) 2-1, New Zealand (h) 1-1, Honduras (h) 0-0, Kyrgyzstan (h) 4-0, Kyrgyzstan (h) 2-0, Palestine (h) 0-0, Oman (n) 4-1, Saudi Arabia (n) 1-0, Uzbekistan (n) 2-1, Korea DPR (n) 2-1, Australia (a) 0-2, Haiti (h) 2-2, Tunisia (h) 1-1, Bhutan (a) 6-0.

CHINESE TAIPEI

Chinese Taipei Football Association, Room 210, 2F, 55 Chang Chi Street, Tatung, Taipei 10363.
Founded: 1936. *FIFA:* 1954; *AFC:* 1954. *National Colours:* All blue with white trim.
International matches 2014–15
Philippines (a) 1-5, Palestine (n) 7-3, Cambodia (a) 0-2, Guam (h) 1-2, Hong Kong (h) 0-1, Korea DPR (n) 0-0, Brunei (h) 0-1, Brunei (a) 2-0, Thailand (h) 0-2.

GUAM

Guam Football Association, PO Box 20008, Barrigada, Guam 96921.
Founded: 1975. *FIFA:* 1996; *AFC:* 1996. *National Colours:* Blue shirts with white sleeves, blue shorts, blue socks.
International matches 2014–15
Macau (a) 2-0, Mongolia (h) 2-0, Northern Mariana Islands† (h) 5-0, Chinese Taipei (a) 2-1, Korea DPR (n) 1-5, Hong Kong (n) 0-0, Hong Kong (a) 0-1, Singapore (a) 2-2, Turkmenistan (h) 1-0, India (h) 2-1.

HONG KONG

Hong Kong Football Association Ltd, 55 Fat Kwong Street, Ho Man Tin, Kowloon, Hong Kong.
Founded: 1914. *FIFA:* 1954; *AFC:* 1954. *National Colours:* All red with white trim.
International matches 2014–15
Vietnam (a) 1-3, Singapore (a) 0-0, Singapore (h) 2-1, Argentina (h) 0-7, Korea DPR (n) 1-2, Chinese Taipei (a) 1-0, Guam (n) 0-0, Guam (h) 1-0, Malaysia (a) 0-0, Bhutan (h) 7-0, Maldives (h) 2-0.

INDIA

All India Football Federation, Football House, Sector 19, Phase 1 Dwarka, New Delhi 110075.
Founded: 1937. *FIFA:* 1948; *AFC:* 1954. *National Colours:* Sky blue and navy shirts, navy shorts, sky blue and navy socks.
International matches 2014–15
Palestine (h) 2-3, Nepal (h) 2-0, Nepal (a) 0-0, Oman (h) 1-2, Guam (a) 1-2.

INDONESIA

Football Association of Indonesia, Gelora Bung Karno Pintu X-XI, PO Box 2305, Senayan, Jakarta 10023.
Founded: 1930. *FIFA:* 1952; *AFC:* 1954. *National Colours:* Red shirts with green trim, red shorts, red socks.
International matches 2014–15
Qatar (a) 2-2, Yemen (h) 0-0, Malaysia (h) 2-0, Cambodia (h) 1-0, Syria (h) 0-2, Vietnam (a) 2-2, Philippines (n) 0-4, Laos (n) 5-1, Cameroon (h) 0-1, Myanmar (h) 2-1.

IRAN

Football Federation IR Iran, No. 4 Third St., Seoul Avenue, Tehran 19958-73591.
Founded: 1920. *FIFA:* 1948; *AFC:* 1954. *National Colours:* All white.
International matches 2014–15
Korea Republic (h) 1-0, Iraq (n) 1-0, Bahrain (n) 2-0, Qatar (n) 1-0, UAE (n) 1-0, Iraq (n) 3-3 (7-6p), Chile (n) 2-0, Sweden (a) 1-3, Uzbekistan (a) 1-0, Turkmenistan (a) 1-1.

IRAQ

Iraq Football Association, Al-Shaab Stadium, PO Box 484, Baghdad.
Founded: 1948. *FIFA:* 1950; *AFC:* 1970. *National Colours:* All white.
International matches 2014–15
Peru (n) 0-2, Yemen (n) 1-1, Bahrain (a) 0-0, Kuwait (n) 0-1, Oman (n) 1-1, UAE (n) 0-2, Kuwait (n) 1-1, Uzbekistan (n) 1-0, Uzbekistan (n) 0-0, Iran (n) 0-1, Jordan (n) 1-0, Japan (n) 0-1, Palestine (n) 2-0, Iran (n) 3-3 (6-7p), Korea Republic (n) 0-2, UAE (n) 2-3, Congo DR (n) 2-1, Congo DR (n) 1-0, Japan (a) 0-4.

JAPAN

Japan Football Association, JFA House, Football Ave., Bunkyo-ku, Tokyo 113-8311.
Founded: 1921. *FIFA:* 1929, rejoined 1950; *AFC:* 1954. *National Colours:* Blue shirts, white shorts, blue socks.
International matches 2014–15
Uruguay (h) 0-2, Venezuela (h) 3-0 (after 2-2 draw; match awarded to Japan), Jamaica (h) 1-0, Brazil (n) 0-4, Honduras (h) 6-0, Australia (h) 2-1, Palestine (n) 4-0, Iraq (n) 1-0, Jordan (n) 2-0, UAE (n) 1-1 (4-5p), Tunisia (h) 2-0, Uzbekistan (h) 5-1, Iraq (h) 4-0, Singapore (h) 0-0.

JORDAN

Jordan Football Association, PO Box 962024, Al-Hussein Youth City, Amman 11196.
Founded: 1949. *FIFA:* 1956; *AFC:* 1970. *National Colours:* All white with red trim.
International matches 2014–15
Uzbekistan (a) 0-2, China PR (a) 1-1, Kuwait (h) 0-1, Kuwait (h) 1-1, Korea Republic (h) 0-1, Estonia (a) 0-1, Uzbekistan (n) 1-2, UAE (n) 0-1, Bahrain (n) 0-1, Iraq (n) 0-1, Palestine (n) 5-1, Japan (n) 0-2, Syria (h) 0-1, Saudi Arabia (a) 1-2, Lebanon (h) 0-0, Kuwait (n) 2-2, Tajikistan (a) 3-1, Trinidad & Tobago (h) 3-0.

KOREA DPR

DPR Korea Football Association, Kumsongdong, Kwangbok Street, Mangyongdae, PO Box 818, Pyongyang.
Founded: 1945. *FIFA:* 1958; *AFC:* 1974. *National Colours:* All red.
International matches 2014–15
Kuwait (n) 0-1, Bahrain (a) 2-2, Qatar (a) 1-3, Hong Kong (n) 2-1, Guam (n) 5-1, Chinese Taipei (a) 0-0, Uzbekistan (n) 0-1, Saudi Arabia (n) 1-4, China PR (n) 1-2, Vietnam (a) 1-1, Thailand (a) 1-0, Yemen (n) 1-0, Uzbekistan (h) 4-2.

KOREA REPUBLIC

Korea Football Association, KFA House 21, Gyeonghuigung-gil 46, Jongno-Gu, Seoul 110-062.
Founded: 1933, 1948. *FIFA:* 1948; *AFC:* 1954. *National Colours:* Red shirts, blue shorts, red socks.
International matches 2014–15
Venezuela (h) 3-1, Uruguay (h) 0-1, Paraguay (n) 2-0, Costa Rica (h) 1-3, Jordan (a) 1-0, Iran (a) 0-1, Saudi Arabia (n) 2-0, Oman (n) 1-0, Kuwait (n) 1-0, Australia (a) 1-0, Uzbekistan (n) 2-0, Iraq (n) 2-0, Australia (a) 1-2, Uzbekistan (h) 1-1, New Zealand (h) 1-0, UAE (n) 3-0, Myanmar (n) 2-0.

KUWAIT

Kuwait Football Association, Block 5, Street 101, Building 141A, Jabriya, PO Box Hawalli 4020, Kuwait 32071.
Founded: 1952. *FIFA:* 1964; *AFC:* 1964. *National Colours:* All blue with white trim.
International matches 2014–15
China PR (a) 1-3, Bahrain (h) 0-1, Jordan (a) 1-0, Jordan (a) 1-1, Korea DPR (n) 1-0, Yemen (n) 1-1, Iraq (n) 1-0, UAE (n) 2-2, Oman (n) 0-5, Iraq (n) 1-1, Australia (a) 1-4, Korea Republic (n) 0-1, Oman (n) 0-1, Colombia (n) 1-3, Jordan (n) 2-2, Lebanon (a) 1-0.

KYRGYZSTAN

Football Federation of Kyrgyz Republic, Mederova Street 1 'B', PO Box 1484, Bishkek 720082.
Founded: 1992. *FIFA:* 1994; *AFC:* 1994. *National Colours:* Red shirts, red shorts, red socks with yellow tops.

International matches 2014–15
Kazakhstan (a) 1-7, China PR (a) 0-4, China PR (a) 0-2, Bangladesh (a) 3-1, Australia (h) 1-2.

LAOS
Lao Football Federation, FIFA Training Centre, Ban Houayhong, Chanthabuly, PO Box 1800, Vientiane 856-21.
Founded: 1951. *FIFA:* 1952; *AFC:* 1968. *National Colours:* All red with white trim.
International matches 2014–15
Cambodia (h) 3-2, Brunei (h) 4-2, Timor-Leste (h) 2-0, Myanmar (h) 1-2, Singapore (a) 0-2, Philippines (n) 1-4, Vietnam (a) 0-3, Indonesia (n) 1-5, Afghanistan (h) 0-2, Cambodia (a) 1-1, Myanmar (h) 2-2, Lebanon (h) 0-2.

LEBANON
Association Libanaise de Football, Verdun Street, Bristol Radwan Centre, PO Box 4732, Beirut.
Founded: 1933. *FIFA:* 1936; *AFC:* 1964. *National Colours:* All red.
International matches 2014–15
Qatar (a) 0-5, Saudi Arabia (a) 1-1, UAE (n) 2-3, Syria (h) 2-2, Jordan (a) 0-0, Kuwait (h) 0-1, Laos (a) 2-0.

MACAU
Associacao de Futebol de Macau, Avenida Wai Leong, Taipa University of Science and Technology, Football Field Block 1, Taipa.
Founded: 1939. *FIFA:* 1978; *AFC:* 1978. *National Colours:* White shirts, black shorts, green socks.
International matches 2014–15
Guam (a) 0-0, Northern Mariana Islands† (n) 1-2, Mongolia (n) 3-2, Singapore (h) 2-2, Cambodia (a) 0-3, Cambodia (h) 1-1.

MALAYSIA
Football Association of Malaysia, 3rd Floor, Wisma FAM, Jalan SS5A/9, Kelana Jaya, Petaling Jaya 47301, Selangor Darul Ehsan.
Founded: 1933. *FIFA:* 1954; *AFC:* 1954. *National Colours:* Yellow and black shirts, black shorts, black socks.
International matches 2014–15
Tajikistan (a) 1-4, Indonesia (a) 0-2, Cambodia (h) 4-1, Syria (h) 0-3, Vietnam (a) 1-3, Myanmar (n) 0-0, Thailand (n) 2-3, Singapore (a) 3-1, Vietnam (h) 1-2, Vietnam (a) 4-2, Thailand (a) 0-2, Thailand (h) 3-2, Oman (a) 0-6, Hong Kong (h) 0-0, Timor-Leste (h) 1-1, Palestine (h) 0-6.

MALDIVES
Football Association of Maldives, FAM House, Ujaalahingun, Male 20388.
Founded: 1982. *FIFA:* 1986; *AFC:* 1984. *National Colours:* Red and white shirts, white shorts, red socks.
International matches 2014–15
Tajikistan (h) 0-2, Qatar (h) 0-1, Hong Kong (a) 0-2.

MONGOLIA
Mongolian Football Federation, PO Box 259, 15th Khoroo, Khan-Uul, Ulan Bator 210646.
Founded: 1959. *FIFA:* 1998; *AFC:* 1998. *National Colours:* Red shirts, blue shorts, red socks.
International matches 2014–15
Northern Mariana Islands† (n) 4-0, Guam (a) 0-2, Macau (n) 2-3, Timor-Leste (a) 1-4, Timor-Leste (h) 0-1.

MYANMAR
Myanmar Football Federation, National Football Training Centre, Waizayanta Road, Thuwunna, Thingankyun Township, Yangon 11070.
Founded: 1947. *FIFA:* 1948; *AFC:* 1954. *National Colours:* All red.
International matches 2014–15
Palestine (n) 4-1, Philippines (a) 3-2, Timor-Leste (n) 0-0, Brunei (n) 3-1, Cambodia (n) 1-0, Laos (a) 2-1, Malaysia (n) 0-0, Singapore (n) 2-4, Thailand (n) 0-2, Indonesia (a) 1-2, Cambodia (n) 0-0, Korea Republic (n) 0-2.

NEPAL
All Nepal Football Association, ANFA House, Satdobato, Lalitpur-17, PO Box 12582, Kathmandu.
Founded: 1951. *FIFA:* 1972; *AFC:* 1954. *National Colours:* All red with white trim.
International matches 2014–15
Philippines (n) 0-3, India (a) 0-2, India (h) 0-0.

OMAN
Oman Football Association, Seeb Sports Stadium, PO Box 3462, 112 Ruwi, Muscat.
Founded: 1978. *FIFA:* 1980; *AFC:* 1980. *National Colours:* All red.
International matches 2014–15
Republic of Ireland (a) 0-2, Kosovo‡ (a) 0-1, Costa Rica (h) 3-4, Uruguay (h) 0-3, Yemen (h) 2-0, UAE (n) 0-0, Iraq (n) 1-1, Kuwait (n) 5-0, Qatar (n) 1-3, UAE (n) 0-1, Qatar (n) 2-2, China PR (n) 1-4, Korea Republic (n) 0-1, Australia (a) 0-4, Kuwait (n) 1-0, Malaysia (h) 6-0, Algeria (n) 1-4, Bahrain (a) 0-0, Syria (h) 1-2, India (a) 2-1.

PAKISTAN
Pakistan Football Federation, PFF Football House, Ferozepur Road, Lahore 54600, Punjab.
Founded: 1947. *FIFA:* 1948; *AFC:* 1954. *National Colours:* All green and white.
International matches 2014–15
Palestine (h) 0-2, Afghanistan (h) 2-1, Yemen (n) 1-3, Yemen (n) 0-0.

PALESTINE
Palestinian Football Association, Nr. Faisal Al-Husseini Stadium, PO Box 4373, Jerusalem-al-Ram.
Founded: 1928. *FIFA:* 1998; *AFC:* 1998. *National Colours:* All red with white trim.
International matches 2014–15
Myanmar (n) 1-4, Chinese Taipei (n) 7-3, India (a) 3-2, Pakistan (a) 2-0, Saudi Arabia (a) 0-2, Vietnam (a) 3-1, Uzbekistan (n) 0-1, China PR (a) 0-0, Japan (n) 0-4, Jordan (n) 1-5, Iraq (n) 0-2, Saudi Arabia (a) 2-3, Malaysia (a) 6-0.

PHILIPPINES
Philippine Football Federation, 27 Danny Floro–corner Capt. Henry Javier Streets, Oranbo, Pasig City 1600.
Founded: 1907. *FIFA:* 1930; *AFC:* 1954. *National Colours:* All blue with white trim.
International matches 2014–15
Chinese Taipei (h) 5-1, Myanmar (h) 2-3, Papua New Guinea (h) 5-0, Nepal (n) 3-0, Cambodia (h) 3-0, Laos (n) 4-1, Indonesia (n) 4-0, Vietnam (a) 1-3, Thailand (h) 0-0, Thailand (a) 0-3, Bahrain (a) 1-2, Bahrain (h) 2-1, Yemen (n) 2-0.

QATAR
Qatar Football Association, 28th Floor, Al Bidda Tower, Corniche Street, West Bay, PO Box 5333, Doha.
Founded: 1960. *FIFA:* 1972; *AFC:* 1974. *National Colours:* All burgundy.
International matches 2014–15
Indonesia (h) 2-2, Morocco (a) 0-0, Peru (h) 0-2, Uzbekistan (h) 3-0, Lebanon (h) 5-0, Australia (h) 1-0, Korea DPR (h) 3-1, Saudi Arabia (a) 1-1, Yemen (n) 0-0, Bahrain (n) 0-0, Oman (n) 3-1, Saudi Arabia (a) 2-1, Estonia (h) 3-0, Oman (n) 2-2, UAE (n) 1-4, Iran (n) 0-1, Bahrain (n) 1-2, Algeria (n) 1-0, Slovenia (n) 1-0, Northern Ireland (n) 1-1, Scotland (a) 0-1, Maldives (a) 1-0.

SAUDI ARABIA
Saudi Arabian Football Federation, Al Mather Quarter, Prince Faisal Bin Fahad Street, PO Box 5844, Riyadh 11432.
Founded: 1956. *FIFA:* 1956; *AFC:* 1972. *National Colours:* White shirts with green trim, white shorts, white socks.
International matches 2014–15
Australia (n) 2-3, Uruguay (h) 1-1, Lebanon (h) 1-1, Palestine (h) 2-0, Qatar (h) 1-1, Bahrain (h) 3-0, Yemen (h) 1-0, UAE (h) 3-2, Qatar (h) 1-2, Bahrain (n) 1-4, Korea Republic (n) 0-2, China PR (n) 0-1, Korea DPR (n) 4-1, Uzbekistan (n) 1-3, Jordan (n) 2-1, Palestine (h) 3-2.

SINGAPORE
Football Association of Singapore, Jalan Besar Stadium, 100 Tyrwhitt Road, Singapore 207542.
Founded: 1892. *FIFA:* 1956; *AFC:* 1954. *National Colours:* All red.
International matches 2014–15
Papua New Guinea (h) 2-1, Hong Kong (h) 0-0, Hong Kong (a) 1-2, Macau (a) 2-2, Bahrain (a) 0-2, Laos (h) 2-0, Cambodia (h) 4-2, Thailand (h) 1-2, Myanmar (h) 4-2, Malaysia (h) 1-3, Thailand (a) 0-2, Guam (h) 2-2, Bangladesh (a) 2-1, Brunei (h) 5-1, Cambodia (a) 4-0, Japan (a) 0-0.

SRI LANKA

Football Federation of Sri Lanka, 100/9 Independence Avenue, Colombo 07.
Founded: 1939. *FIFA:* 1952; *AFC:* 1954. *National Colours:* All red with white trim.
International matches 2014–15
Seychelles (a) 2-1, Seychelles (a) 0-3, Bangladesh (a) 1-1, Bangladesh (a) 0-1, Bhutan (h) 0-1, Bhutan (a) 1-2.

SYRIA

Syrian Arab Federation for Football, Al Faihaa Sports Complex, PO Box 421, Damascus.
Founded: 1936. *FIFA:* 1937; *AFC:* 1970. *National Colours:* All red.
International matches 2014–15
Malaysia (a) 3-0, Indonesia (a) 2-0, Jordan (a) 1-0, Tajikistan (a) 3-2, Lebanon (a) 2-2, Oman (a) 2-1, Afghanistan (a) 6-0.

TAJIKISTAN

Tajikistan Football Federation, 14/3 Ayni Street, Dushanbe 734 025.
Founded: 1936. *FIFA:* 1994; *AFC:* 1994. *National Colours:* Red, white and green shirts, white and red shorts, red and green socks.
International matches 2014–15
Malaysia (h) 4-1, Kazakhstan (a) 1-2, Belarus (a) 1-6, Maldives (a) 2-0, Syria (h) 2-3, Jordan (h) 1-3, Bangladesh (a) 1-1.

THAILAND

Football Association of Thailand, National Stadium, Gate 3, Rama 1 Road, Patumwan, Bangkok 10330.
Founded: 1916. *FIFA:* 1925; *AFC:* 1954. *National Colours:* All red.
International matches 2014–15
China PR (a) 0-3, New Zealand (h) 2-0, Singapore (h) 2-1, Malaysia (a) 3-2, Myanmar (n) 2-0, Philippines (a) 0-0, Philippines (h) 3-0, Malaysia (h) 2-0, Malaysia (a) 2-3, Singapore (h) 2-0, Cameroon (h) 2-3, Korea DPR (h) 0-1, Vietnam (h) 1-0, Bahrain (h) 1-1, Chinese Taipei (a) 2-0.

TIMOR-LESTE

Federacao Futebol de Timor-Leste, Campo Democracia, Avenida Bairo Formosa, Dili.
Founded: 2002. *FIFA:* 2005; *AFC:* 2005. *National Colours:* Red shirts with black trim, red shorts, red socks.
International matches 2014–15
Brunei (n) 4-2, Myanmar (n) 0-0, Cambodia (n) 2-3, Laos (a) 0-2, Mongolia (h) 4-1, Mongolia (a) 1-0, Malaysia (a) 1-1, UAE (n) 0-1.

TURKMENISTAN

Football Federation of Turkmenistan, Stadium Kopetdag, 245 A. Niyazov Street, Ashgabat 744 001.
Founded: 1992. *FIFA:* 1994; *AFC:* 1994. *National Colours:* All white.
International matches 2014–15
Afghanistan (n) 1-3, Philippines (n) 0-2, Guam (a) 0-1, Iran (h) 1-1.

UNITED ARAB EMIRATES

United Arab Emirates Football Association, Zayed Sports City, PO Box 916, Abu Dhabi.
Founded: 1971. *FIFA:* 1974; *AFC:* 1974. *National Colours:* All white with red trim.
International matches 2014–15
Norway (a) 0-0, Lithuania (n) 1-1, Paraguay (n) 0-0, Australia (h) 0-4, Uzbekistan (h) 0-4, Lebanon (n) 3-2, Oman (n) 0-0, Kuwait (n) 2-2, Iraq (n) 2-0, Saudi Arabia (a) 2-3, Oman (n) 1-0, Jordan (n) 1-0, Qatar (n) 4-1, Bahrain (n) 2-1, Iran (n) 0-1, Japan (n) 1-1 (5-4p), Australia (a) 0-2, Iraq (n) 3-2, Saudi Arabia (a) 2-3, Korea Republic (n) 0-3, Timor-Leste (n) 1-0.

UZBEKISTAN

Uzbekistan Football Federation, Massiv Almazar Furkat Street 15/1, Tashkent 700 003.
Founded: 1946. *FIFA:* 1994; *AFC:* 1994. *National Colours:* All white with blue trim.
International matches 2014–15
Azerbaijan (a) 0-0, Jordan (h) 2-0, New Zealand (h) 3-1, Qatar (a) 0-3, Bahrain (n) 0-0, UAE (a) 4-0, Palestine (n) 1-0, Jordan (n) 2-1, Iraq (n) 1-0, Iraq (n) 0-0, Korea DPR (n) 1-0, China PR (n) 1-2, Saudi Arabia (n) 3-1, Korea Republic (n) 0-2, Korea Republic (a) 1-1, Japan (a) 1-5, Iran (h) 0-1, Korea DPR (a) 2-4.

VIETNAM

Vietnam Football Federation, Le Quang Dao Street, Phu Do Ward, Nam Tu Liem District, Hanoi 844.
Founded: 1960 (NV). *FIFA:* 1952 (SV), 1964 (NV); *AFC:* 1954 (SV), 1978 (SRV). *National Colours:* All red.
International matches 2014–15
Hong Kong (h) 3-1, Palestine (h) 1-3, Malaysia (h) 3-1, Indonesia (h) 2-2, Laos (h) 3-0, Philippines (h) 3-1, Malaysia (a) 2-1, Malaysia (h) 2-4, Korea DPR (h) 1-1, Thailand (a) 0-1.

YEMEN

Yemen Football Association, Quarter of Sport Al Jeraf (Ali Mohsen Al-Muraisi Stadium), PO Box 908, Al-Thawra City, Sana'a.
Founded: 1940 (SY), 1962 (NY). *FIFA:* 1967 (SY), 1980 (NY); *AFC:* 1972 (SY), 1980 (NY). *National Colours:* Red shirts, white shorts, black socks.
International matches 2014–15
Indonesia (a) 2-2, Iraq (n) 1-1, Kuwait (n) 1-1, Oman (a) 0-2, Bahrain (n) 0-0, Qatar (n) 0-0, Saudi Arabia (a) 0-1, Pakistan (n) 3-1, Pakistan (n) 0-0, Korea DPR (n) 0-1, Philippines (n) 0-2.

NORTH AND CENTRAL AMERICA AND CARIBBEAN (CONCACAF)

ANGUILLA

Anguilla Football Association, 2 Queen Elizabeth Avenue, PO Box 1318, The Valley, AI-2640.
Founded: 1990. *FIFA:* 1996; *CONCACAF:* 1996. *National Colours:* Turquoise and white shirts, orange and blue and shorts, turquoise and orange socks.
International matches 2014–15
Antigua & Barbuda (a) 0-6, St Vincent/Grenadines (n) 0-4, Dominican Republic (n) 0-10, Nicaragua (a) 0-5, Nicaragua (h) 0-3.

ANTIGUA & BARBUDA

Antigua & Barbuda Football Association, Ground Floor, Sydney Walling Stand, Antigua Recreation Ground, PO Box 773, St John's.
Founded: 1928. *FIFA:* 1970; *CONCACAF:* 1972. *National Colours:* Yellow shirts with black, red and blue stripe, yellow shorts, yellow socks.
International matches 2014–15
Anguilla (h) 6-0, Dominican Republic (h) 2-1, St Vincent/Grenadines (h) 2-1, St Lucia (n) 2-1, Dominican Republic (n) 0-0, Trinidad & Tobago (a) 0-1, Haiti (n) 2-2, Jamaica (a) 0-3, Martinique† (n) 0-2, Dominica (h) 1-0, British Virgin Islands (h) 1-0, St Lucia (h) 1-3, St Lucia (h) 4-1.

ARUBA

Arubaanse Voetbal Bond, Technical Centre Angel Botta, Shaba 24, PO Box 376, Noord.
Founded: 1932. *FIFA:* 1988; *CONCACAF:* 1986. *National Colours:* Yellow shirts with sky blue sleeves, yellow shorts, yellow socks.
International matches 2014–15
Curacao (n) 0-0 (5-3p), Barbados (h) 0-2, Barbados (a) 0-1.

BAHAMAS

Bahamas Football Association, Rosetta Street, PO Box N-8434, Nassau, NP.
Founded: 1967. *FIFA:* 1968; *CONCACAF:* 1981. *National Colours:* Yellow shirts, black shorts, yellow socks.
International matches 2014–15
Bermuda (h) 0-5, Bermuda (a) 0-3.

BARBADOS

Barbados Football Association, Bottom Floor, ABC Marble Complex, PO Box 1362, Fontabelle, St Michael.
Founded: 1910. *FIFA:* 1968; *CONCACAF:* 1967. *National Colours:* Gold shirts with royal blue sleeves, gold shorts, white socks with gold tops.
International matches 2014–15
Suriname (n) 1-1, Martinique† (a) 2-3, Bonaire† (n) 4-1, St Kitts & Nevis (n) 3-2, Haiti (a) 2-4, French Guiana† (n) 0-2, Guyana (h) 2-2, St Vincent/Grenadines (h) 2-2, US Virgin Islands (h) 0-1, US Virgin Islands (a) 4-0, St Kitts & Nevis (h) 1-3, Aruba (a) 2-0, Aruba (h) 1-0.

BELIZE

Football Federation of Belize, 26 Hummingbird Highway, Belmopan, PO Box 1742, Belize City.

Founded: 1980. *FIFA:* 1986; *CONCACAF:* 1986. *National Colours:* Blue shirts with white trim, red shorts, blue socks with white tops.
International matches 2014–15
Honduras (n) 0-2, Guatemala (n) 1-2, El Salvador (n) 0-2, Cayman Islands (h) 0-0, Cayman Islands (a) 1-1, Dominican Republic (a) 2-1, Dominican Republic (h) 3-0.

BERMUDA
Bermuda Football Association, 48 Cedar Avenue, PO Box HM 745, Hamilton HM11.
Founded: 1928. *FIFA:* 1962; *CONCACAF:* 1967. *National Colours:* All red.
International matches 2014–15
Grenada (h) 2-2, Grenada (h) 2-0, Bahamas (a) 5-0, Bahamas (h) 3-0, Puerto Rico (h) 1-1, Guatemala (a) 0-0, Guatemala (h) 0-1.

BRITISH VIRGIN ISLANDS
British Virgin Islands Football Association, Botanic Station, Road Town, PO Box 4269, Tortola VG 1110.
Founded: 1974. *FIFA:* 1996; *CONCACAF:* 1996. *National Colours:* Green shirts with gold trim, gold shorts, green socks.
International matches 2014–15
St Vincent/Grenadines (h) 0-6, Antigua & Barbuda (a) 0-1, Dominica (a) 2-3, Dominica (a) 0-0.

US VIRGIN ISLANDS
USVI Soccer Federation Inc., 498D Strawberry, PO Box 2346, Christiansted, St Croix 00851.
Founded: 1987. *FIFA:* 1998; *CONCACAF:* 1987. *National Colours:* Gold shirts with royal blue trim, gold shorts, gold socks.
International matches 2014–15
Barbados (a) 1-0, Barbados (h) 0-4.

CANADA
Canadian Soccer Association, Place Soccer Canada, 237 Metcalfe Street, Ottawa, Ontario K2P 1R2.
Founded: 1912. *FIFA:* 1912; *CONCACAF:* 1961. *National Colours:* All red.
International matches 2014–15
Jamaica (h) 3-1, Colombia (n) 0-1, Panama (a) 0-0, Iceland (n) 1-2, Iceland (n) 1-1, Guatemala (n) 1-0, Puerto Rico (a) 3-0, Dominica (a) 2-0, Dominica (h) 4-0.

CAYMAN ISLANDS
Cayman Islands Football Association, PO Box 178, Poindexter Road, Prospect, George Town, Grand Cayman KY1-1104.
Founded: 1966. *FIFA:* 1992; *CONCACAF:* 1990. *National Colours:* Red and white shirts, red shorts, red socks with white tops.
International matches 2014–15
Belize (a) 0-0, Belize (h) 1-1, Dominican Republic (a) 0-6.

COSTA RICA
Federacion Costarricense de Futbol, 600 mts sur del Cruce de la Panasonic, San Rafael de Alajuela, Radial a Santa Ana, San Jose 670-1000.
Founded: 1921. *FIFA:* 1927; *CONCACAF:* 1961. *National Colours:* Red shirts, blue shorts, white socks.
International matches 2014–15
Nicaragua (n) 3-0, Panama (n) 2-2, Guatemala (n) 2-1, Oman (a) 4-3, Korea Republic (a) 3-1, Uruguay (h) 3-3 (7-6p), Paraguay (h) 0-0, Panama (a) 1-2, Colombia (n) 0-1, Spain (a) 1-2, Mexico (n) 2-2.

CUBA
Asociacion de Futbol de Cuba, Estadio Pedro Marrero Escuela Nacional de Futbol – Mario Lopez, Avenida 41 no. 44 y 46, La Habana.
Founded: 1924. *FIFA:* 1932; *CONCACAF:* 1961. *National Colours:* All red.
International matches 2014–15
Panama (a) 0-4, Guatemala (a) 0-1, French Guiana† (n) 1-1, Curacao (n) 3-2, Trinidad & Tobago (n) 0-0, Haiti (n) 1-2, Dominican Republic (a) 3-0, Jamaica (a) 0-3, Curacao (a) 0-0, Curacao (h) 1-1.

CURACAO
Curacao Football Federation, Bonamweg 49, PO Box 341, Willemstad.
Founded: 1921 (Netherlands Antilles), 2010. *FIFA:* 1932, 2010; *CONCACAF:* 1961, 2010. *National Colours:* All blue.

International matches 2014–15
Puerto Rico (a) 2-2, Grenada (n) 2-1, French Guiana† (n) 0-0, Martinique† (n) 1-1, St Vincent/Grenadines (n) 0-1, Guadeloupe† (a) 1-0, Trinidad & Tobago (n) 2-3, Cuba (n) 2-3, French Guiana† (n) 1-4, Aruba (n) 2-0 (3-5p), Montserrat (h) 2-1, Montserrat (a) 2-2, Trinidad & Tobago (h) 1-0, Cuba (h) 0-0, Cuba (a) 1-1.

DOMINICA
Dominica Football Association, Patrick John Football House, Bath Estate, PO Box 1080, Roseau.
Founded: 1970. *FIFA:* 1994; *CONCACAF:* 1994. *National Colours:* Emerald green shirts with black sleeves, black shorts, emerald green socks.
International matches 2014–15
Guyana (n) 0-0, St Kitts & Nevis (a) 0-5, St Lucia (n) 1-2, Antigua & Barbuda (a) 0-1, British Virgin Islands (h) 3-2, British Virgin Islands (h) 0-0, St Lucia (a) 1-1, Grenada (a) 2-1, St Vincent/Grenadines (a) 0-1, Canada (h) 0-2, Canada (a) 0-4.

DOMINICAN REPUBLIC
Federacion Dominicana de Futbol, Centro Olimpico Juan Pablo Duarte, Apartado Postal 1953, Santo Domingo.
Founded: 1953. *FIFA:* 1958; *CONCACAF:* 1964. *National Colours:* All navy blue.
International matches 2014–15
El Salvador (a) 0-2, St Vincent/Grenadines (n) 0-1, Antigua & Barbuda (n) 1-2, Anguilla (n) 10-0, Trinidad & Tobago (a) 1-6, Antigua & Barbuda (n) 0-0, St Lucia (n) 3-2, Cuba (h) 0-3, Cayman Islands (h) 6-0, Belize (h) 1-2, Belize (a) 0-3.

EL SALVADOR
Federacion Salvadorena de Futbol, Avenida Jose Matias Delgado, Frente al Centro Espanol Colonia Escalon, Zona 10, San Salvador 1029.
Founded: 1935. *FIFA:* 1938; *CONCACAF:* 1961. *National Colours:* All blue.
International matches 2014–15
Dominican Republic (h) 2-0, Guatemala (n) 1-2, Honduras (n) 1-0, Belize (n) 2-0, Panama (n) 0-1, Colombia (n) 0-3, Ecuador (n) 1-5, Panama (h) 1-3, Nicaragua (a) 2-0, Argentina (n) 0-2, Guatemala (n) 0-0, Honduras (n) 0-2, Chile (a) 0-1, St Kitts & Nevis (a) 2-2, St Kitts & Nevis (h) 4-1.

GRENADA
Grenada Football Association, National Stadium, PO Box 326, St George's.
Founded: 1924. *FIFA:* 1978; *CONCACAF:* 1969. *National Colours:* Yellow shirts, yellow shorts, green socks.
International matches 2014–15
French Guiana† (n) 1-1, Curacao (n) 1-2, Puerto Rico (a) 2-2, Bermuda (a) 2-2, Bermuda (a) 0-2, Guyana (a) 0-2, St Vincent/Grenadines (h) 2-3, Dominica (h) 1-2, St Lucia (a) 2-0, Puerto Rico (a) 0-1, Puerto Rico (h) 2-0.

GUATEMALA
Federacion Nacional de Futbol de Guatemala, 2a Calle 15-57, Zona 15, Boulevard Vista Hermosa, Guatemala City 01015.
Founded: 1919. *FIFA:* 1946; *CONCACAF:* 1961. *National Colours:* Blue shirts with white sash, blue shorts, blue socks.
International matches 2014–15
Nicaragua (n) 3-0, Cuba (h) 1-0, El Salvador (n) 2-1, Belize (n) 2-1, Honduras (n) 2-0, Costa Rica (n) 1-2, Peru (a) 0-1, Canada (n) 0-1, El Salvador (n) 0-0, Mexico (a) 0-3, Uruguay (a) 1-5, Bermuda (h) 0-0, Bermuda (a) 1-0, USA (a) 0-4.

GUYANA
Guyana Football Federation, Lot 17, Dadanawa Street Section 'K', Campbellville, PO Box 10727, Georgetown.
Founded: 1902. *FIFA:* 1970; *CONCACAF:* 1961. *National Colours:* Green shirts with white trim, green shorts, green socks.
International matches 2014–15
Dominica (n) 0-0, St Lucia (n) 0-2, St Kitts & Nevis (a) 0-2, Barbados (a) 2-2, St Lucia (h) 2-0, Grenada (h) 2-0, Suriname (a) 0-1, St Vincent/Grenadines (a) 2-2, St Vincent/Grenadines (h) 4-4.

HAITI
Federation Haitienne de Football, Stade Sylvio Cator, Rue Oswald Durand, Port-au-Prince.
Founded: 1904. *FIFA:* 1933; *CONCACAF:* 1961. *National*

Colours: Blue shirts, red shorts, blue socks.
International matches 2014–15
Kosovo‡ (a) 0-0*, Chile (n) 0-1, French Guiana† (h) 2-2, Barbados (h) 4-2, St Kitts & Nevis (h) 0-0, Antigua & Barbuda (n) 2-2, Martinique† (n) 3-0, Jamaica (a) 0-2, Cuba (n) 2-1, China PR (a) 2-2.
* *Played 05.03.2014, result omitted from last edition.*

HONDURAS

Federacion Nacional Autonoma de Futbol de Honduras, Colonia Florencia Norte, Edificio Plaza America Ave. Roble, 1 y 2 Nivle, PO Box 827, Tegucigalpa 504.
Founded: 1935. *FIFA:* 1946; *CONCACAF:* 1961. *National Colours:* All white.
International matches 2014–15
Belize (n) 2-0, El Salvador (n) 0-1, Guatemala (n) 0-2, Nicaragua (n) 1-0, Mexico (a) 0-2, USA (a) 1-1, Japan (a) 0-6, China PR (a) 0-0, Venezuela (h) 2-3, Venezuela (a) 1-2, French Guiana† (a) 1-3, French Guiana† (h) 3-0, El Salvador (n) 2-0, Paraguay (a) 2-2, Brazil (a) 0-1, Mexico (n) 0-0.

JAMAICA

Jamaica Football Federation Ltd, 20 St Lucia Crescent, Kingston 5.
Founded: 1910. *FIFA:* 1962; *CONCACAF:* 1963. *National Colours:* Gold shirts, black shorts, gold socks with green tops.
International matches 2014–15
Canada (a) 1-3, Japan (a) 0-1, Martinique† (h) 1-1, Antigua & Barbuda (h) 3-0, Haiti (h) 2-0, Trinidad & Tobago (n) 0-0 (4-3p), Venezuela (h) 2-1, Cuba (h) 3-0, Uruguay (n) 0-1, Paraguay (n) 0-1, Brazil (n) 0-1.

MEXICO

Federacion Mexicana de Futbol Asociacion, A.C., Colima No. 373, Colonia Roma, Delegacion Cuauhtemoc, Mexico DF 06700.
Founded: 1927. *FIFA:* 1929; *CONCACAF:* 1961. *National Colours:* All black with green trim.
International matches 2014–15
Chile (n) 0-0, Bolivia (n) 1-0, Honduras (h) 2-0, Panama (n) 1-0, Netherlands (a) 3-2, Belarus (a) 2-3, Ecuador (n) 1-0, Paraguay (n) 1-0, USA (a) 0-2, Guatemala (h) 3-0, Peru (a) 1-1, Brazil (a) 0-2, Bolivia (n) 0-0, Chile (a) 3-3, Ecuador (n) 1-2, Costa Rica (n) 2-2, Honduras (n) 0-0.

MONTSERRAT

Montserrat Football Association Inc., PO Box 505, Blakes, Montserrat.
Founded: 1994. *FIFA:* 1996; *CONCACAF:* 1996. *National Colours:* Black shirts with red stripes, black shorts, black socks.
International matches 2014–15
Curacao (a) 1-2, Curacao (h) 2-2.

NICARAGUA

Federacion Nicaraguense de Futbol, Porton Principal del Hospital Bautista 1 Cuadra Abajo, 1 Cuadra al Sur y 1/2 Cuadra Abajo, Apartado Postal 976, Managua.
Founded: 1931. *FIFA:* 1950; *CONCACAF:* 1961. *National Colours:* All blue.
International matches 2014–15
Guatemala (n) 0-3, Costa Rica (n) 0-3, Panama (n) 0-2, Honduras (n) 0-1, El Salvador (h) 0-2, Anguilla (h) 5-0, Anguilla (a) 3-0, Suriname (h) 1-0, Suriname (a) 3-1.

PANAMA

Federacion Panamena de Futbol, Ciudad Deportiva Irving Saladino, Corregimiento de Juan Diaz, Apartado Postal 0827-00391, Zona 8, Panama City.
Founded: 1937. *FIFA:* 1938; *CONCACAF:* 1961. *National Colours:* All red.
International matches 2014–15
Peru (a) 0-3, Cuba (h) 4-0, Costa Rica (n) 2-2, Nicaragua (n) 2-0, El Salvador (n) 1-0, Mexico (a) 0-1, El Salvador (a) 3-1, Canada (h) 0-0, USA (a) 0-2, Trinidad & Tobago (a) 1-0, Costa Rica (h) 2-1, Ecuador (h) 1-1, Ecuador (a) 0-4.

PUERTO RICO

Federacion Puertorriquena de Futbol, PO Box 367567, San Juan 00936.
Founded: 1940. *FIFA:* 1960; *CONCACAF:* 1961. *National Colours:* Red and white striped shirts, blue shorts, blue socks.
International matches 2014–15
Curacao (h) 2-2, French Guiana† (h) 1-2, Grenada (h) 2-2, Canada (h) 0-3, Bermuda (a) 1-1, Grenada (h) 1-0, Grenada (h) 0-2.

ST KITTS & NEVIS

St Kitts & Nevis Football Association, PO Box 465, Lozack Road, Basseterre.
Founded: 1932. *FIFA:* 1992; *CONCACAF:* 1992. *National Colours:* Green and red shirts, red shorts, green socks.
International matches 2014–15
St Lucia (h) 0-0, Dominica (h) 5-0, Guyana (h) 2-0, Barbados (n) 2-3, French Guiana† (n) 2-1, Haiti (a) 0-0, Turks & Caicos Islands (h) 6-2, Turks & Caicos Islands (a) 6-2, Barbados (a) 3-1, El Salvador (h) 2-2, El Salvador (a) 1-4.

ST LUCIA

St Lucia National Football Association, Barnard Hill, PO Box 255, Castries.
Founded: 1979. *FIFA:* 1988; *CONCACAF:* 1986. *National Colours:* Sky blue shirts with yellow sleeves, sky blue shorts, white socks.
International matches 2014–15
St Kitts & Nevis (a) 0-0, Guyana (n) 2-0, Dominica (n) 2-1, Antigua & Barbuda (n) 1-2, Trinidad & Tobago (a) 0-2, Dominican Republic (n) 2-3, Guyana (a) 0-2, Dominica (h) 1-1, St Vincent/Grenadines (h) 1-2, Grenada (h) 0-2, Antigua & Barbuda (a) 3-1, Antigua & Barbuda (a) 1-4.

ST VINCENT & THE GRENADINES

St Vincent & the Grenadines Football Federation, PO Box 1278, Nichols Building (2nd Floor), Bentinck Square, Victoria Park, Kingstown.
Founded: 1979. *FIFA:* 1988; *CONCACAF:* 1986. *National Colours:* Yellow shirts, blue shorts, blue socks.
International matches 2014–15
Dominican Republic (n) 1-0, Anguilla (n) 4-0, Antigua & Barbuda (a) 1-2, British Virgin Islands (a) 6-0, Guadeloupe† (a) 1-3, Curacao (n) 1-0, Martinique† (n) 3-4, Barbados (a) 2-2, Grenada (a) 3-2, St Lucia (a) 2-1, Dominica (h) 1-0, Guyana (h) 2-2, Guyana (a) 4-4.

SURINAME

Surinaamse Voetbal Bond, Letitia Vriesdelaan 7, PO Box 1223, Paramaribo.
Founded: 1920. *FIFA:* 1929; *CONCACAF:* 1961. *National Colours:* White shirts with green cuffs, white shorts, white socks.
International matches 2014–15
Barbados (n) 1-1, Bonaire† (n) 2-3, Martinique† (a) 0-0, Guyana (h) 1-0, Nicaragua (a) 0-1, Nicaragua (h) 1-3.

TRINIDAD & TOBAGO

Trinidad & Tobago Football Association, 24–26 Dundonald Street, PO Box 400, Port of Spain.
Founded: 1908. *FIFA:* 1964; *CONCACAF:* 1962. *National Colours:* Red shirts with black trim, black shorts with red trim, red socks.
International matches 2014–15
El Salvador (n) 2-2, Haiti (n) 0-2, Honduras (n) 2-0, Mexico (n) 0-1, UAE (n) 3-3 (6-7p), Saudi Arabia (a) 3-1, New Zealand (h) 0-0, Jamaica (a) 1-0, Jamaica (n) 2-0, Argentina (a) 0-3, Iran (n) 0-2. Dominican Republic (h) 6-1, St Lucia (h) 2-0, Antigua & Barbuda (h) 1-0, Curacao (n) 3-2, French Guiana† (n) 4-2, Cuba (n) 0-0, Jamaica (a) 0-0 (3-4p), Panama (h) 0-1, Curacao (a) 0-1, Jordan (a) 0-3.

TURKS & CAICOS ISLANDS

Turks & Caicos Islands Football Association, TCIFA National Academy, Venetian Road, PO Box 626, Providenciales.
Founded: 1996. *FIFA:* 1998; *CONCACAF:* 1996. *National Colours:* All white.
International matches 2014–15
St Kitts & Nevis (a) 2-6, St Kitts & Nevis (h) 2-6.

UNITED STATES

US Soccer Federation, US Soccer House, 1801 S. Prairie Avenue, Chicago, IL 60616.
Founded: 1913. *FIFA:* 1914; *CONCACAF:* 1961. *National Colours:* All white.
International matches 2014–15
Czech Republic (a) 1-0, Ecuador (h) 1-1, Honduras (h) 1-1, Colombia (n) 1-2, Republic of Ireland (a) 1-4, Chile (a) 2-3, Panama (h) 2-0, Denmark (a) 2-3, Switzerland (a) 1-1, Mexico (h) 2-0, Netherlands (a) 4-3, Germany (a) 2-1, Guatemala (h) 4-0.

OCEANIA (OFC)

AMERICAN SAMOA
Football Federation American Samoa, PO Box 982 413, Pago Pago AS 96799.
Founded: 1984. *FIFA:* 1998; *OFC:* 1998. *National Colours:* Navy blue shirts, red shorts, white socks.
International matches 2014–15
None played.

COOK ISLANDS
Cook Islands Football Association, Matavera Main Road, PO Box 29, Avarua, Rarotonga.
Founded: 1971. *FIFA:* 1994; *OFC:* 1994. *National Colours:* Green shirts with white trim, green shorts, white socks.
International matches 2014–15
None played.

FIJI
Fiji Football Association, PO Box 2514, Government Buildings, Suva.
Founded: 1938. *FIFA:* 1964; *OFC:* 1966. *National Colours:* White shirts, black shorts, white socks.
International matches 2014–15
Vanuatu (n) 1-1.

NEW CALEDONIA
Federation Caledonienne de Football, 7 bis, Rue Suffren Quartien latin, BP 560, Noumea 99845.
Founded: 1928. *FIFA:* 2004; *OFC:* 2004. *National Colours:* Grey shirts, red shorts, grey socks.
International matches 2014–15
Papua New Guinea (a) 1-0.

NEW ZEALAND
New Zealand Football, PO Box 301-043, Albany, Auckland.
Founded: 1891. *FIFA:* 1948; *OFC:* 1966. *National Colours:* All white.
International matches 2014–15
Uzbekistan (a) 1-3, China PR (a) 1-1, Thailand (a) 0-2, Korea Republic (a) 0-1.

PAPUA NEW GUINEA
Papua New Guinea Football Association, PO Box 957, Lae 411, Morobe Province.
Founded: 1962. *FIFA:* 1966; *OFC:* 1966. *National Colours:* Red shirts with black trim, red shorts, yellow socks.
International matches 2014–15
Singapore (h) 1-2, Philippines (h) 0-5, New Caledonia (h) 0-1.

SAMOA
Football Federation Samoa, PO Box 1682, Tuanimato, Apia.
Founded: 1968. *FIFA:* 1986; *OFC:* 1986. *National Colours:* Blue, white and red shirts, blue and white shorts, red and blue socks.
International matches 2014–15
None played.

SOLOMON ISLANDS
Solomon Islands Football Federation, Allan Boso Complex, Panatina Academy, PO Box 584, Honiara.
Founded: 1978. *FIFA:* 1988; *OFC:* 1988. *National Colours:* Green, gold and blue shirts, blue and white shorts, white and blue socks.
International matches 2014–15
None played.

TAHITI
Federation Tahitienne de Football, Rue Gerald Coppenrath, Complexe de Fautaua, PO Box 50358, Pirae 98716.
Founded: 1989. *FIFA:* 1990; *OFC:* 1990. *National Colours:* White shirts with red trim, white shorts, white socks.
International matches 2014–15
None played.

TONGA
Tonga Football Association, Loto-Tonga Soka Centre, Valungafulu Road, Atele, PO Box 852, Nuku'alofa.
Founded: 1965. *FIFA:* 1994; *OFC:* 1994. *National Colours:* All red.
International matches 2014–15
None played.

VANUATU
Vanuatu Football Federation, VFF House, Lini Highway, PO Box 266, Port Vila.
Founded: 1934. *FIFA:* 1988; *OFC:* 1988. *National Colours:* Gold and white shirts with green sleeves, green shorts, black socks with white tops.
International matches 2014–15
Fiji (n) 1-1.

AFRICA (CAF)

ALGERIA
Federation Algerienne De Football, Chemin Ahmed Ouaked, BP 39, Dely-Ibrahim, Algiers 16000.
Founded: 1962. *FIFA:* 1963; *CAF:* 1964. *National Colours:* All white.
International matches 2014–15
Ethiopia (a) 2-1, Mali (h) 1-0, Malawi (a) 2-0, Malawi (h) 3-0, Ethiopia (h) 3-1, Mali (a) 0-2, Tunisia (a) 1-1, South Africa (n) 3-1, Ghana (n) 0-1, Senegal (n) 2-0, Ivory Coast (n) 1-3, Qatar (a) 0-1, Oman (n) 4-1, Seychelles (h) 4-0.

ANGOLA
Federacao Angolana de Futetbol, Senado de Compl. da Cidadela Desportiva, BP 3449, Luanda.
Founded: 1979. *FIFA:* 1980; *CAF:* 1980. *National Colours:* Red shirts with yellow trim, black shorts, red socks.
International matches 2014–15
Ethiopia (h) 1-0, Botswana (h) 0-0, Gabon (a) 0-1, Burkina Faso (h) 0-3, Lesotho (a) 0-0, Lesotho (h) 4-0, Gabon (h) 0-0, Burkina Faso (a) 1-1, Ivory Coast (a) 0-2, Central African Republic (h) 4-0, South Africa (a) 1-2, Swaziland (a) 2-2, Swaziland (h) 2-0.

BENIN
Federation Beninoise de Football, Rue du boulevard Djassain, BP 112, 3-eme Arrondissement de Porto-Novo 01.
Founded: 1962. *FIFA:* 1962; *CAF:* 1962. *National Colours:* All yellow.
International matches 2014–15
Malawi (h) 1-0, Malawi (a) 0-1 (3-4p), Tanzania (a) 1-4, Morocco (a) 1-6, Equatorial Guinea (a) 1-1.

BOTSWANA
Botswana Football Association, PO Box 1396, Gaborone.
Founded: 1970. *FIFA:* 1978; *CAF:* 1976. *National Colours:* Blue, white and black shirts, blue shorts, blue socks.
International matches 2014–15
Lesotho (h) 2-0, Guinea-Bissau (h) 2-0, Guinea-Bissau (a) 1-1, Angola (a) 0-0, Tunisia (a) 1-2, Senegal (h) 0-2, Zimbabwe (h) 1-0, Egypt (h) 0-2, Egypt (a) 0-2, Tunisia (h) 0-0, Senegal (a) 0-3, Burkina Faso (a) 0-2, Lesotho (h) 2-0, Mozambique (h) 1-2, South Africa (a) 0-0 (7-6p), Mozambique (n) 1-2, Madagascar (n) 1-2, Uganda (a) 0-2, Lesotho (a) 0-0, Lesotho (h) 1-1.

BURKINA FASO
Federation Burkinabe de Foot-Ball, Centre Technique National Ouaga 2000, BP 57, Ouagadougou 01.
Founded: 1960. *FIFA:* 1964; *CAF:* 1964. *National Colours:* Green shirts with red sleeves, green shorts, green socks.
International matches 2014–15
Lesotho (h) 2-0, Angola (a) 3-0, Gabon (a) 0-2, Gabon (h) 1-1, Lesotho (a) 1-0, Angola (h) 1-1, Swaziland (n) 5-1, Botswana (n) 2-0, Equatorial Guinea (a) 0-0, Congo (n) 1-2, Kazakhstan (a) 0-0, Cameroon (n) 2-3, Comoros (h) 2-0.

BURUNDI
Federation de Football du Burundi, Avenue Muyinga, BP 3426, Bujumbura.
Founded: 1948. *FIFA:* 1972; *CAF:* 1972. *National Colours:* All red with white trim.
International matches 2014–15
Kenya (a) 0-0, Tanzania (h) 2-0, Mauritius (a) 2-2, Senegal (a) 1-3, Djibouti (a) 2-1, Djibouti (h) 2-0.

CAMEROON
Federation Camerounaise de Football, Avenue du 27 aout 1940, Tsinga-Yaounde, BP 1116, Yaounde.
Founded: 1959. *FIFA:* 1962; *CAF:* 1963. *National Colours:* Green shirts, red shorts, yellow socks.

International matches 2014–15
Congo DR (a) 2-0, Ivory Coast (h) 4-1, Sierra Leone (h) 0-0, Sierra Leone (h) 2-0, Congo DR (h) 1-0, Ivory Coast (a) 0-0, Congo DR (h) 1-1, South Africa (n) 1-1, Mali (n) 1-1, Guinea (n) 1-1, Ivory Coast (n) 0-1, Indonesia (a) 1-0, Thailand (a) 3-2, Burkina Faso (n) 3-2, Congo DR (n) 1-1, Mauritania (h) 1-0.

CAPE VERDE ISLANDS
Federacao Caboverdiana de Futebol, Praia Cabo Verde, FCF CX, PO Box 234, Praia.
Founded: 1982. *FIFA:* 1986; *CAF:* 2000. *National Colours:* All blue with white trim.
International matches 2014–15
Niger (a) 3-1, Zambia (h) 2-1, Mozambique (a) 0-2, Mozambique (h) 1-0, Niger (h) 3-1, Zambia (a) 0-1, Congo (n) 3-2, Tunisia (n) 1-1, Congo DR (n) 0-0, Zambia (n) 0-0, Portugal (a) 2-0, Sao Tome & Principe (h) 7-1.

CENTRAL AFRICAN REPUBLIC
Federation Centrafricaine de Football, Avenue des Martyrs, BP 344, Bangui.
Founded: 1961. *FIFA:* 1964; *CAF:* 1965. *National Colours:* All white with blue trim.
International matches 2014–15
Morocco (a) 0-4, Angola (a) 0-4.

CHAD
Federation Tchadienne de Football, BP 886, N'Djamena.
Founded: 1962. *FIFA:* 1964; *CAF:* 1964. *National Colours:* Blue shirts, yellow shorts, red socks.
International matches 2014–15
Nigeria (a) 0-2.

COMOROS
Federation Comorienne de Football, Route d'Itsandra, BP 798, Moroni.
Founded: 1979. *FIFA:* 2005; *CAF:* 2003. *National Colours:* All green.
International matches 2014–15
Burkina Faso (a) 0-2, Zimbabwe (a) 0-2, Zimbabwe (h) 0-0.

CONGO
Federation Congolaise de Football, 80 Rue Eugene Etienne, Centre Ville, BP Box 11, Brazzaville 00 242.
Founded: 1962. *FIFA:* 1964; *CAF:* 1965. *National Colours:* Green shirts, yellow shorts, red socks.
International matches 2014–15
Rwanda (h) 2-0, Rwanda (a) 0-2 (3-4p), Nigeria (a) 3-2, Sudan (h) 2-0, South Africa (h) 0-2, South Africa (a) 0-0, Nigeria (h) 0-2, Sudan (a) 1-0, Cape Verde Islands (n) 2-3, Equatorial Guinea (a) 1-1, Gabon (n) 1-0, Burkina Faso (n) 2-1, Congo DR (n) 2-4, Kenya (n) 1-1.

CONGO DR
Federation Congolaise de Football-Association, 31 Avenue de la Justice Kinshasa-Gombe, BP 1284, Kinshasa 1.
Founded: 1919. *FIFA:* 1964; *CAF:* 1964. *National Colours:* Blue shirts with red sleeves, blue shorts, blue socks.
International matches 2014–15
Cameroon (h) 0-2, Sierra Leone (h) 2-0, Ivory Coast (h) 1-2, Ivory Coast (a) 4-3, Cameroon (a) 0-1, Sierra Leone (h) 3-1, Cameroon (a) 1-1, Zambia (n) 1-1, Cape Verde Islands (n) 0-0, Tunisia (n) 1-1, Congo (n) 4-2, Ivory Coast (n) 1-3, Equatorial Guinea (a) 0-0 (4-2p), Iraq (n) 1-2, Iraq (n) 0-1, Cameroon (n) 1-1, Madagascar (h) 2-1.

DJIBOUTI
Federation Djiboutienne de Football, Centre Technique National, BP 2694, Ville de Djibouti.
Founded: 1979. *FIFA:* 1994; *CAF:* 1994. *National Colours:* Green shirts, white shorts, blue socks.
International matches 2014–15
Tunisia (a) 1-8, Burundi (h) 1-2, Burundi (a) 0-2.

EGYPT
Egyptian Football Association, 5 Gabalaya Street, Gezira El Borg Post Office, Cairo.
Founded: 1921. *FIFA:* 1923; *CAF:* 1957. *National Colours:* Red shirts with white trim, white shorts, black socks.
International matches 2014–15
Kenya (h) 1-0, Senegal (a) 0-2, Tunisia (h) 0-1, Botswana (a) 2-0, Botswana (h) 2-0, Senegal (h) 0-1, Tunisia (a) 1-2, Equatorial Guinea (h) 2-0, Malawi (h) 2-1, Tanzania (h) 3-0.

EQUATORIAL GUINEA
Federacion Ecuatoguineana de Futbol, Avenida de Hassan II, Apartado de correo 1017, Malabo.
Founded: 1957. *FIFA:* 1986; *CAF:* 1986. *National Colours:* All red.
International matches 2014–15
Congo (h) 1-1, Burkina Faso (h) 0-0, Gabon (h) 2-0, Tunisia (h) 2-1, Ghana (h) 0-3, Congo DR (h) 0-0 (2-4p), Egypt (a) 0-2, Ivory Coast (a) 1-1, Andorra (a) 1-0, Benin (h) 1-1.

ERITREA
Eritrean National Football Federation, Sematat Avenue 29–31, PO Box 3665, Asmara.
Founded: 1996. *FIFA:* 1998; *CAF:* 1998. *National Colours:* Blue shirts, red shorts, green socks.
International matches 2014–15
None played.

ETHIOPIA
Ethiopia Football Federation, Addis Ababa Stadium, PO Box 1080, Addis Ababa.
Founded: 1943. *FIFA:* 1952; *CAF:* 1957. *National Colours:* Green shirts, yellow shorts, red socks.
International matches 2014–15
Angola (a) 0-1, Algeria (h) 1-2, Malawi (a) 2-3, Mali (h) 0-2, Mali (a) 3-2, Uganda (a) 0-3, Algeria (a) 1-3, Malawi (h) 0-0, Zambia (h) 0-1, Lesotho (h) 2-1, Kenya (h) 2-0, Kenya (a) 0-0.

GABON
Federation Gabonaise de Football, BP 181, Libreville.
Founded: 1962. *FIFA:* 1966; *CAF:* 1967. *National Colours:* Yellow shirts, blue shorts with yellow trim, blue socks with yellow tops.
International matches 2014–15
Rwanda (h) 0-1, Rwanda (a) 0-1, Angola (h) 1-0, Lesotho (a) 1-1, Burkina Faso (h) 2-0, Burkina Faso (a) 1-1, Angola (a) 0-0, Lesotho (h) 4-2, Senegal (a) 0-1, Burkina Faso (n) 2-0, Congo (n) 0-1, Equatorial Guinea (a) 0-2, Mali (n) 4-3, Belarus (n) 0-0, Niger (a) 1-2, Ivory Coast (h) 0-0.

GAMBIA
Gambia Football Association, Kafining Layout, Bakau, PO Box 523, Banjul.
Founded: 1952. *FIFA:* 1968; *CAF:* 1966. *National Colours:* Red shirts, blue shorts, green socks.
International matches 2014–15
Mauritania (h) 1-0, Uganda (a) 1-1, South Africa (a) 0-0, Senegal (a) 1-3, Senegal (h) 0-1.

GHANA
Ghana Football Association, General Secretariat, South East Ridge, PO Box AN 19338, Accra.
Founded: 1957. *FIFA:* 1958; *CAF:* 1958. *National Colours:* All white.
International matches 2014–15
Uganda (h) 1-1, Togo (a) 3-2, Guinea (n) 1-1, Guinea (h) 3-1, Uganda (a) 0-1, Togo (h) 3-1, Senegal (n) 1-2, Algeria (n) 1-0, South Africa (n) 2-1, Guinea (n) 3-0, Equatorial Guinea (a) 3-0, Ivory Coast (n) 0-0 (8-9p), Senegal (n) 1-2, Mali (n) 1-1, Madagascar (n) 1-2, Zambia (n) 0-3, Togo (h) 1-0, Mauritius (h) 7-1.

GUINEA
Federation Guineenne de Football, Annexe 1 du Palais du Peuple, PO Box 3645, Conakry.
Founded: 1960. *FIFA:* 1962; *CAF:* 1963. *National Colours:* Red shirts, yellow shorts, green socks.
International matches 2014–15
Togo (n) 2-1, Uganda (a) 0-2, Ghana (n) 1-1, Ghana (n) 1-3, Togo (a) 4-1, Uganda (n) 2-0, Senegal (n) 2-5, Ivory Coast (a) 1-1, Cameroon (n) 1-1, Mali (n) 1-1, Guinea (n) 0-3, Swaziland (n) 1-2, Liberia (n) 3-1.

GUINEA-BISSAU
Federacao de Futebol da Guine-Bissau, Alto Bandim (Nova Sede), BP 375, Bissau 1035.
Founded: 1974. *FIFA:* 1986; *CAF:* 1986. *National Colours:* Red shirts with green and yellow trim, red shorts, red socks.
International matches 2014–15
Botswana (a) 0-2, Botswana (h) 1-1, Zambia (a) 0-0, Mali (h) 1-1.

IVORY COAST
Federation Ivoirienne de Football, Treichville Avenue 1, 01, BP 1202, Abidjan 01.
Founded: 1960. *FIFA:* 1964; *CAF:* 1960. *National Colours:* All orange.

International matches 2014–15
Sierra Leone (h) 2-1, Cameroon (a) 1-4, Congo DR (a) 2-1, Congo DR (h) 3-4, Zambia (a) 1-1, Sierra Leone (h) 5-1, Cameroon (h) 0-0, South Africa (a) 0-2, Nigeria (n) 1-0, Sweden (n) 0-2, Guinea (n) 1-1, Mali (n) 1-1, Cameroon (n) 1-0, Algeria (n) 3-1, Congo DR (n) 3-1, Ghana (n) 0-0 (9-8p), Angola (h) 2-0, Equatorial Guinea (h) 1-1, Gabon (a) 0-0.

KENYA

Football Kenya Federation, Nyayo Sports Complex, Kasarani, PO Box 12705, 00400 Nairobi.
Founded: 1960 (KFF); 2011 (FKF). *FIFA:* 1960 (2012); *CAF:* 1968 (2012). *National Colours:* All red.
International matches 2014–15
Burundi (h) 0-0, Lesotho (a) 0-1, Lesotho (h) 0-0, Egypt (a) 0-1, Morocco (a) 0-3, Seychelles (a) 2-0, South Sudan (h) 2-0, Congo (a) 1-1, Ethiopia (a) 0-2, Ethiopia (h) 0-0.

LESOTHO

Lesotho Football Association, Bambatha Tsita Sports Arena, Old Polo Ground, PO Box 1879, Maseru 100.
Founded: 1932. *FIFA:* 1964; *CAF:* 1964. *National Colours:* Blue shirts, green shorts, white socks.
International matches 2014–15
Botswana (a) 0-2, Kenya (h) 1-0, Kenya (a) 0-0, Burkina Faso (a) 0-2, Gabon (h) 1-1, Angola (h) 0-0, Angola (a) 0-4, Burkina Faso (h) 0-1, Gabon (a) 2-4, Botswana (h) 0-2, South Africa (h) 0-0, South Africa (h) 1-1, Madagascar (h) 1-2, Swaziland (h) 0-2, Tanzania (n) 1-0, Ethiopia (a) 1-2, Botswana (h) 0-0, Botswana (a) 1-1.

LIBERIA

Liberia Football Association, Professional Building, Benson Street, PO Box 10-1066, Monrovia 1000.
Founded: 1936. *FIFA:* 1964; *CAF:* 1960. *National Colours:* Red and white shirts with black trim, red shorts, red socks with blue.
International matches 2014–15
Togo (a) 1-2, Guinea (n) 1-3.

LIBYA

Libyan Football Federation, General Sports Federation Building, Sports City, Goriji, PO Box 5137, Tripoli.
Founded: 1962. *FIFA:* 1964; *CAF:* 1965. *National Colours:* Red shirts, black shorts, black socks.
International matches 2014–15
Morocco (n) 0-3, Mali (a) 2-2, Morocco (a) 0-1, Tunisia (n) 1-0, Morocco (a) 0-3.

MADAGASCAR

Federation Malagasy de Football, 29 Rue de Russie Isoraka, PO Box 4409, Antananarivo 101.
Founded: 1961. *FIFA:* 1964; *CAF:* 1963. *National Colours:* All green and white.
International matches 2014–15
Lesotho (a) 2-1, Tanzania (h) 2-0, Swaziland (n) 1-1, Ghana (n) 2-1, Namibia (n) 2-3, Botswana (n) 2-1, Congo DR (a) 1-2.

MALAWI

Football Association of Malawi, Chiwembe Technical Centre, Off Chiwembe Road, PO Box 51657, Limbe.
Founded: 1966. *FIFA:* 1968; *CAF:* 1968. *National Colours:* All red.
International matches 2014–15
Mozambique (h) 1-1, Uganda (a) 0-0, Benin (a) 0-1, Benin (h) 1-0 (4-3p), Mali (a) 0-2, Ethiopia (h) 3-2, Algeria (h) 0-2, Algeria (a) 0-3, Mali (h) 2-0, Ethiopia (a) 0-0, Tanzania (a) 1-1, Zambia (a) 0-2, Mozambique (n) 2-2, South Africa (a) 0-0 (5-4p), Zambia (n) 1-0, Egypt (a) 1-2, Zimbabwe (h) 1-2.

MALI

Federation Malienne de Football, Avenue du Mali, Hamdallaye ACI 2000, BP 1020, Bamako 0000.
Founded: 1960. *FIFA:* 1964; *CAF:* 1963. *National Colours:* All yellow.
International matches 2014–15
Malawi (h) 2-0, Algeria (a) 0-1, Ethiopia (a) 2-0, Ethiopia (h) 2-3, Malawi (a) 0-2, Algeria (h) 2-0, Cameroon (n) 1-1, Ivory Coast (n) 1-1, Guinea (n) 1-1, Gabon (n) 3-4, Ghana (n) 1-1, Libya (h) 2-2, South Sudan (h) 2-0, Guinea-Bissau (a) 1-1.

MAURITANIA

Federation de Foot-Ball de la Rep. Islamique de Mauritanie, Route de l'Espoire, BP 566, Nouakchott.
Founded: 1961. *FIFA:* 1970; *CAF:* 1968. *National Colours:* All green with yellow trim.

International matches 2014–15
Uganda (a) 0-2, Uganda (h) 0-1, Gambia (a) 0-1, Niger (h) 2-0, Cameroon (a) 0-1, Sierra Leone (h) 2-1, Sierra Leone (h) 2-0.

MAURITIUS

Mauritius Football Association, Sepp Blatter House, Trianon.
Founded: 1952. *FIFA:* 1964; *CAF:* 1963. *National Colours:* All white with red trim.
International matches 2014–15
Burundi (h) 2-2, Togo (h) 1-1, Zimbabwe (a) 0-2, Namibia (a) 0-2, Seychelles (a) 1-0, Ghana (a) 1-7, South Africa (a) 0-3.

MOROCCO

Federation Royale Marocaine de Football, 51 bis, Avenue Ibn Sina, Agdal BP 51, Rabat 10 000.
Founded: 1955. *FIFA:* 1960; *CAF:* 1959. *National Colours:* Red shirts with green trim, white shorts, red socks with green trim.
International matches 2014–15
Qatar (h) 0-0, Libya (h) 3-0, Central African Republic (h) 4-0, Kenya (h) 3-0, Benin (h) 6-1, Uruguay (h) 0-1, Libya (h) 1-0, Tunisia (h) 1-1, Libya (h) 3-0.

MOZAMBIQUE

Federacao Mocambicana de Futebol, Avenida Samora Machel 11, Caixa Postal 1467, Maputo.
Founded: 1976. *FIFA:* 1980; *CAF:* 1980. *National Colours:* Red shirts, black shorts, black socks with red tops.
International matches 2014–15
Tanzania (a) 2-2, Tanzania (h) 2-1, Zambia (a) 0-0, Niger (h) 1-1, Cape Verde Islands (h) 2-0, Cape Verde Islands (a) 0-1, Zambia (h) 0-1, Niger (n) 1-1, Botswana (n) 2-1, Malawi (n) 2-2, Botswana (n) 2-1, Namibia (n) 0-2, Rwanda (h) 0-1, Seychelles (a) 5-1, Seychelles (a) 4-0.

NAMIBIA

Namibia Football Association, Richard Kamuhuka Str., Soccer House, Katutura, PO Box 1345, Windhoek 9000.
Founded: 1990. *FIFA:* 1992; *CAF:* 1992. *National Colours:* All red.
International matches 2014–15
Swaziland (h) 1-1, Seychelles (h) 0-0, Mauritius (h) 2-0, Zimbabwe (h) 4-1, Zambia (n) 0-0 (5-4p), Madagascar (n) 3-2, Mozambique (n) 2-0, Niger (a) 0-1, Zambia (h) 2-1, Zambia (a) 1-2 (5-6p).

NIGER

Federation Nigerienne de Football, Avenue Francois Mitterand, BP 10299, Niamey.
Founded: 1961. *FIFA:* 1964; *CAF:* 1964. *National Colours:* White shirts, white shorts, orange socks.
International matches 2014–15
Uganda (h) 2-0, Cape Verde Islands (h) 1-3, Mozambique (a) 1-1, Zambia (h) 0-0, Zambia (a) 0-3, Cape Verde Islands (a) 1-3, Mozambique (h) 1-1, Mauritania (a) 0-2, Gabon (h) 2-1, Namibia (h) 1-0.

NIGERIA

Nigeria Football Federation, Plot 2033, Olusegun Obasanjo Way, Zone 7, Wuse Abuja, PO Box 5101 Garki, Abuja.
Founded: 1945. *FIFA:* 1960; *CAF:* 1960. *National Colours:* All green with white trim.
International matches 2014–15
Congo (h) 2-3, South Africa (a) 0-0, Sudan (a) 0-1, Sudan (h) 3-1, Congo (a) 2-0, South Africa (h) 2-2, Ivory Coast (n) 0-1, Uganda (h) 0-1, South Africa (a) 1-1, Chad (h) 2-0.

RWANDA

Federation Rwandaise de Football Association, BP 2000, Kigali.
Founded: 1972. *FIFA:* 1978; *CAF:* 1976. *National Colours:* Green and yellow hooped shirts, blue shorts, green socks.
International matches 2014–15
Gabon (h) 1-0, Congo (a) 0-2, Gabon (a) 1-0, Congo (h) 2-0 (4-3p), Zambia (a) 0-2, Tanzania (h) 2-0, Mozambique (a) 1-0.

SAO TOME & PRINCIPE

Federacao Santomense de Futebol, Rua Ex-Joao de Deus No. QXXIII-426/26, BP 440, Sao Tome.
Founded: 1975. *FIFA:* 1986; *CAF:* 1986. *National Colours:* Green and red shirts, black shorts, green socks.

International matches 2014–15
Cape Verde Islands (a) 1-7.

SENEGAL
Federation Senegalaise de Football, VDN Ouest-Foire en face du Cicesi, BP 13021, Dakar.
Founded: 1960. *FIFA:* 1964; *CAF:* 1964. *National Colours:* All white with yellow trim.
International matches 2014–15
Egypt (h) 2-0, Botswana (a) 2-0, Tunisia (h) 0-0, Tunisia (a) 0-1, Egypt (a) 1-0, Botswana (h) 3-0, Gabon (n) 1-0, Guinea (n) 5-2, Ghana (n) 2-1, South Africa (n) 1-1, Algeria (n) 0-2, Ghana (n) 2-1, Burundi (h) 3-1, Gambia (h) 3-1, Gambia (a) 1-0.

SEYCHELLES
Seychelles Football Federation, Maison Football, Roche Caiman, PO Box 843, Mahe.
Founded: 1979. *FIFA:* 1986; *CAF:* 1986. *National Colours:* Red shirts, blue shorts, blue socks.
International matches 2014–15
Uganda (a) 0-1, Sierra Leone (a) 0-2, Sri Lanka (h) 1-2, Sri Lanka (h) 3-0, Kenya (a) 0-2, Namibia (h) 0-0, Zimbabwe (h) 0-1, Mauritius (h) 0-1, Algeria (h) 0-4, Mozambique (a) 1-5, Mozambique (h) 0-4.

SIERRA LEONE
Sierra Leone Football Association, 21 Battery Street, Kingtom, PO Box 672, Freetown.
Founded: 1960. *FIFA:* 1960; *CAF:* 1960. *National Colours:* Green shirts, white shorts, blue socks.
International matches 2014–15
Seychelles (h) 2-0, Ivory Coast (a) 1-2, Congo DR (a) 0-2, Cameroon (a) 0-0, Cameroon (a) 0-2, Ivory Coast (a) 1-5, Congo DR (a) 1-3, Sudan (a) 0-1, Mauritania (a) 1-2, Mauritania (a) 0-2.

SOMALIA
Somali Football Federation, Mogadishu BN 03040 (DHL only).
Founded: 1951. *FIFA:* 1962; *CAF:* 1968. *National Colours:* All blue with white trim.
International matches 2014–15
None played.

SOUTH AFRICA
South African Football Association, 76 Nasrec Road, Nasrec, Johannesburg 2000.
Founded: 1991. *FIFA:* 1992; *CAF:* 1992. *National Colours:* Yellow shirts with green trim, green shorts with yellow trim, yellow socks with green tops.
International matches 2014–15
Sudan (a) 3-0, Nigeria (h) 0-0, Congo (a) 2-0, Congo (h) 0-0, Sudan (h) 2-1, Nigeria (a) 2-2, Ivory Coast (h) 2-0, Zambia (h) 1-0, Cameroon (n) 1-1, Algeria (n) 1-3, Senegal (n) 1-1, Ghana (n) 1-2, Swaziland (a) 3-1, Nigeria (h) 1-1, Lesotho (a) 0-0, Lesotho (a) 1-1, Botswana (h) 0-0 (6-7p), Malawi (h) 0-0 (4-5p), Gambia (h) 0-0, Angola (h) 2-1, Mauritius (h) 3-0.

SOUTH SUDAN
South Sudan Football Association, Juba National Stadium, Hai Himra, Talata, Juba.
Founded: 2011. *FIFA:* 2012; *CAF:* 2012. *National Colours:* All blue.
International matches 2014–15
Kenya (a) 0-2, Mali (a) 0-3.

SUDAN
Sudan Football Association, Baladia Street, PO Box 437, 11111 Khartoum.
Founded: 1936. *FIFA:* 1948; *CAF:* 1957. *National Colours:* All red.
International matches 2014–15
Zambia (a) 1-3, South Africa (h) 0-3, Congo (a) 0-2, Nigeria (h) 1-0, Nigeria (a) 1-3, South Africa (a) 1-2, Congo (h) 0-1, Sierra Leone (h) 1-0.

SWAZILAND
National Football Association of Swaziland, Sigwaca House, Plot 582, Sheffield Road, PO Box 641, Mbabane H100.
Founded: 1968. *FIFA:* 1978; *CAF:* 1976. *National Colours:* Blue and red shirts, blue shorts, blue socks.
International matches 2014–15
Namibia (a) 1-1, Zimbabwe (h) 0-2, Tanzania (h) 1-1, Burkina Faso (n) 1-5, South Africa (h) 1-3, Tanzania (a) 1-0, Lesotho (a) 2-0, Madagascar (n) 1-1, Guinea (n) 2-1, Angola (h) 2-2, Angola (a) 0-2.

TANZANIA
Tanzania Football Federation, Karume Memorial Stadium, Uhuru/Shauri Moyo Road, PO Box 1574, Ilala/Dar Es Salaam.
Founded: 1930. *FIFA:* 1964; *CAF:* 1964. *National Colours:* Blue shirts, black shorts, blue socks.
International matches 2014–15
Mozambique (h) 2-2, Mozambique (a) 1-2, Burundi (a) 0-2, Benin (h) 4-1, Swaziland (a) 1-1, Malawi (h) 1-1, Swaziland (h) 0-1, Madagascar (a) 0-2, Lesotho (n) 0-1, Rwanda (a) 0-2, Egypt (a) 0-3, Uganda (h) 0-3, Uganda (a) 1-1.

TOGO
Federation Togolaise de Football, Route de Kegoue, BP 05, Lome.
Founded: 1960. *FIFA:* 1964; *CAF:* 1964. *National Colours:* Yellow shirts, green shorts, yellow socks.
International matches 2014–15
Guinea (n) 1-2, Ghana (h) 2-3, Uganda (a) 1-0, Uganda (h) 1-0, Guinea (h) 1-4, Ghana (a) 1-3, Mauritius (a) 1-1, Ghana (a) 0-1, Liberia (h) 2-1.

TUNISIA
Federation Tunisienne de Football, Stade Annexe d'El Menzah, Cite Olympique, El Menzah 1003.
Founded: 1957. *FIFA:* 1960; *CAF:* 1960. *National Colours:* All white with red trim.
International matches 2014–15
Botswana (h) 2-1, Egypt (a) 1-0, Senegal (a) 0-0, Senegal (h) 1-0, Botswana (a) 0-0, Egypt (h) 2-1, Algeria (h) 1-1, Cape Verde Islands (n) 1-1, Zambia (n) 2-1, Congo DR (n) 1-1, Equatorial Guinea (a) 1-2, Japan (a) 0-2, China PR (a) 1-1, Djibouti (h) 8-1, Morocco (a) 1-1, Libya (n) 0-1.

UGANDA
Federation of Uganda Football Associations, FUFA House, Plot No. 879, Wakaliga Road, Mengo, PO Box 22518, Kampala.
Founded: 1924. *FIFA:* 1960; *CAF:* 1960. *National Colours:* Yellow shirts, black shorts, yellow socks.
International matches 2014–15
Seychelles (h) 1-0, Malawi (h) 0-0, Mauritania (h) 2-0, Mauritania (a) 1-0, Niger (a) 0-2, Ghana (a) 1-1, Guinea (h) 2-0, Togo (h) 0-1, Togo (a) 0-1, Ethiopia (h) 3-0, Ghana (h) 1-0, Guinea (n) 0-2, Nigeria (a) 1-0, Gambia (h) 1-1, Botswana (h) 2-0, Tanzania (a) 3-0, Tanzania (h) 1-1.

ZAMBIA
Football Association of Zambia, Football House, Alick Nkhata Road, Long Acres, PO Box 34751, Lusaka.
Founded: 1929. *FIFA:* 1964; *CAF:* 1964. *National Colours:* Green shirts, green shorts, green and orange socks.
International matches 2014–15
Sudan (h) 3-1, Mozambique (h) 0-0, Cape Verde Islands (a) 1-2, Niger (a) 0-0, Niger (h) 3-0, Ivory Coast (h) 1-1, Mozambique (a) 1-0, Cape Verde Islands (h) 1-0, South Africa (a) 0-1, Congo DR (n) 1-1, Tunisia (n) 1-2, Cape Verde Islands (n) 0-0, Rwanda (h) 2-0, Malawi (h) 2-0, Namibia (n) 0-0 (4-5p), Ghana (n) 3-0, Malawi (n) 0-1, Ethiopia (a) 1-0, Guinea-Bissau (h) 0-0, Namibia (a) 1-2, Namibia (h) 2-1 (6-5p).

ZIMBABWE
Zimbabwe Football Association, ZIFA House, 53 Livingstone Avenue, PO Box CY 114, Causeway, Harare.
Founded: 1965. *FIFA:* 1965; *CAF:* 1980. *National Colours:* Gold shirts, gold shorts, green socks.
International matches 2014–15
Botswana (a) 0-1, Swaziland (a) 2-0, Mauritius (h) 2-0, Seychelles (a) 1-0, Namibia (a) 1-4, Malawi (a) 2-1, Comoros (h) 2-0, Comoros (a) 0-0.

EURO 2016 QUALIFYING COMPETITION

■ *Denotes player sent off.*

GROUP A

Tuesday, 9 September 2014
Czech Republic (1) 2 *(Dockal 22, Pilar 90)*
Holland (0) 1 *(de Vrij 55)*   17,946
Czech Republic: (442) Cech; Kaderabek, Prochazka,
Kadlec M, Limbersky; Dockal, Darida, Krejci (Pilar 66),
Vacha (Kolar 81); Rosicky, Lafata (Vydra 72).
Holland: (532) Cillessen; Janmaat, Veltman (Narsingh
39), de Vrij, Martins Indi, Blind; Wijnaldum, Sneijder, de
Jong; van Persie, Depay.
Referee: Gianluca Rocchi.

Iceland (1) 3 *(Bodvarsson 18, Sigurdsson G 76,*
Sigthorsson 78)
Turkey (0) 0   7000
Iceland: (442) Halldorsson; Bjarnason T, Arnason,
Sigurdsson R, Skulason A; Bjarnason B (Gislason 70),
Gunnarsson, Sigurdsson G (Skulason O 89),
Hallfredsson; Bodvarsson (Kjartansson 90), Sigthorsson.
Turkey: (343) Kivrak; Toprak■, Topal (Calhanoglu 77),
Gulum; Gonul, Emre, Inan (Tufan 65), Erkin; Adin
(Pektemek 64), Yilmaz, Turan.
Referee: Ivan Bebek.

Kazakhstan (0) 0
Latvia (0) 0   10,000
Kazakhstan: (523) Sidelnikov; Miroshnichenko S,
Vorotnikov, Abdulin, Logvinenko, Shomko; Bogdanov,
Smakov; Nuserbaev (Dzholchiev 73), Islamkhan
(Nurgaliev 82), Khizhnichenko.
Latvia: (442) Kolinko; Gabovs, Bulvitis, Gorkss,
Maksimenko; Kovalovs, Zjuzins, Lazdins (Fertovs 27),
Laizans; Sabala, Rudnevs (Visnakovs E 79).
Referee: Ivan Kruzliak.

Friday, 10 October 2014
Holland (0) 3 *(Huntelaar 62, Afellay 82, van Persie 89 (pen))*
Kazakhstan (1) 1 *(Abdulin 18)*   45,000
Holland: (433) Cillessen; van der Wiel, de Vrij, Martins
Indi (Fer 81), Blind; Sneijder, de Jong (Huntelaar 56),
Afellay; Robben, van Persie, Lens.
Kazakhstan: (541) Mokin; Miroshnichenko D,
Dmitrenko (Gorman 72), Vorotnikov, Abdulin,
Suyumbayev; Dzholchiev■, Bogdanov, Karpovich
(Korobkin 79), Shomko; Khizhnichenko (Nurgaliev 90).
Referee: Matej Jug.

Latvia (0) 0
Iceland (0) 3 *(Sigurdsson G 66, Gunnarsson 77,*
Gislason 90)   6354
Latvia: (352) Kolinko; Bulvitis, Dubra, Gabovs; Gorkss,
Morozs, Kovalovs (Visnakovs A 81), Rugins (Freimanis
63), Fertovs; Sabala (Visnakovs E 81), Rudnevs■.
Iceland: (442) Halldorsson; Sigurdsson R, Arnason,
Skulason A, Bjarnason B; Sigurdsson G (Skulason O 80),
Gunnarsson, Bjarnason T, Hallfredsson (Gislason 87);
Bodvarsson (Finnbogason 78), Sigthorsson.
Referee: Robert Schorgenhofer.

Turkey (1) 1 *(Bulut 8)*
Czech Republic (1) 2 *(Sivok 16, Dockal 58)*   25,000
Turkey: (433) Zengin; Gonul, Topal, Kaya, Erkin; Tufan,
Inan (Ozyakup 79), Turan; Sahan (Demir 66), Bulut,
Tore (Adin 68).
Czech Republic: (4231) Cech; Kaderabek, Sivok, Kadlec
M, Limbersky; Darida, Vacha; Dockal (Plasil 90),
Rosicky, Krejci (Pilar 68); Lafata (Vydra 84).
Referee: Jonas Eriksson.

Monday, 13 October 2014
Iceland (2) 2 *(Sigurdsson G 10 (pen), 42)*
Holland (0) 0   10,000
Iceland: (442) Halldorsson; Bjarnason T, Arnason,
Sigurdsson R, Skulason A (Saevarsson 46); Bjarnason B,
Gunnarsson, Sigurdsson G, Hallfredsson; Bodvarsson
(Gislason 89), Sigthorsson.
Holland: (433) Cillessen; van der Wiel, de Vrij, Martins
Indi, Blind; Afellay (Fer 78), de Jong, Sneijder
(Huntelaar 46); Robben, van Persie, Lens (Promes 68).
Referee: Carlos Velasco Carballo.

Kazakhstan (0) 2 *(Logvinenko 84, 90)*
Czech Republic (2) 4 *(Dockal 13, Lafata 44, Krejci 56,*
Necid 88)   24,000
Kazakhstan: (532) Sidelnikov; Miroshnichenko D
(Beisebekov 83), Vorotnikov, Abdulin, Logvinenko,
Shomko; Tagybergen, Karpovich (Konysbayev 57),
Islamkhan; Nuserbaev, Khizhnichenko (Nurgaliev 70).
Czech Republic: (4411) Cech; Kaderabek, Sivok
(Prochazka 81), Kadlec M, Limbersky; Dockal, Vacha,
Darida, Krejci (Pilar 69); Kolar; Lafata (Necid 79).
Referee: Mattias Gestranius.

Latvia (0) 1 *(Sabala 54 (pen))*
Turkey (0) 1 *(Kisa 47)*   6432
Latvia: (4411) Kolinko; Gabovs (Freimanis■ 37), Dubra,
Gorkss, Kurakins; Ikaunieks, Zjuzins (Morozs 83),
Fertovs, Visnakovs A; Sabala; Visnakovs E (Rakels 79).
Turkey: (4321) Babacan; Gonul, Topal, Kaya, Erkin;
Tufan, Ozyakup (Kisa 40), Turan; Sahan (Sari 59), Tore
(Altintop 70); Bulut.
Referee: Bobby Madden.

Sunday, 16 November 2014
Czech Republic (1) 2 *(Kaderabek 45, Bodvarsson 61 (og))*
Iceland (1) 1 *(Sigurdsson R 9)*   11,354
Czech Republic: (4411) Cech; Kaderabek, Sivok, Kadlec
M, Pudil; Dockal, Plasil, Darida, Krejci (Pilar 65);
Rosicky (Prochazka 90); Lafata (Necid 81).
Iceland: (442) Halldorsson; Bjarnason T (Saevarsson 63),
Sigurdsson R, Arnason, Skulason A; Hallfredsson
(Gislason 64), Sigurdsson G, Gunnarsson, Bjarnason B
(Gudmundsson 77); Bodvarsson, Sigthorsson.
Referee: Wolfgang Stark.

Holland (3) 6 *(van Persie 6, Robben 35, 82,*
Huntelaar 42, 89, Bruma 78)
Latvia (0) 0   50,000
Holland: (433) Cillessen; van der Wiel, Bruma, de Vrij,
Willems; Afellay (Depay 69), Blind (Clasie 20), Sneijder;
Robben, Huntelaar, van Persie (Wijnaldum 79).
Latvia: (4411) Kolinko; Gabovs, Dubra, Gorkss,
Kurakins; Ikaunieks (Laizans 46), Zjuzins (Cauna 54),
Fertovs, Visnakovs A; Sabala; Visnakovs E (Rudnevs 70).
Referee: Liran Liany.

Turkey (2) 3 *(Yilmaz 27 (pen), 29, Aziz 83)*
Kazakhstan (0) 1 *(Smakov 87 (pen))*   27,547
Turkey: (532) Babacan; Tufan, Aziz, Inan, Kaya, Erkin;
Sen (Tore 80), Turan, Sahan (Ekici 84); Bulut (Topal 74),
Yilmaz.
Kazakhstan: (343) Mokin; Gorman, Abdulin (Maliy 76),
Logvinenko; Lunin (Shchetkin 73), Tagybergen, Smakov,
Shomko; Konysbayev, Khizhnichenko (Nurgaliev 82),
Islamkhan.
Referee: Aleksei Eskov.

Saturday, 28 March 2015
Czech Republic (0) 1 *(Pilar 90)*
Latvia (1) 1 *(Visnakovs A 30)*   13,700
Czech Republic: (4231) Cech; Gebre Selassie, Kadlec M,
Prochazka, Limbersky; Darida, Plasil (Pilar 46); Dockal,
Rosicky, Krejci (Necid 57); Lafata (Kadlec V 81).
Latvia: (442) Vanins; Dubra, Gorkss, Freimanis,
Maksimenko; Laizans (Ikaunieks 66), Visnakovs A (Fertovs
81), Tarasovs, Zjuzins (Zigajevs 87); Sabala, Rakels.
Referee: Javier Estrada Fernandez.

Holland (0) 1 *(Huntelaar 90)*
Turkey (1) 1 *(Yilmaz 37)*   49,500
Holland: (433) Cillessen; van der Wiel, de Vrij, Martins
Indi (Willems 77), Blind; Wijnaldum (Narsingh 46), de
Jong (Dost 63), Sneijder; Afellay, Huntelaar, Depay.
Turkey: (433) Babacan; Gonul, Aziz (Gulum 69), Balta,
Erkin; Tufan, Topal, Inan; Tore, Yilmaz (Kazim-
Richards 79), Sen (Calhanoglu 60).
Referee: Felix Brych.

Kazakhstan (0) 0
Iceland (2) 3 *(Gudjohnsen 20, Bjarnason B 33, 90)* 13,182
Kazakhstan: (541) Sidelnikov; Gorman (Kuantayev 67),
Vorotnikov, Abdulin (Shchetkin 80), Loginovskiy,
Suyumbayev; Islamkhan, Tagybergen, Smakov,
Nurgaliev (Konysbayev 55); Tazhimbetov.
Iceland: (442) Halldorsson; Saevarsson, Arnason,
Sigurdsson R, Skulason A; Bjarnason B, Gunnarsson
(Hallfredsson 72), Sigurdsson G, Gudmundsson;
Gudjohnsen (Finnbogason 83), Sigthorsson (Bodvarsson
70).
Referee: Tasos Sidiropoulos.

Friday, 12 June 2015
Iceland (0) 2 *(Gunnarsson 60, Sigthorsson 76)*
Czech Republic (0) 1 *(Dockal 55)*   15,500
Iceland: (442) Halldorsson; Saevarsson, Sigurdsson R,
Arnason, Skulason A; Bjarnason B, Sigurdsson G,
Gunnarsson, Hallfredsson (Bodvarsson 63);
Gudmundsson, Sigthorsson (Gislason 90).
Czech Republic: (442) Cech; Kaderabek, Prochazka,
Sivok, Limbersky; Dockal (Darida 84), Rosicky, Pilar
(Krejci 68), Plasil; Vacha (Skoda 79), Necid.
Referee: William Collum.

Kazakhstan (0) 0
Turkey (0) 1 *(Turan 83)*   12,000
Kazakhstan: (541) Pokatilov; Maliy, Gorman
(Tagybergen 78), Abdulin, Logvinenko, Shomko;
Smakov (Beisebekov 67), Konysbayev, Islamkhan
(Kukeev 85), Schmidtgal; Khizhnichenko.
Turkey: (433) Babacan; Kaya (Tasdemir 75), Balta, Aziz,
Gonul; Tufan (Bulut 65), Calhanoglu, Inan; Turan, Topal
(Sen 46), Yilmaz.
Referee: Michael Oliver.

Latvia (0) 0
Holland (0) 2 *(Wijnaldum 67, Narsingh 71)*   9500
Latvia: (442) Vanins; Gorkss, Freimanis (Gabovs 37),
Maksimenko, Jagodinskis; Visnakovs A (Karasausks 75),
Ikaunieks, Tarasovs, Zjuzins; Sabala (Visnakovs E 61),
Rakels.
Holland: (433) Cillessen; van der Wiel, de Vrij, Martins
Indi, Willems (Janmaat 77); Blind, Sneijder, Narsingh;
Huntelaar, van Persie (Wijnaldum 63), Depay (Lens 87).
Referee: Svein Oddvar Moen.

Group A Table	P	W	D	L	F	A	GD	Pts
Iceland	6	5	0	1	14	3	11	15
Czech Republic	6	4	1	1	12	8	4	13
Netherlands	6	3	1	2	13	6	7	10
Turkey	6	2	2	2	7	8	-1	8
Latvia	6	0	3	3	2	13	-11	3
Kazakhstan	6	0	1	5	4	14	-10	1

GROUP B

Tuesday, 9 September 2014
Andorra (1) 1 *(Lima 6 (pen))*
Wales (1) 2 *(Bale 22, 81)*   10,000
Andorra: (442) Pol; Garcia E, Lima, Maneiro, Rubio;
Vales, Peppe (Vieira 52), Ayala (Sanchez Soto 86),
Martinez (Sonejae 83); Lorenzo, Riera.
Wales: (442) Hennessey; Gunter, Taylor N, Chester,
Davies; Williams A, Allen, King (Williams G 76),
Ramsey (Huws 90); Bale, Church (Ledley 62).
Referee: Slavko Vincic.

Bosnia-Herzegovina (1) 1 *(Ibisevic 6)*
Cyprus (1) 2 *(Christofi 45, 73)*   12,000
Bosnia-Herzegovina: (4132) Begovic; Vrsajevic, Bicakcic,
Sunjic, Lulic; Besic; Prcic (Hajrovic 61), Pjanic, Susic
(Medunjanin 61); Dzeko, Ibisevic.
Cyprus: (4411) Georgallides; Kyriakou, Merkis, Junior,
Antoniades; Efrem (Alexandrou 71), Nicolaou, Laban,
Aloneftis (Charalambous 46); Makridis (Sielis 83);
Christofi.
Referee: Yevhen Aranovskiy.

Friday, 10 October 2014
Belgium (3) 6 *(De Bruyne 31 (pen), 34, Chadli 37,
Origi 58, Mertens 65, 68)*
Andorra (0) 0   40,000
Belgium: (451) Courtois; Alderweireld, Kompany
(Pocognoli 55), Lombaerts, Vertonghen; Chadli (Fellaini
61), Nainggolan, Defour, De Bruyne, Mertens; Origi
(Lukaku 66).
Andorra: (4231) Pol; San Nicolas, Garcia E, Lima,
Maneiro; Ayala, Vales; Rubio (Lorenzo 61), Vieira,
Martinez (Moreno 77); Riera (Garcia M 71).
Referee: Serhiy Boiko.

Cyprus (0) 1 *(Makridis 67)*
Israel (2) 2 *(Damari 38, Ben Haim II 45)*   19,164
Cyprus: (4411) Georgallides; Stylianou (Kyriakou 46),
Merkis, Junior, Antoniades; Charalambidis (Sotiriou 46),
Nicolaou, Laban, Makris (Alexandrou 69); Makridis;
Christofi.
Israel: (4141) Martziano; Meshumar, Ben Haim, Tibi,
Ben Haroush; Yeini; Vermouth (Biton 83), Natcho,
Zahavi, Ben Haim II (Rafaelov 74); Damari (Shechter
69).
Referee: Daniele Orsato.

Wales (0) 0
Bosnia-Herzegovina (0) 0   30,741
Wales: (541) Hennessey; Gunter, Chester, Williams A,
Davies, Taylor N; King, Williams J (Williams G 82),
Ledley, Bale; Church (Robson-Kanu 65).
Bosnia-Herzegovina: (433) Begovic; Hadzic, Sunjic,
Mujdza, Besic; Lulic, Susic, Medunjanin; Ibisevic
(Hajrovic 83), Pjanic, Dzeko.
Referee: Vladislav Bezborodov.

Monday, 13 October 2014
Andorra (1) 1 *(Lima 15 (pen))*
Israel (2) 4 *(Damari 3, 41, 81, Hemed 90 (pen))* 800
Andorra: (4231) Pol; Maneiro, Lima (Ayala 40), Garcia
E, Rubio (Pujol 69); Vieira, Vales; Lorenzo, Peppe
(Toscano 83), Martinez; Riera.
Israel: (4141) Martziano; Meshumar, Ben Haim, Tibi,
Twatha; Biton; Vermouth (Shechter 65), Natcho, Zahavi
(Rafaelov 70), Ben Haim II; Damari (Hemed 84).
Referee: Cristian Balaj.

Bosnia-Herzegovina (1) 1 *(Dzeko 28)*
Belgium (0) 1 *(Nainggolan 51)*   12,000
Bosnia-Herzegovina: (442) Begovic; Mujdza, Hadzic,
Sunjic, Lulic; Pjanic, Besic, Medunjanin, Susic (Visca 72);
Ibisevic, Dzeko.
Belgium: (433) Courtois; Vertonghen, Lombaerts,
Kompany, Alderweireld; De Bruyne, Defour (Fellaini
77), Nainggolan; Lukaku (Mertens 57), Hazard, Origi.
Referee: Luca Banti.

Wales (2) 2 *(Cotterill 13, Robson-Kanu 23)*
Cyprus (1) 1 *(Laban 36)*   26,000
Wales: (451) Hennessey; Gunter, Williams A, Chester,
Taylor N; Williams G (Edwards 58), King■, Bale, Ledley,
Robson-Kanu (Taylor J 84); Church (Cotterill 6).
Cyprus: (4411) Kissas; Kyriakou, Merkis, Junior (Angeli
29 (Papathanasiou 85)), Antoniades; Efrem, Nicolaou
(Alexandrou 68), Laban, Sotiriou; Makridis; Christofi.
Referee: Manuel Grafe.

Sunday, 16 November 2014
Belgium (0) 0
Wales (0) 0   55,000
Belgium: (451) Courtois; Alderweireld, Lombaerts, Vertonghen, Van Damme; Witsel, De Bruyne, Fellaini, Hazard, Chadli (Benteke 62); Origi (Mertens 73 (Januzaj 89)).
Wales: (433) Hennessey; Gunter, Taylor N, Chester, Williams A; Allen, Ramsey, Bale; Ledley, Cotterill (Williams G 46), Robson-Kanu (Huws 90).
Referee: Pavel Kralovec.

Cyprus (3) 5 *(Merkis 9, Efrem 31, 42, 60, Christofi 87 (pen))*
Andorra (0) 0   6000
Cyprus: (442) Georgallides; Merkis, Angeli, Demetriou, Antoniades; Efrem (Laifis 78), Mitidis (Kolokoudias 63), Nicolaou, Laban; Christofi, Aloneftis (Makris 46).
Andorra: (4411) Pol; Rubio (Rodrigues 73), Garcia E, Lima (Rodriguez 49), Garcia M; Martinez, Vieira (Ayala 46), Vales, Lorenzo; Pujol; Riera.
Referee: Mark Clattenburg.

Israel (2) 3 *(Vermouth 36, Damari 45, Zahavi 70)*
Bosnia-Herzegovina (0) 0   32,000
Israel: (451) Martziano; Ben Haroush (Davidadze 78), Tibi, Ben Haim II, Meshumar; Yeini, Vermouth (Rafaelov 70), Natcho (Biton 74), Damari, Zahavi; Ben Haim.
Bosnia-Herzegovina: (451) Begovic; Hadzic, Spahic, Sunjic■, Mujdza (Visca 46); Besic (Prcic 46), Lulic, Medunjanin, Hajrovic, Pjanic (Cimirot 62); Kvrzic.
Referee: Antonio Miguel Mateu Lahoz.

Saturday, 28 March 2015
Andorra (0) 0
Bosnia-Herzegovina (1) 3 *(Dzeko 13, 49, 62)*   2500
Andorra: (4231) Pol; San Nicolas, Vales, Lima, Garcia M; Sonejee, Vieira; Clemente (Martinez 54), Rodriguez, Lorenzo (Rubio 85); Gomez (Riera 59).
Bosnia-Herzegovina: (442) Begovic; Mujdza, Spahic, Vranjes (Cocalic 73), Zukanovic; Visca, Besic, Pjanic, Lulic (Medunjanin 77); Ibisevic (Djuric 67), Dzeko.
Referee: Istvan Vad.

Belgium (2) 5 *(Fellaini 21, 66, Benteke 35, Hazard 67, Batshuayi 80)*
Cyprus (0) 0   45,000
Belgium: (4231) Courtois; Alderweireld, Kompany, Lombaerts, Vertonghen; Nainggolan, Witsel; De Bruyne, Fellaini (Carrasco 69), Hazard (Mertens 70); Benteke (Batshuayi 77).
Cyprus: (4231) Kissas; Kyriakou, Merkis, Laifis, Antoniades; Makris (Eleftheriou 71), Nicolaou; Laban (Economides 57), Sotiriou, Makridis (Kastanos 84); Mitidis.
Referee: Ovidiu Alin Hategan.

Israel (0) 0
Wales (1) 3 *(Ramsey 45, Bale 50, 77)*   30,200
Israel: (433) Marciano; Dgani, Ben Haim II, Tibi■, Ben Haroush; Natcho, Yeini, Zahavi (Sahar 70); Rafaelov, Ben Haim (Biton 60), Damari (Hemed 44).
Wales: (352) Hennessey; Collins, Williams A, Davies; Gunter, Allen, Ledley (Vaughan 47), Ramsey (MacDonald 85), Taylor N; Bale, Robson-Kanu (Vokes 69).
Referee: Milorad Mazic.

Tuesday, 31 March 2015
Israel (0) 0
Belgium (1) 1 *(Fellaini 10)*   33,000
Israel: (433) Marciano; Dgani, Ben Haim II, Gershon, Ben Haroush (Barda 84); Yeini (Rafaelov 66), Biton, Natcho; Zahavi, Hemed (Ben Haim 46), Sahar.
Belgium: (433) Courtois; Alderweireld, Kompany■, Lombaerts, Vertonghen; Fellaini, Nainggolan (Origi 86), Witsel; De Bruyne, Benteke (Denayer 66), Hazard (Chadli 63).
Referee: Mark Clattenburg.

Friday, 12 June 2015
Andorra (1) 1 *(Junior 2 (og))*
Cyprus (2) 3 *(Mitidis 14, 45, 53)*   1000
Andorra: (4411) Pol; Rubio, Rodrigues, Vales, Garcia M; Rebes (Peppe 79), Ayala (Sonejee 60), Rodriguez, Moreno (Lima 67); Martinez; Sanchez.
Cyprus: (4231) Georgallides; Demetriou, Sielis, Junior, Antoniades; Nicolaou, Laban (Economides 75); Christofi (Alexandrou 81), Makridis (Kastanos 88), Efrem; Mitidis.
Referee: Tobias Welz.

Bosnia-Herzegovina (2) 3 *(Visca 42, 76, Dzeko 45 (pen))*
Israel (1) 1 *(Ben Haim II 41)*   15,000
Bosnia-Herzegovina: (442) Begovic; Spahic, Kolasinac, Vranjes, Lulic (Hadzic 85); Besic, Medunjanin, Pjanic (Ibisevic 88), Mujdza; Visca (Hajrovic 80), Dzeko.
Israel: (433) Marciano; Ben Haim, Gershon, Dgani, Ben Haroush; Biton (Kahat 80), Natcho, Zahavi; Yeini (Damari 46), Ben Haim II, Sahar (Buzaglo 62).
Referee: Ruddy Buquet.

Wales (1) 1 *(Bale 25)*
Belgium (0) 0   33,280
Wales: (3142) Hennessey; Gunter, Williams A, Chester; Richards; Ledley, Taylor N, Allen, Ramsey; Robson-Kanu (King 90), Bale (Vokes 87).
Belgium: (433) Courtois; Alderweireld (Carrasco 76), Denayer, Lombaerts, Vertonghen; Mertens (Lukaku 46), Nainggolan, Witsel; De Bruyne, Benteke, Hazard.
Referee: Felix Brych.

Group B Table	P	W	D	L	F	A	GD	Pts
Wales	6	4	2	0	8	2	6	14
Belgium	6	3	2	1	13	2	11	11
Israel	6	3	0	3	10	9	1	9
Cyprus	6	3	0	3	12	11	1	9
Bosnia & Herzegovina	6	2	2	2	8	7	1	8
Andorra	6	0	0	6	3	23	−20	0

GROUP C

Monday, 8 September 2014
Luxembourg (1) 1 *(Gerson 42)*
Belarus (0) 1 *(Dragun 78)*   3000
Luxembourg: (442) Joubert; Janisch, Philipps, Schnell, Jans; Da Mota Alves (Laterza 67), Gerson, Martins Pereira, Holter (Payal 76); Bensi, Turpel (Luisi 63).
Belarus: (4141) Gutor; Shitov, Martynovich, Filipenko, Veretilo (Stasevich 62); Olekhnovich (Aleksiyevich 77); Kalachev, Kislyak (Kornilenko 73), Krivets, Balanovich; Dragun.
Referee: Gediminas Mazeika.

Spain (3) 5 *(Sergio Ramos 16 (pen), Alcacer 17, Busquets 45, Silva 50, Pedro 90)*
FYR Macedonia (1) 1 *(Ibraimi 28 (pen))*   16,000
Spain: (433) Casillas; Juanfran, Sergio Ramos (Bartra 68), Albiol, Jordi Alba; Busquets, Fabregas, Koke (Munir 77); Pedro, Alcacer (Isco 57), Silva.
FYR Macedonia: (541) Pacovski; Ristovski, Mojsov, Sikov, Cuculi, Alioski (Demiri 46); Ibraimi, Spirovski (Radeski 64), Trajkovski, Abdurahimi (Velkovski 74); Jahovic.
Referee: Tasos Sidiropoulos.

Ukraine (0) 0
Slovakia (1) 1 *(Mak 17)*   42,000
Ukraine: (451) Pyatov; Shevchuk, Kucher, Rakitskiy, Fedetskiy; Kovalchuk (Bezus 66), Stepanenko, Gusev (Gromov 81), Edmar, Yarmolenko; Zozulya.
Slovakia: (4411) Kozacik; Hubocan, Durica, Gyomber, Pekarik; Weiss (Stoch 67), Hamsik, Kucka, Mak (Duris 90); Pecovsky; Nemec (Kiss 63).
Referee: Craig Thomson.

Thursday, 9 October 2014

Belarus (0) 0

Ukraine (0) 2 *(Martynovich 82 (og), Sydorchuk 90)* 10,500

Belarus: (541) Zhevnov; Palyakow, Verkhovtsov, Martynovich (Savitskiy 87), Filipenko, Balanovich; Kalachev, Krivets, Dragun, Stasevich (Kislyak 46); Gordeichuk (Kornilenko 78).

Ukraine: (433) Pyatov; Fedetskiy, Kucher, Khacheridi, Shevchuk; Stepanenko, Edmar (Budkivskiy 79), Rotan (Sydorchuk 64); Yarmolenko, Zozulya (Tymoschuk 90), Konoplyanka.

Referee: Pol van Boekel.

FYR Macedonia (1) 3 *(Trajkovski 20, Jahovic 66 (pen), Abdurahimi 90)*

Luxembourg (2) 2 *(Bensi 39, Turpel 44)* 7000

FYR Macedonia: (4411) Pacovski; Ristovski, Sikov, Mojsov, Cuculi (Alioski 46); Muarem (Jahovic 60), Ademi, Demiri, Trajkovski; Ibraimi (Abdurahimi 46); Kostovski.

Luxembourg: (541) Joubert; Jans, Philipps, Chanot, Gerson, Janisch; Martins Pereira, Mutsch, Turpel (Deville 70), Da Mota Alves (Holter 63); Bensi (Laterza 75).

Referee: Paolo Mazzoleni.

Slovakia (1) 2 *(Kucka 17, Stoch 87)*

Spain (0) 1 *(Alcacer 82)* 9478

Slovakia: (433) Kozacik; Skrtel, Durica, Pekarik, Hubocan; Pecovsky, Gyomber, Kucka (Kiss 83); Mak (Stoch 61), Hamsik, Weiss (Duris 54).

Spain: (4411) Casillas; Pique, Albiol (Pedro 58), Juanfran (Cazorla 81), Jordi Alba; Busquets, Koke, Silva (Alcacer 71), Fabregas; Iniesta; Costa.

Referee: Bjorn Kuipers.

Sunday, 12 October 2014

Belarus (0) 1 *(Kalachev 79)*

Slovakia (0) 3 *(Hamsik 65, 84, Sestak 90)* 4500

Belarus: (4231) Zhevnov; Shitov (Stasevich 76), Martynovich, Filipenko (Palyakow 55), Bordachev; Verkhovtsov, Dragun; Kalachev, Krivets, Balanovich; Bressan (Gordeichuk 46).

Slovakia: (4231) Kozacik; Pekarik, Skrtel, Durica, Gyomber; Pecovsky, Kucka (Kiss 85); Mak (Sestak 62), Hamsik, Weiss (Stoch 80); Nemec.

Referee: Serge Gumienny.

Luxembourg (0) 0

Spain (2) 4 *(Silva 27, Alcacer 42, Costa 69, Bernat 88)* 8500

Luxembourg: (442) Joubert; Mutsch (Deville 86), Chanot, Martins Pereira (Turpel 60), Philipps; Janisch, Jans, Gerson, Holter; Da Mota Alves (Payal 75), Bensi.

Spain: (442) De Gea; Pique, Bartra, Jordi Alba, Carvajal; Busquets, Iniesta (Bernat 72), Koke, Silva (Pedro 71); Alcacer, Costa (Rodrigo 83).

Referee: Pawel Gil.

Ukraine (1) 1 *(Sydorchuk 45)*

FYR Macedonia (0) 0 33,900

Ukraine: (433) Pyatov; Khacheridi, Kucher, Shevchuk, Fedetskiy; Stepanenko, Rotan (Tymoschuk 90), Sydorchuk (Edmar 90); Yarmolenko, Konoplyanka, Zozulya (Budkivskiy 77).

FYR Macedonia: (442) Pacovski; Alioski, Damcevski, Sikov, Ristovski; Ademi, Gligorov (Stojkov 85), Abdurahimi, Trajkovski; Jahovic (Velkovski 62), Ivanovski (Kostovski 70).

Referee: Sebastien Delferiere.

Saturday, 15 November 2014

FYR Macedonia (0) 0

Slovakia (2) 2 *(Kucka 25, Nemec 38)* 6000

FYR Macedonia: (442) Pacovski; Ristovski, Sikov, Mojsov, Alioski; Abdurahimi, Ademi, Demiri (Babunski 74), Trajkovski; Velkovski (Ivanovski 70), Stojkov (Kostovski 46).

Slovakia: (4231) Kozacik; Pekarik (Svento 46), Skrtel, Durica, Hubocan; Pecovsky, Kucka (Kiss 55); Weiss (Duris 78), Hamsik, Stoch; Nemec.

Referee: Pedro Proenca.

Luxembourg (0) 0

Ukraine (1) 3 *(Yarmolenko 33, 53, 56)* 4379

Luxembourg: (451) Joubert; Jans, Schnell, Chanot, Janisch; Martins Pereira (Da Mota Alves 54), Gerson, Mutsch, Holter, Bensi (Joachim 63); Turpel (Deville 77).

Ukraine: (442) Pyatov; Fedetskiy, Rakitskiy, Khacheridi, Shevchuk; Sydorchuk, Tymoschuk, Konoplyanka (Morozyuk 77), Yarmolenko; Zozulya (Budkivskiy 72), Oliynyk (Kovalchuk 85).

Referee: Kristinn Jakobsson.

Spain (2) 3 *(Isco 18, Busquets 19, Pedro 55)*

Belarus (0) 0 19,249

Spain: (442) Casillas; Juanfran, Pique, Sergio Ramos, Jordi Alba; Cazorla (Callejon 69), Busquets (Bruno 46), Koke, Isco (Morata 80); Pedro, Alcacer.

Belarus: (532) Zhevnov; Matsveychyk, Politevich, Martynovich (Bordachev 30), Yanushkevich, Balanovich; Kalachev, Dragun, Nekhaychik; Krivets (Kislyak 80), Kornilenko (Signevich 66).

Referee: Kenn Hansen.

Friday, 27 March 2015

FYR Macedonia (1) 1 *(Trajkovski 9)*

Belarus (1) 2 *(Kalachev 44, Kornilenko 82)* 4000

FYR Macedonia: (442) Pacovski; Ristovski, Sikov, Markoski, Georgievski; Ibraimi, Hasani, Polozani (Bardhi 30), Trajkovski; Velkoski (Todorovski B 63), Abdurahimi (Blazevski 75).

Belarus: (4141) Zhevnov; Shitov, Martynovich, Filipenko, Bordachev; Maewski (Putsila 80); Kalachev, Hleb (Dragun 87), Kislyak, Stasevich (Nekhaychik 90); Kornilenko.

Referee: Anthony Taylor.

Slovakia (3) 3 *(Nemec 10, Weiss 21, Pekarik 40)*

Luxembourg (0) 0 9524

Slovakia: (4231) Kozacik; Pekarik, Skrtel, Durica, Hubocan; Weiss (Mak 71), Stoch (Sestak 80); Hamsik, Kucka (Hrosovsky 59), Pecovsky; Nemec.

Luxembourg: (4231) Joubert; Jans, Schnell, Chanot, Mutsch; Gerson, Holter (Da Mota Alves 51); Philipps, Bensi (Laterza 78), Joachim; Deville (Payal 64).

Referee: Stephan Studer.

Spain (1) 1 *(Morata 28)*

Ukraine (0) 0 45,000

Spain: (4141) Casillas; Juanfran, Pique, Sergio Ramos, Jordi Alba (Bernat 78); Busquets; Silva, Koke, Iniesta (Cazorla 74), Isco; Morata (Pedro 65).

Ukraine: (4231) Pyatov; Fedetskiy, Khacheridi, Kucher, Shevchuk; Tymoschuk, Rotan; Konoplyanka, Stepanenko (Garmash 76), Yarmolenko; Zozulya (Kravets 32 (Budkivskiy 90)).

Referee: Cuneyt Cakir.

Sunday, 14 June 2015

Belarus (0) 0

Spain (1) 1 *(Silva 45)* 13,000

Belarus: (442) Gorbunov; Martynovich, Shitov, Bordachev, Filipenko; Valadzko (Stasevich 81), Hleb (Putsila 89), Kislyak (Dragun 78), Nekhaychik; Maewski, Kornilenko.

Spain: (442) Casillas; Juanfran, Pique, Sergio Ramos, Jordi Alba; Silva (Bernat 85), Busquets, Fabregas (Isco 75), Cazorla; Pedro (Vitolo 64), Morata.

Referee: Robert Schorgenhofer.

Slovakia (2) 2 *(Salata 8, Hamsik 38)*

FYR Macedonia (0) 1 *(Ademi 69)* 11,000

Slovakia: (4231) Kozacik; Pekarik, Skrtel, Salata, Hubocan; Kucka (Hrosovsky 73), Pecovsky; Mak, Hamsik (Duda 80), Weiss; Nemec (Holosko 84).

FYR Macedonia: (4231) Pacovski; Todorovski A, Mojsov, Dimitrovski, Zuta; Trajcevski, Ademi; Ibraimi (Abdurahimi 89), Hasani, Muarem (Velkoski 82); Trajkovski (Ivanovski 56).

Referee: Kenn Hansen.

Ukraine (0) 3 *(Kravets 49, Garmash 58, Konoplyanka 86)*
Luxembourg (0) 0   32,000

Ukraine: (451) Pyatov; Morozyuk, Khacheridi, Shevchuk, Rakitskiy (Kucher 76); Yarmolenko, Stepanenko, Konoplyanka, Rotan (Garmash 45), Sydorchuk; Kravets (Seleznyov 71).
Luxembourg: (442) Joubert; Chanot, Schnell, Malget, Jans; Holter (Philipps 75), Payal, Gerson, Mutsch; Da Mota Alves (Deville 69), Turpel (Bensi 52).
Referee: Arnold Hunter.

Group C Table	P	W	D	L	F	A	GD	Pts
Slovakia	6	6	0	0	13	3	10	18
Spain	6	5	0	1	15	3	12	15
Ukraine	6	4	0	2	9	2	7	12
Belarus	6	1	1	4	4	11	–7	4
FYR Macedonia	6	1	0	5	6	14	–8	3
Luxembourg	6	0	1	5	3	17	–14	1

GROUP D

Sunday, 7 September 2014
Georgia (1) 1 *(Okriashvili 38)*
Republic of Ireland (1) 2 *(McGeady 23, 90)*   40,000

Georgia: (4141) Loria (Kvaskhvadze 46); Lobjanidze, Kvirkvelia S, Khubutia, Kvirkvelia D; Kashia; Kankava, Daushvili, Ananidze (Targamadze 62), Okriashvili (Mchedlidze 88); Gelashvili.
Republic of Ireland: (4141) Forde; Coleman, O'Shea, Wilson, Ward; McCarthy (Meyler 90); Whelan, Walters, Keane (Long 75), McGeady; Quinn (Brady 76).
Referee: Kevin Blom.

Germany (1) 2 *(Muller 18, 70)*
Scotland (0) 1 *(Anya 66)*   60,209

Germany: (4231) Neuer; Rudy, Howedes, Boateng, Durm; Kroos, Kramer, Gotze, Reus (Ginter 90); Schurrle (Podolski 84); Muller.
Scotland: (442) Marshall; Hutton, Martin R, Whittaker, Hanley; Mulgrew■, Morrison, Fletcher D (McArthur 58), Bannan (Fletcher S 58); Anya, Naismith (Maloney 82).
Referee: Svein Oddvar Moen.

Gibraltar (0) 0
Poland (1) 7 *(Grosicki 11, 47, Lewandowski 50, 53, 86, 90, Szukala 58)*   3000

Gibraltar: (451) Perez J; Wiseman, Chipolina J, Artell (Payas 87), Chipolina R; Casciaro L, Bado, Casciaro R, Walker, Perez B; Casciaro K (Priestley 62).
Poland: (442) Szczesny; Olkowski, Szukala, Glik, Wawrzyniak; Grosicki (Starzynski 78), Krychowiak, Klich (Maczynski 71), Rybus; Milik (Sobota 71), Lewandowski.
Referee: Stefan Johannesson.

Saturday, 11 October 2014
Poland (0) 2 *(Milik 51, Mila 88)*
Germany (0) 0   57,500

Poland: (442) Szczesny; Szukala, Jodlowiec, Wawrzyniak (Jedrzejczyk 84), Glik; Piszczek, Krychowiak, Grosicki (Sobota 71), Rybus; Milik (Mila 77), Lewandowski.
Germany: (4231) Neuer; Hummels, Durm, Rudiger (Kruse 83); Boateng, Bellarabi, Kroos; Gotze, Kramer (Draxler 72), Schurrle (Podolski 78); Muller.
Referee: Pedro Proenca.

Republic of Ireland (3) 7 *(Keane 6, 14, 18 (pen), McClean 46, 53, Perez J 51 (og), Hoolahan 56)*
Gibraltar (0) 0   18,500

Republic of Ireland: (442) Forde; Meyler, O'Shea, Wilson, Ward (Brady 70); McGeady, Hendrick, Gibson, McClean; Hoolahan (Doyle 63); Keane (Murphy 63).
Gibraltar: (451) Perez J (Robba 60); Wiseman, Casciaro R, Chipolina R (Santos 58), Chipolina J; Perez B, Bado (Guilling 46), Payas, Walker, Gosling; Casciaro L.
Referee: Leontios Trattou.

Scotland (1) 1 *(Khubutia 28 (og))*
Georgia (0) 0   48,000

Scotland: (433) Marshall; Robertson, Martin R, Hanley, Hutton; Maloney, Brown, Anya; Fletcher S (Martin C 90), Morrison, Naismith (McArthur 80).
Georgia: (442) Loria; Lobjanidze, Khubutia, Kvirkvelia D (Okriashvili 46), Kvirkvelia S; Daushvili, Grigalava, Kazaishvili (Chanturia 80), Kankava; Gelashvili, Papava (Dzaria 70).
Referee: Miroslav Zelinka.

Tuesday, 14 October 2014
Germany (0) 1 *(Kroos 71)*
Republic of Ireland (0) 1 *(O'Shea 90)*   52,000

Germany: (4231) Neuer; Rudiger, Boateng, Hummels, Durm; Ginter (Podolski 46), Kroos; Bellarabi (Rudy 86), Gotze, Draxler (Kruse 70); Muller.
Republic of Ireland: (442) Forde; Meyler, O'Shea, Wilson, Ward; McGeady, Quinn (Hoolahan 76), Whelan (Hendrick 53), McClean; Walters, Keane (Gibson 62).
Referee: Damir Skomina.

Gibraltar (0) 0
Georgia (2) 3 *(Gelashvili 9, Okriashvili 20, Kankava 69)*   600

Gibraltar: (451) Robba; Garcia, Wiseman, Santos (Chipolina R 76), Chipolina J; Guilling (Gosling 75), Perez B, Casciaro R, Walker, Casciaro K (Priestley 46); Casciaro L.
Georgia: (4231) Loria; Lobjanidze, Khubutia, Kvirkvelia S, Grigalava; Kankava, Dzaria; Okriashvili, Ananidze (Ebralidze 80), Chanturia (Dvalishvili 76); Gelashvili (Papunashvili 67).
Referee: Harald Lechner.

Poland (1) 2 *(Maczynski 11, Milik 76)*
Scotland (1) 2 *(Maloney 18, Naismith 57)*   55,197

Poland: (442) Szczesny; Piszczek, Szukala, Glik, Jedrzejczyk (Zyro 89), Maczynski, Krychowiak, Sobota (Mila 63); Lewandowski, Milik.
Scotland: (442) Marshall; Hutton, Martin R, Greer, Whittaker; Maloney, Morrison, Brown, Anya; Fletcher S (Fletcher D 70), Naismith (Martin C 70).
Referee: Alberto Undiano Mallenco.

Friday, 14 November 2014
Georgia (0) 0
Poland (0) 4 *(Glik 51, Krychowiak 71, Mila 73, Milik 90)*   18,000

Georgia: (4231) Loria; Lobjanidze, Kvirkvelia S, Khubutia, Grigalava; Daushvili, Kashia; Ananidze (Okriashvili 59), Kankava, Kobakhidze (Dzalamidze 88); Mchedlidze (Chanturia 68).
Poland: (4231) Szczesny; Piszczek, Szukala, Glik, Jedrzejczyk; Krychowiak, Maczynski (Jodlowiec 66); Grosicki (Rybus 69), Milik, Mila (Linetty 86); Lewandowski.
Referee: Paolo Tagliavento.

Germany (3) 4 *(Muller 11, 29, Gotze 38, Santos 67 (og))*
Gibraltar (0) 0   44,380

Germany: (3142) Neuer; Durm (Hector 71), Boateng, Mustafi; Kroos (Bender 79); Gotze, Khedira (Volland 60), Podolski, Kruse; Muller, Bellarabi.
Gibraltar: (451) Robba; Garcia, Artell, Wiseman, Casciaro R; Chipolina J, Perez B (Priestley 90), Chipolina R, Sergeant (Santos 58), Walker; Casciaro L (Casciaro K 71).
Referee: Alexandru Dan Tudor.

Scotland (0) 1 *(Maloney 74)*
Republic of Ireland (0) 0   60,000

Scotland: (4411) Marshall; Whittaker, Martin R, Hanley, Robertson; Maloney, Mulgrew, Brown, Anya (Fletcher D 88); Naismith; Fletcher S (Martin C 56).
Republic of Ireland: (442) Forde; Coleman, Keogh, O'Shea, Ward; McGeady, Hendrick (Keane 78), Gibson (Quinn 69), McClean; Walters, Long (Brady 68).
Referee: Milorad Mazic.

Sunday, 29 March 2015

Georgia (0) 0

Germany (2) 2 *(Reus 39, Muller 44)* 54,549

Georgia: (451) Loria; Lobjanidze, Kvirkvelia S, Amisulashvili (Dvali 4), Kashia; Navalovski, Kobakhidze, Kankava, Makharadze (Kenia 63), Okriashvili (Chanturia 47); Mchedlidze.

Germany: (4231) Neuer; Rudy, Boateng, Hummels, Hector; Schweinsteiger, Kroos; Muller (Schurrle 86), Ozil, Reus; Gotze (Podolski 87).

Referee: Clement Turpin.

Republic of Ireland (0) 1 *(Long 90)*

Poland (1) 1 *(Peszko 26)* 50,500

Republic of Ireland: (442) Given; Coleman, O'Shea, Wilson, Brady; Hoolahan, Whelan (Long 83), McCarthy, McGeady (McClean 68); Keane, Walters.

Poland: (442) Fabianski; Olkowski, Szukala, Glik, Wawrzyniak; Peszko (Kucharczyk 87), Krychowiak, Jodlowiec, Rybus; Lewandowski, Milik (Mila 83).

Referee: Jonas Eriksson.

Scotland (4) 6 *(Maloney 18 (pen), 34 (pen), Fletcher S 29, 77, 90, Naismith 39)*

Gibraltar (1) 1 *(Casciaro L 19)* 34,255

Scotland: (352) Marshall; Martin R, Hutton, Robertson; Anya (Bannan 74), Brown, Morrison, Maloney, Ritchie (Greer 46); Fletcher S, Naismith (Rhodes 65).

Gibraltar: (451) Robba; Wiseman, Artell (Garcia 53), Casciaro R, Chipolina J; Walker, Payas, Chipolina R (Gosling 73), Bardon (Duarte 82), Priestley; Casciaro L.

Referee: Mattias Gestranius.

Saturday, 13 June 2015

Gibraltar (0) 0

Germany (1) 7 *(Schurrle 28, 65, 71, Kruse 47, 81, Gundogan 51, Bellarabi 57)* 7467

Gibraltar: (442) Perez J; Garcia, Chipolina R, Casciaro R, Chipolina J; Gosling, Walker, Payas (Sergeant 83), Casciaro K (Bosio 78); Casciaro L, Priestley (Coombes 61).

Germany: (352) Weidenfeller; Rudy, Boateng, Hector; Herrmann (Podolski 56), Ozil, Schweinsteiger, Gundogan (Khedira 67), Bellarabi; Gotze (Kruse 35), Schurrle.

Referee: Clayton Pisani.

Poland (0) 4 *(Milik 61, Lewandowski 89, 90, 90)*

Georgia (0) 0 5600

Poland: (442) Fabianski; Piszczek, Szukala, Pazdan (Komorowski 90), Rybus; Grosicki (Jodlowiec 78), Krychowiak, Maczynski, Peszko (Blaszczykowski 64); Lewandowski, Milik.

Georgia: (541) Loria; Lobjanidze, Kashia, Amisulashvili, Dvali, Navalovski; Okriashvili (Daushvili 46), Ananidze, Kobakhidze (Tskhadadze 75), Kazaishvili; Vatsadze (Chanturia 63).

Referee: Aleksei Kulbakov.

Republic of Ireland (1) 1 *(Walters 39)*

Scotland (0) 1 *(O'Shea 46 (og))* 49,063

Republic of Ireland: (442) Given; Coleman, O'Shea, Wilson, Brady; Hendrick, Whelan (McClean 68), McCarthy, Hoolahan (Keane 73); Walters, Murphy (Long 80).

Scotland: (4231) Marshall; Hutton, Martin R, Mulgrew, Forsyth; Ritchie (Anya 45), Brown (McArthur 85); Morrison, Naismith (Berra 90), Maloney; Fletcher S.

Referee: Nicola Rizzoli.

Group D Table	P	W	D	L	F	A	GD	Pts
Poland	6	4	2	0	20	3	17	14
Germany	6	4	1	1	16	4	12	13
Scotland	6	3	2	1	12	6	6	11
Republic of Ireland	6	2	3	1	12	5	7	9
Georgia	6	1	0	5	4	13	-9	3
Gibraltar	6	0	0	6	1	34	-33	0

GROUP E

Monday, 8 September 2014

Estonia (0) 1 *(Purje 86)*

Slovenia (0) 0 14,000

Estonia: (451) Pareiko; Teniste (Jaager 71), Morozov, Klavan, Kallaste; Antonov (Kams 67), Vunk, Mets, Lindpere (Purje 84), Zenjov; Anier.

Slovenia: (433) Handanovic; Struna, Cesar, Samardzic, Brecko; Kurtic, Rotman (Lazarevic 89), Kampl; Stevanovic■, Ilicic (Birsa 62), Novakovic.

Referee: Szymon Marciniak.

San Marino (0) 0

Lithuania (2) 2 *(Matulevicius 5, Novikovas 36)* 986

San Marino: (532) Simoncini A; Vitaioli F, Simoncini D, Brolli, Bonini (Buscarini 87), Battistini; Gasperoni A, Tosi (Cervellini 56), Vitaioli M; Hirsch (Stefanelli 76), Selva.

Lithuania: (4231) Arlauskis; Freidgeimas, Kijanskas, Zaliukas, Slavickas; Chvedukas, Panka (Vicius 66); Cernych (Kuklys 89), Kalonas, Novikovas; Matulevicius (Stankevicius 85).

Referee: Libor Kovank.

Switzerland (0) 0

England (0) 2 *(Welbeck 59, 90)* 35,500

Switzerland: (433) Sommer; Lichtsteiner, von Bergen, Djourou, Rodriguez; Behrami, Inler, Xhaka (Dzemaili 74); Shaqiri, Seferovic, Mehmedi (Drmic 64).

England: (4312) Hart; Stones, Cahill, Jones (Jagielka 77), Baines; Wilshere (Milner 73), Henderson, Delph; Sterling; Welbeck, Rooney (Lambert 90).

Referee: Cuneyt Cakir.

Thursday, 9 October 2014

England (2) 5 *(Jagielka 24, Rooney 43 (pen), Welbeck 49, Townsend 72, Della Valle 77 (og))*

San Marino (0) 0 55,990

England: (433) Hart; Chambers, Cahill, Jagielka, Gibbs; Henderson (Oxlade-Chamberlain 46), Milner, Wilshere; Welbeck (Townsend 66), Rooney, Sterling (Lallana 46).

San Marino: (541) Simoncini A; Palazzi (Buscarini 73), Vitaioli F, Della Valle, Brolli, Battistini; Hirsch, Tosi (Gasperoni L 63), Chiaruzzi, Vitaioli M; Selva (Rinaldi 87).

Referee: Marcin Borski.

Lithuania (0) 1 *(Mikoliunas 76)*

Estonia (0) 0 4800

Lithuania: (4411) Arlauskis; Vaitkunas, Freidgeimas, Kijanskas, Andriuskevicius; Novikovas, Vicius, Panka, Cernych; Kalonas (Mikoliunas 63); Matulevicius (Beniusis 90).

Estonia: (4141) Pareiko; Kallaste■, Klavan, Barengrub, Jaager; Mets; Antonov, Vunk (Purje 80), Lindpere (Vassiljev 77), Zenjov (Ojamaa 64); Anier.

Referee: Carlos Clos Gomez.

Slovenia (0) 1 *(Novakovic 80 (pen))*

Switzerland (0) 0 8500

Slovenia: (4312) Handanovic; Brecko, Ilic, Cesar, Struna; Birsa (Lazarevic 55), Mertelj, Kirm (Pecnik 72); Kampl; Ljubijankic (Kurtic 46), Novakovic.

Switzerland: (442) Sommer; Lichtsteiner, Djourou, Senderos (von Bergen 70), Rodriguez; Shaqiri, Behrami, Inler (Kasami 81), Xhaka; Seferovic, Drmic (Mehmedi 73).

Referee: Wolfgang Stark.

Sunday, 12 October 2014

Estonia (0) 0

England (0) 1 *(Rooney 73)* 9692

Estonia: (4141) Pareiko; Jaager, Morozov, Klavan■, Pikk; Mets; Antonov, Vunk (Kruglov 83), Vassiljev (Lindpere 46), Zenjov (Ojamaa 79); Anier.

England: (442) Hart; Chambers, Cahill, Jagielka, Baines; Henderson (Sterling 46), Wilshere, Delph (Oxlade-Chamberlain 61), Lallana; Welbeck (Lambert 80), Rooney.

Referee: Marijo Strahonja.

Lithuania (0) 0
Slovenia (2) 2 *(Novakovic 33, 37)* 4000
Lithuania: (442) Arlauskis; Vaitkunas, Freidgeimas, Kijanskas, Andriuskevicius; Novikovas, Zulpa, Panka (Vicius 32), Cernych; Chvedukas (Mikoliunas 75), Matulevicius.
Slovenia: (4132) Handanovic; Brecko, Ilic, Cesar, Struna; Stevanovic (Mertelj 46); Pecnik (Birsa 66), Kurtic, Kirm (Lazarevic 86); Kampl, Novakovic.
Referee: Michail Koukoulakis.

Tuesday, 14 October 2014
San Marino (0) 0
Switzerland (3) 4 *(Seferovic 10, 23, Dzemaili 30, Shaqiri 79)* 5700
San Marino: (541) Simoncini A; Bonini, Vitaioli F (Cervellini 17), Della Valle, Brolli, Battistini; Palazzi, Gasperoni A (Gasperoni L 70), Chiaruzzi, Vitaioli M (Hirsch 61); Stefanelli.
Switzerland: (41212) Sommer; Rodriguez, Djourou, von Bergen, Lichtsteiner (Widmer 59); Xhaka; Dzemaili, Kasami (Barnetta 72); Shaqiri; Drmic (Mehmedi 46), Seferovic.
Referee: Tony Chapron.

Saturday, 15 November 2014
England (0) 3 *(Rooney 59 (pen), Welbeck 65, 72)*
Slovenia (0) 1 *(Henderson 57 (og))* 90,000
England: (433) Hart; Clyne, Cahill, Jagielka (Smalling 89), Gibbs; Henderson, Wilshere, Lallana (Milner 79); Welbeck, Rooney, Sterling (Oxlade-Chamberlain 84).
Slovenia: (4141) Handanovic; Brecko, Cesar, Ilic, Struna; Kirm (Ljubijankic 77); Birsa (Lazarevic 62), Kampl, Kurtic (Rotman 75), Mertelj; Novakovic.
Referee: Olegario Benquerenca.

San Marino (0) 0
Estonia (0) 0 759
San Marino: (541) Simoncini A; Bonini, Vitaioli F, Simoncini D, Brolli, Palazzi; Hirsch (Battistini 60), Chiaruzzi, Tosi, Vitaioli M (Golinucci E 77); Selva (Rinaldi 83).
Estonia: (442) Aksalu; Teniste, Morozov, Artjunin (Teever 74), Kruglov; Antonov, Dmitrijev (Lindpere 46), Mets, Vassiljev; Ojamaa (Anier 62), Zenjov.
Referee: Felix Brych.

Switzerland (0) 4 *(Schar Arlauskis 66 (og), 68, Shaqiri 80, 90)*
Lithuania (0) 0 16,050
Switzerland: (433) Sommer; Moubandje (Fernandes 75), Schar, Djourou, Lichtsteiner; Dzemaili, Inler, Behrami; Mehmedi (Drmic 63), Shaqiri, Seferovic (Schonbachler 83).
Lithuania: (451) Arlauskis; Vaitkunas (Borovskij 64), Freidgeimas, Kijanskas, Andriuskevicius; Cernych, Vicius (Eliosius 83), Chvedukas, Zulpa, Novikovas (Kazlauskas 87); Matulevicius.
Referee: Svein Oddvar Moen.

Friday, 27 March 2015
England (2) 4 *(Rooney 7, Welbeck 45, Sterling 58, Kane 73)*
Lithuania (0) 0 83,671
England: (433) Hart; Clyne, Cahill, Jones, Baines; Henderson (Barkley 71); Carrick, Delph; Sterling, Welbeck (Walcott 77), Rooney (Kane 71).
Lithuania: (532) Arlauskis; Freidgeimas, Kijanskas, Mikuckis (Stankevicius 66), Zaliukas, Andriuskevicius (Slavickas 83); Zulpa, Mikoliunas (Kazlauskas 88), Chvedukas; Cernych, Matulevicius.
Referee: Pavel Kralovec.

Slovenia (1) 6 *(Ilicic 10, Kampl 49, Struna 50, Novakovic 52, Lazarevic 73, Ilic 88)*
San Marino (0) 0 8300
Slovenia: (433) Handanovic; Brecko (Stojanovic 76), Ilic, Cesar, Struna; Birsa, Kurtic, Kirm (Lazarevic 60); Ilicic (Beric 72), Kampl, Novakovic.
San Marino: (541) Benedettini; Bonini, Brolli, Simoncini D, Tosi (Battistini 56), Della Valle (Vitaioli F 77); Hirsch (Golinucci A 83), Mazza, Vitaioli M, Selva; Palazzi.
Referee: Oliver Drachta.

Switzerland (2) 3 *(Schar 17, Xhaka 27, Seferovic 80)*
Estonia (0) 0 14,000
Switzerland: (4312) Sommer; Lichtsteiner (Widmer 77), Schar, Djourou, Rodriguez; Behrami, Inler, Xhaka (Frei 88); Shaqiri; Seferovic, Drmic (Stocker 62).
Estonia: (442) Pareiko; Teniste, Jaager, Klavan, Kallaste; Vassiljev, Dmitrijev (Kruglov 62), Mets, Antonov; Zenjov (Alliku 87), Anier (Ojamaa 56).
Referee: Danny Makkelie.

Sunday, 14 June 2015
Estonia (1) 2 *(Zenjov 35, 63)*
San Marino (0) 0 6131
Estonia: (4141) Aksalu; Teniste, Mets, Klavan, Kallaste; Dmitrijev; Alliku, Lindpere (Kruglov 84), Vassiljev (Antonov 78), Zenjov (Teever 89); Purje.
San Marino: (541) Simoncini A; Bonini, Brolli, Della Valle, Palazzi, Battistini; Hirsch, Tosi (Cervellini 71), Gasperoni L, Vitaioli M (Bianchi 89); Rinaldi (Stefanelli 79).
Referee: Ivan Kruzliak.

Lithuania (0) 1 *(Cernych 64)*
Switzerland (0) 2 *(Drmic 69, Shaqiri 84)* 4786
Lithuania: (4411) Zubas; Vaitkunas, Mikuckis, Klimavicius, Andriuskevicius; Cesnauskis (Luksa 85), Panka, Zulpa (Chvedukas 61), Cernych; Slivka (Vicius 76); Matulevicius.
Switzerland: (433) Sommer; Lichtsteiner, Schar, Djourou, Rodriguez; Behrami, Inler (Dzemaili 58), Xhaka; Seferovic (Mehmedi 58), Shaqiri, Drmic (Embolo 82).
Referee: Craig Thomson.

Slovenia (1) 2 *(Novakovic 37, Pecnik 84)*
England (0) 3 *(Wilshere 57, 73, Rooney 86)* 15,500
Slovenia: (4411) Handanovic; Brecko, Ilic, Cesar, Jokic; Ilicic (Birsa 61), Mertelj, Kurtic (Lazarevic 79), Kirm (Pecnik 72); Kampl; Novakovic.
England: (451) Hart; Jones (Lallana 46), Cahill, Smalling, Gibbs; Sterling, Henderson, Wilshere, Delph (Clyne 85), Townsend (Walcott 75); Rooney.
Referee: Alberto Undiano Mallenco.

Group E Table	P	W	D	L	F	A	GD	Pts
England	6	6	0	0	18	3	15	18
Switzerland	6	4	0	2	13	4	9	12
Slovenia	6	3	0	3	12	7	5	9
Estonia	6	2	1	3	4	2	2	7
Lithuania	6	2	0	4	4	12	–8	6
San Marino	6	0	1	5	0	19	–19	1

GROUP F

Sunday, 7 September 2014
Faroe Islands (1) 1 *(Holst 41)*
Finland (0) 3 *(Riski 53, 79, Eremenko 83)* 3300
Faroe Islands: (4141) Nielsen; Naes, Faero, Nattestad, Davidsen V; Benjaminsen; Hansson, Jakobsen (Baldvinsson 56), Sorensen (Jonsson 76), Holst; Klettskard (Edmundsson 46).
Finland: (4141) Maenpaa; Arkivuo, Moisander, Toivio, Uronen (Markkanen 76); Sparv; Hetemaj, Riski, Eremenko, Ring; Pukki (Pohjanpalo 89).
Referee: Lee Evans.

Greece (0) 0
Romania (1) 1 *(Marica 10 (pen))* 173
Greece: (433) Karnezis; Manolas, Torosidis, Papastathopoulos, Holebas; Mantalos (Christodoulopoulos 65), Samaris (Kone 65), Tachtsidis; Mitroglou, Samaras (Diamantakos 46), Salpingidis.
Romania: (433) Tatarusanu; Rat, Tamas, Chiriches, Grigore; Hoban (Prepelita 84), Chipciu (Torje 90), Pintilii; Maxim (Enache 67), Marica■, Stancu.
Referee: Mark Clattenburg.
Behind closed doors.

Hungary (0) 1 *(Priskin 75)*
Northern Ireland (0) 2 *(McGinn 81, Lafferty 88)*   12,000
Hungary: (343) Gulacsi; Vanczak, Liptak, Juhasz;
Gyurcso (Lovrencsics 59), Varga, Tozser, Balogh; Rudolf
(Kovacs 70), Nikolic (Priskin 46), Dzsudzsak.
Northern Ireland: (442) Carroll; McLaughlin C, McAuley
(Cathcart 72), Hughes, Brunt; Evans C, Davis, Norwood
(McKay 79), Baird; Ward (McGinn 66), Lafferty K.
Referee: Deniz Aytekin.

Saturday, 11 October 2014
Finland (0) 1 *(Hurme 55)*
Greece (1) 1 *(Karelis 24)*   23,500
Finland: (433) Maenpaa; Arkivuo, Moisander, Toivio,
Hurme; Ring, Sparv, Hetemaj (Hamalainen 46);
Eremenko, Riski (Tainio 88), Pukki (Pohjanpalo 70).
Greece: (433) Karnezis; Vyntra, Papastathopoulos,
Manolas, Torosidis; Samaris, Tachtsidis, Maniatis; Karelis
(Samaras 81), Athanasiadis (Mitroglou 84), Mavrias
(Moras 70).
Referee: David Fernandez Borbalan.

Northern Ireland (2) 2 *(McAuley 6, Lafferty K 20)*
Faroe Islands (0) 0   10,500
Northern Ireland: (451) Carroll; McLaughlin C, McAuley
(McCullough 56), Hughes, Ferguson; McGinn (McCourt
67), Davis, Baird, Norwood, Ward; Lafferty K (Magennis
83).
Faroe Islands: (433) Nielsen; Gregersen, Nattestad,
Justinussen (Bartalstovu 90), Davidsen V; Naes,
Benjaminsen, Hansson; Holst (Olsen B 81),
Edmundsson, Klettskard (Hansen A 75).
Referee: Alon Yefet.

Romania (1) 1 *(Rusescu 45)*
Hungary (0) 1 *(Dzsudzsak 82)*   54,000
Romania: (4231) Tatarusanu; Chiriches, Goian (Gardos
5), Grigore, Rat; Pintilii, Hoban; Maxim (Stancu 84),
Chipciu, Sanmartean (Tanase 66); Rusescu.
Hungary: (4231) Kiraly; Varga, Korcsmar, Juhasz, Kadar;
Gera (Tozser 77), Elek; Lovrencsics (Simon K 63),
Dzsudzsak, Stieber (Nikolic 46); Szalai.
Referee: William Collum.

Tuesday, 14 October 2014
Faroe Islands (0) 0
Hungary (1) 1 *(Szalai 21)*   2000
Faroe Islands: (451) Nielsen; Nattestad, Gregersen,
Davidsen V, Naes; Benjaminsen, Holst (Bartalstovu 69),
Hansson, Edmundsson (Hansen A 75), Olsen B;
Vatnhamar (Sorensen 81).
Hungary: (451) Dibusz; Korhut, Juhasz, Varga, Kadar;
Simon K, Nikolic (Fiola 46), Gera, Szalai (Priskin 83),
Dzsudzsak; Tozser (Kalmar 73).
Referee: Aleksei Kulbakov.

Finland (0) 0
Romania (0) 2 *(Stancu 54, 83)*   20,000
Finland: (433) Maenpaa; Hurme, Toivio, Arkivuo,
Moisander; Ring■, Sparv, Hetemaj (Pohjanpalo 64);
Hamalainen (Markkanen 74), Pukki (Riski 46),
Eremenko.
Romania: (4411) Tatarusanu; Luchin, Chiriches, Grigore,
Rat; Torje, Hoban, Pintilii, Tanase (Enache 85); Chipciu
(Sanmartean 49); Stancu (Rusescu 86).
Referee: Paolo Tagliavento.

Greece (0) 0
Northern Ireland (1) 2 *(Ward 9, Lafferty K 51)*   24,000
Greece: (442) Karnezis; Torosidis, Papastathopoulos,
Manolas, Vyntra (Stafylidis 16); Karelis, Tachtsidis,
Maniatis, Samaras (Salpingidis 67); Athanasiadis
(Samaris 46), Mitroglou.
Northern Ireland: (451) Carroll; McLaughlin C, McAuley,
Hughes, Ferguson (Reeves 78); Evans C, Davis, Baird,
Norwood, Ward (McGivern 59); Lafferty K (Magennis
72).
Referee: Stephane Lannoy.

Friday, 14 November 2014
Greece (0) 0
Faroe Islands (0) 1 *(Edmundsson 61)*   7000
Greece: (4231) Karnezis; Torosidis, Manolas, Moras,
Karabelas (Mantalos 78); Maniatis, Samaris; Karelis
(Mavrias 62), Kone, Christodoulopoulos; Gekas
(Athanasiadis 46).
Faroe Islands: (451) Nielsen; Naes, Gregersen, Nattestad,
Davidsen V; Vatnhamar, Olsen B (Olsen K 88),
Benjaminsen, Hansson, Holst (Justinussen 75);
Edmundsson (Faero 85).
Referee: Nicola Rizzoli.

Hungary (0) 1 *(Gera 84)*
Finland (0) 0   19,500
Hungary: (451) Kiraly; Lang, Kadar, Fiola, Juhasz (Forro
57); Elek, Tozser, Dzsudzsak, Simon K (Lovrencsics 77),
Gera; Szalai (Nikolic 63).
Finland: (451) Hradecky; Moisander, Uronen, Hurme,
Toivio; Eremenko, Hetemaj, Sparv, Halsti (Markkanen
87), Hamalainen (Riski 82); Pukki (Pohjanpalo 65).
Referee: Clement Turpin.

Romania (0) 2 *(Papp 74, 79)*
Northern Ireland (0) 0   40,000
Romania: (4231) Tatarusanu; Papp, Chiriches, Grigore,
Rat; Pintilii, Sanmartean; Torje (Hoban 81), Chipciu,
Tanase (Maxim 58); Stancu (Keseru 46).
Northern Ireland: (451) Carroll; McLaughlin C,
McGivern, McAuley, Baird; Hughes, Brunt, Evans C
(McKay 78), Norwood, McGinn (Clingan 63); Lafferty K.
Referee: Jonas Eriksson.

Sunday, 29 March 2015
Hungary (0) 0
Greece (0) 0   22,000
Hungary: (4231) Kiraly; Juhasz, Kadar, De Almeida,
Elek (Pinter 70); Tozser, Stieber; Gera, Dzsudzsak,
Lovrencsics; Szalai (Nikolic 67).
Greece: (433) Karnezis; Papadopoulos, Papastathopoulos,
Manolas, Torosidis; Stafylidis, Kone (Katsouranis 77),
Samaris; Fetfatzidis (Gianniotas 77), Christodoulopoulos
(Fortounis 69), Athanasiadis.
Referee: Sergei Karasev.

Northern Ireland (2) 2 *(Lafferty K 33, 38)*
Finland (0) 1 *(Sadik 90)*   10,264
Northern Ireland: (433) Carroll; McLaughlin C, Evans J,
McAuley, Brunt; Davis (Evans C 46), Baird, Norwood;
McGinn (Dallas 64), Lafferty K (Magennis 79), Ward.
Finland: (433) Hradecky; Sorsa, Toivio (Arajuuri 46),
Moisander, Uronen; Ring, Sparv, Mattila; Hamalainen
(Pohjanpalo 42), Pukki (Sadik 70), Eremenko.
Referee: Szymon Marciniak.

Romania (1) 1 *(Keseru 21)*
Faroe Islands (0) 0   14,000
Romania: (4411) Pantilimon; Papp, Chiriches, Grigore,
Rat; Popa (Torje 71), Pintilii, Sanmartean (Prepelita 85),
Maxim; Rusescu (Tanase 60); Keseru.
Faroe Islands: (4141) Nielsen; Davidsen J, Nattestad,
Gregersen, Davidsen V; Faero (Olsen A 74); Holst,
Olsen B (Sorensen 80), Jakobsen (Joensen 79),
Vatnhamar; Edmundsson.
Referee: Artur Soraes Dias.

Saturday, 13 June 2015
Faroe Islands (1) 2 *(Hansson 32, Olsen B 69)*
Greece (0) 1 *(Papastathopoulos 84)*   4741
Faroe Islands: (4141) Nielsen; Hansen B, Gregersen,
Nattestad, Sorensen (Davidsen J 12); Benjaminsen; Holst
(Faero 74), Hansson, Olsen B, Vatnhamar; Edmundsson
(Joensen 90).
Greece: (433) Karnezis; Torosidis, Papastathopoulos,
Manolas, Stafylidis; Kone (Fountas 80), Samaris,
Christodoulopoulos (Ninis 46); Karelis, Mitroglou,
Fetfatzidis (Kolovos 71).
Referee: Tom Harald Hagen.

Finland (0) 0
Hungary (0) 1 *(Stieber 82)*   20,434
Finland: (4321) Hradecky; Arkivuo, Halsti, Moisander, Raitala; Mattila (Pohjanpalo 85), Sparv, Hetemaj; Hamalainen, Eremenko; Pukki (Riski 46).
Hungary: (4411) Kiraly; Fiola, Juhasz, Lang, Kadar; Stieber, Priskin (Nemeth 46), Tozser, Dzsudzsak (Simon A 88); Gera; Szalai (Nikolic 77).
Referee: Matej Jug.

Northern Ireland (0) 0
Romania (0) 0   10,000
Northern Ireland: (4321) McGovern; McLaughlin C, McAuley, Evans J (Cathcart 79), Brunt; Ward (Evans C 79), Norwood, Davis; Baird, Dallas; Lafferty K.
Romania: (442) Tatarusanu; Papp, Sepsi, Chiriches, Grigore; Chipciu (Stancu 61), Pintilii, Torje, Prepelita; Keseru (Andone 72), Maxim (Tamas 90).
Referee: Carlos Velasco Carballo.

Group F Table	P	W	D	L	F	A	GD	Pts
Romania	6	4	2	0	7	1	6	14
Northern Ireland	6	4	1	1	8	4	4	13
Hungary	6	3	2	1	5	3	2	11
Faroe Islands	6	2	0	4	4	8	–4	6
Finland	6	1	1	4	5	8	–3	4
Greece	6	0	2	4	2	7	–5	2

GROUP G

Monday, 8 September 2014
Austria (1) 1 *(Alaba 7 (pen))*
Sweden (1) 1 *(Zengin 12)*   48,500
Austria: (4231) Almer; Klein, Dragovic, Hinteregger, Fuchs; Baumgartlinger, Alaba; Harnik (Lazaro 86), Junuzovic (Leitgeb 77), Arnautovic; Janko (Okotie 69).
Sweden: (433) Isaksson; Bengtsson, Granqvist, Antonsson, Olsson; Larsson, Kallstrom (Wernbloom 85), Ekdal; Durmaz (Elmander 72), Ibrahimovic, Zengin.
Referee: Pavel Kralovec.

Montenegro (1) 2 *(Vucinic 45, Tomasevic 73)*
Moldova (0) 0   8750
Montenegro: (442) Poleksic; Volkov (Balic 46), Tomasevic, Simic, Savic; Bozovic V, Nikolic, Zverotic, Beqiraj (Jovovic 65); Vucinic, Damjanovic (Vukcevic N 81).
Moldova: (4411) Cebanu; Racu, Epureanu, Armas, Golovatenco; Antoniuc A (Antoniuc M 54), Ionita, Gheorghiev (Cebotaru 81), Dedov; Sidorenco (Posmac 68); Alexeev.
Referee: Aleksei Kulbakov.

Russia (1) 4 *(Buchel M 4 (og), Burgmeier 50 (og), Kombarov 55 (pen), Dzjuba 65)*
Liechtenstein (0) 0   11,236
Russia: (442) Akinfeev (Lodygin 72); Smolnikov, Berezutski, Ignashevich, Kombarov; Samedov, Glushakov, Dzagoev (Ozdoev 64), Cheryshev; Kokorin, Kerzhakov (Dzjuba 46).
Liechtenstein: (451) Jehle; Quintans (Wolfinger 87), Frick, Wieser, Burgmeier; Polverino (Gubser 73), Christen (Brandle 64), Yildiz, Buchel M, Hasler; Salanovic.
Referee: Sebastian Delferiere.

Thursday, 9 October 2014
Liechtenstein (0) 0
Montenegro (0) 0   2790
Liechtenstein: (532) Jehle (Bicer 62); Kaufmann, Quintans (Kuhne 80), Burgmeier, Frick, Wieser (Christen 44); Buchel M, Hasler, Polverino; Salanovic, Yildiz.
Montenegro: (433) Poleksic; Pavicevic, Jovanovic, Tomasevic, Simic; Zverotic, Vukcevic S (Nikolic 57), Jovovic; Jovetic (Grbic 74), Beqiraj (Vucinic 46), Damjanovic.
Referee: Lee Evans.

Moldova (1) 1 *(Dedov 29 (pen))*
Austria (1) 2 *(Alaba 14 (pen), Janko 52)*   10,000
Moldova: (442) Cebanu; Armas, Epureanu, Golovatenco, Jardan; Erhan (Patras 87), Cojocari (Antoniuc A 66), Gatcan, Ionita; Dedov, Picusciac (Sidorenco 46).
Austria: (442) Almer; Dragovic, Fuchs, Alaba, Prodl; Klein, Junuzovic (Ilsanker 86), Baumgartlinger, Arnautovic (Leitgeb 79); Sabitzer (Harnik 47), Janko■.
Referee: Manuel de Sousa.

Sweden (0) 1 *(Toivonen 50)*
Russia (1) 1 *(Kokorin 11)*   44,000
Sweden: (433) Isaksson; Bengtsson, Granqvist, Antonsson, Olsson; Kallstrom (Wernbloom 86), Larsson, Durmaz; Bahoui (Kacaniklic 79), Toivonen (Elmander 57), Zengin.
Russia: (4411) Akinfeev; Smolnikov, Berezutski, Ignashevich, Kombarov (Granat 88); Samedov (Grigorev 73), Glushakov, Fayzulin (Dzagoev 87), Kokorin; Shatov; Dzjuba.
Referee: Nicola Rizzoli.

Sunday, 12 October 2014
Austria (1) 1 *(Okotie 24)*
Montenegro (0) 0   34,000
Austria: (442) Almer; Klein, Dragovic, Hinteregger, Fuchs; Harnik, Baumgartlinger, Alaba, Arnautovic (Hinterseer 62); Junuzovic (Ilsanker 77), Okotie (Lazaro 82).
Montenegro: (4231) Poleksic; Savic, Simic, Basa, Volkov; Zverotic (Jovovic 70), Nikolic; Beqiraj, Vukcevic S (Jovetic 46), Bozovic V (Damjanovic 76); Vucinic.
Referee: Bas Nijhuis.

Russia (0) 1 *(Dzjuba 74 (pen))*
Moldova (0) 1 *(Epureanu 75)*   42,000
Russia: (433) Akinfeev; Parshivlyuk, Ignashevich, Granat, Berezutski; Glushakov, Dzagoev, Cheryshev (Poloz 63); Ionov (Shchennikov 76), Kerzhakov (Ozdoev 46), Dzjuba.
Moldova: (541) Cebanu; Armas, Epureanu, Golovatenco, Jardan, Erhan; Cojocari (Racu 78), Gatcan, Ionita, Dedov (Sidorenco 83); Picusciac (Patras 47).
Referee: Kristinn Jakobsson.

Sweden (1) 2 *(Zengin 34, Durmaz 46)*
Liechtenstein (0) 0   22,528
Sweden: (442) Isaksson; Antonsson, Granqvist, Olsson, Bengtsson; Ekdal (Bahoui 74), Kallstrom, Forsberg (Hrgota 66), Durmaz; Zengin, Elmander (Wernbloom 79).
Liechtenstein: (442) Bicer; Kaufmann, Frick, Quintans, Burgmeier; Christen (Kuhne 77), Buchel M (Wolfinger 83), Hasler, Polverino; Yildiz (Brandle 27), Salanovic.
Referee: Gediminas Mazeika.

Saturday, 15 November 2014
Austria (0) 1 *(Okotie 73)*
Russia (0) 0   53,000
Austria: (4411) Almer; Klein, Dragovic (Prodl 86), Hinteregger, Fuchs; Harnik, Leitgeb, Ilsanker, Arnautovic (Sabitzer 90); Junuzovic; Janko (Okotie 59).
Russia: (451) Akinfeev; Parshivlyuk, Berezutski, Ignashevich, Kombarov; Cheryshev (Ionov 55), Shirokov, Glushakov, Fayzulin (Dzjuba 75), Shatov (Dzagoev 81); Kokorin.
Referee: Martin Atkinson.

Moldova (0) 0
Liechtenstein (0) 1 *(Burgmeier 74)*   6000
Moldova: (343) Cebanu; Golovatenco, Epureanu, Armas; Racu, Gatcan, Cojocari (Spataru 56), Patras (Suvorov 75); Ginsari, Ionita, Dedov.
Liechtenstein: (4321) Buchel B; Quintans (Kieber 89), Kaufmann, Wieser, Burgmeier; Christen, Polverino, Brandle (Kuhne 62); Buchel M (Gubser 88), Hasler; Salanovic.
Referee: Mattias Gestranius.

Montenegro (0) 1 *(Jovetic 81 (pen))*

Sweden (1) 1 *(Ibrahimovic 9)* 15,000

Montenegro: (442) Bozovic M; Savic, Basa, Tomasevic (Jankovic 76), Volkov; Jovovic, Zverotic, Vukcevic N, Bozovic V (Bakic 46); Jovetic, Damjanovic (Beqiraj 66).

Sweden: (433) Isaksson; Lustig (Wendt 46), Granqvist, Antonsson, Bengtsson; Ekdal, Kallstrom, Durmaz; Forsberg (Larsson 62), Ibrahimovic, Zengin (Thelin 85).

Referee: William Collum.

Friday, 27 March 2015

Liechtenstein (0) 0

Austria (2) 5 *(Harnik 14, Janko 16, Alaba 59, Junuzovic 74, Arnautovic 90)* 6127

Liechtenstein: (451) Jehle; Quintans (Salanovic 55), Frick, Kaufmann, Oehri; Christen (Kuhne 83), Buchel M (Gubser 88), Polverino, Wieser, Burgmeier; Hasler.

Austria: (4411) Almer; Klein, Dragovic, Hinteregger, Fuchs; Harnik (Sabitzer 72), Baumgartlinger, Alaba, Arnautovic; Junuzovic (Leitgeb 82); Janko (Djuricin 76).

Referee: Felix Zwayer.

Moldova (0) 0

Sweden (0) 2 *(Ibrahimovic 46, 85 (pen))* 10,500

Moldova: (532) Cebanu; Armas, Epureanu, Golovatenco, Racu, Bolohan; Ionita (Cojocari 36), Gatcan, Andronic (Frunza 70); Dedov, Boghiu (Gheorghiev 86).

Sweden: (442) Isaksson; Bengtsson, Granqvist■, Olsson, Johansson; Larsson (Forsberg 81), Ekdal, Kallstrom, Zengin (Wernbloom 86); Ibrahimovic, Thelin (Berg 69).

Referee: Ivan Bebek.

Montenegro (0) 0

Russia (0) 0

Montenegro: (4231) Poleksic; Zverotic, Simic, Basa, Balic (Bakic 46); Kascelan, Vukcevic N; Marusic, Volkov, Jovetic; Vucinic.

Russia: (4321) Akinfeev (Lodygin 1); Smolnikov, Berezutski, Ignashevich, Kombarov; Shirokov, Denisov, Dzagoev (Torbinski 46); Zhirkov, Shatov; Kokorin.

Match abandoned. Russia awarded 3-0 win

Referee: Deniz Aytekin.

Sunday, 14 June 2015

Liechtenstein (1) 1 *(Wieser 20)*

Moldova (1) 1 *(Boghiu 43)* 2080

Liechtenstein: (433) Jehle; Yildiz, Frick, Kaufmann, Oehri (Kuhne 41); Buchel M (Gubser 69), Polverino, Wieser; Christen, Erne (Brandle 83), Burgmeier.

Moldova: (334) Cebanu; Racu, Epureanu (Carp 46), Armas; Dedov, Cojocari, Erhan; Gatcan, Patras (Antoniuc M 89), Boghiu, Cheptene (Milinceanu 35).

Referee: Libor Kovank.

Russia (0) 0

Austria (1) 1 *(Janko 33)* 38,000

Russia: (451) Akinfeev; Smolnikov, Berezutski (Chernov 12), Novoseltsev, Kombarov (Kerzhakov 71); Shatov, Shirokov, Glushakov, Ivanov (Miranchuk 46), Zhirkov; Kokorin.

Austria: (4231) Almer; Klein, Dragovic, Hinteregger, Fuchs; Ilsanker, Baumgartlinger; Harnik (Sabitzer 65), Junuzovic (Prodl 87), Arnautovic; Janko (Okotie 76).

Referee: Milorad Mazic.

Sweden (3) 3 *(Berg 37, Ibrahimovic 40, 44)*

Montenegro (0) 1 *(Damjanovic 64 (pen))* 50,000

Sweden: (442) Isaksson; Bengtsson, Johansson, Milosevic, Wendt; Larsson, Kallstrom (Wernbloom 72), Ekdal, Zengin (Forsberg 65); Ibrahimovic (Toivonen 90), Berg.

Montenegro: (4231) Poleksic; Zverotic (Saveljich 58), Savic, Simic (Balic 75), Tomasevic; Vukcevic N, Kascelan (Boljevic 46); Marusic, Mugosa, Beqiraj; Damjanovic.

Referee: Huseyin Gocek.

Group G Table	P	W	D	L	F	A	GD	Pts
Austria	6	5	1	0	11	2	9	16
Sweden	6	3	3	0	10	4	6	12
Russia	6	2	2	2	9	4	5	8
Montenegro	6	1	2	3	4	8	-4	5
Liechtenstein	6	1	2	3	2	12	-10	5
Moldova	6	0	2	4	3	9	-6	2

GROUP H

Tuesday, 9 September 2014

Azerbaijan (0) 1 *(Nazarov 53)*

Bulgaria (1) 2 *(Mitsanski 14, Hristov 86)* 25,000

Azerbaijan: (4231) Agayev K; Shukurov, Sadygov, Guseynov, Budak (Nadirov 89); Garayev, Abishov (Guliyev 73); Nazarov, Aliyev, Javadov (Abdullayev 46); Dadasov.

Bulgaria: (4231) Stoyanov; Manolev, Bodurov, Popov A, Minev V; Dyakov, Iliev (Nedelev 73); Milanov G, Gadzhev, Aleksandrov M (Hristov 82); Mitsanski (Galabinov 57).

Referee: Alon Yefet.

Croatia (0) 2 *(Modric 46, Kramaric 81)*

Malta (0) 0 12,000

Croatia: (451) Subasic; Milic, Corluka, Lovren, Srna; Rakitic, Halilovic (Kramaric 67), Modric, Brozovic, Kovacic (Jelavic 46); Mandzukic (Olic 79).

Malta: (442) Hogg; Borg■, Agius, Camilleri, Fenech R (Scicluna 87); Failla, Fenech P, Muscat R (Kristensen 76), Muscat Z; Mifsud (Bezzina 33), Schembri.

Referee: Vladislav Bezborodov.

Norway (0) 0

Italy (1) 2 *(Zaza 16, Bonucci 62)* 26,265

Norway: (442) Nyland; Elabdellaoui, Forren, Nordtveit, Skjelbred (Pedersen 75); Jenssen (Tettey 70), Daehli, Johansen, Flo; King, Nielsen (Elyounoussi T 50).

Italy: (442) Buffon; Darmian (Pasqual 61), Astori, Ranocchia, Bonucci; De Sciglio, Giaccherini, Florenzi (Poli 86), De Rossi; Zaza (Destro 83), Immobile.

Referee: Milorad Mazic.

Friday, 10 October 2014

Bulgaria (0) 0

Croatia (1) 1 *(Bodurov 36 (og))* 30,000

Bulgaria: (442) Stoyanov; Minev I, Popov A, Zanev (Iliev 46), Bodurov; Manolev, Milanov G, Gadzhev (Tonev 69), Dyakov; Mitsanski (Galabinov 46), Popov I.

Croatia: (442) Subasic; Corluka, Srna, Vida, Pranjic; Perisic, Rakitic (Kovacic 80), Modric, Brozovic, Mandzukic, Olic.

Referee: Antonio Miguel Mateu Lahoz.

Italy (1) 2 *(Chiellini 44, 81)*

Azerbaijan (0) 1 *(Chiellini 77 (og))* 30,000

Italy: (532) Buffon; Darmian (Candreva 81), Ranocchia, Bonucci, Chiellini, De Sciglio; Florenzi (Giovinco 78), Pirlo (Aquilani 73), Marchisio; Zaza, Immobile.

Azerbaijan: (442) Agayev K; Allahverdiev, Guseynov, Sadygov, Qirtimov (Ramaldanov 46); Abdullayev, Garayev, Amirguliev (Nadirov 86), Nazarov; Dadasov (Huseynov 59), Aliyev.

Referee: Huseyin Gocek.

Malta (0) 0

Norway (2) 3 *(Daehli 22, King 25, 49)* 3000

Malta: (352) Hogg; Muscat Z, Agius, Camilleri; Fenech P, Muscat R, Fenech R (Grioli 70), Briffa (Kristensen 70); Failla; Mifsud, Schembri (Vella 85).

Norway: (433) Nyland; Elabdellaoui, Nordtveit, Forren, Linnes; Skjelbred (Samuelsen 61), Johansen, Tettey (Singh 77); King (Nielsen 74), Daehli, Elyounoussi T.

Referee: Antony Gautier.

Monday, 13 October 2014

Croatia (4) 6 *(Kramaric 11, Perisic 34, 45, Brozovic 45, Modric 56 (pen), Sadygov 61 (og))*

Azerbaijan (0) 0 15,000

Croatia: (442) Subasic; Srna, Corluka, Vida, Pranjic; Brozovic, Rakitic, Modric (Halilovic 59), Kovacic (Perisic 24); Kramaric (Olic 76), Mandzukic.

Azerbaijan: (442) Agayev K; Medvedev, Sadygov, Guseynov, Allahverdiev (Guliyev 66); Abdullayev, Garayev (Ramazanov 30 (Huseynov 41)), Ramaldanov, Nazarov; Amirguliev, Aliyev.

Referee: Stephan Studer.

Malta (0) 0
Italy (1) 1 *(Pelle 24)* 16,942

Malta: (352) Hogg; Muscat Z, Agius, Camilleri; Mintoff (Baldacchino 72), Muscat R, Failla (Bezzina 90), Briffa, Fenech P; Mifsud■, Schembri (Cohen 85).
Italy: (352) Buffon; Darmian, Bonucci■, Chiellini; Candreva, Verratti, Pasqual, Florenzi (Aquilani 59), Marchisio; Immobile (Giovinco 65), Pelle (Ogbonna 76).
Referee: Ovidiu Alin Hategan.

Norway (1) 2 *(Elyounoussi T 13, Nielsen 71)*
Bulgaria (1) 1 *(Bodurov 43)* 18,990

Norway: (433) Nyland; Elabdellaoui, Linnes, Forren, Nordtveit; Tettey, Skjelbred, Daehli (Odegaard 63); Johansen, King (Nielsen 58), Elyounoussi T (Samuelsen 83).
Bulgaria: (442) Mihailov; Popov A, Bodurov, Minev V, Manolev (Minev I 68); Milanov G, Tonev, Dyakov, Iliev (Aleksandrov M 76); Popov I, Hristov (Galabinov 55).
Referee: Olegario Benquerenca.

Sunday, 16 November 2014

Azerbaijan (0) 0
Norway (1) 1 *(Nordtveit 25)* 8000

Azerbaijan: (433) Agayev S; Shukurov, Yunuszade, Sadygov, Medvedev; Amirguliev, Imamverdiyev (Nazarov 70), Abishov (Qarayev 65); Abdullayev, Aliyev, Javadov.
Norway: (4231) Nyland; Elabdellaoui, Nordtveit, Forren, Hogli; Johansen, Tettey; Daehli (Samuelsen 57), Elyounoussi T (Gulbrandsen 90), Skjelbred; Nielsen (Soderlund 72).
Referee: Yevhen Aranovskiy.

Bulgaria (1) 1 *(Galabinov 6)*
Malta (0) 1 *(Failla 50 (pen))* 1000

Bulgaria: (4231) Stoyanov; Terziev, Minev V, Bodurov, Manolev; Milanov G (Marquinhos 58), Iliev (Tonev 71); Galabinov (Mitsanski 58), Dyakov, Aleksandrov M; Popov I.
Malta: (532) Hogg; Camilleri, Muscat Z, Caruana, Agius, Failla (Bezzina 80); Briffa, Muscat R, Fenech P; Schembri (Fenech R 78), Farrugia (Vella 90).
Referee: Martin Strombergsson.

Italy (1) 1 *(Candreva 11)*
Croatia (1) 1 *(Perisic 15)* 55,000

Italy: (352) Buffon; Darmian, Ranocchia, Chiellini; De Sciglio, Candreva, De Rossi, Marchisio, Pasqual (Soriano 27); Immobile (El Shaarawy 52), Zaza (Pelle 63).
Croatia: (4411) Subasic; Srna, Corluka, Vida, Pranjic; Perisic, Modric (Kovacic 27), Brozovic (Badelj 86), Olic (Kramaric 69); Rakitic; Mandzukic.
Referee: Bjorn Kuipers.

Saturday, 28 March 2015

Azerbaijan (1) 2 *(Huseynov 4, Nazarov 90)*
Malta (0) 0 14,600

Azerbaijan: (4141) Agayev K; Medvedev, Guseynov, Sadygov, Dashdemirov; Qarayev; Alaskarov (Gurbanov 23), Amirguliev, Huseynov, Ismayilov (Nazarov 70); Nadirov (Eddy 80).
Malta: (4411) Hogg; Caruana, Camilleri (Muscat Z 36), Agius, Bezzina (Pisani 46); Fenech P, Borg, Schembri (Fenech R 82), Muscat R; Briffa; Effiong.
Referee: Halis Ozkahya.

Bulgaria (2) 2 *(Popov I 11, Mitsanski 17)*
Italy (1) 2 *(Minev I 4 (og), Eder 84)* 6000

Bulgaria: (4231) Mihailov; Manolev, Bodurov, Aleksandrov A, Minev I; Gadzhev, Dyakov; Milanov I (Vasilev V 88), Popov I (Slavchev 85), Aleksandrov M; Mitsanski (Rubinov 73).
Italy: (352) Sirigu; Barzagli, Bonucci, Chiellini; Antonelli (Gabbiadini 77), Candreva, Verratti, Bertolacci (Soriano 71), Darmian; Zaza (Eder 58), Immobile.
Referee: Damir Skomina.

Croatia (1) 5 *(Brozovic 30, Perisic 54, Olic 66, Schildenfeld 87, Pranjic 90)*
Norway (0) 1 *(Tettey 81)* 22,000

Croatia: (4411) Subasic; Srna, Corluka■, Vida, Pranjic; Perisic, Brozovic, Modric, Olic (Kramaric 70); Rakitic (Schildenfeld 75); Mandzukic (Badelj 88).
Norway: (4411) Nyland; Hogli, Forren, Nordtveit, Linnes; Skjelbred (Samuelsen 19), Johansen, Tettey, Daehli (Nielsen 61); Elyounoussi T (Abdellaoue 80); Odegaard.
Referee: Carlos Velasco Carballo.

Friday, 12 June 2015

Croatia (1) 1 *(Mandzukic 11)*
Italy (1) 1 *(Candreva 36 (pen))* 75

Croatia: (442) Subasic; Srna■, Vida, Schildenfeld, Pranjic (Vrsaljko 72); Perisic, Rakitic, Brozovic, Olic (Rebic 46); Kovacic (Leovac 90), Mandzukic.
Italy: (442) Buffon (Sirigu 46); De Silvestri (De Sciglio 27), Bonucci, Astori, Darmian; Candreva, Parolo, Pirlo, Marchisio; El Shaarawy (Ranocchia 80), Pelle.
Referee: Martin Atkinson.
(Behind closed doors)

Malta (0) 0
Bulgaria (0) 1 *(Popov I 56)* 3924

Malta: (442) Haber; Muscat A (Herrera 63), Agius, Camilleri, Muscat Z; Fenech P, Briffa (Schembri 75), Muscat R, Failla; Mifsud (Cohen 84), Effiong.
Bulgaria: (4321) Mitrev; Bandalovski, Aleksandrov A, Bodurov, Minev I; Gadzhev, Popov I (Chochev 80), Dyakov; Manolev, Aleksandrov M (Malinov 75); Mitsanski (Vasilev R 89).
Referee: Aleksandar Stavrev.

Norway (0) 0
Azerbaijan (0) 0 21,228

Norway: (442) Nyland; Elabdellaoui, Forren, Hovland, Hogli; Odegaard, Johansen, Nordtveit, Skjelbred (Helland 55); King (Diomande 79), Soderlund (Eikrem 68).
Azerbaijan: (433) Agayev K; Medvedev, Guseynov, Sadygov, Dashdemirov; Huseynov, Qarayev, Amirguliev; Ismayilov, Gurbanov (Nadirov 81), Nazarov (Kurbanov 90).
Referee: Pawel Gil.

Group H Table	P	W	D	L	F	A	GD	Pts
Croatia	6	4	2	0	16	3	13	14
Italy	6	3	3	0	9	5	4	12
Norway	6	3	1	2	7	8	–1	10
Bulgaria	6	2	2	2	7	7	0	8
Azerbaijan	6	1	1	4	4	11	–7	4
Malta	6	0	1	5	1	10	–9	1

GROUP I

Sunday, 7 September 2014

Denmark (0) 2 *(Hojbjerg 65, Kahlenberg 80)*
Armenia (0) 1 *(Mkhitaryan 49)* 20,144

Denmark: (4411) Schmeichel; Ankersen, Kjaer (Okore 57), Bjelland, Boilesen; Schone (Vibe 56), Kvist Jorgensen (Kahlenberg 74), Hojbjerg, Krohn-Dehli; Eriksen; Bendtner.
Armenia: (532) Berezovsky; Hovhannisyan, Haroyan, Arzumanyan (Voskanyan 66) Mkoyan, Hayrapetyan; Hovsepyan, Yedigaryan, Mkhitaryan (Pizzelli 71); Manucharyan (Dashyan 84), Ghazaryan.
Referee: Alexandru Dan Tudor.

Portugal (0) 0
Albania (0) 1 *(Balaj 52)* 23,205

Portugal: (433) Rui Patricio; Joao Pereira, Pepe, Ricardo Costa (Veloso 73), Fabio Coentrao; Joao Moutinho, William Carvalho (Ricardo Horta 56), Andre Gomes; Vieirinha (Ivan Cavaleiro 46), Eder, Nani.
Albania: (451) Berisha; Hisaj, Cana, Mavraj, Agolli; Roshi, Xhaka, Kukeli (Kace 66), Abrashi, Lenjani (Lila 75); Balaj (Cikalleshi 81).
Referee: Ruddy Buquet.

Saturday, 11 October 2014

Albania (1) 1 *(Lenjani 38)*

Denmark (0) 1 *(Vibe 81)* 12,800

Albania: (442) Berisha; Hisaj, Cana, Mavraj, Agolli; Abrashi, Kukeli, Xhaka (Rama 82), Lila (Curri 87); Balaj (Cikalleshi 69), Lenjani.
Denmark: (433) Schmeichel; Ankersen (Bech 71), Kjaer, Bjelland, Boilesen; Hojbjerg (Kahlenberg 79), Kvist Jorgensen, Eriksen; Poulsen Y (Vibe 46), Bendtner, Krohn-Dehli.
Referee: Viktor Kassai.

Armenia (0) 1 *(Arzumanyan 73)*

Serbia (0) 1 *(Tosic Z 90)* 7500

Armenia: (343) Berezovsky; Hovhannisyan, Haroyan, Arzumanyan; Voskanyan, Mkrtchyan (Hovsepyan 52), Yedigaryan, Hayrapetyan; Pizzelli (Karapetyan 84), Sarkisov, Manucharyan (Dashyan 66).
Serbia: (4231) Stojkovic; Ivanovic, Mitrovic S, Nastasic, Kolarov; Tosic Z, Gudelj (Mitrovic A 74); Matic, Markovic (Kuzmanovic 26), Tadic; Djordjevic (Lazovic 70).
Referee: Tom Harald Hagen.

Tuesday, 14 October 2014

Denmark (0) 0

Portugal (0) 1 *(Ronaldo 90)* 36,562

Denmark: (4231) Schmeichel; Jacobsen, Kjaer, Agger, Boilesen (Poulsen S 58); Hojbjerg, Kvist Jorgensen; Vibe (Bech 46), Eriksen (Kahlenberg 84), Krohn-Dehli; Bendtner.
Portugal: (433) Rui Patricio; Cedric Soares, Carvalho, Pepe, Eliseu; Joao Moutinho, William Carvalho, Tiago (Quaresma 84); Ronaldo, Danny (Eder 77), Nani (Joao Mario 68).
Referee: Felix Brych.

Serbia (0) 0

Albania (0) 0

Serbia: (541) Stojkovic; Nastasic, Ivanovic, Kolarov, Mitrovic S, Tosic Z; Gudelj, Matic, Tadic, Djuricic; Lazovic.
Albania: (361) Berisha; Lila, Hisaj, Agolli; Mavraj, Lenjani, Xhaka, Cana, Kukeli, Abrashi; Balaj.
Match abandoned. Albania awarded 3-0 win
Referee: Martin Atkinson.

Friday, 14 November 2014

Portugal (0) 1 *(Ronaldo 71)*

Armenia (0) 0 21,042

Portugal: (442) Rui Patricio; Bosingwa, Pepe, Carvalho, Guerreiro; Nani (William Carvalho 88), Joao Moutinho, Tiago, Ronaldo; Postiga (Eder 56), Danny (Quaresma 70).
Armenia: (541) Berezovsky; Hovhannisyan, Haroyan, Arzumanyan, Voskanyan, Hayrapetyan; Mkrtchyan, Mkhitaryan (Pizzelli 83), Yedigaryan (Sarkisov 77), Ghazaryan (Manucharyan 62); Movsisyan.
Referee: Tasos Sidiropoulos.

Serbia (1) 1 *(Tosic Z 4)*

Denmark (0) 3 *(Bendtner 61, 85, Kjaer 63)* 0

Serbia: (4411) Stojkovic; Ivanovic, Bisevac, Mitrovic S, Tosic D; Tosic Z, Gudelj (Mitrovic A 66), Matic, Tadic (Markovic 71); Djuricic (Kuzmanovic 66); Lazovic.
Denmark: (451) Schmeichel; Ankersen (Jacobsen 70), Kjaer, Bjelland, Vibe, Kahlenberg (Rasmussen 88), Kvist Jorgensen, Eriksen, Krohn-Dehli; Bendtner (Poulsen Y 88).
Referee: Cuneyt Cakir.
Behind closed doors.

Sunday, 29 March 2015

Albania (0) 2 *(Mavraj 77, Gashi 81)*

Armenia (1) 1 *(Movsisyan 4)* 12,300

Albania: (433) Berisha; Hisaj, Cana, Mavraj, Agolli; Xhaka, Kukeli, Roshi (Salihi 68); Abrashi (Lenjani 46), Cikalleshi, Memushaj (Gashi 46).
Armenia: (433) Berezovsky; Hambardzumyan■, Arzumanyan, Andonian, Hayrapetyan; Yedigaryan (Korian 84), Manucharyan (Hovhannisyan 67), Mkhitaryan; Pizzelli (Haroyan 82), Ghazaryan, Movsisyan.
Referee: David Fernandez Borbalan.

Portugal (1) 2 *(Carvalho 10, Fabio Coentrao 63)*

Serbia (0) 1 *(Matic 61)* 58,430

Portugal: (433) Rui Patricio; Bosingwa, Bruno Alves, Carvalho (Fonte 16), Eliseu; William Carvalho, Fabio Coentrao (Quaresma 78); Nani, Danny (William Carvalho 85), Ronaldo.
Serbia: (4411) Stojkovic; Basta, Ivanovic, Nastasic, Kolarov; Markovic (Djuricic 65), Petrovic, Matic, Tadic (Tosic Z 78); Ljajic (Skuletic 85); Mitrovic A.
Referee: Christian Brocchi.

Saturday, 13 June 2015

Armenia (1) 2 *(Pizzelli 14, Mkoyan 73)*

Portugal (1) 3 *(Ronaldo 29 (pen), 55, 58)* 15,000

Armenia: (4141) Berezovsky; Mkoyan, Arzumanyan, Andonian, Hayrapetyan; Mkrtchyan (Hovsepyan 29); Hovhannisyan (Ozbiliz 61), Mkhitaryan, Pizzelli, Ghazaryan; Sarkisov (Korian 74).
Portugal: (433) Rui Patricio; Bruno Alves, Fabio Coentrao (Adrien Silva 74), Carvalho (Fonte 79), Eliseu; Joao Moutinho, Danny (William Carvalho 63), Tiago■; Ronaldo, Vieirinha, Nani.
Referee: Sergio Gumienny.

Denmark (1) 2 *(Poulsen Y 13, Poulsen J 87)*

Serbia (0) 0 30,887

Denmark: (433) Schmeichel; Kjaer, Agger, Jacobsen, Poulsen S; Kvist Jorgensen (Christensen 77), Eriksen, Hojbjerg; Krohn-Dehli (Poulsen J 60), Bendtner, Poulsen Y (Vibe 73).
Serbia: (451) Stojkovic; Nastasic, Ivanovic, Kolarov, Maksimovic; Tosic Z (Kostic 66), Matic, Fejsa, Markovic, Mitrovic A (Skuletic 90); Ljajic (Djuricic 81).
Referee: Bjorn Kuipers.

Group I Table	P	W	D	L	F	A	GD	Pts
Portugal	5	4	0	1	7	4	3	12
Albania	4	3	1	0	7	2	5	10
Denmark	5	3	1	1	8	4	4	10
Armenia	5	0	1	4	5	9	-4	1
Serbia*	5	0	1	4	3	11	-8	-2

**Serbia deducted 3 points.*

Competition still being played.

THE WORLD CUP 1930–2014

Year	Winners v Runners-up		Venue	Attendance	Referee
1930	Uruguay v Argentina	4-2	Montevideo	68,346	J. Langenus (Belgium)
	Winning Coach: Alberto Suppici				
1934	Italy v Czechoslovakia	2-1*	Rome	55,000	I. Eklind (Sweden)
	Winning Coach: Vittorio Pozzo				
1938	Italy v Hungary	4-2	Paris	45,000	G. Capdeville (France)
	Winning Coach: Vittorio Pozzo				
1950	Uruguay v Brazil	2-1	Rio de Janeiro	173,850	G. Reader (England)
	Winning Coach: Juan Lopez				
1954	West Germany v Hungary	3-2	Berne	62,500	W. Ling (England)
	Winning Coach: Sepp Herberger				
1958	Brazi v Sweden	5-2	Stockholm	49,737	M. Guigue (France)
	Winning Coach: Vicente Feola				
1962	Brazil v Czechoslovakia	3-1	Santiago	68,679	N. Latychev (USSR)
	Winning Coach: Aymore Moreira				
1966	England v West Germany	4-2*	Wembley	96,924	G. Dienst (Sweden)
	Winning Coach: Alf Ramsey				
1970	Brazil v Italy	4-1	Mexico City	107,412	R. Glockner (East Germany)
	Winning Coach: Mario Zagallo				
1974	West Germany v Netherlands	2-1	Munich	78,200	J. Taylor (England)
	Winning Coach: Helmut Schon				
1978	Argentina v Netherlands	3-1*	Buenos Aires	71,483	S. Gonella (Italy)
	Winning Coach: Cesar Luis Menotti				
1982	Italy v West Germany	3-1	Madrid	90,000	A. C. Coelho (Brazil)
	Winning Coach: Enzo Bearzot				
1986	Argentina v West Germany	3-2	Mexico City	114,600	R. A. Filho (Brazil)
	Winning Coach: Carlos Bilardo				
1990	West Germany v Argentina	1-0	Rome	73,603	E. C. Mendez (Mexico)
	Winning Coach: Franz Beckenbauer				
1994	Brazil v Italy	0-0*	Los Angeles	94,194	S. Puhl (Hungary)
	Brazil won 3-2 on penalties.				
	Winning Coach: Carlos Alberto Parreira				
1998	France v Brazil	3-0	St-Denis	80,000	S. Belqola (Morocco)
	Winning Coach: Aime Jacquet				
2002	Brazil v Germany	2-0	Yokohama	69,029	P. Collina (Italy)
	Winning Coach: Luiz Felipe Scolari				
2006	Italy v France	1-1*	Berlin	69,000	H. Elizondo (Argentina)
	Italy won 5-3 on penalties.				
	Winning Coach: Marcello Lippi				
2010	Spain v Netherlands	1-0	Johannesburg	84,490	H. Webb (England)
	Winning Coach: Vicente del Bosque				
2014	Germany v Argentina	1-0*	Rio de Janeiro	74,738	N. Rizzoli (Italy)
	Winning Coach: Joachim Low				

(*After extra time)

GOALSCORING AND ATTENDANCES IN WORLD CUP FINAL ROUNDS

Year	Venue	Games	Goals (av)	Attendance (av)
1930	Uruguay	18	70 (3.9)	590,549 (32,808)
1934	Italy	17	70 (4.1)	363,000 (21,352)
1938	France	18	84 (4.7)	375,700 (20,872)
1950	Brazil	22	88 (4.0)	1,045,246 (47,511)
1954	Switzerland	26	140 (5.4)	768,607 (29,562)
1958	Sweden	35	126 (3.6)	819,810 (23,423)
1962	Chile	32	89 (2.8)	893,172 (27,912)
1966	England	32	89 (2.8)	1,563,135 (48,848)
1970	Mexico	32	95 (3.0)	1,603,975 (50,124)
1974	West Germany	38	97 (2.6)	1,865,753 (49,098)
1978	Argentina	38	102 (2.7)	1,545,791 (40,678)
1982	Spain	52	146 (2.8)	2,109,723 (40,571)
1986	Mexico	52	132 (2.5)	2,394,031 (46,039)
1990	Italy	52	115 (2.2)	2,516,215 (48,388)
1994	USA	52	141 (2.7)	3,587,538 (68,991)
1998	France	64	171 (2.7)	2,785,100 (43,517)
2002	Japan/S. Korea	64	161 (2.5)	2,705,197 (42,268)
2006	Germany	64	147 (2.3)	3,359,439 (52,491)
2010	South Africa	64	145 (2.3)	3,178,856 (49,669)
2014	Brazil	64	171 (2.7)	3,367,727 (52,621)
Total		836	2379 (2.8)	37,438,564 (44,783)

LEADING GOALSCORERS

Year	Player	Goals
1930	Guillermo Stabile (Argentina)	8
1934	Oldrich Nejedly (Czechoslovakia)	5
1938	Leonidas da Silva (Brazil)	7
1950	Ademir (Brazil)	8
1954	Sandor Kocsis (Hungary)	11
1958	Just Fontaine (France)	13
1962	Valentin Ivanov (USSR), Leonel Sanchez (Chile), Garrincha (Brazil), Vava (Brazil), Florian Albert (Hungary), Drazen Jerkovic (Yugoslavia)	4
1966	Eusebio (Portugal)	9
1970	Gerd Muller (West Germany)	10
1974	Grzegorz Lato (Poland)	7
1978	Mario Kempes (Argentina)	6
1982	Paolo Rossi (Italy)	6
1986	Gary Lineker (England)	6
1990	Salvatore Schillaci (Italy)	6
1994	Oleg Salenko (Russia)	6
	Hristo Stoichkov (Bulgaria)	6
1998	Davor Suker (Croatia)	6
2002	Ronaldo (Brazil)	8
2006	Miroslav Klose (Germany)	5
2010	Thomas Muller (Germany), David Villa (Spain), Wesley Sneijder (Netherlands), Diego Forlan (Uruguay)	5
2014	James Rodriguez (Colombia)	6

EUROPEAN FOOTBALL CHAMPIONSHIP
1960–2012
(formerly EUROPEAN NATIONS' CUP)

Year	Winners v Runners-up		Venue	Attendance	Referee
1960	USSR v Yugoslavia	2-1*	Paris	17,966	A. E. Ellis (England)
	Winning Coach: Gavriil Kachalin				
1964	Spain v USSR	2-1	Madrid	79,115	A. E. Ellis (England)
	Winning Coach: Jose Villalonga				
1968	Italy v Yugoslavia	1-1	Rome	68,817	G. Dienst (Switzerland)
Replay	Italy v Yugoslavia	2-0	Rome	32,866	J. M. O. de Mendibil (Spain)
	Winning Coach: Ferruccio Valcareggi				
1972	West Germany v USSR	3-0	Brussels	43,066	F. Marschall (Austria)
	Winning Coach: Helmut Schon				
1976	Czechoslovakia v West Germany	2-2	Belgrade	30,790	S. Gonella (Italy)
	Czechoslovakia won 5-3 on penalties.				
	Winning Coach: Vaclav Jezek				
1980	West Germany v Belgium	2-1	Rome	47,860	N. Rainea (Romania)
	Winning Coach: Jupp Derwall				
1984	France v Spain	2-0	Paris	47,368	V. Christov (Slovakia)
	Winning Coach: Michel Hidalgo				
1988	Netherlands v USSR	2-0	Munich	62,770	M. Vautrot (France)
	Winning Coach: Rinus Michels				
1992	Denmark v Germany	2-0	Gothenburg	37,800	B. Galler (Switzerland)
	Winning Coach: Richard Moller Nielsen				
1996	Germany v Czech Republic	2-1*	Wembley	73,611	P. Pairetto (Italy)
	Germany won on sudden death 'golden goal'.				
	Winning Coach: Berti Vogts				
2000	France v Italy	2-1*	Rotterdam	48,200	A. Frisk (Sweden)
	France won on sudden death 'golden goal'.				
	Winning Coach: Roger Lemerre				
2004	Greece v Portugal	1-0	Lisbon	62,865	M. Merk (Germany)
	Winning Coach: Otto Rehhagel				
2008	Spain v Germany	1-0	Vienna	51,428	R. Rosetti (Italy)
	Winning Coach: Luis Aragones				
2012	Spain v Italy	4-0	Kiev	63,170	P. Proenca (Portugal)
	Winning Coach: Vicente del Bosque				

OLYMPIC FOOTBALL PAST MEDALLISTS
1896–2012

* No official tournament. ** No official tournament but gold medal later awarded by IOC.

1896 Athens*
1 Denmark
2 Greece

1900 Paris*
1 Great Britain
2 France

1904 St Louis**
1 Canada
2 USA

1908 London
1 Great Britain
2 Denmark
3 Netherlands

1912 Stockholm
1 England
2 Denmark
3 Netherlands

1920 Antwerp
1 Belgium
2 Spain
3 Netherlands

1924 Paris
1 Uruguay
2 Switzerland
3 Sweden

1928 Amsterdam
1 Uruguay
2 Argentina
3 Italy

1932 Los Angeles
no tournament

1936 Berlin
1 Italy
2 Austria
3 Norway

1948 London
1 Sweden
2 Yugoslavia
3 Denmark

1952 Helsinki
1 Hungary
2 Yugoslavia
3 Sweden

1956 Melbourne
1 USSR
2 Yugoslavia
3 Bulgaria

1960 Rome
1 Yugoslavia
2 Denmark
3 Hungary

1964 Tokyo
1 Hungary
2 Czechoslovakia
3 East Germany

1968 Mexico City
1 Hungary
2 Bulgaria
3 Japan

1972 Munich
1 Poland
2 Hungary
3 E Germany/USSR

1976 Montreal
1 East Germany
2 Poland
3 USSR

1980 Moscow
1 Czechoslovakia
2 East Germany
3 USSR

1984 Los Angeles
1 France
2 Brazil
3 Yugoslavia

1988 Seoul
1 USSR
2 Brazil
3 West Germany

1992 Barcelona
1 Spain
2 Poland
3 Ghana

1996 Atlanta
1 Nigeria
2 Argentina
3 Brazil

2000 Sydney
1 Cameroon
2 Spain
3 Chile

2004 Athens
1 Argentina
2 Paraguay
3 Italy

2008 Beijing
1 Argentina
2 Nigeria
3 Brazil

2012 London
1 Mexico
2 Brazil
3 South Korea

BRITISH AND IRISH INTERNATIONAL RESULTS 1872–2015

Note: In the results that follow, wc=World Cup, ec=European Championship, ui=Umbro International Trophy. tf = Tournoi de France. nc = Nations Cup. Northern Ireland played as Ireland before 1921. *After extra time.

ENGLAND v SCOTLAND

Played: 112; England won 47, Scotland won 41, Drawn 24. Goals: England 198, Scotland 172.

Year	Date	Venue	E	S
1872	30 Nov	Glasgow	0	0
1873	8 Mar	Kennington Oval	4	2
1874	7 Mar	Glasgow	1	2
1875	6 Mar	Kennington Oval	2	2
1876	4 Mar	Glasgow	0	3
1877	3 Mar	Kennington Oval	1	3
1878	2 Mar	Glasgow	2	7
1879	5 Apr	Kennington Oval	5	4
1880	13 Mar	Glasgow	4	5
1881	12 Mar	Kennington Oval	1	6
1882	11 Mar	Glasgow	1	5
1883	10 Mar	Sheffield	2	3
1884	15 Mar	Glasgow	0	1
1885	21 Mar	Kennington Oval	1	1
1886	31 Mar	Glasgow	1	1
1887	19 Mar	Blackburn	2	3
1888	17 Mar	Glasgow	5	0
1889	13 Apr	Kennington Oval	2	3
1890	5 Apr	Glasgow	1	1
1891	6 Apr	Blackburn	2	1
1892	2 Apr	Glasgow	4	1
1893	1 Apr	Richmond	5	2
1894	7 Apr	Glasgow	2	2
1895	6 Apr	Everton	3	0
1896	4 Apr	Glasgow	1	2
1897	3 Apr	Crystal Palace	1	2
1898	2 Apr	Glasgow	3	1
1899	8 Apr	Aston Villa	2	1
1900	7 Apr	Glasgow	1	4
1901	30 Mar	Crystal Palace	2	2
1902	3 Mar	Aston Villa	2	2
1903	4 Apr	Sheffield	1	2
1904	9 Apr	Glasgow	1	0
1905	1 Apr	Crystal Palace	1	0
1906	7 Apr	Glasgow	1	2
1907	6 Apr	Newcastle	1	1
1908	4 Apr	Glasgow	1	1
1909	3 Apr	Crystal Palace	2	0
1910	2 Apr	Glasgow	0	2
1911	1 Apr	Everton	1	1
1912	23 Mar	Glasgow	1	1
1913	5 Apr	Chelsea	1	0
1914	14 Apr	Glasgow	1	3
1920	10 Apr	Sheffield	5	4
1921	9 Apr	Glasgow	0	3
1922	8 Apr	Aston Villa	0	1
1923	14 Apr	Glasgow	2	2
1924	12 Apr	Wembley	1	1
1925	4 Apr	Glasgow	0	2
1926	17 Apr	Manchester	0	1
1927	2 Apr	Glasgow	2	1
1928	31 Mar	Wembley	1	5
1929	13 Apr	Glasgow	0	1
1930	5 Apr	Wembley	5	2
1931	28 Mar	Glasgow	0	2
1932	9 Apr	Wembley	3	0
1933	1 Apr	Glasgow	1	2
1934	14 Apr	Wembley	3	0
1935	6 Apr	Glasgow	0	2
1936	4 Apr	Wembley	1	1
1937	17 Apr	Glasgow	1	3
1938	9 Apr	Wembley	0	1
1939	15 Apr	Glasgow	2	1
1947	12 Apr	Wembley	1	1
1948	10 Apr	Glasgow	2	0
1949	9 Apr	Wembley	1	3
wc1950	15 Apr	Glasgow	1	0
1951	14 Apr	Wembley	2	3
1952	5 Apr	Glasgow	2	1
1953	18 Apr	Wembley	2	2
wc1954	3 Apr	Glasgow	4	2
1955	2 Apr	Wembley	7	2
1956	14 Apr	Glasgow	1	1
1957	6 Apr	Wembley	2	1
1958	19 Apr	Glasgow	4	0
1959	11 Apr	Wembley	1	0
1960	9 Apr	Glasgow	1	1
1961	15 Apr	Wembley	9	3
1962	14 Apr	Glasgow	0	2
1963	6 Apr	Wembley	1	2
1964	11 Apr	Glasgow	0	1
1965	10 Apr	Wembley	2	2
1966	2 Apr	Glasgow	4	3
ec1967	15 Apr	Wembley	2	3
ec1968	24 Jan	Glasgow	1	1
1969	10 May	Wembley	4	1
1970	25 Apr	Glasgow	0	0
1971	22 May	Wembley	3	1
1972	27 May	Glasgow	1	0
1973	14 Feb	Glasgow	5	0
1973	19 May	Wembley	1	0
1974	18 May	Glasgow	0	2
1975	24 May	Wembley	5	1
1976	15 May	Glasgow	1	2
1977	4 June	Wembley	1	2
1978	20 May	Glasgow	1	0
1979	26 May	Wembley	3	1
1980	24 May	Glasgow	2	0
1981	23 May	Wembley	0	1
1982	29 May	Glasgow	1	0
1983	1 June	Wembley	2	0
1984	26 May	Glasgow	1	1
1985	25 May	Glasgow	0	1
1986	23 Apr	Wembley	2	1
1987	23 May	Glasgow	0	0
1988	21 May	Wembley	1	0
1989	27 May	Glasgow	2	0
ec1996	15 June	Wembley	2	0
ec1999	13 Nov	Glasgow	2	0
ec1999	17 Nov	Wembley	0	1
2013	14 Aug	Wembley	3	2
2014	18 Nov	Hampden	3	1

ENGLAND v WALES

Played: 101; England won 66, Wales won 14, Drawn 21. Goals: England 245, Wales 90.

Year	Date	Venue	E	W
1879	18 Jan	Kennington Oval	2	1
1880	15 Mar	Wrexham	3	2
1881	26 Feb	Blackburn	0	1
1882	13 Mar	Wrexham	3	5
1883	3 Feb	Kennington Oval	5	0
1884	17 Mar	Wrexham	4	0
1885	14 Mar	Blackburn	1	1
1886	29 Mar	Wrexham	3	1
1887	26 Feb	Kennington Oval	4	0
1888	4 Feb	Crewe	5	1
1889	23 Feb	Stoke	4	1
1890	15 Mar	Wrexham	3	1
1891	7 May	Sunderland	4	1
1892	5 Mar	Wrexham	2	0
1893	13 Mar	Stoke	6	0
1894	12 Mar	Wrexham	5	1

Year	Date	Venue	E	W
1895	18 Mar	Queen's Club, Kensington	1	1
1896	16 Mar	Cardiff	9	1
1897	29 Mar	Sheffield	4	0
1898	28 Mar	Wrexham	3	0
1899	20 Mar	Bristol	4	0
1900	26 Mar	Cardiff	1	1
1901	18 Mar	Newcastle	6	0
1902	3 Mar	Wrexham	0	0
1903	2 Mar	Portsmouth	2	1
1904	29 Feb	Wrexham	2	2
1905	27 Mar	Liverpool	3	1
1906	19 Mar	Cardiff	1	0
1907	18 Mar	Fulham	1	1
1908	16 Mar	Wrexham	7	1
1909	15 Mar	Nottingham	2	0
1910	14 Mar	Cardiff	1	0
1911	13 Mar	Millwall	3	0
1912	11 Mar	Wrexham	2	0
1913	17 Mar	Bristol	4	3
1914	16 Mar	Cardiff	2	0
1920	15 Mar	Highbury	1	2
1921	14 Mar	Cardiff	0	0
1922	13 Mar	Liverpool	1	0
1923	5 Mar	Cardiff	2	2
1924	3 Mar	Blackburn	1	2
1925	28 Feb	Swansea	2	1
1926	1 Mar	Crystal Palace	1	3
1927	12 Feb	Wrexham	3	3
1927	28 Nov	Burnley	1	2
1928	17 Nov	Swansea	3	2
1929	20 Nov	Chelsea	6	0
1930	22 Nov	Wrexham	4	0
1931	18 Nov	Liverpool	3	1
1932	16 Nov	Wrexham	0	0
1933	15 Nov	Newcastle	1	2
1934	29 Sept	Cardiff	4	0
1936	5 Feb	Wolverhampton	1	2
1936	17 Oct	Cardiff	1	2
1937	17 Nov	Middlesbrough	2	1
1938	22 Oct	Cardiff	2	4
1946	13 Nov	Manchester	3	0
1947	18 Oct	Cardiff	3	0
1948	10 Nov	Aston Villa	1	0
wc1949	15 Oct	Cardiff	4	1
1950	15 Nov	Sunderland	4	2
1951	20 Oct	Cardiff	1	1
1952	12 Nov	Wembley	5	2
wc1953	10 Oct	Cardiff	4	1
1954	10 Nov	Wembley	3	2
1955	27 Oct	Cardiff	1	2
1956	14 Nov	Wembley	3	1
1957	19 Oct	Cardiff	4	0
1958	26 Nov	Aston Villa	2	2
1959	17 Oct	Cardiff	1	1
1960	23 Nov	Wembley	5	1
1961	14 Oct	Cardiff	1	1
1962	21 Oct	Wembley	4	0
1963	12 Oct	Cardiff	4	0
1964	18 Nov	Wembley	2	1
1965	2 Oct	Cardiff	0	0
ec1966	16 Nov	Wembley	5	1
ec1967	21 Oct	Cardiff	3	0
1969	7 May	Wembley	2	1
1970	18 Apr	Cardiff	1	1
1971	19 May	Wembley	0	0
1972	20 May	Cardiff	3	0
wc1972	15 Nov	Cardiff	1	0
wc1973	24 Jan	Wembley	1	1
1973	15 May	Wembley	3	0
1974	11 May	Cardiff	2	0
1975	21 May	Wembley	2	2
1976	24 Mar	Wrexham	2	1
1976	8 May	Cardiff	1	0
1977	31 May	Wembley	0	1
1978	3 May	Cardiff	3	1
1979	23 May	Wembley	0	0
1980	17 May	Wrexham	1	4
1981	20 May	Wembley	0	0
1982	27 Apr	Cardiff	1	0
1983	23 Feb	Wembley	2	1
1984	2 May	Wrexham	0	1
wc2004	9 Oct	Old Trafford	2	0
wc2005	3 Sept	Cardiff	1	0
ec2011	26 Mar	Cardiff	2	0
ec2011	6 Sept	Wembley	1	0

ENGLAND v NORTHERN IRELAND

Played: 98; England won 75, Northern Ireland won 7, Drawn 16. Goals: England 323, Northern Ireland 81.

Year	Date	Venue	E	NI
1882	18 Feb	Belfast	13	0
1883	24 Feb	Liverpool	7	0
1884	23 Feb	Belfast	8	1
1885	28 Feb	Manchester	4	0
1886	13 Mar	Belfast	6	1
1887	5 Feb	Sheffield	7	0
1888	31 Mar	Belfast	5	1
1889	2 Mar	Everton	6	1
1890	15 Mar	Belfast	9	1
1891	7 Mar	Wolverhampton	6	1
1892	5 Mar	Belfast	2	0
1893	25 Feb	Birmingham	6	1
1894	3 Mar	Belfast	2	2
1895	9 Mar	Derby	9	0
1896	7 Mar	Belfast	2	0
1897	20 Feb	Nottingham	6	0
1898	5 Mar	Belfast	3	2
1899	18 Feb	Sunderland	13	2
1900	17 Mar	Dublin	2	0
1901	9 Mar	Southampton	3	0
1902	22 Mar	Belfast	1	0
1903	14 Feb	Wolverhampton	4	0
1904	12 Mar	Belfast	3	1
1905	25 Feb	Middlesbrough	1	1
1906	17 Feb	Belfast	5	0
1907	16 Feb	Everton	1	0
1908	15 Feb	Belfast	3	1
1909	13 Feb	Bradford	4	0
1910	12 Feb	Belfast	1	1
1911	11 Feb	Derby	2	1
1912	10 Feb	Dublin	6	1
1913	15 Feb	Belfast	1	2
1914	14 Feb	Middlesbrough	0	3
1919	25 Oct	Belfast	1	1
1920	23 Oct	Sunderland	2	0
1921	22 Oct	Belfast	1	1
1922	21 Oct	West Bromwich	2	0
1923	20 Oct	Belfast	1	2
1924	22 Oct	Everton	3	1
1925	24 Oct	Belfast	0	0
1926	20 Oct	Liverpool	3	3
1927	22 Oct	Belfast	0	2
1928	22 Oct	Everton	2	1
1929	19 Oct	Belfast	3	0
1930	20 Oct	Sheffield	5	1
1931	17 Oct	Belfast	6	2
1932	17 Oct	Blackpool	1	0
1933	14 Oct	Belfast	3	0
1935	6 Feb	Everton	2	1
1935	19 Oct	Belfast	3	1
1936	18 Nov	Stoke	3	1
1937	23 Oct	Belfast	5	1
1938	16 Nov	Manchester	7	0
1946	28 Sept	Belfast	7	2
1947	5 Nov	Everton	2	2
1948	9 Oct	Belfast	6	2
wc1949	16 Nov	Manchester	9	2
1950	7 Oct	Belfast	4	1
1951	14 Nov	Aston Villa	2	0
1952	4 Oct	Belfast	2	2
wc1953	11 Nov	Everton	3	1
1954	2 Oct	Belfast	2	0
1955	2 Nov	Wembley	3	0
1956	10 Oct	Belfast	1	1

			E	NI					E	NI
1957	6 Nov	Wembley	2	3		1975	17 May	Belfast	0	0
1958	4 Oct	Belfast	3	3		1976	11 May	Wembley	4	0
1959	18 Nov	Wembley	2	1		1977	28 May	Belfast	2	1
1960	8 Oct	Belfast	5	2		1978	16 May	Wembley	1	0
1961	22 Nov	Wembley	1	1		EC1979	7 Feb	Wembley	4	0
1962	20 Oct	Belfast	3	1		1979	19 May	Belfast	2	0
1963	20 Nov	Wembley	8	3		EC1979	17 Oct	Belfast	5	1
1964	3 Oct	Belfast	4	3		1980	20 May	Wembley	1	1
1965	10 Nov	Wembley	2	1		1982	23 Feb	Wembley	4	0
EC1966	20 Oct	Belfast	2	0		1983	28 May	Belfast	0	0
EC1967	22 Nov	Wembley	2	0		1984	24 Apr	Wembley	1	0
1969	3 May	Belfast	3	1		wc1985	27 Feb	Belfast	1	0
1970	21 Apr	Wembley	3	1		wc1985	13 Nov	Wembley	0	0
1971	15 May	Belfast	1	0		EC1986	15 Oct	Wembley	3	0
1972	23 May	Wembley	0	1		EC1987	1 Apr	Belfast	2	0
1973	12 May	Everton	2	1		wc2005	26 Mar	Old Trafford	4	0
1974	15 May	Wembley	1	0		wc2005	7 Sept	Belfast	0	1

SCOTLAND v WALES

Played: 107; Scotland won 61, Wales won 23, Drawn 23. Goals: Scotland 243, Wales 124.

			S	W					S	W
1876	25 Mar	Glasgow	4	0		1934	21 Nov	Aberdeen	3	2
1877	5 Mar	Wrexham	2	0		1935	5 Oct	Cardiff	1	1
1878	23 Mar	Glasgow	9	0		1936	2 Dec	Dundee	1	2
1879	7 Apr	Wrexham	3	0		1937	30 Oct	Cardiff	1	2
1880	3 Apr	Glasgow	5	1		1938	9 Nov	Tynecastle	3	2
1881	14 Mar	Wrexham	5	1		1946	19 Oct	Wrexham	1	3
1882	25 Mar	Glasgow	5	0		1947	12 Nov	Glasgow	1	2
1883	12 Mar	Wrexham	3	0		1948	23 Oct	Cardiff	3	1
1884	29 Mar	Glasgow	4	1		wc1949	9 Nov	Glasgow	2	0
1885	23 Mar	Wrexham	8	1		1950	21 Oct	Cardiff	3	1
1886	10 Apr	Glasgow	4	1		1951	14 Nov	Glasgow	0	1
1887	21 Mar	Wrexham	2	0		1952	18 Oct	Cardiff	2	1
1888	10 Mar	Easter Road	5	1		wc1953	4 Nov	Glasgow	3	3
1889	15 Apr	Wrexham	0	0		1954	16 Oct	Cardiff	1	0
1890	22 Mar	Paisley	5	0		1955	9 Nov	Glasgow	2	0
1891	21 Mar	Wrexham	4	3		1956	20 Oct	Cardiff	2	2
1892	26 Mar	Tynecastle	6	1		1957	13 Nov	Glasgow	1	1
1893	18 Mar	Wrexham	8	0		1958	18 Oct	Cardiff	3	0
1894	24 Mar	Kilmarnock	5	2		1959	4 Nov	Glasgow	1	1
1895	23 Mar	Wrexham	2	2		1960	20 Oct	Cardiff	0	2
1896	21 Mar	Dundee	4	0		1961	8 Nov	Glasgow	2	0
1897	20 Mar	Wrexham	2	2		1962	20 Oct	Cardiff	3	2
1898	19 Mar	Motherwell	5	2		1963	20 Nov	Glasgow	2	1
1899	18 Mar	Wrexham	6	0		1964	3 Oct	Cardiff	2	3
1900	3 Feb	Aberdeen	5	2		EC1965	24 Nov	Glasgow	4	1
1901	2 Mar	Wrexham	1	1		EC1966	22 Oct	Cardiff	1	1
1902	15 Mar	Greenock	5	1		1967	22 Nov	Glasgow	3	2
1903	9 Mar	Cardiff	1	0		1969	3 May	Wrexham	5	3
1904	12 Mar	Dundee	1	1		1970	22 Apr	Glasgow	0	0
1905	6 Mar	Wrexham	1	3		1971	15 May	Cardiff	0	0
1906	3 Mar	Tynecastle	0	2		1972	24 May	Glasgow	1	0
1907	4 Mar	Wrexham	0	1		1973	12 May	Wrexham	2	0
1908	7 Mar	Dundee	2	1		1974	14 May	Glasgow	2	0
1909	1 Mar	Wrexham	2	3		1975	17 May	Cardiff	2	2
1910	5 Mar	Kilmarnock	1	0		1976	6 May	Glasgow	3	1
1911	6 Mar	Cardiff	2	2		wc1976	17 Nov	Glasgow	1	0
1912	2 Mar	Tynecastle	1	0		1977	28 May	Wrexham	0	0
1913	3 Mar	Wrexham	0	0		wc1977	12 Oct	Liverpool	2	0
1914	28 Feb	Glasgow	0	0		1978	17 May	Glasgow	1	1
1920	26 Feb	Cardiff	1	1		1979	19 May	Cardiff	0	3
1921	12 Feb	Aberdeen	2	1		1980	21 May	Glasgow	1	0
1922	4 Feb	Wrexham	1	2		1981	16 May	Swansea	0	2
1923	17 Mar	Paisley	2	0		1982	24 May	Glasgow	1	0
1924	16 Feb	Cardiff	0	2		1983	28 May	Cardiff	2	0
1925	14 Feb	Tynecastle	3	1		1984	28 Feb	Glasgow	2	1
1925	31 Oct	Cardiff	3	0		wc1985	27 Mar	Glasgow	0	1
1926	30 Oct	Glasgow	3	0		wc1985	10 Sept	Cardiff	1	1
1927	29 Oct	Wrexham	2	2		1997	27 May	Kilmarnock	0	1
1928	27 Oct	Glasgow	4	2		2004	18 Feb	Cardiff	0	4
1929	26 Oct	Cardiff	4	2		2009	14 Nov	Cardiff	0	3
1930	25 Oct	Glasgow	1	1		NC2011	25 May	Dublin	3	1
1931	31 Oct	Wrexham	3	2		wc2012	12 Oct	Cardiff	1	2
1932	26 Oct	Tynecastle	2	5		wc2013	22 Mar	Glasgow	1	2
1933	4 Oct	Cardiff	2	3						

SCOTLAND v NORTHERN IRELAND

Played: 96; Scotland won 64, Northern Ireland won 15, Drawn 17. Goals: Scotland 261, Northern Ireland 81.

Year	Date	Venue	S	NI		Year	Date	Venue	S	NI
1884	26 Jan	Belfast	5	0		1935	13 Nov	Tynecastle	2	1
1885	14 Mar	Glasgow	8	2		1936	31 Oct	Belfast	3	1
1886	20 Mar	Belfast	7	2		1937	10 Nov	Aberdeen	1	1
1887	19 Feb	Glasgow	4	1		1938	8 Oct	Belfast	2	0
1888	24 Mar	Belfast	10	2		1946	27 Nov	Glasgow	0	0
1889	9 Mar	Glasgow	7	0		1947	4 Oct	Belfast	0	2
1890	29 Mar	Belfast	4	1		1948	17 Nov	Glasgow	3	2
1891	28 Mar	Glasgow	2	1		wc1949	1 Oct	Belfast	8	2
1892	19 Mar	Belfast	3	2		1950	1 Nov	Glasgow	6	1
1893	25 Mar	Glasgow	6	1		1951	6 Oct	Belfast	3	0
1894	31 Mar	Belfast	2	1		1952	5 Nov	Glasgow	1	1
1895	30 Mar	Glasgow	3	1		wc1953	3 Oct	Belfast	3	1
1896	28 Mar	Belfast	3	3		1954	3 Nov	Glasgow	2	2
1897	27 Mar	Glasgow	5	1		1955	8 Oct	Belfast	1	2
1898	26 Mar	Belfast	3	0		1956	7 Nov	Glasgow	1	0
1899	25 Mar	Glasgow	9	1		1957	5 Oct	Belfast	1	1
1900	3 Mar	Belfast	3	0		1958	5 Nov	Glasgow	2	2
1901	23 Feb	Glasgow	11	0		1959	3 Oct	Belfast	4	0
1902	1 Mar	Belfast	5	1		1960	9 Nov	Glasgow	5	2
1902	9 Aug	Belfast	3	0		1961	7 Oct	Belfast	6	1
1903	21 Mar	Glasgow	0	2		1962	7 Nov	Glasgow	5	1
1904	26 Mar	Dublin	1	1		1963	12 Oct	Belfast	1	2
1905	18 Mar	Glasgow	4	0		1964	25 Nov	Glasgow	3	2
1906	17 Mar	Dublin	1	0		1965	2 Oct	Belfast	2	3
1907	16 Mar	Glasgow	3	0		1966	16 Nov	Glasgow	2	1
1908	14 Mar	Dublin	5	0		1967	21 Oct	Belfast	0	1
1909	15 Mar	Glasgow	5	0		1969	6 May	Glasgow	1	1
1910	19 Mar	Belfast	0	1		1970	18 Apr	Belfast	1	0
1911	18 Mar	Glasgow	2	0		1971	18 May	Glasgow	0	1
1912	16 Mar	Belfast	4	1		1972	20 May	Glasgow	2	0
1913	15 Mar	Dublin	2	1		1973	16 May	Glasgow	1	2
1914	14 Mar	Belfast	1	1		1974	11 May	Glasgow	0	1
1920	13 Mar	Glasgow	3	0		1975	20 May	Glasgow	3	0
1921	26 Feb	Belfast	2	0		1976	8 May	Glasgow	3	0
1922	4 Mar	Glasgow	2	1		1977	1 June	Glasgow	3	0
1923	3 Mar	Belfast	1	0		1978	13 May	Glasgow	1	1
1924	1 Mar	Glasgow	2	0		1979	22 May	Glasgow	1	0
1925	28 Feb	Belfast	3	0		1980	17 May	Belfast	0	1
1926	27 Feb	Glasgow	4	0		wc1981	25 Mar	Glasgow	1	1
1927	26 Feb	Belfast	2	0		1981	19 May	Glasgow	2	0
1928	25 Feb	Glasgow	0	1		wc1981	14 Oct	Belfast	0	0
1929	23 Feb	Belfast	7	3		1982	28 Apr	Belfast	1	1
1930	22 Feb	Glasgow	3	1		1983	24 May	Glasgow	0	0
1931	21 Feb	Belfast	0	0		1983	13 Dec	Belfast	0	2
1931	19 Sept	Glasgow	3	1		1992	19 Feb	Glasgow	1	0
1932	12 Sept	Belfast	4	0		2008	20 Aug	Glasgow	0	0
1933	16 Sept	Glasgow	1	2		NC2011	9 Feb	Dublin	3	0
1934	20 Oct	Belfast	1	2		2015	25 Mar	Hampden	1	0

WALES v NORTHERN IRELAND

Played: 94; Wales won 44, Northern Ireland won 27, Drawn 23. Goals: Wales 189, Northern Ireland 131.

Year	Date	Venue	W	NI		Year	Date	Venue	W	NI
1882	25 Feb	Wrexham	7	1		1905	18 Apr	Belfast	2	2
1883	17 Mar	Belfast	1	1		1906	2 Apr	Wrexham	4	4
1884	9 Feb	Wrexham	6	0		1907	23 Feb	Belfast	3	2
1885	11 Apr	Belfast	8	2		1908	11 Apr	Aberdare	0	1
1886	27 Feb	Wrexham	5	0		1909	20 Mar	Belfast	3	2
1887	12 Mar	Belfast	1	4		1910	11 Apr	Wrexham	4	1
1888	3 Mar	Wrexham	11	0		1911	28 Jan	Belfast	2	1
1889	27 Apr	Belfast	3	1		1912	13 Apr	Cardiff	2	3
1890	8 Feb	Shrewsbury	5	2		1913	18 Jan	Belfast	1	0
1891	7 Feb	Belfast	2	7		1914	19 Jan	Wrexham	1	2
1892	27 Feb	Bangor	1	1		1920	14 Feb	Belfast	2	2
1893	8 Apr	Belfast	3	4		1921	9 Apr	Swansea	2	1
1894	24 Feb	Swansea	4	1		1922	4 Apr	Belfast	1	1
1895	16 Mar	Belfast	2	2		1923	14 Apr	Wrexham	0	3
1896	29 Feb	Wrexham	6	1		1924	15 Mar	Belfast	1	0
1897	6 Mar	Belfast	3	4		1925	18 Apr	Wrexham	0	0
1898	19 Feb	Llandudno	0	1		1926	13 Feb	Belfast	0	3
1899	4 Mar	Belfast	0	1		1927	9 Apr	Cardiff	2	2
1900	24 Feb	Llandudno	2	0		1928	4 Feb	Belfast	2	1
1901	23 Mar	Belfast	1	0		1929	2 Feb	Wrexham	2	2
1902	22 Mar	Cardiff	0	3		1930	1 Feb	Belfast	0	7
1903	28 Mar	Belfast	0	2		1931	22 Apr	Wrexham	3	2
1904	21 Mar	Bangor	0	1		1931	5 Dec	Belfast	0	4

			W	NI
1932	7 Dec	Wrexham	4	1
1933	4 Nov	Belfast	1	1
1935	27 Mar	Wrexham	3	1
1936	11 Mar	Belfast	2	3
1937	17 Mar	Wrexham	4	1
1938	16 Mar	Belfast	0	1
1939	15 Mar	Wrexham	3	1
1947	16 Apr	Belfast	1	2
1948	10 Mar	Wrexham	2	0
1949	9 Mar	Belfast	2	0
wc1950	8 Mar	Wrexham	0	0
1951	7 Mar	Belfast	2	1
1952	19 Mar	Swansea	3	0
1953	15 Apr	Belfast	3	2
wc1954	31 Mar	Wrexham	1	2
1955	20 Apr	Belfast	3	2
1956	11 Apr	Cardiff	1	1
1957	10 Apr	Belfast	0	0
1958	16 Apr	Cardiff	1	1
1959	22 Apr	Belfast	1	4
1960	6 Apr	Wrexham	3	2
1961	12 Apr	Belfast	5	1
1962	11 Apr	Cardiff	4	0
1963	3 Apr	Belfast	4	1

			W	NI
1964	15 Apr	Swansea	2	3
1965	31 Mar	Belfast	5	0
1966	30 Mar	Cardiff	1	4
EC1967	12 Apr	Belfast	0	0
EC1968	28 Feb	Wrexham	2	0
1969	10 May	Belfast	0	0
1970	25 Apr	Swansea	1	0
1971	22 May	Belfast	0	1
1972	27 May	Wrexham	0	0
1973	19 May	Everton	0	1
1974	18 May	Wrexham	1	0
1975	23 May	Belfast	0	1
1976	14 May	Swansea	1	0
1977	3 June	Belfast	1	1
1978	19 May	Wrexham	1	0
1979	25 May	Belfast	1	1
1980	23 May	Cardiff	0	1
1982	27 May	Wrexham	3	0
1983	31 May	Belfast	1	0
1984	22 May	Swansea	1	1
wc2004	8 Sept	Cardiff	2	2
wc2005	8 Oct	Belfast	3	2
2007	6 Feb	Belfast	0	0
NC2011	27 May	Dublin	2	0

OTHER BRITISH INTERNATIONAL RESULTS 1908–2015

ENGLAND

			E	A
v ALBANIA			**E**	**A**
wc1989	8 Mar	Tirana	2	0
wc1989	26 Apr	Wembley	5	0
wc2001	28 Mar	Tirana	3	1
wc2001	5 Sept	Newcastle	2	0
v ALGERIA			**E**	**A**
wc2010	18 June	Cape Town	0	0
v ANDORRA			**E**	**A**
EC2006	2 Sept	Old Trafford	5	0
EC2007	28 Mar	Barcelona	3	0
wc2008	6 Sept	Barcelona	2	0
wc2009	10 June	Wembley	6	0
v ARGENTINA			**E**	**A**
1951	9 May	Wembley	2	1
1953	17 May	Buenos Aires	0	0
(abandoned after 21 mins)				
wc1962	2 June	Rancagua	3	1
1964	6 June	Rio de Janeiro	0	1
wc1966	23 July	Wembley	1	0
1974	22 May	Wembley	2	2
1977	12 June	Buenos Aires	1	1
1980	13 May	Wembley	3	1
wc1986	22 June	Mexico City	1	2
1991	25 May	Wembley	2	2
wc1998	30 June	St Etienne	2	2
2000	23 Feb	Wembley	0	0
wc2002	7 June	Sapporo	1	0
2005	12 Nov	Geneva	3	2
v AUSTRALIA			**E**	**A**
1980	31 May	Sydney	2	1
1983	11 June	Sydney	0	0
1983	15 June	Brisbane	1	0
1983	18 June	Melbourne	1	1
1991	1 June	Sydney	1	0
2003	12 Feb	West Ham	1	3
v AUSTRIA			**E**	**A**
1908	6 June	Vienna	6	1
1908	8 June	Vienna	11	1
1909	1 June	Vienna	8	1
1930	14 May	Vienna	0	0
1932	7 Dec	Chelsea	4	3
1936	6 May	Vienna	1	2
1951	28 Nov	Wembley	2	2
1952	25 May	Vienna	3	2
wc1958	15 June	Boras	2	2
1961	27 May	Vienna	1	3
1962	4 Apr	Wembley	3	1
1965	20 Oct	Wembley	2	3

			E	A
1967	27 May	Vienna	1	0
1973	26 Sept	Wembley	7	0
1979	13 June	Vienna	3	4
wc2004	4 Sept	Vienna	2	2
wc2005	8 Oct	Old Trafford	1	0
2007	16 Nov	Vienna	1	0
v AZERBAIJAN			**E**	**A**
wc2004	13 Oct	Baku	1	0
wc2005	30 Mar	Newcastle	2	0
v BELARUS			**E**	**B**
wc2008	15 Oct	Minsk	3	1
wc2009	14 Oct	Wembley	3	0
v BELGIUM			**E**	**B**
1921	21 May	Brussels	2	0
1923	19 Mar	Highbury	6	1
1923	1 Nov	Antwerp	2	2
1924	8 Dec	West Bromwich	4	0
1926	24 May	Antwerp	5	3
1927	11 May	Brussels	9	1
1928	19 May	Antwerp	3	1
1929	11 May	Brussels	5	1
1931	16 May	Brussels	4	1
1936	9 May	Brussels	2	3
1947	21 Sept	Brussels	5	2
1950	18 May	Brussels	4	1
1952	26 Nov	Wembley	5	0
wc1954	17 June	Basle	4	4*
1964	21 Oct	Wembley	2	2
1970	25 Feb	Brussels	3	1
EC1980	12 June	Turin	1	1
wc1990	27 June	Bologna	1	0*
1998	29 May	Casablanca	0	0
1999	10 Oct	Sunderland	2	1
2012	2 June	Wembley	1	0
v BOHEMIA			**E**	**B**
1908	13 June	Prague	4	0
v BRAZIL			**E**	**B**
1956	9 May	Wembley	4	2
wc1958	11 June	Gothenburg	0	0
1959	13 May	Rio de Janeiro	0	2
wc1962	10 June	Vina del Mar	1	3
1963	8 May	Wembley	1	1
1964	30 May	Rio de Janeiro	1	5
1969	12 June	Rio de Janeiro	1	2
wc1970	7 June	Guadalajara	0	1
1976	23 May	Los Angeles	0	1
1977	8 June	Rio de Janeiro	0	0

			E	B
1978	19 Apr	Wembley	1	1
1981	12 May	Wembley	0	1
1984	10 June	Rio de Janeiro	2	0
1987	19 May	Wembley	1	1
1990	28 Mar	Wembley	1	0
1992	17 May	Wembley	1	1
1993	13 June	Washington	1	1
uı1995	11 June	Wembley	1	3
tf1997	10 June	Paris	0	1
2000	27 May	Wembley	1	1
wc2002	21 June	Shizuoka	1	2
2007	1 June	Wembley	1	1
2009	14 Nov	Doha	0	1
2013	6 Feb	Wembley	2	1
2013	2 June	Rio de Janeiro	2	2

v BULGARIA

			E	B
wc1962	7 June	Rancagua	0	0
1968	11 Dec	Wembley	1	1
1974	1 June	Sofia	1	0
EC1979	6 June	Sofia	3	0
EC1979	22 Nov	Wembley	2	0
1996	27 Mar	Wembley	1	0
EC1998	10 Oct	Wembley	0	0
EC1999	9 June	Sofia	1	1
EC2010	3 Sept	Wembley	4	0
EC2011	2 Sept	Sofia	3	0

v CAMEROON

			E	C*
wc1990	1 July	Naples	3	2*
1991	6 Feb	Wembley	2	0
1997	15 Nov	Wembley	2	0
2002	26 May	Kobe	2	2

v CANADA

			E	C
1986	24 May	Burnaby	1	0

v CHILE

			E	C
wc1950	25 June	Rio de Janeiro	2	0
1953	24 May	Santiago	2	1
1984	17 June	Santiago	0	0
1989	23 May	Wembley	0	0
1998	11 Feb	Wembley	0	2
2013	15 Nov	Wembley	0	2

v CHINA

			E	C
1996	23 May	Beijing	3	0

v CIS

			E	C
1992	29 Apr	Moscow	2	2

v COLOMBIA

			E	C
1970	20 May	Bogota	4	0
1988	24 May	Wembley	1	1
1995	6 Sept	Wembley	0	0
wc1998	26 June	Lens	2	0
2005	31 May	New Jersey	3	2

v COSTA RICA

			E	C
wc2014	26 June	Belo Horizonte	0	0

v CROATIA

			E	C
1996	24 Apr	Wembley	0	0
2003	20 Aug	Ipswich	3	1
EC2004	21 June	Lisbon	4	2
EC2006	11 Oct	Zagreb	0	2
EC2007	21 Nov	Wembley	2	3
wc2008	10 Sept	Zagreb	4	1
wc2009	9 Sept	Wembley	5	1

v CYPRUS

			E	C
EC1975	16 Apr	Wembley	5	0
EC1975	11 May	Limassol	1	0

v CZECHOSLOVAKIA

			E	C
1934	16 May	Prague	1	2
1937	1 Dec	Tottenham	5	4
1963	29 May	Bratislava	4	2
1966	2 Nov	Wembley	0	0
wc1970	11 June	Guadalajara	1	0
1973	27 May	Prague	1	1
EC1974	30 Oct	Wembley	3	0
EC1975	30 Oct	Bratislava	1	2
1978	29 Nov	Wembley	1	0
wc1982	20 June	Bilbao	2	0
1990	25 Apr	Wembley	4	2
1992	25 Mar	Prague	2	2

v CZECH REPUBLIC

			E	C
1998	18 Nov	Wembley	2	0
2008	20 Aug	Wembley	2	2

v DENMARK

			E	D
1948	26 Sept	Copenhagen	0	0
1955	2 Oct	Copenhagen	5	1
wc1956	5 Dec	Wolverhampton	5	2
wc1957	15 May	Copenhagen	4	1
1966	3 July	Copenhagen	2	0
EC1978	20 Sept	Copenhagen	4	3
EC1979	12 Sept	Wembley	1	0
EC1982	22 Sept	Copenhagen	2	2
EC1983	21 Sept	Wembley	0	1
1988	14 Sept	Wembley	1	0
1989	7 June	Copenhagen	1	1
1990	15 May	Wembley	1	0
EC1992	11 June	Malmo	0	0
1994	9 Mar	Wembley	1	0
wc2002	15 June	Niigata	3	0
2003	16 Nov	Old Trafford	2	3
2005	17 Aug	Copenhagen	1	4
2011	9 Feb	Copenhagen	2	1
2014	5 Mar	Wembley	1	0

v ECUADOR

			E	Ec
1970	24 May	Quito	2	0
wc2006	25 June	Stuttgart	1	0
2014	4 June	Miami	2	2

v EGYPT

			E	Eg
1986	29 Jan	Cairo	4	0
wc1990	21 June	Cagliari	1	0
2010	3 Mar	Wembley	3	1

v ESTONIA

			E	Es
EC2007	6 June	Tallinn	3	0
EC2007	13 Oct	Wembley	3	0
EC2014	12 Oct	Tallinn	1	0

v FIFA

			E	FIFA
1938	26 Oct	Highbury	3	0
1953	21 Oct	Wembley	4	4
1963	23 Oct	Wembley	2	1

v FINLAND

			E	F
1937	20 May	Helsinki	8	0
1956	20 May	Helsinki	5	1
1966	26 June	Helsinki	3	0
wc1976	13 June	Helsinki	4	1
wc1976	13 Oct	Wembley	2	1
1982	3 June	Helsinki	4	1
wc1984	17 Oct	Wembley	5	0
wc1985	22 May	Helsinki	1	1
1992	3 June	Helsinki	2	1
wc2000	11 Oct	Helsinki	0	0
wc2001	24 Mar	Liverpool	2	1

v FRANCE

			E	F
1923	10 May	Paris	4	1
1924	17 May	Paris	3	1
1925	21 May	Paris	3	2
1927	26 May	Paris	6	0
1928	17 May	Paris	5	1
1929	9 May	Paris	4	1
1931	14 May	Paris	2	5
1933	6 Dec	Tottenham	4	1
1938	26 May	Paris	4	2
1947	3 May	Highbury	3	0
1949	22 May	Paris	3	1
1951	3 Oct	Highbury	2	2
1955	15 May	Paris	0	1
1957	27 Nov	Wembley	4	0
EC1962	3 Oct	Sheffield	1	1
EC1963	27 Feb	Paris	2	5
wc1966	20 July	Wembley	2	0
1969	12 Mar	Wembley	5	0
wc1982	16 June	Bilbao	3	1
1984	29 Feb	Paris	0	2
1992	19 Feb	Wembley	2	0
EC1992	14 June	Malmo	0	0
tf1997	7 June	Montpellier	1	0
1999	10 Feb	Wembley	0	2
2000	2 Sept	Paris	1	1
EC2004	13 June	Lisbon	1	2
2008	26 Mar	Paris	0	1
2010	17 Nov	Paris	1	2
EC2012	11 June	Donetsk	1	1

		v GEORGIA	E	G
wc1996	9 Nov	Tbilisi	2	0
wc1997	30 Apr	Wembley	2	0

		v GERMANY	E	G
1930	10 May	Berlin	3	3
1935	4 Dec	Tottenham	3	0
1938	14 May	Berlin	6	3
1991	11 Sept	Wembley	0	1
1993	19 June	Detroit	1	2
EC1996	26 June	Wembley	1	1*
EC2000	17 June	Charleroi	1	0
wc2000	7 Oct	Wembley	0	1
wc2001	1 Sept	Munich	5	1
2007	22 Aug	Wembley	1	2
2008	19 Nov	Berlin	2	1
wc2010	27 June	Bloemfontein	1	4
2013	19 Nov	Wembley	0	1

		v EAST GERMANY	E	EG
1963	2 June	Leipzig	2	1
1970	25 Nov	Wembley	3	1
1974	29 May	Leipzig	1	1
1984	12 Sept	Wembley	1	0

		v WEST GERMANY	E	WG
1954	1 Dec	Wembley	3	1
1956	26 May	Berlin	3	1
1965	12 May	Nuremberg	1	0
1966	23 Feb	Wembley	1	0
wc1966	30 July	Wembley	4	2*
1968	1 June	Hanover	0	1
wc1970	14 June	Leon	2	3*
EC1972	29 Apr	Wembley	1	3
EC1972	13 May	Berlin	0	0
1975	12 Mar	Wembley	2	0
1978	22 Feb	Munich	1	2
wc1982	29 June	Madrid	0	0
1982	13 Oct	Wembley	1	2
1985	12 June	Mexico City	3	0
1987	9 Sept	Dusseldorf	1	3
wc1990	4 July	Turin	1	1*

		v GHANA	E	G
2011	29 Mar	Wembley	1	1

		v GREECE	E	G
EC1971	21 Apr	Wembley	3	0
EC1971	1 Dec	Piraeus	2	0
EC1982	17 Nov	Salonika	3	0
EC1983	30 Mar	Wembley	0	0
1989	8 Feb	Athens	2	1
1994	17 May	Wembley	5	0
wc2001	6 June	Athens	2	0
wc2001	6 Oct	Old Trafford	2	2
2006	16 Aug	Old Trafford	4	0

		v HONDURAS	E	H
2014	7 June	Miami	0	0

		v HUNGARY	E	H
1908	10 June	Budapest	7	0
1909	29 May	Budapest	4	2
1909	31 May	Budapest	8	2
1934	10 May	Budapest	1	2
1936	2 Dec	Highbury	6	2
1953	25 Nov	Wembley	3	6
1954	23 May	Budapest	1	7
1960	22 May	Budapest	0	2
wc1962	31 May	Rancagua	1	2
1965	5 May	Wembley	1	0
1978	24 May	Wembley	4	1
wc1981	6 June	Budapest	3	1
wc1982	18 Nov	Wembley	1	0
EC1983	27 Apr	Wembley	2	0
EC1983	12 Oct	Budapest	3	0
1988	27 Apr	Budapest	0	0
1990	12 Sept	Wembley	1	0
1992	12 May	Budapest	1	0
1996	18 May	Wembley	3	0
1999	28 Apr	Budapest	1	1
2006	30 May	Old Trafford	3	1
2010	11 Aug	Wembley	2	1

		v ICELAND	E	I
1982	2 June	Reykjavik	1	1
2004	5 June	City of Manchester	6	1
EC2007	24 Mar	Tel Aviv	0	0

		v ISRAEL	E	I
1986	26 Feb	Ramat Gan	2	1
1988	17 Feb	Tel Aviv	0	0
EC2007	24 Mar	Tel Aviv	0	0
EC2007	8 Sept	Wembley	3	0

		v ITALY	E	I
1933	13 May	Rome	1	1
1934	14 Nov	Highbury	3	2
1939	13 May	Milan	2	2
1948	16 May	Turin	4	0
1949	30 Nov	Tottenham	2	0
1952	18 May	Florence	1	1
1959	6 May	Wembley	2	2
1961	24 May	Rome	3	2
1973	14 June	Turin	0	2
1973	14 Nov	Wembley	0	1
1976	28 May	New York	3	2
wc1976	17 Nov	Rome	0	2
wc1977	16 Nov	Wembley	2	0
EC1980	15 June	Turin	0	1
1985	6 June	Mexico City	1	2
1989	15 Nov	Wembley	0	0
wc1990	7 July	Bari	1	2
wc1997	12 Feb	Wembley	0	1
TF1997	4 June	Nantes	2	0
wc1997	11 Oct	Rome	0	0
2000	15 Nov	Turin	0	1
2002	27 Mar	Leeds	1	2
EC2012	24 June	Kiev	0	0
2012	15 Aug	Berne	2	1
wc2014	14 June	Manaus	1	2
2015	31 Mar	Turin	1	1

		v JAMAICA	E	J
2006	3 June	Old Trafford	6	0

		v JAPAN	E	J
UI1995	3 June	Wembley	2	1
2004	1 June	City of Manchester	1	1
2010	30 May	Graz	2	1

		v KAZAKHSTAN	E	K
wc2008	11 Oct	Wembley	5	1
wc2009	6 June	Almaty	4	0

		v KOREA REPUBLIC	E	KR
2002	21 May	Seoguipo	1	1

		v KUWAIT	E	K
wc1982	25 June	Bilbao	1	0

		v LIECHTENSTEIN	E	L
EC2003	29 Mar	Vaduz	2	0
EC2003	10 Sept	Old Trafford	2	0

		v LITHUANIA	E	L
EC2015	27 Mar	Wembley	4	0

		v LUXEMBOURG	E	L
1927	21 May	Esch-sur-Alzette	5	2
wc1960	19 Oct	Luxembourg	9	0
wc1961	28 Sept	Highbury	4	1
wc1977	30 Mar	Wembley	5	0
wc1977	12 Oct	Luxembourg	2	0
EC1982	15 Dec	Wembley	9	0
EC1983	16 Nov	Luxembourg	4	0
EC1998	14 Oct	Luxembourg	3	0
EC1999	4 Sept	Wembley	6	0

		v MACEDONIA	E	M
EC2002	16 Oct	Southampton	2	2
EC2003	6 Sept	Skopje	2	1
EC2006	6 Sept	Skopje	1	0
EC2006	7 Oct	Old Trafford	0	0

		v MALAYSIA	E	M
1991	12 June	Kuala Lumpur	4	2

		v MALTA	E	M
EC1971	3 Feb	Valletta	1	0
EC1971	12 May	Wembley	5	0
2000	3 June	Valletta	2	1

v MEXICO		E	M
1959	24 May	Mexico City	1	2
1961	10 May	Wembley	8	0
wc1966	16 July	Wembley	2	0
1969	1 June	Mexico City	0	0
1985	9 June	Mexico City	0	1
1986	17 May	Los Angeles	3	0
1997	29 Mar	Wembley	2	0
2001	25 May	Derby	4	0
2010	24 May	Wembley	3	1

v MOLDOVA		E	M
wc1996	1 Sept	Chisinau	3	0
wc1997	10 Sept	Wembley	4	0
wc2012	7 Sept	Chisinau	5	0
wc2013	6 Sept	Wembley	4	0

v MONTENEGRO		E	M
EC1989	8 Mar	Tirana	2	0
2010	12 Oct	Wembley	0	0
EC2011	7 Oct	Podgorica	2	2
wc2013	26 Mar	Podgorica	1	1
wc2013	11 Oct	Wembley	4	1

v MOROCCO		E	M
wc1986	6 June	Monterrey	0	0
1998	27 May	Casablanca	1	0

v NETHERLANDS		E	N
1935	18 May	Amsterdam	1	0
1946	27 Nov	Huddersfield	8	2
1964	9 Dec	Amsterdam	1	1
1969	5 Nov	Amsterdam	1	0
1970	14 Jun	Wembley	0	0
1977	9 Feb	Wembley	0	2
1982	25 May	Wembley	2	0
1988	23 Mar	Wembley	2	2
EC1988	15 June	Dusseldorf	1	3
wc1990	16 June	Cagliari	0	0
2005	9 Feb	Villa Park	0	0
wc1993	28 Apr	Wembley	2	2
wc1993	13 Oct	Rotterdam	0	2
EC1996	18 June	Wembley	4	1
2001	15 Aug	Tottenham	0	2
2002	13 Feb	Amsterdam	1	1
2006	15 Nov	Amsterdam	1	1
2009	12 Aug	Amsterdam	2	2
2012	29 Feb	Wembley	2	3

v NEW ZEALAND		E	NZ
1991	3 June	Auckland	1	0
1991	8 June	Wellington	2	0

v NIGERIA		E	N
1994	16 Nov	Wembley	1	0
wc2002	12 June	Osaka	0	0

v NORWAY		E	N
1937	14 May	Oslo	6	0
1938	9 Nov	Newcastle	4	0
1949	18 May	Oslo	4	1
1966	29 June	Oslo	6	1
wc1980	10 Sept	Wembley	4	0
wc1981	9 Sept	Oslo	1	2
wc1992	14 Oct	Wembley	1	1
wc1993	2 June	Oslo	0	2
1994	22 May	Wembley	0	0
1995	11 Oct	Oslo	0	0
2012	26 May	Oslo	1	0
2014	3 Sept	Wembley	1	0

v PARAGUAY		E	P
wc1986	18 June	Mexico City	3	0
2002	17 Apr	Liverpool	4	0
wc2006	10 June	Frankfurt	1	0

v PERU		E	P
1959	17 May	Lima	1	4
1962	20 May	Lima	4	0
2014	30 May	Wembley	3	0

v POLAND		E	P
1966	5 Jan	Everton	1	1
1966	5 July	Chorzow	1	0
wc1973	6 June	Chorzow	0	2
wc1973	17 Oct	Wembley	1	1
wc1986	11 June	Monterrey	3	0
wc1989	3 June	Wembley	3	0
wc1989	11 Oct	Katowice	0	0
EC1990	17 Oct	Wembley	2	0
EC1991	13 Nov	Poznan	1	1
wc1993	29 May	Katowice	1	1
wc1993	8 Sept	Wembley	3	0
wc1996	9 Oct	Wembley	2	1
wc1997	31 May	Katowice	2	0
EC1999	27 Mar	Wembley	3	1
EC1999	8 Sept	Warsaw	0	0
wc2004	8 Sept	Katowice	2	1
wc2005	12 Oct	Old Trafford	2	1
wc2012	17 Oct	Warsaw	1	1
wc2013	15 Oct	Wembley	2	0

v PORTUGAL		E	P
1947	25 May	Lisbon	10	0
1950	14 May	Lisbon	5	3
1951	19 May	Everton	5	2
1955	22 May	Oporto	1	3
1958	7 May	Wembley	2	1
wc1961	21 May	Lisbon	1	1
wc1961	25 Oct	Wembley	2	0
1964	17 May	Lisbon	4	3
1964	4 June	São Paulo	1	1
wc1966	26 July	Wembley	2	1
1969	10 Dec	Wembley	1	0
1974	3 Apr	Lisbon	0	0
EC1974	20 Nov	Wembley	0	0
EC1975	19 Nov	Lisbon	1	1
wc1986	3 June	Monterrey	0	1
1995	12 Dec	Wembley	1	1
1998	22 Apr	Wembley	3	0
EC2000	12 June	Eindhoven	2	3
2002	7 Sept	Villa Park	1	1
2004	18 Feb	Faro	1	1
EC2004	24 June	Lisbon	2	2*
wc2006	1 July	Gelsenkirchen	0	0

v REPUBLIC OF IRELAND		E	RI
1946	30 Sept	Dublin	1	0
1949	21 Sept	Everton	0	2
wc1957	8 May	Wembley	5	1
wc1957	19 May	Dublin	1	1
1964	24 May	Dublin	3	1
1976	8 Sept	Wembley	1	1
EC1978	25 Oct	Dublin	1	1
EC1980	6 Feb	Wembley	2	0
1985	26 Mar	Wembley	2	1
EC1988	12 June	Stuttgart	0	1
wc1990	11 June	Cagliari	1	1
EC1990	14 Nov	Dublin	1	1
EC1991	27 Mar	Wembley	1	1
1995	15 Feb	Dublin	0	1
(abandoned after 27 mins)				
2013	29 May	Wembley	1	1
2015	7 June	Dublin	0	0

v ROMANIA		E	R
1939	24 May	Bucharest	2	0
1968	6 Nov	Bucharest	0	0
1969	15 Jan	Wembley	1	1
wc1970	2 June	Guadalajara	1	0
wc1980	15 Oct	Bucharest	1	2
wc1981	29 April	Wembley	0	0
wc1985	1 May	Bucharest	0	0
wc1985	11 Sept	Wembley	1	1
1994	12 Oct	Wembley	1	1
wc1998	22 June	Toulouse	1	2
EC2000	20 June	Charleroi	2	3

v RUSSIA		E	R
EC2007	12 Sept	Wembley	3	0
EC2007	17 Oct	Moscow	1	2

v SAN MARINO		E	SM
wc1992	17 Feb	Wembley	6	0
wc1993	17 Nov	Bologna	7	1
wc2012	12 Oct	Wembley	5	0
wc2013	22 Mar	Serravalle	8	0
EC2014	9 Oct	Wembley	5	0

v SAUDI ARABIA		E	SA
1988	16 Nov	Riyadh	1	1
1998	23 May	Wembley	0	0

v SERBIA-MONTENEGRO		E	SM
2003	3 June	Leicester	2	1

			E	S
v SLOVAKIA				
EC2002	12 Oct	Bratislava	2	1
EC2003	11 June	Middlesbrough	2	1
2009	28 Mar	Wembley	4	0
v SLOVENIA			E	S
2009	5 Sept	Wembley	2	1
WC2010	23 June	Port Elizabeth	1	0
EC2014	15 Nov	Wembley	3	1
EC2015	14 June	Ljubljana	3	2
v SOUTH AFRICA			E	SA
1997	24 May	Old Trafford	2	1
2003	22 May	Durban	2	1
v SPAIN			E	S
1929	15 May	Madrid	3	4
1931	9 Dec	Highbury	7	1
WC1950	2 July	Rio de Janeiro	0	1
1955	18 May	Madrid	1	1
1955	30 Nov	Wembley	4	1
1960	15 May	Madrid	0	3
1960	26 Oct	Wembley	4	2
1965	8 Dec	Madrid	2	0
1967	24 May	Wembley	2	0
EC1968	3 Apr	Wembley	1	0
EC1968	8 May	Madrid	2	1
1980	26 Mar	Barcelona	2	0
EC1980	18 June	Naples	2	1
1981	25 Mar	Wembley	1	2
WC1982	5 July	Madrid	0	0
1987	18 Feb	Madrid	4	2
1992	9 Sept	Santander	0	1
EC 1996	22 June	Wembley	0	0
2001	28 Feb	Villa Park	3	0
2004	17 Nov	Madrid	0	1
2007	7 Feb	Old Trafford	0	1
2009	11 Feb	Seville	0	2
2011	12 Nov	Wembley	1	0
v SWEDEN			E	S
1923	21 May	Stockholm	4	2
1923	24 May	Stockholm	3	1
1937	17 May	Stockholm	4	0
1947	19 Nov	Highbury	4	2
1949	13 May	Stockholm	1	3
1956	16 May	Stockholm	0	0
1959	28 Oct	Wembley	2	3
1965	16 May	Gothenburg	2	1
1968	22 May	Wembley	3	1
1979	10 June	Stockholm	0	0
1986	10 Sept	Stockholm	0	1
WC1988	19 Oct	Wembley	0	0
WC1989	6 Sept	Stockholm	0	0
EC1992	17 June	Stockholm	1	2
UI1995	8 June	Leeds	3	3
EC1998	5 Sept	Stockholm	1	2
EC1999	5 June	Wembley	0	0
2001	10 Nov	Old Trafford	1	1
WC2002	2 June	Saitama	1	1
2004	31 Mar	Gothenburg	0	1
WC2006	20 June	Cologne	2	2
2011	15 Nov	Wembley	1	0
EC2012	15 June	Kiev	3	2
2012	14 Nov	Stockholm	2	4
v SWITZERLAND			E	S
1933	20 May	Berne	4	0
1938	21 May	Zurich	1	2
1947	18 May	Zurich	0	1
1948	2 Dec	Highbury	6	0
1952	28 May	Zurich	3	0
WC1954	20 June	Berne	2	0
1962	9 May	Wembley	3	1
1963	5 June	Basle	8	1
EC1971	13 Oct	Basle	3	2
EC1971	10 Nov	Wembley	1	1
1975	3 Sept	Basle	2	1
1977	7 Sept	Wembley	0	0
WC1980	19 Nov	Wembley	2	1
WC1981	30 May	Basle	1	2
1988	28 May	Lausanne	1	0
1995	15 Nov	Wembley	3	1
EC1996	8 June	Wembley	1	1
1998	25 Mar	Berne	1	1
EC2004	17 June	Coimbra	3	0

			E	S
2008	6 Feb	Wembley	2	1
EC1989	8 Mar	Tirana	2	0
EC2010	7 Sept	Basle	3	1
EC2011	4 June	Wembley	2	2
EC2014	8 Sept	Basel	2	0
v TRINIDAD & TOBAGO			E	TT
WC2006	15 June	Nuremberg	2	0
2008	2 June	Port of Spain	3	0
v TUNISIA			E	T
1990	2 June	Tunis	1	1
WC1998	15 June	Marseilles	2	0
v TURKEY			E	T
WC1984	14 Nov	Istanbul	8	0
WC1985	16 Oct	Wembley	5	0
EC1987	29 Apr	Izmir	0	0
EC1987	14 Oct	Wembley	8	0
EC1991	1 May	Izmir	1	0
EC1991	16 Oct	Wembley	1	0
WC1992	18 Nov	Wembley	4	0
WC1993	31 Mar	Izmir	2	0
EC2003	2 Apr	Sunderland	2	0
EC2003	11 Oct	Istanbul	0	0
v UKRAINE			E	U
2000	31 May	Wembley	2	0
2004	18 Aug	Newcastle	3	0
WC2009	1 Apr	Wembley	2	1
WC2009	10 Oct	Dnepr	0	1
EC2012	19 June	Donetsk	1	0
WC2012	11 Sept	Wembley	1	1
WC2013	10 Sept	Kiev	0	0
v URUGUAY			E	U
1953	31 May	Montevideo	1	2
WC1954	26 June	Basle	2	4
1964	6 May	Wembley	2	1
WC1966	11 July	Wembley	0	0
1969	8 June	Montevideo	2	1
1977	15 June	Montevideo	0	0
1984	13 June	Montevideo	0	2
1990	22 May	Wembley	1	2
1995	29 Mar	Wembley	0	0
2006	1 Mar	Liverpool	2	1
WC2014	19 June	Sao Paulo	1	2
v USA			E	USA
WC1950	29 June	Belo Horizonte	0	1
1953	8 June	New York	6	3
1959	28 May	Los Angeles	8	1
1964	27 May	New York	10	0
1985	16 June	Los Angeles	5	0
1993	9 June	Foxboro	0	2
1994	7 Sept	Wembley	2	0
2005	28 May	Chicago	2	1
2008	28 May	Wembley	2	0
WC2010	12 June	Rustenburg	1	1
v USSR			E	USSR
1958	18 May	Moscow	1	1
WC1958	8 June	Gothenburg	2	2
WC1958	17 June	Gothenburg	0	1
1958	22 Oct	Wembley	5	0
1967	6 Dec	Wembley	2	2
EC1968	8 June	Rome	2	0
1973	10 June	Moscow	2	1
1984	2 June	Wembley	0	2
1986	26 Mar	Tbilisi	1	0
EC1988	18 June	Frankfurt	1	3
1991	21 May	Wembley	3	1
v YUGOSLAVIA			E	Y
1939	18 May	Belgrade	1	2
1950	22 Nov	Highbury	2	2
1954	16 May	Belgrade	0	1
1956	28 Nov	Wembley	3	0
1958	11 May	Belgrade	0	5
1960	11 May	Wembley	3	3
1965	9 May	Belgrade	1	1
1966	4 May	Wembley	2	0
EC1968	5 June	Florence	0	1
1972	11 Oct	Wembley	1	1
1974	5 June	Belgrade	2	2
EC1986	12 Nov	Wembley	2	0
EC1987	11 Nov	Belgrade	4	1
1989	13 Dec	Wembley	2	1

SCOTLAND

v ARGENTINA			S	A
1977	18 June	Buenos Aires	1	1
1979	2 June	Glasgow	1	3
1990	28 Mar	Glasgow	1	0
2008	19 Nov	Glasgow	0	1

v AUSTRALIA			S	A
wc1985	20 Nov	Glasgow	2	0
wc1985	4 Dec	Melbourne	0	0
1996	27 Mar	Glasgow	1	0
2000	15 Nov	Glasgow	0	2
2012	15 Aug	Easter Road	3	1

v AUSTRIA			S	A
1931	16 May	Vienna	0	5
1933	29 Nov	Glasgow	2	2
1937	9 May	Vienna	1	1
1950	13 Dec	Glasgow	0	1
1951	27 May	Vienna	0	4
wc1954	16 June	Zurich	0	1
1955	19 May	Vienna	4	1
1956	2 May	Glasgow	1	1
1960	29 May	Vienna	1	4
1963	8 May	Glasgow	4	1
(abandoned after 79 mins)				
wc1968	6 Nov	Glasgow	2	1
wc1969	5 Nov	Vienna	0	2
EC1978	20 Sept	Vienna	2	3
EC1979	17 Oct	Glasgow	1	1
1994	20 Apr	Vienna	2	1
wc1996	31 Aug	Vienna	0	0
wc1997	2 Apr	Celtic Park	2	0
2003	30 Apr	Glasgow	0	2
2005	17 Aug	Graz	2	2
2007	30 May	Vienna	1	0

v BELARUS			S	B
wc1997	8 June	Minsk	1	0
wc1997	7 Sept	Aberdeen	4	1
wc2005	8 June	Minsk	0	0
wc2005	8 Oct	Glasgow	0	1

v BELGIUM			S	B
1946	23 Jan	Glasgow	2	2
1947	18 May	Brussels	1	2
1948	28 Apr	Glasgow	2	0
1951	20 May	Brussels	5	0
EC1971	3 Feb	Liege	0	3
EC1971	10 Nov	Aberdeen	1	0
1974	1 June	Brussels	1	2
EC1979	21 Nov	Brussels	0	2
EC1979	19 Dec	Brussels	1	3
EC1982	15 Dec	Brussels	2	3
EC1983	12 Oct	Glasgow	1	1
EC1987	1 Apr	Brussels	1	4
EC1987	14 Oct	Glasgow	2	0
wc2001	24 Mar	Glasgow	2	2
wc2001	5 Sept	Brussels	0	2
wc2012	16 Oct	Brussels	0	2
wc2013	6 Sept	Glasgow	0	2

v BOSNIA-HERZEGOVINA			S	BH
EC1999	4 Sept	Sarajevo	2	1
EC1999	5 Oct	Ibrox	1	0

v BRAZIL			S	B
1966	25 June	Glasgow	1	1
1972	5 July	Rio de Janeiro	0	1
1973	30 June	Glasgow	0	1
wc1974	18 June	Frankfurt	0	0
1977	23 June	Rio de Janeiro	0	2
wc1982	18 June	Seville	1	4
1987	26 May	Glasgow	0	2
wc1990	20 June	Turin	0	1
wc1998	10 June	St Denis	1	2
2011	27 Mar	Emirates	0	2

v BULGARIA			S	B
1978	22 Feb	Glasgow	2	1
EC1986	10 Sept	Glasgow	0	0
EC1987	11 Nov	Sofia	1	0
EC1990	14 Nov	Sofia	1	1
EC1991	27 Mar	Glasgow	1	1
2006	11 May	Kobe	5	1

v CANADA			S	C
1983	12 June	Vancouver	2	0
1983	16 June	Edmonton	3	0
1983	20 June	Toronto	2	0
1992	21 May	Toronto	3	1
2002	15 Oct	Easter Road	3	1

v CHILE			S	C
1977	15 June	Santiago	4	2
1989	30 May	Glasgow	2	0

v CIS			S	C
EC1992	18 June	Norrkoping	3	0

v COLOMBIA			S	C
1988	17 May	Glasgow	0	0
1996	29 May	Miami	0	1
1998	23 May	New York	2	2

v COSTA RICA			S	CR
wc1990	11 June	Genoa	0	1

v CROATIA			S	C
wc2000	11 Oct	Zagreb	1	1
wc2001	1 Sept	Glasgow	0	0
2008	26 Mar	Glasgow	1	1
wc2013	7 June	Zagreb	1	0
wc2013	15 Oct	Glasgow	2	0

v CYPRUS			S	C
wc1968	11 Dec	Nicosia	5	0
wc1969	17 May	Glasgow	8	0
wc1989	8 Feb	Limassol	3	2
wc1989	26 Apr	Glasgow	2	1
2011	11 Nov	Larnaca	2	1

v CZECHOSLOVAKIA			S	C
1937	15 May	Prague	3	1
1937	8 Dec	Glasgow	5	0
wc1961	14 May	Bratislava	0	4
wc1961	26 Sept	Glasgow	3	2
wc1961	29 Nov	Brussels	2	4*
1972	2 July	Porto Alegre	0	0
wc1973	26 Sept	Glasgow	2	1
wc1973	17 Oct	Bratislava	0	1
wc1976	13 Oct	Prague	0	2
wc1977	21 Sept	Glasgow	3	1

v CZECH REPUBLIC			S	C
EC1999	31 Mar	Glasgow	1	2
EC1999	9 June	Prague	2	3
2008	30 May	Prague	1	3
2010	3 Mar	Glasgow	1	0
EC2010	8 Oct	Prague	0	1
EC2011	3 Sept	Glasgow	2	2

v DENMARK			S	D
1951	12 May	Glasgow	3	1
1952	25 May	Copenhagen	2	1
1968	16 Oct	Copenhagen	1	0
EC1970	11 Nov	Glasgow	1	0
EC1971	9 June	Copenhagen	0	1
wc1972	18 Oct	Copenhagen	4	1
wc1972	15 Nov	Glasgow	2	0
EC1975	3 Sept	Copenhagen	1	0
EC1975	29 Oct	Glasgow	3	1
wc1986	4 June	Nezahualcoyotl	0	1
1996	24 Apr	Copenhagen	0	2
1998	25 Mar	Ibrox	0	1
2002	21 Aug	Copenhagen	0	1
2004	28 Apr	Copenhagen	0	1
2011	10 Aug	Glasgow	2	1

v ECUADOR			S	E
1995	24 May	Toyama	2	1

v EGYPT			S	E
1990	16 May	Aberdeen	1	3

v ESTONIA			S	E
wc1993	19 May	Tallinn	3	0
wc1993	2 June	Aberdeen	3	1
wc1997	11 Feb	Monaco	0	0
wc1997	29 Mar	Kilmarnock	2	0
EC1998	10 Oct	Tynecastle	3	2
EC1999	8 Sept	Tallinn	0	0

			S	E
2004	27 May	Tallinn	1	0
2013	6 Feb	Aberdeen	1	0

v FAROE ISLANDS			S	F
EC1994	12 Oct	Glasgow	5	1
EC1995	7 June	Toftir	2	0
EC1998	14 Oct	Aberdeen	2	1
EC1999	5 June	Toftir	1	1
EC2002	7 Sept	Toftir	2	2
EC2003	6 Sept	Glasgow	3	1
EC2006	2 Sept	Celtic Park	6	0
EC2007	6 June	Toftir	2	0
2010	16 Nov	Aberdeen	3	0

v FINLAND			S	F
1954	25 May	Helsinki	2	1
wc1964	21 Oct	Glasgow	3	1
wc1965	27 May	Helsinki	2	1
1976	8 Sept	Glasgow	6	0
1992	25 Mar	Glasgow	1	1
EC1994	7 Sept	Helsinki	2	0
EC1995	6 Sept	Glasgow	1	0
1998	22 Apr	Easter Road	1	1

v FRANCE			S	F
1930	18 May	Paris	2	0
1932	8 May	Paris	3	1
1948	23 May	Paris	0	3
1949	27 Apr	Glasgow	2	0
1950	27 May	Paris	1	0
1951	16 May	Glasgow	1	0
wc1958	15 June	Orebro	1	2
1984	1 June	Marseilles	0	2
wc1989	8 Mar	Glasgow	2	0
wc1989	11 Oct	Paris	0	3
1997	12 Nov	St Etienne	1	2
2000	29 Mar	Glasgow	0	2
2002	27 Mar	Paris	0	5
EC2006	7 Oct	Glasgow	1	0
EC2007	12 Sept	Paris	1	0

v GEORGIA			S	G
EC2007	24 Mar	Glasgow	2	1
EC2007	17 Oct	Tbilisi	0	2
EC2014	11 Oct	Ibrox	1	0

v GERMANY			S	G
1929	1 June	Berlin	1	1
1936	14 Oct	Glasgow	2	0
EC1992	15 June	Norrkoping	0	2
1993	24 Mar	Glasgow	0	1
1999	28 Apr	Bremen	1	0
EC2003	7 June	Glasgow	1	1
EC2003	10 Sept	Dortmund	1	2
EC2014	7 Sept	Dortmund	1	2

v EAST GERMANY			S	EG
1974	30 Oct	Glasgow	3	0
1977	7 Sept	East Berlin	0	1
EC1982	13 Oct	Glasgow	2	0
EC1983	16 Nov	Halle	1	2
1985	16 Oct	Glasgow	0	0
1990	25 Apr	Glasgow	0	1

v WEST GERMANY			S	WG
1957	22 May	Stuttgart	3	1
1959	6 May	Glasgow	3	2
1964	12 May	Hanover	2	2
wc1969	16 Apr	Glasgow	1	1
wc1969	22 Oct	Hamburg	2	3
1973	14 Nov	Glasgow	1	1
1974	27 Mar	Frankfurt	1	2
wc1986	8 June	Queretaro	1	2

v GIBRALTAR			S	G
EC2015	29 Mar	Hampden	6	1

v GREECE			S	G
EC1994	18 Dec	Athens	0	1
EC1995	16 Aug	Glasgow	1	0

v HONG KONG XI			S	HK
†2002	23 May	Hong Kong	4	0

†*match not recognised by FIFA*

v HUNGARY			S	H
1938	7 Dec	Ibrox	3	1
1954	8 Dec	Glasgow	2	4
1955	29 May	Budapest	1	3
1958	7 May	Glasgow	1	1
1960	5 June	Budapest	3'	3
1980	31 May	Budapest	1	3
1987	9 Sept	Glasgow	2	0
2004	18 Aug	Glasgow	0	3

v ICELAND			S	I
wc1984	17 Oct	Glasgow	3	0
wc1985	28 May	Reykjavik	1	0
EC2002	12 Oct	Reykjavik	2	0
EC2003	29 Mar	Glasgow	2	1
wc2008	10 Sept	Reykjavik	2	1
wc2009	1 Apr	Glasgow	2	1

v IRAN			S	I
wc1978	7 June	Cordoba	1	1

v ISRAEL			S	I
wc1981	25 Feb	Tel Aviv	1	0
wc1981	28 Apr	Glasgow	3	1
1986	28 Jan	Tel Aviv	1	0

v ITALY			S	I
1931	20 May	Rome	0	3
wc1965	9 Nov	Glasgow	1	0
wc1965	7 Dec	Naples	0	3
1988	22 Dec	Perugia	0	2
wc1992	18 Nov	Ibrox	0	0
wc1993	13 Oct	Rome	1	3
wc2005	26 Mar	Milan	0	2
wc2005	3 Sept	Glasgow	1	1
EC2007	28 Mar	Bari	0	2
EC2007	17 Nov	Glasgow	1	2

v JAPAN			S	J
1995	21 May	Hiroshima	0	0
2006	13 May	Saitama	0	0
2009	10 Oct	Yokohama	0	2

v KOREA REPUBLIC			S	KR
2002	16 May	Busan	1	4

v LATVIA			S	L
wc1996	5 Oct	Riga	2	0
wc1997	11 Oct	Celtic Park	2	0
wc2000	2 Sept	Riga	1	0
wc2001	6 Oct	Glasgow	2	1

v LIECHTENSTEIN			S	L
EC2010	7 Sept	Glasgow	2	1
EC2011	8 Oct	Vaduz	1	0

v LITHUANIA			S	L
EC1998	5 Sept	Vilnius	0	0
EC1999	9 Oct	Glasgow	3	0
EC2003	2 Apr	Kaunas	0	1
EC2003	11 Oct	Glasgow	1	0
EC2006	6 Sept	Kaunas	2	1
EC2007	8 Sept	Glasgow	3	1
EC2010	3 Sept	Kaunas	0	0
EC2011	6 Sept	Glasgow	1	0

v LUXEMBOURG			S	L
1947	24 May	Luxembourg	6	0
EC1986	12 Nov	Glasgow	3	0
EC1987	2 Dec	Esch	0	0
2012	14 Nov	Luxembourg	2	1

v MACEDONIA			S	M
wc2008	6 Sept	Skopje	0	1
wc2009	5 Sept	Glasgow	2	0
wc2012	11 Sept	Glasgow	1	1
wc2013	10 Sept	Skopje	2	1

v MALTA			S	M
1988	22 Mar	Valletta	1	1
1990	28 May	Valletta	2	1
wc1993	17 Feb	Ibrox	3	0
wc1993	17 Nov	Valletta	2	0
1997	1 June	Valletta	3	2

v MOLDOVA			S	M
wc2004	13 Oct	Chisinau	1	1
wc2005	4 June	Glasgow	2	0

v MOROCCO			S	M
wc1998	23 June	St Etienne	0	3

v NETHERLANDS			S	N
1929	4 June	Amsterdam	2	0
1938	21 May	Amsterdam	3	1
1959	27 May	Amsterdam	2	1
1966	11 May	Glasgow	0	3

			S	N
1968	30 May	Amsterdam	0	0
1971	1 Dec	Amsterdam	1	2
wc1978	11 June	Mendoza	3	2
1982	23 Mar	Glasgow	2	1
1986	29 Apr	Eindhoven	0	0
EC1992	12 June	Gothenburg	0	1
1994	23 Mar	Glasgow	0	1
1994	27 May	Utrecht	1	3
EC1996	10 June	Villa Park	0	0
2000	26 Apr	Arnhem	0	0
EC2003	15 Nov	Glasgow	1	0
EC2003	19 Nov	Amsterdam	0	6
wc2009	28 Mar	Amsterdam	0	3
wc2009	9 Sept	Glasgow	0	1

	v NEW ZEALAND		S	NZ
wc1982	15 June	Malaga	5	2
2003	27 May	Tynecastle	1	1

	v NIGERIA		S	N
2002	17 Apr	Aberdeen	1	2
2014	28 May	Craven Cottage	2	2

	v NORWAY		S	N
1929	26 May	Oslo	7	3
1954	5 May	Glasgow	1	0
1954	19 May	Oslo	1	1
1963	4 June	Bergen	3	4
1963	7 Nov	Glasgow	6	1
1974	6 June	Oslo	2	1
EC1978	25 Oct	Glasgow	3	2
EC1979	7 June	Oslo	4	0
wc1988	14 Sept	Oslo	2	1
wc1989	15 Nov	Glasgow	1	1
1992	3 June	Oslo	0	0
wc1998	16 June	Bordeaux	1	1
2003	20 Aug	Oslo	0	0
wc2004	9 Oct	Glasgow	0	1
wc2005	7 Sept	Oslo	2	1
wc2008	11 Oct	Glasgow	0	0
wc2009	12 Aug	Oslo	0	4
2013	19 Nov	Molde	1	0

	v PARAGUAY		S	P
wc1958	11 June	Norrkoping	2	3

	v PERU		S	P
1972	26 Apr	Glasgow	2	0
wc1978	3 June	Cordoba	1	3
1979	12 Sept	Glasgow	1	1

	v POLAND		S	P
1958	1 June	Warsaw	2	1
1960	4 May	Glasgow	2	3
wc1965	23 May	Chorzow	1	1
wc1965	13 Oct	Glasgow	1	2
1980	28 May	Poznan	0	1
1990	19 May	Glasgow	1	1
2001	25 Apr	Bydgoszcz	1	1
2014	5 Mar	Warsaw	1	0
EC2014	14 Oct	Warsaw	2	2

	v PORTUGAL		S	P
1950	21 May	Lisbon	2	2
1955	4 May	Glasgow	3	0
1959	3 June	Lisbon	0	1
1966	18 June	Glasgow	0	1
EC1971	21 Apr	Lisbon	0	2
EC1971	13 Oct	Glasgow	2	1
1975	13 May	Glasgow	1	0
EC1978	29 Nov	Lisbon	0	1
EC1980	26 Mar	Glasgow	4	1
wc1980	15 Oct	Glasgow	0	0
wc1981	18 Nov	Lisbon	1	2
wc1992	14 Oct	Ibrox	0	0
wc1993	28 Apr	Lisbon	0	5
2002	20 Nov	Braga	0	2

	v QATAR		S	Q
2015	5 June	Easter Road	1	0

	v REPUBLIC OF IRELAND		S	RI
wc1961	3 May	Glasgow	4	1
wc1961	7 May	Dublin	3	0
1963	9 June	Dublin	0	1
1969	21 Sept	Dublin	1	1
EC1986	15 Oct	Dublin	0	0
EC1987	18 Feb	Glasgow	0	1
2000	30 May	Dublin	2	1

			S	RI
2003	12 Feb	Glasgow	0	2
NC2011	29 May	Dublin	0	1
EC2014	14 Nov	Hampden	1	0
EC2015	13 June	Dublin	1	1

	v ROMANIA		S	R
EC1975	1 June	Bucharest	1	1
EC1975	17 Dec	Glasgow	1	1
1986	26 Mar	Glasgow	3	0
EC1990	12 Sept	Glasgow	2	1
EC1991	16 Oct	Bucharest	0	1
2004	31 Mar	Glasgow	1	2

	v RUSSIA		S	R
EC1994	16 Nov	Glasgow	1	1
EC1995	29 Mar	Moscow	0	0

	v SAN MARINO		S	SM
EC1991	1 May	Serravalle	2	0
EC1991	13 Nov	Glasgow	4	0
EC1995	26 Apr	Serravalle	2	0
EC1995	15 Nov	Glasgow	5	0
wc2000	7 Oct	Serravalle	2	0
wc2001	28 Mar	Glasgow	4	0

	v SAUDI ARABIA		S	SA
1988	17 Feb	Riyadh	2	2

	v SERBIA		S	Se
wc2012	8 Sept	Glasgow	0	0
wc2013	26 Mar	Novi Sad	0	2

	v SLOVENIA		S	Sl
wc2004	8 Sept	Glasgow	0	0
wc2005	12 Oct	Celje	3	0
2012	29 Feb	Koper	1	1

	v SOUTH AFRICA		S	SA
2002	20 May	Hong Kong	0	2
2007	22 Aug	Aberdeen	1	0

	v SPAIN		S	Sp
wc1957	8 May	Glasgow	4	2
wc1957	26 May	Madrid	1	4
1963	13 June	Madrid	6	2
1965	8 May	Glasgow	0	0
EC1974	20 Nov	Glasgow	1	2
EC1975	5 Feb	Valencia	1	1
1982	24 Feb	Valencia	0	3
wc1984	14 Nov	Glasgow	3	1
wc1985	27 Feb	Seville	0	1
1988	27 Apr	Madrid	0	0
2004	3 Sept	Valencia	1	1

Match abandoned after 60 minutes; floodlight failure.

			S	Sp
EC2010	12 Oct	Glasgow	2	3
EC2011	11 Oct	Alicante	1	3

	v SWEDEN		S	Sw
1952	30 May	Stockholm	1	3
1953	6 May	Glasgow	1	2
1975	16 Apr	Gothenburg	1	1
1977	27 Apr	Glasgow	3	1
wc1980	10 Sept	Stockholm	1	0
wc1981	9 Sept	Glasgow	2	0
wc1990	16 June	Genoa	2	1
1995	11 Oct	Stockholm	0	2
wc1996	10 Nov	Ibrox	1	0
wc1997	30 Apr	Gothenburg	1	2
2004	17 Nov	Easter Road	1	4
2010	11 Aug	Stockholm	0	3

	v SWITZERLAND		S	Sw
1931	24 May	Geneva	3	2
1946	15 May	Glasgow	3	1
1948	17 May	Berne	1	2
1950	26 Apr	Glasgow	3	1
wc1957	19 May	Basle	2	1
wc1957	6 Nov	Glasgow	3	2
1973	22 June	Berne	0	1
1976	7 Apr	Glasgow	1	0
EC1982	17 Nov	Berne	0	2
EC1983	30 May	Glasgow	2	2
EC1990	17 Oct	Glasgow	2	1
EC1991	11 Sept	Berne	2	2
wc1992	9 Sept	Berne	1	3
wc1993	8 Sept	Aberdeen	1	1
wc1996	18 June	Villa Park	1	0
2006	1 Mar	Glasgow	1	3

		v TRINIDAD & TOBAGO	S	TT
2004	30 May	Easter Road	4	1

		v TURKEY	S	T
1960	8 June	Ankara	2	4

		v UKRAINE	S	U
EC2006	11 Oct	Kiev	0	2
EC2007	13 Oct	Glasgow	3	1

		v URUGUAY	S	U
wc1954	19 June	Basle	0	7
1962	2 May	Glasgow	2	3
1983	21 Sept	Glasgow	2	0
wc1986	13 June	Nezahualcoyotl	0	0

		v USA	S	USA
1952	30 Apr	Glasgow	6	0
1992	17 May	Denver	1	0
1996	26 May	New Britain	1	2
1998	30 May	Washington	0	0
2005	12 Nov	Glasgow	1	1

			S	USA
2012	26 May	Jacksonville	1	5
2013	15 Nov	Glasgow	0	0

		v USSR	S	USSR
1967	10 May	Glasgow	0	2
1971	14 June	Moscow	0	1
wc1982	22 June	Malaga	2	2
1991	6 Feb	Ibrox	0	1

		v YUGOSLAVIA	S	Y
1955	15 May	Belgrade	2	2
1956	21 Nov	Glasgow	2	0
wc1958	8 June	Vasteras	1	1
1972	29 June	Belo Horizonte	2	2
wc1974	22 June	Frankfurt	1	1
1984	12 Sept	Glasgow	6	1
wc1988	19 Oct	Glasgow	1	1
wc1989	6 Sept	Zagreb	1	3

		v ZAIRE	S	Z
wc1974	14 June	Dortmund	2	0

WALES

		v ALBANIA	W	A
EC1994	7 Sept	Cardiff	2	0
EC1995	15 Nov	Tirana	1	1

		v ANDORRA	W	A
EC2014	9 Sept	La Vella	2	1

		v ARGENTINA	W	A
1992	3 June	Tokyo	0	1
2002	13 Feb	Cardiff	1	1

		v ARMENIA	W	A
wc2001	24 Mar	Erevan	2	2
wc2001	1 Sept	Cardiff	0	0

		v AUSTRALIA	W	A
2011	10 Aug	Cardiff	1	2

		v AUSTRIA	W	A
1954	9 May	Vienna	0	2
1955	23 Nov	Wrexham	1	2
EC1974	4 Sept	Vienna	1	2
1975	19 Nov	Wrexham	1	0
1992	29 Apr	Vienna	1	1
EC2005	26 Mar	Cardiff	0	2
EC2005	30 Mar	Vienna	0	1
2013	6 Feb	Swansea	2	1

		v AZERBAIJAN	W	A
EC2002	20 Nov	Baku	2	0
EC2003	29 Mar	Cardiff	4	0
wc2004	4 Sept	Baku	1	1
wc2005	12 Oct	Cardiff	2	0
wc2008	6 Sept	Cardiff	1	0
wc2009	6 June	Baku	1	0

		v BELARUS	W	B
EC1998	14 Oct	Cardiff	3	2
EC1999	4 Sept	Minsk	2	1
wc2000	2 Sept	Minsk	1	2
wc2001	6 Oct	Cardiff	1	0

		v BELGIUM	W	B
1949	22 May	Liege	1	3
1949	23 Nov	Cardiff	5	1
EC1990	17 Oct	Cardiff	3	1
EC1991	27 Mar	Brussels	1	1
wc1992	18 Nov	Brussels	0	2
wc1993	31 Mar	Cardiff	2	0
wc1997	29 Mar	Cardiff	1	2
wc1997	11 Oct	Brussels	2	3
wc2012	7 Sept	Cardiff	0	2
wc2013	15 Oct	Brussels	1	1
EC2014	16 Nov	Brussels	0	0
EC2015	12 June	Cardiff	1	0

		v BOSNIA-HERZEGOVINA	W	BH
2003	12 Feb	Cardiff	2	2
2012	15 Aug	Llanelli	0	2
EC2014	10 Oct	Cardiff	0	0

		v BRAZIL	W	B
wc1958	19 June	Gothenburg	0	1
1962	12 May	Rio de Janeiro	1	3
1962	16 May	São Paulo	1	3
1966	14 May	Rio de Janeiro	1	3
1966	18 May	Belo Horizonte	0	1
1983	12 June	Cardiff	1	1
1991	11 Sept	Cardiff	1	0
1997	12 Nov	Brasilia	0	3
2000	23 May	Cardiff	0	3
2006	5 Sept	Cardiff	0	2

		v BULGARIA	W	B
EC1983	27 Apr	Wrexham	1	0
EC1983	16 Nov	Sofia	0	1
EC1994	14 Dec	Cardiff	0	3
EC1995	29 Mar	Sofia	1	3
2006	15 Aug	Swansea	0	0
2007	22 Aug	Burgas	1	0
EC2010	8 Oct	Cardiff	0	1
EC2011	12 Oct	Sofia	1	0

		v CANADA	W	C
1986	10 May	Toronto	0	2
1986	20 May	Vancouver	3	0
2004	30 May	Wrexham	1	0

		v CHILE	W	C
1966	22 May	Santiago	0	2
2014	4 June	Valparaiso	0	2

		v COSTA RICA	W	CR
1990	20 May	Cardiff	1	0
2012	29 Feb	Cardiff	0	1

		v CROATIA	W	C
2002	21 Aug	Varazdin	1	1
2010	23 May	Osijek	0	2
wc2012	16 Oct	Osijek	0	2
wc2013	26 Mar	Swansea	1	2

		v CYPRUS	W	C
wc1992	14 Oct	Limassol	1	0
wc1993	13 Oct	Cardiff	2	0
2005	16 Nov	Limassol	0	1
EC2006	11 Oct	Cardiff	3	1
EC2007	13 Oct	Nicosia	1	3
EC2014	13 Oct	Cardiff	2	1

		v CZECHOSLOVAKIA	W	C
wc1957	1 May	Cardiff	1	0
wc1957	26 May	Prague	0	2
EC1971	21 Apr	Swansea	1	3
EC1971	27 Oct	Prague	0	1
wc1977	30 Mar	Wrexham	3	0
wc1977	16 Nov	Prague	0	1
wc1980	19 Nov	Cardiff	1	0
wc1981	9 Sept	Prague	0	2
EC1987	29 Apr	Wrexham	1	1
EC1987	11 Nov	Prague	0	2

			W	C
wc1993	28 Apr	Ostrava†	1	1
wc1993	8 Sept	Cardiff†	2	2

†*Czechoslovakia played as RCS (Republic of Czechs and Slovaks).*

v CZECH REPUBLIC			W	CR
2002	27 Mar	Cardiff	0	0
EC2006	2 Sept	Teplice	1	2
EC2007	2 June	Cardiff	0	0

v DENMARK			W	D
wc1964	21 Oct	Copenhagen	0	1
wc1965	1 Dec	Wrexham	4	2
EC1987	9 Sept	Cardiff	1	0
EC1987	14 Oct	Copenhagen	0	1
1990	11 Sept	Copenhagen	0	1
EC1998	10 Oct	Copenhagen	2	1
EC1999	9 June	Liverpool	0	2
2008	19 Nov	Brondby	1	0

v ESTONIA			W	E
1994	23 May	Tallinn	2	1
2009	29 May	Llanelli	1	0

v FAROE ISLANDS			W	F
wc1992	9 Sept	Cardiff	6	0
wc1993	6 June	Toftir	3	0

v FINLAND			W	F
EC1971	26 May	Helsinki	1	0
EC1971	13 Oct	Swansea	3	0
EC1987	10 Sept	Helsinki	1	1
EC1987	1 Apr	Wrexham	4	0
wc1988	19 Oct	Swansea	2	2
wc1989	6 Sept	Helsinki	0	1
2000	29 Mar	Cardiff	1	2
EC2002	7 Sept	Helsinki	2	0
EC2003	10 Sept	Cardiff	1	1
wc2009	28 Mar	Cardiff	0	2
wc2009	10 Oct	Helsinki	1	2
2013	16 Nov	Cardiff	1	1

v FRANCE			W	F
1933	25 May	Paris	1	1
1939	20 May	Paris	1	2
1953	14 May	Paris	1	6
1982	2 June	Toulouse	1	0

v GEORGIA			W	G
EC1994	16 Nov	Tbilisi	0	5
EC1995	7 June	Cardiff	0	1
2008	20 Aug	Swansea	1	2

v GERMANY			W	G
EC1995	26 Apr	Dusseldorf	1	1
EC1995	11 Oct	Cardiff	1	2
2002	14 May	Cardiff	1	0
EC2007	8 Sept	Cardiff	0	2
EC2007	21 Nov	Frankfurt	0	0
wc2008	15 Oct	Moenchengladbach	0	1
wc2009	1 Apr	Cardiff	0	2

v EAST GERMANY			W	EG
wc1957	19 May	Leipzig	1	2
wc1957	25 Sept	Cardiff	4	1
wc1969	16 Apr	Dresden	1	2
wc1969	22 Oct	Cardiff	1	3

v WEST GERMANY			W	WG
1968	8 May	Cardiff	1	1
1969	26 Mar	Frankfurt	1	1
1976	6 Oct	Cardiff	0	2
1977	14 Dec	Dortmund	1	1
EC1979	2 May	Wrexham	0	2
EC1979	17 Oct	Cologne	1	5
wc1989	31 May	Cardiff	0	0
wc1989	15 Nov	Cologne	1	2
EC1991	5 June	Cardiff	1	0
EC1991	16 Oct	Nuremberg	1	4

v GREECE			W	G
wc1964	9 Dec	Athens	0	2
wc1965	17 Mar	Cardiff	4	1

v HUNGARY			W	H
wc1958	8 June	Sanviken	1	1
wc1958	17 June	Stockholm	2	1
1961	28 May	Budapest	2	3
EC1962	7 Nov	Budapest	1	3
EC1963	20 Mar	Cardiff	1	1
EC1974	30 Oct	Cardiff	2	0
EC1975	16 Apr	Budapest	2	1
1985	16 Oct	Cardiff	0	3
2004	31 Mar	Budapest	2	1
2005	9 Feb	Cardiff	2	0

v ICELAND			W	I
wc1980	2 June	Reykjavik	4	0
wc1981	14 Oct	Swansea	2	2
wc1984	12 Sept	Reykjavik	0	1
wc1984	14 Nov	Cardiff	2	1
1991	1 May	Cardiff	1	0
2008	28 May	Reykjavik	1	0
2014	5 Mar	Cardiff	3	1

v IRAN			W	I
1978	18 Apr	Teheran	1	0

v ISRAEL			W	I
wc1958	15 Jan	Tel Aviv	2	0
wc1958	5 Feb	Cardiff	2	0
1984	10 June	Tel Aviv	0	0
1989	8 Feb	Tel Aviv	3	3
EC2015	28 Mar	Haifa	3	0

v ITALY			W	I
1965	1 May	Florence	1	4
wc1968	23 Oct	Cardiff	0	1
wc1969	4 Nov	Rome	1	4
1988	4 June	Brescia	1	0
1996	24 Jan	Terni	0	3
EC1998	5 Sept	Liverpool	0	2
EC1999	5 June	Bologna	0	4
EC2002	16 Oct	Cardiff	2	1
EC2003	6 Sept	Milan	0	4

v JAMAICA			W	J
1998	25 Mar	Cardiff	0	0

v JAPAN			W	J
1992	7 June	Matsuyama	1	0

v KUWAIT			W	K
1977	6 Sept	Wrexham	0	0
1977	20 Sept	Kuwait	0	0

v LATVIA			W	L
2004	18 Aug	Riga	2	0

v LIECHTENSTEIN			W	L
2006	14 Nov	Swansea	4	0
wc2008	11 Oct	Cardiff	2	0
wc2009	14 Oct	Vaduz	2	0

v LUXEMBOURG			W	L
EC1974	20 Nov	Swansea	5	0
EC1975	1 May	Luxembourg	3	1
EC1990	14 Nov	Luxembourg	1	0
EC1991	13 Nov	Cardiff	1	0
2008	26 Mar	Luxembourg	2	0
2010	11 Aug	Llanelli	5	1

v MALTA			W	M
EC1978	25 Oct	Wrexham	7	0
EC1979	2 June	Valletta	2	0
1988	1 June	Valletta	3	2
1998	3 June	Valletta	3	0

v MACEDONIA			W	M
wc2013	6 Sept	Skopje	1	2
wc2013	11 Oct	Cardiff	1	0

v MEXICO			W	M
wc1958	11 June	Stockholm	1	1
1962	22 May	Mexico City	1	2
2012	27 May	New Jersey	0	2

v MOLDOVA			W	M
EC1994	12 Oct	Kishinev	2	3
EC1995	6 Sept	Cardiff	1	0

v MONTENEGRO			W	M
2009	12 Aug	Podgorica	1	2
EC2010	3 Sept	Podgorica	0	1
EC2011	2 Sept	Cardiff	2	1

v NETHERLANDS			W	N
wc1988	14 Sept	Amsterdam	0	1
wc1989	11 Oct	Wrexham	1	2
1992	30 May	Utrecht	0	4
wc1996	5 Oct	Cardiff	1	3
wc1996	9 Nov	Eindhoven	1	7
2008	1 June	Rotterdam	0	2
2014	4 June	Amsterdam	0	2

v NEW ZEALAND			W	NZ
2007	26 May	Wrexham	2	2

v NORWAY			W	N
EC1982	22 Sept	Swansea	1	0
EC1983	21 Sept	Oslo	0	0
1984	6 June	Trondheim	0	1
1985	26 Feb	Wrexham	1	1
1985	5 June	Bergen	2	4
1994	9 Mar	Cardiff	1	3
wc2000	7 Oct	Cardiff	1	1
wc2001	5 Sept	Oslo	2	3
2004	27 May	Oslo	0	0
2008	6 Feb	Wrexham	3	0
2011	12 Nov	Cardiff	4	1

v PARAGUAY			W	P
2006	1 Mar	Cardiff	0	0

v POLAND			W	P
wc1973	28 Mar	Cardiff	2	0
wc1973	26 Sept	Katowice	0	3
1991	29 May	Radom	0	0
wc2000	11 Oct	Warsaw	0	0
wc2001	2 June	Cardiff	1	2
wc2004	13 Oct	Cardiff	2	3
wc2005	7 Sept	Warsaw	0	1
2009	11 Feb	Vila Real	0	1

v PORTUGAL			W	P
1949	15 May	Lisbon	2	3
1951	12 May	Cardiff	2	1
2000	2 June	Chaves	0	3

v QATAR			W	Q
2000	23 Feb	Doha	1	0

v REPUBLIC OF IRELAND			W	RI
1960	28 Sept	Dublin	3	2
1979	11 Sept	Swansea	2	1
1981	24 Feb	Dublin	3	1
1986	26 Mar	Dublin	1	0
1990	28 Mar	Dublin	0	1
1991	6 Feb	Wrexham	0	3
1992	19 Feb	Dublin	1	0
1993	17 Feb	Dublin	1	2
1997	11 Feb	Cardiff	0	0
EC2007	24 Mar	Dublin	0	1
EC2007	17 Nov	Cardiff	2	2
NC2011	8 Feb	Dublin	0	3
2013	14 Aug	Cardiff	0	0

v ROMANIA			W	R
EC1970	11 Nov	Cardiff	0	0
EC1971	24 Nov	Bucharest	0	2
1983	12 Oct	Wrexham	5	0
wc1992	20 May	Bucharest	1	5
wc1993	17 Nov	Cardiff	1	2

v RUSSIA			W	R
EC2003	15 Nov	Moscow	0	0
EC2003	19 Nov	Cardiff	0	1
wc2008	10 Sept	Moscow	1	2
wc2009	9 Sept	Cardiff	1	3

v SAN MARINO			W	SM
wc1996	2 June	Serravalle	5	0
wc1996	31 Aug	Cardiff	6	0
EC2007	28 Mar	Cardiff	3	0
EC2007	17 Oct	Serravalle	2	1

v SAUDI ARABIA			W	SA
1986	25 Feb	Dahran	2	1

v SERBIA			W	S
wc2012	11 Sept	Novi Sad	1	6
wc2013	10 Sept	Cardiff	0	3

v SERBIA-MONTENEGRO			W	SM
EC2003	20 Aug	Belgrade	0	1
EC2003	11 Oct	Cardiff	2	3

v SLOVAKIA			W	S
EC2006	7 Oct	Cardiff	1	5
EC2007	12 Sept	Trnava	5	2

v SLOVENIA			W	Sl
2005	17 Aug	Swansea	0	0

v SPAIN			W	S
wc1961	19 Apr	Cardiff	1	2
wc1961	18 May	Madrid	1	1
1982	24 Mar	Valencia	1	1
wc1984	17 Oct	Seville	0	3
wc1985	30 Apr	Wrexham	3	0

v SWEDEN			W	S
wc1958	15 June	Stockholm	0	0
1988	27 Apr	Stockholm	1	4
1989	26 Apr	Wrexham	0	2
1990	25 Apr	Stockholm	2	4
1994	20 Apr	Wrexham	0	2
2010	3 Mar	Swansea	0	1

v SWITZERLAND			W	S
1949	26 May	Berne	0	4
1951	16 May	Wrexham	3	2
1996	24 Apr	Lugano	0	2
EC1999	31 Mar	Zurich	0	2
EC1999	9 Oct	Wrexham	0	2
EC2010	12 Oct	Basle	1	4
EC2011	8 Oct	Swansea	2	0

v TRINIDAD & TOBAGO			W	TT
2006	27 May	Graz	2	1

v TUNISIA			W	T
1998	6 June	Tunis	0	4

v TURKEY			W	T
EC1978	29 Nov	Wrexham	1	0
EC1979	21 Nov	Izmir	0	1
wc1980	15 Oct	Cardiff	4	0
wc1981	25 Mar	Ankara	1	0
wc1996	14 Dec	Cardiff	0	0
wc1997	20 Aug	Istanbul	4	6

v REST OF UNITED KINGDOM			W	RUK
1951	5 Dec	Cardiff	3	2
1969	28 July	Cardiff	0	1

v UKRAINE			W	U
wc2001	28 Mar	Cardiff	1	1
wc2001	6 June	Kiev	1	1

v URUGUAY			W	U
1986	21 Apr	Wrexham	0	0

v USA			W	USA
2003	27 May	San Jose	0	2

v USSR			W	USSR
wc1965	30 May	Moscow	1	2
wc1965	27 Oct	Cardiff	2	1
wc1981	30 May	Wrexham	0	0
wc1981	18 Nov	Tbilisi	0	3
1987	18 Feb	Swansea	0	0

v YUGOSLAVIA			W	Y
1953	21 May	Belgrade	2	5
1954	22 Nov	Cardiff	1	3
EC1976	24 Apr	Zagreb	0	2
EC1976	22 May	Cardiff	1	1
EC1982	15 Dec	Titograd	4	4
EC1983	14 Dec	Cardiff	1	1
1988	23 Mar	Swansea	1	2

NORTHERN IRELAND

v ALBANIA

			NI	A
wc1965	7 May	Belfast	4	1
wc1965	24 Nov	Tirana	1	1
EC1982	15 Dec	Tirana	0	0
EC1983	27 Apr	Belfast	1	0
wc1992	9 Sept	Belfast	3	0
wc1993	17 Feb	Tirana	2	1
wc1996	14 Dec	Belfast	2	0
wc1997	10 Sept	Zurich	0	1
2010	3 Mar	Tirana	0	1

v ALGERIA

			NI	A
wc1986	3 June	Guadalajara	1	1

v ARGENTINA

			NI	A
wc1958	11 June	Halmstad	1	3

v ARMENIA

			NI	A
wc1996	5 Oct	Belfast	1	1
wc1997	30 Apr	Erevan	0	0
EC2003	29 Mar	Erevan	0	1
EC2003	10 Sept	Belfast	0	1

v AUSTRALIA

			NI	A
1980	11 June	Sydney	2	1
1980	15 June	Melbourne	1	1
1980	18 June	Adelaide	2	1

v AUSTRIA

			NI	A
wc1982	1 July	Madrid	2	2
EC1982	13 Oct	Vienna	0	2
EC1983	21 Sept	Belfast	3	1
EC1990	14 Nov	Vienna	0	0
EC1991	16 Oct	Belfast	2	1
EC1994	12 Oct	Vienna	2	1
EC1995	15 Nov	Belfast	5	3
wc2004	13 Oct	Belfast	3	3
wc2005	12 Oct	Vienna	0	2

v AZERBAIJAN

			NI	A
wc2004	9 Oct	Baku	0	0
wc2005	3 Sept	Belfast	2	0
wc2012	14 Nov	Belfast	1	1
wc2013	11 Oct	Baku	0	2

v BARBADOS

			NI	B
2004	30 May	Waterford	1	1

v BELGIUM

			NI	B
wc1976	10 Nov	Liege	0	2
wc1977	16 Nov	Belfast	3	0
1997	11 Feb	Belfast	3	0

v BRAZIL

			NI	B
wc1986	12 June	Guadalajara	0	3

v BULGARIA

			NI	B
wc1972	18 Oct	Sofia	0	3
wc1973	26 Sept	Sheffield	0	0
EC1978	29 Nov	Sofia	2	0
EC1979	2 May	Belfast	2	0
wc2001	28 Mar	Sofia	3	4
wc2001	2 June	Belfast	0	1
2008	6 Feb	Belfast	0	1

v CANADA

			NI	C
1995	22 May	Edmonton	0	2
1999	27 Apr	Belfast	1	1
2005	9 Feb	Belfast	0	1

v CHILE

			NI	C
1989	26 May	Belfast	0	1
1995	25 May	Edmonton	1	2
2010	30 May	Chillan	0	1
2014	4 June	Valparaiso	0	2

v COLOMBIA

			NI	C
1994	4 June	Boston	0	2

v CYPRUS

			NI	C
EC1971	3 Feb	Nicosia	3	0
EC1971	21 Apr	Belfast	5	0
EC1973	14 Feb	Nicosia	0	1
wc1973	8 May	London	3	0

			NI	C
2002	21 Aug	Belfast	0	0
2014	5 Mar	Nicosia	0	0

v CZECHOSLOVAKIA

			NI	C
wc1958	8 June	Halmstad	1	0
wc1958	17 June	Malmo	2	1*

*After extra time

v CZECH REPUBLIC

			NI	C
wc2001	24 Mar	Belfast	0	1
wc2001	6 June	Teplice	1	3
wc2008	10 Sept	Belfast	0	0
wc2009	14 Oct	Prague	0	0

v DENMARK

			NI	D
EC1978	25 Oct	Belfast	2	1
EC1979	6 June	Copenhagen	0	4
1986	26 Mar	Belfast	1	1
EC1990	17 Oct	Belfast	1	1
EC1991	13 Nov	Odense	1	2
wc1992	18 Nov	Belfast	0	1
wc1993	13 Oct	Copenhagen	0	1
wc2000	7 Oct	Belfast	1	1
wc2001	1 Sept	Copenhagen	1	1
EC2006	7 Oct	Copenhagen	0	0
EC2007	17 Nov	Belfast	2	1

v ESTONIA

			NI	E
2004	31 Mar	Tallinn	1	0
2006	1 Mar	Belfast	1	0
EC2011	6 Sept	Tallinn	1	4
EC2011	7 Oct	Belfast	1	2

v FAROE ISLANDS

			NI	F
EC1991	1 May	Belfast	1	1
EC1991	11 Sept	Landskrona	5	0
EC2010	12 Oct	Toftir	1	1
EC2011	10 Aug	Belfast	4	0
EC2014	11 Oct	Belfast	2	0

v FINLAND

			NI	F
wc1984	27 May	Pori	0	1
wc1984	14 Nov	Belfast	2	1
EC1998	10 Oct	Belfast	1	0
EC1998	9 Oct	Helsinki	1	4
2003	12 Feb	Belfast	0	1
2006	16 Aug	Helsinki	2	1
2012	15 Aug	Belfast	3	3
EC2015	29 Mar	Belfast	2	1

v FRANCE

			NI	F
1928	21 Feb	Paris	0	4
1951	12 May	Belfast	2	2
1952	11 Nov	Paris	1	3
wc1958	19 June	Norrkoping	0	4
1982	24 Mar	Paris	0	4
wc1982	4 July	Madrid	1	4
1986	26 Feb	Paris	0	0
1988	27 Apr	Belfast	0	0
1999	18 Aug	Belfast	0	1

v GEORGIA

			NI	G
2008	26 Mar	Belfast	4	1

v GERMANY

			NI	G
1992	2 June	Bremen	1	1
1996	29 May	Belfast	1	1
wc1996	9 Nov	Nuremberg	1	1
wc1997	20 Aug	Belfast	1	3
EC1999	27 Mar	Belfast	0	3
EC1999	8 Sept	Dortmund	0	4
2005	4 June	Belfast	1	4

v WEST GERMANY

			NI	WG
wc1958	15 June	Malmo	2	2
wc1960	26 Oct	Belfast	3	4
wc1961	10 May	Hamburg	1	2
1966	7 May	Belfast	0	2
1977	27 Apr	Cologne	0	5
EC1982	17 Nov	Belfast	1	0
EC1983	16 Nov	Hamburg	1	0

v GREECE		NI	G
wc1961	3 May	Athens	1	2
wc1961	17 Oct	Belfast	2	0
1988	17 Feb	Athens	2	3
EC2003	2 Apr	Belfast	0	2
EC2003	11 Oct	Athens	0	1
EC2014	14 Oct	Piraeus	2	0

v HONDURAS		NI	H
wc1982	21 June	Zaragoza	1	1

v HUNGARY		NI	H
wc1988	19 Oct	Budapest	0	1
wc1989	6 Sept	Belfast	1	2
2000	26 Apr	Belfast	0	1
2008	19 Nov	Belfast	0	2
EC2014	7 Sept	Budapest	2	1

v ICELAND		NI	I
wc1977	11 June	Reykjavik	0	1
wc1977	21 Sept	Belfast	2	0
wc2000	11 Oct	Reykjavik	0	1
wc2001	5 Sept	Belfast	3	0
EC2006	2 Sept	Belfast	0	3
EC2007	12 Sept	Reykjavik	1	2

v ISRAEL		NI	I
1968	10 Sept	Jaffa	3	2
1976	3 Mar	Tel Aviv	1	1
wc1980	26 Mar	Tel Aviv	0	0
wc1981	18 Nov	Belfast	1	0
1984	16 Oct	Belfast	3	0
1987	18 Feb	Tel Aviv	1	1
2009	12 Aug	Belfast	1	1
wc2013	26 Mar	Belfast	0	2
wc2013	15 Oct	Tel Aviv	1	1

v ITALY		`NI	I
wc1957	25 Apr	Rome	0	1
1957	4 Dec	Belfast	2	2
wc1958	15 Jan	Belfast	2	1
1961	25 Apr	Bologna	2	3
1997	22 Jan	Palermo	0	2
2003	3 June	Campobasso	0	2
2009	6 June	Pisa	0	3
EC2010	8 Oct	Belfast	0	0
EC2011	11 Oct	Pescara	0	3

v LATVIA		NI	L
wc1993	2 June	Riga	2	1
wc1993	8 Sept	Belfast	2	0
EC1995	26 Apr	Riga	1	0
EC1995	7 June	Belfast	1	2
EC2006	11 Oct	Belfast	1	0
EC2007	8 Sept	Riga	0	1

v LIECHTENSTEIN		NI	L
EC1994	20 Apr	Belfast	4	1
EC1995	11 Oct	Eschen	4	0
2002	27 Mar	Vaduz	0	0
EC2007	24 Mar	Vaduz	4	1
EC2007	22 Aug	Belfast	3	1

v LITHUANIA		NI	L
wc1992	28 Apr	Belfast	2	2
wc1993	25 May	Vilnius	1	0

v LUXEMBOURG		NI	L
2000	23 Feb	Luxembourg	3	1
wc2012	11 Sept	Belfast	1	1
wc2013	10 Sept	Luxembourg	2	3

v MALTA		NI	M
wc1988	21 May	Belfast	3	0
wc1989	26 Apr	Valletta	2	0
2000	28 Mar	Valletta	3	0
wc2000	2 Sept	Belfast	1	0
wc2001	6 Oct	Valletta	1	0
2005	17 Aug	Ta'Qali	1	1
2013	6 Feb	Ta'Qali	0	0

v MEXICO		NI	M
1966	22 June	Belfast	4	1
1994	11 June	Miami	0	3

v MOLDOVA		NI	M
EC1998	18 Nov	Belfast	2	2
EC1999	31 Mar	Chisinau	0	0

v MONTENEGRO		NI	M
2010	11 Aug	Podgorica	0	2

v MOROCCO		NI	M
1986	23 Apr	Belfast	2	1
2010	17 Nov	Belfast	1	1

v NETHERLANDS		NI	N
1962	9 May	Rotterdam	0	4
wc1965	17 Mar	Rotterdam	2	1
wc1965	7 Apr	Rotterdam	0	0
wc1976	13 Oct	Rotterdam	2	2
wc1977	12 Oct	Belfast	0	1
2012	2 June	Amsterdam	0	6

v NORWAY		NI	N
1922	25 May	Bergen	1	2
EC1974	4 Sept	Oslo	1	2
EC1975	29 Oct	Belfast	3	0
1990	27 Mar	Belfast	2	3
1996	27 Mar	Belfast	0	2
2001	28 Feb	Belfast	0	4
2004	18 Feb	Belfast	1	4
2012	29 Feb	Belfast	0	3

v POLAND		NI	P
EC1962	10 Oct	Katowice	2	0
EC1962	28 Nov	Belfast	2	0
1988	23 Mar	Belfast	1	1
1991	5 Feb	Belfast	3	1
2002	13 Feb	Limassol	1	4
EC2004	4 Sept	Belfast	0	3
EC2005	30 Mar	Warsaw	0	1
wc2009	28 Mar	Belfast	3	2
wc2009	5 Sept	Chorzow	1	1

v PORTUGAL		NI	P
wc1957	16 Jan	Lisbon	1	1
wc1957	1 May	Belfast	3	0
wc1973	28 Mar	Coventry	1	1
wc1973	14 Nov	Lisbon	1	1
wc1980	19 Nov	Lisbon	0	1
wc1981	29 Apr	Belfast	1	0
EC1994	7 Sept	Belfast	1	2
EC1995	3 Sept	Lisbon	1	1
wc1997	29 Mar	Belfast	0	0
wc1997	11 Oct	Lisbon	0	1
2005	15 Nov	Belfast	1	1
wc2012	16 Oct	Porto	1	1
wc2013	6 Sept	Belfast	2	4

v QATAR		NI	Q
2015	31 May	Crewe	1	1

v REPUBLIC OF IRELAND		NI	RI
EC1978	20 Sept	Dublin	0	0
EC1979	21 Nov	Belfast	1	0
wc1988	14 Sept	Belfast	0	0
wc1989	11 Oct	Dublin	0	3
wc1993	31 Mar	Dublin	0	3
wc1993	17 Nov	Belfast	1	1
EC1994	16 Nov	Belfast	0	4
EC1995	29 Mar	Dublin	1	1
1999	29 May	Dublin	1	0
NC2011	24 May	Dublin	0	5

v ROMANIA		NI	R
wc1984	12 Sept	Belfast	3	2
wc1985	16 Oct	Bucharest	1	0
1994	23 Mar	Chicago	2	0
2006	27 May	Chicago	0	2
EC2014	14 Nov	Bucharest	0	2
EC2015	13 June	Belfast	0	0

v RUSSIA		NI	R
wc2012	7 Sept Moscow	0	2
wc2013	14 Aug Belfast	1	0

v SAN MARINO		NI	SM
wc2008	15 Oct Belfast	4	0
wc2009	11 Feb Serravalle	3	0

v ST KITTS & NEVIS		NI	SK
2004	2 June Basseterre	2	0

v SERBIA		NI	S
2009	14 Nov Belfast	0	1
ec2011	25 Mar Belgrade	1	2
ec2011	2 Sept Belfast	0	1

v SERBIA-MONTENEGRO		NI	SM
2004	28 Apr Belfast	1	1

v SLOVAKIA		NI	S
1998	25 Mar Belfast	1	0
wc2008	6 Sept Bratislava	1	2
wc2009	9 Sept Belfast	0	2

v SLOVENIA		NI	S
wc2008	11 Oct Maribor	0	2
wc2009	1 Apr Belfast	1	0
ec2010	3 Sept Maribor	1	0
ec2011	29 Mar Belfast	0	0

v SOUTH AFRICA		NI	SA
1924	24 Sept Belfast	1	2

v SPAIN		NI	S
1958	15 Oct Madrid	2	6
1963	30 May Bilbao	1	1
1963	30 Oct Belfast	0	1
ec1970	11 Nov Seville	0	3
ec1972	16 Feb Hull	1	1
wc1982	25 June Valencia	1	0
1985	27 Mar Palma	0	0
wc1986	7 June Guadalajara	1	2
wc1988	21 Dec Seville	0	4
wc1989	8 Feb Belfast	0	2
wc1992	14 Oct Belfast	0	0
wc1993	28 Apr Seville	1	3
1998	2 June Santander	1	4
2002	17 Apr Belfast	0	5
ec2002	12 Oct Albacete	0	3
ec2003	11 June Belfast	0	0
ec2006	6 Sept Belfast	3	2
ec2007	21 Nov Las Palmas	0	1

v SWEDEN		NI	S
ec1974	30 Oct Solna	2	0
ec1975	3 Sept Belfast	1	2
wc1980	15 Oct Belfast	3	0
wc1981	3 June Solna	0	1
1996	24 Apr Belfast	1	2

		NI	S
ec2007	28 Mar Belfast	2	1
ec2007	17 Oct Stockholm	1	1

v SWITZERLAND		NI	S
wc1964	14 Oct Belfast	1	0
wc1964	14 Nov Lausanne	1	2
1998	22 Apr Belfast	1	0
2004	18 Aug Zurich	0	0

v THAILAND		NI	T
1997	21 May Bangkok	0	0

v TRINIDAD & TOBAGO		NI	TT
2004	6 June Bacolet	3	0

v TURKEY		NI	T
wc1968	23 Oct Belfast	4	1
wc1968	11 Dec Istanbul	3	0
2013	15 Nov Adana	0	1
ec1983	30 Mar Belfast	2	1
ec1983	12 Oct Ankara	0	1
wc1985	1 May Belfast	2	0
wc1985	11 Sept Izmir	0	0
ec1986	12 Nov Izmir	0	0
ec1987	11 Nov Belfast	1	0
ec1998	5 Sept Istanbul	0	3
ec1999	4 Sept Belfast	0	3
2010	26 May New Britain	0	2
2013	15 Nov Adana	0	1

v UKRAINE		NI	U
wc1996	31 Aug Belfast	0	1
wc1997	2 Apr Kiev	1	2
ec2002	16 Oct Belfast	0	0
ec2003	6 Sept Donetsk	0	0

v URUGUAY		NI	U
1964	29 Apr Belfast	3	0
1990	18 May Belfast	1	0
2006	21 May New Jersey	0	1
2014	30 May Montevideo	0	1

v USSR		NI	USSR
wc1969	19 Sept Belfast	0	0
wc1969	22 Oct Moscow	0	2
ec1971	22 Sept Moscow	0	1
ec1971	13 Oct Belfast	1	1

v YUGOSLAVIA		NI	Y
ec1975	16 Mar Belfast	1	0
ec1975	19 Nov Belgrade	0	1
wc1982	17 June Zaragoza	0	0
ec1987	29 Apr Belfast	1	2
ec1987	14 Oct Sarajevo	0	3
ec1990	12 Sept Belfast	0	2
ec1991	27 Mar Belgrade	1	4
2000	16 Aug Belfast	1	2

REPUBLIC OF IRELAND

v ALBANIA		RI	A
wc1992	26 May Dublin	2	0
wc1993	26 May Tirana	2	1
ec2003	2 Apr Tirana	0	0
ec2003	7 June Dublin	2	1
1998	22 Apr Dublin	0	2
2010	11 Aug Dublin	0	1

†Not considered a full international.

v ALGERIA		RI	A
1982	28 Apr Algiers	0	2
2010	28 May Dublin	3	0

v ANDORRA		RI	A
wc2001	28 Mar Barcelona	3	0
wc2001	25 Apr Dublin	3	1
ec2010	7 Sept Dublin	3	1
ec2011	7 Oct Andorra La Vella	2	0

v ARMENIA		RI	A
ec2010	3 Sept Erevan	1	0
ec2011	11 Oct Dublin	2	1

v AUSTRALIA		RI	A
2003	19 Aug Dublin	2	1
2009	12 Aug Limerick	0	3

v ARGENTINA		RI	A
1951	13 May Dublin	0	1
†1979	29 May Dublin	0	0
1980	16 May Dublin	0	1

v AUSTRIA		RI	A
1952	7 May Vienna	0	6
1953	25 Mar Dublin	4	0
1958	14 Mar Vienna	1	3
wc2013	10 Sept Vienna	0	1
1962	8 Apr Dublin	2	3
ec1963	25 Sept Vienna	0	0

			RI	A
EC1963	13 Oct	Dublin	3	2
1966	22 May	Vienna	0	1
1968	10 Nov	Dublin	2	2
EC1971	30 May	Dublin	1	4
EC1971	10 Oct	Linz	0	6
EC1995	11 June	Dublin	1	3
EC1995	6 Sept	Vienna	1	3
wc2013	26 Mar	Dublin	2	2
wc2013	10 Sept	Vienna	0	1

v BELGIUM

			RI	B
1928	12 Feb	Liege	4	2
1929	30 Apr	Dublin	4	0
1930	11 May	Brussels	3	1
wc1934	25 Feb	Dublin	4	4
1949	24 Apr	Dublin	0	2
1950	10 May	Brussels	1	5
1965	24 Mar	Dublin	0	2
1966	25 May	Liege	3	2
wc1980	15 Oct	Dublin	1	1
wc1981	25 Mar	Brussels	0	1
EC1986	10 Sept	Brussels	2	2
EC1987	29 Apr	Dublin	0	0
wc1997	29 Oct	Dublin	1	1
wc1997	16 Nov	Brussels	1	2

v BOLIVIA

			RI	B
1994	24 May	Dublin	1	0
1996	15 June	New Jersey	3	0
2007	26 May	Boston	1	1

v BOSNIA-HERZEGOVINA

			RI	BH
2012	26 May	Dublin	1	0

v BRAZIL

			RI	B
1974	5 May	Rio de Janeiro	1	2
1982	27 May	Uberlandia	0	7
1987	23 May	Dublin	1	0
2004	18 Feb	Dublin	0	0
2008	6 Feb	Dublin	0	1
2010	2 Mar	Emirates	0	2

v BULGARIA

			RI	B
wc1977	1 June	Sofia	1	2
wc1977	12 Oct	Dublin	0	0
EC1979	19 May	Sofia	0	1
EC1979	17 Oct	Dublin	3	0
wc1987	1 Apr	Sofia	1	2
wc1987	14 Oct	Dublin	2	0
2004	18 Aug	Dublin	1	1
wc2009	28 Mar	Dublin	1	1
wc2009	6 June	Sofia	1	1

v CAMEROON

			RI	C
wc2002	1 June	Niigata	1	1

v CANADA

			RI	C
2003	18 Nov	Dublin	3	0

v CHILE

			RI	C
1960	30 Mar	Dublin	2	0
1972	21 June	Recife	1	2
1974	12 May	Santiago	2	1
1982	22 May	Santiago	0	1
1991	22 May	Dublin	1	1
2006	24 May	Dublin	0	1

v CHINA

			RI	C
1984	3 June	Sapporo	1	0
2005	29 Mar	Dublin	1	0

v COLOMBIA

			RI	C
2008	29 May	Fulham	1	0

v COSTA RICA

			RI	C
2014	6 June	Philadephia	1	1

v CROATIA

			RI	C
1996	2 June	Dublin	2	2
EC1998	5 Sept	Dublin	2	0
EC1999	4 Sept	Zagreb	0	1
2001	15 Aug	Dublin	2	2
2004	16 Nov	Dublin	1	0
2011	10 Aug	Dublin	0	0
EC2012	10 June	Poznan	1	3

v CYPRUS

			RI	C
wc1980	26 Mar	Nicosia	3	2
wc1980	19 Nov	Dublin	6	0
wc2001	24 Mar	Nicosia	4	0
wc2001	6 Oct	Dublin	4	0
wc2004	4 Sept	Dublin	3	0
wc2005	8 Oct	Nicosia	1	0
EC2006	7 Oct	Nicosia	2	5
EC2007	17 Oct	Dublin	1	1
2008	15 Oct	Dublin	1	0
wc2009	5 Sept	Nicosia	2	1

v CZECHOSLOVAKIA

			RI	C
1938	18 May	Prague	2	2
EC1959	5 Apr	Dublin	2	0
EC1959	10 May	Bratislava	0	4
wc1961	8 Oct	Dublin	1	3
wc1961	29 Oct	Prague	1	7
EC1967	21 May	Dublin	0	2
EC1967	22 Nov	Prague	2	1
wc1969	4 May	Dublin	1	2
wc1969	7 Oct	Prague	0	3
1979	26 Sept	Prague	1	4
1981	29 Apr	Dublin	3	1
1986	27 May	Reykjavik	1	0

v CZECH REPUBLIC

			RI	C
1994	5 June	Dublin	1	3
1996	24 Apr	Prague	0	2
1998	25 Mar	Olomouc	1	2
2000	23 Feb	Dublin	3	2
2004	31 Mar	Dublin	2	1
EC2006	11 Oct	Dublin	1	1
EC2007	12 Sept	Prague	0	1
2012	29 Feb	Dublin	1	1

v DENMARK

			RI	D
wc1956	3 Oct	Dublin	2	1
wc1957	2 Oct	Copenhagen	2	0
wc1968	4 Dec	Dublin	1	1
(abandoned after 51 mins)				
wc1969	27 May	Copenhagen	0	2
wc1969	15 Oct	Dublin	1	1
EC1978	24 May	Copenhagen	3	3
EC1979	2 May	Dublin	2	0
wc1984	14 Nov	Copenhagen	0	3
wc1985	13 Nov	Dublin	1	4
wc1992	14 Oct	Copenhagen	0	0
wc1993	28 Apr	Dublin	1	1
2002	27 Mar	Dublin	3	0
2007	22 Aug	Copenhagen	4	0

v ECUADOR

			RI	E
1972	19 June	Natal	3	2
2007	23 May	New Jersey	1	1

v EGYPT

			RI	E
wc1990	17 June	Palermo	0	0

v ENGLAND

			RI	E
1946	30 Sept	Dublin	0	1
1949	21 Sept	Everton	2	0
wc1957	8 May	Wembley	1	5
wc1957	19 May	Dublin	1	1
1964	24 May	Dublin	1	3
1976	8 Sept	Wembley	1	1
EC1978	25 Oct	Dublin	1	1
EC1980	6 Feb	Wembley	0	2
1985	26 Mar	Wembley	1	2
EC1988	12 June	Stuttgart	1	0
wc1990	11 June	Cagliari	1	1
EC1990	14 Nov	Dublin	1	1
EC1991	27 Mar	Wembley	1	1
1995	15 Feb	Dublin	1	0
(abandoned after 27 mins)				
2013	29 May	Wembley	1	1
2015	7 June	Dublin	0	0

v ESTONIA

			RI	E
wc2000	11 Oct	Dublin	2	0
wc2001	6 June	Tallinn	2	0
EC2011	11 Nov	Tallinn	4	0
EC2011	15 Nov	Dublin	1	1

v FAROE ISLANDS

			RI	F
EC2004	13 Oct	Dublin	2	0
EC2005	8 June	Toftir	2	0
WC2012	16 Oct	Torshavn	4	1
WC2013	7 June	Dublin	3	0

v FINLAND

			RI	F
WC1949	8 Sept	Dublin	3	0
WC1949	9 Oct	Helsinki	1	1
1990	16 May	Dublin	1	1
2000	15 Nov	Dublin	3	0
2002	21 Aug	Helsinki	3	0

v FRANCE

			RI	F
1937	23 May	Paris	2	0
1952	16 Nov	Dublin	1	1
WC1953	4 Oct	Dublin	3	5
WC1953	25 Nov	Paris	0	1
WC1972	15 Nov	Dublin	2	1
WC1973	19 May	Paris	1	1
WC1976	17 Nov	Paris	0	2
WC1977	30 Mar	Dublin	1	0
WC1980	28 Oct	Paris	0	2
WC1981	14 Oct	Dublin	3	2
1989	7 Feb	Dublin	0	0
WC2004	9 Oct	Paris	0	0
WC2005	7 Sept	Dublin	0	1
WC2009	14 Nov	Dublin	0	1
WC2009	18 Nov	Paris	1	1

v GEORGIA

			RI	G
EC2003	29 Mar	Tbilisi	2	1
EC2003	11 June	Dublin	2	0
WC2008	6 Sept	Mainz	2	1
WC2009	11 Feb	Dublin	2	1
2013	2 June	Dublin	3	0
EC2014	7 Sept	Tbilisi	2	1

v GERMANY

			RI	G
1935	8 May	Dortmund	1	3
1936	17 Oct	Dublin	5	2
1939	23 May	Bremen	1	1
1994	29 May	Hanover	2	0
WC2002	5 June	Ibaraki	1	1
EC2006	2 Sept	Stuttgart	0	1
EC2007	13 Oct	Dublin	0	0
WC2012	12 Oct	Dublin	1	6
WC2013	11 Oct	Cologne	0	3
EC2014	14 Oct	Gelsenkirchen	1	1

v WEST GERMANY

			RI	WG
1951	17 Oct	Dublin	3	2
1952	4 May	Cologne	0	3
1955	28 May	Hamburg	1	2
1956	25 Nov	Dublin	3	0
1960	11 May	Dusseldorf	1	0
1966	4 May	Dublin	0	4
1970	9 May	Berlin	1	2
1975	1 Mar	Dublin	1	0†
1979	22 May	Dublin	1	3
1981	21 May	Bremen	0	3†
1989	6 Sept	Dublin	1	1

†*v West Germany 'B'*

v GIBRALTAR

			RI	G
EC2014	11 Oct	Dublin	7	0

v GREECE

			RI	G
2000	26 Apr	Dublin	0	1
2002	20 Nov	Athens	0	0
2012	14 Nov	Dublin	0	1

v HUNGARY

			RI	H
1934	15 Dec	Dublin	2	4
1936	3 May	Budapest	3	3
1936	6 Dec	Dublin	2	3
1939	19 Mar	Cork	2	2
1939	18 May	Budapest	2	2
WC1969	8 June	Dublin	1	2
WC1969	5 Nov	Budapest	0	4
WC1989	8 Mar	Budapest	0	0
WC1989	4 June	Dublin	2	0
1991	11 Sept	Gyor	2	1
2012	4 June	Budapest	0	0

v ICELAND

			RI	I
EC1962	12 Aug	Dublin	4	2
EC1962	2 Sept	Reykjavik	1	1
EC1982	13 Oct	Dublin	2	0
EC1983	21 Sept	Reykjavik	3	0
1986	25 May	Reykjavik	2	1
WC1996	10 Nov	Dublin	0	0
WC1997	6 Sept	Reykjavik	4	2

v IRAN

			RI	I
1972	18 June	Recife	2	1
WC2001	10 Nov	Dublin	2	0
WC2001	15 Nov	Tehran	0	1

v N. IRELAND

			RI	NI
EC1978	20 Sept	Dublin	0	0
EC1979	21 Nov	Belfast	0	1
WC1988	14 Sept	Belfast	0	0
WC1989	11 Oct	Dublin	3	0
WC1993	31 Mar	Dublin	3	0
WC1993	17 Nov	Belfast	1	1
EC1994	16 Nov	Belfast	4	0
EC1995	29 Mar	Dublin	1	1
1999	29 May	Dublin	0	1
NC2011	24 May	Dublin	5	0

v ISRAEL

			RI	I
1984	4 Apr	Tel Aviv	0	3
1985	27 May	Tel Aviv	0	0
1987	10 Nov	Dublin	5	0
EC2005	26 Mar	Tel Aviv	1	1
EC2005	4 June	Dublin	2	2

v ITALY

			RI	I
1926	21 Mar	Turin	0	3
1927	23 Apr	Dublin	1	2
EC1970	8 Dec	Rome	0	3
EC1971	10 May	Dublin	1	2
1985	5 Feb	Dublin	1	2
WC1990	30 June	Rome	0	1
1992	4 June	Foxboro	0	2
WC1994	18 June	New York	1	0
2005	17 Aug	Dublin	1	2
WC2009	1 Apr	Bari	1	1
WC2009	10 Oct	Dublin	2	2
2011	7 June	Liege	2	0
EC2012	18 June	Poznan	0	2
2014	31 May	Craven Cottage	0	0

v JAMAICA

			RI	J
2004	2 June	Charlton	1	0

v KAZAKHSTAN

			RI	K
WC2012	7 Sept	Astana	2	1
WC2013	15 Oct	Dublin	3	1

v LATVIA

			RI	L
WC1992	9 Sept	Dublin	4	0
WC1993	2 June	Riga	2	1
EC1994	7 Sept	Riga	3	0
EC1995	11 Oct	Dublin	2	1
2013	15 Nov	Dublin	3	0

v LIECHTENSTEIN

			RI	L
EC1994	12 Oct	Dublin	4	0
EC1995	3 June	Eschen	0	0
WC1996	31 Aug	Eschen	5	0
WC1997	21 May	Dublin	5	0

v LITHUANIA

			RI	L
WC1993	16 June	Vilnius	1	0
WC1993	8 Sept	Dublin	2	0
WC1997	20 Aug	Dublin	0	0
WC1997	10 Sept	Vilnius	2	1

v LUXEMBOURG

			RI	L
1936	9 May	Luxembourg	5	1
WC1953	28 Oct	Dublin	4	0
WC1954	7 Mar	Luxembourg	1	0
EC1987	28 May	Luxembourg	2	0
EC1987	9 Sept	Dublin	2	1

v MACEDONIA			RI	M
wc1996	9 Oct	Dublin	3	0
wc1997	2 Apr	Skopje	2	3
EC1999	9 June	Dublin	1	0
EC1999	9 Oct	Skopje	1	1
EC2011	26 Mar	Dublin	2	1
EC2011	4 June	Podgorica	2	0

v MALTA			RI	M
EC1983	30 Mar	Valletta	1	0
EC1983	16 Nov	Dublin	8	0
wc1989	28 May	Dublin	2	0
wc1989	15 Nov	Valletta	2	0
1990	2 June	Valletta	3	0
EC1998	14 Oct	Dublin	5	0
EC1999	8 Sept	Valletta	3	2

v MEXICO			RI	M
1984	8 Aug	Dublin	0	0
wc1994	24 June	Orlando	1	2
1996	13 June	New Jersey	2	2
1998	23 May	Dublin	0	0
2000	4 June	Chicago	2	2

v MONTENEGRO			RI	M
wc2008	10 Sept	Podgorica	0	0
wc2009	14 Oct	Dublin	0	0

v MOROCCO			RI	M
1990	12 Sept	Dublin	1	0

v NETHERLANDS			RI	N
1932	8 May	Amsterdam	2	0
1934	8 Apr	Amsterdam	2	5
1935	8 Dec	Dublin	3	5
1955	1 May	Dublin	1	0
1956	10 May	Rotterdam	4	1
wc1980	10 Sept	Dublin	2	1
wc1981	9 Sept	Rotterdam	2	2
EC1982	22 Sept	Rotterdam	1	2
EC1983	12 Oct	Dublin	2	3
EC1988	18 June	Gelsenkirchen	0	1
wc1990	21 June	Palermo	1	1
1994	20 Apr	Tilburg	1	0
wc1994	4 July	Orlando	0	2
EC1995	13 Dec	Liverpool	0	2
1996	4 June	Rotterdam	1	3
wc2000	2 Sept	Amsterdam	2	2
wc2001	1 Sept	Dublin	1	0
2004	5 June	Amsterdam	1	0
2006	16 Aug	Dublin	0	4

v NIGERIA			RI	N
2002	16 May	Dublin	1	2
2004	29 May	Charlton	0	3
2009	29 May	Fulham	1	1

v NORWAY			RI	N
wc1937	10 Oct	Oslo	2	3
wc1937	7 Nov	Dublin	3	3
1950	26 Nov	Dublin	2	2
1951	30 May	Oslo	3	2
1954	8 Nov	Dublin	2	1
1955	25 May	Oslo	3	1
1960	6 Nov	Dublin	3	1
1964	13 May	Oslo	4	1
1973	6 June	Oslo	1	1
1976	24 Mar	Dublin	3	0
1978	21 May	Oslo	0	0
wc1984	17 Oct	Oslo	0	1
wc1985	1 May	Dublin	0	0
1988	1 June	Oslo	0	0
wc1994	28 June	New York	0	0
2003	30 Apr	Dublin	1	0
2008	20 Aug	Oslo	1	1
2010	17 Nov	Dublin	1	2

v OMAN			RI	O
2012	11 Sept	London	4	1
2014	3 Sept	Dublin	2	0

v PARAGUAY			RI	P
1999	10 Feb	Dublin	2	0
2010	25 May	Dublin	2	1

v POLAND			RI	P
1938	22 May	Warsaw	0	6
1938	13 Nov	Dublin	3	2
1958	11 May	Katowice	2	2
1958	5 Oct	Dublin	2	2
1964	10 May	Kracow	1	3
1964	25 Oct	Dublin	3	2
1968	15 May	Dublin	2	2
1968	30 Oct	Katowice	0	1
1970	6 May	Dublin	1	2
1970	23 Sept	Dublin	0	2
1973	16 May	Wroclaw	0	2
1973	21 Oct	Dublin	1	0
1976	26 May	Poznan	2	0
1977	24 Apr	Dublin	0	0
1978	12 Apr	Lodz	0	3
1981	23 May	Bydgoszcz	0	3
1984	23 May	Dublin	0	0
1986	12 Nov	Warsaw	0	1
1988	22 May	Dublin	3	1
EC1991	1 May	Dublin	0	0
EC1991	16 Oct	Poznan	3	3
2004	28 Apr	Bydgoszcz	0	0
2013	19 Nov	Poznan	0	0
2008	19 Nov	Dublin	2	3
2013	6 Feb	Dublin	2	0
2013	19 Nov	Poznan	0	0
EC2015	29 Mar	Dublin	1	1

v PORTUGAL			RI	P
1946	16 June	Lisbon	1	3
1947	4 May	Dublin	0	2
1948	23 May	Lisbon	0	2
1949	22 May	Dublin	1	0
1972	25 June	Recife	1	2
1992	7 June	Boston	2	0
EC1995	26 Apr	Dublin	1	0
EC1995	15 Nov	Lisbon	0	3
1996	29 May	Dublin	0	0
wc2000	7 Oct	Lisbon	1	1
wc2001	2 June	Dublin	1	1
2005	9 Feb	Dublin	1	0
2014	10 June	New Jersey	1	5

v ROMANIA			RI	R
1988	23 Mar	Dublin	2	0
wc1990	25 June	Genoa	0	0*
wc1997	30 Apr	Bucharest	0	1
wc1997	11 Oct	Dublin	1	1
2004	27 May	Dublin	1	0

v RUSSIA			RI	R
1994	23 Mar	Dublin	0	0
1996	27 Mar	Dublin	0	2
2002	13 Feb	Dublin	2	0
EC2002	7 Sept	Moscow	2	4
EC2003	6 Sept	Dublin	1	1
EC2010	8 Oct	Dublin	2	3
EC2011	6 Sept	Moscow	0	0

v SAN MARINO			RI	SM
EC2006	15 Nov	Dublin	5	0
EC2007	7 Feb	Serravalle	2	1

v SAUDI ARABIA			RI	SA
wc2002	11 June	Yokohama	3	0

v SCOTLAND			RI	S
wc1961	3 May	Glasgow	1	4
wc1961	7 May	Dublin	0	3
1963	9 June	Dublin	1	0
1969	21 Sept	Dublin	1	1
EC1986	15 Oct	Dublin	0	0
EC1987	18 Feb	Glasgow	1	0
2000	30 May	Dublin	1	2
2003	12 Feb	Glasgow	2	0
NC2011	29 May	Dublin	1	0
EC2014	14 Nov	Hampden	0	1
EC2015	13 June	Dublin	1	1

v SERBIA		RI	S
2008	24 May	Dublin	1	1
2012	15 Aug	Belgrade	0	0
2014	5 Mar	Dublin	1	2

v SLOVAKIA			RI	S
EC2007	28 Mar	Dublin	1	0
EC2007	8 Sept	Bratislava	2	2
EC2010	12 Oct	Zilina	1	1
EC2011	2 Sept	Dublin	0	0

v SOUTH AFRICA			RI	SA
2000	11 June	New Jersey	2	1
2009	8 Sept	Limerick	1	0

v SPAIN			RI	S
1931	26 Apr	Barcelona	1	1
1931	13 Dec	Dublin	0	5
1946	23 June	Madrid	1	0
1947	2 Mar	Dublin	3	2
1948	30 May	Barcelona	1	2
1949	12 June	Dublin	1	4
1952	1 June	Madrid	0	6
1955	27 Nov	Dublin	2	2
EC1964	11 Mar	Seville	1	5
EC1964	8 Apr	Dublin	0	2
WC1965	5 May	Dublin	1	0
WC1965	27 Oct	Seville	1	4
WC1965	10 Nov	Paris	0	1

v SPAIN			RI	S
EC1966	23 Oct	Dublin	0	0
EC1966	7 Dec	Valencia	0	2
1977	9 Feb	Dublin	0	1
EC1982	17 Nov	Dublin	3	3
EC1983	27 Apr	Zaragoza	0	2
1985	26 May	Cork	0	0
WC1988	16 Nov	Seville	0	2
WC1989	26 Apr	Dublin	1	0
WC1992	18 Nov	Seville	0	0
WC1993	13 Oct	Dublin	1	3
WC2002	16 June	Suwon	1	1
EC2012	14 June	Gdansk	0	4
2013	11 June	New York	0	2

v SWEDEN			RI	S
WC1949	2 June	Stockholm	1	3
WC1949	13 Nov	Dublin	1	3
1959	1 Nov	Dublin	3	2
1960	18 May	Malmo	1	4
EC1970	14 Oct	Dublin	1	1
EC1970	28 Oct	Malmo	0	1
1999	28 Apr	Dublin	2	0
2006	1 Mar	Dublin	3	0
WC2013	22 Mar	Stockholm	0	0
WC2013	6 Sept	Dublin	1	2

v SWITZERLAND			RI	S
1935	5 May	Basle	0	1
1936	17 Mar	Dublin	1	0
1937	17 May	Berne	1	0
1938	18 Sept	Dublin	4	0
1948	5 Dec	Dublin	0	1
EC1975	11 May	Dublin	2	1
EC1975	21 May	Berne	0	1
1980	30 Apr	Dublin	2	0
WC1985	2 June	Dublin	3	0
WC1985	11 Sept	Berne	0	0
1992	25 Mar	Dublin	2	1
EC2002	16 Oct	Dublin	1	2
EC2003	11 Oct	Basle	0	2
WC2004	8 Sept	Basle	1	1
WC2005	12 Oct	Dublin	0	0

v TRINIDAD & TOBAGO			RI	TT
1982	30 May	Port of Spain	1	2

v TUNISIA			RI	T
1988	19 Oct	Dublin	4	0

v TURKEY			RI	T
EC1966	16 Nov	Dublin	2	1
EC1967	22 Feb	Ankara	1	2
EC1974	20 Nov	Izmir	1	1
EC1975	29 Oct	Dublin	4	0
2014	25 May	Dublin	1	2
1976	13 Oct	Ankara	3	3
1978	5 Apr	Dublin	4	2
1990	26 May	Izmir	0	0
EC1990	17 Oct	Dublin	5	0
EC1991	13 Nov	Istanbul	3	1
EC2000	13 Nov	Dublin	1	1
EC2000	17 Nov	Bursa	0	0
2003	9 Sept	Dublin	2	2
2014	25 May	Dublin	1	2

v URUGUAY			RI	U
1974	8 May	Montevideo	0	2
1986	23 Apr	Dublin	1	1
2011	29 Mar	Dublin	2	3

v USA			RI	USA
1979	29 Oct	Dublin	3	2
1991	1 June	Boston	1	1
1992	29 Apr	Dublin	4	1
1992	30 May	Washington	1	3
1996	9 June	Boston	1	2
2000	6 June	Boston	1	1
2002	17 Apr	Dublin	2	1
2014	18 Nov	Dublin	4	1

v USSR			RI	USSR
WC1972	18 Oct	Dublin	1	2
WC1973	13 May	Moscow	0	1
EC1974	30 Oct	Dublin	3	0
EC1975	18 May	Kiev	1	2
WC1984	12 Sept	Dublin	1	0
WC1985	16 Oct	Moscow	0	2
EC1988	15 June	Hanover	1	1
1990	25 Apr	Dublin	1	0

v WALES			RI	W
1960	28 Sept	Dublin	2	3
1979	11 Sept	Swansea	1	2
1981	24 Feb	Dublin	1	3
1986	26 Mar	Dublin	0	1
1990	28 Mar	Dublin	1	0
1991	6 Feb	Wrexham	3	0
1992	19 Feb	Dublin	0	1
1993	17 Feb	Dublin	2	1
1997	11 Feb	Cardiff	0	0
EC2007	24 Mar	Dublin	1	0
EC2007	17 Nov	Cardiff	2	2
NC2011	8 Feb	Dublin	3	0
2013	14 Aug	Cardiff	0	0

v YUGOSLAVIA			RI	Y
1955	19 Sept	Dublin	1	4
1988	27 Apr	Dublin	2	0
EC1998	18 Nov	Belgrade	0	1
EC1999	1 Sept	Dublin	2	1

OTHER BRITISH AND IRISH INTERNATIONAL MATCHES 2014–15

FRIENDLIES

■ *Denotes player sent off.*

ENGLAND

Wednesday, 3 September 2014
England (0) 1 *(Rooney 68 (pen))*
Norway (0) 0   40,181
England: (442) Hart; Stones (Chambers 81), Jones, Cahill (Jagielka 84), Baines; Oxlade-Chamberlain (Milner 69), Henderson, Wilshere (Delph 69), Sterling; Rooney (Welbeck 69), Sturridge (Lambert 89).
Norway: (433) Nyland; Elabdellaoui, Nordtveit, Forren, Linnes (Flo 36); Skjelbred (Elyounoussi M 69), Johansen, Jenssen (Pedersen 87); Daehli (Konradsen 57), King (Nielsen 76), Elyounoussi T (Kamara 78).
Referee: Jorge Sousa.

Tuesday, 18 November 2014
Scotland (0) 1 *(Robertson 83)*
England (1) 3 *(Oxlade-Chamberlain 32, Rooney 47, 85)*
                                                   55,000
Scotland: (442) Marshall (Gordon 46); Whittaker, Martin R, Hanley (May 66), Robertson; Maloney (Russell 81), Mulgrew, Brown (Fletcher D 46), Anya (Bannan 61); Martin C (Morrison 46), Naismith.
England: (442) Forster; Clyne, Cahill (Jagielka 46), Smalling, Shaw (Gibbs 66); Oxlade-Chamberlain (Lambert 80), Wilshere (Barkley 87), Downing (Lallana 46); Milner; Welbeck (Sterling 66), Rooney.
Referee: Jonas Eriksson.

Tuesday, 31 March 2015
Italy (1) 1 *(Pelle 29)*
England (0) 1 *(Townsend 79)*   35,000
Italy: (352) Buffon; Bonucci, Ranocchia, Chiellini (Moretti 72); Darmian (Antonelli 73), Soriano, Valdifiori (Verratti 67), Parolo, Florenzi (Abate 60); Eder (Vazquez 60), Pelle (Immobile 60).
England: (4231) Hart; Clyne (Walker 46), Smalling (Carrick 44), Jagielka, Gibbs (Bertrand 88); Jones, Delph (Townsend 70); Walcott (Barkley 55), Rooney, Henderson (Mason 74); Kane.
Referee: Felix Brych.

Sunday, 7 June 2015
Republic of Ireland (0) 0
England (0) 0   43,486
Republic of Ireland: (442) Westwood (Given 61); Coleman, O'Shea (McShane 71), Wilson, Brady; Whelan (Arter 63), McCarthy (McClean 46), Hendrick, McGoldrick (Long 46); Murphy (Walters 56), McGeady.
England: (451) Hart; Jones, Smalling, Cahill (Jagielka 74), Bertrand; Milner, Henderson, Wilshere (Barkley 66), Sterling (Townsend 66), Lallana (Walcott 83); Rooney (Vardy 75).
Referee: Arnold Hunter.

SCOTLAND

Wednesday, 25 March 2015
Scotland (0) 1 *(Berra 85)*
Northern Ireland (0) 0   28,000
Scotland: (433) Gordon (McGregor 46); Whittaker (Russell 78), Greer, Martin R (Naismith 46), Forsyth; McArthur (Morrison 62), Fletcher D, Ritchie; Maloney (Berra 46), Fletcher S (Rhodes 62), Anya.
Northern Ireland: (442) McGovern; Lafferty D, Evans J (McCullough 80), Baird (Hodson 58), Dallas; Reeves (Davis 69), McNair, Hughes, Norwood (McLaughlin R 69); Magennis (McKay 75), Grigg (McCourt 58).
Referee: Martin Atkinson.

Friday, 5 June 2015
Scotland (1) 1 *(Ritchie 41)*
Qatar (0) 0   14,270
Scotland: (433) Marshall (Gordon 46); Forsyth, Greer, Mulgrew, Maloney (Adam 60); Brown (Fletcher D 59), McArthur (Morrison 46), Anya; Ritchie, Naismith (Griffiths 59), Forrest (Russell 74).
Qatar: (352) Lecomte; Hassan A, Kasola, Yasser; Asadalla (Mohammed 66), Hatem (Mukhtar 54), Abdullah (Ismail 78), Boudiaf, El Sayed; Muntari (Ilyas 78), Al Haidous (Hassan M 86).
Referee: Sebastien Delferiere.

NORTHERN IRELAND

Sunday, 31 May 2015
Northern Ireland (0) 1 *(Dallas 46)*
Qatar (0) 1 *(Boudiaf 70)*   3022
Northern Ireland: (4231) Carroll (McGovern 46); McLaughlin C, Hughes (Evans J 61), McNair (Magennis 82), Lafferty D; Cathcart, Evans C; McGinn (Ward 61), Norwood, Dallas (McCourt 73); Grigg (Boyce 73).
Qatar: (433) Lecomte; Traore (Hassan A 55), Kasola, Ismail, Musa; Yasser, Hatem (Boudiaf 56), El Sayed; Siddiq (Asadalla 65), Mohammad (Al Haidous 56), Muntari (Jeddo 81).
Referee: Michael Oliver.

REPUBLIC OF IRELAND

Wednesday, 3 September 2014
Republic of Ireland (1) 2 *(Doyle 20, Pearce 81)*
Oman (0) 0   14,376
Republic of Ireland: (4411) Given (Elliot 45); Meyler (Murphy 85), Keogh, Pearce, Ward; Pilkington (McGeady 59), Gibson (Whelan 70), Quinn, Brady; Hoolahan (Keane 59); Doyle (Long 59).
Oman: (442) Al Habsi; Al Mukhaini, Al Maskari, Mudhafar (Al-Busaidi 60), Al Owaisi; Al Musalami (Al Muqbali 81), Al Farsi, Saleh (Al Maashari 87), Al Hosni (Al Hadhri 76); Hardan (Abdul Karim 60), Al-Qasmi (Al Jabri 60).
Referee: Ilias Spathas.

Tuesday, 18 November 2014
Republic of Ireland (1) 4 *(Pilkington 8, Brady 56, 88, McClean 82)*
USA (1) 1 *(Diskerud 39)*   23,000
Republic of Ireland: (442) Given (Elliot 86); Christie, Pearce, Clark, Brady; Pilkington (McClean 64), Quinn, Meyler, Stokes (McGeady 60); McGoldrick (Long 78), Murphy (Hendrick 78).
USA: (442) Hamid; Johnson, Cameron, Besler, Chandler (Morris 77); Beckerman (Ream 90), Bedoya, Diskerud (Rubin 77), Morales (Garza 64); Wondolowski (Wood 46), Altidore.
Referee: Pawel Raczkowski.

BRITISH AND IRISH INTERNATIONAL APPEARANCES 1872–2015

This is a list of full international appearances by Englishmen, Irishmen, Scotsmen and Welshmen in matches against the Home Countries and against foreign nations. It does not include unofficial matches against Commonwealth and Empire countries. The year indicated refers to the player's international debut season; i.e. 2015 is the 2014–15 season. **Bold** type indicates players who have made an international appearance in season 2014–15.

As at July 2015.

ENGLAND

Abbott, W. 1902 (Everton)	1
A'Court, A. 1958 (Liverpool)	5
Adams, T. A. 1987 (Arsenal)	66
Adcock, H. 1929 (Leicester C)	5
Agbonlahor, G. 2009 (Aston Villa)	3
Alcock, C. W. 1875 (Wanderers)	1
Alderson, J. T. 1923 (Crystal Palace)	1
Aldridge, A. 1888 (WBA, Walsall Town Swifts)	2
Allen, A. 1888 (Aston Villa)	1
Allen, A. 1960 (Stoke C)	3
Allen, C. 1984 (QPR, Tottenham H)	5
Allen, H. 1888 (Wolverhampton W)	5
Allen, J. P. 1934 (Portsmouth)	2
Allen, R. 1952 (WBA)	5
Alsford, W. J. 1935 (Tottenham H)	1
Amos, A. 1885 (Old Carthusians)	2
Anderson, R. D. 1879 (Old Etonians)	1
Anderson, S. 1962 (Sunderland)	2
Anderson, V. A. 1979 (Nottingham F, Arsenal, Manchester U)	30
Anderton, D. R. 1994 (Tottenham H)	30
Angus, J. 1961 (Burnley)	1
Armfield, J. C. 1959 (Blackpool)	43
Armitage, G. H. 1926 (Charlton Ath)	1
Armstrong, D. 1980 (Middlesbrough, Southampton)	3
Armstrong, K. 1955 (Chelsea)	1
Arnold, J. 1933 (Fulham)	1
Arthur, J. W. H. 1885 (Blackburn R)	7
Ashcroft, J. 1906 (Woolwich Arsenal)	3
Ashmore, G. S. 1926 (WBA)	1
Ashton, C. T. 1926 (Corinthians)	1
Ashton, D. 2008 (West Ham U)	1
Ashurst, W. 1923 (Notts Co)	5
Astall, G. 1956 (Birmingham C)	2
Astle, J. 1969 (WBA)	5
Aston, J. 1949 (Manchester U)	17
Athersmith, W. C. 1892 (Aston Villa)	12
Atyeo, P. J. W. 1956 (Bristol C)	6
Austin, S. W. 1926 (Manchester C)	1
Bach, P. 1899 (Sunderland)	1
Bache, J. W. 1903 (Aston Villa)	7
Baddeley, T. 1903 (Wolverhampton W)	5
Bagshaw, J. J. 1920 (Derby Co)	1
Bailey, G. R. 1985 (Manchester U)	2
Bailey, H. P. 1908 (Leicester Fosse)	5
Bailey, M. A. 1964 (Charlton Ath)	2
Bailey, N. C. 1878 (Clapham R)	19
Baily, E. F. 1950 (Tottenham H)	9
Bain, J. 1877 (Oxford University)	1
Baines, L. J. 2010 (Everton)	**30**
Baker, A. 1928 (Arsenal)	1
Baker, B. H. 1921 (Everton, Chelsea)	2
Baker, J. H. 1960 (Hibernian, Arsenal)	8
Ball, A. J. 1965 (Blackpool, Everton, Arsenal)	72
Ball, J. 1928 (Bury)	1
Ball, M. J. 2001 (Everton)	1
Balmer, W. 1905 (Everton)	1
Bamber, J. 1921 (Liverpool)	1
Bambridge, A. L. 1881 (Swifts)	3
Bambridge, E. C. 1879 (Swifts)	18
Bambridge, E. H. 1876 (Swifts)	1
Banks, G. 1963 (Leicester C, Stoke C)	73
Banks, H. E. 1901 (Millwall)	1
Banks, T. 1958 (Bolton W)	6
Bannister, W. 1901 (Burnley, Bolton W)	2
Barclay, R. 1932 (Sheffield U)	3

Bardsley, D. J. 1993 (QPR)	2
Barham, M. 1983 (Norwich C)	2
Barkas, S. 1936 (Manchester C)	5
Barker, J. 1935 (Derby Co)	11
Barker, R. 1872 (Herts Rangers)	1
Barker, R. R. 1895 (Casuals)	1
Barkley, R. 2013 (Everton)	**13**
Barlow, R. J. 1955 (WBA)	1
Barmby, N. J. 1995 (Tottenham H, Middlesbrough, Everton, Liverpool)	23
Barnes, J. 1983 (Watford, Liverpool)	79
Barnes, P. S. 1978 (Manchester C, WBA, Leeds U)	22
Barnet, H. H. 1882 (Royal Engineers)	1
Barrass, M. W. 1952 (Bolton W)	3
Barrett, A. F. 1930 (Fulham)	1
Barrett, E. D. 1991 (Oldham Ath, Aston Villa)	3
Barrett, J. W. 1929 (West Ham U)	1
Barry, G. 2000 (Aston Villa, Manchester C)	53
Barry, L. 1928 (Leicester C)	5
Barson, F. 1920 (Aston Villa)	1
Barton, J. 1890 (Blackburn R)	1
Barton, J. 2007 (Manchester C)	1
Barton, P. H. 1921 (Birmingham)	7
Barton, W. D. 1995 (Wimbledon, Newcastle U)	3
Bassett, W. I. 1888 (WBA)	16
Bastard, S. R. 1880 (Upton Park)	1
Bastin, C. S. 1932 (Arsenal)	21
Batty, D. 1991 (Leeds U, Blackburn R, Newcastle U, Leeds U)	42
Baugh, R. 1886 (Stafford Road, Wolverhampton W)	2
Bayliss, A. E. J. M. 1891 (WBA)	1
Baynham, R. L. 1956 (Luton T)	3
Beardsley, P. A. 1986 (Newcastle U, Liverpool, Newcastle U)	59
Beasant, D. J. 1990 (Chelsea)	2
Beasley, A. 1939 (Huddersfield T)	1
Beats, W. E. 1901 (Wolverhampton W)	2
Beattie, J. S. 2003 (Southampton)	5
Beattie, T. K. 1975 (Ipswich T)	9
Beckham, D. R. J. 1997 (Manchester U, Real Madrid, LA Galaxy)	115
Becton, F. 1895 (Preston NE, Liverpool)	2
Bedford, H. 1923 (Blackpool)	2
Bell, C. 1968 (Manchester C)	48
Bennett, W. 1901 (Sheffield U)	2
Benson, R. W. 1913 (Sheffield U)	1
Bent, D. A. 2006 (Charlton Ath, Tottenham H, Sunderland, Aston Villa)	13
Bentley, D. M. 2008 (Blackburn R, Tottenham H)	7
Bentley, R. T. F. 1949 (Chelsea)	12
Beresford, J. 1934 (Aston Villa)	1
Berry, A. 1909 (Oxford University)	1
Berry, J. J. 1953 (Manchester U)	4
Bertrand, R. 2013 (Chelsea)	**4**
Bestall, J. G. 1935 (Grimsby T)	1
Betmead, H. A. 1937 (Grimsby T)	1
Betts, M. P. 1877 (Old Harrovians)	1
Betts, W. 1889 (Sheffield W)	1
Beverley, J. 1884 (Blackburn R)	3
Birkett, R. H. 1879 (Clapham R)	1
Birkett, R. J. E. 1936 (Middlesbrough)	1
Birley, F. H. 1874 (Oxford University, Wanderers)	2
Birtles, G. 1980 (Nottingham F)	3
Bishop, S. M. 1927 (Leicester C)	4
Blackburn, F. 1901 (Blackburn R)	3
Blackburn, G. F. 1924 (Aston Villa)	1
Blenkinsop, E. 1928 (Sheffield W)	26
Bliss, H. 1921 (Tottenham H)	1

Blissett, L. L. 1983 (Watford, AC Milan) 14
Blockley, J. P. 1973 (Arsenal) 1
Bloomer, S. 1895 (Derby Co, Middlesbrough) 23
Blunstone, F. 1955 (Chelsea) 5
Bond, R. 1905 (Preston NE, Bradford C) 8
Bonetti, P. P. 1966 (Chelsea) 7
Bonsor, A. G. 1873 (Wanderers) 2
Booth, F. 1905 (Manchester C) 1
Booth, T. 1898 (Blackburn R, Everton) 2
Bothroyd, J. 2011 (Cardiff C) 1
Bould, S. A. 1994 (Arsenal) 2
Bowden, E. R. 1935 (Arsenal) 6
Bower, A. G. 1924 (Corinthians) 5
Bowers, J. W. 1934 (Derby Co) 3
Bowles, S. 1974 (QPR) 5
Bowser, S. 1920 (WBA) 1
Bowyer, L. D. 2003 (Leeds U) 1
Boyer, P. J. 1976 (Norwich C) 1
Boyes, W. 1935 (WBA, Everton) 3
Boyle, T. W. 1913 (Burnley) 1
Brabrook, P. 1958 (Chelsea) 3
Bracewell, P. W. 1985 (Everton) 3
Bradford, G. R. W. 1956 (Bristol R) 1
Bradford, J. 1924 (Birmingham) 12
Bradley, W. 1959 (Manchester U) 3
Bradshaw, F. 1908 (Sheffield W) 1
Bradshaw, T. H. 1897 (Liverpool) 1
Bradshaw, W. 1910 (Blackburn R) 4
Brann, G. 1886 (Swifts) 3
Brawn, W. F. 1904 (Aston Villa) 2
Bray, J. 1935 (Manchester C) 6
Brayshaw, E. 1887 (Sheffield W) 1
Bridge, W. M. 2002 (Southampton, Chelsea,
  Manchester C) 36
Bridges, B. J. 1965 (Chelsea) 4
Bridgett, A. 1905 (Sunderland) 11
Brindle, T. 1880 (Darwen) 2
Brittleton, J. T. 1912 (Sheffield W) 5
Britton, C. S. 1935 (Everton) 9
Broadbent, P. F. 1958 (Wolverhampton W) 7
Broadis, I. A. 1952 (Manchester C, Newcastle U) 14
Brockbank, J. 1872 (Cambridge University) 1
Brodie, J. B. 1889 (Wolverhampton W) 3
Bromilow, T. G. 1921 (Liverpool) 5
Bromley-Davenport, W. E. 1884 (Oxford University) 2
Brook, E. F. 1930 (Manchester C) 18
Brooking, T. D. 1974 (West Ham U) 47
Brooks, J. 1957 (Tottenham H) 3
Broome, F. H. 1938 (Aston Villa) 7
Brown, A. 1882 (Aston Villa) 3
Brown, A. 1971 (WBA) 1
Brown, A. S. 1904 (Sheffield U) 2
Brown, G. 1927 (Huddersfield T, Aston Villa) 9
Brown, J. 1881 (Blackburn R) 5
Brown, J. H. 1927 (Sheffield W) 6
Brown, K. 1960 (West Ham U) 1
Brown, W. 1924 (West Ham U) 1
Brown, W. M. 1999 (Manchester U) 23
Bruton, J. 1928 (Burnley) 3
Bryant, W. I. 1925 (Clapton) 1
Buchan, C. M. 1913 (Sunderland) 6
Buchanan, W. S. 1876 (Clapham R) 1
Buckley, F. C. 1914 (Derby Co) 1
Bull, S. G. 1989 (Wolverhampton W) 13
Bullock, F. E. 1921 (Huddersfield T) 1
Bullock, N. 1923 (Bury) 3
Burgess, H. 1904 (Manchester C) 4
Burgess, H. 1931 (Sheffield W) 4
Burnup, C. J. 1896 (Cambridge University) 1
Burrows, H. 1934 (Sheffield W) 3
Burton, F. E. 1889 (Nottingham F) 1
Bury, L. 1877 (Cambridge University, Old Etonians) 2
Butcher, T. 1980 (Ipswich T, Rangers) 77
Butland, J. 2013 (Birmingham C) 1
Butler, J. D. 1925 (Arsenal) 1
Butler, W. 1924 (Bolton W) 1
Butt, N. 1997 (Manchester U, Newcastle U) 39
Byrne, G. 1963 (Liverpool) 2
Byrne, J. J. 1962 (Crystal Palace, West Ham U) 11
Byrne, R. W. 1954 (Manchester U) 33

Cahill, G. J. 2011 (Bolton W, Chelsea) 36
Callaghan, I. R. 1966 (Liverpool) 4
Calvey, J. 1902 (Nottingham F) 1
Campbell, A. F. 1929 (Blackburn R, Huddersfield T) 8
Campbell, F. L. 2012 (Sunderland) 1
Campbell, S. 1996 (Tottenham H, Arsenal, Portsmouth)
  73
Camsell, G. H. 1929 (Middlesbrough) 9
Capes, A. J. 1903 (Stoke) 1
Carr, J. 1905 (Newcastle U) 2
Carr, J. 1920 (Middlesbrough) 2
Carr, W. H. 1875 (Owlerton, Sheffield) 1
Carragher, J. L. 1999 (Liverpool) 38
**Carrick, M. 2001 (West Ham U, Tottenham H,
  Manchester U)** 33
Carroll, A. T. 2011 (Newcastle U, Liverpool) 9
Carson, S. P. 2008 (Liverpool, WBA) 4
Carter, H. S. 1934 (Sunderland, Derby Co) 13
Carter, J. H. 1926 (WBA) 3
Catlin, A. E. 1937 (Sheffield W) 5
Caulker, S. A. 2013 (Tottenham H) 1
Chadwick, A. 1900 (Southampton) 2
Chadwick, E. 1891 (Everton) 7
Chamberlain, M. 1983 (Stoke C) 8
Chambers, H. 1921 (Liverpool) 8
Chambers, C. 2015 (Arsenal) 3
Channon, M. R. 1973 (Southampton, Manchester C) 46
Charles, G. A. 1991 (Nottingham F) 2
Charlton, J. 1965 (Leeds U) 35
Charlton, R. 1958 (Manchester U) 106
Charnley, R. O. 1963 (Blackpool) 1
Charsley, C. C. 1893 (Small Heath) 1
Chedgzoy, S. 1920 (Everton) 8
Chenery, C. J. 1872 (Crystal Palace) 3
Cherry, T. J. 1976 (Leeds U) 27
Chilton, A. 1951 (Manchester U) 2
Chippendale, H. 1894 (Blackburn R) 1
Chivers, M. 1971 (Tottenham H) 24
Christian, E. 1879 (Old Etonians) 1
Clamp, E. 1958 (Wolverhampton W) 4
Clapton, D. R. 1959 (Arsenal) 1
Clare, T. 1889 (Stoke) 4
Clarke, A. J. 1970 (Leeds U) 19
Clarke, H. A. 1954 (Tottenham H) 1
Clay, T. 1920 (Tottenham H) 4
Clayton, R. 1956 (Blackburn R) 35
Clegg, J. C. 1872 (Sheffield W) 1
Clegg, W. E. 1873 (Sheffield W, Sheffield Alb) 2
Clemence, R. N. 1973 (Liverpool, Tottenham H) 61
Clement, D. T. 1976 (QPR) 5
Cleverley, T. W. 2013 (Manchester U) 13
Clough, B. H. 1960 (Middlesbrough) 2
Clough, N. H. 1989 (Nottingham F) 14
Clyne, N. E. 2015 (Southampton) 5
Coates, R. 1970 (Burnley, Tottenham H) 4
Cobbold, W. N. 1883 (Cambridge University,
  Old Carthusians) 9
Cock, J. G. 1920 (Huddersfield T, Chelsea) 2
Cockburn, H. 1947 (Manchester U) 13
Cohen, G. R. 1964 (Fulham) 37
Cole, A. 2001 (Arsenal, Chelsea) 107
Cole, A. A. 1995 (Manchester U) 15
Cole, C. 2009 (West Ham U) 7
Cole, J. J. 2001 (West Ham U, Chelsea) 56
Colclough, H. 1914 (Crystal Palace) 1
Coleman, E. H. 1921 (Dulwich Hamlet) 1
Coleman, J. 1907 (Woolwich Arsenal) 1
Collymore, S. V. 1995 (Nottingham F, Aston Villa) 3
Common, A. 1904 (Sheffield U, Middlesbrough) 3
Compton, L. H. 1951 (Arsenal) 2
Conlin, J. 1906 (Bradford C) 1
Connelly, J. M. 1960 (Burnley, Manchester U) 20
Cook, T. E. R. 1925 (Brighton) 1
Cooper, C. T. 1995 (Nottingham F) 2
Cooper, N. C. 1893 (Cambridge University) 1
Cooper, T. 1928 (Derby Co) 15
Cooper, T. 1969 (Leeds U) 20
Coppell, S. J. 1978 (Manchester U) 42
Copping, W. 1933 (Leeds U, Arsenal, Leeds U) 20
Corbett, B. O. 1901 (Corinthians) 1
Corbett, R. 1903 (Old Malvernians) 1

Jezzard, B. A. G. 1954 (Fulham) 2
Johnson, A. 2005 (Crystal Palace, Everton) 8
Johnson, A. 2010 (Manchester C) 12
Johnson, D. E. 1975 (Ipswich T, Liverpool) 8
Johnson, E. 1880 (Saltley College, Stoke) 2
Johnson, G. M. C. 2004 (Chelsea, Portsmouth, Liverpool) 54
Johnson, J. A. 1937 (Stoke C) 5
Johnson, S. A. M. 2001 (Derby Co) 1
Johnson, T. C. F. 1926 (Manchester C, Everton) 5
Johnson, W. H. 1900 (Sheffield U) 6
Johnston, H. 1947 (Blackpool) 10
Jones, A. 1882 (Walsall Swifts, Great Lever) 3
Jones, H. 1923 (Nottingham F) 1
Jones, H. 1927 (Blackburn R) 6
Jones, M. D. 1965 (Sheffield U, Leeds U) 3
Jones, P. A. 2012 (Manchester U) 17
Jones, R. 1992 (Liverpool) 8
Jones, W. 1901 (Bristol C) 1
Jones, W. H. 1950 (Liverpool) 2
Joy, B. 1936 (Casuals) 1

Kail, E. I. L. 1929 (Dulwich Hamlet) 3
Kane, H. E. 2015 (Tottenham H) 2
Kay, A. H. 1963 (Everton) 1
Kean, F. W. 1923 (Sheffield W, Bolton W) 9
Keegan, J. K. 1973 (Liverpool, SV Hamburg, Southampton) 63
Keen, E. R. L. 1933 (Derby Co) 4
Kelly, M. R. 2012 (Liverpool) 1
Kelly, R. 1920 (Burnley, Sunderland, Huddersfield T) 14
Kennedy, A. 1984 (Liverpool) 2
Kennedy, R. 1976 (Liverpool) 17
Kenyon-Slaney, W. S. 1873 (Wanderers) 1
Keown, M. R. 1992 (Everton, Arsenal) 43
Kevan, D. T. 1957 (WBA) 14
Kidd, B. 1970 (Manchester U) 2
King, L. B. 2002 (Tottenham H) 21
King, R. S. 1882 (Oxford University) 1
Kingsford, R. K. 1874 (Wanderers) 1
Kingsley, M. 1901 (Newcastle U) 1
Kinsey, G. 1892 (Wolverhampton W, Derby Co) 4
Kirchen, A. J. 1937 (Arsenal) 3
Kirkland, C. E. 2007 (Liverpool) 1
Kirton, W. J. 1922 (Aston Villa) 1
Knight, A. E. 1920 (Portsmouth) 1
Knight, Z. 2005 (Fulham) 2
Knowles, C. 1968 (Tottenham H) 4
Konchesky, P. M. 2003 (Charlton Ath, West Ham U) 2

Labone, B. L. 1963 (Everton) 26
Lallana, A. D. 2013 (Southampton, Liverpool) 15
Lambert, R. L. 2013 (Southampton, Liverpool) 11
Lampard, F. J. 2000 (West Ham U, Chelsea) 106
Lampard, F. R. G. 1973 (West Ham U) 2
Langley, E. J. 1958 (Fulham) 3
Langton, R. 1947 (Blackburn R, Preston NE, Bolton W) 11
Latchford, R. D. 1978 (Everton) 12
Latheron, E. G. 1913 (Blackburn R) 2
Lawler, C. 1971 (Liverpool) 4
Lawton, T. 1939 (Everton, Chelsea, Notts Co) 23
Leach, T. 1931 (Sheffield W) 2
Leake, A. 1904 (Aston Villa) 5
Lee, E. A. 1904 (Southampton) 1
Lee, F. H. 1969 (Manchester C) 27
Lee, J. 1951 (Derby Co) 1
Lee, R. M. 1995 (Newcastle U) 21
Lee, S. 1983 (Liverpool) 14
Leighton, J. E. 1886 (Nottingham F) 1
Lennon, A. J. 2006 (Tottenham H) 21
Lescott, J. P. 2008 (Everton, Manchester C) 26
Le Saux, G. P. 1994 (Blackburn R, Chelsea) 36
Le Tissier, M. P. 1994 (Southampton) 8
Lilley, H. E. 1892 (Sheffield U) 1
Linacre, H. J. 1905 (Nottingham F) 2
Lindley, T. 1886 (Cambridge University, Nottingham F) 13
Lindsay, A. 1974 (Liverpool) 4
Lindsay, W. 1877 (Wanderers) 1

Lineker, G. 1984 (Leicester C, Everton, Barcelona, Tottenham H) 80
Lintott, E. H. 1908 (QPR, Bradford C) 7
Lipsham, H. B. 1902 (Sheffield U) 1
Little, B. 1975 (Aston Villa) 1
Livermore, J. C. 2013 (Tottenham H) 1
Lloyd, L. V. 1971 (Liverpool, Nottingham F) 4
Lockett, A. 1903 (Stoke) 1
Lodge, L. V. 1894 (Cambridge University, Corinthians) 5
Lofthouse, J. M. 1885 (Blackburn R, Accrington, Blackburn R) 7
Lofthouse, N. 1951 (Bolton W) 33
Longworth, E. 1920 (Liverpool) 5
Lowder, A. 1889 (Wolverhampton W) 1
Lowe, E. 1947 (Aston Villa) 3
Lucas, T. 1922 (Liverpool) 3
Luntley, E. 1880 (Nottingham F) 2
Lyttelton, Hon. A. 1877 (Cambridge University) 1
Lyttelton, Hon. E. 1878 (Cambridge University) 1

Mabbutt, G. 1983 (Tottenham H) 16
Macaulay, R. H. 1881 (Cambridge University) 1
McCall, J. 1913 (Preston NE) 5
McCann, G. P. 2001 (Sunderland) 1
McDermott, T. 1978 (Liverpool) 25
McDonald, C. A. 1958 (Burnley) 8
Macdonald, M. 1972 (Newcastle U) 14
McFarland, R. L. 1971 (Derby Co) 28
McGarry, W. H. 1954 (Huddersfield T) 4
McGuinness, W. 1959 (Manchester U) 2
McInroy, A. 1927 (Sunderland) 1
McMahon, S. 1988 (Liverpool) 17
McManaman, S. 1995 (Liverpool, Real Madrid) 37
McNab, R. 1969 (Arsenal) 4
McNeal, R. 1914 (WBA) 2
McNeil, M. 1961 (Middlesbrough) 9
Macrae, S. 1883 (Notts Co) 5
Maddison, F. B. 1872 (Oxford University) 1
Madeley, P. E. 1971 (Leeds U) 24
Magee, T. P. 1923 (WBA) 5
Makepeace, H. 1906 (Everton) 4
Male, C. G. 1935 (Arsenal) 19
Mannion, W. J. 1947 (Middlesbrough) 26
Mariner, P. 1977 (Ipswich T, Arsenal) 35
Marsden, J. T. 1891 (Darwen) 1
Marsden, W. 1930 (Sheffield W) 3
Marsh, R. W. 1972 (QPR, Manchester C) 9
Marshall, T. 1880 (Darwen) 2
Martin, A. 1981 (West Ham U) 17
Martin, H. 1914 (Sunderland) 1
Martyn, A. N. 1992 (Crystal Palace, Leeds U) 23
Marwood, B. 1989 (Arsenal) 1
Maskrey, H. M. 1908 (Derby Co) 1
Mason, C. 1887 (Wolverhampton W) 3
Mason, R. G. 2015 (Tottenham H) 1
Matthews, R. D. 1956 (Coventry C) 5
Matthews, S. 1935 (Stoke C, Blackpool) 54
Matthews, V. 1928 (Sheffield U) 2
Maynard, W. J. 1872 (1st Surrey Rifles) 2
Meadows, J. 1955 (Manchester C) 1
Medley, L. D. 1951 (Tottenham H) 6
Meehan, T. 1924 (Chelsea) 1
Melia, J. 1963 (Liverpool) 2
Mercer, D. W. 1923 (Sheffield U) 2
Mercer, J. 1939 (Everton) 5
Merrick, G. H. 1952 (Birmingham C) 23
Merson, P. C. 1992 (Arsenal, Middlesbrough, Aston Villa) 21
Metcalfe, V. 1951 (Huddersfield T) 2
Mew, J. W. 1921 (Manchester U) 1
Middleditch, B. 1897 (Corinthians) 1
Milburn, J. E. T. 1949 (Newcastle U) 13
Miller, B. G. 1961 (Burnley) 1
Miller, H. S. 1923 (Charlton Ath) 1
Mills, D. J. 2001 (Leeds U) 19
Mills, G. R. 1938 (Chelsea) 3
Mills, M. D. 1973 (Ipswich T) 42
Milne, G. 1963 (Liverpool) 14
Milner, J. P. 2010 (Aston Villa, Manchester C) 54
Milton, C. A. 1952 (Arsenal) 1
Milward, A. 1891 (Everton) 4

Mitchell, C. 1880 (Upton Park) 5
Mitchell, J. F. 1925 (Manchester C) 1
Moffat, H. 1913 (Oldham Ath) 1
Molyneux, G. 1902 (Southampton) 4
Moon, W. R. 1888 (Old Westminsters) 7
Moore, H. T. 1883 (Notts Co) 2
Moore, J. 1923 (Derby Co) 1
Moore, R. F. 1962 (West Ham U) 108
Moore, W. G. B. 1923 (West Ham U) 1
Mordue, J. 1912 (Sunderland) 2
Morice, C. J. 1872 (Barnes) 1
Morley, A. 1982 (Aston Villa) 6
Morley, H. 1910 (Notts Co) 1
Morren, T. 1898 (Sheffield U) 1
Morris, F. 1920 (WBA) 2
Morris, J. 1949 (Derby Co) 3
Morris, W. W. 1939 (Wolverhampton W) 3
Morse, H. 1879 (Notts Co) 1
Mort, T. 1924 (Aston Villa) 3
Morten, A. 1873 (Crystal Palace) 1
Mortensen, S. H. 1947 (Blackpool) 25
Morton, J. R. 1938 (West Ham U) 1
Mosforth, W. 1877 (Sheffield W, Sheffield Alb, Sheffield W) 9
Moss, F. 1922 (Aston Villa) 5
Moss, F. 1934 (Arsenal) 4
Mosscrop, E. 1914 (Burnley) 2
Mozley, B. 1950 (Derby Co) 3
Mullen, J. 1947 (Wolverhampton W) 12
Mullery, A. P. 1965 (Tottenham H) 35
Murphy, D. B. 2002 (Liverpool) 9

Neal, P. G. 1976 (Liverpool) 50
Needham, E. 1894 (Sheffield U) 16
Neville, G. A. 1995 (Manchester U) 85
Neville, P. J. 1996 (Manchester U, Everton) 59
Newton, K. R. 1966 (Blackburn R, Everton) 27
Nicholls, J. 1954 (WBA) 2
Nicholson, W. E. 1951 (Tottenham H) 1
Nish, D. J. 1973 (Derby Co) 5
Norman, M. 1962 (Tottenham H) 23
Nugent, D. J. 2007 (Preston NE) 1
Nuttall, H. 1928 (Bolton W) 3

Oakley, W. J. 1895 (Oxford University, Corinthians) 16
O'Dowd, J. P. 1932 (Chelsea) 3
O'Grady, M. 1963 (Huddersfield T, Leeds U) 2
Ogilvie, R. A. M. M. 1874 (Clapham R) 1
Oliver, L. F. 1929 (Fulham) 1
Olney, B. A. 1928 (Aston Villa) 2
Osborne, F. R. 1923 (Fulham, Tottenham H) 4
Osborne, R. 1928 (Leicester C) 1
Osgood, P. L. 1970 (Chelsea) 4
Osman, J. 2013 (Everton) 2
Osman, R. 1980 (Ipswich T) 11
Ottaway, C. J. 1872 (Oxford University) 2
Owen, J. R. B. 1874 (Sheffield) 1
Owen, M. J. 1998 (Liverpool, Real Madrid, Newcastle U) 89
Owen, S. W. 1954 (Luton T) 3
Oxlade-Chamberlain, A. M. D. 2012 (Arsenal) 20

Page, L. A. 1927 (Burnley) 7
Paine, T. L. 1963 (Southampton) 19
Pallister, G. A. 1988 (Middlesbrough, Manchester U) 22
Palmer, C. L. 1992 (Sheffield W) 18
Pantling, H. H. 1924 (Sheffield U) 1
Paravicini, P. J. de 1883 (Cambridge University) 3
Parker, P. A. 1989 (QPR, Manchester U) 19
Parker, S. M. 2004 (Charlton Ath, Chelsea, Newcastle U, West Ham U, Tottenham H) 18
Parker, T. R. 1925 (Southampton) 1
Parkes, P. B. 1974 (QPR) 1
Parkinson, J. 1910 (Liverpool) 2
Parlour, R. 1999 (Arsenal) 10
Parr, P. C. 1882 (Oxford University) 1
Parry, E. H. 1879 (Old Carthusians) 3
Parry, R. A. 1960 (Bolton W) 2
Patchitt, B. C. A. 1923 (Corinthians) 2
Pawson, F. W. 1883 (Cambridge University, Swifts) 2
Payne, J. 1937 (Luton T) 1

Peacock, A. 1962 (Middlesbrough, Leeds U) 6
Peacock, J. 1929 (Middlesbrough) 3
Pearce, S. 1987 (Nottingham F, West Ham U) 78
Pearson, H. F. 1932 (WBA) 1
Pearson, J. H. 1892 (Crewe Alex) 1
Pearson, J. S. 1976 (Manchester U) 15
Pearson, S. C. 1948 (Manchester U) 8
Pease, W. H. 1927 (Middlesbrough) 1
Pegg, D. 1957 (Manchester U) 1
Pejic, M. 1974 (Stoke C) 4
Pelly, F. R. 1893 (Old Foresters) 3
Pennington, J. 1907 (WBA) 25
Pentland, F. B. 1909 (Middlesbrough) 5
Perry, C. 1890 (WBA) 3
Perry, T. 1898 (WBA) 1
Perry, W. 1956 (Blackpool) 3
Perryman, S. 1982 (Tottenham H) 1
Peters, M. 1966 (West Ham U, Tottenham H) 67
Phelan, M. C. 1990 (Manchester U) 1
Phillips, K. 1999 (Sunderland) 8
Phillips, L. H. 1952 (Portsmouth) 3
Pickering, F. 1964 (Everton) 3
Pickering, J. 1933 (Sheffield U) 1
Pickering, N. 1983 (Sunderland) 1
Pike, T. M. 1886 (Cambridge University) 1
Pilkington, B. 1955 (Burnley) 1
Plant, J. 1900 (Bury) 1
Platt, D. 1990 (Aston Villa, Bari, Juventus, Sampdoria, Arsenal) 62
Plum, S. L. 1923 (Charlton Ath) 1
Pointer, R. 1962 (Burnley) 3
Porteous, T. S. 1891 (Sunderland) 1
Powell, C. G. 2001 (Charlton Ath) 5
Priest, A. E. 1900 (Sheffield U) 1
Prinsep, J. F. M. 1879 (Clapham R) 1
Puddefoot, S. C. 1926 (Blackburn R) 2
Pye, J. 1950 (Wolverhampton W) 1
Pym, R. H. 1925 (Bolton W) 3

Quantrill, A. 1920 (Derby Co) 4
Quixall, A. 1954 (Sheffield W) 5

Radford, J. 1969 (Arsenal) 2
Raikes, G. B. 1895 (Oxford University) 4
Ramsey, A. E. 1949 (Southampton, Tottenham H) 32
Rawlings, A. 1921 (Preston NE) 1
Rawlings, W. E. 1922 (Southampton) 2
Rawlinson, J. F. P. 1882 (Cambridge University) 1
Rawson, H. E. 1875 (Royal Engineers) 2
Rawson, W. S. 1875 (Oxford University) 2
Read, A. 1921 (Tufnell Park) 1
Reader, J. 1894 (WBA) 1
Reaney, P. 1969 (Leeds U) 3
Redknapp, J. F. 1996 (Liverpool) 17
Reeves, K. P. 1980 (Norwich C, Manchester C) 2
Regis, C. 1982 (WBA, Coventry C) 5
Reid, P. 1985 (Everton) 13
Revie, D. G. 1955 (Manchester C) 6
Reynolds, J. 1892 (WBA, Aston Villa) 8
Richards, C. H. 1898 (Nottingham F) 1
Richards, G. H. 1909 (Derby Co) 1
Richards, J. P. 1973 (Wolverhampton W) 1
Richards, M. 2007 (Manchester C) 13
Richardson, J. R. 1933 (Newcastle U) 2
Richardson, K. 1994 (Aston Villa) 1
Richardson, K. E. 2005 (Manchester U) 8
Richardson, W. G. 1935 (WBA) 1
Rickaby, S. 1954 (WBA) 1
Ricketts, M. B. 2002 (Bolton W) 1
Rigby, A. 1927 (Blackburn R) 5
Rimmer, E. J. 1930 (Sheffield W) 4
Rimmer, J. J. 1976 (Arsenal) 1
Ripley, S. E. 1994 (Blackburn R) 2
Rix, G. 1981 (Arsenal) 17
Robb, G. 1954 (Tottenham H) 1
Roberts, C. 1905 (Manchester U) 3
Roberts, F. 1925 (Manchester C) 4
Roberts, G. 1983 (Tottenham H) 6
Roberts, H. 1931 (Arsenal) 1
Roberts, H. 1931 (Millwall) 1
Roberts, R. 1887 (WBA) 3

Roberts, W. T. 1924 (Preston NE)	2
Robinson, J. 1937 (Sheffield W)	4
Robinson, J. W. 1897 (Derby Co, New Brighton Tower, Southampton)	11
Robinson, P. W. 2003 (Leeds U, Tottenham H, Blackburn R)	41
Robson, B. 1980 (WBA, Manchester U)	90
Robson, R. 1958 (WBA)	20
Rocastle, D. 1989 (Arsenal)	14
Rodriguez, J. E. 2013 (Southampton)	1
Rodwell, J. 2012 (Everton)	3
Rooney, W. M. 2003 (Everton, Manchester U)	**105**
Rose, W. C. 1884 (Swifts, Preston NE, Wolverhampton W)	5
Rostron, T. 1881 (Darwen)	2
Rowe, A. 1934 (Tottenham H)	1
Rowley, J. F. 1949 (Manchester U)	6
Rowley, W. 1889 (Stoke)	2
Royle, J. 1971 (Everton, Manchester C)	6
Ruddlesdin, H. 1904 (Sheffield W)	3
Ruddock, N. 1995 (Liverpool)	1
Ruddy, J. T. G. 2013 (Norwich C)	1
Ruffell, J. W. 1926 (West Ham U)	6
Russell, B. B. 1883 (Royal Engineers)	1
Rutherford, J. 1904 (Newcastle U)	11
Sadler, D. 1968 (Manchester U)	4
Sagar, C. 1900 (Bury)	2
Sagar, E. 1936 (Everton)	4
Salako, J. A. 1991 (Crystal Palace)	5
Sandford, E. A. 1933 (WBA)	1
Sandilands, R. R. 1892 (Old Westminsters)	5
Sands, J. 1880 (Nottingham F)	1
Sansom, K. G. 1979 (Crystal Palace, Arsenal)	86
Saunders, F. E. 1888 (Swifts)	1
Savage, A. H. 1876 (Crystal Palace)	1
Sayer, J. 1887 (Stoke)	1
Scales, J. R. 1995 (Liverpool)	3
Scattergood, E. 1913 (Derby Co)	1
Schofield, J. 1892 (Stoke)	3
Scholes, P. 1997 (Manchester U)	66
Scott, L. 1947 (Arsenal)	17
Scott, W. R. 1937 (Brentford)	1
Seaman, D. A. 1989 (QPR, Arsenal)	75
Seddon, J. 1923 (Bolton W)	6
Seed, J. M. 1921 (Tottenham H)	5
Settle, J. 1899 (Bury, Everton)	6
Sewell, J. 1952 (Sheffield W)	6
Sewell, W. R. 1924 (Blackburn R)	1
Shackleton, L. F. 1949 (Sunderland)	5
Sharp, J. 1903 (Everton)	2
Sharpe, L. S. 1991 (Manchester U)	8
Shaw, G. E. 1932 (WBA)	1
Shaw, G. L. 1959 (Sheffield U)	5
Shaw, L. P. H. 2014 (Southampton, Manchester U)	**4**
Shawcross, R. J. 2013 (Stoke C)	1
Shea, D. 1914 (Blackburn R)	2
Shearer, A. 1992 (Southampton, Blackburn R, Newcastle U)	63
Shellito, K. J. 1963 (Chelsea)	1
Shelton A. 1889 (Notts Co)	6
Shelton, C. 1888 (Notts Rangers)	1
Shelvey, J. 2013 (Liverpool)	1
Shepherd, A. 1906 (Bolton W, Newcastle U)	2
Sheringham, E. P. 1993 (Tottenham H, Manchester U, Tottenham H)	51
Sherwood, T. A. 1999 (Tottenham H)	3
Shilton, P. L. 1971 (Leicester C, Stoke C, Nottingham F, Southampton, Derby Co)	125
Shimwell, E. 1949 (Blackpool)	1
Shorey, N. 2007 (Reading)	2
Shutt, G. 1886 (Stoke)	1
Silcock, J. 1921 (Manchester U)	3
Sillett, R. P. 1955 (Chelsea)	3
Simms, E. 1922 (Luton T)	1
Simpson, J. 1911 (Blackburn R)	8
Sinclair, T. 2002 (West Ham U, Manchester C)	12
Sinton, A. 1992 (QPR, Sheffield W)	12
Slater, W. J. 1955 (Wolverhampton W)	12
Smalley, T. 1937 (Wolverhampton W)	1
Smalling, C. L. 2012 (Manchester U)	**18**

Smart, T. 1921 (Aston Villa)	5
Smith, A. 1891 (Nottingham F)	3
Smith, A. 2001 (Leeds U, Manchester U, Newcastle U)	19
Smith, A. K. 1872 (Oxford University)	1
Smith, A. M. 1989 (Arsenal)	13
Smith, B. 1921 (Tottenham H)	2
Smith, C. E. 1876 (Crystal Palace)	1
Smith, G. O. 1893 (Oxford University, Old Carthusians, Corinthians)	20
Smith, H. 1905 (Reading)	4
Smith, J. 1920 (WBA)	2
Smith, Joe 1913 (Bolton W)	5
Smith, J. C. R. 1939 (Millwall)	2
Smith, J. W. 1932 (Portsmouth)	3
Smith, Leslie 1939 (Brentford)	1
Smith, Lionel 1951 (Arsenal)	6
Smith, R. A. 1961 (Tottenham H)	15
Smith, S. 1895 (Aston Villa)	1
Smith, S. C. 1936 (Leicester C)	1
Smith, T. 1960 (Birmingham C)	2
Smith, T. 1971 (Liverpool)	1
Smith, W. H. 1922 (Huddersfield T)	3
Sorby, T. H. 1879 (Thursday Wanderers, Sheffield)	1
Southgate, G. 1996 (Aston Villa, Middlesbrough)	57
Southworth, J. 1889 (Blackburn R)	3
Sparks, F. J. 1879 (Herts Rangers, Clapham R)	3
Spence, J. W. 1926 (Manchester U)	2
Spence, R. 1936 (Chelsea)	2
Spencer, C. W. 1924 (Newcastle U)	2
Spencer, H. 1897 (Aston Villa)	6
Spiksley, F. 1893 (Sheffield W)	7
Spilsbury, B. W. 1885 (Cambridge University)	3
Spink, N. 1983 (Aston Villa)	1
Spouncer, W. A. 1900 (Nottingham F)	1
Springett, R. D. G. 1960 (Sheffield W)	33
Sproston, B. 1937 (Leeds U, Tottenham H, Manchester C)	11
Squire, R. T. 1886 (Cambridge University)	3
Stanbrough, M. H. 1895 (Old Carthusians)	1
Staniforth, R. 1954 (Huddersfield T)	8
Starling, R. W. 1933 (Sheffield W, Aston Villa)	2
Statham, D. J. 1983 (WBA)	3
Steele, F. C. 1937 (Stoke C)	6
Stein, B. 1984 (Luton T)	1
Stephenson, C. 1924 (Huddersfield T)	1
Stephenson, G. T. 1928 (Derby Co, Sheffield W)	3
Stephenson, J. E. 1938 (Leeds U)	2
Stepney, A. C. 1968 (Manchester U)	1
Sterland, M. 1989 (Sheffield W)	1
Sterling, R. S. 2013 (Liverpool)	**16**
Steven, T. M. 1985 (Everton, Rangers, Marseille)	36
Stevens, G. A. 1985 (Tottenham H)	7
Stevens, M. G. 1985 (Everton, Rangers)	46
Stewart, J. 1907 (Sheffield W, Newcastle U)	3
Stewart, P. A. 1992 (Tottenham H)	3
Stiles, N. P. 1965 (Manchester U)	28
Stoker, J. 1933 (Birmingham)	3
Stone, S. B. 1996 (Nottingham F)	9
Stones, J. 2014 (Everton)	**4**
Storer, H. 1924 (Derby Co)	2
Storey, P. E. 1971 (Arsenal)	19
Storey-Moore, I. 1970 (Nottingham F)	1
Strange, A. H. 1930 (Sheffield W)	20
Stratford, A. H. 1874 (Wanderers)	1
Streten, B. 1950 (Luton T)	1
Sturgess, A. 1911 (Sheffield U)	2
Sturridge, D. A. 2012 (Chelsea, Liverpool)	**16**
Summerbee, M. G. 1968 (Manchester C)	8
Sunderland, A. 1980 (Arsenal)	1
Sutcliffe, J. W. 1893 (Bolton W, Millwall)	5
Sutton, C. R. 1998 (Blackburn R)	1
Swan, P. 1960 (Sheffield W)	19
Swepstone, H. A. 1880 (Pilgrims)	6
Swift, F. V. 1947 (Manchester C)	19
Tait, G. 1881 (Birmingham Excelsior)	1
Talbot, B. 1977 (Ipswich T, Arsenal)	6
Tambling, R. V. 1963 (Chelsea)	3
Tate, J. T. 1931 (Aston Villa)	3
Taylor, E. 1954 (Blackpool)	1
Taylor, E. H. 1923 (Huddersfield T)	8

Worthington, F. S. 1974 (Leicester C)   8
Wreford-Brown, C. 1889 (Oxford University, Old
  Carthusians)   4
Wright, E. G. D. 1906 (Cambridge University)   1
Wright, I. E. 1991 (Crystal Palace, Arsenal,
  West Ham U)   33
Wright, J. D. 1939 (Newcastle U)   1
Wright, M. 1984 (Southampton, Derby Co,
  Liverpool)   45
Wright, R. I. 2000 (Ipswich T, Arsenal)   2
Wright, T. J. 1968 (Everton)   11
Wright, W. A. 1947 (Wolverhampton W)   105

Wright-Phillips, S. C. 2005 (Manchester C, Chelsea,
  Manchester C)   36
Wylie, J. G. 1878 (Wanderers)   1

Yates, J. 1889 (Burnley)   1
York, R. E. 1922 (Aston Villa)   2
Young, A. 1933 (Huddersfield T)   9
Young, A. S. 2008 (Aston Villa, Manchester U)   30
Young, G. M. 1965 (Sheffield W)   1
Young, L. P. 2005 (Charlton Ath)   7
Zaha, D. W. A. 2013 (Manchester U)   2
Zamora, R. L. 2011 (Fulham)   2

NORTHERN IRELAND

Addis, D. J. 1922 (Cliftonville)   1
Aherne, T. 1947 (Belfast Celtic, Luton T)   4
Alexander, T. E. 1895 (Cliftonville)   1
Allan, C. 1936 (Cliftonville)   1
Allen, J. 1887 (Limavady)   1
Anderson, J. 1925 (Distillery)   1
Anderson, T. 1973 (Manchester U, Swindon T,
  Peterborough U)   22
Anderson, W. 1898 (Linfield, Cliftonville)   4
Andrews, W. 1908 (Glentoran, Grimsby T)   3
Armstrong, G. J. 1977 (Tottenham H, Watford,
  Real Mallorca, WBA, Chesterfield)   63

**Baird, C. P. 2003 (Southampton, Fulham, Reading,
  Burnley, WBA)**   **72**
Baird, G. 1896 (Distillery)   3
Baird, H. C. 1939 (Huddersfield T)   1
Balfe, J. 1909 (Shelbourne)   2
Bambrick, J. 1929 (Linfield, Chelsea)   11
Banks, S. J. 1937 (Cliftonville)   1
Barr, H. H. 1962 (Linfield, Coventry C)   3
Barron, J. H. 1894 (Cliftonville)   7
Barry, J. 1888 (Cliftonville)   3
Barry, J. 1900 (Bohemians)   1
Barton, A. J. 2011 (Preston NE)   1
Baxter, R. A. 1887 (Distillery)   1
Baxter, S. N. 1887 (Cliftonville)   1
Bennett, L. V. 1889 (Dublin University)   1
Best, G. 1964 (Manchester U, Fulham)   37
Bingham, W. L. 1951 (Sunderland, Luton T, Everton,
  Port Vale)   56
Black, K. T. 1988 (Luton T, Nottingham F)   30
Black, T. 1901 (Glentoran)   1
Blair, H. 1928 (Portadown, Swansea T)   4
Blair, J. 1907 (Cliftonville)   5
Blair, R. V. 1975 (Oldham Ath)   5
Blanchflower, J. 1954 (Manchester U)   12
Blanchflower, R. D. 1950 (Barnsley, Aston Villa,
  Tottenham H)   56
Blayney, A. 2006 (Doncaster R, Linfield)   5
Bookman, L. J. O. 1914 (Bradford C, Luton T)   4
Bothwell, a. W. 1926 (Ards)   5
Bowler, G. C. 1950 (Hull C)   3
Boyce, L. 2011 (Werder Bremen, Ross Co)   **5**
Boyle, P. 1901 (Sheffield U)   5
Braithwaite, R. M. 1962 (Linfield, Middlesbrough)   10
Braniff, K. R. 2010 (Portadown)   2
Breen, T. 1935 (Belfast Celtic, Manchester U)   9
Brennan, B. 1912 (Bohemians)   1
Brennan, R. A. 1949 (Luton T, Birmingham C, Fulham) 5
Briggs, W. R. 1962 (Manchester U, Swansea T)   2
Brisby, D. 1891 (Distillery)   1
Brolly, T. H. 1937 (Millwall)   4
Brookes, E. A. 1920 (Shelbourne)   1
Brotherston, N. 1980 (Blackburn R)   27
Brown, J. 1921 (Glenavon, Tranmere R)   3
Brown, J. 1935 (Wolverhampton W, Coventry C,
  Birmingham C)   10
Brown, N. M. 1887 (Limavady)   1
Brown, W. G. 1926 (Glenavon)   1
Browne, F. 1887 (Cliftonville)   5
Browne, R. J. 1936 (Leeds U)   6
Bruce, A. 1925 (Belfast Celtic)   1
Bruce, A. S. 2013 (Hull C)   2

Bruce, W. 1961 (Glentoran)   2
Brunt, C. 2005 (Sheffield W, WBA)   **50**
Bryan, M. A. 2010 (Watford)   2
Buckle, H. R. 1903 (Cliftonville, Sunderland, Bristol R) 3
Buckle, J. 1882 (Cliftonville)   1
Burnett, J. 1894 (Distillery, Glentoran)   5
Burnison, J. 1901 (Distillery)   2
Burnison, S. 1908 (Distillery, Bradford, Distillery)   8
Burns, J. 1923 (Glenavon)   1
Burns, W. 1925 (Glentoran)   1
Butler, M. P. 1939 (Blackpool)   1

Camp, L. M. J. 2011 (Nottingham F)   9
Campbell, A. C. 1963 (Crusaders)   2
Campbell, D. A. 1986 (Nottingham F, Charlton Ath)   10
Campbell, James 1897 (Cliftonville)   14
Campbell, John 1896 (Cliftonville)   1
Campbell, J. P. 1951 (Fulham)   2
Campbell, R. M. 1982 (Bradford C)   2
Campbell, W. G. 1968 (Dundee)   6
Capaldi, A. C. 2004 (Plymouth Arg, Cardiff C)   22
Carey, J. J. 1947 (Manchester U)   7
Carroll, E. 1925 (Glenavon)   1
**Carroll, R. E. 1997 (Wigan Ath, Manchester U,
  West Ham U, Olympiacos, Notts Co)**   **41**
Carson, J. G. 2011 (Ipswich T)   4
Carson, S. 2009 (Coleraine)   1
Casement, C. 2009 (Ipswich T)   1
Casey, T. 1955 (Newcastle U, Portsmouth)   12
Caskey, W. 1979 (Derby Co, Tulsa Roughnecks)   8
Cassidy, T. 1971 (Newcastle U, Burnley)   24
Cathcart, C. G. 2011 (Blackpool, Watford)   **21**
Caughey, M. 1986 (Linfield)   2
Chambers, R. J. 1921 (Distillery, Bury, Nottingham F) 12
Chatton, H. A. 1925 (Partick Thistle)   3
Christian, J. 1889 (Linfield)   1
Clarke, C. J. 1986 (Bournemouth, Southampton, QPR,
  Portsmouth)   38
Clarke, R. 1901 (Belfast Celtic)   2
Cleary, J. 1982 (Glentoran)   5
Clements, D. 1965 (Coventry C, Sheffield W, Everton,
  New York Cosmos)   48
**Clingan, S. G. 2006 (Nottingham F, Norwich C,
  Coventry C, Kilmarnock)**   **39**
Clugston, J. 1888 (Cliftonville)   14
Clyde, M. G. 2005 (Wolverhampton W)   3
Coates, C. 2009 (Crusaders)   6
Cochrane, D. 1939 (Leeds U)   12
Cochrane, G. 1903 (Cliftonville)   1
Cochrane, G. T. 1976 (Coleraine, Burnley,
  Middlesbrough, Gillingham)   26
Cochrane, M. 1898 (Distillery, Leicester Fosse)   8
Collins, F. 1922 (Celtic)   1
Collins, R. 1922 (Cliftonville)   1
Condy, J. 1882 (Distillery)   3
Connell, T. E. 1978 (Coleraine)   1
Connor, J. 1901 (Glentoran, Belfast Celtic)   13
Connor, M. J. 1903 (Brentford, Fulham)   3
Cook, W. 1933 (Celtic, Everton)   15
Cooke, S. 1889 (Belfast YMCA, Cliftonville)   3
Coote, A. 1999 (Norwich C)   6
Coulter, J. 1934 (Belfast Celtic, Everton, Grimsby T,
  Chelmsford C)   11
Cowan, J. 1970 (Newcastle U)   1

Cowan, T. S. 1925 (Queen's Island) 1
Coyle, F. 1956 (Coleraine, Nottingham F) 4
Coyle, L. 1989 (Derry C) 1
Coyle, R. I. 1973 (Sheffield W) 5
Craig, A. B. 1908 (Rangers, Morton) 9
Craig, D. J. 1967 (Newcastle U) 25
Craigan, S. J. 2003 (Partick Thistle, Motherwell) 54
Crawford, A. 1889 (Distillery, Cliftonville) 7
Croft, T. 1922 (Queen's Island) 3
Crone, R. 1889 (Distillery) 4
Crone, W. 1882 (Distillery) 12
Crooks, W. J. 1922 (Manchester U) 1
Crossan, E. 1950 (Blackburn R) 3
Crossan, J. A. 1960 (Sparta-Rotterdam, Sunderland,
 Manchester C, Middlesbrough) 24
Crothers, C. 1907 (Distillery) 1
Cumming, L. 1929 (Huddersfield T, Oldham Ath) 3
Cunningham, W. 1892 (Ulster) 4
Cunningham, W. E. 1951 (St Mirren, Leicester C,
 Dunfermline Ath) 30
Curran, S. 1926 (Belfast Celtic) 4
Curran, J. J. 1922 (Glenavon, Pontypridd, Glenavon) 5
Cush, W. W. 1951 (Glenavon, Leeds U, Portadown) 26

Dallas, S. A, 2011 (Crusaders, Brentford) **5**
Dalrymple, J. 1922 (Distillery) 1
Dalton, W. 1888 (YMCA, Linfield) 11
D'Arcy, S. D. 1952 (Chelsea, Brentford) 5
Darling, J. 1897 (Linfield) 22
Davey, H. H. 1926 (Reading, Portsmouth) 5
Davis, S. 2005 (Aston Villa, Fulham, Rangers,
 Southampton) **74**
Davis, T. L. 1937 (Oldham Ath) 1
Davison, A. J. 1996 (Bolton W, Bradford C, Grimsby T) 3
Davison, J. R. 1882 (Cliftonville) 8
Dennison, R. 1988 (Wolverhampton W) 18
Devine, A. O. 1886 (Limavady) 4
Devine, J. 1990 (Glentoran) 1
Dickson, D. 1970 (Coleraine) 4
Dickson, T. A. 1957 (Linfield) 1
Dickson, W. 1951 (Chelsea, Arsenal) 12
Diffin, W. J. 1931 (Belfast Celtic) 1
Dill, A. H. 1882 (Knock, Down Ath, Cliftonville) 9
Doherty, I. 1901 (Belfast Celtic) 1
Doherty, J. 1928 (Portadown) 1
Doherty, J. 1933 (Cliftonville) 1
Doherty, L. 1985 (Linfield) 2
Doherty, M. 1938 (Derry C) 1
Doherty, P. D. 1935 (Blackpool, Manchester C, Derby
 Co, Huddersfield T, Doncaster R) 16
Doherty, T. E. 2003 (Bristol C) 9
Donaghey, B. 1903 (Belfast Celtic) 1
Donaghy, M. M. 1980 (Luton T, Manchester U, Chelsea) 91
Donnelly, L. 1913 (Distillery) 1
Donnelly, L. F. P. 2014 (Fulham) 1
Donnelly, M. 2009 (Crusaders) 1
Doran, J. F. 1921 (Brighton) 3
Dougan, A. D. 1958 (Portsmouth, Blackburn R,
 Aston Villa, Leicester C, Wolverhampton W) 43
Douglas, J. P. 1947 (Belfast Celtic) 1
Dowd, H. O. 1974 (Glenavon, Sheffield W) 3
Dowie, I. 1990 (Luton T, West Ham U, Southampton,
 C Palace, West Ham U, QPR) 59
Duff, M. J. 2002 (Cheltenham T, Burnley) 24
Duggan, H. A. 1930 (Leeds U) 8
Dunlop, G. 1985 (Linfield) 4
Dunne, J. 1928 (Sheffield U) 7

Eames, W. L. E. 1885 (Dublin University) 3
Eglington, T. J. 1947 (Everton) 6
Elder, A. R. 1960 (Burnley, Stoke C) 40
Elleman, A. R. 1889 (Cliftonville) 2
Elliott, S. 2001 (Motherwell, Hull C) 39
Elwood, J. H. 1929 (Bradford) 2
Emerson, W. 1920 (Glentoran, Burnley) 11
English, S. 1933 (Rangers) 2
Enright, J. 1912 (Leeds C) 1
Evans, C. J. 2009 (Manchester U, Hull C, Blackburn R) **29**
Evans, J. G. 2007 (Manchester U) **42**

Falloon, E. 1931 (Aberdeen) 2
Farquharson, T. G. 1923 (Cardiff C) 7
Farrell, P. 1901 (Distillery) 2
Farrell, P. 1938 (Hibernian) 1
Farrell, P. D. 1947 (Everton) 7
Feeney, J. M. 1947 (Linfield, Swansea T) 2
Feeney, W. 1976 (Glentoran) 1
Feeney, W. J. 2002 (Bournemouth, Luton T, Cardiff C,
 Oldham Ath, Plymouth Arg) 46
Ferguson, G. 1999 (Linfield) 5
Ferguson, S. K. 2009 (Newcastle U) **18**
Ferguson, W. 1966 (Linfield) 2
Ferris, J. 1920 (Belfast Celtic, Chelsea, Belfast Celtic) 6
Ferris, R. O. 1950 (Birmingham C) 3
Fettis, A. W. 1992 (Hull C, Nottingham F, Blackburn R)
 25
Finney, T. 1975 (Sunderland, Cambridge U) 14
Fitzpatrick, J. C. 1896 (Bohemians) 2
Flack, H. 1929 (Burnley) 1
Fleming, J. G. 1987 (Nottingham F, Manchester C,
 Barnsley) 31
Forbes, G. 1888 (Limavady, Distillery) 3
Forde, J. T. 1959 (Ards) 4
Foreman, T. A. 1899 (Cliftonville) 1
Forsythe, J. 1888 (YMCA) 2
Fox, W. T. 1887 (Ulster) 2
Frame, T. 1925 (Linfield) 1
Fulton, R. P. 1928 (Larne, Belfast Celtic) 21

Gaffikin, G. 1890 (Linfield Ath) 15
Galbraith, W. 1890 (Distillery) 1
Gallagher, P. 1920 (Celtic, Falkirk) 11
Gallogly, C. 1951 (Huddersfield T) 2
Gara, A. 1902 (Preston NE) 3
Gardiner, A. 1930 (Cliftonville) 5
Garrett, J. 1925 (Distillery) 1
Garrett, R. 2009 (Linfield) 5
Gaston, R. 1969 (Oxford U) 1
Gaukrodger, G. 1895 (Linfield) 1
Gault, M. 2008 (Linfield) 1
Gaussen, A. D. 1884 (Moyola Park, Magherafelt) 6
Geary, J. 1931 (Glentoran) 2
Gibb, J. T. 1884 (Wellington Park, Cliftonville) 10
Gibb, T. J. 1936 (Cliftonville) 1
Gibson W. K. 1894 (Cliftonville) 14
Gillespie, K. R. 1995 (Manchester U, Newcastle U,
 Blackburn R, Leicester C, Sheffield U) 86
Gillespie, S. 1886 (Hertford) 6
Gillespie, W. 1889 (West Down) 1
Gillespie, W. 1913 (Sheffield U) 25
Goodall, A. L. 1899 (Derby Co, Glossop) 10
Goodbody, M. F. 1889 (Dublin University) 2
Gordon, H. 1895 (Linfield) 3
Gordon R. W. 1891 (Linfield) 7
Gordon, T. 1894 (Linfield) 2
Gorman, R. J. 2010 (Wolverhampton W) 9
Gorman, W. C. 1947 (Brentford) 4
Gough, J. 1925 (Queen's Island) 1
Gowdy, J. 1920 (Glentoran, Queen's Island, Falkirk) 6
Gowdy, W. A. 1932 (Hull C, Sheffield W, Linfield,
 Hibernian) 6
Graham, W. G. L. 1951 (Doncaster R) 14
Gray, P. 1993 (Luton T, Sunderland, Nancy, Luton T,
 Burnley, Oxford U) 26
Greer, W. 1909 (QPR) 3
Gregg, H. 1954 (Doncaster R, Manchester U) 25
Griffin, D. J. 1996 (St Johnstone, Dundee U,
 Stockport Co) 29
Grigg, W. D. 2012 (Walsall, Brentford,
 Milton Keynes D) **7**

Hall, G. 1897 (Distillery) 1
Halligan, W. 1911 (Derby Co, Wolverhampton W) 2
Hamill, M. 1912 (Manchester U, Belfast Celtic,
 Manchester C) 7
Hamill, R. 1999 (Glentoran) 1
Hamilton, B. 1969 (Linfield, Ipswich T, Everton,
 Millwall, Swindon T) 50
Hamilton, G. 2003 (Portadown) 5
Hamilton, J. 1882 (Knock) 2
Hamilton, R. 1928 (Rangers) 5

Hamilton, W. D. 1885 (Dublin Association) 1
Hamilton, W. J. 1885 (Dublin Association) 1
Hamilton, W. J. 1908 (Distillery) 1
Hamilton, W. R. 1978 (QPR, Burnley, Oxford U) 41
Hampton, H. 1911 (Bradford C) 9
Hanna, J. 1912 (Nottingham F) 2
Hanna, J. D. 1899 (Royal Artillery, Portsmouth) 1
Hannon, D. J. 1908 (Bohemians) 6
Harkin, J. T. 1968 (Southport, Shrewsbury T) 5
Harland, A. I. 1922 (Linfield) 2
Harris, J. 1921 (Cliftonville, Glenavon) 2
Harris, V. 1906 (Shelbourne, Everton) 20
Harvey, M. 1961 (Sunderland) 34
Hastings, J. 1882 (Knock, Ulster) 7
Hatton, S. 1963 (Linfield) 2
Hayes, W. E. 1938 (Huddersfield T) 4
Healy, D. J. 2000 (Manchester U, Preston NE, Leeds U,
   Fulham, Sunderland, Rangers, Bury) 95
Healy, P. J. 1982 (Coleraine, Glentoran) 4
Hegan, D. 1970 (WBA, Wolverhampton W) 7
Henderson, J. 1885 (Ulster) 3
Hewison, G. 1885 (Moyola Park) 2
Hill, C. F. 1990 (Sheffield U, Leicester C, Trelleborg,
   Northampton T) 27
Hill, M. J. 1959 (Norwich C, Everton) 7
Hinton, E. 1947 (Fulham, Millwall) 7
Hodson, L. J. S. 2011 (Watford, Milton Keynes D) 15
Holmes, S. P. 2002 (Wrexham) 1
Hopkins, J. 1926 (Brighton) 1
Horlock, K. 1995 (Swindon T, Manchester C) 32
Houston, J. 1912 (Linfield, Everton) 6
Houston, W. 1933 (Linfield) 1
Houston, W. J. 1885 (Moyola Park) 2
Hughes, A. W. 1998 (Newcastle U, Aston Villa, Fulham,
   QPR, Brighton & HA) 96
Hughes, J. 2006 (Lincoln C) 2
Hughes, M. A. 2006 (Oldham Ath) 2
Hughes, M. E. 1992 (Manchester C, Strasbourg,
   West Ham U, Wimbledon, Crystal Palace) 71
Hughes, P. A. 1987 (Bury) 3
Hughes, W. 1951 (Bolton W) 1
Humphries, W. M. 1962 (Ards, Coventry C, Swansea T)
   14
Hunter, A. 1905 (Distillery, Belfast Celtic) 8
Hunter, A. 1970 (Blackburn R, Ipswich T) 53
Hunter, B. V. 1995 (Wrexham, Reading) 15
Hunter, R. J. 1884 (Cliftonville) 3
Hunter, V. 1962 (Coleraine) 2

Ingham, M. G. 2005 (Sunderland, Wrexham) 3
Irvine, R. J. 1962 (Linfield, Stoke C) 8
Irvine, R. W. 1922 (Everton, Portsmouth,
   Connah's Quay, Derry C) 15
Irvine, W. J. 1963 (Burnley, Preston NE,
   Brighton & HA) 23
Irving, S. J. 1923 (Dundee, Cardiff C, Chelsea) 18

Jackson, T. A. 1969 (Everton, Nottingham F,
   Manchester U) 35
Jamison, J. 1976 (Glentoran) 1
Jenkins, I. 1997 (Chester C, Dundee U) 6
Jennings, P. A. 1964 (Watford, Tottenham H, Arsenal,
   Tottenham H) 119
Johnson, D. M. 1999 (Blackburn R, Birmingham C) 56
Johnston, H. 1927 (Portadown) 1
Johnston, R. S. 1882 (Distillery) 5
Johnston, R. S. 1905 (Distillery) 1
Johnston, S. 1890 (Linfield) 4
Johnston, W. 1885 (Oldpark) 2
Johnston, W. C. 1962 (Glenavon, Oldham Ath) 2
Jones, J. 1930 (Linfield, Hibernian, Glenavon) 23
Jones, J. 1956 (Glenavon) 3
Jones, S. 1934 (Distillery, Blackpool) 2
Jones, S. G. 2003 (Crewe Alex, Burnley) 29
Jordan, T. 1895 (Linfield) 2

Kavanagh, P. J. 1930 (Celtic) 1
Keane, T. R. 1949 (Swansea T) 1
Kearns, A. 1900 (Distillery) 6
Kee, P. V. 1990 (Oxford U, Ards) 9
Keith, R. M. 1958 (Newcastle U) 23

Kelly, H. R. 1950 (Fulham, Southampton) 4
Kelly, J. 1896 (Glentoran) 1
Kelly, J. 1932 (Derry C) 11
Kelly, P. J. 1921 (Manchester C) 1
Kelly, P. M. 1950 (Barnsley) 1
Kennedy, A. L. 1923 (Arsenal) 2
Kennedy, P. H. 1999 (Watford, Wigan Ath) 20
Kernaghan, N. 1936 (Belfast Celtic) 3
Kirk, A. R. 2000 (Hearts, Boston U, Northampton T,
   Dunfermline Ath) 11
Kirkwood, H. 1904 (Cliftonville) 1
Kirwan, J. 1900 (Tottenham H, Chelsea, Clyde) 17

Lacey, W. 1909 (Everton, Liverpool, New Brighton) 23
Lafferty, D. P. 2012 (Burnley) 12
Lafferty, K. 2006 (Burnley, Rangers, FC Sion, Palermo) 43
Lawrie, J. 2009 (Port Vale) 3
Lawther, R. 1888 (Glentoran) 2
Lawther, W. I. 1960 (Sunderland, Blackburn R) 4
Leatham, J. 1939 (Belfast Celtic) 1
Ledwidge, J. J. 1906 (Shelbourne) 2
Lemon, J. 1886 (Glentoran, Belfast YMCA) 3
Lennon, N. F. 1994 (Crewe Alex, Leicester C, Celtic) 40
Leslie, W. 1887 (YMCA) 1
Lewis, J. 1899 (Glentoran, Distillery) 4
Little, A. 2009 (Rangers) 9
Lockhart, H. 1884 (Rossall School) 1
Lockhart, N. H. 1947 (Linfield, Coventry C, Aston Villa) 8
Lomas, S. M. 1994 (Manchester C, West Ham U) 45
Loyal, J. 1891 (Clarence) 1
Lutton, R. J. 1970 (Wolverhampton W, West Ham U) 6
Lynas, R. 1925 (Cliftonville) 1
Lyner, D. R. 1920 (Glentoran, Manchester U,
   Kilmarnock) 6
Lytle, J. 1898 (Glentoran) 1

McAdams, W. J. 1954 (Manchester C, Bolton W,
   Leeds U) 15
McAlery, J. M. 1882 (Cliftonville) 2
McAlinden, J. 1938 (Belfast Celtic, Portsmouth,
   Southend U) 4
McAllen, J. 1898 (Linfield) 9
McAlpine, S. 1901 (Cliftonville) 1
McArdle, R. A. 2010 (Rochdale, Aberdeen, Bradford C) 7
McArthur, A. 1886 (Distillery) 1
McAuley, G. 2005 (Lincoln C, Leicester C, Ipswich T,
   WBA) 53
McAuley, J. L. 1911 (Huddersfield T) 6
McAuley, P. 1900 (Belfast Celtic) 1
McBride, S. D. 1991 (Glenavon) 4
McCabe, J. J. 1949 (Leeds U) 6
McCabe, W. 1891 (Ulster) 1
McCambridge, J. 1930 (Ballymena, Cardiff C) 4
McCandless, J. 1912 (Bradford) 5
McCandless, W. 1920 (Linfield, Rangers) 9
McCann, G. S. 2002 (West Ham U, Cheltenham T,
   Barnsley, Scunthorpe U, Peterborough U) 39
McCann, P. 1910 (Belfast Celtic, Glentoran) 7
McCarthy, J. D. 1996 (Port Vale, Birmingham C) 18
McCartney, A. 1903 (Ulster, Linfield, Everton,
   Belfast Celtic, Glentoran) 15
McCartney, G. 2002 (Sunderland, West Ham U,
   Sunderland) 34
McCashin, J. W. 1896 (Cliftonville) 5
McCavana, W. T. 1955 (Coleraine) 3
McCaw, J. H. 1927 (Linfield) 6
McClatchey, J. 1886 (Distillery) 3
McClatchey, T. 1895 (Distillery) 1
McCleary, J. W. 1955 (Cliftonville) 1
McCleery, W. 1922 (Cliftonville, Linfield) 10
McClelland, J. 1980 (Mansfield T, Rangers, Watford,
   Leeds U) 53
McClelland, J. T. 1961 (Arsenal, Fulham) 6
McCluggage, A. 1922 (Cliftonville, Bradford, Burnley) 13
McClure, G. 1907 (Cliftonville, Distillery) 4
McConnell, E. 1904 (Cliftonville, Glentoran, Sunderland,
   Sheffield W) 12
McConnell, P. 1928 (Doncaster R, Southport) 2
McConnell, W. G. 1912 (Bohemians) 6
McConnell, W. H. 1925 (Reading) 8
McCourt, F. J. 1952 (Manchester C) 6

McCourt, P. J. 2002 (Rochdale, Celtic, Barnsley,
Brighton & HA)   **17**
McCoy, R. K. 1987 (Coleraine)   1
McCoy, S. 1896 (Distillery)   1
McCracken, E. 1928 (Barking)   1
McCracken, R. 1921 (Crystal Palace)   4
McCracken, R. 1922 (Linfield)   1
McCracken, W. R. 1902 (Distillery, Newcastle U, Hull C)
  16
McCreery, D. 1976 (Manchester U, QPR,
  Tulsa Roughnecks, Newcastle U, Hearts)   67
McCrory, S. 1958 (Southend U)   1
McCullough, K. 1935 (Belfast Celtic, Manchester C)   5
McCullough, L. 2014 (Doncaster R)   **4**
McCullough, W. J. 1961 (Arsenal, Millwall)   10
McCurdy, C. 1980 (Linfield)   1
McDonald, A. 1986 (QPR)   52
McDonald, R. 1930 (Rangers)   2
McDonnell, J. 1911 (Bohemians)   4
McElhinney, G. M. A. 1984 (Bolton W)   6
McEvilly, L. R. 2002 (Rochdale)   1
McFaul, W. S. 1967 (Linfield, Newcastle U)   6
McGarry, J. K. 1951 (Cliftonville)   3
McGaughey, M. 1985 (Linfield)   1
McGibbon, P. C. G. 1995 (Manchester U, Wigan Ath)   7
McGinn, N. 2009 (Celtic, Aberdeen)   **36**
McGivern, R. 2009 (Manchester C, Hibernian,
Port Vale)   **23**
McGovern, M. 2010 (Ross Co, Hamilton A)   **4**
McGrath, R. C. 1974 (Tottenham H, Manchester U)   21
McGregor, S. 1921 (Glentoran)   1
McGrillen, J. 1924 (Clyde, Belfast Celtic)   2
McGuire, E. 1907 (Distillery)   1
McGuire, J. 1928 (Linfield)   1
McIlroy, H. 1906 (Cliftonville)   1
McIlroy, J. 1952 (Burnley, Stoke C)   55
McIlroy, S. B. 1972 (Manchester U, Stoke C,
  Manchester C)   88
McIlvenny, P. 1924 (Distillery)   1
McIlvenny, H. 1890 (Distillery, Ulster)   2
McKay, W. R. 2013 (Inverness CT, Wigan Ath)   **10**
McKeag, W. 1968 (Glentoran)   2
McKeague, T. 1925 (Glentoran)   1
McKee, F. W. 1906 (Cliftonville, Belfast Celtic)   2
McKelvey, H. 1901 (Glentoran)   2
McKenna, J. 1950 (Huddersfield T)   7
McKenzie, H. 1922 (Distillery)   1
McKenzie, R. 1967 (Airdrieonians)   1
McKeown, N. 1892 (Linfield)   7
McKie, H. 1895 (Cliftonville)   3
Mackie, J. A. 1923 (Arsenal, Portsmouth)   3
McKinney, D. 1921 (Hull C, Bradford C)   2
McKinney, V. J. 1966 (Falkirk)   1
McKnight, A. D. 1988 (Celtic, West Ham U)   10
McKnight, J. 1912 (Preston NE, Glentoran)   2
McLaughlin, C. G. 2012 (Preston NE, Fleetwood T)   **10**
McLaughlin, J. C. 1962 (Shrewsbury T, Swansea C)   12
McLaughlin, R. 2014 (Liverpool)   **3**
McLean, B. S. 2006 (Rangers)   1
McLean, T. 1885 (Limavady)   1
McMahon, G. J. 1995 (Tottenham H, Stoke C)   17
McMahon, J. 1934 (Bohemians)   1
McMaster, G. 1897 (Glentoran)   3
McMichael, A. 1950 (Newcastle U)   40
McMillan, G. 1903 (Distillery)   2
McMillan, S. T. 1963 (Manchester U)   2
McMillen, W. S. 1934 (Manchester U, Chesterfield)   7
McMordie, A. S. 1969 (Middlesbrough)   21
McMorran, E. J. 1947 (Belfast Celtic, Barnsley,
  Doncaster R)   15
McMullan, D. 1926 (Liverpool)   3
McNair, P. J. C. 2015 (Manchester U)   **2**
McNally, B. A. 1986 (Shrewsbury T)   5
McNinch, J. 1931 (Ballymena)   3
McPake, J. 2012 (Coventry C)   1
McParland, P. J. 1954 (Aston Villa, Wolverhampton W)   34
McQuoid, J. J. B. 2011 (Millwall)   5
McShane, J. 1899 (Cliftonville)   4
McVeigh, P. M. 1999 (Tottenham H, Norwich C)   20
McVicker, J. 1888 (Linfield, Glentoran)   2
McWha, W. B. R. 1882 (Knock, Cliftonville)   7

Madden, O. 1938 (Norwich C)   1
Magee, G. 1885 (Wellington Park)   3
Magennis, J. B. D. 2010 (Cardiff C, Aberdeen,
St Mirren, Kilmarnock)   **12**
Magill, E. J. 1962 (Arsenal, Brighton & HA)   26
Magilton, J. 1991 (Oxford U, Southampton, Sheffield W,
  Ipswich T)   52
Maginnis, H. 1900 (Linfield)   8
Mahood, J. 1926 (Belfast Celtic, Ballymena)   9
Mannus, A. 2004 (Linfield, St Johnstone)   7
Manderson, R. 1920 (Rangers)   5
Mansfield, J. 1901 (Dublin Freebooters)   1
Martin, C. 1882 (Cliftonville)   3
Martin, C. 1925 (Bo'ness)   1
Martin, C. J. 1947 (Glentoran, Leeds U, Aston Villa)   6
Martin, D. K. 1934 (Belfast Celtic, Wolverhampton W,
  Nottingham F)   10
Mathieson, A. 1921 (Luton T)   2
Maxwell, J. 1902 (Linfield, Glentoran, Belfast Celtic)   7
Meek, H. L. 1925 (Glentoran)   1
Mehaffy, J. A. C. 1922 (Queen's Island)   1
Meldon, P. A. 1899 (Dublin Freebooters)   2
Mercer, H. V. A. 1908 (Linfield)   1
Mercer, J. T. 1898 (Distillery, Linfield, Distillery,
  Derby Co)   12
Millar, W. 1932 (Barrow)   2
Miller, J. 1929 (Middlesbrough)   3
Milligan, D. 1939 (Chesterfield)   1
Milne, R. G. 1894 (Linfield)   28
Mitchell, E. J. 1933 (Cliftonville, Glentoran)   2
Mitchell, W. 1932 (Distillery, Chelsea)   15
Molyneux, T. B. 1883 (Ligoniel, Cliftonville)   11
Montgomery, F. J. 1955 (Coleraine)   1
Moore, C. 1949 (Glentoran)   1
Moore, P. 1933 (Aberdeen)   1
Moore, R. 1891 (Linfield Ath)   3
Moore, R. L. 1887 (Ulster)   2
Moore, W. 1923 (Falkirk)   1
Moorhead, F. W. 1885 (Dublin University)   1
Moorhead, G. 1923 (Linfield)   4
Moran, J. 1912 (Leeds C)   1
Moreland, V. 1979 (Derby Co)   6
Morgan, G. F. 1922 (Linfield, Nottingham F)   8
Morgan, S. 1972 (Port Vale, Aston Villa, Brighton & HA,
  Sparta Rotterdam)   18
Morrison, R. 1891 (Linfield Ath)   2
Morrison, T. 1895 (Glentoran, Burnley)   7
Morrogh, D. 1896 (Bohemians)   1
Morrow, S. J. 1990 (Arsenal, QPR)   39
Morrow, W. J. 1883 (Moyola Park)   3
Muir, R. 1885 (Oldpark)   2
Mulgrew, J. 2010 (Linfield)   2
Mulholland, T. S. 1906 (Belfast Celtic)   2
Mullan, G. 1983 (Glentoran)   4
Mulligan, J. 1921 (Manchester C)   1
Mulryne, P. P. 1997 (Manchester U, Norwich C,
  Cardiff C)   27
Murdock, C. J. 2000 (Preston NE, Hibernian,
  Crewe Alex, Rotherham U)   34
Murphy, J. 1910 (Bradford C)   3
Murphy, N. 1905 (QPR)   3
Murray, J. M. 1910 (Motherwell, Sheffield W)   3

Napier, R. J. 1966 (Bolton W)   1
Neill, W. J. T. 1961 (Arsenal, Hull C)   59
Nelis, P. 1923 (Nottingham F)   1
Nelson, S. 1970 (Arsenal, Brighton & HA)   51
Nicholl, C. J. 1975 (Aston Villa, Southampton,
  Grimsby T)   51
Nicholl, H. 1902 (Belfast Celtic)   3
Nicholl, J. M. 1976 (Manchester U, Toronto Blizzard,
  Sunderland, Toronto Blizzard, Rangers,
  Toronto Blizzard, WBA)   73
Nicholson, J. J. 1961 (Manchester U, Huddersfield T)   41
Nixon, R. 1914 (Linfield)   1
Nolan, I. R. 1997 (Sheffield W, Bradford C, Wigan Ath)
  18
Nolan-Whelan, J. V. 1901 (Dublin Freebooters)   5
Norwood, O. J. 2011 (Manchester U, Huddersfield T,
Reading)   **25**

SCOTLAND

Brazil, A. 1980 (Ipswich T, Tottenham H) 13
Breckenridge, T. 1888 (Hearts) 1
Bremner, D. 1976 (Hibernian) 1
Bremner, W. J. 1965 (Leeds U) 54
Brennan, F. 1947 (Newcastle U) 7
Breslin, B. 1897 (Hibernian) 1
Brewster, G. 1921 (Everton) 1
Bridcutt, L. 2013 (Brighton & HA) 1
Broadfoot, K. 2009 (Rangers) 4
Brogan, J. 1971 (Celtic) 4
Brown, A. 1890 (St Mirren) 2
Brown, A. 1904 (Middlesbrough) 1
Brown, A. D. 1950 (East Fife, Blackpool) 14
Brown, G. C. P. 1931 (Rangers) 19
Brown, H. 1947 (Partick Thistle) 3
Brown, J. B. 1939 (Clyde) 1
Brown, J. G. 1975 (Sheffield U) 1
Brown, R. 1884 (Dumbarton) 2
Brown, R. 1890 (Cambuslang) 1
Brown, R. 1947 (Rangers) 3
Brown, R. jun. 1885 (Dumbarton) 1
Brown, S. 2006 (Hibernian, Celtic) 45
Brown, W. D. F. 1958 (Dundee, Tottenham H) 28
Browning, J. 1914 (Celtic) 1
Brownlie, J. 1909 (Third Lanark) 16
Brownlie, J. 1971 (Hibernian) 7
Bruce, D. 1890 (Vale of Leven) 1
Bruce, R. F. 1934 (Middlesbrough) 1
Bryson, C. 2011 (Kilmarnock, Derby Co) 2
Buchan, M. M. 1972 (Aberdeen, Manchester U) 34
Buchanan, J. 1889 (Cambuslang) 1
Buchanan, J. 1929 (Rangers) 2
Buchanan, P. S. 1938 (Chelsea) 1
Buchanan, R. 1891 (Abercorn) 1
Buckley, P. 1954 (Aberdeen) 3
Buick, A. 1902 (Hearts) 2
Burchill, M. J. 2000 (Celtic) 6
Burke, C. 2006 (Rangers, Birmingham C) 7
Burley, C. W. 1995 (Chelsea, Celtic, Derby Co) 46
Burley, G. E. 1979 (Ipswich T) 11
Burns, F. 1970 (Manchester U) 1
Burns, K. 1974 (Birmingham C, Nottingham F) 20
Burns, T. 1981 (Celtic) 8
Busby, M. W. 1934 (Manchester C) 1

Cairns, T. 1920 (Rangers) 8
Calderhead, D. 1889 (Q of S Wanderers) 1
Calderwood, C. 1995 (Tottenham H) 36
Calderwood, R. 1885 (Cartvale) 3
Caldow, E. 1957 (Rangers) 40
Caldwell, G. 2002 (Newcastle U, Hibernian, Celtic,
  Wigan Ath) 55
Caldwell, S. 2001 (Newcastle U, Sunderland,
  Burnley,Wigan Ath) 12
Callaghan, P. 1900 (Hibernian) 1
Callaghan, W. 1970 (Dunfermline Ath) 2
Cameron, C. 1999 (Hearts, Wolverhampton W) 28
Cameron, J. 1886 (Rangers) 1
Cameron, J. 1896 (Queen's Park) 1
Cameron, J. 1904 (St Mirren, Chelsea) 2
Campbell, C. 1874 (Queen's Park) 13
Campbell, H. 1889 (Renton) 1
Campbell, Jas 1913 (Sheffield W) 1
Campbell, J. 1880 (South Western) 1
Campbell, J. 1891 (Kilmarnock) 2
Campbell, John 1893 (Celtic) 12
Campbell, John 1899 (Rangers) 4
Campbell, K. 1920 (Liverpool, Partick Thistle) 8
Campbell, P. 1878 (Rangers) 2
Campbell, P. 1898 (Morton) 1
Campbell, R. 1947 (Falkirk, Chelsea) 5
Campbell, W. 1947 (Morton) 5
Canero, P. 2004 (Leicester C) 1
Carabine, J. 1938 (Third Lanark) 3
Carr, W. M. 1970 (Coventry C) 6
Cassidy, J. 1921 (Celtic) 4
Chalmers, S. 1965 (Celtic) 5
Chalmers, W. 1885 (Rangers) 1
Chalmers, W. S. 1929 (Queen's Park) 1
Chambers, T. 1894 (Hearts) 1
Chaplin, G. D. 1908 (Dundee) 1

Cheyne, A. G. 1929 (Aberdeen) 5
Christie, A. J. 1898 (Queen's Park) 3
Christie, R. M. 1884 (Queen's Park) 1
Clark, J. 1966 (Celtic) 4
Clark, R. B. 1968 (Aberdeen) 17
Clarke, S. 1988 (Chelsea) 6
Clarkson, D. 2008 (Motherwell) 2
Cleland, J. 1891 (Royal Albert) 1
Clements, R. 1891 (Leith Ath) 1
Clunas, W. L. 1924 (Sunderland) 2
Collier, W. 1922 (Raith R) 1
Collins, J. 1988 (Hibernian, Celtic, Monaco, Everton) 58
Collins, R. Y. 1951 (Celtic, Everton, Leeds U) 31
Collins, T. 1909 (Hearts) 1
Colman, D. 1911 (Aberdeen) 4
Colquhoun, E. P. 1972 (Sheffield U) 9
Colquhoun, J. 1988 (Hearts) 2
Combe, J. R. 1948 (Hibernian) 3
Commons, K. 2009 (Derby Co, Celtic) 12
Conn, A. 1956 (Hearts) 1
Conn, A. 1975 (Tottenham H) 2
Connachan, E. D. 1962 (Dunfermline Ath) 2
Connelly, G. 1974 (Celtic) 2
Connolly, J. 1973 (Everton) 1
Connor, J. 1886 (Airdrieonians) 1
Connor, J. 1930 (Sunderland) 4
Connor, R. 1986 (Dundee, Aberdeen) 4
Conway, C. 2010 (Dundee U, Cardiff C) 7
Cook, W. L. 1934 (Bolton W) 3
Cooke, C. 1966 (Dundee, Chelsea) 16
Cooper, D. 1980 (Rangers, Motherwell) 22
Cormack, P. B. 1966 (Hibernian, Nottingham F) 9
Cowan, J. 1896 (Aston Villa) 3
Cowan, J. 1948 (Morton) 25
Cowan, W, D. 1924 (Newcastle U) 1
Cowie, D. 1953 (Dundee) 20
Cowie, D. M. 2010 (Watford, Cardiff C) 10
Cox, C. J. 1948 (Hearts) 1
Cox, S. 1949 (Rangers) 24
Craig, A. 1929 (Motherwell) 3
Craig, J. 1977 (Celtic) 1
Craig, J. P. 1968 (Celtic) 1
Craig, T. 1927 (Rangers) 8
Craig, T. B. 1976 (Newcastle U) 1
Crainey, S. D. 2002 (Celtic, Southampton, Blackpool) 12
Crapnell, J. 1929 (Airdrieonians) 9
Crawford, D. 1894 (St Mirren, Rangers) 3
Crawford, J. 1932 (Queen's Park) 5
Crawford, S. 1995 (Raith R, Dunfermline Ath,
  Plymouth Arg) 25
Crerand, P. T. 1961 (Celtic, Manchester U) 16
Cringan, W. 1920 (Celtic) 5
Crosbie, J. A. 1920 (Ayr U, Birmingham) 2
Croal, J. A. 1913 (Falkirk) 3
Cropley, A. J. 1972 (Hibernian) 2
Cross, J. H. 1903 (Third Lanark) 1
Cruickshank, J. 1964 (Hearts) 6
Crum, J. 1936 (Celtic) 2
Cullen, M. J. 1956 (Luton T) 1
Cumming, D. S. 1938 (Middlesbrough) 1
Cumming, J. 1955 (Hearts) 9
Cummings, G. 1935 (Partick Thistle, Aston Villa) 9
Cummings, W. 2002 (Chelsea) 1
Cunningham, A. N. 1920 (Rangers) 12
Cunningham, W. C. 1954 (Preston NE) 8
Curran, H. P. 1970 (Wolverhampton W) 5

Dailly, C. 1997 (Derby Co, Blackburn R, West Ham U,
  Rangers) 67
Dalglish, K. 1972 (Celtic, Liverpool) 102
Davidson, C. I. 1999 (Blackburn R, Leicester C,
  Preston NE) 19
Davidson, D. 1878 (Queen's Park) 5
Davidson, J. A. 1954 (Partick Thistle) 8
Davidson, M. 2013 (St Johnstone) 1
Davidson, S. 1921 (Middlesbrough) 1
Dawson, A. 1980 (Rangers) 5
Dawson, J. 1935 (Rangers) 14
Deans, J. 1975 (Celtic) 2
Delaney, J. 1936 (Celtic, Manchester U) 13
Devine, A. 1910 (Falkirk) 1

Devlin, P. J. 2003 (Birmingham C) 10
Dewar, G. 1888 (Dumbarton) 2
Dewar, N. 1932 (Third Lanark) 3
Dick, J. 1959 (West Ham U) 1
Dickie, M. 1897 (Rangers) 3
Dickov, P. 2001 (Manchester C, Leicester C,
  Blackburn R) 10
Dickson, W. 1888 (Dundee Strathmore) 1
Dickson, W. 1970 (Kilmarnock) 5
Divers, J. 1895 (Celtic) 1
Divers, J. 1939 (Celtic) 1
Dixon, P. A. 2013 (Huddersfield T) 3
Dobie, R. S. 2002 (WBA) 6
Docherty, T. H. 1952 (Preston NE, Arsenal) 25
Dodds, D. 1984 (Dundee U) 2
Dodds, J. 1914 (Celtic) 3
Dodds, W. 1997 (Aberdeen, Dundee U, Rangers) 26
Doig, J. E. 1887 (Arbroath, Sunderland) 5
Donachie, W. 1972 (Manchester C) 35
Donaldson, A. 1914 (Bolton W) 6
Donnachie, J. 1913 (Oldham Ath) 3
Donnelly, S. 1997 (Celtic) 10
Dorrans, G. 2010 (WBA) 10
Dougal, J. 1939 (Preston NE) 1
Dougall, C. 1947 (Birmingham C) 1
Dougan, R. 1950 (Hearts) 1
Douglas, A. 1911 (Chelsea) 1
Douglas, J. 1880 (Renfrew) 1
Douglas, R. 2002 (Celtic, Leicester C) 19
Dowds, P. 1892 (Celtic) 1
Downie, R. 1892 (Third Lanark) 1
Doyle, D. 1892 (Celtic) 8
Doyle, J. 1976 (Ayr U) 1
Drummond, J. 1892 (Falkirk, Rangers) 14
Dunbar, M. 1886 (Cartvale) 1
Duncan, A. 1975 (Hibernian) 6
Duncan, D. 1933 (Derby Co) 14
Duncan, D. M. 1948 (East Fife) 3
Duncan, J. 1878 (Alexandra Ath) 2
Duncan, J. 1926 (Leicester C) 1
Duncanson, J. 1947 (Rangers) 1
Dunlop, J. 1890 (St Mirren) 1
Dunlop, W. 1906 (Liverpool) 1
Dunn, J. 1925 (Hibernian, Everton) 6
Durie, G. S. 1988 (Chelsea, Tottenham H, Rangers) 43
Durrant, I. 1988 (Rangers, Kilmarnock) 20
Dykes, J. 1938 (Hearts) 2

Easson, J. F. 1931 (Portsmouth) 3
Elliott, M. S. 1998 (Leicester C) 18
Ellis, J. 1892 (Mossend Swifts) 1
Evans, A. 1982 (Aston Villa) 4
Evans, R. 1949 (Celtic, Chelsea) 48
Ewart, J. 1921 (Bradford C) 1
Ewing, T. 1958 (Partick Thistle) 2

Farm, G. N. 1953 (Blackpool) 10
Ferguson, B. 1999 (Rangers, Blackburn R, Rangers) 45
Ferguson, D. 1988 (Rangers) 2
Ferguson, D. 1992 (Dundee U, Everton) 7
Ferguson, I. 1989 (Rangers) 9
Ferguson, J. 1874 (Vale of Leven) 6
Ferguson, R. 1966 (Kilmarnock) 7
Fernie, W. 1954 (Celtic) 12
Findlay, R. 1898 (Kilmarnock) 1
Fitchie, T. T. 1905 (Woolwich Arsenal, Queen's Park) 4
Flavell, R. 1947 (Airdrieonians) 2
Fleck, R. 1990 (Norwich C) 4
Fleming, C. 1954 (East Fife) 1
Fleming, J. W. 1929 (Rangers) 3
Fleming, R. 1886 (Morton) 1
Fletcher, D. B. 2004 (Manchester U, WBA) **68**
Fletcher, S. K. 2008 (Hibernian, Burnley,
  Wolverhampton W, Sunderland) **21**
Forbes, A. R. 1947 (Sheffield U, Arsenal) 14
Forbes, J. 1884 (Vale of Leven) 5
Ford, D. 1974 (Hearts) 3
Forrest, J. 1958 (Motherwell) 1
Forrest, J. 1966 (Rangers, Aberdeen) 5
Forrest, J. 2011 (Celtic) **10**
Forsyth, A. 1972 (Partick Thistle, Manchester U) 10

Forsyth, C. 2014 (Derby Co) **4**
Forsyth, R. C. 1964 (Kilmarnock) 4
Forsyth, T. 1971 (Motherwell, Rangers) 22
Fox, D. J. 2010 (Burnley, Southampton) 4
Foyers, R. 1893 (St Bernards) 2
Fraser, D. M. 1968 (WBA) 2
Fraser, J. 1891 (Moffat) 1
Fraser, M. J. E. 1880 (Queen's Park) 5
Fraser, J. 1907 (Dundee) 1
Fraser, W. 1955 (Sunderland) 2
Freedman, D. A. 2002 (Crystal Palace) 2
Fulton, W. 1884 (Abercorn) 1
Fyfe, J. H. 1895 (Third Lanark) 1

Gabriel, J. 1961 (Everton) 2
Gallacher, H. K. 1924 (Airdrieonians, Newcastle U,
  Chelsea, Derby Co) 20
Gallacher, K. W. 1988 (Dundee U, Coventry C,
  Blackburn R, Newcastle U) 53
Gallacher, P. 1935 (Sunderland) 1
Gallacher, P. 2002 (Dundee U) 8
Gallagher, P. 2004 (Blackburn R) 1
Galloway, M. 1992 (Celtic) 1
Galt, J. H. 1908 (Rangers) 2
Gardiner, I. 1958 (Motherwell) 1
Gardner, D. R. 1897 (Third Lanark) 1
Gardner, R. 1872 (Queen's Park, Clydesdale) 5
Gemmell, T. 1955 (St Mirren) 2
Gemmell, T. 1966 (Celtic) 18
Gemmill, A. 1971 (Derby Co, Nottingham F,
  Birmingham C) 43
Gemmill, S. 1995 (Nottingham F, Everton) 26
Gibb, W. 1873 (Clydesdale) 1
Gibson, D. W. 1963 (Leicester C) 7
Gibson, J. D. 1926 (Partick Thistle, Aston Villa) 8
Gibson, N. 1895 (Rangers, Partick Thistle) 14
Gilchrist, J. E. 1922 (Celtic) 1
Gilhooley, M. 1922 (Hull C) 1
Gilks, M. 2013 (Blackpool) 3
Gillespie, G. 1880 (Rangers, Queen's Park) 7
Gillespie, G. T. 1988 (Liverpool) 13
Gillespie, Jas 1898 (Third Lanark) 1
Gillespie, John 1896 (Queen's Park) 1
Gillespie, R. 1927 (Queen's Park) 4
Gillick, T. 1937 (Everton) 5
Gilmour, J. 1931 (Dundee) 1
Gilzean, A. J. 1964 (Dundee, Tottenham H) 22
Glass, S. 1999 (Newcastle U) 1
Glavin, R. 1977 (Celtic) 1
Glen, A. 1956 (Aberdeen) 2
Glen, R. 1895 (Renton, Hibernian) 3
Goodwillie, D. 2011 (Dundee U, Blackburn R) 3
Goram, A. L. 1986 (Oldham Ath, Hibernian, Rangers) 43
Gordon, C. A. 2004 (Hearts, Sunderland, Celtic) **43**
Gordon, J. E. 1912 (Rangers) 10
Gossland, J. 1884 (Rangers) 1
Goudie, J. 1884 (Abercorn) 1
Gough, C. R. 1983 (Dundee U, Tottenham H, Rangers) 61
Gould, J. 2000 (Celtic) 2
Gourlay, J. 1886 (Cambuslang) 2
Govan, J. 1948 (Hibernian) 6
Gow, D. R. 1888 (Rangers) 1
Gow, J. J. 1885 (Queen's Park) 1
Gow, J. R. 1888 (Rangers) 1
Graham, A. 1978 (Leeds U) 11
Graham, G. 1972 (Arsenal, Manchester U) 12
Graham, J. 1884 (Annbank) 1
Graham, J. A. 1921 (Arsenal) 1
Grant, J. 1959 (Hibernian) 2
Grant, P. 1989 (Celtic) 2
Gray, A. 1903 (Hibernian) 1
Gray, A. D. 2003 (Bradford C) 2
Gray, A. M. 1976 (Aston Villa, Wolverhampton W,
  Everton) 20
Gray, D. 1929 (Rangers) 10
Gray, E. 1969 (Leeds U) 12
Gray, F. T. 1976 (Leeds U, Nottingham F, Leeds U) 32
Gray, W. 1886 (Pollokshields Ath) 1
Green, A. 1971 (Blackpool, Newcastle U) 6
Greer, G. 2013 (Brighton & HA) **8**
Greig, J. 1964 (Rangers) 44

Lambie, J. A. 1886 (Queen's Park) — 3
Lambie, W. A. 1892 (Queen's Park) — 9
Lamont, W. 1885 (Pilgrims) — 1
Lang, A. 1880 (Dumbarton) — 1
Lang, J. J. 1876 (Clydesdale, Third Lanark) — 2
Latta, A. 1888 (Dumbarton) — 2
Law, D. 1959 (Huddersfield T, Manchester C, Torino, Manchester U, Manchester C) — 55
Law, G. 1910 (Rangers) — 3
Law, T. 1928 (Chelsea) — 2
Lawrence, J. 1911 (Newcastle U) — 1
Lawrence, T. 1963 (Liverpool) — 3
Lawson, D. 1923 (St Mirren) — 1
Leckie, R. 1872 (Queen's Park) — 1
Leggat, G. 1956 (Aberdeen, Fulham) — 18
Leighton, J. 1983 (Aberdeen, Manchester U, Hibernian, Aberdeen) — 91
Lennie, W. 1908 (Aberdeen) — 2
Lennox, R. 1967 (Celtic) — 10
Leslie, L. G. 1961 (Airdrieonians) — 5
Levein, C. 1990 (Hearts) — 16
Liddell, W. 1947 (Liverpool) — 28
Liddle, D. 1931 (East Fife) — 3
Lindsay, D. 1903 (St Mirren) — 1
Lindsay, J. 1880 (Dumbarton) — 8
Lindsay, J. 1888 (Renton) — 3
Linwood, A. B. 1950 (Clyde) — 1
Little, R. J. 1953 (Rangers) — 1
Livingstone, G. T. 1906 (Manchester C, Rangers) — 2
Lochhead, A. 1889 (Third Lanark) — 1
Logan, J. 1891 (Ayr) — 1
Logan, T. 1913 (Falkirk) — 1
Logie, J. T. 1953 (Arsenal) — 1
Loney, W. 1910 (Celtic) — 2
Long, H. 1947 (Clyde) — 1
Longair, W. 1894 (Dundee) — 1
Lorimer, P. 1970 (Leeds U) — 21
Love, A. 1931 (Aberdeen) — 3
Low, A. 1934 (Falkirk) — 1
Low, J. 1891 (Cambuslang) — 1
Low, T. P. 1897 (Rangers) — 1
Low, W. L. 1911 (Newcastle U) — 5
Lowe, J. 1887 (St Bernards) — 1
Lundie, J. 1886 (Hibernian) — 1
Lyall, J. 1905 (Sheffield W) — 1

McAdam, J. 1880 (Third Lanark) — 1
McAllister, B. 1997 (Wimbledon) — 3
McAllister, G. 1990 (Leicester C, Leeds U, Coventry C) — 57
McAllister, J. R. 2004 (Livingston) — 1
Macari, L. 1972 (Celtic, Manchester U) — 24
McArthur, D. 1895 (Celtic) — 3
McArthur, J. 2011 (Wigan Ath, Crystal Palace) — 20
McAtee, A. 1913 (Celtic) — 1
McAulay, J. 1884 (Arthurlie) — 1
McAulay, J. D. 1882 (Dumbarton) — 9
McAulay, R. 1932 (Rangers) — 2
Macauley, A. R. 1947 (Brentford, Arsenal) — 7
McAvennie, F. 1986 (West Ham U, Celtic) — 5
McBain, E. 1894 (St Mirren) — 1
McBain, N. 1922 (Manchester U, Everton) — 3
McBride, J. 1967 (Celtic) — 2
McBride, P. 1904 (Preston NE) — 6
McCall, A. 1888 (Renton) — 1
McCall, A. S. M. 1990 (Everton, Rangers) — 40
McCall, J. 1886 (Renton) — 5
McCalliog, J. 1967 (Sheffield W, Wolverhampton W) — 5
McCallum, N. 1888 (Renton) — 1
McCann, N. 1999 (Hearts, Rangers, Southampton) — 26
McCann, R. J. 1959 (Motherwell) — 5
McCartney, W. 1902 (Hibernian) — 1
McClair, B. 1987 (Celtic, Manchester U) — 30
McClory, A. 1927 (Motherwell) — 3
McCloy, P. 1924 (Ayr U) — 1
McCloy, P. 1973 (Rangers) — 4
McCoist, A. 1986 (Rangers, Kilmarnock) — 61
McColl, I. M. 1950 (Rangers) — 14
McColl, R. S. 1896 (Queen's Park, Newcastle U, Queen's Park) — 13
McColl, W. 1895 (Renton) — 1

McCombie, A. 1903 (Sunderland, Newcastle U) — 4
McCorkindale, J. 1891 (Partick Thistle) — 1
McCormack, R. 2008 (Motherwell, Cardiff C, Leeds U) — 11
McCormick, R. 1886 (Abercorn) — 1
McCrae, D. 1929 (St Mirren) — 2
McCreadie, A. 1893 (Rangers) — 2
McCreadie, E. G. 1965 (Chelsea) — 23
McCulloch, D. 1935 (Hearts, Brentford, Derby Co) — 7
McCulloch, L. 2005 (Wigan Ath, Rangers) — 18
MacDonald, A. 1976 (Rangers) — 1
McDonald, J. 1886 (Edinburgh University) — 1
McDonald, J. 1956 (Sunderland) — 2
MacDougall, E. J. 1975 (Norwich C) — 7
McDougall, J. 1877 (Vale of Leven) — 5
McDougall, J. 1926 (Airdrieonians) — 1
McDougall, J. 1931 (Liverpool) — 2
McEveley, J. 2008 (Derby Co) — 3
McFadden, J. 2002 (Motherwell, Everton, Birmingham C) — 48
McFadyen, W. 1934 (Motherwell) — 2
Macfarlane, A. 1904 (Dundee) — 5
Macfarlane, W. 1947 (Hearts) — 1
McFarlane, R. 1896 (Greenock Morton) — 1
McGarr, E. 1970 (Aberdeen) — 2
McGarvey, F. P. 1979 (Liverpool, Celtic) — 7
McGeoch, A. 1876 (Dumbreck) — 4
McGhee, J. 1886 (Hibernian) — 1
McGhee, M. 1983 (Aberdeen) — 4
McGinlay, J. 1994 (Bolton W) — 13
McGonagle, W. 1933 (Celtic) — 6
McGrain, D. 1973 (Celtic) — 62
McGregor, A. J. 2007 (Rangers, Besiktas, Hull C) — 33
McGregor, J. C. 1877 (Vale of Leven) — 4
McGrory, J. 1928 (Celtic) — 7
McGrory, J. E. 1965 (Kilmarnock) — 3
McGuire, W. 1881 (Beith) — 2
McGurk, F. 1934 (Birmingham) — 1
McHardy, H. 1885 (Rangers) — 1
McInally, A. 1989 (Aston Villa, Bayern Munich) — 8
McInally, J. 1987 (Dundee U) — 10
McInally, T. B. 1926 (Celtic) — 2
McInnes, D. 2003 (WBA) — 2
McInnes, T. 1889 (Cowlairs) — 1
McIntosh, W. 1905 (Third Lanark) — 1
McIntyre, A. 1878 (Vale of Leven) — 2
McIntyre, H. 1880 (Rangers) — 1
McIntyre, J. 1884 (Rangers) — 1
MacKay, D. 1959 (Celtic) — 14
Mackay, D. C. 1957 (Hearts, Tottenham H) — 22
Mackay, G. 1988 (Hearts) — 4
Mackay, M. 2004 (Norwich C) — 5
McKay, J. 1924 (Blackburn R) — 1
McKay, R. 1928 (Newcastle U) — 1
McKean, R. 1976 (Rangers) — 1
McKenzie, D. 1938 (Brentford) — 1
Mackenzie, J. A. 1954 (Partick Thistle) — 9
McKeown, M. 1889 (Celtic) — 2
McKie, J. 1898 (East Stirling) — 1
McKillop, T. R. 1938 (Rangers) — 1
McKimmie, S. 1989 (Aberdeen) — 40
McKinlay, D. 1922 (Liverpool) — 2
McKinlay, T. 1996 (Celtic) — 22
McKinlay, W. 1994 (Dundee U, Blackburn R) — 29
McKinnon, A. 1874 (Queen's Park) — 1
McKinnon, R. 1966 (Rangers) — 28
McKinnon, R. 1994 (Motherwell) — 3
MacKinnon, W. 1883 (Dumbarton) — 9
MacKinnon, W. W. 1872 (Queen's Park) — 9
McLaren, A. 1929 (St Johnstone) — 5
McLaren, A. 1947 (Preston NE) — 4
McLaren, A. 1992 (Hearts, Rangers) — 24
McLaren, A. 2001 (Kilmarnock) — 1
McLaren, J. 1888 (Hibernian, Celtic) — 3
McLean, A. 1926 (Celtic) — 4
McLean, D. 1896 (St Bernards) — 2
McLean, D. 1912 (Sheffield W) — 1
McLean, G. 1968 (Dundee) — 1
McLean, T. 1969 (Kilmarnock) — 6
McLeish, A. 1980 (Aberdeen) — 77
McLeod, D. 1905 (Celtic) — 4
McLeod, J. 1888 (Dumbarton) — 5

MacLeod, J. M. 1961 (Hibernian)	4	Menzies, A. 1906 (Hearts)	1
MacLeod, M. 1985 (Celtic, Borussia Dortmund,		Mercer, R. 1912 (Hearts)	2
Hibernian)	20	Middleton, R. 1930 (Cowdenbeath)	1
McLeod, W. 1886 (Cowlairs)	1	Millar, J. 1897 (Rangers)	3
McLintock, A. 1875 (Vale of Leven)	3	Millar, J. 1963 (Rangers)	2
McLintock, F. 1963 (Leicester C, Arsenal)	9	Miller, A. 1939 (Hearts)	1
McLuckie, J. S. 1934 (Manchester C)	1	Miller, C. 2001 (Dundee U)	1
McMahon, A. 1892 (Celtic)	6	Miller, J. 1931 (St Mirren)	5
McManus, S. 2007 (Celtic, Middlesbrough)	26	Miller, K. 2001 (Rangers, Wolverhampton W, Celtic,	
McMenemy, J. 1905 (Celtic)	12	Derby Co, Rangers, Bursaspor, Cardiff C, Vancouver	
McMenemy, J. 1934 (Motherwell)	1	Whitecaps)	69
McMillan, I. L. 1952 (Airdrieonians, Rangers)	6	Miller, L. 2006 (Dundee U, Aberdeen)	3
McMillan, J. 1897 (St Bernards)	1	Miller, P. 1882 (Dumbarton)	3
McMillan, T. 1887 (Dumbarton)	1	Miller, T. 1920 (Liverpool, Manchester U)	3
McMullan, J. 1920 (Partick Thistle, Manchester C)	16	Miller, W. 1876 (Third Lanark)	1
McNab, A. 1921 (Morton)	2	Miller, W. 1947 (Celtic)	6
McNab, A. 1937 (Sunderland, WBA)	2	Miller, W. 1975 (Aberdeen)	65
McNab, C. D. 1931 (Dundee)	6	Mills, W. 1936 (Aberdeen)	3
McNab, J. S. 1923 (Liverpool)	1	Milne, J. V. 1938 (Middlesbrough)	2
McNair, A. 1906 (Celtic)	15	Mitchell, D. 1890 (Rangers)	5
McNamara, J. 1997 (Celtic, Wolverhampton W)	33	Mitchell, J. 1908 (Kilmarnock)	3
McNamee, D. 2004 (Livingston)	4	Mitchell, R. C. 1951 (Newcastle U)	2
McNaught, W. 1951 (Raith R)	5	Mochan, N. 1954 (Celtic)	3
McNaughton, K. 2002 (Aberdeen, Cardiff C)	4	Moir, W. 1950 (Bolton W)	1
McNeill, W. 1961 (Celtic)	29	Moncur, R. 1968 (Newcastle U)	16
McNiel, H. 1874 (Queen's Park)	10	Morgan, H. 1898 (St Mirren, Liverpool)	2
McNiel, M. 1876 (Rangers)	2	Morgan, W. 1968 (Burnley, Manchester U)	21
McPhail, J. 1950 (Celtic)	5	Morris, D. 1923 (Raith R)	6
McPhail, R. 1927 (Airdrieonians, Rangers)	17	Morris, H. 1950 (East Fife)	1
McPherson, D. 1892 (Kilmarnock)	1	**Morrison, J. C. 2008 (WBA)**	**39**
McPherson, D. 1989 (Hearts, Rangers)	27	Morrison, T. 1927 (St Mirren)	1
McPherson, J. 1875 (Clydesdale)	1	Morton, A. L. 1920 (Queen's Park, Rangers)	31
McPherson, J. 1879 (Vale of Leven)	8	Morton, H. A. 1929 (Kilmarnock)	2
McPherson, J. 1888 (Kilmarnock, Cowlairs, Rangers)	9	Mudie, J. K. 1957 (Blackpool)	17
McPherson, J. 1891 (Hearts)	1	Muir, W. 1907 (Dundee)	1
McPherson, R. 1882 (Arthurlie)	1	Muirhead, T. A. 1922 (Rangers)	8
McQueen, G. 1974 (Leeds U, Manchester U)	30	**Mulgrew, C. P. 2012 (Celtic)**	**18**
McQueen, M. 1890 (Leith Ath)	2	Mulhall, G. 1960 (Aberdeen, Sunderland)	3
McRorie, D. M. 1931 (Morton)	1	Munro, A. D. 1937 (Hearts, Blackpool)	3
McSpadyen, A. 1939 (Partick Thistle)	2	Munro, F. M. 1971 (Wolverhampton W)	9
McStay, P. 1984 (Celtic)	76	Munro, I. 1979 (St Mirren)	7
McStay, W. 1921 (Celtic)	13	Munro, N. 1888 (Abercorn)	2
McSwegan, G. 2000 (Hearts)	2	Murdoch, J. 1931 (Motherwell)	1
McTavish, J. 1910 (Falkirk)	1	Murdoch, R. 1966 (Celtic)	12
McWattie, G. C. 1901 (Queen's Park)	2	Murphy, F. 1938 (Celtic)	1
McWilliam, P. 1905 (Newcastle U)	8	Murray, I. 2003 (Hibernian, Rangers)	6
Mackay-Steven, G. 2013 (Dundee U)	1	Murray, J. 1895 (Renton)	1
Mackail-Smith, C. 2011 (Peterborough U,		Murray, J. 1958 (Hearts)	5
Brighton & HA)	7	Murray, J. W. 1890 (Vale of Leven)	1
Mackie, J. C. 2011 (QPR)	9	Murray, P. 1896 (Hibernian)	2
Madden, J. 1893 (Celtic)	2	Murray, S. 1972 (Aberdeen)	1
Maguire, C. 2011 (Aberdeen)	2	Murty, G. S. 2004 (Reading)	4
Main, F. R. 1938 (Rangers)	1	Mutch, G. 1938 (Preston NE)	1
Main, J. 1909 (Hibernian)	1		
Maley, W. 1893 (Celtic)	2	**Naismith, S. J. 2007 (Kilmarnock, Rangers, Everton)**	**38**
Maloney, S. R. 2006 (Celtic, Aston Villa, Celtic,		Napier, C. E. 1932 (Celtic, Derby Co)	5
Wigan Ath, Chicago Fire)	**41**	Narey, D. 1977 (Dundee U)	35
Malpas, M. 1984 (Dundee U)	55	Naysmith, G. A. 2000 (Hearts, Everton, Sheffield U)	46
Marshall, D. J. 2005 (Celtic, Cardiff C)	**19**	Neil, R. G. 1896 (Hibernian, Rangers)	2
Marshall, G. 1992 (Celtic)	1	Neill, R. W. 1876 (Queen's Park)	5
Marshall, H. 1899 (Celtic)	2	Neilson, R. 2007 (Hearts)	1
Marshall, J. 1885 (Third Lanark)	4	Nellies, P. 1913 (Hearts)	2
Marshall, J. 1921 (Middlesbrough, Llanelly)	7	Nelson, J. 1925 (Cardiff C)	4
Marshall, J. 1932 (Rangers)	3	Nevin, P. K. F. 1986 (Chelsea, Everton, Tranmere R)	28
Marshall, R. W. 1892 (Rangers)	2	Niblo, T. D. 1904 (Aston Villa)	1
Martin, B. 1995 (Motherwell)	2	Nibloe, J. 1929 (Kilmarnock)	11
Martin, C. H. 2014 (Derby Co)	**5**	Nicholas, C. 1983 (Celtic, Arsenal, Aberdeen)	20
Martin, F. 1954 (Aberdeen)	6	Nicholson, B. 2001 (Dunfermline Ath)	3
Martin, N. 1965 (Hibernian, Sunderland)	3	Nicol, S. 1985 (Liverpool)	27
Martin, R. K. A. 2011 (Norwich C)	**19**	Nisbet, J. 1929 (Ayr U)	3
Martis, J. 1961 (Motherwell)	1	Niven, J. B. 1885 (Moffat)	1
Mason, J. 1949 (Third Lanark)	7		
Massie, A. 1932 (Hearts, Aston Villa)	18	O'Connor, G. 2002 (Hibernian, Lokomotiv Moscow,	
Masson, D. S. 1976 (QPR, Derby Co)	17	Birmingham C)	16
Mathers, D. 1954 (Partick Thistle)	1	O'Donnell, F. 1937 (Preston NE, Blackpool)	6
Matteo, D. 2001 (Leeds U)	6	O'Donnell, P. 1994 (Motherwell)	1
Maxwell, W. S. 1898 (Stoke C)	1	Ogilvie, D. H. 1934 (Motherwell)	1
May, J. 1906 (Rangers)	5	O'Hare, J. 1970 (Derby Co)	13
May, S. 2015 (Sheffield W)	**1**	O'Neil, B. 1996 (Celtic, Wolfsburg, Derby Co,	
Meechan, P. 1896 (Celtic)	1	Preston NE)	7
Meiklejohn, D. D. 1922 (Rangers)	15	O'Neil, J. 2001 (Hibernian)	1

Ormond, W. E. 1954 (Hibernian) — 6
O'Rourke, F. 1907 (Airdrieonians) — 1
Orr, J. 1892 (Kilmarnock) — 1
Orr, R. 1902 (Newcastle U) — 2
Orr, T. 1952 (Morton) — 2
Orr, W. 1900 (Celtic) — 3
Orrock, R. 1913 (Falkirk) — 1
Oswald, J. 1889 (Third Lanark, St Bernards, Rangers) — 3

Parker, A. H. 1955 (Falkirk, Everton) — 15
Parlane, D. 1973 (Rangers) — 12
Parlane, R. 1878 (Vale of Leven) — 3
Paterson, G. D. 1939 (Celtic) — 1
Paterson, J. 1920 (Leicester C) — 1
Paterson, J. 1931 (Cowdenbeath) — 3
Paton, A. 1952 (Motherwell) — 2
Paton, D. 1896 (St Bernards) — 1
Paton, M. 1883 (Dumbarton) — 5
Paton, R. 1879 (Vale of Leven) — 2
Patrick, J. 1897 (St Mirren) — 2
Paul, H. McD. 1909 (Queen's Park) — 3
Paul, W. 1888 (Partick Thistle) — 3
Paul, W. 1891 (Dykebar) — 1
Pearson, S. P. 2004 (Motherwell, Celtic, Derby Co) — 10
Pearson, T. 1947 (Newcastle U) — 2
Penman, A. 1966 (Dundee) — 1
Pettigrew, W. 1976 (Motherwell) — 5
Phillips, J. 1877 (Queen's Park) — 3
Phillips, M. 2012 (Blackpool) — 2
Plenderleith, J. B. 1961 (Manchester C) — 1
Porteous, W. 1903 (Hearts) — 1
Pressley, S. J. 2000 (Hearts) — 32
Pringle, C. 1921 (St Mirren) — 1
Provan, D. 1964 (Rangers) — 5
Provan, D. 1980 (Celtic) — 10
Pursell, P. 1914 (Queen's Park) — 1

Quashie, N. F. 2004 (Portsmouth, Southampton, WBA) — 14
Quinn, J. 1905 (Celtic) — 11
Quinn, P. 1961 (Motherwell) — 4

Rae, G. 2001 (Dundee, Rangers, Cardiff C) — 14
Rae, J. 1889 (Third Lanark) — 2
Raeside, J. S. 1906 (Third Lanark) — 1
Raisbeck, A. G. 1900 (Liverpool) — 8
Rankin, G. 1890 (Vale of Leven) — 2
Rankin, R. 1929 (St Mirren) — 3
Redpath, W. 1949 (Motherwell) — 9
Reid, J. G. 1914 (Airdrieonians) — 3
Reid, R. 1938 (Brentford) — 2
Reid, W. 1911 (Rangers) — 9
Reilly, L. 1949 (Hibernian) — 38
Rennie, H. G. 1900 (Hearts, Hibernian) — 13
Renny-Tailyour, H. W. 1873 (Royal Engineers) — 1
Rhind, A. 1872 (Queen's Park) — 1
Rhodes, J. L. 2012 (Huddersfield T, Blackburn R) — 13
Richmond, A. 1906 (Queen's Park) — 1
Richmond, J. T. 1877 (Clydesdale, Queen's Park) — 3
Ring, T. 1953 (Clyde) — 12
Rioch, B. D. 1975 (Derby Co, Everton, Derby Co) — 24
Riordan, D. G. 2006 (Hibernian) — 3
Ritchie, A. 1891 (East Stirlingshire) — 1
Ritchie, H. 1923 (Hibernian) — 3
Ritchie, J. 1897 (Queen's Park) — 1
Ritchie, M. T. 2015 (Bournemouth) — 4
Ritchie, P. S. 1999 (Hearts, Bolton W, Walsall) — 7
Ritchie, W. 1962 (Rangers) — 1
Robb, D. T. 1971 (Aberdeen) — 5
Robb, W. 1926 (Rangers, Hibernian) — 5
Robertson, A. 1955 (Clyde) — 2
Robertson, A. 2014 (Dundee U, Hull C) — 6
Robertson, D. 1992 (Rangers) — 3
Robertson, G. 1910 (Motherwell, Sheffield W) — 4
Robertson, G. 1938 (Kilmarnock) — 1
Robertson, H. 1962 (Dundee) — 1
Robertson, J. 1931 (Dundee) — 2
Robertson, J. 1991 (Hearts) — 16
Robertson, J. N. 1978 (Nottingham F, Derby Co) — 28
Robertson, J. G. 1965 (Tottenham H) — 1
Robertson, J. T. 1898 (Everton, Southampton, Rangers) — 16
Robertson, P. 1903 (Dundee) — 1

Robertson, S. 2009 (Dundee U) — 2
Robertson, T. 1889 (Queen's Park) — 4
Robertson, T. 1898 (Hearts) — 1
Robertson, W. 1887 (Dumbarton) — 2
Robinson, R. 1974 (Dundee) — 4
Robson, B. G. G. 2008 (Dundee U, Celtic, Middlesbrough) — 17
Ross, M. 2002 (Rangers) — 13
Rough, A. 1976 (Partick Thistle, Hibernian) — 53
Rougvie, D. 1984 (Aberdeen) — 1
Rowan, A. 1880 (Caledonian, Queen's Park) — 2
Russell, D. 1895 (Hearts, Celtic) — 6
Russell, J. 1890 (Cambuslang) — 1
Russell, J. S. S. 2015 (Derby Co) — 3
Russell, W. F. 1924 (Airdrieonians) — 2
Rutherford, E. 1948 (Rangers) — 1

St John, I. 1959 (Motherwell, Liverpool) — 21
Saunders, S. 2011 (Motherwell) — 1
Sawers, W. 1895 (Dundee) — 1
Scarff, P. 1931 (Celtic) — 1
Schaedler, E. 1974 (Hibernian) — 1
Scott, A. S. 1957 (Rangers, Everton) — 16
Scott, J. 1966 (Hibernian) — 1
Scott, J. 1971 (Dundee) — 2
Scott, M. 1898 (Airdrieonians) — 1
Scott, R. 1894 (Airdrieonians) — 1
Scoular, J. 1951 (Portsmouth) — 9
Sellar, W. 1885 (Battlefield, Queen's Park) — 9
Semple, W. 1886 (Cambuslang) — 1
Severin, S. D. 2002 (Hearts, Aberdeen) — 15
Shankly, W. 1938 (Preston NE) — 5
Sharp, G. M. 1985 (Everton) — 12
Sharp, J. 1904 (Dundee, Woolwich Arsenal, Fulham) — 5
Shaw, D. 1947 (Hibernian) — 8
Shaw, F. W. 1884 (Pollokshields Ath) — 2
Shaw, J. 1947 (Rangers) — 4
Shearer, D. 1994 (Aberdeen) — 7
Shearer, R. 1961 (Rangers) — 4
Shinnie, A. M. 2013 (Inverness CT) — 1
Sillars, D. C. 1891 (Queen's Park) — 5
Simpson, J. 1895 (Third Lanark) — 3
Simpson, J. 1935 (Rangers) — 14
Simpson, N. 1983 (Aberdeen) — 5
Simpson, R. C. 1967 (Celtic) — 5
Sinclair, G. L. 1910 (Hearts) — 3
Sinclair, J. W. E. 1966 (Leicester C) — 1
Skene, L. H. 1904 (Queen's Park) — 1
Sloan, T. 1904 (Third Lanark) — 1
Smellie, R. 1887 (Queen's Park) — 6
Smith, A. 1898 (Rangers) — 20
Smith, D. 1966 (Aberdeen, Rangers) — 2
Smith, G. 1947 (Hibernian) — 18
Smith, H. G. 1988 (Hearts) — 3
Smith, J. 1924 (Ayr U) — 1
Smith, J. 1935 (Rangers) — 2
Smith, J. 1968 (Aberdeen, Newcastle U) — 4
Smith, J. 2003 (Celtic) — 2
Smith, J. E. 1959 (Celtic) — 2
Smith, Jas 1872 (Queen's Park) — 1
Smith, John 1877 (Mauchline, Edinburgh University, Queen's Park) — 10
Smith, N. 1897 (Rangers) — 12
Smith, R. 1872 (Queen's Park) — 2
Smith, T. M. 1934 (Kilmarnock, Preston NE) — 2
Snodgrass, R. 2011 (Leeds U, Norwich C) — 15
Somers, P. 1905 (Celtic) — 4
Somers, W. S. 1879 (Third Lanark, Queen's Park) — 3
Somerville, G. 1886 (Queen's Park) — 1
Souness, G. J. 1975 (Middlesbrough, Liverpool, Sampdoria) — 54
Speedie, D. R. 1985 (Chelsea, Coventry C) — 10
Speedie, F. 1903 (Rangers) — 3
Speirs, J. H. 1908 (Rangers) — 1
Spencer, J. 1995 (Chelsea, QPR) — 14
Stanton, P. 1966 (Hibernian) — 16
Stark, J. 1909 (Rangers) — 2
Steel, W. 1947 (Morton, Derby Co, Dundee) — 30
Steele, D. M. 1923 (Huddersfield) — 3
Stein, C. 1969 (Rangers, Coventry C) — 21
Stephen, J. F. 1947 (Bradford) — 2

Stevenson, G. 1928 (Motherwell)	12
Stewart, A. 1888 (Queen's Park)	2
Stewart, A. 1894 (Third Lanark)	1
Stewart, D. 1888 (Dumbarton)	1
Stewart, D. 1893 (Queen's Park)	3
Stewart, D. S. 1978 (Leeds U)	1
Stewart, G. 1906 (Hibernian, Manchester C)	4
Stewart, J. 1977 (Kilmarnock, Middlesbrough)	2
Stewart, M. J. 2002 (Manchester U, Hearts)	4
Stewart, R. 1981 (West Ham U)	10
Stewart, W. G. 1898 (Queen's Park)	2
Stockdale, R. K. 2002 (Middlesbrough)	5
Storrier, D. 1899 (Celtic)	3
Strachan, G. D. 1980 (Aberdeen, Manchester U, Leeds U)	50
Sturrock, P. 1981 (Dundee U)	20
Sullivan, N. 1997 (Wimbledon, Tottenham H)	28
Summers, W. 1926 (St Mirren)	1
Symon, J. S. 1939 (Rangers)	1
Tait, T. S. 1911 (Sunderland)	1
Taylor, J. 1872 (Queen's Park)	6
Taylor, J. D. 1892 (Dumbarton, St Mirren)	4
Taylor, W. 1892 (Hearts)	1
Teale, G. 2006 (Wigan Ath, Derby Co)	13
Telfer, P. N. 2000 (Coventry C)	1
Telfer, W. 1933 (Motherwell)	2
Telfer, W. D. 1954 (St Mirren)	1
Templeton, R. 1902 (Aston Villa, Newcastle U, Woolwich Arsenal, Kilmarnock)	11
Thompson, S. 2002 (Dundee U, Rangers)	16
Thomson, A. 1886 (Arthurlie)	1
Thomson, A. 1889 (Third Lanark)	1
Thomson, A. 1909 (Airdrieonians)	1
Thomson, A. 1926 (Celtic)	3
Thomson, C. 1904 (Hearts, Sunderland)	21
Thomson, C. 1937 (Sunderland)	1
Thomson, D. 1920 (Dundee)	1
Thomson, J. 1930 (Celtic)	4
Thomson, J. J. 1872 (Queen's Park)	3
Thomson, J. R. 1933 (Everton)	1
Thomson, K. 2009 (Rangers, Middlesbrough)	3
Thomson, R. 1932 (Celtic)	1
Thomson, R. W. 1927 (Falkirk)	1
Thomson, S. 1884 (Rangers)	2
Thomson, W. 1892 (Dumbarton)	4
Thomson, W. 1896 (Dundee)	1
Thomson, W. 1980 (St Mirren)	7
Thornton, W. 1947 (Rangers)	7
Toner, W. 1959 (Kilmarnock)	2
Townsley, T. 1926 (Falkirk)	1
Troup, A. 1920 (Dundee, Everton)	5
Turnbull, E. 1948 (Hibernian)	8
Turner, T. 1884 (Arthurlie)	1
Turner, W. 1885 (Pollokshields Ath)	2
Ure, J. F. 1962 (Dundee, Arsenal)	11
Urquhart, D. 1934 (Hibernian)	1
Vallance, T. 1877 (Rangers)	7
Venters, A. 1934 (Cowdenbeath, Rangers)	3
Waddell, T. S. 1891 (Queen's Park)	6
Waddell, W. 1947 (Rangers)	17
Wales, H. M. 1933 (Motherwell)	1
Walker, A. 1988 (Celtic)	3
Walker, F. 1922 (Third Lanark)	1
Walker, G. 1930 (St Mirren)	4
Walker, J. 1895 (Hearts, Rangers)	5

Walker, J. 1911 (Swindon T)	9
Walker, J. N. 1993 (Hearts, Partick Thistle)	2
Walker, R. 1900 (Hearts)	29
Walker, T. 1935 (Hearts)	20
Walker, W. 1909 (Clyde)	2
Wallace, I. A. 1978 (Coventry C)	3
Wallace, L. 2010 (Hearts, Rangers)	8
Wallace, R. 2010 (Preston NE)	1
Wallace, W. S. B. 1965 (Hearts, Celtic)	7
Wardhaugh, J. 1955 (Hearts)	2
Wark, J. 1979 (Ipswich T, Liverpool)	28
Watson, A. 1881 (Queen's Park)	3
Watson, J. 1903 (Sunderland, Middlesbrough)	6
Watson, J. 1948 (Motherwell, Huddersfield T)	2
Watson, J. A. K. 1878 (Rangers)	1
Watson, P. R. 1934 (Blackpool)	1
Watson, R. 1971 (Motherwell)	1
Watson, W. 1898 (Falkirk)	1
Watt, F. 1889 (Kilbirnie)	4
Watt, W. W. 1887 (Queen's Park)	1
Waugh, W. 1938 (Hearts)	1
Webster, A. 2003 (Hearts, Dundee U, Hearts)	28
Weir, A. 1959 (Motherwell)	6
Weir, D. G. 1997 (Hearts, Everton, Rangers)	69
Weir, J. 1887 (Third Lanark)	1
Weir, J. B. 1872 (Queen's Park)	4
Weir, P. 1980 (St Mirren, Aberdeen)	6
White, John 1922 (Albion R, Hearts)	2
White, J. A. 1959 (Falkirk, Tottenham H)	22
White, W. 1907 (Bolton W)	2
Whitelaw, A. 1887 (Vale of Leven)	2
Whittaker, S. G. 2010 (Rangers, Norwich C)	**29**
Whyte, D. 1988 (Celtic, Middlesbrough, Aberdeen)	12
Wilkie, L. 2002 (Dundee)	11
Williams, G. 2002 (Nottingham F)	5
Wilson, A. 1907 (Sheffield W)	6
Wilson, A. 1954 (Portsmouth)	1
Wilson, A. N. 1920 (Dunfermline, Middlesbrough)	12
Wilson, D. 1900 (Queen's Park)	1
Wilson, D. 1913 (Oldham Ath)	1
Wilson, D. 1961 (Rangers)	22
Wilson, D. 2011 (Liverpool)	5
Wilson, G. W. 1904 (Hearts, Everton, Newcastle U)	6
Wilson, Hugh 1890 (Newmilns, Sunderland, Third Lanark)	4
Wilson, I. A. 1987 (Leicester C, Everton)	5
Wilson, J. 1888 (Vale of Leven)	4
Wilson, M. 2011 (Celtic)	1
Wilson, P. 1926 (Celtic)	4
Wilson, P. 1975 (Celtic)	1
Wilson, R. P. 1972 (Arsenal)	2
Winters, R. 1999 (Aberdeen)	1
Wiseman, W. 1927 (Queen's Park)	2
Wood, G. 1979 (Everton, Arsenal)	4
Woodburn, W. A. 1947 (Rangers)	24
Wotherspoon, D. N. 1872 (Queen's Park)	2
Wright, K. 1992 (Hibernian)	1
Wright, S. 1993 (Aberdeen)	2
Wright, T. 1953 (Sunderland)	3
Wylie, T. G. 1890 (Rangers)	1
Yeats, R. 1965 (Liverpool)	2
Yorston, B. C. 1931 (Aberdeen)	1
Yorston, H. 1955 (Aberdeen)	1
Young, A. 1905 (Everton)	2
Young, A. 1960 (Hearts, Everton)	8
Young, G. L. 1947 (Rangers)	53
Young, J. 1906 (Celtic)	1
Younger, T. 1955 (Hibernian, Liverpool)	24

WALES

Adams, H. 1882 (Berwyn R, Druids) 4
Aizlewood, M. 1986 (Charlton Ath, Leeds U, Bradford
C, Bristol C, Cardiff C) 39
Allchurch, I. J. 1951 (Swansea T, Newcastle U, Cardiff
C, Swansea T) 68
Allchurch, L. 1955 (Swansea T, Sheffield U) 11
Allen, B. W. 1951 (Coventry C) 2
Allen, J. M. 2009 (Swansea C, Liverpool) 21
Allen, M. 1986 (Watford, Norwich C, Millwall,
Newcastle U) 14
Arridge, S. 1892 (Bootle, Everton, New Brighton Tower) 8
Astley, D. J. 1931 (Charlton Ath, Aston Villa, Derby Co,
Blackpool) 13
Atherton, R. W. 1899 (Hibernian, Middlesbrough) 9

Bailiff, W. E. 1913 (Llanelly) 4
Baker, C. W. 1958 (Cardiff C) 7
Baker, W. G. 1948 (Cardiff C) 1
**Bale, G. F. 2006 (Southampton, Tottenham H,
Real Madrid) 50**
Bamford, T. 1931 (Wrexham) 5
Barnard, D. S. 1998 (Barnsley, Grimsby T) 22
Barnes, W. 1948 (Arsenal) 22
Bartley, T. 1898 (Glossop NE) 1
Bastock, A. M. 1892 (Shrewsbury T) 1
Beadles, G. H. 1925 (Cardiff C) 2
Bell, W. S. 1881 (Shrewsbury Engineers, Crewe Alex) 5
Bellamy, C. D. 1998 (Norwich C, Coventry C,
Newcastle U, Blackburn R, Liverpool, West Ham U,
Manchester C, Liverpool, Cardiff C) 78
Bennion, S. R. 1926 (Manchester U) 10
Berry, G. F. 1979 (Wolverhampton W, Stoke C) 5
Blackmore, C. G. 1985 (Manchester U, Middlesbrough) 39
Blake, D. J. 2011 (Cardiff C, Crystal Palace) 14
Blake, N. A. 1994 (Sheffield U, Bolton W, Blackburn R,
Wolverhampton W) 29
Blew, H. 1899 (Wrexham) 22
Boden, T. 1880 (Wrexham) 1
Bodin, P. J. 1990 (Swindon T, Crystal Palace,
Swindon T) 23
Boulter, L. M. 1939 (Brentford) 1
Bowdler, H. E. 1893 (Shrewsbury T) 1
Bowdler, J. C. H. 1890 (Shrewsbury T,
Wolverhampton W, Shrewsbury T) 4
Bowen, D. L. 1955 (Arsenal) 19
Bowen, E. 1880 (Druids) 2
Bowen, J. P. 1994 (Swansea C, Birmingham C) 2
Bowen, M. R. 1986 (Tottenham H, Norwich C,
West Ham U) 41
Bowsher, S. J. 1929 (Burnley) 1
Boyle, T. 1981 (Crystal Palace) 1
Bradley, M. S. 2010 (Walsall) 1
Britten, T. J. 1878 (Parkgrove, Presteigne) 2
Brookes, S. J. 1900 (Llandudno) 2
Brown, A. I. 1926 (Aberdare Ath) 1
Brown, J. R. 2006 (Gillingham, Blackburn R, Aberdeen)
3
Browning, M. T. 1996 (Bristol R, Huddersfield T) 5
Bryan, T. 1886 (Oswestry) 2
Buckland, T. 1899 (Bangor) 1
Burgess, W. A. R. 1947 (Tottenham H) 32
Burke, T. 1883 (Wrexham, Newton Heath) 8
Burnett, T. B. 1877 (Ruabon) 1
Burton, A. D. 1963 (Norwich C, Newcastle U) 9
Butler, J. 1893 (Chirk) 3
Butler, W. T. 1900 (Druids) 2

Cartwright, L. 1974 (Coventry C, Wrexham) 7
Carty, T. See McCarthy (Wrexham).
Challen, J. B. 1887 (Corinthians, Wellingborough GS) 4
Chapman, T. 1894 (Newtown, Manchester C, Grimsby T)
7
Charles, J. M. 1981 (Swansea C, QPR, Oxford U) 19
Charles, M. 1955 (Swansea T, Arsenal, Cardiff C) 31
Charles, W. J. 1950 (Leeds U, Juventus, Leeds U,
Cardiff C) 38
Chester, J. G. 2014 (Hull C) 6

Church, S. R. 2009 (Reading, Charlton Ath) 29
Clarke, R. J. 1949 (Manchester C) 22
Coleman, C. 1992 (Crystal Palace, Blackburn R, Fulham) 32
Collier, D. J. 1921 (Grimsby T) 1
Collins, D. L. 2005 (Sunderland, Stoke C) 12
Collins, J. M. 2004 (Cardiff C, West Ham U, Aston Villa,
West Ham U) 44
Collins, W. S. 1931 (Llanelly) 1
Collison, J. D. 2008 (West Ham U) 16
Conde, C. 1884 (Chirk) 3
Cook, F. C. 1925 (Newport Co, Portsmouth) 8
Cornforth, J. M. 1995 (Swansea C) 2
**Cotterill, D. R. G. B. 2006 (Bristol C, Wigan Ath,
Sheffield U, Swansea C, Doncaster R,
Birmingham C) 22**
Coyne, D. 1996 (Tranmere R, Grimsby T, Leicester C,
Burnley, Tranmere R) 16
Crofts, A. L. 2006 (Gillingham, Brighton & HA,
Norwich C, Brighton & HA, Bolton W) 27
Crompton, W. 1931 (Wrexham) 3
Cross, E. A. 1876 (Wrexham) 2
Crosse, K. 1879 (Druids) 3
Crossley, M. G. 1997 (Nottingham F, Middlesbrough,
Fulham) 8
Crowe, V. H. 1959 (Aston Villa) 16
Cumner, R. H. 1939 (Arsenal) 3
Curtis, A. T. 1976 (Swansea C, Leeds U, Swansea C,
Southampton, Cardiff C) 35
Curtis, E. R. 1928 (Cardiff C, Birmingham) 3

Daniel, R. W. 1951 (Arsenal, Sunderland) 21
Darvell, S. 1897 (Oxford University) 2
Davies, A. 1876 (Wrexham) 2
Davies, A. 1904 (Druids, Middlesbrough) 2
Davies, A. 1983 (Manchester U, Newcastle U,
Swansea C, Bradford C) 13
Davies, A. O. 1885 (Barmouth, Swifts, Wrexham,
Crewe Alex) 9
Davies, A. R. 2006 (Yeovil T) 1
Davies, A. T. 1891 (Shrewsbury T) 1
Davies, B. T. 2013 (Swansea C, Tottenham H) 13
Davies, C. 1972 (Charlton Ath) 1
Davies, C. M. 2006 (Oxford U, Verona, Oldham Ath,
Barnsley) 7
Davies, D. 1904 (Bolton W) 3
Davies, D. C. 1899 (Brecon, Hereford) 2
Davies, D. W. 1912 (Treharris, Oldham Ath) 2
Davies, E. Lloyd 1904 (Stoke, Northampton T) 16
Davies, E. R. 1953 (Newcastle U) 6
Davies, G. 1980 (Fulham, Manchester C) 16
Davies, Rev. H. 1928 (Wrexham) 1
Davies, Idwal 1923 (Liverpool Marine) 1
Davies, J. E. 1885 (Oswestry) 1
Davies, Jas 1878 (Wrexham) 1
Davies, John 1879 (Wrexham) 1
Davies, Jos 1888 (Newton Heath, Wolverhampton W) 7
Davies, Jos 1889 (Everton, Chirk, Ardwick, Sheffield U,
Manchester C, Millwall, Reading) 11
Davies, J. P. 1883 (Druids) 2
Davies, Ll. 1907 (Wrexham, Everton, Wrexham) 13
Davies, L. S. 1922 (Cardiff C) 23
Davies, O. 1890 (Wrexham) 1
Davies, R. 1883 (Wrexham) 3
Davies, R. 1885 (Druids) 1
Davies, R. O. 1892 (Wrexham) 2
Davies, R. T. 1964 (Norwich C, Southampton,
Portsmouth) 29
Davies, R. W. 1964 (Bolton W, Newcastle U, Manchester
C, Manchester U, Blackpool) 34
Davies, S. 2001 (Tottenham H, Everton, Fulham) 58
Davies, S. I. 1996 (Manchester U) 1
Davies, Stanley 1920 (Preston NE, Everton, WBA,
Rotherham U) 18
Davies, T. 1886 (Oswestry) 1
Davies, T. 1903 (Druids) 4
Davies, W. 1884 (Wrexham) 1
Davies, W. 1924 (Swansea T, Cardiff C, Notts Co) 17

Davies, William 1903 (Wrexham, Blackburn R) 11
Davies, W. C. 1908 (Crystal Palace, WBA,
Crystal Palace) 4
Davies, W. D. 1975 (Everton, Wrexham, Swansea C) 52
Davies, W. H. 1876 (Oswestry) 4
Davis, G. 1978 (Wrexham) 3
Davis, W. O. 1913 (Millwall Ath) 5
Day, A. 1934 (Tottenham H) 1
Deacy, N. 1977 (PSV Eindhoven, Beringen) 12
Dearson, D. J. 1939 (Birmingham) 3
Delaney, M. A. 2000 (Aston Villa) 36
Derrett, S. C. 1969 (Cardiff C) 4
Dewey, F. T. 1931 (Cardiff Corinthians) 2
Dibble, A. 1986 (Luton T, Manchester C) 3
Dorman, A. 2010 (St Mirren, Crystal Palace) 3
Doughty, J. 1886 (Druids, Newton Heath) 8
Doughty, R. 1888 (Newton Heath) 2
Duffy, R. M. 2006 (Portsmouth) 13
Dummett, P. 2014 (Newcastle U) 1
Durban, A. 1966 (Derby Co) 27
Dwyer, P. J. 1978 (Cardiff C) 10

Eardley, N. 2008 (Oldham Ath, Blackpool) 16
Earnshaw, R. 2002 (Cardiff C, WBA, Norwich C,
Derby Co, Nottingham F, Cardiff C) 59
Easter, J. M. 2007 (Wycombe W, Plymouth Arg,
Milton Keynes D, Crystal Palace, Millwall) 12
Eastwood, F. 2008 (Wolverhampton W, Coventry C) 11
Edwards, C. 1878 (Wrexham) 1
Edwards, C. N. H. 1996 (Swansea C) 1
Edwards, D. A. 2008 (Luton T, Wolverhampton W) 27
Edwards, G. 1947 (Birmingham C, Cardiff C) 12
Edwards, H. 1878 (Wrexham Civil Service, Wrexham) 8
Edwards, J. H. 1876 (Wanderers) 1
Edwards, J. H. 1895 (Oswestry) 3
Edwards, J. H. 1898 (Aberystwyth) 1
Edwards, L. T. 1957 (Charlton Ath) 2
Edwards, R. I. 1978 (Chester, Wrexham) 4
Edwards, R. O. 2003 (Aston Villa, Wolverhampton W) 15
Edwards, R. W. 1998 (Bristol C) 4
Edwards, T. 1932 (Linfield) 1
Egan, W. 1892 (Chirk) 1
Ellis, B. 1932 (Motherwell) 6
Ellis, E. 1931 (Nunhead, Oswestry) 3
Emanuel, W. J. 1973 (Bristol C) 2
England, H. M. 1962 (Blackburn R, Tottenham H) 44
Evans, B. C. 1972 (Swansea C, Hereford U) 7
Evans, C. M. 2008 (Manchester C, Sheffield U) 13
Evans, D. G. 1926 (Reading, Huddersfield T) 4
Evans, H. P. 1922 (Cardiff C) 6
Evans, I. 1976 (Crystal Palace) 13
Evans, J. 1893 (Oswestry) 3
Evans, J. 1912 (Cardiff C) 8
Evans, J. H. 1922 (Southend U) 4
Evans, Len 1927 (Aberdare Ath, Cardiff C,
Birmingham) 4
Evans, M. 1884 (Oswestry) 1
Evans, P. S. 2002 (Brentford, Bradford C) 2
Evans, R. 1902 (Clapton) 1
Evans, R. E. 1906 (Wrexham, Aston Villa, Sheffield U) 10
Evans, R. O. 1902 (Wrexham, Blackburn R, Coventry C) 10
Evans, R. S. 1964 (Swansea T) 1
Evans, S. J. 2007 (Wrexham) 7
Evans, T. J. 1927 (Clapton Orient, Newcastle U) 4
Evans, W. 1933 (Tottenham H) 6
Evans, W. A. W. 1876 (Oxford University) 2
Evans, W. G. 1890 (Bootle, Aston Villa) 3
Evelyn, E. C. 1887 (Crusaders) 1
Eyton-Jones, J. A. 1883 (Wrexham) 4

Farmer, G. 1885 (Oswestry) 2
Felgate, D. 1984 (Lincoln C) 1
Finnigan, R. J. 1930 (Wrexham) 1
Fletcher, C. N. 2004 (Bournemouth, West Ham U,
Crystal Palace) 36
Flynn, B. 1975 (Burnley, Leeds U, Burnley) 66
Ford, T. 1947 (Swansea T, Aston Villa, Sunderland,
Cardiff C) 38

Foulkes, H. E. 1932 (WBA) 1
Foulkes, W. I. 1952 (Newcastle U) 11
Foulkes, W. T. 1884 (Oswestry) 2
Fowler, J. 1925 (Swansea T) 6
Freestone, R. 2000 (Swansea C) 1

Gabbidon, D. L. 2002 (Cardiff C, West Ham U,
QPR, Crystal Palace) 49
Garner, G. 2006 (Leyton Orient) 1
Garner, J. 1896 (Aberystwyth) 1
Giggs, R. J. 1992 (Manchester U) 64
Giles, D. C. 1980 (Swansea C, Crystal Palace) 12
Gillam, S. G. 1889 (Wrexham, Shrewsbury, Clapton) 5
Glascodine, G. 1879 (Wrexham) 1
Glover, E. M. 1932 (Grimsby T) 7
Godding, G. 1923 (Wrexham) 2
Godfrey, B. C. 1964 (Preston NE) 3
Goodwin, U. 1881 (Ruthin) 1
Goss, J. 1991 (Norwich C) 9
Gough, R. T. 1883 (Oswestry White Star) 1
Gray, A. 1924 (Oldham Ath, Manchester C,
Manchester Central, Tranmere R, Chester) 24
Green, A. W. 1901 (Aston Villa, Notts Co, Nottingham F) 8
Green, C. R. 1965 (Birmingham C) 15
Green, G. H. 1938 (Charlton Ath) 4
Green, R. M. 1998 (Wolverhampton W) 2
Grey, Dr W. 1876 (Druids) 2
Griffiths, A. T. 1971 (Wrexham) 17
Griffiths, F. J. 1900 (Blackpool) 2
Griffiths, G. 1887 (Chirk) 1
Griffiths, J. H. 1953 (Swansea T) 1
Griffiths, L. 1902 (Wrexham) 1
Griffiths, M. W. 1947 (Leicester C) 11
Griffiths, P. 1884 (Chirk) 6
Griffiths, P. H. 1932 (Everton) 1
Griffiths, T. P. 1927 (Everton, Bolton W, Middlesbrough,
Aston Villa) 21
**Gunter, C. R. 2007 (Cardiff C, Tottenham H,
Nottingham F, Reading) 59**

Hall, G. D. 1988 (Chelsea) 9
Hallam, J. 1889 (Oswestry) 1
Hanford, H. 1934 (Swansea T, Sheffield W) 7
Harrington, A. C. 1956 (Cardiff C) 11
Harris, C. S. 1976 (Leeds U) 24
Harris, W. C. 1954 (Middlesbrough) 6
Harrison, W. C. 1899 (Wrexham) 5
Hartson, J. 1995 (Arsenal, West Ham U, Wimbledon,
Coventry C, Celtic) 51
Haworth, S. O. 1997 (Cardiff C, Coventry C) 5
Hayes, A. 1890 (Wrexham) 2
**Hennessey, W. R. 2007 (Wolverhampton W,
Crystal Palace) 49**
Hennessey, W. T. 1962 (Birmingham C, Nottingham F,
Derby Co) 39
Hersee, A. M. 1886 (Bangor) 2
Hersee, R. 1886 (Llandudno) 1
Hewitt, R. 1958 (Cardiff C) 5
Hewitt, T. J. 1911 (Wrexham, Chelsea, South Liverpool) 8
Heywood, D. 1879 (Druids) 1
Hibbott, H. 1880 (Newtown Excelsior, Newtown) 3
Higham, G. G. 1878 (Oswestry) 2
Hill, M. R. 1972 (Ipswich T) 2
Hockey, T. 1972 (Sheffield U, Norwich C, Aston Villa) 9
Hoddinott, T. F. 1921 (Watford) 2
Hodges, G. 1984 (Wimbledon, Newcastle U, Watford,
Sheffield U) 18
Hodgkinson, A. V. 1908 (Southampton) 1
Holden, A. 1984 (Chester C) 1
Hole, B. G. 1963 (Cardiff C, Blackburn R, Aston Villa,
Swansea C) 30
Hole, W. J. 1921 (Swansea T) 9
Hollins, D. M. 1962 (Newcastle U) 11
Hopkins, I. J. 1935 (Brentford) 12
Hopkins, J. 1983 (Fulham, Crystal Palace) 16
Hopkins, M. 1956 (Tottenham H) 34
Horne, B. 1988 (Portsmouth, Southampton, Everton,
Birmingham C) 59

MacDonald, S. B. 2011 (Swansea C, Bournemouth) 2
McCarthy, T. P. 1889 (Wrexham) 1
McMillan, R. 1881 (Shrewsbury Engineers) 2
Maguire, G. T. 1990 (Portsmouth) 7
Mahoney, J. F. 1968 (Stoke C, Middlesbrough, Swansea C) 51
Mardon, P. J. 1996 (WBA) 1
Margetson, M. W. 2004 (Cardiff C) 1
Marriott, A. 1996 (Wrexham) 5
Martin, T. J. 1930 (Newport Co) 1
Marustik, C. 1982 (Swansea C) 6
Mates, J. 1891 (Chirk) 3
Matthews, A. J. 2011 (Cardiff C, Celtic) 12
Matthews, R. W. 1921 (Liverpool, Bristol C, Bradford) 3
Matthews, W. 1905 (Chester) 2
Matthias, J. S. 1896 (Brymbo, Shrewsbury T, Wolverhampton W) 5
Matthias, T. J. 1914 (Wrexham) 12
Mays, A. W. 1929 (Wrexham) 1
Medwin, T. C. 1953 (Swansea T, Tottenham H) 30
Melville, A. K. 1990 (Swansea C, Oxford U, Sunderland, Fulham, West Ham U) 65
Meredith, S. 1900 (Chirk, Stoke, Leyton) 8
Meredith, W. H. 1895 (Manchester C, Manchester U) 48
Mielczarek, R. 1971 (Rotherham U) 1
Millership, H. 1920 (Rotherham Co) 6
Millington, A. H. 1963 (WBA, Crystal Palace, Peterborough U, Swansea C) 21
Mills, T. J. 1934 (Clapton Orient, Leicester C) 4
Mills-Roberts, R. H. 1885 (St Thomas' Hospital, Preston NE, Llanberis) 8
Moore, G. 1960 (Cardiff C, Chelsea, Manchester U, Northampton T, Charlton Ath) 21
Morgan, C. 2007 (Milton Keynes D, Peterborough U, Preston NE) 23
Morgan, J. R. 1877 (Cambridge University, Derby School Staff) 10
Morgan, J. T. 1905 (Wrexham) 1
Morgan-Owen, H. 1902 (Oxford University, Corinthians) 4
Morgan-Owen, M. M. 1897 (Oxford University, Corinthians) 13
Morison, S. W. 2011 (Millwall, Norwich C) 20
Morley, E. J. 1925 (Swansea T, Clapton Orient) 4
Morris, A. G. 1896 (Aberystwyth, Swindon T, Nottingham F) 21
Morris, C. 1900 (Chirk, Derby Co, Huddersfield T) 27
Morris, E. 1893 (Chirk) 3
Morris, H. 1894 (Sheffield U, Manchester C, Grimsby T) 3
Morris, J. 1887 (Oswestry) 1
Morris, J. 1898 (Chirk) 1
Morris, R. 1900 (Chirk, Shrewsbury T) 6
Morris, R. 1902 (Newtown, Druids, Liverpool, Leeds C, Grimsby T, Plymouth Arg) 11
Morris, S. 1937 (Birmingham) 5
Morris, W. 1947 (Burnley) 5
Moulsdale, J. R. B. 1925 (Corinthians) 1
Murphy, J. P. 1933 (WBA) 15
Myhill, G. O. 2008 (Hull C, WBA) 19

Nardiello, D. 1978 (Coventry C) 2
Nardiello, D. A. 2007 (Barnsley, QPR) 3
Neal, J. E. 1931 (Colwyn Bay) 2
Neilson, A. B. 1992 (Newcastle U, Southampton) 5
Newnes, J. 1926 (Nelson) 1
Newton, L. F. 1912 (Cardiff Corinthians) 1
Nicholas, D. S. 1923 (Stoke, Swansea T) 3
Nicholas, P. 1979 (Crystal Palace, Arsenal, Crystal Palace, Luton T, Aberdeen, Chelsea, Watford) 73
Nicholls, J. 1924 (Newport Co, Cardiff C) 4
Niedzwiecki, E. A. 1985 (Chelsea) 2
Nock, W. 1897 (Newtown) 1
Nogan, L. M. 1992 (Watford, Reading) 2
Norman, A. J. 1986 (Hull C) 5
Nurse, M. T. G. 1960 (Swansea T, Middlesbrough) 12
Nyatanga, L. J. 2006 (Derby Co, Bristol C) 34

O'Callaghan, E. 1929 (Tottenham H) 11
Oliver, A. 1905 (Bangor, Blackburn R) 2

Oster, J. M. 1998 (Everton, Sunderland) 13
O'Sullivan, P. A. 1973 (Brighton & HA) 3
Owen, D. 1879 (Oswestry) 1
Owen, E. 1884 (Ruthin Grammar School) 3
Owen, G. 1888 (Chirk, Newton Heath, Chirk) 4
Owen, J. 1892 (Newton Heath) 1
Owen, T. 1879 (Oswestry) 1
Owen, Trevor 1899 (Crewe Alex) 2
Owen, W. 1884 (Chirk) 16
Owen, W. P. 1880 (Ruthin) 12
Owens, J. 1902 (Wrexham) 1

Page, M. E. 1971 (Birmingham C) 28
Page, R. J. 1997 (Watford, Sheffield U, Cardiff C, Coventry C) 41
Palmer, D. 1957 (Swansea T) 3
Parris, J. E. 1932 (Bradford) 1
Parry, B. J. 1951 (Swansea T) 1
Parry, C. 1891 (Everton, Newtown) 13
Parry, E. 1922 (Liverpool) 5
Parry, M. 1901 (Liverpool) 16
Parry, P. I. 2004 (Cardiff C) 12
Parry, T. D. 1900 (Oswestry) 7
Parry, W. 1895 (Newtown) 1
Partridge, D. W. 2005 (Motherwell, Bristol C) 7
Pascoe, C. 1984 (Swansea C, Sunderland) 10
Paul, R. 1949 (Swansea T, Manchester C) 33
Peake, E. 1908 (Aberystwyth, Liverpool) 11
Peers, E. J. 1914 (Wolverhampton W, Port Vale) 12
Pembridge, M. A. 1992 (Luton T, Derby Co, Sheffield W, Benfica, Everton, Fulham) 54
Perry, E. 1938 (Doncaster R) 3
Perry, J. 1994 (Cardiff C) 1
Phennah, E. 1878 (Civil Service) 1
Phillips, C. 1931 (Wolverhampton W, Aston Villa) 13
Phillips, D. 1984 (Plymouth Arg, Manchester C, Coventry C, Norwich C, Nottingham F) 62
Phillips, L. 1971 (Cardiff C, Aston Villa, Swansea C, Charlton Ath) 58
Phillips, T. J. S. 1973 (Chelsea) 4
Phoenix, H. 1882 (Wrexham) 1
Pipe, D. R. 2003 (Coventry C) 1
Poland, G. 1939 (Wrexham) 2
Pontin, K. 1980 (Cardiff C) 2
Powell, A. 1947 (Leeds U, Everton, Birmingham C) 8
Powell, D. 1968 (Wrexham, Sheffield U) 11
Powell, I. V. 1947 (QPR, Aston Villa) 8
Powell, J. 1878 (Druids, Bolton W, Newton Heath) 15
Powell, Seth 1885 (Oswestry, WBA) 7
Price, H. 1907 (Aston Villa, Burton U, Wrexham) 5
Price, J. 1877 (Wrexham) 12
Price, L. P. 2006 (Ipswich T, Derby Co, Crystal Palace) 11
Price, P. 1980 (Luton T, Tottenham H) 25
Pring, K. D. 1966 (Rotherham U) 3
Pritchard, H. K. 1985 (Bristol C) 1
Pryce-Jones, A. W. 1895 (Newtown) 1
Pryce-Jones, W. E. 1887 (Cambridge University) 5
Pugh, A. 1889 (Rhostyllen) 1
Pugh, D. H. 1896 (Wrexham, Lincoln C) 7
Pugsley, J. 1930 (Charlton Ath) 1
Pullen, W. J. 1926 (Plymouth Arg) 1

Ramsey, A. J. 2009 (Arsenal) 34
Rankmore, F. E. J. 1966 (Peterborough U) 1
Ratcliffe, K. 1981 (Everton, Cardiff C) 59
Rea, J. C. 1894 (Aberystwyth) 9
Ready, K. 1997 (QPR) 5
Reece, G. I. 1966 (Sheffield U, Cardiff C) 29
Reed, W. G. 1955 (Ipswich T) 2
Rees, A. 1984 (Birmingham C) 1
Rees, J. M. 1992 (Luton T) 1
Rees, R. R. 1965 (Coventry C, WBA, Nottingham F) 39
Rees, W. 1949 (Cardiff C, Tottenham H) 4
Ribeiro, C. M. 2010 (Bristol C) 2
Richards, A. 1932 (Barnsley) 1
Richards, A. D. J. 2012 (Swansea C) 5
Richards, D. 1931 (Wolverhampton W, Brentford, Birmingham) 21

Richards, G. 1899 (Druids, Oswestry, Shrewsbury T) 6
Richards, R. W. 1920 (Wolverhampton W, West Ham U, Mold) 9
Richards, S. V. 1947 (Cardiff C) 1
Richards, W. E. 1933 (Fulham) 1
Ricketts, S. D. 2005 (Swansea C, Hull C, Bolton W, Wolverhampton W) 52
Roach, J. 1885 (Oswestry) 1
Robbins, W. W. 1931 (Cardiff C, WBA) 11
Roberts, A. M. 1993 (QPR) 2
Roberts, D. F. 1973 (Oxford U, Hull C) 17
Roberts, G. W. 2000 (Tranmere R) 9
Roberts, I. W. 1990 (Watford, Huddersfield T, Leicester C, Norwich C) 15
Roberts, Jas 1913 (Wrexham) 2
Roberts, J. 1879 (Corwen, Berwyn R) 7
Roberts, J. 1881 (Ruthin) 2
Roberts, J. 1906 (Bradford C) 2
Roberts, J. G. 1971 (Arsenal, Birmingham C) 22
Roberts, J. H. 1949 (Bolton W) 1
Roberts, N. W. 2000 (Wrexham, Wigan Ath) 4
Roberts, P. S. 1974 (Portsmouth) 4
Roberts, R. 1884 (Druids, Bolton W, Preston NE) 9
Roberts, R. 1886 (Wrexham) 3
Roberts, R. 1891 (Rhos, Crewe Alex) 2
Roberts, R. L. 1890 (Chester) 1
Roberts, S. W. 2005 (Wrexham) 1
Roberts, W. 1879 (Llangollen, Berwyn R) 6
Roberts, W. 1883 (Rhyl) 1
Roberts, W. 1886 (Wrexham) 4
Roberts, W. H. 1882 (Ruthin, Rhyl) 6
Robinson, C. P. 2000 (Wolverhampton W, Portsmouth, Sunderland, Norwich C, Toronto Lynx) 52
Robinson, J. R. C. 1996 (Charlton Ath) 30
Robson-Kanu, T. H. 2010 (Reading) **26**
Rodrigues, P. J. 1965 (Cardiff C, Leicester C, Sheffield W) 40
Rogers, J. P. 1896 (Wrexham) 3
Rogers, W. 1931 (Wrexham) 2
Roose, L. R. 1900 (Aberystwyth, London Welsh, Stoke, Everton, Stoke, Sunderland) 24
Rouse, R. V. 1959 (Crystal Palace) 1
Rowlands, A. C. 1914 (Tranmere R) 1
Rowley, T. 1959 (Tranmere R) 1
Rush, I. 1980 (Liverpool, Juventus, Liverpool) 73
Russell, M. R. 1912 (Merthyr T, Plymouth Arg) 23

Sabine, H. W. 1887 (Oswestry) 1
Saunders, D. 1986 (Brighton & HA, Oxford U, Derby Co, Liverpool, Aston Villa, Galatasaray, Nottingham F, Sheffield U, Benfica, Bradford C) 75
Savage, R. W. 1996 (Crewe Alex, Leicester C, Birmingham C) 39
Savin, G. 1878 (Oswestry) 1
Sayer, P. A. 1977 (Cardiff C) 7
Scrine, F. H. 1950 (Swansea T) 2
Sear, C. R. 1963 (Manchester C) 1
Shaw, E. G. 1882 (Oswestry) 3
Sherwood, A. T. 1947 (Cardiff C, Newport Co) 41
Shone, W. W. 1879 (Oswestry) 1
Shortt, W. W. 1947 (Plymouth Arg) 12
Showers, D. 1975 (Cardiff C) 2
Sidlow, C. 1947 (Liverpool) 7
Sisson, H. 1885 (Wrexham Olympic) 3
Slatter, N. 1983 (Bristol R, Oxford U) 22
Smallman, D. P. 1974 (Wrexham, Everton) 7
Southall, N. 1982 (Everton) 92
Speed, G. A. 1990 (Leeds U, Everton, Newcastle U, Bolton W) 85
Sprake, G. 1964 (Leeds U, Birmingham C) 37
Stansfield, F. 1949 (Cardiff C) 1
Stevenson, B. 1978 (Leeds U, Birmingham C) 15
Stevenson, N. 1982 (Swansea C) 4
Stitfall, R. F. 1953 (Cardiff C) 2
Stock, B. B. 2010 (Doncaster R) 3
Sullivan, D. 1953 (Cardiff C) 17
Symons, C. J. 1992 (Portsmouth, Manchester C, Fulham, Crystal Palace) 37

Tapscott, D. R. 1954 (Arsenal, Cardiff C) 14
Taylor, G. K. 1996 (Crystal Palace, Sheffield U, Burnley, Nottingham F) 15
Taylor, J. 1898 (Wrexham) 1
Taylor, J. W. T. 2015 (Reading) **1**
Taylor, N. J. 2010 (Wrexham, Swansea C) **22**
Taylor, O. D. S. 1893 (Newtown) 4
Thatcher, B. D. 2004 (Leicester C, Manchester C) 7
Thomas, C. 1899 (Druids) 2
Thomas, D. A. 1957 (Swansea T) 2
Thomas, D. S. 1948 (Fulham) 4
Thomas, E. 1925 (Cardiff Corinthians) 1
Thomas, G. 1885 (Wrexham) 2
Thomas, H. 1927 (Manchester U) 1
Thomas, Martin R. 1987 (Newcastle U) 1
Thomas, Mickey 1977 (Wrexham, Manchester U, Everton, Brighton & HA, Stoke C, Chelsea, WBA) 51
Thomas, R. J. 1967 (Swindon T, Derby Co, Cardiff C) 50
Thomas, T. 1898 (Bangor) 2
Thomas, W. R. 1931 (Newport Co) 2
Thomson, D. 1876 (Druids) 1
Thomson, G. F. 1876 (Druids) 2
Toshack, J. B. 1969 (Cardiff C, Liverpool, Swansea C) 40
Townsend, W. 1887 (Newtown) 2
Trainer, H. 1895 (Wrexham) 3
Trainer, J. 1887 (Bolton W, Preston NE) 20
Trollope, P. J. 1997 (Derby Co, Fulham, Coventry C, Northampton T) 9
Tudur-Jones, O. 2008 (Swansea C, Norwich C, Hibernian) 7
Turner, H. G. 1937 (Charlton Ath) 8
Turner, J. 1892 (Wrexham) 1
Turner, R. E. 1891 (Wrexham) 2
Turner, W. H. 1887 (Wrexham) 5

Van Den Hauwe, P. W. R. 1985 (Everton) 13
Vaughan, D. O. 2003 (Crewe Alex, Real Sociedad, Blackpool, Sunderland, Nottingham F) **39**
Vaughan, Jas 1893 (Druids) 4
Vaughan, John 1879 (Oswestry, Druids, Bolton W) 11
Vaughan, J. O. 1885 (Rhyl) 4
Vaughan, N. 1983 (Newport Co, Cardiff C) 10
Vaughan, T. 1885 (Rhyl) 1
Vearncombe, G. 1958 (Cardiff C) 2
Vernon, T. R. 1957 (Blackburn R, Everton, Stoke C) 32
Villars, A. K. 1974 (Cardiff C) 3
Vizard, E. T. 1911 (Bolton W) 22
Vokes, S. M. 2008 (Bournemouth, Wolverhampton W, Burnley) **33**

Walley, J. T. 1971 (Watford) 1
Walsh, I. P. 1980 (Crystal Palace, Swansea C) 18
Ward, D. 1959 (Bristol R, Cardiff C) 2
Ward, D. 2000 (Notts Co, Nottingham F) 5
Warner, J. 1937 (Swansea T, Manchester U) 2
Warren, F. W. 1929 (Cardiff C, Middlesbrough, Hearts) 6
Watkins, A. E. 1898 (Leicester Fosse, Aston Villa, Millwall) 5
Watkins, W. M. 1902 (Stoke, Aston Villa, Sunderland, Stoke) 10
Webster, C. 1957 (Manchester U) 4
Weston, R. D. 2000 (Arsenal, Cardiff C) 7
Whatley, W. J. 1939 (Tottenham H) 2
White, P. F. 1896 (London Welsh) 2
Wilcock, A. R. 1890 (Oswestry) 1
Wilding, J. 1885 (Wrexham Olympians, Bootle, Wrexham) 9
Williams, A. 1994 (Reading, Wolverhampton W, Reading) 13
Williams, A. E. 2008 (Stockport Co, Swansea C) **51**
Williams, A. L. 1931 (Wrexham) 1
Williams, A. P. 1998 (Southampton) 2
Williams, B. 1930 (Bristol C) 1
Williams, B. D. 1928 (Swansea T, Everton) 10
Williams, D. G. 1988 (Derby Co, Ipswich T) 13
Williams, D. M. 1986 (Norwich C) 5
Williams, D. R. 1921 (Merthyr T, Sheffield W, Manchester U) 8
Williams, E. 1893 (Crewe Alex) 2
Williams, E. 1901 (Druids) 5

REPUBLIC OF IRELAND

Desmond, P. 1950 (Middlesbrough) 4
Devine, J. 1980 (Arsenal, Norwich C) 13
Doherty, G. M. T. 2000 (Luton T, Tottenham H, Norwich C) 34
Donnelly, J. 1935 (Dundalk) 10
Donnelly, T. 1938 (Drumcondra, Shamrock R) 2
Donovan, D. C. 1955 (Everton) 5
Donovan, T. 1980 (Aston Villa) 2
Douglas, J. 2004 (Blackburn R, Leeds U) 8
Dowdall, C. 1928 (Fordsons, Barnsley, Cork) 3
Doyle, C. 1959 (Shelbourne) 1
Doyle, Colin 2007 (Birmingham C) 1
Doyle, D. 1926 (Shamrock R) 1
Doyle, K. E. 2006 (Reading, Wolverhampton W) **61**
Doyle, L. 1932 (Dolphin) 1
Doyle, M. P. 2004 (Coventry C) 1
Duff, D. A. 1998 (Blackburn R, Chelsea, Newcastle U, Fulham) 100
Duffy, B. 1950 (Shamrock R) 1
Duffy, S. P. M. 2014 (Everton) 1
Duggan, H. A. 1927 (Leeds U, Newport Co) 5
Dunne, A. P. 1962 (Manchester U, Bolton W) 33
Dunne, J. 1930 (Sheffield U, Arsenal, Southampton, Shamrock R) 15
Dunne, J. C. 1971 (Fulham) 1
Dunne, L. 1935 (Manchester C) 2
Dunne, P. A. J. 1965 (Manchester U) 5
Dunne, R. P. 2000 (Everton, Manchester C, Aston Villa, QPR) 80
Dunne, S. 1953 (Luton T) 15
Dunne, T. 1956 (St Patrick's Ath) 3
Dunning, P. 1971 (Shelbourne) 2
Dunphy, E. M. 1966 (York C, Millwall) 23
Dwyer, N. M. 1960 (West Ham U, Swansea T) 14

Eccles, P. 1986 (Shamrock R) 1
Egan, R. 1929 (Dundalk) 1
Eglington, T. J. 1946 (Shamrock R, Everton) 24
Eliot, R. 2014 (Newcastle U) **3**
Elliott, S. W. 2005 (Sunderland) 9
Ellis, P. 1935 (Bohemians) 7
Evans, M. J. 1998 (Southampton) 1

Fagan, E. 1973 (Shamrock R) 1
Fagan, F. 1955 (Manchester C, Derby Co) 8
Fagan, J. 1926 (Shamrock R) 1
Fahey, K. D. 2010 (Birmingham C) 16
Fairclough, M. 1982 (Dundalk) 2
Fallon, S. 1951 (Celtic) 8
Fallon, W. J. 1935 (Notts Co, Sheffield W) 9
Farquharson, T. G. 1929 (Cardiff C) 4
Farrell, P. 1937 (Hibernian) 2
Farrell, P. D. 1946 (Shamrock R, Everton) 28
Farrelly, G. 1996 (Aston Villa, Everton, Bolton W) 6
Feenan, J. J. 1937 (Sunderland) 2
Finnan, S. 2000 (Fulham, Liverpool, Espanyol) 53
Finucane, A. 1967 (Limerick) 11
Fitzgerald, F. J. 1955 (Waterford) 2
Fitzgerald, P. J. 1961 (Leeds U, Chester) 5
Fitzpatrick, K. 1970 (Limerick) 1
Fitzsimons, A. G. 1950 (Middlesbrough, Lincoln C) 26
Fleming, C. 1996 (Middlesbrough) 10
Flood, J. J. 1926 (Shamrock R) 5
Fogarty, A. 1960 (Sunderland, Hartlepools U) 11
Folan, C. C. 2009 (Hull C) 7
Foley, D. J. 2000 (Watford) 6
Foley, J. 1934 (Cork, Celtic) 7
Foley, K. P. 2009 (Wolverhampton W) 8
Foley, M. 1926 (Shelbourne) 1
Foley, T. C. 1964 (Northampton T) 9
Forde, D. 2011 (Millwall) **23**
Foy, T. 1938 (Shamrock R) 2
Fullam, J. 1961 (Preston NE, Shamrock R) 11
Fullam, R. 1926 (Shamrock R) 2

Gallagher, C. 1967 (Celtic) 2
Gallagher, M. 1954 (Hibernian) 1
Gallagher, P. 1932 (Falkirk) 1

Galvin, A. 1983 (Tottenham H, Sheffield W, Swindon T) 29
Gamble, J. 2007 (Cork C) 2
Gannon, E. 1949 (Notts Co, Sheffield W, Shelbourne) 14
Gannon, M. 1972 (Shelbourne) 1
Gaskins, P. 1934 (Shamrock R, St James' Gate) 7
Gavin, J. T. 1950 (Norwich C, Tottenham H, Norwich C) 7
Geoghegan, M. 1937 (St James' Gate) 2
Gibbons, A. 1952 (St Patrick's Ath) 4
Gibson, D. T. D. 2008 (Manchester U, Everton) **25**
Gilbert, R. 1966 (Shamrock R) 1
Giles, C. 1951 (Doncaster R) 1
Giles, M. J. 1960 (Manchester U, Leeds U, WBA, Shamrock R) 59
Given, S. J. J. 1996 (Blackburn R, Newcastle U, Manchester C, Aston Villa) **130**
Givens, D. J. 1969 (Manchester U, Luton T, QPR, Birmingham C, Neuchatel X) 56
Gleeson, S. M. 2007 (Wolverhampton W) 2
Glen, W. 1927 (Shamrock R) 8
Glynn, D. 1952 (Drumcondra) 2
Godwin, T. F. 1949 (Shamrock R, Leicester C, Bournemouth) 13
Golding, J. 1928 (Shamrock R) 2
Goodman, J. 1997 (Wimbledon) 4
Goodwin, J. 2003 (Stockport Co) 1
Gorman, W. C. 1936 (Bury, Brentford) 13
Grace, J. 1926 (Drumcondra) 1
Grealish, A. 1976 (Orient, Luton T, Brighton & HA, WBA) 45
Green, P. J. 2010 (Derby Co, Leeds U) 20
Gregg, E. 1978 (Bohemians) 8
Griffith, R. 1935 (Walsall) 1
Grimes, A. A. 1978 (Manchester U, Coventry C, Luton T) 18

Hale, A. 1962 (Aston Villa, Doncaster R, Waterford) 14
Hamilton, T. 1959 (Shamrock R) 2
Hand, E. K. 1969 (Portsmouth) 20
Harrington, W. 1936 (Cork) 5
Harte, I. P. 1996 (Leeds U, Levante) 64
Hartnett, J. B. 1949 (Middlesbrough) 2
Haverty, J. 1956 (Arsenal, Blackburn R, Millwall, Celtic, Bristol R, Shelbourne) 32
Hayes, A. W. P. 1979 (Southampton) 1
Hayes, W. E. 1947 (Huddersfield T) 2
Hayes, W. J. 1949 (Limerick) 2
Healey, R. 1977 (Cardiff C) 2
Healy, C. 2002 (Celtic, Sunderland) 13
Heighway, S. D. 1971 (Liverpool, Minnesota K) 34
Henderson, B. 1948 (Drumcondra) 2
Henderson, W. C. P. 2006 (Brighton & HA, Preston NE) 6
Hendrick, J. P. 2013 (Derby Co) **13**
Hennessy, J. 1965 (Shelbourne, St Patrick's Ath) 5
Herrick, J. 1972 (Cork Hibernians, Shamrock R) 3
Higgins, J. 1951 (Birmingham C) 1
Holland, M. R. 2000 (Ipswich T, Charlton Ath) 49
Holmes, J. 1971 (Coventry C, Tottenham H, Vancouver Whitecaps) 30
Hoolahan, W. 2008 (Blackpool, Norwich C) **20**
Horlacher, A. F. 1930 (Bohemians) 7
Houghton, R. J. 1986 (Oxford U, Liverpool, Aston Villa, Crystal Palace, Reading) 73
Howlett, G. 1984 (Brighton & HA) 1
Hoy, M. 1938 (Dundalk) 6
Hughton, C. 1980 (Tottenham H, West Ham U) 53
Hunt, N. 2009 (Reading) 3
Hunt, S. P. 2007 (Reading, Hull C, Wolverhampton W) 39
Hurley, C. J. 1957 (Millwall, Sunderland, Bolton W) 40
Hutchinson, F. 1935 (Drumcondra) 2

Ireland S .J. 2006 (Manchester C) 6
Irwin, D. J. 1991 (Manchester U) 56

Jordan, D. 1937 (Wolverhampton W) 2
Jordan, W. 1934 (Bohemians) 2

Kavanagh, G. A. 1998 (Stoke C, Cardiff C, Wigan Ath) 16
Kavanagh, P. J. 1931 (Celtic) 2
Keane, R. D. 1998 (Wolverhampton W, Coventry C, Internazionale, Leeds U, Tottenham H, Liverpool, Tottenham H, LA Galaxy) 140
Keane, R. M. 1991 (Nottingham F, Manchester U) 67
Keane, T. R. 1949 (Swansea T) 4
Kearin, M. 1972 (Shamrock R) 1
Kearns, F. T. 1954 (West Ham U) 1
Kearns, M. 1971 (Oxford U, Walsall, Wolverhampton W) 18
Kelly, A. T. 1993 (Sheffield U, Blackburn R) 34
Kelly, D. T. 1988 (Walsall, West Ham U, Leicester C, Newcastle U, Wolverhampton W, Sunderland, Tranmere R) 26
Kelly, G. 1994 (Leeds U) 52
Kelly, J. 1932 (Derry C) 4
Kelly, J. A. 1957 (Drumcondra, Preston NE) 47
Kelly, J. P. V. 1961 (Wolverhampton W) 5
Kelly, M. J. 1988 (Portsmouth) 4
Kelly, N. 1954 (Nottingham F) 1
Kelly, S. M. 2006 (Tottenham H, Birmingham C, Fulham, Reading) 38
Kendrick, J. 1927 (Everton, Dolphin) 4
Kenna, J. J. 1995 (Blackburn R) 27
Kennedy, M. F. 1986 (Portsmouth) 2
Kennedy, M. J. 1996 (Liverpool, Wimbledon, Manchester C, Wolverhampton W) 34
Kennedy, W. 1932 (St James' Gate) 3
Kenny, P. 2004 (Sheffield U) 7
Keogh, A. D. 2007 (Wolverhampton W, Millwall) 30
Keogh, J. 1966 (Shamrock R) 1
Keogh, R. J. 2013 (Derby Co) 7
Keogh, S. 1959 (Shamrock R) 1
Kernaghan, A. N. 1993 (Middlesbrough, Manchester C) 22
Kiely, D. L. 2000 (Charlton Ath, WBA) 11
Kiernan, F. W. 1951 (Shamrock R, Southampton) 5
Kilbane, K. D. 1998 (WBA, Sunderland, Everton, Wigan Ath, Hull C) 110
Kinnear, J. P. 1967 (Tottenham H, Brighton & HA) 26
Kinsella, J. 1928 (Shelbourne) 1
Kinsella, M. A. 1998 (Charlton Ath, Aston Villa, WBA) 48
Kinsella, O. 1932 (Shamrock R) 2
Kirkland, A. 1927 (Shamrock R) 1

Lacey, W. 1927 (Shelbourne) 3
Langan, D. 1978 (Derby Co, Birmingham C, Oxford U) 26
Lapira, J. 2007 (Notre Dame) 1
Lawler, J. F. 1953 (Fulham) 8
Lawlor, J. C. 1949 (Drumcondra, Doncaster R) 3
Lawlor, M. 1971 (Shamrock R) 5
Lawrence, L. 2009 (Stoke C, Portsmouth) 15
Lawrenson, M. 1977 (Preston NE, Brighton & HA, Liverpool) 39
Lee, A. D. 2003 (Rotherham U, Cardiff C, Ipswich T) 10
Leech, M. 1969 (Shamrock R) 8
Lennon, C. 1935 (St James' Gate) 3
Lennox, G. 1931 (Dolphin) 2
Long, S. P. 2007 (Reading, WBA, Hull C, Southampton) 54
Lowry, D. 1962 (St Patrick's Ath) 1
Lunn, R. 1939 (Dundalk) 2
Lynch, J. 1934 (Cork Bohemians) 1

McAlinden, J. 1946 (Portsmouth) 2
McAteer, J. W. 1994 (Bolton W, Liverpool, Blackburn R, Sunderland) 52
McCann, J. 1957 (Shamrock R) 1
McCarthy, J. 1926 (Bohemians) 3
McCarthy, J. 2010 (Wigan Ath, Everton) 27
McCarthy, M. 1932 (Shamrock R) 1
McCarthy, M. 1984 (Manchester C, Celtic, Lyon, Millwall) 57
McClean, J. J. 2012 (Sunderland, Wigan Ath) 30
McConville, T. 1972 (Dundalk, Waterford) 6

McDonagh, Jacko 1984 (Shamrock R) 3
McDonagh, J. 1981 (Everton, Bolton W, Notts Co, Wichita Wings) 25
McEvoy, M. A. 1961 (Blackburn R) 17
McGeady, A. J. 2004 (Celtic, Spartak Moscow, Everton) 76
McGee, P. 1978 (QPR, Preston NE) 15
McGoldrick, D. J. 2015 (Ipswich T) 2
McGoldrick, E. J. 1992 (Crystal Palace, Arsenal) 15
McGowan, D. 1949 (West Ham U) 3
McGowan, J. 1947 (Cork U) 1
McGrath, M. 1958 (Blackburn R, Bradford) 22
McGrath, P. 1985 (Manchester U, Aston Villa, Derby Co) 83
McGuire, W. 1936 (Bohemians) 1
Macken, A. 1977 (Derby Co) 1
Macken J. P. 2005 (Manchester C) 1
McKenzie, G. 1938 (Southend U) 9
Mackey, G. 1957 (Shamrock R) 3
McLoughlin, A. F. 1990 (Swindon T, Southampton, Portsmouth) 42
McLoughlin, F. 1930 (Fordsons, Cork) 2
McMillan, W. 1946 (Belfast Celtic) 2
McNally, J. B. 1959 (Luton T) 3
McPhail, S. 2000 (Leeds U) 10
McShane, P. D. 2007 (WBA, Sunderland, Hull C) 32
Madden, O. 1936 (Cork) 1
Madden, P. 2013 (Scunthorpe U) 1
Maguire, J. 1929 (Shamrock R) 1
Mahon, A. J. 2000 (Tranmere R) 2
Malone, G. 1949 (Shelbourne) 1
Mancini, T. J. 1974 (QPR, Arsenal) 5
Martin, C. 1927 (Bo'ness) 1
Martin, C. J. 1946 (Glentoran, Leeds U, Aston Villa) 30
Martin, M. P. 1972 (Bohemians, Manchester U, WBA, Newcastle U) 52
Maybury, A. 1998 (Leeds U, Hearts, Leicester C) 10
Meagan, M. K. 1961 (Everton, Huddersfield T, Drogheda) 17
Meehan, P. 1934 (Drumcondra) 1
Meyler, D. J. 2013 (Sunderland, Hull C) 13
Miller, L. W. P. 2004 (Celtic, Manchester U, Sunderland, Hibernian) 21
Milligan, M. J. 1992 (Oldham Ath) 1
Monahan, P. 1935 (Sligo R) 2
Mooney, J. 1965 (Shamrock R) 2
Moore, A. 1996 (Middlesbrough) 8
Moore, P. 1931 (Shamrock R, Aberdeen, Shamrock R) 9
Moran, K. 1980 (Manchester U, Sporting Gijon, Blackburn R) 71
Moroney, T. 1948 (West Ham U, Evergreen U) 12
Morris, C. B. 1988 (Celtic, Middlesbrough) 35
Morrison, C. H. 2002 (Crystal Palace, Birmingham C, Crystal Palace) 36
Moulson, C. 1936 (Lincoln C, Notts Co) 5
Moulson, G. B. 1948 (Lincoln C) 3
Muckian, C. 1978 (Drogheda U) 1
Muldoon, T. 1927 (Aston Villa) 1
Mulligan, P. M. 1969 (Shamrock R, Chelsea, Crystal Palace, WBA, Shamrock R) 50
Munroe, L. 1954 (Shamrock R) 1
Murphy, A. 1956 (Clyde) 1
Murphy, B. 1986 (Bohemians) 1
Murphy, D. 2007 (Sunderland, Ipswich T) 16
Murphy, J. 1980 (Crystal Palace) 3
Murphy, J. 2004 (WBA, Scunthorpe U) 2
Murphy, P. M. 2007 (Carlisle U) 1
Murray, T. 1950 (Dundalk) 1

Newman, W. 1969 (Shelbourne) 1
Nolan. E. W. 2009 (Preston NE) 3
Nolan, R. 1957 (Shamrock R) 10

O'Brien, A. 2007 (Newcastle U) 5
O'Brien, A. J. 2001 (Newcastle U, Portsmouth) 26
O'Brien, F. 1980 (Philadelphia F) 3
O'Brien J. M. 2006 (Bolton W, West Ham U) 5
O'Brien, L. 1986 (Shamrock R, Manchester U, Newcastle U, Tranmere R) 16

O'Brien, M. T. 1927 (Derby Co, Walsall, Norwich C, Watford) | 4
O'Brien, R. 1976 (Notts Co) | 5
O'Byrne, L. B. 1949 (Shamrock R) | 1
O'Callaghan, B. R. 1979 (Stoke C) | 6
O'Callaghan, K. 1981 (Ipswich T, Portsmouth) | 21
O'Cearuill, J. 2007 (Arsenal) | 2
O'Connell, A. 1967 (Dundalk, Bohemians) | 2
O'Connor, T. 1950 (Shamrock R) | 4
O'Connor, T. 1968 (Fulham, Dundalk, Bohemians) | 7
O'Dea, D. 2010 (Celtic, Toronto, Metalurh Donetsk) | 20
O'Driscoll, J. F. 1949 (Swansea T) | 3
O'Driscoll, S. 1982 (Fulham) | 3
O'Farrell, F. 1952 (West Ham U, Preston NE) | 9
O'Flanagan, K. P. 1938 (Bohemians, Arsenal) | 10
O'Flanagan, M. 1947 (Bohemians) | 1
O'Halloran, S. E. 2007 (Aston Villa) | 2
O'Hanlon, K. G. 1988 (Rotherham U) | 1
O'Kane, P. 1935 (Bohemians) | 3
O'Keefe, E. 1981 (Everton, Port Vale) | 5
O'Keefe, T. 1934 (Cork, Waterford) | 3
O'Leary, D. 1977 (Arsenal) | 68
O'Leary, P. 1980 (Shamrock R) | 7
O'Mahoney, M. T. 1938 (Bristol R) | 6
O'Neill, F. S. 1962 (Shamrock R) | 20
O'Neill, J. 1952 (Everton) | 17
O'Neill, J. 1961 (Preston NE) | 1
O'Neill, K. P. 1996 (Norwich C, Middlesbrough) | 13
O'Neill, W. 1936 (Dundalk) | 11
O'Regan, K. 1984 (Brighton & HA) | 4
O'Reilly, J. 1932 (Brideville, Aberdeen, Brideville, St James' Gate) | 20
O'Reilly, J. 1946 (Cork U) | 2
O'Shea, J. F. 2002 (Manchester U, Sunderland) | **103**

Pearce, A. J. 2013 (Reading) | **6**
Peyton, G. 1977 (Fulham, Bournemouth, Everton) | 33
Peyton, N. 1957 (Shamrock R, Leeds U) | 6
Phelan, T. 1992 (Wimbledon, Manchester C, Chelsea, Everton, Fulham) | 42
Pilkington, A. N. J. 2013 (Norwich C, Cardiff C) | **8**
Potter, D. M. 2007 (Wolverhampton W) | 5

Quinn, A. 2003 (Sheffield W, Sheffield U) | 8
Quinn, B. S. 2000 (Coventry C) | 4
Quinn, N. J. 1986 (Arsenal, Manchester C, Sunderland) | 91
Quinn, S. 2013 (Hull C) | **12**

Randolf, D. E. 2013 (Motherwell) | 2
Reid, A. M. 2004 (Nottingham F, Tottenham H, Charlton Ath, Sunderland, Nottingham F) | 29
Reid, C. 1931 (Brideville) | 1
Reid, S. J. 2002 (Millwall, Blackburn R) | 23
Richardson, D. J. 1972 (Shamrock R, Gillingham) | 3
Rigby, A. 1935 (St James' Gate) | 3
Ringstead, A. 1951 (Sheffield U) | 20
Robinson, J. 1928 (Bohemians, Dolphin) | 2
Robinson, M. 1981 (Brighton & HA, Liverpool, QPR) | 24
Roche, P. J. 1972 (Shelbourne, Manchester U) | 8
Rogers, E. 1968 (Blackburn R, Charlton Ath) | 19
Rowlands, M. C. 2004 (QPR) | 5
Ryan, G. 1978 (Derby Co, Brighton & HA) | 18
Ryan, R. A. 1950 (WBA, Derby Co) | 16

Sadlier, R. T. 2002 (Millwall) | 1
Sammon, C. 2013 (Derby Co) | 9
Savage, D. P. T. 1996 (Millwall) | 5
Saward, P. 1954 (Millwall, Aston Villa, Huddersfield T) | 18
Scannell, T. 1954 (Southend U) | 1
Scully, P. J. 1989 (Arsenal) | 1
Sheedy, K. 1984 (Everton, Newcastle U) | 46
Sheridan, C. 2010 (Celtic, CSKA Sofia) | 3
Sheridan, J. J. 1988 (Leeds U, Sheffield W) | 34
Slaven, B. 1990 (Middlesbrough) | 7
Sloan, J. W. 1946 (Arsenal) | 2
Smyth, M. 1969 (Shamrock R) | 1
Squires, J. 1934 (Shelbourne) | 1
Stapleton, F. 1977 (Arsenal, Manchester U, Ajax, Le Havre, Blackburn R) | 71
Staunton, S. 1989 (Liverpool, Aston Villa, Liverpool, Aston Villa) | 102
St Ledger-Hall, S. P. 2009 (Preston NE, Leicester C) | 37
Stevenson, A. E. 1932 (Dolphin, Everton) | 7
Stokes, A. 2007 (Sunderland, Celtic) | **9**
Strahan, F. 1964 (Shelbourne) | 5
Sullivan, J. 1928 (Fordsons) | 1
Swan, M. M. G. 1960 (Drumcondra) | 1
Synnott, N. 1978 (Shamrock R) | 3

Taylor, T. 1959 (Waterford) | 1
Thomas, P. 1974 (Waterford) | 2
Thompson, J. 2004 (Nottingham F) | 1
Townsend, A. D. 1989 (Norwich C, Chelsea, Aston Villa, Middlesbrough) | 70
Traynor, T. J. 1954 (Southampton) | 8
Treacy, K. 2011 (Preston NE, Burnley) | 6
Treacy, R. C. P. 1966 (WBA, Charlton Ath, Swindon T, Preston NE, WBA, Shamrock R) | 42
Tuohy, L. 1956 (Shamrock R, Newcastle U, Shamrock R) | 8
Turner, C. J. 1936 (Southend U, West Ham U) | 10
Turner, P. 1963 (Celtic) | 2

Vernon, J. 1946 (Belfast Celtic) | 2

Waddock, G. 1980 (QPR, Millwall) | 21
Walsh, D. J. 1946 (Linfield, WBA, Aston Villa) | 20
Walsh, J. 1982 (Limerick) | 1
Walsh, M. 1976 (Blackpool, Everton, QPR, Porto) | 21
Walsh, M. 1982 (Everton) | 4
Walsh, W. 1947 (Manchester C) | 9
Walters, J. R. 2011 (Stoke C) | **33**
Ward, S. R. 2011 (Wolverhampton W) | **29**
Waters, J. 1977 (Grimsby T) | 2
Watters, F. 1926 (Shelbourne) | 1
Weir, E. 1939 (Clyde) | 3
Westwood, K. 2009 (Coventry C, Sunderland, Sheffield W) | **18**
Whelan, G. D. 2008 (Stoke C) | **64**
Whelan, R. 1964 (St Patrick's Ath) | 2
Whelan, R. 1981 (Liverpool, Southend U) | 53
Whelan, W. 1956 (Manchester U) | 4
White, J. J. 1928 (Bohemians) | 1
Whittaker, R. 1959 (Chelsea) | 1
Williams, J. 1938 (Shamrock R) | 1
Wilson, M. D. 2011 (Stoke C) | **23**

BRITISH AND IRISH INTERNATIONAL GOALSCORERS 1872–2015

Where two players with the same surname and initials have appeared for the same country, and one or both have scored, they have been distinguished by reference to the club which appears *first* against their name in the international appearances section.

Bold type indicates players who have scored international goals in season 2014–15.

ENGLAND

Name	Goals
A'Court, A.	1
Adams, T. A.	5
Adcock, H.	1
Alcock, C. W.	1
Allen, A.	3
Allen, R.	2
Amos, A.	1
Anderson, V.	2
Anderton, D. R.	7
Astall, G.	1
Athersmith, W. C.	3
Atyeo, P. J. W.	5
Bache, J. W.	4
Bailey, N. C.	2
Baily, E. F.	5
Baines, L. J.	1
Baker, J. H.	3
Ball, A. J.	8
Bambridge, A. L.	1
Bambridge, E. C.	11
Barclay, R.	2
Barmby, N. J.	4
Barnes, J.	11
Barnes, P. S.	4
Barry, G.	3
Barton, J.	1
Bassett, W. I.	8
Bastin, C. S.	12
Beardsley, P. A.	9
Beasley, A.	1
Beattie, T. K.	1
Beckham, D. R. J.	17
Becton, F.	2
Bedford, H.	1
Bell, C.	9
Bent, D. A.	4
Bentley, R. T. F.	9
Bishop, S. M.	1
Blackburn, F.	1
Blissett, L.	3
Bloomer, S.	28
Bond, R.	2
Bonsor, A. G.	1
Bowden, E. R.	1
Bowers, J. W.	2
Bowles, S.	1
Bradford, G. R. W.	1
Bradford, J.	7
Bradley, W.	2
Bradshaw, F.	3
Brann, G.	1
Bridge, W. M.	1
Bridges, B. J.	1
Bridgett, A.	3
Brindle, T.	1
Britton, C. S.	1
Broadbent, P. F.	2
Broadis, I. A.	8
Brodie, J. B.	1
Bromley-Davenport, W.	2
Brook, E. F.	10
Brooking, T. D.	5
Brooks, J.	2
Broome, F. H.	3
Brown, A.	4
Brown, A. S.	1
Brown, G.	5
Brown, J.	3
Brown, W.	1
Brown, W. M.	1
Buchan, C. M.	4
Bull, S. G.	4
Bullock, N.	2
Burgess, H.	4
Butcher, T.	3
Byrne, J. J.	8
Cahill, G.	3
Campbell, S. J.	1
Camsell, G. H.	18
Carroll, A. T.	2
Carter, H. S.	7
Carter, J. H.	4
Caulker, S. A.	1
Chadwick, E.	3
Chamberlain, M.	1
Chambers, H.	5
Channon, M. R.	21
Charlton, J.	6
Charlton, R.	49
Chenery, C. J.	1
Chivers, M.	13
Clarke, A. J.	10
Cobbold, W. N.	6
Cock, J. G.	2
Cole, A.	1
Cole, J. J.	10
Common, A.	2
Connelly, J. M.	7
Coppell, S. J.	7
Cotterill, G. H.	2
Cowans, G.	2
Crawford, R.	1
Crawshaw, T. H.	1
Crayston, W. J.	1
Creek, F. N. S.	1
Crooks, S. D.	7
Crouch, P. J.	22
Currey, E. S.	2
Currie, A. W.	3
Cursham, A. W.	2
Cursham, H. A.	5
Daft, H. B.	3
Davenport, J. K.	2
Davis, G.	1
Davis, H.	1
Day, S. H.	2
Dean, W. R.	18
Defoe, J. C.	19
Devey, J. H. G.	1
Dewhurst, F.	11
Dix, W. R.	1
Dixon, K. M.	4
Dixon, L. M.	1
Dorrell, A. R.	1
Douglas, B.	11
Drake, E. J.	6
Ducat, A.	1
Dunn, A. T. B.	2
Eastham, G.	2
Edwards, D.	5
Ehiogu, U.	1
Elliott, W. H.	3
Evans, R. E.	1
Ferdinand, L.	5
Ferdinand, R. G.	3
Finney, T.	30
Fleming, H. J.	9
Flowers, R.	10
Forman, Frank	1
Forman, Fred	3
Foster, R. E.	3
Fowler, R. B.	7
Francis, G. C. J.	3
Francis, T.	12
Freeman, B. C.	3
Froggatt, J.	2
Froggatt, R.	2
Galley, T.	1
Gascoigne, P. J.	10
Geary, F.	3
Gerrard, S. G.	21
Gibbins, W. V. T.	3
Gilliatt, W. E.	3
Goddard, P.	1
Goodall, J.	12
Goodyer, A. C.	1
Gosling, R. C.	2
Goulden, L. A.	4
Grainger, C.	3
Greaves, J.	44
Grosvenor, A. T.	2
Gunn, W.	1
Haines, J. T. W.	2
Hall, G. W.	9
Halse, H. J.	2
Hampson, J.	5
Hampton, H.	2
Hancocks, J.	2
Hardman, H. P.	1
Harris, S. S.	2
Hassall, H. W.	4
Hateley, M.	9
Haynes, J. N.	18
Hegan, K. E.	4
Henfrey, A. G.	2
Heskey, E. W.	7
Hilsdon, G. R.	14
Hine, E. W.	4
Hinton, A. T.	1
Hirst, D. E.	1
Hitchens, G. A.	5
Hobbis, H. H. F.	1
Hoddle, G.	8
Hodgetts, D.	1
Hodgson, G.	1
Holley, G. H.	8
Houghton, W. E.	5
Howell, R.	1
Hughes, E. W.	1
Hulme, J. H. A.	4
Hunt, G. S.	1
Hunt, R.	18
Hunter, N.	2
Hurst, G. C.	24
Ince, P. E. C.	2
Jack, D. N. B.	3
Jagielka, P. N.	**3**
Jeffers, F.	1
Jenas, J. A.	1
Johnson, A.	2
Johnson, D. E.	6
Johnson, E.	2
Johnson, G. M. C.	1
Johnson, J. A.	2
Johnson, T. C. F.	5
Johnson, W. H.	1
Kail, E. I. L.	2
Kane, H. E.	**1**
Kay, A. H.	1
Keegan, J. K.	21
Kelly, R.	8
Kennedy, R.	3
Kenyon-Slaney, W. S.	2
Keown, M. R.	2
Kevan, D. T.	8
Kidd, B.	1
King, L. B.	2
Kingsford, R. K.	1
Kirchen, A. J.	2
Kirton, W. J.	1
Lambert, R. L.	3
Lampard, F. J.	29
Langton, R.	1
Latchford, R. D.	5
Latheron, E. G.	1
Lawler, C.	1
Lawton, T.	22
Lee, F.	10
Lee, J.	1
Lee, R. M.	2
Lee, S.	2
Lescott, J.	1
Le Saux, G. P.	1
Lindley, T.	14
Lineker, G.	48
Lofthouse, J. M.	3
Lofthouse, N.	30
Hon. A. Lyttelton	1
Mabbutt, G.	1
Macdonald, M.	6
Mannion, W. J.	11
Mariner, P.	13
Marsh, R. W.	1
Matthews, S.	11
Matthews, V.	1
McCall, J.	1
McDermott, T.	3
McManaman, S.	3
Medley, L. D.	1
Melia, J.	1
Mercer, D. W.	1
Merson, P. C.	3
Milburn, J. E. T.	10
Miller, H. S.	1
Mills, G. R.	3
Milner, J. P.	1
Milward, A.	3
Mitchell, C.	5
Moore, J.	1
Moore, R. F.	2
Moore, W. G. B.	2
Morren, T.	1
Morris, F.	1
Morris, J.	3
Mortensen, S. H.	23
Morton, J. R.	1
Mosforth, W.	3
Mullen, J.	6
Mullery, A. P.	1
Murphy, D. B	1
Neal, P. G.	5
Needham, E.	3

Name	
Pyper, James	2
Pyper, John	1
Quinn, J. M.	12
Quinn, S. J.	4
Reynolds, J.	1
Rowland, K.	1
Rowley, R. W. M.	2
Rushe, F.	1
Sheridan, J.	2
Sherrard, J.	1
Sherrard, W. C.	1
Shields, J.	5
Simpson, W. J.	5
Sloan, H. A. de B.	4
Smyth, S.	5
Spence, D. W.	3
Sproule, I.	1
Stanfield, O. M.	11
Stevenson, A. E.	5
Stewart, I.	2
Taggart, G. P.	7
Thompson, F. W.	2
Torrans, S.	1
Tully, C. P.	3
Turner, A.	1
Walker, J.	1
Walsh, D. J.	5
Ward, J. J.	**2**
Welsh, E.	1
Whiteside, N.	9
Whiteside, T.	1
Whitley, Jeff	2
Williams, J. R.	1
Williams, M. S.	1
Williamson, J.	1
Wilson, D. J.	1
Wilson, K. J.	6
Wilson, S. J.	7
Wilton, J. M.	2
Young, S.	1

N.B. In 1914 Young goal should be credited to Gillespie W v Wales

SCOTLAND

Name	
Aitken, R. *(Celtic)*	1
Aitken, R. *(Dumbarton)*	1
Aitkenhead, W. A. C.	2
Alexander, D.	1
Allan, D. S.	4
Allan, J.	1
Anderson, F.	1
Anderson, W.	4
Andrews, P.	1
Anya, I.	**2**
Archibald, A.	1
Archibald, S.	4
Baird, D.	2
Baird, J. C.	2
Baird, S.	2
Bannon, E.	1
Barbour, A.	1
Barker, J. B.	4
Battles, B. Jr	1
Bauld, W.	2
Baxter, J. C.	3
Beattie, C.	1
Bell, J.	5
Bennett, A.	1
Berra, C. D.	**3**
Berry, D.	1
Bett, J.	1
Beveridge, W. W.	1
Black, A.	3
Black, D.	1

Name	
Bone, J.	1
Booth, S.	6
Boyd, K	7
Boyd, R.	2
Boyd, T.	1
Boyd, W. G.	1
Brackenridge, T.	1
Brand, R.	8
Brazil, A.	1
Bremner, W. J.	3
Broadfoot, K.	1
Brown, A. D.	6
Brown, S.	4
Buchanan, P. S.	1
Buchanan, R.	1
Buckley, P.	1
Buick, A.	2
Burke, C.	2
Burley, C. W.	3
Burns, K.	1
Cairns, T.	1
Caldwell, G.	2
Calderwood, C.	1
Calderwood, R.	2
Caldow, E.	4
Cameron, C.	2
Campbell, C.	1
Campbell, John *(Celtic)*	5
Campbell, John *(Rangers)*	4
Campbell, J. (South Western)	1
Campbell, P.	2
Campbell, R.	1
Cassidy, J.	1
Chalmers, S.	3
Chambers, T.	1
Cheyne, A. G.	4
Christie, A. J.	1
Clarkson, D.	1
Clunas, W. L.	1
Collins, J.	12
Collins, R. Y.	10
Combe, J. R.	1
Commons, K.	2
Conn, A.	1
Cooper, D.	6
Craig, J.	1
Craig, T.	1
Crawford, S.	4
Cunningham, A. N.	5
Curran, H. P.	1
Dailly, C.	6
Dalglish, K.	30
Davidson, D.	1
Davidson, J. A.	1
Delaney, J.	3
Devine, A.	1
Dewar, G.	1
Dewar, N.	4
Dickov, P.	1
Dickson, W.	4
Divers, J.	1
Dobie, R. S.	1
Docherty, T. H.	1
Dodds, D.	1
Dodds, W.	7
Donaldson, A.	1
Donnachie, J.	1
Dougall, J.	1
Drummond, J.	2
Dunbar, M.	1
Duncan, D.	7
Duncan, D. M.	1
Duncan, J.	1
Dunn, J.	2
Durie, G. S.	7
Easson, J. F.	1
Elliott, M. S.	1

Name	
Ellis, J.	1
Ferguson, B.	3
Ferguson, J.	6
Fernie, W.	1
Fitchie, T. T.	1
Flavell, R.	2
Fleming, C.	2
Fleming, J. W.	3
Fletcher, D.	5
Fletcher, S. K.	**4**
Fraser, M. J. E.	3
Freedman, D. A.	1
Gallacher, H. K.	23
Gallacher, K. W.	9
Gallacher, P.	1
Galt, J. H.	1
Gemmell, T. *(St Mirren)*	1
Gemmell, T. *(Celtic)*	1
Gemmill, A.	8
Gemmill, S.	1
Gibb, W.	1
Gibson, D. W.	3
Gibson, J. D.	1
Gibson, N.	1
Gillespie, Jas.	3
Gillick, T.	3
Gilzean, A. J.	12
Goodwillie, D.	1
Gossland, J.	2
Goudie, J.	1
Gough, C. R.	6
Gourlay, J.	1
Graham, A.	2
Graham, G.	3
Gray, A.	7
Gray, E.	3
Gray, F.	1
Greig, J.	3
Groves, W.	4
Hamilton, G.	4
Hamilton, J. (Queen's Park)	3
Hamilton, R. C.	15
Hanley, G. C.	1
Harper, J. M.	2
Hartley, P. J.	1
Harrower, W.	5
Hartford, R. A.	4
Heggie, C. W	4
Henderson, J. G.	1
Henderson, W.	5
Hendry, E. C. J.	3
Herd, D. G.	3
Herd, G.	1
Hewie, J. D.	2
Higgins, A. *(Newcastle U)*	1
Higgins, A. *(Kilmarnock)*	1
Highet, T. C.	1
Holt, G.J.	1
Holton, J. A.	2
Hopkin, D.	2
Houliston, W.	2
Howie, H.	1
Howie, J.	2
Hughes, J.	1
Hunter, W.	1
Hutchison, D.	6
Hutchison, T.	1
Hutton, J.	1
Hyslop, T.	1
Imrie, W. N.	1
Jackson, A.	8
Jackson, C.	1
Jackson, D.	4
James, A. W.	4

Name	
Jardine, A.	1
Jenkinson, T.	1
Jess, E.	2
Johnston, A.	2
Johnston, L. H.	1
Johnston, M.	14
Johnstone, D.	2
Johnstone, J.	4
Johnstone, Jas.	1
Johnstone, R.	10
Johnstone, W.	1
Jordan, J.	11
Kay, J. L.	5
Keillor, A.	3
Kelly, J.	1
Kelso, R.	1
Ker, G.	10
King, A.	1
King, J.	1
Kinnear, D.	1
Kyle, K.	1
Lambert, P.	1
Lambie, J.	1
Lambie, W. A.	5
Lang, J. J.	2
Latta, A.	2
Law, D.	30
Leggat, G.	8
Lennie, W.	1
Lennox, R.	3
Liddell, W.	6
Lindsay, J.	6
Linwood, A. B.	1
Logan, J.	1
Lorimer, P.	4
Love, A.	1
Low, J. *(Cambuslang)*	1
Lowe, J. *(St Bernards)*	1
Macari, L.	5
MacDougall, E. J.	3
MacFarlane, A.	1
MacLeod, M.	1
Mackay, D. C.	4
Mackay, G.	1
MacKenzie, J. A.	1
Mackail-Smith, C.	1
Mackie, J. C.	2
MacKinnon, W. W.	5
Madden, J.	5
Maloney, S. R.	**6**
Marshall, H.	1
Marshall, J.	1
Mason, J.	4
Massie, A.	1
Masson, D. S.	5
McAdam, J.	1
McAllister, G.	5
McArthur, J.	1
McAulay, J. D.	1
McAvennie, F.	1
McCall, J.	1
McCall, S. M.	1
McCalliog, J.	1
McCallum, N.	1
McCann, N.	3
McClair, B. J.	2
McCoist, A.	19
McColl, R. S.	13
McCormack, R.	2
McCulloch, D.	3
McCulloch, L.	1
McDougall, J.	1
McFadden, J.	15*
McFadyen, W.	2
McGhee, M.	2
McGinlay, J.	4
McGregor, J.	1
McGrory, J.	6
McGuire, W.	1

* The Scottish FA officially changed Robsons's goal against Iceland on 10 September 2008 to McFadden.

McInally, A.	3	Ring, T.	2
McInnes, T.	2	Rioch, B. D.	6
McKie, J.	2	Ritchie, J.	1
McKimmie. S.	1	**Ritchie, M. T.**	**1**
McKinlay, W.	4	Ritchie, P. S.	1
McKinnon, A.	1	Robertson, A. *(Clyde)*	2
McKinnon, R.	1	**Robertson, A.**	
McLaren, A.	4	*(Dundee U)*	**1**
McLaren, J.	1	Robertson, J.	3
McLean, A.	1	Robertson, J. N.	8
McLean, T.	1	Robertson, J. T.	2
McLintock, F.	1	Robertson, T.	1
McMahon, A.	6	Robertson, W.	1
McManus, S.	2	Russell, D.	1
McMenemy, J.	5		
McMillan, I. L.	2	Scott, A. S.	5
McNeill, W.	3	Sellar, W.	4
McNiel, H.	5	Sharp, G.	1
McPhail, J.	3	Shaw, F. W.	1
McPhail, R.	7	Shearer, D.	2
McPherson, J.		Simpson, J.	1
(Kilmarnock)	7	Smith, A.	5
McPherson, J.		Smith, G.	4
(Vale of Leven)	1	Smith, J.	1
McPherson, R.	1	Smith, John	13
McQueen, G.	5	Snodgrass, R.	3
McStay, P.	9	Somerville, G.	1
McSwegan, G.	1	Souness, G. J.	4
Meiklejohn, D. D.	3	Speedie, F.	2
Millar, J.	2	St John, I.	9
Miller, K.	18	Steel, W.	12
Miller, T.	2	Stein, C.	10
Miller, W.	1	Stevenson, G.	4
Mitchell, R. C.	1	Stewart, A.	1
Morgan, W.	1	Stewart, R.	1
Morris, D.	1	Stewart, W. E.	1
Morris, H.	3	Strachan, G.	5
Morrison, J. C.	3	Sturrock, P.	3
Morton, A. L.	5		
Mudie, J. K.	9	Taylor, J. D.	1
Mulgrew, C. P.	2	Templeton, R.	1
Mulhall, G.	1	Thompson, S.	3
Munro, A. D.	1	Thomson, A.	1
Munro, N.	2	Thomson, C.	4
Murdoch, R.	5	Thomson, R.	1
Murphy, F.	1	Thomson, W.	1
Murray, J.	1	Thornton, W.	1
Napier, C. E.	3	Waddell, T. S.	1
Narey, D.	1	Waddell, W.	6
Naismith, S. J.	**5**	Walker, J.	1
Naysmith, G. A.	1	Walker, R.	7
Neil, R. G.	2	Walker, T.	9
Nevin, P. K. F.	5	Wallace, I. A.	1
Nicholas, C.	5	Wark, J.	7
Nisbet, J.	2	Watson, J. A. K.	1
		Watt, F.	2
O'Connor, G.	4	Watt, W. W.	1
O'Donnell, F.	2	Webster, A.	1
O'Hare, J.	5	Weir, A.	1
Ormond, W. E.	2	Weir, D.	1
O'Rourke, F.	1	Weir, J. B.	2
Orr, R.	1	White, J. A.	3
Orr, T.	1	Wilkie, L.	1
Oswald, J.	1	Wilson, A. *(Sheffield W)*	2
Own goals	21	Wilson, A. N.	
		(Dunfermline Ath)	13
Parlane, D.	1	Wilson, D. *(Liverpool)*	1
Paul, H. McD.	2	Wilson, D.	
Paul, W.	5	*(Queen's Park)*	2
Pettigrew, W.	2	Wilson, D. *(Rangers)*	9
Provan, D.	1	Wilson, H.	1
		Wylie, T. G.	1
Quashie, N. F.	1		
Quinn, J.	7	Young, A.	5
Quinn, P.	1		
		WALES	
Rankin, G.	2	Allchurch, I. J.	23
Rankin, R.	2	Allen, M.	3
Reid, W.	4	Astley, D. J.	12
Reilly, L.	22	Atherton, R. W.	2
Renny-Tailyour, H. W.	1		
Rhodes, J. L.	3	**Bale, G. F.**	**17**
Richmond, J. T.	1	Bamford, T.	1

Barnes, W.	1	Hopkins, I. J.	2
Bellamy, C. D.	19	Horne, B.	2
Blackmore, C. G.	1	Howell, E. G.	3
Blake, D.	1	Hughes, L. M.	16
Blake, N. A.	4		
Bodin, P. J.	3	James, E.	2
Boulter, L. M.	1	James, L.	10
Bowdler, J. C. H.	3	James, R.	7
Bowen, D. L.	1	Jarrett, R. H.	3
Bowen, M.	3	Jenkyns, C. A.	1
Boyle, T.	1	Jones, A.	1
Bryan, T.	1	Jones, Bryn	6
Burgess, W. A. R.	1	Jones, B. S.	2
Burke, T.	1	Jones, Cliff	16
Butler, W. T.	1	Jones, C. W.	1
		Jones, D. E.	1
Chapman, T.	2	Jones, Evan	1
Charles, J.	1	Jones, H.	1
Charles, M.	6	Jones, I.	1
Charles, W. J.	15	Jones, J. L.	1
Church, S. R.	2	Jones, J. O.	1
Clarke, R. J.	5	Jones, J. P.	1
Coleman, C.	4	Jones, Leslie J.	1
Collier, D. J.	1	Jones, R. A.	2
Collins, J.	3	Jones, W. L.	6
Cotterill, D. R. G. B.	**2**		
Crosse, K.	1	Keenor, F. C.	2
Cumner, R. H.	1	King, A. P.	2
Curtis, A.	6	Koumas, J.	10
Curtis, E. R.	3	Krzywicki, R. L.	1
Davies, D. W.	1	Ledley, J. C.	3
Davies, E. Lloyd	1	Leek, K.	5
Davies, G.	2	Lewis, B.	4
Davies, L. S.	6	Lewis, D. M.	2
Davies, R. T.	9	Lewis, W.	8
Davies, R. W.	6	Lewis, W. L.	3
Davies, Simon	6	Llewelyn, C. M	1
Davies, Stanley	5	Lovell, S.	1
Davies, W.	6	Lowrie, G.	2
Davies, W. H.	1		
Davies, William	5	Mahoney, J. F.	1
Davis, W. O.	1	Mays, A. W.	1
Deacy, N.	4	Medwin, T. C.	6
Doughty, J.	6	Melville, A. K	3
Doughty, R.	2	Meredith, W. H.	11
Durban, A.	2	Mills, T. J.	1
Dwyer, P.	2	Moore, G.	1
		Morgan, J. R.	2
Earnshaw, R.	16	Morgan-Owen, H.	1
Eastwood, F.	4	Morgan-Owen, M. M.	2
Edwards, D. A.	3	Morison, S.	1
Edwards, G.	2	Morris, A. G.	9
Edwards, R. I.	4	Morris, H.	2
England, H. M.	4	Morris, R.	1
Evans, C.	2	Morris, S.	1
Evans, I.	1		
Evans, J.	1	Nicholas, P.	2
Evans, R. E.	2		
Evans, W.	1	O'Callaghan, E.	3
Eyton-Jones, J. A.	1	O'Sullivan, P. A.	1
		Owen, G.	2
Fletcher, C.	1	Owen, W.	4
Flynn, B.	7	Owen, W. P.	6
Ford, T.	23	Own goals	14
Foulkes, W. I.	1		
Fowler, J.	3	Palmer, D.	3
		Parry, P. I.	1
Giles, D.	2	Parry, T. D.	3
Giggs, R. J.	12	Paul, R.	1
Glover, E. M.	7	Peake, E.	1
Godfrey, B. C.	2	Pembridge, M.	6
Green, A. W.	3	Perry, E.	1
Griffiths, A. T.	6	Phillips, C.	5
Griffiths, M. W.	2	Phillips, D.	2
Griffiths, T. P.	3	Powell, A.	1
		Powell, D.	1
Harris, C. S.	1	Price, J.	4
Hartson, J.	14	Price, P.	1
Hersee, R.	1	Pryce-Jones, W. E.	3
Hewitt, R.	1	Pugh, D. H.	1
Hockey, T.	1		
Hodges, G.	2	**Ramsay, A. J.**	**9**
Hole, W. J.	1	Reece, G. I.	2

Rees, R. R.	3
Richards, R. W.	1
Roach, J.	2
Robbins, W. W.	4
Roberts, J. *(Corwen)*	1
Roberts, Jas.	1
Roberts, P. S.	1
Roberts, R. *(Druids)*	1
Roberts, W. *(Llangollen)*	1
	2
Roberts, W. *(Wrexham)*	1
Roberts, W. H.	1
Robinson, C. P.	1
Robinson, J. R. C.	3
Robson-Kanu, T. H.	**2**
Rush, I.	28
Russell, M. R.	1
Sabine, H. W.	1
Saunders, D.	22
Savage, R. W.	2
Shaw, E. G.	2
Sisson, H.	4
Slatter, N.	2
Smallman, D. P.	1
Speed, G. A.	7
Symons, C. J.	2
Tapscott, D. R.	4
Taylor, G. K.	1
Thomas, M.	4
Thomas, T.	1
Toshack, J. B.	12
Trainer, H.	2
Vaughan, D. O.	1
Vaughan, John	2
Vernon, T. R.	8
Vizard, E. T.	1
Vokes, S. M.	6
Walsh, I.	7
Warren, F. W.	3
Watkins, W. M.	4
Wilding, J.	4
Williams, A.	1
Williams, D. R.	2
Williams, G. E.	1
Williams, G. G.	1
Williams, W.	1
Woosnam, A. P.	3
Wynn, G. A.	1
Yorath, T. C.	2
Young, E.	1

REPUBLIC OF IRELAND

Aldridge, J.	19
Ambrose, P.	1
Anderson, J.	1
Andrews, K.	3
Barrett, G.	2
Bermingham, P.	1
Bradshaw, P.	4
Brady, L.	9
Brady, R.	**3**
Breen, G.	7
Brown, J.	1
Byrne, D.	1
Byrne, J.	4
Cantwell, N.	14
Carey, J.	3
Carroll, T.	1
Cascarino, A.	19
Clark, C.	1
Coad, P.	3
Connolly, D. J.	9
Conroy, T.	2
Conway, J.	3
Cox, S. R.	4
Coyne, T.	6
Cummins, G.	5
Curtis, D.	8
Daly, G.	13
Davis, T.	4
Dempsey, J.	1
Dennehy, M.	2
Doherty, G. M. T.	4
Donnelly, J.	4
Donnelly, T.	1
Doyle, K. E.	**14**
Duff, D. A.	8
Duffy, B.	1
Duggan, H.	1
Dunne, J.	13
Dunne, L.	1
Dunne, R. P.	8
Eglington, T.	2
Elliott, S. W.	1
Ellis, P.	1
Fagan, F.	5
Fahey, K.	3
Fallon, S.	2
Fallon, W.	2
Farrell, P.	3
Finnan, S.	2
Fitzgerald, P.	2
Fitzgerald, J.	1
Fitzsimons, A.	7
Flood, J. J.	4
Fogarty, A.	3
Foley, D.	2
Fullam, J.	1
Fullam, R.	1
Galvin, A.	1
Gavin, J.	2
Geoghegan, M.	2
Gibson, D. T. D.	1
Giles, J.	5
Givens, D.	19
Glynn, D.	1
Grealish, T.	8
Green, P. J.	1
Grimes, A. A.	1
Hale, A.	2
Hand, E.	2
Harte, I. P.	11
Haverty, J.	3
Healy, C.	1
Holland, M. R.	5
Holmes, J.	1
Hoolahan, W.	**2**
Horlacher, A.	2
Houghton, R.	6
Hughton, C.	1
Hunt, S. P.	1
Hurley, C.	2
Ireland, S. J.	4
Irwin, D.	4
Jordan, D.	1
Kavanagh, G. A.	1
Keane, R. D.	**65**
Keane, R. M.	9
Kelly, D.	9
Kelly, G.	2
Kelly, J.	2
Kennedy, M.	4
Keogh, A.	2
Keogh, R. J.	1
Kernaghan, A. N.	1
Kilbane, K. D.	8
Kinsella, M. A.	3
Lacey, W.	1
Lawrence, L.	2
Lawrenson, M.	5
Leech, M.	2
Long, S. P.	**12**
McAteer, J. W.	3
McCann, J.	1
McCarthy, M.	2
McClean, J. J.	**4**
McEvoy, A.	6
McGeady, A. G.	**5**
McGee, P.	4
McGrath, P.	8
McLoughlin, A. F.	2
McPhail, S. J. P.	1
Mancini, T.	1
Martin, C.	6
Martin, M.	4
Miller, L. W. P.	1
Mooney, J.	1
Moore, P.	7
Moran, K.	6
Morrison, C. H.	9
Moroney, T.	1
Mulligan, P.	1
O'Brien, A. J.	1
O'Callaghan, K.	1
O'Connor, T.	2
O'Dea, D.	1
O'Farrell, F.	2
O'Flanagan, K.	3
O'Keefe, E.	1
O'Leary, D. A.	1
O'Neill, F.	1
O'Neill, K. P.	4
O'Reilly, J. *(Brideville)*	2
O'Reilly, J. *(Cork)*	1
O'Shea, J. F.	**3**
Own goals	14
Pearce, A. J.	**2**
Pilkington, A. N. J.	**1**
Quinn, N.	21
Reid, A. M.	4
Reid, S. J.	2
Ringstead, A.	7
Robinson, M.	4
Rogers, E.	5
Ryan, G.	1
Ryan, R.	3
St Ledger-Hall, S.	3
Sheedy, K.	9
Sheridan, J.	5
Slaven, B.	1
Sloan, J.	1
Squires, J.	1
Stapleton, F.	20
Staunton, S.	7
Strahan, J.	1
Sullivan, J.	1
Townsend, A. D.	7
Treacy, R.	5
Touhy, L.	4
Waddock, G.	3
Walsh, D.	5
Walsh, M.	3
Walters, J. R.	**6**
Ward, S.	2
Waters, J.	1
White, J. J.	2
Whelan, G. D.	2
Whelan, R.	3
Wilson, M. D.	1

BRITISH AND IRISH INTERNATIONAL MANAGERS

England
Walter Winterbottom 1946–1962 (after period as coach); Alf Ramsey 1963–1974; Joe Mercer (caretaker) 1974; Don Revie 1974–1977; Ron Greenwood 1977–1982; Bobby Robson 1982–1990; Graham Taylor 1990–1993; Terry Venables (coach) l994–1996; Glenn Hoddle 1996–1999; Kevin Keegan 1999–2000; Sven-Goran Eriksson 2001–2006; Steve McClaren 2006–2007; Fabio Capello 2008–2012; Roy Hodgson from May 2012.

Northern Ireland
Peter Doherty 1951–1952; Bertie Peacock 1962–1967; Billy Bingham 1967–1971; Terry Neill 1971–1975; Dave Clements (player-manager) 1975–1976; Danny Blanchflower 1976–1979; Billy Bingham 1980–1994; Bryan Hamilton 1994–1998; Lawrie McMenemy 1998–1999; Sammy McIlroy 2000–2003; Lawrie Sanchez 2004–2007; Nigel Worthington 2007–2011; Michael O'Neill from December 2011.

Scotland (since 1967)
Bobby Brown 1967–1971; Tommy Docherty 1971–1972; Willie Ormond 1973–1977; Ally MacLeod 1977–1978; Jock Stein 1978–1985; Alex Ferguson (caretaker) 1985–1986 Andy Roxburgh (coach) 1986–1993; Craig Brown 1993–2001; Berti Vogts 2002–2004; Walter Smith 2004–2007; Alex McLeish 2007; George Burley 2008–2009; Craig Levein 2009–2012; Gordon Strachan from February 2013.

Wales (since 1974)
Mike Smith 1974–1979; Mike England 1980–1988; David Williams (caretaker) 1988; Terry Yorath 1988–1993; John Toshack 1994 for one match; Mike Smith 1994–1995; Bobby Gould 1995–1999; Mark Hughes 1999–2004; John Toshack 2004–2010; Gary Speed 2010–2011; Chris Coleman from January 2012.

Republic of Ireland
Liam Tuohy 1971–1972; Johnny Giles 1973–1980 (after period as player-manager); Eoin Hand 1980–1985; Jack Charlton 1986–1996; Mick McCarthy 1996–2002; Brian Kerr 2003–2006; Steve Staunton 2006–2007; Giovanni Trapattoni 2008–2013; Martin O'Neill from November 2013.

Manager Michael O'Neill orchestrated Northern Ireland's promising Euro 2016 Championships qualifying campaign.
(Andreas Papakonstaninou/Demotix/Press Association Images)

SOUTH AMERICA

COPA SUDAMERICANA 2014

FIRST ROUND – SOUTH ZONE FIRST LEG

Huachipato v San Jose	3-1
Universitario v Iquique	2-0
Deportivo Capiata v Danubio	3-1
Rentistas v Cerro Porteno	0-2
General Diaz v Cobresal	2-1
Nacional Potosi v Libertad	1-0
Universidad Catolica v River Plate	0-1
Penarol v Jorge Wilstermann	2-0

FIRST ROUND – SOUTH ZONE SECOND LEG (agg)

San Jose v Huachipato	2-3 (3-6)
Iquique v Universitario	1-0 (1-2)
Danubio v Deportivo Capiata	2-2 (3-5)
Cerro Porteno v Rentistas	0-1 (2-1)
Cobresal v General Diaz	2-2 (3-4)
Libertad v Nacional Potosi	3-0 (3-1)
River Plate v Universidad Catolica	3-0 (4-0)
Jorge Wilstermann v Penarol	0-4 (0-6)

FIRST ROUND – NORTH ZONE FIRST LEG

Inti Gas v Caracas	0-1
Barcelona v Alianza Lima	3-0
Deportivo La Guaira v Atletico Nacional	1-1
Aguilas Doradas v Emelec	1-1
UTC v Deportivo Cali	0-0
Millonarios v Universidad Cesar Vallejo	1-2
Trujillanos v Independiente del Valle	0-1
Universidad Catolica v Deportivo Anzoategui	1-1

FIRST ROUND – NORTH ZONE SECOND LEG (agg)

Caracas v Inti Gas	1-0 (2-0)
Alianza Lima v Barcelona	0-0 (0-3)
Atletico Nacional v Deportivo La Guaira	1-0 (2-1)
Emelec v Aguilas Doradas	2-1 (3-2)
Deportivo Cali v UTC	3-0 (3-0)
Universidad Cesar Vallejo v Millonarios	2-2 (4-3)
Independiente del Valle v Trujillanos	1-1 (2-1)
Deportivo Anzoategui v Universidad Catolica	1-1 (2-2)
Universidad Catolica won 5-4 on penalties.	

SECOND ROUND – FIRST LEG

Sport Recife v Vitoria	0-1
Deportivo Capiata v Caracas	1-1
Godoy Cruz v River Plate	0-1
Huachipato v Universidad Catolica	2-0
Fluminense v Goias	2-1
Penarol v Deportivo Cali	2-2
Universitario v Universidad Cesar Vallejo	2-2
Internacional v Bahia	0-2
Independiente del Valle v Cerro Porteno	1-0
Gimnasia y Esgrima v Estudiantes	0-0
Emelec v River Plate	2-1
Criciuma v Sao Paulo	2-1
Barcelona v Libertad	1-0
Rosario Central v Boca Juniors	1-1
Atletico Nacional v General Diaz	0-2

SECOND ROUND – SECOND LEG (agg)

Vitoria v Sport Recife	2-1 (3-1)
Caracas v Deportivo Capiata	1-3 (2-4)
River Plate v Godoy Cruz	2-0 (3-0)
Universidad Catolica v Huachipato	1-0 (1-2)

Goias v Fluminense	1-0 (2-2)
Goias won on away goals rule.	
Deportivo Cali v Penarol	0-1 (2-3)
Universidad Cesar Vallejo v Universitario	3-0 (5-2)
Bahia v Internacional	1-1 (3-1)
Cerro Porteno v Independiente del Valle	3-0 (3-1)
Estudiantes v Gimnasia y Esgrima	1-0 (1-0)
River Plate v Emelec	1-1 (2-3)
Sao Paulo v Criciuma	2-0 (3-2)
Libertad v Barcelona	2-0 (2-1)
Boca Juniors v Rosario Central	3-0 (4-1)
General Diaz v Atletico Nacional	1-3 (3-3)
Atletico Nacional won on away goals rule.	

ROUND OF 16 – FIRST LEG

Atletico Nacional v Vitoria	2-2
Boca Juniors v Deportivo Capiata	0-1
Libertad v River Plate	1-3
Sao Paulo v Huachipato	1-0
Emelec v Goias	1-0
Estudiantes v Penarol	2-1
Cerro Porteno v Lanus	2-1
Bahia v Universidad Cesar Vallejo	2-0

ROUND OF 16 – SECOND LEG (agg)

Vitoria v Atletico Nacional	0-1 (2-3)
Deportivo Capiata v Boca Juniors	0-1 (1-1)
Boca Juniors won 4-3 on penalties.	
River Plate v Libertad	2-0 (5-1)
Huachipato v Sao Paulo	2-3 (2-4)
Goias v Emelec	1-0 (1-1)
Emelec won 6-5 on penalties.	
Penarol v Estudiantes	2-1 (3-3)
Estudiantes won 3-1 on penalties.	
Lanus v Cerro Porteno	1-1 (2-3)
Universidad Cesar Vallejo v Bahia	2-0 (2-2)
Universidad Cesar Vallejo won 7-6 on penalties.	

QUARTER-FINALS – FIRST LEG

Atletico Nacional v Universidad Cesar Vallejo	1-0
Boca Juniors v Cerro Porteno	1-0
Estudiantes v River Plate	1-2
Sao Paulo v Emelec	4-2

QUARTER-FINALS – SECOND LEG (agg)

Universidad Cesar Vallejo v Atletico Nacional	0-1 (0-2)
Cerro Porteno v Boca Juniors	1-4 (1-5)
River Plate v Estudiantes	3-2 (5-3)
Emelec v Sao Paulo	3-2 (5-6)

SEMI-FINALS – FIRST LEG

Atletico Nacional v Sao Paulo	1-0
Boca Juniors v River Plate	0-0

SEMI-FINALS – SECOND LEG (agg)

Sao Paulo v Atletico Nacional	1-0 (1-1)
Atletico Nacional won 4-1 on penalties.	
River Plate v Boca Juniors	1-0 (1-0)

FINAL – FIRST LEG

Atletico Nacional v River Plate	1-1

FINAL – SECOND LEG (agg)

River Plate v Atletico Nacional	2-0 (3-1)

RECOPA SUDAMERICANA 2014

FINAL – FIRST LEG

Lanus v Atletico Mineiro	0-1

FINAL – SECOND LEG (agg)

Atletico Mineiro v Lanus	4-3 (5-3)
(aet)	

COPA SANTANDER LIBERTADORES 2014

SEMI-FINALS – FIRST LEG

Nacional Asuncion v Defensor Sporting	2-0
San Lorenzo v Bolivar	5-0

SEMI-FINALS – SECOND LEG (agg)

Defensor Sporting v Nacional Asuncion	1-0 (1-2)
Bolivar v San Lorenzo	1-0 (1-5)

FINAL – FIRST LEG

Nacional Asuncion v San Lorenzo	1-1

FINAL – SECOND LEG (agg)

San Lorenzo v Nacional Asuncion	1-0 (2-1)

COPA SANTANDER LIBERTADORES 2015

FIRST ROUND FIRST LEG
Alianza Lima v Huracan	0–4
Independiente del Valle v Estudiantes	1–0
Deportivo Tachira v Cerro Porteno	2–1
Morelia v The Strongest	1–1
Palestino v Nacional	1–0
Corinthians v Once Caldas	4–0

FIRST ROUND SECOND LEG
		(agg)
Huracan v Alianza Lima	0–0	4–0
Estudiantes v Independiente del Valle	4–0	4–1
Cerro Porteno v Deportivo Tachira	2–2	3–4
The Strongest v Morelia	2–0	3–1
Nacional v Palestino	2–1	2–2
(Palestino won on away goals)		
Once Caldas v Corinthians	1–1	1-5

SECOND ROUND

GROUP 1
Atletico Mineiro v Atlas	0–1
Santa Fe v Colo Colo	3–1
Colo Colo v Atlas	2–0
Santa Fe v Atletico Mineiro	0–1
Atlas v Colo Colo	1–3
Atletico Mineiro v Santa Fe	2–0
Atlas v Atletico Mineiro	1–0
Colo Colo v Santa Fe	0–3
Atletico Mineiro v Colo Colo	2–0
Santa Fe v Atlas	3–1

GROUP 2
Sao Paulo v Danubio	4–0
San Lorenzo v Corinthians	0–1
Danubio v Corinthians	1–2
Sao Paulo v San Lorenzo	1–0
San Lorenzo v Sao Paulo	1–0
Corinthians v Danubio	4–0
Danubio v Sao Paulo	1–2
Corinthians v San Lorenzo	0–0
Sao Paulo v Corinthians	2–0
San Lorenzo v Danubio	0–1

GROUP 3
Mineros de Guayana v Club Universitario	0–1
Cruzeiro v Huracan	0–0
Club Universitario v Huracan	0–0
Mineros de Guayana v Cruzeiro	0–2
Huracan v Club Universitario	1–1
Cruzeiro v Mineros de Guayana	3–0
Huracan v Cruzeiro	3–1
Club Universitario v Mineros de Guayana	2–0
Cruzeiro v Club Universitario	2–0
Mineros de Guayana v Huracan	3–0

GROUP 4
Emelec v The Strongest	3–0
Internacional v Universidad Chile	3–1
Internacional v Emelec	3–2
Universidad Chile v The Strongest	3–1
The Strongest v Universidad Chile	5–3
Emelec v Internacional	1–1
The Strongest v Emelec	1–0
Universidad Chile v Internacional	0–4
Emelec v Universidad Chile	2–0
Internacional v The Strongest	1–0

GROUP 5
Boca Juniors v Wanderers	2–1
Zamora v Palestino	0–1
Wanderers v Palestino	1–0
Boca Juniors v Zamora	5–0
Zamora v Boca Juniors	1–5
Palestino v Wanderers	1–1
Palestino v Zamora	4–0
Wanderers v Boca Juniors	0–3
Boca Juniors v Palestino	2–0
Zamora v Wanderers	0–3

GROUP 6
River Plate v Tigres UANL	1–1
Juan Aurich v San Jose	2–0
San Jose v Tigres UANL	0–1
Juan Aurich v River Plate	1–1
Tigres UANL v San Jose	4–0
River Plate v Juan Aurich	1–1
San Jose v Juan Aurich	1–1
Tigres UANL v River Plate	2–2
Juan Aurich v Tigres UANL	4–5
River Plate v San Jose	3–0

GROUP 7
Barcelona v Libertad	0–1
Atletico Nacional v Estudiantes	1–1
Barcelona v Atletico Nacional	1–2
Libertad v Estudiantes	1–0
Estudiantes v Libertad	1–0
Atletico Nacional v Barcelona	2–3
Estudiantes v Atletico Nacional	0–1
Libertad v Barcelona	1–1
Atletico Nacional v Libertad	4–0
Barcelona v Estudiantes	0–2

GROUP 8
Racing Club v Guarani	4–1
Sporting Cristal v Deportivo Tachira	1–1
Guarani v Deportivo Tachira	5–2
Racing Club v Sporting Cristal	1–2
Sporting Cristal v Racing Club	0–2
Deportivo Tachira v Guarani	1–1
Guarani v Racing Club	2–0
Deportivo Tachira v Sporting Cristal	0–0
Sporting Cristal v Guarani	1–1
Racing Club v Deportivo Tachira	3–2

ROUND OF 16 FIRST LEG
River Plate v Boca Juniors	1–0
Universitario v Tigres UANL	1–2
Atletico Mineiro v Internacional	2–2
Guarani v Corinthians	2–0
Montevideo Wanderers v Racing	1–1
Estudiantes v Santa Fe	2–1
Emelec v Atletico Nacional	2–0
Sao Paulo v Cruzeiro	1–0

ROUND OF 16 SECOND LEG
		(agg)
Boca Juniors v River Plate	0–0	0-1
(Match abandoned due to crowd disturbance.		
Boca Juniors disqualified.)		
Tigres UANL v Universitario	1–1	3-2
Internacional v Atletico Mineiro	1–3	5-3
Corinthians v Guarani	1–0	0-3
Racing v Montevideo Wanderers	1–2	3-2
Santa Fe v Estudiantes	0–2	3-2
Atletico Nacional v Emelec	0–1	1-2
Cruzeiro v Sao Paulo	0–1	1-1
(Cruzeiro won 4-3 on penalties)		

QUARTER-FINALS FIRST LEG
River Plate v Cruzeiro	0–1
Emelec v Tigres UANL	1–0
Santa Fe v Internacional	1–0
Guarani v Racing	1–0

QUARTER-FINALS SECOND LEG
		(agg)
Cruzeiro v River Plate	3–0	1-3
Tigres UANL v Emelec	0–2	2-1
Internacional v Santa Fe	0–2	2-1
Racing v Guarani	0–0	0-1
Competition still being played.		

AFRICA

AFRICAN CUP OF NATIONS 2015

GROUP STAGE

GROUP A

Equatorial Guinea v Congo	1-1
Burkina Faso v Gabon	0-2
Equatorial Guinea v Burkina Faso	0-0
Gabon v Congo	0-1
Congo v Burkina Faso	2-1
Gabon v Equatorial Guinea	0-2

Group A Table	P	W	D	L	F	A	GD	Pts
Congo	3	2	1	0	4	2	2	7
Equatorial Guinea	3	1	2	0	3	1	2	5
Gabon	3	1	0	2	2	3	-1	3
Burkina Faso	3	0	1	2	1	4	-3	1

GROUP B

Zambia v DR Congo	1-1
Tunisia v Cape Verde	1-1
Zambia v Tunisia	1-2
Cape Verde v DR Congo	0-0
DR Congo v Tunisia	1-1
Cape Verde v Zambia	0-0

Group B Table	P	W	D	L	F	A	GD	Pts
Tunisia	3	1	2	0	4	3	1	5
DR Congo	3	0	3	0	2	2	0	3
Cape Verde	3	0	3	0	1	1	0	3
Zambia	3	0	2	1	2	3	-1	2

GROUP C

Ghana v Senegal	1-2
Algeria v South Africa	3-1
Ghana v Algeria	1-0
South Africa v Senegal	1-1
South Africa v Ghana	1-2
Senegal v Algeria	0-2

Group C Table	P	W	D	L	F	A	GD	Pts
Ghana	3	2	0	1	4	3	1	6
Algeria	3	2	0	1	5	2	3	6
Senegal	3	1	1	1	3	4	-1	4
South Africa	3	0	1	2	3	6	-3	1

GROUP D

Ivory Coast v Guinea	1-1
Mali v Cameroon	1-1
Ivory Coast v Mali	1-1
Cameroon v Guinea	1-1
Cameroon v Ivory Coast	0-1
Guinea v Mali	1-1

Group D Table	P	W	D	L	F	A	GD	Pts
Ivory Coast	3	1	2	0	3	2	1	5
Guinea	3	0	3	0	3	3	0	3
Mali	3	0	3	0	3	3	0	3
Cameroon	3	0	2	1	2	3	-1	2

QUARTER-FINALS

Congo v DR Congo	2-4
Tunisia v Equatorial Guinea	1-2
aet.	
Ghana v Guinea	3-0
Ivory Coast v Algeria	3-1

SEMI-FINALS

DR Congo v Ivory Coast	1-3
Ghana v Equatorial Guinea	3-0

MATCH FOR 3RD PLACE

DR Congo v Equatorial Guinea	0-0
aet; DR Congo won 4-2 on penalties.	

FINAL

Ivory Coast v Ghana	0-0
aet; Ivory Coast won 9-8 on penalties.	

NORTH AMERICA

MAJOR LEAGUE SOCCER 2014

EASTERN CONFERENCE	P	W	D	L	F	A	GD	Pts
DC United	34	17	8	9	52	37	15	59
NE Revolution	34	17	4	13	51	46	5	55
Columbus Crew	34	14	10	10	52	42	10	52
New York Red Bulls	34	13	11	10	55	50	5	50
Sporting Kansas City	34	14	7	13	48	41	7	49
Philadelphia Union	34	10	12	12	51	51	0	42
Toronto	34	11	8	15	44	54	-10	41
Houston Dynamo	34	11	6	17	39	58	-19	39
Chicago Fire	34	6	18	10	41	51	-10	36
Montreal Impact	34	6	10	18	38	58	-20	28

WESTERN CONFERENCE	P	W	D	L	F	A	GD	Pts
Seattle Sounders	34	20	4	10	65	50	15	64
LA Galaxy	34	17	10	7	69	37	32	61
Real Salt Lake	34	15	11	8	54	39	15	56
FC Dallas	34	16	6	12	55	45	10	54
Vancouver Whitecaps	34	12	14	8	42	40	2	50
Portland Timbers	34	12	13	9	61	52	9	49
Chivas USA	34	9	6	19	29	61	-32	33
Colorado Rapids	34	8	8	18	43	62	-19	32
San Jose Earthquakes	34	6	12	16	35	50	-15	30

EASTERN KNOCKOUT ROUND

New York Red Bulls v Sporting Kansas City	2-1

WESTERN KNOCKOUT ROUND

FC Dallas v Vancouver Whitecaps	2-1

EASTERN SEMI-FINALS – FIRST LEG

New York Red Bulls v DC United	2-0
Columbus Crew v New England Revolution	2-4

EASTERN SEMI-FINALS – SECOND LEG

DC United v New York Red Bulls	2-1 (2-3)
New England Revolution v Columbus Crew	3-1 (7-3)

WESTERN SEMI-FINALS – FIRST LEG

FC Dallas v Seattle Sounders	1-1
Real Salt Lake v LA Galaxy	0-0

WESTERN SEMI-FINALS – SECOND LEG

Seattle Sounders v FC Dallas	0-0 (1-1)
Seattle Sounders won on away goals rule.	
LA Galaxy v Real Salt Lake	5-0 (5-0)

EASTERN CHAMPIONSHIP – FIRST LEG

New York Red Bulls v New England Revolution	1-2

EASTERN CHAMPIONSHIP – SECOND LEG

New England Revolution v New York Red Bulls	2-2 (4-3)

WESTERN CHAMPIONSHIP – FIRST LEG

LA Galaxy v Seattle Sounders	1-0

WESTERN CHAMPIONSHIP – SECOND LEG

Seattle Sounders v LA Galaxy	2-1 (2-2)
LA Galaxy won on away goals rule.	

MLS CUP FINAL 2014, Sunday 7 December 2014

LA Galaxy (0) 2 *(Zardes 52, Keane 111)*

New England Revolution (0) 1 *(Tierney 79)*

LA Galaxy: (442) Penedo; De La Garza, Gonzalez, Leonardo, Rogers (Gargan 91); Ishizaki (Gordon 91), Sarvas, Juninho (Husidic 96), Donovan; Keane, Zardes.
New England Revolution: (4231) Shuttleworth; Tierney, Goncalves, Soares, Farrell; Jones, Caldwell (Kobayashi 58); Rowe, Nguyen (Dorman 90), Bunbury; Davies (Mullins 72).
aet. Referee: Mark Geiger.

UEFA UNDER-21 CHAMPIONSHIP 2013–15

QUALIFYING ROUND

GROUP 1

Wales v Moldova	1-0
Lithuania v San Marino	2-1
Finland v Lithuania	2-2
San Marino v Moldova	0-3
Wales v Finland	1-5
San Marino v Lithuania	0-1
Lithuania v Finland	0-1
England v Moldova	1-0
San Marino v Wales	1-0
Finland v England	1-1
Moldova v Wales	0-0
San Marino v England	0-4
Wales v Lithuania	2-0
Wales v San Marino	4-0
Moldova v Finland	1-0
England v Lithuania	5-0
England v Finland	3-0
Moldova v San Marino	2-0
Moldova v Lithuania	3-0
England v San Marino	9-0
England v Wales	1-0
San Marino v Finland	0-0
Wales v England	1-3
Finland v Moldova	1-0
Lithuania v Moldova	0-3
Lithuania v England	0-1
Finland v Wales	2-2
Lithuania v Wales	1-1
Moldova v England	0-3
Finland v San Marino	5-0

Group 1 Table	P	W	D	L	F	A	GD	Pts
England	10	9	1	0	31	2	29	28
Finland	10	4	4	2	17	10	7	16
Moldova	10	5	1	4	12	6	6	16
Wales	10	3	3	4	12	13	–1	12
Lithuania	10	2	2	6	6	19	–13	8
San Marino	10	1	1	8	2	30	–28	4

GROUP 2

Andorra v Russia	0-3
Bulgaria v Andorra	3-0
Andorra v Bulgaria	0-3
Estonia v Denmark	0-1
Estonia v Andorra	1-1
Slovenia v Estonia	0-1
Russia v Slovenia	2-1
Bulgaria v Estonia	1-1
Denmark v Andorra	6-0
Russia v Bulgaria	3-1
Slovenia v Denmark	2-2
Bulgaria v Russia	3-3
Denmark v Slovenia	2-2
Russia v Denmark	0-2
Slovenia v Bulgaria	2-1
Slovenia v Russia	0-1
Andorra v Estonia	0-2
Bulgaria v Denmark	2-3
Bulgaria v Slovenia	1-5
Andorra v Denmark	0-2
Russia v Estonia	1-0
Denmark v Estonia	8-0
Andorra v Slovenia	0-5
Estonia v Russia	1-2
Slovenia v Andorra	5-0
Estonia v Bulgaria	2-2
Denmark v Russia	4-2
Estonia v Slovenia	1-7
Denmark v Bulgaria	7-1
Russia v Andorra	5-0

Group 2 Table	P	W	D	L	F	A	GD	Pts
Denmark	10	8	2	0	37	9	28	26
Russia	10	7	1	2	22	12	10	22
Slovenia	10	5	2	3	29	11	18	17
Bulgaria	10	2	3	5	18	26	–8	9
Estonia	10	2	3	5	9	23	–14	9
Andorra	10	0	1	9	1	35	–34	1

GROUP 3

Scotland v Luxembourg	3-0
Luxembourg v Slovakia	1-7
Luxembourg v Georgia	0-3
Netherlands v Scotland	4-0
Luxembourg v Netherlands	0-1
Slovakia v Georgia	1-0
Georgia v Netherlands	0-6
Scotland v Slovakia	2-1
Georgia v Scotland	2-1
Slovakia v Luxembourg	3-0
Slovakia v Netherlands	2-2
Scotland v Georgia	1-1
Georgia v Slovakia	1-3
Georgia v Luxembourg	1-1
Awarded as forfeit win 3-0 to Luxembourg	
Scotland v Netherlands	1-6
Netherlands v Luxembourg	3-1
Netherlands v Georgia	0-1
Slovakia v Scotland	1-1
Luxembourg v Scotland	0-3
Netherlands v Slovakia	0-1

Group 3 Table	P	W	D	L	F	A	GD	Pts
Slovakia	8	5	2	1	19	7	12	17
Netherlands	8	5	1	2	22	6	16	16
Scotland	8	3	2	3	12	15	–3	11
Georgia	8	3	1	4	8	15	–7	10
Luxembourg	8	1	0	7	5	23	–18	3

GROUP 4

Albania v Hungary	1-2
Bosnia & Herzegovina v Albania	4-1
Albania v Austria	0-1
Hungary v Bosnia & Herzegovina	4-1
Austria v Spain	2-6
Bosnia & Herzegovina v Austria	0-2
Spain v Albania	4-0
Hungary v Austria	0-2
Spain v Bosnia & Herzegovina	3-2
Spain v Hungary	1-0
Albania v Bosnia & Herzegovina	0-1
Hungary v Albania	0-2
Bosnia & Herzegovina v Spain	1-6
Albania v Spain	0-2
Austria v Hungary	4-2
Austria v Albania	1-3
Hungary v Spain	0-1
Austria v Bosnia & Herzegovina	2-0
Bosnia & Herzegovina v Hungary	1-4
Spain v Austria	1-1

Group 4 Table	P	W	D	L	F	A	GD	Pts
Spain	8	7	1	0	24	6	18	22
Austria	8	5	1	2	15	12	3	16
Hungary	8	3	0	5	12	13	–1	9
Bosnia & Herzegovina	8	2	0	6	10	22	–12	6
Albania	8	2	0	6	7	15	–8	6

GROUP 5

Latvia v Liechtenstein	4-0
Liechtenstein v Croatia	0-5
Latvia v Switzerland	0-2
Ukraine v Croatia	0-2
Liechtenstein v Switzerland	0-6
Croatia v Liechtenstein	4-0
Latvia v Ukraine	1-5
Switzerland v Croatia	0-2
Croatia v Switzerland	0-2
Liechtenstein v Latvia	0-2
Switzerland v Ukraine	1-2
Croatia v Latvia	3-1
Switzerland v Liechtenstein	5-1
Croatia v Ukraine	1-1
Liechtenstein v Ukraine	2-5
Ukraine v Latvia	2-1
Latvia v Croatia	1-3
Ukraine v Switzerland	2-0
Ukraine v Liechtenstein	3-0
Switzerland v Latvia	7-1

Group 5 Table	P	W	D	L	F	A	GD	Pts
Croatia	8	6	1	1	20	5	15	19
Ukraine	8	6	1	1	20	8	12	19
Switzerland	8	5	0	3	23	8	15	15
Latvia	8	2	0	6	11	22	–11	6
Liechtenstein	8	0	0	8	3	34	–31	0

GROUP 6

Faroe Islands v Romania	2-2
Montenegro v Faroe Islands	3-0
Faroe Islands v Republic of Ireland	1-4
Faroe Islands v Germany	0-3
Republic of Ireland v Germany	0-4
Montenegro v Romania	3-2
Germany v Montenegro	2-0
Romania v Republic of Ireland	0-0
Republic of Ireland v Romania	0-1
Germany v Faroe Islands	3-2
Republic of Ireland v Faroe Islands	5-2
Montenegro v Germany	1-1
Montenegro v Republic of Ireland	0-0
Romania v Germany	2-2
Romania v Faroe Islands	3-1
Republic of Ireland v Montenegro	1-2
Romania v Montenegro	4-3
Germany v Republic of Ireland	2-0
Germany v Romania	8-0
Faroe Islands v Montenegro	1-0

Group 6 Table	P	W	D	L	F	A	GD	Pts
Germany	8	6	2	0	25	5	20	20
Romania	8	3	3	2	14	19	–5	12
Montenegro	8	3	2	3	12	11	1	11
Republic of Ireland	8	2	2	4	10	12	–2	8
Faroe Islands	8	1	1	6	9	23	–14	4

GROUP 7

Poland v Malta	2-0
Poland v Turkey	3-1
Turkey v Malta	4-0
Sweden v Poland	3-1
Greece v Malta	5-0
Turkey v Sweden	2-2
Turkey v Greece	1-0
Poland v Sweden	2-0
Malta v Greece	0-4
Turkey v Poland	1-0
Greece v Sweden	5-1
Malta v Poland	1-5
Poland v Greece	3-1
Sweden v Malta	5-0
Malta v Sweden	1-2
Greece v Turkey	2-1
Malta v Turkey	0-3
Sweden v Greece	3-0
Sweden v Turkey	4-3
Greece v Poland	3-17

Group 3 Table	P	W	D	L	F	A	GD	Pts
Sweden	8	5	1	2	20	14	6	16
Greece	8	5	0	3	20	10	10	15
Poland	8	5	0	3	17	10	7	15
Turkey	8	4	1	3	16	11	5	13
Malta	8	0	0	8	2	30	–28	0

GROUP 8

Azerbaijan v FYR Macedonia	0-0
Portugal v Norway	5-1
Israel v Azerbaijan	7-2
Norway v FYR Macedonia	2-1
Norway v Azerbaijan	1-3
Portugal v Israel	3-0
Azerbaijan v Portugal	0-2
Norway v Israel	1-3
Israel v Norway	4-1
FYR Macedonia v Azerbaijan	1-0
Israel v Portugal	3-4
FYR Macedonia v Norway	1-3
Portugal v FYR Macedonia	2-0
FYR Macedonia v Portugal	0-1
Azerbaijan v Norway	0-1
FYR Macedonia v Israel	0-3
Azerbaijan v Israel	3-0
Norway v Portugal	1-2
Israel v FYR Macedonia	2-1
Portugal v Azerbaijan	3-1

Group 8 Table	P	W	D	L	F	A	GD	Pts
Portugal	8	8	0	0	22	6	16	24
Israel	8	5	0	3	22	15	7	15
Norway	8	3	0	5	11	19	–8	9
Azerbaijan	8	2	1	5	9	15	–6	7
FYR Macedonia	8	1	1	6	4	13	–9	4

GROUP 9

Belgium v Cyprus	2-0
Cyprus v Northern Ireland	3-0
Serbia v Cyprus	2-1
Italy v Belgium	1-3
Cyprus v Italy	0-2
Belgium v Northern Ireland	1-0
Northern Ireland v Belgium	0-1
Cyprus v Serbia	2-1
Belgium v Italy	0-1
Serbia v Northern Ireland	3-1
Italy v Northern Ireland	3-0
Serbia v Belgium	2-2
Serbia v Italy	1-0
Northern Ireland v Cyprus	1-0
Northern Ireland v Italy	0-2
Belgium v Serbia	0-3
Cyprus v Belgium	0-6
Italy v Serbia	3-2
Northern Ireland v Serbia	1-4
Italy v Cyprus	7-1

Group 9 Table	P	W	D	L	F	A	GD	Pts
Italy	8	6	0	2	19	7	12	18
Serbia	8	5	1	2	18	10	8	16
Belgium	8	5	1	2	15	7	8	16
Cyprus	8	2	0	6	7	21	–14	6
Northern Ireland	8	1	0	7	3	17	–14	3

GROUP 10

Belarus v Iceland	1-2
Armenia v Iceland	1-2
Belarus v Kazakhstan	0-1
Kazakhstan v Armenia	0-1
Iceland v Belarus	4-1
France v Kazakhstan	5-0
Belarus v France	1-2
Iceland v Kazakhstan	2-0
Kazakhstan v Belarus	1-2
Armenia v France	1-4
Armenia v Kazakhstan	1-2
Iceland v France	3-4
France v Armenia	6-0
Belarus v Armenia	0-1
France v Belarus	1-0
Kazakhstan v Iceland	3-2
Iceland v Armenia	4-0
Kazakhstan v France	1-5
France v Iceland	1-1
Armenia v Belarus	2-1

Group 10 Table	P	W	D	L	F	A	GD	Pts
France	8	7	1	0	28	7	21	22
Iceland	8	5	1	2	20	11	9	16
Kazakhstan	8	3	0	5	8	18	–10	9
Armenia	8	3	0	5	7	19	–12	9
Belarus	8	1	0	7	6	14	–8	3

PLAY-OFFS FIRST LEG

Netherlands v Portugal	0-2
Slovakia v Italy	1-1
Serbia v Spain	0-0
Ukraine v Germany	0-3
Denmark v Iceland	0-0
England v Croatia	2-1
France v Sweden	2-0

PLAY-OFFS SECOND LEG

		(agg)
Italy v Slovakia	3-1	(4-2)
Croatia v England	1-2	(2-4)
Portugal v Netherlands	5-4	(7-4)
Germany v Ukraine	2-0	(5-0)
Spain v Serbia	1-2	(1-2)
Iceland v Denmark	1-1	(1-1)
Denmark won on away goals		
Sweden v France	4-1	(4-3)

UEFA UNDER-21 CHAMPIONSHIP 2013–15

FINALS IN CZECH REPUBLIC

■ *Denotes player sent off.*

GROUP A

Wednesday, 17 June 2015

Czech Rep (1) 1 *(Kaderabek 35)*
Denmark (0) 2 *(Vestergaard 56, Sisto 84)*

Czech Rep: (451) Koubek; Kaderabek, Brabec, Baranek (Janos 82), Hybs; Frydek, Prikryl (Travnik 62), Petrak, Zmrhal, Krejci (Skalak 76); Kliment.
Denmark: (433) Jensen; Scholz, Sorensen (Christensen L 25), Vestergaard, Knudsen; Christensen A, Thomsen, Hojbjerg; Poulsen, Fischer (Sisto 57), Falk Jensen (Berggren 89).

Germany (1) 1 *(Can 17)*
Serbia (1) 1 *(Djuricic 8)*

Germany: (4231) ter Stegen; Korb, Ginter, Knoche, Gunter■; Can, Leitner (Kimmich 46); Volland, Meyer (Bittencourt 76), Younes; Hofmann P (Schulz 71).
Serbia: (4231) Dmitrovic; Stojkovic, Spajic, Pantic, Petrovic; Brasanac, Causic; Jojic (Milunovic 90), Djuricic, Srnic (Cavric 78); Pesic (Trujic 90).

Saturday, 20 June 2015

Germany (1) 3 *(Volland 32, 48, Ginter 53)*
Denmark (0) 0

Germany: (451) ter Stegen; Korb, Ginter, Heintz, Schulz; Bittencourt (Gnabry 80), Can (Geis 77), Kimmich, Younes, Meyer; Volland (Klaus 82).
Denmark: (433) Jensen; Scholz, Christensen A, Vestergaard, Knudsen; Jonsson (Norgaard 77), Christensen L, Thomsen; Poulsen (Bech 61), Sisto (Fischer 72), Brock-Madsen.

Serbia (0) 0
Czech Rep (2) 4 *(Kliment 8, 21, 56, Frydek 59)*

Serbia: (442) Dmitrovic; Stojkovic (Petkovic 46), Spajic, Pantic, Petrovic; Jojic (Milunovic 85), Causic (Kovacevic 63), Brasanac, Srnic; Djuricic, Pesic.
Czech Rep: (442) Koubek; Kaderabek, Brabec, Kalas, Hybs; Skalak (Masopust 74), Petrak, Zmrhal, Frydek; Kadlec (Travnik 29), Kliment (Prikryl 81).

Tuesday, 23 June 2015

Czech Rep (0) 1 *(Krejci 66)*
Germany (0) 1 *(Schulz 55)*

Czech Rep: (442) Koubek; Kaderabek, Brabec, Kalas, Hybs; Skalak (Masopust 61), Petrak, Zmrhal, Frydek (Prikryl 79); Travnik (Krejci 59), Kliment.
Germany: (442) ter Stegen; Korb, Ginter, Heintz, Gunter; Younes (Bittencourt 64), Can, Kimmich, Schulz (Hofmann P 90); Meyer (Malli 82), Volland.

Denmark (1) 2 *(Falk Jensen 21, Fischer 47)*
Serbia (0) 0

Denmark: (433) Jensen; Scholz, Christensen A, Vestergaard, Durmisi; Jonsson, Thomsen, Hojbjerg (Norgaard 89); Poulsen, Fischer (Christensen L 66), Falk Jensen (Bech 85).
Serbia: (433) Dmitrovic; Petkovic, Spajic, Cirkovic (Pantic 81), Petrovic; Kovacevic, Causic, Cavric (Milunovic 59); Djuricic, Jojic (Trujic 66), Pesic.

Group A Table	P	W	D	L	F	A	GD	Pts
Denmark	3	2	0	1	4	4	0	6
Germany	3	1	2	0	5	2	3	5
Czech Republic	3	1	1	1	6	5	1	4
Serbia	3	0	1	2	1	7	–6	1

GROUP B

Thursday, 18 June 2015

England (0) 0
Portugal (0) 1 *(Joao Mario 57)*

England: (4231) Butland; Jenkinson, Moore, Gibson, Garbutt; Ward-Prowse (Hughes 54), Chalobah; Redmond, Carroll (Pritchard 79), Lingard (Ings 73); Kane.
Portugal: (433) Jose Sa; Ricardo Esgaio, Tiago Ilori, Paulo Oliveira, Guerreiro; Sergio Oliveira, William Carvalho, Joao Mario (Ruben Neves 85); Ivan Cavaleiro (Medeiros 73), Bernardo Silva, Ricardo Pereira (Carlos Mane 79).

Italy (1) 1 *(Berardi 29 (pen))*
Sweden (0) 2 *(Guidetti 56, Thelin 86 (pen))*

Italy: (433) Bardi; Battocchio (Verdi 60), Sturaro■, Viviani, Baselli (Cataldi 68); Berardi, Belotti (Trotta 77), Zappacosta; Sabelli, Rugani, Bianchetti.
Sweden: (442) Carlgren; Baffo, Milosevic■, Helander, Augustinsson; Khalili, Lewicki, Hiljemark, Larsson (Lindelof 46); Guidetti (Ishak 76), Thelin.

Sunday, 21 June 2015

Italy (0) 0
Portugal (0) 0

Italy: (433) Bardi; Zappacosta, Rugani, Romagnoli, Biraghi; Benassi, Crisetig (Trotta 76), Cataldi; Berardi, Belotti (Viviani 85), Battocchio (Bernardeschi 62).
Portugal: (4132) Jose Sa; Ricardo Esgaio, Paulo Oliveira, Tiago Ilori, Guerreiro; William Carvalho; Joao Mario (Toze 81), Bernardo Silva (Medeiros 78), Sergio Oliveira; Rafa S (Paciencia 54), Carlos Mane.

Sweden (0) 0
England (0) 1 *(Lingard 85)*

Sweden: (442) Carlgren; Lindelof, Baffo, Helander, Augustinsson; Khalili (Quaison 87), Hiljemark, Lewicki, Tibbling (Larsson 78); Guidetti (Ishak 81), Thelin.
England: (442) Butland; Jenkinson, Moore, Gibson, Garbutt; Redmond, Hughes (Ings 46), Chalobah, Pritchard (Lingard 55); Carroll (Loftus-Cheek 73), Kane.

Wednesday, 24 June 2015

England (0) 1 *(Redmond 90)*
Italy (2) 3 *(Belotti 25, Benassi 27, 72)*

England: (4231) Butland; Jenkinson, Stones, Gibson, Garbutt; Chalobah, Forster-Caskey (Loftus-Cheek 63); Redmond, Ings, Lingard; Kane.
Italy: (433) Bardi; Zappacosta (Viviani 83), Rugani, Romagnoli, Biraghi; Benassi, Crisetig, Cataldi; Berardi (Sabelli 62), Belotti, Trotta (Verdi 75).

Portugal (0) 1 *(Paciencia 82)*
Sweden (0) 1 *(Tibbling 89)*

Portugal: (433) Jose Sa; Ricardo Esgaio, Tiago Ilori (Tobias Figueiredo 29), Paulo Oliveira, Guerreiro; William Carvalho, Sergio Oliveira, Bernardo Silva; Joao Mario, Ivan Cavaleiro (Paciencia 57), Ricardo Pereira (Medeiros 73).
Sweden: (442) Carlgren; Lindelof, Milosevic, Augustinsson, Baffo (Helander 80); Lewicki, Hiljemark, Khalili (Quaison 83), Hrgota (Tibbling 52); Guidetti, Thelin.

Group B Table	P	W	D	L	F	A	GD	Pts
Portugal	3	1	2	0	2	1	1	5
Sweden	3	1	1	1	3	3	0	4
Italy	3	1	1	1	4	3	1	4
England	3	1	0	2	2	4	–2	3

SEMI-FINALS

Saturday, 27 June 2015

Denmark (0) 1 *(Bech 63)*

Sweden (2) 4 *(Guidetti 22 (pen), Tibbling 26, Quaison 83, Hiljemark 90)*

Denmark: (433) Jensen; Scholz, Christensen A, Vestergaard, Knudsen; Jonsson (Christensen L 57), Thomsen, Hojbjerg; Bech (Fischer 90), Poulsen, Falk Jensen (Sisto 65).

Sweden: (442) Carlgren; Lindelof, Milosevic, Helander, Augustinsson; Tibbling (Quaison 72), Hiljemark, Lewicki, Khalili; Thelin (Larsson 90), Guidetti (Ishak 60).

Portugal (3) 5 *(Bernardo Silva 25, Ricardo Pereira 33, Ivan Cavaleiro 45, Joao Mario 46, Ricardo Horta 71)*

Germany (0) 0

Portugal: (433) Jose Sa; Ricardo Esgaio, Paulo Oliveira, Tobias Figueiredo, Guerreiro (Joao Cancelo 64); Joao Mario, William Carvalho, Sergio Oliveira; Ricardo Pereira, Bernardo Silva (Rafa S 50), Ivan Cavaleiro (Ricardo Horta 71).

Germany: (4411) ter Stegen; Korb (Klaus 87), Ginter, Heintz, Gunter; Younes, Can, Kimmich, Schulz (Bittencourt▪ 50); Geis (Meyer 46); Volland.

FINAL

Tuesday, 30 June 2015

Sweden (0) 0

Portugal (0) 0

Sweden: (442) Carlgren; Lindelof, Milosevic, Helander (Baffo 46), Augustinsson; Lewicki, Hiljemark, Khalili, Tibbling (Quaison 65); Guidetti, Thelin.

Portugal: (442) Jose Sa; Ricardo Esgaio, Tiago Ilori, Paulo Oliveira, Guerreiro; William Carvalho, Sergio Oliveira (Toze 54), Bernardo Silva, Joao Mario; Ivan Cavaleiro (Medeiros 61), Ricardo Pereira (Paciencia 70).

aet; Sweden won 4-3 on penalties.

FIFA UNDER-20 WORLD CUP 2015

FINALS IN NEW ZEALAND

GROUP A

New Zealand v Ukraine							0-0
USA v Myanmar							2-1
Myanmar v Ukraine							0-6
New Zealand v USA							0-4
Ukraine v USA							3-0
Myanmar v New Zealand							1-5

Group A Table	P	W	D	L	F	A	GD	Pts
Ukraine	3	2	1	0	9	0	9	7
USA	3	2	0	1	6	4	2	6
New Zealand	3	1	1	1	5	5	0	4
Myanmar	3	0	0	3	2	13	–11	0

GROUP B

Argentina v Panama	2-2
Ghana v Austria	1-1
Austria v Panama	2-1
Argentina v Ghana	2-3
Panama v Ghana	0-1
Austria v Argentina	0-0

Group B Table	P	W	D	L	F	A	GD	Pts
Ghana	3	2	1	0	5	3	2	7
Austria	3	1	2	0	3	2	1	5
Argentina	3	0	2	1	4	5	–1	2
Panama	3	0	1	2	3	5	–2	1

GROUP C

Qatar v Colombia	0-1
Portugal v Senegal	3-0
Qatar v Portugal	0-4
Senegal v Colombia	1-1
Colombia v Portugal	1-3
Senegal v Qatar	2-1

Group C Table	P	W	D	L	F	A	GD	Pts
Portugal	3	3	0	0	10	1	9	9
Colombia	3	1	1	1	3	4	–1	4
Senegal	3	1	1	1	3	5	–2	4
Qatar	3	0	0	3	1	7	–6	0

GROUP D

Mexico v Mali	0-2
Uruguay v Serbia	1-0
Mexico v Uruguay	2-1
Serbia v Mali	2-0
Serbia v Mexico	2-0
Mali v Uruguay	1-1

Group D Table	P	W	D	L	F	A	GD	Pts
Serbia	3	2	0	1	4	1	3	6
Mali	3	1	1	1	3	3	0	4
Uruguay	3	1	1	1	3	3	0	4
Mexico	3	1	0	2	2	5	–3	3

GROUP E

| Nigeria v Brazil | 2-4 |
| Korea DPR v Hungary | 1-5 |

Nigeria v Korea DPR	4-0
Hungary v Brazil	1-2
Hungary v Nigeria	0-2
Brazil v Korea DPR	3-0

Group E Table	P	W	D	L	F	A	GD	Pts
Brazil	3	3	0	0	9	3	6	9
Nigeria	3	2	0	1	8	4	4	6
Hungary	3	1	0	2	6	5	1	3
Korea DPR	3	0	0	3	1	12	–11	0

GROUP F

Germany v Fiji	8-1
Uzbekistan v Honduras	3-4
Honduras v Fiji	0-3
Germany v Uzbekistan	3-0
Honduras v Germany	1-5
Fiji v Uzbekistan	0-3

Group F Table	P	W	D	L	F	A	GD	Pts
Germany	3	3	0	0	16	2	14	9
Uzbekistan	3	1	0	2	6	7	–1	3
Honduras	3	1	0	2	5	11	–6	3
Fiji	3	1	0	2	4	11	–7	3

ROUND OF 16

| Ghana v Mali | 0-3 |
| Serbia v Hungary | 2-1 |

(aet; 1-1 at end of normal time)

| USA v Colombia | 1-0 |
| Ukraine v Senegal | 1-1 |

(aet; Senegal won 3-1 on penalties)

Austria v Uzbekistan	0-2
Germany v Nigeria	1-0
Portugal v New Zealand	2-1
Brazil v Uruguay	0-0

(aet; Brazil won 5-4 on penalties)

QUARTER-FINALS

| Brazil v Portugal | 0-0 |

(aet; Brazil won 3-1 on penalties)

| Mali v Germany | 1-1 |

(aet; Mali won 4-3 on penalties)

| USA v Serbia | 0-0 |

(aet; Serbia won 6-5 on penalties)

| Uzbekistan v Senegal | 0-1 |

SEMI-FINALS

| Brazil v Senegal | 5-0 |
| Serbia v Mali | 2-1 |

(aet; 1-1 at end of normal time)

THIRD PLACE PLAY-OFF

| Senegal v Mali | 1-3 |

FINAL

| Brazil v Serbia | 1-2 |

(aet; 1-1 at end of normal time)

UEFA UNDER-19 CHAMPIONSHIP 2013–14

FINALS IN HUNGARY

GROUP A

Portugal v Israel	3-0
Hungary v Austria	1-3
Austria v Israel	3-0
Hungary v Portugal	1-6
Israel v Hungary	1-2
Austria v Portugal	1-2

Group A Table	P	W	D	L	F	A	GD	Pts
Portugal	3	3	0	0	11	2	9	9
Austria	3	2	0	1	7	3	4	6
Hungary	3	1	0	2	4	10	–6	3
Israel	3	0	0	3	1	8	–7	0

GROUP B

Ukraine v Serbia	1-1
Bulgaria v Germany	0-3
Germany v Serbia	2-2
Bulgaria v Ukraine	0-1
Serbia v Bulgaria	1-0
Germany v Ukraine	2-0

Group B Table	P	W	D	L	F	A	GD	Pts
Germany	3	2	1	0	7	2	5	7
Serbia	3	1	2	0	4	3	1	5
Ukraine	3	1	1	1	2	3	–1	4
Bulgaria	3	0	0	3	0	5	–5	0

SEMI-FINALS

| Germany v Austria | 4-0 |
| Portugal v Serbia | 0-0 |

Portugal won 4-3 on penalties.

FINAL

| Portugal v Germany | 0-1 |

UEFA UNDER-19 CHAMPIONSHIP 2014–15

QUALIFYING ROUND

GROUP 1 (LUXEMBOURG)

England v Belarus	3-0
Belgium v Luxembourg	4-0
Luxembourg v England	0-8
Belgium v Belarus	3-2
England v Belgium	4-2
Belarus v Luxembourg	2-2

Group 1 Table	P	W	D	L	F	A	GD	Pts
England	3	3	0	0	15	2	13	9
Belgium	3	2	0	1	9	6	3	6
Belarus	3	0	1	2	4	8	–4	1
Luxembourg	3	0	1	2	2	14	–12	1

GROUP 2 (LATVIA)

Germany v Kazakhstan	6-0
Austria v Latvia	1-0
Austria v Kazakhstan	1-0
Latvia v Germany	0-3
Germany v Austria	1-5
Kazakhstan v Latvia	0-3

Group 2 Table	P	W	D	L	F	A	GD	Pts
Austria	3	3	0	0	7	1	6	9
Germany	3	2	0	1	10	5	5	6
Latvia	3	1	0	2	3	4	–1	3
Kazakhstan	3	0	0	3	10	10	–10	0

GROUP 3 (CROATIA)

Turkey v Iceland	7-3
Croatia v Estonia	1-0
Turkey v Estonia	0-0
Iceland v Croatia	1-4
Croatia v Turkey	0-0
Estonia v Iceland	3-0

Group 3 Table	P	W	D	L	F	A	GD	Pts
Croatia	3	2	1	0	5	1	4	7
Turkey	3	1	2	0	7	3	4	5
Estonia	3	1	1	1	3	1	2	4
Iceland	3	0	0	3	4	14	–10	0

GROUP 4 (HUNGARY)

Slovakia v Slovenia	2-1
Hungary v Azerbaijan	1-1
Slovakia v Azerbaijan	4-1
Slovenia v Hungary	1-1
Hungary v Slovakia	0-3
Azerbaijan v Slovenia	3-2

Group 4 Table	P	W	D	L	F	A	GD	Pts
Slovakia	3	3	0	0	9	2	7	9
Azerbaijan	3	1	1	1	5	7	–2	4
Hungary	3	0	2	1	2	5	–3	2
Slovenia	3	0	1	2	4	6	–2	1

GROUP 5 (NORTHERN IRELAND)

Czech Republic v Northern Ireland	2-0
Russia v Faroe Islands	7-0
Russia v Northern Ireland	5-2
Faroe Islands v Czech Republic	0-2
Czech Republic v Russia	0-2
Northern Ireland v Faroe Islands	3-0

Group 5 Table	P	W	D	L	F	A	GD	Pts
Russia	3	3	0	0	15	2	13	9
Czech Republic	3	2	0	1	4	3	1	6
Northern Ireland	3	1	0	2	5	7	–2	3
Faroe Islands	3	0	0	3	0	12	–12	0

GROUP 6 (REPUBLIC OF IRELAND)

Switzerland v Gibraltar	8-0
Republic of Ireland v Malta	1-0
Republic of Ireland v Gibraltar	4-1
Malta v Switzerland	1-7
Switzerland v Republic of Ireland	1-1
Gibraltar v Malta	1-3

Group 6 Table	P	W	D	L	F	A	GD	Pts
Switzerland	3	2	1	0	16	2	14	7
Republic of Ireland	3	2	1	0	6	2	4	7
Malta	3	1	0	2	4	9	–5	3
Gibraltar	3	0	0	3	2	15	–13	0

GROUP 7 (PORTUGAL)

Denmark v Albania	1-0
Portugal v Wales	2-1
Denmark v Wales	4-0
Albania v Portugal	1-4
Portugal v Denmark	2-1
Wales v Albania	2-1

Group 7 Table	P	W	D	L	F	A	GD	Pts
Portugal	3	3	0	0	8	3	5	9
Denmark	3	2	0	1	6	2	4	6
Wales	3	1	0	2	3	7	–4	3
Albania	3	0	0	3	2	7	–5	0

GROUP 8 (ISRAEL)

Ukraine v Sweden	2-2
Israel v Bulgaria	2-1
Sweden v Israel	1-0
Ukraine v Bulgaria	5-1
Israel v Ukraine	0-5
Bulgaria v Sweden	1-5

Group 8 Table	P	W	D	L	F	A	GD	Pts
Ukraine	3	2	1	0	12	3	9	7
Sweden	3	2	1	0	8	3	5	7
Israel	3	1	0	2	2	7	–5	3
Bulgaria	3	0	0	3	3	12	–9	0

GROUP 9 (SERBIA)

| Italy v Armenia | 3-0 |
| Serbia v San Marino | 4-0 |

Italy v San Marino   6-0
Armenia v Serbia   0-1
Serbia v Italy   1-3
San Marino v Armenia   0-2

Group 9 Table

	P	W	D	L	F	A	GD	Pts
Italy	3	3	0	0	12	1	11	9
Serbia	3	2	0	1	6	3	3	6
Armenia	3	1	0	2	2	4	–2	3
San Marino	3	0	0	3	0	12	–12	0

GROUP 10 (POLAND)

Netherlands v Andorra   7-0
Poland v Moldova   4-1
Netherlands v Moldova   3-0
Andorra v Poland   0-3
Poland v Netherlands   1-2
Moldova v Andorra   2-1

Group 10 Table

	P	W	D	L	F	A	GD	Pts
Netherlands	3	3	0	0	12	1	11	9
Poland	3	2	0	1	8	3	5	6
Moldova	3	1	0	2	3	8	–5	3
Andorra	3	0	0	3	1	12	–11	0

GROUP 11 (GEORGIA)

Romania v Cyprus   0-1
Georgia v Montenegro   0-2
Romania v Montenegro   0-1
Cyprus v Georgia   1-3
Georgia v Romania   3-1
Montenegro v Cyprus   6-3

ELITE ROUND

GROUP 1 (GEORGIA)

Portugal v Turkey   6-1
Spain v Georgia   4-1
Spain v Turkey   5-0
Georgia v Portugal   2-3
Portugal v Spain   0-4
Turkey v Georgia   1-2

Group 1 Table

	P	W	D	L	F	A	GD	Pts
Spain	3	3	0	0	13	1	12	9
Portugal	3	2	0	1	9	7	2	6
Georgia	3	1	0	2	5	8	–3	3
Turkey	3	0	0	3	2	13	–11	0

GROUP 2 (GERMANY)

Slovakia v Germany   1-1
Republic of Ireland v Czech Republic 0-1
Germany v Republic of Ireland   3-2
Slovakia v Czech Republic   3-0
Republic of Ireland v Slovakia   2-2
Czech Republic v Germany   0-6

Group 2 Table

	P	W	D	L	F	A	GD	Pts
Germany	3	2	1	0	10	3	7	7
Slovakia	3	1	2	0	6	3	3	5
Czech Republic	3	1	0	2	1	9	–8	3
Republic of Ireland	3	0	1	2	4	6	–2	1

GROUP 3 (SWEDEN)

Sweden v Lithuania   1-0
Russia v Belgium   1-0
Russia v Lithuania   6-0
Belgium v Sweden   2-0
Sweden v Russia   1-3
Lithuania v Belgium   2-2

Group 3 Table

	P	W	D	L	F	A	GD	Pts
Russia	3	3	0	0	10	1	9	9
Belgium	3	1	1	1	4	3	1	4
Lithuania	3	0	2	1	3	9	–6	2
Sweden	3	0	1	2	2	6	–4	1

GROUP 4 (NETHERLANDS)

Switzerland v Norway   0-1
Netherlands v Serbia   1-0
Serbia v Switzerland   3-1
Netherlands v Norway   1-1
Switzerland v Netherlands   0-4
Norway v Serbia   2-4

Group 11 Table

	P	W	D	L	F	A	GD	Pts
Montenegro	3	3	0	0	9	3	6	9
Georgia	3	2	0	1	6	4	2	6
Cyprus	3	1	0	2	5	9	–4	3
Romania	3	0	0	3	1	5	–4	0

GROUP 12 (FYR MACEDONIA)

Bosnia & Herzegovina v Liechtenstein   5-0
France v FYR Macedonia   2-1
Bosnia & Herzegovina v FYR Macedonia   1-1
Liechtenstein v France   0-6
France v Bosnia & Herzegovina   0-0
FYR Macedonia v Liechtenstein   5-1

Group 12 Table

	P	W	D	L	F	A	GD	Pts
France	3	2	1	0	8	1	7	7
Bosnia & Herzegovina	3	1	2	0	6	1	5	5
FYR Macedonia	3	1	1	1	7	4	3	4
Liechtenstein	3	0	0	3	1	16	–15	0

GROUP 13 (LITHUANIA)

Scotland v Finland   2-2
Norway v Lithuania   2-0
Norway v Finland   0-0
Lithuania v Scotland   0-0
Scotland v Norway   1-1
Finland v Lithuania   0-3

Group 13 Table

	P	W	D	L	F	A	GD	Pts
Norway	3	1	2	0	3	1	2	5
Lithuania	3	1	1	1	3	2	1	4
Scotland	3	0	3	0	3	3	0	3
Finland	3	0	2	1	2	5	–3	2

Group 4 Table

	P	W	D	L	F	A	GD	Pts
Netherlands	3	2	1	0	6	1	5	7
Serbia	3	2	0	1	7	4	3	6
Norway	3	1	1	1	4	5	–1	4
Switzerland	3	0	0	3	1	8	–7	0

GROUP 5 (BOSNIA & HERZEGOVINA)

Montenegro v Poland   2-1
Ukraine v Bosnia & Herzegovina   1-1
Montenegro v Bosnia & Herzegovina   1-0
Poland v Ukraine   2-4
Ukraine v Montenegro   2-0
Bosnia & Herzegovina v Poland   2-0

Group 5 Table

	P	W	D	L	F	A	GD	Pts
Ukraine	3	2	1	0	7	3	4	7
Montenegro	3	2	0	1	3	0	6	6
Bosnia & Herzegovina	3	1	1	1	3	2	1	4
Poland	3	0	0	3	3	8	–5	0

GROUP 6 (AUSTRIA)

Italy v Croatia   2-2
Austria v Scotland   1-2
Italy v Scotland   0-0
Croatia v Austria   0-2
Austria v Italy   2-1
Scotland v Croatia   1-1

Group 6 Table

	P	W	D	L	F	A	GD	Pts
Austria	3	2	0	1	5	3	2	6
Scotland	3	1	2	0	3	2	1	5
Italy	3	0	2	1	4	4	–1	2
Croatia	3	0	2	1	3	5	–2	2

GROUP 7 (FRANCE)

England v Denmark   3-2
France v Azerbaijan   2-0
Denmark v France   0-2
England v Azerbaijan   1-0
France v England   2-1
Azerbaijan v Denmark   0-3

Group 7 Table

	P	W	D	L	F	A	GD	Pts
France	3	3	0	0	6	1	5	9
England	3	2	0	1	5	4	1	6
Denmark	3	1	0	2	5	0	3	3
Azerbaijan	3	0	0	3	0	6	–6	0

Final Tournament in Greece 19–30 July 2015.

UEFA UNDER-17 CHAMPIONSHIP 2014–15

QUALIFYING ROUND

GROUP 1 (REPUBIC OF IRELAND)

Scotland v Faroe Islands	4-0
Republic of Ireland v Gibraltar	5-0
Scotland v Gibraltar	4-0
Faroe Islands v Republic of Ireland	2-4
Republic of Ireland v Scotland	0-0
Gibraltar v Faroe Islands	0-0

Group 1 Table	P	W	D	L	F	A	GD	Pts
Scotland	3	2	1	0	8	0	8	7
Republic of Ireland	3	2	1	0	9	2	7	7
Faroe Islands	3	0	1	2	2	8	–6	1
Gibraltar	3	0	1	2	0	9	–9	1

GROUP 2 (GEORGIA)

Poland v Estonia	4-0
Georgia v Liechtenstein	3-0
Poland v Liechtenstein	4-0
Estonia v Georgia	1-2
Georgia v Poland	0-1
Liechtenstein v Estonia	0-2

Group 2 Table	P	W	D	L	F	A	GD	Pts
Poland	3	3	0	0	9	0	9	9
Georgia	3	2	0	1	5	2	3	6
Estonia	3	1	0	2	3	6	–3	3
Liechtenstein	3	0	0	3	0	9	–9	0

GROUP 3 (MOLDOVA)

Iceland v Moldova	0-0
Italy v Armenia	3-0
Iceland v Armenia	2-0
Moldova v Italy	0-3
Italy v Iceland	1-1
Armenia v Moldova	0-4

Group 3 Table	P	W	D	L	F	A	GD	Pts
Italy	3	2	1	0	7	1	6	7
Iceland	3	1	2	0	3	1	2	5
Moldova	3	1	1	1	4	3	1	4
Armenia	3	0	0	3	0	9	–9	0

GROUP 4 (CYPRUS)

England v Cyprus	4-1
France v FYR Macedonia	3-0
England v FYR Macedonia	1-0
Cyprus v France	0-4
France v England	1-3
FYR Macedonia v Cyprus	1-2

Group 4 Table	P	W	D	L	F	A	GD	Pts
England	3	3	0	0	8	2	6	9
France	3	2	0	1	8	3	5	6
Cyprus	3	1	0	2	3	9	–6	3
FYR Macedonia	3	0	0	3	1	6	–5	0

GROUP 5 (LATVIA)

Ukraine v Greece	0-0
Sweden v Latvia	2-1
Greece v Sweden	0-0
Ukraine v Latvia	0-0
Sweden v Ukraine	0-0
Latvia v Greece	0-1

Group 5 Table	P	W	D	L	F	A	GD	Pts
Sweden	3	1	2	0	2	1	1	5
Greece	3	1	2	0	1	0	1	5
Ukraine	3	0	3	0	0	0	0	3
Latvia	3	0	1	2	1	3	–2	1

GROUP 6 (SLOVENIA)

Turkey v Slovenia	0-5
Portugal v Northern Ireland	3-0
Turkey v Northern Ireland	3-4
Slovenia v Portugal	0-1
Portugal v Turkey	1-0
Northern Ireland v Slovenia	0-0

Group 6 Table	P	W	D	L	F	A	GD	Pts
Portugal	3	3	0	0	5	0	5	9
Slovenia	3	1	1	1	5	1	4	4
Northern Ireland	3	1	1	1	4	6	–2	4
Turkey	3	0	0	3	3	10	–7	0

GROUP 7 (HUNGARY)

Croatia v Kazakhstan	8-1
Hungary v Israel	1-0
Croatia v Israel	0-0
Kazakhstan v Hungary	0-1
Hungary v Croatia	1-2
Israel v Kazakhstan	6-0

Group 7 Table	P	W	D	L	F	A	GD	Pts
Croatia	3	2	1	0	10	2	8	7
Hungary	3	2	0	1	2	1	1	6
Israel	3	1	1	1	6	1	5	4
Kazakhstan	3	0	0	3	1	15	–14	0

GROUP 8 (SERBIA)

Serbia v Malta	1-0
Netherlands v Finland	2-0
Serbia v Finland	1-0
Malta v Netherlands	0-1
Netherlands v Serbia	1-0
Finland v Malta	2-1

Group 8 Table	P	W	D	L	F	A	GD	Pts
Netherlands	3	3	0	0	4	0	4	9
Serbia	3	2	0	1	2	1	1	6
Finland	3	1	0	2	2	4	–2	3
Malta	3	0	0	3	1	4	–3	0

GROUP 9 (ALBANIA)

Austria v San Marino	2-0
Norway v Albania	3-0
San Marino v Norway	0-4
Austria v Albania	2-0
Norway v Austria	0-2
Albania v San Marino	5-1

Group 9 Table	P	W	D	L	F	A	GD	Pts
Austria	3	3	0	0	6	0	6	9
Norway	3	2	0	1	7	2	5	6
Albania	3	1	0	2	5	6	–1	3
San Marino	3	0	0	3	1	11	–10	0

GROUP 10 (BELGIUM)

Switzerland v Bosnia & Herzegovina	0-1
Belgium v Azerbaijan	3-0
Belgium v Bosnia & Herzegovina	4-1
Azerbaijan v Switzerland	2-1
Switzerland v Belgium	1-0
Bosnia & Herzegovina v Azerbaijan	1-1

Bosnia & Herzegovina won 4-3 on penalties.

Group 10 Table	P	W	D	L	F	A	GD	Pts
Belgium	3	2	0	1	7	2	5	6
Azerbaijan	3	1	1	1	3	5	–2	4
Bosnia & Herzegovina	3	1	1	1	3	5	–2	4
Switzerland	3	1	0	2	2	3	–1	3

GROUP 11 (SLOVAKIA)

Slovakia v Luxembourg	1-0
Spain v Lithuania	2-1
Slovakia v Lithuania	2-0
Luxembourg v Spain	0-3
Spain v Slovakia	3-1
Lithuania v Luxembourg	0-3

Group 11 Table	P	W	D	L	F	A	GD	Pts
Spain	3	3	0	0	8	2	6	9
Slovakia	3	2	0	1	4	3	1	6
Luxembourg	3	1	0	2	3	4	–1	3
Lithuania	3	0	0	3	1	7	–6	0

GROUP 12 (ANDORRA)

Czech Republic v Romania	2-1
Denmark v Andorra	3-1
Romania v Denmark	6-1
Czech Republic v Andorra	1-0
Denmark v Czech Republic	0-1
Andorra v Romania	0-1

Group 12 Table	P	W	D	L	F	A	GD	Pts
Czech Republic	3	3	0	0	4	1	3	9
Romania	3	2	0	1	8	3	5	6
Denmark	3	1	0	2	4	8	–4	3
Andorra	3	0	0	3	1	5	–4	0

GROUP 13 (BELARUS)

Russia v Wales	0-0
Belarus v Montenegro	1-0
Russia v Montenegro	2-0
Wales v Belarus	1-2
Belarus v Russia	1-2
Montenegro v Wales	1-2

Group 13 Table	P	W	D	L	F	A	GD	Pts
Russia	3	2	1	0	4	1	3	7
Belarus	3	2	0	1	4	3	1	6
Wales	3	1	1	1	3	3	0	4
Montenegro	3	0	0	3	1	5	-4	0

ELITE ROUND

GROUP 1 (SPAIN)

France v Israel	1-0	Spain v Sweden		2-0
Sweden v France	1-7	Spain v Israel		0-0
France v Spain	1-1	Israel v Sweden		2-0

Group 1 Table	P	W	D	L	F	A	GD	Pts
France	3	2	1	0	9	2	7	7
Spain	3	1	2	0	3	1	2	5
Israel	3	1	1	1	2	1	1	4
Sweden	3	0	0	3	1	11	-10	0

GROUP 2 (AZERBAIJAN)

Portugal v Serbia	0-0	Croatia v Azerbaijan	4-0
Serbia v Croatia	0-3	Portugal v Azerbaijan	3-0
Croatia v Portugal	1-0	Azerbaijan v Serbia	0-4

Group 2 Table	P	W	D	L	F	A	GD	Pts
Croatia	3	3	0	0	8	0	8	9
Portugal	3	1	1	1	3	1	2	4
Serbia	3	1	1	1	4	3	1	4
Azerbaijan	3	0	0	3	0	11	-11	0

GROUP 3 (NETHERLANDS)

Belgium v Northern Ireland	4-0
Netherlands v Georgia	2-0
Georgia v Belgium	0-4
Netherlands v Northern Ireland	1-1
Belgium v Netherlands	0-0
Northern Ireland v Georgia	2-4

Group 3 Table	P	W	D	L	F	A	GD	Pts
Belgium	3	2	1	0	8	0	8	7
Netherlands	3	1	2	0	3	1	2	5
Georgia	3	1	0	2	4	8	-4	3
Northern Ireland	3	0	1	2	3	9	-6	1

GROUP 4 (POLAND)

Republic of Ireland v Greece	2-2
Poland v Belarus	0-2
Belarus v Republic of Ireland	1-3
Poland v Greece	0-1
Republic of Ireland v Poland	0-1
Greece v Belarus	0-0

Group 4 Table	P	W	D	L	F	A	GD	Pts
Greece	3	1	2	0	3	2	1	5
Republic of Ireland	3	1	1	1	5	4	1	4
Belarus	3	1	1	1	3	3	0	4
Poland	3	1	0	2	1	3	-2	3

GROUP 5 (RUSSIA)

Austria v Iceland	1-0	Russia v Wales	0-0
Austria v Wales	3-2	Iceland v Russia	0-4
Russia v Austria	1-1	Wales v Iceland	1-0

Group 5 Table	P	W	D	L	F	A	GD	Pts
Austria	3	2	1	0	5	3	2	7
Russia	3	1	2	0	5	1	4	5
Wales	3	1	1	1	3	3	0	4
Iceland	3	0	0	3	0	6	-6	0

GROUP 6 (ENGLAND)

England v Norway	3-1	Romania v Slovenia	0-3
Norway v Romania	2-0	England v Slovenia	3-1
Romania v England	1-2	Slovenia v Norway	1-0

Group 6 Table	P	W	D	L	F	A	GD	Pts
England	3	3	0	0	8	3	5	9
Slovenia	3	2	0	1	5	3	2	6
Norway	3	1	0	2	3	4	-1	3
Romania	3	0	0	3	1	7	-6	0

GROUP 7 (HUNGARY)

Scotland v Bosnia & Herzegovina	2-0
Czech Republic v Hungary	1-0
Czech Republic v Bosnia & Herzegovina	2-2
Hungary v Scotland	0-0
Scotland v Czech Republic	0-1
Bosnia & Herzegovina v Hungary	2-1

Group 7 Table	P	W	D	L	F	A	GD	Pts
Czech Republic	3	2	1	0	4	2	2	7
Scotland	3	1	1	1	2	1	1	4
Bosnia & Herzegovina	3	1	1	1	4	5	-1	4
Hungary	3	0	1	2	1	3	-2	1

GROUP 8 (GERMANY)

Germany v Slovakia	3-0	Italy v Ukraine	1-0
Germany v Ukraine	3-0	Slovakia v Italy	0-2
Italy v Germany	2-2	Ukraine v Slovakia	1-2

Group 8 Table	P	W	D	L	F	A	GD	Pts
Germany	3	2	1	0	8	2	6	7
Italy	3	2	1	0	5	2	3	7
Slovakia	3	1	0	2	2	6	-4	3
Ukraine	3	0	0	3	1	6	-5	0

FINAL TOURNAMENT (BULGARIA)

GROUP A

Spain v Austria	1-1	Bulgaria v Croatia	0-2
Croatia v Austria	1-0	Bulgaria v Spain	1-2
Austria v Bulgaria	1-1	Croatia v Spain	0-0

Group A Table	P	W	D	L	F	A	GD	Pts
Croatia	3	2	1	0	3	0	3	7
Spain	3	1	2	0	3	2	1	5
Austria	3	0	2	1	2	3	-1	2
Bulgaria	3	0	1	2	2	5	-3	1

GROUP B

Czech Republic v Slovenia	1-0	Belgium v Germany	0-2
Czech Republic v Belgium	0-3	Slovenia v Germany	0-1
Germany v Czech Republic	4-0	Slovenia v Belgium	0-1

Group B Table	P	W	D	L	F	A	GD	Pts
Germany	3	3	0	0	7	0	7	9
Belgium	3	2	0	1	4	2	2	6
Czech Republic	3	1	0	2	1	7	-6	3
Slovenia	3	0	0	3	0	3	-3	0

GROUP C

Greece v Russia	2-2	Scotland v France	0-5
Russia v France	0-1	Greece v Scotland	1-0
France v Greece	1-0	Russia v Scotland	2-0

Group C Table	P	W	D	L	F	A	GD	Pts
France	3	3	0	0	7	0	7	9
Russia	3	1	1	1	4	3	1	4
Greece	3	1	1	1	3	3	0	4
Scotland	3	0	0	3	0	8	-8	0

GROUP D

Republic of Ireland v Netherlands	0-0
Italy v England	0-1
Republic of Ireland v Italy	0-2
Netherlands v England	1-1
England v Republic of Ireland	1-0
Netherlands v Italy	1-1

Group D Table	P	W	D	L	F	A	GD	Pts
England	3	2	1	0	3	1	2	7
Italy	3	1	1	1	3	2	1	4
Netherlands	3	0	3	0	2	2	0	3
Republic of Ireland	3	0	1	2	0	3	-3	1

QUARTER-FINALS

Croatia v Belgium	1-1
Belgium won 5-3 on penalties.	
Germany v Spain	0-0
Germany won 4-2 on penalties.	
England v Russia	0-1
France v Italy	3-0

FIFA WORLD CUP PLAY-OFFS

Croatia v Italy	1-0
Spain v England	0-0
England won 5-3 on penalties.	

SEMI-FINALS

Belgium v France	1-1
France won 2-1 on penalties.	
Germany v Russia	1-0

FINAL

France v Germany	4-1

UEFA YOUTH LEAGUE 2014–15

GROUP A

Juventus v Malmo	2-0
Olympiacos v Atletico Madrid	1-2
Atletico Madrid v Juventus	1-0
Malmo v Olympiacos	1-3
Atletico Madrid v Malmo	3-1
Olympiacos v Juventus	1-1
Juventus v Olympiacos	0-3
Malmo v Atletico Madrid	1-2
Atletico Madrid v Olympiacos	0-2
Malmo v Juventus	2-2
Olympiacos v Malmo	2-0
Juventus v Atletico Madrid	0-3

GROUP B

Liverpool v Ludogorets Razgrad	4-0
Real Madrid v FC Basel	2-0
Ludogorets Razgrad v Real Madrid	0-3
FC Basel v Liverpool	3-2
Ludogorets Razgrad v FC Basel	0-5
Liverpool v Real Madrid	3-2
FC Basel v Ludogorets Razgrad	6-0
Real Madrid v Liverpool	4-1
Ludogorets Razgrad v Liverpool	0-3
FC Basel v Real Madrid	3-2
Liverpool v FC Basel	3-0
Real Madrid v Ludogorets Razgrad	6-0

GROUP C

Monaco v Bayer Leverkusen	3-1
Benfica v Zenit St Petersburg	0-0
Zenit St Petersburg v Monaco	0-3
Bayer Leverkusen v Benfica	2-3
Bayer Leverkusen v Zenit St Petersburg	1-4
Monaco v Benfica	0-1
Zenit St Petersburg v Bayer Leverkusen	0-3
Benfica v Monaco	3-0
Zenit St Petersburg v Benfica	5-1
Bayer Leverkusen v Monaco	4-0
Monaco v Zenit St Petersburg	1-3
Benfica v Bayer Leverkusen	4-1

GROUP D

Galatasaray v Anderlecht	3-0
Borussia Dortmund v Arsenal	0-2
Arsenal v Galatasaray	5-1
Anderlecht v Borussia Dortmund	5-0
Anderlecht v Arsenal	4-3
Galatasaray v Borussia Dortmund	3-2
Arsenal v Anderlecht	1-2
Borussia Dortmund v Galatasaray	5-2
Anderlecht v Galatasaray	3-0

Match abandoned due to Galatasaray fans setting off fireworks after 90+5 minutes with Anderlecht leading 2-0. UEFA ruled that Galatasaray forfeited the match and awarded Anderlecht a 3-0 win.

Arsenal v Borussia Dortmund	1-0
Galatasaray v Arsenal	1-3
Borussia Dortmund v Anderlecht	1-1

GROUP E

Roma v CSKA Moscow	3-1
Bayern Munich v Manchester C	1-4
CSKA Moscow v Bayern Munich	3-1
Manchester C v Roma	2-1
CSKA Moscow v Manchester C	0-2
Roma v Bayern Munich	1-0
Bayern Munich v Roma	3-2
Manchester C v CSKA Moscow	4-2
CSKA Moscow v Roma	0-2
Manchester C v Bayern Munich	6-0
Roma v Manchester C	0-4
Bayern Munich v CSKA Moscow	3-2

GROUP F

Barcelona v APOEL Nicosia	3-0
Ajax v Paris Saint-Germain	6-1
APOEL Nicosia v Ajax	0-0
Paris Saint-Germain v Barcelona	2-2
Barcelona v Ajax	2-2
APOEL Nicosia v Paris Saint-Germain	0-3
Ajax v Barcelona	1-0
Paris Saint-Germain v APOEL Nicosia	6-0
APOEL Nicosia v Barcelona	2-3
Paris Saint-Germain v Ajax	3-6
Ajax v APOEL Nicosia	4-1
Barcelona v Paris Saint-Germain	0-0

GROUP G

Maribor v Sporting Lisbon	1-3
Chelsea v Schalke 04	4-1
Schalke 04 v Maribor	5-0
Sporting Lisbon v Chelsea	0-5
Schalke 04 v Sporting Lisbon	3-0
Chelsea v Maribor	2-0
Maribor v Chelsea	0-7
Sporting Lisbon v Schalke 04	2-3
Sporting Lisbon v Maribor	3-2
Schalke 04 v Chelsea	2-0
Maribor v Schalke 04	1-5
Chelsea v Sporting Lisbon	6-0

GROUP H

Porto v BATE Borisov	2-0
Athletic Bilbao v Shakhtar Donetsk	0-2
Shakhtar Donetsk v Porto	1-1
BATE Borisov v Athletic Bilbao	1-2
Porto v Athletic Bilbao	2-0
BATE Borisov v Shakhtar Donetsk	1-4
Athletic Bilbao v Porto	3-1
Shakhtar Donetsk v BATE Borisov	1-0
BATE Borisov v Porto	0-0
Shakhtar Donetsk v Athletic Bilbao	6-0
Porto v Shakhtar Donetsk	1-1
Athletic Bilbao v BATE Borisov	4-0

ROUND OF 16

Atletico Madrid v Arsenal	1-0
Real Madrid v Porto	1-1

Porto won 3-1 on penalties.

Shakhtar Donetsk v Olympiacos	1-1

Shakhtar Donetsk won 5-4 on penalties.

Anderlecht v Barcelona	1-0
Benfica v Liverpool	2-1
Manchester C v Schalke 04	1-1

Manchester C won 3-1 on penalties.

Ajax v Roma	0-0

Roma won 6-5 on penalties.

Chelsea v Zenit St Petersburg	3-1

QUARTER-FINALS

Chelsea v Atletico Madrid	2-0
Benfica v Shakhtar Donetsk	1-1

Shakhtar Donetsk won 5-4 on penalties.

Roma v Manchester C	2-1
Anderlecht v Porto	5-0

SEMI-FINALS

Anderlecht v Shakhtar Donetsk	1-3
Roma v Chelsea	0-4

FINAL

Nyon, Monday 13 April 2015

Shakhtar Donetsk (1) 2 *(Christensen 37 (og), Kovalenko 90)*

Chelsea (1) 3 *(Brown 7, 55, Solanke 47)*

Shakhtar Donetsk: Kudryk; Kyryukhantsev, Sahutkin, Matviyenko, Vachiberadze, Pikhalonok, Shtander (Kovalenko 71), Hladchenko, Arendaruk (Merkushov 78), Boryachuk, Zubkov.

Chelsea: Collins; Aina, Christensen, Clarke-Salter, Dasilva, Colkett, Musonda (Abraham 85), Boga (Palmer 71), Brown, Loftus-Cheek, Solanke.

Referee: Serdar Gozubuyuk (Netherlands).

ENGLAND UNDER-21 RESULTS 1976–2015

EC *UEFA Competition for Under-21 Teams*

Year	Date		Venue	Eng	Alb
			v ALBANIA		
EC1989	Mar	7	Shkroda	2	1
EC1989	April	25	Ipswich	2	0
EC2001	Mar	27	Tirana	1	0
EC2001	Sept	4	Middlesbrough	5	0

			v ANGOLA	Eng	Ang
1995	June	10	Toulon	1	0
1996	May	28	Toulon	0	2

			v ARGENTINA	Eng	Arg
1998	May	18	Toulon	0	2
2000	Feb	22	Fulham	1	0

			v AUSTRIA	Eng	Aus
1994	Oct	11	Kapfenberg	3	1
1995	Nov	14	Middlesbrough	2	1
EC2004	Sept	3	Krems	2	0
EC2005	Oct	7	Leeds	1	2
2013	June	26	Brighton	4	0

			v AZERBAIJAN	Eng	Az
EC2004	Oct	12	Baku	0	0
EC2005	Mar	29	Middlesbrough	2	0
2009	June	8	Milton Keynes	7	0
EC2011	Sept	1	Watford	6	0
EC2012	Sept	6	Baku	2	0

			v BELARUS	Eng	Bel
2015	Jun	11	Barnsley	1	0

			v BELGIUM	Eng	Bel
1994	June	5	Marseille	2	1
1996	May	24	Toulon	1	0
EC2011	Nov	14	Mons	1	2
EC2012	Feb	29	Middlesbrough	4	0

			v BRAZIL	Eng	B
1993	June	11	Toulon	0	0
1995	June	6	Toulon	0	2
1996	June	1	Toulon	1	2

			v BULGARIA	Eng	Bul
EC1979	June	5	Pernik	3	1
EC1979	Nov	20	Leicester	5	0
1989	June	5	Toulon	2	3
EC1998	Oct	9	West Ham	1	0
EC1999	June	8	Vratsa	1	0
EC2007	Sept	11	Sofia	2	0
EC2007	Nov	16	Milton Keynes	2	0

			v CROATIA	Eng	Cro
1996	Apr	23	Sunderland	0	1
2003	Aug	19	West Ham	0	3
EC2014	Oct	10	Wolverhampton	2	1
EC2014	Oct	14	Vinkovci	2	1

			v CZECHOSLOVAKIA	Eng	Cz
1990	May	28	Toulon	2	1
1992	May	26	Toulon	1	2
1993	June	9	Toulon	1	1

			v CZECH REPUBLIC	Eng	CzR
1998	Nov	17	Ipswich	0	1
EC2007	June	11	Arnhem	0	0
2008	Nov	18	Bramall Lane	2	0
EC2011	June	19	Viborg	1	2
2015	Mar	27	Prague	1	0

			v DENMARK	Eng	Den
EC1978	Sept	19	Hvidovre	2	1
EC1979	Sept	11	Watford	1	0
EC1982	Sept	21	Hvidovre	4	1
EC1983	Sept	20	Norwich	4	1
EC1986	Mar	12	Copenhagen	1	0
EC1986	Mar	26	Manchester	1	1
1988	Sept	13	Watford	0	0
1994	Mar	8	Brentford	1	0
1999	Oct	8	Bradford	4	1
2005	Aug	16	Herning	1	0
2011	Mar	24	Viborg	4	0

			v EQUADOR	Eng	E
2009	Feb	10	Malaga	2	3

			v FINLAND	Eng	Fin
EC1977	May	26	Helsinki	1	0
EC1977	Oct	12	Hull	8	1
			D	Eng	Fin
EC1984	Oct	16	Southampton	2	0
EC1985	May	21	Mikkeli	1	3
EC2000	Oct	10	Valkeakoski	2	2
EC2001	Mar	23	Barnsley	4	0
EC2009	June	15	Halmstad	2	1
EC2013	Sept	9	Tampere	1	1
EC2013	Nov	14	Milton Keynes	3	0

			v FRANCE	Eng	Fra
EC1984	Feb	28	Sheffield	6	1
EC1984	Mar	28	Rouen	1	0
1987	June	11	Toulon	0	2
EC1988	April	13	Besancon	2	4
EC1988	April	27	Highbury	2	2
1988	June	12	Toulon	2	4
1990	May	23	Toulon	7	3
1991	June	3	Toulon	1	0
1992	May	28	Toulon	0	0
1993	June	15	Toulon	1	0
1994	May	31	Aubagne	0	3
1995	June	10	Toulon	0	2
1998	May	14	Toulon	1	1
1999	Feb	9	Derby	2	1
EC2005	Nov	11	Tottenham	1	1
EC2005	Nov	15	Nancy	1	2
2009	Mar	31	Nottingham	0	2
2014	Nov	17	Paris	2	3

			v GEORGIA	Eng	Geo
EC1996	Nov	8	Batumi	1	0
EC1997	April	29	Charlton	0	0
2000	Aug	31	Middlesbrough	6	1

			v GERMANY	Eng	Ger
1991	Sept	10	Scunthorpe	2	1
EC2000	Oct	6	Derby	1	1
EC2001	Aug	31	Frieburg	2	1
2005	Mar	25	Hull	2	2
2005	Sept	6	Mainz	1	1
EC2006	Oct	6	Coventry	1	0
EC2006	Oct	10	Leverkusen	2	0
EC2009	June	22	Halmstad	1	1
EC2009	June	29	Malmo	0	4
2010	Nov	16	Wiesbaden	0	2
2015	Mar	30	Middlesbrough	3	2

			v EAST GERMANY	Eng	EG
EC1980	April	16	Sheffield	1	2
EC1980	April	23	Jena	0	1

			v WEST GERMANY	Eng	WG
EC1982	Sept	21	Sheffield	3	1
EC1982	Oct	12	Bremen	2	3
1987	Sept	8	Ludenscheid	0	2

			v GREECE	Eng	Gre
EC1982	Nov	16	Piraeus	0	1
EC1983	Mar	29	Portsmouth	2	1
1989	Feb	7	Patras	0	1
EC1997	Nov	13	Heraklion	0	2
EC1997	Dec	17	Norwich	4	2
EC2001	June	5	Athens	1	3
EC2001	Oct	5	Ewood Park	2	1
EC2009	Sept	8	Tripoli	1	1
EC2010	Mar	3	Doncaster	1	2

			v HUNGARY	Eng	Hun
EC1981	June	5	Keszthely	2	1
EC1981	Nov	17	Nottingham	2	0
EC1983	April	26	Newcastle	1	0
EC1983	Oct	11	Nyiregyhaza	2	0
1990	Sept	11	Southampton	3	1
1992	May	12	Budapest	2	2
1999	April	27	Budapest	2	2

v ICELAND

				Eng	Ice
2011	Mar	28	Preston	1	2
EC2011	Oct	6	Reykjavik	3	0
EC2011	Nov	10	Colchester	5	0

v ISRAEL

				Eng	Isr
1985	Feb	27	Tel Aviv	2	1
2011	Sept	5	Barnsley	4	1
EC2013	June	11	Jerusalem	0	1

v ITALY

				Eng	Italy
EC1978	Mar	8	Manchester	2	1
EC1978	April	5	Rome	0	0
EC1984	April	18	Manchester	3	1
EC1984	May	2	Florence	0	1
EC1986	April	9	Pisa	0	2
EC1986	April	23	Swindon	1	1
EC1997	Feb	12	Bristol	1	0
EC1997	Oct	10	Rieti	1	0
EC2000	May	27	Bratislava	0	2
2000	Nov	14	Monza*	0	0
2002	Mar	26	Valley Parade	1	1
EC2002	May	20	Basle	1	2
2003	Feb	11	Pisa	0	1
2007	Mar	24	Wembley	3	3
EC2007	June	14	Arnhem	2	2
2011	Feb	8	Empoli	0	1
EC2013	June	5	Tel Aviv	0	1
EC2015	Jun	24	Olomouc	1	3

Abandoned 11 mins; fog.

v LATVIA

				Eng	Lat
1995	April	25	Riga	1	0
1995	June	7	Burnley	4	0

v LITHUANIA

				Eng	Lith
EC2009	Nov	17	Vilnius	0	0
EC2010	Sept	7	Colchester	3	0
EC2013	Oct	15	Ipswich	5	0
EC2014	Sept	5	Zaliakalnis	1	0

v LUXEMBOURG

				Eng	Lux
EC1998	Oct	13	Greven Macher	5	0
EC1999	Sept	3	Reading	5	0

v MACEDONIA

				Eng	M
EC2002	Oct	15	Reading	3	1
EC2003	Sept	5	Skopje	1	1
EC2009	Sept	4	Prilep	2	1
EC2009	Oct	9	Coventry	6	3

v MALAYSIA

				Eng	Mal
1995	June	8	Toulon	2	0

v MEXICO

				Eng	Mex
1988	June	5	Toulon	2	1
1991	May	29	Toulon	6	0
1992	May	25	Toulon	1	1
2001	May	24	Leicester	3	0

v MOLDOVA

				Eng	Mol
EC1996	Aug	31	Chisinau	2	0
EC1997	Sept	9	Wycombe	1	0
EC2006	Aug	15	Ipswich	2	2
EC2013	Sept	5	Reading	1	0
EC2014	Sept	9	Tiraspol	3	0

v MONTENEGRO

				Eng	M
EC2007	Sept	7	Podgorica	3	0
EC2007	Oct	12	Leicester	1	0

v MOROCCO

				Eng	Mor
1987	June	7	Toulon	2	0
1988	June	9	Toulon	1	0

v NETHERLANDS

				Eng	N
EC1993	April	27	Portsmouth	3	0
EC1993	Oct	12	Utrecht	1	1
2001	Aug	14	Reading	4	0
EC2001	Nov	9	Utrecht	2	2
EC2001	Nov	13	Derby	1	0
2004	Feb	17	Hull	3	2
2005	Feb	8	Derby	1	2
2006	Nov	14	Alkmaar	1	0
EC2007	June	20	Heerenveen	1	1
2009	Aug	11	Groningen	0	0

v NORTHERN IRELAND

				Eng	NI
2012	Nov	13	Blackpool	2	0

v NORWAY

				Eng	Nor
EC1977	June	1	Bergen	2	1
EC1977	Sept	6	Brighton	6	0
1980	Sept	9	Southampton	3	0
1981	Sept	8	Drammen	0	0
EC1992	Oct	13	Peterborough	0	2
EC1993	June	1	Stavanger	1	1
1995	Oct	10	Stavanger	2	2
2006	Feb	28	Reading	3	1
2009	Mar	27	Sandefjord	5	0
2011	June	5	Southampton	2	0
EC2011	Oct	10	Drammen	2	1
EC2012	Sept	10	Chesterfield	1	0
EC2013	June	8	Petah Tikva	1	3

v POLAND

				Eng	Pol
EC1982	Mar	17	Warsaw	2	1
EC1982	April	7	West Ham	2	2
EC1989	June	2	Plymouth	2	1
EC1989	Oct	10	Jastrzebie	3	1
EC1990	Oct	16	Tottenham	0	1
EC1991	Nov	12	Pila	1	2
EC1993	May	28	Zdroj	4	1
EC1993	Sept	7	Millwall	1	2
EC1996	Oct	8	Wolverhampton	0	0
EC1997	May	30	Katowice	1	1
EC1999	Mar	26	Southampton	5	0
EC1999	Sept	7	Plock	1	3
EC2004	Sept	7	Rybnik	3	1
EC2005	Oct	11	Hillsborough	4	1
2008	Mar	25	Wolverhampton	0	0

v PORTUGAL

				Eng	Por
1987	June	13	Toulon	0	0
1990	May	21	Toulon	0	1
1993	June	7	Toulon	2	0
1994	June	7	Toulon	2	0
EC1994	Sept	6	Leicester	0	0
1995	Sept	2	Lisbon	0	2
1996	May	30	Toulon	1	3
2000	Apr	16	Stoke	0	1
EC2002	May	22	Zurich	1	3
EC2003	Mar	28	Rio Major	2	4
EC2003	Sept	9	Everton	1	2
EC2008	Nov	20	Agueda	1	1
2008	Sept	5	Wembley	2	0
EC2009	Nov	14	Wembley	1	0
EC2010	Sept	3	Barcelos	1	0
2014	Nov	13	Burnley	3	1
EC2015	Jun	18	Uherske Hradiste	0	1

v REPUBLIC OF IRELAND

				Eng	RoI
1981	Feb	25	Liverpool	1	0
1985	Mar	25	Portsmouth	3	2
1989	June	9	Toulon	0	0
EC1990	Nov	13	Cork	3	0
EC1991	Mar	26	Brentford	3	0
1994	Nov	15	Newcastle	1	0
1995	Mar	27	Dublin	2	0
EC2007	Oct	16	Cork	3	0
EC2008	Feb	5	Southampton	3	0

v ROMANIA

				Eng	Rom
EC1980	Oct	14	Ploesti	0	4
EC1981	April	28	Swindon	3	0
EC1985	April	30	Brasov	0	0
EC1985	Sept	10	Ipswich	3	0
2007	Aug	21	Bristol	1	1
EC2010	Oct	8	Norwich	2	1
EC2010	Oct	12	Botosani	0	0
2013	Mar	21	Wycombe	3	0

v RUSSIA

				Eng	Rus
1994	May	30	Bandol	2	0

v SAN MARINO

				Eng	SM
EC1993	Feb	16	Luton	6	0
EC1993	Nov	17	San Marino	4	0
EC2013	Oct	10	San Marino	4	0
EC2013	Nov	15	Shrewsbury	9	0

v SCOTLAND

				Eng	Sco
1977	April	27	Sheffield	1	0
EC1980	Feb	12	Coventry	2	1
EC1980	Mar	4	Aberdeen	0	0
EC1982	April	19	Glasgow	1	0
EC1982	April	28	Manchester	1	1
EC1988	Feb	16	Aberdeen	1	0
EC1988	Mar	22	Nottingham	1	0

				Eng	*Sco*
1993	June	13	Toulon	1	0
2013	Aug	13	Sheffield	6	0

v SENEGAL				*Eng*	*Sen*
1989	June	7	Toulon	6	1
1991	May	27	Toulon	2	1

v SERBIA				*Eng*	*Ser*
EC2007	June	17	Nijmegen	2	0
EC2012	Oct	12	Norwich	1	0
EC2012	Oct	16	Krusevac	1	0

v SERBIA-MONTENEGRO				*Eng*	*S-M*
2003	June	2	Hull	3	2

v SLOVAKIA				*Eng*	*Slo*
EC2002	June	1	Bratislava	0	2
EC2002	Oct	11	Trnava	4	0
EC2003	June	10	Sunderland	2	0
2007	June	5	Norwich	5	0

v SLOVENIA				*Eng*	*Slo*
2000	Feb	12	Nova Gorica	1	0
2008	Aug	19	Hull	2	1

v SOUTH AFRICA				*Eng*	*SA*
1998	May	16	Toulon	3	1

v SPAIN				*Eng*	*Spa*
EC1984	May	17	Seville	1	0
EC1984	May	24	Sheffield	2	0
1987	Feb	18	Burgos	2	1
1992	Sept	8	Burgos	1	0
2001	Feb	27	Birmingham	0	4
2004	Nov	16	Alcala	0	1
2007	Feb	6	Derby	2	2
EC2009	June	18	Gothenburg	2	0
EC2011	June	12	Herning	1	1

v SWEDEN				*Eng*	*Swe*
1979	June	9	Vasteras	2	1
1986	Sept	9	Ostersund	1	1
EC1988	Oct	18	Coventry	1	1
EC1989	Sept	5	Uppsala	0	1
EC1998	Sept	4	Sundvall	2	0
EC1999	June	4	Huddersfield	3	0
2004	Mar	30	Kristiansund	2	2
EC2009	June	26	Gothenburg	3	3
2013	Feb	5	Walsall	4	0
EC2015	Jun	21	Olomouc	1	0

v SWITZERLAND				*Eng*	*Swit*
EC1980	Nov	18	Ipswich	5	0
EC1981	May	31	Neuenburg	1	0
1988	May	28	Lausanne	1	1

				Eng	*Swit*
1996	April	1	Swindon	0	0
1998	Mar	24	Brugglifeld	0	2
EC2002	May	17	Zurich	2	1
EC2006	Sept	6	Lucerne	3	2

v TURKEY				*Eng*	*Tur*
EC1984	Nov	13	Bursa	0	0
EC1985	Oct	15	Bristol	3	0
EC1987	April	28	Izmir	0	0
EC1987	Oct	13	Sheffield	1	1
EC1991	April	30	Izmir	2	2
1991	Oct	15	Reading	2	0
EC1992	Nov	17	Orient	0	1
EC1993	Mar	30	Izmir	0	0
EC2000	May	29	Bratislava	6	0
EC2003	April	1	Newcastle	1	1
EC2003	Oct	10	Istanbul	0	1

v UKRAINE				*Eng*	*Uk*
2004	Aug	17	Middlesbrough	3	1
EC2011	June	15	Herning	0	0

v USA				*Eng*	*USA*
1989	June	11	Toulon	0	2
1994	June	2	Toulon	3	0

v USSR				*Eng*	*USSR*
1987	June	9	Toulon	0	0
1988	June	7	Toulon	1	0
1990	May	25	Toulon	2	1
1991	May	31	Toulon	2	1

v UZBEKISTAN				*Eng*	*Uzb*
2010	Aug	10	Bristol	2	0

v WALES				*Eng*	*Wales*
1976	Dec	15	Wolverhampton	0	0
1979	Feb	6	Swansea	1	0
1990	Dec	5	Tranmere	0	0
EC2004	Oct	8	Blackburn	2	0
EC2005	Sept	2	Wrexham	4	0
2008	May	5	Wrexham	2	0
EC2008	Oct	10	Cardiff	3	2
EC2008	Oct	14	Villa Park	2	2
EC2013	Mar	5	Derby	1	0
EC2013	May	19	Swansea	3	1

v YUGOSLAVIA				*Eng*	*Yugo*
EC1978	April	19	Novi Sad	1	2
EC1978	May	2	Manchester	1	1
1986	Nov	11	Peterborough	1	1
EC1987	Nov	10	Zemun	5	1
EC2000	Mar	29	Barcelona	3	0
2002	Sept	6	Bolton	1	1

UEFA REGIONS' CUP 2014–15

FINALS IN REPUBLIC OF IRELAND

GROUP A

South Moravia v Tuzla	1-0
Eastern Region IRL v Ankara	2-0
Eastern Region IRL v South Moravia	2-0
Ankara v Tuzla	2-1
Tuzla v Eastern Region IRL	1-2
Ankara v South Moravia	4-2

Group A Table	P	W	D	L	F	A	GD	Pts
Eastern Region IRL	3	3	0	0	6	1	5	9
Ankara	3	2	0	1	6	5	1	6
South Moravia	3	1	0	2	3	6	–3	3
Tuzla	3	0	0	3	2	5	–3	0

GROUP B

Zagreb v Dolnoslaski	4-0
Eastern Region NIR v Wurttemberg	2-2
Zagreb v Eastern Region NIR	3-1
Dolnoslaski v Wurttemberg	0-1
Wurttemberg v Zagreb	1-2
Dolnoslaski v Eastern Region NIR	1-2

Group B Table	P	W	D	L	F	A	GD	Pts
Zagreb	3	3	0	0	9	2	7	9
Wurttemberg	3	1	1	1	4	4	0	4
Eastern Region NIR	3	1	1	1	5	6	–1	4
Dolnoslaski	3	0	0	3	1	7	–6	0

FINAL

Eastern Region IRL v Zagreb	1-0

BRITISH AND IRISH UNDER-21 TEAMS 2014–15

■ *Denotes player sent off.*

ENGLAND

FRIENDLIES

Thursday, 13 November 2014

England (2) 3 *(Ings 6, 58, Jenkinson 44)*

Portugal (0) 1 *(Bernardo Silva 48)* 10,711

England: (433) Butland; Jenkinson, Keane, Gibson, Garbutt (Robinson 80); Ince, Hughes (Chalobah 56), Forster-Caskey; Carroll, Ings (Bamford 79), Redmond (Pritchard 73).

Portugal: (442) Rui Silva; Ricardo Esgaio (Joao Cancelo 46), Frederico Venancio, Rafa A (Bruno Gaspar 83), Tobias Figueiredo; Ruben Neves (Teixeira 85), Bernardo Silva (Rafa S 85), Bruno Fernandes (Joao Teixeira 69), Ruben Pinto (Fabio Sturgeon 69); Ricardo Pereira (Ricardo Horta 46), Bruma (Carlos Mane 69).

Monday, 17 November 2014

France (2) 3 *(Sanogo 29, 44, Coman 73)*

England (2) 2 *(Kane 20, 22)* 5000

France: (433) Areola; Laporte, Conte, Mendy, Gbamin; Tolisso (Sanson 74), Imbula (Bakayoko 64), Veretout; Ntep, Sanogo, Thauvin (Coman 63).

England: (433) Bond; Keane, Garbutt, Gibson (Jenkinson 42), Lascelles, Chalobah (Forster-Caskey 33), Carroll, Pritchard (Ings 46); Ince, Kane (Wilson 65), Redmond.

Friday, 27 March 2015

Czech Rep (0) 0

England (0) 1 *(Carroll 47)* 5126

Czech Rep: (442) Pavlenka; Kalas, Hanousek, Holes, Stronati; Frydek (Masopust 61), Petrak (Takacs 70), Zmrhal, Travnik (Houska 83); Vydra (Prikryl 71), Skalak.

England: (433) Bettinelli; Chambers (Jenkinson 63), Moore (Stones 70), Keane, Targett (Garbutt 46); Forster-Caskey, Pritchard (Lingard 62), Ward-Prowse; Carroll (Hughes 52), Woodrow (Ings 62), Redmond.

Monday, 30 March 2015

England (1) 3 *(Lingard 35, Redmond 79, Ward-Prowse 82)*

Germany (1) 2 *(Hofmann P 15, 50)* 30,178

England: (442) Bond; Jenkinson, Garbutt, Stones, Gibson (Keane 77); Lingard, Forster-Caskey (Chambers 85), Ward-Prowse, Hughes (Pritchard 66); Redmond, Ings.

Germany: (442) ter Stegen; Knoche, Korb, Gunter, Ginter; Bittencourt (Gnabry 46), Leitner (Kimmich 46), Can, Younes (Malli 77); Meyer (Schulz 46), Hofmann P.

Thursday, 11 June 2015

England (0) 1 *(Gibson 83)*

Belarus (0) 0 15,207

England: (442) Butland (Bond 69); Jenkinson, Garbutt, Stones (Chambers 46), Gibson; Ward-Prowse (Chalobah 70), Carroll (Forster-Caskey 70), Hughes (Loftus-Cheek 46), Redmond (Ings 59); Berahino (Kane 59), Pritchard (Lingard 69).

Belarus: (442) Vasilyuchek; Ignatenko, Yablonskiy, Zolotov■, Yanchenko (Klimovich 76); Korzun (Pavlyukovets 87), Leshka (Yeudakimau 46), Lebedzeu (Milevsky 63), Yarotski (Shibun 64); Karpovich, Poznyak.

EURO UNDER-21 CHAMPIONSHIP 2013–15
QUALIFYING GROUP 1

Friday, 5 September 2014

Lithuania (0) 0

England (0) 1 *(Kane 81)* 3000

Lithuania: (451) Svedkauskas; Snapkauskas, Bagdanavicius, Janusevskij, Baravykas; Veliulis, Verbickas (Dapkus 75), Birskys (Grigaravicius 79), Baranauskas E (Tamulevicius 84), Norvilas; Baranauskas L.

England: (433) Butland; Keane, Garbutt, Gibson (Kane 64); Moore; Chalobah, Ward-Prowse, Carroll; Ince (Hughes 79), Redmond (Pritchard 79), Berahino.

Tuesday, 9 September 2014

Moldova (0) 0

England (1) 3 *(Berahino 16, 52, Kane 85)* 2500

Moldova: (532) Koselev; Gheorghiu, Jardan, Focsa, Bogdan (Matei 46), Zasavitchi; Rata (Graur 89), Anton, Mirza; Milinceanu (Spataru 58), Dima.

England: (433) Bond; Moore, Keane, Garbutt (Blackett 82), Lascelles; Forster-Caskey, Carroll, Redmond (Ings 82); Hughes, Berahino (Pritchard 87), Kane.

EURO UNDER-21 CHAMPIONSHIP 2013–15
QUALIFYING PLAY-OFF

Friday, 10 October 2014

England (0) 2 *(Kane 58, Berahino 85 (pen))*

Croatia (1) 1 *(Livaja 13)* 23,107

England: (433) Butland; Keane (Dier 45), Moore, Gibson, Shaw; Hughes (Ince 56), Forster-Caskey, Carroll; Redmond, Berahino, Kane.

Croatia: (433) Livakovic; Zuparic, Datkovic, Mitrovic, Milic (Milos 89); Coric (Pasalic 63), Bradaric, Pavicic; Pjaca, Rebic, Livaja (Bagaric 70).

Tuesday, 14 October 2014

Croatia (1) 1 *(Livaja 38)*

England (1) 2 *(Moore 9, Hughes 73)* 6000

Croatia: (433) Livakovic; Milos, Datkovic, Mitrovic, Milic; Pasalic (Caktas 67), Halilovic (Misic 79), Bradaric; Pjaca, Livaja, Rebic (Bagaric 33).

England: (433) Butland; Dier, Moore, Gibson, Shaw; Hughes, Forster-Caskey, Carroll; Redmond (Ince 85), Kane, Berahino.

NORTHERN IRELAND

EURO UNDER-21 CHAMPIONSHIP 2013–15
QUALIFYING GROUP 9

Tuesday, 9 September 2014

N Ireland (0) 1 *(Brobbel 67)*

Serbia (2) 4 *(Pesic 34, Srnic 36, 56, Kostic 58)* 285

N Ireland: (442) Johns; Dummigan, Conlan (Burns 80), Sendles-White, Harney; McNair (McGeehan 83), Winchester, Doherty (Millar 58), Brobbel; Gray, Duffy.

Serbia: (442) Dmitrovic; Petkovic, Pantic, Petrovic, Veljkovic; Mijailovic, Kostic, Radoja (Milinkovic-Savic 86), Srnic (Stojkovic 90); Pesic, Cavric (Djurdjevic 68).

SCOTLAND

FRIENDLIES

Tuesday, 18 November 2014

Switzerland (1) 1 *(Araz 44)*

Scotland (0) 1 *(King C 90)* 837

Switzerland: (4231) Salvi (Pelloni 74); Janko (Krasniqi 74), Wuthrich, Angha (Tarashaj 63), Untersee; Araz, Rodriguez (Akanji 63); Corbaz (Khelifi 46), Bertone, Embolo; Frey.

Scotland: (4231) Hamilton (Henly 56); Fraser M (Naismith 72), Hendrie, Findlay, McGhee; Slater, Fulton (Handling 56); King A (King C 80), Gauld, Fraser R (Christie 72); McManus (Cardwell 72).

Thursday, 26 March 2015

Hungary (0) 1 *(Szenes Bence 62)*

Scotland (0) 2 *(Shankland 85, 90)* 250

Hungary: (442) Nagy (Csaba 75); Szilagyi, Eperjesi (Angyal 68), Baki (Csato 68), Hangya (Jagodics 46); Kocsis, Novak (Martin 46), Lorinczy (Szenes Bence 60), Sos Bence (Prosser 60); Markvart (Gobar 46), Bese (Pesti 46).

Scotland: (442) Hamilton; Paterson (Hyam 46), McGhee, Findlay (Love 46), Handling (King B 63); Nicholson (Shankland 46), Fraser R, Gauld (Smith 76), McFadzean (Kingsley 63); McGinn (O'Hara 76), McManus (Christie 46).

EURO UNDER-21 CHAMPIONSHIP 2013–15
QUALIFYING GROUP 3

Thursday, 4 September 2014
Slovakia (0) 1 *(Duda 90)*
Scotland (0) 1 *(Fraser R 67)* 1263
Slovakia: (451) Rusov; Pauschek, Ninaj, Hudak, Teixeira; Rusnak (Meszaros 66), Hrosovsky, Duda, Lasik (Lobotka 83), Schranz; Zrelak.
Scotland: (433) Archer; Jack, McGhee, Findlay, Robertson (Hendrie 26); Slater, Macleod, McGinn; Fraser R (McKenzie 82), May, Gauld (Fraser M 88).

Monday, 8 September 2014
Luxembourg (0) 0
Scotland (2) 3 *(Gauld 32, 63, Macleod 36)* 800
Luxembourg: (442) Frising; Mastrangelo, Vogel, Dragovic (Bechtold 12), Da Graca Dias; Mersch (Agovic E 68), Agovic D, Todorovic, Borges (Roulez 58); Couto Pinto, Lascak.
Scotland: (442) Hamilton; Jack, McGhee, Findlay, Hendrie; Macleod (Christie 72), Slater (Fraser M 63), McGinn, Fraser R; May, Gauld (McKenzie 85).

WALES

EURO UNDER-21 CHAMPIONSHIP 2013–15
QUALIFYING GROUP 1

Friday, 5 September 2014
Finland (1) 2 *(Lod 19, Vayrynen 87)*
Wales (0) 2 *(Burns 65, Evans L 69)* 5096
Finland: (433) Gotte; Hatakka (Saksela 83), Rexhepi, Vaisanen, O'Shaughnessy; Brechtel (Kabashi 74), Lam, Kamara; Skrabb (Hertsi 67), Vayrynen, Lod.
Wales: (4411) Ward; Jones, Ray, Walsh, Fox; Edwards, Sheehan, Evans L, Harrison (Hedges 65); O'Sullivan; Burns.

Tuesday, 9 September 2014
Lithuania (0) 1 *(Tamulevicius 81)*
Wales (0) 1 *(Evans L 90)* 550
Lithuania: (4231) Svedkauskas; Girdvainis, Bagdanavicius, Janusevskij, Baravykas; Veliulis (Gedminas 56), Verbickas; Birskys, Baranauskas E (Tamulevicius 48), Norvilas; Baranauskas L (Dapkus 69).
Wales: (4321) Ward; Fox, Williams, Walsh, Hewitt; Sheehan, Edwards (Evans J 58), Evans L; O'Sullivan (Wharton 74), Hedges; Reid (Harrison 62).

EURO UNDER-21 CHAMPIONSHIP 2015–17
QUALIFYING GROUP 5

Tuesday, 31 March 2015
Wales (3) 3 *(O'Sullivan 9, 13, Yorwerth 25)*
Bulgaria (0) 1 *(Kolev 51)* 1175
Wales: (442) Dibble; Jones, Yorwerth, Wright (Smith 55), Sheehan; Evans L, John, O'Sullivan (Weeks 46), Hedges; Burns, Harrison (Wilson 82).

Bulgaria: (541) Lyubenov; Galabov, Popadiyn, Terziev, Vasilev (Rasim 46), Marin; Malinov, Kolev, Iliev, Chunchukov (Angelov 46); Despodov (Vutov 70).

REPUBLIC OF IRELAND

FRIENDLIES

Thursday, 9 October 2014
Norway (2) 4 *(Elyounoussi 27, Berisha 33, Strand 53, Hansen 56)*
Republic of Ireland (0) 1 *(Browne 76 (pen))* 503
Norway: (442) Dyngeland (Vestly Heigre 46); Hoibraten (Granli 46), Gronner (Bergan 46), Grogaard (Hansen 46), Ovenstad (Trondsen 46); Fossum (Omoijuanfo 46), Haraldseid (Vindheim 46), Elyounoussi (Aursnes 46), Skaanes (Strand 46); Finne, Berisha.
Republic of Ireland: (442) Lawlor (Rogers 60); O'Connell, Griffin, Connors (McEvoy 46), Sweeney (Kavanagh 46); Long, Hoban, Lenihan (Watkins-Clark 46); Sadlier (Browne 46); Byrne J, Byrne S (Roberts 60).

EURO UNDER-21 CHAMPIONSHIP 2013–15
QUALIFYING GROUP 6

Friday, 5 September 2014
Germany (0) 2 *(Hofmann P 47, Hofmann J 50)*
Republic of Ireland (0) 0 3969
Germany: (4411) Horn; Korb, Can, Knoche, Gunter; Bittencourt, Geis, Leitner, Schulz (Hofmann J 46); Younes (Kachunga 74); Hofmann P (Arnold 65).
Republic of Ireland: (4231) Lawlor; Long, Hoban, Watkins-Clark, Griffin; Byrne J (Sweeney 60), Lenihan; Sadlier (Garmston 65), Grealish, Connors; Wilkinson.

EURO UNDER-21 CHAMPIONSHIP 2015–17
QUALIFYING GROUP 2

Thursday, 26 March 2015
Republic of Ireland (1) 1 *(Connolly 31)*
Andorra (0) 0 1500
Republic of Ireland: (442) Rogers; Kavanagh, Rea, Hoban, Connors; Lenihan, McEvoy (Browne 86), O'Dowda, Byrne J; Wilkinson (Goodwin 72), Connolly (Maguire 90).
Andorra: (442) Pinto; Gresa (Pomares 76), Rubio (Nazzaro 54), Rebes, Llovera; Reyes, Sanchez, Ferre, Rodriguez; Matos (Villagrasa 68), Alaez.

ENGLAND C 2014–15

INTERNATIONAL CHALLENGE TROPHY
Istanbul, 14 October 2014
Turkey A2 (2) 2 *(Colak 45, 71)*
England C (0) 0
England C: Kitscha; Halls, Dunkley, Roberts, Brown, Pearson (Roberts 70), Gallagher (Comley 74), Payne, Norwood, Moult (Burrow 64), Frear.

Halifax, 18 November 2014
England C (2) 4 *(Bogle 5, Beautyman 42, Yiadom 66, James 79)*
Estonia U23 (1) 2 *(Lepistu 32, Kase 84)* 2388
England C: Hall; Halls, Dunkley, Parkes, Brown, Yiadom, James (Pearson 85), Nolan (Gallagher 80), Frear, Beautyman (Jennings 80), Bogle (Burrow 67).

FRIENDLY MATCH
Larnaca, 17 February 2015
Cyprus U21 (0) 2 *(Charalambos 58, Adamos 60)*
England C (1) 1 *(Yiadom 22)*
England C: Coughlin (Kitscha 46); Bolton (Halls 46), Roberts, Parkes, Brown, Yiadom, Pearson (Woodyard 46), James (Lewis 46), Frear, Norwood (Payne 46), Burrow

BRITISH UNDER-21 APPEARANCES 1976–2015

Bold type indicates players who made an international appearance in season 2014–15.

ENGLAND

Ablett, G. 1988 (Liverpool)	1
Adams, N. 1987 (Everton)	1
Adams, T. A. 1985 (Arsenal)	5
Addison, M. 2010 (Derby Co)	1
Afobe, B. T. 2012 (Arsenal)	2
Agbonlahor, G. 2007 (Aston Villa)	16
Albrighton, M. K. 2011 (Aston Villa)	8
Allen, B. 1992 (QPR)	8
Allen, C. 1980 (QPR, Crystal Palace)	3
Allen, C. A. 1995 (Oxford U)	2
Allen, M. 1987 (QPR)	2
Allen, P. 1985 (West Ham U, Tottenham H)	3
Allen, R. W. 1998 (Tottenham H)	3
Alnwick, B. R. 2008 (Tottenham H)	1
Ambrose, D. P. F. 2003 (Ipswich T, Newcastle U, Charlton Ath)	10
Ameobi, F. 2001 (Newcastle U)	19
Ameobi, S. 2012 (Newcastle U)	5
Amos, B. P. 2012 (Manchester U)	3
Anderson, V. A. 1978 (Nottingham F)	1
Anderton, D. R. 1993 (Tottenham H)	12
Andrews, I. 1987 (Leicester C)	1
Ardley, N. C. 1993 (Wimbledon)	10
Ashcroft, L. 1992 (Preston NE)	1
Ashton, D. 2004 (Crewe Alex, Norwich C)	9
Atherton, P. 1992 (Coventry C)	1
Atkinson, B. 1991 (Sunderland)	6
Awford, A. T. 1993 (Portsmouth)	9
Bailey, G. R. 1979 (Manchester U)	14
Baines, L. J. 2005 (Wigan Ath)	16
Baker, G. E. 1981 (Southampton)	2
Baker, N. L. 2011 (Aston Villa)	3
Ball, M. J. 1999 (Everton)	7
Bamford, P. J. 2013 (Chelsea)	**2**
Bannister, D. 1982 (Sheffield W)	1
Barker, S. 1985 (Blackburn R)	4
Barkley, R. 2012 (Everton)	5
Barmby, N. J. 1994 (Tottenham H, Everton)	4
Barnes, J. 1983 (Watford)	2
Barnes, P. S. 1977 (Manchester C)	9
Barrett, E. D. 1990 (Oldham Ath)	4
Barry, G. 1999 (Aston Villa)	27
Barton, J. 2004 (Manchester C)	2
Bart-Williams, C. G. 1993 (Sheffield W)	16
Batty, D. 1988 (Leeds U)	7
Bazeley, D. S. 1992 (Watford)	1
Beagrie, P. 1988 (Sheffield U)	2
Beardsmore, R. 1989 (Manchester U)	5
Beattie, J. S. 1999 (Southampton)	5
Beckham, D. R. J. 1995 (Manchester U)	9
Berahino, S. 2013 (WBA)	**11**
Bennett, J. 2011 (Middlesbrough)	3
Bennett, R. 2012 (Norwich C)	2
Bent, D. A. 2003 (Ipswich T, Charlton Ath)	14
Bent, M. N. 1998 (Crystal Palace)	2
Bentley, D. M. 2004 (Arsenal, Blackburn R)	8
Beeston, C 1988 (Stoke C)	1
Benjamin, T. J. 2001 (Leicester C)	1
Bertrand, R. 2009 (Chelsea)	16
Bertschin, K. E. 1977 (Birmingham C)	3
Bettinelli, M. 2015 (Fulham)	**1**
Birtles, G. 1980 (Nottingham F)	2
Blackett, T. N. 2014 (Manchester U)	**1**
Blackstock, D. A. 2008 (QPR)	2
Blackwell, D. R. 1991 (Wimbledon)	6
Blake, M. A. 1990 (Aston Villa)	8
Blissett, L. L. 1979 (Watford)	4
Bond, J. H. 2013 (Watford)	**5**
Booth, A. D. 1995 (Huddersfield T)	3
Bothroyd, J. 2001 (Coventry C)	1
Bowyer, L. D. 1996 (Charlton Ath, Leeds U)	13
Bracewell, P. 1983 (Stoke C)	13
Bradbury, L. M. 1997 (Portsmouth, Manchester C)	3
Bramble, T. M. 2001 (Ipswich T, Newcastle U)	10
Branch, P. M. 1997 (Everton)	1
Bradshaw, P. W. 1977 (Wolverhampton W)	4
Breacker, T. 1986 (Luton T)	2

Brennan, M. 1987 (Ipswich T)	5
Bridge, W. M. 1999 (Southampton)	8
Bridges, M. 1997 (Sunderland, Leeds U)	3
Briggs, M. 2012 (Fulham)	2
Brightwell, I. 1989 (Manchester C)	4
Briscoe, L. S. 1996 (Sheffield W)	5
Brock, K. 1984 (Oxford U)	4
Broomes, M. C. 1997 (Blackburn R)	2
Brown, M. R. 1996 (Manchester C)	4
Brown, W. M. 1999 (Manchester U)	8
Bull, S. G. 1989 (Wolverhampton W)	5
Bullock, M. J. 1998 (Barnsley)	1
Burrows, D. 1989 (WBA, Liverpool)	7
Butcher, T. I. 1979 (Ipswich T)	7
Butland, J. 2012 (Birmingham C, Stoke C)	**28**
Butt, N. 1995 (Manchester U)	7
Butters, G. 1989 (Tottenham H)	3
Butterworth, I. 1985 (Coventry C, Nottingham F)	8
Bywater, S. 2001 (West Ham U)	6
Cadamarteri, D. L. 1999 (Everton)	3
Caesar, G. 1987 (Arsenal)	3
Cahill, G. J. 2007 (Aston Villa)	3
Callaghan, N. 1983 (Watford)	9
Camp, L. M. J. 2005 (Derby Co)	5
Campbell, A. P. 2000 (Middlesbrough)	4
Campbell, F. L. 2008 (Manchester U)	14
Campbell, K. J. 1991 (Arsenal)	4
Campbell, S. 1994 (Tottenham)	11
Carbon, M. P. 1996 (Derby Co)	4
Carr, C. 1985 (Fulham)	1
Carr, F. 1987 (Nottingham F)	9
Carragher, J. L. 1997 (Liverpool)	27
Carroll, A. T. 2010 (Newcastle U)	5
Carroll, T. J. 2013 (Tottenham H)	**17**
Carlisle, C. J. 2001 (QPR)	3
Carrick, M. 2001 (West Ham U)	14
Carson, S. P. 2004 (Leeds U, Liverpool)	29
Casper, C. M. 1995 (Manchester U)	1
Caton, T. 1982 (Manchester C)	14
Cattermole, L. B. 2008 (Middlesbrough, Wigan Ath, Sunderland)	16
Caulker, S. R. 2011 (Tottenham H)	10
Chadwick, L. H. 2000 (Manchester U)	13
Challis, T. M. 1996 (QPR)	2
Chalobah, N. N. 2012 (Chelsea)	**21**
Chamberlain, M. 1983 (Stoke C)	4
Chambers, C. 2015 (Arsenal)	**3**
Chaplow, R. D. 2004 (Burnley)	3
Chapman, L. 1981 (Stoke C)	1
Charles, G. A. 1991 (Nottingham F)	4
Chettle, S. 1988 (Nottingham F)	12
Chopra, R. M. 2004 (Newcastle U)	1
Clark, L. R. 1992 (Newcastle U)	11
Clarke, P. M. 2003 (Everton)	8
Christie, M. N. 2001 (Derby Co)	11
Clegg, M. J. 1998 (Manchester U)	2
Clemence, S. N. 1999 (Tottenham H)	1
Cleverley, T. W. 2010 (Manchester U)	16
Clough, N. H. 1986 (Nottingham F)	15
Clyne, N. E. 2012 (Crystal Palace)	8
Cole, A. 2001 (Arsenal)	4
Cole, A. A. 1992 (Arsenal, Bristol C, Newcastle U)	8
Cole, C. 2003 (Chelsea)	19
Cole, J. J. 2000 (West Ham U)	8
Coney, D. 1985 (Fulham)	4
Connor, T. 1987 (Brighton & HA)	1
Cooke, R. 1986 (Tottenham H)	1
Cooke, T. J. 1996 (Manchester U)	4
Cooper, C. T. 1988 (Middlesbrough)	8
Cork, J. F. P. 2009 (Chelsea)	13
Corrigan, J. T. 1978 (Manchester C)	3
Cort, C. E. R. 1999 (Wimbledon)	12
Cottee, A. R. 1985 (West Ham U)	8
Couzens, A. J. 1995 (Leeds U)	3
Cowans, G. S. 1979 (Aston Villa)	5
Cox, N. J. 1993 (Aston Villa)	6
Cranie, M. J. 2008 (Portsmouth)	16

Cranson, I. 1985 (Ipswich T) — 5
Cresswell, R. P. W. 1999 (York C, Sheffield W) — 4
Croft, G. 1995 (Grimsby T) — 4
Crooks, G. 1980 (Stoke C) — 4
Crossley, M. G. 1990 (Nottingham F) — 3
Crouch, P. J. 2002 (Portsmouth, Aston Villa) — 5
Cundy, J. V. 1991 (Chelsea) — 3
Cunningham, L. 1977 (WBA) — 6
Curbishley, L. C. 1981 (Birmingham C) — 1
Curtis, J. C. K. 1998 (Manchester U) — 16

Daniel, P. W. 1977 (Hull C) — 7
Dann, S. 2008 (Coventry C) — 2
Davenport, C. R. P. 2005 (Tottenham H) — 8
Davies, A. J. 2004 (Middlesbrough) — 1
Davies, C. E. 2006 (WBA) — 3
Davies, K. C. 1998 (Southampton, Blackburn R, Southampton) — 3
Davis, K. G. 1995 (Luton T) — 3
Davis, P. 1982 (Arsenal) — 11
Davis, S. 2001 (Fulham) — 11
Dawson, C. 2012 (WBA) — 15
Dawson, M. R. 2003 (Nottingham F, Tottenham H) — 13
Day, C. N. 1996 (Tottenham H, Crystal Palace) — 6
D'Avray, M. 1984 (Ipswich T) — 2
Deehan, J. M. 1977 (Aston Villa) — 7
Defoe, J. C. 2001 (West Ham U) — 23
Delfouneso, N. 2010 (Aston Villa) — 17
Delph, F. 2009 (Leeds U, Aston Villa) — 4
Dennis, M. E. 1980 (Birmingham C) — 3
Derbyshire, M. A. 2007 (Blackburn R) — 14
Dichio, D. S. E. 1996 (QPR) — 1
Dickens, A. 1985 (West Ham U) — 1
Dicks, J. 1988 (West Ham U) — 4
Dier, E. J. E. 2013 (Sporting Lisbon, Tottenham H) — **6**
Digby, F. 1987 (Swindon T) — 5
Dillon, K. P. 1981 (Birmingham C) — 1
Dixon, K. M. 1985 (Chelsea) — 1
Dobson, A. 1989 (Coventry C) — 4
Dodd, J. R. 1991 (Southampton) — 8
Donowa, L. 1985 (Norwich C) — 3
Dorigo, A. R. 1987 (Aston Villa) — 11
Downing, S. 2004 (Middlesbrough) — 8
Dozzell, J. 1987 (Ipswich T) — 9
Draper, M. A. 1991 (Notts Co) — 3
Driver, A. 2009 (Hearts) — 1
Duberry, M. W. 1997 (Chelsea) — 5
Dunn, D. J. I. 1999 (Blackburn R) — 20
Duxbury, M. 1981 (Manchester U) — 7
Dyer, B. A. 1994 (Crystal Palace) — 10
Dyer, K. C. 1998 (Ipswich T, Newcastle U) — 11
Dyson, P. I. 1981 (Coventry C) — 4

Eadie, D. M. 1994 (Norwich C) — 7
Ebanks-Blake, S. 2009 (Wolverhampton W) — 1
Ebbrell, J. 1989 (Everton) — 14
Edghill, R. A. 1994 (Manchester C) — 3
Ehiogu, U. 1992 (Aston Villa) — 15
Elliott, P. 1985 (Luton T) — 3
Elliott, R. J. 1996 (Newcastle U) — 2
Elliott, S. W. 1998 (Derby Co) — 3
Etherington, N. 2002 (Tottenham H) — 3
Euell, J. J. 1998 (Wimbledon) — 6
Evans, R. 2003 (Chelsea) — 2

Fairclough, C. 1985 (Nottingham F, Tottenham H) — 7
Fairclough, D. 1977 (Liverpool) — 1
Fashanu, J. 1980 (Norwich C, Nottingham F) — 11
Fear, P. 1994 (Wimbledon) — 3
Fenton, G. A. 1995 (Aston Villa) — 1
Fenwick, T. W. 1981 (Crystal Palace, QPR) — 11
Ferdinand, A. J. 2005 (West Ham U) — 17
Ferdinand, R. G. 1997 (West Ham U) — 5
Fereday, W. 1985 (QPR) — 5
Fielding, F. D. 2009 (Blackburn R) — 12
Flanagan, J. 2012 (Liverpool) — 3
Flitcroft, G. W. 1993 (Manchester C) — 10
Flowers, T. D. 1987 (Southampton) — 3
Ford, M. 1996 (Leeds U) — 2
Forster, N. M. 1995 (Brentford) — 4
Forsyth, M. 1988 (Derby Co) — 1
Forster-Caskey, J. D. 2014 (Brighton & HA) — **10**
Foster, S. 1980 (Brighton & HA) — 1
Fowler, R. B. 1994 (Liverpool) — 8
Fox, D. J. 2008 (Coventry C) — 1

Froggatt, S. J. 1993 (Aston Villa) — 2
Futcher, P. 1977 (Luton T, Manchester C) — 11

Gabbiadini, M. 1989 (Sunderland) — 2
Gale, A. 1982 (Fulham) — 1
Gallen, K. A. 1995 (QPR) — 4
Garbutt, L. S. 2014 (Everton) — **11**
Gardner, A. 2002 (Tottenham H) — 1
Gardner, C. 2008 (Aston Villa) — 14
Gardner, G. 2012 (Aston Villa) — 5
Gascoigne, P. J. 1987 (Newcastle U) — 13
Gayle, H. 1984 (Birmingham C) — 3
Gernon, T. 1983 (Ipswich T) — 1
Gerrard, P. W. 1993 (Oldham Ath) — 18
Gerrard, S. G. 2000 (Liverpool) — 4
Gibbs, K. J. R. 2009 (Arsenal) — 15
Gibbs, N. 1987 (Watford) — 5
Gibson, B. J. 2014 (Middlesbrough) — **10**
Gibson, C. 1982 (Aston Villa) — 1
Gilbert, W. A. 1979 (Crystal Palace) — 11
Goddard, P. 1981 (West Ham U) — 8
Gordon, D. 1987 (Norwich C) — 4
Gordon, D. D. 1994 (Crystal Palace) — 13
Gosling, D. 2010 (Everton, Newcastle U) — 3
Grant, A. J. 1996 (Everton) — 1
Grant, L. A. 2003 (Derby Co) — 4
Granville, D. P. 1997 (Chelsea) — 3
Gray, A. 1988 (Aston Villa) — 2
Greening, J. 1999 (Manchester U, Middlesbrough) — 18
Griffin, A. 1999 (Newcastle U) — 3
Guppy, S. A. 1998 (Leicester C) — 1

Haigh, P. 1977 (Hull C) — 1
Hall, M. T. J. 1997 (Coventry C) — 8
Hall, R. A. 1992 (Southampton) — 11
Hamilton, D. V. 1997 (Newcastle U) — 1
Hammill, A. 2010 (Wolverhampton W) — 1
Harding, D. A. 2005 (Brighton & HA) — 4
Hardyman, P. 1985 (Portsmouth) — 2
Hargreaves, O. 2001 (Bayern Munich) — 3
Harley, J. 2000 (Chelsea) — 3
Hart, C. 2007 (Manchester C) — 21
Hateley, M. 1982 (Coventry C, Portsmouth) — 10
Hayes, M. 1987 (Arsenal) — 3
Hazell, R. J. 1979 (Wolverhampton W) — 1
Heaney, N. A. 1992 (Arsenal) — 6
Heath, A. 1981 (Stoke C, Everton) — 8
Heaton, T. D. 2008 (Manchester U) — 3
Henderson, J. B. 2011 (Sunderland, Liverpool) — 27
Hendon, I. M. 1992 (Tottenham H) — 7
Hendrie, L. A. 1996 (Aston Villa) — 13
Hesford, I. 1981 (Blackpool) — 7
Heskey, E. W. I. 1997 (Leicester C, Liverpool) — 16
Hilaire, V. 1980 (Crystal Palace) — 9
Hill, D. R. L. 1995 (Tottenham H) — 4
Hillier, D. 1991 (Arsenal) — 1
Hinchcliffe, A. 1989 (Manchester C) — 1
Hines, Z. 2010 (West Ham U) — 2
Hinshelwood, P. A. 1978 (Crystal Palace) — 2
Hirst, D. E. 1988 (Sheffield W) — 7
Hislop, N. S. 1998 (Newcastle U) — 1
Hoddle, G. 1977 (Tottenham H) — 12
Hodge, S. B. 1983 (Nottingham F, Aston Villa) — 8
Hodgson, D. J. 1981 (Middlesbrough) — 6
Holdsworth, D. 1989 (Watford) — 1
Holland, C. J. 1995 (Newcastle U) — 10
Holland, P. 1995 (Mansfield T) — 4
Holloway, D. 1998 (Sunderland) — 1
Horne, B. 1989 (Millwall) — 5
Howe, E. J. F. 1998 (Bournemouth) — 2
Howson, J. M. 2011 (Leeds U) — 1
Hoyte, J. R. 2004 (Arsenal) — 18
Hucker, P. 1984 (QPR) — 2
Huckerby, D. 1997 (Coventry C) — 4
Huddlestone, T. A. 2005 (Derby Co, Tottenham H) — 33
Hughes, S. J. 1997 (Arsenal) — 8
Hughes, W. J. 2012 (Derby Co) — **17**
Humphreys, R. J. 1997 (Sheffield W) — 3
Hunt, N. B. 2004 (Bolton W) — 10

Impey, A. R. 1993 (QPR) — 1
Ince, P. E. C. 1989 (West Ham U) — 2
Ince, T. C. 2012 (Blackpool, Hull C) — **18**
Ings, D. W. J. 2013 (Burnley) — **13**

Jackson, M. A. 1992 (Everton) 10
Jagielka, P. N. 2003 (Sheffield U) 6
James, D. B. 1991 (Watford) 10
James, J. C. 1990 (Luton T) 2
Jansen, M. B. 1999 (Crystal Palace, Blackburn R) 4
Jeffers, F. 2000 (Everton, Arsenal) 16
Jemson, N. B. 1991 (Nottingham F) 1
Jenas, J. A. 2002 (Newcastle U) 9
Jenkinson, C. D. 2013 (Arsenal) **14**
Jerome, C. 2006 (Cardiff C, Birmingham C) 10
Joachim, J. K. 1994 (Leicester C) 9
Johnson, A. 2008 (Middlesbrough) 19
Johnson, G. M. C. 2003 (West Ham U, Chelsea) 14
Johnson, M. 2008 (Manchester C) 2
Johnson, S. A. M. 1999 (Crewe Alex, Derby Co,
  Leeds U) 15
Johnson, T. 1991 (Notts Co, Derby Co) 7
Johnston, C. P. 1981 (Middlesbrough) 2
Jones, D. R. 1977 (Everton) 1
Jones, C. H. 1978 (Tottenham H) 1
Jones, D. F. L. 2004 (Manchester U) 1
Jones, P. A. 2011 (Blackburn R) 9
Jones, R. 1993 (Liverpool) 2

Kane, H. E. 2013 (Tottenham H) **14**
Keane, M. V. 2013 (Manchester U, Burnley) **16**
Keane, W. D. 2012 (Manchester U) 3
Keegan, G. A. 1977 (Manchester C) 1
Kelly, M. R. 2011 (Liverpool) 8
Kenny, W. 1993 (Everton) 1
Keown, M. R. 1987 (Aston Villa) 8
Kerslake, D. 1986 (QPR) 1
Kightly, M. J. 2008 (Wolverhampton W) 7
Kilcline, B. 1983 (Notts C) 2
Kilgallon, M. 2004 (Leeds U) 5
King, A. E. 1977 (Everton) 2
King, L. B. 2000 (Tottenham H) 12
Kirkland, C. E. 2001 (Coventry C, Liverpool) 8
Kitson, P. 1991 (Leicester C, Derby Co) 7
Knight, A. 1983 (Portsmouth) 2
Knight, I. 1987 (Sheffield W) 2
Knight, Z. 2002 (Fulham) 4
Konchesky, P. M. 2002 (Charlton Ath) 15
Kozluk, R. 1998 (Derby Co) 2

Lake, P. 1989 (Manchester C) 5
Lallana, A. D. 2009 (Southampton) 1
Lampard, F. J. 1998 (West Ham U) 19
Langley, T. W. 1978 (Chelsea) 1
Lansbury, H. G. 2010 (Arsenal, Nottingham F) 16
Lascelles, J. 2014 (Newcastle U) **2**
Leadbitter, G. 2008 (Sunderland) 3
Lee, D. J. 1990 (Chelsea) 10
Lee, R. M. 1986 (Charlton Ath) 2
Lee, S. 1981 (Liverpool) 6
Lees, T. J. 2012 (Leeds U) 6
Lennon, A. J. 2006 (Tottenham H) 5
Le Saux, G. P. 1990 (Chelsea) 4
Lescott, J. P. 2003 (Wolverhampton W) 2
Lewis, J. P. 2008 (Peterborough U) 5
Lingard, J. E. 2013 (Manchester U) **11**
Lita, L. H. 2005 (Bristol C, Reading) 9
Loach, S. J. 2009 (Watford) 14
Loftus-Cheek, R. I. 2015 (Chelsea) **3**
Lowe, D. 1988 (Ipswich T) 2
Lowe, J. J. 2012 (Blackburn R) 11
Lukic, J. 1981 (Leeds U) 7
Lund, G. 1985 (Grimsby T) 3

McCall, S. H. 1981 (Ipswich T) 6
McCarthy, A. S. 2011 (Reading) 3
McDonald, N. 1987 (Newcastle U) 5
McEachran, J. M. 2011 (Chelsea) 13
McEveley, J. 2003 (Blackburn R) 1
McGrath, L. 1986 (Coventry C) 1
MacKenzie, S. 1982 (WBA) 3
McLeary, A. 1988 (Millwall) 1
McLeod, I. M. 2006 (Milton Keynes D) 1
McMahon, S. 1981 (Everton, Aston Villa) 6
McManaman, S. 1991 (Liverpool) 7
Mabbutt, G. 1982 (Bristol R, Tottenham H) 7
Maguire, J. H. 2012 (Sheffield U) 1
Makin, C. 1994 (Oldham Ath) 5
Mancienne, M. I. 2008 (Chelsea) 30
Marney, D. E. 2005 (Tottenham H) 1
Marriott, A. 1992 (Nottingham F) 1

Marsh, S. T. 1998 (Oxford U) 1
Marshall, A. J. 1995 (Norwich C) 4
Marshall, B. 2012 (Leicester C) 2
Marshall, L. K. 1999 (Norwich C) 1
Martin, L. 1989 (Manchester U) 2
Martyn, A. N. 1988 (Bristol R) 11
Matteo, D. 1994 (Liverpool) 4
Mattock, J. W. 2008 (Leicester C) 5
Matthew, D. 1990 (Chelsea) 9
May, A. 1986 (Manchester C) 1
Mee, B. 2011 (Manchester C) 2
Merson, P. C. 1989 (Arsenal) 4
Middleton, J. 1977 (Nottingham F, Derby Co) 3
Miller, A. 1988 (Arsenal) 4
Mills, D. J. 1999 (Charlton Ath, Leeds U) 14
Mills, G. R. 1981 (Nottingham F) 2
Milner, J. P. 2004 (Leeds U, Newcastle U, Aston Villa) 46
Mimms, R. 1985 (Rotherham U, Everton) 3
Minto, S. C. 1991 (Charlton Ath) 6
Moore, I. 1996 (Tranmere R, Nottingham F) 7
Moore, L. 2012 (Leicester C) **10**
Moore, L. I. 2006 (Aston Villa) 5
Moran, S. 1982 (Southampton) 2
Morgan, S. 1987 (Leicester C) 2
Morris, J. 1997 (Chelsea) 7
Morrison, R. R. 2013 (West Ham U) 4
Mortimer, P. 1989 (Charlton Ath) 2
Moses, A. P. 1997 (Barnsley) 2
Moses, R. M. 1981 (WBA, Manchester U) 8
Moses, V. 2011 (Wigan Ath) 1
Mountfield, D. 1984 (Everton) 1
Muamba, F. N. 2008 (Birmingham C, Bolton W) 33
Muggleton, C. D. 1990 (Leicester C) 1
Mullins, H. I. 1999 (Crystal Palace) 3
Murphy, D. B. 1998 (Liverpool) 4
Murray, P. 1997 (QPR) 1
Murray, M. W. 2003 (Wolverhampton W) 5
Mutch, A. 1989 (Wolverhampton W) 1
Mutch, J. J. E. S. 2011 (Birmingham C) 1
Myers. A. 1995 (Chelsea) 4

Naughton, K. 2009 (Sheffield U, Tottenham H) 9
Naylor, L. M. 2000 (Wolverhampton W) 3
Nethercott, S. H. 1994 (Tottenham H) 8
Neville, P. J. 1995 (Manchester U) 7
Newell, M. 1986 (Luton T) 4
Newton, A. L. 2001 (West Ham U) 1
Newton, E. J. I. 1993 (Chelsea) 2
Newton, S. O. 1997 (Charlton Ath) 3
Nicholls, A. 1994 (Plymouth Arg) 1
Noble, M. J. 2007 (West Ham U) 20
Nolan, K. A. J. 2003 (Bolton W) 1
Nugent, D. J. 2006 (Preston NE) 14

Oakes, M. C. 1994 (Aston Villa) 6
Oakes, S. J. 1993 (Luton T) 1
Oakley, M. 1997 (Southampton) 4
O'Brien, A. J. 1999 (Bradford C) 1
O'Connor, J. 1996 (Everton) 3
O'Hara, J. D. 2008 (Tottenham H) 7
Oldfield, D. 1989 (Luton T) 1
Olney, I. A. 1990 (Aston Villa) 10
O'Neil, G. P. 2005 (Portsmouth) 9
Onuoha, C. 2006 (Manchester C) 21
Ord, R. J. 1991 (Sunderland) 3
Osman, R. C. 1979 (Ipswich T) 7
Owen, G. A. 1977 (Manchester C, WBA) 22
Owen, M. J. 1998 (Liverpool) 1
Oxlade-Chamberlain, A. M. D. 2011 (Southampton,
  Arsenal) 8

Painter, I. 1986 (Stoke C) 1
Palmer, C. L. 1989 (Sheffield W) 4
Parker, G. 1986 (Hull C, Nottingham F) 6
Parker, P. A. 1985 (Fulham) 8
Parker, S. M. 2001 (Charlton Ath) 12
Parkes, P. B. F. 1979 (QPR) 1
Parkin, S. 1987 (Stoke C) 5
Parlour, R. 1992 (Arsenal) 12
Parnaby, S. 2003 (Middlesbrough) 4
Peach, D. S. 1977 (Southampton) 6
Peake, A. 1982 (Leicester C) 1
Pearce, I. A. 1995 (Blackburn R) 3
Pearce, S. 1987 (Nottingham F) 1
Pennant, J. 2001 (Arsenal) 24
Pickering N. 1983 (Sunderland, Coventry C) 15

Platt, D. 1988 (Aston Villa) 3
Plummer, C. S. 1996 (QPR) 5
Pollock, J. 1995 (Middlesbrough) 3
Porter, G. 1987 (Watford) 12
Potter, G. S. 1997 (Southampton) 1
Powell, N. E. 2012 (Manchester U) 2
Pressman, K. 1989 (Sheffield W) 1
Pritchard, A. D. 2014 (Tottenham H) 9
Proctor, M. 1981 (Middlesbrough, Nottingham F) 4
Prutton, D. T. 2001 (Nottingham F, Southampton) 25
Purse, D. J. 1998 (Birmingham C) 2

Quashie, N. F. 1997 (QPR) 4
Quinn, W. R. 1998 (Sheffield U) 2

Ramage, C. D. 1991 (Derby Co) 3
Ranson, R. 1980 (Manchester C) 10
Redknapp, J. F. 1993 (Liverpool) 19
Redmond, N. D. J. 2013 (Birmingham C, Norwich C) 22
Redmond, S. 1988 (Manchester C) 14
Reeves, K. P. 1978 (Norwich C, Manchester C) 10
Regis, C. 1979 (WBA) 6
Reid, N. S. 1981 (Manchester C) 6
Reid, P. 1977 (Bolton W) 6
Reo-Coker, N. S. A. 2004 (Wimbledon, West Ham U) 23
Richards, D. I. 1995 (Wolverhampton W) 4
Richards, J. P. 1977 (Wolverhampton W) 2
Richards, M. 2007 (Manchester C) 15
Richards, M. L. 2005 (Ipswich T) 1
Richardson, K. E. 2005 (Manchester U) 12
Rideout, P. 1985 (Aston Villa, Bari) 5
Ridgewell, L. M. 2004 (Aston Villa) 8
Riggott, C. M. 2001 (Derby Co) 8
Ripley, S. E. 1988 (Middlesbrough) 8
Ritchie, A. 1982 (Brighton & HA) 1
Rix, G. 1978 (Arsenal) 7
Roberts, A. J. 1995 (Millwall, Crystal Palace) 5
Roberts, B. J. 1997 (Middlesbrough) 1
Robins, M. G. 1990 (Manchester U) 6
Robinson, J. 2012 (Liverpool, QPR) 10
Robinson, P. P. 1999 (Watford) 3
Robinson, P. W. 2000 (Leeds U) 11
Robson, B. 1979 (WBA) 7
Robson, S. 1984 (Arsenal, West Ham U) 8
Rocastle, D. 1987 (Arsenal) 14
Roche, L. P. 2001 (Manchester U) 1
Rodger, G. 1987 (Coventry C) 4
Rodriguez, J. E. 2011 (Burnley) 1
Rodwell, J. 2009 (Everton) 21
Rogers, A. 1998 (Nottingham F) 3
Rosario, R. 1987 (Norwich C) 4
Rose, D. L. 2009 (Tottenham H) 29
Rose, M. 1997 (Arsenal) 2
Rosenior, L. J. 2005 (Fulham) 7
Routledge, W. 2005 (Crystal Palace, Tottenham H) 12
Rowell, G. 1977 (Sunderland) 1
Rudd, D. T. 2013 (Norwich C) 1
Ruddock, N. 1989 (Southampton) 4
Rufus, R. R. 1996 (Charlton Ath) 6
Ryan, J. 1983 (Oldham Ath) 1
Ryder, S. H. 1995 (Walsall) 3

Samuel, J. 2002 (Aston Villa) 7
Samways, V. 1988 (Tottenham H) 5
Sansom, K. G. 1979 (Crystal Palace) 8
Scimeca, R. 1996 (Aston Villa) 9
Scowcroft, J. B. 1997 (Ipswich T) 5
Seaman, D. A. 1985 (Birmingham C) 10
Sears, F. D. 2010 (West Ham U) 3
Sedgley, S. 1987 (Coventry C, Tottenham H) 11
Sellars, S. 1988 (Blackburn R) 3
Selley, I. 1994 (Arsenal) 3
Serrant, C. 1998 (Oldham Ath) 2
Sharpe, L. S. 1989 (Manchester U) 8
Shaw, L. P. H. 2013 (Southampton, Manchester U) 5
Shaw, G. R. 1981 (Aston Villa) 7
Shawcross, R. J. 2008 (Stoke C) 2
Shearer, A. 1991 (Southampton) 11
Shelton, G. 1985 (Sheffield W) 1
Shelvey, J. 2012 (Liverpool, Swansea C) 13
Sheringham, E. P. 1988 (Millwall) 1
Sheron, M. N. 1992 (Manchester C) 16
Sherwood, T. A. 1990 (Norwich C) 4
Shipperley, N. J. 1994 (Chelsea, Southampton) 7
Sidwell, S. J. 2003 (Reading) 5
Simonsen, S. P. A. 1998 (Tranmere R, Everton) 4

Simpson, P. 1986 (Manchester C) 5
Sims, S. 1977 (Leicester C) 10
Sinclair, S. A. 2011 (Swansea C) 7
Sinclair, T. 1994 (QPR, West Ham U) 5
Sinnott, L. 1985 (Watford) 1
Slade, S. A. 1996 (Tottenham H) 4
Slater, S. I. 1990 (West Ham U) 3
Small, B. 1993 (Aston Villa) 12
Smalling, C. L. 2010 (Fulham, Manchester U) 14
Smith, A. 2000 (Leeds U) 10
Smith, A. J. 2012 (Tottenham H) 11
Smith, D. 1988 (Coventry C) 10
Smith, M. 1981 (Sheffield W) 5
Smith, M. 1995 (Sunderland) 1
Smith, T. W. 2001 (Watford) 1
Snodin, I. 1985 (Doncaster R) 4
Soares, T. J. 2006 (Crystal Palace) 4
Sordell, M. A. 2012 (Watford, Bolton W) 14
Spence, J. 2011 (West Ham U) 1
Stanislaus, F. J. 2010 (West Ham U) 2
Statham, B. 1988 (Tottenham H) 3
Statham, D. J. 1978 (WBA) 6
Stead, J. G. 2004 (Blackburn R, Sunderland) 11
Stearman, R. J. 2009 (Wolverhampton W) 4
Steele, J. 2011 (Middlesbrough) 7
Stein, B. 1984 (Luton T) 3
Sterland, M. 1984 (Sheffield W) 7
Sterling, R. S. 2012 (Liverpool) 8
Steven, T. M. 1985 (Everton) 2
Stevens, G. A. 1983 (Brighton & HA, Tottenham H) 8
Stewart, J. 2003 (Leicester C) 1
Stewart, P. 1988 (Manchester C) 1
Stockdale, R. K. 2001 (Middlesbrough) 1
Stones, J. 2013 (Everton) 12
Stuart, G. C. 1990 (Chelsea) 5
Stuart, J. C. 1996 (Charlton Ath) 4
Sturridge, D. A. 2010 (Chelsea) 15
Suckling, P. 1986 (Coventry C, Manchester C, Crystal Palace) 10
Summerbee, N. J. 1993 (Swindon T) 3
Sunderland, A. 1977 (Wolverhampton W) 1
Surman, A. R. E. 2008 (Southampton) 4
Sutch, D. 1992 (Norwich C) 4
Sutton, C. R. 1993 (Norwich C) 13
Swindlehurst, D. 1977 (Crystal Palace) 1

Talbot, B. 1977 (Ipswich T) 1
Targett, M. R. 2015 (Southampton) 1
Taylor, A. D. 2007 (Middlesbrough) 13
Taylor, M. 2001 (Blackburn R) 1
Taylor, M. S. 2003 (Portsmouth) 3
Taylor, R. A. 2006 (Wigan Ath) 4
Taylor, S. J. 2002 (Arsenal) 3
Taylor, S. V. 2004 (Newcastle U) 29
Terry, J. G. 2001 (Chelsea) 9
Thatcher, B. D. 1996 (Millwall, Wimbledon) 4
Thelwell, A. A. 2001 (Tottenham H) 1
Thirlwell, P. 2001 (Sunderland) 1
Thomas, D. 1981 (Coventry C, Tottenham H) 7
Thomas, J. W. 2006 (Charlton Ath) 2
Thomas, M. 1986 (Luton T) 3
Thomas, M. L. 1988 (Arsenal) 12
Thomas, R. E. 1990 (Watford) 1
Thompson, A. 1995 (Bolton W) 2
Thompson, D. A. 1997 (Liverpool) 7
Thompson, G. L. 1981 (Coventry C) 6
Thorn, A. 1988 (Wimbledon) 5
Thornley, B. L. 1996 (Manchester U) 3
Thorpe, T. J. 2013 (Manchester U) 1
Tiler, C. 1990 (Barnsley, Nottingham F) 13
Tomkins, J. O. C. 2009 (West Ham U) 10
Tonge, M. W. E. 2004 (Sheffield U) 1
Townsend, A. D. 2012 (Tottenham H) 3
Trippier, K. J. 2011 (Manchester C) 2

Unsworth, D. G. 1995 (Everton) 6
Upson, M. J. 1999 (Arsenal) 11

Vassell, D. 1999 (Aston Villa) 11
Vaughan, J. O. 2007 (Everton) 4
Venison, B. 1983 (Sunderland) 10
Vernazza, P. A. P. 2001 (Arsenal, Watford) 2
Vinnicombe, C. 1991 (Rangers) 12

Waddle, C. R. 1985 (Newcastle U) 1
Waghorn, M. T. 2012 (Leicester C) 5

Walcott, T. J. 2007 (Arsenal) — 21
Wallace, D. L. 1983 (Southampton) — 14
Wallace, Ray 1989 (Southampton) — 4
Wallace, Rod 1989 (Southampton) — 11
Walker, D. 1985 (Nottingham F) — 7
Walker, I. M. 1991 (Tottenham H) — 9
Walker, K. 2010 (Tottenham H) — 7
Walsh, G. 1988 (Manchester U) — 2
Walsh, P. A. 1983 (Luton T) — 4
Walters, K. 1984 (Aston Villa) — 9
Ward, P. 1978 (Brighton & HA) — 2
Ward-Prowse, J. M. E. 2013 (Southampton) — **13**
Warhurst, P. 1991 (Oldham Ath, Sheffield W) — 8
Watson, B. 2007 (Crystal Palace) — 1
Watson, D. 1984 (Norwich C) — 7
Watson, D. N. 1994 (Barnsley) — 1
Watson, G. 1991 (Sheffield W) — 2
Watson, S. C. 1993 (Newcastle U) — 12
Weaver, N. J. 2000 (Manchester C) — 10
Webb, N. J. 1985 (Portsmouth, Nottingham F) — 3
Welbeck, D. 2009 (Manchester U) — 14
Welsh, J. J. 2004 (Liverpool, Hull C) — 8
Wheater, D. J. 2008 (Middlesbrough) — 11
Whelan, P. J. 1993 (Ipswich T) — 3
Whelan, N. 1995 (Leeds U) — 2
Whittingham, P. 2004 (Aston Villa, Cardiff C) — 17
White, D. 1988 (Manchester C) — 6
Whyte, C. 1982 (Arsenal) — 4
Wickham, C. N. R. 2011 (Ipswich T, Sunderland) — 17
Wicks, S. 1982 (QPR) — 1

Wilkins, R. C. 1977 (Chelsea) — 1
Wilkinson, P. 1985 (Grimsby T, Everton) — 4
Williams, D. 1998 (Sunderland) — 2
Williams, P. 1989 (Charlton Ath) — 4
Williams, P. D. 1991 (Derby Co) — 6
Williams, S. C. 1977 (Southampton) — 14
Wilshere, J. A. 2010 (Arsenal) — 7
Wilson, C. E. G. 2014 (Bournemouth) — **1**
Wilson, M. A. 2001 (Manchester U, Middlesbrough) — 6
Winterburn, N. 1986 (Wimbledon) — 1
Wisdom, A. 2012 (Liverpool) — 10
Wise, D. F. 1988 (Wimbledon) — 1
Woodcook, A. S. 1978 (Nottingham F) — 2
Woodgate, J. S. 2000 (Leeds U) — 1
Woodhouse, C. 1999 (Sheffield U) — 4
Woodrow, C. 2014 (Fulham) — **1**
Woods, C. C. E. 1979 (Nottingham F, QPR, Norwich C) — 6
Wright, A. G. 1993 (Blackburn R) — 2
Wright, M. 1983 (Southampton) — 4
Wright, R. I. 1997 (Ipswich T) — 15
Wright, S. J. 2001 (Liverpool) — 10
Wright, W. 1979 (Everton) — 6
Wright-Phillips, S. C. 2002 (Manchester C) — 6

Yates, D. 1989 (Notts Co) — 5
Young, A. 2007 (Watford, Aston Villa) — 10
Young, L. P. 1999 (Tottenham H, Charlton Ath) — 12

Zaha, D. W. A. 2012 (Crystal Palace, Manchester U) — 13
Zamora, R. L. 2002 (Brighton & HA) — 6

NORTHERN IRELAND

Allen, C. 2009 (Lisburn Distillery) — 1
Armstrong, D. T. 2007 (Hearts) — 1

Bagnall, L. 2011 (Sunderland) — 1
Bailie, N. 1990 (Linfield) — 2
Baird, C. P. 2002 (Southampton) — 6
Ball, D. 2013 (Tottenham H) — 2
Ball, M. 2011 (Norwich C) — 5
Beatty, S. 1990 (Chelsea, Linfield) — 2
Black, J. 2003 (Tottenham H) — 1
Black, K. T. 1990 (Luton T) — 1
Black, R. Z. 2002 (Morecambe) — 1
Blackledge, G. 1978 (Portadown) — 1
Blake, R. G. 2011 (Brentford) — 2
Blayney, A. 2003 (Southampton) — 4
Boyce, L. 2010 (Cliftonville, Werder Bremen) — 8
Boyle, W. S. 1998 (Leeds U) — 7
Braniff, K. R. 2002 (Millwall) — 11
Breeze, J. 2011 (Wigan Ath) — 4
Brennan, C. 2013 (Kilmarnock) — 7
Brobbel, R. 2013 (Middlesbrough) — **9**
Brotherston, N. 1978 (Blackburn R) — 1
Browne, G. 2003 (Manchester C) — 5
Brunt, C. 2005 (Sheffield W) — 2
Bryan, M. A. 2010 (Watford) — 4
Buchanan, D. T. H. 2006 (Bury) — 15
Buchanan, W. B. 2002 (Bolton W, Lisburn Distillery) — 5
Burns, A. 2014 (Linfield) — **1**
Burns, L. 1998 (Port Vale) — 13

Callaghan, A. 2006 (Limavady U, Ballymena U, Derry C) — 15
Campbell, S. 2003 (Ballymena U) — 1
Capaldi, A. C. 2002 (Birmingham C, Plymouth Arg) — 14
Carlisle, W. T. 2000 (Crystal Palace) — 9
Carroll, R. E. 1998 (Wigan Ath) — 11
Carson, J. G. 2011 (Ipswich T, York C) — 12
Carson, S. 2000 (Rangers, Dundee U) — 2
Carson, T. 2007 (Sunderland) — 15
Carvill, M. D. 2008 (Wrexham, Linfield) — 8
Casement, C. 2007 (Ipswich T, Dundee) — 18
Cathcart, C. 2007 (Manchester U) — 15
Catney, R. 2007 (Lisburn Distillery) — 1
Chapman, A. 2008 (Sheffield U, Oxford U) — 7
Clarke, L. 2003 (Peterborough U) — 1
Clarke, R. 2006 (Newry C) — 7
Clarke, R. D. J. 1999 (Portadown) — 5
Clingan, S. G. 2003 (Wolverhampton W, Nottingham F) — 11
Close, B. 2002 (Middlesbrough) — 10
Clucas, M. S. 2011 (Preston NE, Bristol R) — 11
Clyde, M. G. 2002 (Wolverhampton W) — 5
Colligan, L. 2009 (Ballymena U) — 1

Conlan, L. 2013 (Burnley) — **4**
Connell, T. E. 1978 (Coleraine) — 1
Coote, A. 1998 (Norwich C) — 12
Convery, J. 2000 (Celtic) — 4

Dallas, S. 2012 (Crusaders, Brentford) — 2
Davey, H. 2004 (UCD) — 3
Davis, S. 2004 (Aston Villa) — 3
Devine, D. 1994 (Omagh T) — 1
Devine, D. G. 2011 (Preston NE) — 2
Devine, J. 1990 (Glentoran) — 1
Devlin, C. 2011 (Manchester U, unattached, Cliftonville) — 11
Dickson, H. 2002 (Wigan Ath) — 1
Doherty, J. E. 2014 (Watford) — **1**
Doherty, M. 2007 (Hearts) — 2
Dolan, J. 2000 (Millwall) — 6
Donaghy, M. M. 1978 (Larne) — 1
Donnelly, L. 2012 (Fulham) — 6
Donnelly, M. 2007 (Sheffield U, Crusaders) — 5
Donnelly, R. 2013 (Swansea C) — 1
Dowie, I. 1990 (Luton T) — 1
Drummond, W. 2011 (Rangers) — 2
Dudgeon, J. P. 2010 (Manchester U) — 4
Duff, S. 2003 (Cheltenham T) — 1
Duffy, M. 2014 (Derry C) — **1**
Duffy, S. P. M. 2010 (Everton) — 3
Dummigan, C. 2014 (Burnley) — **1**

Elliott, S. 1999 (Glentoran) — 3
Ervin, J. 2005 (Linfield) — 2
Evans, C. J. 2009 (Manchester U) — 10
Evans, J. 2006 (Manchester U) — 3

Feeney, L. 1998 (Linfield, Rangers) — 8
Feeney, W. 2002 (Bournemouth) — 8
Ferguson, M. 2000 (Glentoran) — 2
Ferguson, S. 2009 (Newcastle U) — 11
Fitzgerald, D. 1998 (Rangers) — 4
Flanagan, T. M. 2012 (Milton Keynes D) — 1
Flynn, J. J. 2009 (Blackburn R, Ross Co) — 11
Fordyce, D. T. 2007 (Portsmouth, Glentoran) — 12
Friars, E. C. 2005 (Notts Co) — 7
Friars, S. M. 1998 (Liverpool, Ipswich T) — 21

Garrett, R. 2007 (Stoke C, Linfield) — 14
Gault, M. 2005 (Linfield) — 2
Gibb, S. 2009 (Falkirk, Drogheda U) — 2
Gilfillan, B. J. 2005 (Gretna, Peterhead) — 9
Gillespie, K. R. 1994 (Manchester U) — 1
Glendinning, M. 1994 (Bangor) — 1
Glendinning, R. 2012 (Linfield) — 3

Gorman, R. J. 2012 (Wolverhampton W, Leyton Orient) 4
Graham, G. L. 1999 (Crystal Palace) 5
Graham, R. S. 1999 (QPR) 15
Gray, J. P. 2012 (Accrington S) 11
Gray, P. 1990 (Luton T) 1
Griffin, D. J. 1998 (St Johnstone) 10
Grigg, W. D. 2011 (Walsall) 10

Hamilton, G. 2000 (Blackburn R, Portadown) 12
Hamilton, W. R. 1978 (Linfield) 1
Hanley, N. 2011 (Linfield) 1
Harkin, M. P. 2000 (Wycombe W) 9
Harney, J. J. 2014 (West Ham U) 1
Harvey, J. 1978 (Arsenal) 1
Hawe, S. 2001 (Blackburn R) 2
Hayes, T. 1978 (Luton T) 1
Hazley, M. 2007 (Stoke C) 3
Healy, D. J. 1999 (Manchester U) 8
Hegarty, C. 2011 (Rangers) 7
Herron, C. J. 2003 (QPR) 2
Higgins, R. 2006 (Derry C) 1
Hodson, L. J. S. 2010 (Watford) 10
Holmes, S. 2000 (Manchester C, Wrexham) 13
Howland, D. 2007 (Birmingham C) 4
Hughes, J. 2006 (Lincoln C) 7
Hughes, M. A. 2003 (Tottenham H, Oldham Ath) 12
Hughes, M. E. 1990 (Manchester C) 1
Hunter, M. 2002 (Glentoran) 1

Ingham, M. G. 2001 (Sunderland) 4

Jarvis, D. 2010 (Aberdeen) 2
Johns, C. 2014 (Southampton) 1
Johnson, D. M. 1998 (Blackburn R) 11
Johnston, B. 1978 (Cliftonville) 1
Julian, A. A. 2005 (Brentford) 1

Kane, A. M. 2008 (Blackburn R) 5
Kane, M. 2012 (Glentoran) 1
Kee, B. R. 2010 (Leicester C, Torquay U, Burton Alb) 10
Kee, P. V. 1990 (Oxford U) 1
Kelly, D. 2000 (Derry C) 11
Kelly, N. 1990 (Oldham Ath) 1
Kirk, A. R. 1999 (Hearts) 9
Knowles, J. 2012 (Blackburn R) 2

Lafferty, D. 2009 (Celtic) 6
Lafferty, K. 2006 (Burnley) 2
Lavery, C. 2011 (Ipswich T, Sheffield W) 7
Lawrie, J. 2009 (Port Vale, AFC Telford U) 9
Lennon, N. F. 1990 (Manchester C, Crewe Alex) 2
Lester, C. 2013 (Bolton W) 1
Lindsay, K. 2006 (Larne) 1
Little, A. 2009 (Rangers) 6
Lowry, P. 2009 (Institute, Linfield) 6
Lund, M. 2011 (Stoke C) 4
Lyttle, G. 1998 (Celtic, Peterborough U) 8

Magee, J. 1994 (Bangor) 1
Magee, J. 2009 (Lisburn Distillery) 1
Magennis, J. B. D. 2010 (Cardiff C, Aberdeen) 16
Magilton, J. 1990 (Liverpool) 1
Magnay, C. 2010 (Chelsea) 1
Matthews, N. P. 1990 (Blackpool) 1
McAlinden, L. J. 2012 (Wolverhampton W) 3
McAllister, M. 2007 (Dungannon Swifts) 4
McArdle, R. A. 2006 (Sheffield W, Rochdale) 19
McAreavey, P. 2000 (Swindon T) 7
McBride, J. 1994 (Glentoran) 1
McCaffrey, D. 2006 (Hibernian) 8
McCallion, E. 1998 (Coleraine) 1
McCann, G. S. 2000 (West Ham U) 11
McCann, P. 2003 (Portadown) 1
McCann, R. 2002 (Rangers, Linfield) 2
McCartan, S. V. 2013 (Accrington S) 3
McCartney, G. 2001 (Sunderland) 5
McCashin, S. 2011 (Jerez Industrial, unattached) 2
McChrystal, M. 2005 (Derry C) 9
McClean, J. 2010 (Derry C) 3
McClure, M. 2012 (Wycombe W) 1
McCourt, P. J. 2002 (Rochdale, Derry C) 8
McCoy, R. K. 1990 (Coleraine) 1
McCreery, D. 1978 (Manchester U) 1
McCullough, L. 2013 (Doncaster R) 6
McEleney, S. 2012 (Derry C) 2
McElroy, P. 2013 (Hull C) 1

McEvilly, L. R. 2003 (Rochdale) 9
McFlynn, T. M. 2000 (QPR, Woking, Margate) 19
McGeehan, C. 2013 (Norwich C) 3
McGibbon, P. C. G. 1994 (Manchester U) 1
McGivern, R. 2010 (Manchester C) 6
McGlinchey, B. 1998 (Manchester C, Port Vale,
  Gillingham) 14
McGovern, M. 2005 (Celtic) 10
McGowan, M. V. 2006 (Clyde) 2
McGurk, A. 2010 (Aston Villa) 1
McIlroy, T. 1994 (Linfield) 1
McKay, W. 2009 (Leicester C, Northampton T) 7
McKenna, K. 2007 (Tottenham H) 6
McKeown, R. 2012 (Kilmarnock) 12
McKnight, P. 1998 (Rangers) 3
McLaughlin, C. G. 2010 (Preston NE, Fleetwood T) 7
McLaughlin, P. 2010 (Newcastle U, York C) 10
McLaughlin, R. 2012 (Liverpool) 1
McLean, B. S. 2006 (Rangers) 1
McLean, J. 2009 (Derry C) 4
McLellan, M. 2012 (Preston NE) 1
McMahon, G. J. 2002 (Tottenham H) 1
McMenamin, L. A. 2009 (Sheffield W) 4
McNair, P. J. C. 2014 (Manchester U) 2
McNally, P. 2013 (Celtic) 1
McQuilken, J. 2009 (Tescoma Zlin) 1
McQuoid, J. J. B. 2009 (Bournemouth) 8
McVeigh, A. 2002 (Ayr U) 1
McVeigh, P. M. 1998 (Tottenham H) 11
McVey, K. 2006 (Coleraine) 8
Meenan, D. 2007 (Finn Harps, Monaghan U) 3
Melaugh, G. M. 2002 (Aston Villa, Glentoran) 11
Millar, K. S. 2011 (Oldham Ath, Linfield) 11
Millar, W. P. 1990 (Port Vale) 1
Miskelly, D. T. 2000 (Oldham Ath) 10
Mitchell, A. 2012 (Rangers) 3
Moreland, V. 1978 (Glentoran) 1
Morgan, D. 2012 (Nottingham F) 4
Morgan, M. P. T. 1999 (Preston NE) 1
Morris, E. J. 2002 (WBA, Glentoran) 8
Morrison, O. 2001 (Sheffield W, Sheffield U) 7
Morrow, A. 2001 (Northampton T) 1
Morrow, S. 2005 (Hibernian) 4
Mulgrew, J. 2007 (Linfield) 10
Mulryne, P. P. 1999 (Manchester U, Norwich C) 5
Murray, W. 1978 (Linfield) 1
Murtagh, C. 2005 (Hearts) 1

Nicholl, J. M. 1978 (Manchester U) 1
Nixon, C. 2000 (Glentoran) 1
Nolan, L. J. 2014 (Crewe Alex) 1
Norwood, O. J. 2010 (Manchester U) 11

O'Connor, M. J. 2008 (Crewe Alex) 3
O'Hara, G. 1994 (Leeds U) 1
O'Kane, E. 2009 (Everton, Torquay U) 4
O'Neill, J. P. 1978 (Leicester C) 1
O'Neill, M. A. M. 1994 (Hibernian) 1
O'Neill, S. 2009 (Ballymena U) 4

Paterson, M. A. 2007 (Stoke C) 2
Paterson, D. J. 1994 (Crystal Palace) 1

Quinn, S. J. 1994 (Blackpool) 1

Ramsey, C. 2011 (Portadown) 3
Ramsey, K. 2006 (Institute) 1
Reid, J. T. 2013 (Exeter C) 1
Robinson, S. 1994 (Tottenham H) 1

Scullion, D. 2006 (Dungannon Swifts) 8
Sendles-White J. 2013 (QPR) 8
Sharpe, R. 2013 (Derby Co) 3
Shiels, D. 2005 (Hibernian) 6
Shields, S. P. 2013 (Dagenham & R) 2
Shroot, R. 2009 (Harrow B, Birmingham C) 4
Simms, G. 2001 (Hartlepool U) 14
Skates, G. 2000 (Blackburn R) 4
Sloan, T. 1978 (Ballymena U) 1
Smylie, D. 2006 (Newcastle U, Livingston) 1
Stewart, S. 2009 (Aberdeen) 1
Stewart, T. 2006 (Wolverhampton W, Linfield) 19

Taylor, J. 2007 (Hearts, Glentoran) 10
Taylor, M. S. 1998 (Fulham) 1
Teggart, N. 2005 (Sunderland) 2

Tempest, G. 2013 (Notts Co)	6
Thompson, A. L. 2011 (Watford)	11
Thompson, P. 2006 (Linfield)	4
Toner, C. 2000 (Tottenham H, Leyton Orient)	17
Tuffey, J. 2007 (Partick Thistle)	13
Turner, C. 2007 (Sligo R, Bohemians)	12
Ward, J. J. 2006 (Aston Villa, Chesterfield)	7
Ward, M. 2006 (Dungannon Swifts)	1
Ward, S. 2005 (Glentoran)	10

Waterman, D. G. 1998 (Portsmouth)	14
Waterworth, A. 2008 (Lisburn Distillery, Hamilton A)	7
Webb, S. M. 2004 (Ross Co, St Johnstone, Ross Co)	6
Weir, R. J. 2009 (Sunderland)	8
Wells, D. P. 1999 (Barry T)	1
Whitley, J. 1998 (Manchester C)	17
Willis, P. 2006 (Liverpool)	1
Winchester, C. 2011 (Oldham Ath)	**13**
Winchester, J. 2013 (Kilmarnock)	1

SCOTLAND

Adam, C. G. 2006 (Rangers)	5
Adam, G. 2011 (Rangers)	6
Adams, J. 2007 (Kilmarnock)	1
Aitken, R. 1977 (Celtic)	16
Albiston, A. 1977 (Manchester U)	5
Alexander, N. 1997 (Stenhousemuir, Livingston)	10
Allan, S. 2012 (WBA)	10
Anderson, I. 1997 (Dundee, Toulouse)	15
Anderson, R. 1997 (Aberdeen)	15
Andrews, M. 2011 (East Stirling)	1
Anthony, M. 1997 (Celtic)	3
Archdeacon, O. 1987 (Celtic)	1
Archer, J. G. 2012 (Tottenham H)	**14**
Archibald, A. 1998 (Partick Thistle)	5
Archibald, S. 1980 (Aberdeen, Tottenham H)	5
Arfield, S. 2008 (Falkirk, Huddersfield T)	17
Armstrong, S. 2011 (Dundee U)	20
Bagen, D. 1997 (Kilmarnock)	4
Bain, K. 1993 (Dundee)	4
Baker, M. 1993 (St Mirren)	10
Baltacha, S. S. 2000 (St Mirren)	3
Bannan, B. 2009 (Aston Villa)	10
Bannigan, S. 2013 (Partick Thistle)	3
Bannon, E. J. 1979 (Hearts, Chelsea, Dundee U)	7
Barclay, J. 2011 (Falkirk)	1
Beattie, C. 2004 (Celtic)	7
Beattie, J. 1992 (St Mirren)	4
Beaumont, D. 1985 (Dundee U)	1
Bell, D. 1981 (Aberdeen)	2
Bernard, P. R. J. 1992 (Oldham Ath)	15
Berra, C. 2005 (Hearts)	6
Bett, J. 1981 (Rangers)	7
Black, E. 1983 (Aberdeen)	8
Blair, A. 1980 (Coventry C, Aston Villa)	5
Bollan, G. 1992 (Dundee U, Rangers)	17
Bonar, P. 1997 (Raith R)	4
Booth, C. 2011 (Hibernian)	4
Booth, S. 1991 (Aberdeen)	14
Bowes, M. J. 1992 (Dunfermline Ath)	1
Bowman, D. 1985 (Hearts)	1
Boyack, S. 1997 (Rangers)	1
Boyd, K. 2003 (Kilmarnock)	8
Boyd, T. 1987 (Motherwell)	5
Brazil, A. 1978 (Hibernian)	1
Brazil, A. 1979 (Ipswich T)	8
Brebner, G. I. 1997 (Manchester U, Reading, Hibernian)	18
Brighton, T. 2005 (Rangers, Clyde)	7
Broadfoot, K. 2005 (St Mirren)	5
Brough, J. 1981 (Hearts)	1
Brown, A. H. 2004 (Hibernian)	1
Brown, S. 2005 (Hibernian)	10
Browne, P. 1997 (Raith R)	1
Bryson, C. 2006 (Clyde)	1
Buchan, J. 1997 (Aberdeen)	13
Burchill, M. J. 1998 (Celtic)	15
Burke, A. 1997 (Kilmarnock)	4
Burke, C. 2004 (Rangers)	3
Burley, C. W. 1992 (Chelsea)	7
Burley, G. E. 1977 (Ipswich T)	5
Burns, H. 1985 (Rangers)	2
Burns, T. 1977 (Celtic)	5
Caddis, P. 2008 (Celtic, Dundee U, Celtic, Swindon T)	13
Cairney, T. 2011 (Hull C)	6
Caldwell, G. 2000 (Newcastle U)	19
Caldwell, S. 2001 (Newcastle U)	4
Cameron, G. 2008 (Dundee U)	3
Campbell, R. 2008 (Hibernian)	6
Campbell, S. 1989 (Dundee)	3
Campbell, S. P. 1998 (Leicester C)	15

Canero, P. 2000 (Kilmarnock)	17
Cardwell, H. 2014 (Reading)	**1**
Carey, L. A. 1998 (Bristol C)	1
Carrick, D. 2012 (Hearts)	1
Casey, J. 1978 (Celtic)	1
Chalmers, J. 2014 (Celtic)	1
Christie, M. 1992 (Dundee)	3
Christie, R. 2014 (Inverness CT)	**3**
Clark, R. B. 1977 (Aberdeen)	3
Clarke, S. 1984 (St Mirren)	8
Clarkson, D. 2004 (Motherwell)	13
Cleland, A. 1990 (Dundee U)	11
Cole, D. 2011 (Rangers)	2
Collins, J. 1988 (Hibernian)	8
Collins, N. 2005 (Sunderland)	7
Connolly, P. 1991 (Dundee U)	3
Connor, R. 1981 (Ayr U)	2
Conroy, D. 2007 (Celtic)	4
Considine, A. 2007 (Aberdeen)	5
Cooper, D. 1977 (Clydebank, Rangers)	6
Cooper, N. 1982 (Aberdeen)	13
Coutts, P. A. 2009 (Peterborough U, Preston NE)	7
Crabbe, S. 1990 (Hearts)	2
Craig, M. 1998 (Aberdeen)	2
Craig, T. 1977 (Newcastle U)	1
Crainey, S. D. 2000 (Celtic)	7
Crainie, D. 1983 (Celtic)	1
Crawford, S. 1994 (Raith R)	19
Creaney, G. 1991 (Celtic)	11
Cummings, W. 2000 (Chelsea)	8
Cuthbert, S. 2007 (Celtic, St Mirren)	13
Dailly, C. 1991 (Dundee U)	34
Dalglish, P. 1999 (Newcastle U, Norwich C)	6
Dargo, C. 1998 (Raith R)	10
Davidson, C. I. 1997 (St Johnstone)	2
Davidson, H. N. 2000 (Dundee U)	3
Davidson, M. 2011 (St Johnstone)	1
Dawson, A. 1979 (Rangers)	8
Deas, P. A. 1997 (St Johnstone)	2
Dempster, J. 2004 (Rushden & D)	1
Dennis, S. 1992 (Raith R)	1
Diamond, A. 2004 (Aberdeen)	12
Dickov, P. 1992 (Arsenal)	4
Dixon, P. 2008 (Dundee)	2
Dodds, D. 1978 (Dundee U)	1
Dods, D. 1997 (Hibernian)	5
Doig, C. R. 2000 (Nottingham F)	13
Donald, G. S. 1992 (Hibernian)	3
Donnelly, S. 1994 (Celtic)	11
Dorrans, G. 2007 (Livingston)	6
Dow, A. 1993 (Dundee, Chelsea)	3
Dowie, A. J. 2003 (Rangers, Partick Thistle)	14
Duff, J. 2009 (Inverness CT)	1
Duff, S. 2003 (Dundee U)	9
Duffie, K. 2011 (Falkirk)	6
Duffy, D. A. 2005 (Falkirk, Hull C)	8
Duffy, J. 1987 (Dundee)	1
Durie, G. S. 1987 (Chelsea)	4
Durrant, I. 1987 (Rangers)	4
Doyle, J. 1981 (Partick Thistle)	1
Easton, B. 2009 (Hamilton A)	3
Easton, C. 1997 (Dundee U)	21
Edwards, M. 2012 (Rochdale)	1
Elliot, B. 1998 (Celtic)	2
Elliot, C. 2006 (Hearts)	9
Esson, R. 2000 (Aberdeen)	7
Fagan, S. M. 2005 (Motherwell)	1
Ferguson, B. 1997 (Rangers)	12
Ferguson, D. 1987 (Rangers)	5

Ferguson, D. 1992 (Dundee U)	7
Ferguson, D. 1992 (Manchester U)	5
Ferguson, I. 1983 (Dundee)	4
Ferguson, I. 1987 (Clyde, St Mirren, Rangers)	6
Ferguson, R. 1977 (Hamilton A)	1
Feruz, I. 2012 (Chelsea)	4
Findlay, S. 2012 (Celtic)	**11**
Findlay, W. 1991 (Hibernian)	5
Fitzpatrick, A. 1977 (St Mirren)	5
Fitzpatrick, M. 2007 (Motherwell)	4
Flannigan, C. 1993 (Clydebank)	1
Fleck, J. 2009 (Rangers)	4
Fleck, R. 1987 (Rangers, Norwich C)	6
Fleming, G. 2008 (Gretna)	1
Fletcher, D. B. 2003 (Manchester U)	2
Fletcher, S. 2007 (Hibernian)	7
Forrest, J. 2011 (Celtic)	4
Foster, R. M. 2005 (Aberdeen)	5
Fotheringham, M. M. 2004 (Dundee)	3
Fowler, J. 2002 (Kilmarnock)	3
Foy, R. A. 2004 (Liverpool)	5
Fraser, M. 2012 (Celtic)	**5**
Fraser, R. 2013 (Aberdeen, Bournemouth)	**8**
Fraser, S. T. 2000 (Luton T)	4
Freedman, D. A. 1995 (Barnet, Crystal Palace)	8
Fridge, L. 1989 (St Mirren)	2
Fullarton, J. 1993 (St Mirren)	17
Fulton, J. 2014 (Swansea C)	**1**
Fulton, M. 1980 (St Mirren)	5
Fulton, S. 1991 (Celtic)	7
Fyvie, F. 2012 (Wigan Ath)	8
Gallacher, K. W. 1987 (Dundee U)	7
Gallacher, P. 1999 (Dundee U)	7
Gallacher, S. 2009 (Rangers)	2
Gallagher, P. 2003 (Blackburn R)	11
Galloway, M. 1989 (Hearts, Celtic)	2
Gardiner, J. 1993 (Hibernian)	1
Gauld, R. 2013 (Dundee U, Sporting Lisbon)	**5**
Geddes, R. 1982 (Dundee)	5
Gemmill, S. 1992 (Nottingham F)	4
Germaine, G. 1997 (WBA)	1
Gilles, R. 1997 (St Mirren)	7
Gillespie, G. T. 1979 (Coventry C)	8
Glass, S. 1995 (Aberdeen)	11
Glover, L. 1988 (Nottingham F)	3
Goodwillie, D. 2009 (Dundee U)	9
Goram, A. L. 1987 (Oldham Ath)	1
Gordon, C. S. 2003 (Hearts)	5
Gough, C. R. 1983 (Dundee U)	5
Graham, D. 1998 (Rangers)	8
Grant, P. 1985 (Celtic)	10
Gray, D. P. 2009 (Manchester U)	2
Gray, S. 1987 (Aberdeen)	1
Gray S. 1995 (Celtic)	7
Griffiths, L. 2010 (Dundee, Wolverhampton W)	11
Grimmer, J. 2014 (Fulham)	1
Gunn, B. 1984 (Aberdeen)	9
Hagen, D. 1992 (Rangers)	8
Hamill, J. 2008 (Kilmarnock)	11
Hamilton, B. 1989 (St Mirren)	4
Hamilton, J. 1995 (Dundee, Hearts)	14
Hamilton, J. 2014 (Hearts)	**3**
Hammell, S. 2001 (Motherwell)	11
Handling, D. 2014 (Hibernian)	**3**
Handyside, P. 1993 (Grimsby T)	7
Hanley, G. 2011 (Blackburn R)	1
Hanlon, P. 2009 (Hibernian)	23
Hannah, D. 1993 (Dundee U)	16
Harper, K. 1995 (Hibernian)	7
Hartford, R. A. 1977 (Manchester C)	1
Hartley, P. J. 1997 (Millwall)	1
Hegarty, P. 1987 (Dundee U)	6
Hendrie, S. 2014 (West Ham U)	**3**
Hendry, J. 1992 (Tottenham H)	1
Henly, J. 2014 (Reading)	**1**
Herron, J. 2012 (Celtic)	2
Hetherston, B. 1997 (St Mirren)	1
Hewitt, J. 1982 (Aberdeen)	6
Hogg, G. 1984 (Manchester U)	4
Holt, J. 2012 (Hearts)	7
Hood, G. 1993 (Ayr U)	3
Horn, R. 1997 (Hearts)	6
Howie, S. 1993 (Cowdenbeath)	5
Hughes, R. D. 1999 (Bournemouth)	9

Hughes, S. 2002 (Rangers)	12
Hunter, G. 1987 (Hibernian)	3
Hunter, P. 1989 (East Fife)	3
Hutton, A. 2004 (Rangers)	7
Hutton, K. 2011 (Rangers)	1
Hyam, D. 2015 (Reading)	**1**
Inman, B. 2011 (Newcastle U)	2
Irvine, G. 2006 (Celtic)	2
Jack, R. 2012 (Aberdeen)	**19**
James, K. F. 1997 (Falkirk)	1
Jardine, I. 1979 (Kilmarnock)	1
Jess, E. 1990 (Aberdeen)	14
Johnson, G. I. 1992 (Dundee U)	6
Johnston, A. 1994 (Hearts)	3
Johnston, F. 1993 (Falkirk)	1
Johnston, M. 1984 (Partick Thistle, Watford)	3
Jordan, A. J. 2000 (Bristol C)	3
Jupp, D. A. 1995 (Fulham)	9
Kelly, L. 2012 (Kilmarnock)	9
Kelly, S. 2014 (St Mirren)	1
Kennedy, J. 2003 (Celtic)	15
Kennedy, M. 2012 (Kilmarnock)	1
Kenneth, G. 2008 (Dundee U)	8
Kerr, B. 2003 (Newcastle U)	14
Kerr, F. 2012 (Birmingham C)	3
Kerr, M. 2001 (Kilmarnock)	1
Kerr, S. 1993 (Celtic)	10
Kettings, C. D. 2012 (Blackpool)	3
King, A. 2014 (Swansea C)	**1**
King, B. 2015 (Hearts)	**1**
King, C. M. 2014 (Norwich C)	**1**
Kingsley, S. 2015 (Swansea C)	**1**
Kinniburgh, W. D. 2004 (Motherwell)	3
Kirkwood, D. 1990 (Hearts)	1
Kyle, K. 2001 (Sunderland)	12
Lambert, P. 1991 (St Mirren)	11
Langfield, J. 2000 (Dundee)	2
Lappin, S. 2004 (St Mirren)	10
Lauchlan, J. 1998 (Kilmarnock)	11
Lavety, B. 1993 (St Mirren)	9
Lavin, G. 1993 (Watford)	7
Lawson, P. 2004 (Celtic)	10
Leighton, J. 1982 (Aberdeen)	1
Lennon, S. 2008 (Rangers)	6
Levein, C. 1985 (Hearts)	2
Leven, P. 2005 (Kilmarnock)	2
Liddell, A. M. 1994 (Barnsley)	12
Lindsey, J. 1979 (Motherwell)	1
Locke, G. 1994 (Hearts)	10
Love, D. 2015 (Manchester U)	**1**
Love, G. 1995 (Hibernian)	1
Loy, R. 2009 (Dunfermline Ath, Rangers)	5
Lynch, S. 2003 (Celtic, Preston NE)	13
McAllister, G. 1990 (Leicester C)	1
McAllister, R. 2008 (Inverness CT)	2
McAlpine, H. 1983 (Dundee U)	5
McAnespie, K. 1998 (St Johnstone)	4
McArthur, J. 2008 (Hamilton A)	2
McAuley, S. 1993 (St Johnstone)	1
McAvennie, F. 1982 (St Mirren)	5
McBride, J. 1981 (Everton)	1
McBride, J. P. 1998 (Celtic)	2
McCabe, R. 2012 (Rangers, Sheffield W)	3
McCall, A. S. M. 1988 (Bradford C, Everton)	2
McCann, K. 2008 (Hibernian)	4
McCann, N. 1994 (Dundee)	9
McClair, B. 1984 (Celtic)	8
McCluskey, G. 1979 (Celtic)	6
McCluskey, S. 1997 (St Johnstone)	14
McCoist, A. 1984 (Rangers)	1
McConnell, I. 1997 (Clyde)	1
McCormack, D. 2008 (Hibernian)	1
McCormack, R. 2006 (Rangers, Motherwell, Cardiff C)	13
McCracken, D. 2002 (Dundee U)	5
McCulloch, A. 1981 (Kilmarnock)	1
McCulloch, I. 1982 (Notts Co)	2
McCulloch, L. 1997 (Motherwell)	14
McCunnie, J. 2001 (Dundee U, Ross Co, Dunfermline Ath)	20
MacDonald, A. 2011 (Burnley)	6
MacDonald, J. 1980 (Rangers)	8

MacDonald, J. 2007 (Hearts) 11
McDonald, C. 1995 (Falkirk) 5
McDonald, K. 2008 (Dundee, Burnley) 14
McEwan, C. 1997 (Clyde, Raith R) 17
McEwan, D. 2003 (Livingston) 2
McFadden, J. 2003 (Motherwell) 7
McFadzean C. 2015 (Sheffield U) 1
McFarlane, D. 1997 (Hamilton A) 3
McGarry, S. 1997 (St Mirren) 3
McGarvey, F. P. 1977 (St Mirren, Celtic) 3
McGarvey, S. 1982 (Manchester U) 4
McGeough, D. 2012 (Celtic) 10
McGhee, J. 2013 (Hearts) 10
McGhee, M. 1981 (Aberdeen) 1
McGinn, J. 2014 (St Mirren) 5
McGinn, S. 2009 (St Mirren, Watford) 8
McGinnis, G. 1985 (Dundee U) 1
McGlinchey, M. R. 2007 (Celtic) 1
McGregor, A. 2003 (Rangers) 6
McGregor, C. W. 2013 (Celtic) 5
McGrillen, P. 1994 (Motherwell) 2
McGuire, D. 2002 (Aberdeen) 2
McHattie, K. 2012 (Hearts) 6
McInally, J. 1989 (Dundee U) 1
McKay, B. 2012 (Rangers) 1
McKay, B. 2013 (Hearts) 1
McKean, K. 2011 (St Mirren) 1
McKenzie, R. 2013 (Kilmarnock) 4
McKenzie, R. 1997 (Hearts) 2
McKimmie, S. 1985 (Aberdeen) 3
McKinlay, T. 1984 (Dundee) 6
McKinlay, W. 1989 (Dundee U) 6
McKinnon, R. 1991 (Dundee U) 6
McLaren, A, 1989 (Hearts) 11
McLaren, A. 1993 (Dundee U) 4
McLaughlin, B. 1995 (Celtic) 8
McLaughlin, J. 1981 (Morton) 10
McLean, E. 2008 (Dundee U, St Johnstone) 2
McLean, S. 2003 (Rangers) 4
McLeish, A. 1978 (Aberdeen) 6
McLean, K. 2012 (St Mirren) 11
MacLeod, A. 1979 (Hibernian) 3
McLeod, J. 1989 (Dundee U) 2
MacLeod, L. 2012 (Rangers) 8
MacLeod, M. 1979 (Dumbarton, Celtic) 5
McManus, D. J. 2014 (Aberdeen) 2
McManus, T. 2001 (Hibernian) 14
McMillan, S. 1997 (Motherwell) 4
McNab, N. 1978 (Tottenham H) 1
McNally, M. 1991 (Celtic) 2
McNamara, J. 1994 (Dunfermline Ath, Celtic) 12
McNaughton, K. 2002 (Aberdeen) 1
McNeil, A. 2007 (Hibernian) 1
McNichol, J. 1979 (Brentford) 1
McNiven, D. 1977 (Leeds U) 3
McNiven, S. A. 1996 (Oldham Ath) 1
McParland, A. 2003 (Celtic) 1
McPhee, S. 2002 (Port Vale) 1
McPherson, D. 1984 (Rangers, Hearts) 4
McQuilken, J. 1993 (Celtic) 2
McStay, P. 1983 (Celtic) 5
McWhirter, N. 1991 (St Mirren) 1
Mackay-Steven, G. 2012 (Dundee U) 3
Maguire, C. 2009 (Aberdeen) 12
Main, A. 1988 (Dundee U) 3
Malcolm, R. 2001 (Rangers) 1
Maloney, S. 2002 (Celtic) 21
Malpas, M. 1983 (Dundee U) 8
Marr, B. 2011 (Ross Co) 1
Marshall, D. J. 2004 (Celtic) 10
Marshall, S. R. 1995 (Arsenal) 5
Martin, A. 2009 (Leeds U, Ayr U) 12
Mason, G. R. 1999 (Manchester C, Dunfermline Ath) 2
Mathieson, D. 1997 (Queen of the South) 3
May, E. 1989 (Hibernian) 2
May, S. 2013 (St Johnstone, Sheffield W) 8
Meldrum, C. 1996 (Kilmarnock) 6
Melrose, J. 1977 (Partick Thistle) 3
Millar, M, 2009 (Celtic) 1
Miller, C. 1995 (Rangers) 8
Miller, J. 1987 (Aberdeen, Celtic) 7
Miller, K. 2000 (Hibernian, Rangers) 7
Miller, W. 1991 (Hibernian) 7
Miller, W. F. 1978 (Aberdeen) 2
Milne, K. 2000 (Hearts) 1
Milne, R. 1982 (Dundee U) 3

Mitchell, C. 2008 (Falkirk) 7
Money, I. C. 1987 (St Mirren) 3
Montgomery, N. A. 2003 (Sheffield U) 2
Morrison, S. A. 2004 (Aberdeen, Dunfermline Ath) 12
Muir, L. 1977 (Hibernian) 1
Mulgrew, C. P. 2006 (Celtic, Wolverhampton W, Aberdeen) 14
Murphy, J. 2009 (Motherwell) 13
Murray, H. 2000 (St Mirren) 3
Murray, I. 2001 (Hibernian) 15
Murray, N. 1993 (Rangers) 16
Murray, R. 1993 (Bournemouth) 1
Murray, S. 2004 (Kilmarnock) 2

Narey, D. 1977 (Dundee U) 4
Naismith, J. 2014 (St Mirren) 1
Naismith, S. J. 2006 (Kilmarnock, Rangers) 15
Naysmith, G. A. 1997 (Hearts) 22
Neilson, R. 2000 (Hearts) 1
Ness, J, 2011 (Rangers) 2
Nevin, P. 1985 (Chelsea) 5
Nicholas, C. 1981 (Celtic, Arsenal) 6
Nicholson, B. 1999 (Rangers) 7
Nicholson, S. 2015 (Hearts) 1
Nicol, S. 1981 (Ayr U, Liverpool) 14
Nisbet, S. 1989 (Rangers) 5
Noble, D. J. 2003 (West Ham U) 2
Notman, A. M. 1999 (Manchester U) 10

O'Brien, B. 1999 (Blackburn R, Livingston) 6
O'Connor, G. 2003 (Hibernian) 8
O'Donnell, P. 1992 (Motherwell) 8
O'Donnell, S. 2013 (Partick Thistle) 1
O'Halloran, M. 2012 (Bolton W) 2
O'Hara, M. 2015 (Kilmarnock) 1
O'Leary, R. 2008 (Kilmarnock) 2
O'Neil, B. 1992 (Celtic) 7
O'Neil, J. 1991 (Dundee U) 1
O'Neill, M. 1995 (Clyde) 6
Orr, N. 1978 (Morton) 7

Palmer, L. J. 2011 (Sheffield W) 8
Park, C. 2012 (Middlesbrough) 1
Parker, K. 2001 (St Johnstone) 1
Parlane, D. 1977 (Rangers) 1
Paterson, C. 1981 (Hibernian) 2
Paterson, C. 2012 (Hearts) 8
Paterson, J. 1997 (Dundee U) 9
Pawlett, P. 2012 (Aberdeen) 7
Payne, G. 1978 (Dundee U) 3
Peacock, L. A. 1997 (Carlisle U) 3
Pearce, A. J. 2008 (Reading) 1
Pearson, S. P. 2003 (Motherwell) 8
Perry, R. 2010 (Rangers, Falkirk, Rangers) 16
Pressley, S. J. 1993 (Rangers, Coventry C, Dundee U) 26
Provan, D. 1977 (Kilmarnock) 1
Prunty, B. 2004 (Aberdeen) 6

Quinn, P. C. 2004 (Motherwell) 3
Quinn, R. 2006 (Celtic) 9

Rae, A. 1991 (Millwall) 8
Rae, G. 1999 (Dundee) 6
Redford, I. 1981 (Rangers) 6
Reid, B. 1991 (Rangers) 4
Reid, C. 1993 (Hibernian) 3
Reid, M. 1982 (Celtic) 2
Reid, R. 1977 (St Mirren) 3
Reilly, A. 2004 (Wycombe W) 1
Renicks, S. 1997 (Hamilton A) 1
Reynolds, M. 2007 (Motherwell) 9
Rhodes, J. L. 2011 (Huddersfield T) 8
Rice, B. 1985 (Hibernian) 1
Richardson, L. 1980 (St Mirren) 2
Ridgers, M. 2012 (Hearts) 5
Riordan, D. G. 2004 (Hibernian) 5
Ritchie, A. 1980 (Morton) 2
Ritchie, P. S. 1996 (Hearts) 7
Robertson, A. 1991 (Rangers) 1
Robertson, A. 2013 (Dundee U) 3
Robertson, C. 1977 (Rangers) 1
Robertson, C. 2012 (Aberdeen) 10
Robertson, D. 1987 (Aberdeen) 7
Robertson, D. 2007 (Dundee U) 4
Robertson, G. A. 2004 (Nottingham F, Rotherham U) 15
Robertson, H. 1994 (Aberdeen) 2

Robertson, J. 1985 (Hearts)	2	Stillie, D. 1995 (Aberdeen)	14
Robertson, L. 1993 (Rangers)	3	Strachan, G. D. 1998 (Coventry C)	7
Robertson, S. 1998 (St Johnstone)	2	Sturrock, P. 1977 (Dundee U)	9
Roddie, A. 1992 (Aberdeen)	5	Sweeney, P. H. 2004 (Millwall)	8
Ross, G. 2007 (Dunfermline Ath)	1	Sweeney, S. 1991 (Clydebank)	7
Ross, N. 2011 (Inverness CT)	2		
Ross, T. W. 1977 (Arsenal)	1	Tapping, C. 2013 (Hearts)	1
Rowson, D. 1997 (Aberdeen)	5	Tarrant, N. K. 1999 (Aston Villa)	5
Russell, J. 2011 (Dundee U)	11	Teale, G. 1997 (Clydebank, Ayr U)	6
Russell, R. 1978 (Rangers)	3	Telfer, P. N. 1993 (Luton T)	3
		Templeton, D. 2011 (Hearts)	2
Salton, D. B. 1992 (Luton T)	6	Thomas, K. 1993 (Hearts)	8
Samson, C. I. 2004 (Kilmarnock)	6	Thompson, S. 1997 (Dundee U)	12
Saunders, S. 2011 (Motherwell)	2	Thomson, C. 2011 (Hearts)	2
Scobbie, T. 2008 (Falkirk)	12	Thomson, K. 2005 (Hibernian)	6
Scott, M. 2006 (Livingston)	1	Thomson, W. 1977 (Partick Thistle, St Mirren)	10
Scott, P. 1994 (St Johnstone)	4	Tolmie, J. 1980 (Morton)	1
Scougall, S. 2012 (Livingston, Sheffield U)	2	Tortolano, J. 1987 (Hibernian)	2
Scrimgour, D. 1997 (St Mirren)	3	Toshney, L. 2012 (Celtic)	5
Seaton, A. 1998 (Falkirk)	1	Turner, I. 2005 (Everton)	6
Severin, S. D. 2000 (Hearts)	10	Tweed, S. 1993 (Hibernian)	3
Shankland, L. 2015 (Aberdeen)	**1**		
Shannon, R. 1987 (Dundee)	7	Wales, G. 2000 (Hearts)	1
Sharp, G. M. 1982 (Everton)	1	Walker, A. 1988 (Celtic)	1
Sharp, R. 1990 (Dunfermline Ath)	4	Walker, J. 2013 (Hearts)	1
Sheerin, P. 1996 (Southampton)	1	Wallace, I. A. 1978 (Coventry C)	1
Shields, G. 1997 (Rangers)	2	Wallace, L. 2007 (Hearts)	10
Shinnie, A. 2009 (Dundee, Rangers)	3	Wallace, M. 2012 (Huddersfield T)	4
Shinnie, G. 2012 (Inverness CT)	2	Wallace, R. 2004 (Celtic, Sunderland)	4
Simmons, S. 2003 (Hearts)	1	Walsh, C. 1984 (Nottingham F)	5
Simpson, N. 1982 (Aberdeen)	11	Wark, J. 1977 (Ipswich T)	8
Sinclair, C. 1977 (Dumbarton)	1	Watson, A. 1981 (Aberdeen)	4
Skilling, M. 1993 (Kilmarnock)	2	Watson, K. 1977 (Rangers)	2
Slater, C. 2014 (Kilmarnock)	**5**	Watt, A. 2012 (Celtic)	9
Smith, B. M. 1992 (Celtic)	5	Watt, M. 1991 (Aberdeen)	12
Smith, C. 2008 (St Mirren)	2	Watt. S. M. 2005 (Chelsea)	5
Smith, C. 2015 (Aberdeen)	**1**	Webster, A. 2003 (Hearts)	2
Smith, D. 2012 (Hearts)	4	Whiteford, A. 1997 (St Johnstone)	1
Smith, D. L. 2006 (Motherwell)	2	Whittaker, S. G. 2005 (Hibernian)	18
Smith, G. 1978 (Rangers)	1	Whyte, D. 1987 (Celtic)	9
Smith, G. 2004 (Rangers)	8	Wilkie, L. 2000 (Dundee)	6
Smith, H. G. 1987 (Hearts)	2	Will, J. A. 1992 (Arsenal)	3
Smith, S. 2007 (Rangers)	1	Williams, G. 2002 (Nottingham F)	9
Sneddon, A. 1979 (Celtic)	1	Wilson, D. 2011 (Liverpool, Hearts)	13
Snodgrass, R. 2008 (Livingston)	2	Wilson, M. 2004 (Dundee U, Celtic)	19
Soutar, D. 2003 (Dundee)	11	Wilson, S. 1999 (Rangers)	7
Speedie, D. R. 1985 (Chelsea)	1	Wilson, T. 1983 (St Mirren)	1
Spencer, J. 1991 (Rangers)	3	Wilson, T. 1988 (Nottingham F)	4
Stanton, P. 1977 (Hibernian)	1	Winnie, D. 1988 (St Mirren)	1
Stanton, S. 2014 (Hibernian)	1	Woods, M. 2006 (Sunderland)	2
Stark, W. 1985 (Aberdeen)	1	Wotherspoon, D. 2011 (Hibernian)	16
Stephen, R. 1983 (Dundee)	1	Wright, P. 1989 (Aberdeen, QPR)	3
Stevens, G. 1977 (Motherwell)	1	Wright, S. 1991 (Aberdeen)	14
Stevenson, L. 2008 (Hibernian)	8	Wright, T. 1987 (Oldham Ath)	1
Stewart, C. 2002 (Kilmarnock)	1	Wylde, G. 2011 (Rangers)	7
Stewart, J. 1978 (Kilmarnock, Middlesbrough)	3		
Stewart, M. J. 2000 (Manchester U)	17	Young, Darren 1997 (Aberdeen)	8
Stewart, R. 1979 (Dundee U, West Ham U)	12	Young, Derek 2000 (Aberdeen)	5

WALES

Adams, N. W. 2008 (Bury, Leicester C)	5	Bond, J. H. 2011 (Watford)	1
Alfei, D. M. 2010 (Swansea C)	13	Bowen, J. P. 1993 (Swansea C)	5
Aizlewood, M. 1979 (Luton T)	2	Bowen, M. R. 1983 (Tottenham H)	3
Allen, J. M. 2008 (Swansea C)	13	Boyle, T. 1982 (Crystal Palace)	1
Anthony, B. 2005 (Cardiff C)	8	Brace, D. P. 1995 (Wrexham)	6
		Bradley, M. S. 2007 (Walsall)	17
Baddeley, L. M. 1996 (Cardiff C)	2	Bradshaw, T. 2012 (Shrewsbury T)	8
Balcombe, S. 1982 (Leeds U)	1	Brough, M. 2003 (Notts Co)	3
Bale, G. 2006 (Southampton, Tottenham H)	4	Brown, J. D. 2008 (Cardiff C)	6
Barnhouse, D. J. 1995 (Swansea C)	3	Brown, R. 2003 (Gillingham)	7
Basey, G. W. 2009 (Charlton Ath)	1	Brown, T. A. F. 2011 (Ipswich T, Rotherham U,	
Bater, P. T. 1977 (Bristol R)	2	Aldershot T)	10
Beevers, L. J. 2005 (Boston U, Lincoln C)	7	**Burns, W. 2013 (Bristol C)**	**11**
Bellamy, C. D. 1996 (Norwich C)	4	Byrne, M. T. 2003 (Bolton W)	1
Bender, T. J. 2011 (Colchester U)	4		
Birchall, A. S. 2003 (Arsenal, Mansfield T)	12	Calliste, R. T. 2005 (Manchester U, Liverpool)	15
Bird, A. 1993 (Cardiff C)	6	Carpenter, R. E. 2005 (Burnley)	1
Blackmore, C. 1984 (Manchester U)	3	Cassidy, A. 2011 (Wolverhampton W)	8
Blake, D. J. 2007 (Cardiff C)	14	Cegielski, W. 1977 (Wrexham)	2
Blake, N. A. 1991 (Cardiff C)	5	Chamberlain, E. C. 2010 (Leicester C)	9
Blaney, S. D. 1997 (West Ham U)	3	Chapple, S. R. 1992 (Swansea C)	2
Bloom, J. 2011 (Falkirk)	1	Charles, J. M. 1979 (Swansea C)	8
Bodin, B. P. 2010 (Swindon T, Torquay U)	21	Church, S. R. 2008 (Reading)	15
Bodin, P. J. 1983 (Cardiff C)	1	Clark, J. 1978 (Manchester U, Derby Co)	2

Coates, J. S. 1996 (Swansea C) 5
Coleman, C. 1990 (Swansea C) 3
Collins, J. M. 2003 (Cardiff C) 7
Collins, M. J. 2007 (Fulham, Swansea C) 2
Collison, D. J. 2008 (West Ham U) 7
Cornell, D. J. 2010 (Swansea C) 4
Cotterill, D. R. G. B. 2005 (Bristol C, Wigan Ath) 11
Coyne, D. 1992 (Tranmere R) 7
Craig, N. L. 2009 (Everton) 4
Critchell, K. A. R. 2005 (Southampton) 3
Crofts, A. L. 2005 (Gillingham) 10
Crowell, M. T. 2004 (Wrexham) 7
Curtis, A. T. 1977 (Swansea C) 1

Davies, A. 1982 (Manchester U) 6
Davies, A. G. 2006 (Cambridge U) 6
Davies, A. R. 2005 (Southampton, Yeovil T) 14
Davies, C. M. 2005 (Oxford U, Verona, Oldham Ath) 9
Davies, D. 1999 (Barry C) 2
Davies, G. M. 1993 (Hereford U, Crystal Palace) 7
Davies, I. C. 1978 (Norwich C) 1
Davies, L. 2005 (Bangor C) 1
Davies, R. J. 2006 (WBA) 4
Davies, S. 1999 (Peterborough U, Tottenham H) 10
Dawson, C. 2013 (Leeds U) 2
Day, R. 2000 (Manchester C, Mansfield T) 11
Deacy, N. 1977 (PSV Eindhoven) 1
De-Vulgt, L. S. 2002 (Swansea C) 2
Dibble, A. 1983 (Cardiff C) 3
Dibble, C. 2014 (Barnsley) 1
Doble, R. A. 2010 (Southampton) 10
Doughty, M. E. 2012 (QPR) 1
Doyle, S. C. 1979 (Preston NE, Huddersfield T) 7
Duffy, R. M. 2005 (Portsmouth) 7
Dummett, P. 2011 (Newcastle U) 3
Dwyer, P. J. 1979 (Cardiff C) 1

Eardley, N. 2007 (Oldham Ath, Blackpool) 11
Earnshaw, R. 1999 (Cardiff C) 10
Easter, D. J. 2006 (Cardiff C) 1
Ebdon, M. 1990 (Everton) 2
Edwards, C. N. H. 1996 (Swansea C) 7
Edwards, D. A. 2006 (Shrewsbury T, Luton T, Wolverhampton W) 9
Edwards, G. D. R. 2012 (Swansea C) 6
Edwards, R. I. 1977 (Chester) 2
Edwards, R. W. 1991 (Bristol C) 13
Evans, A. 1977 (Bristol R) 1
Evans, C. 2007 (Manchester C, Sheffield U) 13
Evans, J. 2014 (Fulham) 1
Evans, K. 1999 (Leeds U, Cardiff C) 4
Evans, L. 2013 (Wolverhampton W) 7
Evans, P. S. 1996 (Shrewsbury T) 1
Evans, S. J. 2001 (Crystal Palace) 2
Evans, T. 1995 (Cardiff C) 1

Fish, N. 2005 (Cardiff C) 2
Fleetwood, S. 2005 (Cardiff C) 5
Flynn, C. P. 2007 (Crewe Alex) 1
Folland, R. W. 2000 (Oxford U) 1
Foster, M. G. 1993 (Tranmere R) 1
Fowler, L. A. 2003 (Coventry C, Huddersfield T) 9
Fox, M. A. 2013 (Charlton Ath) 6
Freeman, K. 2012 (Nottingham F, Derby Co) 15
Freestone, R. 1990 (Chelsea) 1

Gabbidon, D. L. 1999 (WBA, Cardiff C) 17
Gale, D. 1983 (Swansea C) 2
Gall, K. A. 2002 (Bristol R, Yeovil T) 8
Gibson, N. D. 1999 (Tranmere R, Sheffield W) 11
Giggs, R. J. 1991 (Manchester U) 1
Gilbert, P. 2005 (Plymouth Arg) 12
Giles, D. C. 1977 (Cardiff C, Swansea C, Crystal Palace) 4
Giles, P. 1982 (Cardiff C) 3
Graham, D. 1991 (Manchester U) 1
Green, R. M. 1998 (Wolverhampton W) 16
Griffith, C. 1990 (Cardiff C) 1
Griffiths, P. 1991 (Shrewsbury T) 1
Grubb, D. 2007 (Bristol C) 1
Gunter, C. 2006 (Cardiff C, Tottenham H) 8

Haldane, L. O. 2007 (Bristol R) 1
Hall, G. D. 1990 (Chelsea) 1
Harrison, E. W. 2013 (Bristol R) 5
Hartson, J. 1994 (Luton T, Arsenal) 9

Haworth, S. O. 1997 (Cardiff C, Coventry C, Wigan Ath) 12
Hedges, R. P. 2014 (Swansea C) 3
Henley, A. 2012 (Blackburn R) 3
Hennessey, W. R. 2006 (Wolverhampton W) 6
Hewitt, E. J. 2012 (Macclesfield T, Ipswich T) 10
Hillier, I. M. 2001 (Tottenham H, Luton T) 5
Hodges, G. 1983 (Wimbledon) 5
Holden, A. 1984 (Chester C) 1
Holloway, C. D. 1999 (Exeter C) 2
Hopkins, J. 1982 (Fulham) 5
Hopkins, S. A. 1999 (Wrexham) 1
Howells, J. 2012 (Luton T) 5
Huggins, D. S. 1996 (Bristol C) 1
Hughes, D. 2005 (Kaiserslautern, Regensburg) 2
Hughes, D. R. 1994 (Southampton) 1
Hughes, I. 1992 (Bury) 11
Hughes, L. M. 1983 (Manchester U) 5
Hughes, R. D. 1996 (Aston Villa, Shrewsbury T) 13
Hughes, W. 1977 (WBA) 3
Huws, E. W. 2012 (Manchester C) 6

Isgrove, L. J. 2013 (Southampton) 6

Jackett, K. 1981 (Watford) 2
Jacobson, J. M. 2006 (Cardiff C, Bristol R) 15
James, L. R. S. 2006 (Southampton) 10
James, R. M. 1977 (Swansea C) 3
Jarman, L. 1996 (Cardiff C) 10
Jeanne, L. C. 1999 (QPR) 8
Jelleyman, G. A. 1999 (Peterborough U) 1
Jenkins, L. D. 1998 (Swansea C) 9
Jenkins, S. R. 1993 (Swansea C) 2
John, D. C. 2014 (Cardiff C) 3
Jones, C. T. 2007 (Swansea C) 1
Jones, E. P. 2000 (Blackpool) 1
Jones, F. 1981 (Wrexham) 1
Jones, G. W. 2014 (Plymouth Arg) 2
Jones, J. A. 2001 (Swansea C) 3
Jones, L. 1982 (Cardiff C) 3
Jones, M. A. 2004 (Wrexham) 4
Jones, M. G. 1998 (Leeds U) 7
Jones, P. L. 1992 (Liverpool) 12
Jones, R. 2011 (AFC Wimbledon) 1
Jones, R. A. 1994 (Sheffield W) 3
Jones, S. 2005 (Swansea C) 1
Jones, V. 1979 (Bristol R) 2

Kendall, L. M. 2001 (Crystal Palace) 2
Kendall, M. 1978 (Tottenham H) 1
Kenworthy, J. R. 1994 (Tranmere R) 3
King, A. 2008 (Leicester C) 11
Knott, G. R. 1996 (Tottenham H) 1

Law, B. J. 1990 (QPR) 2
Lawless, A. 2006 (Torquay U) 1
Lawrence, T. 2013 (Manchester U) 8
Ledley, J. C. 2005 (Cardiff C) 5
Letheran, G. 1977 (Leeds U) 2
Letheran, K. C. 2006 (Swansea C) 1
Lewis, D. 1982 (Swansea C) 9
Lewis, J. 1983 (Cardiff C) 1
Llewellyn, C. M. 1998 (Norwich C) 14
Loveridge, J. 1982 (Swansea C) 3
Low, J. D. 1999 (Bristol R, Cardiff C) 1
Lowndes, S. R. 1979 (Newport Co, Millwall) 4
Lucas, L. P. 2011 (Swansea C) 19

MacDonald, S. B. 2006 (Swansea C) 25
McCarthy, A. J. 1994 (QPR) 3
McDonald, C. 2006 (Cardiff C) 3
Mackin, L. 2006 (Wrexham) 1
Maddy, P. 1982 (Cardiff C) 1
Margetson, M. W. 1992 (Manchester C) 7
Martin, A. P. 1999 (Crystal Palace) 1
Martin, D. A. 2006 (Notts Co) 1
Marustik, C. 1982 (Swansea C) 7
Matthews, A. J. 2010 (Cardiff C) 5
Maxwell, C. 2009 (Wrexham) 16
Maxwell, L. J. 1999 (Liverpool, Cardiff C) 14
Meades, J. 2012 (Cardiff C) 4
Meaker, M. J. 1994 (QPR) 2
Melville, A. K. 1990 (Swansea C, Oxford U) 2
Micallef, C. 1982 (Cardiff C) 3
Morgan, A. M. 1995 (Tranmere R) 4
Morgan, C. 2004 (Wrexham, Milton Keynes D) 12

FA SCHOOLS AND YOUTH GAMES 2014–15

ENGLAND UNDER-16

FRIENDLIES

Burton, 20 August 2014
Game played in 4 separate periods of 30 minutes.
England (2) 3 *(Taylor-Crossdale 3, 46, N'Lundalu 102)*
Belgium (0) 4 *(Verlinden 67, Bongiovanni 77, 85, Boufus 115)*
England (1st half): Thompson J; Sterling, Williams (Willock 52), Bola, Brown, Dozzell, Gilmour, Bennett, Bishiru, Arlott-John, Taylor-Crossdale.
England (2nd half): Dyche; Moore, Tanganga, Thompson L, Dasilva, Ebuzoemu, Bailey, Nelson, Mount, Willock (Taylor-Crossdale 113), N'Lundalu.

UEFA DEVELOPMENT U17 TOURNAMENT

Burton, 16 February 2015
England (2) 2 *(Talyor-Crossdale 4, Heaney 16)*
Switzerland (2) 3 *(Kamaraj 37, 44, Zeqiri 38)*
England: Ashby-Hammond (Yates 25); Sterling (Chalobah 41), Francis, Tanganga, Neufville, Dozzell, Slattery (Scully 74), Mount (Diallo 64), Bennetts (Simmonds 74), Taylor-Crossdale (Campbell 52), Heaney.

Burton, 18 February 2015
England (0) 0
Slovakia (0) 0
England: Thompson J; Sterling, Chalobah, Thompson L, Brown, Diallo, Dozzell (Mount 65), Scully, Leko (Bennetts 65), Simmonds, Campbell (Taylor-Crossdale 65).
England won 4-3 on penalties.

Burton, 21 February 2015
England (0) 1 *(Taylor-Crossdale 49)*
France (0) 1 *(Konate 78)*
England: Thompson J (Yates 55); Sterling (Japhet 41), Neufville (Brown 41), Chalobah, Francis (Thompson L 41), Diallo (Scully 65), Slattery, Mount, Taylor-Crossdale (Simmonds 65), Bennetts (Heaney 55), Leko (Dozzell 73).
England won 4-3 on penalties.

SKY SPORTS VICTORY SHIELD

Bangor, 31 October 2014
Wales (0) 1 *(Angel 43)*
England (0) 0
Wales: Coughlan; Dasilva, Williams, Angel, Jefferies, Smallcombe, Proctor (Phillips 59), Smith (Ampadu 63), Roberts (Evans 73), Woodburn, Cullen
England: Ashby-Hammond; Sterling, Tanganga (Thompson L 41), Bola, Neufville, Gilmour (Diallo 64), Slattery, Mount, Bennetts (Heaney 55), Taylor-Crossdale (Simmonds 75), Leko.

Dungannon, 7 November 2014
Northern Ireland (0) 0
England (1) 1 *(Dozzell 34)*
England: Sandford, Sterling, Brown, Dozzell, Chalobah (Tanganga 60), Thompson L, Lewis, Diallo, Simmonds (N'Lundulu 68), Bishiru, Heaney (Willock 68).

Yeovil, 20 November 2014
England (1) 2 *(Willock 27, Taylor-Crossdale 52)*
Scotland (0) 1 *(Thompson 46)*   4733
England: Ashby-Hammond; Chalobahm (Mount 64), Neufville, Tanganga, Bola, Slattery, Gilmour (Dozzell 41), Willock (Lewis 64), Leko (Bashiru 64), N'Lundulu (Taylor-Crossdale 41), Nelson.
Scotland: McAdams; Freeman, Meredith, Baur, Gallacher, Burt (Middleton 74), Barjonas (Thomson 41), Marku (Connelly 63), Rudden, Aitchison (McLennan 56), Adamson.

MONTAIGU TOURNAMENT

St Jean de Monts, 31 March 2015
England (0) 4 *(Taylor-Crossdale 49, Mount 54, 73 (pen), Bennetts 80)*
Mexico (1) 1
England: Thompson J; 2 Sterling, Chalobah, Bola, Brown (Francis 66), 8 Slattery, Diallo, Leko (Dozzell 71), Mount, Nelson (Bennetts 78), Taylor-Crossdale (Ennis 78).

St Jean de Monts, 2 April 2015
England (0) 1 *(Nelson 73)*
Turkey (0) 0
England: Ashby-Hammond; Lattie, Sterling (Nelson 41), Francis, Chalobah (Brown 41), Gilmour, Diallo (Slattery 41), Dozzell, Bennetts, Ennis, Mount (Brown 41).

La Mothe-Acard, 4 April 2015
Ivory Coast (0) 1 *(78)*
England (1) 1 *(Sterling 32)*
England: Thompson J (Ashby-Hammond 69); Sterling, Chalobah (Lattie 41), Francis, Brown, Slattery, Diallo (Ennis 20), Dozzell, Taylor-Crossdale, Mount (Leko 69), Nelson (Gilmour 55).

Montaigu, Vendee, 6 April 2015
France (0) 1 *(Tshilumba 80)*
England (1) 3 *(Nelson 30, Bennetts 48, Taylor-Crossdale)*
England: Thompson J; Sterling, Chalobah, Bola, Francis (Brown 41), Dozzell, Slattery, Bennetts (Ennis 60), Taylor-Crossdale (Lattie 73), Mount, Nelson (Gilmour 65).

ENGLAND UNDER-17

NORDIC TOURNAMENT

Norre Aaby, 28 July 2014
England (2) 5 *(Dhanda 25, Muskwe 37, 54, Edwards M 44, 49)*
Iceland (0) 1 *(Hilmarsson 69)*
England: Ashby-Hammond (Huffer 74); Arnold, Oxford (Johnson 46), Francis (Leko 68), Neufville (Slattery 46), Kane (Wright 46), Diallo, Edwards K, Edwards M (Cantwell 62), Dhanda (N'Mecha 62), Muskwe.

Kolding, 29 July 2014
Finland (1) 1 *(Lingman 31)*
England (1) 1 *(Cantwell 36)*
England: Huffer; Arnold, Oxford, Johnson, Neufville (Francis 69), Kane, Wright, Slattery (Edwards M 40), Cantwell (Dhanda 40), N'Mecha (Muskwe 52), Leko (Diallo 59).

Kolding, 31 July 2014

England (0) 0

Sweden (2) 3 *(Kamana 2, 13, Elfstrom 55)*

England: Huffer; Arnold (Francis 59), Johnson, Oxford, Neufville, Kane, Wright, Edwards K (Diallo 50), Edwards M (N'Mecha 70), Dhanda (Cantwell 64), Leko (Muskwe 50).

THIRD PLACE PLAY-OFF

Kolding, 2 August 2014

England (0) 0

Denmark (0) 1 *(Rojkjaer 68 (pen))*   489

England: Ashby-Hammond; Arnold (Wright 46), Johnson, Oxford, Francis, Kane, Slattery, Diallo (Edwards M 54), Cantwell (Edwards K 65), Leko (Dhanda 65), Muskwe.

FA INTERNATIONAL TOURNAMENT

Kidderminster, 27 August 2014

England (1) 1 *(Hinds 34)*

Czech Republic (0) 1 *(Miker 71)*   1224

England: Woolston; Yates, Humphreys, Collinge (Johnson 74), DaSilva, Wright, Patching (Davies 63), Holland (Ndukwu 63), Maddox (Gribben 70), Willock, Hinds (Hector-Ingram 63).

Chesterfield, 29 August 2014

England (0) 1 *(Ndukwu 42)*

Portugal (1) 2 *(Moreto 14, Tavares 73)*   1073

England: Oxborough; Yates (Collinge 40), Humphreys, Johnson, Coulson (DaSilva 57), Wright (Maddox 40), Davies, Gribben, Patching (Holland 57), Ndukwu (Willock 78), Hector-Ingram (Hinds 72).

Burton, 31 August 2014

England (3) 4 *(Holland 13, Hinds 18, 63, Hector-Ingram 23)*

Italy (1) 3 *(Matarese 11, Llamas Acuna 48, Mazzocchi 78)*

England: Woolston (Oxborough 72); Yates (DaSilva 40), Johnson, Collinge, Coulson, Davies (Wright 57), Maddox (Patching 40), Holland (Gribben 40), Hinds, Willock, Hector-Ingram (Ndukwu 40).

2015 EUROPEAN CHAMPIONSHIP

QUALIFYING ROUND

Kouklia, 25 October 2014

Cyprus (0) 1 *(Papakonstantinou 80 (pen))*

England (1) 4 *(Ndukwu 13, 45, 58, Edwards M 61)*

England: Woolston; Yates, Oxford, Humphreys, DaSilva, Davies (Collinge 64), Patching, Holland (Wakefield 55), Edwards M, Willock (Maddox 60), Ndukwu.

Paphos, 27 October 2014

England (1) 1 *(N'mecha 14)*

Macedonia (0) 0

England: Woolston; Yates, Humphreys, Collinge, Coulson, Davies, Kane, Wakefield (Holland 56), Maddox (Patching 72), Ndukwu, N'mecha (Willock 62).

Paphos, 30 October 2014

England (2) 3 *(Willock 30, Patching 39, DaSilva 69)*

France 0) 1 *(Karamoh 62)*

England: Woolston; Yates, Oxford, Collinge, DaSilva, Davies, Patching (N'mecha 36), Holland, Edwards M (Kane 66), Willock (Coulson 66), Ndukwu.

ELITE ROUND GROUP 6 (ENGLAND)

Burton, 21 March 2015

England (1) 3 *(Wright 3, Collinge 57, Ndukwu 62)*

Norway (1) 1 *(Risa 11)*   650

England: Woolston; Yates, Oxford, 6 Collinge, Edun, Davies, Wright, Holland (Sterling 77), Willock (Edwards M 72), Ndukwu, Ugbo (Nmecha 68).

Chesterfield, 23 March 2015

England (3) 3 *(Oxford 20, Holland 36, Rom 38 (og))*

Slovenia (0) 1 *(Mlaka 65)*   3126

England: Woolston, Yates, Oxford, Suliman, DaSilva, Davies, Wright, Holland (Nmecha 64), Willock (Patching 48), Ndukwu (Edwards M 54), Sterling.

Burton, 26 March 2015

Romania (1) 1 *(Petre 13)*

England (1) 2 *(Ugbo 7, 53)*   452

England: Huffer; Yates (Oxford 68), Collinge, Suliman, Edun, Davies, Patching, Wright (DaSilva 40), Edwards M, Nmecha, Ugbo (Willock 60).

FINALS (BULGARIA) GROUP D

Burgas, 7 May 2015

Italy (0) 0

England (0) 1 *(Edwards 47)*   2530

England: Woolston; Yates, Oxford, Collinge, DaSilva, Kane, Davies (Arnold 74), Holland, Willock, Ndukwu (Edwards M 41), Mavididi (Ugbo 64).

Stara Zagora, 10 May 2015

Netherlands (0) 1 *(Boultam 56 (pen))*

England (1) 1 *(Fosu-Mensa 18 (og))*   1063

England: Woolston; Yates, Oxford, Collinge, Dasilva, Arnold, Kane, Edun (Wright 77), Edwards M (Ndukwu 62), Willock, Mavididi (Ugbo 55).

Stara Zagora, 13 May 2015

England (0) 1 *(Edwards 71)*

Republic of Ireland (0) 0   974

England: Woolston; Yates, Oxford, Collinge (Suliman 49), Dasilva, Kane, Wright, Holland, Edwards M, Ndukwu (Willock 41), Ugbo (Mavididi 72).

QUARTER-FINALS

Burgas, 16 May 2015

Russia (1) 1 *(Tataev 29)*

England (0) 0   2085

England: Woolston; Yates, Oxford, Collinge (Suliman 64), Dasilva, Kane, Davies, Holland (Edun 60), Edwards M, Willock, Mavididi (Ugbo 69).

WORLD CUP, CHILE 2015 PLAY-OFF QUALIFIER

Sliven, 19 May 2015

Spain (0) 0

England (0) 0   984

England: Woolston (Huffer 77); Yates, Oxford, Suliman, Dasilva, Arnold (Wright 60), Davies, Kane, Edwards M, Willock, Ndukwu (Ugbo 65).

England won 5-3 on penalties.

NIKE U17 INTERNATIONAL TOURNAMENT

Sarasota, 28 November 2014

USA (2) 3 *(Zendejas 11, Pulisic 40 (pen), 48)*

England (0) 1 *(Wright 90)*

England: Whiteman; Yates (Wright 80), Collinge (Oxford 70), Humphreys, Edun, Davies (Stabana 80), Patching, Holland (Ugbo 70), N'mecha (Phillips 61), Ndukwu, Hector-Ingram.

Sarasota, 30 November 2014

England (1) 2 *(Ndukwu 43, Phillips 90)*

Brazil (0) 2 *(Lincoln 84, Evander 87)*

England: Woolston; Arnold! (82), Suliman, Oxford, Edun (Yates 46), Phillips, Wright, Davies (Collinge 46), Edwards M (Hector-Ingram 88), Ugbo (Stabana 84), Ndukwu.

Sarasota, 2 December 2014
England (1) 2 *(Ugbo 29, Hector-Ingram 76)*
Australia (0) 1 *(Joice 57)*
England: Whiteman (Woolston 45); Stabana, Suliman, Humphreys (Collinge 68), Edun (Yates 75), Phillips, Wright (Patching 45), Ugbo, Edwards M (Davies 58), Holland, N'mecha (Hector-Ingram 58).

ALGARVE TOURNAMENT
Parchal, 13 February 2015
England (0) 0
Netherlands (5) 7 *(Fernandes 5, Humphreys (og) 10, Bijleveld 13, Dilrosum 18, 39, 79, Grot 70)*
England: Oxborough; Stabana, Sulliman, Humphreys, Coulson, Nabay (Collinge 41), Wright (Ronan 41), Holland, Gribben, Ndukwu (Green 71), Hector-Ingram (N'mecha 62).

Ferreiras, 15 February 2015
Portugal (0) 1 *(Vieira 55)*
England (1) 1 *(Sterling 26)*
England: Huffer; Yates, Humphreys (Suliman 41), Collinge, Edun, Patching, Green (Gribbin 62), Ronan (Nabay 41), Edwards M (Wright 62), N'mecha (Hector-Ingram 70), Sterling (Ndukwu 73).

Faro, 17 February 2015
Germany (2) 2 *(Schmidt 8, Dorsch 16)*
England (0) 0
England: Huffer (Oxborough 67); Yates (Stabana 67), Coulson (Edun 41), Oxford, Suliman, Patching (N'mecha 59), Gribbin (Holland 50), Wright (Green 50), Edwards M (Collinge 59), Sterling, Ndukwu (Hector-Ingram 41).

ENGLAND UNDER-18

FRIENDLIES
Leigh, 3 September 2014
England (3) 4 *(Armstrong 24, 43, Sims 38, Mitchell 51)*
Netherlands (1) 1 *(Slabbekoorn)*
England: Howes; Egbo, Fry, Taylor Moore (Rossiter 59), Connolly, Cook (Ojo 45), Ledson (Clarke-Salter 59), Sims (Kenny 81), Cooke, Mitchell (Tafari Moore 66), Armstrong (Solanke 66).

Bury, 5 September 2014
England (1) 3 *(Connolly 42, 76, Solanke 56)*
Netherlands (0) 1 *(Da Cruz 62)*
England: Woodman; Tafari Moore, Clarke-Salter (Dael Fry 63), Taylor Moore, Connolly (Egbo 89), Ledson, Kenny, Onomah (Sims 70), Solanke, Armstrong (Cooke 89), Ojo (Mitchell 89).

Caorle, 24 September 2014
Italy (0) 2 *(Edera 56, Minelli 58)*
England (0) 0
England: Woodman (Lewis 86); Waler-Peters, Fry, Clarke-Salter (Adarabioyo 61), Lowe, Walsh, Connolly, Mahoney (Fox 61), Cooke (Abraham 66), Mitchell (Dowell 66), Solanke.

Gdynia, 15 November 2014
Poland (1) 2 *(Walski 42, Olczyk 74)*
England (0) 3 *(Connolly 50, Maitland-Niles 60, Armstrong 69)*
England: Woodman; Waler-Peters, Taylor Moore, Adarabioyo, Connolly, Ledson, Maitland-Niles, Ahearne-Grant (Solanke 79), Rashford (Onomah 79), Sims (Ojo 70), Armstrong.

Gdansk, 17 November 2014
Poland (1) 1 *(Pytlik 10)*
England (1) 4 *(Solanke 11, Ledson 50, Oje 52, 71)*
England: Howes; Connolly (Walker-Peters 72), Taylor Moore, Clarke-Salter, Lowe, Walsh, Ledson (Maitland-Niles 72), Onomah (Sims 83), Ojo (Rashford 83), Armstrong (Ahearne-Grant 58), Solanke.

Burton, 26 March 2015
England (0) 1 *(Armstrong 48)*
Switzerland (0) 0
England: Norman; Kenny, Adarabioyo (Clarke-Salter 46), Taylor Moore, Connolly, Ledson, Reed (Maitland-Niles 81), Sims (Chapman 81), Ojo (Onomah 64), Armstrong, Solanke (Abraham 64).

Walsall, 28 March 2015
England (3) 6 *(Taylor Moore 4, Armstrong 16, 38, Abraham 18, 88, Solanke 85)*
Switzerland (0) 1 *(Ajeti 51)*
England: Howes; Walker-Peters, Taylor Moore, Clarke-Salter, Lowe, Amos, Maitland-Niles (Sims 85), Onomah (Reed 50), Chapman (Ojo 67), Armstrong (Solanke 50), Abraham.

Moscow, 8 June 2015
Russia (0) 0
England (0) 2 *(Armstrong 63 (pen), Roberts 67)*
England: Woodman; Walker-Peters, Fry, Adarabioyo, Connolly, Walsh, Reed, Barlaser, Roberts (Ojo 70), Armstrong (Ahearne-Grant 85), Abraham.

Moscow, 10 June 2015
Russia (1) 2 *(Melkaze 8, Arinov 90)*
England (0) 1 *(Ojo 80)*
England: Woodman (Norman 46); Connolly (Walker-Peters 64), Adarabioyo (Fry 46), Moore, Lowe, Amos, Reed (Barlaser 57), Dowell (Abraham 70), Ojo, Armstrong (Roberts 64), Ahearne-Grant.

ENGLAND UNDER-19

FRIENDLIES
Oberhausen, 8 September 2014
Germany (0) 1 *(Werner 59)*
England (1) 1 *(Fewster 35)*
England: Gunn; Smith-Brown (Whatmough 69), Gomez, Galloway, Chilwell (Aina 59), Morris, Alli (Winks 69), Colkett (Loftus-Cheek 59), Kiwomya (Gray 59), Roberts (Barker 59), Fewster.

Rotherham, 14 November 2014
England (2) 3 *(Brown 15, 20, Loftus-Cheek 64)*
Italy (0) 0   9125
England: Gunn (Smith 76); Aina (Dickie 72), Galloway, Smith-Brown, Chilwell (Bryan 72), Morris (Winks 62), Alli (Colkett 62), Loftus-Cheek, Barker, Brown (Fewster 72), Roberts.

2015 EUROPEAN CHAMPIONSHIP
QUALIFYING ROUND (LUXEMBOURG)
Grevenmacher, 10 October 2014

England (1) 3 *(Loftus-Cheek 30, Roberts 53, Fewster 66 (pen))*

Belarus (0) 0   180
England: Woodman; Smith-Brown, Aina, Galloway, Chilwell, Alli (Winks 73), Morris, Loftus-Cheek (Colkett 78), Roberts, Brown (Fewster 56), Barker.

Luxembourg City, 12 October 2014

Luxembourg (0) 0

England (5) 8 *(Loftus-Cheek 7, 50, Colkett 13, Barker 21 (pen), 44, Roberts 24 (pen), 90, Fewster 88)*   852
England: Smith; Aina, Burke, Galloway (Dickie 46), Smith-Brown, Colkett, Winks, Loftus-Cheek (Morris 67), Roberts, Fewster, Barker (Kiwomya 46).

Luxembourg City, 15 October 2014

England (2) 4 *(Roberts 9, Fewster 31, 85, Barker 81)*

Belgium (1) 2 *(Cools 16, Oulare 65)*   450
England: Woodman; Smith-Brown, Aina, Galloway, Chilwell, Alli (Colkett 82), Morris, Loftus-Cheek, Roberts, Fewster (Kiwomya 87), Barker (Winks 82).

ENGLAND UNDER-20

FRIENDLIES
Telford, 5 September 2014

England (0) 6 *(Aarons 54, Josh Murphy 71, Robinson 73, 89, Baker 78 (pen), Thomas 85)*

Romania (0) 0
England: Walton (Pym 79); Hayden, Ball, Facey (Jones 79), Targett, Baker (Harrop 79), Swift (Reed 63), Robinson, Aarons (Grimes 79), Ibe (Josh Murphy 63), Akpom (Thomas 63).

Bournemouth, 12 November 2014

England (1) 2 *(Akpom 15, Cargill 85)*

Canada (0) 2 *(Petrasso 48, Hamilton 90)*   6986
England: Pym; Facey (Ball 23), Jones (Hause 45), Cargill, Targett (Reed 46), Digby, Baker (Josh Murphy 61), Harrop (Thomas 61), Grimes, Akpom (Wilson 61), Swift (Ibe 61).

Coimbra, 17 November 2014

Portugal (0) 1 *(Martins 60)*   **England (1) 1** *(Targett 29)*
England: Walton; Iorfa, Ball, Hause, Targett, Baker, Reed, Harrop (Akpom 69), Josh Murphy, Wilson, Ibe (Thomas 59).
England won 4-3 on penalties.

Barnet, 25 March 2015

England (0) 1 *(Akpom 79 (pen))* **Mexico (0) 1** *(Ramirez 48)*
England: Walton; Iorfa, Cargill, Hause, Odubajo, Baker (Swift 69), Hanson (Reed 74), Osborn (Grimes 69), Barmby, Akpom, Robinson.
England won 4-2 on penalties.

Plymouth, 29 March 2015

England (1) 2 *(Swift 44, Thomas 68)*

USA (0) 1 *(Tall 76)*   11,406
England: Pickford; Obubajo (Robinson 66), Ball, Turnbull, Toffolo, Reed, Grimes, Stephens, Mowatt (Akpom 79), Swift (Hanson 88), Thomas.

FOUR NATIONS TOURNAMENT
Heerenveen, 9 October 2014

Germany (0) 0   **England (1) 1** *(Sule 34 (og))*
England: Pym; Hayden, Ball, Hause, Targett, Reed (Rothwell 84), Grimes, Digby, Thomas, Akpom, Robinson.

Heerenveen, 11 October 2014

Netherlands (1) 2 *(de Wijs 30, Vloet 80 (pen))*

England (1) 3 *(Long 45, Akpom 89, 90)*
England: Walton; Hayden (Akpom 87), Ball (Robinson 75), Jones, Dabo (Hause 61), Houghton, Pearson (Reed 90), Rothwell, Jacob Murphy (Thomas 87), Swift, Long.

ELITE ROUND GROUP 7 (FRANCE)
Bayeux, 26 March 2015

England (2) 3 *(Brown 33, Pedersen M (og), Smith-Brown 82)*

Denmark (2) 2 *(Ingvartsen 6, Skov 41)*   1359
England: Gunn; Smith-Brown, Chilwell, Winks, Galloway, Gomez, Roberts (Aina 87), Loftus-Cheek, Brown, Colkett, Gray.

Bayeux, 28 March 2015

England (1) 1 *(Smith-Brown 37)*

Azerbajan (0) 0   1394
England: Woodman; Aina, Gomez, Galloway, Smith-Brown, Kuhl, Cook (Colkett 79), Roberts (Gray 67), Loftus-Cheek, Kiwomya, Fewster (Brown 83).

Saint Lo, 31 March 2015

France (1) 2 *(Guirassy 31, Cornet 50)*

England (1) 1 *(Roberts 80)*   3372
England: Gunn; Smith-Brown (Aina 76), Gomez, Galloway, Chilwell, Winks, Roberts, Loftus-Cheek, Colkett (Fewster 82), Gray, Brown.

TOULON TOURNAMENT
Besancon, 28 May 2015

England (2) 3 *(Gray 8, Watmore 24, Akpom 78)*

Morocco (3) 3 *(Hajhouj 13, Bencharki 14, 39)*
England: Walton; Iorfa, Stephens, Cargill (Odubajo 46), Hause, Grimes, Baker, Hanson (Reed 46), Watmore (Akpom 63), Wilson (Robinson 73), Gray.

Besancon, 30 May 2015

England (1) 2 *(Akpom 10, Robinson 50)*

Ivory Coast (0) 1 *(Kone 77)*
England: Pickford; Odubajo, Stephens, Hause, Hayden (Gray 64), Grimes, Reed, Watmore (Aarons 73), Robinson (Baker 66), Akpom (Wilson 70), Thomas.

Aubagne, 3 June 2015

Mexico (1) 2 *(Bueno 42, Zuniga 70)*

England (1) 1 *(Watmore 15)*
England: Pickford; Iorfa (Wilson 77), Stephens, Hause, Odubajo, Swift (Baker 61), Reed, Grimes, Watmore (Robinson 61), Akpom, Gray (Aarons 61).

Besancon, 5 June 2015

England (1) 3 *(Aarons 39, Baker 51, Zheng Wei (og) 59)*

China (0) 1 *(Guo Yi 54)*
England: Walton; Hayden, Cargill (Hause 55), Stephens, Odubajo, Hanson (Reed 62), Baker, Swift, Robinson, Akpom, Aarons (Watmore 55).

3RD/4TH PLACE PLAY-OFF
Toulon, 7 June 2015

England (1) 1 *(Hause 10)*

USA (1) 2 *(Hernandez 8 (pen), Joya 66 (pen))*
England: Walton (Pickford 41); Stephens (Baker 75), Cargill, Hause, Iorfa, Grimes, Hanson (Reed 63), Watmore, Swift, Aarons (Robinson 49), Thomas (Akpom 49).

SCHOOLS FOOTBALL 2014–15

BOODLES INDEPENDENT SCHOOLS FA CUP 2014–15

After extra time.

PRELIMINARY ROUND

Hurstpierpoint v Box Hill	1-3
Sherborne v Lingfield Notre Dame	2-3
Stockport GS v Cheadle Hulme	3-0

FIRST ROUND

ACS Cobham v Haberdashers' Aske's	1-3
Aldenham v Forest	2-3
Bedales v Latymer Upper	0-12
Birkdale v John Lyon	2-0
Bournemouth Collegiate v Bede's	1-6
Box Hill v Colfe's	2-4
Bradfield v Norwich	10-0
Brentwood v Alleyn's	5-1
Bury GS v Harrow	0-1
Chigwell v Trinity	1-3
City of London v Whitgift	3-4*
Dover College v Eton	0-9
Dulwich College v Frensham Heights	5-0
Grammar School at Leeds v Ackworth	3-0
Hampton v Oldham Hulme GS	11-0
Highgate v Ibstock Place	3-2
Hill House v Wolverhampton GS	3-4
KES Witley v Lingfield Notre Dame	1-0
King's School, Chester v Canford	5-0
Lancing v The Harrodian	3-1*
LVS Ascot v Shrewsbury	0-6
Malvern v St. Bede's College	0-5
Manchester GS v Charterhouse	2-3
Millfield v The Grange	2-0
Repton v Ardingly	0-1
RGS Newcastle v Bolton	0-1
Royal Russell v Haileybury	0-2
St. Columba's v Winchester	0-1
St. John's School, Leatherhead v St. Edmund's, Canterbury	8-1
Stockport GS v Tonbridge	1-2
University College School v Kimbolton	3-1
Westminster v Bedford Modern	0-2

SECOND ROUND

Ardingly v KES Witley	12-0
Bedford Modern v Bradfield	1-7
Bolton v St. Bede's College	0-1
Brentwood v King's School, Chester	1-0
Charterhouse v Winchester	2-0
Forest v Colfe's	7-1
Grammar School at Leeds v Dulwich College	2-2*
(Dulwich College won 4-3 on penalties)	
Haberdashers' Aske's v Wolverhampton GS	3-1
Hampton v Millfield	2-1
Highgate v Birkdale	9-1
Lancing v Latymer Upper	2-4

Shrewsbury v Harrow	3-2
St. John's School, Leatherhead v Bede's	0-5
Tonbridge v Haileybury	6-1
Trinity v University College School	4-2
Whitgift v Eton	2-0

THIRD ROUND

Ardingly v Charterhouse	2-2*
(Ardingly won 3-1 on penalties)	
Bede's v Hampton	1-2
Dulwich College v Forest	1-0
Highgate v Shrewsbury	4-3
Latymer Upper v Brentwood	4-0
Tonbridge v St. Bede's College	1-2
Trinity v Haberdashers' Aske's	3-1
Whitgift v Bradfield	1-3

FOURTH ROUND

Bradfield v Highgate	2-0
Hampton v Trinity	3-0
Latymer Upper v Ardingly	1-2
St Bede's College v Dulwich College	0-1

SEMI-FINALS

Bradfield v Ardingly	1-3
Dulwich v Hampton	0-6

FINAL (at Milton Keynes Dons FC)

Ardingly (1) 4 *(Holmes, Hayes-Brown, Adomakoh, Cassidy)*
Hampton (0) 1 *(Heywood)*

Ardingly: D. Bonilla-Rasmussen, G. Southgate, A. Summerfield, M. Penfold, M. Price, J. Adomokoh, C. Holman, O. Haynes-Brown, C. Meegan, T. Webb, F. Wood.
Substitutes: T. Cassidy, M. Makepeace, O. McConnell, O. Pleasants, D. Adomokoh.
Hampton: G. Roberts, T. Godfray, H. Simmons, C. Selwood, H. Heywood, M. Wisdom, T. Phillipson, O. Brightman, J. Parrott, C. Parmiter, D. Sparks.
Substitutes: C. Mears, C. Seth, L. Smith, O. Mayhew, C. Bloomer.
Referee: H. Webb (Yorkshire).

INVESTEC ISFA U15 CUP FINAL

Hampton v Manchester Grammar School	3-2*
(at Burton Albion FC)	

INVESTEC ISFA U13 CUP FINAL

Whitgift v City of London	4-0
(at Burton Albion FC)	

UNIVERSITY FOOTBALL 2015

131st UNIVERSITY MATCH

(Sunday 8 March 2015, at Abbey Stadium, Cambridge, attendance 1351)

Cambridge (1) 1   Oxford (0) 1

Oxford won 6-5 on penalties

Cambridge: Warne; Longden, Hilton, Wolstenhulme, Crooks, Rawson (Painter 67), Grubic (Gorringe 90), Hickey, May, Forde, Gaskell (Yerolemou 90).
Scorer: Forde 35.

Oxford: Szreter; Gomarsall (Oulton 84), Hokinson, Moneke, Dark, Tsaptsinos (Essman 73), Smith M (Tunningley 61), Smith W, Tozer, Rubenstein, Beck-Friis.
Scorer: Rubeinstein 75.

Referee: Neil Swarbrick (Lancashire).

Oxford have won 51 games, Cambridge 50 games and 30 drawn.   Oxford have scored 206 goals, Cambridge 205 goals.

WOMEN'S SUPER LEAGUE 2014

FA WOMEN'S SUPER LEAGUE 1 TABLE 2014

	P	W	D	L	F	A	GD	Pts
Liverpool Ladies	14	7	5	2	19	10	9	26
Chelsea Ladies	14	8	2	4	23	16	7	26
Birmingham C Ladies	14	7	4	3	20	14	6	25
Arsenal Ladies	14	6	3	5	24	21	3	21
Manchester C Women	14	6	1	7	13	16	−3	19
Notts Co Ladies	14	4	6	4	12	8	4	18
Bristol Academy Women	14	5	1	8	18	24	−6	16
Everton Ladies	14	0	4	10	10	30	−20	4

FA WOMEN'S SUPER LEAGUE 2 TABLE 2014

	P	W	D	L	F	A	GD	Pts
Sunderland Ladies	18	15	2	1	47	15	32	47
Doncaster R Belles	18	14	3	1	56	14	42	45
Reading Women	18	13	2	3	60	21	39	41
Aston Villa Ladies	18	9	3	6	25	26	−1	30
Yeovil T Ladies	18	6	4	8	27	26	1	22
Durham Women	18	5	3	10	19	32	−13	18
Watford Ladies	18	5	3	10	22	37	−15	18
Millwall Lionesses	18	4	3	11	20	36	−16	15
Oxford U Women	18	3	3	12	16	44	−28	12
London Bees	18	2	2	14	16	57	−41	8

WOMEN'S SUPER LEAGUE CONTINENTAL CUP 2014

GROUP 1

Arsenal Ladies v Watford Ladies	3-0
London Bees v Millwall Lionesses	0-0
Reading Women v Chelsea Ladies	1-2
Millwall Lionesses v Reading Women	1-1
Watford Ladies v Chelsea Ladies	1-5
Chelsea Ladies v Millwall Lionesses	4-0
London Bees v Watford Ladies	1-3
Reading Women v Arsenal Ladies	2-0
Arsenal Ladies v Chelsea Ladies	3-0
London Bees v Reading Women	1-8
Watford Ladies v Millwall Lionesses	1-2
Arsenal Ladies v London Bees	7-0
Reading Women v Watford Ladies	A-W
Chelsea Ladies v London Bees	13-0
Millwall Lionesses v Arsenal Ladies	0-4

Group 1 Table	P	W	D	L	F	A	GD	Pts
Chelsea Ladies	5	4	0	1	24	5	19	12
Arsenal Ladies	5	4	0	1	17	2	15	12
Watford Ladies	5	2	0	3	5	11	−6	6
Millwall Lionesses	5	1	2	2	3	10	−7	5
Reading Women (−3)	5	2	1	2	12	4	8	4
London Bees	5	0	1	4	2	31	−29	1

GROUP 2

Liverpool Ladies v Everton Ladies	0-0
Sunderland Ladies v Durham Women	3-0
Doncaster R Belles v Manchester C Women	2-1
Liverpool Ladies v Sunderland Ladies	6-0
Durham Women v Doncaster R Belles	1-3
Manchester C Women v Everton Ladies	1-0
Everton Ladies v Durham Women	3-0
Manchester C Women v Liverpool Ladies	2-1
Doncaster R Belles v Sunderland Ladies	0-2
Durham Women v Liverpool Ladies	1-7
Everton Ladies v Doncaster R Belles	3-1
Manchester C Women v Sunderland Ladies	2-0
Liverpool Ladies v Doncaster R Belles	3-2
Durham Women v Manchester C Women	0-3
Sunderland Ladies v Everton Ladies	0-2

Group 2 Table	P	W	D	L	F	A	GD	Pts
Manchester C Women	5	4	0	1	9	3	6	12
Liverpool Ladies	5	3	1	1	17	5	12	10
Everton Ladies	5	3	1	1	8	2	6	10
Doncaster R Belles	5	2	0	3	8	10	−2	6
Sunderland Ladies	5	2	0	3	5	10	−5	6
Durham Women	5	0	0	5	2	19	−17	0

GROUP 3

Notts Co Ladies v Aston Villa Ladies	5-0
Bristol Academy Women v Oxford U Women	9-2
Yeovil T Ladies v Birmingham C Ladies	1-2
Notts Co Ladies v Bristol Academy Women	1-1
Yeovil T Ladies v Aston Villa Ladies	2-0
Aston Villa Ladies v Birmingham C Ladies	0-2
Bristol Academy Women v Yeovil T Ladies	0-0
Oxford U Women v Notts Co Ladies	0-4
Birmingham C Ladies v Oxford U Women	2-0
Bristol Academy Women v Aston Villa Ladies	2-1
Birmingham C Ladies v Notts Co Ladies	0-2
Oxford U Women v Yeovil T Ladies	0-2
Yeovil T Ladies v Notts Co Ladies	0-4
Aston Villa Ladies v Oxford U Women	1-0
Birmingham C Ladies v Bristol Academy Women	0-5

Group 3 Table	P	W	D	L	F	A	GD	Pts
Notts Co Ladies	5	4	1	0	16	1	15	13
Bristol Academy Women	5	3	2	0	17	4	13	11
Birmingham C Ladies	5	3	0	2	6	8	−2	9
Yeovil T Ladies	5	2	1	2	5	6	−1	7
Aston Villa Ladies	5	1	0	4	2	11	−9	3
Oxford U Women	5	0	0	5	2	18	−16	0

SEMI–FINALS

Arsenal Ladies v Notts Co Ladies	2-0
Manchester C Women v Chelsea Ladies	1-0

FINAL

Arsenal Ladies v Manchester C Women	0-1

FA WOMEN'S PREMIER LEAGUE 2014–15

FA WOMEN'S PREMIER LEAGUE NORTHERN DIVISION 2014–15

		Total						Home					Away					
		P	W	D	L	F	A	W	D	L	F	A	W	D	L	F	A	GD	Pts
1	Sheffield Ladies	22	19	1	2	76	19	11	0	0	44	8	8	1	2	32	11	57	58
2	Coventry C*	22	18	2	2	64	16	9	1	1	34	9	9	1	1	30	7	48	50
3	Blackburn R	22	13	3	6	46	34	9	0	2	28	14	4	3	4	18	20	12	42
4	Bradford C	22	11	6	5	49	28	4	5	2	27	13	7	1	3	22	15	21	39
5	Huddersfield T	22	8	5	9	53	65	2	4	5	25	32	6	1	4	28	33	-12	29
6	Derby Co	22	8	3	11	45	56	6	0	5	24	24	2	3	6	21	32	-11	27
7	Stoke C	22	8	2	12	38	38	6	1	4	18	14	2	1	8	20	24	0	26
8	Preston NE	22	7	5	10	41	46	2	3	6	19	29	5	2	4	22	17	-5	26
9	Nottingham F	22	7	2	13	34	52	4	1	6	14	22	3	1	7	20	30	-18	23
10	Sporting Club Alb	22	5	6	11	23	36	1	3	7	10	20	4	3	4	13	16	-13	21
11	Newcastle U	22	5	5	12	33	50	2	3	6	15	23	3	2	6	18	27	-17	20
12	Wolverhampton W	22	2	2	18	17	79	2	0	9	12	41	0	2	9	5	38	-62	8

*Coventry C deducted 6 points.

FA WOMEN'S PREMIER LEAGUE SOUTHERN DIVISION 2014–15

		Total						Home					Away					
		P	W	D	L	F	A	W	D	L	F	A	W	D	L	F	A	GD	Pts
1	Portsmouth Ladies	22	18	2	2	62	25	9	1	1	31	14	9	1	1	31	11	37	56
2	Brighton & HA	22	17	2	3	63	22	10	0	1	31	8	7	2	2	32	14	41	53
3	Charlton Ath	22	15	3	4	88	34	9	1	1	51	13	6	2	3	37	21	54	48
4	Cardiff C	22	14	3	5	69	26	7	2	2	31	10	7	1	3	38	16	43	45
5	Tottenham H	22	12	3	7	60	40	7	2	2	37	17	5	1	5	23	23	20	39
6	West Ham U	22	10	5	7	39	30	4	3	4	20	15	6	2	3	19	15	9	35
7	Lewes	22	6	3	13	31	37	2	2	7	10	15	4	1	6	21	22	-6	21
8	Copsewood	22	6	2	14	22	66	4	1	6	11	28	2	1	8	11	38	-44	20
9	QPR*	22	6	4	12	28	42	3	2	6	15	22	3	2	6	13	20	-14	19
10	Plymouth Arg	22	4	6	12	25	60	4	3	4	16	23	0	3	8	9	37	-35	18
11	Gillingham	22	4	3	15	28	65	3	1	7	17	33	1	2	8	11	32	-37	15
12	Keynsham T	22	1	2	19	26	94	1	1	9	15	58	0	1	10	11	36	-68	5

*QPR deducted 3 points.

WOMEN'S PREMIER LEAGUE CUP 2014–15

PRELIMINARY ROUND

*After extra time.

Cambridge v QPR	1-4
Denham U v Charlton Ath	0-3
Tottenham H v Tranmere R	1-0

Byes: Keynsham T, Steel City W, Nottingham F, Leicester C Women, Portsmouth Ladies, Mossley Hill, Wolverhampton W, Sheffield Ladies, Forest Green R, Blackburn R, C & K Basildon, Sporting Club Alb, Bradford C, Newcastle U, Morecambe, Derby Co, Brighton & HA, Plymouth Arg, Luton T, Norton & Stockton Ancient, Mansfield T, Ipswich T, Guiseley Vixens, Cardiff C, Lewes, FC Reedswood, Gillingham, Coventry C.

FIRST ROUND

Derby Co v Brighton & HA	0-4
Forest Green R v Blackburn R	0-7
Gillingham v Coventry C	0-2
Guiseley Vixens v Cardiff C	0-9
Keynsham T (walkover) v Steel City W	
Lewes v Reedswood	3-0
Mansfield T v Ipswich T	2-3
Mossley Hill v Wolverhampton W	3-2*
Newcastle U v Morecambe	2-1
Norton & Stockton Ancient v Charlton Ath	0-7
Nottingham F v Leicester C	3-1
Plymouth Arg v Luton T	5-0
Portsmouth Ladies v Larkhall Ath	7-1
QPR v C & K Basildon	1-1
C & K Basildon won 9-8 on penalties.	
Sheffield Ladies v Tottenham H	1-0
Sporting Club Alb v Bradford C	1-0

SECOND ROUND

C & K Basildon v Sporting Club Alb	2-0
Ipswich T v Cardiff C	0-9
Keynsham T v Nottingham F	1-2
Lewes v Coventry C	3-6
Newcastle U v Brighton & HA	0-1*
Portsmouth Ladies v Mossley Hill	6-1
Sheffield Ladies v Blackburn R	4-0
Plymouth Arg v Charlton Ath	1-7

QUARTER-FINALS

Brighton & HA v Charlton Ath	0-2
Cardiff C v Coventry C	4-3*
Sheffield Ladies v C & K Basildon	5-0
Nottingham F v Portsmouth Ladies	2-3

SEMI-FINALS

Charlton Ath v Cardiff C	2-0
Portsmouth Ladies v Sheffield Ladies	0-2

FA WOMEN'S PREMIER LEAGUE CUP FINAL 2015

Nuneaton, Sunday 3 May 2015

Charlton Ath (0) 0

Sheffield Ladies (0) 0

Charlton Ath: Lynch; Flack, Dixson, Paye (Southgate 106), Coombs, Clifford, Pittuck, Shepherd, Whinnett (Howlett 95), Graham, Harrison.
Sheffield Ladies: Wallhead; Murphy, Cox, Ashton, Goodman, Lee, Parkin (Michalska 50), Ward (Beanland 96), Johnson, Giampalma, McIver (Gilliatt 74).
aet; Charlton Ath won 4-2 on penalties.

THE FA WOMEN'S CUP 2014–15

*After extra time.

PRELIMINARY ROUND

Rutherford v Prudhoe T	4-1
(Tie awarded to Prudhoe T - Rutherford removed)	
Lowick U v Blyth T Lions	6-7*
(5-5 at the end of normal time)	
Birtley St Joseph v Tynedale	2-7
Brighouse T v Keighley Oaks	10-1
Wakefield Ladies v Malet Lambert	3-5
Carlisle U v CMB Ladies	2-3
Rise Park v Long Eaton U	1-5
Nettleham v Arnold T	13-0
Oadby & Wigston v Dronfield T	2-1
Coventrians v The New Saints	0-4
March T U v Roade	1-7
Raunds T v Kettering T	4-2*
(2-2 at the end of normal time)	
Sandy v Rothwell Corinthians	0-1
AFC Sudbury Ladies v Lowestoft T	1-12
Colchester T (walkover) v Takeley (withdrawn)	
Bury T v Brentwood T	1-1*
(Brentwood T won 4-3 on penalties)	
Sawbridgeworth T v Stevenage	1-0
KIKK U v Barking	2-3
Chesham U v Old Actonians	0-8
Leverstock Green v Headington	6-0
London Corinthians v South Park	12-1
Burgess Hill v Abbey Rangers	4-2
Surrey Eagles v Battersea & Wandsworth	1-2
Regents Park Rangers v Carshalton Ath	0-5
Hassocks v Eastbourne	0-1
Poole T v Aldershot T	4-0
Southampton Women v Fleet T	2-3
Brislington v Downend Flyers	0-2
Bristol Ladies Union v Truro C	0-1
Wootton Bassett T v Ilminster T	2-4
Frome T v Cheltenham Civil Service	2-0
Bridgwater T v Launceston	6-0

FIRST ROUND QUALIFYING

Kader Ladies v York C	0-6
Tynedale v Forest Hall	12-0
Peterlee RA v Prudhoe T	4-2
Birtley T v Middlesbrough Lionesses	4-2
Boldon v Blyth T Lions	4-3
Whitley Bay v Ashington Woodhorn Lane	6-0
Ossett Alb v Wetherby Ath	3-8*
(3-3 at the end of normal time)	
Malet Lambert v Farsley Ladies	0-3
Sheffield W v Handsworth	4-1
Brighouse Ath v Brighouse T	0-2
Hull C v Bradford Park Avenue	12-0
Woolton v Middleton Ath	2-1
Blackpool Wren R v CMB Ladies	10-1
Bury Girls & Ladies v Burnley Ladies	2-8
Merseyrail Bootle v Chester C	10-0
Mersey Girls v Workington Reds	2-1
Blackpool Ladies v Penrith Ladies	2-3*
(2-2 at the end of normal time)	
City of Manchester v Accrington Girls & Ladies	4-8
Crewe Alexandra v Birkenhead	5-2
Ruddington Village v Oadby & Wigston	6-5
Sandiacre T v Nettleham	0-5
West Bridgford v Long Eaton U	0-3
Teversal v Ellistown	0-7
Walsall v Malvern T	3-0
Leamington Lions v The New Saints	1-3
Allscott v Lye T	5-4*
(2-2 at the end of normal time)	
Stone Dominoes v Bilbrook	3-4
Brereton T v Crusaders	2-3
Kenilworth T v Coventry Ladies Development	1-0
Wyrley v Folly Lane	2-2*
(Wyrley won 3-2 on penalties)	
Burton Alb v Bedworth U	10-1
Newmarket T v Wymondham T	0-2
Rothwell Corinthians v Peterborough Northern Star	0-3
Great Shelford v Roade	7-3
Bar Hill v Huntingdon T	4-0
Fulbourn Institute v Raunds T	2-4

Stewarts & Lloyds Corby v Burton Park W	1-2
Brentwood T v West Billericay	2-1
Southendian v Colchester T	2-3
Lowestoft T v Billericay T	8-3
Haringey Bor v Long Lane	2-4
Barking v Sherrardswood	5-1
Garston v Colney Heath	1-3
Royston T v Sawbridgeworth T	4-0
Offley & Stopsley v Harvesters	6-0
Banbury U v Oxford C	0-3
Woodley U v Old Actonians	1-3
Brentford WFC v Hemel Hempstead T	9-2
Wealdstone v AFC Dunstable Ladies	3-2
Colne Valley v Maidenhead U	1-6
Newbury v Ascot U	1-0
Kidlington v Marlow	5-3
Leighton U Vixens v Leverstock Green	2-0
Bexhill U v Carshalton Ath	0-2
AFC Wimbledon Ladies v Fulham Foundation	4-7
London Corinthians v Eastbourne	6-0
Crawley Wasps v Worthing T	9-0
AFC Wimbledon Ladies Development v Rottingdean	
Village	3-0
Parkwood Rangers v Aylesford	2-1
Dartford Royals v Chertsey T	6-0
Maidstone U (walkover) v Battersea & Wandsworth	
(failed to fulfil fixture)	
Herne Bay v Anchorians	3-1
Eastbourne T v Burgess Hill T	7-0
Parley Sports v New Forest	10-3
Christchurch v Fleet T	2-1
Poole T v Basingstoke T	4-3*
(3-3 at the end of normal time)	
Torquay U v Ilminster	5-1
Frome T v Truro C	2-4
Swindon Spitfires v Downend Flyers	2-1*
(1-1 at the end of normal time)	
Pen Mill v Bridgwater T	0-5

SECOND ROUND QUALIFYING

Boldon v Peterlee RA	1-2
Birtley T v Tynedale	0-5
York C v Whitley Bay	0-1
Blackpool Wren R v Merseyrail Bootle	3-0
Accrington Girls & Ladies v Wetherby Ath	5-3
Hull C v Brighouse T	2-0
Farsley Ladies v Sheffield W	1-3
Woolton v Penrith Ladies	1-0
Burnley Ladies v Mersey Girls	2-1
Crewe Alexandra v Nettleham	3-1
The New Saints v Walsall	3-0
Ellistown v Wyrley	4-3*
(2-2 at the end of normal time)	
Raunds T v Crusaders	0-2
Allscott v Burton Alb	0-1
Bilbrook v Kenilworth T	3-0
Long Eaton U v Ruddington Village	1-5
Wymondham T v Great Shelford	2-0
Colchester T v Brentwood T	2-0
Burton Park W v Offley & Stopsley	4-1
Leighton U Vixens v Colney Heath	4-1
Lowestoft T v Wealdstone	8-0
Barking v Royston T	4-0*
(0-0 at the end of normal time)	
Peterborough Northern Star v Bar Hill	2-0*
(first tie 1-2, ordered to be replayed; 0-0 at 90 minutes)	
Long Lane v Brentford WFC	5-4
London Corinthians v Fulham Foundation	3-2
Carshalton Ath v Maidstone U	5-2
Eastbourne T v Parkwood Rangers	3-1
Crawley Wasps v Herne Bay	0-1
AFC Wimbledon Ladies Development v	
Dartford Royals	3-0
Maidenhead U v Old Actonians	2-2*
(Maidenhead U won 3-2 on penalties)	
Poole T v Oxford C	1-2*
(1-1 at the end of normal time)	
Christchurch v Parley Sports	1-4
Bridgwater T v Newbury	4-2
Torquay U (walkover) v Kidlington (withdrawn)	
Truro C v Swindon Spitfires	1-3

THIRD ROUND QUALIFYING

Morecambe v Burnley Ladies	4-3*
(3-3 at the end of normal time)	
Steel C W v Mossley Hill	3-4
Hull C v Chester-le-Street T	4-1
Whitley Bay v Liverpool Marshalls Feds	1-2
Guiseley Ladies (walkover) v Peterlee RA (unable to fulfil fixture)	
Chorley v Tynedale	10-1
Sheffield U Community v Woolton	2-0
Leeds v Tranmere R	2-0
Stockport Co v Accrington Girls & Ladies	4-0
Curzon Ashton v Norton & Stockton Ancients	2-6
Blackpool Wren R v Middlesbrough	6-2
Rotherham U v Sheffield W	8-0
Ruddington Village v Loughborough Foxes	2-13
The New Saints v Leafield Ath	2-0
Crewe Alexandra v Loughborough Students	3-5
Burton Park W v Leicester C Ladies	0-1*
(0-0 at the end of normal time)	
FC Reedswood Ladies v Burton Alb	4-0
Leicester C Women v Crusaders	7-0
Radcliffe Olympic v Ellistown	5-0
Mansfield T v Bilbrook	2-1
C&K Basildon v Barking	3-1
Norwich C v Lowestoft T	1-5
Ipswich T v Colchester T	2-1
Peterborough Northern Star v Milton Keynes Dons	1-2
Wymondham T v Cambridge Women's	1-4*
(1-1 at the end of normal time)	
Leighton U Vixens v Luton T	1-6
Crystal Palace v AFC Wimbledon Ladies Development	3-1*
(1-1 at the end of normal time)	
Long Lane v Herne Bay	0-4
Enfield T v Carshalton Ath	3-3*
(Carshalton Ath won 3-0 on penalties)	
Maidenhead U v Shanklin	3-0
London Corinthians v Denham U	4-0
Eastbourne T v Gosport Bor	5-0
Forest Green R v Oxford C	10-1
Larkhall Ath v Bridgwater T	5-0
Cheltenham T v St Nicholas	2-1
Parley Sports v Exeter C	3-5
Southampton Saints v Swindon Spitfires	2-0
Torquay U v Swindon T	2-4

FIRST ROUND

Chorley v Rotherham U	5-2
Liverpool Marshalls Feds v Stockport Co	3-0
Morecambe v Norton & Stockton Ancients	5-2
Blackpool Wren R v Sheffield U Community	2-3
Hull C v Mossley Hill	3-2
Leeds v Guiseley Ladies	1-0
Loughborough Students v Leicester C Women	0-1
The New Saints v Loughborough Foxes	5-2
Radcliffe Olympic v Mansfield T	3-1
Leicester C Ladies v FC Reedswood Ladies	1-4
Crystal Palace v Milton Keynes Dons	2-0
Bedford v Ipswich T	0-1
Luton T v Cambridge Women's	1-0
Eastbourne T v Chichester C	1-1*
(Eastbourne T won 5-4 on penalties)	
London Corinthians v Lowestoft T	2-3
C&K Basildon v Maidenhead U	5-2
Herne Bay v Carshalton Ath	0-1
Forest Green R v Southampton Saints	2-0
Cheltenham T v Exeter C	1-2
Larkhall Ath v Swindon T	0-0*
(Swindon T won 5-4 on penalties)	

SECOND ROUND

Morecambe v Sheffield U Community	4-2
Nottingham F v Preston NE	1-3
Coventry C v Leeds	3-1
Radcliffe Olympic v Hull C	3-1
Sporting Club Alb v Stoke C	0-2
Blackburn R v Liverpool Marshalls Feds	13-2
The New Saints v Derby Co	3-5
Chorley v FC Reedswood Ladies	2-3
Wolverhampton W v Newcastle U	2-1

Bradford C v Huddersfield T	3-2
Leicester C Women v Sheffield Ladies	0-8
Charlton Ath v Cardiff C	3-2*
(2-2 at the end of normal time)	
Forest Green R v Keynsham T	2-4*
(2-2 at the end of normal time)	
Gillingham v Portsmouth Ladies	0-5
Lowestoft T v Luton T	2-1
Crystal Palace v Ipswich T	2-0
Eastbourne T v QPR	1-0
Swindon T (removed) v Carshalton Ath (walkover)	
Plymouth Argyle v C&K Basildon	2-3
Exeter C v Lewes	1-3
Tottenham Hotspur v Copsewood Coventry	2-1*
(1-1 at the end of normal time)	
Brighton & Hove Alb v West Ham U	6-2

THIRD ROUND

Oxford U v Coventry C	0-3
Blackburn R v Portsmouth Ladies	4-5
Doncaster R Belles v London Bees	3-0
Yeovil T v Lewes	4-1
Radcliffe Olympic v Durham Women's	2-0
Bradford C v FC Reedswood Ladies	5-0
Aston Villa v Sunderland	2-1
Morecambe v Stoke C	2-3
Carshalton Ath v Keynsham T	2-5
Millwall Lionesses v Lowestoft T	3-0
Crystal Palace v Reading Women	0-3
(Tie awarded to Crystal Palace – Reading Women removed)	
Charlton Ath v Wolverhampton W	2-0
C&K Basildon v Sheffield Ladies	0-5
Eastbourne T v Derby Co	2-4*
(2-2 at the end of normal time)	
Tottenham H v Preston NE	5-1
Watford v Brighton & HA	2-1

FOURTH ROUND

Watford v Keynsham T	2-1
Charlton Ath v Crystal Palace	3-3*
(Charlton Ath won 4-2 on penalties)	
Sheffield Ladies v Radcliffe Olympic	4-0
Aston Villa v Yeovil T	2-1*
(1-1 at the end of normal time)	
Portsmouth Ladies v Millwall Lionesses	1-4
Derby Co v Tottenham H	0-3
Stoke C v Coventry C	1-3
Bradford C v Doncaster R Belles	1-2

FIFTH ROUND

Chelsea v Watford	6-0
Coventry C v Charlton Ath	1-2
Manchester C v Doncaster R Belles	3-1
Millwall Lionesses v Arsenal	0-7
Birmingham C v Liverpool	3-1
Aston Villa v Sheffield Ladies	2-0
Notts Co v Tottenham H	4-0
Everton v Bristol Academy	2-1*
(1-1 at the end of normal time)	

SIXTH ROUND

Manchester C v Birmingham C	3-1
Notts Co v Aston Villa	5-1
Everton v Charlton Ath	1-1*
(Everton won 4-3 on penalties)	
Arsenal v Chelsea	1-2

SEMI-FINALS

Chelsea v Manchester C	1-0
Everton v Notts Co	0-3

FA WOMEN'S CUP FINAL 2015

Wembley, Saturday 1 August

Chelsea v Notts Co

UEFA WOMEN'S CHAMPIONS LEAGUE 2014–15

After extra time.

QUALIFYING ROUND – GROUP 1 (LATVIA)

FC Zurich Frauen v Minsk	1-1
Konak Belediyespor v Rigas Futbola skola	11-0
Minsk v Konak Belediyespor	1-2
FC Zurich Frauen v Rigas Futbola skola	2-0
Konak Belediyespor v FC Zurich Frauen	0-4
Rigas Futbola skola v Minsk	0-7

Group 1 Table	P	W	D	L	F	A	GD	Pts
FC Zurich Frauen	3	2	1	0	7	1	6	7
Konak Belediyespor	3	2	0	1	13	5	8	6
Minsk	3	1	1	1	9	3	6	4
Rigas Futbola skola	3	0	0	3	0	20	–20	0

GROUP 2 ROMANIA

NSA Sofia v Hibernians	5-0
Olimpia Cluj Napoca v Raheny U	1-2
Raheny U v NSA Sofia	2-0
Olimpia Cluj Napoca v Hibernians	5-0
NSA Sofia v Olimpia Cluj Napoca	1-4
Hibernians v Raheny U	1-2

Group 2 Table	P	W	D	L	F	A	GD	Pts
Raheny U	3	3	0	0	6	2	4	9
Olimpia Cluj Napoca	3	2	0	1	10	3	7	6
NSA Sofia	3	1	0	2	6	6	0	3
Hibernians	3	0	0	3	1	12	–11	0

GROUP 3 (MONTENEGRO)

MTK Hungaria v Parnu Jalgpalliklubi	3-0
ZNK Pomurje v Ekonomist	4-0
MTK Hungaria v Ekonomist	1-0
Parnu Jalgpalliklubi v ZNK Pomurje	0-4
ZNK Pomurje v MTK Hungaria	1-2
Ekonomist v Parnu Jalgpalliklubi	1-2

Group 3 Table	P	W	D	L	F	A	GD	Pts
MTK Hungaria	3	3	0	0	6	1	5	9
ZNK Pomurje	3	2	0	1	9	2	7	6
Parnu Jalgpalliklubi	3	1	0	2	2	8	–6	3
Ekonomist	3	0	0	3	1	7	–6	0

GROUP 4 (SCOTLAND)

Kharkiv v Glentoran Belfast U	5-0
Glasgow C v Union Nove Zamky	5-0
Union Nove Zamky v Kharkiv	1-3
Glasgow C v Glentoran Belfast U	1-0
Kharkiv v Glasgow C	0-4
Glentoran Belfast U v Union Nove Zamky	5-2

Group 4 Table	P	W	D	L	F	A	GD	Pts
Glasgow C	3	3	0	0	10	1	9	9
Kharkiv	3	2	0	1	8	5	3	6
Glentoran Belfast U	3	1	0	2	5	8	–3	3
Union Nove Zamky	3	0	0	3	3	13	–10	0

GROUP 5 (CROATIA)

ZFK Spartak Subotica v Amazones Dramas	3-0
ZNK Osijek v SS-11 Goliador-Real	12-0
ZFK Spartak Subotica v SS-11 Goliador-Real	19-0
Amazones Dramas v ZNK Osijek	1-3
ZNK Osijek v ZFK Spartak Subotica	1-0
SS-11 Goliador-Real v Amazones Dramas	0-11

Group 5 Table	P	W	D	L	F	A	GD	Pts
ZNK Osijek	3	3	0	0	16	1	15	9
ZFK Spartak Subotica	3	2	0	1	22	1	21	6
Amazones Dramas	3	1	0	2	12	6	6	3
SS-11 Goliador-Real	3	0	0	3	0	42	–42	0

GROUP 6 (LITHUANIA)

Klaksvikar Itrottarfelag v Vllaznia	1-2
Apollon Ladies v Gintra Universitetas	3-1
Apollon Ladies v Vllaznia	0-0
Gintra Universitetas v Klaksvikar Itrottarfelag	2-0
Klaksvikar Itrottarfelag v Apollon Ladies	1-3
Vllaznia v Gintra Universitetas	0-5

Group 6 Table	P	W	D	L	F	A	GD	Pts
Apollon Ladies	3	2	1	0	6	2	4	7
Gintra Universitetas	3	2	0	1	8	3	5	6
Vllaznia	3	1	1	1	2	6	–4	4
Klaksvikar Itrottarfelag	3	0	0	3	2	7	–5	0

GROUP 7 (BOSNIA & HERZEGOVINA)

SFK 2000 Sarajevo v KKPK Medyk Konin	0-3
Aland U v ZFK Kocani	4-0
SFK 2000 Sarajevo v ZFK Kocani	7-0
KKPK Medyk Konin v Aland U	7-0
Aland U v SFK 2000 Sarajevo	0-1
ZFK Kocani v KKPK Medyk Konin	1-11

Group 7 Table	P	W	D	L	F	A	GD	Pts
KKPK Medyk Konin	3	3	0	0	21	1	20	9
SFK 2000 Sarajevo	3	2	0	1	8	3	5	6
Aland U	3	1	0	2	4	8	–4	3
ZFK Kocani	3	0	0	3	1	22	–21	0

GROUP 8 (PORTUGAL)

Standard Liege v Clube Atletico Ouriense	0-1
ASA Tel-Aviv University v Cardiff Met Ladies	2-0
Standard Liege v Cardiff Met Ladies	10-0
Clube Atletico Ouriense v ASA Tel-Aviv University	2-1
ASA Tel-Aviv University v Standard Liege	0-1
Cardiff Met Ladies v Clube Atletico Ouriense	2-1

Group 8 Table	P	W	D	L	F	A	GD	Pts
Clube Atletico Ouriense	3	2	0	1	4	3	1	6
Standard Liege	3	2	0	1	11	1	10	6
ASA Tel-Aviv University	3	1	0	2	3	3	0	3
Cardiff Met Ladies	3	1	0	2	2	13	–11	3

ROUND OF 32 FIRST LEG

BIIK-Kazygurt v Frankfurt	2-2
Ryazan-VDV v Rosengard	1-3
Apollon Ladies v Brondby	1-0
KKPK Medyk Konin v Glasgow C	2-0
Gintra Universitetas v Sparta Prague	1-1
Stabaek v Wolfsburg	0-1
MTK Hungaria v Neulengbach	1-2
ZNK Osijek v FC Zurich Frauen	2-5
Slavia Prague v Barcelona	0-1
ZNK Pomurje v Torres	2-4
Twente v Paris Saint-Germain	1-2
Liverpool v Linkoping	2-1
Clube Atletico Ouriense v Fortuna	0-3
Stjarnan v Zvezda 2005	2-5
Brescia v Lyon	0-5
Raheny U v Bristol Academy	0-4

ROUND OF 32 SECOND LEG

		Agg
Fortuna v Clube Atletico Ouriense	6-0	9-0
Sparta Prague v Gintra Universitetas	1-1*	2-2
Gintra Universitetas won 5-4 on penalties.		
Neulengbach v MTK Hungaria	2-2*	4-3
FC Zurich Frauen v ZNK Osijek	2-0	7-2
Barcelona v Slavia Praha	3-0	4-0
Rosengard v Ryazan-VDV	2-0	5-1
Lyon v Brescia	9-0	14-0
Glasgow C v KKPK Medyk Konin	3-0*	3-2
Torres v ZNK Pomurje	3-1	7-3
Paris Saint-Germain v Twente	1-0	3-1
Frankfurt v BIIK-Kazygurt	4-0	6-2
Zvezda 2005 v Stjarnan	3-1	8-3
Wolfsburg v Stabaek	2-1	3-1
Brondby v Apollon Ladies	3-1*	3-2
Linkoping v Liverpool	3-0	4-2
Bristol Academy v Raheny U	2-1	6-1

ROUND OF 16 FIRST LEG

Rosengard v Fortuna	2-1
Linkoping v Zvezda 2005	5-0
Paris Saint-Germain v Lyon	1-1
Barcelona v Bristol Academy	0-1
Frankfurt v Torres	5-0
Brondby v Gintra Universitetas	5-0
Neulengbach v Wolfsburg	0-4
FC Zurich Frauen v Glasgow C	2-1

ROUND OF 16 SECOND LEG

		Agg
Torres v Frankfurt	0-4	0-9
Gintra Universitetas v Brondby	2-0	2-5
Wolfsburg v Neulengbach	7-0	11-0
Lyon v Paris Saint-Germain	0-1	1-2
Glasgow C v FC Zurich Frauen	4-2	5-4
Zvezda 2005 v Linkoping	3-0	3-5

| Fortuna v Rosengard | 0-2 | 1-4 |
| Bristol Academy v Barcelona | 1-1 | 2-1 |

QUARTER-FINALS FIRST LEG

Bristol Academy v Frankfurt		0-5
Linkoping v Brondby		0-1
Glasgow C v Paris Saint-Germain		0-2
Wolfsburg v Rosengard		1-1

QUARTER-FINALS SECOND LEG Agg

Brondby v Linkoping	1-1	2-1
Rosengard v Wolfsburg	3-3	4-4
Wolfsburg won on away goals.		
Paris Saint-Germain v Glasgow C	5-0	7-0
Frankfurt v Bristol Academy	7-0	12-0

SEMI-FINALS FIRST LEG

| Wolfsburg v Paris Saint-Germain | 0-2 |
| Frankfurt v Brondby | 7-0 |

SEMI-FINALS SECOND LEG Agg

| Brondby v Frankfurt | 0-6 | 0-13 |
| Paris Saint-Germain v Wolfsburg | 1-2 | 3-2 |

WOMEN'S UEFA CHAMPIONS LEAGUE FINAL 2015

Berlin, Thursday 14 May 2015

Frankfurt (1) 2 *(Sasic 32, Islacker 90)*

Paris Saint-Germain (1) 1 *(Delie 40)*   17,147

Frankfurt: Schumann; Kuznik, Priessen, Hendrich, Schmidt (Huth 79), Laudehr (Ando 87), Marozsan, Boquete, Garefrekes, Crnogorcevic (Islacker 66), Sasic.
Paris Saint-Germain: Kiedrzynek; Delannoy, Krahn, Houara-D'Hommeaux, Boulleau (Henning 60), Kaci, Cruz Trana, Alushi (Georges 58), Delie, Asllani (Sarr 90), Dali.
Referee: Esther Staubli.

FIFA WOMEN'S WORLD CUP CANADA 2015

EUROPEAN QUALIFICATION

Malta, Albania, Faroe Islands and Montenegro qualified from a Preliminary Round.

QUALIFYING ROUND

GROUP 1

Germany v Russia	9-0
Republic of Ireland v Slovakia	2-0
Croatia v Republic of Ireland	1-1
Slovakia v Slovenia	1-3
Croatia v Slovakia	0-1
Slovenia v Germany	0-13
Slovenia v Republic of Ireland	0-3
Germany v Croatia	4-0
Slovakia v Russia	0-2
Slovakia v Germany	0-6
Croatia v Germany	0-8
Russia v Slovenia	4-1
Republic of Ireland v Germany	2-3
Russia v Croatia	1-0
Germany v Slovenia	4-0
Republic of Ireland v Russia	1-3
Germany v Slovakia	9-1
Slovenia v Croatia	0-3
Slovenia v Russia	1-2
Republic of Ireland v Croatia	1-0
Russia v Republic of Ireland	0-0
Slovakia v Croatia	1-1
Republic of Ireland v Slovenia	2-0
Russia v Slovakia	3-1
Russia v Germany	1-4
Croatia v Slovenia	1-0
Slovakia v Republic of Ireland	0-1
Slovenia v Slovakia	2-1
Croatia v Russia	1-3
Germany v Republic of Ireland	2-0

Group 1 Table	P	W	D	L	F	A	GD	Pts
Germany	10	10	0	0	62	4	58	30
Russia	10	7	1	2	19	18	1	22
Republic of Ireland	10	5	2	3	13	9	4	17
Croatia	10	2	2	6	7	20	–13	8
Slovenia	10	2	0	8	7	34	–27	6
Slovakia	10	1	1	8	6	29	–23	4

GROUP 2

FYR Macedonia v Romania	1-9
Estonia v Italy	1-5
Italy v Romania	1-0
FYR Macedonia v Czech Republic	1-3
Spain v Estonia	6-0
FYR Macedonia v Estonia	0-2
Romania v Czech Republic	0-0
Spain v Italy	2-0
Spain v Romania	1-0
Spain v Czech Republic	3-2
Italy v Czech Republic	6-1
Spain v FYR Macedonia	12-0
Italy v Spain	0-0

FYR Macedonia v Spain	0-10
Romania v Italy	1-2
Czech Republic v Estonia	6-0
Czech Republic v Romania	0-0
FYR Macedonia v Italy	0-11
Estonia v Spain	0-5
Czech Republic v Italy	0-4
Estonia v FYR Macedonia	1-1
Czech Republic v FYR Macedonia	5-2
Estonia v Romania	0-2
Estonia v Czech Republic	1-4
Romania v FYR Macedonia	6-1
Romania v Spain	0-2
Italy v Estonia	4-0
Italy v FYR Macedonia	15-0
Czech Republic v Spain	0-1
Romania v Estonia	0-3
Estonia awarded match 3-0. Original match ended 2-0 to Romania	

Group 2 Table	P	W	D	L	F	A	GD	Pts
Spain	10	9	1	0	42	2	40	28
Italy	10	8	1	1	48	5	43	25
Czech Republic	10	4	2	4	21	18	3	14
Romania	10	3	2	5	18	11	7	11
Estonia	10	2	1	7	8	33	–25	7
FYR Macedonia	10	0	1	9	6	74	–68	1

GROUP 3

Switzerland v Serbia	9-0
Iceland v Switzerland	0-2
Serbia v Denmark	1-1
Israel v Malta	2-0
Serbia v Iceland	1-2
Denmark v Switzerland	0-1
Malta v Denmark	0-5
Israel v Serbia	3-1
Israel v Switzerland	0-5
Malta v Serbia	0-3
Switzerland v Malta	11-0
Israel v Iceland	0-1
Malta v Iceland	0-8
Switzerland v Denmark	1-1
Malta v Israel	0-3 (f)
Switzerland v Iceland	3-0
Denmark v Serbia	3-1
Switzerland v Israel	9-0
Serbia v Malta	5-0
Denmark v Iceland	1-1
Israel v Denmark	0-5
Serbia v Switzerland	0-7
Iceland v Malta	5-0
Serbia v Israel	3-0
Iceland v Denmark	0-1
Denmark v Malta	8-0
Iceland v Israel	3-0
Malta v Switzerland	0-5
Denmark v Israel	0-1
Iceland v Serbia	9-1

Group 3 Table	P	W	D	L	F	A	GD	Pts
Switzerland	10	9	1	0	53	1	52	28
Iceland	10	6	1	3	29	9	20	19
Denmark	10	5	3	2	25	6	19	18
Israel	10	4	0	6	9	27	−18	12
Serbia	10	3	1	6	16	34	−18	10
Malta	10	0	0	10	0	55	−55	0

GROUP 4

Sweden v Poland	2-0
Faroe Islands v Scotland	2-7
Poland v Faroe Islands	6-0
Scotland v Bosnia & Herzegovina	7-0
Bosnia & Herzegovina v Sweden	0-1
Scotland v Northern Ireland	2-0
Northern Ireland v Bosnia & Herzegovina	0-0
Poland v Scotland	0-4
Sweden v Faroe Islands	5-0
Northern Ireland v Poland	0-3
Scotland v Poland	2-0
Faroe Islands v Bosnia & Herzegovina	1-1
Northern Ireland v Sweden	0-4
Bosnia & Herzegovina v Scotland	1-3
Faroe Islands v Northern Ireland	0-0
Faroe Islands v Poland	0-3
Sweden v Northern Ireland	3-0
Bosnia & Herzegovina v Northern Ireland	1-0
Scotland v Sweden	1-3
Bosnia & Herzegovina v Poland	1-1
Faroe Islands v Sweden	0-5
Northern Ireland v Scotland	0-2
Bosnia & Herzegovina v Faroe Islands	2-0
Poland v Sweden	0-4
Sweden v Bosnia & Herzegovina	3-0
Poland v Northern Ireland	4-0
Scotland v Faroe Islands	9-0
Sweden v Scotland	2-0
Poland v Bosnia & Herzegovina	3-1
Northern Ireland v Faroe Islands	3-0

Group 4 Table	P	W	D	L	F	A	GD	Pts
Sweden	10	10	0	0	32	1	31	30
Scotland	10	8	0	2	37	8	29	24
Poland	10	5	1	4	20	14	6	16
Bosnia & Herzegovina	10	2	3	5	7	19	−12	9
Northern Ireland	10	1	2	7	3	19	−16	5
Faroe Islands	10	0	2	8	3	41	−38	2

GROUP 5

Belgium v Albania	2-0
Norway v Belgium	4-1
Greece v Portugal	1-5
Albania v Netherlands	0-4
Greece v Belgium	1-7
Norway v Albania	7-0
Portugal v Netherlands	0-7
Albania v Greece	1-0
Netherlands v Norway	1-2
Belgium v Portugal	4-1
Netherlands v Greece	7-0
Netherlands v Belgium	1-1
Portugal v Albania	7-1
Greece v Norway	0-5
Albania v Belgium	0-6
Greece v Netherlands	0-6
Portugal v Greece	1-0
Netherlands v Albania	10-1
Belgium v Norway	1-2
Norway v Portugal	2-0
Belgium v Netherlands	0-2
Norway v Greece	6-0
Albania v Portugal	0-3
Portugal v Norway	0-2
Albania v Norway	0-11
Belgium v Greece	11-0
Netherlands v Portugal	3-2
Greece v Albania	4-0
Norway v Netherlands	0-2
Portugal v Belgium	0-1

Group 5 Table	P	W	D	L	F	A	GD	Pts
Norway	10	9	0	1	41	5	36	27
Netherlands	10	8	1	1	43	6	37	25
Belgium	10	6	1	3	34	11	23	19
Portugal	10	4	0	6	19	21	−2	12
Greece	10	1	0	9	6	49	−43	3
Albania	10	1	0	9	3	54	−51	3

GROUP 6

England v Belarus	6-0
Wales v Belarus	1-0
England v Turkey	8-0
Belarus v Montenegro	3-1
England v Wales	2-0
Montenegro v Ukraine	1-4
Montenegro v Wales	0-3
Turkey v England	0-4
Turkey v Montenegro	3-1
Turkey v Ukraine	0-1
Turkey v Wales	1-5
England v Montenegro	9-0
Wales v Ukraine	1-1
Montenegro v Belarus	1-7
Belarus v Turkey	1-2
Wales v Montenegro	4-0
England v Ukraine	4-0
Wales v Turkey	1-0
Belarus v England	0-3
Ukraine v Montenegro	7-0
Montenegro v Turkey	2-3
Ukraine v England	1-2
Belarus v Wales	0-3
Ukraine v Belarus	8-0
Belarus v Ukraine	1-3
Wales v England	0-4
Ukraine v Turkey	8-0
Turkey v Belarus	3-0
Ukraine v Wales	1-0
Montenegro v England	0-10

Group 6 Table	P	W	D	L	F	A	GD	Pts
England	10	10	0	0	52	1	51	30
Ukraine	10	7	1	2	34	9	25	22
Wales	10	6	1	3	18	9	9	19
Turkey	10	4	0	6	12	31	−19	12
Belarus	10	2	0	8	12	31	−19	6
Montenegro	10	0	0	10	6	53	−47	0

GROUP 7

Kazakhstan v Finland	0-2
Austria v Bulgaria	4-0
Kazakhstan v France	0-4
Finland v Austria	2-1
Bulgaria v Kazakhstan	1-1
Hungary v Austria	0-3
Hungary v Bulgaria	4-0
Finland v Kazakhstan	1-0
Austria v France	1-3
Hungary v Kazakhstan	4-1
Bulgaria v France	0-10
France v Bulgaria	14-0
Bulgaria v Austria	1-6
Hungary v Finland	0-4
France v Kazakhstan	7-0
France v Austria	3-1
Finland v Hungary	4-0
Kazakhstan v Bulgaria	4-1
France v Hungary	4-0
Kazakhstan v Hungary	1-2
Austria v Finland	3-1
Finland v Bulgaria	4-0
Kazakhstan v Austria	0-3
Hungary v France	0-4
Bulgaria v Finland	0-8
Finland v France	0-2
Austria v Hungary	4-3
Bulgaria v Hungary	0-7
France v Finland	3-1
Austria v Kazakhstan	5-1

Group 7 Table	P	W	D	L	F	A	GD	Pts
France	10	10	0	0	54	3	51	30
Austria	10	7	0	3	31	14	17	21
Finland	10	7	0	3	27	9	18	21
Hungary	10	4	0	6	20	25	−5	12
Kazakhstan	10	1	1	8	8	30	−22	4
Bulgaria	10	0	1	9	3	62	−59	1

PLAY-OFF SEMI-FINALS FIRST LEG

Italy v Ukraine	2-1
Scotland v Netherlands	1-2

PLAY-OFF SEMI-FINALS SECOND LEG

		(agg)
Ukraine v Italy	2-2	(3-4)
Netherlands v Scotland	2-0	(4-1)

FIFA WOMEN'S WORLD CUP 2015

FINALS IN CANADA

*After extra time.

GROUP A

Canada v China	1-0
New Zealand v Netherlands	0-1
Canada v New Zealand	0-0
China v Netherlands	1-0
China v New Zealand	2-2
Netherlands v Canada	1-1

Group A Table	P	W	D	L	F	A	GD	Pts
Canada	3	1	2	0	2	1	1	5
China	3	1	1	1	3	3	0	4
Netherlands	3	1	1	1	2	2	0	4
New Zealand	3	0	2	1	2	3	–1	2

GROUP B

Norway v Thailand	4-0
Germany v Ivory Coast	10-0
Germany v Norway	1-1
Ivory Coast v Thailand	2-3
Thailand v Germany	0-4
Ivory Coast v Norway	1-3

Group B Table	P	W	D	L	F	A	GD	Pts
Germany	3	2	1	0	15	1	14	7
Norway	3	2	1	0	8	2	6	7
Thailand	3	1	0	2	3	10	–7	3
Ivory Coast	3	0	0	3	3	16	–13	0

GROUP C

Japan v Switzerland	1-0
Cameroon v Ecuador	6-0
Switzerland v Ecuador	10-1
Japan v Cameroon	2-1
Ecuador v Japan	0-1
Switzerland v Cameroon	1-2

Group C Table	P	W	D	L	F	A	GD	Pts
Japan	3	3	0	0	4	1	3	9
Cameroon	3	2	0	1	9	3	6	6
Switzerland	3	1	0	2	11	4	7	3
Ecuador	3	0	0	3	1	17	–16	0

GROUP D

Sweden v Nigeria	3-3
USA v Australia	3-1
Australia v Nigeria	2-0
USA v Sweden	0-0
Nigeria v USA	0-1
Australia v Sweden	1-1

Group D Table	P	W	D	L	F	A	GD	Pts
USA	3	2	1	0	4	1	3	7
Australia	3	1	1	1	4	4	0	4
Sweden	3	0	3	0	4	4	0	3
Nigeria	3	0	1	2	3	6	–3	1

GROUP E

Spain v Costa Rica	1-1
Brazil v Korea Republic	2-0
Brazil v Spain	1-0
Korea Republic v Costa Rica	2-2
Korea Republic v Spain	2-1
Costa Rica v Brazil	0-1

Group E Table	P	W	D	L	F	A	GD	Pts
Brazil	3	3	0	0	4	0	4	9
Korea Republic	3	1	1	1	4	5	–1	4
Costa Rica	3	0	2	1	3	4	–1	2
Spain	3	0	1	2	2	4	–2	1

GROUP F

France v England	1-0
Colombia v Mexico	1-1
France v Colombia	0-2
England v Mexico	2-1
Mexico v France	0-5
England v Colombia	2-1

Group F Table	P	W	D	L	F	A	GD	Pts
France	3	2	0	1	6	2	4	6
England	3	2	0	1	4	3	1	6
Colombia	3	1	1	1	4	3	1	4
Mexico	3	0	1	2	2	8	–6	1

ROUND OF 16

Germany v Sweden	4-1
China v Cameroon	1-0
Brazil v Australia	0-1
France v Korea Republic	3-0
Canada v Switzerland	1-0
Norway v England	1-2
USA v Colombia	2-0
Japan v Netherlands	2-1

QUARTER-FINALS

Germany v France	1-1*
Germany won 5-4 on penalties.	
China v USA	0-1
Australia v Japan	0-1
England v Canada	2-1

SEMI-FINALS

USA v Germany	2-0
Japan v England	2-1

THIRD PLACE PLAY-OFF

Germany v England	0-1*

FINAL

Vancouver, 4 July 2015

USA (4) 5 *(Lloyd 3, 5, 16, Holiday 14, Heath 54)*

Japan (1) 2 *(Ogimi 17, Johnston 52 (og))*   53,431

USA: Solo; Sauerbrunn, Lloyd, Krieger, Holiday, Morgan (Rampone 86), Brian, Rapinoe (O'Hara 61), Heath (Wambach 79), Johnston, Klingenberg.
Japan: Kaihori; Iwashimizu (Sawa 33), Kumagai, Sameshima, Sakaguchi, Miyama, Kawasumi (Sugasawa 39), Ohno (Iwabuchi 60), Utsugi, Ogimi, Ariyoshi.
Referee: Kateryna Monzul (Ukraine).

ENGLAND WOMEN'S INTERNATIONALS 2014–15

■ *Denotes player sent off.*

FRIENDLIES

Hartlepool, 3 August 2014

England (1) 4 *(Carney 36, 80, Kirby 53, Sanderson 68)*
Sweden (0) 0   4547
England: Bardsley; Scott A, Houghton, Bronze (Bassett 71), Stokes (Greenwood 76), Williams (Scott J 76), Nobbs, Carney, Kirby (Duggan 61), Taylor (Aluko 61), Sanderson.

Wembley, 23 November 2014

England (0) 0
Germany (3) 3 *(Scott A 6 (og), Sasic 12, 45)*   45,619
England: Bardsley; Scott A (Potter 84), Houghton, Bronze (Bassett 90), Stokes (Greenwood 84), Nobbs, Williams (Scott J 71), Carney, Sanderson (Taylor 80), Duggan, Aluko (Kirby 62).

Milton Keynes, 13 February 2015

England (0) 0
USA (1) 1 *(Morgan 25)*   14,369
England: Bardsley; Scott A, Houghton, Bassett (Clarke 90), Stokes (Greenwood 90), Nobbs (Williams 81), Potter (Aluko 79), Scott J, Carney, Taylor (Sanderson 81), Kirby.

Manchester, 9 April 2015

England (2) 2 *(Taylor 1, Kirby 10)*
China (1) 1 *(Shanshan 17)*   5665
England: Chamberlain; Scott A, Bassett, Greenwood, Rafferty (Stoney 72), Nobbs, Williams, Scott J (White 90), Moore (Duggan 62), Taylor (Sanderson 79), Kirby (Aluko 72).

Ontario, 30 May 2015

Canada (1) 1 *(Schmidt 23)*
England (0) 0
England: Bardsley; Bronze, Houghton, Stoney, Rafferty (Greenwood 61), Duggan, Scott J, Chapman (Kirby 73), Carney (Moore 83), Sanderson (Aluko 61), White (Williams 61).

FIFA WORLD CUP 2015 QUALIFIERS

Cardiff, 21 August 2014

Wales (0) 0
England (4) 4 *(Carney 16, Aluko 39, Bassett 44, Sanderson 45)*   3581
England: Bardsley; Scott A, Houghton, Bassett, Stokes, Nobbs, Williams (Kirby 63), Carney (Scott J 68), Sanderson, Duggan, Aluko (Taylor 61).
England qualify for World Cup.

Petrovac, 17 September 2014

Montenegro (0) 0 *(Bjelica■ 86)*
England (4) 10 *(Aluko 8, 31, 63, Carney 22, 51, Bronze 37, Duggan 56, 90, Greenwood 90, Potter 90)*
England: Telford; Bronze, Greenwood, Williams, Bonner, Bassett (Potter 57), Nobbs (Scott J 46), Carney, Sanderson (Dowie 64), Duggan, Aluko.

CYPRUS CUP 2015 – GROUP B

Larnaca, 4 March 2015

Finland (0) 1 *(Saari 89 (pen))*
England (1) 3 *(Sanderson 21, Aluko 66, Clarke 83)*
England: Telford; Stokes, Bonner■, Bassett (Scott A 62), Greenwood, Moore, Williams, Potter, Clarke, Aluko, Sanderson.

Nicosia, 6 March 2015

Australia (0) 0
England (2) 3 *(Taylor 8, 17, 83)*
England: Bardsley; Scott A (Turner 88), Houghton (Potter 90), Bassett, Greenwood, Nobbs, Scott J (Williams 60), Chapman, Carney, Taylor, Kirby (Sanderson 71).

Nicosia, 9 March 2015

Netherlands (1) 1 *(Miedema 18)*
England (1) 1 *(42)*
England: Bardsley; Turner (Scott A 63), Bonner, Greenwood, Stokes, Moore (Williams 83), Chapman, Potter, Nobbs (Bassett 63), Kirby (Taylor 69), Aluko.

CYPRUS CUP FINAL 2015

Larnaca, 11 March 2015

England (0) 1 *(Sanderson 67)*
Canada (0) 0
England: Chamberlain; Scott A, Bassett, Greenwood, Rafferty (Bonner 68), Nobbs, Scott J (Chapman 68), Williams, Carney (Kirby 90), Taylor (Moore 88), Sanderson.

FIFA WORLD CUP 2015 FINALS IN CANADA

GROUP F

Moncton, 9 June 2015

France (1) 1 *(Le Sommer 29)*
England (0) 0   11,686
England: Bardsley, Scott A (Kirby 69), Houghton, Bassett, Rafferty, Williams, White (Duggan 60), Scott J, Chapman (Moore 76), Bronze, Aluko.

Moncton, 13 June 2015

England (0) 2 *(Kirby 71, Carney 82)*
Mexico (0) 1 *(Obarra 90)*   13,138
England: Bardsley; Bronze (Scott A 85), Houghton, Bassett, Rafferty (Greenwood 53), Scott J (Carney 66), Williams, Moore, Kirby, Aluko, Duggan.

Montreal, 17 June 2015

England (2) 2 *(Carney 15, Williams 38 (pen))*
Colombia (0) 1 *(Amdrade 90)*   13,862
England: Bardsley; Scott A, Houghton, Stoney, Greenwood, Nobbs, Williams, Moore, Carney (Sanderson 56), Duggan (Taylor 81), Kirby (Potter 66).

ROUND OF 16

Ottawa, 22 June 2015

Norway (0) 1 *(Gulbrandsen 54)*
England (0) 2 *(Houghton 61, Bronze 76)*   19,829
England: Bardsley, Bronze, Houghton, Bassett, Rafferty, Moore, Williams, Chapman, Carney, Duggan (Taylor 63), Kirby (Scott J 54).

QUARTER-FINAL

Vancouver, 27 June 2015

Canada (1) 1 *(Sinclair 42)*
England (2) 2 *(Taylor 11, Bronze 4)*   54,027
England: Bardsley (Chamberlain 52); Bronze, Houghton, Bassett, Rafferty, Moore, Williams (White 79), Scott J, Chapman, Carney (Stoney 90), Taylor.

SEMI-FINAL

Edmonton, 1 July 2015

Japan (1) 2 *(Miyama 33 (pen), Bassett 90 (og))*
England (1) 1 *(Williams 40 (pen))*   31,467
England: Bardsley; Bronze (Scott A 75), Houghton, Bassett, Rafferty, Moore, Williams (Carney 75), Scott J, Chapman, Duggan, Taylor (White 60).

THIRD PLACE PLAY-OFF

Edmonton, 4 July 2015

Germany (0) 0
England (0) 1 *(Williams 108 (pen))*   21,483
England: Bardsley; Houghton, Bassett, Potter, Bronze, Williams (Stoney 111), Chapman (Sanderson 80), Greenwood, Scott J, White (Aluko 61), Carney.
aet.

ENGLAND WOMEN'S INTERNATIONAL MATCHES 1972–2015

Note: In the results that follow, WC = World Cup; EC = European (UEFA) Championships; M = Mundialito; CC = Cyprus Cup; AC = Algarve Cup. * = After extra time. Games were organised by the Women's Football Association from 1971 to 1992 and the Football Association from 1993 to date.

v ARGENTINA

wc2007	17 Sept	Chengdu	6-1

v AUSTRALIA

2003	3 Sept	Burnley	1-0
cc2015	6 Mar	Nicosia	3-0

v AUSTRIA

wc2005	1 Sept	Amstetten	4-1
wc2006	20 Apr	Gillingham	4-0
wc2010	25 Mar	Shepherd's Bush	3-0
wc2010	21 Aug	Krems	4-0

v BELARUS

EC2007	27 Oct	Walsall	4-0
EC2008	8 May	Minsk	6-1
wc2013	21 Sept	Bournemouth	6-0
wc2014	14 June	Minsk	3-0

v BELGIUM

1978	31 Oct	Southampton	3-0
1980	1 May	Ostende	1-2
M1984	20 Aug	Jesolo	1-1
M1984	25 Aug	Caorle	2-1
1989	14 May	Epinal	2-0
EC1990	17 Mar	Ypres	3-0
EC1990	7 Apr	Sheffield	1-0
EC1993	6 Nov	Koksijde	3-0
EC1994	13 Mar	Nottingham	6-0

v CANADA

wc1995	6 June	Helsingborg	3-2
2003	19 May	Montreal	0-4
2003	22 May	Ottawa	0-4
cc2009	12 Mar	Nicosia	3-1
cc 2010	27 Feb	Nicosia	0-1
cc 2011	7 Mar	Nicosia	0-2
cc 2013	13 Mar	Nicosia	1-0
2013	7 Apr	Rotherham	1-0
cc2014	10 Mar	Nicosia	2-0
cc2015	11 Mar	Larnaca	1-0
2015	29 May	Hamilton	0-1
wc2015	27 June	Vancouver	2-1

v CHINA

AC2005	15 Mar	Guia	0-0*
2007	26 Jan	Guangzhou	0-2
2015	9 Apr	Manchester	2-1

v COLOMBIA

wc2015	17 June	Montreal	2-1

v CROATIA

EC1995	19 Nov	Charlton	5-0
EC1996	18 Apr	Osijek	2-0
EC2012	31 Mar	Vrbovec	6-0
EC2012	19 Sept	Walsall	3-0

v CZECH REPUBLIC

2005	26 May	Walsall	4-1
EC2008	20 Mar	Doncaster	0-0
EC2008	28 Sept	Prague	5-1

v DENMARK

1979	19 May	Hvidovre	1-3
1979	13 Sept	Hull	2-2
1981	9 Sept	Tokyo	0-1
EC1984	8 Apr	Crewe	2-1
EC1984	28 Apr	Hjorring	1-0
M1985	19 Aug	Caorle	0-1
EC1987	8 Nov	Blackburn	2-1
EC1988	8 May	Herning	0-2
1991	28 June	Nordby	0-0
1991	30 June	Nordby	3-3
1999	22 Aug	Odense	1-0
2001	23 Aug	Northampton	0-3
2004	19 Feb	Portsmouth	2-0
EC2005	8 June	Blackburn	1-2
2009	22 July	Swindon	1-0

v FINLAND

1979	19 July	Sorrento	3-1
EC1987	25 Oct	Kirkkonummi	2-1
EC1988	4 Sept	Millwall	1-1
EC1989	1 Oct	Brentford	0-0
EC1990	29 Sept	Tampere	0-0
2000	28 Sept	Leyton	2-1
EC2005	5 June	Manchester	3-2
2009	9 Feb	Larnaca	2-2
2009	11 Feb	Larnaca	4-1
EC2009	3 Sept	Turku	3-2
cc2012	28 Feb	Nicosia	3-1
cc2014	7 Mar	Larnaca	3-0
cc2015	4 Mar	Larnaca	3-1

v FRANCE

1973	22 Apr	Brion	3-0
1974	7 Nov	Wimbledon	2-0
1977	26 Feb	Longjumeau	0-0
M1988	22 July	Riva del Garda	1-1
1998	15 Feb	Alencon	2-3
1999	15 Sept	Yeovil	0-1
2000	16 Aug	Marseilles	0-1
wc2002	17 Oct	Crystal Palace	0-1
wc2002	16 Nov	St Etienne	0-1
wc2006	26 Mar	Blackburn	0-0
wc2006	30 Sept	Rennes	1-1
cc2009	7 Mar	Paralimni	2-2
wc2011	9 July	Leverkusen	1-1*
cc2012	4 Mar	Paralimni	0-3
2012	20 Oct	Paris	2-2
EC2013	18 July	Linkoping	0-3
cc2014	12 Mar	Nicosia	0-2
wc2015	9 June	Moncton	0-1

v GERMANY

EC1990	25 Nov	High Wycombe	1-4
EC1990	16 Dec	Bochum	0-2
EC1994	11 Dec	Watford	1-4
EC1995	23 Feb	Bochum	1-2
wc1995	13 June	Vasteras	0-3
1997	27 Feb	Preston	4-6
wc1997	25 Sept	Dessau	0-3
wc1998	8 Mar	Millwall	0-1
EC2001	30 June	Jena	0-3
wc2001	27 Sept	Kassel	1-3
wc2002	19 May	Crystal Palace	0-1
2003	11 Sept	Darmstadt	0-4
2006	25 Oct	Aalen	1-5
2007	30 Jan	Guangzhou	0-0
wc2007	14 Sept	Shanghai	0-0
2008	17 July	Unterhaching	0-3
EC2009	10 Sept	Helsinki	2-6
2014	23 Nov	Wembley	0-3
wc2015	4 July	Vancouver	1-0*

v HUNGARY

wc2005	27 Oct	Tapolca	13-0
wc2006	11 May	Southampton	2-0

v ICELAND

EC1992	17 May	Yeovil	4-0
EC1992	19 July	Kopavogur	2-1
EC1994	8 Oct	Reykjavik	2-1
EC1994	30 Oct	Brighton	2-1
wc2002	16 Sept	Reykjavik	2-2
wc2002	22 Sept	Birmingham	1-0
2004	14 May	Peterborough	1-0
2006	9 Mar	Norwich	1-0
2007	17 May	Southend	4-0
2009	16 July	Colchester	0-2

v ITALY

1976	2 June	Rome	0-2
1976	4 June	Cesena	1-2
1977	15 Nov	Wimbledon	1-0
1979	25 July	Naples	1-3
1982	11 June	Pescara	0-2
M1984	24 Aug	Jesolo	1-1
M1985	20 Aug	Caorle	1-1
M1985	25 Aug	Caorle	3-2
EC1987	13 June	Drammen	1-2
M1988	30 July	Arco di Trento	2-1
1989	1 Nov	High Wycombe	1-1
1990	18 Aug	Wembley	1-4
EC1992	17 Oct	Solofra	2-3
EC1992	7 Nov	Rotherham	0-3
1995	25 Jan	Florence	1-1
EC1995	1 Nov	Sunderland	1-1
EC1996	16 Mar	Cosenza	1-2
1997	23 Apr	Turin	0-2
1998	21 Apr	West Bromwich	1-2
1999	26 May	Bologna	1-4
2003	25 Feb	Viareggio	0-1
2005	17 Feb	Milton Keynes	4-1
EC2009	25 Aug	Lahti	1-2
cc2010	3 Mar	Nicosia	3-2
cc2011	2 Mar	Larnaca	2-0
cc2012	6 Mar	Paralimni	1-3
cc 2013	6 Mar	Nicosia	4-2
EC 2014	5 Mar	Larnaca	2-0

v JAPAN

1981	6 Sept	Kobe	4-0
wc2007	11 Sept	Shanghai	2-2
wc2011	5 July	Augsburg	2-0
2013	26 June	Burton	1-1
wc2015	1 July	Edmonton	1-2

v MALTA

wc2009	25 Oct	Blackpool	8-0
wc2010	20 May	Ta'Qali	6-0

v MEXICO

AC2005	13 Mar	Lagos	5-0
wc2011	27 June	Wolfsburg	1-1
wc2015	13 June	Moncton	2-1

v MONTENEGRO

wc2014	5 Apr	Brighton	9-0
wc2014	17 Sept	Petrovac	10-0

v NETHERLANDS

1973	9 Nov	Reading	1-0
1974	31 May	Groningen	0-3
1976	2 May	Blackpool	2-0
1978	30 Sept	Vlissingen	1-3
1989	13 May	Epinal	0-0
wc1997	30 Oct	West Ham	1-0
wc1998	23 May	Waalwijk	1-2
wc2001	4 Nov	Grimsby	0-0
wc2002	23 Mar	Den Haag	4-1
2004	18 Sept	Heerhugowaard	2-1

2004	22 Sept	Tuitjenhoorn	1-0
wc2005	17 Nov	Zwolle	1-0
wc2006	31 Aug	Charlton	4-0
2007	14 Mar	Swindon	0-1
EC2009	6 Sept	Tampere	2-1*
EC2011	27 Oct	Zwolle	0-0
EC2012	17 June	Salford	1-0
cc2015	9 Mar	Nicosia	1-1

v NEW ZEALAND

2010	21 Oct	Suwon	0-0
wc2011	1 July	Dresden	2-1
cc2013	11 Mar	Larnaca	3-1

v NIGERIA

wc1995	10 June	Karlstad	3-2
2002	23 July	Norwich	0-1
2004	22 Apr	Reading	0-3

v NORTHERN IRELAND

1973	7 Sept	Bath	5-1
EC1982	19 Sept	Crewe	7-1
EC1983	14 May	Belfast	4-0
EC1985	25 May	Antrim	8-1
EC1986	16 Mar	Blackburn	10-0
1987	11 Apr	Leeds	6-0
AC2005	9 Mar	Paderne	4-0
EC2007	13 May	Gillingham	4-0
EC2008	6 Mar	Lurgan	2-0

v NORWAY

1981	25 Oct	Cambridge	0-3
EC 1988	21 Aug	Kleppe	0-2
EC 1988	18 Sept	Blackburn	1-3
EC 1990	27 May	Kleppe	0-2
EC 1990	2 Sept	Old Trafford	0-0
wc1995	8 June	Karlstad	3-2
1997	8 June	Lillestrom	0-4
wc1998	14 May	Oldham	1-2
wc1998	15 Aug	Lillestrom	0-2
EC2000	7 Mar	Norwich	0-3
EC2000	4 June	Moss	0-8
AC2002	1 Mar	Albufeira	1-3
2005	6 May	Barnsley	1-0
2008	14 Feb	Larnaca	2-1
2009	23 Apr	Shrewsbury	3-0
2014	17 Jan	La Manga	1-1
wc2015	22 June	Ottawa	2-1

v PORTUGAL

EC1996	11 Feb	Benavente	5-0
EC1996	19 May	Brentford	3-0
EC2000	20 Feb	Barnsley	2-0
EC2000	22 Apr	Sacavem	2-2
wc2001	24 Nov	Gafanha da Nazare	1-1
wc2002	24 Feb	Portsmouth	3-0
AC2005	11 Mar	Faro	4-0

v REPUBLIC OF IRELAND

1978	2 May	Exeter	6-1
1981	2 May	Dublin	5-0
EC1982	7 Nov	Dublin	1-0
EC1983	11 Sept	Reading	6-0
EC1985	22 Sept	Cork	6-0
EC1986	27 Apr	Reading	4-0
1987	29 Mar	Dublin	1-0

v ROMANIA

EC1998	12 Sept	Campina	4-1
EC1998	11 Oct	High Wycombe	2-1

v RUSSIA

EC2001	24 June	Jena	1-1
2003	21 Oct	Moscow	2-2
2004	19 Aug	Bristol	1-2
2007	8 Mar	Milton Keynes	6-0
EC2009	28 Aug	Helsinki	3-2
EC2013	15 July	Linkoping	1-1

v SCOTLAND

1972	18 Nov	Greenock	3-2
1973	23 June	Nuneaton	8-0
1976	23 May	Enfield	5-1
1977	29 May	Dundee	1-2
EC1982	3 Oct	Dumbarton	4-0
EC1983	22 May	Leeds	2-0
EC1985	17 Mar	Preston	4-0
EC1986	12 Oct	Kirkcaldy	3-1
1989	30 Apr	Kirkcaldy	3-0
1990	6 May	Paisley	4-0
1990	12 May	Wembley	4-0
1991	20 Apr	High Wycombe	5-0
EC1992	17 Apr	Walsall	1-0
EC1992	23 Aug	Perth	2-0
1997	9 Mar	Sheffield	6-0
1997	23 Aug	Livingston	4-0
2001	27 May	Bolton	1-0
AC2002	7 Mar	Quarteira	4-1
2003	13 Nov	Preston	5-0
2005	21 Apr	Tranmere	2-1
2007	11 Mar	High Wycombe	1-0
cc2009	10 Mar	Larnaca	3-0
cc2011	4 Mar	Nicosia	0-2
cc2013	8 Mar	Larnaca	4-4

v SERBIA

EC2011	17 Sept	Belgrade	2-2
EC2011	23 Nov	Doncaster	2-0

v SLOVENIA

EC1993	25 Sept	Ljubljana	10-0
EC1994	17 Apr	Brentford	10-0
EC2011	22 Sept	Swindon	4-0
EC2012	21 June	Velenje	4-0

v SOUTH AFRICA

cc2009	5 Mar	Larnaca	6-0
cc 2010	24 Feb	Larnaca	1-0

v SOUTH KOREA

2010	19 Oct	Suwon	0-0
cc2011	9 Mar	Larnaca	2-0

v SPAIN

EC1993	19 Dec	Osuna	0-0
EC1994	20 Feb	Bradford	0-0
EC1996	8 Sept	Montilla	1-2
EC1996	29 Sept	Tranmere	1-1
2001	22 Mar	Luton	4-2
EC2007	25 Nov	Shrewsbury	1-0
EC2008	2 Oct	Zamora	2-2
wc2010	1 Apr	Millwall	1-0
wc2010	19 June	Aranda de Duero	2-2
EC2013	12 July	Linkoping	2-3

v SWEDEN

1975	15 June	Gothenborg	0-2
1975	7 Sept	Wimbledon	1-3
1979	27 July	Scafati	0-0*
1980	17 Sept	Leicester	1-1
1982	26 May	Kinna	1-1
1983	30 Oct	Charlton	2-2
EC1984	12 May	Gothenburg	0-1
EC1984	27 May	Luton	1-0
EC1987	11 June	Moss	2-3*
1989	23 May	Wembley	0-2
1995	13 May	Halmstad	0-4
1998	26 July	Dagenham	0-1
EC2001	27 June	Jena	0-4
2002	25 Jan	La Manga	0-5
AC2002	5 Mar	Lagos	3-6
EC2005	11 June	Blackburn	0-1

2006	7 Feb	Larnaca	0-0
2006	9 Feb	Achna	1-1
2008	12 Feb	Larnaca	0-2
EC2009	31 Aug	Turku	1-1
2011	17 May	Oxford	2-0
2013	4 July	Ljungskile	1-4
2014	3 Aug	Hartlepool	4-0

v SWITZERLAND

1975	19 Apr	Basel	3-1
1977	28 Apr	Hull	9-1
1979	23 July	Sorrento	2-0
EC1999	16 Oct	Zofingen	3-0
EC2000	13 May	Bristol	1-0
cc2010	1 Mar	Nicosia	2-2
wc2010	12 Sept	Shrewsbury	2-0
wc2010	16 Sept	Wohlen	3-2
cc2012	1 Mar	Larnaca	1-0

v TURKEY

wc2009	26 Nov	Izmir	3-0
wc2010	29 July	Walsall	3-0
wc2013	26 Sept	Portsmouth	8-0
wc2013	31 Oct	Adana	4-0

v UKRAINE

EC2000	30 Oct	Kiev	2-1
EC2000	28 Nov	Leyton	2-0
wc2014	8 May	Shrewsbury	4-0
wc2014	19 June	Lviv	2-1

v USA

M1985	23 Aug	Caorle	3-1
M1988	27 July	Riva del Garda	2-0
1990	9 Aug	Blaine	0-3
1991	25 May	Hirson	1-3
1997	9 May	San Jose	0-5
1997	11 May	Portland	0-6
AC2002	3 Mar	Ferreiras	0-2
2003	17 May	Birmingham (Alabama)	0-6
2007	28 Jan	Guangzhou	1-1
wc2007	22 Sept	Tianjin	0-3
2011	2 Apr	Leyton	2-1
2015	13 Feb	Milton Keynes	0-1

v USSR

1990	11 Aug	Blaine	1-1
1991	20 July	Dmitrov	2-1
1991	21 July	Kashira	2-0
1991	7 Sept	Southampton	2-0
1991	8 Sept	Brighton	1-3

v WALES

1974	17 Mar	Slough	5-0
1976	22 May	Bedford	4-0
1976	17 Oct	Ebbw Vale	2-1
1977	18 Sept	Warminster	5-0
1980	1 June	Warminster	6-1
1985	17 Aug	Ramsey (Isle of Man)	6-0
wc2013	26 Oct	Millwall	2-0
wc2014	21 Aug	Cardiff	4-0

v WEST GERMANY

M1984	22 Aug	Jesolo	0-2
1990	5 Aug	Blaine	1-3

OTHER MATCHES

v ITALY B

1984	27 Aug	Monfalcone	3-1
M1988	20 July	Riva del Garda	3-0

v USA B

1990	7 Aug	Blaine	1-0

NON-LEAGUE TABLES 2014–15

EVO-STIK NORTHERN PREMIER LEAGUE 2014–15

			Total				Home					Away						
		P	W	D	L	F	A	W	D	L	F	A	W	D	L	F	A	GD	Pts
1	FC United of Manchester	46	26	14	6	78	37	16	6	1	48	18	10	8	5	30	19	41	92
2	Workington	46	27	9	10	63	39	15	5	3	35	16	12	4	7	28	23	24	90
3	Ashton U	46	24	12	10	75	54	14	5	4	41	24	10	7	6	34	30	21	84
4	Curzon Ashton¶	46	23	14	9	79	46	15	4	4	49	22	8	10	5	30	24	33	83
5	Ilkeston	46	22	15	9	79	56	10	9	4	37	27	12	6	5	42	29	23	81
6	Blyth Spartans	46	21	16	9	84	54	12	7	4	37	22	9	9	5	47	32	30	79
7	Barwell	46	22	9	15	69	62	13	4	6	38	28	9	5	9	31	34	7	75
8	Skelmersdale U	46	21	10	15	58	48	12	5	6	35	26	9	5	9	23	22	10	73
9	Rushall Olympic	46	21	9	16	76	64	10	6	7	37	31	11	3	9	39	33	12	72
10	Buxton	46	18	16	12	69	57	8	7	8	41	34	10	9	4	28	23	12	70
11	Halesowen T	46	13	20	13	56	48	8	10	5	33	24	5	10	8	23	24	8	59
12	Grantham T	46	15	14	17	64	72	8	8	7	31	33	7	6	10	33	39	–8	59
13	Whitby T	46	14	16	16	56	63	8	9	6	28	26	6	7	10	28	37	–7	58
14	Matlock T	46	15	11	20	57	60	8	6	9	31	30	7	5	11	26	30	–3	56
15	Nantwich T	46	16	7	23	61	76	10	4	9	33	33	6	3	14	28	43	–15	55
16	Stourbridge	46	14	11	21	59	72	9	7	7	34	29	5	4	14	25	43	–13	53
17	Ramsbottom U	46	15	8	23	66	80	7	5	11	35	39	8	3	12	31	41	–14	53
18	King's Lynn T	46	14	10	22	60	81	10	2	11	25	30	4	8	11	35	51	–21	52
19	Frickley Ath	46	12	14	20	60	73	6	6	9	32	31	6	8	11	28	42	–13	50
20	Stamford	46	13	11	22	56	75	9	4	10	30	35	4	7	12	26	40	–19	50
21	Marine	46	11	16	19	58	69	7	8	8	28	28	4	8	11	30	41	–11	49
22	Witton Alb	46	14	7	25	58	86	9	4	10	35	41	5	3	15	23	45	–28	49
23	Trafford	46	6	15	25	58	93	2	8	13	30	44	4	7	12	28	49	–35	33
24	Belper T	46	6	14	26	62	96	5	7	11	39	47	1	7	15	23	49	–34	32

¶Curzon Ashton promoted via play-offs.

EVO-STIK NORTHERN PREMIER LEAGUE DIVISION 1 NORTH 2014–15

		P	W	D	L	F	A	W	D	L	F	A	W	D	L	F	A	GD	Pts
1	Salford C	42	30	5	7	92	42	17	2	2	54	20	13	3	5	38	22	50	95
2	Darlington 1883¶	42	28	7	7	99	37	16	3	2	57	14	12	4	5	42	23	62	91
3	Bamber Bridge	42	25	8	9	88	58	14	3	4	45	30	11	5	5	43	28	30	83
4	Northwich Victoria	42	25	7	10	75	39	12	5	4	40	17	13	2	6	35	22	36	82
5	Spennymoor T	42	22	11	9	76	45	13	5	3	45	25	9	6	6	31	20	31	77
6	Scarborough Ath	42	23	6	13	80	61	14	1	6	43	25	9	5	7	37	36	19	75
7	Mossley	42	23	6	13	79	63	12	2	7	40	29	11	4	6	39	34	16	75
8	Harrogate Railway Ath	42	19	10	13	85	75	11	5	5	42	27	8	5	8	43	48	10	67
9	Warrington T	42	19	8	15	65	55	10	5	6	32	25	9	3	9	33	30	10	65
10	Droylsden	42	20	3	19	98	84	13	2	6	52	30	7	1	13	46	54	14	63
11	Lancaster C	42	18	8	16	65	53	10	3	8	38	25	8	5	8	27	28	12	62
12	Farsley	42	18	7	17	73	64	12	5	4	44	24	6	2	13	29	40	9	61
13	Clitheroe	42	14	10	18	73	81	8	7	6	35	34	6	3	12	38	47	–8	52
14	Brighouse T	42	14	9	19	64	81	9	3	9	39	45	5	6	10	25	36	–17	51
15	Burscough	42	12	12	18	62	73	6	5	10	36	38	6	7	8	26	35	–11	48
16	Kendal T	42	12	10	20	81	92	8	5	8	47	42	4	5	12	34	50	–11	46
17	Ossett Alb*	42	13	7	22	49	72	8	3	10	29	35	5	4	12	20	37	–23	43
18	Ossett T	42	12	6	24	48	83	9	2	10	28	31	3	4	14	20	52	–35	42
19	Radcliffe Bor	42	8	11	23	49	91	6	7	8	32	44	2	4	15	17	47	–42	35
20	Prescot Cables	42	7	12	23	47	86	5	9	7	28	30	2	3	16	19	56	–39	33
21	New Mills	42	6	7	29	56	107	3	3	15	29	55	3	4	14	27	52	–51	25
22	Padiham	42	6	6	30	50	112	4	3	14	25	49	2	3	16	25	63	–62	24

*Ossett Albion deducted 3 points for fielding an ineligible player. ¶Darlington 1883 promoted via play-offs.

EVO-STIK NORTHERN PREMIER LEAGUE DIVISION 1 SOUTH 2014–15

		P	W	D	L	F	A	W	D	L	F	A	W	D	L	F	A	GD	Pts
1	Mickleover Sports	42	31	5	6	105	40	16	2	3	48	15	15	3	3	57	25	65	98
2	Leek T	42	28	5	9	91	38	13	4	4	51	17	15	1	5	40	21	53	89
3	Newcastle T	42	27	6	9	92	46	15	3	4	47	22	12	4	5	45	24	46	87
4	Sutton Coldfield T¶	42	25	8	9	75	41	15	4	2	46	18	10	4	7	29	23	34	83
5	Gresley	42	25	6	11	96	51	16	4	1	54	17	9	2	10	42	34	45	81
6	Stafford Rangers	42	23	12	7	68	33	11	9	1	35	13	12	3	6	33	20	35	81
7	Spalding U	42	23	10	9	84	41	16	2	3	47	16	7	8	6	37	25	43	79
8	Tividale	42	20	11	11	65	43	10	4	7	34	24	10	7	4	31	19	22	71
9	Lincoln U	42	19	9	14	72	55	9	5	7	42	28	10	4	7	30	27	17	66
10	Coalville T	42	19	4	19	76	71	13	2	6	48	27	6	2	13	28	44	5	61
11	Norton U	42	19	4	19	79	75	11	2	8	43	35	8	2	11	36	40	4	61
12	Romulus	42	18	7	17	69	65	9	4	8	35	32	9	3	9	34	33	4	61
13	Chasetown	42	14	9	19	60	64	9	5	7	36	34	5	4	12	24	30	–4	51
14	Loughborough Dynamo	42	13	9	20	71	87	7	3	11	43	51	6	6	9	28	36	–16	48
15	Sheffield	42	14	6	22	74	93	9	0	12	39	50	5	6	10	35	43	–19	48
16	Goole	42	12	10	20	53	66	8	5	8	32	29	4	5	12	21	37	–13	46
17	Stocksbridge Park Steels	42	10	11	21	53	84	5	8	8	29	34	5	3	13	24	50	–31	41
18	Carlton T	42	11	6	25	52	79	8	2	11	27	23	3	4	14	25	46	–27	39
19	Market Drayton T	42	11	4	27	66	109	6	2	13	35	56	5	2	14	31	53	–43	37
20	Kidsgrove Ath	42	9	9	24	48	96	5	5	11	20	38	4	4	13	28	58	–48	36
21	Rainworth Miners Welfare	42	8	6	28	46	91	3	3	15	25	44	5	3	13	21	47	–45	30
22	Brigg T	42	3	3	36	26	153	2	3	16	12	60	1	0	20	14	93	–127	12

¶Sutton Coldfield T promoted via play-offs.

EVO-STIK SOUTHERN PREMIER LEAGUE 2014–15

			Total					Home					Away						
		P	W	D	L	F	A	W	D	L	F	A	W	D	L	F	A	GD	Pts
1	Corby T	44	29	7	8	86	47	14	5	3	43	22	15	2	5	43	25	39	94
2	Poole T	44	28	7	9	84	35	16	3	3	44	14	12	4	6	40	21	49	91
3	Truro C¶	44	27	5	12	83	58	16	2	4	50	26	11	3	8	33	32	25	86
4	Hungerford T	44	22	13	9	64	36	13	8	1	31	8	9	5	8	33	28	28	79
5	St Neots T	44	20	16	8	82	58	13	3	6	51	34	7	13	2	31	24	24	76
6	Redditch U	44	21	12	11	73	44	10	6	6	33	22	11	6	5	40	22	29	75
7	Weymouth	44	22	7	15	71	71	13	4	6	43	26	9	1	12	28	45	0	73
8	Cirencester T	44	20	12	12	77	54	9	8	5	44	33	11	4	7	33	21	23	72
9	Hitchin T	44	20	10	14	78	63	12	5	5	40	25	8	5	9	38	38	15	70
10	Paulton R	44	18	10	16	65	62	11	6	5	39	28	7	4	11	26	34	3	64
11	Chippenham T	44	16	13	15	54	54	10	5	7	30	22	6	8	8	24	32	0	61
12	Chesham U	44	16	12	16	79	72	9	4	9	41	38	7	8	7	38	34	7	60
13	Cambridge C	44	14	15	15	71	62	8	8	6	38	27	6	7	9	33	35	9	57
14	Dunstable T	44	16	9	19	71	78	7	2	13	38	52	9	7	6	33	26	-7	57
15	Bideford	44	16	7	21	66	85	10	4	8	37	30	6	3	13	29	55	-19	55
16	Slough T	44	13	12	19	66	88	7	6	9	33	45	6	6	10	33	43	-22	51
17	Dorchester T	44	14	8	22	63	74	9	5	8	31	28	5	3	14	32	46	-11	50
18	Histon	44	13	10	21	53	74	10	7	5	36	25	3	3	16	17	49	-21	49
19	Biggleswade T	44	11	12	21	57	75	8	5	9	36	42	3	7	12	21	33	-18	45
20	Frome T	44	10	11	23	49	80	7	4	11	26	33	3	7	12	23	47	-31	41
21	Banbury U	44	9	10	25	53	86	6	5	11	27	37	3	5	14	26	49	-33	37
22	Arlesey T	44	10	6	28	43	84	5	4	13	20	36	5	2	15	23	48	-41	36
23	Burnham*	44	5	8	31	41	89	3	5	14	22	43	2	3	17	19	46	-48	20

*Hereford U folded, record expunged. *Burnham deducted 3 points for fielding an ineligible player.*
¶Truro C promoted via play-offs.

EVO-STIK SOUTHERN LEAGUE DIVISION 1 CENTRAL 2014–15

		P	W	D	L	F	A	W	D	L	F	A	W	D	L	F	A	GD	Pts
1	Kettering T	42	30	5	7	90	36	18	1	2	52	15	12	4	5	38	21	54	95
2	Royston T	42	27	3	12	74	50	15	3	3	36	17	12	0	9	38	33	24	84
3	Aylesbury	42	25	7	10	81	46	16	2	3	53	23	9	5	7	28	23	35	82
4	Bedworth U¶	42	25	4	13	85	55	12	3	6	42	24	13	1	7	43	31	30	79
5	Barton T	42	23	9	10	83	53	13	4	4	40	25	10	5	6	43	28	30	78
6	Rugby T	42	22	7	13	78	51	13	3	5	40	21	9	4	8	38	30	27	73
7	Hanwell T	42	21	5	16	71	60	11	1	9	38	33	10	4	7	33	27	11	68
8	Godalming T	42	18	10	14	67	62	9	6	6	34	30	9	4	8	33	32	5	64
9	St Ives T	42	16	12	14	70	77	10	6	5	38	27	6	6	9	32	50	-7	60
10	Northwood	42	15	12	15	60	61	11	5	5	35	23	4	7	10	25	38	-1	57
11	Marlow	42	15	12	15	58	59	8	6	7	31	30	7	6	8	27	29	-1	57
12	Uxbridge	42	15	10	17	71	69	7	6	8	42	41	8	4	9	29	28	2	55
13	Aylesbury U	42	15	8	19	66	80	7	5	9	37	40	8	3	10	29	40	-14	53
14	Potters Bar T	42	16	2	24	68	77	10	0	11	34	38	6	2	13	34	39	-9	50
15	Egham T	42	14	8	20	64	81	7	7	7	33	33	7	1	13	31	48	-17	50
16	Chalfont St Peter	42	11	15	16	60	66	8	6	7	34	33	3	9	9	26	33	-6	48
17	Bedford T	42	13	8	21	62	72	6	4	11	24	34	7	4	10	38	38	-10	47
18	Leighton T	42	10	13	19	52	71	4	7	10	25	38	6	6	9	27	33	-19	43
19	Daventry T	42	12	6	24	47	77	8	4	9	27	38	4	2	15	20	39	-30	42
20	Beaconsfield SYCOB	42	8	16	18	62	75	5	7	9	30	33	3	9	9	32	42	-13	40
21	North Greenford U	42	8	11	23	55	97	7	5	9	34	47	1	6	14	21	50	-42	35
22	AFC Hayes	42	8	7	27	39	88	6	4	11	23	38	2	3	16	16	50	-49	31

¶Bedworth U promoted via play-offs.

EVO-STIK SOUTHERN LEAGUE DIVISION 1 SOUTH & WEST 2014–15

		P	W	D	L	F	A	W	D	L	F	A	W	D	L	F	A	GD	Pts
1	Merthyr T	42	32	6	4	122	34	17	2	2	80	18	15	4	2	42	16	88	102
2	Evesham U	42	27	10	5	94	36	13	5	3	44	16	14	5	2	50	20	58	91
3	Stratford T¶	42	28	5	9	82	40	16	2	3	51	20	12	3	6	31	20	42	89
4	Taunton T	42	24	8	10	71	42	13	4	4	28	20	11	4	6	43	22	29	80
5	Larkhall Ath	42	23	8	11	82	50	12	6	3	42	22	11	2	8	40	28	32	77
6	Yate T	42	21	9	12	79	52	12	4	5	40	23	9	5	7	39	29	27	72
7	Didcot T	42	20	11	11	95	66	11	6	4	49	29	9	5	7	46	37	29	71
8	North Leigh	42	18	13	11	99	58	11	5	5	55	24	7	8	6	44	34	41	67
9	Cinderford T	42	19	10	13	79	48	12	6	3	44	22	7	4	10	35	26	31	67
10	Mangotsfield U	42	20	7	15	73	58	13	4	4	48	20	7	3	11	25	38	15	67
11	Shortwood U	42	17	14	11	77	55	10	6	5	37	22	7	8	6	40	33	22	65
12	Bridgwater T	42	17	11	14	67	59	7	6	8	35	32	10	5	6	32	27	8	62
13	Wimborne T	42	18	7	17	71	68	8	4	9	37	33	10	3	8	34	35	3	61
14	Swindon Supermarine	42	17	5	20	81	79	10	1	10	42	36	7	4	10	39	43	2	56
15	AFC Totton	42	16	5	21	65	75	9	4	8	41	34	7	1	13	24	41	-10	53
16	Tiverton T	42	13	10	19	60	69	9	4	8	41	32	4	6	11	19	37	-9	49
17	Sholing*	42	11	10	21	48	75	9	4	8	33	34	2	6	13	15	41	-27	43
18	Clevedon T*	42	10	8	26	54	111	5	3	13	31	52	5	5	13	23	59	-57	38
19	Fleet T	42	8	8	26	49	97	7	5	9	26	37	1	3	17	23	60	-48	32
20	Wantage T	42	8	4	30	43	100	5	3	10	25	50	3	1	20	18	50	-57	28
21	Bishop's Cleeve	42	6	4	32	52	143	4	2	15	27	65	2	2	17	25	78	-91	22
22	Bashley	42	5	3	36	20	148	0	4	17	11	62	5	1	19	9	86	-128	8

*¶Stratford T promoted via play-offs. *Demoted after failing ground grading.*

RYMAN ISTHMIAN PREMIER LEAGUE 2014–15

		P	W	D	L	F	A	W	D	L	F	A	W	D	L	F	A	GD	Pts
				Total						*Home*					*Away*				
1	Maidstone U	46	29	11	6	85	41	18	4	1	50	20	11	7	5	35	21	44	98
2	Hendon	46	27	14	5	82	55	17	5	1	45	24	10	9	4	37	31	27	95
3	Margate¶	46	25	10	11	94	58	14	5	4	50	28	11	5	7	44	30	36	85
4	Dulwich Hamlet	46	21	13	12	66	51	13	6	4	40	24	8	7	8	26	27	15	76
5	Metropolitan Police	46	21	12	13	72	51	16	4	3	42	16	5	8	10	30	35	21	75
6	Grays Ath	46	22	8	16	70	57	12	5	6	34	23	10	3	10	36	34	13	74
7	Enfield T*	46	24	4	18	70	56	16	1	6	42	26	8	3	12	28	30	14	73
8	Billericay T	46	20	8	18	73	65	12	4	7	47	28	8	4	11	26	37	8	68
9	Leiston	46	18	13	15	73	58	9	6	8	36	23	9	7	7	37	35	15	67
10	Leatherhead	46	19	10	17	72	62	11	3	9	34	26	8	7	8	38	36	10	67
11	Kingstonian	46	18	13	15	63	56	7	9	7	31	27	11	4	8	32	29	7	67
12	Wingate & Finchley	46	20	7	19	72	70	12	4	7	40	25	8	3	12	32	45	2	67
13	East Thurrock U	46	17	15	14	66	71	9	10	4	27	25	8	5	10	39	46	-5	66
14	Bognor Regis T	46	17	12	17	71	64	11	5	7	44	28	6	7	10	27	36	7	63
15	Hampton & Richmond	46	16	9	21	62	79	11	3	9	35	42	5	6	12	27	37	-17	57
16	Harrow Bor	46	15	8	23	64	77	9	5	9	39	36	6	3	14	25	41	-13	53
17	Canvey Island	46	14	11	21	61	77	8	6	9	36	41	6	5	12	25	36	-16	53
18	VCD Ath	46	14	11	21	53	70	8	6	9	29	36	6	5	12	24	34	-17	53
19	Lewes	46	14	11	21	45	67	9	6	8	28	30	5	5	13	17	37	-22	53
20	Tonbridge Angels	46	13	13	20	63	67	9	6	8	39	30	4	7	12	24	37	-4	52
21	Peacehaven & Telscombe	46	13	9	24	58	85	8	4	11	35	42	5	5	13	23	43	-27	48
22	Witham T	46	9	15	22	61	84	7	8	8	35	34	2	7	14	26	50	-23	42
23	AFC Hornchurch	46	10	10	26	46	70	5	9	9	19	25	5	1	17	27	45	-24	40
24	Bury T	46	7	11	28	35	86	5	5	13	21	40	2	6	15	14	46	-51	32

*Enfield T deducted 3 points for fielding an ineligible player. ¶Margate promoted via play-offs.

RYMAN ISTHMIAN LEAGUE DIVISION 1 NORTH 2014–15

		P	W	D	L	F	A	W	D	L	F	A	W	D	L	F	A	GD	Pts
1	Needham Market	46	33	5	8	101	41	18	2	3	58	21	15	3	5	43	20	60	104
2	Harlow T	46	31	10	5	108	58	16	5	2	61	28	15	5	3	47	30	50	103
3	AFC Sudbury	46	28	6	12	89	51	14	2	7	49	30	14	4	5	40	21	38	90
4	Brentwood T¶	46	25	10	11	83	63	10	6	7	40	36	15	4	4	43	27	20	85
5	Thurrock	46	25	9	12	104	57	14	3	6	56	27	11	6	6	48	30	47	84
6	Brightlingsea Regent	46	25	7	14	88	57	13	4	6	42	20	12	3	8	46	37	31	82
7	Dereham T	46	25	6	15	82	63	14	3	6	45	26	11	3	9	37	37	19	81
8	Wroxham	46	23	10	13	97	58	12	6	5	55	23	11	4	8	42	35	39	79
9	Aveley	46	21	7	18	86	75	11	4	8	44	39	10	3	10	42	36	11	70
10	Ware	46	16	16	14	76	61	8	6	9	38	31	8	10	5	38	30	15	64
11	Soham T Rangers	46	19	6	21	74	86	12	2	9	45	38	7	4	12	29	48	-12	63
12	Heybridge Swifts	46	17	11	18	70	75	7	10	6	35	37	10	1	12	35	38	-5	62
13	Thamesmead T	46	16	10	20	61	69	12	2	9	34	24	4	8	11	27	45	-8	58
14	Tilbury	46	16	10	20	64	76	10	5	8	33	28	6	5	12	31	48	-12	58
15	Great Wakering R	46	16	10	22	80	87	7	6	10	42	43	7	4	12	38	44	-7	52
16	Cray W	46	14	10	22	77	86	8	5	10	44	46	6	5	12	33	40	-9	52
17	Waltham Abbey	46	14	10	22	76	90	8	4	11	43	49	6	6	11	33	41	-14	52
18	Cheshunt	46	13	13	20	63	78	6	6	11	29	39	7	7	9	34	39	-15	52
19	Maldon & Tiptree	46	13	10	23	57	78	7	7	9	32	37	6	3	14	25	41	-21	49
20	Romford	46	13	9	24	69	99	8	7	8	42	42	5	2	16	27	57	-30	48
21	Chatham T	46	12	11	23	52	75	8	5	10	26	34	4	6	13	26	41	-23	47
22	Barkingside	46	12	9	25	59	98	7	4	12	24	37	5	5	13	35	61	-39	45
23	Redbridge	46	13	6	27	64	111	10	2	11	34	43	3	4	16	30	68	-47	45
24	Burnham Ramblers	46	5	7	34	50	138	3	3	17	31	70	2	4	17	19	68	-88	22

¶Brentwood T promoted via play-offs.

RYMAN ISTHMIAN LEAGUE DIVISION 1 SOUTH 2014–15

		P	W	D	L	F	A	W	D	L	F	A	W	D	L	F	A	GD	Pts
1	Burgess Hill T	46	33	10	3	105	39	18	3	2	59	20	15	7	1	46	19	66	109
2	Folkestone Invicta	46	29	11	6	107	47	18	3	2	57	21	11	8	4	50	26	60	98
3	Faversham T	46	30	7	9	111	52	16	4	3	59	24	14	3	6	52	28	59	97
4	Merstham¶	46	27	12	7	107	51	14	4	5	59	27	13	8	2	48	24	56	93
5	Whyteleafe	46	23	12	11	91	61	9	7	7	40	34	14	5	4	51	27	30	81
6	Worthing	46	22	10	14	92	65	10	6	7	42	36	12	4	7	50	29	27	76
7	Three Bridges	46	21	9	16	94	95	14	4	5	55	38	7	5	11	39	57	-1	72
8	Whitstable T	46	20	11	15	82	77	12	5	6	49	36	8	6	9	33	41	5	71
9	Herne Bay	46	20	9	17	62	65	10	4	9	31	35	10	5	8	31	30	-3	69
10	Guernsey	46	19	7	20	92	94	12	3	8	48	34	7	4	12	44	60	-2	64
11	Tooting & Mitcham U	46	15	14	17	77	66	10	7	6	47	30	5	7	11	30	36	11	59
12	Sittingbourne	46	16	11	19	55	69	7	8	8	26	35	9	3	11	29	34	-14	59
13	Corinthian–Casuals	46	16	10	20	64	82	9	4	10	34	41	7	6	10	30	41	-18	58
14	South Park	46	16	8	22	76	105	9	4	10	37	55	7	4	12	39	50	-29	56
15	Chipstead	46	15	9	22	67	84	8	4	11	36	43	7	5	11	31	41	-17	54
16	Hythe T	46	14	11	21	62	79	8	7	8	44	32	6	4	13	38	47	3	53
17	Walton & Hersham	46	14	11	21	59	76	10	4	9	36	38	4	7	12	23	38	-17	53
18	Walton Casuals	46	16	5	25	62	94	8	3	12	23	38	8	2	13	39	56	-32	53
19	Hastings U	46	12	12	22	57	70	5	9	9	28	35	7	3	13	29	35	-13	48
20	Carshalton Ath	46	13	9	24	61	79	10	4	9	37	30	3	5	15	24	49	-18	48
21	Ramsgate	46	13	9	24	61	86	7	5	11	31	43	6	4	13	30	43	-25	48
22	East Grinstead T	46	13	6	27	55	94	6	3	14	29	48	7	3	13	26	46	-39	45
23	Redhill	46	10	11	25	69	101	6	6	11	34	44	4	5	14	35	57	-32	41
24	Horsham	46	10	6	30	50	107	5	4	14	29	51	5	2	16	21	56	-57	36

¶Merstham promoted via play-offs.

THE FA TROPHY 2014–15

IN PARTNERSHIP WITH CARLSBERG

After extra time.

PRELIMINARY ROUND

Salford C v Prescot Cables	1-2
Brigg T v Padiham	0-0, 2-4
Lancaster C v Bamber Bridge	1-1, 1-5
Harrogate Railway Ath v Spennymoor T	2-3
Clitheroe v Droylsden	3-2
Brighouse T v Ossett T	0-1
Radcliffe Bor v Darlington 1883	0-2
New Mills v Ossett Alb	2-1
Stocksbridge Park Steels v Sheffield	3-4
Warrington T v Mossley	1-2
Kendal T v Northwich Vic	1-2
Burscough v Goole	0-1
Kettering T v Lincoln U	2-1
Coalville T v Mickleover Sports	1-4
Gresley v Tividale	2-0
Newcastle T v Sutton Coldfield T	2-0
Soham T Rangers v Spalding U	1-6
Chasetown v Norton U	5-0
St Ives T v Stratford T	0-1
Rugby T v Stafford Rangers	0-1
Market Drayton T v Rainworth MW	2-2, 3-0
Romulus v Daventry T	2-0
Leek T v Bedworth U	5-2
Loughborough Dynamo v Kidsgrove Ath	6-3
Cray W v Hastings U	2-0
Heybridge Swifts v Herne Bay	6-3
Burgess Hill T v Aveley	1-0
Whitstable T v AFC Sudbury	1-3
Horsham v Sittingbourne	6-2
Three Bridges v Carshalton Ath	4-1
North Greenford U v Chatham T	0-1
Tooting & Mitcham U v Aylesbury	1-2
Cheshunt v South Park	1-5
Guernsey v Barton R	4-0
Chalfont St Peter v AFC Hayes	1-1, 0-1
Ware v Great Wakering R	4-0
Thurrock v Tilbury	4-3
Harlow T v Wroxham	5-2
Walton Casuals v East Grinstead T	0-0, 6-1
Bedford v Chipstead	4-3
Northwood v Waltham Abbey	3-1
Romford v Uxbridge	1-1, 2-2*
(Uxbridge won 4-3 on penalties)	
Potters Bar T v Royston T	2-2, 1-4
Leighton T v Corinthian Casuals	3-3, 3-1
Aylesbury U v Thamesmead T	2-3
Redbridge v Whyteleafe	1-2
Ramsgate v Folkestone Invicta	1-4
Dereham T v Hanwell T	2-1
Brentwood T v Redhill	1-1, 2-1
Beaconsfield SYCOB v Faversham T	0-4
Burnham Ramblers v Brightlingsea Regent	1-5
Hythe T v Maldon & Tiptree	3-0
Needham Market v Walton & Hersham	1-3
Wimborne T v Godalming T	3-2
Tiverton T v Wantage T	2-0
Didcot T v Marlow	3-1
Larkhall Ath v Shortwood U	2-4
Cinderford T v AFC Totton	1-1, 1-3
Egham T v Bridgwater T	2-1
Bashley v Sholing	0-1
Swindon Supermarine v Fleet T	1-2
Clevedon T v Mangotsfield U	0-3
Yate T v North Leigh	1-2
Taunton T v Merthyr T	1-1, 0-1

FIRST QUALIFYING ROUND

Skelmersdale U v Nantwich T	0-2
Sheffield v Witton Alb	0-1
New Mills v Mossley	3-2
Prescot Cables v Goole	2-4
Farsley v Blyth Spartans	0-2
Whitby T v Ramsbottom U	1-2
FC United of Manchester v Padiham	2-0
Frickley Ath v Marine	0-2
Scarborough Ath v Darlington 1883	0-4

Curzon Ashton v Northwich Vic	0-0, 1-0
Buxton v Ashton U	2-0
Clitheroe v Workington	0-2
Ossett T v Trafford	2-2, 0-3
Spennymoor T v Bamber Bridge	3-1
St Neots T v Ilkeston	2-1
Mickleover Sports v Kettering T	3-2
Carlton T v Stourbridge	1-1, 2-4
Corby T v Redditch U	0-1
Loughborough Dynamo v Grantham T	3-1
Belper T v Histon	2-3
Halesowen T v Matlock T	1-1, 4-0
Evesham U v Banbury U	2-2, 0-1
Gresley v Romulus	3-1
Stamford v Barwell	0-1
Chasetown v Newcastle T	2-1
Rushall Olympic v Cambridge C	2-0
Market Drayton T v King's Lynn T	2-2, 1-5
Stratford T v Stafford Rangers	1-0
Leek T v Spalding U	2-2, 2-1
Aylesbury v Merstham	1-2
Walton Casuals v Peacehaven & Telscombe	2-4
Dulwich Hamlet v Chalfont St Peter	3-0
Thamesmead T v Three Bridges	3-1
Metropolitan Police v Billericay T	1-0
Whyteleafe v Dunstable T	3-1
Maidstone U v Walton & Hersham	3-2
Bedford T v Brightlingsea Regent	4-0
Worthing v Chatham T	1-1, 1-0
Horsham v Ware	1-0
Canvey Island v Leatherhead	1-1, 2-2*
(Leatherhead won 6-5 on penalties)	
Folkestone Invicta v Thurrock	3-2
Margate v Slough T	0-2
Arlesey T v Wingate & Finchley	2-1
Uxbridge v Hythe T	6-1
Brentwood T v Biggleswade T	1-1, 2-3
Hampton & Richmond Bor v Grays Ath	0-3
Burgess Hill T v Chesham U	2-0
Northwood v Guernsey	2-2*
(Northwood won 5-3 on penalties)	
Lewes v Harlow T	1-0
Cray W v Faversham T	3-0
VCD Ath v Tonbridge Angels	0-2
Hungerford T v East Thurrock U	1-1, 2-4
Dereham T v Enfield T	1-0
Bognor Regis T v AFC Sudbury	2-2, 1-2
Bury T v Hendon	1-3
Royston T v Witham T	1-2
Burnham v Hitchin T	2-2, 2-0
Barkingside v Kingstonian	3-1
South Park v Heybridge Swifts	1-4
Leiston v Leighton T	2-2, 5-2
AFC Hornchurch v Harrow Bor	2-0
Mangotsfield U v Bishop's Cleeve	5-1
Sholing v Tiverton T	1-0
AFC Totton v Hereford U	1-2
Truro C v Egham T	3-0
Poole T v North Leigh	3-1
Paulton R v Fleet T	3-0
Chippenham T v Frome T	3-1
Merthyr T v Cirencester T	2-0
Weymouth v Shortwood U	1-0
Dorchester T v Wimborne T	1-3
Bideford v Didcot T	3-3, 1-2

SECOND ROUND QUALIFYING

Chasetown v Loughborough Dynamo	4-1
Spennymoor T v Leek T	3-3, 1-0
Rushall Olympic v Stratford T	5-0
Blyth Spartans v Halesowen T	1-1, 0-2
St Neots T v Darlington 1883	3-1
Curzon Ashton v Barwell	1-2
Witton Alb v Workington	3-3, 0-3
King's Lynn T v Stourbridge	3-1
Redditch U v Trafford	5-2
Gresley v Goole	2-0
FC United of Manchester v Buxton	2-0
Nantwich v Ramsbottom U	1-3

Mickleover Sports v New Mills	A-A
(Tie abandoned after 68 mins due to fog, 1-1)	
Mickleover Sports v New Mills	3-1
Banbury U v Marine	3-2
Hereford U v Mangotsfield U	2-0
Witham T v Truro C	0-1
Dereham T v Sholing	A-A
(Tie abandoned after 73 mins due to fog, 1-1)	
Dereham T v Sholing	0-2
Weymouth v Burnham	0-0, 0-0*
(Weymouth won 5-4 on penalties)	
Maidstone U v AFC Sudbury	0-2
Metropolitan Police v Dulwich Hamlet	2-0
Barkingside v Horsham	1-3
Peacehaven & Telscombe v Thamesmead T	4-3
Lewes v Heybridge Swifts	1-1, 3-2
Leiston v Paulton R	3-2
Burgess Hill T v Folkestone Invicta	0-0, 1-0
Slough T v Merthyr T	1-1, 2-3
Biggleswade T v Poole T	1-2
Uxbridge v Didcot T	1-2
Bedford T v Chippenham T	2-1
Whyteleafe v Leatherhead	1-4
AFC Hornchurch v Merstham	4-2
Histon v Cray W	0-2
East Thurrock U v Arlesey T	4-4, 2-1
Hendon v Worthing	4-0
Tonbridge Angels v Grays Ath	2-0
Wimborne T v Northwood	2-1

THIRD ROUND QUALIFYING

Boston U v Workington	2-1
AFC Fylde v Hednesford T	3-2
Gainsborough Trinity v Brackley T	2-1
Stockport Co v Colwyn Bay	2-1
Bradford (Park Avenue) v Leamington	3-1
King's Lynn T v Harrogate T	0-1
Halesowen T v Gresley	2-0
Worcester C v Barrow	3-0
Chorley v Stalybridge Celtic	2-2, 2-1
Tamworth v Hyde	3-4
North Ferriby U v Mickleover Sports	6-2
Spennymoor T v Chasetown	3-0
Barwell v FC United of Manchester	1-1, 2-3
Solihull Moors v Redditch U	2-1
Guiseley v Rushall Olympic	0-0, 2-1
Banbury U v Ramsbottom U	0-3
Sholing v Farnborough	1-2
Concord Rangers v Boreham Wood	4-0
Weymouth v Cray W	3-1
Merthyr T v Didcot T	3-3, 1-2
Bedford T v Weston-super-Mare	0-0, 2-3*
(1-1 at the end of normal time)	
Hayes & Yeading U v Horsham	6-0
Oxford C v Lewes	6-1
Truro C v Hemel Hempstead T	1-2
Tonbridge Angels v Bromley	0-0, 0-3
Bishop's Stortford v Chelmsford C	4-3
Eastbourne Bor v Lowestoft T	1-2
St Neots T v AFC Sudbury	1-1, 0-1
Ebbsfleet U v Hendon	1-0
Maidenhead U v Metropolitan Police	2-1
Basingstoke T v Whitehawk	1-0
Havant & Waterlooville v East Thurrock U	2-1
Peacehaven & Telscombe v Gosport Bor	0-4
Wimborne T v AFC Hornchurch	4-2
St Albans C v Wealdstone	1-1, 0-3
Gloucester C v Bath C	0-0, 1-3*
(1-1 at the end of normal time)	
Staines T v Poole T	3-3, 1-1*
(Poole T won 5-4 on penalties)	
Burgess Hill T v Leatherhead	3-2
Hereford U v Sutton U	1-2
Leiston bye	

FIRST ROUND

Nuneaton T v Grimsby T	0-2
Hyde v Spennymoor T	4-2
Altrincham v Macclesfield T	1-0
AFC Fylde v Gainsborough Trinity	3-0
Guiseley v Chorley	0-2
Lincoln C v Alfreton T	0-2
North Ferriby U v Boston U	1-1, 2-0
Gateshead v Halesowen T	2-0
Worcester C v FC Halifax T	0-1
Southport v Wrexham	1-1, 0-2

Ramsbottom U v Stockport Co	0-3
Bradford (Park Avenue) v Kidderminster H	1-4
AFC Telford U v Chester FC	1-1, 1-1*
(AFC Telford U won 4-3 on penalties)	
FC United of Manchester v Harrogate T	4-0
Aldershot v Burgess Hill T	0-1
Weymouth v Havant & Waterlooville	1-1, 0-5
Bishop's Stortford v Torquay U	0-5
Lowestoft T v Dover Ath	1-3
Ebbsfleet U v Welling U	1-1, 3-2*
(2-2 at the end of normal time)	
Wealdstone v Hayes & Yeading U	1-0
Wimborne T v Oxford C	0-3
Weston-super-Mare v Farnborough	1-3
Dartford v Solihull Moors	2-0
Woking v Eastleigh	2-0
Hemel Hempstead T v Sutton U	3-0
Basingstoke T v Gosport Bor	2-2, 1-2*
(1-1 at the end of normal time)	
Bromley v Leiston	2-0
Forest Green R v Didcot T	2-2, 3-0
Bristol R v Bath C	2-0
Maidenhead U v Poole T	2-1
Braintree T v AFC Sudbury	1-0
Concord Rangers v Barnet	0-0, 6-2

SECOND ROUND

Chorley v FC United of Manchester	3-3, 0-1
Grimsby T v Gateshead	0-0, 2-3*
(2-2 at the end of normal time)	
Stockport Co v Wrexham	2-2, 1-6
FC Halifax T v Alfreton T	5-3
North Ferriby U v Hyde	2-0
AFC Fylde v AFC Telford U	4-0
Kidderminster H v Altrincham	0-1
Wealdstone v Bath C	1-3
Ebbsfleet U v Forest Green R	1-0
Havant & Waterlooville v Dover Ath	0-1
Maidenhead U v Farnborough	2-2, 0-1
Gosport Bor v Braintree T	0-2
Oxford C v Woking	2-2, 1-2
Hemel Hempstead T v Concord Rangers	3-1
Torquay U v Bromley	4-0
Burgess Hill T v Dartford	1-2

THIRD ROUND

Wrexham v Gateshead	1-1, 2-2*
(Wrexham won 5-3 on penalties)	
Braintree T v Ebbsfleet U	1-1, 0-2
FC United of Manchester v AFC Fylde	3-1
Dartford v FC Halifax T	2-2, 1-3
Farnborough v North Ferriby U	0-2
Hemel Hempstead T v Torquay U	0-2
Bath C v Altrincham	1-0
Woking v Dover Ath	3-3, 0-1

FOURTH ROUND

Dover Ath v Bath C	3-3, 1-2
FC Halifax T v Wrexham	0-1
Torquay U v FC United of Manchester	1-0
North Ferriby U v Ebbsfleet U	1-0

SEMI FINALS – FIRST LEG

Bath C v North Ferriby U	2-2
Wrexham v Torquay U	2-1

SEMI FINALS – SECOND LEG

North Ferriby U v Bath C	1-1*
(3-3 on aggregate; North Ferriby U won 4-2 on penalties)	
Torquay U v Wrexham	0-3
(Wrexham won 5-1 on aggregate)	

FA TROPHY FINAL 2015

Wembley, Sunday 29 March

North Ferriby U (0) 3 (King 76 (pen), Kendall 90, 111)

Wrexham (1) 3 (Moult 11, 118, Harris 59)   14,585

North Ferriby U: Nicklin; Topliss, Wilde (Peat 89), King, Wilson, Hone, Clarke, Fry (Kendall 80), Denton, Bolder (Jarman 61), St Juste.
Wrexham: Coughlin; Ashton, Smith, Hudson, Clarke (Bishop 112), Harris, Moult, Keates (Evans 72), Tomassen, Jennings, Morris (York 87).
Referee: Michael Oliver.
aet; North Ferriby U won 5-4 on penalties.

THE FA VASE 2014–15

IN PARTNERSHIP WITH CARLSBERG

*After extra time.

FIRST ROUND QUALIFYING

Colne v Penrith	2-1
Darlington Railway Ath v Sunderland RCA	0-5
South Shields v Willington	1-0
Albion Sports v Bridlington T	5-2
West Allotment Celtic v Eccleshill U	1-0
Silsden v Brandon U	4-0
Holker Old Boys v Norton & Stockton Ancients	3-0
Hebburn T v Marske U	0-2
Daisy Hill v Newton Aycliffe	3-2
Birtley T v Thornaby	2-1
Jarrow Roofing Boldon CA v Ryhope CW	2-3*
(2-2 at the end of normal time)	
Chester-le-Street T v Knaresborough T	3-1
Northallerton T v North Shields	0-1
Consett v Thackley	2-1
Ryton & Crawcrook Alb v Billingham T	1-1, 0-1
Barnoldswick T v Tow Law T	5-1*
(1-1 at the end of normal time)	
Alsager T v Maltby Main	1-3
Oldham Boro v 1874 Northwich	0-2
Staveley MW v Athersley Recreation	1-2
Appleby Frodingham v Ashton T	2-4*
(2-2 at the end of normal time)	
Dronfield T (walkover) v Cammell Laird (removed)	
Rossington Main v AFC Blackpool	2-0
Runcorn T v Glasshoughton Welfare	11-0
Winsford U v Cheadle T	5-0
Irlam v St Helens T	1-2*
(1-1 at the end of normal time)	
Hemsworth MW v Parkgate	3-2
Stockport Sports v Selby T	5-5, 1-3
Squires Gate v AFC Liverpool	2-4
Vauxhall Motors v Rochdale T	1-3
Worsbrough Bridge Ath v Pontefract Collieries	3-2*
(2-2 at the end of normal time)	
Atherton Collieries v Penistone Church	4-0
Shawbury U v Coventry Copsewood	7-1
Dudley Sports v Eccleshall	0-3
Kirby Muxloe v Stafford T	1-0
Studley v Bilston T	3-1
Continental Star v Heath Hayes	3-2
Sporting Khalsa v Wolverhampton Casuals	4-0
Southam U v Wednesfield	1-0*
(0-0 at the end of normal time)	
Ellesmere Rangers v Stone Old Alleynians	2-2, 1-2
Bewdley T v Coventry Sphinx	3-4*
(3-3 at the end of normal time)	
Lichfield C v Alvechurch	4-2*
(2-2 at the end of normal time)	
Cadbury Ath v Bardon Hill Sports	3-4*
(3-3 at the end of normal time)	
Wolverhampton SC v Gornal Ath	0-5
Shifnal T v Racing Club Warwick	2-1
Wellington Amateurs v Pegasus Juniors	0-3
Malvern T v Walsall Wood	2-3
AFC Wulfrunians v Black Country Rangers	3-1
Tipton T v Hinckley	2-1
Stourport Swifts v Bromsgrove Sporting	2-2, 2-3*
(2-2 at the end of normal time)	
Thurnby Nirvana v Greenwood Meadows	2-1
Harborough T v Holbrook Sports	0-1
Stapenhill v South Normanton Ath	0-3
Holwell Sports v Anstey Nomads	4-2
Retford U v Shirebrook T	3-1
Grimsby Bor v Clipstone	0-6
Long Eaton U v Arnold T	3-0
Louth T v Aylestone Park	2-1*
(1-1 at the end of normal time)	
Radford v Blaby & Whetstone Ath	1-2
Cleethorpes T v Loughborough University	5-2
AFC Mansfield v Teversal	3-2
Thetford T v Ely C	2-1
Yaxley v Swaffham T	2-0
Eynesbury R v Mildenhall T	1-1, 0-2
Kirkley & Pakefield v Diss T	2-1
Godmanchester R v St Neots T Youth & Saints	8-0
Bowers & Pitsea v Codicote	4-2

Barking v Stanway R	1-2
Halstead T v FC Broxbourne Bor	1-2*
(1-1 at the end of normal time)	
Wivenhoe T v Takeley	2-1
Hoddesdon T v Sawbridgeworth T	2-1
Cornard U v FC Romania	1-2
Basildon U v Haverhill Bor	0-1
Baldock T v Sporting Bengal U	4-1
Hatfield T v Hertford T	1-2
AFC Kempston R v Sileby Rangers	4-0
CB Hounslow U v AFC Dunstable	1-3
Irchester U v Staines Lammas	2-2, 1-3
(Tie awarded to Irchester U – Staines Lammas withdrawn)	
Oxhey Jets v Bedfont & Feltham	4-1
Cogenhoe U v Bedford	1-2
Burton Park W v Buckingham Ath	2-2, 3-3*
(Burton Park W won 4-2 on penalties)	
Crawley Green v Thrapston T	3-1*
(1-1 at the end of normal time)	
Wootton Blue Cross v Biggleswade U	1-7
Broadfields U v Harefield U	0-6
Northampton Spencer v Wellingborough Whitworths	3-1
Langford v Spelthorne Sports	2-2, 1-4
Berkhamsted v London Tigers	2-1
Potton U v Winslow U	0-0, 2-1
Raunds T v Woodford U	0-2*
(0-0 at the end of normal time)	
Newport Pagnell T v Bugbrooke St Michaels	3-1
New College Swindon v Fleet Spurs	3-3, 4-2*
(2-2 at the end of normal time)	
Cove v Wootton Bassett T	2-3
Flackwell Heath v Ash U	3-2
Fairford T v Reading T	1-2
Alton T v Tadley Calleva	1-2
Cheltenham Saracens v Milton U	1-2
Slimbridge v Kidlington	1-0
Woodley T v Badshot Lea	3-0
Windsor v Shrivenham	3-0
Hartley Wintney v Holyport	3-2
Canterbury C v Banstead Ath	2-4
Southwick v Dorking	3-2
Fisher v Woodstock Sports	4-3*
(3-3 at the end of normal time)	
St Francis Rangers v Oakwood	5-1*
(1-1 at the end of normal time)	
Wick & Barnham U v Haywards Heath T	4-0
Holmesdale v Colliers Wood U	4-5
Glebe v Bexhill U	0-2
Croydon v Phoenix Sports	3-3, 0-1
Ringmer v Saltdean U	4-1
Horley T v Sevenoaks T	3-2
Raynes Park Vale v Crowborough Ath	2-1
Lancing v Mole Valley SCR	4-1
Dorking W v Chichester C	3-0
Newhaven v Greenwich Bor	2-6
Seven Acre & Sidcup v Pagham	0-1
Epsom Ath v Deal T	3-2
Selsey v Corinthian	0-3
Pewsey Vale v Melksham T	0-4
Amesbury T v Hythe & Dibden	3-1
Swanage T & Herston v Downton	2-0
Cribbs v Cowes Sports	0-1
Hamworthy U v Winterbourne U	6-3
Almondsbury UWE v Whitchurch U	2-3
Warminster T v Longwell Green Sports	1-2*
(1-1 at the end of normal time)	
Wincanton T v Bemerton Heath Harlequins	0-5
Andover T v Westbury U	1-0
Lymington T v Romsey T	8-0
Fareham T v Fawley	2-0
Moneyfields v Brockenhurst	4-0
Roman Glass St George v Devizes T	2-1
AFC Portchester v Bitton	2-1
Oldland Abbotonians v Bradford T	1-7
Bridport v Totton & Eling	5-0
Team Solent v Cadbury Heath	3-3, 1-2*
(1-1 at the end of normal time)	
Elmore v Torpoint Ath	0-5

Camelford v St Blazey	0-0, 1-1*
(St Blazey won 5-4 on penalties)	
Plymouth Parkway v Willand R	4-2
Wells C v Brislington	0-2
Welton R v Cheddar	3-2
Barnstaple T v Elburton Villa	5-0
Ashton & Backwell U v Bishop Sutton	2-4
(Tie awarded to Ashton & Backwell U – Bishop Sutton removed)	
AFC St Austell v Porthleven	8-1
Crediton U v Saltash U	0-3
Tavistock v Radstock T	1-2
Buckland Ath v Cullompton Rangers	1-0
Newquay v Bovey Tracey	1-0

SECOND ROUND QUALIFYING

Holker Old Boys v Durham C	1-0*
(0-0 at the end of normal time)	
Whitley Bay v South Shields	4-3
Billingham v Yorkshire Amateur	1-3
AFC Darwen v Washington	4-3
Colne v Heaton Stannington	4-0
Ryhope CW v Barnoldswick T	5-2
Bishop Auckland v Birtley T	4-0
Alnwick T v Pickering T	5-3
Hall Road Rangers v Consett	0-5
Marske v Chester-le-Street T	2-1
West Allotment Celtic v Nelson	1-1, 2-1
Silsden v Garforth T	3-1
Sunderland RCA v Crook T	1-0
Esh Winning v Seaham Red Star	1-12
Daisy Hill v Albion Sports	5-4
Bedlington Terriers v Liversedge	4-0
Stokesley SC v North Shields	2-4
Billingham Synthonia v Celtic Nation	2-2, 2-1
Selby T v Bacup & Rossendale Bor	4-2
Ashton Ath v Shaw Lane Aquaforce	0-1
Armthorpe Welfare v Bootle	1-2
Dronfield T v Maltby Main	3-3, 1-3, 2-0
(First replay abandoned after 88 mins due to serious injury)	
West Didsbury & Chorlton v Rossington Main	2-1
Bottesford T v Rochdale T	2-1
Winsford U v Hemsworth MW	3-0
Chadderton v Abbey Hey	3-1
Widnes v AFC Emley	0-2
St Helens T v Nostell MW	2-0
Atherton Collieries v AFC Liverpool	4-1*
(1-1 at the end of normal time)	
Hallam v Ashton T	1-3
Athersley Recreation v Runcorn T	1-4
Winterton Rangers v Worsbrough Bridge Ath	1-0*
(0-0 at the end of normal time)	
1874 Northwich v Wigan Robin Park	9-0
Southam U v Barnt Green Spartak	2-0
Brocton v Kirby Muxloe	5-4
Walsall Wood v Pershore T	3-0
Nuneaton Griff v Dudley T	3-1
Shawbury U v AFC Bridgnorth	2-3*
(2-2 at the end of normal time)	
Bardon Hill Sports v AFC Wulfrunians	3-3, 0-1
Aston v Lichfield C	2-0
Ellistown & Ibstock U v Bromyard T	4-0
Lye T v Pegasus Juniors	1-2
Stone Old Alleynians v Gornal Ath	0-4
Continental Star v Willenhall T	2-3
Sporting Khalsa v Hanley T	3-3, 1-3
Eccleshall v Atherstone T	3-0
Bolehall Swifts v Cradley T	4-1
Coventry Sphinx v Studley	2-3
Heather St Johns v Rocester	3-4*
(1-1 at the end of normal time)	
Wellington v Shifnal T	3-2
Bromsgrove Sporting v Tipton T	2-1
Heanor T v Holwell Sports	6-1
Blidworth Welfare v Clipstone	4-2
Radcliffe Olympic v Cleethorpes T	1-6
Blaby & Whetstone Ath v Borrowash Vic	1-2
South Normanton Ath v Dunkirk	0-5
Oadby T v Retford U	2-0
Shepshed Dynamo v Barrow T	4-0
Louth T v Gedling MW	1-4
Basford U v Mickleover Royals	0-1
Long Eaton U v Lincoln Moorlands Railway	3-0
Holbrook Sports v AFC Mansfield	1-4

Thurnby Nirvana v Harrowby U	8-4
Sutton T (removed) v Graham St Prims (walkover)	
Belper N v Quorn	2-1*
(1-1 at the end of normal time)	
Kirkley & Pakefield v Newmarket T	2-0
Peterborough Northern Star v Team Bury	6-0
Fakenham T v Mildenhall T	2-1
Walsham Le Willows v Godmanchester R	1-7
Great Yarmouth T v Boston T	1-0
Peterborough Sports v Thetford T	3-1
Holbeach U v Blackstones	2-0
Yaxley v Sleaford T	2-1
Southend Manor v Wivenhoe T	0-1
Whitton U v FC Romania	5-1
Stowmarket T v Eton Manor	0-4
Hertford T v Ilford	5-0
FC Broxbourne Bor v Woodbridge T	1-2
Cockfosters v Hoddesdon T	5-0
Welwyn Garden C v Clapton	3-0
Baldock T v Long Melford	4-3
Ipswich W v Hadley	4-4, 2-1
Haverhill Bor v London Bari	4-1
Stanway R v FC Clacton	4-1
Bowers & Pitsea v Haverhill R	4-0
Debenham LC v Saffron Walden T	1-3
Stansted v London Colney	1-0
Spelthorne Sports v Risborough Rangers	2-1
Holmer Green v Desborough T	2-1
Rothwell Corinthians v Bedfont Sports	0-1
Bedford v AFC Kempston R	0-3
Kings Langley v Burton Park W	2-0
Sun Sports v Potton U	3-0
Biggleswade U v Northampton Spencer	2-2, 0-1
Wembley v Hillingdon Bor	4-2
Stotfold v Southall	1-0
Harefield U v Wellingborough T	3-2*
(2-2 at the end of normal time)	
Newport Pagnell T v Berkhamsted	0-3
Long Buckby v Oxhey Jets	0-2*
(0-0 at the end of normal time)	
Irchester U v Crawley Green	3-1
Tring Ath v Woodford U	2-1
AFC Dunstable v Leverstock Green	5-0
Newbury v Reading T	1-4
Farnham T v Milton U	2-1
Highworth T v Hartley Wintney	2-1*
(1-1 at the end of normal time)	
Windsor v Binfield	4-0
Flackwell Heath v Frimley Green	5-0
Hook Norton v Tadley Calleva	1-0
Chinnor v Henley T	6-2*
(2-2 at the end of normal time)	
Woodley T v Knaphill	0-2
Eversley & California v Tuffley R	3-3*
(Tuffley R won 6-5 on penalties)	
Slimbridge v Oxford C Nomads	6-0
Wootton Bassett T v Abingdon U	2-3*
(1-1 at the end of normal time)	
New College Swindon v Thame U	0-4
Malmesbury Vic v Bracknell T	3-2
Brimscombe & Thrupp v Carterton	5-2
Bexhill U v Rochester U	2-6
Seaford T v Fisher	0-4
Pagham v Worthing U	5-2
Cobham v Lingfield	0-4
Banstead Ath v Mile Oak	2-1*
(1-1 at the end of normal time)	
Raynes Park Vale v Epsom Ath	2-1
Cray Valley (PM) v Horley T	0-2
Hassocks v Broadbridge Heath	2-1
Molesey v Greenwich Bor	1-2
Phoenix Sports v Lancing	1-0
Wick & Barnham U v Arundel	3-3, 1-2
Colliers Wood U v Shoreham	2-0
Southwick v Lordswood	0-3
AFC Croydon Ath v Chessington & Hook U	0-3
Ringmer v St Francis Rangers	3-2*
(2-2 at the end of normal time)	
Loxwood v Steyning T	5-2
Hailsham T v Dorking W	3-2
Beckenham T v Corinthian	3-5
Cadbury Heath v Ringwood T	2-3
Bradford T v Andover T	4-0
Fareham T v Petersfield T	1-0
Sherborne T v New Milton T	1-0
Cowes Sports v Corsham T	4-0

Longwell Green Sports v Amesbury T	3-1
Bemerton Heath Harlequins v Moneyfields	4-3
Verwood T v Roman Glass St George	6-4*
(4-4 at the end of normal time)	
Chippenham Park v Whitchurch U	3-2*
(2-2 at the end of normal time)	
Calne T v Christchurch	2-1
Winchester C v Laverstock & Ford	8-0
Swanage T & Herston v United Services Portsmouth	1-1*
(United Services Portsmouth won 4-3 on penalties)	
AFC Portchester v Hamworthy U	2-1
Bridport v East Cowes Vic Ath	11-0
Melksham T v Bournemouth	8-1
Horndean v Lymington T	1-1, 5-0
Welton R v Hengrove Ath	2-0
Radstock T v Portishead T	3-0
Buckland Ath v Wellington	7-1
St Blazey v Barnstaple T	1-0
Falmouth T v Ashton & Backwell U	3-2
Shepton Mallet v Wadebridge T	7-2
Keynsham T v Plymouth Parkway	2-3
Saltash U v Street	5-3
Torpoint Ath v Newquay	2-3
Brislington v Witheridge	2-2, 1-1*
(Brislington won 3-2 on penalties)	
AFC St Austell (walkover) v Ilfracombe T (removed)	

FIRST ROUND

Colne v Shildon	2-3*
(2-2 at the end of normal time)	
Bootle v Barton T Old Boys	2-5
Dronfield T v Chadderton	2-1
(Tie awarded to Chadderton – Dronfield T removed)	
West Allotment Celtic v Runcorn T	2-4
North Shields v AFC Emley	4-2
Daisy Hill v Atherton Collieries	0-8
1874 Northwich v Ashton T	2-1
Marske U v Winterton Rangers	5-0
Bishop Auckland v Holker Old Boys	3-0
Bottesford T v Ryhope CW	1-1, 1-2
Selby T v Seaham Red Star	2-4
Guisborough T v Billingham Synthonia	3-1
Shaw Lane Aquaforce v Runcorn Linnets	4-1
St Helens T v Yorkshire Amateur	3-1
Sunderland RCA v Handsworth Parramore	1-0
Bedlington Terriers v Whitley Bay	1-4
AFC Darwen v Maine Road	2-0
Winsford U v Tadcaster Alb	2-3
Consett v Silsden	2-1
West Didsbury & Chorlton v Glossop North End	1-2
Gedling MW v AFC Mansfield	0-2
Long Eaton U v Worksop T	0-3
Walsall Wood v AFC Bridgnorth	3-2
Borrowash Vic v Belper U	2-1
Pegasus Juniors v Aston	4-0
Boldmere St Michaels v Thurnby Nirvana	2-4
Rocester v Brocton	3-6
Bromsgrove Sporting v Nuneaton Griff	3-2
Ellistown & Ibstock U v Hanley T	2-1
Blidworth Welfare v Willenhall T	0-2
Southam U v Cleethorpes T	1-5
Shepshed Dynamo v Oadby T	5-0
Mickleover Royals v Eccleshall	3-0
Dunkirk v Graham St Prims	7-2
Gornal Ath v Studley	3-2
AFC Wulfrunians v Heanor T	0-0, 0-3
Wellington v Bolehall Swifts	2-3
Welwyn Garden C v Peterborough Sports	1-2*
(1-1 at the end of normal time)	
Eton Manor v St Margaretsbury	0-1
Deeping Rangers v Wivenhoe T	1-0
Woodbridge T v Huntingdon T	0-3
Irchester U v Fakenham T	0-4
Oxhey Jets v Tower Hamlets	4-1
Kirkley & Pakefield v Colney Heath	2-3
(Tie awarded to Kirkley & Pakefield – Colney Heath removed)	
Saffron Walden T v Whitton U	2-1
Hertford T v Stanway R	1-1*
(Stanway R won 6-5 on penalties)	
Holbeach U v Gorleston	2-0
Sun Sports v Harefield U	3-1
Haringey Bor v Northampton Spencer	1-1, 0-0*
(Northampton Spencer won 4-3 on penalties)	
Berkhamsted v Kings Langley	0-3

Peterborough Northern Star v Stotfold	1-0
AFC Kempston R v Felixstowe & Walton U	3-1
Ipswich W v Cockfosters	1-0
AFC Dunstable v Haverhill Bor	5-2
Enfield 1893 v Tring Ath	0-4
Godmanchester R v Yaxley	0-0, 0-4
Waltham F v Great Yarmouth T	1-2
Wembley v Bowers & Pitsea	3-2
London Colney v Baldock T	2-1
Colliers Wood U v Ringmer	4-3*
(3-3 at the end of normal time)	
Chessington & Hook U v Camberley T	2-1*
(1-1 at the end of normal time)	
Eastbourne T v Erith & Belvedere	1-2*
(1-1 at the end of normal time)	
Hassocks v Corinthian	3-1
Littlehampton T v Guildford C	4-2*
(2-2 at the end of normal time)	
Ashford T (Middlesex) v Loxwood	2-3
Fisher v Crawley Down Gatwick	2-2, 2-2*
(Crawley Down Gatwick won 4-3 on penalties)	
Lingfield v Epsom & Ewell	5-1
Horsham YMCA v Bedfont Sports	3-1
Raynes Park Vale v Westfield	1-3
Chertsey T v Horley T	1-2
Arundel v Phoenix Sports	0-2
Lordswood v Knaphill	0-1
Greenwich Bor v Hailsham T	7-1
Tunbridge Wells v Rochester U	3-1
Erith T v Banstead Ath	4-1
Pagham v Spelthorne Sports	2-1
Thatcham T v Flackwell Heath	1-4
Bradford T v Malmesbury Vic	5-3
Ardley U v Chippenham Park	1-2
Hook Norton v Newport (IW)	0-2
Ringwood T v United Services Portsmouth	1-3
Windsor v Highworth T	1-4
Holmer Green v Ascot U	2-2, 0-7
Verwood T v Fareham T	2-0
Calne T v Bridport	1-2*
(1-1 at the end of normal time)	
Melksham T v Highmoor Ibis	2-1*
(1-1 at the end of normal time)	
Thame U v Chinnor	2-1
Bemerton Heath Harlequins v Cowes Sports	2-0
Winchester C v Horndean	0-3
Farnham T v Abingdon U	3-3, 1-5
AFC Portchester v Reading T	2-1
Folland Sports v Sherborne T	2-1
AFC St Austell v Saltash U	4-0
Plymouth Parkway v Tuffley R	4-1
Buckland Ath v Longwell Green Sports	1-0*
(0-0 at the end of normal time)	
St Blazey v Gillingham T	4-1
Shepton Mallet v Brislington	2-1
Welton R v Brimscombe & Thrupp	3-1
Newquay v Slimbridge	1-3
Odd Down v Falmouth T	4-3
Bristol Manor Farm v Radstock T	3-0
Alnwick T bye	

SECOND ROUND

Bishop Auckland v 1874 Northwich	1-4
Glossop North End v Ryhope CW	3-0
Alnwick T v St Helens T	4-5*
(4-4 at the end of normal time)	
Dunston UTS v Guisborough T	2-1
Newcastle Benfield v Ashington	2-1
Marske U v Barton T Old Boys	4-1
West Auckland T v Shaw Lane Aquaforce	0-3
AFC Darwen v Chadderton	3-5
Shildon v Runcorn T	3-0
Sunderland RCA v North Shields	0-3
Atherton Collieries v Seaham Red Star	1-2
Congleton v Whitley Bay	0-1
Consett v Whickham	8-0
Tadcaster Alb v Morpeth T	2-1
Worksop T v Ellistown & Ibstock U	2-1
Bolehall Swifts v Dunkirk	4-2
Westfields v St Andrews	2-1
Wisbech T v Cleethorpes T	2-1
Thurnby Nirvana v Gornal Ath	4-1
Shepshed Dynamo v AFC Mansfield	2-3*
(1-1 at the end of normal time)	
Heanor T v Coleshill T	4-3

Borrowash Vic v Bromsgrove Sporting	0-5
Mickleover Royals v Willenhall T	2-0
Brocton v Pegasus Juniors	3-1
Causeway U v Walsall Wood	1-5
Sun Sports v Stanway R	0-1
London Colney v Northampton Spencer	3-1
St Margaretsbury v Ipswich W	3-0
Peterborough Sports v Peterborough Northern Star	3-4
Hullbridge Sports v AFC Rushden & Diamonds	1-0
Holbeach U v Huntingdon T	3-2
Norwich U v AFC Kempston R	2-1
Yaxley v Fakenham T	3-0
Deeping Rangers v Oxhey Jets	2-0
AFC Dunstable v Kirkley & Pakefield	3-2
Saffron Walden T v Kings Langley	6-5*
(5-5 at the end of normal time)	
Ampthill T v Tring Ath	1-4
Wembley v Brantham Ath	3-4*
(2-2 at the end of normal time)	
Great Yarmouth T v Hadleigh U	2-0
Erith T v Phoenix Sports	0-3
Lingfield v Chessington & Hook U	5-1
Horndean v Ascot U	0-1
Hassocks v Ashford U	0-7
Hanworth Villa v Knaphill	1-0
Eastbourne U v Horley T	1-3
Horsham YMCA v Erith & Belvedere	1-2
Abingdon T v Littlehampton T	4-4, 3-7
East Preston v Flackwell Heath	0-8
Westfield v Tunbridge Wells	1-5
Pagham v Colliers Wood U	1-2
United Services Portsmouth v AFC Portchester	1-3
Crawley Down Gatwick v Greenwich Bor	1-3
Newport (IW) v Loxwood	3-2
Alresford T v Thame U	3-1
Odd Down v Hallen	3-2
Verwood T v Plymouth Parkway	5-4
Folland Sports v AFC St Austell	2-3
Buckland Ath v Bristol Manor Farm	2-1
Chippenham Park v Bradford T	1-2*
(1-1 at the end of normal time)	
Blackfield & Langley v Bemerton Heath Harlequins	3-0
Melksham T v Slimbridge	2-2, 4-1
Bodmin T v St Blazey	5-2
Highworth T v Bridport	3-0
Shepton Mallet v Welton R	1-0

THIRD ROUND

Whitley Bay v Dunston UTS	1-2
1874 Northwich v Glossop North End	0-3
Shaw Lane Aquaforce v Shildon	3-2
Chadderton v Newcastle Benfield	2-1
Seaham Red Star v North Shields	2-4
St Helens T v Tadcaster Alb	2-4
Consett v Marske U	3-2*
(2-2 at the end of normal time)	
Worksop T v Westfields	2-1
Thurnby Nirvana v Bromsgrove Sporting	2-1
Bolehall Swifts v Brocton	0-5
Mickleover Royals v AFC Mansfield	0-1
Wisbech T v Walsall Wood	2-3
Deeping Rangers v Heanor T	1-2*
(1-1 at the end of normal time)	
Saffron Walden T v AFC Dunstable	1-0
Hullbridge Sports v Great Yarmouth T	1-0
St Margaretsbury v Stanway R	0-2
Peterborough Northern Star v Flackwell Heath	2-3
Tring Ath v Norwich U	0-1
London Colney v Holbeach U	0-1
Brantham Ath v Yaxley	1-3
Hanworth Villa v Erith & Belvedere	0-2
Alresford T v Phoenix Sports	1-2
Horley T v Greenwich Bor	1-3
AFC Portchester v Tunbridge Wells	0-1
Colliers Wood U v Lingfield	9-2
Ascot U v Newport (IW)	3-0
Littlehampton T v Ashford U	3-3, 1-2
Melksham T v Shepton Mallet	3-2

Blackfield & Langley v Highworth T	0-1
AFC St Austell v Verwood T	6-1
Buckland Ath v Bodmin T	1-4
Bradford T v Odd Down	4-3

FOURTH ROUND

Walsall Wood v Shaw Lane Aquaforce	1-1, 1-4
North Shields v Consett	4-1
Thurnby Nirvana v Holbeach U	3-4*
(3-3 at the end of normal time)	
Chadderton v AFC Mansfield	0-5
Worksop T v Glossop North End	0-1*
(0-0 at the end of normal time)	
Heanor T v Dunston UTS	0-1
Tadcaster Alb v Brocton	3-2
Bodmin T v Phoenix Sports	0-2
Stanway R v Saffron Walden T	1-0
Ascot U v Colliers Wood U	4-2*
(2-2 at the end of normal time)	
Bradford T v Melksham T	3-1
Ashford U v Norwich U	0-5
Greenwich Bor v AFC St Austell	2-3
Flackwell Heath v Hullbridge Sports	3-0
Erith & Belvedere v Yaxley	1-0
Highworth T v Tunbridge Wells	1-1, 2-2*
(Highworth T won 4-2 on penalties)	

FIFTH ROUND

Bradford T v Highworth T	0-2
AFC St Austell v Stanway R	2-0
Ascot U v Norwich U	3-0
Shaw Lane Aquaforce v Flackwell Heath	3-2
Glossop North End v Dunston UTS	2-2, 3-1*
(1-1 at the end of normal time)	
Holbeach U v Erith & Belvedere	2-3*
(2-2 at the end of normal time)	
North Shields v Phoenix Sports	4-1
AFC Mansfield v Tadcaster Alb	0-3

SIXTH ROUND

AFC St Austell v Ascot U	3-2
Erith & Belvedere v North Shields	0-2
Shaw Lane Aquaforce v Glossop North End	2-2*, 1-3*
(2-2 at the end of normal time); (1-1 at the end of normal time)	
Highworth T v Tadcaster Alb	1-1*, 0-1
(1-1 at the end of normal time)	

SEMI-FINALS – FIRST LEG

Highworth T v North Shields	0-1
AFC St Austell v Glossop North End	0-2

SEMI-FINALS – SECOND LEG

North Shields v Highworth T	2-0
North Shields won 3-0 on aggregate.	
Glossop North End v AFC St Austell	0-1
Glossop North End won 2-1 on aggregate	

FA VASE FINAL 2015

Wembley, Saturday 9 May 2015

North Shields (0) 2 *(Bainbridge 80, Forster 96)*

Glossop North End (0) 1 *(Bailey 55)* 9674

North Shields: Bannon; Donnison, Grey, Parker, Hughes, McKeown, Richardson, Morris, Holmes (Forster 69), Luccock (Carr 59), Bainbridge (Wrightson 106).
Glossop North End: Hall; Bowler, Russell, Lugsden, Young, Parker, Blackshaw (Grimshaw 69), Hare (Hind 82), Bailey, Moran (White 61), Lugsden.
Referee: Andrew Madley.
aet; 1-1 at the end of normal time.

THE FA YOUTH CUP 2014–15

After extra time.

PRELIMINARY ROUND

Shildon v Seaham Red Star	2-3
Chester-le-Street T v Newton Aycliffe	2-1
Altrincham v Colne	3-0
Irlam v Glossop North End	15-0
Curzon Ashton v Runcorn Linnets	2-1
Chester v Prescot Cables	2-1
Macclesfield T v FC United of Manchester	3-1
Hyde v Ashton Ath	1-2
Ossett T v Staveley MW	1-3
AFC Emley (removed) v Sheffield (walkover)	
Hall Road Rangers v Harrogate T	2-1*
(1-1 at the end of normal time)	
Silsden v Barton T Old Boys	1-5
Thackley v Handsworth Parramore	1-9
North Ferriby U v Guiseley	0-2
Anstey Nomads v Matlock T	2-3
Blaby & Whetstone Ath (withdrawn) v Loughborough Dynamo (walkover)	
Ilkeston (walkover) v Thurnby Nirvana (withdrawn)	
Aylestone Park v Retford U	1-2
Holwell Sports v Gresley	0-7
Coleshill T v Lichfield C	2-0
Worcester v Pegasus Juniors	4-1
Solihull Moors v Stourbridge	2-1
Wednesfield v Rugby T	2-0
Wolverhampton Casuals v Newcastle T	0-2
Leamington v Sutton Coldfield T	2-1
(Tie awarded to Sutton Coldfield T - Leamington withdrawn)	
Bilston T v Tividale	4-1
Malvern T v Hereford U	0-6
Felixstowe & Walton U v Dereham T	0-4
Newmarket T v Walsham Le Willows	2-0
Gorleston v Woodbridge T	1-3
Ipswich W v Fakenham T	4-4*
(Fakenham T won 4-3 on penalties)	
Mildenhall T v Hadleigh U	4-2
Stowmarket T v Soham T Rangers	4-0
Whitton U (withdrawn) v Haverhill R (walkover)	
AFC Dunstable v AFC Rushden & Diamonds	1-2
AFC Kempston R (withdrawn) v Wellingborough T (walkover)	
Bedford T v Bugbrooke St Michaels	0-2
Rothwell Corinthians v Brackley T	1-2
Barkingside v Clapton	1-2
East Thurrock U v Witham T	4-2
Cockfosters v Codicote	2-3
Billericay T v Tower Hamlets	3-4*
(2-2 at the end of normal time)	
Brentwood T v Burnham Ramblers	2-2*
(Brentwood T won 4-3 on penalties)	
Canvey Island v Cheshunt	1-3
Fisher (walkover) v Halstead T (withdrawn)	
Royston T v Romford	4-1
Potters Bar T v Braintree T	4-2
Stanway R v Redbridge	0-1
Concord Rangers v St Albans C	3-1
Hullbridge Sports v Hitchin T	0-8
Wealdstone v Chesham U	6-0
Leverstock Green (walkover) v Oxhey Jets (withdrawn)	
Hayes & Yeading U v Hampton & Richmond Bor	3-0
AFC Hayes v Corinthian Casuals	2-4
Buckingham Ath v Hanworth Villa	2-2*
(Hanworth Villa won 5-4 on penalties)	
Lordswood (withdrawn) v Margate (walkover)	
Tooting & Mitcham U v Folkestone Invicta	1-6
Tonbridge Angels v Dartford	0-3
Herne Bay v Chatham T	3-1
Greenwich Bor v Dover Ath	3-2*
(1-1 at the end of normal time)	
Lingfield v VCD Ath	2-3
Dulwich Hamlet v East Grinstead T	9-0
Bromley v Cray Valley (PM)	3-0
Crawley Down Gatwick v Mile Oak	3-0
Walton & Hersham v Haywards Heath T	5-2
Pagham v Saltdean U	5-1
Arundel v Fareham T	0-4
Knaphill v Littlehampton T	3-3*
(Littlehampton T won 4-3 on penalties)	

Lewes v Chichester C	9-0
Woking v Horsham	7-0
Aldershot T v Oxford C	1-1*
(Oxford C won 5-4 on penalties)	
Cove (withdrawn) v Kidlington (walkover)	
Windsor v Maidenhead U	0-3
Burnham v Thatcham T	2-3
Hartley Wintney v Basingstoke T	1-0
Christchurch v Gillingham T	6-0
Sholing v AFC Portchester	3-0
Petersfield T (walkover) v Salisbury C (removed)	
Bemerton Heath Harlequins v Moneyfields	0-7
Ringwood T v Wimborne T	0-5
Gloucester C v Bristol R	1-0
Chippenham T (walkover) v Merthyr T (withdrawn)	
Bristol Manor Farm v Yate T	2-7
Weston Super Mare v Brislington	8-0
Torquay U v Clevedon T	9-0
Larkhall Ath v Bath C	0-4
Wells C v Tiverton T	4-3

FIRST ROUND QUALIFYING

Chester-le-Street T v Ryton & Crawcrook Alb	4-0
Newcastle Benfield v Consett	10-2
Seaham Red Star (walkover) v Sunderland RCA (withdrawn)	
Darlington 1883 v Gateshead	3-0
Marine v Ashton T	4-1
Ashton Ath v Daisy Hill	2-1
Lancaster C v Nantwich T	3-5*
(3-3 at the end of normal time)	
Vauxhall Motors v Padiham	4-2
AFC Fylde v Witton Alb	5-3
Salford C v Southport	2-2*
(Southport won 5-4 on penalties)	
Bootle v Abbey Hey	0-1
Curzon Ashton v Clitheroe	1-2
AFC Blackpool v Skelmersdale U	0-5
Widnes (withdrawn) v Chester (walkover)	
Macclesfield T v Warrington T	1-2
Wrexham v West Didsbury & Chorlton	6-0
Altrincham v Irlam	3-0
Staveley MW v Handsworth Parramore	2-0
FC Halifax T v Hall Road Rangers	6-1
Pontefract Collieries v Nostell MW	1-4
Farsley v Stocksbridge Park Steels	1-2
Hemsworth MW v Knaresborough T	0-4
Goole v Barton T Old Boys	0-2
Brighouse T v Guiseley	3-3*
(Brighouse T won 4-3 on penalties)	
Ossett Alb v Sheffield	0-3
Grimsby T v Selby T	4-2*
(2-2 at the end of normal time)	
Matlock T v Gresley	1-0
Basford U v Ilkeston	1-0
Heanor T v Grantham T	1-2*
(1-1 at the end of normal time)	
Arnold T (withdrawn) v Lincoln C (walkover)	
Boston U v Teversal	5-2
Mickleover Sports v Retford U	0-3
Stamford v Oadby T	0-3
Dunkirk v Loughborough Dynamo	2-1
St Andrews v Long Eaton U	5-3
Tipton T v Kidderminster H	0-4
Chasetown v Ellesmere Rangers	3-4
Sutton Coldfield T v Coventry Sphinx	1-5*
(1-1 at the end of normal time)	
Nuneaton T v Racing Club Warwick	5-0
Lye T v Stratford T	1-11
AFC Wulfrunians v Boldmere St Michaels	1-1*
(Boldmere St Michaels won 4-3 on penalties)	
Coleshill T v Newcastle T	2-1
Eccleshall v Solihull Moors	1-2
Bedworth U v Worcester C	1-5
Romulus v Dudley Sports	4-1
Wednesfield v Hereford U	1-4
Nuneaton Griff v Bilston T	0-6
Swaffham T v AFC Sudbury	3-5
Wroxham v Newmarket T	4-0
Cornard U v Woodbridge T	0-11
Fakenham T v Long Melford	6-1

Histon v Bury T	1-0
Kirkley & Pakefield v Mildenhall T	4-3
Dereham T v Brantham Ath	5-2
Lowestoft T v Needham Market	0-6
Norwich U v Great Yarmouth T	0-2
Haverhill R v Stowmarket T	3-2*
(2-2 at the end of normal time)	
St Neots T v Brackley T	3-4
Bugbrooke St Michaels v AFC Rushden & Diamonds	5-0
Peterborough Sports (withdrawn) v Barton R (walkover)	
Wellingborough Whitworths v	
Peterborough Northern Star	0-2
St Ives T v Godmanchester R	2-5*
(2-2 at the end of normal time)	
Cogenhoe U v Wellingborough T	2-0
Yaxley v Corby T	2-4
Bowers & Pitsea v Royston T	2-4
Great Wakering R v Chelmsford C	0-10
Potters Bar T v Cheshunt	5-1
Brightlingsea Regent v Enfield T	0-1
Sawbridgeworth T v FC Clacton	2-4
Codicote v Barking	3-1
Waltham Abbey v Saffron Walden T	3-1
Bishop's Stortford v Hitchin T	1-2
Tilbury v Barnet	1-3
Thurrock v Boreham Wood	2-2*
(Boreham Wood won 4-3 on penalties)	
Tower Hamlets v Aveley	5-1
East Thurrock U v Grays Ath	4-2
AFC Hornchurch (walkover) v Heybridge Swifts	
(withdrawn)	
Redbridge v Concord Rangers	1-1*
(Concord Rangers won 5-4 on penalties)	
Ware v Fisher	3-5*
(2-2 at the end of normal time)	
Clapton v Brentwood T	0-6
Wealdstone v Hanworth Villa	7-0
Bedfont Sports v Hayes & Yeading U	2-3
Northwood v Tring Ath	5-3*
(3-3 at the end of normal time)	
Ashford T (Middlesex) v Metropolitan Police	1-6
Kings Langley v Harefield U	1-7
Uxbridge v Corinthian Casuals	4-2
Wingate & Finchley v Newport Pagnell T	2-1
North Greenford U v Leverstock Green	0-5
Berkhamsted v Staines T	1-3
Corinthian v Welling U	1-3
Greenwich Bor v Thamesmead T	1-5
Eastbourne Bor v Ramsgate	2-0
Bromley v Faversham T	9-0
Folkestone Invicta v Ebbsfleet U	0-4
Hastings U v Holmesdale	4-1*
(1-1 at the end of normal time)	
Croydon v Whitstable T	6-1
Eastbourne U v Colliers Wood U	1-7
Carshalton Ath v Maidstone U	1-3
Eastbourne T v Erith & Belvedere	1-3
Dartford v Margate	4-1
Herne Bay v VCD Ath	3-0
Phoenix Sports v Sutton U	0-7
Dulwich Hamlet v Chipstead	3-0
Newhaven v Bognor Regis T	1-3
Lewes v Raynes Park Vale	2-1
Redhill v Woking	2-10
Camberley T v South Park	2-0
Leatherhead v Horley T	4-1
Three Bridges v Westfield	4-6*
(4-4 at the end of normal time)	
Burgess Hill T v Shoreham	7-1
Pagham v Molesey	3-0
Kingstonian v Peacehaven & Telscombe	4-0
Guildford C v Farnham T	0-1
Littlehampton T v Dorking	11-1
Worthing v Whyteleafe	0-2
Crawley Down Gatwick v Walton & Hersham	0-3
Thatcham T v Bracknell T	3-4
Maidenhead U v Hartley Wintney	6-1
Farnborough v Didcot T	1-7
Marlow v Slough T	2-1
Binfield v Thame U	1-0*
(0-0 at the end of normal time)	
Oxford C v Alton T	7-1
Andover T (removed) v Fleet T (walkover)	
Ascot U v Kidlington	2-1
Poole T v Moneyfields	6-1

Petersfield T v Christchurch	3-4*
(3-3 at the end of normal time)	
Team Solent (withdrawn) v Wimborne T (walkover)	
Romsey T v Havant & Waterlooville	0-6
Hamworthy U (walkover) v Dorchester T (withdrawn)	
Bournemouth v Sholing	1-0
AFC Totton v Eastleigh	1-2*
(1-1 at the end of normal time)	
Chippenham T (walkover) v Mangotsfield U (withdrawn)	
Pewsey Vale v Yate T	3-4
Gloucester C v New College Swindon	4-1
Cirencester T v Forest Green R	1-0
Weston-super-Mare v Ashton & Backwell U	3-0
Hengrove Ath v Wells C	1-2
Torquay U v Willand R	6-2
Elmore v Taunton T	3-9
Paulton R v Bath C	0-2

SECOND ROUND QUALIFYING

Seaham Red Star v Darlington 1883	2-1
Newcastle Benfield v Chester-le-Street T	4-1
Grimsby T v Vauxhall Motors	6-0
Marine v Nostell MW	4-2
FC Halifax T v Stocksbridge Park Steels	1-2
Nantwich T v Staveley MW	3-2*
(2-2 at the end of normal time)	
Knaresborough T v Sheffield	1-0
Wrexham v Ashton Ath	0-2
Chester v Irlam	3-5
Skelmersdale U v Warrington T	3-2
Abbey Hey v Barton T Old Boys	3-1
AFC Fylde v Brighouse T	5-3
Clitheroe v Southport	0-2
Matlock T v Boston U	0-2
Oadby T v St Andrews	2-1*
(1-1 at the end of normal time)	
Grantham T v Dunkirk	2-1
Lincoln C v Corby T	2-0
Basford U v Retford U	5-2
Coleshill T v Romulus	3-0
Bilston T v Hereford U	2-1
Ellesmere Rangers v Boldmere St Michaels	2-1*
(1-1 at the end of normal time)	
Worcester C v Stratford T	3-4
Nuneaton T v Coventry Sphinx	3-1
Kidderminster H v Solihull Moors	6-1
AFC Sudbury v Histon	1-0
Dereham T v Great Yarmouth T	3-6
Woodbridge T v Needham Market	0-3
Fakenham T v Haverhill R	3-1
Wroxham v Kirkley & Pakefield	6-1
Peterborough Northern Star v Godmanchester R	5-0
Brackley T v Bugbrooke St Michaels	2-2*
(Brackley T won 7-6 on penalties)	
Barton R v Cogenhoe U	7-2
Brentwood T v Tower Hamlets	2-2*
(Brentwood T won 4-3 on penalties)	
Codicote v Enfield T	1-0
Boreham Wood v Potters Bar T	2-4
Concord Rangers v Fisher	0-2
Hitchin T v Chelmsford C	1-3
Barnet v FC Clacton	11-1
Royston T v East Thurrock U	3-2
Waltham Abbey v AFC Hornchurch	1-6
Wealdstone v Harefield U	2-1
Wingate & Finchley v Staines T	0-4
Northwood v Leverstock Green	3-7
Metropolitan Police v Marlow	8-2
Hayes & Yeading U v Uxbridge	5-2
Bromley v Eastbourne Bor	4-4*
(Eastbourne Bor won 4-1 on penalties)	
Herne Bay v Erith & Belvedere	4-0
Dulwich Hamlet v Ebbsfleet U	1-3
Croydon v Thamesmead T	1-3
Maidstone U v Sutton U	1-1*
(Sutton U won 4-2 on penalties)	
Hastings U v Dartford	2-3
Colliers Wood U v Welling U	0-2
Wimborne T v Fleet T	2-0
Leatherhead v Littlehampton T	4-0
Burgess Hill T v Woking	0-5
Ascot U v Whyteleafe	6-2
Poole T v Chippenham T	3-0
Walton & Hersham v Bournemouth	2-3
Oxford C v Farnham T	2-1*
(1-1 at the end of normal time)	

Didcot T v Binfield	4-0
Maidenhead U v Bognor Regis T	4-3
Pagham v Havant & Waterlooville	0-4
Christchurch v Hamworthy U	1-0
Westfield v Lewes	0-5
Camberley T v Bracknell T	0-2
Kingstonian v Eastleigh	0-6
Gloucester C v Taunton T	4-0
Wells C v Cirencester T	0-2
Weston-super-Mare v Yate T	5-0
Bath C v Torquay U	0-3

THIRD ROUND QUALIFYING

Marine v Nantwich T	0-4
AFC Fylde v Irlam	4-1
Grimsby T v Abbey Hey	1-1*
(Abbey Hey won 4-2 on penalties)	
Stocksbridge Park Steels v Skelmersdale U	3-2
Seaham Red Star v Ashton Ath	4-0
Newcastle Benfield v Southport	2-2*
(Newcastle Benfield won 13-12 on penalties)	
Lincoln C v Oadby T	1-0*
(0-0 at the end of normal time)	
Knaresborough T v Brackley T	2-0
Basford U v Boston U	1-3
Peterborough Northern Star v Grantham T	3-1
Nuneaton v Stratford T	0-5
Kidderminster H v Coleshill T	6-1
Ellesmere Rangers v Bilston T	2-0
Wroxham v Fakenham T	1-2*
(1-1 at the end of normal time)	
Barton R v AFC Sudbury	0-2
Needham Market v Great Yarmouth T	3-0
Fisher v Barnet	1-10
Leverstock Green v AFC Hornchurch	2-1
Potters Bar T v Staines T	8-5
Chelmsford C v Wealdstone	1-4
Brentwood T v Royston T	0-2
Codicote v Metropolitan Police	1-4
Thamesmead T v Herne Bay	1-0
Hayes & Yeading U v Welling U	1-4
Sutton U v Eastbourne Bor	0-2
Dartford v Ebbsfleet U	1-0
Christchurch v Havant & Waterlooville	4-3
Poole T v Woking	2-0
Didcot T v Leatherhead	4-3
Bracknell T v Wimborne T	1-2
Eastleigh v Ascot U	3-2*
(2-2 at the end of normal time)	
Maidenhead U v Lewes	5-2
Bournemouth v Oxford C	0-7
Gloucester C v Torquay U	1-2
Weston-super-Mare v Cirencester T	3-1

FIRST ROUND

Bury v Seaham Red Star	6-1
Scunthorpe U v Bradford C	1-3
Sheffield U v Hartlepool U	3-1
Crewe Alexandra v Preston North End	2-2*
(Crewe Alexandra won 3-0 on penalties)	
AFC Fylde v Newcastle Benfield	2-1
Doncaster R v Morecambe	3-1
Fleetwood T v Accrington Stanley	1-0
Carlisle U v Barnsley	1-2
Rochdale v Nantwich T	9-0
Abbey Hey v York C	0-2*
(0-0 at the end of normal time)	
Oldham Ath v Tranmere R	1-2
Chesterfield v Stocksbridge Park Steels	4-1
Knaresborough T v Northampton T	0-1
Coventry C v Peterborough Northern Star	3-0
Walsall v Burton Alb	1-2
Peterborough U v Notts Co	2-0
Stratford T v Kidderminster H	1-3
Cambridge U v Milton Keynes Dons	2-5
Shrewsbury T v Lincoln C	7-0
Mansfield T v Boston U	2-2*
(Mansfield T won 3-2 on penalties)	
Ellesmere Rangers v Port Vale	1-2*
(1-1 at the end of normal time)	
Gillingham v Eastleigh	4-1
Wealdstone v Dagenham & Redbridge	2-1
Royston T v AFC Sudbury	2-0
Southend U v Leverstock Green	6-0

Eastbourne Bor v Maidenhead U	0-3
Stevenage v Needham Market	4-3
Fakenham T v AFC Wimbledon	0-7
Leyton Orient v Colchester U	1-3
Potters Bar T v Welling U	1-2*
(1-1 at the end of normal time)	
Dartford v Thamesmead T	3-4
Barnet v Metropolitan Police	2-0
Luton T v Didcot T	4-1
Cheltenham T v Weston-super-Mare	4-0
Oxford U v Bristol C	2-1
Poole T v Torquay U	1-2
Christchurch v Swindon T	0-5
Plymouth Argyle v Portsmouth	0-4
Oxford C v Wimborne T	3-2
Exeter C v Newport Co	1-2

SECOND ROUND

AFC Fylde v Chesterfield	1-4
Doncaster R v Peterborough U	4-2
Mansfield T v Northampton T	3-0
Bradford C v Barnsley	2-0
Tranmere R v Shrewsbury T	3-1*
(1-1 at the end of normal time)	
Port Vale v Bury	3-4*
(3-3 at the end of normal time)	
Burton Alb v Kidderminster H	0-1
Fleetwood T v Sheffield U	3-1
Rochdale v Coventry C	3-4
Crewe Alexandra v York C	4-0
Southend U v Barnet	1-0
Maidenhead U v Torquay U	2-2*
(Torquay U won 4-2 on penalties)	
Oxford C v Luton T	2-1
Gillingham v AFC Wimbledon	1-2
Thamesmead T v Portsmouth	3-7
Newport Co v Milton Keynes Dons	4-5*
(4-4 at the end of normal time)	
Oxford U v Swindon T	3-2
Stevenage v Wealdstone	6-0
Colchester U v Cheltenham T	2-1
Royston T v Welling U	2-1

THIRD ROUND

Mansfield T v Tranmere R	2-2*
(Mansfield T won 5-4 on penalties)	
Colchester U v Ipswich T	0-0*
(Ipswich T won 4-2 on penalties)	
Nottingham F v Milton Keynes Dons	3-2*
(2-2 at the end of normal time)	
Leicester C v Wigan Ath	1-0
Oxford C v Royston T	1-3
Arsenal v Reading	1-0
Huddersfield T v Crystal Palace	2-0
Brighton & Hove Alb v Derby Co	0-2
Portsmouth v Bolton W	0-1
Kidderminster H v Blackpool	1-2
Tottenham Hotspur v Blackburn R	4-1
Sunderland v Fleetwood T	4-0
Leeds U v Chelsea	0-2
AFC Wimbledon v Burnley	1-2
Southampton v West Ham U	2-1
Stevenage v Everton	1-2*
(0-0 at the end of normal time)	
Doncaster R v Norwich C	3-1*
(1-1 at the end of normal time)	
Birmingham C v QPR	4-1
AFC Bournemouth v Coventry C	2-3*
(2-2 at the end of normal time)	
Liverpool v Bradford C	2-0
Millwall v Newcastle U	1-3
Manchester C v Oxford U	2-0
Rotherham U v Wolverhampton W	1-2
Southend U v Middlesbrough	3-4*
(2-2 at the end of normal time)	
Manchester U v Bury	1-0
Swansea C v Watford	3-1
Crewe Alexandra v Fulham	2-1
Sheffield W v Stoke C	0-5
Hull C v Brentford	3-2*
(2-2 at the end of normal time)	
West Bromwich Alb v Torquay U	8-1
Chesterfield v Aston Villa	3-2
Charlton Ath v Cardiff C	0-1

FOURTH ROUND

Leicester C v Chesterfield	1-0
Tottenham Hotspur v Wolverhampton W	2-0
Mansfield T v Stoke C	0-3
West Bromwich Alb v Nottingham F	0-3
Manchester U v Hull C	3-0
Crewe Alexandra v Bolton W	5-0
Blackpool v Birmingham C	1-2*
(1-1 at the end of normal time)	
Sunderland v Ipswich T	3-1*
(1-1 at the end of normal time)	
Arsenal v Royston T	2-1
Swansea C v Doncaster R	2-1
Burnley v Cardiff C	3-1
Chelsea v Huddersfield T	6-1
Liverpool v Derby Co	5-2
Manchester C v Coventry C	8-2
Middlesbrough v Newcastle U	2-3
Everton v Southampton	1-1*
(Southampton won 5-4 on penalties)	

FIFTH ROUND

Arsenal v Crewe Alex	2-3
Nottingham F v Burnley	2-0
Liverpool v Birmingham C	2-3
Southampton v Leicester C	0-2
Chelsea v Swansea C	6-0
Sunderland v Newcastle U	0-0*
(Newcastle U won 3-1 on penalties)	
Tottenham H v Manchester U	3-1
Manchester C v Stoke C	1-0

SIXTH ROUND

Leicester C v Birmingham C	2-1
Newcastle U v Chelsea	0-3*
(0-0 at the end of normal time)	
Manchester C v Crewe Alex	6-1
Nottingham F v Tottenham H	1-2

SEMI-FINALS – 1ST LEG

Tottenham H v Chelsea	2-0
Manchester C v Leicester C	3-0

SEMI-FINALS – 2ND LEG

Chelsea v Tottenham H	5-2
(Chelsea won 5-4 on aggregate)	
Leicester C v Manchester C	1-2
(Manchester C won 5-1 on aggregate)	

FA YOUTH CUP FINAL 2015 1ST LEG

Monday, 20 April 2015

Manchester C (1) 1 *(Buckley-Rickets 9)*

Chelsea (2) 3 *(Abraham 7, 20, Solanke 90)* 6421

Manchester C: (4-4-1-1) Haug; Maffeo, Humphreys-Grant, Adarabioyo, Angelino; Nemane, Bryan, Garcia (Dilrosun 86), Barker; Celina; Buckley-Ricketts.
Chelsea: (4-2-3-1) Collins; Aina, Tomori, Clarke-Salter, Dasilva; Sammut, Colkett; Brown (Boga 90), Musonda (Scott 90), Abraham (Palmer 67); Solanke.
Referee: Robert Madley.

FA YOUTH CUP FINAL 2015 2ND LEG

Monday, 27 April 2015

Chelsea (1) 2 *(Brown 20, Abraham 46)*

Manchester C (1) 1 *(Iheanacho 6)* 10,965

Chelsea: (4-3-3) Collins; Aina, Tomori, Clarke-Salter, Dasilva; Boga (Palmer 74), Colkett, Musonda (Ali 84); Abraham (Sammut 68), Solanke, Brown.
Manchester C: (4-5-1) Haug; Maffeo, Adarabioyo, Humphries-Grant, Tasande; Nemane, Bryan, Wood (Alonso 68), Celina, Barker; Iheanacho (Buckley-Ricketts 71).
Chelsea won 5-2 on aggregate.
Referee: Robert Madley.

THE FA COUNTY YOUTH CUP 2014–15

After extra time.

FIRST ROUND

East Riding v Shropshire	8-2
Durham v Birmingham	3-1
Cheshire v West Riding	3-2
Leicestershire & Rutland v Westmorland	4-3
Nottinghamshire v Staffordshire	1-4
Sheffield & Hallamshire v Cumberland	6-0
Norfolk v Northamptonshire	5-0
Bedfordshire v Cambridgeshire	2-3
Huntingdonshire v Oxfordshire	2-1
Jersey v Kent	1-4
Guernsey v London	0-2
Cornwall v Sussex	2-4
Gloucestershire v Hertfordshire	3-2

SECOND ROUND

Isle of Man v Durham	0-4
Sheffield & Hallamshire v Liverpool	2-3
East Riding v Staffordshire	3-2
Derbyshire v Manchester	1-3
Cheshire v Northumberland	4-3
North Riding v Lancashire	0-4
Leicestershire & Rutland v Lincolnshire	4-0
Sussex v Cambridgeshire	2-3
Kent v Huntingdonshire	3-0
Dorset v Worcestershire	2-3
Herefordshire v London	2-7
Devon v Gloucestershire	0-3
Wiltshire v Berks & Bucks	6-1
Norfolk v Suffolk	1-2
Middlesex v Somerset	5-0
Essex v Amateur Football Alliance	3-1

THIRD ROUND

Cheshire v East Riding	1-0
Wiltshire v Middlesex	1-2
London v Durham	2-4
Manchester v Worcestershire	2-4
Essex v Suffolk	0-3
Lancashire v Kent	1-0
Leicestershire & Rutland v Gloucestershire	2-1
Liverpool v Cambridgeshire	2-1

FOURTH ROUND

Suffolk v Lancashire	0-1
Cheshire v Worcestershire	4-1
Leicestershire & Rutland v Liverpool	1-2
Middlesex v Durham	2-1

SEMI-FINALS

Liverpool v Cheshire	1-1*
(Cheshire won 4-2 on penalties)	
Lancashire v Middlesex	1-2

FA COUNTY YOUTH CUP FINAL 2015

Barnet, Sunday 12 April 2015

Middlesex (1) 2 *(Brown 5, Jackson 54)*

Cheshire (0) 3 *(Collins 75, Greenop 80, Evans 83)* 800

Middlesex: De Cruz; Chaibi (McDonnell 61 (Smith 88), Fisher, Keeley, Brown, Pearce, Mbengui, Bersey, Kearney, Sanders (Jarvis 73), Jackson.
Cheshire: Butler; Campion, Livesey (Heathcote 72), Ford, Hughes, Jones, Evans, Booth, Collins, Greenop, Cain (Clancy 62).
Referee: Lee Swarbey.

THE FA SUNDAY CUP 2014–15

After extra time.

FIRST ROUND

Cleator Moor v Winlaton Commercial	2-0
Hetton Lyons Cricket Club v Seaton Carew	8-0
Sunderland Myers v Burradon & New Fordley	0-3
Witton Park Rose & Crown v	
Stockton Hardwick Social	0-1
Sportsmans v Blackhall Hardwick	2-1
Sunderland RCA Grangetown Florists v	
North Ormesby	2-1
The Old Bank v Fantail	2-3
(Tie awarded to The Old Bank – Fantail removed)	
Bolton Woods v King George	0-2
Home & Bargain v Millhouse	3-2
Chapeltown Fforde Grene v Lobster	2-1
Campfield v Poulton Royal	3-2
Allerton v Thornhill Lees	3-1
AFC Blackburn Leisure v Windmill Kestrels	1-3
Pineapple v Canada	3-0
Black Bull v St John Fisher OB	5-4
Thornton U v Dengo U	3-2*
(2-2 at the end of normal time)	
Queens Park v Kirkdale	2-2*
(Queens Park won 4-2 on penalties)	
HT Sports v LIV Supplies	3-5
Hessle Rangers v BRNESC	3-0
The Molly v Alder	0-2
Garston v Mayfair	0-2
Attenborough Cavaliers v AFC Bush	6-1
Bilsthorpe Celtic (withdrawn) v FC Wyvern Arms	
(walkover)	
Sporting Dynamo v OJM	2-4
Quorn Royals 2008 v Gedling Inn	1-2
Wymeswold (withdrawn) v Nuthall (walkover)	
Punchbowl Old Boys v Birstall Stamford	1-5
Albion v Hundred Acre	2-2*
(Albion won 4-2 on penalties)	
Haunchwood Sports v RHP Sports & Social	2-1
Halfway v Thurmaston PWMC	1-2
Phoenix (withdrawn) v Priory Sports (walkover)	
Flamstead End v Upshire	2-1
Nirankari v New Salamis	0-5
AYFCS v Comets Sports Club	1-4
Willesden WMC v NLO	1-5
Green Man v Hammer	1-2*
(1-1 at the end of normal time)	
St Josephs (Luton) v Club Lewsey	3-0
Celtic SC (Luton) v Broadfields U (Sunday)	2-3*
(2-2 at the end of normal time)	
Two Touch v Brache Nation	1-2
North Wembley v FC Houghton Centre	2-1
Belstone (Sunday) v 61 (Sunday)	7-0
Ajax LA v Polonia Reading	4-1
St Helier (withdrawn) v Wrightchoice CSA (walkover)	
AFC Kumazi Strikers v Barnes Alb	0-1
Bar Sol Ona v Lebeqs Tavern Courage	0-3
Avon Plate v The Windmill	0-7

SECOND ROUND

Custys v Black Bull	3-5*
(3-3 at the end of normal time)	
Thornton U v Alder	1-2
Cleator Moor v Hetton Lyons Cricket Club	1-3
Mayfair v Chapeltown Fforde Grene	1-5
Sunderland RCA Grangetown Florists v	
Newton Aycliffe WMC	1-6
Hartlepool Lion Hillcarter v Sportsmans	4-6
Oyster Martyrs v Humbledon Plains Farm	2-4
Allerton v The Old Bank	2-0
Kennelwood v Stockton Hardwick Social	2-1
King George v Pineapple	2-3
Northallerton Police v Home & Bargain	2-4
LIV Supplies v Burradon & New Fordley	4-2
Windmill Kestrels v Campfield	1-1*
(Campfield won 6-5 on penalties)	
Queens Park v Hessle Rangers	1-0
Star & Garter v Attenborough Cavaliers	1-5
Birstall Stamford v West Bowling	2-2*
(West Bowling won 4-3 on penalties)	
OJM v Gedling Inn	4-0

Albion v Black Horse (Redditch)	1-4
Thurmaston PWMC v FC Wyvern Arms	4-3*
(2-2 at the end of normal time)	
Nuthall v Haunchwood Sports	1-1*
(Haunchwood Sports won 4-1 on penalties)	
Broadfields U (Sunday) v NLO	1-2
Queens Head Chesham v AC Sportsman	1-5
Crawley Green (Sunday) v North Wembley	2-0
Comets Sports Club v Belstone (Sunday)	2-3
Hammer v Brache Nation	4-1
The Sheaf v New Salamis	1-5
Flamstead End v St Josephs (Luton)	0-3
Falcons v Priory Sports	3-4
Wrightchoice CSA v The Windmill	0-2
Lambeth All Stars v Emmer Green (Sunday)	4-1
Ajax LA v Barnes Alb	0-5
Lebeqs Tavern Courage v Patricks	5-1

THIRD ROUND

Humbledon Plains Farm v Home & Bargain	1-3
Sportsmans v Hetton Lyons Cricket Club	0-5
Alder v Chapeltown Fforde Grene	1-3
Allerton v LIV Supplies	3-1
Black Bull v West Bowling	1-0
Campfield v Attenborough Cavaliers	4-3*
(3-3 at the end of normal time)	
Kennelwood v Queens Park	2-3
Pineapple v Newton Aycliffe WMC	5-1
Lambeth All Stars v OJM	1-2
AC Sportsman v Lebeqs Tavern Courage	3-1
(Tie abandoned 87 mins, 3-1)	
Crawley Green (Sunday) v Black Horse (Redditch)	2-1
St Josephs (Luton) v The Windmill	1-5
Barnes Alb v Haunchwood Sports	1-0*
(0-0 at the end of normal time)	
New Salamis v Thurmaston PWMC	5-1
Belstone (Sunday) v Priory Sports	0-1
NLO v Hammer	6-3

FOURTH ROUND

Campfield v Pineapple	4-2
Hetton Lyons Cricket Club v	
Chapeltown Fforde Grene	4-7*
(3-3 at the end of normal time)	
Queens Park v Home & Bargain	0-4
Black Bull v Allerton	1-4
Priory Sports v NLO	0-3
New Salamis v Barnes Alb	2-1*
(1-1 at the end of normal time)	
AC Sportsman v OJM	2-5
Crawley Green (Sunday) v The Windmill	4-1

FIFTH ROUND

Home & Bargain v Campfield	1-2
Allerton v Chapeltown Fforde Grene	1-2
Crawley Green (Sunday) v OJM	0-1
NLO v New Salamis	4-4*
(New Salamis won 4-3 on penalties)	

SEMI-FINALS

Campfield v Chapeltown Fforde Grene	2-1
OJM v New Salamis	4-2*
(2-2 at the end of normal time)	

FA SUNDAY CUP FINAL 2015

Ewood Park, Sunday 26 April 2015

Campfield (0) 2 *(Jones (2))*

OJM (0) 0   547

Campfield: Jones R; Michael Williams, Jones D, Todd, Weston, Santangeli, Macellin, Jones S (McArdle), Matthew Williams, Cox, Wright (Nevitt 65).
OJM: Roberts; Nottingham, Jones (Brown 77), Ramsey-Dickson, Turner, Meese, Darkin, Alkenum, Lynch (Benbow 72), Williams, Taylor-Nelson.
Referee: Mark Haywood.

FA PREMIER UNDER-21 LEAGUE 2014–15

THE FA PREMIER UNDER-21 LEAGUE TABLES

DIVISION 1	P	W	D	L	F	A	GD	Pts
1 Manchester U	22	11	7	4	39	23	16	40
2 Liverpool	22	11	3	8	45	35	10	36
3 Chelsea	22	10	5	7	39	27	12	35
4 Sunderland	22	10	5	7	26	24	2	35
5 Manchester C	22	10	3	9	44	40	4	33
6 Leicester C	22	9	5	8	39	37	2	32
7 Norwich C	22	8	8	6	34	32	2	32
8 Southampton	22	9	4	9	32	34	−2	31
9 Tottenham H	22	8	5	9	30	30	0	29
10 Everton	22	8	3	11	32	37	−5	27
11 Fulham	22	6	4	12	27	45	−18	22
12 West Ham U	22	5	2	15	20	43	−23	17

DIVISION 2	P	W	D	L	F	A	GD	Pts
1 Middlesbrough	22	16	2	4	39	23	16	50
2 Reading	22	13	2	7	38	30	8	41
3 Derby Co	22	12	4	6	39	20	19	40
4 Arsenal	22	11	4	7	38	25	13	37
5 WBA	22	10	7	5	37	27	10	37
6 Newcastle U	22	9	5	8	43	39	4	32
7 Aston Villa	22	8	3	11	25	36	−11	27
8 Brighton & HA	22	6	5	11	19	23	−4	23
9 Bolton W	22	5	8	9	26	33	−7	23
10 Blackburn R	22	5	6	11	23	31	−8	21
11 Stoke C	22	4	6	12	23	50	−27	18
12 Wolverhampton W	22	3	8	11	24	37	−13	17

THE FA PREMIER UNDER-21 LEAGUE CUP
*After extra time.

FIRST QUALIFYING ROUND

Wigan Ath v Preston NE	5-0
Burnley v Hull C	0-2
Watford v Peterborough U	1-0
Gillingham v Plymouth Arg	1-0*
AFC Wimbledon v Bournemouth	1-0

SECOND QUALIFYING ROUND

Nottingham F v Wigan Ath	1-3
Sheffield W v Hull C	0-1
Leeds U v Doncaster R	6-0
Birmingham C v Sheffield U	1-3
Huddersfield T v Barnsley	1-0
Bristol C v Watford	1-2*
Cardiff C v Gillingham	0-1
Charlton Ath v AFC Wimbledon	4-0
Millwall v Colchester U	1-1*
Millwall won 6-5 on penalties.	
Ipswich T v Swansea C	2-1

ROUND OF 32

Sheffield U v Stoke C	0-0*
Stoke C won 5-4 on penalties.	
Leicester C v Leeds U	1-2
Manchester C v Sunderland	2-4
Middlesbrough v Hull C	1-0
Bolton W v Wigan Ath	4-4*
Bolton W won 4-1 on penalties.	
Huddersfield T v Everton	2-0
Newcastle U v Crewe Alex	2-1*
Norwich C v Fulham	4-2
West Ham U v Millwall	1-1
West Ham U won 8-7 on penalties.	
Reading v QPR	3-0
Watford v Gillingham	3-2
Charlton Ath v Brighton & HA	1-0
Ipswich T v Southampton	0-1
Wolverhampton W v Aston Villa	0-1
WBA v Derby Co	0-1

ROUND OF 16

Blackburn R v Aston Villa	3-2
Bolton W v Reading	1-3*
Derby Co v Sunderland	0-0*
Derby Co won 4-3 on penalties.	
Huddersfield T v Charlton Ath	0-0*
Huddersfield T won 6-5 on penalties.	
Middlesbrough v Stoke C	1-4
Newcastle U v West Ham U	4-1
Southampton v Norwich C	2-0
Watford v Leeds U	6-1

QUARTER-FINALS

Derby Co v Stoke C	1-0
Huddersfield T v Reading	0-1
Newcastle U v Blackburn R	0-1
Southampton v Watford	3-2

SEMI-FINALS

Southampton v Derby Co	4-2
Blackburn R v Reading	2-1*

FINAL – FIRST LEG

Blackburn R v Southampton	0-0

FINAL – SECOND LEG

Southampton v Blackburn R	2-1*
Southampton won 2-1 on aggregate.	

FA ACADEMY UNDER-18 LEAGUE 2014–15

THE FA PREMIER UNDER-18 LEAGUE TABLES

NORTHERN GROUP	P	W	D	L	F	A	GD	Pts
1 Middlesbrough	22	16	2	4	59	30	29	50
2 Everton	22	13	2	7	49	30	19	41
3 Manchester C	22	12	4	6	45	29	16	40
4 Manchester U	22	12	2	8	29	24	5	38
5 Wolverhampton W	22	11	4	7	38	36	2	37
6 Derby Co	22	8	9	5	47	36	11	33
7 Liverpool	22	8	5	9	51	51	0	29
8 Sunderland	22	8	5	9	33	35	−2	29
9 Newcastle U	22	6	3	13	36	50	−14	21
10 Blackburn R	22	5	5	12	31	50	−19	20
11 Stoke C	22	5	4	13	23	39	−16	19
12 Bolton W	22	3	5	14	22	53	−31	14

SOUTHERN GROUP	P	W	D	L	F	A	GD	Pts
1 Chelsea	22	15	3	4	69	35	34	48
2 Tottenham H	22	11	5	6	49	38	11	38
3 Aston Villa	22	11	5	6	49	48	1	38
4 WBA	22	10	4	8	36	39	−3	34
5 Reading	22	10	3	9	39	37	2	33
6 West Ham U	22	9	5	8	45	35	10	32
7 Leicester C	22	10	2	10	36	29	7	32
8 Brighton & HA	22	8	3	11	37	41	−4	27
9 Fulham	22	8	3	11	34	45	−11	27
10 Southampton	22	6	5	11	28	34	−6	23
11 Arsenal	22	6	5	11	33	42	−9	23
12 Norwich C	22	5	3	14	19	51	−32	18

THE FA PREMIER UNDER-18 FINAL PHASE

GROUP 1	P	W	D	L	F	A	GD	Pts
1 Middlesbrough	7	5	1	1	17	10	7	16
2 Everton	7	4	2	1	17	7	10	14
3 Chelsea	7	4	1	2	18	14	4	13
4 Manchester U	7	3	2	2	9	8	1	11
5 WBA	7	3	0	4	17	15	2	9
6 Aston Villa	7	2	2	3	10	17	−7	8
7 Manchester C	7	1	1	5	9	17	−8	4
8 Tottenham H	7	1	1	5	12	21	−9	4

GROUP 2	P	W	D	L	F	A	GD	Pts
1 Sunderland	7	4	2	1	9	5	4	14
2 Reading	7	4	1	2	10	6	4	13
3 Wolverhampton W	7	3	3	1	16	5	11	10
4 Derby Co	7	4	0	3	10	10	0	10
5 Leicester C	7	3	0	4	14	13	1	9
6 West Ham U	7	2	1	4	6	10	−4	9
7 Liverpool	7	2	1	4	12	17	−5	7
8 Brighton & HA	7	1	2	4	9	20	−11	5

GROUP 3	P	W	D	L	F	A	GD	Pts
1 Stoke C	7	4	2	1	18	11	7	14
2 Blackburn R	7	4	2	1	13	8	5	14
3 Newcastle U	7	3	1	3	14	9	5	10
4 Southampton	7	3	1	3	10	12	−2	10
5 Fulham	7	3	2	2	13	11	2	9
6 Bolton W	7	2	3	2	9	10	−1	9
7 Norwich C	7	2	1	4	11	15	−4	7
8 Arsenal	7	1	1	5	10	22	−12	4

FINAL THIRD DEVELOPMENT LEAGUE 2014–15

West Division

		P	W	D	L	F	A	GD	Pts
1	Port Vale	12	8	1	3	29	16	13	25
2	Wigan Ath	12	8	1	3	25	20	5	25
3	Walsall	12	6	2	4	28	10	18	20
4	Tranmere R	12	3	5	4	22	20	2	14
5	Morecambe	12	4	2	6	19	31	–12	14
6	Shrewsbury T	12	3	3	6	18	27	–9	12
7	Wrexham	12	2	2	8	16	33	–17	8

East Division

		P	W	D	L	F	A	GD	Pts
1	Hull C	14	11	0	3	33	14	19	33
2	Gateshead	14	8	1	5	27	17	10	25
3	Doncaster R	14	8	1	5	24	17	7	25
4	Scunthorpe U	14	6	1	7	36	29	7	19
5	Hartlepool U	14	5	3	6	31	33	–2	18
6	Rotherham U	14	4	4	6	21	25	–4	16
7	Burton Alb	14	4	3	7	17	28	–11	15
8	Mansfield T	14	2	3	9	15	41	–26	9

South Division

		P	W	D	L	F	A	GD	Pts
1	Luton T	14	10	2	2	41	14	27	32
2	Portsmouth	14	6	5	3	32	26	6	23
3	AFC Wimbledon	14	6	3	5	25	23	2	21
4	Gillingham	14	6	2	6	28	29	–1	20
5	Cambridge U	14	6	2	6	24	31	–7	20
6	Bournemouth	14	5	3	6	37	28	9	18
7	Peterborough U	14	6	0	8	24	35	–11	18
8	Leyton Orient	14	2	1	11	16	41	–25	7

FINAL THIRD DEVELOPMENT LEAGUE CUP 2014–15

Northern Group A

		P	W	D	L	F	A	GD	Pts
1	Port Vale	3	2	0	1	6	2	4	6
2	Shrewsbury T	3	2	0	1	4	4	0	6
3	Walsall	3	1	1	1	4	3	1	4
4	Stoke C	3	0	1	2	1	6	–5	1

Northern Group B

		P	W	D	L	F	A	GD	Pts
1	Derby Co	4	3	1	0	11	2	9	10
2	Huddersfield T	4	2	1	1	8	6	2	7
3	Rotherham U	4	2	0	2	10	6	4	6
4	Doncaster R	4	1	2	1	6	6	0	5
5	Mansfield T	4	0	0	4	3	18	–15	0

Northern Group C

		P	W	D	L	F	A	GD	Pts
1	Middlesbrough	4	4	0	0	10	5	5	12
2	Hull C	4	3	0	1	8	6	2	9
3	Gateshead	4	1	0	3	7	9	–2	3
4	Hartlepool U	4	1	0	3	5	7	–2	3
5	Scunthorpe U	4	1	0	3	8	11	–3	3

Northern Group D

		P	W	D	L	F	A	GD	Pts
1	Wigan Ath	3	2	1	0	9	4	5	7
2	Fleetwood T	3	2	1	0	6	1	5	7
3	Morecambe	3	1	0	2	7	8	–1	3
4	Tranmere R	3	0	0	3	1	10	–9	0

Northern Final
Port Vale v Middlesbrough – 4th August 2015

Southern Group A

		P	W	D	L	F	A	GD	Pts
1	Cambridge U	5	3	1	1	12	6	6	10
2	Milton Keynes D	5	3	0	2	10	8	2	9
3	AFC Wimbledon	5	2	2	1	5	2	3	8
4	Brighton & HA	5	1	3	1	4	5	–1	6
5	Luton T	5	1	1	3	8	9	–1	4
6	Gillingham	5	1	1	3	3	12	–9	4

Southern Group B

		P	W	D	L	F	A	GD	Pts
1	Portsmouth	4	2	2	0	16	8	8	8
2	Newport Co	4	2	1	1	11	5	6	7
3	Plymouth Arg	4	2	1	1	8	8	0	7
4	Cheltenham T	4	1	0	3	5	10	–5	3
5	Bristol C	4	1	0	3	7	16	–9	3

Southern Cup Draw
Milton Keynes D v Newport Co
Portsmouth v Cambridge U

FOOTBALL LEAGUE YOUTH ALLIANCE 2014–15

NORTH WEST

		P	W	D	L	F	A	GD	Pts
1	Bury	30	20	5	5	67	32	35	65
2	Wigan Ath	30	19	7	4	70	27	43	64
3	Rochdale	30	20	3	7	70	41	29	63
4	Tranmere R	30	14	8	8	50	46	4	50
5	Walsall	30	14	6	10	41	31	10	48
6	Preston NE	30	13	8	9	54	31	23	47
7	Oldham Ath	30	14	3	13	60	48	12	45
8	Blackpool	30	13	6	11	47	43	4	45
9	Burnley	30	12	8	10	62	56	6	44
10	Port Vale	30	13	4	13	52	46	6	43
11	Wrexham	30	12	5	13	54	56	–2	41
12	Shrewsbury T	30	8	8	14	56	60	–4	32
13	Carlisle U	30	6	10	14	36	64	–28	28
14	Accrington S	30	8	4	18	35	66	–31	28
15	Fleetwood T	30	8	0	22	24	57	–33	24
16	Morecambe	30	3	1	26	24	98	–74	10

NORTH EAST

		P	W	D	L	F	A	GD	Pts
1	Bradford C	24	17	4	3	61	27	34	55
2	Doncaster R	24	14	7	3	57	21	36	49
3	Chesterfield	24	14	3	7	48	28	20	45
4	Hull C	24	11	6	7	47	37	10	39
5	Lincoln C	24	11	6	7	43	40	3	39
6	Notts Co	24	11	4	9	44	35	9	37
7	Grimsby T	24	11	4	9	39	40	–1	37
8	Mansfield T	24	9	5	10	44	46	–2	32
9	Scunthorpe U	24	7	6	11	33	45	–12	27
10	Rotherham U	24	7	5	12	35	40	–5	26
11	Burton Alb	24	5	6	13	39	64	–25	21
12	Hartlepool U	24	5	2	17	42	63	–21	17
13	York C	24	3	4	17	22	68	–46	13

SOUTH WEST

		P	W	D	L	F	A	GD	Pts
1	Bournemouth	18	13	3	2	36	19	17	42
2	Plymouth Arg	18	10	4	4	43	27	16	34
3	Swindon T	18	9	3	6	43	34	9	30
4	Portsmouth	18	8	4	6	42	32	10	28
5	Exeter C	18	8	2	8	30	29	1	26
6	Bristol R	18	6	6	6	29	25	4	24
7	Oxford U	18	7	1	10	27	32	–5	22
8	Cheltenham T	18	7	1	10	30	42	–12	22
9	Torquay U	18	3	4	11	25	43	–18	13
10	Newport Co	18	3	4	11	27	49	–22	13

SOUTH EAST

		P	W	D	L	F	A	GD	Pts
1	Barnet	24	17	3	4	82	51	31	54
2	Milton Keynes D	24	15	3	6	78	52	26	48
3	Peterborough U	24	14	5	5	62	36	26	47
4	Luton T	24	12	8	4	50	29	21	44
5	Southend U	24	10	7	7	49	45	4	37
6	Watford	24	10	6	8	66	51	15	36
7	Stevenage	24	9	5	10	46	47	–1	32
8	Leyton Orient	24	8	6	10	35	42	–7	30
9	AFC Wimbledon	24	7	6	11	41	47	–6	27
10	Northampton T	24	6	9	9	40	50	–10	27
11	Cambridge U	24	5	4	15	35	58	–23	19
12	Gillingham	24	4	4	16	35	64	–29	16
13	Dagenham & R	24	4	4	16	29	76	–47	16

MERIT LEAGUE 1

		P	W	D	L	F	A	GD	Pts
1	Plymouth Arg	11	8	3	0	23	6	17	27
2	Luton T	11	7	3	1	20	8	12	24
3	Barnet	11	6	1	4	29	18	11	19
4	Watford	11	6	1	4	19	14	5	19
5	Peterborough U	11	6	1	4	19	19	0	19
6	Stevenage	11	5	3	3	21	17	4	18
7	Portsmouth	11	5	2	4	12	20	–8	17
8	Bournemouth	11	4	2	5	21	28	–7	14
9	Exeter C	11	4	1	6	22	20	2	13
10	Milton Keynes D	11	3	1	7	21	26	–5	10
11	Southend U	11	2	1	8	13	21	–8	7
12	Swindon T	11	0	1	10	12	35	–23	1

MERIT LEAGUE 2

		P	W	D	L	F	A	GD	Pts
1	Leyton Orient	10	9	0	1	30	9	21	27
2	Bristol R	10	8	2	0	23	6	17	26
3	Gillingham	10	5	1	4	19	22	–3	16
4	AFC Wimbledon	10	3	5	2	18	14	4	14
5	Dagenham & R	10	4	2	4	21	18	3	14
6	Northampton T	10	4	2	4	11	14	–3	14
7	Cambridge U	10	4	1	5	15	18	–3	13
8	Cheltenham T	10	3	3	4	11	12	–1	12
9	Torquay U	10	3	1	6	16	19	–3	10
10	Oxford U	10	0	0	7	14	23	–9	9
11	Newport Co	10	0	1	9	4	27	–23	1

IMPORTANT ADDRESSES

The Football Association: Wembley Stadium, P.O. Box 1966, London SW1P 9EQ. *0844 980 8200*

Scotland: Hampden Park, Glasgow G42 9AY. *0141 616 6000*

Northern Ireland (Irish FA): Chief Executive, 20 Windsor Avenue, Belfast BT9 6EG. *028 9066 9458*

Wales: 11/12 Neptune Court, Vanguard Way, Cardiff CF24 5PJ. *029 2043 5830*

Republic of Ireland National Sports Campus, Abbotstown, Dublin 15. *00 353 1 8999 500*

International Federation (FIFA): Strasse 20, P.O. Box 8044, Zurich, Switzerland. *00 41 43 222 7777. Fax: 00 41 222 7878*

Union of European Football Associations: Secretary, Route de Geneve 46, P.O. Box 1260, Nyon 2, Switzerland. *Fax: 00 41 848 00 2727*

THE LEAGUES

The Premier League: Nic Coward, 30 Gloucester Place, London W1U 8PL. *0207 864 9000*

The Football League: Andy Williamson, Unit 5, Edward VII Quay, Navigation Way, Preston, Lancashire PR2 2YF. *0844 463 1888. Fax 0870 442 0 1188*

Football Conference: D. Strudwick, 4th Floor, Wellington House, 31–34 Waterloo Street, Birmingham B2 5TJ. *0121 214 1950*

Scottish Premier League: Hampden Park, Somerville Drive, Glasgow G42 9OE. *0141 620 4140*

The Scottish League: Hampden Park, Glasgow G42 9EB. *0141 620 4160*

Football League of Ireland: D. Crowther, 80 Merrion Square, Dublin 2. *00 353 1 6765 120*

Southern League: J. Mills, Sansome Lodge, 4–6 Sansome Walk, Worcester WR1 1LH. *01905 330 444*

Northern Premier League: Ms A. Firth, 23 High Lane, Norton Tower, Halifax, W. Yorkshire HX2 0NW. *01422 410 691*

Isthmian League: Ms K. Discipline, The Base, Dartford Business Park, Victoria Park, Dartford, Kent DA1 5FS. *01322 314 999*

Eastern Counties League: N. Spurling, 16 Thanet Road, Ipswich, Suffolk IP4 5LB. *07855 279 062*

Essex Senior League: Secretary: K. Wilmot, 35 Cecil Road, Walthamstow, London E17 5DH. *07540 441 829*

Hellenic League: B. King, 7 Stoneleigh Drive, Carterton, Oxon OX18 1EE. *0845 260 6644*

Kent Invicta League: John Moules, 25 Braidwood Avenue, Erith, Kent DA8 1EH. *01322 408 557*

Midland League: N. Wood, 30 Glaisdale Road, Hall Green, Birmingham B28 8PX. *07967 440 007*

North West Counties League: J. Deal, 24 The Pastures, Crossens, Southport PR9 8RH. *07713 622 210*

Northern Counties East: B. Gould, 42 Thirlmere Drive, Dronfield, Derbyshire S18 2HW. *07773 653 238*

Northern League: T. Golightly, 85 Park Road North, Chester-le-Street, Co. Durham DH3 3SA. *0191 388 2056*

Spartan South Midlands League: M. Mitchell, 26 Leighton Court, Dunstable, Beds LU6 1EW. *07710 455 409*

Sussex County League: Ms K. Scott, Llandilo, Old Lane, Crowborough TN6 2AF. *07788 737 061*

United Counties League: Ms W. Newey, 4 Wulfric Square, Bretton, Peterborough PE3 8RF. *01733 330 056*

Wessex League: J. Gorman, 6 Overton House, London Road, Overton, Hants RG25 3TP. *01256 770 059*

Western League: K.A. Clarke, 32 Westmead Lane, Chippenham, Wilts SN15 3HZ. *07790 002 279*

Combined Counties League: M.J. Bidmead, 55 Grange Road, Chessington, Surrey KT9 1EZ. *0208 397 4834*

West Midlands League: N.R. Juggins, 14 Badger Way, Blackwell, Bromsgrove, Worcs B60 1EX. *07977 422 362.*

South West Peninsula League: P. Hiscox, 45a Serge Court, The Quay, Exeter, Devon EX2 4EB. *07788 897 706*

Southern Counties East League: T. Day, 27 Mill View Road, Herne Bay, Kent CT6 7JF. *07789 655 768*

OTHER USEFUL ADDRESSES

Amateur Football Alliance: M. Brown, Unit 3, 7 Wenlock Road, London N1 7SL. *0208 733 2613*

Association of Football Badge Collectors: K. Wilkinson, 18 Hinton St, Fairfield, Liverpool L6 3AR. *0151 260 0554*

Association of Provincial Football Supporters Clubs in London: Tina A. Robertson, 45 Durham Avenue, Heston, Middlesex TW5 0HG. *0208 843 9854*

British Universities Sports Association: Karen Rothery, Chief Executive: BUSA, 20–24 King's Bench Street, London SE1 0QX. *0207 633 5080*

English Schools FA: J. Read, 4 Parker Court, Staffordshire Technology Park, Stafford ST18 0WP. *01785 785 970*

Extra Time and Backpass Retro Football Magazine: Greystones, Beechgrove, Kington, Herefordshire HR5 3RH. *0330 606 1417*

Fields In Trust: 2nd Floor, 15 Crinian Street, London N1 9SQ. *0207 427 2110*

Football Foundation: Whittinghton House, 19–30 Alfred Place, London WC1E 7EA. *0845 345 4555*

Football Postcard Collectors Club: PRO: Bryan Horsnell, 275 Overdown Road, Tilehurst, Reading RG31 6NX. *0118 942 4448 (and fax)*

Football Safety Officers Association: John Newsham, FSOA Ltd, Suite 17, Blackburn Rovers Enterprise Centre, Ewood Park, Blackburn BB2 4JF. *01254 841 771.*

Institute of Football Management and Administration: St George's Park, Newborough, Needwood, Burton on Trent DE13 9PD. *0128 357 6350*

Institute of Groundsmanship: 28 Stratford Office Village, Walker Avenue, Wolverton, Milton Keynes MK12 5TW. *01908 312 511*

League Managers Association: St George's Park, Newborough Road, Needwood, Burton on Trent DE13 9PD. *0128 357 6350*

Professional Footballers' Association: G. Taylor, 20 Oxford Court, Bishopsgate, Off Lower Moseley Street, Manchester M2 3WQ. *0161 236 0575*

Programme Monthly & Football Collectable Magazine: 11 Tannington Terrace, London N5 1LE. *020 7359 8687*

Programme Promotions: 21 Roughwood Close, Watford WD17 3HN. *01923 861 468*
Web: www.footballprogrammes.com

Referees' Association: A.W.S. Smith, Unit 12, Ensign Business Centre, Westwood Way, Westwood Heath, Coventry CV4 8JA. *024 7642 0360*

Scottish Football Historians Association: John Lister, 46 Milton Road, Kirkcaldy, Fife KY1 1TL. *01592 268 718*

Sir Norman Chester Centre for Football Research: Department of Sociology, University of Leicester, University Road LE1 7RH. *0116 252 2741/5.*

Soccer Nostalgia: G. Wallis, Albion Chambers, 1 Albion Road, Birchington, Kent CT7 9DN. *01303 275 432.*

Sport England: Sport Park, 3 Oakwood Drive, Loughborough, Leicestershire. *08458 508 508*

Sports Grounds Safety Authority: East Wing, 3rd Floor, Fleetbank House, 2–6 Salisbury Square, London EC4Y 8JX. *0207 930 6693*

Sports Turf Research Institute: St Ives Estate, Harden, Bingley, West Yorkshire BD16 1AU. *01274 565 131*

The Football Supporters' Federation: 1 Ashmore Terrace, Stockton Road, Sunderland, Tyne and Wear SR2 7DE. *0330 440 0044*

The Ninety-Two Club: Mr M. Kimberley, The Ninety-Two Club, 153 Hayes Lane, Kenley, Surrey CR8 5HP.

UK Programme Collectors Club: PM Publications, 38 Lowther Road, Norwich NR4 6QW. *01603 449 237*

Women's Football Conference: Mike Appleby, Wembley Stadium, PO Box 1966, London SW1P 9EQ. *0844 980 8200*

FOOTBALL CLUB CHAPLAINCY

Kenny, an established Premiership midfielder, and his wife, were both hoping for a baby, but the longed-for pregnancy never materialised. 'I'd certainly speak to Edward about this.' Edward is the long-serving honorary chaplain at the club Kenny had left in a multi-million pound transfer some two years earlier.

'You could phone him,' suggested Kenny's wife, and the player did just that, a few days later after training. Edward was surprised to hear from Kenny, but was extremely sympathetic and promised his prayers. Some weeks later Edward was in London attending an overnight conference, and met a clerical friend whose parish was a dozen miles or so from the club for which Kenny now plays, though only a couple from the troubled star's new home. Edward felt that he should share the issue and seek his friend's help, provided the footballer agreed.

There was an immediate rapport between the trio when they all met: a positive, relaxed bond developed between the couple and the parson, who dropped into their home as occasion allowed.

Three years on, Kenny is his club's skipper, he and his wife are the proud parents of twin daughters, and, at the star's initiative, though with the good will of the club's physio and manager, and following an informal get together, the club is about to invite the nearby parson to become its honorary chaplain.

THE REV

OFFICIAL CHAPLAINS TO FA PREMIERSHIP AND FOOTBALL LEAGUE CLUBS

Aston Villa – Rev Ken Baker
Barnsley – Rev Peter Amos
Birmingham C – Rev Kirk McAtear
Blackburn R – Rev Ken Howles
Blackpool – Rev Michael Ward
Bolton W – Mr Phil Mason
Bournemouth – Rev Andy Rimmer
Bradford C – Rev Andy Grieff
Bristol C – Rev Derek Cleave
Burnley – Rev Mark Hirst
Burton Alb – Rev Phil Pusey
Bury – Rev David Ottley
Cambridge U – Rev Stuart Wood
Cardiff C – Rev Dr John Weaver
Carlisle U – Rev Alun Jones
Charlton Ath – Rev Matt Baker
Cheltenham T – Rev Malcolm Allen
Chesterfield – Rev Jim McGlade
Crawley T – Rev Gary Simmons
Crewe Alex – Rev Phil Howell
Crystal Palace – Rev Chris Roe
Dagenham & R – Rev Keiran Bush
Derby Co – Rev Tony Luke
Doncaster R – Rev Barry Miller
Everton – Co-Chaplains Rev Henry Corbett and
  Rev Harry Ross
Fleetwood T – Rev George Ayoma
Fulham – Rev Gary Piper
Gillingham – Rev Richard Hayton
Hull C – Rev Allen Bagshawe
Ipswich T – Rev Kevan McCormack
Leeds U – Rev Dave Niblock
Leicester C – Rev Andrew Hulley
Leyton Orient – Rev Alan Comfort
Liverpool – Rev Bill Bygroves
Luton T – Rev Alan West
Manchester C – Rev Peter Horlock
Manchester U – Rev John Boyers
Mansfield T – Rev Ray Shaw

Millwall – Rev Canon Owen Beament
Newcastle U Academy – Rev Glyn Evans
Newport Co – Rev Keith Beardmore
Northampton T – Rev Andrew Dunlop
Norwich C – Rev Albert Cadmore
Nottingham F – Rev Steve Silvester
Notts Co – Rev Liam O'Boyle
Oldham Ath – Rev John Simmons
Oxford U – Rev Hedley Feast
Peterborough U – Rev Richard Longfoot
Plymouth Arg – Rev Arthur Goode
Port Vale – Rev John Hibberts
Portsmouth – Co-Chaplains Mr Mick Mellows
  and Rev Jonathan Jeffrey
Preston NE – Rev Chris Nelson
QPR – Co-Chaplains Rev Cameron Collington
  and Rev Bob Mayo
Reading – Rev Steven Prince
Scunthorpe U – Rev Alan Wright
Sheffield U – Rev Baz Gascoyne
Sheffield W Academy – Rev Malcolm Drew
Shrewsbury T – Rev Christopher Deakin
Southampton – Rev Andy Bowerman
Southend U – Co-Chaplains Rev Stu Alleway
  and Rev Mike Lodge
Sunderland – Father Marc Lyden-Smith
Swansea C – Rev Kevin Johns
Swansea C Academy – Rev Eirian Wyn
Swindon T – Rev Simon Stevenette
Torquay U – Rev Tim Smith
Walsall – Rev Peter Hart
Watford – Rev Clive Ross
West Ham U – Rev Alan Bolding
Wolverhampton W – Co-Chaplains Rev David
  Wright and Mr Steve Davies
Wycombe W – Rev John Roberts
Yeovil T – Rev Jim Pearce
York C – Rev Paul Deo

The chaplains hope that those who read this page will see the value and benefit of chaplaincy work in football and will take appropriate steps to spread the word where this is possible. They would also like to thank the editors of the Football Yearbook for their continued support for this specialist and growing area of work.

For further information, please contact: Sports Chaplaincy UK, The Avenue Methodist Church, Wincham Road, Sale, Cheshire M33 4PL. Telephone: 0800 181 4051 or email: admin@sportschaplaincy.org.uk. Website: www.sportschaplaincy.org.uk

OBITUARIES

Dexter Adams (Born Handsworth, Birmingham, April 1925. Died Stamford, Lincs, 31 January 2015.) Dexter Adams was a centre half who was a significant figure in the amateur game in the 1950s. A regular in the England line-up between 1951 and 1954, he won 18 caps and captained the side on occasions. He played his club football with Hendon, making over 300 appearances and leading them to success in the 1955 FA Amateur Cup final.

Paul Aldread (Born Mansfield, 6 November 1946. Died Sutton-in-Ashfield, Notts, 14 August 2014.) Paul Aldread was a forward with Mansfield Town in the mid-1960s, making 12 first-team appearances during his time at Field Mill. He later played in the Southern League for Corby Town.

Ron Austin (Born Milton, Kent, 21 August 1920. Died Sittingbourne, Kent, 28 December 2014.) Ron Austin was an attacking player who made 6 wartime appearances for Rotherham United whilst stationed in the RAF nearby during the war. On demobilisation he returned to Kent and he continued his career through to the end of the 1950s with a string of non-league clubs.

Eric Bakie (Born Edinburgh, 8 April 1928. Died Edinburgh, 13 May 2015.) Eric Bakie was a wing half who began his senior career with Aberdeen before moving on to Dunfermline Athletic in the summer of 1951. He stayed at East End Park until December 1956, making over 100 League and Cup appearances before concluding his senior career at St Johnstone. As a youngster he won representative honours for the Scotland NABC team.

Alex Bain (Born Edinburgh, 7 January 1936. Died November 2014.) Alex Bain was a centre forward who developed with Bobby Ancell's Babes at Motherwell before Bill Shankly signed him for Huddersfield Town in August 1957. He enjoyed an excellent scoring record at first-team level with all his clubs (42 goals from 96 league games north and south of the border) although rarely a regular. He went on to play for Chesterfield, Falkirk (two spells) and Bournemouth.

Eric Barber (Born Dublin, 18 January 1942. Died USA, 20 August 2014.) Eric Barber is one of the all-time greats for Shelbourne for whom he is the club's all-time record League of Ireland goalscorer with 126 goals from 219 appearances, achieved in three separate spells between 1958 and 1980. He also had spells away from home with Birmingham City, Chicago Spurs, Kansas City Spurs and in Austria with Wiener SC. He won two full caps for the Republic of Ireland.

Harold Barlow (Born Manchester, 25 October 1925. Died Shropshire, 10 September 2014.) Harold Barlow spent the early post-war years on the books of Crewe Alexandra. A wing half, he made 27 first-team appearances before moving to non-league Mossley in January 1952. He later became a leading Crown Green bowler winning county representative honours.

Peter Barnes (Born St Albans, 29 June 1938. Died Bushey, Herts, 7 October 2014.) Peter Barnes was a part-time professional with Watford between 1957 and 1963. A wing half, he made 10 first-team appearances and later played for Banbury United.

Jim Barrett (Junior) (Born West Ham, 5 November 1930. Died 20 October 2014.) Inside forward Jim Barrett, junior, was the son of a West Ham legend, also Jim, who came up through the ranks with the Hammers. In December 1957 he moved on to Nottingham Forest, where he was a member of the team promoted in 1956–57 before concluding his career with Birmingham City. In total he made over 200 senior appearances, scoring 99 goals. He later worked on the backroom staff at Upton Park and then Millwall.

John Barton (Born Orrell, 27 April 1942. Died Orrell, 21 September 2014.) Goalkeeper John Barton was just 16 years old when he made his debut for Preston North End at Highbury in December 1958. Although mostly a reserve at Deepdale he moved on to Blackburn in the summer of 1966 and was ever-present for Rovers in 1966–67. He made a total of 126 senior appearances before leaving the game in 1972.

John Baxter (Born 5 October 1936. Died 12 December 2014.) John Baxter was a solid and consistent wing half who made over 200 appearances for Hibernian between 1957 and 1966. He also played for Falkirk and Clydebank, gaining a cap for Scotland U23s against Wales in 1958.

Don Bennett (Born Wakefield, 18 December 1933. Died 12 June 2014.) Don Bennett spent several seasons on the books of Arsenal in the 1950s without breaking into the first team. He fared better after signing for Coventry City where he featured regularly at right back, making 77 senior appearances before moving to Hereford United in the summer of 1962. Don was better known as a cricketer, making almost 400 First Class appearances for Middlesex between 1950 and 1968 scoring over 10,000 runs and taking 784 wickets. He stayed at Middlesex as first team coach (1969–1997) and afterwards was on the committee, serving as President in 2007.

John Best (Born Liverpool, 11 July 1940. Died Ireland, 5 October 2014.) John Best made 7 appearances for Tranmere Rovers in the 1960–61 season and later emigrated to the United States where he developed a successful career. He was capped for the USA national team and played for a number of clubs including Philadelphia Spartans, Cleveland Stokers and Dallas Tornado before becoming the first-ever coach of Seattle Sounders.

Ken Birch (Born Birkenhead, 31 December 1933. Died 24 April 2015.) Wing half Ken Birch made over 80 senior appearances for Everton and Southampton in the 1950s before moving into non-league football. He went on to captain the Bangor City team that won the Welsh Cup in 1962 and took Napoli to a replay in the following season's European Cup Winners' Cup tie.

Bob Bishop (Born Southminster, Essex. 12 May 1921. Died 24 December 2014.) Bob Bishop was on the books of Luton Town during World War Two, making two appearances in the emergency competitions in 1943–44. He later became a significant figure for Abbey United and Cambridge United in the 1950s.

Tony Blake (Born Cofton Hackett, Worcs, 26 February 1927. Died 31 October 2014.) Defender Tony Blake made 2 appearances for Birmingham City in the 1949–50 season and later moved on to Gillingham where he played a further 10 games before injury ended his career.

Frank Borghi (Born St Louis, USA, 9 April 1925. Died St Louis, USA, 2 February 2015.) Frank Borghi won world-wide fame as the United States goalkeeper in the team that defeated England 1-0 in the 1950 World Cup finals. A former minor league baseball player he won 9 caps for the USA and helped the Simpkins-Ford club of St Louis to success in the US Open Cup in 1948 and 1950.

Jeff Bourne (Born Linton, Burton-upon-Trent, 19 June 1948. Died 30 July 2014.) Forward Jeff Bourne was never a regular in the best part of six seasons with Derby County, although he made a contribution to the 1974–75 Football League championship season. He later had spells with Crystal Palace and Sheffield United and also spent time in the United States with a number of clubs including Dallas Tornado, Atlanta Chiefs and Seattle Sounders.

Barry Brayton (Born Carlisle, 29 September 1938. Died 20 January 2015.) Barry Brayton was a skilful winger who joined Carlisle United straight from school. He scored one of the goals that helped defeat Chester in May 1962 to clinch the club's first promotion and went on to feature regularly in the team that were Third Division champions in 1964–65. He later played for Workington and non-league Netherfield before leaving football.

Jim Briscoe (Born Swinton, Yorkshire, 14 October 1923. Died Stevenage, 27 August 2014.) Forward Jim Briscoe made a number of appearances for Raith Rovers during the emergency competitions of World War Two, later featuring for Sheffield Wednesday in the 1946–47 season. After leaving Hillsborough he played in the Kent League for both Ramsgate and Margate. He was later on the committee at Ramsgate before becoming commercial manager of Stevenage Town in 1967. At the time of his death he was president of the Stevenage Supporters' Association.

Jimmy Brown, MBE (Born 24 September 1931. Died Dublin, 8 December 2014.) Jimmy Brown won Scottish Junior international honours, playing against Ireland in December 1953, and went on to make 2 appearances for Queen's Park before injury ended his football career. He became a legendary figure in Scottish cricket, winning 85 caps between 1953 and 1973 and captaining the team on over 50 occasions. He was awarded the MBE in 1974 for services to Scottish cricket.

Joe Brown (Born Cramlington, Northumberland, 26 April 1939. Died Burnley, 30 October 2014.) Wing half Joe Brown was on the books of both Middlesbrough and Burnley in the early post-war period, making a handful of appearances for each club. He signed for Bournemouth in the summer of 1954 and over the next six seasons he made over 200 appearances and featured in the team that reached the FA Cup sixth round in 1956–57. After a brief spell at Aldershot he joined the backroom staff at Burnley, serving as manager from January 1976 to February 1977.

Jim Bullions (Born Dennyloanhead, Stirlingshire, 12 March 1924. Died June 2014.) Jim Bullions was the youngest member of the Derby County team that defeated Charlton Athletic to win the 1946 FA Cup final. In November 1947 he joined Leeds United but spent much of his time playing in the Central League. Later at Shrewsbury he was a key figure in the club's early days as a Football League club, making over 100 first-team appearances in four seasons.

John Burn (Born South Shields, 21 January 1930. Died 31 January 2015.) John Burn was a goalkeeper who spent time on the books of Chelsea and Chesterfield without breaking into the first team. He enjoyed a season of regular first-team football with Carlisle United and then made the move to non-league football. During his time with South Shields he featured in famous FA Cup victories over Crewe Alexandra (1958–59) and Chesterfield (1959–60).

Gerry Burrell (Born Portadown, 6 September 1924. Died 25 October 2014.) Winger Gerry Burrell developed in Irish League football during the war before moving to St Mirren in August 1947. He went on to play for Dundee, Huddersfield Town (where he played regular First Division football) and Chesterfield before returning to Northern Ireland. He remained involved in the game and worked as a scout and youth development officer for Linfield between 1976 and 1996.

Jeno Buzanszky (Born Ujdombovar, Hungary 4 May 1925. Died Esztergom, Hungary, 11 January 2015.) Jeno Buzanszky was a defender who was the last surviving member of Hungary's 'Golden' team of the early 1950s. He featured in the two great victories over England and was a member of the team defeated by West Germany in the 1954 World Cup finals, winning 49 caps in total. He won an Olympic Gold medal with the Magyars in 1952.

Jimmy Cain (Born Fishburn, Co Durham, 29 December 1933. Died 9 May 2015.) After an unproductive spell with Bristol City, wing half Jimmy Cain returned to the North East, signing for South Shields. He was a member of the Mariners' team that defeated Crewe Alexandra 5-0 in an FA Cup tie in 1958–59, and then spent the 1960–61 and 1961–62 seasons as a part-timer with Hartlepools United, making 30 Football League appearances.

Jim Cairns (Born Lisburn, Northern Ireland, 12 September 1938. Died Blackpool, 3 November 2014.) Jim Cairns was an inside forward who appeared in the Irish League for Glentoran, Linfield and Crusaders between 1953 and 1966. A Schools and Youth international, he won representative honours for the Irish League against the Football League in October 1962. Whilst at Linfield he was a member of teams that won the Irish League (1960–61) and Irish Cup (1963).

Harry Callaghan (Born Glasgow, 20 March 1929. Died Paisley, 25 July 2014.) Harry Callaghan won international honours for Scotland Amateurs in the 1953–54 season before joining Ipswich Town in September 1954. He struggled to break into the first team at Portman Road, making a solitary Football League appearance at Swansea in December 1954.

Johnny Campbell (Born West Wylam, Northumberland, 23 July 1928. Died February 2015.) Johnny Campbell was an outside left who enjoyed six years of regular first-team football with Gateshead. He was a member of the team that defeated Liverpool, Hull and Plymouth to reach the FA Cup sixth round in 1952–53 only to go down to a single-goal defeat to Bolton in front of a record crowd at Redheugh Park.

Danny Canning (Born Penrhiwceiber, Glamorgan, 21 February 1926. Died Pentlepoir, Pembrokeshire, 30 June 2014.) Danny Canning was a goalkeeper who gained Division Three South winners' medals with both Cardiff City (1946–47) and Swansea Town (1948–49). In total he made over 130 Football League appearances, also featuring briefly with Nottingham Forest.

Joe Carr (Born circa 1932. Died May 2015.) Winger Joe Carr spent nine seasons on the books of St Johnstone making over 200 competitive appearances before leaving to spend the 1962–63 season with Dumbarton. One of the few players to enjoy a sustained period with the club at this time, he was later inducted into Saints' Hall of Fame.

Matt Carson (Born Coatbridge, 11 October 1934. Died Australia, May 2015.) Matt Carson was a tall centre forward who enjoyed an excellent scoring record with Albion Rovers between March 1956 and November 1958. He hit 75 goals in 107 competitive appearances, including 42 in 1956–57, before becoming Southern League club Cheltenham Town's record signing. Spells with Boston United and Kidderminster Harriers followed before he emigrated to Australia.

Sir Philip Carter, CBE (Born Glasgow, 8 May 1927. Died Oxton, Cheshire, 23 April 2015.) Philip Carter watched Everton as a young boy and went on to become chairman of the club during two separate spells (1978 to 1991 and 1998 to 2006). The Toffees were particularly successful in his first period at the helm winning the European Cup Winners' Cup in 1985, two Football League titles and an FA Cup. He was also chairman of the Football League from 1986 to 1988 and played a significant role in the creation of the Premier League in 1992.

Don Clark (Born Bristol, 25 October 1917. Died 14 August 2014.) Don Clark was a centre forward who signed for Bristol City in May 1937 and went on to make his first-team debut towards the end of the 1938–39 season. After featuring regularly during wartime he returned to action as a prolific goalscorer when peacetime football resumed in 1946–47 and his total of 36 League goals scored that season remains a club record. A knee injury suffered in 1949 effectively ended his career.

Ken Clayton (Born Preston, 6 April 1933. Died 26 November 2014.) Ken Clayton signed professional forms for Blackburn Rovers shortly after his 17th birthday, but had to wait until November 1952 for his first-team debut. He was

more or less a regular at left half from the start of the 1955–56 season, with his younger brother Ron taking the right-half berth. His career was effectively ended after he suffered a broken leg in April 1957.

Albert Cochran (Born Ebbw Vale, 26 November 1939. Died 24 January 2015.) Albert Cochran was a goalkeeper who was on the books of Plymouth Argyle as a youngster without breaking into the first team. At Leyton Orient his only senior appearance came in the final game of the 1960–61 season. He later signed for Folkestone Town, where he was a member of the team that reached the FA Cup third round in 1965–66.

Geoff Coffin (Born Chester, 17 August 1924. Died Chester, 12 March 2015.) Centre forward Geoff Coffin served in the Navy during World War Two, before signing for Chester in May 1947. He broke into the first team at Sealand Road soon afterwards and over the next eight years made more than 150 appearances, occasionally playing at centre half. Geoff later moved on to play for Ellesmere Port Town.

Sammy Conn (Born Lanark, 26 October 1961. Died Ayr, 17 August 2014.) A goalscoring midfield player, Sammy Conn began his senior career with Falkirk in the 1980–81 season. He enjoyed a successful career in Scotland over the next 17 years, turning out for Albion Rovers, Clydebank, Airdrieonians and Cowdenbeath, making a total of more than 500 senior appearances, including over 100 for both Albion and Airdrieonians. His early death was due to motor neurone disease.

Geoff Cox (Born Arley, Warwickshire, 30 November 1934. Died 30 October 2014.) Geoff Cox began his career with Birmingham City, featuring both at inside forward and on the wing. In December 1957 he moved on to Torquay United where he was a regular in the line-up for the best part of a decade, making over 250 first-team appearances. He featured in both the 1959–60 and 1965–66 promotion teams.

Frank Cruickshank (Born Polmont, Stirlingshire, 20 November 1931. Died 20 January 2015.) Frank Cruickshank was serving in the RAF when he signed for Notts County in January 1950, but it was not until the 1955–56 season that he established himself for the Magpies. He was ever-present in 1958–59, but then shortly afterwards a knee injury ended his senior career, although he later played in non-league football for Cheltenham Town, Cambridge City and Newmarket Town.

Roger Darvell (Born High Wycombe, 10 February 1931. Died Banbury, 21 October 2014.) Centre half Roger Darvell began his career with Charlton Athletic but never made it to the first team at The Valley and it was with Gillingham that he made his senior debut. However, it was only during a spell at Southport that he featured regularly in first-team football, making 256 appearances for the Sandgrounders between 1958 and 1965 before moving on to Banbury United.

John Divers (Born Clydebank, 8 March 1940. Died Clydebank, 23 September 2014.) John Divers was a skilful inside forward who made over 200 appearances for Celtic in the ten years from 1956. Although it was not a successful period for the Hoops he was capped three times by the Scottish League representative XI. He subsequently had a spell with Partick Thistle before retiring from the game to pursue a career as a teacher.

Bill Dodd (Born Bedlington, Northumberland, 30 September 1936. Died Reedley, Burnley, 14 January 2015.) Bill Dodd was a big old-fashioned style centre forward who joined Burnley from Whitley Bay as a youngster. However, although he played regularly for the reserve and A teams at Turf Moor he failed to break into the first team. He went on to make a solitary Football League appearance for Workington before returning to East Lancashire to play for Rossendale United.

Hugh Doherty (Born Buncrana, Co Donegal, 5 May 1921. Died 29 September 2014.) Hugh Doherty was a winger who played in Irish football for Derry City and Dundalk during World War Two, signing for Celtic in August 1946. He managed 4 first-team appearances at Parkhead and later had spells with Blackpool (where he failed to break into the first team) and Raith Rovers. Hugh was then active for many years in grassroots football in Donegal, and became a town councillor and JP in Buncrana.

Kyle Doherty (Born 13 September 1995. Died Manchester, 1 January 2015.) Midfielder Kyle Doherty was an U20s player with Stenhousemuir who was included in the first-team squad on one occasion in 2014–15 when he was an unused substitute against Ayr United on 30 August. He also featured in the season's Stirlingshire Cup games. His tragic death came after he had travelled to Manchester to celebrate the New Year.

Harry Dowd (Born Salford, 4 July 1938. Died 7 April 2015.) Goalkeeper Harry Dowd made his debut for Manchester City in December 1961 and established himself in the line-up shortly after the start of the 1962–63 season. He went on to make over 200 appearances for City, scoring in the 1-1 draw with Bury in February 1964 when he broke a thumb and continued as an outfield player, with no substitutes available. A highlight was gaining an FA Cup winners' medal with City in 1969. He later spent four years with Oldham Athletic, contributing to their success in winning the Third Division title in 1973–74.

Jimmy Duncan (Born Glasgow, 10 December 1930. Died Glasgow, 1 December 2014.) Winger Jimmy Duncan was unable to establish himself during four seasons with Celtic and it was not until he moved on to Albion Rovers in August 1958, following spells at St Mirren and Dundee United, that he experienced regular first-team football. The two seasons spent with the Coatbridge club were his only prolonged exposure to first-team football, although he managed more than 100 senior appearances in the Scottish game.

Jimmy Dunn (Born Edinburgh, 25 November 1923. Died 31 December 2014.) Inside forward Jimmy Dunn was one of many teenagers signed by Wolves during the war. He went on to make over 100 first-team appearances and featured in all six FA Cup ties in 1949, including the final when the team defeated Leicester City to win the trophy. He moved on to Derby County before a knee injury forced him to leave the senior game. He later returned as trainer and coach to West Bromwich Albion with whom he enjoyed a second successful Wembley trip in 1949.

Tommy Dunne (Born Dublin, 1932. Died Rathgar, Dublin, 15 May 2015.) Defender Tommy Dunne was best known for his spell with St Patrick's Athletic from 1954 to 1964, which saw him win back-to-back League of Ireland titles in 1954–55 and 1955–56 and captain the team to success in the FAI Cup on two occasions (1959 and 1961). He also played with Shamrock Rovers, Sligo Rovers, Dundalk and Transport. Tommy won 3 full caps for the Republic of Ireland and also appeared for the League of Ireland representative side.

Dennis Durham (Born East Halton, Lincs, 26 September 1923. Died Beverley, 26 August 2014.) Dennis Durham was a left half who joined Hull City in 1947 but it was not until the 1952–53 season that he established himself as a regular in the first team. He went on to make over 250 first-team appearances and was a member of the side that won promotion to the old Second Division in 1958–59.

John Dutchman (Born Harrogate, 8 October 1925. Died 22 June 2014.) John Dutchman was an inside forward who played a handful of games for Leeds United as a teenager during the war before studying at Cambridge University. He went on to a career in teaching firstly at Glasgow Academy (during which time he made 7 appearances for Queen's

Park) and then at Chigwell School. He played for Pegasus, gaining an FA Amateur Cup winners' medal in 1951, and Corinthian Casuals, representing England Amateurs on 2 occasions.

Jim Dyson (Born Ryhope, Co Durham, 16 February 1935. Died 12 July 2014.) Jim Dyson was a goalkeeper who spent three seasons on the books of Hartlepools United in the mid-1950s, holding his place throughout the 1955–56 season when the team finished fourth in Division Three North. He later switched codes to rugby union, serving as a member of the Durham County RFU Committee from 1995 and as President in 2010–11.

Bill Ellerington (Born Southampton, 30 June 1923. Died North Baddesley, Hants, 4 April 2015.) Bill Ellerington captained the England Schools team in 1937 and for a while was on the books of Sunderland. After the war he turned professional with Southampton where he went on to make some 238 appearances at full back. He also gained 2 full caps for England. After retiring as a player he remained on the backroom staff at The Dell for many years.

Paddy Fagan (Born Dublin, 7 June 1930. Died 19 November 2014.) Winger Paddy Fagan joined Hull City from League of Ireland club Transport in March 1951. A skilful winger able to unlock opposition defences, he soon moved on to Manchester City for whom he made 165 competitive appearances and gained an FA Cup runners-up medal in 1955. He was not in the team the following season when City lifted the trophy and eventually moved on to Derby County for a final season and a bit of League action. He won 8 full caps for the Republic of Ireland.

John Fantham (Born Sheffield, 6 February 1939. Died June 2014.) Inside forward John Fantham joined Sheffield Wednesday as a 17-year-old in October 1956 and went on to become one of the club's best known players of the 1960s. He made over 400 first-team appearances, helping Wednesday win the Division Two title in 1958–59 and then finish runners-up to Tottenham Hotspur in the top flight in 1960–61. He also won an FA Cup runners-up medal in 1966. He led the club's scoring charts on five separate occasions and is their leading post-war goalscorer. John won a full England cap against Luxembourg in 1961 and also won representative honours for England U23s and the Football League. He concluded his career with a couple of seasons at Rotherham.

Bill Farmer (Born Guernsey, 24 November 1927. Died Corby, 2 July 2014.) Goalkeeper Bill Farmer is one of only a few players from the Channel Islands to feature in senior football. He signed for Nottingham Forest, helping the club's reserve team to the Midland League title in 1952–53 and he was mostly with the second string apart from the 1954–55 season. After a spell in non-league with Brush Sports he spent a season at Oldham, where he played a few matches at the start of the campaign before losing his place.

Brian Farmer (Born Rowley Regis, Worcs, 29 July 1933. Died 1 June 2014.) Brian Farmer took over the right back slot for Birmingham City following the tragic death of Jeff Hall in 1959 and kept his place until losing out to Stan Lynn at the start of the 1961–62 season. Soon afterwards he moved on to Bournemouth where he added almost 150 senior appearances before leaving the senior game.

Willie Finlay (Born Auchterderran, Fife, 9 April 1926. Died Fife, 4 September 2014.) Centre half Willie Finlay joined East Fife from Bowhill Rovers in August 1946 and spent a decade with the club at a time when they were highly successful. He helped them to win the Division B title in 1946–47 and the League Cup on three occasions, making almost 400 appearances before switching to Clyde in 1956. He enjoyed further success with the Bully Wee: two Second Division titles topped by a Scottish Cup final victory over Hibernian in 1958. He concluded his career at Raith Rovers.

Malcolm Finlayson (Born Alexandria, Dunbartonshire, 14 June 1930. Died Dudley, 26 November 2014.) Malcolm Finlayson was a big, brave goalkeeper who signed for Millwall from Renfrew Juniors towards the end of the 1947–48 season. He went on to make over 200 appearances for the Lions before joining Wolverhampton Wanderers in August 1956. He succeeded the legendary Bert Williams as first choice and enjoyed immediate success, helping Wolves to back-to-back Football League titles in 1957–58 and 1958–59 followed by FA Cup success in 1960. After making over 200 appearances for the Molineux club he retired in 1964.

Gerry Fitchet (Born Dundee, 1935. Died Brechin, 24 November 2014.) A product of Brechin Victoria, Gerry Fitchet spent 18 months in the seniors with Brechin City, making 27 first-team appearances to the end of the 1961–62 season. He later had a spell in Australia with the George Cross club of Melbourne.

Alex Forbes (Born Dundee, 21 January 1925. Died Johannesburg, South Africa, 28 July 2014.) Alex Forbes was a hard-tackling left half who won 14 caps for Scotland between 1947 and 1952. He joined Sheffield United from Dundee Juniors North End in September 1944, but it was for his time at Arsenal between 1948 and 1956 that he was best known. He helped the Gunners win the Football League title in 1947–48 and the FA Cup in 1950, also featuring in the team that lost to Newcastle United in the 1952 final. After brief spells with Leyton Orient and Fulham he moved to South Africa where he coached a number of clubs.

Reg Foulkes (Born Shrewsbury, 23 February 1923. Died November 2014.) Reg Foulkes was a solid centre half who was capable of providing leadership at the back to all his teams. A wartime player with Birmingham and Walsall, he distinguished himself with the Saddlers in the immediate post-war period. Sold to Norwich City in the summer of 1950, he added a further 238 League and Cup appearances during his stay at Carrow Road before becoming player-manager of Wisbech Town.

Harry Frame (Born 1 November 1932. Died Christchurch, New Zealand, 14 April 2015.) Harry Frame was a wing half who spent most of the 1950s on the books of East Fife, although he managed just a handful of first-team appearances. He appeared more regularly during a season with Brechin City in 1957–58, helping them to reach the semi-finals of the Scottish League Cup, although he missed the last-four clash with Rangers. He later emigrated to New Zealand.

George Francis (Born Acton, 4 February 1934. Died Slough, 22 October 2014.) Centre forward George Francis joined Brentford as a youngster, winning a regular first-team place in the 1956–57 season. A regular goalscorer alongside striking partner Jim Towers, his tally of 136 League and Cup goals is the second-best in the club's history. He had two spells at Griffin Park, separated by a few months at Queens Park Rangers, finishing off at Gillingham where he featured in the team that won the Division Four title in 1963–64.

Ken Furphy (Born Stockton, 28 May 1931. Died Teignmouth, Devon, 17 January 2015.) Ken Furphy signed for Everton as a teenager but failed to make the first team at Goodison Park. However, his career flourished after joining Darlington and he went on to make more than 500 Football League appearances in a 15-year career in the lower divisions. At both Workington and Watford he worked as player-manager, gaining promotions with both and taking the Hornets to a first-ever place in the FA Cup semi-final. After retiring as a player he managed Blackburn Rovers and Sheffield United and took charge of several NASL teams, including a brief spell with New York Cosmos during the time when Pele was playing for them.

Milan Galic (Born Bosanko Grahovo, Yugoslavia, 8 March 1938. Died Belgrade, 13 September 2014.) Milan Galic was a prolific goalscorer in 1960s football, firstly with Partizan Belgrade and then with Standard Liege and Reims. He won

55 caps for Yugoslavia, gaining a Gold Medal at the 1960 Olympics as a member of the team that defeated Denmark and also featuring in the team that lost out to USSR in the first-ever European Championship final.

Tony Gallego (Born San Sebastian, Spain, 2 June 1924. Died 3 May 2015.) Tony Gallego arrived in England along with his brother Joe as a refugee from the Spanish Civil War. A goalkeeper with Cambridge Town (now Cambridge City) he helped the club reach the FA Cup first round for the first time in their history in 1946–47, then signed for Norwich City in March 1947. Tony made a single first-team appearance for the Canaries at home to Britol Rovers and eventually returned to Cambridge where this time he joined Abbey United, remaining through their name change to Cambridge United.

Martin Garratt (Born York, 22 February 1980. Died Middlesbrough, 24 October 2014.) Martin Garratt was a skilful left-sided midfield player who developed with York City, featuring regularly in the 1998–99 season. Thereafter he had spells with Mansfield Town, St Patrick's Athletic from the League of Ireland, and Lincoln City without establishing himself as a first-team player. He died in tragic circumstances at the age of 34.

Jim Geddes (Born circa 1930. Died 11 July 2014.) Wing half Jim Geddes joined Motherwell from Forth Wanderers in November 1952 and spent three seasons as understudy to Charlie Cox at Fir Park, making just 6 first-team appearances. He subsequently joined Southern League club Cheltenham Town where he spent a further six years, helping the Robins to success in the Southern League Cup in 1957–58.

Peter Gledstone (Born Ferndown, Dorset, 4 May 1934. Died 30 December 2014.) Peter Gledstone was a left back who developed with Bournemouth Gas Works before joining Bournemouth in November 1955. First-choice for three seasons, he went on to make over 100 appearances during his stay at Dean Court. After retiring from football he emigrated, firstly to New Zealand and then Australia.

Harry Gordon (Born Glasgow, 10 December 1931. Died 29 July 2014.) Harry Gordon was a wing half who spent six seasons with Bury having joined from Petershill Juniors. Although he made his debut in August 1952 he was never a regular in the first team, making a total of 21 League appearances before moving on to Buxton.

James Alexander Gordon (Born Edinburgh, 10 February 1936. Died Reading, 18 August 2014.) James Alexander Gordon was a broadcaster who read the classified football results for the BBC's *Sports Report* radio programme for 40 years from 1973. He developed a unique style using inflections and stresses to indicate to the listener whether the result was a home win, away win or draw.

Charlie Gough (Born Glasgow, 21 May 1939. Died Cape Town, South Africa, 3 April 2015.) Left half Charlie Gough made 6 first-team appearances for Charlton Athletic at the start of the 1964–65 season before losing his place. He emigrated to South Africa in January 1965, enjoying considerable success with the Highlands Park club of Johannesburg. He was the father of the Rangers and Scotland star Richard Gough.

Bill Gray (Born Binley, Coventry, 3 December 1931. Died 18 July 2014.) Right half Bill Gray developed with the Coventry City nursery club Modern Machine Tools, signing for City in December 1948. In a six-year stay at Highfield Road he made 2 first-team appearances, both in October 1951, before moving on to Kettering Town.

Dave Groombridge (Born Norbury, Surrey, 30 April 1930. Died Camberley, Surrey, January 2015.) Goalkeeper Dave Groombridge developed with Arsenal nursery club Chase of Chertsey and then Hayes before joining Leyton Orient. He spent a decade on the books at Brisbane Road, although for much of that time he was a second choice. He made a total of 142 senior appearances before a knee injury ended his career.

Gyula Grosics (Born Dorog, Hungary, 4 February 1926. Died Budapest, 13 June 2014.) Goalkeeper Gyula Grosics was a member of the great Hungary team of the 1950s, winning 86 international caps between 1947 and 1962. He was a World Cup finalist in 1954 and an Olympic Gold Medalist in 1952. He also played in the two great victories over England in the early 1950s. At club level his best years were with Honved and Tatabanya Banyasz.

Vic Groves (Born Stepney, London, 5 November 1932. Died January 2015.) Vic Groves was a prominent amateur player in the early 1950s with Leytonstone and Walthamstow before turning professional with Leyton Orient. He got off to a great start in the 1955–56 season, netting 9 goals in his first 8 games, and this earned him a move to Arsenal. Vic had four seasons as a regular with the Gunners, making over 200 appearances, and also appeared for the London FA team in the very first Inter Cities Fairs Cup final against Barcelona. He was capped 3 times for England Amateurs and also won England B and U23 representative honours.

Fred Grubb (Born Dundee, 12 May 1937. Died 16 December 2014.) Fred Grubb joined Dundee United from St Mary's Youth Club but managed just one senior appearance, featuring at centre half against Morton in April 1956. He later graduated from St Andrews University and became a GP firstly in Chesterfield and then in Stretford where he was in practice for 26 years and retired in 1990.

Ken Hale (Born Blyth, Northumberland, 18 September 1939. Died 5 January 2015.) Ken Hale was a powerful inside forward who made his debut for Newcastle at the age of 18. A versatile playmaker, he moved on to Coventry City to become part of the Sky Blue Revolution, gaining a Division Three champions' medal in 1963–64. He also played a role in Oxford's Division Three success in 1968–69 before concluding his career with Darlington and Halifax, bringing his total of Football League appearances to more than 400. He later had a spell as manager of Hartlepool United.

Ernie Hannigan (Born Glasgow, 23 January 1943. Died Perth, Australia, May 2015.) Winger Ernie Hannigan joined Queen of the South as a teenager and made over 100 first-team appearances before moving on to Preston North End. Next stop was Coventry where he helped the Sky Blues avoid relegation in their first season in the top flight before returning to Scotland. He played football around the world – New York Cosmos (USA), Eastern (Hong Kong) and Stirling City (Western Australia) all featuring on his CV.

Chris Harker (Born Shiremoor, Northumberland, 29 June 1937. Died Darlington, 5 September 2014.) Chris Harker was a goalkeeper best known for his time at Bury between 1961 and 1967 for whom he made 178 Football League appearances, all in the old Second Division. His career had begun at Newcastle, where he made a solitary first-team appearance, and he arrived at Gigg Lane via a spell with Aberdeen. Afterwards he was briefly at Grimsby Town before finishing with two ever-present seasons for Rochdale.

Roy Hartle (Born Catshill, Worcs, 4 October 1931. Died Bolton, 5 November 2014.) Roy Hartle was a powerful full back who became a regular for Bolton Wanderers in the 1955–56 season and performed consistently over the next 10 seasons, when he missed just 20 games. He gained an FA Cup winners' medal in 1958 and in the same year played for the Football League against the Irish League, his only major representative honour. He made a total of 499 first-team appearances before leaving in 1966. In the late 1960s he was a Conservative councillor on Bolton Borough Council.

Willie Harvey (Born Clydebank, 23 November 1929. Died June 2014.) Willie Harvey was a traditional-style inside forward best known for his time with Kilmarnock between 1951 and 1958 for whom he scored 66 goals in just over 200

appearances. He went on to play for Dunfermline Athletic, Bradford Park Avenue and Arbroath and also spent time in the Irish League with Bangor City and Derry City.

Harold Hassall (Born Tyldesley, Lancashire, 4 March 1929. Died 30 January 2015.) Harold Hassall won international honours while on the books of Huddersfield Town and this earned him a transfer to Bolton Wanderers, who paid a then club record fee of £27,000 for his services. A goalscoring forward, he went on to play in the 1953 FA Cup final, but suffered a serious knee injury on 1 January 1955 and did not play again. He won 5 caps for England and appeared 3 times for the Football League representative side. He later worked as a coach for the FA and then as a PE lecturer, while from 1981 to 1985 he was secretary of the Amateur Swimming Association.

Ken Hawkes (Born Easington, Co Durham, 6 May 1933. Died 2 February 2015.) Ken Hawkes was a left back who joined Luton Town from Shotton Colliery, eventually breaking into the first team at Kenilworth Road after completing his National Service. He featured in all the Hatters' FA Cup ties in 1958–59, including the defeat at Wembley by Nottingham Forest in the final. He was then beset by injuries leading to a departure to Peterborough where his problems continued.

Adie Hayes (Born Norwich, 22 May 1978. Died 18 August 2014.) Adie Hayes started out as a 14-year-old at Cambridge United and was later a Trainee before signing professional forms in July 1996. A midfielder, he made 39 appearances for the U's before moving on to Kettering Town in the summer of 1998. He continued to play in the non-league game up until the end of 2011, turning out for AFC Sudbury in the 2005 FA Vase final. His early death was as a result of a brain tumour.

Willie Hayes (Born Ballyneety, Co Limerick, 30 March 1928. Died Torquay, 26 August 2014.) Goalkeeper Willie Hayes joined Limerick as a teenager and was capped for the Republic of Ireland against Belgium in April 1949, the club's first international cap. In July 1950 he moved on to Wrexham where he spent a season mostly in the reserves, then after a spell in non-league with Ellesmere Port he returned to senior football with Torquay United. He made 69 appearances for the Gulls and was their first choice 'keeper for 12 months from March 1953.

Sir Jack Hayward, OBE (Born Wolverhampton, 14 June 1923. Died Fort Lauderdale, USA, 13 January 2015.) Jack Hayward took over as owner and chairman of Wolverhampton Wanderers in May 1990 and remained in control until August 2007. A great benefactor to the club he financed the modernisation of the Molineux ground and was at the helm when they gained promotion to the Premier League via the play-offs in 2002–03.

Ron Henry (Born Shoreditch, London, 17 August 1934. Died Harpenden, Herts, 27 December 2014.) Ron Henry was a dependable left back who signed for Tottenham Hotspur after completing his National Service, eventually establishing himself in the side towards the end of 1959. He was then rarely absent over the following seasons, being ever present in the 1960–61 double-winning side. He went on to gain a second FA Cup winners' medal in 1961–62 and the following season was a member of the team that lifted the European Cup Winners' Cup. A member of the Tottenham team which completed the double in 1960–61 and gained further winners' medals in the FA Cup (1962) and European Cup Winners' Cup (1963). He was capped for England against France in February 1963.

Iain Hesford (Born Ndola, Zambia, 4 March 1960. Died 18 November 2014.) Goalkeeper Iain Hesford made over 200 appearances for Blackpool and 500 in total in a career that spanned the period 1977 to 1992. He helped Sunderland win the old Third Division title in 1987–88 and also turned out for Hull City and Maidstone United in the Football League. He also won 7 caps for England at U23 level. He was from a sporting family: his father kept goal for Huddersfield Town in the 1938 FA Cup final while brothers Bob, jnr (capped for England at rugby union) and Steve (rugby league) were both top-class sportsmen.

John Hewie (Born Pretoria, South Africa, 13 December 1927. Died Kirton, near Boston, Lincs, 11 May 2015.) John Hewie was a versatile left-sided defender who joined Charlton Athletic in October 1949, one of several South Africans to make the journey to The Valley around this time. He graduated to the first team at the start of the 1951–52 season and went on to play a total 530 games, his final appearance being against Bolton Wanderers in January 1966. He appeared in all 11 shirts for the Addicks, including a run of 4 games (none of which was lost) as emergency goalkeeper in April 1962. He also won 19 caps for Scotland, featuring in the 1958 World Cup finals.

Peter Hill (Born Heanor, Derbys, 8 August 1931. Died 8 January 2015.) Peter Hill was a pacy inside forward and later winger who progressed from the Coventry City nursery club Modern Machines to first-team football whilst still a teenager. He went on to make over 300 senior appearances during his stay at Highfield Road, where he was one of the few players to retain a constant presence throughout the 1950s. He later spent five years with the club as trainer.

Ken Hodder (Born Stockport, 20 August 1930. Died 3 March 2015.) Ken Hodder was a centre half who spent his entire career with Stockport County, signing professional forms in March 1949. He progressed to the first team in 1952 and went on to make 272 League and Cup appearances, including a run of 101 consecutive games . His career ended after he suffered a broken leg shortly after the start of the 1963–64 season.

Derek Hogg (Born Norton on Tees, Co Durham, 4 November 1950. Died 4 November 2014.) Winger Derek Hogg made over 300 senior appearances in a career that saw him play for Leicester City, West Bromwich Albion and Cardiff City. Signed by the Foxes from Chorley in October 1952 he became a first-team regular in the 1954–55 season and in 1956–57 he helped the team win the Division Two title. Tricky and able to play on either flank (although mostly a left winger), he also won representative honours for the Football League against the Scottish League in October 1955.

Pat Holton (Born Hamilton, 23 December 1935. Died 19 December 2014.) Pat Holton was a defender who developed in Lanarkshire Junior football before joining Hamilton Academical. Some fine performances earned him a move to Motherwell where he became one of the Ancell Babes. He later spent an unproductive period in England with Chelsea and Southend United before eventually returning to play for the Accies and he was an ever-present in the team that won promotion from Division Two in 1964–65.

Jack Hughes (Born West Bromwich, 13 September 1929. Died 23 February 2015.) Jack Hughes was an inside forward who spent three seasons on the books of Walsall in the early 1950s making 44 appearances. He later played for a number of local teams including Stourbridge and Evesham.

Jackie Hunter (Born Leith, circa 1930. Died Edinburgh, 4 June 2014.) Jackie Hunter was a powerful forward who made over 100 appearances for Motherwell in a 10-year spell to 1958. A highlight was scoring four in a 12-1 win over Dundee United in January 1954, the Fir Park club's biggest Scottish League victory. He wound down his career with spells at Dundee United and Forfar Athletic.

Jackie Hutton (Born Bellshill, Lanarkshire, 23 April 1944. Died Belfast, 20 May 2015.) Winger Jackie Hutton joined Hamilton Academical from Wishaw Juniors in March 1962 and went on to enjoy several seasons of first-team football with over 100 senior appearances in a career that also saw him turn out for Scunthorpe United and St Mirren. He

moved to Northern Ireland in 1967, winning two Irish League titles with Glentoran, while he helped Portadown win the All-Ireland Texaco Cup in 1973–74. He concluded his playing career at Cliftonville before turning to management.

Klas Ingesson (Born Odeshog, Sweden, 20 August 1968. Died Odeshog, Sweden, 29 October 2014.) Klas Ingesson was a midfield player who played for several clubs across Europe, notably IFK Gothenburg, Bari and Bologna. He made 18 Premier League appearances for Sheffield Wednesday between September 1994 and the end of 1995. He won 57 caps for Sweden and was a member of the team that finished in third place at the 1994 World Cup finals. At the time of his death, from cancer, he was manager of Swedish club IF Elfsborg.

Bill Jackman (Born Royston, South Yorkshire, 1924. Died 7 May 2015.) Bill Jackman was a winger who made 14 wartime appearances for Wolverhampton Wanderers, also featuring as a guest for Swindon Town. He later spent six years with Worcester City and when his playing days were over he joined the club's backroom staff, combining his football duties with teaching. His grandson Danny Jackman has played for Stockport County, Gillingham and Northampton Town in the Football League.

Albert Jackson (Born Manchester, 12 September 1943. Died Oldham, 2 December 2014.) Albert Jackson was on Manchester United's books as a youngster, then gained Football League experience with Oldham Athletic. Although mostly used as a centre forward during his time at Boundary Park, he earned a reputation as a powerful, no-nonsense defender in non-league football, firstly with Bangor City and then Wigan Athletic, captaining the Latics on their first Wembley visit for the FA Trophy final in 1973. He was in his 30s when invited to play in the NASL for Dallas Tornado, taking extended leave from his employment in an Oldham engineering factory to do so.

Keith James (Born Hillingdon 18 August 1961. Died December 2014.) Keith James was an England youth international who made his senior debut for Portsmouth whilst still a trainee. However, the attacking right back never managed to break into regular first-team football during his time at Fratton Park. He later enjoyed an extensive career in non-league football with multiple clubs, playing in FA Vase finals for Southall (runners-up in 1986) and Yeading (winners in 1990).

Andy Jardine (Born Paisley, 25 November 1935. Died Paisley, 4 July 2014.) Full back Andy Jardine was a loyal servant to Dumbarton between 1957 and 1967, known for his defensive partnership with Tommy Govan, the pair playing together on more than 300 occasions. Andy holds the club record of 298 Scottish League appearances whilst his total of 364 League and Cup games is third in the all-time list.

David Jones (Born Swansea, 3 March 1945. Died Swansea, 29 June 2014.) David Jones was a goalkeeper who joined Swansea Town in December 1955 after serving in the Army with the REME. He was mainly a reserve during his time at the Vetch Field, making just 3 Football League appearances. He moved on to Yeovil Town in the summer of 1958 where he stayed nine seasons, playing more than 350 games and featuring in the side that won the Southern League title in 1963–64.

Jimmy Jones (Born Birkenhead, 3 August 1927. Died Horncastle, Lincs, 5 May 2015.) Goalkeeper Jimmy Jones started out with Everton, but it was only when he joined New Brighton in the summer of 1950 that he experienced first-team football. He was Lincoln City's first-choice 'keeper in the 1951–52 season and went on to play for Accrington Stanley and Rochdale, taking his total of Football League appearances beyond the 300 mark.

Ken Jones (Born Llanelli, 16 April 1926. Died 20 March 2015.) Full back Ken Jones joined Coventry City from Welsh League club Llanelly Town in November 1949 and spent seven years on the books at Highfield Road. He was mostly a reserve apart from 1954–55 when he featured regularly in the line-up. He later switched to non-league football with Lockheed Leamington.

Peter Kearns (Born Wellingborough, 26 March 1937. Died Weymouth, 6 July 2014.) Inside forward Peter Kearns made over 60 appearances for Plymouth Argyle between 1956 and 1961 before joining Corby Town. He developed as a goalscorer with the Southern League club and was snapped up by Aldershot in December 1962. He went on to score 70 goals from 206 League and Cup appearances before finishing off with a spell at Lincoln City.

Andy King (Born Newmilns, Ayrshire, 23 July 1942. Died Kilmarnock, 23 February 2015.) Andy King was a solid full back who spent his entire senior career with Kilmarnock. A former Scottish Youth international, he established himself in the side in 1963–64 and when Killie won the Scottish League title the following season he missed just one game. He remained a fixture in the right-back slot until the end of the 1969–70 season, clocking up more than 300 first-team appearances. He was capped 3 times by Scotland U23s.

Andy King (Born Luton, 14 August 1956. Died 27 May 2015.) Andy King was an influential midfield player notably in two spells at Everton (1976 to 1980 and 1982 to 1984) where he is remembered for a spectacular goal that decided the Merseyside derby match in October 1978. His career had begun as an apprentice with Luton Town, and he also spent time with West Bromwich Albion, Wolverhampton Wanderers and Aldershot. He gained 2 caps for England U21s. Andy was later manager of a number of clubs including Swindon Town, Mansfield Town and Grays Athletic. At the time of his death, a result of a reported heart attack, he was working as a scout for Milton Keynes Dons.

Barrie King (Born West Drayton, Middlesex, 4 July 1940. Died Adelaide, Australia, 29 March 2015.) Barrie King was a half back who starred for St Albans City and Hitchin Town in the early 1960s, winning 7 England Amateur caps. In the summer of 1965 he became Barnet's first signed professional when he joined them for the start of their inaugural season in the Southern League. He went on to make over 400 appearances for Barnet and played for them in the 1972 FA Trophy final. He later emigrated to Australia and went on to represent South Australia at Lawn Bowls.

Ray King (Born Amble, Northumberland, 15 August 1924. Died Bangkok, Thailand, 19 July 2014.) Ray King was a goalkeeper who developed with Newcastle United, with whom he made a number of wartime appearances. He moved on to Leyton Orient, where he made a single appearance and then via Ashington to Port Vale. A key figure for Vale between 1949 and 1957, he enjoyed a tremendous season in 1953–54 when the club reached the semi-final of the FA Cup and won the Division Three North title, for good measure Ray was also capped for England B against Switzerland.

Joe Kinkead (Born Dunmurry, Co Antrim, 27 May 1933. Died 10 March 2015.) Joe Kinkead was a goalkeeper who played for Distillery, Linfield, Larne and Glenavon between 1949 and 1966. He was capped by Northern Ireland at Schoolboy and Youth levels and won 2 Amateur international caps in the 1961–62 season. He was later manager of Ards, Glenavon and the Northern Ireland Youth team.

Bobby Kinloch (Born Govan, Glasgow, 1935. Died Edinburgh, 27 August 2014.) Inside forward Bobby Kinloch signed for Hibernian in November 1959 and did well during his time at Easter Road, scoring 25 goals from 34 competitive appearances. Thereafter his career never really took off during spells with Morton, Berwick Rangers, Raith Rovers and Dunfermline Athletic, plus time in Canada with Toronto City and Hamilton Steelers.

Royce Kirkham (Born Ollerton, Notts, 17 October 1937. Died 24 January 2015.) Royce Kirkham managed just a solitary first-team appearance for Notts County, stepping in at right back for the visit to Doncaster Rovers in December 1956. His football career was ended after he suffered a broken leg and he later joined the Nottingham City Police force. He served 30 years as a police officer, retiring with the rank of superintendent.

Johnny Knox (Born Dunfermline, 21 January 1935. Died Cowdenbeath, 9 June 2014.) Inside forward Johnny Knox developed with Kelty Rangers and then Cowdenbeath, for whom he made 30 appearances. He was still only 18 when transferred to Preston North End in the summer of 1955, but failed to make the grade at Deepdale. Back in Scotland he joined Queen of the South before concluding his career at Cowdenbeath once again.

Eric Lacey (Born Circa 1924. Died March 2015.) Eric Lacey was a full back who won 2 caps for England Schools in 1937. He went on to sign for Barnsley, firstly as an amateur and, from January 1942 as a professional, making 5 wartime appearances for the club.

Roy Law (Born Croydon, 29 September 1937. Died 10 October 2014.) Roy Law was a centre half who won 19 caps for England Amateurs and also featured on 2 occasions for Great Britain in the qualifying games for the 1964 Olympics. At club level he joined Wimbledon as an amateur in 1958 and stayed through until 1972, by which time they had joined the professional ranks. He is the club's record appearance maker (644 games) and captained the side to victory in the FA Amateur Cup in 1963.

Trevor Lewis (Born Blackwood, Monmouthshire, 6 January 1921. Died 12 April 2015.) Trevor Lewis was a winger who lost the best years of his career to the war. He was 27 when he signed for Coventry City and in five years at Highfield Road he was mostly a reserve. He moved on to Gillingham early in 1953 and held down a place until the end of that season before again being restricted to a role as deputy.

Jack Leyfield (Born Handbridge, Cheshire, 5 August 1923. Died Guildford, Surrey 21 December 2014.) Jack Leyfield made wartime appearances for Chester and Darlington before joining Wrexham for the first season of peacetime football. He was used as a utility player at the Racecourse Ground and then spent a season with Southport where he played at wing half and inside forward. He subsequently continued his career in Cheshire non-league football.

Garry Liddell (Born Bannockburn, Stirlingshire, 27 August 1954. Died Denny, Stirlingshire, 29 April 2015.) Garry Liddell was a striker who progressed from the apprentice ranks to a professional contract with Leeds United in September 1971, but with competition for places at Elland Road tough he made just a handful of appearances. He moved on to Grimsby Town in March 1977 where despite twice recovering from a broken leg he helped them gain back-to-back promotions in 1978–79 and 1979–80. He concluded his career with spells at Hearts and Doncaster Rovers before his career was ended due to a neck injury.

Billy Liggett (Born Portadown, 20 June 1925. Died Connecticut, USA, 10 January 2015.) Billy Liggett was a defender who made close on 100 appearances for Linfield between 1945 and 1951 and then spent five years with Glenavon. He was an Irish Cup winner with Linfield in 1948 and won an Irish League Championship medal with Glenavon in 1951–52. He also represented the Irish League on three occasions.

Danny Light (Born Chiswick, Middlesex, 10 July 1948. Died 20 October 2014.) Winger Danny Light burst on the scene at Crystal Palace at the very end of the 1966–67 season, scoring two on his debut against Hull City and adding another the following Saturday against promoted Wolverhampton Wanderers. Unable to fulfil the promise shown, he moved on to Colchester United for two seasons of fairly regular first-team football then played for a number of clubs in the Southern League, notably Dartford.

Roy Little (Born Manchester, 1 June 1931. Died January 2015.) Roy Little was a dependable left back who made over 180 first-team appearances and played in two FA Cup finals for Manchester City, gaining a winners' medal in 1956 when they defeated Birmingham City 3-1. He later spent several years in the south of England, firstly with Brighton & Hove Albion and Crystal Palace and later as player-manager of Dover Athletic.

Wil Lloyd (Born 1945. Died 29 September 2014.) Wil Lloyd was a forward who scored almost 150 goals in a lengthy career with Aberystwyth Town and also played for Llanidloes Town. He won 8 caps for Wales Amateurs.

Jack Lornie (Born Aberdeen, 2 March 1939. Died Inverness, 16 December 2014.) Jack Lornie was something of a young prodigy, gaining schoolboy caps for Scotland and winning the Scottish Junior Cup with Banks O'Dee in 1957. However, his career never quite took off at Leicester City although he was a regular scorer for the reserves. He moved on to Luton Town, then spent time with Carlisle United and Tranmere Rovers before returning to Scotland where he played Highland League football for Ross County, later going on to manage the club.

Roy McCrohan (Born Reading, 22 September 1930. Died 3 March 2015.) Wing half Roy McCrohan started out with Reading but was unable to establish himself in the side and in August 1951 he joined Norwich City in a player exchange. He stayed 11 years at Carrow Road, making over 400 appearances. He was a member of the team that reached the FA Cup semi-final in 1958–59 and was ever present the following season when the Canaries won promotion to Division Two. He concluded his career with spells at Colchester United and Bristol Rovers.

Walter McFarland (Born 1945. Died 16 August 2014.) Walter McFarland spent 14 years with Crusaders, captaining the team that won the Irish League title. He featured in a number of European games and gained a single cap for Northern Ireland Amateurs against Wales in May 1968. He was also a judo competitor of a high standard, winning a silver medal at the World Veterans' championship in 1999, while he was also an All-Ireland and World Masters Champion.

Jimmy McGill (Born Glasgow, 27 November 1946. Died 25 March 2015.) Jimmy McGill was a busy midfield player who made his debut in senior football with Arsenal. He went on to make over 150 appearances for both Huddersfield Town and Hull City, helping the Terriers win promotion to the top flight in 1969–70 when he was ever present. He finished his senior career with a spell at Halifax Town.

Bertie McGonigal (Born Cookstown, Co Tyrone, 2 May 1942. Died 12 September 2014.) Bertie McGonigal was a goalkeeper with Glentoran before joining Brighton & Hove Albion in February 1962 where he made 62 senior appearances. He later played in South Africa with Cape Town City before returning home to sign for Linfield. He was twice capped for the Irish League representative side.

Stuart McGrady (Born Irvine, Ayrshire, 8 April 1985. Died Ayr, 28 February 2015.) Stuart McGrady was a versatile player who began his career as a youngster with Ayr United. He broke into the first team but then moved on to Junior outfit Cumnock only to return to the seniors for a second time when he signed for Queen's Park. At the time of his death he was captain of Maybole Juniors and had played for the team in the afternoon before passing away in his sleep that night.

Ian McGraw (Born Glasgow, 30 August 1926. Died Leicester, 27 October 2014.) Goalkeeper Ian McGraw broke into the Arbroath first team at the start of the 1948–49 season and such was his form that within a matter of months he had

been sold to Leicester City. He made a promising start at Filbert Street, but then suffered a broken finger which kept him out of the 1949 FA Cup final. Complications set in leading to amputation of the finger and this effectively ended his senior career.

Dave Mackay (Born Musselburgh, East Lothian, 14 November 1934. Died Nottingham, 2 March 2015.) Dave Mackay was one of the great players in British football during the post-war period. A barrel-chested left half, his gritty determination and powerful tackle often marked him out as one of the game's hard men, but he also possessed excellent distribution and an astute football brain. He made his name in Scotland with Hearts, helping the Tynecastle club two League Cups, a Scottish Cup and, in 1957–58, captaining the side to the League title. He enjoyed further success with Tottenham Hotspur where he was a member of the famous double team of 1960–61 and two further FA Cup successes. In the twilight of his career he helped Derby County win the Division Two title in 1968–69, when he was joint Footballer of the Year with Tony Book. He won 22 caps for Scotland. Later as a manager he took Derby to the Football League title, and had spells with a number of clubs including Nottingham Forest, Walsall, Doncaster Rovers and Birmingham City.

Tony McNamara (Born Liverpool, 3 October 1929. Died May 2015.) Tony McNamara was a tall right winger who made over 100 appearances for Everton between 1951 and 1957. He created history when he became the first player to appear in all four divisions within a 12-month period, achieving the feat between October 1957 and September 1958 with the Toffees, Liverpool, Crewe Alexandra and Bury. He left senior football soon afterwards.

John McPhee (Born Motherwell, 21 November 1937. Died Hambleton, near Poulton-le-Fylde, Lancs, 4 January 2015.) John McPhee was a hard-working half back who possessed a powerful tackle. He spent his formative years with Motherwell before moving south to Blackpool where he made almost 300 League and Cup appearances and was the club's first-ever used substitute, as well as being Player of the Year on two occasions. He finished his career on a high, helping Southport win promotion from Division Four in 1972–73.

Albert McPherson (Born Salford, 8 July 1927. Died 11 January 2015.) Albert McPherson was a solid centre half who developed in Manchester junior football and after completing his National Service signed for Bury. Unable to break into the Shakers' first team he left for Stalybridge Celtic before Walsall manager Major Frank Buckley spotted him and signed him up. He was rarely absent in 10 seasons at Fellows Park, helping the club gain successive promotions in 1959–60 and 1960–61 and playing over 350 games. He later worked on the backroom staff at West Bromwich Albion for many years.

Tom McQueen (Born West Calder, West Lothian, 21 February 1929. Died February 2015.) Goalkeeper Tom McQueen made his debut in senior football for Leith Athletic but spent several seasons playing principally as back-up. He saw regular first-team action with both Accrington Stanley (1954 to 1957) and Berwick Rangers (1957 to 1960), taking his tally of senior appearances close to the 200-mark before retiring. His son Gordon McQueen later won international honours for Scotland as a defender.

Danny Malloy (Born Longcroft, Stirlingshire, 6 November 1930. Died Larbert, Stirlingshire, 14 January 2015.) Danny Malloy joined Dundee from Camelon Juniors and after two years of National Service he returned to gain a regular first-team place. He became known as a powerful, no-nonsense centre half and after being sold to Cardiff City he led the Bluebirds to promotion to the old First Division in 1959–60. He made over 200 appearances during his stay in south Wales and after a season as player-manager of Doncaster he returned to Scotland to end his career with Clyde. Danny won representative honours for the Scottish League and was also capped by Scotland B.

Valery Mezague (Born Marseille, 8 December 1983. Died Toulon, 15 November 2014.) Valery Mezague was a midfield player who developed with the Montpellier club in France. He spent the 2004–05 season on loan with Portsmouth, making 11 Premier League appearances and subsequently played for Sochaux, Vannes and in Greece with Panetolikos. He returned to England for the second half of 2012–13 with Bury and was on the books of Sporting Toulon at the time of his sudden death. He won 7 caps for Cameroon.

Ralph Miller (Born Slough, 22 June 1941. Died 2014.) Ralph Miller joined Charlton Athletic from Slough and had a brief run of games at right back for the Addicks in the first half of 1964–65 before moving on to Gillingham at the end of the season. A versatile player, he mostly featured for the Kent club at right half then moved on to Bournemouth where he was used at left back. He went on to make over 200 senior appearances before joining Weymouth.

Arnold Mitchell (Born Rotherham, 1 December 1929. Died 18 October 2014.) Arnold Mitchell made a solitary appearance for Notts County in September 1951 on the right wing before joining Exeter City. An attacking player in his early days with the Grecians, he settled down at wing half and went on to create a new club record of 495 Football League appearances. Arnold captained the club to promotion from Division Four in 1963–64 and remained a first-team regular through to the 1965–66 season.

Gus Moffat (Born Carluke, Lanarkshire, 15 May 1948. Died Ontario, Canada, 11 February 2015.) Gus Moffat signed as a teenager for Southampton but became homesick and returned to Lanarkshire, joining Motherwell. On 13 August 1966 he created a piece of history by became the first substitute to score a goal in senior Scottish football after coming on at half-time in the League Cup tie at Dunfermline and scoring in the 71st minute. In 1968 he moved to Canada and he continued to play in North America for over a decade, most notably with Detroit Express. In January 1990 he launched the Detroit Rockers with the former Wrexham player Brian Tinnion.

Ian Moir (Born Aberdeen, 30 April 1943. Died 27 March 2015.) Ian Moir was a tricky winger who developed with Manchester United in the early 1960s, making 45 Division One appearances. He moved on to Blackpool in February 1965 and then Chester. However, he is best remembered for his two spells with Wrexham which yielded over 150 appearances. He helped the club win promotion from the Fourth Division in 1969–70. He also spent a season with Shrewsbury Town.

Steve Mokone (Born Doornfontein, South Africa, 23 March 1932. Died Washington DC, USA, 20 March 2015.) Steve 'Kalamazoo' Mokone was an exciting winger who became the first black South African to play professional football in Europe. Signed by Coventry City from Pretoria Home Stars, he made four first-team appearances before moving to the Netherlands where he became a star with Heracles of Almelo. In a career that saw him play across Europe, he also had brief associations with Cardiff City and Barnsley. In later life he lived in the United States where he gained a PhD in psychology and became an assistant professor at Rochester University in New York State. He was also active in the anti-apartheid movement.

Arthur Montford (Born Glasgow, 25 May 1929. Died Milngavie, Dunbartonshire, 25 November 2014.) Arthur Montford was a journalist and broadcaster who worked for the *Greenock Telegraph*, *Glasgow Evening News*, *Daily Record* and *Glasgow Evening Times* before joining STV in 1957. He subsequently presented the *Scotsport* television programme for 32 years. Arthur was also a director of Morton FC and later honorary vice-president of the club.

Bernard Moore (Born Brighton, 18 December 1923. Died Putnoe, Bedford, 20 July 2014.) Brian Moore was an inside or centre forward who started his career with Brighton & Hove Albion before dropping into non-league with Hastings United. He scored prolifically, earning a move to Luton Town and then a return to Brighton. However he was perhaps best known for his performances with Southern League Bedford Town, famously scoring an equalising goal at Highbury to take Arsenal to a replay in their FA Cup tie in January 1956.

Eddie Moran (Born Cleland, Lanarkshire, 20 July 1930. Died Stockport, 1 July 2014.) Eddie Moran was a skilful inside forward who signed for Leicester City in September 1947. He managed just a short run of appearances during his time at Filbert Street, but did well in a six-year spell with Stockport County. After signing for a then club record fee (£5,000) he made over 100 first-team appearances. Eddie later had spells with Rochdale and Crewe Alexandra before a knee injury brought his career to a close. He is the older brother of John Moran, below.

John Moran (Born Cleland, Lanarkshire, 9 March 1933. Died Netherton, Wishaw, Lanarkshire, 8 April 2015.) John Moran was one of three brothers who all played professional football in England. Signed by Derby County in November 1954, he made two first-team appearances shortly after signing and the following season added a single League Cup outing for St Mirren. Away from football he was involved in local politics as a Labour councillor for 28 years, serving on Motherwell District Council and later on North Lanarkshire Council.

Geoff Morris (Born Birmingham, 8 February 1949. Died Shrewsbury, 16 February 2015.) Geoff Morris was just 16 when he made his senior debut for Walsall, making him the club's youngest-ever player. A winger and later wide midfield player, he finished as the Saddlers' top scorer in 1971–72, making close on 20 appearances during his stay. He was later at Shrewsbury Town, helping the club gain promotion from the Fourth Division in 1974–75. On leaving senior football he played for Kidderminster Harriers and had a spell in Australia with Brisbane Lions.

Sam Morris (Born Warrington 12 February 1930. Died 20 December 2014.) Sam Morris was a half back who was given his debut by Chester in January 1952 and his next two appearances were in the FA Cup ties against First Division Chelsea. The Sealand Road club drew at Stamford Bridge and then went down 3-2 at home in front of a record crowd. In a remarkable start to his career, his following game produced the club's record defeat: 11-2 to Oldham Athletic. Sam was in and out of the side over the next few seasons, gaining a Welsh Cup runners-up medal in 1955 before injury curtailed his career.

Eddie Mulheron (Born 3 May 1942. Died 20 March 2015.) Eddie Mulheron was a solid and dependable full back who joined Clyde in July 1963 and stayed for nine seasons, making over 250 appearances. He emigrated to South Africa where he lived for the next 40 years initially playing for Durban United, then turning to coaching with Manning Rangers after he had received a lifetime ban following an on-field incident.

Andy Murphy (Born 29 July 1939. Died 5 November 2014.) Andy Murphy was on Celtic's books as a teenager but was unable to break into the first team and moved on to Raith Rovers in the summer of 1959. He made his senior debut during his time in Kirkcaldy but it was not until he arrived at Albion Rovers in June 1960 that he experienced regular first-team action. He remained with the Coatbridge club until the end of the 1968–69 season, making 288 League and Cup appearances.

Archie Murphy (Born 21 March 1933. Died Livingston, West Lothian, 29 October 2014.) Left half Archie Murphy joined Alloa Athletic from Armadale Thistle in September 1956 and quickly established himself in the line-up. He went on to make over 200 appearances over the next six seasons before moving on to Cowdenbeath.

John Neal (Born Seaham, Co Durham, 3 April 1932. Died 23 November 2014.) John Neal was a full back who made over 350 appearances in a career with Hull City, Swindon Town, Aston Villa and Southend United between 1949 and 1966. His best years were probably at Villa Park, where he gained promotion to the top flight in 1959–60 and won a Football League Cup winners' medal the following season. He went on to become a respected manager, winning promotion with Wrexham in 1969–70 and taking them to the quarter-finals of the European Cup Winners' Cup in 1975–76. Four years in charge of Middlesbrough followed before he took over at Chelsea, leading them to Division Two success in 1983–84.

Willie Neil (Born Airdrie, 22 May 1939. Died Edinburgh, 22 September 2014.) Willie Neil was a centre half who began with Airdrieonians before joining Queen's Park in 1961. He made 400 appearances during his time with the club, also gaining 14 caps for Scotland Amateurs and playing for the Great Britain Olympic team.

Kenny Parry (Born 21 December 1975. Died Glasgow, 24 April 2015.) Kenny Parry had a brief association with the senior game, making five appearances as a full back for Albion Rovers in the 1994–95 season. He collapsed while playing for Carluke Rovers over-35s and died later in hospital.

Pat Partridge, BEM (Born Billingham, 30 June 1933. Died 31 October 2014.) Pat Partridge was a well-known referee who was on the Football League list from 1966 to 1981 and took charge of a number of important games including the 1975 FA Cup final, the 1976 World Club Championship final; the 1977 European Cup Winners' Cup final and the 1978 Football League Cup Final. He also refereed at the 1978 World Cup finals and the 1980 European Championship finals.

Alex Paterson (Born circa 1935. Died July 2014.) Alex Paterson was the centre of a major controversy on his debut for Stirling Albion against Rangers in August 1954. The Ibrox club's Willie Woodburn was sent off in the final minute of the League Cup tie for fouling him, resulting in a sine die suspension. A young winger, Alex went on to make 24 first-team appearances for Stirling before leaving the senior game.

Bert Patrick (Born Kilsyth, Lanarkshire, 26 April 1946. Died Kilsyth, Lanarkshire, March 2015.) Bert Patrick was a full back who spent eight seasons on the books of Preston North End after signing in August 1963. Although mostly a reserve during his time at Deepdale, he made 50 Football League appearances, featuring regularly in the second half of 1967–68. He later had a season with Barrow before returning north of the border.

Tommy Preston (Born Edinburgh, 23 October 1932. Died Edinburgh, 16 April 2015.) Tommy Preston was an inside forward who made over 300 appearances for Hibernian during a career that spanned the period 1953 to 1964. He gained a Scottish Cup runners-up medal in 1958 and featured in a dozen European ties, including the 4-0 victory over Rot Weiss Essen in September 1955, the very first European Cup tie played by a British club.

Don Ratcliffe (Born Newcastle-under-Lyme, Staffs, 13 November 1934. Died 19 October 2014.) Winger Don Ratcliffe spent 10 seasons on the books of Stoke City, winning a regular first-team place from September 1957 and going on to feature in all 42 League matches in 1962–63 when the Potters won promotion to the top flight. In total he made over 450 senior appearances, also playing with Middlesbrough, Darlington and Crewe Alexandra.

Tim Rawlings (Born Coleshill, Warwickshire, 4 November 1932. Died 28 September 2014.) Tim Rawlings was a hardworking wing half who spent time on the books of West Bromwich Albion without breaking into the first team. He

signed for Walsall in the 1956 close season and went on to make more than 200 appearances during his stay, helping them win consecutive promotions in 1959–60 and 1960–61. He finished off with a couple of seasons at Port Vale.

Sammy Reid (Born Motherwell, 13 October 1939. Died Wishaw, Lanarkshire, 9 November 2014.) Sammy Reid was a clever inside forward who started out as one of Bobby Ancell's Motherwell Babes. Later he became Bill Shankly's first signing for Liverpool, although he never made the first team at Anfield, and also turned out for Falkirk, Clyde, Berwick Rangers and Dumbarton. He created a piece of history in January 1967 when his goal for Berwick famously dismissed Rangers from the Scottish Cup.

Derek Robertson (Born Glasgow, 12 February 1949. Died 29 January 2015.) Goalkeeper Derek Robertson was capped for Scotland at Juvenile level, moving up to Petershill Juniors and then to the seniors with St Johnstone, becoming manager Willie Ormond's first signing for the club. He spent 13 years at Muirton Park, making more than 250 appearances before injuries finally took their toll and he retired from the game.

Billy Ronson (Born Fleetwood, 22 January 1957. Died Perry Hall, Maryland, USA, 8 April 2015.) Billy Ronson was an inspirational midfield player who made his name with Blackpool before being sold to Cardiff City for a then club record fee. He later spent time with Wrexham and Barnsley before emigrating to the United States where he played for several seasons in indoor soccer.

Peter Rushworth (Born Bristol, 12 April 1927. Died 8 November 2014.) Wing half Peter Rushworth had a spell on the books of Leicester City without breaking into the first team before joining Bournemouth in the summer of 1953. He went on to make 88 first-team appearances for the Cherries over the next four seasons before moving on to Salisbury.

John Sadler (Born Maltby, Yorkshire, 21 June 1940. Died Toulouse, France, 19 May 2015.) John Sadler was a journalist who came to prominence as the *Sun's* Northern football correspondent in the 1960s. He went on to become that newspaper's chief sportswriter for over 25 years, covering the period 1976 to 1992, and was known for his tag-line "The man who gives it to you straight".

Gerry Sears (Born Arkwright Town, Derbys, 13 January 1935. Died Chesterfield, 11 September 2014.) Gerry Sears came up through the ranks with Chesterfield, signing professional forms in January 1952. Although his early games were played on the left wing, it was at left back that he established himself in the side, featuring regularly throughout 10 seasons from 1958–59. He made 412 Football League appearances and a further 43 in Cup ties with the Spireites, his only senior club.

Ivor Seemley (Born Sheffield, 30 June 1929. Died 1 November 2014.) Ivor Seemley was a left back who spent nine seasons on the books of Sheffield Wednesday, principally as a reserve. A highlight came when he featured in the 1954 FA Cup semi-final against Preston North End. He went on to enjoy four seasons of regular first-team football – two with Stockport County and two with Chesterfield – before leaving senior football.

Jim Sharkey (Born 12 February 1934. Died 19 October 2014.) Jim Sharkey was a ball-playing inside forward who did well early on with Celtic but by November 1957 he had moved on to Airdrieonians. In a four-year stay with the Onians he made over 100 first-team appearances then concluded his senior career with Raith Rovers before moving on to play in the Southern League with Cambridge United.

Nick Sharkey (Born Helensburgh, Dunbartonshire, 4 May 1943. Died 8 February 2015.) Nick Sharkey was a small but lively forward who enjoyed the best of his career at Sunderland where in six years he scored 62 goals, a rate of more than a goal every other game. He holds a share in the record individual goals tally for the club after netting five times in a 7-1 win over Norwich City in March 1963. He made little impact during a spell with Leicester City but at Mansfield Town he was an important figure in the team that reached the FA Cup quarter-finals, scoring in the giant killing victory over West Ham United. Nick won 2 caps for Scotland U23s.

Leslie Silver OBE (Born Walthamstow, London, 22 January 1925. Died 29 December 2014.) Leslie Silver was a successful local businessman who joined the board of Leeds United in 1981, serving as chairman between 1983 and 1996. During his period the club won the Football League title in 1991–92, the last occasion before the Premier League was introduced.

Frank Slynn (Born Birmingham 10 February 1924. Died Strensall, York 12 November 2014.) Frank Slynn made 46 appearances for Sheffield Wednesday in the early post-war years. Featuring on either wing he was a regular in the side until a broken leg disrupted his career. He later had spells with both Bury and Walsall in the early 1950s, although by this time he was a left half and occasional left back.

Alan Sproates (Born Houghton le Spring, Co Durham, 30 June 1944. Died California, USA, 5 February 2015.) Alan Sproates was a skilful midfield player who was an apprentice with Sunderland before joining Swindon where he received an introduction to senior football. It was at Darlington between 1965 and 1974 where he shone, helping the team win promotion in his first season and making over 300 appearances. On leaving Scunthorpe United he spent time in Australia before emigrating to the United States.

Alfredo di Stefano (Born Buenos Aires, 4 July 1926. Died Madrid, 7 July 2014.) Alfredo di Stefano was one of the all-time greats of world football. A centre forward with a huge presence on the field he began his career in Argentina with River Plate. A strike of players led to a move to the breakaway league in Colombia where he played for Millonarios. In 1953 the Colombian FA joined FIFA and Alfredo moved on to Real Madrid. Here he was one of the great stars of an all-conquering team that won the first five European Cups and eight Spanish titles in an 11-year run. The team almost certainly peaked in the 7-3 European Cup final win over Eintracht Frankfurt at Hampden in 1960. After a brief spell with Espanyol he retired as a player and went into coaching. He is one of the few players to have represented three countries in international football: Argentina, Colombia and Spain.

Len Stephenson (Born Blackpool, 14 July 1930. Died 29 September 2014.) Centre forward Len Stephenson was principally a reserve in almost seven years with Blackpool, but saw more first-team action after signing for Port Vale in March 1955. He finished as Vale's leading scorer in 1955–56 then moved on for a final season in senior football with Oldham Athletic.

Morris Stevenson (Born Tranent, East Lothian, 16 April 1943. Died Edinburgh, 22 July 2014.) Morris Stevenson was a traditional ball-playing inside forward who started out at Motherwell in August 1960. After a spell with Hibernian he moved on to Morton and enjoyed the best seasons of his career in Greenock as a member of the team that won the Division Two title in 1963–64 and reached the League Cup final. He later won a second promotion with Morton before moving south for what proved to be a disappointing time at Luton. Morris concluded his career back in Scotland with Dundee United and Berwick Rangers.

Jim Storrie (Born Kirkintilloch, Dunbartonshire, 31 March 1940. Died Kilsyth, Lanarkshire, 11 November 2014.) Jim Storrie was a powerful, hard-working forward who developed with Airdrieonians, with whom he scored 66 goals in just

118 League and Cup appearances, helping them to a semi-final place in the Scottish Cup in 1960–61. Don Revie brought him to Leeds in June 1962 and he netted 25 goals in his first season at Elland Road. He again led the club's scoring charts in 1964–65, when he also gained an FA Cup runners-up medal. Jim went on to play for Aberdeen, Rotherham United, Portsmouth and St Mirren before ending his playing career. He later had a spell as manager of St Johnstone.

Dave Stratton (Born Dundee, 1927. Died 25 April 2015.) Dave Stratton was a full back who developed with Elmwood Juniors, signing for Dundee United in September 1949. A student, he made over 50 first-team appearances during his time at Tannadice Park and also won 3 caps for Scotland Amateurs.

Eddie Stuart (Born Johannesburg, South Africa, 12 May 1931. Died Wrexham, 4 November 2014.) Eddie Stuart was a hard-tackling full back who joined Wolverhampton Wanderers from the Rangers club of Johannesburg. He went on to make over 300 first-team appearances and was a regular in the side that won back-to-back Football League titles in 1957–58 and 1958–59. He later played for Stoke City, Tranmere Rovers and Stockport County, where he was a near ever-present in the side that won the Division Four title in 1966–67.

Ron Suart (Born Kendal, 18 November 1920. Died 25 March 2015.) Ron Suart was a left back who made over 300 appearances for Blackpool and Blackburn Rovers in the immediate post-war period, twice featuring in FA Cup semi-finals. He spent the 1955–56 season as player-manager of Wigan Athletic before taking over as manager of Scunthorpe United, leading them to the Division Three North championship in 1957–58. He was then manager of Blackpool (May 1958 to January 1967), leaving a few months before they were relegated from the top flight. He then spent 16 years with the backroom staff at Chelsea, where he was briefly manager (October 1974 to April 1975).

Jordan Tabor (Born Oxford, 9 September 1990. Died Antalya, Turkey, 23 July 2014.) Jordan Tabor was a defender and central midfield player who developed through the youth set-up at Chelsea. His only experience of senior football came during a spell as a non-contract player with Cheltenham Town at the start of the 2009–10 season when he featured in a Football League Trophy game against Torquay. He died in tragic circumstances whilst on holiday in Turkey.

David Taylor (Born Forfar, 15 March 1954. Died Glasgow, 24 June 2014.) David Taylor was chief executive of the Scottish FA between 1999 and June 2007. From June 2007 to October 2009 he was General Secretary of UEFA and then became CEO of the UEFA Events company and adviser on corporate business affairs to UEFA. He played both Junior football (for Forfar East End) and amateur football, appearing at Hampden Park for Westerlands AFC when they won the West of Scotland Amateur Cup in 1982.

Dai Thomas (Born Abercregan, Port Talbot, 1 August 1926. Died November 2014.) Dai Thomas joined Swansea Town as an inside forward in August 1948, later converting to full back. He made over 300 appearances during his time at the Vetch Field, also winning 2 full caps for Wales. He finished his senior career with a couple of seasons at Newport County before joining Southern League club Hereford United.

Malcolm Thompson (Born Beverley, 19 October 1946. Died Hull, 24 October 2014.) Centre forward Malcolm Thompson spent two-and-a-half seasons on the books of Hartlepools United, scoring 9 goals from 49 appearances. After moving on to Scarborough he went on to score the winning goal in extra time in the 1973 FA Trophy final against Wigan Athletic. Latterly he was associated with the Hessle Rangers club for 20 years.

Tommy Todd (Born Stonehouse, Lanarkshire, 1 June 1926. Died 2014.) Tommy Todd came to prominence as a teenager, scoring twice as Burnbank Athletic defeated Cambuslang Rangers in the replayed Scottish Junior Cup final in 1944–45 (he had also scored in the first tie). He later enjoyed a productive spell as a centre or inside forward for Hamilton, but in England, where he played for Crewe Alexandra, Derby County and Rochdale, he found it difficult to gain regular first-team football despite a good goals record when selected.

Ian Towers (Born Blackhill, Co Durham, 11 October 1940. Died Cape Town, South Africa, January 2015.) Ian Towers was a winger who joined Burnley, then one of the best clubs in the country, as a teenager. It was not until the departure of John Connelly that he won a regular place in the line-up and soon afterwards he was on his way to Oldham Athletic. He went on to add over 150 appearances in the lower divisions for the Latics and then Bury before emigrating to South Africa where he played for Cape Town City and remained for the rest of his life.

Ray Treacy (Born Dublin, 18 June 1946. Died Dublin, 10 April 2015.) Ray Treacy was a busy, hard-working forward who won 42 caps for the Republic of Ireland between 1966 and 1980. He was perhaps best known for a four-year spell with Charlton Athletic, for whom he made over 150 appearances, but he also spent time with West Bromwich Albion, Swindon Town and Preston North End before returning to Ireland with Shamrock Rovers. He subsequently went into management, leading Shamrock to the League of Ireland title in 1973–74.

Geoff Truett (Born Forest Gate, London, 23 May 1935. Died 5 January 2015.) Geoff Truett was a winger who played for Wycombe Wanderers in the 1957 FA Amateur Cup final before turning professional with Crystal Palace. However, during five seasons at Selhurst Park he was never a first-team regular and he eventually left in the summer of 1962, signing for Tonbridge. He spent 18 seasons with the Kent club for whom he became the first player to make more than 500 appearances.

Chris Turner (Born St Neots, Cambs, 3 April 1951. Died Wisbech, Cambs, 27 April 2015.) Chris Turner was one of the most significant figures in the history of Peterborough United. A commanding central defender, he made over 300 appearances, captaining the team that won the Division Four title in 1973–74. He took his tally of senior games beyond 500 with spells at Luton Town, Cambridge United and Southend United, whilst he also played in the NASL with Connecticut Bicentennials and New England Teamen. He went on to manage Cambridge and then returned to Peterborough in a similar role, leading the club to successive promotions to the second tier. At the end of 1992 he headed a consortium that bought the club and occupied a number of different positions before eventually leaving in May 2001.

Dave Walker (Born Colne, Lancs, 15 October 1941. Died 21 April 2015.) Dave Walker was a hard-tackling wing half who spent his formative years with Burnley. However, after six seasons and just 40 first-team outings he chose to move on, signing for Ted Bates at Southampton. He helped Saints win promotion to the top flight in his first season and played over 200 games before leaving in February 1974 for a brief spell with Cape Town City in South Africa.

Billy Walsh (Born Horden, Co Durham, 4 December 1923. Died Gold Coast, Queensland, Australia, 2014.) Centre half Billy Walsh was on Sunderland's books in the years immediately after the war ended. In seven seasons with the Wearside club he made 105 first-team appearances and later played for Northampton Town and Darlington before emigrating to Australia.

Jimmy Walsh (Born Blairhall, Fife, 3 December 1930. Died Leicester, 6 August 2014.) A lively forward, Jimmy Walsh was a member of the Celtic team that won their first League title in 16 years in 1953–54, while in October 1956, very shortly before being sold to Leicester City, he gained a League Cup winners prize. Whilst at Filbert Street Jimmy

earned an FA Cup runners-up medal as a member of the team that lost out in the 1961 final. His final statistics for the Foxes were impressive: 91 goals from 199 appearances.

Tom Whalen (Born Dumbarton, 9 September 1931. Died Newark, California, USA 21 September 2014.) Tom Whalen was one of the stars of the Dumbarton team of the late 1950s, remembered for setting up many of the chances that enabled Hughie Gallacher to set a club record for goalscoring. In 1961 he emigrated to San Francisco where he continued his football career with San Francisco Scots.

Colin Whitaker (Born Leeds, 14 June 1932. Died 1 May 2015.) Colin Whitaker was a flying winger who started out with Sheffield Wednesday. In June 1956 he joined Shrewsbury Town and he was an ever-present in three of his four full seasons, missing out in 1957–58 when he was sidelined with a broken leg. Thereafter his journeys took him to Queens Park Rangers, Rochdale, Oldham and Barrow before he left senior football in 1964. Colin also played Minor Counties cricket for Shropshire.

David Whyte (Born Greenwich, London, 20 April 1971. Died 9 September 2014.) Striker David Whyte started out with Crystal Palace but he was best known for his time with Charlton Athletic between 1994 and 1997 where he made over 100 appearances (many as a substitute) and topped the club's scoring charts in 1994–95 with 21 League and Cup goals. Later he had spells with Ipswich Town, Bristol Rovers and Southend United before leaving full-time football.

Eddie Wilcox (Born Blaengarw, Glamorgan, 24 March 1927. Died 11 January 2015.) Eddie Wilcox was a forward early in his career, developing with Oxford City in wartime football before stepping up to the professionals with West Bromwich Albion. He was mostly a reserve at The Hawthorns, leaving to join Worcester City where he became something of a legendary figure. Converting to a role as a defender he made over 350 appearances and appeared in the team that famously defeated Liverpool 2-1 in an FA Cup third round tie in January 1959.

Freddie Willcox (Born St Helens, 23 October 1922. Died Liverpool, 22 January 2015.) Freddie Wilcox was a right back who signed amateur forms for Everton just before the outbreak of war and eventually resumed his career with Chester during peacetime. He featured fairly regularly in the side in 1947–48, but then suffered a broken leg which brought his senior career to an end although he later played for South Liverpool.

Dave Williams (Born Newport, 1 March 1942. Died 23 February 2015.) Dave Williams was a pacy full back who was a regular for Newport County for around 10 seasons. He later played for local team Spencer Works before returning to Somerton Park in a coaching capacity. After the original club folded he was involved with the revived organisation in a number of roles, including as a director for a time, and he also acted as kit man for the FA Wales international teams.

Harold Williams (Born Briton Ferry, Glamorgan, 17 June 1924. Died 12 September 2014.) Harold Williams signed for Newport County after being demobbed at the end of the war and was already a full international for Wales when Leeds United bought him in the summer of 1949. A flying winger he made over 200 appearances during his stay at Elland Road, returning briefly to Newport in March 1957 before going back to Yorkshire to conclude his career with Bradford Park Avenue. He won 4 caps for Wales.

Jimmy Williamson (Born 1928. Died Dunkeld, Perthshire, 20 February 2015.) Jimmy Williamson spent four seasons on the books of Dunfermline Athletic after signing from Blairgowrie Juniors. Mostly a centre half, he was never quite able to establish himself in the line-up at East End Park. He later had a brief spell with Montrose before moving on to play for Vale of Atholl in the North Perthshire League. He was believed to be Dunfermline's oldest surviving player at the time of his death.

Sammy Wilson (Born Glasgow, 16 December 1931. Died Glasgow, 8 November 2014.) Sammy Wilson began his senior career at St Mirren and after being released at the end of the 1956–57 season he was snapped up by Celtic. At Parkhead he formed a useful partnership up front with Billy McPhail, scoring 46 goals from 59 appearances. The most significant of these was the opening goal in the 1957–58 League Cup final, when Celtic beat Rangers 7-1. He later tried his luck in England with Millwall and Northampton Town before concluding his career in the Highland League with Ross County and Brora Rangers.

Brian Wood (Born Hamworthy, Dorset, 8 December 1940. Died Woodbridge, Suffolk, 5 July 2014.) Centre half Brian Wood made over 500 senior appearances despite twice suffering a broken leg. After making his debut with Crystal Palace in December 1961, he was a near ever-present in the 1963–64 promotion team. He went on to play for Leyton Orient and Colchester United before finishing with a six-year spell at Workington.

Matt Woods (Born Skelmersdale, Lancs, 1 November 1931. Died, 26 September 2014.) Matt Woods made his debut in senior football with Everton, but it was only after moving on to Blackburn Rovers in November 1956 that he received regular first-team football. He went on to establish himself as an inspirational centre half at Ewood Park, making over 250 appearances and gaining an FA Cup runners-up medal in 1960. He left for a two-year spell in Australia, returning to play for Luton Town and then Stockport County, leading the Hatters to the Division Four title in 1966–67. Later he had a spell as manager of Stockport County (April 1970 to December 1971).

Alan Woodward (Born Chapeltown, South Yorkshire, 7 September 1946. Died Glenpool, Oklahoma, USA, 21 May 2015.) Alan Woodward was an exciting winger with one of the most powerful shots in the game. He joined Sheffield United and spent 15 years at Bramall Lane making over 600 first-team appearances, including a run of 148 consecutive Football League games between 1968 and 1972. He is the club's record post-war goalscorer with a total of 183. He subsequently played for Tulsa Roughnecks in the NASL, settling in Oklahoma where he was active in coaching.

Roger Wosahlo (Born Cambridge, 11 September 1947. Died 10 January 2015.) Roger Wosahlo was an England Schools international, subsequently joining the staff at Stamford Bridge. However, in six seasons he failed to establish himself in English football, also playing for Ipswich Town and Peterborough United, before emigrating to South Africa where he enjoyed a productive spell with the Rangers club of Johannesburg, for whom he was a regular goalscorer. He later spent over 25 years working with Ipswich Wanderers.

Ante Zanetic (Born Korcula, Yugoslavia, 18 November 1936. Died Unanderra, New South Wales, Australia, 18 December 2014.) Ante Zanetic was a midfield player with Hajduk Split who won international honours with Yugoslavia, gaining a Gold Medal at the 1960 Olympic Games and also featuring in the team that lost out in the final of the first-ever European Championships. Shortly afterwards he defected to the West, rebuilding his career in Belgium with Club Brugge and Racing White.

Ian Nannestad

THE FOOTBALL RECORDS

BRITISH FOOTBALL RECORDS

ALL-TIME PREMIER LEAGUE CHAMPIONSHIP SEASONS ON POINTS AVERAGE

	Team	Season	P	W	D	L	F	A	Pts	Pts Av
1	Chelsea	2004–05	38	29	8	1	72	15	95	2.50
2	Manchester U	1999–2000	38	28	7	3	97	45	91	2.39
3	Chelsea	2005–06	38	29	4	5	72	22	91	2.39
4	Arsenal	2003–04	38	26	12	0	73	26	90	2.36
	Manchester U	2008–09	38	28	6	4	68	24	90	2.36
6	Manchester C	2011–12	38	28	5	5	93	29	89	2.34
	Manchester U	2006–07	38	28	5	5	83	27	89	2.34
	Manchester U	2012–13	38	28	5	5	86	43	89	2.34
9	Arsenal	2001–02	38	26	9	3	79	36	87	2.28
	Manchester U	2007–08	38	27	6	5	80	22	87	2.28
	Chelsea	2014–15	38	26	9	3	73	32	87	2.28
12	Chelsea	2009–10	38	27	5	6	103	32	86	2.26
	Manchester C	2013–14	38	27	5	6	102	37	86	2.26
14	Manchester U	1993–94	42	27	11	4	80	38	92	2.19
15	Manchester U	2002–03	38	25	8	5	74	34	83	2.18
16	Manchester U	1995–96	38	25	7	6	73	35	82	2.15
17	Blackburn R	1994–95	42	27	8	7	80	39	89	2.11
18	Manchester U	2000–01	38	24	8	6	79	31	80	2.10
	Manchester U	2010–11	38	23	11	4	78	37	80	2.10
20	Manchester U	1998–99	38	22	13	3	80	37	79	2.07
21	Arsenal	1997–98	38	23	9	6	68	33	78	2.05
22	Manchester U	1992–93	42	24	12	6	67	31	84	2.00
23	Manchester U	1996–97	38	21	12	5	76	44	75	1.97

PREMIER LEAGUE EVER-PRESENT CLUBS

	P	W	D	L	F	A	Pts
Manchester U	886	567	185	134	1753	784	1886
Arsenal	886	482	230	174	1556	832	1676
Chelsea	886	474	224	188	1501	841	1646
Liverpool	886	440	221	225	1460	894	1541
Tottenham H	886	355	226	305	1251	1170	1291
Everton	886	321	253	312	1138	1108	1216
Aston Villa	886	313	267	306	1090	1110	1206

TOP TEN PREMIERSHIP APPEARANCES

1	Giggs, Ryan	632	6	Heskey, Emile	516
2	Lampard, Frank	609	7	Schwarzer, Mark	514
3	James, David	572	8	Carragher, Jamie	508
4	Barry, Gareth	562	9	Neville, Phil	505
5	Speed, Gary	534	10=	Ferdinand, Rio and Gerrard, Steven	504

TOP TEN PREMIERSHIP GOALSCORERS

1	Shearer, Alan	260	6	Fowler, Robbie	163
2	Cole, Andy	187	7	Owen, Michael	150
3	Rooney, Wayne	185	8	Ferdinand, Les	149
4	Lampard, Frank	177	9	Sheringham, Teddy	146
5	Henry, Thierry	175	10	van Persie, Robin	144

SCOTTISH PREMIER LEAGUE SINCE 1998–99

	P	W	D	L	F	A	Pts
Celtic	642	472	93	77	1490	495	1509
Rangers	528	364	93	71	1123	418	1175
Aberdeen	642	233	157	254	761	856	850
Hearts	604	239	147	218	778	735	849
Motherwell	642	227	142	273	810	962	823
Kilmarnock	642	211	159	272	774	936	792
Dundee U	642	206	177	259	797	951	780
Hibernian	568	191	145	232	743	812	718

DOMESTIC LANDMARKS

AUGUST 2014
16 Sam Allardyce became only the fifth manager to reach 400 Premier League matches as manager when his West Ham side lost 0-1 to Tottenham Hotspur on the opening day of the new Premier League season.

SEPTEMBER 2014
14 Wayne Rooney became the youngest player in the Premier League to reach 175 goals. He scored Manchester United's third goal in their 4-0 victory over Queens Park Rangers.

OCTOBER 2014
10 Richard Dunne's 67th minute own goal against Liverpool was a record 10th in the Premier League.

NOVEMBER 2014
8 Sunderland's Sebastian Larsson scored the 23,000th goal in Premier League history with a superb curling free-kick against Everton at the Stadium of Light. Leighton Baines later equalised from the penalty spot as the match ended 1-1.
15 Wayne Rooney won his 100th cap in the Euro 2016 qualifying match against Slovenia at Wembley. Rooney equalised with a second half penalty, his 44th goal for his country, after Slovenia had gone ahead in the 57th minute. England ran out winners 3-1 to maintain their 100 per cent record in the 2016 qualifiers.
22 Leon Osman marked his 400th appearance for Everton with the winning goal in the 2-1 defeat of West Ham at Goodison Park. It was Osman's 55th goal for the Toffees.
29 Hull City manager Steve Bruce's 700th game as a manager ended in a 3-0 defeat at the hands of Manchester United at Old Trafford.

DECEMBER 2014
13 Chelsea manager Jose Mourinho set a new Premier League record by becoming the manager to reach 400 Premier League points in the fewest matches. Chelsea's 2-0 victory over Hull City took Mourinho's points tally to 401 in 174 matches. His closest rival, Sir Alex Ferguson reached 400 points in 191 matches.
17 The FA Cup match between Worcester City and Scunthorpe United became the longest penalty shoot-out in FA Cup history. Scunthorpe won the shoot-out 14-13 after the match had ended 1-1 after extra time.

FEBRUARY 2015
1 Aston Villa made club history in their 5-0 drubbing by Arsenal at the Emirates. It was the 6th successive game in which they had failed to score.

MARCH 2015
7 Tottenham's Harry Kane scored for the sixth Premier League away game in succession becoming only the fourth player to achieve the feat. His double helped Spurs to a 2-1 London derby win over QPR at Loftus Road.
9 Arsenal's 2-1 win at Manchester United in the FA Cup means they have reached the semi-final 28 times, one ahead of Manchester United.
22 Hull City scored two goals in 74 seconds against Chelsea at the KC Stadium, a Premier League record.

APRIL 2015
4 Charlie Adam scored a record-breaking 65 yards strike for Stoke City against Chelsea in the Premier League at the Brittania Stadium.
10 England Women's Under 19s replay their European Championship match against Norway after the original game ended in controversy in the 96th minute. England were awarded a penalty which Leah Williamson scored, but the referee incorrectly awarded a free-kick to Norway rather than a re-taken penalty, after encroachment by an England player. Norway saw out the remainder of the game to win 2-1. UEFA ordered the match to be replayed starting at the 96th minute. Williamson held her nerve to score the penalty and England qualified on goal difference after the 2-2 draw.
18 Arsenal reach the FA Cup final for a record 19th time beating Reading at Wembley in the semi-final. Alexis Sanchez scored twice as the Gunners ran out 2-1 winners after extra-time.
19 Christian Eriksen became the first Danish player to score 10 goals in the Premier League in a season when scoring Tottenham's second goal in the 3-1 Premier League defeat of Newcastle United at St James' Park.

MAY 2015
2 AFC Bournemouth became champions of the Sky Bet Football League Championship and are promoted to the Premier League for the first time in their history. They will be the 47th different club to appear in the Premier League.
4 Chelsea Ladies will play Notts County Ladies in the first women's FA Cup Final to be played at Wembley on 1 August 2015.
11 Sky Bet Football League Play-off match between Swindon Town and Sheffield United saw 10 goals scored in a 5-5 draw, two more than had ever been scored in the play-off match. Swindon went through to the Wembley final with a 7-6 aggregate win.
   Yannick Bolasie became the first Crystal Palace player to score a Premier League hat-trick with his 11-minute treble against Sunderland at the Stadium of Light. Palace ran out 4-1 winners.
16 Sadio Mane scored a hat-trick in 176 first-half seconds (2 minutes 56 seconds) in Southampton's 6-1 thrashing of Aston Villa in the Premier League at St Mary's. It was the fastest hat-trick in Premier League history surpassing Robbie Fowler's 4 minute 33 second hat-trick against Arsenal in 1994.
   In the same game Southampton became the first Premier League team to score five goals in the first half of a match and five goals in the second half of a match in the same season. The five second-half goals came in the 8-0 home victory against Sunderland in October.
24 Petr Cech made his 333rd and final Premier League appearance for Chelsea in the final match of the season, a 3-1 victory against Sunderland at Stamford Bridge.
   Stoke City's Peter Crouch second his 47th headed goal in his side's 6-1 defeat of Liverpool to beat Alan Shearer's record of 46.
   Jermaine Beckford scored a Wembley hat-trick as Preston NE beat Swindon Town 4-0 in the Sky Bet League One Play-off final. It was 10th time lucky for Preston after nine previous failed play-off campaigns.

JULY 2015
4 England Women defeat Germany for the first time in 21 attempts to finish third in the World Cup in Canada.

EUROPEAN CUP AND CHAMPIONS LEAGUE RECORDS

MOST WINS BY CLUB

Real Madrid	10	1956, 1957, 1958, 1959, 1960, 1966, 1998, 2000, 2002, 2014.
AC Milan	7	1963, 1969, 1989, 1990, 1994, 2003, 2007.
Bayern Munich	5	1974, 1975, 1976, 2001, 2013.
Liverpool	5	1977, 1978, 1981, 1984, 2005.
Barcelona	5	1992, 2006, 2009, 2011, 2015.

MOST APPEARANCES IN FINAL
Real Madrid 13; AC Milan 11; Bayern Munich 10

MOST FINAL APPEARANCES PER COUNTRY
Italy 27 (12 wins, 15 defeats)
Spain 25 (15 wins, 10 defeats)
England 19 (12 wins, 7 defeats)
Germany 17 (7 wins, 10 defeats)

MOST CHAMPIONS LEAGUE/EUROPEAN CUP APPEARANCES
157 Xavi (Barcelona)
152 Iker Casillas (Real Madrid)
151 Ryan Giggs (Manchester U)
144 Raul (Real Madrid, Schalke)
139 Paolo Maldini (AC Milan)
130 Clarence Seedorf (Ajax, Real Madrid, Internazionale, AC Milan)
130 Paul Scholes (Manchester U)
128 Roberto Carlos (Internazionale, Real Madrid, Fenerbahce)
120 Carles Puyol (Barcelona)
119 Cristiano Ronaldo (Manchester U, Real Madrid)
116 Andriy Shevchenko (Dynamo Kyiv, AC Milan, Chelsea)

MOST WINS WITH DIFFERENT CLUBS
Clarence Seedorf (Ajax) 1995; (Real Madrid) 1998; (AC Milan) 2003, 2007.

MOST WINNERS MEDALS
6 Francisco Gento (Real Madrid) 1956, 1957, 1958, 1959, 1960, 1966.
5 Alfredo Di Stefano (Real Madrid) 1956, 1957, 1958, 1959, 1960.
5 Jose Maria Zarraga (Real Madrid) 1956, 1957, 1958, 1959, 1960.
5 Paolo Maldini (AC Milan) 1989, 1990, 1994, 2003, 2007.

CHAMPIONS LEAGUE BIGGEST WINS
HJK Helsinki 10, Bangor C 0 19.7.2011
Liverpool 8 Besiktas 0 6.11.2007

MOST SUCCESSIVE CHAMPIONS LEAGUE APPEARANCES
Manchester U (England) 18: 1996–97 to 2013–14.

MOST SUCCESSIVE EUROPEAN CUP APPEARANCES
Real Madrid (Spain) 15: 1955–56 to 1969–70.

MOST SUCCESSIVE WINS IN THE CHAMPIONS LEAGUE
Barcelona (Spain) 11: 2002–03.

LONGEST UNBEATEN RUN IN THE CHAMPIONS LEAGUE
Manchester U (England) 25: 2007–08 to 2009 (Final).

MOST GOALS OVERALL
78 Cristiano Ronaldo (Manchester U, Real Madrid).
77 Lionel Messi (Barcelona).
71 Raul (Real Madrid, Schalke).
60 Ruud van Nistelrooy (PSV Eindhoven, Manchester U, Real Madrid).
58 Andriy Shevchenko (Dynamo Kyiv, AC Milan, Chelsea, Dynamo Kyiv).
51 Thierry Henry (Monaco, Arsenal, Barcelona).
50 Filippo Inzaghi (Juventus, AC Milan).
49 Alfredo Di Stefano (Real Madrid).
47 Eusebio (Benfica).
44 Alessandro Del Piero (Juventus).
44 Didier Drogba (Marseille, Chelsea).
42 Zlatan Ibrahimovic (Ajax, Juventus, Inter Milan, Barcelona, AC Milan, Paris Saint-Germain).
42 Karim Benzema (Lyon, Real Madrid).

MOST GOALS IN CHAMPIONS LEAGUE MATCH
5 Lionel Messi, Barcelona v Bayer Leverkusen (25, 42, 49, 58, 84 mins) (7-1), 7.3.2012.
5 Luiz Adriano, Shaktar Donetsk v BATE (28, 36, 40, 44, 82 (0-7), 21.10.2014.

MOST GOALS IN ONE SEASON
17 Cristiano Ronaldo 2013–14
14 Jose Altafini 1962–63
14 Ruud van Nistelrooy 2002–03
14 Lionel Messi 2011–12

MOST GOALS SCORED IN FINALS
7 Alfredo Di Stefano (Real Madrid), 1956 (1), 1957 (1 pen), 1958 (1), 1959 (1), 1960 (3).
7 Ferenc Puskas (Real Madrid), 1960 (4), 1962 (3).

HIGHEST SCORE IN A EUROPEAN CUP MATCH
European Cup
14 Feyenoord (Netherlands) 12, KR Reykjavik (Iceland) 2 *(First Round First Leg 1969–70)*
Champions League
11 Monaco 8, Deportivo La Coruna 3 5.11.2003

HIGHEST AGGREGATE IN A EUROPEAN CUP MATCH
Benfica (Portugal) 18, Dudelange (Luxembourg) 0
8-0 (h), 10-0 (a) *(Preliminary Round 1965–66)*

FASTEST GOALS SCORED IN CHAMPIONS LEAGUE

10.2 sec	Roy Makaay for Bayern Munich v Real Madrid, 7.3.2007.
11.0 sec	Jonas for Valencia v Bayer Leverkusen, 1.11.2011.
20.07 sec	Gilberto Silva for Arsenal at PSV Eindhoven, 25.9.2002.
20.12 sec	Alessandro Del Piero for Juventus at Manchester U, 1.10.1997.

YOUNGEST CHAMPIONS LEAGUE GOALSCORER
Peter Ofori-Quaye for Olympiacos v Rosenborg at 17 years 195 days in 1997–98.

FASTEST HAT-TRICK SCORED IN CHAMPIONS LEAGUE
Bafetimbi Gomis, 8 mins for Lyon in Dinamo Zagreb v Lyon (1-7) 7.12.2001

FIRST TEAM TO SCORE SEVEN GOALS
Paris Saint-Germain 7, Rosenborg 2 24.10.2000

MOST GOALS BY A GOALKEEPER
Hans-Jorg Butt (for three different clubs)
Hamburg 13.9.2000, Bayer Leverkusen 12.5.2002, Bayern Munich 8.12.2009 – all achieved against Juventus.

LANDMARK GOALS CHAMPIONS LEAGUE
1st Daniel Amokachi, Club Brugge v CSKA Moscow 17 minutes 25.11.1992
1,000th Dmitri Khokhlov, PSV Eindhoven v Benfica 41 minutes 9.12.1998
5,000th Luisao, Benfica v Hapoel Tel Aviv 21 minutes 14.9.2010

HIGHEST SCORING DRAW
Hamburg 4, Juventus 4 13.9.2000
Chelsea 4, Liverpool 4 14.4.2009

MOST CLEAN SHEETS
10: Arsenal 2005–06 (995 minutes with two goalkeepers Manuel Almunia 347 minutes and Jens Lehmann 648 minutes).

EUROPEAN CUP AND CHAMPIONS LEAGUE RECORDS – continued

CHAMPIONS LEAGUE ATTENDANCES AND GOALS FROM GROUP STAGES ONWARDS

Season	Attendances	Average	Goals	Games
1992–93	873,251	34,930	56	25
1993–94	1,202,289	44,529	71	27
1994–95	2,328,515	38,172	140	61
1995–96	1,874,316	30,726	159	61
1996–97	2,093,228	34,315	161	61
1997–98	2,868,271	33,744	239	85
1998–99	3,608,331	42,451	238	85
1999–2000	5,490,709	34,973	442	157
2000–01	5,773,486	36,774	449	157
2001–02	5,417,716	34,508	393	157
2002–03	6,461,112	41,154	431	157
2003–04	4,611,214	36,890	309	125
2004–05	4,946,820	39,575	331	125
2005–06	5,291,187	42,330	285	125
2006–07	5,591,463	44,732	309	125
2007–08	5,454,718	43,638	330	125
2008–09	5,003,754	40,030	329	125
2009–10	5,295,708	42,366	320	125
2010–11	5,474,654	43,797	355	125
2011–12	5,225,363	41,803	345	125
2012–13	5,773,366	46,187	368	125
2013–14	5,713,049	45,704	362	125
2014–15	5,207,592	42,685	361	125

HIGHEST AVERAGE ATTENDANCE IN ONE EUROPEAN CUP SEASON
1959–60 50,545 from a total attendance of 2,780,000.

GREATEST COMEBACKS
Werder Bremen beat Anderlecht 5-3 after being three goals down in 33 minutes on 8.12.1993. They scored five goals in 23 second-half minutes.

Deportivo La Coruna beat Paris Saint-Germain 4-3 after being three goals down in 55 minutes on 7.3.2001. They scored four goals in 27 second-half minutes.

Liverpool after being three goals down to AC Milan in the first half on 25.5.2005 in the Champions League Final. They scored three goals in five second-half minutes and won the penalty shoot-out after extra time 3-2.

Liverpool three goals down to FC Basel in 29 minutes on 12.11.2002. They scored three second half goals in 24 minutes to draw 3-3.

MOST SUCCESSFUL MANAGER
Bob Paisley 3 wins, 1977, 1978, 1981 (Liverpool); Carlo Ancelotti 3 wins, 2002–03, 2006–07 (AC Milan), 2013–14 (Real Madrid).

REINSTATED WINNERS EXCLUDED FROM NEXT COMPETITION
1993 Marseille originally stripped of title. This was rescinded but they were not allowed to compete the following season.

EUROPEAN LANDMARKS 2014–15

SEPTEMBER 2014
8 Zlatan Ibrahimovic won his 100th cap for Sweden in the 1-1 draw with Austria in Vienna.
30 Francesco Totti became the oldest goal scorer in Champions League history at the age of 38 years and 3 days. His strike was a 23rd minute equaliser in the Group E match against Manchester City at the Etihad Stadium, the match ending 1-1.

OCTOBER 2014
4 Barcelona goalkeeper Claudio Bravo made La Liga history by going 630 minutes without conceding a goal after his team won 2-0 at Rayo Vallecano. The previous record holder was also a Barca keeper, Pedro Maria Artola whose record of 560 minutes had stood since 1978.

NOVEMBER 2014
5 Lionel Messi equalled Raul's all-time Champions League goal scoring record. He scored his 71st Champions League goal in Barcelona's 2-0 Group F victory at Ajax.
14 Former West Ham United player Razvan Rat won his 100th cap for Romania in their Euro 2016 qualifier against Finland in Helsinki. Captain Rat celebrated a 2-0 victory for Romania.
16 Daniele Rossi won his 100th cap for Italy in the Euro 2016 qualifier against Croatia. The Roma midfielder helped his country to a 1-1 draw.
21 Didier Drogba scored his 44th goal making him leading African goal scorer in Champions League with his penalty in the 6-0 defeat of Maribor at Stamford Bridge. It was also his first goal for Chelsea since his return to the Bridge.
22 Lionel Messi breaks yet another La Liga record by becoming the all-time top scorer in the Spanish league. His hat-trick against Sevilla in Barcelona's 5-1 victory to reach 253 goals to surpass Telmo Zarra's record which had stood for 59 years.
26 Barcelona's Lionel Messi became the all-time Champions League top goalscorer after scoring a hat-trick in Barca's 0-4 victory at Apoel Nicosia. His total goals in the competition increased to 74, three clear of previous record holder Raul. It was Messi's 5th hat-trick in the competition – another record.
27 Adriano became the first player to score back-to-back hat-tricks in the Champions League in his side's 5-0 crushing of BATE Borisov.

DECEMBER 2014
9 Real Madrid recorded their 19th successive victory in all competitions, a new record for a Spanish club. The 4-0 thumping of Ludogorets came in the final game of Group B in the Champions League at the Bernabeu.
10 Andreas Iniesta made his 100th Champions League appearance for Barcelona in their 3-1 home victory over Paris Saint-Germain. The victory meant Barcelona finished top of Group F ahead of Paris Saint-Germain in second place.

MARCH 2015
10 Cristiano Ronaldo's 77th and 78th Champions League strikes in Real Madrid's 3-4 defeat to Shalke 04 in the round of 16, nudged him one ahead of rival Lionel Messi in the all-time Champions League goalscorer records.
11 Olexandr Kucher received the fastest red card in Champions League history after only 3 minutes. His Shakhtar Donetsk side lost 7-0 to Bayern Munich in the Allianz Arena.
29 Gilbratar scored their first competitive goal when policeman Lee Casciaro scored against Scotland at Hampden Park. He equalized Shaun Maloney's 18th-minute penalty. Steven Fletcher scored a hat-trick for Scotland in their 6-1 success, the first Scotland hat-trick for 46 years when Colin Stein scored four against Cyprus.

MAY 2015
12 Barcelona's Xavi made his 150th appearance in the Champions League semi-final second leg clash with Bayern Munich. Xavi was a 75th minute substitute as the Germans won the match 3-2, but Barcelona progressed to the final 5-3 on aggregate after the first leg had finished 3-0.
13 Real Madrid's Iker Casillas made his 150th Champions League appearance as Juventus secured a 3-2 aggregate win in the Bernabeu. Former Madrid player Alvaro Marota's equaliser saw the Italians through to the Champions League final.

TOP TEN PREMIER LEAGUE AVERAGE ATTENDANCES 2014–15

1	Manchester U	75,335
2	Arsenal	58,142
3	Newcastle U	50,359
4	Manchester C	45,365
5	Liverpool	44,658
6	Sunderland	43,157
7	Chelsea	41,546
8	Everton	38,405
9	Tottenham H	35,727
10	West Ham U	34,871

TOP TEN FOOTBALL LEAGUE AVERAGE ATTENDANCES 2014–15

1	Derby Co	29,231
2	Norwich C	26,342
3	Brighton & HA	25,644
4	Leeds U	24,051
5	Nottingham F	23,492
6	Wolverhampton W	22,418
7	Sheffield W	21,992
8	Cardiff C	21,123
9	Ipswich T	19,602
10	Middlesbrough	19,562

TOP TEN AVERAGE ATTENDANCES

1	Manchester U	2006–07	75,826
2	Manchester U	2007–08	75,691
3	Manchester U	2012–13	75,530
4	Manchester U	2011–12	75,387
5	Manchester U	2014–15	75,335
6	Manchester U	2008–09	75,308
7	Manchester U	2013–14	75,207
8	Manchester U	2010–11	75,109
9	Manchester U	2009–10	74,863
10	Manchester U	2005–06	68,765

TOP TEN AVERAGE WORLD CUP FINAL CROWDS

1	In USA	1994	68,991
2	In Brazil	2014	52,621
3	In Germany	2006	52,491
4	In Mexico	1970	50,124
5	In South Africa	2010	49,669
6	In West Germany	1974	49,098
7	In England	1966	48,847
8	In Italy	1990	48,388
9	In Brazil	1950	47,511
10	In Mexico	1986	46,039

TOP TEN ALL-TIME ENGLAND CAPS

1	Peter Shilton	125
2	David Beckham	115
3	Steven Gerrard	114
4	Bobby Moore	108
5	Ashley Cole	107
6	Bobby Charlton	106
	Frank Lampard	106
8	Billy Wright	105
	Wayne Rooney	105
10	Bryan Robson	90

TOP TEN ALL-TIME ENGLAND GOALSCORERS

1	Bobby Charlton	49
2	Gary Lineker	48
	Wayne Rooney	48
4	Jimmy Greaves	44
5	Michael Owen	40
	Tom Finney	30
6	Nat Lofthouse	30
	Alan Shearer	30
9	Vivian Woodward	29
	Frank Lampard	29

GOALKEEPING RECORDS
(without conceding a goal)

FA PREMIER LEAGUE
Edwin van der Sar (Manchester U) in 1,311 minutes during the 2008–09 season.

FOOTBALL LEAGUE
Steve Death (Reading) 1,103 minutes from 24 March to 18 August 1979.

SCOTTISH PREMIER LEAGUE
Fraser Forster (Celtic) in 1,215 minutes from 6 December 2013 to 25 February 2014.

MOST CLEAN SHEETS IN A SEASON
Petr Cech (Chelsea) 24 2004–05

MOST CLEAN SHEETS OVERALL IN PREMIER LEAGUE
David James (Liverpool, Aston Villa, West Ham U, Manchester C and Portsmouth) 170 games.

MOST GOALS FOR IN A SEASON

		Goals	Games
FA PREMIER LEAGUE			
2009–10	Chelsea	103	38
FOOTBALL LEAGUE			
Division 4			
1960–61	Peterborough U	134	46
SCOTTISH PREMIER LEAGUE			
2003–04	Celtic	105	38
SCOTTISH LEAGUE			
Division 2			
1937–38	Raith R	142	34

MOST GOALS AGAINST IN A SEASON

		Goals	Games
FA PREMIER LEAGUE			
1993–94	Swindon T	100	42
FOOTBALL LEAGUE			
Division 2			
1898–99	Darwen	141	34
SCOTTISH PREMIER LEAGUE			
1999–2000	Aberdeen	83	36
SCOTTISH LEAGUE			
Division 2			
1931–32	Edinburgh C	146	38

MOST LEAGUE GOALS IN A SEASON

		Goals	Games
FA PREMIER LEAGUE			
1993–94	Andy Cole (Newcastle U)	34	40
1994–95	Alan Shearer (Blackburn R)	34	42
FOOTBALL LEAGUE			
Division 1			
1927–28	Dixie Dean (Everton)	60	39
Division 2			
1926–27	George Camsell (Middlesbrough)	59	37
Division 3(S)			
1936–37	Joe Payne (Luton T)	55	39
Division 3(N)			
1936–37	Ted Harston (Mansfield T)	55	41
Division 3			
1959–60	Derek Reeves (Southampton)	39	46
Division 4			
1960–61	Terry Bly (Peterborough U)	52	46
FA CUP			
1887–88	Jimmy Ross (Preston NE)	20	8
LEAGUE CUP			
1986–87	Clive Allen (Tottenham H)	12	9
SCOTTISH PREMIER LEAGUE			
2000–01	Henrik Larsson (Celtic)	35	37
SCOTTISH LEAGUE			
Division 1			
1931–32	William McFadyen (Motherwell)	52	34
Division 2			
1927–28	Jim Smith (Ayr U)	66	38

MOST FA CUP FINAL GOALS

Ian Rush (Liverpool) 5: 1986(2), 1989(2), 1992(1)

SCORED IN EVERY PREMIERSHIP GAME

Arsenal 2001–02: 38 matches

FEWEST GOALS FOR IN A SEASON

		Goals	Games
FA PREMIER LEAGUE			
2007–08	Derby Co	20	38
FOOTBALL LEAGUE			
Division 2			
1899–1900	Loughborough T	18	34
SCOTTISH PREMIER LEAGUE			
2010–11	St Johnstone	23	38
SCOTTISH LEAGUE			
New Division 1			
1980–81	Stirling Alb	18	39

FEWEST GOALS AGAINST IN A SEASON

		Goals	Games
FA PREMIER LEAGUE			
2004–05	Chelsea	15	38
FOOTBALL LEAGUE			
Division 1			
1978–79	Liverpool	16	42
SCOTTISH PREMIER LEAGUE			
2001–02	Celtic	18	38
SCOTTISH LEAGUE			
Division 1			
1913–14	Celtic	14	38

MOST LEAGUE GOALS IN A CAREER

	Goals	Games	Season
FOOTBALL LEAGUE			
Arthur Rowley			
WBA	4	24	1946–48
Fulham	27	56	1948–50
Leicester C	251	303	1950–58
Shrewsbury T	152	236	1958–65
	434	619	
SCOTTISH LEAGUE			
Jimmy McGrory			
Celtic	1	3	1922–23
Clydebank	13	30	1923–24
Celtic	396	375	1924–38
	410	408	

MOST HAT-TRICKS

Career
37: Dixie Dean (Tranmere R, Everton, Notts Co, England)

Division 1 (one season post-war)
6: Jimmy Greaves (Chelsea), 1960–61

Three for one team in one match
West, Spouncer, Hooper, Nottingham F v Leicester Fosse, Division 1, 21 April 1909
Loasby, Smith, Wells, Northampton T v Walsall, Division 3S, 5 Nov 1927
Bowater, Hoyland, Readman, Mansfield T v Rotherham U, Division 3N, 27 Dec 1932
Barnes, Ambler, Davies, Wrexham v Hartlepools U, Division 4, 3 March 1962
Adcock, Stewart, White, Manchester C v Huddersfield T, Division 2, 7 Nov 1987

MOST CUP GOALS IN A CAREER

FA CUP (pre-Second World War)
Henry Cursham 48 (Notts Co)

FA CUP (post-war)
Ian Rush 43 (Chester, Liverpool)

LEAGUE CUP
Geoff Hurst 49 (West Ham U, Stoke C)
Ian Rush 49 (Chester, Liverpool, Newcastle U)

GOALS PER GAME (Football League to 1991–92)

Goals per game	Division 1		Division 2		Division 3		Division 4		Division 3(S)		Division 3(N)	
	Games	Goals	Games	Goals	Games	Goals	Games	Goals	Games	Goals	Games	Goals
0	2465	0	2665	0	1446	0	1438	0	997	0	803	0
1	5606	5606	5836	5836	3225	3225	3106	3106	2073	2073	1914	1914
2	8275	16550	8609	17218	4569	9138	4441	8882	3314	6628	2939	5878
3	7731	23193	7842	23526	3784	11352	4041	12123	2996	8988	2922	8766
4	6229	24920	5897	23588	2837	11348	2784	11136	2445	9780	2410	9640
5	3752	18755	3634	18170	1566	7830	1506	7530	1554	7770	1599	7995
6	2137	12822	2007	12042	769	4614	786	4716	870	5220	930	5580
7	1092	7644	1001	7007	357	2499	336	2352	451	3157	461	3227
8	542	4336	376	3008	135	1080	143	1144	209	1672	221	1768
9	197	1773	164	1476	64	576	35	315	76	684	102	918
10	83	830	68	680	13	130	8	80	33	330	45	450
11	37	407	19	209	2	22	7	77	15	165	15	165
12	12	144	17	204	1	12	0	0	7	84	8	96
13	4	52	4	52	0	0	0	0	2	26	4	52
14	2	28	1	14	0	0	0	0	0	0	0	0
17	0	0	0	0	0	0	0	0	0	0	1	17
	38164	117061	38140	113030	18768	51826	18631	51461	15042	46577	14374	46466

Extensive research by statisticians has unearthed seven results from the early years of the Football League which differ from the original scores. These are 26 January 1889 Wolverhampton W 5 Everton 0 (not 4-0), 16 March 1889 Notts Co 3 Derby Co 5 (not 2-5), 4 January 1896 Arsenal 5 Loughborough 0 (not 6-0), 28 November 1896 Leicester Fosse 4 Walsall 2 (not 4-1), 21 April 1900 Burslem Port Vale 2 Lincoln C 1 (not 2-0), 25 December 1902 Glossop NE 3 Stockport Co 0 (not 3-1), 26 April 1913 Hull C 2 Leicester C 0 (not 2-1).

GOALS PER GAME (from 1992–93)

Goals per game	Premier		Championship/Div 1		League One/Div 2		League Two/Div 3	
	Games	Goals	Games	Goals	Games	Goals	Games	Goals
0	769	0	1040	0	981	0	1017	0
1	1653	1653	2377	2377	2380	2380	2429	2429
2	2186	4372	3215	6430	3233	6466	3176	6352
3	1886	5658	2714	8142	2772	8316	2719	8157
4	1309	5236	1761	7044	1784	7136	1652	6608
5	655	3275	953	4765	936	4680	853	4265
6	317	1902	431	2586	383	2298	364	2184
7	131	917	144	1008	158	1106	142	994
8	61	488	46	368	46	368	47	376
9	13	117	8	72	18	162	19	171
10	5	50	5	50	5	50	5	50
11	1	11	2	22	0	0	3	33
	8986	23679	12696	32864	12696	32962	12426	31619

New Overall Totals (since 1992)		Totals (up to 1991–92)		Complete Overall Totals (since 1888–89)	
Games	46774	Games	143119	Games	189893
Goals	121124	Goals	426421	Goals	547545

A CENTURY OF LEAGUE AND CUP GOALS IN CONSECUTIVE SEASONS

George Camsell	League	Cup	Season
Middlesbrough	59	5	1926–27
(101 goals)	33	4	1927–28

(Camsell's cup goals were all scored in the FA Cup.)

Steve Bull			
Wolverhampton W	34	18	1987–88
(102 goals)	37	13	1988–89

(Bull had 12 in the Sherpa Van Trophy, 3 Littlewoods Cup, 3 FA Cup in 1987–88; 11 Sherpa Van Trophy, 2 Littlewoods Cup in 1988–89.)

PENALTIES

Most in a season (individual)

Division 1	Goals	Season
Francis Lee (Manchester C)	13	1971–72

Most awarded in one game

Five   Crystal Palace (4 – 1 scored, 3 missed)
v Brighton & HA (1 scored), Div 2   1988–89

Most saved in a season

Division 1
Paul Cooper (Ipswich T)   8 (of 10)   1979–80

MOST GOALS IN A GAME

FA PREMIER LEAGUE
4 Mar 1995   Andy Cole (Manchester U)
             5 goals v Ipswich T
19 Sept 1999 Alan Shearer (Newcastle U)
             5 goals v Sheffield W
22 Nov 2009 Jermain Defoe (Tottenham H)
             5 goals v Wigan Ath
27 Nov 2010 Dimitar Berbatov (Manchester U)
             5 goals v Blackburn R

FOOTBALL LEAGUE
Division 1
14 Dec 1935 Ted Drake (Arsenal) 7 goals v Aston Villa
Division 2
5 Feb 1955   Tommy Briggs (Blackburn R)
             7 goals v Bristol R
23 Feb 1957 Neville Coleman (Stoke C) 7 goals v
             Lincoln C
Division 3(S)
13 Apr 1936 Joe Payne (Luton T) 10 goals v Bristol R
Division 3(N)
26 Dec 1935 Bunny Bell (Tranmere R)
             9 goals v Oldham Ath
Division 3
24 Apr 1965 Barrie Thomas (Scunthorpe U)
             5 goals v Luton T
20 Nov 1965 Keith East (Swindon T)
             5 goals v Mansfield T
16 Sept 1969 Steve Earle (Fulham) 5 goals v Halifax T
2 Oct 1971   Alf Wood (Shrewsbury T)
             5 goals v Blackburn R
10 Sept 1983 Tony Caldwell (Bolton W)
             5 goals v Walsall
4 May 1987   Andy Jones (Port Vale)
             5 goals v Newport Co
3 Apr 1990   Steve Wilkinson (Mansfield T)
             5 goals v Birmingham C
5 Sept 1998 Giuliano Grazioli (Peterborough U)
             5 goals v Barnet
6 Apr 2002   Lee Jones (Wrexham)
             5 goals v Cambridge U
Division 4
26 Dec 1962 Bert Lister (Oldham Ath)
             6 goals v Southport

FA CUP
20 Nov 1971 Ted MacDougall (Bournemouth)
             9 goals v Margate (*1st Round*)

LEAGUE CUP
25 Oct 1989 Frankie Bunn (Oldham Ath)
             6 goals v Scarborough

SCOTTISH LEAGUE
Premier Division
17 Nov 1984 Paul Sturrock (Dundee U)
             5 goals v Morton
Premier League
23 Aug 1996 Marco Negri (Rangers) 5 goals v
             Dundee U
4 Nov 2000   Kenny Miller (Rangers) 5 goals v
             St Mirren
25 Sept 2004 Kris Boyd (Kilmarnock) 5 goals v
             Dundee U
30 Dec 2009 Kris Boyd (Rangers) 5 goals v
             Dundee U
13 May 2012 Gary Hooper (Celtic) 5 goals v Hearts
Division 1
14 Sept 1928 Jimmy McGrory (Celtic)
             8 goals v Dunfermline Ath
Division 2
1 Oct 1927   Owen McNally (Arthurlie)
             8 goals v Armadale
2 Jan 1930   Jim Dyet (King's Park)
             8 goals v Forfar Ath
18 Apr 1936 John Calder (Morton)
             8 goals v Raith R
20 Aug 1937 Norman Hayward (Raith R)
             8 goals v Brechin C

SCOTTISH CUP
12 Sept 1885 John Petrie (Arbroath)
             13 goals v Bon Accord (*1st Round*)

LONGEST SEQUENCE OF CONSECUTIVE DEFEATS

	Team	Games
FOOTBALL LEAGUE		
Division 2		
1898–99	Darwen	18

LONGEST UNBEATEN SEQUENCE

	Team	Games
FA PREMIER LEAGUE		
May 2003–Oct 2004	Arsenal	49
FOOTBALL LEAGUE – League 1		
Jan 2011–Nov 2011	Huddersfield T	43

LONGEST UNBEATEN CUP SEQUENCE

Liverpool	25 rounds	League/Milk Cup	1980–84

LONGEST UNBEATEN SEQUENCE IN A SEASON

	Team	Games
FA PREMIER LEAGUE		
2003–04	Arsenal	38
FOOTBALL LEAGUE – Division 1		
1920–21	Burnley	30
SCOTTISH PREMIER LEAGUE		
2003–04	Celtic	32

LONGEST UNBEATEN START TO A SEASON

	Team	Games
FA PREMIER LEAGUE		
2003–04	Arsenal	38
FOOTBALL LEAGUE – Division 1		
1973–74	Leeds U	29
1987–88	Liverpool	29

LONGEST SEQUENCE WITHOUT A WIN IN A SEASON

	Team	Games
FA PREMIER LEAGUE		
2007–08	Derby Co	32
FOOTBALL LEAGUE	Team	Games
Division 2		
1983–84	Cambridge U	31

LONGEST SEQUENCE WITHOUT A WIN FROM SEASON'S START

	Team	Games
FOOTBALL LEAGUE		
Division 4		
1970–71	Newport Co	25

LONGEST SEQUENCE OF CONSECUTIVE SCORING (individual)

FA PREMIER LEAGUE		
Ruud van Nistelrooy		
(Manchester U)	15 in 10 games	2003–04
FOOTBALL LEAGUE RECORD		
Tom Phillipson		
(Wolverhampton W)	23 in 13 games	1926–27

LONGEST WINNING SEQUENCE

	Team	Games
FA PREMIER LEAGUE		
2001–02 and 2002–03	Arsenal	14
FOOTBALL LEAGUE – Division 2		
1904–05	Manchester U	14
1905–06	Bristol C	14
1950–51	Preston NE	14
FROM SEASON'S START – Division 3		
1985–86	Reading	13
SCOTTISH PREMIER LEAGUE		
2003–04	Celtic	25

HIGHEST WINS

Highest win in a First-Class Match
(*Scottish Cup 1st Round*)
Arbroath   36 Bon Accord   0   12 Sept 1885

Highest win in an International Match
England   13 Ireland   0   18 Feb 1882

Highest win in an FA Cup Match
Preston NE   26 Hyde U   0   15 Oct 1887
(*1st Round*)

Highest win in a League Cup Match
West Ham U   10 Bury   0   25 Oct 1983
(*2nd Round, 2nd Leg*)
Liverpool   10 Fulham   0   23 Sept 1986
(*2nd Round, 1st Leg*)

Highest win in an FA Premier League Match
Manchester U   9 Ipswich T   0   4 Mar 1995
Tottenham H   9 Wigan Ath   1   22 Nov 2009

Highest win in a Football League Match
Division 2 – highest home win
Newcastle U   13 Newport Co   0   5 Oct 1946
Division 3(N) – highest home win
Stockport Co   13 Halifax T   0   6 Jan 1934
Division 2 – highest away win
Burslem Port Vale 0 Sheffield U   10   10 Dec 1892

Highest wins in a Scottish League Match
Scottish Premier League – highest home win
Celtic   9 Aberdeen   0   6 Nov 2010
Scottish Division 2 – highest home win
Airdrieonians   15 Dundee Wanderers 1   1 Dec 1894
Scottish Premier League – away win
Hamilton A   0 Celtic   8   5 Nov 1988

MOST HOME WINS IN A SEASON

Brentford won all 21 games in Division 3(S), 1929–30

RECORD AWAY WINS IN A SEASON

Doncaster R won 18 of 21 games in Division 3(N), 1946–47

CONSECUTIVE AWAY WINS

FA PREMIER LEAGUE
Arsenal 12 games 2012–13, 2013–14.

FOOTBALL LEAGUE
Division 1
Tottenham H 10 games (1959–60 (2), 1960–61 (8))

HIGHEST AGGREGATE SCORES

FA PREMIER LEAGUE
Portsmouth   7 Reading   4   29 Sept 2007
Highest Aggregate Score England
Division 3(N)
Tranmere R   13 Oldham Ath   4   26 Dec 1935
Highest Aggregate Score Scotland
Division 2
Airdrieonians   15 Dundee Wanderers 1   1 Dec 1894

MOST WINS IN A SEASON

		Wins	Games
FA PREMIER LEAGUE			
2004–05	Chelsea	29	38
2005–06	Chelsea	29	38
FOOTBALL LEAGUE			
Division 3(N)			
1946–47	Doncaster R	33	42
SCOTTISH PREMIER LEAGUE			
2001–02	Celtic	33	38
SCOTTISH LEAGUE			
Division 1			
1920–21	Rangers	35	42

FEWEST WINS IN A SEASON

		Wins	Games
FA PREMIER LEAGUE			
2007–08	Derby Co	1	38
FOOTBALL LEAGUE			
Division 2			
1899–1900	Loughborough T	1	34
SCOTTISH PREMIER LEAGUE			
1998–99	Dunfermline Ath	4	36
SCOTTISH LEAGUE			
Division 1			
1891–92	Vale of Leven	0	22

UNDEFEATED AT HOME OVERALL

Liverpool 85 games (63 League, 9 League Cup, 7 European, 6 FA Cup), Jan 1978–Jan 1981

UNDEFEATED AT HOME LEAGUE

Chelsea 86 games, March 2004–October 2008

UNDEFEATED AWAY

Arsenal 19 games, FA Premier League 2001–02 and 2003–04 (only Preston NE with 11 in 1888–89 had previously remained unbeaten away) in the top flight.

MOST POINTS IN A SEASON
(three points for a win)

		Points	Games
FA PREMIER LEAGUE			
2004–05	Chelsea	95	38
FOOTBALL LEAGUE			
Championship			
2005–06	Reading	106	46
SCOTTISH PREMIER LEAGUE			
2001–02	Celtic	103	38
SCOTTISH LEAGUE			
League One			
2013–14	Rangers	102	36

MOST POINTS IN A SEASON
(under old system of two points for a win)

		Points	Games
FOOTBALL LEAGUE			
Division 4			
1975–76	Lincoln C	74	46
SCOTTISH LEAGUE			
Division 1			
1920–21	Rangers	76	42

FEWEST POINTS IN A SEASON

		Points	Games
FA PREMIER LEAGUE			
2007–08	Derby Co	11	38
FOOTBALL LEAGUE			
Division 2			
1904–05	Doncaster R	8	34
1899–1900	Loughborough T	8	34
SCOTTISH PREMIER LEAGUE			
2007–08	Gretna	13	38
SCOTTISH LEAGUE			
Division 1			
1954–55	Stirling Alb	6	30

NO DEFEATS IN A SEASON

FA PREMIER LEAGUE
2003–04   Arsenal   won 26, drew 12

FOOTBALL LEAGUE
Division 1
1888–89   Preston NE   won 18, drew 4
Division 2
1893–94   Liverpool   won 22, drew 6

SCOTTISH LEAGUE DIVISION 1
1898–99   Rangers   won 18
League One
2013–14   Rangers   won 33, drew 3

ONE DEFEAT IN A SEASON

FA PREMIER LEAGUE		*Defeats*	*Games*
2004–05	Chelsea	1	38

FOOTBALL LEAGUE			
Division 1			
1990–91	Arsenal	1	38

SCOTTISH PREMIER LEAGUE			
2001–02	Celtic	1	38
2013–14	Celtic	1	38

SCOTTISH LEAGUE			
Premier Division			
Division 1			
1920–21	Rangers	1	42
Division 2			
1956–57	Clyde	1	36
1962–63	Morton	1	36
1967–68	St Mirren	1	36
New Division 1			
2011–12	Ross Co	1	36
New Division 2			
1975–76	Raith R	1	26

MOST DEFEATS IN A SEASON

FA PREMIER LEAGUE		*Defeats*	*Games*
1994–95	Ipswich T	29	42
2005–06	Sunderland	29	38
2007–08	Derby Co	29	38

FOOTBALL LEAGUE			
Division 3			
1997–98	Doncaster R	34	46

SCOTTISH PREMIER LEAGUE			
2005–06	Livingston	28	38

SCOTTISH LEAGUE			
New Division 1			
1992–93	Cowdenbeath	34	44

SENDINGS-OFF

SEASON
451 (League alone)   2003–04
(Before rescinded cards taken into account)

DAY
19 (League)   13 Dec 2003

FA CUP FINAL
Kevin Moran, Manchester U v Everton   1985
Jose Antonio Reyes, Arsenal v Manchester U   2005

QUICKEST
FA Premier League
Andreas Johansson, Wigan Ath v Arsenal 7 May 2006
and Keith Gillespie, Sheffield U v Reading 20 January
2007 both in 10 seconds
Football League
Walter Boyd, Swansea C v Darlington, Div 3 as
substitute in zero seconds   23 Nov 1999

MOST IN ONE GAME
Five: Chesterfield (2) v Plymouth Arg (3) 22 Feb 1997
Five: Wigan Ath (1) v Bristol R (4)   2 Dec 1997
Five: Exeter C (3) v Cambridge U (2)   23 Nov 2002

MOST IN ONE TEAM
Wigan Ath (1) v Bristol R (4)   2 Dec 1997
Hereford U (4) v Northampton T (0)   6 Sept 1992

MOST DRAWN GAMES IN A SEASON

FA PREMIER LEAGUE		*Draws*	*Games*
1993–94	Manchester C	18	42
1993–94	Sheffield U	18	42
1994–95	Southampton	18	42

FOOTBALL LEAGUE			
Division 1			
1978–79	Norwich C	23	42
Division 3			
1997–98	Cardiff C	23	46
1997–98	Hartlepool U	23	46
Division 4			
1986–87	Exeter C	23	46

SCOTTISH PREMIER LEAGUE			
1998–99	Dunfermline Ath	16	38

SCOTTISH LEAGUE			
Premier Division			
1993–94	Aberdeen	21	44
New Division 1			
1986–87	East Fife	21	44

MOST SUCCESSFUL MANAGERS

Sir Alex Ferguson CBE
Manchester U
1986–2013, 25 major trophies:
13 Premier League, 5 FA Cup, 4 League Cup,
2 Champions League, 1 Cup-Winners' Cup.

Aberdeen
1976–86, 9 major trophies:
3 League, 4 Scottish Cup, 1 League Cup, 1 Cup-
Winners' Cup.

Bob Paisley – Liverpool
1974–83, 13 major trophies:
6 League, 3 European Cup, 3 League Cup, 1 UEFA
Cup.

Bill Struth – Rangers
1920–54, 30 major trophies:
18 League, 10 Scottish Cup, 2 League Cup

LEAGUE CHAMPIONSHIP HAT-TRICKS

Huddersfield T	1923–24 to 1925–26
Arsenal	1932–33 to 1934–35
Liverpool	1981–82 to 1983–84
Manchester U	1998–99 to 2000–01
Manchester U	2006–07 to 2008–09

MOST FA CUP MEDALS

Ashley Cole 7 (Arsenal 2002, 2003, 2005, Chelsea
2007, 2009, 2010, 2012)

MOST LEAGUE MEDALS

Ryan Giggs (Manchester U) 13: 1993, 1994, 1996, 1997,
1999, 2000, 2001, 2003, 2007, 2008, 2009, 2011 and 2013.

MOST SENIOR MATCHES

1,390 Peter Shilton (1,005 League, 86 FA Cup, 102
League Cup, 125 Internationals, 13 Under-23, 4
Football League XI, 20 European Cup, 7 Texaco Cup,
5 Simod Cup, 4 European Super Cup, 4 UEFA Cup, 3
Screen Sport Super Cup, 3 Zenith Data Systems Cup,
2 Autoglass Trophy, 2 Charity Shield, 2 Full Members
Cup, 1 Anglo-Italian Cup, 1 Football League play-offs,
1 World Club Championship)

MOST LEAGUE APPEARANCES
(750+ matches)

1,005 Peter Shilton (286 Leicester C, 110 Stoke C, 202 Nottingham F, 188 Southampton, 175 Derby Co, 34 Plymouth Arg, 1 Bolton W, 9 Leyton Orient) 1966–97

931 Tony Ford (355 Grimsby T, 9 Sunderland (loan), 112 Stoke C, 114 WBA, 68 Grimsby T, 5 Bradford C (loan), 76 Scunthorpe U, 103 Mansfield T, 89 Rochdale) 1975–2002

909 Graeme Armstrong (204 Stirling A, 83 Berwick R, 353 Meadowbank Thistle, 268 Stenhousemuir, 1 Alloa Ath) 1975–2001

863 Tommy Hutchison (165 Blackpool, 314 Coventry C, 46 Manchester C, 92 Burnley, 178 Swansea C, 68 Alloa Ath) 1965–91

833 Graham Alexander (159 Scunthorpe U, 150 Luton T, 370 Preston NE, 154 Burnley) 1990–2012

824 Terry Paine (713 Southampton, 111 Hereford U) 1957–77

790 Neil Redfearn (35 Bolton W, 10 Lincoln C (loan), 90 Lincoln C, 46 Doncaster R, 57 Crystal Palace, 24 Watford, 62 Oldham Ath, 292 Barnsley, 30 Charlton Ath, 17 Bradford C, 22 Wigan Ath, 42 Halifax T, 54 Boston U, 9 Rochdale) 1982–2004

788 David James (89 Watford, 214 Liverpool, 67 Aston Villa, 91 West Ham U, 93 Manchester C, 134 Portsmouth, 81 Bristol C, 19 Bournemouth) 1988–2013

782 Robbie James (484 Swansea C, 48 Stoke C, 87 QPR, 23 Leicester C, 89 Bradford C, 51 Cardiff C) 1973–94

777 Alan Oakes (565 Manchester C, 211 Chester C, 1 Port Vale) 1959–84

774 Dave Beasant (340 Wimbledon, 20 Newcastle U, 133 Chelsea, 6 Grimsby T (loan), 4 Wolverhampton W (loan), 88 Southampton, 139 Nottingham F, 27 Portsmouth, 1 Tottenham H (loan), 16 Brighton & HA) 1979–2003

771 John Burridge (27 Workington, 134 Blackpool, 65 Aston Villa, 6 Southend U (loan), 88 Crystal Palace, 39 QPR, 74 Wolverhampton W, 6 Derby Co (loan), 109 Sheffield U, 62 Southampton, 67 Newcastle U, 65 Hibernian, 3 Scarborough, 4 Lincoln C, 3 Aberdeen, 3 Dumbarton, 3 Falkirk, 4 Manchester C, 3 Darlington, 6 Queen of the S) 1968–96

770 John Trollope (all for Swindon T) 1960–80†

764 Jimmy Dickinson (all for Portsmouth) 1946–65

763 Stuart McCall (395 Bradford C, 103 Everton, 194 Rangers, 71 Sheffield U) 1982–2004

761 Roy Sproson (all for Port Vale) 1950–72

760 Mick Tait (64 Oxford U, 106 Carlisle U, 33 Hull C, 240 Portsmouth, 99 Reading, 79 Darlington, 139 Hartlepool U) 1975–97

758 Ray Clemence (48 Scunthorpe U, 470 Liverpool, 240 Tottenham H) 1966–87

758 Billy Bonds (95 Charlton Ath, 663 West Ham U) 1964–88

757 Pat Jennings (48 Watford, 472 Tottenham H, 237 Arsenal) 1963–86

757 Frank Worthington (171 Huddersfield T, 210 Leicester C, 84 Bolton W, 75 Birmingham C, 32 Leeds U, 19 Sunderland, 34 Southampton, 31 Brighton & HA, 59 Tranmere R, 23 Preston NE, 19 Stockport Co) 1966–88

752 Wayne Allison (84 Halifax T, 7 Watford, 195 Bristol C, 101 Swindon T, 74 Huddersfield T, 103 Tranmere R, 73 Sheffield U, 115 Chesterfield) 1987–2008

† record for one club

CONSECUTIVE

401 Harold Bell (401 Tranmere R; 459 in all games) 1946–55

YOUNGEST PLAYERS

FA Premier League appearance
Matthew Briggs, 16 years 65 days, Fulham v Middlesbrough, 13.5.2007

FA Premier League scorer
James Vaughan, 16 years 271 days, Everton v Crystal Palace 10.4.2005

Football League appearance
Reuben Noble-Lazarus 15 years 45 days, Barnsley v Ipswich T, FL Championship 30.9.2008

Football League scorer
Ronnie Dix, 15 years 180 days, Bristol Rovers v Norwich C, Division 3S, 3.3.1928

Division 1 appearance
Derek Forster, 15 years 185 days, Sunderland v Leicester C, 22.8.1964

Division 1 scorer
Jason Dozzell, 16 years 57 days as substitute Ipswich T v Coventry C, 4.2.1984

Division 1 hat-tricks
Alan Shearer, 17 years 240 days, Southampton v Arsenal, 9.4.88
Jimmy Greaves, 17 years 10 months, Chelsea v Portsmouth, 25.12.1957

FA Cup appearance (any round)
Andy Awford, 15 years 88 days as substitute Worcester City v Boreham Wood, 3rd Qual. rd, 10.10.1987

FA Cup appearance (competition rounds)
Brendan Galloway, 15 years 240 days, Milton Keynes D v Nantwich T, 12.11.2011

FA Cup Final appearance
Curtis Weston, 17 years 119 days, Millwall v Manchester U, 22.5.2004

FA Cup Final scorer
Norman Whiteside, 17 years 18 days, Manchester United v Brighton & HA, 1983

FA Cup Final captain
David Nish, 21 years 212 days, Leicester C v Manchester U, 1969

League Cup appearance
Chris Coward, 16 years 30 days, Stockport Co v Sheffield W, 2005

League Cup Final scorer
Norman Whiteside, 17 years 324 days, Manchester U v Liverpool, 1983

League Cup Final captain
Barry Venison, 20 years 7 months 8 days, Sunderland v Norwich C, 1985

Scottish Premier League appearance
Scott Robinson, 16 years 45 days, Hearts v Inverness CT, 26.4.2008

Scottish Football League appearance
Jordan Allan, 14 years 189 days, Airdrie U v Livingston, 26.4.2013

Scottish Premier League scorer
Fraser Fyvie, 16 years 306 days, Aberdeen v Hearts, 27.1.2010

OLDEST PLAYERS

FA Premier League appearance
John Burridge, 43 years 5 months, Manchester C v QPR, 14.5.1995

Football League appearance
Neil McBain, 52 years 4 months, New Brighton v Hartlepools U, Div 3N, 15.3.47 (McBain was New Brighton's manager and had to play in an emergency)

Division 1 appearance
Stanley Matthews, 50 years 5 days, Stoke C v Fulham, 6.2.65

INTERNATIONAL RECORDS

MOST GOALS IN AN INTERNATIONAL

Record/World Cup	Archie Thompson (Australia) 13 goals v American Samoa	11.4.2001
England	Howard Vaughton (Aston Villa) 5 goals v Ireland, at Belfast Steve Bloomer (Derby Co) 5 goals v Wales, at Cardiff Willie Hall (Tottenham H) 5 goals v Ireland, at Old Trafford Malcolm Macdonald (Newcastle U) 5 goals v Cyprus, at Wembley	18.2.1882 16.3.1896 16.11.1938 16.4.1975
Northern Ireland	Joe Bambrick (Linfield) 6 goals v Wales, at Belfast	1.2.1930
Wales	John Price (Wrexham) 4 goals v Ireland, at Wrexham Mel Charles (Cardiff C) 4 goals v Ireland, at Cardiff Ian Edwards (Chester) 4 goals v Malta, at Wrexham	25.2.1882 11.4.1962 25.10.1978
Scotland	Alexander Higgins (Kilmarnock) 4 goals v Ireland, at Hampden Park Charles Heggie (Rangers) 4 goals v Ireland, at Belfast William Dickson (Dundee Strathmore) 4 goals v Ireland, at Belfast William Paul (Partick Thistle) 4 goals v Wales, at Paisley Jake Madden (Celtic) 4 goals v Wales, at Wrexham Duke McMahon (Celtic) 4 goals v Ireland, at Celtic Park Bob Hamilton (Rangers) 4 goals v Ireland, at Celtic Park Jimmy Quinn (Celtic) 4 goals v Ireland, at Dublin Hughie Gallacher (Newcastle U) 4 goals v Ireland, at Belfast Billy Steel (Dundee) 4 goals v N. Ireland, at Hampden Park Denis Law (Manchester U) 4 goals v N. Ireland, at Hampden Park Denis Law (Manchester U) 4 goals v Norway, at Hampden Park Colin Stein (Rangers) 4 goals v Cyprus, at Hampden Park	14.3.1885 20.3.1886 24.3.1888 22.3.1890 18.3.1893 23.2.1901 23.2.1901 14.3.1908 23.2.1929 1.11.1950 7.11.1962 7.11.1963 17.5.1969

MOST GOALS IN AN INTERNATIONAL CAREER

		Goals	Games
England	Bobby Charlton (Manchester U)	49	106
Scotland	Denis Law (Huddersfield T, Manchester C, Torino, Manchester U) Kenny Dalglish (Celtic, Liverpool)	30 30	55 102
Northern Ireland	David Healy (Manchester U, Preston NE, Leeds U, Fulham, Sunderland, Rangers)	35	93
Wales	Ian Rush (Liverpool, Juventus)	28	73
Republic of Ireland	Robbie Keane (Wolverhampton W, Coventry C, Internazionale, Leeds U, Tottenham H, Liverpool, Tottenham H, LA Galaxy)	65	140

HIGHEST SCORES

World Cup Match	Australia	31	American Samoa	0	2001
European Championship	San Marino	0	Germany	13	2006
Olympic Games	Denmark Germany	17 16	France USSR	1 0	1908 1912
Olympic Qualifying Tournament	Vanuatu	46	Micronesia	0	2015
Other International Match	Libya	21	Oman	0	1966
	Abandoned after 80 minutes as Oman refused to play on.				
European Cup	Feyenoord	12	KR Reykjavik	2	1969
European Cup-Winners' Cup	Sporting Lisbon	16	Apoel Nicosia	1	1963
Fairs & UEFA Cups	Ajax	14	Red Boys	0	1984

GOALSCORING RECORDS

World Cup Final	Geoff Hurst (England) 3 goals v West Germany	1966
World Cup Final tournament	Just Fontaine (France) 13 goals	1958
World Cup career	Miroslav Klose (Germany) 16 goals	2002, 2006, 2010, 2014
Career	Artur Friedenreich (Brazil) 1,329 goals Pele (Brazil) 1,281 goals Franz 'Bimbo' Binder (Austria, Germany) 1,006 goals	1910–30 *1956–78 1930–50
World Cup Finals fastest	Hakan Sukur (Turkey) 10.8 secs v South Korea	2002

Pele subsequently scored two goals in Testimonial matches making his total 1,283.

MOST CAPPED INTERNATIONALS IN THE BRITISH ISLES

England	Peter Shilton	125 appearances	1970–90
Northern Ireland	Pat Jennings	119 appearances	1964–86
Scotland	Kenny Dalglish	102 appearances	1971–86
Wales	Neville Southall	92 appearances	1982–97
Republic of Ireland	Robbie Keane	140 appearances	1998–2015

THE FA BARCLAYS PREMIER LEAGUE AND FOOTBALL LEAGUE FIXTURES 2015–16

Sky Sports   All fixtures subject to change.

Sunday, 2 August 2015
FA Community Shield
Chelsea v Arsenal

Friday, 7 August 2015
Sky Bet Championship
Brighton & HA v Nottingham F* (7.45)

Saturday, 8 August 2015
Barclays Premier League
Bournemouth v Aston Villa
Chelsea v Swansea C* (5.30)
Everton v Watford
Leicester C v Sunderland
Manchester U v Tottenham H (12.45)
Norwich C v Crystal Palace

Sky Bet Championship
Birmingham C v Reading
Blackburn R v Wolverhampton W
Bolton W v Derby Co
Brentford v Ipswich T
Cardiff C v Fulham
Charlton Ath v QPR
Hull C v Huddersfield T
Leeds U v Burnley* (12.30)
Preston NE v Middlesbrough
Rotherham U v Milton Keynes D
Sheffield W v Bristol C

Sky Bet League One
Burton Alb v Scunthorpe U
Chesterfield v Barnsley
Colchester U v Blackpool
Coventry C v Wigan Ath
Crewe Alex v Port Vale
Doncaster R v Bury
Fleetwood T v Southend U
Gillingham v Sheffield U
Rochdale v Peterborough U
Shrewsbury T v Millwall
Swindon T v Bradford C
Walsall v Oldham Ath

Sky Bet League Two
AFC Wimbledon v Plymouth Arg
Accrington S v Luton T
Bristol R v Northampton T
Cambridge U v Newport Co
Exeter C v Yeovil T
Hartlepool U v Morecambe
Leyton Orient v Barnet
Mansfield T v Carlisle U
Oxford U v Crawley T
Portsmouth v Dagenham & R
Stevenage v Notts Co
Wycombe W v York C

Sunday, 9 August 2015
Barclays Premier League
Arsenal v West Ham U* (1.30)
Newcastle U v Southampton (1.30)
Stoke C v Liverpool* (4.00)

Monday, 10 August 2015
Barclays Premier League
WBA v Manchester C* (8.00)

Friday, 14 August 2015
Barclays Premier League
Aston Villa v Manchester U* (7.45)

Saturday, 15 August 2015
Barclays Premier League
Southampton v Everton (12.45)
Sunderland v Norwich C

Swansea C v Newcastle U
Tottenham H v Stoke C
Watford v WBA
West Ham U v Leicester C

Sky Bet Championship
Bristol C v Brentford
Burnley v Birmingham C
Derby Co v Charlton Ath
Fulham v Brighton & HA
Huddersfield T v Blackburn R
Ipswich T v Sheffield W
Middlesbrough v Bolton W
Milton Keynes D v Preston NE
Nottingham F v Rotherham U
QPR v Cardiff C
Reading v Leeds U

Sky Bet League One
Barnsley v Burton Alb
Blackpool v Rochdale
Bradford C v Shrewsbury T
Bury v Swindon T
Millwall v Coventry C
Oldham Ath v Fleetwood T
Peterborough U v Colchester U
Port Vale v Gillingham
Scunthorpe U v Crewe Alex
Sheffield U v Chesterfield
Southend U v Walsall
Wigan Ath v Doncaster R

Sky Bet League Two
Barnet v Wycombe W
Carlisle U v Cambridge U
Crawley T v AFC Wimbledon
Dagenham & R v Leyton Orient
Luton T v Oxford U
Morecambe v Accrington S
Newport Co v Stevenage
Northampton T v Exeter C
Notts Co v Mansfield T
Plymouth Arg v Portsmouth
Yeovil T v Bristol R
York C v Hartlepool U

Sunday, 16 August 2015
Barclays Premier League
Crystal Palace v Arsenal* (1.30)
Manchester C v Chelsea* (4.00)

Sky Bet Championship
Wolverhampton W v Hull C* (12.00)

Monday, 17 August 2015
Barclays Premier League
Liverpool v Bournemouth* (8.00)

Tuesday, 18 August 2015
Sky Bet Championship
Blackburn R v Cardiff C
Brentford v Birmingham C
Bristol C v Leeds U
Derby Co v Middlesbrough
Huddersfield T v Brighton & HA
Hull C v Fulham
Ipswich T v Burnley
Milton Keynes D v Bolton W
Nottingham F v Charlton Ath
Rotherham U v Preston NE
Sheffield W v Reading
Wolverhampton W v QPR

Sky Bet League One
Blackpool v Burton Alb
Bradford C v Gillingham

Bury v Fleetwood T
Colchester U v Oldham Ath
Coventry C v Crewe Alex
Doncaster R v Southend U
Millwall v Barnsley
Peterborough U v Sheffield U
Rochdale v Walsall
Shrewsbury T v Chesterfield
Swindon T v Port Vale
Wigan Ath v Scunthorpe U

Sky Bet League Two
AFC Wimbledon v Cambridge U
Accrington S v Mansfield T
Barnet v Northampton T
Crawley T v Portsmouth
Dagenham & R v Exeter C
Hartlepool U v Newport Co
Leyton Orient v Stevenage
Luton T v Bristol R
Morecambe v Wycombe W
Oxford U v Notts Co
Plymouth Arg v Carlisle U
York C v Yeovil T

Friday, 21 August 2015
Sky Bet Championship
Birmingham C v Derby Co* (7.45)

Saturday, 22 August 2015
Barclays Premier League
Crystal Palace v Aston Villa
Leicester C v Tottenham H
Manchester U v Newcastle U (12.45
Norwich C v Stoke C
Sunderland v Swansea C
West Ham U v Bournemouth

Sky Bet Championship
Bolton W v Nottingham F
Brighton & HA v Blackburn R
Burnley v Brentford
Cardiff C v Wolverhampton W
Charlton Ath v Hull C
Fulham v Huddersfield T
Leeds U v Sheffield W* (12.30)
Middlesbrough v Bristol C
Preston NE v Ipswich T
QPR v Rotherham U
Reading v Milton Keynes D

Sky Bet League One
Barnsley v Bradford C
Burton Alb v Peterborough U
Chesterfield v Rochdale
Crewe Alex v Bury
Fleetwood T v Colchester U
Gillingham v Wigan Ath
Oldham Ath v Shrewsbury T
Port Vale v Doncaster R
Scunthorpe U v Millwall
Sheffield U v Blackpool
Southend U v Swindon T
Walsall v Coventry C

Sky Bet League Two
Bristol R v Barnet
Cambridge U v Crawley T
Carlisle U v AFC Wimbledon
Exeter C v York C
Mansfield T v Oxford U
Newport Co v Leyton Orient
Northampton T v Plymouth Arg
Notts Co v Accrington S
Portsmouth v Morecambe

Stevenage v Hartlepool U
Wycombe W v Dagenham & R
Yeovil T v Luton T

Sunday, 23 August 2015
Barclays Premier League
WBA v Chelsea* (1.30)
Everton v Manchester C* (4.00)
Watford v Southampton (4.00)

Monday, 24 August 2015
Barclays Premier League
Arsenal v Liverpool* (8.00)

Friday, 28 August 2015
Sky Bet Championship
Blackburn R v Bolton W* (7.45)

Saturday, 29 August 2015
Barclays Premier League
Aston Villa v Sunderland
Bournemouth v Leicester C
Chelsea v Crystal Palace
Liverpool v West Ham U
Manchester C v Watford
Newcastle U v Arsenal (12.45)
Stoke C v WBA
Tottenham H v Everton* (5.30)

Sky Bet Championship
Brentford v Reading
Bristol C v Burnley
Derby Co v Leeds U* (12.05)
Huddersfield T v QPR
Hull C v Preston NE
Ipswich T v Brighton & HA
Milton Keynes D v Birmingham C
Nottingham F v Cardiff C
Rotherham U v Fulham
Sheffield W v Middlesbrough
Wolverhampton W v Charlton Ath

Sky Bet League One
Blackpool v Walsall
Bradford C v Port Vale
Bury v Oldham Ath
Colchester U v Scunthorpe U
Coventry C v Southend U
Doncaster R v Fleetwood T
Millwall v Chesterfield
Peterborough U v Gillingham
Rochdale v Barnsley
Shrewsbury T v Burton Alb
Swindon T v Sheffield U
Wigan Ath v Crewe Alex

Sky Bet League Two
AFC Wimbledon v Exeter C
Accrington S v Northampton T
Barnet v Cambridge U
Crawley T v Wycombe W
Dagenham & R v Stevenage
Hartlepool U v Carlisle U
Leyton Orient v Bristol R
Luton T v Portsmouth
Morecambe v Notts Co
Oxford U v Yeovil T
Plymouth Arg v Newport Co
York C v Mansfield T

Sunday, 30 August 2015
Barclays Premier League
Southampton v Norwich C* (1.30)
Swansea C v Manchester U* (4.00)

Saturday, 5 September 2015
Sky Bet League One
Barnsley v Shrewsbury T
Chesterfield v Wigan Ath
Crewe Alex v Swindon T
Fleetwood T v Rochdale
Gillingham v Doncaster R
Oldham Ath v Bradford C
Port Vale v Millwall
Scunthorpe U v Blackpool
Sheffield U v Colchester U

Southend U v Peterborough U* (12.30)
Walsall v Bury

Sky Bet League Two
Cambridge U v Luton T
Carlisle U v Barnet
Exeter C v Leyton Orient
Mansfield T v AFC Wimbledon
Newport Co v York C
Northampton T v Dagenham & R
Notts Co v Crawley T
Portsmouth v Accrington S
Stevenage v Plymouth Arg
Wycombe W v Hartlepool U
Yeovil T v Morecambe

Sunday, 6 September 2015
Sky Bet League One
Burton Alb v Coventry C* (2.30)

Sky Bet League Two
Bristol R v Oxford U* (12.15)

Friday, 11 September 2015
Sky Bet Championship
Reading v Ipswich T* (8.00)

Saturday, 12 September 2015
Barclays Premier League
Arsenal v Stoke C
Crystal Palace v Manchester C
Everton v Chelsea (12.45)
Manchester U v Liverpool* (5.30)
Norwich C v Bournemouth
Watford v Swansea C
WBA v Southampton

Sky Bet Championship
Birmingham C v Bristol C
Bolton W v Wolverhampton W
Brighton & HA v Hull C
Burnley v Sheffield W
Cardiff C v Huddersfield T
Charlton Ath v Rotherham U
Fulham v Blackburn R
Leeds U v Brentford
Middlesbrough v Milton Keynes D
Preston NE v Derby Co
QPR v Nottingham F

Sky Bet League One
Barnsley v Swindon T
Burton Alb v Rochdale
Chesterfield v Colchester U
Crewe Alex v Millwall
Fleetwood T v Bradford C
Gillingham v Blackpool
Oldham Ath v Peterborough U
Port Vale v Wigan Ath
Scunthorpe U v Coventry C
Sheffield U v Bury
Southend U v Shrewsbury T
Walsall v Doncaster R

Sky Bet League Two
Bristol R v Accrington S
Cambridge U v Leyton Orient
Carlisle U v Dagenham & R
Exeter C v Hartlepool U
Mansfield T v Crawley T
Newport Co v Morecambe
Northampton T v Oxford U
Notts Co v Luton T
Portsmouth v Barnet
Stevenage v York C
Wycombe W v Plymouth Arg
Yeovil T v AFC Wimbledon

Sunday, 13 September 2015
Barclays Premier League
Sunderland v Tottenham H* (1.30)
Leicester C v Aston Villa* (4.00)

Monday, 14 September 2015
Barclays Premier League
West Ham U v Newcastle U* (8.00)

Tuesday, 15 September 2015
Sky Bet Championship
Birmingham C v Nottingham F
Bolton W v Sheffield W
Brighton & HA v Rotherham U
Burnley v Milton Keynes D
Cardiff C v Hull C
Charlton Ath v Huddersfield T
Fulham v Wolverhampton W
Leeds U v Ipswich T
Middlesbrough v Brentford
Preston NE v Bristol C
QPR v Blackburn R
Reading v Derby Co

Saturday, 19 September 2015
Barclays Premier League
Aston Villa v WBA
Bournemouth v Sunderland
Chelsea v Arsenal (12.45)
Manchester C v West Ham U* (5.30)
Newcastle U v Watford
Stoke C v Leicester C
Swansea C v Everton

Sky Bet Championship
Blackburn R v Charlton Ath
Brentford v Preston NE
Bristol C v Reading
Derby Co v Burnley
Huddersfield T v Bolton W
Hull C v QPR
Ipswich T v Birmingham C
Milton Keynes D v Leeds U
Nottingham F v Middlesbrough* (12.30)
Rotherham U v Cardiff C
Sheffield W v Fulham
Wolverhampton W v Brighton & HA

Sky Bet League One
Blackpool v Barnsley
Bradford C v Sheffield U
Bury v Port Vale
Colchester U v Gillingham
Coventry C v Chesterfield
Doncaster R v Oldham Ath
Millwall v Southend U
Peterborough U v Walsall
Rochdale v Scunthorpe U
Shrewsbury T v Crewe Alex
Swindon T v Burton Alb
Wigan Ath v Fleetwood T

Sky Bet League Two
AFC Wimbledon v Notts Co
Accrington S v Exeter C
Barnet v Stevenage
Crawley T v Yeovil T
Dagenham & R v Newport Co
Hartlepool U v Cambridge U
Leyton Orient v Wycombe W
Luton T v Mansfield T
Morecambe v Northampton T
Oxford U v Portsmouth
Plymouth Arg v Bristol R
York C v Carlisle U

Sunday, 20 September 2015
Barclays Premier League
Tottenham H v Crystal Palace* (1.30)
Southampton v Manchester U* (4.00)
Liverpool v Norwich C (4.00)

Friday, 25 September 2015
Sky Bet Championship
Fulham v QPR* (7.45)

Saturday, 26 September 2015
Barclays Premier League
Leicester C v Arsenal
Liverpool v Aston Villa
Manchester U v Sunderland
Newcastle U v Chelsea* (5.30)
Southampton v Swansea C
Stoke C v Bournemouth
Tottenham H v Manchester C (12.45)
West Ham U v Norwich C

Sky Bet Championship
Birmingham C v Rotherham U
Bolton W v Brighton & HA
Brentford v Sheffield W
Burnley v Reading
Cardiff C v Charlton Ath
Huddersfield T v Nottingham F
Hull C v Blackburn R
Ipswich T v Bristol C
Middlesbrough v Leeds U
Milton Keynes D v Derby Co
Preston NE v Wolverhampton W

Sky Bet League One
Barnsley v Gillingham
Bradford C v Peterborough U
Bury v Coventry C
Chesterfield v Burton Alb
Fleetwood T v Port Vale
Millwall v Rochdale
Oldham Ath v Wigan Ath
Sheffield U v Doncaster R
Shrewsbury T v Blackpool
Southend U v Scunthorpe U
Swindon T v Colchester U
Walsall v Crewe Alex

Sky Bet League Two
Barnet v Dagenham & R
Bristol R v Portsmouth
Cambridge U v Stevenage
Carlisle U v Newport Co
Crawley T v Accrington S
Exeter C v Wycombe W
Luton T v AFC Wimbledon
Mansfield T v Plymouth Arg
Northampton T v Leyton Orient
Notts Co v York C
Oxford U v Morecambe
Yeovil T v Hartlepool U

Sunday, 27 September 2015
Barclays Premier League
Watford v Crystal Palace* (4.00)

Monday, 28 September 2015
Barclays Premier League
WBA v Everton* (8.00)

Tuesday, 29 September 2015
Sky Bet League One
Blackpool v Chesterfield
Burton Alb v Sheffield U
Colchester U v Bradford C
Coventry C v Barnsley
Crewe Alex v Southend U
Doncaster R v Swindon T
Gillingham v Fleetwood T
Peterborough U v Bury
Port Vale v Oldham Ath
Rochdale v Shrewsbury T
Scunthorpe U v Walsall
Wigan Ath v Millwall

Sky Bet League Two
AFC Wimbledon v Northampton T
Accrington S v Yeovil T
Dagenham & R v Notts Co
Hartlepool U v Bristol R
Leyton Orient v Carlisle U
Morecambe v Luton T
Newport Co v Crawley T
Plymouth Arg v Barnet
Portsmouth v Exeter C
Stevenage v Mansfield T
Wycombe W v Cambridge U
York C v Oxford U

Friday, 2 October 2015
Sky Bet Championship
Rotherham U v Burnley* (7.45)

Saturday, 3 October 2015
Barclays Premier League
Arsenal v Manchester U
Aston Villa v Stoke C
Bournemouth v Watford

Chelsea v Southampton
Crystal Palace v WBA
Everton v Liverpool
Manchester C v Newcastle U
Norwich C v Leicester C
Sunderland v West Ham U
Swansea C v Tottenham H

Sky Bet Championship
Blackburn R v Ipswich T
Brighton & HA v Cardiff C
Bristol C v Milton Keynes D
Charlton Ath v Fulham
Derby Co v Brentford
Leeds U v Birmingham C
Nottingham F v Hull C
QPR v Bolton W
Reading v Middlesbrough
Sheffield W v Preston NE
Wolverhampton W v Huddersfield T*
  (12.30)

Sky Bet League One
Blackpool v Swindon T
Burton Alb v Southend U
Colchester U v Bury
Coventry C v Shrewsbury T
Crewe Alex v Chesterfield
Doncaster R v Barnsley
Gillingham v Oldham Ath
Peterborough U v Millwall
Port Vale v Sheffield U
Rochdale v Bradford C
Scunthorpe U v Fleetwood T
Wigan Ath v Walsall

Sky Bet League Two
AFC Wimbledon v Barnet
Accrington S v Oxford U
Dagenham & R v Mansfield T
Hartlepool U v Luton T
Leyton Orient v Notts Co
Morecambe v Bristol R
Newport Co v Exeter C
Plymouth Arg v Crawley T
Portsmouth v Yeovil T
Stevenage v Carlisle U
Wycombe W v Northampton T
York C v Cambridge U

Saturday, 10 October 2015
Sky Bet League One
Barnsley v Crewe Alex
Bradford C v Blackpool
Bury v Wigan Ath
Chesterfield v Gillingham
Fleetwood T v Coventry C
Millwall v Doncaster R
Oldham Ath v Scunthorpe U
Sheffield U v Rochdale
Shrewsbury T v Colchester U
Southend U v Port Vale
Swindon T v Peterborough U
Walsall v Burton Alb

Sky Bet League Two
Barnet v Accrington S
Bristol R v Wycombe W
Cambridge U v Portsmouth
Carlisle U v Morecambe
Crawley T v Leyton Orient
Exeter C v Stevenage
Luton T v York C
Mansfield T v Newport Co
Northampton T v Hartlepool U
Notts Co v Plymouth Arg
Oxford U v AFC Wimbledon
Yeovil T v Dagenham & R

Saturday, 17 October 2015
Barclays Premier League
Chelsea v Aston Villa
Crystal Palace v West Ham U
Everton v Manchester U
Manchester C v Bournemouth
Newcastle U v Norwich C
Southampton v Leicester C

Swansea C v Stoke C
Tottenham H v Liverpool
Watford v Arsenal
WBA v Sunderland

Sky Bet Championship
Birmingham C v QPR
Brentford v Rotherham U
Bristol C v Nottingham F
Burnley v Bolton W
Derby Co v Wolverhampton W
Ipswich T v Huddersfield T
Leeds U v Brighton & HA
Middlesbrough v Fulham
Milton Keynes D v Blackburn R
Preston NE v Cardiff C
Reading v Charlton Ath
Sheffield W v Hull C

Sky Bet League One
Bury v Rochdale
Coventry C v Blackpool
Crewe Alex v Gillingham
Doncaster R v Bradford C
Fleetwood T v Burton Alb
Millwall v Swindon T
Oldham Ath v Sheffield U
Port Vale v Peterborough U
Scunthorpe U v Shrewsbury T
Southend U v Barnsley
Walsall v Chesterfield
Wigan Ath v Colchester U

Sky Bet League Two
AFC Wimbledon v Morecambe
Barnet v York C
Cambridge U v Northampton T
Carlisle U v Exeter C
Crawley T v Luton T
Dagenham & R v Hartlepool U
Leyton Orient v Oxford U
Mansfield T v Bristol R
Newport Co v Portsmouth
Notts Co v Yeovil T
Plymouth Arg v Accrington S
Stevenage v Wycombe W

Tuesday, 20 October 2015
Sky Bet Championship
Blackburn R v Derby Co
Bolton W v Birmingham C
Brighton & HA v Bristol C
Cardiff C v Middlesbrough
Charlton Ath v Preston NE
Fulham v Leeds U
Huddersfield T v Milton Keynes D
Hull C v Ipswich T
Nottingham F v Burnley
QPR v Sheffield W
Rotherham U v Reading
Wolverhampton W v Brentford

Sky Bet League One
Barnsley v Walsall
Blackpool v Millwall
Bradford C v Bury
Burton Alb v Crewe Alex
Chesterfield v Southend U
Colchester U v Port Vale
Gillingham v Scunthorpe U
Peterborough U v Wigan Ath
Rochdale v Coventry C
Sheffield U v Fleetwood T
Shrewsbury T v Doncaster R
Swindon T v Oldham Ath

Sky Bet League Two
Accrington S v AFC Wimbledon
Bristol R v Notts Co
Exeter C v Cambridge U
Hartlepool U v Barnet
Luton T v Leyton Orient
Morecambe v Crawley T
Northampton T v Carlisle U
Oxford U v Plymouth Arg
Portsmouth v Stevenage
Wycombe W v Newport Co

Yeovil T v Mansfield T
York C v Dagenham & R

Saturday, 24 October 2015
Barclays Premier League
Arsenal v Everton
Aston Villa v Swansea C
Bournemouth v Tottenham H
Leicester C v Crystal Palace
Liverpool v Southampton
Manchester U v Manchester C
Norwich C v WBA
Stoke C v Watford
Sunderland v Newcastle U
West Ham U v Chelsea

Sky Bet Championship
Blackburn R v Burnley
Bolton W v Leeds U
Brighton & HA v Preston NE
Cardiff C v Bristol C
Charlton Ath v Brentford
Fulham v Reading
Huddersfield T v Derby Co
Hull C v Birmingham C
Nottingham F v Ipswich T
QPR v Milton Keynes D
Rotherham U v Sheffield W
Wolverhampton W v Middlesbrough

Sky Bet League One
Barnsley v Fleetwood T
Blackpool v Crewe Alex
Bradford C v Wigan Ath
Burton Alb v Port Vale
Chesterfield v Scunthorpe U
Colchester U v Walsall
Gillingham v Southend U
Peterborough U v Doncaster R
Rochdale v Oldham Ath
Sheffield U v Millwall
Shrewsbury T v Bury
Swindon T v Coventry C

Sky Bet League Two
Accrington S v Dagenham & R
Bristol R v Newport Co
Exeter C v Notts Co
Hartlepool U v Crawley T
Luton T v Plymouth Arg
Morecambe v Leyton Orient
Northampton T v Stevenage
Oxford U v Barnet
Portsmouth v Mansfield T
Wycombe W v Carlisle U
Yeovil T v Cambridge U
York C v AFC Wimbledon

Saturday, 31 October 2015
Barclays Premier League
Chelsea v Liverpool
Crystal Palace v Manchester U
Everton v Sunderland
Manchester C v Norwich C
Newcastle U v Stoke C
Southampton v Bournemouth
Swansea C v Arsenal
Tottenham H v Aston Villa
Watford v West Ham U
WBA v Leicester C

Sky Bet Championship
Birmingham C v Wolverhampton W
Brentford v QPR
Bristol C v Fulham
Burnley v Huddersfield T
Derby Co v Rotherham U
Ipswich T v Cardiff C
Leeds U v Blackburn R
Middlesbrough v Charlton Ath
Milton Keynes D v Hull C
Preston NE v Bolton W
Reading v Brighton & HA
Sheffield W v Nottingham F

Sky Bet League One
Bury v Blackpool
Coventry C v Peterborough U
Crewe Alex v Sheffield U
Doncaster R v Colchester U
Fleetwood T v Chesterfield
Millwall v Bradford C
Oldham Ath v Burton Alb
Port Vale v Shrewsbury T
Scunthorpe U v Barnsley
Southend U v Rochdale
Walsall v Gillingham
Wigan Ath v Swindon T

Sky Bet League Two
AFC Wimbledon v Hartlepool U
Barnet v Exeter C
Cambridge U v Bristol R
Carlisle U v Yeovil T
Crawley T v York C
Dagenham & R v Luton T
Leyton Orient v Accrington S
Mansfield T v Wycombe W
Newport Co v Northampton T
Notts Co v Portsmouth
Plymouth Arg v Morecambe
Stevenage v Oxford U

Tuesday, 3 November 2015
Sky Bet Championship
Birmingham C v Blackburn R
Brentford v Hull C
Bristol C v Wolverhampton W
Burnley v Fulham
Derby Co v QPR
Ipswich T v Bolton W
Leeds U v Cardiff C
Middlesbrough v Rotherham U
Milton Keynes D v Charlton Ath
Preston NE v Nottingham F
Reading v Huddersfield T
Sheffield W v Brighton & HA

Saturday, 7 November 2015
Barclays Premier League
Arsenal v Tottenham H
Aston Villa v Manchester C
Bournemouth v Newcastle U
Leicester C v Watford
Liverpool v Crystal Palace
Manchester U v WBA
Norwich C v Swansea C
Stoke C v Chelsea
Sunderland v Southampton
West Ham U v Everton

Sky Bet Championship
Blackburn R v Brentford
Bolton W v Bristol C
Brighton & HA v Milton Keynes D
Cardiff C v Reading
Charlton Ath v Sheffield W
Fulham v Birmingham C
Huddersfield T v Leeds U
Hull C v Middlesbrough
Nottingham F v Derby Co
QPR v Preston NE
Rotherham U v Ipswich T
Wolverhampton W v Burnley

Saturday, 14 November 2015
Sky Bet League One
Barnsley v Port Vale
Blackpool v Doncaster R
Bradford C v Crewe Alex
Burton Alb v Millwall
Chesterfield v Oldham Ath
Colchester U v Coventry C
Gillingham v Bury
Peterborough U v Fleetwood T
Rochdale v Wigan Ath
Sheffield U v Southend U
Shrewsbury T v Walsall
Swindon T v Scunthorpe U

Sky Bet League Two
Accrington S v Newport Co
Bristol R v Carlisle U
Exeter C v Crawley T
Hartlepool U v Leyton Orient
Luton T v Barnet
Morecambe v Dagenham & R
Northampton T v Mansfield T
Oxford U v Cambridge U
Portsmouth v AFC Wimbledon
Wycombe W v Notts Co
Yeovil T v Stevenage
York C v Plymouth Arg

Saturday, 21 November 2015
Barclays Premier League
Chelsea v Norwich C
Crystal Palace v Sunderland
Everton v Aston Villa
Manchester C v Liverpool
Newcastle U v Leicester C
Southampton v Stoke C
Swansea C v Bournemouth
Tottenham H v West Ham U
Watford v Manchester U
WBA v Arsenal

Sky Bet Championship
Birmingham C v Charlton Ath
Brentford v Nottingham F
Bristol C v Hull C
Burnley v Brighton & HA
Derby Co v Cardiff C
Ipswich T v Wolverhampton W
Leeds U v Rotherham U
Middlesbrough v QPR
Milton Keynes D v Fulham
Preston NE v Blackburn R
Reading v Bolton W
Sheffield W v Huddersfield T

Sky Bet League One
Bury v Burton Alb
Coventry C v Gillingham
Crewe Alex v Peterborough U
Doncaster R v Rochdale
Fleetwood T v Swindon T
Millwall v Colchester U
Oldham Ath v Barnsley
Port Vale v Chesterfield
Scunthorpe U v Bradford C
Southend U v Blackpool
Walsall v Sheffield U
Wigan Ath v Shrewsbury T

Sky Bet League Two
AFC Wimbledon v Wycombe W
Barnet v Morecambe
Cambridge U v Accrington S
Carlisle U v Portsmouth
Crawley T v Bristol R
Dagenham & R v Oxford U
Leyton Orient v York C
Mansfield T v Hartlepool U
Newport Co v Yeovil T
Notts Co v Northampton T
Plymouth Arg v Exeter C
Stevenage v Luton T

Tuesday, 24 November 2015
Sky Bet League One
Bradford C v Coventry C
Bury v Scunthorpe U
Colchester U v Crewe Alex
Doncaster R v Chesterfield
Fleetwood T v Millwall
Gillingham v Rochdale
Oldham Ath v Southend U
Peterborough U v Barnsley
Port Vale v Blackpool
Sheffield U v Shrewsbury T
Swindon T v Walsall
Wigan Ath v Burton Alb

Sky Bet League Two
AFC Wimbledon v Dagenham & R
Accrington S v Hartlepool U

Bristol R v Stevenage
Crawley T v Northampton T
Luton T v Carlisle U
Mansfield T v Exeter C
Morecambe v Cambridge U
Notts Co v Barnet
Oxford U v Newport Co
Plymouth Arg v Leyton Orient
Portsmouth v York C
Yeovil T v Wycombe W

Saturday, 28 November 2015
Barclays Premier League
Aston Villa v Watford
Bournemouth v Everton
Crystal Palace v Newcastle U
Leicester C v Manchester U
Liverpool v Swansea C
Manchester C v Southampton
Norwich C v Arsenal
Sunderland v Stoke C
Tottenham H v Chelsea
West Ham U v WBA

Sky Bet Championship
Blackburn R v Sheffield W
Bolton W v Brentford
Brighton & HA v Birmingham C
Cardiff C v Burnley
Charlton Ath v Ipswich T
Fulham v Preston NE
Huddersfield T v Middlesbrough
Hull C v Derby Co
Nottingham F v Reading
QPR v Leeds U
Rotherham U v Bristol C
Wolverhampton W v Milton Keynes D

Sky Bet League One
Barnsley v Sheffield U
Blackpool v Fleetwood T
Burton Alb v Colchester U
Chesterfield v Swindon T
Coventry C v Doncaster R
Crewe Alex v Oldham Ath
Millwall v Bury
Rochdale v Port Vale
Scunthorpe U v Peterborough U
Shrewsbury T v Gillingham
Southend U v Wigan Ath
Walsall v Bradford C

Sky Bet League Two
Barnet v Mansfield T
Cambridge U v Notts Co
Carlisle U v Crawley T
Dagenham & R v Plymouth Arg
Exeter C v Bristol R
Hartlepool U v Oxford U
Leyton Orient v AFC Wimbledon
Newport Co v Luton T
Northampton T v Yeovil T
Stevenage v Morecambe
Wycombe W v Portsmouth
York C v Accrington S

Saturday, 5 December 2015
Barclays Premier League
Arsenal v Sunderland
Chelsea v Bournemouth
Everton v Crystal Palace
Manchester U v West Ham U
Newcastle U v Liverpool
Southampton v Aston Villa
Stoke C v Manchester C
Swansea C v Leicester C
Watford v Norwich C
WBA v Tottenham H

Sky Bet Championship
Birmingham C v Huddersfield T
Bolton W v Cardiff C
Brentford v Milton Keynes D
Brighton & HA v Charlton Ath
Bristol C v Blackburn R
Burnley v Preston NE

Ipswich T v Middlesbrough
Leeds U v Hull C
Nottingham F v Fulham
Reading v QPR
Rotherham U v Wolverhampton W
Sheffield W v Derby Co

Saturday, 12 December 2015
Barclays Premier League
Aston Villa v Arsenal
Bournemouth v Manchester U
Crystal Palace v Southampton
Leicester C v Chelsea
Liverpool v WBA
Manchester C v Swansea C
Norwich C v Everton
Sunderland v Watford
Tottenham H v Newcastle U
West Ham U v Stoke C

Sky Bet Championship
Blackburn R v Rotherham U
Cardiff C v Sheffield W
Charlton Ath v Leeds U
Derby Co v Brighton & HA
Fulham v Brentford
Huddersfield T v Bristol C
Hull C v Bolton W
Middlesbrough v Birmingham C
Milton Keynes D v Ipswich T
Preston NE v Reading
QPR v Burnley
Wolverhampton W v Nottingham F

Sky Bet League One
Bradford C v Southend U
Bury v Chesterfield
Colchester U v Barnsley
Doncaster R v Crewe Alex
Fleetwood T v Walsall
Gillingham v Burton Alb
Oldham Ath v Millwall
Peterborough U v Shrewsbury T
Port Vale v Scunthorpe U
Sheffield U v Coventry C
Swindon T v Rochdale
Wigan Ath v Blackpool

Sky Bet League Two
AFC Wimbledon v Stevenage
Accrington S v Wycombe W
Bristol R v York C
Crawley T v Dagenham & R
Luton T v Northampton T
Mansfield T v Leyton Orient
Morecambe v Exeter C
Notts Co v Newport Co
Oxford U v Carlisle U
Plymouth Arg v Cambridge U
Portsmouth v Hartlepool U
Yeovil T v Barnet

Tuesday, 15 December 2015
Sky Bet Championship
Blackburn R v Nottingham F
Cardiff C v Brentford
Charlton Ath v Bolton W
Derby Co v Bristol C
Fulham v Ipswich T
Huddersfield T v Rotherham U
Hull C v Reading
Middlesbrough v Burnley
Milton Keynes D v Sheffield W
Preston NE v Birmingham C
QPR v Brighton & HA
Wolverhampton W v Leeds U

Saturday, 19 December 2015
Barclays Premier League
Arsenal v Manchester C
Chelsea v Sunderland
Everton v Leicester C
Manchester U v Norwich C
Newcastle U v Aston Villa
Southampton v Tottenham H
Stoke C v Crystal Palace

Swansea C v West Ham U
Watford v Liverpool
WBA v Bournemouth

Sky Bet Championship
Birmingham C v Cardiff C
Bolton W v Fulham
Brentford v Huddersfield T
Brighton & HA v Middlesbrough
Bristol C v QPR
Burnley v Charlton Ath
Ipswich T v Derby Co
Leeds U v Preston NE
Nottingham F v Milton Keynes D
Reading v Blackburn R
Rotherham U v Hull C
Sheffield W v Wolverhampton W

Sky Bet League One
Barnsley v Wigan Ath
Blackpool v Peterborough U
Burton Alb v Doncaster R
Chesterfield v Bradford C
Coventry C v Oldham Ath
Crewe Alex v Fleetwood T
Millwall v Gillingham
Rochdale v Colchester U
Scunthorpe U v Sheffield U
Shrewsbury T v Swindon T
Southend U v Bury
Walsall v Port Vale

Sky Bet League Two
Barnet v Crawley T
Cambridge U v Mansfield T
Carlisle U v Notts Co
Dagenham & R v Bristol R
Exeter C v Luton T
Hartlepool U v Plymouth Arg
Leyton Orient v Yeovil T
Newport Co v AFC Wimbledon
Northampton T v Portsmouth
Stevenage v Accrington S
Wycombe W v Oxford U
York C v Morecambe

Saturday, 26 December 2015
Barclays Premier League
Aston Villa v West Ham U
Bournemouth v Crystal Palace
Chelsea v Watford
Liverpool v Leicester C
Manchester C v Sunderland
Newcastle U v Everton
Southampton v Arsenal
Stoke C v Manchester U
Swansea C v WBA
Tottenham H v Norwich C

Sky Bet Championship
Blackburn R v Middlesbrough
Brentford v Brighton & HA
Bristol C v Charlton Ath
Derby Co v Fulham
Huddersfield T v Preston NE
Hull C v Burnley
Ipswich T v QPR
Milton Keynes D v Cardiff C
Nottingham F v Leeds U
Rotherham U v Bolton W
Sheffield W v Birmingham C
Wolverhampton W v Reading

Sky Bet League One
Blackpool v Oldham Ath
Bradford C v Burton Alb
Bury v Barnsley
Colchester U v Southend U
Coventry C v Port Vale
Doncaster R v Scunthorpe U
Millwall v Walsall
Peterborough U v Chesterfield
Rochdale v Crewe Alex
Shrewsbury T v Fleetwood T
Swindon T v Gillingham
Wigan Ath v Sheffield U

Sky Bet League Two
AFC Wimbledon v Bristol R
Accrington S v Carlisle U
Barnet v Newport Co
Crawley T v Stevenage
Dagenham & R v Cambridge U
Hartlepool U v Notts Co
Leyton Orient v Portsmouth
Luton T v Wycombe W
Morecambe v Mansfield T
Oxford U v Exeter C
Plymouth Arg v Yeovil T
York C v Northampton T

Monday, 28 December 2015
Barclays Premier League
Arsenal v Bournemouth
Crystal Palace v Swansea C
Everton v Stoke C
Leicester C v Manchester C
Manchester U v Chelsea
Norwich C v Aston Villa
Sunderland v Liverpool
Watford v Tottenham H
WBA v Newcastle U
West Ham U v Southampton

Sky Bet Championship
Birmingham C v Milton Keynes D
Bolton W v Blackburn R
Brighton & HA v Ipswich T
Burnley v Bristol C
Cardiff C v Nottingham F
Charlton Ath v Wolverhampton W
Fulham v Rotherham U
Leeds U v Derby Co
Middlesbrough v Sheffield W
Preston NE v Hull C
QPR v Huddersfield T
Reading v Brentford

Sky Bet League One
Barnsley v Blackpool
Burton Alb v Swindon T
Chesterfield v Coventry C
Crewe Alex v Shrewsbury T
Fleetwood T v Wigan Ath
Gillingham v Colchester U
Oldham Ath v Doncaster R
Port Vale v Bury
Scunthorpe U v Rochdale
Sheffield U v Bradford C
Southend U v Millwall
Walsall v Peterborough U

Sky Bet League Two
Bristol R v Leyton Orient
Cambridge U v Barnet
Carlisle U v Hartlepool U
Exeter C v AFC Wimbledon
Mansfield T v York C
Newport Co v Plymouth Arg
Northampton T v Accrington S
Notts Co v Morecambe
Portsmouth v Luton T
Stevenage v Dagenham & R
Wycombe W v Crawley T
Yeovil T v Oxford U

Saturday, 2 January 2016
Barclays Premier League
Arsenal v Newcastle U
Crystal Palace v Chelsea
Everton v Tottenham H
Leicester C v Bournemouth
Manchester U v Swansea C
Norwich C v Southampton
Sunderland v Aston Villa
Watford v Manchester C
WBA v Stoke C
West Ham U v Liverpool

Sky Bet Championship
Birmingham C v Brentford
Bolton W v Huddersfield T
Brighton & HA v Wolverhampton W
Burnley v Ipswich T

Cardiff C v Blackburn R
Charlton Ath v Nottingham F
Fulham v Sheffield W
Leeds U v Milton Keynes D
Middlesbrough v Derby Co
Preston NE v Rotherham U
QPR v Hull C
Reading v Bristol C

Sky Bet League One
Barnsley v Millwall
Burton Alb v Blackpool
Chesterfield v Shrewsbury T
Crewe Alex v Coventry C
Fleetwood T v Bury
Gillingham v Bradford C
Oldham Ath v Colchester U
Port Vale v Swindon T
Scunthorpe U v Wigan Ath
Sheffield U v Peterborough U
Southend U v Doncaster R
Walsall v Rochdale

Sky Bet League Two
Bristol R v Luton T
Cambridge U v AFC Wimbledon
Carlisle U v Plymouth Arg
Exeter C v Dagenham & R
Mansfield T v Accrington S
Newport Co v Hartlepool U
Northampton T v Barnet
Notts Co v Oxford U
Portsmouth v Crawley T
Stevenage v Leyton Orient
Wycombe W v Morecambe
Yeovil T v York C

Saturday, 9 January 2016
Sky Bet League One
Blackpool v Sheffield U
Bradford C v Barnsley
Bury v Crewe Alex
Colchester U v Fleetwood T
Coventry C v Walsall
Doncaster R v Port Vale
Millwall v Scunthorpe U
Peterborough U v Burton Alb
Rochdale v Chesterfield
Shrewsbury T v Oldham Ath
Swindon T v Southend U
Wigan Ath v Gillingham

Sky Bet League Two
AFC Wimbledon v Carlisle U
Accrington S v Notts Co
Barnet v Bristol R
Crawley T v Cambridge U
Dagenham & R v Wycombe W
Hartlepool U v Stevenage
Leyton Orient v Newport Co
Luton T v Yeovil T
Morecambe v Portsmouth
Oxford U v Mansfield T
Plymouth Arg v Northampton T
York C v Exeter C

Tuesday, 12 January 2016
Barclays Premier League
Aston Villa v Crystal Palace
Bournemouth v West Ham U
Liverpool v Arsenal
Swansea C v Sunderland

Sky Bet Championship
Blackburn R v QPR
Brentford v Middlesbrough
Bristol C v Preston NE
Derby Co v Reading
Huddersfield T v Charlton Ath
Hull C v Cardiff C
Ipswich T v Leeds U
Milton Keynes D v Burnley
Nottingham F v Birmingham C
Rotherham U v Brighton & HA
Sheffield W v Bolton W
Wolverhampton W v Fulham

Wednesday, 13 January 2016
Barclays Premier League
Chelsea v WBA
Manchester C v Everton
Newcastle U v Manchester U
Southampton v Watford
Stoke C v Norwich C
Tottenham H v Leicester C

Saturday, 16 January 2016
Barclays Premier League
Aston Villa v Leicester C
Bournemouth v Norwich C
Chelsea v Everton
Liverpool v Manchester U
Manchester C v Crystal Palace
Newcastle U v West Ham U
Southampton v WBA
Stoke C v Arsenal
Swansea C v Watford
Tottenham H v Sunderland

Sky Bet Championship
Blackburn R v Brighton & HA
Brentford v Burnley
Bristol C v Middlesbrough
Derby Co v Birmingham C
Huddersfield T v Fulham
Hull C v Charlton Ath
Ipswich T v Preston NE
Milton Keynes D v Reading
Nottingham F v Bolton W
Rotherham U v QPR
Sheffield W v Leeds U
Wolverhampton W v Cardiff C

Sky Bet League One
Blackpool v Scunthorpe U
Bradford C v Oldham Ath
Bury v Walsall
Colchester U v Sheffield U
Coventry C v Burton Alb
Doncaster R v Gillingham
Millwall v Port Vale
Peterborough U v Southend U
Rochdale v Fleetwood T
Shrewsbury T v Barnsley
Swindon T v Crewe Alex
Wigan Ath v Chesterfield

Sky Bet League Two
AFC Wimbledon v Mansfield T
Accrington S v Portsmouth
Barnet v Carlisle U
Crawley T v Notts Co
Dagenham & R v Northampton T
Hartlepool U v Wycombe W
Leyton Orient v Exeter C
Luton T v Cambridge U
Morecambe v Yeovil T
Oxford U v Bristol R
Plymouth Arg v Stevenage
York C v Newport Co

Saturday, 23 January 2016
Barclays Premier League
Arsenal v Chelsea
Crystal Palace v Tottenham H
Everton v Swansea C
Leicester C v Stoke C
Manchester U v Southampton
Norwich C v Liverpool
Sunderland v Bournemouth
Watford v Newcastle U
WBA v Aston Villa
West Ham U v Manchester C

Sky Bet Championship
Birmingham C v Ipswich T
Bolton W v Milton Keynes D
Brighton & HA v Huddersfield T
Burnley v Derby Co
Cardiff C v Rotherham U
Charlton Ath v Blackburn R
Fulham v Hull C
Leeds U v Bristol C

Middlesbrough v Nottingham F
Preston NE v Brentford
QPR v Wolverhampton W
Reading v Sheffield W

Sky Bet League One
Barnsley v Rochdale
Burton Alb v Shrewsbury T
Chesterfield v Millwall
Crewe Alex v Wigan Ath
Fleetwood T v Doncaster R
Gillingham v Peterborough U
Oldham Ath v Bury
Port Vale v Bradford C
Scunthorpe U v Colchester U
Sheffield U v Swindon T
Southend U v Coventry C
Walsall v Blackpool

Sky Bet League Two
Bristol R v Plymouth Arg
Cambridge U v Hartlepool U
Carlisle U v York C
Exeter C v Accrington S
Mansfield T v Luton T
Newport Co v Dagenham & R
Northampton T v Morecambe
Notts Co v AFC Wimbledon
Portsmouth v Oxford U
Stevenage v Barnet
Wycombe W v Leyton Orient
Yeovil T v Crawley T

Saturday, 30 January 2016
Sky Bet Championship
Blackburn R v Fulham
Brentford v Leeds U
Bristol C v Birmingham C
Derby Co v Preston NE
Huddersfield T v Cardiff C
Hull C v Brighton & HA
Ipswich T v Reading
Milton Keynes D v Middlesbrough
Nottingham F v QPR
Rotherham U v Charlton Ath
Sheffield W v Burnley
Wolverhampton W v Bolton W

Sky Bet League One
Blackpool v Gillingham
Bradford C v Fleetwood T
Bury v Sheffield U
Colchester U v Chesterfield
Coventry C v Scunthorpe U
Doncaster R v Walsall
Millwall v Crewe Alex
Peterborough U v Oldham Ath
Rochdale v Burton Alb
Shrewsbury T v Southend U
Swindon T v Barnsley
Wigan Ath v Port Vale

Sky Bet League Two
AFC Wimbledon v Yeovil T
Accrington S v Bristol R
Barnet v Portsmouth
Crawley T v Mansfield T
Dagenham & R v Carlisle U
Hartlepool U v Exeter C
Leyton Orient v Cambridge U
Luton T v Notts Co
Morecambe v Newport Co
Oxford U v Northampton T
Plymouth Arg v Wycombe W
York C v Stevenage

Tuesday, 2 February 2016
Barclays Premier League
Arsenal v Southampton
Crystal Palace v Bournemouth
Leicester C v Liverpool
Manchester U v Stoke C
Norwich C v Tottenham H
Sunderland v Manchester C
Watford v Chelsea
WBA v Swansea C
West Ham U v Aston Villa

Wednesday, 3 February 2016
Barclays Premier League
Everton v Newcastle U

Saturday, 6 February 2016
Barclays Premier League
Aston Villa v Norwich C
Bournemouth v Arsenal
Chelsea v Manchester U
Liverpool v Sunderland
Manchester C v Leicester C
Newcastle U v WBA
Southampton v West Ham U
Stoke C v Everton
Swansea C v Crystal Palace
Tottenham H v Watford

Sky Bet Championship
Birmingham C v Sheffield W
Bolton W v Rotherham U
Brighton & HA v Brentford
Burnley v Hull C
Cardiff C v Milton Keynes D
Charlton Ath v Bristol C
Fulham v Derby Co
Leeds U v Nottingham F
Middlesbrough v Blackburn R
Preston NE v Huddersfield T
QPR v Ipswich T
Reading v Wolverhampton W

Sky Bet League One
Barnsley v Bury
Burton Alb v Bradford C
Chesterfield v Peterborough U
Crewe Alex v Rochdale
Fleetwood T v Shrewsbury T
Gillingham v Swindon T
Oldham Ath v Blackpool
Port Vale v Coventry C
Scunthorpe U v Doncaster R
Sheffield U v Wigan Ath
Southend U v Colchester U
Walsall v Millwall

Sky Bet League Two
Bristol R v AFC Wimbledon
Cambridge U v Dagenham & R
Carlisle U v Accrington S
Exeter C v Oxford U
Mansfield T v Morecambe
Newport Co v Barnet
Northampton T v York C
Notts Co v Hartlepool U
Portsmouth v Leyton Orient
Stevenage v Crawley T
Wycombe W v Luton T
Yeovil T v Plymouth Arg

Saturday, 13 February 2016
Barclays Premier League
Arsenal v Leicester C
Aston Villa v Liverpool
Bournemouth v Stoke C
Chelsea v Newcastle U
Crystal Palace v Watford
Everton v WBA
Manchester C v Tottenham H
Norwich C v West Ham U
Sunderland v Manchester U
Swansea C v Southampton

Sky Bet Championship
Blackburn R v Hull C
Brighton & HA v Bolton W
Bristol C v Ipswich T
Charlton Ath v Cardiff C
Derby Co v Milton Keynes D
Leeds U v Middlesbrough
Nottingham F v Huddersfield T
QPR v Fulham
Reading v Burnley
Rotherham U v Birmingham C
Sheffield W v Brentford
Wolverhampton W v Preston NE

Sky Bet League One
Blackpool v Shrewsbury T
Burton Alb v Chesterfield
Colchester U v Swindon T
Coventry C v Bury
Crewe Alex v Walsall
Doncaster R v Sheffield U
Gillingham v Barnsley
Peterborough U v Bradford C
Port Vale v Fleetwood T
Rochdale v Millwall
Scunthorpe U v Southend U
Wigan Ath v Oldham Ath

Sky Bet League Two
AFC Wimbledon v Luton T
Accrington S v Crawley T
Dagenham & R v Barnet
Hartlepool U v Yeovil T
Leyton Orient v Northampton T
Morecambe v Oxford U
Newport Co v Carlisle U
Plymouth Arg v Mansfield T
Portsmouth v Bristol R
Stevenage v Cambridge U
Wycombe W v Exeter C
York C v Notts Co

Saturday, 20 February 2016
Sky Bet Championship
Birmingham C v Leeds U
Bolton W v QPR
Brentford v Derby Co
Burnley v Rotherham U
Cardiff C v Brighton & HA
Fulham v Charlton Ath
Huddersfield T v Wolverhampton W
Hull C v Nottingham F
Ipswich T v Blackburn R
Middlesbrough v Reading
Milton Keynes D v Bristol C
Preston NE v Sheffield W

Sky Bet League One
Barnsley v Doncaster R
Bradford C v Rochdale
Bury v Colchester U
Chesterfield v Crewe Alex
Fleetwood T v Scunthorpe U
Millwall v Peterborough U
Oldham Ath v Gillingham
Sheffield U v Port Vale
Shrewsbury T v Coventry C
Southend U v Burton Alb
Swindon T v Blackpool
Walsall v Wigan Ath

Sky Bet League Two
Barnet v AFC Wimbledon
Bristol R v Morecambe
Cambridge U v York C
Carlisle U v Stevenage
Crawley T v Plymouth Arg
Exeter C v Newport Co
Luton T v Hartlepool U
Mansfield T v Dagenham & R
Northampton T v Wycombe W
Notts Co v Leyton Orient
Oxford U v Accrington S
Yeovil T v Portsmouth

Tuesday, 23 February 2016
Sky Bet Championship
Birmingham C v Bolton W
Brentford v Wolverhampton W
Bristol C v Brighton & HA
Burnley v Nottingham F
Derby Co v Blackburn R
Ipswich T v Hull C
Leeds U v Fulham
Middlesbrough v Cardiff C
Milton Keynes D v Huddersfield T
Preston NE v Charlton Ath
Reading v Rotherham U
Sheffield W v QPR

Saturday, 27 February 2016
Barclays Premier League
Leicester C v Norwich C
Liverpool v Everton
Manchester U v Arsenal
Newcastle U v Manchester C
Southampton v Chelsea
Stoke C v Aston Villa
Tottenham H v Swansea C
Watford v Bournemouth
WBA v Crystal Palace
West Ham U v Sunderland

Sky Bet Championship
Blackburn R v Milton Keynes D
Bolton W v Burnley
Brighton & HA v Leeds U
Cardiff C v Preston NE
Charlton Ath v Reading
Fulham v Middlesbrough
Huddersfield T v Ipswich T
Hull C v Sheffield W
Nottingham F v Bristol C
QPR v Birmingham C
Rotherham U v Brentford
Wolverhampton W v Derby Co

Sky Bet League One
Blackpool v Bradford C
Burton Alb v Walsall
Colchester U v Shrewsbury T
Coventry C v Fleetwood T
Crewe Alex v Barnsley
Doncaster R v Millwall
Gillingham v Chesterfield
Peterborough U v Swindon T
Port Vale v Southend U
Rochdale v Sheffield U
Scunthorpe U v Oldham Ath
Wigan Ath v Bury

Sky Bet League Two
AFC Wimbledon v Oxford U
Accrington S v Barnet
Dagenham & R v Yeovil T
Hartlepool U v Northampton T
Leyton Orient v Crawley T
Morecambe v Carlisle U
Newport Co v Mansfield T
Plymouth Arg v Notts Co
Portsmouth v Cambridge U
Stevenage v Exeter C
Wycombe W v Bristol R
York C v Luton T

Tuesday, 1 March 2016
Barclays Premier League
Arsenal v Swansea C
Aston Villa v Everton
Bournemouth v Southampton
Leicester C v WBA
Liverpool v Manchester C
Manchester U v Watford
Norwich C v Chelsea
Sunderland v Crystal Palace
West Ham U v Tottenham H

Sky Bet League One
Barnsley v Coventry C
Bradford C v Colchester U
Bury v Peterborough U
Chesterfield v Blackpool
Fleetwood T v Gillingham
Millwall v Wigan Ath
Oldham Ath v Port Vale
Sheffield U v Burton Alb
Shrewsbury T v Rochdale
Southend U v Crewe Alex
Swindon T v Doncaster R
Walsall v Scunthorpe U

Sky Bet League Two
Barnet v Plymouth Arg
Bristol R v Hartlepool U
Cambridge U v Wycombe W
Carlisle U v Leyton Orient
Crawley T v Newport Co

Exeter C v Portsmouth
Luton T v Morecambe
Mansfield T v Stevenage
Northampton T v AFC Wimbledon
Notts Co v Dagenham & R
Oxford U v York C
Yeovil T v Accrington S

Wednesday, 2 March 2016
Barclays Premier League
Stoke C v Newcastle U

Saturday, 5 March 2016
Barclays Premier League
Chelsea v Stoke C
Crystal Palace v Liverpool
Everton v West Ham U
Manchester C v Aston Villa
Newcastle U v Bournemouth
Southampton v Sunderland
Swansea C v Norwich C
Tottenham H v Arsenal
Watford v Leicester C
WBA v Manchester U

Sky Bet Championship
Birmingham C v Hull C
Brentford v Charlton Ath
Bristol C v Cardiff C
Burnley v Blackburn R
Derby Co v Huddersfield T
Ipswich T v Nottingham F
Leeds U v Bolton W
Middlesbrough v Wolverhampton W
Milton Keynes D v QPR
Preston NE v Brighton & HA
Reading v Fulham
Sheffield W v Rotherham U

Sky Bet League One
Bury v Bradford C
Coventry C v Rochdale
Crewe Alex v Burton Alb
Doncaster R v Shrewsbury T
Fleetwood T v Sheffield U
Millwall v Blackpool
Oldham Ath v Swindon T
Port Vale v Colchester U
Scunthorpe U v Gillingham
Southend U v Chesterfield
Walsall v Barnsley
Wigan Ath v Peterborough U

Sky Bet League Two
AFC Wimbledon v Accrington S
Barnet v Hartlepool U
Cambridge U v Exeter C
Carlisle U v Northampton T
Crawley T v Morecambe
Dagenham & R v York C
Leyton Orient v Luton T
Mansfield T v Yeovil T
Newport Co v Wycombe W
Notts Co v Bristol R
Plymouth Arg v Oxford U
Stevenage v Portsmouth

Tuesday, 8 March 2016
Sky Bet Championship
Blackburn R v Birmingham C
Bolton W v Ipswich T
Brighton & HA v Sheffield W
Cardiff C v Leeds U
Charlton Ath v Milton Keynes D
Fulham v Burnley
Huddersfield T v Reading
Hull C v Brentford
Nottingham F v Preston NE
QPR v Derby Co
Rotherham U v Middlesbrough
Wolverhampton W v Bristol C

Saturday, 12 March 2016
Barclays Premier League
Arsenal v WBA
Aston Villa v Tottenham H
Bournemouth v Swansea C

Leicester C v Newcastle U
Liverpool v Chelsea
Manchester U v Crystal Palace
Norwich C v Manchester C
Stoke C v Southampton
Sunderland v Everton
West Ham U v Watford

Sky Bet Championship
Blackburn R v Leeds U
Bolton W v Preston NE
Brighton & HA v Reading
Cardiff C v Ipswich T
Charlton Ath v Middlesbrough
Fulham v Bristol C
Huddersfield T v Burnley
Hull C v Milton Keynes D
Nottingham F v Sheffield W
QPR v Brentford
Rotherham U v Derby Co
Wolverhampton W v Birmingham C

Sky Bet League One
Barnsley v Southend U
Blackpool v Coventry C
Bradford C v Doncaster R
Burton Alb v Fleetwood T
Chesterfield v Walsall
Colchester U v Wigan Ath
Gillingham v Crewe Alex
Peterborough U v Port Vale
Rochdale v Bury
Sheffield U v Oldham Ath
Shrewsbury T v Scunthorpe U
Swindon T v Millwall

Sky Bet League Two
Accrington S v Plymouth Arg
Bristol R v Mansfield T
Exeter C v Carlisle U
Hartlepool U v Dagenham & R
Luton T v Crawley T
Morecambe v AFC Wimbledon
Northampton T v Cambridge U
Oxford U v Leyton Orient
Portsmouth v Newport Co
Wycombe W v Stevenage
Yeovil T v Notts Co
York C v Barnet

Saturday, 19 March 2016
Barclays Premier League
Chelsea v West Ham U
Crystal Palace v Leicester C
Everton v Arsenal
Manchester C v Manchester U
Newcastle U v Sunderland
Southampton v Liverpool
Swansea C v Aston Villa
Tottenham H v Bournemouth
Watford v Stoke C
WBA v Norwich C

Sky Bet Championship
Birmingham C v Fulham
Brentford v Blackburn R
Bristol C v Bolton W
Burnley v Wolverhampton W
Derby Co v Nottingham F
Ipswich T v Rotherham U
Leeds U v Huddersfield T
Middlesbrough v Hull C
Milton Keynes D v Brighton & HA
Preston NE v QPR
Reading v Cardiff C
Sheffield W v Charlton Ath

Sky Bet League One
Bury v Shrewsbury T
Coventry C v Swindon T
Crewe Alex v Blackpool
Doncaster R v Peterborough U
Fleetwood T v Barnsley
Millwall v Sheffield U
Oldham Ath v Rochdale
Port Vale v Burton Alb
Scunthorpe U v Chesterfield

Southend U v Gillingham
Walsall v Colchester U
Wigan Ath v Bradford C

Saturday, 26 March 2016
Sky Bet League One
Barnsley v Scunthorpe U
Blackpool v Bury
Bradford C v Millwall
Burton Alb v Oldham Ath
Chesterfield v Fleetwood T
Colchester U v Doncaster R
Gillingham v Walsall
Peterborough U v Coventry C
Rochdale v Southend U
Sheffield U v Crewe Alex
Shrewsbury T v Port Vale
Swindon T v Wigan Ath

Sky Bet League Two
Accrington S v Leyton Orient
Bristol R v Cambridge U
Exeter C v Barnet
Hartlepool U v AFC Wimbledon
Luton T v Dagenham & R
Morecambe v Plymouth Arg
Northampton T v Newport Co
Oxford U v Stevenage
Portsmouth v Notts Co
Wycombe W v Mansfield T
Yeovil T v Carlisle U
York C v Crawley T

Monday, 28 March 2016
Sky Bet League One
Bury v Gillingham
Coventry C v Colchester U
Crewe Alex v Bradford C
Doncaster R v Blackpool
Fleetwood T v Peterborough U
Millwall v Burton Alb
Oldham Ath v Chesterfield
Port Vale v Barnsley
Scunthorpe U v Swindon T
Southend U v Sheffield U
Walsall v Shrewsbury T
Wigan Ath v Rochdale

Sky Bet League Two
AFC Wimbledon v Portsmouth
Barnet v Luton T
Cambridge U v Oxford U
Carlisle U v Bristol R
Crawley T v Exeter C
Dagenham & R v Morecambe
Leyton Orient v Hartlepool U
Mansfield T v Northampton T
Newport Co v Accrington S
Notts Co v Wycombe W
Plymouth Arg v York C
Stevenage v Yeovil T

Saturday, 2 April 2016
Barclays Premier League
Arsenal v Watford
Aston Villa v Chelsea
Bournemouth v Manchester C
Leicester C v Southampton
Liverpool v Tottenham H
Manchester U v Everton
Norwich C v Newcastle U
Stoke C v Swansea C

Sunderland v WBA
West Ham U v Crystal Palace

Sky Bet Championship
Blackburn R v Preston NE
Bolton W v Reading
Brighton & HA v Burnley
Cardiff C v Derby Co
Charlton Ath v Birmingham C
Fulham v Milton Keynes D
Huddersfield T v Sheffield W
Hull C v Bristol C
Nottingham F v Brentford
QPR v Middlesbrough
Rotherham U v Leeds U
Wolverhampton W v Ipswich T

Sky Bet League One
Barnsley v Oldham Ath
Blackpool v Southend U
Bradford C v Scunthorpe U
Burton Alb v Bury
Chesterfield v Port Vale
Colchester U v Millwall
Gillingham v Coventry C
Peterborough U v Crewe Alex
Rochdale v Doncaster R
Sheffield U v Walsall
Shrewsbury T v Wigan Ath
Swindon T v Fleetwood T

Sky Bet League Two
Accrington S v Cambridge U
Bristol R v Crawley T
Exeter C v Plymouth Arg
Hartlepool U v Mansfield T
Luton T v Stevenage
Morecambe v Barnet
Northampton T v Notts Co
Oxford U v Dagenham & R
Portsmouth v Carlisle U
Wycombe W v AFC Wimbledon
Yeovil T v Newport Co
York C v Leyton Orient

Tuesday, 5 April 2016
Sky Bet Championship
Birmingham C v Brighton & HA
Brentford v Bolton W
Bristol C v Rotherham U
Burnley v Cardiff C
Derby Co v Hull C
Ipswich T v Charlton Ath
Leeds U v QPR
Middlesbrough v Huddersfield T
Milton Keynes D v Wolverhampton W
Preston NE v Fulham
Reading v Nottingham F
Sheffield W v Blackburn R

Saturday, 9 April 2016
Barclays Premier League
Aston Villa v Bournemouth
Crystal Palace v Norwich C
Liverpool v Stoke C
Manchester C v WBA
Southampton v Newcastle U
Sunderland v Leicester C
Swansea C v Chelsea
Tottenham H v Manchester U
Watford v Everton
West Ham U v Arsenal

Sky Bet Championship
Bristol C v Sheffield W
Burnley v Leeds U
Derby Co v Bolton W
Fulham v Cardiff C
Huddersfield T v Hull C
Ipswich T v Brentford
Middlesbrough v Preston NE
Milton Keynes D v Rotherham U
Nottingham F v Brighton & HA
QPR v Charlton Ath
Reading v Birmingham C
Wolverhampton W v Blackburn R

Sky Bet League One
Barnsley v Chesterfield
Blackpool v Colchester U
Bradford C v Swindon T
Bury v Doncaster R
Millwall v Shrewsbury T
Oldham Ath v Walsall
Peterborough U v Rochdale
Port Vale v Crewe Alex
Scunthorpe U v Burton Alb
Sheffield U v Gillingham
Southend U v Fleetwood T
Wigan Ath v Coventry C

Sky Bet League Two
Barnet v Leyton Orient
Carlisle U v Mansfield T
Crawley T v Oxford U
Dagenham & R v Portsmouth
Luton T v Accrington S
Morecambe v Hartlepool U
Newport Co v Cambridge U
Northampton T v Bristol R
Notts Co v Stevenage
Plymouth Arg v AFC Wimbledon
Yeovil T v Exeter C
York C v Wycombe W

Saturday, 16 April 2016
Barclays Premier League
Arsenal v Crystal Palace
Bournemouth v Liverpool
Chelsea v Manchester C
Everton v Southampton
Leicester C v West Ham U
Manchester U v Aston Villa
Newcastle U v Swansea C
Norwich C v Sunderland
Stoke C v Tottenham H
WBA v Watford

Sky Bet Championship
Birmingham C v Burnley
Blackburn R v Huddersfield T
Bolton W v Middlesbrough
Brentford v Bristol C
Brighton & HA v Fulham
Cardiff C v QPR
Charlton Ath v Derby Co
Hull C v Wolverhampton W
Leeds U v Reading
Preston NE v Milton Keynes D
Rotherham U v Nottingham F
Sheffield W v Ipswich T

Sky Bet League One
Burton Alb v Barnsley
Chesterfield v Sheffield U
Colchester U v Peterborough U
Coventry C v Millwall
Crewe Alex v Scunthorpe U
Doncaster R v Wigan Ath
Fleetwood T v Oldham Ath
Gillingham v Port Vale
Rochdale v Blackpool
Shrewsbury T v Bradford C
Swindon T v Bury
Walsall v Southend U

Sky Bet League Two
AFC Wimbledon v Crawley T
Accrington S v Morecambe
Bristol R v Yeovil T
Cambridge U v Carlisle U
Exeter C v Northampton T
Hartlepool U v York C
Leyton Orient v Dagenham & R
Mansfield T v Notts Co
Oxford U v Luton T
Portsmouth v Plymouth Arg
Stevenage v Newport Co
Wycombe W v Barnet

Tuesday, 19 April 2016
Sky Bet Championship
Birmingham C v Preston NE
Bolton W v Charlton Ath

Brentford v Cardiff C
Brighton & HA v QPR
Bristol C v Derby Co
Burnley v Middlesbrough
Ipswich T v Fulham
Leeds U v Wolverhampton W
Nottingham F v Blackburn R
Reading v Hull C
Rotherham U v Huddersfield T
Sheffield W v Milton Keynes D

Sky Bet League One
Barnsley v Peterborough U
Blackpool v Port Vale
Burton Alb v Wigan Ath
Chesterfield v Doncaster R
Coventry C v Bradford C
Crewe Alex v Colchester U
Millwall v Fleetwood T
Rochdale v Gillingham
Scunthorpe U v Bury
Shrewsbury T v Sheffield U
Southend U v Oldham Ath
Walsall v Swindon T

Sky Bet League Two
Barnet v Notts Co
Cambridge U v Morecambe
Carlisle U v Luton T
Dagenham & R v AFC Wimbledon
Exeter C v Mansfield T
Hartlepool U v Accrington S
Leyton Orient v Plymouth Arg
Newport Co v Oxford U
Northampton T v Crawley T
Stevenage v Bristol R
Wycombe W v Yeovil T
York C v Portsmouth

Saturday, 23 April 2016
Barclays Premier League
Aston Villa v Southampton
Bournemouth v Chelsea
Crystal Palace v Everton
Leicester C v Swansea C
Liverpool v Newcastle U
Manchester C v Stoke C
Norwich C v Watford
Sunderland v Arsenal
Tottenham H v WBA
West Ham U v Manchester U

Sky Bet Championship
Blackburn R v Bristol C
Cardiff C v Bolton W
Charlton Ath v Brighton & HA
Derby Co v Sheffield W
Fulham v Nottingham F
Huddersfield T v Birmingham C
Hull C v Leeds U
Middlesbrough v Ipswich T
Milton Keynes D v Brentford
Preston NE v Burnley
QPR v Reading
Wolverhampton W v Rotherham U

Sky Bet League One
Bradford C v Walsall
Bury v Millwall
Colchester U v Burton Alb
Doncaster R v Coventry C
Fleetwood T v Blackpool
Gillingham v Shrewsbury T

Oldham Ath v Crewe Alex
Peterborough U v Scunthorpe U
Port Vale v Rochdale
Sheffield U v Barnsley
Swindon T v Chesterfield
Wigan Ath v Southend U

Sky Bet League Two
AFC Wimbledon v Leyton Orient
Accrington S v York C
Bristol R v Exeter C
Crawley T v Carlisle U
Luton T v Newport Co
Mansfield T v Barnet
Morecambe v Stevenage
Notts Co v Cambridge U
Oxford U v Hartlepool U
Plymouth Arg v Dagenham & R
Portsmouth v Wycombe W
Yeovil T v Northampton T

Saturday, 30 April 2016
Barclays Premier League
Arsenal v Norwich C
Chelsea v Tottenham H
Everton v Bournemouth
Manchester U v Leicester C
Newcastle U v Crystal Palace
Southampton v Manchester C
Stoke C v Sunderland
Swansea C v Liverpool
Watford v Aston Villa
WBA v West Ham U

Sky Bet Championship
Birmingham C v Middlesbrough
Bolton W v Hull C
Brentford v Fulham
Brighton & HA v Derby Co
Bristol C v Huddersfield T
Burnley v QPR
Ipswich T v Milton Keynes D
Leeds U v Charlton Ath
Nottingham F v Wolverhampton W
Reading v Preston NE
Rotherham U v Blackburn R
Sheffield W v Cardiff C

Sky Bet League One
Barnsley v Colchester U
Blackpool v Wigan Ath
Burton Alb v Gillingham
Chesterfield v Bury
Coventry C v Sheffield U
Crewe Alex v Doncaster R
Millwall v Oldham Ath
Rochdale v Swindon T
Scunthorpe U v Port Vale
Shrewsbury T v Peterborough U
Southend U v Bradford C
Walsall v Fleetwood T

Sky Bet League Two
Barnet v Yeovil T
Cambridge U v Plymouth Arg
Carlisle U v Oxford U
Dagenham & R v Crawley T
Exeter C v Morecambe
Hartlepool U v Portsmouth
Leyton Orient v Mansfield T
Newport Co v Notts Co
Northampton T v Luton T
Stevenage v AFC Wimbledon

Wycombe W v Accrington S
York C v Bristol R

Saturday, 7 May 2016
Barclays Premier League
Aston Villa v Newcastle U
Bournemouth v WBA
Crystal Palace v Stoke C
Leicester C v Everton
Liverpool v Watford
Manchester C v Arsenal
Norwich C v Manchester U
Sunderland v Chelsea
Tottenham H v Southampton
West Ham U v Swansea C

Sky Bet Championship
Blackburn R v Reading
Cardiff C v Birmingham C
Charlton Ath v Burnley
Derby Co v Ipswich T
Fulham v Bolton W
Huddersfield T v Brentford
Hull C v Rotherham U
Middlesbrough v Brighton & HA
Milton Keynes D v Nottingham F
Preston NE v Leeds U
QPR v Bristol C
Wolverhampton W v Sheffield W

Sky Bet League Two
AFC Wimbledon v Newport Co
Accrington S v Stevenage
Bristol R v Dagenham & R
Crawley T v Barnet
Luton T v Exeter C
Mansfield T v Cambridge U
Morecambe v York C
Notts Co v Carlisle U
Oxford U v Wycombe W
Plymouth Arg v Hartlepool U
Portsmouth v Northampton T
Yeovil T v Leyton Orient

Sunday, 8 May 2016
Sky Bet League One
Bradford C v Chesterfield
Bury v Southend U
Colchester U v Rochdale
Doncaster R v Burton Alb
Fleetwood T v Crewe Alex
Gillingham v Millwall
Oldham Ath v Coventry C
Peterborough U v Blackpool
Port Vale v Walsall
Sheffield U v Scunthorpe U
Swindon T v Shrewsbury T
Wigan Ath v Barnsley

Sunday, 15 May 2016
Barclays Premier League
Arsenal v Aston Villa
Chelsea v Leicester C
Everton v Norwich C
Manchester U v Bournemouth
Newcastle U v Tottenham H
Southampton v Crystal Palace
Stoke C v West Ham U
Swansea C v Manchester C
Watford v Sunderland
WBA v Liverpool

CONFERENCE PREMIER FIXTURES 2015–16

Saturday, 8 August 2015
Aldershot T v Gateshead
Altrincham v Forest Green R
Barrow v Dover Ath
Boreham Wood v FC Halifax T
Bromley v Wrexham
Chester FC v Braintree T
Kidderminster H v Grimsby T
Lincoln C v Cheltenham T
Southport v Eastleigh
Torquay U v Macclesfield T
Tranmere R v Woking
Welling U v Guiseley

Tuesday, 11 August 2015
Braintree T v Lincoln C
Cheltenham T v Aldershot T
Dover Ath v Kidderminster H
Eastleigh v Boreham Wood
FC Halifax T v Chester FC
Forest Green R v Welling U
Gateshead v Tranmere R
Grimsby T v Barrow
Guiseley v Altrincham
Macclesfield T v Southport
Woking v Bromley
Wrexham v Torquay U

Saturday, 15 August 2015
Braintree T v Tranmere R
Cheltenham T v Southport
Dover Ath v Chester FC
Eastleigh v Lincoln C
FC Halifax T v Torquay U
Forest Green R v Barrow
Gateshead v Boreham Wood
Grimsby T v Bromley
Guiseley v Kidderminster H
Macclesfield T v Welling U
Woking v Altrincham
Wrexham v Aldershot T

Tuesday, 18 August 2015
Aldershot T v Dover Ath
Altrincham v Grimsby T
Barrow v Guiseley
Boreham Wood v Forest Green R
Bromley v Braintree T
Chester FC v Cheltenham T
Kidderminster H v Wrexham
Lincoln C v Macclesfield T
Southport v Gateshead
Torquay U v Woking
Tranmere R v FC Halifax T
Welling U v Eastleigh

Saturday, 22 August 2015
Braintree T v Southport
Cheltenham T v Barrow
Dover Ath v Altrincham
Eastleigh v Macclesfield T
FC Halifax T v Bromley
Forest Green R v Lincoln C
Gateshead v Kidderminster H
Grimsby T v Torquay U
Guiseley v Aldershot T
Tranmere R v Boreham Wood
Woking v Chester FC
Wrexham v Welling U

Saturday, 29 August 2015
Aldershot T v Eastleigh
Altrincham v Tranmere R
Barrow v Southport
Boreham Wood v Woking
Bromley v Dover Ath
Guiseley v Gateshead
Kidderminster H v Forest Green R
Lincoln C v Grimsby T
Macclesfield T v Chester FC
Torquay U v Cheltenham T
Welling U v Braintree T
Wrexham v FC Halifax T

Monday, 31 August 2015
Braintree T v Aldershot T
Cheltenham T v Wrexham
Chester FC v Guiseley
Dover Ath v Boreham Wood
Eastleigh v Torquay U
FC Halifax T v Barrow
Forest Green R v Bromley
Gateshead v Lincoln C
Grimsby T v Macclesfield T
Southport v Altrincham
Tranmere R v Kidderminster H
Woking v Welling U

Saturday, 5 September 2015
Aldershot T v FC Halifax T
Altrincham v Cheltenham T
Barrow v Eastleigh
Boreham Wood v Grimsby T
Bromley v Gateshead
Chester FC v Forest Green R
Kidderminster H v Braintree T
Lincoln C v Wrexham
Macclesfield T v Woking
Southport v Dover Ath
Torquay U v Guiseley
Welling U v Tranmere R

Saturday, 12 September 2015
Braintree T v Barrow
Bromley v Macclesfield T
Cheltenham T v Dover Ath
Eastleigh v Gateshead
FC Halifax T v Kidderminster H
Forest Green R v Southport
Grimsby T v Aldershot T
Guiseley v Woking
Lincoln C v Boreham Wood
Tranmere R v Chester FC
Welling U v Torquay U
Wrexham v Altrincham

Tuesday, 15 September 2015
Aldershot T v Welling U
Altrincham v Eastleigh
Barrow v Lincoln C
Boreham Wood v Bromley
Cheltenham T v Macclesfield T
Chester FC v Grimsby T
Dover Ath v Braintree T
Gateshead v Wrexham
Guiseley v FC Halifax T
Kidderminster H v Torquay U
Southport v Tranmere R
Woking v Forest Green R

Saturday, 19 September 2015
Altrincham v Braintree T
Barrow v Aldershot T
Boreham Wood v Wrexham
Chester FC v Eastleigh
Dover Ath v Guiseley
FC Halifax T v Southport
Gateshead v Welling U
Grimsby T v Tranmere R
Kidderminster H v Lincoln C
Macclesfield T v Forest Green R
Torquay U v Bromley
Woking v Cheltenham T

Tuesday, 22 September 2015
Braintree T v Woking
Bromley v Kidderminster H
Eastleigh v Dover Ath
FC Halifax T v Gateshead
Forest Green R v Cheltenham T
Guiseley v Southport
Lincoln C v Altrincham
Macclesfield T v Barrow
Torquay U v Boreham Wood
Tranmere R v Aldershot T
Welling U v Chester FC
Wrexham v Grimsby T

Saturday, 26 September 2015
Aldershot T v Macclesfield T
Barrow v Kidderminster H
Boreham Wood v Altrincham
Braintree T v Guiseley
Bromley v Chester FC
Cheltenham T v Tranmere R
Dover Ath v Woking
Forest Green R v Gateshead
Lincoln C v Torquay U
Southport v Grimsby T
Welling U v FC Halifax T
Wrexham v Eastleigh

Saturday, 3 October 2015
Altrincham v Barrow
Chester FC v Wrexham
Eastleigh v Braintree T
FC Halifax T v Cheltenham T
Gateshead v Dover Ath
Grimsby T v Forest Green R
Guiseley v Lincoln C
Kidderminster H v Welling U
Macclesfield T v Boreham Wood
Torquay U v Aldershot T
Tranmere R v Bromley
Woking v Southport

Tuesday, 6 October 2015
Aldershot T v Forest Green R
Altrincham v FC Halifax T
Barrow v Chester FC
Cheltenham T v Braintree T
Grimsby T v Gateshead
Guiseley v Macclesfield T
Kidderminster H v Boreham Wood
Torquay U v Dover Ath
Welling U v Bromley
Wrexham v Tranmere R

Saturday, 10 October 2015
Aldershot T v Altrincham
Boreham Wood v Welling U

Braintree T v Grimsby T
Bromley v Barrow
Chester FC v Lincoln C
Dover Ath v Wrexham
FC Halifax T v Woking
Forest Green R v Guiseley
Gateshead v Cheltenham T
Macclesfield T v Kidderminster H
Southport v Torquay U
Tranmere R v Eastleigh

Tuesday, 13 October 2015
Altrincham v Kidderminster H
Boreham Wood v Aldershot T
Braintree T v Dover Ath
Bromley v Cheltenham T
Eastleigh v Forest Green R
Grimsby T v FC Halifax T
Macclesfield T v Gateshead
Southport v Chester FC
Tranmere R v Barrow
Welling U v Lincoln C
Woking v Torquay U
Wrexham v Guiseley

Saturday, 17 October 2015
Aldershot T v Bromley
Barrow v Welling U
Cheltenham T v Eastleigh
Chester FC v FC Halifax T
Dover Ath v Macclesfield T
Forest Green R v Tranmere R
Gateshead v Altrincham
Guiseley v Boreham Wood
Kidderminster H v Southport
Lincoln C v Braintree T
Torquay U v Grimsby T
Woking v Wrexham

Saturday, 31 October 2015
Altrincham v Torquay U
Boreham Wood v Gateshead
Braintree T v Macclesfield T
Eastleigh v FC Halifax T
Forest Green R v Chester FC
Grimsby T v Cheltenham T
Guiseley v Welling U
Kidderminster H v Woking
Lincoln C v Bromley
Southport v Aldershot T
Tranmere R v Dover Ath
Wrexham v Barrow

Tuesday, 10 November 2015
Aldershot T v Lincoln C
Barrow v Grimsby T
Bromley v Boreham Wood
Cheltenham T v Guiseley
Chester FC v Kidderminster H
Dover Ath v Eastleigh
Gateshead v Southport
Macclesfield T v Altrincham
Torquay U v Wrexham
Welling U v Forest Green R
Woking v Braintree T

Saturday, 14 November 2015
Barrow v Torquay U
Boreham Wood v Chester FC
Bromley v Altrincham
FC Halifax T v Braintree T
Forest Green R v Dover Ath
Grimsby T v Welling U
Guiseley v Eastleigh

Kidderminster H v Aldershot T
Lincoln C v Tranmere R
Southport v Cheltenham T
Woking v Macclesfield T
Wrexham v Gateshead

Saturday, 21 November 2015
Aldershot T v Wrexham
Altrincham v Boreham Wood
Braintree T v Kidderminster H
Cheltenham T v Forest Green R
Chester FC v Woking
Dover Ath v Barrow
Eastleigh v Grimsby T
Gateshead v FC Halifax T
Macclesfield T v Bromley
Torquay U v Lincoln C
Tranmere R v Guiseley
Welling U v Southport

Tuesday, 24 November 2015
Boreham Wood v Lincoln C
Chester FC v Dover Ath
Guiseley v Barrow
Woking v Tranmere R

Saturday, 28 November 2015
Aldershot T v Cheltenham T
Barrow v Woking
Boreham Wood v Tranmere R
Braintree T v Torquay U
Eastleigh v Southport
FC Halifax T v Dover Ath
Forest Green R v Altrincham
Gateshead v Chester FC
Grimsby T v Kidderminster H
Guiseley v Bromley
Lincoln C v Welling U
Wrexham v Macclesfield T

Saturday, 5 December 2015
Altrincham v Wrexham
Barrow v Boreham Wood
Bromley v Grimsby T
Cheltenham T v Chester FC
Dover Ath v Aldershot T
FC Halifax T v Guiseley
Kidderminster H v Gateshead
Macclesfield T v Eastleigh
Southport v Forest Green R
Torquay U v Welling U
Tranmere R v Braintree T
Woking v Lincoln C

Saturday, 19 December 2015
Aldershot T v Guiseley
Braintree T v Wrexham
Cheltenham T v Altrincham
Chester FC v Torquay U
Eastleigh v Kidderminster H
FC Halifax T v Tranmere R
Forest Green R v Boreham Wood
Gateshead v Woking
Grimsby T v Dover Ath
Lincoln C v Barrow
Southport v Bromley
Welling U v Macclesfield T

Saturday, 26 December 2015
Aldershot T v Woking
Altrincham v Chester FC
Barrow v Gateshead
Boreham Wood v Braintree T
Bromley v Eastleigh

Guiseley v Grimsby T
Kidderminster H v Cheltenham T
Lincoln C v FC Halifax T
Macclesfield T v Tranmere R
Torquay U v Forest Green R
Welling U v Dover Ath
Wrexham v Southport

Monday, 28 December 2015
Braintree T v Welling U
Cheltenham T v Torquay U
Chester FC v Macclesfield T
Dover Ath v Bromley
Eastleigh v Aldershot T
FC Halifax T v Wrexham
Forest Green R v Kidderminster H
Gateshead v Guiseley
Grimsby T v Lincoln C
Southport v Barrow
Tranmere R v Altrincham
Woking v Boreham Wood

Saturday, 2 January 2016
Braintree T v Boreham Wood
Cheltenham T v Kidderminster H
Chester FC v Altrincham
Dover Ath v Welling U
Eastleigh v Bromley
FC Halifax T v Lincoln C
Forest Green R v Torquay U
Gateshead v Barrow
Grimsby T v Guiseley
Southport v Wrexham
Tranmere R v Macclesfield T
Woking v Aldershot T

Saturday, 9 January 2016
Aldershot T v Chester FC
Altrincham v Gateshead
Barrow v Tranmere R
Boreham Wood v Cheltenham T
Bromley v Southport
Guiseley v Forest Green R
Kidderminster H v Eastleigh
Lincoln C v Dover Ath
Macclesfield T v FC Halifax T
Torquay U v Braintree T
Welling U v Grimsby T
Wrexham v Woking

Saturday, 23 January 2016
Boreham Wood v Eastleigh
Bromley v Tranmere R
Chester FC v Southport
Dover Ath v Cheltenham T
Forest Green R v Braintree T
Grimsby T v Altrincham
Kidderminster H v Guiseley
Macclesfield T v Aldershot T
Torquay U v Gateshead
Welling U v Barrow
Woking v FC Halifax T
Wrexham v Lincoln C

Tuesday, 26 January 2016
Altrincham v Woking

Saturday, 30 January 2016
Aldershot T v Kidderminster H
Altrincham v Dover Ath
Braintree T v Chester FC
Cheltenham T v Bromley
Eastleigh v Wrexham
FC Halifax T v Welling U

Forest Green R v Macclesfield T
Gateshead v Grimsby T
Lincoln C v Guiseley
Southport v Boreham Wood
Tranmere R v Torquay U
Woking v Barrow

Saturday, 6 February 2016
Barrow v Cheltenham T
Boreham Wood v Kidderminster H
Braintree T v Gateshead
Bromley v FC Halifax T
Chester FC v Aldershot T
Dover Ath v Southport
Grimsby T v Woking
Guiseley v Tranmere R
Lincoln C v Eastleigh
Macclesfield T v Torquay U
Welling U v Altrincham
Wrexham v Forest Green R

Tuesday, 9 February 2016
Tranmere R v Southport

Saturday, 13 February 2016
Aldershot T v Tranmere R
Altrincham v Lincoln C
Cheltenham T v Welling U
Dover Ath v Gateshead
Eastleigh v Barrow
FC Halifax T v Forest Green R
Grimsby T v Boreham Wood
Kidderminster H v Macclesfield T
Southport v Braintree T
Torquay U v Chester FC
Woking v Guiseley
Wrexham v Bromley

Tuesday, 16 February 2016
Gateshead v Eastleigh
Torquay U v FC Halifax T

Saturday, 20 February 2016
Altrincham v Guiseley
Barrow v Braintree T
Boreham Wood v Torquay U
Bromley v Woking
FC Halifax T v Grimsby T
Forest Green R v Eastleigh
Gateshead v Aldershot T
Kidderminster H v Chester FC
Lincoln C v Southport
Macclesfield T v Dover Ath
Tranmere R v Cheltenham T
Welling U v Wrexham

Tuesday, 23 February 2016
Braintree T v FC Halifax T
Lincoln C v Forest Green R
Southport v Macclesfield T
Wrexham v Kidderminster H

Saturday, 27 February 2016
Barrow v Forest Green R
Cheltenham T v Gateshead
Chester FC v Tranmere R
Dover Ath v Lincoln C
Eastleigh v Woking
FC Halifax T v Boreham Wood
Grimsby T v Southport
Guiseley v Braintree T
Kidderminster H v Bromley
Macclesfield T v Wrexham
Torquay U v Altrincham
Welling U v Aldershot T

Tuesday, 1 March 2016
Aldershot T v Grimsby T
Bromley v Welling U
Eastleigh v Cheltenham T

Saturday, 5 March 2016
Altrincham v Macclesfield T
Boreham Wood v Barrow
Braintree T v Eastleigh
Chester FC v Bromley
Forest Green R v Grimsby T
Guiseley v Wrexham
Lincoln C v Aldershot T
Southport v FC Halifax T
Torquay U v Kidderminster H
Tranmere R v Gateshead
Welling U v Cheltenham T
Woking v Dover Ath

Saturday, 12 March 2016
Aldershot T v Torquay U
Barrow v Altrincham
Bromley v Guiseley
Cheltenham T v Woking
Dover Ath v Tranmere R
Eastleigh v Chester FC
Gateshead v Forest Green R
Grimsby T v Braintree T
Kidderminster H v FC Halifax T
Macclesfield T v Lincoln C
Southport v Welling U
Wrexham v Boreham Wood

Saturday, 19 March 2016
Altrincham v Aldershot T
Barrow v Bromley
Boreham Wood v Macclesfield T
Braintree T v Cheltenham T
FC Halifax T v Eastleigh
Guiseley v Dover Ath
Lincoln C v Kidderminster H
Torquay U v Southport
Tranmere R v Forest Green R
Welling U v Gateshead
Woking v Grimsby T
Wrexham v Chester FC

Saturday, 26 March 2016
Braintree T v Bromley
Cheltenham T v Boreham Wood
Chester FC v Barrow
Dover Ath v Torquay U
Eastleigh v Welling U
FC Halifax T v Altrincham
Forest Green R v Aldershot T
Gateshead v Macclesfield T
Grimsby T v Wrexham
Southport v Guiseley
Tranmere R v Lincoln C
Woking v Kidderminster H

Monday, 28 March 2016
Aldershot T v Braintree T
Altrincham v Southport
Barrow v FC Halifax T
Boreham Wood v Dover Ath
Bromley v Forest Green R
Guiseley v Chester FC
Kidderminster H v Tranmere R
Lincoln C v Gateshead
Macclesfield T v Grimsby T
Torquay U v Eastleigh
Welling U v Woking
Wrexham v Cheltenham T

Saturday, 2 April 2016
Aldershot T v Barrow
Bromley v Lincoln C
Cheltenham T v Grimsby T
Chester FC v Boreham Wood
Dover Ath v FC Halifax T
Eastleigh v Guiseley
Forest Green R v Wrexham
Gateshead v Torquay U
Kidderminster H v Altrincham
Macclesfield T v Braintree T
Southport v Woking
Tranmere R v Welling U

Saturday, 9 April 2016
Altrincham v Bromley
Barrow v Macclesfield T
Boreham Wood v Southport
Braintree T v Forest Green R
FC Halifax T v Aldershot T
Grimsby T v Eastleigh
Guiseley v Cheltenham T
Lincoln C v Chester FC
Torquay U v Tranmere R
Welling U v Kidderminster H
Woking v Gateshead
Wrexham v Dover Ath

Saturday, 16 April 2016
Aldershot T v Boreham Wood
Bromley v Torquay U
Cheltenham T v FC Halifax T
Chester FC v Welling U
Dover Ath v Grimsby T
Eastleigh v Altrincham
Forest Green R v Woking
Gateshead v Braintree T
Kidderminster H v Barrow
Macclesfield T v Guiseley
Southport v Lincoln C
Tranmere R v Wrexham

Saturday, 23 April 2016
Aldershot T v Southport
Altrincham v Welling U
Boreham Wood v Guiseley
Eastleigh v Tranmere R
Forest Green R v FC Halifax T
Gateshead v Bromley
Grimsby T v Chester FC
Kidderminster H v Dover Ath
Lincoln C v Woking
Macclesfield T v Cheltenham T
Torquay U v Barrow
Wrexham v Braintree T

Saturday, 30 April 2016
Barrow v Wrexham
Braintree T v Altrincham
Bromley v Aldershot T
Cheltenham T v Lincoln C
Chester FC v Gateshead
Dover Ath v Forest Green R
FC Halifax T v Macclesfield T
Guiseley v Torquay U
Southport v Kidderminster H
Tranmere R v Grimsby T
Welling U v Boreham Wood
Woking v Eastleigh

THE SCOTTISH PREMIER LEAGUE AND SCOTTISH LEAGUE FIXTURES 2015–16

Sky Sports   All fixtures subject to change.

Saturday, 1 August 2015
Ladbrokes Scottish Premiership
Celtic v Ross Co* (12.45)
Hamilton A v Partick Thistle
Hearts v St Johnstone
Inverness CT v Motherwell
Kilmarnock v Dundee

Sunday, 2 August 2015
Ladbrokes Scottish Premiership
Dundee U v Aberdeen* (3.30)

Saturday, 8 August 2015
Ladbrokes Scottish Premiership
Aberdeen v Kilmarnock
Dundee v Hearts
Motherwell v Dundee U
Partick Thistle v Celtic
Ross Co v Hamilton A
St Johnstone v Inverness CT

Ladbrokes Scottish Championship
Dumbarton v Hibernian
Morton v Falkirk
Queen of South v Alloa Ath
Raith R v Livingston
Rangers v St Mirren

Ladbrokes Scottish League 1
Airdrieonians v Forfar Ath
Albion R v Ayr U
Brechin C v Dunfermline Ath
Cowdenbeath v Stranraer
Peterhead v Stenhousemuir

Ladbrokes Scottish League 2
Arbroath v Elgin C
Berwick R v Montrose
East Stirlingshire v East Fife
Queen's Park v Annan Ath
Stirling Alb v Clyde

Wednesday, 12 August 2015
Ladbrokes Scottish Premiership
Aberdeen v Hamilton A
Dundee U v Dundee
Hearts v Motherwell
Inverness CT v Partick Thistle
Kilmarnock v Celtic
St Johnstone v Ross Co

Saturday, 15 August 2015
Ladbrokes Scottish Premiership
Celtic v Inverness CT
Dundee v St Johnstone
Hamilton A v Dundee U
Motherwell v Aberdeen
Partick Thistle v Kilmarnock
Ross Co v Hearts

Ladbrokes Scottish Championship
Alloa Ath v Rangers
Falkirk v Raith R
Hibernian v Morton
Livingston v Queen of South
St Mirren v Dumbarton

Ladbrokes Scottish League 1
Ayr U v Brechin C
Dunfermline Ath v Cowdenbeath
Forfar Ath v Albion R
Stenhousemuir v Airdrieonians
Stranraer v Peterhead

Ladbrokes Scottish League 2
Annan Ath v Stirling Alb
Clyde v Queen's Park
East Fife v Berwick R
Elgin C v East Stirlingshire
Montrose v Arbroath

Saturday, 22 August 2015
Ladbrokes Scottish Premiership
Aberdeen v Dundee
Dundee U v Celtic
Hearts v Partick Thistle
Inverness CT v Hamilton A
Kilmarnock v Ross Co
St Johnstone v Motherwell

Ladbrokes Scottish Championship
Dumbarton v Queen of South
Livingston v Falkirk
Morton v St Mirren
Raith R v Alloa Ath
Rangers v Hibernian

Ladbrokes Scottish League 1
Brechin C v Airdrieonians
Cowdenbeath v Albion R
Forfar Ath v Stenhousemuir
Peterhead v Dunfermline Ath
Stranraer v Ayr U

Ladbrokes Scottish League 2
Arbroath v Queen's Park
East Fife v Elgin C
East Stirlingshire v Annan Ath
Montrose v Clyde
Stirling Alb v Berwick R

Saturday, 29 August 2015
Ladbrokes Scottish Premiership
Celtic v St Johnstone
Dundee v Inverness CT
Hamilton A v Hearts
Motherwell v Kilmarnock
Partick Thistle v Aberdeen
Ross Co v Dundee U

Ladbrokes Scottish Championship
Alloa Ath v Morton
Falkirk v Dumbarton
Hibernian v Raith R
Queen of South v Rangers
St Mirren v Livingston

Ladbrokes Scottish League 1
Airdrieonians v Peterhead
Albion R v Brechin C
Ayr U v Forfar Ath
Dunfermline Ath v Stranraer
Stenhousemuir v Cowdenbeath

Ladbrokes Scottish League 2
Annan Ath v Montrose
Berwick R v Arbroath
Clyde v East Stirlingshire
Elgin C v Stirling Alb
Queen's Park v East Fife

Saturday, 5 September 2015
Ladbrokes Scottish Championship
Dumbarton v Alloa Ath
Falkirk v Hibernian
Livingston v Morton
Queen of South v St Mirren
Rangers v Raith R

Ladbrokes Scottish League 1
Airdrieonians v Cowdenbeath
Ayr U v Stenhousemuir
Forfar Ath v Dunfermline Ath
Peterhead v Albion R
Stranraer v Brechin C

Ladbrokes Scottish League 2
Annan Ath v East Fife
Arbroath v Clyde
Berwick R v Queen's Park
East Stirlingshire v Stirling Alb
Montrose v Elgin C

Saturday, 12 September 2015
Ladbrokes Scottish Premiership
Aberdeen v Celtic
Dundee U v Kilmarnock
Inverness CT v Hearts
Motherwell v Ross Co
Partick Thistle v Dundee
St Johnstone v Hamilton A

Ladbrokes Scottish Championship
Hibernian v Alloa Ath
Morton v Dumbarton
Raith R v Queen of South
Rangers v Livingston
St Mirren v Falkirk

Ladbrokes Scottish League 1
Albion R v Airdrieonians
Brechin C v Forfar Ath
Cowdenbeath v Peterhead
Dunfermline Ath v Ayr U
Stenhousemuir v Stranraer

Ladbrokes Scottish League 2
Clyde v Annan Ath
East Fife v Arbroath
Elgin C v Berwick R
Queen's Park v East Stirlingshire
Stirling Alb v Montrose

Saturday, 19 September 2015
Ladbrokes Scottish Premiership
Celtic v Dundee
Dundee U v Inverness CT
Hamilton A v Motherwell
Hearts v Aberdeen
Kilmarnock v St Johnstone
Ross Co v Partick Thistle

Ladbrokes Scottish Championship
Alloa Ath v Falkirk
Dumbarton v Rangers
Livingston v Hibernian
Queen of South v Morton
St Mirren v Raith R

Ladbrokes Scottish League 1
Airdrieonians v Ayr U
Cowdenbeath v Forfar Ath
Peterhead v Brechin C
Stenhousemuir v Dunfermline Ath
Stranraer v Albion R

Ladbrokes Scottish League 2
Arbroath v Stirling Alb
Berwick R v Annan Ath
East Fife v Clyde
Montrose v East Stirlingshire
Queen's Park v Elgin C

Saturday, 26 September 2015
Ladbrokes Scottish Premiership
Celtic v Hearts
Dundee v Ross Co
Inverness CT v Aberdeen
Kilmarnock v Hamilton A
Motherwell v Partick Thistle
St Johnstone v Dundee U

Ladbrokes Scottish Championship
Alloa Ath v Livingston
Falkirk v Queen of South
Hibernian v St Mirren
Morton v Rangers
Raith R v Dumbarton

Ladbrokes Scottish League 1
Albion R v Stenhousemuir
Ayr U v Peterhead
Brechin C v Cowdenbeath
Dunfermline Ath v Airdrieonians
Forfar Ath v Stranraer

Ladbrokes Scottish League 2
Annan Ath v Elgin C
Clyde v Berwick R
East Stirlingshire v Arbroath
Montrose v East Fife
Stirling Alb v Queen's Park

Saturday, 3 October 2015
Ladbrokes Scottish Premiership
Aberdeen v St Johnstone
Dundee v Motherwell
Hamilton A v Celtic
Hearts v Kilmarnock
Partick Thistle v Dundee U
Ross Co v Inverness CT

Ladbrokes Scottish Championship
Dumbarton v Livingston
Queen of South v Hibernian
Raith R v Morton
Rangers v Falkirk
St Mirren v Alloa Ath

Ladbrokes Scottish League 1
Airdrieonians v Stranraer
Ayr U v Cowdenbeath
Dunfermline Ath v Albion R
Peterhead v Forfar Ath
Stenhousemuir v Brechin C

Ladbrokes Scottish League 2
Arbroath v Annan Ath
Berwick R v East Stirlingshire
East Fife v Stirling Alb
Elgin C v Clyde
Queen's Park v Montrose

Saturday, 17 October 2015
Ladbrokes Scottish Premiership
Dundee U v Hearts
Hamilton A v Dundee
Kilmarnock v Inverness CT
Motherwell v Celtic
Ross Co v Aberdeen
St Johnstone v Partick Thistle

Ladbrokes Scottish Championship
Alloa Ath v Raith R
Falkirk v Morton
Hibernian v Dumbarton
Livingston v St Mirren
Rangers v Queen of South

Ladbrokes Scottish League 1
Airdrieonians v Brechin C
Albion R v Peterhead
Cowdenbeath v Stenhousemuir
Forfar Ath v Ayr U
Stranraer v Dunfermline Ath

Ladbrokes Scottish League 2
Annan Ath v Queen's Park
Arbroath v Montrose
Berwick R v East Fife
Clyde v Stirling Alb
East Stirlingshire v Elgin C

Saturday, 24 October 2015
Ladbrokes Scottish Premiership
Aberdeen v Motherwell
Celtic v Dundee U
Dundee v Kilmarnock
Hearts v Ross Co
Inverness CT v St Johnstone
Partick Thistle v Hamilton A

Ladbrokes Scottish Championship
Dumbarton v Falkirk
Morton v Alloa Ath
Queen of South v Livingston
Raith R v Hibernian
St Mirren v Rangers

Ladbrokes Scottish League 1
Brechin C v Albion R
Dunfermline Ath v Forfar Ath
Peterhead v Airdrieonians
Stenhousemuir v Ayr U
Stranraer v Cowdenbeath

Saturday, 31 October 2015
Ladbrokes Scottish Premiership
Celtic v Aberdeen
Dundee U v Ross Co
Hamilton A v St Johnstone
Inverness CT v Dundee
Kilmarnock v Motherwell
Partick Thistle v Hearts

Ladbrokes Scottish Championship
Alloa Ath v Queen of South
Dumbarton v Morton
Falkirk v St Mirren

Hibernian v Rangers
Livingston v Raith R

Ladbrokes Scottish League 1
Airdrieonians v Albion R
Ayr U v Stranraer
Cowdenbeath v Dunfermline Ath
Forfar Ath v Brechin C
Stenhousemuir v Peterhead

Ladbrokes Scottish League 2
East Fife v Annan Ath
Elgin C v Arbroath
Montrose v Berwick R
Queen's Park v Clyde
Stirling Alb v East Stirlingshire

Saturday, 7 November 2015
Ladbrokes Scottish Premiership
Aberdeen v Dundee U
Dundee v Partick Thistle
Hearts v Hamilton A
Motherwell v Inverness CT
Ross Co v Celtic
St Johnstone v Kilmarnock

Ladbrokes Scottish Championship
Morton v Livingston
Queen of South v Dumbarton
Raith R v Falkirk
Rangers v Alloa Ath
St Mirren v Hibernian

Ladbrokes Scottish League 1
Albion R v Cowdenbeath
Brechin C v Ayr U
Dunfermline Ath v Peterhead
Forfar Ath v Airdrieonians
Stranraer v Stenhousemuir

Ladbrokes Scottish League 2
Arbroath v East Fife
Berwick R v Stirling Alb
Clyde v Montrose
East Stirlingshire v Queen's Park
Elgin C v Annan Ath

Saturday, 14 November 2015
Ladbrokes Scottish Championship
Falkirk v Alloa Ath
Hibernian v Livingston
Morton v Queen of South
Raith R v St Mirren
Rangers v Dumbarton

Ladbrokes Scottish League 1
Airdrieonians v Dunfermline Ath
Ayr U v Albion R
Cowdenbeath v Brechin C
Peterhead v Stranraer
Stenhousemuir v Forfar Ath

Ladbrokes Scottish League 2
Annan Ath v Berwick R
Clyde v Elgin C
East Fife v East Stirlingshire
Montrose v Queen's Park
Stirling Alb v Arbroath

Saturday, 21 November 2015
Ladbrokes Scottish Premiership
Celtic v Kilmarnock
Dundee U v St Johnstone
Hamilton A v Aberdeen

Hearts v Dundee
Partick Thistle v Inverness CT
Ross Co v Motherwell

Ladbrokes Scottish Championship
Alloa Ath v Hibernian
Dumbarton v Raith R
Livingston v Rangers
Queen of South v Falkirk
St Mirren v Morton

Ladbrokes Scottish League 1
Albion R v Dunfermline Ath
Ayr U v Airdrieonians
Brechin C v Stenhousemuir
Peterhead v Cowdenbeath
Stranraer v Forfar Ath

Ladbrokes Scottish League 2
Annan Ath v Arbroath
Berwick R v Clyde
East Stirlingshire v Montrose
Elgin C v East Fife
Queen's Park v Stirling Alb

Saturday, 28 November 2015
Ladbrokes Scottish Premiership
Aberdeen v Ross Co
Dundee U v Hamilton A
Inverness CT v Celtic
Kilmarnock v Partick Thistle
Motherwell v Hearts
St Johnstone v Dundee

Saturday, 5 December 2015
Ladbrokes Scottish Premiership
Celtic v Hamilton A
Dundee v Aberdeen
Hearts v Inverness CT
Kilmarnock v Dundee U
Partick Thistle v Motherwell
Ross Co v St Johnstone

Ladbrokes Scottish Championship
Alloa Ath v Dumbarton
Falkirk v Livingston
Morton v Hibernian
Raith R v Rangers
St Mirren v Queen of South

Ladbrokes Scottish League 1
Airdrieonians v Stenhousemuir
Albion R v Stranraer
Cowdenbeath v Ayr U
Dunfermline Ath v Brechin C
Forfar Ath v Peterhead

Ladbrokes Scottish League 2
Arbroath v Berwick R
East Fife v Queen's Park
East Stirlingshire v Clyde
Montrose v Annan Ath
Stirling Alb v Elgin C

Saturday, 12 December 2015
Ladbrokes Scottish Premiership
Aberdeen v Hearts
Dundee U v Partick Thistle
Hamilton A v Ross Co
Inverness CT v Kilmarnock
Motherwell v Dundee
St Johnstone v Celtic

Ladbrokes Scottish Championship
Dumbarton v St Mirren
Hibernian v Falkirk
Livingston v Alloa Ath
Queen of South v Raith R
Rangers v Morton

Ladbrokes Scottish League 1
Ayr U v Dunfermline Ath
Brechin C v Peterhead
Forfar Ath v Cowdenbeath
Stenhousemuir v Albion R
Stranraer v Airdrieonians

Ladbrokes Scottish League 2
Annan Ath v East Stirlingshire
Berwick R v Elgin C
Clyde v East Fife
Montrose v Stirling Alb
Queen's Park v Arbroath

Saturday, 19 December 2015
Ladbrokes Scottish Premiership
Celtic v Motherwell
Dundee v Hamilton A
Inverness CT v Dundee U
Kilmarnock v Aberdeen
Partick Thistle v Ross Co
St Johnstone v Hearts

Ladbrokes Scottish Championship
Alloa Ath v St Mirren
Falkirk v Rangers
Hibernian v Queen of South
Livingston v Dumbarton
Morton v Raith R

Ladbrokes Scottish League 1
Albion R v Forfar Ath
Brechin C v Stranraer
Cowdenbeath v Airdrieonians
Dunfermline Ath v Stenhousemuir
Peterhead v Ayr U

Ladbrokes Scottish League 2
Clyde v Arbroath
East Fife v Montrose
East Stirlingshire v Berwick R
Elgin C v Queen's Park
Stirling Alb v Annan Ath

Saturday, 26 December 2015
Ladbrokes Scottish Premiership
Aberdeen v Inverness CT
Dundee U v Motherwell
Hamilton A v Kilmarnock
Hearts v Celtic
Partick Thistle v St Johnstone
Ross Co v Dundee

Ladbrokes Scottish Championship
Falkirk v Dumbarton
Queen of South v Morton
Raith R v Alloa Ath
Rangers v Hibernian
St Mirren v Livingston

Ladbrokes Scottish League 1
Airdrieonians v Peterhead
Ayr U v Brechin C
Cowdenbeath v Albion R
Forfar Ath v Dunfermline Ath
Stenhousemuir v Stranraer

Ladbrokes Scottish League 2
Annan Ath v Clyde
Arbroath v East Stirlingshire
Elgin C v Montrose
Queen's Park v Berwick R
Stirling Alb v East Fife

Wednesday, 30 December 2015
Ladbrokes Scottish Premiership
Aberdeen v Partick Thistle
Dundee v Celtic
Hamilton A v Inverness CT
Hearts v Dundee U
Motherwell v St Johnstone
Ross Co v Kilmarnock

Saturday, 2 January 2016
Ladbrokes Scottish Premiership
Celtic v Partick Thistle
Dundee v Dundee U
Inverness CT v Ross Co
Kilmarnock v Hearts
Motherwell v Hamilton A
St Johnstone v Aberdeen

Ladbrokes Scottish Championship
Alloa Ath v Falkirk
Dumbarton v Rangers
Hibernian v Raith R
Livingston v Queen of South
Morton v St Mirren

Ladbrokes Scottish League 1
Albion R v Airdrieonians
Brechin C v Forfar Ath
Dunfermline Ath v Cowdenbeath
Peterhead v Stenhousemuir
Stranraer v Ayr U

Ladbrokes Scottish League 2
Berwick R v Annan Ath
Clyde v Queen's Park
East Fife v Elgin C
East Stirlingshire v Stirling Alb
Montrose v Arbroath

Saturday, 9 January 2016
Ladbrokes Scottish League 2
Arbroath v Elgin C
East Fife v Berwick R
Montrose v East Stirlingshire
Queen's Park v Annan Ath
Stirling Alb v Clyde

Saturday, 16 January 2016
Ladbrokes Scottish Premiership
Dundee U v Celtic
Hearts v Motherwell
Kilmarnock v Inverness CT
Partick Thistle v Dundee
Ross Co v Aberdeen
St Johnstone v Hamilton A

Ladbrokes Scottish Championship
Alloa Ath v Morton
Dumbarton v Queen of South
Falkirk v Hibernian
Rangers v Livingston
St Mirren v Raith R

Ladbrokes Scottish League 1
Airdrieonians v Forfar Ath
Ayr U v Cowdenbeath

Dunfermline Ath v Albion R
Stenhousemuir v Brechin C
Stranraer v Peterhead

Ladbrokes Scottish League 2
Annan Ath v East Fife
Berwick R v Arbroath
Clyde v East Stirlingshire
Elgin C v Stirling Alb
Queen's Park v Montrose

Saturday, 23 January 2016
Ladbrokes Scottish Premiership
Aberdeen v Dundee
Celtic v St Johnstone
Dundee U v Kilmarnock
Hamilton A v Hearts
Inverness CT v Partick Thistle
Motherwell v Ross Co

Ladbrokes Scottish Championship
Hibernian v St Mirren
Livingston v Falkirk
Morton v Rangers
Queen of South v Alloa Ath
Raith R v Dumbarton

Ladbrokes Scottish League 1
Albion R v Ayr U
Brechin C v Airdrieonians
Cowdenbeath v Stranraer
Forfar Ath v Stenhousemuir
Peterhead v Dunfermline Ath

Ladbrokes Scottish League 2
Arbroath v Annan Ath
East Stirlingshire v East Fife
Elgin C v Berwick R
Montrose v Clyde
Stirling Alb v Queen's Park

Saturday, 30 January 2016
Ladbrokes Scottish Premiership
Aberdeen v Celtic
Dundee v Motherwell
Kilmarnock v Hamilton A
Partick Thistle v Dundee U
Ross Co v Hearts
St Johnstone v Inverness CT

Ladbrokes Scottish Championship
Dumbarton v Livingston
Hibernian v Morton
Raith R v Queen of South
Rangers v Falkirk
St Mirren v Alloa Ath

Ladbrokes Scottish League 1
Ayr U v Stenhousemuir
Cowdenbeath v Forfar Ath
Dunfermline Ath v Airdrieonians
Peterhead v Albion R
Stranraer v Brechin C

Ladbrokes Scottish League 2
Annan Ath v Elgin C
Berwick R v Queen's Park
East Fife v Clyde
East Stirlingshire v Arbroath
Stirling Alb v Montrose

Saturday, 6 February 2016
Ladbrokes Scottish League 1
Airdrieonians v Cowdenbeath

Albion R v Brechin C
Ayr U v Peterhead
Forfar Ath v Stranraer
Stenhousemuir v Dunfermline Ath

Ladbrokes Scottish League 2
Arbroath v Stirling Alb
Berwick R v East Stirlingshire
Clyde v Annan Ath
Montrose v East Fife
Queen's Park v Elgin C

Saturday, 13 February 2016
Ladbrokes Scottish Premiership
Celtic v Ross Co
Dundee v St Johnstone
Hamilton A v Dundee U
Hearts v Partick Thistle
Inverness CT v Aberdeen
Motherwell v Kilmarnock

Ladbrokes Scottish Championship
Alloa Ath v Rangers
Falkirk v Raith R
Livingston v Hibernian
Morton v Dumbarton
Queen of South v St Mirren

Ladbrokes Scottish League 1
Brechin C v Cowdenbeath
Dunfermline Ath v Ayr U
Peterhead v Forfar Ath
Stenhousemuir v Airdrieonians
Stranraer v Albion R

Ladbrokes Scottish League 2
Annan Ath v Montrose
East Fife v Arbroath
Elgin C v Clyde
Queen's Park v East Stirlingshire
Stirling Alb v Berwick R

Saturday, 20 February 2016
Ladbrokes Scottish Premiership
Celtic v Inverness CT
Dundee U v Hearts
Kilmarnock v Dundee
Partick Thistle v Aberdeen
Ross Co v Hamilton A
St Johnstone v Motherwell

Ladbrokes Scottish Championship
Hibernian v Alloa Ath
Morton v Falkirk
Queen of South v Rangers
Raith R v Livingston
St Mirren v Dumbarton

Ladbrokes Scottish League 1
Airdrieonians v Stranraer
Albion R v Stenhousemuir
Ayr U v Forfar Ath
Brechin C v Dunfermline Ath
Cowdenbeath v Peterhead

Ladbrokes Scottish League 2
Arbroath v Queen's Park
Clyde v Berwick R
East Fife v Stirling Alb
East Stirlingshire v Annan Ath
Montrose v Elgin C

Saturday, 27 February 2016
Ladbrokes Scottish Premiership
Aberdeen v St Johnstone
Dundee v Inverness CT
Hamilton A v Celtic
Hearts v Kilmarnock
Motherwell v Partick Thistle
Ross Co v Dundee U

Ladbrokes Scottish Championship
Alloa Ath v Livingston
Dumbarton v Hibernian
Falkirk v Queen of South
Raith R v Morton
Rangers v St Mirren

Ladbrokes Scottish League 1
Airdrieonians v Ayr U
Dunfermline Ath v Stranraer
Forfar Ath v Albion R
Peterhead v Brechin C
Stenhousemuir v Cowdenbeath

Ladbrokes Scottish League 2
Annan Ath v Stirling Alb
Arbroath v Clyde
Berwick R v Montrose
Elgin C v East Stirlingshire
Queen's Park v East Fife

Tuesday, 1 March 2016
Ladbrokes Scottish Championship
Livingston v Morton
Queen of South v Hibernian
Rangers v Raith R
St Mirren v Falkirk

Wednesday, 2 March 2016
Ladbrokes Scottish Premiership
Celtic v Dundee
Dundee U v Aberdeen
Hamilton A v Motherwell
Inverness CT v Hearts
Kilmarnock v Ross Co
St Johnstone v Partick Thistle

Ladbrokes Scottish Championship
Dumbarton v Alloa Ath

Saturday, 5 March 2016
Ladbrokes Scottish Championship
Falkirk v Alloa Ath
Hibernian v Rangers
Livingston v Dumbarton
Morton v Queen of South
Raith R v St Mirren

Ladbrokes Scottish League 1
Albion R v Peterhead
Brechin C v Ayr U
Cowdenbeath v Airdrieonians
Dunfermline Ath v Stenhousemuir
Stranraer v Forfar Ath

Ladbrokes Scottish League 2
Annan Ath v Clyde
East Stirlingshire v Montrose
Elgin C v East Fife
Queen's Park v Berwick R
Stirling Alb v Arbroath

Saturday, 12 March 2016
Ladbrokes Scottish Premiership
Aberdeen v Kilmarnock

Dundee v Hearts
Inverness CT v Hamilton A
Motherwell v Dundee U
Partick Thistle v Celtic
St Johnstone v Ross Co

Ladbrokes Scottish Championship
Alloa Ath v Raith R
Dumbarton v Falkirk
Hibernian v Livingston
Rangers v Morton
St Mirren v Queen of South

Ladbrokes Scottish League 1
Airdrieonians v Brechin C
Albion R v Stranraer
Ayr U v Dunfermline Ath
Forfar Ath v Cowdenbeath
Stenhousemuir v Peterhead

Ladbrokes Scottish League 2
Arbroath v East Stirlingshire
Berwick R v Stirling Alb
Clyde v Elgin C
East Fife v Annan Ath
Montrose v Queen's Park

Saturday, 19 March 2016
Ladbrokes Scottish Premiership
Dundee U v Dundee
Hamilton A v Partick Thistle
Hearts v St Johnstone
Kilmarnock v Celtic
Motherwell v Aberdeen
Ross Co v Inverness CT

Ladbrokes Scottish Championship
Falkirk v Rangers
Livingston v St Mirren
Morton v Alloa Ath
Queen of South v Dumbarton
Raith R v Hibernian

Ladbrokes Scottish League 1
Brechin C v Albion R
Cowdenbeath v Dunfermline Ath
Forfar Ath v Ayr U
Peterhead v Airdrieonians
Stranraer v Stenhousemuir

Ladbrokes Scottish League 2
Annan Ath v Berwick R
East Stirlingshire v Clyde
Elgin C v Montrose
Queen's Park v Arbroath
Stirling Alb v East Fife

Saturday, 26 March 2016
Ladbrokes Scottish Championship
Alloa Ath v St Mirren
Falkirk v Livingston
Hibernian v Dumbarton
Morton v Raith R
Rangers v Queen of South

Ladbrokes Scottish League 1
Airdrieonians v Albion R
Ayr U v Stranraer

Dunfermline Ath v Brechin C
Peterhead v Cowdenbeath
Stenhousemuir v Forfar Ath

Ladbrokes Scottish League 2
Berwick R v Elgin C
Clyde v Arbroath
East Fife v Queen's Park
Montrose v Annan Ath
Stirling Alb v East Stirlingshire

Saturday, 2 April 2016
Ladbrokes Scottish Premiership
Aberdeen v Hamilton A
Celtic v Hearts
Dundee v Ross Co
Inverness CT v Motherwell
Partick Thistle v Kilmarnock
St Johnstone v Dundee U

Ladbrokes Scottish Championship
Dumbarton v Morton
Livingston v Alloa Ath
Queen of South v Falkirk
Raith R v Rangers
St Mirren v Hibernian

Ladbrokes Scottish League 1
Albion R v Dunfermline Ath
Brechin C v Stenhousemuir
Cowdenbeath v Ayr U
Forfar Ath v Peterhead
Stranraer v Airdrieonians

Ladbrokes Scottish League 2
Arbroath v East Fife
Clyde v Montrose
East Stirlingshire v Berwick R
Elgin C v Annan Ath
Queen's Park v Stirling Alb

Saturday, 9 April 2016
Ladbrokes Scottish Premiership
Dundee U v Inverness CT
Hamilton A v Dundee
Hearts v Aberdeen
Kilmarnock v St Johnstone
Motherwell v Celtic
Ross Co v Partick Thistle

Ladbrokes Scottish Championship
Alloa Ath v Hibernian
Falkirk v St Mirren
Morton v Livingston
Queen of South v Raith R
Rangers v Dumbarton

Ladbrokes Scottish League 1
Airdrieonians v Stenhousemuir
Ayr U v Albion R
Cowdenbeath v Brechin C
Dunfermline Ath v Forfar Ath
Peterhead v Stranraer

Ladbrokes Scottish League 2
Annan Ath v Arbroath
Berwick R v Clyde
East Fife v Montrose

East Stirlingshire v Queen's Park
Stirling Alb v Elgin C

Saturday, 16 April 2016
Ladbrokes Scottish Championship
Alloa Ath v Queen of South
Dumbarton v Raith R
Hibernian v Falkirk
Livingston v Rangers
St Mirren v Morton

Ladbrokes Scottish League 1
Albion R v Cowdenbeath
Brechin C v Peterhead
Forfar Ath v Airdrieonians
Stenhousemuir v Ayr U
Stranraer v Dunfermline Ath

Ladbrokes Scottish League 2
Annan Ath v East Stirlingshire
Arbroath v Berwick R
Clyde v East Fife
Elgin C v Queen's Park
Montrose v Stirling Alb

Saturday, 23 April 2016
Ladbrokes Scottish Championship
Dumbarton v St Mirren
Morton v Hibernian
Queen of South v Livingston
Raith R v Falkirk
Rangers v Alloa Ath

Ladbrokes Scottish League 1
Airdrieonians v Dunfermline Ath
Albion R v Forfar Ath
Brechin C v Stranraer
Cowdenbeath v Stenhousemuir
Peterhead v Ayr U

Ladbrokes Scottish League 2
Arbroath v Montrose
Berwick R v East Fife
East Stirlingshire v Elgin C
Queen's Park v Clyde
Stirling Alb v Annan Ath

Saturday, 30 April 2016
Ladbrokes Scottish Championship
Alloa Ath v Dumbarton
Falkirk v Morton
Hibernian v Queen of South
Livingston v Raith R
St Mirren v Rangers

Ladbrokes Scottish League 1
Ayr U v Airdrieonians
Dunfermline Ath v Peterhead
Forfar Ath v Brechin C
Stenhousemuir v Albion R
Stranraer v Cowdenbeath

Ladbrokes Scottish League 2
Annan Ath v Queen's Park
Clyde v Stirling Alb
East Fife v East Stirlingshire
Elgin C v Arbroath
Montrose v Berwick R

FOOTBALL ASSOCIATION FIXTURES 2015–16

JULY 2015

7 Tuesday	UEFA Champions League 1Q(2)
8 Wednesday	UEFA Champions League 1Q(2)
9 Thursday	UEFA Europa League 1Q(2)
14 Tuesday	UEFA Champions League 2Q(1)
15 Wednesday	UEFA Champions League 2Q(1)
16 Thursday	UEFA Europa League 2Q(1)
21 Tuesday	UEFA Champions League 2Q(2)
22 Wednesday	UEFA Champions League 2Q(2)
23 Thursday	UEFA Europa League 2Q(2)
28 Tuesday	UEFA Champions League 3Q(1)
29 Wednesday	UEFA Champions League 3Q(1)
30 Thursday	UEFA Europa League 3Q(1)

AUGUST 2015

1 Saturday	FA Women's Cup Final (2014–15)
2 Sunday	FA Community Shield
4 Tuesday	UEFA Champions League 3Q(2)
5 Wednesday	UEFA Champions League 3Q(2)
6 Thursday	UEFA Europa League 3Q(2)
8 Saturday	Premier League Commences
	Football League Commences
	National League Commences
11 Tuesday	UEFA Super Cup
	Football League Cup 1
15 Saturday	FA Cup EP
18 Tuesday	UEFA Champions League Qualifying Play-Off(1)
19 Wednesday	UEFA Champions League Qualifying Play-Off(1)
20 Thursday	UEFA Europa League Qualifying Play-Off(1)
25 Tuesday	UEFA Champions League Qualifying Play-Off(2)
26 Wednesday	UEFA Champions League Qualifying Play-Off(2)
	Football League Cup 2
27 Thursday	UEFA Europa League Qualifying Play-Off(2)
29 Saturday	FA Cup P

SEPTEMBER 2015

2 Wednesday	Football League Trophy 1
5 Saturday	San Marino v England – EURO 2016 Qualifier
	FA Vase 1Q
7 Monday	FA Youth Cup P†
8 Tuesday	England v Switzerland – EURO 2016 Qualifier
12 Saturday	FA Cup 1Q
15 Tuesday	UEFA Champions League MD1
16 Wednesday	UEFA Champions League MD1
17 Thursday	UEFA Europa League MD1
21 Monday	FA Youth Cup 1Q†
23 Wednesday	Football League Cup 3
26 Saturday	FA Cup 2Q
29 Tuesday	UEFA Champions League MD2
30 Wednesday	UEFA Champions League MD2

OCTOBER 2015

1 Thursday	UEFA Europa League MD2
3 Saturday	FA Trophy P
	FA Vase 2Q
5 Monday	FA Youth Cup 2Q†
7 Wednesday	Football League Trophy 2
9 Friday	England v Estonia – EURO 2016 Qualifier
10 Saturday	FA Cup 3Q
	FA County Youth Cup 1*
12 Monday	Lithuania v England – EURO 2016 Qualifier
18 Sunday	FA Sunday Cup 1
19 Monday	FA Youth Cup 3Q†
20 Tuesday	UEFA Champions League MD3
21 Wednesday	UEFA Champions League MD3
22 Thursday	UEFA Europa League MD3
24 Saturday	FA Cup 4Q
28 Wednesday	Football League Cup 4
31 Saturday	FA Trophy 1Q
	FA Vase 1P

NOVEMBER 2015

3 Tuesday	UEFA Champions League MD4
4 Wednesday	UEFA Champions League MD4
5 Thursday	UEFA Europa League MD4
7 Saturday	FA Cup 1P
	FA Youth Cup 1P*
	FA County Youth Cup 2*
11 Wednesday	Football League Trophy QF
13 Friday	Possible England International
14 Saturday	FA Trophy 2Q
15 Sunday	FA Sunday Cup 2
17 Tuesday	Possible England International
21 Saturday	FA Vase 2P
	FA Youth Cup 2P*
24 Tuesday	UEFA Champions League MD5
25 Wednesday	UEFA Champions League MD5
26 Thursday	UEFA Europa League MD5
28 Saturday	FA Trophy 3Q

DECEMBER 2015

2 Wednesday	Football League Cup 5
5 Saturday	FA Cup 2P
8 Tuesday	UEFA Champions League MD6
9 Wednesday	UEFA Champions League MD6
	Football League Trophy SF
10 Thursday	UEFA Europa League MD6
12 Saturday	FA Trophy 1P
	FA Vase 3P
	FA County Youth Cup 3*
13 Sunday	FA Sunday Cup 3
19 Saturday	FA Youth Cup 3P*
25 Friday	Christmas Day
26 Saturday	Boxing Day

JANUARY 2016

1 Friday	New Year's Day
6 Wednesday	Football League Cup SF(1)
9 Saturday	FA Cup 3P
	FA Vase 4P
12 Wednesday	Football League Trophy AF(1)
16 Saturday	FA Trophy 2P
	FA Youth Cup 4P*
17 Sunday	FA Sunday Cup 4
23 Saturday	FA County Youth Cup 4*
27 Wednesday	Football League Cup SF(2)
	Football League Trophy AF(2)
30 Saturday	FA Cup 4P
	FA Vase 5P

FEBRUARY 2016

6 Saturday	FA Trophy 3P
	FA Youth Cup 5P*
14 Sunday	FA Sunday Cup 5
16 Tuesday	UEFA Champions League 16(1)
17 Wednesday	UEFA Champions League 16(1)
18 Thursday	UEFA Europa League 32(1)
20 Saturday	FA Cup 5P
	FA Vase 6P
23 Tuesday	UEFA Champions League 16(1)
24 Wednesday	UEFA Champions League 16(1)
25 Thursday	UEFA Europa League 32(2)
27 Saturday	FA Trophy 4P
	FA Youth Cup 6P*
	FA County Youth Cup SF*
28 Sunday	Football League Cup Final

MARCH 2016

8 Tuesday	UEFA Champions League 16(2)
9 Wednesday	UEFA Champions League 16(2)
10 Thursday	UEFA Europa League 16(1)
12 Saturday	FA Cup 6P
	FA Trophy SF(1)
	FA Vase SF(1)
13 Sunday	FA Sunday Cup SF
15 Tuesday	UEFA Champions League 16(2)
16 Wednesday	UEFA Champions League 16(2)
17 Thursday	UEFA Europa League 16(2)
19 Saturday	FA Trophy SF(2)
	FA Vase SF(2)
	FA Youth Cup SF(1)*
25 Friday	Good Friday
28 Monday	Bank Holiday

APRIL 2016

3 Sunday	Football League Trophy Final
5 Tuesday	UEFA Champions League QF(1)
6 Wednesday	UEFA Champions League QF(1)
7 Thursday	UEFA Europa League QF(1)
9 Saturday	FA Youth Cup SF(2)*
	FA County Youth Cup Final *(prov)*

12 Tuesday	UEFA Champions League QF(2)
13 Wednesday	UEFA Champions League QF(2)
14 Thursday	UEFA Europa League QF(2)
17 Sunday	FA Sunday Cup Final *(prov)*
23 Saturday	FA Cup SF
24 Sunday	FA Cup SF
26 Tuesday	UEFA Champions League SF(1)
27 Wednesday	UEFA Champions League SF(1)
28 Thursday	UEFA Europa League SF(1)
30 Saturday	National League Ends

MAY 2016

2 Monday	Bank Holiday
3 Tuesday	UEFA Champions League SF(2)
4 Wednesday	UEFA Champions League SF(2)
	Football Conference SF Play Offs to Sunday 8
5 Thursday	UEFA Europa League SF(2)
7 Saturday	Football League Ends
12 Thursday	Football League Play-Off Semi-Finals to Friday 20
14 Saturday	National League North & South Promotion Finals
15 Sunday	End of Premier League
	National League Premier Div Promotion Final
18 Wednesday	UEFA Europa League Final
20 Friday	End of Football League Play-Off's
21 Saturday	FA Cup Final
22 Sunday	FA Trophy Final
	FA Vase Final
28 Saturday	UEFA Champions League Final
	Football League Championship Play-Off Final
29 Sunday	Football League 1 Play-Off Final
30 Monday	Football League 2 Play-Off Final

JUNE 2016

10 Friday	UEFA EURO 2016 commences

JULY 2016

Sun 10 July	UEFA EURO 2016 Final

FA Youth Cup Final 1st & 2nd Leg – dates to be confirmed
FA Women's Cup Dates – to be confirmed
*closing date of round
†week commencing

STOP PRESS

SUMMER TRANSFER DIARY 2015

England Women reach World Cup Semi-Finals, but fall to Japan ... Tinkerman Ranieri new Leicester City manager after Nigel Pearson sacked ... Manchester City sign Raheem Sterling from Liverpool for a new club record and highest ever transfer fee for an English player of £44,000,000 (rising to £49,000,000) ... Palace break record for Cabaye – £10,000,000 ... West Ham through first qualifying round in Europa League ... Turkish delight as RVP heads to Fenerbahce ... Delph double U-turn takes him from Villa to Manchester City ... Benteke to Liverpool in pipeline.

Reported fees only, otherwise Free or Undisclosed.

2 June: **Dedryck Boyata** Manchester C to Celtic – £1.5m; **Richard Brindley** Rotherham U to Colchester U; **Leon Clarke** Wolverhampton W to Bury; **Barry Corr** Southend U to Cambridge U; **Tim Erlandsson** Halmstads to Nottingham F; **Josh Lelan** Derby Co to Northampton; **Cameron McGeehan** Norwich C to Luton T; **Jim McNulty** Bury to Rochdale; **Bobby Olejnik** Peterborough U to Exeter C; **Rhys Sharpe** Derby Co to Notts Co.
3 June: **Christian Fuchs** Schalke to Leicester C; **Nathan Thomas** Motherwell to Mansfield T.
4 June: **Giedrius Arlauskis** Steaua Bucharest to Watford; **James Milner** Manchester C to Liverpool.
5 June: **Chris Beardsley** Stevenage to Mansfield T; **Tom Cleverley** Manchester U to Everton; **Callum Reilly** Birmingham C to Burton Alb; **Marley Watkins** Inverness CT to Barnsley.
6 June: **Sylvan Ebanks-Blake** Preston NE to Chesterfield; **Shaun Whalley** Luton T to Shrewsbury T.
8 June: **Lewis Alessandra** Plymouth Arg to Rochdale; **Jermaine Beckford** Bolton W to Preston NE; **Darren Bent** Aston Villa to Derby Co; **Lee Collins** Northampton T to Mansfield T; **Colin Doyle** Birmingham C to Blackpool; **Adam Dugdale** Tranmere R to Morecambe; **Danny Ings** Burnley to Liverpool; **Peter Murphy** Wycombe W to Morecambe; **Alex Pearce** Reading to Derby Co; **Aaron Wildig** Shrewsbury T to Morecambe; **Harry Worley** Stevenage to Hartlepool U.
9 June: **Andre Ayew** Marseille to Swansea C; **Sean Clohessy** Colchester U to Leyton Orient; **Charlie Horton** Cardiff C to Leeds U; **Sammy Moore** AFC Wimbledon to Leyton Orient; **Tom Pope** Port Vale to Bury.
10 June: **Chris Dagnall** Leyton Orient to Kerala Blasters; **Lee Erwin** Motherwell to Leeds U; **Charlie Goode** Hendon to Scunthorpe U; **Pedro Obiang** Sampdoria to West Ham U; **Thorsten Stuckmann** Preston NE to Doncaster R; **Aidy White** Leeds U to Rotherham U.
11 June: **Gavin Hoyte** Gillingham to Barnet; **Scott Laird** Preston NE to Scunthorpe U; **Brad Potts** Carlisle U to Blackpool; **George Swan** Wolverhampton W to York C; **Shaun Whalley** Luton T to Shrewsbury T; **Ryan Williams** Morecambe to Brentford.
12 June: **Adam Bogdan** Bolton W to Liverpool; **Jake Carroll** Huddersfield T to Hartlepool U; **Scott Carson** Wigan Ath to Derby Co; **Memphis Depay** PSV Eindhoven to Man U; **Jay Emmanuel-Thomas** Bristol C to QPR; **Kyle Letheren** Dundee to Blackpool; **Joe Mattock** Sheffield W to Rotherham U; **Craig Morgan** Rotherham U to Wigan Ath; **Elliot Omozusi** Leyton Orient to Cambridge U; **Sam Slocombe** Scunthorpe U to Oxford U; **Adel Taarabt** QPR to Benfica; **Craig Westcarr** Portsmouth to Mansfield T.
15 June: **Luke Berry** Cambridge U to Barnsley; **Calum Butcher** Dundee U to Burton Alb; **Trevor Carson** Cheltenham T to Hartlepool U; **Bradley Garmston** WBA to Gillingham; **Darren Holden** Hartlepool U to Ross Co; **Sam Kelly** Norwich C to Port Vale; **Clark Robertson** Aberdeen to Blackpool; **Ryan Sellers** Bolton W to Wycombe W; **Enda Stevens** Aston Villa to Portsmouth; **Remie Streete** Newcastle U to Port Vale; **Garry Thompson** Notts Co to Wycombe W; **Ben Williamson** Port Vale to Gillingham.
16 June: **Joselu** Hannover to Stoke C – £5.75m; **Juanmi** Malaga to Southampton – £5m; **Paul Gallagher** Leicester C to Preston NE; **Jamie Mackie** Nottingham F to QPR; **Rob Milsom** Rotherham U to Notts Co; **Matt Tootle** Crewe Alex to Shrewsbury T.
17 June: **Jack Compton** Hartlepool U to Yeovil T; **Matt Dolan** Bradford C to Yeovil T; **Christophe Lepoint** Charlton Ath to SV Zulte Waregem; **Micah Richards** Manchester C to Aston Villa; **Gary Roberts** Chesterfield to Portsmouth; **Jimmy Ryan** Chesterfield to Fleetwood T.
18 June: **Semi Ajayi** Arsenal to Cardiff C; **Sam Foley** Yeovil T to Port Vale; **Jonathan Franks** Hartlepool U to Ross Co; **Cedric Soares** Sporting Lisbon to Southampton – £4.7m; **Simon Walton** Stevenage to Crawley T; **Andreas Weimann** Aston Villa to Derby Co.
19 June: **Chris Baird** WBA to Derby Co; **Darius Charles** Stevenage to Burton Alb; **George Green** Everton to Oldham Ath; **Gael Kakuta** Chelsea to Sevilla; **Marc Laird** Tranmere R to Yeovil T; **Andy Lonergan** Bolton W to Fulham; **Paul McCallum** West Ham U to Leyton Orient; **Ben Pringle** Rotherham U to Fulham; **Franck Tabanou** St Etienne to Swansea C; **Ben Tozer** Northampton T to Yeovil T; **Kieran Trippier** Burnley to Tottenham H; **Blair Turgott** Coventry C to Leyton Orient; **Andy Williams** Swindon T to Doncaster R.
20 June: **Joe Gomez** Charlton Ath to Liverpool – £3.5m.
22 June: **Matthew Briggs** Millwall to Colchester U; **Jordan Gibbons** QPR to Yeovil T; **Nicky Hunt** Accrington S to Mansfield T; **Rob Kiernan** Wigan Ath to Rangers; **Matthew Lowton** Aston Villa to Burnley; **James McClean** Wigan Ath to WBA – £1.5m; **Youssouf Mulumbu** WBA to Norwich C; **Maarten Stekelenburg** Fulham to Southampton; **Yacouba Sylla** Aston Villa to Rennes.
23 June: **Jordan Archer** Tottenham H to Millwall; **Patrick Bauer** Maritimo to Charlton Ath; **James Berrett** Yeovil T to Hartlepool U; **Jake Cassidy** Wolverhampton W to Oldham Ath; **Bira Dembele** Stevenage to Barnet; **Shamir Fenelon** Brighton & HA to Crawley T; **Scott Flinders** Hartlepool U to York C; **Shaun Jeffers** Newport Co to Yeovil T; **Joe Martin** Gillingham to Millwall; **Jon Meades** Oxford U to Wimbledon; **Kristoffer Nordfeldt** Heerenveen to Swansea C; **Liam Rosenior** Hull C to Brighton & HA; **Dean Whitehead** Middlesbrough to Huddersfield T; **Josh Yorwerth** Cardiff C to Ipswich T.
24 June: **Sol Bamba** Palermo to Leeds U; **Adam Barton** Coventry C to Portsmouth; **Junior Brown** Mansfield T to Shrewsbury T; **Roberto Firmino** Hoffenheim to Liverpool – £29m; **Tomer Hemed** Almeria to Brighton & HA; **John Herron** Celtic to Blackpool; **Bastien Hery** Rochdale to Carlisle U; **Robert Huth** Stoke C to Leicester C; **Brian Jensen** Crawley T to Mansfield T; **Adam McGurk** Burton Alb to Portsmouth; **Steven Schumacher** Fleetwood T to Stevenage; **Scott Shearer** Crewe Alex to Mansfield T; **Omar Sowunmi** Ipswich T to Yeovil T.
25 June: **Yoann Barbet** Chamois Niortais to Brentford; **Christian Burgess** Peterborough U to Portsmouth; **Lewis Buxton** Sheffield W to Rotherham U; **Danny Carr** Huddersfield T to Cambridge U; **Gerard Deulofeu** Barcelona to Everton – £4.3m; **Jabo Ibehre** Colchester U to Carlisle U; **Darryl Lachman** FC Twente to Sheffield W; **Gary Sawyer** Leyton Orient to Plymouth Arg; **Gill Swerts** NAC Breda to Notts Co.
26 June: **Lewis Baker** Chelsea to Vitesse Arnhem; **Tom Cairney** Blackburn R to Fulham; **Jason Davidson** WBA to Huddersfield T; **Ryan Fraser** Bournemouth to Ipswich T; **Tom Hopper** Leicester C to Scunthorpe U; **Tyrone Mings** Ipswich T to Bournemouth; **Shinji Okazaki** Mainz to Leicester C – £7m subject to work permit; **Dimitri Payet** Marseille to West Ham U; **Brett Pitman** Bournemouth to Ipswich T; **Adam Smith** Leicester C to Northampton T; **Anthony Stewart** Crewe Alex to Wycombe W; **Danny Ward** Liverpool to Aberdeen.
27 June: **Billy Kee** Scunthorpe U to Accrington S; **Adam Legzdins** Leyton Orient to Birmingham C; **Billy Paynter** Carlisle U to Hartlepool U.
29 June: **Kari Arnason** Rotherham U to Malmo; **El Hadji Ba** Sunderland to Charlton Ath; **Petr Cech** Chelsea to Arsenal –

£10m; **Ross Etheridge** Derby Co to Accrington S; **Jake Jervis** Ross Co to Plymouth Arg; **Josh McQuoid** Bournemouth to Luton T; **Tom Naylor** Derby Co to Burton Alb; **Paulinho** Tottenham H to Guangzhou Evergrande – £9.9m; **Orlando Sa** Legia Warsaw to Reading.

30 June: **Angelo Balanta** Bristol R to Carlisle U; **George Baldock** Milton Keynes D to Oxford U; **Jason Banton** Plymouth Arg to Wycombe W; **Simon Church** Charlton Ath to Milton Keynes D; **Cody Cropper** Southampton to Milton Keynes D; **Mark Cullen** Luton T to Blackpool – £180,000 rising; **Donervon Daniels** WBA to Wigan Ath; **Andrew Davies** Bradford C to Ross Co; **Steven Davies** Blackpool to Bradford; **Dale Jennings** Barnsley to Milton Keynes D; **Louis Laing** Nottingham F to Motherwell; **Chris Lines** Port Vale to Bristol R; **Gary MacKenzie** Blackpool to Doncaster R; **Alfie Mawson** Brentford to Barnsley; **Alexander McQueen** Tottenham H to Carlisle U; **Jacob Mellis** Blackpool to Bury; **Nyron Nosworthy** Blackpool to Dagenham & R; **Stephen Quinn** Hull C to Reading; **Oriol Riera** Wigan Ath to Deportivo La Coruna; **Chris Robertson** Port Vale to Ross Co; **Danny Rowe** Rotherham U to Wycombe W; **Vincent Sasso** Braga to Sheffield W; **Timmy Thiele** Borussia Dortmund to Burton Alb; **Lars Veldwijk** Nottingham F to PEC Zwolle; **Gregg Wylde** St Mirren to Plymouth Arg.

1 July: **David Amoo** Carlisle U to Partick Th; **Ben Amos** Manchester U to Bolton W; **Stephen Arthurworrey** Fulham to Yeovil T; **Andy Barcham** Portsmouth to AFC Wimbledon; **Nathaniel Clyne** Southampton to Liverpool – £12.5m; **Sebastian Coates** Liverpool to Sunderland; **Jason Demetriou** Anorthosis Famagusta to Walsall; **Ryan Dickson** Crawley T to Yeovil T; **Sylvain Distin** Everton to Bournemouth; **Eder** Sporting Braga to Swansea C; **Lewis Holtby** Tottenham H to Hamburg; **Saidy Janko** Manchester U to Celtic; **Konstantin Kerschbaumer** FC Admira Wacker Modling to Brentford; **Tomasz Kuszczak** Wolverhampton W to Birmingham C; **Gary Madine** Sheffield W to Bolton W; **Simon Makienok** Palermo to Charlton Ath; **Paddy McCourt** Brighton & HA to Luton T; **Matt Mills** Bolton W to Nottingham F; **Jason Mooney** York C to Accrington S; **Josh Morris** Blackburn R to Bradford C; **Magnus Okuonghae** Colchester U to Luton T; **Matej Vydra** Udinese to Watford; **Chris Wood** Leicester C to Leeds U.

2 July: **Andreas Bjelland** FC Twente to Brentford – £2.1m; **Gaetan Bong** Wigan Ath to Brighton & HA; **Ryan Clarke** Oxford U to Northampton T; **Andy Delort** Wigan Ath to Caen; **Max Ehmer** QPR to Gillingham; **Tom Elliott** Cambridge U to AFC Wimbledon; **Neil Etheridge** Charlton Ath to Walsall; **Jose Holebas** Roma to Watford – £1.8m; **Emmanuel Ledesma** Middlesbrough to Rotherham U; **Ainsley Maitland-Niles** Arsenal to Ipswich T; **Paul McShane** Hull C to Reading; **David Mooney** Leyton Orient to Southend U; **Brandon Ormonde-Ottewill** Arsenal to Swindon T; **Karleigh Osborne** Bristol C to AFC Wimbledon; **Sebastian Polter** FSV Mainz to QPR; **Jazz Richards** Swansea C to Fulham; **Jon Stead** Huddersfield T to Notts Co; **Jamie Ward** Derby Co to Nottingham F; **Luke Williams** Middlesbrough to Scunthorpe U.

4 July: **Mawouna Amevor** Go Ahead Eagles to Notts Co; **Sam Beasant** Stevenage to Cambridge U; **Jonathan Bond** Watford to Reading; **Troy Brown** Cheltenham T to Exeter C; **Jamie Burrows** Rangers to Yeovil T; **Graham Carey** Ross Co to Plymouth Arg; **Conor Coady** Huddersfield T to Wolverhampton W; **Danny Collins** Nottingham F to Rotherham U; **Tony Craig** Brentford to Millwall; **Mark Duffy** Birmingham C to Burton Alb; **George Elokobi** Oldham Ath to Colchester U; **Radamel Falcao** Monaco to Chelsea; **Danny Green** Milton Keynes D to Luton T; **Jack Hunt** Crystal Palace to Sheffield W; **Thomas Ince** Hull C to Derby Co – £4.75m; **Tony McMahon** Blackpool to Bradford C; **Mario Pasalic** Chelsea to Monaco; **Lukas Podolski** Arsenal to Galatasaray – £1.8m; **Max Power** Tranmere R to Wigan Ath – tribunal; **Tom Thorpe** Manchester U to Rotherham U; **Anthony Wordsworth** Ipswich T to Southend U.

6 July: **Alex Baptiste** Bolton W to Middlesbrough; **Billy Bingham** Dagenham & R to Crewe Alex; **Adam Campbell** Newcastle U to Notts Co; **Etienne Capoue** Tottenham H to Watford; **Richard Chaplow** Millwall to Doncaster R; **Kyle De Silva** Crystal Palace to Notts Co; **Michael Doyle** Sheffield U to Portsmouth; **Joe Edwards** Yeovil T to Colchester U; **Greg Halford** Nottingham F to Rotherham U; **Niki Maenpaa** VVV-Venlo to Brighton & HA; **Remi Matthews** Norwich C to Burton Alb; **Nani** Manchester U to Fenerbahce – £4.25m; **Eddie Nolan** Scunthorpe U to York C; **Sanmi Odelusi** Bolton W to Wigan Ath; **Derik Osede** Real Madrid to Bolton W; **Kudus Oyenuga** Dundee U to Hartlepool U; **Ollie Palmer** Mansfield T to Leyton Orient; **Sam Ricketts** Wolverhampton W to Coventry C; **Josh Simpson** Crawley T to Plymouth Arg; **Genaro Snijders** FC Oss to Notts Co; **Enes Unal** Bursaspor to Manchester C.

7 July: **Sammy Ameobi** Newcastle U to Cardiff C; **Craig Davies** Bolton W to Wigan Ath; **Julian Jenner** Disogyor to Notts Co; **Cuco Martina** FC Twente to Southampton; **Jamie O'Hara** Blackpool to Fulham; **Bryan Ruiz** Fulham to Sporting Lisbon; **Jayden Stockley** Bournemouth to Portsmouth; **Jelle Vossen** Genk to Burnley.

8 July: **Toby Alderweireld** Atletico Madrid to Tottenham H; **Jon Ashton** Stevenage to Crawley T; **Graham Burke** Aston Villa to Notts Co; **Eggert Jonsson** FC Vestsjaelland to Fleetwood T; **Filip Valencic** Monza to Notts Co; **Romain Vincelot** Leyton Orient to Coventry C; **Shaun Batt** Leyton Orient to Barnet.

10 July: **Yohan Cabaye** Paris Saint-Germain to Crystal Palace – £10m; **David Cornell** Swansea C to Oldham Ath; **Kyle Dempsey** Carlisle U to Huddersfield T; **Shay Given** Aston Villa to Stoke C; **Idrissa Gueye** Lille to Aston Villa; **Marco Matias** Nacional to Sheffield W; **Josh McEachran** Chelsea to Brentford – £750,000; **Jamie Ness** Stoke C to Scunthorpe U; **Steven Nzonzi** Stoke C to Sevilla – £7m; **Mark O'Brien** Derby Co to Luton T; **Angelo Ogbonna** Juventus to West Ham U – £10m; **Lewis Price** Crystal Palace to Sheffield U; **Jack Redshaw** Morecambe to Blackpool; **Ross Wallace** Burnley to Sheffield W.

11 July: **Valon Behrami** Hamburg to Watford; **Matteo Darmian** Torino to Manchester U – £12.7m; **John Guidetti** Manchester City to Celta Vigo; **Georginio Wijnaldum** PSV Eindhoven to Newcastle U – £14.5m.

12 July: **Glen Johnson** Liverpool to Stoke C.

13 July: **Asmir Begovic** Stoke C to Chelsea – £8m; **Filippo Costa** Chievo to Bournemouth; **Peter Denton** Rotherham U to Hartlepool U; **Coll Donaldson** QPR to Dundee U; **Aaron Hughes** Brighton & HA to Melbourne C; **Ollie McBurnie** Bradford C to Swansea C; **Danny Pugh** Coventry C to Bury; **Morgan Schneiderlin** Southampton to Manchester U – £25m; **Bastian Schweinsteiger** Bayern Munich to Manchester U – £14.4m; **Drissa Traore** Notts Co to Swindon T.

14 July: **Ali Al-Habsi** Wigan Ath to Reading; **Ryan Bird** Cambridge U to Yeovil T; **David Fox** Colchester U to Crewe Alex; **Will Grigg** Brentford to Wigan Ath; **Mark Marshall** Port Vale to Bradford C; **Allan Nyom** Udinese to Watford; **Lyle Taylor** Scunthorpe U to AFC Wimbledon; **Raheem Sterling** Liverpool to Manchester C – £44m (rising to £49m); **Robin van Persie** Manchester U to Fenerbahce; **Martyn Woolford** Millwall to Sheffield U.

15 July: **Jordy Clasie** Feyenoord to Southampton – £8m; **Jeff Hughes** Fleetwood T to Cambridge U; **Jeremain Lens** Dynamo Kiev to Sunderland – £8m; **Scott Loach** Rotherham U to Notts Co; **Moha El Ouriachi** Barcelona to Stoke C; **Ross Turnbull** Barnsley to Leeds U.

16 July: **Younes Kaboul** Tottenham H to Sunderland; **Stewart Downing** West Ham U to Middlesbrough – £5.5m; **Milan Lalkovic** Barnsley to Walsall; **Matt McClure** Wycombe to Dagenham & R; **Lewis McGugan** Watford to Sheffield W; **Josh Passley** Fulham to Dagenham & R.

17 July: **Fabian Delph** Aston Villa to Manchester C – £8m; **Cristian Benavente** Castilla to MK Dons; **Wes Fogden** Portsmouth to Yeovil T; **Fraser Franks** Luton T to Stevenage; **Jordy Hiwula** Manchester C to Huddersfield T; **Conor Newton** Rotherham U to Cambridge U.

18 July: **Jordan Amavi** Nice to Aston Villa; **Anthony O'Connor** Plymouth Arg to Burton Alb.

19 July: **Patrick Roberts** Fulham to Manchester C.

20 July: **Lee Angol** Luton T to Peterborough U; **Wesley Atkinson** WBA to Notts Co; **Tjaronn Chery** FC Groningen to QPR; **Jonathan Kodjia** Angers SCO to Bristol C – £2.1m; **AJ Leitch-Smith** Yeovil T to Port Vale; **Kieran Sadlier** St Mirren to Peterborough U; **Aaron Taylor-Sinclair** Wigan Ath to Doncaster R.

21 July: **Aleksandar Mitrovic** Anderlecht to Newcastle U – £13m; **Ahmed Kashi** Metz to Charlton Ath; **Bangaly-Fode Koita** Caen to Blackburn R; **Sacha Petschi** CA Bastia to Blackburn R; **Benjamin Stambouli** Tottenham H to Paris Saint-Germain – £6m.

Compiler's pick: **Callum Garrett**, Cleveland Hall Boys Club, Gateshead – 2014–15 under-13 player of the season; 2013–14 under-12 player of the season; 2012–13 under-11 player of the season; 2011–12 under-10 player of the season.

Now you can buy any of these other bestselling sports titles from your bookshop or *direct from the publisher.*

FREE P&P AND UK DELIVERY
(Overseas and Ireland £3.50 per book)

The Secret Player	Anonymous	£8.99
Champions League Dreams	Rafa Benitez	£8.99
Bend it Like Bullard	Jimmy Bullard	£8.99
My Autobiography	Dan Carter	£20.00
Lions Tales	Matt Dawson	£8.99
My Story	Sven-Göran Eriksson	£8.99
My Liverpool Story	Steven Gerrard	£16.99
The Didi Man	Dietmar Hamann	£9.99
Vegas Tales	Ricky Hatton	£20.00
Football Clichés	Adam Hurrey	£12.99
Bomb: My Autobiography	Adam Jones	£20.00
Jeffanory	Jeff Stelling	£9.99
Crossing the Line: My Story	Luis Suarez	£8.99
Tuffers' Alternative Guide to the Ashes	Phil Tufnell	£8.99
Tuffers' Cricket Tales	Phil Tufnell	£9.99
Where Am I?: My Autobiography	Phil Tufnell	£20.00
The Gaffer	Neil Warnock	£8.99

TO ORDER SIMPLY CALL THIS NUMBER

01235 400 414

or visit our website:
www.headline.co.uk

Prices and availability subject to change without notice.